D1467732

SEASHORE STYLE

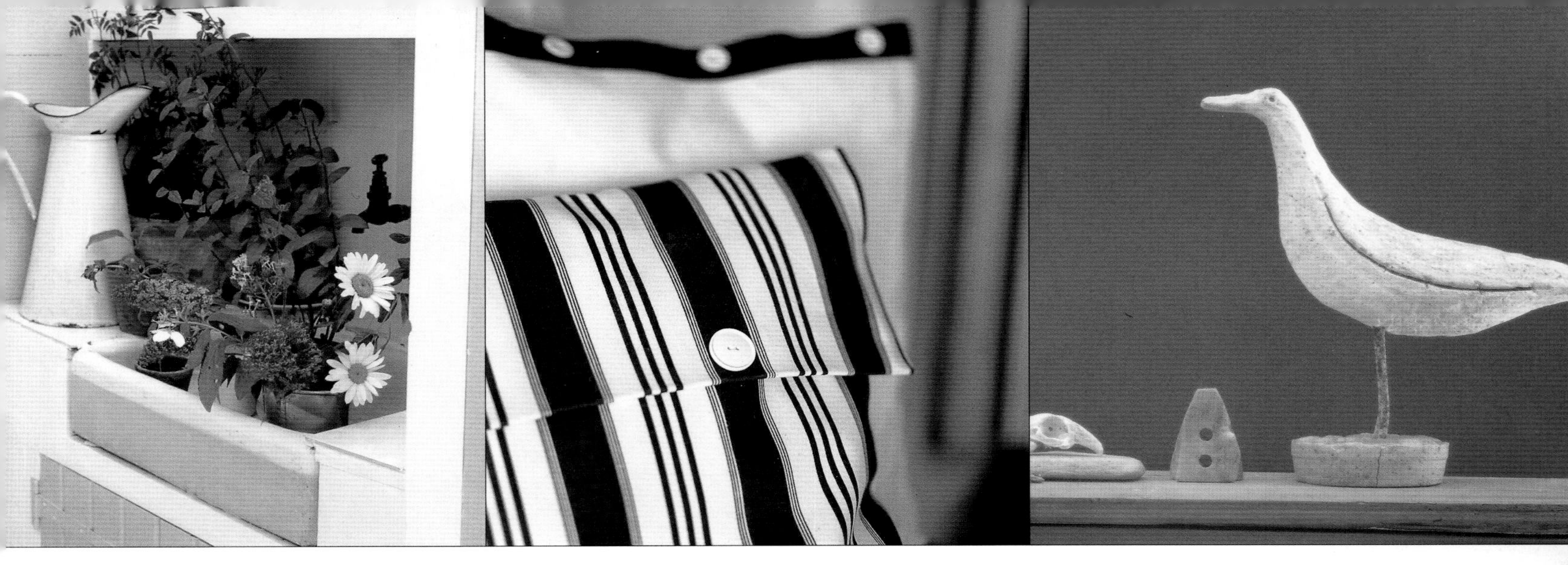

SEASHORE STYLE

Decorative ideas inspired by the spirit of the seashore

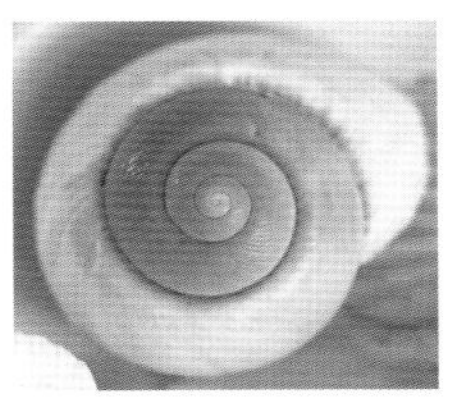

ANDREA SPENCER
Photography by Spike Powell

LORENZ BOOKS
NEW YORK • LONDON • SYDNEY • BATH

First published in the UK in 1997 by Lorenz Books

This edition published in the USA by Lorenz Books
an imprint of
Anness Publishing Inc.
27 West 20th Street
New York, New York 10011

ISBN 1 85967 378 3

Publisher: Joanna Lorenz
Project Editor: Judith Simons
Designer: Lisa Tai
Photographer: Spike Powell
Stylist: Andrea Spencer

Printed and bound in Hong Kong

1 3 5 7 9 10 8 6 4 2

Special Photography: p. 1, 8, Polly Wreford, p. 16, top Adrian Taylor, p. 27, bottom Graham Rae, p. 55, left Tim Imrie, pp. 104 left, 106, 130 right, 132 top, 133, Debbie Patterson

CONTENTS

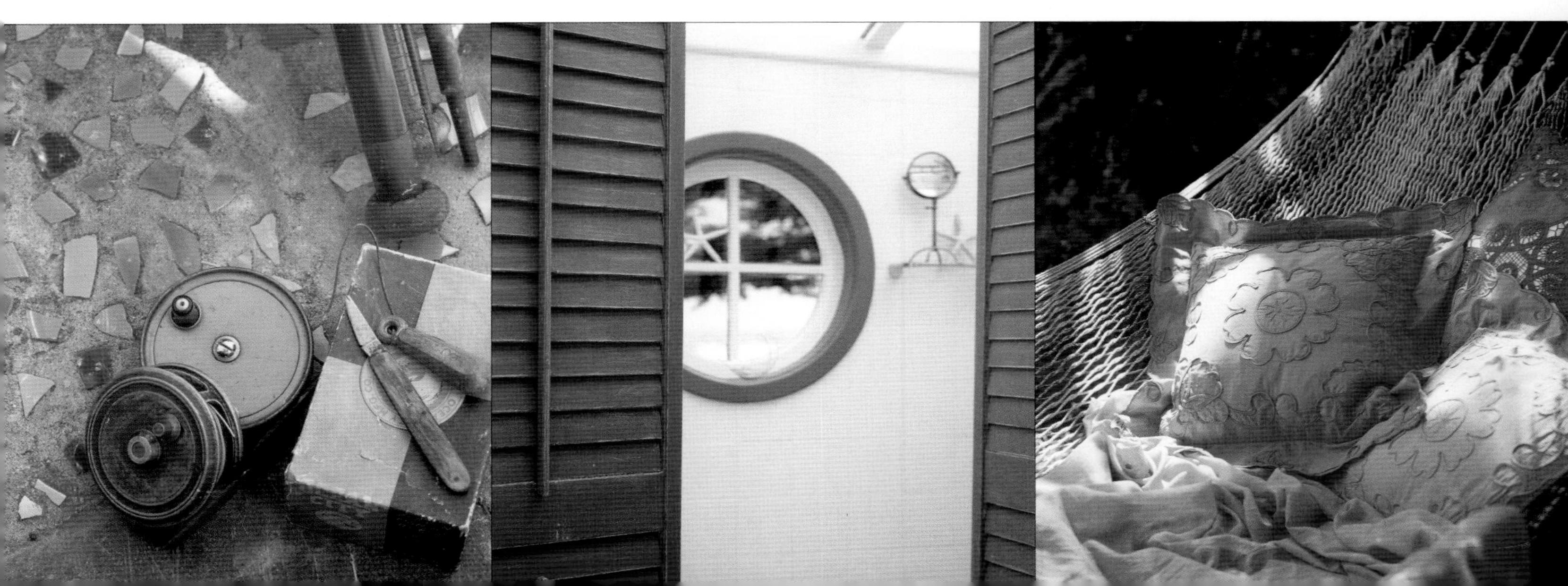

Introduction

coastline
pebbles
boats
driftwood
wind
shells
waves
beach huts
sand
breakwater
shingle
life belts

The essence of seashore style is the sea itself, stirring powerful, evocative memories of childhood vacations. Every summer our cities empty and we head *en masse* for the coast. To walk across the beach to the water's edge is one of the great joys in life. As our cares and everyday concerns evaporate, we enter a new world of light and space, distance and energy – a world where the elements rule, and wind and waves create an ever-changing environment. Dipping our toes in the ocean, we gaze in wonder at the horizon. Picking up a pebble, we marvel at its shape and pattern and, sensing it to be somehow precious, slip it into a pocket. Squinting into a rock pool, we spy movement and suddenly are children again. By introducing the style of the seashore into our homes, we can bring back these memories and recapture the invigorating sensation of mental and physical well-being that we experience by the sea.

coastline

boats

driftwood

wind

pebbles

Introduction

As the pace of living speeds up, it becomes more essential for people to create a harmonious home environment. Seashore style fulfills such a need – it is a style that can work anywhere, be it a beach hut or a simple cottage, a traditionally understated period room or a fresher approach in modern surroundings.

Seashore style uses materials that improve with the passing of time, and furniture and furnishings that are simple, practical and above all comfortable. Matte, chalky seascape colors are featured, as are uneven surfaces and distressed patterns that evoke the ebb and flow of the shoreline. Wood and stone blend harmoniously with each other and with unpretentious canvas, calico and muslin. Wicker, jute, raffia and rope are combined with seashells and driftwood to create a balanced, down-to-earth living space and to provide a restful backdrop for day-to-day existence. Seashore style is calm, easy on the eye, and provides a welcome antidote to life in the fast lane. It is about appreciating the natural environment, taking the time to savor the here-and-now aspects of life.

So, take a stroll along the shoreline and seek your inspiration from nature's treasures at the water's edge. Use the colors, textures and natural gifts of the sea as creative themes for beautifying your surroundings. Arrange the mementos from your seaside strolls around your home and let them serve as a reminder of happy, peaceful days spent by the sea.

Left: *Natural materials are at the heart of seashore style. Driftwood and feathers form a striking centerpiece, and shells look attractive arranged in a bowl, sewn onto a napkin, or attached to the front of a flowerpot.*

Right, clockwise from top left: *A splendid wrought-iron veranda in traditional seashore style; a jaunty weather vane with elaborate curlicues; the weathered color of life preservers; a weather-beaten doorway, painted in familiar seaside colors; old wood fish-packing crates with rope handles; a sailor-like knot.*

KATI
YH 127 • SOUTHWO

wind

coastline

waves

driftwood

shells

Seaside Evocations

All seaside homes have an inherent simplicity that imbues the atmosphere with a sense of tranquillity. However, architectural styles do vary around the coastlines of the world, depending on the local climate and resources. The gray stone cottages of the Brittany coast are quite different from the dazzling whitewashed exteriors of the Mediterranean, or the wood houses of the Baltic and Atlantic.

Nordic Style

As would be expected from a country almost surrounded by water, Scandinavian interiors are intimately bound up with the all-pervasive blues of seas, lakes and sky. In a country where trees are plentiful, and workable stone scarce, it is no surprise to find that the majority of the population lives in wood or timber-framed houses. In the past, furniture and utensils were made of wood, as were the tools used to build boats and sleds. Planked walls were the preferred building choice and, although painted colors have been used for decoration since Viking times, it was not until the eighteenth century that color was widely used for cottage interiors, on walls and built-in furniture. Many old cottages still have walls honeycombed with cupboard beds – the one nearest the hearth used to be reserved for old or ailing members of the family. Winters are cold, harsh and long, and

Left: *Found tinware makes an impromptu vase.*

Right: *Bleached floorboards, simple wood furniture and whitewashed walls: the essence of Nordic style is its simplicity. Here, a beach towel hangs drying over a wood-burning stove.*

Below: *An elegant, old-fashioned shelter on the seafront promenade. You can almost hear the band playing in the distance.*

the summer evenings are sometimes cool, so wood-burning stoves and fireplaces are still an integral part of every home.

Simpler household interiors were painted predominantly in one color, often a slate blue-green with a few prized pieces of furniture spectacularly decorated. Gray used to be a popular choice, partly because it was considered fashionable and partly because the ingredients were relatively inexpensive. The clear matte colors indigenous to Scandinavia come from distemper and limewash and, being organic paints, they let the surface breathe and gently weather over the years. Wood floors take on a subtly distressed look over the decades as floorboards are bleached by repeated scrubbing with wet silver sand.

Atlantic Style

Battered by the heavy seas and blasted by the icy winds that whistle off the Atlantic, the isolated east coast of the United States became a haven for rich nineteenth-century Americans who built summer homes there to escape from the stiflingly hot cities and to enjoy the quiet and cool sea air. Wood is the indigenous building material, so these houses were mainly built of clapboard. Although residences initially appeared to be large, much of the space was taken up by the wide surrounding verandas, providing shade and a pleasant place to sit in the evening cool.

Today, we view light as an absolute must for our continued health and well-being. The sunnier the day, the brighter

Above: *A row of beach huts is an essential element in the traditional British seaside. Whether freshly painted or faded and peeling, they always look attractive.*

the room, and the better our frame of mind. Nineteenth-century Americans, in keeping with the dominant fashion at that time, influenced by the Victorians in England, decorated their homes in rather somber colors, with lots of solid mahogany furniture in every room and heavy curtains draping the windows to keep interiors cool. This was typical of many turn-of-the-century homes, where protection from the sun and heat was deemed more important than ventilation. However, nowadays things have changed. Modern interiors are painted white to enhance the architectural detail and to reflect available light; windows are left free of cumbersome drapes so inhabitants can enjoy the invigorating offshore breezes. Furniture is kept simple and is either left bare or painted with soft whites or subtle seascape colors. Exterior wood is left in its natural state to reflect light from sunrise to sunset.

English Seaside Style

In many coastal towns in England, houses are brightly painted in carnival colors that soften as they fade in the sun. This creates a pretty patchwork effect that is accentuated by flowerpots and window boxes, decorative ironwork and old-fashioned verandas. Piers, esplanades and the old "grand" hotels add to the atmosphere. The north of England has a distinctive seaside style, with buckets and spades, kiss-me-quick hats, donkey rides on the beach and "naughty" postcards. At Saint Ives in Cornwall, in southern England, the exceptional quality of the light has inspired countless artists.

Mediterranean Style

The light in Greece is legendary – it has an almost luminous quality that seems to bring out the intensity of color everywhere. The dazzling sunlight and azure of the crystal-clear water are the basis for many interior schemes where three colors predominate: white, blue and ochre. White, a symbol of purity and cleanliness, is seen in the whitewashed façades that are repainted annually. Blue, the color of the ocean, from aquas to turquoise to navy, is used on windows, doors and furniture. Ochre, the color of earth, terra cotta and stone, is an ever-present background.

Once inhabited by modest farmers or fishermen, the tiny island houses, with thick whitewashed stone walls, plank floors and painted wood ceilings, have a simplicity and charm all their own, and they have become as much in demand as vacation homes by those wanting to escape the rat race and opt for a simpler life. Overhanging wood balconies and exterior stone staircases are piled on top of each other in intricate patterns on the densely populated hillsides, and donkey tracks lined with pebbles or whitewashed stones snake through the villages.

Above: *Houses and boats cluster together in this Italian seaside town. Vines provide shelter from the sun on roof terraces.*

Left: *These Greek whitewashed buildings take on a soft pink and orange glow in the evening sunlight.*

High walls pierced by arches provide areas of vital shade at different times of day, and sun-loving plants sit on top of them or in huge terra cotta pots in courtyards. Doors are a symbol of Greek hospitality, and they are usually made of wood, crowned with decorative flowers and brightly painted or topped with carved stone. Many such entrances open onto luscious gardens, some of which are decorated with Kroklai, a beautiful mosaic of black and white pebbles traditionally used in the gardens, courtyards and house interiors on the island of Rhodes. There is also a huge range of crafted tables, benches and chairs all used for dining outside.

In summer, doors and windows are kept tightly shuttered against the heat of the day, and even fabric and furnishings are kept to a bare minimum to make the most of the cool air generated by thick stone floors and walls.

Italian Mediterranean homes also emphasize cool interiors, and geometric-patterned marble floors are popular. Houses are stacked almost randomly, interspersed with roof terraces, laundry lines and small gardens. The French Riviera, in contrast, is lined with grand villas, hotels and apartments, and luxury yachts are anchored offshore. Houses in the old French ports are still traditional, however, with shuttered windows leading out to balconies full of flowers.

Pacific and Caribbean Style

Pacific style centers on the islands of the South Seas, fanned by balmy northeast trade winds. Ventilation and shelter from the sun are the main priorities, as well as protection from dramatic tropical storms. Houses are often improvised out of bamboo, corrugated iron and whatever is at hand. Cane awnings shade the sun's rays and giant fans stir the air. Warm, vivid colors look good in the bright sunlight.

Caribbean style also draws heavily on tropical influences. Colors are strong and vibrant, life is lived in the slow lane, fans stir the still air and there is an element of make do with what you have got, as all manner of materials are used within the home – from corrugated iron to tar paper.

Above right: *Thatched roofs are a feature of Pacific style: here, they blend wonderfully with the prettily painted beach huts.*

Right: *Decorative woodwork on the roof of this West Indian home is reminiscent of waves, and the shaping on the veranda brings the sun and its rays to mind.*

floors

shutters

paving

walls

plaster

Inspirational Elements

True seashore style re-creates the natural beauty of the ocean in your home. It can be as simple as displaying your beachcombing finds on a windowsill, or as complex as drawing on maritime themes to decorate an entire room.

Natural Elements

Take a stroll along the shoreline and you will find a beachcomber's treasure trove that provides an endless source of inspiration for decorative treatments. Found objects need very little arranging – the simpler the better.

Scoop up a handful of smooth pebbles and look closely at their intricate patterning and veining. Large worn stones look beautiful when casually displayed on shelves, but also can do duty as paperweights, doorstops, hearthside companions, or as a tiny shingled beach around the base of a vase or piece of driftwood. Examine pieces of glass worn almost translucent by the sands of time and see them transformed into tiny jewels. Place shells along windowsills so they catch the light, fill glass tanks to overflowing with favorite shells or arrange a selection

Above: *Driftwood can serve equally well as a natural sculpture or as firewood.*

Top and left: *The seashore abounds with wildlife – sturdy plants cling to the cliffs and sandy crabs scuttle along wooden jetties.*

Above: *Pebbles worn smooth by the ocean have a symmetry and charm that make them perennial favorites as vacation souvenirs and keepsakes.*

Right: *The remains of an old breakwater create strange shapes in the shallows.*

around beautiful mirrors and curtain edgings. Small strands of seaweed may be used to create a charming seascape around the edge of a mirror: The paler variety looks especially stunning when made into a tiny wreath.

Driftwood, worn by the relentless pounding of the sea, becomes a sculpture fit to grace a mantelpiece. Weathered driftwood, with curls of peeling paint still adhering to its contours, can be fashioned into shelves hung from lengths of worn rope. Larger pieces can be crafted into furniture.

Take a closer look at wonderful rusting anchors and weather vanes. Collect shells, driftwood, pebbles and other treasures, and use them as a reminder of the patterns of natural decorating that are the very essence of the seashore.

Seascape Colors

Color is the easiest and most inexpensive way to transform your home. It can make rooms appear smaller or more spacious, and also give an air of vibrancy and vitality.

Re-create the luminous quality of the sea in the Mediterranean or the Aegean, turning from blue to jade-green as the water hits a sunlit patch of sand, a clear blue English sky with the whiteness of a gull in sharp contrast, or the red and blue hulls of Italian fishing boats as they are tossed around on the waves.

Blue is expansive, like the sea and sky, and it can create calm meditative spaces. Yellow is warming and positive like the sun. Red makes us stop in our tracks and so should be

Above : *The sun gives a rosy glow to the sky and shoreline of this Californian beach as it sets over the ocean.*

Right: *Few views are more relaxing than the sight of moored boats bobbing gently in safe waters, as in this Greek island harbor.*

Left: *The bright primary colors on this life preserver and dinghy are pleasing to the eye and would also work well in the color scheme for a child's bedroom.*

ΝΣΤΑΝΤΙΝΟΣ
1386

Above left: *Natural materials such as wood and rope weather beautifully. Bleached blues and off-whites are central colors in seashore style.*
Above right: *Alliums grow in abundance on the cliffs: they too are a lovely faded color.*
Below left and right: *Old fishing nets, floats and life preservers can be incorporated in interiors.*

used merely as an accent to inject life. Look at how colors are changed by other colors and by the light in which they are seen. Pale colors create a feeling of light and space, while darker tones provide shade and suggest a more somber mood. Walls painted white keep houses cool, and reflect the sparkling light from the sea and sky.

Develop a color palette that works best for you by looking at the landscape and seascape and amassing a collection of treasures that please you. Display them on a windowsill or by a fireplace in the room you are thinking of decorating and note how the colors work together – try a selection of glass worn smooth by the sea in brilliant blues, aquas and greens, the reds and shocking pinks of geraniums set on a cerulean blue cloth, or even chalky white stones and matte white shells juxtaposed with rope and rusty metal.

Charmingly Distressed

Think of the simple seaside huts with weather-beaten timbers, dotted along the coastline where land meets sea. Note how the strong colors have been faded by the elements, and use these as a

Above left and right: *Layers of paint are stripped away by the elements, creating subtle color effects on wooden surfaces.*
Below left and right: *The seashore offers strong textural contrasts – fresh white daisies against a piece of old wood, and thick coils of net.*

basis for a scheme. Look at fibers and textures found at the seashore and see how beautiful they have become with the passage of time: salt-faded fishing nets in soft aquas; life preservers worn to a delicate shade of pink; deep blues that have become almost lavender; hulls of boats weathered by the pounding of the sea where successive layers of paint are still visible. Emulate these soft colors and flaking paint on chairs and chests of drawers, and distress wood to echo the sun-bleached silver-gray found on exposed buildings and verandas.

When decorating your home, observe how beach huts and fishermen's huts differ in their finishes – a beach hut generally has brightly colored paintwork, while the wood on a fisherman's hut is left to weather gradually, unadorned. Get inspiration for your decorative ideas from the planking used horizontally or vertically, and look closely at how struts of wood work together to form the ribs of the interiors of boats.

Examine pebbles and shingle, which are often inlaid into walls and floors in subtle colors and intricate designs. The most unexpected things, such as small, smooth stones, can be turned into objects of infinite beauty. Copy the intricate knots and

splicing of seafarers to fashion your own tie-backs and chair trims. Note the fine ironwork used on weather vanes, piers, bandstands and shelters and use them as inspiration for shelf brackets, gates or table bases.

Exteriors

As anyone who lives by the coast will tell you, exterior maintenance is a priority, and durable paint is the answer. Traditionally, coastal dwellers relied on whitewash to withstand the ravages of sea, salt air and storms, although in later years, more vivid treatments became popular. Armed with a paintbrush and a bright color, householders embark on the annual ritual of preserving, protecting and promoting their homes. The stark whites of the Mediterranean are in marked contrast to some areas of England and northern Europe where woodwork painted in seaside blues, sunshine yellows and vivid reds stands out wonderfully against the dark gray stone exteriors. Individual expression is key and, while many schemes show a disregard for color coordination, collectively these brave statements create a brash carnival quality that is every bit as much a part of seashore style as their more subtle counterparts.

Cheerful displays of flowering plants are often found by doorways and in seafront gardens. Choose plants that can withstand the strong sea breezes, salty air and sandy soil found near the coast. Prettily patterned weatherboarding, decked verandas and frontages decorated with simply patterned pebbles add interest, as does the spectacular ironwork found on piers and promenade shelters.

Left: *The seagull's plaintive cry is one of the most evocative of all seaside sounds. This traditional white wood building has an unusually grand frontage.*

Below: *Weathering adds character to the beams on an old wood door, set in the whitewashed stone wall of a fishing village. Cheerful flowering plants in pots add a touch of color.*

Top: *A shelter on a promenade serves as a refuge from sea spray.*

Above: *The paintwork on these beach huts mirrors the blue and white of the sea and sky.*

Left: *Cobblestones look wonderful on outdoor surfaces such as patios and garden paths.*

floors
shutters
paving
wall
plaster

Rooms with Sea Views

You do not need to live by the seaside to give your home a seashore feel. Model boats on windowsills, shuttered windows and seafaring pictures all conjure up the ambience of the ocean. Decorate table settings with shells, or paint seaside motifs onto a tabletop. Make the most of a sunny day or starry night and move into the patio or garden and imagine yourself by the water's edge. Put up a beach parasol, or create a shaded area with a canopy made from canvas or sailcloth.

Rooms for Eating

In the kitchen, shelves and cupboards are a must to keep everything shipshape, so display your china and glass on open shelves or keep it dust-free behind glazed doors. Natural-looking shelves can be made from reclaimed timber such as old

Above: *Quarry tiles are a perfect natural contrast in this all-white kitchen. Accessories such as driftwood fish and a model sailing boat give an immediate seaside feel.*

Left: *Display your favorite china, glass and seashore finds on a simple homemade dresser. Attach tongue-and-groove boarding to the wall before putting up the shelves.*

Right: *A tiny beach hut veranda is an idyllic setting for enjoying a leisurely meal.*

Left: *Toy boats look wonderful in windows, with the light shining through the sails. Choose the boat to fit the size of the window.*

Below left: *The bathroom is the ideal place to display a collection of shells and other seaside finds.*

Below right: *A simple touch like this navy-and-white striped roller towel gives an instant nautical feel.*

floorboards, scaffolding boards or driftwood. Paint them with a colorwash in off-white or chalky blue. Where possible, leave windows unadorned and line windowsills with displays of beautiful old model boats, shells and other seashore finds intermingled with fresh herbs and scented flowers.

Tongue-and-groove boarding is a familiar feature in many seaside homes and it is also an ideal surface for kitchens and dining rooms. Not only does it imbue a room with a certain warmth but it is also architecturally interesting, can hide a multitude of sins and has good insulating properties. Painted a soft white, it looks clean and fresh rather than cold or clinical.

Stone, tiled or wooden floors combine most successfully with all colors and they can easily be mopped and wiped in case of spills. To soften hard surfaces, use rag rugs or runners in toning colors.

Natural floor coverings would also suit the seashore style and there is a large selection – coir, jute, seagrass and sisal are all hardwearing. They can be fitted or, if you prefer, you can buy individual beach mats bound with colored cotton tape.

Rooms for Sleeping

Of all the rooms in the house, the bedroom should be the most tranquil and relaxing. An all-white room is beautifully romantic and immediately conjures up images of fine voile curtains wafting in the sea breezes, filmy mosquito nets loosely knotted over inviting beds dressed in cool, crisp linens, and shutters keeping out the scorching heat of the midday sun.

An all-white room is not necessarily everybody's idea of heaven, and soft colors look glorious too. Chalky pinks and blues, aquas and delicate greens are all very relaxing choices for a bedroom. So introduce spots of color in softly distressed seaside shades on chests of drawers, wicker furniture and even bed linen. Color is completely personal, and creating the right shade is purely a matter of experimenting, but it is worth remembering that colors change dramatically as the light in the room changes. For instance, a wood floor in full sunlight can cast a warm glow around an all-white room. To avoid disappointment, first paint colors onto a piece of board or pin a piece of paper to the wall before starting – watch what happens to the color in different lights throughout the day.

Rooms for Bathing

Bathrooms, although functional, can be leisurely and luxurious rooms – somewhere to unwind and soak away your cares after a hard day. If the space is large enough, install a comfortable chair, have heated rails to warm towels, install good lighting and, above all, make sure that bottles, lotions and potions are within arm's reach of the bath and shower.

Shells are the perfect foil in this watery world: arrange them along the windowsill so they catch the light, and fill shelves with displays of coral and other mementos of days by the sea. Make fine muslin curtains for cupboard doors and decorate them with tiny shells. Create a chair-rail using strips of rope with shells and pebbles attached, or introduce a simple line around the wall with clam shells. If you want to go totally overboard, you could cover all the walls with shells, thus turning your bathroom into a delightful underwater grotto.

Above right: *This ornate headboard is made even more charming by the gently peeling paint.*

Right: *Create a vacation fantasy by suspending a canopy in the shape of a beach hut over seaside-striped bed linen.*

Above: *A navy-blue painted dresser makes a stunning background for modern blue-and-white china.*

Left: *A wonderfully cluttered harbormaster's office decorated in shades of blue.*

Below: *Painted canvas floorcloths are a traditional and practical floor covering. This one shows a knotted rope design.*

Above: *A useful corner for storing oilskins, boots and hats, ready for wet and windy weather.*

Above: *A room with a view needs very little extra decoration – keep the windows simple and uncluttered.*

Rooms for Living

Make the sitting room the most inviting place in the home. It should be a harmonious, comfortable space that is the center of family life; used for relaxing, playing with the children, entertaining and perhaps even eating.

White is the perfect foil for most colors and creates a neutral and timeless backdrop for furniture and furnishings. Think of white paint washed over brick, tongue-and-groove planking or rough plaster with its straightforward simplicity. Planked wood as a wall or floor surface is both evocative of seaside interiors and visually pleasing. It provides a robust waterproof surface when painted, is interesting to look at and can easily be wiped over with a damp cloth. Salvage yards are often a good source of old wood or floorboards which simply need sanding and sealing or painting.

You can introduce a textural dimension and depth by adopting traditional methods of application such as colorwashing, distressing and aging. Soft, matte seascape colors provide cool, tranquil backgrounds, while bold, luminous colors brushed onto walls with diluted latex paint create an interesting textured finish that is reminiscent of hotter Mediterranean climes.

Whatever background you choose, avid beachcombers and seaside collectors have little difficulty in decorating their home, as their many acquisitions add interest to every corner. Not only do natural displays provide a focal point, but they are also a wonderful conversation piece, bringing vitality to a room. Remember, too, that display areas often work more effectively when collections are grouped according to a theme. Balance complementary and contrasting colors and textures, or assemble objects with a common denominator of provenance, shape or material.

Make the most of every available ray of light, and dress windows, if required, to enhance their architectural interest and beauty. Fabrics such as voiles and muslins allow the maximum light to permeate the room and, if window treatments are kept fairly plain, seashells, twists of straw and rope can all be used to give a little extra definition.

Seashore Surfaces

walls

floors

paving

shutters

wood

plaster

paint

tiles

mosaic

distressed

lime

decking

Beach huts are the ultimate seashore dwellings. Identical and simple in shape, the colors of their faded paintwork give each one a distinctive character. Sturdy white bargeboarding outside and tongue-and-groove matchboarding inside create the snug atmosphere of a ship's cabin. Painted white or colorwashed, the interior looks faintly nautical. A combination of sun-bleached fabrics, weather-beaten furniture and touches of maritime color immediately bring to mind the look of a coastal dwelling. By the sea, the elements take their toll on even the most robust surfaces and materials. Strong winds, sunlight and salt spray gradually distress exteriors to create the weathered effects that are typical of seashore style, and so fashionable in interior design. Wood fades to a ghost of its former self, paintwork peels, metal rusts and fabrics fade softly. Enjoy the subtle gradations of tone, texture and color.

floors

shutters

paving

walls

plaster

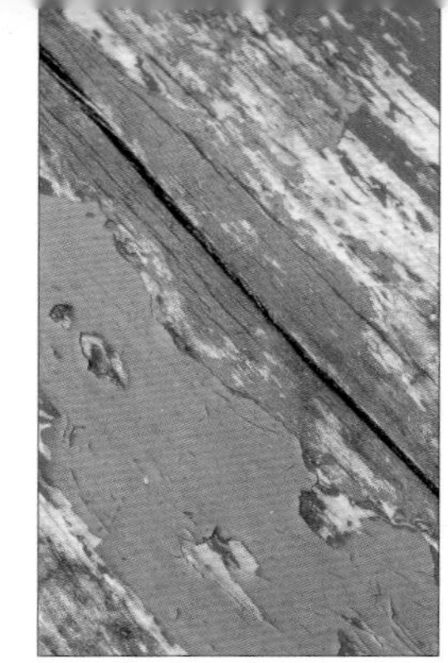

Seashore Surfaces

Walls and floors form the shell of our living space, so it is essential that they create an atmosphere that is both harmonious and comforting. There are many ways of creating a tranquil seashore scheme – the calm neutrality and simplicity of white on white, pale distressed wood, stone and matting are all fine examples. Natural wall treatments have a certain tactile quality that provides an added dimension, from the faintest blush of whitewash over rough plaster to robust matchboard cladding.

Injections of color can provide instant shortcuts to link a room with nature – from the gentle seashore shades of misty blue, gray-green and sand to the earthy ochres, rich terracottas and the vivid aqua-blues that bring the Greek skies and sea right into your home. Paint suppliers offer a staggeringly large range of colors in different finishes. Even a plain matte color painted on the wall can provide an ideal backdrop for a seashore theme.

Broken color and distressed or aging paint can create informal and interesting walls and woodwork. Part of the charm of natural pigments is their soft, slightly patchy look. Like other natural materials, such finishes age well, fading gently in sunlight. However, care should be taken if using organic paints, such as limewash, which is extremely caustic, or distemper, which is chemically incompatible with modern paint. Apply over fresh plaster or onto a surface that has been completely stripped of previous finishes to prevent flaking.

Above: *A simple display of gnarled wood branches contrasts beautifully with the smooth metal surface of an old galvanized bucket.*

Above: *Use a small window to frame a still life of shells or coral.*

Right: *Distressed surfaces work well together. The pot was washed with paint then decorated with string and glass from the beach.*

Above: *The horizontals and verticals of old fencing and weatherboarding suggest ideas for interior woodwork.*

Left: *Soft blue and white is the perfect seaside color scheme. The white daisies give a fresh Scandinavian feel.*

Below left: *This fish mosaic makes a colorful, eye-catching focal point for an otherwise rough or uneven floor.*

Below: *The faded colors and texture on this fishing box and tackle are ideal inspiration for distressing walls or furniture.*

Take time when considering how to treat your flooring, as it acts as the background for furniture and decoration. Wood boards are the perfect foil for a seaside look, as they are long-lasting and take on a beautiful patina with age. Give them a soft pine look with a coat of matte varnish, or create a chalky white finish by applying either liming paste or a wash of diluted latex paint sealed with matte varnish. Although floorboards are warmer and more yielding underfoot than tiles or stone, weathered stone flags do have a timeless quality, and can provide a practical – and hardwearing – solution for areas that connect interior spaces with the outdoors.

Ceramic and mosaic floor and wall tiles now come in an impressive palette of colors and finishes and give surfaces a luminous and interesting quality. One wonderful idea to evoke the seashore is to embed small fragments of tiles, smooth rounded stones, pebbles or shells into wet concrete to create an original design or border of your choosing.

Above right: *Broken shards of blue and turquoise tiles have been set in concrete to make a simple floor surface. Choose harmonious colors, break the tiles into tiny pieces and set in wet concrete. Old china plates can also be used.*

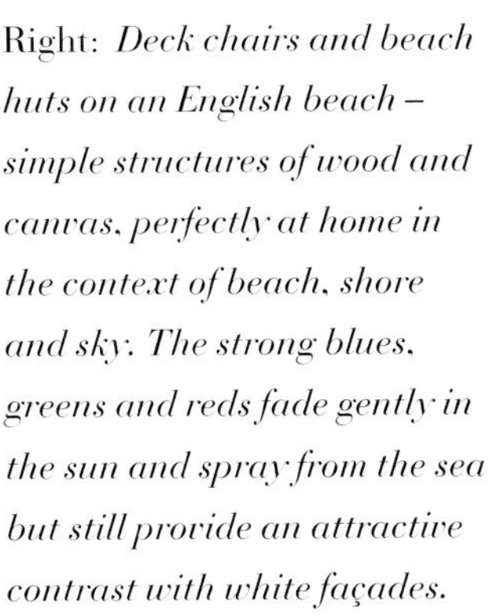

Right: *Deck chairs and beach huts on an English beach – simple structures of wood and canvas, perfectly at home in the context of beach, shore and sky. The strong blues, greens and reds fade gently in the sun and spray from the sea but still provide an attractive contrast with white façades.*

Mediterranean hues: *colorwashed walls*

Use this carefree colorwashing technique to create a wall with a difference. It is ideal for covering large, uneven surfaces quickly and easily, and by choosing colors reminiscent of the sea, an authentic ocean mood can be evoked in no time. Not only can you experiment with color, but you can also try different textures – apply the paint with a sponge, cloth, wallpaper brush, bunch of long feathers or a wide household brush and you will get a different result each time. Pale colors work best on a white or off-white base to give the feeling of a casually applied wash. However, you can achieve a stronger look and more Mediterranean effect, as here, by using a dark shade for your base with an even darker tone over the top.

You will need:

- **Latex paint, in two shades of blue, one slightly darker than the other**
- **Paintbrush**
- **Paint bucket**
- **Natural sponge**
- **Soft cloth (optional)**

1 Apply two coats of the lighter blue to cover the surface totally. Let dry thoroughly.

2 Dilute the darker shade of paint in the proportion 1:1 with water and apply it with a sponge in a circular motion.

3 Rub over the edges with a soft cloth or sponge to avoid seams.

4 Finally, dab paint in areas that are too light or show marks.

Sunbleached: *crackle glaze shutters*

Crackle glaze is an excellent medium for aging new doors, shutters or even furniture. It is easy to apply, and when sealed with a matte varnish it provides a permanent finish with an air of dignified age. The crackle glaze itself should always be applied between two layers of water-based latex paint. This sandwich of paint–glaze–paint allows the surface of the glaze to crack and split, creating a peeled patina reminiscent of aging paint. Once all three layers have been applied, the shutter should be sealed with a natural varnish such as shellac.

YOU WILL NEED:

- **Cloths**
- **Sandpaper**
- **Latex paint, in aqua-green and blue**
- **Paintbrush**
- **Crackle glaze**

1 Dust and clean the wood shutter to prepare it for treatment.

2 Rub down the surface of the shutter with sandpaper to provide a key, then buff it up with a soft cloth.

3 Apply two coats of aqua-green paint to the shutter, letting it dry thoroughly between coats.

4 Apply a thin coat of crackle glaze all over the surface of the shutter and let it dry thoroughly.

5 Water down some blue paint in the proportion 2:1, water to paint, and apply it to the surface. Let dry and crack.

6 Gently sand over the blue paint to distress and to let the crackle glaze and aqua-green paint show through.

Aqua cladding: *tongue-and-groove wall*

Tongue-and-groove boarding is the perfect way to create an instant seashore feeling within your home. It is warm to the touch, architecturally interesting and can conceal walls that are in poor condition. However, do not use this technique on walls that are damp. Boarding or planking can be used throughout the home and, once painted, provides a waterproof surface ideal even for the bathroom. If you do not want to cover walls, then use it on the ceiling where it looks just as attractive. After attaching them, either leave the boards natural, varnish them or paint them in a matte color. Make sure you buy enough boarding to complete the work – if you have to use a few boards from another batch, the machine used to shape the tongues and grooves may not be set to exactly the same tolerance, and the seams might not fit.

You will need:

- **Tape measure**
- **Felt-tip marker**
- **Drill**
- **Hammer**
- **Wall plugs**
- **Level**
- **2 x 1 inch planed or sawed softwood battens**
- **Screwdriver**
- **2 inch screws**
- **Tongue-and-groove boards**
- **Tenon saw**
- **1½ inch panel pins**
- **Hammer**
- **Sandpaper**
- **Latex paint, in two shades of aqua**
- **Paintbrush**
- **Cloth**

1 Measure and mark positions 16 inches apart down the wall for the battens. Drill holes in the wall on the marked positions.

2 Hammer wall plugs into the drilled holes.

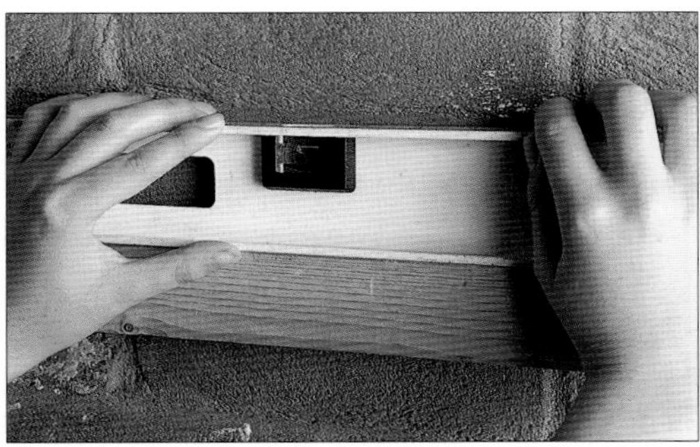

3 Using a level, align each batten to produce a vertical flat plane across the wall.

4 Mark the positions for the screws on the battens and drill the holes.

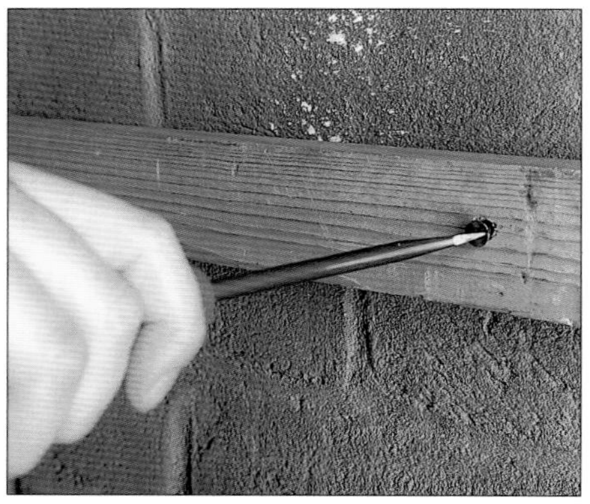

5 Attach the battens firmly to the wall with the screws.

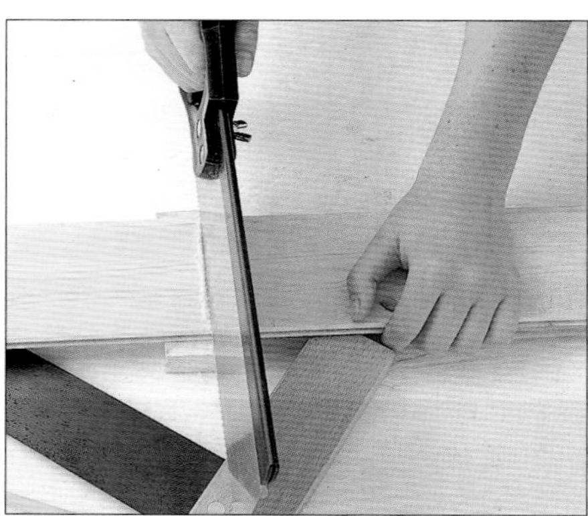

6 Mark out the tongue-and-groove boards with the marker and cut them to length using a tenon saw.

7 With the grooved edge against the left-hand wall, plumb the first board with a level.

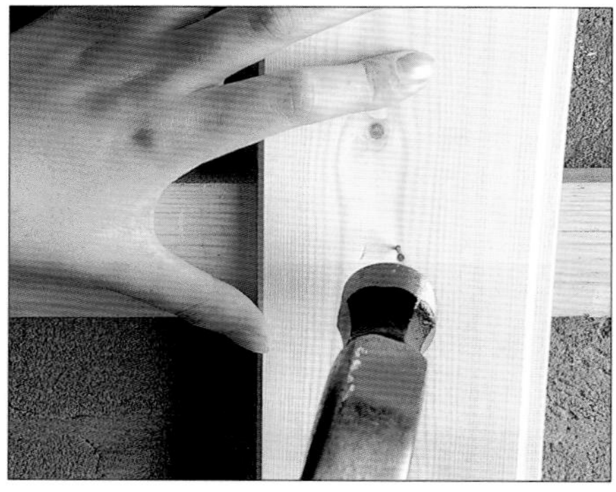

8 Nail the board to the battens through the center of the face using panel pins. Use 1½ inch pins when attaching boards directly to a timber-framed wall.

9 Slide the next board onto the tongue, protecting the edge while you tap it in place with a hammer. Attach the board to the battens: drive a pin through the inner corner of the tongue at an angle. Sink the head below the surface with a hammer. Slide on the next board to hide the wood attachment and repeat to cover the entire wall. Sand the holes until they are even.

10 Dilute a pale aqua latex paint with water in the proportion 1:1 and brush it onto the surface evenly.

11 Wipe off any excess paint with a dry cloth. Let dry thoroughly.

12 Apply a darker shade of aqua by brushing it on in random strokes.

13 Wipe off any excess paint with a soft cloth and let dry thoroughly.

Washed out: *decking and floorboards*

Floorboards are the perfect starting point for a seaside interior, as they bring to mind ships' decking and beach huts. Liming the boards creates a soft, weathered look that is reminiscent of a Scandinavian interior. This effect can also be achieved by simply bleaching the boards and scrubbing them vigorously every time you clean them – this leaves the boards looking fresh, but you must be prepared to scrub them on a regular basis to avoid any staining and darkening. One quick and effective way to whiten boards is to apply a coat of diluted latex paint or a mixture of white pigment and linseed oil. Alternatively, you could sand, then wax or seal the boards (in their natural state) with several coats of matte or gloss transparent sealer. There are, of course, many other ways of decorating floors, such as with checkerboard designs and eye-catching shell-motif borders, so here are a few examples to get you thinking about revitalizing your floors.

Limed Boards

You will need:

- **Wire brush**
- **Liming paste**
- **Fine steel wool**
- **Fine, clear paste wax**
- **Soft cloths**

1 Stroke the floorboards with a wire brush, working gently in the direction of the grain.

2 Apply the liming paste with some fine steel wool, making sure you fill in the grain as you work.

3 Working on one small area at a time, rub the liming paste into the boards in a circular motion. Let dry thoroughly.

4 Remove the excess by rubbing in some clear paste wax with a soft cloth. Buff the surface with a soft cloth to produce a dull sheen. ➤

"Bleached" Boards
(see opposite page)

YOU WILL NEED:

- **Small tube of white zinc pigment or tint**
- **Raw linseed oil**
- **Mixing bowl**
- **Spoon, for mixing paint**
- **Cloth**
- **Matte varnish**
- **Wide paintbrush**

1 Mix the tube of zinc into the linseed oil. About 3¼ pints of the mixture covers 25 square yards.

2 Apply the zinc mixture to the floorboards with a cloth, rubbing against the grain to start with.

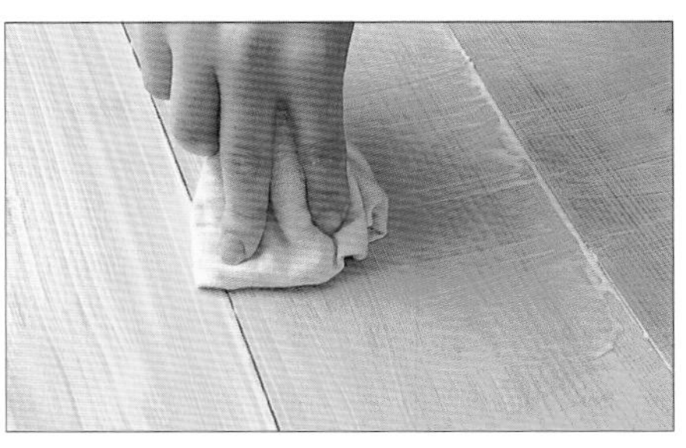

3 Work the mixture into the floorboards, rubbing with the grain. Let dry thoroughly.

4 Seal with a matte natural varnish, or just apply another layer of white zinc when the first treatment wears away.

Whitewashed Boards

YOU WILL NEED:

- **White latex paint**
- **Mixing bowl**
- **Measuring cups**
- **Spoon, for mixing paint**
- **Wide paintbrush**
- **Sandpaper**

1 Dilute the white latex paint with cold water.

2 Using a wide paintbrush, brush the whitewash over the floorboards lightly and evenly. Let dry thoroughly.

3 Finally, rub the surface of the painted floorboards gently with sandpaper to give an aged effect.

Pebble-dashed: *stone and pebble paving*

Pebbles, cobbles and stone have all been used the world over to create beautifully classic yet hardwearing floors. Many floors, such as those found on the Greek islands, are fashioned into incredible mosaic designs. Others, sometimes seen in old houses owned by ships' captains, depict nautical subjects such as an anchor or a ship and compass. The simple checkerboard design here looks stunning in its simplicity and is, in fact, not at all difficult to create. So, forget about the more traditional paving ideas available and try bringing this real feel of the seaside to your feet as you walk about your home.

YOU WILL NEED:

- **Sharp sand**
- **Cement**
- **Straightedge**
- **Tiles**
- **Hammer**
- **Pebbles**
- **Soft brush**
- **Watering can, with a fine spray nozzle**

1 Mix equal quantities of sharp sand and cement. Pour this dry mortar onto the flat surface to be paved. Using a straightedge, level it out until it is smooth. Remove a small quantity so that the mixture does not overflow as you work.

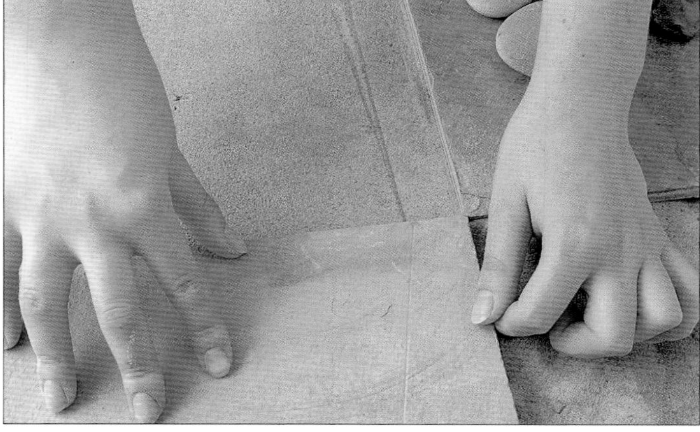

2 Position the tiles, creating alternate squares in a checkerboard effect, making sure they are absolutely square. Hammer them firmly into position and check that once the pebbles are inserted the floor will be level.

3 Arrange your pebbles in a pleasing design, then press them firmly into place. If necessary, hammer them in.

4 Brush dry mortar evenly over the finished surface. Using a watering can, dampen the surface. As the mortar absorbs the moisture, it will set hard.

Seascape Fabrics

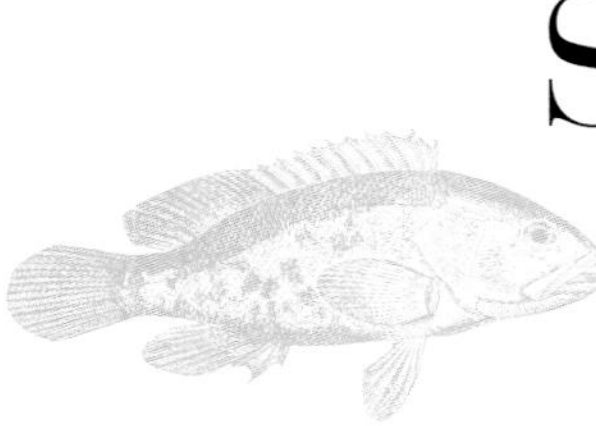

curtains

bed linen

cushions

table linen

embroidered

dyed

painted

muslins

blinds

ginghams

flags

striped

The sound of fabric caught by the wind recalls being on a sailing boat at sea or listening to windsocks in a yacht marina on shore. In summer, leave windows open to the sun and sky, and allow unlined curtains to blow free. Lightweight cottons, voile and muslin will lift gently with the slightest breeze and your spirits will lift with them. Seashore fabrics are best kept simple – natural linens, cottons and canvas, with blue-and-white stripes, or ginghams and checks to give bold accents of pattern. Spacious interiors with predominantly white surfaces can be transformed by judicious spots of color – faded fabrics in washed-out greens, blues and pinks create an atmospheric quality that brings to mind respectively the sea, sky and sun. Modern fabrics incorporating natural fibers such as hemp and raffia fit in well with the seaside theme. For an instant nautical look, fly the flag in royal blue, navy, white and red.

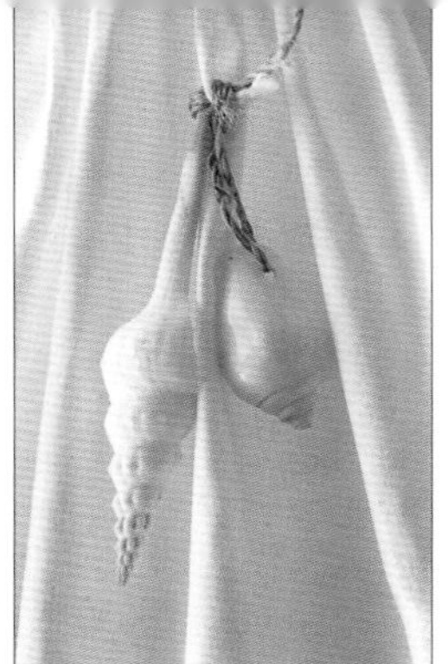

Seascape Fabrics

Natural fabrics such as cotton, canvas, linen and muslin, offer a wide range of textures, weights and finishes to act as a basis for creative work. From the coolness of linen to the translucence of muslin and the firmness of heavier-weight canvas, many different techniques can be used. Fabrics can be fashioned into simple swathed curtains with delicate shell edgings, or constructed into a nautical striped canvas hanging that resembles a ship's awning. Remember that it is often the simpler colors and fabrics that work best.

White linen is timelessly elegant, cool and refreshing and it is beautiful when draped on beds or tables. The popularity of linen has risen enormously over the past few years and, although it is quite expensive, it is a hardwearing fabric, which makes it a perfect choice for curtains, sofa covers and cushions. Pure cotton is the most versatile of all furnishing materials – it is soft, strong, hardwearing and fairly inexpensive, so calico and voile can be used in large quantities. Muslin has been used for centuries as a way of diffusing light, and a swath draped over a pole must be the simplest and easiest of all window treatments. Muslin can simply be tied, looped, clipped or laced onto a pole or rod to make a striking feature of the way it is hung.

Stiffer cottons that block the light, such as cotton duck, canvas or ticking, are equally affordable and hang well. However, they look most attractive when rigged up like sails, lashing the material onto a pole or rod with a rope threaded through eyelets. Chandlers and yachting stores supply a huge range of ropes, pulleys and cleats that can be pressed into service to create an authentic nautical look. Thinking laterally, you can also use other items such as lengths of driftwood or bamboo as poles.

Cushions, chair covers and throws are not essential, but provide an instant way of adding warmth and comfort to a

Left: *Make simple curtains for a bathroom cabinet or window by stitching knots of raffia and string and small shells onto white voile.*

Right: *Mosquito nets give an instant image of romantic tropical shores. Stitch a few delicate starfish and seahorses to the net.*

Left: *A pretty checked duvet cover is left out to air in the warm summer sun and sea breeze on a veranda of a beach house. Soft blue and white cottons are the essence of seashore style. Large checks and ginghams mix well with smaller ones and with stripes.*

room. They are relatively inexpensive to make and are a good starting point for a less experienced dressmaker to work with. Choose your fabrics to correspond with the seasons. In summer, work with whites, aquas and blues, which are reminiscent of seas and skies in tropical climes. In winter, make colors warmer and more comforting with cosy navy-blue blankets and coordinating cushions, or muted blues and greens for soft furnishings. Light fires and lanterns to cast a glorious warm glow over the scene, and don thick fishermen's sweaters and woolly ribbed socks for complete seashore ambience.

One of the simplest ways to add a nautical look to a room is by using cotton flags. Make them into cushion covers or

Above: *Dress up simple muslin curtains with a pretty shell edging. Thread the shells first on a length of wire so they are easy to remove when the curtains are washed.*

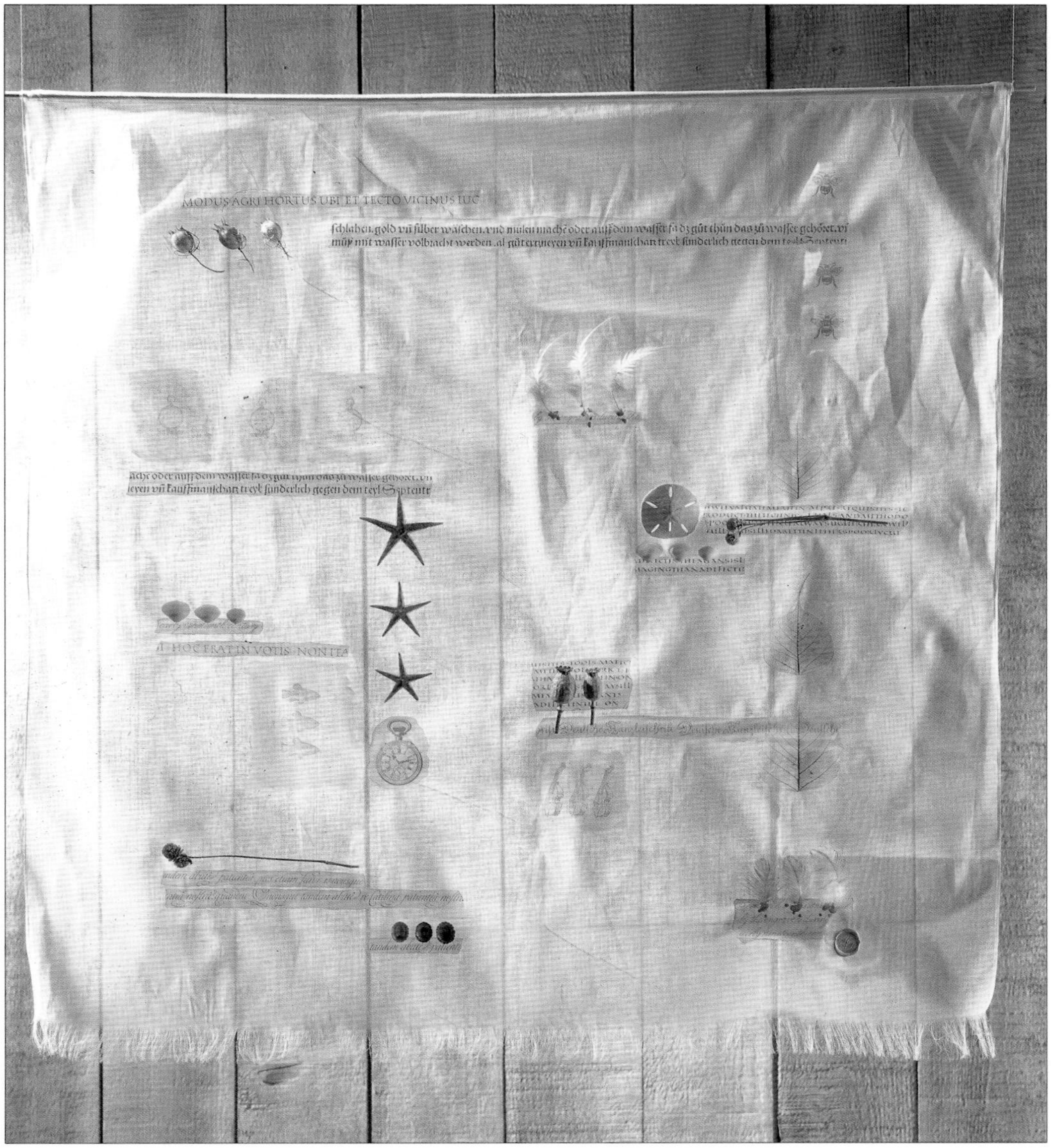

Left: *This ethereal screen is made of stiffened muslin embellished with a combination of shells, starfish, feathers and dried seedheads. The tongue-and-groove wall in the background reinforces the maritime theme.*

sew several flags into a giant patchwork bedspread, backed with blue or red cotton lining. Add a layer of batting in the middle for warmth on chilly nights, if desired. You can also make your own simple flags. Felt is the ideal fabric for these, as it is easy to work with and never frays. Use multi-colored flags to decorate the top of a blind or a cupboard – or as jaunty bunting around a child's room.

Heavy deck-chair canvas comes in many delightful colors, so use it not only for deck chairs but also to cover cushions and director's chairs, or to make blinds. If the fabric piece is not wide enough for your window, then simply attach eyelets down the sides of two separate panels. Lace both panels together to form a larger fabric piece that is not only a more suitable width to function as a blind, but also has a visually interesting central section.

Left: *Multi-colored flags provide startling splashes of color against a clear blue sky and inspiration for interiors—for example, to brighten up a child's room.*

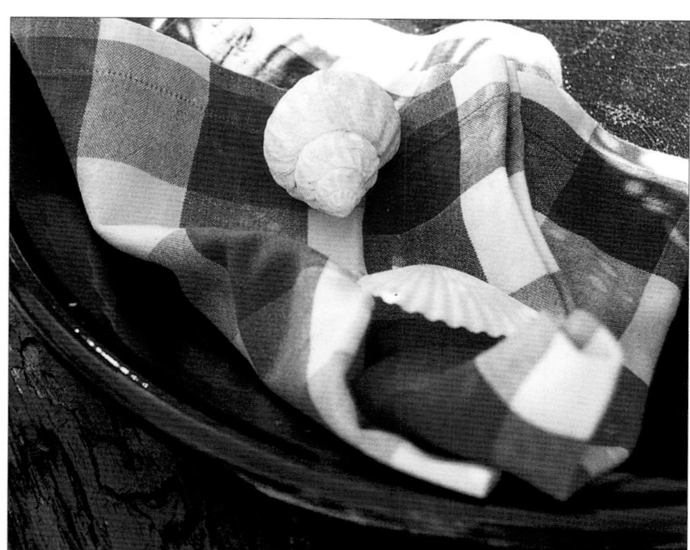

Above: *Blue-and-white fabrics look wonderful bleached by strong sunlight. The effect is very Scandinavian.*

Left: *A royal-blue and white striped towel spells instant summer-by-the-seaside, even in the most suburban bathroom.*

Right: *Give cushions a bold nautical look by inserting brass rivets at regular intervals around the edges and threading them with white cord or rope. Make the holes in minutes with a hole punch.*

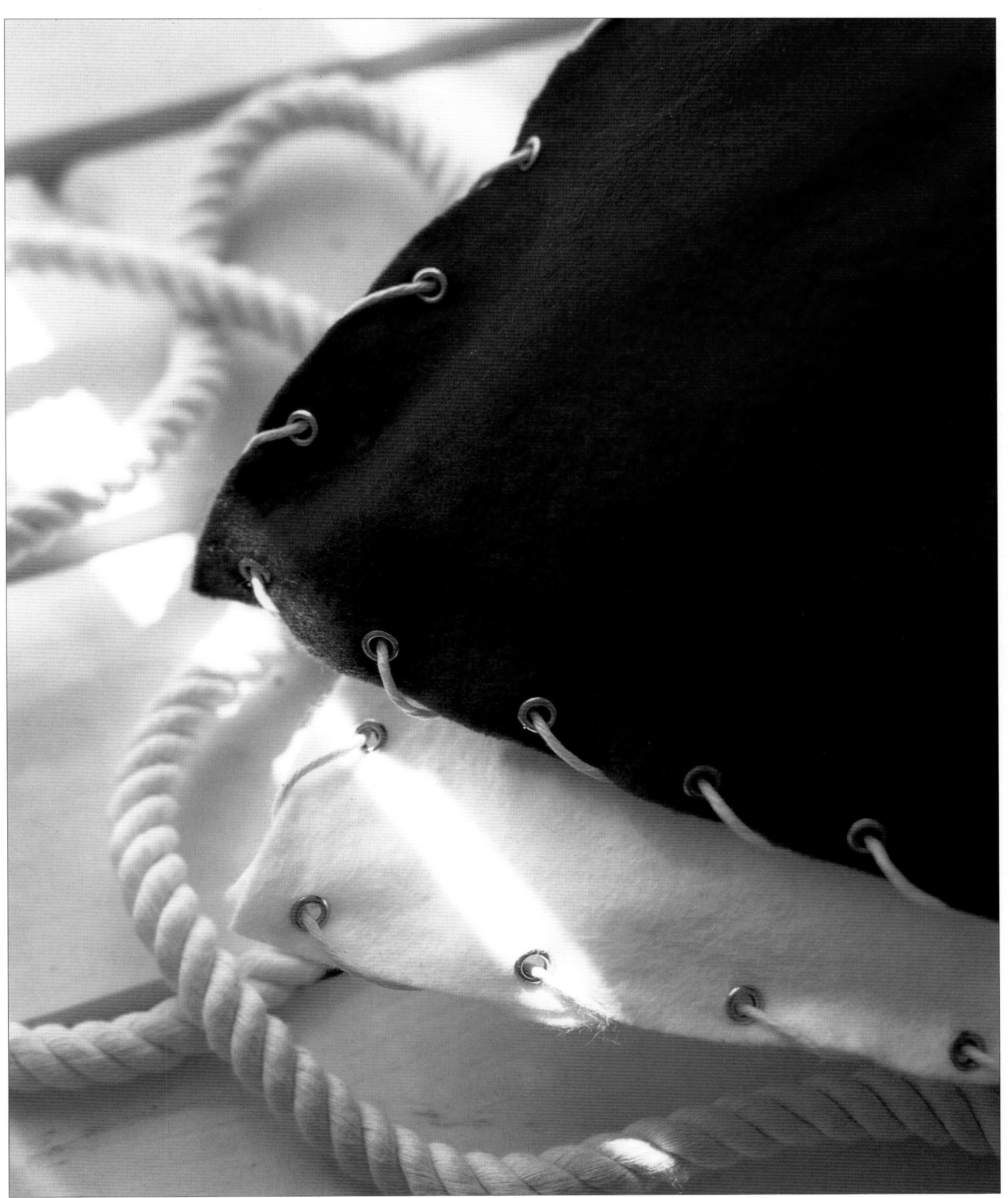

Shoreline dining: *shell and driftwood tablecloth*

Transform a crisp linen cloth into a three-dimensional work of art by adorning it with tiny bundles of driftwood and delicately colored shells. This tablecloth creates a beautiful setting for an outdoor dinner party on a summer's evening, and is bound to remind all guests of happy times by the sea. All the adornments are wired on so they can be removed easily when the cloth needs washing. As a stunning centerpiece for your table, mussel shells filled with wax and used as candles are hard to beat. Or fill a large glass dish with water, place white shells and stones at the bottom and float candles or flowers on the top for a romantic setting. As a *pièce de résistance*, make an ice bowl with tiny shells set within the ice and fill with shrimps, prawns or even oysters for a real seafood treat.

You will need:
- **Pieces of driftwood**
- **Craft knife**
- **Jute string**
- **Jeweler's wire**
- **Scissors**
- **Glue gun and sticks**
- **Shells**
- **Drill (optional)**

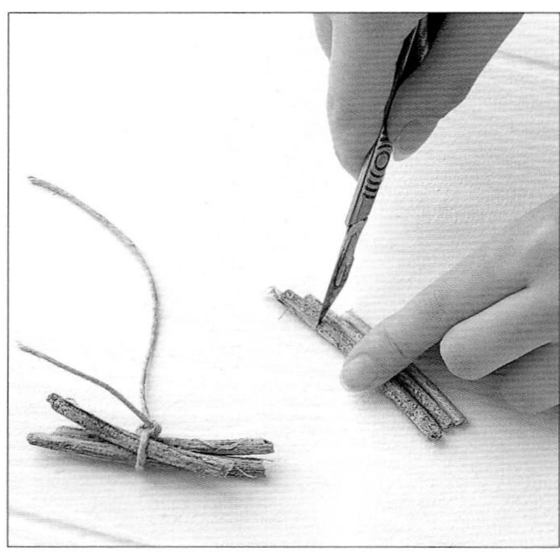

1 Cut the driftwood to length with a craft knife, about 1½–2 inches.

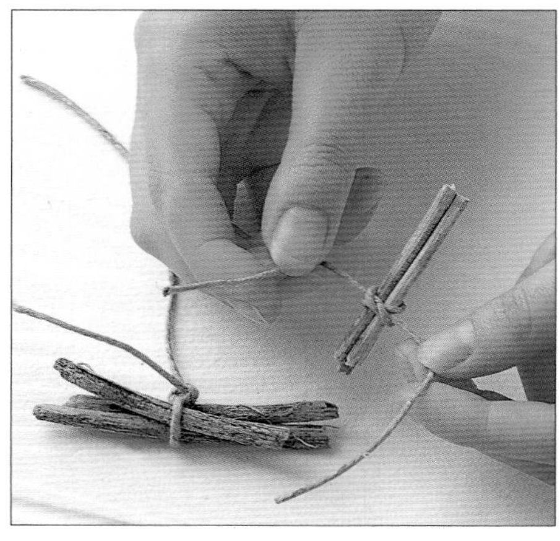

2 Tie the lengths in small bundles with jute string and knot tightly to hold them firm.

3 Take the jeweler's wire and cut it into 2½ inch lengths.

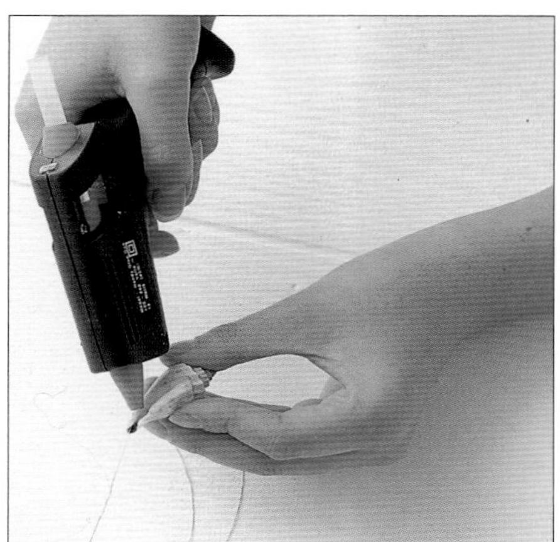

4 Using a glue gun, place a spot of glue onto a shell and press the jeweler's wire firmly into position, until the glue sets and the wire has bonded firmly with the shell.

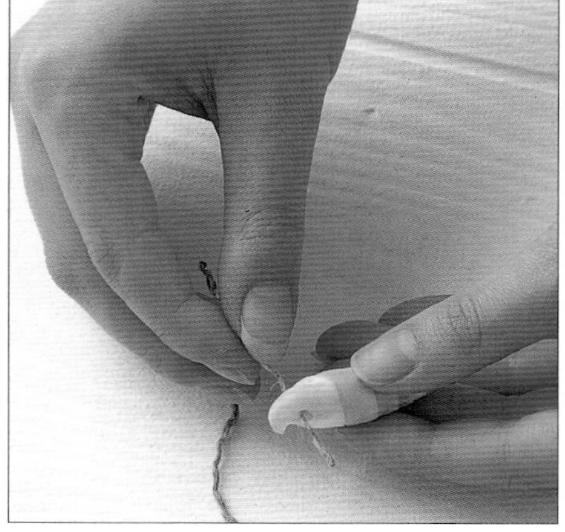

5 If the shells are pre-drilled, or if you have drilled them yourself, a piece of string can be threaded through and knotted in the same way as the driftwood bundles.

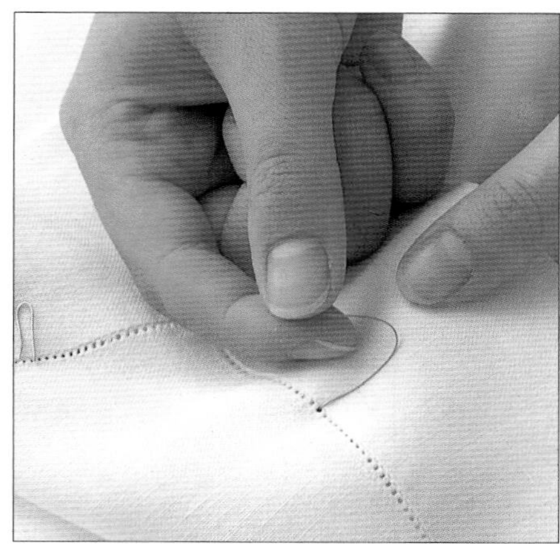

6 To attach the bundles and shells with string to the cloth, thread a piece of wire under the string and secure it firmly. Thread the wire through the piquéed edge and wind into a "U" shape to hold it firm.

Seafarers' luggage: *duffel bag*

A perennial favorite, the duffel bag is reminiscent of seafaring folk leaving the safety of the land for their travels and adventures on the water. Here, a hardwearing white cotton drill is decorated with small strips of driftwood gathered from along the shore. Canvas makes a good alternative fabric. Choose a color that suits your taste – a deep navy, vibrant red or the vivid turquoise and aqua-blues of hotter climes would all work just as well as a brilliant white or soft cream. All age groups love this kind of bag, and you will soon find that everybody is excited to fill it with their personal treasures as they head for the beach during the long days of the summer months.

YOU WILL NEED:

- **Plate**
- **Cotton drill or canvas**
- **Pencil or tailor's chalk**
- **Scissors**
- **Tape measure**
- **Dressmaker's pins**
- **Needle and matching thread**
- **Eyelet pack**
- **Hammer**
- **Masking or yachting tape**
- **Cord**
- **Piece of driftwood**

1 Decide what size you want your bag to be. To make the base, draw around a plate onto your fabric, using a pale pencil or tailor's chalk. Cut out the shape, allowing ⅝ inch for the seam.

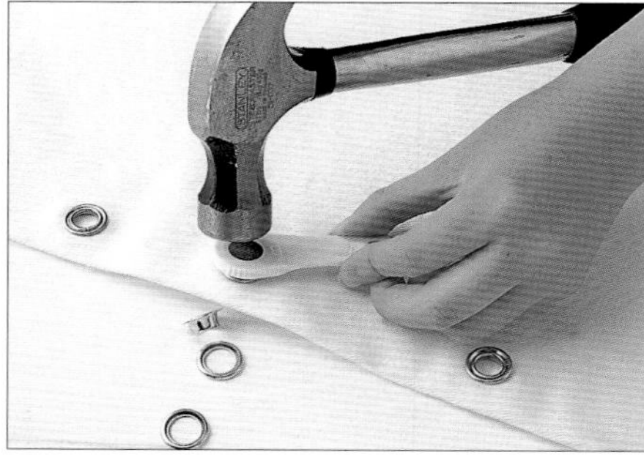

2 Measure out the side of the bag to give the depth you want, again allowing for seams and a top turnover, and cut it out. Turn over the top of the bag, pin it down and hem along it. Mark evenly spaced positions for the eyelets. Attach the eyelets along the top hem and hammer into place.

3 Next, make a small cotton or canvas tag on the base of the bag to hold the drawstring cord.

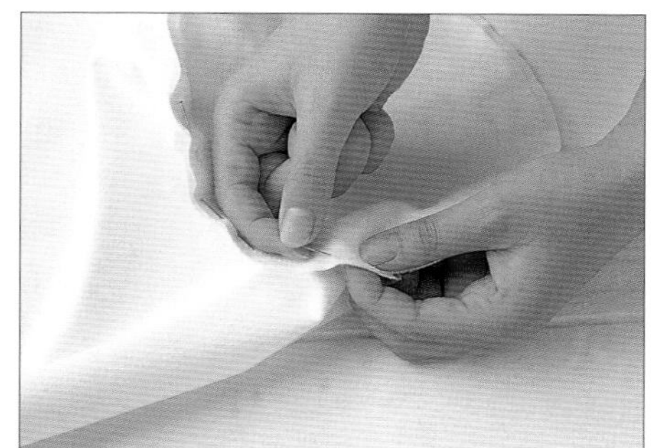

4 Pin, baste and sew the base of the duffel bag to the side.

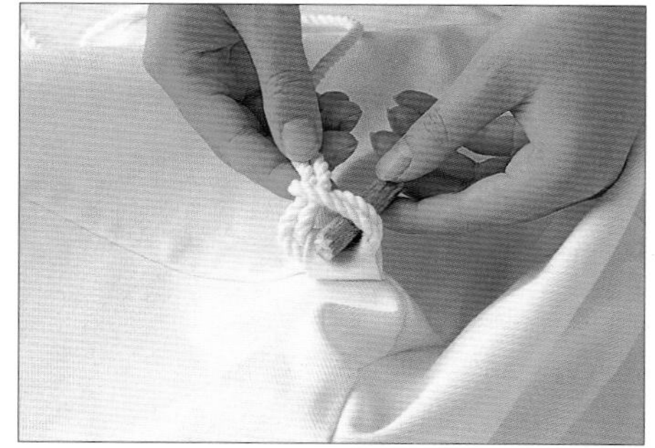

5 Fasten masking or yachting tape to the end of the cord to prevent it from fraying. Fold the cord in half and loop through the tag. Thread the two ends through the loop and pull it up in a hitch knot to secure it firmly to the tag. Poke the driftwood piece through the knot.

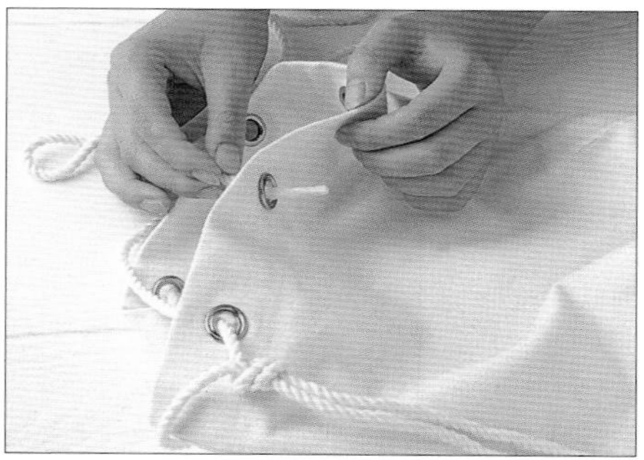

6 Knot the pieces of rope at the top of the bag before threading them through the eyelets. Thread the rope through all the eyelets to complete the drawstring.

Seaside stripes: *beach hut curtain and cushions*

This is a wonderfully simple hanging that can be adapted to suit any room or decorative style. Here, a striped canvas is hung from a bamboo pole to hide deck chairs and other beach paraphernalia from view. Alternatives include using calico for a sitting room, muslin for a bedroom, ginghams for a kitchen and a cheerful striped deck-chair fabric for a child's room. In order to see the hanging clearly, fullness of fabric is not required, so the project is extremely economical. Stylish buttoned cushions scattered casually through the room coordinate with the canvas hanging to complete the fresh beach hut style.

Curtain

YOU WILL NEED:

- **Tape measure**
- **Canvas**
- **Scissors**
- **Dressmaker's pins**
- **Needle and basting thread**
- **Matching sewing thread**
- **Dressmaker's pencil**
- **Eyelet pack**
- **Hammer**

1 Measure the width and drop of your window or area you wish to curtain off and cut the fabric to size. Turn under a 2-inch hem on the top and bottom. Pin, tack and sew using two lines of stitching.

2 Measure 1 inch in from either edge at the top of the curtain and mark the position for the first eyelets. Divide the remaining width of fabric into regular intervals for the eyelets, allowing about 5 inches of space between each one. Mark the positions.

➤

3 Attach the eyelets, following the manufacturer's instructions.

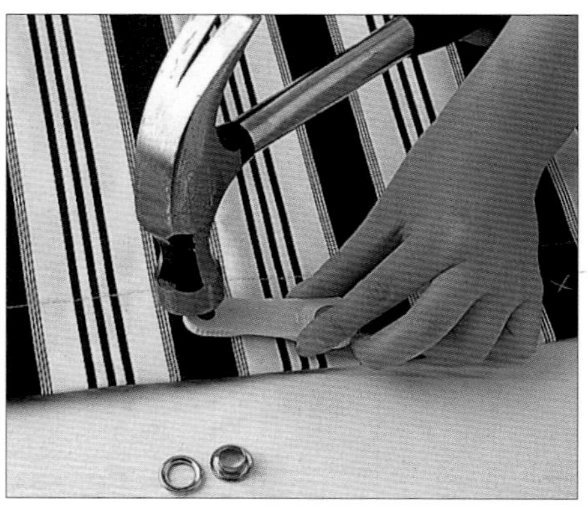

4 On a flat surface, hammer the eyelets firmly into place.

Striped Cushions *(see opposite page, front)*

YOU WILL NEED:

- **Scissors**
- **Fabric**
- **Tape measure**
- **Cushion pads**
- **Needle and matching thread**
- **Velcro tabs**
- **Buttons**

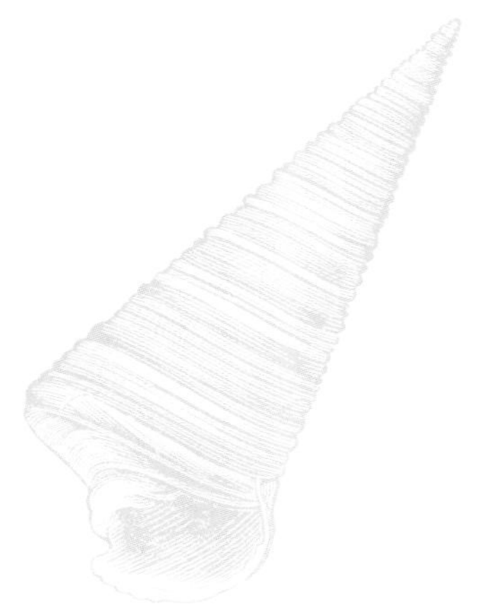

1 Cut a length of fabric two-and-a-half times the length of the cushion, plus a seam allowance. Fold over the fabric for twice the length of the cushion pad, leaving the extra half-length for the flap. Sew the seams.

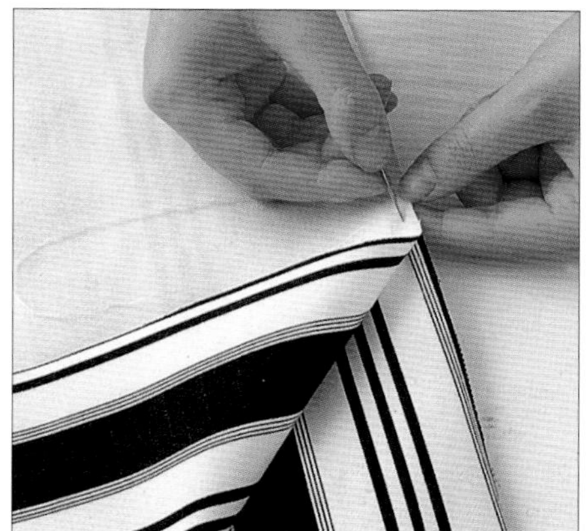

2 Sew down both edges of the flap and trim the corners. Attach Velcro tabs along the length.

3 Sew buttons along the outside of the cushion flap. Insert the cushion pad, then turn the flap over and fasten with Velcro.

Button Cushions *(see right, back)*

You will need:

- **Tape measure**
- **Cushion pads**
- **Fabric**
- **Scissors**
- **Needle and matching thread**
- **1 yard cotton tape, ⅝ inch wide**
- **Buttons**

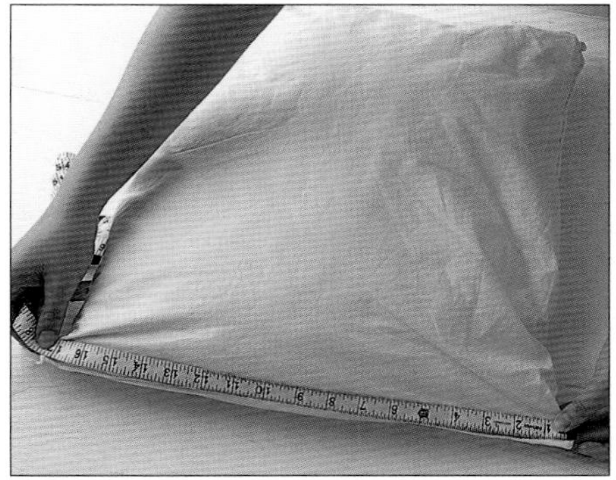

1 Measure the cushion pad and cut the fabric to size. You need twice the length plus 1-inch seams and once the width plus ⅝-inch side seams.

2 Turn under a hem at each end of the fabric and sew along on the right side. Pin the tape in place.

3 Baste and sew the tape in position on the right side.

4 With wrong sides together, fold the fabric in half and attach the side seams.

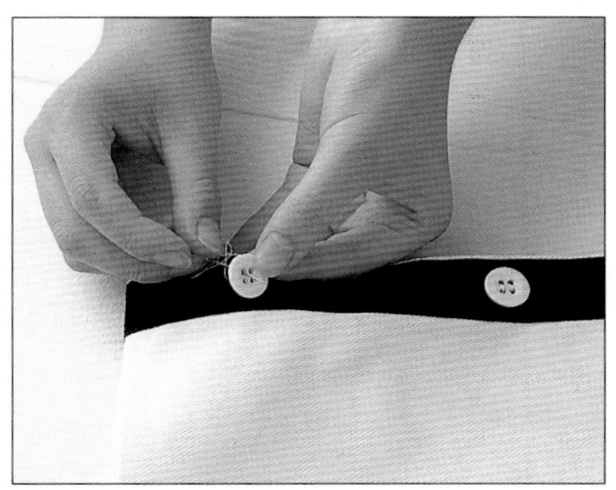

5 Mark positions for the buttons and sew them in place.

Ocean blue: *dyed linens*

Using dyes must be one of the quickest, easiest and most fun ways of transforming a piece of fabric. Dyes can refresh tired whites and pale colors and revitalize jaded and worn clothes and linens. Instead of casting out your old favorites, just apply a bit of imagination and some fabric dye and before you know it you will have created a whole new look. Here, a piece of muslin is tie-dyed to give it the pretty aqua color of the ocean stretching into the distance. Coordinating cushions are dyed to match. If you want to create a darker ocean feel in your home, choose a dark blue dye and imitate the ambience of a more dramatic shoreline.

YOU WILL NEED:

- **Muslin**
- **Needle and matching thread**
- **String**
- **Fabric dye**
- **Glass bead or marble (optional)**

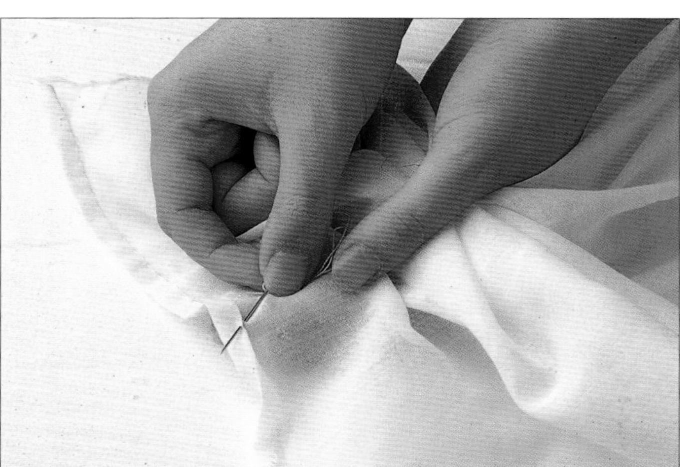

1 Turn under a double hem and slip stitch around the muslin to neaten the edges.

2 On a flat surface, fold the hemmed muslin fabric in half, then fold it in half again.

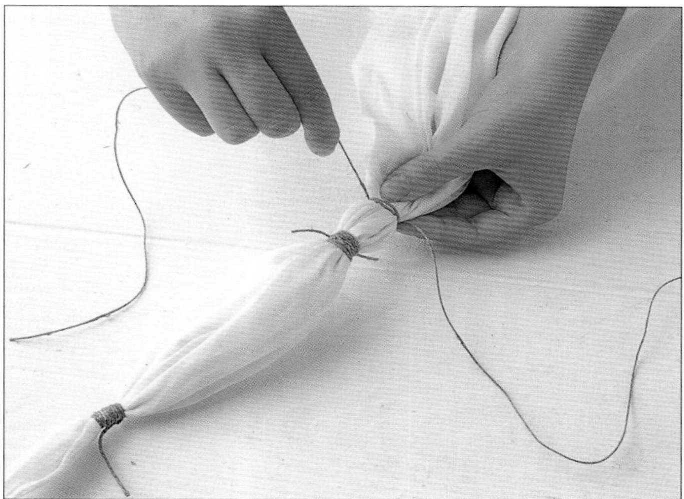

3 Taking the center point of the folding, squeeze the muslin together tightly and bind around it with string so when the fabric is dyed, these areas (which will form circles) will be paler. Dye the fabric following the manufacturer's instructions.

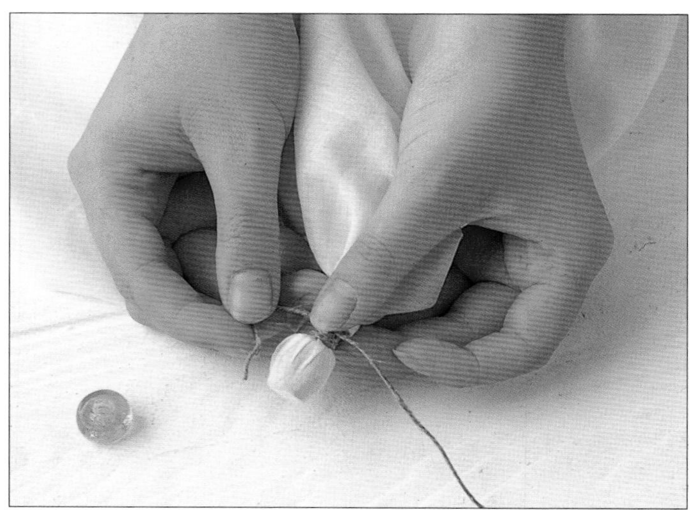

4 To make smaller circles, tie a glass bead or marble into the corners and bind around tightly before dyeing.

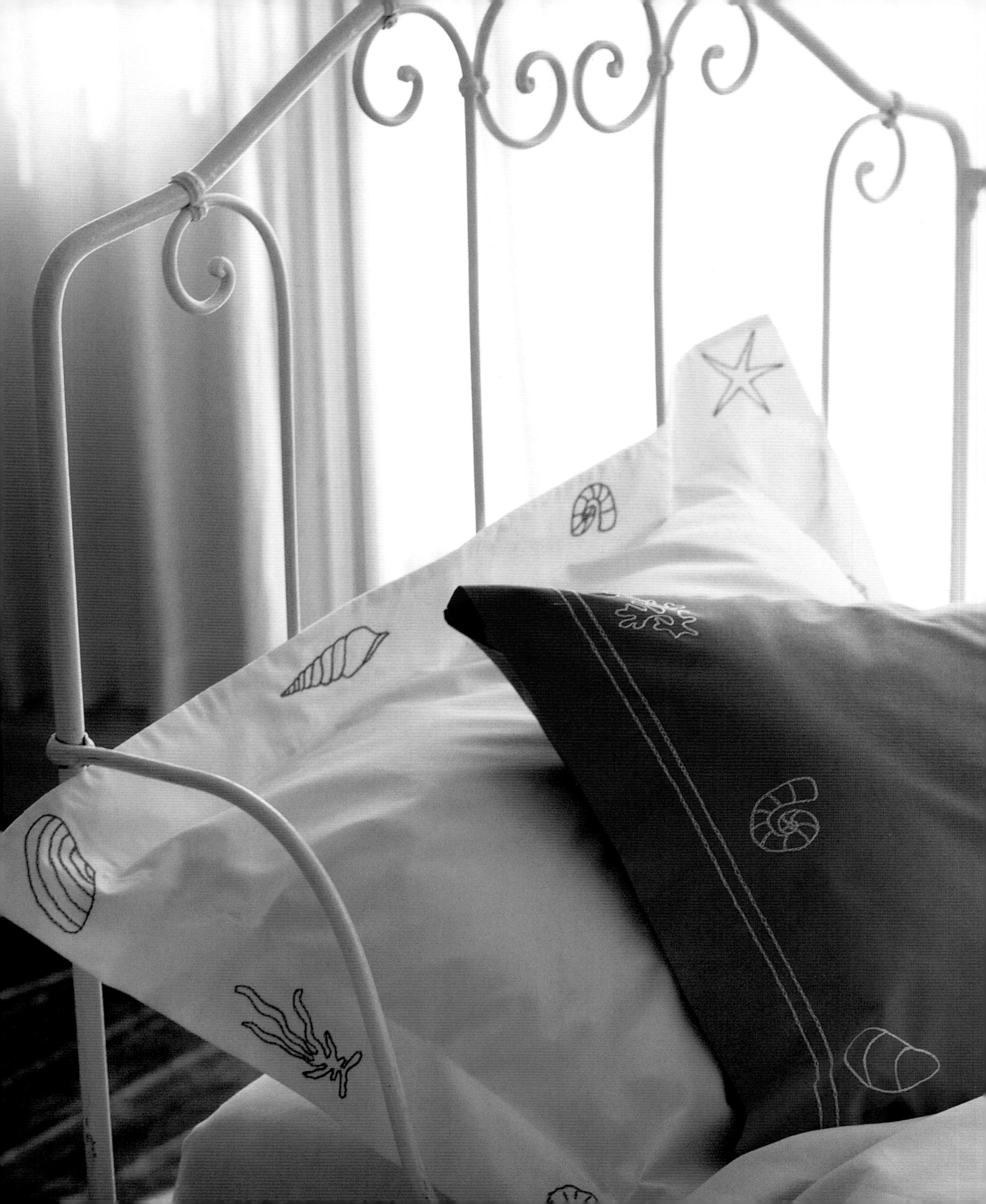

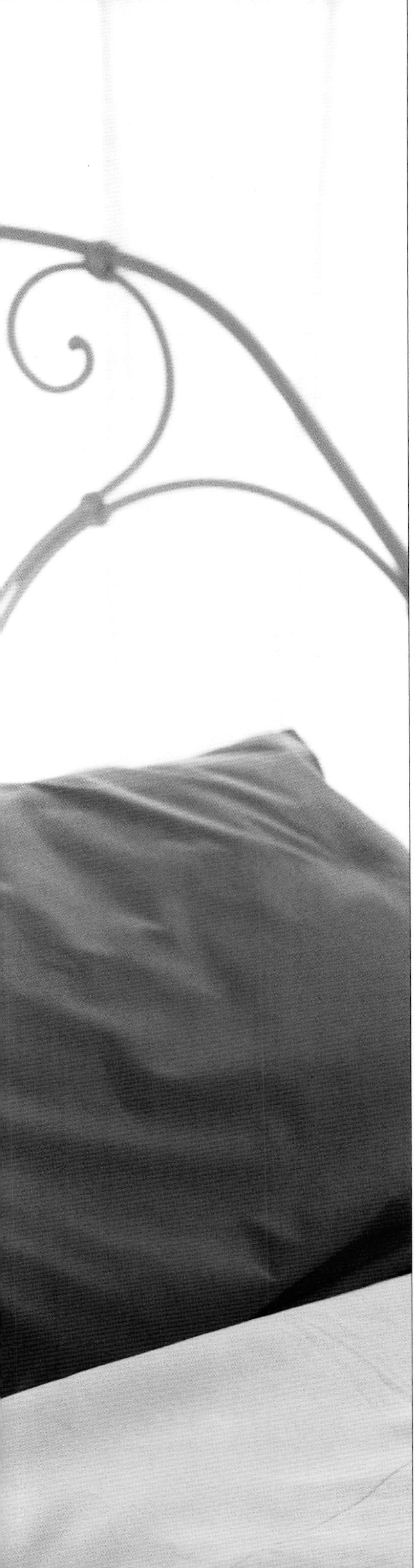

Seashore dreams: *embroidered pillowcases*

Fall asleep to the sound of the seashore with pillowcases that are guaranteed to evoke blue skies, drifts of clouds, and waves with tiny foaming edges. The co-ordinating blue-and-white scheme is gloriously fresh; a chain stitch and a single strand of thread give a deliciously delicate feel to the embroidery of the sea creatures and shells adorning the pillowcases. Use a shade of deep sky-blue on the crispest of white linens and set off the blue of the other pillowcase with snowy white stitching. Keep an eye out for pictures of shells, fish, mermaids or even lighthouses with which to decorate your pillows and experiment with different sizes to see whether you prefer a single image in one corner, a border around the edge of the pillowcase or perhaps one image in the center of the pillowcase.

You will need:

- **Pencil**
- **Thin cardboard**
- **Tracing paper**
- **Pillowcase**
- **Scissors**
- **Dressmaker's pins**
- **Dressmaker's carbon paper**
- **Dressmaker's pencil**
- **Needle and embroidery floss**
- **Ruler**
- **Cord (optional)**

1 Copy the templates from the back of the book onto cardboard, or trace your own.

2 Scale the images up or down to suit the size of your pillowcase design.

3 Copy the images onto tracing paper and cut them out. Arrange them around the edge of the pillowcase until the desired effect is achieved. ➤

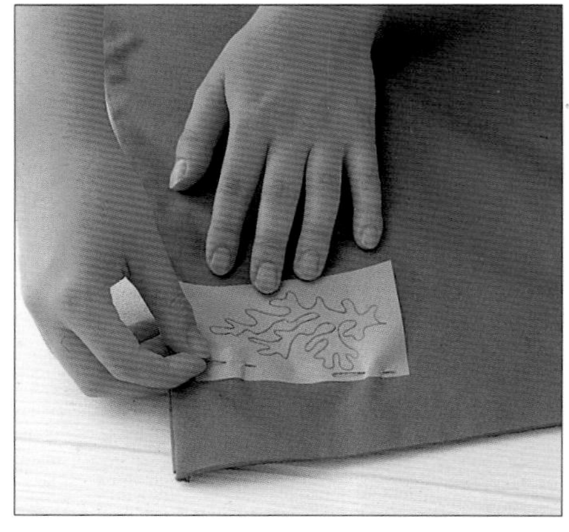

4 Pin the pieces of tracing paper in place once you are happy with the design.

5 Next, pin sheets of dressmaker's carbon paper under the tracing paper in the marked positions.

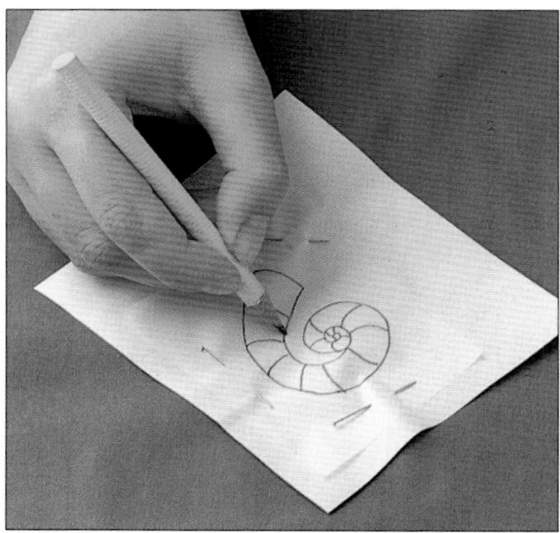

6 Trace over the images with a dressmaker's pencil to leave a clear outline on the fabric.

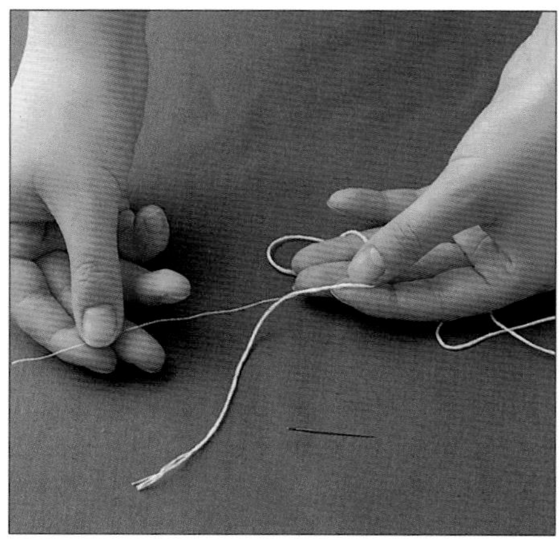

7 Separate your embroidery floss into single strands to work the chain stitch.

8 Start the chain stitch by making a loop and pushing the needle into the fabric on the line of the image.

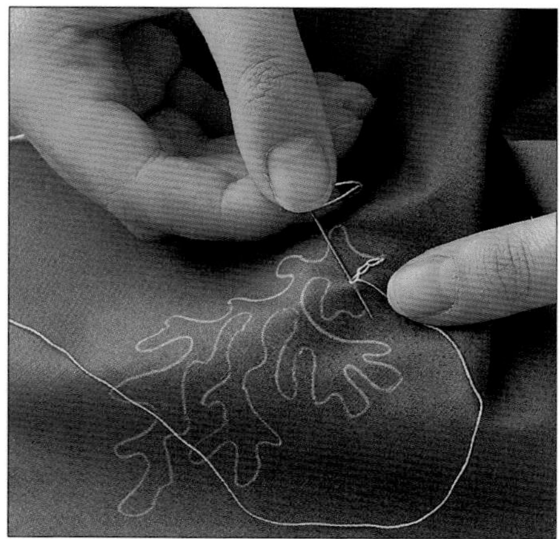

9 Push through into the center of the loop, following the line of the image.

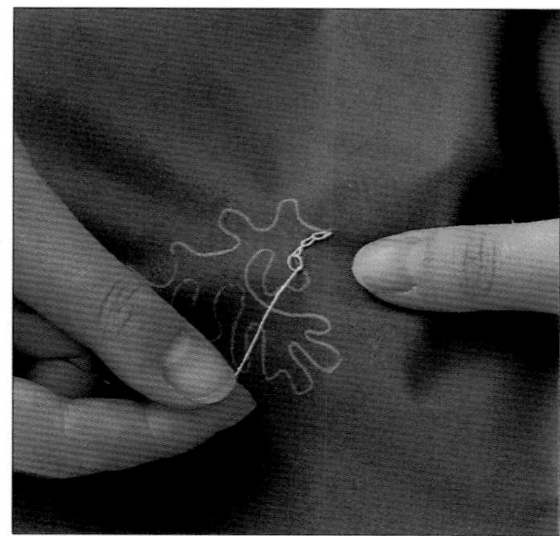

10 Pull the thread taut. Always try to keep stitch lengths and tautness of thread even throughout the embroidery.

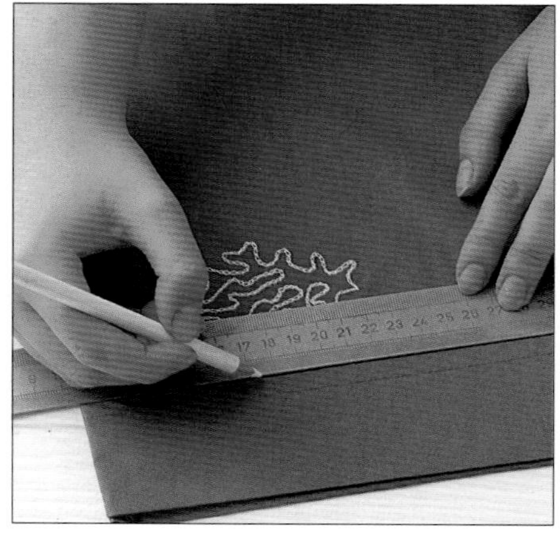

11 Mark an edging with a ruler for the top of the pillowcase.

12 Finish the edge of the pillowcase with a simple line of cord or with a double row of chain stitch.

Blue and white: *bench cushion*

This novel idea transforms everyday dish towels into a wonderfully comfortable padded seat. The crisp white and blue colors are evocative of the seaside, and they give a truly fresh feel to these generous cushions. This technique is used on mattresses in many countries, such as Greece, where they are often filled with cotton or natural horsehair. However, a cheaper and just as effective alternative is batting or wads of cotton. Once you have made your cushion, experiment with it: use it indoors or out, or make a few cushions and stack them on a window recess to make an inviting seat.

YOU WILL NEED:

- **2 cotton dish towels**
- **Scissors**
- **Dressmaker's pins**
- **Needle and basting thread**
- **Batting**
- **Matching cotton thread**
- **6-inch pieces of embroidery floss**
- **Quilting needle**

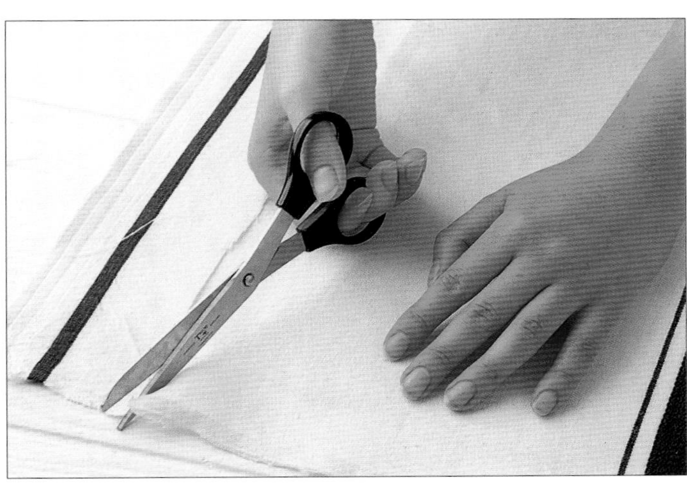

1 Cut one dish towel down to form the base of the cushion cover. The other dish towel forms the top and sides.

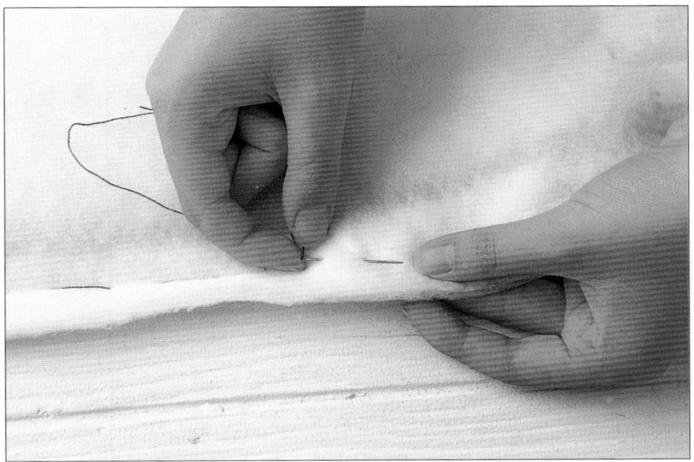

2 Pin and baste a thin layer of batting to the wrong side of both dish towels.

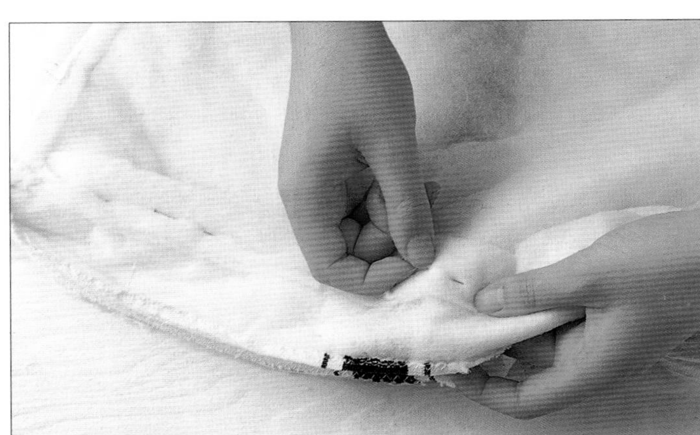

3 Put the dish towels right sides together and sew the top section to the bottom section. Leave a gap open at one end so it can be filled with batting.

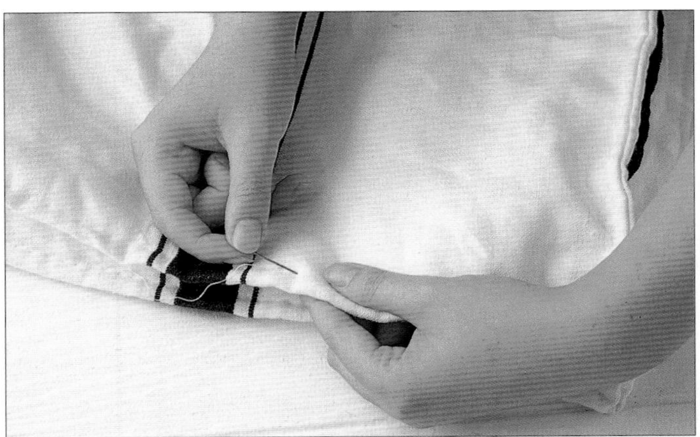

4 On the right-hand side, make a seam allowance of ¾ inch by pinching 1 inch of fabric into a raised section. Pin, baste, fill the cushion with batting and sew with a running stitch. ➤

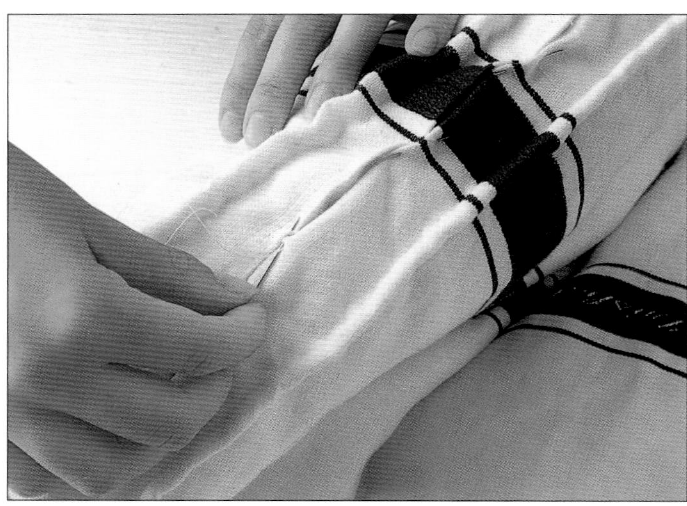

5 Fill with batting and stitch the opening closed.

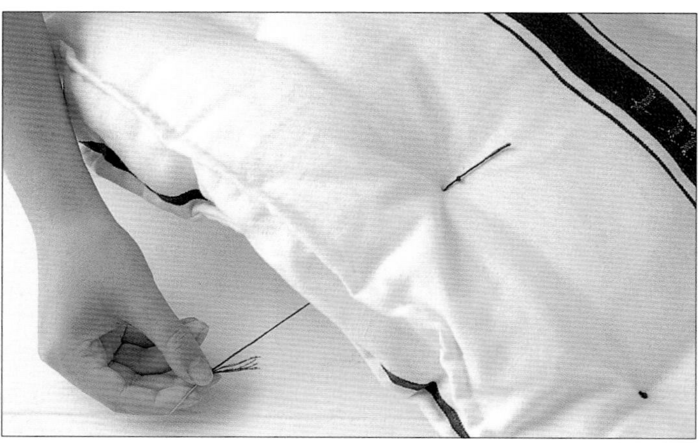

6 Mark the positions of the quilting points on the top and bottom of the cushion. Double knot the embroidery floss at the end and thread it onto a thick quilting needle. At each of the marked quilting points, thread right through the cushion.

7 Double back the thread through the cushion and knot again. Attach decorative knots on the top with a small stitch.

Watery motifs: *shower curtain*

Give your shower room a feel of the great outdoors with this refreshing scene of starfish, shells and seaweed swaying gently, as though rocked by an ocean current. The clear shower curtain provides a watery backdrop for you to create your very own seaside mood with whatever marine motifs you choose. The example shown here uses a monochromatic, crisp scheme, but you could work equally well with warm, bright, vivid colors to give the project a lively Mediterranean feel.

YOU WILL NEED:

- **Pencil**
- **Paper**
- **Clear plastic shower curtain**
- **Scissors**
- **Masking tape**
- **White waterproof paint**
- **Paintbrush**

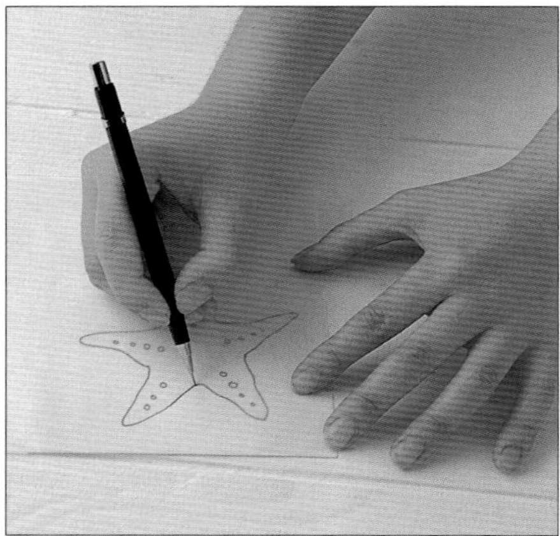

1 Copy the templates from the back of the book or, alternatively, trace your own design onto paper.

2 Reduce or enlarge the images to fit your chosen design for the shower curtain.

3 Cut out the paper templates or designs and arrange them on the shower curtain as desired.

4 Position the paper templates on a large tabletop in the desired pattern and secure them in place with masking tape. Use a table with a tough surface that will not be harmed by the masking tape.

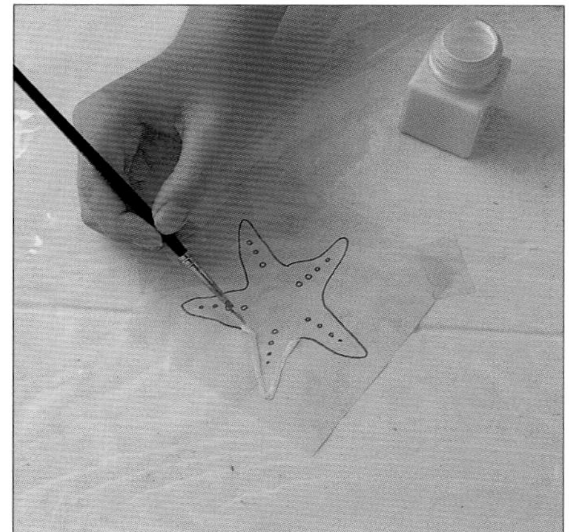

5 Place the shower curtain on top of the images and tape it down firmly. Using white waterproof paint, carefully paint the images onto the shower curtain surface. Let dry thoroughly before hanging up.

Seaside Furniture

shelves chairs tables mosaics rope timber storage bedheads string wicker pallets planks

Beachcombing is the inspiration and the theme when you decide to furnish a room in seashore style. Steamer trunks and wicker laundry hampers have an evocative seafaring charm and serve as flexible storage containers for bedding, blankets or toys. Planks of reclaimed timber and driftwood make rugged chairs and cupboards, full of character. Hunt through thrift stores and junkyards for old furniture, floorboards, wood crates and pallets, all of which can be stripped and varnished or painted. Alternatively, you can imitate the beautiful silvers and whites of aged, weatherworn wood by distressing modern furniture. Transform a damaged or dull tabletop with a painted shell design, or collect real shells and use them to create a richly encrusted surface. Authentic seashore-style chairs are those specifically designed for lazy days in the sun – wicker chairs, director's chairs and, of course, traditional deck chairs with striped canvas.

Seaside Furniture

The simple elegance of wood and whitewash is a timeless solution for seaside homes where mismatched pieces of furniture work well against a backdrop of single-color walls and flooring. One or two well-chosen pieces from different periods can blend happily with thrift-store finds and serve as the foundation for a spontaneous and personal look.

Wood cane and wicker both have a warm, tactile quality – distressed director's chairs make wonderful outdoor or indoor seating, while wood dining tables, rattan side tables, wicker hampers and wood trunks all help create the sort of unselfconscious, informal arrangements that evoke an easy, natural environment.

Furniture made from reclaimed timber can be elegant as well as kind to the environment, and one way of guaranteeing yourself such an individual product is to patronize the work of young furniture designers who use natural materials such as driftwood in their contemporary pieces. Commissioning a piece of furniture is not necessarily expensive, and being involved in the whole process, perhaps even specifying the materials and giving pointers to the possible design, is bound

Above: *Transform a nest of tables, purchased at a thrift store, with a layer of seashells. The long razor shells make a perfect edging.*

Left: *Paint a simple metal tabletop with a shell design, then wash over the top to give a faded look. Varnish the surface to protect it.*

Right: *Reclaimed timber makes a wonderfully stocky cupboard. Leave the original weatherworn tones of the wood or paint it in bright primary colors.*

Above: *This half-chair, half-sculpture, made from driftwood and fencing, suits this outdoor setting but would look equally striking in a spacious modern interior.*

Below: *The subtle shades of worn painted timbers blend beautifully. To achieve this effect on new painting, sand back to the wood in areas.*

Left: *This elegant Edwardian-style structure is a windbreak-and-awning in one. It rolls up for easy transport.*

Right: *Director's chairs are the upscale version of the traditional folding deck chair. They are stylish enough to use indoors.*

to increase your appreciation of a piece as well as giving you the satisfaction of supporting individual artisans.

Mosaic makes a wonderful surface on furniture, and the palette of colors available in this art is exquisite. Either commission a mosaic artist to fashion a pictorial design for you, or choose something much more simple and use the technique to create your own piece.

If you are an amateur carpenter, then rough wood pallets can come into their own without too much difficulty – craft them into interesting headboards and pretty shelves. Search

Below: *Wicker chairs also look equally good indoors or out. Add a large comfortable cushion embroidered with a nautical motif.*

Above: *The reclaimed timbers in this striking wardrobe have been simply used as they are, complete with nails sticking out.*

Left: *This unusual kitchen cupboard has cathedral-style decorative doors, but inside the shelves are very practical.*

Right: *Even a grandfather-style clock can be made from odd pieces of wood, giving a new twist to an old look.*

junkyards, thrift stores and flea markets for interesting pieces of furniture that can be renovated. Just strip away any previous coats of paint or varnish, then oil or wax the wood. Finish them off with a wash of water-based paint for a matte distressed effect, or apply a wash of white paint tinted with ochre to produce a faded chalky finish. Alternatively, you could apply sea-greens, blues and soft reds with their cheerful appeal reminiscent of faded beach houses, boats and fishing nets.

To enliven tired wicker furniture, paint it pure brilliant white – this is most definitely a color that will remind you of seashore verandas and the simple, clean lines of beach huts. You can find old chairs and other creaking wicker pieces at thrift or antique stores.

Stack old tea chests, open ends facing out, for an instant storage unit, or turn them upside down for a makeshift table. In addition, you can use their wood to craft a small cupboard.

Flotsam storage: *packing-crate shelves*

These charmingly rustic shelves are created from a cast-off pallet but you could use an orange crate. Pallets can be picked up easily and very cheaply at lumberyards, or you might even find an abandoned one for free at a dump or by a trash can. The charm of these shelves is that they have a rather naive quality, so there is no need to worry if the edges are a bit rough or uneven – that is all part of the effect. To finish off the shelves, wash them with a diluted latex paint in the color scheme of your choice: Try strong Mediterranean colors for a child's bedroom or a bathroom or a soft gray-blue for a sophisticated touch of the American east coast. The end result is the ideal storage solution for toiletries in the bathroom, an array of spices in the kitchen, or seashore finds such as shells and pebbles in a child's room.

You will need:

- **Pallet or orange crate**
- **Ruler**
- **Pencil**
- **Saw**
- **Wood glue**
- **Hammer**
- **Nails**
- **Sandpaper**
- **Length of square-edged dowel**
- **Drill (optional)**
- **String (optional)**

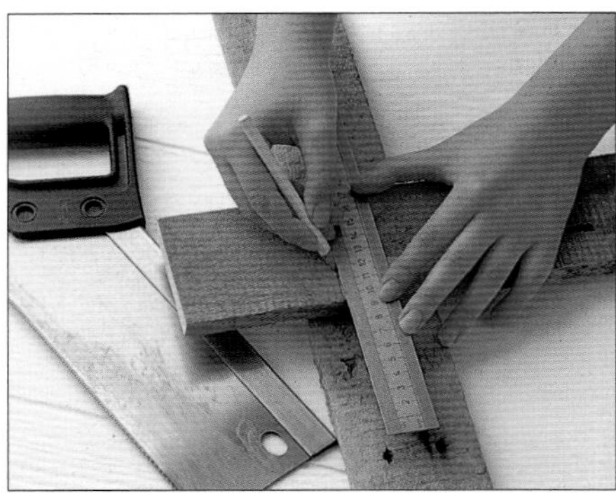

1 Decide what size you want your shelves to be. Measure and cut the shelf and back to the same size as the pallet or crate. Saw two small pieces for the side sections.

2 Run a line of strong wood glue down the back edge of the base of the shelf. Press the two pieces of wood firmly together to create a right angle. Let dry thoroughly.

3 Insert the end-pieces into the right angles at either end of the shelf, and hammer three nails in each side to hold firmly in place.

4 Sand the wood down to create a smooth surface as a key for the paint.

5 Take the length of dowel and secure it in position with nails to form a rail across the front of the shelf.

6 For another style of shelf, drill a hole through each end-piece and thread a piece of string through, knotting the string at each end to secure.

Té
MARCA REGISTRADA
PALAS

Nautical seating: *string and driftwood*

Transform a simple chair into something quite special by binding it with string, attaching pieces of driftwood collected from the beach. Awkward seams are decorated with strips of flotsam and jetsam, and two "horns" give the finishing effect to the chair back. Making or changing furniture is just a matter of using what is at hand. String is hardwearing, cheap and gives furniture a tactile quality. Other decorations for the chair could include shells incorporated into the design instead of driftwood, or perhaps a piece of coral to add color. Try to view furniture as a work of art rather than a functional object, and adapt your chair to suit your mood. Tables, shelves, stools and cupboards can all be adorned with beachcombing finds – it really is just a matter of gathering pieces from the seaside and making them work as a harmonious whole.

YOU WILL NEED:

- **Jute or garden string**
- **Scissors**
- **Glue gun and sticks**
- **Chair**
- **Pieces of driftwood**
- **Fine gauge fishermen's netting (optional)**
- **Staple gun and staples (optional)**

1 Take the jute or garden string, cut it into manageable lengths and roll these into small balls.

2 Glue the end of a ball of string firmly to the top of the chair to secure the end. You will need to do this each time you begin a new ball.

3 Run a thin line of glue up the back of the chair to secure the string while you are working. Pull the string taut while you wrap it around the chair, making sure it does not overlap and twist.

4 To decorate the struts on the back of the chair, wrap the string over a bunch of driftwood pieces at the seam. Wind one way to secure it, then wind back again. ➤

5 Make two crisscross patterns along the middle of the chair strut to decorate. Hold them in place with glue.

6 To attach the driftwood pieces to the top of the chair, apply some glue along them.

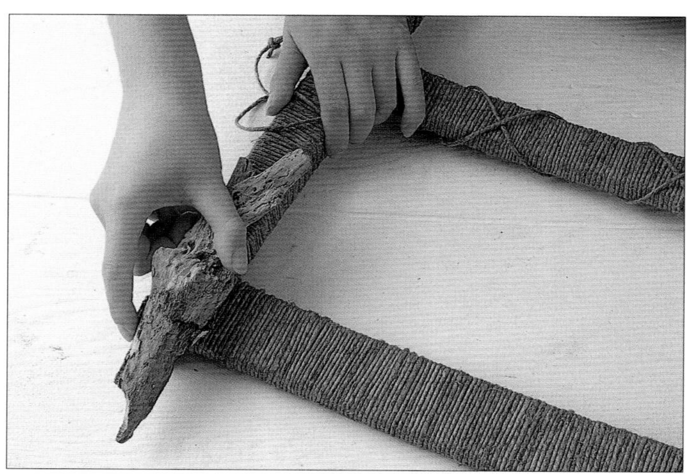

7 Position the driftwood pieces on the chair as desired.

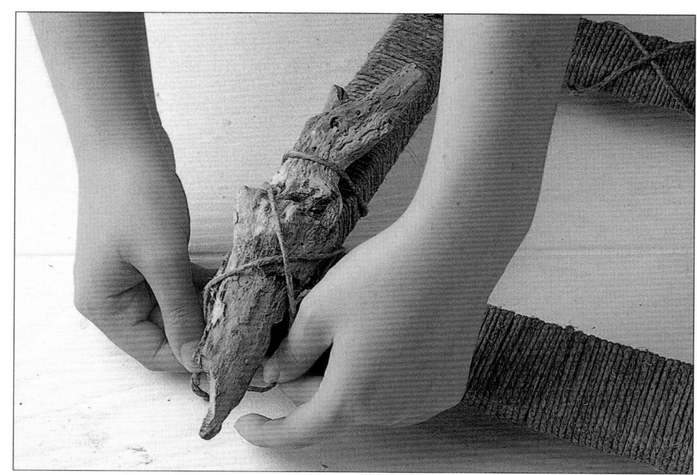

8 Bind secure driftwood pieces in place with string. To finish off, knot the string and bind it underneath.

9 As a variation, you could upholster the seat of the chair with netting. Take a piece of fishermen's netting and fold it in half.

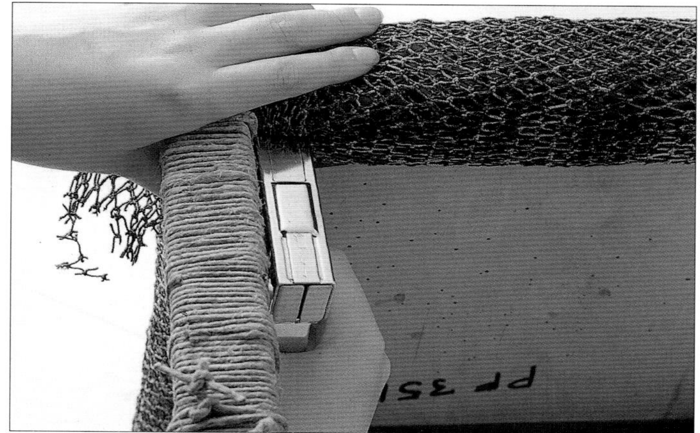

10 Secure the netting firmly to the underneath of the chair seat with a staple gun.

Seascape colors: *mosaic table*

This mosaic table provides a stunning focal point for any room. It evokes fresh sea breezes sweeping in off the water, and it would work equally well inside or out of doors. Mosaics are currently experiencing a tremendous revival and they provide an opportunity to create wonderful designs, from the simple swirls shown here to intricately decorated panels. Glass mosaic squares come in a huge range of colors, from muted matte shades of gray-greens and blues to searing primaries and shiny metallics. Provided you keep the shape and design simple, the whole process can be completed by even the most inexperienced mosaic creators.

YOU WILL NEED:

- **Piece of plywood**
- **Jigsaw**
- **Sharp knife**
- **White glue**
- **Paintbrushes**
- **Pencil**
- **Protective goggles**
- **Tile cutters**
- **Vitreous glass squares, in various colors**
- **Cement-based tile-adhesive powder**
- **Soft brush**
- **Plant sprayer**
- **Cloths**
- **Rubber gloves**
- **Fine sandpaper**

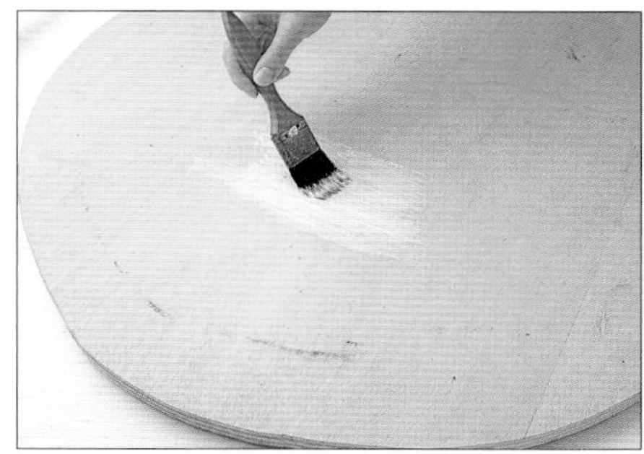

1 Cut the plywood to the desired shape for your table. Scour it with a sharp knife and prime it with a coat of diluted white glue. Let dry thoroughly.

2 Draw swirls radiating from the center for the design on the table pictured here, or create your own design.

3 Wearing protective goggles, use tile cutters to cut white glass squares into quarters. Use different densities of white to add interest to the design.

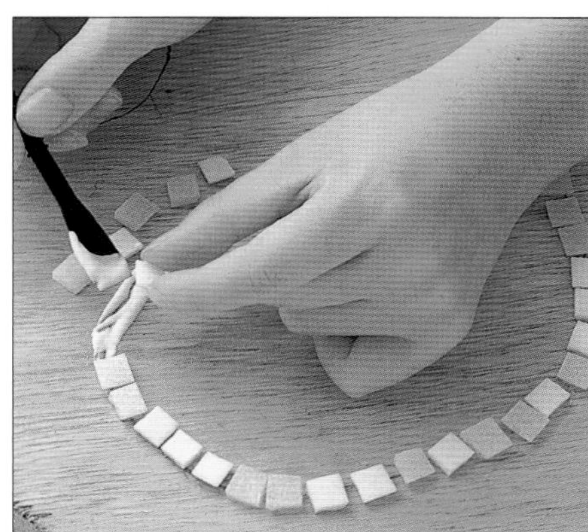

4 Put white glue along the pencil line swirls, then position the white glass on them, smooth side up.

5 Select your colors for the areas between the white lines. Here, browns and sand colors form the edge, while blues, greens and whites form the central areas. Spread out your selected colors to see if the combinations work.

6 Cut your chosen squares into quarters, using the tile cutters and wearing protective goggles.

7 Glue the central pieces to the tabletop with white glue.

8 To finish off the edge, glue pieces around the border of the table. Let dry thoroughly overnight.

9 Sprinkle dry cement-based tile-adhesive powder on the mosaic surface and spread it over using a soft brush. Make sure all the spaces between the tile pieces are filled.

10 Spray water over the mosaic, making sure all the cement is wet. Wipe away any excess with a cloth.

11 Mix some cement-based tile-adhesive powder with water and, wearing rubber gloves, rub it into the edges of the table with your fingers. Let dry overnight.

12 Rub off any excess cement with fine sandpaper and polish the table with a soft cloth.

Duckboarding: *bath mat*

Duckboarding brings to mind boats, marinas and luxurious days spent beside a pool with the sound of splashing water in the background. This duckboard bath mat is made from strips of wood and can be used either in the shower or as a mat on which to step out of the bath. If you are feeling even more adventurous, then create a whole floor in a similar fashion, but position the slats a little closer together. This would make a highly original surface for a bathroom, and coming out of the bath to feel the smooth wood underfoot is a treat most people would enjoy. Use a hardwood to withstand water, and make sure that it is treated with a water-resistant matte yachting varnish when finished to help preserve it.

YOU WILL NEED:

- **Hardwood slats, 2 x 1 inch**
- **Saw**
- **Sandpaper**
- **Ruler**
- **Pencil**
- **Bradawl**
- **Wood glue**
- **Brass screws**
- **Screwdriver**
- **Matte yachting varnish**
- **Paintbrush**

1 Decide on the size of your bath mat. Allowing for 1 inch between slats, figure out how many slats you need. Cut the wood to size. Sand the ends of the pieces.

2 Cut two lengths of wood to act as the cross-pieces onto which all the slats are attached. Mark them at regular intervals where the slats will be.

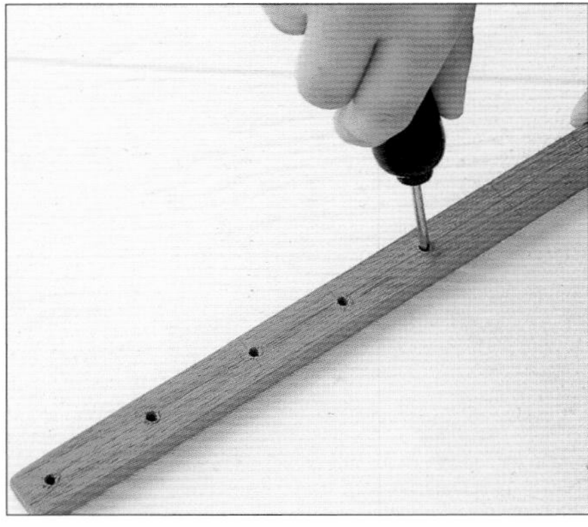

3 Using a bradawl, make holes for the brass screws in the center of the marks.

4 Mark on the back of each end of the wood slats where the cross-pieces will go. Place a small amount of wood glue on these marks.

5 Position the cross-pieces on top of the slats, matching up all the marks. Secure them in place with brass screws. Finish the mat with a coat of yachting varnish.

Sea-weathered effects: *director's chair*

If you are one of those people who dislikes the fresh, clean look of a newly painted surface, then this aging treatment is the one for you to try. It instantly transforms furniture from new to old, imbuing pieces with an interesting weathered quality in next to no time, thus allowing them to blend into their surroundings. Getting away from a beautifully flat, pristine paint surface and acquiring an old, worn look makes an object more comfortable to live with and more relaxing to look at. Here, by using an aging technique, a basic director's chair is given a whole new dimension. Changing the vivid cover for one with a soft, rather washed-out stripe also adds to the overall effect of a comfortable seaside life.

YOU WILL NEED:

- **Director's chair**
- **Scrubbing brush**
- **Bucket**
- **Soapy water**
- **Cloth**
- **Masking tape**
- **White candle**
- **Latex paint, in pale blue and white**
- **Paintbrushes**
- **Paint bucket**
- **Sandpaper**
- **Matte varnish**

1 Remove the cover from the chair and rub off any excess dirt from the frame with the scrubbing brush.

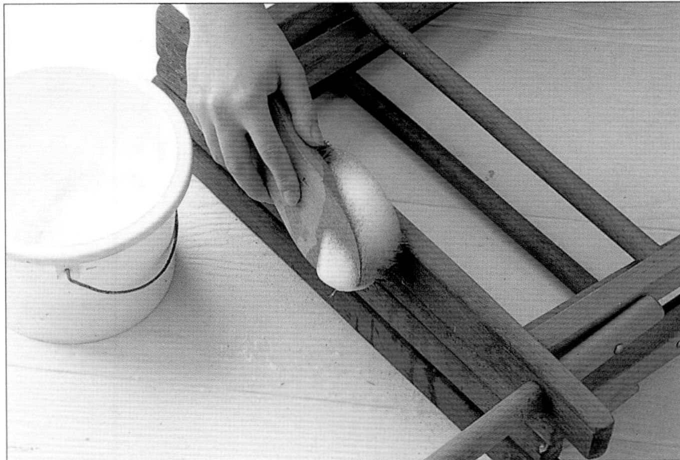

2 Scrub the chair clean with the scrubbing brush and soapy water.

3 Wipe the chair down with a clean, dry cloth and then let it dry thoroughly.

4 Put masking tape over all the metal attachments on the chair.

➤

5 Rub the chair with a candle to deposit wax on the surface, concentrating on the edges and corners. The heavier the wax deposit, the more distressed it will look.

6 Dilute the pale blue latex paint in the proportion 3:1 with water in the paint bucket.

7 Apply a coat of paint all over the chair. Let dry thoroughly.

8 Rub over the paint with sandpaper to reveal the wood underneath, then rub the chair all over with the candle again.

9 Dilute the white paint 3:1 with water.

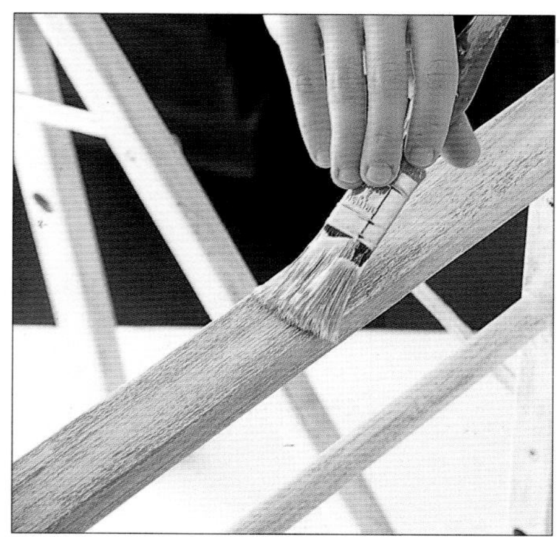

10 Apply a coat of white paint over the chair. Let dry thoroughly.

11 Rub over the paint with sandpaper to reveal the wood in some parts and the blue paint in others.

12 Seal the chair using a matte varnish to protect the surface. When dry, replace the chair cover.

Sea-washed: *simple shelving*

Create a stunning hanging shelf using a single floorboard. Wood stain and a wash of white latex paint give the surface a distressed finish. Knotted rope is the perfect partner to blend with the distressed wood and give a real nautical air. Neutral displays look wonderful when decorated with simple twigs, strings of seashells and feathers, all gathered from the beach. If you are looking for something more vibrant, just paint or stain the shelves in a brighter Mediterranean color, or you could use warm blues and gray-greens to create a shelf more akin to an Atlantic coastline.

You will need:

- **Floorboard or plank of wood**
- **Pencil**
- **Ruler**
- **Saw**
- **Drill**
- **Sandpaper**
- **Wood stain**
- **Cloths**
- **White latex paint**
- **Paintbrush**
- **Paint bucket**
- **Matte varnish (optional)**
- **4 lengths rope**
- **Masking tape**
- **Glue gun and sticks**

1 Cut the floorboard or wood plank into three pieces of equal length, depending on how long you want your shelves to be. Each piece should be 1 inch wider than the next.

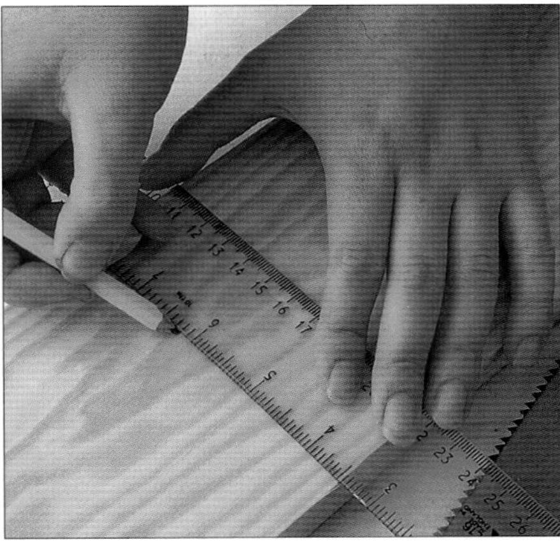

2 Using a pencil and ruler, measure and mark two holes at each end of the three shelf pieces. They should all align where you want the rope to go through.

3 Drill holes through the marks you have made on each of the three pieces of wood. Rub down the wood with sandpaper to make sure it is smooth.

4 Wipe the stain evenly over the pieces of shelving using a clean cloth. Let dry thoroughly.

5 Dilute the white paint in the proportion 4:1 with water, and apply a thin wash to the shelves.

6 Using a soft, absorbent cloth, rub away most of the white paint to leave a distressed look. ➤

7 Varnish the wood with a matte varnish, if desired, to prevent staining once in use.

8 Take two lengths of rope and wind masking tape around the ends. Knot one end of each rope and thread the other ends through the two holes on one end of the widest shelf. Mark two positions on the rope at the desired height on the middle shelf and tie a knot.

9 *Thread the rope through the middle shelf. Mark two positions with masking tape at the height you want the top shelf to hang. Tie a secure knot.*

10 *Thread the rope through the top shelf. Using a glue gun, glue all the knots to the holes to secure the shelves.*

11 *Knot the rope firmly at the top of the third shelf as shown, and glue it firmly in place.*

Rustic planks: *pallet headboard*

The next time you see a pallet abandoned on the roadside, do not just walk past it – take a closer look at it and consider whether it is worth taking it home to fashion into a unique piece of furniture. Here, a pallet was rescued and transformed into a headboard for a bed. It could also have ended up as a cupboard, shelves or even a tabletop. With a quick coat of paint, the crude wood becomes an object that would be equally at home in a modern apartment or a beach hut by the sea. The pallet retains its natural roughness due to the different widths of the planks and nail holes, but the end effect is one of charm and tranquillity.

YOU WILL NEED:

- **Pallet**
- **Pliers**
- **Ruler**
- **Pencil**
- **Saw**
- **Nails**
- **Hammer**
- **Coarse grade sandpaper**
- **White latex paint**
- **Paintbrush**
- **Paint kettle**
- **Matte varnish (optional)**

1 Remove the nails and struts of wood from the pallet.

2 Decide on the size of the headboard, then measure and cut the wood to size.

3 Make a support for the headboard by nailing four pieces of wood together, plus a piece attached centrally for stability.

4 Nail the varying widths of wood to this frame to form the front of the headboard. Sand down all the wood to prevent splinters from forming.

5 Paint the headboard with two coats of watered-down white paint so the grain shows through. If desired, finish the headboard with a coat of matte varnish.

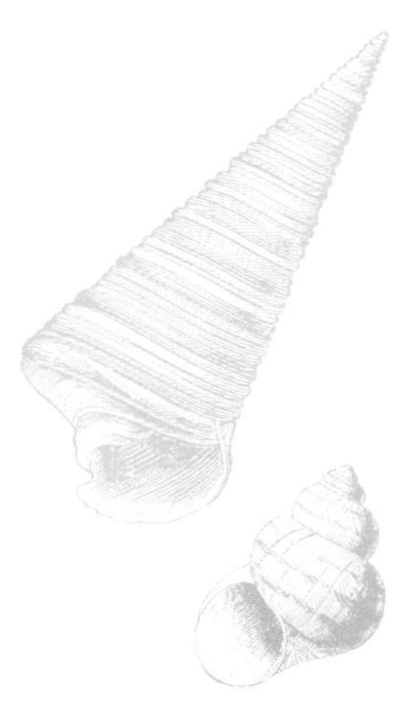

Shoreline Details

lamps

screens

mirrors

candles

pictures

frames

pots

trimmings

tie-backs

blinds

driftwood

shells

In a simple interior, details add a personal note and breathe life into a room. Make the most of *objets trouvés* brought back as souvenirs from trips to the seaside. Collecting shells and pebbles at the beach is even more addictive if you know that you are going to use them later. Even the sculptural shapes of humble driftwood reappear in the home as functional and very modern objects. The roughness of rope, jute and raffia lends yet another note of character and texture that is strongly reminiscent of ships and the sea. Picture and mirror frames can be decorated in a variety of ways – covered with shells for a Victorian look, or with a striking blue-and-white china mosaic improvised from broken or chipped tiles and china. A plain wood picture frame is also very typical of seashore style. Distress the wood first, then glue on small fish or model boats picked up at a fishing-tackle or toy store.

Shoreline Details

Natural treasures such as seashells, starfish, stones, coral and driftwood can be bought at stores, but it is somehow missing the point to buy them. If you cannot find the shells you need, then use only those you know to be byproducts of the fishing industry, such as mussel or oyster shells. Shells and coral on sale at craft stores were harvested when the animal was still alive – this is why they look so uniformly shiny and free from imperfection. Excessive harvesting has driven some species to the brink of extinction.

The delight of discovery is one of the earliest and most enduring of life's pleasures, and it gives found objects a special meaning. Knowing on which beach you unearthed your prize enhances the delight of a found object. Most of us return from vacations or weekends away with pockets and backpacks stuffed with finds. Instead of simply discarding

Above: *Fill plain glass containers with creamy white shells and sea-smoothed pebbles.*

Left: *Use shells, stones and other* objets trouvés *for a subtle display that is pleasing to the eye.*

Right: *For a quick and easy blind, simply fringe the edge of a raffia mat. Add a small piece of driftwood as a blind pull.*

Left: *Enliven a plain picture frame with gilded seashore motifs.*

Right: *To distress a wood frame, apply crackle glaze over a layer of paint. When the glaze has dried, paint in a different color and the bottom color will show through.*

Below: *Make a fish skeleton out of strips of driftwood, with a rivet for the eye. Glue onto a large piece of wood and hang on the wall.*

such mementos, you can easily incorporate them into your surroundings and enjoy their elemental qualities and associations long after your return.

Accessories and soft furnishings form an integral part of interior design, so use them to reflect your personal tastes and surround yourself with things that you like. Think about rooms without pictures, flowers or decorative objects of any kind – they can be beautiful spaces but they lack character and a sense of being inhabited. Give your decorative ideas a prominent place in your home and they will attract and hold onlookers' attention.

To stamp your personality on a room, you could simply adorn a brown paper lampshade with a fringe of pebbles and set it at a jaunty angle, or decorate an existing plain mirror with a host of seashore finds – the end result will grace any bathroom and reflect back every bit of available light. Use souvenirs from seaside strolls and fishing trips to make a decorative window screen to diffuse the streaming summer sun or to disguise a less-than-picturesque view.

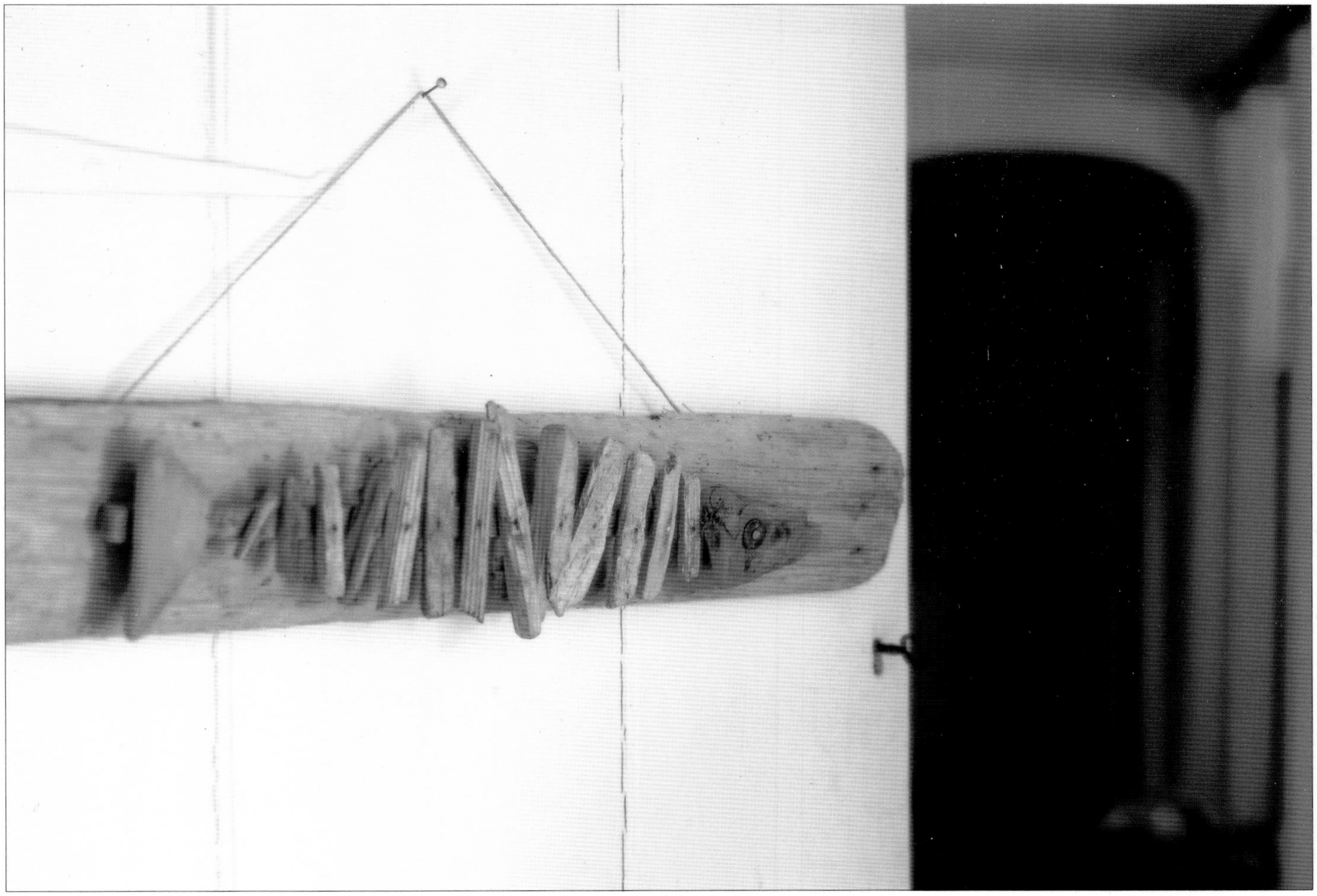

The scope for decoration is boundless, and materials are plentiful and free. Found objects can form an integral part of any natural display. Play color against color, texture against texture. Turn simple strips of driftwood into quirky candlesticks complete with feathered hands, and experiment with different arrangements and locations to keep the effect fresh, spontaneous and lively.

Above: *Cover a mirror frame with a rich collection of shells and coral, glued in position.*

Above: *This beautiful simple laundry bag is made of white linen, decorated with a few delicate shells.*

Below: *Mediterranean pots make a strong statement in a garden or sitting room. The soft blues are reminiscent of sea and sky.*

Right: *Broken or chipped tiles and china can find new life as the basis for a mosaic to decorate a box or the frame of a mirror. Here, toning shades of blue evoke a seashore theme, as do the contrasting white starfish shapes.*

Sea-tumbled trimmings: *pebble lampshade*

Bring a touch of class and a quirky seaside style to a simple brown paper lampshade. Using pebbles worn smooth by sea waters and picked up at the beach, you can create a work of art that is truly individual. All natural materials work harmoniously together, so pebbles and raffia combined with brown paper are absolutely perfect. Here, a curvaceous metal frame adds a jaunty seaside angle to the shade – an additional option would be to bind the metal stem with string to give it an even more natural feel.

YOU WILL NEED:

- **Raffia**
- **Small pebbles**
- **Glue gun and sticks**
- **Paper lampshade**
- **Scissors**

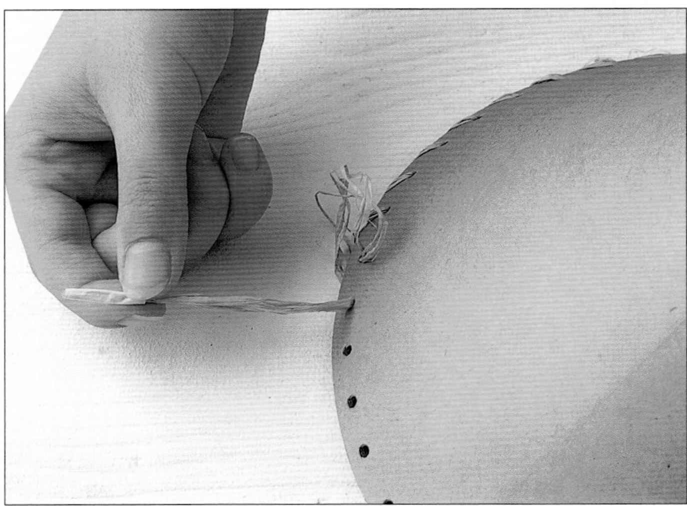

1 Thread the raffia through the top and bottom edges of the lampshade instead of the ribbon.

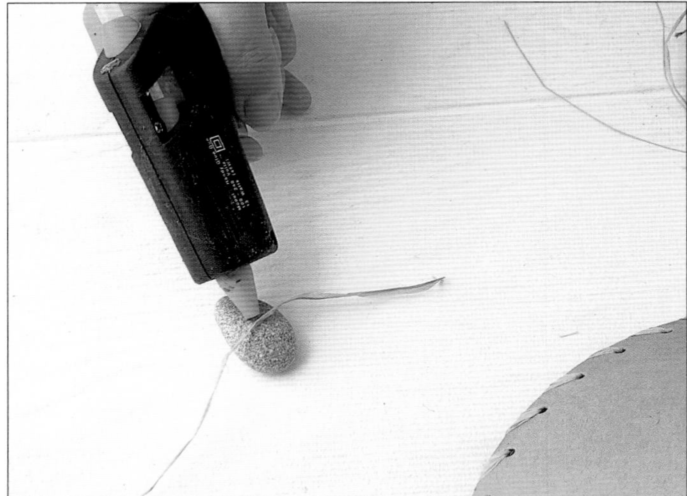

2 Pull thin strips of raffia apart and position the pieces on the pebbles. Glue them together.

3 Tie the raffia and pebbles in neat knots.

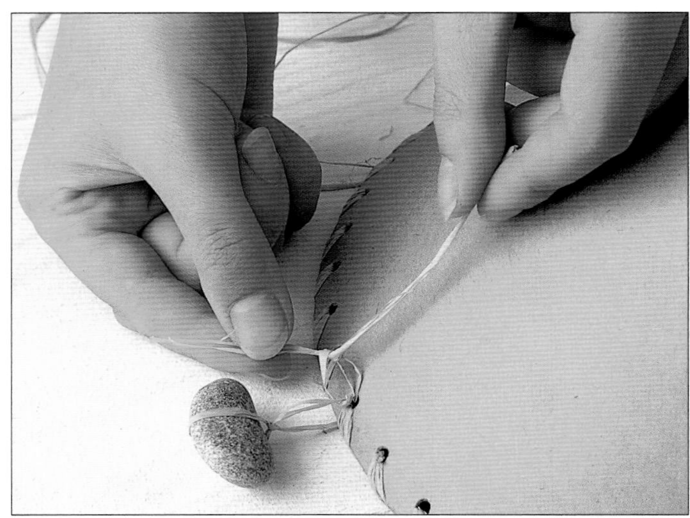

4 Hang the stones all around the lampshade, knotting the pebbles in place. Trim the loose ends of the raffia.

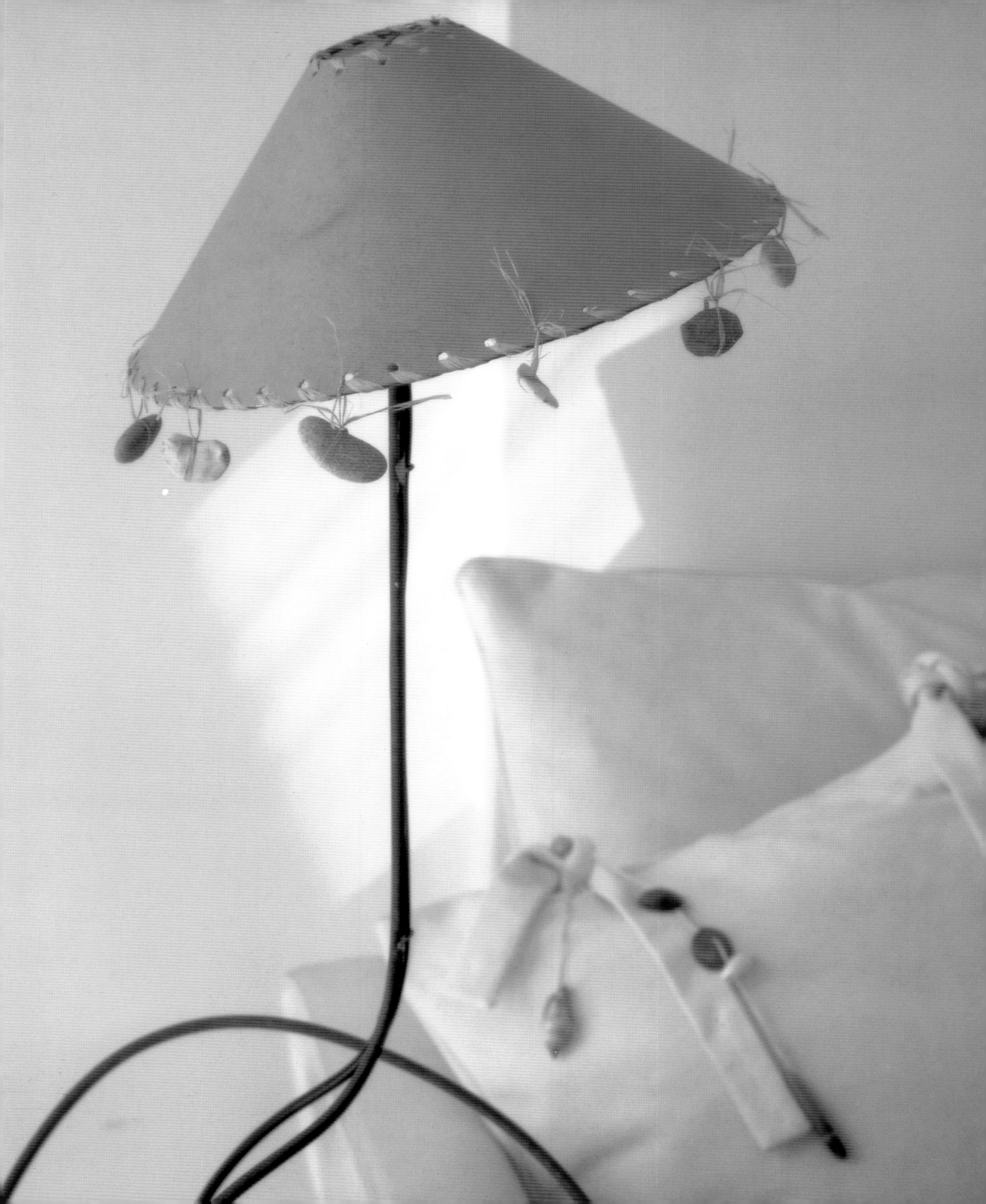

Sand and shells: *shelf edging*

Make the perfect seaside setting by introducing a shelf edging that is not only reminiscent of the waves of the sea in its shape but is coated with a fine spray of sand and decorated with the prettiest of shells. This makes an ideal bathroom or bedroom addition and also works very effectively in any kitchen area. Living rooms could benefit too, as the alcoves beside a fireplace can be fitted with four shelves on either side and each shelf can be decorated with a different design. Small stones could be used for one, a collection of wonderful colored glass worn smooth by the action of the sea could make another, or shells, as here – there are many options. A more ornate design such as rolling waves could also be used, but this would need to be cut with a jigsaw. If you do not want to go to the trouble of cutting your own shaped shelf edging, there are many available in a variety of designs, all in untreated timber so you can simply buy the edging, paint it and decorate it as you see appropriate.

YOU WILL NEED:

- **Piece of plywood**
- **Dinner plate**
- **Pencil**
- **Saw or jigsaw**
- **Fine sandpaper**
- **White latex paint**
- **Paintbrushes**
- **White glue or spray mount**
- **Silver sand**
- **Glue gun and sticks**
- **Shells**

1 Take the plywood and, using the edge of a dinner plate, mark a scalloped edging. Use a side plate or even a saucer for smaller edging.

2 Using a saw or jigsaw, cut out your shelf-edge design and sand the edges smooth with fine sandpaper.

3 Apply a coat of white latex paint to the edging. Let dry thoroughly.

4 Apply a coat of white glue to the edging, or spray it with spray mount to cover the surface evenly.

5 While still tacky, sprinkle a fine layer of silver sand to cover the whole shelf. It does not matter if it goes on a little patchy, as this is part of the charm. Let dry.

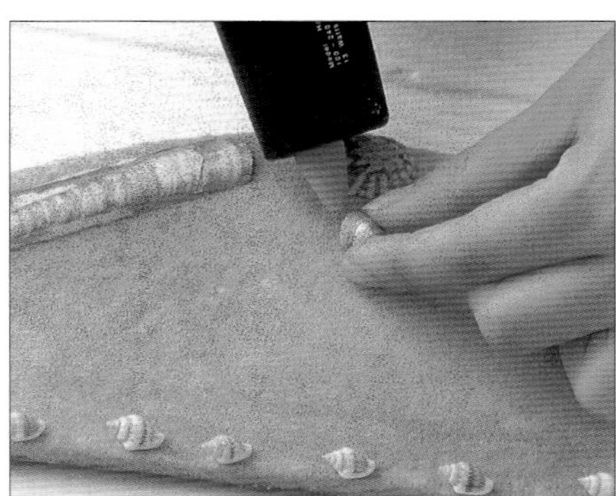

6 Using a glue gun, glue shells onto the edging to make an attractive design.

Seaside finds: *window screen*

This is an ideal screen for any window that is not overlooked, as its main purpose is to act as a fascinating decorative foil. It would make a stunning hanging in the watery world of the bathroom, in an attic bedroom or in a small window in a hallway. It is a unique way of displaying seashore finds, such as worn glass, shells and stones, and newer items, such as fishing floats, weights and lures (with their hooks removed). Everything is attached with near-invisible fishing line so the screen appears to be floating in mid-air within the window space. The more you gaze at it, the more the image of the sea comes to mind.

You will need:

- **Seaside finds, such as glass, shells and fishing tackle**
- **Fishing line**
- **Glue gun and sticks (optional)**
- **Bradawl**
- **Piece of dowel**
- **Hooks and rings**

1 On a flat surface, lay out your selection of seaside objects in a design of your choice.

2 Tie the objects onto lengths of fishing line, either making holes and knotting them or attaching them with a glue gun.

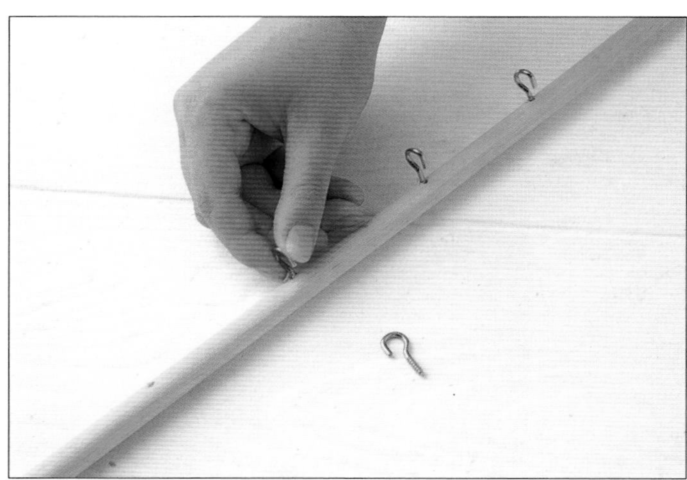

3 Using a bradawl, make holes in the dowel at regular intervals and insert hooks.

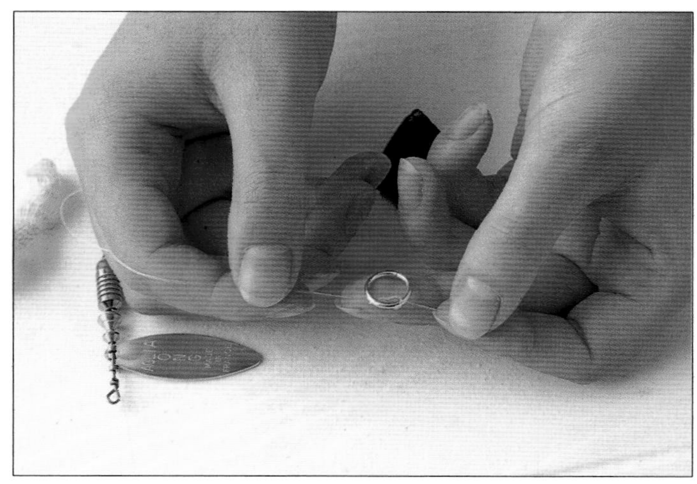

4 Attach the rings onto the ends of the decorated lines and hang them from the hooks on the dowel.

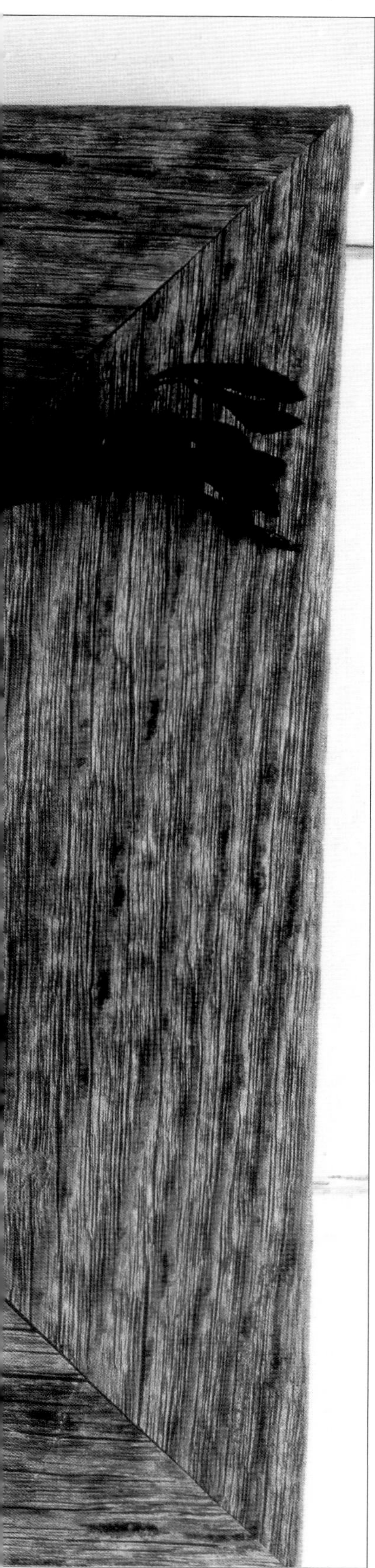

Set sail: *framed boat picture*

Dress up an old frame and create your very own work of art, without even needing to be able to draw. Again, it is largely a matter of searching the beach or seashore for interesting pebbles, seaweed and pieces of driftwood. The recycled picture frame used here works particularly well as it has a driftwood appearance to begin with. These types of frames are fairly widely available both in natural wood and woods that have been washed with a soft gray-blue or gray-green pigment. If you cannot find one, you can always buy a simple wood frame or buy a stretcher (these are simple wood struts in varying sizes that slot together to make an instant frame and are available at art stores). This can either be painted, or a selection of driftwood could be glued around the edge for a particularly interesting finish.

YOU WILL NEED:

- **String**
- **Scissors**
- **Picture frame in recycled timber**
- **Thick cardboard**
- **Fiber pot, from garden center**
- **Pebble**
- **Glue gun and sticks**
- **Seaweed**

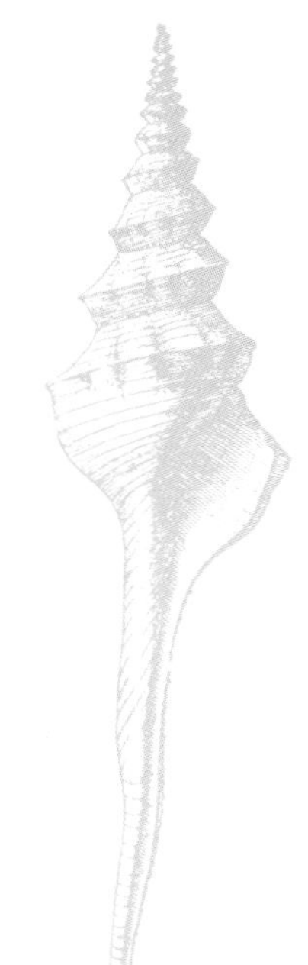

1 Cut a length of string and wind it around the top and bottom of the frame to make a casual yet interesting design. Tie to secure. Cut a piece of cardboard to act as a backing.

2 For the boat picture, tear the fiber pot into small pieces to make the sail shapes. ➤

3 Lay out your pebble and sails to make sure they balance.

4 Arrange the pebble and sails on the backing cardboard and glue them firmly in position.

5 Experiment to see where the seaweed looks most attractive.

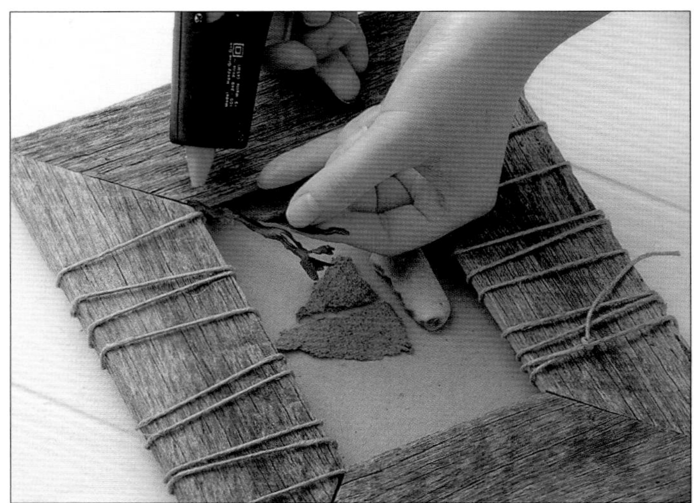

6 Glue the seaweed in position.

Left: *The natural beauty of driftwood is an invaluable inspiration. The texture and color provide practical ideas for decorating frames, while the strange, sculpted shapes of branches that have been battered by the elements can be re-created in miniature for a naturally abstract picture.*

Seaside views: *shell mirror*

This is the perfect way either to dress up an existing mirror or to create a very special one of your own. It makes a wonderful gift, and all sea-loving friends are bound to be enchanted by the mixture of sand and seashells. Any shape of mirror is suitable for this treatment that is a beautiful addition to any bathroom, bedroom or hallway: rectangular and oval mirrors are especially effective. When finished, position the shell-encrusted mirror on the wall so it reflects every patch of blue there is and allows sunlight to bounce off it and light up the room.

You will need:

- **Tape measure**
- **Mirror**
- **Piece of hardboard**
- **Hanging hook**
- **Glue gun and sticks**
- **White glue**
- **Paper**
- **Sand**
- **Cardboard (optional)**
- **Shells – scallop, mussels; smaller shells; drilled; tiny shells; and razor**
- **Twine**
- **Tweezers**
- **Seaweed**

1 Measure the mirror and cut a piece of hardboard slightly larger all around to allow for the decorative border. Attach a hanging hook to the back of the hardboard.

2 Attach the mirror to the hardboard using a glue gun.

3 Coat the hardboard border with white glue and, using the paper as a funnel, sprinkle it with sand to create a seaside background.

4 If needed, attach a piece of cardboard in the center of the top of the mirror to support a central shell. ➤

5 Decide upon your design and position the central shell and some mussel shells on the top.

6 Position some mussel shells around the edge of the frame and attach them securely with a glue gun.

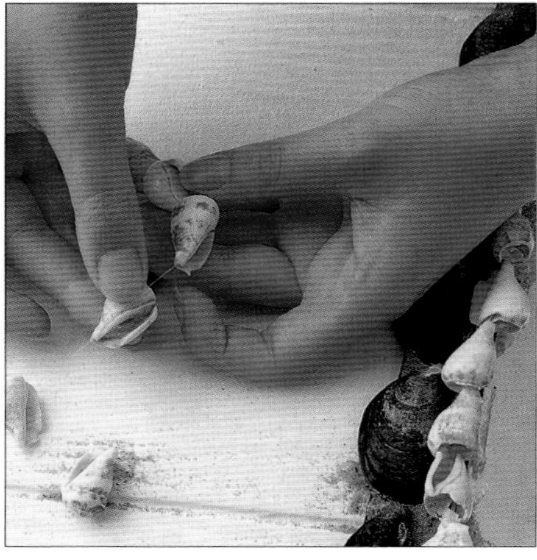

7 Thread smaller shells on twine and attach a length around the edge of the border.

8 Glue tiny shells in position inside the outer row of mussel shells.

9 Glue another layer of mussel shells onto the inner edge, attaching them to the surface of the mirror itself.

10 Glue razor shells in place on the bottom edge of the mirror to form a "V" shape.

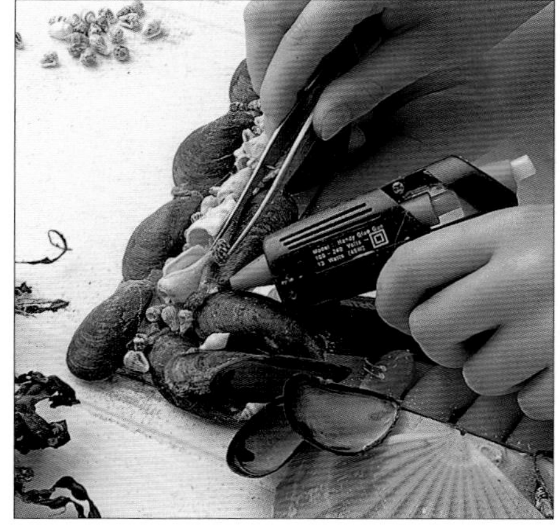

11 Using tweezers, position tiny shells in between all the edging shells to cover any of the mirror under the edge. Glue in place.

12 To finish, position strands of seaweed where required and glue them in place with the glue gun.

Nautical knots: *curtain tie-back*

Take a tip from able-bodied seamen and create a stunning tie-back from a length of rope and a simple slip stitch. The only technical skill required is a basic knowledge of how to knit. The tassel is secured by "whipping," a well-known seafaring term for binding ropes together using twine or string. Fasten the tie-back with a simple cleat decorated with a single pebble to give an even stronger seafaring feel. This type of curtain treatment looks terrific when used with cream calico or linen fabric – muslin would look beautiful too, but you might need to use a finer gauge of rope.

YOU WILL NEED:

- **1–1½ yard length rope**
- **Dressmaker's pin**
- **Jute string**
- **Scissors**

1 Tie a knot in the end of a length of rope. Work a chain stitch in the rope; this is the same technique as casting on with one needle and one finger for knitting, i.e. make two loops.

2 Thread one loop through the other loop, tightening as you go.

3 To make the tassel, unravel the end of the rope and fluff it out by running a dressmaker's pin down the unraveled sections to separate out the fibers.

4 Bind jute string around the rope end using a whip knot. Make a loop at the bottom and top ends of the string, leaving a tail of about 3 inches at the bottom end.

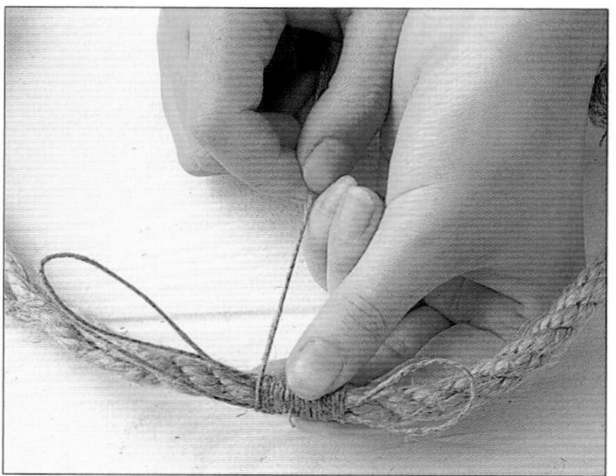

5 From the top, start to whip around the rope with the string, leaving both loops visible. Whip as closely and as tightly as possible, keeping the string bound closely together and working with an even tension.

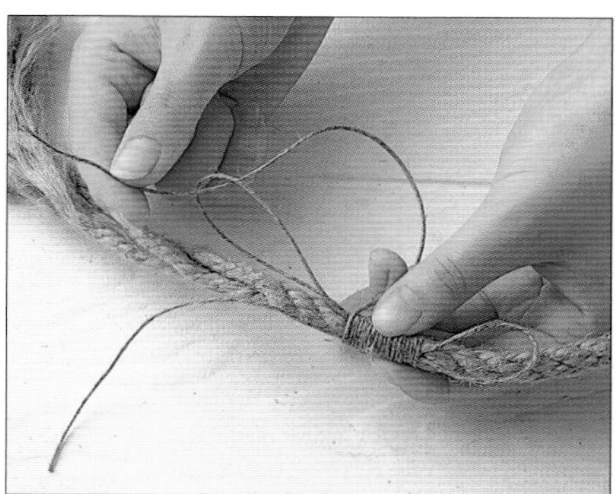

6 To finish, thread the string through the lower loop and pull the loop at the other end. As you pull harder, the other end of the string pulls through. Snip off the ends of the string to neaten.

Sculpted by the waves: *driftwood candlestick*

Create a truly original, artistic candlestick by amalgamating various items from the beach, such as birds' feathers and bits of wood or fishing tackle. The end result will delight all onlookers, and it radiates a certain spirit of its own. Remember, though, that lit candles must never be left unattended – and especially in this instance with driftwood and feathers providing the base. Because of the sculptural nature of this particular piece, it could happily stand on its own as an art object without being lit.

YOU WILL NEED:
- **2–3 pieces driftwood**
- **Glue gun and sticks**
- **Florist's wire**
- **2 feathers**
- **Craft knife**
- **Candle**

1 Use two or three pieces of driftwood to form a pleasing candlestick base. Using a glue gun, fix the driftwood pieces together.

2 When dry, bind a piece of wire around the cross-section and fashion it into two candelabra-shaped arms.

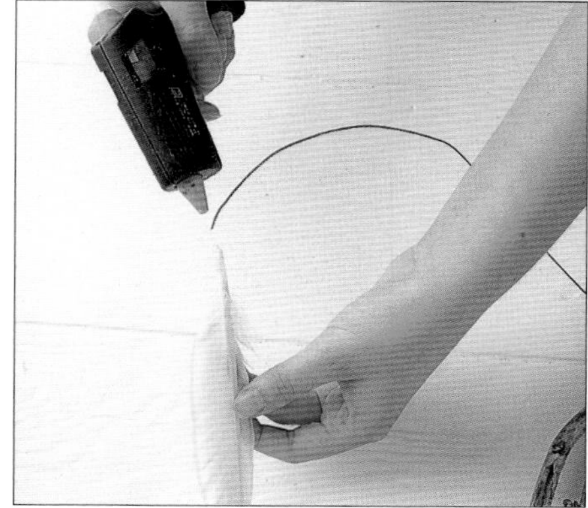

3 Attach the feathers to the arm ends by placing a dot of glue on the ends of the wire and inserting these into the quills.

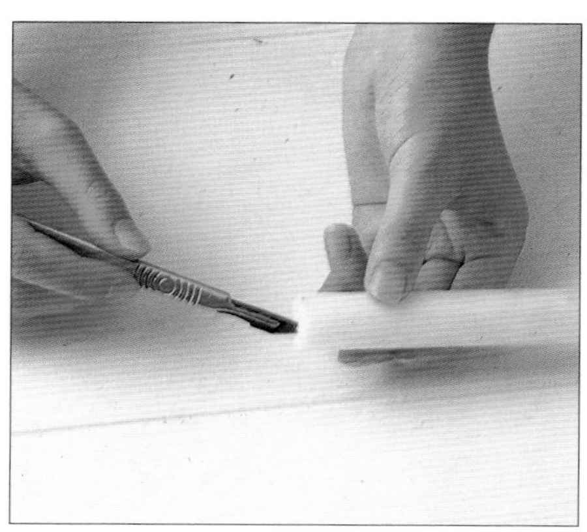

4 Using a craft knife, make a small hole in the end of a candle to stabilize it in the candle holder.

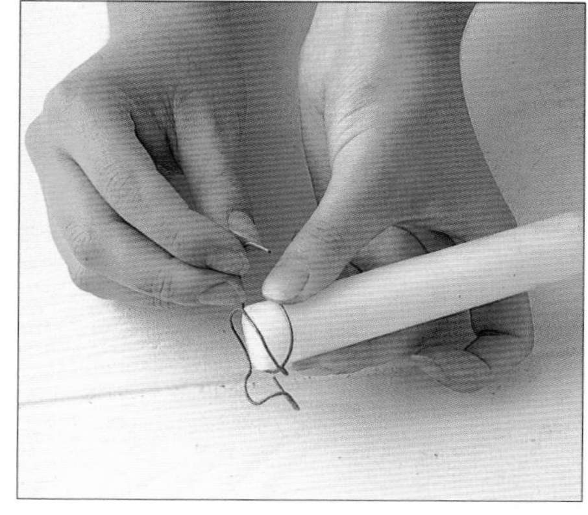

5 Cut a short length of wire and wind it around the base of the candle.

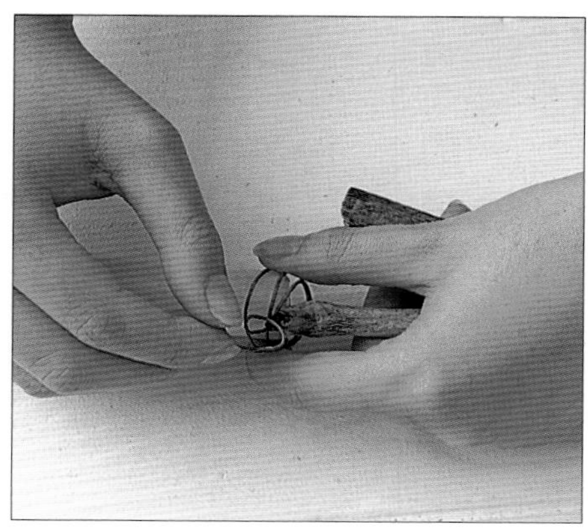

6 Insert a small piece of the driftwood candle holder up into the base of the candle and secure by tightening up the wire. Do not let the candle burn down to its driftwood anchor.

Sea Accessories

ceramics

books

boats

glassware

china

boxes

lanterns

games

pots

placenames

trays

bottles

Accessories can add color and style to every part of your home. Create a series of still-life effects within the home by rearranging favorite accessories to suit your mood, the season and the occasion. In the daytime, place decorative glasses and bottles in vivid blues and greens on a sunny windowsill so they catch the light. Display cheerfully spotted blue cups and saucers on a kitchen shelf or dresser. For dinner guests, bring out shell candles and hurricane lamps, and continue the seashore theme by setting the table with pebble place cards. Give a fresh look to traditional crafts by painting plain glass and china with your own seashore motifs, or decorating trays and boxes with fish or shell découpage in bright modern colors. The ideal solution for a collection of small disparate objects is to bring them all together in a sand garden, which you can revise and add to after each new visit to the seaside.

Sea Accessories

Seaside and country walks can yield all manner of unusual and beautiful objects discarded by humans and nature alike. Sculptural branches and twigs, pine cones, acorns, seeds and seed heads, a wide variety of leaves, seaweed, old rope, pebbles, starfish and seashells all can be gathered together to form the basis of your craft materials. Once collected, they can be transformed into a wealth of attractive and original decorative objects that make wonderful accessories for the home.

Other decorative ideas can be crafted from everyday items found just about anywhere. For example, if you have got a simple wood box, just paint it in the color of your choice, then decorate it with a cornucopia of shells, or turn glasses and vases into display cases overflowing with seashore finds. Likewise, you could decorate plain carafes, storage jars and white china with stunning seaside designs, or make a striking statement on a windowsill with a row of colored glass and antique bottles.

Above: *Delight your guests with personalized pebble place cards.*

Left: *This cast concrete seagull, found at a tag sale, is a fun addition to the most conventional mantelpiece or shelf. The shoreline pebbles reinforce the nautical theme of the display.*

Right: *Set the breakfast table with an ethnic embroidered napkin and scarlet geraniums, and imagine you are on a Greek island.*

Above: *Tin lanterns are imported today from many countries. Mix different shapes and sizes for magical summer evenings.*

Below: *To make lovely individual candles, place a night-light in each mussel shell, then fill the shell with melted candle wax.*

By using your surroundings as inspiration you can achieve quite impressive results with the materials available. To turn a plain wood box into a painted aquarium with exotic fish floating on the surface, cut out pictures of marine animals from a book or magazine and attach them to the box's surface using a découpage technique. Découpage is also ideal for screens, walls or even pieces of furniture, and images such as birds, shells, lighthouses and boats all can be used to evoke a seashore mood.

Inexpensive woven baskets, available at garden centers, make ideal containers for kitchens, bathrooms or bedrooms. They are already decorative and usually can be made even more so by adding lengths of tiny shell necklaces in a zigzag design. Found objects can form an integral part of natural displays, as in a sand garden with a rugged frame constructed from reclaimed timber and filled with flotsam from the beach. A tiny piece of driftwood can be used to craft a small sailing boat, while a simple shell and garden pot becomes a pretty sailing vessel.

Right: *The flames from floating candles cast soft reflections in the water, reminiscent of night-time fishing boats at sea.*

Far right: *Glue small shells onto the covers of colorful notebooks and decorate a terra-cotta pot to match.*

Creating special items for the home can be as economical as it is satisfying, and there is often no need to visit specialty craft suppliers when focusing on a seashore theme – use pieces of cast-off garden twine or household string to make schools of fish and jaunty anchors on handmade notepaper and sturdy book covers.

Group together old bottles found on the shore and place a candle in each to illuminate an informal supper. Another wonderful idea is to make your own lanterns from simple tin cans. Remove the labels and place a piece of wood in each can for a brace. Using a sharp implement such as a bradawl, make tiny pin pricks in a design all over the surface. When you light your lantern, the candlelight will flicker through.

Right: *Decorate a window box or planter with mussel shells and fill with plants in toning colors.*

Above: *Stitch rows of shells onto a wicker basket for a beautiful contrast of texture.*

Left: *Gift-wrap herbs or small presents in fabric bags tied with string and decorated with shells and driftwood.*

Right: *This elaborate outdoor display uses candles, starfish, sand and driftwood to dramatic effect.*

Marineware: *painted carafe*

Add another dimension to a plain glass carafe by painting stunning seaside scenes directly onto the glass. Pieces of seaweed, shell images and starfish are all suitable images. If you want to create a special seaside setting for a particular dinner party, simply paint on the images with white latex paint and they can be washed off at the end of the evening. Alternatively, use glass paint and create a range of stylish natural glassware in tune with a seashore way of life. Do not restrict yourself to just one carafe – make a display of matching glassware with a variety of glasses and pitchers in all shapes and sizes.

YOU WILL NEED:

- **Carafe**
- **Lint-free cotton**
- **Alcohol**
- **Pencil**
- **Paper**
- **Tracing paper**
- **Masking tape**
- **Carbon paper**
- **Felt tip marker**
- **White glass paint**
- **Paintbrush**

1 Wipe the surface of the glass with lint-free cotton and alcohol to make the surface absolutely clean.

2 Draw your designs, either using the templates at the back of the book or your own freehand illustrations.

3 Transfer your designs to tracing paper.

4 Using masking tape, stick your designs around the carafe, placing a piece of carbon paper underneath the tracing paper. Draw around the outline with a sharp marker so the outline is transferred to the glass.

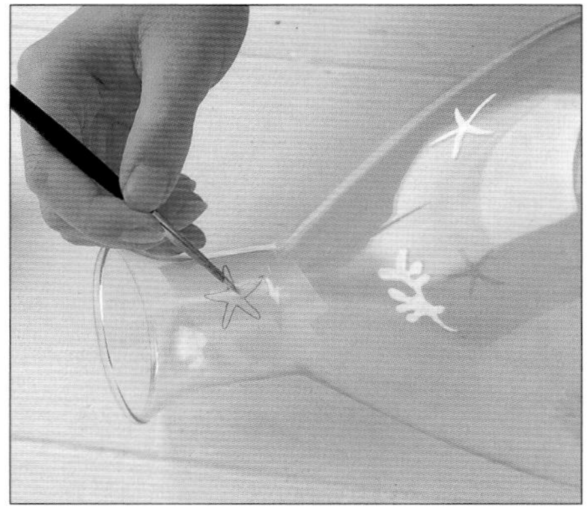

5 Paint the outlines and fill in the designs with white glass paint.

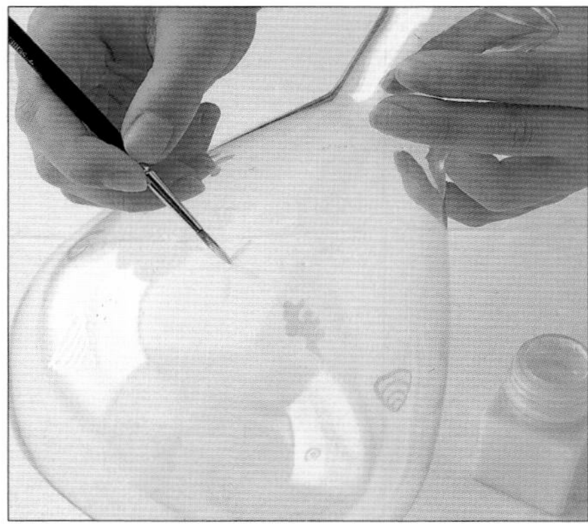

6 Alternatively, place the image inside the carafe or on the other side of the glass and paint the image through the glass.

Dining by the sea: *painted china*

Fine white china is beautiful in its own right, but here is a way of injecting color and adding another dimension to a plain white dinner set. If you are throwing a special dinner party and are committed to going all out, then embellish additional decorative plates and soup bowls for each setting using latex paint – although these items should not be used for food. The paint can be wiped off the next day. However, if you use a ceramic paint, tableware can be decorated permanently. Small images of shells and starfish look delicate, use just one maritime motif around a plate and have each place setting completely unique. Likewise, if the images are enlarged on a photocopier, a central image on each plate can look great. Experiment with different sizes – just copy each image a few times, then play around with the sizes to see which you find the most pleasing.

You will need:

- **Tracing paper**
- **Pencil**
- **Scissors**
- **China plates and soup bowls**
- **Lint-free cotton**
- **Alcohol**
- **Ruler**
- **Carbon paper**
- **Masking tape**
- **Blue ceramic paint**
- **Fine paintbrush**

1 Copy the template from the back of the book onto tracing paper, or make a template of your own design. Cut the shapes out with sharp scissors.

2 Wipe the surface of the plate with lint-free cotton and alcohol to make the surface absolutely clean.

3 Find and mark the middle of the plate with a ruler and pencil.

4 Section the plate into eight equal parts and mark up the eight sections.

5 Try various design options with your templates to see which one you find the most pleasing.

6 Cut carbon paper into small pieces to fit your templates.

7 Place the carbon paper under the template designs on the plate and stick them down with masking tape to secure.

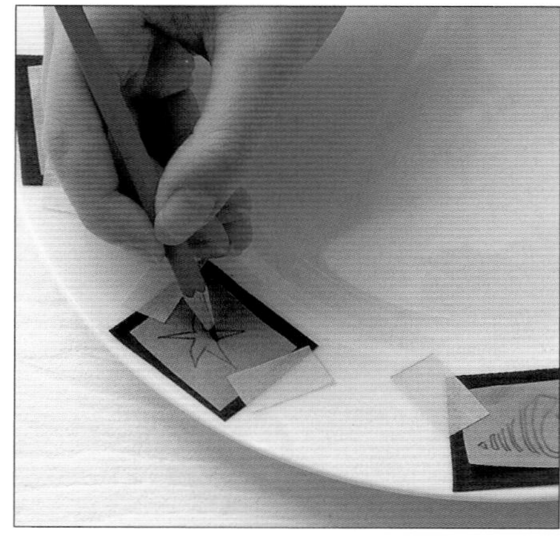

8 Trace around the template outlines with a sharp pencil, then remove the tape and templates.

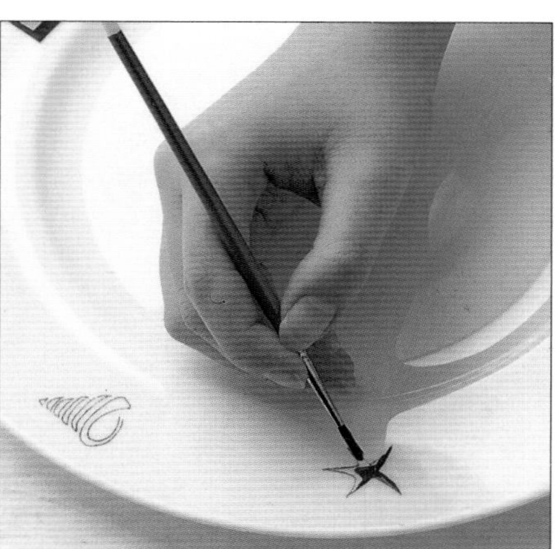

9 Paint in the shapes carefully using ceramic paint. Let dry thoroughly.

10 Mark, trace and paint the design in the center of the soup bowl.

11 Add small dots on the handles of the bowl. Let dry thoroughly.

12 Remove the pencil marks from the china before using.

Letters from afar: *notepaper and book*

There is nothing more flattering or personal than receiving notepaper, stationery and notebooks that have been handcrafted. Making paper is not difficult, but it can be a time-consuming affair. However, it is extremely easy to decorate ready-bought paper, and it is wonderful to incorporate motifs such as anchors or fish, for example, that bring the seaside to mind. Using pale cream paper and natural string creates a gift that is elegant in its simplicity.

Book

YOU WILL NEED:

- **Thick garden twine**
- **Pieces of driftwood**
- **Glue gun and sticks**
- **Notebook**

1 Tie a piece of thick garden twine to each end of a piece of driftwood. Knot in place.

2 Tie more sticks to the twine to form a line, pulling it taut at the top and bottom.

3 To make the book cover, glue the row of driftwood in position to the notebook.

4 Tie the pieces of twine at the ends to complete the book.

➤

Envelope and Notepaper

You will need:

- **Paper**
- **Single-hole punch**
- **White glue**
- **String**
- **Pieces of driftwood**
- **Scissors**

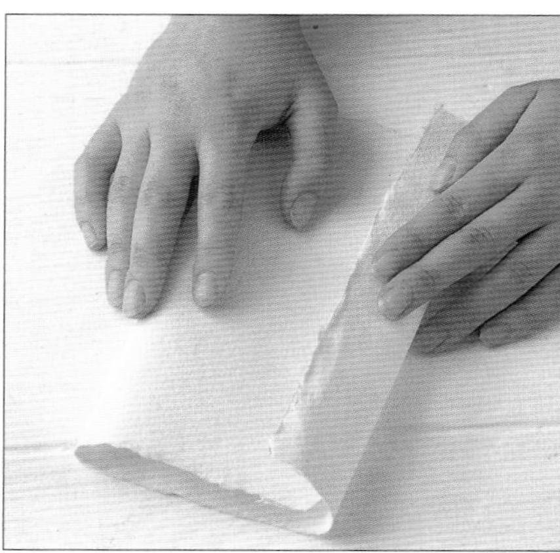

1 To make the envelope, fold over a piece of paper, leaving a shorter edge to fold down as the flap of the envelope (about one-eighth of the paper).

2 Punch six holes for the string: two on the flap and four on the back of the envelope, as shown.

3 Put white glue along the sides of the envelope and glue it down.

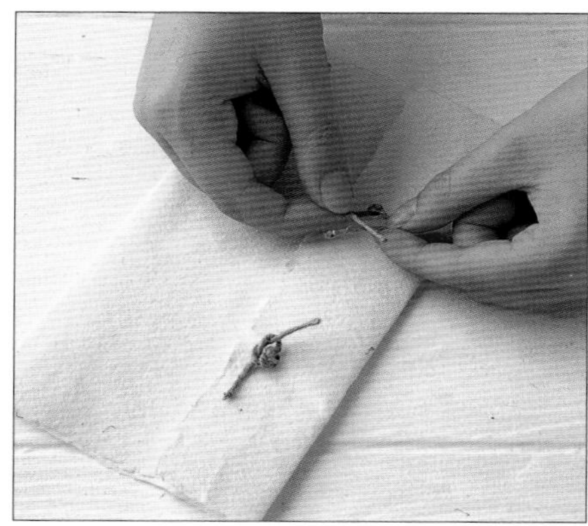

4 Thread pieces of string through the holes and knot them in place.

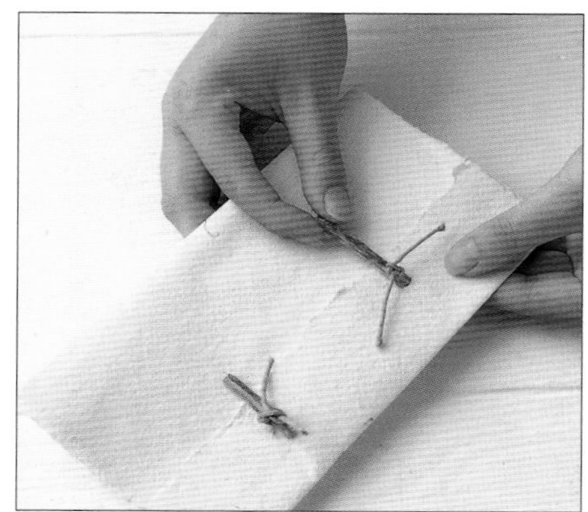

5 Slip pieces of driftwood under the string to decorate.

6 To make the fish for the notepaper, cut a small piece of string and cross the ends over to form a fish shape. Cut a thin strip for the end of the tail. Glue the fish on the paper to secure it.

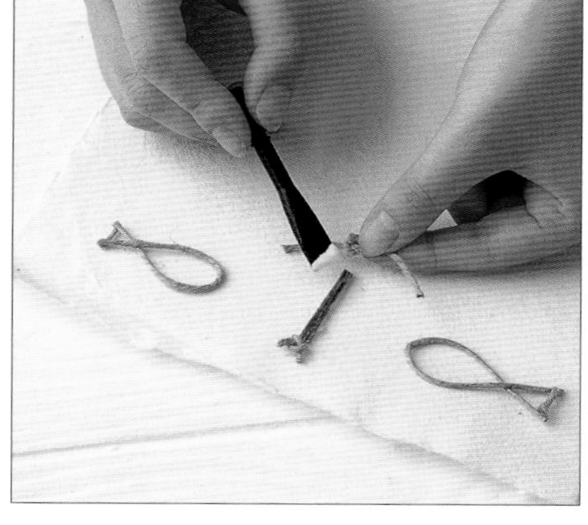

7 To make the anchor, knot a piece of string in the center and bend up the ends to form a base. Glue a single piece of driftwood for the upright, then glue everything in place.

Shell-encrusted: *decorative box*

Turn a simple wood box into a special gift with the addition of a little paint and a motif made from shells and driftwood. Once thought to be rather *outré*, shell boxes have now made a big comeback and are considered attractive and desirable, in a rather kitschy sort of way. Making a shell box is really quite straightforward – just choose a charming selection of bits and pieces and arrange them as you like. Choose a motif that you feel is suitable, such as an urn, crescent, horn or anchor, then draw the shape and fill it with tiny shells. If you run out of shells, fill the spaces with seeds, beans or pulses. As long as the coloring matches, then anything goes.

YOU WILL NEED:

- **Wood box**
- **Black latex paint**
- **Paintbrush**
- **Thick cardboard**
- **Craft knife**
- **Saucer**
- **Small shells**
- **Glue gun and sticks**
- **Pieces of driftwood**
- **Florist's wire**

1 Paint a wood box with an even coat of black latex paint. Let dry thoroughly.

2 Cut out a crescent from thick cardboard, using a saucer to make the shape.

3 Position small shells to form a pattern on the cardboard crescent and glue them in position using a glue gun.

4 Make the base for the urn from driftwood and shells, breaking them into even-size pieces. Glue them in position on the lid of the box.

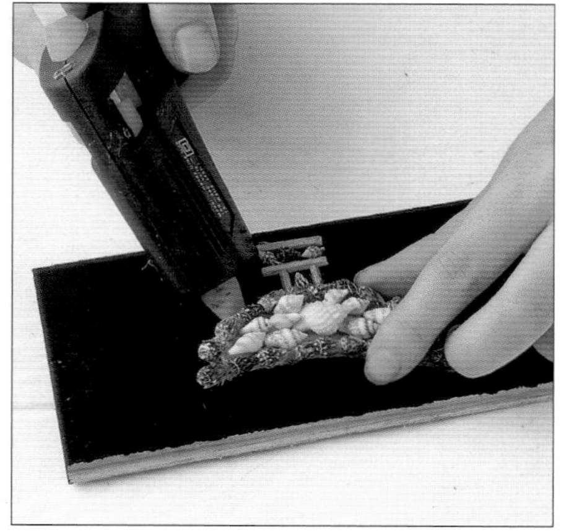

5 Position the crescent of shells over the urn base and glue in place.

6 Wind pieces of wire around a paintbrush to form handles for the urn. Glue them in place.

11 Position and glue the paper motifs on the tray as desired. Varnish over the motifs on the tray, giving it at least three coats.

12 Cut two lengths of rope for the handles and tape the ends with masking tape. Push the rope through the holes.

13 Knot the ends of the rope securely to hold the handles in place.

Cast adrift: *driftwood boat*

Scour the beach for pieces of interestingly shaped driftwood and other flotsam and jetsam – it is a delightful and extremely therapeutic way to spend a day at the beach. Sort through your finds and choose shapes that would instantly make a boat or a fish. You will be amazed at just how many uses there are for a humble piece of driftwood, given a little imagination and creativity. Fashion your discoveries into shapes, and within hours you could even have your own flotilla. If you are feeling a little more industrious, you could cut out the simple shape of a fish and mount it onto a stand made from a gloriously shaped beach find. Visually delightful when displayed on a windowsill or on a shelf in the kitchen or bathroom, you can keep your finds as a memento of a happy beach vacation or give them as lovely presents to friends.

YOU WILL NEED:

- **Beach finds**
- **Drill**
- **Craft knife**
- **Glue gun and sticks**
- **Flotsam or fiber pot**

1 Decide how you want your boat to look, then mark the position for the mast. Using a fairly small drill bit, make a hole in the driftwood.

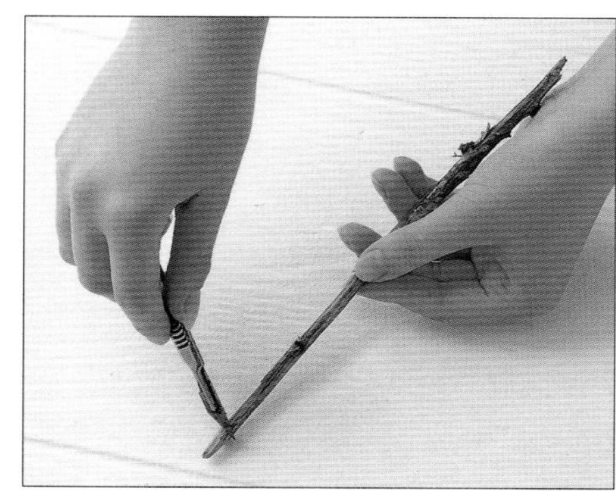

2 Take the piece you will be using for the mast and file down the end to a slight point with a craft knife (remember to cut away from yourself to avoid accidents).

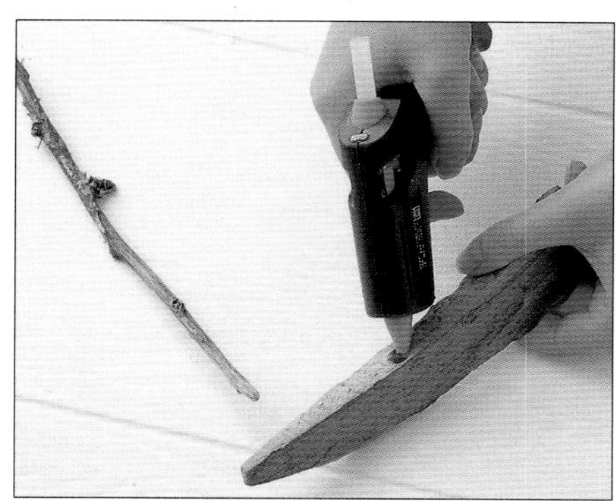

3 Squeeze glue into the drilled hole and attach the mast in place. Let dry thoroughly.

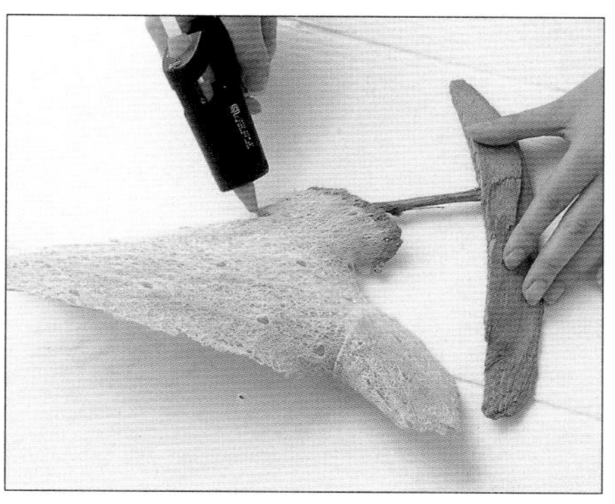

4 For the sail, attach the flotsam or torn-up fiber pot to the mast. If desired, use pieces of seaweed strung up to look like rigging.

Beach style: *sand gardens*

Create your very own container gardens using the most unusual of plantings. Instead of pansies and daisies, grow small clumps of marram grass. Make pleasing patterns in the boxes with shells and coral. Broken tiles and stones alongside pieces of cork can be fashioned into a garden with an almost Japanese simplicity that would look at home anywhere, from a city apartment to a beach cottage. Here, a selection of smaller boxes is used, but you could just as easily make a larger garden, support it on bricks, fill it, then cover the top with glass to make a delightful coffee table that is a focal point with its shoreline view.

YOU WILL NEED:

- **1 yard x ⅝ inch piece wood**
- **Ruler**
- **Pencil**
- **Saw**
- **Wood glue**
- **Piece of hardboard or plywood, 10 inches square**
- **Hammer**
- **Panel pins**
- **Sand**
- **Broken china, shells or seaside finds**

1 Cut the piece of wood into four pieces, two 10 inches and two 9 inches long, to form the square sides of the box for the sand garden.

2 Run a line of wood glue around the edge of the hardboard or plywood piece and position the wood sides on this, with the same-size pieces facing each other. Let dry thoroughly.

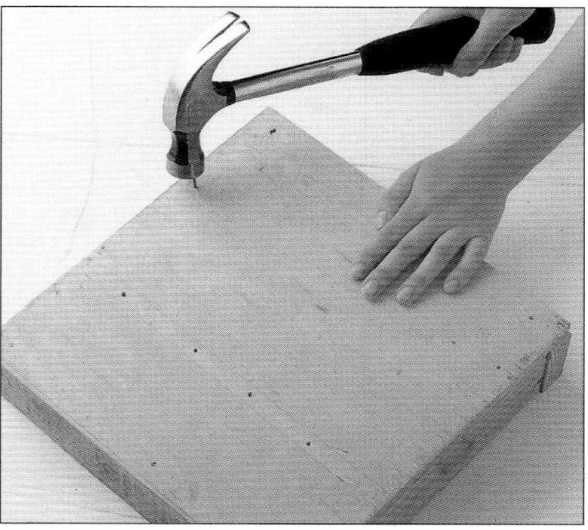

3 Turn the box over and hammer in panel pins all the way around.

4 Fill the box with dry sand.

5 Work out your preferred design on the surface of the sand.

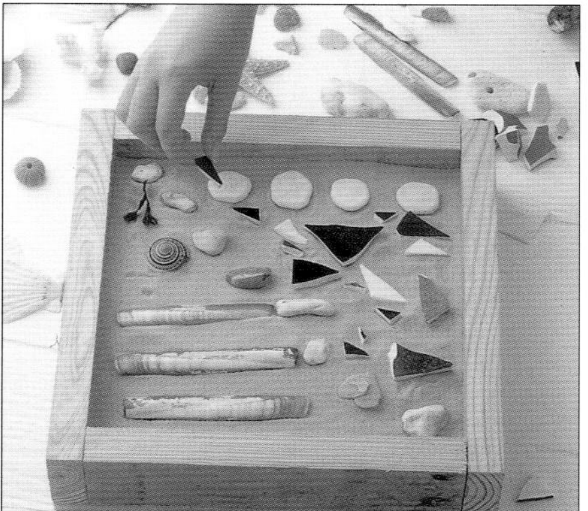

6 You could use pieces of broken china like mosaics and mix them with razor shells and sand dollars.

Seaside games: *bag of dominoes*

Hessian has a wonderful tactile quality, is extremely inexpensive and can be used for any manner of things. Here, it is used to great effect to make a drawstring bag, filled with domino-painted pebbles. It is a fun idea that could be made either as a gift or while on vacation. The bag is easy to make, and children will really enjoy finding and marking up stones as dominoes. Jute or hessian bags are also perfect for holding marbles, dice or Chinese checkers.

You will need:

- **Hessian, ½ yard**
- **Scissors**
- **Large-eyed tapestry needle**
- **Jute garden twine**
- **Pebbles**
- **Fine black felt-tip marker**

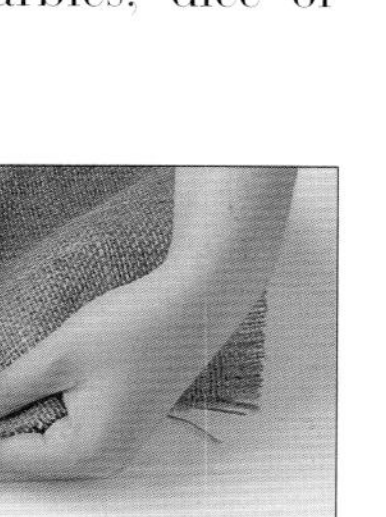

1 Decide what size you want your bag to be; it will have to be reasonably big because of the number of dominoes. Cut the hessian to twice the length required and fold the fabric in half. Pull some threads from the loosely woven hessian to use for sewing up the bag.

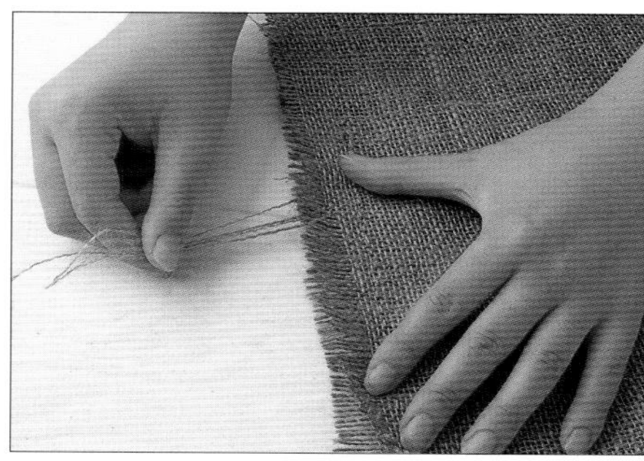

2 Put the wrong sides together and, using the tapestry needle and hessian threads, slip stitch the opening down the sides and across the bottom. Then fray the sides by pulling out two to three strands to leave a fringed edging.

3 Draw down three threads 1½–2 inches from the bag's top edge and again 1 inch below this. Thread twine through the bottom line, picking up three strands at a time, to form the drawstring. Knot the ends so they will not fray.

4 Mark domino dots on the pebbles with a marker and place them in the bag. Do not make the pebbles too big or the bag will be very heavy.

Templates

The templates on these pages can be used at this size or scaled up or down, using either a grid system or a photocopier. For the grid system, trace the template and draw a grid of evenly spaced squares over your tracing. To scale up, draw a larger grid onto another piece of paper. Copy the outline onto the second grid by taking each square individually and drawing the relevant part of the outline in the larger square. Finally, draw over the lines to make sure they are continuous. To trace the templates, you will need a pencil, tracing paper and scissors.

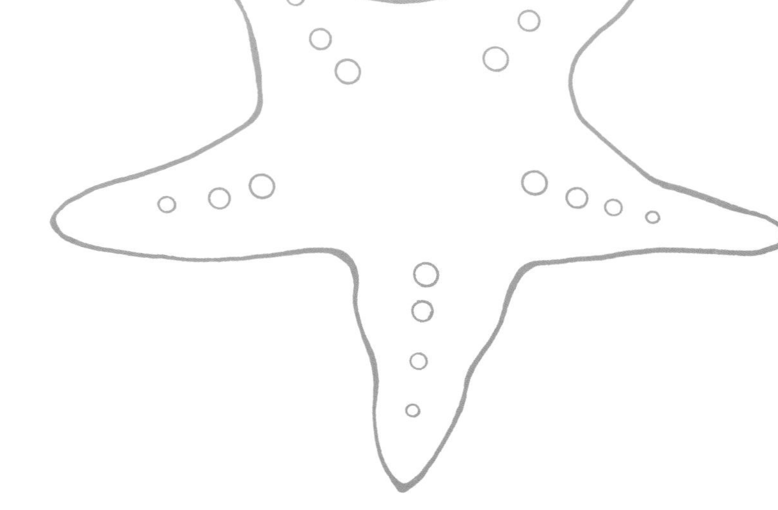

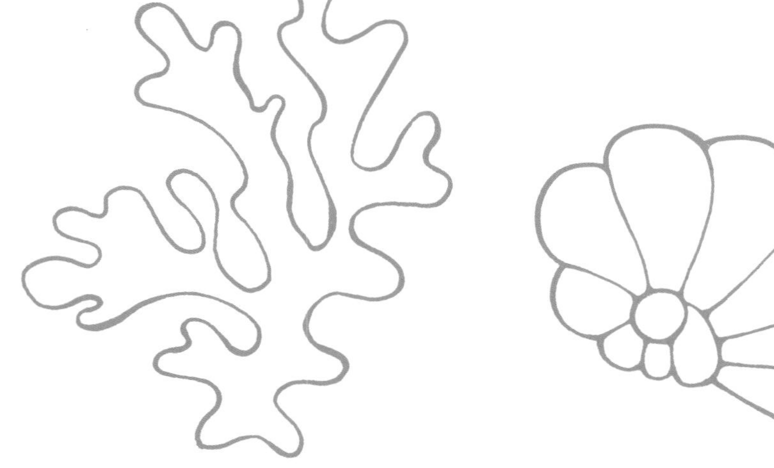

Shower curtain, pp. 74-5

Glass carafe, pp. 134–5

China, pp. 136–8

Embroidered pillowcases, pp. 68–9

Acknowledgments

Bazar
82 Golborne Road
London W10 5BS
Tel: 0181 969 6262
(headboard p. 27, windbreak p. 76, squid vase p. 157)

Bombay Duck
16 Malton Road
London W10 5UP
Tel: 0181 964 8882
(Glasses, p. 91)

Decorative Living
55 New Kings Road
London SW6 4SE
Tel: 0171 736 5623

Yves DeLorme
Tel: 01296 994 980

Dylon International Ltd.
Consumer Advice Line: 0181 663 4296
(Dye for linens, pp. 66–7)

The Finishing Touch & Design Ltd.
Marsh Mills
Luck Lane
Huddersfield HD3 4AB
Tel: 01484 514463
(Bed linen, pp. 100-1)

Harley & Co. Antiques
295 Lillie Road
London SW6 7LL
Tel: 0171 381 5277
(Shell tables, p. 78, mirror and pots, p. 108)

The Kasbah
8 Southampton Street
London WC2E 7HA
Tel: 0171 240 3538
(Lanterns, p. 130)

Malabar
Unit 31-33, South Bank Business Centre
Ponton Road
London SW8 5BL
(Fabrics, pp. 50–1)

The Mulberry Home Collection
41–42 New Bond Street
London W1Y 9HB
Tel. enquiries: 01749 340594
(Cushions, p. 80, director's chairs, p. 80–1)

The Nursery Window
83 Walton Street
London SW3 2HP
Tel: 0171 581 3358

Josephine Ryan Antiques
320 Lillie Road
London SW6 7PA
Tel: 0171 381 6003

Project Contributors

Thanks to Helen Baird for the mosaic table on p. 111 and the mosaic bowl and mirror on p. 109; Emma Harding for the floor cloth on p. 28 and the tray on p. 146; Mandy Pritty for the muslin seashore screen on p. 55; Jonty Henshall for the driftwood beach chair on p.79, the reclaimed timber cupboard on p.79, the kitchen cupboard on p. 82, the wood wardrobe on p. 82 and the grandfather clock on p. 83; Andrew Ewing for the lamp base on p. 111.

Acknowledgments

Many thanks to the Reeves family for their hospitality and for the use of their home, Judith Botten for her charming beach house, Alison Davis for her assistance in hand modeling, Sacha Cohen for her paint techniques, Pam Grinsted for her beautiful sewing of duffel bags and beach house curtains and cushions, and Pat Istead for her superb needlework on the bench cushions. Special thanks to Charles Shirvell, without whose creativity, patience and skill many of the projects would not have been possible; and to James Duncan for the step photography. A huge thank you to Spike Powell for his beautiful photographs.

Picture Acknowledgments

The publishers would like to thank the following for photographs used in this book: Spectrum Color Library: p. 8 and p. 17: stones on the beach; p. 2 and p. 12: beach huts reflected in water; p. 22: doorway, Casares, Spain; Superstock: p. 14: Ia, Santorini, Greece; Riomaggiore, Italy; p. 18: Redondo Beach, California; p. 19: Mykonos, Cyclades Islands, Greece; p. 29-30: harbor town of Yialos, Symi, Greece; Marie Claire Maison: p. 11: Nordic summer cottage (photographer I. Snitt, stylist D. Rozenztroch); Julian Nieman: p.15: veranda, Anguilla, West Indies; beach hut, Sri Lanka. © Julian Nieman; Maggy Howarth: p. 34, pebble fish mosaic.

Index

Page numbers in *italic* refer to illustrations

Sala
James

The Comparative Guide to American Hospitals

Volume 3

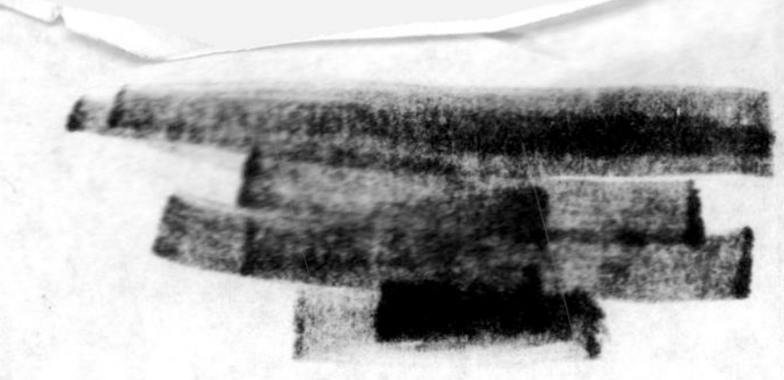

The Comparative Guide to American Hospitals

Volume 3

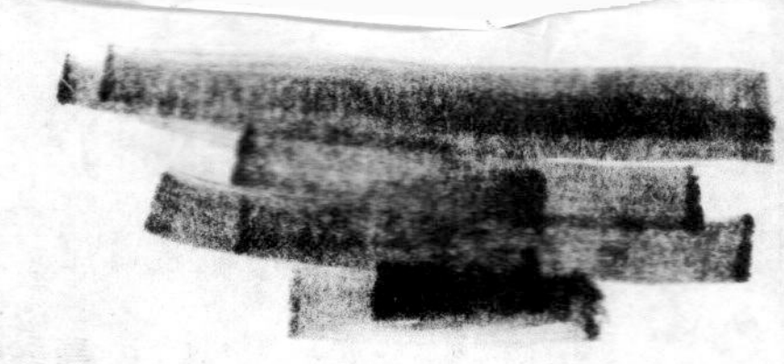

Third Edition

The Comparative Guide to American Hospitals

Volume 3: Central Region

4,693 Hospitals with Key Personnel and 49 Quality Measures Relating to Heart Attack, Heart Failure, Pneumonia, Childhood Asthma, Surgical Care, Medical Imaging and Patient Experience

---

A SEDGWICK PRESS Book

Grey House Publishing

PUBLISHER: Leslie Mackenzie
EDITOR: David Garoogian
EDITORIAL DIRECTOR: Laura Mars
PRODUCTION MANAGER: Kristen Thatcher
MARKETING DIRECTOR: Jessica Moody

A Sedgewick Press Book
Grey House Publishing, Inc.
4919 Route 22
Amenia, NY 12501
518.789.8700
FAX 845.373.6390
www.greyhouse.com
e-mail: books @greyhouse.com

Third Edition

Printed in Canada

Comparative guide to American hospitals. Vol. 3, Central region; [ed. David Garoogian]. — 3rd ed. (2011)

v. ; cm.

Includes index.
"4,693 Hospitals with Key Personnel and 49 Quality Measures Relating to Heart Attack, Heart Failure, Pneumonia, Childhood Asthma, Surgical Care, Medical Imaging and Patient Experience."

1. Hospitals--United States--Directories. 2. Hospitals--United States--Periodicals. 3. Hospitals--Ratings--United States--Statistics--Periodicals. 4. Myocardial infarction--Hospitals--United States--Directories. 5. Heart failure--Hospitals--United States--Directories. 6. Pneumonia--Hospitals--United States--Directories. I. Garoogian, David.

RA977 .C66
610/.025

4-Volume Set	ISBN: 978-1-59237-838-8
Volume 1	ISBN: 978-1-59237-839-5
Volume 2	ISBN: 978-1-59237-840-1
Volume 3	**ISBN: 978-1-59237-841-8**
Volume 4	ISBN: 978-1-59237-842-5

Table of Contents

Introduction

This is the third edition of *The Comparative Guide to American Hospitals*. It reports on how 4,693 hospitals—**310 more than last edition**—in America measure up when caring for patients with a number of specific conditions. The second edition reported on **Heart Attacks, Heart Failure, Pneumonia** and **Surgical Care**. This third edition includes additional data on **Childhood Asthma, Medical Imaging** and **Patients' Hospital Experiences.** Also new is an appendix on **30-Day Readmission Rates**.

This work is based on a Federal study (Hospital Compare) in which short-term acute care and critical access hospitals around the country voluntarily report on quality measures to receive an incentive payment established by the Medicare Prescription Drug, Improvement and Modernization Act of 2003. Each hospital in this edition is rated on 49 recognized quality measures—**25 more than last edition**—and is compared to both state and national averages.

In *The Comparative Guide to American Hospitals,* the data is organized, sorted and ranked by our editors. It is this organization and ranking that makes *The Comparative Guide to American Hospitals* a unique and valuable tool to the health care consumer. Data is presented in such a way as to inform and educate the user, who can then put the facts into a meaningful context as hospitals are evaluated state by state.

Due to the increased data, and the regional use of such data, this edition is comprised of four regional volumes—**Eastern, Southern, Central** and **Western**. In addition to comprehensive **hospital rankings and profiles** for all states in the region, each volume includes a **State-by-State Statistical Summary**.

In addition to the data from Hospital Compare, each hospital profile in *The Comparative Guide to American Hospitals* is comprised of value-added data from Grey House's *Directory of Hospital Personnel*. This critical contact data includes fax numbers, web sites, email addresses, and number of beds plus **23,685 key contact names—2,995 more names** than last edition. In addition, each state chapter includes **State Hospital Rankings**.

Section One: State Hospital Rankings & State Profiles

The first section of each regional volume of *The Comparative Guide to American Hospitals* is arranged alphabetically by state. Each state chapter starts with a ranking section, unique to Grey House, that ranks hospitals in that state on how often they meet each of the accepted quality protocols. This first section:

- **Evaluates 49 Quality Measures:** The quality measures ranked in *The Comparative Guide to American Hospitals* are based on accepted, effective treatments supported by the Centers for Medicare & Medical Services of the US Department of Health & Human Services and the Hospital Quality Alliance (HQA)—a public/private collaboration established to promote on hospital quality of care. HQA represents consumers, hospitals, doctors, employers, accrediting organizations and Federal agencies.
- **Examines Critical Conditions: Heart Attack Care** measures include angiotensin converting enzyme inhibitor (ACE inhibitor) or angiotensin receptor blocker (ARB) for left ventricular systolic dysfunction (LVSD), aspirin at arrival and discharge, beta blocker at discharge, fibrinolytic medication timing, percutaneous coronary intervention (PCI) within 90 minutes of arrival, and smoking cessation advice or counseling; **Chest Pain/Possible Heart Attack Care *(NEW)*** measures include aspirin at arrival, median time to ECG, median time to transfer, and fibrinolytic medication timing; **Heart Failure Care** measures include angiotensin converting enzyme (ACE) inhibitor or angiotensin receptor blocker (ARB) for left ventricular systolic dysfunction (LVSD), discharge instructions given, evaluation of left ventricular systolic (LVS) function, and smoking cessation advice or counseling; **Pneumonia Care** measures include appropriate initial antibiotic, blood culture timing, influenza vaccination, initial antibiotic timing, pneumococcal vaccination, and smoking cessation advice or counseling; **Surgical Care** measures include appropriate venous thromboembolism prophylaxis (VTP) within 24 hours ***(NEW)***, appropriate hair removal ***(NEW)***, appropriate beta blocker usage ***(NEW)***, controlled postoperative blood glucose ***(NEW)***, prophylactic antibiotic timing, prophylactic antibiotic selection, prophylactic antibiotic stopped, recommended

venous thromboembolism prophylaxis (VTP) ordered *(NEW)*, and urinary catheter removal *(NEW)*; **Children's Asthma Care** *(NEW)* measures include receiving systemic corticosteroids, receiving home management plan, and receiving reliever medication.

- **Examines the Use of Medical Imaging** *(NEW)*: MRI for low back pain, follow-up mammogram/ultrasound, combination abdominal CT scan, and combination chest CT scan.
- **Summarizes the Survey of Patients' Hospital Experiences** *(NEW)*
HCAHPS (Hospital Consumer Assessment of Healthcare Providers and Systems) is a national, standardized survey of hospital patients. HCAHPS (pronounced "H-caps") was created to publicly report the patient's perspective of hospital care. The survey asks a random sample of recently discharged patients about important aspects of their hospital experience. The HCAHPS results allow consumers to make fair and objective comparisons between hospitals, and of individual hospitals to state and national benchmarks, on ten important measures of patients' perspectives of care:
    - How do patients rate the hospital overall?
    - How often did doctors communicate well with patients?
    - How often did nurses communicate well with patients?
    - How often did patients receive help quickly from hospital staff?
    - How often did staff explain about medicines before giving them to patients?
    - How often was patients' pain well controlled?
    - How often was the area around patients' rooms kept quiet at night?
    - How often were the patients' rooms and bathrooms kept clean?
    - Were patients given information about what to do during their recovery at home?
    - Would patients recommend the hospital to friends and family?

Following the ranking section, hospital profiles are listed first by city, then alpha within city. Profiles include name, address, phone, fax, web site, hospital type and ownership, number of beds, and whether the hospital provides emergency services. Further, each profile includes an average of five key medical contacts—representing not only the facility's top administration but also the physicians specifically responsible for the care of heart, pneumonia, and asthma patients, as well as surgical care. Again, these data points are unique to *The Comparative Guide to American Hospitals*, and complete the picture for health care consumers searching for quality care.

Section Two: Statistical Summary, Appendixes & Index

The second section of *The Comparative Guide to American Hospitals* includes:

- **Regional State-by-State Statistical Summary Tables** show at a glance how hospitals in the same state score and compare with each other. Hospitals are arranged alphabetically by state.
- **Appendix A: 30-Day Mortality Charts** Unique to Grey House, the Mortality Charts again, take data and organize it in a helpful, informative way for the reader. It lists hospitals nationwide that are "better" or "worse" than the national average, plus a State Summary of Hospital Mortality Rates.
- **Appendix B: 30-Day Readmission Charts** ***(another unique, NEW element)*** lists hospitals nationwide that are "better" or "worse" than the national average, plus a State Summary of Hospital Readmission Rates.
- **Appendix C: Glossary of Terms** provides a list of 50 medical terms to make the best use possible of the data in this edition.
- **Regional Hospital Profile Index** lists hospitals alphabetically, including city and state.

This completely revised third edition of *The Comparative Guide to American Hospitals* is a valuable guide for the entire medical community, with more hospitals, more criteria measures and more key executives than the last edition. It offers an indispensable snapshot of how hospitals measure up, not only to established "best practices," but also to each other.

We welcome your comments to this edition.

USER'S GUIDE

The listing to the right illustrates the kind of information that is or might be included in a Hospital Profile. Each numbered item of information is described in the paragraphs following the example.

❶ **Saint Claire Regional Medical Center**
222 Medical Circle — Phone: 606-783-6500
Morehead, KY 40351 — Fax: 606-783-6503
E-mail: mjneff@st-claire.org
URL: www.st-claire.org
Type: Acute Care Hospitals — Emergency Services: Yes
Ownership: Voluntary Non-Profit - Church — Beds: 159

❷ **Key Personnel:**
CEO/President. . . . . Mark J Neff
Cardiac Laboratory. . . . . Charlotte Lewis
Chief of Medical Staff. . . . . Will Mehlan, MD
Infection Control. . . . . Charlette Kinney
Operating Room. . . . . Lisa Amburgery
Pediatric In-Patient Care . . . . Nancy Maggard
Quality Assurance . . . . Linda Fultz
Radiology. . . . . Charles Butler

❸ Measure	Cases	This Hosp.	State Avg.	U.S. Avg.
❹ **Heart Attack Care**				
ACE Inhibitor or ARB for LVSD[1]	14	79%	94%	96%
Aspirin at Arrival	84	100%	98%	99%
Aspirin at Discharge	72	96%	99%	98%
Beta Blocker at Discharge	73	99%	98%	98%
Fibrinolytic Medication Timing	0	-	60%	55%
PCI Within 90 Minutes of Arrival[1]	10	100%	88%	90%
Smoking Cessation Advice	36	97%	100%	99%
❺ **Chest Pain/Possible Heart Attack Care**				
Aspirin at Arrival	85	99%	95%	95%
Average Time to ECG (minutes)	95	1	7	8
Average Time to Transfer (minutes)[1]	4	54	65	61
Fibrinolytic Medication Timing[1]	3	33%	62%	54%
❻ **Heart Failure Care**				
ACE Inhibitor or ARB for LVSD	49	96%	91%	94%
Discharge Instructions	104	88%	82%	88%
Evaluation of LVS Function	129	97%	96%	98%
Smoking Cessation Advice	30	97%	98%	98%
❼ **Pneumonia Care**				
Appropriate Initial Antibiotic	106	92%	90%	92%
Blood Culture Timing	216	92%	95%	96%
Influenza Vaccine	113	96%	92%	91%
Initial Antibiotic Timing	196	97%	95%	95%
Pneumococcal Vaccine	183	91%	94%	93%
Smoking Cessation Advice	108	97%	98%	97%
❽ **Surgical Care Improvement Project**				
Appropriate VTP Within 24 Hours[2]	92	96%	91%	92%
Appropriate Hair Removal[2]	196	99%	99%	99%
Appropriate Beta Blocker Usage[2]	78	92%	93%	93%
Controlled Postoperative Blood Glucose[2]	0	-	94%	93%
Prophylactic Antibiotic Timing[2]	118	88%	97%	97%
Prophylactic Antibiotic Timing (Outpatient)	80	91%	92%	92%
Prophylactic Antibiotic Selection[2]	119	97%	98%	97%
Prophylactic Antibiotic Select. (Outpatient)	117	91%	93%	94%
Prophylactic Antibiotic Stopped[2]	116	90%	94%	94%
Recommended VTP Ordered[2]	92	98%	94%	94%
Urinary Catheter Removal[2]	42	71%	89%	90%
❾ **Children's Asthma Care**				
Received Systemic Corticosteroids[1]	4	100%	-	100%
Received Home Management Plan[1]	5	80%	-	71%
Received Reliever Medication[1]	5	100%	-	100%
❿ **Use of Medical Imaging**				
Combination Abdominal CT Scan	700	0.616	0.160	0.191
Combination Chest CT Scan	463	0.039	0.054	0.054
Follow-up Mammogram/Ultrasound	756	7.9%	7.9%	8.4%
MRI for Low Back Pain	143	43.4%	35.6%	32.7%
⓫ **Survey of Patients' Hospital Experiences**				
Area Around Room 'Always' Quiet at Night	300+	49%	-	58%
Doctors 'Always' Communicated Well	300+	85%	-	80%
Home Recovery Information Given	300+	83%	-	82%
Hospital Given 9 or 10 on 10 Point Scale	300+	62%	-	67%
Meds 'Always' Explained Before Given	300+	64%	-	60%
Nurses 'Always' Communicated Well	300+	80%	-	76%
Pain 'Always' Well Controlled	300+	71%	-	69%
Room and Bathroom 'Always' Clean	300+	71%	-	71%
Timely Help 'Always' Received	300+	64%	-	64%
Would Definitely Recommend Hospital	300+	66%	-	69%

➊ **Hospital Name and Record Header:** hospital name; street address; phone; fax; e-mail; URL; hospital type; ownership; emergency services (Yes/No); and number of beds.

➋ **Key Personnel:** includes the names of key personnel primarily related to the conditions covered in this publication.

➌ **Hospital Compare Data:** each table contains data covering fourty-nine measures contained in the Hospital Compare database. There are five columns:

Measure: the fourty-nine quality measures reported.

There are eleven possible footnotes:

1. *The number of cases is too small (<25) to reliably tell how well a hospital is performing.*
For each measure, the rate is the percent of patients for whom the treatment is appropriate. Where these numbers are small (fewer than 25 patients), the calculated rate may not accurately predict the hospital's future performance. As the quality data base is expanded to a full rolling four quarters of data for each measure, the number of cases used to determine hospitals' rates will likely increase, thereby increasing the reliability and stability of the rates. Note: This footnote does not necessarily reflect hospital size or overall patient volume.

2. *The hospital indicated that the data submitted for this measure were based on a sample of cases.*
A rate may be based upon the total number of cases treated by a hospital, or for a facility with a large caseload, a rate may be based on a random sample of the cases the hospital treated. This footnote indicates that a hospital chose to submit data for a sample of its total cases (following specific rules for how to the select the cases).

3. *Data was collected during a shorter time period (fewer quarters) than the maximum possible time for this measure (one quarter equals three months.).*
Each rate reflects the care given over a specific time period, up to a maximum of four quarters during a 12 month period. The number of quarters of data available is determined by when hospitals first began to report data using a specific measure. For example, for the ten measures in the "Starter Set", the maximum number of quarters for which a hospital could have provided data is four quarters. For measures added more recently, the maximum will be fewer than four quarters. This footnote indicates that the hospital's rate was based on data from fewer than the maximum possible number of quarters that the measure was generally collected.

4. *Inaccurate information submitted and suppressed for one or more quarters.*
Hospitals are required to submit accurate, reportable data to the Centers for Medicare and Medicaid Services (CMS). The rates for these measures were calculated by excluding data that had been suppressed for one or more quarters because they were identified as inaccurate.

5. *No data is available from the hospital for this measure.*
Hospitals volunteer to provide data for reporting on Hospital Compare. This footnote is applied when the hospital did not submit any cases for a measure or if they suppressed their data from public reporting.

6. *Fewer than 100 patients completed the HCAHPS survey. Use these rates with caution, as the number of surveys may be too low to reliably assess hospital performance.*
The number of completed surveys the hospital or its vendor provided to CMS is less than 100.

7. *Survey results are based on less than 12 months of survey data.*
This footnote is applied when HCAHPS results are based on less than 12 months of survey data.

8. *Survey results are not available for this period.*
This footnote is applied when a hospital did not participate in HCAHPS, did not collect sufficient HCAHPS data for public reporting purposes, or chose to suppress their HCAHPS results.

9. *No patients were eligible for the HCAHPS Survey.*
This footnote is applied when a hospital has no patients eligible to participate in the HCAHPS survey.

10. *A state average was not calculated because too few hospitals in the state submitted data.*
This footnote is applied when too few hospitals submitted data.

11. *There were discrepancies in the data collection process.*
This footnote is applied when there have been deviations from HCAHPS data collection protocols. CMS is working with survey vendors and/or hospitals to correct this situation.

Cases: the size of the data sample (number of patients) for each hospital and quality measure. In addition, the notation "0" is applied when a hospital provided care to patients with a condition, such as pneumonia, but the cases that the hospital submitted did not meet the specific criteria for being included in the calculation of the measure.

This Hospital: the performance rate that the hospital achieved for each quality measure. This value is expressed as a percentage of the sample size that was measured. The performance rate is calculated by dividing the numerator by the denominator. The denominator is the sum of all eligible cases (as defined in the measure specifications) submitted to the QIO Clinical Data Warehouse for the reporting period. The numerator is the sum of all eligible cases submitted for the same reporting period where the recommended care was provided.

State Average: the average rate for all hospitals reporting data in the state the hospital is located in.
U.S. Average: the average rate for all hospitals reporting nationwide.

Note: Beginning in December 2010, state and national averages for the process of care measures are calculated by summing the cases in the state or nation that "passed" the measure (Numerator) and dividing that sum by the number of cases in the state or national Denominator. For the national and state averages, a simple average was constructed where the numerator was the sum of all non-excluded hospitals' scores and the denominator was the total number of hospitals, each calculated at either the national or individual state level. For the process and survey measures, the national and state averages are calculated before excluding suppressed rates and are not recalculated using only published rates as was done prior to September 2009. Acute Care-VA Medical Centers are not included in the calculation of the national and state comparison rates.

The children's asthma care national and state averages are calculated differently. The average rate for all healthcare organizations in the nation that provide results for a measure. The average rate is calculated by dividing the total number of patients who had the recommended care provided for a measure by the total number of patients who met the inclusion and exclusion criteria for that measure in the nation for the timeframe being reported.

❹ Heart Attack Care

Every year, about one million people suffer a heart attack (acute myocardial infarction or AMI). AMI is among the leading causes of hospital admission for Medicare beneficiaries, age 65 and older.

Scientific evidence indicates that the following process of care measures represent the best practices for the treatment of AMI. Higher scores are better.

- **ACE Inhibitor or ARB for LVSD** - AMI patients with left ventricular systolic dysfunction (LVSD) and without angiotensin converting enzyme inhibitor (ACE inhibitor) contraindications or angiotensin receptor blocker (ARB) contraindications who are prescribed an ACE inhibitor or an ARB at hospital discharge.
- **Aspirin at Arrival** - Acute myocardial infarction (AMI) patients without aspirin contraindications who received aspirin within 24 hours before or after hospital arrival.
- **Aspirin at Discharge** - AMI patients without aspirin contraindications who were prescribed aspirin at hospital discharge.
- **Beta Blocker at Discharge** - AMI patients without beta-blocker contraindications who were prescribed a beta-blocker at hospital discharge.
- **Fibrinolytic Medication Timing** - AMI patients receiving fibrinolytic therapy during the hospital stay and having a time from hospital arrival to fibrinolysis of 30 minutes or less.
- **PCI Within 90 Minutes of Arrival** - AMI patients receiving Percutaneous Coronary Intervention (PCI) during the hospital stay with a time from hospital arrival to PCI of 90 minutes or less.
- **Smoking Cessation Advice** - AMI patients with a history of smoking cigarettes, who are given smoking cessation advice or counseling during a hospital stay.

❺ Chest Pain/Possible Heart Attack Care

These are all outpatient measures. Higher scores are better.

- **Aspirin at Arrival** - Acute myocardial infarction (AMI) patients without aspirin contraindications who received aspirin within 24 hours before or after hospital arrival.
- **Median Time to ECG** - Median number of minutes before outpatients with heart attack (or with chest pain that suggest a possible heart attack) got an ECG (a lower number of minutes is better).
- **Median Time to Transfer** - Median number of minutes before outpatients with heart attack who needed specialized care were transferred to another hospital (a lower number of minutes is better).

- **Fibrinolytic Medication Timing** - AMI patients receiving fibrinolytic therapy during the hospital stay and having a time from hospital arrival to fibrinolysis of 30 minutes or less.

❻ Heart Failure Care

Heart failure is the most common hospital admission diagnosis in patients age 65 or older, accounting for more than 700,000 hospitalizations among Medicare beneficiaries every year. It is associated with severe functional impairments and high rates of mortality and morbidity.

Substantial scientific evidence indicates that the following process of care measures represent the best practices for the treatment of heart failure. Higher scores are better.

- **ACE Inhibitor or ARB for LVSD** - Heart failure patients with left ventricular systolic dysfunction (LVSD) and without angiotensin converting enzyme inhibitor (ACE inhibitor) contraindications or angiotensin receptor blocker (ARB) contraindications who are prescribed an ACE inhibitor or an ARB at hospital discharge.
- **Discharge Instructions** - Heart failure patients discharged home with written instructions or educational material given to patient or care giver at discharge or during the hospital stay addressing all of the following: activity level, diet, discharge medications, follow-up appointment, weight monitoring, and what to do if symptoms worsen.
- **Evaluation of LVS Function** - Heart failure patients with documentation in the hospital record that an evaluation of the left ventricular systolic (LVS) function was performed before arrival, during hospitalization, or is planned for after discharge.
- **Smoking Cessation Advice** - Heart failure patients with a history of smoking cigarettes, who are given smoking cessation advice or counseling during a hospital stay.

❼ Pneumonia Care

Community acquired pneumonia is a major contributor to illness and mortality in the United States, causing four million episodes of illness and nearly one million hospital admissions each year.

Scientific evidence indicates that the following process of care measures represent the best practices for the treatment of community-acquired pneumonia. Higher scores are better.

- **Appropriate Initial Antibiotic** - Immunocompetent patients with pneumonia who receive an initial antibiotic regimen that is consistent with current guidelines.
- **Blood Culture Timing** - Pneumonia patients whose initial emergency room blood culture specimen was collected prior to first hospital dose of antibiotics.
- **Influenza Vaccination** - Pneumonia patients age 50 years and older, hospitalized during October, November, December, January, or February who were screened for influenza vaccine status and were vaccinated prior to discharge, if indicated.
- **Initial Antibiotic Timing** - Pneumonia inpatients who receive antibiotics within 6 hours of hospital arrival. Evidence shows better outcomes for administration times less than four hours.
- **Pneumococcal Vaccination** - Pneumonia inpatients age 65 and older who were screened for pneumococcal vaccine status and were administered the vaccine prior to discharge, if indicated.
- **Smoking Cessation Advice** - Pneumonia patients with a history of smoking cigarettes, who are given smoking cessation advice or counseling during a hospital stay.

❽ Surgical Care Improvement Project

Hospitals can reduce the risk of complications like wound infection or blood clots in surgery patients by giving the right treatments at the right time. For example, studies show a strong association of reduced incidence of post-operative infection with administration of antibiotics within the one hour prior to surgery. After the incision is closed, however, studies show that prolonged administration of prophylaxis with antibiotics may increase the risk of certain other infections at no additional benefit to the surgical patient.

Scientific evidence indicates that the following process of care measures represent the best practices for the prevention of infections after selected surgeries (colon surgery, hip and knee arthroplasty, abdominal and vaginal hysterectomy, cardiac surgery (including coronary artery bypass grafts (CABG)) and vascular surgery). Higher scores are better.

- **Appropriate VTP Within 24 Hours** - Surgery patients who received appropriate venous thromboembolism prophylaxis (VTP) within 24 Hours prior to surgical incision time to 24 hours after surgery end time.
- **Appropriate Hair Removal** - Surgery patients with appropriate surgical site hair removal. No hair removal, or hair removal with clippers or depilatory is considered appropriate. Shaving is considered inappropriate.
- **Appropriate Beta Blocker Usage** - Surgery patients who were taking heart drugs called beta blockers before coming to the hospital, who were kept on the beta blockers during the period just before and after their surgery.
- **Controlled Postoperative Blood Glucose** - Cardiac surgery patients with controlled 6 A.M. blood glucose (= 200 mg/dL) on postoperative day one (POD 1) and postoperative day two (POD 2) with surgery end date being postoperative day zero (POD 0).
- **Prophylactic Antibiotic Timing** - Surgical inpatients who received prophylactic antibiotics within 1 hour prior to surgical incision.
- **Prophylactic Antibiotic Timing (Outpatient)** - Surgical outpatients who received prophylactic antibiotics within 1 hour prior to surgical incision.
- **Prophylactic Antibiotic Selection** - Surgical inpatients who received the recommended antibiotics for their particular type of surgery.
- **Prophylactic Antibiotic Selection (Outpatient)** - Surgical outpatients who received the recommended antibiotics for their particular type of surgery.
- **Prophylactic Antibiotic Stopped** - Surgical patients whose prophylactic antibiotics were discontinued within 24 hours after surgery end time.
- **Recommended VTP Ordered** - Surgery patients with recommended venous thromboembolism prophylaxis (VTP) ordered anytime from hospital arrival to 48 hours after surgery end time.
- **Urinary Catheters Removal** - Inpatients whose urinary catheters were removed within 2 days after surgery to reduce the risk of infections. Shows the percent of surgery patients whose urinary catheters were removed on the first or second day after surgery.

❾ Children's Asthma Care

Asthma is the most common chronic disease in children and a major cause of morbidity and increased health care expenditures nationally (Adams, et al., 2001). For children, asthma is one of the most frequent reasons for admission to hospitals (McCormick, et al., 1999). Other researchers noted that there are approximately 200,000 admissions for childhood asthma in the United States annually, representing more than $3 billion dollars in healthcare costs (Silber, et al., 2003). Under-treatment and/or inappropriate treatment of asthma are recognized as major contributors to asthma morbidity and mortality.

- **Received Systemic Corticosteroids** - Use of systemic Corticosteroid Medication in pediatric patients admitted for inpatient treatment of asthma.
- **Received Home Management Plan** - An assessment that there is documentation in the medical record that a Home Management Plan of Care (HMPC) document was given to the pediatric asthma patient/caregiver.
- **Received Reliever Medication** - Use of relievers in pediatric patients admitted for inpatient treatment of asthma.

❿ Use of Medical Imaging

"Medical imaging" is the name for tests that create images of various parts of the body to screen for or diagnose medical conditions. Examples of medical imaging include CT scans, MRIs, and mammograms. The measures on use of medical imaging give you information about how hospitals use medical imaging tests for outpatients based on the following: 1) Protecting patients' safety, such as keeping patients' exposure to radiation and other risks as low as possible; 2) Following up properly when screening tests such as mammograms show a possible problem; 3) Avoiding the risk, stress, and cost of doing imaging tests that patients may not need.

The measures of medical imaging are based on Medicare claims data. CMS compiles this information from claims for patients in Original (fee-for-service) Medicare. It does not include people in Medicare Advantage plans or people who do not have Medicare. The information is limited to medical imaging facilities that are part of a hospital or associated with a hospital. These facilities can be inside or near the hospital, or in a different location. The information only includes medical imaging done on outpatients. Medical imaging tests done for patients who have been admitted to the hospital as inpatients aren't included.

- **MRI for Low Back Pain** (NQF Endorsed, October 2008) - This measure calculates the percentage of patients who had an MRI of the Lumbar Spine with a diagnosis of low back pain without Medicare claims-based evidence of antecedent conservative therapy. If a number is high, it may mean the facility is doing too many unnecessary MRIs for low back pain.

- **Follow-up Mammogram/Ultrasound** (Not NQF Endorsed at this time) - This measure calculates the percentage of patients with mammography screening studies done in the outpatient hospital setting that are followed within 45 days by a diagnostic mammography or ultrasound of the breast study in an outpatient or office setting. A number that is much lower than 8% may mean there's not enough follow-up. A number much higher than 14% may mean there's too much unnecessary follow-up.

- **Combination Abdominal CT Scan** (Not NQF Endorsed at this time) - This measure calculates the ratio of CT abdomen studies that are performed both with/without contrast out of all CT abdomen studies performed (those with contrast, those without contrast, and those with both). The range for this measure is 0 to 1. A number very close to 1 may mean that too many patients are being given a combination (double) scan when a single scan is all they need.

- **Combination Chest CT Scan** (NQF Endorsed, October 2008) - This measure calculates the ratio of CT thorax studies that are performed with and without contrast out of all CT thorax studies performed (those with contrast, those without contrast, and those with both). The range for this measure is 0 to 1. A number very close to 1 may mean that too many patients are being given a combination (double) scan when a single scan is all they need.

The National Quality Forum (NQF) is an independent organization created to develop and implement a strategy for health care quality measurement and public reporting. The NQF brings together stakeholders from throughout the healthcare industry to jointly decide which quality measures meet industry standards and are suitable for reporting on Hospital Compare. While NQF endorses the quality measures, it does not monitor or review the data that are collected from and about hospitals.

NQF considers several factors when deciding whether a quality measure should be reported: 1) Whether it addresses an aspect of care or treatment that improves people's health or well-being; 2) Whether it can be measured accurately and reliably in different hospitals; 3) Whether the information can be used to improve the quality of care or to inform patients' decisions about where to go for care.

⓫ Survey of Patients' Hospital Experiences (HCAHPS)

HCAHPS (Hospital Consumer Assessment of Healthcare Providers and Systems) is a national, standardized survey of hospital patients. HCAHPS (pronounced "H-caps") was created to publicly report the patient's perspective of hospital care. The survey asks a random sample of recently discharged patients about important aspects of their hospital experience. The HCAHPS results allow consumers to make fair and objective comparisons between hospitals, and of individual hospitals to state and national benchmarks, on ten important measures of patients' perspectives of care.

HCAHPS was developed by a partnership of public and private organizations. Development of the survey was funded by the Federal government, specifically the Centers for Medicare & Medicaid Services (CMS) and the Agency for Healthcare Research and Quality (AHRQ). For more on HCAHPS information, please visit the official HCAHPS website: www.hcahpsonline.org

What questions are on the survey?

The HCAHPS survey asks patients to give feedback about topics for which they are the best source of information. The survey asks patients to answer questions about their experiences in the hospital. To make sure the HCAHPS survey data is meaningful; patients only answer questions about topics with which they have experience. The HCAHPS survey asks patients to answer questions related to ten topics. The topics and questions are listed in the table below.

HCAHPS Topic Text	HCAHPS Answer Description
How do patients rate the hospital overall?	*Patients who gave a rating of 9 or 10 (high)*
	Patients who gave a rating of 7 or 8 (medium)
	Patients who gave a rating of 6 or lower (low)
How often did doctors communicate well with patients?	*Doctors always communicated well*
	Doctors usually communicated well
	Doctors sometimes or never communicated well

HCAHPS Topic Text	HCAHPS Answer Description
How often did nurses communicate well with patients?	*Nurses always communicated well*
	Nurses usually communicated well
	Nurses sometimes or never communicated well
How often did patients receive help quickly from hospital staff?	*Patients always received help as soon as they wanted*
	Patients usually received help as soon as they wanted
	Patients sometimes or never received help as soon as they wanted
How often did staff explain about medicines before giving them to patients?	*Staff always explained*
	Staff usually explained
	Staff sometimes or never explained
How often was patients' pain well controlled?	*Pain was always well controlled*
	Pain was usually well controlled
	Pain was sometimes or never well controlled
How often was the area around patients' rooms kept quiet at night?	*Always quiet at night*
	Usually quiet at night
	Sometimes or never quiet at night
How often were the patients' rooms and bathrooms kept clean?	*Room was always clean*
	Room was usually clean
	Room was sometimes or never clean
Were patients given information about what to do during their recovery at home?	*YES, staff did give patients this information*
	NO, staff did not give patients this information
Would patients recommend the hospital to friends and family?	*YES, patients would definitely recommend the hospital*
	YES, patients would probably recommend the hospital
	NO, patients would not recommend the hospital (they probably would not or definitely would not recommend it)

Note: Answers in italics are measures included in this book.

How many patients were surveyed for each hospital and how were they selected?

The goal is for each hospital to get at least 300 completed patient surveys per year. In general, the more patients that respond to a hospital's survey, the more the results shown on this website will reflect the experiences of all the patients who used that hospital. Patients are randomly selected to participate in the HCAHPS survey. Hospitals are not allowed to choose which patients are selected.

Which hospitals participate in the HCAHPS survey?

All short-term, acute care, non-specialty hospitals are invited to participate in the HCAHPS survey. Most hospitals choose to participate. Hospitals that treat only certain types of patients or medical problems, called specialty hospitals, are not included in the HCAHPS survey. Examples include psychiatric hospitals or children's hospitals. Children's hospitals are not included because the HCAHPS survey asks about adult care only.

How is HCAHPS survey data collected?

HCAHPS survey data must be collected by organizations that are trained by the Federal government in HCAHPS survey data collection procedures. Hospitals can choose to conduct the survey in one of four ways: by mail, by telephone, by mail and telephone, or by active interactive voice recognition (IVR). Regardless of how the survey is conducted, all patients answer the same questions. Patients complete the HCAHPS survey after they leave the hospital.

Confidence Intervals

The table below enables the user to calculate confidence intervals for each reported measure.

Confidence intervals can be used to estimate the precision of the calculated rates for an individual hospital. A confidence interval is the range of values, within which an estimated value or rate is likely to fall. A confidence interval is a statistical determination of the degree of certainty associated with an estimated value. As can be seen in the table of estimated values (below), large differences between individual hospitals' rates may be significant, and small differences between hospitals are usually not significant.

The smaller the sample size, the greater the difference in rates must be order for that difference to be statistically meaningful. Also, as sample size varies between hospitals, it is difficult to precisely compare their rates, without considering the confidence intervals.

Over time, as the quality data base is expanded, a full four quarters of data will ultimately be available, so the number of cases used to determine hospitals' rates will likely increase, thereby increasing the reliability and stability of the rates.

Estimating Confidence Intervals for the Quality Measures: Estimated Values for Proportion Data

Sample Size	Observed Rate								
	10%	20%	30%	40%	50%	60%	70%	80%	90%
< 25	*	*	24.9	26.6	27.2	26.6	24.9	*	*
25 - 75	8.3	11.1	12.7	13.6	13.9	13.6	12.7	11.1	8.3
76 - 125	5.9	7.8	9.0	9.6	9.8	9.6	9.0	7.8	5.9
126 - 175	4.8	6.4	7.3	7.8	8.0	7.8	7.3	6.4	4.8
176 - 225	4.2	5.5	6.4	6.8	6.9	6.8	6.4	5.5	4.2
226 -275	3.7	5.0	5.7	6.1	6.2	6.1	5.7	5.0	3.7
276+	2.9	3.9	4.5	4.8	4.9	4.8	4.5	3.9	2.9

*Source: CMS/OCSQ/QIG. The values in the table are the approximate amount to add and subtract from the observed rate to estimate a 95 percent confidence interval for the given sample size. (Interpolation between the values in the table is appropriate.) * Estimates of an interval in these cells exceed the natural limits for proportions.*

Data Sources

The statistical information in this book comes from data downloaded from www.hospitalcompare.hhs.gov, a website tool developed by the Centers for Medicare & Medicaid Services (CMS). Process of Care (Heart Attack, Chest Pain/Possible Heart Attack, Heart Failure, Pneumonia, Surgical Care Improvment Project, Children's Asthma) and HCAHPS measures cover data collected April 2009 through March 2010. Use of Medical Imaging measures cover January 2008 through December 2008. Outcome of Care measures (Mortality and Readmission Rates) covers July 2006 through June 2009. *Source: www.hospitalcompare.hhs.gov, Centers for Medicare & Medicaid Services (CMS), an agency of the U.S. Department of Health and Human Services (DHHS) along with the Hospital Quality Alliance (HQA).*

Key personnel, fax numbers, e-mail addresses, URLs, and number of beds come from *Directory of Hospital Personnel, 2011,* Grey House Publishing.

Heart Attack Care

1. ACE Inhibitor or ARB for LVSD

Hospital Name	City	Rate	Cases
Advocate Christ Hospital & Medical Center[2]	Oak Lawn	100%	55
Advocate Condell Medical Center	Libertyville	100%	32
Advocate Good Samaritan Hospital	Downers Grove	100%	52
Advocate Good Shepherd Hospital	Barrington	100%	31
Advocate Lutheran General Hospital	Park Ridge	100%	43
Advocate South Suburban Hospital	Hazel Crest	100%	27
Elmhurst Memorial Hospital[2]	Elmhurst	100%	38
Genesis Medical Center Illini Campus	Silvis	100%	77
John H Stroger Jr Hospital[2]	Chicago	100%	34
Louis A Weiss Memorial Hospital	Chicago	100%	25
Loyola Gottlieb Memorial Hospital	Melrose Park	100%	44
Loyola University Medical Center	Maywood	100%	33
Our Lady of the Resurrection Medical Center	Chicago	100%	29
Provena St Joseph Medical Center	Joliet	100%	49
Resurrection Medical Center	Chicago	100%	41
Saint Elizabeth Hospital	Belleville	100%	38
St Mary & Elizabeth Med Ctr-Div Campus	Chicago	100%	25
Silver Cross Hospital	Joliet	100%	47
Memorial Hospital	Belleville	99%	68
Memorial Hospital of Carbondale	Carbondale	99%	74
Saint Francis Medical Center	Peoria	99%	77
Saint Johns Hospital	Springfield	99%	116
Decatur Memorial Hospital	Decatur	98%	57
Edward Hospital	Naperville	98%	44
Macneal Hospital	Berwyn	98%	45
Methodist Medical Center of Illinois	Peoria	98%	41
Mount Sinai Hospital Medical Center	Chicago	98%	44
Swedish American Hospital	Rockford	98%	42
Swedish Covenant Hospital	Chicago	98%	61
Trinity Rock Island	Rock Island	98%	62
Blessing Hospital	Quincy	97%	30
Central Dupage Hospital	Winfield	97%	34
Copley Memorial Hospital	Aurora	97%	29
Rockford Memorial Hospital	Rockford	97%	30
The University of Chicago Medical Center	Chicago	97%	38
Evanston Hospital	Evanston	96%	50
Mercy Hospital and Medical Center	Chicago	96%	48
Northwestern Memorial Hospital	Chicago	96%	46
Saint Anthony Medical Center	Rockford	96%	45
Vista Medical Center East	Waukegan	96%	25
St James Hospital-Olympia Fields	Olympia Fields	95%	56
Alexian Brothers Medical Center	Elk Grove Vlg	94%	49
Memorial Medical Center	Springfield	94%	77
Palos Community Hospital[2]	Palos Heights	94%	33
Rush University Medical Center	Chicago	94%	35
Good Samaritan Regional Health Center	Mount Vernon	93%	54
Carle Foundation Hospital[2]	Urbana	92%	60
Ingalls Memorial Hospital[2]	Harvey	92%	40
Metrosouth Medical Center	Blue Island	92%	36
Centegra Health System - McHenry Hospital	Mchenry	91%	34
Northwest Community Hospital	Arlington Hgts	91%	33
Provena Covenant Medical Center - Urbana	Urbana	88%	41
Holy Cross Hospital[2]	Chicago	69%	32

2. Aspirin at Arrival

Hospital Name	City	Rate	Cases
Adventist Bolingbrook Hospital	Bolingbrook	100%	84
Adventist La Grange Memorial Hospital	La Grange	100%	134
Advocate Condell Medical Center	Libertyville	100%	221
Advocate Good Samaritan Hospital	Downers Grove	100%	240
Advocate Good Shepherd Hospital	Barrington	100%	210
Advocate Illinois Masonic Medical Center	Chicago	100%	127
Advocate Lutheran General Hospital	Park Ridge	100%	255
Advocate South Suburban Hospital	Hazel Crest	100%	148
Alton Memorial Hospital	Alton	100%	95
Blessing Hospital	Quincy	100%	212
CGH Medical Center	Sterling	100%	80
Decatur Memorial Hospital	Decatur	100%	172
Edward Hospital	Naperville	100%	214
Elmhurst Memorial Hospital[2]	Elmhurst	100%	213
Fhn Memorial Hospital	Freeport	100%	65
Galesburg Cottage Hospital	Galesburg	100%	35
Gateway Regional Medical Center	Granite City	100%	91
Hinsdale Hospital	Hinsdale	100%	89
J Brown VA Med Ctr-VA Chicago Healthcare	Chicago	100%	43
Lake Forest Hospital	Lake Forest	100%	53
Little Company of Mary Hospital	Evergreen Park	100%	109
Louis A Weiss Memorial Hospital	Chicago	100%	109
Loyola University Medical Center	Maywood	100%	157
Macneal Hospital	Berwyn	100%	209
Metrosouth Medical Center	Blue Island	100%	110
Morris Hospital & Healthcare Centers	Morris	100%	81
Norwegian-American Hospital	Chicago	100%	37
Our Lady of the Resurrection Medical Center	Chicago	100%	224
Proctor Hospital	Peoria	100%	66
Provena St Marys Hospital	Kankakee	100%	57
Rush University Medical Center	Chicago	100%	90
Saint Alexius Medical Center	Hoffman Estates	100%	173
Saint Johns Hospital	Springfield	100%	158
Saint Joseph Medical Center	Bloomington	100%	111
St Mary & Elizabeth Med Ctr-Div Campus	Chicago	100%	159
Saint Marys Hospital	Centralia	100%	48
Sherman Hospital	Elgin	100%	161
Skokie Hospital	Skokie	100%	120
Swedish American Hospital	Rockford	100%	218
Trinity Rock Island	Rock Island	100%	252
The University of Chicago Medical Center	Chicago	100%	96
West Suburban Medical Center	Oak Park	100%	74
Advocate Christ Hospital & Medical Center[2]	Oak Lawn	99%	256
Advocate Trinity Hospital	Chicago	99%	167
Alexian Brothers Medical Center	Elk Grove Vlg	99%	213
Bromenn Healthcare	Normal	99%	159
Carle Foundation Hospital[2]	Urbana	99%	161
Centegra Health System - McHenry Hospital	Mchenry	99%	226
Central Dupage Hospital	Winfield	99%	190
Copley Memorial Hospital	Aurora	99%	182
Delnor Community Hospital	Geneva	99%	100
Evanston Hospital	Evanston	99%	412
Ingalls Memorial Hospital[2]	Harvey	99%	201
John H Stroger Jr Hospital[2]	Chicago	99%	178
Loyola Gottlieb Memorial Hospital	Melrose Park	99%	174
Memorial Medical Center	Springfield	99%	344
Methodist Medical Center of Illinois	Peoria	99%	116
Mount Sinai Hospital Medical Center	Chicago	99%	115
Northwest Community Hospital	Arlington Hgts	99%	390
Northwestern Memorial Hospital	Chicago	99%	294
Palos Community Hospital[2]	Palos Heights	99%	276
Provena St Joseph Medical Center	Joliet	99%	309
Resurrection Medical Center	Chicago	99%	342
Rockford Memorial Hospital	Rockford	99%	161
Saint Anthony Medical Center	Rockford	99%	222
Saint Francis Medical Center	Peoria	99%	217
St James Hospital-Olympia Fields	Olympia Fields	99%	306
Saint Joseph Hospital	Chicago	99%	68
Silver Cross Hospital	Joliet	99%	192
Genesis Medical Center Illini Campus	Silvis	98%	115
Good Samaritan Regional Health Center	Mount Vernon	98%	141
Heartland Regional Medical Center	Marion	98%	56
Katherine Shaw Bethea Hospital	Dixon	98%	54
Kishwaukee Community Hospital	Dekalb	98%	65
Memorial Hospital	Belleville	98%	301
Memorial Hospital of Carbondale	Carbondale	98%	119
Pekin Memorial Hospital	Pekin	98%	41
Provena Mercy Medical Center	Aurora	98%	110
RHC St Francis Hospital	Evanston	98%	106
Saint Elizabeth Hospital	Belleville	98%	170
Saint Mary Medical Center	Galesburg	98%	40
Saint Marys Hospital[2]	Decatur	98%	47
University of Illinois Hospital	Chicago	98%	59
Vista Medical Center East	Waukegan	98%	132
Westlake Community Hospital	Melrose Park	98%	41
Adventist Glenoaks	Glendale Hghts	97%	37
Herrin Hospital	Herrin	97%	29
Hines VA Medical Center	Hines	97%	36
Mercy Hospital and Medical Center	Chicago	97%	194
Provena United Samaritans Med Ctr-Logan	Danville	97%	69
Riverside Medical Center	Kankakee	97%	113
Sarah Bush Lincoln Health Center	Mattoon	97%	37
Anderson Hospital	Maryville	96%	113
Provena-Saint Joseph Hospital	Elgin	96%	125
Rush Oak Park Hospital	Oak Park	96%	25
Saint Anthony's Health Center	Alton	96%	45
Swedish Covenant Hospital	Chicago	96%	275
Centegra Health Sys-Woodstock Hospital	Woodstock	95%	59
Provena Covenant Medical Center - Urbana	Urbana	93%	90
Touchette Regional Hospital	Centreville	92%	26
Holy Cross Hospital[2]	Chicago	90%	105
Saint Marys Hospital	Streator	89%	28
South Shore Hospital	Chicago	84%	38

3. Aspirin at Discharge

Hospital Name	City	Rate	Cases
Adventist Bolingbrook Hospital	Bolingbrook	100%	68
Adventist Glenoaks	Glendale Hghts	100%	26
Adventist La Grange Memorial Hospital	La Grange	100%	117
Advocate Christ Hospital & Medical Center[2]	Oak Lawn	100%	305
Advocate Condell Medical Center	Libertyville	100%	215
Advocate Good Samaritan Hospital	Downers Grove	100%	226
Advocate Good Shepherd Hospital	Barrington	100%	217
Advocate Illinois Masonic Medical Center	Chicago	100%	173
Advocate South Suburban Hospital	Hazel Crest	100%	126
Advocate Trinity Hospital	Chicago	100%	112
Alexian Brothers Medical Center	Elk Grove Vlg	100%	249
Alton Memorial Hospital	Alton	100%	80
Blessing Hospital	Quincy	100%	247
Carle Foundation Hospital[2]	Urbana	100%	278
Centegra Health Sys-Woodstock Hospital	Woodstock	100%	25
Central Dupage Hospital	Winfield	100%	198
Decatur Memorial Hospital	Decatur	100%	220
Delnor Community Hospital	Geneva	100%	86
Elmhurst Memorial Hospital[2]	Elmhurst	100%	201
Gateway Regional Medical Center	Granite City	100%	73
Good Samaritan Regional Health Center	Mount Vernon	100%	274
Hines VA Medical Center	Hines	100%	33
Hinsdale Hospital	Hinsdale	100%	94
J Brown VA Med Ctr-VA Chicago Healthcare	Chicago	100%	42
Katherine Shaw Bethea Hospital	Dixon	100%	50
Little Company of Mary Hospital	Evergreen Park	100%	81
Loyola Gottlieb Memorial Hospital	Melrose Park	100%	157
Loyola University Medical Center	Maywood	100%	178
Methodist Medical Center of Illinois	Peoria	100%	211
Morris Hospital & Healthcare Centers	Morris	100%	67
Mount Sinai Hospital Medical Center	Chicago	100%	153
Our Lady of the Resurrection Medical Center	Chicago	100%	182
Pekin Memorial Hospital	Pekin	100%	29
Proctor Hospital	Peoria	100%	67
Provena Mercy Medical Center	Aurora	100%	118
Provena St Joseph Medical Center	Joliet	100%	296
Provena St Marys Hospital	Kankakee	100%	50
RHC St Francis Hospital	Evanston	100%	101
Saint Alexius Medical Center	Hoffman Estates	100%	144
Saint Elizabeth Hospital	Belleville	100%	229
Saint Francis Medical Center	Peoria	100%	547
Saint Johns Hospital	Springfield	100%	559
Saint Joseph Hospital	Chicago	100%	74
Saint Joseph Medical Center	Bloomington	100%	145
St Mary & Elizabeth Med Ctr-Div Campus	Chicago	100%	157
Saint Marys Hospital	Centralia	100%	31
Silver Cross Hospital	Joliet	100%	176
Swedish American Hospital	Rockford	100%	233
Westlake Community Hospital	Melrose Park	100%	37
Advocate Lutheran General Hospital	Park Ridge	99%	241
Anderson Hospital	Maryville	99%	97
Bromenn Healthcare	Normal	99%	165
CGH Medical Center	Sterling	99%	69
Copley Memorial Hospital	Aurora	99%	183
Edward Hospital	Naperville	99%	231
Evanston Hospital	Evanston	99%	392
Genesis Medical Center Illini Campus	Silvis	99%	113
Louis A Weiss Memorial Hospital	Chicago	99%	95
Memorial Hospital	Belleville	99%	285
Memorial Hospital of Carbondale	Carbondale	99%	394
Memorial Medical Center	Springfield	99%	520
Palos Community Hospital[2]	Palos Heights	99%	254
Resurrection Medical Center	Chicago	99%	314
Riverside Medical Center	Kankakee	99%	104
Rockford Memorial Hospital	Rockford	99%	220
Rush University Medical Center	Chicago	99%	128
Saint Anthony Medical Center	Rockford	99%	258
St James Hospital-Olympia Fields	Olympia Fields	99%	288
Sherman Hospital	Elgin	99%	162
Skokie Hospital	Skokie	99%	106
Trinity Rock Island	Rock Island	99%	391
The University of Chicago Medical Center	Chicago	99%	137
Centegra Health System - McHenry Hospital	Mchenry	98%	290
Fhn Memorial Hospital	Freeport	98%	58
Ingalls Memorial Hospital[2]	Harvey	98%	196
John H Stroger Jr Hospital[2]	Chicago	98%	189
Lake Forest Hospital	Lake Forest	98%	43
Macneal Hospital	Berwyn	98%	185
Northwestern Memorial Hospital	Chicago	98%	299
Swedish Covenant Hospital	Chicago	98%	248
University of Illinois Hospital	Chicago	98%	80
Heartland Regional Medical Center	Marion	97%	78
Northwest Community Hospital	Arlington Hgts	97%	349
Provena Covenant Medical Center - Urbana	Urbana	97%	190
Saint Marys Hospital[2]	Decatur	97%	34
Galesburg Cottage Hospital	Galesburg	96%	28
Metrosouth Medical Center	Blue Island	96%	107
Saint Mary Medical Center	Galesburg	96%	26
Kishwaukee Community Hospital	Dekalb	95%	58
Provena-Saint Joseph Hospital	Elgin	95%	124
Saint Anthony's Health Center	Alton	95%	42
Mercy Hospital and Medical Center	Chicago	94%	180
Vista Medical Center East	Waukegan	94%	122
West Suburban Medical Center	Oak Park	89%	57
Provena United Samaritans Med Ctr-Logan	Danville	88%	32
Holy Cross Hospital[2]	Chicago	83%	89

4. Beta Blocker at Discharge

Hospital Name	City	Rate	Cases
Adventist La Grange Memorial Hospital	La Grange	100%	114
Advocate Christ Hospital & Medical Center[2]	Oak Lawn	100%	295
Advocate Condell Medical Center	Libertyville	100%	201
Advocate Good Samaritan Hospital	Downers Grove	100%	224
Advocate Good Shepherd Hospital	Barrington	100%	214

NOTE: Hospital profiles are in alphabetical order by state, then city, then hospital within the city; Rankings exclude hospitals with less than 25 cases except for patient surveys which excludes hospitals with less than 100 cases; (a) 100–299 cases; (1) The number of cases is too small to be sure how well a hospital is performing; (2) The hospital indicated that the data submitted for this measure were based on a sample of cases; (3) Data was collected during a shorter time period (fewer quarters) than the maximum possible time for this measure; (4) Suppressed for one or more quarters by CMS; (5) No data is available from the hospital for this measure; (6) Fewer than 100 patients completed the HCAHPS survey. Use these rates with caution, as the number of surveys may be too low to reliably assess hospital performance; (7) Survey results are based on less than 12 months of data; (8) Survey results are not available for this reporting period; (9) No or very few patients were eligible for the HCAHPS survey. The scores shown, if any, reflect a very small number of surveys; (10) A state average was not calculated because too few hospitals in the state submitted data; (11) There were discrepancies in the data collection process; Please refer to the User's Guide for a full explanation of data.

Hospital Name	City	Rate	Cases
Advocate Illinois Masonic Medical Center	Chicago	100%	169
Advocate Lutheran General Hospital	Park Ridge	100%	236
Advocate South Suburban Hospital	Hazel Crest	100%	133
Advocate Trinity Hospital	Chicago	100%	112
Alton Memorial Hospital	Alton	100%	84
Anderson Hospital	Maryville	100%	97
Copley Memorial Hospital	Aurora	100%	179
Decatur Memorial Hospital	Decatur	100%	224
Delnor Community Hospital	Geneva	100%	89
Elmhurst Memorial Hospital[2]	Elmhurst	100%	196
Galesburg Cottage Hospital	Galesburg	100%	28
Gateway Regional Medical Center	Granite City	100%	60
Genesis Medical Center Illini Campus	Silvis	100%	105
Good Samaritan Regional Health Center	Mount Vernon	100%	269
Hines VA Medical Center	Hines	100%	27
Katherine Shaw Bethea Hospital	Dixon	100%	45
Kishwaukee Community Hospital	Dekalb	100%	55
Lake Forest Hospital	Lake Forest	100%	41
Little Company of Mary Hospital	Evergreen Park	100%	79
Loyola Gottlieb Memorial Hospital	Melrose Park	100%	171
Methodist Medical Center of Illinois	Peoria	100%	212
Morris Hospital & Healthcare Centers	Morris	100%	66
Mount Sinai Hospital Medical Center	Chicago	100%	130
Our Lady of the Resurrection Medical Center	Chicago	100%	165
Palos Community Hospital[2]	Palos Heights	100%	241
Pekin Memorial Hospital	Pekin	100%	30
Proctor Hospital	Peoria	100%	68
Provena St Marys Hospital	Kankakee	100%	48
Rockford Memorial Hospital	Rockford	100%	219
Saint Johns Hospital	Springfield	100%	546
Saint Joseph Hospital	Chicago	100%	64
St Mary & Elizabeth Med Ctr-Div Campus	Chicago	100%	160
Saint Mary Medical Center	Galesburg	100%	26
Saint Marys Hospital	Centralia	100%	34
Sarah Bush Lincoln Health Center	Mattoon	100%	25
Sherman Hospital	Elgin	100%	164
Swedish American Hospital	Rockford	100%	229
Adventist Bolingbrook Hospital	Bolingbrook	99%	70
Alexian Brothers Medical Center	Elk Grove Vlg	99%	245
Carle Foundation Hospital[2]	Urbana	99%	270
Central Dupage Hospital	Winfield	99%	192
CGH Medical Center	Sterling	99%	67
Edward Hospital	Naperville	99%	222
Evanston Hospital	Evanston	99%	384
Hinsdale Hospital	Hinsdale	99%	101
John H Stroger Jr Hospital[2]	Chicago	99%	184
Louis A Weiss Memorial Hospital	Chicago	99%	104
Loyola University Medical Center	Maywood	99%	167
Memorial Hospital	Belleville	99%	279
Memorial Hospital of Carbondale	Carbondale	99%	383
Memorial Medical Center	Springfield	99%	495
Northwest Community Hospital	Arlington Hgts	99%	339
Provena St Joseph Medical Center	Joliet	99%	299
Saint Alexius Medical Center	Hoffman Estates	99%	146
Saint Elizabeth Hospital	Belleville	99%	224
Saint Francis Medical Center	Peoria	99%	541
St James Hospital-Olympia Fields	Olympia Fields	99%	304
Saint Joseph Medical Center	Bloomington	99%	140
Silver Cross Hospital	Joliet	99%	171
Bromenn Healthcare	Normal	98%	161
Fhn Memorial Hospital	Freeport	98%	58
Ingalls Memorial Hospital[2]	Harvey	98%	198
J Brown VA Med Ctr-VA Chicago Healthcare	Chicago	98%	40
Macneal Hospital	Berwyn	98%	186
Northwestern Memorial Hospital	Chicago	98%	281
Provena Mercy Medical Center	Aurora	98%	121
Provena United Samaritans Med Ctr-Logan	Danville	98%	48
Provena-Saint Joseph Hospital	Elgin	98%	121
Resurrection Medical Center	Chicago	98%	293
Rush University Medical Center	Chicago	98%	122
Trinity Rock Island	Rock Island	98%	364
The University of Chicago Medical Center	Chicago	98%	131
Centegra Health System - McHenry Hospital	Mchenry	97%	299
Heartland Regional Medical Center	Marion	97%	78
Provena Covenant Medical Center - Urbana	Urbana	97%	192
Westlake Community Hospital	Melrose Park	97%	39
Blessing Hospital	Quincy	96%	236
Mercy Hospital and Medical Center	Chicago	96%	167
Riverside Medical Center	Kankakee	96%	106
University of Illinois Hospital	Chicago	96%	79
West Suburban Medical Center	Oak Park	96%	69
Saint Anthony Medical Center	Rockford	95%	254
Saint Anthony's Health Center	Alton	95%	43
Saint Marys Hospital[2]	Decatur	95%	38
Vista Medical Center East	Waukegan	95%	125
Skokie Hospital	Skokie	94%	103
Swedish Covenant Hospital	Chicago	94%	249
Centegra Health Sys-Woodstock Hospital	Woodstock	93%	28
Metrosouth Medical Center	Blue Island	91%	103
RHC St Francis Hospital	Evanston	88%	96
Holy Cross Hospital[2]	Chicago	84%	86

6. PCI Within 90 Minutes of Arrival

Hospital Name	City	Rate	Cases
Advocate Christ Hospital & Medical Center[2]	Oak Lawn	100%	45
Advocate Condell Medical Center	Libertyville	100%	62
Loyola University Medical Center	Maywood	100%	30
Saint Elizabeth Hospital	Belleville	100%	29
Saint Johns Hospital	Springfield	100%	43
Memorial Medical Center	Springfield	99%	71
Advocate Good Samaritan Hospital	Downers Grove	98%	61
Advocate Lutheran General Hospital	Park Ridge	98%	50
Alexian Brothers Medical Center	Elk Grove Vlg	98%	58
Saint Francis Medical Center	Peoria	98%	50
Blessing Hospital	Quincy	97%	32
Copley Memorial Hospital	Aurora	97%	35
Decatur Memorial Hospital	Decatur	97%	31
Elmhurst Memorial Hospital[2]	Elmhurst	97%	33
Memorial Hospital of Carbondale	Carbondale	97%	29
Evanston Hospital	Evanston	96%	82
Macneal Hospital	Berwyn	96%	45
St Mary & Elizabeth Med Ctr-Div Campus	Chicago	96%	27
Sherman Hospital	Elgin	96%	49
Bromenn Healthcare	Normal	94%	31
Delnor Community Hospital	Geneva	94%	33
Memorial Hospital	Belleville	94%	34
Riverside Medical Center	Kankakee	94%	36
Silver Cross Hospital	Joliet	94%	50
Advocate Good Shepherd Hospital	Barrington	93%	41
Methodist Medical Center of Illinois	Peoria	93%	27
Northwest Community Hospital	Arlington Hgts	93%	59
Provena-Saint Joseph Hospital	Elgin	93%	27
Saint Alexius Medical Center	Hoffman Estates	93%	41
Swedish American Hospital	Rockford	93%	43
Palos Community Hospital[2]	Palos Heights	92%	48
Northwestern Memorial Hospital	Chicago	91%	45
Trinity Rock Island	Rock Island	91%	45
Adventist La Grange Memorial Hospital	La Grange	90%	31
Central Dupage Hospital	Winfield	89%	53
Provena St Joseph Medical Center	Joliet	88%	56
Rockford Memorial Hospital	Rockford	87%	31
Our Lady of the Resurrection Medical Center	Chicago	86%	36
Edward Hospital	Naperville	85%	33
Resurrection Medical Center	Chicago	84%	63
Metrosouth Medical Center	Blue Island	81%	27
Centegra Health System - McHenry Hospital	Mchenry	80%	50
Saint Anthony Medical Center	Rockford	80%	50
Kishwaukee Community Hospital	Dekalb	76%	25
Saint Joseph Medical Center	Bloomington	73%	33

7. Smoking Cessation Advice

Hospital Name	City	Rate	Cases
Adventist Bolingbrook Hospital	Bolingbrook	100%	30
Adventist La Grange Memorial Hospital	La Grange	100%	44
Advocate Christ Hospital & Medical Center[2]	Oak Lawn	100%	109
Advocate Condell Medical Center	Libertyville	100%	76
Advocate Good Samaritan Hospital	Downers Grove	100%	55
Advocate Good Shepherd Hospital	Barrington	100%	73
Advocate Illinois Masonic Medical Center	Chicago	100%	64
Advocate Lutheran General Hospital	Park Ridge	100%	61
Advocate South Suburban Hospital	Hazel Crest	100%	53
Alexian Brothers Medical Center	Elk Grove Vlg	100%	85
Alton Memorial Hospital	Alton	100%	31
Anderson Hospital	Maryville	100%	30
Blessing Hospital	Quincy	100%	82
Bromenn Healthcare	Normal	100%	66
Carle Foundation Hospital[2]	Urbana	100%	101
Central Dupage Hospital	Winfield	100%	54
Copley Memorial Hospital	Aurora	100%	77
Decatur Memorial Hospital	Decatur	100%	86
Edward Hospital	Naperville	100%	61
Elmhurst Memorial Hospital[2]	Elmhurst	100%	48
Evanston Hospital	Evanston	100%	70
Gateway Regional Medical Center	Granite City	100%	30
Genesis Medical Center Illini Campus	Silvis	100%	37
Good Samaritan Regional Health Center	Mount Vernon	100%	121
Heartland Regional Medical Center	Marion	100%	33
Ingalls Memorial Hospital[2]	Harvey	100%	65
John H Stroger Jr Hospital[2]	Chicago	100%	82
Kishwaukee Community Hospital	Dekalb	100%	26
Louis A Weiss Memorial Hospital	Chicago	100%	37
Loyola Gottlieb Memorial Hospital	Melrose Park	100%	51
Loyola University Medical Center	Maywood	100%	55
Macneal Hospital	Berwyn	100%	61
Memorial Hospital	Belleville	100%	78
Mercy Hospital and Medical Center	Chicago	100%	55
Methodist Medical Center of Illinois	Peoria	100%	97
Metrosouth Medical Center	Blue Island	100%	37
Morris Hospital & Healthcare Centers	Morris	100%	28
Mount Sinai Hospital Medical Center	Chicago	100%	67
Northwestern Memorial Hospital	Chicago	100%	72
Our Lady of the Resurrection Medical Center	Chicago	100%	50
Palos Community Hospital[2]	Palos Heights	100%	75
Provena Mercy Medical Center	Aurora	100%	34
Provena St Joseph Medical Center	Joliet	100%	78
Provena-Saint Joseph Hospital	Elgin	100%	40
Resurrection Medical Center	Chicago	100%	75
Rockford Memorial Hospital	Rockford	100%	80
Saint Alexius Medical Center	Hoffman Estates	100%	54
Saint Anthony Medical Center	Rockford	100%	84
Saint Elizabeth Hospital	Belleville	100%	88
Saint Francis Medical Center	Peoria	100%	209
St James Hospital-Olympia Fields	Olympia Fields	100%	84
Saint Johns Hospital	Springfield	100%	228
Saint Joseph Medical Center	Bloomington	100%	65
Sherman Hospital	Elgin	100%	50
Silver Cross Hospital	Joliet	100%	53
Swedish American Hospital	Rockford	100%	86
Swedish Covenant Hospital	Chicago	100%	49
Trinity Rock Island	Rock Island	100%	135
The University of Chicago Medical Center	Chicago	100%	44
University of Illinois Hospital	Chicago	100%	33
Vista Medical Center East	Waukegan	100%	49
West Suburban Medical Center	Oak Park	100%	32
Centegra Health System - McHenry Hospital	Mchenry	99%	102
Memorial Hospital of Carbondale	Carbondale	99%	169
Memorial Medical Center	Springfield	99%	183
Provena Covenant Medical Center - Urbana	Urbana	99%	87
Advocate Trinity Hospital	Chicago	98%	46
Northwest Community Hospital	Arlington Hgts	98%	66
Rush University Medical Center	Chicago	98%	40
St Mary & Elizabeth Med Ctr-Div Campus	Chicago	98%	54
Riverside Medical Center	Kankakee	97%	39
Holy Cross Hospital[2]	Chicago	90%	40

Chest Pain/Possible Heart Attack Care

8. Aspirin at Arrival

Hospital Name	City	Rate	Cases
Crossroads Community Hospital	Mount Vernon	100%	47
Fhn Memorial Hospital	Freeport	100%	35
Galesburg Cottage Hospital	Galesburg	100%	70
Gateway Regional Medical Center	Granite City	100%	42
Genesis Medical Center Illini Campus	Silvis	100%	35
Illinois Valley Community Hospital	Peru	100%	52
Lake Forest Hospital	Lake Forest	100%	33
Memorial Hospital	Chester	100%	41
OSF Holy Family Medical Center	Monmouth	100%	33
Ottawa Reg Hosp & Healthcare Ctr	Ottawa	100%	70
Our Lady of the Resurrection Medical Center	Chicago	100%	32
Provident Hospital of Chicago	Chicago	100%	35
Saint Josephs Hospital	Breese	100%	86
St Mary & Elizabeth Med Ctr-Div Campus	Chicago	100%	78
Saint Marys Hospital	Decatur	100%	40
Saint Marys Hospital	Streator	100%	46
Vista Medical Center West	Waukegan	100%	105
Anderson Hospital	Maryville	98%	86
CGH Medical Center	Sterling	98%	89
Clay County Hospital	Flora	98%	58
Hardin County General Hospital	Rosiclare	98%	50
Red Bud Regional Hospital	Red Bud	98%	93
Saint Margarets Hospital	Spring Valley	98%	45
Saint Mary Medical Center	Galesburg	98%	105
Abraham Lincoln Memorial Hospital	Lincoln	97%	191
Alton Memorial Hospital	Alton	97%	68
Greenville Regional Hospital	Greenville	97%	32
Harrisburg Medical Center	Harrisburg	97%	129
Herrin Hospital	Herrin	96%	157
Swedish American Hospital	Rockford	96%	50
Union County Hospital	Anna	96%	82
Fairfield Memorial Hospital	Fairfield	95%	76
Graham Hospital Association	Canton	95%	76
Oak Forest Hospital	Oak Forest	95%	37
Saint Anthonys Memorial Hospital	Effingham	95%	187
Saint Bernard Hospital	Chicago	95%	100
Saint James Hospital	Pontiac	95%	99
Sarah Bush Lincoln Health Center	Mattoon	95%	176
Centegra Health Sys-Woodstock Hospital	Woodstock	94%	51
Jersey Community Hospital	Jerseyville	94%	65
McDonough District Hospital	Macomb	94%	81
Passavant Area Hospital	Jacksonville	94%	298
Pekin Memorial Hospital	Pekin	94%	54
Saint Marys Hospital	Centralia	94%	131
Wabash General Hospital	Mount Carmel	94%	71
Ingalls Memorial Hospital	Harvey	93%	46
Shelby Memorial Hospital	Shelbyville	92%	62
St James Hospital-Olympia Fields	Olympia Fields	90%	31
Provena United Samaritans Med Ctr-Logan	Danville	89%	128
Richland Memorial Hospital	Olney	83%	36
Swedish Covenant Hospital	Chicago	82%	49
Palos Community Hospital	Palos Heights	76%	29
The University of Chicago Medical Center	Chicago	71%	34

NOTE: Hospital profiles are in alphabetical order by state, then city, then hospital within the city; Rankings exclude hospitals with less than 25 cases except for patient surveys which excludes hospitals with less than 100 cases; (a) 100–299 cases; (1) The number of cases is too small to be sure how well a hospital is performing; (2) The hospital indicated that the data submitted for this measure were based on a sample of cases; (3) Data was collected during a shorter time period (fewer quarters) than the maximum possible time for this measure; (4) Suppressed for one or more quarters by CMS; (5) No data is available from the hospital for this measure; (6) Fewer than 100 patients completed the HCAHPS survey. Use these rates with caution, as the number of surveys may be too low to reliably assess hospital performance; (7) Survey results are based on less than 12 months of data; (8) Survey results are not available for this reporting period; (9) No or very few patients were eligible for the HCAHPS survey. The scores shown, if any, reflect a very small number of surveys; (10) A state average was not calculated because too few hospitals in the state submitted data; (11) There were discrepancies in the data collection process; Please refer to the User's Guide for a full explanation of data.

9. Median Time to ECG (minutes)

Hospital Name	City	Min.	Cases
Palos Community Hospital	Palos Heights	0	29
Saint Bernard Hospital	Chicago	0	104
Anderson Hospital	Maryville	1	87
Crossroads Community Hospital	Mount Vernon	2	49
Herrin Hospital	Herrin	2	164
Our Lady of the Resurrection Medical Center	Chicago	3	31
Abraham Lincoln Memorial Hospital	Lincoln	4	197
Illinois Valley Community Hospital	Peru	4	55
Centegra Health Sys-Woodstock Hospital	Woodstock	5	53
Harrisburg Medical Center	Harrisburg	5	134
Ottawa Reg Hosp & Healthcare Ctr	Ottawa	5	75
Pekin Memorial Hospital	Pekin	5	55
Alton Memorial Hospital	Alton	6	65
Fhn Memorial Hospital	Freeport	6	35
Genesis Medical Center Illini Campus	Silvis	6	39
Jersey Community Hospital	Jerseyville	6	68
Lake Forest Hospital	Lake Forest	6	40
Memorial Hospital	Chester	6	44
OSF Holy Family Medical Center	Monmouth	6	35
Red Bud Regional Hospital	Red Bud	6	98
St James Hospital-Olympia Fields	Olympia Fields	6	34
Saint Margarets Hospital	Spring Valley	6	48
St Mary & Elizabeth Med Ctr-Div Campus	Chicago	6	81
Shelby Memorial Hospital	Shelbyville	6	66
Swedish American Hospital	Rockford	6	50
Good Samaritan Regional Health Center	Mount Vernon	6	26
Hardin County General Hospital	Rosiclare	7	55
McDonough District Hospital	Macomb	7	85
Saint Josephs Hospital	Breese	7	88
Saint Marys Hospital	Streator	7	46
Galesburg Cottage Hospital	Galesburg	8	74
Saint James Hospital	Pontiac	8	105
Saint Marys Hospital	Centralia	8	138
Swedish Covenant Hospital	Chicago	8	54
Wabash General Hospital	Mount Carmel	8	72
CGH Medical Center	Sterling	9	90
Graham Hospital Association	Canton	9	76
Saint Mary Medical Center	Galesburg	9	107
Union County Hospital	Anna	9	83
Fairfield Memorial Hospital	Fairfield	10	82
Ingalls Memorial Hospital	Harvey	10	46
Gateway Regional Medical Center	Granite City	11	46
Greenville Regional Hospital	Greenville	11	33
Provena United Samaritans Med Ctr-Logan	Danville	11	129
Sarah Bush Lincoln Health Center	Mattoon	11	182
Saint Anthonys Memorial Hospital	Effingham	12	193
Saint Marys Hospital	Decatur	12	42
Vista Medical Center West	Waukegan	13	111
Passavant Area Hospital	Jacksonville	14	301
Clay County Hospital	Flora	15	54
The University of Chicago Medical Center	Chicago	15	35
Oak Forest Hospital	Oak Forest	16	37
Richland Memorial Hospital	Olney	20	37
Provident Hospital of Chicago	Chicago	103	37

10. Median Time to Transfer (minutes)

Hospital Name	City	Min.	Cases
Anderson Hospital	Maryville	45	31
Passavant Area Hospital	Jacksonville	53	29

Heart Failure Care

12. ACE Inhibitor or ARB for LVSD

Hospital Name	City	Rate	Cases
Advocate Christ Hospital & Medical Center[2]	Oak Lawn	100%	115
Advocate Condell Medical Center	Libertyville	100%	107
Advocate Good Samaritan Hospital	Downers Grove	100%	161
Central Dupage Hospital	Winfield	100%	106
Delnor Community Hospital	Geneva	100%	44
Gateway Regional Medical Center	Granite City	100%	44
Hines VA Medical Center	Hines	100%	121
Jackson Park Hospital	Chicago	100%	159
Katherine Shaw Bethea Hospital	Dixon	100%	27
Lake Forest Hospital	Lake Forest	100%	46
Little Company of Mary Hospital[2]	Evergreen Park	100%	93
Loretto Hospital	Chicago	100%	46
Loyola Gottlieb Memorial Hospital	Melrose Park	100%	79
Methodist Medical Center of Illinois	Peoria	100%	106
North Chicago VA Medical Center	North Chicago	100%	34
Northwest Community Hospital[2]	Arlington Hgts	100%	52
Our Lady of the Resurrection Medical Center	Chicago	100%	71
Pekin Memorial Hospital	Pekin	100%	33
Proctor Hospital	Peoria	100%	40
Rockford Memorial Hospital	Rockford	100%	73
Saint Johns Hospital[2]	Springfield	100%	112
St Mary & Elizabeth Med Ctr-Div Campus	Chicago	100%	134
Saint Marys Hospital	Centralia	100%	47
Saint Marys Hospital[2]	Decatur	100%	55
Sarah Bush Lincoln Health Center	Mattoon	100%	52
The University of Chicago Medical Center[2]	Chicago	100%	123
Adventist La Grange Memorial Hospital	La Grange	99%	81
Advocate Lutheran General Hospital	Park Ridge	99%	187
Advocate South Suburban Hospital[2]	Hazel Crest	99%	133
Advocate Trinity Hospital	Chicago	99%	171
Macneal Hospital	Berwyn	99%	137
Provena St Joseph Medical Center[2]	Joliet	99%	93
Rush University Medical Center[2]	Chicago	99%	155
Adventist Bolingbrook Hospital	Bolingbrook	98%	61
Advocate Illinois Masonic Medical Center[2]	Chicago	98%	124
Carle Foundation Hospital[2]	Urbana	98%	119
Copley Memorial Hospital	Aurora	98%	63
Elmhurst Memorial Hospital[2]	Elmhurst	98%	90
Heartland Regional Medical Center	Marion	98%	62
John H Stroger Jr Hospital[2]	Chicago	98%	134
Louis A Weiss Memorial Hospital	Chicago	98%	103
Loyola University Medical Center	Maywood	98%	261
Memorial Hospital	Belleville	98%	182
Memorial Medical Center	Springfield	98%	183
Northwestern Memorial Hospital	Chicago	98%	318
Oak Forest Hospital[2]	Oak Forest	98%	110
Palos Community Hospital[2]	Palos Heights	98%	48
Silver Cross Hospital	Joliet	98%	128
Trinity Rock Island[2]	Rock Island	98%	82
Bromenn Healthcare	Normal	97%	92
CGH Medical Center	Sterling	97%	36
Fhn Memorial Hospital	Freeport	97%	59
J Brown VA Med Ctr-VA Chicago Healthcare	Chicago	97%	154
Provident Hospital of Chicago[2]	Chicago	97%	152
Saint Francis Medical Center	Peoria	97%	183
Swedish American Hospital	Rockford	97%	132
Anderson Hospital	Maryville	96%	79
Kishwaukee Community Hospital	Dekalb	96%	52
Provena St Marys Hospital	Kankakee	96%	56
Saint Mary Medical Center	Galesburg	96%	45
Sherman Hospital	Elgin	96%	71
Vista Medical Center East	Waukegan	96%	103
Edward Hospital	Naperville	95%	143
Evanston Hospital	Evanston	95%	231
Ingalls Memorial Hospital[2]	Harvey	95%	95
Mount Sinai Hospital Medical Center	Chicago	95%	157
Saint Anthonys Memorial Hospital	Effingham	95%	41
University of Illinois Hospital[2]	Chicago	95%	132
VA Illiana Healthcare System - Danville	Danville	95%	39
Advocate Good Shepherd Hospital	Barrington	94%	72
Alexian Brothers Medical Center	Elk Grove Vlg	94%	137
Alton Memorial Hospital	Alton	94%	72
Genesis Medical Center Illini Campus	Silvis	94%	70
Good Samaritan Regional Health Center	Mount Vernon	94%	67
Saint Joseph Hospital	Chicago	94%	63
Saint Joseph Medical Center	Bloomington	94%	66
Touchette Regional Hospital	Centreville	94%	69
Westlake Community Hospital	Melrose Park	94%	82
Marion Illinois VA Medical Center	Marion	93%	57
Saint Anthony's Health Center	Alton	93%	46
West Suburban Medical Center[2]	Oak Park	93%	126
Centegra Health System - McHenry Hospital	Mchenry	92%	90
Mercy Hospital and Medical Center[2]	Chicago	92%	168
Provena United Samaritans Med Ctr-Logan	Danville	92%	96
Riverside Medical Center	Kankakee	92%	86
Rush Oak Park Hospital	Oak Park	92%	61
Saint Alexius Medical Center	Hoffman Estates	92%	64
St James Hospital-Olympia Fields	Olympia Fields	92%	276
Skokie Hospital	Skokie	92%	79
South Shore Hospital	Chicago	92%	64
Swedish Covenant Hospital	Chicago	92%	171
Adventist Glenoaks	Glendale Hghts	91%	34
Saint Elizabeth Hospital[2]	Belleville	91%	134
Decatur Memorial Hospital[2]	Decatur	90%	147
Morris Hospital & Healthcare Centers	Morris	90%	48
Provena Covenant Medical Center - Urbana	Urbana	89%	104
Saint Anthony Medical Center	Rockford	89%	94
Hinsdale Hospital	Hinsdale	88%	75
Memorial Hospital of Carbondale	Carbondale	88%	76
Passavant Area Hospital[2]	Jacksonville	88%	26
Resurrection Medical Center	Chicago	87%	142
RHC St Francis Hospital	Evanston	87%	84
Saint Anthony Hospital	Chicago	87%	69
Metrosouth Medical Center	Blue Island	85%	253
Norwegian-American Hospital	Chicago	85%	87
Blessing Hospital	Quincy	84%	89
Jersey Community Hospital	Jerseyville	84%	25
McDonough District Hospital	Macomb	84%	31
Holy Cross Hospital[2]	Chicago	83%	164
Herrin Hospital	Herrin	82%	50
Provena Mercy Medical Center[2]	Aurora	80%	76
Saint Bernard Hospital	Chicago	80%	122
Graham Hospital Association	Canton	77%	35
Provena-Saint Joseph Hospital	Elgin	74%	68
Thorek Memorial Hospital	Chicago	71%	34
Roseland Community Hospital[2]	Chicago	70%	101
Sacred Heart Hospital	Chicago	68%	34

13. Discharge Instructions

Hospital Name	City	Rate	Cases
Elmhurst Memorial Hospital[2]	Elmhurst	100%	229
Harrisburg Medical Center[2]	Harrisburg	100%	67
Jackson Park Hospital	Chicago	100%	270
J Brown VA Med Ctr-VA Chicago Healthcare	Chicago	100%	259
Loretto Hospital	Chicago	100%	101
Saint Francis Hospital	Litchfield	100%	25
Saint James Hospital	Pontiac	100%	25
St Mary & Elizabeth Med Ctr-Div Campus	Chicago	100%	330
Saint Marys Hospital	Centralia	100%	147
Taylorville Memorial Hospital	Taylorville	100%	43
Advocate Christ Hospital & Medical Center[2]	Oak Lawn	99%	255
Advocate Good Samaritan Hospital	Downers Grove	99%	337
Advocate Lutheran General Hospital	Park Ridge	99%	374
Marion Illinois VA Medical Center	Marion	99%	135
Saint Joseph Hospital	Chicago	99%	195
Decatur Memorial Hospital[2]	Decatur	98%	312
Hines VA Medical Center	Hines	98%	248
Lake Forest Hospital	Lake Forest	98%	146
Louis A Weiss Memorial Hospital	Chicago	98%	203
Mount Sinai Hospital Medical Center	Chicago	98%	275
Perry Memorial Hospital	Princeton	98%	44
Roseland Community Hospital[2]	Chicago	98%	239
Saint Bernard Hospital	Chicago	98%	314
Saint Joseph Medical Center	Bloomington	98%	124
Advocate Illinois Masonic Medical Center[2]	Chicago	97%	233
Copley Memorial Hospital	Aurora	97%	203
Hoopeston Community Memorial Hospital	Hoopeston	97%	32
Northwestern Memorial Hospital	Chicago	97%	768
Trinity Rock Island[2]	Rock Island	97%	207
Alexian Brothers Medical Center	Elk Grove Vlg	96%	398
Central Dupage Hospital	Winfield	96%	338
Evanston Hospital	Evanston	96%	695
Jersey Community Hospital	Jerseyville	96%	54
Provena Covenant Medical Center - Urbana	Urbana	96%	228
Provident Hospital of Chicago[2]	Chicago	96%	266
Saint Alexius Medical Center	Hoffman Estates	96%	277
Saint Joseph Memorial Hospital	Murphysboro	96%	26
Sarah Bush Lincoln Health Center	Mattoon	96%	173
Sherman Hospital	Elgin	96%	268
Centegra Health System - McHenry Hospital	Mchenry	95%	260
Genesis Medical Center Illini Campus	Silvis	95%	140
Macneal Hospital	Berwyn	95%	306
Northwest Community Hospital[2]	Arlington Hgts	95%	189
Pekin Memorial Hospital	Pekin	95%	92
Provena Mercy Medical Center[2]	Aurora	95%	147
Good Samaritan Regional Health Center	Mount Vernon	94%	163
Loyola University Medical Center	Maywood	94%	601
Memorial Medical Center	Springfield	94%	444
Metrosouth Medical Center	Blue Island	94%	521
Our Lady of the Resurrection Medical Center	Chicago	94%	249
RHC St Francis Hospital	Evanston	94%	224
Riverside Medical Center	Kankakee	94%	173
Saint Anthony Medical Center	Rockford	94%	215
West Suburban Medical Center[2]	Oak Park	94%	288
Advocate South Suburban Hospital[2]	Hazel Crest	93%	260
Blessing Hospital	Quincy	93%	223
Katherine Shaw Bethea Hospital	Dixon	93%	91
Methodist Medical Center of Illinois	Peoria	93%	238
North Chicago VA Medical Center	North Chicago	93%	68
Advocate Condell Medical Center	Libertyville	92%	325
Ingalls Memorial Hospital[2]	Harvey	92%	257
Proctor Hospital	Peoria	92%	95
Saint Johns Hospital[2]	Springfield	92%	244
Centegra Health Sys-Woodstock Hospital	Woodstock	91%	79
Hamilton Memorial Hospital District	Mcleansboro	91%	32
Oak Forest Hospital[2]	Oak Forest	91%	202
Wabash General Hospital	Mount Carmel	91%	34
Advocate Good Shepherd Hospital	Barrington	90%	218
Clay County Hospital	Flora	90%	29
Delnor Community Hospital	Geneva	90%	149
Palos Community Hospital[2]	Palos Heights	90%	207
Saint Josephs Hospital[2]	Breese	90%	30
Saint Marys Hospital	Streator	90%	51
Thorek Memorial Hospital	Chicago	90%	89
Vista Medical Center East	Waukegan	90%	282
Crossroads Community Hospital	Mount Vernon	89%	28
Galesburg Cottage Hospital	Galesburg	89%	56
Mercy Hospital and Medical Center[2]	Chicago	89%	275
Morris Hospital & Healthcare Centers	Morris	89%	143
Rockford Memorial Hospital	Rockford	89%	193
Saint Mary Medical Center	Galesburg	89%	72
Silver Cross Hospital	Joliet	89%	312
Swedish American Hospital	Rockford	89%	311
Carle Foundation Hospital[2]	Urbana	88%	244

NOTE: Hospital profiles are in alphabetical order by state, then city, then hospital within the city; Rankings exclude hospitals with less than 25 cases except for patient surveys which excludes hospitals with less than 100 cases; (a) 100–299 cases; (1) The number of cases is too small to be sure how well a hospital is performing; (2) The hospital indicated that the data submitted for this measure were based on a sample of cases; (3) Data was collected during a shorter time period (fewer quarters) than the maximum possible time for this measure; (4) Suppressed for one or more quarters by CMS; (5) No data is available from the hospital for this measure; (6) Fewer than 100 patients completed the HCAHPS survey. Use these rates with caution, as the number of surveys may be too low to reliably assess hospital performance; (7) Survey results are based on less than 12 months of data; (8) Survey results are not available for this reporting period; (9) No or very few patients were eligible for the HCAHPS survey. The scores shown, if any, reflect a very small number of surveys; (10) A state average was not calculated because too few hospitals in the state submitted data; (11) There were discrepancies in the data collection process; Please refer to the User's Guide for a full explanation of data.

Hospital Name	City	Rate	Cases
Gateway Regional Medical Center	Granite City	88%	137
Graham Hospital Association	Canton	88%	60
Saint Marys Hospital[2]	Decatur	88%	165
Advocate Trinity Hospital	Chicago	87%	386
Fhn Memorial Hospital	Freeport	87%	100
Loyola Gottlieb Memorial Hospital	Melrose Park	87%	275
Provena United Samaritans Med Ctr-Logan	Danville	87%	197
St James Hospital-Olympia Fields	Olympia Fields	87%	655
Swedish Covenant Hospital	Chicago	87%	341
The University of Chicago Medical Center[2]	Chicago	87%	254
Edward Hospital	Naperville	86%	336
Salem Township Hospital	Salem	86%	28
VA Illiana Healthcare System - Danville	Danville	86%	73
Kewanee Hospital	Kewanee	85%	27
Memorial Hospital	Belleville	85%	492
Saint Francis Medical Center	Peoria	85%	385
CGH Medical Center	Sterling	84%	179
Little Company of Mary Hospital[2]	Evergreen Park	84%	263
Ottawa Reg Hosp & Healthcare Ctr	Ottawa	84%	56
Westlake Community Hospital	Melrose Park	84%	170
Bromenn Healthcare	Normal	83%	185
Provena St Joseph Medical Center[2]	Joliet	83%	239
Rush Oak Park Hospital	Oak Park	83%	152
Saint Anthonys Memorial Hospital	Effingham	83%	139
Saint Elizabeth Hospital[2]	Belleville	83%	379
Union County Hospital	Anna	83%	29
Alton Memorial Hospital	Alton	82%	171
Anderson Hospital	Maryville	82%	167
Passavant Area Hospital[2]	Jacksonville	82%	82
Adventist La Grange Memorial Hospital	La Grange	81%	243
Rush University Medical Center[2]	Chicago	81%	283
Crawford Memorial Hospital	Robinson	80%	30
Hinsdale Hospital	Hinsdale	79%	163
Illinois Valley Community Hospital	Peru	79%	61
Provena St Marys Hospital	Kankakee	79%	102
Saint Anthony Hospital	Chicago	79%	123
Kishwaukee Community Hospital	Dekalb	78%	117
Resurrection Medical Center	Chicago	78%	393
Saint Anthony's Health Center	Alton	78%	117
Saint Margarets Hospital	Spring Valley	78%	55
Memorial Hospital	Chester	76%	29
Provena-Saint Joseph Hospital	Elgin	75%	151
Skokie Hospital	Skokie	71%	196
Herrin Hospital	Herrin	70%	141
Richland Memorial Hospital	Olney	70%	57
Touchette Regional Hospital	Centreville	70%	159
John H Stroger Jr Hospital[2]	Chicago	69%	300
Shelby Memorial Hospital	Shelbyville	68%	31
Memorial Hospital of Carbondale	Carbondale	67%	178
Norwegian-American Hospital	Chicago	67%	159
South Shore Hospital	Chicago	66%	183
Holy Cross Hospital[2]	Chicago	65%	291
McDonough District Hospital	Macomb	63%	49
Adventist Glenoaks	Glendale Hghts	61%	54
Iroquois Memorial Hospital	Watseka	60%	52
Heartland Regional Medical Center	Marion	59%	116
Adventist Bolingbrook Hospital	Bolingbrook	56%	142
University of Illinois Hospital[2]	Chicago	55%	252
Sacred Heart Hospital	Chicago	34%	132

14. Evaluation of LVS Function

Hospital Name	City	Rate	Cases
Adventist La Grange Memorial Hospital	La Grange	100%	327
Advocate Christ Hospital & Medical Center[2]	Oak Lawn	100%	344
Advocate Condell Medical Center	Libertyville	100%	428
Advocate Good Samaritan Hospital	Downers Grove	100%	456
Advocate Good Shepherd Hospital	Barrington	100%	314
Advocate Illinois Masonic Medical Center[2]	Chicago	100%	307
Advocate Lutheran General Hospital	Park Ridge	100%	518
Advocate South Suburban Hospital[2]	Hazel Crest	100%	314
Alexian Brothers Medical Center	Elk Grove Vlg	100%	497
Alton Memorial Hospital	Alton	100%	226
Anderson Hospital	Maryville	100%	249
Bromenn Healthcare	Normal	100%	245
Carle Foundation Hospital[2]	Urbana	100%	300
Central Dupage Hospital	Winfield	100%	415
CGH Medical Center	Sterling	100%	219
Crossroads Community Hospital	Mount Vernon	100%	38
Delnor Community Hospital	Geneva	100%	203
Edward Hospital	Naperville	100%	434
Elmhurst Memorial Hospital[2]	Elmhurst	100%	308
Evanston Hospital	Evanston	100%	993
Fairfield Memorial Hospital	Fairfield	100%	29
Fhn Memorial Hospital	Freeport	100%	164
Gateway Regional Medical Center	Granite City	100%	160
Genesis Medical Center Illini Campus	Silvis	100%	214
Good Samaritan Regional Health Center	Mount Vernon	100%	193
Hamilton Memorial Hospital District	Mcleansboro	100%	52
Hardin County General Hospital	Rosiclare	100%	29
Hillsboro Area Hospital	Hillsboro	100%	33
Hines VA Medical Center	Hines	100%	271
Hinsdale Hospital	Hinsdale	100%	249
Jackson Park Hospital	Chicago	100%	302
J Brown VA Med Ctr-VA Chicago Healthcare	Chicago	100%	288
Katherine Shaw Bethea Hospital	Dixon	100%	131
Lake Forest Hospital	Lake Forest	100%	179
Little Company of Mary Hospital[2]	Evergreen Park	100%	327
Loretto Hospital	Chicago	100%	141
Louis A Weiss Memorial Hospital	Chicago	100%	275
Loyola Gottlieb Memorial Hospital	Melrose Park	100%	335
Loyola University Medical Center	Maywood	100%	690
Macneal Hospital	Berwyn	100%	379
Marion Illinois VA Medical Center	Marion	100%	143
Mason District Hospital	Havana	100%	26
Memorial Hospital	Chester	100%	41
Memorial Medical Center	Springfield	100%	557
Mendota Community Hospital	Mendota	100%	35
Methodist Medical Center of Illinois	Peoria	100%	310
Metrosouth Medical Center	Blue Island	100%	588
Morris Hospital & Healthcare Centers	Morris	100%	183
North Chicago VA Medical Center	North Chicago	100%	73
Northwest Community Hospital[2]	Arlington Hgts	100%	306
Northwestern Memorial Hospital	Chicago	100%	852
Our Lady of the Resurrection Medical Center	Chicago	100%	414
Palos Community Hospital[2]	Palos Heights	100%	266
Pekin Memorial Hospital	Pekin	100%	111
Proctor Hospital	Peoria	100%	145
Provena Covenant Medical Center - Urbana	Urbana	100%	284
Provena St Marys Hospital	Kankakee	100%	125
Provident Hospital of Chicago[2]	Chicago	100%	276
Red Bud Regional Hospital	Red Bud	100%	41
Resurrection Medical Center	Chicago	100%	609
Rockford Memorial Hospital	Rockford	100%	270
Rush University Medical Center[2]	Chicago	100%	298
Saint Alexius Medical Center	Hoffman Estates	100%	397
Saint Francis Medical Center	Peoria	100%	492
Saint James Hospital	Pontiac	100%	35
Saint Johns Hospital[2]	Springfield	100%	295
Saint Joseph Hospital	Chicago	100%	280
Saint Joseph Memorial Hospital	Murphysboro	100%	35
Saint Margarets Hospital	Spring Valley	100%	91
St Mary & Elizabeth Med Ctr-Div Campus	Chicago	100%	391
Saint Mary Medical Center	Galesburg	100%	109
Saint Marys Hospital	Centralia	100%	204
Saint Marys Hospital[2]	Decatur	100%	227
Sarah Bush Lincoln Health Center	Mattoon	100%	234
Silver Cross Hospital	Joliet	100%	420
Swedish American Hospital	Rockford	100%	426
Thorek Memorial Hospital	Chicago	100%	129
The University of Chicago Medical Center[2]	Chicago	100%	280
University of Illinois Hospital[2]	Chicago	100%	271
VA Illiana Healthcare System - Danville	Danville	100%	73
Westlake Community Hospital	Melrose Park	100%	213
Adventist Bolingbrook Hospital	Bolingbrook	99%	175
Advocate Trinity Hospital	Chicago	99%	439
Blessing Hospital	Quincy	99%	351
Centegra Health System - McHenry Hospital	Mchenry	99%	331
Copley Memorial Hospital	Aurora	99%	275
Decatur Memorial Hospital[2]	Decatur	99%	407
Galesburg Cottage Hospital	Galesburg	99%	102
Heartland Regional Medical Center	Marion	99%	136
Herrin Hospital	Herrin	99%	177
Ingalls Memorial Hospital[2]	Harvey	99%	307
Kishwaukee Community Hospital	Dekalb	99%	154
McDonough District Hospital	Macomb	99%	91
Memorial Hospital	Belleville	99%	603
Memorial Hospital of Carbondale	Carbondale	99%	213
Mount Sinai Hospital Medical Center	Chicago	99%	302
Norwegian-American Hospital	Chicago	99%	210
Provena St Joseph Medical Center[2]	Joliet	99%	307
Saint Anthony Medical Center	Rockford	99%	301
St James Hospital-Olympia Fields	Olympia Fields	99%	806
Saint Joseph Medical Center	Bloomington	99%	163
Swedish Covenant Hospital	Chicago	99%	467
Trinity Rock Island[2]	Rock Island	99%	288
Vista Medical Center East	Waukegan	99%	342
West Suburban Medical Center[2]	Oak Park	99%	316
Clay County Hospital	Flora	98%	44
Methodist Hospital of Chicago	Chicago	98%	48
Oak Forest Hospital[2]	Oak Forest	98%	202
RHC St Francis Hospital	Evanston	98%	304
Riverside Medical Center	Kankakee	98%	222
Saint Anthony's Health Center	Alton	98%	165
Saint Anthonys Memorial Hospital	Effingham	98%	178
Saint Elizabeth Hospital[2]	Belleville	98%	456
Saint Josephs Hospital[2]	Breese	98%	47
Sherman Hospital	Elgin	98%	342
Taylorville Memorial Hospital	Taylorville	98%	63
John H Stroger Jr Hospital[2]	Chicago	97%	308
Provena United Samaritans Med Ctr-Logan	Danville	97%	275
Rochelle Community Hospital	Rochelle	97%	30
Saint Anthony Hospital	Chicago	97%	140
Saint Bernard Hospital	Chicago	97%	345
Skokie Hospital	Skokie	97%	318
Adventist Glenoaks	Glendale Hghts	96%	78
Centegra Health Sys-Woodstock Hospital	Woodstock	96%	121
Mercy Hospital and Medical Center[2]	Chicago	96%	307
Provena Mercy Medical Center[2]	Aurora	96%	197
Saint Marys Hospital	Streator	96%	84
Touchette Regional Hospital	Centreville	96%	171
Valley West Community Hospital	Sandwich	96%	26
Holy Cross Hospital[2]	Chicago	95%	302
Ottawa Reg Hosp & Healthcare Ctr	Ottawa	95%	79
Paris Community Hospital	Paris	95%	39
Passavant Area Hospital[2]	Jacksonville	95%	123
Union County Hospital	Anna	95%	37
Harrisburg Medical Center[2]	Harrisburg	94%	100
Illinois Valley Community Hospital	Peru	94%	82
Rush Oak Park Hospital	Oak Park	94%	196
Wabash General Hospital	Mount Carmel	93%	54
Iroquois Memorial Hospital	Watseka	92%	79
Crawford Memorial Hospital	Robinson	91%	46
Lawrence County Memorial Hospital	Lawrenceville	91%	46
Provena-Saint Joseph Hospital	Elgin	90%	210
Saint Joseph's Hospital	Highland	90%	30
Kewanee Hospital	Kewanee	89%	45
Richland Memorial Hospital	Olney	89%	87
Sacred Heart Hospital	Chicago	89%	144
Shelby Memorial Hospital	Shelbyville	89%	91
South Shore Hospital	Chicago	89%	235
Pana Community Hospital	Pana	88%	33
Graham Hospital Association	Canton	86%	108
Roseland Community Hospital[2]	Chicago	86%	259
Fayette County Hospital[3]	Vandalia	85%	26
Jersey Community Hospital	Jerseyville	85%	86
Hoopeston Community Memorial Hospital	Hoopeston	82%	39
Saint Francis Hospital	Litchfield	82%	40
Perry Memorial Hospital	Princeton	81%	59
Marshall Browning Hospital	Du Quoin	64%	28
Salem Township Hospital	Salem	62%	45
OSF Holy Family Medical Center[3]	Monmouth	53%	30

15. Smoking Cessation Advice

Hospital Name	City	Rate	Cases
Adventist La Grange Memorial Hospital	La Grange	100%	32
Advocate Christ Hospital & Medical Center[2]	Oak Lawn	100%	52
Advocate Condell Medical Center	Libertyville	100%	48
Advocate Good Samaritan Hospital	Downers Grove	100%	43
Advocate Good Shepherd Hospital	Barrington	100%	41
Advocate Illinois Masonic Medical Center[2]	Chicago	100%	76
Advocate Lutheran General Hospital	Park Ridge	100%	49
Advocate South Suburban Hospital[2]	Hazel Crest	100%	85
Advocate Trinity Hospital	Chicago	100%	119
Alexian Brothers Medical Center	Elk Grove Vlg	100%	44
Alton Memorial Hospital	Alton	100%	42
Blessing Hospital	Quincy	100%	49
Carle Foundation Hospital[2]	Urbana	100%	44
Central Dupage Hospital	Winfield	100%	61
Copley Memorial Hospital	Aurora	100%	46
Decatur Memorial Hospital[2]	Decatur	100%	54
Delnor Community Hospital	Geneva	100%	33
Edward Hospital	Naperville	100%	48
Elmhurst Memorial Hospital[2]	Elmhurst	100%	37
Gateway Regional Medical Center	Granite City	100%	48
Genesis Medical Center Illini Campus	Silvis	100%	25
Good Samaritan Regional Health Center	Mount Vernon	100%	34
Heartland Regional Medical Center	Marion	100%	25
Herrin Hospital	Herrin	100%	31
Hines VA Medical Center	Hines	100%	61
Ingalls Memorial Hospital[2]	Harvey	100%	48
Jackson Park Hospital	Chicago	100%	134
J Brown VA Med Ctr-VA Chicago Healthcare	Chicago	100%	102
Katherine Shaw Bethea Hospital	Dixon	100%	25
Kishwaukee Community Hospital	Dekalb	100%	25
Little Company of Mary Hospital[2]	Evergreen Park	100%	66
Loretto Hospital	Chicago	100%	41
Louis A Weiss Memorial Hospital	Chicago	100%	70
Loyola Gottlieb Memorial Hospital	Melrose Park	100%	40
Macneal Hospital	Berwyn	100%	52
Memorial Hospital	Belleville	100%	114
Memorial Medical Center	Springfield	100%	95
Mercy Hospital and Medical Center[2]	Chicago	100%	62
Methodist Medical Center of Illinois	Peoria	100%	69
Morris Hospital & Healthcare Centers	Morris	100%	26
Mount Sinai Hospital Medical Center	Chicago	100%	124
North Chicago VA Medical Center	North Chicago	100%	32
Northwestern Memorial Hospital	Chicago	100%	149
Norwegian-American Hospital	Chicago	100%	54
Our Lady of the Resurrection Medical Center	Chicago	100%	67
Palos Community Hospital[2]	Palos Heights	100%	30
Provena Covenant Medical Center - Urbana	Urbana	100%	52

NOTE: Hospital profiles are in alphabetical order by state, then city, then hospital within the city; Rankings exclude hospitals with less than 25 cases except for patient surveys which excludes hospitals with less than 100 cases; (a) 100–299 cases; (1) The number of cases is too small to be sure how well a hospital is performing; (2) The hospital indicated that the data submitted for this measure were based on a sample of cases; (3) Data was collected during a shorter time period (fewer quarters) than the maximum possible time for this measure; (4) Suppressed for one or more quarters by CMS; (5) No data is available from the hospital for this measure; (6) Fewer than 100 patients completed the HCAHPS survey. Use these rates with caution, as the number of surveys may be too low to reliably assess hospital performance; (7) Survey results are based on less than 12 months of data; (8) Survey results are not available for this reporting period; (9) No or very few patients were eligible for the HCAHPS survey. The scores shown, if any, reflect a very small number of surveys; (10) A state average was not calculated because too few hospitals in the state submitted data; (11) There were discrepancies in the data collection process; Please refer to the User's Guide for a full explanation of data.

Hospital Name	City	Rate	Cases
Provena Mercy Medical Center[2]	Aurora	100%	26
Provena St Marys Hospital	Kankakee	100%	37
Resurrection Medical Center	Chicago	100%	49
RHC St Francis Hospital	Evanston	100%	44
Rockford Memorial Hospital	Rockford	100%	60
Rush Oak Park Hospital	Oak Park	100%	32
Saint Alexius Medical Center	Hoffman Estates	100%	44
Saint Anthony Medical Center	Rockford	100%	26
Saint Anthony's Health Center	Alton	100%	28
Saint Bernard Hospital	Chicago	100%	162
Saint Francis Medical Center	Peoria	100%	108
St James Hospital-Olympia Fields	Olympia Fields	100%	153
Saint Johns Hospital[2]	Springfield	100%	91
Saint Joseph Hospital	Chicago	100%	26
Saint Joseph Medical Center	Bloomington	100%	30
St Mary & Elizabeth Med Ctr-Div Campus	Chicago	100%	85
Saint Marys Hospital	Centralia	100%	30
Saint Marys Hospital[2]	Decatur	100%	44
Sarah Bush Lincoln Health Center	Mattoon	100%	50
Silver Cross Hospital	Joliet	100%	67
Swedish American Hospital	Rockford	100%	96
Trinity Rock Island[2]	Rock Island	100%	36
University of Illinois Hospital[2]	Chicago	100%	72
Vista Medical Center East	Waukegan	100%	71
Westlake Community Hospital	Melrose Park	100%	36
John H Stroger Jr Hospital[2]	Chicago	99%	94
Metrosouth Medical Center	Blue Island	99%	97
Provident Hospital of Chicago[2]	Chicago	99%	122
West Suburban Medical Center[2]	Oak Park	99%	106
Anderson Hospital	Maryville	98%	45
Centegra Health System - McHenry Hospital	Mchenry	98%	49
Loyola University Medical Center	Maywood	98%	132
Memorial Hospital of Carbondale	Carbondale	98%	44
Oak Forest Hospital[2]	Oak Forest	98%	62
Provena United Samaritans Med Ctr-Logan	Danville	98%	46
Roseland Community Hospital[2]	Chicago	98%	93
Saint Elizabeth Hospital[2]	Belleville	98%	66
Sherman Hospital	Elgin	98%	49
South Shore Hospital	Chicago	98%	44
Swedish Covenant Hospital	Chicago	98%	56
The University of Chicago Medical Center[2]	Chicago	98%	48
Holy Cross Hospital[2]	Chicago	97%	106
Provena-Saint Joseph Hospital	Elgin	97%	37
Saint Anthonys Memorial Hospital	Effingham	97%	31
Touchette Regional Hospital	Centreville	97%	75
Evanston Hospital	Evanston	96%	85
Rush University Medical Center[2]	Chicago	94%	53
Adventist Bolingbrook Hospital	Bolingbrook	92%	26
Riverside Medical Center	Kankakee	92%	40
Saint Mary Medical Center	Galesburg	85%	26

Pneumonia Care

16. Appropriate Initial Antibiotic

Hospital Name	City	Rate	Cases
Gateway Regional Medical Center	Granite City	100%	50
Proctor Hospital[2]	Peoria	100%	106
Advocate Illinois Masonic Medical Center[2]	Chicago	98%	60
Hillsboro Area Hospital	Hillsboro	98%	42
McDonough District Hospital	Macomb	98%	41
Rockford Memorial Hospital	Rockford	98%	178
Sherman Hospital	Elgin	98%	133
Adventist La Grange Memorial Hospital	La Grange	97%	148
Advocate South Suburban Hospital[2]	Hazel Crest	97%	75
Bromenn Healthcare	Normal	97%	94
Delnor Community Hospital	Geneva	97%	127
Evanston Hospital[2]	Evanston	97%	106
Genesis Medical Center Illini Campus	Silvis	97%	102
Hardin County General Hospital	Rosiclare	97%	37
Hoopeston Community Memorial Hospital	Hoopeston	97%	30
John & Mary Kirby Hospital	Monticello	97%	35
Methodist Medical Center of Illinois	Peoria	97%	149
North Chicago VA Medical Center	North Chicago	97%	62
Northwestern Memorial Hospital	Chicago	97%	135
Thorek Memorial Hospital	Chicago	97%	36
Trinity Rock Island[2]	Rock Island	97%	71
Union County Hospital	Anna	97%	36
Westlake Community Hospital	Melrose Park	97%	35
Adventist Bolingbrook Hospital	Bolingbrook	96%	110
Advocate Condell Medical Center[2]	Libertyville	96%	85
Advocate Good Samaritan Hospital[2]	Downers Grove	96%	142
Central Dupage Hospital	Winfield	96%	189
Mount Sinai Hospital Medical Center	Chicago	96%	95
Ottawa Reg Hosp & Healthcare Ctr	Ottawa	96%	103
Our Lady of the Resurrection Medical Center	Chicago	96%	130
Resurrection Medical Center	Chicago	96%	180
Saint Francis Medical Center	Peoria	96%	217
Saint Joseph Memorial Hospital	Murphysboro	96%	28
VA Illiana Healthcare System - Danville	Danville	96%	25
Advocate Christ Hospital & Medical Center[2]	Oak Lawn	95%	65
Advocate Good Shepherd Hospital	Barrington	95%	101
Carle Foundation Hospital[2]	Urbana	95%	78
Edward Hospital	Naperville	95%	248
Galesburg Cottage Hospital	Galesburg	95%	60
Hines VA Medical Center	Hines	95%	66
Katherine Shaw Bethea Hospital	Dixon	95%	44
Lake Forest Hospital	Lake Forest	95%	114
Memorial Hospital	Belleville	95%	235
Memorial Hospital[2]	Chester	95%	43
Mercy Hospital and Medical Center[2]	Chicago	95%	77
Provident Hospital of Chicago[2]	Chicago	95%	131
Saint Alexius Medical Center	Hoffman Estates	95%	165
St Mary & Elizabeth Med Ctr-Div Campus	Chicago	95%	208
Saint Marys Hospital[2]	Streator	95%	65
Blessing Hospital	Quincy	94%	234
Clay County Hospital	Flora	94%	49
Little Company of Mary Hospital[2]	Evergreen Park	94%	82
Northwest Community Hospital[2]	Arlington Hgts	94%	83
Oak Forest Hospital	Oak Forest	94%	49
Silver Cross Hospital	Joliet	94%	193
Swedish American Hospital	Rockford	94%	170
Advocate Lutheran General Hospital	Park Ridge	93%	150
Advocate Trinity Hospital	Chicago	93%	143
Anderson Hospital[2]	Maryville	93%	103
Carlinville Area Hospital	Carlinville	93%	29
Centegra Health Sys-Woodstock Hospital	Woodstock	93%	99
CGH Medical Center	Sterling	93%	89
Elmhurst Memorial Hospital[2]	Elmhurst	93%	82
Good Samaritan Regional Health Center	Mount Vernon	93%	107
Loyola University Medical Center	Maywood	93%	92
Memorial Hospital of Carbondale	Carbondale	93%	61
Palos Community Hospital[2]	Palos Heights	93%	82
Passavant Area Hospital	Jacksonville	93%	135
Red Bud Regional Hospital	Red Bud	93%	42
Saint Marys Hospital	Centralia	93%	84
Sarah Bush Lincoln Health Center	Mattoon	93%	105
Sparta Community Hospital	Sparta	93%	44
Copley Memorial Hospital	Aurora	92%	119
Fhn Memorial Hospital	Freeport	92%	91
Graham Hospital Association	Canton	92%	36
J Brown VA Med Ctr-VA Chicago Healthcare	Chicago	92%	51
Kewanee Hospital	Kewanee	92%	36
Provena United Samaritans Med Ctr-Logan	Danville	92%	147
Saint James Hospital	Pontiac	92%	48
Saint Mary Medical Center	Galesburg	92%	142
Decatur Memorial Hospital[2]	Decatur	91%	187
Macneal Hospital	Berwyn	91%	150
Memorial Medical Center	Springfield	91%	291
Pekin Memorial Hospital	Pekin	91%	119
Abraham Lincoln Memorial Hospital	Lincoln	90%	31
Gibson Community Hospital[2]	Gibson City	90%	42
Ingalls Memorial Hospital[2]	Harvey	90%	94
Kishwaukee Community Hospital	Dekalb	90%	93
St James Hospital-Olympia Fields[2]	Olympia Fields	90%	121
Skokie Hospital	Skokie	90%	93
Adventist Glenoaks	Glendale Hghts	89%	27
Alexian Brothers Medical Center	Elk Grove Vlg	89%	202
Crossroads Community Hospital	Mount Vernon	89%	56
Richland Memorial Hospital	Olney	89%	62
Saint Anthonys Memorial Hospital	Effingham	89%	117
Saint Joseph Hospital	Chicago	89%	75
Saint Josephs Hospital	Breese	89%	72
Swedish Covenant Hospital	Chicago	89%	189
Touchette Regional Hospital	Centreville	89%	44
Crawford Memorial Hospital	Robinson	88%	26
Herrin Hospital	Herrin	88%	95
Louis A Weiss Memorial Hospital	Chicago	88%	52
Loyola Gottlieb Memorial Hospital	Melrose Park	88%	69
Marion Illinois VA Medical Center	Marion	88%	80
Provena St Joseph Medical Center[2]	Joliet	88%	77
Provena-Saint Joseph Hospital[2]	Elgin	88%	77
Saint Bernard Hospital	Chicago	88%	120
Saint Joseph Medical Center	Bloomington	88%	101
Saint Margarets Hospital	Spring Valley	88%	40
Saint Marys Hospital[2]	Decatur	88%	104
West Suburban Medical Center[2]	Oak Park	88%	86
Alton Memorial Hospital[2]	Alton	87%	187
Centegra Health System - McHenry Hospital	Mchenry	87%	141
Provena Covenant Medical Center - Urbana	Urbana	87%	92
Saint Johns Hospital[2]	Springfield	87%	61
Hinsdale Hospital	Hinsdale	86%	120
Provena Mercy Medical Center[2]	Aurora	86%	94
Saint Elizabeth Hospital[2]	Belleville	86%	199
Saint Joseph's Hospital	Highland	86%	29
Wabash General Hospital[2]	Mount Carmel	86%	50
Heartland Regional Medical Center	Marion	85%	68
Iroquois Memorial Hospital	Watseka	85%	84
Metrosouth Medical Center	Blue Island	85%	120
Perry Memorial Hospital	Princeton	85%	40
Saint Anthony's Health Center	Alton	85%	92
Saint Anthony Hospital	Chicago	84%	75
Saint Francis Hospital	Litchfield	84%	38
Greenville Regional Hospital	Greenville	83%	30
Jersey Community Hospital	Jerseyville	83%	83
Norwegian-American Hospital	Chicago	83%	71
Riverside Medical Center	Kankakee	83%	108
Rush Oak Park Hospital	Oak Park	83%	58
Saint Anthony Medical Center	Rockford	83%	115
Ferrell Hospital Community Foundations	Eldorado	82%	28
Rush University Medical Center[2]	Chicago	82%	40
University of Illinois Hospital[2]	Chicago	82%	51
Vista Medical Center East	Waukegan	82%	93
Morris Hospital & Healthcare Centers[2]	Morris	80%	103
Provena St Marys Hospital[2]	Kankakee	80%	84
Illinois Valley Community Hospital	Peru	79%	67
Harrisburg Medical Center[2]	Harrisburg	78%	93
Loretto Hospital	Chicago	78%	55
Rochelle Community Hospital	Rochelle	78%	27
Taylorville Memorial Hospital	Taylorville	77%	48
Holy Cross Hospital[2]	Chicago	76%	72
RHC St Francis Hospital	Evanston	75%	173
Salem Township Hospital	Salem	72%	25
John H Stroger Jr Hospital[2]	Chicago	70%	121
South Shore Hospital	Chicago	67%	45
Roseland Community Hospital[2]	Chicago	66%	118
Jackson Park Hospital[2]	Chicago	11%	152

17. Blood Culture Timing

Hospital Name	City	Rate	Cases
Adventist La Grange Memorial Hospital	La Grange	100%	266
Advocate Good Shepherd Hospital	Barrington	100%	234
Advocate Illinois Masonic Medical Center[2]	Chicago	100%	145
Advocate Lutheran General Hospital	Park Ridge	100%	267
Clay County Hospital	Flora	100%	68
Crossroads Community Hospital	Mount Vernon	100%	70
Edward Hospital	Naperville	100%	438
Fairfield Memorial Hospital	Fairfield	100%	28
Gateway Regional Medical Center	Granite City	100%	113
Genesis Medical Center Illini Campus	Silvis	100%	161
Good Samaritan Regional Health Center	Mount Vernon	100%	135
Herrin Hospital	Herrin	100%	119
Hines VA Medical Center	Hines	100%	129
Jackson Park Hospital[2]	Chicago	100%	82
J Brown VA Med Ctr-VA Chicago Healthcare	Chicago	100%	71
Katherine Shaw Bethea Hospital	Dixon	100%	70
Little Company of Mary Hospital[2]	Evergreen Park	100%	116
Memorial Hospital[2]	Chester	100%	33
Mendota Community Hospital	Mendota	100%	31
North Chicago VA Medical Center	North Chicago	100%	72
Our Lady of the Resurrection Medical Center	Chicago	100%	159
Resurrection Medical Center	Chicago	100%	452
Richland Memorial Hospital	Olney	100%	69
Rochelle Community Hospital	Rochelle	100%	32
Saint Joseph Medical Center	Bloomington	100%	88
Saint Joseph Memorial Hospital	Murphysboro	100%	43
Saint Josephs Hospital	Breese	100%	89
St Mary & Elizabeth Med Ctr-Div Campus	Chicago	100%	352
Saint Marys Hospital	Centralia	100%	142
Saint Marys Hospital[2]	Streator	100%	93
Sherman Hospital	Elgin	100%	235
VA Illiana Healthcare System - Danville	Danville	100%	29
Westlake Community Hospital	Melrose Park	100%	73
Adventist Glenoaks	Glendale Hghts	99%	89
Advocate Condell Medical Center[2]	Libertyville	99%	135
Advocate Good Samaritan Hospital[2]	Downers Grove	99%	227
Alexian Brothers Medical Center	Elk Grove Vlg	99%	306
Alton Memorial Hospital[2]	Alton	99%	271
Blessing Hospital	Quincy	99%	438
Centegra Health System - McHenry Hospital	Mchenry	99%	230
Delnor Community Hospital	Geneva	99%	105
Elmhurst Memorial Hospital[2]	Elmhurst	99%	151
Galesburg Cottage Hospital	Galesburg	99%	116
Heartland Regional Medical Center	Marion	99%	115
Methodist Medical Center of Illinois	Peoria	99%	194
Mount Sinai Hospital Medical Center	Chicago	99%	203
Northwestern Memorial Hospital	Chicago	99%	401
Proctor Hospital[2]	Peoria	99%	200
Red Bud Regional Hospital	Red Bud	99%	69
Rockford Memorial Hospital	Rockford	99%	324
Saint Alexius Medical Center	Hoffman Estates	99%	329
Saint Anthony Hospital	Chicago	99%	128
Saint Mary Medical Center	Galesburg	99%	176
Trinity Rock Island[2]	Rock Island	99%	125
Adventist Bolingbrook Hospital	Bolingbrook	98%	162
Advocate Christ Hospital & Medical Center[2]	Oak Lawn	98%	54
Carle Foundation Hospital[2]	Urbana	98%	99
Central Dupage Hospital	Winfield	98%	215
CGH Medical Center	Sterling	98%	126
Decatur Memorial Hospital[2]	Decatur	98%	301
Evanston Hospital[2]	Evanston	98%	180
Hardin County General Hospital	Rosiclare	98%	57

NOTE: Hospital profiles are in alphabetical order by state, then city, then hospital within the city; Rankings exclude hospitals with less than 25 cases except for patient surveys which excludes hospitals with less than 100 cases; (a) 100–299 cases; (1) The number of cases is too small to be sure how well a hospital is performing; (2) The hospital indicated that the data submitted for this measure were based on a sample of cases; (3) Data was collected during a shorter time period (fewer quarters) than the maximum possible time for this measure; (4) Suppressed for one or more quarters by CMS; (5) No data is available from the hospital for this measure; (6) Fewer than 100 patients completed the HCAHPS survey. Use these rates with caution, as the number of surveys may be too low to reliably assess hospital performance; (7) Survey results are based on less than 12 months of data; (8) Survey results are not available for this reporting period; (9) No or very few patients were eligible for the HCAHPS survey. The scores shown, if any, reflect a very small number of surveys; (10) A state average was not calculated because too few hospitals in the state submitted data; (11) There were discrepancies in the data collection process; Please refer to the User's Guide for a full explanation of data.

Ingalls Memorial Hospital[2]	Harvey	98%	123
Louis A Weiss Memorial Hospital	Chicago	98%	201
Oak Forest Hospital	Oak Forest	98%	56
Pekin Memorial Hospital	Pekin	98%	250
RHC St Francis Hospital	Evanston	98%	422
Riverside Medical Center	Kankakee	98%	235
Saint Anthony Medical Center	Rockford	98%	212
Saint Elizabeth Hospital[2]	Belleville	98%	277
Saint Joseph Hospital	Chicago	98%	149
Saint Margarets Hospital	Spring Valley	98%	49
The University of Chicago Medical Center[2]	Chicago	98%	53
University of Illinois Hospital[2]	Chicago	98%	130
Advocate South Suburban Hospital[2]	Hazel Crest	97%	58
Advocate Trinity Hospital	Chicago	97%	202
Anderson Hospital[2]	Maryville	97%	189
Copley Memorial Hospital	Aurora	97%	154
Fhn Memorial Hospital	Freeport	97%	145
Gibson Community Hospital[2]	Gibson City	97%	38
Graham Hospital Association	Canton	97%	66
Hillsboro Area Hospital	Hillsboro	97%	30
Hinsdale Hospital	Hinsdale	97%	243
Jersey Community Hospital	Jerseyville	97%	116
Kishwaukee Community Hospital	Dekalb	97%	101
Lake Forest Hospital	Lake Forest	97%	207
Lawrence County Memorial Hospital	Lawrenceville	97%	30
Loyola Gottlieb Memorial Hospital	Melrose Park	97%	78
Memorial Medical Center	Springfield	97%	390
Provena Covenant Medical Center - Urbana	Urbana	97%	148
Saint Bernard Hospital	Chicago	97%	245
Silver Cross Hospital	Joliet	97%	241
Vista Medical Center East	Waukegan	97%	113
West Suburban Medical Center[2]	Oak Park	97%	176
Abraham Lincoln Memorial Hospital	Lincoln	96%	53
Centegra Health Sys-Woodstock Hospital	Woodstock	96%	154
Crawford Memorial Hospital	Robinson	96%	47
John & Mary Kirby Hospital	Monticello	96%	45
Loyola University Medical Center	Maywood	96%	255
Marion Illinois VA Medical Center	Marion	96%	112
McDonough District Hospital	Macomb	96%	51
Memorial Hospital of Carbondale	Carbondale	96%	106
Pana Community Hospital	Pana	96%	25
Rush Oak Park Hospital	Oak Park	96%	56
Saint Anthony's Health Center	Alton	96%	142
St James Hospital-Olympia Fields[2]	Olympia Fields	96%	274
Saint Johns Hospital[2]	Springfield	96%	53
Touchette Regional Hospital	Centreville	96%	51
Union County Hospital	Anna	96%	57
Loretto Hospital	Chicago	95%	101
Macneal Hospital	Berwyn	95%	235
Memorial Hospital	Belleville	95%	375
Ottawa Reg Hosp & Healthcare Ctr	Ottawa	95%	155
Saint James Hospital	Pontiac	95%	61
Sarah Bush Lincoln Health Center	Mattoon	95%	99
Skokie Hospital	Skokie	95%	88
Swedish Covenant Hospital	Chicago	95%	356
Bromenn Healthcare	Normal	94%	216
Holy Cross Hospital[2]	Chicago	94%	103
Kewanee Hospital	Kewanee	94%	49
Morris Hospital & Healthcare Centers[2]	Morris	94%	156
Passavant Area Hospital	Jacksonville	94%	227
Perry Memorial Hospital	Princeton	94%	52
Provena-Saint Joseph Hospital[2]	Elgin	94%	129
Rush University Medical Center[2]	Chicago	94%	109
Saint Anthonys Memorial Hospital	Effingham	94%	161
Saint Marys Hospital[2]	Decatur	94%	144
Swedish American Hospital	Rockford	94%	261
Thorek Memorial Hospital	Chicago	94%	71
Valley West Community Hospital	Sandwich	94%	31
Illinois Valley Community Hospital	Peru	93%	82
Mercy Hospital and Medical Center[2]	Chicago	93%	130
Northwest Community Hospital[2]	Arlington Hgts	93%	149
Palos Community Hospital[2]	Palos Heights	93%	144
Greenville Regional Hospital	Greenville	92%	52
Metrosouth Medical Center	Blue Island	92%	173
Provena St Marys Hospital[2]	Kankakee	92%	145
Provena United Samaritans Med Ctr-Logan	Danville	92%	174
Saint Francis Medical Center	Peoria	92%	310
Provena St Joseph Medical Center[2]	Joliet	91%	111
Iroquois Memorial Hospital	Watseka	90%	122
Saint Francis Hospital	Litchfield	90%	49
Wabash General Hospital[2]	Mount Carmel	90%	51
Norwegian-American Hospital	Chicago	89%	98
Provena Mercy Medical Center[2]	Aurora	89%	170
Taylorville Memorial Hospital	Taylorville	89%	90
Methodist Hospital of Chicago	Chicago	88%	113
Salem Township Hospital	Salem	88%	32
John H Stroger Jr Hospital[2]	Chicago	87%	166
South Shore Hospital	Chicago	85%	100
Provident Hospital of Chicago[2]	Chicago	83%	151
Shelby Memorial Hospital	Shelbyville	79%	38
Harrisburg Medical Center[2]	Harrisburg	78%	93
Roseland Community Hospital[2]	Chicago	75%	77
Hoopeston Community Memorial Hospital	Hoopeston	70%	57

18. Influenza Vaccine

Hospital Name	City	Rate	Cases
Abraham Lincoln Memorial Hospital	Lincoln	100%	39
Advocate Condell Medical Center[2]	Libertyville	100%	89
Advocate Good Shepherd Hospital	Barrington	100%	132
Anderson Hospital[2]	Maryville	100%	98
Fairfield Memorial Hospital	Fairfield	100%	30
Hillsboro Area Hospital	Hillsboro	100%	36
J Brown VA Med Ctr-VA Chicago Healthcare	Chicago	100%	72
Little Company of Mary Hospital[2]	Evergreen Park	100%	79
Loretto Hospital	Chicago	100%	51
Our Lady of the Resurrection Medical Center	Chicago	100%	164
Saint Joseph Memorial Hospital	Murphysboro	100%	31
Saint Marys Hospital	Centralia	100%	142
The University of Chicago Medical Center[2]	Chicago	100%	55
Advocate Christ Hospital & Medical Center[2]	Oak Lawn	99%	110
Advocate Illinois Masonic Medical Center[2]	Chicago	99%	79
Advocate Lutheran General Hospital	Park Ridge	99%	201
Advocate South Suburban Hospital[2]	Hazel Crest	99%	86
Advocate Trinity Hospital	Chicago	99%	143
Delnor Community Hospital	Geneva	99%	132
Galesburg Cottage Hospital	Galesburg	99%	104
Pekin Memorial Hospital	Pekin	99%	123
Saint Joseph Hospital	Chicago	99%	111
Saint Marys Hospital[2]	Decatur	99%	106
Silver Cross Hospital	Joliet	99%	232
Thorek Memorial Hospital	Chicago	99%	74
Evanston Hospital[2]	Evanston	98%	129
Good Samaritan Regional Health Center	Mount Vernon	98%	125
Hines VA Medical Center	Hines	98%	112
Katherine Shaw Bethea Hospital	Dixon	98%	56
Louis A Weiss Memorial Hospital	Chicago	98%	112
Memorial Hospital	Belleville	98%	222
Methodist Medical Center of Illinois	Peoria	98%	182
Proctor Hospital[2]	Peoria	98%	125
Rush Oak Park Hospital	Oak Park	98%	58
Saint Alexius Medical Center	Hoffman Estates	98%	250
Saint James Hospital	Pontiac	98%	47
Saint Marys Hospital[2]	Streator	98%	90
Sherman Hospital	Elgin	98%	129
Taylorville Memorial Hospital	Taylorville	98%	81
Vista Medical Center East	Waukegan	98%	119
Adventist Bolingbrook Hospital	Bolingbrook	97%	87
Advocate Good Samaritan Hospital[2]	Downers Grove	97%	167
Carle Foundation Hospital[2]	Urbana	97%	75
Crawford Memorial Hospital	Robinson	97%	31
Edward Hospital	Naperville	97%	277
Hardin County General Hospital	Rosiclare	97%	36
Provena St Joseph Medical Center[2]	Joliet	97%	73
Provident Hospital of Chicago[2]	Chicago	97%	67
Riverside Medical Center	Kankakee	97%	142
Saint Bernard Hospital	Chicago	97%	86
Saint Josephs Hospital	Breese	97%	70
Fhn Memorial Hospital	Freeport	96%	92
Gateway Regional Medical Center	Granite City	96%	51
Genesis Medical Center Illini Campus	Silvis	96%	111
Gibson Community Hospital[2]	Gibson City	96%	25
Graham Hospital Association	Canton	96%	46
Loyola Gottlieb Memorial Hospital	Melrose Park	96%	99
Passavant Area Hospital	Jacksonville	96%	141
Saint Joseph's Hospital	Highland	96%	25
Blessing Hospital	Quincy	95%	291
Elmhurst Memorial Hospital[2]	Elmhurst	95%	100
Iroquois Memorial Hospital	Watseka	95%	64
Palos Community Hospital[2]	Palos Heights	95%	93
Red Bud Regional Hospital	Red Bud	95%	38
St Mary & Elizabeth Med Ctr-Div Campus	Chicago	95%	149
Clay County Hospital	Flora	94%	35
Jersey Community Hospital	Jerseyville	94%	64
Morris Hospital & Healthcare Centers[2]	Morris	94%	111
Northwest Community Hospital[2]	Arlington Hgts	94%	94
Saint Anthony Medical Center	Rockford	94%	143
Saint Elizabeth Hospital	Belleville	94%	200
Bromenn Healthcare	Normal	93%	145
CGH Medical Center	Sterling	93%	107
Copley Memorial Hospital	Aurora	93%	81
Harrisburg Medical Center[2]	Harrisburg	93%	91
Illinois Valley Community Hospital	Peru	93%	67
Lake Forest Hospital	Lake Forest	93%	99
McDonough District Hospital	Macomb	93%	60
Northwestern Memorial Hospital	Chicago	93%	274
Union County Hospital	Anna	93%	42
VA Illiana Healthcare System - Danville	Danville	93%	29
Decatur Memorial Hospital[2]	Decatur	92%	216
Provena St Marys Hospital[2]	Kankakee	92%	77
RHC St Francis Hospital	Evanston	92%	255
Saint Anthonys Memorial Hospital	Effingham	92%	107
Saint Francis Medical Center	Peoria	92%	288
Skokie Hospital	Skokie	92%	119
Swedish American Hospital	Rockford	92%	176
Adventist Glenoaks	Glendale Hghts	91%	35
Macneal Hospital	Berwyn	91%	150
Rockford Memorial Hospital	Rockford	91%	221
Saint Margarets Hospital	Spring Valley	91%	54
Saint Mary Medical Center	Galesburg	91%	137
Trinity Rock Island[2]	Rock Island	91%	94
Adventist La Grange Memorial Hospital	La Grange	90%	160
Central Dupage Hospital	Winfield	90%	174
Memorial Hospital	Chester	90%	39
Ottawa Reg Hosp & Healthcare Ctr	Ottawa	90%	120
Resurrection Medical Center	Chicago	90%	268
St James Hospital-Olympia Fields[2]	Olympia Fields	90%	147
Saint Joseph Medical Center	Bloomington	90%	104
Alton Memorial Hospital[2]	Alton	89%	167
Crossroads Community Hospital	Mount Vernon	89%	46
Loyola University Medical Center	Maywood	89%	158
Provena Covenant Medical Center - Urbana	Urbana	89%	125
Touchette Regional Hospital	Centreville	89%	27
Herrin Hospital	Herrin	88%	144
Hinsdale Hospital	Hinsdale	88%	142
Kewanee Hospital	Kewanee	88%	41
Memorial Medical Center	Springfield	88%	311
Memorial Hospital of Carbondale	Carbondale	87%	106
Provena Mercy Medical Center[2]	Aurora	87%	86
Ingalls Memorial Hospital[2]	Harvey	86%	84
Provena United Samaritans Med Ctr-Logan	Danville	86%	175
Alexian Brothers Medical Center	Elk Grove Vlg	85%	256
Marion Illinois VA Medical Center	Marion	85%	79
Saint Anthony's Health Center	Alton	85%	117
Wabash General Hospital	Mount Carmel	85%	48
Westlake Community Hospital	Melrose Park	85%	54
Fayette County Hospital[3]	Vandalia	84%	31
Heartland Regional Medical Center	Marion	83%	107
Metrosouth Medical Center	Blue Island	83%	120
West Suburban Medical Center[2]	Oak Park	83%	78
Salem Township Hospital	Salem	81%	26
Sarah Bush Lincoln Health Center	Mattoon	81%	135
John & Mary Kirby Hospital	Monticello	79%	28
Methodist Hospital of Chicago	Chicago	79%	89
Saint Johns Hospital[2]	Springfield	79%	84
Ferrell Hospital Community Foundations	Eldorado	78%	27
Mount Sinai Hospital Medical Center	Chicago	78%	54
Provena-Saint Joseph Hospital[2]	Elgin	78%	85
Rush University Medical Center[2]	Chicago	78%	50
Swedish Covenant Hospital	Chicago	78%	267
Centegra Health System - McHenry Hospital	Mchenry	75%	152
Kishwaukee Community Hospital	Dekalb	75%	105
Norwegian-American Hospital	Chicago	74%	50
Centegra Health Sys-Woodstock Hospital	Woodstock	73%	104
Perry Memorial Hospital	Princeton	72%	47
University of Illinois Hospital[2]	Chicago	72%	68
Richland Memorial Hospital	Olney	71%	89
Holy Cross Hospital[2]	Chicago	68%	56
Saint Anthony Hospital	Chicago	68%	66
John H Stroger Jr Hospital[2]	Chicago	59%	68
Jackson Park Hospital[2]	Chicago	58%	53
Shelby Memorial Hospital	Shelbyville	54%	35
Mercy Hospital and Medical Center[2]	Chicago	51%	91
South Shore Hospital	Chicago	23%	62
Roseland Community Hospital	Chicago	16%	77

19. Initial Antibiotic Timing

Hospital Name	City	Rate	Cases
Advocate Good Shepherd Hospital	Barrington	100%	201
Advocate Illinois Masonic Medical Center[2]	Chicago	100%	113
Advocate South Suburban Hospital[2]	Hazel Crest	100%	141
Gibson Community Hospital[2]	Gibson City	100%	50
Hamilton Memorial Hospital District	Mcleansboro	100%	27
Hillsboro Area Hospital	Hillsboro	100%	51
Katherine Shaw Bethea Hospital	Dixon	100%	85
Lawrence County Memorial Hospital	Lawrenceville	100%	36
Mason District Hospital	Havana	100%	26
Methodist Medical Center of Illinois	Peoria	100%	224
Paris Community Hospital	Paris	100%	39
Passavant Area Hospital	Jacksonville	100%	210
Red Bud Regional Hospital	Red Bud	100%	67
Silver Cross Hospital	Joliet	100%	346
Wabash General Hospital[2]	Mount Carmel	100%	64
Adventist La Grange Memorial Hospital	La Grange	99%	310
Advocate Good Samaritan Hospital[2]	Downers Grove	99%	236
Advocate Lutheran General Hospital	Park Ridge	99%	280
Blessing Hospital	Quincy	99%	436
Centegra Health Sys-Woodstock Hospital	Woodstock	99%	158
Copley Memorial Hospital	Aurora	99%	173
Crossroads Community Hospital	Mount Vernon	99%	75
Decatur Memorial Hospital[2]	Decatur	99%	289
Delnor Community Hospital	Geneva	99%	213

NOTE: Hospital profiles are in alphabetical order by state, then city, then hospital within the city; Rankings exclude hospitals with less than 25 cases except for patient surveys which excludes hospitals with less than 100 cases; (a) 100–299 cases; (1) The number of cases is too small to be sure how well a hospital is performing; (2) The hospital indicated that the data submitted for this measure were based on a sample of cases; (3) Data was collected during a shorter time period (fewer quarters) than the maximum possible time for this measure; (4) Suppressed for one or more quarters by CMS; (5) No data is available from the hospital for this measure; (6) Fewer than 100 patients completed the HCAHPS survey. Use these rates with caution, as the number of surveys may be too low to reliably assess hospital performance; (7) Survey results are based on less than 12 months of data; (8) Survey results are not available for this reporting period; (9) No or very few patients were eligible for the HCAHPS survey. The scores shown, if any, reflect a very small number of surveys; (10) A state average was not calculated because too few hospitals in the state submitted data; (11) There were discrepancies in the data collection process; Please refer to the User's Guide for a full explanation of data.

Evanston Hospital[2]	Evanston	99%	165
Fhn Memorial Hospital	Freeport	99%	141
Galesburg Cottage Hospital	Galesburg	99%	108
Gateway Regional Medical Center	Granite City	99%	99
Jersey Community Hospital	Jerseyville	99%	108
Ottawa Reg Hosp & Healthcare Ctr	Ottawa	99%	171
Our Lady of the Resurrection Medical Center	Chicago	99%	246
Pekin Memorial Hospital	Pekin	99%	231
Proctor Hospital[2]	Peoria	99%	184
Abraham Lincoln Memorial Hospital	Lincoln	98%	54
Advocate Christ Hospital & Medical Center[2]	Oak Lawn	98%	140
Advocate Condell Medical Center[2]	Libertyville	98%	156
Carle Foundation Hospital[2]	Urbana	98%	126
Central Dupage Hospital	Winfield	98%	249
Genesis Medical Center Illini Campus	Silvis	98%	161
Good Samaritan Regional Health Center	Mount Vernon	98%	171
Graham Hospital Association	Canton	98%	65
Hardin County General Hospital	Rosiclare	98%	57
Kewanee Hospital	Kewanee	98%	47
Lake Forest Hospital	Lake Forest	98%	158
Little Company of Mary Hospital[2]	Evergreen Park	98%	143
Louis A Weiss Memorial Hospital	Chicago	98%	176
Northwest Community Hospital[2]	Arlington Hgts	98%	156
Richland Memorial Hospital	Olney	98%	92
Riverside Medical Center	Kankakee	98%	220
Saint Anthony Medical Center	Rockford	98%	190
Saint Josephs Hospital	Breese	98%	99
Saint Margarets Hospital	Spring Valley	98%	102
St Mary & Elizabeth Med Ctr-Div Campus	Chicago	98%	329
Saint Mary Medical Center	Galesburg	98%	217
Saint Marys Hospital	Centralia	98%	206
Saint Marys Hospital[2]	Streator	98%	120
Skokie Hospital	Skokie	98%	172
Sparta Community Hospital	Sparta	98%	53
The University of Chicago Medical Center[2]	Chicago	98%	44
Adventist Glenoaks	Glendale Hghts	97%	65
Alton Memorial Hospital[2]	Alton	97%	279
Carlinville Area Hospital	Carlinville	97%	31
Clay County Hospital	Flora	97%	74
Edward Hospital	Naperville	97%	439
Harrisburg Medical Center[2]	Harrisburg	97%	154
Hinsdale Hospital	Hinsdale	97%	217
Illini Community Hospital	Pittsfield	97%	33
Morris Hospital & Healthcare Centers[2]	Morris	97%	151
North Chicago VA Medical Center	North Chicago	97%	70
Palos Community Hospital[2]	Palos Heights	97%	129
Provena St Marys Hospital[2]	Kankakee	97%	151
Resurrection Medical Center	Chicago	97%	406
RHC St Francis Hospital	Evanston	97%	385
Rochelle Community Hospital	Rochelle	97%	38
Saint Anthony's Health Center	Alton	97%	148
Saint Joseph Hospital	Chicago	97%	146
Sarah Bush Lincoln Health Center	Mattoon	97%	184
Trinity Rock Island[2]	Rock Island	97%	128
Valley West Community Hospital	Sandwich	97%	35
Westlake Community Hospital	Melrose Park	97%	69
Adventist Bolingbrook Hospital	Bolingbrook	96%	164
Alexian Brothers Medical Center	Elk Grove Vlg	96%	320
Centegra Health System - McHenry Hospital	Mchenry	96%	246
Elmhurst Memorial Hospital[2]	Elmhurst	96%	136
Greenville Regional Hospital	Greenville	96%	51
Macneal Hospital	Berwyn	96%	223
Memorial Hospital[2]	Chester	96%	54
Mount Sinai Hospital Medical Center	Chicago	96%	135
Northwestern Memorial Hospital	Chicago	96%	359
Perry Memorial Hospital	Princeton	96%	74
Provena-Saint Joseph Hospital[2]	Elgin	96%	125
Saint Elizabeth Hospital[2]	Belleville	96%	343
Saint Francis Medical Center	Peoria	96%	386
Saint Joseph Medical Center	Bloomington	96%	128
Union County Hospital	Anna	96%	55
VA Illiana Healthcare System - Danville	Danville	96%	45
Anderson Hospital[2]	Maryville	95%	161
CGH Medical Center	Sterling	95%	168
Fayette County Hospital[3]	Vandalia	95%	42
Heartland Regional Medical Center	Marion	95%	117
Hines VA Medical Center	Hines	95%	132
Illinois Valley Community Hospital	Peru	95%	95
Ingalls Memorial Hospital[2]	Harvey	95%	146
Loyola Gottlieb Memorial Hospital	Melrose Park	95%	141
Memorial Hospital	Belleville	95%	345
Memorial Hospital of Carbondale	Carbondale	95%	127
Memorial Medical Center	Springfield	95%	532
Rockford Memorial Hospital	Rockford	95%	348
Saint James Hospital	Pontiac	95%	61
St James Hospital-Olympia Fields[2]	Olympia Fields	95%	289
Saint Marys Hospital[2]	Decatur	95%	153
Sherman Hospital	Elgin	95%	219
Swedish American Hospital	Rockford	95%	263
Swedish Covenant Hospital	Chicago	95%	296
Taylorville Memorial Hospital	Taylorville	95%	119
West Suburban Medical Center[2]	Oak Park	95%	161
Advocate Trinity Hospital	Chicago	94%	203
Provena Covenant Medical Center - Urbana	Urbana	94%	157
Provena United Samaritans Med Ctr-Logan	Danville	94%	218
Rush University Medical Center[2]	Chicago	94%	96
Saint Alexius Medical Center	Hoffman Estates	94%	290
Saint Anthony Hospital	Chicago	94%	124
Vista Medical Center East	Waukegan	94%	168
Hoopeston Community Memorial Hospital	Hoopeston	93%	27
Iroquois Memorial Hospital	Watseka	93%	118
John & Mary Kirby Hospital	Monticello	93%	45
Kishwaukee Community Hospital	Dekalb	93%	137
McDonough District Hospital	Macomb	93%	70
Provena Mercy Medical Center[2]	Aurora	93%	157
Saint Anthonys Memorial Hospital	Effingham	93%	170
Thorek Memorial Hospital	Chicago	93%	69
Touchette Regional Hospital	Centreville	93%	58
Fairfield Memorial Hospital	Fairfield	92%	36
Herrin Hospital	Herrin	92%	177
Provena St Joseph Medical Center[2]	Joliet	92%	139
Rush Oak Park Hospital	Oak Park	92%	91
Saint Bernard Hospital	Chicago	92%	298
Ferrell Hospital Community Foundations	Eldorado	91%	34
Loyola University Medical Center	Maywood	91%	219
Mercy Hospital and Medical Center[2]	Chicago	91%	148
Metrosouth Medical Center	Blue Island	91%	201
University of Illinois Hospital[2]	Chicago	91%	139
Bromenn Healthcare	Normal	90%	194
Saint Francis Hospital	Litchfield	90%	52
Saint Joseph's Hospital	Highland	90%	31
Saint Johns Hospital[2]	Springfield	89%	88
Loretto Hospital	Chicago	88%	113
Shelby Memorial Hospital	Shelbyville	88%	43
Jackson Park Hospital[2]	Chicago	87%	172
J Brown VA Med Ctr-VA Chicago Healthcare	Chicago	87%	93
Methodist Hospital of Chicago	Chicago	87%	148
Oak Forest Hospital	Oak Forest	87%	45
South Shore Hospital	Chicago	83%	109
Holy Cross Hospital[2]	Chicago	81%	119
Norwegian-American Hospital	Chicago	81%	118
Provident Hospital of Chicago[2]	Chicago	79%	156
Roseland Community Hospital[2]	Chicago	76%	143
John H Stroger Jr Hospital[2]	Chicago	65%	190

20. Pneumococcal Vaccine

Hospital Name	City	Rate	Cases
Adventist Glenoaks	Glendale Hghts	100%	41
Crossroads Community Hospital	Mount Vernon	100%	70
Delnor Community Hospital	Geneva	100%	226
Fairfield Memorial Hospital	Fairfield	100%	35
Good Samaritan Regional Health Center	Mount Vernon	100%	164
Hillsboro Area Hospital	Hillsboro	100%	52
Loretto Hospital	Chicago	100%	59
Mason District Hospital	Havana	100%	30
Memorial Hospital	Belleville	100%	299
Our Lady of the Resurrection Medical Center	Chicago	100%	223
Saint James Hospital	Pontiac	100%	54
Saint Josephs Hospital	Breese	100%	92
Saint Marys Hospital	Centralia	100%	180
Saint Marys Hospital[2]	Decatur	100%	127
Sarah Bush Lincoln Health Center	Mattoon	100%	174
Taylorville Memorial Hospital	Taylorville	100%	146
Vista Medical Center East	Waukegan	100%	144
Advocate Christ Hospital & Medical Center[2]	Oak Lawn	99%	167
Advocate Condell Medical Center[2]	Libertyville	99%	132
Advocate Good Shepherd Hospital	Barrington	99%	211
Advocate Lutheran General Hospital	Park Ridge	99%	305
Advocate South Suburban Hospital[2]	Hazel Crest	99%	133
Hines VA Medical Center	Hines	99%	149
J Brown VA Med Ctr-VA Chicago Healthcare	Chicago	99%	80
Red Bud Regional Hospital	Red Bud	99%	70
Riverside Medical Center	Kankakee	99%	190
Saint Alexius Medical Center	Hoffman Estates	99%	355
Silver Cross Hospital	Joliet	99%	293
Trinity Rock Island[2]	Rock Island	99%	142
Abraham Lincoln Memorial Hospital	Lincoln	98%	63
Advocate Trinity Hospital	Chicago	98%	168
Galesburg Cottage Hospital	Galesburg	98%	111
Gateway Regional Medical Center	Granite City	98%	62
Genesis Medical Center Illini Campus	Silvis	98%	133
Hardin County General Hospital	Rosiclare	98%	51
Methodist Medical Center of Illinois	Peoria	98%	257
Passavant Area Hospital	Jacksonville	98%	172
Pekin Memorial Hospital	Pekin	98%	188
Provena-Saint Joseph Hospital[2]	Elgin	98%	121
Saint Joseph Hospital	Chicago	98%	145
Saint Marys Hospital[2]	Streator	98%	115
Thorek Memorial Hospital	Chicago	98%	81
Union County Hospital	Anna	98%	57
Advocate Eureka Hospital	Eureka	97%	32
Advocate Illinois Masonic Medical Center[2]	Chicago	97%	92
Crawford Memorial Hospital	Robinson	97%	33
Edward Hospital	Naperville	97%	408
Evanston Hospital[2]	Evanston	97%	194
Iroquois Memorial Hospital	Watseka	97%	117
Mendota Community Hospital	Mendota	97%	31
Proctor Hospital[2]	Peoria	97%	195
Saint Joseph Medical Center	Bloomington	97%	129
Saint Joseph Memorial Hospital	Murphysboro	97%	38
The University of Chicago Medical Center[2]	Chicago	97%	58
VA Illiana Healthcare System - Danville	Danville	97%	32
Adventist Bolingbrook Hospital	Bolingbrook	96%	109
Advocate Good Samaritan Hospital[2]	Downers Grove	96%	258
Blessing Hospital	Quincy	96%	405
CGH Medical Center	Sterling	96%	139
Hamilton Memorial Hospital District	Mcleansboro	96%	27
Illini Community Hospital	Pittsfield	96%	28
Ingalls Memorial Hospital[2]	Harvey	96%	90
Katherine Shaw Bethea Hospital	Dixon	96%	79
Lake Forest Hospital	Lake Forest	96%	137
Little Company of Mary Hospital[2]	Evergreen Park	96%	143
Louis A Weiss Memorial Hospital	Chicago	96%	171
Loyola Gottlieb Memorial Hospital	Melrose Park	96%	112
Macneal Hospital	Berwyn	96%	208
Morris Hospital & Healthcare Centers[2]	Morris	96%	160
Ottawa Reg Hosp & Healthcare Ctr	Ottawa	96%	149
St Mary & Elizabeth Med Ctr-Div Campus	Chicago	96%	181
Carle Foundation Hospital[2]	Urbana	95%	110
Fhn Memorial Hospital	Freeport	95%	126
Gibson Community Hospital[2]	Gibson City	95%	40
Loyola University Medical Center	Maywood	95%	217
Marion Illinois VA Medical Center	Marion	95%	85
Northwestern Memorial Hospital	Chicago	95%	301
Saint Mary Medical Center	Galesburg	95%	181
Sherman Hospital	Elgin	95%	187
Alexian Brothers Medical Center	Elk Grove Vlg	94%	378
Elmhurst Memorial Hospital[2]	Elmhurst	94%	143
Palos Community Hospital[2]	Palos Heights	94%	152
Paris Community Hospital	Paris	94%	35
Rush Oak Park Hospital	Oak Park	94%	84
Saint Anthony Medical Center	Rockford	94%	222
Saint Elizabeth Hospital[2]	Belleville	94%	263
Saint Margarets Hospital	Spring Valley	94%	82
Adventist La Grange Memorial Hospital	La Grange	93%	274
Anderson Hospital[2]	Maryville	93%	140
Bromenn Healthcare	Normal	93%	191
Clay County Hospital	Flora	93%	54
Illinois Valley Community Hospital	Peru	93%	108
McDonough District Hospital	Macomb	93%	84
Memorial Hospital[2]	Chester	93%	44
Provena United Samaritans Med Ctr-Logan	Danville	93%	240
St James Hospital-Olympia Fields[2]	Olympia Fields	93%	197
Swedish American Hospital	Rockford	93%	227
Central Dupage Hospital	Winfield	92%	212
Copley Memorial Hospital	Aurora	92%	119
Kishwaukee Community Hospital	Dekalb	92%	147
RHC St Francis Hospital	Evanston	92%	333
Rockford Memorial Hospital	Rockford	92%	289
Saint Anthony's Health Center	Alton	92%	154
Valley West Community Hospital	Sandwich	92%	26
Carlinville Area Hospital	Carlinville	91%	33
Ferrell Hospital Community Foundations	Eldorado	91%	35
Harrisburg Medical Center[2]	Harrisburg	91%	127
Memorial Medical Center	Springfield	91%	507
Mount Sinai Hospital Medical Center	Chicago	91%	101
Provena St Marys Hospital[2]	Kankakee	91%	101
Resurrection Medical Center	Chicago	91%	412
Saint Francis Medical Center	Peoria	91%	380
Westlake Community Hospital	Melrose Park	91%	58
Decatur Memorial Hospital[2]	Decatur	90%	292
Graham Hospital Association	Canton	90%	60
Herrin Hospital	Herrin	90%	177
John & Mary Kirby Hospital	Monticello	90%	41
Memorial Hospital of Carbondale	Carbondale	90%	119
Saint Bernard Hospital	Chicago	90%	126
Alton Memorial Hospital[2]	Alton	89%	228
Hinsdale Hospital	Hinsdale	89%	240
Northwest Community Hospital[2]	Arlington Hgts	89%	141
Provena St Joseph Medical Center[2]	Joliet	89%	124
Saint Anthonys Memorial Hospital	Effingham	89%	179
Swedish Covenant Hospital	Chicago	89%	369
Fayette County Hospital[3]	Vandalia	88%	33
Heartland Regional Medical Center	Marion	88%	152
Kewanee Hospital	Kewanee	88%	48
Richland Memorial Hospital	Olney	88%	114
Jersey Community Hospital	Jerseyville	87%	94
Skokie Hospital	Skokie	86%	199
West Suburban Medical Center[2]	Oak Park	86%	91
Metrosouth Medical Center	Blue Island	85%	159
Provena Covenant Medical Center - Urbana	Urbana	85%	168
Saint Joseph's Hospital	Highland	85%	33

NOTE: Hospital profiles are in alphabetical order by state, then city, then hospital within the city; Rankings exclude hospitals with less than 25 cases except for patient surveys which excludes hospitals with less than 100 cases; (a) 100–299 cases; (1) The number of cases is too small to be sure how well a hospital is performing; (2) The hospital indicated that the data submitted for this measure were based on a sample of cases; (3) Data was collected during a shorter time period (fewer quarters) than the maximum possible time for this measure; (4) Suppressed for one or more quarters by CMS; (5) No data is available from the hospital for this measure; (6) Fewer than 100 patients completed the HCAHPS survey. Use these rates with caution, as the number of surveys may be too low to reliably assess hospital performance; (7) Survey results are based on less than 12 months of data; (8) Survey results are not available for this reporting period; (9) No or very few patients were eligible for the HCAHPS survey. The scores shown, if any, reflect a very small number of surveys; (10) A state average was not calculated because too few hospitals in the state submitted data; (11) There were discrepancies in the data collection process; Please refer to the User's Guide for a full explanation of data.

Hospital Name	City	Rate	Cases
Holy Cross Hospital[2]	Chicago	84%	86
Provident Hospital of Chicago[2]	Chicago	84%	44
University of Illinois Hospital[2]	Chicago	84%	76
Provena Mercy Medical Center[2]	Aurora	83%	115
Rush University Medical Center[2]	Chicago	80%	74
Saint Johns Hospital[2]	Springfield	80%	123
Wabash General Hospital[2]	Mount Carmel	79%	78
Hoopeston Community Memorial Hospital	Hoopeston	78%	49
Lawrence County Memorial Hospital	Lawrenceville	76%	25
Greenville Regional Hospital	Greenville	74%	47
Methodist Hospital of Chicago	Chicago	74%	90
Centegra Health System - McHenry Hospital	Mchenry	73%	211
Saint Francis Hospital	Litchfield	70%	47
Rochelle Community Hospital	Rochelle	68%	34
Perry Memorial Hospital	Princeton	67%	66
Saint Anthony Hospital	Chicago	66%	76
Jackson Park Hospital[2]	Chicago	63%	52
Centegra Health Sys-Woodstock Hospital	Woodstock	62%	135
Salem Township Hospital	Salem	62%	34
Norwegian-American Hospital	Chicago	60%	48
Shelby Memorial Hospital	Shelbyville	51%	53
John H Stroger Jr Hospital[2]	Chicago	42%	36
Mercy Hospital and Medical Center[2]	Chicago	37%	128
Roseland Community Hospital[2]	Chicago	19%	85
South Shore Hospital	Chicago	19%	84

21. Smoking Cessation Advice

Hospital Name	City	Rate	Cases
Adventist Bolingbrook Hospital	Bolingbrook	100%	45
Adventist La Grange Memorial Hospital	La Grange	100%	47
Advocate Condell Medical Center[2]	Libertyville	100%	40
Advocate Good Samaritan Hospital[2]	Downers Grove	100%	72
Advocate Good Shepherd Hospital	Barrington	100%	58
Advocate Lutheran General Hospital	Park Ridge	100%	63
Advocate South Suburban Hospital[2]	Hazel Crest	100%	54
Alton Memorial Hospital[2]	Alton	100%	105
Anderson Hospital[2]	Maryville	100%	76
Blessing Hospital	Quincy	100%	160
Bromenn Healthcare	Normal	100%	38
Carle Foundation Hospital[2]	Urbana	100%	51
Central Dupage Hospital	Winfield	100%	80
Copley Memorial Hospital	Aurora	100%	55
Crossroads Community Hospital	Mount Vernon	100%	27
Decatur Memorial Hospital[2]	Decatur	100%	92
Delnor Community Hospital	Geneva	100%	40
Elmhurst Memorial Hospital[2]	Elmhurst	100%	35
Evanston Hospital[2]	Evanston	100%	34
Galesburg Cottage Hospital	Galesburg	100%	36
Gateway Regional Medical Center	Granite City	100%	54
Good Samaritan Regional Health Center	Mount Vernon	100%	59
Heartland Regional Medical Center	Marion	100%	59
Hines VA Medical Center	Hines	100%	78
Ingalls Memorial Hospital[2]	Harvey	100%	51
Jackson Park Hospital[2]	Chicago	100%	61
Katherine Shaw Bethea Hospital	Dixon	100%	30
Lake Forest Hospital	Lake Forest	100%	34
Little Company of Mary Hospital[2]	Evergreen Park	100%	49
Loretto Hospital	Chicago	100%	36
Loyola Gottlieb Memorial Hospital	Melrose Park	100%	31
Loyola University Medical Center	Maywood	100%	68
Macneal Hospital	Berwyn	100%	83
Marion Illinois VA Medical Center	Marion	100%	50
Mercy Hospital and Medical Center[2]	Chicago	100%	69
Methodist Medical Center of Illinois	Peoria	100%	106
Metrosouth Medical Center	Blue Island	100%	67
Mount Sinai Hospital Medical Center	Chicago	100%	107
North Chicago VA Medical Center	North Chicago	100%	33
Norwegian-American Hospital	Chicago	100%	34
Our Lady of the Resurrection Medical Center	Chicago	100%	101
Passavant Area Hospital	Jacksonville	100%	62
Provena Covenant Medical Center - Urbana	Urbana	100%	73
Provena Mercy Medical Center[2]	Aurora	100%	47
Provena St Joseph Medical Center[2]	Joliet	100%	45
Provena St Marys Hospital[2]	Kankakee	100%	70
Provena United Samaritans Med Ctr-Logan	Danville	100%	85
RHC St Francis Hospital	Evanston	100%	64
Rockford Memorial Hospital	Rockford	100%	120
Roseland Community Hospital[2]	Chicago	100%	54
Rush Oak Park Hospital	Oak Park	100%	28
Saint Alexius Medical Center	Hoffman Estates	100%	112
Saint Anthony Hospital	Chicago	100%	40
Saint Anthony Medical Center	Rockford	100%	71
Saint Francis Medical Center	Peoria	100%	203
Saint James Hospital	Pontiac	100%	30
St James Hospital-Olympia Fields[2]	Olympia Fields	100%	100
Saint Johns Hospital[2]	Springfield	100%	73
Saint Joseph Hospital	Chicago	100%	34
Saint Joseph Medical Center	Bloomington	100%	62
Saint Josephs Hospital	Breese	100%	32
St Mary & Elizabeth Med Ctr-Div Campus	Chicago	100%	138
Saint Marys Hospital	Centralia	100%	86
Saint Marys Hospital[2]	Decatur	100%	54
Sarah Bush Lincoln Health Center	Mattoon	100%	74
Silver Cross Hospital	Joliet	100%	125
Swedish American Hospital	Rockford	100%	133
Swedish Covenant Hospital	Chicago	100%	64
Taylorville Memorial Hospital	Taylorville	100%	30
The University of Chicago Medical Center[2]	Chicago	100%	35
University of Illinois Hospital[2]	Chicago	100%	54
West Suburban Medical Center[2]	Oak Park	100%	71
Advocate Trinity Hospital	Chicago	99%	82
Alexian Brothers Medical Center	Elk Grove Vlg	99%	93
Edward Hospital	Naperville	99%	113
Memorial Hospital	Belleville	99%	143
Northwestern Memorial Hospital	Chicago	99%	149
Pekin Memorial Hospital	Pekin	99%	68
Resurrection Medical Center	Chicago	99%	73
Saint Anthony's Health Center	Alton	99%	73
J Brown VA Med Ctr-VA Chicago Healthcare	Chicago	98%	62
Morris Hospital & Healthcare Centers[2]	Morris	98%	61
Provident Hospital of Chicago[2]	Chicago	98%	108
Vista Medical Center East	Waukegan	98%	62
CGH Medical Center	Sterling	97%	38
Harrisburg Medical Center[2]	Harrisburg	97%	31
Hinsdale Hospital	Hinsdale	97%	38
John H Stroger Jr Hospital[2]	Chicago	97%	102
Memorial Medical Center	Springfield	97%	231
Saint Bernard Hospital	Chicago	97%	102
Advocate Christ Hospital & Medical Center[2]	Oak Lawn	96%	50
Advocate Illinois Masonic Medical Center[2]	Chicago	96%	57
Centegra Health System - McHenry Hospital	Mchenry	96%	85
Genesis Medical Center Illini Campus	Silvis	96%	51
Herrin Hospital	Herrin	96%	92
Jersey Community Hospital	Jerseyville	96%	26
Louis A Weiss Memorial Hospital	Chicago	96%	56
Sherman Hospital	Elgin	96%	74
Thorek Memorial Hospital	Chicago	96%	25
Touchette Regional Hospital	Centreville	96%	25
Trinity Rock Island[2]	Rock Island	96%	50
Centegra Health Sys-Woodstock Hospital	Woodstock	95%	56
Memorial Hospital of Carbondale	Carbondale	95%	84
Proctor Hospital[2]	Peoria	95%	40
Rush University Medical Center[2]	Chicago	95%	38
Saint Elizabeth Hospital[2]	Belleville	95%	128
Kishwaukee Community Hospital	Dekalb	94%	32
Palos Community Hospital[2]	Palos Heights	94%	35
Saint Anthonys Memorial Hospital	Effingham	94%	67
Ottawa Reg Hosp & Healthcare Ctr	Ottawa	93%	55
Provena-Saint Joseph Hospital[2]	Elgin	92%	36
Saint Mary Medical Center	Galesburg	92%	77
Methodist Hospital of Chicago	Chicago	91%	101
Iroquois Memorial Hospital	Watseka	90%	29
Richland Memorial Hospital	Olney	89%	36
Riverside Medical Center	Kankakee	88%	77
Saint Marys Hospital[2]	Streator	88%	43
Fhn Memorial Hospital	Freeport	86%	37
Holy Cross Hospital[2]	Chicago	81%	48

Surgical Care Improvement Project

22. Appropriate VTP Within 24 Hours

Hospital Name	City	Rate	Cases
Advocate Trinity Hospital[2]	Chicago	100%	147
Fairfield Memorial Hospital	Fairfield	100%	30
Katherine Shaw Bethea Hospital	Dixon	100%	95
Provident Hospital of Chicago[2]	Chicago	100%	39
Sherman Hospital	Elgin	100%	320
Skokie Hospital[2]	Skokie	100%	153
Central Dupage Hospital[2]	Winfield	99%	95
Evanston Hospital[2]	Evanston	99%	537
Galesburg Cottage Hospital	Galesburg	99%	115
Gateway Regional Medical Center	Granite City	99%	100
J Brown VA Med Ctr-VA Chicago Healthcare[2]	Chicago	99%	136
Little Company of Mary Hospital[2]	Evergreen Park	99%	240
Provena St Joseph Medical Center[2]	Joliet	99%	190
Saint Marys Hospital	Centralia	99%	121
The University of Chicago Medical Center[2]	Chicago	99%	195
West Suburban Medical Center[2]	Oak Park	99%	146
Advocate Christ Hospital & Medical Center[2]	Oak Lawn	98%	212
Advocate Good Shepherd Hospital[2]	Barrington	98%	153
Advocate South Suburban Hospital[2]	Hazel Crest	98%	159
Delnor Community Hospital[2]	Geneva	98%	172
Macneal Hospital[2]	Berwyn	98%	258
Our Lady of the Resurrection Medical Center	Chicago	98%	202
Saint Margarets Hospital	Spring Valley	98%	81
Saint Marys Hospital	Streator	98%	89
Thorek Memorial Hospital	Chicago	98%	41
Wabash General Hospital	Mount Carmel	98%	51
Advocate Good Samaritan Hospital[2]	Downers Grove	97%	203
Advocate Illinois Masonic Medical Center[2]	Chicago	97%	217
Alexian Brothers Medical Center[2]	Elk Grove Vlg	97%	269
Anderson Hospital[2]	Maryville	97%	228
Genesis Medical Center Illini Campus[2]	Silvis	97%	134
Good Samaritan Regional Health Center	Mount Vernon	97%	237
Hines VA Medical Center[2]	Hines	97%	78
Illinois Valley Community Hospital	Peru	97%	71
Loyola University Medical Center[2]	Maywood	97%	175
Pekin Memorial Hospital	Pekin	97%	153
Rush University Medical Center[2]	Chicago	97%	193
Saint Alexius Medical Center[2]	Hoffman Estates	97%	209
University of Illinois Hospital[2]	Chicago	97%	222
Adventist La Grange Memorial Hospital[2]	La Grange	96%	178
Advocate Lutheran General Hospital[2]	Park Ridge	96%	211
CGH Medical Center[2]	Sterling	96%	242
Edward Hospital	Naperville	96%	635
Graham Hospital Association	Canton	96%	69
Louis A Weiss Memorial Hospital[2]	Chicago	96%	171
Mount Sinai Hospital Medical Center[2]	Chicago	96%	110
Saint Mary Medical Center	Galesburg	96%	181
Silver Cross Hospital[2]	Joliet	96%	178
Westlake Community Hospital	Melrose Park	96%	75
Alton Memorial Hospital	Alton	95%	134
Blessing Hospital	Quincy	95%	245
Carle Foundation Hospital[2]	Urbana	95%	130
Hinsdale Hospital[2]	Hinsdale	95%	144
Memorial Hospital[2]	Belleville	95%	208
Memorial Hospital of Carbondale[2]	Carbondale	95%	378
Sarah Bush Lincoln Health Center	Mattoon	95%	171
Advocate Condell Medical Center[2]	Libertyville	94%	189
Copley Memorial Hospital[2]	Aurora	94%	199
Northwestern Memorial Hospital[2]	Chicago	94%	200
Saint Anthonys Memorial Hospital	Effingham	94%	364
Adventist Glenoaks	Glendale Hghts	93%	43
Decatur Memorial Hospital[2]	Decatur	93%	294
Heartland Regional Medical Center[2]	Marion	93%	186
Memorial Medical Center[2]	Springfield	93%	194
Saint Francis Medical Center[2]	Peoria	93%	436
St James Hospital-Olympia Fields[2]	Olympia Fields	93%	269
St Mary & Elizabeth Med Ctr-Div Campus[2]	Chicago	93%	202
Elmhurst Memorial Hospital[2]	Elmhurst	92%	213
Hammond Henry Hospital	Geneseo	92%	38
Iroquois Memorial Hospital	Watseka	92%	25
Methodist Medical Center of Illinois[2]	Peoria	92%	184
Midwestern Region Medical Center	Zion	92%	187
Ottawa Reg Hosp & Healthcare Ctr	Ottawa	92%	92
Proctor Hospital[2]	Peoria	92%	140
Provena St Marys Hospital[2]	Kankakee	92%	134
RHC St Francis Hospital[2]	Evanston	92%	335
Saint Marys Hospital[2]	Decatur	92%	144
Vista Medical Center East[2]	Waukegan	92%	123
Fhn Memorial Hospital[2]	Freeport	91%	115
Ingalls Memorial Hospital[2]	Harvey	91%	138
Lake Forest Hospital	Lake Forest	91%	268
Morris Hospital & Healthcare Centers	Morris	91%	92
Northwest Community Hospital[2]	Arlington Hgts	91%	182
Palos Community Hospital[2]	Palos Heights	91%	233
Saint Joseph Medical Center	Bloomington	91%	172
Crossroads Community Hospital[2]	Mount Vernon	90%	51
Herrin Hospital	Herrin	90%	173
Holy Cross Hospital[2]	Chicago	89%	142
John H Stroger Jr Hospital[2]	Chicago	89%	204
McDonough District Hospital	Macomb	89%	45
Saint Bernard Hospital	Chicago	89%	65
Saint Joseph Hospital[2]	Chicago	89%	152
Saint Josephs Hospital	Breese	89%	53
Adventist Bolingbrook Hospital	Bolingbrook	88%	83
Mercy Hospital and Medical Center	Chicago	88%	248
Metrosouth Medical Center	Blue Island	88%	185
Rush Oak Park Hospital	Oak Park	88%	181
Swedish American Hospital[2]	Rockford	88%	286
Centegra Health Sys-Woodstock Hospital[2]	Woodstock	87%	162
Provena-Saint Joseph Hospital[2]	Elgin	87%	191
Saint James Hospital	Pontiac	87%	55
Bromenn Healthcare[2]	Normal	86%	204
Kishwaukee Community Hospital	Dekalb	86%	138
Rockford Memorial Hospital	Rockford	86%	254
Saint Anthony's Health Center	Alton	86%	80
Provena Mercy Medical Center[2]	Aurora	85%	158
Resurrection Medical Center[2]	Chicago	85%	213
Trinity Rock Island[2]	Rock Island	85%	136
Saint Anthony Medical Center[2]	Rockford	84%	256
Saint Elizabeth Hospital[2]	Belleville	84%	180
Riverside Medical Center[2]	Kankakee	83%	127
Loyola Gottlieb Memorial Hospital[2]	Melrose Park	81%	192
Swedish Covenant Hospital[2]	Chicago	81%	160
Centegra Health System - McHenry Hospital[2]	Mchenry	78%	235
Saint Johns Hospital[2]	Springfield	78%	161
Saint Joseph's Hospital	Highland	78%	27
Provena Covenant Medical Center - Urbana[2]	Urbana	77%	180
Passavant Area Hospital[2]	Jacksonville	74%	105
Saint Anthony Hospital	Chicago	74%	53

NOTE: Hospital profiles are in alphabetical order by state, then city, then hospital within the city; Rankings exclude hospitals with less than 25 cases except for patient surveys which excludes hospitals with less than 100 cases; (a) 100–299 cases; (1) The number of cases is too small to be sure how well a hospital is performing; (2) The hospital indicated that the data submitted for this measure were based on a sample of cases; (3) Data was collected during a shorter time period (fewer quarters) than the maximum possible time for this measure; (4) Suppressed for one or more quarters by CMS; (5) No data is available from the hospital for this measure; (6) Fewer than 100 patients completed the HCAHPS survey. Use these rates with caution, as the number of surveys may be too low to reliably assess hospital performance; (7) Survey results are based on less than 12 months of data; (8) Survey results are not available for this reporting period; (9) No or very few patients were eligible for the HCAHPS survey. The scores shown, if any, reflect a very small number of surveys; (10) A state average was not calculated because too few hospitals in the state submitted data; (11) There were discrepancies in the data collection process; Please refer to the User's Guide for a full explanation of data.

Hospital Name	City	Rate	Cases
Gibson Community Hospital	Gibson City	73%	37
Perry Memorial Hospital	Princeton	73%	33
Provena United Samaritans Med Ctr-Logan[2]	Danville	73%	139
Richland Memorial Hospital	Olney	69%	29
Sacred Heart Hospital	Chicago	68%	37
Touchette Regional Hospital	Centreville	68%	28
Valley West Community Hospital	Sandwich	61%	33
South Shore Hospital	Chicago	59%	34
Norwegian-American Hospital	Chicago	42%	43
Saint Francis Hospital	Litchfield	33%	39
Roseland Community Hospital	Chicago	21%	39

23. Appropriate Hair Removal

Hospital Name	City	Rate	Cases
Abraham Lincoln Memorial Hospital	Lincoln	100%	64
Adventist Glenoaks	Glendale Hghts	100%	90
Adventist La Grange Memorial Hospital[2]	La Grange	100%	411
Advocate Christ Hospital & Medical Center[2]	Oak Lawn	100%	741
Advocate Condell Medical Center[2]	Libertyville	100%	609
Advocate Good Samaritan Hospital[2]	Downers Grove	100%	612
Advocate Good Shepherd Hospital[2]	Barrington	100%	594
Advocate Illinois Masonic Medical Center[2]	Chicago	100%	607
Advocate Lutheran General Hospital[2]	Park Ridge	100%	641
Advocate South Suburban Hospital[2]	Hazel Crest	100%	415
Advocate Trinity Hospital[2]	Chicago	100%	402
Alexian Brothers Medical Center[2]	Elk Grove Vlg	100%	728
Alton Memorial Hospital	Alton	100%	333
Anderson Hospital[2]	Maryville	100%	512
Blessing Hospital	Quincy	100%	663
Bromenn Healthcare[2]	Normal	100%	771
Carle Foundation Hospital[2]	Urbana	100%	604
Centegra Health System - McHenry Hospital[2]	Mchenry	100%	758
Centegra Health Sys-Woodstock Hospital[2]	Woodstock	100%	622
Central Dupage Hospital[2]	Winfield	100%	553
Copley Memorial Hospital[2]	Aurora	100%	840
Crawford Memorial Hospital	Robinson	100%	54
Decatur Memorial Hospital[2]	Decatur	100%	809
Delnor Community Hospital[2]	Geneva	100%	466
Edward Hospital	Naperville	100%	1858
Elmhurst Memorial Hospital[2]	Elmhurst	100%	543
Evanston Hospital[2]	Evanston	100%	1658
Fairfield Memorial Hospital	Fairfield	100%	43
Fhn Memorial Hospital[2]	Freeport	100%	429
Galesburg Cottage Hospital	Galesburg	100%	244
Gateway Regional Medical Center	Granite City	100%	255
Genesis Medical Center Illini Campus[2]	Silvis	100%	422
Good Samaritan Regional Health Center	Mount Vernon	100%	647
Graham Hospital Association	Canton	100%	215
Hammond Henry Hospital	Geneseo	100%	111
Harrisburg Medical Center	Harrisburg	100%	34
Heartland Regional Medical Center[2]	Marion	100%	483
Herrin Hospital	Herrin	100%	277
Hines VA Medical Center[2]	Hines	100%	252
Hinsdale Hospital[2]	Hinsdale	100%	440
Illinois Valley Community Hospital	Peru	100%	248
Ingalls Memorial Hospital[2]	Harvey	100%	452
Iroquois Memorial Hospital	Watseka	100%	87
Jersey Community Hospital	Jerseyville	100%	49
Katherine Shaw Bethea Hospital	Dixon	100%	290
Kewanee Hospital	Kewanee	100%	50
Lake Forest Hospital	Lake Forest	100%	822
Little Company of Mary Hospital[2]	Evergreen Park	100%	478
Loretto Hospital	Chicago	100%	32
Louis A Weiss Memorial Hospital[2]	Chicago	100%	412
Loyola Gottlieb Memorial Hospital[2]	Melrose Park	100%	428
Loyola University Medical Center[2]	Maywood	100%	576
McDonough District Hospital	Macomb	100%	107
Memorial Hospital[2]	Belleville	100%	647
Memorial Hospital of Carbondale[2]	Carbondale	100%	1084
Memorial Medical Center[2]	Springfield	100%	1051
Mercy Harvard Hospital	Harvard	100%	47
Mercy Hospital and Medical Center	Chicago	100%	618
Methodist Hospital of Chicago	Chicago	100%	32
Methodist Medical Center of Illinois[2]	Peoria	100%	906
Midwestern Region Medical Center	Zion	100%	210
Morris Hospital & Healthcare Centers	Morris	100%	321
Mount Sinai Hospital Medical Center[2]	Chicago	100%	306
Northwestern Memorial Hospital[2]	Chicago	100%	711
Norwegian-American Hospital	Chicago	100%	92
Ottawa Reg Hosp & Healthcare Ctr	Ottawa	100%	214
Our Lady of the Resurrection Medical Center	Chicago	100%	353
Palos Community Hospital[2]	Palos Heights	100%	632
Passavant Area Hospital[2]	Jacksonville	100%	353
Pekin Memorial Hospital	Pekin	100%	357
Proctor Hospital[2]	Peoria	100%	793
Provena Covenant Medical Center - Urbana[2]	Urbana	100%	617
Provena Mercy Medical Center[2]	Aurora	100%	636
Provena St Joseph Medical Center[2]	Joliet	100%	615
Provena St Marys Hospital[2]	Kankakee	100%	411
Provena United Samaritans Med Ctr-Logan[2]	Danville	100%	253
Provident Hospital of Chicago[2]	Chicago	100%	85
Red Bud Regional Hospital[2]	Red Bud	100%	42
Resurrection Medical Center[2]	Chicago	100%	620
Richland Memorial Hospital	Olney	100%	105
Rockford Memorial Hospital	Rockford	100%	1032
Rush University Medical Center[2]	Chicago	100%	624
Sacred Heart Hospital	Chicago	100%	89
Saint Alexius Medical Center[2]	Hoffman Estates	100%	466
Saint Anthony Medical Center[2]	Rockford	100%	1204
Saint Anthony's Health Center	Alton	100%	307
Saint Bernard Hospital	Chicago	100%	115
Saint Francis Medical Center[2]	Peoria	100%	1769
Saint James Hospital	Pontiac	100%	154
Saint Johns Hospital[2]	Springfield	100%	711
Saint Joseph Hospital[2]	Chicago	100%	515
Saint Joseph Medical Center	Bloomington	100%	750
Saint Joseph's Hospital	Highland	100%	37
Saint Josephs Hospital	Breese	100%	123
St Mary & Elizabeth Med Ctr-Div Campus[2]	Chicago	100%	458
Saint Mary Medical Center	Galesburg	100%	347
Saint Marys Hospital	Centralia	100%	288
Saint Marys Hospital[2]	Decatur	100%	336
Saint Marys Hospital	Streator	100%	173
Sarah Bush Lincoln Health Center	Mattoon	100%	520
Sherman Hospital	Elgin	100%	884
Silver Cross Hospital[2]	Joliet	100%	679
Skokie Hospital[2]	Skokie	100%	518
Swedish American Hospital[2]	Rockford	100%	1210
Thorek Memorial Hospital	Chicago	100%	79
Touchette Regional Hospital	Centreville	100%	70
Trinity Rock Island[2]	Rock Island	100%	512
The University of Chicago Medical Center[2]	Chicago	100%	571
University of Illinois Hospital[2]	Chicago	100%	420
Valley West Community Hospital	Sandwich	100%	69
Vista Medical Center East[2]	Waukegan	100%	510
Wabash General Hospital	Mount Carmel	100%	74
West Suburban Medical Center[2]	Oak Park	100%	461
Westlake Community Hospital	Melrose Park	100%	175
Adventist Bolingbrook Hospital	Bolingbrook	99%	149
CGH Medical Center[2]	Sterling	99%	444
Crossroads Community Hospital[2]	Mount Vernon	99%	188
J Brown VA Med Ctr-VA Chicago Healthcare[2]	Chicago	99%	177
Kishwaukee Community Hospital	Dekalb	99%	382
RHC St Francis Hospital[2]	Evanston	99%	572
Riverside Medical Center[2]	Kankakee	99%	517
Rush Oak Park Hospital	Oak Park	99%	378
Saint Anthony Hospital	Chicago	99%	107
Saint Anthonys Memorial Hospital	Effingham	99%	921
Saint Elizabeth Hospital[2]	Belleville	99%	485
St James Hospital-Olympia Fields[2]	Olympia Fields	99%	702
Saint Margarets Hospital	Spring Valley	99%	335
Holy Cross Hospital[2]	Chicago	98%	215
John H Stroger Jr Hospital[2]	Chicago	98%	453
Provena-Saint Joseph Hospital[2]	Elgin	98%	416
Swedish Covenant Hospital[2]	Chicago	98%	421
Taylorville Memorial Hospital	Taylorville	98%	50
South Shore Hospital	Chicago	97%	78
Macneal Hospital[2]	Berwyn	96%	738
Gibson Community Hospital	Gibson City	92%	106
Jackson Park Hospital	Chicago	91%	47
Metrosouth Medical Center	Blue Island	91%	532
Saint Francis Hospital	Litchfield	85%	48
Northwest Community Hospital[2]	Arlington Hgts	84%	670
Perry Memorial Hospital	Princeton	78%	49
Roseland Community Hospital	Chicago	69%	96

24. Appropriate Beta Blocker Usage

Hospital Name	City	Rate	Cases
Alton Memorial Hospital	Alton	100%	92
Crossroads Community Hospital[2]	Mount Vernon	100%	49
Decatur Memorial Hospital[2]	Decatur	100%	284
Evanston Hospital[2]	Evanston	100%	461
Gateway Regional Medical Center	Granite City	100%	46
Genesis Medical Center Illini Campus[2]	Silvis	100%	98
Hines VA Medical Center[2]	Hines	100%	143
Illinois Valley Community Hospital	Peru	100%	81
J Brown VA Med Ctr-VA Chicago Healthcare[2]	Chicago	100%	59
Katherine Shaw Bethea Hospital	Dixon	100%	86
Ottawa Reg Hosp & Healthcare Ctr	Ottawa	100%	44
Our Lady of the Resurrection Medical Center	Chicago	100%	59
Provena St Joseph Medical Center[2]	Joliet	100%	220
Saint Marys Hospital[2]	Decatur	100%	91
Saint Marys Hospital	Streator	100%	60
Skokie Hospital[2]	Skokie	100%	161
Westlake Community Hospital	Melrose Park	100%	36
Advocate Condell Medical Center[2]	Libertyville	99%	201
Advocate Lutheran General Hospital[2]	Park Ridge	99%	233
Alexian Brothers Medical Center[2]	Elk Grove Vlg	99%	278
Edward Hospital	Naperville	99%	570
Elmhurst Memorial Hospital[2]	Elmhurst	99%	171
Saint Marys Hospital	Centralia	99%	81
Advocate Good Shepherd Hospital[2]	Barrington	98%	243
Advocate South Suburban Hospital[2]	Hazel Crest	98%	126
Carle Foundation Hospital[2]	Urbana	98%	261
Central Dupage Hospital[2]	Winfield	98%	182
Little Company of Mary Hospital[2]	Evergreen Park	98%	118
Memorial Hospital[2]	Belleville	98%	251
Sherman Hospital	Elgin	98%	293
Adventist Bolingbrook Hospital	Bolingbrook	97%	33
Adventist La Grange Memorial Hospital[2]	La Grange	97%	138
Advocate Good Samaritan Hospital[2]	Downers Grove	97%	198
Centegra Health System - McHenry Hospital[2]	Mchenry	97%	275
Delnor Community Hospital[2]	Geneva	97%	145
Memorial Medical Center[2]	Springfield	97%	440
Saint Anthony's Health Center	Alton	97%	91
Trinity Rock Island[2]	Rock Island	97%	184
Advocate Illinois Masonic Medical Center[2]	Chicago	96%	182
Good Samaritan Regional Health Center	Mount Vernon	96%	231
Hinsdale Hospital[2]	Hinsdale	96%	120
Macneal Hospital[2]	Berwyn	96%	248
Rockford Memorial Hospital	Rockford	96%	349
Saint Mary Medical Center	Galesburg	96%	103
Swedish American Hospital[2]	Rockford	96%	380
Swedish Covenant Hospital[2]	Chicago	96%	127
Vista Medical Center East[2]	Waukegan	96%	123
Advocate Trinity Hospital[2]	Chicago	95%	129
Ingalls Memorial Hospital[2]	Harvey	95%	130
Methodist Medical Center of Illinois[2]	Peoria	95%	289
Saint Anthony Medical Center[2]	Rockford	95%	450
St Mary & Elizabeth Med Ctr-Div Campus[2]	Chicago	95%	133
Silver Cross Hospital[2]	Joliet	95%	153
Copley Memorial Hospital[2]	Aurora	94%	274
Fhn Memorial Hospital[2]	Freeport	94%	133
Galesburg Cottage Hospital	Galesburg	94%	82
Lake Forest Hospital	Lake Forest	94%	181
Northwest Community Hospital[2]	Arlington Hgts	94%	225
Saint Anthonys Memorial Hospital	Effingham	94%	268
Saint Elizabeth Hospital[2]	Belleville	94%	189
Sarah Bush Lincoln Health Center	Mattoon	94%	147
The University of Chicago Medical Center[2]	Chicago	94%	159
West Suburban Medical Center[2]	Oak Park	94%	115
Advocate Christ Hospital & Medical Center[2]	Oak Lawn	93%	303
Centegra Health Sys-Woodstock Hospital[2]	Woodstock	93%	167
Herrin Hospital	Herrin	93%	102
Morris Hospital & Healthcare Centers	Morris	93%	85
Pekin Memorial Hospital	Pekin	93%	84
Saint Johns Hospital[2]	Springfield	93%	301
University of Illinois Hospital[2]	Chicago	93%	135
Louis A Weiss Memorial Hospital[2]	Chicago	92%	133
Anderson Hospital[2]	Maryville	91%	119
Proctor Hospital[2]	Peoria	91%	270
Provena-Saint Joseph Hospital[2]	Elgin	91%	134
Riverside Medical Center[2]	Kankakee	91%	196
Saint Alexius Medical Center[2]	Hoffman Estates	91%	101
Bromenn Healthcare[2]	Normal	90%	196
Loyola Gottlieb Memorial Hospital[2]	Melrose Park	90%	118
Memorial Hospital of Carbondale[2]	Carbondale	90%	414
Provena St Marys Hospital[2]	Kankakee	90%	84
Saint Joseph Medical Center	Bloomington	90%	237
Kishwaukee Community Hospital	Dekalb	89%	115
Loyola University Medical Center[2]	Maywood	89%	245
Rush Oak Park Hospital	Oak Park	89%	110
Saint Margarets Hospital	Spring Valley	89%	100
Blessing Hospital	Quincy	88%	208
Graham Hospital Association	Canton	88%	51
Heartland Regional Medical Center[2]	Marion	88%	155
Mount Sinai Hospital Medical Center[2]	Chicago	88%	74
Provena Mercy Medical Center[2]	Aurora	87%	207
Wabash General Hospital	Mount Carmel	87%	31
Northwestern Memorial Hospital[2]	Chicago	86%	222
Resurrection Medical Center[2]	Chicago	86%	230
Saint James Hospital	Pontiac	86%	51
Palos Community Hospital[2]	Palos Heights	85%	207
Gibson Community Hospital	Gibson City	84%	31
St James Hospital-Olympia Fields[2]	Olympia Fields	84%	225
Saint Joseph Hospital[2]	Chicago	84%	143
John H Stroger Jr Hospital[2]	Chicago	83%	132
Midwestern Region Medical Center	Zion	83%	35
Rush University Medical Center[2]	Chicago	83%	175
Provena Covenant Medical Center - Urbana[2]	Urbana	82%	215
Provena United Samaritans Med Ctr-Logan[2]	Danville	82%	85
CGH Medical Center[2]	Sterling	81%	149
Saint Francis Medical Center[2]	Peoria	78%	622
Holy Cross Hospital[2]	Chicago	77%	61
RHC St Francis Hospital[2]	Evanston	73%	136
McDonough District Hospital	Macomb	72%	29
Metrosouth Medical Center	Blue Island	70%	159
Passavant Area Hospital[2]	Jacksonville	70%	110
Mercy Hospital and Medical Center	Chicago	59%	180

NOTE: Hospital profiles are in alphabetical order by state, then city, then hospital within the city; Rankings exclude hospitals with less than 25 cases except for patient surveys which excludes hospitals with less than 100 cases; (a) 100–299 cases; (1) The number of cases is too small to be sure how well a hospital is performing; (2) The hospital indicated that the data submitted for this measure were based on a sample of cases; (3) Data was collected during a shorter time period (fewer quarters) than the maximum possible time for this measure; (4) Suppressed for one or more quarters by CMS; (5) No data is available from the hospital for this measure; (6) Fewer than 100 patients completed the HCAHPS survey. Use these rates with caution, as the number of surveys may be too low to reliably assess hospital performance; (7) Survey results are based on less than 12 months of data; (8) Survey results are not available for this reporting period; (9) No or very few patients were eligible for the HCAHPS survey. The scores shown, if any, reflect a very small number of surveys; (10) A state average was not calculated because too few hospitals in the state submitted data; (11) There were discrepancies in the data collection process; Please refer to the User's Guide for a full explanation of data.

25. Controlled Postoperative Blood Glucose

Hospital Name	City	Rate	Cases
Adventist La Grange Memorial Hospital[2]	La Grange	100%	55
Advocate Good Shepherd Hospital[2]	Barrington	100%	134
Central Dupage Hospital[2]	Winfield	100%	105
Advocate Condell Medical Center[2]	Libertyville	99%	120
Bromenn Healthcare[2]	Normal	99%	67
Elmhurst Memorial Hospital[2]	Elmhurst	99%	112
Evanston Hospital[2]	Evanston	99%	225
Advocate Good Samaritan Hospital[2]	Downers Grove	98%	132
Copley Memorial Hospital[2]	Aurora	98%	97
Good Samaritan Regional Health Center	Mount Vernon	98%	52
Memorial Hospital[2]	Belleville	98%	125
Provena-Saint Joseph Hospital[2]	Elgin	98%	43
Sherman Hospital	Elgin	98%	101
Vista Medical Center East[2]	Waukegan	98%	45
Loyola Gottlieb Memorial Hospital[2]	Melrose Park	97%	64
Mount Sinai Hospital Medical Center[2]	Chicago	97%	34
Palos Community Hospital[2]	Palos Heights	97%	133
Centegra Health System - McHenry Hospital[2]	Mchenry	96%	136
Edward Hospital	Naperville	96%	211
Memorial Hospital of Carbondale[2]	Carbondale	96%	201
Methodist Medical Center of Illinois[2]	Peoria	96%	135
Northwestern Memorial Hospital[2]	Chicago	96%	144
Resurrection Medical Center[2]	Chicago	96%	127
Advocate Christ Hospital & Medical Center[2]	Oak Lawn	95%	145
Blessing Hospital	Quincy	95%	85
Decatur Memorial Hospital[2]	Decatur	95%	97
Alexian Brothers Medical Center[2]	Elk Grove Vlg	94%	141
Memorial Medical Center[2]	Springfield	94%	248
Proctor Hospital[2]	Peoria	94%	66
Saint Johns Hospital[2]	Springfield	94%	180
Trinity Rock Island[2]	Rock Island	94%	114
The University of Chicago Medical Center[2]	Chicago	94%	121
Saint Joseph Hospital[2]	Chicago	93%	58
Swedish American Hospital[2]	Rockford	93%	163
Swedish Covenant Hospital[2]	Chicago	93%	72
Advocate Lutheran General Hospital[2]	Park Ridge	92%	108
Hines VA Medical Center[2]	Hines	92%	108
Mercy Hospital and Medical Center	Chicago	92%	84
Skokie Hospital[2]	Skokie	92%	53
Carle Foundation Hospital[2]	Urbana	91%	137
Northwest Community Hospital[2]	Arlington Hgts	91%	160
Provena Mercy Medical Center[2]	Aurora	91%	159
Saint Anthony Medical Center[2]	Rockford	91%	182
St Mary & Elizabeth Med Ctr-Div Campus[2]	Chicago	91%	54
Advocate Illinois Masonic Medical Center[2]	Chicago	90%	86
Provena Covenant Medical Center - Urbana[2]	Urbana	90%	106
Ingalls Memorial Hospital[2]	Harvey	89%	37
Loyola University Medical Center[2]	Maywood	89%	138
Riverside Medical Center[2]	Kankakee	89%	121
Rockford Memorial Hospital	Rockford	89%	149
Rush University Medical Center[2]	Chicago	89%	90
Hinsdale Hospital[2]	Hinsdale	88%	77
Macneal Hospital[2]	Berwyn	88%	80
Provena St Joseph Medical Center[2]	Joliet	88%	133
St James Hospital-Olympia Fields[2]	Olympia Fields	88%	99
Saint Elizabeth Hospital[2]	Belleville	87%	113
University of Illinois Hospital[2]	Chicago	85%	52
Saint Francis Medical Center[2]	Peoria	84%	351
John H Stroger Jr Hospital[2]	Chicago	83%	92
RHC St Francis Hospital[2]	Evanston	83%	64
Saint Joseph Medical Center	Bloomington	80%	87
West Suburban Medical Center[2]	Oak Park	78%	41
Metrosouth Medical Center	Blue Island	47%	79

26. Prophylactic Antibiotic Timing

Hospital Name	City	Rate	Cases
Adventist Glenoaks	Glendale Hghts	100%	35
Advocate Good Samaritan Hospital[2]	Downers Grove	100%	439
Advocate Lutheran General Hospital[2]	Park Ridge	100%	460
Advocate Trinity Hospital[2]	Chicago	100%	256
Decatur Memorial Hospital[2]	Decatur	100%	583
Genesis Medical Center Illini Campus[2]	Silvis	100%	313
Katherine Shaw Bethea Hospital	Dixon	100%	197
Kewanee Hospital	Kewanee	100%	29
Red Bud Regional Hospital[2]	Red Bud	100%	35
Saint Marys Hospital	Centralia	100%	168
Silver Cross Hospital[2]	Joliet	100%	509
Thorek Memorial Hospital	Chicago	100%	43
Valley West Community Hospital	Sandwich	100%	35
Advocate Christ Hospital & Medical Center[2]	Oak Lawn	99%	488
Advocate Illinois Masonic Medical Center[2]	Chicago	99%	432
Advocate South Suburban Hospital[2]	Hazel Crest	99%	295
Central Dupage Hospital[2]	Winfield	99%	391
Copley Memorial Hospital[2]	Aurora	99%	669
Crossroads Community Hospital[2]	Mount Vernon	99%	146
Elmhurst Memorial Hospital[2]	Elmhurst	99%	368
Evanston Hospital[2]	Evanston	99%	1123
Fhn Memorial Hospital[2]	Freeport	99%	291
Gateway Regional Medical Center	Granite City	99%	202
Little Company of Mary Hospital[2]	Evergreen Park	99%	283
Methodist Medical Center of Illinois[2]	Peoria	99%	715
Mount Sinai Hospital Medical Center[2]	Chicago	99%	172
Ottawa Reg Hosp & Healthcare Ctr	Ottawa	99%	143
Passavant Area Hospital[2]	Jacksonville	99%	276
Proctor Hospital[2]	Peoria	99%	630
Resurrection Medical Center[2]	Chicago	99%	434
Rockford Memorial Hospital	Rockford	99%	575
Saint Alexius Medical Center[2]	Hoffman Estates	99%	309
St Mary & Elizabeth Med Ctr-Div Campus[2]	Chicago	99%	297
Saint Marys Hospital	Streator	99%	113
Sherman Hospital	Elgin	99%	552
Swedish American Hospital[2]	Rockford	99%	942
The University of Chicago Medical Center[2]	Chicago	99%	377
University of Illinois Hospital[2]	Chicago	99%	275
Vista Medical Center East[2]	Waukegan	99%	361
West Suburban Medical Center[2]	Oak Park	99%	322
Abraham Lincoln Memorial Hospital	Lincoln	98%	41
Advocate Condell Medical Center[2]	Libertyville	98%	425
Advocate Good Shepherd Hospital[2]	Barrington	98%	425
Alexian Brothers Medical Center[2]	Elk Grove Vlg	98%	481
Alton Memorial Hospital	Alton	98%	239
Delnor Community Hospital[2]	Geneva	98%	317
Galesburg Cottage Hospital	Galesburg	98%	171
Hammond Henry Hospital	Geneseo	98%	88
Hines VA Medical Center	Hines	98%	158
Lake Forest Hospital	Lake Forest	98%	640
Loyola University Medical Center[2]	Maywood	98%	381
Macneal Hospital[2]	Berwyn	98%	539
Memorial Hospital[2]	Belleville	98%	421
Memorial Medical Center[2]	Springfield	98%	842
Morris Hospital & Healthcare Centers	Morris	98%	244
Palos Community Hospital[2]	Palos Heights	98%	415
Provena St Marys Hospital[2]	Kankakee	98%	285
Saint Anthony Medical Center[2]	Rockford	98%	964
Saint James Hospital	Pontiac	98%	105
Saint Joseph Medical Center	Bloomington	98%	541
Saint Mary Medical Center	Galesburg	98%	231
Saint Marys Hospital[2]	Decatur	98%	235
Sarah Bush Lincoln Health Center	Mattoon	98%	382
Skokie Hospital[2]	Skokie	98%	347
Taylorville Memorial Hospital	Taylorville	98%	45
Touchette Regional Hospital	Centreville	98%	44
Trinity Rock Island[2]	Rock Island	98%	357
Adventist La Grange Memorial Hospital[2]	La Grange	97%	283
Blessing Hospital	Quincy	97%	405
Bromenn Healthcare[2]	Normal	97%	543
CGH Medical Center[2]	Sterling	97%	307
Edward Hospital	Naperville	97%	1228
Ingalls Memorial Hospital[2]	Harvey	97%	332
Louis A Weiss Memorial Hospital[2]	Chicago	97%	245
Loyola Gottlieb Memorial Hospital[2]	Melrose Park	97%	306
Memorial Hospital of Carbondale[2]	Carbondale	97%	714
Metrosouth Medical Center	Blue Island	97%	383
Northwestern Memorial Hospital[2]	Chicago	97%	437
Our Lady of the Resurrection Medical Center	Chicago	97%	149
Pekin Memorial Hospital	Pekin	97%	227
Provena St Joseph Medical Center[2]	Joliet	97%	477
Provena-Saint Joseph Hospital[2]	Elgin	97%	264
RHC St Francis Hospital[2]	Evanston	97%	364
Riverside Medical Center[2]	Kankakee	97%	352
Saint Francis Medical Center[2]	Peoria	97%	1417
Saint Johns Hospital[2]	Springfield	97%	510
Saint Joseph Hospital[2]	Chicago	97%	389
Saint Josephs Hospital	Breese	97%	79
Anderson Hospital[2]	Maryville	96%	362
Good Samaritan Regional Health Center	Mount Vernon	96%	502
Heartland Regional Medical Center[2]	Marion	96%	316
Illinois Valley Community Hospital	Peru	96%	200
Iroquois Memorial Hospital	Watseka	96%	69
Mercy Harvard Hospital	Harvard	96%	26
Provena United Samaritans Med Ctr-Logan[2]	Danville	96%	155
Rush Oak Park Hospital	Oak Park	96%	211
Rush University Medical Center[2]	Chicago	96%	397
Saint Anthony's Health Center	Alton	96%	239
Westlake Community Hospital	Melrose Park	96%	109
Carle Foundation Hospital[2]	Urbana	95%	422
Graham Hospital Association	Canton	95%	131
Hinsdale Hospital[2]	Hinsdale	95%	309
J Brown VA Med Ctr-VA Chicago Healthcare	Chicago	95%	83
Norwegian-American Hospital	Chicago	95%	40
Provena Covenant Medical Center - Urbana[2]	Urbana	95%	438
Centegra Health System - McHenry Hospital[2]	Mchenry	94%	557
Gibson Community Hospital	Gibson City	94%	82
McDonough District Hospital	Macomb	94%	70
Midwestern Region Medical Center	Zion	94%	71
Saint Elizabeth Hospital[2]	Belleville	94%	313
St James Hospital-Olympia Fields[2]	Olympia Fields	94%	424
Centegra Health Sys-Woodstock Hospital[2]	Woodstock	93%	491
John H Stroger Jr Hospital[2]	Chicago	93%	268
Provena Mercy Medical Center[2]	Aurora	93%	470
Provident Hospital of Chicago[2]	Chicago	93%	67
Saint Joseph's Hospital	Highland	93%	27
Swedish Covenant Hospital[2]	Chicago	93%	271
Wabash General Hospital	Mount Carmel	93%	67
Herrin Hospital	Herrin	92%	198
Saint Margarets Hospital	Spring Valley	92%	242
Holy Cross Hospital[2]	Chicago	91%	123
Kishwaukee Community Hospital	Dekalb	91%	269
Mercy Hospital and Medical Center	Chicago	91%	382
Saint Anthonys Memorial Hospital	Effingham	91%	690
Richland Memorial Hospital	Olney	90%	84
Adventist Bolingbrook Hospital	Bolingbrook	89%	79
Saint Bernard Hospital	Chicago	89%	38
Jersey Community Hospital	Jerseyville	88%	32
Saint Francis Hospital	Litchfield	88%	50
Crawford Memorial Hospital	Robinson	87%	46
Northwest Community Hospital[2]	Arlington Hgts	87%	487
Saint Anthony Hospital	Chicago	85%	46
Sacred Heart Hospital	Chicago	56%	43
South Shore Hospital	Chicago	38%	39

27. Prophylactic Antibiotic Timing (Outpatient)

Hospital Name	City	Rate	Cases
Iroquois Memorial Hospital	Watseka	100%	31
Advocate Illinois Masonic Medical Center	Chicago	99%	401
Advocate Lutheran General Hospital	Park Ridge	99%	730
Copley Memorial Hospital	Aurora	99%	303
Evanston Hospital	Evanston	99%	623
Genesis Medical Center Illini Campus	Silvis	99%	108
Saint Joseph Medical Center	Bloomington	99%	189
Delnor Community Hospital	Geneva	98%	109
Edward Hospital	Naperville	98%	474
Rockford Memorial Hospital	Rockford	98%	361
Saint Mary Medical Center	Galesburg	98%	47
Sarah Bush Lincoln Health Center	Mattoon	98%	122
Vista Medical Center East	Waukegan	98%	162
Advocate Christ Hospital & Medical Center	Oak Lawn	97%	728
Advocate Good Shepherd Hospital	Barrington	97%	396
Advocate South Suburban Hospital	Hazel Crest	97%	220
Alexian Brothers Medical Center	Elk Grove Vlg	97%	518
Central Dupage Hospital	Winfield	97%	490
Fairfield Memorial Hospital	Fairfield	97%	36
Galesburg Cottage Hospital	Galesburg	97%	108
Gateway Regional Medical Center	Granite City	97%	73
Loyola Gottlieb Memorial Hospital	Melrose Park	97%	62
Morris Hospital & Healthcare Centers	Morris	97%	292
Northwestern Memorial Hospital	Chicago	97%	561
Saint Marys Hospital[3]	Decatur	97%	111
Silver Cross Hospital	Joliet	97%	378
Skokie Hospital	Skokie	97%	192
Trinity Rock Island	Rock Island	97%	478
Advocate Good Samaritan Hospital	Downers Grove	96%	323
Anderson Hospital	Maryville	96%	288
Decatur Memorial Hospital	Decatur	96%	406
Elmhurst Memorial Hospital	Elmhurst	96%	167
Hinsdale Hospital	Hinsdale	96%	278
John H Stroger Jr Hospital	Chicago	96%	141
Katherine Shaw Bethea Hospital	Dixon	96%	84
Lake Forest Hospital	Lake Forest	96%	327
Little Company of Mary Hospital	Evergreen Park	96%	242
Mercy Harvard Hospital[3]	Harvard	96%	26
Midwestern Region Medical Center	Zion	96%	28
Palos Community Hospital	Palos Heights	96%	224
Passavant Area Hospital	Jacksonville	96%	70
Swedish American Hospital	Rockford	96%	312
Memorial Hospital of Carbondale	Carbondale	95%	452
Methodist Medical Center of Illinois	Peoria	95%	337
Provena Covenant Medical Center - Urbana	Urbana	95%	286
Resurrection Medical Center	Chicago	95%	199
West Suburban Medical Center	Oak Park	95%	142
Advocate Condell Medical Center	Libertyville	94%	446
Advocate Trinity Hospital	Chicago	94%	115
Alton Memorial Hospital	Alton	94%	142
Heartland Regional Medical Center	Marion	94%	207
Ingalls Memorial Hospital	Harvey	94%	107
Memorial Medical Center	Springfield	94%	655
Saint Alexius Medical Center	Hoffman Estates	94%	321
Adventist La Grange Memorial Hospital	La Grange	93%	155
Carle Foundation Hospital	Urbana	93%	435
CGH Medical Center	Sterling	93%	57
Good Samaritan Regional Health Center	Mount Vernon	93%	193
Loyola University Medical Center	Maywood	93%	268
Provident Hospital of Chicago	Chicago	93%	72
Riverside Medical Center	Kankakee	93%	381
Rush University Medical Center	Chicago	93%	414
Saint Anthony Medical Center	Rockford	93%	369
Saint Johns Hospital	Springfield	93%	428
Saint Joseph Hospital	Chicago	93%	161
Saint Margarets Hospital	Spring Valley	93%	44

NOTE: Hospital profiles are in alphabetical order by state, then city, then hospital within the city; Rankings exclude hospitals with less than 25 cases except for patient surveys which excludes hospitals with less than 100 cases; (a) 100–299 cases; (1) The number of cases is too small to be sure how well a hospital is performing; (2) The hospital indicated that the data submitted for this measure were based on a sample of cases; (3) Data was collected during a shorter time period (fewer quarters) than the maximum possible time for this measure; (4) Suppressed for one or more quarters by CMS; (5) No data is available from the hospital for this measure; (6) Fewer than 100 patients completed the HCAHPS survey. Use these rates with caution, as the number of surveys may be too low to reliably assess hospital performance; (7) Survey results are based on less than 12 months of data; (8) Survey results are not available for this reporting period; (9) No or very few patients were eligible for the HCAHPS survey. The scores shown, if any, reflect a very small number of surveys; (10) A state average was not calculated because too few hospitals in the state submitted data; (11) There were discrepancies in the data collection process; Please refer to the User's Guide for a full explanation of data.

Thorek Memorial Hospital	Chicago	93%	27
Fhn Memorial Hospital	Freeport	92%	92
Graham Hospital Association	Canton	92%	80
Memorial Hospital	Belleville	92%	494
Methodist Hospital of Chicago	Chicago	92%	36
Provena St Marys Hospital	Kankakee	92%	199
Saint Francis Medical Center	Peoria	92%	320
Proctor Hospital	Peoria	91%	123
Saint Elizabeth Hospital	Belleville	91%	179
St Mary & Elizabeth Med Ctr-Div Campus	Chicago	91%	198
Crossroads Community Hospital	Mount Vernon	90%	48
Metrosouth Medical Center	Blue Island	90%	278
Northwest Community Hospital	Arlington Hgts	90%	350
Provena St Joseph Medical Center	Joliet	90%	378
Bromenn Healthcare	Normal	89%	229
Illinois Valley Community Hospital	Peru	89%	136
Blessing Hospital	Quincy	88%	271
Ottawa Reg Hosp & Healthcare Ctr	Ottawa	88%	57
Our Lady of the Resurrection Medical Center	Chicago	88%	98
Saint Anthony Hospital	Chicago	88%	120
Saint Anthony's Health Center	Alton	88%	49
Saint Marys Hospital	Streator	88%	67
The University of Chicago Medical Center	Chicago	88%	286
University of Illinois Hospital	Chicago	88%	200
Kishwaukee Community Hospital	Dekalb	86%	123
Provena Mercy Medical Center	Aurora	86%	174
Adventist Bolingbrook Hospital	Bolingbrook	85%	111
Richland Memorial Hospital	Olney	85%	26
Saint Josephs Hospital	Breese	85%	39
Westlake Community Hospital	Melrose Park	85%	93
Mount Sinai Hospital Medical Center	Chicago	84%	74
RHC St Francis Hospital	Evanston	82%	73
Rush Oak Park Hospital	Oak Park	82%	40
Centegra Health System - McHenry Hospital	Mchenry	81%	163
Herrin Hospital	Herrin	81%	37
Norwegian-American Hospital	Chicago	81%	43
St James Hospital-Olympia Fields	Olympia Fields	81%	265
McDonough District Hospital	Macomb	80%	45
Mercy Hospital and Medical Center	Chicago	80%	148
Provena United Samaritans Med Ctr-Logan	Danville	79%	48
Saint Marys Hospital	Centralia	79%	52
Provena-Saint Joseph Hospital	Elgin	78%	109
Adventist Glenoaks	Glendale Hghts	77%	31
Centegra Health Sys-Woodstock Hospital	Woodstock	77%	84
Louis A Weiss Memorial Hospital	Chicago	76%	147
Swedish Covenant Hospital	Chicago	76%	142
Holy Cross Hospital	Chicago	74%	58
Macneal Hospital	Berwyn	74%	388
Sacred Heart Hospital	Chicago	73%	44
Saint Anthonys Memorial Hospital	Effingham	68%	76
Sherman Hospital	Elgin	65%	220
Touchette Regional Hospital	Centreville	6%	36

28. Prophylactic Antibiotic Selection

Hospital Name	City	Rate	Cases
Abraham Lincoln Memorial Hospital	Lincoln	100%	42
Adventist Glenoaks	Glendale Hghts	100%	35
Advocate South Suburban Hospital[2]	Hazel Crest	100%	298
Edward Hospital	Naperville	100%	1240
Gateway Regional Medical Center	Granite City	100%	203
Hinsdale Hospital[2]	Hinsdale	100%	313
Illinois Valley Community Hospital	Peru	100%	200
Taylorville Memorial Hospital	Taylorville	100%	45
Advocate Good Shepherd Hospital[2]	Barrington	99%	436
Alton Memorial Hospital	Alton	99%	242
Carle Foundation Hospital[2]	Urbana	99%	446
Central Dupage Hospital[2]	Winfield	99%	394
Crossroads Community Hospital[2]	Mount Vernon	99%	146
Decatur Memorial Hospital[2]	Decatur	99%	588
Elmhurst Memorial Hospital[2]	Elmhurst	99%	375
Gibson Community Hospital	Gibson City	99%	83
Good Samaritan Regional Health Center	Mount Vernon	99%	510
Heartland Regional Medical Center[2]	Marion	99%	318
Hines VA Medical Center	Hines	99%	158
Ingalls Memorial Hospital[2]	Harvey	99%	335
Katherine Shaw Bethea Hospital	Dixon	99%	198
McDonough District Hospital	Macomb	99%	70
Methodist Medical Center of Illinois[2]	Peoria	99%	728
Northwestern Memorial Hospital[2]	Chicago	99%	451
Ottawa Reg Hosp & Healthcare Ctr	Ottawa	99%	145
Proctor Hospital[2]	Peoria	99%	634
Saint Anthony Medical Center[2]	Rockford	99%	974
Saint James Hospital	Pontiac	99%	108
St James Hospital-Olympia Fields[2]	Olympia Fields	99%	429
Saint Johns Hospital[2]	Springfield	99%	518
Saint Mary Medical Center	Galesburg	99%	234
Saint Marys Hospital	Centralia	99%	168
Silver Cross Hospital[2]	Joliet	99%	509
Skokie Hospital[2]	Skokie	99%	350
Trinity Rock Island[2]	Rock Island	99%	366
The University of Chicago Medical Center[2]	Chicago	99%	386
Adventist La Grange Memorial Hospital[2]	La Grange	98%	283
Advocate Condell Medical Center[2]	Libertyville	98%	429
Advocate Good Samaritan Hospital[2]	Downers Grove	98%	442
Advocate Trinity Hospital[2]	Chicago	98%	256
Evanston Hospital[2]	Evanston	98%	1132
Genesis Medical Center Illini Campus[2]	Silvis	98%	312
J Brown VA Med Ctr-VA Chicago Healthcare	Chicago	98%	86
Lake Forest Hospital	Lake Forest	98%	642
Little Company of Mary Hospital[2]	Evergreen Park	98%	285
Louis A Weiss Memorial Hospital[2]	Chicago	98%	245
Macneal Hospital[2]	Berwyn	98%	559
Memorial Hospital[2]	Belleville	98%	426
Memorial Medical Center[2]	Springfield	98%	847
Metrosouth Medical Center	Blue Island	98%	389
Morris Hospital & Healthcare Centers	Morris	98%	245
Palos Community Hospital[2]	Palos Heights	98%	423
Provena-Saint Joseph Hospital[2]	Elgin	98%	265
Resurrection Medical Center[2]	Chicago	98%	445
Rockford Memorial Hospital	Rockford	98%	593
Rush Oak Park Hospital	Oak Park	98%	212
Saint Francis Medical Center[2]	Peoria	98%	1430
Saint Joseph Medical Center	Bloomington	98%	546
Saint Margarets Hospital	Spring Valley	98%	241
Swedish American Hospital[2]	Rockford	98%	956
Thorek Memorial Hospital	Chicago	98%	43
Touchette Regional Hospital	Centreville	98%	45
Advocate Christ Hospital & Medical Center[2]	Oak Lawn	97%	499
Advocate Illinois Masonic Medical Center[2]	Chicago	97%	435
Advocate Lutheran General Hospital[2]	Park Ridge	97%	464
Anderson Hospital[2]	Maryville	97%	368
Blessing Hospital	Quincy	97%	412
Bromenn Healthcare[2]	Normal	97%	545
Centegra Health System - McHenry Hospital[2]	Mchenry	97%	559
Centegra Health Sys-Woodstock Hospital[2]	Woodstock	97%	492
Copley Memorial Hospital[2]	Aurora	97%	675
Galesburg Cottage Hospital	Galesburg	97%	172
Iroquois Memorial Hospital	Watseka	97%	69
Kewanee Hospital	Kewanee	97%	29
Provena Mercy Medical Center[2]	Aurora	97%	478
Provena St Marys Hospital[2]	Kankakee	97%	284
Riverside Medical Center[2]	Kankakee	97%	359
Saint Alexius Medical Center[2]	Hoffman Estates	97%	311
Saint Anthonys Memorial Hospital	Effingham	97%	695
Saint Josephs Hospital	Breese	97%	79
Saint Marys Hospital[2]	Decatur	97%	236
Sarah Bush Lincoln Health Center	Mattoon	97%	387
Sherman Hospital	Elgin	97%	555
University of Illinois Hospital[2]	Chicago	97%	282
Vista Medical Center East[2]	Waukegan	97%	363
Alexian Brothers Medical Center[2]	Elk Grove Vlg	96%	487
CGH Medical Center[2]	Sterling	96%	307
Delnor Community Hospital[2]	Geneva	96%	316
Loyola University Medical Center[2]	Maywood	96%	387
Mercy Harvard Hospital	Harvard	96%	26
Midwestern Region Medical Center	Zion	96%	71
Mount Sinai Hospital Medical Center[2]	Chicago	96%	175
Passavant Area Hospital[2]	Jacksonville	96%	278
Pekin Memorial Hospital	Pekin	96%	229
Provena Covenant Medical Center - Urbana[2]	Urbana	96%	442
RHC St Francis Hospital[2]	Evanston	96%	367
Rush University Medical Center[2]	Chicago	96%	398
Saint Anthony's Health Center	Alton	96%	242
Saint Joseph's Hospital	Highland	96%	27
St Mary & Elizabeth Med Ctr-Div Campus[2]	Chicago	96%	297
Saint Marys Hospital	Streator	96%	113
Graham Hospital Association	Canton	95%	134
Herrin Hospital	Herrin	95%	198
Northwest Community Hospital[2]	Arlington Hgts	95%	488
Provena United Samaritans Med Ctr-Logan[2]	Danville	95%	155
Provident Hospital of Chicago[2]	Chicago	95%	66
Richland Memorial Hospital	Olney	95%	80
Saint Elizabeth Hospital[2]	Belleville	95%	317
Fhn Memorial Hospital[2]	Freeport	94%	292
Memorial Hospital of Carbondale[2]	Carbondale	94%	718
Mercy Hospital and Medical Center	Chicago	94%	382
Our Lady of the Resurrection Medical Center	Chicago	94%	150
Provena St Joseph Medical Center[2]	Joliet	94%	479
Red Bud Regional Hospital[2]	Red Bud	94%	35
Saint Joseph Hospital[2]	Chicago	94%	392
West Suburban Medical Center[2]	Oak Park	94%	326
Westlake Community Hospital	Melrose Park	94%	110
Hammond Henry Hospital	Geneseo	93%	88
Wabash General Hospital	Mount Carmel	93%	67
John H Stroger Jr Hospital[2]	Chicago	92%	266
Adventist Bolingbrook Hospital	Bolingbrook	91%	77
Crawford Memorial Hospital	Robinson	91%	47
Holy Cross Hospital[2]	Chicago	91%	124
Jersey Community Hospital	Jerseyville	91%	32
Kishwaukee Community Hospital	Dekalb	91%	266
Loyola Gottlieb Memorial Hospital[2]	Melrose Park	91%	305
Valley West Community Hospital	Sandwich	91%	35
Sacred Heart Hospital	Chicago	90%	42
Swedish Covenant Hospital[2]	Chicago	90%	274
Saint Francis Hospital	Litchfield	86%	50
Norwegian-American Hospital	Chicago	85%	39
Saint Anthony Hospital	Chicago	85%	46
Saint Bernard Hospital	Chicago	82%	38
South Shore Hospital	Chicago	80%	40

29. Prophylactic Antibiotic Selection (Outpatient)

Hospital Name	City	Rate	Cases
Thorek Memorial Hospital	Chicago	100%	25
Advocate South Suburban Hospital	Hazel Crest	99%	219
Fhn Memorial Hospital	Freeport	99%	142
Hinsdale Hospital	Hinsdale	99%	272
Katherine Shaw Bethea Hospital	Dixon	99%	81
Little Company of Mary Hospital	Evergreen Park	99%	239
Mount Sinai Hospital Medical Center	Chicago	99%	208
Saint Anthonys Memorial Hospital	Effingham	99%	71
Saint Joseph Medical Center	Bloomington	99%	189
Saint Marys Hospital[3]	Decatur	99%	145
Adventist La Grange Memorial Hospital	La Grange	98%	149
Advocate Condell Medical Center	Libertyville	98%	442
Advocate Good Samaritan Hospital	Downers Grove	98%	317
Advocate Good Shepherd Hospital	Barrington	98%	391
Advocate Illinois Masonic Medical Center	Chicago	98%	476
Advocate Lutheran General Hospital	Park Ridge	98%	727
Central Dupage Hospital	Winfield	98%	483
Decatur Memorial Hospital	Decatur	98%	394
Edward Hospital	Naperville	98%	470
Ingalls Memorial Hospital	Harvey	98%	104
Memorial Hospital of Carbondale	Carbondale	98%	438
Saint Alexius Medical Center	Hoffman Estates	98%	316
Saint Anthony's Health Center	Alton	98%	112
Vista Medical Center East	Waukegan	98%	166
Anderson Hospital	Maryville	97%	283
Copley Memorial Hospital	Aurora	97%	301
Genesis Medical Center Illini Campus	Silvis	97%	107
Lake Forest Hospital	Lake Forest	97%	327
McDonough District Hospital	Macomb	97%	36
Methodist Hospital of Chicago	Chicago	97%	33
Northwestern Memorial Hospital	Chicago	97%	554
Norwegian-American Hospital	Chicago	97%	36
Palos Community Hospital	Palos Heights	97%	222
Provena-Saint Joseph Hospital	Elgin	97%	118
Rockford Memorial Hospital	Rockford	97%	357
Saint Marys Hospital	Streator	97%	63
Swedish American Hospital	Rockford	97%	307
Advocate Trinity Hospital	Chicago	96%	113
Blessing Hospital	Quincy	96%	248
Bromenn Healthcare	Normal	96%	213
Centegra Health System - McHenry Hospital	Mchenry	96%	150
Crossroads Community Hospital	Mount Vernon	96%	85
Gateway Regional Medical Center	Granite City	96%	72
Kishwaukee Community Hospital	Dekalb	96%	117
Mercy Harvard Hospital[3]	Harvard	96%	26
Metrosouth Medical Center	Blue Island	96%	261
Midwestern Region Medical Center	Zion	96%	28
Ottawa Reg Hosp & Healthcare Ctr	Ottawa	96%	53
Saint Johns Hospital	Springfield	96%	423
St Mary & Elizabeth Med Ctr-Div Campus	Chicago	96%	184
Silver Cross Hospital	Joliet	96%	371
Skokie Hospital	Skokie	96%	191
Advocate Christ Hospital & Medical Center	Oak Lawn	95%	723
Alexian Brothers Medical Center	Elk Grove Vlg	95%	515
Jersey Community Hospital	Jerseyville	95%	39
Loyola Gottlieb Memorial Hospital	Melrose Park	95%	60
Memorial Hospital	Belleville	95%	499
Provena Covenant Medical Center - Urbana	Urbana	95%	276
Provena St Joseph Medical Center	Joliet	95%	361
Saint Anthony Medical Center	Rockford	95%	363
Saint Joseph Hospital	Chicago	95%	154
Alton Memorial Hospital	Alton	94%	144
Centegra Health Sys-Woodstock Hospital	Woodstock	94%	71
Evanston Hospital	Evanston	94%	619
Saint Elizabeth Hospital	Belleville	94%	207
Saint Josephs Hospital	Breese	94%	34
The University of Chicago Medical Center	Chicago	94%	486
University of Illinois Hospital	Chicago	94%	223
Carle Foundation Hospital	Urbana	93%	434
Heartland Regional Medical Center	Marion	93%	213
Illinois Valley Community Hospital	Peru	93%	132
Loyola University Medical Center	Maywood	93%	486
Memorial Medical Center	Springfield	93%	648
Methodist Medical Center of Illinois	Peoria	93%	329
Provena St Marys Hospital	Kankakee	93%	191
Saint Mary Medical Center	Galesburg	93%	46
Galesburg Cottage Hospital	Galesburg	92%	106
Our Lady of the Resurrection Medical Center	Chicago	92%	90
Provena United Samaritans Med Ctr-Logan	Danville	92%	38

NOTE: Hospital profiles are in alphabetical order by state, then city, then hospital within the city; Rankings exclude hospitals with less than 25 cases except for patient surveys which excludes hospitals with less than 100 cases; (a) 100–299 cases; (1) The number of cases is too small to be sure how well a hospital is performing; (2) The hospital indicated that the data submitted for this measure were based on a sample of cases; (3) Data was collected during a shorter time period (fewer quarters) than the maximum possible time for this measure; (4) Suppressed for one or more quarters by CMS; (5) No data is available from the hospital for this measure; (6) Fewer than 100 patients completed the HCAHPS survey. Use these rates with caution, as the number of surveys may be too low to reliably assess hospital performance; (7) Survey results are based on less than 12 months of data; (8) Survey results are not available for this reporting period; (9) No or very few patients were eligible for the HCAHPS survey. The scores shown, if any, reflect a very small number of surveys; (10) A state average was not calculated because too few hospitals in the state submitted data; (11) There were discrepancies in the data collection process; Please refer to the User's Guide for a full explanation of data.

Riverside Medical Center	Kankakee	92%	378
Rush Oak Park Hospital	Oak Park	92%	37
Trinity Rock Island	Rock Island	92%	475
West Suburban Medical Center	Oak Park	92%	138
Elmhurst Memorial Hospital	Elmhurst	91%	163
Herrin Hospital	Herrin	91%	33
Saint Anthony Hospital	Chicago	91%	106
Delnor Community Hospital	Geneva	90%	109
Good Samaritan Regional Health Center	Mount Vernon	90%	191
Saint Francis Medical Center	Peoria	90%	315
Adventist Glenoaks	Glendale Hghts	89%	27
Graham Hospital Association	Canton	89%	75
Resurrection Medical Center	Chicago	89%	196
Saint Margarets Hospital	Spring Valley	89%	44
Adventist Bolingbrook Hospital	Bolingbrook	88%	108
Northwest Community Hospital	Arlington Hgts	88%	366
Proctor Hospital	Peoria	88%	117
RHC St Francis Hospital	Evanston	88%	67
Rush University Medical Center	Chicago	88%	406
Sacred Heart Hospital	Chicago	88%	42
Saint Marys Hospital	Centralia	88%	42
Sarah Bush Lincoln Health Center	Mattoon	88%	122
Westlake Community Hospital	Melrose Park	88%	84
John H Stroger Jr Hospital	Chicago	87%	140
Provena Mercy Medical Center	Aurora	87%	171
Provident Hospital of Chicago	Chicago	87%	77
Fairfield Memorial Hospital	Fairfield	86%	36
Morris Hospital & Healthcare Centers	Morris	86%	319
St James Hospital-Olympia Fields	Olympia Fields	86%	246
CGH Medical Center	Sterling	85%	55
Swedish Covenant Hospital	Chicago	85%	117
Iroquois Memorial Hospital	Watseka	84%	31
Louis A Weiss Memorial Hospital	Chicago	84%	257
Mercy Hospital and Medical Center	Chicago	83%	134
Sherman Hospital	Elgin	82%	220
Passavant Area Hospital	Jacksonville	80%	69
Macneal Hospital	Berwyn	79%	317
Holy Cross Hospital	Chicago	73%	49

30. Prophylactic Antibiotic Stopped

Hospital Name	City	Rate	Cases
Abraham Lincoln Memorial Hospital	Lincoln	100%	40
Hines VA Medical Center	Hines	100%	155
Sherman Hospital	Elgin	100%	503
Evanston Hospital[2]	Evanston	99%	1080
Fhn Memorial Hospital[2]	Freeport	99%	276
Gateway Regional Medical Center	Granite City	99%	202
Little Company of Mary Hospital[2]	Evergreen Park	99%	247
Saint Marys Hospital	Centralia	99%	152
Advocate Christ Hospital & Medical Center[2]	Oak Lawn	98%	461
Advocate Good Samaritan Hospital[2]	Downers Grove	98%	425
Advocate Illinois Masonic Medical Center[2]	Chicago	98%	406
Elmhurst Memorial Hospital[2]	Elmhurst	98%	354
Our Lady of the Resurrection Medical Center	Chicago	98%	135
Provident Hospital of Chicago[2]	Chicago	98%	64
Saint Alexius Medical Center[2]	Hoffman Estates	98%	284
Silver Cross Hospital[2]	Joliet	98%	480
Swedish American Hospital[2]	Rockford	98%	883
The University of Chicago Medical Center[2]	Chicago	98%	352
Vista Medical Center East[2]	Waukegan	98%	348
Adventist Glenoaks	Glendale Hghts	97%	34
Advocate South Suburban Hospital[2]	Hazel Crest	97%	271
Carle Foundation Hospital[2]	Urbana	97%	413
Central Dupage Hospital[2]	Winfield	97%	375
Decatur Memorial Hospital[2]	Decatur	97%	572
Galesburg Cottage Hospital	Galesburg	97%	161
Ingalls Memorial Hospital[2]	Harvey	97%	321
J Brown VA Med Ctr-VA Chicago Healthcare	Chicago	97%	79
Katherine Shaw Bethea Hospital	Dixon	97%	153
Macneal Hospital[2]	Berwyn	97%	513
Memorial Medical Center[2]	Springfield	97%	813
Methodist Medical Center of Illinois[2]	Peoria	97%	679
Saint James Hospital	Pontiac	97%	95
Saint Johns Hospital[2]	Springfield	97%	482
Thorek Memorial Hospital	Chicago	97%	36
Trinity Rock Island[2]	Rock Island	97%	352
University of Illinois Hospital[2]	Chicago	97%	259
Wabash General Hospital	Mount Carmel	97%	65
West Suburban Medical Center[2]	Oak Park	97%	318
Advocate Condell Medical Center[2]	Libertyville	96%	398
Advocate Good Shepherd Hospital[2]	Barrington	96%	416
Advocate Lutheran General Hospital[2]	Park Ridge	96%	434
Alton Memorial Hospital	Alton	96%	226
CGH Medical Center[2]	Sterling	96%	303
Delnor Community Hospital[2]	Geneva	96%	304
Edward Hospital	Naperville	96%	1167
Genesis Medical Center Illini Campus[2]	Silvis	96%	305
Lake Forest Hospital	Lake Forest	96%	638
Louis A Weiss Memorial Hospital[2]	Chicago	96%	231
Memorial Hospital[2]	Belleville	96%	409
Mercy Harvard Hospital	Harvard	96%	26
Passavant Area Hospital[2]	Jacksonville	96%	263
Saint Anthony Medical Center[2]	Rockford	96%	943
Saint Anthonys Memorial Hospital	Effingham	96%	666
Saint Margarets Hospital	Spring Valley	96%	227
Skokie Hospital[2]	Skokie	96%	343
Alexian Brothers Medical Center[2]	Elk Grove Vlg	95%	414
Bromenn Healthcare[2]	Normal	95%	521
Pekin Memorial Hospital	Pekin	95%	219
Rush University Medical Center[2]	Chicago	95%	379
Adventist La Grange Memorial Hospital[2]	La Grange	94%	270
Blessing Hospital	Quincy	94%	383
Centegra Health Sys-Woodstock Hospital[2]	Woodstock	94%	481
Good Samaritan Regional Health Center	Mount Vernon	94%	476
Hinsdale Hospital[2]	Hinsdale	94%	292
Iroquois Memorial Hospital	Watseka	94%	65
Kishwaukee Community Hospital	Dekalb	94%	257
Loyola University Medical Center[2]	Maywood	94%	370
Metrosouth Medical Center	Blue Island	94%	355
Mount Sinai Hospital Medical Center[2]	Chicago	94%	155
Northwestern Memorial Hospital[2]	Chicago	94%	416
Proctor Hospital[2]	Peoria	94%	623
Provena St Marys Hospital[2]	Kankakee	94%	271
Red Bud Regional Hospital[2]	Red Bud	94%	35
St Mary & Elizabeth Med Ctr-Div Campus[2]	Chicago	94%	287
Valley West Community Hospital	Sandwich	94%	35
Westlake Community Hospital	Melrose Park	94%	90
Advocate Trinity Hospital[2]	Chicago	93%	245
Anderson Hospital[2]	Maryville	93%	347
Copley Memorial Hospital[2]	Aurora	93%	656
Gibson Community Hospital	Gibson City	93%	82
Graham Hospital Association	Canton	93%	128
Hammond Henry Hospital	Geneseo	93%	87
John H Stroger Jr Hospital[2]	Chicago	93%	257
Memorial Hospital of Carbondale[2]	Carbondale	93%	679
Northwest Community Hospital[2]	Arlington Hgts	93%	457
Palos Community Hospital[2]	Palos Heights	93%	401
Resurrection Medical Center[2]	Chicago	93%	416
Rockford Memorial Hospital	Rockford	93%	547
St James Hospital-Olympia Fields[2]	Olympia Fields	93%	391
Saint Mary Medical Center	Galesburg	93%	218
Saint Marys Hospital	Streator	93%	110
Sarah Bush Lincoln Health Center	Mattoon	93%	349
Illinois Valley Community Hospital	Peru	92%	200
Loyola Gottlieb Memorial Hospital[2]	Melrose Park	92%	295
Ottawa Reg Hosp & Healthcare Ctr	Ottawa	92%	136
Provena Covenant Medical Center - Urbana[2]	Urbana	92%	418
Saint Anthony's Health Center	Alton	92%	225
Saint Francis Medical Center[2]	Peoria	92%	1372
Saint Marys Hospital[2]	Decatur	92%	221
Crossroads Community Hospital[2]	Mount Vernon	91%	140
Provena Mercy Medical Center[2]	Aurora	91%	429
Rush Oak Park Hospital	Oak Park	91%	202
Saint Joseph Medical Center	Bloomington	91%	514
Touchette Regional Hospital	Centreville	91%	44
Jersey Community Hospital	Jerseyville	90%	31
Mercy Hospital and Medical Center	Chicago	90%	366
Midwestern Region Medical Center	Zion	90%	63
Saint Josephs Hospital	Breese	90%	78
RHC St Francis Hospital[2]	Evanston	89%	332
Saint Elizabeth Hospital[2]	Belleville	89%	299
Saint Joseph Hospital[2]	Chicago	89%	381
Swedish Covenant Hospital[2]	Chicago	89%	259
Taylorville Memorial Hospital	Taylorville	89%	44
Centegra Health System - McHenry Hospital[2]	Mchenry	88%	536
Herrin Hospital	Herrin	88%	183
Morris Hospital & Healthcare Centers	Morris	88%	242
Richland Memorial Hospital	Olney	88%	76
Provena-Saint Joseph Hospital[2]	Elgin	87%	247
Riverside Medical Center[2]	Kankakee	87%	328
South Shore Hospital	Chicago	87%	39
McDonough District Hospital	Macomb	86%	66
Provena St Joseph Medical Center[2]	Joliet	86%	441
Provena United Samaritans Med Ctr-Logan[2]	Danville	84%	148
Heartland Regional Medical Center[2]	Marion	82%	292
Kewanee Hospital	Kewanee	82%	28
Saint Joseph's Hospital	Highland	81%	27
Holy Cross Hospital[2]	Chicago	79%	121
Saint Bernard Hospital	Chicago	78%	36
Crawford Memorial Hospital	Robinson	74%	46
Saint Anthony Hospital	Chicago	66%	44
Adventist Bolingbrook Hospital	Bolingbrook	64%	75
Norwegian-American Hospital	Chicago	64%	36
Saint Francis Hospital	Litchfield	60%	50
Sacred Heart Hospital	Chicago	57%	42

31. Recommended VTP Ordered

Hospital Name	City	Rate	Cases
Advocate Trinity Hospital[2]	Chicago	100%	147
Central Dupage Hospital[2]	Winfield	100%	95
Fairfield Memorial Hospital	Fairfield	100%	30
Katherine Shaw Bethea Hospital	Dixon	100%	95
Little Company of Mary Hospital[2]	Evergreen Park	100%	240
Provident Hospital of Chicago[2]	Chicago	100%	39
Sherman Hospital	Elgin	100%	320
Skokie Hospital[2]	Skokie	100%	153
Wabash General Hospital	Mount Carmel	100%	51
Advocate Christ Hospital & Medical Center[2]	Oak Lawn	99%	212
Advocate Lutheran General Hospital[2]	Park Ridge	99%	211
Advocate South Suburban Hospital[2]	Hazel Crest	99%	159
Delnor Community Hospital[2]	Geneva	99%	172
Evanston Hospital[2]	Evanston	99%	537
Gateway Regional Medical Center	Granite City	99%	100
Genesis Medical Center Illini Campus[2]	Silvis	99%	135
Hinsdale Hospital[2]	Hinsdale	99%	144
J Brown VA Med Ctr-VA Chicago Healthcare[2]	Chicago	99%	136
Macneal Hospital[2]	Berwyn	99%	258
Midwestern Region Medical Center	Zion	99%	187
Mount Sinai Hospital Medical Center[2]	Chicago	99%	110
Our Lady of the Resurrection Medical Center	Chicago	99%	202
Provena St Joseph Medical Center[2]	Joliet	99%	190
Saint Margarets Hospital	Spring Valley	99%	81
Saint Marys Hospital	Streator	99%	89
The University of Chicago Medical Center[2]	Chicago	99%	195
University of Illinois Hospital[2]	Chicago	99%	222
West Suburban Medical Center[2]	Oak Park	99%	146
Advocate Good Samaritan Hospital[2]	Downers Grove	98%	203
Advocate Good Shepherd Hospital[2]	Barrington	98%	153
Alexian Brothers Medical Center[2]	Elk Grove Vlg	98%	269
Crossroads Community Hospital[2]	Mount Vernon	98%	51
Galesburg Cottage Hospital	Galesburg	98%	117
Louis A Weiss Memorial Hospital[2]	Chicago	98%	171
Loyola University Medical Center[2]	Maywood	98%	175
Mercy Hospital and Medical Center	Chicago	98%	248
Northwestern Memorial Hospital[2]	Chicago	98%	200
Rush University Medical Center[2]	Chicago	98%	193
Saint Alexius Medical Center[2]	Hoffman Estates	98%	209
Saint Anthony's Health Center	Alton	98%	80
Saint Marys Hospital	Centralia	98%	122
Thorek Memorial Hospital	Chicago	98%	41
Adventist La Grange Memorial Hospital[2]	La Grange	97%	178
Advocate Illinois Masonic Medical Center[2]	Chicago	97%	217
Anderson Hospital[2]	Maryville	97%	228
Edward Hospital	Naperville	97%	635
Fhn Memorial Hospital[2]	Freeport	97%	115
Good Samaritan Regional Health Center	Mount Vernon	97%	238
Hines VA Medical Center[2]	Hines	97%	78
Memorial Hospital[2]	Belleville	97%	209
Memorial Medical Center[2]	Springfield	97%	194
Pekin Memorial Hospital	Pekin	97%	153
St James Hospital-Olympia Fields[2]	Olympia Fields	97%	270
Saint Mary Medical Center	Galesburg	97%	182
Silver Cross Hospital[2]	Joliet	97%	179
Alton Memorial Hospital	Alton	96%	134
CGH Medical Center[2]	Sterling	96%	242
Copley Memorial Hospital[2]	Aurora	96%	199
Heartland Regional Medical Center[2]	Marion	96%	186
Holy Cross Hospital[2]	Chicago	96%	142
Illinois Valley Community Hospital	Peru	96%	72
Ingalls Memorial Hospital[2]	Harvey	96%	138
Ottawa Reg Hosp & Healthcare Ctr	Ottawa	96%	92
Proctor Hospital[2]	Peoria	96%	140
Saint Francis Medical Center[2]	Peoria	96%	436
Westlake Community Hospital	Melrose Park	96%	75
Blessing Hospital	Quincy	95%	246
Carle Foundation Hospital[2]	Urbana	95%	130
Hammond Henry Hospital	Geneseo	95%	38
Memorial Hospital of Carbondale[2]	Carbondale	95%	384
Methodist Medical Center of Illinois[2]	Peoria	95%	184
Resurrection Medical Center[2]	Chicago	95%	213
RHC St Francis Hospital[2]	Evanston	95%	335
Saint Anthony Medical Center[2]	Rockford	95%	256
St Mary & Elizabeth Med Ctr-Div Campus[2]	Chicago	95%	202
Sarah Bush Lincoln Health Center	Mattoon	95%	173
Vista Medical Center East[2]	Waukegan	95%	123
Advocate Condell Medical Center[2]	Libertyville	94%	189
Elmhurst Memorial Hospital[2]	Elmhurst	94%	213
Herrin Hospital	Herrin	94%	173
Northwest Community Hospital[2]	Arlington Hgts	94%	182
Palos Community Hospital[2]	Palos Heights	94%	234
Saint Anthonys Memorial Hospital	Effingham	94%	367
Trinity Rock Island[2]	Rock Island	94%	136
Decatur Memorial Hospital[2]	Decatur	93%	294
Graham Hospital Association	Canton	93%	71
Lake Forest Hospital	Lake Forest	93%	268
Rush Oak Park Hospital	Oak Park	93%	182
Saint Marys Hospital[2]	Decatur	93%	145
Swedish American Hospital[2]	Rockford	93%	287
Adventist Bolingbrook Hospital	Bolingbrook	92%	83
Iroquois Memorial Hospital	Watseka	92%	25
Morris Hospital & Healthcare Centers	Morris	92%	92

NOTE: Hospital profiles are in alphabetical order by state, then city, then hospital within the city; Rankings exclude hospitals with less than 25 cases except for patient surveys which excludes hospitals with less than 100 cases; (a) 100–299 cases; (1) The number of cases is too small to be sure how well a hospital is performing; (2) The hospital indicated that the data submitted for this measure were based on a sample of cases; (3) Data was collected during a shorter time period (fewer quarters) than the maximum possible time for this measure; (4) Suppressed for one or more quarters by CMS; (5) No data is available from the hospital for this measure; (6) Fewer than 100 patients completed the HCAHPS survey. Use these rates with caution, as the number of surveys may be too low to reliably assess hospital performance; (7) Survey results are based on less than 12 months of data; (8) Survey results are not available for this reporting period; (9) No or very few patients were eligible for the HCAHPS survey. The scores shown, if any, reflect a very small number of surveys; (10) A state average was not calculated because too few hospitals in the state submitted data; (11) There were discrepancies in the data collection process; Please refer to the User's Guide for a full explanation of data.

Hospital Name	City	Rate	Cases
Provena St Marys Hospital[2]	Kankakee	92%	134
Rockford Memorial Hospital	Rockford	92%	259
Saint Joseph Hospital[2]	Chicago	92%	152
Saint Joseph Medical Center	Bloomington	92%	172
Adventist Glenoaks	Glendale Hghts	91%	44
Kishwaukee Community Hospital	Dekalb	91%	138
Provena-Saint Joseph Hospital[2]	Elgin	91%	191
Saint Elizabeth Hospital[2]	Belleville	91%	180
Bromenn Healthcare[2]	Normal	89%	204
John H Stroger Jr Hospital[2]	Chicago	89%	204
McDonough District Hospital	Macomb	89%	46
Metrosouth Medical Center	Blue Island	89%	185
Saint James Hospital	Pontiac	89%	55
Saint Josephs Hospital	Breese	89%	53
Centegra Health Sys-Woodstock Hospital[2]	Woodstock	88%	162
Provena United Samaritans Med Ctr-Logan[2]	Danville	88%	139
Loyola Gottlieb Memorial Hospital[2]	Melrose Park	86%	194
Saint Johns Hospital[2]	Springfield	86%	161
Centegra Health System - McHenry Hospital[2]	Mchenry	85%	236
Provena Mercy Medical Center[2]	Aurora	85%	158
Swedish Covenant Hospital[2]	Chicago	84%	160
Riverside Medical Center[2]	Kankakee	83%	127
Saint Bernard Hospital	Chicago	83%	70
Provena Covenant Medical Center - Urbana[2]	Urbana	82%	180
Saint Joseph's Hospital	Highland	81%	27
Sacred Heart Hospital	Chicago	78%	40
Richland Memorial Hospital	Olney	77%	30
Passavant Area Hospital[2]	Jacksonville	76%	106
Gibson Community Hospital	Gibson City	73%	37
Perry Memorial Hospital	Princeton	73%	33
Valley West Community Hospital	Sandwich	73%	33
Saint Anthony Hospital	Chicago	72%	54
Touchette Regional Hospital	Centreville	66%	29
Norwegian-American Hospital	Chicago	51%	47
South Shore Hospital	Chicago	41%	49
Saint Francis Hospital	Litchfield	33%	39
Roseland Community Hospital	Chicago	15%	55
Jackson Park Hospital	Chicago	0%	30

32. Urinary Catheter Removal

Hospital Name	City	Rate	Cases
Hines VA Medical Center[2]	Hines	100%	138
Illinois Valley Community Hospital	Peru	100%	96
J Brown VA Med Ctr-VA Chicago Healthcare[2]	Chicago	100%	79
Katherine Shaw Bethea Hospital	Dixon	100%	31
Little Company of Mary Hospital[2]	Evergreen Park	100%	66
Saint James Hospital	Pontiac	100%	47
Saint Margarets Hospital	Spring Valley	100%	102
Saint Marys Hospital	Centralia	100%	45
Advocate South Suburban Hospital[2]	Hazel Crest	99%	69
Galesburg Cottage Hospital	Galesburg	99%	81
Gateway Regional Medical Center	Granite City	99%	69
Silver Cross Hospital[2]	Joliet	99%	167
Skokie Hospital[2]	Skokie	99%	150
Evanston Hospital[2]	Evanston	98%	260
Hinsdale Hospital[2]	Hinsdale	98%	80
Morris Hospital & Healthcare Centers	Morris	98%	100
Mount Sinai Hospital Medical Center[2]	Chicago	98%	43
Pekin Memorial Hospital	Pekin	98%	98
Advocate Good Shepherd Hospital[2]	Barrington	97%	137
Advocate Lutheran General Hospital[2]	Park Ridge	97%	116
Louis A Weiss Memorial Hospital[2]	Chicago	97%	117
Provena St Marys Hospital[2]	Kankakee	97%	119
Trinity Rock Island[2]	Rock Island	97%	62
Wabash General Hospital	Mount Carmel	97%	29
Advocate Illinois Masonic Medical Center[2]	Chicago	96%	106
Central Dupage Hospital[2]	Winfield	96%	100
Herrin Hospital	Herrin	96%	89
Macneal Hospital[2]	Berwyn	96%	190
Methodist Medical Center of Illinois[2]	Peoria	96%	233
Proctor Hospital[2]	Peoria	96%	291
Saint Anthonys Memorial Hospital	Effingham	96%	274
Carle Foundation Hospital[2]	Urbana	95%	106
Ingalls Memorial Hospital[2]	Harvey	95%	78
Loyola University Medical Center[2]	Maywood	95%	142
Provena St Joseph Medical Center[2]	Joliet	95%	124
Saint Anthony's Health Center	Alton	95%	93
Saint Mary Medical Center	Galesburg	95%	106
Copley Memorial Hospital[2]	Aurora	94%	249
Decatur Memorial Hospital[2]	Decatur	94%	238
Gibson Community Hospital	Gibson City	94%	47
Graham Hospital Association	Canton	94%	54
Lake Forest Hospital	Lake Forest	94%	248
Our Lady of the Resurrection Medical Center	Chicago	94%	47
Rush Oak Park Hospital	Oak Park	94%	124
Saint Marys Hospital[2]	Decatur	94%	48
Advocate Condell Medical Center[2]	Libertyville	93%	125
Centegra Health Sys-Woodstock Hospital[2]	Woodstock	93%	146
Kishwaukee Community Hospital	Dekalb	93%	90
Memorial Medical Center[2]	Springfield	93%	219
Saint Johns Hospital[2]	Springfield	93%	199
Saint Marys Hospital	Streator	93%	45
Vista Medical Center East	Waukegan	93%	101
Adventist Bolingbrook Hospital	Bolingbrook	92%	26
Anderson Hospital[2]	Maryville	92%	72
Loyola Gottlieb Memorial Hospital[2]	Melrose Park	92%	96
Ottawa Reg Hosp & Healthcare Ctr	Ottawa	92%	39
Riverside Medical Center[2]	Kankakee	92%	111
Saint Joseph Hospital[2]	Chicago	92%	38
West Suburban Medical Center[2]	Oak Park	92%	49
Advocate Good Samaritan Hospital[2]	Downers Grove	91%	82
Alexian Brothers Medical Center[2]	Elk Grove Vlg	91%	158
Crossroads Community Hospital	Mount Vernon	91%	35
Edward Hospital	Naperville	91%	555
Saint Alexius Medical Center[2]	Hoffman Estates	91%	94
Saint Joseph Medical Center	Bloomington	91%	163
University of Illinois Hospital[2]	Chicago	91%	85
Rush University Medical Center[2]	Chicago	89%	110
St Mary & Elizabeth Med Ctr-Div Campus[2]	Chicago	89%	54
Swedish American Hospital[2]	Rockford	89%	164
Memorial Hospital of Carbondale[2]	Carbondale	88%	246
Provena-Saint Joseph Hospital[2]	Elgin	88%	50
Advocate Trinity Hospital[2]	Chicago	87%	46
St James Hospital-Olympia Fields[2]	Olympia Fields	87%	70
Advocate Christ Hospital & Medical Center[2]	Oak Lawn	86%	111
Saint Francis Medical Center[2]	Peoria	86%	439
Bromenn Healthcare[2]	Normal	85%	81
CGH Medical Center[2]	Sterling	85%	117
Memorial Hospital[2]	Belleville	85%	146
Saint Anthony Medical Center[2]	Rockford	85%	97
Delnor Community Hospital[2]	Geneva	84%	50
Elmhurst Memorial Hospital[2]	Elmhurst	84%	99
Mercy Hospital and Medical Center	Chicago	84%	138
Metrosouth Medical Center	Blue Island	84%	128
Northwestern Memorial Hospital[2]	Chicago	84%	192
Adventist La Grange Memorial Hospital[2]	La Grange	83%	99
Alton Memorial Hospital	Alton	83%	109
Provena Covenant Medical Center - Urbana[2]	Urbana	83%	163
Northwest Community Hospital[2]	Arlington Hgts	82%	147
The University of Chicago Medical Center[2]	Chicago	82%	130
Good Samaritan Regional Health Center	Mount Vernon	81%	31
Heartland Regional Medical Center	Marion	81%	42
Resurrection Medical Center[2]	Chicago	81%	118
Palos Community Hospital[2]	Palos Heights	79%	84
Centegra Health System - McHenry Hospital[2]	Mchenry	74%	214
Saint Josephs Hospital	Breese	72%	25
Sarah Bush Lincoln Health Center	Mattoon	72%	75
Blessing Hospital	Quincy	70%	79
Provena Mercy Medical Center[2]	Aurora	70%	184
Rockford Memorial Hospital	Rockford	70%	127
Saint Elizabeth Hospital[2]	Belleville	70%	89
John H Stroger Jr Hospital[2]	Chicago	66%	47
Swedish Covenant Hospital[2]	Chicago	66%	82
Provena United Samaritans Med Ctr-Logan[2]	Danville	65%	26
RHC St Francis Hospital[2]	Evanston	63%	78
Holy Cross Hospital[2]	Chicago	39%	36

Children's Asthma Care

33. Received Systemic Corticosteroids

Hospital Name	City	Rate	Cases
The University of Chicago Medical Center[2]	Chicago	100%	239
Saint Johns Hospital	Springfield	99%	88
Loyola University Medical Center	Maywood	97%	38

34. Received Home Management Plan of Care

Hospital Name	City	Rate	Cases
Loyola University Medical Center	Maywood	81%	37
Saint Johns Hospital	Springfield	60%	88
The University of Chicago Medical Center[2]	Chicago	7%	239

35. Received Reliever Medication

Hospital Name	City	Rate	Cases
Loyola University Medical Center	Maywood	100%	38
Saint Johns Hospital	Springfield	100%	88
The University of Chicago Medical Center[2]	Chicago	100%	239

Use of Medical Imaging

36. Combination Abdominal CT Scan

Hospital Name	City	Ratio	Cases
Provident Hospital of Chicago	Chicago	0.000	70
Touchette Regional Hospital	Centreville	0.000	71
Carle Foundation Hospital	Urbana	0.009	233
Provena Covenant Medical Center - Urbana	Urbana	0.010	305
South Shore Hospital	Chicago	0.013	78
Holy Cross Hospital	Chicago	0.016	306
Loretto Hospital	Chicago	0.022	46
Passavant Area Hospital	Jacksonville	0.026	498
Saint Anthony Hospital	Chicago	0.028	106
Mercy Harvard Hospital	Harvard	0.033	92
Taylorville Memorial Hospital	Taylorville	0.034	357
Shelby Memorial Hospital	Shelbyville	0.037	161
Genesis Medical Center Illini Campus	Silvis	0.044	362
Decatur Memorial Hospital	Decatur	0.045	2382
Kishwaukee Community Hospital	Dekalb	0.046	457
Advocate Trinity Hospital	Chicago	0.049	389
Advocate Lutheran General Hospital	Park Ridge	0.058	2202
Palos Community Hospital	Palos Heights	0.059	1969
Swedish American Hospital	Rockford	0.059	1062
Trinity Rock Island	Rock Island	0.059	1113
Blessing Hospital	Quincy	0.061	526
Saint Marys Hospital	Decatur	0.062	513
Copley Memorial Hospital	Aurora	0.066	785
Saint Mary Medical Center	Galesburg	0.068	472
Norwegian-American Hospital	Chicago	0.072	181
Saint James Hospital	Pontiac	0.072	416
Fhn Memorial Hospital	Freeport	0.073	508
Metrosouth Medical Center	Blue Island	0.074	457
Jackson Park Hospital[1]	Chicago	0.075	53
Saint Anthony Medical Center	Rockford	0.076	1154
Sarah Bush Lincoln Health Center	Mattoon	0.076	828
The University of Chicago Medical Center	Chicago	0.076	3622
Mendota Community Hospital	Mendota	0.077	235
Illini Community Hospital	Pittsfield	0.080	188
Provena Mercy Medical Center	Aurora	0.080	388
Adventist Glenoaks	Glendale Hghts	0.081	124
Ingalls Memorial Hospital	Harvey	0.082	1471
Silver Cross Hospital	Joliet	0.082	672
Advocate Christ Hospital & Medical Center	Oak Lawn	0.087	1349
Memorial Hospital	Chester	0.090	211
Northwest Community Hospital	Arlington Hgts	0.090	3470
Morris Hospital & Healthcare Centers	Morris	0.092	649
Adventist La Grange Memorial Hospital	La Grange	0.093	873
Memorial Medical Center	Springfield	0.093	1873
Advocate South Suburban Hospital	Hazel Crest	0.094	732
Pekin Memorial Hospital	Pekin	0.094	682
Heartland Regional Medical Center	Marion	0.095	518
Rockford Memorial Hospital	Rockford	0.098	697
Adventist Bolingbrook Hospital	Bolingbrook	0.101	159
Abraham Lincoln Memorial Hospital	Lincoln	0.102	459
Memorial Hospital	Belleville	0.102	1377
Herrin Hospital	Herrin	0.107	1080
Louis A Weiss Memorial Hospital	Chicago	0.109	549
Memorial Hospital of Carbondale	Carbondale	0.112	721
Alton Memorial Hospital	Alton	0.114	888
Mercy Hospital and Medical Center	Chicago	0.118	619
Ottawa Reg Hosp & Healthcare Ctr	Ottawa	0.118	509
Advocate Illinois Masonic Medical Center	Chicago	0.122	641
Advocate Good Shepherd Hospital	Barrington	0.125	999
Little Company of Mary Hospital	Evergreen Park	0.125	977
Illinois Valley Community Hospital	Peru	0.126	405
Saint Joseph Hospital	Chicago	0.129	458
Swedish Covenant Hospital	Chicago	0.132	1085
Saint Margarets Hospital	Spring Valley	0.134	276
Saint Joseph Memorial Hospital	Murphysboro	0.136	396
Provena St Marys Hospital	Kankakee	0.137	510
Macneal Hospital	Berwyn	0.140	608
Rush University Medical Center	Chicago	0.140	328
Saint Francis Medical Center	Peoria	0.142	1625
Resurrection Medical Center	Chicago	0.144	1585
Mount Sinai Hospital Medical Center	Chicago	0.146	328
Elmhurst Memorial Hospital	Elmhurst	0.155	1591
Advocate Good Samaritan Hospital	Downers Grove	0.156	1183
Riverside Medical Center	Kankakee	0.165	901
Anderson Hospital	Maryville	0.197	656
Northwestern Memorial Hospital	Chicago	0.201	4159
St Mary & Elizabeth Med Ctr-Div Campus	Chicago	0.201	671
Saint Josephs Hospital	Breese	0.204	275
Union County Hospital	Anna	0.207	276
St James Hospital-Olympia Fields	Olympia Fields	0.208	711
Loyola University Medical Center	Maywood	0.214	2704
Gateway Regional Medical Center	Granite City	0.217	309
Westlake Community Hospital	Melrose Park	0.219	224
Methodist Medical Center of Illinois	Peoria	0.224	1116
West Suburban Medical Center	Oak Park	0.229	528
University of Illinois Hospital	Chicago	0.232	788
Evanston Hospital	Evanston	0.236	5038
Loyola Gottlieb Memorial Hospital	Melrose Park	0.237	603
Provena-Saint Joseph Hospital	Elgin	0.240	563
Hinsdale Hospital	Hinsdale	0.241	909
Sherman Hospital	Elgin	0.243	787
Red Bud Regional Hospital	Red Bud	0.250	204
Saint Anthony's Health Center	Alton	0.310	491
Hardin County General Hospital	Rosiclare	0.318	85
Central Dupage Hospital	Winfield	0.324	1480
CGH Medical Center	Sterling	0.337	600
Saint Alexius Medical Center	Hoffman Estates	0.337	962
Roseland Community Hospital	Chicago	0.350	60

NOTE: Hospital profiles are in alphabetical order by state, then city, then hospital within the city; Rankings exclude hospitals with less than 25 cases except for patient surveys which excludes hospitals with less than 100 cases; (a) 100–299 cases; (1) The number of cases is too small to be sure how well a hospital is performing; (2) The hospital indicated that the data submitted for this measure were based on a sample of cases; (3) Data was collected during a shorter time period (fewer quarters) than the maximum possible time for this measure; (4) Suppressed for one or more quarters by CMS; (5) No data is available from the hospital for this measure; (6) Fewer than 100 patients completed the HCAHPS survey. Use these rates with caution, as the number of surveys may be too low to reliably assess hospital performance; (7) Survey results are based on less than 12 months of data; (8) Survey results are not available for this reporting period; (9) No or very few patients were eligible for the HCAHPS survey. The scores shown, if any, reflect a very small number of surveys; (10) A state average was not calculated because too few hospitals in the state submitted data; (11) There were discrepancies in the data collection process; Please refer to the User's Guide for a full explanation of data.

Provena St Joseph Medical Center	Joliet	0.360	1073
RHC St Francis Hospital	Evanston	0.380	626
Advocate Condell Medical Center	Libertyville	0.397	1271
Our Lady of the Resurrection Medical Center	Chicago	0.399	501
Provena United Samaritans Med Ctr-Logan	Danville	0.411	474
Crossroads Community Hospital	Mount Vernon	0.413	208
Wabash General Hospital	Mount Carmel	0.420	212
Saint Johns Hospital	Springfield	0.460	755
Skokie Hospital	Skokie	0.464	317
Rush Oak Park Hospital	Oak Park	0.468	325
Saint Elizabeth Hospital	Belleville	0.484	826
Methodist Hospital of Chicago	Chicago	0.494	81
Iroquois Memorial Hospital	Watseka	0.495	218
Alexian Brothers Medical Center	Elk Grove Vlg	0.520	1701
Harrisburg Medical Center	Harrisburg	0.526	390
Jersey Community Hospital	Jerseyville	0.527	256
Fairfield Memorial Hospital	Fairfield	0.533	390
Delnor Community Hospital	Geneva	0.561	974
Saint Marys Hospital	Streator	0.566	274
Clay County Hospital	Flora	0.567	263
Vista Medical Center East	Waukegan	0.569	861
Katherine Shaw Bethea Hospital	Dixon	0.592	326
Saint Bernard Hospital	Chicago	0.607	112
Good Samaritan Regional Health Center	Mount Vernon	0.612	737
John H Stroger Jr Hospital	Chicago	0.631	740
Sacred Heart Hospital	Chicago	0.632	57
Proctor Hospital	Peoria	0.675	425
Bromenn Healthcare	Normal	0.682	446
Centegra Health System - McHenry Hospital	Mchenry	0.699	933
OSF Holy Family Medical Center	Monmouth	0.699	73
Richland Memorial Hospital	Olney	0.702	238
Galesburg Cottage Hospital	Galesburg	0.704	247
Centegra Health Sys-Woodstock Hospital	Woodstock	0.711	523
Edward Hospital	Naperville	0.715	1754
Graham Hospital Association	Canton	0.719	366
Saint Joseph Medical Center	Bloomington	0.722	324
Saint Marys Hospital	Centralia	0.728	691
McDonough District Hospital	Macomb	0.733	330
Lake Forest Hospital	Lake Forest	0.739	983
Saint Anthonys Memorial Hospital	Effingham	0.751	995
Greenville Regional Hospital	Greenville	0.773	375
Advocate Eureka Hospital	Eureka	0.806	124
Thorek Memorial Hospital	Chicago	0.834	181
Midwestern Region Medical Center	Zion	0.974	694

37. Combination Chest CT Scan

Hospital Name	City	Ratio	Cases
Carle Foundation Hospital	Urbana	0.000	171
Holy Cross Hospital	Chicago	0.000	218
Jackson Park Hospital[1]	Chicago	0.000	44
Loretto Hospital[1]	Chicago	0.000	25
Memorial Hospital	Chester	0.000	115
Metrosouth Medical Center	Blue Island	0.000	445
Midwestern Region Medical Center	Zion	0.000	760
Norwegian-American Hospital	Chicago	0.000	57
Provident Hospital of Chicago[1]	Chicago	0.000	42
Saint Bernard Hospital	Chicago	0.000	79
Sarah Bush Lincoln Health Center	Mattoon	0.000	612
Touchette Regional Hospital	Centreville	0.000	50
Union County Hospital	Anna	0.000	130
Westlake Community Hospital	Melrose Park	0.000	124
Northwestern Memorial Hospital	Chicago	0.001	4348
Saint Anthony Medical Center	Rockford	0.001	1032
The University of Chicago Medical Center	Chicago	0.001	4244
Blessing Hospital	Quincy	0.002	426
Swedish American Hospital	Rockford	0.002	1002
Fhn Memorial Hospital	Freeport	0.003	353
Rockford Memorial Hospital	Rockford	0.003	682
Taylorville Memorial Hospital	Taylorville	0.003	310
Decatur Memorial Hospital	Decatur	0.006	1876
Provena Covenant Medical Center - Urbana	Urbana	0.006	162
Rush Oak Park Hospital	Oak Park	0.006	177
Saint Anthonys Memorial Hospital	Effingham	0.006	642
Saint Joseph Hospital	Chicago	0.006	316
Adventist La Grange Memorial Hospital	La Grange	0.007	703
Passavant Area Hospital	Jacksonville	0.007	299
St Mary & Elizabeth Med Ctr-Div Campus	Chicago	0.007	151
Louis A Weiss Memorial Hospital	Chicago	0.008	475
Pekin Memorial Hospital	Pekin	0.008	532
Palos Community Hospital	Palos Heights	0.010	2265
Hinsdale Hospital	Hinsdale	0.011	704
Illinois Valley Community Hospital	Peru	0.011	285
Saint Marys Hospital	Decatur	0.011	369
Saint Mary Medical Center	Galesburg	0.012	343
Shelby Memorial Hospital	Shelbyville	0.012	86
Illini Community Hospital	Pittsfield	0.013	153
John H Stroger Jr Hospital	Chicago	0.013	78
Kishwaukee Community Hospital	Dekalb	0.013	311
Ingalls Memorial Hospital	Harvey	0.014	1451
Morris Hospital & Healthcare Centers	Morris	0.015	459
Anderson Hospital	Maryville	0.016	793
Loyola University Medical Center	Maywood	0.016	2392
Central Dupage Hospital	Winfield	0.017	1469
Memorial Medical Center	Springfield	0.017	1692
Saint Anthony Hospital	Chicago	0.017	60
Alton Memorial Hospital	Alton	0.018	509
Swedish Covenant Hospital	Chicago	0.018	786
Alexian Brothers Medical Center	Elk Grove Vlg	0.019	1477
Advocate Good Shepherd Hospital	Barrington	0.020	909
Heartland Regional Medical Center	Marion	0.021	282
Ottawa Reg Hosp & Healthcare Ctr	Ottawa	0.022	408
Little Company of Mary Hospital	Evergreen Park	0.023	887
Abraham Lincoln Memorial Hospital	Lincoln	0.025	315
Centegra Health Sys-Woodstock Hospital	Woodstock	0.025	317
Copley Memorial Hospital	Aurora	0.025	487
Northwest Community Hospital	Arlington Hgts	0.025	2628
Saint Francis Medical Center	Peoria	0.027	1262
Gateway Regional Medical Center	Granite City	0.029	205
Memorial Hospital of Carbondale	Carbondale	0.029	385
Mendota Community Hospital	Mendota	0.029	140
Clay County Hospital	Flora	0.032	218
Saint Margarets Hospital	Spring Valley	0.032	217
Advocate Illinois Masonic Medical Center	Chicago	0.034	528
Advocate Lutheran General Hospital	Park Ridge	0.036	1767
Methodist Medical Center of Illinois	Peoria	0.036	881
Provena St Marys Hospital	Kankakee	0.037	271
Advocate Christ Hospital & Medical Center	Oak Lawn	0.038	1483
Saint James Hospital	Pontiac	0.039	279
Evanston Hospital	Evanston	0.040	5565
Elmhurst Memorial Hospital	Elmhurst	0.041	1321
South Shore Hospital	Chicago	0.041	49
Fairfield Memorial Hospital	Fairfield	0.042	238
Provena Mercy Medical Center	Aurora	0.045	222
Centegra Health System - McHenry Hospital	Mchenry	0.046	659
Silver Cross Hospital	Joliet	0.048	681
University of Illinois Hospital	Chicago	0.048	794
Rush University Medical Center	Chicago	0.050	160
Mercy Harvard Hospital	Harvard	0.051	78
Saint Josephs Hospital	Breese	0.051	217
Advocate South Suburban Hospital	Hazel Crest	0.052	497
Adventist Glenoaks	Glendale Hghts	0.053	57
Advocate Trinity Hospital	Chicago	0.053	246
Memorial Hospital	Belleville	0.053	941
Trinity Rock Island	Rock Island	0.069	763
Mount Sinai Hospital Medical Center	Chicago	0.072	250
Saint Anthony's Health Center	Alton	0.072	207
Advocate Good Samaritan Hospital	Downers Grove	0.073	1155
Herrin Hospital	Herrin	0.074	679
Jersey Community Hospital	Jerseyville	0.078	90
Saint Joseph Memorial Hospital	Murphysboro	0.078	115
Mercy Hospital and Medical Center	Chicago	0.083	336
Resurrection Medical Center	Chicago	0.093	1079
Adventist Bolingbrook Hospital[1]	Bolingbrook	0.095	63
Genesis Medical Center Illini Campus	Silvis	0.100	261
St James Hospital-Olympia Fields	Olympia Fields	0.109	548
Macneal Hospital	Berwyn	0.125	506
Loyola Gottlieb Memorial Hospital	Melrose Park	0.135	325
Sherman Hospital	Elgin	0.147	620
Riverside Medical Center	Kankakee	0.169	485
Saint Johns Hospital	Springfield	0.169	813
Provena St Joseph Medical Center	Joliet	0.171	914
Provena United Samaritans Med Ctr-Logan	Danville	0.171	456
Saint Alexius Medical Center	Hoffman Estates	0.175	936
Good Samaritan Regional Health Center	Mount Vernon	0.187	422
Saint Marys Hospital	Centralia	0.195	430
Saint Elizabeth Hospital	Belleville	0.200	715
Roseland Community Hospital[1]	Chicago	0.211	38
McDonough District Hospital	Macomb	0.217	373
West Suburban Medical Center	Oak Park	0.233	352
Provena-Saint Joseph Hospital	Elgin	0.236	394
Our Lady of the Resurrection Medical Center	Chicago	0.272	334
Red Bud Regional Hospital	Red Bud	0.278	115
Thorek Memorial Hospital	Chicago	0.319	94
Methodist Hospital of Chicago	Chicago	0.329	73
RHC St Francis Hospital	Evanston	0.330	454
Advocate Condell Medical Center	Libertyville	0.338	932
CGH Medical Center	Sterling	0.341	384
Delnor Community Hospital	Geneva	0.357	770
Crossroads Community Hospital	Mount Vernon	0.375	96
Iroquois Memorial Hospital	Watseka	0.393	122
Wabash General Hospital	Mount Carmel	0.403	144
Richland Memorial Hospital	Olney	0.429	210
Bromenn Healthcare	Normal	0.476	590
Sacred Heart Hospital	Chicago	0.529	34
Proctor Hospital	Peoria	0.532	278
Katherine Shaw Bethea Hospital	Dixon	0.538	195
Vista Medical Center East	Waukegan	0.551	615
Saint Marys Hospital	Streator	0.560	234
Skokie Hospital	Skokie	0.593	204
Saint Joseph Medical Center	Bloomington	0.615	351
Harrisburg Medical Center	Harrisburg	0.654	301
Galesburg Cottage Hospital	Galesburg	0.677	229
Greenville Regional Hospital	Greenville	0.679	243
Lake Forest Hospital	Lake Forest	0.682	737
Advocate Eureka Hospital	Eureka	0.684	95
Edward Hospital	Naperville	0.698	1439
Graham Hospital Association	Canton	0.732	246
Hardin County General Hospital[1]	Rosiclare	0.743	35
OSF Holy Family Medical Center[1]	Monmouth	0.839	62

38. Follow-up Mammogram/Ultrasound

Hospital Name	City	Rate	Cases
Fairfield Memorial Hospital	Fairfield	0.5%	365
Graham Hospital Association	Canton	1.6%	500
Holy Cross Hospital	Chicago	1.9%	526
Alton Memorial Hospital	Alton	2.0%	1181
Richland Memorial Hospital	Olney	2.2%	224
South Shore Hospital	Chicago	2.2%	179
Roseland Community Hospital	Chicago	2.9%	68
Centegra Health Sys-Woodstock Hospital	Woodstock	3.4%	860
Saint Bernard Hospital	Chicago	3.6%	112
Midwestern Region Medical Center	Zion	3.9%	205
OSF Holy Family Medical Center	Monmouth	4.0%	300
University of Illinois Hospital	Chicago	4.1%	701
Mercy Hospital and Medical Center	Chicago	4.2%	1510
Saint Anthony Hospital	Chicago	4.3%	209
Vista Medical Center East	Waukegan	4.3%	1916
Central Dupage Hospital	Winfield	4.4%	2668
Evanston Hospital	Evanston	4.4%	9551
Advocate Eureka Hospital	Eureka	4.5%	222
Bromenn Healthcare	Normal	4.8%	1164
Galesburg Cottage Hospital	Galesburg	4.8%	705
Centegra Health System - McHenry Hospital	Mchenry	5.2%	1336
Harrisburg Medical Center	Harrisburg	5.3%	695
Passavant Area Hospital	Jacksonville	5.3%	1016
Saint Joseph Medical Center	Bloomington	5.3%	525
Mount Sinai Hospital Medical Center	Chicago	5.4%	411
Saint Marys Hospital	Streator	5.5%	860
Mercy Harvard Hospital	Harvard	5.6%	89
Provena St Joseph Medical Center	Joliet	5.6%	2201
St Mary & Elizabeth Med Ctr-Div Campus	Chicago	5.6%	481
Fhn Memorial Hospital	Freeport	5.8%	1016
Sarah Bush Lincoln Health Center	Mattoon	5.8%	1535
Illinois Valley Community Hospital	Peru	5.9%	746
The University of Chicago Medical Center	Chicago	6.0%	2377
Rush Oak Park Hospital	Oak Park	6.1%	890
Saint Marys Hospital	Decatur	6.1%	919
Advocate Lutheran General Hospital	Park Ridge	6.2%	3625
Saint Marys Hospital	Centralia	6.2%	728
Louis A Weiss Memorial Hospital	Chicago	6.3%	571
West Suburban Medical Center	Oak Park	6.3%	160
Herrin Hospital	Herrin	6.4%	1111
Clay County Hospital	Flora	6.5%	385
Gateway Regional Medical Center	Granite City	6.5%	525
Good Samaritan Regional Health Center	Mount Vernon	6.5%	910
McDonough District Hospital	Macomb	6.5%	642
Saint Mary Medical Center	Galesburg	6.6%	1323
Wabash General Hospital	Mount Carmel	6.6%	211
Illini Community Hospital	Pittsfield	6.7%	330
St James Hospital-Olympia Fields	Olympia Fields	6.7%	1319
Touchette Regional Hospital	Centreville	6.7%	223
Hardin County General Hospital	Rosiclare	6.8%	88
Sherman Hospital	Elgin	6.8%	1663
Saint Margarets Hospital	Spring Valley	6.9%	563
Loyola University Medical Center	Maywood	7.0%	2282
Morris Hospital & Healthcare Centers	Morris	7.0%	788
Blessing Hospital	Quincy	7.1%	1554
Jackson Park Hospital	Chicago	7.1%	99
Loyola Gottlieb Memorial Hospital	Melrose Park	7.1%	1288
Memorial Hospital of Carbondale	Carbondale	7.2%	1923
Memorial Medical Center	Springfield	7.2%	3066
Alexian Brothers Medical Center	Elk Grove Vlg	7.3%	2615
Copley Memorial Hospital	Aurora	7.3%	725
Saint Anthony's Health Center	Alton	7.3%	871
Swedish Covenant Hospital	Chicago	7.3%	1556
Taylorville Memorial Hospital	Taylorville	7.3%	641
Saint Joseph Hospital	Chicago	7.4%	1035
Mendota Community Hospital	Mendota	7.5%	334
Saint Josephs Hospital	Breese	7.5%	612
Abraham Lincoln Memorial Hospital	Lincoln	7.7%	427
Northwest Community Hospital	Arlington Hgts	7.7%	5143
Norwegian-American Hospital	Chicago	7.7%	287
Sacred Heart Hospital	Chicago	7.7%	195
Advocate Christ Hospital & Medical Center	Oak Lawn	7.8%	2229
Advocate Illinois Masonic Medical Center	Chicago	7.8%	982
Crossroads Community Hospital	Mount Vernon	7.9%	453
Kishwaukee Community Hospital	Dekalb	7.9%	508
Heartland Regional Medical Center	Marion	8.0%	425
Adventist Glenoaks	Glendale Hghts	8.1%	111
Saint Alexius Medical Center	Hoffman Estates	8.1%	1166
Skokie Hospital	Skokie	8.1%	2398

NOTE: Hospital profiles are in alphabetical order by state, then city, then hospital within the city; Rankings exclude hospitals with less than 25 cases except for patient surveys which excludes hospitals with less than 100 cases; (a) 100–299 cases; (1) The number of cases is too small to be sure how well a hospital is performing; (2) The hospital indicated that the data submitted for this measure were based on a sample of cases; (3) Data was collected during a shorter time period (fewer quarters) than the maximum possible time for this measure; (4) Suppressed for one or more quarters by CMS; (5) No data is available from the hospital for this measure; (6) Fewer than 100 patients completed the HCAHPS survey. Use these rates with caution, as the number of surveys may be too low to reliably assess hospital performance; (7) Survey results are based on less than 12 months of data; (8) Survey results are not available for this reporting period; (9) No or very few patients were eligible for the HCAHPS survey. The scores shown, if any, reflect a very small number of surveys; (10) A state average was not calculated because too few hospitals in the state submitted data; (11) There were discrepancies in the data collection process; Please refer to the User's Guide for a full explanation of data.

Hospital Name	City	Rate	Cases
Riverside Medical Center	Kankakee	8.2%	1741
Silver Cross Hospital	Joliet	8.3%	942
Northwestern Memorial Hospital	Chicago	8.4%	3743
Memorial Hospital	Chester	8.5%	235
Westlake Community Hospital	Melrose Park	8.5%	435
Ingalls Memorial Hospital	Harvey	8.6%	2589
Loretto Hospital[1]	Chicago	8.6%	58
Saint Anthony Medical Center	Rockford	8.7%	1381
Saint Francis Medical Center	Peoria	8.7%	4488
Swedish American Hospital	Rockford	8.7%	2740
Union County Hospital	Anna	8.7%	358
Proctor Hospital	Peoria	8.9%	440
Advocate Good Shepherd Hospital	Barrington	9.0%	1483
Provena St Marys Hospital	Kankakee	9.0%	679
Rush University Medical Center	Chicago	9.0%	2038
Saint Anthonys Memorial Hospital	Effingham	9.1%	1567
Decatur Memorial Hospital	Decatur	9.2%	3058
Jersey Community Hospital	Jerseyville	9.2%	346
Provena Covenant Medical Center - Urbana	Urbana	9.2%	338
Our Lady of the Resurrection Medical Center	Chicago	9.3%	924
Macneal Hospital	Berwyn	9.4%	1330
Advocate South Suburban Hospital	Hazel Crest	9.7%	1087
CGH Medical Center	Sterling	10.1%	503
Provena-Saint Joseph Hospital	Elgin	10.2%	768
Saint James Hospital	Pontiac	10.2%	783
Genesis Medical Center Illini Campus	Silvis	10.3%	847
Methodist Hospital of Chicago	Chicago	10.3%	116
Memorial Hospital	Belleville	10.4%	1803
Hinsdale Hospital	Hinsdale	10.6%	3031
Metrosouth Medical Center	Blue Island	10.7%	671
Trinity Rock Island	Rock Island	10.9%	2177
Palos Community Hospital	Palos Heights	11.2%	2785
Edward Hospital	Naperville	11.4%	2536
Advocate Good Samaritan Hospital	Downers Grove	11.6%	2270
Iroquois Memorial Hospital	Watseka	11.7%	409
Adventist Bolingbrook Hospital	Bolingbrook	11.8%	187
Little Company of Mary Hospital	Evergreen Park	11.9%	1729
Methodist Medical Center of Illinois	Peoria	12.0%	2032
Anderson Hospital	Maryville	12.2%	755
Adventist La Grange Memorial Hospital	La Grange	12.3%	1600
Delnor Community Hospital	Geneva	12.4%	1093
Saint Johns Hospital	Springfield	12.4%	1812
Advocate Trinity Hospital	Chicago	12.7%	880
Elmhurst Memorial Hospital	Elmhurst	13.0%	2231
RHC St Francis Hospital	Evanston	14.2%	1123
Advocate Condell Medical Center	Libertyville	14.5%	1460
Lake Forest Hospital	Lake Forest	14.9%	2527
Katherine Shaw Bethea Hospital	Dixon	15.1%	819
Resurrection Medical Center	Chicago	15.1%	2446
Pekin Memorial Hospital	Pekin	15.7%	739
Saint Elizabeth Hospital	Belleville	16.0%	1446
Red Bud Regional Hospital	Red Bud	16.2%	303
Provena Mercy Medical Center	Aurora	16.3%	443
Thorek Memorial Hospital	Chicago	17.9%	173
Provena United Samaritans Med Ctr-Logan	Danville	18.2%	335
Shelby Memorial Hospital	Shelbyville	19.0%	195
Ottawa Reg Hosp & Healthcare Ctr	Ottawa	21.0%	352

39. MRI for Low Back Pain

Hospital Name	City	Rate	Cases
Sacred Heart Hospital[1]	Chicago	15.0%	60
Saint Joseph Memorial Hospital[1]	Murphysboro	19.4%	31
Shelby Memorial Hospital[1]	Shelbyville	20.0%	25
Thorek Memorial Hospital[1]	Chicago	22.2%	36
Memorial Hospital[1]	Chester	22.6%	31
Saint Anthony Hospital[1]	Chicago	24.1%	29
Gateway Regional Medical Center	Granite City	24.5%	98
Pekin Memorial Hospital	Pekin	24.6%	118
Genesis Medical Center Illini Campus	Silvis	25.4%	71
Provena Covenant Medical Center - Urbana	Urbana	25.4%	59
Heartland Regional Medical Center	Marion	26.3%	80
Vista Medical Center East	Waukegan	26.6%	128
Louis A Weiss Memorial Hospital	Chicago	27.0%	126
Ottawa Reg Hosp & Healthcare Ctr	Ottawa	27.6%	127
Hinsdale Hospital	Hinsdale	27.7%	137
Provena St Joseph Medical Center	Joliet	27.9%	330
Katherine Shaw Bethea Hospital	Dixon	28.2%	117
Saint Joseph Medical Center	Bloomington	28.2%	103
Provena Mercy Medical Center	Aurora	28.3%	106
Saint Mary Medical Center	Galesburg	28.5%	123
Metrosouth Medical Center	Blue Island	28.8%	59
Blessing Hospital	Quincy	28.9%	121
Centegra Health Sys-Woodstock Hospital	Woodstock	28.9%	121
Loyola University Medical Center	Maywood	28.9%	377
Northwestern Memorial Hospital	Chicago	29.5%	774
Lake Forest Hospital	Lake Forest	29.6%	233
Our Lady of the Resurrection Medical Center	Chicago	29.7%	74
Saint James Hospital	Pontiac	29.7%	101
Rockford Memorial Hospital	Rockford	29.8%	248
Provena St Marys Hospital	Kankakee	30.4%	112
Delnor Community Hospital	Geneva	30.7%	140
Anderson Hospital	Maryville	30.9%	139
Holy Cross Hospital[1]	Chicago	31.0%	42
McDonough District Hospital	Macomb	31.0%	58
Northwest Community Hospital	Arlington Hgts	31.0%	575
Alexian Brothers Medical Center	Elk Grove Vlg	31.1%	235
Evanston Hospital	Evanston	31.1%	1226
Advocate Lutheran General Hospital	Park Ridge	31.2%	247
Methodist Medical Center of Illinois	Peoria	31.3%	310
Saint Margarets Hospital	Spring Valley	31.6%	76
Centegra Health System - McHenry Hospital	Mchenry	31.7%	249
Illinois Valley Community Hospital	Peru	31.8%	179
Illini Community Hospital[1]	Pittsfield	32.0%	25
Little Company of Mary Hospital	Evergreen Park	32.0%	103
CGH Medical Center	Sterling	32.1%	137
Adventist La Grange Memorial Hospital	La Grange	32.2%	143
Mendota Community Hospital[1]	Mendota	32.5%	40
University of Illinois Hospital	Chicago	32.5%	154
Advocate Good Samaritan Hospital	Downers Grove	32.7%	156
Edward Hospital	Naperville	32.8%	341
Memorial Hospital	Belleville	32.8%	268
Elmhurst Memorial Hospital	Elmhurst	32.9%	471
Morris Hospital & Healthcare Centers	Morris	32.9%	164
Riverside Medical Center	Kankakee	32.9%	426
Saint Anthony's Health Center	Alton	33.0%	88
Jersey Community Hospital	Jerseyville	33.3%	51
Saint Elizabeth Hospital	Belleville	33.3%	114
Fhn Memorial Hospital	Freeport	33.6%	143
Mercy Hospital and Medical Center	Chicago	33.6%	140
Ingalls Memorial Hospital	Harvey	33.7%	323
Swedish American Hospital	Rockford	33.7%	252
Memorial Medical Center	Springfield	33.8%	391
Saint Marys Hospital	Streator	33.8%	80
Saint Francis Medical Center	Peoria	34.0%	350
Provena-Saint Joseph Hospital	Elgin	34.3%	70
Sarah Bush Lincoln Health Center	Mattoon	34.3%	181
Central Dupage Hospital	Winfield	34.5%	220
Union County Hospital[1]	Anna	34.5%	29
Advocate Good Shepherd Hospital	Barrington	34.6%	104
Saint Alexius Medical Center	Hoffman Estates	34.6%	156
Advocate South Suburban Hospital	Hazel Crest	34.7%	95
Copley Memorial Hospital	Aurora	34.7%	95
Proctor Hospital	Peoria	34.7%	95
Saint Joseph Hospital	Chicago	34.9%	83
Advocate Condell Medical Center	Libertyville	35.0%	197
Bromenn Healthcare	Normal	35.0%	120
The University of Chicago Medical Center	Chicago	35.1%	285
Adventist Bolingbrook Hospital[1]	Bolingbrook	35.3%	34
Saint Marys Hospital	Decatur	35.3%	187
Silver Cross Hospital	Joliet	35.5%	211
Saint Anthonys Memorial Hospital	Effingham	35.6%	160
Saint Anthony Medical Center	Rockford	35.8%	193
Swedish Covenant Hospital	Chicago	35.9%	281
Sherman Hospital	Elgin	36.0%	100
Advocate Trinity Hospital	Chicago	36.5%	63
Loyola Gottlieb Memorial Hospital	Melrose Park	36.5%	189
St Mary & Elizabeth Med Ctr-Div Campus	Chicago	36.7%	109
Provena United Samaritans Med Ctr-Logan	Danville	37.0%	208
Resurrection Medical Center	Chicago	37.2%	352
Kishwaukee Community Hospital[1]	Dekalb	37.5%	40
West Suburban Medical Center	Oak Park	37.5%	64
Advocate Christ Hospital & Medical Center	Oak Lawn	37.6%	117
Saint Josephs Hospital	Breese	37.7%	53
Westlake Community Hospital[1]	Melrose Park	37.9%	29
Galesburg Cottage Hospital	Galesburg	38.1%	84
John H Stroger Jr Hospital[1]	Chicago	38.2%	34
St James Hospital-Olympia Fields	Olympia Fields	38.2%	123
Decatur Memorial Hospital	Decatur	38.3%	626
Crossroads Community Hospital[1]	Mount Vernon	38.5%	26
Advocate Illinois Masonic Medical Center	Chicago	39.2%	143
Saint Marys Hospital	Centralia	39.6%	106
Saint Johns Hospital	Springfield	40.0%	160
Passavant Area Hospital	Jacksonville	41.5%	135
Memorial Hospital of Carbondale	Carbondale	41.7%	127
Good Samaritan Regional Health Center	Mount Vernon	41.8%	122
Advocate Eureka Hospital[1]	Eureka	41.9%	31
RHC St Francis Hospital	Evanston	42.0%	69
Wabash General Hospital[1]	Mount Carmel	42.4%	33
OSF Holy Family Medical Center	Monmouth	42.6%	47
Herrin Hospital	Herrin	43.7%	167
Greenville Regional Hospital[1]	Greenville	44.8%	29
Fairfield Memorial Hospital	Fairfield	45.7%	35
Abraham Lincoln Memorial Hospital	Lincoln	47.8%	90
Iroquois Memorial Hospital	Watseka	48.5%	33
Graham Hospital Association	Canton	50.5%	95
Mount Sinai Hospital Medical Center[1]	Chicago	60.7%	28
Taylorville Memorial Hospital	Taylorville	66.3%	80

Survey of Patients' Hospital Experiences

40. Area Around Room 'Always' Quiet at Night

Hospital Name	City	Rate	Cases
Kewanee Hospital[11]	Kewanee	74%	(a)
Rochelle Community Hospital	Rochelle	73%	(a)
Valley West Community Hospital	Sandwich	73%	300+
Saint Josephs Hospital	Breese	69%	300+
Provident Hospital of Chicago	Chicago	68%	300+
Provena St Joseph Medical Center	Joliet	67%	300+
Adventist Bolingbrook Hospital	Bolingbrook	66%	300+
Provena United Samaritans Med Ctr-Logan	Danville	66%	300+
Gibson Community Hospital	Gibson City	65%	300+
Pinckneyville Community Hospital	Pinckneyville	65%	(a)
Provena-Saint Joseph Hospital	Elgin	65%	300+
Saint Francis Hospital	Litchfield	65%	300+
Abraham Lincoln Memorial Hospital	Lincoln	64%	(a)
Delnor Community Hospital	Geneva	64%	300+
Illini Community Hospital	Pittsfield	64%	(a)
Mercy Hospital and Medical Center	Chicago	64%	300+
Northwestern Memorial Hospital	Chicago	64%	300+
Richland Memorial Hospital	Olney	64%	300+
Touchette Regional Hospital	Centreville	64%	(a)
Jersey Community Hospital	Jerseyville	63%	300+
OSF Holy Family Medical Center	Monmouth	63%	(a)
Rush Oak Park Hospital	Oak Park	63%	300+
Saint Joseph Medical Center	Bloomington	63%	300+
Saint Joseph Memorial Hospital	Murphysboro	63%	(a)
Union County Hospital	Anna	63%	(a)
Adventist La Grange Memorial Hospital	La Grange	62%	300+
Edward Hospital	Naperville	62%	300+
Oak Forest Hospital	Oak Forest	62%	300+
Saint Marys Hospital	Centralia	62%	300+
Sherman Hospital	Elgin	62%	300+
Provena St Marys Hospital	Kankakee	61%	300+
Alton Memorial Hospital	Alton	60%	300+
Greenville Regional Hospital	Greenville	60%	(a)
Hammond Henry Hospital	Geneseo	60%	300+
Memorial Hospital of Carbondale	Carbondale	60%	300+
Methodist Medical Center of Illinois	Peoria	60%	300+
Midwestern Region Medical Center	Zion	60%	300+
Provena Covenant Medical Center - Urbana	Urbana	60%	300+
Salem Township Hospital	Salem	60%	(a)
West Suburban Medical Center	Oak Park	60%	300+
Saint Joseph's Hospital	Highland	59%	(a)
Saint Marys Hospital	Decatur	59%	300+
Advocate Trinity Hospital	Chicago	58%	300+
Bromenn Healthcare	Normal	58%	300+
Illinois Valley Community Hospital	Peru	58%	300+
Saint Bernard Hospital	Chicago	58%	300+
St Mary & Elizabeth Med Ctr-Div Campus	Chicago	58%	300+
Carlinville Area Hospital	Carlinville	57%	(a)
Evanston Hospital	Evanston	57%	300+
Louis A Weiss Memorial Hospital	Chicago	57%	300+
Mendota Community Hospital	Mendota	57%	300+
Morris Hospital & Healthcare Centers	Morris	57%	300+
Provena Mercy Medical Center	Aurora	57%	300+
Red Bud Regional Hospital	Red Bud	57%	(a)
Roseland Community Hospital	Chicago	57%	300+
Sacred Heart Hospital	Chicago	57%	300+
Saint Mary Medical Center	Galesburg	57%	300+
Crawford Memorial Hospital	Robinson	56%	(a)
Decatur Memorial Hospital	Decatur	56%	300+
Galesburg Cottage Hospital	Galesburg	56%	300+
McDonough District Hospital	Macomb	56%	300+
Memorial Hospital	Belleville	56%	300+
Proctor Hospital	Peoria	56%	300+
Saint Marys Hospital	Streator	56%	300+
Sarah Bush Lincoln Health Center	Mattoon	56%	300+
Silver Cross Hospital	Joliet	56%	300+
South Shore Hospital	Chicago	56%	300+
CGH Medical Center	Sterling	55%	300+
Harrisburg Medical Center	Harrisburg	55%	300+
John H Stroger Jr Hospital	Chicago	55%	300+
Katherine Shaw Bethea Hospital	Dixon	55%	300+
Kishwaukee Community Hospital	Dekalb	55%	300+
Passavant Area Hospital	Jacksonville	55%	300+
Rockford Memorial Hospital	Rockford	55%	300+
Swedish American Hospital	Rockford	55%	300+
University of Illinois Hospital	Chicago	55%	300+
Westlake Community Hospital[11]	Melrose Park	55%	300+
Advocate Lutheran General Hospital	Park Ridge	54%	300+
Fhn Memorial Hospital	Freeport	54%	300+
Gateway Regional Medical Center	Granite City	54%	300+
Genesis Medical Center Illini Campus	Silvis	54%	300+
Iroquois Memorial Hospital	Watseka	54%	300+
Saint Anthony's Health Center	Alton	54%	300+
Saint Johns Hospital	Springfield	54%	300+
Alexian Brothers Medical Center	Elk Grove Vlg	53%	300+
Hillsboro Area Hospital	Hillsboro	53%	(a)
Loyola University Medical Center	Maywood	53%	300+

NOTE: Hospital profiles are in alphabetical order by state, then city, then hospital within the city; Rankings exclude hospitals with less than 25 cases except for patient surveys which excludes hospitals with less than 100 cases; (a) 100–299 cases; (1) The number of cases is too small to be sure how well a hospital is performing; (2) The hospital indicated that the data submitted for this measure were based on a sample of cases; (3) Data was collected during a shorter time period (fewer quarters) than the maximum possible time for this measure; (4) Suppressed for one or more quarters by CMS; (5) No data is available from the hospital for this measure; (6) Fewer than 100 patients completed the HCAHPS survey. Use these rates with caution, as the number of surveys may be too low to reliably assess hospital performance; (7) Survey results are based on less than 12 months of data; (8) Survey results are not available for this reporting period; (9) No or very few patients were eligible for the HCAHPS survey. The scores shown, if any, reflect a very small number of surveys; (10) A state average was not calculated because too few hospitals in the state submitted data; (11) There were discrepancies in the data collection process; Please refer to the User's Guide for a full explanation of data.

Hospital Name	City	Rate	Cases
Rush University Medical Center	Chicago	53%	300+
Saint Anthonys Memorial Hospital	Effingham	53%	300+
Saint James Hospital	Pontiac	53%	300+
Saint Margarets Hospital	Spring Valley	53%	300+
Advocate South Suburban Hospital	Hazel Crest	52%	300+
Copley Memorial Hospital	Aurora	52%	300+
Crossroads Community Hospital	Mount Vernon	52%	300+
Heartland Regional Medical Center	Marion	52%	300+
Lake Forest Hospital	Lake Forest	52%	300+
Methodist Hospital of Chicago	Chicago	52%	(a)
Ottawa Reg Hosp & Healthcare Ctr	Ottawa	52%	300+
Saint Elizabeth Hospital	Belleville	52%	300+
Saint Joseph Hospital	Chicago	52%	300+
Thorek Memorial Hospital	Chicago	52%	300+
Adventist Glenoaks	Glendale Hghts	51%	300+
Anderson Hospital	Maryville	51%	300+
Central Dupage Hospital	Winfield	51%	300+
Ingalls Memorial Hospital	Harvey	51%	300+
Little Company of Mary Hospital	Evergreen Park	51%	300+
Metrosouth Medical Center	Blue Island	51%	300+
Riverside Medical Center	Kankakee	51%	300+
Advocate Good Samaritan Hospital	Downers Grove	50%	300+
Carle Foundation Hospital	Urbana	50%	300+
Good Samaritan Regional Health Center	Mount Vernon	50%	300+
Macneal Hospital	Berwyn	50%	300+
Pekin Memorial Hospital	Pekin	50%	300+
Shelby Memorial Hospital	Shelbyville	50%	(a)
Trinity Rock Island	Rock Island	50%	300+
Advocate Christ Hospital & Medical Center	Oak Lawn	49%	300+
Advocate Illinois Masonic Medical Center	Chicago	49%	300+
Elmhurst Memorial Hospital	Elmhurst	49%	300+
Graham Hospital Association	Canton	49%	300+
Hinsdale Hospital	Hinsdale	49%	300+
Holy Cross Hospital	Chicago	49%	300+
Loyola Gottlieb Memorial Hospital	Melrose Park	49%	300+
Mount Sinai Hospital Medical Center	Chicago	49%	300+
Saint Francis Medical Center	Peoria	49%	300+
St James Hospital-Olympia Fields	Olympia Fields	49%	300+
Herrin Hospital	Herrin	48%	300+
Jackson Park Hospital	Chicago	48%	300+
Loretto Hospital	Chicago	48%	(a)
Skokie Hospital	Skokie	48%	300+
The University of Chicago Medical Center	Chicago	48%	300+
Vista Medical Center East	Waukegan	48%	300+
Advocate Condell Medical Center	Libertyville	45%	300+
Blessing Hospital	Quincy	45%	300+
Centegra Health Sys-Woodstock Hospital	Woodstock	45%	300+
Saint Anthony Medical Center	Rockford	45%	300+
Taylorville Memorial Hospital	Taylorville	45%	300+
Advocate Good Shepherd Hospital	Barrington	44%	300+
Saint Anthony Hospital	Chicago	44%	300+
Memorial Medical Center	Springfield	43%	300+
Palos Community Hospital	Palos Heights	43%	300+
Our Lady of the Resurrection Medical Center	Chicago	42%	300+
RHC St Francis Hospital	Evanston	42%	300+
Saint Alexius Medical Center	Hoffman Estates	42%	300+
Centegra Health System - McHenry Hospital	Mchenry	41%	300+
Swedish Covenant Hospital	Chicago	41%	300+
Norwegian-American Hospital	Chicago	40%	300+
Resurrection Medical Center	Chicago	40%	300+
Northwest Community Hospital	Arlington Hgts	39%	300+

41. Doctors 'Always' Communicated Well

Hospital Name	City	Rate	Cases
Abraham Lincoln Memorial Hospital	Lincoln	91%	(a)
Illinois Valley Community Hospital	Peru	88%	300+
Pinckneyville Community Hospital	Pinckneyville	88%	(a)
Salem Township Hospital	Salem	88%	(a)
Hammond Henry Hospital	Geneseo	87%	300+
Crawford Memorial Hospital	Robinson	86%	(a)
Gibson Community Hospital	Gibson City	86%	300+
Mendota Community Hospital	Mendota	86%	300+
Saint Josephs Hospital	Breese	86%	300+
Saint Margarets Hospital	Spring Valley	86%	300+
Carlinville Area Hospital	Carlinville	85%	(a)
Herrin Hospital	Herrin	85%	300+
Illini Community Hospital	Pittsfield	85%	(a)
Midwestern Region Medical Center	Zion	85%	300+
Morris Hospital & Healthcare Centers	Morris	85%	300+
Provena United Samaritans Med Ctr-Logan	Danville	85%	300+
Richland Memorial Hospital	Olney	85%	300+
Sarah Bush Lincoln Health Center	Mattoon	85%	300+
Union County Hospital	Anna	85%	(a)
Valley West Community Hospital	Sandwich	85%	300+
Alton Memorial Hospital	Alton	84%	300+
Galesburg Cottage Hospital	Galesburg	84%	300+
Graham Hospital Association	Canton	84%	300+
Kewanee Hospital[11]	Kewanee	84%	(a)
McDonough District Hospital	Macomb	84%	300+
Red Bud Regional Hospital	Red Bud	84%	(a)
Saint James Hospital	Pontiac	84%	300+
Saint Joseph's Hospital	Highland	84%	(a)
Taylorville Memorial Hospital	Taylorville	84%	300+
Katherine Shaw Bethea Hospital	Dixon	83%	300+
Saint Francis Hospital	Litchfield	83%	300+
Saint Joseph Medical Center	Bloomington	83%	300+
Saint Mary Medical Center	Galesburg	83%	300+
Crossroads Community Hospital	Mount Vernon	82%	300+
Edward Hospital	Naperville	82%	300+
Rochelle Community Hospital	Rochelle	82%	(a)
Saint Marys Hospital	Centralia	82%	300+
Westlake Community Hospital[11]	Melrose Park	82%	300+
Bromenn Healthcare	Normal	81%	300+
Carle Foundation Hospital	Urbana	81%	300+
Delnor Community Hospital	Geneva	81%	300+
Elmhurst Memorial Hospital	Elmhurst	81%	300+
Jersey Community Hospital	Jerseyville	81%	300+
Kishwaukee Community Hospital	Dekalb	81%	300+
Lake Forest Hospital	Lake Forest	81%	300+
Pekin Memorial Hospital	Pekin	81%	300+
Saint Joseph Memorial Hospital	Murphysboro	81%	(a)
Saint Marys Hospital	Streator	81%	300+
University of Illinois Hospital	Chicago	81%	300+
Advocate Good Samaritan Hospital	Downers Grove	80%	300+
Alexian Brothers Medical Center	Elk Grove Vlg	80%	300+
Anderson Hospital	Maryville	80%	300+
Central Dupage Hospital	Winfield	80%	300+
CGH Medical Center	Sterling	80%	300+
Genesis Medical Center Illini Campus	Silvis	80%	300+
Harrisburg Medical Center	Harrisburg	80%	300+
Macneal Hospital	Berwyn	80%	300+
Memorial Hospital of Carbondale	Carbondale	80%	300+
Mercy Hospital and Medical Center	Chicago	80%	300+
Methodist Medical Center of Illinois	Peoria	80%	300+
Palos Community Hospital	Palos Heights	80%	300+
Passavant Area Hospital	Jacksonville	80%	300+
Provena St Marys Hospital	Kankakee	80%	300+
Provident Hospital of Chicago	Chicago	80%	300+
Saint Anthonys Memorial Hospital	Effingham	80%	300+
Shelby Memorial Hospital	Shelbyville	80%	(a)
Touchette Regional Hospital	Centreville	80%	(a)
West Suburban Medical Center	Oak Park	80%	300+
Copley Memorial Hospital	Aurora	79%	300+
Gateway Regional Medical Center	Granite City	79%	300+
John H Stroger Jr Hospital	Chicago	79%	300+
Little Company of Mary Hospital	Evergreen Park	79%	300+
Loyola Gottlieb Memorial Hospital	Melrose Park	79%	300+
Proctor Hospital	Peoria	79%	300+
Provena Covenant Medical Center - Urbana	Urbana	79%	300+
Rush Oak Park Hospital	Oak Park	79%	300+
Saint Alexius Medical Center	Hoffman Estates	79%	300+
Saint Johns Hospital	Springfield	79%	300+
The University of Chicago Medical Center	Chicago	79%	300+
Adventist La Grange Memorial Hospital	La Grange	78%	300+
Advocate Good Shepherd Hospital	Barrington	78%	300+
Advocate Lutheran General Hospital	Park Ridge	78%	300+
Advocate South Suburban Hospital	Hazel Crest	78%	300+
Blessing Hospital	Quincy	78%	300+
Centegra Health Sys-Woodstock Hospital	Woodstock	78%	300+
Decatur Memorial Hospital	Decatur	78%	300+
Good Samaritan Regional Health Center	Mount Vernon	78%	300+
Hillsboro Area Hospital	Hillsboro	78%	(a)
Iroquois Memorial Hospital	Watseka	78%	300+
Memorial Hospital	Belleville	78%	300+
Memorial Medical Center	Springfield	78%	300+
Metrosouth Medical Center	Blue Island	78%	300+
Oak Forest Hospital	Oak Forest	78%	300+
Ottawa Reg Hosp & Healthcare Ctr	Ottawa	78%	300+
Riverside Medical Center	Kankakee	78%	300+
Saint Anthony's Health Center	Alton	78%	300+
Saint Francis Medical Center	Peoria	78%	300+
Saint Joseph Hospital	Chicago	78%	300+
Silver Cross Hospital	Joliet	78%	300+
Trinity Rock Island	Rock Island	78%	300+
Advocate Christ Hospital & Medical Center	Oak Lawn	77%	300+
Advocate Illinois Masonic Medical Center	Chicago	77%	300+
Centegra Health System - McHenry Hospital	Mchenry	77%	300+
Evanston Hospital	Evanston	77%	300+
Louis A Weiss Memorial Hospital	Chicago	77%	300+
Loyola University Medical Center	Maywood	77%	300+
Northwestern Memorial Hospital	Chicago	77%	300+
OSF Holy Family Medical Center	Monmouth	77%	(a)
Provena Mercy Medical Center	Aurora	77%	300+
Provena St Joseph Medical Center	Joliet	77%	300+
Provena-Saint Joseph Hospital	Elgin	77%	300+
Saint Anthony Hospital	Chicago	77%	300+
Saint Elizabeth Hospital	Belleville	77%	300+
St Mary & Elizabeth Med Ctr-Div Campus	Chicago	77%	300+
Saint Marys Hospital	Decatur	77%	300+
Swedish American Hospital	Rockford	77%	300+
Fhn Memorial Hospital	Freeport	76%	300+
Hinsdale Hospital	Hinsdale	76%	300+
Rush University Medical Center	Chicago	76%	300+
Sacred Heart Hospital	Chicago	76%	300+
Saint Anthony Medical Center	Rockford	76%	300+
Adventist Bolingbrook Hospital	Bolingbrook	75%	300+
Heartland Regional Medical Center	Marion	75%	300+
Ingalls Memorial Hospital	Harvey	75%	300+
Resurrection Medical Center	Chicago	75%	300+
Roseland Community Hospital	Chicago	75%	300+
St James Hospital-Olympia Fields	Olympia Fields	75%	300+
Vista Medical Center East	Waukegan	75%	300+
Advocate Condell Medical Center	Libertyville	74%	300+
Advocate Trinity Hospital	Chicago	74%	300+
Greenville Regional Hospital	Greenville	74%	(a)
Mount Sinai Hospital Medical Center	Chicago	74%	300+
Rockford Memorial Hospital	Rockford	74%	300+
Sherman Hospital	Elgin	74%	300+
Skokie Hospital	Skokie	74%	300+
Swedish Covenant Hospital	Chicago	74%	300+
Adventist Glenoaks	Glendale Hghts	73%	300+
RHC St Francis Hospital	Evanston	73%	300+
Methodist Hospital of Chicago	Chicago	72%	(a)
Our Lady of the Resurrection Medical Center	Chicago	72%	300+
Northwest Community Hospital	Arlington Hgts	71%	300+
Thorek Memorial Hospital	Chicago	71%	300+
Saint Bernard Hospital	Chicago	70%	300+
South Shore Hospital	Chicago	70%	300+
Loretto Hospital	Chicago	69%	(a)
Holy Cross Hospital	Chicago	68%	300+
Jackson Park Hospital	Chicago	68%	300+
Norwegian-American Hospital	Chicago	66%	300+

42. Home Recovery Information Given

Hospital Name	City	Rate	Cases
Pinckneyville Community Hospital	Pinckneyville	95%	(a)
Gibson Community Hospital	Gibson City	91%	300+
Midwestern Region Medical Center	Zion	91%	300+
McDonough District Hospital	Macomb	90%	300+
Saint James Hospital	Pontiac	90%	300+
Abraham Lincoln Memorial Hospital	Lincoln	89%	(a)
Central Dupage Hospital	Winfield	89%	300+
Crawford Memorial Hospital	Robinson	89%	(a)
Saint Mary Medical Center	Galesburg	89%	300+
Sarah Bush Lincoln Health Center	Mattoon	89%	300+
Bromenn Healthcare	Normal	88%	300+
Illinois Valley Community Hospital	Peru	88%	300+
Carlinville Area Hospital	Carlinville	87%	(a)
Centegra Health Sys-Woodstock Hospital	Woodstock	87%	300+
Herrin Hospital	Herrin	87%	300+
Illini Community Hospital	Pittsfield	87%	(a)
Mendota Community Hospital	Mendota	87%	300+
OSF Holy Family Medical Center	Monmouth	87%	(a)
Proctor Hospital	Peoria	87%	300+
Provena United Samaritans Med Ctr-Logan	Danville	87%	300+
Provena-Saint Joseph Hospital	Elgin	87%	300+
Richland Memorial Hospital	Olney	87%	300+
Rochelle Community Hospital	Rochelle	87%	(a)
Saint Marys Hospital	Centralia	87%	300+
Blessing Hospital	Quincy	86%	300+
Centegra Health System - McHenry Hospital	Mchenry	86%	300+
Decatur Memorial Hospital	Decatur	86%	300+
Delnor Community Hospital	Geneva	86%	300+
Good Samaritan Regional Health Center	Mount Vernon	86%	300+
Katherine Shaw Bethea Hospital	Dixon	86%	300+
Memorial Hospital of Carbondale	Carbondale	86%	300+
Methodist Medical Center of Illinois	Peoria	86%	300+
Morris Hospital & Healthcare Centers	Morris	86%	300+
Saint Joseph Memorial Hospital	Murphysboro	86%	(a)
Trinity Rock Island	Rock Island	86%	300+
Adventist La Grange Memorial Hospital	La Grange	85%	300+
Advocate Lutheran General Hospital	Park Ridge	85%	300+
Galesburg Cottage Hospital	Galesburg	85%	300+
Ottawa Reg Hosp & Healthcare Ctr	Ottawa	85%	300+
Saint Joseph's Hospital	Highland	85%	(a)
Saint Josephs Hospital	Breese	85%	300+
Saint Margarets Hospital	Spring Valley	85%	300+
Saint Marys Hospital	Streator	85%	300+
Advocate Christ Hospital & Medical Center	Oak Lawn	84%	300+
Alton Memorial Hospital	Alton	84%	300+
CGH Medical Center	Sterling	84%	300+
Crossroads Community Hospital	Mount Vernon	84%	300+
Edward Hospital	Naperville	84%	300+
Genesis Medical Center Illini Campus	Silvis	84%	300+
Passavant Area Hospital	Jacksonville	84%	300+
Pekin Memorial Hospital	Pekin	84%	300+
Provena Covenant Medical Center - Urbana	Urbana	84%	300+
Provena Mercy Medical Center	Aurora	84%	300+
Provena St Joseph Medical Center	Joliet	84%	300+
Provena St Marys Hospital	Kankakee	84%	300+
Red Bud Regional Hospital	Red Bud	84%	(a)

NOTE: Hospital profiles are in alphabetical order by state, then city, then hospital within the city; Rankings exclude hospitals with less than 25 cases except for patient surveys which excludes hospitals with less than 100 cases; (a) 100–299 cases; (1) The number of cases is too small to be sure how well a hospital is performing; (2) The hospital indicated that the data submitted for this measure were based on a sample of cases; (3) Data was collected during a shorter time period (fewer quarters) than the maximum possible time for this measure; (4) Suppressed for one or more quarters by CMS; (5) No data is available from the hospital for this measure; (6) Fewer than 100 patients completed the HCAHPS survey. Use these rates with caution, as the number of surveys may be too low to reliably assess hospital performance; (7) Survey results are based on less than 12 months of data; (8) Survey results are not available for this reporting period; (9) No or very few patients were eligible for the HCAHPS survey. The scores shown, if any, reflect a very small number of surveys; (10) A state average was not calculated because too few hospitals in the state submitted data; (11) There were discrepancies in the data collection process; Please refer to the User's Guide for a full explanation of data.

Saint Anthony's Health Center	Alton	84%	300+
Advocate Good Samaritan Hospital	Downers Grove	83%	300+
Advocate Good Shepherd Hospital	Barrington	83%	300+
Alexian Brothers Medical Center	Elk Grove Vlg	83%	300+
Carle Foundation Hospital	Urbana	83%	300+
Elmhurst Memorial Hospital	Elmhurst	83%	300+
Graham Hospital Association	Canton	83%	300+
Greenville Regional Hospital	Greenville	83%	(a)
Hammond Henry Hospital	Geneseo	83%	300+
Hinsdale Hospital	Hinsdale	83%	300+
Iroquois Memorial Hospital	Watseka	83%	300+
Lake Forest Hospital	Lake Forest	83%	300+
Riverside Medical Center	Kankakee	83%	300+
Rush University Medical Center	Chicago	83%	300+
Saint Francis Medical Center	Peoria	83%	300+
Saint Joseph Medical Center	Bloomington	83%	300+
Salem Township Hospital	Salem	83%	(a)
West Suburban Medical Center	Oak Park	83%	300+
Adventist Bolingbrook Hospital	Bolingbrook	82%	300+
Copley Memorial Hospital	Aurora	82%	300+
Kewanee Hospital[11]	Kewanee	82%	(a)
Loyola University Medical Center	Maywood	82%	300+
Saint Anthony Medical Center	Rockford	82%	300+
Sherman Hospital	Elgin	82%	300+
Anderson Hospital	Maryville	81%	300+
Evanston Hospital	Evanston	81%	300+
Hillsboro Area Hospital	Hillsboro	81%	(a)
Kishwaukee Community Hospital	Dekalb	81%	300+
Macneal Hospital	Berwyn	81%	300+
Palos Community Hospital	Palos Heights	81%	300+
Rockford Memorial Hospital	Rockford	81%	300+
Saint Alexius Medical Center	Hoffman Estates	81%	300+
Saint Anthonys Memorial Hospital	Effingham	81%	300+
Saint Elizabeth Hospital	Belleville	81%	300+
Saint Francis Hospital	Litchfield	81%	300+
Saint Johns Hospital	Springfield	81%	300+
Saint Joseph Hospital	Chicago	81%	300+
Saint Marys Hospital	Decatur	81%	300+
Swedish American Hospital	Rockford	81%	300+
University of Illinois Hospital	Chicago	81%	300+
Valley West Community Hospital	Sandwich	81%	300+
Adventist Glenoaks	Glendale Hghts	80%	300+
Advocate Illinois Masonic Medical Center	Chicago	80%	300+
Fhn Memorial Hospital	Freeport	80%	300+
Heartland Regional Medical Center	Marion	80%	300+
Memorial Hospital	Belleville	80%	300+
Memorial Medical Center	Springfield	80%	300+
Swedish Covenant Hospital	Chicago	80%	300+
The University of Chicago Medical Center	Chicago	80%	300+
Advocate South Suburban Hospital	Hazel Crest	79%	300+
Jersey Community Hospital	Jerseyville	79%	300+
Little Company of Mary Hospital	Evergreen Park	79%	300+
Mercy Hospital and Medical Center	Chicago	79%	300+
Our Lady of the Resurrection Medical Center	Chicago	79%	300+
Resurrection Medical Center	Chicago	79%	300+
RHC St Francis Hospital	Evanston	79%	300+
Westlake Community Hospital[11]	Melrose Park	79%	300+
Harrisburg Medical Center	Harrisburg	78%	300+
St Mary & Elizabeth Med Ctr-Div Campus	Chicago	78%	300+
Silver Cross Hospital	Joliet	78%	300+
Gateway Regional Medical Center	Granite City	77%	300+
Loyola Gottlieb Memorial Hospital	Melrose Park	77%	300+
Northwest Community Hospital	Arlington Hgts	77%	300+
Northwestern Memorial Hospital	Chicago	77%	300+
Oak Forest Hospital	Oak Forest	77%	300+
Touchette Regional Hospital	Centreville	77%	(a)
Union County Hospital	Anna	77%	(a)
Advocate Condell Medical Center	Libertyville	76%	300+
Ingalls Memorial Hospital	Harvey	76%	300+
Mount Sinai Hospital Medical Center	Chicago	76%	300+
Provident Hospital of Chicago	Chicago	76%	300+
Taylorville Memorial Hospital	Taylorville	76%	300+
Louis A Weiss Memorial Hospital	Chicago	75%	300+
Rush Oak Park Hospital	Oak Park	75%	300+
St James Hospital-Olympia Fields	Olympia Fields	75%	300+
Thorek Memorial Hospital	Chicago	75%	300+
John H Stroger Jr Hospital	Chicago	74%	300+
Shelby Memorial Hospital	Shelbyville	74%	(a)
Vista Medical Center East	Waukegan	74%	300+
Saint Anthony Hospital	Chicago	73%	300+
Skokie Hospital	Skokie	73%	300+
Saint Bernard Hospital	Chicago	72%	300+
Methodist Hospital of Chicago	Chicago	71%	(a)
Metrosouth Medical Center	Blue Island	71%	300+
Holy Cross Hospital	Chicago	70%	300+
Norwegian-American Hospital	Chicago	70%	300+
Sacred Heart Hospital	Chicago	70%	300+
Advocate Trinity Hospital	Chicago	69%	300+
Roseland Community Hospital	Chicago	66%	300+
Jackson Park Hospital	Chicago	61%	300+
Loretto Hospital	Chicago	58%	(a)
South Shore Hospital	Chicago	56%	300+

43. Hospital Given 9 or 10 on 10 Point Scale

Hospital Name	City	Rate	Cases
Midwestern Region Medical Center	Zion	86%	300+
Gibson Community Hospital	Gibson City	83%	300+
Rochelle Community Hospital	Rochelle	82%	(a)
Saint Josephs Hospital	Breese	81%	300+
Central Dupage Hospital	Winfield	79%	300+
Hammond Henry Hospital	Geneseo	78%	300+
Morris Hospital & Healthcare Centers	Morris	78%	300+
Illini Community Hospital	Pittsfield	77%	(a)
Methodist Medical Center of Illinois	Peoria	77%	300+
Northwestern Memorial Hospital	Chicago	77%	300+
Saint Marys Hospital	Centralia	77%	300+
Carlinville Area Hospital	Carlinville	76%	(a)
Carle Foundation Hospital	Urbana	75%	300+
Delnor Community Hospital	Geneva	75%	300+
Illinois Valley Community Hospital	Peru	75%	300+
Saint Joseph Medical Center	Bloomington	75%	300+
Saint Joseph Memorial Hospital	Murphysboro	75%	(a)
Saint Mary Medical Center	Galesburg	75%	300+
Salem Township Hospital	Salem	75%	(a)
Bromenn Healthcare	Normal	74%	300+
Edward Hospital	Naperville	74%	300+
Memorial Hospital of Carbondale	Carbondale	74%	300+
Provena St Marys Hospital	Kankakee	74%	300+
Abraham Lincoln Memorial Hospital	Lincoln	73%	(a)
Katherine Shaw Bethea Hospital	Dixon	73%	300+
Lake Forest Hospital	Lake Forest	73%	300+
Proctor Hospital	Peoria	73%	300+
Sarah Bush Lincoln Health Center	Mattoon	73%	300+
Advocate Lutheran General Hospital	Park Ridge	72%	300+
Genesis Medical Center Illini Campus	Silvis	72%	300+
Herrin Hospital	Herrin	72%	300+
OSF Holy Family Medical Center	Monmouth	72%	(a)
Red Bud Regional Hospital	Red Bud	72%	(a)
Saint Joseph's Hospital	Highland	72%	(a)
Advocate Good Samaritan Hospital	Downers Grove	71%	300+
Alexian Brothers Medical Center	Elk Grove Vlg	71%	300+
Alton Memorial Hospital	Alton	71%	300+
Richland Memorial Hospital	Olney	71%	300+
Riverside Medical Center	Kankakee	71%	300+
Silver Cross Hospital	Joliet	71%	300+
Valley West Community Hospital	Sandwich	71%	300+
Evanston Hospital	Evanston	70%	300+
Hillsboro Area Hospital	Hillsboro	70%	(a)
Memorial Hospital	Belleville	70%	300+
Rush University Medical Center	Chicago	70%	300+
Saint Anthony Medical Center	Rockford	70%	300+
Saint Francis Hospital	Litchfield	70%	300+
Saint James Hospital	Pontiac	70%	300+
Saint Johns Hospital	Springfield	69%	300+
Jersey Community Hospital	Jerseyville	68%	300+
Mendota Community Hospital	Mendota	68%	300+
Mercy Hospital and Medical Center	Chicago	68%	300+
Passavant Area Hospital	Jacksonville	68%	300+
Pekin Memorial Hospital	Pekin	68%	300+
Provena United Samaritans Med Ctr-Logan	Danville	68%	300+
Provena-Saint Joseph Hospital	Elgin	68%	300+
Saint Francis Medical Center	Peoria	68%	300+
Taylorville Memorial Hospital	Taylorville	68%	300+
Copley Memorial Hospital	Aurora	67%	300+
Decatur Memorial Hospital	Decatur	67%	300+
Good Samaritan Regional Health Center	Mount Vernon	67%	300+
Graham Hospital Association	Canton	67%	300+
Kishwaukee Community Hospital	Dekalb	67%	300+
Provena St Joseph Medical Center	Joliet	67%	300+
Saint Anthony Hospital	Chicago	67%	300+
St Mary & Elizabeth Med Ctr-Div Campus	Chicago	67%	300+
Sherman Hospital	Elgin	67%	300+
Westlake Community Hospital[11]	Melrose Park	67%	300+
Adventist La Grange Memorial Hospital	La Grange	66%	300+
Advocate Christ Hospital & Medical Center	Oak Lawn	66%	300+
Advocate Good Shepherd Hospital	Barrington	66%	300+
CGH Medical Center	Sterling	66%	300+
Loyola University Medical Center	Maywood	66%	300+
Pinckneyville Community Hospital	Pinckneyville	66%	(a)
Saint Alexius Medical Center	Hoffman Estates	66%	300+
Saint Anthony's Health Center	Alton	66%	300+
Saint Anthonys Memorial Hospital	Effingham	66%	300+
Swedish American Hospital	Rockford	66%	300+
Advocate Illinois Masonic Medical Center	Chicago	65%	300+
Blessing Hospital	Quincy	65%	300+
Centegra Health System - McHenry Hospital	Mchenry	65%	300+
Harrisburg Medical Center	Harrisburg	65%	300+
Hinsdale Hospital	Hinsdale	65%	300+
Iroquois Memorial Hospital	Watseka	65%	300+
Little Company of Mary Hospital	Evergreen Park	65%	300+
McDonough District Hospital	Macomb	65%	300+
Memorial Medical Center	Springfield	65%	300+
Provena Covenant Medical Center - Urbana	Urbana	65%	300+
Centegra Health Sys-Woodstock Hospital	Woodstock	64%	300+
Crawford Memorial Hospital	Robinson	64%	(a)
Saint Joseph Hospital	Chicago	64%	300+
Adventist Bolingbrook Hospital	Bolingbrook	63%	300+
Crossroads Community Hospital	Mount Vernon	63%	300+
Elmhurst Memorial Hospital	Elmhurst	63%	300+
Methodist Hospital of Chicago	Chicago	63%	(a)
Palos Community Hospital	Palos Heights	63%	300+
Rockford Memorial Hospital	Rockford	63%	300+
Union County Hospital	Anna	63%	(a)
The University of Chicago Medical Center	Chicago	63%	300+
West Suburban Medical Center	Oak Park	63%	300+
Galesburg Cottage Hospital	Galesburg	62%	300+
Greenville Regional Hospital	Greenville	62%	(a)
Kewanee Hospital[11]	Kewanee	62%	(a)
Louis A Weiss Memorial Hospital	Chicago	62%	300+
Ottawa Reg Hosp & Healthcare Ctr	Ottawa	62%	300+
Saint Margarets Hospital	Spring Valley	62%	300+
Saint Marys Hospital	Decatur	62%	300+
Trinity Rock Island	Rock Island	62%	300+
Advocate South Suburban Hospital	Hazel Crest	61%	300+
Anderson Hospital	Maryville	61%	300+
Fhn Memorial Hospital	Freeport	61%	300+
Ingalls Memorial Hospital	Harvey	61%	300+
Macneal Hospital	Berwyn	61%	300+
Provena Mercy Medical Center	Aurora	61%	300+
Saint Marys Hospital	Streator	61%	300+
Rush Oak Park Hospital	Oak Park	60%	300+
Oak Forest Hospital	Oak Forest	59%	300+
University of Illinois Hospital	Chicago	59%	300+
Advocate Condell Medical Center	Libertyville	58%	300+
Northwest Community Hospital	Arlington Hgts	58%	300+
RHC St Francis Hospital	Evanston	58%	300+
Loyola Gottlieb Memorial Hospital	Melrose Park	57%	300+
Saint Elizabeth Hospital	Belleville	57%	300+
St James Hospital-Olympia Fields	Olympia Fields	57%	300+
Gateway Regional Medical Center	Granite City	56%	300+
Shelby Memorial Hospital	Shelbyville	56%	(a)
Swedish Covenant Hospital	Chicago	56%	300+
Heartland Regional Medical Center	Marion	55%	300+
Resurrection Medical Center	Chicago	55%	300+
Advocate Trinity Hospital	Chicago	54%	300+
Metrosouth Medical Center	Blue Island	54%	300+
John H Stroger Jr Hospital	Chicago	52%	300+
Vista Medical Center East	Waukegan	52%	300+
Adventist Glenoaks	Glendale Hghts	51%	300+
Mount Sinai Hospital Medical Center	Chicago	51%	300+
Provident Hospital of Chicago	Chicago	51%	300+
Skokie Hospital	Skokie	51%	300+
Our Lady of the Resurrection Medical Center	Chicago	49%	300+
Thorek Memorial Hospital	Chicago	48%	300+
Touchette Regional Hospital	Centreville	48%	(a)
Sacred Heart Hospital	Chicago	47%	300+
Holy Cross Hospital	Chicago	45%	300+
Norwegian-American Hospital	Chicago	45%	300+
Roseland Community Hospital	Chicago	43%	300+
Saint Bernard Hospital	Chicago	43%	300+
Loretto Hospital	Chicago	41%	(a)
South Shore Hospital	Chicago	41%	300+
Jackson Park Hospital	Chicago	31%	300+

44. Meds 'Always' Explained Before Given

Hospital Name	City	Rate	Cases
Saint Josephs Hospital	Breese	73%	300+
Illinois Valley Community Hospital	Peru	72%	300+
Rochelle Community Hospital	Rochelle	72%	(a)
Hammond Henry Hospital	Geneseo	71%	300+
Crawford Memorial Hospital	Robinson	69%	(a)
Illini Community Hospital	Pittsfield	69%	(a)
Midwestern Region Medical Center	Zion	69%	300+
Saint Joseph Memorial Hospital	Murphysboro	69%	(a)
Carlinville Area Hospital	Carlinville	68%	(a)
Gibson Community Hospital	Gibson City	68%	300+
Sarah Bush Lincoln Health Center	Mattoon	68%	300+
University of Illinois Hospital	Chicago	68%	300+
Saint Mary Medical Center	Galesburg	67%	300+
Abraham Lincoln Memorial Hospital	Lincoln	66%	(a)
Kewanee Hospital[11]	Kewanee	66%	(a)
Pinckneyville Community Hospital	Pinckneyville	66%	(a)
Salem Township Hospital	Salem	66%	(a)
Hillsboro Area Hospital	Hillsboro	65%	(a)
Methodist Medical Center of Illinois	Peoria	65%	300+
Herrin Hospital	Herrin	64%	300+
Richland Memorial Hospital	Olney	64%	300+
Saint Joseph Medical Center	Bloomington	64%	300+
Saint Margarets Hospital	Spring Valley	64%	300+
Saint Marys Hospital	Centralia	64%	300+
Carle Foundation Hospital	Urbana	63%	300+

NOTE: Hospital profiles are in alphabetical order by state, then city, then hospital within the city; Rankings exclude hospitals with less than 25 cases except for patient surveys which excludes hospitals with less than 100 cases; (a) 100–299 cases; (1) The number of cases is too small to be sure how well a hospital is performing; (2) The hospital indicated that the data submitted for this measure were based on a sample of cases; (3) Data was collected during a shorter time period (fewer quarters) than the maximum possible time for this measure; (4) Suppressed for one or more quarters by CMS; (5) No data is available from the hospital for this measure; (6) Fewer than 100 patients completed the HCAHPS survey. Use these rates with caution, as the number of surveys may be too low to reliably assess hospital performance; (7) Survey results are based on less than 12 months of data; (8) Survey results are not available for this reporting period; (9) No or very few patients were eligible for the HCAHPS survey. The scores shown, if any, reflect a very small number of surveys; (10) A state average was not calculated because too few hospitals in the state submitted data; (11) There were discrepancies in the data collection process; Please refer to the User's Guide for a full explanation of data.

CGH Medical Center	Sterling	63%	300+
Delnor Community Hospital	Geneva	63%	300+
Good Samaritan Regional Health Center	Mount Vernon	63%	300+
Memorial Hospital of Carbondale	Carbondale	63%	300+
Mendota Community Hospital	Mendota	63%	300+
Provena United Samaritans Med Ctr-Logan	Danville	63%	300+
Saint Francis Hospital	Litchfield	63%	300+
Saint James Hospital	Pontiac	63%	300+
Saint Joseph's Hospital	Highland	63%	(a)
Valley West Community Hospital	Sandwich	63%	300+
Advocate Good Samaritan Hospital	Downers Grove	62%	300+
Edward Hospital	Naperville	62%	300+
Jersey Community Hospital	Jerseyville	62%	300+
Katherine Shaw Bethea Hospital	Dixon	62%	300+
Taylorville Memorial Hospital	Taylorville	62%	300+
West Suburban Medical Center	Oak Park	62%	300+
Advocate Illinois Masonic Medical Center	Chicago	61%	300+
Advocate Lutheran General Hospital	Park Ridge	61%	300+
Alexian Brothers Medical Center	Elk Grove Vlg	61%	300+
Fhn Memorial Hospital	Freeport	61%	300+
Iroquois Memorial Hospital	Watseka	61%	300+
Morris Hospital & Healthcare Centers	Morris	61%	300+
Ottawa Reg Hosp & Healthcare Ctr	Ottawa	61%	300+
Provena St Marys Hospital	Kankakee	61%	300+
Riverside Medical Center	Kankakee	61%	300+
Saint Anthony Medical Center	Rockford	61%	300+
Saint Anthony's Health Center	Alton	61%	300+
Saint Anthonys Memorial Hospital	Effingham	61%	300+
Silver Cross Hospital	Joliet	61%	300+
Trinity Rock Island	Rock Island	61%	300+
Union County Hospital	Anna	61%	(a)
Advocate Christ Hospital & Medical Center	Oak Lawn	60%	300+
Advocate Good Shepherd Hospital	Barrington	60%	300+
Blessing Hospital	Quincy	60%	300+
Centegra Health System - McHenry Hospital	Mchenry	60%	300+
Central Dupage Hospital	Winfield	60%	300+
Copley Memorial Hospital	Aurora	60%	300+
Elmhurst Memorial Hospital	Elmhurst	60%	300+
Graham Hospital Association	Canton	60%	300+
Passavant Area Hospital	Jacksonville	60%	300+
Rush University Medical Center	Chicago	60%	300+
Saint Marys Hospital	Streator	60%	300+
Westlake Community Hospital[11]	Melrose Park	60%	300+
Advocate South Suburban Hospital	Hazel Crest	59%	300+
Centegra Health Sys-Woodstock Hospital	Woodstock	59%	300+
Galesburg Cottage Hospital	Galesburg	59%	300+
Genesis Medical Center Illini Campus	Silvis	59%	300+
McDonough District Hospital	Macomb	59%	300+
Memorial Hospital	Belleville	59%	300+
Northwestern Memorial Hospital	Chicago	59%	300+
Palos Community Hospital	Palos Heights	59%	300+
Pekin Memorial Hospital	Pekin	59%	300+
Provena Covenant Medical Center - Urbana	Urbana	59%	300+
Provident Hospital of Chicago	Chicago	59%	300+
Red Bud Regional Hospital	Red Bud	59%	(a)
Saint Alexius Medical Center	Hoffman Estates	59%	300+
Saint Francis Medical Center	Peoria	59%	300+
Saint Johns Hospital	Springfield	59%	300+
Saint Joseph Hospital	Chicago	59%	300+
Shelby Memorial Hospital	Shelbyville	59%	(a)
Swedish American Hospital	Rockford	59%	300+
Alton Memorial Hospital	Alton	58%	300+
Lake Forest Hospital	Lake Forest	58%	300+
Loyola University Medical Center	Maywood	58%	300+
Macneal Hospital	Berwyn	58%	300+
Oak Forest Hospital	Oak Forest	58%	300+
Provena Mercy Medical Center	Aurora	58%	300+
Provena-Saint Joseph Hospital	Elgin	58%	300+
Crossroads Community Hospital	Mount Vernon	57%	300+
Gateway Regional Medical Center	Granite City	57%	300+
Harrisburg Medical Center	Harrisburg	57%	300+
Kishwaukee Community Hospital	Dekalb	57%	300+
Loyola Gottlieb Memorial Hospital	Melrose Park	57%	300+
Mercy Hospital and Medical Center	Chicago	57%	300+
Metrosouth Medical Center	Blue Island	57%	300+
Rush Oak Park Hospital	Oak Park	57%	300+
Sherman Hospital	Elgin	57%	300+
Advocate Trinity Hospital	Chicago	56%	300+
Bromenn Healthcare	Normal	56%	300+
Decatur Memorial Hospital	Decatur	56%	300+
Evanston Hospital	Evanston	56%	300+
Louis A Weiss Memorial Hospital	Chicago	56%	300+
Memorial Medical Center	Springfield	56%	300+
Mount Sinai Hospital Medical Center	Chicago	56%	300+
Rockford Memorial Hospital	Rockford	56%	300+
St James Hospital-Olympia Fields	Olympia Fields	56%	300+
The University of Chicago Medical Center	Chicago	56%	300+
Anderson Hospital	Maryville	55%	300+
Little Company of Mary Hospital	Evergreen Park	55%	300+
Adventist Glenoaks	Glendale Hghts	54%	300+
Adventist La Grange Memorial Hospital	La Grange	54%	300+
Advocate Condell Medical Center	Libertyville	54%	300+
Hinsdale Hospital	Hinsdale	54%	300+
Proctor Hospital	Peoria	54%	300+
Provena St Joseph Medical Center	Joliet	54%	300+
Resurrection Medical Center	Chicago	54%	300+
Saint Marys Hospital	Decatur	54%	300+
Adventist Bolingbrook Hospital	Bolingbrook	53%	300+
Greenville Regional Hospital	Greenville	53%	(a)
Ingalls Memorial Hospital	Harvey	53%	300+
Our Lady of the Resurrection Medical Center	Chicago	53%	300+
Heartland Regional Medical Center	Marion	52%	300+
John H Stroger Jr Hospital	Chicago	52%	300+
OSF Holy Family Medical Center	Monmouth	52%	(a)
Saint Anthony Hospital	Chicago	52%	300+
Saint Elizabeth Hospital	Belleville	52%	300+
St Mary & Elizabeth Med Ctr-Div Campus	Chicago	52%	300+
Vista Medical Center East	Waukegan	52%	300+
Northwest Community Hospital	Arlington Hgts	51%	300+
Sacred Heart Hospital	Chicago	51%	300+
Saint Bernard Hospital	Chicago	51%	300+
Swedish Covenant Hospital	Chicago	51%	300+
Touchette Regional Hospital	Centreville	51%	(a)
Skokie Hospital	Skokie	49%	300+
RHC St Francis Hospital	Evanston	48%	300+
South Shore Hospital	Chicago	48%	300+
Holy Cross Hospital	Chicago	47%	300+
Roseland Community Hospital	Chicago	47%	300+
Thorek Memorial Hospital	Chicago	46%	300+
Jackson Park Hospital	Chicago	45%	300+
Methodist Hospital of Chicago	Chicago	45%	(a)
Loretto Hospital	Chicago	41%	(a)
Norwegian-American Hospital	Chicago	40%	300+

45. Nurses 'Always' Communicated Well

Hospital Name	City	Rate	Cases
Saint Josephs Hospital	Breese	87%	300+
Illinois Valley Community Hospital	Peru	86%	300+
Carlinville Area Hospital	Carlinville	85%	(a)
Illini Community Hospital	Pittsfield	85%	(a)
Saint Marys Hospital	Centralia	85%	300+
Hammond Henry Hospital	Geneseo	84%	300+
Rochelle Community Hospital	Rochelle	84%	(a)
Saint Joseph Memorial Hospital	Murphysboro	84%	(a)
Saint Joseph's Hospital	Highland	84%	(a)
Salem Township Hospital	Salem	84%	(a)
Mendota Community Hospital	Mendota	83%	300+
Methodist Medical Center of Illinois	Peoria	83%	300+
Crawford Memorial Hospital	Robinson	82%	(a)
Gibson Community Hospital	Gibson City	82%	300+
Katherine Shaw Bethea Hospital	Dixon	82%	300+
Morris Hospital & Healthcare Centers	Morris	82%	300+
Pinckneyville Community Hospital	Pinckneyville	82%	(a)
Sarah Bush Lincoln Health Center	Mattoon	82%	300+
Valley West Community Hospital	Sandwich	82%	300+
Abraham Lincoln Memorial Hospital	Lincoln	81%	(a)
Central Dupage Hospital	Winfield	81%	300+
Hillsboro Area Hospital	Hillsboro	81%	(a)
Saint Mary Medical Center	Galesburg	81%	300+
Alton Memorial Hospital	Alton	80%	300+
Carle Foundation Hospital	Urbana	80%	300+
Delnor Community Hospital	Geneva	80%	300+
Good Samaritan Regional Health Center	Mount Vernon	80%	300+
Midwestern Region Medical Center	Zion	80%	300+
Provena United Samaritans Med Ctr-Logan	Danville	80%	300+
Saint Alexius Medical Center	Hoffman Estates	80%	300+
Saint James Hospital	Pontiac	80%	300+
Saint Joseph Medical Center	Bloomington	80%	300+
Advocate Christ Hospital & Medical Center	Oak Lawn	79%	300+
Alexian Brothers Medical Center	Elk Grove Vlg	79%	300+
Blessing Hospital	Quincy	79%	300+
Bromenn Healthcare	Normal	79%	300+
Graham Hospital Association	Canton	79%	300+
Jersey Community Hospital	Jerseyville	79%	300+
Memorial Hospital of Carbondale	Carbondale	79%	300+
Provena St Marys Hospital	Kankakee	79%	300+
Red Bud Regional Hospital	Red Bud	79%	(a)
Richland Memorial Hospital	Olney	79%	300+
Riverside Medical Center	Kankakee	79%	300+
Saint Francis Hospital	Litchfield	79%	300+
Advocate Good Samaritan Hospital	Downers Grove	78%	300+
Edward Hospital	Naperville	78%	300+
Herrin Hospital	Herrin	78%	300+
Iroquois Memorial Hospital	Watseka	78%	300+
McDonough District Hospital	Macomb	78%	300+
Memorial Hospital	Belleville	78%	300+
Oak Forest Hospital	Oak Forest	78%	300+
Ottawa Reg Hosp & Healthcare Ctr	Ottawa	78%	300+
Provena Covenant Medical Center - Urbana	Urbana	78%	300+
Silver Cross Hospital	Joliet	78%	300+
Taylorville Memorial Hospital	Taylorville	78%	300+
Advocate Good Shepherd Hospital	Barrington	77%	300+
Centegra Health System - McHenry Hospital	Mchenry	77%	300+
Genesis Medical Center Illini Campus	Silvis	77%	300+
Greenville Regional Hospital	Greenville	77%	(a)
Macneal Hospital	Berwyn	77%	300+
Mercy Hospital and Medical Center	Chicago	77%	300+
OSF Holy Family Medical Center	Monmouth	77%	(a)
Pekin Memorial Hospital	Pekin	77%	300+
Rush University Medical Center	Chicago	77%	300+
Saint Francis Medical Center	Peoria	77%	300+
Saint Margarets Hospital	Spring Valley	77%	300+
Westlake Community Hospital[11]	Melrose Park	77%	300+
Advocate Lutheran General Hospital	Park Ridge	76%	300+
Centegra Health Sys-Woodstock Hospital	Woodstock	76%	300+
Fhn Memorial Hospital	Freeport	76%	300+
Harrisburg Medical Center	Harrisburg	76%	300+
Palos Community Hospital	Palos Heights	76%	300+
Passavant Area Hospital	Jacksonville	76%	300+
Saint Anthony Medical Center	Rockford	76%	300+
Saint Marys Hospital	Streator	76%	300+
Sherman Hospital	Elgin	76%	300+
Swedish American Hospital	Rockford	76%	300+
Advocate Illinois Masonic Medical Center	Chicago	75%	300+
Advocate South Suburban Hospital	Hazel Crest	75%	300+
Elmhurst Memorial Hospital	Elmhurst	75%	300+
Kewanee Hospital[11]	Kewanee	75%	(a)
Kishwaukee Community Hospital	Dekalb	75%	300+
Lake Forest Hospital	Lake Forest	75%	300+
Little Company of Mary Hospital	Evergreen Park	75%	300+
Memorial Medical Center	Springfield	75%	300+
Shelby Memorial Hospital	Shelbyville	75%	(a)
Union County Hospital	Anna	75%	(a)
CGH Medical Center	Sterling	74%	300+
Copley Memorial Hospital	Aurora	74%	300+
Crossroads Community Hospital	Mount Vernon	74%	300+
Decatur Memorial Hospital	Decatur	74%	300+
Evanston Hospital	Evanston	74%	300+
Loyola Gottlieb Memorial Hospital	Melrose Park	74%	300+
Provena Mercy Medical Center	Aurora	74%	300+
Saint Anthony's Health Center	Alton	74%	300+
Saint Anthonys Memorial Hospital	Effingham	74%	300+
Saint Johns Hospital	Springfield	74%	300+
Advocate Trinity Hospital	Chicago	73%	300+
Anderson Hospital	Maryville	73%	300+
Galesburg Cottage Hospital	Galesburg	73%	300+
Loyola University Medical Center	Maywood	73%	300+
Northwestern Memorial Hospital	Chicago	73%	300+
Proctor Hospital	Peoria	73%	300+
Provena St Joseph Medical Center	Joliet	73%	300+
Provena-Saint Joseph Hospital	Elgin	73%	300+
Gateway Regional Medical Center	Granite City	72%	300+
Louis A Weiss Memorial Hospital	Chicago	72%	300+
Rockford Memorial Hospital	Rockford	72%	300+
Rush Oak Park Hospital	Oak Park	72%	300+
St James Hospital-Olympia Fields	Olympia Fields	72%	300+
Trinity Rock Island	Rock Island	72%	300+
The University of Chicago Medical Center	Chicago	71%	300+
Adventist La Grange Memorial Hospital	La Grange	70%	300+
Advocate Condell Medical Center	Libertyville	70%	300+
Hinsdale Hospital	Hinsdale	70%	300+
Metrosouth Medical Center	Blue Island	70%	300+
Saint Elizabeth Hospital	Belleville	70%	300+
Saint Joseph Hospital	Chicago	70%	300+
Saint Marys Hospital	Decatur	70%	300+
Touchette Regional Hospital	Centreville	70%	(a)
West Suburban Medical Center	Oak Park	70%	300+
Ingalls Memorial Hospital	Harvey	69%	300+
Provident Hospital of Chicago	Chicago	69%	300+
Resurrection Medical Center	Chicago	69%	300+
RHC St Francis Hospital	Evanston	69%	300+
University of Illinois Hospital	Chicago	69%	300+
Heartland Regional Medical Center	Marion	68%	300+
Northwest Community Hospital	Arlington Hgts	68%	300+
Skokie Hospital	Skokie	68%	300+
St Mary & Elizabeth Med Ctr-Div Campus	Chicago	67%	300+
Adventist Bolingbrook Hospital	Bolingbrook	66%	300+
Our Lady of the Resurrection Medical Center	Chicago	66%	300+
Saint Anthony Hospital	Chicago	65%	300+
Swedish Covenant Hospital	Chicago	65%	300+
Adventist Glenoaks	Glendale Hghts	64%	300+
Saint Bernard Hospital	Chicago	64%	300+
Holy Cross Hospital	Chicago	63%	300+
Mount Sinai Hospital Medical Center	Chicago	63%	300+
South Shore Hospital	Chicago	63%	300+
Vista Medical Center East	Waukegan	63%	300+
John H Stroger Jr Hospital	Chicago	62%	300+
Sacred Heart Hospital	Chicago	62%	300+
Methodist Hospital of Chicago	Chicago	60%	(a)
Roseland Community Hospital	Chicago	60%	300+
Thorek Memorial Hospital	Chicago	60%	300+
Loretto Hospital	Chicago	59%	(a)

NOTE: Hospital profiles are in alphabetical order by state, then city, then hospital within the city; Rankings exclude hospitals with less than 25 cases except for patient surveys which excludes hospitals with less than 100 cases; (a) 100–299 cases; (1) The number of cases is too small to be sure how well a hospital is performing; (2) The hospital indicated that the data submitted for this measure were based on a sample of cases; (3) Data was collected during a shorter time period (fewer quarters) than the maximum possible time for this measure; (4) Suppressed for one or more quarters by CMS; (5) No data is available from the hospital for this measure; (6) Fewer than 100 patients completed the HCAHPS survey. Use these rates with caution, as the number of surveys may be too low to reliably assess hospital performance; (7) Survey results are based on less than 12 months of data; (8) Survey results are not available for this reporting period; (9) No or very few patients were eligible for the HCAHPS survey. The scores shown, if any, reflect a very small number of surveys; (10) A state average was not calculated because too few hospitals in the state submitted data; (11) There were discrepancies in the data collection process; Please refer to the User's Guide for a full explanation of data.

Hospital Name	City	Rate	Cases
Jackson Park Hospital	Chicago	54%	300+
Norwegian-American Hospital	Chicago	52%	300+

46. Pain 'Always' Well Controlled

Hospital Name	City	Rate	Cases
Carlinville Area Hospital	Carlinville	83%	(a)
Pinckneyville Community Hospital	Pinckneyville	81%	(a)
Saint Joseph's Hospital	Highland	80%	(a)
Saint Marys Hospital	Centralia	80%	300+
Midwestern Region Medical Center	Zion	79%	300+
Rochelle Community Hospital	Rochelle	79%	(a)
Red Bud Regional Hospital	Red Bud	78%	(a)
Saint Josephs Hospital	Breese	78%	300+
Gibson Community Hospital	Gibson City	77%	300+
Abraham Lincoln Memorial Hospital	Lincoln	76%	(a)
Illini Community Hospital	Pittsfield	76%	(a)
Illinois Valley Community Hospital	Peru	76%	300+
Valley West Community Hospital	Sandwich	76%	300+
Hammond Henry Hospital	Geneseo	75%	300+
Katherine Shaw Bethea Hospital	Dixon	75%	300+
Methodist Medical Center of Illinois	Peoria	75%	300+
Richland Memorial Hospital	Olney	75%	300+
Salem Township Hospital	Salem	75%	(a)
Bromenn Healthcare	Normal	74%	300+
Crawford Memorial Hospital	Robinson	74%	(a)
Morris Hospital & Healthcare Centers	Morris	74%	300+
Central Dupage Hospital	Winfield	73%	300+
Good Samaritan Regional Health Center	Mount Vernon	73%	300+
McDonough District Hospital	Macomb	73%	300+
Passavant Area Hospital	Jacksonville	73%	300+
Saint James Hospital	Pontiac	73%	300+
Saint Mary Medical Center	Galesburg	73%	300+
Sarah Bush Lincoln Health Center	Mattoon	73%	300+
Advocate Christ Hospital & Medical Center	Oak Lawn	72%	300+
Alton Memorial Hospital	Alton	72%	300+
Edward Hospital	Naperville	72%	300+
Hillsboro Area Hospital	Hillsboro	72%	(a)
Iroquois Memorial Hospital	Watseka	72%	300+
Jersey Community Hospital	Jerseyville	72%	300+
Memorial Hospital of Carbondale	Carbondale	72%	300+
Mendota Community Hospital	Mendota	72%	300+
Provena St Joseph Medical Center	Joliet	72%	300+
Provena St Marys Hospital	Kankakee	72%	300+
Saint Joseph Memorial Hospital	Murphysboro	72%	(a)
Westlake Community Hospital[11]	Melrose Park	72%	300+
CGH Medical Center	Sterling	71%	300+
Delnor Community Hospital	Geneva	71%	300+
Genesis Medical Center Illini Campus	Silvis	71%	300+
Macneal Hospital	Berwyn	71%	300+
Provena United Samaritans Med Ctr-Logan	Danville	71%	300+
Saint Alexius Medical Center	Hoffman Estates	71%	300+
Saint Francis Hospital	Litchfield	71%	300+
Saint Joseph Medical Center	Bloomington	71%	300+
Silver Cross Hospital	Joliet	71%	300+
University of Illinois Hospital	Chicago	71%	300+
Advocate Good Samaritan Hospital	Downers Grove	70%	300+
Advocate Lutheran General Hospital	Park Ridge	70%	300+
Blessing Hospital	Quincy	70%	300+
Carle Foundation Hospital	Urbana	70%	300+
Centegra Health System - McHenry Hospital	Mchenry	70%	300+
Centegra Health Sys-Woodstock Hospital	Woodstock	70%	300+
Herrin Hospital	Herrin	70%	300+
Kewanee Hospital[11]	Kewanee	70%	(a)
Memorial Hospital	Belleville	70%	300+
Palos Community Hospital	Palos Heights	70%	300+
Pekin Memorial Hospital	Pekin	70%	300+
Provena Covenant Medical Center - Urbana	Urbana	70%	300+
Provena-Saint Joseph Hospital	Elgin	70%	300+
Riverside Medical Center	Kankakee	70%	300+
Rush Oak Park Hospital	Oak Park	70%	300+
Saint Marys Hospital	Streator	70%	300+
Swedish American Hospital	Rockford	70%	300+
Taylorville Memorial Hospital	Taylorville	70%	300+
Advocate Good Shepherd Hospital	Barrington	69%	300+
Advocate Illinois Masonic Medical Center	Chicago	69%	300+
Alexian Brothers Medical Center	Elk Grove Vlg	69%	300+
Copley Memorial Hospital	Aurora	69%	300+
Crossroads Community Hospital	Mount Vernon	69%	300+
Greenville Regional Hospital	Greenville	69%	(a)
Kishwaukee Community Hospital	Dekalb	69%	300+
Lake Forest Hospital	Lake Forest	69%	300+
Little Company of Mary Hospital	Evergreen Park	69%	300+
Loyola Gottlieb Memorial Hospital	Melrose Park	69%	300+
Mercy Hospital and Medical Center	Chicago	69%	300+
Northwestern Memorial Hospital	Chicago	69%	300+
Oak Forest Hospital	Oak Forest	69%	300+
Proctor Hospital	Peoria	69%	300+
Saint Anthony Medical Center	Rockford	69%	300+
Saint Francis Medical Center	Peoria	69%	300+
Union County Hospital	Anna	69%	(a)
Advocate South Suburban Hospital	Hazel Crest	68%	300+
Advocate Trinity Hospital	Chicago	68%	300+
Elmhurst Memorial Hospital	Elmhurst	68%	300+
Graham Hospital Association	Canton	68%	300+
Harrisburg Medical Center	Harrisburg	68%	300+
Ottawa Reg Hosp & Healthcare Ctr	Ottawa	68%	300+
Rush University Medical Center	Chicago	68%	300+
Sherman Hospital	Elgin	68%	300+
West Suburban Medical Center	Oak Park	68%	300+
Anderson Hospital	Maryville	67%	300+
Evanston Hospital	Evanston	67%	300+
Loyola University Medical Center	Maywood	67%	300+
Memorial Medical Center	Springfield	67%	300+
OSF Holy Family Medical Center	Monmouth	67%	(a)
Saint Anthony's Health Center	Alton	67%	300+
St James Hospital-Olympia Fields	Olympia Fields	67%	300+
Trinity Rock Island	Rock Island	67%	300+
Adventist La Grange Memorial Hospital	La Grange	66%	300+
Decatur Memorial Hospital	Decatur	66%	300+
Galesburg Cottage Hospital	Galesburg	66%	300+
Hinsdale Hospital	Hinsdale	66%	300+
Ingalls Memorial Hospital	Harvey	66%	300+
Louis A Weiss Memorial Hospital	Chicago	66%	300+
Provident Hospital of Chicago	Chicago	66%	300+
Saint Anthonys Memorial Hospital	Effingham	66%	300+
Saint Johns Hospital	Springfield	66%	300+
Saint Margarets Hospital	Spring Valley	66%	300+
Advocate Condell Medical Center	Libertyville	65%	300+
Fhn Memorial Hospital	Freeport	65%	300+
Shelby Memorial Hospital	Shelbyville	65%	(a)
The University of Chicago Medical Center	Chicago	65%	300+
Northwest Community Hospital	Arlington Hgts	64%	300+
Resurrection Medical Center	Chicago	64%	300+
Rockford Memorial Hospital	Rockford	64%	300+
Sacred Heart Hospital	Chicago	64%	300+
Saint Elizabeth Hospital	Belleville	64%	300+
St Mary & Elizabeth Med Ctr-Div Campus	Chicago	64%	300+
Adventist Bolingbrook Hospital	Bolingbrook	63%	300+
Heartland Regional Medical Center	Marion	63%	300+
John H Stroger Jr Hospital	Chicago	63%	300+
Metrosouth Medical Center	Blue Island	63%	300+
Provena Mercy Medical Center	Aurora	63%	300+
RHC St Francis Hospital	Evanston	63%	300+
Saint Joseph Hospital	Chicago	63%	300+
Gateway Regional Medical Center	Granite City	62%	300+
Our Lady of the Resurrection Medical Center	Chicago	62%	300+
Saint Marys Hospital	Decatur	62%	300+
Adventist Glenoaks	Glendale Hghts	61%	300+
Mount Sinai Hospital Medical Center	Chicago	61%	300+
Vista Medical Center East	Waukegan	61%	300+
Saint Anthony Hospital	Chicago	60%	300+
Swedish Covenant Hospital	Chicago	60%	300+
Touchette Regional Hospital	Centreville	60%	(a)
Saint Bernard Hospital	Chicago	59%	300+
Roseland Community Hospital	Chicago	57%	300+
Skokie Hospital	Skokie	57%	300+
South Shore Hospital	Chicago	57%	300+
Thorek Memorial Hospital	Chicago	56%	300+
Holy Cross Hospital	Chicago	55%	300+
Norwegian-American Hospital	Chicago	52%	300+
Loretto Hospital	Chicago	50%	(a)
Methodist Hospital of Chicago	Chicago	50%	(a)
Jackson Park Hospital	Chicago	49%	300+

47. Room and Bathroom 'Always' Clean

Hospital Name	City	Rate	Cases
Carlinville Area Hospital	Carlinville	89%	(a)
Saint Joseph Memorial Hospital	Murphysboro	88%	(a)
Salem Township Hospital	Salem	88%	(a)
Rochelle Community Hospital	Rochelle	87%	(a)
Saint Joseph's Hospital	Highland	86%	(a)
Saint Josephs Hospital	Breese	85%	300+
Saint Marys Hospital	Centralia	85%	300+
Illini Community Hospital	Pittsfield	84%	(a)
Kewanee Hospital[11]	Kewanee	84%	(a)
Illinois Valley Community Hospital	Peru	83%	300+
Saint Francis Hospital	Litchfield	83%	300+
OSF Holy Family Medical Center	Monmouth	82%	(a)
McDonough District Hospital	Macomb	81%	300+
Jersey Community Hospital	Jerseyville	80%	300+
Mendota Community Hospital	Mendota	80%	300+
Abraham Lincoln Memorial Hospital	Lincoln	79%	(a)
Centegra Health Sys-Woodstock Hospital	Woodstock	79%	300+
Crawford Memorial Hospital	Robinson	79%	(a)
Iroquois Memorial Hospital	Watseka	79%	300+
Saint James Hospital	Pontiac	79%	300+
Shelby Memorial Hospital	Shelbyville	79%	(a)
Valley West Community Hospital	Sandwich	79%	300+
CGH Medical Center	Sterling	78%	300+
Gibson Community Hospital	Gibson City	78%	300+
Hammond Henry Hospital	Geneseo	78%	300+
Methodist Medical Center of Illinois	Peoria	78%	300+
Morris Hospital & Healthcare Centers	Morris	78%	300+
Pinckneyville Community Hospital	Pinckneyville	78%	(a)
Alexian Brothers Medical Center	Elk Grove Vlg	77%	300+
Methodist Hospital of Chicago	Chicago	77%	(a)
Ottawa Reg Hosp & Healthcare Ctr	Ottawa	77%	300+
Saint Joseph Medical Center	Bloomington	77%	300+
Saint Marys Hospital	Streator	77%	300+
Centegra Health System - McHenry Hospital	Mchenry	76%	300+
Herrin Hospital	Herrin	76%	300+
Kishwaukee Community Hospital	Dekalb	76%	300+
Memorial Hospital of Carbondale	Carbondale	76%	300+
Passavant Area Hospital	Jacksonville	76%	300+
Taylorville Memorial Hospital	Taylorville	76%	300+
Delnor Community Hospital	Geneva	75%	300+
Good Samaritan Regional Health Center	Mount Vernon	75%	300+
Katherine Shaw Bethea Hospital	Dixon	75%	300+
Provena St Marys Hospital	Kankakee	75%	300+
Red Bud Regional Hospital	Red Bud	75%	(a)
Saint Mary Medical Center	Galesburg	75%	300+
Graham Hospital Association	Canton	74%	300+
Midwestern Region Medical Center	Zion	74%	300+
Sherman Hospital	Elgin	74%	300+
Advocate Lutheran General Hospital	Park Ridge	73%	300+
Alton Memorial Hospital	Alton	73%	300+
Blessing Hospital	Quincy	73%	300+
Hillsboro Area Hospital	Hillsboro	73%	(a)
Hinsdale Hospital	Hinsdale	73%	300+
Lake Forest Hospital	Lake Forest	73%	300+
Provena-Saint Joseph Hospital	Elgin	73%	300+
Saint Anthony Medical Center	Rockford	73%	300+
Saint Margarets Hospital	Spring Valley	73%	300+
Sarah Bush Lincoln Health Center	Mattoon	73%	300+
Advocate Good Shepherd Hospital	Barrington	72%	300+
Anderson Hospital	Maryville	72%	300+
Macneal Hospital	Berwyn	72%	300+
Pekin Memorial Hospital	Pekin	72%	300+
Saint Francis Medical Center	Peoria	72%	300+
Swedish American Hospital	Rockford	72%	300+
Union County Hospital	Anna	72%	(a)
Advocate Good Samaritan Hospital	Downers Grove	71%	300+
Bromenn Healthcare	Normal	71%	300+
Crossroads Community Hospital	Mount Vernon	71%	300+
Harrisburg Medical Center	Harrisburg	71%	300+
Louis A Weiss Memorial Hospital	Chicago	71%	300+
Mercy Hospital and Medical Center	Chicago	71%	300+
Saint Anthony's Health Center	Alton	71%	300+
Saint Anthonys Memorial Hospital	Effingham	71%	300+
Silver Cross Hospital	Joliet	71%	300+
Adventist Bolingbrook Hospital	Bolingbrook	70%	300+
Adventist La Grange Memorial Hospital	La Grange	70%	300+
Advocate Illinois Masonic Medical Center	Chicago	70%	300+
Central Dupage Hospital	Winfield	70%	300+
Genesis Medical Center Illini Campus	Silvis	70%	300+
Greenville Regional Hospital	Greenville	70%	(a)
Saint Alexius Medical Center	Hoffman Estates	70%	300+
Westlake Community Hospital[11]	Melrose Park	70%	300+
Advocate Condell Medical Center	Libertyville	69%	300+
Evanston Hospital	Evanston	69%	300+
Fhn Memorial Hospital	Freeport	69%	300+
Loyola Gottlieb Memorial Hospital	Melrose Park	69%	300+
Memorial Hospital	Belleville	69%	300+
Proctor Hospital	Peoria	69%	300+
Riverside Medical Center	Kankakee	69%	300+
Rockford Memorial Hospital	Rockford	69%	300+
Trinity Rock Island	Rock Island	69%	300+
Edward Hospital	Naperville	68%	300+
Northwestern Memorial Hospital	Chicago	68%	300+
Saint Johns Hospital	Springfield	68%	300+
Advocate Christ Hospital & Medical Center	Oak Lawn	67%	300+
Advocate Trinity Hospital	Chicago	67%	300+
Provena Mercy Medical Center	Aurora	67%	300+
Advocate South Suburban Hospital	Hazel Crest	66%	300+
Carle Foundation Hospital	Urbana	66%	300+
Galesburg Cottage Hospital	Galesburg	66%	300+
Heartland Regional Medical Center	Marion	66%	300+
Palos Community Hospital	Palos Heights	66%	300+
Provena Covenant Medical Center - Urbana	Urbana	66%	300+
Provena United Samaritans Med Ctr-Logan	Danville	66%	300+
Rush Oak Park Hospital	Oak Park	66%	300+
West Suburban Medical Center	Oak Park	66%	300+
Adventist Glenoaks	Glendale Hghts	65%	300+
Copley Memorial Hospital	Aurora	65%	300+
Decatur Memorial Hospital	Decatur	65%	300+
Little Company of Mary Hospital	Evergreen Park	65%	300+
Loyola University Medical Center	Maywood	65%	300+
Metrosouth Medical Center	Blue Island	65%	300+
Oak Forest Hospital	Oak Forest	65%	300+
Provena St Joseph Medical Center	Joliet	65%	300+
Saint Bernard Hospital	Chicago	65%	300+

NOTE: Hospital profiles are in alphabetical order by state, then city, then hospital within the city; Rankings exclude hospitals with less than 25 cases except for patient surveys which excludes hospitals with less than 100 cases; (a) 100–299 cases; (1) The number of cases is too small to be sure how well a hospital is performing; (2) The hospital indicated that the data submitted for this measure were based on a sample of cases; (3) Data was collected during a shorter time period (fewer quarters) than the maximum possible time for this measure; (4) Suppressed for one or more quarters by CMS; (5) No data is available from the hospital for this measure; (6) Fewer than 100 patients completed the HCAHPS survey. Use these rates with caution, as the number of surveys may be too low to reliably assess hospital performance; (7) Survey results are based on less than 12 months of data; (8) Survey results are not available for this reporting period; (9) No or very few patients were eligible for the HCAHPS survey. The scores shown, if any, reflect a very small number of surveys; (10) A state average was not calculated because too few hospitals in the state submitted data; (11) There were discrepancies in the data collection process; Please refer to the User's Guide for a full explanation of data.

Hospital Name	City	Rate	Cases
St James Hospital-Olympia Fields	Olympia Fields	65%	300+
Saint Joseph Hospital	Chicago	65%	300+
Thorek Memorial Hospital	Chicago	65%	300+
Our Lady of the Resurrection Medical Center	Chicago	64%	300+
Provident Hospital of Chicago	Chicago	64%	300+
Richland Memorial Hospital	Olney	64%	300+
Touchette Regional Hospital	Centreville	64%	(a)
University of Illinois Hospital	Chicago	64%	300+
RHC St Francis Hospital	Evanston	63%	300+
St Mary & Elizabeth Med Ctr-Div Campus	Chicago	63%	300+
Elmhurst Memorial Hospital	Elmhurst	62%	300+
Gateway Regional Medical Center	Granite City	62%	300+
Ingalls Memorial Hospital	Harvey	62%	300+
Sacred Heart Hospital	Chicago	62%	300+
Saint Marys Hospital	Decatur	62%	300+
Holy Cross Hospital	Chicago	61%	300+
Northwest Community Hospital	Arlington Hgts	61%	300+
Roseland Community Hospital	Chicago	61%	300+
Rush University Medical Center	Chicago	61%	300+
South Shore Hospital	Chicago	61%	300+
Memorial Medical Center	Springfield	60%	300+
Skokie Hospital	Skokie	60%	300+
The University of Chicago Medical Center	Chicago	60%	300+
Saint Anthony Hospital	Chicago	58%	300+
Saint Elizabeth Hospital	Belleville	58%	300+
Loretto Hospital	Chicago	57%	(a)
Swedish Covenant Hospital	Chicago	57%	300+
Vista Medical Center East	Waukegan	57%	300+
Jackson Park Hospital	Chicago	56%	300+
Norwegian-American Hospital	Chicago	56%	300+
Resurrection Medical Center	Chicago	54%	300+
Mount Sinai Hospital Medical Center	Chicago	53%	300+
John H Stroger Jr Hospital	Chicago	52%	300+

48. Timely Help 'Always' Received

Hospital Name	City	Rate	Cases
Rochelle Community Hospital	Rochelle	85%	(a)
Illini Community Hospital	Pittsfield	79%	(a)
Illinois Valley Community Hospital	Peru	79%	300+
Saint Joseph Memorial Hospital	Murphysboro	79%	(a)
Pinckneyville Community Hospital	Pinckneyville	78%	(a)
Saint Marys Hospital	Centralia	78%	300+
Hammond Henry Hospital	Geneseo	77%	300+
Mendota Community Hospital	Mendota	77%	300+
Jersey Community Hospital	Jerseyville	76%	300+
Saint James Hospital	Pontiac	76%	300+
Gibson Community Hospital	Gibson City	75%	300+
OSF Holy Family Medical Center	Monmouth	75%	(a)
Saint Mary Medical Center	Galesburg	75%	300+
Crawford Memorial Hospital	Robinson	74%	(a)
Katherine Shaw Bethea Hospital	Dixon	73%	300+
Salem Township Hospital	Salem	73%	(a)
Abraham Lincoln Memorial Hospital	Lincoln	72%	(a)
Iroquois Memorial Hospital	Watseka	72%	300+
McDonough District Hospital	Macomb	72%	300+
Morris Hospital & Healthcare Centers	Morris	72%	300+
Saint Josephs Hospital	Breese	72%	300+
Valley West Community Hospital	Sandwich	72%	300+
Carlinville Area Hospital	Carlinville	71%	(a)
Hillsboro Area Hospital	Hillsboro	70%	(a)
Pekin Memorial Hospital	Pekin	70%	300+
Sarah Bush Lincoln Health Center	Mattoon	70%	300+
CGH Medical Center	Sterling	69%	300+
Midwestern Region Medical Center	Zion	69%	300+
Ottawa Reg Hosp & Healthcare Ctr	Ottawa	69%	300+
Richland Memorial Hospital	Olney	69%	300+
Good Samaritan Regional Health Center	Mount Vernon	68%	300+
Methodist Medical Center of Illinois	Peoria	68%	300+
Saint Marys Hospital	Streator	68%	300+
Graham Hospital Association	Canton	67%	300+
Oak Forest Hospital	Oak Forest	67%	300+
Provena St Marys Hospital	Kankakee	67%	300+
Riverside Medical Center	Kankakee	67%	300+
Saint Joseph Medical Center	Bloomington	67%	300+
Swedish American Hospital	Rockford	67%	300+
Memorial Hospital of Carbondale	Carbondale	66%	300+
Saint Alexius Medical Center	Hoffman Estates	66%	300+
Saint Francis Hospital	Litchfield	66%	300+
Saint Joseph's Hospital	Highland	66%	(a)
Centegra Health System - McHenry Hospital	Mchenry	65%	300+
Centegra Health Sys-Woodstock Hospital	Woodstock	65%	300+
Central Dupage Hospital	Winfield	65%	300+
Herrin Hospital	Herrin	65%	300+
Advocate Christ Hospital & Medical Center	Oak Lawn	64%	300+
Advocate Good Samaritan Hospital	Downers Grove	64%	300+
Carle Foundation Hospital	Urbana	64%	300+
Delnor Community Hospital	Geneva	64%	300+
Harrisburg Medical Center	Harrisburg	64%	300+
Provena United Samaritans Med Ctr-Logan	Danville	64%	300+
Taylorville Memorial Hospital	Taylorville	64%	300+
Alexian Brothers Medical Center	Elk Grove Vlg	63%	300+
Genesis Medical Center Illini Campus	Silvis	63%	300+
Macneal Hospital	Berwyn	63%	300+
Saint Anthony Medical Center	Rockford	63%	300+
Union County Hospital	Anna	63%	(a)
Advocate Illinois Masonic Medical Center	Chicago	62%	300+
Blessing Hospital	Quincy	62%	300+
Greenville Regional Hospital	Greenville	62%	(a)
Provena Covenant Medical Center - Urbana	Urbana	62%	300+
Saint Anthonys Memorial Hospital	Effingham	62%	300+
Silver Cross Hospital	Joliet	62%	300+
Alton Memorial Hospital	Alton	61%	300+
Memorial Hospital	Belleville	61%	300+
Passavant Area Hospital	Jacksonville	61%	300+
Saint Johns Hospital	Springfield	61%	300+
University of Illinois Hospital	Chicago	61%	300+
Westlake Community Hospital[11]	Melrose Park	61%	300+
Advocate Lutheran General Hospital	Park Ridge	60%	300+
Anderson Hospital	Maryville	60%	300+
Bromenn Healthcare	Normal	60%	300+
Edward Hospital	Naperville	60%	300+
Little Company of Mary Hospital	Evergreen Park	60%	300+
Palos Community Hospital	Palos Heights	60%	300+
Saint Margarets Hospital	Spring Valley	60%	300+
Shelby Memorial Hospital	Shelbyville	60%	(a)
Advocate Good Shepherd Hospital	Barrington	59%	300+
Advocate South Suburban Hospital	Hazel Crest	59%	300+
Fhn Memorial Hospital	Freeport	59%	300+
Lake Forest Hospital	Lake Forest	59%	300+
Louis A Weiss Memorial Hospital	Chicago	59%	300+
Northwestern Memorial Hospital	Chicago	59%	300+
Proctor Hospital	Peoria	59%	300+
Rush Oak Park Hospital	Oak Park	59%	300+
Rush University Medical Center	Chicago	59%	300+
Saint Anthony's Health Center	Alton	59%	300+
Sherman Hospital	Elgin	59%	300+
Decatur Memorial Hospital	Decatur	58%	300+
Galesburg Cottage Hospital	Galesburg	58%	300+
Hinsdale Hospital	Hinsdale	58%	300+
Kishwaukee Community Hospital	Dekalb	58%	300+
Loyola Gottlieb Memorial Hospital	Melrose Park	58%	300+
Adventist La Grange Memorial Hospital	La Grange	57%	300+
Crossroads Community Hospital	Mount Vernon	57%	300+
Elmhurst Memorial Hospital	Elmhurst	57%	300+
Kewanee Hospital[11]	Kewanee	57%	(a)
Memorial Medical Center	Springfield	57%	300+
Metrosouth Medical Center	Blue Island	57%	300+
RHC St Francis Hospital	Evanston	57%	300+
Saint Francis Medical Center	Peoria	57%	300+
Advocate Trinity Hospital	Chicago	56%	300+
Copley Memorial Hospital	Aurora	56%	300+
Evanston Hospital	Evanston	56%	300+
Heartland Regional Medical Center	Marion	56%	300+
Mercy Hospital and Medical Center	Chicago	56%	300+
Our Lady of the Resurrection Medical Center	Chicago	56%	300+
Red Bud Regional Hospital	Red Bud	56%	(a)
Adventist Bolingbrook Hospital	Bolingbrook	55%	300+
Adventist Glenoaks	Glendale Hghts	55%	300+
Advocate Condell Medical Center	Libertyville	55%	300+
Provena Mercy Medical Center	Aurora	55%	300+
Provena St Joseph Medical Center	Joliet	55%	300+
St James Hospital-Olympia Fields	Olympia Fields	55%	300+
Saint Joseph Hospital	Chicago	55%	300+
St Mary & Elizabeth Med Ctr-Div Campus	Chicago	55%	300+
The University of Chicago Medical Center	Chicago	55%	300+
Gateway Regional Medical Center	Granite City	54%	300+
Loyola University Medical Center	Maywood	54%	300+
Northwest Community Hospital	Arlington Hgts	54%	300+
Provena-Saint Joseph Hospital	Elgin	54%	300+
Provident Hospital of Chicago	Chicago	53%	300+
Saint Marys Hospital	Decatur	53%	300+
Saint Anthony Hospital	Chicago	52%	300+
Saint Elizabeth Hospital	Belleville	52%	300+
Ingalls Memorial Hospital	Harvey	51%	300+
Resurrection Medical Center	Chicago	51%	300+
Rockford Memorial Hospital	Rockford	51%	300+
Saint Bernard Hospital	Chicago	51%	300+
John H Stroger Jr Hospital	Chicago	50%	300+
Swedish Covenant Hospital	Chicago	50%	300+
Skokie Hospital	Skokie	49%	300+
Trinity Rock Island	Rock Island	49%	300+
West Suburban Medical Center	Oak Park	49%	300+
Sacred Heart Hospital	Chicago	47%	300+
South Shore Hospital	Chicago	47%	300+
Touchette Regional Hospital	Centreville	47%	(a)
Vista Medical Center East	Waukegan	47%	300+
Holy Cross Hospital	Chicago	46%	300+
Norwegian-American Hospital	Chicago	44%	300+
Thorek Memorial Hospital	Chicago	44%	300+
Mount Sinai Hospital Medical Center	Chicago	42%	300+
Loretto Hospital	Chicago	39%	(a)
Methodist Hospital of Chicago	Chicago	39%	(a)
Jackson Park Hospital	Chicago	38%	300+
Roseland Community Hospital	Chicago	38%	300+

49. Would Definitely Recommend Hospital

Hospital Name	City	Rate	Cases
Midwestern Region Medical Center	Zion	91%	300+
Saint Josephs Hospital	Breese	83%	300+
Saint Mary Medical Center	Galesburg	83%	300+
Memorial Hospital of Carbondale	Carbondale	82%	300+
Morris Hospital & Healthcare Centers	Morris	82%	300+
Northwestern Memorial Hospital	Chicago	82%	300+
Central Dupage Hospital	Winfield	81%	300+
Edward Hospital	Naperville	81%	300+
Gibson Community Hospital	Gibson City	81%	300+
Methodist Medical Center of Illinois	Peoria	81%	300+
Carle Foundation Hospital	Urbana	80%	300+
Rochelle Community Hospital	Rochelle	79%	(a)
Saint Joseph Memorial Hospital	Murphysboro	79%	(a)
Abraham Lincoln Memorial Hospital	Lincoln	78%	(a)
Alton Memorial Hospital	Alton	78%	300+
Bromenn Healthcare	Normal	78%	300+
Herrin Hospital	Herrin	78%	300+
Proctor Hospital	Peoria	78%	300+
Riverside Medical Center	Kankakee	78%	300+
Saint Joseph Medical Center	Bloomington	78%	300+
Advocate Good Samaritan Hospital	Downers Grove	77%	300+
Alexian Brothers Medical Center	Elk Grove Vlg	77%	300+
Delnor Community Hospital	Geneva	77%	300+
Hammond Henry Hospital	Geneseo	77%	300+
Illinois Valley Community Hospital	Peru	77%	300+
Katherine Shaw Bethea Hospital	Dixon	77%	300+
Mercy Hospital and Medical Center	Chicago	77%	300+
Provena St Marys Hospital	Kankakee	77%	300+
Advocate Lutheran General Hospital	Park Ridge	76%	300+
Evanston Hospital	Evanston	76%	300+
Lake Forest Hospital	Lake Forest	76%	300+
Rush University Medical Center	Chicago	76%	300+
Saint Marys Hospital	Centralia	76%	300+
Genesis Medical Center Illini Campus	Silvis	75%	300+
Memorial Hospital	Belleville	74%	300+
Memorial Medical Center	Springfield	74%	300+
Richland Memorial Hospital	Olney	74%	300+
Sarah Bush Lincoln Health Center	Mattoon	74%	300+
Carlinville Area Hospital	Carlinville	73%	(a)
Copley Memorial Hospital	Aurora	73%	300+
Decatur Memorial Hospital	Decatur	73%	300+
Provena Covenant Medical Center - Urbana	Urbana	73%	300+
Saint Anthony Medical Center	Rockford	73%	300+
Saint Johns Hospital	Springfield	73%	300+
Sherman Hospital	Elgin	73%	300+
Advocate Good Shepherd Hospital	Barrington	72%	300+
Good Samaritan Regional Health Center	Mount Vernon	72%	300+
Loyola University Medical Center	Maywood	72%	300+
Provena-Saint Joseph Hospital	Elgin	72%	300+
Salem Township Hospital	Salem	72%	(a)
Silver Cross Hospital	Joliet	72%	300+
Swedish American Hospital	Rockford	72%	300+
Valley West Community Hospital	Sandwich	72%	300+
Saint Francis Medical Center	Peoria	71%	300+
Saint James Hospital	Pontiac	71%	300+
Saint Joseph's Hospital	Highland	71%	(a)
Adventist La Grange Memorial Hospital	La Grange	70%	300+
Provena St Joseph Medical Center	Joliet	70%	300+
The University of Chicago Medical Center	Chicago	70%	300+
Advocate Illinois Masonic Medical Center	Chicago	69%	300+
Anderson Hospital	Maryville	69%	300+
Illini Community Hospital	Pittsfield	69%	(a)
Kishwaukee Community Hospital	Dekalb	69%	300+
Saint Marys Hospital	Decatur	69%	300+
Advocate Christ Hospital & Medical Center	Oak Lawn	68%	300+
Centegra Health System - McHenry Hospital	Mchenry	68%	300+
Centegra Health Sys-Woodstock Hospital	Woodstock	68%	300+
Elmhurst Memorial Hospital	Elmhurst	68%	300+
Hinsdale Hospital	Hinsdale	68%	300+
Palos Community Hospital	Palos Heights	68%	300+
Saint Alexius Medical Center	Hoffman Estates	68%	300+
Saint Anthony's Health Center	Alton	68%	300+
Taylorville Memorial Hospital	Taylorville	68%	300+
Little Company of Mary Hospital	Evergreen Park	67%	300+
Red Bud Regional Hospital	Red Bud	67%	(a)
Rockford Memorial Hospital	Rockford	67%	300+
Saint Anthonys Memorial Hospital	Effingham	67%	300+
Saint Joseph Hospital	Chicago	67%	300+
Saint Margarets Hospital	Spring Valley	67%	300+
CGH Medical Center	Sterling	66%	300+
Oak Forest Hospital	Oak Forest	66%	300+
OSF Holy Family Medical Center	Monmouth	66%	(a)
St Mary & Elizabeth Med Ctr-Div Campus	Chicago	66%	300+
Westlake Community Hospital[11]	Melrose Park	66%	300+

NOTE: Hospital profiles are in alphabetical order by state, then city, then hospital within the city; Rankings exclude hospitals with less than 25 cases except for patient surveys which excludes hospitals with less than 100 cases; (a) 100–299 cases; (1) The number of cases is too small to be sure how well a hospital is performing; (2) The hospital indicated that the data submitted for this measure were based on a sample of cases; (3) Data was collected during a shorter time period (fewer quarters) than the maximum possible time for this measure; (4) Suppressed for one or more quarters by CMS; (5) No data is available from the hospital for this measure; (6) Fewer than 100 patients completed the HCAHPS survey. Use these rates with caution, as the number of surveys may be too low to reliably assess hospital performance; (7) Survey results are based on less than 12 months of data; (8) Survey results are not available for this reporting period; (9) No or very few patients were eligible for the HCAHPS survey. The scores shown, if any, reflect a very small number of surveys; (10) A state average was not calculated because too few hospitals in the state submitted data; (11) There were discrepancies in the data collection process; Please refer to the User's Guide for a full explanation of data.

Adventist Bolingbrook Hospital	Bolingbrook	65%	300+
Ingalls Memorial Hospital	Harvey	65%	300+
Mendota Community Hospital	Mendota	65%	300+
Northwest Community Hospital	Arlington Hgts	65%	300+
Pekin Memorial Hospital	Pekin	65%	300+
Saint Anthony Hospital	Chicago	65%	300+
Blessing Hospital	Quincy	64%	300+
Hillsboro Area Hospital	Hillsboro	64%	(a)
Macneal Hospital	Berwyn	64%	300+
McDonough District Hospital	Macomb	64%	300+
Passavant Area Hospital	Jacksonville	64%	300+
Provena Mercy Medical Center	Aurora	64%	300+
Rush Oak Park Hospital	Oak Park	64%	300+
Saint Francis Hospital	Litchfield	64%	300+
Trinity Rock Island	Rock Island	64%	300+
Advocate South Suburban Hospital	Hazel Crest	63%	300+
Louis A Weiss Memorial Hospital	Chicago	63%	300+
Ottawa Reg Hosp & Healthcare Ctr	Ottawa	63%	300+
Saint Marys Hospital	Streator	63%	300+
University of Illinois Hospital	Chicago	63%	300+
Advocate Condell Medical Center	Libertyville	62%	300+
Crossroads Community Hospital	Mount Vernon	62%	300+
Greenville Regional Hospital	Greenville	62%	(a)
Jersey Community Hospital	Jerseyville	62%	300+
RHC St Francis Hospital	Evanston	62%	300+
Galesburg Cottage Hospital	Galesburg	61%	300+
Graham Hospital Association	Canton	61%	300+
Harrisburg Medical Center	Harrisburg	61%	300+
John H Stroger Jr Hospital	Chicago	61%	300+
Pinckneyville Community Hospital	Pinckneyville	61%	(a)
Saint Elizabeth Hospital	Belleville	61%	300+
Swedish Covenant Hospital	Chicago	61%	300+
West Suburban Medical Center	Oak Park	61%	300+
Crawford Memorial Hospital	Robinson	60%	(a)
Iroquois Memorial Hospital	Watseka	60%	300+
Loyola Gottlieb Memorial Hospital	Melrose Park	60%	300+
Methodist Hospital of Chicago	Chicago	60%	(a)
Skokie Hospital	Skokie	60%	300+
Resurrection Medical Center	Chicago	59%	300+
St James Hospital-Olympia Fields	Olympia Fields	58%	300+
Metrosouth Medical Center	Blue Island	57%	300+
Union County Hospital	Anna	57%	(a)
Adventist Glenoaks	Glendale Hghts	56%	300+
Kewanee Hospital[11]	Kewanee	56%	(a)
Fhn Memorial Hospital	Freeport	55%	300+
Provena United Samaritans Med Ctr-Logan	Danville	55%	300+
Sacred Heart Hospital	Chicago	55%	300+
Gateway Regional Medical Center	Granite City	53%	300+
Provident Hospital of Chicago	Chicago	53%	300+
Touchette Regional Hospital	Centreville	53%	(a)
Advocate Trinity Hospital	Chicago	52%	300+
Heartland Regional Medical Center	Marion	52%	300+
Mount Sinai Hospital Medical Center	Chicago	52%	300+
Our Lady of the Resurrection Medical Center	Chicago	51%	300+
Vista Medical Center East	Waukegan	48%	300+
Thorek Memorial Hospital	Chicago	47%	300+
Norwegian-American Hospital	Chicago	44%	300+
Shelby Memorial Hospital	Shelbyville	44%	(a)
Holy Cross Hospital	Chicago	43%	300+
Roseland Community Hospital	Chicago	40%	300+
Loretto Hospital	Chicago	39%	(a)
Saint Bernard Hospital	Chicago	39%	300+
South Shore Hospital	Chicago	38%	300+
Jackson Park Hospital	Chicago	30%	300+

NOTE: Hospital profiles are in alphabetical order by state, then city, then hospital within the city; Rankings exclude hospitals with less than 25 cases except for patient surveys which excludes hospitals with less than 100 cases; (a) 100–299 cases; (1) The number of cases is too small to be sure how well a hospital is performing; (2) The hospital indicated that the data submitted for this measure were based on a sample of cases; (3) Data was collected during a shorter time period (fewer quarters) than the maximum possible time for this measure; (4) Suppressed for one or more quarters by CMS; (5) No data is available from the hospital for this measure; (6) Fewer than 100 patients completed the HCAHPS survey. Use these rates with caution, as the number of surveys may be too low to reliably assess hospital performance; (7) Survey results are based on less than 12 months of data; (8) Survey results are not available for this reporting period; (9) No or very few patients were eligible for the HCAHPS survey. The scores shown, if any, reflect a very small number of surveys; (10) A state average was not calculated because too few hospitals in the state submitted data; (11) There were discrepancies in the data collection process; Please refer to the User's Guide for a full explanation of data.

Mercer County Hospital

409 NW 9th Avenue
Aledo, IL 61231
URL: www.mercerhospital.org
Type: Critical Access Hospitals
Ownership: Voluntary Non-Profit - Other
Phone: 309-582-5301
Emergency Services: Yes
Beds: 22

Key Personnel:
Administrator . . . . Ted Rogalski

Measure	Cases	This Hosp.	State Avg.	U.S. Avg.
Heart Attack Care				
ACE Inhibitor or ARB for LVSD[5]	0	-	96%	96%
Aspirin at Arrival[5]	0	-	99%	99%
Aspirin at Discharge[5]	0	-	99%	98%
Beta Blocker at Discharge[5]	0	-	98%	98%
Fibrinolytic Medication Timing[5]	0	-	50%	55%
PCI Within 90 Minutes of Arrival[5]	0	-	90%	90%
Smoking Cessation Advice[5]	0	-	100%	99%
Chest Pain/Possible Heart Attack Care				
Aspirin at Arrival	-	-	95%	95%
Median Time to ECG (minutes)	-	-	8	8
Median Time to Transfer (minutes)	-	-	57	61
Fibrinolytic Medication Timing	-	-	33%	54%
Heart Failure Care				
ACE Inhibitor or ARB for LVSD[5]	0	-	94%	94%
Discharge Instructions[5]	0	-	89%	88%
Evaluation of LVS Function[5]	0	-	98%	98%
Smoking Cessation Advice[5]	0	-	99%	98%
Pneumonia Care				
Appropriate Initial Antibiotic[5]	0	-	90%	92%
Blood Culture Timing[5]	0	-	97%	96%
Influenza Vaccine[5]	0	-	91%	91%
Initial Antibiotic Timing[5]	0	-	96%	95%
Pneumococcal Vaccine[5]	0	-	92%	93%
Smoking Cessation Advice[5]	0	-	98%	97%
Surgical Care Improvement Project				
Appropriate VTP Within 24 Hours[5]	0	-	92%	92%
Appropriate Hair Removal[5]	0	-	99%	99%
Appropriate Beta Blocker Usage[5]	0	-	92%	93%
Controlled Postoperative Blood Glucose[5]	0	-	92%	93%
Prophylactic Antibiotic Timing[5]	0	-	97%	97%
Prophylactic Antibiotic Timing (Outpatient)	-	-	93%	92%
Prophylactic Antibiotic Selection[5]	0	-	97%	97%
Prophylactic Antibiotic Select. (Outpatient)	-	-	94%	94%
Prophylactic Antibiotic Stopped[5]	0	-	94%	94%
Recommended VTP Ordered[5]	0	-	94%	94%
Urinary Catheter Removal[5]	0	-	89%	90%
Children's Asthma Care				
Received Systemic Corticosteroids	-	-	-	100%
Received Home Management Plan	-	-	-	71%
Received Reliever Medication	-	-	-	100%
Use of Medical Imaging				
Combination Abdominal CT Scan	-	-	0.246	0.191
Combination Chest CT Scan	-	-	0.098	0.054
Follow-up Mammogram/Ultrasound	-	-	8.4%	8.4%
MRI for Low Back Pain	-	-	33.4%	32.7%
Survey of Patients' Hospital Experiences				
Area Around Room 'Always' Quiet at Night[8]	-	-	-	58%
Doctors 'Always' Communicated Well[8]	-	-	-	80%
Home Recovery Information Given[8]	-	-	-	82%
Hospital Given 9 or 10 on 10 Point Scale[8]	-	-	-	67%
Meds 'Always' Explained Before Given[8]	-	-	-	60%
Nurses 'Always' Communicated Well[8]	-	-	-	76%
Pain 'Always' Well Controlled[8]	-	-	-	69%
Room and Bathroom 'Always' Clean[8]	-	-	-	71%
Timely Help 'Always' Received[8]	-	-	-	64%
Would Definitely Recommend Hospital[8]	-	-	-	69%

Alton Memorial Hospital

One Memorial Drive
Alton, IL 62002
URL: www.altonmemorialhospital.org
Type: Acute Care Hospitals
Ownership: Voluntary Non-Profit - Private
Phone: 618-463-7300
Fax: 618-463-7850
Emergency Services: Yes
Beds: 222

Key Personnel:
CEO/President. . . . . Dave Braasch

Measure	Cases	This Hosp.	State Avg.	U.S. Avg.
Heart Attack Care				
ACE Inhibitor or ARB for LVSD[1]	11	91%	96%	96%
Aspirin at Arrival	95	100%	99%	99%
Aspirin at Discharge	80	100%	99%	98%
Beta Blocker at Discharge	84	100%	98%	98%
Fibrinolytic Medication Timing[1]	1	100%	50%	55%
PCI Within 90 Minutes of Arrival[1]	3	100%	90%	90%
Smoking Cessation Advice	31	100%	100%	99%
Chest Pain/Possible Heart Attack Care				
Aspirin at Arrival	68	97%	95%	95%
Median Time to ECG (minutes)	65	6	8	8
Median Time to Transfer (minutes)[1,3]	5	51	57	61
Fibrinolytic Medication Timing	0	-	33%	54%
Heart Failure Care				
ACE Inhibitor or ARB for LVSD	72	94%	94%	94%
Discharge Instructions	171	82%	89%	88%
Evaluation of LVS Function	226	100%	98%	98%
Smoking Cessation Advice	42	100%	99%	98%
Pneumonia Care				
Appropriate Initial Antibiotic[2]	187	87%	90%	92%
Blood Culture Timing[2]	271	99%	97%	96%
Influenza Vaccine[2]	167	89%	91%	91%
Initial Antibiotic Timing[2]	279	97%	96%	95%
Pneumococcal Vaccine[2]	228	89%	92%	93%
Smoking Cessation Advice[2]	105	100%	98%	97%
Surgical Care Improvement Project				
Appropriate VTP Within 24 Hours	134	95%	92%	92%
Appropriate Hair Removal	333	100%	99%	99%
Appropriate Beta Blocker Usage	92	100%	92%	93%
Controlled Postoperative Blood Glucose	0	-	92%	93%
Prophylactic Antibiotic Timing	239	98%	97%	97%
Prophylactic Antibiotic Timing (Outpatient)	142	94%	93%	92%
Prophylactic Antibiotic Selection	242	99%	97%	97%
Prophylactic Antibiotic Select. (Outpatient)	144	94%	94%	94%
Prophylactic Antibiotic Stopped	226	96%	94%	94%
Recommended VTP Ordered	134	96%	94%	94%
Urinary Catheter Removal	109	83%	89%	90%
Children's Asthma Care				
Received Systemic Corticosteroids	-	-	-	100%
Received Home Management Plan	-	-	-	71%
Received Reliever Medication	-	-	-	100%
Use of Medical Imaging				
Combination Abdominal CT Scan	888	0.114	0.246	0.191
Combination Chest CT Scan	509	0.018	0.098	0.054
Follow-up Mammogram/Ultrasound	1,181	2.0%	8.4%	8.4%
MRI for Low Back Pain[1]	3	33.3%	33.4%	32.7%
Survey of Patients' Hospital Experiences				
Area Around Room 'Always' Quiet at Night	300+	60%	-	58%
Doctors 'Always' Communicated Well	300+	84%	-	80%
Home Recovery Information Given	300+	84%	-	82%
Hospital Given 9 or 10 on 10 Point Scale	300+	71%	-	67%
Meds 'Always' Explained Before Given	300+	58%	-	60%
Nurses 'Always' Communicated Well	300+	80%	-	76%
Pain 'Always' Well Controlled	300+	72%	-	69%
Room and Bathroom 'Always' Clean	300+	73%	-	71%
Timely Help 'Always' Received	300+	61%	-	64%
Would Definitely Recommend Hospital	300+	78%	-	69%

Saint Anthony's Health Center

St Anthony's Way
Alton, IL 62002
URL: www.sahc.org
Type: Acute Care Hospitals
Ownership: Voluntary Non-Profit - Church
Phone: 618-465-2571
Fax: 618-474-4860
Emergency Services: Yes
Beds: 192

Key Personnel:
CEO/President. . . . . E J Kuiper
Cardiac Laboratory. . . . . Pamela Kratovil
Chief of Medical Staff . . . . Salvador LoBianco, MD
Quality Assurance . . . . Susan Hornsey
Emergency Room . . . . Karen Marzluf

Measure	Cases	This Hosp.	State Avg.	U.S. Avg.
Heart Attack Care				
ACE Inhibitor or ARB for LVSD[1]	6	83%	96%	96%
Aspirin at Arrival	45	96%	99%	99%
Aspirin at Discharge	42	95%	99%	98%
Beta Blocker at Discharge	43	95%	98%	98%
Fibrinolytic Medication Timing	0	-	50%	55%
PCI Within 90 Minutes of Arrival[1]	7	86%	90%	90%
Smoking Cessation Advice[1]	12	100%	100%	99%
Chest Pain/Possible Heart Attack Care				
Aspirin at Arrival[1]	21	95%	95%	95%
Median Time to ECG (minutes)[1]	22	12	8	8
Median Time to Transfer (minutes)[1]	9	62	57	61
Fibrinolytic Medication Timing	0	-	33%	54%
Heart Failure Care				
ACE Inhibitor or ARB for LVSD	46	93%	94%	94%
Discharge Instructions	117	78%	89%	88%
Evaluation of LVS Function	165	98%	98%	98%
Smoking Cessation Advice	28	100%	99%	98%
Pneumonia Care				
Appropriate Initial Antibiotic	92	85%	90%	92%
Blood Culture Timing	142	96%	97%	96%
Influenza Vaccine	117	85%	91%	91%
Initial Antibiotic Timing	148	97%	96%	95%
Pneumococcal Vaccine	154	92%	92%	93%
Smoking Cessation Advice	73	99%	98%	97%
Surgical Care Improvement Project				
Appropriate VTP Within 24 Hours	80	86%	92%	92%
Appropriate Hair Removal	307	100%	99%	99%
Appropriate Beta Blocker Usage	91	97%	92%	93%
Controlled Postoperative Blood Glucose	0	-	92%	93%
Prophylactic Antibiotic Timing	239	96%	97%	97%
Prophylactic Antibiotic Timing (Outpatient)	49	88%	93%	92%
Prophylactic Antibiotic Selection	242	96%	97%	97%
Prophylactic Antibiotic Select. (Outpatient)	112	98%	94%	94%
Prophylactic Antibiotic Stopped	225	92%	94%	94%
Recommended VTP Ordered	80	98%	94%	94%
Urinary Catheter Removal	93	95%	89%	90%
Children's Asthma Care				
Received Systemic Corticosteroids	-	-	-	100%
Received Home Management Plan	-	-	-	71%
Received Reliever Medication	-	-	-	100%
Use of Medical Imaging				
Combination Abdominal CT Scan	491	0.310	0.246	0.191
Combination Chest CT Scan	207	0.072	0.098	0.054
Follow-up Mammogram/Ultrasound	871	7.3%	8.4%	8.4%
MRI for Low Back Pain	88	33.0%	33.4%	32.7%
Survey of Patients' Hospital Experiences				
Area Around Room 'Always' Quiet at Night	300+	54%	-	58%
Doctors 'Always' Communicated Well	300+	78%	-	80%
Home Recovery Information Given	300+	84%	-	82%
Hospital Given 9 or 10 on 10 Point Scale	300+	66%	-	67%
Meds 'Always' Explained Before Given	300+	61%	-	60%
Nurses 'Always' Communicated Well	300+	74%	-	76%
Pain 'Always' Well Controlled	300+	67%	-	69%
Room and Bathroom 'Always' Clean	300+	71%	-	71%
Timely Help 'Always' Received	300+	59%	-	64%
Would Definitely Recommend Hospital	300+	68%	-	69%

NOTE: Hospital profiles are in alphabetical order by state, then city, then hospital within the city; Rankings exclude hospitals with less than 25 cases except for patient surveys which excludes hospitals with less than 100 cases; (a) 100–299 cases; (1) The number of cases is too small to be sure how well a hospital is performing; (2) The hospital indicated that the data submitted for this measure were based on a sample of cases; (3) Data was collected during a shorter time period (fewer quarters) than the maximum possible time for this measure; (4) Suppressed for one or more quarters by CMS; (5) No data is available from the hospital for this measure; (6) Fewer than 100 patients completed the HCAHPS survey. Use these rates with caution, as the number of surveys may be too low to reliably assess hospital performance; (7) Survey results are based on less than 12 months of data; (8) Survey results are not available for this reporting period; (9) No or very few patients were eligible for the HCAHPS survey. The scores shown, if any, reflect a very small number of surveys; (10) A state average was not calculated because too few hospitals in the state submitted data; (11) There were discrepancies in the data collection process; Please refer to the User's Guide for a full explanation of data.

Union County Hospital

517 North Main Street
Anna, IL 62906
Type: Critical Access Hospitals
Ownership: Proprietary

Phone: 618-833-4511
Fax: 618-833-4183
Emergency Services: Yes
Beds: 58

Key Personnel:

CEO/President. . . . . James R Farris
Chief of Medical Staff. . . . . Deanna St Germain, DO
Operating Room. . . . . Paula Parr, RN
Quality Assurance . . . . Tonia Capel, RN
Radiology. . . . . Peter Wories
Emergency Room . . . . Judy Lewis, RN

Measure	Cases	This Hosp.	State Avg.	U.S. Avg.
Heart Attack Care				
ACE Inhibitor or ARB for LVSD[3]	0	-	96%	96%
Aspirin at Arrival[3,1]	1	100%	99%	99%
Aspirin at Discharge[1,3]	1	100%	99%	98%
Beta Blocker at Discharge[1,3]	1	100%	98%	98%
Fibrinolytic Medication Timing[3]	0	-	50%	55%
PCI Within 90 Minutes of Arrival[3]	0	-	90%	90%
Smoking Cessation Advice[3]	0	-	100%	99%
Chest Pain/Possible Heart Attack Care				
Aspirin at Arrival	82	96%	95%	95%
Median Time to ECG (minutes)	83	9	8	8
Median Time to Transfer (minutes)[1]	14	42	57	61
Fibrinolytic Medication Timing	0	-	33%	54%
Heart Failure Care				
ACE Inhibitor or ARB for LVSD[1]	17	88%	94%	94%
Discharge Instructions	29	83%	89%	88%
Evaluation of LVS Function	37	95%	98%	98%
Smoking Cessation Advice[1]	11	100%	99%	98%
Pneumonia Care				
Appropriate Initial Antibiotic	36	97%	90%	92%
Blood Culture Timing	57	96%	97%	96%
Influenza Vaccine	42	93%	91%	91%
Initial Antibiotic Timing	55	96%	96%	95%
Pneumococcal Vaccine	57	98%	92%	93%
Smoking Cessation Advice[1]	20	100%	98%	97%
Surgical Care Improvement Project				
Appropriate VTP Within 24 Hours[3]	0	-	92%	92%
Appropriate Hair Removal[1,3]	1	100%	99%	99%
Appropriate Beta Blocker Usage[3]	0	-	92%	93%
Controlled Postoperative Blood Glucose[3]	0	-	92%	93%
Prophylactic Antibiotic Timing[1,3]	1	100%	97%	97%
Prophylactic Antibiotic Timing (Outpatient)[1,3]	4	100%	93%	92%
Prophylactic Antibiotic Selection[1,3]	1	100%	97%	97%
Prophylactic Antibiotic Select. (Outpatient)[1,3]	4	100%	94%	94%
Prophylactic Antibiotic Stopped[1,3]	1	100%	94%	94%
Recommended VTP Ordered[3]	0	-	94%	94%
Urinary Catheter Removal[3]	0	-	89%	90%
Children's Asthma Care				
Received Systemic Corticosteroids	-	-	-	100%
Received Home Management Plan	-	-	-	71%
Received Reliever Medication	-	-	-	100%
Use of Medical Imaging				
Combination Abdominal CT Scan	276	0.207	0.246	0.191
Combination Chest CT Scan	130	0.000	0.098	0.054
Follow-up Mammogram/Ultrasound	358	8.7%	8.4%	8.4%
MRI for Low Back Pain[1]	29	34.5%	33.4%	32.7%
Survey of Patients' Hospital Experiences				
Area Around Room 'Always' Quiet at Night	(a)	63%	-	58%
Doctors 'Always' Communicated Well	(a)	85%	-	80%
Home Recovery Information Given	(a)	77%	-	82%
Hospital Given 9 or 10 on 10 Point Scale	(a)	63%	-	67%
Meds 'Always' Explained Before Given	(a)	61%	-	60%
Nurses 'Always' Communicated Well	(a)	75%	-	76%
Pain 'Always' Well Controlled	(a)	69%	-	69%
Room and Bathroom 'Always' Clean	(a)	72%	-	71%
Timely Help 'Always' Received	(a)	63%	-	64%
Would Definitely Recommend Hospital	(a)	57%	-	69%

Northwest Community Hospital

800 W Central Road
Arlington Heights, IL 60005
URL: www.nch.org
Type: Acute Care Hospitals
Ownership: Voluntary Non-Profit - Other

Phone: 847-618-1000
Fax: 847-618-5509
Emergency Services: Yes
Beds: 488

Key Personnel:

CEO/President. . . . . Bruce K Crowther
Cardiac Laboratory. . . . . Gilbert Sita, MD
Chief of Medical Staff. . . . . Donald E Pochly
Infection Control. . . . . Karen Gormen
Operating Room. . . . . Mark Levin, MD
Pediatric In-Patient Care . . . . Timothy Geleske, MD
Quality Assurance . . . . Joyce McComb
Radiology. . . . . Clifford Wolf, MD

Measure	Cases	This Hosp.	State Avg.	U.S. Avg.
Heart Attack Care				
ACE Inhibitor or ARB for LVSD	33	91%	96%	96%
Aspirin at Arrival	390	99%	99%	99%
Aspirin at Discharge	349	97%	99%	98%
Beta Blocker at Discharge	339	99%	98%	98%
Fibrinolytic Medication Timing	0	-	50%	55%
PCI Within 90 Minutes of Arrival	59	93%	90%	90%
Smoking Cessation Advice	66	98%	100%	99%
Chest Pain/Possible Heart Attack Care				
Aspirin at Arrival[1]	7	57%	95%	95%
Median Time to ECG (minutes)[1]	7	4	8	8
Median Time to Transfer (minutes)[5]	0	-	57	61
Fibrinolytic Medication Timing[5]	0	-	33%	54%
Heart Failure Care				
ACE Inhibitor or ARB for LVSD[2]	52	100%	94%	94%
Discharge Instructions[2]	189	95%	89%	88%
Evaluation of LVS Function[2]	306	100%	98%	98%
Smoking Cessation Advice[1,2]	18	100%	99%	98%
Pneumonia Care				
Appropriate Initial Antibiotic[2]	83	94%	90%	92%
Blood Culture Timing[2]	149	93%	97%	96%
Influenza Vaccine[2]	94	94%	91%	91%
Initial Antibiotic Timing[2]	156	98%	96%	95%
Pneumococcal Vaccine[2]	141	89%	92%	93%
Smoking Cessation Advice[1,2]	22	82%	98%	97%
Surgical Care Improvement Project				
Appropriate VTP Within 24 Hours[2]	182	91%	92%	92%
Appropriate Hair Removal[2]	670	84%	99%	99%
Appropriate Beta Blocker Usage[2]	225	94%	92%	93%
Controlled Postoperative Blood Glucose[2]	160	91%	92%	93%
Prophylactic Antibiotic Timing[2]	487	87%	97%	97%
Prophylactic Antibiotic Timing (Outpatient)	350	90%	93%	92%
Prophylactic Antibiotic Selection[2]	488	95%	97%	97%
Prophylactic Antibiotic Select. (Outpatient)	366	88%	94%	94%
Prophylactic Antibiotic Stopped[2]	457	93%	94%	94%
Recommended VTP Ordered[2]	182	94%	94%	94%
Urinary Catheter Removal[2]	147	82%	89%	90%
Children's Asthma Care				
Received Systemic Corticosteroids	-	-	-	100%
Received Home Management Plan	-	-	-	71%
Received Reliever Medication	-	-	-	100%
Use of Medical Imaging				
Combination Abdominal CT Scan	3,470	0.090	0.246	0.191
Combination Chest CT Scan	2,628	0.025	0.098	0.054
Follow-up Mammogram/Ultrasound	5,143	7.7%	8.4%	8.4%
MRI for Low Back Pain	575	31.0%	33.4%	32.7%
Survey of Patients' Hospital Experiences				
Area Around Room 'Always' Quiet at Night	300+	39%	-	58%
Doctors 'Always' Communicated Well	300+	71%	-	80%
Home Recovery Information Given	300+	77%	-	82%
Hospital Given 9 or 10 on 10 Point Scale	300+	58%	-	67%
Meds 'Always' Explained Before Given	300+	51%	-	60%
Nurses 'Always' Communicated Well	300+	68%	-	76%
Pain 'Always' Well Controlled	300+	64%	-	69%
Room and Bathroom 'Always' Clean	300+	61%	-	71%
Timely Help 'Always' Received	300+	54%	-	64%
Would Definitely Recommend Hospital	300+	65%	-	69%

Copley Memorial Hospital

2000 Ogden Avenue
Aurora, IL 60504
E-mail: clord@rsh.net
URL: www.rushcopley.com
Type: Acute Care Hospitals
Ownership: Government - Local

Phone: 630-978-6200
Fax: 630-978-6888
Emergency Services: Yes
Beds: 183

Key Personnel:

CEO/President. . . . . Barry C Finn, MBA CPA
Chief of Medical Staff. . . . . Steven B Lowenthal, MD
Infection Control. . . . . Maria Montero
Operating Room. . . . . David Reinhaft
Pediatric In-Patient Care . . . . Janet Smith, RN
Quality Assurance . . . . Lisa Brady, MS
Radiology. . . . . Syed A Akbar

Measure	Cases	This Hosp.	State Avg.	U.S. Avg.
Heart Attack Care				
ACE Inhibitor or ARB for LVSD	29	97%	96%	96%
Aspirin at Arrival	182	99%	99%	99%
Aspirin at Discharge	183	99%	99%	98%
Beta Blocker at Discharge	179	100%	98%	98%
Fibrinolytic Medication Timing	0	-	50%	55%
PCI Within 90 Minutes of Arrival	35	97%	90%	90%
Smoking Cessation Advice	77	100%	100%	99%
Chest Pain/Possible Heart Attack Care				
Aspirin at Arrival[1,3]	12	92%	95%	95%
Median Time to ECG (minutes)[1,3]	11	7	8	8
Median Time to Transfer (minutes)[5]	0	-	57	61
Fibrinolytic Medication Timing[3]	0	-	33%	54%
Heart Failure Care				
ACE Inhibitor or ARB for LVSD	63	98%	94%	94%
Discharge Instructions	203	97%	89%	88%
Evaluation of LVS Function	275	99%	98%	98%
Smoking Cessation Advice	46	100%	99%	98%
Pneumonia Care				
Appropriate Initial Antibiotic	119	92%	90%	92%
Blood Culture Timing	154	97%	97%	96%
Influenza Vaccine	81	93%	91%	91%
Initial Antibiotic Timing	173	99%	96%	95%
Pneumococcal Vaccine	119	92%	92%	93%
Smoking Cessation Advice	55	100%	98%	97%
Surgical Care Improvement Project				
Appropriate VTP Within 24 Hours[2]	199	94%	92%	92%
Appropriate Hair Removal[2]	840	100%	99%	99%
Appropriate Beta Blocker Usage[2]	274	94%	92%	93%
Controlled Postoperative Blood Glucose[2]	97	98%	92%	93%
Prophylactic Antibiotic Timing[2]	669	99%	97%	97%
Prophylactic Antibiotic Timing (Outpatient)	303	99%	93%	92%
Prophylactic Antibiotic Selection[2]	675	97%	97%	97%
Prophylactic Antibiotic Select. (Outpatient)	301	97%	94%	94%
Prophylactic Antibiotic Stopped[2]	656	93%	94%	94%
Recommended VTP Ordered[2]	199	96%	94%	94%
Urinary Catheter Removal[2]	249	94%	89%	90%
Children's Asthma Care				
Received Systemic Corticosteroids	-	-	-	100%
Received Home Management Plan	-	-	-	71%
Received Reliever Medication	-	-	-	100%
Use of Medical Imaging				
Combination Abdominal CT Scan	785	0.066	0.246	0.191
Combination Chest CT Scan	487	0.025	0.098	0.054
Follow-up Mammogram/Ultrasound	725	7.3%	8.4%	8.4%
MRI for Low Back Pain	95	34.7%	33.4%	32.7%
Survey of Patients' Hospital Experiences				
Area Around Room 'Always' Quiet at Night	300+	52%	-	58%
Doctors 'Always' Communicated Well	300+	79%	-	80%
Home Recovery Information Given	300+	82%	-	82%
Hospital Given 9 or 10 on 10 Point Scale	300+	67%	-	67%
Meds 'Always' Explained Before Given	300+	60%	-	60%
Nurses 'Always' Communicated Well	300+	74%	-	76%
Pain 'Always' Well Controlled	300+	69%	-	69%
Room and Bathroom 'Always' Clean	300+	65%	-	71%
Timely Help 'Always' Received	300+	56%	-	64%
Would Definitely Recommend Hospital	300+	73%	-	69%

NOTE: Hospital profiles are in alphabetical order by state, then city, then hospital within the city; Rankings exclude hospitals with less than 25 cases except for patient surveys which excludes hospitals with less than 100 cases; (a) 100–299 cases; (1) The number of cases is too small to be sure how well a hospital is performing; (2) The hospital indicated that the data submitted for this measure were based on a sample of cases; (3) Data was collected during a shorter time period (fewer quarters) than the maximum possible time for this measure; (4) Suppressed for one or more quarters by CMS; (5) No data is available from the hospital for this measure; (6) Fewer than 100 patients completed the HCAHPS survey. Use these rates with caution, as the number of surveys may be too low to reliably assess hospital performance; (7) Survey results are based on less than 12 months of data; (8) Survey results are not available for this reporting period; (9) No or very few patients were eligible for the HCAHPS survey. The scores shown, if any, reflect a very small number of surveys; (10) A state average was not calculated because too few hospitals in the state submitted data; (11) There were discrepancies in the data collection process; Please refer to the User's Guide for a full explanation of data.

Provena Mercy Medical Center

1325 N Highland Avenue Phone: 630-859-2222
Aurora, IL 60506 Fax: 630-801-2608
URL: www.provena.org/mercy
Type: Acute Care Hospitals Emergency Services: Yes
Ownership: Voluntary Non-Profit - Church Beds: 356

Key Personnel:
CEO/President. . . . . Teresa Stokes
Chief of Medical Staff. . . . . Michael Loebach, MD
Infection Control. . . . . Kathy Hettinger
Operating Room. . . . . Kathleen Satchel, RN
Radiology. . . . . EH Dolin, MD
Anesthesiology. . . . . HF Tsang, MD
Emergency Room . . . . James Kolka, MD

Measure	Cases	This Hosp.	State Avg.	U.S. Avg.
Heart Attack Care				
ACE Inhibitor or ARB for LVSD[1]	21	95%	96%	96%
Aspirin at Arrival	110	98%	99%	99%
Aspirin at Discharge	118	100%	99%	98%
Beta Blocker at Discharge	121	98%	98%	98%
Fibrinolytic Medication Timing	0	-	50%	55%
PCI Within 90 Minutes of Arrival[1]	22	73%	90%	90%
Smoking Cessation Advice	34	100%	100%	99%
Chest Pain/Possible Heart Attack Care				
Aspirin at Arrival[1]	5	80%	95%	95%
Median Time to ECG (minutes)[1]	5	9	8	8
Median Time to Transfer (minutes)[5]	0	-	57	61
Fibrinolytic Medication Timing[3]	0	-	33%	54%
Heart Failure Care				
ACE Inhibitor or ARB for LVSD[2]	76	80%	94%	94%
Discharge Instructions[2]	147	95%	89%	88%
Evaluation of LVS Function[2]	197	96%	98%	98%
Smoking Cessation Advice[2]	26	100%	99%	98%
Pneumonia Care				
Appropriate Initial Antibiotic[2]	94	86%	90%	92%
Blood Culture Timing[2]	170	89%	97%	96%
Influenza Vaccine[2]	86	87%	91%	91%
Initial Antibiotic Timing[2]	157	93%	96%	95%
Pneumococcal Vaccine[2]	115	83%	92%	93%
Smoking Cessation Advice[2]	47	100%	98%	97%
Surgical Care Improvement Project				
Appropriate VTP Within 24 Hours[2]	158	85%	92%	92%
Appropriate Hair Removal[2]	636	100%	99%	99%
Appropriate Beta Blocker Usage[2]	207	87%	92%	93%
Controlled Postoperative Blood Glucose[2]	159	91%	92%	93%
Prophylactic Antibiotic Timing[2]	470	93%	97%	97%
Prophylactic Antibiotic Timing (Outpatient)	174	86%	93%	92%
Prophylactic Antibiotic Selection[2]	478	97%	97%	97%
Prophylactic Antibiotic Select. (Outpatient)	171	87%	94%	94%
Prophylactic Antibiotic Stopped[2]	429	91%	94%	94%
Recommended VTP Ordered[2]	158	85%	94%	94%
Urinary Catheter Removal[2]	184	70%	89%	90%
Children's Asthma Care				
Received Systemic Corticosteroids	-	-	-	100%
Received Home Management Plan	-	-	-	71%
Received Reliever Medication	-	-	-	100%
Use of Medical Imaging				
Combination Abdominal CT Scan	388	0.080	0.246	0.191
Combination Chest CT Scan	222	0.045	0.098	0.054
Follow-up Mammogram/Ultrasound	443	16.3%	8.4%	8.4%
MRI for Low Back Pain	106	28.3%	33.4%	32.7%
Survey of Patients' Hospital Experiences				
Area Around Room 'Always' Quiet at Night	300+	57%	-	58%
Doctors 'Always' Communicated Well	300+	77%	-	80%
Home Recovery Information Given	300+	84%	-	82%
Hospital Given 9 or 10 on 10 Point Scale	300+	61%	-	67%
Meds 'Always' Explained Before Given	300+	58%	-	60%
Nurses 'Always' Communicated Well	300+	74%	-	76%
Pain 'Always' Well Controlled	300+	63%	-	69%
Room and Bathroom 'Always' Clean	300+	67%	-	71%
Timely Help 'Always' Received	300+	55%	-	64%
Would Definitely Recommend Hospital	300+	64%	-	69%

Advocate Good Shepherd Hospital

450 West Highway 22 Phone: 847-381-9600
Barrington, IL 60010 Fax: 847-842-4060
URL: www.advocatehealth.com
Type: Acute Care Hospitals Emergency Services: Yes
Ownership: Voluntary Non-Profit - Church Beds: 154

Key Personnel:
CEO/President. . . . . Karen Lambert
Quality Assurance . . . . Mike Wiegel
Radiology. . . . . Sebouh Guevikia, MD

Measure	Cases	This Hosp.	State Avg.	U.S. Avg.
Heart Attack Care				
ACE Inhibitor or ARB for LVSD	31	100%	96%	96%
Aspirin at Arrival	210	100%	99%	99%
Aspirin at Discharge	217	100%	99%	98%
Beta Blocker at Discharge	214	100%	98%	98%
Fibrinolytic Medication Timing	0	-	50%	55%
PCI Within 90 Minutes of Arrival	41	93%	90%	90%
Smoking Cessation Advice	73	100%	100%	99%
Chest Pain/Possible Heart Attack Care				
Aspirin at Arrival[1,3]	1	100%	95%	95%
Median Time to ECG (minutes)[1,3]	1	9	8	8
Median Time to Transfer (minutes)[5]	0	-	57	61
Fibrinolytic Medication Timing[5]	0	-	33%	54%
Heart Failure Care				
ACE Inhibitor or ARB for LVSD	72	94%	94%	94%
Discharge Instructions	218	90%	89%	88%
Evaluation of LVS Function	314	100%	98%	98%
Smoking Cessation Advice	41	100%	99%	98%
Pneumonia Care				
Appropriate Initial Antibiotic	101	95%	90%	92%
Blood Culture Timing	234	100%	97%	96%
Influenza Vaccine	132	100%	91%	91%
Initial Antibiotic Timing	201	100%	96%	95%
Pneumococcal Vaccine	211	99%	92%	93%
Smoking Cessation Advice	58	100%	98%	97%
Surgical Care Improvement Project				
Appropriate VTP Within 24 Hours[2]	153	98%	92%	92%
Appropriate Hair Removal[2]	594	100%	99%	99%
Appropriate Beta Blocker Usage[2]	243	98%	92%	93%
Controlled Postoperative Blood Glucose[2]	134	100%	92%	93%
Prophylactic Antibiotic Timing[2]	425	98%	97%	97%
Prophylactic Antibiotic Timing (Outpatient)	396	97%	93%	92%
Prophylactic Antibiotic Selection[2]	436	99%	97%	97%
Prophylactic Antibiotic Select. (Outpatient)	391	98%	94%	94%
Prophylactic Antibiotic Stopped[2]	416	96%	94%	94%
Recommended VTP Ordered[2]	153	98%	94%	94%
Urinary Catheter Removal[2]	137	97%	89%	90%
Children's Asthma Care				
Received Systemic Corticosteroids	-	-	-	100%
Received Home Management Plan	-	-	-	71%
Received Reliever Medication	-	-	-	100%
Use of Medical Imaging				
Combination Abdominal CT Scan	999	0.125	0.246	0.191
Combination Chest CT Scan	909	0.020	0.098	0.054
Follow-up Mammogram/Ultrasound	1,483	9.0%	8.4%	8.4%
MRI for Low Back Pain	104	34.6%	33.4%	32.7%
Survey of Patients' Hospital Experiences				
Area Around Room 'Always' Quiet at Night	300+	44%	-	58%
Doctors 'Always' Communicated Well	300+	78%	-	80%
Home Recovery Information Given	300+	83%	-	82%
Hospital Given 9 or 10 on 10 Point Scale	300+	66%	-	67%
Meds 'Always' Explained Before Given	300+	60%	-	60%
Nurses 'Always' Communicated Well	300+	77%	-	76%
Pain 'Always' Well Controlled	300+	69%	-	69%
Room and Bathroom 'Always' Clean	300+	72%	-	71%
Timely Help 'Always' Received	300+	59%	-	64%
Would Definitely Recommend Hospital	300+	72%	-	69%

Memorial Hospital

4500 Memorial Drive Phone: 618-233-7750
Belleville, IL 62226 Fax: 618-257-6911
E-mail: info@memhosp.com
URL: www.memhosp.com
Type: Acute Care Hospitals Emergency Services: Yes
Ownership: Voluntary Non-Profit - Private Beds: 313

Key Personnel:
CEO/President. . . . . Mark J Turner
Chief of Medical Staff. . . . . William Casperson MD
Infection Control. . . . . Kathy Harms
Operating Room. . . . . Brian Johnson RN
Quality Assurance . . . . Kerry Wrigley
Anesthesiology. . . . . Paul Sander MD
Emergency Room . . . . Thomas Byrne MD
Intensive Care Unit. . . . . Kim Howell

Measure	Cases	This Hosp.	State Avg.	U.S. Avg.
Heart Attack Care				
ACE Inhibitor or ARB for LVSD	68	99%	96%	96%
Aspirin at Arrival	301	98%	99%	99%
Aspirin at Discharge	285	99%	99%	98%
Beta Blocker at Discharge	279	99%	98%	98%
Fibrinolytic Medication Timing	0	-	50%	55%
PCI Within 90 Minutes of Arrival	34	94%	90%	90%
Smoking Cessation Advice	78	100%	100%	99%
Chest Pain/Possible Heart Attack Care				
Aspirin at Arrival[1]	20	100%	95%	95%
Median Time to ECG (minutes)[1]	21	2	8	8
Median Time to Transfer (minutes)[5]	0	-	57	61
Fibrinolytic Medication Timing[3]	0	-	33%	54%
Heart Failure Care				
ACE Inhibitor or ARB for LVSD	182	98%	94%	94%
Discharge Instructions	492	85%	89%	88%
Evaluation of LVS Function	603	99%	98%	98%
Smoking Cessation Advice	114	100%	99%	98%
Pneumonia Care				
Appropriate Initial Antibiotic	235	95%	90%	92%
Blood Culture Timing	375	95%	97%	96%
Influenza Vaccine	222	98%	91%	91%
Initial Antibiotic Timing	345	95%	96%	95%
Pneumococcal Vaccine	299	100%	92%	93%
Smoking Cessation Advice	143	99%	98%	97%
Surgical Care Improvement Project				
Appropriate VTP Within 24 Hours[2]	208	95%	92%	92%
Appropriate Hair Removal[2]	647	100%	99%	99%
Appropriate Beta Blocker Usage[2]	251	98%	92%	93%
Controlled Postoperative Blood Glucose[2]	125	98%	92%	93%
Prophylactic Antibiotic Timing[2]	421	98%	97%	97%
Prophylactic Antibiotic Timing (Outpatient)	494	92%	93%	92%
Prophylactic Antibiotic Selection[2]	426	98%	97%	97%
Prophylactic Antibiotic Select. (Outpatient)	499	95%	94%	94%
Prophylactic Antibiotic Stopped[2]	409	96%	94%	94%
Recommended VTP Ordered[2]	209	97%	94%	94%
Urinary Catheter Removal[2]	146	85%	89%	90%
Children's Asthma Care				
Received Systemic Corticosteroids	-	-	-	100%
Received Home Management Plan	-	-	-	71%
Received Reliever Medication	-	-	-	100%
Use of Medical Imaging				
Combination Abdominal CT Scan	1,377	0.102	0.246	0.191
Combination Chest CT Scan	941	0.053	0.098	0.054
Follow-up Mammogram/Ultrasound	1,803	10.4%	8.4%	8.4%
MRI for Low Back Pain	268	32.8%	33.4%	32.7%
Survey of Patients' Hospital Experiences				
Area Around Room 'Always' Quiet at Night	300+	56%	-	58%
Doctors 'Always' Communicated Well	300+	78%	-	80%
Home Recovery Information Given	300+	80%	-	82%
Hospital Given 9 or 10 on 10 Point Scale	300+	70%	-	67%
Meds 'Always' Explained Before Given	300+	59%	-	60%
Nurses 'Always' Communicated Well	300+	78%	-	76%
Pain 'Always' Well Controlled	300+	70%	-	69%
Room and Bathroom 'Always' Clean	300+	69%	-	71%
Timely Help 'Always' Received	300+	61%	-	64%
Would Definitely Recommend Hospital	300+	74%	-	69%

NOTE: Hospital profiles are in alphabetical order by state, then city, then hospital within the city; Rankings exclude hospitals with less than 25 cases except for patient surveys which excludes hospitals with less than 100 cases; (a) 100–299 cases; (1) The number of cases is too small to be sure how well a hospital is performing; (2) The hospital indicated that the data submitted for this measure were based on a sample of cases; (3) Data was collected during a shorter time period (fewer quarters) than the maximum possible time for this measure; (4) Suppressed for one or more quarters by CMS; (5) No data is available from the hospital for this measure; (6) Fewer than 100 patients completed the HCAHPS survey. Use these rates with caution, as the number of surveys may be too low to reliably assess hospital performance; (7) Survey results are based on less than 12 months of data; (8) Survey results are not available for this reporting period; (9) No or very few patients were eligible for the HCAHPS survey. The scores shown, if any, reflect a very small number of surveys; (10) A state average was not calculated because too few hospitals in the state submitted data; (11) There were discrepancies in the data collection process; Please refer to the User's Guide for a full explanation of data.

Saint Elizabeth Hospital

211 S Third St
Belleville, IL 62222
Phone: 618-234-2120
Fax: 618-222-4650
URL: www.steliz.org
Type: Acute Care Hospitals
Emergency Services: No
Ownership: Voluntary Non-Profit - Church
Beds: 498

Key Personnel:
Chief of Medical Staff.......... Salil Gupta MD
Infection Control.............. Laura Stollard
Operating Room.............. Andrea Spalter
Pediatric In-Patient Care .... Salil Gupta MD
Quality Assurance .... Lana Peters
Radiology.................. Paul Schroeder MD
Emergency Room .... Paul Saba
Intensive Care Unit........... Terry Brown

Measure	Cases	This Hosp.	State Avg.	U.S. Avg.
Heart Attack Care				
ACE Inhibitor or ARB for LVSD	38	100%	96%	96%
Aspirin at Arrival	170	98%	99%	99%
Aspirin at Discharge	229	100%	99%	98%
Beta Blocker at Discharge	224	99%	98%	98%
Fibrinolytic Medication Timing	0	-	50%	55%
PCI Within 90 Minutes of Arrival	29	100%	90%	90%
Smoking Cessation Advice	88	100%	100%	99%
Chest Pain/Possible Heart Attack Care				
Aspirin at Arrival[1]	9	89%	95%	95%
Median Time to ECG (minutes)[1]	10	0	8	8
Median Time to Transfer (minutes)[5]	0	-	57	61
Fibrinolytic Medication Timing[5]	0	-	33%	54%
Heart Failure Care				
ACE Inhibitor or ARB for LVSD[2]	134	91%	94%	94%
Discharge Instructions[2]	379	83%	89%	88%
Evaluation of LVS Function[2]	456	98%	98%	98%
Smoking Cessation Advice[2]	66	98%	99%	98%
Pneumonia Care				
Appropriate Initial Antibiotic[2]	199	86%	90%	92%
Blood Culture Timing[2]	277	98%	97%	96%
Influenza Vaccine	200	94%	91%	91%
Initial Antibiotic Timing[2]	343	96%	96%	95%
Pneumococcal Vaccine[2]	263	94%	92%	93%
Smoking Cessation Advice[2]	128	95%	98%	97%
Surgical Care Improvement Project				
Appropriate VTP Within 24 Hours[2]	180	84%	92%	92%
Appropriate Hair Removal[2]	485	99%	99%	99%
Appropriate Beta Blocker Usage[2]	189	94%	92%	93%
Controlled Postoperative Blood Glucose[2]	113	87%	92%	93%
Prophylactic Antibiotic Timing[2]	313	94%	97%	97%
Prophylactic Antibiotic Timing (Outpatient)	179	91%	93%	92%
Prophylactic Antibiotic Selection[2]	317	95%	97%	97%
Prophylactic Antibiotic Select. (Outpatient)	207	94%	94%	94%
Prophylactic Antibiotic Stopped[2]	299	89%	94%	94%
Recommended VTP Ordered[2]	180	91%	94%	94%
Urinary Catheter Removal[2]	89	70%	89%	90%
Children's Asthma Care				
Received Systemic Corticosteroids	-	-	-	100%
Received Home Management Plan	-	-	-	71%
Received Reliever Medication	-	-	-	100%
Use of Medical Imaging				
Combination Abdominal CT Scan	826	0.484	0.246	0.191
Combination Chest CT Scan	715	0.200	0.098	0.054
Follow-up Mammogram/Ultrasound	1,446	16.0%	8.4%	8.4%
MRI for Low Back Pain	114	33.3%	33.4%	32.7%
Survey of Patients' Hospital Experiences				
Area Around Room 'Always' Quiet at Night	300+	52%	-	58%
Doctors 'Always' Communicated Well	300+	77%	-	80%
Home Recovery Information Given	300+	81%	-	82%
Hospital Given 9 or 10 on 10 Point Scale	300+	57%	-	67%
Meds 'Always' Explained Before Given	300+	52%	-	60%
Nurses 'Always' Communicated Well	300+	70%	-	76%
Pain 'Always' Well Controlled	300+	64%	-	69%
Room and Bathroom 'Always' Clean	300+	58%	-	71%
Timely Help 'Always' Received	300+	52%	-	64%
Would Definitely Recommend Hospital	300+	61%	-	69%

Macneal Hospital

3249 South Oak Park Avenue
Berwyn, IL 60402
Phone: 708-783-9100
Fax: 708-783-3489
URL: www.macneal.com
Type: Acute Care Hospitals
Emergency Services: Yes
Ownership: Proprietary
Beds: 400

Key Personnel:
CEO/President............... Brian Lemon
Cardiac Laboratory............ Donald Dickson
Chief of Medical Staff.......... Gary Wainer
Emergency Room .... Brian Fchurgin

Measure	Cases	This Hosp.	State Avg.	U.S. Avg.
Heart Attack Care				
ACE Inhibitor or ARB for LVSD	45	98%	96%	96%
Aspirin at Arrival	209	100%	99%	99%
Aspirin at Discharge	185	98%	99%	98%
Beta Blocker at Discharge	186	98%	98%	98%
Fibrinolytic Medication Timing	0	-	50%	55%
PCI Within 90 Minutes of Arrival	45	96%	90%	90%
Smoking Cessation Advice	61	100%	100%	99%
Chest Pain/Possible Heart Attack Care				
Aspirin at Arrival[1,3]	2	100%	95%	95%
Median Time to ECG (minutes)[1,3]	2	6	8	8
Median Time to Transfer (minutes)[5]	0	-	57	61
Fibrinolytic Medication Timing[5]	0	-	33%	54%
Heart Failure Care				
ACE Inhibitor or ARB for LVSD	137	99%	94%	94%
Discharge Instructions	306	95%	89%	88%
Evaluation of LVS Function	379	100%	98%	98%
Smoking Cessation Advice	52	100%	99%	98%
Pneumonia Care				
Appropriate Initial Antibiotic	150	91%	90%	92%
Blood Culture Timing	235	95%	97%	96%
Influenza Vaccine	150	91%	91%	91%
Initial Antibiotic Timing	223	96%	96%	95%
Pneumococcal Vaccine	208	96%	92%	93%
Smoking Cessation Advice	83	100%	98%	97%
Surgical Care Improvement Project				
Appropriate VTP Within 24 Hours[2]	258	98%	92%	92%
Appropriate Hair Removal[2]	738	96%	99%	99%
Appropriate Beta Blocker Usage[2]	248	96%	92%	93%
Controlled Postoperative Blood Glucose[2]	80	88%	92%	93%
Prophylactic Antibiotic Timing[2]	539	98%	97%	97%
Prophylactic Antibiotic Timing (Outpatient)	388	74%	93%	92%
Prophylactic Antibiotic Selection[2]	559	98%	97%	97%
Prophylactic Antibiotic Select. (Outpatient)	317	79%	94%	94%
Prophylactic Antibiotic Stopped[2]	513	97%	94%	94%
Recommended VTP Ordered[2]	258	99%	94%	94%
Urinary Catheter Removal[2]	190	96%	89%	90%
Children's Asthma Care				
Received Systemic Corticosteroids	-	-	-	100%
Received Home Management Plan	-	-	-	71%
Received Reliever Medication	-	-	-	100%
Use of Medical Imaging				
Combination Abdominal CT Scan	608	0.140	0.246	0.191
Combination Chest CT Scan	506	0.125	0.098	0.054
Follow-up Mammogram/Ultrasound	1,330	9.4%	8.4%	8.4%
MRI for Low Back Pain[1]	8	25.0%	33.4%	32.7%
Survey of Patients' Hospital Experiences				
Area Around Room 'Always' Quiet at Night	300+	50%	-	58%
Doctors 'Always' Communicated Well	300+	80%	-	80%
Home Recovery Information Given	300+	81%	-	82%
Hospital Given 9 or 10 on 10 Point Scale	300+	61%	-	67%
Meds 'Always' Explained Before Given	300+	58%	-	60%
Nurses 'Always' Communicated Well	300+	77%	-	76%
Pain 'Always' Well Controlled	300+	71%	-	69%
Room and Bathroom 'Always' Clean	300+	72%	-	71%
Timely Help 'Always' Received	300+	63%	-	64%
Would Definitely Recommend Hospital	300+	64%	-	69%

Saint Joseph Medical Center

2200 E Washington
Bloomington, IL 61701
Phone: 309-662-3311
Fax: 309-662-7665
Type: Acute Care Hospitals
Emergency Services: Yes
Ownership: Voluntary Non-Profit - Church
Beds: 182

Key Personnel:
CEO/President............... Kenneth Natzke
Chief of Medical Staff.......... Herbert Weiser, MD
Operating Room.............. Marsha Reeves
Pediatric Ambulatory Care ...... Mark Ulbrich, MD
Pediatric In-Patient Care ...... Mark Ulbrich, MD
Quality Assurance .... Kathy Haig
Radiology.................. James McGee, MD

Measure	Cases	This Hosp.	State Avg.	U.S. Avg.
Heart Attack Care				
ACE Inhibitor or ARB for LVSD[1]	22	91%	96%	96%
Aspirin at Arrival	111	100%	99%	99%
Aspirin at Discharge	145	100%	99%	98%
Beta Blocker at Discharge	140	99%	98%	98%
Fibrinolytic Medication Timing	0	-	50%	55%
PCI Within 90 Minutes of Arrival	33	73%	90%	90%
Smoking Cessation Advice	65	100%	100%	99%
Chest Pain/Possible Heart Attack Care				
Aspirin at Arrival[1,3]	2	50%	95%	95%
Median Time to ECG (minutes)[1,3]	2	12	8	8
Median Time to Transfer (minutes)[5]	0	-	57	61
Fibrinolytic Medication Timing[5]	0	-	33%	54%
Heart Failure Care				
ACE Inhibitor or ARB for LVSD	66	94%	94%	94%
Discharge Instructions	124	98%	89%	88%
Evaluation of LVS Function	163	99%	98%	98%
Smoking Cessation Advice	30	100%	99%	98%
Pneumonia Care				
Appropriate Initial Antibiotic	101	88%	90%	92%
Blood Culture Timing	88	100%	97%	96%
Influenza Vaccine	104	90%	91%	91%
Initial Antibiotic Timing	128	96%	96%	95%
Pneumococcal Vaccine	129	97%	92%	93%
Smoking Cessation Advice	62	100%	98%	97%
Surgical Care Improvement Project				
Appropriate VTP Within 24 Hours	172	91%	92%	92%
Appropriate Hair Removal	750	100%	99%	99%
Appropriate Beta Blocker Usage	237	90%	92%	93%
Controlled Postoperative Blood Glucose	87	80%	92%	93%
Prophylactic Antibiotic Timing	541	98%	97%	97%
Prophylactic Antibiotic Timing (Outpatient)	189	99%	93%	92%
Prophylactic Antibiotic Selection	546	98%	97%	97%
Prophylactic Antibiotic Select. (Outpatient)	189	99%	94%	94%
Prophylactic Antibiotic Stopped	514	91%	94%	94%
Recommended VTP Ordered	172	92%	94%	94%
Urinary Catheter Removal	163	91%	89%	90%
Children's Asthma Care				
Received Systemic Corticosteroids	-	-	-	100%
Received Home Management Plan	-	-	-	71%
Received Reliever Medication	-	-	-	100%
Use of Medical Imaging				
Combination Abdominal CT Scan	324	0.722	0.246	0.191
Combination Chest CT Scan	351	0.615	0.098	0.054
Follow-up Mammogram/Ultrasound	525	5.3%	8.4%	8.4%
MRI for Low Back Pain	103	28.2%	33.4%	32.7%
Survey of Patients' Hospital Experiences				
Area Around Room 'Always' Quiet at Night	300+	63%	-	58%
Doctors 'Always' Communicated Well	300+	83%	-	80%
Home Recovery Information Given	300+	83%	-	82%
Hospital Given 9 or 10 on 10 Point Scale	300+	75%	-	67%
Meds 'Always' Explained Before Given	300+	64%	-	60%
Nurses 'Always' Communicated Well	300+	80%	-	76%
Pain 'Always' Well Controlled	300+	71%	-	69%
Room and Bathroom 'Always' Clean	300+	77%	-	71%
Timely Help 'Always' Received	300+	67%	-	64%
Would Definitely Recommend Hospital	300+	78%	-	69%

NOTE: Hospital profiles are in alphabetical order by state, then city, then hospital within the city; Rankings exclude hospitals with less than 25 cases except for patient surveys which excludes hospitals with less than 100 cases; (a) 100–299 cases; (1) The number of cases is too small to be sure how well a hospital is performing; (2) The hospital indicated that the data submitted for this measure were based on a sample of cases; (3) Data was collected during a shorter time period (fewer quarters) than the maximum possible time for this measure; (4) Suppressed for one or more quarters by CMS; (5) No data is available from the hospital for this measure; (6) Fewer than 100 patients completed the HCAHPS survey. Use these rates with caution, as the number of surveys may be too low to reliably assess hospital performance; (7) Survey results are based on less than 12 months of data; (8) Survey results are not available for this reporting period; (9) No or very few patients were eligible for the HCAHPS survey. The scores shown, if any, reflect a very small number of surveys; (10) A state average was not calculated because too few hospitals in the state submitted data; (11) There were discrepancies in the data collection process; Please refer to the User's Guide for a full explanation of data.

Metrosouth Medical Center

12935 S Gregory
Blue Island, IL 60406
Phone: 708-597-2000
Fax: 708-389-9480
URL: www.stfrancisblueisland.com
Type: Acute Care Hospitals
Emergency Services: Yes
Ownership: Proprietary
Beds: 410

Key Personnel:
CEO/President. . . . . Colleen Kannaday
Chief of Medical Staff . . . . Kurt Erickson, MD
Infection Control. . . . . Robert Fliegelman, MD
Operating Room. . . . . Nancy Kasper, RN
Radiology. . . . . Vicki McFarlane
Emergency Room . . . . Daniel Kowalzyk, MD

Measure	Cases	This Hosp.	State Avg.	U.S. Avg.
Heart Attack Care				
ACE Inhibitor or ARB for LVSD	36	92%	96%	96%
Aspirin at Arrival	110	100%	99%	99%
Aspirin at Discharge	107	96%	99%	98%
Beta Blocker at Discharge	103	91%	98%	98%
Fibrinolytic Medication Timing	0	-	50%	55%
PCI Within 90 Minutes of Arrival	27	81%	90%	90%
Smoking Cessation Advice	37	100%	100%	99%
Chest Pain/Possible Heart Attack Care				
Aspirin at Arrival[1]	14	100%	95%	95%
Median Time to ECG (minutes)[1]	15	8	8	8
Median Time to Transfer (minutes)[5]	0	-	57	61
Fibrinolytic Medication Timing[5]	0	-	33%	54%
Heart Failure Care				
ACE Inhibitor or ARB for LVSD	253	85%	94%	94%
Discharge Instructions	521	94%	89%	88%
Evaluation of LVS Function	588	100%	98%	98%
Smoking Cessation Advice	97	99%	99%	98%
Pneumonia Care				
Appropriate Initial Antibiotic	120	85%	90%	92%
Blood Culture Timing	173	92%	97%	96%
Influenza Vaccine	120	83%	91%	91%
Initial Antibiotic Timing	201	91%	96%	95%
Pneumococcal Vaccine	159	85%	92%	93%
Smoking Cessation Advice	67	100%	98%	97%
Surgical Care Improvement Project				
Appropriate VTP Within 24 Hours	185	88%	92%	92%
Appropriate Hair Removal	532	91%	99%	99%
Appropriate Beta Blocker Usage	159	70%	92%	93%
Controlled Postoperative Blood Glucose	79	47%	92%	93%
Prophylactic Antibiotic Timing	383	97%	97%	97%
Prophylactic Antibiotic Timing (Outpatient)	278	90%	93%	92%
Prophylactic Antibiotic Selection	389	98%	97%	97%
Prophylactic Antibiotic Select. (Outpatient)	261	96%	94%	94%
Prophylactic Antibiotic Stopped	355	94%	94%	94%
Recommended VTP Ordered	185	89%	94%	94%
Urinary Catheter Removal	128	84%	89%	90%
Children's Asthma Care				
Received Systemic Corticosteroids	-	-	-	100%
Received Home Management Plan	-	-	-	71%
Received Reliever Medication	-	-	-	100%
Use of Medical Imaging				
Combination Abdominal CT Scan	457	0.074	0.246	0.191
Combination Chest CT Scan	445	0.000	0.098	0.054
Follow-up Mammogram/Ultrasound	671	10.7%	8.4%	8.4%
MRI for Low Back Pain	59	28.8%	33.4%	32.7%
Survey of Patients' Hospital Experiences				
Area Around Room 'Always' Quiet at Night	300+	51%	-	58%
Doctors 'Always' Communicated Well	300+	78%	-	80%
Home Recovery Information Given	300+	71%	-	82%
Hospital Given 9 or 10 on 10 Point Scale	300+	54%	-	67%
Meds 'Always' Explained Before Given	300+	57%	-	60%
Nurses 'Always' Communicated Well	300+	70%	-	76%
Pain 'Always' Well Controlled	300+	63%	-	69%
Room and Bathroom 'Always' Clean	300+	65%	-	71%
Timely Help 'Always' Received	300+	57%	-	64%
Would Definitely Recommend Hospital	300+	57%	-	69%

Adventist Bolingbrook Hospital

500 Remington Boulevard
Bolingbrook, IL 60440
Phone: 630-226-8100
URL: www.keepingyouwell.com
Type: Acute Care Hospitals
Emergency Services: Yes
Ownership: Voluntary Non-Profit - Private

Measure	Cases	This Hosp.	State Avg.	U.S. Avg.
Heart Attack Care				
ACE Inhibitor or ARB for LVSD[1]	10	80%	96%	96%
Aspirin at Arrival	84	100%	99%	99%
Aspirin at Discharge	68	100%	99%	98%
Beta Blocker at Discharge	70	99%	98%	98%
Fibrinolytic Medication Timing	0	-	50%	55%
PCI Within 90 Minutes of Arrival[1]	20	95%	90%	90%
Smoking Cessation Advice	30	100%	100%	99%
Chest Pain/Possible Heart Attack Care				
Aspirin at Arrival[1]	11	73%	95%	95%
Median Time to ECG (minutes)[1]	10	9	8	8
Median Time to Transfer (minutes)[5]	0	-	57	61
Fibrinolytic Medication Timing[5]	0	-	33%	54%
Heart Failure Care				
ACE Inhibitor or ARB for LVSD	61	98%	94%	94%
Discharge Instructions	142	56%	89%	88%
Evaluation of LVS Function	175	99%	98%	98%
Smoking Cessation Advice	26	92%	99%	98%
Pneumonia Care				
Appropriate Initial Antibiotic	110	96%	90%	92%
Blood Culture Timing	162	98%	97%	96%
Influenza Vaccine	87	97%	91%	91%
Initial Antibiotic Timing	164	96%	96%	95%
Pneumococcal Vaccine	109	96%	92%	93%
Smoking Cessation Advice	45	100%	98%	97%
Surgical Care Improvement Project				
Appropriate VTP Within 24 Hours	83	88%	92%	92%
Appropriate Hair Removal	149	99%	99%	99%
Appropriate Beta Blocker Usage	33	97%	92%	93%
Controlled Postoperative Blood Glucose	0	-	92%	93%
Prophylactic Antibiotic Timing	79	89%	97%	97%
Prophylactic Antibiotic Timing (Outpatient)	111	85%	93%	92%
Prophylactic Antibiotic Selection	77	91%	97%	97%
Prophylactic Antibiotic Select. (Outpatient)	108	88%	94%	94%
Prophylactic Antibiotic Stopped	75	64%	94%	94%
Recommended VTP Ordered	83	92%	94%	94%
Urinary Catheter Removal	26	92%	89%	90%
Children's Asthma Care				
Received Systemic Corticosteroids	-	-	-	100%
Received Home Management Plan	-	-	-	71%
Received Reliever Medication	-	-	-	100%
Use of Medical Imaging				
Combination Abdominal CT Scan	159	0.101	0.246	0.191
Combination Chest CT Scan[1]	63	0.095	0.098	0.054
Follow-up Mammogram/Ultrasound	187	11.8%	8.4%	8.4%
MRI for Low Back Pain[1]	34	35.3%	33.4%	32.7%
Survey of Patients' Hospital Experiences				
Area Around Room 'Always' Quiet at Night	300+	66%	-	58%
Doctors 'Always' Communicated Well	300+	75%	-	80%
Home Recovery Information Given	300+	82%	-	82%
Hospital Given 9 or 10 on 10 Point Scale	300+	63%	-	67%
Meds 'Always' Explained Before Given	300+	53%	-	60%
Nurses 'Always' Communicated Well	300+	66%	-	76%
Pain 'Always' Well Controlled	300+	63%	-	69%
Room and Bathroom 'Always' Clean	300+	70%	-	71%
Timely Help 'Always' Received	300+	55%	-	64%
Would Definitely Recommend Hospital	300+	65%	-	69%

Saint Josephs Hospital

9515 Holy Cross Ln
Breese, IL 62230
Phone: 618-526-4511
Fax: 618-526-8022
E-mail: phinton@sjh.hshs.org
URL: www.stjoebreese.com
Type: Acute Care Hospitals
Emergency Services: Yes
Ownership: Voluntary Non-Profit - Church
Beds: 85

Key Personnel:
CEO/President. . . . . Jacolyn Schlautman
Operating Room. . . . . Renato Rivera, RN
Quality Assurance . . . . Jan Robert, RN
Radiology. . . . . Thomas Doyle

Measure	Cases	This Hosp.	State Avg.	U.S. Avg.
Heart Attack Care				
ACE Inhibitor or ARB for LVSD[3]	0	-	96%	96%
Aspirin at Arrival[1,3]	1	100%	99%	99%
Aspirin at Discharge[3]	0	-	99%	98%
Beta Blocker at Discharge[3]	0	-	98%	98%
Fibrinolytic Medication Timing[3]	0	-	50%	55%
PCI Within 90 Minutes of Arrival[3]	0	-	90%	90%
Smoking Cessation Advice[3]	0	-	100%	99%
Chest Pain/Possible Heart Attack Care				
Aspirin at Arrival	86	100%	95%	95%
Median Time to ECG (minutes)	88	7	8	8
Median Time to Transfer (minutes)[1]	9	40	57	61
Fibrinolytic Medication Timing	0	-	33%	54%
Heart Failure Care				
ACE Inhibitor or ARB for LVSD[1,2]	15	87%	94%	94%
Discharge Instructions[2]	30	90%	89%	88%
Evaluation of LVS Function[2]	47	98%	98%	98%
Smoking Cessation Advice[1,2]	6	100%	99%	98%
Pneumonia Care				
Appropriate Initial Antibiotic	72	89%	90%	92%
Blood Culture Timing	89	100%	97%	96%
Influenza Vaccine	70	97%	91%	91%
Initial Antibiotic Timing	99	98%	96%	95%
Pneumococcal Vaccine	92	100%	92%	93%
Smoking Cessation Advice	32	100%	98%	97%
Surgical Care Improvement Project				
Appropriate VTP Within 24 Hours	53	89%	92%	92%
Appropriate Hair Removal	123	100%	99%	99%
Appropriate Beta Blocker Usage[1]	21	100%	92%	93%
Controlled Postoperative Blood Glucose	0	-	92%	93%
Prophylactic Antibiotic Timing	79	97%	97%	97%
Prophylactic Antibiotic Timing (Outpatient)	39	85%	93%	92%
Prophylactic Antibiotic Selection	79	97%	97%	97%
Prophylactic Antibiotic Select. (Outpatient)	34	94%	94%	94%
Prophylactic Antibiotic Stopped	78	90%	94%	94%
Recommended VTP Ordered	53	89%	94%	94%
Urinary Catheter Removal	25	72%	89%	90%
Children's Asthma Care				
Received Systemic Corticosteroids	-	-	-	100%
Received Home Management Plan	-	-	-	71%
Received Reliever Medication	-	-	-	100%
Use of Medical Imaging				
Combination Abdominal CT Scan	275	0.204	0.246	0.191
Combination Chest CT Scan	217	0.051	0.098	0.054
Follow-up Mammogram/Ultrasound	612	7.5%	8.4%	8.4%
MRI for Low Back Pain	53	37.7%	33.4%	32.7%
Survey of Patients' Hospital Experiences				
Area Around Room 'Always' Quiet at Night	300+	69%	-	58%
Doctors 'Always' Communicated Well	300+	86%	-	80%
Home Recovery Information Given	300+	85%	-	82%
Hospital Given 9 or 10 on 10 Point Scale	300+	81%	-	67%
Meds 'Always' Explained Before Given	300+	73%	-	60%
Nurses 'Always' Communicated Well	300+	87%	-	76%
Pain 'Always' Well Controlled	300+	78%	-	69%
Room and Bathroom 'Always' Clean	300+	85%	-	71%
Timely Help 'Always' Received	300+	72%	-	64%
Would Definitely Recommend Hospital	300+	83%	-	69%

NOTE: Hospital profiles are in alphabetical order by state, then city, then hospital within the city; Rankings exclude hospitals with less than 25 cases except for patient surveys which excludes hospitals with less than 100 cases; (a) 100–299 cases; (1) The number of cases is too small to be sure how well a hospital is performing; (2) The hospital indicated that the data submitted for this measure were based on a sample of cases; (3) Data was collected during a shorter time period (fewer quarters) than the maximum possible time for this measure; (4) Suppressed for one or more quarters by CMS; (5) No data is available from the hospital for this measure; (6) Fewer than 100 patients completed the HCAHPS survey. Use these rates with caution, as the number of surveys may be too low to reliably assess hospital performance; (7) Survey results are based on less than 12 months of data; (8) Survey results are not available for this reporting period; (9) No or very few patients were eligible for the HCAHPS survey. The scores shown, if any, reflect a very small number of surveys; (10) A state average was not calculated because too few hospitals in the state submitted data; (11) There were discrepancies in the data collection process; Please refer to the User's Guide for a full explanation of data.

Graham Hospital Association

210 West Walnut Street
Canton, IL 61520
Phone: 309-647-5240
Fax: 309-649-5197
URL: www.grahamhospital.org
Type: Acute Care Hospitals
Emergency Services: Yes
Ownership: Voluntary Non-Profit - Other
Beds: 124

Key Personnel:
CEO/President. . . . . D Ray Slaubaugh
Chief of Medical Staff . . . . Shirley Frantz, MD
Operating Room. . . . . Mary Ahn
Quality Assurance . . . . Carol Welch

Measure	Cases	This Hosp.	State Avg.	U.S. Avg.
Heart Attack Care				
ACE Inhibitor or ARB for LVSD[1,3]	2	100%	96%	96%
Aspirin at Arrival[1,3]	8	88%	99%	99%
Aspirin at Discharge[1,3]	3	100%	99%	98%
Beta Blocker at Discharge[1,3]	3	100%	98%	98%
Fibrinolytic Medication Timing[3]	0	-	50%	55%
PCI Within 90 Minutes of Arrival[3]	0	-	90%	90%
Smoking Cessation Advice[3]	0	-	100%	99%
Chest Pain/Possible Heart Attack Care				
Aspirin at Arrival	76	95%	95%	95%
Median Time to ECG (minutes)	76	9	8	8
Median Time to Transfer (minutes)[1]	19	58	57	61
Fibrinolytic Medication Timing	0	-	33%	54%
Heart Failure Care				
ACE Inhibitor or ARB for LVSD	35	77%	94%	94%
Discharge Instructions	60	88%	89%	88%
Evaluation of LVS Function	108	86%	98%	98%
Smoking Cessation Advice[1]	8	88%	99%	98%
Pneumonia Care				
Appropriate Initial Antibiotic	36	92%	90%	92%
Blood Culture Timing	66	97%	97%	96%
Influenza Vaccine	46	96%	91%	91%
Initial Antibiotic Timing	65	98%	96%	95%
Pneumococcal Vaccine	60	90%	92%	93%
Smoking Cessation Advice[1]	19	95%	98%	97%
Surgical Care Improvement Project				
Appropriate VTP Within 24 Hours	69	96%	92%	92%
Appropriate Hair Removal	215	100%	99%	99%
Appropriate Beta Blocker Usage	51	88%	92%	93%
Controlled Postoperative Blood Glucose	0	-	92%	93%
Prophylactic Antibiotic Timing	131	95%	97%	97%
Prophylactic Antibiotic Timing (Outpatient)	80	92%	93%	92%
Prophylactic Antibiotic Selection	134	95%	97%	97%
Prophylactic Antibiotic Select. (Outpatient)	75	89%	94%	94%
Prophylactic Antibiotic Stopped	128	93%	94%	94%
Recommended VTP Ordered	71	93%	94%	94%
Urinary Catheter Removal	54	94%	89%	90%
Children's Asthma Care				
Received Systemic Corticosteroids	-	-	-	100%
Received Home Management Plan	-	-	-	71%
Received Reliever Medication	-	-	-	100%
Use of Medical Imaging				
Combination Abdominal CT Scan	366	0.719	0.246	0.191
Combination Chest CT Scan	246	0.732	0.098	0.054
Follow-up Mammogram/Ultrasound	500	1.6%	8.4%	8.4%
MRI for Low Back Pain	95	50.5%	33.4%	32.7%
Survey of Patients' Hospital Experiences				
Area Around Room 'Always' Quiet at Night	300+	49%	-	58%
Doctors 'Always' Communicated Well	300+	84%	-	80%
Home Recovery Information Given	300+	83%	-	82%
Hospital Given 9 or 10 on 10 Point Scale	300+	67%	-	67%
Meds 'Always' Explained Before Given	300+	60%	-	60%
Nurses 'Always' Communicated Well	300+	79%	-	76%
Pain 'Always' Well Controlled	300+	68%	-	69%
Room and Bathroom 'Always' Clean	300+	74%	-	71%
Timely Help 'Always' Received	300+	67%	-	64%
Would Definitely Recommend Hospital	300+	61%	-	69%

Memorial Hospital of Carbondale

405 W Jackson
Carbondale, IL 62902
Phone: 618-549-0721
Fax: 618-529-0449
URL: www.sih.net
Type: Acute Care Hospitals
Emergency Services: Yes
Ownership: Voluntary Non-Profit - Private
Beds: 150

Key Personnel:
CEO/President. . . . . George Maroney
Chief of Medical Staff . . . . Marshall Ryan
Operating Room. . . . . R Judson Brewer
Emergency Room . . . . Kent Arnold

Measure	Cases	This Hosp.	State Avg.	U.S. Avg.
Heart Attack Care				
ACE Inhibitor or ARB for LVSD	74	99%	96%	96%
Aspirin at Arrival	119	98%	99%	99%
Aspirin at Discharge	394	99%	99%	98%
Beta Blocker at Discharge	383	99%	98%	98%
Fibrinolytic Medication Timing	0	-	50%	55%
PCI Within 90 Minutes of Arrival	29	97%	90%	90%
Smoking Cessation Advice	169	99%	100%	99%
Chest Pain/Possible Heart Attack Care				
Aspirin at Arrival[5]	0	-	95%	95%
Median Time to ECG (minutes)[5]	0	-	8	8
Median Time to Transfer (minutes)[5]	0	-	57	61
Fibrinolytic Medication Timing[5]	0	-	33%	54%
Heart Failure Care				
ACE Inhibitor or ARB for LVSD	76	88%	94%	94%
Discharge Instructions	178	67%	89%	88%
Evaluation of LVS Function	213	99%	98%	98%
Smoking Cessation Advice	44	98%	99%	98%
Pneumonia Care				
Appropriate Initial Antibiotic	61	93%	90%	92%
Blood Culture Timing	106	96%	97%	96%
Influenza Vaccine	106	87%	91%	91%
Initial Antibiotic Timing	127	95%	96%	95%
Pneumococcal Vaccine	119	90%	92%	93%
Smoking Cessation Advice	84	95%	98%	97%
Surgical Care Improvement Project				
Appropriate VTP Within 24 Hours[2]	378	95%	92%	92%
Appropriate Hair Removal[2]	1,084	100%	99%	99%
Appropriate Beta Blocker Usage[2]	414	90%	92%	93%
Controlled Postoperative Blood Glucose[2]	201	96%	92%	93%
Prophylactic Antibiotic Timing[2]	714	97%	97%	97%
Prophylactic Antibiotic Timing (Outpatient)	452	95%	93%	92%
Prophylactic Antibiotic Selection[2]	718	94%	97%	97%
Prophylactic Antibiotic Select. (Outpatient)	438	98%	94%	94%
Prophylactic Antibiotic Stopped[2]	679	93%	94%	94%
Recommended VTP Ordered[2]	384	95%	94%	94%
Urinary Catheter Removal[2]	246	88%	89%	90%
Children's Asthma Care				
Received Systemic Corticosteroids	-	-	-	100%
Received Home Management Plan	-	-	-	71%
Received Reliever Medication	-	-	-	100%
Use of Medical Imaging				
Combination Abdominal CT Scan	721	0.112	0.246	0.191
Combination Chest CT Scan	385	0.029	0.098	0.054
Follow-up Mammogram/Ultrasound	1,923	7.2%	8.4%	8.4%
MRI for Low Back Pain	127	41.7%	33.4%	32.7%
Survey of Patients' Hospital Experiences				
Area Around Room 'Always' Quiet at Night	300+	60%	-	58%
Doctors 'Always' Communicated Well	300+	80%	-	80%
Home Recovery Information Given	300+	86%	-	82%
Hospital Given 9 or 10 on 10 Point Scale	300+	74%	-	67%
Meds 'Always' Explained Before Given	300+	63%	-	60%
Nurses 'Always' Communicated Well	300+	79%	-	76%
Pain 'Always' Well Controlled	300+	72%	-	69%
Room and Bathroom 'Always' Clean	300+	76%	-	71%
Timely Help 'Always' Received	300+	66%	-	64%
Would Definitely Recommend Hospital	300+	82%	-	69%

Carlinville Area Hospital

1001 Morgan Street
Carlinville, IL 62626
Phone: 217-854-3141
Fax: 217-854-7861
Type: Critical Access Hospitals
Emergency Services: Yes
Ownership: Voluntary Non-Profit - Private
Beds: 33

Key Personnel:
CEO/President. . . . . Steve Hannah
Operating Room. . . . . Rosie Arnett
Quality Assurance . . . . Nick Tex
Emergency Room . . . . Robert England, MD

Measure	Cases	This Hosp.	State Avg.	U.S. Avg.
Heart Attack Care				
ACE Inhibitor or ARB for LVSD[1]	1	100%	96%	96%
Aspirin at Arrival[1]	4	75%	99%	99%
Aspirin at Discharge[1]	2	50%	99%	98%
Beta Blocker at Discharge[1]	3	67%	98%	98%
Fibrinolytic Medication Timing[5]	0	-	50%	55%
PCI Within 90 Minutes of Arrival[5]	0	-	90%	90%
Smoking Cessation Advice	0	-	100%	99%
Chest Pain/Possible Heart Attack Care				
Aspirin at Arrival	-	-	95%	95%
Median Time to ECG (minutes)	-	-	8	8
Median Time to Transfer (minutes)	-	-	57	61
Fibrinolytic Medication Timing	-	-	33%	54%
Heart Failure Care				
ACE Inhibitor or ARB for LVSD[1]	3	100%	94%	94%
Discharge Instructions[1]	8	88%	89%	88%
Evaluation of LVS Function[1]	19	89%	98%	98%
Smoking Cessation Advice	0	-	99%	98%
Pneumonia Care				
Appropriate Initial Antibiotic	29	93%	90%	92%
Blood Culture Timing[1]	24	88%	97%	96%
Influenza Vaccine[1]	20	95%	91%	91%
Initial Antibiotic Timing	31	97%	96%	95%
Pneumococcal Vaccine	33	91%	92%	93%
Smoking Cessation Advice[1]	5	100%	98%	97%
Surgical Care Improvement Project				
Appropriate VTP Within 24 Hours[5]	0	-	92%	92%
Appropriate Hair Removal[5]	0	-	99%	99%
Appropriate Beta Blocker Usage[5]	0	-	92%	93%
Controlled Postoperative Blood Glucose[5]	0	-	92%	93%
Prophylactic Antibiotic Timing[5]	0	-	97%	97%
Prophylactic Antibiotic Timing (Outpatient)	-	-	93%	92%
Prophylactic Antibiotic Selection[5]	0	-	97%	97%
Prophylactic Antibiotic Select. (Outpatient)	-	-	94%	94%
Prophylactic Antibiotic Stopped[5]	0	-	94%	94%
Recommended VTP Ordered[5]	0	-	94%	94%
Urinary Catheter Removal[5]	0	-	89%	90%
Children's Asthma Care				
Received Systemic Corticosteroids	-	-	-	100%
Received Home Management Plan	-	-	-	71%
Received Reliever Medication	-	-	-	100%
Use of Medical Imaging				
Combination Abdominal CT Scan	-	-	0.246	0.191
Combination Chest CT Scan	-	-	0.098	0.054
Follow-up Mammogram/Ultrasound	-	-	8.4%	8.4%
MRI for Low Back Pain	-	-	33.4%	32.7%
Survey of Patients' Hospital Experiences				
Area Around Room 'Always' Quiet at Night	(a)	57%	-	58%
Doctors 'Always' Communicated Well	(a)	85%	-	80%
Home Recovery Information Given	(a)	87%	-	82%
Hospital Given 9 or 10 on 10 Point Scale	(a)	76%	-	67%
Meds 'Always' Explained Before Given	(a)	68%	-	60%
Nurses 'Always' Communicated Well	(a)	85%	-	76%
Pain 'Always' Well Controlled	(a)	83%	-	69%
Room and Bathroom 'Always' Clean	(a)	89%	-	71%
Timely Help 'Always' Received	(a)	71%	-	64%
Would Definitely Recommend Hospital	(a)	73%	-	69%

NOTE: Hospital profiles are in alphabetical order by state, then city, then hospital within the city; Rankings exclude hospitals with less than 25 cases except for patient surveys which excludes hospitals with less than 100 cases; (a) 100–299 cases; (1) The number of cases is too small to be sure how well a hospital is performing; (2) The hospital indicated that the data submitted for this measure were based on a sample of cases; (3) Data was collected during a shorter time period (fewer quarters) than the maximum possible time for this measure; (4) Suppressed for one or more quarters by CMS; (5) No data is available from the hospital for this measure; (6) Fewer than 100 patients completed the HCAHPS survey. Use these rates with caution, as the number of surveys may be too low to reliably assess hospital performance; (7) Survey results are based on less than 12 months of data; (8) Survey results are not available for this reporting period; (9) No or very few patients were eligible for the HCAHPS survey. The scores shown, if any, reflect a very small number of surveys; (10) A state average was not calculated because too few hospitals in the state submitted data; (11) There were discrepancies in the data collection process; Please refer to the User's Guide for a full explanation of data.

Thomas H Boyd Memorial Hospital

800 School St
Carrollton, IL 62016
Type: Critical Access Hospitals
Ownership: Voluntary Non-Profit - Private
Phone: 217-942-6946
Fax: 217-942-6091
Emergency Services: Yes
Beds: 65

Key Personnel:
CEO/President. . . . . Deborah Campbell
Cardiac Laboratory. . . . . Terry Grooms
Chief of Medical Staff. . . . . August Adams
Operating Room. . . . . Judy Brannan
Quality Assurance . . . . Jenny Clough
Emergency Room . . . . Renan Mapue

Measure	Cases	This Hosp.	State Avg.	U.S. Avg.
Heart Attack Care				
ACE Inhibitor or ARB for LVSD[3]	0	-	96%	96%
Aspirin at Arrival[3]	0	-	99%	99%
Aspirin at Discharge[3]	0	-	99%	98%
Beta Blocker at Discharge[3]	0	-	98%	98%
Fibrinolytic Medication Timing[3]	0	-	50%	55%
PCI Within 90 Minutes of Arrival[3]	0	-	90%	90%
Smoking Cessation Advice[3]	0	-	100%	99%
Chest Pain/Possible Heart Attack Care				
Aspirin at Arrival	-	-	95%	95%
Median Time to ECG (minutes)	-	-	8	8
Median Time to Transfer (minutes)	-	-	57	61
Fibrinolytic Medication Timing	-	-	33%	54%
Heart Failure Care				
ACE Inhibitor or ARB for LVSD	0	-	94%	94%
Discharge Instructions[1]	7	14%	89%	88%
Evaluation of LVS Function[1]	15	0%	98%	98%
Smoking Cessation Advice[1]	1	100%	99%	98%
Pneumonia Care				
Appropriate Initial Antibiotic[1,2,3]	9	44%	90%	92%
Blood Culture Timing[1,2,3]	6	83%	97%	96%
Influenza Vaccine[1,3]	2	100%	91%	91%
Initial Antibiotic Timing[1,2,3]	13	92%	96%	95%
Pneumococcal Vaccine[1,2,3]	16	56%	92%	93%
Smoking Cessation Advice[1,2,3]	5	80%	98%	97%
Surgical Care Improvement Project				
Appropriate VTP Within 24 Hours[5]	0	-	92%	92%
Appropriate Hair Removal[5]	0	-	99%	99%
Appropriate Beta Blocker Usage[5]	0	-	92%	93%
Controlled Postoperative Blood Glucose[5]	0	-	92%	93%
Prophylactic Antibiotic Timing[5]	0	-	97%	97%
Prophylactic Antibiotic Timing (Outpatient)	-	-	93%	92%
Prophylactic Antibiotic Selection[5]	0	-	97%	97%
Prophylactic Antibiotic Select. (Outpatient)	-	-	94%	94%
Prophylactic Antibiotic Stopped[5]	0	-	94%	94%
Recommended VTP Ordered[5]	0	-	94%	94%
Urinary Catheter Removal[5]	0	-	89%	90%
Children's Asthma Care				
Received Systemic Corticosteroids	-	-	-	100%
Received Home Management Plan	-	-	-	71%
Received Reliever Medication	-	-	-	100%
Use of Medical Imaging				
Combination Abdominal CT Scan	-	-	0.246	0.191
Combination Chest CT Scan	-	-	0.098	0.054
Follow-up Mammogram/Ultrasound	-	-	8.4%	8.4%
MRI for Low Back Pain	-	-	33.4%	32.7%
Survey of Patients' Hospital Experiences				
Area Around Room 'Always' Quiet at Night[8]	-	-	-	58%
Doctors 'Always' Communicated Well[8]	-	-	-	80%
Home Recovery Information Given[8]	-	-	-	82%
Hospital Given 9 or 10 on 10 Point Scale[8]	-	-	-	67%
Meds 'Always' Explained Before Given[8]	-	-	-	60%
Nurses 'Always' Communicated Well[8]	-	-	-	76%
Pain 'Always' Well Controlled[8]	-	-	-	69%
Room and Bathroom 'Always' Clean[8]	-	-	-	71%
Timely Help 'Always' Received[8]	-	-	-	64%
Would Definitely Recommend Hospital[8]	-	-	-	69%

Saint Marys Hospital

400 North Pleasant Avenue
Centralia, IL 62801
URL: www.stmarys-goodsamaritan.com
Type: Acute Care Hospitals
Ownership: Voluntary Non-Profit - Church
Phone: 618-436-8000
Fax: 618-436-8046
Emergency Services: Yes
Beds: 276

Key Personnel:
CEO/President. . . . . James W Sanger
Cardiac Laboratory. . . . . Trecy Siscus
Chief of Medical Staff . . . . Tom Martin, MD
Operating Room. . . . . James Jeffers, RN
Pediatric Ambulatory Care . . . . . . Nazir Ahmad, MD
Pediatric In-Patient Care . . . . Nazir Ahmad, MD
Quality Assurance . . . . Mary Lynn Szperra
Radiology. . . . . Richard Rudman, MD

Measure	Cases	This Hosp.	State Avg.	U.S. Avg.
Heart Attack Care				
ACE Inhibitor or ARB for LVSD[1]	3	100%	96%	96%
Aspirin at Arrival	48	100%	99%	99%
Aspirin at Discharge	31	100%	99%	98%
Beta Blocker at Discharge	34	100%	98%	98%
Fibrinolytic Medication Timing	0	-	50%	55%
PCI Within 90 Minutes of Arrival	0	-	90%	90%
Smoking Cessation Advice[1]	8	100%	100%	99%
Chest Pain/Possible Heart Attack Care				
Aspirin at Arrival	131	94%	95%	95%
Median Time to ECG (minutes)	138	8	8	8
Median Time to Transfer (minutes)[1,3]	10	48	57	61
Fibrinolytic Medication Timing	0	-	33%	54%
Heart Failure Care				
ACE Inhibitor or ARB for LVSD	47	100%	94%	94%
Discharge Instructions	147	100%	89%	88%
Evaluation of LVS Function	204	100%	98%	98%
Smoking Cessation Advice	30	100%	99%	98%
Pneumonia Care				
Appropriate Initial Antibiotic	84	93%	90%	92%
Blood Culture Timing	142	100%	97%	96%
Influenza Vaccine	142	100%	91%	91%
Initial Antibiotic Timing	206	98%	96%	95%
Pneumococcal Vaccine	180	100%	92%	93%
Smoking Cessation Advice	86	100%	98%	97%
Surgical Care Improvement Project				
Appropriate VTP Within 24 Hours	121	99%	92%	92%
Appropriate Hair Removal	288	100%	99%	99%
Appropriate Beta Blocker Usage	81	99%	92%	93%
Controlled Postoperative Blood Glucose	0	-	92%	93%
Prophylactic Antibiotic Timing	168	100%	97%	97%
Prophylactic Antibiotic Timing (Outpatient)	52	79%	93%	92%
Prophylactic Antibiotic Selection	168	99%	97%	97%
Prophylactic Antibiotic Select. (Outpatient)	42	88%	94%	94%
Prophylactic Antibiotic Stopped	152	99%	94%	94%
Recommended VTP Ordered	122	98%	94%	94%
Urinary Catheter Removal	45	100%	89%	90%
Children's Asthma Care				
Received Systemic Corticosteroids	-	-	-	100%
Received Home Management Plan	-	-	-	71%
Received Reliever Medication	-	-	-	100%
Use of Medical Imaging				
Combination Abdominal CT Scan	691	0.728	0.246	0.191
Combination Chest CT Scan	430	0.195	0.098	0.054
Follow-up Mammogram/Ultrasound	728	6.2%	8.4%	8.4%
MRI for Low Back Pain	106	39.6%	33.4%	32.7%
Survey of Patients' Hospital Experiences				
Area Around Room 'Always' Quiet at Night	300+	62%	-	58%
Doctors 'Always' Communicated Well	300+	82%	-	80%
Home Recovery Information Given	300+	87%	-	82%
Hospital Given 9 or 10 on 10 Point Scale	300+	77%	-	67%
Meds 'Always' Explained Before Given	300+	64%	-	60%
Nurses 'Always' Communicated Well	300+	85%	-	76%
Pain 'Always' Well Controlled	300+	80%	-	69%
Room and Bathroom 'Always' Clean	300+	85%	-	71%
Timely Help 'Always' Received	300+	78%	-	64%
Would Definitely Recommend Hospital	300+	76%	-	69%

Touchette Regional Hospital

5900 Bond Avenue
Centreville, IL 62207
URL: www.touchette.org
Type: Acute Care Hospitals
Ownership: Voluntary Non-Profit - Private
Phone: 618-332-3060
Fax: 618-332-5256
Emergency Services: Yes
Beds: 114

Key Personnel:
CEO/President. . . . . Robert Klutts
Chief of Medical Staff . . . . Jose Ramon
Infection Control. . . . . Pat Giacin
Operating Room. . . . . Patricia Clark
Quality Assurance . . . . Rich Hampson
Radiology. . . . . David Hunter
Emergency Room . . . . Louis Gary

Measure	Cases	This Hosp.	State Avg.	U.S. Avg.
Heart Attack Care				
ACE Inhibitor or ARB for LVSD[1]	1	100%	96%	96%
Aspirin at Arrival	26	92%	99%	99%
Aspirin at Discharge[1]	10	100%	99%	98%
Beta Blocker at Discharge[1]	9	67%	98%	98%
Fibrinolytic Medication Timing[1]	2	0%	50%	55%
PCI Within 90 Minutes of Arrival	0	-	90%	90%
Smoking Cessation Advice[1]	4	100%	100%	99%
Chest Pain/Possible Heart Attack Care				
Aspirin at Arrival[1]	17	100%	95%	95%
Median Time to ECG (minutes)[1]	18	9	8	8
Median Time to Transfer (minutes)[3]	0	-	57	61
Fibrinolytic Medication Timing[1]	2	0%	33%	54%
Heart Failure Care				
ACE Inhibitor or ARB for LVSD	69	94%	94%	94%
Discharge Instructions	159	70%	89%	88%
Evaluation of LVS Function	171	96%	98%	98%
Smoking Cessation Advice	75	97%	99%	98%
Pneumonia Care				
Appropriate Initial Antibiotic	44	89%	90%	92%
Blood Culture Timing	51	96%	97%	96%
Influenza Vaccine	27	89%	91%	91%
Initial Antibiotic Timing	58	93%	96%	95%
Pneumococcal Vaccine[1]	18	83%	92%	93%
Smoking Cessation Advice	25	96%	98%	97%
Surgical Care Improvement Project				
Appropriate VTP Within 24 Hours	28	68%	92%	92%
Appropriate Hair Removal	70	100%	99%	99%
Appropriate Beta Blocker Usage[1]	8	75%	92%	93%
Controlled Postoperative Blood Glucose	0	-	92%	93%
Prophylactic Antibiotic Timing	44	98%	97%	97%
Prophylactic Antibiotic Timing (Outpatient)	36	6%	93%	92%
Prophylactic Antibiotic Selection	45	98%	97%	97%
Prophylactic Antibiotic Select. (Outpatient)[1]	9	78%	94%	94%
Prophylactic Antibiotic Stopped	44	91%	94%	94%
Recommended VTP Ordered	29	66%	94%	94%
Urinary Catheter Removal[1]	8	75%	89%	90%
Children's Asthma Care				
Received Systemic Corticosteroids	-	-	-	100%
Received Home Management Plan	-	-	-	71%
Received Reliever Medication	-	-	-	100%
Use of Medical Imaging				
Combination Abdominal CT Scan	71	0.000	0.246	0.191
Combination Chest CT Scan	50	0.000	0.098	0.054
Follow-up Mammogram/Ultrasound	223	6.7%	8.4%	8.4%
MRI for Low Back Pain[1]	9	44.4%	33.4%	32.7%
Survey of Patients' Hospital Experiences				
Area Around Room 'Always' Quiet at Night	(a)	64%	-	58%
Doctors 'Always' Communicated Well	(a)	80%	-	80%
Home Recovery Information Given	(a)	77%	-	82%
Hospital Given 9 or 10 on 10 Point Scale	(a)	48%	-	67%
Meds 'Always' Explained Before Given	(a)	51%	-	60%
Nurses 'Always' Communicated Well	(a)	70%	-	76%
Pain 'Always' Well Controlled	(a)	60%	-	69%
Room and Bathroom 'Always' Clean	(a)	64%	-	71%
Timely Help 'Always' Received	(a)	47%	-	64%
Would Definitely Recommend Hospital	(a)	53%	-	69%

NOTE: Hospital profiles are in alphabetical order by state, then city, then hospital within the city; Rankings exclude hospitals with less than 25 cases except for patient surveys which excludes hospitals with less than 100 cases; (a) 100–299 cases; (1) The number of cases is too small to be sure how well a hospital is performing; (2) The hospital indicated that the data submitted for this measure were based on a sample of cases; (3) Data was collected during a shorter time period (fewer quarters) than the maximum possible time for this measure; (4) Suppressed for one or more quarters by CMS; (5) No data is available from the hospital for this measure; (6) Fewer than 100 patients completed the HCAHPS survey. Use these rates with caution, as the number of surveys may be too low to reliably assess hospital performance; (7) Survey results are based on less than 12 months of data; (8) Survey results are not available for this reporting period; (9) No or very few patients were eligible for the HCAHPS survey. The scores shown, if any, reflect a very small number of surveys; (10) A state average was not calculated because too few hospitals in the state submitted data; (11) There were discrepancies in the data collection process; Please refer to the User's Guide for a full explanation of data.

Memorial Hospital

1900 State Street Phone: 618-826-4581
Chester, IL 62233 Fax: 618-826-4813
URL: www.mhchester.com
Type: Critical Access Hospitals Emergency Services: Yes
Ownership: Govt - Hospital Dist/Auth Beds: 25

Key Personnel:

CEO/President. . . . . Steven A Hayes
Chief of Medical Staff . . . . Allen Liefer, MD
Infection Control. . . . . Machelle Kureker
Operating Room. . . . . Patricia Nanney, RN
Radiology. . . . . Joseph Dugan
Emergency Room . . . . Mary Rosendohl, RN
Intensive Care Unit. . . . . Karen Wolf

Measure	Cases	This Hosp.	State Avg.	U.S. Avg.
Heart Attack Care				
ACE Inhibitor or ARB for LVSD[3]	0	-	96%	96%
Aspirin at Arrival[1,3]	1	100%	99%	99%
Aspirin at Discharge[1,3]	1	100%	99%	98%
Beta Blocker at Discharge[1,3]	1	100%	98%	98%
Fibrinolytic Medication Timing[3]	0	-	50%	55%
PCI Within 90 Minutes of Arrival[5]	0	-	90%	90%
Smoking Cessation Advice[3]	0	-	100%	99%
Chest Pain/Possible Heart Attack Care				
Aspirin at Arrival	41	100%	95%	95%
Median Time to ECG (minutes)	44	6	8	8
Median Time to Transfer (minutes)[1,3]	1	68	57	61
Fibrinolytic Medication Timing	0	-	33%	54%
Heart Failure Care				
ACE Inhibitor or ARB for LVSD[1]	10	100%	94%	94%
Discharge Instructions	29	76%	89%	88%
Evaluation of LVS Function	41	100%	98%	98%
Smoking Cessation Advice[1]	7	100%	99%	98%
Pneumonia Care				
Appropriate Initial Antibiotic[2]	43	95%	90%	92%
Blood Culture Timing[2]	33	100%	97%	96%
Influenza Vaccine	39	90%	91%	91%
Initial Antibiotic Timing[2]	54	96%	96%	95%
Pneumococcal Vaccine[2]	44	93%	92%	93%
Smoking Cessation Advice[1,2]	13	100%	98%	97%
Surgical Care Improvement Project				
Appropriate VTP Within 24 Hours[1]	10	100%	92%	92%
Appropriate Hair Removal[1]	22	100%	99%	99%
Appropriate Beta Blocker Usage[1]	9	78%	92%	93%
Controlled Postoperative Blood Glucose[5]	0	-	92%	93%
Prophylactic Antibiotic Timing[1]	18	89%	97%	97%
Prophylactic Antibiotic Timing (Outpatient)[1]	21	52%	93%	92%
Prophylactic Antibiotic Selection[1]	18	100%	97%	97%
Prophylactic Antibiotic Select. (Outpatient)[1]	17	88%	94%	94%
Prophylactic Antibiotic Stopped[1]	17	100%	94%	94%
Recommended VTP Ordered[1]	10	100%	94%	94%
Urinary Catheter Removal[1]	4	100%	89%	90%
Children's Asthma Care				
Received Systemic Corticosteroids	-	-	-	100%
Received Home Management Plan	-	-	-	71%
Received Reliever Medication	-	-	-	100%
Use of Medical Imaging				
Combination Abdominal CT Scan	211	0.090	0.246	0.191
Combination Chest CT Scan	115	0.000	0.098	0.054
Follow-up Mammogram/Ultrasound	235	8.5%	8.4%	8.4%
MRI for Low Back Pain[1]	31	22.6%	33.4%	32.7%
Survey of Patients' Hospital Experiences				
Area Around Room 'Always' Quiet at Night[8]	-	-	-	58%
Doctors 'Always' Communicated Well[8]	-	-	-	80%
Home Recovery Information Given[8]	-	-	-	82%
Hospital Given 9 or 10 on 10 Point Scale[8]	-	-	-	67%
Meds 'Always' Explained Before Given[8]	-	-	-	60%
Nurses 'Always' Communicated Well[8]	-	-	-	76%
Pain 'Always' Well Controlled[8]	-	-	-	69%
Room and Bathroom 'Always' Clean[8]	-	-	-	71%
Timely Help 'Always' Received[8]	-	-	-	64%
Would Definitely Recommend Hospital[8]	-	-	-	69%

Advocate Illinois Masonic Medical Center

836 West Wellington Avenue Phone: 773-975-1600
Chicago, IL 60657 Fax: 773-296-8119
URL: www.advocatehealth.com/immc
Type: Acute Care Hospitals Emergency Services: Yes
Ownership: Voluntary Non-Profit - Church Beds: 370

Key Personnel:

CEO/President. . . . . Susan Lopez
Patient Relations . . . . Ellen Donovan

Measure	Cases	This Hosp.	State Avg.	U.S. Avg.
Heart Attack Care				
ACE Inhibitor or ARB for LVSD[1]	20	100%	96%	96%
Aspirin at Arrival	127	100%	99%	99%
Aspirin at Discharge	173	100%	99%	98%
Beta Blocker at Discharge	169	100%	98%	98%
Fibrinolytic Medication Timing[1]	1	100%	50%	55%
PCI Within 90 Minutes of Arrival[1]	13	85%	90%	90%
Smoking Cessation Advice	64	100%	100%	99%
Chest Pain/Possible Heart Attack Care				
Aspirin at Arrival[1,3]	1	0%	95%	95%
Median Time to ECG (minutes)[1,3]	1	0	8	8
Median Time to Transfer (minutes)[5]	0	-	57	61
Fibrinolytic Medication Timing[5]	0	-	33%	54%
Heart Failure Care				
ACE Inhibitor or ARB for LVSD[2]	124	98%	94%	94%
Discharge Instructions[2]	233	97%	89%	88%
Evaluation of LVS Function[2]	307	100%	98%	98%
Smoking Cessation Advice[2]	76	100%	99%	98%
Pneumonia Care				
Appropriate Initial Antibiotic[2]	60	98%	90%	92%
Blood Culture Timing[2]	145	100%	97%	96%
Influenza Vaccine[2]	79	99%	91%	91%
Initial Antibiotic Timing[2]	113	100%	96%	95%
Pneumococcal Vaccine[2]	92	97%	92%	93%
Smoking Cessation Advice[2]	57	96%	98%	97%
Surgical Care Improvement Project				
Appropriate VTP Within 24 Hours[2]	217	97%	92%	92%
Appropriate Hair Removal[2]	607	100%	99%	99%
Appropriate Beta Blocker Usage[2]	182	96%	92%	93%
Controlled Postoperative Blood Glucose[2]	86	90%	92%	93%
Prophylactic Antibiotic Timing[2]	432	99%	97%	97%
Prophylactic Antibiotic Timing (Outpatient)	401	99%	93%	92%
Prophylactic Antibiotic Selection[2]	435	97%	97%	97%
Prophylactic Antibiotic Select. (Outpatient)	476	98%	94%	94%
Prophylactic Antibiotic Stopped[2]	406	98%	94%	94%
Recommended VTP Ordered[2]	217	97%	94%	94%
Urinary Catheter Removal[2]	106	96%	89%	90%
Children's Asthma Care				
Received Systemic Corticosteroids	-	-	-	100%
Received Home Management Plan	-	-	-	71%
Received Reliever Medication	-	-	-	100%
Use of Medical Imaging				
Combination Abdominal CT Scan	641	0.122	0.246	0.191
Combination Chest CT Scan	528	0.034	0.098	0.054
Follow-up Mammogram/Ultrasound	982	7.8%	8.4%	8.4%
MRI for Low Back Pain	143	39.2%	33.4%	32.7%
Survey of Patients' Hospital Experiences				
Area Around Room 'Always' Quiet at Night	300+	49%	-	58%
Doctors 'Always' Communicated Well	300+	77%	-	80%
Home Recovery Information Given	300+	80%	-	82%
Hospital Given 9 or 10 on 10 Point Scale	300+	65%	-	67%
Meds 'Always' Explained Before Given	300+	61%	-	60%
Nurses 'Always' Communicated Well	300+	75%	-	76%
Pain 'Always' Well Controlled	300+	69%	-	69%
Room and Bathroom 'Always' Clean	300+	70%	-	71%
Timely Help 'Always' Received	300+	62%	-	64%
Would Definitely Recommend Hospital	300+	69%	-	69%

Advocate Trinity Hospital

2320 E 93rd St Phone: 773-967-2000
Chicago, IL 60617 Fax: 773-967-4209
URL: www.advocatehealth.com/trin
Type: Acute Care Hospitals Emergency Services: Yes
Ownership: Voluntary Non-Profit - Church

Key Personnel:

CEO/President. . . . . Anthony Munroe
Radiology. . . . . Ari Mintz

Measure	Cases	This Hosp.	State Avg.	U.S. Avg.
Heart Attack Care				
ACE Inhibitor or ARB for LVSD[1]	18	100%	96%	96%
Aspirin at Arrival	167	99%	99%	99%
Aspirin at Discharge	112	100%	99%	98%
Beta Blocker at Discharge	112	100%	98%	98%
Fibrinolytic Medication Timing	0	-	50%	55%
PCI Within 90 Minutes of Arrival[1]	12	100%	90%	90%
Smoking Cessation Advice	46	98%	100%	99%
Chest Pain/Possible Heart Attack Care				
Aspirin at Arrival[1]	16	88%	95%	95%
Median Time to ECG (minutes)[1]	17	9	8	8
Median Time to Transfer (minutes)[1,3]	1	136	57	61
Fibrinolytic Medication Timing[3]	0	-	33%	54%
Heart Failure Care				
ACE Inhibitor or ARB for LVSD	171	99%	94%	94%
Discharge Instructions	386	87%	89%	88%
Evaluation of LVS Function	439	99%	98%	98%
Smoking Cessation Advice	119	100%	99%	98%
Pneumonia Care				
Appropriate Initial Antibiotic	143	93%	90%	92%
Blood Culture Timing	202	97%	97%	96%
Influenza Vaccine	143	99%	91%	91%
Initial Antibiotic Timing	203	94%	96%	95%
Pneumococcal Vaccine	168	98%	92%	93%
Smoking Cessation Advice	82	99%	98%	97%
Surgical Care Improvement Project				
Appropriate VTP Within 24 Hours[2]	147	100%	92%	92%
Appropriate Hair Removal[2]	402	100%	99%	99%
Appropriate Beta Blocker Usage[2]	129	95%	92%	93%
Controlled Postoperative Blood Glucose[2]	0	-	92%	93%
Prophylactic Antibiotic Timing[2]	256	100%	97%	97%
Prophylactic Antibiotic Timing (Outpatient)	115	94%	93%	92%
Prophylactic Antibiotic Selection[2]	256	98%	97%	97%
Prophylactic Antibiotic Select. (Outpatient)	113	96%	94%	94%
Prophylactic Antibiotic Stopped[2]	245	93%	94%	94%
Recommended VTP Ordered[2]	147	100%	94%	94%
Urinary Catheter Removal[2]	46	87%	89%	90%
Children's Asthma Care				
Received Systemic Corticosteroids	-	-	-	100%
Received Home Management Plan	-	-	-	71%
Received Reliever Medication	-	-	-	100%
Use of Medical Imaging				
Combination Abdominal CT Scan	389	0.049	0.246	0.191
Combination Chest CT Scan	246	0.053	0.098	0.054
Follow-up Mammogram/Ultrasound	880	12.7%	8.4%	8.4%
MRI for Low Back Pain	63	36.5%	33.4%	32.7%
Survey of Patients' Hospital Experiences				
Area Around Room 'Always' Quiet at Night	300+	58%	-	58%
Doctors 'Always' Communicated Well	300+	74%	-	80%
Home Recovery Information Given	300+	69%	-	82%
Hospital Given 9 or 10 on 10 Point Scale	300+	54%	-	67%
Meds 'Always' Explained Before Given	300+	56%	-	60%
Nurses 'Always' Communicated Well	300+	73%	-	76%
Pain 'Always' Well Controlled	300+	68%	-	69%
Room and Bathroom 'Always' Clean	300+	67%	-	71%
Timely Help 'Always' Received	300+	56%	-	64%
Would Definitely Recommend Hospital	300+	52%	-	69%

NOTE: Hospital profiles are in alphabetical order by state, then city, then hospital within the city; Rankings exclude hospitals with less than 25 cases except for patient surveys which excludes hospitals with less than 100 cases; (a) 100–299 cases; (1) The number of cases is too small to be sure how well a hospital is performing; (2) The hospital indicated that the data submitted for this measure were based on a sample of cases; (3) Data was collected during a shorter time period (fewer quarters) than the maximum possible time for this measure; (4) Suppressed for one or more quarters by CMS; (5) No data is available from the hospital for this measure; (6) Fewer than 100 patients completed the HCAHPS survey. Use these rates with caution, as the number of surveys may be too low to reliably assess hospital performance; (7) Survey results are based on less than 12 months of data; (8) Survey results are not available for this reporting period; (9) No or very few patients were eligible for the HCAHPS survey. The scores shown, if any, reflect a very small number of surveys; (10) A state average was not calculated because too few hospitals in the state submitted data; (11) There were discrepancies in the data collection process; Please refer to the User's Guide for a full explanation of data.

Holy Cross Hospital

2701 W 68th Street
Chicago, IL 60629
URL: www.holycrosshospital.org
Type: Acute Care Hospitals
Ownership: Voluntary Non-Profit - Church
Phone: 773-471-8000
Fax: 773-884-8013
Emergency Services: Yes
Beds: 244

Key Personnel:
CEO/President. . . . . Brian Lemon
Chief of Medical Staff. . . . . Chin Waung
Operating Room. . . . . Suzanne Rich
Quality Assurance . . . . Michael Jucius
Emergency Room . . . . Ann Reninger, RN

Measure	Cases	This Hosp.	State Avg.	U.S. Avg.
Heart Attack Care				
ACE Inhibitor or ARB for LVSD[2]	32	69%	96%	96%
Aspirin at Arrival[2]	105	90%	99%	99%
Aspirin at Discharge[2]	89	83%	99%	98%
Beta Blocker at Discharge[2]	86	84%	98%	98%
Fibrinolytic Medication Timing[1,2]	1	0%	50%	55%
PCI Within 90 Minutes of Arrival[1,2]	14	14%	90%	90%
Smoking Cessation Advice[2]	40	90%	100%	99%
Chest Pain/Possible Heart Attack Care				
Aspirin at Arrival[1]	20	85%	95%	95%
Median Time to ECG (minutes)[1]	21	7	8	8
Median Time to Transfer (minutes)[3]	0	-	57	61
Fibrinolytic Medication Timing[3]	0	-	33%	54%
Heart Failure Care				
ACE Inhibitor or ARB for LVSD[2]	164	83%	94%	94%
Discharge Instructions[2]	291	65%	89%	88%
Evaluation of LVS Function[2]	302	95%	98%	98%
Smoking Cessation Advice[2]	106	97%	99%	98%
Pneumonia Care				
Appropriate Initial Antibiotic[2]	72	76%	90%	92%
Blood Culture Timing[2]	103	94%	97%	96%
Influenza Vaccine[2]	56	68%	91%	91%
Initial Antibiotic Timing[2]	119	81%	96%	95%
Pneumococcal Vaccine[2]	86	84%	92%	93%
Smoking Cessation Advice[2]	48	81%	98%	97%
Surgical Care Improvement Project				
Appropriate VTP Within 24 Hours[2]	142	89%	92%	92%
Appropriate Hair Removal[2]	215	98%	99%	99%
Appropriate Beta Blocker Usage[2]	61	77%	92%	93%
Controlled Postoperative Blood Glucose[2]	0	-	92%	93%
Prophylactic Antibiotic Timing[2]	123	91%	97%	97%
Prophylactic Antibiotic Timing (Outpatient)	58	74%	93%	92%
Prophylactic Antibiotic Selection[2]	124	91%	97%	97%
Prophylactic Antibiotic Select. (Outpatient)	49	73%	94%	94%
Prophylactic Antibiotic Stopped[2]	121	79%	94%	94%
Recommended VTP Ordered[2]	142	96%	94%	94%
Urinary Catheter Removal[2]	36	39%	89%	90%
Children's Asthma Care				
Received Systemic Corticosteroids	-	-	-	100%
Received Home Management Plan	-	-	-	71%
Received Reliever Medication	-	-	-	100%
Use of Medical Imaging				
Combination Abdominal CT Scan	306	0.016	0.246	0.191
Combination Chest CT Scan	218	0.000	0.098	0.054
Follow-up Mammogram/Ultrasound	526	1.9%	8.4%	8.4%
MRI for Low Back Pain[1]	42	31.0%	33.4%	32.7%
Survey of Patients' Hospital Experiences				
Area Around Room 'Always' Quiet at Night	300+	49%	-	58%
Doctors 'Always' Communicated Well	300+	68%	-	80%
Home Recovery Information Given	300+	70%	-	82%
Hospital Given 9 or 10 on 10 Point Scale	300+	45%	-	67%
Meds 'Always' Explained Before Given	300+	47%	-	60%
Nurses 'Always' Communicated Well	300+	63%	-	76%
Pain 'Always' Well Controlled	300+	55%	-	69%
Room and Bathroom 'Always' Clean	300+	61%	-	71%
Timely Help 'Always' Received	300+	46%	-	64%
Would Definitely Recommend Hospital	300+	43%	-	69%

Jackson Park Hospital

7531 S Stony Island Ave
Chicago, IL 60649
URL: www.jacksonparkhospital.org
Type: Acute Care Hospitals
Ownership: Voluntary Non-Profit - Private
Phone: 773-947-7500
Fax: 773-947-7791
Emergency Services: Yes
Beds: 336

Key Personnel:
CEO/President. . . . . Peter Friedell
Cardiac Laboratory. . . . . D Kumar, MD
Chief of Medical Staff . . . . Michael A Wilczynski, MD
Infection Control. . . . . Martha Lyons, RN
Quality Assurance . . . . Rosemary Albright
Intensive Care Unit. . . . . Produb David, RN
Patient Relations . . . . Magdalene Armstead, MSN RN

Measure	Cases	This Hosp.	State Avg.	U.S. Avg.
Heart Attack Care				
ACE Inhibitor or ARB for LVSD[1]	2	100%	96%	96%
Aspirin at Arrival[1]	23	100%	99%	99%
Aspirin at Discharge[1]	10	100%	99%	98%
Beta Blocker at Discharge[1]	10	100%	98%	98%
Fibrinolytic Medication Timing	0	-	50%	55%
PCI Within 90 Minutes of Arrival	0	-	90%	90%
Smoking Cessation Advice	0	-	100%	99%
Chest Pain/Possible Heart Attack Care				
Aspirin at Arrival[5]	0	-	95%	95%
Median Time to ECG (minutes)[5]	0	-	8	8
Median Time to Transfer (minutes)[5]	0	-	57	61
Fibrinolytic Medication Timing[5]	0	-	33%	54%
Heart Failure Care				
ACE Inhibitor or ARB for LVSD	159	100%	94%	94%
Discharge Instructions	270	100%	89%	88%
Evaluation of LVS Function	302	100%	98%	98%
Smoking Cessation Advice	134	100%	99%	98%
Pneumonia Care				
Appropriate Initial Antibiotic[2]	152	11%	90%	92%
Blood Culture Timing[2]	82	100%	97%	96%
Influenza Vaccine[2]	53	58%	91%	91%
Initial Antibiotic Timing[2]	172	87%	96%	95%
Pneumococcal Vaccine[2]	52	63%	92%	93%
Smoking Cessation Advice[2]	61	100%	98%	97%
Surgical Care Improvement Project				
Appropriate VTP Within 24 Hours	0	-	92%	92%
Appropriate Hair Removal	47	91%	99%	99%
Appropriate Beta Blocker Usage[1]	2	50%	92%	93%
Controlled Postoperative Blood Glucose	0	-	92%	93%
Prophylactic Antibiotic Timing[1]	17	6%	97%	97%
Prophylactic Antibiotic Timing (Outpatient)[5]	0	-	93%	92%
Prophylactic Antibiotic Selection[1]	15	73%	97%	97%
Prophylactic Antibiotic Select. (Outpatient)[5]	0	-	94%	94%
Prophylactic Antibiotic Stopped[1]	15	80%	94%	94%
Recommended VTP Ordered	30	0%	94%	94%
Urinary Catheter Removal	0	-	89%	90%
Children's Asthma Care				
Received Systemic Corticosteroids	-	-	-	100%
Received Home Management Plan	-	-	-	71%
Received Reliever Medication	-	-	-	100%
Use of Medical Imaging				
Combination Abdominal CT Scan[1]	53	0.075	0.246	0.191
Combination Chest CT Scan[1]	44	0.000	0.098	0.054
Follow-up Mammogram/Ultrasound	99	7.1%	8.4%	8.4%
MRI for Low Back Pain[5]	0	-	33.4%	32.7%
Survey of Patients' Hospital Experiences				
Area Around Room 'Always' Quiet at Night	300+	48%	-	58%
Doctors 'Always' Communicated Well	300+	68%	-	80%
Home Recovery Information Given	300+	61%	-	82%
Hospital Given 9 or 10 on 10 Point Scale	300+	31%	-	67%
Meds 'Always' Explained Before Given	300+	45%	-	60%
Nurses 'Always' Communicated Well	300+	54%	-	76%
Pain 'Always' Well Controlled	300+	49%	-	69%
Room and Bathroom 'Always' Clean	300+	56%	-	71%
Timely Help 'Always' Received	300+	38%	-	64%
Would Definitely Recommend Hospital	300+	30%	-	69%

Jesse Brown VA Medical Center - VA Chicago Healthcare

820 S Damen Street
Chicago, IL 60612
URL: www.va.gov
Type: Acute Care-Veterans Administration
Ownership: Government - Federal
Phone: 312-569-8387
Fax: 312-569-6188
Emergency Services: No
Beds: 337

Key Personnel:
CEO/President. . . . . Richard Centron
Operating Room. . . . . Darlene Rzepka, RN
Quality Assurance . . . . James Curry
Radiology. . . . . Edwin April, MD

Measure	Cases	This Hosp.	State Avg.	U.S. Avg.
Heart Attack Care				
ACE Inhibitor or ARB for LVSD[1]	6	83%	96%	96%
Aspirin at Arrival	43	100%	99%	99%
Aspirin at Discharge	42	100%	99%	98%
Beta Blocker at Discharge	40	98%	98%	98%
Fibrinolytic Medication Timing[5]	0	-	50%	55%
PCI Within 90 Minutes of Arrival[1]	7	86%	90%	90%
Smoking Cessation Advice[1]	20	100%	100%	99%
Chest Pain/Possible Heart Attack Care				
Aspirin at Arrival	-	-	95%	95%
Median Time to ECG (minutes)	-	-	8	8
Median Time to Transfer (minutes)	-	-	57	61
Fibrinolytic Medication Timing	-	-	33%	54%
Heart Failure Care				
ACE Inhibitor or ARB for LVSD	154	97%	94%	94%
Discharge Instructions	259	100%	89%	88%
Evaluation of LVS Function	288	100%	98%	98%
Smoking Cessation Advice	102	100%	99%	98%
Pneumonia Care				
Appropriate Initial Antibiotic	51	92%	90%	92%
Blood Culture Timing	71	100%	97%	96%
Influenza Vaccine	72	100%	91%	91%
Initial Antibiotic Timing	93	87%	96%	95%
Pneumococcal Vaccine	80	99%	92%	93%
Smoking Cessation Advice	62	98%	98%	97%
Surgical Care Improvement Project				
Appropriate VTP Within 24 Hours[2]	136	99%	92%	92%
Appropriate Hair Removal[2]	177	99%	99%	99%
Appropriate Beta Blocker Usage[2]	59	100%	92%	93%
Controlled Postoperative Blood Glucose[2,5]	0	-	92%	93%
Prophylactic Antibiotic Timing	83	95%	97%	97%
Prophylactic Antibiotic Timing (Outpatient)	-	-	93%	92%
Prophylactic Antibiotic Selection	86	98%	97%	97%
Prophylactic Antibiotic Select. (Outpatient)	-	-	94%	94%
Prophylactic Antibiotic Stopped	79	97%	94%	94%
Recommended VTP Ordered[2]	136	99%	94%	94%
Urinary Catheter Removal[2]	79	100%	89%	90%
Children's Asthma Care				
Received Systemic Corticosteroids	-	-	-	100%
Received Home Management Plan	-	-	-	71%
Received Reliever Medication	-	-	-	100%
Use of Medical Imaging				
Combination Abdominal CT Scan	-	-	0.246	0.191
Combination Chest CT Scan	-	-	0.098	0.054
Follow-up Mammogram/Ultrasound	-	-	8.4%	8.4%
MRI for Low Back Pain	-	-	33.4%	32.7%
Survey of Patients' Hospital Experiences				
Area Around Room 'Always' Quiet at Night	-	-	-	58%
Doctors 'Always' Communicated Well	-	-	-	80%
Home Recovery Information Given	-	-	-	82%
Hospital Given 9 or 10 on 10 Point Scale	-	-	-	67%
Meds 'Always' Explained Before Given	-	-	-	60%
Nurses 'Always' Communicated Well	-	-	-	76%
Pain 'Always' Well Controlled	-	-	-	69%
Room and Bathroom 'Always' Clean	-	-	-	71%
Timely Help 'Always' Received	-	-	-	64%
Would Definitely Recommend Hospital	-	-	-	69%

NOTE: Hospital profiles are in alphabetical order by state, then city, then hospital within the city; Rankings exclude hospitals with less than 25 cases except for patient surveys which excludes hospitals with less than 100 cases; (a) 100–299 cases; (1) The number of cases is too small to be sure how well a hospital is performing; (2) The hospital indicated that the data submitted for this measure were based on a sample of cases; (3) Data was collected during a shorter time period (fewer quarters) than the maximum possible time for this measure; (4) Suppressed for one or more quarters by CMS; (5) No data is available from the hospital for this measure; (6) Fewer than 100 patients completed the HCAHPS survey. Use these rates with caution, as the number of surveys may be too low to reliably assess hospital performance; (7) Survey results are based on less than 12 months of data; (8) Survey results are not available for this reporting period; (9) No or very few patients were eligible for the HCAHPS survey. The scores shown, if any, reflect a very small number of surveys; (10) A state average was not calculated because too few hospitals in the state submitted data; (11) There were discrepancies in the data collection process; Please refer to the User's Guide for a full explanation of data.

John H Stroger Jr Hospital

1901 W Harrison St
Chicago, IL 60612
URL: cookcountygov.com
Phone: 312-864-6000
Fax: 312-864-9725
Type: Acute Care Hospitals
Ownership: Government - Local
Emergency Services: Yes
Beds: 464

Key Personnel:
CEO/President. . . . . Lacy L Thomas
Chief of Medical Staff . . . . Stephen Hamburger, MD
Infection Control. . . . . Robert Weinstein, MD
Operating Room. . . . . Brenda White
Quality Assurance . . . . Margaret Martin
Intensive Care Unit. . . . . Mary O'Flaherty

Measure	Cases	This Hosp.	State Avg.	U.S. Avg.
Heart Attack Care				
ACE Inhibitor or ARB for LVSD[2]	34	100%	96%	96%
Aspirin at Arrival[2]	178	99%	99%	99%
Aspirin at Discharge[2]	189	98%	99%	98%
Beta Blocker at Discharge[2]	184	99%	98%	98%
Fibrinolytic Medication Timing[2]	0	-	50%	55%
PCI Within 90 Minutes of Arrival[1,2]	7	71%	90%	90%
Smoking Cessation Advice[2]	82	100%	100%	99%
Chest Pain/Possible Heart Attack Care				
Aspirin at Arrival[5]	0	-	95%	95%
Median Time to ECG (minutes)[5]	0	-	8	8
Median Time to Transfer (minutes)[5]	0	-	57	61
Fibrinolytic Medication Timing[5]	0	-	33%	54%
Heart Failure Care				
ACE Inhibitor or ARB for LVSD[2]	134	98%	94%	94%
Discharge Instructions[2]	300	69%	89%	88%
Evaluation of LVS Function[2]	308	97%	98%	98%
Smoking Cessation Advice[2]	94	99%	99%	98%
Pneumonia Care				
Appropriate Initial Antibiotic[2]	121	70%	90%	92%
Blood Culture Timing[2]	166	87%	97%	96%
Influenza Vaccine[2]	68	59%	91%	91%
Initial Antibiotic Timing[2]	190	65%	96%	95%
Pneumococcal Vaccine[2]	36	42%	92%	93%
Smoking Cessation Advice[2]	102	97%	98%	97%
Surgical Care Improvement Project				
Appropriate VTP Within 24 Hours[2]	204	89%	92%	92%
Appropriate Hair Removal[2]	453	98%	99%	99%
Appropriate Beta Blocker Usage[2]	132	83%	92%	93%
Controlled Postoperative Blood Glucose[2]	92	83%	92%	93%
Prophylactic Antibiotic Timing[2]	268	93%	97%	97%
Prophylactic Antibiotic Timing (Outpatient)	141	96%	93%	92%
Prophylactic Antibiotic Selection[2]	266	92%	97%	97%
Prophylactic Antibiotic Select. (Outpatient)	140	87%	94%	94%
Prophylactic Antibiotic Stopped[2]	257	93%	94%	94%
Recommended VTP Ordered[2]	204	89%	94%	94%
Urinary Catheter Removal[2]	47	66%	89%	90%
Children's Asthma Care				
Received Systemic Corticosteroids	-	-	-	100%
Received Home Management Plan	-	-	-	71%
Received Reliever Medication	-	-	-	100%
Use of Medical Imaging				
Combination Abdominal CT Scan	740	0.631	0.246	0.191
Combination Chest CT Scan	78	0.013	0.098	0.054
Follow-up Mammogram/Ultrasound[5]	0	-	8.4%	8.4%
MRI for Low Back Pain[1]	34	38.2%	33.4%	32.7%
Survey of Patients' Hospital Experiences				
Area Around Room 'Always' Quiet at Night	300+	55%	-	58%
Doctors 'Always' Communicated Well	300+	79%	-	80%
Home Recovery Information Given	300+	74%	-	82%
Hospital Given 9 or 10 on 10 Point Scale	300+	52%	-	67%
Meds 'Always' Explained Before Given	300+	52%	-	60%
Nurses 'Always' Communicated Well	300+	62%	-	76%
Pain 'Always' Well Controlled	300+	63%	-	69%
Room and Bathroom 'Always' Clean	300+	52%	-	71%
Timely Help 'Always' Received	300+	50%	-	64%
Would Definitely Recommend Hospital	300+	61%	-	69%

Loretto Hospital

645 South Central Ave
Chicago, IL 60644
URL: www.lorettohospital.org
Phone: 773-626-4300
Fax: 773-626-2613
Type: Acute Care Hospitals
Ownership: Proprietary
Emergency Services: No
Beds: 189

Key Personnel:
CEO/President. . . . . Steve Drucker
Chief of Medical Staff . . . . Dr. Humid M Humayum, MD
Infection Control. . . . . Omar Jrab
Operating Room. . . . . Mary Frolik
Ambulatory Care . . . . Dr. Deen Gaddam
Emergency Room . . . . Patricia Lindeman

Measure	Cases	This Hosp.	State Avg.	U.S. Avg.
Heart Attack Care				
ACE Inhibitor or ARB for LVSD	0	-	96%	96%
Aspirin at Arrival[1]	12	92%	99%	99%
Aspirin at Discharge[1]	2	100%	99%	98%
Beta Blocker at Discharge[1]	3	100%	98%	98%
Fibrinolytic Medication Timing	0	-	50%	55%
PCI Within 90 Minutes of Arrival	0	-	90%	90%
Smoking Cessation Advice	0	-	100%	99%
Chest Pain/Possible Heart Attack Care				
Aspirin at Arrival[1,3]	12	92%	95%	95%
Median Time to ECG (minutes)[1,3]	13	15	8	8
Median Time to Transfer (minutes)[3]	0	-	57	61
Fibrinolytic Medication Timing[1,3]	1	0%	33%	54%
Heart Failure Care				
ACE Inhibitor or ARB for LVSD	46	100%	94%	94%
Discharge Instructions	101	100%	89%	88%
Evaluation of LVS Function	141	100%	98%	98%
Smoking Cessation Advice	41	100%	99%	98%
Pneumonia Care				
Appropriate Initial Antibiotic	55	78%	90%	92%
Blood Culture Timing	101	95%	97%	96%
Influenza Vaccine	51	100%	91%	91%
Initial Antibiotic Timing	113	88%	96%	95%
Pneumococcal Vaccine	59	100%	92%	93%
Smoking Cessation Advice	36	100%	98%	97%
Surgical Care Improvement Project				
Appropriate VTP Within 24 Hours[1]	18	67%	92%	92%
Appropriate Hair Removal	32	100%	99%	99%
Appropriate Beta Blocker Usage[1]	7	86%	92%	93%
Controlled Postoperative Blood Glucose	0	-	92%	93%
Prophylactic Antibiotic Timing[1]	5	40%	97%	97%
Prophylactic Antibiotic Timing (Outpatient)[1]	24	75%	93%	92%
Prophylactic Antibiotic Selection[1]	6	83%	97%	97%
Prophylactic Antibiotic Select. (Outpatient)[1]	19	95%	94%	94%
Prophylactic Antibiotic Stopped[1]	4	100%	94%	94%
Recommended VTP Ordered[1]	19	63%	94%	94%
Urinary Catheter Removal[1]	1	100%	89%	90%
Children's Asthma Care				
Received Systemic Corticosteroids	-	-	-	100%
Received Home Management Plan	-	-	-	71%
Received Reliever Medication	-	-	-	100%
Use of Medical Imaging				
Combination Abdominal CT Scan	46	0.022	0.246	0.191
Combination Chest CT Scan[1]	25	0.000	0.098	0.054
Follow-up Mammogram/Ultrasound[1]	58	8.6%	8.4%	8.4%
MRI for Low Back Pain[5]	0	-	33.4%	32.7%
Survey of Patients' Hospital Experiences				
Area Around Room 'Always' Quiet at Night	(a)	48%	-	58%
Doctors 'Always' Communicated Well	(a)	69%	-	80%
Home Recovery Information Given	(a)	58%	-	82%
Hospital Given 9 or 10 on 10 Point Scale	(a)	41%	-	67%
Meds 'Always' Explained Before Given	(a)	41%	-	60%
Nurses 'Always' Communicated Well	(a)	59%	-	76%
Pain 'Always' Well Controlled	(a)	50%	-	69%
Room and Bathroom 'Always' Clean	(a)	57%	-	71%
Timely Help 'Always' Received	(a)	39%	-	64%
Would Definitely Recommend Hospital	(a)	39%	-	69%

Louis A Weiss Memorial Hospital

4646 N Marine Drive
Chicago, IL 60640
E-mail: cboykin@weisshospital.org
URL: www.weisshospital.org
Phone: 773-878-8700
Fax: 773-564-5359
Type: Acute Care Hospitals
Ownership: Proprietary
Emergency Services: No
Beds: 357

Key Personnel:
CEO/President. . . . . Tracey Rogers
Chief of Medical Staff . . . . Stuart Kraussn, MD
Infection Control. . . . . David Balling, MD
Operating Room. . . . . Marc Adajar
Quality Assurance . . . . Chris Brady, RN
Radiology. . . . . Hiroyuki Abe, MD
Anesthesiology. . . . . Kenneth Rodino, MD
Emergency Room . . . . Leo Dilan, MD

Measure	Cases	This Hosp.	State Avg.	U.S. Avg.
Heart Attack Care				
ACE Inhibitor or ARB for LVSD	25	100%	96%	96%
Aspirin at Arrival	109	100%	99%	99%
Aspirin at Discharge	95	99%	99%	98%
Beta Blocker at Discharge	104	99%	98%	98%
Fibrinolytic Medication Timing	0	-	50%	55%
PCI Within 90 Minutes of Arrival[1]	12	83%	90%	90%
Smoking Cessation Advice	37	100%	100%	99%
Chest Pain/Possible Heart Attack Care				
Aspirin at Arrival[3]	0	-	95%	95%
Median Time to ECG (minutes)[3]	0	-	8	8
Median Time to Transfer (minutes)[5]	0	-	57	61
Fibrinolytic Medication Timing[5]	0	-	33%	54%
Heart Failure Care				
ACE Inhibitor or ARB for LVSD	103	98%	94%	94%
Discharge Instructions	203	98%	89%	88%
Evaluation of LVS Function	275	100%	98%	98%
Smoking Cessation Advice	70	100%	99%	98%
Pneumonia Care				
Appropriate Initial Antibiotic	52	88%	90%	92%
Blood Culture Timing	201	98%	97%	96%
Influenza Vaccine	112	98%	91%	91%
Initial Antibiotic Timing	176	98%	96%	95%
Pneumococcal Vaccine	171	96%	92%	93%
Smoking Cessation Advice	56	96%	98%	97%
Surgical Care Improvement Project				
Appropriate VTP Within 24 Hours[2]	171	96%	92%	92%
Appropriate Hair Removal[2]	412	100%	99%	99%
Appropriate Beta Blocker Usage[2]	133	92%	92%	93%
Controlled Postoperative Blood Glucose[1,2]	23	83%	92%	93%
Prophylactic Antibiotic Timing[2]	245	97%	97%	97%
Prophylactic Antibiotic Timing (Outpatient)	147	76%	93%	92%
Prophylactic Antibiotic Selection[2]	245	98%	97%	97%
Prophylactic Antibiotic Select. (Outpatient)	257	84%	94%	94%
Prophylactic Antibiotic Stopped[2]	231	96%	94%	94%
Recommended VTP Ordered[2]	171	98%	94%	94%
Urinary Catheter Removal[2]	117	97%	89%	90%
Children's Asthma Care				
Received Systemic Corticosteroids	-	-	-	100%
Received Home Management Plan	-	-	-	71%
Received Reliever Medication	-	-	-	100%
Use of Medical Imaging				
Combination Abdominal CT Scan	549	0.109	0.246	0.191
Combination Chest CT Scan	475	0.008	0.098	0.054
Follow-up Mammogram/Ultrasound	571	6.3%	8.4%	8.4%
MRI for Low Back Pain	126	27.0%	33.4%	32.7%
Survey of Patients' Hospital Experiences				
Area Around Room 'Always' Quiet at Night	300+	57%	-	58%
Doctors 'Always' Communicated Well	300+	77%	-	80%
Home Recovery Information Given	300+	75%	-	82%
Hospital Given 9 or 10 on 10 Point Scale	300+	62%	-	67%
Meds 'Always' Explained Before Given	300+	56%	-	60%
Nurses 'Always' Communicated Well	300+	72%	-	76%
Pain 'Always' Well Controlled	300+	66%	-	69%
Room and Bathroom 'Always' Clean	300+	71%	-	71%
Timely Help 'Always' Received	300+	59%	-	64%
Would Definitely Recommend Hospital	300+	63%	-	69%

NOTE: Hospital profiles are in alphabetical order by state, then city, then hospital within the city; Rankings exclude hospitals with less than 25 cases except for patient surveys which excludes hospitals with less than 100 cases; (a) 100–299 cases; (1) The number of cases is too small to be sure how well a hospital is performing; (2) The hospital indicated that the data submitted for this measure were based on a sample of cases; (3) Data was collected during a shorter time period (fewer quarters) than the maximum possible time for this measure; (4) Suppressed for one or more quarters by CMS; (5) No data is available from the hospital for this measure; (6) Fewer than 100 patients completed the HCAHPS survey. Use these rates with caution, as the number of surveys may be too low to reliably assess hospital performance; (7) Survey results are based on less than 12 months of data; (8) Survey results are not available for this reporting period; (9) No or very few patients were eligible for the HCAHPS survey. The scores shown, if any, reflect a very small number of surveys; (10) A state average was not calculated because too few hospitals in the state submitted data; (11) There were discrepancies in the data collection process; Please refer to the User's Guide for a full explanation of data.

Mercy Hospital and Medical Center

2525 S Michigan Ave   Phone: 312-567-2000
Chicago, IL 60616
E-mail: mercy@mercy-chicago.org
URL: www.mercy-chicago.org
Type: Acute Care Hospitals   Emergency Services: Yes
Ownership: Voluntary Non-Profit - Church   Beds: 507

Key Personnel:
CEO/President. . . . . Sheila Lyne RSM
Cardiac Laboratory. . . . . Karen Walker
Infection Control. . . . . Jean Kirk RN
Operating Room. . . . . Mary Alice Ledenmeyer
Pediatric Ambulatory Care . . . . . . Jere Freidman MD
Pediatric In-Patient Care . . . . . . Jere Freidman MD
Quality Assurance . . . . Nancy Hill Davis
Radiology. . . . . Shahrooz Sepahdari MD

Measure	Cases	This Hosp.	State Avg.	U.S. Avg.
Heart Attack Care				
ACE Inhibitor or ARB for LVSD	48	96%	96%	96%
Aspirin at Arrival	194	97%	99%	99%
Aspirin at Discharge	180	94%	99%	98%
Beta Blocker at Discharge	167	96%	98%	98%
Fibrinolytic Medication Timing	0	-	50%	55%
PCI Within 90 Minutes of Arrival[1]	16	56%	90%	90%
Smoking Cessation Advice	55	100%	100%	99%
Chest Pain/Possible Heart Attack Care				
Aspirin at Arrival[5]	0	-	95%	95%
Median Time to ECG (minutes)[5]	0	-	8	8
Median Time to Transfer (minutes)[5]	0	-	57	61
Fibrinolytic Medication Timing[5]	0	-	33%	54%
Heart Failure Care				
ACE Inhibitor or ARB for LVSD[2]	168	92%	94%	94%
Discharge Instructions[2]	275	89%	89%	88%
Evaluation of LVS Function[2]	307	96%	98%	98%
Smoking Cessation Advice[2]	62	100%	99%	98%
Pneumonia Care				
Appropriate Initial Antibiotic[2]	77	95%	90%	92%
Blood Culture Timing[2]	130	93%	97%	96%
Influenza Vaccine[2]	91	51%	91%	91%
Initial Antibiotic Timing[2]	148	91%	96%	95%
Pneumococcal Vaccine[2]	128	37%	92%	93%
Smoking Cessation Advice[2]	69	100%	98%	97%
Surgical Care Improvement Project				
Appropriate VTP Within 24 Hours	248	88%	92%	92%
Appropriate Hair Removal	618	100%	99%	99%
Appropriate Beta Blocker Usage	180	59%	92%	93%
Controlled Postoperative Blood Glucose	84	92%	92%	93%
Prophylactic Antibiotic Timing	382	91%	97%	97%
Prophylactic Antibiotic Timing (Outpatient)	148	80%	93%	92%
Prophylactic Antibiotic Selection	382	94%	97%	97%
Prophylactic Antibiotic Select. (Outpatient)	134	83%	94%	94%
Prophylactic Antibiotic Stopped	366	90%	94%	94%
Recommended VTP Ordered	248	98%	94%	94%
Urinary Catheter Removal	138	84%	89%	90%
Children's Asthma Care				
Received Systemic Corticosteroids	-	-	-	100%
Received Home Management Plan	-	-	-	71%
Received Reliever Medication	-	-	-	100%
Use of Medical Imaging				
Combination Abdominal CT Scan	619	0.118	0.246	0.191
Combination Chest CT Scan	336	0.083	0.098	0.054
Follow-up Mammogram/Ultrasound	1,510	4.2%	8.4%	8.4%
MRI for Low Back Pain	140	33.6%	33.4%	32.7%
Survey of Patients' Hospital Experiences				
Area Around Room 'Always' Quiet at Night	300+	64%	-	58%
Doctors 'Always' Communicated Well	300+	80%	-	80%
Home Recovery Information Given	300+	79%	-	82%
Hospital Given 9 or 10 on 10 Point Scale	300+	68%	-	67%
Meds 'Always' Explained Before Given	300+	57%	-	60%
Nurses 'Always' Communicated Well	300+	77%	-	76%
Pain 'Always' Well Controlled	300+	69%	-	69%
Room and Bathroom 'Always' Clean	300+	71%	-	71%
Timely Help 'Always' Received	300+	56%	-	64%
Would Definitely Recommend Hospital	300+	77%	-	69%

Methodist Hospital of Chicago

5025 N Paulina Street   Phone: 773-271-9040
Chicago, IL 60640   Fax: 773-989-1348
URL: www.methodistchicago.org
Type: Acute Care Hospitals   Emergency Services: Yes
Ownership: Voluntary Non-Profit - Church   Beds: 198

Key Personnel:
CEO/President. . . . . Steven Dahl
Chief of Medical Staff. . . . . Irzing Tracer, MD
Quality Assurance . . . . Eleanor Wolrfram

Measure	Cases	This Hosp.	State Avg.	U.S. Avg.
Heart Attack Care				
ACE Inhibitor or ARB for LVSD[1]	2	100%	96%	96%
Aspirin at Arrival[1]	11	100%	99%	99%
Aspirin at Discharge[1]	7	100%	99%	98%
Beta Blocker at Discharge[1]	6	67%	98%	98%
Fibrinolytic Medication Timing	0	-	50%	55%
PCI Within 90 Minutes of Arrival	0	-	90%	90%
Smoking Cessation Advice[1]	1	100%	100%	99%
Chest Pain/Possible Heart Attack Care				
Aspirin at Arrival[3]	0	-	95%	95%
Median Time to ECG (minutes)[3]	0	-	8	8
Median Time to Transfer (minutes)[5]	0	-	57	61
Fibrinolytic Medication Timing[5]	0	-	33%	54%
Heart Failure Care				
ACE Inhibitor or ARB for LVSD[1]	13	92%	94%	94%
Discharge Instructions[1]	6	50%	89%	88%
Evaluation of LVS Function	48	98%	98%	98%
Smoking Cessation Advice[1]	17	100%	99%	98%
Pneumonia Care				
Appropriate Initial Antibiotic[1]	9	56%	90%	92%
Blood Culture Timing	113	88%	97%	96%
Influenza Vaccine	89	79%	91%	91%
Initial Antibiotic Timing	148	87%	96%	95%
Pneumococcal Vaccine	90	74%	92%	93%
Smoking Cessation Advice	101	91%	98%	97%
Surgical Care Improvement Project				
Appropriate VTP Within 24 Hours[1]	23	83%	92%	92%
Appropriate Hair Removal	32	100%	99%	99%
Appropriate Beta Blocker Usage[1]	11	91%	92%	93%
Controlled Postoperative Blood Glucose	0	-	92%	93%
Prophylactic Antibiotic Timing[1]	6	50%	97%	97%
Prophylactic Antibiotic Timing (Outpatient)	36	92%	93%	92%
Prophylactic Antibiotic Selection[1]	8	88%	97%	97%
Prophylactic Antibiotic Select. (Outpatient)	33	97%	94%	94%
Prophylactic Antibiotic Stopped[1]	6	83%	94%	94%
Recommended VTP Ordered[1]	23	83%	94%	94%
Urinary Catheter Removal	0	-	89%	90%
Children's Asthma Care				
Received Systemic Corticosteroids	-	-	-	100%
Received Home Management Plan	-	-	-	71%
Received Reliever Medication	-	-	-	100%
Use of Medical Imaging				
Combination Abdominal CT Scan	81	0.494	0.246	0.191
Combination Chest CT Scan	73	0.329	0.098	0.054
Follow-up Mammogram/Ultrasound	116	10.3%	8.4%	8.4%
MRI for Low Back Pain[1]	2	50.0%	33.4%	32.7%
Survey of Patients' Hospital Experiences				
Area Around Room 'Always' Quiet at Night	(a)	52%	-	58%
Doctors 'Always' Communicated Well	(a)	72%	-	80%
Home Recovery Information Given	(a)	71%	-	82%
Hospital Given 9 or 10 on 10 Point Scale	(a)	63%	-	67%
Meds 'Always' Explained Before Given	(a)	45%	-	60%
Nurses 'Always' Communicated Well	(a)	60%	-	76%
Pain 'Always' Well Controlled	(a)	50%	-	69%
Room and Bathroom 'Always' Clean	(a)	77%	-	71%
Timely Help 'Always' Received	(a)	39%	-	64%
Would Definitely Recommend Hospital	(a)	60%	-	69%

Mount Sinai Hospital Medical Center

15th Street at California   Phone: 773-257-6751
Chicago, IL 60608   Fax: 773-257-6208
URL: www.sinai.org
Type: Acute Care Hospitals   Emergency Services: No
Ownership: Voluntary Non-Profit - Private   Beds: 432

Key Personnel:
Chief of Medical Staff . . . . Jack Garon MD
Infection Control. . . . . Jan Lepenski
Operating Room. . . . . Sue McKenna
Quality Assurance . . . . Robert Tarver
Radiology. . . . . Randy Boberg
Anesthesiology. . . . . John Vazquez MD
Emergency Room . . . . Leslie Zun MD
Intensive Care Unit. . . . . Barbara Shields-Johnson

Measure	Cases	This Hosp.	State Avg.	U.S. Avg.
Heart Attack Care				
ACE Inhibitor or ARB for LVSD	44	98%	96%	96%
Aspirin at Arrival	115	99%	99%	99%
Aspirin at Discharge	153	100%	99%	98%
Beta Blocker at Discharge	130	100%	98%	98%
Fibrinolytic Medication Timing	0	-	50%	55%
PCI Within 90 Minutes of Arrival[1]	16	50%	90%	90%
Smoking Cessation Advice	67	100%	100%	99%
Chest Pain/Possible Heart Attack Care				
Aspirin at Arrival[3]	0	-	95%	95%
Median Time to ECG (minutes)[3]	0	-	8	8
Median Time to Transfer (minutes)[5]	0	-	57	61
Fibrinolytic Medication Timing[5]	0	-	33%	54%
Heart Failure Care				
ACE Inhibitor or ARB for LVSD	157	95%	94%	94%
Discharge Instructions	275	98%	89%	88%
Evaluation of LVS Function	302	99%	98%	98%
Smoking Cessation Advice	124	100%	99%	98%
Pneumonia Care				
Appropriate Initial Antibiotic	95	96%	90%	92%
Blood Culture Timing	203	99%	97%	96%
Influenza Vaccine	54	78%	91%	91%
Initial Antibiotic Timing	135	96%	96%	95%
Pneumococcal Vaccine	101	91%	92%	93%
Smoking Cessation Advice	107	100%	98%	97%
Surgical Care Improvement Project				
Appropriate VTP Within 24 Hours[2]	110	96%	92%	92%
Appropriate Hair Removal[2]	306	100%	99%	99%
Appropriate Beta Blocker Usage[2]	74	88%	92%	93%
Controlled Postoperative Blood Glucose[2]	34	97%	92%	93%
Prophylactic Antibiotic Timing[2]	172	99%	97%	97%
Prophylactic Antibiotic Timing (Outpatient)	74	84%	93%	92%
Prophylactic Antibiotic Selection[2]	175	96%	97%	97%
Prophylactic Antibiotic Select. (Outpatient)	208	99%	94%	94%
Prophylactic Antibiotic Stopped[2]	155	94%	94%	94%
Recommended VTP Ordered[2]	110	99%	94%	94%
Urinary Catheter Removal[2]	43	98%	89%	90%
Children's Asthma Care				
Received Systemic Corticosteroids	-	-	-	100%
Received Home Management Plan	-	-	-	71%
Received Reliever Medication	-	-	-	100%
Use of Medical Imaging				
Combination Abdominal CT Scan	328	0.146	0.246	0.191
Combination Chest CT Scan	250	0.072	0.098	0.054
Follow-up Mammogram/Ultrasound	411	5.4%	8.4%	8.4%
MRI for Low Back Pain[1]	28	60.7%	33.4%	32.7%
Survey of Patients' Hospital Experiences				
Area Around Room 'Always' Quiet at Night	300+	49%	-	58%
Doctors 'Always' Communicated Well	300+	74%	-	80%
Home Recovery Information Given	300+	76%	-	82%
Hospital Given 9 or 10 on 10 Point Scale	300+	51%	-	67%
Meds 'Always' Explained Before Given	300+	56%	-	60%
Nurses 'Always' Communicated Well	300+	63%	-	76%
Pain 'Always' Well Controlled	300+	61%	-	69%
Room and Bathroom 'Always' Clean	300+	53%	-	71%
Timely Help 'Always' Received	300+	42%	-	64%
Would Definitely Recommend Hospital	300+	52%	-	69%

NOTE: Hospital profiles are in alphabetical order by state, then city, then hospital within the city; Rankings exclude hospitals with less than 25 cases except for patient surveys which excludes hospitals with less than 100 cases; (a) 100–299 cases; (1) The number of cases is too small to be sure how well a hospital is performing; (2) The hospital indicated that the data submitted for this measure were based on a sample of cases; (3) Data was collected during a shorter time period (fewer quarters) than the maximum possible time for this measure; (4) Suppressed for one or more quarters by CMS; (5) No data is available from the hospital for this measure; (6) Fewer than 100 patients completed the HCAHPS survey. Use these rates with caution, as the number of surveys may be too low to reliably assess hospital performance; (7) Survey results are based on less than 12 months of data; (8) Survey results are not available for this reporting period; (9) No or very few patients were eligible for the HCAHPS survey. The scores shown, if any, reflect a very small number of surveys; (10) A state average was not calculated because too few hospitals in the state submitted data; (11) There were discrepancies in the data collection process; Please refer to the User's Guide for a full explanation of data.

Northwestern Memorial Hospital

251 E Huron St | Phone: 312-926-2000
Chicago, IL 60611 | Fax: 312-926-3858
URL: www.nmh.org
Type: Acute Care Hospitals | Emergency Services: Yes
Ownership: Voluntary Non-Profit - Private | Beds: 744

Key Personnel:
CEO/President. . . . . Dean M Harrison
Cardiac Laboratory. . . . . Alan Kadish, MD
Chief of Medical Staff. . . . . John Clarke, MD
Infection Control. . . . . Steve Wolinsky, MD
Operating Room. . . . . Michael Langerfeld
Pediatric Ambulatory Care . . . . . . Martin Myers, MD
Quality Assurance . . . . Laura Lingl
Radiology. . . . . Eric Russell, MD

Measure	Cases	This Hosp.	State Avg.	U.S. Avg.
Heart Attack Care				
ACE Inhibitor or ARB for LVSD	46	96%	96%	96%
Aspirin at Arrival	294	99%	99%	99%
Aspirin at Discharge	299	98%	99%	98%
Beta Blocker at Discharge	281	98%	98%	98%
Fibrinolytic Medication Timing	0	-	50%	55%
PCI Within 90 Minutes of Arrival	45	91%	90%	90%
Smoking Cessation Advice	72	100%	100%	99%
Chest Pain/Possible Heart Attack Care				
Aspirin at Arrival[5]	0	-	95%	95%
Median Time to ECG (minutes)[5]	0	-	8	8
Median Time to Transfer (minutes)[5]	0	-	57	61
Fibrinolytic Medication Timing[5]	0	-	33%	54%
Heart Failure Care				
ACE Inhibitor or ARB for LVSD	318	98%	94%	94%
Discharge Instructions	768	97%	89%	88%
Evaluation of LVS Function	852	100%	98%	98%
Smoking Cessation Advice	149	100%	99%	98%
Pneumonia Care				
Appropriate Initial Antibiotic	135	97%	90%	92%
Blood Culture Timing	401	99%	97%	96%
Influenza Vaccine	274	93%	91%	91%
Initial Antibiotic Timing	359	96%	96%	95%
Pneumococcal Vaccine	301	95%	92%	93%
Smoking Cessation Advice	149	99%	98%	97%
Surgical Care Improvement Project				
Appropriate VTP Within 24 Hours[2]	200	94%	92%	92%
Appropriate Hair Removal[2]	711	100%	99%	99%
Appropriate Beta Blocker Usage[2]	222	86%	92%	93%
Controlled Postoperative Blood Glucose[2]	144	96%	92%	93%
Prophylactic Antibiotic Timing[2]	437	97%	97%	97%
Prophylactic Antibiotic Timing (Outpatient)	561	97%	93%	92%
Prophylactic Antibiotic Selection[2]	451	99%	97%	97%
Prophylactic Antibiotic Select. (Outpatient)	554	97%	94%	94%
Prophylactic Antibiotic Stopped[2]	416	94%	94%	94%
Recommended VTP Ordered[2]	200	98%	94%	94%
Urinary Catheter Removal[2]	192	84%	89%	90%
Children's Asthma Care				
Received Systemic Corticosteroids	-	-	-	100%
Received Home Management Plan	-	-	-	71%
Received Reliever Medication	-	-	-	100%
Use of Medical Imaging				
Combination Abdominal CT Scan	4,159	0.201	0.246	0.191
Combination Chest CT Scan	4,348	0.001	0.098	0.054
Follow-up Mammogram/Ultrasound	3,743	8.4%	8.4%	8.4%
MRI for Low Back Pain	774	29.5%	33.4%	32.7%
Survey of Patients' Hospital Experiences				
Area Around Room 'Always' Quiet at Night	300+	64%	-	58%
Doctors 'Always' Communicated Well	300+	77%	-	80%
Home Recovery Information Given	300+	77%	-	82%
Hospital Given 9 or 10 on 10 Point Scale	300+	77%	-	67%
Meds 'Always' Explained Before Given	300+	59%	-	60%
Nurses 'Always' Communicated Well	300+	73%	-	76%
Pain 'Always' Well Controlled	300+	69%	-	69%
Room and Bathroom 'Always' Clean	300+	68%	-	71%
Timely Help 'Always' Received	300+	59%	-	64%
Would Definitely Recommend Hospital	300+	82%	-	69%

Norwegian-American Hospital

1044 N Francisco Ave | Phone: 773-292-8200
Chicago, IL 60622 | Fax: 773-278-3531
URL: www.nahospital.org
Type: Acute Care Hospitals | Emergency Services: Yes
Ownership: Voluntary Non-Profit - Private | Beds: 200

Key Personnel:
CEO/President. . . . . Michael E Haley
Chief of Medical Staff . . . . Jose De Leon, MD
Operating Room. . . . . Rose Garcia, RN
Pediatric In-Patient Care . . . . Henry Munez, MD
Quality Assurance . . . . James McCracken
Emergency Room . . . . Lilia Charpe, RN

Measure	Cases	This Hosp.	State Avg.	U.S. Avg.
Heart Attack Care				
ACE Inhibitor or ARB for LVSD[1]	3	100%	96%	96%
Aspirin at Arrival	37	100%	99%	99%
Aspirin at Discharge[1]	24	96%	99%	98%
Beta Blocker at Discharge[1]	24	83%	98%	98%
Fibrinolytic Medication Timing	0	-	50%	55%
PCI Within 90 Minutes of Arrival[1]	7	14%	90%	90%
Smoking Cessation Advice[1]	9	100%	100%	99%
Chest Pain/Possible Heart Attack Care				
Aspirin at Arrival[1,3]	3	100%	95%	95%
Median Time to ECG (minutes)[1,3]	3	2	8	8
Median Time to Transfer (minutes)[1,3]	1	300	57	61
Fibrinolytic Medication Timing[3]	0	-	33%	54%
Heart Failure Care				
ACE Inhibitor or ARB for LVSD	87	85%	94%	94%
Discharge Instructions	159	67%	89%	88%
Evaluation of LVS Function	210	99%	98%	98%
Smoking Cessation Advice	54	100%	99%	98%
Pneumonia Care				
Appropriate Initial Antibiotic	71	83%	90%	92%
Blood Culture Timing	98	89%	97%	96%
Influenza Vaccine	50	74%	91%	91%
Initial Antibiotic Timing	118	81%	96%	95%
Pneumococcal Vaccine	48	60%	92%	93%
Smoking Cessation Advice	34	100%	98%	97%
Surgical Care Improvement Project				
Appropriate VTP Within 24 Hours	43	42%	92%	92%
Appropriate Hair Removal	92	100%	99%	99%
Appropriate Beta Blocker Usage[1]	9	56%	92%	93%
Controlled Postoperative Blood Glucose	0	-	92%	93%
Prophylactic Antibiotic Timing	40	95%	97%	97%
Prophylactic Antibiotic Timing (Outpatient)	43	81%	93%	92%
Prophylactic Antibiotic Selection	39	85%	97%	97%
Prophylactic Antibiotic Select. (Outpatient)	36	97%	94%	94%
Prophylactic Antibiotic Stopped	36	64%	94%	94%
Recommended VTP Ordered	47	51%	94%	94%
Urinary Catheter Removal[1]	6	67%	89%	90%
Children's Asthma Care				
Received Systemic Corticosteroids	-	-	-	100%
Received Home Management Plan	-	-	-	71%
Received Reliever Medication	-	-	-	100%
Use of Medical Imaging				
Combination Abdominal CT Scan	181	0.072	0.246	0.191
Combination Chest CT Scan	57	0.000	0.098	0.054
Follow-up Mammogram/Ultrasound	287	7.7%	8.4%	8.4%
MRI for Low Back Pain[1]	15	26.7%	33.4%	32.7%
Survey of Patients' Hospital Experiences				
Area Around Room 'Always' Quiet at Night	300+	40%	-	58%
Doctors 'Always' Communicated Well	300+	66%	-	80%
Home Recovery Information Given	300+	70%	-	82%
Hospital Given 9 or 10 on 10 Point Scale	300+	45%	-	67%
Meds 'Always' Explained Before Given	300+	40%	-	60%
Nurses 'Always' Communicated Well	300+	52%	-	76%
Pain 'Always' Well Controlled	300+	52%	-	69%
Room and Bathroom 'Always' Clean	300+	56%	-	71%
Timely Help 'Always' Received	300+	44%	-	64%
Would Definitely Recommend Hospital	300+	44%	-	69%

Our Lady of the Resurrection Medical Center

5645 W Addison | Phone: 773-282-7000
Chicago, IL 60634 | Fax: 773-794-8353
URL: www.reshealth.org
Type: Acute Care Hospitals | Emergency Services: Yes
Ownership: Voluntary Non-Profit - Church | Beds: 264

Key Personnel:
CEO/President. . . . . John Short
Cardiac Laboratory. . . . . Sue Schaub
Chief of Medical Staff. . . . . Shirish Shah, MD
Infection Control. . . . . Ann Marie Ogle, RN
Operating Room. . . . . Crystal Mobley, RN
Quality Assurance . . . . George Einhorn

Measure	Cases	This Hosp.	State Avg.	U.S. Avg.
Heart Attack Care				
ACE Inhibitor or ARB for LVSD	29	100%	96%	96%
Aspirin at Arrival	224	100%	99%	99%
Aspirin at Discharge	182	100%	99%	98%
Beta Blocker at Discharge	165	100%	98%	98%
Fibrinolytic Medication Timing	0	-	50%	55%
PCI Within 90 Minutes of Arrival	36	86%	90%	90%
Smoking Cessation Advice	50	100%	100%	99%
Chest Pain/Possible Heart Attack Care				
Aspirin at Arrival	32	100%	95%	95%
Median Time to ECG (minutes)	31	3	8	8
Median Time to Transfer (minutes)[5]	0	-	57	61
Fibrinolytic Medication Timing[3]	0	-	33%	54%
Heart Failure Care				
ACE Inhibitor or ARB for LVSD	71	100%	94%	94%
Discharge Instructions	249	94%	89%	88%
Evaluation of LVS Function	414	100%	98%	98%
Smoking Cessation Advice	67	100%	99%	98%
Pneumonia Care				
Appropriate Initial Antibiotic	130	96%	90%	92%
Blood Culture Timing	159	100%	97%	96%
Influenza Vaccine	164	100%	91%	91%
Initial Antibiotic Timing	246	99%	96%	95%
Pneumococcal Vaccine	223	100%	92%	93%
Smoking Cessation Advice	101	100%	98%	97%
Surgical Care Improvement Project				
Appropriate VTP Within 24 Hours	202	98%	92%	92%
Appropriate Hair Removal	353	100%	99%	99%
Appropriate Beta Blocker Usage	59	100%	92%	93%
Controlled Postoperative Blood Glucose	0	-	92%	93%
Prophylactic Antibiotic Timing	149	97%	97%	97%
Prophylactic Antibiotic Timing (Outpatient)	98	88%	93%	92%
Prophylactic Antibiotic Selection	150	94%	97%	97%
Prophylactic Antibiotic Select. (Outpatient)	90	92%	94%	94%
Prophylactic Antibiotic Stopped	135	98%	94%	94%
Recommended VTP Ordered	202	99%	94%	94%
Urinary Catheter Removal	47	94%	89%	90%
Children's Asthma Care				
Received Systemic Corticosteroids	-	-	-	100%
Received Home Management Plan	-	-	-	71%
Received Reliever Medication	-	-	-	100%
Use of Medical Imaging				
Combination Abdominal CT Scan	501	0.399	0.246	0.191
Combination Chest CT Scan	334	0.272	0.098	0.054
Follow-up Mammogram/Ultrasound	924	9.3%	8.4%	8.4%
MRI for Low Back Pain	74	29.7%	33.4%	32.7%
Survey of Patients' Hospital Experiences				
Area Around Room 'Always' Quiet at Night	300+	42%	-	58%
Doctors 'Always' Communicated Well	300+	72%	-	80%
Home Recovery Information Given	300+	79%	-	82%
Hospital Given 9 or 10 on 10 Point Scale	300+	49%	-	67%
Meds 'Always' Explained Before Given	300+	53%	-	60%
Nurses 'Always' Communicated Well	300+	66%	-	76%
Pain 'Always' Well Controlled	300+	62%	-	69%
Room and Bathroom 'Always' Clean	300+	64%	-	71%
Timely Help 'Always' Received	300+	56%	-	64%
Would Definitely Recommend Hospital	300+	51%	-	69%

NOTE: Hospital profiles are in alphabetical order by state, then city, then hospital within the city; Rankings exclude hospitals with less than 25 cases except for patient surveys which excludes hospitals with less than 100 cases; (a) 100–299 cases; (1) The number of cases is too small to be sure how well a hospital is performing; (2) The hospital indicated that the data submitted for this measure were based on a sample of cases; (3) Data was collected during a shorter time period (fewer quarters) than the maximum possible time for this measure; (4) Suppressed for one or more quarters by CMS; (5) No data is available from the hospital for this measure; (6) Fewer than 100 patients completed the HCAHPS survey. Use these rates with caution, as the number of surveys may be too low to reliably assess hospital performance; (7) Survey results are based on less than 12 months of data; (8) Survey results are not available for this reporting period; (9) No or very few patients were eligible for the HCAHPS survey. The scores shown, if any, reflect a very small number of surveys; (10) A state average was not calculated because too few hospitals in the state submitted data; (11) There were discrepancies in the data collection process; Please refer to the User's Guide for a full explanation of data.

Provident Hospital of Chicago

500 E 51st St
Chicago, IL 60615
Phone: 312-572-2000
Fax: 312-572-2796
URL: www.providentfoundation.org
Type: Acute Care Hospitals
Emergency Services: Yes
Ownership: Government - Local
Beds: 243
Key Personnel:
Chief of Medical Staff . . . . James Myles
Quality Assurance . . . . Joseph Coty

Measure	Cases	This Hosp.	State Avg.	U.S. Avg.
Heart Attack Care				
ACE Inhibitor or ARB for LVSD[1]	1	100%	96%	96%
Aspirin at Arrival[1]	11	100%	99%	99%
Aspirin at Discharge[1]	4	100%	99%	98%
Beta Blocker at Discharge[1]	4	100%	98%	98%
Fibrinolytic Medication Timing	0	-	50%	55%
PCI Within 90 Minutes of Arrival	0	-	90%	90%
Smoking Cessation Advice[1]	1	100%	100%	99%
Chest Pain/Possible Heart Attack Care				
Aspirin at Arrival	35	100%	95%	95%
Median Time to ECG (minutes)	37	103	8	8
Median Time to Transfer (minutes)[1,3]	3	771	57	61
Fibrinolytic Medication Timing[1]	1	0%	33%	54%
Heart Failure Care				
ACE Inhibitor or ARB for LVSD[2]	152	97%	94%	94%
Discharge Instructions[2]	266	96%	89%	88%
Evaluation of LVS Function[2]	276	100%	98%	98%
Smoking Cessation Advice[2]	122	99%	99%	98%
Pneumonia Care				
Appropriate Initial Antibiotic[2]	131	95%	90%	92%
Blood Culture Timing[2]	151	83%	97%	96%
Influenza Vaccine[2]	67	97%	91%	91%
Initial Antibiotic Timing[2]	156	79%	96%	95%
Pneumococcal Vaccine[2]	44	84%	92%	93%
Smoking Cessation Advice[2]	108	98%	98%	97%
Surgical Care Improvement Project				
Appropriate VTP Within 24 Hours[2]	39	100%	92%	92%
Appropriate Hair Removal[2]	85	100%	99%	99%
Appropriate Beta Blocker Usage[1,2]	6	100%	92%	93%
Controlled Postoperative Blood Glucose[1,2]	1	100%	92%	93%
Prophylactic Antibiotic Timing[2]	67	93%	97%	97%
Prophylactic Antibiotic Timing (Outpatient)	72	93%	93%	92%
Prophylactic Antibiotic Selection[2]	66	95%	97%	97%
Prophylactic Antibiotic Select. (Outpatient)	77	87%	94%	94%
Prophylactic Antibiotic Stopped[2]	64	98%	94%	94%
Recommended VTP Ordered[2]	39	100%	94%	94%
Urinary Catheter Removal[1,2]	2	100%	89%	90%
Children's Asthma Care				
Received Systemic Corticosteroids	-	-	-	100%
Received Home Management Plan	-	-	-	71%
Received Reliever Medication	-	-	-	100%
Use of Medical Imaging				
Combination Abdominal CT Scan	70	0.000	0.246	0.191
Combination Chest CT Scan[1]	42	0.000	0.098	0.054
Follow-up Mammogram/Ultrasound[1]	4	0.0%	8.4%	8.4%
MRI for Low Back Pain[5]	0	-	33.4%	32.7%
Survey of Patients' Hospital Experiences				
Area Around Room 'Always' Quiet at Night	300+	68%	-	58%
Doctors 'Always' Communicated Well	300+	80%	-	80%
Home Recovery Information Given	300+	76%	-	82%
Hospital Given 9 or 10 on 10 Point Scale	300+	51%	-	67%
Meds 'Always' Explained Before Given	300+	59%	-	60%
Nurses 'Always' Communicated Well	300+	69%	-	76%
Pain 'Always' Well Controlled	300+	66%	-	69%
Room and Bathroom 'Always' Clean	300+	64%	-	71%
Timely Help 'Always' Received	300+	53%	-	64%
Would Definitely Recommend Hospital	300+	53%	-	69%

Resurrection Medical Center

7435 W Talcott Avenue
Chicago, IL 60631
Phone: 773-774-8000
Fax: 773-792-9926
URL: www.reshealthcare.org
Type: Acute Care Hospitals
Emergency Services: Yes
Ownership: Voluntary Non-Profit - Church
Beds: 434
Key Personnel:
CEO/President. . . . . Sandra Brue
Chief of Medical Staff . . . . Rosa Cubria
Infection Control. . . . . Marcia Beckerdite
Operating Room. . . . . Debbie Serwa
Pediatric Ambulatory Care . . . . Kathy Nierzwicki, RN
Quality Assurance . . . . Vicky Malone
Radiology. . . . . John McGreevy

Measure	Cases	This Hosp.	State Avg.	U.S. Avg.
Heart Attack Care				
ACE Inhibitor or ARB for LVSD	41	100%	96%	96%
Aspirin at Arrival	342	99%	99%	99%
Aspirin at Discharge	314	99%	99%	98%
Beta Blocker at Discharge	293	98%	98%	98%
Fibrinolytic Medication Timing	0	-	50%	55%
PCI Within 90 Minutes of Arrival	63	84%	90%	90%
Smoking Cessation Advice	75	100%	100%	99%
Chest Pain/Possible Heart Attack Care				
Aspirin at Arrival[1]	16	94%	95%	95%
Median Time to ECG (minutes)[1]	17	9	8	8
Median Time to Transfer (minutes)[5]	0	-	57	61
Fibrinolytic Medication Timing[3]	0	-	33%	54%
Heart Failure Care				
ACE Inhibitor or ARB for LVSD	142	87%	94%	94%
Discharge Instructions	393	78%	89%	88%
Evaluation of LVS Function	609	100%	98%	98%
Smoking Cessation Advice	49	100%	99%	98%
Pneumonia Care				
Appropriate Initial Antibiotic	180	96%	90%	92%
Blood Culture Timing	452	100%	97%	96%
Influenza Vaccine	268	90%	91%	91%
Initial Antibiotic Timing	406	97%	96%	95%
Pneumococcal Vaccine	412	91%	92%	93%
Smoking Cessation Advice	73	99%	98%	97%
Surgical Care Improvement Project				
Appropriate VTP Within 24 Hours[2]	213	85%	92%	92%
Appropriate Hair Removal[2]	620	100%	99%	99%
Appropriate Beta Blocker Usage[2]	230	86%	92%	93%
Controlled Postoperative Blood Glucose[2]	127	96%	92%	93%
Prophylactic Antibiotic Timing[2]	434	99%	97%	97%
Prophylactic Antibiotic Timing (Outpatient)	199	95%	93%	92%
Prophylactic Antibiotic Selection[2]	445	98%	97%	97%
Prophylactic Antibiotic Select. (Outpatient)	196	89%	94%	94%
Prophylactic Antibiotic Stopped[2]	416	93%	94%	94%
Recommended VTP Ordered[2]	213	95%	94%	94%
Urinary Catheter Removal[2]	118	81%	89%	90%
Children's Asthma Care				
Received Systemic Corticosteroids	-	-	-	100%
Received Home Management Plan	-	-	-	71%
Received Reliever Medication	-	-	-	100%
Use of Medical Imaging				
Combination Abdominal CT Scan	1,585	0.144	0.246	0.191
Combination Chest CT Scan	1,079	0.093	0.098	0.054
Follow-up Mammogram/Ultrasound	2,446	15.1%	8.4%	8.4%
MRI for Low Back Pain	352	37.2%	33.4%	32.7%
Survey of Patients' Hospital Experiences				
Area Around Room 'Always' Quiet at Night	300+	40%	-	58%
Doctors 'Always' Communicated Well	300+	75%	-	80%
Home Recovery Information Given	300+	79%	-	82%
Hospital Given 9 or 10 on 10 Point Scale	300+	55%	-	67%
Meds 'Always' Explained Before Given	300+	54%	-	60%
Nurses 'Always' Communicated Well	300+	69%	-	76%
Pain 'Always' Well Controlled	300+	64%	-	69%
Room and Bathroom 'Always' Clean	300+	54%	-	71%
Timely Help 'Always' Received	300+	51%	-	64%
Would Definitely Recommend Hospital	300+	59%	-	69%

Roseland Community Hospital

45 W 111th Street
Chicago, IL 60628
Phone: 773-995-3000
Fax: 773-995-1052
URL: www.roselandhospital.org
Type: Acute Care Hospitals
Emergency Services: Yes
Ownership: Voluntary Non-Profit - Other
Beds: 162
Key Personnel:
CEO/President. . . . . Donald C Sibery
Operating Room. . . . . Gladys Williams
Quality Assurance . . . . Mary Walker

Measure	Cases	This Hosp.	State Avg.	U.S. Avg.
Heart Attack Care				
ACE Inhibitor or ARB for LVSD[1]	9	56%	96%	96%
Aspirin at Arrival[1]	23	87%	99%	99%
Aspirin at Discharge[1]	20	85%	99%	98%
Beta Blocker at Discharge[1]	20	80%	98%	98%
Fibrinolytic Medication Timing	0	-	50%	55%
PCI Within 90 Minutes of Arrival	0	-	90%	90%
Smoking Cessation Advice[1]	7	86%	100%	99%
Chest Pain/Possible Heart Attack Care				
Aspirin at Arrival[1]	24	88%	95%	95%
Median Time to ECG (minutes)[1]	24	36	8	8
Median Time to Transfer (minutes)[5]	0	-	57	61
Fibrinolytic Medication Timing[3]	0	-	33%	54%
Heart Failure Care				
ACE Inhibitor or ARB for LVSD[2]	101	70%	94%	94%
Discharge Instructions[2]	239	98%	89%	88%
Evaluation of LVS Function[2]	259	86%	98%	98%
Smoking Cessation Advice[2]	93	98%	99%	98%
Pneumonia Care				
Appropriate Initial Antibiotic[2]	118	66%	90%	92%
Blood Culture Timing[2]	77	75%	97%	96%
Influenza Vaccine	77	16%	91%	91%
Initial Antibiotic Timing[2]	143	76%	96%	95%
Pneumococcal Vaccine[2]	85	19%	92%	93%
Smoking Cessation Advice[2]	54	100%	98%	97%
Surgical Care Improvement Project				
Appropriate VTP Within 24 Hours	39	21%	92%	92%
Appropriate Hair Removal	96	69%	99%	99%
Appropriate Beta Blocker Usage[1]	10	80%	92%	93%
Controlled Postoperative Blood Glucose	0	-	92%	93%
Prophylactic Antibiotic Timing[1]	19	89%	97%	97%
Prophylactic Antibiotic Timing (Outpatient)[1,3]	2	0%	93%	92%
Prophylactic Antibiotic Selection[1]	18	83%	97%	97%
Prophylactic Antibiotic Select. (Outpatient)[3]	0	-	94%	94%
Prophylactic Antibiotic Stopped[1]	18	94%	94%	94%
Recommended VTP Ordered	55	15%	94%	94%
Urinary Catheter Removal[1]	20	45%	89%	90%
Children's Asthma Care				
Received Systemic Corticosteroids	-	-	-	100%
Received Home Management Plan	-	-	-	71%
Received Reliever Medication	-	-	-	100%
Use of Medical Imaging				
Combination Abdominal CT Scan	60	0.350	0.246	0.191
Combination Chest CT Scan[1]	38	0.211	0.098	0.054
Follow-up Mammogram/Ultrasound	68	2.9%	8.4%	8.4%
MRI for Low Back Pain[5]	0	-	33.4%	32.7%
Survey of Patients' Hospital Experiences				
Area Around Room 'Always' Quiet at Night	300+	57%	-	58%
Doctors 'Always' Communicated Well	300+	75%	-	80%
Home Recovery Information Given	300+	66%	-	82%
Hospital Given 9 or 10 on 10 Point Scale	300+	43%	-	67%
Meds 'Always' Explained Before Given	300+	47%	-	60%
Nurses 'Always' Communicated Well	300+	60%	-	76%
Pain 'Always' Well Controlled	300+	57%	-	69%
Room and Bathroom 'Always' Clean	300+	61%	-	71%
Timely Help 'Always' Received	300+	38%	-	64%
Would Definitely Recommend Hospital	300+	40%	-	69%

NOTE: Hospital profiles are in alphabetical order by state, then city, then hospital within the city; Rankings exclude hospitals with less than 25 cases except for patient surveys which excludes hospitals with less than 100 cases; (a) 100–299 cases; (1) The number of cases is too small to be sure how well a hospital is performing; (2) The hospital indicated that the data submitted for this measure were based on a sample of cases; (3) Data was collected during a shorter time period (fewer quarters) than the maximum possible time for this measure; (4) Suppressed for one or more quarters by CMS; (5) No data is available from the hospital for this measure; (6) Fewer than 100 patients completed the HCAHPS survey. Use these rates with caution, as the number of surveys may be too low to reliably assess hospital performance; (7) Survey results are based on less than 12 months of data; (8) Survey results are not available for this reporting period; (9) No or very few patients were eligible for the HCAHPS survey. The scores shown, if any, reflect a very small number of surveys; (10) A state average was not calculated because too few hospitals in the state submitted data; (11) There were discrepancies in the data collection process; Please refer to the User's Guide for a full explanation of data.

Rush University Medical Center

1653 West Congress Parkway
Chicago, IL 60612
URL: www.ruch.edu
Type: Acute Care Hospitals
Ownership: Voluntary Non-Profit - Private

Phone: 312-942-5000
Fax: 312-942-8021
Emergency Services: Yes
Beds: 618

Key Personnel:

CEO/President. . . . . Larry M Goodman, MD
Chief of Medical Staff. . . . . David A Ansell, MD
Infection Control. . . . . Gorden Trenholme, MD
Pediatric In-Patient Care . . . . . . Samuel P Gotoff, MD
Quality Assurance . . . . Susan O'Leary
Radiology. . . . . Jerry Petasnick, MD
Emergency Room . . . . Paul K Hanashiro, MD
Intensive Care Unit. . . . . Joan Mathien, RN

Measure	Cases	This Hosp.	State Avg.	U.S. Avg.
Heart Attack Care				
ACE Inhibitor or ARB for LVSD	35	94%	96%	96%
Aspirin at Arrival	90	100%	99%	99%
Aspirin at Discharge	128	99%	99%	98%
Beta Blocker at Discharge	122	98%	98%	98%
Fibrinolytic Medication Timing	0	-	50%	55%
PCI Within 90 Minutes of Arrival[1]	13	100%	90%	90%
Smoking Cessation Advice	40	98%	100%	99%
Chest Pain/Possible Heart Attack Care				
Aspirin at Arrival[5]	0	-	95%	95%
Median Time to ECG (minutes)[5]	0	-	8	8
Median Time to Transfer (minutes)[5]	0	-	57	61
Fibrinolytic Medication Timing[5]	0	-	33%	54%
Heart Failure Care				
ACE Inhibitor or ARB for LVSD[2]	155	99%	94%	94%
Discharge Instructions[2]	283	81%	89%	88%
Evaluation of LVS Function[2]	298	100%	98%	98%
Smoking Cessation Advice[2]	53	94%	99%	98%
Pneumonia Care				
Appropriate Initial Antibiotic[2]	40	82%	90%	92%
Blood Culture Timing[2]	109	94%	97%	96%
Influenza Vaccine[2]	50	78%	91%	91%
Initial Antibiotic Timing[2]	96	94%	96%	95%
Pneumococcal Vaccine[2]	74	80%	92%	93%
Smoking Cessation Advice[2]	38	95%	98%	97%
Surgical Care Improvement Project				
Appropriate VTP Within 24 Hours[2]	193	97%	92%	92%
Appropriate Hair Removal[2]	624	100%	99%	99%
Appropriate Beta Blocker Usage[2]	175	83%	92%	93%
Controlled Postoperative Blood Glucose[2]	90	89%	92%	93%
Prophylactic Antibiotic Timing[2]	397	96%	97%	97%
Prophylactic Antibiotic Timing (Outpatient)	414	93%	93%	92%
Prophylactic Antibiotic Selection[2]	398	96%	97%	97%
Prophylactic Antibiotic Select. (Outpatient)	406	88%	94%	94%
Prophylactic Antibiotic Stopped[2]	379	95%	94%	94%
Recommended VTP Ordered[2]	193	98%	94%	94%
Urinary Catheter Removal[2]	110	89%	89%	90%
Children's Asthma Care				
Received Systemic Corticosteroids	-	-	-	100%
Received Home Management Plan	-	-	-	71%
Received Reliever Medication	-	-	-	100%
Use of Medical Imaging				
Combination Abdominal CT Scan	328	0.140	0.246	0.191
Combination Chest CT Scan	160	0.050	0.098	0.054
Follow-up Mammogram/Ultrasound	2,038	9.0%	8.4%	8.4%
MRI for Low Back Pain[1]	16	6.3%	33.4%	32.7%
Survey of Patients' Hospital Experiences				
Area Around Room 'Always' Quiet at Night	300+	53%	-	58%
Doctors 'Always' Communicated Well	300+	76%	-	80%
Home Recovery Information Given	300+	83%	-	82%
Hospital Given 9 or 10 on 10 Point Scale	300+	70%	-	67%
Meds 'Always' Explained Before Given	300+	60%	-	60%
Nurses 'Always' Communicated Well	300+	77%	-	76%
Pain 'Always' Well Controlled	300+	68%	-	69%
Room and Bathroom 'Always' Clean	300+	61%	-	71%
Timely Help 'Always' Received	300+	59%	-	64%
Would Definitely Recommend Hospital	300+	76%	-	69%

Sacred Heart Hospital

3240 W Franklin Blvd
Chicago, IL 60624
URL: www.sacredheartchicago.com
Type: Acute Care Hospitals
Ownership: Voluntary Non-Profit - Private

Phone: 773-722-3020
Fax: 773-722-5535
Emergency Services: No
Beds: 119

Key Personnel:

CEO/President. . . . . Edward J Novak
Cardiac Laboratory. . . . . Mike Napper
Infection Control. . . . . Helen Sethurama
Quality Assurance . . . . Holly Gaunt
Patient Relations . . . . Madonna Mikaitis, R

Measure	Cases	This Hosp.	State Avg.	U.S. Avg.
Heart Attack Care				
ACE Inhibitor or ARB for LVSD[3]	0	-	96%	96%
Aspirin at Arrival[1,3]	2	50%	99%	99%
Aspirin at Discharge[1,3]	1	0%	99%	98%
Beta Blocker at Discharge[1,3]	2	50%	98%	98%
Fibrinolytic Medication Timing[3]	0	-	50%	55%
PCI Within 90 Minutes of Arrival[3]	0	-	90%	90%
Smoking Cessation Advice[3]	0	-	100%	99%
Chest Pain/Possible Heart Attack Care				
Aspirin at Arrival[5]	0	-	95%	95%
Median Time to ECG (minutes)[5]	0	-	8	8
Median Time to Transfer (minutes)[5]	0	-	57	61
Fibrinolytic Medication Timing[5]	0	-	33%	54%
Heart Failure Care				
ACE Inhibitor or ARB for LVSD	34	68%	94%	94%
Discharge Instructions	132	34%	89%	88%
Evaluation of LVS Function	144	89%	98%	98%
Smoking Cessation Advice[1]	23	87%	99%	98%
Pneumonia Care				
Appropriate Initial Antibiotic[1]	6	83%	90%	92%
Blood Culture Timing[1]	5	100%	97%	96%
Influenza Vaccine[1]	5	80%	91%	91%
Initial Antibiotic Timing[1]	11	55%	96%	95%
Pneumococcal Vaccine[1]	9	89%	92%	93%
Smoking Cessation Advice[1]	2	100%	98%	97%
Surgical Care Improvement Project				
Appropriate VTP Within 24 Hours	37	68%	92%	92%
Appropriate Hair Removal	89	100%	99%	99%
Appropriate Beta Blocker Usage[1]	16	88%	92%	93%
Controlled Postoperative Blood Glucose	0	-	92%	93%
Prophylactic Antibiotic Timing	43	56%	97%	97%
Prophylactic Antibiotic Timing (Outpatient)	44	73%	93%	92%
Prophylactic Antibiotic Selection	42	90%	97%	97%
Prophylactic Antibiotic Select. (Outpatient)	42	88%	94%	94%
Prophylactic Antibiotic Stopped	42	57%	94%	94%
Recommended VTP Ordered	40	78%	94%	94%
Urinary Catheter Removal[1]	10	50%	89%	90%
Children's Asthma Care				
Received Systemic Corticosteroids	-	-	-	100%
Received Home Management Plan	-	-	-	71%
Received Reliever Medication	-	-	-	100%
Use of Medical Imaging				
Combination Abdominal CT Scan	57	0.632	0.246	0.191
Combination Chest CT Scan	34	0.529	0.098	0.054
Follow-up Mammogram/Ultrasound	195	7.7%	8.4%	8.4%
MRI for Low Back Pain[1]	60	15.0%	33.4%	32.7%
Survey of Patients' Hospital Experiences				
Area Around Room 'Always' Quiet at Night	300+	57%	-	58%
Doctors 'Always' Communicated Well	300+	76%	-	80%
Home Recovery Information Given	300+	70%	-	82%
Hospital Given 9 or 10 on 10 Point Scale	300+	47%	-	67%
Meds 'Always' Explained Before Given	300+	51%	-	60%
Nurses 'Always' Communicated Well	300+	62%	-	76%
Pain 'Always' Well Controlled	300+	64%	-	69%
Room and Bathroom 'Always' Clean	300+	62%	-	71%
Timely Help 'Always' Received	300+	47%	-	64%
Would Definitely Recommend Hospital	300+	55%	-	69%

Saint Anthony Hospital

2875 West 19th Street
Chicago, IL 60623
URL: www.cath-health.org
Type: Acute Care Hospitals
Ownership: Voluntary Non-Profit - Church

Phone: 773-521-1710
Fax: 773-521-7902
Emergency Services: Yes
Beds: 183

Key Personnel:

CEO/President. . . . . Kathleen K DeVine
Cardiac Laboratory. . . . . Fran Washington
Chief of Medical Staff. . . . . Rolando Lara, MD
Infection Control. . . . . Julie Sammarco
Operating Room. . . . . Oscar Herbas
Pediatric In-Patient Care . . . . . . Denisse Roque-Leon
Quality Assurance . . . . Tom Forbes

Measure	Cases	This Hosp.	State Avg.	U.S. Avg.
Heart Attack Care				
ACE Inhibitor or ARB for LVSD[1]	2	100%	96%	96%
Aspirin at Arrival[1]	19	95%	99%	99%
Aspirin at Discharge[1]	8	100%	99%	98%
Beta Blocker at Discharge[1]	7	100%	98%	98%
Fibrinolytic Medication Timing	0	-	50%	55%
PCI Within 90 Minutes of Arrival	0	-	90%	90%
Smoking Cessation Advice[1]	1	100%	100%	99%
Chest Pain/Possible Heart Attack Care				
Aspirin at Arrival[1]	23	100%	95%	95%
Median Time to ECG (minutes)[1]	23	13	8	8
Median Time to Transfer (minutes)[1,3]	1	49	57	61
Fibrinolytic Medication Timing[1]	2	50%	33%	54%
Heart Failure Care				
ACE Inhibitor or ARB for LVSD	69	87%	94%	94%
Discharge Instructions	123	79%	89%	88%
Evaluation of LVS Function	140	97%	98%	98%
Smoking Cessation Advice[1]	24	100%	99%	98%
Pneumonia Care				
Appropriate Initial Antibiotic	75	84%	90%	92%
Blood Culture Timing	128	99%	97%	96%
Influenza Vaccine	66	68%	91%	91%
Initial Antibiotic Timing	124	94%	96%	95%
Pneumococcal Vaccine	76	66%	92%	93%
Smoking Cessation Advice	40	100%	98%	97%
Surgical Care Improvement Project				
Appropriate VTP Within 24 Hours	53	74%	92%	92%
Appropriate Hair Removal	107	99%	99%	99%
Appropriate Beta Blocker Usage[1]	12	83%	92%	93%
Controlled Postoperative Blood Glucose	0	-	92%	93%
Prophylactic Antibiotic Timing	46	85%	97%	97%
Prophylactic Antibiotic Timing (Outpatient)	120	88%	93%	92%
Prophylactic Antibiotic Selection	46	85%	97%	97%
Prophylactic Antibiotic Select. (Outpatient)	106	91%	94%	94%
Prophylactic Antibiotic Stopped	44	66%	94%	94%
Recommended VTP Ordered	54	72%	94%	94%
Urinary Catheter Removal[1]	5	80%	89%	90%
Children's Asthma Care				
Received Systemic Corticosteroids	-	-	-	100%
Received Home Management Plan	-	-	-	71%
Received Reliever Medication	-	-	-	100%
Use of Medical Imaging				
Combination Abdominal CT Scan	106	0.028	0.246	0.191
Combination Chest CT Scan	60	0.017	0.098	0.054
Follow-up Mammogram/Ultrasound	209	4.3%	8.4%	8.4%
MRI for Low Back Pain[1]	29	24.1%	33.4%	32.7%
Survey of Patients' Hospital Experiences				
Area Around Room 'Always' Quiet at Night	300+	44%	-	58%
Doctors 'Always' Communicated Well	300+	77%	-	80%
Home Recovery Information Given	300+	73%	-	82%
Hospital Given 9 or 10 on 10 Point Scale	300+	67%	-	67%
Meds 'Always' Explained Before Given	300+	52%	-	60%
Nurses 'Always' Communicated Well	300+	65%	-	76%
Pain 'Always' Well Controlled	300+	60%	-	69%
Room and Bathroom 'Always' Clean	300+	58%	-	71%
Timely Help 'Always' Received	300+	52%	-	64%
Would Definitely Recommend Hospital	300+	65%	-	69%

NOTE: Hospital profiles are in alphabetical order by state, then city, then hospital within the city; Rankings exclude hospitals with less than 25 cases except for patient surveys which excludes hospitals with less than 100 cases; (a) 100–299 cases; (1) The number of cases is too small to be sure how well a hospital is performing; (2) The hospital indicated that the data submitted for this measure were based on a sample of cases; (3) Data was collected during a shorter time period (fewer quarters) than the maximum possible time for this measure; (4) Suppressed for one or more quarters by CMS; (5) No data is available from the hospital for this measure; (6) Fewer than 100 patients completed the HCAHPS survey. Use these rates with caution, as the number of surveys may be too low to reliably assess hospital performance; (7) Survey results are based on less than 12 months of data; (8) Survey results are not available for this reporting period; (9) No or very few patients were eligible for the HCAHPS survey. The scores shown, if any, reflect a very small number of surveys; (10) A state average was not calculated because too few hospitals in the state submitted data; (11) There were discrepancies in the data collection process; Please refer to the User's Guide for a full explanation of data.

Saint Bernard Hospital

326 W 64th St
Chicago, IL 60621
E-mail: info@stbh.org
URL: www.stbernardhospital.com
Type: Acute Care Hospitals
Ownership: Voluntary Non-Profit - Church

Phone: 773-962-3900
Fax: 773-962-0034
Emergency Services: No
Beds: 183

Key Personnel:
CEO/President. . . . . Guy Alton
Chief of Medical Staff . . . . Rogelio Cave
Quality Assurance . . . . Roland Abellera
Radiology. . . . . James Beckett
Patient Relations . . . . Roland Campbell

Measure	Cases	This Hosp.	State Avg.	U.S. Avg.
Heart Attack Care				
ACE Inhibitor or ARB for LVSD[1]	3	100%	96%	96%
Aspirin at Arrival[1]	23	96%	99%	99%
Aspirin at Discharge[1]	12	75%	99%	98%
Beta Blocker at Discharge[1]	12	75%	98%	98%
Fibrinolytic Medication Timing	0	-	50%	55%
PCI Within 90 Minutes of Arrival	0	-	90%	90%
Smoking Cessation Advice[1]	4	100%	100%	99%
Chest Pain/Possible Heart Attack Care				
Aspirin at Arrival	100	95%	95%	95%
Median Time to ECG (minutes)	104	0	8	8
Median Time to Transfer (minutes)[1]	22	104	57	61
Fibrinolytic Medication Timing	0	-	33%	54%
Heart Failure Care				
ACE Inhibitor or ARB for LVSD	122	80%	94%	94%
Discharge Instructions	314	98%	89%	88%
Evaluation of LVS Function	345	97%	98%	98%
Smoking Cessation Advice	162	100%	99%	98%
Pneumonia Care				
Appropriate Initial Antibiotic	120	88%	90%	92%
Blood Culture Timing	245	97%	97%	96%
Influenza Vaccine	86	97%	91%	91%
Initial Antibiotic Timing	298	92%	96%	95%
Pneumococcal Vaccine	126	90%	92%	93%
Smoking Cessation Advice	102	97%	98%	97%
Surgical Care Improvement Project				
Appropriate VTP Within 24 Hours	65	89%	92%	92%
Appropriate Hair Removal	115	100%	99%	99%
Appropriate Beta Blocker Usage[1]	10	100%	92%	93%
Controlled Postoperative Blood Glucose	0	-	92%	93%
Prophylactic Antibiotic Timing	38	89%	97%	97%
Prophylactic Antibiotic Timing (Outpatient)[1]	10	10%	93%	92%
Prophylactic Antibiotic Selection	38	82%	97%	97%
Prophylactic Antibiotic Select. (Outpatient)[1]	1	100%	94%	94%
Prophylactic Antibiotic Stopped	36	78%	94%	94%
Recommended VTP Ordered	70	83%	94%	94%
Urinary Catheter Removal[1]	5	60%	89%	90%
Children's Asthma Care				
Received Systemic Corticosteroids	-	-	-	100%
Received Home Management Plan	-	-	-	71%
Received Reliever Medication	-	-	-	100%
Use of Medical Imaging				
Combination Abdominal CT Scan	112	0.607	0.246	0.191
Combination Chest CT Scan	79	0.000	0.098	0.054
Follow-up Mammogram/Ultrasound	112	3.6%	8.4%	8.4%
MRI for Low Back Pain[5]	0	-	33.4%	32.7%
Survey of Patients' Hospital Experiences				
Area Around Room 'Always' Quiet at Night	300+	58%	-	58%
Doctors 'Always' Communicated Well	300+	70%	-	80%
Home Recovery Information Given	300+	72%	-	82%
Hospital Given 9 or 10 on 10 Point Scale	300+	43%	-	67%
Meds 'Always' Explained Before Given	300+	51%	-	60%
Nurses 'Always' Communicated Well	300+	64%	-	76%
Pain 'Always' Well Controlled	300+	59%	-	69%
Room and Bathroom 'Always' Clean	300+	65%	-	71%
Timely Help 'Always' Received	300+	51%	-	64%
Would Definitely Recommend Hospital	300+	39%	-	69%

Saint Joseph Hospital

2900 North Lake Shore Drive
Chicago, IL 60657
URL: www.res-health.org
Type: Acute Care Hospitals
Ownership: Voluntary Non-Profit - Church

Phone: 773-665-3000
Fax: 773-665-6502
Emergency Services: Yes
Beds: 492

Key Personnel:
CEO/President. . . . . Ronald Struxness
Cardiac Laboratory. . . . . Kathy Pyme
Chief of Medical Staff . . . . Andrew Gorchynky
Quality Assurance . . . . Margaret Heinrich
Radiology. . . . . Howard Gerard, MD
Anesthesiology. . . . . Cathy Watt, MD
Emergency Room . . . . Geoffery Grassle
Hemotology Center . . . . Leon Dragon

Measure	Cases	This Hosp.	State Avg.	U.S. Avg.
Heart Attack Care				
ACE Inhibitor or ARB for LVSD[1]	9	100%	96%	96%
Aspirin at Arrival	68	99%	99%	99%
Aspirin at Discharge	74	100%	99%	98%
Beta Blocker at Discharge	64	100%	98%	98%
Fibrinolytic Medication Timing	0	-	50%	55%
PCI Within 90 Minutes of Arrival[1]	13	69%	90%	90%
Smoking Cessation Advice[1]	14	100%	100%	99%
Chest Pain/Possible Heart Attack Care				
Aspirin at Arrival[5]	0	-	95%	95%
Median Time to ECG (minutes)[5]	0	-	8	8
Median Time to Transfer (minutes)[5]	0	-	57	61
Fibrinolytic Medication Timing[5]	0	-	33%	54%
Heart Failure Care				
ACE Inhibitor or ARB for LVSD	63	94%	94%	94%
Discharge Instructions	195	99%	89%	88%
Evaluation of LVS Function	280	100%	98%	98%
Smoking Cessation Advice	26	100%	99%	98%
Pneumonia Care				
Appropriate Initial Antibiotic	75	89%	90%	92%
Blood Culture Timing	149	98%	97%	96%
Influenza Vaccine	111	99%	91%	91%
Initial Antibiotic Timing	146	97%	96%	95%
Pneumococcal Vaccine	145	98%	92%	93%
Smoking Cessation Advice	34	100%	98%	97%
Surgical Care Improvement Project				
Appropriate VTP Within 24 Hours[2]	152	89%	92%	92%
Appropriate Hair Removal[2]	515	100%	99%	99%
Appropriate Beta Blocker Usage[2]	143	84%	92%	93%
Controlled Postoperative Blood Glucose[2]	58	93%	92%	93%
Prophylactic Antibiotic Timing[2]	389	97%	97%	97%
Prophylactic Antibiotic Timing (Outpatient)	161	93%	93%	92%
Prophylactic Antibiotic Selection[2]	392	94%	97%	97%
Prophylactic Antibiotic Select. (Outpatient)	154	95%	94%	94%
Prophylactic Antibiotic Stopped[2]	381	89%	94%	94%
Recommended VTP Ordered[2]	152	92%	94%	94%
Urinary Catheter Removal[2]	38	92%	89%	90%
Children's Asthma Care				
Received Systemic Corticosteroids	-	-	-	100%
Received Home Management Plan	-	-	-	71%
Received Reliever Medication	-	-	-	100%
Use of Medical Imaging				
Combination Abdominal CT Scan	458	0.129	0.246	0.191
Combination Chest CT Scan	316	0.006	0.098	0.054
Follow-up Mammogram/Ultrasound	1,035	7.4%	8.4%	8.4%
MRI for Low Back Pain	83	34.9%	33.4%	32.7%
Survey of Patients' Hospital Experiences				
Area Around Room 'Always' Quiet at Night	300+	52%	-	58%
Doctors 'Always' Communicated Well	300+	78%	-	80%
Home Recovery Information Given	300+	81%	-	82%
Hospital Given 9 or 10 on 10 Point Scale	300+	64%	-	67%
Meds 'Always' Explained Before Given	300+	59%	-	60%
Nurses 'Always' Communicated Well	300+	70%	-	76%
Pain 'Always' Well Controlled	300+	63%	-	69%
Room and Bathroom 'Always' Clean	300+	65%	-	71%
Timely Help 'Always' Received	300+	55%	-	64%
Would Definitely Recommend Hospital	300+	67%	-	69%

Saint Mary & Elizabeth Medical Center-Division Campus

2233 W Division St
Chicago, IL 60622
URL: www.reshealth.org
Type: Acute Care Hospitals
Ownership: Voluntary Non-Profit - Church

Phone: 312-633-5896
Fax: 312-770-2392
Emergency Services: Yes
Beds: 387

Key Personnel:
CEO/President. . . . . Margaret McDermott
Cardiac Laboratory. . . . . John Sedivy
Chief of Medical Staff . . . . Hugo Velrade, MD
Infection Control . . . . Pat Alexander, RN
Operating Room. . . . . Gail Alkovich
Quality Assurance . . . . Patti Graham, RN
Radiology. . . . . William Plos

Measure	Cases	This Hosp.	State Avg.	U.S. Avg.
Heart Attack Care				
ACE Inhibitor or ARB for LVSD	25	100%	96%	96%
Aspirin at Arrival	159	100%	99%	99%
Aspirin at Discharge	157	100%	99%	98%
Beta Blocker at Discharge	160	100%	98%	98%
Fibrinolytic Medication Timing	0	-	50%	55%
PCI Within 90 Minutes of Arrival	27	96%	90%	90%
Smoking Cessation Advice	54	98%	100%	99%
Chest Pain/Possible Heart Attack Care				
Aspirin at Arrival	78	100%	95%	95%
Median Time to ECG (minutes)	81	6	8	8
Median Time to Transfer (minutes)[1,3]	1	27	57	61
Fibrinolytic Medication Timing[3]	0	-	33%	54%
Heart Failure Care				
ACE Inhibitor or ARB for LVSD	134	100%	94%	94%
Discharge Instructions	330	100%	89%	88%
Evaluation of LVS Function	391	100%	98%	98%
Smoking Cessation Advice	85	100%	99%	98%
Pneumonia Care				
Appropriate Initial Antibiotic	208	95%	90%	92%
Blood Culture Timing	352	100%	97%	96%
Influenza Vaccine	149	95%	91%	91%
Initial Antibiotic Timing	329	98%	96%	95%
Pneumococcal Vaccine	181	96%	92%	93%
Smoking Cessation Advice	138	100%	98%	97%
Surgical Care Improvement Project				
Appropriate VTP Within 24 Hours[2]	202	93%	92%	92%
Appropriate Hair Removal[2]	458	100%	99%	99%
Appropriate Beta Blocker Usage[2]	133	95%	92%	93%
Controlled Postoperative Blood Glucose[2]	54	91%	92%	93%
Prophylactic Antibiotic Timing[2]	297	99%	97%	97%
Prophylactic Antibiotic Timing (Outpatient)	198	91%	93%	92%
Prophylactic Antibiotic Selection[2]	297	96%	97%	97%
Prophylactic Antibiotic Select. (Outpatient)	184	96%	94%	94%
Prophylactic Antibiotic Stopped[2]	287	94%	94%	94%
Recommended VTP Ordered[2]	202	95%	94%	94%
Urinary Catheter Removal[2]	54	89%	89%	90%
Children's Asthma Care				
Received Systemic Corticosteroids	-	-	-	100%
Received Home Management Plan	-	-	-	71%
Received Reliever Medication	-	-	-	100%
Use of Medical Imaging				
Combination Abdominal CT Scan	671	0.201	0.246	0.191
Combination Chest CT Scan	151	0.007	0.098	0.054
Follow-up Mammogram/Ultrasound	481	5.6%	8.4%	8.4%
MRI for Low Back Pain	109	36.7%	33.4%	32.7%
Survey of Patients' Hospital Experiences				
Area Around Room 'Always' Quiet at Night	300+	58%	-	58%
Doctors 'Always' Communicated Well	300+	77%	-	80%
Home Recovery Information Given	300+	78%	-	82%
Hospital Given 9 or 10 on 10 Point Scale	300+	67%	-	67%
Meds 'Always' Explained Before Given	300+	52%	-	60%
Nurses 'Always' Communicated Well	300+	67%	-	76%
Pain 'Always' Well Controlled	300+	64%	-	69%
Room and Bathroom 'Always' Clean	300+	63%	-	71%
Timely Help 'Always' Received	300+	55%	-	64%
Would Definitely Recommend Hospital	300+	66%	-	69%

NOTE: Hospital profiles are in alphabetical order by state, then city, then hospital within the city; Rankings exclude hospitals with less than 25 cases except for patient surveys which excludes hospitals with less than 100 cases; (a) 100–299 cases; (1) The number of cases is too small to be sure how well a hospital is performing; (2) The hospital indicated that the data submitted for this measure were based on a sample of cases; (3) Data was collected during a shorter time period (fewer quarters) than the maximum possible time for this measure; (4) Suppressed for one or more quarters by CMS; (5) No data is available from the hospital for this measure; (6) Fewer than 100 patients completed the HCAHPS survey. Use these rates with caution, as the number of surveys may be too low to reliably assess hospital performance; (7) Survey results are based on less than 12 months of data; (8) Survey results are not available for this reporting period; (9) No or very few patients were eligible for the HCAHPS survey. The scores shown, if any, reflect a very small number of surveys; (10) A state average was not calculated because too few hospitals in the state submitted data; (11) There were discrepancies in the data collection process; Please refer to the User's Guide for a full explanation of data.

South Shore Hospital

8012 South Crandon Avenue
Chicago, IL 60617
URL: www.southshorehospital.com
Type: Acute Care Hospitals
Ownership: Voluntary Non-Profit - Private
Phone: 773-768-0810
Fax: 773-768-8154
Emergency Services: Yes
Beds: 170

Key Personnel:
CEO/President. . . . . Jesus M Ong
Operating Room. . . . . Flortina McCoo, RN
Quality Assurance . . . . Marisel Pineda
Radiology. . . . . Tim Williams
Emergency Room . . . . Jackie Levandowski, RN
Patient Relations . . . . Leslie M. Rogers

Measure	Cases	This Hosp.	State Avg.	U.S. Avg.
Heart Attack Care				
ACE Inhibitor or ARB for LVSD[1]	2	100%	96%	96%
Aspirin at Arrival	38	84%	99%	99%
Aspirin at Discharge[1]	16	94%	99%	98%
Beta Blocker at Discharge[1]	19	89%	98%	98%
Fibrinolytic Medication Timing	0	-	50%	55%
PCI Within 90 Minutes of Arrival	0	-	90%	90%
Smoking Cessation Advice[1]	8	88%	100%	99%
Chest Pain/Possible Heart Attack Care				
Aspirin at Arrival[1,3]	5	100%	95%	95%
Median Time to ECG (minutes)[1,3]	5	13	8	8
Median Time to Transfer (minutes)[5]	0	-	57	61
Fibrinolytic Medication Timing[3]	0	-	33%	54%
Heart Failure Care				
ACE Inhibitor or ARB for LVSD	64	92%	94%	94%
Discharge Instructions	183	66%	89%	88%
Evaluation of LVS Function	235	89%	98%	98%
Smoking Cessation Advice	44	98%	99%	98%
Pneumonia Care				
Appropriate Initial Antibiotic	45	67%	90%	92%
Blood Culture Timing	100	85%	97%	96%
Influenza Vaccine	62	23%	91%	91%
Initial Antibiotic Timing	109	83%	96%	95%
Pneumococcal Vaccine	84	19%	92%	93%
Smoking Cessation Advice[1]	19	100%	98%	97%
Surgical Care Improvement Project				
Appropriate VTP Within 24 Hours	34	59%	92%	92%
Appropriate Hair Removal	78	97%	99%	99%
Appropriate Beta Blocker Usage[1]	12	92%	92%	93%
Controlled Postoperative Blood Glucose	0	-	92%	93%
Prophylactic Antibiotic Timing	39	38%	97%	97%
Prophylactic Antibiotic Timing (Outpatient)[1,3]	13	85%	93%	92%
Prophylactic Antibiotic Selection	40	80%	97%	97%
Prophylactic Antibiotic Select. (Outpatient)[1,3]	14	100%	94%	94%
Prophylactic Antibiotic Stopped	39	87%	94%	94%
Recommended VTP Ordered	49	41%	94%	94%
Urinary Catheter Removal[1]	10	20%	89%	90%
Children's Asthma Care				
Received Systemic Corticosteroids	-	-	-	100%
Received Home Management Plan	-	-	-	71%
Received Reliever Medication	-	-	-	100%
Use of Medical Imaging				
Combination Abdominal CT Scan	78	0.013	0.246	0.191
Combination Chest CT Scan	49	0.041	0.098	0.054
Follow-up Mammogram/Ultrasound	179	2.2%	8.4%	8.4%
MRI for Low Back Pain[5]	0	-	33.4%	32.7%
Survey of Patients' Hospital Experiences				
Area Around Room 'Always' Quiet at Night	300+	56%	-	58%
Doctors 'Always' Communicated Well	300+	70%	-	80%
Home Recovery Information Given	300+	56%	-	82%
Hospital Given 9 or 10 on 10 Point Scale	300+	41%	-	67%
Meds 'Always' Explained Before Given	300+	48%	-	60%
Nurses 'Always' Communicated Well	300+	63%	-	76%
Pain 'Always' Well Controlled	300+	57%	-	69%
Room and Bathroom 'Always' Clean	300+	61%	-	71%
Timely Help 'Always' Received	300+	47%	-	64%
Would Definitely Recommend Hospital	300+	38%	-	69%

Swedish Covenant Hospital

5145 N California Ave
Chicago, IL 60625
Type: Acute Care Hospitals
Ownership: Voluntary Non-Profit - Church
Phone: 773-878-8200
Fax: 773-878-6152
Emergency Services: Yes
Beds: 330

Key Personnel:
CEO/President. . . . . Mark Newton
Cardiac Laboratory. . . . . Jerrad Shapiro
Chief of Medical Staff. . . . . Albert Saporta, MD
Operating Room. . . . . Mary Shehan
Pediatric Ambulatory Care . . . . . . Roberto Espinosa, MD
Pediatric In-Patient Care . . . . Roberto Espinosa, MD
Quality Assurance . . . . Janis Rueping
Radiology. . . . . Bruce Silver, MD

Measure	Cases	This Hosp.	State Avg.	U.S. Avg.
Heart Attack Care				
ACE Inhibitor or ARB for LVSD	61	98%	96%	96%
Aspirin at Arrival	275	96%	99%	99%
Aspirin at Discharge	248	98%	99%	98%
Beta Blocker at Discharge	249	94%	98%	98%
Fibrinolytic Medication Timing	0	-	50%	55%
PCI Within 90 Minutes of Arrival[1]	22	86%	90%	90%
Smoking Cessation Advice	49	100%	100%	99%
Chest Pain/Possible Heart Attack Care				
Aspirin at Arrival	49	82%	95%	95%
Median Time to ECG (minutes)	54	8	8	8
Median Time to Transfer (minutes)[1,3]	1	62	57	61
Fibrinolytic Medication Timing[3]	0	-	33%	54%
Heart Failure Care				
ACE Inhibitor or ARB for LVSD	171	92%	94%	94%
Discharge Instructions	341	87%	89%	88%
Evaluation of LVS Function	467	99%	98%	98%
Smoking Cessation Advice	56	98%	99%	98%
Pneumonia Care				
Appropriate Initial Antibiotic	189	89%	90%	92%
Blood Culture Timing	356	95%	97%	96%
Influenza Vaccine	267	78%	91%	91%
Initial Antibiotic Timing	296	95%	96%	95%
Pneumococcal Vaccine	369	89%	92%	93%
Smoking Cessation Advice	64	100%	98%	97%
Surgical Care Improvement Project				
Appropriate VTP Within 24 Hours[2]	160	81%	92%	92%
Appropriate Hair Removal[2]	421	98%	99%	99%
Appropriate Beta Blocker Usage[2]	127	96%	92%	93%
Controlled Postoperative Blood Glucose[2]	72	93%	92%	93%
Prophylactic Antibiotic Timing[2]	271	93%	97%	97%
Prophylactic Antibiotic Timing (Outpatient)	142	76%	93%	92%
Prophylactic Antibiotic Selection[2]	274	90%	97%	97%
Prophylactic Antibiotic Select. (Outpatient)	117	85%	94%	94%
Prophylactic Antibiotic Stopped[2]	259	89%	94%	94%
Recommended VTP Ordered[2]	160	84%	94%	94%
Urinary Catheter Removal[2]	82	66%	89%	90%
Children's Asthma Care				
Received Systemic Corticosteroids	-	-	-	100%
Received Home Management Plan	-	-	-	71%
Received Reliever Medication	-	-	-	100%
Use of Medical Imaging				
Combination Abdominal CT Scan	1,085	0.132	0.246	0.191
Combination Chest CT Scan	786	0.018	0.098	0.054
Follow-up Mammogram/Ultrasound	1,556	7.3%	8.4%	8.4%
MRI for Low Back Pain	281	35.9%	33.4%	32.7%
Survey of Patients' Hospital Experiences				
Area Around Room 'Always' Quiet at Night	300+	41%	-	58%
Doctors 'Always' Communicated Well	300+	74%	-	80%
Home Recovery Information Given	300+	80%	-	82%
Hospital Given 9 or 10 on 10 Point Scale	300+	56%	-	67%
Meds 'Always' Explained Before Given	300+	51%	-	60%
Nurses 'Always' Communicated Well	300+	65%	-	76%
Pain 'Always' Well Controlled	300+	60%	-	69%
Room and Bathroom 'Always' Clean	300+	57%	-	71%
Timely Help 'Always' Received	300+	50%	-	64%
Would Definitely Recommend Hospital	300+	61%	-	69%

Thorek Memorial Hospital

850 W Irving Park Rd
Chicago, IL 60613
URL: www.thorek.org
Type: Acute Care Hospitals
Ownership: Voluntary Non-Profit - Other
Phone: 312-525-6780
Fax: 773-975-6703
Emergency Services: Yes
Beds: 218

Key Personnel:
Chief of Medical Staff. . . . . Jagan Mohan, MD
Operating Room. . . . . Gregory Nacopoulos
Quality Assurance . . . . John Danielson
Radiology. . . . . Peter Berger, MD
Emergency Room . . . . Effie Heale

Measure	Cases	This Hosp.	State Avg.	U.S. Avg.
Heart Attack Care				
ACE Inhibitor or ARB for LVSD[1]	2	50%	96%	96%
Aspirin at Arrival[1]	21	95%	99%	99%
Aspirin at Discharge[1]	9	78%	99%	98%
Beta Blocker at Discharge[1]	9	67%	98%	98%
Fibrinolytic Medication Timing	0	-	50%	55%
PCI Within 90 Minutes of Arrival	0	-	90%	90%
Smoking Cessation Advice[1]	1	100%	100%	99%
Chest Pain/Possible Heart Attack Care				
Aspirin at Arrival[1,3]	1	100%	95%	95%
Median Time to ECG (minutes)[1,3]	1	12	8	8
Median Time to Transfer (minutes)[5]	0	-	57	61
Fibrinolytic Medication Timing[5]	0	-	33%	54%
Heart Failure Care				
ACE Inhibitor or ARB for LVSD	34	71%	94%	94%
Discharge Instructions	89	90%	89%	88%
Evaluation of LVS Function	129	100%	98%	98%
Smoking Cessation Advice[1]	23	91%	99%	98%
Pneumonia Care				
Appropriate Initial Antibiotic	36	97%	90%	92%
Blood Culture Timing	71	94%	97%	96%
Influenza Vaccine	74	99%	91%	91%
Initial Antibiotic Timing	69	93%	96%	95%
Pneumococcal Vaccine	81	98%	92%	93%
Smoking Cessation Advice	25	96%	98%	97%
Surgical Care Improvement Project				
Appropriate VTP Within 24 Hours	41	98%	92%	92%
Appropriate Hair Removal	79	100%	99%	99%
Appropriate Beta Blocker Usage[1]	14	86%	92%	93%
Controlled Postoperative Blood Glucose	0	-	92%	93%
Prophylactic Antibiotic Timing	43	100%	97%	97%
Prophylactic Antibiotic Timing (Outpatient)	27	93%	93%	92%
Prophylactic Antibiotic Selection	43	98%	97%	97%
Prophylactic Antibiotic Select. (Outpatient)	25	100%	94%	94%
Prophylactic Antibiotic Stopped	36	97%	94%	94%
Recommended VTP Ordered	41	98%	94%	94%
Urinary Catheter Removal[1]	4	100%	89%	90%
Children's Asthma Care				
Received Systemic Corticosteroids	-	-	-	100%
Received Home Management Plan	-	-	-	71%
Received Reliever Medication	-	-	-	100%
Use of Medical Imaging				
Combination Abdominal CT Scan	181	0.834	0.246	0.191
Combination Chest CT Scan	94	0.319	0.098	0.054
Follow-up Mammogram/Ultrasound	173	17.9%	8.4%	8.4%
MRI for Low Back Pain[1]	36	22.2%	33.4%	32.7%
Survey of Patients' Hospital Experiences				
Area Around Room 'Always' Quiet at Night	300+	52%	-	58%
Doctors 'Always' Communicated Well	300+	71%	-	80%
Home Recovery Information Given	300+	75%	-	82%
Hospital Given 9 or 10 on 10 Point Scale	300+	48%	-	67%
Meds 'Always' Explained Before Given	300+	46%	-	60%
Nurses 'Always' Communicated Well	300+	60%	-	76%
Pain 'Always' Well Controlled	300+	56%	-	69%
Room and Bathroom 'Always' Clean	300+	65%	-	71%
Timely Help 'Always' Received	300+	44%	-	64%
Would Definitely Recommend Hospital	300+	47%	-	69%

NOTE: Hospital profiles are in alphabetical order by state, then city, then hospital within the city; Rankings exclude hospitals with less than 25 cases except for patient surveys which excludes hospitals with less than 100 cases; (a) 100–299 cases; (1) The number of cases is too small to be sure how well a hospital is performing; (2) The hospital indicated that the data submitted for this measure were based on a sample of cases; (3) Data was collected during a shorter time period (fewer quarters) than the maximum possible time for this measure; (4) Suppressed for one or more quarters by CMS; (5) No data is available from the hospital for this measure; (6) Fewer than 100 patients completed the HCAHPS survey. Use these rates with caution, as the number of surveys may be too low to reliably assess hospital performance; (7) Survey results are based on less than 12 months of data; (8) Survey results are not available for this reporting period; (9) No or very few patients were eligible for the HCAHPS survey. The scores shown, if any, reflect a very small number of surveys; (10) A state average was not calculated because too few hospitals in the state submitted data; (11) There were discrepancies in the data collection process; Please refer to the User's Guide for a full explanation of data.

The University of Chicago Medical Center

5841 South Maryland
Chicago, IL 60637
URL: www.uchospitals.edu
Type: Acute Care Hospitals
Ownership: Voluntary Non-Profit - Private
Phone: 773-702-1000
Fax: 773-702-9005
Emergency Services: Yes
Beds: 662

Key Personnel:
Pediatric In-Patient Care .... Kim Taaca, MD
Quality Assurance .... Krista Curell
Radiology.................. Richard Baron, MD
Ambulatory Care .... Laurence Dry
Anesthesiology............... David Glick

Measure	Cases	This Hosp.	State Avg.	U.S. Avg.
Heart Attack Care				
ACE Inhibitor or ARB for LVSD	38	97%	96%	96%
Aspirin at Arrival	96	100%	99%	99%
Aspirin at Discharge	137	99%	99%	98%
Beta Blocker at Discharge	131	98%	98%	98%
Fibrinolytic Medication Timing	0	-	50%	55%
PCI Within 90 Minutes of Arrival[1]	18	94%	90%	90%
Smoking Cessation Advice	44	100%	100%	99%
Chest Pain/Possible Heart Attack Care				
Aspirin at Arrival	34	71%	95%	95%
Median Time to ECG (minutes)	35	15	8	8
Median Time to Transfer (minutes)[5]	0	-	57	61
Fibrinolytic Medication Timing[5]	0	-	33%	54%
Heart Failure Care				
ACE Inhibitor or ARB for LVSD[2]	123	100%	94%	94%
Discharge Instructions[2]	254	87%	89%	88%
Evaluation of LVS Function[2]	280	100%	98%	98%
Smoking Cessation Advice[2]	48	98%	99%	98%
Pneumonia Care				
Appropriate Initial Antibiotic[1,2]	18	94%	90%	92%
Blood Culture Timing[2]	53	98%	97%	96%
Influenza Vaccine[2]	55	100%	91%	91%
Initial Antibiotic Timing[2]	44	98%	96%	95%
Pneumococcal Vaccine[2]	58	97%	92%	93%
Smoking Cessation Advice[2]	35	100%	98%	97%
Surgical Care Improvement Project				
Appropriate VTP Within 24 Hours[2]	195	99%	92%	92%
Appropriate Hair Removal[2]	571	100%	99%	99%
Appropriate Beta Blocker Usage[2]	159	94%	92%	93%
Controlled Postoperative Blood Glucose[2]	121	94%	92%	93%
Prophylactic Antibiotic Timing[2]	377	99%	97%	97%
Prophylactic Antibiotic Timing (Outpatient)	286	88%	93%	92%
Prophylactic Antibiotic Selection[2]	386	99%	97%	97%
Prophylactic Antibiotic Select. (Outpatient)	486	94%	94%	94%
Prophylactic Antibiotic Stopped[2]	352	98%	94%	94%
Recommended VTP Ordered[2]	195	99%	94%	94%
Urinary Catheter Removal[2]	130	82%	89%	90%
Children's Asthma Care				
Received Systemic Corticosteroids[2]	239	100%	-	100%
Received Home Management Plan[2]	239	7%	-	71%
Received Reliever Medication[2]	239	100%	-	100%
Use of Medical Imaging				
Combination Abdominal CT Scan	3,622	0.076	0.246	0.191
Combination Chest CT Scan	4,244	0.001	0.098	0.054
Follow-up Mammogram/Ultrasound	2,377	6.0%	8.4%	8.4%
MRI for Low Back Pain	285	35.1%	33.4%	32.7%
Survey of Patients' Hospital Experiences				
Area Around Room 'Always' Quiet at Night	300+	48%	-	58%
Doctors 'Always' Communicated Well	300+	79%	-	80%
Home Recovery Information Given	300+	80%	-	82%
Hospital Given 9 or 10 on 10 Point Scale	300+	63%	-	67%
Meds 'Always' Explained Before Given	300+	56%	-	60%
Nurses 'Always' Communicated Well	300+	71%	-	76%
Pain 'Always' Well Controlled	300+	65%	-	69%
Room and Bathroom 'Always' Clean	300+	60%	-	71%
Timely Help 'Always' Received	300+	55%	-	64%
Would Definitely Recommend Hospital	300+	70%	-	69%

University of Illinois Hospital

1740 West Taylor St Suite 1400
Chicago, IL 60612
URL: www.uic.edu
Type: Acute Care Hospitals
Ownership: Government - State
Phone: 312-996-3900
Fax: 312-996-7049
Emergency Services: No
Beds: 570

Key Personnel:
CEO/President.............. John DeNardo
Chief of Medical Staff.......... Lawrence Frohman, MD
Infection Control.............. James L Cook, MD
Operating Room............. Barbara Vela
Pediatric Ambulatory Care ...... George R Honig, MD
Pediatric In-Patient Care ...... George R Honig, MD
Quality Assurance .... Debra Krause
Radiology.................. Mahmood Mafee, MD

Measure	Cases	This Hosp.	State Avg.	U.S. Avg.
Heart Attack Care				
ACE Inhibitor or ARB for LVSD[1]	18	94%	96%	96%
Aspirin at Arrival	59	98%	99%	99%
Aspirin at Discharge	80	98%	99%	98%
Beta Blocker at Discharge	79	96%	98%	98%
Fibrinolytic Medication Timing	0	-	50%	55%
PCI Within 90 Minutes of Arrival[1]	15	80%	90%	90%
Smoking Cessation Advice	33	100%	100%	99%
Chest Pain/Possible Heart Attack Care				
Aspirin at Arrival[1,3]	1	100%	95%	95%
Median Time to ECG (minutes)[1,3]	1	349	8	8
Median Time to Transfer (minutes)[5]	0	-	57	61
Fibrinolytic Medication Timing[5]	0	-	33%	54%
Heart Failure Care				
ACE Inhibitor or ARB for LVSD[2]	132	95%	94%	94%
Discharge Instructions[2]	252	55%	89%	88%
Evaluation of LVS Function[2]	271	100%	98%	98%
Smoking Cessation Advice[2]	72	100%	99%	98%
Pneumonia Care				
Appropriate Initial Antibiotic[2]	51	82%	90%	92%
Blood Culture Timing[2]	130	98%	97%	96%
Influenza Vaccine[2]	68	72%	91%	91%
Initial Antibiotic Timing[2]	139	91%	96%	95%
Pneumococcal Vaccine[2]	76	84%	92%	93%
Smoking Cessation Advice[2]	54	100%	98%	97%
Surgical Care Improvement Project				
Appropriate VTP Within 24 Hours[2]	222	97%	92%	92%
Appropriate Hair Removal[2]	420	100%	99%	99%
Appropriate Beta Blocker Usage[2]	135	93%	92%	93%
Controlled Postoperative Blood Glucose[2]	52	85%	92%	93%
Prophylactic Antibiotic Timing[2]	275	99%	97%	97%
Prophylactic Antibiotic Timing (Outpatient)	200	88%	93%	92%
Prophylactic Antibiotic Selection[2]	282	97%	97%	97%
Prophylactic Antibiotic Select. (Outpatient)	223	94%	94%	94%
Prophylactic Antibiotic Stopped[2]	259	97%	94%	94%
Recommended VTP Ordered[2]	222	99%	94%	94%
Urinary Catheter Removal[2]	85	91%	89%	90%
Children's Asthma Care				
Received Systemic Corticosteroids	-	-	-	100%
Received Home Management Plan	-	-	-	71%
Received Reliever Medication	-	-	-	100%
Use of Medical Imaging				
Combination Abdominal CT Scan	788	0.232	0.246	0.191
Combination Chest CT Scan	794	0.048	0.098	0.054
Follow-up Mammogram/Ultrasound	701	4.1%	8.4%	8.4%
MRI for Low Back Pain	154	32.5%	33.4%	32.7%
Survey of Patients' Hospital Experiences				
Area Around Room 'Always' Quiet at Night	300+	55%	-	58%
Doctors 'Always' Communicated Well	300+	81%	-	80%
Home Recovery Information Given	300+	81%	-	82%
Hospital Given 9 or 10 on 10 Point Scale	300+	59%	-	67%
Meds 'Always' Explained Before Given	300+	68%	-	60%
Nurses 'Always' Communicated Well	300+	69%	-	76%
Pain 'Always' Well Controlled	300+	71%	-	69%
Room and Bathroom 'Always' Clean	300+	64%	-	71%
Timely Help 'Always' Received	300+	61%	-	64%
Would Definitely Recommend Hospital	300+	63%	-	69%

Dr John Warner Hospital

422 W White St
Clinton, IL 61727
URL: www.djwhospital.org
Type: Critical Access Hospitals
Ownership: Voluntary Non-Profit - Other
Phone: 217-935-9571
Fax: 217-937-5244
Emergency Services: Yes
Beds: 25

Key Personnel:
CEO/President................ Earl N. Sheehy
Chief of Medical Staff.......... Dr Tricia Scerba
Infection Control.............. Heidi Coook
Operating Room.............. Brenda Saubert
Quality Assurance .... Kathy Isaac
Ambulatory Care .... Karen Welch
Emergency Room .... Heidi Cook
Intensive Care Unit............ Brenda Lehman

Measure	Cases	This Hosp.	State Avg.	U.S. Avg.
Heart Attack Care				
ACE Inhibitor or ARB for LVSD[5]	0	-	96%	96%
Aspirin at Arrival[5]	0	-	99%	99%
Aspirin at Discharge[5]	0	-	99%	98%
Beta Blocker at Discharge[5]	0	-	98%	98%
Fibrinolytic Medication Timing[5]	0	-	50%	55%
PCI Within 90 Minutes of Arrival[5]	0	-	90%	90%
Smoking Cessation Advice[5]	0	-	100%	99%
Chest Pain/Possible Heart Attack Care				
Aspirin at Arrival	-	-	95%	95%
Median Time to ECG (minutes)	-	-	8	8
Median Time to Transfer (minutes)	-	-	57	61
Fibrinolytic Medication Timing	-	-	33%	54%
Heart Failure Care				
ACE Inhibitor or ARB for LVSD[5]	0	-	94%	94%
Discharge Instructions[5]	0	-	89%	88%
Evaluation of LVS Function[5]	0	-	98%	98%
Smoking Cessation Advice[5]	0	-	99%	98%
Pneumonia Care				
Appropriate Initial Antibiotic[5]	0	-	90%	92%
Blood Culture Timing[5]	0	-	97%	96%
Influenza Vaccine[5]	0	-	91%	91%
Initial Antibiotic Timing[5]	0	-	96%	95%
Pneumococcal Vaccine[5]	0	-	92%	93%
Smoking Cessation Advice[5]	0	-	98%	97%
Surgical Care Improvement Project				
Appropriate VTP Within 24 Hours[5]	0	-	92%	92%
Appropriate Hair Removal[5]	0	-	99%	99%
Appropriate Beta Blocker Usage[5]	0	-	92%	93%
Controlled Postoperative Blood Glucose[5]	0	-	92%	93%
Prophylactic Antibiotic Timing[5]	0	-	97%	97%
Prophylactic Antibiotic Timing (Outpatient)	0	-	93%	92%
Prophylactic Antibiotic Selection[5]	0	-	97%	97%
Prophylactic Antibiotic Select. (Outpatient)	0	-	94%	94%
Prophylactic Antibiotic Stopped[5]	0	-	94%	94%
Recommended VTP Ordered[5]	0	-	94%	94%
Urinary Catheter Removal[5]	0	-	89%	90%
Children's Asthma Care				
Received Systemic Corticosteroids	-	-	-	100%
Received Home Management Plan	-	-	-	71%
Received Reliever Medication	-	-	-	100%
Use of Medical Imaging				
Combination Abdominal CT Scan	-	-	0.246	0.191
Combination Chest CT Scan	-	-	0.098	0.054
Follow-up Mammogram/Ultrasound	-	-	8.4%	8.4%
MRI for Low Back Pain	-	-	33.4%	32.7%
Survey of Patients' Hospital Experiences				
Area Around Room 'Always' Quiet at Night[8]	-	-	-	58%
Doctors 'Always' Communicated Well[8]	-	-	-	80%
Home Recovery Information Given[8]	-	-	-	82%
Hospital Given 9 or 10 on 10 Point Scale[8]	-	-	-	67%
Meds 'Always' Explained Before Given[8]	-	-	-	60%
Nurses 'Always' Communicated Well[8]	-	-	-	76%
Pain 'Always' Well Controlled[8]	-	-	-	69%
Room and Bathroom 'Always' Clean[8]	-	-	-	71%
Timely Help 'Always' Received[8]	-	-	-	64%
Would Definitely Recommend Hospital[8]	-	-	-	69%

NOTE: Hospital profiles are in alphabetical order by state, then city, then hospital within the city; Rankings exclude hospitals with less than 25 cases except for patient surveys which excludes hospitals with less than 100 cases; (a) 100–299 cases; (1) The number of cases is too small to be sure how well a hospital is performing; (2) The hospital indicated that the data submitted for this measure were based on a sample of cases; (3) Data was collected during a shorter time period (fewer quarters) than the maximum possible time for this measure; (4) Suppressed for one or more quarters by CMS; (5) No data is available from the hospital for this measure; (6) Fewer than 100 patients completed the HCAHPS survey. Use these rates with caution, as the number of surveys may be too low to reliably assess hospital performance; (7) Survey results are based on less than 12 months of data; (8) Survey results are not available for this reporting period; (9) No or very few patients were eligible for the HCAHPS survey. The scores shown, if any, reflect a very small number of surveys; (10) A state average was not calculated because too few hospitals in the state submitted data; (11) There were discrepancies in the data collection process; Please refer to the User's Guide for a full explanation of data.

Provena United Samaritans Medical Center - Logan

812 N Logan
Danville, IL 61832
Phone: 217-443-5000
Fax: 217-443-1965
URL: www.provena.org/usmc
Type: Acute Care Hospitals
Emergency Services: Yes
Ownership: Voluntary Non-Profit - Church
Beds: 210

Key Personnel:
CEO/President. . . . . David Bertauski
Chief of Medical Staff . . . . Charanjit Rakalla, MD
Infection Control. . . . . JoAnne Guyman, RN
Pediatric In-Patient Care . . . . Ray Maciejewski, MD
Radiology. . . . . Prasad Devabhak
Emergency Room . . . . Mary Miller, RN
Hemotology Center . . . . J Labyog, MD
Intensive Care Unit. . . . . Sharon Tuggle

Measure	Cases	This Hosp.	State Avg.	U.S. Avg.
Heart Attack Care				
ACE Inhibitor or ARB for LVSD[1]	12	92%	96%	96%
Aspirin at Arrival	69	97%	99%	99%
Aspirin at Discharge	32	88%	99%	98%
Beta Blocker at Discharge	48	98%	98%	98%
Fibrinolytic Medication Timing	0	-	50%	55%
PCI Within 90 Minutes of Arrival	0	-	90%	90%
Smoking Cessation Advice[1]	7	100%	100%	99%
Chest Pain/Possible Heart Attack Care				
Aspirin at Arrival	128	89%	95%	95%
Median Time to ECG (minutes)	129	11	8	8
Median Time to Transfer (minutes)[1]	21	64	57	61
Fibrinolytic Medication Timing[1]	11	18%	33%	54%
Heart Failure Care				
ACE Inhibitor or ARB for LVSD	96	92%	94%	94%
Discharge Instructions	197	87%	89%	88%
Evaluation of LVS Function	275	97%	98%	98%
Smoking Cessation Advice	46	98%	99%	98%
Pneumonia Care				
Appropriate Initial Antibiotic	147	92%	90%	92%
Blood Culture Timing	174	92%	97%	96%
Influenza Vaccine	175	86%	91%	91%
Initial Antibiotic Timing	218	94%	96%	95%
Pneumococcal Vaccine	240	93%	92%	93%
Smoking Cessation Advice	85	100%	98%	97%
Surgical Care Improvement Project				
Appropriate VTP Within 24 Hours[2]	139	73%	92%	92%
Appropriate Hair Removal[2]	253	100%	99%	99%
Appropriate Beta Blocker Usage[2]	85	82%	92%	93%
Controlled Postoperative Blood Glucose[2]	0	-	92%	93%
Prophylactic Antibiotic Timing[2]	155	96%	97%	97%
Prophylactic Antibiotic Timing (Outpatient)	48	79%	93%	92%
Prophylactic Antibiotic Selection[2]	155	95%	97%	97%
Prophylactic Antibiotic Select. (Outpatient)	38	92%	94%	94%
Prophylactic Antibiotic Stopped[2]	148	84%	94%	94%
Recommended VTP Ordered[2]	139	88%	94%	94%
Urinary Catheter Removal[2]	26	65%	89%	90%
Children's Asthma Care				
Received Systemic Corticosteroids	-	-	-	100%
Received Home Management Plan	-	-	-	71%
Received Reliever Medication	-	-	-	100%
Use of Medical Imaging				
Combination Abdominal CT Scan	474	0.411	0.246	0.191
Combination Chest CT Scan	456	0.171	0.098	0.054
Follow-up Mammogram/Ultrasound	335	18.2%	8.4%	8.4%
MRI for Low Back Pain	208	37.0%	33.4%	32.7%
Survey of Patients' Hospital Experiences				
Area Around Room 'Always' Quiet at Night	300+	66%	-	58%
Doctors 'Always' Communicated Well	300+	85%	-	80%
Home Recovery Information Given	300+	87%	-	82%
Hospital Given 9 or 10 on 10 Point Scale	300+	68%	-	67%
Meds 'Always' Explained Before Given	300+	63%	-	60%
Nurses 'Always' Communicated Well	300+	80%	-	76%
Pain 'Always' Well Controlled	300+	71%	-	69%
Room and Bathroom 'Always' Clean	300+	66%	-	71%
Timely Help 'Always' Received	300+	64%	-	64%
Would Definitely Recommend Hospital	300+	55%	-	69%

VA Illiana Healthcare System - Danville

1900 E. Main
Danville, IL 61832
Phone: 217-554-3000
Fax: 217-554-4552
URL: www.va.gov
Type: Acute Care-Veterans Administration
Emergency Services: No
Ownership: Government - Federal
Beds: 361

Key Personnel:
CEO/President. . . . . Romero Zamberletti
Chief of Medical Staff . . . . Uma Sekar, MD
Quality Assurance . . . . Kim Gibson
Radiology. . . . . M Gai, MD
Patient Relations . . . . Kim Grossman

Measure	Cases	This Hosp.	State Avg.	U.S. Avg.
Heart Attack Care				
ACE Inhibitor or ARB for LVSD[5]	0	-	96%	96%
Aspirin at Arrival[5]	0	-	99%	99%
Aspirin at Discharge[5]	0	-	99%	98%
Beta Blocker at Discharge[5]	0	-	98%	98%
Fibrinolytic Medication Timing[5]	0	-	50%	55%
PCI Within 90 Minutes of Arrival[5]	0	-	90%	90%
Smoking Cessation Advice[5]	0	-	100%	99%
Chest Pain/Possible Heart Attack Care				
Aspirin at Arrival	-	-	95%	95%
Median Time to ECG (minutes)	-	-	8	8
Median Time to Transfer (minutes)	-	-	57	61
Fibrinolytic Medication Timing	-	-	33%	54%
Heart Failure Care				
ACE Inhibitor or ARB for LVSD	39	95%	94%	94%
Discharge Instructions	73	86%	89%	88%
Evaluation of LVS Function	73	100%	98%	98%
Smoking Cessation Advice[1]	23	100%	99%	98%
Pneumonia Care				
Appropriate Initial Antibiotic	25	96%	90%	92%
Blood Culture Timing	29	100%	97%	96%
Influenza Vaccine	29	93%	91%	91%
Initial Antibiotic Timing	45	96%	96%	95%
Pneumococcal Vaccine	32	97%	92%	93%
Smoking Cessation Advice[1]	23	100%	98%	97%
Surgical Care Improvement Project				
Appropriate VTP Within 24 Hours[1,2]	12	100%	92%	92%
Appropriate Hair Removal[1,2]	20	100%	99%	99%
Appropriate Beta Blocker Usage[1,2]	11	100%	92%	93%
Controlled Postoperative Blood Glucose[2,5]	0	-	92%	93%
Prophylactic Antibiotic Timing[1]	14	86%	97%	97%
Prophylactic Antibiotic Timing (Outpatient)	-	-	93%	92%
Prophylactic Antibiotic Selection[1]	14	100%	97%	97%
Prophylactic Antibiotic Select. (Outpatient)	-	-	94%	94%
Prophylactic Antibiotic Stopped[1]	13	92%	94%	94%
Recommended VTP Ordered[1,2]	12	100%	94%	94%
Urinary Catheter Removal[1,2]	3	67%	89%	90%
Children's Asthma Care				
Received Systemic Corticosteroids	-	-	-	100%
Received Home Management Plan	-	-	-	71%
Received Reliever Medication	-	-	-	100%
Use of Medical Imaging				
Combination Abdominal CT Scan	-	-	0.246	0.191
Combination Chest CT Scan	-	-	0.098	0.054
Follow-up Mammogram/Ultrasound	-	-	8.4%	8.4%
MRI for Low Back Pain	-	-	33.4%	32.7%
Survey of Patients' Hospital Experiences				
Area Around Room 'Always' Quiet at Night	-	-	-	58%
Doctors 'Always' Communicated Well	-	-	-	80%
Home Recovery Information Given	-	-	-	82%
Hospital Given 9 or 10 on 10 Point Scale	-	-	-	67%
Meds 'Always' Explained Before Given	-	-	-	60%
Nurses 'Always' Communicated Well	-	-	-	76%
Pain 'Always' Well Controlled	-	-	-	69%
Room and Bathroom 'Always' Clean	-	-	-	71%
Timely Help 'Always' Received	-	-	-	64%
Would Definitely Recommend Hospital	-	-	-	69%

Decatur Memorial Hospital

2300 North Edward Street
Decatur, IL 62526
Phone: 217-877-8121
Fax: 217-876-6118
URL: www.dmhcares.org
Type: Acute Care Hospitals
Emergency Services: Yes
Ownership: Voluntary Non-Profit - Other
Beds: 314

Key Personnel:
CEO/President. . . . . Kenneth Smithmier
Chief of Medical Staff . . . . Jame L Wade, MD
Infection Control. . . . . Alma Miller, RN
Operating Room. . . . . Sally Hodges
Pediatric In-Patient Care . . . . MA Arzon, MD
Quality Assurance . . . . Beth Paul, RN
Radiology. . . . . G Richard Locke, MD
Intensive Care Unit. . . . . Michael Zia, MD

Measure	Cases	This Hosp.	State Avg.	U.S. Avg.
Heart Attack Care				
ACE Inhibitor or ARB for LVSD	57	98%	96%	96%
Aspirin at Arrival	172	100%	99%	99%
Aspirin at Discharge	220	100%	99%	98%
Beta Blocker at Discharge	224	100%	98%	98%
Fibrinolytic Medication Timing	0	-	50%	55%
PCI Within 90 Minutes of Arrival	31	97%	90%	90%
Smoking Cessation Advice	86	100%	100%	99%
Chest Pain/Possible Heart Attack Care				
Aspirin at Arrival[5]	0	-	95%	95%
Median Time to ECG (minutes)[5]	0	-	8	8
Median Time to Transfer (minutes)[5]	0	-	57	61
Fibrinolytic Medication Timing[5]	0	-	33%	54%
Heart Failure Care				
ACE Inhibitor or ARB for LVSD[2]	147	90%	94%	94%
Discharge Instructions[2]	312	98%	89%	88%
Evaluation of LVS Function[2]	407	99%	98%	98%
Smoking Cessation Advice[2]	54	100%	99%	98%
Pneumonia Care				
Appropriate Initial Antibiotic[2]	187	91%	90%	92%
Blood Culture Timing[2]	301	98%	97%	96%
Influenza Vaccine[2]	216	92%	91%	91%
Initial Antibiotic Timing[2]	289	99%	96%	95%
Pneumococcal Vaccine[2]	292	90%	92%	93%
Smoking Cessation Advice[2]	92	100%	98%	97%
Surgical Care Improvement Project				
Appropriate VTP Within 24 Hours[2]	294	93%	92%	92%
Appropriate Hair Removal[2]	809	100%	99%	99%
Appropriate Beta Blocker Usage[2]	284	100%	92%	93%
Controlled Postoperative Blood Glucose[2]	97	95%	92%	93%
Prophylactic Antibiotic Timing[2]	583	100%	97%	97%
Prophylactic Antibiotic Timing (Outpatient)	406	96%	93%	92%
Prophylactic Antibiotic Selection[2]	588	99%	97%	97%
Prophylactic Antibiotic Select. (Outpatient)	394	98%	94%	94%
Prophylactic Antibiotic Stopped[2]	572	97%	94%	94%
Recommended VTP Ordered[2]	294	93%	94%	94%
Urinary Catheter Removal[2]	238	94%	89%	90%
Children's Asthma Care				
Received Systemic Corticosteroids	-	-	-	100%
Received Home Management Plan	-	-	-	71%
Received Reliever Medication	-	-	-	100%
Use of Medical Imaging				
Combination Abdominal CT Scan	2,382	0.045	0.246	0.191
Combination Chest CT Scan	1,876	0.006	0.098	0.054
Follow-up Mammogram/Ultrasound	3,058	9.2%	8.4%	8.4%
MRI for Low Back Pain	626	38.3%	33.4%	32.7%
Survey of Patients' Hospital Experiences				
Area Around Room 'Always' Quiet at Night	300+	56%	-	58%
Doctors 'Always' Communicated Well	300+	78%	-	80%
Home Recovery Information Given	300+	86%	-	82%
Hospital Given 9 or 10 on 10 Point Scale	300+	67%	-	67%
Meds 'Always' Explained Before Given	300+	56%	-	60%
Nurses 'Always' Communicated Well	300+	74%	-	76%
Pain 'Always' Well Controlled	300+	66%	-	69%
Room and Bathroom 'Always' Clean	300+	65%	-	71%
Timely Help 'Always' Received	300+	58%	-	64%
Would Definitely Recommend Hospital	300+	73%	-	69%

NOTE: Hospital profiles are in alphabetical order by state, then city, then hospital within the city; Rankings exclude hospitals with less than 25 cases except for patient surveys which excludes hospitals with less than 100 cases; (a) 100–299 cases; (1) The number of cases is too small to be sure how well a hospital is performing; (2) The hospital indicated that the data submitted for this measure were based on a sample of cases; (3) Data was collected during a shorter time period (fewer quarters) than the maximum possible time for this measure; (4) Suppressed for one or more quarters by CMS; (5) No data is available from the hospital for this measure; (6) Fewer than 100 patients completed the HCAHPS survey. Use these rates with caution, as the number of surveys may be too low to reliably assess hospital performance; (7) Survey results are based on less than 12 months of data; (8) Survey results are not available for this reporting period; (9) No or very few patients were eligible for the HCAHPS survey. The scores shown, if any, reflect a very small number of surveys; (10) A state average was not calculated because too few hospitals in the state submitted data; (11) There were discrepancies in the data collection process; Please refer to the User's Guide for a full explanation of data.

Saint Marys Hospital

1800 E Lake Shore Dr
Decatur, IL 62521
URL: www.stmarys-hospital.com
Type: Acute Care Hospitals
Ownership: Voluntary Non-Profit - Private
Phone: 217-464-7000
Fax: 217-464-1616
Emergency Services: Yes
Beds: 371

Key Personnel:

CEO/President. . . . . Anthony D Pfitzer
Chief of Medical Staff. . . . . D Patel, MD
Coronary Care . . . . Glen Griesheim, RN
Pediatric Ambulatory Care . . . . . G Chiligiris, MD
Quality Assurance . . . . Gayla Hislope
Anesthesiology. . . . . John Furry, MD
Emergency Room . . . . Phillip Barnell, MD
Intensive Care Unit. . . . . Steven Arnold, MD

Measure	Cases	This Hosp.	State Avg.	U.S. Avg.
Heart Attack Care				
ACE Inhibitor or ARB for LVSD[1,2]	9	100%	96%	96%
Aspirin at Arrival[2]	47	98%	99%	99%
Aspirin at Discharge[2]	34	97%	99%	98%
Beta Blocker at Discharge[2]	38	95%	98%	98%
Fibrinolytic Medication Timing[2]	0	-	50%	55%
PCI Within 90 Minutes of Arrival[2]	0	-	90%	90%
Smoking Cessation Advice[1,2]	9	100%	100%	99%
Chest Pain/Possible Heart Attack Care				
Aspirin at Arrival	40	100%	95%	95%
Median Time to ECG (minutes)	42	12	8	8
Median Time to Transfer (minutes)[1,3]	5	91	57	61
Fibrinolytic Medication Timing	0	-	33%	54%
Heart Failure Care				
ACE Inhibitor or ARB for LVSD[2]	55	100%	94%	94%
Discharge Instructions[2]	165	88%	89%	88%
Evaluation of LVS Function[2]	227	100%	98%	98%
Smoking Cessation Advice[2]	44	100%	99%	98%
Pneumonia Care				
Appropriate Initial Antibiotic[2]	104	88%	90%	92%
Blood Culture Timing[2]	144	94%	97%	96%
Influenza Vaccine[2]	106	99%	91%	91%
Initial Antibiotic Timing[2]	153	95%	96%	95%
Pneumococcal Vaccine[2]	127	100%	92%	93%
Smoking Cessation Advice[2]	54	100%	98%	97%
Surgical Care Improvement Project				
Appropriate VTP Within 24 Hours[2]	144	92%	92%	92%
Appropriate Hair Removal[2]	336	100%	99%	99%
Appropriate Beta Blocker Usage[2]	91	100%	92%	93%
Controlled Postoperative Blood Glucose[2]	0	-	92%	93%
Prophylactic Antibiotic Timing[2]	235	98%	97%	97%
Prophylactic Antibiotic Timing (Outpatient)[3]	111	97%	93%	92%
Prophylactic Antibiotic Selection[2]	236	97%	97%	97%
Prophylactic Antibiotic Select. (Outpatient)[3]	145	99%	94%	94%
Prophylactic Antibiotic Stopped[2]	221	92%	94%	94%
Recommended VTP Ordered[2]	145	93%	94%	94%
Urinary Catheter Removal[2]	48	94%	89%	90%
Children's Asthma Care				
Received Systemic Corticosteroids	-	-	-	100%
Received Home Management Plan	-	-	-	71%
Received Reliever Medication	-	-	-	100%
Use of Medical Imaging				
Combination Abdominal CT Scan	513	0.062	0.246	0.191
Combination Chest CT Scan	369	0.011	0.098	0.054
Follow-up Mammogram/Ultrasound	919	6.1%	8.4%	8.4%
MRI for Low Back Pain	187	35.3%	33.4%	32.7%
Survey of Patients' Hospital Experiences				
Area Around Room 'Always' Quiet at Night	300+	59%	-	58%
Doctors 'Always' Communicated Well	300+	77%	-	80%
Home Recovery Information Given	300+	81%	-	82%
Hospital Given 9 or 10 on 10 Point Scale	300+	62%	-	67%
Meds 'Always' Explained Before Given	300+	54%	-	60%
Nurses 'Always' Communicated Well	300+	70%	-	76%
Pain 'Always' Well Controlled	300+	62%	-	69%
Room and Bathroom 'Always' Clean	300+	62%	-	71%
Timely Help 'Always' Received	300+	53%	-	64%
Would Definitely Recommend Hospital	300+	69%	-	69%

Kishwaukee Community Hospital

One Kish Hospital Drive
Dekalb, IL 60115
URL: www.kishhospital.org
Type: Acute Care Hospitals
Ownership: Voluntary Non-Profit - Private
Phone: 815-756-1521
Fax: 815-756-7665
Emergency Services: Yes
Beds: 172

Key Personnel:

CEO/President. . . . . Kevin Poorten
Chief of Medical Staff. . . . . Pamela Duffy
Operating Room. . . . . Stephen R Goldman
Pediatric Ambulatory Care . . . . . . Suzanne Cook, MD
Pediatric In-Patient Care . . . . Suzanne Cook, MD
Quality Assurance . . . . Brad Copple
Radiology. . . . . Thomas R Cain, MD
Patient Relations . . . . Pamela Duffy

Measure	Cases	This Hosp.	State Avg.	U.S. Avg.
Heart Attack Care				
ACE Inhibitor or ARB for LVSD[1]	5	80%	96%	96%
Aspirin at Arrival	65	98%	99%	99%
Aspirin at Discharge	58	95%	99%	98%
Beta Blocker at Discharge	55	100%	98%	98%
Fibrinolytic Medication Timing[1]	1	0%	50%	55%
PCI Within 90 Minutes of Arrival	25	76%	90%	90%
Smoking Cessation Advice	26	100%	100%	99%
Chest Pain/Possible Heart Attack Care				
Aspirin at Arrival[1]	19	95%	95%	95%
Median Time to ECG (minutes)[1]	20	20	8	8
Median Time to Transfer (minutes)[5]	0	-	57	61
Fibrinolytic Medication Timing[3]	0	-	33%	54%
Heart Failure Care				
ACE Inhibitor or ARB for LVSD	52	96%	94%	94%
Discharge Instructions	117	78%	89%	88%
Evaluation of LVS Function	154	99%	98%	98%
Smoking Cessation Advice	25	100%	99%	98%
Pneumonia Care				
Appropriate Initial Antibiotic	93	90%	90%	92%
Blood Culture Timing	101	97%	97%	96%
Influenza Vaccine	105	75%	91%	91%
Initial Antibiotic Timing	137	93%	96%	95%
Pneumococcal Vaccine	147	92%	92%	93%
Smoking Cessation Advice	32	94%	98%	97%
Surgical Care Improvement Project				
Appropriate VTP Within 24 Hours	138	86%	92%	92%
Appropriate Hair Removal	382	99%	99%	99%
Appropriate Beta Blocker Usage	115	89%	92%	93%
Controlled Postoperative Blood Glucose	0	-	92%	93%
Prophylactic Antibiotic Timing	269	91%	97%	97%
Prophylactic Antibiotic Timing (Outpatient)	123	86%	93%	92%
Prophylactic Antibiotic Selection	266	91%	97%	97%
Prophylactic Antibiotic Select. (Outpatient)	117	96%	94%	94%
Prophylactic Antibiotic Stopped	257	94%	94%	94%
Recommended VTP Ordered	138	91%	94%	94%
Urinary Catheter Removal	90	93%	89%	90%
Children's Asthma Care				
Received Systemic Corticosteroids	-	-	-	100%
Received Home Management Plan	-	-	-	71%
Received Reliever Medication	-	-	-	100%
Use of Medical Imaging				
Combination Abdominal CT Scan	457	0.046	0.246	0.191
Combination Chest CT Scan	311	0.013	0.098	0.054
Follow-up Mammogram/Ultrasound	508	7.9%	8.4%	8.4%
MRI for Low Back Pain[1]	40	37.5%	33.4%	32.7%
Survey of Patients' Hospital Experiences				
Area Around Room 'Always' Quiet at Night	300+	55%	-	58%
Doctors 'Always' Communicated Well	300+	81%	-	80%
Home Recovery Information Given	300+	81%	-	82%
Hospital Given 9 or 10 on 10 Point Scale	300+	67%	-	67%
Meds 'Always' Explained Before Given	300+	57%	-	60%
Nurses 'Always' Communicated Well	300+	75%	-	76%
Pain 'Always' Well Controlled	300+	69%	-	69%
Room and Bathroom 'Always' Clean	300+	76%	-	71%
Timely Help 'Always' Received	300+	58%	-	64%
Would Definitely Recommend Hospital	300+	69%	-	69%

Katherine Shaw Bethea Hospital

403 E 1st St
Dixon, IL 61021
Type: Acute Care Hospitals
Ownership: Voluntary Non-Profit - Other
Phone: 815-288-5531
Emergency Services: Yes

Key Personnel:

CEO/President. . . . . Darryl Vandervort

Measure	Cases	This Hosp.	State Avg.	U.S. Avg.
Heart Attack Care				
ACE Inhibitor or ARB for LVSD[1]	8	100%	96%	96%
Aspirin at Arrival	54	98%	99%	99%
Aspirin at Discharge	50	100%	99%	98%
Beta Blocker at Discharge	45	100%	98%	98%
Fibrinolytic Medication Timing[1]	2	100%	50%	55%
PCI Within 90 Minutes of Arrival[1]	4	75%	90%	90%
Smoking Cessation Advice[1]	19	100%	100%	99%
Chest Pain/Possible Heart Attack Care				
Aspirin at Arrival[1,3]	15	100%	95%	95%
Median Time to ECG (minutes)[1,3]	15	10	8	8
Median Time to Transfer (minutes)[3]	0	-	57	61
Fibrinolytic Medication Timing[1,3]	2	50%	33%	54%
Heart Failure Care				
ACE Inhibitor or ARB for LVSD	27	100%	94%	94%
Discharge Instructions	91	93%	89%	88%
Evaluation of LVS Function	131	100%	98%	98%
Smoking Cessation Advice	25	100%	99%	98%
Pneumonia Care				
Appropriate Initial Antibiotic	44	95%	90%	92%
Blood Culture Timing	70	100%	97%	96%
Influenza Vaccine	56	98%	91%	91%
Initial Antibiotic Timing	85	100%	96%	95%
Pneumococcal Vaccine	79	96%	92%	93%
Smoking Cessation Advice	30	100%	98%	97%
Surgical Care Improvement Project				
Appropriate VTP Within 24 Hours	95	100%	92%	92%
Appropriate Hair Removal	290	100%	99%	99%
Appropriate Beta Blocker Usage	86	100%	92%	93%
Controlled Postoperative Blood Glucose	0	-	92%	93%
Prophylactic Antibiotic Timing	197	100%	97%	97%
Prophylactic Antibiotic Timing (Outpatient)	84	96%	93%	92%
Prophylactic Antibiotic Selection	198	99%	97%	97%
Prophylactic Antibiotic Select. (Outpatient)	81	99%	94%	94%
Prophylactic Antibiotic Stopped	153	97%	94%	94%
Recommended VTP Ordered	95	100%	94%	94%
Urinary Catheter Removal	31	100%	89%	90%
Children's Asthma Care				
Received Systemic Corticosteroids	-	-	-	100%
Received Home Management Plan	-	-	-	71%
Received Reliever Medication	-	-	-	100%
Use of Medical Imaging				
Combination Abdominal CT Scan	326	0.592	0.246	0.191
Combination Chest CT Scan	195	0.538	0.098	0.054
Follow-up Mammogram/Ultrasound	819	15.1%	8.4%	8.4%
MRI for Low Back Pain	117	28.2%	33.4%	32.7%
Survey of Patients' Hospital Experiences				
Area Around Room 'Always' Quiet at Night	300+	55%	-	58%
Doctors 'Always' Communicated Well	300+	83%	-	80%
Home Recovery Information Given	300+	86%	-	82%
Hospital Given 9 or 10 on 10 Point Scale	300+	73%	-	67%
Meds 'Always' Explained Before Given	300+	62%	-	60%
Nurses 'Always' Communicated Well	300+	82%	-	76%
Pain 'Always' Well Controlled	300+	75%	-	69%
Room and Bathroom 'Always' Clean	300+	75%	-	71%
Timely Help 'Always' Received	300+	73%	-	64%
Would Definitely Recommend Hospital	300+	77%	-	69%

NOTE: Hospital profiles are in alphabetical order by state, then city, then hospital within the city; Rankings exclude hospitals with less than 25 cases except for patient surveys which excludes hospitals with less than 100 cases; (a) 100–299 cases; (1) The number of cases is too small to be sure how well a hospital is performing; (2) The hospital indicated that the data submitted for this measure were based on a sample of cases; (3) Data was collected during a shorter time period (fewer quarters) than the maximum possible time for this measure; (4) Suppressed for one or more quarters by CMS; (5) No data is available from the hospital for this measure; (6) Fewer than 100 patients completed the HCAHPS survey. Use these rates with caution, as the number of surveys may be too low to reliably assess hospital performance; (7) Survey results are based on less than 12 months of data; (8) Survey results are not available for this reporting period; (9) No or very few patients were eligible for the HCAHPS survey. The scores shown, if any, reflect a very small number of surveys; (10) A state average was not calculated because too few hospitals in the state submitted data; (11) There were discrepancies in the data collection process; Please refer to the User's Guide for a full explanation of data.

Advocate Good Samaritan Hospital

3815 Highland Avenue
Downers Grove, IL 60515
Phone: 630-275-5900
Fax: 630-963-8605
URL: www.advocatehealth.com/gsam
Type: Acute Care Hospitals
Emergency Services: Yes
Ownership: Voluntary Non-Profit - Church
Beds: 327

Key Personnel:
CEO/President. . . . . Jon Bruss
Chief of Medical Staff. . . . . Timothy Payne
Pediatric In-Patient Care . . . . Gus Rousonebs, MD
Radiology. . . . . R William Wayne, LVN

Measure	Cases	This Hosp.	State Avg.	U.S. Avg.
Heart Attack Care				
ACE Inhibitor or ARB for LVSD	52	100%	96%	96%
Aspirin at Arrival	240	100%	99%	99%
Aspirin at Discharge	226	100%	99%	98%
Beta Blocker at Discharge	224	100%	98%	98%
Fibrinolytic Medication Timing	0	-	50%	55%
PCI Within 90 Minutes of Arrival	61	98%	90%	90%
Smoking Cessation Advice	55	100%	100%	99%
Chest Pain/Possible Heart Attack Care				
Aspirin at Arrival[1,3]	2	100%	95%	95%
Median Time to ECG (minutes)[1,3]	2	21	8	8
Median Time to Transfer (minutes)[5]	0	-	57	61
Fibrinolytic Medication Timing[5]	0	-	33%	54%
Heart Failure Care				
ACE Inhibitor or ARB for LVSD	161	100%	94%	94%
Discharge Instructions	337	99%	89%	88%
Evaluation of LVS Function	456	100%	98%	98%
Smoking Cessation Advice	43	100%	99%	98%
Pneumonia Care				
Appropriate Initial Antibiotic[2]	142	96%	90%	92%
Blood Culture Timing[2]	227	99%	97%	96%
Influenza Vaccine[2]	167	97%	91%	91%
Initial Antibiotic Timing[2]	236	99%	96%	95%
Pneumococcal Vaccine[2]	258	96%	92%	93%
Smoking Cessation Advice[2]	72	100%	98%	97%
Surgical Care Improvement Project				
Appropriate VTP Within 24 Hours[2]	203	97%	92%	92%
Appropriate Hair Removal[2]	612	100%	99%	99%
Appropriate Beta Blocker Usage[2]	198	97%	92%	93%
Controlled Postoperative Blood Glucose[2]	132	98%	92%	93%
Prophylactic Antibiotic Timing[2]	439	100%	97%	97%
Prophylactic Antibiotic Timing (Outpatient)	323	96%	93%	92%
Prophylactic Antibiotic Selection[2]	442	98%	97%	97%
Prophylactic Antibiotic Select. (Outpatient)	317	98%	94%	94%
Prophylactic Antibiotic Stopped[2]	425	98%	94%	94%
Recommended VTP Ordered[2]	203	98%	94%	94%
Urinary Catheter Removal[2]	82	91%	89%	90%
Children's Asthma Care				
Received Systemic Corticosteroids	-	-	-	100%
Received Home Management Plan	-	-	-	71%
Received Reliever Medication	-	-	-	100%
Use of Medical Imaging				
Combination Abdominal CT Scan	1,183	0.156	0.246	0.191
Combination Chest CT Scan	1,155	0.073	0.098	0.054
Follow-up Mammogram/Ultrasound	2,270	11.6%	8.4%	8.4%
MRI for Low Back Pain	156	32.7%	33.4%	32.7%
Survey of Patients' Hospital Experiences				
Area Around Room 'Always' Quiet at Night	300+	50%	-	58%
Doctors 'Always' Communicated Well	300+	80%	-	80%
Home Recovery Information Given	300+	83%	-	82%
Hospital Given 9 or 10 on 10 Point Scale	300+	71%	-	67%
Meds 'Always' Explained Before Given	300+	62%	-	60%
Nurses 'Always' Communicated Well	300+	78%	-	76%
Pain 'Always' Well Controlled	300+	70%	-	69%
Room and Bathroom 'Always' Clean	300+	71%	-	71%
Timely Help 'Always' Received	300+	64%	-	64%
Would Definitely Recommend Hospital	300+	77%	-	69%

Marshall Browning Hospital

900 North Washington Street
Du Quoin, IL 62832
Phone: 618-542-2146
Fax: 618-542-4756
URL: www.marshallbrowninghospital.com
Type: Critical Access Hospitals
Emergency Services: Yes
Ownership: Voluntary Non-Profit - Private
Beds: 25

Key Personnel:
CEO/President. . . . . William J Huff

Measure	Cases	This Hosp.	State Avg.	U.S. Avg.
Heart Attack Care				
ACE Inhibitor or ARB for LVSD[3]	0	-	96%	96%
Aspirin at Arrival[1,3]	1	100%	99%	99%
Aspirin at Discharge[1,3]	1	100%	99%	98%
Beta Blocker at Discharge[1,3]	1	100%	98%	98%
Fibrinolytic Medication Timing[3]	0	-	50%	55%
PCI Within 90 Minutes of Arrival[3]	0	-	90%	90%
Smoking Cessation Advice[3]	0	-	100%	99%
Chest Pain/Possible Heart Attack Care				
Aspirin at Arrival	-	-	95%	95%
Median Time to ECG (minutes)	-	-	8	8
Median Time to Transfer (minutes)	-	-	57	61
Fibrinolytic Medication Timing	-	-	33%	54%
Heart Failure Care				
ACE Inhibitor or ARB for LVSD[1]	9	67%	94%	94%
Discharge Instructions[1]	20	55%	89%	88%
Evaluation of LVS Function	28	64%	98%	98%
Smoking Cessation Advice[1]	3	33%	99%	98%
Pneumonia Care				
Appropriate Initial Antibiotic[1]	14	79%	90%	92%
Blood Culture Timing[1]	22	95%	97%	96%
Influenza Vaccine[1]	18	61%	91%	91%
Initial Antibiotic Timing[1]	15	80%	96%	95%
Pneumococcal Vaccine[1]	22	23%	92%	93%
Smoking Cessation Advice[1]	6	50%	98%	97%
Surgical Care Improvement Project				
Appropriate VTP Within 24 Hours[5]	0	-	92%	92%
Appropriate Hair Removal[5]	0	-	99%	99%
Appropriate Beta Blocker Usage[5]	0	-	92%	93%
Controlled Postoperative Blood Glucose[5]	0	-	92%	93%
Prophylactic Antibiotic Timing[5]	0	-	97%	97%
Prophylactic Antibiotic Timing (Outpatient)	-	-	93%	92%
Prophylactic Antibiotic Selection[5]	0	-	97%	97%
Prophylactic Antibiotic Select. (Outpatient)	-	-	94%	94%
Prophylactic Antibiotic Stopped[5]	0	-	94%	94%
Recommended VTP Ordered[5]	0	-	94%	94%
Urinary Catheter Removal[5]	0	-	89%	90%
Children's Asthma Care				
Received Systemic Corticosteroids	-	-	-	100%
Received Home Management Plan	-	-	-	71%
Received Reliever Medication	-	-	-	100%
Use of Medical Imaging				
Combination Abdominal CT Scan	-	-	0.246	0.191
Combination Chest CT Scan	-	-	0.098	0.054
Follow-up Mammogram/Ultrasound	-	-	8.4%	8.4%
MRI for Low Back Pain	-	-	33.4%	32.7%
Survey of Patients' Hospital Experiences				
Area Around Room 'Always' Quiet at Night[8]	-	-	-	58%
Doctors 'Always' Communicated Well[8]	-	-	-	80%
Home Recovery Information Given[8]	-	-	-	82%
Hospital Given 9 or 10 on 10 Point Scale[8]	-	-	-	67%
Meds 'Always' Explained Before Given[8]	-	-	-	60%
Nurses 'Always' Communicated Well[8]	-	-	-	76%
Pain 'Always' Well Controlled[8]	-	-	-	69%
Room and Bathroom 'Always' Clean[8]	-	-	-	71%
Timely Help 'Always' Received[8]	-	-	-	64%
Would Definitely Recommend Hospital[8]	-	-	-	69%

Saint Anthonys Memorial Hospital

503 N Maple Street
Effingham, IL 62401
Phone: 217-342-2121
Fax: 217-347-1563
E-mail: hospital@effingham.net
URL: www.stanthonyshospital.org
Type: Acute Care Hospitals
Emergency Services: Yes
Ownership: Voluntary Non-Profit - Church
Beds: 146

Key Personnel:
CEO/President. . . . . Daneial J Woods
Coronary Care . . . . Sharyn Phillips
Infection Control. . . . . Kim Howell
Operating Room. . . . . Ruben Boyajian
Pediatric In-Patient Care . . . . Sharyn Phillips
Quality Assurance . . . . Mark Finley
Radiology. . . . . Marily Boone

Measure	Cases	This Hosp.	State Avg.	U.S. Avg.
Heart Attack Care				
ACE Inhibitor or ARB for LVSD[1]	8	75%	96%	96%
Aspirin at Arrival[1]	19	84%	99%	99%
Aspirin at Discharge[1]	20	85%	99%	98%
Beta Blocker at Discharge[1]	20	95%	98%	98%
Fibrinolytic Medication Timing	0	-	50%	55%
PCI Within 90 Minutes of Arrival	0	-	90%	90%
Smoking Cessation Advice[1]	2	100%	100%	99%
Chest Pain/Possible Heart Attack Care				
Aspirin at Arrival	187	95%	95%	95%
Median Time to ECG (minutes)	193	12	8	8
Median Time to Transfer (minutes)[3]	0	-	57	61
Fibrinolytic Medication Timing[1]	1	0%	33%	54%
Heart Failure Care				
ACE Inhibitor or ARB for LVSD	41	95%	94%	94%
Discharge Instructions	139	83%	89%	88%
Evaluation of LVS Function	178	98%	98%	98%
Smoking Cessation Advice	31	97%	99%	98%
Pneumonia Care				
Appropriate Initial Antibiotic	117	89%	90%	92%
Blood Culture Timing	161	94%	97%	96%
Influenza Vaccine	107	92%	91%	91%
Initial Antibiotic Timing	170	93%	96%	95%
Pneumococcal Vaccine	179	89%	92%	93%
Smoking Cessation Advice	67	94%	98%	97%
Surgical Care Improvement Project				
Appropriate VTP Within 24 Hours	364	94%	92%	92%
Appropriate Hair Removal	921	99%	99%	99%
Appropriate Beta Blocker Usage	268	94%	92%	93%
Controlled Postoperative Blood Glucose	0	-	92%	93%
Prophylactic Antibiotic Timing	690	91%	97%	97%
Prophylactic Antibiotic Timing (Outpatient)	76	68%	93%	92%
Prophylactic Antibiotic Selection	695	97%	97%	97%
Prophylactic Antibiotic Select. (Outpatient)	71	99%	94%	94%
Prophylactic Antibiotic Stopped	666	96%	94%	94%
Recommended VTP Ordered	367	94%	94%	94%
Urinary Catheter Removal	274	96%	89%	90%
Children's Asthma Care				
Received Systemic Corticosteroids	-	-	-	100%
Received Home Management Plan	-	-	-	71%
Received Reliever Medication	-	-	-	100%
Use of Medical Imaging				
Combination Abdominal CT Scan	995	0.751	0.246	0.191
Combination Chest CT Scan	642	0.006	0.098	0.054
Follow-up Mammogram/Ultrasound	1,567	9.1%	8.4%	8.4%
MRI for Low Back Pain	160	35.6%	33.4%	32.7%
Survey of Patients' Hospital Experiences				
Area Around Room 'Always' Quiet at Night	300+	53%	-	58%
Doctors 'Always' Communicated Well	300+	80%	-	80%
Home Recovery Information Given	300+	81%	-	82%
Hospital Given 9 or 10 on 10 Point Scale	300+	66%	-	67%
Meds 'Always' Explained Before Given	300+	61%	-	60%
Nurses 'Always' Communicated Well	300+	74%	-	76%
Pain 'Always' Well Controlled	300+	66%	-	69%
Room and Bathroom 'Always' Clean	300+	71%	-	71%
Timely Help 'Always' Received	300+	62%	-	64%
Would Definitely Recommend Hospital	300+	67%	-	69%

NOTE: Hospital profiles are in alphabetical order by state, then city, then hospital within the city; Rankings exclude hospitals with less than 25 cases except for patient surveys which excludes hospitals with less than 100 cases; (a) 100–299 cases; (1) The number of cases is too small to be sure how well a hospital is performing; (2) The hospital indicated that the data submitted for this measure were based on a sample of cases; (3) Data was collected during a shorter time period (fewer quarters) than the maximum possible time for this measure; (4) Suppressed for one or more quarters by CMS; (5) No data is available from the hospital for this measure; (6) Fewer than 100 patients completed the HCAHPS survey. Use these rates with caution, as the number of surveys may be too low to reliably assess hospital performance; (7) Survey results are based on less than 12 months of data; (8) Survey results are not available for this reporting period; (9) No or very few patients were eligible for the HCAHPS survey. The scores shown, if any, reflect a very small number of surveys; (10) A state average was not calculated because too few hospitals in the state submitted data; (11) There were discrepancies in the data collection process; Please refer to the User's Guide for a full explanation of data.

Ferrell Hospital Community Foundations

1201 Pine Street Phone: 618-273-3361
Eldorado, IL 62930 Fax: 618-273-2571
Type: Critical Access Hospitals Emergency Services: Yes
Ownership: Proprietary Beds: 51

Key Personnel:
CEO/President. . . . . William Hartley
Chief of Medical Staff. . . . . Eliott Partirdge
Operating Room. . . . . Samir F Abdo
Radiology. . . . . Tina Murray
Emergency Room . . . . Jackie Tripp

Measure	Cases	This Hosp.	State Avg.	U.S. Avg.
Heart Attack Care				
ACE Inhibitor or ARB for LVSD	0	-	96%	96%
Aspirin at Arrival[1]	1	100%	99%	99%
Aspirin at Discharge	0	-	99%	98%
Beta Blocker at Discharge	0	-	98%	98%
Fibrinolytic Medication Timing	0	-	50%	55%
PCI Within 90 Minutes of Arrival	0	-	90%	90%
Smoking Cessation Advice	0	-	100%	99%
Chest Pain/Possible Heart Attack Care				
Aspirin at Arrival	-	-	95%	95%
Median Time to ECG (minutes)	-	-	8	8
Median Time to Transfer (minutes)	-	-	57	61
Fibrinolytic Medication Timing	-	-	33%	54%
Heart Failure Care				
ACE Inhibitor or ARB for LVSD[1]	2	50%	94%	94%
Discharge Instructions[1]	15	27%	89%	88%
Evaluation of LVS Function[1]	19	58%	98%	98%
Smoking Cessation Advice[1]	4	75%	99%	98%
Pneumonia Care				
Appropriate Initial Antibiotic	28	82%	90%	92%
Blood Culture Timing[1]	10	90%	97%	96%
Influenza Vaccine	27	78%	91%	91%
Initial Antibiotic Timing	34	91%	96%	95%
Pneumococcal Vaccine	35	91%	92%	93%
Smoking Cessation Advice[1]	21	90%	98%	97%
Surgical Care Improvement Project				
Appropriate VTP Within 24 Hours[1,3]	1	100%	92%	92%
Appropriate Hair Removal[1,3]	1	0%	99%	99%
Appropriate Beta Blocker Usage[5]	0	-	92%	93%
Controlled Postoperative Blood Glucose[3]	0	-	92%	93%
Prophylactic Antibiotic Timing[1,3]	1	0%	97%	97%
Prophylactic Antibiotic Timing (Outpatient)	-	-	93%	92%
Prophylactic Antibiotic Selection[1,3]	1	0%	97%	97%
Prophylactic Antibiotic Select. (Outpatient)	-	-	94%	94%
Prophylactic Antibiotic Stopped[1,3]	1	100%	94%	94%
Recommended VTP Ordered[1,3]	1	100%	94%	94%
Urinary Catheter Removal[5]	0	-	89%	90%
Children's Asthma Care				
Received Systemic Corticosteroids	-	-	-	100%
Received Home Management Plan	-	-	-	71%
Received Reliever Medication	-	-	-	100%
Use of Medical Imaging				
Combination Abdominal CT Scan	-	-	0.246	0.191
Combination Chest CT Scan	-	-	0.098	0.054
Follow-up Mammogram/Ultrasound	-	-	8.4%	8.4%
MRI for Low Back Pain	-	-	33.4%	32.7%
Survey of Patients' Hospital Experiences				
Area Around Room 'Always' Quiet at Night[8]	-	-	-	58%
Doctors 'Always' Communicated Well[8]	-	-	-	80%
Home Recovery Information Given[8]	-	-	-	82%
Hospital Given 9 or 10 on 10 Point Scale[8]	-	-	-	67%
Meds 'Always' Explained Before Given[8]	-	-	-	60%
Nurses 'Always' Communicated Well[8]	-	-	-	76%
Pain 'Always' Well Controlled[8]	-	-	-	69%
Room and Bathroom 'Always' Clean[8]	-	-	-	71%
Timely Help 'Always' Received[8]	-	-	-	64%
Would Definitely Recommend Hospital[8]	-	-	-	69%

Provena-Saint Joseph Hospital

77 N Airlite Street Phone: 847-695-3200
Elgin, IL 60123 Fax: 847-622-2070
URL: www.provenasaintjoeph.com
Type: Acute Care Hospitals Emergency Services: Yes
Ownership: Voluntary Non-Profit - Church Beds: 260

Key Personnel:
CEO/President. . . . . William McDonald
Cardiac Laboratory. . . . . Jeff Berchner
Chief of Medical Staff . . . . Charles Carallo, MD
Infection Control. . . . . Kathy Hogan
Operating Room. . . . . Feli Bayani
Quality Assurance . . . . Carol Fodge
Radiology. . . . . Laurie Schachtner

Measure	Cases	This Hosp.	State Avg.	U.S. Avg.
Heart Attack Care				
ACE Inhibitor or ARB for LVSD[1]	18	83%	96%	96%
Aspirin at Arrival	125	96%	99%	99%
Aspirin at Discharge	124	95%	99%	98%
Beta Blocker at Discharge	121	98%	98%	98%
Fibrinolytic Medication Timing	0	-	50%	55%
PCI Within 90 Minutes of Arrival	27	93%	90%	90%
Smoking Cessation Advice	40	100%	100%	99%
Chest Pain/Possible Heart Attack Care				
Aspirin at Arrival[1,3]	2	100%	95%	95%
Median Time to ECG (minutes)[1,3]	2	2	8	8
Median Time to Transfer (minutes)[5]	0	-	57	61
Fibrinolytic Medication Timing[5]	0	-	33%	54%
Heart Failure Care				
ACE Inhibitor or ARB for LVSD	68	74%	94%	94%
Discharge Instructions	151	75%	89%	88%
Evaluation of LVS Function	210	90%	98%	98%
Smoking Cessation Advice	37	97%	99%	98%
Pneumonia Care				
Appropriate Initial Antibiotic[2]	77	88%	90%	92%
Blood Culture Timing[2]	129	94%	97%	96%
Influenza Vaccine[2]	85	78%	91%	91%
Initial Antibiotic Timing[2]	125	96%	96%	95%
Pneumococcal Vaccine[2]	121	98%	92%	93%
Smoking Cessation Advice[2]	36	92%	98%	97%
Surgical Care Improvement Project				
Appropriate VTP Within 24 Hours[2]	191	87%	92%	92%
Appropriate Hair Removal[2]	416	98%	99%	99%
Appropriate Beta Blocker Usage[2]	134	91%	92%	93%
Controlled Postoperative Blood Glucose[2]	43	98%	92%	93%
Prophylactic Antibiotic Timing[2]	264	97%	97%	97%
Prophylactic Antibiotic Timing (Outpatient)	109	78%	93%	92%
Prophylactic Antibiotic Selection[2]	265	98%	97%	97%
Prophylactic Antibiotic Select. (Outpatient)	118	97%	94%	94%
Prophylactic Antibiotic Stopped[2]	247	87%	94%	94%
Recommended VTP Ordered[2]	191	91%	94%	94%
Urinary Catheter Removal[2]	50	88%	89%	90%
Children's Asthma Care				
Received Systemic Corticosteroids	-	-	-	100%
Received Home Management Plan	-	-	-	71%
Received Reliever Medication	-	-	-	100%
Use of Medical Imaging				
Combination Abdominal CT Scan	563	0.240	0.246	0.191
Combination Chest CT Scan	394	0.236	0.098	0.054
Follow-up Mammogram/Ultrasound	768	10.2%	8.4%	8.4%
MRI for Low Back Pain	70	34.3%	33.4%	32.7%
Survey of Patients' Hospital Experiences				
Area Around Room 'Always' Quiet at Night	300+	65%	-	58%
Doctors 'Always' Communicated Well	300+	77%	-	80%
Home Recovery Information Given	300+	87%	-	82%
Hospital Given 9 or 10 on 10 Point Scale	300+	68%	-	67%
Meds 'Always' Explained Before Given	300+	58%	-	60%
Nurses 'Always' Communicated Well	300+	73%	-	76%
Pain 'Always' Well Controlled	300+	70%	-	69%
Room and Bathroom 'Always' Clean	300+	73%	-	71%
Timely Help 'Always' Received	300+	54%	-	64%
Would Definitely Recommend Hospital	300+	72%	-	69%

Sherman Hospital

1425 North Randall Road Phone: 847-742-9800
Elgin, IL 60123 Fax: 847-429-2035
URL: www.shermanhealth.com
Type: Acute Care Hospitals Emergency Services: Yes
Ownership: Voluntary Non-Profit - Other Beds: 353

Key Personnel:
CEO/President. . . . . Richard B Floyd, FACHE
Chief of Medical Staff. . . . . Edgar Feldman, MD, FACS
Infection Control. . . . . Sallie Rivera, RN
Operating Room. . . . . Paula Bergschneider
Pediatric Ambulatory Care . . . . . . Patrick Esposito, MD
Pediatric In-Patient Care . . . . Patrick Esposito, MD
Quality Assurance . . . . Barbara Giardino
Radiology. . . . . Debbie Petges

Measure	Cases	This Hosp.	State Avg.	U.S. Avg.
Heart Attack Care				
ACE Inhibitor or ARB for LVSD[1]	20	100%	96%	96%
Aspirin at Arrival	161	100%	99%	99%
Aspirin at Discharge	162	99%	99%	98%
Beta Blocker at Discharge	164	100%	98%	98%
Fibrinolytic Medication Timing	0	-	50%	55%
PCI Within 90 Minutes of Arrival	49	96%	90%	90%
Smoking Cessation Advice	50	100%	100%	99%
Chest Pain/Possible Heart Attack Care				
Aspirin at Arrival[1,3]	2	100%	95%	95%
Median Time to ECG (minutes)[1,3]	3	10	8	8
Median Time to Transfer (minutes)[5]	0	-	57	61
Fibrinolytic Medication Timing[5]	0	-	33%	54%
Heart Failure Care				
ACE Inhibitor or ARB for LVSD	71	96%	94%	94%
Discharge Instructions	268	96%	89%	88%
Evaluation of LVS Function	342	98%	98%	98%
Smoking Cessation Advice	49	98%	99%	98%
Pneumonia Care				
Appropriate Initial Antibiotic	133	98%	90%	92%
Blood Culture Timing	235	100%	97%	96%
Influenza Vaccine	129	98%	91%	91%
Initial Antibiotic Timing	219	95%	96%	95%
Pneumococcal Vaccine	187	95%	92%	93%
Smoking Cessation Advice	74	96%	98%	97%
Surgical Care Improvement Project				
Appropriate VTP Within 24 Hours	320	100%	92%	92%
Appropriate Hair Removal	884	100%	99%	99%
Appropriate Beta Blocker Usage	293	98%	92%	93%
Controlled Postoperative Blood Glucose	101	98%	92%	93%
Prophylactic Antibiotic Timing	552	99%	97%	97%
Prophylactic Antibiotic Timing (Outpatient)	220	65%	93%	92%
Prophylactic Antibiotic Selection	555	97%	97%	97%
Prophylactic Antibiotic Select. (Outpatient)	220	82%	94%	94%
Prophylactic Antibiotic Stopped	503	100%	94%	94%
Recommended VTP Ordered	320	100%	94%	94%
Urinary Catheter Removal[1]	24	100%	89%	90%
Children's Asthma Care				
Received Systemic Corticosteroids	-	-	-	100%
Received Home Management Plan	-	-	-	71%
Received Reliever Medication	-	-	-	100%
Use of Medical Imaging				
Combination Abdominal CT Scan	787	0.243	0.246	0.191
Combination Chest CT Scan	620	0.147	0.098	0.054
Follow-up Mammogram/Ultrasound	1,663	6.8%	8.4%	8.4%
MRI for Low Back Pain	100	36.0%	33.4%	32.7%
Survey of Patients' Hospital Experiences				
Area Around Room 'Always' Quiet at Night	300+	62%	-	58%
Doctors 'Always' Communicated Well	300+	74%	-	80%
Home Recovery Information Given	300+	82%	-	82%
Hospital Given 9 or 10 on 10 Point Scale	300+	67%	-	67%
Meds 'Always' Explained Before Given	300+	57%	-	60%
Nurses 'Always' Communicated Well	300+	76%	-	76%
Pain 'Always' Well Controlled	300+	68%	-	69%
Room and Bathroom 'Always' Clean	300+	74%	-	71%
Timely Help 'Always' Received	300+	59%	-	64%
Would Definitely Recommend Hospital	300+	73%	-	69%

NOTE: Hospital profiles are in alphabetical order by state, then city, then hospital within the city; Rankings exclude hospitals with less than 25 cases except for patient surveys which excludes hospitals with less than 100 cases; (a) 100–299 cases; (1) The number of cases is too small to be sure how well a hospital is performing; (2) The hospital indicated that the data submitted for this measure were based on a sample of cases; (3) Data was collected during a shorter time period (fewer quarters) than the maximum possible time for this measure; (4) Suppressed for one or more quarters by CMS; (5) No data is available from the hospital for this measure; (6) Fewer than 100 patients completed the HCAHPS survey. Use these rates with caution, as the number of surveys may be too low to reliably assess hospital performance; (7) Survey results are based on less than 12 months of data; (8) Survey results are not available for this reporting period; (9) No or very few patients were eligible for the HCAHPS survey. The scores shown, if any, reflect a very small number of surveys; (10) A state average was not calculated because too few hospitals in the state submitted data; (11) There were discrepancies in the data collection process; Please refer to the User's Guide for a full explanation of data.

Alexian Brothers Medical Center

800 W Biesterfield Rd
Elk Grove Village, IL 60007
URL: www.alexian.org
Type: Acute Care Hospitals
Ownership: Voluntary Non-Profit - Church

Phone: 847-437-5500
Fax: 847-981-5766
Emergency Services: Yes
Beds: 483

Key Personnel:

CEO/President. . . . . John Werrbach
Cardiac Laboratory. . . . . Paul J. Grunenwald
Chief of Medical Staff . . . . Barry Glick, MD
Infection Control. . . . . Laura Marconnet
Pediatric In-Patient Care . . . . Patsy Buckberg
Radiology. . . . . Steve Jung
Emergency Room . . . . Rick Stephani, CHRM
Intensive Care Unit. . . . . Debra Perrin-Davis

Measure	Cases	This Hosp.	State Avg.	U.S. Avg.
Heart Attack Care				
ACE Inhibitor or ARB for LVSD	49	94%	96%	96%
Aspirin at Arrival	213	99%	99%	99%
Aspirin at Discharge	249	100%	99%	98%
Beta Blocker at Discharge	245	99%	98%	98%
Fibrinolytic Medication Timing	0	-	50%	55%
PCI Within 90 Minutes of Arrival	58	98%	90%	90%
Smoking Cessation Advice	85	100%	100%	99%
Chest Pain/Possible Heart Attack Care				
Aspirin at Arrival[1,3]	4	100%	95%	95%
Median Time to ECG (minutes)[1,3]	4	5	8	8
Median Time to Transfer (minutes)[5]	0	-	57	61
Fibrinolytic Medication Timing[5]	0	-	33%	54%
Heart Failure Care				
ACE Inhibitor or ARB for LVSD	137	94%	94%	94%
Discharge Instructions	398	96%	89%	88%
Evaluation of LVS Function	497	100%	98%	98%
Smoking Cessation Advice	44	100%	99%	98%
Pneumonia Care				
Appropriate Initial Antibiotic	202	89%	90%	92%
Blood Culture Timing	306	99%	97%	96%
Influenza Vaccine	256	85%	91%	91%
Initial Antibiotic Timing	320	96%	96%	95%
Pneumococcal Vaccine	378	94%	92%	93%
Smoking Cessation Advice	93	99%	98%	97%
Surgical Care Improvement Project				
Appropriate VTP Within 24 Hours[2]	269	97%	92%	92%
Appropriate Hair Removal[2]	728	100%	99%	99%
Appropriate Beta Blocker Usage[2]	278	99%	92%	93%
Controlled Postoperative Blood Glucose[2]	141	94%	92%	93%
Prophylactic Antibiotic Timing[2]	481	98%	97%	97%
Prophylactic Antibiotic Timing (Outpatient)	518	97%	93%	92%
Prophylactic Antibiotic Selection[2]	487	96%	97%	97%
Prophylactic Antibiotic Select. (Outpatient)	515	95%	94%	94%
Prophylactic Antibiotic Stopped[2]	414	95%	94%	94%
Recommended VTP Ordered[2]	269	98%	94%	94%
Urinary Catheter Removal[2]	158	91%	89%	90%
Children's Asthma Care				
Received Systemic Corticosteroids	-	-	-	100%
Received Home Management Plan	-	-	-	71%
Received Reliever Medication	-	-	-	100%
Use of Medical Imaging				
Combination Abdominal CT Scan	1,701	0.520	0.246	0.191
Combination Chest CT Scan	1,477	0.019	0.098	0.054
Follow-up Mammogram/Ultrasound	2,615	7.3%	8.4%	8.4%
MRI for Low Back Pain	235	31.1%	33.4%	32.7%
Survey of Patients' Hospital Experiences				
Area Around Room 'Always' Quiet at Night	300+	53%	-	58%
Doctors 'Always' Communicated Well	300+	80%	-	80%
Home Recovery Information Given	300+	83%	-	82%
Hospital Given 9 or 10 on 10 Point Scale	300+	71%	-	67%
Meds 'Always' Explained Before Given	300+	61%	-	60%
Nurses 'Always' Communicated Well	300+	79%	-	76%
Pain 'Always' Well Controlled	300+	69%	-	69%
Room and Bathroom 'Always' Clean	300+	77%	-	71%
Timely Help 'Always' Received	300+	63%	-	64%
Would Definitely Recommend Hospital	300+	77%	-	69%

Elmhurst Memorial Hospital

200 Berteau Ave
Elmhurst, IL 60126
URL: www.emhc.org
Type: Acute Care Hospitals
Ownership: Voluntary Non-Profit - Other

Phone: 630-833-1400
Fax: 630-782-7844
Emergency Services: Yes
Beds: 427

Key Personnel:

CEO/President. . . . . Leo F Fronza, Jr
Chief of Medical Staff . . . . Lawrence Barr, MD
Infection Control. . . . . Patricia Funderburk
Operating Room. . . . . Diane Drugas, MD
Pediatric In-Patient Care . . . . . . Edward Pont, MD
Quality Assurance . . . . Craig Grothaus
Radiology. . . . . Aloyzas Pakalniskis, MD
Emergency Room . . . . Fred Jacobs, MD

Measure	Cases	This Hosp.	State Avg.	U.S. Avg.
Heart Attack Care				
ACE Inhibitor or ARB for LVSD[2]	38	100%	96%	96%
Aspirin at Arrival[2]	213	100%	99%	99%
Aspirin at Discharge[2]	201	100%	99%	98%
Beta Blocker at Discharge[2]	196	100%	98%	98%
Fibrinolytic Medication Timing[2]	0	-	50%	55%
PCI Within 90 Minutes of Arrival[2]	33	97%	90%	90%
Smoking Cessation Advice[2]	48	100%	100%	99%
Chest Pain/Possible Heart Attack Care				
Aspirin at Arrival[3]	0	-	95%	95%
Median Time to ECG (minutes)[3]	0	-	8	8
Median Time to Transfer (minutes)[5]	0	-	57	61
Fibrinolytic Medication Timing[5]	0	-	33%	54%
Heart Failure Care				
ACE Inhibitor or ARB for LVSD[2]	90	98%	94%	94%
Discharge Instructions[2]	229	100%	89%	88%
Evaluation of LVS Function[2]	308	100%	98%	98%
Smoking Cessation Advice[2]	37	100%	99%	98%
Pneumonia Care				
Appropriate Initial Antibiotic[2]	82	93%	90%	92%
Blood Culture Timing[2]	151	99%	97%	96%
Influenza Vaccine[2]	100	95%	91%	91%
Initial Antibiotic Timing[2]	136	96%	96%	95%
Pneumococcal Vaccine[2]	143	94%	92%	93%
Smoking Cessation Advice[2]	35	100%	98%	97%
Surgical Care Improvement Project				
Appropriate VTP Within 24 Hours[2]	213	92%	92%	92%
Appropriate Hair Removal[2]	543	100%	99%	99%
Appropriate Beta Blocker Usage[2]	171	99%	92%	93%
Controlled Postoperative Blood Glucose[2]	112	99%	92%	93%
Prophylactic Antibiotic Timing[2]	368	99%	97%	97%
Prophylactic Antibiotic Timing (Outpatient)	167	96%	93%	92%
Prophylactic Antibiotic Selection[2]	375	99%	97%	97%
Prophylactic Antibiotic Select. (Outpatient)	163	91%	94%	94%
Prophylactic Antibiotic Stopped[2]	354	98%	94%	94%
Recommended VTP Ordered[2]	213	94%	94%	94%
Urinary Catheter Removal[2]	99	84%	89%	90%
Children's Asthma Care				
Received Systemic Corticosteroids	-	-	-	100%
Received Home Management Plan	-	-	-	71%
Received Reliever Medication	-	-	-	100%
Use of Medical Imaging				
Combination Abdominal CT Scan	1,591	0.155	0.246	0.191
Combination Chest CT Scan	1,321	0.041	0.098	0.054
Follow-up Mammogram/Ultrasound	2,231	13.0%	8.4%	8.4%
MRI for Low Back Pain	471	32.9%	33.4%	32.7%
Survey of Patients' Hospital Experiences				
Area Around Room 'Always' Quiet at Night	300+	49%	-	58%
Doctors 'Always' Communicated Well	300+	81%	-	80%
Home Recovery Information Given	300+	83%	-	82%
Hospital Given 9 or 10 on 10 Point Scale	300+	63%	-	67%
Meds 'Always' Explained Before Given	300+	60%	-	60%
Nurses 'Always' Communicated Well	300+	75%	-	76%
Pain 'Always' Well Controlled	300+	68%	-	69%
Room and Bathroom 'Always' Clean	300+	62%	-	71%
Timely Help 'Always' Received	300+	57%	-	64%
Would Definitely Recommend Hospital	300+	68%	-	69%

Advocate Eureka Hospital

101 S Major St
Eureka, IL 61530
E-mail: webmaster@bromenn.org
URL: www.eurekahospital.org
Type: Critical Access Hospitals
Ownership: Voluntary Non-Profit - Private

Phone: 309-467-2371
Fax: 309-467-2880
Emergency Services: Yes
Beds: 25

Key Personnel:

CEO/President. . . . . Roger S Hunt
Chief of Medical Staff . . . . Steven K Jones, DO
Coronary Care . . . . Jeff Williams
Infection Control. . . . . Henrietta Iwema, RN
Operating Room. . . . . Steve Holman
Quality Assurance . . . . Jane Ulrich
Anesthesiology. . . . . Rodney T McCalla, MD
Emergency Room . . . . Jeff Williams

Measure	Cases	This Hosp.	State Avg.	U.S. Avg.
Heart Attack Care				
ACE Inhibitor or ARB for LVSD[5]	0	-	96%	96%
Aspirin at Arrival[5]	0	-	99%	99%
Aspirin at Discharge[5]	0	-	99%	98%
Beta Blocker at Discharge[5]	0	-	98%	98%
Fibrinolytic Medication Timing[5]	0	-	50%	55%
PCI Within 90 Minutes of Arrival[5]	0	-	90%	90%
Smoking Cessation Advice[5]	0	-	100%	99%
Chest Pain/Possible Heart Attack Care				
Aspirin at Arrival[1]	21	100%	95%	95%
Median Time to ECG (minutes)[1]	21	4	8	8
Median Time to Transfer (minutes)[1]	2	118	57	61
Fibrinolytic Medication Timing	0	-	33%	54%
Heart Failure Care				
ACE Inhibitor or ARB for LVSD[1]	10	90%	94%	94%
Discharge Instructions[1]	9	78%	89%	88%
Evaluation of LVS Function[1]	23	100%	98%	98%
Smoking Cessation Advice[1]	1	100%	99%	98%
Pneumonia Care				
Appropriate Initial Antibiotic[1]	16	100%	90%	92%
Blood Culture Timing[1]	21	100%	97%	96%
Influenza Vaccine[1]	19	95%	91%	91%
Initial Antibiotic Timing[1]	24	100%	96%	95%
Pneumococcal Vaccine	32	97%	92%	93%
Smoking Cessation Advice[1]	4	100%	98%	97%
Surgical Care Improvement Project				
Appropriate VTP Within 24 Hours[5]	0	-	92%	92%
Appropriate Hair Removal[5]	0	-	99%	99%
Appropriate Beta Blocker Usage[5]	0	-	92%	93%
Controlled Postoperative Blood Glucose[5]	0	-	92%	93%
Prophylactic Antibiotic Timing[5]	0	-	97%	97%
Prophylactic Antibiotic Timing (Outpatient)[5]	0	-	93%	92%
Prophylactic Antibiotic Selection[5]	0	-	97%	97%
Prophylactic Antibiotic Select. (Outpatient)[5]	0	-	94%	94%
Prophylactic Antibiotic Stopped[5]	0	-	94%	94%
Recommended VTP Ordered[5]	0	-	94%	94%
Urinary Catheter Removal[5]	0	-	89%	90%
Children's Asthma Care				
Received Systemic Corticosteroids	-	-	-	100%
Received Home Management Plan	-	-	-	71%
Received Reliever Medication	-	-	-	100%
Use of Medical Imaging				
Combination Abdominal CT Scan	124	0.806	0.246	0.191
Combination Chest CT Scan	95	0.684	0.098	0.054
Follow-up Mammogram/Ultrasound	222	4.5%	8.4%	8.4%
MRI for Low Back Pain[1]	31	41.9%	33.4%	32.7%
Survey of Patients' Hospital Experiences				
Area Around Room 'Always' Quiet at Night[8]	-	-	-	58%
Doctors 'Always' Communicated Well[8]	-	-	-	80%
Home Recovery Information Given[8]	-	-	-	82%
Hospital Given 9 or 10 on 10 Point Scale[8]	-	-	-	67%
Meds 'Always' Explained Before Given[8]	-	-	-	60%
Nurses 'Always' Communicated Well[8]	-	-	-	76%
Pain 'Always' Well Controlled[8]	-	-	-	69%
Room and Bathroom 'Always' Clean[8]	-	-	-	71%
Timely Help 'Always' Received[8]	-	-	-	64%
Would Definitely Recommend Hospital[8]	-	-	-	69%

NOTE: Hospital profiles are in alphabetical order by state, then city, then hospital within the city; Rankings exclude hospitals with less than 25 cases except for patient surveys which excludes hospitals with less than 100 cases; (a) 100–299 cases; (1) The number of cases is too small to be sure how well a hospital is performing; (2) The hospital indicated that the data submitted for this measure were based on a sample of cases; (3) Data was collected during a shorter time period (fewer quarters) than the maximum possible time for this measure; (4) Suppressed for one or more quarters by CMS; (5) No data is available from the hospital for this measure; (6) Fewer than 100 patients completed the HCAHPS survey. Use these rates with caution, as the number of surveys may be too low to reliably assess hospital performance; (7) Survey results are based on less than 12 months of data; (8) Survey results are not available for this reporting period; (9) No or very few patients were eligible for the HCAHPS survey. The scores shown, if any, reflect a very small number of surveys; (10) A state average was not calculated because too few hospitals in the state submitted data; (11) There were discrepancies in the data collection process; Please refer to the User's Guide for a full explanation of data.

Evanston Hospital

2650 Ridge Ave
Evanston, IL 60201
URL: www.enh.org
Type: Acute Care Hospitals
Ownership: Voluntary Non-Profit - Other
Phone: 847-432-8000
Fax: 847-570-5243
Emergency Services: Yes
Beds: 635

Key Personnel:
CEO/President. . . . . Mark Neaman
Chief of Medical Staff . . . . Arnold Wagner
Infection Control. . . . . Kay O'Connor, RN
Operating Room. . . . . Bill Duffy
Quality Assurance . . . . Emma Hooks
Radiology. . . . . Russell Zage

Measure	Cases	This Hosp.	State Avg.	U.S. Avg.
Heart Attack Care				
ACE Inhibitor or ARB for LVSD	50	96%	96%	96%
Aspirin at Arrival	412	99%	99%	99%
Aspirin at Discharge	392	99%	99%	98%
Beta Blocker at Discharge	384	99%	98%	98%
Fibrinolytic Medication Timing	0	-	50%	55%
PCI Within 90 Minutes of Arrival	82	96%	90%	90%
Smoking Cessation Advice	70	100%	100%	99%
Chest Pain/Possible Heart Attack Care				
Aspirin at Arrival[5]	0	-	95%	95%
Median Time to ECG (minutes)[5]	0	-	8	8
Median Time to Transfer (minutes)[5]	0	-	57	61
Fibrinolytic Medication Timing[5]	0	-	33%	54%
Heart Failure Care				
ACE Inhibitor or ARB for LVSD	231	95%	94%	94%
Discharge Instructions	695	96%	89%	88%
Evaluation of LVS Function	993	100%	98%	98%
Smoking Cessation Advice	85	96%	99%	98%
Pneumonia Care				
Appropriate Initial Antibiotic[2]	106	97%	90%	92%
Blood Culture Timing[2]	180	98%	97%	96%
Influenza Vaccine[2]	129	98%	91%	91%
Initial Antibiotic Timing[2]	165	99%	96%	95%
Pneumococcal Vaccine[2]	194	97%	92%	93%
Smoking Cessation Advice[2]	34	100%	98%	97%
Surgical Care Improvement Project				
Appropriate VTP Within 24 Hours[2]	537	99%	92%	92%
Appropriate Hair Removal[2]	1,658	100%	99%	99%
Appropriate Beta Blocker Usage[2]	461	100%	92%	93%
Controlled Postoperative Blood Glucose[2]	225	99%	92%	93%
Prophylactic Antibiotic Timing[2]	1,123	99%	97%	97%
Prophylactic Antibiotic Timing (Outpatient)	623	99%	93%	92%
Prophylactic Antibiotic Selection[2]	1,132	98%	97%	97%
Prophylactic Antibiotic Select. (Outpatient)	619	94%	94%	94%
Prophylactic Antibiotic Stopped[2]	1,080	99%	94%	94%
Recommended VTP Ordered[2]	537	99%	94%	94%
Urinary Catheter Removal[2]	260	98%	89%	90%
Children's Asthma Care				
Received Systemic Corticosteroids	-	-	-	100%
Received Home Management Plan	-	-	-	71%
Received Reliever Medication	-	-	-	100%
Use of Medical Imaging				
Combination Abdominal CT Scan	5,038	0.236	0.246	0.191
Combination Chest CT Scan	5,565	0.040	0.098	0.054
Follow-up Mammogram/Ultrasound	9,551	4.4%	8.4%	8.4%
MRI for Low Back Pain	1,226	31.1%	33.4%	32.7%
Survey of Patients' Hospital Experiences				
Area Around Room 'Always' Quiet at Night	300+	57%	-	58%
Doctors 'Always' Communicated Well	300+	77%	-	80%
Home Recovery Information Given	300+	81%	-	82%
Hospital Given 9 or 10 on 10 Point Scale	300+	70%	-	67%
Meds 'Always' Explained Before Given	300+	56%	-	60%
Nurses 'Always' Communicated Well	300+	74%	-	76%
Pain 'Always' Well Controlled	300+	67%	-	69%
Room and Bathroom 'Always' Clean	300+	69%	-	71%
Timely Help 'Always' Received	300+	56%	-	64%
Would Definitely Recommend Hospital	300+	76%	-	69%

RHC St Francis Hospital

355 Ridge Ave
Evanston, IL 60202
URL: www.reshealth.org
Type: Acute Care Hospitals
Ownership: Voluntary Non-Profit - Church
Phone: 847-316-4000
Fax: 847-316-4500
Emergency Services: Yes
Beds: 445

Key Personnel:
CEO/President. . . . . Jeffrey Murphy
Chief of Medical Staff . . . . Ann Kinnealey, MD
Infection Control. . . . . Chris Costas, MD
Operating Room. . . . . Pamela Bemaung, RN
Pediatric Ambulatory Care . . . . . . Chris Costas, MD
Pediatric In-Patient Care . . . . . . Chris Costas, MD
Quality Assurance . . . . Lori Biala-Smith
Radiology. . . . . Thomas Cronin, MD

Measure	Cases	This Hosp.	State Avg.	U.S. Avg.
Heart Attack Care				
ACE Inhibitor or ARB for LVSD[1]	13	69%	96%	96%
Aspirin at Arrival	106	98%	99%	99%
Aspirin at Discharge	101	100%	99%	98%
Beta Blocker at Discharge	96	88%	98%	98%
Fibrinolytic Medication Timing	0	-	50%	55%
PCI Within 90 Minutes of Arrival[1]	24	88%	90%	90%
Smoking Cessation Advice[1]	24	100%	100%	99%
Chest Pain/Possible Heart Attack Care				
Aspirin at Arrival[1,3]	4	100%	95%	95%
Median Time to ECG (minutes)[1,3]	4	8	8	8
Median Time to Transfer (minutes)[5]	0	-	57	61
Fibrinolytic Medication Timing[5]	0	-	33%	54%
Heart Failure Care				
ACE Inhibitor or ARB for LVSD	84	87%	94%	94%
Discharge Instructions	224	94%	89%	88%
Evaluation of LVS Function	304	98%	98%	98%
Smoking Cessation Advice	44	100%	99%	98%
Pneumonia Care				
Appropriate Initial Antibiotic	173	75%	90%	92%
Blood Culture Timing	422	98%	97%	96%
Influenza Vaccine	255	92%	91%	91%
Initial Antibiotic Timing	385	97%	96%	95%
Pneumococcal Vaccine	333	92%	92%	93%
Smoking Cessation Advice	64	100%	98%	97%
Surgical Care Improvement Project				
Appropriate VTP Within 24 Hours[2]	335	92%	92%	92%
Appropriate Hair Removal[2]	572	99%	99%	99%
Appropriate Beta Blocker Usage[2]	136	73%	92%	93%
Controlled Postoperative Blood Glucose[2]	64	83%	92%	93%
Prophylactic Antibiotic Timing[2]	364	97%	97%	97%
Prophylactic Antibiotic Timing (Outpatient)	73	82%	93%	92%
Prophylactic Antibiotic Selection[2]	367	96%	97%	97%
Prophylactic Antibiotic Select. (Outpatient)	67	88%	94%	94%
Prophylactic Antibiotic Stopped[2]	332	89%	94%	94%
Recommended VTP Ordered[2]	335	95%	94%	94%
Urinary Catheter Removal[2]	78	63%	89%	90%
Children's Asthma Care				
Received Systemic Corticosteroids	-	-	-	100%
Received Home Management Plan	-	-	-	71%
Received Reliever Medication	-	-	-	100%
Use of Medical Imaging				
Combination Abdominal CT Scan	626	0.380	0.246	0.191
Combination Chest CT Scan	454	0.330	0.098	0.054
Follow-up Mammogram/Ultrasound	1,123	14.2%	8.4%	8.4%
MRI for Low Back Pain	69	42.0%	33.4%	32.7%
Survey of Patients' Hospital Experiences				
Area Around Room 'Always' Quiet at Night	300+	42%	-	58%
Doctors 'Always' Communicated Well	300+	73%	-	80%
Home Recovery Information Given	300+	79%	-	82%
Hospital Given 9 or 10 on 10 Point Scale	300+	58%	-	67%
Meds 'Always' Explained Before Given	300+	48%	-	60%
Nurses 'Always' Communicated Well	300+	69%	-	76%
Pain 'Always' Well Controlled	300+	63%	-	69%
Room and Bathroom 'Always' Clean	300+	63%	-	71%
Timely Help 'Always' Received	300+	57%	-	64%
Would Definitely Recommend Hospital	300+	62%	-	69%

Little Company of Mary Hospital

2800 W 95th St
Evergreen Park, IL 60805
URL: www.lcmh.org
Type: Acute Care Hospitals
Ownership: Voluntary Non-Profit - Church
Phone: 708-422-6200
Fax: 708-229-6733
Emergency Services: Yes
Beds: 487

Key Personnel:
Cardiac Laboratory. . . . . Kathy Paul
Chief of Medical Staff . . . . Kent Armruster MD
Infection Control. . . . . Carol Hoffman
Operating Room. . . . . Marilyn Coonin
Pediatric Ambulatory Care . . . . . . Hassan Alzan MD
Radiology. . . . . George Saprenza
Emergency Room . . . . Michael O'Mara DO
Intensive Care Unit. . . . . Jim Boyle

Measure	Cases	This Hosp.	State Avg.	U.S. Avg.
Heart Attack Care				
ACE Inhibitor or ARB for LVSD[1]	22	100%	96%	96%
Aspirin at Arrival	109	100%	99%	99%
Aspirin at Discharge	81	100%	99%	98%
Beta Blocker at Discharge	79	100%	98%	98%
Fibrinolytic Medication Timing	0	-	50%	55%
PCI Within 90 Minutes of Arrival[1]	18	94%	90%	90%
Smoking Cessation Advice[1]	20	100%	100%	99%
Chest Pain/Possible Heart Attack Care				
Aspirin at Arrival[1]	7	71%	95%	95%
Median Time to ECG (minutes)[1]	8	4	8	8
Median Time to Transfer (minutes)[5]	0	-	57	61
Fibrinolytic Medication Timing[5]	0	-	33%	54%
Heart Failure Care				
ACE Inhibitor or ARB for LVSD[2]	93	100%	94%	94%
Discharge Instructions[2]	263	84%	89%	88%
Evaluation of LVS Function[2]	327	100%	98%	98%
Smoking Cessation Advice[2]	66	100%	99%	98%
Pneumonia Care				
Appropriate Initial Antibiotic[2]	82	94%	90%	92%
Blood Culture Timing[2]	116	100%	97%	96%
Influenza Vaccine[2]	79	100%	91%	91%
Initial Antibiotic Timing[2]	143	98%	96%	95%
Pneumococcal Vaccine[2]	143	96%	92%	93%
Smoking Cessation Advice[2]	49	100%	98%	97%
Surgical Care Improvement Project				
Appropriate VTP Within 24 Hours[2]	240	99%	92%	92%
Appropriate Hair Removal[2]	478	100%	99%	99%
Appropriate Beta Blocker Usage[2]	118	98%	92%	93%
Controlled Postoperative Blood Glucose[2]	0	-	92%	93%
Prophylactic Antibiotic Timing[2]	283	99%	97%	97%
Prophylactic Antibiotic Timing (Outpatient)	242	96%	93%	92%
Prophylactic Antibiotic Selection[2]	285	98%	97%	97%
Prophylactic Antibiotic Select. (Outpatient)	239	99%	94%	94%
Prophylactic Antibiotic Stopped[2]	247	99%	94%	94%
Recommended VTP Ordered[2]	240	100%	94%	94%
Urinary Catheter Removal[2]	66	100%	89%	90%
Children's Asthma Care				
Received Systemic Corticosteroids	-	-	-	100%
Received Home Management Plan	-	-	-	71%
Received Reliever Medication	-	-	-	100%
Use of Medical Imaging				
Combination Abdominal CT Scan	977	0.125	0.246	0.191
Combination Chest CT Scan	887	0.023	0.098	0.054
Follow-up Mammogram/Ultrasound	1,729	11.9%	8.4%	8.4%
MRI for Low Back Pain	103	32.0%	33.4%	32.7%
Survey of Patients' Hospital Experiences				
Area Around Room 'Always' Quiet at Night	300+	51%	-	58%
Doctors 'Always' Communicated Well	300+	79%	-	80%
Home Recovery Information Given	300+	79%	-	82%
Hospital Given 9 or 10 on 10 Point Scale	300+	65%	-	67%
Meds 'Always' Explained Before Given	300+	55%	-	60%
Nurses 'Always' Communicated Well	300+	75%	-	76%
Pain 'Always' Well Controlled	300+	69%	-	69%
Room and Bathroom 'Always' Clean	300+	65%	-	71%
Timely Help 'Always' Received	300+	60%	-	64%
Would Definitely Recommend Hospital	300+	67%	-	69%

NOTE: Hospital profiles are in alphabetical order by state, then city, then hospital within the city; Rankings exclude hospitals with less than 25 cases except for patient surveys which excludes hospitals with less than 100 cases; (a) 100–299 cases; (1) The number of cases is too small to be sure how well a hospital is performing; (2) The hospital indicated that the data submitted for this measure were based on a sample of cases; (3) Data was collected during a shorter time period (fewer quarters) than the maximum possible time for this measure; (4) Suppressed for one or more quarters by CMS; (5) No data is available from the hospital for this measure; (6) Fewer than 100 patients completed the HCAHPS survey. Use these rates with caution, as the number of surveys may be too low to reliably assess hospital performance; (7) Survey results are based on less than 12 months of data; (8) Survey results are not available for this reporting period; (9) No or very few patients were eligible for the HCAHPS survey. The scores shown, if any, reflect a very small number of surveys; (10) A state average was not calculated because too few hospitals in the state submitted data; (11) There were discrepancies in the data collection process; Please refer to the User's Guide for a full explanation of data.

Fairfield Memorial Hospital

303 N W 11th Street
Fairfield, IL 62837
Phone: 618-842-2611
Fax: 618-842-2011
URL: www.fairfieldob.com
Type: Critical Access Hospitals
Emergency Services: Yes
Ownership: Voluntary Non-Profit - Private
Beds: 80

Key Personnel:

CEO/President. . . . . Michale Brown
Chief of Medical Staff. . . . . Patrick Molt
Infection Control. . . . . Hazel Best, RN
Quality Assurance . . . . Frances Strange
Radiology. . . . . Enrique Bouffar III
Emergency Room . . . . Bo Schneider, MD

Measure	Cases	This Hosp.	State Avg.	U.S. Avg.
Heart Attack Care				
ACE Inhibitor or ARB for LVSD[1]	1	100%	96%	96%
Aspirin at Arrival[1]	10	80%	99%	99%
Aspirin at Discharge[1]	6	50%	99%	98%
Beta Blocker at Discharge[1]	6	50%	98%	98%
Fibrinolytic Medication Timing	0	-	50%	55%
PCI Within 90 Minutes of Arrival	0	-	90%	90%
Smoking Cessation Advice	0	-	100%	99%
Chest Pain/Possible Heart Attack Care				
Aspirin at Arrival	76	95%	95%	95%
Median Time to ECG (minutes)	82	10	8	8
Median Time to Transfer (minutes)[3]	0	-	57	61
Fibrinolytic Medication Timing[3]	0	-	33%	54%
Heart Failure Care				
ACE Inhibitor or ARB for LVSD[1]	11	55%	94%	94%
Discharge Instructions[1]	16	75%	89%	88%
Evaluation of LVS Function	29	100%	98%	98%
Smoking Cessation Advice[1]	2	50%	99%	98%
Pneumonia Care				
Appropriate Initial Antibiotic[1]	22	73%	90%	92%
Blood Culture Timing	28	100%	97%	96%
Influenza Vaccine	30	100%	91%	91%
Initial Antibiotic Timing	36	92%	96%	95%
Pneumococcal Vaccine	35	100%	92%	93%
Smoking Cessation Advice[1]	10	100%	98%	97%
Surgical Care Improvement Project				
Appropriate VTP Within 24 Hours	30	100%	92%	92%
Appropriate Hair Removal	43	100%	99%	99%
Appropriate Beta Blocker Usage[5]	0	-	92%	93%
Controlled Postoperative Blood Glucose	0	-	92%	93%
Prophylactic Antibiotic Timing[1]	21	100%	97%	97%
Prophylactic Antibiotic Timing (Outpatient)	36	97%	93%	92%
Prophylactic Antibiotic Selection[1]	22	100%	97%	97%
Prophylactic Antibiotic Select. (Outpatient)	36	86%	94%	94%
Prophylactic Antibiotic Stopped[1]	21	100%	94%	94%
Recommended VTP Ordered	30	100%	94%	94%
Urinary Catheter Removal[1]	4	75%	89%	90%
Children's Asthma Care				
Received Systemic Corticosteroids	-	-	-	100%
Received Home Management Plan	-	-	-	71%
Received Reliever Medication	-	-	-	100%
Use of Medical Imaging				
Combination Abdominal CT Scan	390	0.533	0.246	0.191
Combination Chest CT Scan	238	0.042	0.098	0.054
Follow-up Mammogram/Ultrasound	365	0.5%	8.4%	8.4%
MRI for Low Back Pain	35	45.7%	33.4%	32.7%
Survey of Patients' Hospital Experiences				
Area Around Room 'Always' Quiet at Night[8]	-	-	-	58%
Doctors 'Always' Communicated Well[8]	-	-	-	80%
Home Recovery Information Given[8]	-	-	-	82%
Hospital Given 9 or 10 on 10 Point Scale[8]	-	-	-	67%
Meds 'Always' Explained Before Given[8]	-	-	-	60%
Nurses 'Always' Communicated Well[8]	-	-	-	76%
Pain 'Always' Well Controlled[8]	-	-	-	69%
Room and Bathroom 'Always' Clean[8]	-	-	-	71%
Timely Help 'Always' Received[8]	-	-	-	64%
Would Definitely Recommend Hospital[8]	-	-	-	69%

Clay County Hospital

911 Stacy Burk Drive
Flora, IL 62839
Phone: 618-662-2131
Fax: 618-662-1486
E-mail: cchdas@wabash.net
URL: www.claycountyhospital.org
Type: Critical Access Hospitals
Emergency Services: Yes
Ownership: Voluntary Non-Profit - Other
Beds: 18

Key Personnel:

CEO/President. . . . . Steven H Lipstein
Chief of Medical Staff. . . . . Jennifer Maneja
Quality Assurance . . . . Mike Anderson
Radiology. . . . . Preecha Tawjareon
Emergency Room . . . . Eileen Enlow, RN

Measure	Cases	This Hosp.	State Avg.	U.S. Avg.
Heart Attack Care				
ACE Inhibitor or ARB for LVSD	0	-	96%	96%
Aspirin at Arrival[1]	11	91%	99%	99%
Aspirin at Discharge[1]	4	100%	99%	98%
Beta Blocker at Discharge[1]	3	100%	98%	98%
Fibrinolytic Medication Timing	0	-	50%	55%
PCI Within 90 Minutes of Arrival	0	-	90%	90%
Smoking Cessation Advice[1]	1	100%	100%	99%
Chest Pain/Possible Heart Attack Care				
Aspirin at Arrival	58	98%	95%	95%
Median Time to ECG (minutes)	54	15	8	8
Median Time to Transfer (minutes)[5]	0	-	57	61
Fibrinolytic Medication Timing	0	-	33%	54%
Heart Failure Care				
ACE Inhibitor or ARB for LVSD[1]	11	91%	94%	94%
Discharge Instructions	29	90%	89%	88%
Evaluation of LVS Function	44	98%	98%	98%
Smoking Cessation Advice[1]	5	100%	99%	98%
Pneumonia Care				
Appropriate Initial Antibiotic	49	94%	90%	92%
Blood Culture Timing	68	100%	97%	96%
Influenza Vaccine	35	94%	91%	91%
Initial Antibiotic Timing	74	97%	96%	95%
Pneumococcal Vaccine	54	93%	92%	93%
Smoking Cessation Advice[1]	19	100%	98%	97%
Surgical Care Improvement Project				
Appropriate VTP Within 24 Hours[1,3]	7	100%	92%	92%
Appropriate Hair Removal[1,3]	7	100%	99%	99%
Appropriate Beta Blocker Usage[3]	0	-	92%	93%
Controlled Postoperative Blood Glucose[3]	0	-	92%	93%
Prophylactic Antibiotic Timing[1,3]	3	100%	97%	97%
Prophylactic Antibiotic Timing (Outpatient)[1]	6	33%	93%	92%
Prophylactic Antibiotic Selection[1,3]	3	67%	97%	97%
Prophylactic Antibiotic Select. (Outpatient)[1]	4	100%	94%	94%
Prophylactic Antibiotic Stopped[1,3]	3	67%	94%	94%
Recommended VTP Ordered[1,3]	7	100%	94%	94%
Urinary Catheter Removal[1]	2	100%	89%	90%
Children's Asthma Care				
Received Systemic Corticosteroids	-	-	-	100%
Received Home Management Plan	-	-	-	71%
Received Reliever Medication	-	-	-	100%
Use of Medical Imaging				
Combination Abdominal CT Scan	263	0.567	0.246	0.191
Combination Chest CT Scan	218	0.032	0.098	0.054
Follow-up Mammogram/Ultrasound	385	6.5%	8.4%	8.4%
MRI for Low Back Pain[1]	12	33.3%	33.4%	32.7%
Survey of Patients' Hospital Experiences				
Area Around Room 'Always' Quiet at Night[8]	-	-	-	58%
Doctors 'Always' Communicated Well[8]	-	-	-	80%
Home Recovery Information Given[8]	-	-	-	82%
Hospital Given 9 or 10 on 10 Point Scale[8]	-	-	-	67%
Meds 'Always' Explained Before Given[8]	-	-	-	60%
Nurses 'Always' Communicated Well[8]	-	-	-	76%
Pain 'Always' Well Controlled[8]	-	-	-	69%
Room and Bathroom 'Always' Clean[8]	-	-	-	71%
Timely Help 'Always' Received[8]	-	-	-	64%
Would Definitely Recommend Hospital[8]	-	-	-	69%

Fhn Memorial Hospital

1045 West Stephenson Street
Freeport, IL 61032
Phone: 815-235-4131
Fax: 815-599-6417
E-mail: wecare@fhn.org
URL: www.fhn.org
Type: Acute Care Hospitals
Emergency Services: Yes
Ownership: Voluntary Non-Profit - Private
Beds: 194

Key Personnel:

CEO/President. . . . . Michael Perry
Chief of Medical Staff. . . . . Alan Esker
Operating Room. . . . . Barry Barnes
Radiology. . . . . Gustavo Espinosa

Measure	Cases	This Hosp.	State Avg.	U.S. Avg.
Heart Attack Care				
ACE Inhibitor or ARB for LVSD[1]	12	100%	96%	96%
Aspirin at Arrival	65	100%	99%	99%
Aspirin at Discharge	58	98%	99%	98%
Beta Blocker at Discharge	58	98%	98%	98%
Fibrinolytic Medication Timing	0	-	50%	55%
PCI Within 90 Minutes of Arrival[1]	5	100%	90%	90%
Smoking Cessation Advice[1]	13	100%	100%	99%
Chest Pain/Possible Heart Attack Care				
Aspirin at Arrival	35	100%	95%	95%
Median Time to ECG (minutes)	35	6	8	8
Median Time to Transfer (minutes)[1,3]	8	61	57	61
Fibrinolytic Medication Timing[1]	3	33%	33%	54%
Heart Failure Care				
ACE Inhibitor or ARB for LVSD	59	97%	94%	94%
Discharge Instructions	100	87%	89%	88%
Evaluation of LVS Function	164	100%	98%	98%
Smoking Cessation Advice[1]	16	75%	99%	98%
Pneumonia Care				
Appropriate Initial Antibiotic	91	92%	90%	92%
Blood Culture Timing	145	97%	97%	96%
Influenza Vaccine	92	96%	91%	91%
Initial Antibiotic Timing	141	99%	96%	95%
Pneumococcal Vaccine	126	95%	92%	93%
Smoking Cessation Advice	37	86%	98%	97%
Surgical Care Improvement Project				
Appropriate VTP Within 24 Hours[2]	115	91%	92%	92%
Appropriate Hair Removal[2]	429	100%	99%	99%
Appropriate Beta Blocker Usage[2]	133	94%	92%	93%
Controlled Postoperative Blood Glucose[2]	0	-	92%	93%
Prophylactic Antibiotic Timing[2]	291	99%	97%	97%
Prophylactic Antibiotic Timing (Outpatient)	92	92%	93%	92%
Prophylactic Antibiotic Selection[2]	292	94%	97%	97%
Prophylactic Antibiotic Select. (Outpatient)	142	99%	94%	94%
Prophylactic Antibiotic Stopped[2]	276	99%	94%	94%
Recommended VTP Ordered[2]	115	97%	94%	94%
Urinary Catheter Removal[1]	21	95%	89%	90%
Children's Asthma Care				
Received Systemic Corticosteroids	-	-	-	100%
Received Home Management Plan	-	-	-	71%
Received Reliever Medication	-	-	-	100%
Use of Medical Imaging				
Combination Abdominal CT Scan	508	0.073	0.246	0.191
Combination Chest CT Scan	353	0.003	0.098	0.054
Follow-up Mammogram/Ultrasound	1,016	5.8%	8.4%	8.4%
MRI for Low Back Pain	143	33.6%	33.4%	32.7%
Survey of Patients' Hospital Experiences				
Area Around Room 'Always' Quiet at Night	300+	54%	-	58%
Doctors 'Always' Communicated Well	300+	76%	-	80%
Home Recovery Information Given	300+	80%	-	82%
Hospital Given 9 or 10 on 10 Point Scale	300+	61%	-	67%
Meds 'Always' Explained Before Given	300+	61%	-	60%
Nurses 'Always' Communicated Well	300+	76%	-	76%
Pain 'Always' Well Controlled	300+	65%	-	69%
Room and Bathroom 'Always' Clean	300+	69%	-	71%
Timely Help 'Always' Received	300+	59%	-	64%
Would Definitely Recommend Hospital	300+	55%	-	69%

NOTE: Hospital profiles are in alphabetical order by state, then city, then hospital within the city; Rankings exclude hospitals with less than 25 cases except for patient surveys which excludes hospitals with less than 100 cases; (a) 100–299 cases; (1) The number of cases is too small to be sure how well a hospital is performing; (2) The hospital indicated that the data submitted for this measure were based on a sample of cases; (3) Data was collected during a shorter time period (fewer quarters) than the maximum possible time for this measure; (4) Suppressed for one or more quarters by CMS; (5) No data is available from the hospital for this measure; (6) Fewer than 100 patients completed the HCAHPS survey. Use these rates with caution, as the number of surveys may be too low to reliably assess hospital performance; (7) Survey results are based on less than 12 months of data; (8) Survey results are not available for this reporting period; (9) No or very few patients were eligible for the HCAHPS survey. The scores shown, if any, reflect a very small number of surveys; (10) A state average was not calculated because too few hospitals in the state submitted data; (11) There were discrepancies in the data collection process; Please refer to the User's Guide for a full explanation of data.

Midwest Medical Center

One Medical Center Drive
Galena, IL 61036
Phone: 815-777-1340
Type: Critical Access Hospitals
Emergency Services: Yes
Ownership: Voluntary Non-Profit - Private

Measure	Cases	This Hosp.	State Avg.	U.S. Avg.
Heart Attack Care				
ACE Inhibitor or ARB for LVSD[5]	0	-	96%	96%
Aspirin at Arrival[5]	0	-	99%	99%
Aspirin at Discharge[5]	0	-	99%	98%
Beta Blocker at Discharge[5]	0	-	98%	98%
Fibrinolytic Medication Timing[5]	0	-	50%	55%
PCI Within 90 Minutes of Arrival[5]	0	-	90%	90%
Smoking Cessation Advice[5]	0	-	100%	99%
Chest Pain/Possible Heart Attack Care				
Aspirin at Arrival	-	-	95%	95%
Median Time to ECG (minutes)	-	-	8	8
Median Time to Transfer (minutes)	-	-	57	61
Fibrinolytic Medication Timing	-	-	33%	54%
Heart Failure Care				
ACE Inhibitor or ARB for LVSD[5]	0	-	94%	94%
Discharge Instructions[5]	0	-	89%	88%
Evaluation of LVS Function[5]	0	-	98%	98%
Smoking Cessation Advice[5]	0	-	99%	98%
Pneumonia Care				
Appropriate Initial Antibiotic[1,3]	1	100%	90%	92%
Blood Culture Timing[1,3]	3	67%	97%	96%
Influenza Vaccine[5]	0	-	91%	91%
Initial Antibiotic Timing[1,3]	6	100%	96%	95%
Pneumococcal Vaccine[1,3]	5	80%	92%	93%
Smoking Cessation Advice[1,3]	1	0%	98%	97%
Surgical Care Improvement Project				
Appropriate VTP Within 24 Hours[5]	0	-	92%	92%
Appropriate Hair Removal[5]	0	-	99%	99%
Appropriate Beta Blocker Usage[5]	0	-	92%	93%
Controlled Postoperative Blood Glucose[5]	0	-	92%	93%
Prophylactic Antibiotic Timing[5]	0	-	97%	97%
Prophylactic Antibiotic Timing (Outpatient)	-	-	93%	92%
Prophylactic Antibiotic Selection[5]	0	-	97%	97%
Prophylactic Antibiotic Select. (Outpatient)	-	-	94%	94%
Prophylactic Antibiotic Stopped[5]	0	-	94%	94%
Recommended VTP Ordered[5]	0	-	94%	94%
Urinary Catheter Removal[5]	0	-	89%	90%
Children's Asthma Care				
Received Systemic Corticosteroids	-	-	-	100%
Received Home Management Plan	-	-	-	71%
Received Reliever Medication	-	-	-	100%
Use of Medical Imaging				
Combination Abdominal CT Scan	-	-	0.246	0.191
Combination Chest CT Scan	-	-	0.098	0.054
Follow-up Mammogram/Ultrasound	-	-	8.4%	8.4%
MRI for Low Back Pain	-	-	33.4%	32.7%
Survey of Patients' Hospital Experiences				
Area Around Room 'Always' Quiet at Night[8]	-	-	-	58%
Doctors 'Always' Communicated Well[8]	-	-	-	80%
Home Recovery Information Given[8]	-	-	-	82%
Hospital Given 9 or 10 on 10 Point Scale[8]	-	-	-	67%
Meds 'Always' Explained Before Given[8]	-	-	-	60%
Nurses 'Always' Communicated Well[8]	-	-	-	76%
Pain 'Always' Well Controlled[8]	-	-	-	69%
Room and Bathroom 'Always' Clean[8]	-	-	-	71%
Timely Help 'Always' Received[8]	-	-	-	64%
Would Definitely Recommend Hospital[8]	-	-	-	69%

Galesburg Cottage Hospital

695 N Kellogg St
Galesburg, IL 61401
Phone: 309-345-4555
Fax: 309-343-2393
URL: www.cottagehospital.com
Type: Acute Care Hospitals
Emergency Services: Yes
Ownership: Proprietary
Beds: 170

Key Personnel:
CEO/President. . . . . Kenneth Hutchenrider
Cardiac Laboratory. . . . . Johanna Steller
Chief of Medical Staff . . . . Mark Daus, MD
Coronary Care . . . . Deb Rickard
Infection Control. . . . . Linda Newcomb
Operating Room. . . . . Alan Willis
Radiology. . . . . Jared Browning

Measure	Cases	This Hosp.	State Avg.	U.S. Avg.
Heart Attack Care				
ACE Inhibitor or ARB for LVSD[1]	3	100%	96%	96%
Aspirin at Arrival	35	100%	99%	99%
Aspirin at Discharge	28	96%	99%	98%
Beta Blocker at Discharge	28	100%	98%	98%
Fibrinolytic Medication Timing	0	-	50%	55%
PCI Within 90 Minutes of Arrival	0	-	90%	90%
Smoking Cessation Advice[1]	7	100%	100%	99%
Chest Pain/Possible Heart Attack Care				
Aspirin at Arrival	70	100%	95%	95%
Median Time to ECG (minutes)	74	8	8	8
Median Time to Transfer (minutes)[1,3]	4	62	57	61
Fibrinolytic Medication Timing[1]	3	33%	33%	54%
Heart Failure Care				
ACE Inhibitor or ARB for LVSD[1]	22	95%	94%	94%
Discharge Instructions	56	89%	89%	88%
Evaluation of LVS Function	102	99%	98%	98%
Smoking Cessation Advice[1]	19	100%	99%	98%
Pneumonia Care				
Appropriate Initial Antibiotic	60	95%	90%	92%
Blood Culture Timing	116	99%	97%	96%
Influenza Vaccine	104	99%	91%	91%
Initial Antibiotic Timing	108	99%	96%	95%
Pneumococcal Vaccine	111	98%	92%	93%
Smoking Cessation Advice	36	100%	98%	97%
Surgical Care Improvement Project				
Appropriate VTP Within 24 Hours	115	99%	92%	92%
Appropriate Hair Removal	244	100%	99%	99%
Appropriate Beta Blocker Usage	82	94%	92%	93%
Controlled Postoperative Blood Glucose	0	-	92%	93%
Prophylactic Antibiotic Timing	171	98%	97%	97%
Prophylactic Antibiotic Timing (Outpatient)	108	97%	93%	92%
Prophylactic Antibiotic Selection	172	97%	97%	97%
Prophylactic Antibiotic Select. (Outpatient)	106	92%	94%	94%
Prophylactic Antibiotic Stopped	161	97%	94%	94%
Recommended VTP Ordered	117	98%	94%	94%
Urinary Catheter Removal	81	99%	89%	90%
Children's Asthma Care				
Received Systemic Corticosteroids	-	-	-	100%
Received Home Management Plan	-	-	-	71%
Received Reliever Medication	-	-	-	100%
Use of Medical Imaging				
Combination Abdominal CT Scan	247	0.704	0.246	0.191
Combination Chest CT Scan	229	0.677	0.098	0.054
Follow-up Mammogram/Ultrasound	705	4.8%	8.4%	8.4%
MRI for Low Back Pain	84	38.1%	33.4%	32.7%
Survey of Patients' Hospital Experiences				
Area Around Room 'Always' Quiet at Night	300+	56%	-	58%
Doctors 'Always' Communicated Well	300+	84%	-	80%
Home Recovery Information Given	300+	85%	-	82%
Hospital Given 9 or 10 on 10 Point Scale	300+	62%	-	67%
Meds 'Always' Explained Before Given	300+	59%	-	60%
Nurses 'Always' Communicated Well	300+	73%	-	76%
Pain 'Always' Well Controlled	300+	66%	-	69%
Room and Bathroom 'Always' Clean	300+	66%	-	71%
Timely Help 'Always' Received	300+	58%	-	64%
Would Definitely Recommend Hospital	300+	61%	-	69%

Saint Mary Medical Center

3333 North Seminary
Galesburg, IL 61401
Phone: 309-344-3161
Fax: 309-344-9494
URL: www.osfhealthcare.org
Type: Acute Care Hospitals
Emergency Services: Yes
Ownership: Voluntary Non-Profit - Church
Beds: 156

Key Personnel:
CEO/President. . . . . Richard Kowalski
Coronary Care . . . . Rosie Friend
Infection Control. . . . . Bonnie Fransene
Operating Room. . . . . Julia Nielsen
Pediatric In-Patient Care . . . . Carrie Hagen
Anesthesiology. . . . . Gary Daligowski
Emergency Room . . . . Cathy Anderson
Intensive Care Unit. . . . . Rosie Friend

Measure	Cases	This Hosp.	State Avg.	U.S. Avg.
Heart Attack Care				
ACE Inhibitor or ARB for LVSD[1]	7	100%	96%	96%
Aspirin at Arrival	40	98%	99%	99%
Aspirin at Discharge	26	96%	99%	98%
Beta Blocker at Discharge	26	100%	98%	98%
Fibrinolytic Medication Timing	0	-	50%	55%
PCI Within 90 Minutes of Arrival	0	-	90%	90%
Smoking Cessation Advice[1]	5	100%	100%	99%
Chest Pain/Possible Heart Attack Care				
Aspirin at Arrival	105	98%	95%	95%
Median Time to ECG (minutes)	107	9	8	8
Median Time to Transfer (minutes)[1]	24	59	57	61
Fibrinolytic Medication Timing[1]	3	33%	33%	54%
Heart Failure Care				
ACE Inhibitor or ARB for LVSD	45	96%	94%	94%
Discharge Instructions	72	89%	89%	88%
Evaluation of LVS Function	109	100%	98%	98%
Smoking Cessation Advice	26	85%	99%	98%
Pneumonia Care				
Appropriate Initial Antibiotic	142	92%	90%	92%
Blood Culture Timing	176	99%	97%	96%
Influenza Vaccine	137	91%	91%	91%
Initial Antibiotic Timing	217	98%	96%	95%
Pneumococcal Vaccine	181	95%	92%	93%
Smoking Cessation Advice	77	92%	98%	97%
Surgical Care Improvement Project				
Appropriate VTP Within 24 Hours	181	96%	92%	92%
Appropriate Hair Removal	347	100%	99%	99%
Appropriate Beta Blocker Usage	103	96%	92%	93%
Controlled Postoperative Blood Glucose	0	-	92%	93%
Prophylactic Antibiotic Timing	231	98%	97%	97%
Prophylactic Antibiotic Timing (Outpatient)	47	98%	93%	92%
Prophylactic Antibiotic Selection	234	99%	97%	97%
Prophylactic Antibiotic Select. (Outpatient)	46	93%	94%	94%
Prophylactic Antibiotic Stopped	218	93%	94%	94%
Recommended VTP Ordered	182	97%	94%	94%
Urinary Catheter Removal	106	95%	89%	90%
Children's Asthma Care				
Received Systemic Corticosteroids	-	-	-	100%
Received Home Management Plan	-	-	-	71%
Received Reliever Medication	-	-	-	100%
Use of Medical Imaging				
Combination Abdominal CT Scan	472	0.068	0.246	0.191
Combination Chest CT Scan	343	0.012	0.098	0.054
Follow-up Mammogram/Ultrasound	1,323	6.6%	8.4%	8.4%
MRI for Low Back Pain	123	28.5%	33.4%	32.7%
Survey of Patients' Hospital Experiences				
Area Around Room 'Always' Quiet at Night	300+	57%	-	58%
Doctors 'Always' Communicated Well	300+	83%	-	80%
Home Recovery Information Given	300+	89%	-	82%
Hospital Given 9 or 10 on 10 Point Scale	300+	75%	-	67%
Meds 'Always' Explained Before Given	300+	67%	-	60%
Nurses 'Always' Communicated Well	300+	81%	-	76%
Pain 'Always' Well Controlled	300+	73%	-	69%
Room and Bathroom 'Always' Clean	300+	75%	-	71%
Timely Help 'Always' Received	300+	75%	-	64%
Would Definitely Recommend Hospital	300+	83%	-	69%

NOTE: Hospital profiles are in alphabetical order by state, then city, then hospital within the city; Rankings exclude hospitals with less than 25 cases except for patient surveys which excludes hospitals with less than 100 cases; (a) 100–299 cases; (1) The number of cases is too small to be sure how well a hospital is performing; (2) The hospital indicated that the data submitted for this measure were based on a sample of cases; (3) Data was collected during a shorter time period (fewer quarters) than the maximum possible time for this measure; (4) Suppressed for one or more quarters by CMS; (5) No data is available from the hospital for this measure; (6) Fewer than 100 patients completed the HCAHPS survey. Use these rates with caution, as the number of surveys may be too low to reliably assess hospital performance; (7) Survey results are based on less than 12 months of data; (8) Survey results are not available for this reporting period; (9) No or very few patients were eligible for the HCAHPS survey. The scores shown, if any, reflect a very small number of surveys; (10) A state average was not calculated because too few hospitals in the state submitted data; (11) There were discrepancies in the data collection process; Please refer to the User's Guide for a full explanation of data.

Hammond Henry Hospital

600 N College Avenue Phone: 309-944-6431
Geneseo, IL 61254 Fax: 309-944-5299
E-mail: hhh@hammondhenry.com
URL: www.hammondhenry.com
Type: Critical Access Hospitals Emergency Services: Yes
Ownership: Govt - Hospital Dist/Auth Beds: 105

Key Personnel:
CEO/President............... Bradley Solberg
Chief of Medical Staff.......... L Gumidyala
Infection Control.............. Geri Egert
Operating Room............. Yogin Parikh
Quality Assurance .... Geri Egert
Emergency Room .... Lokanathum Gumadyala, MD
Intensive Care Unit............ Karen Crossman
Patient Relations .... Diane Swaggen

Measure	Cases	This Hosp.	State Avg.	U.S. Avg.
Heart Attack Care				
ACE Inhibitor or ARB for LVSD[5]	0	-	96%	96%
Aspirin at Arrival[5]	0	-	99%	99%
Aspirin at Discharge[5]	0	-	99%	98%
Beta Blocker at Discharge[5]	0	-	98%	98%
Fibrinolytic Medication Timing[5]	0	-	50%	55%
PCI Within 90 Minutes of Arrival[5]	0	-	90%	90%
Smoking Cessation Advice[5]	0	-	100%	99%
Chest Pain/Possible Heart Attack Care				
Aspirin at Arrival	-	-	95%	95%
Median Time to ECG (minutes)	-	-	8	8
Median Time to Transfer (minutes)	-	-	57	61
Fibrinolytic Medication Timing	-	-	33%	54%
Heart Failure Care				
ACE Inhibitor or ARB for LVSD[5]	0	-	94%	94%
Discharge Instructions[5]	0	-	89%	88%
Evaluation of LVS Function[5]	0	-	98%	98%
Smoking Cessation Advice[5]	0	-	99%	98%
Pneumonia Care				
Appropriate Initial Antibiotic[5]	0	-	90%	92%
Blood Culture Timing[5]	0	-	97%	96%
Influenza Vaccine[5]	0	-	91%	91%
Initial Antibiotic Timing[5]	0	-	96%	95%
Pneumococcal Vaccine[5]	0	-	92%	93%
Smoking Cessation Advice[5]	0	-	98%	97%
Surgical Care Improvement Project				
Appropriate VTP Within 24 Hours	38	92%	92%	92%
Appropriate Hair Removal	111	100%	99%	99%
Appropriate Beta Blocker Usage[5]	0	-	92%	93%
Controlled Postoperative Blood Glucose	0	-	92%	93%
Prophylactic Antibiotic Timing	88	98%	97%	97%
Prophylactic Antibiotic Timing (Outpatient)	-	-	93%	92%
Prophylactic Antibiotic Selection	88	93%	97%	97%
Prophylactic Antibiotic Select. (Outpatient)	-	-	94%	94%
Prophylactic Antibiotic Stopped	87	93%	94%	94%
Recommended VTP Ordered	38	95%	94%	94%
Urinary Catheter Removal[1]	9	33%	89%	90%
Children's Asthma Care				
Received Systemic Corticosteroids	-	-	-	100%
Received Home Management Plan	-	-	-	71%
Received Reliever Medication	-	-	-	100%
Use of Medical Imaging				
Combination Abdominal CT Scan	-	-	0.246	0.191
Combination Chest CT Scan	-	-	0.098	0.054
Follow-up Mammogram/Ultrasound	-	-	8.4%	8.4%
MRI for Low Back Pain	-	-	33.4%	32.7%
Survey of Patients' Hospital Experiences				
Area Around Room 'Always' Quiet at Night	300+	60%	-	58%
Doctors 'Always' Communicated Well	300+	87%	-	80%
Home Recovery Information Given	300+	83%	-	82%
Hospital Given 9 or 10 on 10 Point Scale	300+	78%	-	67%
Meds 'Always' Explained Before Given	300+	71%	-	60%
Nurses 'Always' Communicated Well	300+	84%	-	76%
Pain 'Always' Well Controlled	300+	75%	-	69%
Room and Bathroom 'Always' Clean	300+	78%	-	71%
Timely Help 'Always' Received	300+	77%	-	64%
Would Definitely Recommend Hospital	300+	77%	-	69%

Delnor Community Hospital

300 Randall Rd Phone: 630-208-3000
Geneva, IL 60134 Fax: 630-208-3478
E-mail: info@delnor.com
URL: www.delnor.com
Type: Acute Care Hospitals Emergency Services: Yes
Ownership: Voluntary Non-Profit - Other Beds: 118

Key Personnel:
CEO/President............... Craig A Livermore
Operating Room.............. Paul Batty
Pediatric Ambulatory Care ...... Cathy Brill
Pediatric In-Patient Care .... Cathy Brill
Quality Assurance .... Linda Adams
Radiology.................... Sidney Jain

Measure	Cases	This Hosp.	State Avg.	U.S. Avg.
Heart Attack Care				
ACE Inhibitor or ARB for LVSD[1]	10	100%	96%	96%
Aspirin at Arrival	100	99%	99%	99%
Aspirin at Discharge	86	100%	99%	98%
Beta Blocker at Discharge	89	100%	98%	98%
Fibrinolytic Medication Timing	0	-	50%	55%
PCI Within 90 Minutes of Arrival	33	94%	90%	90%
Smoking Cessation Advice[1]	23	100%	100%	99%
Chest Pain/Possible Heart Attack Care				
Aspirin at Arrival[1]	12	100%	95%	95%
Median Time to ECG (minutes)[1]	12	6	8	8
Median Time to Transfer (minutes)[5]	0	-	57	61
Fibrinolytic Medication Timing[3]	0	-	33%	54%
Heart Failure Care				
ACE Inhibitor or ARB for LVSD	44	100%	94%	94%
Discharge Instructions	149	90%	89%	88%
Evaluation of LVS Function	203	100%	98%	98%
Smoking Cessation Advice	33	100%	99%	98%
Pneumonia Care				
Appropriate Initial Antibiotic	127	97%	90%	92%
Blood Culture Timing	105	99%	97%	96%
Influenza Vaccine	132	99%	91%	91%
Initial Antibiotic Timing	213	99%	96%	95%
Pneumococcal Vaccine	226	100%	92%	93%
Smoking Cessation Advice	40	100%	98%	97%
Surgical Care Improvement Project				
Appropriate VTP Within 24 Hours[2]	172	98%	92%	92%
Appropriate Hair Removal[2]	466	100%	99%	99%
Appropriate Beta Blocker Usage[2]	145	97%	92%	93%
Controlled Postoperative Blood Glucose[2]	0	-	92%	93%
Prophylactic Antibiotic Timing[2]	317	98%	97%	97%
Prophylactic Antibiotic Timing (Outpatient)	109	98%	93%	92%
Prophylactic Antibiotic Selection[2]	316	96%	97%	97%
Prophylactic Antibiotic Select. (Outpatient)	109	90%	94%	94%
Prophylactic Antibiotic Stopped[2]	304	96%	94%	94%
Recommended VTP Ordered[2]	172	99%	94%	94%
Urinary Catheter Removal[2]	50	84%	89%	90%
Children's Asthma Care				
Received Systemic Corticosteroids	-	-	-	100%
Received Home Management Plan	-	-	-	71%
Received Reliever Medication	-	-	-	100%
Use of Medical Imaging				
Combination Abdominal CT Scan	974	0.561	0.246	0.191
Combination Chest CT Scan	770	0.357	0.098	0.054
Follow-up Mammogram/Ultrasound	1,093	12.4%	8.4%	8.4%
MRI for Low Back Pain	140	30.7%	33.4%	32.7%
Survey of Patients' Hospital Experiences				
Area Around Room 'Always' Quiet at Night	300+	64%	-	58%
Doctors 'Always' Communicated Well	300+	81%	-	80%
Home Recovery Information Given	300+	86%	-	82%
Hospital Given 9 or 10 on 10 Point Scale	300+	75%	-	67%
Meds 'Always' Explained Before Given	300+	63%	-	60%
Nurses 'Always' Communicated Well	300+	80%	-	76%
Pain 'Always' Well Controlled	300+	71%	-	69%
Room and Bathroom 'Always' Clean	300+	75%	-	71%
Timely Help 'Always' Received	300+	64%	-	64%
Would Definitely Recommend Hospital	300+	77%	-	69%

Gibson Community Hospital

1120 N Melvin Street Phone: 217-784-4251
Gibson City, IL 60936 Fax: 217-784-2610
URL: www.gibsonhospital.org
Type: Critical Access Hospitals Emergency Services: Yes
Ownership: Voluntary Non-Profit - Other Beds: 82

Key Personnel:
CEO/President................ Rob Schmitt
Infection Control.............. Becki Garard
Operating Room............... Eric Kivisto
Quality Assurance .... Sylvia Day
Radiology.................... Daniel Ha
Anesthesiology............... Roger Birky
Emergency Room .... Almuhannad Alfrhan
Intensive Care Unit............ Brenda Standerfer

Measure	Cases	This Hosp.	State Avg.	U.S. Avg.
Heart Attack Care				
ACE Inhibitor or ARB for LVSD[5]	0	-	96%	96%
Aspirin at Arrival[5]	0	-	99%	99%
Aspirin at Discharge[5]	0	-	99%	98%
Beta Blocker at Discharge[5]	0	-	98%	98%
Fibrinolytic Medication Timing[5]	0	-	50%	55%
PCI Within 90 Minutes of Arrival[5]	0	-	90%	90%
Smoking Cessation Advice[5]	0	-	100%	99%
Chest Pain/Possible Heart Attack Care				
Aspirin at Arrival	-	-	95%	95%
Median Time to ECG (minutes)	-	-	8	8
Median Time to Transfer (minutes)	-	-	57	61
Fibrinolytic Medication Timing	-	-	33%	54%
Heart Failure Care				
ACE Inhibitor or ARB for LVSD[1]	6	83%	94%	94%
Discharge Instructions[1]	8	100%	89%	88%
Evaluation of LVS Function[1]	16	100%	98%	98%
Smoking Cessation Advice[1]	2	100%	99%	98%
Pneumonia Care				
Appropriate Initial Antibiotic[2]	42	90%	90%	92%
Blood Culture Timing[2]	38	97%	97%	96%
Influenza Vaccine[2]	25	96%	91%	91%
Initial Antibiotic Timing[2]	50	100%	96%	95%
Pneumococcal Vaccine[2]	40	95%	92%	93%
Smoking Cessation Advice[1,2]	13	92%	98%	97%
Surgical Care Improvement Project				
Appropriate VTP Within 24 Hours	37	73%	92%	92%
Appropriate Hair Removal	106	92%	99%	99%
Appropriate Beta Blocker Usage	31	84%	92%	93%
Controlled Postoperative Blood Glucose	0	-	92%	93%
Prophylactic Antibiotic Timing	82	94%	97%	97%
Prophylactic Antibiotic Timing (Outpatient)	-	-	93%	92%
Prophylactic Antibiotic Selection	83	99%	97%	97%
Prophylactic Antibiotic Select. (Outpatient)	-	-	94%	94%
Prophylactic Antibiotic Stopped	82	93%	94%	94%
Recommended VTP Ordered	37	73%	94%	94%
Urinary Catheter Removal	47	94%	89%	90%
Children's Asthma Care				
Received Systemic Corticosteroids	-	-	-	100%
Received Home Management Plan	-	-	-	71%
Received Reliever Medication	-	-	-	100%
Use of Medical Imaging				
Combination Abdominal CT Scan	-	-	0.246	0.191
Combination Chest CT Scan	-	-	0.098	0.054
Follow-up Mammogram/Ultrasound	-	-	8.4%	8.4%
MRI for Low Back Pain	-	-	33.4%	32.7%
Survey of Patients' Hospital Experiences				
Area Around Room 'Always' Quiet at Night	300+	65%	-	58%
Doctors 'Always' Communicated Well	300+	86%	-	80%
Home Recovery Information Given	300+	91%	-	82%
Hospital Given 9 or 10 on 10 Point Scale	300+	83%	-	67%
Meds 'Always' Explained Before Given	300+	68%	-	60%
Nurses 'Always' Communicated Well	300+	82%	-	76%
Pain 'Always' Well Controlled	300+	77%	-	69%
Room and Bathroom 'Always' Clean	300+	78%	-	71%
Timely Help 'Always' Received	300+	75%	-	64%
Would Definitely Recommend Hospital	300+	81%	-	69%

NOTE: Hospital profiles are in alphabetical order by state, then city, then hospital within the city; Rankings exclude hospitals with less than 25 cases except for patient surveys which excludes hospitals with less than 100 cases; (a) 100–299 cases; (1) The number of cases is too small to be sure how well a hospital is performing; (2) The hospital indicated that the data submitted for this measure were based on a sample of cases; (3) Data was collected during a shorter time period (fewer quarters) than the maximum possible time for this measure; (4) Suppressed for one or more quarters by CMS; (5) No data is available from the hospital for this measure; (6) Fewer than 100 patients completed the HCAHPS survey. Use these rates with caution, as the number of surveys may be too low to reliably assess hospital performance; (7) Survey results are based on less than 12 months of data; (8) Survey results are not available for this reporting period; (9) No or very few patients were eligible for the HCAHPS survey. The scores shown, if any, reflect a very small number of surveys; (10) A state average was not calculated because too few hospitals in the state submitted data; (11) There were discrepancies in the data collection process; Please refer to the User's Guide for a full explanation of data.

Adventist Glenoaks

701 Winthrop Avenue
Glendale Heights, IL 60139
URL: www.keepingyouwell.com
Type: Acute Care Hospitals
Ownership: Voluntary Non-Profit - Other
Phone: 630-545-6160
Fax: 630-545-3920
Emergency Services: Yes
Beds: 186

Key Personnel:
CEO/President. . . . . Brinsley Lewis
Cardiac Laboratory. . . . . Richard Kenney
Chief of Medical Staff. . . . . Lisa Wohl, MD
Infection Control. . . . . Darlene Gallagher
Operating Room. . . . . Judy Papendorf
Quality Assurance . . . . Chris Rendl
Radiology. . . . . Patricia Lee

Measure	Cases	This Hosp.	State Avg.	U.S. Avg.
Heart Attack Care				
ACE Inhibitor or ARB for LVSD[1]	4	100%	96%	96%
Aspirin at Arrival	37	97%	99%	99%
Aspirin at Discharge	26	100%	99%	98%
Beta Blocker at Discharge[1]	24	100%	98%	98%
Fibrinolytic Medication Timing	0	-	50%	55%
PCI Within 90 Minutes of Arrival[1]	5	100%	90%	90%
Smoking Cessation Advice[1]	10	100%	100%	99%
Chest Pain/Possible Heart Attack Care				
Aspirin at Arrival[1,3]	3	100%	95%	95%
Median Time to ECG (minutes)[1,3]	3	0	8	8
Median Time to Transfer (minutes)[5]	0	-	57	61
Fibrinolytic Medication Timing[5]	0	-	33%	54%
Heart Failure Care				
ACE Inhibitor or ARB for LVSD	34	91%	94%	94%
Discharge Instructions	54	61%	89%	88%
Evaluation of LVS Function	78	96%	98%	98%
Smoking Cessation Advice[1]	16	100%	99%	98%
Pneumonia Care				
Appropriate Initial Antibiotic	27	89%	90%	92%
Blood Culture Timing	89	99%	97%	96%
Influenza Vaccine	35	91%	91%	91%
Initial Antibiotic Timing	65	97%	96%	95%
Pneumococcal Vaccine	41	100%	92%	93%
Smoking Cessation Advice[1]	17	100%	98%	97%
Surgical Care Improvement Project				
Appropriate VTP Within 24 Hours	43	93%	92%	92%
Appropriate Hair Removal	90	100%	99%	99%
Appropriate Beta Blocker Usage[1]	20	55%	92%	93%
Controlled Postoperative Blood Glucose	0	-	92%	93%
Prophylactic Antibiotic Timing	35	100%	97%	97%
Prophylactic Antibiotic Timing (Outpatient)	31	77%	93%	92%
Prophylactic Antibiotic Selection	35	100%	97%	97%
Prophylactic Antibiotic Select. (Outpatient)	27	89%	94%	94%
Prophylactic Antibiotic Stopped	34	97%	94%	94%
Recommended VTP Ordered	44	91%	94%	94%
Urinary Catheter Removal[1]	10	60%	89%	90%
Children's Asthma Care				
Received Systemic Corticosteroids	-	-	-	100%
Received Home Management Plan	-	-	-	71%
Received Reliever Medication	-	-	-	100%
Use of Medical Imaging				
Combination Abdominal CT Scan	124	0.081	0.246	0.191
Combination Chest CT Scan	57	0.053	0.098	0.054
Follow-up Mammogram/Ultrasound	111	8.1%	8.4%	8.4%
MRI for Low Back Pain[1]	20	40.0%	33.4%	32.7%
Survey of Patients' Hospital Experiences				
Area Around Room 'Always' Quiet at Night	300+	51%	-	58%
Doctors 'Always' Communicated Well	300+	73%	-	80%
Home Recovery Information Given	300+	80%	-	82%
Hospital Given 9 or 10 on 10 Point Scale	300+	51%	-	67%
Meds 'Always' Explained Before Given	300+	54%	-	60%
Nurses 'Always' Communicated Well	300+	64%	-	76%
Pain 'Always' Well Controlled	300+	61%	-	69%
Room and Bathroom 'Always' Clean	300+	65%	-	71%
Timely Help 'Always' Received	300+	55%	-	64%
Would Definitely Recommend Hospital	300+	56%	-	69%

Gateway Regional Medical Center

2100 Madison Avenue
Granite City, IL 62040
URL: www.sehs.com
Type: Acute Care Hospitals
Ownership: Proprietary
Phone: 618-798-3175
Fax: 618-798-3853
Emergency Services: Yes
Beds: 393

Key Personnel:
Chief of Medical Staff. . . . . K Konzen, MD
Infection Control. . . . . Ruth Ann Gabriel
Operating Room. . . . . Wesley Harris
Pediatric Ambulatory Care . . . . . . S Ahmad, MD
Pediatric In-Patient Care . . . . S Ahmad, MD
Quality Assurance . . . . Marcia Walker
Radiology. . . . . Karen Aderholdt, MD

Measure	Cases	This Hosp.	State Avg.	U.S. Avg.
Heart Attack Care				
ACE Inhibitor or ARB for LVSD[1]	11	100%	96%	96%
Aspirin at Arrival	91	100%	99%	99%
Aspirin at Discharge	73	100%	99%	98%
Beta Blocker at Discharge	60	100%	98%	98%
Fibrinolytic Medication Timing	0	-	50%	55%
PCI Within 90 Minutes of Arrival[1]	1	100%	90%	90%
Smoking Cessation Advice	30	100%	100%	99%
Chest Pain/Possible Heart Attack Care				
Aspirin at Arrival	42	100%	95%	95%
Median Time to ECG (minutes)	46	11	8	8
Median Time to Transfer (minutes)[1]	2	58	57	61
Fibrinolytic Medication Timing[1]	1	100%	33%	54%
Heart Failure Care				
ACE Inhibitor or ARB for LVSD	44	100%	94%	94%
Discharge Instructions	137	88%	89%	88%
Evaluation of LVS Function	160	100%	98%	98%
Smoking Cessation Advice	48	100%	99%	98%
Pneumonia Care				
Appropriate Initial Antibiotic	50	100%	90%	92%
Blood Culture Timing	113	100%	97%	96%
Influenza Vaccine	51	96%	91%	91%
Initial Antibiotic Timing	99	99%	96%	95%
Pneumococcal Vaccine	62	98%	92%	93%
Smoking Cessation Advice	54	100%	98%	97%
Surgical Care Improvement Project				
Appropriate VTP Within 24 Hours	100	99%	92%	92%
Appropriate Hair Removal	255	100%	99%	99%
Appropriate Beta Blocker Usage	46	100%	92%	93%
Controlled Postoperative Blood Glucose	0	-	92%	93%
Prophylactic Antibiotic Timing	202	99%	97%	97%
Prophylactic Antibiotic Timing (Outpatient)	73	97%	93%	92%
Prophylactic Antibiotic Selection	203	100%	97%	97%
Prophylactic Antibiotic Select. (Outpatient)	72	96%	94%	94%
Prophylactic Antibiotic Stopped	202	99%	94%	94%
Recommended VTP Ordered	100	99%	94%	94%
Urinary Catheter Removal	69	99%	89%	90%
Children's Asthma Care				
Received Systemic Corticosteroids	-	-	-	100%
Received Home Management Plan	-	-	-	71%
Received Reliever Medication	-	-	-	100%
Use of Medical Imaging				
Combination Abdominal CT Scan	309	0.217	0.246	0.191
Combination Chest CT Scan	205	0.029	0.098	0.054
Follow-up Mammogram/Ultrasound	525	6.5%	8.4%	8.4%
MRI for Low Back Pain	98	24.5%	33.4%	32.7%
Survey of Patients' Hospital Experiences				
Area Around Room 'Always' Quiet at Night	300+	54%	-	58%
Doctors 'Always' Communicated Well	300+	79%	-	80%
Home Recovery Information Given	300+	77%	-	82%
Hospital Given 9 or 10 on 10 Point Scale	300+	56%	-	67%
Meds 'Always' Explained Before Given	300+	57%	-	60%
Nurses 'Always' Communicated Well	300+	72%	-	76%
Pain 'Always' Well Controlled	300+	62%	-	69%
Room and Bathroom 'Always' Clean	300+	62%	-	71%
Timely Help 'Always' Received	300+	54%	-	64%
Would Definitely Recommend Hospital	300+	53%	-	69%

Greenville Regional Hospital

200 Healthcare Dr
Greenville, IL 62246
Type: Acute Care Hospitals
Ownership: Voluntary Non-Profit - Other
Phone: 618-664-1230
Fax: 618-664-9750
Emergency Services: Yes
Beds: 50

Key Personnel:
CEO/President. . . . . Morris Bond
Quality Assurance . . . . Alisa Beck
Emergency Room . . . . Sara McPeak

Measure	Cases	This Hosp.	State Avg.	U.S. Avg.
Heart Attack Care				
ACE Inhibitor or ARB for LVSD[3]	0	-	96%	96%
Aspirin at Arrival[1,3]	1	100%	99%	99%
Aspirin at Discharge[1,3]	1	100%	99%	98%
Beta Blocker at Discharge[1,3]	2	50%	98%	98%
Fibrinolytic Medication Timing[3]	0	-	50%	55%
PCI Within 90 Minutes of Arrival[3]	0	-	90%	90%
Smoking Cessation Advice[3]	0	-	100%	99%
Chest Pain/Possible Heart Attack Care				
Aspirin at Arrival	32	97%	95%	95%
Median Time to ECG (minutes)	33	11	8	8
Median Time to Transfer (minutes)[1,3]	2	47	57	61
Fibrinolytic Medication Timing[1]	1	0%	33%	54%
Heart Failure Care				
ACE Inhibitor or ARB for LVSD[1]	7	57%	94%	94%
Discharge Instructions[1]	12	100%	89%	88%
Evaluation of LVS Function[1]	20	90%	98%	98%
Smoking Cessation Advice[1]	2	100%	99%	98%
Pneumonia Care				
Appropriate Initial Antibiotic	30	83%	90%	92%
Blood Culture Timing	52	92%	97%	96%
Influenza Vaccine[1]	23	70%	91%	91%
Initial Antibiotic Timing	51	96%	96%	95%
Pneumococcal Vaccine	47	74%	92%	93%
Smoking Cessation Advice[1]	11	91%	98%	97%
Surgical Care Improvement Project				
Appropriate VTP Within 24 Hours[1]	10	50%	92%	92%
Appropriate Hair Removal[1]	13	92%	99%	99%
Appropriate Beta Blocker Usage[1]	3	67%	92%	93%
Controlled Postoperative Blood Glucose	0	-	92%	93%
Prophylactic Antibiotic Timing[1]	6	67%	97%	97%
Prophylactic Antibiotic Timing (Outpatient)[1,3]	6	83%	93%	92%
Prophylactic Antibiotic Selection[1]	7	43%	97%	97%
Prophylactic Antibiotic Select. (Outpatient)[1,3]	6	50%	94%	94%
Prophylactic Antibiotic Stopped[1]	6	100%	94%	94%
Recommended VTP Ordered[1]	10	50%	94%	94%
Urinary Catheter Removal[1]	1	100%	89%	90%
Children's Asthma Care				
Received Systemic Corticosteroids	-	-	-	100%
Received Home Management Plan	-	-	-	71%
Received Reliever Medication	-	-	-	100%
Use of Medical Imaging				
Combination Abdominal CT Scan	375	0.773	0.246	0.191
Combination Chest CT Scan	243	0.679	0.098	0.054
Follow-up Mammogram/Ultrasound[5]	0	-	8.4%	8.4%
MRI for Low Back Pain[1]	29	44.8%	33.4%	32.7%
Survey of Patients' Hospital Experiences				
Area Around Room 'Always' Quiet at Night	(a)	60%	-	58%
Doctors 'Always' Communicated Well	(a)	74%	-	80%
Home Recovery Information Given	(a)	83%	-	82%
Hospital Given 9 or 10 on 10 Point Scale	(a)	62%	-	67%
Meds 'Always' Explained Before Given	(a)	53%	-	60%
Nurses 'Always' Communicated Well	(a)	77%	-	76%
Pain 'Always' Well Controlled	(a)	69%	-	69%
Room and Bathroom 'Always' Clean	(a)	70%	-	71%
Timely Help 'Always' Received	(a)	62%	-	64%
Would Definitely Recommend Hospital	(a)	62%	-	69%

NOTE: Hospital profiles are in alphabetical order by state, then city, then hospital within the city; Rankings exclude hospitals with less than 25 cases except for patient surveys which excludes hospitals with less than 100 cases; (a) 100–299 cases; (1) The number of cases is too small to be sure how well a hospital is performing; (2) The hospital indicated that the data submitted for this measure were based on a sample of cases; (3) Data was collected during a shorter time period (fewer quarters) than the maximum possible time for this measure; (4) Suppressed for one or more quarters by CMS; (5) No data is available from the hospital for this measure; (6) Fewer than 100 patients completed the HCAHPS survey. Use these rates with caution, as the number of surveys may be too low to reliably assess hospital performance; (7) Survey results are based on less than 12 months of data; (8) Survey results are not available for this reporting period; (9) No or very few patients were eligible for the HCAHPS survey. The scores shown, if any, reflect a very small number of surveys; (10) A state average was not calculated because too few hospitals in the state submitted data; (11) There were discrepancies in the data collection process; Please refer to the User's Guide for a full explanation of data.

Harrisburg Medical Center

100 Doctor Warren Tuttle Dr
Harrisburg, IL 62946
Phone: 618-253-7671
Fax: 618-252-7274
E-mail: cchatterton@harrisburgmed.org
Type: Acute Care Hospitals
Emergency Services: Yes
Ownership: Voluntary Non-Profit - Other
Beds: 86

Key Personnel:

CEO/President. . . . . Vince Ashley
Chief of Medical Staff. . . . . Vinay Mehta, MD
Infection Control. . . . . Brenda Duckworth, RN
Operating Room. . . . . Linda Murphy, RN
Quality Assurance . . . . Danny Lampley
Radiology. . . . . H T Youssef, MD

Measure	Cases	This Hosp.	State Avg.	U.S. Avg.
Heart Attack Care				
ACE Inhibitor or ARB for LVSD[1]	2	100%	96%	96%
Aspirin at Arrival[1]	16	100%	99%	99%
Aspirin at Discharge[1]	9	100%	99%	98%
Beta Blocker at Discharge[1]	7	100%	98%	98%
Fibrinolytic Medication Timing	0	-	50%	55%
PCI Within 90 Minutes of Arrival	0	-	90%	90%
Smoking Cessation Advice[1]	1	100%	100%	99%
Chest Pain/Possible Heart Attack Care				
Aspirin at Arrival	129	97%	95%	95%
Median Time to ECG (minutes)	134	5	8	8
Median Time to Transfer (minutes)[1,3]	4	26	57	61
Fibrinolytic Medication Timing	0	-	33%	54%
Heart Failure Care				
ACE Inhibitor or ARB for LVSD[1,2]	19	100%	94%	94%
Discharge Instructions[2]	67	100%	89%	88%
Evaluation of LVS Function[2]	100	94%	98%	98%
Smoking Cessation Advice[1,2]	12	100%	99%	98%
Pneumonia Care				
Appropriate Initial Antibiotic[2]	93	78%	90%	92%
Blood Culture Timing[2]	93	78%	97%	96%
Influenza Vaccine[2]	91	93%	91%	91%
Initial Antibiotic Timing[2]	154	97%	96%	95%
Pneumococcal Vaccine[2]	127	91%	92%	93%
Smoking Cessation Advice[2]	31	97%	98%	97%
Surgical Care Improvement Project				
Appropriate VTP Within 24 Hours[1]	18	56%	92%	92%
Appropriate Hair Removal	34	100%	99%	99%
Appropriate Beta Blocker Usage[1]	7	71%	92%	93%
Controlled Postoperative Blood Glucose	0	-	92%	93%
Prophylactic Antibiotic Timing[1]	21	90%	97%	97%
Prophylactic Antibiotic Timing (Outpatient)[3]	0	-	93%	92%
Prophylactic Antibiotic Selection[1]	20	80%	97%	97%
Prophylactic Antibiotic Select. (Outpatient)[3]	0	-	94%	94%
Prophylactic Antibiotic Stopped[1]	20	100%	94%	94%
Recommended VTP Ordered[1]	18	56%	94%	94%
Urinary Catheter Removal[1]	2	100%	89%	90%
Children's Asthma Care				
Received Systemic Corticosteroids	-	-	-	100%
Received Home Management Plan	-	-	-	71%
Received Reliever Medication	-	-	-	100%
Use of Medical Imaging				
Combination Abdominal CT Scan	390	0.526	0.246	0.191
Combination Chest CT Scan	301	0.654	0.098	0.054
Follow-up Mammogram/Ultrasound	695	5.3%	8.4%	8.4%
MRI for Low Back Pain[5]	0	-	33.4%	32.7%
Survey of Patients' Hospital Experiences				
Area Around Room 'Always' Quiet at Night	300+	55%	-	58%
Doctors 'Always' Communicated Well	300+	80%	-	80%
Home Recovery Information Given	300+	78%	-	82%
Hospital Given 9 or 10 on 10 Point Scale	300+	65%	-	67%
Meds 'Always' Explained Before Given	300+	57%	-	60%
Nurses 'Always' Communicated Well	300+	76%	-	76%
Pain 'Always' Well Controlled	300+	68%	-	69%
Room and Bathroom 'Always' Clean	300+	71%	-	71%
Timely Help 'Always' Received	300+	64%	-	64%
Would Definitely Recommend Hospital	300+	61%	-	69%

Mercy Harvard Hospital

901 Grant Street
Harvard, IL 60033
Phone: 815-943-5431
Fax: 815-943-2493
E-mail: custserv@mhsjvl.org
URL: www.mercyhealthsystem.org
Type: Critical Access Hospitals
Emergency Services: Yes
Ownership: Voluntary Non-Profit - Private
Beds: 46

Key Personnel:

CEO/President. . . . . Dan Colby
Chief of Medical Staff. . . . . Joseph Levenstein, MD
Radiology. . . . . Leon F DeJongh
Emergency Room . . . . Brian Aldred, MD
Patient Relations . . . . Connie Secor, RN

Measure	Cases	This Hosp.	State Avg.	U.S. Avg.
Heart Attack Care				
ACE Inhibitor or ARB for LVSD[5]	0	-	96%	96%
Aspirin at Arrival[5]	0	-	99%	99%
Aspirin at Discharge[5]	0	-	99%	98%
Beta Blocker at Discharge[5]	0	-	98%	98%
Fibrinolytic Medication Timing[5]	0	-	50%	55%
PCI Within 90 Minutes of Arrival[5]	0	-	90%	90%
Smoking Cessation Advice[5]	0	-	100%	99%
Chest Pain/Possible Heart Attack Care				
Aspirin at Arrival[1,3]	16	100%	95%	95%
Median Time to ECG (minutes)[1,3]	17	6	8	8
Median Time to Transfer (minutes)[1,3]	2	42	57	61
Fibrinolytic Medication Timing[3]	0	-	33%	54%
Heart Failure Care				
ACE Inhibitor or ARB for LVSD[1,3]	6	100%	94%	94%
Discharge Instructions[1,3]	15	100%	89%	88%
Evaluation of LVS Function[1,3]	24	100%	98%	98%
Smoking Cessation Advice[1,3]	2	50%	99%	98%
Pneumonia Care				
Appropriate Initial Antibiotic[1,3]	12	100%	90%	92%
Blood Culture Timing[1,3]	15	100%	97%	96%
Influenza Vaccine[1]	17	100%	91%	91%
Initial Antibiotic Timing[1,3]	17	94%	96%	95%
Pneumococcal Vaccine[1,3]	13	92%	92%	93%
Smoking Cessation Advice[1,3]	4	100%	98%	97%
Surgical Care Improvement Project				
Appropriate VTP Within 24 Hours[1]	19	89%	92%	92%
Appropriate Hair Removal	47	100%	99%	99%
Appropriate Beta Blocker Usage[1]	7	86%	92%	93%
Controlled Postoperative Blood Glucose	0	-	92%	93%
Prophylactic Antibiotic Timing	26	96%	97%	97%
Prophylactic Antibiotic Timing (Outpatient)[3]	26	96%	93%	92%
Prophylactic Antibiotic Selection	26	96%	97%	97%
Prophylactic Antibiotic Select. (Outpatient)[3]	26	96%	94%	94%
Prophylactic Antibiotic Stopped	26	96%	94%	94%
Recommended VTP Ordered[1]	19	89%	94%	94%
Urinary Catheter Removal[1]	20	100%	89%	90%
Children's Asthma Care				
Received Systemic Corticosteroids	-	-	-	100%
Received Home Management Plan	-	-	-	71%
Received Reliever Medication	-	-	-	100%
Use of Medical Imaging				
Combination Abdominal CT Scan	92	0.033	0.246	0.191
Combination Chest CT Scan	78	0.051	0.098	0.054
Follow-up Mammogram/Ultrasound	89	5.6%	8.4%	8.4%
MRI for Low Back Pain[1]	5	60.0%	33.4%	32.7%
Survey of Patients' Hospital Experiences				
Area Around Room 'Always' Quiet at Night[8]	-	-	-	58%
Doctors 'Always' Communicated Well[8]	-	-	-	80%
Home Recovery Information Given[8]	-	-	-	82%
Hospital Given 9 or 10 on 10 Point Scale[8]	-	-	-	67%
Meds 'Always' Explained Before Given[8]	-	-	-	60%
Nurses 'Always' Communicated Well[8]	-	-	-	76%
Pain 'Always' Well Controlled[8]	-	-	-	69%
Room and Bathroom 'Always' Clean[8]	-	-	-	71%
Timely Help 'Always' Received[8]	-	-	-	64%
Would Definitely Recommend Hospital[8]	-	-	-	69%

Ingalls Memorial Hospital

One Ingalls Drive
Harvey, IL 60426
Phone: 708-333-2300
Fax: 708-915-2707
URL: www.ingalls.org
Type: Acute Care Hospitals
Emergency Services: Yes
Ownership: Voluntary Non-Profit - Private
Beds: 326

Key Personnel:

CEO/President. . . . . Kurt Johnson

Measure	Cases	This Hosp.	State Avg.	U.S. Avg.
Heart Attack Care				
ACE Inhibitor or ARB for LVSD[2]	40	92%	96%	96%
Aspirin at Arrival[2]	201	99%	99%	99%
Aspirin at Discharge[2]	196	98%	99%	98%
Beta Blocker at Discharge[2]	198	98%	98%	98%
Fibrinolytic Medication Timing[2]	0	-	50%	55%
PCI Within 90 Minutes of Arrival[1,2]	20	100%	90%	90%
Smoking Cessation Advice[2]	65	100%	100%	99%
Chest Pain/Possible Heart Attack Care				
Aspirin at Arrival	46	93%	95%	95%
Median Time to ECG (minutes)	46	10	8	8
Median Time to Transfer (minutes)[1]	6	32	57	61
Fibrinolytic Medication Timing	0	-	33%	54%
Heart Failure Care				
ACE Inhibitor or ARB for LVSD[2]	95	95%	94%	94%
Discharge Instructions[2]	257	92%	89%	88%
Evaluation of LVS Function[2]	307	99%	98%	98%
Smoking Cessation Advice[2]	48	100%	99%	98%
Pneumonia Care				
Appropriate Initial Antibiotic[2]	94	90%	90%	92%
Blood Culture Timing[2]	123	98%	97%	96%
Influenza Vaccine[2]	84	86%	91%	91%
Initial Antibiotic Timing[2]	146	95%	96%	95%
Pneumococcal Vaccine[2]	90	96%	92%	93%
Smoking Cessation Advice[2]	51	100%	98%	97%
Surgical Care Improvement Project				
Appropriate VTP Within 24 Hours[2]	138	91%	92%	92%
Appropriate Hair Removal[2]	452	100%	99%	99%
Appropriate Beta Blocker Usage[2]	130	95%	92%	93%
Controlled Postoperative Blood Glucose[2]	37	89%	92%	93%
Prophylactic Antibiotic Timing[2]	332	97%	97%	97%
Prophylactic Antibiotic Timing (Outpatient)	107	94%	93%	92%
Prophylactic Antibiotic Selection[2]	335	99%	97%	97%
Prophylactic Antibiotic Select. (Outpatient)	104	98%	94%	94%
Prophylactic Antibiotic Stopped[2]	321	97%	94%	94%
Recommended VTP Ordered[2]	138	96%	94%	94%
Urinary Catheter Removal[2]	78	95%	89%	90%
Children's Asthma Care				
Received Systemic Corticosteroids	-	-	-	100%
Received Home Management Plan	-	-	-	71%
Received Reliever Medication	-	-	-	100%
Use of Medical Imaging				
Combination Abdominal CT Scan	1,471	0.082	0.246	0.191
Combination Chest CT Scan	1,451	0.014	0.098	0.054
Follow-up Mammogram/Ultrasound	2,589	8.6%	8.4%	8.4%
MRI for Low Back Pain	323	33.7%	33.4%	32.7%
Survey of Patients' Hospital Experiences				
Area Around Room 'Always' Quiet at Night	300+	51%	-	58%
Doctors 'Always' Communicated Well	300+	75%	-	80%
Home Recovery Information Given	300+	76%	-	82%
Hospital Given 9 or 10 on 10 Point Scale	300+	61%	-	67%
Meds 'Always' Explained Before Given	300+	53%	-	60%
Nurses 'Always' Communicated Well	300+	69%	-	76%
Pain 'Always' Well Controlled	300+	66%	-	69%
Room and Bathroom 'Always' Clean	300+	62%	-	71%
Timely Help 'Always' Received	300+	51%	-	64%
Would Definitely Recommend Hospital	300+	65%	-	69%

NOTE: Hospital profiles are in alphabetical order by state, then city, then hospital within the city; Rankings exclude hospitals with less than 25 cases except for patient surveys which excludes hospitals with less than 100 cases; (a) 100–299 cases; (1) The number of cases is too small to be sure how well a hospital is performing; (2) The hospital indicated that the data submitted for this measure were based on a sample of cases; (3) Data was collected during a shorter time period (fewer quarters) than the maximum possible time for this measure; (4) Suppressed for one or more quarters by CMS; (5) No data is available from the hospital for this measure; (6) Fewer than 100 patients completed the HCAHPS survey. Use these rates with caution, as the number of surveys may be too low to reliably assess hospital performance; (7) Survey results are based on less than 12 months of data; (8) Survey results are not available for this reporting period; (9) No or very few patients were eligible for the HCAHPS survey. The scores shown, if any, reflect a very small number of surveys; (10) A state average was not calculated because too few hospitals in the state submitted data; (11) There were discrepancies in the data collection process; Please refer to the User's Guide for a full explanation of data.

Mason District Hospital

615 North Promenade St
Havana, IL 62644
Phone: 309-543-4431
Fax: 309-543-8523
E-mail: hwolin@fgi.net
URL: www.masondistricthospital.org
Type: Critical Access Hospitals
Emergency Services: Yes
Ownership: Govt - Hospital Dist/Auth
Beds: 48

Key Personnel:
Chief of Medical Staff . . . . Tad A Yetter
Infection Control . . . . Lori Canada
Operating Room. . . . . Darci Bull, RN
Quality Assurance . . . . Gail Behrends
Emergency Room . . . . Rhonda Hine, RN

Measure	Cases	This Hosp.	State Avg.	U.S. Avg.
Heart Attack Care				
ACE Inhibitor or ARB for LVSD[3]	0	-	96%	96%
Aspirin at Arrival[3]	0	-	99%	99%
Aspirin at Discharge[3]	0	-	99%	98%
Beta Blocker at Discharge[3]	0	-	98%	98%
Fibrinolytic Medication Timing[3]	0	-	50%	55%
PCI Within 90 Minutes of Arrival[3]	0	-	90%	90%
Smoking Cessation Advice[3]	0	-	100%	99%
Chest Pain/Possible Heart Attack Care				
Aspirin at Arrival	-	-	95%	95%
Median Time to ECG (minutes)	-	-	8	8
Median Time to Transfer (minutes)	-	-	57	61
Fibrinolytic Medication Timing	-	-	33%	54%
Heart Failure Care				
ACE Inhibitor or ARB for LVSD[1]	7	100%	94%	94%
Discharge Instructions[1]	12	92%	89%	88%
Evaluation of LVS Function	26	100%	98%	98%
Smoking Cessation Advice[1]	3	100%	99%	98%
Pneumonia Care				
Appropriate Initial Antibiotic[1]	19	100%	90%	92%
Blood Culture Timing[1]	8	88%	97%	96%
Influenza Vaccine[1]	16	100%	91%	91%
Initial Antibiotic Timing	26	100%	96%	95%
Pneumococcal Vaccine	30	100%	92%	93%
Smoking Cessation Advice[1]	6	83%	98%	97%
Surgical Care Improvement Project				
Appropriate VTP Within 24 Hours[1,3]	3	100%	92%	92%
Appropriate Hair Removal[1,3]	4	100%	99%	99%
Appropriate Beta Blocker Usage[5]	0	-	92%	93%
Controlled Postoperative Blood Glucose[3]	0	-	92%	93%
Prophylactic Antibiotic Timing[1,3]	2	100%	97%	97%
Prophylactic Antibiotic Timing (Outpatient)	-	-	93%	92%
Prophylactic Antibiotic Selection[1,3]	2	100%	97%	97%
Prophylactic Antibiotic Select. (Outpatient)	-	-	94%	94%
Prophylactic Antibiotic Stopped[1,3]	2	100%	94%	94%
Recommended VTP Ordered[1,3]	3	100%	94%	94%
Urinary Catheter Removal[3]	0	-	89%	90%
Children's Asthma Care				
Received Systemic Corticosteroids	-	-	-	100%
Received Home Management Plan	-	-	-	71%
Received Reliever Medication	-	-	-	100%
Use of Medical Imaging				
Combination Abdominal CT Scan	-	-	0.246	0.191
Combination Chest CT Scan	-	-	0.098	0.054
Follow-up Mammogram/Ultrasound	-	-	8.4%	8.4%
MRI for Low Back Pain	-	-	33.4%	32.7%
Survey of Patients' Hospital Experiences				
Area Around Room 'Always' Quiet at Night[6]	<100	58%	-	58%
Doctors 'Always' Communicated Well[6]	<100	87%	-	80%
Home Recovery Information Given[6]	<100	89%	-	82%
Hospital Given 9 or 10 on 10 Point Scale[6]	<100	88%	-	67%
Meds 'Always' Explained Before Given[6]	<100	72%	-	60%
Nurses 'Always' Communicated Well[6]	<100	87%	-	76%
Pain 'Always' Well Controlled[6]	<100	76%	-	69%
Room and Bathroom 'Always' Clean[6]	<100	85%	-	71%
Timely Help 'Always' Received[6]	<100	81%	-	64%
Would Definitely Recommend Hospital	<100	83%	-	69%

Advocate South Suburban Hospital

17800 S Kedzie Ave
Hazel Crest, IL 60429
Phone: 708-799-8000
Fax: 773-967-4217
E-mail: maureen.daugherty@advocatehealth.com
URL: www.advocatehealth.com
Type: Acute Care Hospitals
Emergency Services: Yes
Ownership: Voluntary Non-Profit - Church
Beds: 291

Key Personnel:
CEO/President. . . . . Pat Martin
Chief of Medical Staff . . . . Asta Kelly, MD
Operating Room. . . . . Cynthia Newell
Quality Assurance . . . . Mary Lange
Radiology. . . . . J Nayden, MD
Emergency Room . . . . Diane Warbuton
Intensive Care Unit. . . . . Donna Gurley

Measure	Cases	This Hosp.	State Avg.	U.S. Avg.
Heart Attack Care				
ACE Inhibitor or ARB for LVSD	27	100%	96%	96%
Aspirin at Arrival	148	100%	99%	99%
Aspirin at Discharge	126	100%	99%	98%
Beta Blocker at Discharge	133	100%	98%	98%
Fibrinolytic Medication Timing	0	-	50%	55%
PCI Within 90 Minutes of Arrival[1]	19	100%	90%	90%
Smoking Cessation Advice	53	100%	100%	99%
Chest Pain/Possible Heart Attack Care				
Aspirin at Arrival[1]	7	71%	95%	95%
Median Time to ECG (minutes)[1]	7	4	8	8
Median Time to Transfer (minutes)[5]	0	-	57	61
Fibrinolytic Medication Timing[5]	0	-	33%	54%
Heart Failure Care				
ACE Inhibitor or ARB for LVSD[2]	133	99%	94%	94%
Discharge Instructions[2]	260	93%	89%	88%
Evaluation of LVS Function[2]	314	100%	98%	98%
Smoking Cessation Advice[2]	85	100%	99%	98%
Pneumonia Care				
Appropriate Initial Antibiotic[2]	75	97%	90%	92%
Blood Culture Timing[2]	58	97%	97%	96%
Influenza Vaccine[2]	86	99%	91%	91%
Initial Antibiotic Timing[2]	141	100%	96%	95%
Pneumococcal Vaccine[2]	133	99%	92%	93%
Smoking Cessation Advice[2]	54	100%	98%	97%
Surgical Care Improvement Project				
Appropriate VTP Within 24 Hours[2]	159	98%	92%	92%
Appropriate Hair Removal[2]	415	100%	99%	99%
Appropriate Beta Blocker Usage[2]	126	98%	92%	93%
Controlled Postoperative Blood Glucose[2]	0	-	92%	93%
Prophylactic Antibiotic Timing[2]	295	99%	97%	97%
Prophylactic Antibiotic Timing (Outpatient)	220	97%	93%	92%
Prophylactic Antibiotic Selection[2]	298	100%	97%	97%
Prophylactic Antibiotic Select. (Outpatient)	219	99%	94%	94%
Prophylactic Antibiotic Stopped[2]	271	97%	94%	94%
Recommended VTP Ordered[2]	159	99%	94%	94%
Urinary Catheter Removal[2]	69	99%	89%	90%
Children's Asthma Care				
Received Systemic Corticosteroids	-	-	-	100%
Received Home Management Plan	-	-	-	71%
Received Reliever Medication	-	-	-	100%
Use of Medical Imaging				
Combination Abdominal CT Scan	732	0.094	0.246	0.191
Combination Chest CT Scan	497	0.052	0.098	0.054
Follow-up Mammogram/Ultrasound	1,087	9.7%	8.4%	8.4%
MRI for Low Back Pain	95	34.7%	33.4%	32.7%
Survey of Patients' Hospital Experiences				
Area Around Room 'Always' Quiet at Night	300+	52%	-	58%
Doctors 'Always' Communicated Well	300+	78%	-	80%
Home Recovery Information Given	300+	79%	-	82%
Hospital Given 9 or 10 on 10 Point Scale	300+	61%	-	67%
Meds 'Always' Explained Before Given	300+	59%	-	60%
Nurses 'Always' Communicated Well	300+	75%	-	76%
Pain 'Always' Well Controlled	300+	68%	-	69%
Room and Bathroom 'Always' Clean	300+	66%	-	71%
Timely Help 'Always' Received	300+	59%	-	64%
Would Definitely Recommend Hospital	300+	63%	-	69%

Herrin Hospital

201 S 14th St
Herrin, IL 62948
Phone: 618-942-2171
Fax: 618-351-4929
URL: www.sih.net
Type: Acute Care Hospitals
Emergency Services: Yes
Ownership: Voluntary Non-Profit - Private
Beds: 102

Key Personnel:
CEO/President. . . . . Jack Buckley
Chief of Medical Staff . . . . Pramote Anantachai, MD
Infection Control . . . . Dottie Throgmorton, RN
Operating Room. . . . . Antoni Kos, RN
Quality Assurance . . . . Paula Alters
Radiology. . . . . James Borders
Emergency Room . . . . Daniel Bercu, MD
Intensive Care Unit. . . . . Dottie Throgmorton, RN

Measure	Cases	This Hosp.	State Avg.	U.S. Avg.
Heart Attack Care				
ACE Inhibitor or ARB for LVSD[1]	7	57%	96%	96%
Aspirin at Arrival	29	97%	99%	99%
Aspirin at Discharge[1]	18	94%	99%	98%
Beta Blocker at Discharge[1]	18	100%	98%	98%
Fibrinolytic Medication Timing	0	-	50%	55%
PCI Within 90 Minutes of Arrival	0	-	90%	90%
Smoking Cessation Advice[1]	6	100%	100%	99%
Chest Pain/Possible Heart Attack Care				
Aspirin at Arrival	157	96%	95%	95%
Median Time to ECG (minutes)	164	2	8	8
Median Time to Transfer (minutes)[1]	24	26	57	61
Fibrinolytic Medication Timing	0	-	33%	54%
Heart Failure Care				
ACE Inhibitor or ARB for LVSD	50	82%	94%	94%
Discharge Instructions	141	70%	89%	88%
Evaluation of LVS Function	177	99%	98%	98%
Smoking Cessation Advice	31	100%	99%	98%
Pneumonia Care				
Appropriate Initial Antibiotic	95	88%	90%	92%
Blood Culture Timing	119	100%	97%	96%
Influenza Vaccine	144	88%	91%	91%
Initial Antibiotic Timing	177	92%	96%	95%
Pneumococcal Vaccine	177	90%	92%	93%
Smoking Cessation Advice	92	96%	98%	97%
Surgical Care Improvement Project				
Appropriate VTP Within 24 Hours	173	90%	92%	92%
Appropriate Hair Removal	277	100%	99%	99%
Appropriate Beta Blocker Usage	102	93%	92%	93%
Controlled Postoperative Blood Glucose	0	-	92%	93%
Prophylactic Antibiotic Timing	198	92%	97%	97%
Prophylactic Antibiotic Timing (Outpatient)	37	81%	93%	92%
Prophylactic Antibiotic Selection	198	95%	97%	97%
Prophylactic Antibiotic Select. (Outpatient)	33	91%	94%	94%
Prophylactic Antibiotic Stopped	183	88%	94%	94%
Recommended VTP Ordered	173	94%	94%	94%
Urinary Catheter Removal	89	96%	89%	90%
Children's Asthma Care				
Received Systemic Corticosteroids	-	-	-	100%
Received Home Management Plan	-	-	-	71%
Received Reliever Medication	-	-	-	100%
Use of Medical Imaging				
Combination Abdominal CT Scan	1,080	0.107	0.246	0.191
Combination Chest CT Scan	679	0.074	0.098	0.054
Follow-up Mammogram/Ultrasound	1,111	6.4%	8.4%	8.4%
MRI for Low Back Pain	167	43.7%	33.4%	32.7%
Survey of Patients' Hospital Experiences				
Area Around Room 'Always' Quiet at Night	300+	48%	-	58%
Doctors 'Always' Communicated Well	300+	85%	-	80%
Home Recovery Information Given	300+	87%	-	82%
Hospital Given 9 or 10 on 10 Point Scale	300+	72%	-	67%
Meds 'Always' Explained Before Given	300+	64%	-	60%
Nurses 'Always' Communicated Well	300+	78%	-	76%
Pain 'Always' Well Controlled	300+	70%	-	69%
Room and Bathroom 'Always' Clean	300+	76%	-	71%
Timely Help 'Always' Received	300+	65%	-	64%
Would Definitely Recommend Hospital	300+	78%	-	69%

NOTE: Hospital profiles are in alphabetical order by state, then city, then hospital within the city; Rankings exclude hospitals with less than 25 cases except for patient surveys which excludes hospitals with less than 100 cases; (a) 100–299 cases; (1) The number of cases is too small to be sure how well a hospital is performing; (2) The hospital indicated that the data submitted for this measure were based on a sample of cases; (3) Data was collected during a shorter time period (fewer quarters) than the maximum possible time for this measure; (4) Suppressed for one or more quarters by CMS; (5) No data is available from the hospital for this measure; (6) Fewer than 100 patients completed the HCAHPS survey. Use these rates with caution, as the number of surveys may be too low to reliably assess hospital performance; (7) Survey results are based on less than 12 months of data; (8) Survey results are not available for this reporting period; (9) No or very few patients were eligible for the HCAHPS survey. The scores shown, if any, reflect a very small number of surveys; (10) A state average was not calculated because too few hospitals in the state submitted data; (11) There were discrepancies in the data collection process; Please refer to the User's Guide for a full explanation of data.

Saint Joseph's Hospital

1515 Main Street
Highland, IL 62249
Phone: 618-654-7421
Fax: 618-654-2012
Type: Critical Access Hospitals
Emergency Services: Yes
Ownership: Voluntary Non-Profit - Church
Beds: 106

Key Personnel:

CEO/President. . . . . Lowell Jones
Chief of Medical Staff . . . . Greg Mirianda
Radiology. . . . . Robert Killian
Anesthesiology. . . . . Brad Bernstein
Emergency Room . . . . Armand Miranda, MD

Measure	Cases	This Hosp.	State Avg.	U.S. Avg.
Heart Attack Care				
ACE Inhibitor or ARB for LVSD[5]	0	-	96%	96%
Aspirin at Arrival[5]	0	-	99%	99%
Aspirin at Discharge[5]	0	-	99%	98%
Beta Blocker at Discharge[5]	0	-	98%	98%
Fibrinolytic Medication Timing[5]	0	-	50%	55%
PCI Within 90 Minutes of Arrival[5]	0	-	90%	90%
Smoking Cessation Advice[5]	0	-	100%	99%
Chest Pain/Possible Heart Attack Care				
Aspirin at Arrival	-	-	95%	95%
Median Time to ECG (minutes)	-	-	8	8
Median Time to Transfer (minutes)	-	-	57	61
Fibrinolytic Medication Timing	-	-	33%	54%
Heart Failure Care				
ACE Inhibitor or ARB for LVSD[1]	6	83%	94%	94%
Discharge Instructions[1]	14	100%	89%	88%
Evaluation of LVS Function	30	90%	98%	98%
Smoking Cessation Advice[1]	3	100%	99%	98%
Pneumonia Care				
Appropriate Initial Antibiotic	29	86%	90%	92%
Blood Culture Timing[1]	23	100%	97%	96%
Influenza Vaccine	25	96%	91%	91%
Initial Antibiotic Timing	31	90%	96%	95%
Pneumococcal Vaccine	33	85%	92%	93%
Smoking Cessation Advice[1]	12	100%	98%	97%
Surgical Care Improvement Project				
Appropriate VTP Within 24 Hours	27	78%	92%	92%
Appropriate Hair Removal	37	100%	99%	99%
Appropriate Beta Blocker Usage[1]	10	50%	92%	93%
Controlled Postoperative Blood Glucose[5]	0	-	92%	93%
Prophylactic Antibiotic Timing	27	93%	97%	97%
Prophylactic Antibiotic Timing (Outpatient)	-	-	93%	92%
Prophylactic Antibiotic Selection	27	96%	97%	97%
Prophylactic Antibiotic Select. (Outpatient)	-	-	94%	94%
Prophylactic Antibiotic Stopped	27	81%	94%	94%
Recommended VTP Ordered	27	81%	94%	94%
Urinary Catheter Removal[1]	15	73%	89%	90%
Children's Asthma Care				
Received Systemic Corticosteroids	-	-	-	100%
Received Home Management Plan	-	-	-	71%
Received Reliever Medication	-	-	-	100%
Use of Medical Imaging				
Combination Abdominal CT Scan	-	-	0.246	0.191
Combination Chest CT Scan	-	-	0.098	0.054
Follow-up Mammogram/Ultrasound	-	-	8.4%	8.4%
MRI for Low Back Pain	-	-	33.4%	32.7%
Survey of Patients' Hospital Experiences				
Area Around Room 'Always' Quiet at Night	(a)	59%	-	58%
Doctors 'Always' Communicated Well	(a)	84%	-	80%
Home Recovery Information Given	(a)	85%	-	82%
Hospital Given 9 or 10 on 10 Point Scale	(a)	72%	-	67%
Meds 'Always' Explained Before Given	(a)	63%	-	60%
Nurses 'Always' Communicated Well	(a)	84%	-	76%
Pain 'Always' Well Controlled	(a)	80%	-	69%
Room and Bathroom 'Always' Clean	(a)	86%	-	71%
Timely Help 'Always' Received	(a)	66%	-	64%
Would Definitely Recommend Hospital	(a)	71%	-	69%

Hillsboro Area Hospital

1200 E Tremont Street
Hillsboro, IL 62049
Phone: 217-532-6111
Fax: 217-532-2726
Type: Critical Access Hospitals
Emergency Services: Yes
Ownership: Voluntary Non-Profit - Private
Beds: 100

Key Personnel:

Chief of Medical Staff . . . . Roger McFarlin, MD
Coronary Care . . . . Deehon Rives
Infection Control. . . . . Kathy Sullivan, RN
Operating Room. . . . . Theresa Rapp
Pediatric In-Patient Care . . . . Deehan Rives
Quality Assurance . . . . Angie Dugan
Radiology. . . . . Patricia Weaver

Measure	Cases	This Hosp.	State Avg.	U.S. Avg.
Heart Attack Care				
ACE Inhibitor or ARB for LVSD	0	-	96%	96%
Aspirin at Arrival[1]	5	80%	99%	99%
Aspirin at Discharge[1]	4	100%	99%	98%
Beta Blocker at Discharge[1]	3	100%	98%	98%
Fibrinolytic Medication Timing	0	-	50%	55%
PCI Within 90 Minutes of Arrival	0	-	90%	90%
Smoking Cessation Advice[1]	1	100%	100%	99%
Chest Pain/Possible Heart Attack Care				
Aspirin at Arrival	-	-	95%	95%
Median Time to ECG (minutes)	-	-	8	8
Median Time to Transfer (minutes)	-	-	57	61
Fibrinolytic Medication Timing	-	-	33%	54%
Heart Failure Care				
ACE Inhibitor or ARB for LVSD[1]	6	100%	94%	94%
Discharge Instructions[1]	21	100%	89%	88%
Evaluation of LVS Function	33	100%	98%	98%
Smoking Cessation Advice[1]	6	100%	99%	98%
Pneumonia Care				
Appropriate Initial Antibiotic	42	98%	90%	92%
Blood Culture Timing	30	97%	97%	96%
Influenza Vaccine	36	100%	91%	91%
Initial Antibiotic Timing	51	100%	96%	95%
Pneumococcal Vaccine	52	100%	92%	93%
Smoking Cessation Advice[1]	14	100%	98%	97%
Surgical Care Improvement Project				
Appropriate VTP Within 24 Hours[3]	0	-	92%	92%
Appropriate Hair Removal[1,3]	1	100%	99%	99%
Appropriate Beta Blocker Usage[1,3]	1	100%	92%	93%
Controlled Postoperative Blood Glucose[3]	0	-	92%	93%
Prophylactic Antibiotic Timing[3]	0	-	97%	97%
Prophylactic Antibiotic Timing (Outpatient)	-	-	93%	92%
Prophylactic Antibiotic Selection[3]	0	-	97%	97%
Prophylactic Antibiotic Select. (Outpatient)	-	-	94%	94%
Prophylactic Antibiotic Stopped[3]	0	-	94%	94%
Recommended VTP Ordered[3]	0	-	94%	94%
Urinary Catheter Removal[5]	0	-	89%	90%
Children's Asthma Care				
Received Systemic Corticosteroids	-	-	-	100%
Received Home Management Plan	-	-	-	71%
Received Reliever Medication	-	-	-	100%
Use of Medical Imaging				
Combination Abdominal CT Scan	-	-	0.246	0.191
Combination Chest CT Scan	-	-	0.098	0.054
Follow-up Mammogram/Ultrasound	-	-	8.4%	8.4%
MRI for Low Back Pain	-	-	33.4%	32.7%
Survey of Patients' Hospital Experiences				
Area Around Room 'Always' Quiet at Night	(a)	53%	-	58%
Doctors 'Always' Communicated Well	(a)	78%	-	80%
Home Recovery Information Given	(a)	81%	-	82%
Hospital Given 9 or 10 on 10 Point Scale	(a)	70%	-	67%
Meds 'Always' Explained Before Given	(a)	65%	-	60%
Nurses 'Always' Communicated Well	(a)	81%	-	76%
Pain 'Always' Well Controlled	(a)	72%	-	69%
Room and Bathroom 'Always' Clean	(a)	73%	-	71%
Timely Help 'Always' Received	(a)	70%	-	64%
Would Definitely Recommend Hospital	(a)	64%	-	69%

Hines VA Medical Center

5th Street & Roosevelt Avenue
Hines, IL 60141
Phone: 708-202-8387
Fax: 708-202-2725
URL: www.visn12.med.va.gov/Hines
Type: Acute Care-Veterans Administration
Emergency Services: No
Ownership: Government - Federal
Beds: 472

Key Personnel:

Chief of Medical Staff . . . . P Fahey, MD
Infection Control. . . . . D Schaaff, MD
Operating Room. . . . . E Pierce, RN
Quality Assurance . . . . L Beverly
Radiology. . . . . Mark VanDrunen, MD
Anesthesiology. . . . . B Kleinmann, MD
Emergency Room . . . . P Murdoch, MD
Intensive Care Unit. . . . . L Rutledge, RN

Measure	Cases	This Hosp.	State Avg.	U.S. Avg.
Heart Attack Care				
ACE Inhibitor or ARB for LVSD[1]	10	100%	96%	96%
Aspirin at Arrival	36	97%	99%	99%
Aspirin at Discharge	33	100%	99%	98%
Beta Blocker at Discharge	27	100%	98%	98%
Fibrinolytic Medication Timing[5]	0	-	50%	55%
PCI Within 90 Minutes of Arrival[1]	5	20%	90%	90%
Smoking Cessation Advice[1]	14	100%	100%	99%
Chest Pain/Possible Heart Attack Care				
Aspirin at Arrival	-	-	95%	95%
Median Time to ECG (minutes)	-	-	8	8
Median Time to Transfer (minutes)	-	-	57	61
Fibrinolytic Medication Timing	-	-	33%	54%
Heart Failure Care				
ACE Inhibitor or ARB for LVSD	121	100%	94%	94%
Discharge Instructions	248	98%	89%	88%
Evaluation of LVS Function	271	100%	98%	98%
Smoking Cessation Advice	61	100%	99%	98%
Pneumonia Care				
Appropriate Initial Antibiotic	66	95%	90%	92%
Blood Culture Timing	129	100%	97%	96%
Influenza Vaccine	112	98%	91%	91%
Initial Antibiotic Timing	132	95%	96%	95%
Pneumococcal Vaccine	149	99%	92%	93%
Smoking Cessation Advice	78	100%	98%	97%
Surgical Care Improvement Project				
Appropriate VTP Within 24 Hours[2]	78	97%	92%	92%
Appropriate Hair Removal[2]	252	100%	99%	99%
Appropriate Beta Blocker Usage[2]	143	100%	92%	93%
Controlled Postoperative Blood Glucose[2]	108	92%	92%	93%
Prophylactic Antibiotic Timing	158	98%	97%	97%
Prophylactic Antibiotic Timing (Outpatient)	-	-	93%	92%
Prophylactic Antibiotic Selection	158	99%	97%	97%
Prophylactic Antibiotic Select. (Outpatient)	-	-	94%	94%
Prophylactic Antibiotic Stopped	155	100%	94%	94%
Recommended VTP Ordered[2]	78	97%	94%	94%
Urinary Catheter Removal[2]	138	100%	89%	90%
Children's Asthma Care				
Received Systemic Corticosteroids	-	-	-	100%
Received Home Management Plan	-	-	-	71%
Received Reliever Medication	-	-	-	100%
Use of Medical Imaging				
Combination Abdominal CT Scan	-	-	0.246	0.191
Combination Chest CT Scan	-	-	0.098	0.054
Follow-up Mammogram/Ultrasound	-	-	8.4%	8.4%
MRI for Low Back Pain	-	-	33.4%	32.7%
Survey of Patients' Hospital Experiences				
Area Around Room 'Always' Quiet at Night	-	-	-	58%
Doctors 'Always' Communicated Well	-	-	-	80%
Home Recovery Information Given	-	-	-	82%
Hospital Given 9 or 10 on 10 Point Scale	-	-	-	67%
Meds 'Always' Explained Before Given	-	-	-	60%
Nurses 'Always' Communicated Well	-	-	-	76%
Pain 'Always' Well Controlled	-	-	-	69%
Room and Bathroom 'Always' Clean	-	-	-	71%
Timely Help 'Always' Received	-	-	-	64%
Would Definitely Recommend Hospital	-	-	-	69%

NOTE: Hospital profiles are in alphabetical order by state, then city, then hospital within the city; Rankings exclude hospitals with less than 25 cases except for patient surveys which excludes hospitals with less than 100 cases; (a) 100–299 cases; (1) The number of cases is too small to be sure how well a hospital is performing; (2) The hospital indicated that the data submitted for this measure were based on a sample of cases; (3) Data was collected during a shorter time period (fewer quarters) than the maximum possible time for this measure; (4) Suppressed for one or more quarters by CMS; (5) No data is available from the hospital for this measure; (6) Fewer than 100 patients completed the HCAHPS survey. Use these rates with caution, as the number of surveys may be too low to reliably assess hospital performance; (7) Survey results are based on less than 12 months of data; (8) Survey results are not available for this reporting period; (9) No or very few patients were eligible for the HCAHPS survey. The scores shown, if any, reflect a very small number of surveys; (10) A state average was not calculated because too few hospitals in the state submitted data; (11) There were discrepancies in the data collection process; Please refer to the User's Guide for a full explanation of data.

Hinsdale Hospital

120 North Oak St Phone: 630-856-9000
Hinsdale, IL 60521 Fax: 630-856-7560
URL: www.keepingyouwell.com
Type: Acute Care Hospitals Emergency Services: Yes
Ownership: Voluntary Non-Profit - Church Beds: 426

Key Personnel:
CEO/President. . . . . Ernie Sadau
Chief of Medical Staff. . . . . Robert Zeck, MD
Quality Assurance . . . . Donita Phillips
Radiology. . . . . Val Lavezzi
Ambulatory Care . . . . Sue Smith
Emergency Room . . . . Sue Smith

Measure	Cases	This Hosp.	State Avg.	U.S. Avg.
Heart Attack Care				
ACE Inhibitor or ARB for LVSD[1]	16	88%	96%	96%
Aspirin at Arrival	89	100%	99%	99%
Aspirin at Discharge	94	100%	99%	98%
Beta Blocker at Discharge	101	99%	98%	98%
Fibrinolytic Medication Timing	0	-	50%	55%
PCI Within 90 Minutes of Arrival[1]	17	100%	90%	90%
Smoking Cessation Advice[1]	23	100%	100%	99%
Chest Pain/Possible Heart Attack Care				
Aspirin at Arrival[5]	0	-	95%	95%
Median Time to ECG (minutes)[5]	0	-	8	8
Median Time to Transfer (minutes)[5]	0	-	57	61
Fibrinolytic Medication Timing[5]	0	-	33%	54%
Heart Failure Care				
ACE Inhibitor or ARB for LVSD	75	88%	94%	94%
Discharge Instructions	163	79%	89%	88%
Evaluation of LVS Function	249	100%	98%	98%
Smoking Cessation Advice[1]	24	100%	99%	98%
Pneumonia Care				
Appropriate Initial Antibiotic	120	86%	90%	92%
Blood Culture Timing	243	97%	97%	96%
Influenza Vaccine	142	88%	91%	91%
Initial Antibiotic Timing	217	97%	96%	95%
Pneumococcal Vaccine	240	89%	92%	93%
Smoking Cessation Advice	38	97%	98%	97%
Surgical Care Improvement Project				
Appropriate VTP Within 24 Hours[2]	144	95%	92%	92%
Appropriate Hair Removal[2]	440	100%	99%	99%
Appropriate Beta Blocker Usage[2]	120	96%	92%	93%
Controlled Postoperative Blood Glucose[2]	77	88%	92%	93%
Prophylactic Antibiotic Timing[2]	309	95%	97%	97%
Prophylactic Antibiotic Timing (Outpatient)	278	96%	93%	92%
Prophylactic Antibiotic Selection[2]	313	100%	97%	97%
Prophylactic Antibiotic Select. (Outpatient)	272	99%	94%	94%
Prophylactic Antibiotic Stopped[2]	292	94%	94%	94%
Recommended VTP Ordered[2]	144	99%	94%	94%
Urinary Catheter Removal[2]	80	98%	89%	90%
Children's Asthma Care				
Received Systemic Corticosteroids	-	-	-	100%
Received Home Management Plan	-	-	-	71%
Received Reliever Medication	-	-	-	100%
Use of Medical Imaging				
Combination Abdominal CT Scan	909	0.241	0.246	0.191
Combination Chest CT Scan	704	0.011	0.098	0.054
Follow-up Mammogram/Ultrasound	3,031	10.6%	8.4%	8.4%
MRI for Low Back Pain	137	27.7%	33.4%	32.7%
Survey of Patients' Hospital Experiences				
Area Around Room 'Always' Quiet at Night	300+	49%	-	58%
Doctors 'Always' Communicated Well	300+	76%	-	80%
Home Recovery Information Given	300+	83%	-	82%
Hospital Given 9 or 10 on 10 Point Scale	300+	65%	-	67%
Meds 'Always' Explained Before Given	300+	54%	-	60%
Nurses 'Always' Communicated Well	300+	70%	-	76%
Pain 'Always' Well Controlled	300+	66%	-	69%
Room and Bathroom 'Always' Clean	300+	73%	-	71%
Timely Help 'Always' Received	300+	58%	-	64%
Would Definitely Recommend Hospital	300+	68%	-	69%

Saint Alexius Medical Center

1555 N Barrington Rd Phone: 847-843-2000
Hoffman Estates, IL 60194 Fax: 847-781-3914
E-mail: linda.baker@stalexius.net
URL: www.alexianbrothershealth.org
Type: Acute Care Hospitals Emergency Services: Yes
Ownership: Voluntary Non-Profit - Church Beds: 331

Key Personnel:
CEO/President. . . . . Edward M Goldberg
Cardiac Laboratory. . . . . Laura Fiaccato
Operating Room. . . . . Barb Cerwin
Pediatric In-Patient Care . . . . Laurie Miller RN
Radiology. . . . . Scott Baker
Emergency Room . . . . Keith Hill RN
Hemotology Center . . . . Carol Pfeifer RN
Intensive Care Unit. . . . . Barb Wallace

Measure	Cases	This Hosp.	State Avg.	U.S. Avg.
Heart Attack Care				
ACE Inhibitor or ARB for LVSD[1]	24	96%	96%	96%
Aspirin at Arrival	173	100%	99%	99%
Aspirin at Discharge	144	100%	99%	98%
Beta Blocker at Discharge	146	99%	98%	98%
Fibrinolytic Medication Timing	0	-	50%	55%
PCI Within 90 Minutes of Arrival	41	93%	90%	90%
Smoking Cessation Advice	54	100%	100%	99%
Chest Pain/Possible Heart Attack Care				
Aspirin at Arrival[1]	11	91%	95%	95%
Median Time to ECG (minutes)[1]	13	7	8	8
Median Time to Transfer (minutes)[1,3]	1	130	57	61
Fibrinolytic Medication Timing[3]	0	-	33%	54%
Heart Failure Care				
ACE Inhibitor or ARB for LVSD	64	92%	94%	94%
Discharge Instructions	277	96%	89%	88%
Evaluation of LVS Function	397	100%	98%	98%
Smoking Cessation Advice	44	100%	99%	98%
Pneumonia Care				
Appropriate Initial Antibiotic	165	95%	90%	92%
Blood Culture Timing	329	99%	97%	96%
Influenza Vaccine	250	98%	91%	91%
Initial Antibiotic Timing	290	94%	96%	95%
Pneumococcal Vaccine	355	99%	92%	93%
Smoking Cessation Advice	112	100%	98%	97%
Surgical Care Improvement Project				
Appropriate VTP Within 24 Hours[2]	209	97%	92%	92%
Appropriate Hair Removal[2]	466	100%	99%	99%
Appropriate Beta Blocker Usage[2]	101	91%	92%	93%
Controlled Postoperative Blood Glucose[2]	0	-	92%	93%
Prophylactic Antibiotic Timing[2]	309	99%	97%	97%
Prophylactic Antibiotic Timing (Outpatient)	321	94%	93%	92%
Prophylactic Antibiotic Selection[2]	311	97%	97%	97%
Prophylactic Antibiotic Select. (Outpatient)	316	98%	94%	94%
Prophylactic Antibiotic Stopped[2]	284	98%	94%	94%
Recommended VTP Ordered[2]	209	98%	94%	94%
Urinary Catheter Removal[2]	94	91%	89%	90%
Children's Asthma Care				
Received Systemic Corticosteroids	-	-	-	100%
Received Home Management Plan	-	-	-	71%
Received Reliever Medication	-	-	-	100%
Use of Medical Imaging				
Combination Abdominal CT Scan	962	0.337	0.246	0.191
Combination Chest CT Scan	936	0.175	0.098	0.054
Follow-up Mammogram/Ultrasound	1,166	8.1%	8.4%	8.4%
MRI for Low Back Pain	156	34.6%	33.4%	32.7%
Survey of Patients' Hospital Experiences				
Area Around Room 'Always' Quiet at Night	300+	42%	-	58%
Doctors 'Always' Communicated Well	300+	79%	-	80%
Home Recovery Information Given	300+	81%	-	82%
Hospital Given 9 or 10 on 10 Point Scale	300+	66%	-	67%
Meds 'Always' Explained Before Given	300+	59%	-	60%
Nurses 'Always' Communicated Well	300+	80%	-	76%
Pain 'Always' Well Controlled	300+	71%	-	69%
Room and Bathroom 'Always' Clean	300+	70%	-	71%
Timely Help 'Always' Received	300+	66%	-	64%
Would Definitely Recommend Hospital	300+	68%	-	69%

Hoopeston Community Memorial Hospital

701 East Orange Street Phone: 217-283-5531
Hoopeston, IL 60942 Fax: 217-283-7991
Type: Critical Access Hospitals Emergency Services: Yes
Ownership: Voluntary Non-Profit - Private Beds: 25

Key Personnel:
CEO/President. . . . . Frank T Caruso
Chief of Medical Staff. . . . . Daesun Oh, MD
Infection Control. . . . . Carole Bond
Operating Room. . . . . Dr San Diego, RN
Quality Assurance . . . . Dianne Vance, LPN
Anesthesiology. . . . . Dennis Birkey, CRNA

Measure	Cases	This Hosp.	State Avg.	U.S. Avg.
Heart Attack Care				
ACE Inhibitor or ARB for LVSD[3]	0	-	96%	96%
Aspirin at Arrival[3]	0	-	99%	99%
Aspirin at Discharge[3]	0	-	99%	98%
Beta Blocker at Discharge[3]	0	-	98%	98%
Fibrinolytic Medication Timing[3]	0	-	50%	55%
PCI Within 90 Minutes of Arrival[3]	0	-	90%	90%
Smoking Cessation Advice[3]	0	-	100%	99%
Chest Pain/Possible Heart Attack Care				
Aspirin at Arrival	-	-	95%	95%
Median Time to ECG (minutes)	-	-	8	8
Median Time to Transfer (minutes)	-	-	57	61
Fibrinolytic Medication Timing	-	-	33%	54%
Heart Failure Care				
ACE Inhibitor or ARB for LVSD[1]	8	88%	94%	94%
Discharge Instructions	32	97%	89%	88%
Evaluation of LVS Function	39	82%	98%	98%
Smoking Cessation Advice[1]	5	100%	99%	98%
Pneumonia Care				
Appropriate Initial Antibiotic	30	97%	90%	92%
Blood Culture Timing	57	70%	97%	96%
Influenza Vaccine[1]	23	100%	91%	91%
Initial Antibiotic Timing	27	93%	96%	95%
Pneumococcal Vaccine	49	78%	92%	93%
Smoking Cessation Advice[1]	11	73%	98%	97%
Surgical Care Improvement Project				
Appropriate VTP Within 24 Hours[1]	3	67%	92%	92%
Appropriate Hair Removal[1]	13	100%	99%	99%
Appropriate Beta Blocker Usage[5]	0	-	92%	93%
Controlled Postoperative Blood Glucose	0	-	92%	93%
Prophylactic Antibiotic Timing[1]	7	100%	97%	97%
Prophylactic Antibiotic Timing (Outpatient)	-	-	93%	92%
Prophylactic Antibiotic Selection[1]	6	100%	97%	97%
Prophylactic Antibiotic Select. (Outpatient)	-	-	94%	94%
Prophylactic Antibiotic Stopped[1]	6	100%	94%	94%
Recommended VTP Ordered[1]	3	67%	94%	94%
Urinary Catheter Removal[1]	9	100%	89%	90%
Children's Asthma Care				
Received Systemic Corticosteroids	-	-	-	100%
Received Home Management Plan	-	-	-	71%
Received Reliever Medication	-	-	-	100%
Use of Medical Imaging				
Combination Abdominal CT Scan	-	-	0.246	0.191
Combination Chest CT Scan	-	-	0.098	0.054
Follow-up Mammogram/Ultrasound	-	-	8.4%	8.4%
MRI for Low Back Pain	-	-	33.4%	32.7%
Survey of Patients' Hospital Experiences				
Area Around Room 'Always' Quiet at Night[8]	-	-	-	58%
Doctors 'Always' Communicated Well[8]	-	-	-	80%
Home Recovery Information Given[8]	-	-	-	82%
Hospital Given 9 or 10 on 10 Point Scale[8]	-	-	-	67%
Meds 'Always' Explained Before Given[8]	-	-	-	60%
Nurses 'Always' Communicated Well[8]	-	-	-	76%
Pain 'Always' Well Controlled[8]	-	-	-	69%
Room and Bathroom 'Always' Clean[8]	-	-	-	71%
Timely Help 'Always' Received[8]	-	-	-	64%
Would Definitely Recommend Hospital[8]	-	-	-	69%

NOTE: Hospital profiles are in alphabetical order by state, then city, then hospital within the city; Rankings exclude hospitals with less than 25 cases except for patient surveys which excludes hospitals with less than 100 cases; (a) 100–299 cases; (1) The number of cases is too small to be sure how well a hospital is performing; (2) The hospital indicated that the data submitted for this measure were based on a sample of cases; (3) Data was collected during a shorter time period (fewer quarters) than the maximum possible time for this measure; (4) Suppressed for one or more quarters by CMS; (5) No data is available from the hospital for this measure; (6) Fewer than 100 patients completed the HCAHPS survey. Use these rates with caution, as the number of surveys may be too low to reliably assess hospital performance; (7) Survey results are based on less than 12 months of data; (8) Survey results are not available for this reporting period; (9) No or very few patients were eligible for the HCAHPS survey. The scores shown, if any, reflect a very small number of surveys; (10) A state average was not calculated because too few hospitals in the state submitted data; (11) There were discrepancies in the data collection process; Please refer to the User's Guide for a full explanation of data.

Hopedale Medical Complex

107 Tremont Street
Hopedale, IL 61747
Phone: 309-449-3321
Type: Critical Access Hospitals
Emergency Services: Yes
Ownership: Voluntary Non-Profit - Private

Measure	Cases	This Hosp.	State Avg.	U.S. Avg.
Heart Attack Care				
ACE Inhibitor or ARB for LVSD[5]	0	-	96%	96%
Aspirin at Arrival[5]	0	-	99%	99%
Aspirin at Discharge[5]	0	-	99%	98%
Beta Blocker at Discharge[5]	0	-	98%	98%
Fibrinolytic Medication Timing[5]	0	-	50%	55%
PCI Within 90 Minutes of Arrival[5]	0	-	90%	90%
Smoking Cessation Advice[5]	0	-	100%	99%
Chest Pain/Possible Heart Attack Care				
Aspirin at Arrival	-	-	95%	95%
Median Time to ECG (minutes)	-	-	8	8
Median Time to Transfer (minutes)	-	-	57	61
Fibrinolytic Medication Timing	-	-	33%	54%
Heart Failure Care				
ACE Inhibitor or ARB for LVSD[5]	0	-	94%	94%
Discharge Instructions[5]	0	-	89%	88%
Evaluation of LVS Function[5]	0	-	98%	98%
Smoking Cessation Advice[5]	0	-	99%	98%
Pneumonia Care				
Appropriate Initial Antibiotic[5]	0	-	90%	92%
Blood Culture Timing[5]	0	-	97%	96%
Influenza Vaccine[5]	0	-	91%	91%
Initial Antibiotic Timing[5]	0	-	96%	95%
Pneumococcal Vaccine[5]	0	-	92%	93%
Smoking Cessation Advice[5]	0	-	98%	97%
Surgical Care Improvement Project				
Appropriate VTP Within 24 Hours[5]	0	-	92%	92%
Appropriate Hair Removal[5]	0	-	99%	99%
Appropriate Beta Blocker Usage[5]	0	-	92%	93%
Controlled Postoperative Blood Glucose[5]	0	-	92%	93%
Prophylactic Antibiotic Timing[5]	0	-	97%	97%
Prophylactic Antibiotic Timing (Outpatient)	-	-	93%	92%
Prophylactic Antibiotic Selection[5]	0	-	97%	97%
Prophylactic Antibiotic Select. (Outpatient)	-	-	94%	94%
Prophylactic Antibiotic Stopped[5]	0	-	94%	94%
Recommended VTP Ordered[5]	0	-	94%	94%
Urinary Catheter Removal[5]	0	-	89%	90%
Children's Asthma Care				
Received Systemic Corticosteroids	-	-	-	100%
Received Home Management Plan	-	-	-	71%
Received Reliever Medication	-	-	-	100%
Use of Medical Imaging				
Combination Abdominal CT Scan	-	-	0.246	0.191
Combination Chest CT Scan	-	-	0.098	0.054
Follow-up Mammogram/Ultrasound	-	-	8.4%	8.4%
MRI for Low Back Pain	-	-	33.4%	32.7%
Survey of Patients' Hospital Experiences				
Area Around Room 'Always' Quiet at Night[8]	-	-	-	58%
Doctors 'Always' Communicated Well[8]	-	-	-	80%
Home Recovery Infomation Given[8]	-	-	-	82%
Hospital Given 9 or 10 on 10 Point Scale[8]	-	-	-	67%
Meds 'Always' Explained Before Given[8]	-	-	-	60%
Nurses 'Always' Communicated Well[8]	-	-	-	76%
Pain 'Always' Well Controlled[8]	-	-	-	69%
Room and Bathroom 'Always' Clean[8]	-	-	-	71%
Timely Help 'Always' Received[8]	-	-	-	64%
Would Definitely Recommend Hospital[8]	-	-	-	69%

Passavant Area Hospital

1600 W Walnut St
Jacksonville, IL 62650
Phone: 217-245-9551
Fax: 217-479-5637
E-mail: info@passavanthospital.com
URL: www.passavanthospital.com
Type: Acute Care Hospitals
Emergency Services: Yes
Ownership: Voluntary Non-Profit - Private
Beds: 173

Key Personnel:
CEO/President. . . . . Chester A Wynn, CPA
Chief of Medical Staff. . . . . Tara Ramsey, MD
Infection Control. . . . . Anne Beck
Operating Room. . . . . Tracy Mills, RN
Quality Assurance . . . . Connie Mudd
Radiology. . . . . Robert Stallworth, MD
Emergency Room . . . . Michael Whitmore, MD
Intensive Care Unit. . . . . Terry Beachamp

Measure	Cases	This Hosp.	State Avg.	U.S. Avg.
Heart Attack Care				
ACE Inhibitor or ARB for LVSD	0	-	96%	96%
Aspirin at Arrival[1]	6	100%	99%	99%
Aspirin at Discharge[1]	3	100%	99%	98%
Beta Blocker at Discharge[1]	3	100%	98%	98%
Fibrinolytic Medication Timing	0	-	50%	55%
PCI Within 90 Minutes of Arrival	0	-	90%	90%
Smoking Cessation Advice[1]	1	100%	100%	99%
Chest Pain/Possible Heart Attack Care				
Aspirin at Arrival	298	94%	95%	95%
Median Time to ECG (minutes)	301	14	8	8
Median Time to Transfer (minutes)	29	53	57	61
Fibrinolytic Medication Timing[1]	1	0%	33%	54%
Heart Failure Care				
ACE Inhibitor or ARB for LVSD[2]	26	88%	94%	94%
Discharge Instructions[2]	82	82%	89%	88%
Evaluation of LVS Function[2]	123	95%	98%	98%
Smoking Cessation Advice[1,2]	23	100%	99%	98%
Pneumonia Care				
Appropriate Initial Antibiotic	135	93%	90%	92%
Blood Culture Timing	227	94%	97%	96%
Influenza Vaccine	141	96%	91%	91%
Initial Antibiotic Timing	210	100%	96%	95%
Pneumococcal Vaccine	172	98%	92%	93%
Smoking Cessation Advice	62	100%	98%	97%
Surgical Care Improvement Project				
Appropriate VTP Within 24 Hours[2]	105	74%	92%	92%
Appropriate Hair Removal[2]	353	100%	99%	99%
Appropriate Beta Blocker Usage[2]	110	70%	92%	93%
Controlled Postoperative Blood Glucose[2]	0	-	92%	93%
Prophylactic Antibiotic Timing[2]	276	99%	97%	97%
Prophylactic Antibiotic Timing (Outpatient)	70	96%	93%	92%
Prophylactic Antibiotic Selection[2]	278	96%	97%	97%
Prophylactic Antibiotic Select. (Outpatient)	69	80%	94%	94%
Prophylactic Antibiotic Stopped[2]	263	96%	94%	94%
Recommended VTP Ordered[2]	106	76%	94%	94%
Urinary Catheter Removal[1,2]	18	78%	89%	90%
Children's Asthma Care				
Received Systemic Corticosteroids	-	-	-	100%
Received Home Management Plan	-	-	-	71%
Received Reliever Medication	-	-	-	100%
Use of Medical Imaging				
Combination Abdominal CT Scan	498	0.026	0.246	0.191
Combination Chest CT Scan	299	0.007	0.098	0.054
Follow-up Mammogram/Ultrasound	1,016	5.3%	8.4%	8.4%
MRI for Low Back Pain	135	41.5%	33.4%	32.7%
Survey of Patients' Hospital Experiences				
Area Around Room 'Always' Quiet at Night	300+	55%	-	58%
Doctors 'Always' Communicated Well	300+	80%	-	80%
Home Recovery Information Given	300+	84%	-	82%
Hospital Given 9 or 10 on 10 Point Scale	300+	68%	-	67%
Meds 'Always' Explained Before Given	300+	60%	-	60%
Nurses 'Always' Communicated Well	300+	76%	-	76%
Pain 'Always' Well Controlled	300+	73%	-	69%
Room and Bathroom 'Always' Clean	300+	76%	-	71%
Timely Help 'Always' Received	300+	61%	-	64%
Would Definitely Recommend Hospital	300+	64%	-	69%

Jersey Community Hospital

400 Maple Summit Road
Jerseyville, IL 62052
Phone: 618-498-6402
Fax: 618-498-8492
Type: Acute Care Hospitals
Emergency Services: Yes
Ownership: Government - Local
Beds: 67

Key Personnel:
CEO/President. . . . . Larry Bear
Chief of Medical Staff. . . . . Susan Vritweiser
Quality Assurance . . . . Nancy Wollenwebber
Emergency Room . . . . Alvina Isringhausen

Measure	Cases	This Hosp.	State Avg.	U.S. Avg.
Heart Attack Care				
ACE Inhibitor or ARB for LVSD[1]	3	67%	96%	96%
Aspirin at Arrival[1]	20	95%	99%	99%
Aspirin at Discharge[1]	16	94%	99%	98%
Beta Blocker at Discharge[1]	16	75%	98%	98%
Fibrinolytic Medication Timing	0	-	50%	55%
PCI Within 90 Minutes of Arrival	0	-	90%	90%
Smoking Cessation Advice[1]	1	100%	100%	99%
Chest Pain/Possible Heart Attack Care				
Aspirin at Arrival	65	94%	95%	95%
Median Time to ECG (minutes)	68	6	8	8
Median Time to Transfer (minutes)[1,3]	1	65	57	61
Fibrinolytic Medication Timing[1]	3	33%	33%	54%
Heart Failure Care				
ACE Inhibitor or ARB for LVSD	25	84%	94%	94%
Discharge Instructions	54	96%	89%	88%
Evaluation of LVS Function	86	85%	98%	98%
Smoking Cessation Advice[1]	9	100%	99%	98%
Pneumonia Care				
Appropriate Initial Antibiotic	83	83%	90%	92%
Blood Culture Timing	116	97%	97%	96%
Influenza Vaccine	64	94%	91%	91%
Initial Antibiotic Timing	108	99%	96%	95%
Pneumococcal Vaccine	94	87%	92%	93%
Smoking Cessation Advice	26	96%	98%	97%
Surgical Care Improvement Project				
Appropriate VTP Within 24 Hours[1]	16	75%	92%	92%
Appropriate Hair Removal	49	100%	99%	99%
Appropriate Beta Blocker Usage[1]	12	83%	92%	93%
Controlled Postoperative Blood Glucose	0	-	92%	93%
Prophylactic Antibiotic Timing	32	88%	97%	97%
Prophylactic Antibiotic Timing (Outpatient)[1]	14	93%	93%	92%
Prophylactic Antibiotic Selection	32	91%	97%	97%
Prophylactic Antibiotic Select. (Outpatient)	39	95%	94%	94%
Prophylactic Antibiotic Stopped	31	90%	94%	94%
Recommended VTP Ordered[1]	17	71%	94%	94%
Urinary Catheter Removal[1]	1	100%	89%	90%
Children's Asthma Care				
Received Systemic Corticosteroids	-	-	-	100%
Received Home Management Plan	-	-	-	71%
Received Reliever Medication	-	-	-	100%
Use of Medical Imaging				
Combination Abdominal CT Scan	256	0.527	0.246	0.191
Combination Chest CT Scan	90	0.078	0.098	0.054
Follow-up Mammogram/Ultrasound	346	9.2%	8.4%	8.4%
MRI for Low Back Pain	51	33.3%	33.4%	32.7%
Survey of Patients' Hospital Experiences				
Area Around Room 'Always' Quiet at Night	300+	63%	-	58%
Doctors 'Always' Communicated Well	300+	81%	-	80%
Home Recovery Information Given	300+	79%	-	82%
Hospital Given 9 or 10 on 10 Point Scale	300+	68%	-	67%
Meds 'Always' Explained Before Given	300+	62%	-	60%
Nurses 'Always' Communicated Well	300+	79%	-	76%
Pain 'Always' Well Controlled	300+	72%	-	69%
Room and Bathroom 'Always' Clean	300+	80%	-	71%
Timely Help 'Always' Received	300+	76%	-	64%
Would Definitely Recommend Hospital	300+	62%	-	69%

NOTE: Hospital profiles are in alphabetical order by state, then city, then hospital within the city; Rankings exclude hospitals with less than 25 cases except for patient surveys which excludes hospitals with less than 100 cases; (a) 100–299 cases; (1) The number of cases is too small to be sure how well a hospital is performing; (2) The hospital indicated that the data submitted for this measure were based on a sample of cases; (3) Data was collected during a shorter time period (fewer quarters) than the maximum possible time for this measure; (4) Suppressed for one or more quarters by CMS; (5) No data is available from the hospital for this measure; (6) Fewer than 100 patients completed the HCAHPS survey. Use these rates with caution, as the number of surveys may be too low to reliably assess hospital performance; (7) Survey results are based on less than 12 months of data; (8) Survey results are not available for this reporting period; (9) No or very few patients were eligible for the HCAHPS survey. The scores shown, if any, reflect a very small number of surveys; (10) A state average was not calculated because too few hospitals in the state submitted data; (11) There were discrepancies in the data collection process; Please refer to the User's Guide for a full explanation of data.

Provena St Joseph Medical Center

333 N Madison Phone: 815-725-7133
Joliet, IL 60435 Fax: 815-741-7121
URL: www.provena.org/stjoes
Type: Acute Care Hospitals Emergency Services: Yes
Ownership: Voluntary Non-Profit - Church Beds: 452

Key Personnel:
CEO/President. . . . . Jeffrey L Brickman FACHE
Infection Control. . . . . Peg Sheehan
Pediatric Ambulatory Care . . . . . . Rhea Simons, MD
Pediatric In-Patient Care . . . . Rhea Simons, MD
Quality Assurance . . . . Lon McPherson, MD
Emergency Room . . . . Rao Kilaru, MD
Patient Relations . . . . Kathleen Mikos

Measure	Cases	This Hosp.	State Avg.	U.S. Avg.
Heart Attack Care				
ACE Inhibitor or ARB for LVSD	49	100%	96%	96%
Aspirin at Arrival	309	99%	99%	99%
Aspirin at Discharge	296	100%	99%	98%
Beta Blocker at Discharge	299	99%	98%	98%
Fibrinolytic Medication Timing	0	-	50%	55%
PCI Within 90 Minutes of Arrival	56	88%	90%	90%
Smoking Cessation Advice	78	100%	100%	99%
Chest Pain/Possible Heart Attack Care				
Aspirin at Arrival[1]	8	100%	95%	95%
Median Time to ECG (minutes)[1]	8	12	8	8
Median Time to Transfer (minutes)[5]	0	-	57	61
Fibrinolytic Medication Timing[5]	0	-	33%	54%
Heart Failure Care				
ACE Inhibitor or ARB for LVSD[2]	93	99%	94%	94%
Discharge Instructions[2]	239	83%	89%	88%
Evaluation of LVS Function[2]	307	99%	98%	98%
Smoking Cessation Advice[1,2]	24	100%	99%	98%
Pneumonia Care				
Appropriate Initial Antibiotic[2]	77	88%	90%	92%
Blood Culture Timing[2]	111	91%	97%	96%
Influenza Vaccine[2]	73	97%	91%	91%
Initial Antibiotic Timing[2]	139	92%	96%	95%
Pneumococcal Vaccine[2]	124	89%	92%	93%
Smoking Cessation Advice[2]	45	100%	98%	97%
Surgical Care Improvement Project				
Appropriate VTP Within 24 Hours[2]	190	99%	92%	92%
Appropriate Hair Removal[2]	615	100%	99%	99%
Appropriate Beta Blocker Usage[2]	220	100%	92%	93%
Controlled Postoperative Blood Glucose[2]	133	88%	92%	93%
Prophylactic Antibiotic Timing[2]	477	97%	97%	97%
Prophylactic Antibiotic Timing (Outpatient)	378	90%	93%	92%
Prophylactic Antibiotic Selection[2]	479	94%	97%	97%
Prophylactic Antibiotic Select. (Outpatient)	361	95%	94%	94%
Prophylactic Antibiotic Stopped[2]	441	86%	94%	94%
Recommended VTP Ordered[2]	190	99%	94%	94%
Urinary Catheter Removal[2]	124	95%	89%	90%
Children's Asthma Care				
Received Systemic Corticosteroids	-	-	-	100%
Received Home Management Plan	-	-	-	71%
Received Reliever Medication	-	-	-	100%
Use of Medical Imaging				
Combination Abdominal CT Scan	1,073	0.360	0.246	0.191
Combination Chest CT Scan	914	0.171	0.098	0.054
Follow-up Mammogram/Ultrasound	2,201	5.6%	8.4%	8.4%
MRI for Low Back Pain	330	27.9%	33.4%	32.7%
Survey of Patients' Hospital Experiences				
Area Around Room 'Always' Quiet at Night	300+	67%	-	58%
Doctors 'Always' Communicated Well	300+	77%	-	80%
Home Recovery Information Given	300+	84%	-	82%
Hospital Given 9 or 10 on 10 Point Scale	300+	67%	-	67%
Meds 'Always' Explained Before Given	300+	54%	-	60%
Nurses 'Always' Communicated Well	300+	73%	-	76%
Pain 'Always' Well Controlled	300+	72%	-	69%
Room and Bathroom 'Always' Clean	300+	65%	-	71%
Timely Help 'Always' Received	300+	55%	-	64%
Would Definitely Recommend Hospital	300+	70%	-	69%

Silver Cross Hospital

1200 Maple Rd Phone: 815-740-1100
Joliet, IL 60432 Fax: 815-740-3561
E-mail: tsimons@silvercross.org
URL: www.silvercross.org
Type: Acute Care Hospitals Emergency Services: Yes
Ownership: Voluntary Non-Profit - Private Beds: 297

Key Personnel:
CEO/President. . . . . Paul Pawlak
Cardiac Laboratory. . . . . Paula Simpson
Chief of Medical Staff . . . . Kishor Ajmere
Infection Control. . . . . Margaret Rodegher
Pediatric In-Patient Care . . . . Peggy Gricus
Quality Assurance . . . . Billie Schimanski
Radiology. . . . . Salwa Asaad

Measure	Cases	This Hosp.	State Avg.	U.S. Avg.
Heart Attack Care				
ACE Inhibitor or ARB for LVSD	47	100%	96%	96%
Aspirin at Arrival	192	99%	99%	99%
Aspirin at Discharge	176	100%	99%	98%
Beta Blocker at Discharge	171	99%	98%	98%
Fibrinolytic Medication Timing	0	-	50%	55%
PCI Within 90 Minutes of Arrival	50	94%	90%	90%
Smoking Cessation Advice	53	100%	100%	99%
Chest Pain/Possible Heart Attack Care				
Aspirin at Arrival[1]	17	94%	95%	95%
Median Time to ECG (minutes)[1]	17	3	8	8
Median Time to Transfer (minutes)[1,3]	1	92	57	61
Fibrinolytic Medication Timing[3]	0	-	33%	54%
Heart Failure Care				
ACE Inhibitor or ARB for LVSD	128	98%	94%	94%
Discharge Instructions	312	89%	89%	88%
Evaluation of LVS Function	420	100%	98%	98%
Smoking Cessation Advice	67	100%	99%	98%
Pneumonia Care				
Appropriate Initial Antibiotic	193	94%	90%	92%
Blood Culture Timing	241	97%	97%	96%
Influenza Vaccine	232	99%	91%	91%
Initial Antibiotic Timing	346	100%	96%	95%
Pneumococcal Vaccine	293	99%	92%	93%
Smoking Cessation Advice	125	100%	98%	97%
Surgical Care Improvement Project				
Appropriate VTP Within 24 Hours[2]	178	96%	92%	92%
Appropriate Hair Removal[2]	679	100%	99%	99%
Appropriate Beta Blocker Usage[2]	153	95%	92%	93%
Controlled Postoperative Blood Glucose[2]	0	-	92%	93%
Prophylactic Antibiotic Timing[2]	509	100%	97%	97%
Prophylactic Antibiotic Timing (Outpatient)	378	97%	93%	92%
Prophylactic Antibiotic Selection[2]	509	99%	97%	97%
Prophylactic Antibiotic Select. (Outpatient)	371	96%	94%	94%
Prophylactic Antibiotic Stopped[2]	480	98%	94%	94%
Recommended VTP Ordered[2]	179	97%	94%	94%
Urinary Catheter Removal[2]	167	99%	89%	90%
Children's Asthma Care				
Received Systemic Corticosteroids	-	-	-	100%
Received Home Management Plan	-	-	-	71%
Received Reliever Medication	-	-	-	100%
Use of Medical Imaging				
Combination Abdominal CT Scan	672	0.082	0.246	0.191
Combination Chest CT Scan	681	0.048	0.098	0.054
Follow-up Mammogram/Ultrasound	942	8.3%	8.4%	8.4%
MRI for Low Back Pain	211	35.5%	33.4%	32.7%
Survey of Patients' Hospital Experiences				
Area Around Room 'Always' Quiet at Night	300+	56%	-	58%
Doctors 'Always' Communicated Well	300+	78%	-	80%
Home Recovery Information Given	300+	78%	-	82%
Hospital Given 9 or 10 on 10 Point Scale	300+	71%	-	67%
Meds 'Always' Explained Before Given	300+	61%	-	60%
Nurses 'Always' Communicated Well	300+	78%	-	76%
Pain 'Always' Well Controlled	300+	71%	-	69%
Room and Bathroom 'Always' Clean	300+	71%	-	71%
Timely Help 'Always' Received	300+	62%	-	64%
Would Definitely Recommend Hospital	300+	72%	-	69%

Provena St Marys Hospital

500 W Court St Phone: 815-937-2490
Kankakee, IL 60901 Fax: 815-937-8772
URL: www.provenastmarys.com
Type: Acute Care Hospitals Emergency Services: Yes
Ownership: Voluntary Non-Profit - Other Beds: 210

Key Personnel:
CEO/President. . . . . George N Miller Jr
Cardiac Laboratory. . . . . Michelle Hardesty
Chief of Medical Staff . . . . Hippen Hammer
Infection Control. . . . . Julie Nehls
Operating Room. . . . . Robert E Brockman, RN
Quality Assurance . . . . Len Winnicki
Emergency Room . . . . Tony Brunello

Measure	Cases	This Hosp.	State Avg.	U.S. Avg.
Heart Attack Care				
ACE Inhibitor or ARB for LVSD[1]	13	100%	96%	96%
Aspirin at Arrival	57	100%	99%	99%
Aspirin at Discharge	50	100%	99%	98%
Beta Blocker at Discharge	48	100%	98%	98%
Fibrinolytic Medication Timing	0	-	50%	55%
PCI Within 90 Minutes of Arrival[1]	17	100%	90%	90%
Smoking Cessation Advice[1]	21	100%	100%	99%
Chest Pain/Possible Heart Attack Care				
Aspirin at Arrival[1]	4	100%	95%	95%
Median Time to ECG (minutes)[1]	5	11	8	8
Median Time to Transfer (minutes)[5]	0	-	57	61
Fibrinolytic Medication Timing[5]	0	-	33%	54%
Heart Failure Care				
ACE Inhibitor or ARB for LVSD	56	96%	94%	94%
Discharge Instructions	102	79%	89%	88%
Evaluation of LVS Function	125	100%	98%	98%
Smoking Cessation Advice	37	100%	99%	98%
Pneumonia Care				
Appropriate Initial Antibiotic[2]	84	80%	90%	92%
Blood Culture Timing[2]	145	92%	97%	96%
Influenza Vaccine[2]	77	92%	91%	91%
Initial Antibiotic Timing[2]	151	97%	96%	95%
Pneumococcal Vaccine[2]	101	91%	92%	93%
Smoking Cessation Advice[2]	70	100%	98%	97%
Surgical Care Improvement Project				
Appropriate VTP Within 24 Hours[2]	134	92%	92%	92%
Appropriate Hair Removal[2]	411	100%	99%	99%
Appropriate Beta Blocker Usage[2]	84	90%	92%	93%
Controlled Postoperative Blood Glucose[2]	0	-	92%	93%
Prophylactic Antibiotic Timing[2]	285	98%	97%	97%
Prophylactic Antibiotic Timing (Outpatient)	199	92%	93%	92%
Prophylactic Antibiotic Selection[2]	284	97%	97%	97%
Prophylactic Antibiotic Select. (Outpatient)	191	93%	94%	94%
Prophylactic Antibiotic Stopped[2]	271	94%	94%	94%
Recommended VTP Ordered[2]	134	92%	94%	94%
Urinary Catheter Removal[2]	119	97%	89%	90%
Children's Asthma Care				
Received Systemic Corticosteroids	-	-	-	100%
Received Home Management Plan	-	-	-	71%
Received Reliever Medication	-	-	-	100%
Use of Medical Imaging				
Combination Abdominal CT Scan	510	0.137	0.246	0.191
Combination Chest CT Scan	271	0.037	0.098	0.054
Follow-up Mammogram/Ultrasound	679	9.0%	8.4%	8.4%
MRI for Low Back Pain	112	30.4%	33.4%	32.7%
Survey of Patients' Hospital Experiences				
Area Around Room 'Always' Quiet at Night	300+	61%	-	58%
Doctors 'Always' Communicated Well	300+	80%	-	80%
Home Recovery Information Given	300+	84%	-	82%
Hospital Given 9 or 10 on 10 Point Scale	300+	74%	-	67%
Meds 'Always' Explained Before Given	300+	61%	-	60%
Nurses 'Always' Communicated Well	300+	79%	-	76%
Pain 'Always' Well Controlled	300+	72%	-	69%
Room and Bathroom 'Always' Clean	300+	75%	-	71%
Timely Help 'Always' Received	300+	67%	-	64%
Would Definitely Recommend Hospital	300+	77%	-	69%

NOTE: Hospital profiles are in alphabetical order by state, then city, then hospital within the city; Rankings exclude hospitals with less than 25 cases except for patient surveys which excludes hospitals with less than 100 cases; (a) 100–299 cases; (1) The number of cases is too small to be sure how well a hospital is performing; (2) The hospital indicated that the data submitted for this measure were based on a sample of cases; (3) Data was collected during a shorter time period (fewer quarters) than the maximum possible time for this measure; (4) Suppressed for one or more quarters by CMS; (5) No data is available from the hospital for this measure; (6) Fewer than 100 patients completed the HCAHPS survey. Use these rates with caution, as the number of surveys may be too low to reliably assess hospital performance; (7) Survey results are based on less than 12 months of data; (8) Survey results are not available for this reporting period; (9) No or very few patients were eligible for the HCAHPS survey. The scores shown, if any, reflect a very small number of surveys; (10) A state average was not calculated because too few hospitals in the state submitted data; (11) There were discrepancies in the data collection process; Please refer to the User's Guide for a full explanation of data.

Riverside Medical Center

350 N Wall St Phone: 815-933-1671
Kankakee, IL 60901 Fax: 815-935-7823
URL: www.riversidehealthcare.org
Type: Acute Care Hospitals Emergency Services: Yes
Ownership: Voluntary Non-Profit - Other Beds: 336

Key Personnel:
CEO/President. . . . . Phil Kambic
Coronary Care . . . . Allen Kelly
Operating Room. . . . . Sandra Kegg, RN
Quality Assurance . . . . Mary Schore
Radiology. . . . . Nicholas Slimuck, MD
Emergency Room . . . . Crystal Allen

Measure	Cases	This Hosp.	State Avg.	U.S. Avg.
Heart Attack Care				
ACE Inhibitor or ARB for LVSD[1]	21	95%	96%	96%
Aspirin at Arrival	113	97%	99%	99%
Aspirin at Discharge	104	99%	99%	98%
Beta Blocker at Discharge	106	96%	98%	98%
Fibrinolytic Medication Timing	0	-	50%	55%
PCI Within 90 Minutes of Arrival	36	94%	90%	90%
Smoking Cessation Advice	39	97%	100%	99%
Chest Pain/Possible Heart Attack Care				
Aspirin at Arrival[1,3]	2	0%	95%	95%
Median Time to ECG (minutes)[1,3]	2	4	8	8
Median Time to Transfer (minutes)[5]	0	-	57	61
Fibrinolytic Medication Timing[5]	0	-	33%	54%
Heart Failure Care				
ACE Inhibitor or ARB for LVSD	86	92%	94%	94%
Discharge Instructions	173	94%	89%	88%
Evaluation of LVS Function	222	98%	98%	98%
Smoking Cessation Advice	40	92%	99%	98%
Pneumonia Care				
Appropriate Initial Antibiotic	108	83%	90%	92%
Blood Culture Timing	235	98%	97%	96%
Influenza Vaccine	142	97%	91%	91%
Initial Antibiotic Timing	220	98%	96%	95%
Pneumococcal Vaccine	190	99%	92%	93%
Smoking Cessation Advice	77	88%	98%	97%
Surgical Care Improvement Project				
Appropriate VTP Within 24 Hours[2]	127	83%	92%	92%
Appropriate Hair Removal[2]	517	99%	99%	99%
Appropriate Beta Blocker Usage[2]	196	91%	92%	93%
Controlled Postoperative Blood Glucose[2]	121	89%	92%	93%
Prophylactic Antibiotic Timing[2]	352	97%	97%	97%
Prophylactic Antibiotic Timing (Outpatient)	381	93%	93%	92%
Prophylactic Antibiotic Selection[2]	359	97%	97%	97%
Prophylactic Antibiotic Select. (Outpatient)	378	92%	94%	94%
Prophylactic Antibiotic Stopped[2]	328	87%	94%	94%
Recommended VTP Ordered[2]	127	83%	94%	94%
Urinary Catheter Removal[2]	111	92%	89%	90%
Children's Asthma Care				
Received Systemic Corticosteroids	-	-	-	100%
Received Home Management Plan	-	-	-	71%
Received Reliever Medication	-	-	-	100%
Use of Medical Imaging				
Combination Abdominal CT Scan	901	0.165	0.246	0.191
Combination Chest CT Scan	485	0.169	0.098	0.054
Follow-up Mammogram/Ultrasound	1,741	8.2%	8.4%	8.4%
MRI for Low Back Pain	426	32.9%	33.4%	32.7%
Survey of Patients' Hospital Experiences				
Area Around Room 'Always' Quiet at Night	300+	51%	-	58%
Doctors 'Always' Communicated Well	300+	78%	-	80%
Home Recovery Information Given	300+	83%	-	82%
Hospital Given 9 or 10 on 10 Point Scale	300+	71%	-	67%
Meds 'Always' Explained Before Given	300+	61%	-	60%
Nurses 'Always' Communicated Well	300+	79%	-	76%
Pain 'Always' Well Controlled	300+	70%	-	69%
Room and Bathroom 'Always' Clean	300+	69%	-	71%
Timely Help 'Always' Received	300+	67%	-	64%
Would Definitely Recommend Hospital	300+	78%	-	69%

Kewanee Hospital

1051 West South Street Phone: 309-853-3361
Kewanee, IL 61443 Fax: 309-854-5209
E-mail: rlindner@kewaneehospital.com
URL: kewaneehospital.com
Type: Critical Access Hospitals Emergency Services: Yes
Ownership: Voluntary Non-Profit - Private Beds: 82

Key Personnel:
CEO/President. . . . . Margaret Gustafson
Chief of Medical Staff . . . . Rick Cernovich, MD
Infection Control. . . . . Brenda Wager
Operating Room. . . . . Karen Swan
Quality Assurance . . . . Colleen Lewis
Anesthesiology. . . . . Keith Barnhill
Emergency Room . . . . Adam Reading
Hemotology Center . . . . Jan Sams

Measure	Cases	This Hosp.	State Avg.	U.S. Avg.
Heart Attack Care				
ACE Inhibitor or ARB for LVSD[3]	0	-	96%	96%
Aspirin at Arrival[3]	0	-	99%	99%
Aspirin at Discharge[1,3]	1	100%	99%	98%
Beta Blocker at Discharge[1,3]	2	50%	98%	98%
Fibrinolytic Medication Timing[3]	0	-	50%	55%
PCI Within 90 Minutes of Arrival[5]	0	-	90%	90%
Smoking Cessation Advice[3]	0	-	100%	99%
Chest Pain/Possible Heart Attack Care				
Aspirin at Arrival	-	-	95%	95%
Median Time to ECG (minutes)	-	-	8	8
Median Time to Transfer (minutes)	-	-	57	61
Fibrinolytic Medication Timing	-	-	33%	54%
Heart Failure Care				
ACE Inhibitor or ARB for LVSD[1]	9	89%	94%	94%
Discharge Instructions	27	85%	89%	88%
Evaluation of LVS Function	45	89%	98%	98%
Smoking Cessation Advice[1]	7	100%	99%	98%
Pneumonia Care				
Appropriate Initial Antibiotic	36	92%	90%	92%
Blood Culture Timing	49	94%	97%	96%
Influenza Vaccine	41	88%	91%	91%
Initial Antibiotic Timing	47	98%	96%	95%
Pneumococcal Vaccine	48	88%	92%	93%
Smoking Cessation Advice[1]	15	93%	98%	97%
Surgical Care Improvement Project				
Appropriate VTP Within 24 Hours[1]	20	100%	92%	92%
Appropriate Hair Removal	50	100%	99%	99%
Appropriate Beta Blocker Usage[1]	13	100%	92%	93%
Controlled Postoperative Blood Glucose[5]	0	-	92%	93%
Prophylactic Antibiotic Timing	29	100%	97%	97%
Prophylactic Antibiotic Timing (Outpatient)	-	-	93%	92%
Prophylactic Antibiotic Selection	29	97%	97%	97%
Prophylactic Antibiotic Select. (Outpatient)	-	-	94%	94%
Prophylactic Antibiotic Stopped	28	82%	94%	94%
Recommended VTP Ordered[1]	20	100%	94%	94%
Urinary Catheter Removal[1]	4	100%	89%	90%
Children's Asthma Care				
Received Systemic Corticosteroids	-	-	-	100%
Received Home Management Plan	-	-	-	71%
Received Reliever Medication	-	-	-	100%
Use of Medical Imaging				
Combination Abdominal CT Scan	-	-	0.246	0.191
Combination Chest CT Scan	-	-	0.098	0.054
Follow-up Mammogram/Ultrasound	-	-	8.4%	8.4%
MRI for Low Back Pain	-	-	33.4%	32.7%
Survey of Patients' Hospital Experiences				
Area Around Room 'Always' Quiet at Night[11]	(a)	74%	-	58%
Doctors 'Always' Communicated Well[11]	(a)	84%	-	80%
Home Recovery Information Given[11]	(a)	82%	-	82%
Hospital Given 9 or 10 on 10 Point Scale[11]	(a)	62%	-	67%
Meds 'Always' Explained Before Given[11]	(a)	66%	-	60%
Nurses 'Always' Communicated Well[11]	(a)	75%	-	76%
Pain 'Always' Well Controlled[11]	(a)	70%	-	69%
Room and Bathroom 'Always' Clean[11]	(a)	84%	-	71%
Timely Help 'Always' Received[11]	(a)	57%	-	64%
Would Definitely Recommend Hospital[11]	(a)	56%	-	69%

Adventist La Grange Memorial Hospital

5101 S Willow Springs Rd Phone: 708-352-1200
La Grange, IL 60525 Fax: 708-245-5627
E-mail: egervain@ahss.org
URL: www.keepingyouwell.com
Type: Acute Care Hospitals Emergency Services: Yes
Ownership: Voluntary Non-Profit - Church Beds: 274

Key Personnel:
CEO/President. . . . . Rick Wright
Chief of Medical Staff . . . . Patrick Quirke, MD
Operating Room. . . . . Lori Kaspar, RN
Pediatric In-Patient Care . . . . . . Marc Freed, DO
Quality Assurance . . . . Sue Cunningham
Radiology. . . . . Timothy N Merrill, MD
Emergency Room . . . . Gail Weimer, RN

Measure	Cases	This Hosp.	State Avg.	U.S. Avg.
Heart Attack Care				
ACE Inhibitor or ARB for LVSD[1]	14	100%	96%	96%
Aspirin at Arrival	134	100%	99%	99%
Aspirin at Discharge	117	100%	99%	98%
Beta Blocker at Discharge	114	100%	98%	98%
Fibrinolytic Medication Timing	0	-	50%	55%
PCI Within 90 Minutes of Arrival	31	90%	90%	90%
Smoking Cessation Advice	44	100%	100%	99%
Chest Pain/Possible Heart Attack Care				
Aspirin at Arrival[1,3]	2	100%	95%	95%
Median Time to ECG (minutes)[1,3]	2	4	8	8
Median Time to Transfer (minutes)[5]	0	-	57	61
Fibrinolytic Medication Timing[5]	0	-	33%	54%
Heart Failure Care				
ACE Inhibitor or ARB for LVSD	81	99%	94%	94%
Discharge Instructions	243	81%	89%	88%
Evaluation of LVS Function	327	100%	98%	98%
Smoking Cessation Advice	32	100%	99%	98%
Pneumonia Care				
Appropriate Initial Antibiotic	148	97%	90%	92%
Blood Culture Timing	266	100%	97%	96%
Influenza Vaccine	160	90%	91%	91%
Initial Antibiotic Timing	310	99%	96%	95%
Pneumococcal Vaccine	274	93%	92%	93%
Smoking Cessation Advice	47	100%	98%	97%
Surgical Care Improvement Project				
Appropriate VTP Within 24 Hours[2]	178	96%	92%	92%
Appropriate Hair Removal[2]	411	100%	99%	99%
Appropriate Beta Blocker Usage[2]	138	97%	92%	93%
Controlled Postoperative Blood Glucose[2]	55	100%	92%	93%
Prophylactic Antibiotic Timing[2]	283	97%	97%	97%
Prophylactic Antibiotic Timing (Outpatient)	155	93%	93%	92%
Prophylactic Antibiotic Selection[2]	283	98%	97%	97%
Prophylactic Antibiotic Select. (Outpatient)	149	98%	94%	94%
Prophylactic Antibiotic Stopped[2]	270	94%	94%	94%
Recommended VTP Ordered[2]	178	97%	94%	94%
Urinary Catheter Removal[2]	99	83%	89%	90%
Children's Asthma Care				
Received Systemic Corticosteroids	-	-	-	100%
Received Home Management Plan	-	-	-	71%
Received Reliever Medication	-	-	-	100%
Use of Medical Imaging				
Combination Abdominal CT Scan	873	0.093	0.246	0.191
Combination Chest CT Scan	703	0.007	0.098	0.054
Follow-up Mammogram/Ultrasound	1,600	12.3%	8.4%	8.4%
MRI for Low Back Pain	143	32.2%	33.4%	32.7%
Survey of Patients' Hospital Experiences				
Area Around Room 'Always' Quiet at Night	300+	62%	-	58%
Doctors 'Always' Communicated Well	300+	78%	-	80%
Home Recovery Information Given	300+	85%	-	82%
Hospital Given 9 or 10 on 10 Point Scale	300+	66%	-	67%
Meds 'Always' Explained Before Given	300+	54%	-	60%
Nurses 'Always' Communicated Well	300+	70%	-	76%
Pain 'Always' Well Controlled	300+	66%	-	69%
Room and Bathroom 'Always' Clean	300+	70%	-	71%
Timely Help 'Always' Received	300+	57%	-	64%
Would Definitely Recommend Hospital	300+	70%	-	69%

NOTE: Hospital profiles are in alphabetical order by state, then city, then hospital within the city; Rankings exclude hospitals with less than 25 cases except for patient surveys which excludes hospitals with less than 100 cases; (a) 100–299 cases; (1) The number of cases is too small to be sure how well a hospital is performing; (2) The hospital indicated that the data submitted for this measure were based on a sample of cases; (3) Data was collected during a shorter time period (fewer quarters) than the maximum possible time for this measure; (4) Suppressed for one or more quarters by CMS; (5) No data is available from the hospital for this measure; (6) Fewer than 100 patients completed the HCAHPS survey. Use these rates with caution, as the number of surveys may be too low to reliably assess hospital performance; (7) Survey results are based on less than 12 months of data; (8) Survey results are not available for this reporting period; (9) No or very few patients were eligible for the HCAHPS survey. The scores shown, if any, reflect a very small number of surveys; (10) A state average was not calculated because too few hospitals in the state submitted data; (11) There were discrepancies in the data collection process; Please refer to the User's Guide for a full explanation of data.

Lake Forest Hospital

660 N Westmoreland Road
Lake Forest, IL 60045
Phone: 847-234-5600
Fax: 847-535-7846
URL: www.lakeforesthospital.com
Type: Acute Care Hospitals
Emergency Services: Yes
Ownership: Voluntary Non-Profit - Other
Beds: 261

Key Personnel:
CEO/President. . . . . William Ries

Measure	Cases	This Hosp.	State Avg.	U.S. Avg.
Heart Attack Care				
ACE Inhibitor or ARB for LVSD[1]	7	100%	96%	96%
Aspirin at Arrival	53	100%	99%	99%
Aspirin at Discharge	43	98%	99%	98%
Beta Blocker at Discharge	41	100%	98%	98%
Fibrinolytic Medication Timing	0	-	50%	55%
PCI Within 90 Minutes of Arrival[1]	10	80%	90%	90%
Smoking Cessation Advice[1]	10	100%	100%	99%
Chest Pain/Possible Heart Attack Care				
Aspirin at Arrival	33	100%	95%	95%
Median Time to ECG (minutes)	40	6	8	8
Median Time to Transfer (minutes)[1,3]	3	28	57	61
Fibrinolytic Medication Timing[3]	0	-	33%	54%
Heart Failure Care				
ACE Inhibitor or ARB for LVSD	46	100%	94%	94%
Discharge Instructions	146	98%	89%	88%
Evaluation of LVS Function	179	100%	98%	98%
Smoking Cessation Advice[1]	8	100%	99%	98%
Pneumonia Care				
Appropriate Initial Antibiotic	114	95%	90%	92%
Blood Culture Timing	207	97%	97%	96%
Influenza Vaccine	99	93%	91%	91%
Initial Antibiotic Timing	158	98%	96%	95%
Pneumococcal Vaccine	137	96%	92%	93%
Smoking Cessation Advice	34	100%	98%	97%
Surgical Care Improvement Project				
Appropriate VTP Within 24 Hours	268	91%	92%	92%
Appropriate Hair Removal	822	100%	99%	99%
Appropriate Beta Blocker Usage	181	94%	92%	93%
Controlled Postoperative Blood Glucose	0	-	92%	93%
Prophylactic Antibiotic Timing	640	98%	97%	97%
Prophylactic Antibiotic Timing (Outpatient)	327	96%	93%	92%
Prophylactic Antibiotic Selection	642	98%	97%	97%
Prophylactic Antibiotic Select. (Outpatient)	327	97%	94%	94%
Prophylactic Antibiotic Stopped	638	96%	94%	94%
Recommended VTP Ordered	268	93%	94%	94%
Urinary Catheter Removal	248	94%	89%	90%
Children's Asthma Care				
Received Systemic Corticosteroids	-	-	-	100%
Received Home Management Plan	-	-	-	71%
Received Reliever Medication	-	-	-	100%
Use of Medical Imaging				
Combination Abdominal CT Scan	983	0.739	0.246	0.191
Combination Chest CT Scan	737	0.682	0.098	0.054
Follow-up Mammogram/Ultrasound	2,527	14.9%	8.4%	8.4%
MRI for Low Back Pain	233	29.6%	33.4%	32.7%
Survey of Patients' Hospital Experiences				
Area Around Room 'Always' Quiet at Night	300+	52%	-	58%
Doctors 'Always' Communicated Well	300+	81%	-	80%
Home Recovery Information Given	300+	83%	-	82%
Hospital Given 9 or 10 on 10 Point Scale	300+	73%	-	67%
Meds 'Always' Explained Before Given	300+	58%	-	60%
Nurses 'Always' Communicated Well	300+	75%	-	76%
Pain 'Always' Well Controlled	300+	69%	-	69%
Room and Bathroom 'Always' Clean	300+	73%	-	71%
Timely Help 'Always' Received	300+	59%	-	64%
Would Definitely Recommend Hospital	300+	76%	-	69%

Lawrence County Memorial Hospital

2200 W State St
Lawrenceville, IL 62439
Phone: 618-943-1000
Fax: 618-943-7230
Type: Critical Access Hospitals
Emergency Services: Yes
Ownership: Government - Local
Beds: 25

Key Personnel:
CEO/President. . . . . Doug Florkowski
Chief of Medical Staff. . . . . Gary Carr, MD
Infection Control. . . . . Deborah Lemeroa, RN
Quality Assurance . . . . Debbie Gregory
Radiology. . . . . Debbie Miller
Anesthesiology. . . . . Tim Williams, DO
Emergency Room . . . . Rita Garvey

Measure	Cases	This Hosp.	State Avg.	U.S. Avg.
Heart Attack Care				
ACE Inhibitor or ARB for LVSD[1,3]	2	100%	96%	96%
Aspirin at Arrival[1,3]	3	100%	99%	99%
Aspirin at Discharge[1,3]	3	100%	99%	98%
Beta Blocker at Discharge[1,3]	2	100%	98%	98%
Fibrinolytic Medication Timing[3]	0	-	50%	55%
PCI Within 90 Minutes of Arrival[3]	0	-	90%	90%
Smoking Cessation Advice[3]	0	-	100%	99%
Chest Pain/Possible Heart Attack Care				
Aspirin at Arrival	-	-	95%	95%
Median Time to ECG (minutes)	-	-	8	8
Median Time to Transfer (minutes)	-	-	57	61
Fibrinolytic Medication Timing	-	-	33%	54%
Heart Failure Care				
ACE Inhibitor or ARB for LVSD[1]	19	100%	94%	94%
Discharge Instructions[1]	24	100%	89%	88%
Evaluation of LVS Function	46	91%	98%	98%
Smoking Cessation Advice[1]	8	100%	99%	98%
Pneumonia Care				
Appropriate Initial Antibiotic[1]	12	50%	90%	92%
Blood Culture Timing	30	97%	97%	96%
Influenza Vaccine[1]	17	94%	91%	91%
Initial Antibiotic Timing	36	100%	96%	95%
Pneumococcal Vaccine	25	76%	92%	93%
Smoking Cessation Advice[1]	5	100%	98%	97%
Surgical Care Improvement Project				
Appropriate VTP Within 24 Hours[5]	0	-	92%	92%
Appropriate Hair Removal[5]	0	-	99%	99%
Appropriate Beta Blocker Usage[5]	0	-	92%	93%
Controlled Postoperative Blood Glucose[5]	0	-	92%	93%
Prophylactic Antibiotic Timing[5]	0	-	97%	97%
Prophylactic Antibiotic Timing (Outpatient)	-	-	93%	92%
Prophylactic Antibiotic Selection[5]	0	-	97%	97%
Prophylactic Antibiotic Select. (Outpatient)	-	-	94%	94%
Prophylactic Antibiotic Stopped[5]	0	-	94%	94%
Recommended VTP Ordered[5]	0	-	94%	94%
Urinary Catheter Removal[5]	0	-	89%	90%
Children's Asthma Care				
Received Systemic Corticosteroids	-	-	-	100%
Received Home Management Plan	-	-	-	71%
Received Reliever Medication	-	-	-	100%
Use of Medical Imaging				
Combination Abdominal CT Scan	-	-	0.246	0.191
Combination Chest CT Scan	-	-	0.098	0.054
Follow-up Mammogram/Ultrasound	-	-	8.4%	8.4%
MRI for Low Back Pain	-	-	33.4%	32.7%
Survey of Patients' Hospital Experiences				
Area Around Room 'Always' Quiet at Night[8]	-	-	-	58%
Doctors 'Always' Communicated Well[8]	-	-	-	80%
Home Recovery Information Given[8]	-	-	-	82%
Hospital Given 9 or 10 on 10 Point Scale[8]	-	-	-	67%
Meds 'Always' Explained Before Given[8]	-	-	-	60%
Nurses 'Always' Communicated Well[8]	-	-	-	76%
Pain 'Always' Well Controlled[8]	-	-	-	69%
Room and Bathroom 'Always' Clean[8]	-	-	-	71%
Timely Help 'Always' Received[8]	-	-	-	64%
Would Definitely Recommend Hospital[8]	-	-	-	69%

Advocate Condell Medical Center

801 S Milwaukee Ave
Libertyville, IL 60048
Phone: 847-990-5200
Fax: 847-362-1721
URL: www.condell.org
Type: Acute Care Hospitals
Emergency Services: Yes
Ownership: Voluntary Non-Profit - Other
Beds: 305

Key Personnel:
CEO/President. . . . . Eugene Pritchard
Cardiac Laboratory. . . . . Vinda Russo
Infection Control. . . . . Emily Bergman
Quality Assurance . . . . Kathleen Mika
Radiology. . . . . Daniel Y Kim
Emergency Room . . . . William E Maloney
Intensive Care Unit. . . . . Sharon Reich

Measure	Cases	This Hosp.	State Avg.	U.S. Avg.
Heart Attack Care				
ACE Inhibitor or ARB for LVSD	32	100%	96%	96%
Aspirin at Arrival	221	100%	99%	99%
Aspirin at Discharge	215	100%	99%	98%
Beta Blocker at Discharge	201	100%	98%	98%
Fibrinolytic Medication Timing	0	-	50%	55%
PCI Within 90 Minutes of Arrival	62	100%	90%	90%
Smoking Cessation Advice	76	100%	100%	99%
Chest Pain/Possible Heart Attack Care				
Aspirin at Arrival[1]	6	100%	95%	95%
Median Time to ECG (minutes)[1]	6	16	8	8
Median Time to Transfer (minutes)[5]	0	-	57	61
Fibrinolytic Medication Timing[5]	0	-	33%	54%
Heart Failure Care				
ACE Inhibitor or ARB for LVSD	107	100%	94%	94%
Discharge Instructions	325	92%	89%	88%
Evaluation of LVS Function	428	100%	98%	98%
Smoking Cessation Advice	48	100%	99%	98%
Pneumonia Care				
Appropriate Initial Antibiotic[2]	85	96%	90%	92%
Blood Culture Timing[2]	135	99%	97%	96%
Influenza Vaccine[2]	89	100%	91%	91%
Initial Antibiotic Timing[2]	156	98%	96%	95%
Pneumococcal Vaccine[2]	132	99%	92%	93%
Smoking Cessation Advice[2]	40	100%	98%	97%
Surgical Care Improvement Project				
Appropriate VTP Within 24 Hours[2]	189	94%	92%	92%
Appropriate Hair Removal[2]	609	100%	99%	99%
Appropriate Beta Blocker Usage[2]	201	99%	92%	93%
Controlled Postoperative Blood Glucose[2]	120	99%	92%	93%
Prophylactic Antibiotic Timing[2]	425	98%	97%	97%
Prophylactic Antibiotic Timing (Outpatient)	446	94%	93%	92%
Prophylactic Antibiotic Selection[2]	429	98%	97%	97%
Prophylactic Antibiotic Select. (Outpatient)	442	98%	94%	94%
Prophylactic Antibiotic Stopped[2]	398	96%	94%	94%
Recommended VTP Ordered[2]	189	94%	94%	94%
Urinary Catheter Removal[2]	125	93%	89%	90%
Children's Asthma Care				
Received Systemic Corticosteroids	-	-	-	100%
Received Home Management Plan	-	-	-	71%
Received Reliever Medication	-	-	-	100%
Use of Medical Imaging				
Combination Abdominal CT Scan	1,271	0.397	0.246	0.191
Combination Chest CT Scan	932	0.338	0.098	0.054
Follow-up Mammogram/Ultrasound	1,460	14.5%	8.4%	8.4%
MRI for Low Back Pain	197	35.0%	33.4%	32.7%
Survey of Patients' Hospital Experiences				
Area Around Room 'Always' Quiet at Night	300+	45%	-	58%
Doctors 'Always' Communicated Well	300+	74%	-	80%
Home Recovery Information Given	300+	76%	-	82%
Hospital Given 9 or 10 on 10 Point Scale	300+	58%	-	67%
Meds 'Always' Explained Before Given	300+	54%	-	60%
Nurses 'Always' Communicated Well	300+	70%	-	76%
Pain 'Always' Well Controlled	300+	65%	-	69%
Room and Bathroom 'Always' Clean	300+	69%	-	71%
Timely Help 'Always' Received	300+	55%	-	64%
Would Definitely Recommend Hospital	300+	62%	-	69%

NOTE: Hospital profiles are in alphabetical order by state, then city, then hospital within the city; Rankings exclude hospitals with less than 25 cases except for patient surveys which excludes hospitals with less than 100 cases; (a) 100–299 cases; (1) The number of cases is too small to be sure how well a hospital is performing; (2) The hospital indicated that the data submitted for this measure were based on a sample of cases; (3) Data was collected during a shorter time period (fewer quarters) than the maximum possible time for this measure; (4) Suppressed for one or more quarters by CMS; (5) No data is available from the hospital for this measure; (6) Fewer than 100 patients completed the HCAHPS survey. Use these rates with caution, as the number of surveys may be too low to reliably assess hospital performance; (7) Survey results are based on less than 12 months of data; (8) Survey results are not available for this reporting period; (9) No or very few patients were eligible for the HCAHPS survey. The scores shown, if any, reflect a very small number of surveys; (10) A state average was not calculated because too few hospitals in the state submitted data; (11) There were discrepancies in the data collection process; Please refer to the User's Guide for a full explanation of data.

Abraham Lincoln Memorial Hospital

315 8th Street
Lincoln, IL 62656
Phone: 217-732-2161
Fax: 217-732-7481
URL: www.almh.org
Type: Critical Access Hospitals
Emergency Services: Yes
Ownership: Voluntary Non-Profit - Private
Beds: 66

Key Personnel:

Chief of Medical Staff.......... Amir John Wahab, MD
Infection Control............. Margaret Evers, RN
Operating Room.............. Debbie Morrow, RN
Quality Assurance .... Kathleen Vipond
Radiology.................... Charles Neal
Anesthesiology............... Gene Quint
Emergency Room .... Larry Pinter, MD
Intensive Care Unit........... Judy Evans

Measure	Cases	This Hosp.	State Avg.	U.S. Avg.
Heart Attack Care				
ACE Inhibitor or ARB for LVSD[3]	0	-	96%	96%
Aspirin at Arrival[1,3]	1	100%	99%	99%
Aspirin at Discharge[1,3]	1	100%	99%	98%
Beta Blocker at Discharge[1,3]	1	100%	98%	98%
Fibrinolytic Medication Timing[3]	0	-	50%	55%
PCI Within 90 Minutes of Arrival[3]	0	-	90%	90%
Smoking Cessation Advice[3]	0	-	100%	99%
Chest Pain/Possible Heart Attack Care				
Aspirin at Arrival	191	97%	95%	95%
Median Time to ECG (minutes)	197	4	8	8
Median Time to Transfer (minutes)	0	-	57	61
Fibrinolytic Medication Timing	0	-	33%	54%
Heart Failure Care				
ACE Inhibitor or ARB for LVSD[1]	3	100%	94%	94%
Discharge Instructions[1]	10	100%	89%	88%
Evaluation of LVS Function[1]	20	100%	98%	98%
Smoking Cessation Advice[1]	1	100%	99%	98%
Pneumonia Care				
Appropriate Initial Antibiotic	31	90%	90%	92%
Blood Culture Timing	53	96%	97%	96%
Influenza Vaccine	39	100%	91%	91%
Initial Antibiotic Timing	54	98%	96%	95%
Pneumococcal Vaccine	63	98%	92%	93%
Smoking Cessation Advice[1]	9	100%	98%	97%
Surgical Care Improvement Project				
Appropriate VTP Within 24 Hours[1]	19	100%	92%	92%
Appropriate Hair Removal	64	100%	99%	99%
Appropriate Beta Blocker Usage[1]	12	100%	92%	93%
Controlled Postoperative Blood Glucose	0	-	92%	93%
Prophylactic Antibiotic Timing	41	98%	97%	97%
Prophylactic Antibiotic Timing (Outpatient)[5]	0	-	93%	92%
Prophylactic Antibiotic Selection	42	100%	97%	97%
Prophylactic Antibiotic Select. (Outpatient)[5]	0	-	94%	94%
Prophylactic Antibiotic Stopped	40	100%	94%	94%
Recommended VTP Ordered[1]	19	100%	94%	94%
Urinary Catheter Removal[1]	16	100%	89%	90%
Children's Asthma Care				
Received Systemic Corticosteroids	-	-	-	100%
Received Home Management Plan	-	-	-	71%
Received Reliever Medication	-	-	-	100%
Use of Medical Imaging				
Combination Abdominal CT Scan	459	0.102	0.246	0.191
Combination Chest CT Scan	315	0.025	0.098	0.054
Follow-up Mammogram/Ultrasound	427	7.7%	8.4%	8.4%
MRI for Low Back Pain	90	47.8%	33.4%	32.7%
Survey of Patients' Hospital Experiences				
Area Around Room 'Always' Quiet at Night	(a)	64%	-	58%
Doctors 'Always' Communicated Well	(a)	91%	-	80%
Home Recovery Information Given	(a)	89%	-	82%
Hospital Given 9 or 10 on 10 Point Scale	(a)	73%	-	67%
Meds 'Always' Explained Before Given	(a)	66%	-	60%
Nurses 'Always' Communicated Well	(a)	81%	-	76%
Pain 'Always' Well Controlled	(a)	76%	-	69%
Room and Bathroom 'Always' Clean	(a)	79%	-	71%
Timely Help 'Always' Received	(a)	72%	-	64%
Would Definitely Recommend Hospital	(a)	78%	-	69%

Saint Francis Hospital

1215 Franciscan Dr
Litchfield, IL 62056
Phone: 217-324-2191
Fax: 217-324-3081
URL: www.stfrancis-litchfield.org
Type: Critical Access Hospitals
Emergency Services: Yes
Ownership: Voluntary Non-Profit - Church
Beds: 25

Key Personnel:

Chief of Medical Staff.......... Timothy Ishmael, MD
Infection Control............. Angie Tefteller, RN
Operating Room.............. D Billiter
Quality Assurance .... Bev Deaton
Radiology.................... Laura Smalley
Emergency Room .... Vicky Fuller, RN
Intensive Care Unit........... Pat Wernsing, RN

Measure	Cases	This Hosp.	State Avg.	U.S. Avg.
Heart Attack Care				
ACE Inhibitor or ARB for LVSD[5]	0	-	96%	96%
Aspirin at Arrival[5]	0	-	99%	99%
Aspirin at Discharge[5]	0	-	99%	98%
Beta Blocker at Discharge[5]	0	-	98%	98%
Fibrinolytic Medication Timing[5]	0	-	50%	55%
PCI Within 90 Minutes of Arrival[5]	0	-	90%	90%
Smoking Cessation Advice[5]	0	-	100%	99%
Chest Pain/Possible Heart Attack Care				
Aspirin at Arrival	-	-	95%	95%
Median Time to ECG (minutes)	-	-	8	8
Median Time to Transfer (minutes)	-	-	57	61
Fibrinolytic Medication Timing	-	-	33%	54%
Heart Failure Care				
ACE Inhibitor or ARB for LVSD[1]	6	100%	94%	94%
Discharge Instructions	25	100%	89%	88%
Evaluation of LVS Function	40	82%	98%	98%
Smoking Cessation Advice[1]	5	80%	99%	98%
Pneumonia Care				
Appropriate Initial Antibiotic	38	84%	90%	92%
Blood Culture Timing	49	90%	97%	96%
Influenza Vaccine[1]	23	70%	91%	91%
Initial Antibiotic Timing	52	90%	96%	95%
Pneumococcal Vaccine	47	70%	92%	93%
Smoking Cessation Advice[1]	22	82%	98%	97%
Surgical Care Improvement Project				
Appropriate VTP Within 24 Hours	39	33%	92%	92%
Appropriate Hair Removal	48	85%	99%	99%
Appropriate Beta Blocker Usage[1]	19	79%	92%	93%
Controlled Postoperative Blood Glucose[5]	0	-	92%	93%
Prophylactic Antibiotic Timing	50	88%	97%	97%
Prophylactic Antibiotic Timing (Outpatient)	-	-	93%	92%
Prophylactic Antibiotic Selection	50	86%	97%	97%
Prophylactic Antibiotic Select. (Outpatient)	-	-	94%	94%
Prophylactic Antibiotic Stopped	50	60%	94%	94%
Recommended VTP Ordered	39	33%	94%	94%
Urinary Catheter Removal[1]	18	56%	89%	90%
Children's Asthma Care				
Received Systemic Corticosteroids	-	-	-	100%
Received Home Management Plan	-	-	-	71%
Received Reliever Medication	-	-	-	100%
Use of Medical Imaging				
Combination Abdominal CT Scan	-	-	0.246	0.191
Combination Chest CT Scan	-	-	0.098	0.054
Follow-up Mammogram/Ultrasound	-	-	8.4%	8.4%
MRI for Low Back Pain	-	-	33.4%	32.7%
Survey of Patients' Hospital Experiences				
Area Around Room 'Always' Quiet at Night	300+	65%	-	58%
Doctors 'Always' Communicated Well	300+	83%	-	80%
Home Recovery Information Given	300+	81%	-	82%
Hospital Given 9 or 10 on 10 Point Scale	300+	70%	-	67%
Meds 'Always' Explained Before Given	300+	63%	-	60%
Nurses 'Always' Communicated Well	300+	79%	-	76%
Pain 'Always' Well Controlled	300+	71%	-	69%
Room and Bathroom 'Always' Clean	300+	83%	-	71%
Timely Help 'Always' Received	300+	66%	-	64%
Would Definitely Recommend Hospital	300+	64%	-	69%

McDonough District Hospital

525 East Grant Street
Macomb, IL 61455
Phone: 309-833-4101
Fax: 309-836-1507
URL: www.mdh.org
Type: Acute Care Hospitals
Emergency Services: Yes
Ownership: Govt - Hospital Dist/Auth
Beds: 113

Key Personnel:

CEO/President................ Stephen R Hopper
Chief of Medical Staff.......... Dr Charles O'Neill
Infection Control............. Carol Rowland-Maguire, RN
Operating Room.............. Linda Sampson
Quality Assurance .... Linda Dace
Radiology.................... Ronald Rigdon, MD

Measure	Cases	This Hosp.	State Avg.	U.S. Avg.
Heart Attack Care				
ACE Inhibitor or ARB for LVSD[1,3]	1	100%	96%	96%
Aspirin at Arrival[1,3]	6	100%	99%	99%
Aspirin at Discharge[1,3]	4	75%	99%	98%
Beta Blocker at Discharge[1,3]	4	100%	98%	98%
Fibrinolytic Medication Timing[3]	0	-	50%	55%
PCI Within 90 Minutes of Arrival[3]	0	-	90%	90%
Smoking Cessation Advice[3]	0	-	100%	99%
Chest Pain/Possible Heart Attack Care				
Aspirin at Arrival	81	94%	95%	95%
Median Time to ECG (minutes)	85	7	8	8
Median Time to Transfer (minutes)[1,3]	3	57	57	61
Fibrinolytic Medication Timing[1]	1	100%	33%	54%
Heart Failure Care				
ACE Inhibitor or ARB for LVSD	31	84%	94%	94%
Discharge Instructions	49	63%	89%	88%
Evaluation of LVS Function	91	99%	98%	98%
Smoking Cessation Advice[1]	9	89%	99%	98%
Pneumonia Care				
Appropriate Initial Antibiotic	41	98%	90%	92%
Blood Culture Timing	51	96%	97%	96%
Influenza Vaccine	60	93%	91%	91%
Initial Antibiotic Timing	70	93%	96%	95%
Pneumococcal Vaccine	84	93%	92%	93%
Smoking Cessation Advice[1]	12	92%	98%	97%
Surgical Care Improvement Project				
Appropriate VTP Within 24 Hours	45	89%	92%	92%
Appropriate Hair Removal	107	100%	99%	99%
Appropriate Beta Blocker Usage	29	72%	92%	93%
Controlled Postoperative Blood Glucose	0	-	92%	93%
Prophylactic Antibiotic Timing	70	94%	97%	97%
Prophylactic Antibiotic Timing (Outpatient)	45	80%	93%	92%
Prophylactic Antibiotic Selection	70	99%	97%	97%
Prophylactic Antibiotic Select. (Outpatient)	36	97%	94%	94%
Prophylactic Antibiotic Stopped	66	86%	94%	94%
Recommended VTP Ordered	46	89%	94%	94%
Urinary Catheter Removal[1]	22	77%	89%	90%
Children's Asthma Care				
Received Systemic Corticosteroids	-	-	-	100%
Received Home Management Plan	-	-	-	71%
Received Reliever Medication	-	-	-	100%
Use of Medical Imaging				
Combination Abdominal CT Scan	330	0.733	0.246	0.191
Combination Chest CT Scan	373	0.217	0.098	0.054
Follow-up Mammogram/Ultrasound	642	6.5%	8.4%	8.4%
MRI for Low Back Pain	58	31.0%	33.4%	32.7%
Survey of Patients' Hospital Experiences				
Area Around Room 'Always' Quiet at Night	300+	56%	-	58%
Doctors 'Always' Communicated Well	300+	84%	-	80%
Home Recovery Information Given	300+	90%	-	82%
Hospital Given 9 or 10 on 10 Point Scale	300+	65%	-	67%
Meds 'Always' Explained Before Given	300+	59%	-	60%
Nurses 'Always' Communicated Well	300+	78%	-	76%
Pain 'Always' Well Controlled	300+	73%	-	69%
Room and Bathroom 'Always' Clean	300+	81%	-	71%
Timely Help 'Always' Received	300+	72%	-	64%
Would Definitely Recommend Hospital	300+	64%	-	69%

NOTE: Hospital profiles are in alphabetical order by state, then city, then hospital within the city; Rankings exclude hospitals with less than 25 cases except for patient surveys which excludes hospitals with less than 100 cases; (a) 100–299 cases; (1) The number of cases is too small to be sure how well a hospital is performing; (2) The hospital indicated that the data submitted for this measure were based on a sample of cases; (3) Data was collected during a shorter time period (fewer quarters) than the maximum possible time for this measure; (4) Suppressed for one or more quarters by CMS; (5) No data is available from the hospital for this measure; (6) Fewer than 100 patients completed the HCAHPS survey. Use these rates with caution, as the number of surveys may be too low to reliably assess hospital performance; (7) Survey results are based on less than 12 months of data; (8) Survey results are not available for this reporting period; (9) No or very few patients were eligible for the HCAHPS survey. The scores shown, if any, reflect a very small number of surveys; (10) A state average was not calculated because too few hospitals in the state submitted data; (11) There were discrepancies in the data collection process; Please refer to the User's Guide for a full explanation of data.

Heartland Regional Medical Center

3333 W De Young
Marion, IL 62959
Phone: 618-998-7000
Type: Acute Care Hospitals
Emergency Services: Yes
Ownership: Proprietary
Beds: 92

Measure	Cases	This Hosp.	State Avg.	U.S. Avg.
Heart Attack Care				
ACE Inhibitor or ARB for LVSD[1]	19	84%	96%	96%
Aspirin at Arrival	56	98%	99%	99%
Aspirin at Discharge	78	97%	99%	98%
Beta Blocker at Discharge	78	97%	98%	98%
Fibrinolytic Medication Timing	0	-	50%	55%
PCI Within 90 Minutes of Arrival[1]	12	83%	90%	90%
Smoking Cessation Advice	33	100%	100%	99%
Chest Pain/Possible Heart Attack Care				
Aspirin at Arrival[1,3]	6	67%	95%	95%
Median Time to ECG (minutes)[1,3]	7	5	8	8
Median Time to Transfer (minutes)[5]	0	-	57	61
Fibrinolytic Medication Timing[3]	0	-	33%	54%
Heart Failure Care				
ACE Inhibitor or ARB for LVSD	62	98%	94%	94%
Discharge Instructions	116	59%	89%	88%
Evaluation of LVS Function	136	99%	98%	98%
Smoking Cessation Advice	25	100%	99%	98%
Pneumonia Care				
Appropriate Initial Antibiotic	68	85%	90%	92%
Blood Culture Timing	115	99%	97%	96%
Influenza Vaccine	107	83%	91%	91%
Initial Antibiotic Timing	117	95%	96%	95%
Pneumococcal Vaccine	152	88%	92%	93%
Smoking Cessation Advice	59	100%	98%	97%
Surgical Care Improvement Project				
Appropriate VTP Within 24 Hours[2]	186	93%	92%	92%
Appropriate Hair Removal[2]	483	100%	99%	99%
Appropriate Beta Blocker Usage[2]	155	88%	92%	93%
Controlled Postoperative Blood Glucose[1,2]	21	90%	92%	93%
Prophylactic Antibiotic Timing[2]	316	96%	97%	97%
Prophylactic Antibiotic Timing (Outpatient)	207	94%	93%	92%
Prophylactic Antibiotic Selection[2]	318	99%	97%	97%
Prophylactic Antibiotic Select. (Outpatient)	213	93%	94%	94%
Prophylactic Antibiotic Stopped[2]	292	82%	94%	94%
Recommended VTP Ordered[2]	186	96%	94%	94%
Urinary Catheter Removal	42	81%	89%	90%
Children's Asthma Care				
Received Systemic Corticosteroids	-	-	-	100%
Received Home Management Plan	-	-	-	71%
Received Reliever Medication	-	-	-	100%
Use of Medical Imaging				
Combination Abdominal CT Scan	518	0.095	0.246	0.191
Combination Chest CT Scan	282	0.021	0.098	0.054
Follow-up Mammogram/Ultrasound	425	8.0%	8.4%	8.4%
MRI for Low Back Pain	80	26.3%	33.4%	32.7%
Survey of Patients' Hospital Experiences				
Area Around Room 'Always' Quiet at Night	300+	52%	-	58%
Doctors 'Always' Communicated Well	300+	75%	-	80%
Home Recovery Information Given	300+	80%	-	82%
Hospital Given 9 or 10 on 10 Point Scale	300+	55%	-	67%
Meds 'Always' Explained Before Given	300+	52%	-	60%
Nurses 'Always' Communicated Well	300+	68%	-	76%
Pain 'Always' Well Controlled	300+	63%	-	69%
Room and Bathroom 'Always' Clean	300+	66%	-	71%
Timely Help 'Always' Received	300+	56%	-	64%
Would Definitely Recommend Hospital	300+	52%	-	69%

Marion Illinois VA Medical Center

2401 West Main
Marion, IL 62959
Phone: 618-997-5311
Fax: 618-998-5667
Type: Acute Care-Veterans Administration
Emergency Services: No
Ownership: Government - Federal
Beds: 39

Key Personnel:
CEO/President. . . . . Arpakorn Kantatan, MD
Chief of Medical Staff . . . . RV Chadaga, MD
Infection Control. . . . . Jan Collins
Operating Room. . . . . Debbie Bertramd
Emergency Room . . . . Betty Dunbar
Intensive Care Unit. . . . . Cheryl Sherrill

Measure	Cases	This Hosp.	State Avg.	U.S. Avg.
Heart Attack Care				
ACE Inhibitor or ARB for LVSD[5]	0	-	96%	96%
Aspirin at Arrival[5]	0	-	99%	99%
Aspirin at Discharge[5]	0	-	99%	98%
Beta Blocker at Discharge[5]	0	-	98%	98%
Fibrinolytic Medication Timing[5]	0	-	50%	55%
PCI Within 90 Minutes of Arrival[5]	0	-	90%	90%
Smoking Cessation Advice[5]	0	-	100%	99%
Chest Pain/Possible Heart Attack Care				
Aspirin at Arrival	-	-	95%	95%
Median Time to ECG (minutes)	-	-	8	8
Median Time to Transfer (minutes)	-	-	57	61
Fibrinolytic Medication Timing	-	-	33%	54%
Heart Failure Care				
ACE Inhibitor or ARB for LVSD	57	93%	94%	94%
Discharge Instructions	135	99%	89%	88%
Evaluation of LVS Function	143	100%	98%	98%
Smoking Cessation Advice[1]	22	100%	99%	98%
Pneumonia Care				
Appropriate Initial Antibiotic	80	88%	90%	92%
Blood Culture Timing	112	96%	97%	96%
Influenza Vaccine	79	85%	91%	91%
Initial Antibiotic Timing[1]	17	94%	96%	95%
Pneumococcal Vaccine	85	95%	92%	93%
Smoking Cessation Advice	50	100%	98%	97%
Surgical Care Improvement Project				
Appropriate VTP Within 24 Hours[2,5]	0	-	92%	92%
Appropriate Hair Removal[2,5]	0	-	99%	99%
Appropriate Beta Blocker Usage[2,5]	0	-	92%	93%
Controlled Postoperative Blood Glucose[2,5]	0	-	92%	93%
Prophylactic Antibiotic Timing[5]	0	-	97%	97%
Prophylactic Antibiotic Timing (Outpatient)	-	-	93%	92%
Prophylactic Antibiotic Selection[5]	0	-	97%	97%
Prophylactic Antibiotic Select. (Outpatient)	-	-	94%	94%
Prophylactic Antibiotic Stopped[5]	0	-	94%	94%
Recommended VTP Ordered[2,5]	0	-	94%	94%
Urinary Catheter Removal[2,5]	0	-	89%	90%
Children's Asthma Care				
Received Systemic Corticosteroids	-	-	-	100%
Received Home Management Plan	-	-	-	71%
Received Reliever Medication	-	-	-	100%
Use of Medical Imaging				
Combination Abdominal CT Scan	-	-	0.246	0.191
Combination Chest CT Scan	-	-	0.098	0.054
Follow-up Mammogram/Ultrasound	-	-	8.4%	8.4%
MRI for Low Back Pain	-	-	33.4%	32.7%
Survey of Patients' Hospital Experiences				
Area Around Room 'Always' Quiet at Night	-	-	-	58%
Doctors 'Always' Communicated Well	-	-	-	80%
Home Recovery Information Given	-	-	-	82%
Hospital Given 9 or 10 on 10 Point Scale	-	-	-	67%
Meds 'Always' Explained Before Given	-	-	-	60%
Nurses 'Always' Communicated Well	-	-	-	76%
Pain 'Always' Well Controlled	-	-	-	69%
Room and Bathroom 'Always' Clean	-	-	-	71%
Timely Help 'Always' Received	-	-	-	64%
Would Definitely Recommend Hospital	-	-	-	69%

Anderson Hospital

6800 State Route 162
Maryville, IL 62062
Phone: 618-288-5711
Fax: 618-288-4088
URL: www.andersonhospital.org
Type: Acute Care Hospitals
Emergency Services: Yes
Ownership: Voluntary Non-Profit - Private
Beds: 130

Key Personnel:
CEO/President. . . . . R Coert Shepard
Chief of Medical Staff. . . . . Rod Greeling, MD
Infection Control. . . . . Doris Driscoll, RN
Operating Room. . . . . Scott A Wong, RN
Pediatric Ambulatory Care . . . . . . Lizabeth Didriksen, MD
Pediatric In-Patient Care . . . . Lizabeth Didriksen, MD
Quality Assurance . . . . Dolores Phelps

Measure	Cases	This Hosp.	State Avg.	U.S. Avg.
Heart Attack Care				
ACE Inhibitor or ARB for LVSD[1]	11	100%	96%	96%
Aspirin at Arrival	113	96%	99%	99%
Aspirin at Discharge	97	99%	99%	98%
Beta Blocker at Discharge	97	100%	98%	98%
Fibrinolytic Medication Timing	0	-	50%	55%
PCI Within 90 Minutes of Arrival[1]	14	86%	90%	90%
Smoking Cessation Advice	30	100%	100%	99%
Chest Pain/Possible Heart Attack Care				
Aspirin at Arrival	86	98%	95%	95%
Median Time to ECG (minutes)	87	1	8	8
Median Time to Transfer (minutes)	31	45	57	61
Fibrinolytic Medication Timing	0	-	33%	54%
Heart Failure Care				
ACE Inhibitor or ARB for LVSD	79	96%	94%	94%
Discharge Instructions	167	82%	89%	88%
Evaluation of LVS Function	249	100%	98%	98%
Smoking Cessation Advice	45	98%	99%	98%
Pneumonia Care				
Appropriate Initial Antibiotic[2]	103	93%	90%	92%
Blood Culture Timing[2]	189	97%	97%	96%
Influenza Vaccine[2]	98	100%	91%	91%
Initial Antibiotic Timing[2]	161	95%	96%	95%
Pneumococcal Vaccine[2]	140	93%	92%	93%
Smoking Cessation Advice[2]	76	100%	98%	97%
Surgical Care Improvement Project				
Appropriate VTP Within 24 Hours[2]	228	97%	92%	92%
Appropriate Hair Removal[2]	512	100%	99%	99%
Appropriate Beta Blocker Usage[2]	119	91%	92%	93%
Controlled Postoperative Blood Glucose[2]	0	-	92%	93%
Prophylactic Antibiotic Timing[2]	362	96%	97%	97%
Prophylactic Antibiotic Timing (Outpatient)	288	96%	93%	92%
Prophylactic Antibiotic Selection[2]	368	97%	97%	97%
Prophylactic Antibiotic Select. (Outpatient)	283	97%	94%	94%
Prophylactic Antibiotic Stopped[2]	347	93%	94%	94%
Recommended VTP Ordered[2]	228	97%	94%	94%
Urinary Catheter Removal[2]	72	92%	89%	90%
Children's Asthma Care				
Received Systemic Corticosteroids	-	-	-	100%
Received Home Management Plan	-	-	-	71%
Received Reliever Medication	-	-	-	100%
Use of Medical Imaging				
Combination Abdominal CT Scan	656	0.197	0.246	0.191
Combination Chest CT Scan	793	0.016	0.098	0.054
Follow-up Mammogram/Ultrasound	755	12.2%	8.4%	8.4%
MRI for Low Back Pain	139	30.9%	33.4%	32.7%
Survey of Patients' Hospital Experiences				
Area Around Room 'Always' Quiet at Night	300+	51%	-	58%
Doctors 'Always' Communicated Well	300+	80%	-	80%
Home Recovery Information Given	300+	81%	-	82%
Hospital Given 9 or 10 on 10 Point Scale	300+	61%	-	67%
Meds 'Always' Explained Before Given	300+	55%	-	60%
Nurses 'Always' Communicated Well	300+	73%	-	76%
Pain 'Always' Well Controlled	300+	67%	-	69%
Room and Bathroom 'Always' Clean	300+	72%	-	71%
Timely Help 'Always' Received	300+	60%	-	64%
Would Definitely Recommend Hospital	300+	69%	-	69%

NOTE: Hospital profiles are in alphabetical order by state, then city, then hospital within the city; Rankings exclude hospitals with less than 25 cases except for patient surveys which excludes hospitals with less than 100 cases; (a) 100–299 cases; (1) The number of cases is too small to be sure how well a hospital is performing; (2) The hospital indicated that the data submitted for this measure were based on a sample of cases; (3) Data was collected during a shorter time period (fewer quarters) than the maximum possible time for this measure; (4) Suppressed for one or more quarters by CMS; (5) No data is available from the hospital for this measure; (6) Fewer than 100 patients completed the HCAHPS survey. Use these rates with caution, as the number of surveys may be too low to reliably assess hospital performance; (7) Survey results are based on less than 12 months of data; (8) Survey results are not available for this reporting period; (9) No or very few patients were eligible for the HCAHPS survey. The scores shown, if any, reflect a very small number of surveys; (10) A state average was not calculated because too few hospitals in the state submitted data; (11) There were discrepancies in the data collection process; Please refer to the User's Guide for a full explanation of data.

Sarah Bush Lincoln Health Center

1000 Health Center Dr | Phone: 217-258-2572
Mattoon, IL 61938 | Fax: 217-258-2111
E-mail: jpierce@sblhs.org
Type: Acute Care Hospitals | Emergency Services: Yes
Ownership: Voluntary Non-Profit - Private | Beds: 202

Key Personnel:
CEO/President.............. Gary L Barnett
Chief of Medical Staff.......... Dr Joseph Burton
Infection Control.............. Ramona Tomshack
Operating Room.............. Carol Ray
Pediatric Ambulatory Care...... Thomas Snowden, MD
Pediatric In-Patient Care....... Thomas Snowden, MD
Quality Assurance............ Cheryl Creasy, RN
Radiology.................. Jon Banas, DO

Measure	Cases	This Hosp.	State Avg.	U.S. Avg.
Heart Attack Care				
ACE Inhibitor or ARB for LVSD[1]	4	100%	96%	96%
Aspirin at Arrival	37	97%	99%	99%
Aspirin at Discharge[1]	20	100%	99%	98%
Beta Blocker at Discharge	25	100%	98%	98%
Fibrinolytic Medication Timing	0	-	50%	55%
PCI Within 90 Minutes of Arrival	0	-	90%	90%
Smoking Cessation Advice[1]	4	100%	100%	99%
Chest Pain/Possible Heart Attack Care				
Aspirin at Arrival	176	95%	95%	95%
Median Time to ECG (minutes)	182	11	8	8
Median Time to Transfer (minutes)[1]	15	71	57	61
Fibrinolytic Medication Timing[1]	4	25%	33%	54%
Heart Failure Care				
ACE Inhibitor or ARB for LVSD	52	100%	94%	94%
Discharge Instructions	173	96%	89%	88%
Evaluation of LVS Function	234	100%	98%	98%
Smoking Cessation Advice	50	100%	99%	98%
Pneumonia Care				
Appropriate Initial Antibiotic	105	93%	90%	92%
Blood Culture Timing	99	95%	97%	96%
Influenza Vaccine	135	81%	91%	91%
Initial Antibiotic Timing	184	97%	96%	95%
Pneumococcal Vaccine	174	100%	92%	93%
Smoking Cessation Advice	74	100%	98%	97%
Surgical Care Improvement Project				
Appropriate VTP Within 24 Hours	171	95%	92%	92%
Appropriate Hair Removal	520	100%	99%	99%
Appropriate Beta Blocker Usage	147	94%	92%	93%
Controlled Postoperative Blood Glucose	0	-	92%	93%
Prophylactic Antibiotic Timing	382	98%	97%	97%
Prophylactic Antibiotic Timing (Outpatient)	122	98%	93%	92%
Prophylactic Antibiotic Selection	387	97%	97%	97%
Prophylactic Antibiotic Select. (Outpatient)	122	88%	94%	94%
Prophylactic Antibiotic Stopped	349	93%	94%	94%
Recommended VTP Ordered	173	95%	94%	94%
Urinary Catheter Removal	75	72%	89%	90%
Children's Asthma Care				
Received Systemic Corticosteroids	-	-	-	100%
Received Home Management Plan	-	-	-	71%
Received Reliever Medication	-	-	-	100%
Use of Medical Imaging				
Combination Abdominal CT Scan	828	0.076	0.246	0.191
Combination Chest CT Scan	612	0.000	0.098	0.054
Follow-up Mammogram/Ultrasound	1,535	5.8%	8.4%	8.4%
MRI for Low Back Pain	181	34.3%	33.4%	32.7%
Survey of Patients' Hospital Experiences				
Area Around Room 'Always' Quiet at Night	300+	56%	-	58%
Doctors 'Always' Communicated Well	300+	85%	-	80%
Home Recovery Information Given	300+	89%	-	82%
Hospital Given 9 or 10 on 10 Point Scale	300+	73%	-	67%
Meds 'Always' Explained Before Given	300+	68%	-	60%
Nurses 'Always' Communicated Well	300+	82%	-	76%
Pain 'Always' Well Controlled	300+	73%	-	69%
Room and Bathroom 'Always' Clean	300+	73%	-	71%
Timely Help 'Always' Received	300+	70%	-	64%
Would Definitely Recommend Hospital	300+	74%	-	69%

Loyola University Medical Center

2160 S 1st Avenue | Phone: 708-216-9000
Maywood, IL 60153 | Fax: 708-216-5690
URL: www.lumc.edu
Type: Acute Care Hospitals | Emergency Services: Yes
Ownership: Voluntary Non-Profit - Private | Beds: 589

Key Personnel:
CEO/President.............. Anthony L Barbato, MD
Cardiac Laboratory............ David Wilber
Chief of Medical Staff.......... Leonard L Vertuno, MD
Infection Control.............. Paul O'Keefe, MD
Operating Room.............. Margaret Vorrier
Pediatric Ambulatory Care...... Joseph Zanga, MD
Quality Assurance............ Jodi Palmer
Radiology.................. Robert E Henkin, MD

Measure	Cases	This Hosp.	State Avg.	U.S. Avg.
Heart Attack Care				
ACE Inhibitor or ARB for LVSD	33	100%	96%	96%
Aspirin at Arrival	157	100%	99%	99%
Aspirin at Discharge	178	100%	99%	98%
Beta Blocker at Discharge	167	99%	98%	98%
Fibrinolytic Medication Timing	0	-	50%	55%
PCI Within 90 Minutes of Arrival	30	100%	90%	90%
Smoking Cessation Advice	55	100%	100%	99%
Chest Pain/Possible Heart Attack Care				
Aspirin at Arrival[5]	0	-	95%	95%
Median Time to ECG (minutes)[5]	0	-	8	8
Median Time to Transfer (minutes)[5]	0	-	57	61
Fibrinolytic Medication Timing[5]	0	-	33%	54%
Heart Failure Care				
ACE Inhibitor or ARB for LVSD	261	98%	94%	94%
Discharge Instructions	601	94%	89%	88%
Evaluation of LVS Function	690	100%	98%	98%
Smoking Cessation Advice	132	98%	99%	98%
Pneumonia Care				
Appropriate Initial Antibiotic	92	93%	90%	92%
Blood Culture Timing	255	96%	97%	96%
Influenza Vaccine	158	89%	91%	91%
Initial Antibiotic Timing	219	91%	96%	95%
Pneumococcal Vaccine	217	95%	92%	93%
Smoking Cessation Advice	68	100%	98%	97%
Surgical Care Improvement Project				
Appropriate VTP Within 24 Hours[2]	175	97%	92%	92%
Appropriate Hair Removal[2]	576	100%	99%	99%
Appropriate Beta Blocker Usage[2]	245	89%	92%	93%
Controlled Postoperative Blood Glucose[2]	138	89%	92%	93%
Prophylactic Antibiotic Timing[2]	381	98%	97%	97%
Prophylactic Antibiotic Timing (Outpatient)	268	93%	93%	92%
Prophylactic Antibiotic Selection[2]	387	96%	97%	97%
Prophylactic Antibiotic Select. (Outpatient)	486	93%	94%	94%
Prophylactic Antibiotic Stopped[2]	370	94%	94%	94%
Recommended VTP Ordered[2]	175	98%	94%	94%
Urinary Catheter Removal[2]	142	95%	89%	90%
Children's Asthma Care				
Received Systemic Corticosteroids	38	97%	-	100%
Received Home Management Plan	37	81%	-	71%
Received Reliever Medication	38	100%	-	100%
Use of Medical Imaging				
Combination Abdominal CT Scan	2,704	0.214	0.246	0.191
Combination Chest CT Scan	2,392	0.016	0.098	0.054
Follow-up Mammogram/Ultrasound	2,282	7.0%	8.4%	8.4%
MRI for Low Back Pain	377	28.9%	33.4%	32.7%
Survey of Patients' Hospital Experiences				
Area Around Room 'Always' Quiet at Night	300+	53%	-	58%
Doctors 'Always' Communicated Well	300+	77%	-	80%
Home Recovery Information Given	300+	82%	-	82%
Hospital Given 9 or 10 on 10 Point Scale	300+	66%	-	67%
Meds 'Always' Explained Before Given	300+	58%	-	60%
Nurses 'Always' Communicated Well	300+	73%	-	76%
Pain 'Always' Well Controlled	300+	67%	-	69%
Room and Bathroom 'Always' Clean	300+	65%	-	71%
Timely Help 'Always' Received	300+	54%	-	64%
Would Definitely Recommend Hospital	300+	72%	-	69%

Centegra Health System - McHenry Hospital

4201 Medical Center Drive | Phone: 815-344-5000
Mchenry, IL 60050 | Fax: 815-759-8094
URL: www.centegra.org
Type: Acute Care Hospitals | Emergency Services: Yes
Ownership: Voluntary Non-Profit - Other | Beds: 196

Key Personnel:
CEO/President.............. Michael S Eesley
Chief of Medical Staff.......... Z Thaddeus Lorenc, MD
Infection Control.............. Pat Kinney
Quality Assurance............ Aaron Shepley
Emergency Room............ Amy Moerschbaecher

Measure	Cases	This Hosp.	State Avg.	U.S. Avg.
Heart Attack Care				
ACE Inhibitor or ARB for LVSD	34	91%	96%	96%
Aspirin at Arrival	226	99%	99%	99%
Aspirin at Discharge	290	98%	99%	98%
Beta Blocker at Discharge	299	97%	98%	98%
Fibrinolytic Medication Timing	0	-	50%	55%
PCI Within 90 Minutes of Arrival	50	80%	90%	90%
Smoking Cessation Advice	102	99%	100%	99%
Chest Pain/Possible Heart Attack Care				
Aspirin at Arrival[1,3]	7	86%	95%	95%
Median Time to ECG (minutes)[1,3]	7	13	8	8
Median Time to Transfer (minutes)[5]	0	-	57	61
Fibrinolytic Medication Timing[5]	0	-	33%	54%
Heart Failure Care				
ACE Inhibitor or ARB for LVSD	90	92%	94%	94%
Discharge Instructions	260	95%	89%	88%
Evaluation of LVS Function	331	99%	98%	98%
Smoking Cessation Advice	49	98%	99%	98%
Pneumonia Care				
Appropriate Initial Antibiotic	141	87%	90%	92%
Blood Culture Timing	230	99%	97%	96%
Influenza Vaccine	152	75%	91%	91%
Initial Antibiotic Timing	246	96%	96%	95%
Pneumococcal Vaccine	211	73%	92%	93%
Smoking Cessation Advice	85	96%	98%	97%
Surgical Care Improvement Project				
Appropriate VTP Within 24 Hours[2]	235	78%	92%	92%
Appropriate Hair Removal[2]	758	100%	99%	99%
Appropriate Beta Blocker Usage[2]	275	97%	92%	93%
Controlled Postoperative Blood Glucose[2]	136	96%	92%	93%
Prophylactic Antibiotic Timing[2]	557	94%	97%	97%
Prophylactic Antibiotic Timing (Outpatient)	163	81%	93%	92%
Prophylactic Antibiotic Selection[2]	559	97%	97%	97%
Prophylactic Antibiotic Select. (Outpatient)	150	96%	94%	94%
Prophylactic Antibiotic Stopped[2]	536	88%	94%	94%
Recommended VTP Ordered[2]	236	85%	94%	94%
Urinary Catheter Removal[2]	214	74%	89%	90%
Children's Asthma Care				
Received Systemic Corticosteroids	-	-	-	100%
Received Home Management Plan	-	-	-	71%
Received Reliever Medication	-	-	-	100%
Use of Medical Imaging				
Combination Abdominal CT Scan	933	0.699	0.246	0.191
Combination Chest CT Scan	659	0.046	0.098	0.054
Follow-up Mammogram/Ultrasound	1,336	5.2%	8.4%	8.4%
MRI for Low Back Pain	249	31.7%	33.4%	32.7%
Survey of Patients' Hospital Experiences				
Area Around Room 'Always' Quiet at Night	300+	41%	-	58%
Doctors 'Always' Communicated Well	300+	77%	-	80%
Home Recovery Information Given	300+	86%	-	82%
Hospital Given 9 or 10 on 10 Point Scale	300+	65%	-	67%
Meds 'Always' Explained Before Given	300+	60%	-	60%
Nurses 'Always' Communicated Well	300+	77%	-	76%
Pain 'Always' Well Controlled	300+	70%	-	69%
Room and Bathroom 'Always' Clean	300+	76%	-	71%
Timely Help 'Always' Received	300+	65%	-	64%
Would Definitely Recommend Hospital	300+	68%	-	69%

NOTE: Hospital profiles are in alphabetical order by state, then city, then hospital within the city; Rankings exclude hospitals with less than 25 cases except for patient surveys which excludes hospitals with less than 100 cases; (a) 100–299 cases; (1) The number of cases is too small to be sure how well a hospital is performing; (2) The hospital indicated that the data submitted for this measure were based on a sample of cases; (3) Data was collected during a shorter time period (fewer quarters) than the maximum possible time for this measure; (4) Suppressed for one or more quarters by CMS; (5) No data is available from the hospital for this measure; (6) Fewer than 100 patients completed the HCAHPS survey. Use these rates with caution, as the number of surveys may be too low to reliably assess hospital performance; (7) Survey results are based on less than 12 months of data; (8) Survey results are not available for this reporting period; (9) No or very few patients were eligible for the HCAHPS survey. The scores shown, if any, reflect a very small number of surveys; (10) A state average was not calculated because too few hospitals in the state submitted data; (11) There were discrepancies in the data collection process; Please refer to the User's Guide for a full explanation of data.

Hamilton Memorial Hospital District

611 S Marshall Avenue | Phone: 618-643-2361
Mcleansboro, IL 62859 | Fax: 618-643-2875
URL: www.mcleansboro.com
Type: Critical Access Hospitals | Emergency Services: Yes
Ownership: Govt - Hospital Dist/Auth | Beds: 85

Key Personnel:
CEO/President. . . . . Randall W Dauby

Measure	Cases	This Hosp.	State Avg.	U.S. Avg.
Heart Attack Care				
ACE Inhibitor or ARB for LVSD[5]	0	-	96%	96%
Aspirin at Arrival[5]	0	-	99%	99%
Aspirin at Discharge[5]	0	-	99%	98%
Beta Blocker at Discharge[5]	0	-	98%	98%
Fibrinolytic Medication Timing[5]	0	-	50%	55%
PCI Within 90 Minutes of Arrival[5]	0	-	90%	90%
Smoking Cessation Advice[5]	0	-	100%	99%
Chest Pain/Possible Heart Attack Care				
Aspirin at Arrival	-	-	95%	95%
Median Time to ECG (minutes)	-	-	8	8
Median Time to Transfer (minutes)	-	-	57	61
Fibrinolytic Medication Timing	-	-	33%	54%
Heart Failure Care				
ACE Inhibitor or ARB for LVSD[1]	13	92%	94%	94%
Discharge Instructions	32	91%	89%	88%
Evaluation of LVS Function	52	100%	98%	98%
Smoking Cessation Advice[1]	7	71%	99%	98%
Pneumonia Care				
Appropriate Initial Antibiotic[1]	22	73%	90%	92%
Blood Culture Timing[1]	13	92%	97%	96%
Influenza Vaccine[1]	22	100%	91%	91%
Initial Antibiotic Timing	27	100%	96%	95%
Pneumococcal Vaccine	27	96%	92%	93%
Smoking Cessation Advice[1]	15	87%	98%	97%
Surgical Care Improvement Project				
Appropriate VTP Within 24 Hours[1,3]	1	100%	92%	92%
Appropriate Hair Removal[1,3]	1	100%	99%	99%
Appropriate Beta Blocker Usage[5]	0	-	92%	93%
Controlled Postoperative Blood Glucose[3]	0	-	92%	93%
Prophylactic Antibiotic Timing[1,3]	1	0%	97%	97%
Prophylactic Antibiotic Timing (Outpatient)	-	-	93%	92%
Prophylactic Antibiotic Selection[1,3]	1	100%	97%	97%
Prophylactic Antibiotic Select. (Outpatient)	-	-	94%	94%
Prophylactic Antibiotic Stopped[1,3]	1	100%	94%	94%
Recommended VTP Ordered[1,3]	1	100%	94%	94%
Urinary Catheter Removal[1,3]	1	100%	89%	90%
Children's Asthma Care				
Received Systemic Corticosteroids	-	-	-	100%
Received Home Management Plan	-	-	-	71%
Received Reliever Medication	-	-	-	100%
Use of Medical Imaging				
Combination Abdominal CT Scan	-	-	0.246	0.191
Combination Chest CT Scan	-	-	0.098	0.054
Follow-up Mammogram/Ultrasound	-	-	8.4%	8.4%
MRI for Low Back Pain	-	-	33.4%	32.7%
Survey of Patients' Hospital Experiences				
Area Around Room 'Always' Quiet at Night[8]	-	-	-	58%
Doctors 'Always' Communicated Well[8]	-	-	-	80%
Home Recovery Information Given[8]	-	-	-	82%
Hospital Given 9 or 10 on 10 Point Scale[8]	-	-	-	67%
Meds 'Always' Explained Before Given[8]	-	-	-	60%
Nurses 'Always' Communicated Well[8]	-	-	-	76%
Pain 'Always' Well Controlled[8]	-	-	-	69%
Room and Bathroom 'Always' Clean[8]	-	-	-	71%
Timely Help 'Always' Received[8]	-	-	-	64%
Would Definitely Recommend Hospital[8]	-	-	-	69%

Loyola Gottlieb Memorial Hospital

701 West North Ave | Phone: 708-450-4924
Melrose Park, IL 60160 | Fax: 708-681-0078
URL: www.gottliebhospital.org
Type: Acute Care Hospitals | Emergency Services: Yes
Ownership: Voluntary Non-Profit - Private | Beds: 250

Key Personnel:
CEO/President. . . . . Pat Cassidy
Chief of Medical Staff. . . . . Dr. Anand Lal
Infection Control. . . . . Cathy Paulas
Operating Room. . . . . Kathy Kozerski, RN
Quality Assurance . . . . Bev McAdam
Radiology. . . . . Ron Shimonis

Measure	Cases	This Hosp.	State Avg.	U.S. Avg.
Heart Attack Care				
ACE Inhibitor or ARB for LVSD	44	100%	96%	96%
Aspirin at Arrival	174	99%	99%	99%
Aspirin at Discharge	157	100%	99%	98%
Beta Blocker at Discharge	171	100%	98%	98%
Fibrinolytic Medication Timing	0	-	50%	55%
PCI Within 90 Minutes of Arrival[1]	23	65%	90%	90%
Smoking Cessation Advice	51	100%	100%	99%
Chest Pain/Possible Heart Attack Care				
Aspirin at Arrival	0	-	95%	95%
Median Time to ECG (minutes)	0	-	8	8
Median Time to Transfer (minutes)[5]	0	-	57	61
Fibrinolytic Medication Timing[5]	0	-	33%	54%
Heart Failure Care				
ACE Inhibitor or ARB for LVSD	79	100%	94%	94%
Discharge Instructions	275	87%	89%	88%
Evaluation of LVS Function	335	100%	98%	98%
Smoking Cessation Advice	40	100%	99%	98%
Pneumonia Care				
Appropriate Initial Antibiotic	69	88%	90%	92%
Blood Culture Timing	78	97%	97%	96%
Influenza Vaccine	99	96%	91%	91%
Initial Antibiotic Timing	141	95%	96%	95%
Pneumococcal Vaccine	112	96%	92%	93%
Smoking Cessation Advice	31	100%	98%	97%
Surgical Care Improvement Project				
Appropriate VTP Within 24 Hours[2]	192	81%	92%	92%
Appropriate Hair Removal[2]	428	100%	99%	99%
Appropriate Beta Blocker Usage[2]	118	90%	92%	93%
Controlled Postoperative Blood Glucose[2]	64	97%	92%	93%
Prophylactic Antibiotic Timing[2]	306	97%	97%	97%
Prophylactic Antibiotic Timing (Outpatient)	62	97%	93%	92%
Prophylactic Antibiotic Selection[2]	305	91%	97%	97%
Prophylactic Antibiotic Select. (Outpatient)	60	95%	94%	94%
Prophylactic Antibiotic Stopped[2]	295	92%	94%	94%
Recommended VTP Ordered[2]	194	86%	94%	94%
Urinary Catheter Removal[2]	96	92%	89%	90%
Children's Asthma Care				
Received Systemic Corticosteroids	-	-	-	100%
Received Home Management Plan	-	-	-	71%
Received Reliever Medication	-	-	-	100%
Use of Medical Imaging				
Combination Abdominal CT Scan	603	0.237	0.246	0.191
Combination Chest CT Scan	325	0.135	0.098	0.054
Follow-up Mammogram/Ultrasound	1,288	7.1%	8.4%	8.4%
MRI for Low Back Pain	189	36.5%	33.4%	32.7%
Survey of Patients' Hospital Experiences				
Area Around Room 'Always' Quiet at Night	300+	49%	-	58%
Doctors 'Always' Communicated Well	300+	79%	-	80%
Home Recovery Information Given	300+	77%	-	82%
Hospital Given 9 or 10 on 10 Point Scale	300+	57%	-	67%
Meds 'Always' Explained Before Given	300+	57%	-	60%
Nurses 'Always' Communicated Well	300+	74%	-	76%
Pain 'Always' Well Controlled	300+	69%	-	69%
Room and Bathroom 'Always' Clean	300+	69%	-	71%
Timely Help 'Always' Received	300+	58%	-	64%
Would Definitely Recommend Hospital	300+	60%	-	69%

Westlake Community Hospital

1225 Lake St | Phone: 708-938-4000
Melrose Park, IL 60160 | Fax: 708-938-7905
URL: www.reshealth.org
Type: Acute Care Hospitals | Emergency Services: Yes
Ownership: Voluntary Non-Profit - Other | Beds: 326

Key Personnel:
CEO/President. . . . . Pat Shehorn
Chief of Medical Staff. . . . . Nabil Saleh
Operating Room. . . . . Julio Jiminez
Pediatric Ambulatory Care . . . . . . Kundankumar Giri, MD
Pediatric In-Patient Care . . . . Kundankumar Giri, MD
Quality Assurance . . . . Paulette Thomas
Radiology. . . . . Robert Liebman, MD
Emergency Room . . . . Steve Meeks

Measure	Cases	This Hosp.	State Avg.	U.S. Avg.
Heart Attack Care				
ACE Inhibitor or ARB for LVSD[1]	7	100%	96%	96%
Aspirin at Arrival	41	98%	99%	99%
Aspirin at Discharge	37	100%	99%	98%
Beta Blocker at Discharge	39	97%	98%	98%
Fibrinolytic Medication Timing	0	-	50%	55%
PCI Within 90 Minutes of Arrival[1]	4	75%	90%	90%
Smoking Cessation Advice[1]	17	100%	100%	99%
Chest Pain/Possible Heart Attack Care				
Aspirin at Arrival[5]	0	-	95%	95%
Median Time to ECG (minutes)[5]	0	-	8	8
Median Time to Transfer (minutes)[5]	0	-	57	61
Fibrinolytic Medication Timing[5]	0	-	33%	54%
Heart Failure Care				
ACE Inhibitor or ARB for LVSD	82	94%	94%	94%
Discharge Instructions	170	84%	89%	88%
Evaluation of LVS Function	213	100%	98%	98%
Smoking Cessation Advice	36	100%	99%	98%
Pneumonia Care				
Appropriate Initial Antibiotic	35	97%	90%	92%
Blood Culture Timing	73	100%	97%	96%
Influenza Vaccine	54	85%	91%	91%
Initial Antibiotic Timing	69	97%	96%	95%
Pneumococcal Vaccine	58	91%	92%	93%
Smoking Cessation Advice[1]	21	100%	98%	97%
Surgical Care Improvement Project				
Appropriate VTP Within 24 Hours	75	96%	92%	92%
Appropriate Hair Removal	175	100%	99%	99%
Appropriate Beta Blocker Usage	36	100%	92%	93%
Controlled Postoperative Blood Glucose[1]	18	78%	92%	93%
Prophylactic Antibiotic Timing	109	96%	97%	97%
Prophylactic Antibiotic Timing (Outpatient)	93	85%	93%	92%
Prophylactic Antibiotic Selection	110	94%	97%	97%
Prophylactic Antibiotic Select. (Outpatient)	84	88%	94%	94%
Prophylactic Antibiotic Stopped	90	94%	94%	94%
Recommended VTP Ordered	75	96%	94%	94%
Urinary Catheter Removal[1]	10	100%	89%	90%
Children's Asthma Care				
Received Systemic Corticosteroids	-	-	-	100%
Received Home Management Plan	-	-	-	71%
Received Reliever Medication	-	-	-	100%
Use of Medical Imaging				
Combination Abdominal CT Scan	224	0.219	0.246	0.191
Combination Chest CT Scan	124	0.000	0.098	0.054
Follow-up Mammogram/Ultrasound	435	8.5%	8.4%	8.4%
MRI for Low Back Pain[1]	29	37.9%	33.4%	32.7%
Survey of Patients' Hospital Experiences				
Area Around Room 'Always' Quiet at Night[11]	300+	55%	-	58%
Doctors 'Always' Communicated Well[11]	300+	82%	-	80%
Home Recovery Information Given[11]	300+	79%	-	82%
Hospital Given 9 or 10 on 10 Point Scale[11]	300+	67%	-	67%
Meds 'Always' Explained Before Given[11]	300+	60%	-	60%
Nurses 'Always' Communicated Well[11]	300+	77%	-	76%
Pain 'Always' Well Controlled[11]	300+	72%	-	69%
Room and Bathroom 'Always' Clean[11]	300+	70%	-	71%
Timely Help 'Always' Received[11]	300+	61%	-	64%
Would Definitely Recommend Hospital[11]	300+	66%	-	69%

NOTE: Hospital profiles are in alphabetical order by state, then city, then hospital within the city; Rankings exclude hospitals with less than 25 cases except for patient surveys which excludes hospitals with less than 100 cases; (a) 100–299 cases; (1) The number of cases is too small to be sure how well a hospital is performing; (2) The hospital indicated that the data submitted for this measure were based on a sample of cases; (3) Data was collected during a shorter time period (fewer quarters) than the maximum possible time for this measure; (4) Suppressed for one or more quarters by CMS; (5) No data is available from the hospital for this measure; (6) Fewer than 100 patients completed the HCAHPS survey. Use these rates with caution, as the number of surveys may be too low to reliably assess hospital performance; (7) Survey results are based on less than 12 months of data; (8) Survey results are not available for this reporting period; (9) No or very few patients were eligible for the HCAHPS survey. The scores shown, if any, reflect a very small number of surveys; (10) A state average was not calculated because too few hospitals in the state submitted data; (11) There were discrepancies in the data collection process; Please refer to the User's Guide for a full explanation of data.

Mendota Community Hospital

1315 Memorial Dr
Mendota, IL 61342
Phone: 815-539-7461
Fax: 815-538-5516
URL: www.mendotahospital.org
Type: Critical Access Hospitals
Emergency Services: Yes
Ownership: Voluntary Non-Profit - Private
Beds: 32

Key Personnel:

Chief of Medical Staff.......... Mary Chin
Operating Room.............. Jason Goliath
Pediatric Ambulatory Care...... Deepak Nathani, MD
Pediatric In-Patient Care....... Deepak Nathani, MD
Quality Assurance............ Janet Lane

Measure	Cases	This Hosp.	State Avg.	U.S. Avg.
Heart Attack Care				
ACE Inhibitor or ARB for LVSD[3]	0	-	96%	96%
Aspirin at Arrival[1,3]	3	100%	99%	99%
Aspirin at Discharge[1,3]	2	100%	99%	98%
Beta Blocker at Discharge[1,3]	2	100%	98%	98%
Fibrinolytic Medication Timing[1,3]	1	0%	50%	55%
PCI Within 90 Minutes of Arrival[3]	0	-	90%	90%
Smoking Cessation Advice[3]	0	-	100%	99%
Chest Pain/Possible Heart Attack Care				
Aspirin at Arrival[5]	0	-	95%	95%
Median Time to ECG (minutes)[5]	0	-	8	8
Median Time to Transfer (minutes)[5]	0	-	57	61
Fibrinolytic Medication Timing[5]	0	-	33%	54%
Heart Failure Care				
ACE Inhibitor or ARB for LVSD[1]	9	100%	94%	94%
Discharge Instructions[1]	22	82%	89%	88%
Evaluation of LVS Function	35	100%	98%	98%
Smoking Cessation Advice[1]	2	100%	99%	98%
Pneumonia Care				
Appropriate Initial Antibiotic[1]	6	83%	90%	92%
Blood Culture Timing	31	100%	97%	96%
Influenza Vaccine[1]	14	100%	91%	91%
Initial Antibiotic Timing[1]	18	100%	96%	95%
Pneumococcal Vaccine	31	97%	92%	93%
Smoking Cessation Advice[1]	3	100%	98%	97%
Surgical Care Improvement Project				
Appropriate VTP Within 24 Hours[1]	19	100%	92%	92%
Appropriate Hair Removal[1]	24	100%	99%	99%
Appropriate Beta Blocker Usage[1]	9	89%	92%	93%
Controlled Postoperative Blood Glucose	0	-	92%	93%
Prophylactic Antibiotic Timing[1]	3	67%	97%	97%
Prophylactic Antibiotic Timing (Outpatient)[5]	0	-	93%	92%
Prophylactic Antibiotic Selection[1]	3	67%	97%	97%
Prophylactic Antibiotic Select. (Outpatient)[5]	0	-	94%	94%
Prophylactic Antibiotic Stopped[1]	3	100%	94%	94%
Recommended VTP Ordered[1]	19	100%	94%	94%
Urinary Catheter Removal[1]	5	100%	89%	90%
Children's Asthma Care				
Received Systemic Corticosteroids	-	-	-	100%
Received Home Management Plan	-	-	-	71%
Received Reliever Medication	-	-	-	100%
Use of Medical Imaging				
Combination Abdominal CT Scan	235	0.077	0.246	0.191
Combination Chest CT Scan	140	0.029	0.098	0.054
Follow-up Mammogram/Ultrasound	334	7.5%	8.4%	8.4%
MRI for Low Back Pain[1]	40	32.5%	33.4%	32.7%
Survey of Patients' Hospital Experiences				
Area Around Room 'Always' Quiet at Night	300+	57%	-	58%
Doctors 'Always' Communicated Well	300+	86%	-	80%
Home Recovery Information Given	300+	87%	-	82%
Hospital Given 9 or 10 on 10 Point Scale	300+	68%	-	67%
Meds 'Always' Explained Before Given	300+	63%	-	60%
Nurses 'Always' Communicated Well	300+	83%	-	76%
Pain 'Always' Well Controlled	300+	72%	-	69%
Room and Bathroom 'Always' Clean	300+	80%	-	71%
Timely Help 'Always' Received	300+	77%	-	64%
Would Definitely Recommend Hospital	300+	65%	-	69%

OSF Holy Family Medical Center

1000 W Harlem Avenue
Monmouth, IL 61462
Phone: 309-734-3141
Fax: 309-734-3029
URL: www.cmchospital.com
Type: Critical Access Hospitals
Emergency Services: Yes
Ownership: Voluntary Non-Profit - Private
Beds: 68

Key Personnel:

CEO/President............... Donald G Brown
Cardiac Laboratory........... Sara Glasnovich
Chief of Medical Staff.......... Ruben Medrano
Operating Room.............. Lisa Morris
Quality Assurance........... Mary Craig, RN
Radiology.................. Byung Hyun
Emergency Room............ Laura Elliott

Measure	Cases	This Hosp.	State Avg.	U.S. Avg.
Heart Attack Care				
ACE Inhibitor or ARB for LVSD[3]	0	-	96%	96%
Aspirin at Arrival[1,3]	1	100%	99%	99%
Aspirin at Discharge[3]	0	-	99%	98%
Beta Blocker at Discharge[3]	0	-	98%	98%
Fibrinolytic Medication Timing[3]	0	-	50%	55%
PCI Within 90 Minutes of Arrival[3]	0	-	90%	90%
Smoking Cessation Advice[3]	0	-	100%	99%
Chest Pain/Possible Heart Attack Care				
Aspirin at Arrival	33	100%	95%	95%
Median Time to ECG (minutes)	35	6	8	8
Median Time to Transfer (minutes)[1,3]	5	60	57	61
Fibrinolytic Medication Timing[1]	3	0%	33%	54%
Heart Failure Care				
ACE Inhibitor or ARB for LVSD[1,3]	6	67%	94%	94%
Discharge Instructions[1,3]	20	90%	89%	88%
Evaluation of LVS Function[3]	30	53%	98%	98%
Smoking Cessation Advice[1,3]	7	100%	99%	98%
Pneumonia Care				
Appropriate Initial Antibiotic[1,3]	2	100%	90%	92%
Blood Culture Timing[1,3]	10	100%	97%	96%
Influenza Vaccine[1]	14	86%	91%	91%
Initial Antibiotic Timing[1,3]	16	100%	96%	95%
Pneumococcal Vaccine[1,3]	19	89%	92%	93%
Smoking Cessation Advice[1,3]	2	50%	98%	97%
Surgical Care Improvement Project				
Appropriate VTP Within 24 Hours[1,3]	9	56%	92%	92%
Appropriate Hair Removal[1,3]	9	100%	99%	99%
Appropriate Beta Blocker Usage[3]	0	-	92%	93%
Controlled Postoperative Blood Glucose[3]	0	-	92%	93%
Prophylactic Antibiotic Timing[1,3]	4	100%	97%	97%
Prophylactic Antibiotic Timing (Outpatient)[1,3]	8	100%	93%	92%
Prophylactic Antibiotic Selection[1,3]	4	100%	97%	97%
Prophylactic Antibiotic Select. (Outpatient)[1,3]	8	100%	94%	94%
Prophylactic Antibiotic Stopped[1,3]	4	75%	94%	94%
Recommended VTP Ordered[1,3]	9	56%	94%	94%
Urinary Catheter Removal[1]	2	50%	89%	90%
Children's Asthma Care				
Received Systemic Corticosteroids	-	-	-	100%
Received Home Management Plan	-	-	-	71%
Received Reliever Medication	-	-	-	100%
Use of Medical Imaging				
Combination Abdominal CT Scan	73	0.699	0.246	0.191
Combination Chest CT Scan[1]	62	0.839	0.098	0.054
Follow-up Mammogram/Ultrasound	300	4.0%	8.4%	8.4%
MRI for Low Back Pain	47	42.6%	33.4%	32.7%
Survey of Patients' Hospital Experiences				
Area Around Room 'Always' Quiet at Night	(a)	63%	-	58%
Doctors 'Always' Communicated Well	(a)	77%	-	80%
Home Recovery Information Given	(a)	87%	-	82%
Hospital Given 9 or 10 on 10 Point Scale	(a)	72%	-	67%
Meds 'Always' Explained Before Given	(a)	52%	-	60%
Nurses 'Always' Communicated Well	(a)	77%	-	76%
Pain 'Always' Well Controlled	(a)	67%	-	69%
Room and Bathroom 'Always' Clean	(a)	82%	-	71%
Timely Help 'Always' Received	(a)	75%	-	64%
Would Definitely Recommend Hospital	(a)	66%	-	69%

John & Mary Kirby Hospital

1111 N State St
Monticello, IL 61856
Phone: 217-762-2115
Fax: 217-762-6267
Type: Critical Access Hospitals
Emergency Services: Yes
Ownership: Voluntary Non-Profit - Private
Beds: 17

Measure	Cases	This Hosp.	State Avg.	U.S. Avg.
Heart Attack Care				
ACE Inhibitor or ARB for LVSD[5]	0	-	96%	96%
Aspirin at Arrival[5]	0	-	99%	99%
Aspirin at Discharge[5]	0	-	99%	98%
Beta Blocker at Discharge[5]	0	-	98%	98%
Fibrinolytic Medication Timing[5]	0	-	50%	55%
PCI Within 90 Minutes of Arrival[5]	0	-	90%	90%
Smoking Cessation Advice[5]	0	-	100%	99%
Chest Pain/Possible Heart Attack Care				
Aspirin at Arrival	-	-	95%	95%
Median Time to ECG (minutes)	-	-	8	8
Median Time to Transfer (minutes)	-	-	57	61
Fibrinolytic Medication Timing	-	-	33%	54%
Heart Failure Care				
ACE Inhibitor or ARB for LVSD[1]	5	100%	94%	94%
Discharge Instructions[1]	5	100%	89%	88%
Evaluation of LVS Function[1]	12	92%	98%	98%
Smoking Cessation Advice[1]	2	100%	99%	98%
Pneumonia Care				
Appropriate Initial Antibiotic	35	97%	90%	92%
Blood Culture Timing	45	96%	97%	96%
Influenza Vaccine	28	79%	91%	91%
Initial Antibiotic Timing	45	93%	96%	95%
Pneumococcal Vaccine	41	90%	92%	93%
Smoking Cessation Advice[1]	10	100%	98%	97%
Surgical Care Improvement Project				
Appropriate VTP Within 24 Hours[5]	0	-	92%	92%
Appropriate Hair Removal[5]	0	-	99%	99%
Appropriate Beta Blocker Usage[5]	0	-	92%	93%
Controlled Postoperative Blood Glucose[5]	0	-	92%	93%
Prophylactic Antibiotic Timing[5]	0	-	97%	97%
Prophylactic Antibiotic Timing (Outpatient)	-	-	93%	92%
Prophylactic Antibiotic Selection[5]	0	-	97%	97%
Prophylactic Antibiotic Select. (Outpatient)	-	-	94%	94%
Prophylactic Antibiotic Stopped[5]	0	-	94%	94%
Recommended VTP Ordered[5]	0	-	94%	94%
Urinary Catheter Removal[5]	0	-	89%	90%
Children's Asthma Care				
Received Systemic Corticosteroids	-	-	-	100%
Received Home Management Plan	-	-	-	71%
Received Reliever Medication	-	-	-	100%
Use of Medical Imaging				
Combination Abdominal CT Scan	-	-	0.246	0.191
Combination Chest CT Scan	-	-	0.098	0.054
Follow-up Mammogram/Ultrasound	-	-	8.4%	8.4%
MRI for Low Back Pain	-	-	33.4%	32.7%
Survey of Patients' Hospital Experiences				
Area Around Room 'Always' Quiet at Night[8]	-	-	-	58%
Doctors 'Always' Communicated Well[8]	-	-	-	80%
Home Recovery Information Given[8]	-	-	-	82%
Hospital Given 9 or 10 on 10 Point Scale[8]	-	-	-	67%
Meds 'Always' Explained Before Given[8]	-	-	-	60%
Nurses 'Always' Communicated Well[8]	-	-	-	76%
Pain 'Always' Well Controlled[8]	-	-	-	69%
Room and Bathroom 'Always' Clean[8]	-	-	-	71%
Timely Help 'Always' Received[8]	-	-	-	64%
Would Definitely Recommend Hospital[8]	-	-	-	69%

NOTE: Hospital profiles are in alphabetical order by state, then city, then hospital within the city; Rankings exclude hospitals with less than 25 cases except for patient surveys which excludes hospitals with less than 100 cases; (a) 100–299 cases; (1) The number of cases is too small to be sure how well a hospital is performing; (2) The hospital indicated that the data submitted for this measure were based on a sample of cases; (3) Data was collected during a shorter time period (fewer quarters) than the maximum possible time for this measure; (4) Suppressed for one or more quarters by CMS; (5) No data is available from the hospital for this measure; (6) Fewer than 100 patients completed the HCAHPS survey. Use these rates with caution, as the number of surveys may be too low to reliably assess hospital performance; (7) Survey results are based on less than 12 months of data; (8) Survey results are not available for this reporting period; (9) No or very few patients were eligible for the HCAHPS survey. The scores shown, if any, reflect a very small number of surveys; (10) A state average was not calculated because too few hospitals in the state submitted data; (11) There were discrepancies in the data collection process; Please refer to the User's Guide for a full explanation of data.

Morris Hospital & Healthcare Centers

150 W High St Phone: 815-942-2932
Morris, IL 60450 Fax: 815-942-3154
URL: www.morrishospital.org
Type: Acute Care Hospitals Emergency Services: Yes
Ownership: Voluntary Non-Profit - Private Beds: 82

Key Personnel:
CEO/President. . . . . Bill Bruce
Chief of Medical Staff. . . . . Sherwin Ritz MD
Radiology. . . . . Jeffrey E Chung
Emergency Room . . . . Sean C Atchison

Measure	Cases	This Hosp.	State Avg.	U.S. Avg.
Heart Attack Care				
ACE Inhibitor or ARB for LVSD[1]	10	100%	96%	96%
Aspirin at Arrival	81	100%	99%	99%
Aspirin at Discharge	67	100%	99%	98%
Beta Blocker at Discharge	66	100%	98%	98%
Fibrinolytic Medication Timing	0	-	50%	55%
PCI Within 90 Minutes of Arrival[1]	18	100%	90%	90%
Smoking Cessation Advice	28	100%	100%	99%
Chest Pain/Possible Heart Attack Care				
Aspirin at Arrival[1]	8	100%	95%	95%
Median Time to ECG (minutes)[1]	8	8	8	8
Median Time to Transfer (minutes)[1,3]	4	76	57	61
Fibrinolytic Medication Timing[3]	0	-	33%	54%
Heart Failure Care				
ACE Inhibitor or ARB for LVSD	48	90%	94%	94%
Discharge Instructions	143	89%	89%	88%
Evaluation of LVS Function	183	100%	98%	98%
Smoking Cessation Advice	26	100%	99%	98%
Pneumonia Care				
Appropriate Initial Antibiotic[2]	103	80%	90%	92%
Blood Culture Timing[2]	156	94%	97%	96%
Influenza Vaccine[2]	111	94%	91%	91%
Initial Antibiotic Timing[2]	151	97%	96%	95%
Pneumococcal Vaccine[2]	160	96%	92%	93%
Smoking Cessation Advice[2]	61	98%	98%	97%
Surgical Care Improvement Project				
Appropriate VTP Within 24 Hours	92	91%	92%	92%
Appropriate Hair Removal	321	100%	99%	99%
Appropriate Beta Blocker Usage	85	93%	92%	93%
Controlled Postoperative Blood Glucose	0	-	92%	93%
Prophylactic Antibiotic Timing	244	98%	97%	97%
Prophylactic Antibiotic Timing (Outpatient)	292	97%	93%	92%
Prophylactic Antibiotic Selection	245	98%	97%	97%
Prophylactic Antibiotic Select. (Outpatient)	319	86%	94%	94%
Prophylactic Antibiotic Stopped	242	88%	94%	94%
Recommended VTP Ordered	92	92%	94%	94%
Urinary Catheter Removal	100	98%	89%	90%
Children's Asthma Care				
Received Systemic Corticosteroids	-	-	-	100%
Received Home Management Plan	-	-	-	71%
Received Reliever Medication	-	-	-	100%
Use of Medical Imaging				
Combination Abdominal CT Scan	649	0.092	0.246	0.191
Combination Chest CT Scan	459	0.015	0.098	0.054
Follow-up Mammogram/Ultrasound	788	7.0%	8.4%	8.4%
MRI for Low Back Pain	164	32.9%	33.4%	32.7%
Survey of Patients' Hospital Experiences				
Area Around Room 'Always' Quiet at Night	300+	57%	-	58%
Doctors 'Always' Communicated Well	300+	85%	-	80%
Home Recovery Information Given	300+	86%	-	82%
Hospital Given 9 or 10 on 10 Point Scale	300+	78%	-	67%
Meds 'Always' Explained Before Given	300+	61%	-	60%
Nurses 'Always' Communicated Well	300+	82%	-	76%
Pain 'Always' Well Controlled	300+	74%	-	69%
Room and Bathroom 'Always' Clean	300+	78%	-	71%
Timely Help 'Always' Received	300+	72%	-	64%
Would Definitely Recommend Hospital	300+	82%	-	69%

Wabash General Hospital

1418 College Drive Phone: 618-262-8621
Mount Carmel, IL 62863 Fax: 618-263-6461
URL: www.wabashgeneral.com
Type: Critical Access Hospitals Emergency Services: Yes
Ownership: Govt - Hospital Dist/Auth Beds: 56

Key Personnel:
CEO/President. . . . . Jay Turvis
Radiology. H Youssef

Measure	Cases	This Hosp.	State Avg.	U.S. Avg.
Heart Attack Care				
ACE Inhibitor or ARB for LVSD[1,3]	2	100%	96%	96%
Aspirin at Arrival[1,3]	5	100%	99%	99%
Aspirin at Discharge[1,3]	4	100%	99%	98%
Beta Blocker at Discharge[1,3]	5	100%	98%	98%
Fibrinolytic Medication Timing[3]	0	-	50%	55%
PCI Within 90 Minutes of Arrival[5]	0	-	90%	90%
Smoking Cessation Advice[3]	0	-	100%	99%
Chest Pain/Possible Heart Attack Care				
Aspirin at Arrival	71	94%	95%	95%
Median Time to ECG (minutes)	72	8	8	8
Median Time to Transfer (minutes)[1,3]	5	72	57	61
Fibrinolytic Medication Timing	0	-	33%	54%
Heart Failure Care				
ACE Inhibitor or ARB for LVSD[1]	15	100%	94%	94%
Discharge Instructions	34	91%	89%	88%
Evaluation of LVS Function	54	93%	98%	98%
Smoking Cessation Advice[1]	9	67%	99%	98%
Pneumonia Care				
Appropriate Initial Antibiotic[2]	50	86%	90%	92%
Blood Culture Timing[2]	51	90%	97%	96%
Influenza Vaccine	48	85%	91%	91%
Initial Antibiotic Timing[2]	64	100%	96%	95%
Pneumococcal Vaccine[2]	78	79%	92%	93%
Smoking Cessation Advice[1,2]	19	95%	98%	97%
Surgical Care Improvement Project				
Appropriate VTP Within 24 Hours	51	98%	92%	92%
Appropriate Hair Removal	74	100%	99%	99%
Appropriate Beta Blocker Usage	31	87%	92%	93%
Controlled Postoperative Blood Glucose	0	-	92%	93%
Prophylactic Antibiotic Timing	67	93%	97%	97%
Prophylactic Antibiotic Timing (Outpatient)[1,3]	10	80%	93%	92%
Prophylactic Antibiotic Selection	67	93%	97%	97%
Prophylactic Antibiotic Select. (Outpatient)[1,3]	8	100%	94%	94%
Prophylactic Antibiotic Stopped	65	97%	94%	94%
Recommended VTP Ordered	51	100%	94%	94%
Urinary Catheter Removal	29	97%	89%	90%
Children's Asthma Care				
Received Systemic Corticosteroids	-	-	-	100%
Received Home Management Plan	-	-	-	71%
Received Reliever Medication	-	-	-	100%
Use of Medical Imaging				
Combination Abdominal CT Scan	212	0.420	0.246	0.191
Combination Chest CT Scan	144	0.403	0.098	0.054
Follow-up Mammogram/Ultrasound	211	6.6%	8.4%	8.4%
MRI for Low Back Pain[1]	33	42.4%	33.4%	32.7%
Survey of Patients' Hospital Experiences				
Area Around Room 'Always' Quiet at Night[8]	-	-	-	58%
Doctors 'Always' Communicated Well[8]	-	-	-	80%
Home Recovery Information Given[8]	-	-	-	82%
Hospital Given 9 or 10 on 10 Point Scale[8]	-	-	-	67%
Meds 'Always' Explained Before Given[8]	-	-	-	60%
Nurses 'Always' Communicated Well[8]	-	-	-	76%
Pain 'Always' Well Controlled[8]	-	-	-	69%
Room and Bathroom 'Always' Clean[8]	-	-	-	71%
Timely Help 'Always' Received[8]	-	-	-	64%
Would Definitely Recommend Hospital[8]	-	-	-	69%

Crossroads Community Hospital

8 Doctors Park Road Phone: 618-244-5500
Mount Vernon, IL 62864 Fax: 618-244-5566
URL: www.crossroadscommnityhospital.com
Type: Acute Care Hospitals Emergency Services: Yes
Ownership: Proprietary Beds: 55

Key Personnel:
CEO/President. . . . . Gregory F Simsniel, RN
Chief of Medical Staff. . . . . Alan Sroehling
Infection Control. . . . . Mike Beirman, RN
Operating Room. . . . . Doris Shields, RN
Quality Assurance . . . . Karen Salamone
Radiology. . . . . Andrew Holz, BS

Measure	Cases	This Hosp.	State Avg.	U.S. Avg.
Heart Attack Care				
ACE Inhibitor or ARB for LVSD[1]	1	100%	96%	96%
Aspirin at Arrival[1]	3	100%	99%	99%
Aspirin at Discharge[1]	3	100%	99%	98%
Beta Blocker at Discharge[1]	2	100%	98%	98%
Fibrinolytic Medication Timing	0	-	50%	55%
PCI Within 90 Minutes of Arrival	0	-	90%	90%
Smoking Cessation Advice	0	-	100%	99%
Chest Pain/Possible Heart Attack Care				
Aspirin at Arrival	47	100%	95%	95%
Median Time to ECG (minutes)	49	2	8	8
Median Time to Transfer (minutes)[1,3]	4	48	57	61
Fibrinolytic Medication Timing	0	-	33%	54%
Heart Failure Care				
ACE Inhibitor or ARB for LVSD[1]	14	100%	94%	94%
Discharge Instructions	28	89%	89%	88%
Evaluation of LVS Function	38	100%	98%	98%
Smoking Cessation Advice[1]	4	100%	99%	98%
Pneumonia Care				
Appropriate Initial Antibiotic	56	89%	90%	92%
Blood Culture Timing	70	100%	97%	96%
Influenza Vaccine	46	89%	91%	91%
Initial Antibiotic Timing	75	99%	96%	95%
Pneumococcal Vaccine	70	100%	92%	93%
Smoking Cessation Advice	27	100%	98%	97%
Surgical Care Improvement Project				
Appropriate VTP Within 24 Hours[2]	51	90%	92%	92%
Appropriate Hair Removal[2]	188	99%	99%	99%
Appropriate Beta Blocker Usage[2]	49	100%	92%	93%
Controlled Postoperative Blood Glucose[2]	0	-	92%	93%
Prophylactic Antibiotic Timing[2]	146	99%	97%	97%
Prophylactic Antibiotic Timing (Outpatient)	48	90%	93%	92%
Prophylactic Antibiotic Selection[2]	146	99%	97%	97%
Prophylactic Antibiotic Select. (Outpatient)	85	96%	94%	94%
Prophylactic Antibiotic Stopped[2]	140	91%	94%	94%
Recommended VTP Ordered[2]	51	98%	94%	94%
Urinary Catheter Removal	35	91%	89%	90%
Children's Asthma Care				
Received Systemic Corticosteroids	-	-	-	100%
Received Home Management Plan	-	-	-	71%
Received Reliever Medication	-	-	-	100%
Use of Medical Imaging				
Combination Abdominal CT Scan	208	0.413	0.246	0.191
Combination Chest CT Scan	96	0.375	0.098	0.054
Follow-up Mammogram/Ultrasound	453	7.9%	8.4%	8.4%
MRI for Low Back Pain[1]	26	38.5%	33.4%	32.7%
Survey of Patients' Hospital Experiences				
Area Around Room 'Always' Quiet at Night	300+	52%	-	58%
Doctors 'Always' Communicated Well	300+	82%	-	80%
Home Recovery Information Given	300+	84%	-	82%
Hospital Given 9 or 10 on 10 Point Scale	300+	63%	-	67%
Meds 'Always' Explained Before Given	300+	57%	-	60%
Nurses 'Always' Communicated Well	300+	74%	-	76%
Pain 'Always' Well Controlled	300+	69%	-	69%
Room and Bathroom 'Always' Clean	300+	71%	-	71%
Timely Help 'Always' Received	300+	57%	-	64%
Would Definitely Recommend Hospital	300+	62%	-	69%

NOTE: Hospital profiles are in alphabetical order by state, then city, then hospital within the city; Rankings exclude hospitals with less than 25 cases except for patient surveys which excludes hospitals with less than 100 cases; (a) 100–299 cases; (1) The number of cases is too small to be sure how well a hospital is performing; (2) The hospital indicated that the data submitted for this measure were based on a sample of cases; (3) Data was collected during a shorter time period (fewer quarters) than the maximum possible time for this measure; (4) Suppressed for one or more quarters by CMS; (5) No data is available from the hospital for this measure; (6) Fewer than 100 patients completed the HCAHPS survey. Use these rates with caution, as the number of surveys may be too low to reliably assess hospital performance; (7) Survey results are based on less than 12 months of data; (8) Survey results are not available for this reporting period; (9) No or very few patients were eligible for the HCAHPS survey. The scores shown, if any, reflect a very small number of surveys; (10) A state average was not calculated because too few hospitals in the state submitted data; (11) There were discrepancies in the data collection process; Please refer to the User's Guide for a full explanation of data.

Good Samaritan Regional Health Center

605 N 12th Street — Phone: 618-242-4600
Mount Vernon, IL 62864 — Fax: 618-242-3196
Type: Acute Care Hospitals — Emergency Services: Yes
Ownership: Voluntary Non-Profit - Church — Beds: 175

Key Personnel:
CEO/President. . . . . Leo F Childers, Jr
Chief of Medical Staff . . . . Jitendra Trivedi, MD
Infection Control. . . . . Jeralee Sargent, RN
Operating Room. . . . . Kevin Claffey, RN
Quality Assurance . . . . Joby Glenn
Radiology. . . . . Henry Chen, MD
Emergency Room . . . . Scott Roustio, MD
Intensive Care Unit. . . . . Darren Bock

Measure	Cases	This Hosp.	State Avg.	U.S. Avg.
Heart Attack Care				
ACE Inhibitor or ARB for LVSD	54	93%	96%	96%
Aspirin at Arrival	141	98%	99%	99%
Aspirin at Discharge	274	100%	99%	98%
Beta Blocker at Discharge	269	100%	98%	98%
Fibrinolytic Medication Timing[1]	1	0%	50%	55%
PCI Within 90 Minutes of Arrival[1]	20	80%	90%	90%
Smoking Cessation Advice	121	100%	100%	99%
Chest Pain/Possible Heart Attack Care				
Aspirin at Arrival[1]	23	91%	95%	95%
Median Time to ECG (minutes)	26	7	8	8
Median Time to Transfer (minutes)[5]	0	-	57	61
Fibrinolytic Medication Timing[3]	0	-	33%	54%
Heart Failure Care				
ACE Inhibitor or ARB for LVSD	67	94%	94%	94%
Discharge Instructions	163	94%	89%	88%
Evaluation of LVS Function	193	100%	98%	98%
Smoking Cessation Advice	34	100%	99%	98%
Pneumonia Care				
Appropriate Initial Antibiotic	107	93%	90%	92%
Blood Culture Timing	135	100%	97%	96%
Influenza Vaccine	125	98%	91%	91%
Initial Antibiotic Timing	171	98%	96%	95%
Pneumococcal Vaccine	164	100%	92%	93%
Smoking Cessation Advice	59	100%	98%	97%
Surgical Care Improvement Project				
Appropriate VTP Within 24 Hours	237	97%	92%	92%
Appropriate Hair Removal	647	100%	99%	99%
Appropriate Beta Blocker Usage	231	96%	92%	93%
Controlled Postoperative Blood Glucose	52	98%	92%	93%
Prophylactic Antibiotic Timing	502	96%	97%	97%
Prophylactic Antibiotic Timing (Outpatient)	193	93%	93%	92%
Prophylactic Antibiotic Selection	510	99%	97%	97%
Prophylactic Antibiotic Select. (Outpatient)	191	90%	94%	94%
Prophylactic Antibiotic Stopped	476	94%	94%	94%
Recommended VTP Ordered	238	97%	94%	94%
Urinary Catheter Removal	31	81%	89%	90%
Children's Asthma Care				
Received Systemic Corticosteroids	-	-	-	100%
Received Home Management Plan	-	-	-	71%
Received Reliever Medication	-	-	-	100%
Use of Medical Imaging				
Combination Abdominal CT Scan	737	0.612	0.246	0.191
Combination Chest CT Scan	422	0.187	0.098	0.054
Follow-up Mammogram/Ultrasound	910	6.5%	8.4%	8.4%
MRI for Low Back Pain	122	41.8%	33.4%	32.7%
Survey of Patients' Hospital Experiences				
Area Around Room 'Always' Quiet at Night	300+	50%	-	58%
Doctors 'Always' Communicated Well	300+	78%	-	80%
Home Recovery Information Given	300+	86%	-	82%
Hospital Given 9 or 10 on 10 Point Scale	300+	67%	-	67%
Meds 'Always' Explained Before Given	300+	63%	-	60%
Nurses 'Always' Communicated Well	300+	80%	-	76%
Pain 'Always' Well Controlled	300+	73%	-	69%
Room and Bathroom 'Always' Clean	300+	75%	-	71%
Timely Help 'Always' Received	300+	68%	-	64%
Would Definitely Recommend Hospital	300+	72%	-	69%

Saint Joseph Memorial Hospital

2 South Hospital Drive — Phone: 618-684-3156
Murphysboro, IL 62966 — Fax: 618-529-0535
E-mail: info@sih.net
URL: www.sih.net
Type: Critical Access Hospitals — Emergency Services: Yes
Ownership: Voluntary Non-Profit - Private — Beds: 59

Key Personnel:
Chief of Medical Staff . . . . Dale Blaise, MD
Infection Control. . . . . Tammy Jurgens
Operating Room. . . . . David Clutts
Quality Assurance . . . . Tammy Jurgens
Anesthesiology. . . . . Louise Vaughn
Emergency Room . . . . Karen Robert
Intensive Care Unit. . . . . Ann Smith, RN

Measure	Cases	This Hosp.	State Avg.	U.S. Avg.
Heart Attack Care				
ACE Inhibitor or ARB for LVSD[1,3]	1	100%	96%	96%
Aspirin at Arrival[1,3]	2	100%	99%	99%
Aspirin at Discharge[3]	0	-	99%	98%
Beta Blocker at Discharge[1,3]	1	100%	98%	98%
Fibrinolytic Medication Timing[3]	0	-	50%	55%
PCI Within 90 Minutes of Arrival[3]	0	-	90%	90%
Smoking Cessation Advice[1,3]	1	100%	100%	99%
Chest Pain/Possible Heart Attack Care				
Aspirin at Arrival[5]	0	-	95%	95%
Median Time to ECG (minutes)[5]	0	-	8	8
Median Time to Transfer (minutes)[5]	0	-	57	61
Fibrinolytic Medication Timing[5]	0	-	33%	54%
Heart Failure Care				
ACE Inhibitor or ARB for LVSD[1]	3	100%	94%	94%
Discharge Instructions	26	96%	89%	88%
Evaluation of LVS Function	35	100%	98%	98%
Smoking Cessation Advice[1]	5	100%	99%	98%
Pneumonia Care				
Appropriate Initial Antibiotic	28	96%	90%	92%
Blood Culture Timing	43	100%	97%	96%
Influenza Vaccine	31	100%	91%	91%
Initial Antibiotic Timing[1]	18	100%	96%	95%
Pneumococcal Vaccine	38	97%	92%	93%
Smoking Cessation Advice[1]	15	100%	98%	97%
Surgical Care Improvement Project				
Appropriate VTP Within 24 Hours[1,3]	3	100%	92%	92%
Appropriate Hair Removal[1,3]	3	100%	99%	99%
Appropriate Beta Blocker Usage[5]	0	-	92%	93%
Controlled Postoperative Blood Glucose[3]	0	-	92%	93%
Prophylactic Antibiotic Timing[1,3]	1	100%	97%	97%
Prophylactic Antibiotic Timing (Outpatient)[5]	0	-	93%	92%
Prophylactic Antibiotic Selection[1,3]	1	100%	97%	97%
Prophylactic Antibiotic Select. (Outpatient)[5]	0	-	94%	94%
Prophylactic Antibiotic Stopped[1,3]	1	100%	94%	94%
Recommended VTP Ordered[1,3]	3	100%	94%	94%
Urinary Catheter Removal[1]	1	100%	89%	90%
Children's Asthma Care				
Received Systemic Corticosteroids	-	-	-	100%
Received Home Management Plan	-	-	-	71%
Received Reliever Medication	-	-	-	100%
Use of Medical Imaging				
Combination Abdominal CT Scan	396	0.136	0.246	0.191
Combination Chest CT Scan	115	0.078	0.098	0.054
Follow-up Mammogram/Ultrasound[5]	0	-	8.4%	8.4%
MRI for Low Back Pain[1]	31	19.4%	33.4%	32.7%
Survey of Patients' Hospital Experiences				
Area Around Room 'Always' Quiet at Night	(a)	63%	-	58%
Doctors 'Always' Communicated Well	(a)	81%	-	80%
Home Recovery Information Given	(a)	86%	-	82%
Hospital Given 9 or 10 on 10 Point Scale	(a)	75%	-	67%
Meds 'Always' Explained Before Given	(a)	69%	-	60%
Nurses 'Always' Communicated Well	(a)	84%	-	76%
Pain 'Always' Well Controlled	(a)	72%	-	69%
Room and Bathroom 'Always' Clean	(a)	88%	-	71%
Timely Help 'Always' Received	(a)	79%	-	64%
Would Definitely Recommend Hospital	(a)	79%	-	69%

Edward Hospital

801 South Washington — Phone: 630-527-3000
Naperville, IL 60540 — Fax: 630-961-4910
URL: www.edward.org
Type: Acute Care Hospitals — Emergency Services: Yes
Ownership: Voluntary Non-Profit - Private — Beds: 179

Key Personnel:
CEO/President. . . . . Pamela Meyer-Davis
Chief of Medical Staff . . . . Glenn Grobe
Infection Control. . . . . Robert Chase, MD
Operating Room. . . . . Mohan Airan
Pediatric Ambulatory Care . . . . . . Timothy Wall
Pediatric In-Patient Care . . . . Timothy Wall
Quality Assurance . . . . Jane Mitchell
Radiology. . . . . Yuk-Pui Li, MD

Measure	Cases	This Hosp.	State Avg.	U.S. Avg.
Heart Attack Care				
ACE Inhibitor or ARB for LVSD	44	98%	96%	96%
Aspirin at Arrival	214	100%	99%	99%
Aspirin at Discharge	231	99%	99%	98%
Beta Blocker at Discharge	222	99%	98%	98%
Fibrinolytic Medication Timing	0	-	50%	55%
PCI Within 90 Minutes of Arrival	33	85%	90%	90%
Smoking Cessation Advice	61	100%	100%	99%
Chest Pain/Possible Heart Attack Care				
Aspirin at Arrival[1]	12	100%	95%	95%
Median Time to ECG (minutes)[1]	11	8	8	8
Median Time to Transfer (minutes)[5]	0	-	57	61
Fibrinolytic Medication Timing[5]	0	-	33%	54%
Heart Failure Care				
ACE Inhibitor or ARB for LVSD	143	95%	94%	94%
Discharge Instructions	336	86%	89%	88%
Evaluation of LVS Function	434	100%	98%	98%
Smoking Cessation Advice	48	100%	99%	98%
Pneumonia Care				
Appropriate Initial Antibiotic	248	95%	90%	92%
Blood Culture Timing	438	100%	97%	96%
Influenza Vaccine	277	97%	91%	91%
Initial Antibiotic Timing	439	97%	96%	95%
Pneumococcal Vaccine	408	97%	92%	93%
Smoking Cessation Advice	113	99%	98%	97%
Surgical Care Improvement Project				
Appropriate VTP Within 24 Hours	635	96%	92%	92%
Appropriate Hair Removal	1,858	100%	99%	99%
Appropriate Beta Blocker Usage	570	99%	92%	93%
Controlled Postoperative Blood Glucose	211	96%	92%	93%
Prophylactic Antibiotic Timing	1,228	97%	97%	97%
Prophylactic Antibiotic Timing (Outpatient)	474	98%	93%	92%
Prophylactic Antibiotic Selection	1,240	100%	97%	97%
Prophylactic Antibiotic Select. (Outpatient)	470	98%	94%	94%
Prophylactic Antibiotic Stopped	1,167	96%	94%	94%
Recommended VTP Ordered	635	97%	94%	94%
Urinary Catheter Removal	555	91%	89%	90%
Children's Asthma Care				
Received Systemic Corticosteroids	-	-	-	100%
Received Home Management Plan	-	-	-	71%
Received Reliever Medication	-	-	-	100%
Use of Medical Imaging				
Combination Abdominal CT Scan	1,754	0.715	0.246	0.191
Combination Chest CT Scan	1,439	0.698	0.098	0.054
Follow-up Mammogram/Ultrasound	2,536	11.4%	8.4%	8.4%
MRI for Low Back Pain	341	32.8%	33.4%	32.7%
Survey of Patients' Hospital Experiences				
Area Around Room 'Always' Quiet at Night	300+	62%	-	58%
Doctors 'Always' Communicated Well	300+	82%	-	80%
Home Recovery Information Given	300+	84%	-	82%
Hospital Given 9 or 10 on 10 Point Scale	300+	74%	-	67%
Meds 'Always' Explained Before Given	300+	62%	-	60%
Nurses 'Always' Communicated Well	300+	78%	-	76%
Pain 'Always' Well Controlled	300+	72%	-	69%
Room and Bathroom 'Always' Clean	300+	68%	-	71%
Timely Help 'Always' Received	300+	60%	-	64%
Would Definitely Recommend Hospital	300+	81%	-	69%

NOTE: Hospital profiles are in alphabetical order by state, then city, then hospital within the city; Rankings exclude hospitals with less than 25 cases except for patient surveys which excludes hospitals with less than 100 cases; (a) 100–299 cases; (1) The number of cases is too small to be sure how well a hospital is performing; (2) The hospital indicated that the data submitted for this measure were based on a sample of cases; (3) Data was collected during a shorter time period (fewer quarters) than the maximum possible time for this measure; (4) Suppressed for one or more quarters by CMS; (5) No data is available from the hospital for this measure; (6) Fewer than 100 patients completed the HCAHPS survey. Use these rates with caution, as the number of surveys may be too low to reliably assess hospital performance; (7) Survey results are based on less than 12 months of data; (8) Survey results are not available for this reporting period; (9) No or very few patients were eligible for the HCAHPS survey. The scores shown, if any, reflect a very small number of surveys; (10) A state average was not calculated because too few hospitals in the state submitted data; (11) There were discrepancies in the data collection process; Please refer to the User's Guide for a full explanation of data.

Bromenn Healthcare

1304 Franklin Avenue — Phone: 309-454-1400
Normal, IL 61761
Type: Acute Care Hospitals — Emergency Services: Yes
Ownership: Voluntary Non-Profit - Church
Key Personnel:
CEO/President. . . . . Roger S Hunt

Measure	Cases	This Hosp.	State Avg.	U.S. Avg.
Heart Attack Care				
ACE Inhibitor or ARB for LVSD[1]	16	100%	96%	96%
Aspirin at Arrival	159	99%	99%	99%
Aspirin at Discharge	165	99%	99%	98%
Beta Blocker at Discharge	161	98%	98%	98%
Fibrinolytic Medication Timing	0	-	50%	55%
PCI Within 90 Minutes of Arrival	31	94%	90%	90%
Smoking Cessation Advice	66	100%	100%	99%
Chest Pain/Possible Heart Attack Care				
Aspirin at Arrival[1,3]	1	100%	95%	95%
Median Time to ECG (minutes)[1,3]	1	1	8	8
Median Time to Transfer (minutes)[5]	0	-	57	61
Fibrinolytic Medication Timing[5]	0	-	33%	54%
Heart Failure Care				
ACE Inhibitor or ARB for LVSD	92	97%	94%	94%
Discharge Instructions	185	83%	89%	88%
Evaluation of LVS Function	245	100%	98%	98%
Smoking Cessation Advice[1]	8	100%	99%	98%
Pneumonia Care				
Appropriate Initial Antibiotic	94	97%	90%	92%
Blood Culture Timing	216	94%	97%	96%
Influenza Vaccine	145	93%	91%	91%
Initial Antibiotic Timing	194	90%	96%	95%
Pneumococcal Vaccine	191	93%	92%	93%
Smoking Cessation Advice	38	100%	98%	97%
Surgical Care Improvement Project				
Appropriate VTP Within 24 Hours[2]	204	86%	92%	92%
Appropriate Hair Removal[2]	771	100%	99%	99%
Appropriate Beta Blocker Usage[2]	196	90%	92%	93%
Controlled Postoperative Blood Glucose[2]	67	99%	92%	93%
Prophylactic Antibiotic Timing[2]	543	97%	97%	97%
Prophylactic Antibiotic Timing (Outpatient)	229	89%	93%	92%
Prophylactic Antibiotic Selection[2]	545	97%	97%	97%
Prophylactic Antibiotic Select. (Outpatient)	213	96%	94%	94%
Prophylactic Antibiotic Stopped[2]	521	95%	94%	94%
Recommended VTP Ordered[2]	204	89%	94%	94%
Urinary Catheter Removal[2]	81	85%	89%	90%
Children's Asthma Care				
Received Systemic Corticosteroids	-	-	-	100%
Received Home Management Plan	-	-	-	71%
Received Reliever Medication	-	-	-	100%
Use of Medical Imaging				
Combination Abdominal CT Scan	446	0.682	0.246	0.191
Combination Chest CT Scan	590	0.476	0.098	0.054
Follow-up Mammogram/Ultrasound	1,164	4.8%	8.4%	8.4%
MRI for Low Back Pain	120	35.0%	33.4%	32.7%
Survey of Patients' Hospital Experiences				
Area Around Room 'Always' Quiet at Night	300+	58%	-	58%
Doctors 'Always' Communicated Well	300+	81%	-	80%
Home Recovery Information Given	300+	88%	-	82%
Hospital Given 9 or 10 on 10 Point Scale	300+	74%	-	67%
Meds 'Always' Explained Before Given	300+	56%	-	60%
Nurses 'Always' Communicated Well	300+	79%	-	76%
Pain 'Always' Well Controlled	300+	74%	-	69%
Room and Bathroom 'Always' Clean	300+	71%	-	71%
Timely Help 'Always' Received	300+	60%	-	64%
Would Definitely Recommend Hospital	300+	78%	-	69%

North Chicago VA Medical Center

3001 Greenbay Road — Phone: 847-688-1900
North Chicago, IL 60064 — Fax: 224-610-3806
URL: www.northchicago.va.gov
Type: Acute Care-Veterans Administration — Emergency Services: No
Ownership: Government - Federal
Key Personnel:
CEO/President. . . . . Patrick L. Sullivan, FACHE
Chief of Medical Staff. . . . . Tariq Hassan, MD
Quality Assurance . . . . Sharon Pusateri
Radiology. . . . . Wonsang Chun, MD
Emergency Room . . . . Frank Maldonado, MD
Intensive Care Unit. . . . . Celestina Bobadilla, RN

Measure	Cases	This Hosp.	State Avg.	U.S. Avg.
Heart Attack Care				
ACE Inhibitor or ARB for LVSD[1]	1	100%	96%	96%
Aspirin at Arrival[1]	11	100%	99%	99%
Aspirin at Discharge[1]	4	100%	99%	98%
Beta Blocker at Discharge[1]	4	100%	98%	98%
Fibrinolytic Medication Timing[5]	0	-	50%	55%
PCI Within 90 Minutes of Arrival[5]	0	-	90%	90%
Smoking Cessation Advice[1]	1	100%	100%	99%
Chest Pain/Possible Heart Attack Care				
Aspirin at Arrival	-	-	95%	95%
Median Time to ECG (minutes)	-	-	8	8
Median Time to Transfer (minutes)	-	-	57	61
Fibrinolytic Medication Timing	-	-	33%	54%
Heart Failure Care				
ACE Inhibitor or ARB for LVSD	34	100%	94%	94%
Discharge Instructions	68	93%	89%	88%
Evaluation of LVS Function	73	100%	98%	98%
Smoking Cessation Advice	32	100%	99%	98%
Pneumonia Care				
Appropriate Initial Antibiotic	62	97%	90%	92%
Blood Culture Timing	72	100%	97%	96%
Influenza Vaccine[1]	23	100%	91%	91%
Initial Antibiotic Timing	70	97%	96%	95%
Pneumococcal Vaccine[1]	24	100%	92%	93%
Smoking Cessation Advice	33	100%	98%	97%
Surgical Care Improvement Project				
Appropriate VTP Within 24 Hours[2,5]	0	-	92%	92%
Appropriate Hair Removal[2,5]	0	-	99%	99%
Appropriate Beta Blocker Usage[2,5]	0	-	92%	93%
Controlled Postoperative Blood Glucose[2,5]	0	-	92%	93%
Prophylactic Antibiotic Timing[5]	0	-	97%	97%
Prophylactic Antibiotic Timing (Outpatient)	-	-	93%	92%
Prophylactic Antibiotic Selection[5]	0	-	97%	97%
Prophylactic Antibiotic Select. (Outpatient)	-	-	94%	94%
Prophylactic Antibiotic Stopped[5]	0	-	94%	94%
Recommended VTP Ordered[2,5]	0	-	94%	94%
Urinary Catheter Removal[2,5]	0	-	89%	90%
Children's Asthma Care				
Received Systemic Corticosteroids	-	-	-	100%
Received Home Management Plan	-	-	-	71%
Received Reliever Medication	-	-	-	100%
Use of Medical Imaging				
Combination Abdominal CT Scan	-	-	0.246	0.191
Combination Chest CT Scan	-	-	0.098	0.054
Follow-up Mammogram/Ultrasound	-	-	8.4%	8.4%
MRI for Low Back Pain	-	-	33.4%	32.7%
Survey of Patients' Hospital Experiences				
Area Around Room 'Always' Quiet at Night	-	-	-	58%
Doctors 'Always' Communicated Well	-	-	-	80%
Home Recovery Information Given	-	-	-	82%
Hospital Given 9 or 10 on 10 Point Scale	-	-	-	67%
Meds 'Always' Explained Before Given	-	-	-	60%
Nurses 'Always' Communicated Well	-	-	-	76%
Pain 'Always' Well Controlled	-	-	-	69%
Room and Bathroom 'Always' Clean	-	-	-	71%
Timely Help 'Always' Received	-	-	-	64%
Would Definitely Recommend Hospital	-	-	-	69%

Oak Forest Hospital

159th & Cicero Avenue — Phone: 708-687-7200
Oak Forest, IL 60452 — Fax: 708-687-7979
URL: www.cchil.org/dom/oak.html
Type: Acute Care Hospitals — Emergency Services: Yes
Ownership: Government - Local — Beds: 600
Key Personnel:
Chief of Medical Staff. . . . . Joseph Durham, MD
Coronary Care . . . . Lorraine Bangayan
Infection Control. . . . . Patricia DeMarais, MD
Quality Assurance . . . . Dave Johnson
Radiology. . . . . Tunisia Pinkley
Emergency Room . . . . Shams Shafiei, MD
Intensive Care Unit. . . . . S Chintanakarn, MD

Measure	Cases	This Hosp.	State Avg.	U.S. Avg.
Heart Attack Care				
ACE Inhibitor or ARB for LVSD	0	-	96%	96%
Aspirin at Arrival[1]	3	67%	99%	99%
Aspirin at Discharge[1]	1	100%	99%	98%
Beta Blocker at Discharge[1]	1	100%	98%	98%
Fibrinolytic Medication Timing	0	-	50%	55%
PCI Within 90 Minutes of Arrival	0	-	90%	90%
Smoking Cessation Advice	0	-	100%	99%
Chest Pain/Possible Heart Attack Care				
Aspirin at Arrival	37	95%	95%	95%
Median Time to ECG (minutes)	37	16	8	8
Median Time to Transfer (minutes)[1,3]	6	162	57	61
Fibrinolytic Medication Timing	0	-	33%	54%
Heart Failure Care				
ACE Inhibitor or ARB for LVSD[2]	110	98%	94%	94%
Discharge Instructions[2]	202	91%	89%	88%
Evaluation of LVS Function[2]	202	98%	98%	98%
Smoking Cessation Advice[2]	62	98%	99%	98%
Pneumonia Care				
Appropriate Initial Antibiotic	49	94%	90%	92%
Blood Culture Timing	56	98%	97%	96%
Influenza Vaccine[1]	17	88%	91%	91%
Initial Antibiotic Timing	45	87%	96%	95%
Pneumococcal Vaccine[1]	7	57%	92%	93%
Smoking Cessation Advice[1]	20	95%	98%	97%
Surgical Care Improvement Project				
Appropriate VTP Within 24 Hours[1]	7	100%	92%	92%
Appropriate Hair Removal[1]	8	100%	99%	99%
Appropriate Beta Blocker Usage	0	-	92%	93%
Controlled Postoperative Blood Glucose	0	-	92%	93%
Prophylactic Antibiotic Timing[1]	2	100%	97%	97%
Prophylactic Antibiotic Timing (Outpatient)[1,3]	12	100%	93%	92%
Prophylactic Antibiotic Selection[1]	2	100%	97%	97%
Prophylactic Antibiotic Select. (Outpatient)[1,3]	12	92%	94%	94%
Prophylactic Antibiotic Stopped[1]	2	100%	94%	94%
Recommended VTP Ordered[1]	7	100%	94%	94%
Urinary Catheter Removal[1]	1	100%	89%	90%
Children's Asthma Care				
Received Systemic Corticosteroids	-	-	-	100%
Received Home Management Plan	-	-	-	71%
Received Reliever Medication	-	-	-	100%
Use of Medical Imaging				
Combination Abdominal CT Scan[1]	18	0.000	0.246	0.191
Combination Chest CT Scan[1]	12	0.083	0.098	0.054
Follow-up Mammogram/Ultrasound[5]	0	-	8.4%	8.4%
MRI for Low Back Pain[5]	0	-	33.4%	32.7%
Survey of Patients' Hospital Experiences				
Area Around Room 'Always' Quiet at Night	300+	62%	-	58%
Doctors 'Always' Communicated Well	300+	78%	-	80%
Home Recovery Information Given	300+	77%	-	82%
Hospital Given 9 or 10 on 10 Point Scale	300+	59%	-	67%
Meds 'Always' Explained Before Given	300+	58%	-	60%
Nurses 'Always' Communicated Well	300+	78%	-	76%
Pain 'Always' Well Controlled	300+	69%	-	69%
Room and Bathroom 'Always' Clean	300+	65%	-	71%
Timely Help 'Always' Received	300+	67%	-	64%
Would Definitely Recommend Hospital	300+	66%	-	69%

NOTE: Hospital profiles are in alphabetical order by state, then city, then hospital within the city; Rankings exclude hospitals with less than 25 cases except for patient surveys which excludes hospitals with less than 100 cases; (a) 100–299 cases; (1) The number of cases is too small to be sure how well a hospital is performing; (2) The hospital indicated that the data submitted for this measure were based on a sample of cases; (3) Data was collected during a shorter time period (fewer quarters) than the maximum possible time for this measure; (4) Suppressed for one or more quarters by CMS; (5) No data is available from the hospital for this measure; (6) Fewer than 100 patients completed the HCAHPS survey. Use these rates with caution, as the number of surveys may be too low to reliably assess hospital performance; (7) Survey results are based on less than 12 months of data; (8) Survey results are not available for this reporting period; (9) No or very few patients were eligible for the HCAHPS survey. The scores shown, if any, reflect a very small number of surveys; (10) A state average was not calculated because too few hospitals in the state submitted data; (11) There were discrepancies in the data collection process; Please refer to the User's Guide for a full explanation of data.

Advocate Christ Hospital & Medical Center

4440 W 95th Street — Phone: 708-684-8000
Oak Lawn, IL 60453 — Fax: 708-864-4440
URL: www.advocatehealth.com
Type: Acute Care Hospitals — Emergency Services: Yes
Ownership: Voluntary Non-Profit - Church — Beds: 64

Key Personnel:
CEO/President. . . . . Kenneth W Lukhard
Radiology. . . . . Sangarappillai Asoka

Measure	Cases	This Hosp.	State Avg.	U.S. Avg.
Heart Attack Care				
ACE Inhibitor or ARB for LVSD[2]	55	100%	96%	96%
Aspirin at Arrival[2]	256	99%	99%	99%
Aspirin at Discharge[2]	305	100%	99%	98%
Beta Blocker at Discharge[2]	295	100%	98%	98%
Fibrinolytic Medication Timing[2]	0	-	50%	55%
PCI Within 90 Minutes of Arrival[2]	45	100%	90%	90%
Smoking Cessation Advice[2]	109	100%	100%	99%
Chest Pain/Possible Heart Attack Care				
Aspirin at Arrival[1]	16	94%	95%	95%
Median Time to ECG (minutes)[1]	17	4	8	8
Median Time to Transfer (minutes)[5]	0	-	57	61
Fibrinolytic Medication Timing[3]	0	-	33%	54%
Heart Failure Care				
ACE Inhibitor or ARB for LVSD[2]	115	100%	94%	94%
Discharge Instructions[2]	255	99%	89%	88%
Evaluation of LVS Function[2]	344	100%	98%	98%
Smoking Cessation Advice[2]	52	100%	99%	98%
Pneumonia Care				
Appropriate Initial Antibiotic[2]	65	95%	90%	92%
Blood Culture Timing[2]	54	98%	97%	96%
Influenza Vaccine[2]	110	99%	91%	91%
Initial Antibiotic Timing[2]	140	98%	96%	95%
Pneumococcal Vaccine[2]	167	99%	92%	93%
Smoking Cessation Advice[2]	50	96%	98%	97%
Surgical Care Improvement Project				
Appropriate VTP Within 24 Hours[2]	212	98%	92%	92%
Appropriate Hair Removal[2]	741	100%	99%	99%
Appropriate Beta Blocker Usage[2]	303	93%	92%	93%
Controlled Postoperative Blood Glucose[2]	145	95%	92%	93%
Prophylactic Antibiotic Timing[2]	488	99%	97%	97%
Prophylactic Antibiotic Timing (Outpatient)	728	97%	93%	92%
Prophylactic Antibiotic Selection[2]	499	97%	97%	97%
Prophylactic Antibiotic Select. (Outpatient)	723	95%	94%	94%
Prophylactic Antibiotic Stopped[2]	461	98%	94%	94%
Recommended VTP Ordered[2]	212	99%	94%	94%
Urinary Catheter Removal[2]	111	86%	89%	90%
Children's Asthma Care				
Received Systemic Corticosteroids	-	-	-	100%
Received Home Management Plan	-	-	-	71%
Received Reliever Medication	-	-	-	100%
Use of Medical Imaging				
Combination Abdominal CT Scan	1,349	0.087	0.246	0.191
Combination Chest CT Scan	1,483	0.038	0.098	0.054
Follow-up Mammogram/Ultrasound	2,229	7.8%	8.4%	8.4%
MRI for Low Back Pain	117	37.6%	33.4%	32.7%
Survey of Patients' Hospital Experiences				
Area Around Room 'Always' Quiet at Night	300+	49%	-	58%
Doctors 'Always' Communicated Well	300+	77%	-	80%
Home Recovery Information Given	300+	84%	-	82%
Hospital Given 9 or 10 on 10 Point Scale	300+	66%	-	67%
Meds 'Always' Explained Before Given	300+	60%	-	60%
Nurses 'Always' Communicated Well	300+	79%	-	76%
Pain 'Always' Well Controlled	300+	72%	-	69%
Room and Bathroom 'Always' Clean	300+	67%	-	71%
Timely Help 'Always' Received	300+	64%	-	64%
Would Definitely Recommend Hospital	300+	68%	-	69%

Rush Oak Park Hospital

520 S Maple Ave — Phone: 708-383-9300
Oak Park, IL 60304 — Fax: 708-660-6658
URL: www.oakparkhospital.org
Type: Acute Care Hospitals — Emergency Services: Yes
Ownership: Voluntary Non-Profit - Church — Beds: 296

Key Personnel:
CEO/President. . . . . Bruce M Elegant
Chief of Medical Staff. . . . . Phillip Paluttis MD
Operating Room. . . . . Diane Vendola
Quality Assurance . . . . Mary Barrie RN
Radiology. . . . . William Mollihan MD
Emergency Room . . . . Daniel Noonan MD

Measure	Cases	This Hosp.	State Avg.	U.S. Avg.
Heart Attack Care				
ACE Inhibitor or ARB for LVSD[1]	4	100%	96%	96%
Aspirin at Arrival	25	96%	99%	99%
Aspirin at Discharge[1]	19	95%	99%	98%
Beta Blocker at Discharge[1]	19	100%	98%	98%
Fibrinolytic Medication Timing	0	-	50%	55%
PCI Within 90 Minutes of Arrival[1]	1	100%	90%	90%
Smoking Cessation Advice[1]	9	100%	100%	99%
Chest Pain/Possible Heart Attack Care				
Aspirin at Arrival[1]	17	100%	95%	95%
Median Time to ECG (minutes)[1]	16	6	8	8
Median Time to Transfer (minutes)[1]	7	35	57	61
Fibrinolytic Medication Timing	0	-	33%	54%
Heart Failure Care				
ACE Inhibitor or ARB for LVSD	61	92%	94%	94%
Discharge Instructions	152	83%	89%	88%
Evaluation of LVS Function	196	94%	98%	98%
Smoking Cessation Advice	32	100%	99%	98%
Pneumonia Care				
Appropriate Initial Antibiotic	58	83%	90%	92%
Blood Culture Timing	56	96%	97%	96%
Influenza Vaccine	58	98%	91%	91%
Initial Antibiotic Timing	91	92%	96%	95%
Pneumococcal Vaccine	84	94%	92%	93%
Smoking Cessation Advice	28	100%	98%	97%
Surgical Care Improvement Project				
Appropriate VTP Within 24 Hours	181	88%	92%	92%
Appropriate Hair Removal	378	99%	99%	99%
Appropriate Beta Blocker Usage	110	89%	92%	93%
Controlled Postoperative Blood Glucose	0	-	92%	93%
Prophylactic Antibiotic Timing	211	96%	97%	97%
Prophylactic Antibiotic Timing (Outpatient)	40	82%	93%	92%
Prophylactic Antibiotic Selection	212	98%	97%	97%
Prophylactic Antibiotic Select. (Outpatient)	37	92%	94%	94%
Prophylactic Antibiotic Stopped	202	91%	94%	94%
Recommended VTP Ordered	182	93%	94%	94%
Urinary Catheter Removal	124	94%	89%	90%
Children's Asthma Care				
Received Systemic Corticosteroids	-	-	-	100%
Received Home Management Plan	-	-	-	71%
Received Reliever Medication	-	-	-	100%
Use of Medical Imaging				
Combination Abdominal CT Scan	325	0.468	0.246	0.191
Combination Chest CT Scan	177	0.006	0.098	0.054
Follow-up Mammogram/Ultrasound	890	6.1%	8.4%	8.4%
MRI for Low Back Pain[1]	1	0.0%	33.4%	32.7%
Survey of Patients' Hospital Experiences				
Area Around Room 'Always' Quiet at Night	300+	63%	-	58%
Doctors 'Always' Communicated Well	300+	79%	-	80%
Home Recovery Information Given	300+	75%	-	82%
Hospital Given 9 or 10 on 10 Point Scale	300+	60%	-	67%
Meds 'Always' Explained Before Given	300+	57%	-	60%
Nurses 'Always' Communicated Well	300+	72%	-	76%
Pain 'Always' Well Controlled	300+	70%	-	69%
Room and Bathroom 'Always' Clean	300+	66%	-	71%
Timely Help 'Always' Received	300+	59%	-	64%
Would Definitely Recommend Hospital	300+	64%	-	69%

West Suburban Medical Center

Erie at Austin Boulevard — Phone: 708-383-6200
Oak Park, IL 60302 — Fax: 708-386-9246
URL: www.wshmc.org
Type: Acute Care Hospitals — Emergency Services: Yes
Ownership: Voluntary Non-Profit - Other — Beds: 258

Key Personnel:
CEO/President. . . . . Jay Kreuzer
Chief of Medical Staff . . . . Roy Horras, MD
Operating Room. . . . . Margaret Zeinthiewicz
Quality Assurance . . . . Christine Clark
Radiology. . . . . Gayle Payonk
Anesthesiology. . . . . Vermeri Murthy, MD
Emergency Room . . . . Sandra Watkins
Patient Relations . . . . Deborah Davisson

Measure	Cases	This Hosp.	State Avg.	U.S. Avg.
Heart Attack Care				
ACE Inhibitor or ARB for LVSD[1]	14	93%	96%	96%
Aspirin at Arrival	74	100%	99%	99%
Aspirin at Discharge	57	89%	99%	98%
Beta Blocker at Discharge	69	96%	98%	98%
Fibrinolytic Medication Timing	0	-	50%	55%
PCI Within 90 Minutes of Arrival[1]	10	50%	90%	90%
Smoking Cessation Advice	32	100%	100%	99%
Chest Pain/Possible Heart Attack Care				
Aspirin at Arrival[1]	5	100%	95%	95%
Median Time to ECG (minutes)[1]	5	9	8	8
Median Time to Transfer (minutes)[5]	0	-	57	61
Fibrinolytic Medication Timing[5]	0	-	33%	54%
Heart Failure Care				
ACE Inhibitor or ARB for LVSD[2]	126	93%	94%	94%
Discharge Instructions[2]	288	94%	89%	88%
Evaluation of LVS Function[2]	316	99%	98%	98%
Smoking Cessation Advice[2]	106	99%	99%	98%
Pneumonia Care				
Appropriate Initial Antibiotic[2]	86	88%	90%	92%
Blood Culture Timing[2]	176	97%	97%	96%
Influenza Vaccine[2]	78	83%	91%	91%
Initial Antibiotic Timing[2]	161	95%	96%	95%
Pneumococcal Vaccine[2]	91	86%	92%	93%
Smoking Cessation Advice[2]	71	100%	98%	97%
Surgical Care Improvement Project				
Appropriate VTP Within 24 Hours[2]	146	99%	92%	92%
Appropriate Hair Removal[2]	461	100%	99%	99%
Appropriate Beta Blocker Usage[2]	115	94%	92%	93%
Controlled Postoperative Blood Glucose[2]	41	78%	92%	93%
Prophylactic Antibiotic Timing[2]	322	99%	97%	97%
Prophylactic Antibiotic Timing (Outpatient)	142	95%	93%	92%
Prophylactic Antibiotic Selection[2]	326	94%	97%	97%
Prophylactic Antibiotic Select. (Outpatient)	138	92%	94%	94%
Prophylactic Antibiotic Stopped[2]	318	97%	94%	94%
Recommended VTP Ordered[2]	146	99%	94%	94%
Urinary Catheter Removal[2]	49	92%	89%	90%
Children's Asthma Care				
Received Systemic Corticosteroids	-	-	-	100%
Received Home Management Plan	-	-	-	71%
Received Reliever Medication	-	-	-	100%
Use of Medical Imaging				
Combination Abdominal CT Scan	528	0.229	0.246	0.191
Combination Chest CT Scan	352	0.233	0.098	0.054
Follow-up Mammogram/Ultrasound	160	6.3%	8.4%	8.4%
MRI for Low Back Pain	64	37.5%	33.4%	32.7%
Survey of Patients' Hospital Experiences				
Area Around Room 'Always' Quiet at Night	300+	60%	-	58%
Doctors 'Always' Communicated Well	300+	80%	-	80%
Home Recovery Information Given	300+	83%	-	82%
Hospital Given 9 or 10 on 10 Point Scale	300+	63%	-	67%
Meds 'Always' Explained Before Given	300+	62%	-	60%
Nurses 'Always' Communicated Well	300+	70%	-	76%
Pain 'Always' Well Controlled	300+	68%	-	69%
Room and Bathroom 'Always' Clean	300+	66%	-	71%
Timely Help 'Always' Received	300+	49%	-	64%
Would Definitely Recommend Hospital	300+	61%	-	69%

NOTE: Hospital profiles are in alphabetical order by state, then city, then hospital within the city; Rankings exclude hospitals with less than 25 cases except for patient surveys which excludes hospitals with less than 100 cases; (a) 100–299 cases; (1) The number of cases is too small to be sure how well a hospital is performing; (2) The hospital indicated that the data submitted for this measure were based on a sample of cases; (3) Data was collected during a shorter time period (fewer quarters) than the maximum possible time for this measure; (4) Suppressed for one or more quarters by CMS; (5) No data is available from the hospital for this measure; (6) Fewer than 100 patients completed the HCAHPS survey. Use these rates with caution, as the number of surveys may be too low to reliably assess hospital performance; (7) Survey results are based on less than 12 months of data; (8) Survey results are not available for this reporting period; (9) No or very few patients were eligible for the HCAHPS survey. The scores shown, if any, reflect a very small number of surveys; (10) A state average was not calculated because too few hospitals in the state submitted data; (11) There were discrepancies in the data collection process; Please refer to the User's Guide for a full explanation of data.

Richland Memorial Hospital

800 East Locust — Phone: 618-395-2131
Olney, IL 62450 — Fax: 618-392-3228
URL: www.richlandmemorial.com
Type: Acute Care Hospitals — Emergency Services: Yes
Ownership: Voluntary Non-Profit - Private — Beds: 135

Key Personnel:
CEO/President. . . . . David Allen
Chief of Medical Staff . . . . Robert Nash, MD
Infection Control. . . . . Penni Kuenstler
Operating Room. . . . . Kathy Cowman
Quality Assurance . . . . Lana Royse
Radiology. . . . . Randy Bishop
Emergency Room . . . . Donna Brown
Intensive Care Unit. . . . . Joan Sager

Measure	Cases	This Hosp.	State Avg.	U.S. Avg.
Heart Attack Care				
ACE Inhibitor or ARB for LVSD[1]	1	100%	96%	96%
Aspirin at Arrival[1]	7	86%	99%	99%
Aspirin at Discharge[1]	6	83%	99%	98%
Beta Blocker at Discharge[1]	6	83%	98%	98%
Fibrinolytic Medication Timing	0	-	50%	55%
PCI Within 90 Minutes of Arrival	0	-	90%	90%
Smoking Cessation Advice[1]	3	67%	100%	99%
Chest Pain/Possible Heart Attack Care				
Aspirin at Arrival	36	83%	95%	95%
Median Time to ECG (minutes)	37	20	8	8
Median Time to Transfer (minutes)[1,3]	5	85	57	61
Fibrinolytic Medication Timing[1]	3	33%	33%	54%
Heart Failure Care				
ACE Inhibitor or ARB for LVSD[1]	24	71%	94%	94%
Discharge Instructions	57	70%	89%	88%
Evaluation of LVS Function	87	89%	98%	98%
Smoking Cessation Advice[1]	8	75%	99%	98%
Pneumonia Care				
Appropriate Initial Antibiotic	62	89%	90%	92%
Blood Culture Timing	69	100%	97%	96%
Influenza Vaccine	89	71%	91%	91%
Initial Antibiotic Timing	92	98%	96%	95%
Pneumococcal Vaccine	114	88%	92%	93%
Smoking Cessation Advice	36	89%	98%	97%
Surgical Care Improvement Project				
Appropriate VTP Within 24 Hours	29	69%	92%	92%
Appropriate Hair Removal	105	100%	99%	99%
Appropriate Beta Blocker Usage[1]	22	68%	92%	93%
Controlled Postoperative Blood Glucose	0	-	92%	93%
Prophylactic Antibiotic Timing	84	90%	97%	97%
Prophylactic Antibiotic Timing (Outpatient)	26	85%	93%	92%
Prophylactic Antibiotic Selection	80	95%	97%	97%
Prophylactic Antibiotic Select. (Outpatient)[1]	24	96%	94%	94%
Prophylactic Antibiotic Stopped	76	88%	94%	94%
Recommended VTP Ordered	30	77%	94%	94%
Urinary Catheter Removal[1]	4	25%	89%	90%
Children's Asthma Care				
Received Systemic Corticosteroids	-	-	-	100%
Received Home Management Plan	-	-	-	71%
Received Reliever Medication	-	-	-	100%
Use of Medical Imaging				
Combination Abdominal CT Scan	238	0.702	0.246	0.191
Combination Chest CT Scan	210	0.429	0.098	0.054
Follow-up Mammogram/Ultrasound	224	2.2%	8.4%	8.4%
MRI for Low Back Pain[1]	24	29.2%	33.4%	32.7%
Survey of Patients' Hospital Experiences				
Area Around Room 'Always' Quiet at Night	300+	64%	-	58%
Doctors 'Always' Communicated Well	300+	85%	-	80%
Home Recovery Information Given	300+	87%	-	82%
Hospital Given 9 or 10 on 10 Point Scale	300+	71%	-	67%
Meds 'Always' Explained Before Given	300+	64%	-	60%
Nurses 'Always' Communicated Well	300+	79%	-	76%
Pain 'Always' Well Controlled	300+	75%	-	69%
Room and Bathroom 'Always' Clean	300+	64%	-	71%
Timely Help 'Always' Received	300+	69%	-	64%
Would Definitely Recommend Hospital	300+	74%	-	69%

Saint James Hospital & Health Center-Olympia Fields

20201 S Crawford Avenue — Phone: 708-747-4000
Olympia Fields, IL 60461 — Fax: 708-756-6763
Type: Acute Care Hospitals — Emergency Services: Yes
Ownership: Proprietary — Beds: 201

Key Personnel:
CEO/President. . . . . Peter J Murphy
Chief of Medical Staff . . . . Aswatch Subram, MD

Measure	Cases	This Hosp.	State Avg.	U.S. Avg.
Heart Attack Care				
ACE Inhibitor or ARB for LVSD	56	95%	96%	96%
Aspirin at Arrival	306	99%	99%	99%
Aspirin at Discharge	288	99%	99%	98%
Beta Blocker at Discharge	304	99%	98%	98%
Fibrinolytic Medication Timing	0	-	50%	55%
PCI Within 90 Minutes of Arrival[1]	20	95%	90%	90%
Smoking Cessation Advice	84	100%	100%	99%
Chest Pain/Possible Heart Attack Care				
Aspirin at Arrival	31	90%	95%	95%
Median Time to ECG (minutes)	34	6	8	8
Median Time to Transfer (minutes)[5]	0	-	57	61
Fibrinolytic Medication Timing[3]	0	-	33%	54%
Heart Failure Care				
ACE Inhibitor or ARB for LVSD	276	92%	94%	94%
Discharge Instructions	655	87%	89%	88%
Evaluation of LVS Function	806	99%	98%	98%
Smoking Cessation Advice	153	100%	99%	98%
Pneumonia Care				
Appropriate Initial Antibiotic[2]	121	90%	90%	92%
Blood Culture Timing[2]	274	96%	97%	96%
Influenza Vaccine[2]	147	90%	91%	91%
Initial Antibiotic Timing[2]	289	95%	96%	95%
Pneumococcal Vaccine[2]	197	93%	92%	93%
Smoking Cessation Advice[2]	100	100%	98%	97%
Surgical Care Improvement Project				
Appropriate VTP Within 24 Hours[2]	269	93%	92%	92%
Appropriate Hair Removal[2]	702	99%	99%	99%
Appropriate Beta Blocker Usage[2]	225	84%	92%	93%
Controlled Postoperative Blood Glucose[2]	99	88%	92%	93%
Prophylactic Antibiotic Timing[2]	424	94%	97%	97%
Prophylactic Antibiotic Timing (Outpatient)	265	81%	93%	92%
Prophylactic Antibiotic Selection[2]	429	99%	97%	97%
Prophylactic Antibiotic Select. (Outpatient)	246	86%	94%	94%
Prophylactic Antibiotic Stopped[2]	391	93%	94%	94%
Recommended VTP Ordered[2]	270	97%	94%	94%
Urinary Catheter Removal[2]	70	87%	89%	90%
Children's Asthma Care				
Received Systemic Corticosteroids	-	-	-	100%
Received Home Management Plan	-	-	-	71%
Received Reliever Medication	-	-	-	100%
Use of Medical Imaging				
Combination Abdominal CT Scan	711	0.208	0.246	0.191
Combination Chest CT Scan	548	0.109	0.098	0.054
Follow-up Mammogram/Ultrasound	1,319	6.7%	8.4%	8.4%
MRI for Low Back Pain	123	38.2%	33.4%	32.7%
Survey of Patients' Hospital Experiences				
Area Around Room 'Always' Quiet at Night	300+	49%	-	58%
Doctors 'Always' Communicated Well	300+	75%	-	80%
Home Recovery Information Given	300+	75%	-	82%
Hospital Given 9 or 10 on 10 Point Scale	300+	57%	-	67%
Meds 'Always' Explained Before Given	300+	56%	-	60%
Nurses 'Always' Communicated Well	300+	72%	-	76%
Pain 'Always' Well Controlled	300+	67%	-	69%
Room and Bathroom 'Always' Clean	300+	65%	-	71%
Timely Help 'Always' Received	300+	55%	-	64%
Would Definitely Recommend Hospital	300+	58%	-	69%

Ottawa Regional Hospital & Healthcare Center

1100 East Norris Drive — Phone: 815-433-3100
Ottawa, IL 61350 — Fax: 815-431-5500
URL: www.community-hospital.org
Type: Acute Care Hospitals — Emergency Services: Yes
Ownership: Voluntary Non-Profit - Private — Beds: 124

Key Personnel:
CEO/President. . . . . Robert I Schmelter
Chief of Medical Staff . . . . Joseph S Kokoszka, MD
Infection Control. . . . . Kerry Gerding
Operating Room. . . . . Caner Celeboglu
Quality Assurance . . . . Marcy Perkunas
Radiology. . . . . Byron Johnson, MD
Emergency Room . . . . Linda Grey, RN
Intensive Care Unit. . . . . Kathy Jakubek, RN

Measure	Cases	This Hosp.	State Avg.	U.S. Avg.
Heart Attack Care				
ACE Inhibitor or ARB for LVSD[5]	0	-	96%	96%
Aspirin at Arrival[5]	0	-	99%	99%
Aspirin at Discharge[5]	0	-	99%	98%
Beta Blocker at Discharge[5]	0	-	98%	98%
Fibrinolytic Medication Timing[5]	0	-	50%	55%
PCI Within 90 Minutes of Arrival[5]	0	-	90%	90%
Smoking Cessation Advice[5]	0	-	100%	99%
Chest Pain/Possible Heart Attack Care				
Aspirin at Arrival	70	100%	95%	95%
Median Time to ECG (minutes)	75	5	8	8
Median Time to Transfer (minutes)[1]	1	102	57	61
Fibrinolytic Medication Timing[1]	8	75%	33%	54%
Heart Failure Care				
ACE Inhibitor or ARB for LVSD[1]	24	83%	94%	94%
Discharge Instructions	56	84%	89%	88%
Evaluation of LVS Function	79	95%	98%	98%
Smoking Cessation Advice[1]	9	89%	99%	98%
Pneumonia Care				
Appropriate Initial Antibiotic	103	96%	90%	92%
Blood Culture Timing	155	95%	97%	96%
Influenza Vaccine	120	90%	91%	91%
Initial Antibiotic Timing	171	99%	96%	95%
Pneumococcal Vaccine	149	96%	92%	93%
Smoking Cessation Advice	55	93%	98%	97%
Surgical Care Improvement Project				
Appropriate VTP Within 24 Hours	92	92%	92%	92%
Appropriate Hair Removal	214	100%	99%	99%
Appropriate Beta Blocker Usage	44	100%	92%	93%
Controlled Postoperative Blood Glucose	0	-	92%	93%
Prophylactic Antibiotic Timing	143	99%	97%	97%
Prophylactic Antibiotic Timing (Outpatient)	57	88%	93%	92%
Prophylactic Antibiotic Selection	145	99%	97%	97%
Prophylactic Antibiotic Select. (Outpatient)	53	96%	94%	94%
Prophylactic Antibiotic Stopped	136	92%	94%	94%
Recommended VTP Ordered	92	96%	94%	94%
Urinary Catheter Removal	39	92%	89%	90%
Children's Asthma Care				
Received Systemic Corticosteroids	-	-	-	100%
Received Home Management Plan	-	-	-	71%
Received Reliever Medication	-	-	-	100%
Use of Medical Imaging				
Combination Abdominal CT Scan	509	0.118	0.246	0.191
Combination Chest CT Scan	408	0.022	0.098	0.054
Follow-up Mammogram/Ultrasound	352	21.0%	8.4%	8.4%
MRI for Low Back Pain	127	27.6%	33.4%	32.7%
Survey of Patients' Hospital Experiences				
Area Around Room 'Always' Quiet at Night	300+	52%	-	58%
Doctors 'Always' Communicated Well	300+	78%	-	80%
Home Recovery Information Given	300+	85%	-	82%
Hospital Given 9 or 10 on 10 Point Scale	300+	62%	-	67%
Meds 'Always' Explained Before Given	300+	61%	-	60%
Nurses 'Always' Communicated Well	300+	78%	-	76%
Pain 'Always' Well Controlled	300+	68%	-	69%
Room and Bathroom 'Always' Clean	300+	77%	-	71%
Timely Help 'Always' Received	300+	69%	-	64%
Would Definitely Recommend Hospital	300+	63%	-	69%

NOTE: Hospital profiles are in alphabetical order by state, then city, then hospital within the city; Rankings exclude hospitals with less than 25 cases except for patient surveys which excludes hospitals with less than 100 cases; (a) 100–299 cases; (1) The number of cases is too small to be sure how well a hospital is performing; (2) The hospital indicated that the data submitted for this measure were based on a sample of cases; (3) Data was collected during a shorter time period (fewer quarters) than the maximum possible time for this measure; (4) Suppressed for one or more quarters by CMS; (5) No data is available from the hospital for this measure; (6) Fewer than 100 patients completed the HCAHPS survey. Use these rates with caution, as the number of surveys may be too low to reliably assess hospital performance; (7) Survey results are based on less than 12 months of data; (8) Survey results are not available for this reporting period; (9) No or very few patients were eligible for the HCAHPS survey. The scores shown, if any, reflect a very small number of surveys; (10) A state average was not calculated because too few hospitals in the state submitted data; (11) There were discrepancies in the data collection process; Please refer to the User's Guide for a full explanation of data.

Palos Community Hospital

12251 South 80th Avenue Phone: 708-923-4000
Palos Heights, IL 60463 Fax: 708-923-4620
URL: www.paloshospital.org
Type: Acute Care Hospitals Emergency Services: Yes
Ownership: Voluntary Non-Profit - Private Beds: 436

Key Personnel:

CEO/President. . . . . Sr Margaret Wright
Cardiac Laboratory. . . . . Julie Callahan
Chief of Medical Staff . . . . Thomas Lavery
Quality Assurance . . . . Nancy Kayse
Emergency Room . . . . Lori Stott

Measure	Cases	This Hosp.	State Avg.	U.S. Avg.
Heart Attack Care				
ACE Inhibitor or ARB for LVSD[2]	33	94%	96%	96%
Aspirin at Arrival[2]	276	99%	99%	99%
Aspirin at Discharge[2]	254	99%	99%	98%
Beta Blocker at Discharge[2]	241	100%	98%	98%
Fibrinolytic Medication Timing[2]	0	-	50%	55%
PCI Within 90 Minutes of Arrival[2]	48	92%	90%	90%
Smoking Cessation Advice[2]	75	100%	100%	99%
Chest Pain/Possible Heart Attack Care				
Aspirin at Arrival	29	76%	95%	95%
Median Time to ECG (minutes)	29	0	8	8
Median Time to Transfer (minutes)[5]	0	-	57	61
Fibrinolytic Medication Timing[5]	0	-	33%	54%
Heart Failure Care				
ACE Inhibitor or ARB for LVSD[2]	48	98%	94%	94%
Discharge Instructions[2]	207	90%	89%	88%
Evaluation of LVS Function[2]	266	100%	98%	98%
Smoking Cessation Advice[2]	30	100%	99%	98%
Pneumonia Care				
Appropriate Initial Antibiotic[2]	82	93%	90%	92%
Blood Culture Timing[2]	144	93%	97%	96%
Influenza Vaccine[2]	93	95%	91%	91%
Initial Antibiotic Timing[2]	129	97%	96%	95%
Pneumococcal Vaccine[2]	152	94%	92%	93%
Smoking Cessation Advice[2]	35	94%	98%	97%
Surgical Care Improvement Project				
Appropriate VTP Within 24 Hours[2]	233	91%	92%	92%
Appropriate Hair Removal[2]	632	100%	99%	99%
Appropriate Beta Blocker Usage[2]	207	85%	92%	93%
Controlled Postoperative Blood Glucose[2]	133	97%	92%	93%
Prophylactic Antibiotic Timing[2]	415	98%	97%	97%
Prophylactic Antibiotic Timing (Outpatient)	224	96%	93%	92%
Prophylactic Antibiotic Selection[2]	423	98%	97%	97%
Prophylactic Antibiotic Select. (Outpatient)	222	97%	94%	94%
Prophylactic Antibiotic Stopped[2]	401	93%	94%	94%
Recommended VTP Ordered[2]	234	94%	94%	94%
Urinary Catheter Removal[2]	84	79%	89%	90%
Children's Asthma Care				
Received Systemic Corticosteroids	-	-	-	100%
Received Home Management Plan	-	-	-	71%
Received Reliever Medication	-	-	-	100%
Use of Medical Imaging				
Combination Abdominal CT Scan	1,969	0.059	0.246	0.191
Combination Chest CT Scan	2,265	0.010	0.098	0.054
Follow-up Mammogram/Ultrasound	2,785	11.2%	8.4%	8.4%
MRI for Low Back Pain[5]	0	-	33.4%	32.7%
Survey of Patients' Hospital Experiences				
Area Around Room 'Always' Quiet at Night	300+	43%	-	58%
Doctors 'Always' Communicated Well	300+	80%	-	80%
Home Recovery Information Given	300+	81%	-	82%
Hospital Given 9 or 10 on 10 Point Scale	300+	63%	-	67%
Meds 'Always' Explained Before Given	300+	59%	-	60%
Nurses 'Always' Communicated Well	300+	76%	-	76%
Pain 'Always' Well Controlled	300+	70%	-	69%
Room and Bathroom 'Always' Clean	300+	66%	-	71%
Timely Help 'Always' Received	300+	60%	-	64%
Would Definitely Recommend Hospital	300+	68%	-	69%

Pana Community Hospital

101 E Ninth Street Phone: 217-562-2131
Pana, IL 62557 Fax: 217-562-6270
Type: Critical Access Hospitals Emergency Services: Yes
Ownership: Voluntary Non-Profit - Private Beds: 44

Key Personnel:

CEO/President. . . . . Roland Carlson
Chief of Medical Staff. . . . . Allen Frigy, MD
Infection Control. . . . . Sheri Trexler
Operating Room. . . . . Nora Washburn, RN

Measure	Cases	This Hosp.	State Avg.	U.S. Avg.
Heart Attack Care				
ACE Inhibitor or ARB for LVSD[5]	0	-	96%	96%
Aspirin at Arrival[5]	0	-	99%	99%
Aspirin at Discharge[5]	0	-	99%	98%
Beta Blocker at Discharge[5]	0	-	98%	98%
Fibrinolytic Medication Timing[5]	0	-	50%	55%
PCI Within 90 Minutes of Arrival[5]	0	-	90%	90%
Smoking Cessation Advice[5]	0	-	100%	99%
Chest Pain/Possible Heart Attack Care				
Aspirin at Arrival	-	-	95%	95%
Median Time to ECG (minutes)	-	-	8	8
Median Time to Transfer (minutes)	-	-	57	61
Fibrinolytic Medication Timing	-	-	33%	54%
Heart Failure Care				
ACE Inhibitor or ARB for LVSD[1]	11	82%	94%	94%
Discharge Instructions[1]	21	81%	89%	88%
Evaluation of LVS Function	33	88%	98%	98%
Smoking Cessation Advice[1]	1	100%	99%	98%
Pneumonia Care				
Appropriate Initial Antibiotic[1]	20	85%	90%	92%
Blood Culture Timing	25	96%	97%	96%
Influenza Vaccine[1]	12	75%	91%	91%
Initial Antibiotic Timing[5]	0	-	96%	95%
Pneumococcal Vaccine[1]	21	81%	92%	93%
Smoking Cessation Advice[1]	9	100%	98%	97%
Surgical Care Improvement Project				
Appropriate VTP Within 24 Hours[5]	0	-	92%	92%
Appropriate Hair Removal[5]	0	-	99%	99%
Appropriate Beta Blocker Usage[5]	0	-	92%	93%
Controlled Postoperative Blood Glucose[5]	0	-	92%	93%
Prophylactic Antibiotic Timing[5]	0	-	97%	97%
Prophylactic Antibiotic Timing (Outpatient)	-	-	93%	92%
Prophylactic Antibiotic Selection[5]	0	-	97%	97%
Prophylactic Antibiotic Select. (Outpatient)	-	-	94%	94%
Prophylactic Antibiotic Stopped[5]	0	-	94%	94%
Recommended VTP Ordered[5]	0	-	94%	94%
Urinary Catheter Removal[5]	0	-	89%	90%
Children's Asthma Care				
Received Systemic Corticosteroids	-	-	-	100%
Received Home Management Plan	-	-	-	71%
Received Reliever Medication	-	-	-	100%
Use of Medical Imaging				
Combination Abdominal CT Scan	-	-	0.246	0.191
Combination Chest CT Scan	-	-	0.098	0.054
Follow-up Mammogram/Ultrasound	-	-	8.4%	8.4%
MRI for Low Back Pain	-	-	33.4%	32.7%
Survey of Patients' Hospital Experiences				
Area Around Room 'Always' Quiet at Night[8]	-	-	-	58%
Doctors 'Always' Communicated Well[8]	-	-	-	80%
Home Recovery Information Given[8]	-	-	-	82%
Hospital Given 9 or 10 on 10 Point Scale[8]	-	-	-	67%
Meds 'Always' Explained Before Given[8]	-	-	-	60%
Nurses 'Always' Communicated Well[8]	-	-	-	76%
Pain 'Always' Well Controlled[8]	-	-	-	69%
Room and Bathroom 'Always' Clean[8]	-	-	-	71%
Timely Help 'Always' Received[8]	-	-	-	64%
Would Definitely Recommend Hospital[8]	-	-	-	69%

Paris Community Hospital

721 E Court Street Phone: 217-465-4141
Paris, IL 61944 Fax: 217-463-2096
URL: www.pariscommunityhospital.com
Type: Critical Access Hospitals Emergency Services: Yes
Ownership: Voluntary Non-Profit - Other Beds: 49

Key Personnel:

CEO/President. . . . . Randy Simmons
Chief of Medical Staff . . . . Daniel R Gilbert, DO
Infection Control. . . . . Tammy Hewitt, RN
Operating Room. . . . . Katrina Conine, RN
Quality Assurance . . . . Robin Gordon
Radiology. . . . . Bruce Houle
Emergency Room . . . . Rachel Woltman, DO
Intensive Care Unit. . . . . Rachel Young, RN

Measure	Cases	This Hosp.	State Avg.	U.S. Avg.
Heart Attack Care				
ACE Inhibitor or ARB for LVSD	0	-	96%	96%
Aspirin at Arrival[1]	3	100%	99%	99%
Aspirin at Discharge[1]	2	50%	99%	98%
Beta Blocker at Discharge	0	-	98%	98%
Fibrinolytic Medication Timing	0	-	50%	55%
PCI Within 90 Minutes of Arrival	0	-	90%	90%
Smoking Cessation Advice	0	-	100%	99%
Chest Pain/Possible Heart Attack Care				
Aspirin at Arrival	-	-	95%	95%
Median Time to ECG (minutes)	-	-	8	8
Median Time to Transfer (minutes)	-	-	57	61
Fibrinolytic Medication Timing	-	-	33%	54%
Heart Failure Care				
ACE Inhibitor or ARB for LVSD[1]	8	100%	94%	94%
Discharge Instructions[1]	17	100%	89%	88%
Evaluation of LVS Function	39	95%	98%	98%
Smoking Cessation Advice[1]	3	100%	99%	98%
Pneumonia Care				
Appropriate Initial Antibiotic[1]	24	88%	90%	92%
Blood Culture Timing[1]	17	100%	97%	96%
Influenza Vaccine[1]	18	94%	91%	91%
Initial Antibiotic Timing	39	100%	96%	95%
Pneumococcal Vaccine	35	94%	92%	93%
Smoking Cessation Advice[1]	15	93%	98%	97%
Surgical Care Improvement Project				
Appropriate VTP Within 24 Hours[1]	6	67%	92%	92%
Appropriate Hair Removal[1]	7	100%	99%	99%
Appropriate Beta Blocker Usage[1]	2	50%	92%	93%
Controlled Postoperative Blood Glucose	0	-	92%	93%
Prophylactic Antibiotic Timing[1]	4	100%	97%	97%
Prophylactic Antibiotic Timing (Outpatient)	-	-	93%	92%
Prophylactic Antibiotic Selection[1]	4	75%	97%	97%
Prophylactic Antibiotic Select. (Outpatient)	-	-	94%	94%
Prophylactic Antibiotic Stopped[1]	4	100%	94%	94%
Recommended VTP Ordered[1]	6	67%	94%	94%
Urinary Catheter Removal[1]	3	100%	89%	90%
Children's Asthma Care				
Received Systemic Corticosteroids	-	-	-	100%
Received Home Management Plan	-	-	-	71%
Received Reliever Medication	-	-	-	100%
Use of Medical Imaging				
Combination Abdominal CT Scan	-	-	0.246	0.191
Combination Chest CT Scan	-	-	0.098	0.054
Follow-up Mammogram/Ultrasound	-	-	8.4%	8.4%
MRI for Low Back Pain	-	-	33.4%	32.7%
Survey of Patients' Hospital Experiences				
Area Around Room 'Always' Quiet at Night[8]	-	-	-	58%
Doctors 'Always' Communicated Well[8]	-	-	-	80%
Home Recovery Information Given[8]	-	-	-	82%
Hospital Given 9 or 10 on 10 Point Scale[8]	-	-	-	67%
Meds 'Always' Explained Before Given[8]	-	-	-	60%
Nurses 'Always' Communicated Well[8]	-	-	-	76%
Pain 'Always' Well Controlled[8]	-	-	-	69%
Room and Bathroom 'Always' Clean[8]	-	-	-	71%
Timely Help 'Always' Received[8]	-	-	-	64%
Would Definitely Recommend Hospital[8]	-	-	-	69%

NOTE: Hospital profiles are in alphabetical order by state, then city, then hospital within the city; Rankings exclude hospitals with less than 25 cases except for patient surveys which excludes hospitals with less than 100 cases; (a) 100–299 cases; (1) The number of cases is too small to be sure how well a hospital is performing; (2) The hospital indicated that the data submitted for this measure were based on a sample of cases; (3) Data was collected during a shorter time period (fewer quarters) than the maximum possible time for this measure; (4) Suppressed for one or more quarters by CMS; (5) No data is available from the hospital for this measure; (6) Fewer than 100 patients completed the HCAHPS survey. Use these rates with caution, as the number of surveys may be too low to reliably assess hospital performance; (7) Survey results are based on less than 12 months of data; (8) Survey results are not available for this reporting period; (9) No or very few patients were eligible for the HCAHPS survey. The scores shown, if any, reflect a very small number of surveys; (10) A state average was not calculated because too few hospitals in the state submitted data; (11) There were discrepancies in the data collection process; Please refer to the User's Guide for a full explanation of data.

Advocate Lutheran General Hospital

1775 Dempster St Phone: 847-723-2210
Park Ridge, IL 60068 Fax: 847-696-2612
URL: www.advocatehealth.com
Type: Acute Care Hospitals Emergency Services: Yes
Ownership: Voluntary Non-Profit - Church

Key Personnel:
CEO/President. . . . . Bruce C Campbell
Chief of Medical Staff . . . . John Sage
Radiology. . . . . John McFadden

Measure	Cases	This Hosp.	State Avg.	U.S. Avg.
Heart Attack Care				
ACE Inhibitor or ARB for LVSD	43	100%	96%	96%
Aspirin at Arrival	255	100%	99%	99%
Aspirin at Discharge	241	99%	99%	98%
Beta Blocker at Discharge	236	100%	98%	98%
Fibrinolytic Medication Timing	0	-	50%	55%
PCI Within 90 Minutes of Arrival	50	98%	90%	90%
Smoking Cessation Advice	61	100%	100%	99%
Chest Pain/Possible Heart Attack Care				
Aspirin at Arrival[1]	4	75%	95%	95%
Median Time to ECG (minutes)[1]	5	7	8	8
Median Time to Transfer (minutes)[5]	0	-	57	61
Fibrinolytic Medication Timing[5]	0	-	33%	54%
Heart Failure Care				
ACE Inhibitor or ARB for LVSD	187	99%	94%	94%
Discharge Instructions	374	99%	89%	88%
Evaluation of LVS Function	518	100%	98%	98%
Smoking Cessation Advice	49	100%	99%	98%
Pneumonia Care				
Appropriate Initial Antibiotic	150	93%	90%	92%
Blood Culture Timing	267	100%	97%	96%
Influenza Vaccine	201	99%	91%	91%
Initial Antibiotic Timing	280	99%	96%	95%
Pneumococcal Vaccine	305	99%	92%	93%
Smoking Cessation Advice	63	100%	98%	97%
Surgical Care Improvement Project				
Appropriate VTP Within 24 Hours[2]	211	96%	92%	92%
Appropriate Hair Removal[2]	641	100%	99%	99%
Appropriate Beta Blocker Usage[2]	233	99%	92%	93%
Controlled Postoperative Blood Glucose[2]	108	92%	92%	93%
Prophylactic Antibiotic Timing[2]	460	100%	97%	97%
Prophylactic Antibiotic Timing (Outpatient)	730	99%	93%	92%
Prophylactic Antibiotic Selection[2]	464	97%	97%	97%
Prophylactic Antibiotic Select. (Outpatient)	727	98%	94%	94%
Prophylactic Antibiotic Stopped[2]	434	96%	94%	94%
Recommended VTP Ordered[2]	211	99%	94%	94%
Urinary Catheter Removal[2]	116	97%	89%	90%
Children's Asthma Care				
Received Systemic Corticosteroids	-	-	-	100%
Received Home Management Plan	-	-	-	71%
Received Reliever Medication	-	-	-	100%
Use of Medical Imaging				
Combination Abdominal CT Scan	2,202	0.058	0.246	0.191
Combination Chest CT Scan	1,767	0.036	0.098	0.054
Follow-up Mammogram/Ultrasound	3,625	6.2%	8.4%	8.4%
MRI for Low Back Pain	247	31.2%	33.4%	32.7%
Survey of Patients' Hospital Experiences				
Area Around Room 'Always' Quiet at Night	300+	54%	-	58%
Doctors 'Always' Communicated Well	300+	78%	-	80%
Home Recovery Information Given	300+	85%	-	82%
Hospital Given 9 or 10 on 10 Point Scale	300+	72%	-	67%
Meds 'Always' Explained Before Given	300+	61%	-	60%
Nurses 'Always' Communicated Well	300+	76%	-	76%
Pain 'Always' Well Controlled	300+	70%	-	69%
Room and Bathroom 'Always' Clean	300+	73%	-	71%
Timely Help 'Always' Received	300+	60%	-	64%
Would Definitely Recommend Hospital	300+	76%	-	69%

Pekin Memorial Hospital

600 South 13th Street Phone: 309-347-1151
Pekin, IL 61554 Fax: 309-347-5453
URL: www.pekinhospital.org
Type: Acute Care Hospitals Emergency Services: Yes
Ownership: Voluntary Non-Profit - Private Beds: 125

Key Personnel:
CEO/President. . . . . Robert Moore
Quality Assurance . . . . Sandy Brooks

Measure	Cases	This Hosp.	State Avg.	U.S. Avg.
Heart Attack Care				
ACE Inhibitor or ARB for LVSD[1]	5	100%	96%	96%
Aspirin at Arrival	41	98%	99%	99%
Aspirin at Discharge	29	100%	99%	98%
Beta Blocker at Discharge	30	100%	98%	98%
Fibrinolytic Medication Timing	0	-	50%	55%
PCI Within 90 Minutes of Arrival	0	-	90%	90%
Smoking Cessation Advice[1]	6	100%	100%	99%
Chest Pain/Possible Heart Attack Care				
Aspirin at Arrival	54	94%	95%	95%
Median Time to ECG (minutes)	55	5	8	8
Median Time to Transfer (minutes)[1]	4	56	57	61
Fibrinolytic Medication Timing	0	-	33%	54%
Heart Failure Care				
ACE Inhibitor or ARB for LVSD	33	100%	94%	94%
Discharge Instructions	92	95%	89%	88%
Evaluation of LVS Function	111	100%	98%	98%
Smoking Cessation Advice[1]	22	100%	99%	98%
Pneumonia Care				
Appropriate Initial Antibiotic	119	91%	90%	92%
Blood Culture Timing	250	98%	97%	96%
Influenza Vaccine	123	99%	91%	91%
Initial Antibiotic Timing	231	99%	96%	95%
Pneumococcal Vaccine	188	98%	92%	93%
Smoking Cessation Advice	68	99%	98%	97%
Surgical Care Improvement Project				
Appropriate VTP Within 24 Hours	153	97%	92%	92%
Appropriate Hair Removal	357	100%	99%	99%
Appropriate Beta Blocker Usage	84	93%	92%	93%
Controlled Postoperative Blood Glucose	0	-	92%	93%
Prophylactic Antibiotic Timing	227	97%	97%	97%
Prophylactic Antibiotic Timing (Outpatient)[1]	19	63%	93%	92%
Prophylactic Antibiotic Selection	229	96%	97%	97%
Prophylactic Antibiotic Select. (Outpatient)[1]	18	94%	94%	94%
Prophylactic Antibiotic Stopped	219	95%	94%	94%
Recommended VTP Ordered	153	97%	94%	94%
Urinary Catheter Removal	98	98%	89%	90%
Children's Asthma Care				
Received Systemic Corticosteroids	-	-	-	100%
Received Home Management Plan	-	-	-	71%
Received Reliever Medication	-	-	-	100%
Use of Medical Imaging				
Combination Abdominal CT Scan	682	0.094	0.246	0.191
Combination Chest CT Scan	532	0.008	0.098	0.054
Follow-up Mammogram/Ultrasound	739	15.7%	8.4%	8.4%
MRI for Low Back Pain	118	24.6%	33.4%	32.7%
Survey of Patients' Hospital Experiences				
Area Around Room 'Always' Quiet at Night	300+	50%	-	58%
Doctors 'Always' Communicated Well	300+	81%	-	80%
Home Recovery Information Given	300+	84%	-	82%
Hospital Given 9 or 10 on 10 Point Scale	300+	68%	-	67%
Meds 'Always' Explained Before Given	300+	59%	-	60%
Nurses 'Always' Communicated Well	300+	77%	-	76%
Pain 'Always' Well Controlled	300+	70%	-	69%
Room and Bathroom 'Always' Clean	300+	72%	-	71%
Timely Help 'Always' Received	300+	70%	-	64%
Would Definitely Recommend Hospital	300+	65%	-	69%

Methodist Medical Center of Illinois

221 N E Glen Oak Ave Phone: 309-672-5522
Peoria, IL 61636 Fax: 309-671-8303
URL: www.mmci.org
Type: Acute Care Hospitals Emergency Services: Yes
Ownership: Voluntary Non-Profit - Other Beds: 330

Key Personnel:
CEO/President. . . . . W Michael Bryant
Cardiac Laboratory. . . . . Jeanine Spain, RN
Chief of Medical Staff . . . . Thomas Mulvey MD
Infection Control. . . . . Linda Barton
Operating Room. . . . . Jeanine Spain
Quality Assurance . . . . Sandy Pryor
Radiology. . . . . Mike Namanny, DO
Patient Relations . . . . Shelley Wilkes

Measure	Cases	This Hosp.	State Avg.	U.S. Avg.
Heart Attack Care				
ACE Inhibitor or ARB for LVSD	41	98%	96%	96%
Aspirin at Arrival	116	99%	99%	99%
Aspirin at Discharge	211	100%	99%	98%
Beta Blocker at Discharge	212	100%	98%	98%
Fibrinolytic Medication Timing	0	-	50%	55%
PCI Within 90 Minutes of Arrival	27	93%	90%	90%
Smoking Cessation Advice	97	100%	100%	99%
Chest Pain/Possible Heart Attack Care				
Aspirin at Arrival[5]	0	-	95%	95%
Median Time to ECG (minutes)[5]	0	-	8	8
Median Time to Transfer (minutes)[5]	0	-	57	61
Fibrinolytic Medication Timing[5]	0	-	33%	54%
Heart Failure Care				
ACE Inhibitor or ARB for LVSD	106	100%	94%	94%
Discharge Instructions	238	93%	89%	88%
Evaluation of LVS Function	310	100%	98%	98%
Smoking Cessation Advice	69	100%	99%	98%
Pneumonia Care				
Appropriate Initial Antibiotic	149	97%	90%	92%
Blood Culture Timing	194	99%	97%	96%
Influenza Vaccine	182	98%	91%	91%
Initial Antibiotic Timing	224	100%	96%	95%
Pneumococcal Vaccine	257	98%	92%	93%
Smoking Cessation Advice	106	100%	98%	97%
Surgical Care Improvement Project				
Appropriate VTP Within 24 Hours[2]	184	92%	92%	92%
Appropriate Hair Removal[2]	906	100%	99%	99%
Appropriate Beta Blocker Usage[2]	289	95%	92%	93%
Controlled Postoperative Blood Glucose[2]	135	96%	92%	93%
Prophylactic Antibiotic Timing[2]	715	99%	97%	97%
Prophylactic Antibiotic Timing (Outpatient)	337	95%	93%	92%
Prophylactic Antibiotic Selection[2]	728	99%	97%	97%
Prophylactic Antibiotic Select. (Outpatient)	329	93%	94%	94%
Prophylactic Antibiotic Stopped[2]	679	97%	94%	94%
Recommended VTP Ordered[2]	184	95%	94%	94%
Urinary Catheter Removal[2]	233	96%	89%	90%
Children's Asthma Care				
Received Systemic Corticosteroids	-	-	-	100%
Received Home Management Plan	-	-	-	71%
Received Reliever Medication	-	-	-	100%
Use of Medical Imaging				
Combination Abdominal CT Scan	1,116	0.224	0.246	0.191
Combination Chest CT Scan	881	0.036	0.098	0.054
Follow-up Mammogram/Ultrasound	2,032	12.0%	8.4%	8.4%
MRI for Low Back Pain	310	31.3%	33.4%	32.7%
Survey of Patients' Hospital Experiences				
Area Around Room 'Always' Quiet at Night	300+	60%	-	58%
Doctors 'Always' Communicated Well	300+	80%	-	80%
Home Recovery Information Given	300+	86%	-	82%
Hospital Given 9 or 10 on 10 Point Scale	300+	77%	-	67%
Meds 'Always' Explained Before Given	300+	65%	-	60%
Nurses 'Always' Communicated Well	300+	83%	-	76%
Pain 'Always' Well Controlled	300+	75%	-	69%
Room and Bathroom 'Always' Clean	300+	78%	-	71%
Timely Help 'Always' Received	300+	68%	-	64%
Would Definitely Recommend Hospital	300+	81%	-	69%

NOTE: Hospital profiles are in alphabetical order by state, then city, then hospital within the city; Rankings exclude hospitals with less than 25 cases except for patient surveys which excludes hospitals with less than 100 cases; (a) 100–299 cases; (1) The number of cases is too small to be sure how well a hospital is performing; (2) The hospital indicated that the data submitted for this measure were based on a sample of cases; (3) Data was collected during a shorter time period (fewer quarters) than the maximum possible time for this measure; (4) Suppressed for one or more quarters by CMS; (5) No data is available from the hospital for this measure; (6) Fewer than 100 patients completed the HCAHPS survey. Use these rates with caution, as the number of surveys may be too low to reliably assess hospital performance; (7) Survey results are based on less than 12 months of data; (8) Survey results are not available for this reporting period; (9) No or very few patients were eligible for the HCAHPS survey. The scores shown, if any, reflect a very small number of surveys; (10) A state average was not calculated because too few hospitals in the state submitted data; (11) There were discrepancies in the data collection process; Please refer to the User's Guide for a full explanation of data.

Proctor Hospital

5409 N Knoxville Ave
Peoria, IL 61614
Phone: 309-691-1000
Fax: 309-689-6062
E-mail: information@proctor.org
URL: www.proctor.org
Type: Acute Care Hospitals
Emergency Services: Yes
Ownership: Voluntary Non-Profit - Private
Beds: 175

Key Personnel:
CEO/President. . . . . Norman H LaConte
Quality Assurance . . . . Angie Moore, MS

Measure	Cases	This Hosp.	State Avg.	U.S. Avg.
Heart Attack Care				
ACE Inhibitor or ARB for LVSD[1]	11	100%	96%	96%
Aspirin at Arrival	66	100%	99%	99%
Aspirin at Discharge	67	100%	99%	98%
Beta Blocker at Discharge	68	100%	98%	98%
Fibrinolytic Medication Timing	0	-	50%	55%
PCI Within 90 Minutes of Arrival[1]	19	95%	90%	90%
Smoking Cessation Advice[1]	20	100%	100%	99%
Chest Pain/Possible Heart Attack Care				
Aspirin at Arrival[5]	0	-	95%	95%
Median Time to ECG (minutes)[5]	0	-	8	8
Median Time to Transfer (minutes)[5]	0	-	57	61
Fibrinolytic Medication Timing[5]	0	-	33%	54%
Heart Failure Care				
ACE Inhibitor or ARB for LVSD	40	100%	94%	94%
Discharge Instructions	95	92%	89%	88%
Evaluation of LVS Function	145	100%	98%	98%
Smoking Cessation Advice[1]	9	100%	99%	98%
Pneumonia Care				
Appropriate Initial Antibiotic[2]	106	100%	90%	92%
Blood Culture Timing[2]	200	99%	97%	96%
Influenza Vaccine[2]	125	98%	91%	91%
Initial Antibiotic Timing[2]	184	99%	96%	95%
Pneumococcal Vaccine[2]	195	97%	92%	93%
Smoking Cessation Advice[2]	40	95%	98%	97%
Surgical Care Improvement Project				
Appropriate VTP Within 24 Hours[2]	140	92%	92%	92%
Appropriate Hair Removal[2]	793	100%	99%	99%
Appropriate Beta Blocker Usage[2]	270	91%	92%	93%
Controlled Postoperative Blood Glucose[2]	66	94%	92%	93%
Prophylactic Antibiotic Timing[2]	630	99%	97%	97%
Prophylactic Antibiotic Timing (Outpatient)	123	91%	93%	92%
Prophylactic Antibiotic Selection[2]	634	99%	97%	97%
Prophylactic Antibiotic Select. (Outpatient)	117	88%	94%	94%
Prophylactic Antibiotic Stopped[2]	623	94%	94%	94%
Recommended VTP Ordered[2]	140	96%	94%	94%
Urinary Catheter Removal[2]	291	96%	89%	90%
Children's Asthma Care				
Received Systemic Corticosteroids	-	-	-	100%
Received Home Management Plan	-	-	-	71%
Received Reliever Medication	-	-	-	100%
Use of Medical Imaging				
Combination Abdominal CT Scan	425	0.675	0.246	0.191
Combination Chest CT Scan	278	0.532	0.098	0.054
Follow-up Mammogram/Ultrasound	440	8.9%	8.4%	8.4%
MRI for Low Back Pain	95	34.7%	33.4%	32.7%
Survey of Patients' Hospital Experiences				
Area Around Room 'Always' Quiet at Night	300+	56%	-	58%
Doctors 'Always' Communicated Well	300+	79%	-	80%
Home Recovery Information Given	300+	87%	-	82%
Hospital Given 9 or 10 on 10 Point Scale	300+	73%	-	67%
Meds 'Always' Explained Before Given	300+	54%	-	60%
Nurses 'Always' Communicated Well	300+	73%	-	76%
Pain 'Always' Well Controlled	300+	69%	-	69%
Room and Bathroom 'Always' Clean	300+	69%	-	71%
Timely Help 'Always' Received	300+	59%	-	64%
Would Definitely Recommend Hospital	300+	78%	-	69%

Saint Francis Medical Center

530 NE Glen Oak Ave
Peoria, IL 61637
Phone: 309-655-2000
Fax: 309-671-8996
URL: www.osfsaintfrancis.org
Type: Acute Care Hospitals
Emergency Services: Yes
Ownership: Voluntary Non-Profit - Church
Beds: 731

Key Personnel:
Cardiac Laboratory. . . . . Delmar Smith
Chief of Medical Staff. . . . . Tim Miller, MD
Infection Control. . . . . Patricia Ham
Operating Room. . . . . Judy Winkler, MD
Pediatric Ambulatory Care . . . . . . Kay Saving, MD
Quality Assurance . . . . Gail Strunk
Radiology. . . . . Gary Zwicky, MD

Measure	Cases	This Hosp.	State Avg.	U.S. Avg.
Heart Attack Care				
ACE Inhibitor or ARB for LVSD	77	99%	96%	96%
Aspirin at Arrival	217	99%	99%	99%
Aspirin at Discharge	547	100%	99%	98%
Beta Blocker at Discharge	541	99%	98%	98%
Fibrinolytic Medication Timing	0	-	50%	55%
PCI Within 90 Minutes of Arrival	50	98%	90%	90%
Smoking Cessation Advice	209	100%	100%	99%
Chest Pain/Possible Heart Attack Care				
Aspirin at Arrival[1,3]	1	0%	95%	95%
Median Time to ECG (minutes)[1,3]	1	17	8	8
Median Time to Transfer (minutes)[5]	0	-	57	61
Fibrinolytic Medication Timing[5]	0	-	33%	54%
Heart Failure Care				
ACE Inhibitor or ARB for LVSD	183	97%	94%	94%
Discharge Instructions	385	85%	89%	88%
Evaluation of LVS Function	492	100%	98%	98%
Smoking Cessation Advice	108	100%	99%	98%
Pneumonia Care				
Appropriate Initial Antibiotic	217	96%	90%	92%
Blood Culture Timing	310	92%	97%	96%
Influenza Vaccine	288	92%	91%	91%
Initial Antibiotic Timing	386	96%	96%	95%
Pneumococcal Vaccine	380	91%	92%	93%
Smoking Cessation Advice	203	100%	98%	97%
Surgical Care Improvement Project				
Appropriate VTP Within 24 Hours[2]	436	93%	92%	92%
Appropriate Hair Removal[2]	1,769	100%	99%	99%
Appropriate Beta Blocker Usage[2]	622	78%	92%	93%
Controlled Postoperative Blood Glucose[2]	351	84%	92%	93%
Prophylactic Antibiotic Timing[2]	1,417	97%	97%	97%
Prophylactic Antibiotic Timing (Outpatient)	320	92%	93%	92%
Prophylactic Antibiotic Selection[2]	1,430	98%	97%	97%
Prophylactic Antibiotic Select. (Outpatient)	315	90%	94%	94%
Prophylactic Antibiotic Stopped[2]	1,372	92%	94%	94%
Recommended VTP Ordered[2]	436	96%	94%	94%
Urinary Catheter Removal[2]	439	86%	89%	90%
Children's Asthma Care				
Received Systemic Corticosteroids	-	-	-	100%
Received Home Management Plan	-	-	-	71%
Received Reliever Medication	-	-	-	100%
Use of Medical Imaging				
Combination Abdominal CT Scan	1,625	0.142	0.246	0.191
Combination Chest CT Scan	1,262	0.027	0.098	0.054
Follow-up Mammogram/Ultrasound	4,488	8.7%	8.4%	8.4%
MRI for Low Back Pain	350	34.0%	33.4%	32.7%
Survey of Patients' Hospital Experiences				
Area Around Room 'Always' Quiet at Night	300+	49%	-	58%
Doctors 'Always' Communicated Well	300+	78%	-	80%
Home Recovery Information Given	300+	83%	-	82%
Hospital Given 9 or 10 on 10 Point Scale	300+	68%	-	67%
Meds 'Always' Explained Before Given	300+	59%	-	60%
Nurses 'Always' Communicated Well	300+	77%	-	76%
Pain 'Always' Well Controlled	300+	69%	-	69%
Room and Bathroom 'Always' Clean	300+	72%	-	71%
Timely Help 'Always' Received	300+	57%	-	64%
Would Definitely Recommend Hospital	300+	71%	-	69%

Illinois Valley Community Hospital

925 West St
Peru, IL 61354
Phone: 815-223-3300
Fax: 815-223-3394
E-mail: prelate@ivch.org
URL: www.ivch.org
Type: Acute Care Hospitals
Emergency Services: Yes
Ownership: Voluntary Non-Profit - Other
Beds: 172

Key Personnel:
Chief of Medical Staff. . . . . Mario Cote, MD
Infection Control. . . . . Deb Patyk
Operating Room. . . . . Elizabeth Soeder
Quality Assurance . . . . Carol Myer
Radiology. . . . . Steven Coventry, MD
Anesthesiology. . . . . Deofil Orteza, MD
Emergency Room . . . . Greg Guard, MD

Measure	Cases	This Hosp.	State Avg.	U.S. Avg.
Heart Attack Care				
ACE Inhibitor or ARB for LVSD[1,2]	2	100%	96%	96%
Aspirin at Arrival[1,2]	7	100%	99%	99%
Aspirin at Discharge[1,2]	5	100%	99%	98%
Beta Blocker at Discharge[1,2]	6	100%	98%	98%
Fibrinolytic Medication Timing[1,2]	1	0%	50%	55%
PCI Within 90 Minutes of Arrival[2]	0	-	90%	90%
Smoking Cessation Advice[2]	0	-	100%	99%
Chest Pain/Possible Heart Attack Care				
Aspirin at Arrival	52	100%	95%	95%
Median Time to ECG (minutes)	55	4	8	8
Median Time to Transfer (minutes)[1]	7	60	57	61
Fibrinolytic Medication Timing[1]	2	50%	33%	54%
Heart Failure Care				
ACE Inhibitor or ARB for LVSD[1]	22	100%	94%	94%
Discharge Instructions	61	79%	89%	88%
Evaluation of LVS Function	82	94%	98%	98%
Smoking Cessation Advice[1]	11	100%	99%	98%
Pneumonia Care				
Appropriate Initial Antibiotic	67	79%	90%	92%
Blood Culture Timing	82	93%	97%	96%
Influenza Vaccine	67	93%	91%	91%
Initial Antibiotic Timing	95	95%	96%	95%
Pneumococcal Vaccine	108	93%	92%	93%
Smoking Cessation Advice[1]	19	100%	98%	97%
Surgical Care Improvement Project				
Appropriate VTP Within 24 Hours	71	97%	92%	92%
Appropriate Hair Removal	248	100%	99%	99%
Appropriate Beta Blocker Usage	81	100%	92%	93%
Controlled Postoperative Blood Glucose	0	-	92%	93%
Prophylactic Antibiotic Timing	200	96%	97%	97%
Prophylactic Antibiotic Timing (Outpatient)	136	89%	93%	92%
Prophylactic Antibiotic Selection	200	100%	97%	97%
Prophylactic Antibiotic Select. (Outpatient)	132	93%	94%	94%
Prophylactic Antibiotic Stopped	200	92%	94%	94%
Recommended VTP Ordered	72	96%	94%	94%
Urinary Catheter Removal	96	100%	89%	90%
Children's Asthma Care				
Received Systemic Corticosteroids	-	-	-	100%
Received Home Management Plan	-	-	-	71%
Received Reliever Medication	-	-	-	100%
Use of Medical Imaging				
Combination Abdominal CT Scan	405	0.126	0.246	0.191
Combination Chest CT Scan	285	0.011	0.098	0.054
Follow-up Mammogram/Ultrasound	746	5.9%	8.4%	8.4%
MRI for Low Back Pain	179	31.8%	33.4%	32.7%
Survey of Patients' Hospital Experiences				
Area Around Room 'Always' Quiet at Night	300+	58%	-	58%
Doctors 'Always' Communicated Well	300+	88%	-	80%
Home Recovery Information Given	300+	88%	-	82%
Hospital Given 9 or 10 on 10 Point Scale	300+	75%	-	67%
Meds 'Always' Explained Before Given	300+	72%	-	60%
Nurses 'Always' Communicated Well	300+	86%	-	76%
Pain 'Always' Well Controlled	300+	76%	-	69%
Room and Bathroom 'Always' Clean	300+	83%	-	71%
Timely Help 'Always' Received	300+	79%	-	64%
Would Definitely Recommend Hospital	300+	77%	-	69%

NOTE: Hospital profiles are in alphabetical order by state, then city, then hospital within the city; Rankings exclude hospitals with less than 25 cases except for patient surveys which excludes hospitals with less than 100 cases; (a) 100–299 cases; (1) The number of cases is too small to be sure how well a hospital is performing; (2) The hospital indicated that the data submitted for this measure were based on a sample of cases; (3) Data was collected during a shorter time period (fewer quarters) than the maximum possible time for this measure; (4) Suppressed for one or more quarters by CMS; (5) No data is available from the hospital for this measure; (6) Fewer than 100 patients completed the HCAHPS survey. Use these rates with caution, as the number of surveys may be too low to reliably assess hospital performance; (7) Survey results are based on less than 12 months of data; (8) Survey results are not available for this reporting period; (9) No or very few patients were eligible for the HCAHPS survey. The scores shown, if any, reflect a very small number of surveys; (10) A state average was not calculated because too few hospitals in the state submitted data; (11) There were discrepancies in the data collection process; Please refer to the User's Guide for a full explanation of data.

Pinckneyville Community Hospital

101 N Walnut
Pinckneyville, IL 62274
Type: Critical Access Hospitals
Ownership: Govt - Hospital Dist/Auth
Phone: 618-357-2187
Fax: 618-357-6740
Emergency Services: Yes
Beds: 85

Key Personnel:
Chief of Medical Staff . . . . Craig Fovard

Measure	Cases	This Hosp.	State Avg.	U.S. Avg.
Heart Attack Care				
ACE Inhibitor or ARB for LVSD[3]	0	-	96%	96%
Aspirin at Arrival[3]	0	-	99%	99%
Aspirin at Discharge[3]	0	-	99%	98%
Beta Blocker at Discharge[3]	0	-	98%	98%
Fibrinolytic Medication Timing[3]	0	-	50%	55%
PCI Within 90 Minutes of Arrival[3]	0	-	90%	90%
Smoking Cessation Advice[3]	0	-	100%	99%
Chest Pain/Possible Heart Attack Care				
Aspirin at Arrival	-	-	95%	95%
Median Time to ECG (minutes)	-	-	8	8
Median Time to Transfer (minutes)	-	-	57	61
Fibrinolytic Medication Timing	-	-	33%	54%
Heart Failure Care				
ACE Inhibitor or ARB for LVSD[1,3]	7	86%	94%	94%
Discharge Instructions[1,3]	8	100%	89%	88%
Evaluation of LVS Function[1,3]	15	93%	98%	98%
Smoking Cessation Advice[1,3]	1	100%	99%	98%
Pneumonia Care				
Appropriate Initial Antibiotic[1]	12	100%	90%	92%
Blood Culture Timing[1]	13	92%	97%	96%
Influenza Vaccine[1]	6	100%	91%	91%
Initial Antibiotic Timing[1]	9	100%	96%	95%
Pneumococcal Vaccine[1]	11	91%	92%	93%
Smoking Cessation Advice[1]	4	100%	98%	97%
Surgical Care Improvement Project				
Appropriate VTP Within 24 Hours[1,3]	1	100%	92%	92%
Appropriate Hair Removal[1,3]	1	100%	99%	99%
Appropriate Beta Blocker Usage[5]	0	-	92%	93%
Controlled Postoperative Blood Glucose[3]	0	-	92%	93%
Prophylactic Antibiotic Timing[3]	0	-	97%	97%
Prophylactic Antibiotic Timing (Outpatient)	-	-	93%	92%
Prophylactic Antibiotic Selection[3]	0	-	97%	97%
Prophylactic Antibiotic Select. (Outpatient)	-	-	94%	94%
Prophylactic Antibiotic Stopped[3]	0	-	94%	94%
Recommended VTP Ordered[1,3]	1	100%	94%	94%
Urinary Catheter Removal[5]	0	-	89%	90%
Children's Asthma Care				
Received Systemic Corticosteroids	-	-	-	100%
Received Home Management Plan	-	-	-	71%
Received Reliever Medication	-	-	-	100%
Use of Medical Imaging				
Combination Abdominal CT Scan	-	-	0.246	0.191
Combination Chest CT Scan	-	-	0.098	0.054
Follow-up Mammogram/Ultrasound	-	-	8.4%	8.4%
MRI for Low Back Pain	-	-	33.4%	32.7%
Survey of Patients' Hospital Experiences				
Area Around Room 'Always' Quiet at Night	(a)	65%	-	58%
Doctors 'Always' Communicated Well	(a)	88%	-	80%
Home Recovery Information Given	(a)	95%	-	82%
Hospital Given 9 or 10 on 10 Point Scale	(a)	66%	-	67%
Meds 'Always' Explained Before Given	(a)	66%	-	60%
Nurses 'Always' Communicated Well	(a)	82%	-	76%
Pain 'Always' Well Controlled	(a)	81%	-	69%
Room and Bathroom 'Always' Clean	(a)	78%	-	71%
Timely Help 'Always' Received	(a)	78%	-	64%
Would Definitely Recommend Hospital	(a)	61%	-	69%

Illini Community Hospital

640 W Washington
Pittsfield, IL 62363
Type: Critical Access Hospitals
Ownership: Voluntary Non-Profit - Private
Phone: 217-285-2113
Fax: 217-285-5090
Emergency Services: Yes
Beds: 37

Measure	Cases	This Hosp.	State Avg.	U.S. Avg.
Heart Attack Care				
ACE Inhibitor or ARB for LVSD[3]	0	-	96%	96%
Aspirin at Arrival[3]	0	-	99%	99%
Aspirin at Discharge[3]	0	-	99%	98%
Beta Blocker at Discharge[3]	0	-	98%	98%
Fibrinolytic Medication Timing[3]	0	-	50%	55%
PCI Within 90 Minutes of Arrival[5]	0	-	90%	90%
Smoking Cessation Advice[3]	0	-	100%	99%
Chest Pain/Possible Heart Attack Care				
Aspirin at Arrival[5]	0	-	95%	95%
Median Time to ECG (minutes)[5]	0	-	8	8
Median Time to Transfer (minutes)[5]	0	-	57	61
Fibrinolytic Medication Timing[5]	0	-	33%	54%
Heart Failure Care				
ACE Inhibitor or ARB for LVSD[1,2,3]	6	83%	94%	94%
Discharge Instructions[1,2,3]	10	70%	89%	88%
Evaluation of LVS Function[1,2,3]	24	88%	98%	98%
Smoking Cessation Advice[1,2,3]	3	100%	99%	98%
Pneumonia Care				
Appropriate Initial Antibiotic[1]	19	95%	90%	92%
Blood Culture Timing[1]	19	95%	97%	96%
Influenza Vaccine[1]	14	100%	91%	91%
Initial Antibiotic Timing	33	97%	96%	95%
Pneumococcal Vaccine	28	96%	92%	93%
Smoking Cessation Advice[1]	8	100%	98%	97%
Surgical Care Improvement Project				
Appropriate VTP Within 24 Hours[1,3]	3	0%	92%	92%
Appropriate Hair Removal[1,3]	7	86%	99%	99%
Appropriate Beta Blocker Usage[5]	0	-	92%	93%
Controlled Postoperative Blood Glucose[5]	0	-	92%	93%
Prophylactic Antibiotic Timing[3]	0	-	97%	97%
Prophylactic Antibiotic Timing (Outpatient)[5]	0	-	93%	92%
Prophylactic Antibiotic Selection[3]	0	-	97%	97%
Prophylactic Antibiotic Select. (Outpatient)[5]	0	-	94%	94%
Prophylactic Antibiotic Stopped[3]	0	-	94%	94%
Recommended VTP Ordered[1,3]	3	0%	94%	94%
Urinary Catheter Removal[3]	0	-	89%	90%
Children's Asthma Care				
Received Systemic Corticosteroids	-	-	-	100%
Received Home Management Plan	-	-	-	71%
Received Reliever Medication	-	-	-	100%
Use of Medical Imaging				
Combination Abdominal CT Scan	188	0.080	0.246	0.191
Combination Chest CT Scan	153	0.013	0.098	0.054
Follow-up Mammogram/Ultrasound	330	6.7%	8.4%	8.4%
MRI for Low Back Pain[1]	25	32.0%	33.4%	32.7%
Survey of Patients' Hospital Experiences				
Area Around Room 'Always' Quiet at Night	(a)	64%	-	58%
Doctors 'Always' Communicated Well	(a)	85%	-	80%
Home Recovery Information Given	(a)	87%	-	82%
Hospital Given 9 or 10 on 10 Point Scale	(a)	77%	-	67%
Meds 'Always' Explained Before Given	(a)	69%	-	60%
Nurses 'Always' Communicated Well	(a)	85%	-	76%
Pain 'Always' Well Controlled	(a)	76%	-	69%
Room and Bathroom 'Always' Clean	(a)	84%	-	71%
Timely Help 'Always' Received	(a)	79%	-	64%
Would Definitely Recommend Hospital	(a)	69%	-	69%

Saint James Hospital

2500 West Reynolds Street
Pontiac, IL 61764
Type: Acute Care Hospitals
Ownership: Voluntary Non-Profit - Church
Phone: 815-842-2828
Fax: 815-842-4912
Emergency Services: Yes
Beds: 89

Key Personnel:
Operating Room. . . . . Rajendra Shrivastav
Emergency Room . . . . Nan Marx

Measure	Cases	This Hosp.	State Avg.	U.S. Avg.
Heart Attack Care				
ACE Inhibitor or ARB for LVSD[3]	0	-	96%	96%
Aspirin at Arrival[1,3]	3	100%	99%	99%
Aspirin at Discharge[1,3]	2	100%	99%	98%
Beta Blocker at Discharge[1,3]	1	100%	98%	98%
Fibrinolytic Medication Timing[3]	0	-	50%	55%
PCI Within 90 Minutes of Arrival[3]	0	-	90%	90%
Smoking Cessation Advice[3]	0	-	100%	99%
Chest Pain/Possible Heart Attack Care				
Aspirin at Arrival	99	95%	95%	95%
Median Time to ECG (minutes)	105	8	8	8
Median Time to Transfer (minutes)[1]	8	54	57	61
Fibrinolytic Medication Timing[1]	2	0%	33%	54%
Heart Failure Care				
ACE Inhibitor or ARB for LVSD[1]	14	100%	94%	94%
Discharge Instructions	25	100%	89%	88%
Evaluation of LVS Function	35	100%	98%	98%
Smoking Cessation Advice[1]	4	100%	99%	98%
Pneumonia Care				
Appropriate Initial Antibiotic	48	92%	90%	92%
Blood Culture Timing	61	95%	97%	96%
Influenza Vaccine	47	98%	91%	91%
Initial Antibiotic Timing	61	95%	96%	95%
Pneumococcal Vaccine	54	100%	92%	93%
Smoking Cessation Advice	30	100%	98%	97%
Surgical Care Improvement Project				
Appropriate VTP Within 24 Hours	55	87%	92%	92%
Appropriate Hair Removal	154	100%	99%	99%
Appropriate Beta Blocker Usage	51	86%	92%	93%
Controlled Postoperative Blood Glucose	0	-	92%	93%
Prophylactic Antibiotic Timing	105	98%	97%	97%
Prophylactic Antibiotic Timing (Outpatient)[1]	24	100%	93%	92%
Prophylactic Antibiotic Selection	108	99%	97%	97%
Prophylactic Antibiotic Select. (Outpatient)[1]	24	100%	94%	94%
Prophylactic Antibiotic Stopped	95	97%	94%	94%
Recommended VTP Ordered	55	89%	94%	94%
Urinary Catheter Removal	47	100%	89%	90%
Children's Asthma Care				
Received Systemic Corticosteroids	-	-	-	100%
Received Home Management Plan	-	-	-	71%
Received Reliever Medication	-	-	-	100%
Use of Medical Imaging				
Combination Abdominal CT Scan	416	0.072	0.246	0.191
Combination Chest CT Scan	279	0.039	0.098	0.054
Follow-up Mammogram/Ultrasound	783	10.2%	8.4%	8.4%
MRI for Low Back Pain	101	29.7%	33.4%	32.7%
Survey of Patients' Hospital Experiences				
Area Around Room 'Always' Quiet at Night	300+	53%	-	58%
Doctors 'Always' Communicated Well	300+	84%	-	80%
Home Recovery Information Given	300+	90%	-	82%
Hospital Given 9 or 10 on 10 Point Scale	300+	70%	-	67%
Meds 'Always' Explained Before Given	300+	63%	-	60%
Nurses 'Always' Communicated Well	300+	80%	-	76%
Pain 'Always' Well Controlled	300+	73%	-	69%
Room and Bathroom 'Always' Clean	300+	79%	-	71%
Timely Help 'Always' Received	300+	76%	-	64%
Would Definitely Recommend Hospital	300+	71%	-	69%

NOTE: Hospital profiles are in alphabetical order by state, then city, then hospital within the city; Rankings exclude hospitals with less than 25 cases except for patient surveys which excludes hospitals with less than 100 cases; (a) 100–299 cases; (1) The number of cases is too small to be sure how well a hospital is performing; (2) The hospital indicated that the data submitted for this measure were based on a sample of cases; (3) Data was collected during a shorter time period (fewer quarters) than the maximum possible time for this measure; (4) Suppressed for one or more quarters by CMS; (5) No data is available from the hospital for this measure; (6) Fewer than 100 patients completed the HCAHPS survey. Use these rates with caution, as the number of surveys may be too low to reliably assess hospital performance; (7) Survey results are based on less than 12 months of data; (8) Survey results are not available for this reporting period; (9) No or very few patients were eligible for the HCAHPS survey. The scores shown, if any, reflect a very small number of surveys; (10) A state average was not calculated because too few hospitals in the state submitted data; (11) There were discrepancies in the data collection process; Please refer to the User's Guide for a full explanation of data.

Perry Memorial Hospital

530 Park Avenue East
Princeton, IL 61356
URL: www.perry-memorial.org
Type: Critical Access Hospitals
Ownership: Government - Local
Phone: 815-875-2811
Fax: 815-872-6006
Emergency Services: Yes
Beds: 98

Key Personnel:
CEO/President. . . . . Robert Senneff
Chief of Medical Staff . . . . E Doran, MD
Quality Assurance . . . . Denise Jackson
Emergency Room . . . . Dr. Earel Belford
Patient Relations . . . . Jeanine Dressler

Measure	Cases	This Hosp.	State Avg.	U.S. Avg.
Heart Attack Care				
ACE Inhibitor or ARB for LVSD[1]	2	100%	96%	96%
Aspirin at Arrival[1]	3	67%	99%	99%
Aspirin at Discharge[1]	4	75%	99%	98%
Beta Blocker at Discharge[1]	5	80%	98%	98%
Fibrinolytic Medication Timing	0	-	50%	55%
PCI Within 90 Minutes of Arrival	0	-	90%	90%
Smoking Cessation Advice	0	-	100%	99%
Chest Pain/Possible Heart Attack Care				
Aspirin at Arrival	-	-	95%	95%
Median Time to ECG (minutes)	-	-	8	8
Median Time to Transfer (minutes)	-	-	57	61
Fibrinolytic Medication Timing	-	-	33%	54%
Heart Failure Care				
ACE Inhibitor or ARB for LVSD[1]	9	78%	94%	94%
Discharge Instructions	44	98%	89%	88%
Evaluation of LVS Function	59	81%	98%	98%
Smoking Cessation Advice[1]	5	40%	99%	98%
Pneumonia Care				
Appropriate Initial Antibiotic	40	85%	90%	92%
Blood Culture Timing	52	94%	97%	96%
Influenza Vaccine	47	72%	91%	91%
Initial Antibiotic Timing	74	96%	96%	95%
Pneumococcal Vaccine	66	67%	92%	93%
Smoking Cessation Advice[1]	18	83%	98%	97%
Surgical Care Improvement Project				
Appropriate VTP Within 24 Hours	33	73%	92%	92%
Appropriate Hair Removal	49	78%	99%	99%
Appropriate Beta Blocker Usage[1]	8	62%	92%	93%
Controlled Postoperative Blood Glucose	0	-	92%	93%
Prophylactic Antibiotic Timing[1]	20	90%	97%	97%
Prophylactic Antibiotic Timing (Outpatient)	-	-	93%	92%
Prophylactic Antibiotic Selection[1]	20	95%	97%	97%
Prophylactic Antibiotic Select. (Outpatient)	-	-	94%	94%
Prophylactic Antibiotic Stopped[1]	19	89%	94%	94%
Recommended VTP Ordered	33	73%	94%	94%
Urinary Catheter Removal[1]	4	100%	89%	90%
Children's Asthma Care				
Received Systemic Corticosteroids	-	-	-	100%
Received Home Management Plan	-	-	-	71%
Received Reliever Medication	-	-	-	100%
Use of Medical Imaging				
Combination Abdominal CT Scan	-	-	0.246	0.191
Combination Chest CT Scan	-	-	0.098	0.054
Follow-up Mammogram/Ultrasound	-	-	8.4%	8.4%
MRI for Low Back Pain	-	-	33.4%	32.7%
Survey of Patients' Hospital Experiences				
Area Around Room 'Always' Quiet at Night[8]	-	-	-	58%
Doctors 'Always' Communicated Well[8]	-	-	-	80%
Home Recovery Information Given[8]	-	-	-	82%
Hospital Given 9 or 10 on 10 Point Scale[8]	-	-	-	67%
Meds 'Always' Explained Before Given[8]	-	-	-	60%
Nurses 'Always' Communicated Well[8]	-	-	-	76%
Pain 'Always' Well Controlled[8]	-	-	-	69%
Room and Bathroom 'Always' Clean[8]	-	-	-	71%
Timely Help 'Always' Received[8]	-	-	-	64%
Would Definitely Recommend Hospital[8]	-	-	-	69%

Blessing Hospital

Broadway at 11th Street
Quincy, IL 62301
E-mail: sfelde@blessinghospital.com
URL: www.blessinghealthsystem.org
Type: Acute Care Hospitals
Ownership: Voluntary Non-Profit - Private
Phone: 217-223-5811
Fax: 217-223-1200
Emergency Services: Yes
Beds: 426

Key Personnel:
CEO/President. . . . . Maureen A Kahn
Cardiac Laboratory. . . . . James Kase
Chief of Medical Staff . . . . Steve Sanders, DO
Infection Control. . . . . Carleen Orton, RN
Operating Room. . . . . William Birsic, RN
Pediatric In-Patient Care . . . . Joan Hynek, RN
Quality Assurance . . . . Tena Jones
Radiology. . . . . Bonnie Kleissle

Measure	Cases	This Hosp.	State Avg.	U.S. Avg.
Heart Attack Care				
ACE Inhibitor or ARB for LVSD	30	97%	96%	96%
Aspirin at Arrival	212	100%	99%	99%
Aspirin at Discharge	247	100%	99%	98%
Beta Blocker at Discharge	236	96%	98%	98%
Fibrinolytic Medication Timing	0	-	50%	55%
PCI Within 90 Minutes of Arrival	32	97%	90%	90%
Smoking Cessation Advice	82	100%	100%	99%
Chest Pain/Possible Heart Attack Care				
Aspirin at Arrival[1,3]	5	100%	95%	95%
Median Time to ECG (minutes)[1,3]	6	8	8	8
Median Time to Transfer (minutes)[5]	0	-	57	61
Fibrinolytic Medication Timing[3]	0	-	33%	54%
Heart Failure Care				
ACE Inhibitor or ARB for LVSD	89	84%	94%	94%
Discharge Instructions	223	93%	89%	88%
Evaluation of LVS Function	351	99%	98%	98%
Smoking Cessation Advice	49	100%	99%	98%
Pneumonia Care				
Appropriate Initial Antibiotic	234	94%	90%	92%
Blood Culture Timing	438	99%	97%	96%
Influenza Vaccine	291	95%	91%	91%
Initial Antibiotic Timing	436	99%	96%	95%
Pneumococcal Vaccine	405	96%	92%	93%
Smoking Cessation Advice	160	100%	98%	97%
Surgical Care Improvement Project				
Appropriate VTP Within 24 Hours	245	95%	92%	92%
Appropriate Hair Removal	663	100%	99%	99%
Appropriate Beta Blocker Usage	208	88%	92%	93%
Controlled Postoperative Blood Glucose	85	95%	92%	93%
Prophylactic Antibiotic Timing	405	97%	97%	97%
Prophylactic Antibiotic Timing (Outpatient)	271	88%	93%	92%
Prophylactic Antibiotic Selection	412	97%	97%	97%
Prophylactic Antibiotic Select. (Outpatient)	248	96%	94%	94%
Prophylactic Antibiotic Stopped	383	94%	94%	94%
Recommended VTP Ordered	246	95%	94%	94%
Urinary Catheter Removal	79	70%	89%	90%
Children's Asthma Care				
Received Systemic Corticosteroids	-	-	-	100%
Received Home Management Plan	-	-	-	71%
Received Reliever Medication	-	-	-	100%
Use of Medical Imaging				
Combination Abdominal CT Scan	526	0.061	0.246	0.191
Combination Chest CT Scan	426	0.002	0.098	0.054
Follow-up Mammogram/Ultrasound	1,554	7.1%	8.4%	8.4%
MRI for Low Back Pain	121	28.9%	33.4%	32.7%
Survey of Patients' Hospital Experiences				
Area Around Room 'Always' Quiet at Night	300+	45%	-	58%
Doctors 'Always' Communicated Well	300+	78%	-	80%
Home Recovery Information Given	300+	86%	-	82%
Hospital Given 9 or 10 on 10 Point Scale	300+	65%	-	67%
Meds 'Always' Explained Before Given	300+	60%	-	60%
Nurses 'Always' Communicated Well	300+	79%	-	76%
Pain 'Always' Well Controlled	300+	70%	-	69%
Room and Bathroom 'Always' Clean	300+	73%	-	71%
Timely Help 'Always' Received	300+	62%	-	64%
Would Definitely Recommend Hospital	300+	64%	-	69%

Red Bud Regional Hospital

325 Spring Street
Red Bud, IL 62278
Type: Critical Access Hospitals
Ownership: Proprietary
Phone: 618-282-3831
Fax: 618-282-6101
Emergency Services: Yes
Beds: 202

Key Personnel:
CEO/President. . . . . Bob Moore
Chief of Medical Staff . . . . Chung Khan
Emergency Room . . . . Steven Elster

Measure	Cases	This Hosp.	State Avg.	U.S. Avg.
Heart Attack Care				
ACE Inhibitor or ARB for LVSD[3]	0	-	96%	96%
Aspirin at Arrival[1,3]	1	100%	99%	99%
Aspirin at Discharge[3]	0	-	99%	98%
Beta Blocker at Discharge[1,3]	1	100%	98%	98%
Fibrinolytic Medication Timing[3]	0	-	50%	55%
PCI Within 90 Minutes of Arrival[3]	0	-	90%	90%
Smoking Cessation Advice[3]	0	-	100%	99%
Chest Pain/Possible Heart Attack Care				
Aspirin at Arrival	93	98%	95%	95%
Median Time to ECG (minutes)	98	6	8	8
Median Time to Transfer (minutes)[1,3]	6	56	57	61
Fibrinolytic Medication Timing[3]	0	-	33%	54%
Heart Failure Care				
ACE Inhibitor or ARB for LVSD[1]	9	89%	94%	94%
Discharge Instructions[1]	17	82%	89%	88%
Evaluation of LVS Function	41	100%	98%	98%
Smoking Cessation Advice[1]	7	100%	99%	98%
Pneumonia Care				
Appropriate Initial Antibiotic	42	93%	90%	92%
Blood Culture Timing	69	99%	97%	96%
Influenza Vaccine	38	95%	91%	91%
Initial Antibiotic Timing	67	100%	96%	95%
Pneumococcal Vaccine	70	99%	92%	93%
Smoking Cessation Advice[1]	4	100%	98%	97%
Surgical Care Improvement Project				
Appropriate VTP Within 24 Hours[1,2]	6	100%	92%	92%
Appropriate Hair Removal[2]	42	100%	99%	99%
Appropriate Beta Blocker Usage[1,2]	7	100%	92%	93%
Controlled Postoperative Blood Glucose[2]	0	-	92%	93%
Prophylactic Antibiotic Timing[2]	35	100%	97%	97%
Prophylactic Antibiotic Timing (Outpatient)[1]	18	94%	93%	92%
Prophylactic Antibiotic Selection[2]	35	94%	97%	97%
Prophylactic Antibiotic Select. (Outpatient)[1]	17	100%	94%	94%
Prophylactic Antibiotic Stopped[2]	35	94%	94%	94%
Recommended VTP Ordered[1,2]	6	100%	94%	94%
Urinary Catheter Removal[1]	2	50%	89%	90%
Children's Asthma Care				
Received Systemic Corticosteroids	-	-	-	100%
Received Home Management Plan	-	-	-	71%
Received Reliever Medication	-	-	-	100%
Use of Medical Imaging				
Combination Abdominal CT Scan	204	0.250	0.246	0.191
Combination Chest CT Scan	115	0.278	0.098	0.054
Follow-up Mammogram/Ultrasound	303	16.2%	8.4%	8.4%
MRI for Low Back Pain[1]	10	30.0%	33.4%	32.7%
Survey of Patients' Hospital Experiences				
Area Around Room 'Always' Quiet at Night	(a)	57%	-	58%
Doctors 'Always' Communicated Well	(a)	84%	-	80%
Home Recovery Information Given	(a)	84%	-	82%
Hospital Given 9 or 10 on 10 Point Scale	(a)	72%	-	67%
Meds 'Always' Explained Before Given	(a)	59%	-	60%
Nurses 'Always' Communicated Well	(a)	79%	-	76%
Pain 'Always' Well Controlled	(a)	78%	-	69%
Room and Bathroom 'Always' Clean	(a)	75%	-	71%
Timely Help 'Always' Received	(a)	56%	-	64%
Would Definitely Recommend Hospital	(a)	67%	-	69%

NOTE: Hospital profiles are in alphabetical order by state, then city, then hospital within the city; Rankings exclude hospitals with less than 25 cases except for patient surveys which excludes hospitals with less than 100 cases; (a) 100–299 cases; (1) The number of cases is too small to be sure how well a hospital is performing; (2) The hospital indicated that the data submitted for this measure were based on a sample of cases; (3) Data was collected during a shorter time period (fewer quarters) than the maximum possible time for this measure; (4) Suppressed for one or more quarters by CMS; (5) No data is available from the hospital for this measure; (6) Fewer than 100 patients completed the HCAHPS survey. Use these rates with caution, as the number of surveys may be too low to reliably assess hospital performance; (7) Survey results are based on less than 12 months of data; (8) Survey results are not available for this reporting period; (9) No or very few patients were eligible for the HCAHPS survey. The scores shown, if any, reflect a very small number of surveys; (10) A state average was not calculated because too few hospitals in the state submitted data; (11) There were discrepancies in the data collection process; Please refer to the User's Guide for a full explanation of data.

Crawford Memorial Hospital

1000 North Allen Street
Robinson, IL 62454
Phone: 618-546-2514
Fax: 618-546-2600
E-mail: debbie.robinson@crawfordmh.org
URL: www.crawfordmh.com
Type: Critical Access Hospitals
Emergency Services: Yes
Ownership: Govt - Hospital Dist/Auth
Beds: 93

Key Personnel:
CEO/President. . . . . Randy Simmons, MHA
Chief of Medical Staff . . . . Michael Elliott, MD
Quality Assurance . . . . Darra Beard

Measure	Cases	This Hosp.	State Avg.	U.S. Avg.
Heart Attack Care				
ACE Inhibitor or ARB for LVSD[1]	2	100%	96%	96%
Aspirin at Arrival[1]	8	100%	99%	99%
Aspirin at Discharge[1]	4	100%	99%	98%
Beta Blocker at Discharge[1]	3	100%	98%	98%
Fibrinolytic Medication Timing	0	-	50%	55%
PCI Within 90 Minutes of Arrival	0	-	90%	90%
Smoking Cessation Advice	0	-	100%	99%
Chest Pain/Possible Heart Attack Care				
Aspirin at Arrival	-	-	95%	95%
Median Time to ECG (minutes)	-	-	8	8
Median Time to Transfer (minutes)	-	-	57	61
Fibrinolytic Medication Timing	-	-	33%	54%
Heart Failure Care				
ACE Inhibitor or ARB for LVSD[1]	13	92%	94%	94%
Discharge Instructions	30	80%	89%	88%
Evaluation of LVS Function	46	91%	98%	98%
Smoking Cessation Advice[1]	3	67%	99%	98%
Pneumonia Care				
Appropriate Initial Antibiotic	26	88%	90%	92%
Blood Culture Timing	47	96%	97%	96%
Influenza Vaccine	31	97%	91%	91%
Initial Antibiotic Timing[5]	0	-	96%	95%
Pneumococcal Vaccine	33	97%	92%	93%
Smoking Cessation Advice[1]	17	88%	98%	97%
Surgical Care Improvement Project				
Appropriate VTP Within 24 Hours[1]	21	81%	92%	92%
Appropriate Hair Removal	54	100%	99%	99%
Appropriate Beta Blocker Usage[5]	0	-	92%	93%
Controlled Postoperative Blood Glucose	0	-	92%	93%
Prophylactic Antibiotic Timing	46	87%	97%	97%
Prophylactic Antibiotic Timing (Outpatient)	-	-	93%	92%
Prophylactic Antibiotic Selection	47	91%	97%	97%
Prophylactic Antibiotic Select. (Outpatient)	-	-	94%	94%
Prophylactic Antibiotic Stopped	46	74%	94%	94%
Recommended VTP Ordered[1]	21	86%	94%	94%
Urinary Catheter Removal[1]	4	50%	89%	90%
Children's Asthma Care				
Received Systemic Corticosteroids	-	-	-	100%
Received Home Management Plan	-	-	-	71%
Received Reliever Medication	-	-	-	100%
Use of Medical Imaging				
Combination Abdominal CT Scan	-	-	0.246	0.191
Combination Chest CT Scan	-	-	0.098	0.054
Follow-up Mammogram/Ultrasound	-	-	8.4%	8.4%
MRI for Low Back Pain	-	-	33.4%	32.7%
Survey of Patients' Hospital Experiences				
Area Around Room 'Always' Quiet at Night	(a)	56%	-	58%
Doctors 'Always' Communicated Well	(a)	86%	-	80%
Home Recovery Information Given	(a)	89%	-	82%
Hospital Given 9 or 10 on 10 Point Scale	(a)	64%	-	67%
Meds 'Always' Explained Before Given	(a)	69%	-	60%
Nurses 'Always' Communicated Well	(a)	82%	-	76%
Pain 'Always' Well Controlled	(a)	74%	-	69%
Room and Bathroom 'Always' Clean	(a)	79%	-	71%
Timely Help 'Always' Received	(a)	74%	-	64%
Would Definitely Recommend Hospital	(a)	60%	-	69%

Rochelle Community Hospital

900 N 2nd St
Rochelle, IL 61068
Phone: 815-562-2181
Fax: 815-562-5474
URL: www.rcha.net
Type: Critical Access Hospitals
Emergency Services: Yes
Ownership: Voluntary Non-Profit - Private
Beds: 42

Key Personnel:
CEO/President. . . . . Greggory Olson
Chief of Medical Staff. . . . . John Prabbaker, MD
Infection Control. . . . . Dorrie Kasman
Quality Assurance . . . . Karen Tracey, RN
Radiology. . . . . Nester S Cuasay
Emergency Room . . . . Janet Lodico, RN

Measure	Cases	This Hosp.	State Avg.	U.S. Avg.
Heart Attack Care				
ACE Inhibitor or ARB for LVSD	0	-	96%	96%
Aspirin at Arrival[1]	4	100%	99%	99%
Aspirin at Discharge[1]	3	100%	99%	98%
Beta Blocker at Discharge[1]	3	100%	98%	98%
Fibrinolytic Medication Timing	0	-	50%	55%
PCI Within 90 Minutes of Arrival	0	-	90%	90%
Smoking Cessation Advice	0	-	100%	99%
Chest Pain/Possible Heart Attack Care				
Aspirin at Arrival	-	-	95%	95%
Median Time to ECG (minutes)	-	-	8	8
Median Time to Transfer (minutes)	-	-	57	61
Fibrinolytic Medication Timing	-	-	33%	54%
Heart Failure Care				
ACE Inhibitor or ARB for LVSD[1]	11	18%	94%	94%
Discharge Instructions[1]	23	91%	89%	88%
Evaluation of LVS Function	30	97%	98%	98%
Smoking Cessation Advice[1]	4	25%	99%	98%
Pneumonia Care				
Appropriate Initial Antibiotic	27	78%	90%	92%
Blood Culture Timing	32	100%	97%	96%
Influenza Vaccine[1]	22	86%	91%	91%
Initial Antibiotic Timing	38	97%	96%	95%
Pneumococcal Vaccine	34	68%	92%	93%
Smoking Cessation Advice[1]	8	75%	98%	97%
Surgical Care Improvement Project				
Appropriate VTP Within 24 Hours[1]	15	93%	92%	92%
Appropriate Hair Removal[1]	22	86%	99%	99%
Appropriate Beta Blocker Usage[5]	0	-	92%	93%
Controlled Postoperative Blood Glucose	0	-	92%	93%
Prophylactic Antibiotic Timing[1]	10	80%	97%	97%
Prophylactic Antibiotic Timing (Outpatient)	-	-	93%	92%
Prophylactic Antibiotic Selection[1]	11	82%	97%	97%
Prophylactic Antibiotic Select. (Outpatient)	-	-	94%	94%
Prophylactic Antibiotic Stopped[1]	9	89%	94%	94%
Recommended VTP Ordered[1]	15	93%	94%	94%
Urinary Catheter Removal[1]	3	100%	89%	90%
Children's Asthma Care				
Received Systemic Corticosteroids	-	-	-	100%
Received Home Management Plan	-	-	-	71%
Received Reliever Medication	-	-	-	100%
Use of Medical Imaging				
Combination Abdominal CT Scan	-	-	0.246	0.191
Combination Chest CT Scan	-	-	0.098	0.054
Follow-up Mammogram/Ultrasound	-	-	8.4%	8.4%
MRI for Low Back Pain	-	-	33.4%	32.7%
Survey of Patients' Hospital Experiences				
Area Around Room 'Always' Quiet at Night	(a)	73%	-	58%
Doctors 'Always' Communicated Well	(a)	82%	-	80%
Home Recovery Information Given	(a)	87%	-	82%
Hospital Given 9 or 10 on 10 Point Scale	(a)	82%	-	67%
Meds 'Always' Explained Before Given	(a)	72%	-	60%
Nurses 'Always' Communicated Well	(a)	84%	-	76%
Pain 'Always' Well Controlled	(a)	79%	-	69%
Room and Bathroom 'Always' Clean	(a)	87%	-	71%
Timely Help 'Always' Received	(a)	85%	-	64%
Would Definitely Recommend Hospital	(a)	79%	-	69%

Trinity Rock Island

2701 17th St
Rock Island, IL 61201
Phone: 309-779-5000
Fax: 309-779-2695
URL: www.trinityqc.com
Type: Acute Care Hospitals
Emergency Services: Yes
Ownership: Voluntary Non-Profit - Other
Beds: 349

Key Personnel:
CEO/President. . . . . Andrea Y Coleman
Chief of Medical Staff. . . . . Harry Wallner, MD
Infection Control. . . . . Marilynn Van Vliete, RN
Operating Room. . . . . Cherie Fulks
Pediatric Ambulatory Care . . . . . . Paulito Juazon, MD
Pediatric In-Patient Care . . . . Paulito Juazon, MD
Quality Assurance . . . . Cheryl Jackson
Radiology. . . . . Craig Tillman, MD

Measure	Cases	This Hosp.	State Avg.	U.S. Avg.
Heart Attack Care				
ACE Inhibitor or ARB for LVSD	62	98%	96%	96%
Aspirin at Arrival	252	100%	99%	99%
Aspirin at Discharge	391	99%	99%	98%
Beta Blocker at Discharge	364	98%	98%	98%
Fibrinolytic Medication Timing	0	-	50%	55%
PCI Within 90 Minutes of Arrival	45	91%	90%	90%
Smoking Cessation Advice	135	100%	100%	99%
Chest Pain/Possible Heart Attack Care				
Aspirin at Arrival[1]	11	82%	95%	95%
Median Time to ECG (minutes)[1]	11	9	8	8
Median Time to Transfer (minutes)[5]	0	-	57	61
Fibrinolytic Medication Timing[3]	0	-	33%	54%
Heart Failure Care				
ACE Inhibitor or ARB for LVSD[2]	82	98%	94%	94%
Discharge Instructions[2]	207	97%	89%	88%
Evaluation of LVS Function[2]	288	99%	98%	98%
Smoking Cessation Advice[2]	36	100%	99%	98%
Pneumonia Care				
Appropriate Initial Antibiotic[2]	71	97%	90%	92%
Blood Culture Timing[2]	125	99%	97%	96%
Influenza Vaccine[2]	94	91%	91%	91%
Initial Antibiotic Timing[2]	128	97%	96%	95%
Pneumococcal Vaccine[2]	142	99%	92%	93%
Smoking Cessation Advice[2]	50	96%	98%	97%
Surgical Care Improvement Project				
Appropriate VTP Within 24 Hours[2]	136	85%	92%	92%
Appropriate Hair Removal[2]	512	100%	99%	99%
Appropriate Beta Blocker Usage[2]	184	97%	92%	93%
Controlled Postoperative Blood Glucose[2]	114	94%	92%	93%
Prophylactic Antibiotic Timing[2]	357	98%	97%	97%
Prophylactic Antibiotic Timing (Outpatient)	478	97%	93%	92%
Prophylactic Antibiotic Selection[2]	366	99%	97%	97%
Prophylactic Antibiotic Select. (Outpatient)	475	92%	94%	94%
Prophylactic Antibiotic Stopped[2]	352	97%	94%	94%
Recommended VTP Ordered[2]	136	94%	94%	94%
Urinary Catheter Removal[2]	62	97%	89%	90%
Children's Asthma Care				
Received Systemic Corticosteroids	-	-	-	100%
Received Home Management Plan	-	-	-	71%
Received Reliever Medication	-	-	-	100%
Use of Medical Imaging				
Combination Abdominal CT Scan	1,113	0.059	0.246	0.191
Combination Chest CT Scan	763	0.069	0.098	0.054
Follow-up Mammogram/Ultrasound	2,177	10.9%	8.4%	8.4%
MRI for Low Back Pain[5]	0	-	33.4%	32.7%
Survey of Patients' Hospital Experiences				
Area Around Room 'Always' Quiet at Night	300+	50%	-	58%
Doctors 'Always' Communicated Well	300+	78%	-	80%
Home Recovery Information Given	300+	86%	-	82%
Hospital Given 9 or 10 on 10 Point Scale	300+	62%	-	67%
Meds 'Always' Explained Before Given	300+	61%	-	60%
Nurses 'Always' Communicated Well	300+	72%	-	76%
Pain 'Always' Well Controlled	300+	67%	-	69%
Room and Bathroom 'Always' Clean	300+	69%	-	71%
Timely Help 'Always' Received	300+	49%	-	64%
Would Definitely Recommend Hospital	300+	64%	-	69%

NOTE: Hospital profiles are in alphabetical order by state, then city, then hospital within the city; Rankings exclude hospitals with less than 25 cases except for patient surveys which excludes hospitals with less than 100 cases; (a) 100–299 cases; (1) The number of cases is too small to be sure how well a hospital is performing; (2) The hospital indicated that the data submitted for this measure were based on a sample of cases; (3) Data was collected during a shorter time period (fewer quarters) than the maximum possible time for this measure; (4) Suppressed for one or more quarters by CMS; (5) No data is available from the hospital for this measure; (6) Fewer than 100 patients completed the HCAHPS survey. Use these rates with caution, as the number of surveys may be too low to reliably assess hospital performance; (7) Survey results are based on less than 12 months of data; (8) Survey results are not available for this reporting period; (9) No or very few patients were eligible for the HCAHPS survey. The scores shown, if any, reflect a very small number of surveys; (10) A state average was not calculated because too few hospitals in the state submitted data; (11) There were discrepancies in the data collection process; Please refer to the User's Guide for a full explanation of data.

Rockford Memorial Hospital

2400 North Rockton Avenue Phone: 815-968-6861
Rockford, IL 61103 Fax: 815-971-6167
URL: www.rhsnet.org
Type: Acute Care Hospitals Emergency Services: Yes
Ownership: Voluntary Non-Profit - Private Beds: 396

Key Personnel:
CEO/President. . . . . Gary Kaatz
Chief of Medical Staff. . . . . Milton Schmitt, MD
Emergency Room . . . . Dennis Veharra, MD

Measure	Cases	This Hosp.	State Avg.	U.S. Avg.
Heart Attack Care				
ACE Inhibitor or ARB for LVSD	30	97%	96%	96%
Aspirin at Arrival	161	99%	99%	99%
Aspirin at Discharge	220	99%	99%	98%
Beta Blocker at Discharge	219	100%	98%	98%
Fibrinolytic Medication Timing	0	-	50%	55%
PCI Within 90 Minutes of Arrival	31	87%	90%	90%
Smoking Cessation Advice	80	100%	100%	99%
Chest Pain/Possible Heart Attack Care				
Aspirin at Arrival[5]	0	-	95%	95%
Median Time to ECG (minutes)[5]	0	-	8	8
Median Time to Transfer (minutes)[5]	0	-	57	61
Fibrinolytic Medication Timing[5]	0	-	33%	54%
Heart Failure Care				
ACE Inhibitor or ARB for LVSD	73	100%	94%	94%
Discharge Instructions	193	89%	89%	88%
Evaluation of LVS Function	270	100%	98%	98%
Smoking Cessation Advice	60	100%	99%	98%
Pneumonia Care				
Appropriate Initial Antibiotic	178	98%	90%	92%
Blood Culture Timing	324	99%	97%	96%
Influenza Vaccine	221	91%	91%	91%
Initial Antibiotic Timing	348	95%	96%	95%
Pneumococcal Vaccine	289	92%	92%	93%
Smoking Cessation Advice	120	100%	98%	97%
Surgical Care Improvement Project				
Appropriate VTP Within 24 Hours	254	86%	92%	92%
Appropriate Hair Removal	1,032	100%	99%	99%
Appropriate Beta Blocker Usage	349	96%	92%	93%
Controlled Postoperative Blood Glucose	149	89%	92%	93%
Prophylactic Antibiotic Timing	575	99%	97%	97%
Prophylactic Antibiotic Timing (Outpatient)	361	98%	93%	92%
Prophylactic Antibiotic Selection	593	98%	97%	97%
Prophylactic Antibiotic Select. (Outpatient)	357	97%	94%	94%
Prophylactic Antibiotic Stopped	547	93%	94%	94%
Recommended VTP Ordered	259	92%	94%	94%
Urinary Catheter Removal	127	70%	89%	90%
Children's Asthma Care				
Received Systemic Corticosteroids	-	-	-	100%
Received Home Management Plan	-	-	-	71%
Received Reliever Medication	-	-	-	100%
Use of Medical Imaging				
Combination Abdominal CT Scan	697	0.098	0.246	0.191
Combination Chest CT Scan	682	0.003	0.098	0.054
Follow-up Mammogram/Ultrasound[5]	0	-	8.4%	8.4%
MRI for Low Back Pain	248	29.8%	33.4%	32.7%
Survey of Patients' Hospital Experiences				
Area Around Room 'Always' Quiet at Night	300+	55%	-	58%
Doctors 'Always' Communicated Well	300+	74%	-	80%
Home Recovery Information Given	300+	81%	-	82%
Hospital Given 9 or 10 on 10 Point Scale	300+	63%	-	67%
Meds 'Always' Explained Before Given	300+	56%	-	60%
Nurses 'Always' Communicated Well	300+	72%	-	76%
Pain 'Always' Well Controlled	300+	64%	-	69%
Room and Bathroom 'Always' Clean	300+	69%	-	71%
Timely Help 'Always' Received	300+	51%	-	64%
Would Definitely Recommend Hospital	300+	67%	-	69%

Saint Anthony Medical Center

5666 East State Street Phone: 815-226-2000
Rockford, IL 61108 Fax: 815-395-5449
URL: www.osfhealth.com
Type: Acute Care Hospitals Emergency Services: Yes
Ownership: Voluntary Non-Profit - Church Beds: 254

Key Personnel:
CEO/President. . . . . David A Schertz
Chief of Medical Staff. . . . . Robert White, MD
Coronary Care. . . . . Brenda Schroeder, RN
Infection Control. . . . . Larry Brown, RN
Operating Room. . . . . Sarah Walder, RN
Pediatric Ambulatory Care . . . . . . Errol C Baptist, MD
Quality Assurance . . . . Susan Taphorn, RN
Radiology. . . . . David Childers

Measure	Cases	This Hosp.	State Avg.	U.S. Avg.
Heart Attack Care				
ACE Inhibitor or ARB for LVSD	45	96%	96%	96%
Aspirin at Arrival	222	99%	99%	99%
Aspirin at Discharge	258	99%	99%	98%
Beta Blocker at Discharge	254	95%	98%	98%
Fibrinolytic Medication Timing	0	-	50%	55%
PCI Within 90 Minutes of Arrival	50	80%	90%	90%
Smoking Cessation Advice	84	100%	100%	99%
Chest Pain/Possible Heart Attack Care				
Aspirin at Arrival[1]	7	100%	95%	95%
Median Time to ECG (minutes)[1]	8	16	8	8
Median Time to Transfer (minutes)[5]	0	-	57	61
Fibrinolytic Medication Timing[5]	0	-	33%	54%
Heart Failure Care				
ACE Inhibitor or ARB for LVSD	94	89%	94%	94%
Discharge Instructions	215	94%	89%	88%
Evaluation of LVS Function	301	99%	98%	98%
Smoking Cessation Advice	26	100%	99%	98%
Pneumonia Care				
Appropriate Initial Antibiotic	115	83%	90%	92%
Blood Culture Timing	212	98%	97%	96%
Influenza Vaccine	143	94%	91%	91%
Initial Antibiotic Timing	190	98%	96%	95%
Pneumococcal Vaccine	222	94%	92%	93%
Smoking Cessation Advice	71	100%	98%	97%
Surgical Care Improvement Project				
Appropriate VTP Within 24 Hours[2]	256	84%	92%	92%
Appropriate Hair Removal[2]	1,204	100%	99%	99%
Appropriate Beta Blocker Usage[2]	450	95%	92%	93%
Controlled Postoperative Blood Glucose[2]	182	91%	92%	93%
Prophylactic Antibiotic Timing[2]	964	98%	97%	97%
Prophylactic Antibiotic Timing (Outpatient)	369	93%	93%	92%
Prophylactic Antibiotic Selection[2]	974	99%	97%	97%
Prophylactic Antibiotic Select. (Outpatient)	363	95%	94%	94%
Prophylactic Antibiotic Stopped[2]	943	96%	94%	94%
Recommended VTP Ordered[2]	256	95%	94%	94%
Urinary Catheter Removal[2]	97	85%	89%	90%
Children's Asthma Care				
Received Systemic Corticosteroids	-	-	-	100%
Received Home Management Plan	-	-	-	71%
Received Reliever Medication	-	-	-	100%
Use of Medical Imaging				
Combination Abdominal CT Scan	1,154	0.076	0.246	0.191
Combination Chest CT Scan	1,032	0.001	0.098	0.054
Follow-up Mammogram/Ultrasound	1,381	8.7%	8.4%	8.4%
MRI for Low Back Pain	193	35.8%	33.4%	32.7%
Survey of Patients' Hospital Experiences				
Area Around Room 'Always' Quiet at Night	300+	45%	-	58%
Doctors 'Always' Communicated Well	300+	76%	-	80%
Home Recovery Information Given	300+	82%	-	82%
Hospital Given 9 or 10 on 10 Point Scale	300+	70%	-	67%
Meds 'Always' Explained Before Given	300+	61%	-	60%
Nurses 'Always' Communicated Well	300+	76%	-	76%
Pain 'Always' Well Controlled	300+	69%	-	69%
Room and Bathroom 'Always' Clean	300+	73%	-	71%
Timely Help 'Always' Received	300+	63%	-	64%
Would Definitely Recommend Hospital	300+	73%	-	69%

Swedish American Hospital

1401 East State Street Phone: 815-968-4400
Rockford, IL 61104 Fax: 815-961-2445
URL: www.swedishamerican.org
Type: Acute Care Hospitals Emergency Services: Yes
Ownership: Voluntary Non-Profit - Other Beds: 357

Key Personnel:
Chief of Medical Staff. . . . . Dr Kathleen Kelly
Infection Control. . . . . Gary Rifkin, MD
Pediatric Ambulatory Care . . . . . . Dr Glen Burress
Quality Assurance . . . . Beverly Merfeld
Radiology. . . . . Dr Marc Bernstein
Anesthesiology. . . . . Dr Timothy Starck
Emergency Room . . . . Dr John Underwood
Intensive Care Unit. . . . . Kathy Arnold

Measure	Cases	This Hosp.	State Avg.	U.S. Avg.
Heart Attack Care				
ACE Inhibitor or ARB for LVSD	42	98%	96%	96%
Aspirin at Arrival	218	100%	99%	99%
Aspirin at Discharge	233	100%	99%	98%
Beta Blocker at Discharge	229	100%	98%	98%
Fibrinolytic Medication Timing	0	-	50%	55%
PCI Within 90 Minutes of Arrival	43	93%	90%	90%
Smoking Cessation Advice	86	100%	100%	99%
Chest Pain/Possible Heart Attack Care				
Aspirin at Arrival	50	96%	95%	95%
Median Time to ECG (minutes)	50	6	8	8
Median Time to Transfer (minutes)[1,3]	1	43	57	61
Fibrinolytic Medication Timing[3]	0	-	33%	54%
Heart Failure Care				
ACE Inhibitor or ARB for LVSD	132	97%	94%	94%
Discharge Instructions	311	89%	89%	88%
Evaluation of LVS Function	426	100%	98%	98%
Smoking Cessation Advice	96	100%	99%	98%
Pneumonia Care				
Appropriate Initial Antibiotic	170	94%	90%	92%
Blood Culture Timing	261	94%	97%	96%
Influenza Vaccine	176	92%	91%	91%
Initial Antibiotic Timing	263	95%	96%	95%
Pneumococcal Vaccine	227	93%	92%	93%
Smoking Cessation Advice	133	100%	98%	97%
Surgical Care Improvement Project				
Appropriate VTP Within 24 Hours[2]	286	88%	92%	92%
Appropriate Hair Removal[2]	1,210	100%	99%	99%
Appropriate Beta Blocker Usage[2]	380	96%	92%	93%
Controlled Postoperative Blood Glucose[2]	163	93%	92%	93%
Prophylactic Antibiotic Timing[2]	942	99%	97%	97%
Prophylactic Antibiotic Timing (Outpatient)	312	96%	93%	92%
Prophylactic Antibiotic Selection[2]	956	98%	97%	97%
Prophylactic Antibiotic Select. (Outpatient)	307	97%	94%	94%
Prophylactic Antibiotic Stopped[2]	883	98%	94%	94%
Recommended VTP Ordered[2]	287	93%	94%	94%
Urinary Catheter Removal[2]	164	89%	89%	90%
Children's Asthma Care				
Received Systemic Corticosteroids	-	-	-	100%
Received Home Management Plan	-	-	-	71%
Received Reliever Medication	-	-	-	100%
Use of Medical Imaging				
Combination Abdominal CT Scan	1,062	0.059	0.246	0.191
Combination Chest CT Scan	1,002	0.002	0.098	0.054
Follow-up Mammogram/Ultrasound	2,740	8.7%	8.4%	8.4%
MRI for Low Back Pain	252	33.7%	33.4%	32.7%
Survey of Patients' Hospital Experiences				
Area Around Room 'Always' Quiet at Night	300+	55%	-	58%
Doctors 'Always' Communicated Well	300+	77%	-	80%
Home Recovery Information Given	300+	81%	-	82%
Hospital Given 9 or 10 on 10 Point Scale	300+	66%	-	67%
Meds 'Always' Explained Before Given	300+	59%	-	60%
Nurses 'Always' Communicated Well	300+	76%	-	76%
Pain 'Always' Well Controlled	300+	70%	-	69%
Room and Bathroom 'Always' Clean	300+	72%	-	71%
Timely Help 'Always' Received	300+	67%	-	64%
Would Definitely Recommend Hospital	300+	72%	-	69%

NOTE: Hospital profiles are in alphabetical order by state, then city, then hospital within the city; Rankings exclude hospitals with less than 25 cases except for patient surveys which excludes hospitals with less than 100 cases; (a) 100–299 cases; (1) The number of cases is too small to be sure how well a hospital is performing; (2) The hospital indicated that the data submitted for this measure were based on a sample of cases; (3) Data was collected during a shorter time period (fewer quarters) than the maximum possible time for this measure; (4) Suppressed for one or more quarters by CMS; (5) No data is available from the hospital for this measure; (6) Fewer than 100 patients completed the HCAHPS survey. Use these rates with caution, as the number of surveys may be too low to reliably assess hospital performance; (7) Survey results are based on less than 12 months of data; (8) Survey results are not available for this reporting period; (9) No or very few patients were eligible for the HCAHPS survey. The scores shown, if any, reflect a very small number of surveys; (10) A state average was not calculated because too few hospitals in the state submitted data; (11) There were discrepancies in the data collection process; Please refer to the User's Guide for a full explanation of data.

Hardin County General Hospital

Ferrell Road
Rosiclare, IL 62982
Phone: 618-285-6634
Fax: 618-285-3564
Type: Critical Access Hospitals
Emergency Services: Yes
Ownership: Voluntary Non-Profit - Private
Beds: 25

Key Personnel:

CEO/President. . . . . Roby Williams
Chief of Medical Staff . . . . Marcos Sunga, MD
Quality Assurance . . . . Jan Donbrow, RN
Radiology. . . . . Alice Kayler
Emergency Room . . . . Marsha Broadway, RN

Measure	Cases	This Hosp.	State Avg.	U.S. Avg.
Heart Attack Care				
ACE Inhibitor or ARB for LVSD[5]	0	-	96%	96%
Aspirin at Arrival[5]	0	-	99%	99%
Aspirin at Discharge[5]	0	-	99%	98%
Beta Blocker at Discharge[5]	0	-	98%	98%
Fibrinolytic Medication Timing[5]	0	-	50%	55%
PCI Within 90 Minutes of Arrival[5]	0	-	90%	90%
Smoking Cessation Advice[5]	0	-	100%	99%
Chest Pain/Possible Heart Attack Care				
Aspirin at Arrival	50	98%	95%	95%
Median Time to ECG (minutes)	55	7	8	8
Median Time to Transfer (minutes)[3]	0	-	57	61
Fibrinolytic Medication Timing[1,3]	3	33%	33%	54%
Heart Failure Care				
ACE Inhibitor or ARB for LVSD[1]	5	100%	94%	94%
Discharge Instructions[1]	19	100%	89%	88%
Evaluation of LVS Function	29	100%	98%	98%
Smoking Cessation Advice[1]	7	100%	99%	98%
Pneumonia Care				
Appropriate Initial Antibiotic	37	97%	90%	92%
Blood Culture Timing	57	98%	97%	96%
Influenza Vaccine	36	97%	91%	91%
Initial Antibiotic Timing	57	98%	96%	95%
Pneumococcal Vaccine	51	98%	92%	93%
Smoking Cessation Advice[1]	18	100%	98%	97%
Surgical Care Improvement Project				
Appropriate VTP Within 24 Hours[5]	0	-	92%	92%
Appropriate Hair Removal[5]	0	-	99%	99%
Appropriate Beta Blocker Usage[5]	0	-	92%	93%
Controlled Postoperative Blood Glucose[5]	0	-	92%	93%
Prophylactic Antibiotic Timing[5]	0	-	97%	97%
Prophylactic Antibiotic Timing (Outpatient)[5]	0	-	93%	92%
Prophylactic Antibiotic Selection[5]	0	-	97%	97%
Prophylactic Antibiotic Select. (Outpatient)[5]	0	-	94%	94%
Prophylactic Antibiotic Stopped[5]	0	-	94%	94%
Recommended VTP Ordered[5]	0	-	94%	94%
Urinary Catheter Removal[5]	0	-	89%	90%
Children's Asthma Care				
Received Systemic Corticosteroids	-	-	-	100%
Received Home Management Plan	-	-	-	71%
Received Reliever Medication	-	-	-	100%
Use of Medical Imaging				
Combination Abdominal CT Scan	85	0.318	0.246	0.191
Combination Chest CT Scan[1]	35	0.743	0.098	0.054
Follow-up Mammogram/Ultrasound	88	6.8%	8.4%	8.4%
MRI for Low Back Pain[1]	22	31.8%	33.4%	32.7%
Survey of Patients' Hospital Experiences				
Area Around Room 'Always' Quiet at Night[8]	-	-	-	58%
Doctors 'Always' Communicated Well[8]	-	-	-	80%
Home Recovery Information Given[8]	-	-	-	82%
Hospital Given 9 or 10 on 10 Point Scale[8]	-	-	-	67%
Meds 'Always' Explained Before Given[8]	-	-	-	60%
Nurses 'Always' Communicated Well[8]	-	-	-	76%
Pain 'Always' Well Controlled[8]	-	-	-	69%
Room and Bathroom 'Always' Clean[8]	-	-	-	71%
Timely Help 'Always' Received[8]	-	-	-	64%
Would Definitely Recommend Hospital[8]	-	-	-	69%

Sarah D Culbertson Memorial Hospital

238 South Congress Street
Rushville, IL 62681
Phone: 217-322-4321
Fax: 217-322-6425
E-mail: CMH@CMHospital.com
URL: www.cmhospital.com
Type: Critical Access Hospitals
Emergency Services: Yes
Ownership: Govt - Hospital Dist/Auth
Beds: 64

Key Personnel:

CEO/President. . . . . David Sniff
Chief of Medical Staff . . . . Lisa Downs, RN
Quality Assurance . . . . Judy Richy
Emergency Room . . . . Lisa Downs, RN

Measure	Cases	This Hosp.	State Avg.	U.S. Avg.
Heart Attack Care				
ACE Inhibitor or ARB for LVSD[5]	0	-	96%	96%
Aspirin at Arrival[5]	0	-	99%	99%
Aspirin at Discharge[5]	0	-	99%	98%
Beta Blocker at Discharge[5]	0	-	98%	98%
Fibrinolytic Medication Timing[5]	0	-	50%	55%
PCI Within 90 Minutes of Arrival[5]	0	-	90%	90%
Smoking Cessation Advice[5]	0	-	100%	99%
Chest Pain/Possible Heart Attack Care				
Aspirin at Arrival	-	-	95%	95%
Median Time to ECG (minutes)	-	-	8	8
Median Time to Transfer (minutes)	-	-	57	61
Fibrinolytic Medication Timing	-	-	33%	54%
Heart Failure Care				
ACE Inhibitor or ARB for LVSD[1]	2	100%	94%	94%
Discharge Instructions[1]	3	67%	89%	88%
Evaluation of LVS Function[1]	8	50%	98%	98%
Smoking Cessation Advice	0	-	99%	98%
Pneumonia Care				
Appropriate Initial Antibiotic[1]	15	100%	90%	92%
Blood Culture Timing[1]	12	100%	97%	96%
Influenza Vaccine[1]	12	58%	91%	91%
Initial Antibiotic Timing[1]	17	94%	96%	95%
Pneumococcal Vaccine[1]	16	88%	92%	93%
Smoking Cessation Advice[1]	8	50%	98%	97%
Surgical Care Improvement Project				
Appropriate VTP Within 24 Hours[3]	0	-	92%	92%
Appropriate Hair Removal[1,3]	3	100%	99%	99%
Appropriate Beta Blocker Usage[5]	0	-	92%	93%
Controlled Postoperative Blood Glucose[3]	0	-	92%	93%
Prophylactic Antibiotic Timing[1,3]	4	25%	97%	97%
Prophylactic Antibiotic Timing (Outpatient)	-	-	93%	92%
Prophylactic Antibiotic Selection[1,3]	4	100%	97%	97%
Prophylactic Antibiotic Select. (Outpatient)	-	-	94%	94%
Prophylactic Antibiotic Stopped[1,3]	4	50%	94%	94%
Recommended VTP Ordered[3]	0	-	94%	94%
Urinary Catheter Removal	0	-	89%	90%
Children's Asthma Care				
Received Systemic Corticosteroids	-	-	-	100%
Received Home Management Plan	-	-	-	71%
Received Reliever Medication	-	-	-	100%
Use of Medical Imaging				
Combination Abdominal CT Scan	-	-	0.246	0.191
Combination Chest CT Scan	-	-	0.098	0.054
Follow-up Mammogram/Ultrasound	-	-	8.4%	8.4%
MRI for Low Back Pain	-	-	33.4%	32.7%
Survey of Patients' Hospital Experiences				
Area Around Room 'Always' Quiet at Night[8]	-	-	-	58%
Doctors 'Always' Communicated Well[8]	-	-	-	80%
Home Recovery Information Given[8]	-	-	-	82%
Hospital Given 9 or 10 on 10 Point Scale[8]	-	-	-	67%
Meds 'Always' Explained Before Given[8]	-	-	-	60%
Nurses 'Always' Communicated Well[8]	-	-	-	76%
Pain 'Always' Well Controlled[8]	-	-	-	69%
Room and Bathroom 'Always' Clean[8]	-	-	-	71%
Timely Help 'Always' Received[8]	-	-	-	64%
Would Definitely Recommend Hospital[8]	-	-	-	69%

Salem Township Hospital

1201 Ricker Drive
Salem, IL 62881
Phone: 618-548-3194
Fax: 618-548-6831
Type: Critical Access Hospitals
Emergency Services: Yes
Ownership: Government - Local
Beds: 46

Key Personnel:

CEO/President. . . . . Rithilli Rennegarve
Chief of Medical Staff . . . . A T Aguilar
Infection Control. . . . . Wilma Gott, RN, B
Operating Room. . . . . S Lakshmanan, RN
Quality Assurance . . . . Sheri Schultz
Radiology. . . . . Preecha Tawjare, MD
Emergency Room . . . . Roberto Garcia
Intensive Care Unit. . . . . P Suppiah, MD

Measure	Cases	This Hosp.	State Avg.	U.S. Avg.
Heart Attack Care				
ACE Inhibitor or ARB for LVSD[5]	0	-	96%	96%
Aspirin at Arrival[5]	0	-	99%	99%
Aspirin at Discharge[5]	0	-	99%	98%
Beta Blocker at Discharge[5]	0	-	98%	98%
Fibrinolytic Medication Timing[5]	0	-	50%	55%
PCI Within 90 Minutes of Arrival[5]	0	-	90%	90%
Smoking Cessation Advice[5]	0	-	100%	99%
Chest Pain/Possible Heart Attack Care				
Aspirin at Arrival	-	-	95%	95%
Median Time to ECG (minutes)	-	-	8	8
Median Time to Transfer (minutes)	-	-	57	61
Fibrinolytic Medication Timing	-	-	33%	54%
Heart Failure Care				
ACE Inhibitor or ARB for LVSD[1]	7	86%	94%	94%
Discharge Instructions	28	86%	89%	88%
Evaluation of LVS Function	45	62%	98%	98%
Smoking Cessation Advice[1]	7	100%	99%	98%
Pneumonia Care				
Appropriate Initial Antibiotic	25	72%	90%	92%
Blood Culture Timing	32	88%	97%	96%
Influenza Vaccine	26	81%	91%	91%
Initial Antibiotic Timing[1]	24	92%	96%	95%
Pneumococcal Vaccine	34	62%	92%	93%
Smoking Cessation Advice[1]	14	93%	98%	97%
Surgical Care Improvement Project				
Appropriate VTP Within 24 Hours[1]	19	100%	92%	92%
Appropriate Hair Removal[1]	21	100%	99%	99%
Appropriate Beta Blocker Usage[5]	0	-	92%	93%
Controlled Postoperative Blood Glucose	0	-	92%	93%
Prophylactic Antibiotic Timing[1]	14	64%	97%	97%
Prophylactic Antibiotic Timing (Outpatient)	-	-	93%	92%
Prophylactic Antibiotic Selection[1]	14	93%	97%	97%
Prophylactic Antibiotic Select. (Outpatient)	-	-	94%	94%
Prophylactic Antibiotic Stopped[1]	12	100%	94%	94%
Recommended VTP Ordered[1]	19	100%	94%	94%
Urinary Catheter Removal[1]	1	100%	89%	90%
Children's Asthma Care				
Received Systemic Corticosteroids	-	-	-	100%
Received Home Management Plan	-	-	-	71%
Received Reliever Medication	-	-	-	100%
Use of Medical Imaging				
Combination Abdominal CT Scan	-	-	0.246	0.191
Combination Chest CT Scan	-	-	0.098	0.054
Follow-up Mammogram/Ultrasound	-	-	8.4%	8.4%
MRI for Low Back Pain	-	-	33.4%	32.7%
Survey of Patients' Hospital Experiences				
Area Around Room 'Always' Quiet at Night	(a)	60%	-	58%
Doctors 'Always' Communicated Well	(a)	88%	-	80%
Home Recovery Information Given	(a)	83%	-	82%
Hospital Given 9 or 10 on 10 Point Scale	(a)	75%	-	67%
Meds 'Always' Explained Before Given	(a)	66%	-	60%
Nurses 'Always' Communicated Well	(a)	84%	-	76%
Pain 'Always' Well Controlled	(a)	75%	-	69%
Room and Bathroom 'Always' Clean	(a)	88%	-	71%
Timely Help 'Always' Received	(a)	73%	-	64%
Would Definitely Recommend Hospital	(a)	72%	-	69%

NOTE: Hospital profiles are in alphabetical order by state, then city, then hospital within the city; Rankings exclude hospitals with less than 25 cases except for patient surveys which excludes hospitals with less than 100 cases; (a) 100–299 cases; (1) The number of cases is too small to be sure how well a hospital is performing; (2) The hospital indicated that the data submitted for this measure were based on a sample of cases; (3) Data was collected during a shorter time period (fewer quarters) than the maximum possible time for this measure; (4) Suppressed for one or more quarters by CMS; (5) No data is available from the hospital for this measure; (6) Fewer than 100 patients completed the HCAHPS survey. Use these rates with caution, as the number of surveys may be too low to reliably assess hospital performance; (7) Survey results are based on less than 12 months of data; (8) Survey results are not available for this reporting period; (9) No or very few patients were eligible for the HCAHPS survey. The scores shown, if any, reflect a very small number of surveys; (10) A state average was not calculated because too few hospitals in the state submitted data; (11) There were discrepancies in the data collection process; Please refer to the User's Guide for a full explanation of data.

Valley West Community Hospital

11 East Pleasant Avenue Phone: 815-786-8484
Sandwich, IL 60548 Fax: 815-786-3705
E-mail: sandhosp@snd.softfarm.com/sandhosp
URL: www.snd.softfarm.com/sandhosp
Type: Critical Access Hospitals Emergency Services: Yes
Ownership: Voluntary Non-Profit - Other Beds: 84

Key Personnel:
CEO/President. . . . . Brad Topple
Chief of Medical Staff. . . . . Martin Brauweiler
Infection Control. . . . . Carol Vignali
Operating Room. . . . . Richard W Mason
Radiology. . . . . Thomas R Cain, MD
Emergency Room . . . . Victor Garber, MD
Intensive Care Unit. . . . . Kris Wyant, RN

Measure	Cases	This Hosp.	State Avg.	U.S. Avg.
Heart Attack Care				
ACE Inhibitor or ARB for LVSD	0	-	96%	96%
Aspirin at Arrival[1]	6	100%	99%	99%
Aspirin at Discharge[1]	4	25%	99%	98%
Beta Blocker at Discharge[1]	4	75%	98%	98%
Fibrinolytic Medication Timing	0	-	50%	55%
PCI Within 90 Minutes of Arrival	0	-	90%	90%
Smoking Cessation Advice	0	-	100%	99%
Chest Pain/Possible Heart Attack Care				
Aspirin at Arrival	-	-	95%	95%
Median Time to ECG (minutes)	-	-	8	8
Median Time to Transfer (minutes)	-	-	57	61
Fibrinolytic Medication Timing	-	-	33%	54%
Heart Failure Care				
ACE Inhibitor or ARB for LVSD[1]	7	100%	94%	94%
Discharge Instructions[1]	22	82%	89%	88%
Evaluation of LVS Function	26	96%	98%	98%
Smoking Cessation Advice[1]	2	50%	99%	98%
Pneumonia Care				
Appropriate Initial Antibiotic[1]	23	100%	90%	92%
Blood Culture Timing	31	94%	97%	96%
Influenza Vaccine[1]	16	81%	91%	91%
Initial Antibiotic Timing	35	97%	96%	95%
Pneumococcal Vaccine	26	92%	92%	93%
Smoking Cessation Advice[1]	9	78%	98%	97%
Surgical Care Improvement Project				
Appropriate VTP Within 24 Hours	33	61%	92%	92%
Appropriate Hair Removal	69	100%	99%	99%
Appropriate Beta Blocker Usage[5]	0	-	92%	93%
Controlled Postoperative Blood Glucose	0	-	92%	93%
Prophylactic Antibiotic Timing	35	100%	97%	97%
Prophylactic Antibiotic Timing (Outpatient)	-	-	93%	92%
Prophylactic Antibiotic Selection	35	91%	97%	97%
Prophylactic Antibiotic Select. (Outpatient)	-	-	94%	94%
Prophylactic Antibiotic Stopped	35	94%	94%	94%
Recommended VTP Ordered	33	73%	94%	94%
Urinary Catheter Removal[1]	11	91%	89%	90%
Children's Asthma Care				
Received Systemic Corticosteroids	-	-	-	100%
Received Home Management Plan	-	-	-	71%
Received Reliever Medication	-	-	-	100%
Use of Medical Imaging				
Combination Abdominal CT Scan	-	-	0.246	0.191
Combination Chest CT Scan	-	-	0.098	0.054
Follow-up Mammogram/Ultrasound	-	-	8.4%	8.4%
MRI for Low Back Pain	-	-	33.4%	32.7%
Survey of Patients' Hospital Experiences				
Area Around Room 'Always' Quiet at Night	300+	73%	-	58%
Doctors 'Always' Communicated Well	300+	85%	-	80%
Home Recovery Information Given	300+	81%	-	82%
Hospital Given 9 or 10 on 10 Point Scale	300+	71%	-	67%
Meds 'Always' Explained Before Given	300+	63%	-	60%
Nurses 'Always' Communicated Well	300+	82%	-	76%
Pain 'Always' Well Controlled	300+	76%	-	69%
Room and Bathroom 'Always' Clean	300+	79%	-	71%
Timely Help 'Always' Received	300+	72%	-	64%
Would Definitely Recommend Hospital	300+	72%	-	69%

Shelby Memorial Hospital

200 S Cedar St Phone: 217-774-3961
Shelbyville, IL 62565 Fax: 217-774-5100
Type: Acute Care Hospitals Emergency Services: Yes
Ownership: Voluntary Non-Profit - Private Beds: 54

Key Personnel:
Chief of Medical Staff . . . . Arnold V Agapito
Infection Control. . . . . Meredith Barnes
Operating Room. . . . . Meredith Barnes
Quality Assurance . . . . Donna Bales, RN
Radiology. . . . . Caroline Rodman, MD
Emergency Room . . . . U Dauz, MD
Intensive Care Unit. . . . . Das Gurujal, MD

Measure	Cases	This Hosp.	State Avg.	U.S. Avg.
Heart Attack Care				
ACE Inhibitor or ARB for LVSD	0	-	96%	96%
Aspirin at Arrival[1]	4	100%	99%	99%
Aspirin at Discharge[1]	2	100%	99%	98%
Beta Blocker at Discharge[1]	2	100%	98%	98%
Fibrinolytic Medication Timing	0	-	50%	55%
PCI Within 90 Minutes of Arrival	0	-	90%	90%
Smoking Cessation Advice	0	-	100%	99%
Chest Pain/Possible Heart Attack Care				
Aspirin at Arrival	62	92%	95%	95%
Median Time to ECG (minutes)	66	6	8	8
Median Time to Transfer (minutes)[1,3]	4	129	57	61
Fibrinolytic Medication Timing[1,3]	4	25%	33%	54%
Heart Failure Care				
ACE Inhibitor or ARB for LVSD[1]	6	67%	94%	94%
Discharge Instructions	31	68%	89%	88%
Evaluation of LVS Function	91	89%	98%	98%
Smoking Cessation Advice[1]	5	100%	99%	98%
Pneumonia Care				
Appropriate Initial Antibiotic[1]	20	90%	90%	92%
Blood Culture Timing	38	79%	97%	96%
Influenza Vaccine	35	54%	91%	91%
Initial Antibiotic Timing	43	88%	96%	95%
Pneumococcal Vaccine	53	51%	92%	93%
Smoking Cessation Advice[1]	8	75%	98%	97%
Surgical Care Improvement Project				
Appropriate VTP Within 24 Hours[5]	0	-	92%	92%
Appropriate Hair Removal[5]	0	-	99%	99%
Appropriate Beta Blocker Usage[5]	0	-	92%	93%
Controlled Postoperative Blood Glucose[5]	0	-	92%	93%
Prophylactic Antibiotic Timing[5]	0	-	97%	97%
Prophylactic Antibiotic Timing (Outpatient)[5]	0	-	93%	92%
Prophylactic Antibiotic Selection[5]	0	-	97%	97%
Prophylactic Antibiotic Select. (Outpatient)[5]	0	-	94%	94%
Prophylactic Antibiotic Stopped[5]	0	-	94%	94%
Recommended VTP Ordered[5]	0	-	94%	94%
Urinary Catheter Removal[5]	0	-	89%	90%
Children's Asthma Care				
Received Systemic Corticosteroids	-	-	-	100%
Received Home Management Plan	-	-	-	71%
Received Reliever Medication	-	-	-	100%
Use of Medical Imaging				
Combination Abdominal CT Scan	161	0.037	0.246	0.191
Combination Chest CT Scan	86	0.012	0.098	0.054
Follow-up Mammogram/Ultrasound	195	19.0%	8.4%	8.4%
MRI for Low Back Pain[1]	25	20.0%	33.4%	32.7%
Survey of Patients' Hospital Experiences				
Area Around Room 'Always' Quiet at Night	(a)	50%	-	58%
Doctors 'Always' Communicated Well	(a)	80%	-	80%
Home Recovery Information Given	(a)	74%	-	82%
Hospital Given 9 or 10 on 10 Point Scale	(a)	56%	-	67%
Meds 'Always' Explained Before Given	(a)	59%	-	60%
Nurses 'Always' Communicated Well	(a)	75%	-	76%
Pain 'Always' Well Controlled	(a)	65%	-	69%
Room and Bathroom 'Always' Clean	(a)	79%	-	71%
Timely Help 'Always' Received	(a)	60%	-	64%
Would Definitely Recommend Hospital	(a)	44%	-	69%

Genesis Medical Center Illini Campus

801 Illini Drive Phone: 309-792-9363
Silvis, IL 61282 Fax: 309-792-4274
Type: Acute Care Hospitals Emergency Services: Yes
Ownership: Government - Local Beds: 150

Key Personnel:
CEO/President. . . . . Charles Bruhn
Cardiac Laboratory. . . . . Andy Nelson
Chief of Medical Staff. . . . . Thomas VonGilliern, MD
Infection Control. . . . . Anne Lewis
Operating Room. . . . . Sandy Freddy
Emergency Room . . . . Janet Eckhart, RN

Measure	Cases	This Hosp.	State Avg.	U.S. Avg.
Heart Attack Care				
ACE Inhibitor or ARB for LVSD	77	100%	96%	96%
Aspirin at Arrival	115	98%	99%	99%
Aspirin at Discharge	113	99%	99%	98%
Beta Blocker at Discharge	105	100%	98%	98%
Fibrinolytic Medication Timing	0	-	50%	55%
PCI Within 90 Minutes of Arrival[1]	21	86%	90%	90%
Smoking Cessation Advice	37	100%	100%	99%
Chest Pain/Possible Heart Attack Care				
Aspirin at Arrival	35	100%	95%	95%
Median Time to ECG (minutes)	39	6	8	8
Median Time to Transfer (minutes)[1,3]	1	127	57	61
Fibrinolytic Medication Timing	0	-	33%	54%
Heart Failure Care				
ACE Inhibitor or ARB for LVSD	70	94%	94%	94%
Discharge Instructions	140	95%	89%	88%
Evaluation of LVS Function	214	100%	98%	98%
Smoking Cessation Advice	25	100%	99%	98%
Pneumonia Care				
Appropriate Initial Antibiotic	102	97%	90%	92%
Blood Culture Timing	161	100%	97%	96%
Influenza Vaccine	111	96%	91%	91%
Initial Antibiotic Timing	161	98%	96%	95%
Pneumococcal Vaccine	133	98%	92%	93%
Smoking Cessation Advice	51	96%	98%	97%
Surgical Care Improvement Project				
Appropriate VTP Within 24 Hours[2]	134	97%	92%	92%
Appropriate Hair Removal[2]	422	100%	99%	99%
Appropriate Beta Blocker Usage[2]	98	100%	92%	93%
Controlled Postoperative Blood Glucose[2]	0	-	92%	93%
Prophylactic Antibiotic Timing[2]	313	100%	97%	97%
Prophylactic Antibiotic Timing (Outpatient)	108	99%	93%	92%
Prophylactic Antibiotic Selection[2]	312	98%	97%	97%
Prophylactic Antibiotic Select. (Outpatient)	107	97%	94%	94%
Prophylactic Antibiotic Stopped[2]	305	96%	94%	94%
Recommended VTP Ordered[2]	135	99%	94%	94%
Urinary Catheter Removal[1,2]	18	94%	89%	90%
Children's Asthma Care				
Received Systemic Corticosteroids	-	-	-	100%
Received Home Management Plan	-	-	-	71%
Received Reliever Medication	-	-	-	100%
Use of Medical Imaging				
Combination Abdominal CT Scan	362	0.044	0.246	0.191
Combination Chest CT Scan	261	0.100	0.098	0.054
Follow-up Mammogram/Ultrasound	847	10.3%	8.4%	8.4%
MRI for Low Back Pain	71	25.4%	33.4%	32.7%
Survey of Patients' Hospital Experiences				
Area Around Room 'Always' Quiet at Night	300+	54%	-	58%
Doctors 'Always' Communicated Well	300+	80%	-	80%
Home Recovery Information Given	300+	84%	-	82%
Hospital Given 9 or 10 on 10 Point Scale	300+	72%	-	67%
Meds 'Always' Explained Before Given	300+	59%	-	60%
Nurses 'Always' Communicated Well	300+	77%	-	76%
Pain 'Always' Well Controlled	300+	71%	-	69%
Room and Bathroom 'Always' Clean	300+	70%	-	71%
Timely Help 'Always' Received	300+	63%	-	64%
Would Definitely Recommend Hospital	300+	75%	-	69%

NOTE: Hospital profiles are in alphabetical order by state, then city, then hospital within the city; Rankings exclude hospitals with less than 25 cases except for patient surveys which excludes hospitals with less than 100 cases; (a) 100–299 cases; (1) The number of cases is too small to be sure how well a hospital is performing; (2) The hospital indicated that the data submitted for this measure were based on a sample of cases; (3) Data was collected during a shorter time period (fewer quarters) than the maximum possible time for this measure; (4) Suppressed for one or more quarters by CMS; (5) No data is available from the hospital for this measure; (6) Fewer than 100 patients completed the HCAHPS survey. Use these rates with caution, as the number of surveys may be too low to reliably assess hospital performance; (7) Survey results are based on less than 12 months of data; (8) Survey results are not available for this reporting period; (9) No or very few patients were eligible for the HCAHPS survey. The scores shown, if any, reflect a very small number of surveys; (10) A state average was not calculated because too few hospitals in the state submitted data; (11) There were discrepancies in the data collection process; Please refer to the User's Guide for a full explanation of data.

Skokie Hospital

9600 Gross Point Road
Skokie, IL 60076
Type: Acute Care Hospitals
Ownership: Voluntary Non-Profit - Other
Phone: 847-677-9600
Fax: 847-933-6439
Emergency Services: Yes
Beds: 268

Key Personnel:
CEO/President. . . . . James Frankenbach
Intensive Care Unit. . . . . Rachelle Eifert

Measure	Cases	This Hosp.	State Avg.	U.S. Avg.
Heart Attack Care				
ACE Inhibitor or ARB for LVSD[1]	17	88%	96%	96%
Aspirin at Arrival	120	100%	99%	99%
Aspirin at Discharge	106	99%	99%	98%
Beta Blocker at Discharge	103	94%	98%	98%
Fibrinolytic Medication Timing	0	-	50%	55%
PCI Within 90 Minutes of Arrival[1]	23	91%	90%	90%
Smoking Cessation Advice[1]	17	100%	100%	99%
Chest Pain/Possible Heart Attack Care				
Aspirin at Arrival[3]	0	-	95%	95%
Median Time to ECG (minutes)[3]	0	-	8	8
Median Time to Transfer (minutes)[5]	0	-	57	61
Fibrinolytic Medication Timing[5]	0	-	33%	54%
Heart Failure Care				
ACE Inhibitor or ARB for LVSD	79	92%	94%	94%
Discharge Instructions	196	71%	89%	88%
Evaluation of LVS Function	318	97%	98%	98%
Smoking Cessation Advice[1]	9	89%	99%	98%
Pneumonia Care				
Appropriate Initial Antibiotic	93	90%	90%	92%
Blood Culture Timing	88	95%	97%	96%
Influenza Vaccine	119	92%	91%	91%
Initial Antibiotic Timing	172	98%	96%	95%
Pneumococcal Vaccine	199	86%	92%	93%
Smoking Cessation Advice[1]	16	94%	98%	97%
Surgical Care Improvement Project				
Appropriate VTP Within 24 Hours[2]	153	100%	92%	92%
Appropriate Hair Removal[2]	518	100%	99%	99%
Appropriate Beta Blocker Usage[2]	161	100%	92%	93%
Controlled Postoperative Blood Glucose[2]	53	92%	92%	93%
Prophylactic Antibiotic Timing[2]	347	98%	97%	97%
Prophylactic Antibiotic Timing (Outpatient)	192	97%	93%	92%
Prophylactic Antibiotic Selection[2]	350	99%	97%	97%
Prophylactic Antibiotic Select. (Outpatient)	191	96%	94%	94%
Prophylactic Antibiotic Stopped[2]	343	96%	94%	94%
Recommended VTP Ordered[2]	153	100%	94%	94%
Urinary Catheter Removal[2]	150	99%	89%	90%
Children's Asthma Care				
Received Systemic Corticosteroids	-	-	-	100%
Received Home Management Plan	-	-	-	71%
Received Reliever Medication	-	-	-	100%
Use of Medical Imaging				
Combination Abdominal CT Scan	317	0.464	0.246	0.191
Combination Chest CT Scan	204	0.593	0.098	0.054
Follow-up Mammogram/Ultrasound	2,398	8.1%	8.4%	8.4%
MRI for Low Back Pain[1]	7	28.6%	33.4%	32.7%
Survey of Patients' Hospital Experiences				
Area Around Room 'Always' Quiet at Night	300+	48%	-	58%
Doctors 'Always' Communicated Well	300+	74%	-	80%
Home Recovery Information Given	300+	73%	-	82%
Hospital Given 9 or 10 on 10 Point Scale	300+	51%	-	67%
Meds 'Always' Explained Before Given	300+	49%	-	60%
Nurses 'Always' Communicated Well	300+	68%	-	76%
Pain 'Always' Well Controlled	300+	57%	-	69%
Room and Bathroom 'Always' Clean	300+	60%	-	71%
Timely Help 'Always' Received	300+	49%	-	64%
Would Definitely Recommend Hospital	300+	60%	-	69%

Sparta Community Hospital

818 E Broadway
Sparta, IL 62286
E-mail: hertzingp@spartahospital.com
URL: www.spartahospital.com
Type: Critical Access Hospitals
Ownership: Govt - Hospital Dist/Auth
Phone: 618-443-2177
Fax: 618-443-1383
Emergency Services: Yes
Beds: 39

Key Personnel:
Chief of Medical Staff. . . . . Wim Sippo, MD
Infection Control. . . . . Donna Chappell, RN
Operating Room. . . . . Janet Zeidler, RN
Quality Assurance . . . . Ruth Holloway
Anesthesiology. . . . . Debbie Weatherspoon
Emergency Room . . . . Sharon Hall, MD

Measure	Cases	This Hosp.	State Avg.	U.S. Avg.
Heart Attack Care				
ACE Inhibitor or ARB for LVSD	0	-	96%	96%
Aspirin at Arrival[1]	2	100%	99%	99%
Aspirin at Discharge[5]	0	-	99%	98%
Beta Blocker at Discharge[5]	0	-	98%	98%
Fibrinolytic Medication Timing	0	-	50%	55%
PCI Within 90 Minutes of Arrival	0	-	90%	90%
Smoking Cessation Advice	0	-	100%	99%
Chest Pain/Possible Heart Attack Care				
Aspirin at Arrival	-	-	95%	95%
Median Time to ECG (minutes)	-	-	8	8
Median Time to Transfer (minutes)	-	-	57	61
Fibrinolytic Medication Timing	-	-	33%	54%
Heart Failure Care				
ACE Inhibitor or ARB for LVSD[5]	0	-	94%	94%
Discharge Instructions[5]	0	-	89%	88%
Evaluation of LVS Function[5]	0	-	98%	98%
Smoking Cessation Advice[1]	4	100%	99%	98%
Pneumonia Care				
Appropriate Initial Antibiotic	44	93%	90%	92%
Blood Culture Timing[1]	21	95%	97%	96%
Influenza Vaccine[5]	0	-	91%	91%
Initial Antibiotic Timing	53	98%	96%	95%
Pneumococcal Vaccine[5]	0	-	92%	93%
Smoking Cessation Advice[1]	20	95%	98%	97%
Surgical Care Improvement Project				
Appropriate VTP Within 24 Hours[5]	0	-	92%	92%
Appropriate Hair Removal[5]	0	-	99%	99%
Appropriate Beta Blocker Usage[5]	0	-	92%	93%
Controlled Postoperative Blood Glucose[5]	0	-	92%	93%
Prophylactic Antibiotic Timing[5]	0	-	97%	97%
Prophylactic Antibiotic Timing (Outpatient)	-	-	93%	92%
Prophylactic Antibiotic Selection[5]	0	-	97%	97%
Prophylactic Antibiotic Select. (Outpatient)	-	-	94%	94%
Prophylactic Antibiotic Stopped[5]	0	-	94%	94%
Recommended VTP Ordered[5]	0	-	94%	94%
Urinary Catheter Removal[5]	0	-	89%	90%
Children's Asthma Care				
Received Systemic Corticosteroids	-	-	-	100%
Received Home Management Plan	-	-	-	71%
Received Reliever Medication	-	-	-	100%
Use of Medical Imaging				
Combination Abdominal CT Scan	-	-	0.246	0.191
Combination Chest CT Scan	-	-	0.098	0.054
Follow-up Mammogram/Ultrasound	-	-	8.4%	8.4%
MRI for Low Back Pain	-	-	33.4%	32.7%
Survey of Patients' Hospital Experiences				
Area Around Room 'Always' Quiet at Night[8]	-	-	-	58%
Doctors 'Always' Communicated Well[8]	-	-	-	80%
Home Recovery Information Given[8]	-	-	-	82%
Hospital Given 9 or 10 on 10 Point Scale[8]	-	-	-	67%
Meds 'Always' Explained Before Given[8]	-	-	-	60%
Nurses 'Always' Communicated Well[8]	-	-	-	76%
Pain 'Always' Well Controlled[8]	-	-	-	69%
Room and Bathroom 'Always' Clean[8]	-	-	-	71%
Timely Help 'Always' Received[8]	-	-	-	64%
Would Definitely Recommend Hospital[8]	-	-	-	69%

Saint Margarets Hospital

600 E 1st St
Spring Valley, IL 61362
E-mail: hrdir@st-margarets.com
Type: Acute Care Hospitals
Ownership: Voluntary Non-Profit - Church
Phone: 815-664-1362
Fax: 815-664-1608
Emergency Services: Yes
Beds: 155

Key Personnel:
CEO/President. . . . . Tim Muntz
Chief of Medical Staff. . . . . Marshal Cummings

Measure	Cases	This Hosp.	State Avg.	U.S. Avg.
Heart Attack Care				
ACE Inhibitor or ARB for LVSD[1,3]	2	100%	96%	96%
Aspirin at Arrival[1,3]	4	100%	99%	99%
Aspirin at Discharge[1,3]	3	100%	99%	98%
Beta Blocker at Discharge[1,3]	3	100%	98%	98%
Fibrinolytic Medication Timing[3]	0	-	50%	55%
PCI Within 90 Minutes of Arrival[3]	0	-	90%	90%
Smoking Cessation Advice[1,3]	1	100%	100%	99%
Chest Pain/Possible Heart Attack Care				
Aspirin at Arrival	45	98%	95%	95%
Median Time to ECG (minutes)	48	6	8	8
Median Time to Transfer (minutes)[1,3]	6	68	57	61
Fibrinolytic Medication Timing[1]	2	50%	33%	54%
Heart Failure Care				
ACE Inhibitor or ARB for LVSD[1]	19	95%	94%	94%
Discharge Instructions	55	78%	89%	88%
Evaluation of LVS Function	91	100%	98%	98%
Smoking Cessation Advice[1]	11	73%	99%	98%
Pneumonia Care				
Appropriate Initial Antibiotic	40	88%	90%	92%
Blood Culture Timing	49	98%	97%	96%
Influenza Vaccine	54	91%	91%	91%
Initial Antibiotic Timing	102	98%	96%	95%
Pneumococcal Vaccine	82	94%	92%	93%
Smoking Cessation Advice[1]	15	87%	98%	97%
Surgical Care Improvement Project				
Appropriate VTP Within 24 Hours	81	98%	92%	92%
Appropriate Hair Removal	335	99%	99%	99%
Appropriate Beta Blocker Usage	100	89%	92%	93%
Controlled Postoperative Blood Glucose	0	-	92%	93%
Prophylactic Antibiotic Timing	242	92%	97%	97%
Prophylactic Antibiotic Timing (Outpatient)	44	93%	93%	92%
Prophylactic Antibiotic Selection	241	98%	97%	97%
Prophylactic Antibiotic Select. (Outpatient)	44	89%	94%	94%
Prophylactic Antibiotic Stopped	227	96%	94%	94%
Recommended VTP Ordered	81	99%	94%	94%
Urinary Catheter Removal	102	100%	89%	90%
Children's Asthma Care				
Received Systemic Corticosteroids	-	-	-	100%
Received Home Management Plan	-	-	-	71%
Received Reliever Medication	-	-	-	100%
Use of Medical Imaging				
Combination Abdominal CT Scan	276	0.134	0.246	0.191
Combination Chest CT Scan	217	0.032	0.098	0.054
Follow-up Mammogram/Ultrasound	563	6.9%	8.4%	8.4%
MRI for Low Back Pain	76	31.6%	33.4%	32.7%
Survey of Patients' Hospital Experiences				
Area Around Room 'Always' Quiet at Night	300+	53%	-	58%
Doctors 'Always' Communicated Well	300+	86%	-	80%
Home Recovery Information Given	300+	85%	-	82%
Hospital Given 9 or 10 on 10 Point Scale	300+	62%	-	67%
Meds 'Always' Explained Before Given	300+	64%	-	60%
Nurses 'Always' Communicated Well	300+	77%	-	76%
Pain 'Always' Well Controlled	300+	66%	-	69%
Room and Bathroom 'Always' Clean	300+	73%	-	71%
Timely Help 'Always' Received	300+	60%	-	64%
Would Definitely Recommend Hospital	300+	67%	-	69%

NOTE: Hospital profiles are in alphabetical order by state, then city, then hospital within the city; Rankings exclude hospitals with less than 25 cases except for patient surveys which excludes hospitals with less than 100 cases; (a) 100–299 cases; (1) The number of cases is too small to be sure how well a hospital is performing; (2) The hospital indicated that the data submitted for this measure were based on a sample of cases; (3) Data was collected during a shorter time period (fewer quarters) than the maximum possible time for this measure; (4) Suppressed for one or more quarters by CMS; (5) No data is available from the hospital for this measure; (6) Fewer than 100 patients completed the HCAHPS survey. Use these rates with caution, as the number of surveys may be too low to reliably assess hospital performance; (7) Survey results are based on less than 12 months of data; (8) Survey results are not available for this reporting period; (9) No or very few patients were eligible for the HCAHPS survey. The scores shown, if any, reflect a very small number of surveys; (10) A state average was not calculated because too few hospitals in the state submitted data; (11) There were discrepancies in the data collection process; Please refer to the User's Guide for a full explanation of data.

Memorial Medical Center

701 N First St Phone: 217-788-3000
Springfield, IL 62781 Fax: 217-788-5594
URL: www.memorialmedical.com
Type: Acute Care Hospitals Emergency Services: Yes
Ownership: Voluntary Non-Profit - Private Beds: 444

Key Personnel:

CEO/President. . . . . Edgar J. Curtis
Chief of Medical Staff. . . . . Robert Vautrain, MD
Coronary Care . . . . Donna Crompton, RN
Infection Control. . . . . Margaret Roth, RN
Operating Room. . . . . Sandy Flattery, RN
Quality Assurance . . . . Todd Riplinger
Radiology. . . . . Kathy Ambs
Patient Relations . . . . Marsha Prater, PhD RN

Measure	Cases	This Hosp.	State Avg.	U.S. Avg.
Heart Attack Care				
ACE Inhibitor or ARB for LVSD	77	94%	96%	96%
Aspirin at Arrival	344	99%	99%	99%
Aspirin at Discharge	520	99%	99%	98%
Beta Blocker at Discharge	495	99%	98%	98%
Fibrinolytic Medication Timing	0	-	50%	55%
PCI Within 90 Minutes of Arrival	71	99%	90%	90%
Smoking Cessation Advice	183	99%	100%	99%
Chest Pain/Possible Heart Attack Care				
Aspirin at Arrival[1,3]	6	100%	95%	95%
Median Time to ECG (minutes)[1,3]	6	20	8	8
Median Time to Transfer (minutes)[5]	0	-	57	61
Fibrinolytic Medication Timing[5]	0	-	33%	54%
Heart Failure Care				
ACE Inhibitor or ARB for LVSD	183	98%	94%	94%
Discharge Instructions	444	94%	89%	88%
Evaluation of LVS Function	557	100%	98%	98%
Smoking Cessation Advice	95	100%	99%	98%
Pneumonia Care				
Appropriate Initial Antibiotic	291	91%	90%	92%
Blood Culture Timing	390	97%	97%	96%
Influenza Vaccine	311	88%	91%	91%
Initial Antibiotic Timing	532	95%	96%	95%
Pneumococcal Vaccine	507	91%	92%	93%
Smoking Cessation Advice	231	97%	98%	97%
Surgical Care Improvement Project				
Appropriate VTP Within 24 Hours[2]	194	93%	92%	92%
Appropriate Hair Removal[2]	1,051	100%	99%	99%
Appropriate Beta Blocker Usage[2]	440	97%	92%	93%
Controlled Postoperative Blood Glucose[2]	248	94%	92%	93%
Prophylactic Antibiotic Timing[2]	842	98%	97%	97%
Prophylactic Antibiotic Timing (Outpatient)	655	94%	93%	92%
Prophylactic Antibiotic Selection[2]	847	98%	97%	97%
Prophylactic Antibiotic Select. (Outpatient)	648	93%	94%	94%
Prophylactic Antibiotic Stopped[2]	813	97%	94%	94%
Recommended VTP Ordered[2]	194	97%	94%	94%
Urinary Catheter Removal[2]	219	93%	89%	90%
Children's Asthma Care				
Received Systemic Corticosteroids	-	-	-	100%
Received Home Management Plan	-	-	-	71%
Received Reliever Medication	-	-	-	100%
Use of Medical Imaging				
Combination Abdominal CT Scan	1,873	0.093	0.246	0.191
Combination Chest CT Scan	1,692	0.017	0.098	0.054
Follow-up Mammogram/Ultrasound	3,066	7.2%	8.4%	8.4%
MRI for Low Back Pain	391	33.8%	33.4%	32.7%
Survey of Patients' Hospital Experiences				
Area Around Room 'Always' Quiet at Night	300+	43%	-	58%
Doctors 'Always' Communicated Well	300+	78%	-	80%
Home Recovery Information Given	300+	80%	-	82%
Hospital Given 9 or 10 on 10 Point Scale	300+	65%	-	67%
Meds 'Always' Explained Before Given	300+	56%	-	60%
Nurses 'Always' Communicated Well	300+	75%	-	76%
Pain 'Always' Well Controlled	300+	67%	-	69%
Room and Bathroom 'Always' Clean	300+	60%	-	71%
Timely Help 'Always' Received	300+	57%	-	64%
Would Definitely Recommend Hospital	300+	74%	-	69%

Saint Johns Hospital

800 E Carpenter St Phone: 217-544-6464
Springfield, IL 62769 Fax: 217-535-3989
URL: www.st-johns.org
Type: Acute Care Hospitals Emergency Services: Yes
Ownership: Voluntary Non-Profit - Church Beds: 742

Key Personnel:

CEO/President. . . . . Bob Ritz
Chief of Medical Staff . . . . Craig Backs MD
Infection Control. . . . . Carol Coleman RN
Radiology. . . . . Pat Hynes
Emergency Room . . . . Amy Jones
Intensive Care Unit. . . . . Betty Meisser

Measure	Cases	This Hosp.	State Avg.	U.S. Avg.
Heart Attack Care				
ACE Inhibitor or ARB for LVSD	116	99%	96%	96%
Aspirin at Arrival	158	100%	99%	99%
Aspirin at Discharge	559	100%	99%	98%
Beta Blocker at Discharge	546	100%	98%	98%
Fibrinolytic Medication Timing	0	-	50%	55%
PCI Within 90 Minutes of Arrival	43	100%	90%	90%
Smoking Cessation Advice	228	100%	100%	99%
Chest Pain/Possible Heart Attack Care				
Aspirin at Arrival[3]	0	-	95%	95%
Median Time to ECG (minutes)[3]	0	-	8	8
Median Time to Transfer (minutes)[5]	0	-	57	61
Fibrinolytic Medication Timing[5]	0	-	33%	54%
Heart Failure Care				
ACE Inhibitor or ARB for LVSD[2]	112	100%	94%	94%
Discharge Instructions[2]	244	92%	89%	88%
Evaluation of LVS Function[2]	295	100%	98%	98%
Smoking Cessation Advice[2]	91	100%	99%	98%
Pneumonia Care				
Appropriate Initial Antibiotic[2]	61	87%	90%	92%
Blood Culture Timing[2]	53	96%	97%	96%
Influenza Vaccine[2]	84	79%	91%	91%
Initial Antibiotic Timing[2]	88	89%	96%	95%
Pneumococcal Vaccine[2]	123	80%	92%	93%
Smoking Cessation Advice[2]	73	100%	98%	97%
Surgical Care Improvement Project				
Appropriate VTP Within 24 Hours[2]	161	78%	92%	92%
Appropriate Hair Removal[2]	711	100%	99%	99%
Appropriate Beta Blocker Usage[2]	301	93%	92%	93%
Controlled Postoperative Blood Glucose[2]	180	94%	92%	93%
Prophylactic Antibiotic Timing[2]	510	97%	97%	97%
Prophylactic Antibiotic Timing (Outpatient)	428	93%	93%	92%
Prophylactic Antibiotic Selection[2]	518	99%	97%	97%
Prophylactic Antibiotic Select. (Outpatient)	423	96%	94%	94%
Prophylactic Antibiotic Stopped[2]	482	97%	94%	94%
Recommended VTP Ordered[2]	161	86%	94%	94%
Urinary Catheter Removal[2]	199	93%	89%	90%
Children's Asthma Care				
Received Systemic Corticosteroids	88	99%	-	100%
Received Home Management Plan	88	60%	-	71%
Received Reliever Medication	88	100%	-	100%
Use of Medical Imaging				
Combination Abdominal CT Scan	755	0.460	0.246	0.191
Combination Chest CT Scan	813	0.169	0.098	0.054
Follow-up Mammogram/Ultrasound	1,812	12.4%	8.4%	8.4%
MRI for Low Back Pain	160	40.0%	33.4%	32.7%
Survey of Patients' Hospital Experiences				
Area Around Room 'Always' Quiet at Night	300+	54%	-	58%
Doctors 'Always' Communicated Well	300+	79%	-	80%
Home Recovery Information Given	300+	81%	-	82%
Hospital Given 9 or 10 on 10 Point Scale	300+	69%	-	67%
Meds 'Always' Explained Before Given	300+	59%	-	60%
Nurses 'Always' Communicated Well	300+	74%	-	76%
Pain 'Always' Well Controlled	300+	66%	-	69%
Room and Bathroom 'Always' Clean	300+	68%	-	71%
Timely Help 'Always' Received	300+	61%	-	64%
Would Definitely Recommend Hospital	300+	73%	-	69%

Community Memorial Hospital

400 Caldwell Phone: 618-635-2200
Staunton, IL 62088 Fax: 618-635-3400
E-mail: mbellovich@stauntonhospital.org
URL: www.stauntonhospital.org
Type: Critical Access Hospitals Emergency Services: Yes
Ownership: Voluntary Non-Profit - Other Beds: 49

Key Personnel:

CEO/President. . . . . Patrick B Heise
Chief of Medical Staff. . . . . Manish Mathur
Infection Control. . . . . Judy Matteson, RN
Operating Room. . . . . Joseph Blazer, RN
Quality Assurance . . . . Judy Matteson, RN
Emergency Room . . . . Roberta Monsholt, RN

Measure	Cases	This Hosp.	State Avg.	U.S. Avg.
Heart Attack Care				
ACE Inhibitor or ARB for LVSD[1]	1	0%	96%	96%
Aspirin at Arrival[1]	8	75%	99%	99%
Aspirin at Discharge[1]	6	83%	99%	98%
Beta Blocker at Discharge[1]	7	86%	98%	98%
Fibrinolytic Medication Timing	0	-	50%	55%
PCI Within 90 Minutes of Arrival	0	-	90%	90%
Smoking Cessation Advice	0	-	100%	99%
Chest Pain/Possible Heart Attack Care				
Aspirin at Arrival	-	-	95%	95%
Median Time to ECG (minutes)	-	-	8	8
Median Time to Transfer (minutes)	-	-	57	61
Fibrinolytic Medication Timing	-	-	33%	54%
Heart Failure Care				
ACE Inhibitor or ARB for LVSD[1,3]	4	50%	94%	94%
Discharge Instructions[1,3]	6	50%	89%	88%
Evaluation of LVS Function[1,3]	8	75%	98%	98%
Smoking Cessation Advice[3]	0	-	99%	98%
Pneumonia Care				
Appropriate Initial Antibiotic[1]	13	92%	90%	92%
Blood Culture Timing[1]	8	62%	97%	96%
Influenza Vaccine[1]	9	89%	91%	91%
Initial Antibiotic Timing[1]	13	100%	96%	95%
Pneumococcal Vaccine[1]	11	73%	92%	93%
Smoking Cessation Advice[1]	6	67%	98%	97%
Surgical Care Improvement Project				
Appropriate VTP Within 24 Hours[1,3]	1	0%	92%	92%
Appropriate Hair Removal[1,3]	7	100%	99%	99%
Appropriate Beta Blocker Usage[5]	0	-	92%	93%
Controlled Postoperative Blood Glucose[3]	0	-	92%	93%
Prophylactic Antibiotic Timing[1,3]	5	20%	97%	97%
Prophylactic Antibiotic Timing (Outpatient)	-	-	93%	92%
Prophylactic Antibiotic Selection[1,3]	4	100%	97%	97%
Prophylactic Antibiotic Select. (Outpatient)	-	-	94%	94%
Prophylactic Antibiotic Stopped[1,3]	4	100%	94%	94%
Recommended VTP Ordered[1,3]	1	0%	94%	94%
Urinary Catheter Removal[3]	0	-	89%	90%
Children's Asthma Care				
Received Systemic Corticosteroids	-	-	-	100%
Received Home Management Plan	-	-	-	71%
Received Reliever Medication	-	-	-	100%
Use of Medical Imaging				
Combination Abdominal CT Scan	-	-	0.246	0.191
Combination Chest CT Scan	-	-	0.098	0.054
Follow-up Mammogram/Ultrasound	-	-	8.4%	8.4%
MRI for Low Back Pain	-	-	33.4%	32.7%
Survey of Patients' Hospital Experiences				
Area Around Room 'Always' Quiet at Night[8]	-	-	-	58%
Doctors 'Always' Communicated Well[8]	-	-	-	80%
Home Recovery Information Given[8]	-	-	-	82%
Hospital Given 9 or 10 on 10 Point Scale[8]	-	-	-	67%
Meds 'Always' Explained Before Given[8]	-	-	-	60%
Nurses 'Always' Communicated Well[8]	-	-	-	76%
Pain 'Always' Well Controlled[8]	-	-	-	69%
Room and Bathroom 'Always' Clean[8]	-	-	-	71%
Timely Help 'Always' Received[8]	-	-	-	64%
Would Definitely Recommend Hospital[8]	-	-	-	69%

NOTE: Hospital profiles are in alphabetical order by state, then city, then hospital within the city; Rankings exclude hospitals with less than 25 cases except for patient surveys which excludes hospitals with less than 100 cases; (a) 100–299 cases; (1) The number of cases is too small to be sure how well a hospital is performing; (2) The hospital indicated that the data submitted for this measure were based on a sample of cases; (3) Data was collected during a shorter time period (fewer quarters) than the maximum possible time for this measure; (4) Suppressed for one or more quarters by CMS; (5) No data is available from the hospital for this measure; (6) Fewer than 100 patients completed the HCAHPS survey. Use these rates with caution, as the number of surveys may be too low to reliably assess hospital performance; (7) Survey results are based on less than 12 months of data; (8) Survey results are not available for this reporting period; (9) No or very few patients were eligible for the HCAHPS survey. The scores shown, if any, reflect a very small number of surveys; (10) A state average was not calculated because too few hospitals in the state submitted data; (11) There were discrepancies in the data collection process; Please refer to the User's Guide for a full explanation of data.

CGH Medical Center

100 East Lefevre Road
Sterling, IL 61081
URL: www.cghmc.com
Type: Acute Care Hospitals
Ownership: Government - Local
Phone: 815-625-0400
Fax: 815-625-4825
Emergency Services: Yes
Beds: 139

Key Personnel:
CEO/President. . . . . Ed Andersen
Chief of Medical Staff. . . . . Angel Biazquez, MD
Infection Control. . . . . Sandra Westbo, RN
Operating Room. . . . . Thomas P McGlone
Pediatric Ambulatory Care . . . . . . Mandrama Herman, MD
Pediatric In-Patient Care . . . . Mandrama Herman, MD
Quality Assurance . . . . Theresa Friel-Draper, RN
Radiology. . . . . Eugene W Brown, MD

Measure	Cases	This Hosp.	State Avg.	U.S. Avg.
Heart Attack Care				
ACE Inhibitor or ARB for LVSD[1]	13	100%	96%	96%
Aspirin at Arrival	80	100%	99%	99%
Aspirin at Discharge	69	99%	99%	98%
Beta Blocker at Discharge	67	99%	98%	98%
Fibrinolytic Medication Timing	0	-	50%	55%
PCI Within 90 Minutes of Arrival[1]	21	81%	90%	90%
Smoking Cessation Advice[1]	24	100%	100%	99%
Chest Pain/Possible Heart Attack Care				
Aspirin at Arrival	89	98%	95%	95%
Median Time to ECG (minutes)	90	9	8	8
Median Time to Transfer (minutes)[1,3]	3	407	57	61
Fibrinolytic Medication Timing[1]	1	0%	33%	54%
Heart Failure Care				
ACE Inhibitor or ARB for LVSD	36	97%	94%	94%
Discharge Instructions	179	84%	89%	88%
Evaluation of LVS Function	219	100%	98%	98%
Smoking Cessation Advice[1]	20	100%	99%	98%
Pneumonia Care				
Appropriate Initial Antibiotic	89	93%	90%	92%
Blood Culture Timing	126	98%	97%	96%
Influenza Vaccine	107	93%	91%	91%
Initial Antibiotic Timing	168	95%	96%	95%
Pneumococcal Vaccine	139	96%	92%	93%
Smoking Cessation Advice	38	97%	98%	97%
Surgical Care Improvement Project				
Appropriate VTP Within 24 Hours[2]	242	96%	92%	92%
Appropriate Hair Removal[2]	444	99%	99%	99%
Appropriate Beta Blocker Usage[2]	149	81%	92%	93%
Controlled Postoperative Blood Glucose[2]	0	-	92%	93%
Prophylactic Antibiotic Timing[2]	307	97%	97%	97%
Prophylactic Antibiotic Timing (Outpatient)	57	93%	93%	92%
Prophylactic Antibiotic Selection[2]	307	96%	97%	97%
Prophylactic Antibiotic Select. (Outpatient)	55	85%	94%	94%
Prophylactic Antibiotic Stopped[2]	303	96%	94%	94%
Recommended VTP Ordered[2]	242	96%	94%	94%
Urinary Catheter Removal[2]	117	85%	89%	90%
Children's Asthma Care				
Received Systemic Corticosteroids	-	-	-	100%
Received Home Management Plan	-	-	-	71%
Received Reliever Medication	-	-	-	100%
Use of Medical Imaging				
Combination Abdominal CT Scan	600	0.337	0.246	0.191
Combination Chest CT Scan	384	0.341	0.098	0.054
Follow-up Mammogram/Ultrasound	503	10.1%	8.4%	8.4%
MRI for Low Back Pain	137	32.1%	33.4%	32.7%
Survey of Patients' Hospital Experiences				
Area Around Room 'Always' Quiet at Night	300+	55%	-	58%
Doctors 'Always' Communicated Well	300+	80%	-	80%
Home Recovery Information Given	300+	84%	-	82%
Hospital Given 9 or 10 on 10 Point Scale	300+	66%	-	67%
Meds 'Always' Explained Before Given	300+	63%	-	60%
Nurses 'Always' Communicated Well	300+	74%	-	76%
Pain 'Always' Well Controlled	300+	71%	-	69%
Room and Bathroom 'Always' Clean	300+	78%	-	71%
Timely Help 'Always' Received	300+	69%	-	64%
Would Definitely Recommend Hospital	300+	66%		69%

Saint Marys Hospital

111 Spring Street
Streator, IL 61364
URL: www.stmaryshospital.org
Type: Acute Care Hospitals
Ownership: Voluntary Non-Profit - Church
Phone: 815-673-2311
Fax: 815-673-4592
Emergency Services: Yes
Beds: 251

Key Personnel:
CEO/President. . . . . Marker Heller
Chief of Medical Staff . . . . Glen Ricca
Operating Room. . . . . Bonnie Ostrem, RN
Pediatric Ambulatory Care . . . . . . Bella Baz, MD
Pediatric In-Patient Care . . . . Bella Baz, MD
Quality Assurance . . . . Walter Wahl
Radiology. . . . . Mark Hilborn, MD
Emergency Room . . . . Susan Taylor, RN

Measure	Cases	This Hosp.	State Avg.	U.S. Avg.
Heart Attack Care				
ACE Inhibitor or ARB for LVSD[1]	1	100%	96%	96%
Aspirin at Arrival	28	89%	99%	99%
Aspirin at Discharge[1]	20	95%	99%	98%
Beta Blocker at Discharge[1]	22	100%	98%	98%
Fibrinolytic Medication Timing	0	-	50%	55%
PCI Within 90 Minutes of Arrival	0	-	90%	90%
Smoking Cessation Advice[1]	2	100%	100%	99%
Chest Pain/Possible Heart Attack Care				
Aspirin at Arrival	46	100%	95%	95%
Median Time to ECG (minutes)	46	7	8	8
Median Time to Transfer (minutes)[1,3]	3	73	57	61
Fibrinolytic Medication Timing[1]	4	25%	33%	54%
Heart Failure Care				
ACE Inhibitor or ARB for LVSD[1]	18	100%	94%	94%
Discharge Instructions	51	90%	89%	88%
Evaluation of LVS Function	84	96%	98%	98%
Smoking Cessation Advice[1]	7	100%	99%	98%
Pneumonia Care				
Appropriate Initial Antibiotic[2]	65	95%	90%	92%
Blood Culture Timing[2]	93	100%	97%	96%
Influenza Vaccine[2]	90	98%	91%	91%
Initial Antibiotic Timing[2]	120	98%	96%	95%
Pneumococcal Vaccine[2]	115	98%	92%	93%
Smoking Cessation Advice[2]	43	88%	98%	97%
Surgical Care Improvement Project				
Appropriate VTP Within 24 Hours	89	98%	92%	92%
Appropriate Hair Removal	173	100%	99%	99%
Appropriate Beta Blocker Usage	60	100%	92%	93%
Controlled Postoperative Blood Glucose	0	-	92%	93%
Prophylactic Antibiotic Timing	113	99%	97%	97%
Prophylactic Antibiotic Timing (Outpatient)	67	88%	93%	92%
Prophylactic Antibiotic Selection	113	96%	97%	97%
Prophylactic Antibiotic Select. (Outpatient)	63	97%	94%	94%
Prophylactic Antibiotic Stopped	110	93%	94%	94%
Recommended VTP Ordered	89	99%	94%	94%
Urinary Catheter Removal	45	93%	89%	90%
Children's Asthma Care				
Received Systemic Corticosteroids	-	-	-	100%
Received Home Management Plan	-	-	-	71%
Received Reliever Medication	-	-	-	100%
Use of Medical Imaging				
Combination Abdominal CT Scan	274	0.566	0.246	0.191
Combination Chest CT Scan	234	0.560	0.098	0.054
Follow-up Mammogram/Ultrasound	860	5.5%	8.4%	8.4%
MRI for Low Back Pain	80	33.8%	33.4%	32.7%
Survey of Patients' Hospital Experiences				
Area Around Room 'Always' Quiet at Night	300+	56%	-	58%
Doctors 'Always' Communicated Well	300+	81%	-	80%
Home Recovery Information Given	300+	85%	-	82%
Hospital Given 9 or 10 on 10 Point Scale	300+	61%	-	67%
Meds 'Always' Explained Before Given	300+	60%	-	60%
Nurses 'Always' Communicated Well	300+	76%	-	76%
Pain 'Always' Well Controlled	300+	70%	-	69%
Room and Bathroom 'Always' Clean	300+	77%	-	71%
Timely Help 'Always' Received	300+	68%		64%
Would Definitely Recommend Hospital	300+	63%	-	69%

Taylorville Memorial Hospital

201 East Pleasant Street
Taylorville, IL 62568
URL: www.svmh.org
Type: Critical Access Hospitals
Ownership: Voluntary Non-Profit - Church
Phone: 217-824-3331
Fax: 217-824-1638
Emergency Services: Yes
Beds: 74

Key Personnel:
CEO/President. . . . . Dan Raab
Chief of Medical Staff . . . . Richard K DelValle
Emergency Room . . . . Matthew Yociss, MD

Measure	Cases	This Hosp.	State Avg.	U.S. Avg.
Heart Attack Care				
ACE Inhibitor or ARB for LVSD[1]	1	100%	96%	96%
Aspirin at Arrival[1]	5	80%	99%	99%
Aspirin at Discharge[1]	2	100%	99%	98%
Beta Blocker at Discharge[1]	2	100%	98%	98%
Fibrinolytic Medication Timing	0	-	50%	55%
PCI Within 90 Minutes of Arrival[5]	0	-	90%	90%
Smoking Cessation Advice	0	-	100%	99%
Chest Pain/Possible Heart Attack Care				
Aspirin at Arrival[1,3]	22	82%	95%	95%
Median Time to ECG (minutes)[1,3]	22	3	8	8
Median Time to Transfer (minutes)[3]	0	-	57	61
Fibrinolytic Medication Timing[3]	0	-	33%	54%
Heart Failure Care				
ACE Inhibitor or ARB for LVSD[1]	24	96%	94%	94%
Discharge Instructions	43	100%	89%	88%
Evaluation of LVS Function	63	98%	98%	98%
Smoking Cessation Advice[1]	9	89%	99%	98%
Pneumonia Care				
Appropriate Initial Antibiotic	48	77%	90%	92%
Blood Culture Timing	90	89%	97%	96%
Influenza Vaccine	81	98%	91%	91%
Initial Antibiotic Timing	119	95%	96%	95%
Pneumococcal Vaccine	146	100%	92%	93%
Smoking Cessation Advice	30	100%	98%	97%
Surgical Care Improvement Project				
Appropriate VTP Within 24 Hours[1]	3	100%	92%	92%
Appropriate Hair Removal	50	98%	99%	99%
Appropriate Beta Blocker Usage[5]	0	-	92%	93%
Controlled Postoperative Blood Glucose	0	-	92%	93%
Prophylactic Antibiotic Timing	45	98%	97%	97%
Prophylactic Antibiotic Timing (Outpatient)[5]	0	-	93%	92%
Prophylactic Antibiotic Selection	45	100%	97%	97%
Prophylactic Antibiotic Select. (Outpatient)[5]	0	-	94%	94%
Prophylactic Antibiotic Stopped	44	89%	94%	94%
Recommended VTP Ordered[1]	3	100%	94%	94%
Urinary Catheter Removal	0	-	89%	90%
Children's Asthma Care				
Received Systemic Corticosteroids	-	-	-	100%
Received Home Management Plan	-	-	-	71%
Received Reliever Medication	-	-	-	100%
Use of Medical Imaging				
Combination Abdominal CT Scan	357	0.034	0.246	0.191
Combination Chest CT Scan	310	0.003	0.098	0.054
Follow-up Mammogram/Ultrasound	641	7.3%	8.4%	8.4%
MRI for Low Back Pain	80	66.3%	33.4%	32.7%
Survey of Patients' Hospital Experiences				
Area Around Room 'Always' Quiet at Night	300+	45%	-	58%
Doctors 'Always' Communicated Well	300+	84%	-	80%
Home Recovery Information Given	300+	76%	-	82%
Hospital Given 9 or 10 on 10 Point Scale	300+	68%	-	67%
Meds 'Always' Explained Before Given	300+	62%	-	60%
Nurses 'Always' Communicated Well	300+	78%	-	76%
Pain 'Always' Well Controlled	300+	70%	-	69%
Room and Bathroom 'Always' Clean	300+	76%	-	71%
Timely Help 'Always' Received	300+	64%	-	64%
Would Definitely Recommend Hospital	300+	68%	-	69%

NOTE: Hospital profiles are in alphabetical order by state, then city, then hospital within the city; Rankings exclude hospitals with less than 25 cases except for patient surveys which excludes hospitals with less than 100 cases; (a) 100–299 cases; (1) The number of cases is too small to be sure how well a hospital is performing; (2) The hospital indicated that the data submitted for this measure were based on a sample of cases; (3) Data was collected during a shorter time period (fewer quarters) than the maximum possible time for this measure; (4) Suppressed for one or more quarters by CMS; (5) No data is available from the hospital for this measure; (6) Fewer than 100 patients completed the HCAHPS survey. Use these rates with caution, as the number of surveys may be too low to reliably assess hospital performance; (7) Survey results are based on less than 12 months of data; (8) Survey results are not available for this reporting period; (9) No or very few patients were eligible for the HCAHPS survey. The scores shown, if any, reflect a very small number of surveys; (10) A state average was not calculated because too few hospitals in the state submitted data; (11) There were discrepancies in the data collection process; Please refer to the User's Guide for a full explanation of data.

Carle Foundation Hospital

611 West Park Street
Urbana, IL 61801
URL: www.carle.com
Type: Acute Care Hospitals
Ownership: Voluntary Non-Profit - Other

Phone: 217-383-3311
Fax: 217-383-3373
Emergency Services: Yes
Beds: 305

Key Personnel:

CEO/President. . . . . James C. Leanard
Chief of Medical Staff. . . . . David Graham, MD
Operating Room. . . . . Sue Cook
Pediatric In-Patient Care . . . . Malcolm Hill, MD
Quality Assurance . . . . LJ Fallon
Radiology. . . . . Jon Hendrickson, MD
Emergency Room . . . . Jay Yambert

Measure	Cases	This Hosp.	State Avg.	U.S. Avg.
Heart Attack Care				
ACE Inhibitor or ARB for LVSD[2]	60	92%	96%	96%
Aspirin at Arrival[2]	161	99%	99%	99%
Aspirin at Discharge[2]	278	100%	99%	98%
Beta Blocker at Discharge[2]	270	99%	98%	98%
Fibrinolytic Medication Timing[2]	0	-	50%	55%
PCI Within 90 Minutes of Arrival[1,2]	19	89%	90%	90%
Smoking Cessation Advice[2]	101	100%	100%	99%
Chest Pain/Possible Heart Attack Care				
Aspirin at Arrival[1,3]	2	100%	95%	95%
Median Time to ECG (minutes)[1,3]	2	60	8	8
Median Time to Transfer (minutes)[5]	0	-	57	61
Fibrinolytic Medication Timing[5]	0	-	33%	54%
Heart Failure Care				
ACE Inhibitor or ARB for LVSD[2]	119	98%	94%	94%
Discharge Instructions[2]	244	88%	89%	88%
Evaluation of LVS Function[2]	300	100%	98%	98%
Smoking Cessation Advice[2]	44	100%	99%	98%
Pneumonia Care				
Appropriate Initial Antibiotic[2]	78	95%	90%	92%
Blood Culture Timing[2]	99	98%	97%	96%
Influenza Vaccine[2]	75	97%	91%	91%
Initial Antibiotic Timing[2]	126	98%	96%	95%
Pneumococcal Vaccine[2]	110	95%	92%	93%
Smoking Cessation Advice[2]	51	100%	98%	97%
Surgical Care Improvement Project				
Appropriate VTP Within 24 Hours[2]	130	95%	92%	92%
Appropriate Hair Removal[2]	604	100%	99%	99%
Appropriate Beta Blocker Usage[2]	261	98%	92%	93%
Controlled Postoperative Blood Glucose[2]	137	91%	92%	93%
Prophylactic Antibiotic Timing[2]	422	95%	97%	97%
Prophylactic Antibiotic Timing (Outpatient)	435	93%	93%	92%
Prophylactic Antibiotic Selection[2]	446	99%	97%	97%
Prophylactic Antibiotic Select. (Outpatient)	434	93%	94%	94%
Prophylactic Antibiotic Stopped[2]	413	97%	94%	94%
Recommended VTP Ordered[2]	130	95%	94%	94%
Urinary Catheter Removal[2]	106	95%	89%	90%
Children's Asthma Care				
Received Systemic Corticosteroids	-	-	-	100%
Received Home Management Plan	-	-	-	71%
Received Reliever Medication	-	-	-	100%
Use of Medical Imaging				
Combination Abdominal CT Scan	233	0.009	0.246	0.191
Combination Chest CT Scan	171	0.000	0.098	0.054
Follow-up Mammogram/Ultrasound[5]	0	-	8.4%	8.4%
MRI for Low Back Pain[1]	4	0.0%	33.4%	32.7%
Survey of Patients' Hospital Experiences				
Area Around Room 'Always' Quiet at Night	300+	50%	-	58%
Doctors 'Always' Communicated Well	300+	81%	-	80%
Home Recovery Information Given	300+	83%	-	82%
Hospital Given 9 or 10 on 10 Point Scale	300+	75%	-	67%
Meds 'Always' Explained Before Given	300+	63%	-	60%
Nurses 'Always' Communicated Well	300+	80%	-	76%
Pain 'Always' Well Controlled	300+	70%	-	69%
Room and Bathroom 'Always' Clean	300+	66%	-	71%
Timely Help 'Always' Received	300+	64%	-	64%
Would Definitely Recommend Hospital	300+	80%	-	69%

Provena Covenant Medical Center - Urbana

1400 West Park Avenue
Urbana, IL 61801
URL: www.provena.org/covenant
Type: Acute Care Hospitals
Ownership: Voluntary Non-Profit - Church

Phone: 217-337-2000
Fax: 217-337-2619
Emergency Services: Yes
Beds: 268

Key Personnel:

CEO/President. . . . . Diane Friedman
Pediatric In-Patient Care . . . . Barbara Michell, MD
Radiology. . . . . Ed Mabry

Measure	Cases	This Hosp.	State Avg.	U.S. Avg.
Heart Attack Care				
ACE Inhibitor or ARB for LVSD	41	88%	96%	96%
Aspirin at Arrival	90	93%	99%	99%
Aspirin at Discharge	190	97%	99%	98%
Beta Blocker at Discharge	192	97%	98%	98%
Fibrinolytic Medication Timing[1]	5	40%	50%	55%
PCI Within 90 Minutes of Arrival[1]	10	90%	90%	90%
Smoking Cessation Advice	87	99%	100%	99%
Chest Pain/Possible Heart Attack Care				
Aspirin at Arrival[1]	8	88%	95%	95%
Median Time to ECG (minutes)[1]	8	5	8	8
Median Time to Transfer (minutes)[5]	0	-	57	61
Fibrinolytic Medication Timing[5]	0	-	33%	54%
Heart Failure Care				
ACE Inhibitor or ARB for LVSD	104	89%	94%	94%
Discharge Instructions	228	96%	89%	88%
Evaluation of LVS Function	284	100%	98%	98%
Smoking Cessation Advice	52	100%	99%	98%
Pneumonia Care				
Appropriate Initial Antibiotic	92	87%	90%	92%
Blood Culture Timing	148	97%	97%	96%
Influenza Vaccine	125	89%	91%	91%
Initial Antibiotic Timing	157	94%	96%	95%
Pneumococcal Vaccine	168	85%	92%	93%
Smoking Cessation Advice	73	100%	98%	97%
Surgical Care Improvement Project				
Appropriate VTP Within 24 Hours[2]	180	77%	92%	92%
Appropriate Hair Removal[2]	617	100%	99%	99%
Appropriate Beta Blocker Usage[2]	215	82%	92%	93%
Controlled Postoperative Blood Glucose[2]	106	90%	92%	93%
Prophylactic Antibiotic Timing[2]	438	95%	97%	97%
Prophylactic Antibiotic Timing (Outpatient)	286	95%	93%	92%
Prophylactic Antibiotic Selection[2]	442	96%	97%	97%
Prophylactic Antibiotic Select. (Outpatient)	276	95%	94%	94%
Prophylactic Antibiotic Stopped[2]	418	92%	94%	94%
Recommended VTP Ordered[2]	180	82%	94%	94%
Urinary Catheter Removal[2]	163	83%	89%	90%
Children's Asthma Care				
Received Systemic Corticosteroids	-	-	-	100%
Received Home Management Plan	-	-	-	71%
Received Reliever Medication	-	-	-	100%
Use of Medical Imaging				
Combination Abdominal CT Scan	305	0.010	0.246	0.191
Combination Chest CT Scan	162	0.006	0.098	0.054
Follow-up Mammogram/Ultrasound	338	9.2%	8.4%	8.4%
MRI for Low Back Pain	59	25.4%	33.4%	32.7%
Survey of Patients' Hospital Experiences				
Area Around Room 'Always' Quiet at Night	300+	60%	-	58%
Doctors 'Always' Communicated Well	300+	79%	-	80%
Home Recovery Information Given	300+	84%	-	82%
Hospital Given 9 or 10 on 10 Point Scale	300+	65%	-	67%
Meds 'Always' Explained Before Given	300+	59%	-	60%
Nurses 'Always' Communicated Well	300+	78%	-	76%
Pain 'Always' Well Controlled	300+	70%	-	69%
Room and Bathroom 'Always' Clean	300+	66%	-	71%
Timely Help 'Always' Received	300+	62%	-	64%
Would Definitely Recommend Hospital	300+	73%	-	69%

Fayette County Hospital

7th and Taylor
Vandalia, IL 62471
Type: Critical Access Hospitals
Ownership: Voluntary Non-Profit - Other

Phone: 618-283-1231
Fax: 618-283-4652
Emergency Services: Yes
Beds: 160

Key Personnel:

CEO/President. . . . . Denich Hucchison
Cardiac Laboratory. . . . . John Cowinjano
Chief of Medical Staff. . . . . Brunch Schwarm

Measure	Cases	This Hosp.	State Avg.	U.S. Avg.
Heart Attack Care				
ACE Inhibitor or ARB for LVSD[3]	0	-	96%	96%
Aspirin at Arrival[1,3]	2	50%	99%	99%
Aspirin at Discharge[1,3]	3	67%	99%	98%
Beta Blocker at Discharge[1,3]	3	67%	98%	98%
Fibrinolytic Medication Timing[3]	0	-	50%	55%
PCI Within 90 Minutes of Arrival[3]	0	-	90%	90%
Smoking Cessation Advice[3]	0	-	100%	99%
Chest Pain/Possible Heart Attack Care				
Aspirin at Arrival	-	-	95%	95%
Median Time to ECG (minutes)	-	-	8	8
Median Time to Transfer (minutes)	-	-	57	61
Fibrinolytic Medication Timing	-	-	33%	54%
Heart Failure Care				
ACE Inhibitor or ARB for LVSD[1,3]	7	57%	94%	94%
Discharge Instructions[1,3]	15	87%	89%	88%
Evaluation of LVS Function[3]	26	85%	98%	98%
Smoking Cessation Advice[1,3]	5	60%	99%	98%
Pneumonia Care				
Appropriate Initial Antibiotic[1,3]	15	73%	90%	92%
Blood Culture Timing[1,3]	15	93%	97%	96%
Influenza Vaccine[3]	31	84%	91%	91%
Initial Antibiotic Timing[3]	42	95%	96%	95%
Pneumococcal Vaccine[3]	33	88%	92%	93%
Smoking Cessation Advice[1,3]	10	80%	98%	97%
Surgical Care Improvement Project				
Appropriate VTP Within 24 Hours[3]	0	-	92%	92%
Appropriate Hair Removal[1,3]	1	100%	99%	99%
Appropriate Beta Blocker Usage[5]	0	-	92%	93%
Controlled Postoperative Blood Glucose[3]	0	-	92%	93%
Prophylactic Antibiotic Timing[1,3]	1	0%	97%	97%
Prophylactic Antibiotic Timing (Outpatient)	-	-	93%	92%
Prophylactic Antibiotic Selection[3]	0	-	97%	97%
Prophylactic Antibiotic Select. (Outpatient)	-	-	94%	94%
Prophylactic Antibiotic Stopped[3]	0	-	94%	94%
Recommended VTP Ordered[3]	0	-	94%	94%
Urinary Catheter Removal[1,3]	1	100%	89%	90%
Children's Asthma Care				
Received Systemic Corticosteroids	-	-	-	100%
Received Home Management Plan	-	-	-	71%
Received Reliever Medication	-	-	-	100%
Use of Medical Imaging				
Combination Abdominal CT Scan	-	-	0.246	0.191
Combination Chest CT Scan	-	-	0.098	0.054
Follow-up Mammogram/Ultrasound	-	-	8.4%	8.4%
MRI for Low Back Pain	-	-	33.4%	32.7%
Survey of Patients' Hospital Experiences				
Area Around Room 'Always' Quiet at Night[8]	-	-	-	58%
Doctors 'Always' Communicated Well[8]	-	-	-	80%
Home Recovery Information Given[8]	-	-	-	82%
Hospital Given 9 or 10 on 10 Point Scale[8]	-	-	-	67%
Meds 'Always' Explained Before Given[8]	-	-	-	60%
Nurses 'Always' Communicated Well[8]	-	-	-	76%
Pain 'Always' Well Controlled[8]	-	-	-	69%
Room and Bathroom 'Always' Clean[8]	-	-	-	71%
Timely Help 'Always' Received[8]	-	-	-	64%
Would Definitely Recommend Hospital[8]	-	-	-	69%

NOTE: Hospital profiles are in alphabetical order by state, then city, then hospital within the city; Rankings exclude hospitals with less than 25 cases except for patient surveys which excludes hospitals with less than 100 cases; (a) 100–299 cases; (1) The number of cases is too small to be sure how well a hospital is performing; (2) The hospital indicated that the data submitted for this measure were based on a sample of cases; (3) Data was collected during a shorter time period (fewer quarters) than the maximum possible time for this measure; (4) Suppressed for one or more quarters by CMS; (5) No data is available from the hospital for this measure; (6) Fewer than 100 patients completed the HCAHPS survey. Use these rates with caution, as the number of surveys may be too low to reliably assess hospital performance; (7) Survey results are based on less than 12 months of data; (8) Survey results are not available for this reporting period; (9) No or very few patients were eligible for the HCAHPS survey. The scores shown, if any, reflect a very small number of surveys; (10) A state average was not calculated because too few hospitals in the state submitted data; (11) There were discrepancies in the data collection process; Please refer to the User's Guide for a full explanation of data.

Iroquois Memorial Hospital

200 Fairman Street
Watseka, IL 60970
Phone: 815-432-5201
Fax: 815-432-7821
E-mail: info@iroquoimemorial.com
URL: www.iroquoismemorial.com
Type: Acute Care Hospitals
Emergency Services: Yes
Ownership: Voluntary Non-Profit - Other
Beds: 94

Key Personnel:
CEO/President. . . . . Steve Leurck
Coronary Care . . . . Peggy Jaskula
Infection Control. . . . . Lou Wonna Bell
Operating Room. . . . . Sharon Hilgendorf
Quality Assurance . . . . Tom McCann
Radiology. . . . . Kenneth Hurst
Intensive Care Unit. . . . . Peggy Jaskula RN
Patient Relations . . . . Terri Fanning

Measure	Cases	This Hosp.	State Avg.	U.S. Avg.
Heart Attack Care				
ACE Inhibitor or ARB for LVSD[1]	3	100%	96%	96%
Aspirin at Arrival[1]	22	91%	99%	99%
Aspirin at Discharge[1]	12	75%	99%	98%
Beta Blocker at Discharge[1]	11	100%	98%	98%
Fibrinolytic Medication Timing[1]	2	100%	50%	55%
PCI Within 90 Minutes of Arrival	0	-	90%	90%
Smoking Cessation Advice[1]	3	67%	100%	99%
Chest Pain/Possible Heart Attack Care				
Aspirin at Arrival[1]	13	100%	95%	95%
Median Time to ECG (minutes)[1]	15	9	8	8
Median Time to Transfer (minutes)[1,3]	1	50	57	61
Fibrinolytic Medication Timing[1,3]	1	100%	33%	54%
Heart Failure Care				
ACE Inhibitor or ARB for LVSD[1]	24	88%	94%	94%
Discharge Instructions	52	60%	89%	88%
Evaluation of LVS Function	79	92%	98%	98%
Smoking Cessation Advice[1]	12	92%	99%	98%
Pneumonia Care				
Appropriate Initial Antibiotic	84	85%	90%	92%
Blood Culture Timing	122	90%	97%	96%
Influenza Vaccine	64	95%	91%	91%
Initial Antibiotic Timing	118	93%	96%	95%
Pneumococcal Vaccine	117	97%	92%	93%
Smoking Cessation Advice	29	90%	98%	97%
Surgical Care Improvement Project				
Appropriate VTP Within 24 Hours	25	92%	92%	92%
Appropriate Hair Removal	87	100%	99%	99%
Appropriate Beta Blocker Usage[1]	24	96%	92%	93%
Controlled Postoperative Blood Glucose	0	-	92%	93%
Prophylactic Antibiotic Timing	69	96%	97%	97%
Prophylactic Antibiotic Timing (Outpatient)	31	100%	93%	92%
Prophylactic Antibiotic Selection	69	97%	97%	97%
Prophylactic Antibiotic Select. (Outpatient)	31	84%	94%	94%
Prophylactic Antibiotic Stopped	65	94%	94%	94%
Recommended VTP Ordered	25	92%	94%	94%
Urinary Catheter Removal[1]	2	100%	89%	90%
Children's Asthma Care				
Received Systemic Corticosteroids	-	-	-	100%
Received Home Management Plan	-	-	-	71%
Received Reliever Medication	-	-	-	100%
Use of Medical Imaging				
Combination Abdominal CT Scan	218	0.495	0.246	0.191
Combination Chest CT Scan	122	0.393	0.098	0.054
Follow-up Mammogram/Ultrasound	409	11.7%	8.4%	8.4%
MRI for Low Back Pain	33	48.5%	33.4%	32.7%
Survey of Patients' Hospital Experiences				
Area Around Room 'Always' Quiet at Night	300+	54%	-	58%
Doctors 'Always' Communicated Well	300+	78%	-	80%
Home Recovery Information Given	300+	83%	-	82%
Hospital Given 9 or 10 on 10 Point Scale	300+	65%	-	67%
Meds 'Always' Explained Before Given	300+	61%	-	60%
Nurses 'Always' Communicated Well	300+	78%	-	76%
Pain 'Always' Well Controlled	300+	72%	-	69%
Room and Bathroom 'Always' Clean	300+	79%	-	71%
Timely Help 'Always' Received	300+	72%	-	64%
Would Definitely Recommend Hospital	300+	60%	-	69%

Vista Medical Center East

1324 North Sheridan Road
Waukegan, IL 60085
Phone: 847-360-4000
Fax: 847-360-4230
URL: www.vistahealth.com
Type: Acute Care Hospitals
Emergency Services: Yes
Ownership: Voluntary Non-Profit - Other
Beds: 299

Key Personnel:
CEO/President. . . . . Timothy Harrington
Quality Assurance . . . . Lora Johnas

Measure	Cases	This Hosp.	State Avg.	U.S. Avg.
Heart Attack Care				
ACE Inhibitor or ARB for LVSD	25	96%	96%	96%
Aspirin at Arrival	132	98%	99%	99%
Aspirin at Discharge	122	94%	99%	98%
Beta Blocker at Discharge	125	95%	98%	98%
Fibrinolytic Medication Timing[1]	2	100%	50%	55%
PCI Within 90 Minutes of Arrival[1]	23	83%	90%	90%
Smoking Cessation Advice	49	100%	100%	99%
Chest Pain/Possible Heart Attack Care				
Aspirin at Arrival[1]	4	75%	95%	95%
Median Time to ECG (minutes)[1]	4	0	8	8
Median Time to Transfer (minutes)[5]	0	-	57	61
Fibrinolytic Medication Timing[5]	0	-	33%	54%
Heart Failure Care				
ACE Inhibitor or ARB for LVSD	103	96%	94%	94%
Discharge Instructions	282	90%	89%	88%
Evaluation of LVS Function	342	99%	98%	98%
Smoking Cessation Advice	71	100%	99%	98%
Pneumonia Care				
Appropriate Initial Antibiotic	93	82%	90%	92%
Blood Culture Timing	113	97%	97%	96%
Influenza Vaccine	119	98%	91%	91%
Initial Antibiotic Timing	168	94%	96%	95%
Pneumococcal Vaccine	144	100%	92%	93%
Smoking Cessation Advice	62	98%	98%	97%
Surgical Care Improvement Project				
Appropriate VTP Within 24 Hours[2]	123	92%	92%	92%
Appropriate Hair Removal[2]	510	100%	99%	99%
Appropriate Beta Blocker Usage[2]	123	96%	92%	93%
Controlled Postoperative Blood Glucose[2]	45	98%	92%	93%
Prophylactic Antibiotic Timing[2]	361	99%	97%	97%
Prophylactic Antibiotic Timing (Outpatient)	162	98%	93%	92%
Prophylactic Antibiotic Selection[2]	363	97%	97%	97%
Prophylactic Antibiotic Select. (Outpatient)	166	98%	94%	94%
Prophylactic Antibiotic Stopped[2]	348	98%	94%	94%
Recommended VTP Ordered[2]	123	95%	94%	94%
Urinary Catheter Removal	101	93%	89%	90%
Children's Asthma Care				
Received Systemic Corticosteroids	-	-	-	100%
Received Home Management Plan	-	-	-	71%
Received Reliever Medication	-	-	-	100%
Use of Medical Imaging				
Combination Abdominal CT Scan	861	0.569	0.246	0.191
Combination Chest CT Scan	615	0.551	0.098	0.054
Follow-up Mammogram/Ultrasound	1,916	4.3%	8.4%	8.4%
MRI for Low Back Pain	128	26.6%	33.4%	32.7%
Survey of Patients' Hospital Experiences				
Area Around Room 'Always' Quiet at Night	300+	48%	-	58%
Doctors 'Always' Communicated Well	300+	75%	-	80%
Home Recovery Information Given	300+	74%	-	82%
Hospital Given 9 or 10 on 10 Point Scale	300+	52%	-	67%
Meds 'Always' Explained Before Given	300+	52%	-	60%
Nurses 'Always' Communicated Well	300+	63%	-	76%
Pain 'Always' Well Controlled	300+	61%	-	69%
Room and Bathroom 'Always' Clean	300+	57%	-	71%
Timely Help 'Always' Received	300+	47%	-	64%
Would Definitely Recommend Hospital	300+	48%	-	69%

Vista Medical Center West

2615 Washington St
Waukegan, IL 60085
Phone: 847-249-3900
Fax: 847-360-4230
URL: www.vistahealth.com
Type: Acute Care Hospitals
Emergency Services: Yes
Ownership: Voluntary Non-Profit - Church
Beds: 388

Key Personnel:
CEO/President. . . . . Timothy J Harrington
Infection Control . . . . Karen VanBuren
Operating Room. . . . . Marianne Finlay
Quality Assurance . . . . Lora Johnas
Radiology. . . . . Elaine Pape, MD
Emergency Room . . . . Denise Tucker, RN
Intensive Care Unit. . . . . Kathy Dumalski
Patient Relations . . . . Mary Anne Yuknay

Measure	Cases	This Hosp.	State Avg.	U.S. Avg.
Heart Attack Care				
ACE Inhibitor or ARB for LVSD[5]	0	-	96%	96%
Aspirin at Arrival[5]	0	-	99%	99%
Aspirin at Discharge[5]	0	-	99%	98%
Beta Blocker at Discharge[5]	0	-	98%	98%
Fibrinolytic Medication Timing[5]	0	-	50%	55%
PCI Within 90 Minutes of Arrival[5]	0	-	90%	90%
Smoking Cessation Advice[5]	0	-	100%	99%
Chest Pain/Possible Heart Attack Care				
Aspirin at Arrival	105	100%	95%	95%
Median Time to ECG (minutes)	111	13	8	8
Median Time to Transfer (minutes)[1,3]	1	101	57	61
Fibrinolytic Medication Timing[3]	0	-	33%	54%
Heart Failure Care				
ACE Inhibitor or ARB for LVSD[5]	0	-	94%	94%
Discharge Instructions[5]	0	-	89%	88%
Evaluation of LVS Function[5]	0	-	98%	98%
Smoking Cessation Advice[5]	0	-	99%	98%
Pneumonia Care				
Appropriate Initial Antibiotic[5]	0	-	90%	92%
Blood Culture Timing[5]	0	-	97%	96%
Influenza Vaccine[5]	0	-	91%	91%
Initial Antibiotic Timing[5]	0	-	96%	95%
Pneumococcal Vaccine[5]	0	-	92%	93%
Smoking Cessation Advice[5]	0	-	98%	97%
Surgical Care Improvement Project				
Appropriate VTP Within 24 Hours[5]	0	-	92%	92%
Appropriate Hair Removal[5]	0	-	99%	99%
Appropriate Beta Blocker Usage[5]	0	-	92%	93%
Controlled Postoperative Blood Glucose[5]	0	-	92%	93%
Prophylactic Antibiotic Timing[5]	0	-	97%	97%
Prophylactic Antibiotic Timing (Outpatient)[5]	0	-	93%	92%
Prophylactic Antibiotic Selection[5]	0	-	97%	97%
Prophylactic Antibiotic Select. (Outpatient)[5]	0	-	94%	94%
Prophylactic Antibiotic Stopped[5]	0	-	94%	94%
Recommended VTP Ordered[5]	0	-	94%	94%
Urinary Catheter Removal[5]	0	-	89%	90%
Children's Asthma Care				
Received Systemic Corticosteroids	-	-	-	100%
Received Home Management Plan	-	-	-	71%
Received Reliever Medication	-	-	-	100%
Use of Medical Imaging				
Combination Abdominal CT Scan[1]	23	0.217	0.246	0.191
Combination Chest CT Scan[1]	2	0.500	0.098	0.054
Follow-up Mammogram/Ultrasound[5]	0	-	8.4%	8.4%
MRI for Low Back Pain[5]	0	-	33.4%	32.7%
Survey of Patients' Hospital Experiences				
Area Around Room 'Always' Quiet at Night[9]	-	-	-	58%
Doctors 'Always' Communicated Well[9]	-	-	-	80%
Home Recovery Information Given[9]	-	-	-	82%
Hospital Given 9 or 10 on 10 Point Scale[9]	-	-	-	67%
Meds 'Always' Explained Before Given[9]	-	-	-	60%
Nurses 'Always' Communicated Well[9]	-	-	-	76%
Pain 'Always' Well Controlled[9]	-	-	-	69%
Room and Bathroom 'Always' Clean[9]	-	-	-	71%
Timely Help 'Always' Received[9]	-	-	-	64%
Would Definitely Recommend Hospital[9]	-	-	-	69%

NOTE: Hospital profiles are in alphabetical order by state, then city, then hospital within the city; Rankings exclude hospitals with less than 25 cases except for patient surveys which excludes hospitals with less than 100 cases; (a) 100–299 cases; (1) The number of cases is too small to be sure how well a hospital is performing; (2) The hospital indicated that the data submitted for this measure were based on a sample of cases; (3) Data was collected during a shorter time period (fewer quarters) than the maximum possible time for this measure; (4) Suppressed for one or more quarters by CMS; (5) No data is available from the hospital for this measure; (6) Fewer than 100 patients completed the HCAHPS survey. Use these rates with caution, as the number of surveys may be too low to reliably assess hospital performance; (7) Survey results are based on less than 12 months of data; (8) Survey results are not available for this reporting period; (9) No or very few patients were eligible for the HCAHPS survey. The scores shown, if any, reflect a very small number of surveys; (10) A state average was not calculated because too few hospitals in the state submitted data; (11) There were discrepancies in the data collection process; Please refer to the User's Guide for a full explanation of data.

Central Dupage Hospital

25 North Winfield Road
Winfield, IL 60190
Phone: 630-682-1600
Fax: 630-933-1300
E-mail: cdh_information@cdh.org
URL: www.cdh.org
Type: Acute Care Hospitals
Emergency Services: Yes
Ownership: Voluntary Non-Profit - Private
Beds: 20

Key Personnel:
CEO/President. . . . . Luke McGuinness
Chief of Medical Staff . . . . Kevin Most

Measure	Cases	This Hosp.	State Avg.	U.S. Avg.
Heart Attack Care				
ACE Inhibitor or ARB for LVSD	34	97%	96%	96%
Aspirin at Arrival	190	99%	99%	99%
Aspirin at Discharge	198	100%	99%	98%
Beta Blocker at Discharge	192	99%	98%	98%
Fibrinolytic Medication Timing	0	-	50%	55%
PCI Within 90 Minutes of Arrival	53	89%	90%	90%
Smoking Cessation Advice	54	100%	100%	99%
Chest Pain/Possible Heart Attack Care				
Aspirin at Arrival[5]	0	-	95%	95%
Median Time to ECG (minutes)[5]	0	-	8	8
Median Time to Transfer (minutes)[5]	0	-	57	61
Fibrinolytic Medication Timing[5]	0	-	33%	54%
Heart Failure Care				
ACE Inhibitor or ARB for LVSD	106	100%	94%	94%
Discharge Instructions	338	96%	89%	88%
Evaluation of LVS Function	415	100%	98%	98%
Smoking Cessation Advice	61	100%	99%	98%
Pneumonia Care				
Appropriate Initial Antibiotic	189	96%	90%	92%
Blood Culture Timing	215	98%	97%	96%
Influenza Vaccine	174	90%	91%	91%
Initial Antibiotic Timing	249	98%	96%	95%
Pneumococcal Vaccine	212	92%	92%	93%
Smoking Cessation Advice	80	100%	98%	97%
Surgical Care Improvement Project				
Appropriate VTP Within 24 Hours[2]	95	99%	92%	92%
Appropriate Hair Removal[2]	553	100%	99%	99%
Appropriate Beta Blocker Usage[2]	182	98%	92%	93%
Controlled Postoperative Blood Glucose[2]	105	100%	92%	93%
Prophylactic Antibiotic Timing[2]	391	99%	97%	97%
Prophylactic Antibiotic Timing (Outpatient)	490	97%	93%	92%
Prophylactic Antibiotic Selection[2]	394	99%	97%	97%
Prophylactic Antibiotic Select. (Outpatient)	483	98%	94%	94%
Prophylactic Antibiotic Stopped[2]	375	97%	94%	94%
Recommended VTP Ordered[2]	95	100%	94%	94%
Urinary Catheter Removal[2]	100	96%	89%	90%
Children's Asthma Care				
Received Systemic Corticosteroids	-	-	-	100%
Received Home Management Plan	-	-	-	71%
Received Reliever Medication	-	-	-	100%
Use of Medical Imaging				
Combination Abdominal CT Scan	1,480	0.324	0.246	0.191
Combination Chest CT Scan	1,469	0.017	0.098	0.054
Follow-up Mammogram/Ultrasound	2,668	4.4%	8.4%	8.4%
MRI for Low Back Pain	220	34.5%	33.4%	32.7%
Survey of Patients' Hospital Experiences				
Area Around Room 'Always' Quiet at Night	300+	51%	-	58%
Doctors 'Always' Communicated Well	300+	80%	-	80%
Home Recovery Information Given	300+	89%	-	82%
Hospital Given 9 or 10 on 10 Point Scale	300+	79%	-	67%
Meds 'Always' Explained Before Given	300+	60%	-	60%
Nurses 'Always' Communicated Well	300+	81%	-	76%
Pain 'Always' Well Controlled	300+	73%	-	69%
Room and Bathroom 'Always' Clean	300+	70%	-	71%
Timely Help 'Always' Received	300+	65%	-	64%
Would Definitely Recommend Hospital	300+	81%	-	69%

Centegra Health System - Woodstock Hospital

3701 Doty Road
Woodstock, IL 60098
Phone: 815-788-5823
Fax: 815-334-3948
Type: Acute Care Hospitals
Emergency Services: Yes
Ownership: Voluntary Non-Profit - Private
Beds: 154

Key Personnel:
CEO/President. . . . . Paul Laubick

Measure	Cases	This Hosp.	State Avg.	U.S. Avg.
Heart Attack Care				
ACE Inhibitor or ARB for LVSD[1]	5	100%	96%	96%
Aspirin at Arrival	59	95%	99%	99%
Aspirin at Discharge	25	100%	99%	98%
Beta Blocker at Discharge	28	93%	98%	98%
Fibrinolytic Medication Timing	0	-	50%	55%
PCI Within 90 Minutes of Arrival	0	-	90%	90%
Smoking Cessation Advice[1]	5	80%	100%	99%
Chest Pain/Possible Heart Attack Care				
Aspirin at Arrival	51	94%	95%	95%
Median Time to ECG (minutes)	53	5	8	8
Median Time to Transfer (minutes)[1]	9	50	57	61
Fibrinolytic Medication Timing	0	-	33%	54%
Heart Failure Care				
ACE Inhibitor or ARB for LVSD[1]	18	89%	94%	94%
Discharge Instructions	79	91%	89%	88%
Evaluation of LVS Function	121	96%	98%	98%
Smoking Cessation Advice[1]	18	94%	99%	98%
Pneumonia Care				
Appropriate Initial Antibiotic	99	93%	90%	92%
Blood Culture Timing	154	96%	97%	96%
Influenza Vaccine	104	73%	91%	91%
Initial Antibiotic Timing	158	99%	96%	95%
Pneumococcal Vaccine	135	62%	92%	93%
Smoking Cessation Advice	56	95%	98%	97%
Surgical Care Improvement Project				
Appropriate VTP Within 24 Hours[2]	162	87%	92%	92%
Appropriate Hair Removal[2]	622	100%	99%	99%
Appropriate Beta Blocker Usage[2]	167	93%	92%	93%
Controlled Postoperative Blood Glucose[2]	0	-	92%	93%
Prophylactic Antibiotic Timing[2]	491	93%	97%	97%
Prophylactic Antibiotic Timing (Outpatient)	84	77%	93%	92%
Prophylactic Antibiotic Selection[2]	492	97%	97%	97%
Prophylactic Antibiotic Select. (Outpatient)	71	94%	94%	94%
Prophylactic Antibiotic Stopped[2]	481	94%	94%	94%
Recommended VTP Ordered[2]	162	88%	94%	94%
Urinary Catheter Removal[2]	146	93%	89%	90%
Children's Asthma Care				
Received Systemic Corticosteroids	-	-	-	100%
Received Home Management Plan	-	-	-	71%
Received Reliever Medication	-	-	-	100%
Use of Medical Imaging				
Combination Abdominal CT Scan	523	0.711	0.246	0.191
Combination Chest CT Scan	317	0.025	0.098	0.054
Follow-up Mammogram/Ultrasound	860	3.4%	8.4%	8.4%
MRI for Low Back Pain	121	28.9%	33.4%	32.7%
Survey of Patients' Hospital Experiences				
Area Around Room 'Always' Quiet at Night	300+	45%	-	58%
Doctors 'Always' Communicated Well	300+	78%	-	80%
Home Recovery Information Given	300+	87%	-	82%
Hospital Given 9 or 10 on 10 Point Scale	300+	64%	-	67%
Meds 'Always' Explained Before Given	300+	59%	-	60%
Nurses 'Always' Communicated Well	300+	76%	-	76%
Pain 'Always' Well Controlled	300+	70%	-	69%
Room and Bathroom 'Always' Clean	300+	79%	-	71%
Timely Help 'Always' Received	300+	65%	-	64%
Would Definitely Recommend Hospital	300+	68%	-	69%

Midwestern Region Medical Center

2520 Elisha Avenue
Zion, IL 60099
Phone: 847-872-4561
Fax: 847-872-6222
E-mail: susan.thomas@mrmc-ctca.com
URL: www.cancercare.com
Type: Acute Care Hospitals
Emergency Services: Yes
Ownership: Proprietary
Beds: 95

Key Personnel:
CEO/President. . . . . Roger Cary
Chief of Medical Staff . . . . Joel Granitk
Infection Control. . . . . Debra Horton
Operating Room. . . . . Sharon Dimitrijevich
Quality Assurance . . . . Carol Lepper
Radiology. . . . . Pakorn Sirijintakarn, MD

Measure	Cases	This Hosp.	State Avg.	U.S. Avg.
Heart Attack Care				
ACE Inhibitor or ARB for LVSD[5]	0	-	96%	96%
Aspirin at Arrival[5]	0	-	99%	99%
Aspirin at Discharge[5]	0	-	99%	98%
Beta Blocker at Discharge[5]	0	-	98%	98%
Fibrinolytic Medication Timing[5]	0	-	50%	55%
PCI Within 90 Minutes of Arrival[5]	0	-	90%	90%
Smoking Cessation Advice[5]	0	-	100%	99%
Chest Pain/Possible Heart Attack Care				
Aspirin at Arrival[1,3]	1	100%	95%	95%
Median Time to ECG (minutes)[1,3]	1	17	8	8
Median Time to Transfer (minutes)[5]	0	-	57	61
Fibrinolytic Medication Timing[5]	0	-	33%	54%
Heart Failure Care				
ACE Inhibitor or ARB for LVSD[1,3]	3	100%	94%	94%
Discharge Instructions[1,3]	3	67%	89%	88%
Evaluation of LVS Function[1,3]	3	100%	98%	98%
Smoking Cessation Advice[1,3]	2	100%	99%	98%
Pneumonia Care				
Appropriate Initial Antibiotic[1]	4	50%	90%	92%
Blood Culture Timing[1]	8	100%	97%	96%
Influenza Vaccine[1]	12	75%	91%	91%
Initial Antibiotic Timing[1]	17	88%	96%	95%
Pneumococcal Vaccine[1]	5	100%	92%	93%
Smoking Cessation Advice[1]	10	90%	98%	97%
Surgical Care Improvement Project				
Appropriate VTP Within 24 Hours	187	92%	92%	92%
Appropriate Hair Removal	210	100%	99%	99%
Appropriate Beta Blocker Usage	35	83%	92%	93%
Controlled Postoperative Blood Glucose	0	-	92%	93%
Prophylactic Antibiotic Timing	71	94%	97%	97%
Prophylactic Antibiotic Timing (Outpatient)	28	96%	93%	92%
Prophylactic Antibiotic Selection	71	96%	97%	97%
Prophylactic Antibiotic Select. (Outpatient)	28	96%	94%	94%
Prophylactic Antibiotic Stopped	63	90%	94%	94%
Recommended VTP Ordered	187	99%	94%	94%
Urinary Catheter Removal[1]	22	45%	89%	90%
Children's Asthma Care				
Received Systemic Corticosteroids	-	-	-	100%
Received Home Management Plan	-	-	-	71%
Received Reliever Medication	-	-	-	100%
Use of Medical Imaging				
Combination Abdominal CT Scan	694	0.974	0.246	0.191
Combination Chest CT Scan	760	0.000	0.098	0.054
Follow-up Mammogram/Ultrasound	205	3.9%	8.4%	8.4%
MRI for Low Back Pain[1]	8	25.0%	33.4%	32.7%
Survey of Patients' Hospital Experiences				
Area Around Room 'Always' Quiet at Night	300+	60%	-	58%
Doctors 'Always' Communicated Well	300+	85%	-	80%
Home Recovery Information Given	300+	91%	-	82%
Hospital Given 9 or 10 on 10 Point Scale	300+	86%	-	67%
Meds 'Always' Explained Before Given	300+	69%	-	60%
Nurses 'Always' Communicated Well	300+	80%	-	76%
Pain 'Always' Well Controlled	300+	79%	-	69%
Room and Bathroom 'Always' Clean	300+	74%	-	71%
Timely Help 'Always' Received	300+	69%	-	64%
Would Definitely Recommend Hospital	300+	91%	-	69%

NOTE: Hospital profiles are in alphabetical order by state, then city, then hospital within the city; Rankings exclude hospitals with less than 25 cases except for patient surveys which excludes hospitals with less than 100 cases; (a) 100–299 cases; (1) The number of cases is too small to be sure how well a hospital is performing; (2) The hospital indicated that the data submitted for this measure were based on a sample of cases; (3) Data was collected during a shorter time period (fewer quarters) than the maximum possible time for this measure; (4) Suppressed for one or more quarters by CMS; (5) No data is available from the hospital for this measure; (6) Fewer than 100 patients completed the HCAHPS survey. Use these rates with caution, as the number of surveys may be too low to reliably assess hospital performance; (7) Survey results are based on less than 12 months of data; (8) Survey results are not available for this reporting period; (9) No or very few patients were eligible for the HCAHPS survey. The scores shown, if any, reflect a very small number of surveys; (10) A state average was not calculated because too few hospitals in the state submitted data; (11) There were discrepancies in the data collection process; Please refer to the User's Guide for a full explanation of data.

Heart Attack Care

1. ACE Inhibitor or ARB for LVSD

Hospital Name	City	Rate	Cases
Community Hospital East	Indianapolis	100%	30
Franciscan St Anthony Health-Michigan City	Michigan City	100%	26
Howard Regional Health System	Kokomo	100%	35
Indiana University Health	Indianapolis	100%	100
Memorial Hospital of South Bend	South Bend	100%	27
Reid Hospital & Health Care Services	Richmond	100%	57
Terre Haute Regional Hospital	Terre Haute	100%	30
Bloomington Hospital	Bloomington	98%	47
St Francis Hosp & Health Ctrs-Indianapolis	Indianapolis	98%	91
Saint Vincent Heart Center of Indiana	Indianapolis	98%	245
Saint Vincent Hospital & Health Services	Indianapolis	98%	80
William N Wishard Memorial Hospital[2]	Indianapolis	98%	42
Ball Memorial Hospital	Muncie	97%	74
Elkhart General Hospital	Elkhart	97%	62
Good Samaritan Hospital	Vincennes	97%	31
Lutheran Hospital of Indiana	Fort Wayne	97%	99
Saint Elizabeth Central	Lafayette	97%	33
Floyd Memorial Hospital and Health Services	New Albany	96%	83
The Indiana Heart Hospital	Indianapolis	96%	73
Union Hospital	Terre Haute	96%	81
Parkview Hospital	Fort Wayne	94%	86
Saint Mary's Medical Center of Evansville	Evansville	94%	68
Community Hospital South	Indianapolis	93%	28
Franciscan St Margaret Health - Hammond	Hammond	93%	42
Methodist Hospitals[2]	Gary	90%	49
Clark Memorial Hospital	Jeffersonville	89%	38
Columbus Regional Hospital	Columbus	89%	36
The Heart Hospital at Deaconess Gateway[3]	Newburgh	89%	27
Deaconess Hospital	Evansville	87%	71
Indiana University Health Arnett Hospital	Lafayette	87%	30

2. Aspirin at Arrival

Hospital Name	City	Rate	Cases
Community Hospital South	Indianapolis	100%	93
Dearborn County Hospital	Lawrenceburg	100%	47
Floyd Memorial Hospital and Health Services	New Albany	100%	257
Howard Regional Health System	Kokomo	100%	112
Indiana University Health Arnett Hospital	Lafayette	100%	147
Indiana University Health North Hospital	Carmel	100%	29
Indianapolis VA Medical Center	Indianapolis	100%	111
IU Health Goshen Hospital	Goshen	100%	54
Laporte Hospital and Health Services	La Porte	100%	107
Porter Valparaiso Hospital Campus	Valparaiso	100%	155
Reid Hospital & Health Care Services	Richmond	100%	286
Riverview Hospital	Noblesville	100%	101
Saint Catherine Hospital	East Chicago	100%	63
Saint Elizabeth Central	Lafayette	100%	98
Saint Elizabeth East	Lafayette	100%	47
Saint Joseph Regional Medical Center	Mishawaka	100%	223
St Joseph's Reg Med Ctr-Plymouth	Plymouth	100%	34
Saint Vincent Heart Center of Indiana	Indianapolis	100%	129
Ball Memorial Hospital	Muncie	99%	241
Bloomington Hospital	Bloomington	99%	277
Columbus Regional Hospital	Columbus	99%	195
Community Hospital East	Indianapolis	99%	113
Elkhart General Hospital	Elkhart	99%	296
Franciscan St Anthony Health - Crown Point	Crown Point	99%	162
Franciscan St Anthony Health-Michigan City	Michigan City	99%	135
Franciscan St Margaret Health - Dyer	Dyer	99%	100
Good Samaritan Hospital	Vincennes	99%	101
Hendricks Regional Health	Danville	99%	72
The Indiana Heart Hospital	Indianapolis	99%	145
Indiana University Health	Indianapolis	99%	357
Parkview Hospital	Fort Wayne	99%	267
St Francis Hosp & Health Ctrs-Indianapolis	Indianapolis	99%	303
Saint Mary Medical Center	Hobart	99%	100
Saint Vincent Dunn Hospital	Bedford	99%	81
Terre Haute Regional Hospital	Terre Haute	99%	76
Comm Hosp of Anderson & Madison County	Anderson	98%	54
Franciscan St Margaret Health - Hammond	Hammond	98%	215
Kosciusko Community Hospital	Warsaw	98%	42
Lutheran Hospital of Indiana	Fort Wayne	98%	225
Memorial Hospital and Health Care Center	Jasper	98%	123
Memorial Hospital of South Bend	South Bend	98%	252
Saint John's Health System[2]	Anderson	98%	46
Saint Joseph Hospital	Fort Wayne	98%	51
Saint Mary's Medical Center of Evansville	Evansville	98%	203
Saint Vincent Hospital & Health Services	Indianapolis	98%	265
Union Hospital	Terre Haute	98%	245
William N Wishard Memorial Hospital[2]	Indianapolis	98%	249
Clark Memorial Hospital	Jeffersonville	97%	167
Marion General Hospital	Marion	97%	39
Community Hospital	Munster	96%	164
Deaconess Hospital	Evansville	96%	261
Indiana University Health West Hospital	Avon	96%	89
The King's Daughters' Hospital	Madison	96%	25
Methodist Hospitals[2]	Gary	94%	215
Bedford Regional Medical Center	Bedford	92%	37

3. Aspirin at Discharge

Hospital Name	City	Rate	Cases
Bloomington Hospital	Bloomington	100%	358
Community Hospital South	Indianapolis	100%	132
Dearborn County Hospital	Lawrenceburg	100%	26
Franciscan St Margaret Health - Dyer	Dyer	100%	93
Hendricks Regional Health	Danville	100%	59
Howard Regional Health System	Kokomo	100%	110
IU Health Goshen Hospital	Goshen	100%	46
Laporte Hospital and Health Services	La Porte	100%	112
Lutheran Hospital of Indiana	Fort Wayne	100%	553
Parkview Hospital	Fort Wayne	100%	555
Porter Valparaiso Hospital Campus	Valparaiso	100%	179
Reid Hospital & Health Care Services	Richmond	100%	350
Riverview Hospital	Noblesville	100%	97
Saint Catherine Hospital	East Chicago	100%	53
Saint Elizabeth East	Lafayette	100%	79
St Francis Hosp & Health Ctrs-Indianapolis	Indianapolis	100%	492
Saint John's Health System[2]	Anderson	100%	25
Saint Joseph Regional Medical Center	Mishawaka	100%	257
Saint Vincent Dunn Hospital	Bedford	100%	92
Saint Vincent Hospital & Health Services	Indianapolis	100%	365
Union Hospital	Terre Haute	100%	321
Ball Memorial Hospital	Muncie	99%	335
Columbus Regional Hospital	Columbus	99%	242
Community Hospital East	Indianapolis	99%	109
Franciscan St Anthony Health - Crown Point	Crown Point	99%	142
Franciscan St Anthony Health-Michigan City	Michigan City	99%	119
Franciscan St Margaret Health - Hammond	Hammond	99%	208
The Heart Hospital at Deaconess Gateway[3]	Newburgh	99%	136
The Indiana Heart Hospital	Indianapolis	99%	352
Indiana University Health	Indianapolis	99%	537
Indiana University Health Arnett Hospital	Lafayette	99%	152
Indiana University Health West Hospital	Avon	99%	70
Indianapolis VA Medical Center	Indianapolis	99%	112
Memorial Hospital and Health Care Center	Jasper	99%	159
Memorial Hospital of South Bend	South Bend	99%	266
Saint Elizabeth Central	Lafayette	99%	167
Saint Joseph Hospital	Fort Wayne	99%	150
Saint Mary's Medical Center of Evansville	Evansville	99%	293
Saint Vincent Heart Center of Indiana	Indianapolis	99%	1064
Terre Haute Regional Hospital	Terre Haute	99%	125
Community Hospital	Munster	98%	153
Deaconess Hospital	Evansville	98%	391
Floyd Memorial Hospital and Health Services	New Albany	98%	298
Good Samaritan Hospital	Vincennes	98%	131
William N Wishard Memorial Hospital[2]	Indianapolis	98%	228
Bedford Regional Medical Center	Bedford	97%	34
Clark Memorial Hospital	Jeffersonville	97%	181
Elkhart General Hospital	Elkhart	97%	329
Indiana University Health North Hospital	Carmel	97%	31
Saint Mary Medical Center	Hobart	95%	93
Methodist Hospitals[2]	Gary	92%	190
Marion General Hospital	Marion	90%	29
Comm Hosp of Anderson & Madison County	Anderson	89%	37

4. Beta Blocker at Discharge

Hospital Name	City	Rate	Cases
Bedford Regional Medical Center	Bedford	100%	33
Bloomington Hospital	Bloomington	100%	357
Community Hospital East	Indianapolis	100%	108
Comm Hosp of Anderson & Madison County	Anderson	100%	49
Community Hospital South	Indianapolis	100%	126
Howard Regional Health System	Kokomo	100%	107
Indiana University Health	Indianapolis	100%	515
Indianapolis VA Medical Center	Indianapolis	100%	111
IU Health Goshen Hospital	Goshen	100%	45
Laporte Hospital and Health Services	La Porte	100%	99
Memorial Hospital of South Bend	South Bend	100%	252
Parkview Hospital	Fort Wayne	100%	547
Porter Valparaiso Hospital Campus	Valparaiso	100%	176
Reid Hospital & Health Care Services	Richmond	100%	338
Riverview Hospital	Noblesville	100%	97
Saint Catherine Hospital	East Chicago	100%	59
Saint Elizabeth Central	Lafayette	100%	163
Saint Elizabeth East	Lafayette	100%	75
St Francis Hosp & Health Ctrs-Indianapolis	Indianapolis	100%	473
Saint John's Health System[2]	Anderson	100%	29
Saint Joseph Hospital	Fort Wayne	100%	145
Saint Vincent Dunn Hospital	Bedford	100%	88
Ball Memorial Hospital	Muncie	99%	323
Franciscan St Anthony Health-Michigan City	Michigan City	99%	113
The Indiana Heart Hospital	Indianapolis	99%	330
Lutheran Hospital of Indiana	Fort Wayne	99%	516
Memorial Hospital and Health Care Center	Jasper	99%	143
Saint Joseph Regional Medical Center	Mishawaka	99%	249
Saint Mary's Medical Center of Evansville	Evansville	99%	287
Saint Vincent Heart Center of Indiana	Indianapolis	99%	1039
Saint Vincent Hospital & Health Services	Indianapolis	99%	350
Terre Haute Regional Hospital	Terre Haute	99%	129
Union Hospital	Terre Haute	99%	314
Clark Memorial Hospital	Jeffersonville	98%	186
Columbus Regional Hospital	Columbus	98%	235
Floyd Memorial Hospital and Health Services	New Albany	98%	273
Franciscan St Margaret Health - Dyer	Dyer	98%	98
Hendricks Regional Health	Danville	98%	53
Indiana University Health Arnett Hospital	Lafayette	98%	145
Franciscan St Anthony Health - Crown Point	Crown Point	97%	149
Saint Mary Medical Center	Hobart	97%	96
Community Hospital	Munster	96%	132
Dearborn County Hospital	Lawrenceburg	96%	26
Franciscan St Margaret Health - Hammond	Hammond	96%	198
Good Samaritan Hospital	Vincennes	96%	135
The Heart Hospital at Deaconess Gateway[3]	Newburgh	96%	139
Deaconess Hospital	Evansville	95%	373
Elkhart General Hospital	Elkhart	95%	296
Indiana University Health West Hospital	Avon	95%	63
Marion General Hospital	Marion	94%	31
William N Wishard Memorial Hospital[2]	Indianapolis	94%	221
Methodist Hospitals[2]	Gary	92%	196
Indiana University Health North Hospital	Carmel	90%	30

6. PCI Within 90 Minutes of Arrival

Hospital Name	City	Rate	Cases
Howard Regional Health System	Kokomo	100%	39
Memorial Hospital of South Bend	South Bend	100%	55
Saint Mary's Medical Center of Evansville	Evansville	100%	44
Columbus Regional Hospital	Columbus	98%	46
Deaconess Hospital	Evansville	98%	55
Elkhart General Hospital	Elkhart	98%	49
Clark Memorial Hospital	Jeffersonville	97%	36
Indiana University Health	Indianapolis	97%	96
Reid Hospital & Health Care Services	Richmond	97%	62
St Francis Hosp & Health Ctrs-Indianapolis	Indianapolis	97%	92
Lutheran Hospital of Indiana	Fort Wayne	96%	45
Saint Elizabeth Central	Lafayette	96%	27
Bloomington Hospital	Bloomington	95%	56
Saint Joseph Regional Medical Center	Mishawaka	95%	44
Floyd Memorial Hospital and Health Services	New Albany	94%	51
Franciscan St Anthony Health - Crown Point	Crown Point	94%	36
The Indiana Heart Hospital	Indianapolis	94%	51
Community Hospital	Munster	93%	28
Community Hospital East	Indianapolis	93%	29
Parkview Hospital	Fort Wayne	93%	60
Riverview Hospital	Noblesville	93%	28
Ball Memorial Hospital	Muncie	92%	60
Good Samaritan Hospital	Vincennes	90%	31
Porter Valparaiso Hospital Campus	Valparaiso	90%	39
Franciscan St Margaret Health - Hammond	Hammond	87%	38
Union Hospital	Terre Haute	87%	46
Community Hospital South	Indianapolis	83%	29
Saint Vincent Hospital & Health Services	Indianapolis	71%	38

7. Smoking Cessation Advice

Hospital Name	City	Rate	Cases
Bloomington Hospital	Bloomington	100%	143
Clark Memorial Hospital	Jeffersonville	100%	78
Columbus Regional Hospital	Columbus	100%	61
Community Hospital	Munster	100%	51
Community Hospital East	Indianapolis	100%	50
Community Hospital South	Indianapolis	100%	61
Elkhart General Hospital	Elkhart	100%	135
Floyd Memorial Hospital and Health Services	New Albany	100%	113
Franciscan St Anthony Health - Crown Point	Crown Point	100%	67
Franciscan St Margaret Health - Dyer	Dyer	100%	33
Howard Regional Health System	Kokomo	100%	55
The Indiana Heart Hospital	Indianapolis	100%	130
Indiana University Health	Indianapolis	100%	221
Laporte Hospital and Health Services	La Porte	100%	46
Lutheran Hospital of Indiana	Fort Wayne	100%	201
Methodist Hospitals[2]	Gary	100%	81
Parkview Hospital	Fort Wayne	100%	216
Porter Valparaiso Hospital Campus	Valparaiso	100%	70
Reid Hospital & Health Care Services	Richmond	100%	114
Riverview Hospital	Noblesville	100%	35
Saint Elizabeth Central	Lafayette	100%	59
Saint Elizabeth East	Lafayette	100%	26
Saint Joseph Hospital	Fort Wayne	100%	70
Saint Joseph Regional Medical Center	Mishawaka	100%	90
Saint Mary's Medical Center of Evansville	Evansville	100%	117
Saint Vincent Dunn Hospital	Bedford	100%	32
Saint Vincent Heart Center of Indiana	Indianapolis	100%	386
Saint Vincent Hospital & Health Services	Indianapolis	100%	100
Terre Haute Regional Hospital	Terre Haute	100%	65
Union Hospital	Terre Haute	100%	115
William N Wishard Memorial Hospital[2]	Indianapolis	100%	132
Ball Memorial Hospital	Muncie	99%	142

NOTE: Hospital profiles are in alphabetical order by state, then city, then hospital within the city; Rankings exclude hospitals with less than 25 cases except for patient surveys which excludes hospitals with less than 100 cases; (a) 100–299 cases; (1) The number of cases is too small to be sure how well a hospital is performing; (2) The hospital indicated that the data submitted for this measure were based on a sample of cases; (3) Data was collected during a shorter time period (fewer quarters) than the maximum possible time for this measure; (4) Suppressed for one or more quarters by CMS; (5) No data is available from the hospital for this measure; (6) Fewer than 100 patients completed the HCAHPS survey. Use these rates with caution, as the number of surveys may be too low to reliably assess hospital performance; (7) Survey results are based on less than 12 months of data; (8) Survey results are not available for this reporting period; (9) No or very few patients were eligible for the HCAHPS survey. The scores shown, if any, reflect a very small number of surveys; (10) A state average was not calculated because too few hospitals in the state submitted data; (11) There were discrepancies in the data collection process; Please refer to the User's Guide for a full explanation of data.

Hospital Name	City	Rate	Cases
Franciscan St Margaret Health - Hammond	Hammond	99%	80
St Francis Hosp & Health Ctrs-Indianapolis	Indianapolis	99%	192
Indiana University Health Arnett Hospital	Lafayette	98%	50
Indianapolis VA Medical Center	Indianapolis	98%	47
Memorial Hospital and Health Care Center	Jasper	98%	63
Memorial Hospital of South Bend	South Bend	98%	96
Deaconess Hospital	Evansville	97%	154
Saint Mary Medical Center	Hobart	97%	38
Good Samaritan Hospital	Vincennes	96%	51
Franciscan St Anthony Health-Michigan City	Michigan City	94%	52
The Heart Hospital at Deaconess Gateway[3]	Newburgh	91%	54

Chest Pain/Possible Heart Attack Care

8. Aspirin at Arrival

Hospital Name	City	Rate	Cases
Dupont Hospital	Fort Wayne	100%	65
IU Health Goshen Hospital	Goshen	100%	71
St Joseph's Reg Med Ctr-Plymouth	Plymouth	100%	44
Comm Hosp of Anderson & Madison County	Anderson	99%	84
Daviess Community Hospital	Washington	99%	77
Dearborn County Hospital	Lawrenceburg	99%	134
The King's Daughters' Hospital	Madison	99%	122
Parkview Lagrange Hospital	Lagrange	99%	75
Union Hospital Clinton	Clinton	99%	148
Bluffton Regional Medical Center	Bluffton	98%	63
Decatur County Memorial Hospital	Greensburg	98%	138
Dukes Memorial Hospital	Peru	98%	172
Johnson Memorial Hospital	Franklin	98%	46
Kosciusko Community Hospital	Warsaw	98%	228
Saint John's Health System	Anderson	98%	113
Cameron Memorial Community Hospital	Angola	97%	153
Deaconess Hospital	Evansville	97%	823
Henry County Memorial Hospital	New Castle	97%	240
Howard Regional Health System	Kokomo	97%	30
Parkview Noble Hospital	Kendallville	97%	96
Parkview Whitley Hospital	Columbia City	97%	158
Saint Francis Hospital and Health Centers	Beech Grove	97%	105
Saint Vincent Dunn Hospital	Bedford	97%	75
Saint Vincent Mercy Hospital	Elwood	97%	60
Sullivan County Community Hospital	Sullivan	97%	132
Dekalb Memorial Hospital	Auburn	96%	112
Major Hospital	Shelbyville	96%	100
Margaret Mary Community Hospital	Batesville	96%	114
Memorial Hospital	Logansport	96%	96
Parkview Huntington Hospital	Huntington	96%	107
Saint Joseph Hospital & Health Center	Kokomo	96%	106
Saint Elizabeth Central	Lafayette	95%	76
Schneck Medical Center	Seymour	95%	170
Fayette Regional Health System	Connersville	94%	97
Harrison County Hospital	Corydon	94%	87
Hendricks Regional Health	Danville	94%	174
Marion General Hospital	Marion	94%	207
Morgan Hospital and Medical Center	Martinsville	94%	50
Saint Francis Hospital Mooresville	Mooresville	94%	171
Hancock Regional Hospital	Greenfield	93%	81
Indiana University Health West Hospital	Avon	93%	56
Saint Vincent Carmel Hospital	Carmel	93%	137
Saint Clare Medical Center	Crawfordsville	92%	165
Witham Health Services	Lebanon	92%	87
Community Hospital North	Indianapolis	91%	131
Saint Elizabeth East	Lafayette	91%	67
Jay County Hospital	Portland	87%	106
Saint Vincent Hospital & Health Services	Indianapolis	87%	60
Starke Memorial Hospital	Knox	83%	66
St Francis Hosp & Health Ctrs-Indianapolis	Indianapolis	67%	70

9. Median Time to ECG (minutes)

Hospital Name	City	Min.	Cases
Johnson Memorial Hospital	Franklin	2	69
Morgan Hospital and Medical Center	Martinsville	2	52
Saint Vincent Mercy Hospital	Elwood	2	72
Saint Vincent Dunn Hospital	Bedford	3	80
Bluffton Regional Medical Center	Bluffton	4	65
Dupont Hospital	Fort Wayne	4	68
Hancock Regional Hospital	Greenfield	4	84
Henry County Memorial Hospital	New Castle	4	268
Kosciusko Community Hospital	Warsaw	4	234
Major Hospital	Shelbyville	4	105
Parkview Noble Hospital	Kendallville	4	100
Sullivan County Community Hospital	Sullivan	4	142
Daviess Community Hospital	Washington	5	83
Deaconess Hospital	Evansville	5	854
IU Health Goshen Hospital	Goshen	5	72
Parkview Lagrange Hospital	Lagrange	5	75
Saint Elizabeth Central	Lafayette	5	80
Union Hospital Clinton	Clinton	5	155
Bedford Regional Medical Center[3]	Bedford	6	25
Cameron Memorial Community Hospital	Angola	6	158
Harrison County Hospital	Corydon	6	97
Howard Regional Health System	Kokomo	6	33
Jay County Hospital	Portland	6	112
Margaret Mary Community Hospital	Batesville	6	118
Marion General Hospital	Marion	6	215
Memorial Hospital	Logansport	6	125
Parkview Whitley Hospital	Columbia City	6	159
Saint Vincent Hospital & Health Services	Indianapolis	6	60
Starke Memorial Hospital	Knox	6	71
Dukes Memorial Hospital	Peru	7	181
Fayette Regional Health System	Connersville	7	102
Saint Francis Hospital and Health Centers	Beech Grove	7	109
St Joseph's Reg Med Ctr-Plymouth	Plymouth	7	45
Saint Vincent Carmel Hospital	Carmel	7	140
Dearborn County Hospital	Lawrenceburg	8	140
Indiana University Health West Hospital	Avon	8	58
The King's Daughters' Hospital	Madison	8	124
Parkview Huntington Hospital	Huntington	8	109
Saint Elizabeth East	Lafayette	8	69
Saint Francis Hospital Mooresville	Mooresville	8	177
Saint John's Health System	Anderson	8	117
Saint Joseph Hospital & Health Center	Kokomo	8	106
Schneck Medical Center	Seymour	8	183
Witham Health Services	Lebanon	8	90
Saint Clare Medical Center	Crawfordsville	9	167
St Francis Hosp & Health Ctrs-Indianapolis	Indianapolis	9	75
Comm Hosp of Anderson & Madison County	Anderson	10	89
Dekalb Memorial Hospital	Auburn	10	115
Hendricks Regional Health	Danville	10	176
Decatur County Memorial Hospital	Greensburg	11	149
Community Hospital North	Indianapolis	12	139

10. Median Time to Transfer (minutes)

Hospital Name	City	Min.	Cases
Deaconess Hospital	Evansville	38	28
Saint Joseph Hospital & Health Center	Kokomo	41	35
Marion General Hospital	Marion	56	40
Hendricks Regional Health	Danville	58	25

Heart Failure Care

12. ACE Inhibitor or ARB for LVSD

Hospital Name	City	Rate	Cases
Comm Hosp of Anderson & Madison County	Anderson	100%	66
Fayette Regional Health System	Connersville	100%	28
Franciscan St Anthony Health-Michigan City	Michigan City	100%	84
Henry County Memorial Hospital	New Castle	100%	38
IU Health Goshen Hospital	Goshen	100%	73
Laporte Hospital and Health Services	La Porte	100%	92
Porter Valparaiso Hospital Campus	Valparaiso	100%	112
Saint Catherine Hospital	East Chicago	100%	75
Saint Joseph Hospital	Fort Wayne	100%	60
Terre Haute Regional Hospital	Terre Haute	100%	56
Indiana University Health	Indianapolis	99%	346
Memorial Hospital of South Bend	South Bend	99%	113
Reid Hospital & Health Care Services	Richmond	99%	97
Howard Regional Health System	Kokomo	98%	41
The Indiana Heart Hospital	Indianapolis	98%	147
Methodist Hospitals[2]	Gary	98%	142
Franciscan St Margaret Health - Hammond[2]	Hammond	97%	115
Indianapolis VA Medical Center	Indianapolis	97%	117
Riverview Hospital	Noblesville	97%	34
Ball Memorial Hospital[2]	Muncie	96%	104
Columbus Regional Hospital	Columbus	96%	98
Parkview Hospital[2]	Fort Wayne	96%	92
Saint Joseph Regional Medical Center	Mishawaka	96%	112
Saint Mary Medical Center[2]	Hobart	96%	113
Union Hospital	Terre Haute	96%	185
Bloomington Hospital	Bloomington	95%	91
Lutheran Hospital of Indiana	Fort Wayne	95%	158
Saint Vincent Hospital & Health Services	Indianapolis	95%	254
Community Hospital[2]	Munster	94%	67
Franciscan St Margaret Health - Dyer	Dyer	94%	77
Kosciusko Community Hospital	Warsaw	94%	36
St Francis Hosp & Health Ctrs-Indianapolis	Indianapolis	94%	145
Community Hospital South	Indianapolis	93%	76
Major Hospital	Shelbyville	93%	28
Community Hospital East	Indianapolis	92%	91
Hendricks Regional Health	Danville	92%	48
Saint Elizabeth Central	Lafayette	92%	80
Saint John's Health System[2]	Anderson	92%	51
Indiana University Health West Hospital	Avon	90%	39
Marion General Hospital	Marion	90%	63
William N Wishard Memorial Hospital	Indianapolis	90%	189
Floyd Memorial Hospital and Health Services	New Albany	89%	95
Saint Mary's Medical Center of Evansville	Evansville	89%	153
Clark Memorial Hospital	Jeffersonville	88%	102
Elkhart General Hospital	Elkhart	87%	237
Franciscan St Anthony Health - Crown Point[2]	Crown Point	87%	83
Good Samaritan Hospital	Vincennes	86%	98
VA Northern Indiana Healthcare Sys-Marion	Marion	85%	26
Memorial Hospital and Health Care Center	Jasper	84%	67
Indiana University Health Arnett Hospital[2]	Lafayette	82%	49
Deaconess Hospital	Evansville	81%	234
Dearborn County Hospital	Lawrenceburg	79%	33
Saint Francis Hospital and Health Centers	Beech Grove	79%	39
Saint Joseph Hospital & Health Center	Kokomo	78%	46
Saint Vincent Heart Center of Indiana	Indianapolis	68%	203

13. Discharge Instructions

Hospital Name	City	Rate	Cases
Bluffton Regional Medical Center	Bluffton	100%	36
Dupont Hospital	Fort Wayne	100%	35
Franciscan St Anthony Health-Michigan City	Michigan City	100%	204
Howard Regional Health System	Kokomo	100%	104
Indianapolis VA Medical Center	Indianapolis	100%	287
Memorial Hospital	Logansport	100%	38
Morgan Hospital and Medical Center	Martinsville	100%	70
Porter Valparaiso Hospital Campus	Valparaiso	100%	252
Saint Joseph Hospital	Fort Wayne	100%	153
Saint Vincent Williamsport Hospital	Williamsport	100%	26
Tipton Hospital	Tipton	100%	26
Ball Memorial Hospital[2]	Muncie	99%	214
The King's Daughters' Hospital	Madison	99%	108
Saint Mary Medical Center[2]	Hobart	99%	234
The Indiana Heart Hospital	Indianapolis	98%	326
Saint Vincent Dunn Hospital	Bedford	98%	55
VA Northern Indiana Healthcare Sys-Marion	Marion	98%	100
Cameron Memorial Community Hospital	Angola	97%	32
Comm Hosp of Anderson & Madison County	Anderson	97%	178
Saint Catherine Hospital	East Chicago	97%	276
William N Wishard Memorial Hospital	Indianapolis	97%	371
Kosciusko Community Hospital	Warsaw	96%	100
Margaret Mary Community Hospital	Batesville	96%	50
Saint Joseph Regional Medical Center	Mishawaka	96%	363
Decatur County Memorial Hospital	Greensburg	95%	39
Henry County Memorial Hospital	New Castle	95%	80
Saint John's Health System[2]	Anderson	95%	110
Bloomington Hospital	Bloomington	94%	189
Franciscan St Margaret Health - Dyer	Dyer	94%	200
Greene County General Hospital	Linton	94%	33
Memorial Hospital of South Bend	South Bend	94%	318
Reid Hospital & Health Care Services	Richmond	94%	277
Saint Clare Medical Center	Crawfordsville	94%	70
Fayette Regional Health System	Connersville	93%	57
Indiana University Health	Indianapolis	92%	731
Riverview Hospital	Noblesville	92%	66
St Joseph's Reg Med Ctr-Plymouth	Plymouth	92%	60
IU Health Goshen Hospital	Goshen	91%	129
Terre Haute Regional Hospital	Terre Haute	91%	173
Floyd Memorial Hospital and Health Services	New Albany	90%	286
Scott Memorial Hospital	Scottsburg	90%	31
Laporte Hospital and Health Services	La Porte	89%	160
Clark Memorial Hospital	Jeffersonville	88%	264
Indiana University Health West Hospital	Avon	88%	108
St Francis Hosp & Health Ctrs-Indianapolis	Indianapolis	88%	394
Saint Vincent Heart Center of Indiana	Indianapolis	88%	383
Schneck Medical Center	Seymour	88%	56
Good Samaritan Hospital	Vincennes	87%	200
Marion General Hospital	Marion	87%	118
Lutheran Hospital of Indiana	Fort Wayne	86%	397
Hendricks Regional Health	Danville	85%	106
Parkview Noble Hospital	Kendallville	85%	41
Bedford Regional Medical Center	Bedford	84%	43
Indiana University Health North Hospital	Carmel	84%	56
Parkview Huntington Hospital	Huntington	84%	37
Union Hospital	Terre Haute	84%	470
Adams Memorial Hospital	Decatur	83%	66
Franciscan St Anthony Health - Crown Point[2]	Crown Point	83%	196
Saint Mary's Medical Center of Evansville	Evansville	83%	327
Community Hospital North	Indianapolis	82%	67
Franciscan St Margaret Health - Hammond[2]	Hammond	82%	293
Parkview Whitley Hospital	Columbia City	81%	26
Dekalb Memorial Hospital	Auburn	79%	38
Saint Elizabeth Central	Lafayette	79%	135
Parkview Hospital[2]	Fort Wayne	78%	223
Saint Catherine Regional Hospital	Charlestown	78%	27
Starke Memorial Hospital	Knox	77%	26
Major Hospital	Shelbyville	76%	51
Community Hospital East	Indianapolis	74%	231
Saint Vincent Randolph Hospital	Winchester	74%	43
Community Hospital[2]	Munster	73%	232
Franciscan Physicians Hospital	Munster	72%	43
Saint Francis Hospital and Health Centers	Beech Grove	72%	85
Community Hospital South	Indianapolis	71%	159
Elkhart General Hospital	Elkhart	70%	417
Memorial Hospital and Health Care Center	Jasper	70%	149
Saint Joseph Hospital & Health Center	Kokomo	70%	82
The Heart Hospital at Deaconess Gateway[3]	Newburgh	69%	54
Columbus Regional Hospital	Columbus	68%	190
Saint Vincent Hospital & Health Services	Indianapolis	68%	629

NOTE: Hospital profiles are in alphabetical order by state, then city, then hospital within the city; Rankings exclude hospitals with less than 25 cases except for patient surveys which excludes hospitals with less than 100 cases; (a) 100–299 cases; (1) The number of cases is too small to be sure how well a hospital is performing; (2) The hospital indicated that the data submitted for this measure were based on a sample of cases; (3) Data was collected during a shorter time period (fewer quarters) than the maximum possible time for this measure; (4) Suppressed for one or more quarters by CMS; (5) No data is available from the hospital for this measure; (6) Fewer than 100 patients completed the HCAHPS survey. Use these rates with caution, as the number of surveys may be too low to reliably assess hospital performance; (7) Survey results are based on less than 12 months of data; (8) Survey results are not available for this reporting period; (9) No or very few patients were eligible for the HCAHPS survey. The scores shown, if any, reflect a very small number of surveys; (10) A state average was not calculated because too few hospitals in the state submitted data; (11) There were discrepancies in the data collection process; Please refer to the User's Guide for a full explanation of data.

Hospital Name	City	Rate	Cases
Saint Elizabeth East	Lafayette	67%	55
Hancock Regional Hospital	Greenfield	66%	53
Dearborn County Hospital	Lawrenceburg	64%	86
Deaconess Hospital	Evansville	63%	548
Johnson Memorial Hospital	Franklin	63%	54
Union Hospital Clinton	Clinton	62%	34
Westview Hospital	Indianapolis	59%	51
Indiana University Health Arnett Hospital[2]	Lafayette	55%	132
Methodist Hospitals[2]	Gary	52%	269
Daviess Community Hospital	Washington	46%	35
Witham Health Services	Lebanon	45%	55

14. Evaluation of LVS Function

Hospital Name	City	Rate	Cases
Bluffton Regional Medical Center	Bluffton	100%	53
Comm Hosp of Anderson & Madison County	Anderson	100%	232
Decatur County Memorial Hospital	Greensburg	100%	67
Dupont Hospital	Fort Wayne	100%	39
Fayette Regional Health System	Connersville	100%	88
Franciscan St Anthony Health-Michigan City	Michigan City	100%	231
Henry County Memorial Hospital	New Castle	100%	111
Indiana University Health	Indianapolis	100%	879
Indiana University Health North Hospital	Carmel	100%	76
Indiana University Health West Hospital	Avon	100%	153
Indianapolis VA Medical Center	Indianapolis	100%	314
IU Health Goshen Hospital	Goshen	100%	185
Laporte Hospital and Health Services	La Porte	100%	212
Major Hospital	Shelbyville	100%	72
Memorial Hospital	Logansport	100%	55
Memorial Hospital of South Bend	South Bend	100%	403
Porter Valparaiso Hospital Campus	Valparaiso	100%	323
Putnam County Hospital	Greencastle	100%	30
Saint Catherine Hospital	East Chicago	100%	338
Saint Joseph Hospital	Fort Wayne	100%	188
Saint Joseph Regional Medical Center	Mishawaka	100%	478
St Joseph's Reg Med Ctr-Plymouth	Plymouth	100%	90
Saint Mary Medical Center[2]	Hobart	100%	270
Saint Vincent Heart Center of Indiana	Indianapolis	100%	447
Terre Haute Regional Hospital	Terre Haute	100%	212
Tipton Hospital	Tipton	100%	48
Union Hospital	Terre Haute	100%	570
Union Hospital Clinton	Clinton	100%	41
Adams Memorial Hospital	Decatur	99%	87
Ball Memorial Hospital[2]	Muncie	99%	301
Bloomington Hospital	Bloomington	99%	262
Clark Memorial Hospital	Jeffersonville	99%	337
Columbus Regional Hospital	Columbus	99%	247
Community Hospital East	Indianapolis	99%	285
Community Hospital South	Indianapolis	99%	211
Elkhart General Hospital	Elkhart	99%	549
Franciscan St Anthony Health - Crown Point[2]	Crown Point	99%	270
Howard Regional Health System	Kokomo	99%	156
The Indiana Heart Hospital	Indianapolis	99%	377
Indiana University Health Arnett Hospital[2]	Lafayette	99%	193
The King's Daughters' Hospital	Madison	99%	143
Kosciusko Community Hospital	Warsaw	99%	150
Margaret Mary Community Hospital	Batesville	99%	74
Marion General Hospital	Marion	99%	189
Methodist Hospitals[2]	Gary	99%	317
Morgan Hospital and Medical Center	Martinsville	99%	88
Parkview Hospital[2]	Fort Wayne	99%	294
Reid Hospital & Health Care Services	Richmond	99%	383
Riverview Hospital	Noblesville	99%	110
Saint Elizabeth East	Lafayette	99%	81
Saint Francis Hospital and Health Centers	Beech Grove	99%	164
St Francis Hosp & Health Ctrs-Indianapolis	Indianapolis	99%	453
VA Northern Indiana Healthcare Sys-Marion	Marion	99%	106
Westview Hospital	Indianapolis	99%	68
Dearborn County Hospital	Lawrenceburg	98%	104
Dekalb Memorial Hospital	Auburn	98%	59
Franciscan Physicians Hospital	Munster	98%	44
Franciscan St Margaret Health - Dyer	Dyer	98%	244
Jasper County Hospital	Rensselaer	98%	41
Lutheran Hospital of Indiana	Fort Wayne	98%	507
Saint Elizabeth Central	Lafayette	98%	195
Saint Vincent Williamsport Hospital	Williamsport	98%	46
William N Wishard Memorial Hospital	Indianapolis	98%	409
Floyd Memorial Hospital and Health Services	New Albany	97%	388
Franciscan St Margaret Health - Hammond[2]	Hammond	97%	333
Harrison County Hospital	Corydon	97%	39
Hendricks Regional Health	Danville	97%	146
Johnson Memorial Hospital	Franklin	97%	75
Saint Francis Hospital Mooresville	Mooresville	97%	32
Saint Mary's Medical Center of Evansville	Evansville	97%	420
Saint Vincent Dunn Hospital	Bedford	97%	88
Schneck Medical Center	Seymour	97%	73
Community Hospital[2]	Munster	96%	295
Hancock Regional Hospital	Greenfield	96%	84
Parkview Huntington Hospital	Huntington	96%	52
Saint Vincent Hospital & Health Services	Indianapolis	96%	832
Bedford Regional Medical Center	Bedford	95%	55
Community Hospital North	Indianapolis	95%	110
Saint John's Health System[2]	Anderson	95%	160
Saint Joseph Hospital & Health Center	Kokomo	95%	122
Daviess Community Hospital	Washington	94%	49
Dukes Memorial Hospital	Peru	94%	31
The Heart Hospital at Deaconess Gateway[3]	Newburgh	94%	70
Memorial Hospital and Health Care Center	Jasper	94%	212
Saint Catherine Regional Hospital	Charlestown	94%	32
Deaconess Hospital	Evansville	93%	729
Good Samaritan Hospital	Vincennes	93%	266
Parkview Noble Hospital	Kendallville	93%	61
Parkview Whitley Hospital	Columbia City	90%	41
Wabash County Hospital	Wabash	90%	39
Saint Vincent Carmel Hospital	Carmel	89%	38
Witham Health Services	Lebanon	89%	75
Saint Vincent Clay Hospital	Brazil	87%	31
Saint Vincent Randolph Hospital	Winchester	86%	44
Saint Clare Medical Center	Crawfordsville	85%	106
Saint Vincent Mercy Hospital	Elwood	84%	25
Cameron Memorial Community Hospital	Angola	83%	47
Scott Memorial Hospital	Scottsburg	83%	29
Saint Mary's Warrick Hospital	Boonville	81%	27
Starke Memorial Hospital	Knox	81%	27
White County Memorial Hospital	Monticello	81%	31
Perry County Memorial Hospital	Tell City	79%	33
Pinnacle Hospital[2]	Crown Point	78%	27
Monroe Hospital	Bloomington	76%	37
Sullivan County Community Hospital	Sullivan	74%	42
Greene County General Hospital	Linton	63%	52

15. Smoking Cessation Advice

Hospital Name	City	Rate	Cases
Ball Memorial Hospital[2]	Muncie	100%	52
Clark Memorial Hospital	Jeffersonville	100%	65
Columbus Regional Hospital	Columbus	100%	45
Community Hospital[2]	Munster	100%	38
Community Hospital East	Indianapolis	100%	75
Comm Hosp of Anderson & Madison County	Anderson	100%	49
Community Hospital South	Indianapolis	100%	44
Dearborn County Hospital	Lawrenceburg	100%	25
Elkhart General Hospital	Elkhart	100%	95
Floyd Memorial Hospital and Health Services	New Albany	100%	63
Franciscan St Anthony Health-Michigan City	Michigan City	100%	52
Franciscan St Margaret Health - Dyer	Dyer	100%	29
Franciscan St Margaret Health - Hammond[2]	Hammond	100%	100
The Indiana Heart Hospital	Indianapolis	100%	60
Indiana University Health	Indianapolis	100%	213
IU Health Goshen Hospital	Goshen	100%	31
Kosciusko Community Hospital	Warsaw	100%	25
Laporte Hospital and Health Services	La Porte	100%	25
Lutheran Hospital of Indiana	Fort Wayne	100%	77
Marion General Hospital	Marion	100%	32
Memorial Hospital of South Bend	South Bend	100%	103
Methodist Hospitals[2]	Gary	100%	81
Parkview Hospital[2]	Fort Wayne	100%	58
Porter Valparaiso Hospital Campus	Valparaiso	100%	36
Reid Hospital & Health Care Services	Richmond	100%	67
Saint Catherine Hospital	East Chicago	100%	66
Saint Elizabeth Central	Lafayette	100%	25
St Francis Hosp & Health Ctrs-Indianapolis	Indianapolis	100%	73
Saint John's Health System[2]	Anderson	100%	34
Saint Joseph Hospital	Fort Wayne	100%	48
Saint Joseph Regional Medical Center	Mishawaka	100%	101
Saint Mary Medical Center[2]	Hobart	100%	26
Saint Mary's Medical Center of Evansville	Evansville	100%	65
Saint Vincent Heart Center of Indiana	Indianapolis	100%	63
Saint Vincent Hospital & Health Services	Indianapolis	100%	125
Terre Haute Regional Hospital	Terre Haute	100%	59
Union Hospital	Terre Haute	100%	67
William N Wishard Memorial Hospital	Indianapolis	99%	169
Franciscan St Anthony Health - Crown Point[2]	Crown Point	98%	46
Indianapolis VA Medical Center	Indianapolis	98%	102
Good Samaritan Hospital	Vincennes	97%	35
Bloomington Hospital	Bloomington	94%	53
Deaconess Hospital	Evansville	90%	183

Pneumonia Care

16. Appropriate Initial Antibiotic

Hospital Name	City	Rate	Cases
Bluffton Regional Medical Center	Bluffton	100%	81
Dekalb Memorial Hospital	Auburn	100%	72
Dupont Hospital	Fort Wayne	100%	47
VA Northern Indiana Healthcare Sys-Marion	Marion	100%	44
Ball Memorial Hospital	Muncie	99%	203
Franciscan St Anthony Health-Michigan City	Michigan City	99%	72
Indiana University Health West Hospital[2]	Avon	99%	73
Margaret Mary Community Hospital	Batesville	99%	67
Indianapolis VA Medical Center	Indianapolis	98%	115
Parkview Lagrange Hospital	Lagrange	98%	44
Parkview Noble Hospital	Kendallville	98%	59
Reid Hospital & Health Care Services	Richmond	98%	291
Dukes Memorial Hospital	Peru	97%	36
Major Hospital	Shelbyville	97%	89
Saint Joseph Regional Medical Center	Mishawaka	97%	230
Schneck Medical Center	Seymour	97%	64
Union Hospital Clinton	Clinton	97%	36
Deaconess Hospital[2]	Evansville	96%	180
The King's Daughters' Hospital	Madison	96%	116
Parkview Hospital[2]	Fort Wayne	96%	91
Parkview Whitley Hospital	Columbia City	96%	50
Saint Mary's Medical Center of Evansville	Evansville	96%	166
Clark Memorial Hospital	Jeffersonville	95%	227
Columbus Regional Hospital	Columbus	95%	144
Franciscan St Margaret Health - Dyer	Dyer	95%	92
IU Health Goshen Hospital[2]	Goshen	95%	104
Kosciusko Community Hospital	Warsaw	95%	97
Marion General Hospital	Marion	95%	127
Saint Vincent Mercy Hospital	Elwood	95%	37
William N Wishard Memorial Hospital[2]	Indianapolis	95%	92
Bloomington Hospital	Bloomington	94%	199
Community Hospital South[2]	Indianapolis	94%	83
Franciscan St Margaret Health - Hammond[2]	Hammond	94%	82
Hancock Regional Hospital[2]	Greenfield	94%	87
Saint Mary's Warrick Hospital	Boonville	94%	34
Terre Haute Regional Hospital	Terre Haute	94%	78
Comm Hosp of Anderson & Madison County[2]	Anderson	93%	100
Fayette Regional Health System	Connersville	93%	97
Floyd Memorial Hospital and Health Services	New Albany	93%	216
Gibson General Hospital	Princeton	93%	29
Henry County Memorial Hospital	New Castle	93%	106
Johnson Memorial Hospital	Franklin	93%	83
Sullivan County Community Hospital	Sullivan	93%	44
Cameron Memorial Community Hospital	Angola	92%	53
Community Hospital East[2]	Indianapolis	92%	91
Dearborn County Hospital	Lawrenceburg	92%	102
Parkview Huntington Hospital	Huntington	92%	59
Saint Catherine Hospital	East Chicago	92%	92
Saint Vincent Randolph Hospital	Winchester	92%	25
Community Hospital[2]	Munster	91%	81
Daviess Community Hospital	Washington	91%	92
Howard Regional Health System	Kokomo	91%	126
Indiana University Health Arnett Hospital[2]	Lafayette	91%	82
Jay County Hospital	Portland	91%	34
Scott Memorial Hospital	Scottsburg	91%	54
Memorial Hospital and Health Care Center[2]	Jasper	90%	97
Porter Valparaiso Hospital Campus	Valparaiso	90%	146
St Joseph's Reg Med Ctr-Plymouth	Plymouth	90%	67
Saint Vincent Dunn Hospital	Bedford	90%	48
Saint Vincent Williamsport Hospital	Williamsport	90%	29
Union Hospital	Terre Haute	90%	238
Community Hospital North[2]	Indianapolis	89%	74
Saint Joseph Hospital	Fort Wayne	89%	38
Elkhart General Hospital	Elkhart	88%	163
Franciscan St Anthony Health - Crown Point[2]	Crown Point	88%	78
Good Samaritan Hospital	Vincennes	88%	120
Saint Clare Medical Center	Crawfordsville	88%	67
Indiana University Health[2]	Indianapolis	87%	45
Witham Health Services	Lebanon	87%	54
Indiana University Health North Hospital	Carmel	86%	49
Laporte Hospital and Health Services	La Porte	86%	93
Lutheran Hospital of Indiana	Fort Wayne	86%	132
Putnam County Hospital	Greencastle	86%	37
Saint Elizabeth Central[2]	Lafayette	86%	71
Tipton Hospital	Tipton	86%	35
White County Memorial Hospital	Monticello	86%	59
Memorial Hospital	Logansport	85%	81
Memorial Hospital of South Bend	South Bend	85%	167
Saint Elizabeth East	Lafayette	85%	46
Saint Joseph Hospital & Health Center	Kokomo	85%	110
Westview Hospital	Indianapolis	85%	34
Riverview Hospital	Noblesville	84%	86
Decatur County Memorial Hospital	Greensburg	83%	29
Saint Vincent Jennings Hospital[3]	North Vernon	83%	30
Adams Memorial Hospital	Decatur	82%	84
Bedford Regional Medical Center	Bedford	82%	56
Jasper County Hospital	Rensselaer	82%	39
Saint Mary Medical Center[2]	Hobart	82%	74
Saint Vincent Frankfort Hospital	Frankfort	82%	44
Starke Memorial Hospital[2]	Knox	82%	39
Wabash County Hospital	Wabash	82%	33
Greene County General Hospital	Linton	81%	27
Harrison County Hospital	Corydon	80%	75
Saint John's Health System[2]	Anderson	80%	91
Hendricks Regional Health	Danville	79%	125
Saint Catherine Regional Hospital	Charlestown	78%	36
Methodist Hospitals[2]	Gary	76%	50
St Francis Hosp & Health Ctrs-Indianapolis	Indianapolis	76%	144
Saint Vincent Hospital & Health Services	Indianapolis	75%	151
Perry County Memorial Hospital	Tell City	72%	36

NOTE: Hospital profiles are in alphabetical order by state, then city, then hospital within the city; Rankings exclude hospitals with less than 25 cases except for patient surveys which excludes hospitals with less than 100 cases; (a) 100–299 cases; (1) The number of cases is too small to be sure how well a hospital is performing; (2) The hospital indicated that the data submitted for this measure were based on a sample of cases; (3) Data was collected during a shorter time period (fewer quarters) than the maximum possible time for this measure; (4) Suppressed for one or more quarters by CMS; (5) No data is available from the hospital for this measure; (6) Fewer than 100 patients completed the HCAHPS survey. Use these rates with caution, as the number of surveys may be too low to reliably assess hospital performance; (7) Survey results are based on less than 12 months of data; (8) Survey results are not available for this reporting period; (9) No or very few patients were eligible for the HCAHPS survey. The scores shown, if any, reflect a very small number of surveys; (10) A state average was not calculated because too few hospitals in the state submitted data; (11) There were discrepancies in the data collection process; Please refer to the User's Guide for a full explanation of data.

Hospital Name	City	Rate	Cases
Saint Francis Hospital and Health Centers[2]	Beech Grove	70%	110
Morgan Hospital and Medical Center	Martinsville	69%	58
Saint Francis Hospital Mooresville	Mooresville	68%	73
Saint Vincent Carmel Hospital	Carmel	57%	51

17. Blood Culture Timing

Hospital Name	City	Rate	Cases
Bluffton Regional Medical Center	Bluffton	100%	92
Cameron Memorial Community Hospital	Angola	100%	42
Dekalb Memorial Hospital	Auburn	100%	70
Dupont Hospital	Fort Wayne	100%	55
Monroe Hospital	Bloomington	100%	39
Reid Hospital & Health Care Services	Richmond	100%	483
Saint Mary Medical Center[2]	Hobart	100%	96
Terre Haute Regional Hospital	Terre Haute	100%	111
VA Northern Indiana Healthcare Sys-Marion	Marion	100%	46
Wabash County Hospital	Wabash	100%	33
Fayette Regional Health System	Connersville	99%	121
Franciscan St Anthony Health-Michigan City	Michigan City	99%	98
Good Samaritan Hospital	Vincennes	99%	156
Indianapolis VA Medical Center	Indianapolis	99%	185
The King's Daughters' Hospital	Madison	99%	134
Major Hospital	Shelbyville	99%	150
Memorial Hospital of South Bend	South Bend	99%	172
Parkview Noble Hospital	Kendallville	99%	72
Saint Elizabeth Central[2]	Lafayette	99%	83
Saint Joseph Hospital & Health Center	Kokomo	99%	167
St Joseph's Reg Med Ctr-Plymouth	Plymouth	99%	72
Schneck Medical Center	Seymour	99%	99
Ball Memorial Hospital	Muncie	98%	328
Columbus Regional Hospital	Columbus	98%	218
Franciscan St Anthony Health - Crown Point[2]	Crown Point	98%	126
Howard Regional Health System	Kokomo	98%	145
Kosciusko Community Hospital	Warsaw	98%	147
Lutheran Hospital of Indiana	Fort Wayne	98%	198
Marion General Hospital	Marion	98%	130
Morgan Hospital and Medical Center	Martinsville	98%	88
Perry County Memorial Hospital	Tell City	98%	45
Saint John's Health System[2]	Anderson	98%	147
Saint Joseph Regional Medical Center	Mishawaka	98%	222
Saint Mary's Medical Center of Evansville	Evansville	98%	240
Westview Hospital	Indianapolis	98%	53
William N Wishard Memorial Hospital[2]	Indianapolis	98%	130
Bedford Regional Medical Center	Bedford	97%	102
Bloomington Hospital	Bloomington	97%	296
Clark Memorial Hospital	Jeffersonville	97%	328
Dukes Memorial Hospital	Peru	97%	36
Floyd Memorial Hospital and Health Services	New Albany	97%	424
Franciscan St Margaret Health - Hammond[2]	Hammond	97%	197
Hancock Regional Hospital[2]	Greenfield	97%	106
Indiana University Health Arnett Hospital[2]	Lafayette	97%	143
Margaret Mary Community Hospital	Batesville	97%	92
Memorial Hospital	Logansport	97%	74
Saint Joseph Hospital	Fort Wayne	97%	39
Tipton Hospital	Tipton	97%	39
Elkhart General Hospital	Elkhart	96%	53
Franciscan St Margaret Health - Dyer	Dyer	96%	155
Henry County Memorial Hospital	New Castle	96%	112
Parkview Whitley Hospital	Columbia City	96%	45
Riverview Hospital	Noblesville	96%	114
Community Hospital North[2]	Indianapolis	95%	132
Deaconess Hospital[2]	Evansville	95%	252
IU Health Goshen Hospital[2]	Goshen	95%	121
Parkview Huntington Hospital	Huntington	95%	56
Saint Clare Medical Center	Crawfordsville	95%	60
Saint Elizabeth East	Lafayette	95%	44
Saint Francis Hospital Mooresville	Mooresville	95%	60
Saint Vincent Hospital & Health Services	Indianapolis	95%	256
Community Hospital East[2]	Indianapolis	94%	131
Community Hospital South[2]	Indianapolis	94%	125
Daviess Community Hospital	Washington	94%	144
Indiana University Health[2]	Indianapolis	94%	103
Indiana University Health North Hospital	Carmel	94%	51
Johnson Memorial Hospital	Franklin	94%	98
Porter Valparaiso Hospital Campus	Valparaiso	94%	259
Saint Catherine Hospital	East Chicago	94%	101
Saint Vincent Dunn Hospital	Bedford	94%	66
Saint Vincent Frankfort Hospital	Frankfort	94%	50
Union Hospital	Terre Haute	94%	139
Community Hospital[2]	Munster	93%	147
Greene County General Hospital	Linton	93%	29
Memorial Hospital and Health Care Center[2]	Jasper	93%	97
Methodist Hospitals[2]	Gary	93%	108
Saint Vincent Randolph Hospital	Winchester	93%	45
Saint Vincent Williamsport Hospital	Williamsport	93%	46
Adams Memorial Hospital	Decatur	92%	87
Dearborn County Hospital	Lawrenceburg	92%	145
Starke Memorial Hospital[2]	Knox	92%	49
Gibson General Hospital	Princeton	91%	47
Laporte Hospital and Health Services	La Porte	91%	179
Putnam County Hospital	Greencastle	91%	66
Hendricks Regional Health	Danville	90%	134
Saint Vincent Mercy Hospital	Elwood	90%	49
White County Memorial Hospital	Monticello	90%	71
Decatur County Memorial Hospital	Greensburg	89%	37
Harrison County Hospital	Corydon	89%	64
Jay County Hospital	Portland	89%	47
Indiana University Health West Hospital[2]	Avon	88%	153
Sullivan County Community Hospital	Sullivan	88%	50
Witham Health Services	Lebanon	87%	82
Saint Francis Hospital and Health Centers[2]	Beech Grove	86%	175
Saint Vincent Carmel Hospital	Carmel	86%	80
Parkview Hospital[2]	Fort Wayne	85%	95
Scott Memorial Hospital	Scottsburg	85%	55
St Francis Hosp & Health Ctrs-Indianapolis	Indianapolis	84%	133
Comm Hosp of Anderson & Madison County[2]	Anderson	83%	75
Jasper County Hospital	Rensselaer	77%	44
Saint Mary's Warrick Hospital	Boonville	73%	30

18. Influenza Vaccine

Hospital Name	City	Rate	Cases
Decatur County Memorial Hospital	Greensburg	100%	28
Dupont Hospital	Fort Wayne	100%	32
Henry County Memorial Hospital	New Castle	100%	78
The King's Daughters' Hospital	Madison	100%	117
Major Hospital	Shelbyville	100%	89
Schneck Medical Center	Seymour	100%	78
Scott Memorial Hospital	Scottsburg	100%	30
Terre Haute Regional Hospital	Terre Haute	100%	103
Bluffton Regional Medical Center	Bluffton	99%	75
Columbus Regional Hospital	Columbus	99%	163
Fayette Regional Health System	Connersville	99%	82
Good Samaritan Hospital	Vincennes	99%	184
Indianapolis VA Medical Center	Indianapolis	99%	131
IU Health Goshen Hospital[2]	Goshen	99%	87
Parkview Hospital[2]	Fort Wayne	99%	91
Reid Hospital & Health Care Services	Richmond	99%	396
Saint Joseph Regional Medical Center	Mishawaka	99%	205
Kosciusko Community Hospital	Warsaw	98%	86
Perry County Memorial Hospital	Tell City	98%	46
Putnam County Hospital	Greencastle	98%	44
Riverview Hospital	Noblesville	98%	99
St Joseph's Reg Med Ctr-Plymouth	Plymouth	98%	65
Saint Mary Medical Center[2]	Hobart	98%	64
Saint Vincent Dunn Hospital	Bedford	98%	55
Comm Hosp of Anderson & Madison County[2]	Anderson	97%	101
Dearborn County Hospital	Lawrenceburg	97%	108
Dekalb Memorial Hospital	Auburn	97%	59
Lutheran Hospital of Indiana	Fort Wayne	97%	189
Parkview Whitley Hospital	Columbia City	97%	32
Saint Joseph Hospital	Fort Wayne	97%	33
Saint Vincent Williamsport Hospital	Williamsport	97%	30
Cameron Memorial Community Hospital	Angola	96%	56
Clark Memorial Hospital	Jeffersonville	96%	258
Parkview Huntington Hospital	Huntington	96%	55
Parkview Noble Hospital	Kendallville	96%	52
Saint Elizabeth East	Lafayette	96%	54
Bedford Regional Medical Center	Bedford	95%	37
Franciscan St Anthony Health - Crown Point[2]	Crown Point	95%	79
Howard Regional Health System	Kokomo	95%	144
Indiana University Health West Hospital[2]	Avon	95%	77
Jay County Hospital	Portland	95%	38
Porter Valparaiso Hospital Campus	Valparaiso	95%	228
Saint Elizabeth Central	Lafayette	95%	85
Saint John's Health System[2]	Anderson	95%	78
VA Northern Indiana Healthcare Sys-Marion	Marion	95%	44
Ball Memorial Hospital	Muncie	94%	279
Bloomington Hospital	Bloomington	94%	227
Community Hospital[2]	Munster	94%	90
Franciscan St Anthony Health-Michigan City	Michigan City	94%	62
Franciscan St Margaret Health - Hammond[2]	Hammond	94%	89
Memorial Hospital	Logansport	94%	64
Saint Joseph Hospital & Health Center	Kokomo	94%	135
Union Hospital	Terre Haute	94%	288
Hendricks Regional Health	Danville	93%	118
Marion General Hospital	Marion	93%	123
Memorial Hospital of South Bend	South Bend	93%	157
Parkview Lagrange Hospital	Lagrange	93%	28
Saint Francis Hospital Mooresville	Mooresville	93%	44
Wabash County Hospital	Wabash	93%	29
Adams Memorial Hospital	Decatur	92%	64
Community Hospital North[2]	Indianapolis	92%	72
Memorial Hospital and Health Care Center[2]	Jasper	92%	93
St Francis Hosp & Health Ctrs-Indianapolis	Indianapolis	92%	112
Saint Mary's Warrick Hospital	Boonville	92%	25
Tipton Hospital	Tipton	92%	37
Hancock Regional Hospital[2]	Greenfield	91%	85
Laporte Hospital and Health Services	La Porte	91%	113
Saint Vincent Frankfort Hospital	Frankfort	91%	35
Westview Hospital	Indianapolis	91%	46
Franciscan St Margaret Health - Dyer	Dyer	90%	98
Indiana University Health Arnett Hospital[2]	Lafayette	90%	89
Saint Francis Hospital and Health Centers[2]	Beech Grove	90%	194
Indiana University Health[2]	Indianapolis	89%	84
Saint Catherine Hospital	East Chicago	89%	71
Saint Mary's Medical Center of Evansville	Evansville	89%	205
Saint Vincent Randolph Hospital	Winchester	89%	28
Saint Vincent Hospital & Health Services	Indianapolis	88%	249
Deaconess Hospital[2]	Evansville	87%	297
Elkhart General Hospital	Elkhart	87%	167
Margaret Mary Community Hospital	Batesville	87%	77
Morgan Hospital and Medical Center	Martinsville	87%	53
Saint Clare Medical Center	Crawfordsville	87%	47
Dukes Memorial Hospital	Peru	86%	37
Community Hospital South[2]	Indianapolis	85%	75
Floyd Memorial Hospital and Health Services	New Albany	85%	325
Harrison County Hospital	Corydon	85%	71
Indiana University Health North Hospital	Carmel	85%	48
Community Hospital East[2]	Indianapolis	84%	73
Johnson Memorial Hospital	Franklin	84%	56
Methodist Hospitals[2]	Gary	84%	83
Daviess Community Hospital	Washington	79%	97
Witham Health Services	Lebanon	79%	48
William N Wishard Memorial Hospital[2]	Indianapolis	77%	47
Saint Vincent Carmel Hospital	Carmel	76%	34
Greene County General Hospital	Linton	74%	27
Jasper County Hospital	Rensselaer	73%	37
Sullivan County Community Hospital	Sullivan	69%	29
Starke Memorial Hospital[2]	Knox	62%	26
White County Memorial Hospital	Monticello	57%	47

19. Initial Antibiotic Timing

Hospital Name	City	Rate	Cases
Bluffton Regional Medical Center	Bluffton	100%	119
Dekalb Memorial Hospital	Auburn	100%	97
Dukes Memorial Hospital	Peru	100%	54
Dupont Hospital	Fort Wayne	100%	50
IU Health Goshen Hospital[2]	Goshen	100%	131
Major Hospital	Shelbyville	100%	135
Margaret Mary Community Hospital	Batesville	100%	95
Parkview Huntington Hospital	Huntington	100%	87
Parkview Lagrange Hospital	Lagrange	100%	49
Saint Francis Hospital Mooresville	Mooresville	100%	86
St Joseph's Reg Med Ctr-Plymouth	Plymouth	100%	103
Saint Vincent Dunn Hospital	Bedford	100%	72
Wabash County Hospital	Wabash	100%	30
Witham Health Services	Lebanon	100%	82
Bedford Regional Medical Center	Bedford	99%	92
Columbus Regional Hospital	Columbus	99%	215
Community Hospital East[2]	Indianapolis	99%	146
Daviess Community Hospital	Washington	99%	122
Fayette Regional Health System	Connersville	99%	143
Henry County Memorial Hospital	New Castle	99%	157
Indiana University Health West Hospital[2]	Avon	99%	122
Johnson Memorial Hospital	Franklin	99%	88
The King's Daughters' Hospital	Madison	99%	188
Memorial Hospital and Health Care Center[2]	Jasper	99%	135
Reid Hospital & Health Care Services	Richmond	99%	452
Saint Clare Medical Center	Crawfordsville	99%	87
Terre Haute Regional Hospital	Terre Haute	99%	112
Bloomington Hospital	Bloomington	98%	287
Cameron Memorial Community Hospital	Angola	98%	90
Decatur County Memorial Hospital	Greensburg	98%	47
Hendricks Regional Health	Danville	98%	174
Parkview Whitley Hospital	Columbia City	98%	58
Saint John's Health System[2]	Anderson	98%	138
Saint Joseph Hospital	Fort Wayne	98%	53
Saint Joseph Regional Medical Center	Mishawaka	98%	373
Schneck Medical Center	Seymour	98%	118
Sullivan County Community Hospital	Sullivan	98%	62
VA Northern Indiana Healthcare Sys-Marion	Marion	98%	52
Ball Memorial Hospital	Muncie	97%	299
Community Hospital North[2]	Indianapolis	97%	125
Deaconess Hospital[2]	Evansville	97%	320
Floyd Memorial Hospital and Health Services	New Albany	97%	376
Franciscan St Anthony Health - Crown Point[2]	Crown Point	97%	145
Franciscan St Anthony Health-Michigan City	Michigan City	97%	113
Franciscan St Margaret Health - Hammond[2]	Hammond	97%	208
Good Samaritan Hospital	Vincennes	97%	195
Indiana University Health[2]	Indianapolis	97%	107
Kosciusko Community Hospital	Warsaw	97%	144
Memorial Hospital	Logansport	97%	114
Parkview Noble Hospital	Kendallville	97%	79
Saint Elizabeth Central[2]	Lafayette	97%	102
White County Memorial Hospital	Monticello	97%	76
Community Hospital[2]	Munster	96%	156
Comm Hosp of Anderson & Madison County[2]	Anderson	96%	155
Elkhart General Hospital	Elkhart	96%	285
Gibson General Hospital	Princeton	96%	45
Indiana University Health Arnett Hospital[2]	Lafayette	96%	135

NOTE: Hospital profiles are in alphabetical order by state, then city, then hospital within the city; Rankings exclude hospitals with less than 25 cases except for patient surveys which excludes hospitals with less than 100 cases; (a) 100–299 cases; (1) The number of cases is too small to be sure how well a hospital is performing; (2) The hospital indicated that the data submitted for this measure were based on a sample of cases; (3) Data was collected during a shorter time period (fewer quarters) than the maximum possible time for this measure; (4) Suppressed for one or more quarters by CMS; (5) No data is available from the hospital for this measure; (6) Fewer than 100 patients completed the HCAHPS survey. Use these rates with caution, as the number of surveys may be too low to reliably assess hospital performance; (7) Survey results are based on less than 12 months of data; (8) Survey results are not available for this reporting period; (9) No or very few patients were eligible for the HCAHPS survey. The scores shown, if any, reflect a very small number of surveys; (10) A state average was not calculated because too few hospitals in the state submitted data; (11) There were discrepancies in the data collection process; Please refer to the User's Guide for a full explanation of data.

Laporte Hospital and Health Services	La Porte	96%	169
Marion General Hospital	Marion	96%	166
Saint Catherine Hospital	East Chicago	96%	120
Saint Mary's Medical Center of Evansville	Evansville	96%	288
Saint Vincent Mercy Hospital	Elwood	96%	54
Saint Vincent Randolph Hospital	Winchester	96%	56
Union Hospital Clinton	Clinton	96%	48
Adams Memorial Hospital	Decatur	95%	95
Community Hospital South[2]	Indianapolis	95%	143
Franciscan St Margaret Health - Dyer	Dyer	95%	155
Greene County General Hospital	Linton	95%	44
Hancock Regional Hospital[2]	Greenfield	95%	132
Harrison County Hospital	Corydon	95%	94
Indiana University Health North Hospital	Carmel	95%	57
Lutheran Hospital of Indiana	Fort Wayne	95%	207
Morgan Hospital and Medical Center	Martinsville	95%	94
Parkview Hospital[2]	Fort Wayne	95%	129
Putnam County Hospital	Greencastle	95%	63
Riverview Hospital	Noblesville	95%	125
Saint Joseph Hospital & Health Center	Kokomo	95%	165
Saint Mary Medical Center[2]	Hobart	95%	128
Saint Vincent Frankfort Hospital	Frankfort	95%	61
Saint Vincent Williamsport Hospital	Williamsport	95%	44
Clark Memorial Hospital	Jeffersonville	94%	315
Dearborn County Hospital	Lawrenceburg	94%	162
Howard Regional Health System	Kokomo	94%	174
Indianapolis VA Medical Center	Indianapolis	94%	195
Memorial Hospital of South Bend	South Bend	94%	236
Saint Catherine Regional Hospital	Charlestown	94%	35
Scott Memorial Hospital	Scottsburg	94%	63
Jasper County Hospital	Rensselaer	93%	54
Methodist Hospitals[2]	Gary	93%	138
Porter Valparaiso Hospital Campus	Valparaiso	93%	247
Saint Elizabeth East	Lafayette	93%	71
Saint Vincent Hospital & Health Services	Indianapolis	93%	260
Starke Memorial Hospital[2]	Knox	93%	54
Union Hospital	Terre Haute	93%	368
William N Wishard Memorial Hospital[2]	Indianapolis	93%	134
Tipton Hospital	Tipton	92%	49
Westview Hospital	Indianapolis	92%	53
Perry County Memorial Hospital	Tell City	91%	58
Saint Vincent Carmel Hospital	Carmel	91%	74
Jay County Hospital	Portland	90%	62
Saint Francis Hospital and Health Centers[2]	Beech Grove	89%	193
St Francis Hosp & Health Ctrs-Indianapolis	Indianapolis	86%	153

20. Pneumococcal Vaccine

Hospital Name	City	Rate	Cases
Bluffton Regional Medical Center	Bluffton	100%	115
Dupont Hospital	Fort Wayne	100%	34
Fayette Regional Health System	Connersville	100%	130
Henry County Memorial Hospital	New Castle	100%	121
Indianapolis VA Medical Center	Indianapolis	100%	155
The King's Daughters' Hospital	Madison	100%	148
Major Hospital	Shelbyville	100%	142
Reid Hospital & Health Care Services	Richmond	100%	527
Saint Joseph Hospital	Fort Wayne	100%	26
Saint Vincent Williamsport Hospital	Williamsport	100%	39
Schneck Medical Center	Seymour	100%	125
Terre Haute Regional Hospital	Terre Haute	100%	95
VA Northern Indiana Healthcare Sys-Marion	Marion	100%	54
Westview Hospital	Indianapolis	100%	50
Bedford Regional Medical Center	Bedford	99%	75
Cameron Memorial Community Hospital	Angola	99%	68
Indiana University Health West Hospital[2]	Avon	99%	123
IU Health Goshen Hospital[2]	Goshen	99%	113
Lutheran Hospital of Indiana	Fort Wayne	99%	198
Parkview Hospital[2]	Fort Wayne	99%	135
Saint Joseph Regional Medical Center	Mishawaka	99%	303
St Joseph's Reg Med Ctr-Plymouth	Plymouth	99%	88
Columbus Regional Hospital	Columbus	98%	210
Dearborn County Hospital	Lawrenceburg	98%	139
Dekalb Memorial Hospital	Auburn	98%	86
Franciscan St Anthony Health - Crown Point[2]	Crown Point	98%	124
Good Samaritan Hospital	Vincennes	98%	194
Kosciusko Community Hospital	Warsaw	98%	112
Memorial Hospital	Logansport	98%	94
Memorial Hospital of South Bend	South Bend	98%	216
Putnam County Hospital	Greencastle	98%	62
Tipton Hospital	Tipton	98%	50
Union Hospital	Terre Haute	98%	351
Union Hospital Clinton	Clinton	98%	40
Bloomington Hospital	Bloomington	97%	299
Comm Hosp of Anderson & Madison County[2]	Anderson	97%	148
Decatur County Memorial Hospital	Greensburg	97%	34
Franciscan St Anthony Health-Michigan City	Michigan City	97%	97
Gibson General Hospital	Princeton	97%	30
Johnson Memorial Hospital	Franklin	97%	79
Parkview Noble Hospital	Kendallville	97%	75
Saint Vincent Dunn Hospital	Bedford	97%	73
Ball Memorial Hospital	Muncie	96%	363
Clark Memorial Hospital	Jeffersonville	96%	278
Howard Regional Health System	Kokomo	96%	167
Memorial Hospital and Health Care Center[2]	Jasper	96%	129
Parkview Whitley Hospital	Columbia City	96%	51
Porter Valparaiso Hospital Campus	Valparaiso	96%	272
Riverview Hospital	Noblesville	96%	123
Saint John's Health System[2]	Anderson	96%	171
Saint Joseph Hospital & Health Center	Kokomo	96%	159
Scott Memorial Hospital	Scottsburg	96%	45
Witham Health Services	Lebanon	96%	52
Floyd Memorial Hospital and Health Services	New Albany	95%	386
Marion General Hospital	Marion	95%	139
Perry County Memorial Hospital	Tell City	95%	60
Dukes Memorial Hospital	Peru	94%	51
Indiana University Health Arnett Hospital[2]	Lafayette	94%	126
Parkview Lagrange Hospital	Lagrange	94%	36
Saint Mary's Medical Center of Evansville	Evansville	94%	271
Saint Vincent Frankfort Hospital	Frankfort	94%	48
Community Hospital[2]	Munster	93%	138
Franciscan St Margaret Health - Hammond[2]	Hammond	93%	117
Laporte Hospital and Health Services	La Porte	93%	146
Morgan Hospital and Medical Center	Martinsville	93%	70
Saint Catherine Hospital	East Chicago	93%	67
Saint Mary Medical Center[2]	Hobart	93%	98
Saint Vincent Randolph Hospital	Winchester	93%	43
Harrison County Hospital	Corydon	92%	104
Indiana University Health[2]	Indianapolis	92%	96
Parkview Huntington Hospital	Huntington	92%	74
Community Hospital North[2]	Indianapolis	91%	114
Community Hospital South[2]	Indianapolis	91%	142
Deaconess Hospital[2]	Evansville	91%	362
Saint Elizabeth Central[2]	Lafayette	91%	131
Saint Francis Hospital and Health Centers[2]	Beech Grove	91%	256
Adams Memorial Hospital	Decatur	90%	97
St Francis Hosp & Health Ctrs-Indianapolis	Indianapolis	90%	154
Community Hospital East[2]	Indianapolis	89%	102
Hancock Regional Hospital[2]	Greenfield	89%	119
Hendricks Regional Health	Danville	89%	159
Jay County Hospital	Portland	89%	47
Saint Catherine Regional Hospital	Charlestown	89%	27
Saint Vincent Hospital & Health Services	Indianapolis	89%	316
Elkhart General Hospital	Elkhart	87%	199
Jasper County Hospital	Rensselaer	87%	53
Saint Elizabeth East	Lafayette	87%	70
William N Wishard Memorial Hospital[2]	Indianapolis	87%	67
Saint Francis Hospital Mooresville	Mooresville	86%	65
Sullivan County Community Hospital	Sullivan	86%	44
Franciscan St Margaret Health - Dyer	Dyer	85%	117
Saint Vincent Carmel Hospital	Carmel	85%	48
White County Memorial Hospital	Monticello	85%	59
Saint Vincent Mercy Hospital	Elwood	84%	44
Wabash County Hospital	Wabash	82%	39
Greene County General Hospital	Linton	80%	45
Indiana University Health North Hospital	Carmel	80%	59
Margaret Mary Community Hospital	Batesville	80%	105
Saint Mary's Warrick Hospital	Boonville	79%	33
Methodist Hospitals[2]	Gary	78%	119
Saint Clare Medical Center	Crawfordsville	78%	69
Starke Memorial Hospital[2]	Knox	76%	25
Daviess Community Hospital	Washington	75%	141
Monroe Hospital	Bloomington	69%	32
Kentuckiana Medical Center[2,3]	Clarksville	48%	25

21. Smoking Cessation Advice

Hospital Name	City	Rate	Cases
Clark Memorial Hospital	Jeffersonville	100%	180
Columbus Regional Hospital	Columbus	100%	120
Community Hospital[2]	Munster	100%	40
Community Hospital East[2]	Indianapolis	100%	54
Community Hospital North[2]	Indianapolis	100%	40
Comm Hosp of Anderson & Madison County[2]	Anderson	100%	67
Community Hospital South[2]	Indianapolis	100%	38
Dearborn County Hospital	Lawrenceburg	100%	76
Dekalb Memorial Hospital	Auburn	100%	42
Fayette Regional Health System	Connersville	100%	79
Franciscan St Anthony Health-Michigan City	Michigan City	100%	53
Franciscan St Margaret Health - Hammond[2]	Hammond	100%	86
Hancock Regional Hospital[2]	Greenfield	100%	44
Hendricks Regional Health	Danville	100%	51
Henry County Memorial Hospital	New Castle	100%	57
Howard Regional Health System	Kokomo	100%	80
Indiana University Health West Hospital[2]	Avon	100%	55
IU Health Goshen Hospital[2]	Goshen	100%	57
Johnson Memorial Hospital	Franklin	100%	31
The King's Daughters' Hospital	Madison	100%	87
Kosciusko Community Hospital	Warsaw	100%	41
Laporte Hospital and Health Services	La Porte	100%	81
Major Hospital	Shelbyville	100%	59
Margaret Mary Community Hospital	Batesville	100%	38
Memorial Hospital	Logansport	100%	43
Methodist Hospitals[2]	Gary	100%	48
Morgan Hospital and Medical Center	Martinsville	100%	30
Parkview Hospital[2]	Fort Wayne	100%	55
Parkview Huntington Hospital	Huntington	100%	31
Parkview Noble Hospital	Kendallville	100%	37
Porter Valparaiso Hospital Campus	Valparaiso	100%	100
Reid Hospital & Health Care Services	Richmond	100%	210
Saint Catherine Hospital	East Chicago	100%	73
Saint Elizabeth Central[2]	Lafayette	100%	39
Saint Elizabeth East	Lafayette	100%	27
Saint Joseph Hospital	Fort Wayne	100%	37
Saint Joseph Hospital & Health Center	Kokomo	100%	76
Saint Joseph Regional Medical Center	Mishawaka	100%	131
St Joseph's Reg Med Ctr-Plymouth	Plymouth	100%	36
Saint Vincent Dunn Hospital	Bedford	100%	26
Saint Vincent Hospital & Health Services	Indianapolis	100%	148
Terre Haute Regional Hospital	Terre Haute	100%	82
Union Hospital	Terre Haute	100%	188
William N Wishard Memorial Hospital[2]	Indianapolis	100%	83
Floyd Memorial Hospital and Health Services	New Albany	99%	186
Lutheran Hospital of Indiana	Fort Wayne	99%	98
Saint Francis Hospital and Health Centers[2]	Beech Grove	99%	115
Saint Mary's Medical Center of Evansville	Evansville	99%	171
Ball Memorial Hospital	Muncie	98%	177
Elkhart General Hospital	Elkhart	98%	122
Franciscan St Anthony Health - Crown Point[2]	Crown Point	98%	47
Memorial Hospital of South Bend	South Bend	98%	94
St Francis Hosp & Health Ctrs-Indianapolis	Indianapolis	98%	58
Saint Mary Medical Center[2]	Hobart	98%	52
Bloomington Hospital	Bloomington	97%	130
Franciscan St Margaret Health - Dyer	Dyer	97%	32
Indiana University Health[2]	Indianapolis	97%	67
Riverview Hospital	Noblesville	97%	35
Westview Hospital	Indianapolis	97%	30
Indianapolis VA Medical Center	Indianapolis	96%	110
Saint John's Health System[2]	Anderson	96%	73
Scott Memorial Hospital	Scottsburg	96%	25
Good Samaritan Hospital	Vincennes	95%	76
Schneck Medical Center	Seymour	94%	53
White County Memorial Hospital	Monticello	94%	33
Deaconess Hospital[2]	Evansville	93%	183
Indiana University Health Arnett Hospital[2]	Lafayette	93%	41
Union Hospital Clinton	Clinton	93%	29
Memorial Hospital and Health Care Center[2]	Jasper	91%	45
Marion General Hospital	Marion	90%	70
Bedford Regional Medical Center	Bedford	89%	37
Starke Memorial Hospital[2]	Knox	89%	27
Witham Health Services	Lebanon	88%	32
VA Northern Indiana Healthcare Sys-Marion	Marion	85%	26
Daviess Community Hospital	Washington	82%	56
Sullivan County Community Hospital	Sullivan	81%	27
Harrison County Hospital	Corydon	80%	40

Surgical Care Improvement Project

22. Appropriate VTP Within 24 Hours

Hospital Name	City	Rate	Cases
Bedford Regional Medical Center	Bedford	100%	53
Bluffton Regional Medical Center	Bluffton	100%	50
Dupont Hospital	Fort Wayne	100%	89
Harrison County Hospital	Corydon	100%	28
Morgan Hospital and Medical Center	Martinsville	100%	33
Parkview Huntington Hospital	Huntington	100%	47
Parkview Lagrange Hospital	Lagrange	100%	30
Terre Haute Regional Hospital	Terre Haute	100%	119
Franciscan St Anthony Health-Michigan City	Michigan City	99%	162
Saint Francis Hospital Mooresville[2]	Mooresville	99%	203
Reid Hospital & Health Care Services	Richmond	98%	230
Saint Francis Hospital and Health Centers[2]	Beech Grove	98%	276
Tipton Hospital	Tipton	98%	47
Fayette Regional Health System	Connersville	97%	30
Indianapolis VA Medical Center[2]	Indianapolis	97%	191
Kosciusko Community Hospital	Warsaw	97%	71
The Ortho Hosp of Lutheran Health Network	Fort Wayne	97%	138
Riverview Hospital	Noblesville	97%	140
Saint Catherine Hospital	East Chicago	97%	119
Community Hospital North[2]	Indianapolis	96%	165
Indiana University Health[2]	Indianapolis	96%	263
Indiana University Health North Hospital[2]	Carmel	96%	72
Major Hospital	Shelbyville	96%	57
Saint Vincent Dunn Hospital	Bedford	96%	27
Hendricks Regional Health	Danville	95%	112
Henry County Memorial Hospital	New Castle	95%	111
St Joseph's Reg Med Ctr-Plymouth	Plymouth	95%	38
Ball Memorial Hospital[2]	Muncie	94%	288
Franciscan St Margaret Health - Dyer	Dyer	94%	208
The King's Daughters' Hospital	Madison	94%	89
Lutheran Hospital of Indiana	Fort Wayne	94%	486
Marion General Hospital	Marion	94%	277

NOTE: Hospital profiles are in alphabetical order by state, then city, then hospital within the city; Rankings exclude hospitals with less than 25 cases except for patient surveys which excludes hospitals with less than 100 cases; (a) 100–299 cases; (1) The number of cases is too small to be sure how well a hospital is performing; (2) The hospital indicated that the data submitted for this measure were based on a sample of cases; (3) Data was collected during a shorter time period (fewer quarters) than the maximum possible time for this measure; (4) Suppressed for one or more quarters by CMS; (5) No data is available from the hospital for this measure; (6) Fewer than 100 patients completed the HCAHPS survey. Use these rates with caution, as the number of surveys may be too low to reliably assess hospital performance; (7) Survey results are based on less than 12 months of data; (8) Survey results are not available for this reporting period; (9) No or very few patients were eligible for the HCAHPS survey. The scores shown, if any, reflect a very small number of surveys; (10) A state average was not calculated because too few hospitals in the state submitted data; (11) There were discrepancies in the data collection process; Please refer to the User's Guide for a full explanation of data.

Hospital Name	City	Rate	Cases
William N Wishard Memorial Hospital[2]	Indianapolis	94%	180
Community Hospital East[2]	Indianapolis	93%	151
Dekalb Memorial Hospital	Auburn	93%	30
Elkhart General Hospital[2]	Elkhart	93%	164
Johnson Memorial Hospital	Franklin	93%	73
St Francis Hosp & Health Ctrs-Indianapolis	Indianapolis	93%	151
Good Samaritan Hospital	Vincennes	92%	168
Parkview Hospital[2]	Fort Wayne	92%	180
Parkview Whitley Hospital	Columbia City	92%	26
Union Hospital	Terre Haute	92%	413
Community Hospital South[2]	Indianapolis	91%	130
Franciscan St Margaret Health - Hammond	Hammond	91%	144
Methodist Hospitals[2]	Gary	91%	186
Saint Joseph Regional Medical Center[2]	Mishawaka	91%	143
Saint Mary's Medical Center of Evansville[2]	Evansville	91%	229
Schneck Medical Center	Seymour	91%	76
Clark Memorial Hospital[2]	Jeffersonville	90%	285
Columbus Regional Hospital	Columbus	90%	192
Hancock Regional Hospital[2]	Greenfield	90%	116
Saint Joseph Hospital	Fort Wayne	90%	39
Saint Vincent Carmel Hospital[2]	Carmel	90%	89
Bloomington Hospital	Bloomington	89%	349
Dearborn County Hospital	Lawrenceburg	89%	118
Indiana University Health West Hospital[2]	Avon	89%	104
Monroe Hospital	Bloomington	89%	27
Franciscan Physicians Hospital	Munster	88%	40
Indiana University Health Arnett Hospital[2]	Lafayette	88%	154
IU Health Goshen Hospital	Goshen	88%	216
Comm Hosp of Anderson & Madison County	Anderson	87%	133
Laporte Hospital and Health Services	La Porte	87%	153
Saint John's Health System[2]	Anderson	86%	104
Saint Vincent Hospital & Health Services[2]	Indianapolis	86%	193
Deaconess Hospital[2]	Evansville	84%	192
Saint Clare Medical Center	Crawfordsville	83%	48
Saint Joseph Hospital & Health Center	Kokomo	83%	83
Memorial Hospital and Health Care Center[2]	Jasper	82%	119
Saint Elizabeth East[2]	Lafayette	82%	185
Westview Hospital	Indianapolis	82%	45
Franciscan St Anthony Health - Crown Point[2]	Crown Point	81%	194
Porter Valparaiso Hospital Campus	Valparaiso	81%	236
Witham Health Services	Lebanon	80%	54
Floyd Memorial Hospital and Health Services	New Albany	79%	234
Memorial Hospital of South Bend[2]	South Bend	79%	217
Saint Mary Medical Center[2]	Hobart	79%	150
Community Hospital[2]	Munster	78%	226
Margaret Mary Community Hospital	Batesville	76%	50
Memorial Hospital	Logansport	74%	27
Howard Regional Health System	Kokomo	73%	84
Daviess Community Hospital	Washington	56%	32

23. Appropriate Hair Removal

Hospital Name	City	Rate	Cases
Ball Memorial Hospital[2]	Muncie	100%	822
Bedford Regional Medical Center	Bedford	100%	131
Bloomington Hospital	Bloomington	100%	1204
Bluffton Regional Medical Center	Bluffton	100%	140
Cameron Memorial Community Hospital	Angola	100%	29
Clark Memorial Hospital[2]	Jeffersonville	100%	642
Columbus Regional Hospital	Columbus	100%	734
Community Hospital[2]	Munster	100%	703
Community Hospital East[2]	Indianapolis	100%	396
Community Hospital North[2]	Indianapolis	100%	442
Comm Hosp of Anderson & Madison County	Anderson	100%	486
Community Hospital South[2]	Indianapolis	100%	457
Daviess Community Hospital	Washington	100%	54
Dearborn County Hospital	Lawrenceburg	100%	261
Decatur County Memorial Hospital	Greensburg	100%	109
Dekalb Memorial Hospital	Auburn	100%	70
Dupont Hospital	Fort Wayne	100%	598
Elkhart General Hospital[2]	Elkhart	100%	933
Floyd Memorial Hospital and Health Services	New Albany	100%	741
Franciscan St Anthony Health - Crown Point[2]	Crown Point	100%	455
Franciscan St Anthony Health-Michigan City	Michigan City	100%	401
Good Samaritan Hospital	Vincennes	100%	604
Hancock Regional Hospital[2]	Greenfield	100%	333
Henry County Memorial Hospital	New Castle	100%	359
Howard Regional Health System	Kokomo	100%	251
The Indiana Heart Hospital[2]	Indianapolis	100%	604
Indiana Orthopaedic Hospital[2]	Indianapolis	100%	236
Indiana University Health[2]	Indianapolis	100%	752
Indiana University Health Arnett Hospital[2]	Lafayette	100%	432
Indiana University Health North Hospital[2]	Carmel	100%	286
Indiana University Health West Hospital[2]	Avon	100%	271
Indianapolis VA Medical Center[2]	Indianapolis	100%	469
IU Health Goshen Hospital	Goshen	100%	585
Jay County Hospital[3]	Portland	100%	31
Johnson Memorial Hospital	Franklin	100%	163
The King's Daughters' Hospital	Madison	100%	203
Kosciusko Community Hospital	Warsaw	100%	321
Lutheran Hospital of Indiana	Fort Wayne	100%	1498
Major Hospital	Shelbyville	100%	148
Marion General Hospital	Marion	100%	498
Memorial Hospital	Logansport	100%	137
Memorial Hospital and Health Care Center[2]	Jasper	100%	631
Methodist Hospitals[2]	Gary	100%	493
Monroe Hospital	Bloomington	100%	183
Morgan Hospital and Medical Center	Martinsville	100%	70
Orthopaedic Hospital at Parkview North[2]	Fort Wayne	100%	269
The Ortho Hosp of Lutheran Health Network	Fort Wayne	100%	1101
Parkview Hospital[2]	Fort Wayne	100%	729
Parkview Huntington Hospital	Huntington	100%	114
Parkview Lagrange Hospital	Lagrange	100%	59
Parkview Whitley Hospital	Columbia City	100%	69
Porter Valparaiso Hospital Campus	Valparaiso	100%	1056
Reid Hospital & Health Care Services	Richmond	100%	819
Riverview Hospital	Noblesville	100%	569
Saint Catherine Hospital	East Chicago	100%	307
Saint Clare Medical Center	Crawfordsville	100%	158
Saint Elizabeth Central[2,3]	Lafayette	100%	273
Saint Elizabeth East[2]	Lafayette	100%	756
Saint Francis Hospital and Health Centers[2]	Beech Grove	100%	744
St Francis Hosp & Health Ctrs-Indianapolis	Indianapolis	100%	863
Saint Francis Hospital Mooresville[2]	Mooresville	100%	811
Saint John's Health System[2]	Anderson	100%	360
Saint Joseph Hospital	Fort Wayne	100%	140
Saint Joseph Hospital & Health Center	Kokomo	100%	295
Saint Joseph Regional Medical Center[2]	Mishawaka	100%	695
St Joseph's Reg Med Ctr-Plymouth	Plymouth	100%	196
Saint Vincent Carmel Hospital[2]	Carmel	100%	303
Saint Vincent Dunn Hospital	Bedford	100%	50
Saint Vincent Heart Center of Indiana[2]	Indianapolis	100%	358
Schneck Medical Center	Seymour	100%	247
Sullivan County Community Hospital	Sullivan	100%	30
Surgical Hospital of Munster[2]	Munster	100%	80
Terre Haute Regional Hospital	Terre Haute	100%	381
Tipton Hospital	Tipton	100%	130
Wabash County Hospital	Wabash	100%	35
Westview Hospital	Indianapolis	100%	132
Witham Health Services	Lebanon	100%	118
The Women's Hospital	Newburgh	100%	189
Deaconess Hospital[2]	Evansville	99%	818
Fayette Regional Health System	Connersville	99%	99
Franciscan Physicians Hospital	Munster	99%	84
Franciscan St Margaret Health - Dyer	Dyer	99%	384
Franciscan St Margaret Health - Hammond	Hammond	99%	416
The Heart Hospital at Deaconess Gateway[2,3]	Newburgh	99%	171
Hendricks Regional Health	Danville	99%	358
Margaret Mary Community Hospital	Batesville	99%	160
Memorial Hospital of South Bend[2]	South Bend	99%	815
Parkview Noble Hospital	Kendallville	99%	85
Physicians' Medical Center[2]	New Albany	99%	152
Saint Mary Medical Center[2]	Hobart	99%	532
Saint Mary's Medical Center of Evansville[2]	Evansville	99%	1429
Saint Vincent Hospital & Health Services[2]	Indianapolis	99%	793
Union Hospital	Terre Haute	99%	1188
William N Wishard Memorial Hospital[2]	Indianapolis	99%	345
Harrison County Hospital	Corydon	98%	42
Laporte Hospital and Health Services	La Porte	98%	472
Putnam County Hospital	Greencastle	98%	40
Kentuckiana Medical Center[2,3]	Clarksville	97%	68
Saint Vincent Frankfort Hospital	Frankfort	94%	31
Adams Memorial Hospital	Decatur	87%	52

24. Appropriate Beta Blocker Usage

Hospital Name	City	Rate	Cases
Ball Memorial Hospital[2]	Muncie	100%	261
Bluffton Regional Medical Center	Bluffton	100%	39
Comm Hosp of Anderson & Madison County	Anderson	100%	138
Dupont Hospital	Fort Wayne	100%	142
Floyd Memorial Hospital and Health Services	New Albany	100%	242
Franciscan Physicians Hospital	Munster	100%	30
Kosciusko Community Hospital	Warsaw	100%	75
William N Wishard Memorial Hospital[2]	Indianapolis	100%	61
Clark Memorial Hospital[2]	Jeffersonville	99%	176
Franciscan St Margaret Health - Dyer	Dyer	99%	107
Indiana University Health North Hospital[2]	Carmel	99%	67
Terre Haute Regional Hospital	Terre Haute	99%	146
Riverview Hospital	Noblesville	98%	178
Saint John's Health System[2]	Anderson	98%	89
Saint Joseph Hospital	Fort Wayne	98%	44
Community Hospital North[2]	Indianapolis	97%	92
Community Hospital South[2]	Indianapolis	97%	116
Fayette Regional Health System	Connersville	97%	29
Franciscan St Margaret Health - Hammond	Hammond	97%	118
Henry County Memorial Hospital	New Castle	97%	177
Indiana Orthopaedic Hospital[2]	Indianapolis	97%	113
Johnson Memorial Hospital	Franklin	97%	35
Kentuckiana Medical Center[2,3]	Clarksville	97%	39
Memorial Hospital and Health Care Center[2]	Jasper	97%	183
The Ortho Hosp of Lutheran Health Network	Fort Wayne	97%	370
Porter Valparaiso Hospital Campus	Valparaiso	97%	331
Saint Clare Medical Center	Crawfordsville	97%	33
Schneck Medical Center	Seymour	97%	65
Tipton Hospital	Tipton	97%	36
Community Hospital East[2]	Indianapolis	96%	103
Good Samaritan Hospital	Vincennes	96%	165
Saint Elizabeth Central[2,3]	Lafayette	96%	91
Bloomington Hospital	Bloomington	95%	379
Columbus Regional Hospital	Columbus	95%	242
Franciscan St Anthony Health-Michigan City	Michigan City	95%	132
The King's Daughters' Hospital	Madison	95%	43
Parkview Huntington Hospital	Huntington	95%	40
Saint Catherine Hospital	East Chicago	95%	78
St Joseph's Reg Med Ctr-Plymouth	Plymouth	95%	42
Saint Vincent Heart Center of Indiana[2]	Indianapolis	95%	184
Elkhart General Hospital[2]	Elkhart	94%	247
Indiana University Health Arnett Hospital[2]	Lafayette	94%	142
Indianapolis VA Medical Center[2]	Indianapolis	94%	272
IU Health Goshen Hospital	Goshen	94%	140
Saint Elizabeth East[2]	Lafayette	94%	205
Saint Joseph Hospital & Health Center	Kokomo	94%	108
Saint Mary Medical Center[2]	Hobart	94%	151
Laporte Hospital and Health Services	La Porte	93%	135
Parkview Hospital[2]	Fort Wayne	93%	280
Reid Hospital & Health Care Services	Richmond	93%	296
Saint Joseph Regional Medical Center[2]	Mishawaka	93%	186
Indiana University Health[2]	Indianapolis	92%	218
Lutheran Hospital of Indiana	Fort Wayne	92%	626
St Francis Hosp & Health Ctrs-Indianapolis	Indianapolis	92%	379
Deaconess Hospital[2]	Evansville	91%	278
Major Hospital	Shelbyville	91%	46
Marion General Hospital	Marion	91%	156
Saint Francis Hospital and Health Centers[2]	Beech Grove	91%	268
Saint Mary's Medical Center of Evansville[2]	Evansville	91%	467
Bedford Regional Medical Center	Bedford	90%	31
Community Hospital[2]	Munster	90%	230
Dearborn County Hospital	Lawrenceburg	90%	71
Methodist Hospitals[2]	Gary	90%	144
Orthopaedic Hospital at Parkview North[2]	Fort Wayne	90%	83
Saint Vincent Carmel Hospital[2]	Carmel	89%	72
Saint Vincent Hospital & Health Services[2]	Indianapolis	89%	323
Union Hospital	Terre Haute	89%	453
Franciscan St Anthony Health - Crown Point[2]	Crown Point	87%	113
The Heart Hospital at Deaconess Gateway[2,3]	Newburgh	87%	95
Westview Hospital	Indianapolis	87%	31
Howard Regional Health System	Kokomo	85%	91
Margaret Mary Community Hospital	Batesville	85%	33
Saint Francis Hospital Mooresville[2]	Mooresville	83%	225
The Indiana Heart Hospital[2]	Indianapolis	81%	333
Witham Health Services	Lebanon	81%	31
Indiana University Health West Hospital[2]	Avon	80%	44
Hendricks Regional Health	Danville	79%	97
Memorial Hospital of South Bend[2]	South Bend	79%	227
Physicians' Medical Center[2]	New Albany	79%	28
Hancock Regional Hospital[2]	Greenfield	69%	99

25. Controlled Postoperative Blood Glucose

Hospital Name	City	Rate	Cases
Saint Elizabeth East[2]	Lafayette	100%	27
Ball Memorial Hospital[2]	Muncie	99%	132
Community Hospital[2]	Munster	98%	151
Saint Catherine Hospital	East Chicago	98%	56
Saint Joseph Hospital	Fort Wayne	98%	42
Elkhart General Hospital[2]	Elkhart	97%	228
Saint Vincent Heart Center of Indiana[2]	Indianapolis	97%	294
Parkview Hospital[2]	Fort Wayne	96%	175
Saint Elizabeth Central[2,3]	Lafayette	96%	46
Bloomington Hospital	Bloomington	95%	144
The Heart Hospital at Deaconess Gateway[2,3]	Newburgh	95%	163
Howard Regional Health System	Kokomo	95%	38
The Indiana Heart Hospital[2]	Indianapolis	95%	349
Indiana University Health[2]	Indianapolis	95%	115
Indiana University Health Arnett Hospital[2]	Lafayette	95%	92
Reid Hospital & Health Care Services	Richmond	95%	165
St Francis Hosp & Health Ctrs-Indianapolis	Indianapolis	95%	401
Union Hospital	Terre Haute	95%	194
Floyd Memorial Hospital and Health Services	New Albany	94%	144
Laporte Hospital and Health Services	La Porte	94%	51
Saint Joseph Regional Medical Center[2]	Mishawaka	94%	140
Terre Haute Regional Hospital	Terre Haute	94%	72
Columbus Regional Hospital	Columbus	93%	56
Franciscan St Anthony Health-Michigan City	Michigan City	93%	29
Indianapolis VA Medical Center[2]	Indianapolis	93%	102
Deaconess Hospital[2]	Evansville	92%	108
Good Samaritan Hospital	Vincennes	92%	51
Kentuckiana Medical Center[2,3]	Clarksville	92%	49
Saint Vincent Hospital & Health Services[2]	Indianapolis	92%	203
Franciscan St Margaret Health - Dyer	Dyer	90%	40
Lutheran Hospital of Indiana	Fort Wayne	89%	350
Riverview Hospital	Noblesville	89%	46

NOTE: Hospital profiles are in alphabetical order by state, then city, then hospital within the city; Rankings exclude hospitals with less than 25 cases except for patient surveys which excludes hospitals with less than 100 cases; (a) 100–299 cases; (1) The number of cases is too small to be sure how well a hospital is performing; (2) The hospital indicated that the data submitted for this measure were based on a sample of cases; (3) Data was collected during a shorter time period (fewer quarters) than the maximum possible time for this measure; (4) Suppressed for one or more quarters by CMS; (5) No data is available from the hospital for this measure; (6) Fewer than 100 patients completed the HCAHPS survey. Use these rates with caution, as the number of surveys may be too low to reliably assess hospital performance; (7) Survey results are based on less than 12 months of data; (8) Survey results are not available for this reporting period; (9) No or very few patients were eligible for the HCAHPS survey. The scores shown, if any, reflect a very small number of surveys; (10) A state average was not calculated because too few hospitals in the state submitted data; (11) There were discrepancies in the data collection process; Please refer to the User's Guide for a full explanation of data.

Hospital Name	City	Rate	Cases
Saint Mary's Medical Center of Evansville[2]	Evansville	89%	186
Memorial Hospital of South Bend[2]	South Bend	87%	164
Methodist Hospitals[2]	Gary	87%	77
Franciscan Physicians Hospital	Munster	85%	26
Porter Valparaiso Hospital Campus	Valparaiso	85%	118
Franciscan St Margaret Health - Hammond	Hammond	83%	92
Franciscan St Anthony Health - Crown Point[2]	Crown Point	77%	66
Saint Mary Medical Center[2]	Hobart	77%	65

26. Prophylactic Antibiotic Timing

Hospital Name	City	Rate	Cases
Clark Memorial Hospital[2]	Jeffersonville	100%	449
Dekalb Memorial Hospital	Auburn	100%	36
Dupont Hospital	Fort Wayne	100%	476
Indiana Orthopaedic Hospital[2]	Indianapolis	100%	168
Kosciusko Community Hospital	Warsaw	100%	244
The Ortho Hosp of Lutheran Health Network	Fort Wayne	100%	947
Saint Catherine Hospital	East Chicago	100%	201
St Joseph's Reg Med Ctr-Plymouth	Plymouth	100%	164
Terre Haute Regional Hospital	Terre Haute	100%	274
Tipton Hospital	Tipton	100%	91
Bluffton Regional Medical Center	Bluffton	99%	101
Columbus Regional Hospital	Columbus	99%	471
Fayette Regional Health System	Connersville	99%	83
Franciscan St Anthony Health - Crown Point[2]	Crown Point	99%	322
Franciscan St Margaret Health - Hammond	Hammond	99%	249
Good Samaritan Hospital	Vincennes	99%	405
Henry County Memorial Hospital	New Castle	99%	276
Howard Regional Health System	Kokomo	99%	165
The Indiana Heart Hospital[2]	Indianapolis	99%	466
Indiana University Health North Hospital[2]	Carmel	99%	215
Indiana University Health West Hospital[2]	Avon	99%	172
Indianapolis VA Medical Center	Indianapolis	99%	346
Reid Hospital & Health Care Services	Richmond	99%	571
Riverview Hospital	Noblesville	99%	403
Saint Clare Medical Center	Crawfordsville	99%	140
Saint Elizabeth East[2]	Lafayette	99%	531
Saint Mary Medical Center[2]	Hobart	99%	367
Schneck Medical Center	Seymour	99%	170
Bedford Regional Medical Center	Bedford	98%	99
Decatur County Memorial Hospital	Greensburg	98%	65
Franciscan Physicians Hospital	Munster	98%	52
Franciscan St Margaret Health - Dyer	Dyer	98%	240
Indiana University Health Arnett Hospital[2]	Lafayette	98%	294
IU Health Goshen Hospital	Goshen	98%	378
The King's Daughters' Hospital	Madison	98%	110
Lutheran Hospital of Indiana	Fort Wayne	98%	687
Margaret Mary Community Hospital	Batesville	98%	120
Methodist Hospitals[2]	Gary	98%	332
Parkview Whitley Hospital	Columbia City	98%	54
Porter Valparaiso Hospital Campus	Valparaiso	98%	764
St Francis Hosp & Health Ctrs-Indianapolis	Indianapolis	98%	575
Saint Francis Hospital Mooresville[2]	Mooresville	98%	597
Saint John's Health System[2]	Anderson	98%	234
Saint Joseph Regional Medical Center[2]	Mishawaka	98%	510
Saint Vincent Heart Center of Indiana[2]	Indianapolis	98%	200
Saint Vincent Hospital & Health Services[2]	Indianapolis	98%	532
William N Wishard Memorial Hospital[2]	Indianapolis	98%	238
Ball Memorial Hospital[2]	Muncie	97%	606
Community Hospital North[2]	Indianapolis	97%	306
Comm Hosp of Anderson & Madison County	Anderson	97%	360
Elkhart General Hospital[2]	Elkhart	97%	691
Hendricks Regional Health	Danville	97%	258
Indiana University Health[2]	Indianapolis	97%	510
Laporte Hospital and Health Services	La Porte	97%	345
Parkview Huntington Hospital	Huntington	97%	96
Parkview Noble Hospital	Kendallville	97%	66
Physicians' Medical Center[2]	New Albany	97%	143
Saint Elizabeth Central[2,3]	Lafayette	97%	225
Saint Francis Hospital and Health Centers[2]	Beech Grove	97%	442
Saint Joseph Hospital & Health Center	Kokomo	97%	228
Saint Vincent Carmel Hospital[2]	Carmel	97%	227
Saint Vincent Frankfort Hospital	Frankfort	97%	29
Union Hospital	Terre Haute	97%	732
Bloomington Hospital	Bloomington	96%	775
Community Hospital East[2]	Indianapolis	96%	248
Floyd Memorial Hospital and Health Services	New Albany	96%	441
Franciscan St Anthony Health-Michigan City	Michigan City	96%	269
Johnson Memorial Hospital	Franklin	96%	102
Marion General Hospital	Marion	96%	359
Monroe Hospital	Bloomington	96%	146
Orthopaedic Hospital at Parkview North[2]	Fort Wayne	96%	201
Saint Joseph Hospital	Fort Wayne	96%	90
Saint Mary's Medical Center of Evansville[2]	Evansville	96%	1122
Community Hospital South[2]	Indianapolis	95%	307
Hancock Regional Hospital[2]	Greenfield	95%	241
Memorial Hospital and Health Care Center[2]	Jasper	95%	507
Parkview Hospital[2]	Fort Wayne	95%	524
Memorial Hospital	Logansport	94%	101
Westview Hospital	Indianapolis	94%	84
The Women's Hospital	Newburgh	94%	141
Community Hospital[2]	Munster	93%	495
Major Hospital	Shelbyville	93%	95
Dearborn County Hospital	Lawrenceburg	92%	181
Memorial Hospital of South Bend[2]	South Bend	92%	591
Parkview Lagrange Hospital	Lagrange	92%	52
Deaconess Hospital[2]	Evansville	91%	552
The Heart Hospital at Deaconess Gateway[2,3]	Newburgh	90%	102
Morgan Hospital and Medical Center	Martinsville	85%	27
Surgical Hospital of Munster[2]	Munster	83%	69
Witham Health Services	Lebanon	71%	92
Kentuckiana Medical Center[2,3]	Clarksville	57%	56

27. Prophylactic Antibiotic Timing (Outpatient)

Hospital Name	City	Rate	Cases
Dukes Memorial Hospital	Peru	100%	46
Dupont Hospital	Fort Wayne	100%	465
Indiana Orthopaedic Hospital	Indianapolis	100%	486
Terre Haute Regional Hospital	Terre Haute	100%	223
The Ortho Hosp of Lutheran Health Network	Fort Wayne	99%	819
Riverview Hospital	Noblesville	99%	177
Saint Elizabeth Central[3]	Lafayette	99%	198
Bluffton Regional Medical Center	Bluffton	98%	42
Indiana University Health North Hospital	Carmel	98%	423
Lutheran Hospital of Indiana	Fort Wayne	98%	1463
Saint Elizabeth East	Lafayette	98%	625
St Joseph's Reg Med Ctr-Plymouth	Plymouth	98%	40
The Women's Hospital	Newburgh	98%	474
Comm Hosp of Anderson & Madison County	Anderson	97%	183
Dekalb Memorial Hospital	Auburn	97%	113
Floyd Memorial Hospital and Health Services	New Albany	97%	327
Good Samaritan Hospital	Vincennes	97%	168
Kosciusko Community Hospital	Warsaw	97%	99
Schneck Medical Center	Seymour	97%	114
Columbus Regional Hospital	Columbus	96%	386
Franciscan St Anthony Health - Crown Point	Crown Point	96%	275
The Indiana Heart Hospital	Indianapolis	96%	330
Indiana University Health West Hospital	Avon	96%	190
Johnson Memorial Hospital	Franklin	96%	96
Major Hospital	Shelbyville	96%	45
Methodist Hospitals	Gary	96%	326
Orthopaedic Hospital at Parkview North	Fort Wayne	96%	347
Parkview Hospital	Fort Wayne	96%	721
Saint Joseph Regional Medical Center	Mishawaka	96%	350
Ball Memorial Hospital	Muncie	95%	504
Bloomington Hospital	Bloomington	95%	851
Franciscan Physicians Hospital	Munster	95%	76
Henry County Memorial Hospital	New Castle	95%	157
Indiana University Health	Indianapolis	95%	783
Saint Joseph Hospital	Fort Wayne	95%	73
Union Hospital	Terre Haute	95%	850
Community Hospital	Munster	94%	589
Saint John's Health System	Anderson	94%	178
Saint Mary Medical Center	Hobart	94%	394
Memorial Hospital	Logansport	93%	126
Reid Hospital & Health Care Services	Richmond	93%	382
Clark Memorial Hospital	Jeffersonville	92%	395
Elkhart General Hospital	Elkhart	92%	290
Parkview Huntington Hospital	Huntington	92%	99
Parkview Noble Hospital	Kendallville	92%	26
Saint Mary's Medical Center of Evansville	Evansville	92%	1292
Hendricks Regional Health	Danville	91%	215
Howard Regional Health System	Kokomo	91%	57
Physicians' Medical Center	New Albany	91%	187
Porter Valparaiso Hospital Campus	Valparaiso	91%	527
Saint Francis Hospital and Health Centers	Beech Grove	91%	267
St Francis Hosp & Health Ctrs-Indianapolis	Indianapolis	91%	653
Saint Joseph Hospital & Health Center	Kokomo	91%	175
The King's Daughters' Hospital	Madison	90%	60
Parkview Whitley Hospital	Columbia City	90%	42
Saint Clare Medical Center	Crawfordsville	90%	51
Saint Vincent Carmel Hospital	Carmel	90%	98
Community Hospital North	Indianapolis	89%	480
Saint Vincent Hospital & Health Services	Indianapolis	89%	913
Westview Hospital	Indianapolis	88%	51
William N Wishard Memorial Hospital	Indianapolis	88%	80
Memorial Hospital of South Bend	South Bend	87%	677
Community Hospital South	Indianapolis	86%	324
Decatur County Memorial Hospital	Greensburg	86%	35
Marion General Hospital	Marion	86%	142
Deaconess Hospital	Evansville	85%	1277
Indiana University Health Arnett Hospital	Lafayette	85%	369
IU Health Goshen Hospital	Goshen	85%	117
Saint Francis Hospital Mooresville	Mooresville	85%	95
Franciscan St Margaret Health - Hammond	Hammond	84%	122
Memorial Hospital and Health Care Center	Jasper	83%	127
Saint Catherine Hospital	East Chicago	83%	87
Fayette Regional Health System	Connersville	81%	43
Hancock Regional Hospital	Greenfield	81%	133
Laporte Hospital and Health Services	La Porte	80%	192
Surgical Hospital of Munster	Munster	80%	30
Cameron Memorial Community Hospital	Angola	79%	39
Franciscan St Margaret Health - Dyer	Dyer	77%	197
Community Hospital East	Indianapolis	76%	364
Margaret Mary Community Hospital	Batesville	75%	68
Saint Vincent Heart Center of Indiana	Indianapolis	74%	349
Dearborn County Hospital	Lawrenceburg	70%	88
The Heart Hospital at Deaconess Gateway[3]	Newburgh	70%	128
Franciscan St Anthony Health-Michigan City	Michigan City	63%	229
Morgan Hospital and Medical Center	Martinsville	38%	72

28. Prophylactic Antibiotic Selection

Hospital Name	City	Rate	Cases
Ball Memorial Hospital[2]	Muncie	100%	613
Bluffton Regional Medical Center	Bluffton	100%	101
Decatur County Memorial Hospital	Greensburg	100%	66
Dupont Hospital	Fort Wayne	100%	477
The Heart Hospital at Deaconess Gateway[2,3]	Newburgh	100%	106
Henry County Memorial Hospital	New Castle	100%	279
Indiana Orthopaedic Hospital[2]	Indianapolis	100%	168
Kentuckiana Medical Center[2,3]	Clarksville	100%	58
The King's Daughters' Hospital	Madison	100%	110
Major Hospital	Shelbyville	100%	95
Orthopaedic Hospital at Parkview North[2]	Fort Wayne	100%	201
The Ortho Hosp of Lutheran Health Network	Fort Wayne	100%	950
Parkview Lagrange Hospital	Lagrange	100%	52
Parkview Whitley Hospital	Columbia City	100%	54
Saint Vincent Heart Center of Indiana[2]	Indianapolis	100%	204
Bloomington Hospital	Bloomington	99%	780
Columbus Regional Hospital	Columbus	99%	469
Comm Hosp of Anderson & Madison County	Anderson	99%	360
Good Samaritan Hospital	Vincennes	99%	413
The Indiana Heart Hospital[2]	Indianapolis	99%	474
Indiana University Health Arnett Hospital[2]	Lafayette	99%	296
Indiana University Health North Hospital[2]	Carmel	99%	219
Indiana University Health West Hospital[2]	Avon	99%	172
Indianapolis VA Medical Center	Indianapolis	99%	358
Lutheran Hospital of Indiana	Fort Wayne	99%	709
Parkview Huntington Hospital	Huntington	99%	96
Parkview Noble Hospital	Kendallville	99%	67
Reid Hospital & Health Care Services	Richmond	99%	584
Saint Catherine Hospital	East Chicago	99%	204
Saint Clare Medical Center	Crawfordsville	99%	142
Saint Elizabeth East[2]	Lafayette	99%	533
St Joseph's Reg Med Ctr-Plymouth	Plymouth	99%	165
Saint Mary's Medical Center of Evansville[2]	Evansville	99%	1136
Saint Vincent Carmel Hospital[2]	Carmel	99%	228
Schneck Medical Center	Seymour	99%	171
Witham Health Services	Lebanon	99%	91
The Women's Hospital	Newburgh	99%	141
Bedford Regional Medical Center	Bedford	98%	99
Clark Memorial Hospital[2]	Jeffersonville	98%	453
Deaconess Hospital[2]	Evansville	98%	556
Dearborn County Hospital	Lawrenceburg	98%	183
Floyd Memorial Hospital and Health Services	New Albany	98%	444
Franciscan Physicians Hospital	Munster	98%	53
Franciscan St Anthony Health-Michigan City	Michigan City	98%	272
Franciscan St Margaret Health - Dyer	Dyer	98%	241
Hancock Regional Hospital[2]	Greenfield	98%	239
Laporte Hospital and Health Services	La Porte	98%	343
Margaret Mary Community Hospital	Batesville	98%	120
Parkview Hospital[2]	Fort Wayne	98%	541
Porter Valparaiso Hospital Campus	Valparaiso	98%	769
Riverview Hospital	Noblesville	98%	402
Saint Elizabeth Central[2,3]	Lafayette	98%	226
Saint Francis Hospital and Health Centers[2]	Beech Grove	98%	442
Saint Francis Hospital Mooresville[2]	Mooresville	98%	597
Saint Joseph Hospital	Fort Wayne	98%	91
Saint Joseph Regional Medical Center[2]	Mishawaka	98%	517
Saint Mary Medical Center[2]	Hobart	98%	365
Terre Haute Regional Hospital	Terre Haute	98%	276
Tipton Hospital	Tipton	98%	90
William N Wishard Memorial Hospital[2]	Indianapolis	98%	241
Community Hospital[2]	Munster	97%	502
Community Hospital North[2]	Indianapolis	97%	308
Franciscan St Margaret Health - Hammond	Hammond	97%	260
Hendricks Regional Health	Danville	97%	258
Indiana University Health[2]	Indianapolis	97%	515
IU Health Goshen Hospital	Goshen	97%	383
Kosciusko Community Hospital	Warsaw	97%	245
Memorial Hospital and Health Care Center[2]	Jasper	97%	508
Monroe Hospital	Bloomington	97%	144
St Francis Hosp & Health Ctrs-Indianapolis	Indianapolis	97%	587
Saint Vincent Frankfort Hospital	Frankfort	97%	29
Saint Vincent Hospital & Health Services[2]	Indianapolis	97%	538
Community Hospital East[2]	Indianapolis	96%	251
Howard Regional Health System	Kokomo	96%	166
Saint John's Health System[2]	Anderson	96%	235
Union Hospital	Terre Haute	96%	731
Community Hospital South[2]	Indianapolis	95%	308

NOTE: Hospital profiles are in alphabetical order by state, then city, then hospital within the city; Rankings exclude hospitals with less than 25 cases except for patient surveys which excludes hospitals with less than 100 cases; (a) 100–299 cases; (1) The number of cases is too small to be sure how well a hospital is performing; (2) The hospital indicated that the data submitted for this measure were based on a sample of cases; (3) Data was collected during a shorter time period (fewer quarters) than the maximum possible time for this measure; (4) Suppressed for one or more quarters by CMS; (5) No data is available from the hospital for this measure; (6) Fewer than 100 patients completed the HCAHPS survey. Use these rates with caution, as the number of surveys may be too low to reliably assess hospital performance; (7) Survey results are based on less than 12 months of data; (8) Survey results are not available for this reporting period; (9) No or very few patients were eligible for the HCAHPS survey. The scores shown, if any, reflect a very small number of surveys; (10) A state average was not calculated because too few hospitals in the state submitted data; (11) There were discrepancies in the data collection process; Please refer to the User's Guide for a full explanation of data.

Elkhart General Hospital[2]	Elkhart	95%	708
Fayette Regional Health System	Connersville	95%	83
Johnson Memorial Hospital	Franklin	95%	101
Dekalb Memorial Hospital	Auburn	94%	36
Franciscan St Anthony Health - Crown Point[2]	Crown Point	94%	326
Marion General Hospital	Marion	94%	361
Memorial Hospital of South Bend[2]	South Bend	94%	598
Saint Joseph Hospital & Health Center	Kokomo	94%	228
Westview Hospital	Indianapolis	94%	82
Methodist Hospitals[2]	Gary	93%	337
Morgan Hospital and Medical Center	Martinsville	93%	28
Saint Vincent Dunn Hospital	Bedford	93%	29
Memorial Hospital	Logansport	91%	102
Physicians' Medical Center[2]	New Albany	87%	143
Surgical Hospital of Munster[2]	Munster	72%	69

29. Prophylactic Antibiotic Selection (Outpatient)

Hospital Name	City	Rate	Cases
Dekalb Memorial Hospital	Auburn	100%	113
The Indiana Heart Hospital	Indianapolis	100%	325
Indiana Orthopaedic Hospital	Indianapolis	100%	486
Major Hospital	Shelbyville	100%	45
The Ortho Hosp of Lutheran Health Network	Fort Wayne	100%	818
Saint Clare Medical Center	Crawfordsville	100%	47
St Joseph's Reg Med Ctr-Plymouth	Plymouth	100%	40
Comm Hosp of Anderson & Madison County	Anderson	99%	184
Dupont Hospital	Fort Wayne	99%	466
Franciscan Physicians Hospital	Munster	99%	75
Kosciusko Community Hospital	Warsaw	99%	97
Lutheran Hospital of Indiana	Fort Wayne	99%	1457
Orthopaedic Hospital at Parkview North	Fort Wayne	99%	344
Saint Elizabeth Central[3]	Lafayette	99%	198
Saint Joseph Regional Medical Center	Mishawaka	99%	340
Ball Memorial Hospital	Muncie	98%	525
Dukes Memorial Hospital	Peru	98%	46
The Heart Hospital at Deaconess Gateway[3]	Newburgh	98%	128
Indiana University Health West Hospital	Avon	98%	186
Saint John's Health System	Anderson	98%	180
Terre Haute Regional Hospital	Terre Haute	98%	223
Columbus Regional Hospital	Columbus	97%	381
Decatur County Memorial Hospital	Greensburg	97%	31
Memorial Hospital	Logansport	97%	121
Parkview Hospital	Fort Wayne	97%	716
Reid Hospital & Health Care Services	Richmond	97%	385
Saint Francis Hospital and Health Centers	Beech Grove	97%	258
Saint Joseph Hospital	Fort Wayne	97%	72
Saint Mary Medical Center	Hobart	97%	390
Westview Hospital	Indianapolis	97%	63
The Women's Hospital	Newburgh	97%	473
Community Hospital	Munster	96%	615
Franciscan St Anthony Health-Michigan City	Michigan City	96%	169
Howard Regional Health System	Kokomo	96%	56
Indiana University Health Arnett Hospital	Lafayette	96%	351
IU Health Goshen Hospital	Goshen	96%	118
Saint Elizabeth East	Lafayette	96%	620
Schneck Medical Center	Seymour	96%	113
Surgical Hospital of Munster	Munster	96%	27
William N Wishard Memorial Hospital	Indianapolis	96%	96
Bloomington Hospital	Bloomington	95%	837
Bluffton Regional Medical Center	Bluffton	95%	42
Cameron Memorial Community Hospital	Angola	95%	38
Elkhart General Hospital	Elkhart	95%	286
Good Samaritan Hospital	Vincennes	95%	166
Henry County Memorial Hospital	New Castle	95%	151
Indiana University Health North Hospital	Carmel	95%	419
Johnson Memorial Hospital	Franklin	95%	94
The King's Daughters' Hospital	Madison	95%	55
Memorial Hospital and Health Care Center	Jasper	95%	110
Parkview Whitley Hospital	Columbia City	95%	41
Porter Valparaiso Hospital Campus	Valparaiso	95%	510
St Francis Hosp & Health Ctrs-Indianapolis	Indianapolis	95%	641
Saint Mary's Medical Center of Evansville	Evansville	95%	1273
Union Hospital	Terre Haute	95%	840
Clark Memorial Hospital	Jeffersonville	94%	377
Marion General Hospital	Marion	94%	133
Riverview Hospital	Noblesville	94%	176
Saint Catherine Hospital	East Chicago	94%	82
Saint Francis Hospital Mooresville	Mooresville	94%	89
Saint Vincent Hospital & Health Services	Indianapolis	94%	872
Community Hospital North	Indianapolis	93%	460
Deaconess Hospital	Evansville	93%	1277
Dearborn County Hospital	Lawrenceburg	93%	134
Hancock Regional Hospital	Greenfield	93%	122
Saint Vincent Carmel Hospital	Carmel	93%	92
Saint Vincent Heart Center of Indiana	Indianapolis	93%	349
Fayette Regional Health System	Connersville	92%	39
Franciscan St Anthony Health - Crown Point	Crown Point	92%	267
Franciscan St Margaret Health - Hammond	Hammond	92%	129
Indiana University Health	Indianapolis	92%	906
Laporte Hospital and Health Services	La Porte	92%	173
Parkview Noble Hospital	Kendallville	92%	25
Community Hospital South	Indianapolis	91%	315
Saint Joseph Hospital & Health Center	Kokomo	90%	169
Floyd Memorial Hospital and Health Services	New Albany	89%	317
Franciscan St Margaret Health - Dyer	Dyer	89%	225
Morgan Hospital and Medical Center	Martinsville	89%	38
Parkview Huntington Hospital	Huntington	89%	92
Hendricks Regional Health	Danville	87%	207
Methodist Hospitals	Gary	86%	323
Community Hospital East	Indianapolis	85%	353
Margaret Mary Community Hospital	Batesville	85%	60
Physicians' Medical Center	New Albany	79%	194
Memorial Hospital of South Bend	South Bend	75%	654

30. Prophylactic Antibiotic Stopped

Hospital Name	City	Rate	Cases
Dupont Hospital	Fort Wayne	100%	461
Monroe Hospital	Bloomington	100%	144
Surgical Hospital of Munster[2]	Munster	100%	69
Bluffton Regional Medical Center	Bluffton	99%	96
Indiana University Health North Hospital[2]	Carmel	99%	207
The Ortho Hosp of Lutheran Health Network	Fort Wayne	99%	932
Physicians' Medical Center[2]	New Albany	99%	143
Reid Hospital & Health Care Services	Richmond	99%	526
Ball Memorial Hospital[2]	Muncie	98%	564
Bedford Regional Medical Center	Bedford	98%	95
Franciscan St Anthony Health-Michigan City	Michigan City	98%	249
Henry County Memorial Hospital	New Castle	98%	266
Memorial Hospital	Logansport	98%	101
Saint Elizabeth East[2]	Lafayette	98%	513
Saint Vincent Heart Center of Indiana[2]	Indianapolis	98%	193
Terre Haute Regional Hospital	Terre Haute	98%	232
Bloomington Hospital	Bloomington	97%	748
Community Hospital East[2]	Indianapolis	97%	243
Community Hospital North[2]	Indianapolis	97%	283
Dekalb Memorial Hospital	Auburn	97%	35
Fayette Regional Health System	Connersville	97%	78
Franciscan St Margaret Health - Hammond	Hammond	97%	236
Good Samaritan Hospital	Vincennes	97%	384
Hancock Regional Hospital[2]	Greenfield	97%	232
Johnson Memorial Hospital	Franklin	97%	98
Kosciusko Community Hospital	Warsaw	97%	237
Orthopaedic Hospital at Parkview North[2]	Fort Wayne	97%	199
Saint Elizabeth Central[2,3]	Lafayette	97%	212
St Francis Hosp & Health Ctrs-Indianapolis	Indianapolis	97%	551
Saint Joseph Hospital	Fort Wayne	97%	87
St Joseph's Reg Med Ctr-Plymouth	Plymouth	97%	159
Saint Vincent Carmel Hospital[2]	Carmel	97%	226
Saint Vincent Frankfort Hospital	Frankfort	97%	29
The Women's Hospital	Newburgh	97%	133
Clark Memorial Hospital[2]	Jeffersonville	96%	431
Columbus Regional Hospital	Columbus	96%	426
Comm Hosp of Anderson & Madison County	Anderson	96%	351
Community Hospital South[2]	Indianapolis	96%	298
Indiana Orthopaedic Hospital[2]	Indianapolis	96%	168
The King's Daughters' Hospital	Madison	96%	107
Laporte Hospital and Health Services	La Porte	96%	326
Parkview Huntington Hospital	Huntington	96%	95
Porter Valparaiso Hospital Campus	Valparaiso	96%	745
Saint Francis Hospital and Health Centers[2]	Beech Grove	96%	412
Saint Joseph Regional Medical Center[2]	Mishawaka	96%	495
Saint Mary's Medical Center of Evansville[2]	Evansville	96%	1107
Schneck Medical Center	Seymour	96%	163
Tipton Hospital	Tipton	96%	90
Westview Hospital	Indianapolis	96%	79
Decatur County Memorial Hospital	Greensburg	95%	62
Franciscan St Margaret Health - Dyer	Dyer	95%	223
Hendricks Regional Health	Danville	95%	254
Indiana University Health[2]	Indianapolis	95%	467
Indianapolis VA Medical Center	Indianapolis	95%	331
Memorial Hospital and Health Care Center[2]	Jasper	95%	491
Memorial Hospital of South Bend[2]	South Bend	95%	573
Parkview Noble Hospital	Kendallville	95%	64
Saint Francis Hospital Mooresville[2]	Mooresville	95%	593
Saint Vincent Hospital & Health Services[2]	Indianapolis	95%	526
Dearborn County Hospital	Lawrenceburg	94%	179
Elkhart General Hospital[2]	Elkhart	94%	655
Parkview Hospital[2]	Fort Wayne	94%	509
Parkview Lagrange Hospital	Lagrange	94%	50
Parkview Whitley Hospital	Columbia City	94%	50
Saint Catherine Hospital	East Chicago	94%	180
William N Wishard Memorial Hospital[2]	Indianapolis	94%	234
The Indiana Heart Hospital[2]	Indianapolis	93%	440
IU Health Goshen Hospital	Goshen	93%	367
Kentuckiana Medical Center[2,3]	Clarksville	93%	56
Lutheran Hospital of Indiana	Fort Wayne	93%	636
Major Hospital	Shelbyville	93%	90
Marion General Hospital	Marion	93%	345
Riverview Hospital	Noblesville	93%	390
Community Hospital[2]	Munster	92%	465
Franciscan Physicians Hospital	Munster	92%	48
Indiana University Health West Hospital[2]	Avon	92%	164
Saint Clare Medical Center	Crawfordsville	92%	140
Saint John's Health System[2]	Anderson	92%	231
Saint Mary Medical Center[2]	Hobart	92%	355
Union Hospital	Terre Haute	92%	674
Witham Health Services	Lebanon	91%	88
Floyd Memorial Hospital and Health Services	New Albany	90%	407
Margaret Mary Community Hospital	Batesville	90%	117
Methodist Hospitals[2]	Gary	90%	317
Indiana University Health Arnett Hospital[2]	Lafayette	88%	269
The Heart Hospital at Deaconess Gateway[2,3]	Newburgh	87%	100
Deaconess Hospital[2]	Evansville	85%	518
Franciscan St Anthony Health - Crown Point[2]	Crown Point	85%	314
Howard Regional Health System	Kokomo	85%	155
Saint Joseph Hospital & Health Center	Kokomo	85%	224
Morgan Hospital and Medical Center	Martinsville	80%	25

31. Recommended VTP Ordered

Hospital Name	City	Rate	Cases
Bedford Regional Medical Center	Bedford	100%	53
Bluffton Regional Medical Center	Bluffton	100%	50
Dekalb Memorial Hospital	Auburn	100%	30
Dupont Hospital	Fort Wayne	100%	89
Harrison County Hospital	Corydon	100%	28
Morgan Hospital and Medical Center	Martinsville	100%	33
Parkview Huntington Hospital	Huntington	100%	47
Parkview Lagrange Hospital	Lagrange	100%	30
St Joseph's Reg Med Ctr-Plymouth	Plymouth	100%	38
Terre Haute Regional Hospital	Terre Haute	100%	119
Franciscan St Anthony Health-Michigan City	Michigan City	99%	162
Indianapolis VA Medical Center[2]	Indianapolis	99%	191
Saint Francis Hospital and Health Centers[2]	Beech Grove	99%	276
Saint Francis Hospital Mooresville[2]	Mooresville	99%	203
The Ortho Hosp of Lutheran Health Network	Fort Wayne	98%	138
Reid Hospital & Health Care Services	Richmond	98%	230
Saint Catherine Hospital	East Chicago	98%	119
Tipton Hospital	Tipton	98%	47
Fayette Regional Health System	Connersville	97%	30
Franciscan St Margaret Health - Dyer	Dyer	97%	208
Franciscan St Margaret Health - Hammond	Hammond	97%	146
Indiana University Health[2]	Indianapolis	97%	264
Kosciusko Community Hospital	Warsaw	97%	71
Riverview Hospital	Noblesville	97%	140
Community Hospital North[2]	Indianapolis	96%	168
Hendricks Regional Health	Danville	96%	112
Indiana University Health North Hospital[2]	Carmel	96%	72
The King's Daughters' Hospital	Madison	96%	89
Lutheran Hospital of Indiana	Fort Wayne	96%	487
Major Hospital	Shelbyville	96%	57
St Francis Hosp & Health Ctrs-Indianapolis	Indianapolis	96%	151
Saint Vincent Dunn Hospital	Bedford	96%	27
Ball Memorial Hospital[2]	Muncie	95%	288
Elkhart General Hospital[2]	Elkhart	95%	164
Henry County Memorial Hospital	New Castle	95%	111
Indiana University Health West Hospital[2]	Avon	95%	104
Johnson Memorial Hospital	Franklin	95%	74
Saint Joseph Hospital	Fort Wayne	95%	39
Union Hospital	Terre Haute	95%	415
William N Wishard Memorial Hospital[2]	Indianapolis	95%	181
Clark Memorial Hospital[2]	Jeffersonville	94%	285
Community Hospital East[2]	Indianapolis	94%	151
Good Samaritan Hospital	Vincennes	94%	168
Methodist Hospitals[2]	Gary	94%	188
Saint Mary's Medical Center of Evansville[2]	Evansville	94%	230
Columbus Regional Hospital	Columbus	93%	192
Dearborn County Hospital	Lawrenceburg	93%	118
Marion General Hospital	Marion	93%	286
Schneck Medical Center	Seymour	93%	76
Community Hospital South[2]	Indianapolis	92%	130
Franciscan Physicians Hospital	Munster	92%	40
Indiana University Health Arnett Hospital[2]	Lafayette	92%	154
Parkview Hospital[2]	Fort Wayne	92%	182
Parkview Whitley Hospital	Columbia City	92%	26
Saint Joseph Regional Medical Center[2]	Mishawaka	92%	143
Hancock Regional Hospital[2]	Greenfield	91%	116
Saint Elizabeth East[2]	Lafayette	91%	185
Bloomington Hospital	Bloomington	90%	351
Deaconess Hospital[2]	Evansville	90%	197
Howard Regional Health System	Kokomo	90%	84
Laporte Hospital and Health Services	La Porte	90%	154
IU Health Goshen Hospital	Goshen	89%	219
Saint Vincent Carmel Hospital[2]	Carmel	88%	92
Comm Hosp of Anderson & Madison County	Anderson	87%	134
Saint Vincent Hospital & Health Services[2]	Indianapolis	87%	194
Monroe Hospital	Bloomington	86%	28
Saint Clare Medical Center	Crawfordsville	86%	49
Saint John's Health System[2]	Anderson	86%	104
Franciscan St Anthony Health - Crown Point[2]	Crown Point	85%	194
Porter Valparaiso Hospital Campus	Valparaiso	85%	236

NOTE: Hospital profiles are in alphabetical order by state, then city, then hospital within the city; Rankings exclude hospitals with less than 25 cases except for patient surveys which excludes hospitals with less than 100 cases; (a) 100–299 cases; (1) The number of cases is too small to be sure how well a hospital is performing; (2) The hospital indicated that the data submitted for this measure were based on a sample of cases; (3) Data was collected during a shorter time period (fewer quarters) than the maximum possible time for this measure; (4) Suppressed for one or more quarters by CMS; (5) No data is available from the hospital for this measure; (6) Fewer than 100 patients completed the HCAHPS survey. Use these rates with caution, as the number of surveys may be too low to reliably assess hospital performance; (7) Survey results are based on less than 12 months of data; (8) Survey results are not available for this reporting period; (9) No or very few patients were eligible for the HCAHPS survey. The scores shown, if any, reflect a very small number of surveys; (10) A state average was not calculated because too few hospitals in the state submitted data; (11) There were discrepancies in the data collection process; Please refer to the User's Guide for a full explanation of data.

Hospital Name	City	Rate	Cases
Community Hospital[2]	Munster	84%	226
Westview Hospital	Indianapolis	84%	45
Saint Joseph Hospital & Health Center	Kokomo	83%	84
Witham Health Services	Lebanon	83%	54
Memorial Hospital and Health Care Center[2]	Jasper	82%	121
Floyd Memorial Hospital and Health Services	New Albany	81%	235
Memorial Hospital of South Bend[2]	South Bend	81%	218
Saint Mary Medical Center[2]	Hobart	81%	151
Margaret Mary Community Hospital	Batesville	76%	50
Memorial Hospital	Logansport	74%	27
Daviess Community Hospital	Washington	56%	32

32. Urinary Catheter Removal

Hospital Name	City	Rate	Cases
Community Hospital South[2]	Indianapolis	100%	79
Monroe Hospital	Bloomington	100%	72
Saint Clare Medical Center	Crawfordsville	100%	55
Terre Haute Regional Hospital	Terre Haute	100%	50
Tipton Hospital	Tipton	100%	44
Elkhart General Hospital[2]	Elkhart	99%	230
Saint Francis Hospital Mooresville[2]	Mooresville	99%	400
Columbus Regional Hospital	Columbus	98%	208
Dupont Hospital	Fort Wayne	98%	60
The Heart Hospital at Deaconess Gateway[2]	Newburgh	98%	99
Henry County Memorial Hospital	New Castle	98%	45
Orthopaedic Hospital at Parkview North[2]	Fort Wayne	98%	110
The Ortho Hosp of Lutheran Health Network	Fort Wayne	98%	132
Riverview Hospital	Noblesville	98%	167
Community Hospital North[2]	Indianapolis	97%	35
Decatur County Memorial Hospital	Greensburg	97%	34
The King's Daughters' Hospital	Madison	97%	32
Saint John's Health System[2]	Anderson	97%	91
Floyd Memorial Hospital and Health Services	New Albany	96%	178
Franciscan St Anthony Health-Michigan City	Michigan City	96%	102
The Indiana Heart Hospital	Indianapolis	96%	226
Indianapolis VA Medical Center[2]	Indianapolis	96%	203
Saint Catherine Hospital	East Chicago	96%	71
St Francis Hosp & Health Ctrs-Indianapolis	Indianapolis	96%	169
William N Wishard Memorial Hospital[2]	Indianapolis	96%	85
Bloomington Hospital	Bloomington	95%	360
Hancock Regional Hospital[2]	Greenfield	95%	62
Marion General Hospital	Marion	95%	42
Reid Hospital & Health Care Services	Richmond	95%	146
Ball Memorial Hospital[2]	Muncie	94%	228
Clark Memorial Hospital[2]	Jeffersonville	94%	156
Comm Hosp of Anderson & Madison County	Anderson	94%	124
Laporte Hospital and Health Services	La Porte	94%	101
Parkview Hospital[2]	Fort Wayne	94%	123
Saint Joseph Regional Medical Center[2]	Mishawaka	94%	87
Saint Mary's Medical Center of Evansville[2]	Evansville	94%	335
Memorial Hospital and Health Care Center[2]	Jasper	93%	92
Good Samaritan Hospital	Vincennes	91%	45
Major Hospital	Shelbyville	91%	44
Saint Elizabeth East[2]	Lafayette	91%	102
Indiana University Health[2]	Indianapolis	90%	146
Physicians' Medical Center[2]	New Albany	90%	41
Hendricks Regional Health	Danville	89%	116
Indiana University Health North Hospital[2]	Carmel	89%	85
Johnson Memorial Hospital	Franklin	88%	33
Saint Francis Hospital and Health Centers	Beech Grove	88%	82
Union Hospital	Terre Haute	88%	267
Community Hospital East[2]	Indianapolis	87%	46
Dearborn County Hospital	Lawrenceburg	87%	54
Saint Joseph Hospital & Health Center	Kokomo	87%	90
Community Hospital[2]	Munster	86%	138
Franciscan St Margaret Health - Dyer	Dyer	86%	37
IU Health Goshen Hospital	Goshen	86%	108
Saint Vincent Heart Center of Indiana[2]	Indianapolis	86%	101
Porter Valparaiso Hospital Campus	Valparaiso	85%	156
Methodist Hospitals[2]	Gary	83%	84
Saint Vincent Hospital & Health Services[2]	Indianapolis	83%	190
Lutheran Hospital of Indiana	Fort Wayne	82%	222
Witham Health Services	Lebanon	82%	28
Deaconess Hospital[2]	Evansville	81%	85
Howard Regional Health System	Kokomo	81%	53
Memorial Hospital of South Bend[2]	South Bend	80%	115
Indiana University Health West Hospital[2]	Avon	79%	70
Saint Mary Medical Center[2]	Hobart	79%	91
Indiana University Health Arnett Hospital[2]	Lafayette	78%	104
Franciscan St Margaret Health - Hammond	Hammond	76%	51
Bedford Regional Medical Center	Bedford	73%	30
Franciscan St Anthony Health - Crown Point[2]	Crown Point	73%	99

Children's Asthma Care

33. Received Systemic Corticosteroids

Hospital Name	City	Rate	Cases
Indiana University Health North Hospital[2]	Carmel	100%	80

34. Received Home Management Plan of Care

Hospital Name	City	Rate	Cases
Indiana University Health North Hospital[2]	Carmel	90%	80

35. Received Reliever Medication

Hospital Name	City	Rate	Cases
Indiana University Health North Hospital[2]	Carmel	100%	80

Use of Medical Imaging

36. Combination Abdominal CT Scan

Hospital Name	City	Ratio	Cases
Parkview Lagrange Hospital	Lagrange	0.011	179
Westview Hospital	Indianapolis	0.012	162
Howard Regional Health System	Kokomo	0.018	856
Bluffton Regional Medical Center	Bluffton	0.022	231
St Joseph's Reg Med Ctr-Plymouth	Plymouth	0.023	432
Saint Mary's Medical Center of Evansville	Evansville	0.024	1366
Columbus Regional Hospital	Columbus	0.025	563
Monroe Hospital	Bloomington	0.029	205
Saint Vincent Dunn Hospital	Bedford	0.030	333
Parkview Noble Hospital	Kendallville	0.031	353
Dukes Memorial Hospital	Peru	0.032	249
Schneck Medical Center	Seymour	0.041	589
Johnson Memorial Hospital	Franklin	0.042	504
Bloomington Hospital	Bloomington	0.044	589
Lutheran Hospital of Indiana	Fort Wayne	0.046	654
Saint Clare Medical Center	Crawfordsville	0.046	539
Deaconess Hospital	Evansville	0.047	1714
Community Hospital of Bremen	Bremen	0.048	83
Union Hospital	Terre Haute	0.050	845
Ball Memorial Hospital	Muncie	0.051	1127
Saint Joseph Regional Medical Center	Mishawaka	0.051	763
Fayette Regional Health System	Connersville	0.053	245
IU Health Goshen Hospital	Goshen	0.056	660
Community Hospital South	Indianapolis	0.058	533
Blackford Community Hospital	Hartford City	0.059	220
Riverview Hospital	Noblesville	0.059	544
Henry County Memorial Hospital	New Castle	0.060	629
Indiana University Health West Hospital	Avon	0.064	623
Saint Francis Hospital and Health Centers	Beech Grove	0.066	455
Elkhart General Hospital	Elkhart	0.067	983
Dupont Hospital	Fort Wayne	0.068	324
Rush Memorial Hospital	Rushville	0.068	191
Saint Elizabeth Central	Lafayette	0.072	594
Comm Hosp of Anderson & Madison County	Anderson	0.075	755
Saint Vincent Hospital & Health Services	Indianapolis	0.078	2054
Indiana University Health North Hospital	Carmel	0.079	419
Hancock Regional Hospital	Greenfield	0.085	600
Saint Joseph Hospital & Health Center	Kokomo	0.091	656
Indiana University Health	Indianapolis	0.093	3827
Witham Health Services	Lebanon	0.094	436
Saint Vincent Carmel Hospital	Carmel	0.096	437
William N Wishard Memorial Hospital	Indianapolis	0.099	750
Indiana University Health Arnett Hospital	Lafayette	0.100	70
Memorial Hospital of South Bend	South Bend	0.103	757
Reid Hospital & Health Care Services	Richmond	0.110	1288
Saint Joseph Hospital	Fort Wayne	0.110	181
Saint John's Health System	Anderson	0.111	915
Saint Vincent Randolph Hospital	Winchester	0.112	233
Saint Francis Hospital Mooresville	Mooresville	0.118	313
The Indiana Heart Hospital	Indianapolis	0.120	92
Morgan Hospital and Medical Center	Martinsville	0.129	271
St Francis Hosp & Health Ctrs-Indianapolis	Indianapolis	0.129	1547
Saint Catherine Regional Hospital	Charlestown	0.146	103
Margaret Mary Community Hospital	Batesville	0.169	344
Jay County Hospital	Portland	0.183	268
Saint Vincent Heart Center of Indiana[1]	Indianapolis	0.205	39
Community Hospital East	Indianapolis	0.210	1135
Terre Haute Regional Hospital	Terre Haute	0.216	361
Saint Vincent Mercy Hospital	Elwood	0.218	211
Community Hospital North	Indianapolis	0.231	888
Cameron Memorial Community Hospital	Angola	0.241	303
Parkview Whitley Hospital	Columbia City	0.262	214
Parkview Huntington Hospital	Huntington	0.263	213
Parkview Hospital	Fort Wayne	0.277	1080
Hendricks Regional Health	Danville	0.292	920
Methodist Hospitals	Gary	0.315	1090
Pinnacle Hospital	Crown Point	0.326	92
Major Hospital	Shelbyville	0.328	393
Community Hospital	Munster	0.333	1973
Franciscan St Anthony Health - Crown Point	Crown Point	0.333	1035
Bedford Regional Medical Center	Bedford	0.354	452
Dekalb Memorial Hospital	Auburn	0.360	344
Sullivan County Community Hospital	Sullivan	0.394	284
Saint Elizabeth East	Lafayette	0.425	1401
Saint Mary Medical Center	Hobart	0.426	940
Franciscan St Anthony Health-Michigan City	Michigan City	0.437	506
Union Hospital Clinton	Clinton	0.438	313
Saint Catherine Hospital	East Chicago	0.453	406
Dearborn County Hospital	Lawrenceburg	0.466	620
Laporte Hospital and Health Services	La Porte	0.479	735
Kosciusko Community Hospital	Warsaw	0.497	493
Good Samaritan Hospital	Vincennes	0.507	1034
Starke Memorial Hospital	Knox	0.543	210
Franciscan St Margaret Health - Hammond	Hammond	0.586	517
Franciscan St Margaret Health - Dyer	Dyer	0.594	424
Decatur County Memorial Hospital	Greensburg	0.612	196
Porter Valparaiso Hospital Campus	Valparaiso	0.629	1328
Memorial Hospital and Health Care Center	Jasper	0.638	937
Floyd Memorial Hospital and Health Services	New Albany	0.648	1127
Marion General Hospital	Marion	0.690	1039
Harrison County Hospital	Corydon	0.704	379
Memorial Hospital	Logansport	0.707	464
Clark Memorial Hospital	Jeffersonville	0.726	1042
The King's Daughters' Hospital	Madison	0.768	603
Saint Vincent Salem Hospital	Salem	0.801	166
Franciscan Physicians Hospital[1]	Munster	0.808	26
Daviess Community Hospital	Washington	0.830	229

37. Combination Chest CT Scan

Hospital Name	City	Ratio	Cases
Dekalb Memorial Hospital	Auburn	0.000	149
Johnson Memorial Hospital	Franklin	0.000	295
Parkview Noble Hospital	Kendallville	0.000	149
Rush Memorial Hospital	Rushville	0.000	92
St Joseph's Reg Med Ctr-Plymouth	Plymouth	0.000	292
Saint Vincent Carmel Hospital	Carmel	0.000	210
Saint Vincent Mercy Hospital	Elwood	0.000	115
Westview Hospital	Indianapolis	0.000	86
Saint Joseph Regional Medical Center	Mishawaka	0.002	465
Saint Mary's Medical Center of Evansville	Evansville	0.002	1285
Saint Vincent Hospital & Health Services	Indianapolis	0.003	1694
Lutheran Hospital of Indiana	Fort Wayne	0.004	459
Saint Francis Hospital and Health Centers	Beech Grove	0.004	257
Columbus Regional Hospital	Columbus	0.005	553
Comm Hosp of Anderson & Madison County	Anderson	0.005	600
Schneck Medical Center	Seymour	0.005	365
Union Hospital	Terre Haute	0.005	421
Reid Hospital & Health Care Services	Richmond	0.006	806
Saint Joseph Hospital & Health Center	Kokomo	0.006	505
Saint Vincent Dunn Hospital	Bedford	0.006	155
Clark Memorial Hospital	Jeffersonville	0.007	1013
Deaconess Hospital	Evansville	0.007	1279
Saint Elizabeth Central	Lafayette	0.007	611
Saint Catherine Hospital	East Chicago	0.008	244
Indiana University Health North Hospital	Carmel	0.009	347
Cameron Memorial Community Hospital	Angola	0.010	205
Elkhart General Hospital	Elkhart	0.010	813
Howard Regional Health System	Kokomo	0.010	1025
Saint Joseph Hospital	Fort Wayne	0.010	98
Indiana University Health	Indianapolis	0.011	3506
Saint Elizabeth East	Lafayette	0.012	1259
Fayette Regional Health System	Connersville	0.013	156
Indiana University Health West Hospital	Avon	0.013	532
IU Health Goshen Hospital	Goshen	0.013	535
Witham Health Services	Lebanon	0.015	331
Blackford Community Hospital	Hartford City	0.016	126
Bloomington Hospital	Bloomington	0.016	255
Riverview Hospital	Noblesville	0.016	435
Community Hospital of Bremen	Bremen	0.019	52
Dukes Memorial Hospital	Peru	0.019	208
Hancock Regional Hospital	Greenfield	0.021	521
Dupont Hospital	Fort Wayne	0.022	182
Saint Vincent Randolph Hospital	Winchester	0.022	139
Indiana University Health Arnett Hospital[1]	Lafayette	0.024	42
Parkview Hospital	Fort Wayne	0.025	730
Memorial Hospital of South Bend	South Bend	0.026	623
Henry County Memorial Hospital	New Castle	0.027	299
Saint John's Health System	Anderson	0.028	928
Monroe Hospital	Bloomington	0.030	99
St Francis Hosp & Health Ctrs-Indianapolis	Indianapolis	0.030	941
Saint Clare Medical Center	Crawfordsville	0.032	312
Franciscan St Margaret Health - Hammond	Hammond	0.033	364
Bluffton Regional Medical Center	Bluffton	0.039	153
Morgan Hospital and Medical Center	Martinsville	0.040	177
Memorial Hospital	Logansport	0.041	290
Sullivan County Community Hospital	Sullivan	0.042	215
Floyd Memorial Hospital and Health Services	New Albany	0.043	889
William N Wishard Memorial Hospital	Indianapolis	0.043	557
Parkview Whitley Hospital	Columbia City	0.045	134
Ball Memorial Hospital	Muncie	0.053	584
Parkview Huntington Hospital	Huntington	0.071	127
Community Hospital South	Indianapolis	0.077	392
The Indiana Heart Hospital	Indianapolis	0.087	173
Dearborn County Hospital	Lawrenceburg	0.089	427
Hendricks Regional Health	Danville	0.107	514
Franciscan St Margaret Health - Dyer	Dyer	0.112	268
Good Samaritan Hospital	Vincennes	0.114	603

NOTE: Hospital profiles are in alphabetical order by state, then city, then hospital within the city; Rankings exclude hospitals with less than 25 cases except for patient surveys which excludes hospitals with less than 100 cases; (a) 100–299 cases; (1) The number of cases is too small to be sure how well a hospital is performing; (2) The hospital indicated that the data submitted for this measure were based on a sample of cases; (3) Data was collected during a shorter time period (fewer quarters) than the maximum possible time for this measure; (4) Suppressed for one or more quarters by CMS; (5) No data is available from the hospital for this measure; (6) Fewer than 100 patients completed the HCAHPS survey. Use these rates with caution, as the number of surveys may be too low to reliably assess hospital performance; (7) Survey results are based on less than 12 months of data; (8) Survey results are not available for this reporting period; (9) No or very few patients were eligible for the HCAHPS survey. The scores shown, if any, reflect a very small number of surveys; (10) A state average was not calculated because too few hospitals in the state submitted data; (11) There were discrepancies in the data collection process; Please refer to the User's Guide for a full explanation of data.

Hospital Name	City	Rate	Cases
Jay County Hospital	Portland	0.115	104
Saint Francis Hospital Mooresville	Mooresville	0.120	184
Harrison County Hospital	Corydon	0.131	222
Terre Haute Regional Hospital	Terre Haute	0.133	256
Major Hospital	Shelbyville	0.143	300
Saint Catherine Regional Hospital	Charlestown	0.143	133
Parkview Lagrange Hospital	Lagrange	0.157	83
Decatur County Memorial Hospital	Greensburg	0.160	119
Community Hospital East	Indianapolis	0.161	974
Margaret Mary Community Hospital	Batesville	0.186	231
Pinnacle Hospital	Crown Point	0.192	73
Community Hospital North	Indianapolis	0.198	774
Community Hospital	Munster	0.300	1384
Saint Vincent Salem Hospital	Salem	0.315	108
Saint Vincent Heart Center of Indiana	Indianapolis	0.327	52
Methodist Hospitals	Gary	0.337	603
Bedford Regional Medical Center	Bedford	0.363	245
Saint Mary Medical Center	Hobart	0.395	851
Kosciusko Community Hospital	Warsaw	0.396	283
Franciscan St Anthony Health - Crown Point	Crown Point	0.445	760
Daviess Community Hospital	Washington	0.500	128
Union Hospital Clinton	Clinton	0.534	178
Starke Memorial Hospital	Knox	0.555	110
Franciscan St Anthony Health-Michigan City	Michigan City	0.556	399
Porter Valparaiso Hospital Campus	Valparaiso	0.583	911
Laporte Hospital and Health Services	La Porte	0.698	504
The King's Daughters' Hospital	Madison	0.765	349
Memorial Hospital and Health Care Center	Jasper	0.775	668
Marion General Hospital	Marion	0.787	601

38. Follow-up Mammogram/Ultrasound

Hospital Name	City	Rate	Cases
Kosciusko Community Hospital	Warsaw	1.2%	660
Franciscan St Anthony Health-Michigan City	Michigan City	2.2%	1210
Westview Hospital	Indianapolis	2.7%	261
Sullivan County Community Hospital	Sullivan	2.8%	211
Bedford Regional Medical Center	Bedford	3.2%	598
Decatur County Memorial Hospital	Greensburg	3.8%	445
The King's Daughters' Hospital	Madison	3.8%	945
Franciscan St Margaret Health - Dyer	Dyer	4.1%	440
Henry County Memorial Hospital	New Castle	4.1%	1010
Community Hospital	Munster	4.3%	2396
Saint Catherine Hospital	East Chicago	4.3%	559
Franciscan St Margaret Health - Hammond	Hammond	4.9%	652
Good Samaritan Hospital	Vincennes	4.9%	1542
Major Hospital	Shelbyville	4.9%	716
Johnson Memorial Hospital	Franklin	5.4%	683
Saint Joseph Hospital	Fort Wayne	5.4%	387
Community Hospital of Bremen	Bremen	5.5%	200
Reid Hospital & Health Care Services	Richmond	5.6%	2179
Fayette Regional Health System	Connersville	5.7%	370
Parkview Whitley Hospital	Columbia City	6.0%	332
Clark Memorial Hospital	Jeffersonville	6.2%	1524
Dukes Memorial Hospital	Peru	6.4%	299
Saint Clare Medical Center	Crawfordsville	6.4%	748
Memorial Hospital of South Bend	South Bend	6.5%	1224
Franciscan Physicians Hospital	Munster	6.7%	60
Saint Francis Hospital Mooresville	Mooresville	6.7%	627
Indiana University Health	Indianapolis	6.8%	3069
Saint Mary Medical Center	Hobart	6.8%	878
Community Hospital South	Indianapolis	7.1%	778
Dearborn County Hospital	Lawrenceburg	7.2%	847
Hancock Regional Hospital	Greenfield	7.2%	1156
Franciscan St Anthony Health - Crown Point	Crown Point	7.4%	1644
Parkview Lagrange Hospital	Lagrange	7.4%	270
Rush Memorial Hospital	Rushville	7.4%	188
Saint Elizabeth Central	Lafayette	7.4%	2043
Saint Vincent Randolph Hospital	Winchester	7.4%	311
Dupont Hospital	Fort Wayne	7.5%	308
Bluffton Regional Medical Center	Bluffton	7.7%	673
Methodist Hospitals	Gary	7.7%	1459
Union Hospital Clinton	Clinton	7.7%	234
Indiana University Health North Hospital	Carmel	7.8%	462
Cameron Memorial Community Hospital	Angola	8.0%	411
Elkhart General Hospital	Elkhart	8.2%	2280
Ball Memorial Hospital	Muncie	8.3%	2460
William N Wishard Memorial Hospital	Indianapolis	8.4%	1353
Floyd Memorial Hospital and Health Services	New Albany	8.5%	1540
IU Health Goshen Hospital	Goshen	8.6%	1448
Community Hospital East	Indianapolis	8.7%	2278
Porter Valparaiso Hospital Campus	Valparaiso	8.7%	1834
St Francis Hosp & Health Ctrs-Indianapolis	Indianapolis	8.8%	2338
Community Hospital North	Indianapolis	9.1%	1178
Howard Regional Health System	Kokomo	9.1%	997
Saint Vincent Hospital & Health Services	Indianapolis	9.1%	2738
Parkview Noble Hospital	Kendallville	9.2%	382
Daviess Community Hospital	Washington	9.3%	452
Hendricks Regional Health	Danville	9.6%	1235
Saint Joseph Hospital & Health Center	Kokomo	9.6%	688
Columbus Regional Hospital	Columbus	9.7%	1283
Riverview Hospital	Noblesville	9.7%	1032
Memorial Hospital	Logansport	9.9%	1017
Harrison County Hospital	Corydon	10.1%	505
Schneck Medical Center	Seymour	10.1%	704
Saint John's Health System	Anderson	10.2%	1805
Memorial Hospital and Health Care Center	Jasper	10.3%	1386
Marion General Hospital	Marion	10.6%	1784
Saint Vincent Carmel Hospital	Carmel	10.8%	427
Dekalb Memorial Hospital	Auburn	11.0%	365
Union Hospital	Terre Haute	11.4%	2073
Saint Vincent Dunn Hospital	Bedford	11.6%	311
Indiana University Health West Hospital	Avon	11.8%	524
Witham Health Services	Lebanon	11.8%	576
Saint Catherine Regional Hospital	Charlestown	11.9%	109
Blackford Community Hospital	Hartford City	12.0%	241
Parkview Huntington Hospital	Huntington	12.1%	338
Terre Haute Regional Hospital	Terre Haute	12.1%	578
Comm Hosp of Anderson & Madison County	Anderson	12.2%	1357
Morgan Hospital and Medical Center	Martinsville	12.9%	420
St Joseph's Reg Med Ctr-Plymouth	Plymouth	13.4%	543
Saint Joseph Regional Medical Center	Mishawaka	14.4%	1262
Margaret Mary Community Hospital	Batesville	14.7%	416
Jay County Hospital	Portland	14.8%	345
Starke Memorial Hospital	Knox	14.9%	175
Saint Vincent Salem Hospital	Salem	16.7%	198
Laporte Hospital and Health Services	La Porte	17.6%	1154
Saint Vincent Mercy Hospital	Elwood	22.2%	329

39. MRI for Low Back Pain

Hospital Name	City	Rate	Cases
Saint Vincent Dunn Hospital[1]	Bedford	18.8%	32
Decatur County Memorial Hospital[1]	Greensburg	22.9%	48
Bloomington Hospital	Bloomington	23.6%	144
Saint Vincent Mercy Hospital[1]	Elwood	23.9%	46
Major Hospital	Shelbyville	27.6%	145
Lutheran Hospital of Indiana[1]	Fort Wayne	28.0%	25
Franciscan St Anthony Health - Crown Point	Crown Point	28.8%	212
William N Wishard Memorial Hospital	Indianapolis	28.9%	190
Cameron Memorial Community Hospital	Angola	29.3%	75
Dearborn County Hospital	Lawrenceburg	29.5%	129
Westview Hospital[1]	Indianapolis	29.8%	47
Dekalb Memorial Hospital[1]	Auburn	30.0%	50
Monroe Hospital	Bloomington	30.4%	56
Saint Clare Medical Center	Crawfordsville	30.5%	128
Community Hospital of Bremen[1]	Bremen	30.6%	36
Union Hospital	Terre Haute	30.7%	215
Franciscan St Margaret Health - Dyer	Dyer	30.8%	133
Franciscan St Margaret Health - Hammond	Hammond	31.0%	116
Riverview Hospital	Noblesville	31.0%	126
Dukes Memorial Hospital	Peru	31.5%	54
Fayette Regional Health System	Connersville	31.5%	73
Good Samaritan Hospital	Vincennes	31.6%	171
Laporte Hospital and Health Services	La Porte	31.8%	296
Bluffton Regional Medical Center	Bluffton	31.9%	94
Floyd Memorial Hospital and Health Services	New Albany	31.9%	188
Indiana Orthopaedic Hospital	Indianapolis	31.9%	141
Witham Health Services	Lebanon	31.9%	94
Saint Catherine Regional Hospital[1]	Charlestown	32.1%	28
Kosciusko Community Hospital	Warsaw	32.3%	198
Saint Vincent Carmel Hospital	Carmel	32.7%	220
Margaret Mary Community Hospital	Batesville	32.8%	61
The Ortho Hosp of Lutheran Health Network	Fort Wayne	32.9%	73
St Francis Hosp & Health Ctrs-Indianapolis	Indianapolis	33.0%	427
Elkhart General Hospital	Elkhart	33.2%	196
Community Hospital East	Indianapolis	34.0%	438
Memorial Hospital and Health Care Center	Jasper	34.0%	159
Johnson Memorial Hospital	Franklin	34.2%	76
Saint Vincent Hospital & Health Services	Indianapolis	34.4%	392
Saint Vincent Randolph Hospital[1]	Winchester	34.4%	32
Indiana University Health West Hospital	Avon	34.5%	145
IU Health Goshen Hospital	Goshen	34.6%	127
Morgan Hospital and Medical Center	Martinsville	34.6%	52
Porter Valparaiso Hospital Campus	Valparaiso	35.1%	350
Community Hospital North	Indianapolis	35.3%	354
Henry County Memorial Hospital	New Castle	35.3%	136
Parkview Noble Hospital	Kendallville	35.3%	102
The King's Daughters' Hospital	Madison	35.4%	82
Community Hospital	Munster	35.5%	341
Parkview Whitley Hospital	Columbia City	35.5%	62
Saint Mary's Medical Center of Evansville	Evansville	35.5%	293
Hancock Regional Hospital	Greenfield	35.6%	160
Columbus Regional Hospital	Columbus	35.7%	84
Reid Hospital & Health Care Services	Richmond	35.9%	348
Dupont Hospital	Fort Wayne	36.0%	75
Methodist Hospitals	Gary	36.0%	136
Daviess Community Hospital	Washington	36.2%	69
Saint Elizabeth East	Lafayette	36.2%	329
Blackford Community Hospital[1]	Hartford City	36.6%	41
Marion General Hospital	Marion	36.9%	244
Saint Mary Medical Center	Hobart	37.0%	184
Franciscan St Anthony Health-Michigan City	Michigan City	37.1%	167
Parkview Huntington Hospital	Huntington	37.1%	62
Saint John's Health System	Anderson	37.4%	270
Memorial Hospital	Logansport	37.5%	144
Comm Hosp of Anderson & Madison County	Anderson	37.7%	199
Hendricks Regional Health	Danville	37.7%	220
Community Hospital South	Indianapolis	38.0%	121
Pinnacle Hospital	Crown Point	38.0%	79
Ball Memorial Hospital	Muncie	38.2%	186
Bedford Regional Medical Center	Bedford	38.6%	83
Saint Francis Hospital Mooresville	Mooresville	39.2%	79
Saint Elizabeth Central[1]	Lafayette	39.3%	28
Deaconess Hospital	Evansville	39.4%	340
Saint Joseph Hospital & Health Center	Kokomo	39.4%	132
Harrison County Hospital	Corydon	39.5%	81
Saint Vincent Salem Hospital	Salem	39.5%	43
Schneck Medical Center	Seymour	40.4%	104
Clark Memorial Hospital	Jeffersonville	40.6%	207
Saint Catherine Hospital	East Chicago	42.0%	112
Indiana University Health	Indianapolis	42.6%	568
Jay County Hospital	Portland	43.1%	51
Parkview Hospital	Fort Wayne	43.5%	177
Starke Memorial Hospital	Knox	44.4%	54
Indiana University Health North Hospital	Carmel	44.6%	83
Parkview Lagrange Hospital	Lagrange	45.2%	42
Saint Francis Hospital and Health Centers	Beech Grove	45.9%	61
Rush Memorial Hospital[1]	Rushville	48.1%	27
Sullivan County Community Hospital	Sullivan	51.2%	43

Survey of Patients' Hospital Experiences

40. Area Around Room 'Always' Quiet at Night

Hospital Name	City	Rate	Cases
Physicians' Medical Center	New Albany	84%	(a)
Indiana Orthopaedic Hospital	Indianapolis	76%	300+
Jay County Hospital	Portland	71%	(a)
The Women's Hospital	Newburgh	69%	300+
Indiana University Health Arnett Hospital	Lafayette	68%	300+
Monroe Hospital	Bloomington	68%	300+
Orthopaedic Hospital at Parkview North	Fort Wayne	68%	300+
Fayette Regional Health System	Connersville	67%	300+
Indiana University Health North Hospital	Carmel	67%	300+
Memorial Hospital and Health Care Center	Jasper	67%	300+
Schneck Medical Center	Seymour	67%	300+
Franciscan Physicians Hospital	Munster	66%	300+
The Indiana Heart Hospital	Indianapolis	66%	300+
The Ortho Hosp of Lutheran Health Network	Fort Wayne	66%	300+
Tipton Hospital	Tipton	66%	300+
Dukes Memorial Hospital	Peru	65%	(a)
Floyd Memorial Hospital and Health Services	New Albany	65%	300+
Saint Francis Hospital Mooresville	Mooresville	65%	300+
Saint Vincent Dunn Hospital	Bedford	65%	300+
Saint Vincent Frankfort Hospital	Frankfort	65%	(a)
Gibson General Hospital	Princeton	64%	(a)
Parkview Whitley Hospital	Columbia City	64%	300+
Sullivan County Community Hospital	Sullivan	64%	(a)
Morgan Hospital and Medical Center	Martinsville	63%	300+
Scott Memorial Hospital	Scottsburg	63%	(a)
Parkview Huntington Hospital	Huntington	62%	300+
Parkview Noble Hospital	Kendallville	62%	300+
Saint Vincent Carmel Hospital	Carmel	62%	300+
Starke Memorial Hospital	Knox	62%	(a)
Community Hospital North	Indianapolis	61%	300+
Parkview Hospital	Fort Wayne	61%	300+
Parkview Lagrange Hospital	Lagrange	61%	(a)
Bluffton Regional Medical Center	Bluffton	60%	300+
Indiana University Health West Hospital	Avon	60%	300+
Saint Joseph Regional Medical Center	Mishawaka	60%	300+
Saint Mary's Medical Center of Evansville	Evansville	60%	300+
Saint Vincent Hospital & Health Services	Indianapolis	60%	300+
Wabash County Hospital	Wabash	60%	(a)
Witham Health Services	Lebanon	60%	300+
Harrison County Hospital	Corydon	59%	300+
Hendricks Regional Health	Danville	59%	300+
Saint Catherine Hospital	East Chicago	59%	300+
Saint Elizabeth East	Lafayette	59%	300+
Cameron Memorial Community Hospital	Angola	58%	300+
Deaconess Hospital	Evansville	58%	300+
Dupont Hospital	Fort Wayne	58%	300+
Franciscan St Margaret Health - Hammond	Hammond	58%	300+
Henry County Memorial Hospital	New Castle	58%	300+
Memorial Hospital	Logansport	58%	300+
Saint Joseph Hospital	Fort Wayne	58%	300+
St Joseph's Reg Med Ctr-Plymouth	Plymouth	58%	300+
Westview Hospital	Indianapolis	58%	300+
Daviess Community Hospital	Washington	57%	300+
Hancock Regional Hospital	Greenfield	57%	300+
Howard Regional Health System	Kokomo	57%	300+
Major Hospital	Shelbyville	57%	300+
Riverview Hospital	Noblesville	57%	300+

NOTE: Hospital profiles are in alphabetical order by state, then city, then hospital within the city; Rankings exclude hospitals with less than 25 cases except for patient surveys which excludes hospitals with less than 100 cases; (a) 100–299 cases; (1) The number of cases is too small to be sure how well a hospital is performing; (2) The hospital indicated that the data submitted for this measure were based on a sample of cases; (3) Data was collected during a shorter time period (fewer quarters) than the maximum possible time for this measure; (4) Suppressed for one or more quarters by CMS; (5) No data is available from the hospital for this measure; (6) Fewer than 100 patients completed the HCAHPS survey. Use these rates with caution, as the number of surveys may be too low to reliably assess hospital performance; (7) Survey results are based on less than 12 months of data; (8) Survey results are not available for this reporting period; (9) No or very few patients were eligible for the HCAHPS survey. The scores shown, if any, reflect a very small number of surveys; (10) A state average was not calculated because too few hospitals in the state submitted data; (11) There were discrepancies in the data collection process; Please refer to the User's Guide for a full explanation of data.

Hospital Name	City	Rate	Cases
Saint Mary Medical Center	Hobart	57%	300+
Saint Vincent Heart Center of Indiana	Indianapolis	57%	300+
William N Wishard Memorial Hospital	Indianapolis	57%	300+
Comm Hosp of Anderson & Madison County	Anderson	56%	300+
Johnson Memorial Hospital	Franklin	56%	300+
Margaret Mary Community Hospital	Batesville	56%	300+
Community Hospital	Munster	55%	300+
Dearborn County Hospital	Lawrenceburg	55%	300+
Dekalb Memorial Hospital	Auburn	55%	300+
Good Samaritan Hospital	Vincennes	55%	300+
Saint Vincent Randolph Hospital	Winchester	55%	(a)
Terre Haute Regional Hospital	Terre Haute	55%	300+
Ball Memorial Hospital	Muncie	54%	300+
Reid Hospital & Health Care Services	Richmond	54%	300+
Clark Memorial Hospital	Jeffersonville	53%	300+
IU Health Goshen Hospital	Goshen	53%	300+
St Francis Hosp & Health Ctrs-Indianapolis	Indianapolis	53%	300+
Saint John's Health System	Anderson	53%	300+
Union Hospital Clinton	Clinton	53%	300+
Elkhart General Hospital	Elkhart	52%	300+
The King's Daughters' Hospital	Madison	52%	300+
Marion General Hospital	Marion	52%	300+
Saint Francis Hospital and Health Centers	Beech Grove	52%	300+
Saint Vincent Williamsport Hospital	Williamsport	52%	(a)
Decatur County Memorial Hospital	Greensburg	51%	(a)
Franciscan St Anthony Health-Michigan City	Michigan City	51%	300+
Indiana University Health	Indianapolis	51%	300+
Kosciusko Community Hospital	Warsaw	51%	300+
Laporte Hospital and Health Services	La Porte	51%	300+
Saint Catherine Regional Hospital	Charlestown	51%	(a)
Saint Clare Medical Center	Crawfordsville	51%	300+
Saint Joseph Hospital & Health Center	Kokomo	50%	300+
Community Hospital East	Indianapolis	49%	300+
Franciscan St Anthony Health - Crown Point	Crown Point	49%	300+
Franciscan St Margaret Health - Dyer	Dyer	49%	300+
Porter Valparaiso Hospital Campus	Valparaiso	49%	300+
Union Hospital	Terre Haute	49%	300+
Bloomington Hospital	Bloomington	47%	300+
Community Hospital South	Indianapolis	47%	300+
Methodist Hospitals	Gary	47%	300+
Saint Elizabeth Central	Lafayette	47%	300+
Saint Vincent Mercy Hospital	Elwood	47%	(a)
Lutheran Hospital of Indiana	Fort Wayne	46%	300+
Saint Vincent Clay Hospital	Brazil	46%	(a)
Bedford Regional Medical Center	Bedford	44%	300+
Columbus Regional Hospital	Columbus	44%	300+
Memorial Hospital of South Bend	South Bend	43%	300+

41. Doctors 'Always' Communicated Well

Hospital Name	City	Rate	Cases
Physicians' Medical Center	New Albany	91%	(a)
Dekalb Memorial Hospital	Auburn	90%	300+
Parkview Whitley Hospital	Columbia City	89%	300+
Harrison County Hospital	Corydon	88%	300+
Indiana Orthopaedic Hospital	Indianapolis	88%	300+
Margaret Mary Community Hospital	Batesville	88%	300+
Saint Vincent Dunn Hospital	Bedford	88%	300+
Tipton Hospital	Tipton	88%	300+
Decatur County Memorial Hospital	Greensburg	87%	(a)
Memorial Hospital and Health Care Center	Jasper	87%	300+
Orthopaedic Hospital at Parkview North	Fort Wayne	87%	300+
Parkview Noble Hospital	Kendallville	87%	300+
Gibson General Hospital	Princeton	85%	(a)
Jay County Hospital	Portland	85%	(a)
Marion General Hospital	Marion	85%	300+
Parkview Huntington Hospital	Huntington	85%	300+
Parkview Lagrange Hospital	Lagrange	85%	(a)
Saint Vincent Clay Hospital	Brazil	85%	(a)
Saint Vincent Frankfort Hospital	Frankfort	85%	(a)
Schneck Medical Center	Seymour	85%	300+
Scott Memorial Hospital	Scottsburg	85%	(a)
Bedford Regional Medical Center	Bedford	84%	300+
Cameron Memorial Community Hospital	Angola	84%	300+
Fayette Regional Health System	Connersville	84%	300+
Johnson Memorial Hospital	Franklin	84%	300+
Monroe Hospital	Bloomington	84%	300+
Parkview Hospital	Fort Wayne	84%	300+
Saint Vincent Carmel Hospital	Carmel	84%	300+
Saint Vincent Heart Center of Indiana	Indianapolis	84%	300+
The Women's Hospital	Newburgh	84%	300+
Columbus Regional Hospital	Columbus	83%	300+
Comm Hosp of Anderson & Madison County	Anderson	83%	300+
Dukes Memorial Hospital	Peru	83%	(a)
Floyd Memorial Hospital and Health Services	New Albany	83%	300+
Good Samaritan Hospital	Vincennes	83%	300+
Hendricks Regional Health	Danville	83%	300+
Henry County Memorial Hospital	New Castle	83%	300+
Major Hospital	Shelbyville	83%	300+
Saint Francis Hospital Mooresville	Mooresville	83%	300+
Saint John's Health System	Anderson	83%	300+
St Joseph's Reg Med Ctr-Plymouth	Plymouth	83%	300+
Saint Mary's Medical Center of Evansville	Evansville	83%	300+
Witham Health Services	Lebanon	83%	300+
Clark Memorial Hospital	Jeffersonville	82%	300+
Community Hospital	Munster	82%	300+
Franciscan St Anthony Health-Michigan City	Michigan City	82%	300+
Hancock Regional Hospital	Greenfield	82%	300+
Howard Regional Health System	Kokomo	82%	300+
Indiana University Health North Hospital	Carmel	82%	300+
The King's Daughters' Hospital	Madison	82%	300+
Kosciusko Community Hospital	Warsaw	82%	300+
Memorial Hospital	Logansport	82%	300+
The Ortho Hosp of Lutheran Health Network	Fort Wayne	82%	300+
Riverview Hospital	Noblesville	82%	300+
Saint Vincent Mercy Hospital	Elwood	82%	(a)
Saint Vincent Randolph Hospital	Winchester	82%	(a)
Saint Vincent Williamsport Hospital	Williamsport	82%	(a)
Terre Haute Regional Hospital	Terre Haute	82%	300+
Westview Hospital	Indianapolis	82%	300+
Franciscan Physicians Hospital	Munster	81%	300+
The Indiana Heart Hospital	Indianapolis	81%	300+
Union Hospital Clinton	Clinton	81%	300+
Ball Memorial Hospital	Muncie	80%	300+
Bloomington Hospital	Bloomington	80%	300+
Daviess Community Hospital	Washington	80%	300+
Memorial Hospital of South Bend	South Bend	80%	300+
Saint Clare Medical Center	Crawfordsville	80%	300+
Saint Elizabeth East	Lafayette	80%	300+
St Francis Hosp & Health Ctrs-Indianapolis	Indianapolis	80%	300+
Saint Joseph Hospital	Fort Wayne	80%	300+
Saint Joseph Hospital & Health Center	Kokomo	80%	300+
Saint Vincent Hospital & Health Services	Indianapolis	80%	300+
Bluffton Regional Medical Center	Bluffton	79%	300+
Dearborn County Hospital	Lawrenceburg	79%	300+
Dupont Hospital	Fort Wayne	79%	300+
Morgan Hospital and Medical Center	Martinsville	79%	300+
Reid Hospital & Health Care Services	Richmond	79%	300+
Saint Joseph Regional Medical Center	Mishawaka	79%	300+
Saint Mary Medical Center	Hobart	79%	300+
Wabash County Hospital	Wabash	79%	(a)
William N Wishard Memorial Hospital	Indianapolis	79%	300+
Indiana University Health West Hospital	Avon	78%	300+
IU Health Goshen Hospital	Goshen	78%	300+
Saint Catherine Hospital	East Chicago	78%	300+
Starke Memorial Hospital	Knox	78%	(a)
Sullivan County Community Hospital	Sullivan	78%	(a)
Community Hospital North	Indianapolis	77%	300+
Deaconess Hospital	Evansville	77%	300+
Franciscan St Anthony Health - Crown Point	Crown Point	77%	300+
Franciscan St Margaret Health - Dyer	Dyer	77%	300+
Porter Valparaiso Hospital Campus	Valparaiso	77%	300+
Community Hospital South	Indianapolis	76%	300+
Lutheran Hospital of Indiana	Fort Wayne	76%	300+
Saint Catherine Regional Hospital	Charlestown	76%	(a)
Elkhart General Hospital	Elkhart	75%	300+
Laporte Hospital and Health Services	La Porte	75%	300+
Saint Elizabeth Central	Lafayette	75%	300+
Union Hospital	Terre Haute	75%	300+
Community Hospital East	Indianapolis	74%	300+
Indiana University Health	Indianapolis	74%	300+
Methodist Hospitals	Gary	74%	300+
Saint Francis Hospital and Health Centers	Beech Grove	73%	300+
Franciscan St Margaret Health - Hammond	Hammond	72%	300+
Indiana University Health Arnett Hospital	Lafayette	72%	300+

42. Home Recovery Information Given

Hospital Name	City	Rate	Cases
Indiana Orthopaedic Hospital	Indianapolis	93%	300+
Hendricks Regional Health	Danville	91%	300+
Orthopaedic Hospital at Parkview North	Fort Wayne	91%	300+
Decatur County Memorial Hospital	Greensburg	90%	(a)
The Ortho Hosp of Lutheran Health Network	Fort Wayne	90%	300+
Parkview Whitley Hospital	Columbia City	90%	300+
Good Samaritan Hospital	Vincennes	89%	300+
Harrison County Hospital	Corydon	89%	300+
Parkview Huntington Hospital	Huntington	89%	300+
Parkview Noble Hospital	Kendallville	89%	300+
Dukes Memorial Hospital	Peru	88%	(a)
Fayette Regional Health System	Connersville	88%	300+
Jay County Hospital	Portland	88%	(a)
Saint Joseph Hospital	Fort Wayne	88%	300+
Terre Haute Regional Hospital	Terre Haute	88%	300+
Tipton Hospital	Tipton	88%	300+
The Women's Hospital	Newburgh	88%	300+
Parkview Hospital	Fort Wayne	87%	300+
Saint Francis Hospital Mooresville	Mooresville	87%	300+
St Joseph's Reg Med Ctr-Plymouth	Plymouth	87%	300+
Saint Mary's Medical Center of Evansville	Evansville	87%	300+
Bluffton Regional Medical Center	Bluffton	86%	300+
Dekalb Memorial Hospital	Auburn	86%	300+
The King's Daughters' Hospital	Madison	86%	300+
Laporte Hospital and Health Services	La Porte	86%	300+
Lutheran Hospital of Indiana	Fort Wayne	86%	300+
Riverview Hospital	Noblesville	86%	300+
Saint Elizabeth East	Lafayette	86%	300+
Saint John's Health System	Anderson	86%	300+
Saint Vincent Dunn Hospital	Bedford	86%	300+
Wabash County Hospital	Wabash	86%	(a)
Bloomington Hospital	Bloomington	85%	300+
Comm Hosp of Anderson & Madison County	Anderson	85%	300+
Dupont Hospital	Fort Wayne	85%	300+
Henry County Memorial Hospital	New Castle	85%	300+
Johnson Memorial Hospital	Franklin	85%	300+
Physicians' Medical Center	New Albany	85%	(a)
St Francis Hosp & Health Ctrs-Indianapolis	Indianapolis	85%	300+
Saint Joseph Regional Medical Center	Mishawaka	85%	300+
Saint Vincent Heart Center of Indiana	Indianapolis	85%	300+
Saint Vincent Mercy Hospital	Elwood	85%	(a)
Ball Memorial Hospital	Muncie	84%	300+
Franciscan St Anthony Health - Crown Point	Crown Point	84%	300+
Major Hospital	Shelbyville	84%	300+
Margaret Mary Community Hospital	Batesville	84%	300+
Memorial Hospital of South Bend	South Bend	84%	300+
Parkview Lagrange Hospital	Lagrange	84%	(a)
Reid Hospital & Health Care Services	Richmond	84%	300+
Saint Elizabeth Central	Lafayette	84%	300+
Saint Mary Medical Center	Hobart	84%	300+
Saint Vincent Williamsport Hospital	Williamsport	84%	(a)
Schneck Medical Center	Seymour	84%	300+
Union Hospital	Terre Haute	84%	300+
Bedford Regional Medical Center	Bedford	83%	300+
Community Hospital	Munster	83%	300+
Franciscan Physicians Hospital	Munster	83%	300+
Hancock Regional Hospital	Greenfield	83%	300+
The Indiana Heart Hospital	Indianapolis	83%	300+
Kosciusko Community Hospital	Warsaw	83%	300+
Marion General Hospital	Marion	83%	300+
Saint Francis Hospital and Health Centers	Beech Grove	83%	300+
Saint Vincent Carmel Hospital	Carmel	83%	300+
Union Hospital Clinton	Clinton	83%	300+
Floyd Memorial Hospital and Health Services	New Albany	82%	300+
Gibson General Hospital	Princeton	82%	(a)
Indiana University Health Arnett Hospital	Lafayette	82%	300+
Indiana University Health North Hospital	Carmel	82%	300+
Saint Vincent Frankfort Hospital	Frankfort	82%	(a)
Saint Vincent Hospital & Health Services	Indianapolis	82%	300+
Saint Vincent Randolph Hospital	Winchester	82%	(a)
William N Wishard Memorial Hospital	Indianapolis	82%	300+
Cameron Memorial Community Hospital	Angola	81%	300+
Daviess Community Hospital	Washington	81%	300+
Howard Regional Health System	Kokomo	81%	300+
IU Health Goshen Hospital	Goshen	81%	300+
Memorial Hospital	Logansport	81%	300+
Porter Valparaiso Hospital Campus	Valparaiso	81%	300+
Scott Memorial Hospital	Scottsburg	81%	(a)
Westview Hospital	Indianapolis	81%	300+
Franciscan St Anthony Health-Michigan City	Michigan City	80%	300+
Indiana University Health	Indianapolis	80%	300+
Indiana University Health West Hospital	Avon	80%	300+
Saint Catherine Hospital	East Chicago	80%	300+
Saint Clare Medical Center	Crawfordsville	80%	300+
Saint Joseph Hospital & Health Center	Kokomo	80%	300+
Sullivan County Community Hospital	Sullivan	80%	(a)
Witham Health Services	Lebanon	80%	300+
Columbus Regional Hospital	Columbus	79%	300+
Community Hospital East	Indianapolis	79%	300+
Community Hospital North	Indianapolis	79%	300+
Methodist Hospitals	Gary	79%	300+
Community Hospital South	Indianapolis	78%	300+
Deaconess Hospital	Evansville	78%	300+
Elkhart General Hospital	Elkhart	78%	300+
Monroe Hospital	Bloomington	78%	300+
Saint Vincent Clay Hospital	Brazil	78%	(a)
Dearborn County Hospital	Lawrenceburg	77%	300+
Memorial Hospital and Health Care Center	Jasper	77%	300+
Morgan Hospital and Medical Center	Martinsville	75%	300+
Clark Memorial Hospital	Jeffersonville	74%	300+
Franciscan St Margaret Health - Dyer	Dyer	74%	300+
Franciscan St Margaret Health - Hammond	Hammond	72%	300+
Starke Memorial Hospital	Knox	71%	(a)
Saint Catherine Regional Hospital	Charlestown	67%	(a)

43. Hospital Given 9 or 10 on 10 Point Scale

Hospital Name	City	Rate	Cases
Indiana Orthopaedic Hospital	Indianapolis	90%	300+
Saint Vincent Heart Center of Indiana	Indianapolis	87%	300+
The Women's Hospital	Newburgh	86%	300+
The Indiana Heart Hospital	Indianapolis	84%	300+
Indiana University Health North Hospital	Carmel	83%	300+
Physicians' Medical Center	New Albany	83%	(a)

NOTE: Hospital profiles are in alphabetical order by state, then city, then hospital within the city; Rankings exclude hospitals with less than 25 cases except for patient surveys which excludes hospitals with less than 100 cases; (a) 100–299 cases; (1) The number of cases is too small to be sure how well a hospital is performing; (2) The hospital indicated that the data submitted for this measure were based on a sample of cases; (3) Data was collected during a shorter time period (fewer quarters) than the maximum possible time for this measure; (4) Suppressed for one or more quarters by CMS; (5) No data is available from the hospital for this measure; (6) Fewer than 100 patients completed the HCAHPS survey. Use these rates with caution, as the number of surveys may be too low to reliably assess hospital performance; (7) Survey results are based on less than 12 months of data; (8) Survey results are not available for this reporting period; (9) No or very few patients were eligible for the HCAHPS survey. The scores shown, if any, reflect a very small number of surveys; (10) A state average was not calculated because too few hospitals in the state submitted data; (11) There were discrepancies in the data collection process; Please refer to the User's Guide for a full explanation of data.

Margaret Mary Community Hospital	Batesville	82%	300+
Hendricks Regional Health	Danville	81%	300+
Saint Vincent Carmel Hospital	Carmel	81%	300+
Tipton Hospital	Tipton	81%	300+
Floyd Memorial Hospital and Health Services	New Albany	80%	300+
Orthopaedic Hospital at Parkview North	Fort Wayne	80%	300+
Parkview Lagrange Hospital	Lagrange	80%	(a)
Dekalb Memorial Hospital	Auburn	79%	300+
Parkview Whitley Hospital	Columbia City	79%	300+
Saint Francis Hospital Mooresville	Mooresville	79%	300+
St Joseph's Reg Med Ctr-Plymouth	Plymouth	79%	300+
Parkview Noble Hospital	Kendallville	78%	300+
Community Hospital	Munster	77%	300+
Dupont Hospital	Fort Wayne	77%	300+
Indiana University Health West Hospital	Avon	77%	300+
Memorial Hospital and Health Care Center	Jasper	77%	300+
Parkview Huntington Hospital	Huntington	77%	300+
Saint Mary's Medical Center of Evansville	Evansville	77%	300+
Saint Vincent Dunn Hospital	Bedford	77%	300+
Saint Vincent Frankfort Hospital	Frankfort	77%	(a)
Saint Vincent Hospital & Health Services	Indianapolis	77%	300+
Franciscan Physicians Hospital	Munster	76%	300+
Good Samaritan Hospital	Vincennes	76%	300+
The Ortho Hosp of Lutheran Health Network	Fort Wayne	76%	300+
Parkview Hospital	Fort Wayne	76%	300+
St Francis Hosp & Health Ctrs-Indianapolis	Indianapolis	76%	300+
Jay County Hospital	Portland	75%	(a)
Lutheran Hospital of Indiana	Fort Wayne	75%	300+
Schneck Medical Center	Seymour	75%	300+
Comm Hosp of Anderson & Madison County	Anderson	74%	300+
Indiana University Health Arnett Hospital	Lafayette	74%	300+
Memorial Hospital of South Bend	South Bend	74%	300+
Monroe Hospital	Bloomington	74%	300+
Saint Mary Medical Center	Hobart	74%	300+
Bluffton Regional Medical Center	Bluffton	73%	300+
Gibson General Hospital	Princeton	73%	(a)
Hancock Regional Hospital	Greenfield	73%	300+
Saint Joseph Hospital & Health Center	Kokomo	73%	300+
Saint Joseph Regional Medical Center	Mishawaka	73%	300+
Scott Memorial Hospital	Scottsburg	73%	(a)
Witham Health Services	Lebanon	73%	300+
Bedford Regional Medical Center	Bedford	72%	300+
Clark Memorial Hospital	Jeffersonville	72%	300+
Community Hospital North	Indianapolis	72%	300+
Johnson Memorial Hospital	Franklin	72%	300+
Major Hospital	Shelbyville	72%	300+
Riverview Hospital	Noblesville	72%	300+
Saint Vincent Mercy Hospital	Elwood	72%	(a)
Columbus Regional Hospital	Columbus	71%	300+
Fayette Regional Health System	Connersville	71%	300+
Harrison County Hospital	Corydon	71%	300+
Henry County Memorial Hospital	New Castle	71%	300+
IU Health Goshen Hospital	Goshen	71%	300+
Reid Hospital & Health Care Services	Richmond	71%	300+
Saint John's Health System	Anderson	71%	300+
Terre Haute Regional Hospital	Terre Haute	71%	300+
Wabash County Hospital	Wabash	71%	(a)
Bloomington Hospital	Bloomington	70%	300+
Saint Catherine Hospital	East Chicago	70%	300+
Union Hospital Clinton	Clinton	70%	300+
William N Wishard Memorial Hospital	Indianapolis	70%	300+
Cameron Memorial Community Hospital	Angola	69%	300+
Marion General Hospital	Marion	69%	300+
Saint Francis Hospital and Health Centers	Beech Grove	69%	300+
Saint Joseph Hospital	Fort Wayne	69%	300+
Ball Memorial Hospital	Muncie	68%	300+
Community Hospital South	Indianapolis	68%	300+
Deaconess Hospital	Evansville	68%	300+
Elkhart General Hospital	Elkhart	68%	300+
Franciscan St Anthony Health - Crown Point	Crown Point	68%	300+
Howard Regional Health System	Kokomo	68%	300+
Saint Vincent Williamsport Hospital	Williamsport	68%	(a)
Franciscan St Anthony Health-Michigan City	Michigan City	67%	300+
Sullivan County Community Hospital	Sullivan	67%	(a)
Westview Hospital	Indianapolis	67%	300+
Saint Elizabeth East	Lafayette	66%	300+
Saint Vincent Randolph Hospital	Winchester	66%	(a)
Union Hospital	Terre Haute	66%	300+
Decatur County Memorial Hospital	Greensburg	65%	(a)
Indiana University Health	Indianapolis	65%	300+
The King's Daughters' Hospital	Madison	65%	300+
Memorial Hospital	Logansport	65%	300+
Saint Elizabeth Central	Lafayette	65%	300+
Dukes Memorial Hospital	Peru	64%	(a)
Franciscan St Margaret Health - Dyer	Dyer	64%	300+
Kosciusko Community Hospital	Warsaw	64%	300+
Laporte Hospital and Health Services	La Porte	64%	300+
Daviess Community Hospital	Washington	63%	300+
Dearborn County Hospital	Lawrenceburg	63%	300+
Saint Vincent Clay Hospital	Brazil	62%	(a)
Community Hospital East	Indianapolis	61%	300+
Morgan Hospital and Medical Center	Martinsville	59%	300+
Saint Clare Medical Center	Crawfordsville	59%	300+
Porter Valparaiso Hospital Campus	Valparaiso	58%	300+
Franciscan St Margaret Health - Hammond	Hammond	56%	300+
Starke Memorial Hospital	Knox	54%	(a)
Saint Catherine Regional Hospital	Charlestown	51%	(a)
Methodist Hospitals	Gary	49%	300+

44. Meds 'Always' Explained Before Given

Hospital Name	City	Rate	Cases
Physicians' Medical Center	New Albany	75%	(a)
Scott Memorial Hospital	Scottsburg	73%	(a)
Indiana Orthopaedic Hospital	Indianapolis	72%	300+
Saint Vincent Dunn Hospital	Bedford	72%	300+
Harrison County Hospital	Corydon	70%	300+
Parkview Noble Hospital	Kendallville	70%	300+
Fayette Regional Health System	Connersville	69%	300+
Parkview Whitley Hospital	Columbia City	69%	300+
Dekalb Memorial Hospital	Auburn	68%	300+
Jay County Hospital	Portland	68%	(a)
Marion General Hospital	Marion	68%	300+
Saint Vincent Frankfort Hospital	Frankfort	68%	(a)
Bedford Regional Medical Center	Bedford	67%	300+
Orthopaedic Hospital at Parkview North	Fort Wayne	67%	300+
Bluffton Regional Medical Center	Bluffton	66%	300+
Community Hospital	Munster	65%	300+
Dukes Memorial Hospital	Peru	65%	(a)
Good Samaritan Hospital	Vincennes	65%	300+
Johnson Memorial Hospital	Franklin	65%	300+
Major Hospital	Shelbyville	65%	300+
Saint Francis Hospital Mooresville	Mooresville	65%	300+
Union Hospital Clinton	Clinton	65%	300+
Clark Memorial Hospital	Jeffersonville	64%	300+
Henry County Memorial Hospital	New Castle	64%	300+
Margaret Mary Community Hospital	Batesville	64%	300+
Memorial Hospital	Logansport	64%	300+
Parkview Hospital	Fort Wayne	64%	300+
Riverview Hospital	Noblesville	64%	300+
St Joseph's Reg Med Ctr-Plymouth	Plymouth	64%	300+
Saint Vincent Williamsport Hospital	Williamsport	64%	(a)
Schneck Medical Center	Seymour	64%	300+
Franciscan Physicians Hospital	Munster	63%	300+
Howard Regional Health System	Kokomo	63%	300+
Memorial Hospital and Health Care Center	Jasper	63%	300+
Saint Catherine Hospital	East Chicago	63%	300+
Saint Mary's Medical Center of Evansville	Evansville	63%	300+
Saint Vincent Heart Center of Indiana	Indianapolis	63%	300+
Saint Vincent Mercy Hospital	Elwood	63%	(a)
Saint Vincent Randolph Hospital	Winchester	63%	(a)
Comm Hosp of Anderson & Madison County	Anderson	62%	300+
Parkview Huntington Hospital	Huntington	62%	300+
Terre Haute Regional Hospital	Terre Haute	62%	300+
Wabash County Hospital	Wabash	62%	(a)
Witham Health Services	Lebanon	62%	300+
Ball Memorial Hospital	Muncie	61%	300+
Cameron Memorial Community Hospital	Angola	61%	300+
Franciscan St Anthony Health-Michigan City	Michigan City	61%	300+
The King's Daughters' Hospital	Madison	61%	300+
Saint Mary Medical Center	Hobart	61%	300+
Saint Vincent Carmel Hospital	Carmel	61%	300+
Saint Vincent Hospital & Health Services	Indianapolis	61%	300+
Hancock Regional Hospital	Greenfield	60%	300+
Hendricks Regional Health	Danville	60%	300+
Morgan Hospital and Medical Center	Martinsville	60%	300+
Saint Joseph Hospital	Fort Wayne	60%	300+
Bloomington Hospital	Bloomington	59%	300+
Decatur County Memorial Hospital	Greensburg	59%	(a)
Floyd Memorial Hospital and Health Services	New Albany	59%	300+
IU Health Goshen Hospital	Goshen	59%	300+
Monroe Hospital	Bloomington	59%	300+
Parkview Lagrange Hospital	Lagrange	59%	(a)
Saint John's Health System	Anderson	59%	300+
Sullivan County Community Hospital	Sullivan	59%	(a)
Tipton Hospital	Tipton	59%	300+
Columbus Regional Hospital	Columbus	58%	300+
Deaconess Hospital	Evansville	58%	300+
Dearborn County Hospital	Lawrenceburg	58%	300+
Gibson General Hospital	Princeton	58%	(a)
The Ortho Hosp of Lutheran Health Network	Fort Wayne	58%	300+
Saint Elizabeth East	Lafayette	58%	300+
St Francis Hosp & Health Ctrs-Indianapolis	Indianapolis	58%	300+
Saint Joseph Hospital & Health Center	Kokomo	58%	300+
William N Wishard Memorial Hospital	Indianapolis	58%	300+
Daviess Community Hospital	Washington	57%	300+
Franciscan St Anthony Health - Crown Point	Crown Point	57%	300+
Indiana University Health Arnett Hospital	Lafayette	57%	300+
Kosciusko Community Hospital	Warsaw	57%	300+
Lutheran Hospital of Indiana	Fort Wayne	57%	300+
Memorial Hospital of South Bend	South Bend	57%	300+
Reid Hospital & Health Care Services	Richmond	57%	300+
Saint Joseph Regional Medical Center	Mishawaka	57%	300+
The Women's Hospital	Newburgh	57%	300+
Indiana University Health	Indianapolis	56%	300+
Indiana University Health North Hospital	Carmel	56%	300+
Laporte Hospital and Health Services	La Porte	56%	300+
Saint Clare Medical Center	Crawfordsville	56%	300+
Saint Francis Hospital and Health Centers	Beech Grove	56%	300+
Community Hospital North	Indianapolis	55%	300+
Dupont Hospital	Fort Wayne	55%	300+
The Indiana Heart Hospital	Indianapolis	55%	300+
Porter Valparaiso Hospital Campus	Valparaiso	55%	300+
Saint Vincent Clay Hospital	Brazil	55%	(a)
Starke Memorial Hospital	Knox	55%	(a)
Community Hospital South	Indianapolis	54%	300+
Elkhart General Hospital	Elkhart	54%	300+
Franciscan St Margaret Health - Dyer	Dyer	54%	300+
Indiana University Health West Hospital	Avon	54%	300+
Saint Elizabeth Central	Lafayette	54%	300+
Union Hospital	Terre Haute	54%	300+
Community Hospital East	Indianapolis	53%	300+
Westview Hospital	Indianapolis	53%	300+
Franciscan St Margaret Health - Hammond	Hammond	52%	300+
Methodist Hospitals	Gary	52%	300+
Saint Catherine Regional Hospital	Charlestown	45%	(a)

45. Nurses 'Always' Communicated Well

Hospital Name	City	Rate	Cases
Indiana Orthopaedic Hospital	Indianapolis	87%	300+
Parkview Whitley Hospital	Columbia City	87%	300+
Scott Memorial Hospital	Scottsburg	87%	(a)
Margaret Mary Community Hospital	Batesville	86%	300+
Wabash County Hospital	Wabash	86%	(a)
Saint Vincent Frankfort Hospital	Frankfort	85%	(a)
Saint Vincent Heart Center of Indiana	Indianapolis	85%	300+
Good Samaritan Hospital	Vincennes	84%	300+
Parkview Huntington Hospital	Huntington	84%	300+
Physicians' Medical Center	New Albany	84%	(a)
Cameron Memorial Community Hospital	Angola	83%	300+
Major Hospital	Shelbyville	83%	300+
Marion General Hospital	Marion	83%	300+
Memorial Hospital and Health Care Center	Jasper	83%	300+
Parkview Hospital	Fort Wayne	83%	300+
Saint Vincent Carmel Hospital	Carmel	83%	300+
Saint Vincent Dunn Hospital	Bedford	83%	300+
Saint Vincent Mercy Hospital	Elwood	83%	(a)
Saint Vincent Williamsport Hospital	Williamsport	83%	(a)
Starke Memorial Hospital	Knox	83%	(a)
Community Hospital	Munster	82%	300+
Fayette Regional Health System	Connersville	82%	300+
Franciscan Physicians Hospital	Munster	82%	300+
Gibson General Hospital	Princeton	82%	(a)
Parkview Noble Hospital	Kendallville	82%	300+
St Joseph's Reg Med Ctr-Plymouth	Plymouth	82%	300+
Schneck Medical Center	Seymour	82%	300+
Tipton Hospital	Tipton	82%	300+
Bluffton Regional Medical Center	Bluffton	81%	300+
Dekalb Memorial Hospital	Auburn	81%	300+
Harrison County Hospital	Corydon	81%	300+
Henry County Memorial Hospital	New Castle	81%	300+
The Indiana Heart Hospital	Indianapolis	81%	300+
Johnson Memorial Hospital	Franklin	81%	300+
Clark Memorial Hospital	Jeffersonville	80%	300+
Franciscan St Anthony Health-Michigan City	Michigan City	80%	300+
Jay County Hospital	Portland	80%	(a)
Memorial Hospital	Logansport	80%	300+
Monroe Hospital	Bloomington	80%	300+
Saint Francis Hospital Mooresville	Mooresville	80%	300+
Saint John's Health System	Anderson	80%	300+
Saint Mary Medical Center	Hobart	80%	300+
Union Hospital Clinton	Clinton	80%	300+
Bedford Regional Medical Center	Bedford	79%	300+
Comm Hosp of Anderson & Madison County	Anderson	79%	300+
Decatur County Memorial Hospital	Greensburg	79%	(a)
Floyd Memorial Hospital and Health Services	New Albany	79%	300+
Hendricks Regional Health	Danville	79%	300+
Howard Regional Health System	Kokomo	79%	300+
Orthopaedic Hospital at Parkview North	Fort Wayne	79%	300+
Parkview Lagrange Hospital	Lagrange	79%	(a)
Saint Catherine Hospital	East Chicago	79%	300+
Saint Mary's Medical Center of Evansville	Evansville	79%	300+
Witham Health Services	Lebanon	79%	300+
The Women's Hospital	Newburgh	79%	300+
Ball Memorial Hospital	Muncie	78%	300+
Hancock Regional Hospital	Greenfield	78%	300+
IU Health Goshen Hospital	Goshen	78%	300+
The King's Daughters' Hospital	Madison	78%	300+
Saint Elizabeth East	Lafayette	78%	300+
Saint Vincent Clay Hospital	Brazil	78%	(a)
Terre Haute Regional Hospital	Terre Haute	78%	300+
Columbus Regional Hospital	Columbus	77%	300+

NOTE: Hospital profiles are in alphabetical order by state, then city, then hospital within the city; Rankings exclude hospitals with less than 25 cases except for patient surveys which excludes hospitals with less than 100 cases; (a) 100–299 cases; (1) The number of cases is too small to be sure how well a hospital is performing; (2) The hospital indicated that the data submitted for this measure were based on a sample of cases; (3) Data was collected during a shorter time period (fewer quarters) than the maximum possible time for this measure; (4) Suppressed for one or more quarters by CMS; (5) No data is available from the hospital for this measure; (6) Fewer than 100 patients completed the HCAHPS survey. Use these rates with caution, as the number of surveys may be too low to reliably assess hospital performance; (7) Survey results are based on less than 12 months of data; (8) Survey results are not available for this reporting period; (9) No or very few patients were eligible for the HCAHPS survey. The scores shown, if any, reflect a very small number of surveys; (10) A state average was not calculated because too few hospitals in the state submitted data; (11) There were discrepancies in the data collection process; Please refer to the User's Guide for a full explanation of data.

Hospital Name	City	Rate	Cases
Dearborn County Hospital	Lawrenceburg	77%	300+
Dukes Memorial Hospital	Peru	77%	(a)
Dupont Hospital	Fort Wayne	77%	300+
Lutheran Hospital of Indiana	Fort Wayne	77%	300+
The Ortho Hosp of Lutheran Health Network	Fort Wayne	77%	300+
Saint Elizabeth Central	Lafayette	77%	300+
St Francis Hosp & Health Ctrs-Indianapolis	Indianapolis	77%	300+
Saint Joseph Regional Medical Center	Mishawaka	77%	300+
Saint Vincent Hospital & Health Services	Indianapolis	77%	300+
Sullivan County Community Hospital	Sullivan	77%	(a)
Indiana University Health Arnett Hospital	Lafayette	76%	300+
Memorial Hospital of South Bend	South Bend	76%	300+
Reid Hospital & Health Care Services	Richmond	76%	300+
Riverview Hospital	Noblesville	76%	300+
Saint Joseph Hospital	Fort Wayne	76%	300+
Bloomington Hospital	Bloomington	75%	300+
Deaconess Hospital	Evansville	75%	300+
Franciscan St Anthony Health - Crown Point	Crown Point	75%	300+
Indiana University Health North Hospital	Carmel	75%	300+
Kosciusko Community Hospital	Warsaw	75%	300+
Laporte Hospital and Health Services	La Porte	75%	300+
Saint Francis Hospital and Health Centers	Beech Grove	75%	300+
Saint Clare Medical Center	Crawfordsville	74%	300+
Saint Joseph Hospital & Health Center	Kokomo	74%	300+
Saint Vincent Randolph Hospital	Winchester	74%	(a)
Community Hospital South	Indianapolis	73%	300+
Elkhart General Hospital	Elkhart	73%	300+
Franciscan St Margaret Health - Dyer	Dyer	73%	300+
Union Hospital	Terre Haute	73%	300+
Porter Valparaiso Hospital Campus	Valparaiso	72%	300+
William N Wishard Memorial Hospital	Indianapolis	72%	300+
Community Hospital North	Indianapolis	71%	300+
Daviess Community Hospital	Washington	71%	300+
Indiana University Health	Indianapolis	71%	300+
Indiana University Health West Hospital	Avon	71%	300+
Morgan Hospital and Medical Center	Martinsville	71%	300+
Westview Hospital	Indianapolis	71%	300+
Franciscan St Margaret Health - Hammond	Hammond	70%	300+
Community Hospital East	Indianapolis	69%	300+
Methodist Hospitals	Gary	68%	300+
Saint Catherine Regional Hospital	Charlestown	68%	(a)

46. Pain 'Always' Well Controlled

Hospital Name	City	Rate	Cases
Parkview Whitley Hospital	Columbia City	81%	300+
Indiana Orthopaedic Hospital	Indianapolis	79%	300+
Margaret Mary Community Hospital	Batesville	79%	300+
Scott Memorial Hospital	Scottsburg	79%	(a)
Good Samaritan Hospital	Vincennes	78%	300+
Wabash County Hospital	Wabash	78%	(a)
Fayette Regional Health System	Connersville	77%	300+
Parkview Hospital	Fort Wayne	77%	300+
Physicians' Medical Center	New Albany	77%	(a)
Saint Vincent Carmel Hospital	Carmel	77%	300+
Saint Vincent Heart Center of Indiana	Indianapolis	77%	300+
Parkview Huntington Hospital	Huntington	76%	300+
Parkview Noble Hospital	Kendallville	76%	300+
Schneck Medical Center	Seymour	76%	300+
Cameron Memorial Community Hospital	Angola	75%	300+
Dekalb Memorial Hospital	Auburn	75%	300+
Dukes Memorial Hospital	Peru	75%	(a)
Jay County Hospital	Portland	75%	(a)
Ball Memorial Hospital	Muncie	74%	300+
Community Hospital	Munster	74%	300+
Franciscan St Anthony Health-Michigan City	Michigan City	74%	300+
Henry County Memorial Hospital	New Castle	74%	300+
Howard Regional Health System	Kokomo	74%	300+
Marion General Hospital	Marion	74%	300+
Memorial Hospital	Logansport	74%	300+
Saint Elizabeth East	Lafayette	74%	300+
St Joseph's Reg Med Ctr-Plymouth	Plymouth	74%	300+
Saint Vincent Mercy Hospital	Elwood	74%	(a)
Union Hospital Clinton	Clinton	74%	300+
Bluffton Regional Medical Center	Bluffton	73%	300+
Clark Memorial Hospital	Jeffersonville	73%	300+
Decatur County Memorial Hospital	Greensburg	73%	(a)
Franciscan Physicians Hospital	Munster	73%	300+
The Indiana Heart Hospital	Indianapolis	73%	300+
Major Hospital	Shelbyville	73%	300+
Monroe Hospital	Bloomington	73%	300+
Parkview Lagrange Hospital	Lagrange	73%	(a)
Saint Francis Hospital Mooresville	Mooresville	73%	300+
Saint Vincent Dunn Hospital	Bedford	73%	300+
Saint Vincent Frankfort Hospital	Frankfort	73%	(a)
Dupont Hospital	Fort Wayne	72%	300+
Hancock Regional Hospital	Greenfield	72%	300+
Memorial Hospital and Health Care Center	Jasper	72%	300+
Memorial Hospital of South Bend	South Bend	72%	300+
Saint Catherine Hospital	East Chicago	72%	300+
Saint Francis Hospital and Health Centers	Beech Grove	72%	300+
Saint Vincent Hospital & Health Services	Indianapolis	72%	300+
Terre Haute Regional Hospital	Terre Haute	72%	300+
Witham Health Services	Lebanon	72%	300+
The Women's Hospital	Newburgh	72%	300+
Bedford Regional Medical Center	Bedford	71%	300+
Columbus Regional Hospital	Columbus	71%	300+
Comm Hosp of Anderson & Madison County	Anderson	71%	300+
Gibson General Hospital	Princeton	71%	(a)
Harrison County Hospital	Corydon	71%	300+
Hendricks Regional Health	Danville	71%	300+
IU Health Goshen Hospital	Goshen	71%	300+
Riverview Hospital	Noblesville	71%	300+
Saint Elizabeth Central	Lafayette	71%	300+
Saint Joseph Hospital	Fort Wayne	71%	300+
Saint Mary Medical Center	Hobart	71%	300+
Tipton Hospital	Tipton	71%	300+
Indiana University Health Arnett Hospital	Lafayette	70%	300+
Indiana University Health North Hospital	Carmel	70%	300+
The King's Daughters' Hospital	Madison	70%	300+
Kosciusko Community Hospital	Warsaw	70%	300+
Lutheran Hospital of Indiana	Fort Wayne	70%	300+
St Francis Hosp & Health Ctrs-Indianapolis	Indianapolis	70%	300+
Saint John's Health System	Anderson	70%	300+
Saint Joseph Regional Medical Center	Mishawaka	70%	300+
Saint Mary's Medical Center of Evansville	Evansville	70%	300+
Saint Vincent Clay Hospital	Brazil	70%	(a)
Bloomington Hospital	Bloomington	69%	300+
Johnson Memorial Hospital	Franklin	69%	300+
The Ortho Hosp of Lutheran Health Network	Fort Wayne	69%	300+
Saint Vincent Randolph Hospital	Winchester	69%	(a)
Saint Vincent Williamsport Hospital	Williamsport	69%	(a)
Sullivan County Community Hospital	Sullivan	69%	(a)
Community Hospital North	Indianapolis	68%	300+
Community Hospital South	Indianapolis	68%	300+
Elkhart General Hospital	Elkhart	68%	300+
Floyd Memorial Hospital and Health Services	New Albany	68%	300+
Franciscan St Anthony Health - Crown Point	Crown Point	68%	300+
Indiana University Health	Indianapolis	68%	300+
Reid Hospital & Health Care Services	Richmond	68%	300+
William N Wishard Memorial Hospital	Indianapolis	68%	300+
Daviess Community Hospital	Washington	67%	300+
Deaconess Hospital	Evansville	67%	300+
Dearborn County Hospital	Lawrenceburg	67%	300+
Laporte Hospital and Health Services	La Porte	67%	300+
Porter Valparaiso Hospital Campus	Valparaiso	67%	300+
Saint Joseph Hospital & Health Center	Kokomo	67%	300+
Starke Memorial Hospital	Knox	67%	(a)
Community Hospital East	Indianapolis	66%	300+
Franciscan St Margaret Health - Dyer	Dyer	66%	300+
Methodist Hospitals	Gary	66%	300+
Morgan Hospital and Medical Center	Martinsville	66%	300+
Orthopaedic Hospital at Parkview North	Fort Wayne	66%	300+
Union Hospital	Terre Haute	65%	300+
Saint Clare Medical Center	Crawfordsville	64%	300+
Westview Hospital	Indianapolis	64%	300+
Indiana University Health West Hospital	Avon	63%	300+
Franciscan St Margaret Health - Hammond	Hammond	62%	300+
Saint Catherine Regional Hospital	Charlestown	57%	(a)

47. Room and Bathroom 'Always' Clean

Hospital Name	City	Rate	Cases
Indiana Orthopaedic Hospital	Indianapolis	89%	300+
Good Samaritan Hospital	Vincennes	87%	300+
Saint Vincent Williamsport Hospital	Williamsport	87%	(a)
Monroe Hospital	Bloomington	85%	300+
Fayette Regional Health System	Connersville	84%	300+
Margaret Mary Community Hospital	Batesville	84%	300+
Memorial Hospital and Health Care Center	Jasper	84%	300+
Reid Hospital & Health Care Services	Richmond	84%	300+
Starke Memorial Hospital	Knox	84%	(a)
Wabash County Hospital	Wabash	84%	(a)
Cameron Memorial Community Hospital	Angola	83%	300+
Sullivan County Community Hospital	Sullivan	83%	(a)
Franciscan Physicians Hospital	Munster	82%	300+
Harrison County Hospital	Corydon	82%	300+
Major Hospital	Shelbyville	82%	300+
Scott Memorial Hospital	Scottsburg	82%	(a)
The Women's Hospital	Newburgh	82%	300+
Tipton Hospital	Tipton	81%	300+
Dearborn County Hospital	Lawrenceburg	80%	300+
Parkview Noble Hospital	Kendallville	80%	300+
Columbus Regional Hospital	Columbus	79%	300+
Dekalb Memorial Hospital	Auburn	79%	300+
Parkview Lagrange Hospital	Lagrange	79%	(a)
Saint Francis Hospital Mooresville	Mooresville	79%	300+
Saint Vincent Clay Hospital	Brazil	79%	(a)
Bluffton Regional Medical Center	Bluffton	78%	300+
Community Hospital	Munster	78%	300+
The Indiana Heart Hospital	Indianapolis	78%	300+
Memorial Hospital	Logansport	78%	300+
Parkview Whitley Hospital	Columbia City	78%	300+
Schneck Medical Center	Seymour	78%	300+
Clark Memorial Hospital	Jeffersonville	77%	300+
Franciscan St Anthony Health - Crown Point	Crown Point	77%	300+
Hendricks Regional Health	Danville	77%	300+
IU Health Goshen Hospital	Goshen	77%	300+
Saint Elizabeth East	Lafayette	77%	300+
Saint John's Health System	Anderson	77%	300+
Saint Mary Medical Center	Hobart	77%	300+
Saint Vincent Heart Center of Indiana	Indianapolis	77%	300+
Bedford Regional Medical Center	Bedford	76%	300+
Daviess Community Hospital	Washington	76%	300+
Hancock Regional Hospital	Greenfield	76%	300+
Riverview Hospital	Noblesville	76%	300+
Gibson General Hospital	Princeton	75%	(a)
Henry County Memorial Hospital	New Castle	75%	300+
Indiana University Health Arnett Hospital	Lafayette	75%	300+
Johnson Memorial Hospital	Franklin	75%	300+
Parkview Huntington Hospital	Huntington	75%	300+
Physicians' Medical Center	New Albany	75%	(a)
Saint Mary's Medical Center of Evansville	Evansville	75%	300+
Saint Vincent Carmel Hospital	Carmel	75%	300+
Union Hospital Clinton	Clinton	75%	300+
Witham Health Services	Lebanon	75%	300+
Indiana University Health West Hospital	Avon	74%	300+
The King's Daughters' Hospital	Madison	74%	300+
Marion General Hospital	Marion	74%	300+
Parkview Hospital	Fort Wayne	74%	300+
Saint Catherine Hospital	East Chicago	74%	300+
Saint Joseph Hospital	Fort Wayne	74%	300+
Saint Vincent Dunn Hospital	Bedford	74%	300+
Saint Vincent Frankfort Hospital	Frankfort	74%	(a)
Terre Haute Regional Hospital	Terre Haute	74%	300+
Comm Hosp of Anderson & Madison County	Anderson	73%	300+
Elkhart General Hospital	Elkhart	73%	300+
Dupont Hospital	Fort Wayne	72%	300+
Franciscan St Margaret Health - Dyer	Dyer	72%	300+
Orthopaedic Hospital at Parkview North	Fort Wayne	72%	300+
The Ortho Hosp of Lutheran Health Network	Fort Wayne	72%	300+
St Francis Hosp & Health Ctrs-Indianapolis	Indianapolis	72%	300+
Saint Joseph Hospital & Health Center	Kokomo	72%	300+
St Joseph's Reg Med Ctr-Plymouth	Plymouth	72%	300+
Saint Vincent Randolph Hospital	Winchester	72%	(a)
Union Hospital	Terre Haute	72%	300+
Floyd Memorial Hospital and Health Services	New Albany	71%	300+
Franciscan St Anthony Health-Michigan City	Michigan City	71%	300+
Jay County Hospital	Portland	71%	(a)
Ball Memorial Hospital	Muncie	70%	300+
Franciscan St Margaret Health - Hammond	Hammond	70%	300+
Howard Regional Health System	Kokomo	70%	300+
Laporte Hospital and Health Services	La Porte	70%	300+
Community Hospital North	Indianapolis	69%	300+
Deaconess Hospital	Evansville	69%	300+
Decatur County Memorial Hospital	Greensburg	69%	(a)
Indiana University Health North Hospital	Carmel	69%	300+
Kosciusko Community Hospital	Warsaw	69%	300+
Saint Francis Hospital and Health Centers	Beech Grove	69%	300+
Lutheran Hospital of Indiana	Fort Wayne	68%	300+
Memorial Hospital of South Bend	South Bend	68%	300+
Saint Clare Medical Center	Crawfordsville	68%	300+
Saint Elizabeth Central	Lafayette	68%	300+
Saint Joseph Regional Medical Center	Mishawaka	68%	300+
Saint Vincent Hospital & Health Services	Indianapolis	68%	300+
Saint Vincent Mercy Hospital	Elwood	68%	(a)
Westview Hospital	Indianapolis	68%	300+
Community Hospital South	Indianapolis	67%	300+
Dukes Memorial Hospital	Peru	67%	(a)
Bloomington Hospital	Bloomington	66%	300+
Morgan Hospital and Medical Center	Martinsville	66%	300+
William N Wishard Memorial Hospital	Indianapolis	66%	300+
Community Hospital East	Indianapolis	65%	300+
Indiana University Health	Indianapolis	63%	300+
Porter Valparaiso Hospital Campus	Valparaiso	63%	300+
Methodist Hospitals	Gary	61%	300+
Saint Catherine Regional Hospital	Charlestown	54%	(a)

48. Timely Help 'Always' Received

Hospital Name	City	Rate	Cases
Physicians' Medical Center	New Albany	83%	(a)
Cameron Memorial Community Hospital	Angola	81%	300+
Wabash County Hospital	Wabash	81%	(a)
Indiana Orthopaedic Hospital	Indianapolis	80%	300+
Parkview Whitley Hospital	Columbia City	79%	300+
Scott Memorial Hospital	Scottsburg	79%	(a)
Saint Vincent Williamsport Hospital	Williamsport	78%	(a)
Dekalb Memorial Hospital	Auburn	77%	300+
Saint Vincent Dunn Hospital	Bedford	77%	300+
Saint Vincent Heart Center of Indiana	Indianapolis	77%	300+
Fayette Regional Health System	Connersville	76%	300+
Franciscan Physicians Hospital	Munster	76%	300+

NOTE: Hospital profiles are in alphabetical order by state, then city, then hospital within the city; Rankings exclude hospitals with less than 25 cases except for patient surveys which excludes hospitals with less than 100 cases; (a) 100–299 cases; (1) The number of cases is too small to be sure how well a hospital is performing; (2) The hospital indicated that the data submitted for this measure were based on a sample of cases; (3) Data was collected during a shorter time period (fewer quarters) than the maximum possible time for this measure; (4) Suppressed for one or more quarters by CMS; (5) No data is available from the hospital for this measure; (6) Fewer than 100 patients completed the HCAHPS survey. Use these rates with caution, as the number of surveys may be too low to reliably assess hospital performance; (7) Survey results are based on less than 12 months of data; (8) Survey results are not available for this reporting period; (9) No or very few patients were eligible for the HCAHPS survey. The scores shown, if any, reflect a very small number of surveys; (10) A state average was not calculated because too few hospitals in the state submitted data; (11) There were discrepancies in the data collection process; Please refer to the User's Guide for a full explanation of data.

Good Samaritan Hospital	Vincennes	76%	300+
Margaret Mary Community Hospital	Batesville	76%	300+
Major Hospital	Shelbyville	75%	300+
Sullivan County Community Hospital	Sullivan	75%	(a)
Union Hospital Clinton	Clinton	75%	300+
The Indiana Heart Hospital	Indianapolis	74%	300+
Jay County Hospital	Portland	74%	(a)
Parkview Huntington Hospital	Huntington	74%	300+
St Joseph's Reg Med Ctr-Plymouth	Plymouth	74%	300+
Saint Vincent Frankfort Hospital	Frankfort	74%	(a)
Gibson General Hospital	Princeton	73%	(a)
Marion General Hospital	Marion	73%	300+
Memorial Hospital	Logansport	73%	300+
The King's Daughters' Hospital	Madison	72%	300+
Orthopaedic Hospital at Parkview North	Fort Wayne	72%	300+
Parkview Noble Hospital	Kendallville	72%	300+
Schneck Medical Center	Seymour	72%	300+
Starke Memorial Hospital	Knox	72%	(a)
Harrison County Hospital	Corydon	71%	300+
Parkview Lagrange Hospital	Lagrange	71%	(a)
Dukes Memorial Hospital	Peru	70%	(a)
IU Health Goshen Hospital	Goshen	70%	300+
Saint Vincent Carmel Hospital	Carmel	70%	300+
Saint Vincent Randolph Hospital	Winchester	70%	(a)
Community Hospital	Munster	69%	300+
Daviess Community Hospital	Washington	69%	300+
Floyd Memorial Hospital and Health Services	New Albany	69%	300+
St Francis Hosp & Health Ctrs-Indianapolis	Indianapolis	69%	300+
Witham Health Services	Lebanon	69%	300+
Bedford Regional Medical Center	Bedford	68%	300+
Dearborn County Hospital	Lawrenceburg	68%	300+
Johnson Memorial Hospital	Franklin	68%	300+
Memorial Hospital and Health Care Center	Jasper	68%	300+
The Ortho Hosp of Lutheran Health Network	Fort Wayne	68%	300+
Parkview Hospital	Fort Wayne	68%	300+
Saint Mary's Medical Center of Evansville	Evansville	68%	300+
Tipton Hospital	Tipton	68%	300+
Bluffton Regional Medical Center	Bluffton	67%	300+
Clark Memorial Hospital	Jeffersonville	67%	300+
Comm Hosp of Anderson & Madison County	Anderson	67%	300+
Decatur County Memorial Hospital	Greensburg	67%	(a)
Franciscan St Anthony Health-Michigan City	Michigan City	67%	300+
Hancock Regional Hospital	Greenfield	67%	300+
Monroe Hospital	Bloomington	67%	300+
Saint Catherine Hospital	East Chicago	67%	300+
Saint John's Health System	Anderson	67%	300+
Terre Haute Regional Hospital	Terre Haute	67%	300+
The Women's Hospital	Newburgh	67%	300+
Henry County Memorial Hospital	New Castle	66%	300+
Memorial Hospital of South Bend	South Bend	66%	300+
Saint Joseph Hospital	Fort Wayne	66%	300+
Saint Mary Medical Center	Hobart	66%	300+
Dupont Hospital	Fort Wayne	65%	300+
Lutheran Hospital of Indiana	Fort Wayne	65%	300+
Saint Vincent Mercy Hospital	Elwood	65%	(a)
Bloomington Hospital	Bloomington	64%	300+
Columbus Regional Hospital	Columbus	64%	300+
Saint Francis Hospital Mooresville	Mooresville	64%	300+
Howard Regional Health System	Kokomo	63%	300+
Laporte Hospital and Health Services	La Porte	63%	300+
Saint Vincent Hospital & Health Services	Indianapolis	63%	300+
Union Hospital	Terre Haute	63%	300+
Hendricks Regional Health	Danville	62%	300+
Morgan Hospital and Medical Center	Martinsville	62%	300+
Riverview Hospital	Noblesville	62%	300+
Saint Joseph Hospital & Health Center	Kokomo	62%	300+
Saint Joseph Regional Medical Center	Mishawaka	62%	300+
Ball Memorial Hospital	Muncie	61%	300+
Community Hospital South	Indianapolis	61%	300+
Elkhart General Hospital	Elkhart	61%	300+
Indiana University Health Arnett Hospital	Lafayette	61%	300+
Saint Clare Medical Center	Crawfordsville	61%	300+
Community Hospital East	Indianapolis	60%	300+
Indiana University Health North Hospital	Carmel	60%	300+
Indiana University Health West Hospital	Avon	60%	300+
Saint Elizabeth East	Lafayette	60%	300+
Saint Vincent Clay Hospital	Brazil	60%	(a)
Deaconess Hospital	Evansville	59%	300+
Reid Hospital & Health Care Services	Richmond	59%	300+
Saint Francis Hospital and Health Centers	Beech Grove	59%	300+
Kosciusko Community Hospital	Warsaw	58%	300+
Saint Elizabeth Central	Lafayette	58%	300+
Franciscan St Margaret Health - Dyer	Dyer	57%	300+
Westview Hospital	Indianapolis	57%	300+
William N Wishard Memorial Hospital	Indianapolis	56%	300+
Community Hospital North	Indianapolis	55%	300+
Franciscan St Anthony Health - Crown Point	Crown Point	55%	300+
Saint Catherine Regional Hospital	Charlestown	54%	(a)
Franciscan St Margaret Health - Hammond	Hammond	53%	300+
Indiana University Health	Indianapolis	52%	300+
Methodist Hospitals	Gary	52%	300+
Porter Valparaiso Hospital Campus	Valparaiso	51%	300+

49. Would Definitely Recommend Hospital

Hospital Name	City	Rate	Cases
Saint Vincent Heart Center of Indiana	Indianapolis	92%	300+
Indiana Orthopaedic Hospital	Indianapolis	91%	300+
The Indiana Heart Hospital	Indianapolis	87%	300+
The Women's Hospital	Newburgh	86%	300+
Margaret Mary Community Hospital	Batesville	85%	300+
Saint Vincent Carmel Hospital	Carmel	85%	300+
Indiana University Health North Hospital	Carmel	84%	300+
Saint Francis Hospital Mooresville	Mooresville	84%	300+
Hendricks Regional Health	Danville	83%	300+
Physicians' Medical Center	New Albany	83%	(a)
Floyd Memorial Hospital and Health Services	New Albany	82%	300+
Orthopaedic Hospital at Parkview North	Fort Wayne	82%	300+
Saint Mary's Medical Center of Evansville	Evansville	82%	300+
Tipton Hospital	Tipton	81%	300+
Community Hospital	Munster	80%	300+
The Ortho Hosp of Lutheran Health Network	Fort Wayne	80%	300+
Saint Mary Medical Center	Hobart	80%	300+
Saint Vincent Hospital & Health Services	Indianapolis	80%	300+
Community Hospital North	Indianapolis	79%	300+
Dupont Hospital	Fort Wayne	79%	300+
Good Samaritan Hospital	Vincennes	79%	300+
St Francis Hosp & Health Ctrs-Indianapolis	Indianapolis	79%	300+
Saint Joseph Hospital & Health Center	Kokomo	79%	300+
Lutheran Hospital of Indiana	Fort Wayne	78%	300+
Memorial Hospital and Health Care Center	Jasper	78%	300+
Parkview Hospital	Fort Wayne	78%	300+
Parkview Whitley Hospital	Columbia City	78%	300+
Schneck Medical Center	Seymour	78%	300+
Comm Hosp of Anderson & Madison County	Anderson	77%	300+
Indiana University Health Arnett Hospital	Lafayette	77%	300+
Indiana University Health West Hospital	Avon	77%	300+
Monroe Hospital	Bloomington	77%	300+
Parkview Noble Hospital	Kendallville	77%	300+
Saint Joseph Regional Medical Center	Mishawaka	77%	300+
St Joseph's Reg Med Ctr-Plymouth	Plymouth	77%	300+
Dekalb Memorial Hospital	Auburn	76%	300+
Memorial Hospital of South Bend	South Bend	76%	300+
Saint John's Health System	Anderson	76%	300+
Parkview Huntington Hospital	Huntington	75%	300+
Parkview Lagrange Hospital	Lagrange	75%	(a)
Bloomington Hospital	Bloomington	74%	300+
Clark Memorial Hospital	Jeffersonville	74%	300+
Franciscan Physicians Hospital	Munster	74%	300+
IU Health Goshen Hospital	Goshen	74%	300+
Jay County Hospital	Portland	74%	(a)
Saint Vincent Dunn Hospital	Bedford	74%	300+
Terre Haute Regional Hospital	Terre Haute	74%	300+
Witham Health Services	Lebanon	74%	300+
Franciscan St Anthony Health - Crown Point	Crown Point	73%	300+
Reid Hospital & Health Care Services	Richmond	73%	300+
Bedford Regional Medical Center	Bedford	72%	300+
Columbus Regional Hospital	Columbus	72%	300+
Deaconess Hospital	Evansville	72%	300+
Hancock Regional Hospital	Greenfield	72%	300+
Major Hospital	Shelbyville	72%	300+
Riverview Hospital	Noblesville	72%	300+
Saint Elizabeth East	Lafayette	72%	300+
Saint Francis Hospital and Health Centers	Beech Grove	72%	300+
Scott Memorial Hospital	Scottsburg	72%	(a)
Sullivan County Community Hospital	Sullivan	72%	(a)
Community Hospital South	Indianapolis	71%	300+
Harrison County Hospital	Corydon	71%	300+
Howard Regional Health System	Kokomo	71%	300+
Johnson Memorial Hospital	Franklin	71%	300+
Saint Catherine Hospital	East Chicago	71%	300+
Union Hospital	Terre Haute	71%	300+
William N Wishard Memorial Hospital	Indianapolis	71%	300+
Bluffton Regional Medical Center	Bluffton	70%	300+
Henry County Memorial Hospital	New Castle	70%	300+
Saint Elizabeth Central	Lafayette	70%	300+
Cameron Memorial Community Hospital	Angola	69%	300+
Elkhart General Hospital	Elkhart	69%	300+
Saint Joseph Hospital	Fort Wayne	69%	300+
Franciscan St Anthony Health-Michigan City	Michigan City	68%	300+
Gibson General Hospital	Princeton	68%	(a)
Indiana University Health	Indianapolis	68%	300+
Saint Vincent Mercy Hospital	Elwood	68%	(a)
Saint Vincent Williamsport Hospital	Williamsport	68%	(a)
Union Hospital Clinton	Clinton	68%	300+
Saint Vincent Frankfort Hospital	Frankfort	67%	(a)
Westview Hospital	Indianapolis	67%	300+
Community Hospital East	Indianapolis	66%	300+
Dukes Memorial Hospital	Peru	66%	(a)
Fayette Regional Health System	Connersville	66%	300+
Laporte Hospital and Health Services	La Porte	66%	300+
Marion General Hospital	Marion	66%	300+
Wabash County Hospital	Wabash	66%	(a)
Ball Memorial Hospital	Muncie	65%	300+
Franciscan St Margaret Health - Dyer	Dyer	65%	300+
Dearborn County Hospital	Lawrenceburg	64%	300+
Decatur County Memorial Hospital	Greensburg	64%	(a)
Memorial Hospital	Logansport	64%	300+
The King's Daughters' Hospital	Madison	62%	300+
Saint Vincent Randolph Hospital	Winchester	61%	(a)
Porter Valparaiso Hospital Campus	Valparaiso	60%	300+
Kosciusko Community Hospital	Warsaw	59%	300+
Saint Clare Medical Center	Crawfordsville	59%	300+
Daviess Community Hospital	Washington	58%	300+
Franciscan St Margaret Health - Hammond	Hammond	57%	300+
Morgan Hospital and Medical Center	Martinsville	57%	300+
Saint Vincent Clay Hospital	Brazil	56%	(a)
Starke Memorial Hospital	Knox	56%	(a)
Methodist Hospitals	Gary	52%	300+
Saint Catherine Regional Hospital	Charlestown	52%	(a)

NOTE: Hospital profiles are in alphabetical order by state, then city, then hospital within the city; Rankings exclude hospitals with less than 25 cases except for patient surveys which excludes hospitals with less than 100 cases; (a) 100–299 cases; (1) The number of cases is too small to be sure how well a hospital is performing; (2) The hospital indicated that the data submitted for this measure were based on a sample of cases; (3) Data was collected during a shorter time period (fewer quarters) than the maximum possible time for this measure; (4) Suppressed for one or more quarters by CMS; (5) No data is available from the hospital for this measure; (6) Fewer than 100 patients completed the HCAHPS survey. Use these rates with caution, as the number of surveys may be too low to reliably assess hospital performance; (7) Survey results are based on less than 12 months of data; (8) Survey results are not available for this reporting period; (9) No or very few patients were eligible for the HCAHPS survey. The scores shown, if any, reflect a very small number of surveys; (10) A state average was not calculated because too few hospitals in the state submitted data; (11) There were discrepancies in the data collection process; Please refer to the User's Guide for a full explanation of data.

Community Hospital of Anderson and Madison County

1515 N Madison Ave
Anderson, IN 46011
Phone: 765-298-4242
URL: www.communityanderson.com
Type: Acute Care Hospitals
Emergency Services: Yes
Ownership: Voluntary Non-Profit - Other

Measure	Cases	This Hosp.	State Avg.	U.S. Avg.
Heart Attack Care				
ACE Inhibitor or ARB for LVSD[1]	16	100%	96%	96%
Aspirin at Arrival	54	98%	98%	99%
Aspirin at Discharge	37	89%	99%	98%
Beta Blocker at Discharge	49	100%	98%	98%
Fibrinolytic Medication Timing	0	-	37%	55%
PCI Within 90 Minutes of Arrival[1]	3	33%	93%	90%
Smoking Cessation Advice[1]	13	100%	99%	99%
Chest Pain/Possible Heart Attack Care				
Aspirin at Arrival	84	99%	95%	95%
Median Time to ECG (minutes)	89	10	6	8
Median Time to Transfer (minutes)[1]	19	41	49	61
Fibrinolytic Medication Timing	0	-	63%	54%
Heart Failure Care				
ACE Inhibitor or ARB for LVSD	66	100%	92%	94%
Discharge Instructions	178	97%	84%	88%
Evaluation of LVS Function	232	100%	98%	98%
Smoking Cessation Advice	49	100%	99%	98%
Pneumonia Care				
Appropriate Initial Antibiotic[2]	100	93%	90%	92%
Blood Culture Timing[2]	75	83%	95%	96%
Influenza Vaccine[2]	101	97%	93%	91%
Initial Antibiotic Timing[2]	155	96%	96%	95%
Pneumococcal Vaccine[2]	148	97%	94%	93%
Smoking Cessation Advice[2]	67	100%	98%	97%
Surgical Care Improvement Project				
Appropriate VTP Within 24 Hours	133	87%	90%	92%
Appropriate Hair Removal	486	100%	100%	99%
Appropriate Beta Blocker Usage	138	100%	93%	93%
Controlled Postoperative Blood Glucose	0	-	93%	93%
Prophylactic Antibiotic Timing	360	97%	97%	97%
Prophylactic Antibiotic Timing (Outpatient)	183	97%	92%	92%
Prophylactic Antibiotic Selection	360	99%	98%	97%
Prophylactic Antibiotic Select. (Outpatient)	184	99%	95%	94%
Prophylactic Antibiotic Stopped	351	96%	95%	94%
Recommended VTP Ordered	134	87%	92%	94%
Urinary Catheter Removal	124	94%	92%	90%
Children's Asthma Care				
Received Systemic Corticosteroids	-	-	-	100%
Received Home Management Plan	-	-	-	71%
Received Reliever Medication	-	-	-	100%
Use of Medical Imaging				
Combination Abdominal CT Scan	755	0.075	0.237	0.191
Combination Chest CT Scan	600	0.005	0.120	0.054
Follow-up Mammogram/Ultrasound	1,357	12.2%	8.3%	8.4%
MRI for Low Back Pain	199	37.7%	35.2%	32.7%
Survey of Patients' Hospital Experiences				
Area Around Room 'Always' Quiet at Night	300+	56%	-	58%
Doctors 'Always' Communicated Well	300+	83%	-	80%
Home Recovery Information Given	300+	85%	-	82%
Hospital Given 9 or 10 on 10 Point Scale	300+	74%	-	67%
Meds 'Always' Explained Before Given	300+	62%	-	60%
Nurses 'Always' Communicated Well	300+	79%	-	76%
Pain 'Always' Well Controlled	300+	71%	-	69%
Room and Bathroom 'Always' Clean	300+	73%	-	71%
Timely Help 'Always' Received	300+	67%	-	64%
Would Definitely Recommend Hospital	300+	77%	-	69%

Saint John's Health System

2015 Jackson St
Anderson, IN 46016
Phone: 765-649-2511
Fax: 765-646-8504
URL: www.stjohnshealthsystem.org
Type: Acute Care Hospitals
Emergency Services: Yes
Ownership: Voluntary Non-Profit - Private
Beds: 225

Key Personnel:
CEO/President. . . . . Tom Van Osdol
Pediatric In-Patient Care . . . . David Beahm, MD
Quality Assurance . . . . Ross Brodhead
Radiology. . . . . Henry Jones, MD
Anesthesiology. . . . . John Vu, MD
Emergency Room . . . . Robert Steele
Intensive Care Unit. . . . . Tracy MCallister

Measure	Cases	This Hosp.	State Avg.	U.S. Avg.
Heart Attack Care				
ACE Inhibitor or ARB for LVSD[1,2]	3	100%	96%	96%
Aspirin at Arrival[2]	46	98%	98%	99%
Aspirin at Discharge[2]	25	100%	99%	98%
Beta Blocker at Discharge[2]	29	100%	98%	98%
Fibrinolytic Medication Timing[2]	0	-	37%	55%
PCI Within 90 Minutes of Arrival[2]	0	-	93%	90%
Smoking Cessation Advice[1,2]	2	100%	99%	99%
Chest Pain/Possible Heart Attack Care				
Aspirin at Arrival	113	98%	95%	95%
Median Time to ECG (minutes)	117	8	6	8
Median Time to Transfer (minutes)[1]	22	400	49	61
Fibrinolytic Medication Timing	0	-	63%	54%
Heart Failure Care				
ACE Inhibitor or ARB for LVSD[2]	51	92%	92%	94%
Discharge Instructions[2]	110	95%	84%	88%
Evaluation of LVS Function[2]	160	95%	98%	98%
Smoking Cessation Advice[2]	34	100%	99%	98%
Pneumonia Care				
Appropriate Initial Antibiotic[2]	91	80%	90%	92%
Blood Culture Timing[2]	147	98%	95%	96%
Influenza Vaccine[2]	78	95%	93%	91%
Initial Antibiotic Timing[2]	138	98%	96%	95%
Pneumococcal Vaccine[2]	171	96%	94%	93%
Smoking Cessation Advice[2]	73	96%	98%	97%
Surgical Care Improvement Project				
Appropriate VTP Within 24 Hours[2]	104	86%	90%	92%
Appropriate Hair Removal[2]	360	100%	100%	99%
Appropriate Beta Blocker Usage[2]	89	98%	93%	93%
Controlled Postoperative Blood Glucose[2]	0	-	93%	93%
Prophylactic Antibiotic Timing[2]	234	98%	97%	97%
Prophylactic Antibiotic Timing (Outpatient)	178	94%	92%	92%
Prophylactic Antibiotic Selection[2]	235	96%	98%	97%
Prophylactic Antibiotic Select. (Outpatient)	180	98%	95%	94%
Prophylactic Antibiotic Stopped[2]	231	92%	95%	94%
Recommended VTP Ordered[2]	104	86%	92%	94%
Urinary Catheter Removal[2]	91	97%	92%	90%
Children's Asthma Care				
Received Systemic Corticosteroids	-	-	-	100%
Received Home Management Plan	-	-	-	71%
Received Reliever Medication	-	-	-	100%
Use of Medical Imaging				
Combination Abdominal CT Scan	915	0.111	0.237	0.191
Combination Chest CT Scan	928	0.028	0.120	0.054
Follow-up Mammogram/Ultrasound	1,805	10.2%	8.3%	8.4%
MRI for Low Back Pain	270	37.4%	35.2%	32.7%
Survey of Patients' Hospital Experiences				
Area Around Room 'Always' Quiet at Night	300+	53%	-	58%
Doctors 'Always' Communicated Well	300+	83%	-	80%
Home Recovery Information Given	300+	86%	-	82%
Hospital Given 9 or 10 on 10 Point Scale	300+	71%	-	67%
Meds 'Always' Explained Before Given	300+	59%	-	60%
Nurses 'Always' Communicated Well	300+	80%	-	76%
Pain 'Always' Well Controlled	300+	70%	-	69%
Room and Bathroom 'Always' Clean	300+	77%	-	71%
Timely Help 'Always' Received	300+	67%	-	64%
Would Definitely Recommend Hospital	300+	76%	-	69%

Cameron Memorial Community Hospital

416 E Maumee Street
Angola, IN 46703
Phone: 260-665-2141
Fax: 260-665-2879
URL: www.cameronmch.com
Type: Critical Access Hospitals
Emergency Services: Yes
Ownership: Voluntary Non-Profit - Private
Beds: 25

Key Personnel:
CEO/President. . . . . Dennis L Knapp
Chief of Medical Staff. . . . . Michael E Holton

Measure	Cases	This Hosp.	State Avg.	U.S. Avg.
Heart Attack Care				
ACE Inhibitor or ARB for LVSD[5]	0	-	96%	96%
Aspirin at Arrival[5]	0	-	98%	99%
Aspirin at Discharge[5]	0	-	99%	98%
Beta Blocker at Discharge[5]	0	-	98%	98%
Fibrinolytic Medication Timing[5]	0	-	37%	55%
PCI Within 90 Minutes of Arrival[5]	0	-	93%	90%
Smoking Cessation Advice[5]	0	-	99%	99%
Chest Pain/Possible Heart Attack Care				
Aspirin at Arrival	153	97%	95%	95%
Median Time to ECG (minutes)	158	6	6	8
Median Time to Transfer (minutes)[1]	24	53	49	61
Fibrinolytic Medication Timing[1]	2	0%	63%	54%
Heart Failure Care				
ACE Inhibitor or ARB for LVSD[1]	10	100%	92%	94%
Discharge Instructions	32	97%	84%	88%
Evaluation of LVS Function	47	83%	98%	98%
Smoking Cessation Advice[1]	6	100%	99%	98%
Pneumonia Care				
Appropriate Initial Antibiotic	53	92%	90%	92%
Blood Culture Timing	42	100%	95%	96%
Influenza Vaccine	56	96%	93%	91%
Initial Antibiotic Timing	90	98%	96%	95%
Pneumococcal Vaccine	68	99%	94%	93%
Smoking Cessation Advice[1]	18	89%	98%	97%
Surgical Care Improvement Project				
Appropriate VTP Within 24 Hours[1]	14	86%	90%	92%
Appropriate Hair Removal	29	100%	100%	99%
Appropriate Beta Blocker Usage[5]	0	-	93%	93%
Controlled Postoperative Blood Glucose	0	-	93%	93%
Prophylactic Antibiotic Timing[1]	12	75%	97%	97%
Prophylactic Antibiotic Timing (Outpatient)	39	79%	92%	92%
Prophylactic Antibiotic Selection[1]	12	100%	98%	97%
Prophylactic Antibiotic Select. (Outpatient)	38	95%	95%	94%
Prophylactic Antibiotic Stopped[1]	11	100%	95%	94%
Recommended VTP Ordered[1]	14	86%	92%	94%
Urinary Catheter Removal[1]	4	75%	92%	90%
Children's Asthma Care				
Received Systemic Corticosteroids	-	-	-	100%
Received Home Management Plan	-	-	-	71%
Received Reliever Medication	-	-	-	100%
Use of Medical Imaging				
Combination Abdominal CT Scan	303	0.241	0.237	0.191
Combination Chest CT Scan	205	0.010	0.120	0.054
Follow-up Mammogram/Ultrasound	411	8.0%	8.3%	8.4%
MRI for Low Back Pain	75	29.3%	35.2%	32.7%
Survey of Patients' Hospital Experiences				
Area Around Room 'Always' Quiet at Night	300+	58%	-	58%
Doctors 'Always' Communicated Well	300+	84%	-	80%
Home Recovery Information Given	300+	81%	-	82%
Hospital Given 9 or 10 on 10 Point Scale	300+	69%	-	67%
Meds 'Always' Explained Before Given	300+	61%	-	60%
Nurses 'Always' Communicated Well	300+	83%	-	76%
Pain 'Always' Well Controlled	300+	75%	-	69%
Room and Bathroom 'Always' Clean	300+	83%	-	71%
Timely Help 'Always' Received	300+	81%	-	64%
Would Definitely Recommend Hospital	300+	69%	-	69%

NOTE: Hospital profiles are in alphabetical order by state, then city, then hospital within the city; Rankings exclude hospitals with less than 25 cases except for patient surveys which excludes hospitals with less than 100 cases; (a) 100–299 cases; (1) The number of cases is too small to be sure how well a hospital is performing; (2) The hospital indicated that the data submitted for this measure were based on a sample of cases; (3) Data was collected during a shorter time period (fewer quarters) than the maximum possible time for this measure; (4) Suppressed for one or more quarters by CMS; (5) No data is available from the hospital for this measure; (6) Fewer than 100 patients completed the HCAHPS survey. Use these rates with caution, as the number of surveys may be too low to reliably assess hospital performance; (7) Survey results are based on less than 12 months of data; (8) Survey results are not available for this reporting period; (9) No or very few patients were eligible for the HCAHPS survey. The scores shown, if any, reflect a very small number of surveys; (10) A state average was not calculated because too few hospitals in the state submitted data; (11) There were discrepancies in the data collection process; Please refer to the User's Guide for a full explanation of data.

Dekalb Memorial Hospital

1316 E Seventh Street
Auburn, IN 46706
Phone: 260-925-4600
Fax: 260-925-4733
E-mail: info@dekalbmemorial.com
URL: www.dekalbmemorial.com
Type: Acute Care Hospitals
Emergency Services: Yes
Ownership: Voluntary Non-Profit - Private
Beds: 47

Key Personnel:

CEO/President. . . . . JM Corey
Chief of Medical Staff. . . . . Khin Mar Oo, MD
Infection Control. . . . . Mary Bigelow, RN
Operating Room. . . . . Jeffrey Justice, RN
Pediatric Ambulatory Care . . . . . . David Marquis, MD
Pediatric In-Patient Care . . . . David Marquis, MD
Quality Assurance . . . . Cheryl Markiton, RN

Measure	Cases	This Hosp.	State Avg.	U.S. Avg.
Heart Attack Care				
ACE Inhibitor or ARB for LVSD[1]	1	100%	96%	96%
Aspirin at Arrival[1]	14	93%	98%	99%
Aspirin at Discharge[1]	13	92%	99%	98%
Beta Blocker at Discharge[1]	14	100%	98%	98%
Fibrinolytic Medication Timing	0	-	37%	55%
PCI Within 90 Minutes of Arrival	0	-	93%	90%
Smoking Cessation Advice[1]	1	100%	99%	99%
Chest Pain/Possible Heart Attack Care				
Aspirin at Arrival	112	96%	95%	95%
Median Time to ECG (minutes)	115	10	6	8
Median Time to Transfer (minutes)[1,3]	3	48	49	61
Fibrinolytic Medication Timing[1]	3	67%	63%	54%
Heart Failure Care				
ACE Inhibitor or ARB for LVSD[1]	11	82%	92%	94%
Discharge Instructions	38	79%	84%	88%
Evaluation of LVS Function	59	98%	98%	98%
Smoking Cessation Advice[1]	7	100%	99%	98%
Pneumonia Care				
Appropriate Initial Antibiotic	72	100%	90%	92%
Blood Culture Timing	70	100%	95%	96%
Influenza Vaccine	59	97%	93%	91%
Initial Antibiotic Timing	97	100%	96%	95%
Pneumococcal Vaccine	86	98%	94%	93%
Smoking Cessation Advice	42	100%	98%	97%
Surgical Care Improvement Project				
Appropriate VTP Within 24 Hours	30	93%	90%	92%
Appropriate Hair Removal	70	100%	100%	99%
Appropriate Beta Blocker Usage[1]	13	92%	93%	93%
Controlled Postoperative Blood Glucose	0	-	93%	93%
Prophylactic Antibiotic Timing	36	100%	97%	97%
Prophylactic Antibiotic Timing (Outpatient)	113	97%	92%	92%
Prophylactic Antibiotic Selection	36	94%	98%	97%
Prophylactic Antibiotic Select. (Outpatient)	113	100%	95%	94%
Prophylactic Antibiotic Stopped	35	97%	95%	94%
Recommended VTP Ordered	30	100%	92%	94%
Urinary Catheter Removal[1]	4	100%	92%	90%
Children's Asthma Care				
Received Systemic Corticosteroids	-	-	-	100%
Received Home Management Plan	-	-	-	71%
Received Reliever Medication	-	-	-	100%
Use of Medical Imaging				
Combination Abdominal CT Scan	344	0.360	0.237	0.191
Combination Chest CT Scan	149	0.000	0.120	0.054
Follow-up Mammogram/Ultrasound	365	11.0%	8.3%	8.4%
MRI for Low Back Pain[1]	50	30.0%	35.2%	32.7%
Survey of Patients' Hospital Experiences				
Area Around Room 'Always' Quiet at Night	300+	55%	-	58%
Doctors 'Always' Communicated Well	300+	90%	-	80%
Home Recovery Information Given	300+	86%	-	82%
Hospital Given 9 or 10 on 10 Point Scale	300+	79%	-	67%
Meds 'Always' Explained Before Given	300+	68%	-	60%
Nurses 'Always' Communicated Well	300+	81%	-	76%
Pain 'Always' Well Controlled	300+	75%	-	69%
Room and Bathroom 'Always' Clean	300+	79%	-	71%
Timely Help 'Always' Received	300+	77%	-	64%
Would Definitely Recommend Hospital	300+	76%	-	69%

Indiana University Health West Hospital

1111 N Ronald Reagan Parkway
Avon, IN 46123
Phone: 317-217-3000
Type: Acute Care Hospitals
Emergency Services: Yes
Ownership: Voluntary Non-Profit - Private

Key Personnel:

CEO/President. . . . . Al Gatmaitan FACHE

Measure	Cases	This Hosp.	State Avg.	U.S. Avg.
Heart Attack Care				
ACE Inhibitor or ARB for LVSD[1]	8	88%	96%	96%
Aspirin at Arrival	89	96%	98%	99%
Aspirin at Discharge	70	99%	99%	98%
Beta Blocker at Discharge	63	95%	98%	98%
Fibrinolytic Medication Timing	0	-	37%	55%
PCI Within 90 Minutes of Arrival	0	-	93%	90%
Smoking Cessation Advice[1]	15	100%	99%	99%
Chest Pain/Possible Heart Attack Care				
Aspirin at Arrival	56	93%	95%	95%
Median Time to ECG (minutes)	58	8	6	8
Median Time to Transfer (minutes)[1,3]	15	43	49	61
Fibrinolytic Medication Timing	0	-	63%	54%
Heart Failure Care				
ACE Inhibitor or ARB for LVSD	39	90%	92%	94%
Discharge Instructions	108	88%	84%	88%
Evaluation of LVS Function	153	100%	98%	98%
Smoking Cessation Advice[1]	15	100%	99%	98%
Pneumonia Care				
Appropriate Initial Antibiotic[2]	73	99%	90%	92%
Blood Culture Timing[2]	153	88%	95%	96%
Influenza Vaccine[2]	77	95%	93%	91%
Initial Antibiotic Timing[2]	122	99%	96%	95%
Pneumococcal Vaccine[2]	123	99%	94%	93%
Smoking Cessation Advice[2]	55	100%	98%	97%
Surgical Care Improvement Project				
Appropriate VTP Within 24 Hours[2]	104	89%	90%	92%
Appropriate Hair Removal[2]	271	100%	100%	99%
Appropriate Beta Blocker Usage[2]	44	80%	93%	93%
Controlled Postoperative Blood Glucose[2]	0	-	93%	93%
Prophylactic Antibiotic Timing[2]	172	99%	97%	97%
Prophylactic Antibiotic Timing (Outpatient)	190	96%	92%	92%
Prophylactic Antibiotic Selection[2]	172	99%	98%	97%
Prophylactic Antibiotic Select. (Outpatient)	186	98%	95%	94%
Prophylactic Antibiotic Stopped[2]	164	92%	95%	94%
Recommended VTP Ordered[2]	104	95%	92%	94%
Urinary Catheter Removal[2]	70	79%	92%	90%
Children's Asthma Care				
Received Systemic Corticosteroids	-	-	-	100%
Received Home Management Plan	-	-	-	71%
Received Reliever Medication	-	-	-	100%
Use of Medical Imaging				
Combination Abdominal CT Scan	623	0.064	0.237	0.191
Combination Chest CT Scan	532	0.013	0.120	0.054
Follow-up Mammogram/Ultrasound	524	11.8%	8.3%	8.4%
MRI for Low Back Pain	145	34.5%	35.2%	32.7%
Survey of Patients' Hospital Experiences				
Area Around Room 'Always' Quiet at Night	300+	60%	-	58%
Doctors 'Always' Communicated Well	300+	78%	-	80%
Home Recovery Information Given	300+	80%	-	82%
Hospital Given 9 or 10 on 10 Point Scale	300+	77%	-	67%
Meds 'Always' Explained Before Given	300+	54%	-	60%
Nurses 'Always' Communicated Well	300+	71%	-	76%
Pain 'Always' Well Controlled	300+	63%	-	69%
Room and Bathroom 'Always' Clean	300+	74%	-	71%
Timely Help 'Always' Received	300+	60%	-	64%
Would Definitely Recommend Hospital	300+	77%	-	69%

Margaret Mary Community Hospital

321 Mitchell Avenue
Batesville, IN 47006
Phone: 812-934-6624
Fax: 812-934-5373
E-mail: mmch@venus.net
URL: www.mmch.org
Type: Critical Access Hospitals
Emergency Services: Yes
Ownership: Voluntary Non-Profit - Private
Beds: 79

Key Personnel:

CEO/President. . . . . Timothy L Putnam
Chief of Medical Staff. . . . . Janet Ford, MD
Infection Control. . . . . Lisa Banks
Operating Room. . . . . Brian Albers
Quality Assurance . . . . Lisa Banks
Radiology. . . . . James Browne

Measure	Cases	This Hosp.	State Avg.	U.S. Avg.
Heart Attack Care				
ACE Inhibitor or ARB for LVSD[5]	0	-	96%	96%
Aspirin at Arrival[5]	0	-	98%	99%
Aspirin at Discharge[5]	0	-	99%	98%
Beta Blocker at Discharge[5]	0	-	98%	98%
Fibrinolytic Medication Timing[5]	0	-	37%	55%
PCI Within 90 Minutes of Arrival[5]	0	-	93%	90%
Smoking Cessation Advice[5]	0	-	99%	99%
Chest Pain/Possible Heart Attack Care				
Aspirin at Arrival	114	96%	95%	95%
Median Time to ECG (minutes)	118	6	6	8
Median Time to Transfer (minutes)[1,3]	6	76	49	61
Fibrinolytic Medication Timing[1]	9	33%	63%	54%
Heart Failure Care				
ACE Inhibitor or ARB for LVSD[1]	14	86%	92%	94%
Discharge Instructions	50	96%	84%	88%
Evaluation of LVS Function	74	99%	98%	98%
Smoking Cessation Advice[1]	13	100%	99%	98%
Pneumonia Care				
Appropriate Initial Antibiotic	67	99%	90%	92%
Blood Culture Timing	92	97%	95%	96%
Influenza Vaccine	77	87%	93%	91%
Initial Antibiotic Timing	95	100%	96%	95%
Pneumococcal Vaccine	105	80%	94%	93%
Smoking Cessation Advice	38	100%	98%	97%
Surgical Care Improvement Project				
Appropriate VTP Within 24 Hours	50	76%	90%	92%
Appropriate Hair Removal	160	99%	100%	99%
Appropriate Beta Blocker Usage	33	85%	93%	93%
Controlled Postoperative Blood Glucose[5]	0	-	93%	93%
Prophylactic Antibiotic Timing	120	98%	97%	97%
Prophylactic Antibiotic Timing (Outpatient)	68	75%	92%	92%
Prophylactic Antibiotic Selection	120	98%	98%	97%
Prophylactic Antibiotic Select. (Outpatient)	60	85%	95%	94%
Prophylactic Antibiotic Stopped	117	90%	95%	94%
Recommended VTP Ordered	50	76%	92%	94%
Urinary Catheter Removal[1]	20	95%	92%	90%
Children's Asthma Care				
Received Systemic Corticosteroids	-	-	-	100%
Received Home Management Plan	-	-	-	71%
Received Reliever Medication	-	-	-	100%
Use of Medical Imaging				
Combination Abdominal CT Scan	344	0.169	0.237	0.191
Combination Chest CT Scan	231	0.186	0.120	0.054
Follow-up Mammogram/Ultrasound	416	14.7%	8.3%	8.4%
MRI for Low Back Pain	61	32.8%	35.2%	32.7%
Survey of Patients' Hospital Experiences				
Area Around Room 'Always' Quiet at Night	300+	56%	-	58%
Doctors 'Always' Communicated Well	300+	88%	-	80%
Home Recovery Information Given	300+	84%	-	82%
Hospital Given 9 or 10 on 10 Point Scale	300+	82%	-	67%
Meds 'Always' Explained Before Given	300+	64%	-	60%
Nurses 'Always' Communicated Well	300+	86%	-	76%
Pain 'Always' Well Controlled	300+	79%	-	69%
Room and Bathroom 'Always' Clean	300+	84%	-	71%
Timely Help 'Always' Received	300+	76%	-	64%
Would Definitely Recommend Hospital	300+	85%	-	69%

NOTE: Hospital profiles are in alphabetical order by state, then city, then hospital within the city; Rankings exclude hospitals with less than 25 cases except for patient surveys which excludes hospitals with less than 100 cases; (a) 100–299 cases; (1) The number of cases is too small to be sure how well a hospital is performing; (2) The hospital indicated that the data submitted for this measure were based on a sample of cases; (3) Data was collected during a shorter time period (fewer quarters) than the maximum possible time for this measure; (4) Suppressed for one or more quarters by CMS; (5) No data is available from the hospital for this measure; (6) Fewer than 100 patients completed the HCAHPS survey. Use these rates with caution, as the number of surveys may be too low to reliably assess hospital performance; (7) Survey results are based on less than 12 months of data; (8) Survey results are not available for this reporting period; (9) No or very few patients were eligible for the HCAHPS survey. The scores shown, if any, reflect a very small number of surveys; (10) A state average was not calculated because too few hospitals in the state submitted data; (11) There were discrepancies in the data collection process; Please refer to the User's Guide for a full explanation of data.

Bedford Regional Medical Center

2900 W 16th St Phone: 812-275-1200
Bedford, IN 47421 Fax: 812-275-1450
E-mail: kellis@kiva.net
URL: www.brmchealthcare.com
Type: Critical Access Hospitals Emergency Services: Yes
Ownership: Voluntary Non-Profit - Private Beds: 49

Key Personnel:
CEO/President. . . . . Bradford W Dykes
Chief of Medical Staff . . . . Cristina Bickford
Radiology. . . . . Steven A Archibald

Measure	Cases	This Hosp.	State Avg.	U.S. Avg.
Heart Attack Care				
ACE Inhibitor or ARB for LVSD[1]	5	100%	96%	96%
Aspirin at Arrival	37	92%	98%	99%
Aspirin at Discharge	34	97%	99%	98%
Beta Blocker at Discharge	33	100%	98%	98%
Fibrinolytic Medication Timing	0	-	37%	55%
PCI Within 90 Minutes of Arrival	0	-	93%	90%
Smoking Cessation Advice[1]	9	89%	99%	99%
Chest Pain/Possible Heart Attack Care				
Aspirin at Arrival[1,3]	23	100%	95%	95%
Median Time to ECG (minutes)[3]	25	6	6	8
Median Time to Transfer (minutes)[1,3]	2	66	49	61
Fibrinolytic Medication Timing[3]	0	-	63%	54%
Heart Failure Care				
ACE Inhibitor or ARB for LVSD[1]	24	79%	92%	94%
Discharge Instructions	43	84%	84%	88%
Evaluation of LVS Function	55	95%	98%	98%
Smoking Cessation Advice[1]	10	100%	99%	98%
Pneumonia Care				
Appropriate Initial Antibiotic	56	82%	90%	92%
Blood Culture Timing	102	97%	95%	96%
Influenza Vaccine	37	95%	93%	91%
Initial Antibiotic Timing	92	99%	96%	95%
Pneumococcal Vaccine	75	99%	94%	93%
Smoking Cessation Advice	37	89%	98%	97%
Surgical Care Improvement Project				
Appropriate VTP Within 24 Hours	53	100%	90%	92%
Appropriate Hair Removal	131	100%	100%	99%
Appropriate Beta Blocker Usage	31	90%	93%	93%
Controlled Postoperative Blood Glucose[3]	0	-	93%	93%
Prophylactic Antibiotic Timing	99	98%	97%	97%
Prophylactic Antibiotic Timing (Outpatient)[1,3]	15	100%	92%	92%
Prophylactic Antibiotic Selection	99	98%	98%	97%
Prophylactic Antibiotic Select. (Outpatient)[1,3]	15	93%	95%	94%
Prophylactic Antibiotic Stopped	95	98%	95%	94%
Recommended VTP Ordered	53	100%	92%	94%
Urinary Catheter Removal	30	73%	92%	90%
Children's Asthma Care				
Received Systemic Corticosteroids	-	-	-	100%
Received Home Management Plan	-	-	-	71%
Received Reliever Medication	-	-	-	100%
Use of Medical Imaging				
Combination Abdominal CT Scan	452	0.354	0.237	0.191
Combination Chest CT Scan	245	0.363	0.120	0.054
Follow-up Mammogram/Ultrasound	598	3.2%	8.3%	8.4%
MRI for Low Back Pain	83	38.6%	35.2%	32.7%
Survey of Patients' Hospital Experiences				
Area Around Room 'Always' Quiet at Night	300+	44%	-	58%
Doctors 'Always' Communicated Well	300+	84%	-	80%
Home Recovery Information Given	300+	83%	-	82%
Hospital Given 9 or 10 on 10 Point Scale	300+	72%	-	67%
Meds 'Always' Explained Before Given	300+	67%	-	60%
Nurses 'Always' Communicated Well	300+	79%	-	76%
Pain 'Always' Well Controlled	300+	71%	-	69%
Room and Bathroom 'Always' Clean	300+	76%	-	71%
Timely Help 'Always' Received	300+	68%	-	64%
Would Definitely Recommend Hospital	300+	72%	-	69%

Saint Vincent Dunn Hospital

1600 23rd Street Phone: 812-275-3331
Bedford, IN 47421 Fax: 812-276-1211
Type: Critical Access Hospitals Emergency Services: Yes
Ownership: Voluntary Non-Profit - Other Beds: 137

Key Personnel:
CEO/President. . . . . D Bruner
Cardiac Laboratory. . . . . Audi Baer
Chief of Medical Staff . . . . RB Kalari
Emergency Room . . . . Rodney Beeler

Measure	Cases	This Hosp.	State Avg.	U.S. Avg.
Heart Attack Care				
ACE Inhibitor or ARB for LVSD[1]	14	100%	96%	96%
Aspirin at Arrival	81	99%	98%	99%
Aspirin at Discharge	92	100%	99%	98%
Beta Blocker at Discharge	88	100%	98%	98%
Fibrinolytic Medication Timing	0	-	37%	55%
PCI Within 90 Minutes of Arrival[1]	21	100%	93%	90%
Smoking Cessation Advice	32	100%	99%	99%
Chest Pain/Possible Heart Attack Care				
Aspirin at Arrival	75	97%	95%	95%
Median Time to ECG (minutes)	80	3	6	8
Median Time to Transfer (minutes)[1]	17	37	49	61
Fibrinolytic Medication Timing	0	-	63%	54%
Heart Failure Care				
ACE Inhibitor or ARB for LVSD[1]	22	95%	92%	94%
Discharge Instructions	55	98%	84%	88%
Evaluation of LVS Function	88	97%	98%	98%
Smoking Cessation Advice[1]	18	94%	99%	98%
Pneumonia Care				
Appropriate Initial Antibiotic	48	90%	90%	92%
Blood Culture Timing	66	94%	95%	96%
Influenza Vaccine	55	98%	93%	91%
Initial Antibiotic Timing	72	100%	96%	95%
Pneumococcal Vaccine	73	97%	94%	93%
Smoking Cessation Advice	26	100%	98%	97%
Surgical Care Improvement Project				
Appropriate VTP Within 24 Hours	27	96%	90%	92%
Appropriate Hair Removal	50	100%	100%	99%
Appropriate Beta Blocker Usage[1]	13	54%	93%	93%
Controlled Postoperative Blood Glucose	0	-	93%	93%
Prophylactic Antibiotic Timing[1]	24	100%	97%	97%
Prophylactic Antibiotic Timing (Outpatient)[1]	23	91%	92%	92%
Prophylactic Antibiotic Selection	29	93%	98%	97%
Prophylactic Antibiotic Select. (Outpatient)[1]	21	81%	95%	94%
Prophylactic Antibiotic Stopped[1]	20	80%	95%	94%
Recommended VTP Ordered	27	96%	92%	94%
Urinary Catheter Removal[1]	5	40%	92%	90%
Children's Asthma Care				
Received Systemic Corticosteroids	-	-	-	100%
Received Home Management Plan	-	-	-	71%
Received Reliever Medication	-	-	-	100%
Use of Medical Imaging				
Combination Abdominal CT Scan	333	0.030	0.237	0.191
Combination Chest CT Scan	155	0.006	0.120	0.054
Follow-up Mammogram/Ultrasound	311	11.6%	8.3%	8.4%
MRI for Low Back Pain[1]	32	18.8%	35.2%	32.7%
Survey of Patients' Hospital Experiences				
Area Around Room 'Always' Quiet at Night	300+	65%	-	58%
Doctors 'Always' Communicated Well	300+	88%	-	80%
Home Recovery Information Given	300+	86%	-	82%
Hospital Given 9 or 10 on 10 Point Scale	300+	77%	-	67%
Meds 'Always' Explained Before Given	300+	72%	-	60%
Nurses 'Always' Communicated Well	300+	83%	-	76%
Pain 'Always' Well Controlled	300+	73%	-	69%
Room and Bathroom 'Always' Clean	300+	74%	-	71%
Timely Help 'Always' Received	300+	77%	-	64%
Would Definitely Recommend Hospital	300+	74%	-	69%

Saint Francis Hospital and Health Centers

1600 Albany Street Phone: 317-783-8133
Beech Grove, IN 46107 Fax: 317-784-4675
URL: www.stfrancis-indy.org
Type: Acute Care Hospitals Emergency Services: Yes
Ownership: Voluntary Non-Profit - Church Beds: 500

Key Personnel:
Cardiac Laboratory. . . . . Paula Phillips
Chief of Medical Staff . . . . Donald Kerner
Infection Control. . . . . Cindy Eagan
Quality Assurance . . . . Doug Gioe
Radiology. . . . . Charisse Mershon
Emergency Room . . . . Claire Roembke, RN

Measure	Cases	This Hosp.	State Avg.	U.S. Avg.
Heart Attack Care				
ACE Inhibitor or ARB for LVSD[1]	2	100%	96%	96%
Aspirin at Arrival[1]	20	95%	98%	99%
Aspirin at Discharge[1]	15	100%	99%	98%
Beta Blocker at Discharge[1]	14	100%	98%	98%
Fibrinolytic Medication Timing	0	-	37%	55%
PCI Within 90 Minutes of Arrival	0	-	93%	90%
Smoking Cessation Advice[1]	1	100%	99%	99%
Chest Pain/Possible Heart Attack Care				
Aspirin at Arrival	105	97%	95%	95%
Median Time to ECG (minutes)	109	7	6	8
Median Time to Transfer (minutes)[1,3]	5	36	49	61
Fibrinolytic Medication Timing	0	-	63%	54%
Heart Failure Care				
ACE Inhibitor or ARB for LVSD	39	79%	92%	94%
Discharge Instructions	85	72%	84%	88%
Evaluation of LVS Function	164	99%	98%	98%
Smoking Cessation Advice[1]	17	100%	99%	98%
Pneumonia Care				
Appropriate Initial Antibiotic[2]	110	70%	90%	92%
Blood Culture Timing[2]	175	86%	95%	96%
Influenza Vaccine[2]	194	90%	93%	91%
Initial Antibiotic Timing[2]	193	89%	96%	95%
Pneumococcal Vaccine[2]	256	91%	94%	93%
Smoking Cessation Advice[2]	115	99%	98%	97%
Surgical Care Improvement Project				
Appropriate VTP Within 24 Hours[2]	276	98%	90%	92%
Appropriate Hair Removal[2]	744	100%	100%	99%
Appropriate Beta Blocker Usage[2]	268	91%	93%	93%
Controlled Postoperative Blood Glucose[2]	0	-	93%	93%
Prophylactic Antibiotic Timing[2]	442	97%	97%	97%
Prophylactic Antibiotic Timing (Outpatient)	267	91%	92%	92%
Prophylactic Antibiotic Selection[2]	442	98%	98%	97%
Prophylactic Antibiotic Select. (Outpatient)	258	97%	95%	94%
Prophylactic Antibiotic Stopped[2]	412	96%	95%	94%
Recommended VTP Ordered[2]	276	99%	92%	94%
Urinary Catheter Removal	82	88%	92%	90%
Children's Asthma Care				
Received Systemic Corticosteroids	-	-	-	100%
Received Home Management Plan	-	-	-	71%
Received Reliever Medication	-	-	-	100%
Use of Medical Imaging				
Combination Abdominal CT Scan	455	0.066	0.237	0.191
Combination Chest CT Scan	257	0.004	0.120	0.054
Follow-up Mammogram/Ultrasound[5]	0	-	8.3%	8.4%
MRI for Low Back Pain	61	45.9%	35.2%	32.7%
Survey of Patients' Hospital Experiences				
Area Around Room 'Always' Quiet at Night	300+	52%	-	58%
Doctors 'Always' Communicated Well	300+	73%	-	80%
Home Recovery Information Given	300+	83%	-	82%
Hospital Given 9 or 10 on 10 Point Scale	300+	69%	-	67%
Meds 'Always' Explained Before Given	300+	56%	-	60%
Nurses 'Always' Communicated Well	300+	75%	-	76%
Pain 'Always' Well Controlled	300+	72%	-	69%
Room and Bathroom 'Always' Clean	300+	69%	-	71%
Timely Help 'Always' Received	300+	59%	-	64%
Would Definitely Recommend Hospital	300+	72%	-	69%

NOTE: Hospital profiles are in alphabetical order by state, then city, then hospital within the city; Rankings exclude hospitals with less than 25 cases except for patient surveys which excludes hospitals with less than 100 cases; (a) 100–299 cases; (1) The number of cases is too small to be sure how well a hospital is performing; (2) The hospital indicated that the data submitted for this measure were based on a sample of cases; (3) Data was collected during a shorter time period (fewer quarters) than the maximum possible time for this measure; (4) Suppressed for one or more quarters by CMS; (5) No data is available from the hospital for this measure; (6) Fewer than 100 patients completed the HCAHPS survey. Use these rates with caution, as the number of surveys may be too low to reliably assess hospital performance; (7) Survey results are based on less than 12 months of data; (8) Survey results are not available for this reporting period; (9) No or very few patients were eligible for the HCAHPS survey. The scores shown, if any, reflect a very small number of surveys; (10) A state average was not calculated because too few hospitals in the state submitted data; (11) There were discrepancies in the data collection process; Please refer to the User's Guide for a full explanation of data.

Bloomington Hospital

601 W Second Street
Bloomington, IN 47403
Phone: 812-353-9555
Fax: 812-353-9321
E-mail: info@bloomingtonhospital.org
URL: bloomingtonhospital.org
Type: Acute Care Hospitals
Emergency Services: Yes
Ownership: Voluntary Non-Profit - Private
Beds: 355

Key Personnel:
CEO/President. . . . . Mark E Moore
Chief of Medical Staff . . . . James Farris MD
Radiology. . . . . Bruce Riley

Measure	Cases	This Hosp.	State Avg.	U.S. Avg.
Heart Attack Care				
ACE Inhibitor or ARB for LVSD	47	98%	96%	96%
Aspirin at Arrival	277	99%	98%	99%
Aspirin at Discharge	358	100%	99%	98%
Beta Blocker at Discharge	357	100%	98%	98%
Fibrinolytic Medication Timing	0	-	37%	55%
PCI Within 90 Minutes of Arrival	56	95%	93%	90%
Smoking Cessation Advice	143	100%	99%	99%
Chest Pain/Possible Heart Attack Care				
Aspirin at Arrival[1,3]	2	100%	95%	95%
Median Time to ECG (minutes)[1,3]	2	8	6	8
Median Time to Transfer (minutes)[5]	0	-	49	61
Fibrinolytic Medication Timing[3]	0	-	63%	54%
Heart Failure Care				
ACE Inhibitor or ARB for LVSD	91	95%	92%	94%
Discharge Instructions	189	94%	84%	88%
Evaluation of LVS Function	262	99%	98%	98%
Smoking Cessation Advice	53	94%	99%	98%
Pneumonia Care				
Appropriate Initial Antibiotic	199	94%	90%	92%
Blood Culture Timing	296	97%	95%	96%
Influenza Vaccine	227	94%	93%	91%
Initial Antibiotic Timing	287	98%	96%	95%
Pneumococcal Vaccine	299	97%	94%	93%
Smoking Cessation Advice	130	97%	98%	97%
Surgical Care Improvement Project				
Appropriate VTP Within 24 Hours	349	89%	90%	92%
Appropriate Hair Removal	1,204	100%	100%	99%
Appropriate Beta Blocker Usage	379	95%	93%	93%
Controlled Postoperative Blood Glucose	144	95%	93%	93%
Prophylactic Antibiotic Timing	775	96%	97%	97%
Prophylactic Antibiotic Timing (Outpatient)	851	95%	92%	92%
Prophylactic Antibiotic Selection	780	99%	98%	97%
Prophylactic Antibiotic Select. (Outpatient)	837	95%	95%	94%
Prophylactic Antibiotic Stopped	748	97%	95%	94%
Recommended VTP Ordered	351	90%	92%	94%
Urinary Catheter Removal	360	95%	92%	90%
Children's Asthma Care				
Received Systemic Corticosteroids	-	-	-	100%
Received Home Management Plan	-	-	-	71%
Received Reliever Medication	-	-	-	100%
Use of Medical Imaging				
Combination Abdominal CT Scan	589	0.044	0.237	0.191
Combination Chest CT Scan	255	0.016	0.120	0.054
Follow-up Mammogram/Ultrasound[5]	0	-	8.3%	8.4%
MRI for Low Back Pain	144	23.6%	35.2%	32.7%
Survey of Patients' Hospital Experiences				
Area Around Room 'Always' Quiet at Night	300+	47%	-	58%
Doctors 'Always' Communicated Well	300+	80%	-	80%
Home Recovery Information Given	300+	85%	-	82%
Hospital Given 9 or 10 on 10 Point Scale	300+	70%	-	67%
Meds 'Always' Explained Before Given	300+	59%	-	60%
Nurses 'Always' Communicated Well	300+	75%	-	76%
Pain 'Always' Well Controlled	300+	69%	-	69%
Room and Bathroom 'Always' Clean	300+	66%	-	71%
Timely Help 'Always' Received	300+	64%	-	64%
Would Definitely Recommend Hospital	300+	74%	-	69%

Monroe Hospital

4011 S Monroe Medical Park Blvd
Bloomington, IN 47403
Phone: 812-825-1111
URL: www.monroehospital.com
Type: Acute Care Hospitals
Emergency Services: Yes
Ownership: Voluntary Non-Profit - Private

Measure	Cases	This Hosp.	State Avg.	U.S. Avg.
Heart Attack Care				
ACE Inhibitor or ARB for LVSD[3]	0	-	96%	96%
Aspirin at Arrival[1,3]	4	75%	98%	99%
Aspirin at Discharge[1,3]	2	100%	99%	98%
Beta Blocker at Discharge[1,3]	2	50%	98%	98%
Fibrinolytic Medication Timing[1,3]	3	33%	37%	55%
PCI Within 90 Minutes of Arrival[3]	0	-	93%	90%
Smoking Cessation Advice[3]	0	-	99%	99%
Chest Pain/Possible Heart Attack Care				
Aspirin at Arrival[1,3]	9	100%	95%	95%
Median Time to ECG (minutes)[1,3]	11	8	6	8
Median Time to Transfer (minutes)[1,3]	3	80	49	61
Fibrinolytic Medication Timing[1,3]	2	0%	63%	54%
Heart Failure Care				
ACE Inhibitor or ARB for LVSD[1]	8	100%	92%	94%
Discharge Instructions[1]	22	59%	84%	88%
Evaluation of LVS Function	37	76%	98%	98%
Smoking Cessation Advice[1]	2	100%	99%	98%
Pneumonia Care				
Appropriate Initial Antibiotic[1]	9	100%	90%	92%
Blood Culture Timing	39	100%	95%	96%
Influenza Vaccine[1]	16	94%	93%	91%
Initial Antibiotic Timing[1]	18	94%	96%	95%
Pneumococcal Vaccine	32	69%	94%	93%
Smoking Cessation Advice[1]	21	100%	98%	97%
Surgical Care Improvement Project				
Appropriate VTP Within 24 Hours	27	89%	90%	92%
Appropriate Hair Removal	183	100%	100%	99%
Appropriate Beta Blocker Usage[1]	14	93%	93%	93%
Controlled Postoperative Blood Glucose	0	-	93%	93%
Prophylactic Antibiotic Timing	146	96%	97%	97%
Prophylactic Antibiotic Timing (Outpatient)[1,3]	13	92%	92%	92%
Prophylactic Antibiotic Selection	144	97%	98%	97%
Prophylactic Antibiotic Select. (Outpatient)[1,3]	13	92%	95%	94%
Prophylactic Antibiotic Stopped	144	100%	95%	94%
Recommended VTP Ordered	28	86%	92%	94%
Urinary Catheter Removal	72	100%	92%	90%
Children's Asthma Care				
Received Systemic Corticosteroids	-	-	-	100%
Received Home Management Plan	-	-	-	71%
Received Reliever Medication	-	-	-	100%
Use of Medical Imaging				
Combination Abdominal CT Scan	205	0.029	0.237	0.191
Combination Chest CT Scan	99	0.030	0.120	0.054
Follow-up Mammogram/Ultrasound[5]	0	-	8.3%	8.4%
MRI for Low Back Pain	56	30.4%	35.2%	32.7%
Survey of Patients' Hospital Experiences				
Area Around Room 'Always' Quiet at Night	300+	68%	-	58%
Doctors 'Always' Communicated Well	300+	84%	-	80%
Home Recovery Information Given	300+	78%	-	82%
Hospital Given 9 or 10 on 10 Point Scale	300+	74%	-	67%
Meds 'Always' Explained Before Given	300+	59%	-	60%
Nurses 'Always' Communicated Well	300+	80%	-	76%
Pain 'Always' Well Controlled	300+	73%	-	69%
Room and Bathroom 'Always' Clean	300+	85%	-	71%
Timely Help 'Always' Received	300+	67%	-	64%
Would Definitely Recommend Hospital	300+	77%	-	69%

Bluffton Regional Medical Center

303 S Main St
Bluffton, IN 46714
Phone: 260-824-3210
Fax: 260-919-3851
URL: www.blufftonregional.com
Type: Acute Care Hospitals
Emergency Services: Yes
Ownership: Proprietary
Beds: 79

Key Personnel:
CEO/President. . . . . Thomas Clark
Radiology. . . . . Brett Hagedorn
Emergency Room . . . . Derrick Williams

Measure	Cases	This Hosp.	State Avg.	U.S. Avg.
Heart Attack Care				
ACE Inhibitor or ARB for LVSD	0	-	96%	96%
Aspirin at Arrival[1]	15	100%	98%	99%
Aspirin at Discharge[1]	13	100%	99%	98%
Beta Blocker at Discharge[1]	14	100%	98%	98%
Fibrinolytic Medication Timing[1]	1	0%	37%	55%
PCI Within 90 Minutes of Arrival	0	-	93%	90%
Smoking Cessation Advice[1]	2	100%	99%	99%
Chest Pain/Possible Heart Attack Care				
Aspirin at Arrival	63	98%	95%	95%
Median Time to ECG (minutes)	65	4	6	8
Median Time to Transfer (minutes)[1]	15	42	49	61
Fibrinolytic Medication Timing	0	-	63%	54%
Heart Failure Care				
ACE Inhibitor or ARB for LVSD[1]	23	100%	92%	94%
Discharge Instructions	36	100%	84%	88%
Evaluation of LVS Function	53	100%	98%	98%
Smoking Cessation Advice[1]	1	100%	99%	98%
Pneumonia Care				
Appropriate Initial Antibiotic	81	100%	90%	92%
Blood Culture Timing	92	100%	95%	96%
Influenza Vaccine	75	99%	93%	91%
Initial Antibiotic Timing	119	100%	96%	95%
Pneumococcal Vaccine	115	100%	94%	93%
Smoking Cessation Advice[1]	23	100%	98%	97%
Surgical Care Improvement Project				
Appropriate VTP Within 24 Hours	50	100%	90%	92%
Appropriate Hair Removal	140	100%	100%	99%
Appropriate Beta Blocker Usage	39	100%	93%	93%
Controlled Postoperative Blood Glucose	0	-	93%	93%
Prophylactic Antibiotic Timing	101	99%	97%	97%
Prophylactic Antibiotic Timing (Outpatient)	42	98%	92%	92%
Prophylactic Antibiotic Selection	101	100%	98%	97%
Prophylactic Antibiotic Select. (Outpatient)	42	95%	95%	94%
Prophylactic Antibiotic Stopped	96	99%	95%	94%
Recommended VTP Ordered	50	100%	92%	94%
Urinary Catheter Removal[1]	17	94%	92%	90%
Children's Asthma Care				
Received Systemic Corticosteroids	-	-	-	100%
Received Home Management Plan	-	-	-	71%
Received Reliever Medication	-	-	-	100%
Use of Medical Imaging				
Combination Abdominal CT Scan	231	0.022	0.237	0.191
Combination Chest CT Scan	153	0.039	0.120	0.054
Follow-up Mammogram/Ultrasound	673	7.7%	8.3%	8.4%
MRI for Low Back Pain	94	31.9%	35.2%	32.7%
Survey of Patients' Hospital Experiences				
Area Around Room 'Always' Quiet at Night	300+	60%	-	58%
Doctors 'Always' Communicated Well	300+	79%	-	80%
Home Recovery Information Given	300+	86%	-	82%
Hospital Given 9 or 10 on 10 Point Scale	300+	73%	-	67%
Meds 'Always' Explained Before Given	300+	66%	-	60%
Nurses 'Always' Communicated Well	300+	81%	-	76%
Pain 'Always' Well Controlled	300+	73%	-	69%
Room and Bathroom 'Always' Clean	300+	78%	-	71%
Timely Help 'Always' Received	300+	67%	-	64%
Would Definitely Recommend Hospital	300+	70%	-	69%

NOTE: Hospital profiles are in alphabetical order by state, then city, then hospital within the city; Rankings exclude hospitals with less than 25 cases except for patient surveys which excludes hospitals with less than 100 cases; (a) 100–299 cases; (1) The number of cases is too small to be sure how well a hospital is performing; (2) The hospital indicated that the data submitted for this measure were based on a sample of cases; (3) Data was collected during a shorter time period (fewer quarters) than the maximum possible time for this measure; (4) Suppressed for one or more quarters by CMS; (5) No data is available from the hospital for this measure; (6) Fewer than 100 patients completed the HCAHPS survey. Use these rates with caution, as the number of surveys may be too low to reliably assess hospital performance; (7) Survey results are based on less than 12 months of data; (8) Survey results are not available for this reporting period; (9) No or very few patients were eligible for the HCAHPS survey. The scores shown, if any, reflect a very small number of surveys; (10) A state average was not calculated because too few hospitals in the state submitted data; (11) There were discrepancies in the data collection process; Please refer to the User's Guide for a full explanation of data.

Saint Mary's Warrick Hospital

1116 Millis Ave Phone: 812-897-4800
Boonville, IN 47601 Fax: 812-897-7375
URL: www.stmarys.org
Type: Critical Access Hospitals Emergency Services: Yes
Ownership: Voluntary Non-Profit - Private Beds: 25

Key Personnel:
CEO/President. . . . . Marc Dooley
Chief of Medical Staff. . . . . David Vaughn
Emergency Room . . . . David Baughn

Measure	Cases	This Hosp.	State Avg.	U.S. Avg.
Heart Attack Care				
ACE Inhibitor or ARB for LVSD[3]	0	-	96%	96%
Aspirin at Arrival[1,3]	1	100%	98%	99%
Aspirin at Discharge[3]	0	-	99%	98%
Beta Blocker at Discharge[3]	0	-	98%	98%
Fibrinolytic Medication Timing[3]	0	-	37%	55%
PCI Within 90 Minutes of Arrival[3]	0	-	93%	90%
Smoking Cessation Advice[3]	0	-	99%	99%
Chest Pain/Possible Heart Attack Care				
Aspirin at Arrival	-	-	95%	95%
Median Time to ECG (minutes)	-	-	6	8
Median Time to Transfer (minutes)	-	-	49	61
Fibrinolytic Medication Timing	-	-	63%	54%
Heart Failure Care				
ACE Inhibitor or ARB for LVSD[1]	13	100%	92%	94%
Discharge Instructions[1]	16	31%	84%	88%
Evaluation of LVS Function	27	81%	98%	98%
Smoking Cessation Advice[1]	2	100%	99%	98%
Pneumonia Care				
Appropriate Initial Antibiotic	34	94%	90%	92%
Blood Culture Timing	30	73%	95%	96%
Influenza Vaccine	25	92%	93%	91%
Initial Antibiotic Timing[5]	0	-	96%	95%
Pneumococcal Vaccine	33	79%	94%	93%
Smoking Cessation Advice[1]	21	71%	98%	97%
Surgical Care Improvement Project				
Appropriate VTP Within 24 Hours[5]	0	-	90%	92%
Appropriate Hair Removal[5]	0	-	100%	99%
Appropriate Beta Blocker Usage[5]	0	-	93%	93%
Controlled Postoperative Blood Glucose[5]	0	-	93%	93%
Prophylactic Antibiotic Timing[5]	0	-	97%	97%
Prophylactic Antibiotic Timing (Outpatient)	-	-	92%	92%
Prophylactic Antibiotic Selection[5]	0	-	98%	97%
Prophylactic Antibiotic Select. (Outpatient)	-	-	95%	94%
Prophylactic Antibiotic Stopped[5]	0	-	95%	94%
Recommended VTP Ordered[5]	0	-	92%	94%
Urinary Catheter Removal[5]	0	-	92%	90%
Children's Asthma Care				
Received Systemic Corticosteroids	-	-	-	100%
Received Home Management Plan	-	-	-	71%
Received Reliever Medication	-	-	-	100%
Use of Medical Imaging				
Combination Abdominal CT Scan	-	-	0.237	0.191
Combination Chest CT Scan	-	-	0.120	0.054
Follow-up Mammogram/Ultrasound	-	-	8.3%	8.4%
MRI for Low Back Pain	-	-	35.2%	32.7%
Survey of Patients' Hospital Experiences				
Area Around Room 'Always' Quiet at Night[8]	-	-	-	58%
Doctors 'Always' Communicated Well[8]	-	-	-	80%
Home Recovery Information Given[8]	-	-	-	82%
Hospital Given 9 or 10 on 10 Point Scale[8]	-	-	-	67%
Meds 'Always' Explained Before Given[8]	-	-	-	60%
Nurses 'Always' Communicated Well[8]	-	-	-	76%
Pain 'Always' Well Controlled[8]	-	-	-	69%
Room and Bathroom 'Always' Clean[8]	-	-	-	71%
Timely Help 'Always' Received[8]	-	-	-	64%
Would Definitely Recommend Hospital[8]	-	-	-	69%

Saint Vincent Clay Hospital

1206 E National Ave Phone: 812-442-2500
Brazil, IN 47834 Fax: 812-442-2605
URL: www.stvincent.org/faccen/clay
Type: Critical Access Hospitals Emergency Services: Yes
Ownership: Voluntary Non-Profit - Private Beds: 58

Key Personnel:
CEO/President. . . . . Jerry Laue
Chief of Medical Staff. . . . . Catherine Brush
Operating Room. . . . . Jamie J Webster
Quality Assurance . . . . Thomas Falen, RN
Emergency Room . . . . R Curtis Oehler, MD

Measure	Cases	This Hosp.	State Avg.	U.S. Avg.
Heart Attack Care				
ACE Inhibitor or ARB for LVSD[3]	0	-	96%	96%
Aspirin at Arrival[1,3]	1	100%	98%	99%
Aspirin at Discharge[3]	0	-	99%	98%
Beta Blocker at Discharge[1,3]	1	100%	98%	98%
Fibrinolytic Medication Timing[3]	0	-	37%	55%
PCI Within 90 Minutes of Arrival[5]	0	-	93%	90%
Smoking Cessation Advice[1,3]	1	100%	99%	99%
Chest Pain/Possible Heart Attack Care				
Aspirin at Arrival	-	-	95%	95%
Median Time to ECG (minutes)	-	-	6	8
Median Time to Transfer (minutes)	-	-	49	61
Fibrinolytic Medication Timing	-	-	63%	54%
Heart Failure Care				
ACE Inhibitor or ARB for LVSD[1]	9	89%	92%	94%
Discharge Instructions[1]	21	100%	84%	88%
Evaluation of LVS Function	31	87%	98%	98%
Smoking Cessation Advice[1]	4	100%	99%	98%
Pneumonia Care				
Appropriate Initial Antibiotic[1]	11	100%	90%	92%
Blood Culture Timing[1]	20	85%	95%	96%
Influenza Vaccine[1]	13	77%	93%	91%
Initial Antibiotic Timing[1]	22	100%	96%	95%
Pneumococcal Vaccine[1]	17	65%	94%	93%
Smoking Cessation Advice[1]	7	57%	98%	97%
Surgical Care Improvement Project				
Appropriate VTP Within 24 Hours[1]	13	92%	90%	92%
Appropriate Hair Removal[1]	21	100%	100%	99%
Appropriate Beta Blocker Usage[1]	3	100%	93%	93%
Controlled Postoperative Blood Glucose[5]	0	-	93%	93%
Prophylactic Antibiotic Timing[1]	8	62%	97%	97%
Prophylactic Antibiotic Timing (Outpatient)	-	-	92%	92%
Prophylactic Antibiotic Selection[1]	12	75%	98%	97%
Prophylactic Antibiotic Select. (Outpatient)	-	-	95%	94%
Prophylactic Antibiotic Stopped[1]	7	57%	95%	94%
Recommended VTP Ordered[1]	13	100%	92%	94%
Urinary Catheter Removal[1]	4	50%	92%	90%
Children's Asthma Care				
Received Systemic Corticosteroids	-	-	-	100%
Received Home Management Plan	-	-	-	71%
Received Reliever Medication	-	-	-	100%
Use of Medical Imaging				
Combination Abdominal CT Scan	-	-	0.237	0.191
Combination Chest CT Scan	-	-	0.120	0.054
Follow-up Mammogram/Ultrasound	-	-	8.3%	8.4%
MRI for Low Back Pain	-	-	35.2%	32.7%
Survey of Patients' Hospital Experiences				
Area Around Room 'Always' Quiet at Night	(a)	46%	-	58%
Doctors 'Always' Communicated Well	(a)	85%	-	80%
Home Recovery Information Given	(a)	78%	-	82%
Hospital Given 9 or 10 on 10 Point Scale	(a)	62%	-	67%
Meds 'Always' Explained Before Given	(a)	55%	-	60%
Nurses 'Always' Communicated Well	(a)	78%	-	76%
Pain 'Always' Well Controlled	(a)	70%	-	69%
Room and Bathroom 'Always' Clean	(a)	79%	-	71%
Timely Help 'Always' Received	(a)	60%	-	64%
Would Definitely Recommend Hospital	(a)	56%	-	69%

Community Hospital of Bremen

1020 High Road Phone: 574-546-2211
Bremen, IN 46506 Fax: 574-546-4312
E-mail: pboard@bremenhospital.com
URL: www.bremenhospital.com
Type: Critical Access Hospitals Emergency Services: Yes
Ownership: Voluntary Non-Profit - Private Beds: 24

Key Personnel:
CEO/President. . . . . Scott Graybill
Chief of Medical Staff. . . . . Carey Gear, MD
Infection Control. . . . . Teresa Brown, RN
Quality Assurance . . . . Dick Balmer
Emergency Room . . . . Carey Gear, MD

Measure	Cases	This Hosp.	State Avg.	U.S. Avg.
Heart Attack Care				
ACE Inhibitor or ARB for LVSD[5]	0	-	96%	96%
Aspirin at Arrival[5]	0	-	98%	99%
Aspirin at Discharge[5]	0	-	99%	98%
Beta Blocker at Discharge[5]	0	-	98%	98%
Fibrinolytic Medication Timing[5]	0	-	37%	55%
PCI Within 90 Minutes of Arrival[5]	0	-	93%	90%
Smoking Cessation Advice[5]	0	-	99%	99%
Chest Pain/Possible Heart Attack Care				
Aspirin at Arrival[5]	0	-	95%	95%
Median Time to ECG (minutes)[5]	0	-	6	8
Median Time to Transfer (minutes)[5]	0	-	49	61
Fibrinolytic Medication Timing[5]	0	-	63%	54%
Heart Failure Care				
ACE Inhibitor or ARB for LVSD[3]	0	-	92%	94%
Discharge Instructions[1,3]	2	100%	84%	88%
Evaluation of LVS Function[1,3]	2	50%	98%	98%
Smoking Cessation Advice[1,3]	2	100%	99%	98%
Pneumonia Care				
Appropriate Initial Antibiotic[1,3]	2	100%	90%	92%
Blood Culture Timing[1,3]	5	100%	95%	96%
Influenza Vaccine[5]	0	-	93%	91%
Initial Antibiotic Timing[1,3]	6	100%	96%	95%
Pneumococcal Vaccine[1,3]	3	100%	94%	93%
Smoking Cessation Advice[1,3]	2	100%	98%	97%
Surgical Care Improvement Project				
Appropriate VTP Within 24 Hours[5]	0	-	90%	92%
Appropriate Hair Removal[5]	0	-	100%	99%
Appropriate Beta Blocker Usage[5]	0	-	93%	93%
Controlled Postoperative Blood Glucose[5]	0	-	93%	93%
Prophylactic Antibiotic Timing[5]	0	-	97%	97%
Prophylactic Antibiotic Timing (Outpatient)[5]	0	-	92%	92%
Prophylactic Antibiotic Selection[5]	0	-	98%	97%
Prophylactic Antibiotic Select. (Outpatient)[5]	0	-	95%	94%
Prophylactic Antibiotic Stopped[5]	0	-	95%	94%
Recommended VTP Ordered[5]	0	-	92%	94%
Urinary Catheter Removal[5]	0	-	92%	90%
Children's Asthma Care				
Received Systemic Corticosteroids	-	-	-	100%
Received Home Management Plan	-	-	-	71%
Received Reliever Medication	-	-	-	100%
Use of Medical Imaging				
Combination Abdominal CT Scan	83	0.048	0.237	0.191
Combination Chest CT Scan	52	0.019	0.120	0.054
Follow-up Mammogram/Ultrasound	200	5.5%	8.3%	8.4%
MRI for Low Back Pain[1]	36	30.6%	35.2%	32.7%
Survey of Patients' Hospital Experiences				
Area Around Room 'Always' Quiet at Night[8]	-	-	-	58%
Doctors 'Always' Communicated Well[8]	-	-	-	80%
Home Recovery Information Given[8]	-	-	-	82%
Hospital Given 9 or 10 on 10 Point Scale[8]	-	-	-	67%
Meds 'Always' Explained Before Given[8]	-	-	-	60%
Nurses 'Always' Communicated Well[8]	-	-	-	76%
Pain 'Always' Well Controlled[8]	-	-	-	69%
Room and Bathroom 'Always' Clean[8]	-	-	-	71%
Timely Help 'Always' Received[8]	-	-	-	64%
Would Definitely Recommend Hospital[8]	-	-	-	69%

NOTE: Hospital profiles are in alphabetical order by state, then city, then hospital within the city; Rankings exclude hospitals with less than 25 cases except for patient surveys which excludes hospitals with less than 100 cases; (a) 100–299 cases; (1) The number of cases is too small to be sure how well a hospital is performing; (2) The hospital indicated that the data submitted for this measure were based on a sample of cases; (3) Data was collected during a shorter time period (fewer quarters) than the maximum possible time for this measure; (4) Suppressed for one or more quarters by CMS; (5) No data is available from the hospital for this measure; (6) Fewer than 100 patients completed the HCAHPS survey. Use these rates with caution, as the number of surveys may be too low to reliably assess hospital performance; (7) Survey results are based on less than 12 months of data; (8) Survey results are not available for this reporting period; (9) No or very few patients were eligible for the HCAHPS survey. The scores shown, if any, reflect a very small number of surveys; (10) A state average was not calculated because too few hospitals in the state submitted data; (11) There were discrepancies in the data collection process; Please refer to the User's Guide for a full explanation of data.

Indiana University Health North Hospital

11700 N Meridian St
Carmel, IN 46032
Phone: 317-688-2000
Type: Acute Care Hospitals
Emergency Services: Yes
Ownership: Proprietary
Key Personnel:
CEO/President. . . . . Jonathan R Goble
Chief of Medical Staff . . . . Lynda Smirz MD

Measure	Cases	This Hosp.	State Avg.	U.S. Avg.
Heart Attack Care				
ACE Inhibitor or ARB for LVSD[1]	11	91%	96%	96%
Aspirin at Arrival	29	100%	98%	99%
Aspirin at Discharge	31	97%	99%	98%
Beta Blocker at Discharge	30	90%	98%	98%
Fibrinolytic Medication Timing	0	-	37%	55%
PCI Within 90 Minutes of Arrival[1]	4	25%	93%	90%
Smoking Cessation Advice[1]	5	100%	99%	99%
Chest Pain/Possible Heart Attack Care				
Aspirin at Arrival[3]	0	-	95%	95%
Median Time to ECG (minutes)[3]	0	-	6	8
Median Time to Transfer (minutes)[5]	0	-	49	61
Fibrinolytic Medication Timing[5]	0	-	63%	54%
Heart Failure Care				
ACE Inhibitor or ARB for LVSD[1]	23	91%	92%	94%
Discharge Instructions	56	84%	84%	88%
Evaluation of LVS Function	76	100%	98%	98%
Smoking Cessation Advice[1]	5	100%	99%	98%
Pneumonia Care				
Appropriate Initial Antibiotic	49	86%	90%	92%
Blood Culture Timing	51	94%	95%	96%
Influenza Vaccine	48	85%	93%	91%
Initial Antibiotic Timing	57	95%	96%	95%
Pneumococcal Vaccine	59	80%	94%	93%
Smoking Cessation Advice[1]	12	100%	98%	97%
Surgical Care Improvement Project				
Appropriate VTP Within 24 Hours[2]	72	96%	90%	92%
Appropriate Hair Removal[2]	286	100%	100%	99%
Appropriate Beta Blocker Usage[2]	67	99%	93%	93%
Controlled Postoperative Blood Glucose[2]	0	-	93%	93%
Prophylactic Antibiotic Timing[2]	215	99%	97%	97%
Prophylactic Antibiotic Timing (Outpatient)	423	98%	92%	92%
Prophylactic Antibiotic Selection[2]	219	99%	98%	97%
Prophylactic Antibiotic Select. (Outpatient)	419	95%	95%	94%
Prophylactic Antibiotic Stopped[2]	207	99%	95%	94%
Recommended VTP Ordered[2]	72	96%	92%	94%
Urinary Catheter Removal[2]	85	89%	92%	90%
Children's Asthma Care				
Received Systemic Corticosteroids[2]	80	100%	-	100%
Received Home Management Plan[2]	80	90%	-	71%
Received Reliever Medication[2]	80	100%	-	100%
Use of Medical Imaging				
Combination Abdominal CT Scan	419	0.079	0.237	0.191
Combination Chest CT Scan	347	0.009	0.120	0.054
Follow-up Mammogram/Ultrasound	422	7.8%	8.3%	8.4%
MRI for Low Back Pain	83	44.6%	35.2%	32.7%
Survey of Patients' Hospital Experiences				
Area Around Room 'Always' Quiet at Night	300+	67%	-	58%
Doctors 'Always' Communicated Well	300+	82%	-	80%
Home Recovery Information Given	300+	82%	-	82%
Hospital Given 9 or 10 on 10 Point Scale	300+	83%	-	67%
Meds 'Always' Explained Before Given	300+	56%	-	60%
Nurses 'Always' Communicated Well	300+	75%	-	76%
Pain 'Always' Well Controlled	300+	70%	-	69%
Room and Bathroom 'Always' Clean	300+	69%	-	71%
Timely Help 'Always' Received	300+	60%	-	64%
Would Definitely Recommend Hospital	300+	84%	-	69%

Saint Vincent Carmel Hospital

13500 N Meridian St
Carmel, IN 46032
Phone: 317-582-7000
URL: www.carmel.stvincent.org
Type: Acute Care Hospitals
Emergency Services: Yes
Ownership: Voluntary Non-Profit - Church
Beds: 100
Key Personnel:
Chief of Medical Staff . . . . Steve Priddy, MD
Operating Room. . . . . Carrie Drummond
Quality Assurance . . . . Cindy Ransford
Anesthesiology. . . . . Steve Priddy, MD
Emergency Room . . . . Kay Darnell
Intensive Care Unit. . . . . Ted Eads

Measure	Cases	This Hosp.	State Avg.	U.S. Avg.
Heart Attack Care				
ACE Inhibitor or ARB for LVSD[1,3]	1	100%	96%	96%
Aspirin at Arrival[1,3]	4	100%	98%	99%
Aspirin at Discharge[1,3]	1	100%	99%	98%
Beta Blocker at Discharge[1,3]	3	100%	98%	98%
Fibrinolytic Medication Timing[3]	0	-	37%	55%
PCI Within 90 Minutes of Arrival[3]	0	-	93%	90%
Smoking Cessation Advice[3]	0	-	99%	99%
Chest Pain/Possible Heart Attack Care				
Aspirin at Arrival	137	93%	95%	95%
Median Time to ECG (minutes)	140	7	6	8
Median Time to Transfer (minutes)[1]	14	70	49	61
Fibrinolytic Medication Timing[1]	2	100%	63%	54%
Heart Failure Care				
ACE Inhibitor or ARB for LVSD[1]	8	100%	92%	94%
Discharge Instructions[1]	20	80%	84%	88%
Evaluation of LVS Function	38	89%	98%	98%
Smoking Cessation Advice[1]	2	100%	99%	98%
Pneumonia Care				
Appropriate Initial Antibiotic	51	57%	90%	92%
Blood Culture Timing	80	86%	95%	96%
Influenza Vaccine	34	76%	93%	91%
Initial Antibiotic Timing	74	91%	96%	95%
Pneumococcal Vaccine	48	85%	94%	93%
Smoking Cessation Advice[1]	14	100%	98%	97%
Surgical Care Improvement Project				
Appropriate VTP Within 24 Hours[2]	89	90%	90%	92%
Appropriate Hair Removal[2]	303	100%	100%	99%
Appropriate Beta Blocker Usage[2]	72	89%	93%	93%
Controlled Postoperative Blood Glucose[2]	0	-	93%	93%
Prophylactic Antibiotic Timing[2]	227	97%	97%	97%
Prophylactic Antibiotic Timing (Outpatient)	98	90%	92%	92%
Prophylactic Antibiotic Selection[2]	228	99%	98%	97%
Prophylactic Antibiotic Select. (Outpatient)	92	93%	95%	94%
Prophylactic Antibiotic Stopped[2]	226	97%	95%	94%
Recommended VTP Ordered[2]	92	88%	92%	94%
Urinary Catheter Removal[1,2]	15	93%	92%	90%
Children's Asthma Care				
Received Systemic Corticosteroids	-	-	-	100%
Received Home Management Plan	-	-	-	71%
Received Reliever Medication	-	-	-	100%
Use of Medical Imaging				
Combination Abdominal CT Scan	437	0.096	0.237	0.191
Combination Chest CT Scan	210	0.000	0.120	0.054
Follow-up Mammogram/Ultrasound	427	10.8%	8.3%	8.4%
MRI for Low Back Pain	220	32.7%	35.2%	32.7%
Survey of Patients' Hospital Experiences				
Area Around Room 'Always' Quiet at Night	300+	62%	-	58%
Doctors 'Always' Communicated Well	300+	84%	-	80%
Home Recovery Information Given	300+	83%	-	82%
Hospital Given 9 or 10 on 10 Point Scale	300+	81%	-	67%
Meds 'Always' Explained Before Given	300+	61%	-	60%
Nurses 'Always' Communicated Well	300+	83%	-	76%
Pain 'Always' Well Controlled	300+	77%	-	69%
Room and Bathroom 'Always' Clean	300+	75%	-	71%
Timely Help 'Always' Received	300+	70%	-	64%
Would Definitely Recommend Hospital	300+	85%	-	69%

Saint Catherine Regional Hospital

2200 Market Street
Charlestown, IN 47111
Phone: 812-256-3301
Fax: 812-256-0201
E-mail: wobertate@altavista.net
Type: Acute Care Hospitals
Emergency Services: No
Ownership: Proprietary
Beds: 96

Measure	Cases	This Hosp.	State Avg.	U.S. Avg.
Heart Attack Care				
ACE Inhibitor or ARB for LVSD	0	-	96%	96%
Aspirin at Arrival[1]	6	67%	98%	99%
Aspirin at Discharge[1]	3	100%	99%	98%
Beta Blocker at Discharge[1]	3	67%	98%	98%
Fibrinolytic Medication Timing[1]	2	0%	37%	55%
PCI Within 90 Minutes of Arrival	0	-	93%	90%
Smoking Cessation Advice[1]	2	100%	99%	99%
Chest Pain/Possible Heart Attack Care				
Aspirin at Arrival[1]	24	100%	95%	95%
Median Time to ECG (minutes)[1]	23	9	6	8
Median Time to Transfer (minutes)[3]	0	-	49	61
Fibrinolytic Medication Timing[1,3]	1	0%	63%	54%
Heart Failure Care				
ACE Inhibitor or ARB for LVSD[1]	15	60%	92%	94%
Discharge Instructions	27	78%	84%	88%
Evaluation of LVS Function	32	94%	98%	98%
Smoking Cessation Advice[1]	7	100%	99%	98%
Pneumonia Care				
Appropriate Initial Antibiotic	36	78%	90%	92%
Blood Culture Timing[1]	22	77%	95%	96%
Influenza Vaccine[1]	23	91%	93%	91%
Initial Antibiotic Timing	35	94%	96%	95%
Pneumococcal Vaccine	27	89%	94%	93%
Smoking Cessation Advice[1]	19	100%	98%	97%
Surgical Care Improvement Project				
Appropriate VTP Within 24 Hours[1]	6	67%	90%	92%
Appropriate Hair Removal[1]	9	78%	100%	99%
Appropriate Beta Blocker Usage[1]	1	100%	93%	93%
Controlled Postoperative Blood Glucose	0	-	93%	93%
Prophylactic Antibiotic Timing[1]	4	25%	97%	97%
Prophylactic Antibiotic Timing (Outpatient)[1,3]	5	0%	92%	92%
Prophylactic Antibiotic Selection[1]	5	40%	98%	97%
Prophylactic Antibiotic Select. (Outpatient)[3]	0	-	95%	94%
Prophylactic Antibiotic Stopped[1]	4	75%	95%	94%
Recommended VTP Ordered[1]	6	67%	92%	94%
Urinary Catheter Removal[1]	1	100%	92%	90%
Children's Asthma Care				
Received Systemic Corticosteroids	-	-	-	100%
Received Home Management Plan	-	-	-	71%
Received Reliever Medication	-	-	-	100%
Use of Medical Imaging				
Combination Abdominal CT Scan	103	0.146	0.237	0.191
Combination Chest CT Scan	133	0.143	0.120	0.054
Follow-up Mammogram/Ultrasound	109	11.9%	8.3%	8.4%
MRI for Low Back Pain[1]	28	32.1%	35.2%	32.7%
Survey of Patients' Hospital Experiences				
Area Around Room 'Always' Quiet at Night	(a)	51%	-	58%
Doctors 'Always' Communicated Well	(a)	76%	-	80%
Home Recovery Information Given	(a)	67%	-	82%
Hospital Given 9 or 10 on 10 Point Scale	(a)	51%	-	67%
Meds 'Always' Explained Before Given	(a)	45%	-	60%
Nurses 'Always' Communicated Well	(a)	68%	-	76%
Pain 'Always' Well Controlled	(a)	57%	-	69%
Room and Bathroom 'Always' Clean	(a)	54%	-	71%
Timely Help 'Always' Received	(a)	54%	-	64%
Would Definitely Recommend Hospital	(a)	52%	-	69%

NOTE: Hospital profiles are in alphabetical order by state, then city, then hospital within the city; Rankings exclude hospitals with less than 25 cases except for patient surveys which excludes hospitals with less than 100 cases; (a) 100–299 cases; (1) The number of cases is too small to be sure how well a hospital is performing; (2) The hospital indicated that the data submitted for this measure were based on a sample of cases; (3) Data was collected during a shorter time period (fewer quarters) than the maximum possible time for this measure; (4) Suppressed for one or more quarters by CMS; (5) No data is available from the hospital for this measure; (6) Fewer than 100 patients completed the HCAHPS survey. Use these rates with caution, as the number of surveys may be too low to reliably assess hospital performance; (7) Survey results are based on less than 12 months of data; (8) Survey results are not available for this reporting period; (9) No or very few patients were eligible for the HCAHPS survey. The scores shown, if any, reflect a very small number of surveys; (10) A state average was not calculated because too few hospitals in the state submitted data; (11) There were discrepancies in the data collection process; Please refer to the User's Guide for a full explanation of data.

Kentuckiana Medical Center

4601 Medical Plaza Way
Clarksville, IN 47129
Phone: 812-280-3300
Type: Acute Care Hospitals
Emergency Services: No
Ownership: Proprietary
Beds: 34
Key Personnel:
CEO .... Chris Staves

Measure	Cases	This Hosp.	State Avg.	U.S. Avg.
Heart Attack Care				
ACE Inhibitor or ARB for LVSD[1,2,3]	7	100%	96%	96%
Aspirin at Arrival[1,2,3]	1	100%	98%	99%
Aspirin at Discharge[1,2,3]	8	100%	99%	98%
Beta Blocker at Discharge[1,2,3]	7	100%	98%	98%
Fibrinolytic Medication Timing[2,3]	0	-	37%	55%
PCI Within 90 Minutes of Arrival[2,3]	0	-	93%	90%
Smoking Cessation Advice[1,2,3]	3	100%	99%	99%
Chest Pain/Possible Heart Attack Care				
Aspirin at Arrival[5]	0	-	95%	95%
Median Time to ECG (minutes)[5]	0	-	6	8
Median Time to Transfer (minutes)[5]	0	-	49	61
Fibrinolytic Medication Timing[5]	0	-	63%	54%
Heart Failure Care				
ACE Inhibitor or ARB for LVSD[1,2,3]	10	100%	92%	94%
Discharge Instructions[1,2,3]	15	100%	84%	88%
Evaluation of LVS Function[1,2,3]	17	82%	98%	98%
Smoking Cessation Advice[1,2,3]	3	100%	99%	98%
Pneumonia Care				
Appropriate Initial Antibiotic[2,3]	0	-	90%	92%
Blood Culture Timing[2,3]	0	-	95%	96%
Influenza Vaccine[1,2,3]	9	44%	93%	91%
Initial Antibiotic Timing[1,2,3]	19	58%	96%	95%
Pneumococcal Vaccine[2,3]	25	48%	94%	93%
Smoking Cessation Advice[1,2,3]	7	71%	98%	97%
Surgical Care Improvement Project				
Appropriate VTP Within 24 Hours[1,2,3]	3	100%	90%	92%
Appropriate Hair Removal[2,3]	68	97%	100%	99%
Appropriate Beta Blocker Usage[2,3]	39	97%	93%	93%
Controlled Postoperative Blood Glucose[2,3]	49	92%	93%	93%
Prophylactic Antibiotic Timing[2,3]	56	57%	97%	97%
Prophylactic Antibiotic Timing (Outpatient)[5]	0	-	92%	92%
Prophylactic Antibiotic Selection[2,3]	58	100%	98%	97%
Prophylactic Antibiotic Select. (Outpatient)[5]	0	-	95%	94%
Prophylactic Antibiotic Stopped[2,3]	56	93%	95%	94%
Recommended VTP Ordered[1,2,3]	3	100%	92%	94%
Urinary Catheter Removal[2]	0	-	92%	90%
Children's Asthma Care				
Received Systemic Corticosteroids	-	-	-	100%
Received Home Management Plan	-	-	-	71%
Received Reliever Medication	-	-	-	100%
Use of Medical Imaging				
Combination Abdominal CT Scan[5]	0	-	0.237	0.191
Combination Chest CT Scan[5]	0	-	0.120	0.054
Follow-up Mammogram/Ultrasound[5]	0	-	8.3%	8.4%
MRI for Low Back Pain[5]	0	-	35.2%	32.7%
Survey of Patients' Hospital Experiences				
Area Around Room 'Always' Quiet at Night[8]	-	-	-	58%
Doctors 'Always' Communicated Well[8]	-	-	-	80%
Home Recovery Information Given[8]	-	-	-	82%
Hospital Given 9 or 10 on 10 Point Scale[8]	-	-	-	67%
Meds 'Always' Explained Before Given[8]	-	-	-	60%
Nurses 'Always' Communicated Well[8]	-	-	-	76%
Pain 'Always' Well Controlled[8]	-	-	-	69%
Room and Bathroom 'Always' Clean[8]	-	-	-	71%
Timely Help 'Always' Received[8]	-	-	-	64%
Would Definitely Recommend Hospital[8]	-	-	-	69%

Union Hospital Clinton

801 S Main St
Clinton, IN 47842
Phone: 765-832-1234
E-mail: prpublic@uhhg.org
URL: www.unionhospitalhealthgroup.org/wcch
Type: Critical Access Hospitals
Emergency Services: Yes
Ownership: Voluntary Non-Profit - Private
Key Personnel:
CEO/President................ Terri Hill

Measure	Cases	This Hosp.	State Avg.	U.S. Avg.
Heart Attack Care				
ACE Inhibitor or ARB for LVSD	0	-	96%	96%
Aspirin at Arrival[1]	1	100%	98%	99%
Aspirin at Discharge	0	-	99%	98%
Beta Blocker at Discharge	0	-	98%	98%
Fibrinolytic Medication Timing	0	-	37%	55%
PCI Within 90 Minutes of Arrival	0	-	93%	90%
Smoking Cessation Advice	0	-	99%	99%
Chest Pain/Possible Heart Attack Care				
Aspirin at Arrival	148	99%	95%	95%
Median Time to ECG (minutes)	155	5	6	8
Median Time to Transfer (minutes)[1]	10	46	49	61
Fibrinolytic Medication Timing	0	-	63%	54%
Heart Failure Care				
ACE Inhibitor or ARB for LVSD[1]	12	100%	92%	94%
Discharge Instructions	34	62%	84%	88%
Evaluation of LVS Function	41	100%	98%	98%
Smoking Cessation Advice[1]	6	100%	99%	98%
Pneumonia Care				
Appropriate Initial Antibiotic	36	97%	90%	92%
Blood Culture Timing[1]	21	90%	95%	96%
Influenza Vaccine[1]	18	100%	93%	91%
Initial Antibiotic Timing	48	96%	96%	95%
Pneumococcal Vaccine	40	98%	94%	93%
Smoking Cessation Advice	29	93%	98%	97%
Surgical Care Improvement Project				
Appropriate VTP Within 24 Hours[1]	13	92%	90%	92%
Appropriate Hair Removal[1]	23	100%	100%	99%
Appropriate Beta Blocker Usage[1]	8	62%	93%	93%
Controlled Postoperative Blood Glucose	0	-	93%	93%
Prophylactic Antibiotic Timing[1]	11	91%	97%	97%
Prophylactic Antibiotic Timing (Outpatient)[5]	0	-	92%	92%
Prophylactic Antibiotic Selection[1]	11	100%	98%	97%
Prophylactic Antibiotic Select. (Outpatient)[5]	0	-	95%	94%
Prophylactic Antibiotic Stopped[1]	11	100%	95%	94%
Recommended VTP Ordered[1]	13	100%	92%	94%
Urinary Catheter Removal[1]	4	75%	92%	90%
Children's Asthma Care				
Received Systemic Corticosteroids	-	-	-	100%
Received Home Management Plan	-	-	-	71%
Received Reliever Medication	-	-	-	100%
Use of Medical Imaging				
Combination Abdominal CT Scan	313	0.438	0.237	0.191
Combination Chest CT Scan	178	0.534	0.120	0.054
Follow-up Mammogram/Ultrasound	234	7.7%	8.3%	8.4%
MRI for Low Back Pain[5]	0	-	35.2%	32.7%
Survey of Patients' Hospital Experiences				
Area Around Room 'Always' Quiet at Night	300+	53%	-	58%
Doctors 'Always' Communicated Well	300+	81%	-	80%
Home Recovery Information Given	300+	83%	-	82%
Hospital Given 9 or 10 on 10 Point Scale	300+	70%	-	67%
Meds 'Always' Explained Before Given	300+	65%	-	60%
Nurses 'Always' Communicated Well	300+	80%	-	76%
Pain 'Always' Well Controlled	300+	74%	-	69%
Room and Bathroom 'Always' Clean	300+	75%	-	71%
Timely Help 'Always' Received	300+	75%	-	64%
Would Definitely Recommend Hospital	300+	68%	-	69%

Parkview Whitley Hospital

353 N Oak St
Columbia City, IN 46725
Phone: 260-248-9301
Fax: 260-248-9107
URL: www.parkview.com
Type: Acute Care Hospitals
Emergency Services: Yes
Ownership: Voluntary Non-Profit - Private
Beds: 45
Key Personnel:
CEO/President............... John Meister
Chief of Medical Staff.......... Dr Jeff Brookes

Measure	Cases	This Hosp.	State Avg.	U.S. Avg.
Heart Attack Care				
ACE Inhibitor or ARB for LVSD[3]	0	-	96%	96%
Aspirin at Arrival[3]	0	-	98%	99%
Aspirin at Discharge[3]	0	-	99%	98%
Beta Blocker at Discharge[3]	0	-	98%	98%
Fibrinolytic Medication Timing[3]	0	-	37%	55%
PCI Within 90 Minutes of Arrival[3]	0	-	93%	90%
Smoking Cessation Advice[3]	0	-	99%	99%
Chest Pain/Possible Heart Attack Care				
Aspirin at Arrival	158	97%	95%	95%
Median Time to ECG (minutes)	159	6	6	8
Median Time to Transfer (minutes)[1]	8	31	49	61
Fibrinolytic Medication Timing[1]	1	100%	63%	54%
Heart Failure Care				
ACE Inhibitor or ARB for LVSD[1]	5	80%	92%	94%
Discharge Instructions	26	81%	84%	88%
Evaluation of LVS Function	41	90%	98%	98%
Smoking Cessation Advice[1]	8	100%	99%	98%
Pneumonia Care				
Appropriate Initial Antibiotic	50	96%	90%	92%
Blood Culture Timing	45	96%	95%	96%
Influenza Vaccine	32	97%	93%	91%
Initial Antibiotic Timing	58	98%	96%	95%
Pneumococcal Vaccine	51	96%	94%	93%
Smoking Cessation Advice[1]	20	100%	98%	97%
Surgical Care Improvement Project				
Appropriate VTP Within 24 Hours	26	92%	90%	92%
Appropriate Hair Removal	69	100%	100%	99%
Appropriate Beta Blocker Usage[1]	19	95%	93%	93%
Controlled Postoperative Blood Glucose	0	-	93%	93%
Prophylactic Antibiotic Timing	54	98%	97%	97%
Prophylactic Antibiotic Timing (Outpatient)	42	90%	92%	92%
Prophylactic Antibiotic Selection	54	100%	98%	97%
Prophylactic Antibiotic Select. (Outpatient)	41	95%	95%	94%
Prophylactic Antibiotic Stopped	50	94%	95%	94%
Recommended VTP Ordered	26	92%	92%	94%
Urinary Catheter Removal[1]	15	100%	92%	90%
Children's Asthma Care				
Received Systemic Corticosteroids	-	-	-	100%
Received Home Management Plan	-	-	-	71%
Received Reliever Medication	-	-	-	100%
Use of Medical Imaging				
Combination Abdominal CT Scan	214	0.262	0.237	0.191
Combination Chest CT Scan	134	0.045	0.120	0.054
Follow-up Mammogram/Ultrasound	332	6.0%	8.3%	8.4%
MRI for Low Back Pain	62	35.5%	35.2%	32.7%
Survey of Patients' Hospital Experiences				
Area Around Room 'Always' Quiet at Night	300+	64%	-	58%
Doctors 'Always' Communicated Well	300+	89%	-	80%
Home Recovery Information Given	300+	90%	-	82%
Hospital Given 9 or 10 on 10 Point Scale	300+	79%	-	67%
Meds 'Always' Explained Before Given	300+	69%	-	60%
Nurses 'Always' Communicated Well	300+	87%	-	76%
Pain 'Always' Well Controlled	300+	81%	-	69%
Room and Bathroom 'Always' Clean	300+	78%	-	71%
Timely Help 'Always' Received	300+	79%	-	64%
Would Definitely Recommend Hospital	300+	78%	-	69%

NOTE: Hospital profiles are in alphabetical order by state, then city, then hospital within the city; Rankings exclude hospitals with less than 25 cases except for patient surveys which excludes hospitals with less than 100 cases; (a) 100–299 cases; (1) The number of cases is too small to be sure how well a hospital is performing; (2) The hospital indicated that the data submitted for this measure were based on a sample of cases; (3) Data was collected during a shorter time period (fewer quarters) than the maximum possible time for this measure; (4) Suppressed for one or more quarters by CMS; (5) No data is available from the hospital for this measure; (6) Fewer than 100 patients completed the HCAHPS survey. Use these rates with caution, as the number of surveys may be too low to reliably assess hospital performance; (7) Survey results are based on less than 12 months of data; (8) Survey results are not available for this reporting period; (9) No or very few patients were eligible for the HCAHPS survey. The scores shown, if any, reflect a very small number of surveys; (10) A state average was not calculated because too few hospitals in the state submitted data; (11) There were discrepancies in the data collection process; Please refer to the User's Guide for a full explanation of data.

Columbus Regional Hospital

2400 E 17th Street
Columbus, IN 47201
URL: www.crh.org
Phone: 812-379-4441
Fax: 812-376-5001
Type: Acute Care Hospitals
Ownership: Government - Local
Emergency Services: Yes
Beds: 225

Key Personnel:

CEO/President. . . . . Douglas Lenord
Chief of Medical Staff . . . . D Sauderman
Infection Control. . . . . Cindy Fields
Quality Assurance . . . . Martha Myers
Radiology. . . . . Martha J Dwenger

Measure	Cases	This Hosp.	State Avg.	U.S. Avg.
Heart Attack Care				
ACE Inhibitor or ARB for LVSD	36	89%	96%	96%
Aspirin at Arrival	195	99%	98%	99%
Aspirin at Discharge	242	99%	99%	98%
Beta Blocker at Discharge	235	98%	98%	98%
Fibrinolytic Medication Timing	0	-	37%	55%
PCI Within 90 Minutes of Arrival	46	98%	93%	90%
Smoking Cessation Advice	61	100%	99%	99%
Chest Pain/Possible Heart Attack Care				
Aspirin at Arrival[1]	16	100%	95%	95%
Median Time to ECG (minutes)[1]	19	2	6	8
Median Time to Transfer (minutes)[5]	0	-	49	61
Fibrinolytic Medication Timing[3]	0	-	63%	54%
Heart Failure Care				
ACE Inhibitor or ARB for LVSD	98	96%	92%	94%
Discharge Instructions	190	68%	84%	88%
Evaluation of LVS Function	247	99%	98%	98%
Smoking Cessation Advice	45	100%	99%	98%
Pneumonia Care				
Appropriate Initial Antibiotic	144	95%	90%	92%
Blood Culture Timing	218	98%	95%	96%
Influenza Vaccine	163	99%	93%	91%
Initial Antibiotic Timing	215	99%	96%	95%
Pneumococcal Vaccine	210	98%	94%	93%
Smoking Cessation Advice	120	100%	98%	97%
Surgical Care Improvement Project				
Appropriate VTP Within 24 Hours	192	90%	90%	92%
Appropriate Hair Removal	734	100%	100%	99%
Appropriate Beta Blocker Usage	242	95%	93%	93%
Controlled Postoperative Blood Glucose	56	93%	93%	93%
Prophylactic Antibiotic Timing	471	99%	97%	97%
Prophylactic Antibiotic Timing (Outpatient)	386	96%	92%	92%
Prophylactic Antibiotic Selection	469	99%	98%	97%
Prophylactic Antibiotic Select. (Outpatient)	381	97%	95%	94%
Prophylactic Antibiotic Stopped	426	96%	95%	94%
Recommended VTP Ordered	192	93%	92%	94%
Urinary Catheter Removal	208	98%	92%	90%
Children's Asthma Care				
Received Systemic Corticosteroids	-	-	-	100%
Received Home Management Plan	-	-	-	71%
Received Reliever Medication	-	-	-	100%
Use of Medical Imaging				
Combination Abdominal CT Scan	563	0.025	0.237	0.191
Combination Chest CT Scan	553	0.005	0.120	0.054
Follow-up Mammogram/Ultrasound	1,283	9.7%	8.3%	8.4%
MRI for Low Back Pain	84	35.7%	35.2%	32.7%
Survey of Patients' Hospital Experiences				
Area Around Room 'Always' Quiet at Night	300+	44%	-	58%
Doctors 'Always' Communicated Well	300+	83%	-	80%
Home Recovery Information Given	300+	79%	-	82%
Hospital Given 9 or 10 on 10 Point Scale	300+	71%	-	67%
Meds 'Always' Explained Before Given	300+	58%	-	60%
Nurses 'Always' Communicated Well	300+	77%	-	76%
Pain 'Always' Well Controlled	300+	71%	-	69%
Room and Bathroom 'Always' Clean	300+	79%	-	71%
Timely Help 'Always' Received	300+	64%	-	64%
Would Definitely Recommend Hospital	300+	72%	-	69%

Fayette Regional Health System

1941 Virginia Ave
Connersville, IN 47331
URL: www.fayettememorial.org
Phone: 765-825-5131
Fax: 765-827-7775
Type: Acute Care Hospitals
Ownership: Voluntary Non-Profit - Private
Emergency Services: Yes
Beds: 140

Key Personnel:

CEO/President. . . . . David R Brandon
Cardiac Laboratory. . . . . Joan Baum, DO
Chief of Medical Staff . . . . Wayne White
Operating Room. . . . . Peggy Stang
Quality Assurance . . . . Betty Klein
Anesthesiology. . . . . Abdul Khan, MD
Emergency Room . . . . Shelley Millor
Intensive Care Unit. . . . . Paula Anderson

Measure	Cases	This Hosp.	State Avg.	U.S. Avg.
Heart Attack Care				
ACE Inhibitor or ARB for LVSD[1]	3	100%	96%	96%
Aspirin at Arrival[1]	15	100%	98%	99%
Aspirin at Discharge[1]	10	100%	99%	98%
Beta Blocker at Discharge[1]	11	100%	98%	98%
Fibrinolytic Medication Timing	0	-	37%	55%
PCI Within 90 Minutes of Arrival	0	-	93%	90%
Smoking Cessation Advice[1]	2	100%	99%	99%
Chest Pain/Possible Heart Attack Care				
Aspirin at Arrival	97	94%	95%	95%
Median Time to ECG (minutes)	102	7	6	8
Median Time to Transfer (minutes)[1]	8	44	49	61
Fibrinolytic Medication Timing	0	-	63%	54%
Heart Failure Care				
ACE Inhibitor or ARB for LVSD	28	100%	92%	94%
Discharge Instructions	57	93%	84%	88%
Evaluation of LVS Function	88	100%	98%	98%
Smoking Cessation Advice[1]	12	100%	99%	98%
Pneumonia Care				
Appropriate Initial Antibiotic	97	93%	90%	92%
Blood Culture Timing	121	99%	95%	96%
Influenza Vaccine	82	99%	93%	91%
Initial Antibiotic Timing	143	99%	96%	95%
Pneumococcal Vaccine	130	100%	94%	93%
Smoking Cessation Advice	79	100%	98%	97%
Surgical Care Improvement Project				
Appropriate VTP Within 24 Hours	30	97%	90%	92%
Appropriate Hair Removal	99	99%	100%	99%
Appropriate Beta Blocker Usage	29	97%	93%	93%
Controlled Postoperative Blood Glucose	0	-	93%	93%
Prophylactic Antibiotic Timing	83	99%	97%	97%
Prophylactic Antibiotic Timing (Outpatient)	43	81%	92%	92%
Prophylactic Antibiotic Selection	83	95%	98%	97%
Prophylactic Antibiotic Select. (Outpatient)	39	92%	95%	94%
Prophylactic Antibiotic Stopped	78	97%	95%	94%
Recommended VTP Ordered	30	97%	92%	94%
Urinary Catheter Removal[1]	22	100%	92%	90%
Children's Asthma Care				
Received Systemic Corticosteroids	-	-	-	100%
Received Home Management Plan	-	-	-	71%
Received Reliever Medication	-	-	-	100%
Use of Medical Imaging				
Combination Abdominal CT Scan	245	0.053	0.237	0.191
Combination Chest CT Scan	156	0.013	0.120	0.054
Follow-up Mammogram/Ultrasound	370	5.7%	8.3%	8.4%
MRI for Low Back Pain	73	31.5%	35.2%	32.7%
Survey of Patients' Hospital Experiences				
Area Around Room 'Always' Quiet at Night	300+	67%	-	58%
Doctors 'Always' Communicated Well	300+	84%	-	80%
Home Recovery Information Given	300+	88%	-	82%
Hospital Given 9 or 10 on 10 Point Scale	300+	71%	-	67%
Meds 'Always' Explained Before Given	300+	69%	-	60%
Nurses 'Always' Communicated Well	300+	82%	-	76%
Pain 'Always' Well Controlled	300+	77%	-	69%
Room and Bathroom 'Always' Clean	300+	84%	-	71%
Timely Help 'Always' Received	300+	76%	-	64%
Would Definitely Recommend Hospital	300+	66%	-	69%

Harrison County Hospital

1141 Hospital Drive NW
Corydon, IN 47112
URL: www.hchin.org
Phone: 812-738-4251
Fax: 812-738-7829
Type: Critical Access Hospitals
Ownership: Government - Local
Emergency Services: Yes
Beds: 68

Key Personnel:

CEO/President. . . . . Steve Taylor
Chief of Medical Staff . . . . Reggie Lyell, MD
Infection Control. . . . . Debra Gibson
Operating Room. . . . . Rashidul Islam, RN
Pediatric Ambulatory Care . . . . . . John Norton, MD
Pediatric In-Patient Care . . . . John Norton, MD
Quality Assurance . . . . Jonell Dailey
Radiology. . . . . Christopher J Day

Measure	Cases	This Hosp.	State Avg.	U.S. Avg.
Heart Attack Care				
ACE Inhibitor or ARB for LVSD[1]	2	0%	96%	96%
Aspirin at Arrival[1]	5	100%	98%	99%
Aspirin at Discharge[1]	4	100%	99%	98%
Beta Blocker at Discharge[1]	4	75%	98%	98%
Fibrinolytic Medication Timing	0	-	37%	55%
PCI Within 90 Minutes of Arrival	0	-	93%	90%
Smoking Cessation Advice[1]	1	0%	99%	99%
Chest Pain/Possible Heart Attack Care				
Aspirin at Arrival	87	94%	95%	95%
Median Time to ECG (minutes)	97	6	6	8
Median Time to Transfer (minutes)[1]	20	57	49	61
Fibrinolytic Medication Timing[1]	1	0%	63%	54%
Heart Failure Care				
ACE Inhibitor or ARB for LVSD[1]	7	100%	92%	94%
Discharge Instructions[1]	23	87%	84%	88%
Evaluation of LVS Function	39	97%	98%	98%
Smoking Cessation Advice[1]	9	100%	99%	98%
Pneumonia Care				
Appropriate Initial Antibiotic	75	80%	90%	92%
Blood Culture Timing	64	89%	95%	96%
Influenza Vaccine	71	85%	93%	91%
Initial Antibiotic Timing	94	95%	96%	95%
Pneumococcal Vaccine	104	92%	94%	93%
Smoking Cessation Advice	40	80%	98%	97%
Surgical Care Improvement Project				
Appropriate VTP Within 24 Hours	28	100%	90%	92%
Appropriate Hair Removal	42	98%	100%	99%
Appropriate Beta Blocker Usage[1]	8	100%	93%	93%
Controlled Postoperative Blood Glucose	0	-	93%	93%
Prophylactic Antibiotic Timing[1]	17	94%	97%	97%
Prophylactic Antibiotic Timing (Outpatient)[1]	22	95%	92%	92%
Prophylactic Antibiotic Selection[1]	19	95%	98%	97%
Prophylactic Antibiotic Select. (Outpatient)[1]	21	100%	95%	94%
Prophylactic Antibiotic Stopped[1]	16	81%	95%	94%
Recommended VTP Ordered	28	100%	92%	94%
Urinary Catheter Removal[1]	13	92%	92%	90%
Children's Asthma Care				
Received Systemic Corticosteroids	-	-	-	100%
Received Home Management Plan	-	-	-	71%
Received Reliever Medication	-	-	-	100%
Use of Medical Imaging				
Combination Abdominal CT Scan	379	0.704	0.237	0.191
Combination Chest CT Scan	222	0.131	0.120	0.054
Follow-up Mammogram/Ultrasound	505	10.1%	8.3%	8.4%
MRI for Low Back Pain	81	39.5%	35.2%	32.7%
Survey of Patients' Hospital Experiences				
Area Around Room 'Always' Quiet at Night	300+	59%	-	58%
Doctors 'Always' Communicated Well	300+	88%	-	80%
Home Recovery Information Given	300+	89%	-	82%
Hospital Given 9 or 10 on 10 Point Scale	300+	71%	-	67%
Meds 'Always' Explained Before Given	300+	70%	-	60%
Nurses 'Always' Communicated Well	300+	81%	-	76%
Pain 'Always' Well Controlled	300+	71%	-	69%
Room and Bathroom 'Always' Clean	300+	82%	-	71%
Timely Help 'Always' Received	300+	71%	-	64%
Would Definitely Recommend Hospital	300+	71%	-	69%

NOTE: Hospital profiles are in alphabetical order by state, then city, then hospital within the city; Rankings exclude hospitals with less than 25 cases except for patient surveys which excludes hospitals with less than 100 cases; (a) 100–299 cases; (1) The number of cases is too small to be sure how well a hospital is performing; (2) The hospital indicated that the data submitted for this measure were based on a sample of cases; (3) Data was collected during a shorter time period (fewer quarters) than the maximum possible time for this measure; (4) Suppressed for one or more quarters by CMS; (5) No data is available from the hospital for this measure; (6) Fewer than 100 patients completed the HCAHPS survey. Use these rates with caution, as the number of surveys may be too low to reliably assess hospital performance; (7) Survey results are based on less than 12 months of data; (8) Survey results are not available for this reporting period; (9) No or very few patients were eligible for the HCAHPS survey. The scores shown, if any, reflect a very small number of surveys; (10) A state average was not calculated because too few hospitals in the state submitted data; (11) There were discrepancies in the data collection process; Please refer to the User's Guide for a full explanation of data.

Saint Clare Medical Center

1710 Lafayette Road
Crawfordsville, IN 47933
URL: www.stclaremedical.org
Type: Acute Care Hospitals
Ownership: Voluntary Non-Profit - Church

Phone: 765-362-2800
Fax: 765-364-9010
Emergency Services: Yes
Beds: 120

Key Personnel:
Chief of Medical Staff. . . . . Jude Momodu
Radiology. . . . . Barry E Allen

Measure	Cases	This Hosp.	State Avg.	U.S. Avg.
Heart Attack Care				
ACE Inhibitor or ARB for LVSD[1]	1	0%	96%	96%
Aspirin at Arrival[1]	5	100%	98%	99%
Aspirin at Discharge[1]	3	100%	99%	98%
Beta Blocker at Discharge[1]	2	100%	98%	98%
Fibrinolytic Medication Timing	0	-	37%	55%
PCI Within 90 Minutes of Arrival	0	-	93%	90%
Smoking Cessation Advice	0	-	99%	99%
Chest Pain/Possible Heart Attack Care				
Aspirin at Arrival	165	92%	95%	95%
Median Time to ECG (minutes)	167	9	6	8
Median Time to Transfer (minutes)[1,3]	6	44	49	61
Fibrinolytic Medication Timing	0	-	63%	54%
Heart Failure Care				
ACE Inhibitor or ARB for LVSD[1]	24	83%	92%	94%
Discharge Instructions	70	94%	84%	88%
Evaluation of LVS Function	106	85%	98%	98%
Smoking Cessation Advice[1]	4	100%	99%	98%
Pneumonia Care				
Appropriate Initial Antibiotic	67	88%	90%	92%
Blood Culture Timing	60	95%	95%	96%
Influenza Vaccine	47	87%	93%	91%
Initial Antibiotic Timing	87	99%	96%	95%
Pneumococcal Vaccine	69	78%	94%	93%
Smoking Cessation Advice[1]	17	100%	98%	97%
Surgical Care Improvement Project				
Appropriate VTP Within 24 Hours	48	83%	90%	92%
Appropriate Hair Removal	158	100%	100%	99%
Appropriate Beta Blocker Usage	33	97%	93%	93%
Controlled Postoperative Blood Glucose	0	-	93%	93%
Prophylactic Antibiotic Timing	140	99%	97%	97%
Prophylactic Antibiotic Timing (Outpatient)	51	90%	92%	92%
Prophylactic Antibiotic Selection	142	99%	98%	97%
Prophylactic Antibiotic Select. (Outpatient)	47	100%	95%	94%
Prophylactic Antibiotic Stopped	140	92%	95%	94%
Recommended VTP Ordered	49	86%	92%	94%
Urinary Catheter Removal	55	100%	92%	90%
Children's Asthma Care				
Received Systemic Corticosteroids	-	-	-	100%
Received Home Management Plan	-	-	-	71%
Received Reliever Medication	-	-	-	100%
Use of Medical Imaging				
Combination Abdominal CT Scan	539	0.046	0.237	0.191
Combination Chest CT Scan	312	0.032	0.120	0.054
Follow-up Mammogram/Ultrasound	748	6.4%	8.3%	8.4%
MRI for Low Back Pain	128	30.5%	35.2%	32.7%
Survey of Patients' Hospital Experiences				
Area Around Room 'Always' Quiet at Night	300+	51%	-	58%
Doctors 'Always' Communicated Well	300+	80%	-	80%
Home Recovery Information Given	300+	80%	-	82%
Hospital Given 9 or 10 on 10 Point Scale	300+	59%	-	67%
Meds 'Always' Explained Before Given	300+	56%	-	60%
Nurses 'Always' Communicated Well	300+	74%	-	76%
Pain 'Always' Well Controlled	300+	64%	-	69%
Room and Bathroom 'Always' Clean	300+	68%	-	71%
Timely Help 'Always' Received	300+	61%	-	64%
Would Definitely Recommend Hospital	300+	59%	-	69%

Franciscan St Anthony Health - Crown Point

1201 S Main St
Crown Point, IN 46307
URL: www.stanthonymedicalcenter.com
Type: Acute Care Hospitals
Ownership: Voluntary Non-Profit - Church

Phone: 219-757-6100
Fax: 219-757-6242
Emergency Services: Yes
Beds: 411

Key Personnel:
CEO/President. . . . . David F Ruskowski
Cardiac Laboratory. . . . . Susan Slivka
Infection Control. . . . . Chris Shakula
Operating Room. . . . . Carla McArdle
Pediatric Ambulatory Care . . . . . . Darlene Sekerez MD
Pediatric In-Patient Care . . . . Darlene Sekerez MD
Quality Assurance . . . . Sharon Werner
Radiology. . . . . Mohammed Abbas MD

Measure	Cases	This Hosp.	State Avg.	U.S. Avg.
Heart Attack Care				
ACE Inhibitor or ARB for LVSD[1]	19	95%	96%	96%
Aspirin at Arrival	162	99%	98%	99%
Aspirin at Discharge	142	99%	99%	98%
Beta Blocker at Discharge	149	97%	98%	98%
Fibrinolytic Medication Timing	0	-	37%	55%
PCI Within 90 Minutes of Arrival	36	94%	93%	90%
Smoking Cessation Advice	67	100%	99%	99%
Chest Pain/Possible Heart Attack Care				
Aspirin at Arrival[5]	0	-	95%	95%
Median Time to ECG (minutes)[5]	0	-	6	8
Median Time to Transfer (minutes)[5]	0	-	49	61
Fibrinolytic Medication Timing[5]	0	-	63%	54%
Heart Failure Care				
ACE Inhibitor or ARB for LVSD[2]	83	87%	92%	94%
Discharge Instructions[2]	196	83%	84%	88%
Evaluation of LVS Function[2]	270	99%	98%	98%
Smoking Cessation Advice[2]	46	98%	99%	98%
Pneumonia Care				
Appropriate Initial Antibiotic[2]	78	88%	90%	92%
Blood Culture Timing[2]	126	98%	95%	96%
Influenza Vaccine[2]	79	95%	93%	91%
Initial Antibiotic Timing[2]	145	97%	96%	95%
Pneumococcal Vaccine[2]	124	98%	94%	93%
Smoking Cessation Advice[2]	47	98%	98%	97%
Surgical Care Improvement Project				
Appropriate VTP Within 24 Hours[2]	194	81%	90%	92%
Appropriate Hair Removal[2]	455	100%	100%	99%
Appropriate Beta Blocker Usage[2]	113	87%	93%	93%
Controlled Postoperative Blood Glucose[2]	66	77%	93%	93%
Prophylactic Antibiotic Timing[2]	322	99%	97%	97%
Prophylactic Antibiotic Timing (Outpatient)	275	96%	92%	92%
Prophylactic Antibiotic Selection[2]	326	94%	98%	97%
Prophylactic Antibiotic Select. (Outpatient)	267	92%	95%	94%
Prophylactic Antibiotic Stopped[2]	314	85%	95%	94%
Recommended VTP Ordered[2]	194	85%	92%	94%
Urinary Catheter Removal[2]	99	73%	92%	90%
Children's Asthma Care				
Received Systemic Corticosteroids	-	-	-	100%
Received Home Management Plan	-	-	-	71%
Received Reliever Medication	-	-	-	100%
Use of Medical Imaging				
Combination Abdominal CT Scan	1,035	0.333	0.237	0.191
Combination Chest CT Scan	760	0.445	0.120	0.054
Follow-up Mammogram/Ultrasound	1,644	7.4%	8.3%	8.4%
MRI for Low Back Pain	212	28.8%	35.2%	32.7%
Survey of Patients' Hospital Experiences				
Area Around Room 'Always' Quiet at Night	300+	49%	-	58%
Doctors 'Always' Communicated Well	300+	77%	-	80%
Home Recovery Information Given	300+	84%	-	82%
Hospital Given 9 or 10 on 10 Point Scale	300+	68%	-	67%
Meds 'Always' Explained Before Given	300+	57%	-	60%
Nurses 'Always' Communicated Well	300+	75%	-	76%
Pain 'Always' Well Controlled	300+	68%	-	69%
Room and Bathroom 'Always' Clean	300+	77%	-	71%
Timely Help 'Always' Received	300+	55%	-	64%
Would Definitely Recommend Hospital	300+	73%	-	69%

Pinnacle Hospital

9301 Connecticut Drive
Crown Point, IN 46307
URL: www.pinnaclehealthcare.net
Type: Acute Care Hospitals
Ownership: Proprietary

Phone: 219-756-2100
Emergency Services: No
Beds: 18

Measure	Cases	This Hosp.	State Avg.	U.S. Avg.
Heart Attack Care				
ACE Inhibitor or ARB for LVSD[5]	0	-	96%	96%
Aspirin at Arrival[5]	0	-	98%	99%
Aspirin at Discharge[5]	0	-	99%	98%
Beta Blocker at Discharge[5]	0	-	98%	98%
Fibrinolytic Medication Timing[5]	0	-	37%	55%
PCI Within 90 Minutes of Arrival[5]	0	-	93%	90%
Smoking Cessation Advice[5]	0	-	99%	99%
Chest Pain/Possible Heart Attack Care				
Aspirin at Arrival[5]	0	-	95%	95%
Median Time to ECG (minutes)[5]	0	-	6	8
Median Time to Transfer (minutes)[5]	0	-	49	61
Fibrinolytic Medication Timing[5]	0	-	63%	54%
Heart Failure Care				
ACE Inhibitor or ARB for LVSD[1,2]	10	60%	92%	94%
Discharge Instructions[1,2]	20	60%	84%	88%
Evaluation of LVS Function[2]	27	78%	98%	98%
Smoking Cessation Advice[1,2]	3	67%	99%	98%
Pneumonia Care				
Appropriate Initial Antibiotic[1]	12	58%	90%	92%
Blood Culture Timing	0	-	95%	96%
Influenza Vaccine[1]	17	76%	93%	91%
Initial Antibiotic Timing[1]	15	73%	96%	95%
Pneumococcal Vaccine[1]	24	67%	94%	93%
Smoking Cessation Advice[1]	3	100%	98%	97%
Surgical Care Improvement Project				
Appropriate VTP Within 24 Hours[1,2]	2	50%	90%	92%
Appropriate Hair Removal[1,2]	18	100%	100%	99%
Appropriate Beta Blocker Usage[1,2]	2	100%	93%	93%
Controlled Postoperative Blood Glucose[2]	0	-	93%	93%
Prophylactic Antibiotic Timing[1,2]	9	78%	97%	97%
Prophylactic Antibiotic Timing (Outpatient)[1]	21	81%	92%	92%
Prophylactic Antibiotic Selection[1,2]	9	89%	98%	97%
Prophylactic Antibiotic Select. (Outpatient)[1]	19	84%	95%	94%
Prophylactic Antibiotic Stopped[1,2]	9	100%	95%	94%
Recommended VTP Ordered[1,2]	2	50%	92%	94%
Urinary Catheter Removal[1]	3	33%	92%	90%
Children's Asthma Care				
Received Systemic Corticosteroids	-	-	-	100%
Received Home Management Plan	-	-	-	71%
Received Reliever Medication	-	-	-	100%
Use of Medical Imaging				
Combination Abdominal CT Scan	92	0.326	0.237	0.191
Combination Chest CT Scan	73	0.192	0.120	0.054
Follow-up Mammogram/Ultrasound[5]	0	-	8.3%	8.4%
MRI for Low Back Pain	79	38.0%	35.2%	32.7%
Survey of Patients' Hospital Experiences				
Area Around Room 'Always' Quiet at Night[8]	-	-	-	58%
Doctors 'Always' Communicated Well[8]	-	-	-	80%
Home Recovery Information Given[8]	-	-	-	82%
Hospital Given 9 or 10 on 10 Point Scale[8]	-	-	-	67%
Meds 'Always' Explained Before Given[8]	-	-	-	60%
Nurses 'Always' Communicated Well[8]	-	-	-	76%
Pain 'Always' Well Controlled[8]	-	-	-	69%
Room and Bathroom 'Always' Clean[8]	-	-	-	71%
Timely Help 'Always' Received[8]	-	-	-	64%
Would Definitely Recommend Hospital[8]	-	-	-	69%

NOTE: Hospital profiles are in alphabetical order by state, then city, then hospital within the city; Rankings exclude hospitals with less than 25 cases except for patient surveys which excludes hospitals with less than 100 cases; (a) 100–299 cases; (1) The number of cases is too small to be sure how well a hospital is performing; (2) The hospital indicated that the data submitted for this measure were based on a sample of cases; (3) Data was collected during a shorter time period (fewer quarters) than the maximum possible time for this measure; (4) Suppressed for one or more quarters by CMS; (5) No data is available from the hospital for this measure; (6) Fewer than 100 patients completed the HCAHPS survey. Use these rates with caution, as the number of surveys may be too low to reliably assess hospital performance; (7) Survey results are based on less than 12 months of data; (8) Survey results are not available for this reporting period; (9) No or very few patients were eligible for the HCAHPS survey. The scores shown, if any, reflect a very small number of surveys; (10) A state average was not calculated because too few hospitals in the state submitted data; (11) There were discrepancies in the data collection process; Please refer to the User's Guide for a full explanation of data.

Hendricks Regional Health

1000 E Main Street
Danville, IN 46122
URL: www.hendricksregional.org
Phone: 317-745-4451
Fax: 317-745-8325
Type: Acute Care Hospitals
Ownership: Government - Local
Emergency Services: Yes
Beds: 141

Key Personnel:

CEO/President. . . . . Dennis W Dawes
Chief of Medical Staff . . . . Gordon Reed
Coronary Care . . . . Jo Morton
Operating Room. . . . . Christopher M Evanson
Pediatric In-Patient Care . . . . . . Deb Case
Radiology. . . . . Mark G Ferrara
Intensive Care Unit. . . . . Jo Morton
Patient Relations . . . . Trudy Tharp

Measure	Cases	This Hosp.	State Avg.	U.S. Avg.
Heart Attack Care				
ACE Inhibitor or ARB for LVSD[1]	22	95%	96%	96%
Aspirin at Arrival	72	99%	98%	99%
Aspirin at Discharge	59	100%	99%	98%
Beta Blocker at Discharge	53	98%	98%	98%
Fibrinolytic Medication Timing	0	-	37%	55%
PCI Within 90 Minutes of Arrival[1]	2	100%	93%	90%
Smoking Cessation Advice[1]	9	100%	99%	99%
Chest Pain/Possible Heart Attack Care				
Aspirin at Arrival	174	94%	95%	95%
Median Time to ECG (minutes)	176	10	6	8
Median Time to Transfer (minutes)	25	58	49	61
Fibrinolytic Medication Timing	0	-	63%	54%
Heart Failure Care				
ACE Inhibitor or ARB for LVSD	48	92%	92%	94%
Discharge Instructions	106	85%	84%	88%
Evaluation of LVS Function	146	97%	98%	98%
Smoking Cessation Advice[1]	22	100%	99%	98%
Pneumonia Care				
Appropriate Initial Antibiotic	125	79%	90%	92%
Blood Culture Timing	134	90%	95%	96%
Influenza Vaccine	118	93%	93%	91%
Initial Antibiotic Timing	174	98%	96%	95%
Pneumococcal Vaccine	159	89%	94%	93%
Smoking Cessation Advice	51	100%	98%	97%
Surgical Care Improvement Project				
Appropriate VTP Within 24 Hours	112	95%	90%	92%
Appropriate Hair Removal	358	99%	100%	99%
Appropriate Beta Blocker Usage	97	79%	93%	93%
Controlled Postoperative Blood Glucose	0	-	93%	93%
Prophylactic Antibiotic Timing	258	97%	97%	97%
Prophylactic Antibiotic Timing (Outpatient)	215	91%	92%	92%
Prophylactic Antibiotic Selection	258	97%	98%	97%
Prophylactic Antibiotic Select. (Outpatient)	207	87%	95%	94%
Prophylactic Antibiotic Stopped	254	95%	95%	94%
Recommended VTP Ordered	112	96%	92%	94%
Urinary Catheter Removal	116	89%	92%	90%
Children's Asthma Care				
Received Systemic Corticosteroids	-	-	-	100%
Received Home Management Plan	-	-	-	71%
Received Reliever Medication	-	-	-	100%
Use of Medical Imaging				
Combination Abdominal CT Scan	920	0.292	0.237	0.191
Combination Chest CT Scan	514	0.107	0.120	0.054
Follow-up Mammogram/Ultrasound	1,235	9.6%	8.3%	8.4%
MRI for Low Back Pain	220	37.7%	35.2%	32.7%
Survey of Patients' Hospital Experiences				
Area Around Room 'Always' Quiet at Night	300+	59%	-	58%
Doctors 'Always' Communicated Well	300+	83%	-	80%
Home Recovery Information Given	300+	91%	-	82%
Hospital Given 9 or 10 on 10 Point Scale	300+	81%	-	67%
Meds 'Always' Explained Before Given	300+	60%	-	60%
Nurses 'Always' Communicated Well	300+	79%	-	76%
Pain 'Always' Well Controlled	300+	71%	-	69%
Room and Bathroom 'Always' Clean	300+	77%	-	71%
Timely Help 'Always' Received	300+	62%	-	64%
Would Definitely Recommend Hospital	300+	83%	-	69%

Adams Memorial Hospital

1100 Mercer Avenue
Decatur, IN 46733
URL: www.adamshospital.com
Phone: 260-724-2145
Fax: 260-728-3865
Type: Critical Access Hospitals
Ownership: Government - Local
Emergency Services: Yes
Beds: 87

Key Personnel:

Cardiac Laboratory. . . . . Ronda Brune
Chief of Medical Staff . . . . Brian Zurcher, MD
Infection Control . . . . Peggy LaFountaine
Anesthesiology. . . . . Donald Advent, MD
Emergency Room . . . . Lesley Scholl, MD

Measure	Cases	This Hosp.	State Avg.	U.S. Avg.
Heart Attack Care				
ACE Inhibitor or ARB for LVSD[1]	5	100%	96%	96%
Aspirin at Arrival[1]	19	100%	98%	99%
Aspirin at Discharge[1]	13	100%	99%	98%
Beta Blocker at Discharge[1]	12	100%	98%	98%
Fibrinolytic Medication Timing[1]	1	0%	37%	55%
PCI Within 90 Minutes of Arrival[3]	0	-	93%	90%
Smoking Cessation Advice[1]	3	33%	99%	99%
Chest Pain/Possible Heart Attack Care				
Aspirin at Arrival	-	-	95%	95%
Median Time to ECG (minutes)	-	-	6	8
Median Time to Transfer (minutes)	-	-	49	61
Fibrinolytic Medication Timing	-	-	63%	54%
Heart Failure Care				
ACE Inhibitor or ARB for LVSD[1]	20	100%	92%	94%
Discharge Instructions	66	83%	84%	88%
Evaluation of LVS Function	87	99%	98%	98%
Smoking Cessation Advice[1]	8	100%	99%	98%
Pneumonia Care				
Appropriate Initial Antibiotic	84	82%	90%	92%
Blood Culture Timing	87	92%	95%	96%
Influenza Vaccine	64	92%	93%	91%
Initial Antibiotic Timing	95	95%	96%	95%
Pneumococcal Vaccine	97	90%	94%	93%
Smoking Cessation Advice[1]	17	100%	98%	97%
Surgical Care Improvement Project				
Appropriate VTP Within 24 Hours[1,3]	13	85%	90%	92%
Appropriate Hair Removal	52	87%	100%	99%
Appropriate Beta Blocker Usage[1,3]	12	50%	93%	93%
Controlled Postoperative Blood Glucose[5]	0	-	93%	93%
Prophylactic Antibiotic Timing[1]	20	55%	97%	97%
Prophylactic Antibiotic Timing (Outpatient)	-	-	92%	92%
Prophylactic Antibiotic Selection[1]	21	86%	98%	97%
Prophylactic Antibiotic Select. (Outpatient)	-	-	95%	94%
Prophylactic Antibiotic Stopped[1]	20	80%	95%	94%
Recommended VTP Ordered[1,3]	17	71%	92%	94%
Urinary Catheter Removal[1]	9	89%	92%	90%
Children's Asthma Care				
Received Systemic Corticosteroids	-	-	-	100%
Received Home Management Plan	-	-	-	71%
Received Reliever Medication	-	-	-	100%
Use of Medical Imaging				
Combination Abdominal CT Scan	-	-	0.237	0.191
Combination Chest CT Scan	-	-	0.120	0.054
Follow-up Mammogram/Ultrasound	-	-	8.3%	8.4%
MRI for Low Back Pain	-	-	35.2%	32.7%
Survey of Patients' Hospital Experiences				
Area Around Room 'Always' Quiet at Night[8]	-	-	-	58%
Doctors 'Always' Communicated Well[8]	-	-	-	80%
Home Recovery Information Given[8]	-	-	-	82%
Hospital Given 9 or 10 on 10 Point Scale[8]	-	-	-	67%
Meds 'Always' Explained Before Given[8]	-	-	-	60%
Nurses 'Always' Communicated Well[8]	-	-	-	76%
Pain 'Always' Well Controlled[8]	-	-	-	69%
Room and Bathroom 'Always' Clean[8]	-	-	-	71%
Timely Help 'Always' Received[8]	-	-	-	64%
Would Definitely Recommend Hospital[8]	-	-	-	69%

Franciscan St Margaret Health - Dyer

24 Joliet Street
Dyer, IN 46311
URL: www.smmhc.com
Phone: 219-865-2141
Fax: 219-864-2585
Type: Acute Care Hospitals
Ownership: Voluntary Non-Profit - Church
Emergency Services: Yes
Beds: 794

Key Personnel:

CEO/President. . . . . Eugene Diamond
Cardiac Laboratory. . . . . Dora Slupsizi
Chief of Medical Staff . . . . R Kanuru, MD
Pediatric In-Patient Care . . . . . . Anne Leus
Quality Assurance . . . . Joanne O'Malley
Radiology. . . . . Wally Grzych

Measure	Cases	This Hosp.	State Avg.	U.S. Avg.
Heart Attack Care				
ACE Inhibitor or ARB for LVSD[1]	16	100%	96%	96%
Aspirin at Arrival	100	99%	98%	99%
Aspirin at Discharge	93	100%	99%	98%
Beta Blocker at Discharge	98	98%	98%	98%
Fibrinolytic Medication Timing	0	-	37%	55%
PCI Within 90 Minutes of Arrival[1]	20	100%	93%	90%
Smoking Cessation Advice	33	100%	99%	99%
Chest Pain/Possible Heart Attack Care				
Aspirin at Arrival[5]	0	-	95%	95%
Median Time to ECG (minutes)[5]	0	-	6	8
Median Time to Transfer (minutes)[5]	0	-	49	61
Fibrinolytic Medication Timing[5]	0	-	63%	54%
Heart Failure Care				
ACE Inhibitor or ARB for LVSD	77	94%	92%	94%
Discharge Instructions	200	94%	84%	88%
Evaluation of LVS Function	244	98%	98%	98%
Smoking Cessation Advice	29	100%	99%	98%
Pneumonia Care				
Appropriate Initial Antibiotic	92	95%	90%	92%
Blood Culture Timing	155	96%	95%	96%
Influenza Vaccine	98	90%	93%	91%
Initial Antibiotic Timing	155	95%	96%	95%
Pneumococcal Vaccine	117	85%	94%	93%
Smoking Cessation Advice	32	97%	98%	97%
Surgical Care Improvement Project				
Appropriate VTP Within 24 Hours	208	94%	90%	92%
Appropriate Hair Removal	384	99%	100%	99%
Appropriate Beta Blocker Usage	107	99%	93%	93%
Controlled Postoperative Blood Glucose	40	90%	93%	93%
Prophylactic Antibiotic Timing	240	98%	97%	97%
Prophylactic Antibiotic Timing (Outpatient)	197	77%	92%	92%
Prophylactic Antibiotic Selection	241	98%	98%	97%
Prophylactic Antibiotic Select. (Outpatient)	225	89%	95%	94%
Prophylactic Antibiotic Stopped	223	95%	95%	94%
Recommended VTP Ordered	208	97%	92%	94%
Urinary Catheter Removal	37	86%	92%	90%
Children's Asthma Care				
Received Systemic Corticosteroids	-	-	-	100%
Received Home Management Plan	-	-	-	71%
Received Reliever Medication	-	-	-	100%
Use of Medical Imaging				
Combination Abdominal CT Scan	424	0.594	0.237	0.191
Combination Chest CT Scan	268	0.112	0.120	0.054
Follow-up Mammogram/Ultrasound	440	4.1%	8.3%	8.4%
MRI for Low Back Pain	133	30.8%	35.2%	32.7%
Survey of Patients' Hospital Experiences				
Area Around Room 'Always' Quiet at Night	300+	49%	-	58%
Doctors 'Always' Communicated Well	300+	77%	-	80%
Home Recovery Information Given	300+	74%	-	82%
Hospital Given 9 or 10 on 10 Point Scale	300+	64%	-	67%
Meds 'Always' Explained Before Given	300+	54%	-	60%
Nurses 'Always' Communicated Well	300+	73%	-	76%
Pain 'Always' Well Controlled	300+	66%	-	69%
Room and Bathroom 'Always' Clean	300+	72%	-	71%
Timely Help 'Always' Received	300+	57%	-	64%
Would Definitely Recommend Hospital	300+	65%	-	69%

NOTE: Hospital profiles are in alphabetical order by state, then city, then hospital within the city; Rankings exclude hospitals with less than 25 cases except for patient surveys which excludes hospitals with less than 100 cases; (a) 100–299 cases; (1) The number of cases is too small to be sure how well a hospital is performing; (2) The hospital indicated that the data submitted for this measure were based on a sample of cases; (3) Data was collected during a shorter time period (fewer quarters) than the maximum possible time for this measure; (4) Suppressed for one or more quarters by CMS; (5) No data is available from the hospital for this measure; (6) Fewer than 100 patients completed the HCAHPS survey. Use these rates with caution, as the number of surveys may be too low to reliably assess hospital performance; (7) Survey results are based on less than 12 months of data; (8) Survey results are not available for this reporting period; (9) No or very few patients were eligible for the HCAHPS survey. The scores shown, if any, reflect a very small number of surveys; (10) A state average was not calculated because too few hospitals in the state submitted data; (11) There were discrepancies in the data collection process; Please refer to the User's Guide for a full explanation of data.

Saint Catherine Hospital

4321 Fir Street
East Chicago, IN 46312
URL: www.comhs.org/stcatherine
Type: Acute Care Hospitals
Ownership: Voluntary Non-Profit - Private
Phone: 219-392-7004
Fax: 219-392-7622
Emergency Services: Yes
Beds: 290

Key Personnel:
Cardiac Laboratory. . . . . Miguel Gambette
Chief of Medical Staff . . . . John Griep
Operating Room. . . . . Lori McBride, RN
Emergency Room . . . . Jeffery Dubnow

Measure	Cases	This Hosp.	State Avg.	U.S. Avg.
Heart Attack Care				
ACE Inhibitor or ARB for LVSD[1]	7	100%	96%	96%
Aspirin at Arrival	63	100%	98%	99%
Aspirin at Discharge	53	100%	99%	98%
Beta Blocker at Discharge	59	100%	98%	98%
Fibrinolytic Medication Timing	0	-	37%	55%
PCI Within 90 Minutes of Arrival[1]	9	89%	93%	90%
Smoking Cessation Advice[1]	22	100%	99%	99%
Chest Pain/Possible Heart Attack Care				
Aspirin at Arrival[1,3]	2	100%	95%	95%
Median Time to ECG (minutes)[1,3]	1	0	6	8
Median Time to Transfer (minutes)[5]	0	-	49	61
Fibrinolytic Medication Timing[5]	0	-	63%	54%
Heart Failure Care				
ACE Inhibitor or ARB for LVSD	75	100%	92%	94%
Discharge Instructions	276	97%	84%	88%
Evaluation of LVS Function	338	100%	98%	98%
Smoking Cessation Advice	66	100%	99%	98%
Pneumonia Care				
Appropriate Initial Antibiotic	92	92%	90%	92%
Blood Culture Timing	101	94%	95%	96%
Influenza Vaccine	71	89%	93%	91%
Initial Antibiotic Timing	120	96%	96%	95%
Pneumococcal Vaccine	67	93%	94%	93%
Smoking Cessation Advice	73	100%	98%	97%
Surgical Care Improvement Project				
Appropriate VTP Within 24 Hours	119	97%	90%	92%
Appropriate Hair Removal	307	100%	100%	99%
Appropriate Beta Blocker Usage	78	95%	93%	93%
Controlled Postoperative Blood Glucose	56	98%	93%	93%
Prophylactic Antibiotic Timing	201	100%	97%	97%
Prophylactic Antibiotic Timing (Outpatient)	87	83%	92%	92%
Prophylactic Antibiotic Selection	204	99%	98%	97%
Prophylactic Antibiotic Select. (Outpatient)	82	94%	95%	94%
Prophylactic Antibiotic Stopped	180	94%	95%	94%
Recommended VTP Ordered	119	98%	92%	94%
Urinary Catheter Removal	71	96%	92%	90%
Children's Asthma Care				
Received Systemic Corticosteroids	-	-	-	100%
Received Home Management Plan	-	-	-	71%
Received Reliever Medication	-	-	-	100%
Use of Medical Imaging				
Combination Abdominal CT Scan	406	0.453	0.237	0.191
Combination Chest CT Scan	244	0.008	0.120	0.054
Follow-up Mammogram/Ultrasound	559	4.3%	8.3%	8.4%
MRI for Low Back Pain	112	42.0%	35.2%	32.7%
Survey of Patients' Hospital Experiences				
Area Around Room 'Always' Quiet at Night	300+	59%	-	58%
Doctors 'Always' Communicated Well	300+	78%	-	80%
Home Recovery Information Given	300+	80%	-	82%
Hospital Given 9 or 10 on 10 Point Scale	300+	70%	-	67%
Meds 'Always' Explained Before Given	300+	63%	-	60%
Nurses 'Always' Communicated Well	300+	79%	-	76%
Pain 'Always' Well Controlled	300+	72%	-	69%
Room and Bathroom 'Always' Clean	300+	74%	-	71%
Timely Help 'Always' Received	300+	67%	-	64%
Would Definitely Recommend Hospital	300+	71%	-	69%

Elkhart General Hospital

600 East Blvd
Elkhart, IN 46514
URL: www.egh.org
Type: Acute Care Hospitals
Ownership: Government - Local
Phone: 574-294-2621
Fax: 574-523-3495
Emergency Services: Yes
Beds: 365

Key Personnel:
CEO/President. . . . . Mary Thornton
Quality Assurance . . . . Jean Putnam
Emergency Room . . . . Colleen Nowlin

Measure	Cases	This Hosp.	State Avg.	U.S. Avg.
Heart Attack Care				
ACE Inhibitor or ARB for LVSD	62	97%	96%	96%
Aspirin at Arrival	296	99%	98%	99%
Aspirin at Discharge	329	97%	99%	98%
Beta Blocker at Discharge	296	95%	98%	98%
Fibrinolytic Medication Timing	0	-	37%	55%
PCI Within 90 Minutes of Arrival	49	98%	93%	90%
Smoking Cessation Advice	135	100%	99%	99%
Chest Pain/Possible Heart Attack Care				
Aspirin at Arrival[1]	11	91%	95%	95%
Median Time to ECG (minutes)[1]	13	11	6	8
Median Time to Transfer (minutes)[5]	0	-	49	61
Fibrinolytic Medication Timing[5]	0	-	63%	54%
Heart Failure Care				
ACE Inhibitor or ARB for LVSD	237	87%	92%	94%
Discharge Instructions	417	70%	84%	88%
Evaluation of LVS Function	549	99%	98%	98%
Smoking Cessation Advice	95	100%	99%	98%
Pneumonia Care				
Appropriate Initial Antibiotic	163	88%	90%	92%
Blood Culture Timing	53	96%	95%	96%
Influenza Vaccine	167	87%	93%	91%
Initial Antibiotic Timing	285	96%	96%	95%
Pneumococcal Vaccine	199	87%	94%	93%
Smoking Cessation Advice	122	98%	98%	97%
Surgical Care Improvement Project				
Appropriate VTP Within 24 Hours[2]	164	93%	90%	92%
Appropriate Hair Removal[2]	933	100%	100%	99%
Appropriate Beta Blocker Usage[2]	247	94%	93%	93%
Controlled Postoperative Blood Glucose[2]	228	97%	93%	93%
Prophylactic Antibiotic Timing[2]	691	97%	97%	97%
Prophylactic Antibiotic Timing (Outpatient)	290	92%	92%	92%
Prophylactic Antibiotic Selection[2]	708	95%	98%	97%
Prophylactic Antibiotic Select. (Outpatient)	286	95%	95%	94%
Prophylactic Antibiotic Stopped[2]	655	94%	95%	94%
Recommended VTP Ordered[2]	164	95%	92%	94%
Urinary Catheter Removal[2]	230	99%	92%	90%
Children's Asthma Care				
Received Systemic Corticosteroids	-	-	-	100%
Received Home Management Plan	-	-	-	71%
Received Reliever Medication	-	-	-	100%
Use of Medical Imaging				
Combination Abdominal CT Scan	983	0.067	0.237	0.191
Combination Chest CT Scan	813	0.010	0.120	0.054
Follow-up Mammogram/Ultrasound	2,280	8.2%	8.3%	8.4%
MRI for Low Back Pain	196	33.2%	35.2%	32.7%
Survey of Patients' Hospital Experiences				
Area Around Room 'Always' Quiet at Night	300+	52%	-	58%
Doctors 'Always' Communicated Well	300+	75%	-	80%
Home Recovery Information Given	300+	78%	-	82%
Hospital Given 9 or 10 on 10 Point Scale	300+	68%	-	67%
Meds 'Always' Explained Before Given	300+	54%	-	60%
Nurses 'Always' Communicated Well	300+	73%	-	76%
Pain 'Always' Well Controlled	300+	68%	-	69%
Room and Bathroom 'Always' Clean	300+	73%	-	71%
Timely Help 'Always' Received	300+	61%	-	64%
Would Definitely Recommend Hospital	300+	69%	-	69%

Saint Vincent Mercy Hospital

1331 South A St
Elwood, IN 46036
URL: www.stvincent.org
Type: Critical Access Hospitals
Ownership: Voluntary Non-Profit - Church
Phone: 765-552-4594
Fax: 765-552-4700
Emergency Services: Yes
Beds: 25

Key Personnel:
CEO/President. . . . . Deborah Rasper, EdD
Chief of Medical Staff . . . . Robert Helm, MD
Infection Control. . . . . Candy Robinson
Operating Room. . . . . Sheryl Miller, RN
Quality Assurance . . . . John D Doyle
Radiology. . . . . Maria S Coutz
Emergency Room . . . . Brad Hayes
Intensive Care Unit. . . . . Tamala Hobbs

Measure	Cases	This Hosp.	State Avg.	U.S. Avg.
Heart Attack Care				
ACE Inhibitor or ARB for LVSD[3]	0	-	96%	96%
Aspirin at Arrival[1,3]	1	100%	98%	99%
Aspirin at Discharge[1,3]	1	100%	99%	98%
Beta Blocker at Discharge[1,3]	1	100%	98%	98%
Fibrinolytic Medication Timing[3]	0	-	37%	55%
PCI Within 90 Minutes of Arrival[5]	0	-	93%	90%
Smoking Cessation Advice[3]	0	-	99%	99%
Chest Pain/Possible Heart Attack Care				
Aspirin at Arrival	60	97%	95%	95%
Median Time to ECG (minutes)	72	2	6	8
Median Time to Transfer (minutes)[3]	0	-	49	61
Fibrinolytic Medication Timing[1]	4	75%	63%	54%
Heart Failure Care				
ACE Inhibitor or ARB for LVSD[1]	9	89%	92%	94%
Discharge Instructions[1]	21	57%	84%	88%
Evaluation of LVS Function	25	84%	98%	98%
Smoking Cessation Advice[1]	3	100%	99%	98%
Pneumonia Care				
Appropriate Initial Antibiotic	37	95%	90%	92%
Blood Culture Timing	49	90%	95%	96%
Influenza Vaccine[1]	24	92%	93%	91%
Initial Antibiotic Timing	54	96%	96%	95%
Pneumococcal Vaccine	44	84%	94%	93%
Smoking Cessation Advice[1]	22	100%	98%	97%
Surgical Care Improvement Project				
Appropriate VTP Within 24 Hours[1]	7	100%	90%	92%
Appropriate Hair Removal[1]	11	100%	100%	99%
Appropriate Beta Blocker Usage[1]	1	100%	93%	93%
Controlled Postoperative Blood Glucose	0	-	93%	93%
Prophylactic Antibiotic Timing[1]	3	67%	97%	97%
Prophylactic Antibiotic Timing (Outpatient)[5]	0	-	92%	92%
Prophylactic Antibiotic Selection[1]	3	100%	98%	97%
Prophylactic Antibiotic Select. (Outpatient)[5]	0	-	95%	94%
Prophylactic Antibiotic Stopped[1]	3	100%	95%	94%
Recommended VTP Ordered[1]	8	88%	92%	94%
Urinary Catheter Removal[1]	1	100%	92%	90%
Children's Asthma Care				
Received Systemic Corticosteroids	-	-	-	100%
Received Home Management Plan	-	-	-	71%
Received Reliever Medication	-	-	-	100%
Use of Medical Imaging				
Combination Abdominal CT Scan	211	0.218	0.237	0.191
Combination Chest CT Scan	115	0.000	0.120	0.054
Follow-up Mammogram/Ultrasound	329	22.2%	8.3%	8.4%
MRI for Low Back Pain[1]	46	23.9%	35.2%	32.7%
Survey of Patients' Hospital Experiences				
Area Around Room 'Always' Quiet at Night	(a)	47%	-	58%
Doctors 'Always' Communicated Well	(a)	82%	-	80%
Home Recovery Information Given	(a)	85%	-	82%
Hospital Given 9 or 10 on 10 Point Scale	(a)	72%	-	67%
Meds 'Always' Explained Before Given	(a)	63%	-	60%
Nurses 'Always' Communicated Well	(a)	83%	-	76%
Pain 'Always' Well Controlled	(a)	74%	-	69%
Room and Bathroom 'Always' Clean	(a)	68%	-	71%
Timely Help 'Always' Received	(a)	65%	-	64%
Would Definitely Recommend Hospital	(a)	68%	-	69%

NOTE: Hospital profiles are in alphabetical order by state, then city, then hospital within the city; Rankings exclude hospitals with less than 25 cases except for patient surveys which excludes hospitals with less than 100 cases; (a) 100–299 cases; (1) The number of cases is too small to be sure how well a hospital is performing; (2) The hospital indicated that the data submitted for this measure were based on a sample of cases; (3) Data was collected during a shorter time period (fewer quarters) than the maximum possible time for this measure; (4) Suppressed for one or more quarters by CMS; (5) No data is available from the hospital for this measure; (6) Fewer than 100 patients completed the HCAHPS survey. Use these rates with caution, as the number of surveys may be too low to reliably assess hospital performance; (7) Survey results are based on less than 12 months of data; (8) Survey results are not available for this reporting period; (9) No or very few patients were eligible for the HCAHPS survey. The scores shown, if any, reflect a very small number of surveys; (10) A state average was not calculated because too few hospitals in the state submitted data; (11) There were discrepancies in the data collection process; Please refer to the User's Guide for a full explanation of data.

Deaconess Hospital

600 Mary St Phone: 812-450-2252
Evansville, IN 47747 Fax: 812-450-6051
URL: www.deaconess.com
Type: Acute Care Hospitals Emergency Services: Yes
Ownership: Voluntary Non-Profit - Private Beds: 400

Key Personnel:
CEO/President. . . . . Wallace Simmons
Cardiac Laboratory. . . . . Joan Fedor-Bassemier
Chief of Medical Staff . . . . James Porter, MD
Coronary Care . . . . Joana Fedor-Bessemier
Infection Control. . . . . Mellodee Montgomery
Operating Room. . . . . Lynn Lingafelter
Quality Assurance . . . . Tom Alvey
Radiology. . . . . Ray Poston

Measure	Cases	This Hosp.	State Avg.	U.S. Avg.
Heart Attack Care				
ACE Inhibitor or ARB for LVSD	71	87%	96%	96%
Aspirin at Arrival	261	96%	98%	99%
Aspirin at Discharge	391	98%	99%	98%
Beta Blocker at Discharge	373	95%	98%	98%
Fibrinolytic Medication Timing[1]	1	0%	37%	55%
PCI Within 90 Minutes of Arrival	55	98%	93%	90%
Smoking Cessation Advice	154	97%	99%	99%
Chest Pain/Possible Heart Attack Care				
Aspirin at Arrival	823	97%	95%	95%
Median Time to ECG (minutes)	854	5	6	8
Median Time to Transfer (minutes)	28	38	49	61
Fibrinolytic Medication Timing	0	-	63%	54%
Heart Failure Care				
ACE Inhibitor or ARB for LVSD	234	81%	92%	94%
Discharge Instructions	548	63%	84%	88%
Evaluation of LVS Function	729	93%	98%	98%
Smoking Cessation Advice	183	90%	99%	98%
Pneumonia Care				
Appropriate Initial Antibiotic[2]	180	96%	90%	92%
Blood Culture Timing[2]	252	95%	95%	96%
Influenza Vaccine[2]	297	87%	93%	91%
Initial Antibiotic Timing[2]	320	97%	96%	95%
Pneumococcal Vaccine[2]	362	91%	94%	93%
Smoking Cessation Advice[2]	183	93%	98%	97%
Surgical Care Improvement Project				
Appropriate VTP Within 24 Hours[2]	192	84%	90%	92%
Appropriate Hair Removal[2]	818	99%	100%	99%
Appropriate Beta Blocker Usage[2]	278	91%	93%	93%
Controlled Postoperative Blood Glucose[2]	108	92%	93%	93%
Prophylactic Antibiotic Timing[2]	552	91%	97%	97%
Prophylactic Antibiotic Timing (Outpatient)	1,277	85%	92%	92%
Prophylactic Antibiotic Selection[2]	556	98%	98%	97%
Prophylactic Antibiotic Select. (Outpatient)	1,277	93%	95%	94%
Prophylactic Antibiotic Stopped[2]	518	85%	95%	94%
Recommended VTP Ordered[2]	197	90%	92%	94%
Urinary Catheter Removal[2]	85	81%	92%	90%
Children's Asthma Care				
Received Systemic Corticosteroids	-	-	-	100%
Received Home Management Plan	-	-	-	71%
Received Reliever Medication	-	-	-	100%
Use of Medical Imaging				
Combination Abdominal CT Scan	1,714	0.047	0.237	0.191
Combination Chest CT Scan	1,279	0.007	0.120	0.054
Follow-up Mammogram/Ultrasound[5]	0	-	8.3%	8.4%
MRI for Low Back Pain	340	39.4%	35.2%	32.7%
Survey of Patients' Hospital Experiences				
Area Around Room 'Always' Quiet at Night	300+	58%	-	58%
Doctors 'Always' Communicated Well	300+	77%	-	80%
Home Recovery Information Given	300+	78%	-	82%
Hospital Given 9 or 10 on 10 Point Scale	300+	68%	-	67%
Meds 'Always' Explained Before Given	300+	58%	-	60%
Nurses 'Always' Communicated Well	300+	75%	-	76%
Pain 'Always' Well Controlled	300+	67%	-	69%
Room and Bathroom 'Always' Clean	300+	69%	-	71%
Timely Help 'Always' Received	300+	59%	-	64%
Would Definitely Recommend Hospital	300+	72%	-	69%

Saint Mary's Medical Center of Evansville

3700 Washington Avenue Phone: 812-485-4000
Evansville, IN 47750 Fax: 812-485-7800
URL: www.stmarys.org
Type: Acute Care Hospitals Emergency Services: Yes
Ownership: Voluntary Non-Profit - Private Beds: 564

Key Personnel:
CEO/President. . . . . R Kenneth Spear, MD
Infection Control. . . . . Donna Bratt
Operating Room. . . . . Lisa McGuire
Pediatric Ambulatory Care . . . . . . Kishor Bhatt, MD
Pediatric In-Patient Care . . . . Kishor Bhatt, MD
Quality Assurance . . . . Marty Runge
Radiology. . . . . Paul Hargan, MD
Emergency Room . . . . Connie Brandes

Measure	Cases	This Hosp.	State Avg.	U.S. Avg.
Heart Attack Care				
ACE Inhibitor or ARB for LVSD	68	94%	96%	96%
Aspirin at Arrival	203	98%	98%	99%
Aspirin at Discharge	293	99%	99%	98%
Beta Blocker at Discharge	287	99%	98%	98%
Fibrinolytic Medication Timing	0	-	37%	55%
PCI Within 90 Minutes of Arrival	44	100%	93%	90%
Smoking Cessation Advice	117	100%	99%	99%
Chest Pain/Possible Heart Attack Care				
Aspirin at Arrival[5]	0	-	95%	95%
Median Time to ECG (minutes)[5]	0	-	6	8
Median Time to Transfer (minutes)[5]	0	-	49	61
Fibrinolytic Medication Timing[5]	0	-	63%	54%
Heart Failure Care				
ACE Inhibitor or ARB for LVSD	153	89%	92%	94%
Discharge Instructions	327	83%	84%	88%
Evaluation of LVS Function	420	97%	98%	98%
Smoking Cessation Advice	65	100%	99%	98%
Pneumonia Care				
Appropriate Initial Antibiotic	166	96%	90%	92%
Blood Culture Timing	240	98%	95%	96%
Influenza Vaccine	205	89%	93%	91%
Initial Antibiotic Timing	288	96%	96%	95%
Pneumococcal Vaccine	271	94%	94%	93%
Smoking Cessation Advice	171	99%	98%	97%
Surgical Care Improvement Project				
Appropriate VTP Within 24 Hours[2]	229	91%	90%	92%
Appropriate Hair Removal[2]	1,429	99%	100%	99%
Appropriate Beta Blocker Usage[2]	467	91%	93%	93%
Controlled Postoperative Blood Glucose[2]	186	89%	93%	93%
Prophylactic Antibiotic Timing[2]	1,122	96%	97%	97%
Prophylactic Antibiotic Timing (Outpatient)	1,292	92%	92%	92%
Prophylactic Antibiotic Selection[2]	1,136	99%	98%	97%
Prophylactic Antibiotic Select. (Outpatient)	1,273	95%	95%	94%
Prophylactic Antibiotic Stopped[2]	1,107	96%	95%	94%
Recommended VTP Ordered[2]	230	94%	92%	94%
Urinary Catheter Removal[2]	335	94%	92%	90%
Children's Asthma Care				
Received Systemic Corticosteroids	-	-	-	100%
Received Home Management Plan	-	-	-	71%
Received Reliever Medication	-	-	-	100%
Use of Medical Imaging				
Combination Abdominal CT Scan	1,366	0.024	0.237	0.191
Combination Chest CT Scan	1,285	0.002	0.120	0.054
Follow-up Mammogram/Ultrasound[5]	0	-	8.3%	8.4%
MRI for Low Back Pain	293	35.5%	35.2%	32.7%
Survey of Patients' Hospital Experiences				
Area Around Room 'Always' Quiet at Night	300+	60%	-	58%
Doctors 'Always' Communicated Well	300+	83%	-	80%
Home Recovery Information Given	300+	87%	-	82%
Hospital Given 9 or 10 on 10 Point Scale	300+	77%	-	67%
Meds 'Always' Explained Before Given	300+	63%	-	60%
Nurses 'Always' Communicated Well	300+	79%	-	76%
Pain 'Always' Well Controlled	300+	70%	-	69%
Room and Bathroom 'Always' Clean	300+	75%	-	71%
Timely Help 'Always' Received	300+	68%	-	64%
Would Definitely Recommend Hospital	300+	82%	-	69%

Dupont Hospital

2520 E Dupont Rd Phone: 260-416-3023
Fort Wayne, IN 46825
URL: www.theduponthospital.com
Type: Acute Care Hospitals Emergency Services: Yes
Ownership: Proprietary Beds: 131

Key Personnel:
CEO/President. . . . . Mike Schatzlein
Quality Assurance . . . . Theresa Herman MD

Measure	Cases	This Hosp.	State Avg.	U.S. Avg.
Heart Attack Care				
ACE Inhibitor or ARB for LVSD	0	-	96%	96%
Aspirin at Arrival[1]	6	100%	98%	99%
Aspirin at Discharge[1]	4	100%	99%	98%
Beta Blocker at Discharge[1]	2	100%	98%	98%
Fibrinolytic Medication Timing	0	-	37%	55%
PCI Within 90 Minutes of Arrival	0	-	93%	90%
Smoking Cessation Advice	0	-	99%	99%
Chest Pain/Possible Heart Attack Care				
Aspirin at Arrival	65	100%	95%	95%
Median Time to ECG (minutes)	68	4	6	8
Median Time to Transfer (minutes)[1]	8	46	49	61
Fibrinolytic Medication Timing	0	-	63%	54%
Heart Failure Care				
ACE Inhibitor or ARB for LVSD[1]	14	100%	92%	94%
Discharge Instructions	35	100%	84%	88%
Evaluation of LVS Function	39	100%	98%	98%
Smoking Cessation Advice[1]	5	100%	99%	98%
Pneumonia Care				
Appropriate Initial Antibiotic	47	100%	90%	92%
Blood Culture Timing	55	100%	95%	96%
Influenza Vaccine	32	100%	93%	91%
Initial Antibiotic Timing	50	100%	96%	95%
Pneumococcal Vaccine	34	100%	94%	93%
Smoking Cessation Advice[1]	17	100%	98%	97%
Surgical Care Improvement Project				
Appropriate VTP Within 24 Hours	89	100%	90%	92%
Appropriate Hair Removal	598	100%	100%	99%
Appropriate Beta Blocker Usage	142	100%	93%	93%
Controlled Postoperative Blood Glucose	0	-	93%	93%
Prophylactic Antibiotic Timing	476	100%	97%	97%
Prophylactic Antibiotic Timing (Outpatient)	465	100%	92%	92%
Prophylactic Antibiotic Selection	477	100%	98%	97%
Prophylactic Antibiotic Select. (Outpatient)	466	99%	95%	94%
Prophylactic Antibiotic Stopped	461	100%	95%	94%
Recommended VTP Ordered	89	100%	92%	94%
Urinary Catheter Removal	60	98%	92%	90%
Children's Asthma Care				
Received Systemic Corticosteroids	-	-	-	100%
Received Home Management Plan	-	-	-	71%
Received Reliever Medication	-	-	-	100%
Use of Medical Imaging				
Combination Abdominal CT Scan	324	0.068	0.237	0.191
Combination Chest CT Scan	182	0.022	0.120	0.054
Follow-up Mammogram/Ultrasound	308	7.5%	8.3%	8.4%
MRI for Low Back Pain	75	36.0%	35.2%	32.7%
Survey of Patients' Hospital Experiences				
Area Around Room 'Always' Quiet at Night	300+	58%	-	58%
Doctors 'Always' Communicated Well	300+	79%	-	80%
Home Recovery Information Given	300+	85%	-	82%
Hospital Given 9 or 10 on 10 Point Scale	300+	77%	-	67%
Meds 'Always' Explained Before Given	300+	55%	-	60%
Nurses 'Always' Communicated Well	300+	77%	-	76%
Pain 'Always' Well Controlled	300+	72%	-	69%
Room and Bathroom 'Always' Clean	300+	72%	-	71%
Timely Help 'Always' Received	300+	65%	-	64%
Would Definitely Recommend Hospital	300+	79%	-	69%

NOTE: Hospital profiles are in alphabetical order by state, then city, then hospital within the city; Rankings exclude hospitals with less than 25 cases except for patient surveys which excludes hospitals with less than 100 cases; (a) 100–299 cases; (1) The number of cases is too small to be sure how well a hospital is performing; (2) The hospital indicated that the data submitted for this measure were based on a sample of cases; (3) Data was collected during a shorter time period (fewer quarters) than the maximum possible time for this measure; (4) Suppressed for one or more quarters by CMS; (5) No data is available from the hospital for this measure; (6) Fewer than 100 patients completed the HCAHPS survey. Use these rates with caution, as the number of surveys may be too low to reliably assess hospital performance; (7) Survey results are based on less than 12 months of data; (8) Survey results are not available for this reporting period; (9) No or very few patients were eligible for the HCAHPS survey. The scores shown, if any, reflect a very small number of surveys; (10) A state average was not calculated because too few hospitals in the state submitted data; (11) There were discrepancies in the data collection process; Please refer to the User's Guide for a full explanation of data.

Lutheran Hospital of Indiana

7950 W Jefferson Boulevard
Fort Wayne, IN 46804
URL: www.lutheranhospital.com
Type: Acute Care Hospitals
Ownership: Voluntary Non-Profit - Private
Phone: 260-435-7001
Fax: 260-435-7640
Emergency Services: Yes
Beds: 435

Key Personnel:
CEO/President. . . . . Thomas D Miller
Chief of Medical Staff . . . . B.V. House, MD

Measure	Cases	This Hosp.	State Avg.	U.S. Avg.
Heart Attack Care				
ACE Inhibitor or ARB for LVSD	99	97%	96%	96%
Aspirin at Arrival	225	98%	98%	99%
Aspirin at Discharge	553	100%	99%	98%
Beta Blocker at Discharge	516	99%	98%	98%
Fibrinolytic Medication Timing	0	-	37%	55%
PCI Within 90 Minutes of Arrival	45	96%	93%	90%
Smoking Cessation Advice	201	100%	99%	99%
Chest Pain/Possible Heart Attack Care				
Aspirin at Arrival[5]	0	-	95%	95%
Median Time to ECG (minutes)[5]	0	-	6	8
Median Time to Transfer (minutes)[5]	0	-	49	61
Fibrinolytic Medication Timing[5]	0	-	63%	54%
Heart Failure Care				
ACE Inhibitor or ARB for LVSD	158	95%	92%	94%
Discharge Instructions	397	86%	84%	88%
Evaluation of LVS Function	507	98%	98%	98%
Smoking Cessation Advice	77	100%	99%	98%
Pneumonia Care				
Appropriate Initial Antibiotic	132	86%	90%	92%
Blood Culture Timing	198	98%	95%	96%
Influenza Vaccine	189	97%	93%	91%
Initial Antibiotic Timing	207	95%	96%	95%
Pneumococcal Vaccine	198	99%	94%	93%
Smoking Cessation Advice	98	99%	98%	97%
Surgical Care Improvement Project				
Appropriate VTP Within 24 Hours	486	94%	90%	92%
Appropriate Hair Removal	1,498	100%	100%	99%
Appropriate Beta Blocker Usage	626	92%	93%	93%
Controlled Postoperative Blood Glucose	350	89%	93%	93%
Prophylactic Antibiotic Timing	687	98%	97%	97%
Prophylactic Antibiotic Timing (Outpatient)	1,463	98%	92%	92%
Prophylactic Antibiotic Selection	709	99%	98%	97%
Prophylactic Antibiotic Select. (Outpatient)	1,457	99%	95%	94%
Prophylactic Antibiotic Stopped	636	93%	95%	94%
Recommended VTP Ordered	487	96%	92%	94%
Urinary Catheter Removal	222	82%	92%	90%
Children's Asthma Care				
Received Systemic Corticosteroids	-	-	-	100%
Received Home Management Plan	-	-	-	71%
Received Reliever Medication	-	-	-	100%
Use of Medical Imaging				
Combination Abdominal CT Scan	654	0.046	0.237	0.191
Combination Chest CT Scan	459	0.004	0.120	0.054
Follow-up Mammogram/Ultrasound[5]	0	-	8.3%	8.4%
MRI for Low Back Pain[1]	25	28.0%	35.2%	32.7%
Survey of Patients' Hospital Experiences				
Area Around Room 'Always' Quiet at Night	300+	46%	-	58%
Doctors 'Always' Communicated Well	300+	76%	-	80%
Home Recovery Information Given	300+	86%	-	82%
Hospital Given 9 or 10 on 10 Point Scale	300+	75%	-	67%
Meds 'Always' Explained Before Given	300+	57%	-	60%
Nurses 'Always' Communicated Well	300+	77%	-	76%
Pain 'Always' Well Controlled	300+	70%	-	69%
Room and Bathroom 'Always' Clean	300+	68%	-	71%
Timely Help 'Always' Received	300+	65%	-	64%
Would Definitely Recommend Hospital	300+	78%	-	69%

Orthopaedic Hospital at Parkview North

11130 Parkview Circle Dr
Fort Wayne, IN 46845
URL: www.parkview.com
Type: Acute Care Hospitals
Ownership: Voluntary Non-Profit - Private
Phone: 260-672-4050
Emergency Services: Yes
Beds: 37

Key Personnel:
President/CEO. . . . . Michael Packnett

Measure	Cases	This Hosp.	State Avg.	U.S. Avg.
Heart Attack Care				
ACE Inhibitor or ARB for LVSD[5]	0	-	96%	96%
Aspirin at Arrival[5]	0	-	98%	99%
Aspirin at Discharge[5]	0	-	99%	98%
Beta Blocker at Discharge[5]	0	-	98%	98%
Fibrinolytic Medication Timing[5]	0	-	37%	55%
PCI Within 90 Minutes of Arrival[5]	0	-	93%	90%
Smoking Cessation Advice[5]	0	-	99%	99%
Chest Pain/Possible Heart Attack Care				
Aspirin at Arrival[5]	0	-	95%	95%
Median Time to ECG (minutes)[5]	0	-	6	8
Median Time to Transfer (minutes)[5]	0	-	49	61
Fibrinolytic Medication Timing[5]	0	-	63%	54%
Heart Failure Care				
ACE Inhibitor or ARB for LVSD[5]	0	-	92%	94%
Discharge Instructions[5]	0	-	84%	88%
Evaluation of LVS Function[5]	0	-	98%	98%
Smoking Cessation Advice[5]	0	-	99%	98%
Pneumonia Care				
Appropriate Initial Antibiotic[5]	0	-	90%	92%
Blood Culture Timing[5]	0	-	95%	96%
Influenza Vaccine[5]	0	-	93%	91%
Initial Antibiotic Timing[5]	0	-	96%	95%
Pneumococcal Vaccine[5]	0	-	94%	93%
Smoking Cessation Advice[5]	0	-	98%	97%
Surgical Care Improvement Project				
Appropriate VTP Within 24 Hours[1,2]	23	100%	90%	92%
Appropriate Hair Removal[2]	269	100%	100%	99%
Appropriate Beta Blocker Usage[2]	83	90%	93%	93%
Controlled Postoperative Blood Glucose[2]	0	-	93%	93%
Prophylactic Antibiotic Timing[2]	201	96%	97%	97%
Prophylactic Antibiotic Timing (Outpatient)	347	96%	92%	92%
Prophylactic Antibiotic Selection[2]	201	100%	98%	97%
Prophylactic Antibiotic Select. (Outpatient)	344	99%	95%	94%
Prophylactic Antibiotic Stopped[2]	199	97%	95%	94%
Recommended VTP Ordered[1,2]	23	100%	92%	94%
Urinary Catheter Removal[2]	110	98%	92%	90%
Children's Asthma Care				
Received Systemic Corticosteroids	-	-	-	100%
Received Home Management Plan	-	-	-	71%
Received Reliever Medication	-	-	-	100%
Use of Medical Imaging				
Combination Abdominal CT Scan[5]	0	-	0.237	0.191
Combination Chest CT Scan[5]	0	-	0.120	0.054
Follow-up Mammogram/Ultrasound[5]	0	-	8.3%	8.4%
MRI for Low Back Pain[5]	0	-	35.2%	32.7%
Survey of Patients' Hospital Experiences				
Area Around Room 'Always' Quiet at Night	300+	68%	-	58%
Doctors 'Always' Communicated Well	300+	87%	-	80%
Home Recovery Information Given	300+	91%	-	82%
Hospital Given 9 or 10 on 10 Point Scale	300+	80%	-	67%
Meds 'Always' Explained Before Given	300+	67%	-	60%
Nurses 'Always' Communicated Well	300+	79%	-	76%
Pain 'Always' Well Controlled	300+	66%	-	69%
Room and Bathroom 'Always' Clean	300+	72%	-	71%
Timely Help 'Always' Received	300+	72%	-	64%
Would Definitely Recommend Hospital	300+	82%	-	69%

The Orthopaedic Hospital of Lutheran Health Network

7952 W Jefferson Blvd
Fort Wayne, IN 46804
URL: www.lutheranhealth.net
Type: Acute Care Hospitals
Ownership: Government - State
Phone: 260-435-2999
Emergency Services: No
Beds: 39

Key Personnel:
CEO . . . . Shelly Miller

Measure	Cases	This Hosp.	State Avg.	U.S. Avg.
Heart Attack Care				
ACE Inhibitor or ARB for LVSD[5]	0	-	96%	96%
Aspirin at Arrival[5]	0	-	98%	99%
Aspirin at Discharge[5]	0	-	99%	98%
Beta Blocker at Discharge[5]	0	-	98%	98%
Fibrinolytic Medication Timing[5]	0	-	37%	55%
PCI Within 90 Minutes of Arrival[5]	0	-	93%	90%
Smoking Cessation Advice[5]	0	-	99%	99%
Chest Pain/Possible Heart Attack Care				
Aspirin at Arrival[5]	0	-	95%	95%
Median Time to ECG (minutes)[5]	0	-	6	8
Median Time to Transfer (minutes)[5]	0	-	49	61
Fibrinolytic Medication Timing[5]	0	-	63%	54%
Heart Failure Care				
ACE Inhibitor or ARB for LVSD[5]	0	-	92%	94%
Discharge Instructions[5]	0	-	84%	88%
Evaluation of LVS Function[5]	0	-	98%	98%
Smoking Cessation Advice[5]	0	-	99%	98%
Pneumonia Care				
Appropriate Initial Antibiotic[5]	0	-	90%	92%
Blood Culture Timing[5]	0	-	95%	96%
Influenza Vaccine[5]	0	-	93%	91%
Initial Antibiotic Timing[5]	0	-	96%	95%
Pneumococcal Vaccine[5]	0	-	94%	93%
Smoking Cessation Advice[5]	0	-	98%	97%
Surgical Care Improvement Project				
Appropriate VTP Within 24 Hours	138	97%	90%	92%
Appropriate Hair Removal	1,101	100%	100%	99%
Appropriate Beta Blocker Usage	370	97%	93%	93%
Controlled Postoperative Blood Glucose	0	-	93%	93%
Prophylactic Antibiotic Timing	947	100%	97%	97%
Prophylactic Antibiotic Timing (Outpatient)	819	99%	92%	92%
Prophylactic Antibiotic Selection	950	100%	98%	97%
Prophylactic Antibiotic Select. (Outpatient)	818	100%	95%	94%
Prophylactic Antibiotic Stopped	932	99%	95%	94%
Recommended VTP Ordered	138	98%	92%	94%
Urinary Catheter Removal	132	98%	92%	90%
Children's Asthma Care				
Received Systemic Corticosteroids	-	-	-	100%
Received Home Management Plan	-	-	-	71%
Received Reliever Medication	-	-	-	100%
Use of Medical Imaging				
Combination Abdominal CT Scan[5]	0	-	0.237	0.191
Combination Chest CT Scan[5]	0	-	0.120	0.054
Follow-up Mammogram/Ultrasound[5]	0	-	8.3%	8.4%
MRI for Low Back Pain	73	32.9%	35.2%	32.7%
Survey of Patients' Hospital Experiences				
Area Around Room 'Always' Quiet at Night	300+	66%	-	58%
Doctors 'Always' Communicated Well	300+	82%	-	80%
Home Recovery Information Given	300+	90%	-	82%
Hospital Given 9 or 10 on 10 Point Scale	300+	76%	-	67%
Meds 'Always' Explained Before Given	300+	58%	-	60%
Nurses 'Always' Communicated Well	300+	77%	-	76%
Pain 'Always' Well Controlled	300+	69%	-	69%
Room and Bathroom 'Always' Clean	300+	72%	-	71%
Timely Help 'Always' Received	300+	68%	-	64%
Would Definitely Recommend Hospital	300+	80%	-	69%

NOTE: Hospital profiles are in alphabetical order by state, then city, then hospital within the city; Rankings exclude hospitals with less than 25 cases except for patient surveys which excludes hospitals with less than 100 cases; (a) 100–299 cases; (1) The number of cases is too small to be sure how well a hospital is performing; (2) The hospital indicated that the data submitted for this measure were based on a sample of cases; (3) Data was collected during a shorter time period (fewer quarters) than the maximum possible time for this measure; (4) Suppressed for one or more quarters by CMS; (5) No data is available from the hospital for this measure; (6) Fewer than 100 patients completed the HCAHPS survey. Use these rates with caution, as the number of surveys may be too low to reliably assess hospital performance; (7) Survey results are based on less than 12 months of data; (8) Survey results are not available for this reporting period; (9) No or very few patients were eligible for the HCAHPS survey. The scores shown, if any, reflect a very small number of surveys; (10) A state average was not calculated because too few hospitals in the state submitted data; (11) There were discrepancies in the data collection process; Please refer to the User's Guide for a full explanation of data.

Parkview Hospital

2200 Randalia Dr
Fort Wayne, IN 46805
Phone: 260-373-4000
Fax: 260-483-1373
E-mail: fdb@parkview.com
URL: www.parkview.com
Type: Acute Care Hospitals
Emergency Services: Yes
Ownership: Voluntary Non-Profit - Private
Beds: 656

Key Personnel:

CEO/President. . . . . Frank D Byrne, MD
Chief of Medical Staff. . . . . Richard Neilsen, MD
Infection Control. . . . . Joan Kennedy, RN
Operating Room. . . . . Katie Smith
Pediatric Ambulatory Care . . . . . . Michael Dick, MD
Pediatric In-Patient Care . . . . . . Michael Dick, MD
Quality Assurance . . . . Sue Ehinger
Radiology. . . . . Claudia Bergdoll

Measure	Cases	This Hosp.	State Avg.	U.S. Avg.
Heart Attack Care				
ACE Inhibitor or ARB for LVSD	86	94%	96%	96%
Aspirin at Arrival	267	99%	98%	99%
Aspirin at Discharge	555	100%	99%	98%
Beta Blocker at Discharge	547	100%	98%	98%
Fibrinolytic Medication Timing[1]	1	0%	37%	55%
PCI Within 90 Minutes of Arrival	60	93%	93%	90%
Smoking Cessation Advice	216	100%	99%	99%
Chest Pain/Possible Heart Attack Care				
Aspirin at Arrival[1,3]	7	100%	95%	95%
Median Time to ECG (minutes)[1,3]	7	5	6	8
Median Time to Transfer (minutes)[5]	0	-	49	61
Fibrinolytic Medication Timing[5]	0	-	63%	54%
Heart Failure Care				
ACE Inhibitor or ARB for LVSD[2]	92	96%	92%	94%
Discharge Instructions[2]	223	78%	84%	88%
Evaluation of LVS Function[2]	294	99%	98%	98%
Smoking Cessation Advice[2]	58	100%	99%	98%
Pneumonia Care				
Appropriate Initial Antibiotic[2]	91	96%	90%	92%
Blood Culture Timing[2]	95	85%	95%	96%
Influenza Vaccine[2]	91	99%	93%	91%
Initial Antibiotic Timing[2]	129	95%	96%	95%
Pneumococcal Vaccine[2]	135	99%	94%	93%
Smoking Cessation Advice[2]	55	100%	98%	97%
Surgical Care Improvement Project				
Appropriate VTP Within 24 Hours[2]	180	92%	90%	92%
Appropriate Hair Removal[2]	729	100%	100%	99%
Appropriate Beta Blocker Usage[2]	280	93%	93%	93%
Controlled Postoperative Blood Glucose[2]	175	96%	93%	93%
Prophylactic Antibiotic Timing[2]	524	95%	97%	97%
Prophylactic Antibiotic Timing (Outpatient)	721	96%	92%	92%
Prophylactic Antibiotic Selection[2]	541	98%	98%	97%
Prophylactic Antibiotic Select. (Outpatient)	716	97%	95%	94%
Prophylactic Antibiotic Stopped[2]	509	94%	95%	94%
Recommended VTP Ordered[2]	182	92%	92%	94%
Urinary Catheter Removal[2]	123	94%	92%	90%
Children's Asthma Care				
Received Systemic Corticosteroids	-	-	-	100%
Received Home Management Plan	-	-	-	71%
Received Reliever Medication	-	-	-	100%
Use of Medical Imaging				
Combination Abdominal CT Scan	1,080	0.277	0.237	0.191
Combination Chest CT Scan	730	0.025	0.120	0.054
Follow-up Mammogram/Ultrasound[5]	0	-	8.3%	8.4%
MRI for Low Back Pain	177	43.5%	35.2%	32.7%
Survey of Patients' Hospital Experiences				
Area Around Room 'Always' Quiet at Night	300+	61%	-	58%
Doctors 'Always' Communicated Well	300+	84%	-	80%
Home Recovery Information Given	300+	87%	-	82%
Hospital Given 9 or 10 on 10 Point Scale	300+	76%	-	67%
Meds 'Always' Explained Before Given	300+	64%	-	60%
Nurses 'Always' Communicated Well	300+	83%	-	76%
Pain 'Always' Well Controlled	300+	77%	-	69%
Room and Bathroom 'Always' Clean	300+	74%	-	71%
Timely Help 'Always' Received	300+	68%	-	64%
Would Definitely Recommend Hospital	300+	78%	-	69%

Saint Joseph Hospital

700 Broadway
Fort Wayne, IN 46802
Phone: 260-425-3000
Fax: 260-425-3013
URL: www.stjoehospital.com
Type: Acute Care Hospitals
Emergency Services: Yes
Ownership: Proprietary
Beds: 191

Key Personnel:

CEO/President. . . . . Kirk Bay
Chief of Medical Staff. . . . . Bryan E Flueckiger
Operating Room. . . . . Bernice Ewing
Quality Assurance . . . . Cheryl Rieves
Emergency Room . . . . Jernice Watson, RN

Measure	Cases	This Hosp.	State Avg.	U.S. Avg.
Heart Attack Care				
ACE Inhibitor or ARB for LVSD[1]	18	100%	96%	96%
Aspirin at Arrival	51	98%	98%	99%
Aspirin at Discharge	150	99%	99%	98%
Beta Blocker at Discharge	145	100%	98%	98%
Fibrinolytic Medication Timing	0	-	37%	55%
PCI Within 90 Minutes of Arrival[1]	14	86%	93%	90%
Smoking Cessation Advice	70	100%	99%	99%
Chest Pain/Possible Heart Attack Care				
Aspirin at Arrival[1,3]	2	100%	95%	95%
Median Time to ECG (minutes)[1,3]	3	6	6	8
Median Time to Transfer (minutes)[5]	0	-	49	61
Fibrinolytic Medication Timing[5]	0	-	63%	54%
Heart Failure Care				
ACE Inhibitor or ARB for LVSD	60	100%	92%	94%
Discharge Instructions	153	100%	84%	88%
Evaluation of LVS Function	188	100%	98%	98%
Smoking Cessation Advice	48	100%	99%	98%
Pneumonia Care				
Appropriate Initial Antibiotic	38	89%	90%	92%
Blood Culture Timing	39	97%	95%	96%
Influenza Vaccine	33	97%	93%	91%
Initial Antibiotic Timing	53	98%	96%	95%
Pneumococcal Vaccine	26	100%	94%	93%
Smoking Cessation Advice	37	100%	98%	97%
Surgical Care Improvement Project				
Appropriate VTP Within 24 Hours	39	90%	90%	92%
Appropriate Hair Removal	140	100%	100%	99%
Appropriate Beta Blocker Usage	44	98%	93%	93%
Controlled Postoperative Blood Glucose	42	98%	93%	93%
Prophylactic Antibiotic Timing	90	96%	97%	97%
Prophylactic Antibiotic Timing (Outpatient)	73	95%	92%	92%
Prophylactic Antibiotic Selection	91	98%	98%	97%
Prophylactic Antibiotic Select. (Outpatient)	72	97%	95%	94%
Prophylactic Antibiotic Stopped	87	97%	95%	94%
Recommended VTP Ordered	39	95%	92%	94%
Urinary Catheter Removal[1]	11	100%	92%	90%
Children's Asthma Care				
Received Systemic Corticosteroids	-	-	-	100%
Received Home Management Plan	-	-	-	71%
Received Reliever Medication	-	-	-	100%
Use of Medical Imaging				
Combination Abdominal CT Scan	181	0.110	0.237	0.191
Combination Chest CT Scan	98	0.010	0.120	0.054
Follow-up Mammogram/Ultrasound	387	5.4%	8.3%	8.4%
MRI for Low Back Pain[1]	9	33.3%	35.2%	32.7%
Survey of Patients' Hospital Experiences				
Area Around Room 'Always' Quiet at Night	300+	58%	-	58%
Doctors 'Always' Communicated Well	300+	80%	-	80%
Home Recovery Information Given	300+	88%	-	82%
Hospital Given 9 or 10 on 10 Point Scale	300+	69%	-	67%
Meds 'Always' Explained Before Given	300+	60%	-	60%
Nurses 'Always' Communicated Well	300+	76%	-	76%
Pain 'Always' Well Controlled	300+	71%	-	69%
Room and Bathroom 'Always' Clean	300+	74%	-	71%
Timely Help 'Always' Received	300+	66%	-	64%
Would Definitely Recommend Hospital	300+	69%	-	69%

Saint Vincent Frankfort Hospital

1300 S Jackson St
Frankfort, IN 46041
Phone: 765-656-3000
Fax: 765-654-6881
URL: www.stvincent.org
Type: Critical Access Hospitals
Emergency Services: Yes
Ownership: Voluntary Non-Profit - Church
Beds: 25

Key Personnel:

CEO/President. . . . . Thomas Crawford, EdD
Chief of Medical Staff. . . . . Stephen D Thorp, MD
Operating Room. . . . . Cindi Mattingly, RN
Quality Assurance . . . . John D Doyle
Radiology. . . . . Stevan A Fritsch, MD
Anesthesiology. . . . . Alexandra Dominik, MD
Emergency Room . . . . James Rudolph, MD
Intensive Care Unit. . . . . Debbie Lineback, RN

Measure	Cases	This Hosp.	State Avg.	U.S. Avg.
Heart Attack Care				
ACE Inhibitor or ARB for LVSD[1,3]	1	100%	96%	96%
Aspirin at Arrival[1,3]	1	100%	98%	99%
Aspirin at Discharge[1,3]	1	100%	99%	98%
Beta Blocker at Discharge[1,3]	1	100%	98%	98%
Fibrinolytic Medication Timing[3]	0	-	37%	55%
PCI Within 90 Minutes of Arrival[5]	0	-	93%	90%
Smoking Cessation Advice[3]	0	-	99%	99%
Chest Pain/Possible Heart Attack Care				
Aspirin at Arrival	-	-	95%	95%
Median Time to ECG (minutes)	-	-	6	8
Median Time to Transfer (minutes)	-	-	49	61
Fibrinolytic Medication Timing	-	-	63%	54%
Heart Failure Care				
ACE Inhibitor or ARB for LVSD[1]	3	100%	92%	94%
Discharge Instructions[1]	11	82%	84%	88%
Evaluation of LVS Function[1]	17	82%	98%	98%
Smoking Cessation Advice[1]	2	100%	99%	98%
Pneumonia Care				
Appropriate Initial Antibiotic	44	82%	90%	92%
Blood Culture Timing	50	94%	95%	96%
Influenza Vaccine	35	91%	93%	91%
Initial Antibiotic Timing	61	95%	96%	95%
Pneumococcal Vaccine	48	94%	94%	93%
Smoking Cessation Advice[1]	11	100%	98%	97%
Surgical Care Improvement Project				
Appropriate VTP Within 24 Hours[1]	22	100%	90%	92%
Appropriate Hair Removal	31	94%	100%	99%
Appropriate Beta Blocker Usage[1]	11	91%	93%	93%
Controlled Postoperative Blood Glucose[5]	0	-	93%	93%
Prophylactic Antibiotic Timing	29	97%	97%	97%
Prophylactic Antibiotic Timing (Outpatient)	-	-	92%	92%
Prophylactic Antibiotic Selection	29	97%	98%	97%
Prophylactic Antibiotic Select. (Outpatient)	-	-	95%	94%
Prophylactic Antibiotic Stopped	29	97%	95%	94%
Recommended VTP Ordered[1]	22	100%	92%	94%
Urinary Catheter Removal[1]	2	0%	92%	90%
Children's Asthma Care				
Received Systemic Corticosteroids	-	-	-	100%
Received Home Management Plan	-	-	-	71%
Received Reliever Medication	-	-	-	100%
Use of Medical Imaging				
Combination Abdominal CT Scan	-	-	0.237	0.191
Combination Chest CT Scan	-	-	0.120	0.054
Follow-up Mammogram/Ultrasound	-	-	8.3%	8.4%
MRI for Low Back Pain	-	-	35.2%	32.7%
Survey of Patients' Hospital Experiences				
Area Around Room 'Always' Quiet at Night	(a)	65%	-	58%
Doctors 'Always' Communicated Well	(a)	85%	-	80%
Home Recovery Information Given	(a)	82%	-	82%
Hospital Given 9 or 10 on 10 Point Scale	(a)	77%	-	67%
Meds 'Always' Explained Before Given	(a)	68%	-	60%
Nurses 'Always' Communicated Well	(a)	85%	-	76%
Pain 'Always' Well Controlled	(a)	73%	-	69%
Room and Bathroom 'Always' Clean	(a)	74%	-	71%
Timely Help 'Always' Received	(a)	74%	-	64%
Would Definitely Recommend Hospital	(a)	67%	-	69%

NOTE: Hospital profiles are in alphabetical order by state, then city, then hospital within the city; Rankings exclude hospitals with less than 25 cases except for patient surveys which excludes hospitals with less than 100 cases; (a) 100–299 cases; (1) The number of cases is too small to be sure how well a hospital is performing; (2) The hospital indicated that the data submitted for this measure were based on a sample of cases; (3) Data was collected during a shorter time period (fewer quarters) than the maximum possible time for this measure; (4) Suppressed for one or more quarters by CMS; (5) No data is available from the hospital for this measure; (6) Fewer than 100 patients completed the HCAHPS survey. Use these rates with caution, as the number of surveys may be too low to reliably assess hospital performance; (7) Survey results are based on less than 12 months of data; (8) Survey results are not available for this reporting period; (9) No or very few patients were eligible for the HCAHPS survey. The scores shown, if any, reflect a very small number of surveys; (10) A state average was not calculated because too few hospitals in the state submitted data; (11) There were discrepancies in the data collection process; Please refer to the User's Guide for a full explanation of data.

Johnson Memorial Hospital

1125 W Jefferson Street
Franklin, IN 46131
URL: www.johnsonmemorial.org
Type: Acute Care Hospitals
Ownership: Government - Local
Phone: 317-736-3300
Fax: 317-738-7894
Emergency Services: Yes
Beds: 161

Key Personnel:
CEO/President . . . . Larry Heydon
Chief of Medical Staff . . . . John Norris, MD
Operating Room . . . . Vickie McCullough
Quality Assurance . . . . Cindy Lewis
Radiology . . . . Richard Buck
Anesthesiology . . . . D Buch, MD
Emergency Room . . . . Carla M Taylor
Intensive Care Unit . . . . Karen Robards

Measure	Cases	This Hosp.	State Avg.	U.S. Avg.
Heart Attack Care				
ACE Inhibitor or ARB for LVSD	0	-	96%	96%
Aspirin at Arrival[1]	12	92%	98%	99%
Aspirin at Discharge[1]	1	100%	99%	98%
Beta Blocker at Discharge[1]	3	100%	98%	98%
Fibrinolytic Medication Timing	0	-	37%	55%
PCI Within 90 Minutes of Arrival	0	-	93%	90%
Smoking Cessation Advice[1]	1	100%	99%	99%
Chest Pain/Possible Heart Attack Care				
Aspirin at Arrival	46	98%	95%	95%
Median Time to ECG (minutes)	69	2	6	8
Median Time to Transfer (minutes)[1]	15	31	49	61
Fibrinolytic Medication Timing	0	-	63%	54%
Heart Failure Care				
ACE Inhibitor or ARB for LVSD[1]	17	88%	92%	94%
Discharge Instructions	54	63%	84%	88%
Evaluation of LVS Function	75	97%	98%	98%
Smoking Cessation Advice[1]	14	100%	99%	98%
Pneumonia Care				
Appropriate Initial Antibiotic	83	93%	90%	92%
Blood Culture Timing	98	94%	95%	96%
Influenza Vaccine	56	84%	93%	91%
Initial Antibiotic Timing	88	99%	96%	95%
Pneumococcal Vaccine	79	97%	94%	93%
Smoking Cessation Advice	31	100%	98%	97%
Surgical Care Improvement Project				
Appropriate VTP Within 24 Hours	73	93%	90%	92%
Appropriate Hair Removal	163	100%	100%	99%
Appropriate Beta Blocker Usage	35	97%	93%	93%
Controlled Postoperative Blood Glucose	0	-	93%	93%
Prophylactic Antibiotic Timing	102	96%	97%	97%
Prophylactic Antibiotic Timing (Outpatient)	96	96%	92%	92%
Prophylactic Antibiotic Selection	101	95%	98%	97%
Prophylactic Antibiotic Select. (Outpatient)	94	95%	95%	94%
Prophylactic Antibiotic Stopped	98	97%	95%	94%
Recommended VTP Ordered	74	95%	92%	94%
Urinary Catheter Removal	33	88%	92%	90%
Children's Asthma Care				
Received Systemic Corticosteroids	-	-	-	100%
Received Home Management Plan	-	-	-	71%
Received Reliever Medication	-	-	-	100%
Use of Medical Imaging				
Combination Abdominal CT Scan	504	0.042	0.237	0.191
Combination Chest CT Scan	295	0.000	0.120	0.054
Follow-up Mammogram/Ultrasound	683	5.4%	8.3%	8.4%
MRI for Low Back Pain	76	34.2%	35.2%	32.7%
Survey of Patients' Hospital Experiences				
Area Around Room 'Always' Quiet at Night	300+	56%	-	58%
Doctors 'Always' Communicated Well	300+	84%	-	80%
Home Recovery Information Given	300+	85%	-	82%
Hospital Given 9 or 10 on 10 Point Scale	300+	72%	-	67%
Meds 'Always' Explained Before Given	300+	65%	-	60%
Nurses 'Always' Communicated Well	300+	81%	-	76%
Pain 'Always' Well Controlled	300+	69%	-	69%
Room and Bathroom 'Always' Clean	300+	75%	-	71%
Timely Help 'Always' Received	300+	68%	-	64%
Would Definitely Recommend Hospital	300+	71%	-	69%

Methodist Hospitals

600 Grant Street
Gary, IN 46402
URL: www.methodisthospital.org
Type: Acute Care Hospitals
Ownership: Government - Local
Phone: 219-886-4601
Fax: 219-886-4592
Emergency Services: Yes
Beds: 469

Key Personnel:
CEO/President . . . . Adolphus Anekwe, MD
Cardiac Laboratory . . . . Nazzal Obaid, MD
Chief of Medical Staff . . . . Bashir Ahmad
Pediatric Ambulatory Care . . . . . . Steve Simpson, MD
Anesthesiology . . . . Michele Sproviero, MD
Emergency Room . . . . Michael McGee, MD

Measure	Cases	This Hosp.	State Avg.	U.S. Avg.
Heart Attack Care				
ACE Inhibitor or ARB for LVSD[2]	49	90%	96%	96%
Aspirin at Arrival[2]	215	94%	98%	99%
Aspirin at Discharge[2]	190	92%	99%	98%
Beta Blocker at Discharge[2]	196	92%	98%	98%
Fibrinolytic Medication Timing[2]	0	-	37%	55%
PCI Within 90 Minutes of Arrival[1,2]	18	28%	93%	90%
Smoking Cessation Advice[2]	81	100%	99%	99%
Chest Pain/Possible Heart Attack Care				
Aspirin at Arrival[5]	0	-	95%	95%
Median Time to ECG (minutes)[5]	0	-	6	8
Median Time to Transfer (minutes)[5]	0	-	49	61
Fibrinolytic Medication Timing[5]	0	-	63%	54%
Heart Failure Care				
ACE Inhibitor or ARB for LVSD[2]	142	98%	92%	94%
Discharge Instructions[2]	269	52%	84%	88%
Evaluation of LVS Function[2]	317	99%	98%	98%
Smoking Cessation Advice[2]	81	100%	99%	98%
Pneumonia Care				
Appropriate Initial Antibiotic[2]	50	76%	90%	92%
Blood Culture Timing[2]	108	93%	95%	96%
Influenza Vaccine[2]	83	84%	93%	91%
Initial Antibiotic Timing[2]	138	93%	96%	95%
Pneumococcal Vaccine[2]	119	78%	94%	93%
Smoking Cessation Advice[2]	48	100%	98%	97%
Surgical Care Improvement Project				
Appropriate VTP Within 24 Hours[2]	186	91%	90%	92%
Appropriate Hair Removal[2]	493	100%	100%	99%
Appropriate Beta Blocker Usage[2]	144	90%	93%	93%
Controlled Postoperative Blood Glucose[2]	77	87%	93%	93%
Prophylactic Antibiotic Timing[2]	332	98%	97%	97%
Prophylactic Antibiotic Timing (Outpatient)	326	96%	92%	92%
Prophylactic Antibiotic Selection[2]	337	93%	98%	97%
Prophylactic Antibiotic Select. (Outpatient)	323	86%	95%	94%
Prophylactic Antibiotic Stopped[2]	317	90%	95%	94%
Recommended VTP Ordered[2]	188	94%	92%	94%
Urinary Catheter Removal[2]	84	83%	92%	90%
Children's Asthma Care				
Received Systemic Corticosteroids	-	-	-	100%
Received Home Management Plan	-	-	-	71%
Received Reliever Medication	-	-	-	100%
Use of Medical Imaging				
Combination Abdominal CT Scan	1,090	0.315	0.237	0.191
Combination Chest CT Scan	603	0.337	0.120	0.054
Follow-up Mammogram/Ultrasound	1,459	7.7%	8.3%	8.4%
MRI for Low Back Pain	136	36.0%	35.2%	32.7%
Survey of Patients' Hospital Experiences				
Area Around Room 'Always' Quiet at Night	300+	47%	-	58%
Doctors 'Always' Communicated Well	300+	74%	-	80%
Home Recovery Information Given	300+	79%	-	82%
Hospital Given 9 or 10 on 10 Point Scale	300+	49%	-	67%
Meds 'Always' Explained Before Given	300+	52%	-	60%
Nurses 'Always' Communicated Well	300+	68%	-	76%
Pain 'Always' Well Controlled	300+	66%	-	69%
Room and Bathroom 'Always' Clean	300+	61%	-	71%
Timely Help 'Always' Received	300+	52%	-	64%
Would Definitely Recommend Hospital	300+	52%	-	69%

IU Health Goshen Hospital

200 High Park Ave
Goshen, IN 46526
E-mail: ksearcy@goshenhealth.com
URL: www.goshenhosp.com
Type: Acute Care Hospitals
Ownership: Voluntary Non-Profit - Other
Phone: 574-533-2141
Fax: 574-535-2859
Emergency Services: Yes
Beds: 115

Key Personnel:
CEO/President . . . . James Dague
Cardiac Laboratory . . . . Scott Ereksen
Chief of Medical Staff . . . . Randy Cammengade
Operating Room . . . . Wil Beachy
Radiology . . . . Jody Barber
Emergency Room . . . . Candes Andersen

Measure	Cases	This Hosp.	State Avg.	U.S. Avg.
Heart Attack Care				
ACE Inhibitor or ARB for LVSD[1]	11	100%	96%	96%
Aspirin at Arrival	54	100%	98%	99%
Aspirin at Discharge	46	100%	99%	98%
Beta Blocker at Discharge	45	100%	98%	98%
Fibrinolytic Medication Timing	0	-	37%	55%
PCI Within 90 Minutes of Arrival[1]	7	100%	93%	90%
Smoking Cessation Advice[1]	16	100%	99%	99%
Chest Pain/Possible Heart Attack Care				
Aspirin at Arrival	71	100%	95%	95%
Median Time to ECG (minutes)	72	5	6	8
Median Time to Transfer (minutes)[1]	19	43	49	61
Fibrinolytic Medication Timing[1]	3	100%	63%	54%
Heart Failure Care				
ACE Inhibitor or ARB for LVSD	73	100%	92%	94%
Discharge Instructions	129	91%	84%	88%
Evaluation of LVS Function	185	100%	98%	98%
Smoking Cessation Advice	31	100%	99%	98%
Pneumonia Care				
Appropriate Initial Antibiotic[2]	104	95%	90%	92%
Blood Culture Timing[2]	121	95%	95%	96%
Influenza Vaccine[2]	87	99%	93%	91%
Initial Antibiotic Timing[2]	131	100%	96%	95%
Pneumococcal Vaccine[2]	113	99%	94%	93%
Smoking Cessation Advice[2]	57	100%	98%	97%
Surgical Care Improvement Project				
Appropriate VTP Within 24 Hours	216	88%	90%	92%
Appropriate Hair Removal	585	100%	100%	99%
Appropriate Beta Blocker Usage	140	94%	93%	93%
Controlled Postoperative Blood Glucose	0	-	93%	93%
Prophylactic Antibiotic Timing	378	98%	97%	97%
Prophylactic Antibiotic Timing (Outpatient)	117	85%	92%	92%
Prophylactic Antibiotic Selection	383	97%	98%	97%
Prophylactic Antibiotic Select. (Outpatient)	118	96%	95%	94%
Prophylactic Antibiotic Stopped	367	93%	95%	94%
Recommended VTP Ordered	219	89%	92%	94%
Urinary Catheter Removal	108	86%	92%	90%
Children's Asthma Care				
Received Systemic Corticosteroids	-	-	-	100%
Received Home Management Plan	-	-	-	71%
Received Reliever Medication	-	-	-	100%
Use of Medical Imaging				
Combination Abdominal CT Scan	660	0.056	0.237	0.191
Combination Chest CT Scan	535	0.013	0.120	0.054
Follow-up Mammogram/Ultrasound	1,448	8.6%	8.3%	8.4%
MRI for Low Back Pain	127	34.6%	35.2%	32.7%
Survey of Patients' Hospital Experiences				
Area Around Room 'Always' Quiet at Night	300+	53%	-	58%
Doctors 'Always' Communicated Well	300+	78%	-	80%
Home Recovery Information Given	300+	81%	-	82%
Hospital Given 9 or 10 on 10 Point Scale	300+	71%	-	67%
Meds 'Always' Explained Before Given	300+	59%	-	60%
Nurses 'Always' Communicated Well	300+	78%	-	76%
Pain 'Always' Well Controlled	300+	71%	-	69%
Room and Bathroom 'Always' Clean	300+	77%	-	71%
Timely Help 'Always' Received	300+	70%	-	64%
Would Definitely Recommend Hospital	300+	74%	-	69%

NOTE: Hospital profiles are in alphabetical order by state, then city, then hospital within the city; Rankings exclude hospitals with less than 25 cases except for patient surveys which excludes hospitals with less than 100 cases; (a) 100–299 cases; (1) The number of cases is too small to be sure how well a hospital is performing; (2) The hospital indicated that the data submitted for this measure were based on a sample of cases; (3) Data was collected during a shorter time period (fewer quarters) than the maximum possible time for this measure; (4) Suppressed for one or more quarters by CMS; (5) No data is available from the hospital for this measure; (6) Fewer than 100 patients completed the HCAHPS survey. Use these rates with caution, as the number of surveys may be too low to reliably assess hospital performance; (7) Survey results are based on less than 12 months of data; (8) Survey results are not available for this reporting period; (9) No or very few patients were eligible for the HCAHPS survey. The scores shown, if any, reflect a very small number of surveys; (10) A state average was not calculated because too few hospitals in the state submitted data; (11) There were discrepancies in the data collection process; Please refer to the User's Guide for a full explanation of data.

Putnam County Hospital

1542 S Bloomington St Phone: 765-655-2620
Greencastle, IN 46135 Fax: 765-655-2625
Type: Critical Access Hospitals Emergency Services: Yes
Ownership: Government - Local Beds: 85

Key Personnel:
CEO/President. . . . . Dennis Weatherford
Cardiac Laboratory. . . . . Douglas Eley
Chief of Medical Staff. . . . . Donna Gennaway
Infection Control. . . . . Suzanne Tucker
Operating Room. . . . . Jodie Wyndham
Quality Assurance . . . . Dennis Weatherford
Radiology. . . . . Paul Sanders
Intensive Care Unit. . . . . Jackie Eitel

Measure	Cases	This Hosp.	State Avg.	U.S. Avg.
Heart Attack Care				
ACE Inhibitor or ARB for LVSD[1]	1	100%	96%	96%
Aspirin at Arrival[1]	4	100%	98%	99%
Aspirin at Discharge[1]	4	100%	99%	98%
Beta Blocker at Discharge[1]	4	100%	98%	98%
Fibrinolytic Medication Timing	0	-	37%	55%
PCI Within 90 Minutes of Arrival	0	-	93%	90%
Smoking Cessation Advice	0	-	99%	99%
Chest Pain/Possible Heart Attack Care				
Aspirin at Arrival	-	-	95%	95%
Median Time to ECG (minutes)	-	-	6	8
Median Time to Transfer (minutes)	-	-	49	61
Fibrinolytic Medication Timing	-	-	63%	54%
Heart Failure Care				
ACE Inhibitor or ARB for LVSD[1]	15	100%	92%	94%
Discharge Instructions[1]	21	100%	84%	88%
Evaluation of LVS Function	30	100%	98%	98%
Smoking Cessation Advice[1]	3	100%	99%	98%
Pneumonia Care				
Appropriate Initial Antibiotic	37	86%	90%	92%
Blood Culture Timing	66	91%	95%	96%
Influenza Vaccine	44	98%	93%	91%
Initial Antibiotic Timing	63	95%	96%	95%
Pneumococcal Vaccine	62	98%	94%	93%
Smoking Cessation Advice[1]	14	93%	98%	97%
Surgical Care Improvement Project				
Appropriate VTP Within 24 Hours[1]	23	87%	90%	92%
Appropriate Hair Removal	40	98%	100%	99%
Appropriate Beta Blocker Usage[1]	3	100%	93%	93%
Controlled Postoperative Blood Glucose[5]	0	-	93%	93%
Prophylactic Antibiotic Timing[1]	19	84%	97%	97%
Prophylactic Antibiotic Timing (Outpatient)	-	-	92%	92%
Prophylactic Antibiotic Selection[1]	19	79%	98%	97%
Prophylactic Antibiotic Select. (Outpatient)	-	-	95%	94%
Prophylactic Antibiotic Stopped[1]	17	76%	95%	94%
Recommended VTP Ordered[1]	23	87%	92%	94%
Urinary Catheter Removal[1]	8	100%	92%	90%
Children's Asthma Care				
Received Systemic Corticosteroids	-	-	-	100%
Received Home Management Plan	-	-	-	71%
Received Reliever Medication	-	-	-	100%
Use of Medical Imaging				
Combination Abdominal CT Scan	-	-	0.237	0.191
Combination Chest CT Scan	-	-	0.120	0.054
Follow-up Mammogram/Ultrasound	-	-	8.3%	8.4%
MRI for Low Back Pain	-	-	35.2%	32.7%
Survey of Patients' Hospital Experiences				
Area Around Room 'Always' Quiet at Night[8]	-	-	-	58%
Doctors 'Always' Communicated Well[8]	-	-	-	80%
Home Recovery Information Given[8]	-	-	-	82%
Hospital Given 9 or 10 on 10 Point Scale[8]	-	-	-	67%
Meds 'Always' Explained Before Given[8]	-	-	-	60%
Nurses 'Always' Communicated Well[8]	-	-	-	76%
Pain 'Always' Well Controlled[8]	-	-	-	69%
Room and Bathroom 'Always' Clean[8]	-	-	-	71%
Timely Help 'Always' Received[8]	-	-	-	64%
Would Definitely Recommend Hospital[8]	-	-	-	69%

Hancock Regional Hospital

801 N State Street Phone: 317-468-4412
Greenfield, IN 46140
URL: www.hancockregional.org
Type: Acute Care Hospitals Emergency Services: Yes
Ownership: Government - Local Beds: 94

Key Personnel:
CEO/President. . . . . Bobby Keen, MD
Chief of Medical Staff . . . . Michael Fletcher, MD
Coronary Care . . . . Tammy Strunk, RN
Operating Room. . . . . Brenda Cole
Radiology. . . . . Lisa Wood
Emergency Room . . . . Judy Hall

Measure	Cases	This Hosp.	State Avg.	U.S. Avg.
Heart Attack Care				
ACE Inhibitor or ARB for LVSD[1]	4	75%	96%	96%
Aspirin at Arrival[1]	24	100%	98%	99%
Aspirin at Discharge[1]	20	100%	99%	98%
Beta Blocker at Discharge[1]	17	100%	98%	98%
Fibrinolytic Medication Timing	0	-	37%	55%
PCI Within 90 Minutes of Arrival[1]	1	0%	93%	90%
Smoking Cessation Advice[1]	3	100%	99%	99%
Chest Pain/Possible Heart Attack Care				
Aspirin at Arrival	81	93%	95%	95%
Median Time to ECG (minutes)	84	4	6	8
Median Time to Transfer (minutes)[1]	9	70	49	61
Fibrinolytic Medication Timing	0	-	63%	54%
Heart Failure Care				
ACE Inhibitor or ARB for LVSD[1]	22	95%	92%	94%
Discharge Instructions	53	66%	84%	88%
Evaluation of LVS Function	84	96%	98%	98%
Smoking Cessation Advice[1]	14	100%	99%	98%
Pneumonia Care				
Appropriate Initial Antibiotic[2]	87	94%	90%	92%
Blood Culture Timing[2]	106	97%	95%	96%
Influenza Vaccine[2]	85	91%	93%	91%
Initial Antibiotic Timing[2]	132	95%	96%	95%
Pneumococcal Vaccine[2]	119	89%	94%	93%
Smoking Cessation Advice[2]	44	100%	98%	97%
Surgical Care Improvement Project				
Appropriate VTP Within 24 Hours[2]	116	90%	90%	92%
Appropriate Hair Removal[2]	333	100%	100%	99%
Appropriate Beta Blocker Usage[2]	99	69%	93%	93%
Controlled Postoperative Blood Glucose[2]	0	-	93%	93%
Prophylactic Antibiotic Timing[2]	241	95%	97%	97%
Prophylactic Antibiotic Timing (Outpatient)	133	81%	92%	92%
Prophylactic Antibiotic Selection[2]	239	98%	98%	97%
Prophylactic Antibiotic Select. (Outpatient)	122	93%	95%	94%
Prophylactic Antibiotic Stopped[2]	232	97%	95%	94%
Recommended VTP Ordered[2]	116	91%	92%	94%
Urinary Catheter Removal[2]	62	95%	92%	90%
Children's Asthma Care				
Received Systemic Corticosteroids	-	-	-	100%
Received Home Management Plan	-	-	-	71%
Received Reliever Medication	-	-	-	100%
Use of Medical Imaging				
Combination Abdominal CT Scan	600	0.085	0.237	0.191
Combination Chest CT Scan	521	0.021	0.120	0.054
Follow-up Mammogram/Ultrasound	1,156	7.2%	8.3%	8.4%
MRI for Low Back Pain	160	35.6%	35.2%	32.7%
Survey of Patients' Hospital Experiences				
Area Around Room 'Always' Quiet at Night	300+	57%	-	58%
Doctors 'Always' Communicated Well	300+	82%	-	80%
Home Recovery Information Given	300+	83%	-	82%
Hospital Given 9 or 10 on 10 Point Scale	300+	73%	-	67%
Meds 'Always' Explained Before Given	300+	60%	-	60%
Nurses 'Always' Communicated Well	300+	78%	-	76%
Pain 'Always' Well Controlled	300+	72%	-	69%
Room and Bathroom 'Always' Clean	300+	76%	-	71%
Timely Help 'Always' Received	300+	67%	-	64%
Would Definitely Recommend Hospital	300+	72%	-	69%

Decatur County Memorial Hospital

720 N Lincoln Street Phone: 812-663-4331
Greensburg, IN 47240 Fax: 812-663-9738
URL: www.dcmh.net
Type: Critical Access Hospitals Emergency Services: Yes
Ownership: Government - Local Beds: 115

Key Personnel:
CEO/President. . . . . William R Alloy FACHE
Infection Control. . . . . Pat Barnes RN
Operating Room. . . . . Jae Riedeman
Radiology. . . . . Barbara Taylor
Anesthesiology. . . . . Sergio Bisono MD
Emergency Room . . . . Michael McCarthy MD
Intensive Care Unit. . . . . Cindy Grote RN

Measure	Cases	This Hosp.	State Avg.	U.S. Avg.
Heart Attack Care				
ACE Inhibitor or ARB for LVSD[1,3]	1	100%	96%	96%
Aspirin at Arrival[1,3]	2	100%	98%	99%
Aspirin at Discharge[1,3]	2	100%	99%	98%
Beta Blocker at Discharge[1,3]	2	100%	98%	98%
Fibrinolytic Medication Timing[3]	0	-	37%	55%
PCI Within 90 Minutes of Arrival[3]	0	-	93%	90%
Smoking Cessation Advice[1,3]	2	50%	99%	99%
Chest Pain/Possible Heart Attack Care				
Aspirin at Arrival	138	98%	95%	95%
Median Time to ECG (minutes)	149	11	6	8
Median Time to Transfer (minutes)[1]	7	88	49	61
Fibrinolytic Medication Timing[1]	4	75%	63%	54%
Heart Failure Care				
ACE Inhibitor or ARB for LVSD[1]	8	88%	92%	94%
Discharge Instructions	39	95%	84%	88%
Evaluation of LVS Function	67	100%	98%	98%
Smoking Cessation Advice[1]	5	100%	99%	98%
Pneumonia Care				
Appropriate Initial Antibiotic	29	83%	90%	92%
Blood Culture Timing	37	89%	95%	96%
Influenza Vaccine	28	100%	93%	91%
Initial Antibiotic Timing	47	98%	96%	95%
Pneumococcal Vaccine	34	97%	94%	93%
Smoking Cessation Advice[1]	22	100%	98%	97%
Surgical Care Improvement Project				
Appropriate VTP Within 24 Hours[1]	22	55%	90%	92%
Appropriate Hair Removal	109	100%	100%	99%
Appropriate Beta Blocker Usage[1]	23	100%	93%	93%
Controlled Postoperative Blood Glucose[3]	0	-	93%	93%
Prophylactic Antibiotic Timing	65	98%	97%	97%
Prophylactic Antibiotic Timing (Outpatient)	35	86%	92%	92%
Prophylactic Antibiotic Selection	66	100%	98%	97%
Prophylactic Antibiotic Select. (Outpatient)	31	97%	95%	94%
Prophylactic Antibiotic Stopped	62	95%	95%	94%
Recommended VTP Ordered[1]	22	59%	92%	94%
Urinary Catheter Removal	34	97%	92%	90%
Children's Asthma Care				
Received Systemic Corticosteroids	-	-	-	100%
Received Home Management Plan	-	-	-	71%
Received Reliever Medication	-	-	-	100%
Use of Medical Imaging				
Combination Abdominal CT Scan	196	0.612	0.237	0.191
Combination Chest CT Scan	119	0.160	0.120	0.054
Follow-up Mammogram/Ultrasound	445	3.8%	8.3%	8.4%
MRI for Low Back Pain[1]	48	22.9%	35.2%	32.7%
Survey of Patients' Hospital Experiences				
Area Around Room 'Always' Quiet at Night	(a)	51%	-	58%
Doctors 'Always' Communicated Well	(a)	87%	-	80%
Home Recovery Information Given	(a)	90%	-	82%
Hospital Given 9 or 10 on 10 Point Scale	(a)	65%	-	67%
Meds 'Always' Explained Before Given	(a)	59%	-	60%
Nurses 'Always' Communicated Well	(a)	79%	-	76%
Pain 'Always' Well Controlled	(a)	73%	-	69%
Room and Bathroom 'Always' Clean	(a)	69%	-	71%
Timely Help 'Always' Received	(a)	67%	-	64%
Would Definitely Recommend Hospital	(a)	64%	-	69%

NOTE: Hospital profiles are in alphabetical order by state, then city, then hospital within the city; Rankings exclude hospitals with less than 25 cases except for patient surveys which excludes hospitals with less than 100 cases; (a) 100–299 cases; (1) The number of cases is too small to be sure how well a hospital is performing; (2) The hospital indicated that the data submitted for this measure were based on a sample of cases; (3) Data was collected during a shorter time period (fewer quarters) than the maximum possible time for this measure; (4) Suppressed for one or more quarters by CMS; (5) No data is available from the hospital for this measure; (6) Fewer than 100 patients completed the HCAHPS survey. Use these rates with caution, as the number of surveys may be too low to reliably assess hospital performance; (7) Survey results are based on less than 12 months of data; (8) Survey results are not available for this reporting period; (9) No or very few patients were eligible for the HCAHPS survey. The scores shown, if any, reflect a very small number of surveys; (10) A state average was not calculated because too few hospitals in the state submitted data; (11) There were discrepancies in the data collection process; Please refer to the User's Guide for a full explanation of data.

Franciscan St Margaret Health - Hammond

5454 Hohman Ave — Phone: 219-932-2300
Hammond, IN 46320 — Fax: 219-933-2585
URL: www.smmhc.com
Type: Acute Care Hospitals — Emergency Services: Yes
Ownership: Voluntary Non-Profit - Church — Beds: 475

Key Personnel:
CEO/President. . . . . Jean Diamond
Chief of Medical Staff. . . . . J Patel
Infection Control. . . . . Sally Bola
Operating Room. . . . . Harvey J Levin, RN
Pediatric Ambulatory Care . . . . . . S Paul
Pediatric In-Patient Care . . . . . . S Paul
Quality Assurance . . . . Jess McHenry
Radiology. . . . . J Marcus Lee

Measure	Cases	This Hosp.	State Avg.	U.S. Avg.
Heart Attack Care				
ACE Inhibitor or ARB for LVSD	42	93%	96%	96%
Aspirin at Arrival	215	98%	98%	99%
Aspirin at Discharge	208	99%	99%	98%
Beta Blocker at Discharge	198	96%	98%	98%
Fibrinolytic Medication Timing	0	-	37%	55%
PCI Within 90 Minutes of Arrival	38	87%	93%	90%
Smoking Cessation Advice	80	99%	99%	99%
Chest Pain/Possible Heart Attack Care				
Aspirin at Arrival[1]	17	94%	95%	95%
Median Time to ECG (minutes)[1]	20	6	6	8
Median Time to Transfer (minutes)[5]	0	-	49	61
Fibrinolytic Medication Timing[5]	0	-	63%	54%
Heart Failure Care				
ACE Inhibitor or ARB for LVSD[2]	115	97%	92%	94%
Discharge Instructions[2]	293	82%	84%	88%
Evaluation of LVS Function[2]	333	97%	98%	98%
Smoking Cessation Advice[2]	100	100%	99%	98%
Pneumonia Care				
Appropriate Initial Antibiotic[2]	82	94%	90%	92%
Blood Culture Timing[2]	197	97%	95%	96%
Influenza Vaccine[2]	89	94%	93%	91%
Initial Antibiotic Timing[2]	208	97%	96%	95%
Pneumococcal Vaccine[2]	117	93%	94%	93%
Smoking Cessation Advice[2]	86	100%	98%	97%
Surgical Care Improvement Project				
Appropriate VTP Within 24 Hours	144	91%	90%	92%
Appropriate Hair Removal	416	99%	100%	99%
Appropriate Beta Blocker Usage	118	97%	93%	93%
Controlled Postoperative Blood Glucose	92	83%	93%	93%
Prophylactic Antibiotic Timing	249	99%	97%	97%
Prophylactic Antibiotic Timing (Outpatient)	122	84%	92%	92%
Prophylactic Antibiotic Selection	260	97%	98%	97%
Prophylactic Antibiotic Select. (Outpatient)	129	92%	95%	94%
Prophylactic Antibiotic Stopped	236	97%	95%	94%
Recommended VTP Ordered	146	97%	92%	94%
Urinary Catheter Removal	51	76%	92%	90%
Children's Asthma Care				
Received Systemic Corticosteroids	-	-	-	100%
Received Home Management Plan	-	-	-	71%
Received Reliever Medication	-	-	-	100%
Use of Medical Imaging				
Combination Abdominal CT Scan	517	0.586	0.237	0.191
Combination Chest CT Scan	364	0.033	0.120	0.054
Follow-up Mammogram/Ultrasound	652	4.9%	8.3%	8.4%
MRI for Low Back Pain	116	31.0%	35.2%	32.7%
Survey of Patients' Hospital Experiences				
Area Around Room 'Always' Quiet at Night	300+	58%	-	58%
Doctors 'Always' Communicated Well	300+	72%	-	80%
Home Recovery Information Given	300+	72%	-	82%
Hospital Given 9 or 10 on 10 Point Scale	300+	56%	-	67%
Meds 'Always' Explained Before Given	300+	52%	-	60%
Nurses 'Always' Communicated Well	300+	70%	-	76%
Pain 'Always' Well Controlled	300+	62%	-	69%
Room and Bathroom 'Always' Clean	300+	70%	-	71%
Timely Help 'Always' Received	300+	53%	-	64%
Would Definitely Recommend Hospital	300+	57%	-	69%

Blackford Community Hospital

410 Pilgrim Boulevard — Phone: 765-348-0300
Hartford City, IN 47348 — Fax: 765-348-0574
URL: www.accesschs.org
Type: Critical Access Hospitals — Emergency Services: Yes
Ownership: Voluntary Non-Profit - Private — Beds: 65

Key Personnel:
CEO/President. . . . . Steve West
Chief of Medical Staff. . . . . Jon Blake, MD
Infection Control. . . . . Jennifer Horsley
Operating Room. . . . . Gail Lewis
Quality Assurance . . . . Nancy Hedden
Emergency Room . . . . Thomas Lee

Measure	Cases	This Hosp.	State Avg.	U.S. Avg.
Heart Attack Care				
ACE Inhibitor or ARB for LVSD	-	-	96%	96%
Aspirin at Arrival	-	-	98%	99%
Aspirin at Discharge	-	-	99%	98%
Beta Blocker at Discharge	-	-	98%	98%
Fibrinolytic Medication Timing	-	-	37%	55%
PCI Within 90 Minutes of Arrival	-	-	93%	90%
Smoking Cessation Advice	-	-	99%	99%
Chest Pain/Possible Heart Attack Care				
Aspirin at Arrival[5]	0	-	95%	95%
Median Time to ECG (minutes)[5]	0	-	6	8
Median Time to Transfer (minutes)[5]	0	-	49	61
Fibrinolytic Medication Timing[5]	0	-	63%	54%
Heart Failure Care				
ACE Inhibitor or ARB for LVSD	-	-	92%	94%
Discharge Instructions	-	-	84%	88%
Evaluation of LVS Function	-	-	98%	98%
Smoking Cessation Advice	-	-	99%	98%
Pneumonia Care				
Appropriate Initial Antibiotic	-	-	90%	92%
Blood Culture Timing	-	-	95%	96%
Influenza Vaccine	-	-	93%	91%
Initial Antibiotic Timing	-	-	96%	95%
Pneumococcal Vaccine	-	-	94%	93%
Smoking Cessation Advice	-	-	98%	97%
Surgical Care Improvement Project				
Appropriate VTP Within 24 Hours	-	-	90%	92%
Appropriate Hair Removal	-	-	100%	99%
Appropriate Beta Blocker Usage	-	-	93%	93%
Controlled Postoperative Blood Glucose	-	-	93%	93%
Prophylactic Antibiotic Timing	-	-	97%	97%
Prophylactic Antibiotic Timing (Outpatient)[5]	0	-	92%	92%
Prophylactic Antibiotic Selection	-	-	98%	97%
Prophylactic Antibiotic Select. (Outpatient)[5]	0	-	95%	94%
Prophylactic Antibiotic Stopped	-	-	95%	94%
Recommended VTP Ordered	-	-	92%	94%
Urinary Catheter Removal	-	-	92%	90%
Children's Asthma Care				
Received Systemic Corticosteroids	-	-	-	100%
Received Home Management Plan	-	-	-	71%
Received Reliever Medication	-	-	-	100%
Use of Medical Imaging				
Combination Abdominal CT Scan	220	0.059	0.237	0.191
Combination Chest CT Scan	126	0.016	0.120	0.054
Follow-up Mammogram/Ultrasound	241	12.0%	8.3%	8.4%
MRI for Low Back Pain[1]	41	36.6%	35.2%	32.7%
Survey of Patients' Hospital Experiences				
Area Around Room 'Always' Quiet at Night	-	-	-	58%
Doctors 'Always' Communicated Well	-	-	-	80%
Home Recovery Information Given	-	-	-	82%
Hospital Given 9 or 10 on 10 Point Scale	-	-	-	67%
Meds 'Always' Explained Before Given	-	-	-	60%
Nurses 'Always' Communicated Well	-	-	-	76%
Pain 'Always' Well Controlled	-	-	-	69%
Room and Bathroom 'Always' Clean	-	-	-	71%
Timely Help 'Always' Received	-	-	-	64%
Would Definitely Recommend Hospital	-	-	-	69%

Saint Mary Medical Center

1500 S Lake Park Avenue — Phone: 219-942-0551
Hobart, IN 46342
Type: Acute Care Hospitals — Emergency Services: Yes
Ownership: Voluntary Non-Profit - Private — Beds: 190

Key Personnel:
CEO/President. . . . . Janice Ryba

Measure	Cases	This Hosp.	State Avg.	U.S. Avg.
Heart Attack Care				
ACE Inhibitor or ARB for LVSD[1]	18	100%	96%	96%
Aspirin at Arrival	100	99%	98%	99%
Aspirin at Discharge	93	95%	99%	98%
Beta Blocker at Discharge	96	97%	98%	98%
Fibrinolytic Medication Timing	0	-	37%	55%
PCI Within 90 Minutes of Arrival[1]	17	71%	93%	90%
Smoking Cessation Advice	38	97%	99%	99%
Chest Pain/Possible Heart Attack Care				
Aspirin at Arrival[1,3]	2	100%	95%	95%
Median Time to ECG (minutes)[1,3]	2	34	6	8
Median Time to Transfer (minutes)[5]	0	-	49	61
Fibrinolytic Medication Timing[5]	0	-	63%	54%
Heart Failure Care				
ACE Inhibitor or ARB for LVSD[2]	113	96%	92%	94%
Discharge Instructions[2]	234	99%	84%	88%
Evaluation of LVS Function[2]	270	100%	98%	98%
Smoking Cessation Advice[2]	26	100%	99%	98%
Pneumonia Care				
Appropriate Initial Antibiotic[2]	74	82%	90%	92%
Blood Culture Timing[2]	96	100%	95%	96%
Influenza Vaccine[2]	64	98%	93%	91%
Initial Antibiotic Timing[2]	128	95%	96%	95%
Pneumococcal Vaccine[2]	98	93%	94%	93%
Smoking Cessation Advice[2]	52	98%	98%	97%
Surgical Care Improvement Project				
Appropriate VTP Within 24 Hours[2]	150	79%	90%	92%
Appropriate Hair Removal[2]	532	99%	100%	99%
Appropriate Beta Blocker Usage[2]	151	94%	93%	93%
Controlled Postoperative Blood Glucose[2]	65	77%	93%	93%
Prophylactic Antibiotic Timing[2]	367	99%	97%	97%
Prophylactic Antibiotic Timing (Outpatient)	394	94%	92%	92%
Prophylactic Antibiotic Selection[2]	365	98%	98%	97%
Prophylactic Antibiotic Select. (Outpatient)	390	97%	95%	94%
Prophylactic Antibiotic Stopped[2]	355	92%	95%	94%
Recommended VTP Ordered[2]	151	81%	92%	94%
Urinary Catheter Removal[2]	91	79%	92%	90%
Children's Asthma Care				
Received Systemic Corticosteroids	-	-	-	100%
Received Home Management Plan	-	-	-	71%
Received Reliever Medication	-	-	-	100%
Use of Medical Imaging				
Combination Abdominal CT Scan	940	0.426	0.237	0.191
Combination Chest CT Scan	851	0.395	0.120	0.054
Follow-up Mammogram/Ultrasound	878	6.8%	8.3%	8.4%
MRI for Low Back Pain	184	37.0%	35.2%	32.7%
Survey of Patients' Hospital Experiences				
Area Around Room 'Always' Quiet at Night	300+	57%	-	58%
Doctors 'Always' Communicated Well	300+	79%	-	80%
Home Recovery Information Given	300+	84%	-	82%
Hospital Given 9 or 10 on 10 Point Scale	300+	74%	-	67%
Meds 'Always' Explained Before Given	300+	61%	-	60%
Nurses 'Always' Communicated Well	300+	80%	-	76%
Pain 'Always' Well Controlled	300+	71%	-	69%
Room and Bathroom 'Always' Clean	300+	77%	-	71%
Timely Help 'Always' Received	300+	66%	-	64%
Would Definitely Recommend Hospital	300+	80%	-	69%

NOTE: Hospital profiles are in alphabetical order by state, then city, then hospital within the city; Rankings exclude hospitals with less than 25 cases except for patient surveys which excludes hospitals with less than 100 cases; (a) 100–299 cases; (1) The number of cases is too small to be sure how well a hospital is performing; (2) The hospital indicated that the data submitted for this measure were based on a sample of cases; (3) Data was collected during a shorter time period (fewer quarters) than the maximum possible time for this measure; (4) Suppressed for one or more quarters by CMS; (5) No data is available from the hospital for this measure; (6) Fewer than 100 patients completed the HCAHPS survey. Use these rates with caution, as the number of surveys may be too low to reliably assess hospital performance; (7) Survey results are based on less than 12 months of data; (8) Survey results are not available for this reporting period; (9) No or very few patients were eligible for the HCAHPS survey. The scores shown, if any, reflect a very small number of surveys; (10) A state average was not calculated because too few hospitals in the state submitted data; (11) There were discrepancies in the data collection process; Please refer to the User's Guide for a full explanation of data.

Parkview Huntington Hospital

2001 Stults Rd
Huntington, IN 46750
URL: www.parkview.com
Type: Acute Care Hospitals
Ownership: Voluntary Non-Profit - Private
Phone: 260-355-3000
Fax: 260-355-3346
Emergency Services: Yes
Beds: 36

Key Personnel:
Chief of Medical Staff.......... Jeffrey Brookes
Quality Assurance .... Mary Johnson, RN
Emergency Room .... Mary Johnson, RN

Measure	Cases	This Hosp.	State Avg.	U.S. Avg.
Heart Attack Care				
ACE Inhibitor or ARB for LVSD[3]	0	-	96%	96%
Aspirin at Arrival[1,3]	1	100%	98%	99%
Aspirin at Discharge[1,3]	1	100%	99%	98%
Beta Blocker at Discharge[1,3]	1	0%	98%	98%
Fibrinolytic Medication Timing[3]	0	-	37%	55%
PCI Within 90 Minutes of Arrival[3]	0	-	93%	90%
Smoking Cessation Advice[3]	0	-	99%	99%
Chest Pain/Possible Heart Attack Care				
Aspirin at Arrival	107	96%	95%	95%
Median Time to ECG (minutes)	109	8	6	8
Median Time to Transfer (minutes)[1,3]	5	42	49	61
Fibrinolytic Medication Timing[1]	1	100%	63%	54%
Heart Failure Care				
ACE Inhibitor or ARB for LVSD[1]	14	100%	92%	94%
Discharge Instructions	37	84%	84%	88%
Evaluation of LVS Function	52	96%	98%	98%
Smoking Cessation Advice[1]	8	100%	99%	98%
Pneumonia Care				
Appropriate Initial Antibiotic	59	92%	90%	92%
Blood Culture Timing	56	95%	95%	96%
Influenza Vaccine	55	96%	93%	91%
Initial Antibiotic Timing	87	100%	96%	95%
Pneumococcal Vaccine	74	92%	94%	93%
Smoking Cessation Advice	31	100%	98%	97%
Surgical Care Improvement Project				
Appropriate VTP Within 24 Hours	47	100%	90%	92%
Appropriate Hair Removal	114	100%	100%	99%
Appropriate Beta Blocker Usage	40	95%	93%	93%
Controlled Postoperative Blood Glucose	0	-	93%	93%
Prophylactic Antibiotic Timing	96	97%	97%	97%
Prophylactic Antibiotic Timing (Outpatient)	99	92%	92%	92%
Prophylactic Antibiotic Selection	96	99%	98%	97%
Prophylactic Antibiotic Select. (Outpatient)	92	89%	95%	94%
Prophylactic Antibiotic Stopped	95	96%	95%	94%
Recommended VTP Ordered	47	100%	92%	94%
Urinary Catheter Removal[1]	19	89%	92%	90%
Children's Asthma Care				
Received Systemic Corticosteroids	-	-	-	100%
Received Home Management Plan	-	-	-	71%
Received Reliever Medication	-	-	-	100%
Use of Medical Imaging				
Combination Abdominal CT Scan	213	0.263	0.237	0.191
Combination Chest CT Scan	127	0.071	0.120	0.054
Follow-up Mammogram/Ultrasound	338	12.1%	8.3%	8.4%
MRI for Low Back Pain	62	37.1%	35.2%	32.7%
Survey of Patients' Hospital Experiences				
Area Around Room 'Always' Quiet at Night	300+	62%	-	58%
Doctors 'Always' Communicated Well	300+	85%	-	80%
Home Recovery Information Given	300+	89%	-	82%
Hospital Given 9 or 10 on 10 Point Scale	300+	77%	-	67%
Meds 'Always' Explained Before Given	300+	62%	-	60%
Nurses 'Always' Communicated Well	300+	84%	-	76%
Pain 'Always' Well Controlled	300+	76%	-	69%
Room and Bathroom 'Always' Clean	300+	75%	-	71%
Timely Help 'Always' Received	300+	74%	-	64%
Would Definitely Recommend Hospital	300+	75%	-	69%

Community Hospital East

1500 N Ritter Ave
Indianapolis, IN 46219
URL: www.ecommunity.com
Type: Acute Care Hospitals
Ownership: Voluntary Non-Profit - Private
Phone: 317-355-5411
Fax: 317-351-7726
Emergency Services: Yes
Beds: 1,025

Key Personnel:
CEO/President.............. Bryan A Mills
Chief of Medical Staff.......... Clif Knight, MD
Infection Control.............. Robert Baker, MD
Pediatric Ambulatory Care ...... Jerrald Smith
Pediatric In-Patient Care .... Jerrald Smith
Quality Assurance .... Ruth Adams
Radiology.................. Michael Mullinix, MD

Measure	Cases	This Hosp.	State Avg.	U.S. Avg.
Heart Attack Care				
ACE Inhibitor or ARB for LVSD	30	100%	96%	96%
Aspirin at Arrival	113	99%	98%	99%
Aspirin at Discharge	109	99%	99%	98%
Beta Blocker at Discharge	108	100%	98%	98%
Fibrinolytic Medication Timing	0	-	37%	55%
PCI Within 90 Minutes of Arrival	29	93%	93%	90%
Smoking Cessation Advice	50	100%	99%	99%
Chest Pain/Possible Heart Attack Care				
Aspirin at Arrival[1]	21	95%	95%	95%
Median Time to ECG (minutes)[1]	22	4	6	8
Median Time to Transfer (minutes)[1,3]	1	159	49	61
Fibrinolytic Medication Timing[3]	0	-	63%	54%
Heart Failure Care				
ACE Inhibitor or ARB for LVSD	91	92%	92%	94%
Discharge Instructions	231	74%	84%	88%
Evaluation of LVS Function	285	99%	98%	98%
Smoking Cessation Advice	75	100%	99%	98%
Pneumonia Care				
Appropriate Initial Antibiotic[2]	91	92%	90%	92%
Blood Culture Timing[2]	131	94%	95%	96%
Influenza Vaccine[2]	73	84%	93%	91%
Initial Antibiotic Timing[2]	146	99%	96%	95%
Pneumococcal Vaccine[2]	102	89%	94%	93%
Smoking Cessation Advice[2]	54	100%	98%	97%
Surgical Care Improvement Project				
Appropriate VTP Within 24 Hours[2]	151	93%	90%	92%
Appropriate Hair Removal[2]	396	100%	100%	99%
Appropriate Beta Blocker Usage[2]	103	96%	93%	93%
Controlled Postoperative Blood Glucose[2]	0	-	93%	93%
Prophylactic Antibiotic Timing[2]	248	96%	97%	97%
Prophylactic Antibiotic Timing (Outpatient)	364	76%	92%	92%
Prophylactic Antibiotic Selection[2]	251	96%	98%	97%
Prophylactic Antibiotic Select. (Outpatient)	353	85%	95%	94%
Prophylactic Antibiotic Stopped[2]	243	97%	95%	94%
Recommended VTP Ordered[2]	151	94%	92%	94%
Urinary Catheter Removal[2]	46	87%	92%	90%
Children's Asthma Care				
Received Systemic Corticosteroids	-	-	-	100%
Received Home Management Plan	-	-	-	71%
Received Reliever Medication	-	-	-	100%
Use of Medical Imaging				
Combination Abdominal CT Scan	1,135	0.210	0.237	0.191
Combination Chest CT Scan	974	0.161	0.120	0.054
Follow-up Mammogram/Ultrasound	2,278	8.7%	8.3%	8.4%
MRI for Low Back Pain	438	34.0%	35.2%	32.7%
Survey of Patients' Hospital Experiences				
Area Around Room 'Always' Quiet at Night	300+	49%	-	58%
Doctors 'Always' Communicated Well	300+	74%	-	80%
Home Recovery Information Given	300+	79%	-	82%
Hospital Given 9 or 10 on 10 Point Scale	300+	61%	-	67%
Meds 'Always' Explained Before Given	300+	53%	-	60%
Nurses 'Always' Communicated Well	300+	69%	-	76%
Pain 'Always' Well Controlled	300+	66%	-	69%
Room and Bathroom 'Always' Clean	300+	65%	-	71%
Timely Help 'Always' Received	300+	60%	-	64%
Would Definitely Recommend Hospital	300+	66%	-	69%

Community Hospital North

7150 Clearvista Drive
Indianapolis, IN 46256
URL: www.ecommunity.com/north
Type: Acute Care Hospitals
Ownership: Voluntary Non-Profit - Private
Phone: 317-621-5335
Fax: 317-621-3627
Emergency Services: Yes
Beds: 282

Key Personnel:
CEO/President.............. William Corley
Chief of Medical Staff.......... Mark Dixon
Radiology.................. Jeff Jackson

Measure	Cases	This Hosp.	State Avg.	U.S. Avg.
Heart Attack Care				
ACE Inhibitor or ARB for LVSD[1]	2	100%	96%	96%
Aspirin at Arrival[1]	6	67%	98%	99%
Aspirin at Discharge[1]	3	100%	99%	98%
Beta Blocker at Discharge[1]	3	67%	98%	98%
Fibrinolytic Medication Timing	0	-	37%	55%
PCI Within 90 Minutes of Arrival	0	-	93%	90%
Smoking Cessation Advice[1]	1	100%	99%	99%
Chest Pain/Possible Heart Attack Care				
Aspirin at Arrival	131	91%	95%	95%
Median Time to ECG (minutes)	139	12	6	8
Median Time to Transfer (minutes)[1]	14	62	49	61
Fibrinolytic Medication Timing	0	-	63%	54%
Heart Failure Care				
ACE Inhibitor or ARB for LVSD[1]	20	75%	92%	94%
Discharge Instructions	67	82%	84%	88%
Evaluation of LVS Function	110	95%	98%	98%
Smoking Cessation Advice[1]	13	100%	99%	98%
Pneumonia Care				
Appropriate Initial Antibiotic[2]	74	89%	90%	92%
Blood Culture Timing[2]	132	95%	95%	96%
Influenza Vaccine[2]	72	92%	93%	91%
Initial Antibiotic Timing[2]	125	97%	96%	95%
Pneumococcal Vaccine[2]	114	91%	94%	93%
Smoking Cessation Advice[2]	40	100%	98%	97%
Surgical Care Improvement Project				
Appropriate VTP Within 24 Hours[2]	165	96%	90%	92%
Appropriate Hair Removal[2]	442	100%	100%	99%
Appropriate Beta Blocker Usage[2]	92	97%	93%	93%
Controlled Postoperative Blood Glucose[1,2]	1	100%	93%	93%
Prophylactic Antibiotic Timing[2]	306	97%	97%	97%
Prophylactic Antibiotic Timing (Outpatient)	480	89%	92%	92%
Prophylactic Antibiotic Selection[2]	308	97%	98%	97%
Prophylactic Antibiotic Select. (Outpatient)	460	93%	95%	94%
Prophylactic Antibiotic Stopped[2]	283	97%	95%	94%
Recommended VTP Ordered[2]	168	96%	92%	94%
Urinary Catheter Removal[2]	35	97%	92%	90%
Children's Asthma Care				
Received Systemic Corticosteroids	-	-	-	100%
Received Home Management Plan	-	-	-	71%
Received Reliever Medication	-	-	-	100%
Use of Medical Imaging				
Combination Abdominal CT Scan	888	0.231	0.237	0.191
Combination Chest CT Scan	774	0.198	0.120	0.054
Follow-up Mammogram/Ultrasound	1,178	9.1%	8.3%	8.4%
MRI for Low Back Pain	354	35.3%	35.2%	32.7%
Survey of Patients' Hospital Experiences				
Area Around Room 'Always' Quiet at Night	300+	61%	-	58%
Doctors 'Always' Communicated Well	300+	77%	-	80%
Home Recovery Information Given	300+	79%	-	82%
Hospital Given 9 or 10 on 10 Point Scale	300+	72%	-	67%
Meds 'Always' Explained Before Given	300+	55%	-	60%
Nurses 'Always' Communicated Well	300+	71%	-	76%
Pain 'Always' Well Controlled	300+	68%	-	69%
Room and Bathroom 'Always' Clean	300+	69%	-	71%
Timely Help 'Always' Received	300+	55%	-	64%
Would Definitely Recommend Hospital	300+	79%	-	69%

NOTE: Hospital profiles are in alphabetical order by state, then city, then hospital within the city; Rankings exclude hospitals with less than 25 cases except for patient surveys which excludes hospitals with less than 100 cases; (a) 100–299 cases; (1) The number of cases is too small to be sure how well a hospital is performing; (2) The hospital indicated that the data submitted for this measure were based on a sample of cases; (3) Data was collected during a shorter time period (fewer quarters) than the maximum possible time for this measure; (4) Suppressed for one or more quarters by CMS; (5) No data is available from the hospital for this measure; (6) Fewer than 100 patients completed the HCAHPS survey. Use these rates with caution, as the number of surveys may be too low to reliably assess hospital performance; (7) Survey results are based on less than 12 months of data; (8) Survey results are not available for this reporting period; (9) No or very few patients were eligible for the HCAHPS survey. The scores shown, if any, reflect a very small number of surveys; (10) A state average was not calculated because too few hospitals in the state submitted data; (11) There were discrepancies in the data collection process; Please refer to the User's Guide for a full explanation of data.

Community Hospital South

1402 E County Line Rd S | Phone: 317-887-7112
Indianapolis, IN 46227 | Fax: 317-887-4670
URL: www.ecommunity.com/south
Type: Acute Care Hospitals | Emergency Services: Yes
Ownership: Voluntary Non-Profit - Private

Key Personnel:
CEO/President. . . . . William Corley
Chief of Medical Staff . . . . Carolyn Waymire
Coronary Care . . . . Kerry Sawin
Infection Control . . . . Gayle Walsh
Operating Room. . . . . Mark Walke
Pediatric Ambulatory Care . . . . . . Sue Sandberg
Quality Assurance . . . . Cleo Burgard
Radiology. . . . . Thomas Belt

Measure	Cases	This Hosp.	State Avg.	U.S. Avg.
Heart Attack Care				
ACE Inhibitor or ARB for LVSD	28	93%	96%	96%
Aspirin at Arrival	93	100%	98%	99%
Aspirin at Discharge	132	100%	99%	98%
Beta Blocker at Discharge	126	100%	98%	98%
Fibrinolytic Medication Timing	0	-	37%	55%
PCI Within 90 Minutes of Arrival	29	83%	93%	90%
Smoking Cessation Advice	61	100%	99%	99%
Chest Pain/Possible Heart Attack Care				
Aspirin at Arrival[1]	12	92%	95%	95%
Median Time to ECG (minutes)[1]	14	6	6	8
Median Time to Transfer (minutes)[1,3]	2	263	49	61
Fibrinolytic Medication Timing[3]	0	-	63%	54%
Heart Failure Care				
ACE Inhibitor or ARB for LVSD	76	93%	92%	94%
Discharge Instructions	159	71%	84%	88%
Evaluation of LVS Function	211	99%	98%	98%
Smoking Cessation Advice	44	100%	99%	98%
Pneumonia Care				
Appropriate Initial Antibiotic[2]	83	94%	90%	92%
Blood Culture Timing[2]	125	94%	95%	96%
Influenza Vaccine[2]	75	85%	93%	91%
Initial Antibiotic Timing[2]	143	95%	96%	95%
Pneumococcal Vaccine[2]	142	91%	94%	93%
Smoking Cessation Advice[2]	38	100%	98%	97%
Surgical Care Improvement Project				
Appropriate VTP Within 24 Hours[2]	130	91%	90%	92%
Appropriate Hair Removal[2]	457	100%	100%	99%
Appropriate Beta Blocker Usage[2]	116	97%	93%	93%
Controlled Postoperative Blood Glucose[2]	0	-	93%	93%
Prophylactic Antibiotic Timing[2]	307	95%	97%	97%
Prophylactic Antibiotic Timing (Outpatient)	324	86%	92%	92%
Prophylactic Antibiotic Selection[2]	308	95%	98%	97%
Prophylactic Antibiotic Select. (Outpatient)	315	91%	95%	94%
Prophylactic Antibiotic Stopped[2]	298	96%	95%	94%
Recommended VTP Ordered[2]	130	92%	92%	94%
Urinary Catheter Removal[2]	79	100%	92%	90%
Children's Asthma Care				
Received Systemic Corticosteroids	-	-	-	100%
Received Home Management Plan	-	-	-	71%
Received Reliever Medication	-	-	-	100%
Use of Medical Imaging				
Combination Abdominal CT Scan	533	0.058	0.237	0.191
Combination Chest CT Scan	392	0.077	0.120	0.054
Follow-up Mammogram/Ultrasound	778	7.1%	8.3%	8.4%
MRI for Low Back Pain	121	38.0%	35.2%	32.7%
Survey of Patients' Hospital Experiences				
Area Around Room 'Always' Quiet at Night	300+	47%	-	58%
Doctors 'Always' Communicated Well	300+	76%	-	80%
Home Recovery Information Given	300+	78%	-	82%
Hospital Given 9 or 10 on 10 Point Scale	300+	68%	-	67%
Meds 'Always' Explained Before Given	300+	54%	-	60%
Nurses 'Always' Communicated Well	300+	73%	-	76%
Pain 'Always' Well Controlled	300+	68%	-	69%
Room and Bathroom 'Always' Clean	300+	67%	-	71%
Timely Help 'Always' Received	300+	61%	-	64%
Would Definitely Recommend Hospital	300+	71%	-	69%

The Indiana Heart Hospital

8075 N Shadeland Ave | Phone: 317-621-8063
Indianapolis, IN 46250 | Fax: 317-621-8111
URL: www.hearthospital.com
Type: Acute Care Hospitals | Emergency Services: Yes
Ownership: Proprietary | Beds: 72

Key Personnel:
CEO/President. . . . . Thomas A Malasto

Measure	Cases	This Hosp.	State Avg.	U.S. Avg.
Heart Attack Care				
ACE Inhibitor or ARB for LVSD	73	96%	96%	96%
Aspirin at Arrival	145	99%	98%	99%
Aspirin at Discharge	352	99%	99%	98%
Beta Blocker at Discharge	330	99%	98%	98%
Fibrinolytic Medication Timing	0	-	37%	55%
PCI Within 90 Minutes of Arrival	51	94%	93%	90%
Smoking Cessation Advice	130	100%	99%	99%
Chest Pain/Possible Heart Attack Care				
Aspirin at Arrival[1]	14	100%	95%	95%
Median Time to ECG (minutes)[1]	15	4	6	8
Median Time to Transfer (minutes)[5]	0	-	49	61
Fibrinolytic Medication Timing[3]	0	-	63%	54%
Heart Failure Care				
ACE Inhibitor or ARB for LVSD	147	98%	92%	94%
Discharge Instructions	326	98%	84%	88%
Evaluation of LVS Function	377	99%	98%	98%
Smoking Cessation Advice	60	100%	99%	98%
Pneumonia Care				
Appropriate Initial Antibiotic[1]	5	80%	90%	92%
Blood Culture Timing[1]	6	100%	95%	96%
Influenza Vaccine[1]	12	92%	93%	91%
Initial Antibiotic Timing[1]	4	100%	96%	95%
Pneumococcal Vaccine[1]	17	88%	94%	93%
Smoking Cessation Advice[1]	6	100%	98%	97%
Surgical Care Improvement Project				
Appropriate VTP Within 24 Hours[1,2]	12	100%	90%	92%
Appropriate Hair Removal[2]	604	100%	100%	99%
Appropriate Beta Blocker Usage[2]	333	81%	93%	93%
Controlled Postoperative Blood Glucose[2]	349	95%	93%	93%
Prophylactic Antibiotic Timing[2]	466	99%	97%	97%
Prophylactic Antibiotic Timing (Outpatient)	330	96%	92%	92%
Prophylactic Antibiotic Selection[2]	474	99%	98%	97%
Prophylactic Antibiotic Select. (Outpatient)	325	100%	95%	94%
Prophylactic Antibiotic Stopped[2]	440	93%	95%	94%
Recommended VTP Ordered[1,2]	12	100%	92%	94%
Urinary Catheter Removal	226	96%	92%	90%
Children's Asthma Care				
Received Systemic Corticosteroids	-	-	-	100%
Received Home Management Plan	-	-	-	71%
Received Reliever Medication	-	-	-	100%
Use of Medical Imaging				
Combination Abdominal CT Scan	92	0.120	0.237	0.191
Combination Chest CT Scan	173	0.087	0.120	0.054
Follow-up Mammogram/Ultrasound[5]	0	-	8.3%	8.4%
MRI for Low Back Pain[5]	0	-	35.2%	32.7%
Survey of Patients' Hospital Experiences				
Area Around Room 'Always' Quiet at Night	300+	66%	-	58%
Doctors 'Always' Communicated Well	300+	81%	-	80%
Home Recovery Information Given	300+	83%	-	82%
Hospital Given 9 or 10 on 10 Point Scale	300+	84%	-	67%
Meds 'Always' Explained Before Given	300+	55%	-	60%
Nurses 'Always' Communicated Well	300+	81%	-	76%
Pain 'Always' Well Controlled	300+	73%	-	69%
Room and Bathroom 'Always' Clean	300+	78%	-	71%
Timely Help 'Always' Received	300+	74%	-	64%
Would Definitely Recommend Hospital	300+	87%	-	69%

Indiana Orthopaedic Hospital

8400 Northwest Blvd | Phone: 317-956-1000
Indianapolis, IN 46278
Type: Acute Care Hospitals | Emergency Services: No
Ownership: Proprietary

Measure	Cases	This Hosp.	State Avg.	U.S. Avg.
Heart Attack Care				
ACE Inhibitor or ARB for LVSD[5]	0	-	96%	96%
Aspirin at Arrival[5]	0	-	98%	99%
Aspirin at Discharge[5]	0	-	99%	98%
Beta Blocker at Discharge[5]	0	-	98%	98%
Fibrinolytic Medication Timing[5]	0	-	37%	55%
PCI Within 90 Minutes of Arrival[5]	0	-	93%	90%
Smoking Cessation Advice[5]	0	-	99%	99%
Chest Pain/Possible Heart Attack Care				
Aspirin at Arrival[5]	0	-	95%	95%
Median Time to ECG (minutes)[5]	0	-	6	8
Median Time to Transfer (minutes)[5]	0	-	49	61
Fibrinolytic Medication Timing[5]	0	-	63%	54%
Heart Failure Care				
ACE Inhibitor or ARB for LVSD[5]	0	-	92%	94%
Discharge Instructions[5]	0	-	84%	88%
Evaluation of LVS Function[5]	0	-	98%	98%
Smoking Cessation Advice[5]	0	-	99%	98%
Pneumonia Care				
Appropriate Initial Antibiotic[5]	0	-	90%	92%
Blood Culture Timing[5]	0	-	95%	96%
Influenza Vaccine[5]	0	-	93%	91%
Initial Antibiotic Timing[5]	0	-	96%	95%
Pneumococcal Vaccine[5]	0	-	94%	93%
Smoking Cessation Advice[5]	0	-	98%	97%
Surgical Care Improvement Project				
Appropriate VTP Within 24 Hours[1,2]	6	100%	90%	92%
Appropriate Hair Removal[2]	236	100%	100%	99%
Appropriate Beta Blocker Usage[2]	113	97%	93%	93%
Controlled Postoperative Blood Glucose[2]	0	-	93%	93%
Prophylactic Antibiotic Timing[2]	168	100%	97%	97%
Prophylactic Antibiotic Timing (Outpatient)	486	100%	92%	92%
Prophylactic Antibiotic Selection[2]	168	100%	98%	97%
Prophylactic Antibiotic Select. (Outpatient)	486	100%	95%	94%
Prophylactic Antibiotic Stopped[2]	168	96%	95%	94%
Recommended VTP Ordered[1,2]	6	100%	92%	94%
Urinary Catheter Removal[1,2]	21	100%	92%	90%
Children's Asthma Care				
Received Systemic Corticosteroids	-	-	-	100%
Received Home Management Plan	-	-	-	71%
Received Reliever Medication	-	-	-	100%
Use of Medical Imaging				
Combination Abdominal CT Scan[1]	1	0.000	0.237	0.191
Combination Chest CT Scan[1]	18	0.000	0.120	0.054
Follow-up Mammogram/Ultrasound[5]	0	-	8.3%	8.4%
MRI for Low Back Pain	141	31.9%	35.2%	32.7%
Survey of Patients' Hospital Experiences				
Area Around Room 'Always' Quiet at Night	300+	76%	-	58%
Doctors 'Always' Communicated Well	300+	88%	-	80%
Home Recovery Information Given	300+	93%	-	82%
Hospital Given 9 or 10 on 10 Point Scale	300+	90%	-	67%
Meds 'Always' Explained Before Given	300+	72%	-	60%
Nurses 'Always' Communicated Well	300+	87%	-	76%
Pain 'Always' Well Controlled	300+	79%	-	69%
Room and Bathroom 'Always' Clean	300+	89%	-	71%
Timely Help 'Always' Received	300+	80%	-	64%
Would Definitely Recommend Hospital	300+	91%	-	69%

NOTE: Hospital profiles are in alphabetical order by state, then city, then hospital within the city; Rankings exclude hospitals with less than 25 cases except for patient surveys which excludes hospitals with less than 100 cases; (a) 100–299 cases; (1) The number of cases is too small to be sure how well a hospital is performing; (2) The hospital indicated that the data submitted for this measure were based on a sample of cases; (3) Data was collected during a shorter time period (fewer quarters) than the maximum possible time for this measure; (4) Suppressed for one or more quarters by CMS; (5) No data is available from the hospital for this measure; (6) Fewer than 100 patients completed the HCAHPS survey. Use these rates with caution, as the number of surveys may be too low to reliably assess hospital performance; (7) Survey results are based on less than 12 months of data; (8) Survey results are not available for this reporting period; (9) No or very few patients were eligible for the HCAHPS survey. The scores shown, if any, reflect a very small number of surveys; (10) A state average was not calculated because too few hospitals in the state submitted data; (11) There were discrepancies in the data collection process; Please refer to the User's Guide for a full explanation of data.

Indiana University Health

1701 N Senate Blvd
Indianapolis, IN 46206
Type: Acute Care Hospitals
Ownership: Voluntary Non-Profit - Private
Phone: 317-962-5900
Fax: 317-962-1867
Emergency Services: Yes
Beds: 1,120

Measure	Cases	This Hosp.	State Avg.	U.S. Avg.
Heart Attack Care				
ACE Inhibitor or ARB for LVSD	100	100%	96%	96%
Aspirin at Arrival	357	99%	98%	99%
Aspirin at Discharge	537	99%	99%	98%
Beta Blocker at Discharge	515	100%	98%	98%
Fibrinolytic Medication Timing	0	-	37%	55%
PCI Within 90 Minutes of Arrival	96	97%	93%	90%
Smoking Cessation Advice	221	100%	99%	99%
Chest Pain/Possible Heart Attack Care				
Aspirin at Arrival[3]	0	-	95%	95%
Median Time to ECG (minutes)[3]	0	-	6	8
Median Time to Transfer (minutes)[5]	0	-	49	61
Fibrinolytic Medication Timing[5]	0	-	63%	54%
Heart Failure Care				
ACE Inhibitor or ARB for LVSD	346	99%	92%	94%
Discharge Instructions	731	92%	84%	88%
Evaluation of LVS Function	879	100%	98%	98%
Smoking Cessation Advice	213	100%	99%	98%
Pneumonia Care				
Appropriate Initial Antibiotic[2]	45	87%	90%	92%
Blood Culture Timing[2]	103	94%	95%	96%
Influenza Vaccine[2]	84	89%	93%	91%
Initial Antibiotic Timing[2]	107	97%	96%	95%
Pneumococcal Vaccine[2]	96	92%	94%	93%
Smoking Cessation Advice[2]	67	97%	98%	97%
Surgical Care Improvement Project				
Appropriate VTP Within 24 Hours[2]	263	96%	90%	92%
Appropriate Hair Removal[2]	752	100%	100%	99%
Appropriate Beta Blocker Usage[2]	218	92%	93%	93%
Controlled Postoperative Blood Glucose[2]	115	95%	93%	93%
Prophylactic Antibiotic Timing[2]	510	97%	97%	97%
Prophylactic Antibiotic Timing (Outpatient)	783	95%	92%	92%
Prophylactic Antibiotic Selection[2]	515	97%	98%	97%
Prophylactic Antibiotic Select. (Outpatient)	906	92%	95%	94%
Prophylactic Antibiotic Stopped[2]	467	95%	95%	94%
Recommended VTP Ordered[2]	264	97%	92%	94%
Urinary Catheter Removal[2]	146	90%	92%	90%
Children's Asthma Care				
Received Systemic Corticosteroids	-	-	-	100%
Received Home Management Plan	-	-	-	71%
Received Reliever Medication	-	-	-	100%
Use of Medical Imaging				
Combination Abdominal CT Scan	3,827	0.093	0.237	0.191
Combination Chest CT Scan	3,506	0.011	0.120	0.054
Follow-up Mammogram/Ultrasound	3,069	6.8%	8.3%	8.4%
MRI for Low Back Pain	568	42.6%	35.2%	32.7%
Survey of Patients' Hospital Experiences				
Area Around Room 'Always' Quiet at Night	300+	51%	-	58%
Doctors 'Always' Communicated Well	300+	74%	-	80%
Home Recovery Information Given	300+	80%	-	82%
Hospital Given 9 or 10 on 10 Point Scale	300+	65%	-	67%
Meds 'Always' Explained Before Given	300+	56%	-	60%
Nurses 'Always' Communicated Well	300+	71%	-	76%
Pain 'Always' Well Controlled	300+	68%	-	69%
Room and Bathroom 'Always' Clean	300+	63%	-	71%
Timely Help 'Always' Received	300+	52%	-	64%
Would Definitely Recommend Hospital	300+	68%	-	69%

Indianapolis VA Medical Center

1481 W. Tenth Street
Indianapolis, IN 46202
URL: www.indianapolis.va.gov
Type: Acute Care-Veterans Administration
Ownership: Government - Federal
Phone: 317-554-0000
Fax: 317-988-2701
Emergency Services: No
Beds: 170

Key Personnel:
CEO/President. . . . . Thomas Mattice
Chief of Medical Staff. . . . . Kenneth E Klotz, MD
Operating Room. . . . . Delores Cikrit, MD
Quality Assurance . . . . Mary Ann Payne
Ambulatory Care . . . . Peter Woodbridge, MD
Anesthesiology. . . . . SS Moorthy, MD
Patient Relations . . . . Ann Barrett

Measure	Cases	This Hosp.	State Avg.	U.S. Avg.
Heart Attack Care				
ACE Inhibitor or ARB for LVSD[1]	13	92%	96%	96%
Aspirin at Arrival	111	100%	98%	99%
Aspirin at Discharge	112	99%	99%	98%
Beta Blocker at Discharge	111	100%	98%	98%
Fibrinolytic Medication Timing[5]	0	-	37%	55%
PCI Within 90 Minutes of Arrival[1]	15	47%	93%	90%
Smoking Cessation Advice	47	98%	99%	99%
Chest Pain/Possible Heart Attack Care				
Aspirin at Arrival	-	-	95%	95%
Median Time to ECG (minutes)	-	-	6	8
Median Time to Transfer (minutes)	-	-	49	61
Fibrinolytic Medication Timing	-	-	63%	54%
Heart Failure Care				
ACE Inhibitor or ARB for LVSD	117	97%	92%	94%
Discharge Instructions	287	100%	84%	88%
Evaluation of LVS Function	314	100%	98%	98%
Smoking Cessation Advice	102	98%	99%	98%
Pneumonia Care				
Appropriate Initial Antibiotic	115	98%	90%	92%
Blood Culture Timing	185	99%	95%	96%
Influenza Vaccine	131	99%	93%	91%
Initial Antibiotic Timing	195	94%	96%	95%
Pneumococcal Vaccine	155	100%	94%	93%
Smoking Cessation Advice	110	96%	98%	97%
Surgical Care Improvement Project				
Appropriate VTP Within 24 Hours[2]	191	97%	90%	92%
Appropriate Hair Removal[2]	469	100%	100%	99%
Appropriate Beta Blocker Usage[2]	272	94%	93%	93%
Controlled Postoperative Blood Glucose[2]	102	93%	93%	93%
Prophylactic Antibiotic Timing	346	99%	97%	97%
Prophylactic Antibiotic Timing (Outpatient)	-	-	92%	92%
Prophylactic Antibiotic Selection	358	99%	98%	97%
Prophylactic Antibiotic Select. (Outpatient)	-	-	95%	94%
Prophylactic Antibiotic Stopped	331	95%	95%	94%
Recommended VTP Ordered[2]	191	99%	92%	94%
Urinary Catheter Removal[2]	203	96%	92%	90%
Children's Asthma Care				
Received Systemic Corticosteroids	-	-	-	100%
Received Home Management Plan	-	-	-	71%
Received Reliever Medication	-	-	-	100%
Use of Medical Imaging				
Combination Abdominal CT Scan	-	-	0.237	0.191
Combination Chest CT Scan	-	-	0.120	0.054
Follow-up Mammogram/Ultrasound	-	-	8.3%	8.4%
MRI for Low Back Pain	-	-	35.2%	32.7%
Survey of Patients' Hospital Experiences				
Area Around Room 'Always' Quiet at Night	-	-	-	58%
Doctors 'Always' Communicated Well	-	-	-	80%
Home Recovery Information Given	-	-	-	82%
Hospital Given 9 or 10 on 10 Point Scale	-	-	-	67%
Meds 'Always' Explained Before Given	-	-	-	60%
Nurses 'Always' Communicated Well	-	-	-	76%
Pain 'Always' Well Controlled	-	-	-	69%
Room and Bathroom 'Always' Clean	-	-	-	71%
Timely Help 'Always' Received	-	-	-	64%
Would Definitely Recommend Hospital	-	-	-	69%

Saint Francis Hospital and Health Centers-Indianapolis

8111 S Emerson Avenue
Indianapolis, IN 46237
URL: www.stfrancishospitals.org
Type: Acute Care Hospitals
Ownership: Voluntary Non-Profit - Church
Phone: 317-865-5001
Fax: 317-783-8152
Emergency Services: Yes

Key Personnel:
CEO/President. . . . . Robert Brody
Chief of Medical Staff. . . . . Alan Gillespie

Measure	Cases	This Hosp.	State Avg.	U.S. Avg.
Heart Attack Care				
ACE Inhibitor or ARB for LVSD	91	98%	96%	96%
Aspirin at Arrival	303	99%	98%	99%
Aspirin at Discharge	492	100%	99%	98%
Beta Blocker at Discharge	473	100%	98%	98%
Fibrinolytic Medication Timing	0	-	37%	55%
PCI Within 90 Minutes of Arrival	92	97%	93%	90%
Smoking Cessation Advice	192	99%	99%	99%
Chest Pain/Possible Heart Attack Care				
Aspirin at Arrival	70	67%	95%	95%
Median Time to ECG (minutes)	75	9	6	8
Median Time to Transfer (minutes)[5]	0	-	49	61
Fibrinolytic Medication Timing[3]	0	-	63%	54%
Heart Failure Care				
ACE Inhibitor or ARB for LVSD	145	94%	92%	94%
Discharge Instructions	394	88%	84%	88%
Evaluation of LVS Function	453	99%	98%	98%
Smoking Cessation Advice	73	100%	99%	98%
Pneumonia Care				
Appropriate Initial Antibiotic	144	76%	90%	92%
Blood Culture Timing	133	84%	95%	96%
Influenza Vaccine	112	92%	93%	91%
Initial Antibiotic Timing	153	86%	96%	95%
Pneumococcal Vaccine	154	90%	94%	93%
Smoking Cessation Advice	58	98%	98%	97%
Surgical Care Improvement Project				
Appropriate VTP Within 24 Hours	151	93%	90%	92%
Appropriate Hair Removal	863	100%	100%	99%
Appropriate Beta Blocker Usage	379	92%	93%	93%
Controlled Postoperative Blood Glucose	401	95%	93%	93%
Prophylactic Antibiotic Timing	575	98%	97%	97%
Prophylactic Antibiotic Timing (Outpatient)	653	91%	92%	92%
Prophylactic Antibiotic Selection	587	97%	98%	97%
Prophylactic Antibiotic Select. (Outpatient)	641	95%	95%	94%
Prophylactic Antibiotic Stopped	551	97%	95%	94%
Recommended VTP Ordered	151	96%	92%	94%
Urinary Catheter Removal	169	96%	92%	90%
Children's Asthma Care				
Received Systemic Corticosteroids	-	-	-	100%
Received Home Management Plan	-	-	-	71%
Received Reliever Medication	-	-	-	100%
Use of Medical Imaging				
Combination Abdominal CT Scan	1,547	0.129	0.237	0.191
Combination Chest CT Scan	941	0.030	0.120	0.054
Follow-up Mammogram/Ultrasound	2,338	8.8%	8.3%	8.4%
MRI for Low Back Pain	427	33.0%	35.2%	32.7%
Survey of Patients' Hospital Experiences				
Area Around Room 'Always' Quiet at Night	300+	53%	-	58%
Doctors 'Always' Communicated Well	300+	80%	-	80%
Home Recovery Information Given	300+	85%	-	82%
Hospital Given 9 or 10 on 10 Point Scale	300+	76%	-	67%
Meds 'Always' Explained Before Given	300+	58%	-	60%
Nurses 'Always' Communicated Well	300+	77%	-	76%
Pain 'Always' Well Controlled	300+	70%	-	69%
Room and Bathroom 'Always' Clean	300+	72%	-	71%
Timely Help 'Always' Received	300+	69%	-	64%
Would Definitely Recommend Hospital	300+	79%	-	69%

NOTE: Hospital profiles are in alphabetical order by state, then city, then hospital within the city; Rankings exclude hospitals with less than 25 cases except for patient surveys which excludes hospitals with less than 100 cases; (a) 100–299 cases; (1) The number of cases is too small to be sure how well a hospital is performing; (2) The hospital indicated that the data submitted for this measure were based on a sample of cases; (3) Data was collected during a shorter time period (fewer quarters) than the maximum possible time for this measure; (4) Suppressed for one or more quarters by CMS; (5) No data is available from the hospital for this measure; (6) Fewer than 100 patients completed the HCAHPS survey. Use these rates with caution, as the number of surveys may be too low to reliably assess hospital performance; (7) Survey results are based on less than 12 months of data; (8) Survey results are not available for this reporting period; (9) No or very few patients were eligible for the HCAHPS survey. The scores shown, if any, reflect a very small number of surveys; (10) A state average was not calculated because too few hospitals in the state submitted data; (11) There were discrepancies in the data collection process; Please refer to the User's Guide for a full explanation of data.

Saint Vincent Heart Center of Indiana

10580 N Meridian St — Phone: 317-583-5000
Indianapolis, IN 46290 — Fax: 317-583-5002
E-mail: marketing@theheathcenter.com
URL: www.theheartcenter.com
Type: Acute Care Hospitals — Emergency Services: Yes
Ownership: Proprietary — Beds: 80
Key Personnel:
CEO/President. . . . . John Stewart
Cardiac Laboratory. . . . . Gregg Elsener
Chief of Medical Staff . . . . William Store

Measure	Cases	This Hosp.	State Avg.	U.S. Avg.
Heart Attack Care				
ACE Inhibitor or ARB for LVSD	245	98%	96%	96%
Aspirin at Arrival	129	100%	98%	99%
Aspirin at Discharge	1,064	99%	99%	98%
Beta Blocker at Discharge	1,039	99%	98%	98%
Fibrinolytic Medication Timing	0	-	37%	55%
PCI Within 90 Minutes of Arrival[1]	20	100%	93%	90%
Smoking Cessation Advice	386	100%	99%	99%
Chest Pain/Possible Heart Attack Care				
Aspirin at Arrival[1]	9	78%	95%	95%
Median Time to ECG (minutes)[1]	12	5	6	8
Median Time to Transfer (minutes)[5]	0	-	49	61
Fibrinolytic Medication Timing[5]	0	-	63%	54%
Heart Failure Care				
ACE Inhibitor or ARB for LVSD	203	68%	92%	94%
Discharge Instructions	383	88%	84%	88%
Evaluation of LVS Function	447	100%	98%	98%
Smoking Cessation Advice	63	100%	99%	98%
Pneumonia Care				
Appropriate Initial Antibiotic[1]	4	100%	90%	92%
Blood Culture Timing[1]	5	100%	95%	96%
Influenza Vaccine[1]	6	17%	93%	91%
Initial Antibiotic Timing[1]	5	100%	96%	95%
Pneumococcal Vaccine[1]	13	46%	94%	93%
Smoking Cessation Advice[1]	1	100%	98%	97%
Surgical Care Improvement Project				
Appropriate VTP Within 24 Hours[2]	0	-	90%	92%
Appropriate Hair Removal[2]	358	100%	100%	99%
Appropriate Beta Blocker Usage[2]	184	95%	93%	93%
Controlled Postoperative Blood Glucose[2]	294	97%	93%	93%
Prophylactic Antibiotic Timing[2]	200	98%	97%	97%
Prophylactic Antibiotic Timing (Outpatient)	349	74%	92%	92%
Prophylactic Antibiotic Selection[2]	204	100%	98%	97%
Prophylactic Antibiotic Select. (Outpatient)	349	93%	95%	94%
Prophylactic Antibiotic Stopped[2]	193	98%	95%	94%
Recommended VTP Ordered[2]	0	-	92%	94%
Urinary Catheter Removal[2]	101	86%	92%	90%
Children's Asthma Care				
Received Systemic Corticosteroids	-	-	-	100%
Received Home Management Plan	-	-	-	71%
Received Reliever Medication	-	-	-	100%
Use of Medical Imaging				
Combination Abdominal CT Scan[1]	39	0.205	0.237	0.191
Combination Chest CT Scan	52	0.327	0.120	0.054
Follow-up Mammogram/Ultrasound[5]	0	-	8.3%	8.4%
MRI for Low Back Pain[1]	17	17.6%	35.2%	32.7%
Survey of Patients' Hospital Experiences				
Area Around Room 'Always' Quiet at Night	300+	57%	-	58%
Doctors 'Always' Communicated Well	300+	84%	-	80%
Home Recovery Information Given	300+	85%	-	82%
Hospital Given 9 or 10 on 10 Point Scale	300+	87%	-	67%
Meds 'Always' Explained Before Given	300+	63%	-	60%
Nurses 'Always' Communicated Well	300+	85%	-	76%
Pain 'Always' Well Controlled	300+	77%	-	69%
Room and Bathroom 'Always' Clean	300+	77%	-	71%
Timely Help 'Always' Received	300+	77%	-	64%
Would Definitely Recommend Hospital	300+	92%	-	69%

Saint Vincent Hospital & Health Services

2001 W 86th Street — Phone: 317-338-7000
Indianapolis, IN 46260 — Fax: 317-338-7005
URL: www.indianapolis.stvincent.org
Type: Acute Care Hospitals — Emergency Services: Yes
Ownership: Voluntary Non-Profit - Church — Beds: 650
Key Personnel:
CEO/President. . . . . Sr Bernice Coreil, DC
Coronary Care . . . . Andrew Allen
Infection Control. . . . . Carolyn Davee
Pediatric In-Patient Care . . . . Edward Aull, MD
Quality Assurance . . . . John D Doyle
Radiology. . . . . Peter D Arfken, MD
Anesthesiology. . . . . Steven R Young, MD

Measure	Cases	This Hosp.	State Avg.	U.S. Avg.
Heart Attack Care				
ACE Inhibitor or ARB for LVSD	80	98%	96%	96%
Aspirin at Arrival	265	98%	98%	99%
Aspirin at Discharge	365	100%	99%	98%
Beta Blocker at Discharge	350	99%	98%	98%
Fibrinolytic Medication Timing	0	-	37%	55%
PCI Within 90 Minutes of Arrival	38	71%	93%	90%
Smoking Cessation Advice	100	100%	99%	99%
Chest Pain/Possible Heart Attack Care				
Aspirin at Arrival	60	87%	95%	95%
Median Time to ECG (minutes)	60	6	6	8
Median Time to Transfer (minutes)[1,3]	3	52	49	61
Fibrinolytic Medication Timing[3]	0	-	63%	54%
Heart Failure Care				
ACE Inhibitor or ARB for LVSD	254	95%	92%	94%
Discharge Instructions	629	68%	84%	88%
Evaluation of LVS Function	832	96%	98%	98%
Smoking Cessation Advice	125	100%	99%	98%
Pneumonia Care				
Appropriate Initial Antibiotic	151	75%	90%	92%
Blood Culture Timing	256	95%	95%	96%
Influenza Vaccine	249	88%	93%	91%
Initial Antibiotic Timing	260	93%	96%	95%
Pneumococcal Vaccine	316	89%	94%	93%
Smoking Cessation Advice	148	100%	98%	97%
Surgical Care Improvement Project				
Appropriate VTP Within 24 Hours[2]	193	86%	90%	92%
Appropriate Hair Removal[2]	793	99%	100%	99%
Appropriate Beta Blocker Usage[2]	323	89%	93%	93%
Controlled Postoperative Blood Glucose[2]	203	92%	93%	93%
Prophylactic Antibiotic Timing[2]	532	98%	97%	97%
Prophylactic Antibiotic Timing (Outpatient)	913	89%	92%	92%
Prophylactic Antibiotic Selection[2]	538	97%	98%	97%
Prophylactic Antibiotic Select. (Outpatient)	872	94%	95%	94%
Prophylactic Antibiotic Stopped[2]	526	95%	95%	94%
Recommended VTP Ordered[2]	194	87%	92%	94%
Urinary Catheter Removal[2]	190	83%	92%	90%
Children's Asthma Care				
Received Systemic Corticosteroids	-	-	-	100%
Received Home Management Plan	-	-	-	71%
Received Reliever Medication	-	-	-	100%
Use of Medical Imaging				
Combination Abdominal CT Scan	2,054	0.078	0.237	0.191
Combination Chest CT Scan	1,694	0.003	0.120	0.054
Follow-up Mammogram/Ultrasound	2,738	9.1%	8.3%	8.4%
MRI for Low Back Pain	392	34.4%	35.2%	32.7%
Survey of Patients' Hospital Experiences				
Area Around Room 'Always' Quiet at Night	300+	60%	-	58%
Doctors 'Always' Communicated Well	300+	80%	-	80%
Home Recovery Information Given	300+	82%	-	82%
Hospital Given 9 or 10 on 10 Point Scale	300+	77%	-	67%
Meds 'Always' Explained Before Given	300+	61%	-	60%
Nurses 'Always' Communicated Well	300+	77%	-	76%
Pain 'Always' Well Controlled	300+	72%	-	69%
Room and Bathroom 'Always' Clean	300+	68%	-	71%
Timely Help 'Always' Received	300+	63%	-	64%
Would Definitely Recommend Hospital	300+	80%	-	69%

Westview Hospital

3630 Guion Rd — Phone: 317-920-7288
Indianapolis, IN 46222 — Fax: 317-920-7551
E-mail: info@westviewhospital.org
URL: www.westviewhospital.org
Type: Acute Care Hospitals — Emergency Services: Yes
Ownership: Voluntary Non-Profit - Private — Beds: 116
Key Personnel:
CEO/President. . . . . Jerry Porter
Quality Assurance . . . . Michele Borten

Measure	Cases	This Hosp.	State Avg.	U.S. Avg.
Heart Attack Care				
ACE Inhibitor or ARB for LVSD[1]	1	100%	96%	96%
Aspirin at Arrival[1]	3	67%	98%	99%
Aspirin at Discharge[1]	2	50%	99%	98%
Beta Blocker at Discharge[1]	2	100%	98%	98%
Fibrinolytic Medication Timing[1]	1	0%	37%	55%
PCI Within 90 Minutes of Arrival	0	-	93%	90%
Smoking Cessation Advice	0	-	99%	99%
Chest Pain/Possible Heart Attack Care				
Aspirin at Arrival[1]	15	87%	95%	95%
Median Time to ECG (minutes)[1]	15	6	6	8
Median Time to Transfer (minutes)[5]	0	-	49	61
Fibrinolytic Medication Timing[3]	0	-	63%	54%
Heart Failure Care				
ACE Inhibitor or ARB for LVSD[1]	15	67%	92%	94%
Discharge Instructions	51	59%	84%	88%
Evaluation of LVS Function	68	99%	98%	98%
Smoking Cessation Advice[1]	15	93%	99%	98%
Pneumonia Care				
Appropriate Initial Antibiotic	34	85%	90%	92%
Blood Culture Timing	53	98%	95%	96%
Influenza Vaccine	46	91%	93%	91%
Initial Antibiotic Timing	53	92%	96%	95%
Pneumococcal Vaccine	50	100%	94%	93%
Smoking Cessation Advice	30	97%	98%	97%
Surgical Care Improvement Project				
Appropriate VTP Within 24 Hours	45	82%	90%	92%
Appropriate Hair Removal	132	100%	100%	99%
Appropriate Beta Blocker Usage	31	87%	93%	93%
Controlled Postoperative Blood Glucose	0	-	93%	93%
Prophylactic Antibiotic Timing	84	94%	97%	97%
Prophylactic Antibiotic Timing (Outpatient)	51	88%	92%	92%
Prophylactic Antibiotic Selection	82	94%	98%	97%
Prophylactic Antibiotic Select. (Outpatient)	63	97%	95%	94%
Prophylactic Antibiotic Stopped	79	96%	95%	94%
Recommended VTP Ordered	45	84%	92%	94%
Urinary Catheter Removal[1]	9	100%	92%	90%
Children's Asthma Care				
Received Systemic Corticosteroids	-	-	-	100%
Received Home Management Plan	-	-	-	71%
Received Reliever Medication	-	-	-	100%
Use of Medical Imaging				
Combination Abdominal CT Scan	162	0.012	0.237	0.191
Combination Chest CT Scan	86	0.000	0.120	0.054
Follow-up Mammogram/Ultrasound	261	2.7%	8.3%	8.4%
MRI for Low Back Pain[1]	47	29.8%	35.2%	32.7%
Survey of Patients' Hospital Experiences				
Area Around Room 'Always' Quiet at Night	300+	58%	-	58%
Doctors 'Always' Communicated Well	300+	82%	-	80%
Home Recovery Information Given	300+	81%	-	82%
Hospital Given 9 or 10 on 10 Point Scale	300+	67%	-	67%
Meds 'Always' Explained Before Given	300+	53%	-	60%
Nurses 'Always' Communicated Well	300+	71%	-	76%
Pain 'Always' Well Controlled	300+	64%	-	69%
Room and Bathroom 'Always' Clean	300+	68%	-	71%
Timely Help 'Always' Received	300+	57%	-	64%
Would Definitely Recommend Hospital	300+	67%	-	69%

NOTE: Hospital profiles are in alphabetical order by state, then city, then hospital within the city; Rankings exclude hospitals with less than 25 cases except for patient surveys which excludes hospitals with less than 100 cases; (a) 100–299 cases; (1) The number of cases is too small to be sure how well a hospital is performing; (2) The hospital indicated that the data submitted for this measure were based on a sample of cases; (3) Data was collected during a shorter time period (fewer quarters) than the maximum possible time for this measure; (4) Suppressed for one or more quarters by CMS; (5) No data is available from the hospital for this measure; (6) Fewer than 100 patients completed the HCAHPS survey. Use these rates with caution, as the number of surveys may be too low to reliably assess hospital performance; (7) Survey results are based on less than 12 months of data; (8) Survey results are not available for this reporting period; (9) No or very few patients were eligible for the HCAHPS survey. The scores shown, if any, reflect a very small number of surveys; (10) A state average was not calculated because too few hospitals in the state submitted data; (11) There were discrepancies in the data collection process; Please refer to the User's Guide for a full explanation of data.

William N Wishard Memorial Hospital

1001 W 10th St
Indianapolis, IN 46202
URL: www.wishard.edu
Phone: 317-630-7592
Fax: 317-630-7678
Type: Acute Care Hospitals
Ownership: Government - Local
Emergency Services: Yes
Beds: 354

Key Personnel:
CEO/President. . . . . Lisa E Harris, MD

Measure	Cases	This Hosp.	State Avg.	U.S. Avg.
Heart Attack Care				
ACE Inhibitor or ARB for LVSD[2]	42	98%	96%	96%
Aspirin at Arrival[2]	249	98%	98%	99%
Aspirin at Discharge[2]	228	98%	99%	98%
Beta Blocker at Discharge[2]	221	94%	98%	98%
Fibrinolytic Medication Timing[2]	0	-	37%	55%
PCI Within 90 Minutes of Arrival[1,2]	10	90%	93%	90%
Smoking Cessation Advice[2]	132	100%	99%	99%
Chest Pain/Possible Heart Attack Care				
Aspirin at Arrival[5]	0	-	95%	95%
Median Time to ECG (minutes)[5]	0	-	6	8
Median Time to Transfer (minutes)[5]	0	-	49	61
Fibrinolytic Medication Timing[5]	0	-	63%	54%
Heart Failure Care				
ACE Inhibitor or ARB for LVSD	189	90%	92%	94%
Discharge Instructions	371	97%	84%	88%
Evaluation of LVS Function	409	98%	98%	98%
Smoking Cessation Advice	169	99%	99%	98%
Pneumonia Care				
Appropriate Initial Antibiotic[2]	92	95%	90%	92%
Blood Culture Timing[2]	130	98%	95%	96%
Influenza Vaccine[2]	47	77%	93%	91%
Initial Antibiotic Timing[2]	134	93%	96%	95%
Pneumococcal Vaccine[2]	67	87%	94%	93%
Smoking Cessation Advice[2]	83	100%	98%	97%
Surgical Care Improvement Project				
Appropriate VTP Within 24 Hours[2]	180	94%	90%	92%
Appropriate Hair Removal[2]	345	99%	100%	99%
Appropriate Beta Blocker Usage[2]	61	100%	93%	93%
Controlled Postoperative Blood Glucose[2]	0	-	93%	93%
Prophylactic Antibiotic Timing[2]	238	98%	97%	97%
Prophylactic Antibiotic Timing (Outpatient)	80	88%	92%	92%
Prophylactic Antibiotic Selection[2]	241	98%	98%	97%
Prophylactic Antibiotic Select. (Outpatient)	96	96%	95%	94%
Prophylactic Antibiotic Stopped[2]	234	94%	95%	94%
Recommended VTP Ordered[2]	181	95%	92%	94%
Urinary Catheter Removal[2]	85	96%	92%	90%
Children's Asthma Care				
Received Systemic Corticosteroids	-	-	-	100%
Received Home Management Plan	-	-	-	71%
Received Reliever Medication	-	-	-	100%
Use of Medical Imaging				
Combination Abdominal CT Scan	750	0.099	0.237	0.191
Combination Chest CT Scan	557	0.043	0.120	0.054
Follow-up Mammogram/Ultrasound	1,353	8.4%	8.3%	8.4%
MRI for Low Back Pain	190	28.9%	35.2%	32.7%
Survey of Patients' Hospital Experiences				
Area Around Room 'Always' Quiet at Night	300+	57%	-	58%
Doctors 'Always' Communicated Well	300+	79%	-	80%
Home Recovery Information Given	300+	82%	-	82%
Hospital Given 9 or 10 on 10 Point Scale	300+	70%	-	67%
Meds 'Always' Explained Before Given	300+	58%	-	60%
Nurses 'Always' Communicated Well	300+	72%	-	76%
Pain 'Always' Well Controlled	300+	68%	-	69%
Room and Bathroom 'Always' Clean	300+	66%	-	71%
Timely Help 'Always' Received	300+	56%	-	64%
Would Definitely Recommend Hospital	300+	71%	-	69%

Memorial Hospital and Health Care Center

800 W 9th Street
Jasper, IN 47546
URL: www.mhhcc.org
Phone: 812-482-2345
Fax: 812-482-0302
Type: Acute Care Hospitals
Ownership: Voluntary Non-Profit - Church
Emergency Services: Yes
Beds: 131

Key Personnel:
CEO/President. . . . . Ray Snowden
Chief of Medical Staff. . . . . Robert Earhard, MD
Coronary Care . . . . Kathy Howell
Infection Control. . . . . Sue Willis, RN
Pediatric Ambulatory Care . . . . . . Suzanne Burgess, RN
Pediatric In-Patient Care . . . . Suzanne Burgess, RN
Quality Assurance . . . . Denise Kaatzal, RN
Radiology. . . . . Elaine Schitter

Measure	Cases	This Hosp.	State Avg.	U.S. Avg.
Heart Attack Care				
ACE Inhibitor or ARB for LVSD[1]	22	77%	96%	96%
Aspirin at Arrival	123	98%	98%	99%
Aspirin at Discharge	159	99%	99%	98%
Beta Blocker at Discharge	143	99%	98%	98%
Fibrinolytic Medication Timing	0	-	37%	55%
PCI Within 90 Minutes of Arrival[1]	18	83%	93%	90%
Smoking Cessation Advice	63	98%	99%	99%
Chest Pain/Possible Heart Attack Care				
Aspirin at Arrival[5]	0	-	95%	95%
Median Time to ECG (minutes)[5]	0	-	6	8
Median Time to Transfer (minutes)[5]	0	-	49	61
Fibrinolytic Medication Timing[5]	0	-	63%	54%
Heart Failure Care				
ACE Inhibitor or ARB for LVSD	67	84%	92%	94%
Discharge Instructions	149	70%	84%	88%
Evaluation of LVS Function	212	94%	98%	98%
Smoking Cessation Advice[1]	22	91%	99%	98%
Pneumonia Care				
Appropriate Initial Antibiotic[2]	97	90%	90%	92%
Blood Culture Timing[2]	97	93%	95%	96%
Influenza Vaccine[2]	93	92%	93%	91%
Initial Antibiotic Timing[2]	135	99%	96%	95%
Pneumococcal Vaccine[2]	129	96%	94%	93%
Smoking Cessation Advice[2]	45	91%	98%	97%
Surgical Care Improvement Project				
Appropriate VTP Within 24 Hours[2]	119	82%	90%	92%
Appropriate Hair Removal[2]	631	100%	100%	99%
Appropriate Beta Blocker Usage[2]	183	97%	93%	93%
Controlled Postoperative Blood Glucose[2]	0	-	93%	93%
Prophylactic Antibiotic Timing[2]	507	95%	97%	97%
Prophylactic Antibiotic Timing (Outpatient)	127	83%	92%	92%
Prophylactic Antibiotic Selection[2]	508	97%	98%	97%
Prophylactic Antibiotic Select. (Outpatient)	110	95%	95%	94%
Prophylactic Antibiotic Stopped[2]	491	95%	95%	94%
Recommended VTP Ordered[2]	121	82%	92%	94%
Urinary Catheter Removal[2]	92	93%	92%	90%
Children's Asthma Care				
Received Systemic Corticosteroids	-	-	-	100%
Received Home Management Plan	-	-	-	71%
Received Reliever Medication	-	-	-	100%
Use of Medical Imaging				
Combination Abdominal CT Scan	937	0.638	0.237	0.191
Combination Chest CT Scan	668	0.775	0.120	0.054
Follow-up Mammogram/Ultrasound	1,386	10.3%	8.3%	8.4%
MRI for Low Back Pain	159	34.0%	35.2%	32.7%
Survey of Patients' Hospital Experiences				
Area Around Room 'Always' Quiet at Night	300+	67%	-	58%
Doctors 'Always' Communicated Well	300+	87%	-	80%
Home Recovery Information Given	300+	77%	-	82%
Hospital Given 9 or 10 on 10 Point Scale	300+	77%	-	67%
Meds 'Always' Explained Before Given	300+	63%	-	60%
Nurses 'Always' Communicated Well	300+	83%	-	76%
Pain 'Always' Well Controlled	300+	72%	-	69%
Room and Bathroom 'Always' Clean	300+	84%	-	71%
Timely Help 'Always' Received	300+	68%	-	64%
Would Definitely Recommend Hospital	300+	78%	-	69%

Clark Memorial Hospital

1220 Missouri Avenue
Jeffersonville, IN 47130
Phone: 812-283-2142
Fax: 812-283-2688
E-mail: paula.lamb@clarkmemorial.org
URL: www.clarkmemorial.org
Type: Acute Care Hospitals
Ownership: Government - Local
Emergency Services: Yes
Beds: 241

Key Personnel:
CEO/President. . . . . Martin Padgett
Chief of Medical Staff. . . . . Warlito A Bautista
Operating Room. . . . . Ruth Schmidt
Quality Assurance . . . . Chad Brough
Radiology. . . . . Asma Ahmad, MD
Emergency Room . . . . Lynn Meuer

Measure	Cases	This Hosp.	State Avg.	U.S. Avg.
Heart Attack Care				
ACE Inhibitor or ARB for LVSD	38	89%	96%	96%
Aspirin at Arrival	167	97%	98%	99%
Aspirin at Discharge	181	97%	99%	98%
Beta Blocker at Discharge	186	98%	98%	98%
Fibrinolytic Medication Timing[1]	1	100%	37%	55%
PCI Within 90 Minutes of Arrival	36	97%	93%	90%
Smoking Cessation Advice	78	100%	99%	99%
Chest Pain/Possible Heart Attack Care				
Aspirin at Arrival[1]	11	91%	95%	95%
Median Time to ECG (minutes)[1]	11	5	6	8
Median Time to Transfer (minutes)[1,3]	1	139	49	61
Fibrinolytic Medication Timing[3]	0	-	63%	54%
Heart Failure Care				
ACE Inhibitor or ARB for LVSD	102	88%	92%	94%
Discharge Instructions	264	88%	84%	88%
Evaluation of LVS Function	337	99%	98%	98%
Smoking Cessation Advice	65	100%	99%	98%
Pneumonia Care				
Appropriate Initial Antibiotic	227	95%	90%	92%
Blood Culture Timing	328	97%	95%	96%
Influenza Vaccine	258	96%	93%	91%
Initial Antibiotic Timing	315	94%	96%	95%
Pneumococcal Vaccine	278	96%	94%	93%
Smoking Cessation Advice	180	100%	98%	97%
Surgical Care Improvement Project				
Appropriate VTP Within 24 Hours[2]	285	90%	90%	92%
Appropriate Hair Removal[2]	642	100%	100%	99%
Appropriate Beta Blocker Usage[2]	176	99%	93%	93%
Controlled Postoperative Blood Glucose[2]	0	-	93%	93%
Prophylactic Antibiotic Timing[2]	449	100%	97%	97%
Prophylactic Antibiotic Timing (Outpatient)	395	92%	92%	92%
Prophylactic Antibiotic Selection[2]	453	98%	98%	97%
Prophylactic Antibiotic Select. (Outpatient)	377	94%	95%	94%
Prophylactic Antibiotic Stopped[2]	431	96%	95%	94%
Recommended VTP Ordered[2]	285	94%	92%	94%
Urinary Catheter Removal[2]	156	94%	92%	90%
Children's Asthma Care				
Received Systemic Corticosteroids	-	-	-	100%
Received Home Management Plan	-	-	-	71%
Received Reliever Medication	-	-	-	100%
Use of Medical Imaging				
Combination Abdominal CT Scan	1,042	0.726	0.237	0.191
Combination Chest CT Scan	1,013	0.007	0.120	0.054
Follow-up Mammogram/Ultrasound	1,524	6.2%	8.3%	8.4%
MRI for Low Back Pain	207	40.6%	35.2%	32.7%
Survey of Patients' Hospital Experiences				
Area Around Room 'Always' Quiet at Night	300+	53%	-	58%
Doctors 'Always' Communicated Well	300+	82%	-	80%
Home Recovery Information Given	300+	74%	-	82%
Hospital Given 9 or 10 on 10 Point Scale	300+	72%	-	67%
Meds 'Always' Explained Before Given	300+	64%	-	60%
Nurses 'Always' Communicated Well	300+	80%	-	76%
Pain 'Always' Well Controlled	300+	73%	-	69%
Room and Bathroom 'Always' Clean	300+	77%	-	71%
Timely Help 'Always' Received	300+	67%	-	64%
Would Definitely Recommend Hospital	300+	74%	-	69%

NOTE: Hospital profiles are in alphabetical order by state, then city, then hospital within the city; Rankings exclude hospitals with less than 25 cases except for patient surveys which excludes hospitals with less than 100 cases; (a) 100–299 cases; (1) The number of cases is too small to be sure how well a hospital is performing; (2) The hospital indicated that the data submitted for this measure were based on a sample of cases; (3) Data was collected during a shorter time period (fewer quarters) than the maximum possible time for this measure; (4) Suppressed for one or more quarters by CMS; (5) No data is available from the hospital for this measure; (6) Fewer than 100 patients completed the HCAHPS survey. Use these rates with caution, as the number of surveys may be too low to reliably assess hospital performance; (7) Survey results are based on less than 12 months of data; (8) Survey results are not available for this reporting period; (9) No or very few patients were eligible for the HCAHPS survey. The scores shown, if any, reflect a very small number of surveys; (10) A state average was not calculated because too few hospitals in the state submitted data; (11) There were discrepancies in the data collection process; Please refer to the User's Guide for a full explanation of data.

Parkview Noble Hospital

401 Sawyer Road
Kendallville, IN 46755
Phone: 260-347-8700
E-mail: mashek4126@aol.com
URL: www.parkview.com
Type: Acute Care Hospitals
Emergency Services: Yes
Ownership: Government - Local
Beds: 66

Key Personnel:
CEO/President. . . . . John Berhow
Chief of Medical Staff . . . . Abdali Jan, MD
Infection Control. . . . . Karen Denny
Operating Room. . . . . Holly Goe
Quality Assurance . . . . Mary Hageman
Emergency Room . . . . Kim Horan
Hemotology Center . . . . Karen Stroman
Intensive Care Unit. . . . . Mindy Kurtz

Measure	Cases	This Hosp.	State Avg.	U.S. Avg.
Heart Attack Care				
ACE Inhibitor or ARB for LVSD[3]	0	-	96%	96%
Aspirin at Arrival[1,3]	4	100%	98%	99%
Aspirin at Discharge[1,3]	4	100%	99%	98%
Beta Blocker at Discharge[1,3]	4	100%	98%	98%
Fibrinolytic Medication Timing[3]	0	-	37%	55%
PCI Within 90 Minutes of Arrival[3]	0	-	93%	90%
Smoking Cessation Advice[1,3]	2	100%	99%	99%
Chest Pain/Possible Heart Attack Care				
Aspirin at Arrival	96	97%	95%	95%
Median Time to ECG (minutes)	100	4	6	8
Median Time to Transfer (minutes)[1,3]	2	46	49	61
Fibrinolytic Medication Timing[1]	3	67%	63%	54%
Heart Failure Care				
ACE Inhibitor or ARB for LVSD[1]	12	67%	92%	94%
Discharge Instructions	41	85%	84%	88%
Evaluation of LVS Function	61	93%	98%	98%
Smoking Cessation Advice[1]	10	100%	99%	98%
Pneumonia Care				
Appropriate Initial Antibiotic	59	98%	90%	92%
Blood Culture Timing	72	99%	95%	96%
Influenza Vaccine	52	96%	93%	91%
Initial Antibiotic Timing	79	97%	96%	95%
Pneumococcal Vaccine	75	97%	94%	93%
Smoking Cessation Advice	37	100%	98%	97%
Surgical Care Improvement Project				
Appropriate VTP Within 24 Hours[1]	20	90%	90%	92%
Appropriate Hair Removal	85	99%	100%	99%
Appropriate Beta Blocker Usage[1]	14	93%	93%	93%
Controlled Postoperative Blood Glucose	0	-	93%	93%
Prophylactic Antibiotic Timing	66	97%	97%	97%
Prophylactic Antibiotic Timing (Outpatient)	26	92%	92%	92%
Prophylactic Antibiotic Selection	67	99%	98%	97%
Prophylactic Antibiotic Select. (Outpatient)	25	92%	95%	94%
Prophylactic Antibiotic Stopped	64	95%	95%	94%
Recommended VTP Ordered[1]	21	86%	92%	94%
Urinary Catheter Removal[1]	12	92%	92%	90%
Children's Asthma Care				
Received Systemic Corticosteroids	-	-	-	100%
Received Home Management Plan	-	-	-	71%
Received Reliever Medication	-	-	-	100%
Use of Medical Imaging				
Combination Abdominal CT Scan	353	0.031	0.237	0.191
Combination Chest CT Scan	149	0.000	0.120	0.054
Follow-up Mammogram/Ultrasound	382	9.2%	8.3%	8.4%
MRI for Low Back Pain	102	35.3%	35.2%	32.7%
Survey of Patients' Hospital Experiences				
Area Around Room 'Always' Quiet at Night	300+	62%	-	58%
Doctors 'Always' Communicated Well	300+	87%	-	80%
Home Recovery Information Given	300+	89%	-	82%
Hospital Given 9 or 10 on 10 Point Scale	300+	78%	-	67%
Meds 'Always' Explained Before Given	300+	70%	-	60%
Nurses 'Always' Communicated Well	300+	82%	-	76%
Pain 'Always' Well Controlled	300+	76%	-	69%
Room and Bathroom 'Always' Clean	300+	80%	-	71%
Timely Help 'Always' Received	300+	72%	-	64%
Would Definitely Recommend Hospital	300+	77%	-	69%

Starke Memorial Hospital

102 E Culver Road
Knox, IN 46534
Phone: 574-772-1100
Fax: 574-772-1144
E-mail: info@starkememorial.com
URL: www.starkememorial.com
Type: Acute Care Hospitals
Emergency Services: Yes
Ownership: Proprietary
Beds: 53

Key Personnel:
CEO/President. . . . . Michael Meadows
Chief of Medical Staff . . . . Patricia Alexander
Coronary Care . . . . Tanya Emory
Quality Assurance . . . . Peggy Madsen
Emergency Room . . . . Kathie Jones, RN

Measure	Cases	This Hosp.	State Avg.	U.S. Avg.
Heart Attack Care				
ACE Inhibitor or ARB for LVSD[3]	0	-	96%	96%
Aspirin at Arrival[1,3]	3	100%	98%	99%
Aspirin at Discharge[1,3]	1	100%	99%	98%
Beta Blocker at Discharge[1,3]	1	100%	98%	98%
Fibrinolytic Medication Timing[3]	0	-	37%	55%
PCI Within 90 Minutes of Arrival[3]	0	-	93%	90%
Smoking Cessation Advice[3]	0	-	99%	99%
Chest Pain/Possible Heart Attack Care				
Aspirin at Arrival	66	83%	95%	95%
Median Time to ECG (minutes)	71	6	6	8
Median Time to Transfer (minutes)[1]	11	67	49	61
Fibrinolytic Medication Timing	0	-	63%	54%
Heart Failure Care				
ACE Inhibitor or ARB for LVSD[1]	8	75%	92%	94%
Discharge Instructions	26	77%	84%	88%
Evaluation of LVS Function	27	81%	98%	98%
Smoking Cessation Advice[1]	8	88%	99%	98%
Pneumonia Care				
Appropriate Initial Antibiotic[2]	39	82%	90%	92%
Blood Culture Timing[2]	49	92%	95%	96%
Influenza Vaccine[2]	26	62%	93%	91%
Initial Antibiotic Timing[2]	54	93%	96%	95%
Pneumococcal Vaccine[2]	25	76%	94%	93%
Smoking Cessation Advice[2]	27	89%	98%	97%
Surgical Care Improvement Project				
Appropriate VTP Within 24 Hours[1]	7	100%	90%	92%
Appropriate Hair Removal[1]	12	100%	100%	99%
Appropriate Beta Blocker Usage[1]	6	100%	93%	93%
Controlled Postoperative Blood Glucose	0	-	93%	93%
Prophylactic Antibiotic Timing[1]	7	86%	97%	97%
Prophylactic Antibiotic Timing (Outpatient)[1]	15	80%	92%	92%
Prophylactic Antibiotic Selection[1]	8	100%	98%	97%
Prophylactic Antibiotic Select. (Outpatient)[1]	14	86%	95%	94%
Prophylactic Antibiotic Stopped[1]	6	67%	95%	94%
Recommended VTP Ordered[1]	7	100%	92%	94%
Urinary Catheter Removal[1]	1	100%	92%	90%
Children's Asthma Care				
Received Systemic Corticosteroids	-	-	-	100%
Received Home Management Plan	-	-	-	71%
Received Reliever Medication	-	-	-	100%
Use of Medical Imaging				
Combination Abdominal CT Scan	210	0.543	0.237	0.191
Combination Chest CT Scan	110	0.555	0.120	0.054
Follow-up Mammogram/Ultrasound	175	14.9%	8.3%	8.4%
MRI for Low Back Pain	54	44.4%	35.2%	32.7%
Survey of Patients' Hospital Experiences				
Area Around Room 'Always' Quiet at Night	(a)	62%	-	58%
Doctors 'Always' Communicated Well	(a)	78%	-	80%
Home Recovery Information Given	(a)	71%	-	82%
Hospital Given 9 or 10 on 10 Point Scale	(a)	54%	-	67%
Meds 'Always' Explained Before Given	(a)	55%	-	60%
Nurses 'Always' Communicated Well	(a)	83%	-	76%
Pain 'Always' Well Controlled	(a)	67%	-	69%
Room and Bathroom 'Always' Clean	(a)	84%	-	71%
Timely Help 'Always' Received	(a)	72%	-	64%
Would Definitely Recommend Hospital	(a)	56%	-	69%

Howard Regional Health System

3500 S Lafountain St
Kokomo, IN 46904
Phone: 765-453-8371
Fax: 765-453-8087
URL: www.howardcommunity.org
Type: Acute Care Hospitals
Emergency Services: Yes
Ownership: Government - Local
Beds: 150

Key Personnel:
CEO/President. . . . . James P Alender
Chief of Medical Staff . . . . Bruce Hughes, MD
Infection Control. . . . . Danel Peterson
Radiology. . . . . William I Babchuk, MD
Anesthesiology. . . . . Marvin Lodde, MD
Emergency Room . . . . Sherif MD, RN

Measure	Cases	This Hosp.	State Avg.	U.S. Avg.
Heart Attack Care				
ACE Inhibitor or ARB for LVSD	35	100%	96%	96%
Aspirin at Arrival	112	100%	98%	99%
Aspirin at Discharge	110	100%	99%	98%
Beta Blocker at Discharge	107	100%	98%	98%
Fibrinolytic Medication Timing	0	-	37%	55%
PCI Within 90 Minutes of Arrival	39	100%	93%	90%
Smoking Cessation Advice	55	100%	99%	99%
Chest Pain/Possible Heart Attack Care				
Aspirin at Arrival	30	97%	95%	95%
Median Time to ECG (minutes)	33	6	6	8
Median Time to Transfer (minutes)[1]	7	51	49	61
Fibrinolytic Medication Timing	0	-	63%	54%
Heart Failure Care				
ACE Inhibitor or ARB for LVSD	41	98%	92%	94%
Discharge Instructions	104	100%	84%	88%
Evaluation of LVS Function	156	99%	98%	98%
Smoking Cessation Advice[1]	24	100%	99%	98%
Pneumonia Care				
Appropriate Initial Antibiotic	126	91%	90%	92%
Blood Culture Timing	145	98%	95%	96%
Influenza Vaccine	144	95%	93%	91%
Initial Antibiotic Timing	174	94%	96%	95%
Pneumococcal Vaccine	167	96%	94%	93%
Smoking Cessation Advice	80	100%	98%	97%
Surgical Care Improvement Project				
Appropriate VTP Within 24 Hours	84	73%	90%	92%
Appropriate Hair Removal	251	100%	100%	99%
Appropriate Beta Blocker Usage	91	85%	93%	93%
Controlled Postoperative Blood Glucose	38	95%	93%	93%
Prophylactic Antibiotic Timing	165	99%	97%	97%
Prophylactic Antibiotic Timing (Outpatient)	57	91%	92%	92%
Prophylactic Antibiotic Selection	166	96%	98%	97%
Prophylactic Antibiotic Select. (Outpatient)	56	96%	95%	94%
Prophylactic Antibiotic Stopped	155	85%	95%	94%
Recommended VTP Ordered	84	90%	92%	94%
Urinary Catheter Removal	53	81%	92%	90%
Children's Asthma Care				
Received Systemic Corticosteroids	-	-	-	100%
Received Home Management Plan	-	-	-	71%
Received Reliever Medication	-	-	-	100%
Use of Medical Imaging				
Combination Abdominal CT Scan	856	0.018	0.237	0.191
Combination Chest CT Scan	1,025	0.010	0.120	0.054
Follow-up Mammogram/Ultrasound	997	9.1%	8.3%	8.4%
MRI for Low Back Pain[1]	12	33.3%	35.2%	32.7%
Survey of Patients' Hospital Experiences				
Area Around Room 'Always' Quiet at Night	300+	57%	-	58%
Doctors 'Always' Communicated Well	300+	82%	-	80%
Home Recovery Information Given	300+	81%	-	82%
Hospital Given 9 or 10 on 10 Point Scale	300+	68%	-	67%
Meds 'Always' Explained Before Given	300+	63%	-	60%
Nurses 'Always' Communicated Well	300+	79%	-	76%
Pain 'Always' Well Controlled	300+	74%	-	69%
Room and Bathroom 'Always' Clean	300+	70%	-	71%
Timely Help 'Always' Received	300+	63%	-	64%
Would Definitely Recommend Hospital	300+	71%	-	69%

NOTE: Hospital profiles are in alphabetical order by state, then city, then hospital within the city; Rankings exclude hospitals with less than 25 cases except for patient surveys which excludes hospitals with less than 100 cases; (a) 100–299 cases; (1) The number of cases is too small to be sure how well a hospital is performing; (2) The hospital indicated that the data submitted for this measure were based on a sample of cases; (3) Data was collected during a shorter time period (fewer quarters) than the maximum possible time for this measure; (4) Suppressed for one or more quarters by CMS; (5) No data is available from the hospital for this measure; (6) Fewer than 100 patients completed the HCAHPS survey. Use these rates with caution, as the number of surveys may be too low to reliably assess hospital performance; (7) Survey results are based on less than 12 months of data; (8) Survey results are not available for this reporting period; (9) No or very few patients were eligible for the HCAHPS survey. The scores shown, if any, reflect a very small number of surveys; (10) A state average was not calculated because too few hospitals in the state submitted data; (11) There were discrepancies in the data collection process; Please refer to the User's Guide for a full explanation of data.

Saint Joseph Hospital & Health Center

1907 W Sycamore St
Kokomo, IN 46904
Phone: 765-456-5300
Fax: 765-456-5779
URL: www.stvincent.org
Type: Acute Care Hospitals
Emergency Services: Yes
Ownership: Voluntary Non-Profit - Church
Beds: 156

Key Personnel:

CEO/President. . . . . Darcy Burghay
Cardiac Laboratory. . . . . Shapor Khosravipour
Chief of Medical Staff . . . . RJ Steele, MD
Operating Room. . . . . Michael B Tempel, RN
Quality Assurance . . . . Polly Jones
Radiology. . . . . Peter D Arfken, MD
Emergency Room . . . . John Ayers

Measure	Cases	This Hosp.	State Avg.	U.S. Avg.
Heart Attack Care				
ACE Inhibitor or ARB for LVSD[1]	2	100%	96%	96%
Aspirin at Arrival[1]	8	100%	98%	99%
Aspirin at Discharge[1]	6	100%	99%	98%
Beta Blocker at Discharge[1]	6	100%	98%	98%
Fibrinolytic Medication Timing	0	-	37%	55%
PCI Within 90 Minutes of Arrival	0	-	93%	90%
Smoking Cessation Advice[1]	1	100%	99%	99%
Chest Pain/Possible Heart Attack Care				
Aspirin at Arrival	106	96%	95%	95%
Median Time to ECG (minutes)	106	8	6	8
Median Time to Transfer (minutes)	35	41	49	61
Fibrinolytic Medication Timing	0	-	63%	54%
Heart Failure Care				
ACE Inhibitor or ARB for LVSD	46	78%	92%	94%
Discharge Instructions	82	70%	84%	88%
Evaluation of LVS Function	122	95%	98%	98%
Smoking Cessation Advice[1]	18	100%	99%	98%
Pneumonia Care				
Appropriate Initial Antibiotic	110	85%	90%	92%
Blood Culture Timing	167	99%	95%	96%
Influenza Vaccine	135	94%	93%	91%
Initial Antibiotic Timing	165	95%	96%	95%
Pneumococcal Vaccine	159	96%	94%	93%
Smoking Cessation Advice	76	100%	98%	97%
Surgical Care Improvement Project				
Appropriate VTP Within 24 Hours	83	83%	90%	92%
Appropriate Hair Removal	295	100%	100%	99%
Appropriate Beta Blocker Usage	108	94%	93%	93%
Controlled Postoperative Blood Glucose	0	-	93%	93%
Prophylactic Antibiotic Timing	228	97%	97%	97%
Prophylactic Antibiotic Timing (Outpatient)	175	91%	92%	92%
Prophylactic Antibiotic Selection	228	94%	98%	97%
Prophylactic Antibiotic Select. (Outpatient)	169	90%	95%	94%
Prophylactic Antibiotic Stopped	224	85%	95%	94%
Recommended VTP Ordered	84	83%	92%	94%
Urinary Catheter Removal	90	87%	92%	90%
Children's Asthma Care				
Received Systemic Corticosteroids	-	-	-	100%
Received Home Management Plan	-	-	-	71%
Received Reliever Medication	-	-	-	100%
Use of Medical Imaging				
Combination Abdominal CT Scan	656	0.091	0.237	0.191
Combination Chest CT Scan	505	0.006	0.120	0.054
Follow-up Mammogram/Ultrasound	688	9.6%	8.3%	8.4%
MRI for Low Back Pain	132	39.4%	35.2%	32.7%
Survey of Patients' Hospital Experiences				
Area Around Room 'Always' Quiet at Night	300+	50%	-	58%
Doctors 'Always' Communicated Well	300+	80%	-	80%
Home Recovery Information Given	300+	80%	-	82%
Hospital Given 9 or 10 on 10 Point Scale	300+	73%	-	67%
Meds 'Always' Explained Before Given	300+	58%	-	60%
Nurses 'Always' Communicated Well	300+	74%	-	76%
Pain 'Always' Well Controlled	300+	67%	-	69%
Room and Bathroom 'Always' Clean	300+	72%	-	71%
Timely Help 'Always' Received	300+	62%	-	64%
Would Definitely Recommend Hospital	300+	79%	-	69%

Laporte Hospital and Health Services

1007 Lincoln Way
La Porte, IN 46350
Phone: 219-326-1234
Fax: 219-326-2509
URL: www.laportehealth.org
Type: Acute Care Hospitals
Emergency Services: Yes
Ownership: Voluntary Non-Profit - Private
Beds: 227

Key Personnel:

CEO/President. . . . . Michael Haley
Chief of Medical Staff . . . . Dabi Baughman
Operating Room. . . . . James Cornwell, RN
Pediatric In-Patient Care . . . . Marwan Saman, MD
Quality Assurance . . . . Leigh E Morris
Radiology. . . . . Edward Neyman

Measure	Cases	This Hosp.	State Avg.	U.S. Avg.
Heart Attack Care				
ACE Inhibitor or ARB for LVSD[1]	22	86%	96%	96%
Aspirin at Arrival	107	100%	98%	99%
Aspirin at Discharge	112	100%	99%	98%
Beta Blocker at Discharge	99	100%	98%	98%
Fibrinolytic Medication Timing[1]	1	0%	37%	55%
PCI Within 90 Minutes of Arrival[1]	20	95%	93%	90%
Smoking Cessation Advice	46	100%	99%	99%
Chest Pain/Possible Heart Attack Care				
Aspirin at Arrival[1,3]	1	100%	95%	95%
Median Time to ECG (minutes)[1,3]	1	15	6	8
Median Time to Transfer (minutes)[5]	0	-	49	61
Fibrinolytic Medication Timing[5]	0	-	63%	54%
Heart Failure Care				
ACE Inhibitor or ARB for LVSD	92	100%	92%	94%
Discharge Instructions	160	89%	84%	88%
Evaluation of LVS Function	212	100%	98%	98%
Smoking Cessation Advice	25	100%	99%	98%
Pneumonia Care				
Appropriate Initial Antibiotic	93	86%	90%	92%
Blood Culture Timing	179	91%	95%	96%
Influenza Vaccine	113	91%	93%	91%
Initial Antibiotic Timing	169	96%	96%	95%
Pneumococcal Vaccine	146	93%	94%	93%
Smoking Cessation Advice	81	100%	98%	97%
Surgical Care Improvement Project				
Appropriate VTP Within 24 Hours	153	87%	90%	92%
Appropriate Hair Removal	472	98%	100%	99%
Appropriate Beta Blocker Usage	135	93%	93%	93%
Controlled Postoperative Blood Glucose	51	94%	93%	93%
Prophylactic Antibiotic Timing	345	97%	97%	97%
Prophylactic Antibiotic Timing (Outpatient)	192	80%	92%	92%
Prophylactic Antibiotic Selection	343	98%	98%	97%
Prophylactic Antibiotic Select. (Outpatient)	173	92%	95%	94%
Prophylactic Antibiotic Stopped	326	96%	95%	94%
Recommended VTP Ordered	154	90%	92%	94%
Urinary Catheter Removal	101	94%	92%	90%
Children's Asthma Care				
Received Systemic Corticosteroids	-	-	-	100%
Received Home Management Plan	-	-	-	71%
Received Reliever Medication	-	-	-	100%
Use of Medical Imaging				
Combination Abdominal CT Scan	735	0.479	0.237	0.191
Combination Chest CT Scan	504	0.698	0.120	0.054
Follow-up Mammogram/Ultrasound	1,154	17.6%	8.3%	8.4%
MRI for Low Back Pain	296	31.8%	35.2%	32.7%
Survey of Patients' Hospital Experiences				
Area Around Room 'Always' Quiet at Night	300+	51%	-	58%
Doctors 'Always' Communicated Well	300+	75%	-	80%
Home Recovery Information Given	300+	86%	-	82%
Hospital Given 9 or 10 on 10 Point Scale	300+	64%	-	67%
Meds 'Always' Explained Before Given	300+	56%	-	60%
Nurses 'Always' Communicated Well	300+	75%	-	76%
Pain 'Always' Well Controlled	300+	67%	-	69%
Room and Bathroom 'Always' Clean	300+	70%	-	71%
Timely Help 'Always' Received	300+	63%	-	64%
Would Definitely Recommend Hospital	300+	66%	-	69%

Indiana University Health Arnett Hospital

5165 Mccarty Lane
Lafayette, IN 47905
Phone: 765-448-8000
URL: iuhealth.org/arnett
Type: Acute Care Hospitals
Emergency Services: Yes
Ownership: Voluntary Non-Profit - Private

Key Personnel:

CEO . . . . Al Gatmaitan

Measure	Cases	This Hosp.	State Avg.	U.S. Avg.
Heart Attack Care				
ACE Inhibitor or ARB for LVSD	30	87%	96%	96%
Aspirin at Arrival	147	100%	98%	99%
Aspirin at Discharge	152	99%	99%	98%
Beta Blocker at Discharge	145	98%	98%	98%
Fibrinolytic Medication Timing	0	-	37%	55%
PCI Within 90 Minutes of Arrival[1]	14	93%	93%	90%
Smoking Cessation Advice	50	98%	99%	99%
Chest Pain/Possible Heart Attack Care				
Aspirin at Arrival[5]	0	-	95%	95%
Median Time to ECG (minutes)[5]	0	-	6	8
Median Time to Transfer (minutes)[5]	0	-	49	61
Fibrinolytic Medication Timing[5]	0	-	63%	54%
Heart Failure Care				
ACE Inhibitor or ARB for LVSD[2]	49	82%	92%	94%
Discharge Instructions[2]	132	55%	84%	88%
Evaluation of LVS Function[2]	193	99%	98%	98%
Smoking Cessation Advice[1,2]	24	96%	99%	98%
Pneumonia Care				
Appropriate Initial Antibiotic[2]	82	91%	90%	92%
Blood Culture Timing[2]	143	97%	95%	96%
Influenza Vaccine[2]	89	90%	93%	91%
Initial Antibiotic Timing[2]	135	96%	96%	95%
Pneumococcal Vaccine[2]	126	94%	94%	93%
Smoking Cessation Advice[2]	41	93%	98%	97%
Surgical Care Improvement Project				
Appropriate VTP Within 24 Hours[2]	154	88%	90%	92%
Appropriate Hair Removal[2]	432	100%	100%	99%
Appropriate Beta Blocker Usage[2]	142	94%	93%	93%
Controlled Postoperative Blood Glucose[2]	92	95%	93%	93%
Prophylactic Antibiotic Timing[2]	294	98%	97%	97%
Prophylactic Antibiotic Timing (Outpatient)	369	85%	92%	92%
Prophylactic Antibiotic Selection[2]	296	99%	98%	97%
Prophylactic Antibiotic Select. (Outpatient)	351	96%	95%	94%
Prophylactic Antibiotic Stopped[2]	269	88%	95%	94%
Recommended VTP Ordered[2]	154	92%	92%	94%
Urinary Catheter Removal[2]	104	78%	92%	90%
Children's Asthma Care				
Received Systemic Corticosteroids	-	-	-	100%
Received Home Management Plan	-	-	-	71%
Received Reliever Medication	-	-	-	100%
Use of Medical Imaging				
Combination Abdominal CT Scan	70	0.100	0.237	0.191
Combination Chest CT Scan[1]	42	0.024	0.120	0.054
Follow-up Mammogram/Ultrasound[5]	0	-	8.3%	8.4%
MRI for Low Back Pain[1]	17	64.7%	35.2%	32.7%
Survey of Patients' Hospital Experiences				
Area Around Room 'Always' Quiet at Night	300+	68%	-	58%
Doctors 'Always' Communicated Well	300+	72%	-	80%
Home Recovery Information Given	300+	82%	-	82%
Hospital Given 9 or 10 on 10 Point Scale	300+	74%	-	67%
Meds 'Always' Explained Before Given	300+	57%	-	60%
Nurses 'Always' Communicated Well	300+	76%	-	76%
Pain 'Always' Well Controlled	300+	70%	-	69%
Room and Bathroom 'Always' Clean	300+	75%	-	71%
Timely Help 'Always' Received	300+	61%	-	64%
Would Definitely Recommend Hospital	300+	77%	-	69%

NOTE: Hospital profiles are in alphabetical order by state, then city, then hospital within the city; Rankings exclude hospitals with less than 25 cases except for patient surveys which excludes hospitals with less than 100 cases; (a) 100–299 cases; (1) The number of cases is too small to be sure how well a hospital is performing; (2) The hospital indicated that the data submitted for this measure were based on a sample of cases; (3) Data was collected during a shorter time period (fewer quarters) than the maximum possible time for this measure; (4) Suppressed for one or more quarters by CMS; (5) No data is available from the hospital for this measure; (6) Fewer than 100 patients completed the HCAHPS survey. Use these rates with caution, as the number of surveys may be too low to reliably assess hospital performance; (7) Survey results are based on less than 12 months of data; (8) Survey results are not available for this reporting period; (9) No or very few patients were eligible for the HCAHPS survey. The scores shown, if any, reflect a very small number of surveys; (10) A state average was not calculated because too few hospitals in the state submitted data; (11) There were discrepancies in the data collection process; Please refer to the User's Guide for a full explanation of data.

Saint Elizabeth Central

1501 Hartford St
Lafayette, IN 47904
URL: www.glhsi.org
Type: Acute Care Hospitals
Ownership: Voluntary Non-Profit - Church
Phone: 765-423-6011
Fax: 765-423-6925
Emergency Services: Yes
Beds: 375

Key Personnel:
CEO/President. . . . . Terrence Wilson
Cardiac Laboratory. . . . . Larry Drummond
Chief of Medical Staff . . . . Donald Edelen, MD
Infection Control. . . . . Patricia Boardman, RN
Operating Room. . . . . Joan Miller, RN
Pediatric In-Patient Care . . . . Marcia Sukits, RN
Quality Assurance . . . . Donald Edelen, MD
Radiology. . . . . Steve Good, MD

Measure	Cases	This Hosp.	State Avg.	U.S. Avg.
Heart Attack Care				
ACE Inhibitor or ARB for LVSD	33	97%	96%	96%
Aspirin at Arrival	98	100%	98%	99%
Aspirin at Discharge	167	99%	99%	98%
Beta Blocker at Discharge	163	100%	98%	98%
Fibrinolytic Medication Timing	0	-	37%	55%
PCI Within 90 Minutes of Arrival	27	96%	93%	90%
Smoking Cessation Advice	59	100%	99%	99%
Chest Pain/Possible Heart Attack Care				
Aspirin at Arrival	76	95%	95%	95%
Median Time to ECG (minutes)	80	5	6	8
Median Time to Transfer (minutes)[3]	0	-	49	61
Fibrinolytic Medication Timing[3]	0	-	63%	54%
Heart Failure Care				
ACE Inhibitor or ARB for LVSD	80	92%	92%	94%
Discharge Instructions	135	79%	84%	88%
Evaluation of LVS Function	195	98%	98%	98%
Smoking Cessation Advice	25	100%	99%	98%
Pneumonia Care				
Appropriate Initial Antibiotic[2]	71	86%	90%	92%
Blood Culture Timing[2]	83	99%	95%	96%
Influenza Vaccine	85	95%	93%	91%
Initial Antibiotic Timing[2]	102	97%	96%	95%
Pneumococcal Vaccine[2]	131	91%	94%	93%
Smoking Cessation Advice[2]	39	100%	98%	97%
Surgical Care Improvement Project				
Appropriate VTP Within 24 Hours[1,2,3]	17	94%	90%	92%
Appropriate Hair Removal[2,3]	273	100%	100%	99%
Appropriate Beta Blocker Usage[2,3]	91	96%	93%	93%
Controlled Postoperative Blood Glucose[2,3]	46	96%	93%	93%
Prophylactic Antibiotic Timing[2,3]	225	97%	97%	97%
Prophylactic Antibiotic Timing (Outpatient)[3]	198	99%	92%	92%
Prophylactic Antibiotic Selection[2,3]	226	98%	98%	97%
Prophylactic Antibiotic Select. (Outpatient)[3]	198	99%	95%	94%
Prophylactic Antibiotic Stopped[2,3]	212	97%	95%	94%
Recommended VTP Ordered[1,2,3]	17	94%	92%	94%
Urinary Catheter Removal[1,3]	19	95%	92%	90%
Children's Asthma Care				
Received Systemic Corticosteroids	-	-	-	100%
Received Home Management Plan	-	-	-	71%
Received Reliever Medication	-	-	-	100%
Use of Medical Imaging				
Combination Abdominal CT Scan	594	0.072	0.237	0.191
Combination Chest CT Scan	611	0.007	0.120	0.054
Follow-up Mammogram/Ultrasound	2,043	7.4%	8.3%	8.4%
MRI for Low Back Pain[1]	28	39.3%	35.2%	32.7%
Survey of Patients' Hospital Experiences				
Area Around Room 'Always' Quiet at Night	300+	47%	-	58%
Doctors 'Always' Communicated Well	300+	75%	-	80%
Home Recovery Information Given	300+	84%	-	82%
Hospital Given 9 or 10 on 10 Point Scale	300+	65%	-	67%
Meds 'Always' Explained Before Given	300+	54%	-	60%
Nurses 'Always' Communicated Well	300+	77%	-	76%
Pain 'Always' Well Controlled	300+	71%	-	69%
Room and Bathroom 'Always' Clean	300+	68%	-	71%
Timely Help 'Always' Received	300+	58%	-	64%
Would Definitely Recommend Hospital	300+	70%	-	69%

Saint Elizabeth East

1701 S Creasy Ln
Lafayette, IN 47905
URL: www.ste.org
Type: Acute Care Hospitals
Ownership: Voluntary Non-Profit - Church
Phone: 765-502-4000
Fax: 765-423-6475
Emergency Services: Yes
Beds: 263

Key Personnel:
CEO/President. . . . . Terry Wilson
Cardiac Laboratory. . . . . Sam Haskett
Infection Control. . . . . Laura Aschenberg
Pediatric In-Patient Care . . . . Marcia Cherry
Quality Assurance . . . . Terry Janssen
Radiology. . . . . Carlos Vasquez
Emergency Room . . . . Wayne O'Connor
Intensive Care Unit. . . . . Carol Bailey

Measure	Cases	This Hosp.	State Avg.	U.S. Avg.
Heart Attack Care				
ACE Inhibitor or ARB for LVSD[1]	10	100%	96%	96%
Aspirin at Arrival	47	100%	98%	99%
Aspirin at Discharge	79	100%	99%	98%
Beta Blocker at Discharge	75	100%	98%	98%
Fibrinolytic Medication Timing[1]	1	100%	37%	55%
PCI Within 90 Minutes of Arrival[1]	13	85%	93%	90%
Smoking Cessation Advice	26	100%	99%	99%
Chest Pain/Possible Heart Attack Care				
Aspirin at Arrival	67	91%	95%	95%
Median Time to ECG (minutes)	69	8	6	8
Median Time to Transfer (minutes)[1,3]	6	46	49	61
Fibrinolytic Medication Timing[3]	0	-	63%	54%
Heart Failure Care				
ACE Inhibitor or ARB for LVSD[1]	23	91%	92%	94%
Discharge Instructions	55	67%	84%	88%
Evaluation of LVS Function	81	99%	98%	98%
Smoking Cessation Advice[1]	12	100%	99%	98%
Pneumonia Care				
Appropriate Initial Antibiotic	46	85%	90%	92%
Blood Culture Timing	44	95%	95%	96%
Influenza Vaccine	54	96%	93%	91%
Initial Antibiotic Timing	71	93%	96%	95%
Pneumococcal Vaccine	70	87%	94%	93%
Smoking Cessation Advice	27	100%	98%	97%
Surgical Care Improvement Project				
Appropriate VTP Within 24 Hours[2]	185	82%	90%	92%
Appropriate Hair Removal[2]	756	100%	100%	99%
Appropriate Beta Blocker Usage[2]	205	94%	93%	93%
Controlled Postoperative Blood Glucose[2]	27	100%	93%	93%
Prophylactic Antibiotic Timing[2]	531	99%	97%	97%
Prophylactic Antibiotic Timing (Outpatient)	625	98%	92%	92%
Prophylactic Antibiotic Selection[2]	533	99%	98%	97%
Prophylactic Antibiotic Select. (Outpatient)	620	96%	95%	94%
Prophylactic Antibiotic Stopped[2]	513	98%	95%	94%
Recommended VTP Ordered[2]	185	91%	92%	94%
Urinary Catheter Removal[2]	102	91%	92%	90%
Children's Asthma Care				
Received Systemic Corticosteroids	-	-	-	100%
Received Home Management Plan	-	-	-	71%
Received Reliever Medication	-	-	-	100%
Use of Medical Imaging				
Combination Abdominal CT Scan	1,401	0.425	0.237	0.191
Combination Chest CT Scan	1,259	0.012	0.120	0.054
Follow-up Mammogram/Ultrasound[1]	1	0.0%	8.3%	8.4%
MRI for Low Back Pain	329	36.2%	35.2%	32.7%
Survey of Patients' Hospital Experiences				
Area Around Room 'Always' Quiet at Night	300+	59%	-	58%
Doctors 'Always' Communicated Well	300+	80%	-	80%
Home Recovery Information Given	300+	86%	-	82%
Hospital Given 9 or 10 on 10 Point Scale	300+	66%	-	67%
Meds 'Always' Explained Before Given	300+	58%	-	60%
Nurses 'Always' Communicated Well	300+	78%	-	76%
Pain 'Always' Well Controlled	300+	74%	-	69%
Room and Bathroom 'Always' Clean	300+	77%	-	71%
Timely Help 'Always' Received	300+	60%	-	64%
Would Definitely Recommend Hospital	300+	72%	-	69%

Parkview Lagrange Hospital

207 N Townline Road
Lagrange, IN 46761
Type: Critical Access Hospitals
Ownership: Government - Federal
Phone: 260-463-9000
Fax: 260-463-3190
Emergency Services: Yes
Beds: 62

Key Personnel:
Chief of Medical Staff . . . . Shashank Kashyap, MD
Infection Control. . . . . Jane Case
Quality Assurance . . . . Diane Barnes
Radiology. . . . . James Wehrenberg, MD
Anesthesiology. . . . . Evan Thompson, MD
Emergency Room . . . . Scott Smith, MD

Measure	Cases	This Hosp.	State Avg.	U.S. Avg.
Heart Attack Care				
ACE Inhibitor or ARB for LVSD	0	-	96%	96%
Aspirin at Arrival[1]	1	100%	98%	99%
Aspirin at Discharge[1]	1	100%	99%	98%
Beta Blocker at Discharge[1]	1	100%	98%	98%
Fibrinolytic Medication Timing	0	-	37%	55%
PCI Within 90 Minutes of Arrival	0	-	93%	90%
Smoking Cessation Advice	0	-	99%	99%
Chest Pain/Possible Heart Attack Care				
Aspirin at Arrival	75	99%	95%	95%
Median Time to ECG (minutes)	75	5	6	8
Median Time to Transfer (minutes)[1,3]	7	58	49	61
Fibrinolytic Medication Timing[1]	1	0%	63%	54%
Heart Failure Care				
ACE Inhibitor or ARB for LVSD[1]	5	60%	92%	94%
Discharge Instructions[1]	13	77%	84%	88%
Evaluation of LVS Function[1]	19	100%	98%	98%
Smoking Cessation Advice[1]	2	100%	99%	98%
Pneumonia Care				
Appropriate Initial Antibiotic	44	98%	90%	92%
Blood Culture Timing[1]	22	100%	95%	96%
Influenza Vaccine	28	93%	93%	91%
Initial Antibiotic Timing	49	100%	96%	95%
Pneumococcal Vaccine	36	94%	94%	93%
Smoking Cessation Advice[1]	13	100%	98%	97%
Surgical Care Improvement Project				
Appropriate VTP Within 24 Hours	30	100%	90%	92%
Appropriate Hair Removal	59	100%	100%	99%
Appropriate Beta Blocker Usage[1]	4	75%	93%	93%
Controlled Postoperative Blood Glucose	0	-	93%	93%
Prophylactic Antibiotic Timing	52	92%	97%	97%
Prophylactic Antibiotic Timing (Outpatient)[1]	20	95%	92%	92%
Prophylactic Antibiotic Selection	52	100%	98%	97%
Prophylactic Antibiotic Select. (Outpatient)[1]	20	100%	95%	94%
Prophylactic Antibiotic Stopped	50	94%	95%	94%
Recommended VTP Ordered	30	100%	92%	94%
Urinary Catheter Removal[1]	10	90%	92%	90%
Children's Asthma Care				
Received Systemic Corticosteroids	-	-	-	100%
Received Home Management Plan	-	-	-	71%
Received Reliever Medication	-	-	-	100%
Use of Medical Imaging				
Combination Abdominal CT Scan	179	0.011	0.237	0.191
Combination Chest CT Scan	83	0.157	0.120	0.054
Follow-up Mammogram/Ultrasound	270	7.4%	8.3%	8.4%
MRI for Low Back Pain	42	45.2%	35.2%	32.7%
Survey of Patients' Hospital Experiences				
Area Around Room 'Always' Quiet at Night	(a)	61%	-	58%
Doctors 'Always' Communicated Well	(a)	85%	-	80%
Home Recovery Information Given	(a)	84%	-	82%
Hospital Given 9 or 10 on 10 Point Scale	(a)	80%	-	67%
Meds 'Always' Explained Before Given	(a)	59%	-	60%
Nurses 'Always' Communicated Well	(a)	79%	-	76%
Pain 'Always' Well Controlled	(a)	73%	-	69%
Room and Bathroom 'Always' Clean	(a)	79%	-	71%
Timely Help 'Always' Received	(a)	71%	-	64%
Would Definitely Recommend Hospital	(a)	75%	-	69%

NOTE: Hospital profiles are in alphabetical order by state, then city, then hospital within the city; Rankings exclude hospitals with less than 25 cases except for patient surveys which excludes hospitals with less than 100 cases; (a) 100–299 cases; (1) The number of cases is too small to be sure how well a hospital is performing; (2) The hospital indicated that the data submitted for this measure were based on a sample of cases; (3) Data was collected during a shorter time period (fewer quarters) than the maximum possible time for this measure; (4) Suppressed for one or more quarters by CMS; (5) No data is available from the hospital for this measure; (6) Fewer than 100 patients completed the HCAHPS survey. Use these rates with caution, as the number of surveys may be too low to reliably assess hospital performance; (7) Survey results are based on less than 12 months of data; (8) Survey results are not available for this reporting period; (9) No or very few patients were eligible for the HCAHPS survey. The scores shown, if any, reflect a very small number of surveys; (10) A state average was not calculated because too few hospitals in the state submitted data; (11) There were discrepancies in the data collection process; Please refer to the User's Guide for a full explanation of data.

Dearborn County Hospital

600 Wilson Creek Rd
Lawrenceburg, IN 47025
E-mail: hhinds@dch.org
URL: www.dhc.org
Phone: 812-537-1010
Fax: 812-537-2897
Type: Acute Care Hospitals
Ownership: Government - Local
Emergency Services: Yes
Beds: 144

Key Personnel:
Chief of Medical Staff.......... Stephen Eliason, MD
Operating Room.............. Connie Cecil
Pediatric Ambulatory Care...... Michael Caudy, MD
Quality Assurance .... Stephanie Craig, RN
Radiology.................. John A Botsford
Anesthesiology............... Joseph Uehlein, MD
Emergency Room .... Ellen McCracken
Intensive Care Unit............ Keri Amberger, RN

Measure	Cases	This Hosp.	State Avg.	U.S. Avg.
Heart Attack Care				
ACE Inhibitor or ARB for LVSD[1]	4	75%	96%	96%
Aspirin at Arrival	47	100%	98%	99%
Aspirin at Discharge	26	100%	99%	98%
Beta Blocker at Discharge	26	96%	98%	98%
Fibrinolytic Medication Timing[1]	6	67%	37%	55%
PCI Within 90 Minutes of Arrival	0	-	93%	90%
Smoking Cessation Advice[1]	7	100%	99%	99%
Chest Pain/Possible Heart Attack Care				
Aspirin at Arrival	134	99%	95%	95%
Median Time to ECG (minutes)	140	8	6	8
Median Time to Transfer (minutes)[1]	2	194	49	61
Fibrinolytic Medication Timing[1]	15	73%	63%	54%
Heart Failure Care				
ACE Inhibitor or ARB for LVSD	33	79%	92%	94%
Discharge Instructions	86	64%	84%	88%
Evaluation of LVS Function	104	98%	98%	98%
Smoking Cessation Advice	25	100%	99%	98%
Pneumonia Care				
Appropriate Initial Antibiotic	102	92%	90%	92%
Blood Culture Timing	145	92%	95%	96%
Influenza Vaccine	108	97%	93%	91%
Initial Antibiotic Timing	162	94%	96%	95%
Pneumococcal Vaccine	139	98%	94%	93%
Smoking Cessation Advice	76	100%	98%	97%
Surgical Care Improvement Project				
Appropriate VTP Within 24 Hours	118	89%	90%	92%
Appropriate Hair Removal	261	100%	100%	99%
Appropriate Beta Blocker Usage	71	90%	93%	93%
Controlled Postoperative Blood Glucose	0	-	93%	93%
Prophylactic Antibiotic Timing	181	92%	97%	97%
Prophylactic Antibiotic Timing (Outpatient)	88	70%	92%	92%
Prophylactic Antibiotic Selection	183	98%	98%	97%
Prophylactic Antibiotic Select. (Outpatient)	134	93%	95%	94%
Prophylactic Antibiotic Stopped	179	94%	95%	94%
Recommended VTP Ordered	118	93%	92%	94%
Urinary Catheter Removal	54	87%	92%	90%
Children's Asthma Care				
Received Systemic Corticosteroids	-	-	-	100%
Received Home Management Plan	-	-	-	71%
Received Reliever Medication	-	-	-	100%
Use of Medical Imaging				
Combination Abdominal CT Scan	620	0.466	0.237	0.191
Combination Chest CT Scan	427	0.089	0.120	0.054
Follow-up Mammogram/Ultrasound	847	7.2%	8.3%	8.4%
MRI for Low Back Pain	129	29.5%	35.2%	32.7%
Survey of Patients' Hospital Experiences				
Area Around Room 'Always' Quiet at Night	300+	55%	-	58%
Doctors 'Always' Communicated Well	300+	79%	-	80%
Home Recovery Information Given	300+	77%	-	82%
Hospital Given 9 or 10 on 10 Point Scale	300+	63%	-	67%
Meds 'Always' Explained Before Given	300+	58%	-	60%
Nurses 'Always' Communicated Well	300+	77%	-	76%
Pain 'Always' Well Controlled	300+	67%	-	69%
Room and Bathroom 'Always' Clean	300+	80%	-	71%
Timely Help 'Always' Received	300+	68%	-	64%
Would Definitely Recommend Hospital	300+	64%	-	69%

Witham Health Services

2605 N Lebanon Stt
Lebanon, IN 46052
URL: www.witham.org
Phone: 765-485-8000
Fax: 765-482-8688
Type: Acute Care Hospitals
Ownership: Government - Local
Emergency Services: Yes
Beds: 80

Key Personnel:
CEO/President.............. Raymond Ingham
Chief of Medical Staff.......... Robert Watt, PhD, MD
Coronary Care............... Cindy Line
Radiology.................. Homer Beltz
Patient Relations .... Diane Feder, RN, MSN

Measure	Cases	This Hosp.	State Avg.	U.S. Avg.
Heart Attack Care				
ACE Inhibitor or ARB for LVSD[1,3]	3	100%	96%	96%
Aspirin at Arrival[1,3]	17	88%	98%	99%
Aspirin at Discharge[1,3]	16	100%	99%	98%
Beta Blocker at Discharge[1,3]	16	88%	98%	98%
Fibrinolytic Medication Timing[3]	0	-	37%	55%
PCI Within 90 Minutes of Arrival[3]	0	-	93%	90%
Smoking Cessation Advice[1,3]	2	100%	99%	99%
Chest Pain/Possible Heart Attack Care				
Aspirin at Arrival	87	92%	95%	95%
Median Time to ECG (minutes)	90	8	6	8
Median Time to Transfer (minutes)[3]	0	-	49	61
Fibrinolytic Medication Timing[3]	0	-	63%	54%
Heart Failure Care				
ACE Inhibitor or ARB for LVSD[1]	11	91%	92%	94%
Discharge Instructions	55	45%	84%	88%
Evaluation of LVS Function	75	89%	98%	98%
Smoking Cessation Advice[1]	5	100%	99%	98%
Pneumonia Care				
Appropriate Initial Antibiotic	54	87%	90%	92%
Blood Culture Timing	82	87%	95%	96%
Influenza Vaccine	48	79%	93%	91%
Initial Antibiotic Timing	82	100%	96%	95%
Pneumococcal Vaccine	52	96%	94%	93%
Smoking Cessation Advice	32	88%	98%	97%
Surgical Care Improvement Project				
Appropriate VTP Within 24 Hours	54	80%	90%	92%
Appropriate Hair Removal	118	100%	100%	99%
Appropriate Beta Blocker Usage	31	81%	93%	93%
Controlled Postoperative Blood Glucose	0	-	93%	93%
Prophylactic Antibiotic Timing	92	71%	97%	97%
Prophylactic Antibiotic Timing (Outpatient)[1]	18	61%	92%	92%
Prophylactic Antibiotic Selection	91	99%	98%	97%
Prophylactic Antibiotic Select. (Outpatient)[1]	14	93%	95%	94%
Prophylactic Antibiotic Stopped	88	91%	95%	94%
Recommended VTP Ordered	54	83%	92%	94%
Urinary Catheter Removal	28	82%	92%	90%
Children's Asthma Care				
Received Systemic Corticosteroids	-	-	-	100%
Received Home Management Plan	-	-	-	71%
Received Reliever Medication	-	-	-	100%
Use of Medical Imaging				
Combination Abdominal CT Scan	436	0.094	0.237	0.191
Combination Chest CT Scan	331	0.015	0.120	0.054
Follow-up Mammogram/Ultrasound	576	11.8%	8.3%	8.4%
MRI for Low Back Pain	94	31.9%	35.2%	32.7%
Survey of Patients' Hospital Experiences				
Area Around Room 'Always' Quiet at Night	300+	60%	-	58%
Doctors 'Always' Communicated Well	300+	83%	-	80%
Home Recovery Information Given	300+	80%	-	82%
Hospital Given 9 or 10 on 10 Point Scale	300+	73%	-	67%
Meds 'Always' Explained Before Given	300+	62%	-	60%
Nurses 'Always' Communicated Well	300+	79%	-	76%
Pain 'Always' Well Controlled	300+	72%	-	69%
Room and Bathroom 'Always' Clean	300+	75%	-	71%
Timely Help 'Always' Received	300+	69%	-	64%
Would Definitely Recommend Hospital	300+	74%	-	69%

Greene County General Hospital

Lone Tree Rd Rr 1 Box 1000
Linton, IN 47441
URL: www.greenecountyhospital.com
Phone: 812-847-5212
Fax: 812-847-6166
Type: Critical Access Hospitals
Ownership: Government - Local
Emergency Services: Yes
Beds: 76

Key Personnel:
CEO/President............... Jonas Uland
Chief of Medical Staff.......... Jitender Bhandari
Infection Control............. Cheryl Corbin
Quality Assurance .... Janet Sweet
Radiology.................. Martina Swaby-Steele, MD
Emergency Room .... Tim Hale
Intensive Care Unit............ Amy Miller

Measure	Cases	This Hosp.	State Avg.	U.S. Avg.
Heart Attack Care				
ACE Inhibitor or ARB for LVSD[3]	0	-	96%	96%
Aspirin at Arrival[1,3]	1	100%	98%	99%
Aspirin at Discharge[3]	0	-	99%	98%
Beta Blocker at Discharge[3]	0	-	98%	98%
Fibrinolytic Medication Timing[3]	0	-	37%	55%
PCI Within 90 Minutes of Arrival[5]	0	-	93%	90%
Smoking Cessation Advice[3]	0	-	99%	99%
Chest Pain/Possible Heart Attack Care				
Aspirin at Arrival	-	-	95%	95%
Median Time to ECG (minutes)	-	-	6	8
Median Time to Transfer (minutes)	-	-	49	61
Fibrinolytic Medication Timing	-	-	63%	54%
Heart Failure Care				
ACE Inhibitor or ARB for LVSD[1]	7	86%	92%	94%
Discharge Instructions	33	94%	84%	88%
Evaluation of LVS Function	52	63%	98%	98%
Smoking Cessation Advice[1]	5	100%	99%	98%
Pneumonia Care				
Appropriate Initial Antibiotic	27	81%	90%	92%
Blood Culture Timing	29	93%	95%	96%
Influenza Vaccine	27	74%	93%	91%
Initial Antibiotic Timing	44	95%	96%	95%
Pneumococcal Vaccine	45	80%	94%	93%
Smoking Cessation Advice[1]	16	94%	98%	97%
Surgical Care Improvement Project				
Appropriate VTP Within 24 Hours[5]	0	-	90%	92%
Appropriate Hair Removal[5]	0	-	100%	99%
Appropriate Beta Blocker Usage[5]	0	-	93%	93%
Controlled Postoperative Blood Glucose[5]	0	-	93%	93%
Prophylactic Antibiotic Timing[5]	0	-	97%	97%
Prophylactic Antibiotic Timing (Outpatient)	-	-	92%	92%
Prophylactic Antibiotic Selection[5]	0	-	98%	97%
Prophylactic Antibiotic Select. (Outpatient)	-	-	95%	94%
Prophylactic Antibiotic Stopped[5]	0	-	95%	94%
Recommended VTP Ordered[5]	0	-	92%	94%
Urinary Catheter Removal[5]	0	-	92%	90%
Children's Asthma Care				
Received Systemic Corticosteroids	-	-	-	100%
Received Home Management Plan	-	-	-	71%
Received Reliever Medication	-	-	-	100%
Use of Medical Imaging				
Combination Abdominal CT Scan	-	-	0.237	0.191
Combination Chest CT Scan	-	-	0.120	0.054
Follow-up Mammogram/Ultrasound	-	-	8.3%	8.4%
MRI for Low Back Pain	-	-	35.2%	32.7%
Survey of Patients' Hospital Experiences				
Area Around Room 'Always' Quiet at Night[8]	-	-	-	58%
Doctors 'Always' Communicated Well[8]	-	-	-	80%
Home Recovery Information Given[8]	-	-	-	82%
Hospital Given 9 or 10 on 10 Point Scale[8]	-	-	-	67%
Meds 'Always' Explained Before Given[8]	-	-	-	60%
Nurses 'Always' Communicated Well[8]	-	-	-	76%
Pain 'Always' Well Controlled[8]	-	-	-	69%
Room and Bathroom 'Always' Clean[8]	-	-	-	71%
Timely Help 'Always' Received[8]	-	-	-	64%
Would Definitely Recommend Hospital[8]	-	-	-	69%

NOTE: Hospital profiles are in alphabetical order by state, then city, then hospital within the city; Rankings exclude hospitals with less than 25 cases except for patient surveys which excludes hospitals with less than 100 cases; (a) 100–299 cases; (1) The number of cases is too small to be sure how well a hospital is performing; (2) The hospital indicated that the data submitted for this measure were based on a sample of cases; (3) Data was collected during a shorter time period (fewer quarters) than the maximum possible time for this measure; (4) Suppressed for one or more quarters by CMS; (5) No data is available from the hospital for this measure; (6) Fewer than 100 patients completed the HCAHPS survey. Use these rates with caution, as the number of surveys may be too low to reliably assess hospital performance; (7) Survey results are based on less than 12 months of data; (8) Survey results are not available for this reporting period; (9) No or very few patients were eligible for the HCAHPS survey. The scores shown, if any, reflect a very small number of surveys; (10) A state average was not calculated because too few hospitals in the state submitted data; (11) There were discrepancies in the data collection process; Please refer to the User's Guide for a full explanation of data.

Memorial Hospital

1101 Michigan Ave
Logansport, IN 46947
Phone: 574-753-7541
E-mail: info@mhlogan.org
URL: www.mhlogan.org
Type: Acute Care Hospitals
Emergency Services: Yes
Ownership: Government - Federal
Beds: 104

Key Personnel:
CEO/President. . . . . Brian Shockney
Chief of Medical Staff . . . . Charles Montgomery, MD
Infection Control. . . . . Sebrena Ide, RN
Operating Room. . . . . Todd Weinstein, RN
Quality Assurance . . . . Kathy Pattee, RN
Radiology. . . . . William Harvey
Intensive Care Unit. . . . . Angela Cleland, RN
Patient Relations . . . . Alice Rothermel

Measure	Cases	This Hosp.	State Avg.	U.S. Avg.
Heart Attack Care				
ACE Inhibitor or ARB for LVSD[1]	1	100%	96%	96%
Aspirin at Arrival[1]	3	100%	98%	99%
Aspirin at Discharge[1]	3	100%	99%	98%
Beta Blocker at Discharge[1]	3	100%	98%	98%
Fibrinolytic Medication Timing	0	-	37%	55%
PCI Within 90 Minutes of Arrival	0	-	93%	90%
Smoking Cessation Advice	0	-	99%	99%
Chest Pain/Possible Heart Attack Care				
Aspirin at Arrival	96	96%	95%	95%
Median Time to ECG (minutes)	125	6	6	8
Median Time to Transfer (minutes)[1]	12	74	49	61
Fibrinolytic Medication Timing[1]	3	33%	63%	54%
Heart Failure Care				
ACE Inhibitor or ARB for LVSD[1]	19	89%	92%	94%
Discharge Instructions	38	100%	84%	88%
Evaluation of LVS Function	55	100%	98%	98%
Smoking Cessation Advice[1]	7	100%	99%	98%
Pneumonia Care				
Appropriate Initial Antibiotic	81	85%	90%	92%
Blood Culture Timing	74	97%	95%	96%
Influenza Vaccine	64	94%	93%	91%
Initial Antibiotic Timing	114	97%	96%	95%
Pneumococcal Vaccine	94	98%	94%	93%
Smoking Cessation Advice	43	100%	98%	97%
Surgical Care Improvement Project				
Appropriate VTP Within 24 Hours	27	74%	90%	92%
Appropriate Hair Removal	137	100%	100%	99%
Appropriate Beta Blocker Usage[1]	7	100%	93%	93%
Controlled Postoperative Blood Glucose	0	-	93%	93%
Prophylactic Antibiotic Timing	101	94%	97%	97%
Prophylactic Antibiotic Timing (Outpatient)	126	93%	92%	92%
Prophylactic Antibiotic Selection	102	91%	98%	97%
Prophylactic Antibiotic Select. (Outpatient)	121	97%	95%	94%
Prophylactic Antibiotic Stopped	101	98%	95%	94%
Recommended VTP Ordered	27	74%	92%	94%
Urinary Catheter Removal[1]	5	40%	92%	90%
Children's Asthma Care				
Received Systemic Corticosteroids	-	-	-	100%
Received Home Management Plan	-	-	-	71%
Received Reliever Medication	-	-	-	100%
Use of Medical Imaging				
Combination Abdominal CT Scan	464	0.707	0.237	0.191
Combination Chest CT Scan	290	0.041	0.120	0.054
Follow-up Mammogram/Ultrasound	1,017	9.9%	8.3%	8.4%
MRI for Low Back Pain	144	37.5%	35.2%	32.7%
Survey of Patients' Hospital Experiences				
Area Around Room 'Always' Quiet at Night	300+	58%	-	58%
Doctors 'Always' Communicated Well	300+	82%	-	80%
Home Recovery Information Given	300+	81%	-	82%
Hospital Given 9 or 10 on 10 Point Scale	300+	65%	-	67%
Meds 'Always' Explained Before Given	300+	64%	-	60%
Nurses 'Always' Communicated Well	300+	80%	-	76%
Pain 'Always' Well Controlled	300+	74%	-	69%
Room and Bathroom 'Always' Clean	300+	78%	-	71%
Timely Help 'Always' Received	300+	73%	-	64%
Would Definitely Recommend Hospital	300+	64%	-	69%

The King's Daughters' Hospital and Health Services

One Kings Daughters Drive
Madison, IN 47250
Phone: 812-265-5211
Fax: 812-265-0680
E-mail: kdh@seida.com
URL: www.kdhhs.org
Type: Acute Care Hospitals
Emergency Services: Yes
Ownership: Voluntary Non-Profit - Private
Beds: 142

Key Personnel:
Chief of Medical Staff . . . . William Estes, MD
Infection Control. . . . . Vikki Conners, RN
Operating Room. . . . . Kathy Brown
Quality Assurance . . . . Judy Gill
Radiology. . . . . Robert Leatherm, MD
Emergency Room . . . . L Bernard
Hemotology Center . . . . Judy Tingle
Intensive Care Unit. . . . . Nick James, RN

Measure	Cases	This Hosp.	State Avg.	U.S. Avg.
Heart Attack Care				
ACE Inhibitor or ARB for LVSD[1]	1	100%	96%	96%
Aspirin at Arrival	25	96%	98%	99%
Aspirin at Discharge[1]	14	100%	99%	98%
Beta Blocker at Discharge[1]	9	89%	98%	98%
Fibrinolytic Medication Timing	0	-	37%	55%
PCI Within 90 Minutes of Arrival	0	-	93%	90%
Smoking Cessation Advice[1]	2	100%	99%	99%
Chest Pain/Possible Heart Attack Care				
Aspirin at Arrival	122	99%	95%	95%
Median Time to ECG (minutes)	124	8	6	8
Median Time to Transfer (minutes)[1,3]	2	154	49	61
Fibrinolytic Medication Timing[1]	12	92%	63%	54%
Heart Failure Care				
ACE Inhibitor or ARB for LVSD[1]	23	96%	92%	94%
Discharge Instructions	108	99%	84%	88%
Evaluation of LVS Function	143	99%	98%	98%
Smoking Cessation Advice[1]	24	100%	99%	98%
Pneumonia Care				
Appropriate Initial Antibiotic	116	96%	90%	92%
Blood Culture Timing	134	99%	95%	96%
Influenza Vaccine	117	100%	93%	91%
Initial Antibiotic Timing	188	99%	96%	95%
Pneumococcal Vaccine	148	100%	94%	93%
Smoking Cessation Advice	87	100%	98%	97%
Surgical Care Improvement Project				
Appropriate VTP Within 24 Hours	89	94%	90%	92%
Appropriate Hair Removal	203	100%	100%	99%
Appropriate Beta Blocker Usage	43	95%	93%	93%
Controlled Postoperative Blood Glucose	0	-	93%	93%
Prophylactic Antibiotic Timing	110	98%	97%	97%
Prophylactic Antibiotic Timing (Outpatient)	60	90%	92%	92%
Prophylactic Antibiotic Selection	110	100%	98%	97%
Prophylactic Antibiotic Select. (Outpatient)	55	95%	95%	94%
Prophylactic Antibiotic Stopped	107	96%	95%	94%
Recommended VTP Ordered	89	96%	92%	94%
Urinary Catheter Removal	32	97%	92%	90%
Children's Asthma Care				
Received Systemic Corticosteroids	-	-	-	100%
Received Home Management Plan	-	-	-	71%
Received Reliever Medication	-	-	-	100%
Use of Medical Imaging				
Combination Abdominal CT Scan	603	0.768	0.237	0.191
Combination Chest CT Scan	349	0.765	0.120	0.054
Follow-up Mammogram/Ultrasound	945	3.8%	8.3%	8.4%
MRI for Low Back Pain	82	35.4%	35.2%	32.7%
Survey of Patients' Hospital Experiences				
Area Around Room 'Always' Quiet at Night	300+	52%	-	58%
Doctors 'Always' Communicated Well	300+	82%	-	80%
Home Recovery Information Given	300+	86%	-	82%
Hospital Given 9 or 10 on 10 Point Scale	300+	65%	-	67%
Meds 'Always' Explained Before Given	300+	61%	-	60%
Nurses 'Always' Communicated Well	300+	78%	-	76%
Pain 'Always' Well Controlled	300+	70%	-	69%
Room and Bathroom 'Always' Clean	300+	74%	-	71%
Timely Help 'Always' Received	300+	72%	-	64%
Would Definitely Recommend Hospital	300+	62%	-	69%

Marion General Hospital

441 N Wabash Ave
Marion, IN 46952
Phone: 765-662-4684
Fax: 765-662-4842
Type: Acute Care Hospitals
Emergency Services: Yes
Ownership: Voluntary Non-Profit - Other
Beds: 191

Key Personnel:
Chief of Medical Staff . . . . Aaron M Fritz
Infection Control. . . . . B Eppler, RN
Operating Room. . . . . Robert Crowell
Quality Assurance . . . . Ruth Masiongale
Radiology. . . . . Sheri L Brinker

Measure	Cases	This Hosp.	State Avg.	U.S. Avg.
Heart Attack Care				
ACE Inhibitor or ARB for LVSD[1]	5	80%	96%	96%
Aspirin at Arrival	39	97%	98%	99%
Aspirin at Discharge	29	90%	99%	98%
Beta Blocker at Discharge	31	94%	98%	98%
Fibrinolytic Medication Timing	0	-	37%	55%
PCI Within 90 Minutes of Arrival[1]	1	100%	93%	90%
Smoking Cessation Advice[1]	4	100%	99%	99%
Chest Pain/Possible Heart Attack Care				
Aspirin at Arrival	207	94%	95%	95%
Median Time to ECG (minutes)	215	6	6	8
Median Time to Transfer (minutes)	40	56	49	61
Fibrinolytic Medication Timing[1]	2	0%	63%	54%
Heart Failure Care				
ACE Inhibitor or ARB for LVSD	63	90%	92%	94%
Discharge Instructions	118	87%	84%	88%
Evaluation of LVS Function	189	99%	98%	98%
Smoking Cessation Advice	32	100%	99%	98%
Pneumonia Care				
Appropriate Initial Antibiotic	127	95%	90%	92%
Blood Culture Timing	130	98%	95%	96%
Influenza Vaccine	123	93%	93%	91%
Initial Antibiotic Timing	166	96%	96%	95%
Pneumococcal Vaccine	139	95%	94%	93%
Smoking Cessation Advice	70	90%	98%	97%
Surgical Care Improvement Project				
Appropriate VTP Within 24 Hours	277	94%	90%	92%
Appropriate Hair Removal	498	100%	100%	99%
Appropriate Beta Blocker Usage	156	91%	93%	93%
Controlled Postoperative Blood Glucose	0	-	93%	93%
Prophylactic Antibiotic Timing	359	96%	97%	97%
Prophylactic Antibiotic Timing (Outpatient)	142	86%	92%	92%
Prophylactic Antibiotic Selection	361	94%	98%	97%
Prophylactic Antibiotic Select. (Outpatient)	133	94%	95%	94%
Prophylactic Antibiotic Stopped	345	93%	95%	94%
Recommended VTP Ordered	286	93%	92%	94%
Urinary Catheter Removal	42	95%	92%	90%
Children's Asthma Care				
Received Systemic Corticosteroids	-	-	-	100%
Received Home Management Plan	-	-	-	71%
Received Reliever Medication	-	-	-	100%
Use of Medical Imaging				
Combination Abdominal CT Scan	1,039	0.690	0.237	0.191
Combination Chest CT Scan	601	0.787	0.120	0.054
Follow-up Mammogram/Ultrasound	1,784	10.6%	8.3%	8.4%
MRI for Low Back Pain	244	36.9%	35.2%	32.7%
Survey of Patients' Hospital Experiences				
Area Around Room 'Always' Quiet at Night	300+	52%	-	58%
Doctors 'Always' Communicated Well	300+	85%	-	80%
Home Recovery Information Given	300+	83%	-	82%
Hospital Given 9 or 10 on 10 Point Scale	300+	69%	-	67%
Meds 'Always' Explained Before Given	300+	68%	-	60%
Nurses 'Always' Communicated Well	300+	83%	-	76%
Pain 'Always' Well Controlled	300+	74%	-	69%
Room and Bathroom 'Always' Clean	300+	74%	-	71%
Timely Help 'Always' Received	300+	73%	-	64%
Would Definitely Recommend Hospital	300+	66%	-	69%

NOTE: Hospital profiles are in alphabetical order by state, then city, then hospital within the city; Rankings exclude hospitals with less than 25 cases except for patient surveys which excludes hospitals with less than 100 cases; (a) 100–299 cases; (1) The number of cases is too small to be sure how well a hospital is performing; (2) The hospital indicated that the data submitted for this measure were based on a sample of cases; (3) Data was collected during a shorter time period (fewer quarters) than the maximum possible time for this measure; (4) Suppressed for one or more quarters by CMS; (5) No data is available from the hospital for this measure; (6) Fewer than 100 patients completed the HCAHPS survey. Use these rates with caution, as the number of surveys may be too low to reliably assess hospital performance; (7) Survey results are based on less than 12 months of data; (8) Survey results are not available for this reporting period; (9) No or very few patients were eligible for the HCAHPS survey. The scores shown, if any, reflect a very small number of surveys; (10) A state average was not calculated because too few hospitals in the state submitted data; (11) There were discrepancies in the data collection process; Please refer to the User's Guide for a full explanation of data.

VA Northern Indiana Healthcare System - Marion

1700 E. 38th Street
Marion, IN 46953
Phone: 765-674-3321
URL: www.northernindiana.va.gov
Type: Acute Care-Veterans Administration
Emergency Services: No
Ownership: Government - Federal

Measure	Cases	This Hosp.	State Avg.	U.S. Avg.
Heart Attack Care				
ACE Inhibitor or ARB for LVSD[5]	0	-	96%	96%
Aspirin at Arrival[5]	0	-	98%	99%
Aspirin at Discharge[5]	0	-	99%	98%
Beta Blocker at Discharge[5]	0	-	98%	98%
Fibrinolytic Medication Timing[5]	0	-	37%	55%
PCI Within 90 Minutes of Arrival[5]	0	-	93%	90%
Smoking Cessation Advice[5]	0	-	99%	99%
Chest Pain/Possible Heart Attack Care				
Aspirin at Arrival	-	-	95%	95%
Median Time to ECG (minutes)	-	-	6	8
Median Time to Transfer (minutes)	-	-	49	61
Fibrinolytic Medication Timing	-	-	63%	54%
Heart Failure Care				
ACE Inhibitor or ARB for LVSD	26	85%	92%	94%
Discharge Instructions	100	98%	84%	88%
Evaluation of LVS Function	106	99%	98%	98%
Smoking Cessation Advice[1]	24	92%	99%	98%
Pneumonia Care				
Appropriate Initial Antibiotic	44	100%	90%	92%
Blood Culture Timing	46	100%	95%	96%
Influenza Vaccine	44	95%	93%	91%
Initial Antibiotic Timing	52	98%	96%	95%
Pneumococcal Vaccine	54	100%	94%	93%
Smoking Cessation Advice	26	85%	98%	97%
Surgical Care Improvement Project				
Appropriate VTP Within 24 Hours[2,5]	0	-	90%	92%
Appropriate Hair Removal[2,5]	0	-	100%	99%
Appropriate Beta Blocker Usage[2,5]	0	-	93%	93%
Controlled Postoperative Blood Glucose[2,5]	0	-	93%	93%
Prophylactic Antibiotic Timing[5]	0	-	97%	97%
Prophylactic Antibiotic Timing (Outpatient)	-	-	92%	92%
Prophylactic Antibiotic Selection[5]	-	-	98%	97%
Prophylactic Antibiotic Select. (Outpatient)	-	-	95%	94%
Prophylactic Antibiotic Stopped[5]	0	-	95%	94%
Recommended VTP Ordered[2,5]	0	-	92%	94%
Urinary Catheter Removal[2,5]	0	-	92%	90%
Children's Asthma Care				
Received Systemic Corticosteroids	-	-	-	100%
Received Home Management Plan	-	-	-	71%
Received Reliever Medication	-	-	-	100%
Use of Medical Imaging				
Combination Abdominal CT Scan	-	-	0.237	0.191
Combination Chest CT Scan	-	-	0.120	0.054
Follow-up Mammogram/Ultrasound	-	-	8.3%	8.4%
MRI for Low Back Pain	-	-	35.2%	32.7%
Survey of Patients' Hospital Experiences				
Area Around Room 'Always' Quiet at Night	-	-	-	58%
Doctors 'Always' Communicated Well	-	-	-	80%
Home Recovery Information Given	-	-	-	82%
Hospital Given 9 or 10 on 10 Point Scale	-	-	-	67%
Meds 'Always' Explained Before Given	-	-	-	60%
Nurses 'Always' Communicated Well	-	-	-	76%
Pain 'Always' Well Controlled	-	-	-	69%
Room and Bathroom 'Always' Clean	-	-	-	71%
Timely Help 'Always' Received	-	-	-	64%
Would Definitely Recommend Hospital	-	-	-	69%

Morgan Hospital and Medical Center

2209 John R Wooden Drive
Martinsville, IN 46151
Phone: 765-349-6500
Fax: 765-349-5411
Type: Acute Care Hospitals
Emergency Services: Yes
Ownership: Government - Local
Beds: 106

Key Personnel:
CEO/President. . . . . Tom Laux
Chief of Medical Staff. . . . . Warren L Gray
Infection Control. . . . . Deanna Skaggs
Operating Room. . . . . Michael D Boyer
Radiology. . . . . Caryn C Anderson
Hemotology Center . . . . Vicki Elliff
Patient Relations . . . . Debra Frenn

Measure	Cases	This Hosp.	State Avg.	U.S. Avg.
Heart Attack Care				
ACE Inhibitor or ARB for LVSD[1]	2	100%	96%	96%
Aspirin at Arrival[1]	14	100%	98%	99%
Aspirin at Discharge[1]	7	100%	99%	98%
Beta Blocker at Discharge[1]	9	100%	98%	98%
Fibrinolytic Medication Timing	0	-	37%	55%
PCI Within 90 Minutes of Arrival	0	-	93%	90%
Smoking Cessation Advice	0	-	99%	99%
Chest Pain/Possible Heart Attack Care				
Aspirin at Arrival	50	94%	95%	95%
Median Time to ECG (minutes)	52	2	6	8
Median Time to Transfer (minutes)[1,3]	1	32	49	61
Fibrinolytic Medication Timing[3]	0	-	63%	54%
Heart Failure Care				
ACE Inhibitor or ARB for LVSD[1]	17	94%	92%	94%
Discharge Instructions	70	100%	84%	88%
Evaluation of LVS Function	88	99%	98%	98%
Smoking Cessation Advice[1]	12	100%	99%	98%
Pneumonia Care				
Appropriate Initial Antibiotic	58	69%	90%	92%
Blood Culture Timing	88	98%	95%	96%
Influenza Vaccine	53	87%	93%	91%
Initial Antibiotic Timing	94	95%	96%	95%
Pneumococcal Vaccine	70	93%	94%	93%
Smoking Cessation Advice	30	100%	98%	97%
Surgical Care Improvement Project				
Appropriate VTP Within 24 Hours	33	100%	90%	92%
Appropriate Hair Removal	70	100%	100%	99%
Appropriate Beta Blocker Usage[1]	15	47%	93%	93%
Controlled Postoperative Blood Glucose	0	-	93%	93%
Prophylactic Antibiotic Timing	27	85%	97%	97%
Prophylactic Antibiotic Timing (Outpatient)	72	38%	92%	92%
Prophylactic Antibiotic Selection	28	93%	98%	97%
Prophylactic Antibiotic Select. (Outpatient)	38	89%	95%	94%
Prophylactic Antibiotic Stopped	25	80%	95%	94%
Recommended VTP Ordered	33	100%	92%	94%
Urinary Catheter Removal[1]	12	100%	92%	90%
Children's Asthma Care				
Received Systemic Corticosteroids	-	-	-	100%
Received Home Management Plan	-	-	-	71%
Received Reliever Medication	-	-	-	100%
Use of Medical Imaging				
Combination Abdominal CT Scan	271	0.129	0.237	0.191
Combination Chest CT Scan	177	0.040	0.120	0.054
Follow-up Mammogram/Ultrasound	420	12.9%	8.3%	8.4%
MRI for Low Back Pain	52	34.6%	35.2%	32.7%
Survey of Patients' Hospital Experiences				
Area Around Room 'Always' Quiet at Night	300+	63%	-	58%
Doctors 'Always' Communicated Well	300+	79%	-	80%
Home Recovery Information Given	300+	75%	-	82%
Hospital Given 9 or 10 on 10 Point Scale	300+	59%	-	67%
Meds 'Always' Explained Before Given	300+	60%	-	60%
Nurses 'Always' Communicated Well	300+	71%	-	76%
Pain 'Always' Well Controlled	300+	66%	-	69%
Room and Bathroom 'Always' Clean	300+	66%	-	71%
Timely Help 'Always' Received	300+	62%	-	64%
Would Definitely Recommend Hospital	300+	57%	-	69%

Franciscan St Anthony Health - Michigan City

301 W Homer St
Michigan City, IN 46360
Phone: 219-879-8511
Fax: 219-877-1684
URL: www.samhc.org
Type: Acute Care Hospitals
Emergency Services: Yes
Ownership: Voluntary Non-Profit - Church
Beds: 310

Key Personnel:
CEO/President. . . . . Bruce Rampage
Cardiac Laboratory. . . . . Linda Rempala
Chief of Medical Staff . . . . James Callaghan, MD
Infection Control. . . . . Janene Gumz-Pulaski
Operating Room. . . . . Maria Petti
Quality Assurance . . . . Gloria Covert
Radiology. . . . . Cheryl Hoas

Measure	Cases	This Hosp.	State Avg.	U.S. Avg.
Heart Attack Care				
ACE Inhibitor or ARB for LVSD	26	100%	96%	96%
Aspirin at Arrival	135	99%	98%	99%
Aspirin at Discharge	119	99%	99%	98%
Beta Blocker at Discharge	113	99%	98%	98%
Fibrinolytic Medication Timing	0	-	37%	55%
PCI Within 90 Minutes of Arrival[1]	20	100%	93%	90%
Smoking Cessation Advice	52	94%	99%	99%
Chest Pain/Possible Heart Attack Care				
Aspirin at Arrival[1]	1	100%	95%	95%
Median Time to ECG (minutes)[1]	2	4	6	8
Median Time to Transfer (minutes)[5]	0	-	49	61
Fibrinolytic Medication Timing[3]	0	-	63%	54%
Heart Failure Care				
ACE Inhibitor or ARB for LVSD	84	100%	92%	94%
Discharge Instructions	204	100%	84%	88%
Evaluation of LVS Function	231	100%	98%	98%
Smoking Cessation Advice	52	100%	99%	98%
Pneumonia Care				
Appropriate Initial Antibiotic	72	99%	90%	92%
Blood Culture Timing	98	99%	95%	96%
Influenza Vaccine	62	94%	93%	91%
Initial Antibiotic Timing	113	97%	96%	95%
Pneumococcal Vaccine	97	97%	94%	93%
Smoking Cessation Advice	53	100%	98%	97%
Surgical Care Improvement Project				
Appropriate VTP Within 24 Hours	162	99%	90%	92%
Appropriate Hair Removal	401	100%	100%	99%
Appropriate Beta Blocker Usage	132	95%	93%	93%
Controlled Postoperative Blood Glucose	29	93%	93%	93%
Prophylactic Antibiotic Timing	269	96%	97%	97%
Prophylactic Antibiotic Timing (Outpatient)	229	63%	92%	92%
Prophylactic Antibiotic Selection	272	98%	98%	97%
Prophylactic Antibiotic Select. (Outpatient)	169	96%	95%	94%
Prophylactic Antibiotic Stopped	249	98%	95%	94%
Recommended VTP Ordered	162	99%	92%	94%
Urinary Catheter Removal	102	96%	92%	90%
Children's Asthma Care				
Received Systemic Corticosteroids	-	-	-	100%
Received Home Management Plan	-	-	-	71%
Received Reliever Medication	-	-	-	100%
Use of Medical Imaging				
Combination Abdominal CT Scan	506	0.437	0.237	0.191
Combination Chest CT Scan	399	0.556	0.120	0.054
Follow-up Mammogram/Ultrasound	1,210	2.2%	8.3%	8.4%
MRI for Low Back Pain	167	37.1%	35.2%	32.7%
Survey of Patients' Hospital Experiences				
Area Around Room 'Always' Quiet at Night	300+	51%	-	58%
Doctors 'Always' Communicated Well	300+	82%	-	80%
Home Recovery Information Given	300+	80%	-	82%
Hospital Given 9 or 10 on 10 Point Scale	300+	67%	-	67%
Meds 'Always' Explained Before Given	300+	61%	-	60%
Nurses 'Always' Communicated Well	300+	80%	-	76%
Pain 'Always' Well Controlled	300+	74%	-	69%
Room and Bathroom 'Always' Clean	300+	71%	-	71%
Timely Help 'Always' Received	300+	67%	-	64%
Would Definitely Recommend Hospital	300+	68%	-	69%

NOTE: Hospital profiles are in alphabetical order by state, then city, then hospital within the city; Rankings exclude hospitals with less than 25 cases except for patient surveys which excludes hospitals with less than 100 cases; (a) 100–299 cases; (1) The number of cases is too small to be sure how well a hospital is performing; (2) The hospital indicated that the data submitted for this measure were based on a sample of cases; (3) Data was collected during a shorter time period (fewer quarters) than the maximum possible time for this measure; (4) Suppressed for one or more quarters by CMS; (5) No data is available from the hospital for this measure; (6) Fewer than 100 patients completed the HCAHPS survey. Use these rates with caution, as the number of surveys may be too low to reliably assess hospital performance; (7) Survey results are based on less than 12 months of data; (8) Survey results are not available for this reporting period; (9) No or very few patients were eligible for the HCAHPS survey. The scores shown, if any, reflect a very small number of surveys; (10) A state average was not calculated because too few hospitals in the state submitted data; (11) There were discrepancies in the data collection process; Please refer to the User's Guide for a full explanation of data.

Saint Joseph Regional Medical Center

5215 Holy Cross Pkwy Phone: 574-335-5000
Mishawaka, IN 46545 Fax: 574-247-5401
URL: www.sjmed.com
Type: Acute Care Hospitals Emergency Services: Yes
Ownership: Voluntary Non-Profit - Private Beds: 125

Key Personnel:
CEO/President. . . . . Lori Terce
Chief of Medical Staff . . . . Norbet Sphear
Emergency Room . . . . Bruce Harley

Measure	Cases	This Hosp.	State Avg.	U.S. Avg.
Heart Attack Care				
ACE Inhibitor or ARB for LVSD[1]	20	100%	96%	96%
Aspirin at Arrival	223	100%	98%	99%
Aspirin at Discharge	257	100%	99%	98%
Beta Blocker at Discharge	249	99%	98%	98%
Fibrinolytic Medication Timing	0	-	37%	55%
PCI Within 90 Minutes of Arrival	44	95%	93%	90%
Smoking Cessation Advice	90	100%	99%	99%
Chest Pain/Possible Heart Attack Care				
Aspirin at Arrival[1]	7	100%	95%	95%
Median Time to ECG (minutes)[1]	7	11	6	8
Median Time to Transfer (minutes)[5]	0	-	49	61
Fibrinolytic Medication Timing[3]	0	-	63%	54%
Heart Failure Care				
ACE Inhibitor or ARB for LVSD	112	96%	92%	94%
Discharge Instructions	363	96%	84%	88%
Evaluation of LVS Function	478	100%	98%	98%
Smoking Cessation Advice	101	100%	99%	98%
Pneumonia Care				
Appropriate Initial Antibiotic	230	97%	90%	92%
Blood Culture Timing	222	98%	95%	96%
Influenza Vaccine	205	99%	93%	91%
Initial Antibiotic Timing	373	98%	96%	95%
Pneumococcal Vaccine	303	99%	94%	93%
Smoking Cessation Advice	131	100%	98%	97%
Surgical Care Improvement Project				
Appropriate VTP Within 24 Hours[2]	143	91%	90%	92%
Appropriate Hair Removal[2]	695	100%	100%	99%
Appropriate Beta Blocker Usage[2]	186	93%	93%	93%
Controlled Postoperative Blood Glucose[2]	140	94%	93%	93%
Prophylactic Antibiotic Timing[2]	510	98%	97%	97%
Prophylactic Antibiotic Timing (Outpatient)	350	96%	92%	92%
Prophylactic Antibiotic Selection[2]	517	98%	98%	97%
Prophylactic Antibiotic Select. (Outpatient)	340	99%	95%	94%
Prophylactic Antibiotic Stopped[2]	495	96%	95%	94%
Recommended VTP Ordered[2]	143	92%	92%	94%
Urinary Catheter Removal[2]	87	94%	92%	90%
Children's Asthma Care				
Received Systemic Corticosteroids	-	-	-	100%
Received Home Management Plan	-	-	-	71%
Received Reliever Medication	-	-	-	100%
Use of Medical Imaging				
Combination Abdominal CT Scan	763	0.051	0.237	0.191
Combination Chest CT Scan	465	0.002	0.120	0.054
Follow-up Mammogram/Ultrasound	1,262	14.4%	8.3%	8.4%
MRI for Low Back Pain[5]	0	-	35.2%	32.7%
Survey of Patients' Hospital Experiences				
Area Around Room 'Always' Quiet at Night	300+	60%	-	58%
Doctors 'Always' Communicated Well	300+	79%	-	80%
Home Recovery Information Given	300+	85%	-	82%
Hospital Given 9 or 10 on 10 Point Scale	300+	73%	-	67%
Meds 'Always' Explained Before Given	300+	57%	-	60%
Nurses 'Always' Communicated Well	300+	77%	-	76%
Pain 'Always' Well Controlled	300+	70%	-	69%
Room and Bathroom 'Always' Clean	300+	68%	-	71%
Timely Help 'Always' Received	300+	62%	-	64%
Would Definitely Recommend Hospital	300+	77%	-	69%

Unity Medical and Surgical Hospital

4455 Edison Lakes Pkwy Phone: 574-231-6800
Mishawaka, IN 46545
URL: physicianshospitalsystem.net
Type: Acute Care Hospitals Emergency Services: No
Ownership: Proprietary

Key Personnel:
President/CEO. . . . . Cameron Gilbert, PhD

Measure	Cases	This Hosp.	State Avg.	U.S. Avg.
Heart Attack Care				
ACE Inhibitor or ARB for LVSD[5]	0	-	96%	96%
Aspirin at Arrival[5]	0	-	98%	99%
Aspirin at Discharge[5]	0	-	99%	98%
Beta Blocker at Discharge[5]	0	-	98%	98%
Fibrinolytic Medication Timing[5]	0	-	37%	55%
PCI Within 90 Minutes of Arrival[5]	0	-	93%	90%
Smoking Cessation Advice[5]	0	-	99%	99%
Chest Pain/Possible Heart Attack Care				
Aspirin at Arrival	-	-	95%	95%
Median Time to ECG (minutes)	-	-	6	8
Median Time to Transfer (minutes)	-	-	49	61
Fibrinolytic Medication Timing	-	-	63%	54%
Heart Failure Care				
ACE Inhibitor or ARB for LVSD[5]	0	-	92%	94%
Discharge Instructions[5]	0	-	84%	88%
Evaluation of LVS Function[5]	0	-	98%	98%
Smoking Cessation Advice[5]	0	-	99%	98%
Pneumonia Care				
Appropriate Initial Antibiotic[5]	0	-	90%	92%
Blood Culture Timing[5]	0	-	95%	96%
Influenza Vaccine[5]	0	-	93%	91%
Initial Antibiotic Timing[5]	0	-	96%	95%
Pneumococcal Vaccine[5]	0	-	94%	93%
Smoking Cessation Advice[5]	0	-	98%	97%
Surgical Care Improvement Project				
Appropriate VTP Within 24 Hours[5]	0	-	90%	92%
Appropriate Hair Removal[5]	0	-	100%	99%
Appropriate Beta Blocker Usage[5]	0	-	93%	93%
Controlled Postoperative Blood Glucose[5]	0	-	93%	93%
Prophylactic Antibiotic Timing[5]	0	-	97%	97%
Prophylactic Antibiotic Timing (Outpatient)	-	-	92%	92%
Prophylactic Antibiotic Selection[5]	0	-	98%	97%
Prophylactic Antibiotic Select. (Outpatient)	-	-	95%	94%
Prophylactic Antibiotic Stopped[5]	0	-	95%	94%
Recommended VTP Ordered[5]	0	-	92%	94%
Urinary Catheter Removal[5]	0	-	92%	90%
Children's Asthma Care				
Received Systemic Corticosteroids	-	-	-	100%
Received Home Management Plan	-	-	-	71%
Received Reliever Medication	-	-	-	100%
Use of Medical Imaging				
Combination Abdominal CT Scan	-	-	0.237	0.191
Combination Chest CT Scan	-	-	0.120	0.054
Follow-up Mammogram/Ultrasound	-	-	8.3%	8.4%
MRI for Low Back Pain	-	-	35.2%	32.7%
Survey of Patients' Hospital Experiences				
Area Around Room 'Always' Quiet at Night[8]	-	-	-	58%
Doctors 'Always' Communicated Well[8]	-	-	-	80%
Home Recovery Information Given[8]	-	-	-	82%
Hospital Given 9 or 10 on 10 Point Scale[8]	-	-	-	67%
Meds 'Always' Explained Before Given[8]	-	-	-	60%
Nurses 'Always' Communicated Well[8]	-	-	-	76%
Pain 'Always' Well Controlled[8]	-	-	-	69%
Room and Bathroom 'Always' Clean[8]	-	-	-	71%
Timely Help 'Always' Received[8]	-	-	-	64%
Would Definitely Recommend Hospital[8]	-	-	-	69%

White County Memorial Hospital

720 S Sixth Street Phone: 574-583-7111
Monticello, IN 47960
E-mail: tcreamer@whitecmh.org
URL: www.whitecmh.org
Type: Critical Access Hospitals Emergency Services: Yes
Ownership: Government - Local Beds: 25

Key Personnel:
CEO/President. . . . . Paul Cardwell
Chief of Medical Staff . . . . David Bailey
Infection Control . . . . Robin Smith
Operating Room. . . . . Joni Diener
Quality Assurance . . . . Dave Ley
Emergency Room . . . . Denise Voetz

Measure	Cases	This Hosp.	State Avg.	U.S. Avg.
Heart Attack Care				
ACE Inhibitor or ARB for LVSD	0	-	96%	96%
Aspirin at Arrival[1]	4	75%	98%	99%
Aspirin at Discharge[1]	4	100%	99%	98%
Beta Blocker at Discharge[1]	4	100%	98%	98%
Fibrinolytic Medication Timing[5]	0	-	37%	55%
PCI Within 90 Minutes of Arrival[5]	0	-	93%	90%
Smoking Cessation Advice[1]	1	100%	99%	99%
Chest Pain/Possible Heart Attack Care				
Aspirin at Arrival	-	-	95%	95%
Median Time to ECG (minutes)	-	-	6	8
Median Time to Transfer (minutes)	-	-	49	61
Fibrinolytic Medication Timing	-	-	63%	54%
Heart Failure Care				
ACE Inhibitor or ARB for LVSD[1]	12	67%	92%	94%
Discharge Instructions[1]	20	95%	84%	88%
Evaluation of LVS Function	31	81%	98%	98%
Smoking Cessation Advice[1]	3	100%	99%	98%
Pneumonia Care				
Appropriate Initial Antibiotic	59	86%	90%	92%
Blood Culture Timing	71	90%	95%	96%
Influenza Vaccine	47	57%	93%	91%
Initial Antibiotic Timing	76	97%	96%	95%
Pneumococcal Vaccine	59	85%	94%	93%
Smoking Cessation Advice	33	94%	98%	97%
Surgical Care Improvement Project				
Appropriate VTP Within 24 Hours[5]	0	-	90%	92%
Appropriate Hair Removal[1]	9	100%	100%	99%
Appropriate Beta Blocker Usage[5]	0	-	93%	93%
Controlled Postoperative Blood Glucose[5]	0	-	93%	93%
Prophylactic Antibiotic Timing[1]	5	60%	97%	97%
Prophylactic Antibiotic Timing (Outpatient)	-	-	92%	92%
Prophylactic Antibiotic Selection[1]	4	100%	98%	97%
Prophylactic Antibiotic Select. (Outpatient)	-	-	95%	94%
Prophylactic Antibiotic Stopped[1]	4	100%	95%	94%
Recommended VTP Ordered[5]	0	-	92%	94%
Urinary Catheter Removal[1]	1	100%	92%	90%
Children's Asthma Care				
Received Systemic Corticosteroids	-	-	-	100%
Received Home Management Plan	-	-	-	71%
Received Reliever Medication	-	-	-	100%
Use of Medical Imaging				
Combination Abdominal CT Scan	-	-	0.237	0.191
Combination Chest CT Scan	-	-	0.120	0.054
Follow-up Mammogram/Ultrasound	-	-	8.3%	8.4%
MRI for Low Back Pain	-	-	35.2%	32.7%
Survey of Patients' Hospital Experiences				
Area Around Room 'Always' Quiet at Night[8]	-	-	-	58%
Doctors 'Always' Communicated Well[8]	-	-	-	80%
Home Recovery Information Given[8]	-	-	-	82%
Hospital Given 9 or 10 on 10 Point Scale[8]	-	-	-	67%
Meds 'Always' Explained Before Given[8]	-	-	-	60%
Nurses 'Always' Communicated Well[8]	-	-	-	76%
Pain 'Always' Well Controlled[8]	-	-	-	69%
Room and Bathroom 'Always' Clean[8]	-	-	-	71%
Timely Help 'Always' Received[8]	-	-	-	64%
Would Definitely Recommend Hospital[8]	-	-	-	69%

NOTE: Hospital profiles are in alphabetical order by state, then city, then hospital within the city; Rankings exclude hospitals with less than 25 cases except for patient surveys which excludes hospitals with less than 100 cases; (a) 100–299 cases; (1) The number of cases is too small to be sure how well a hospital is performing; (2) The hospital indicated that the data submitted for this measure were based on a sample of cases; (3) Data was collected during a shorter time period (fewer quarters) than the maximum possible time for this measure; (4) Suppressed for one or more quarters by CMS; (5) No data is available from the hospital for this measure; (6) Fewer than 100 patients completed the HCAHPS survey. Use these rates with caution, as the number of surveys may be too low to reliably assess hospital performance; (7) Survey results are based on less than 12 months of data; (8) Survey results are not available for this reporting period; (9) No or very few patients were eligible for the HCAHPS survey. The scores shown, if any, reflect a very small number of surveys; (10) A state average was not calculated because too few hospitals in the state submitted data; (11) There were discrepancies in the data collection process; Please refer to the User's Guide for a full explanation of data.

Saint Francis Hospital Mooresville

1201 Hadley Road Phone: 317-831-1160
Mooresville, IN 46158 Fax: 317-831-9315
URL: www.stfrancishospitals.org
Type: Acute Care Hospitals Emergency Services: No
Ownership: Voluntary Non-Profit - Church Beds: 64

Key Personnel:

CEO/President. . . . . Robert J Brody
Chief of Medical Staff. . . . . Alan Gillespie
Radiology. . . . . Katie Lee, RT(T)

Measure	Cases	This Hosp.	State Avg.	U.S. Avg.
Heart Attack Care				
ACE Inhibitor or ARB for LVSD[1]	1	100%	96%	96%
Aspirin at Arrival[1]	7	100%	98%	99%
Aspirin at Discharge[1]	5	100%	99%	98%
Beta Blocker at Discharge[1]	5	100%	98%	98%
Fibrinolytic Medication Timing	0	-	37%	55%
PCI Within 90 Minutes of Arrival	0	-	93%	90%
Smoking Cessation Advice	0	-	99%	99%
Chest Pain/Possible Heart Attack Care				
Aspirin at Arrival	171	94%	95%	95%
Median Time to ECG (minutes)	177	8	6	8
Median Time to Transfer (minutes)[1,3]	7	33	49	61
Fibrinolytic Medication Timing	0	-	63%	54%
Heart Failure Care				
ACE Inhibitor or ARB for LVSD[1]	9	78%	92%	94%
Discharge Instructions[1]	21	76%	84%	88%
Evaluation of LVS Function	32	97%	98%	98%
Smoking Cessation Advice[1]	2	100%	99%	98%
Pneumonia Care				
Appropriate Initial Antibiotic	73	68%	90%	92%
Blood Culture Timing	60	95%	95%	96%
Influenza Vaccine	44	93%	93%	91%
Initial Antibiotic Timing	86	100%	96%	95%
Pneumococcal Vaccine	65	86%	94%	93%
Smoking Cessation Advice[1]	22	100%	98%	97%
Surgical Care Improvement Project				
Appropriate VTP Within 24 Hours[2]	203	99%	90%	92%
Appropriate Hair Removal[2]	811	100%	100%	99%
Appropriate Beta Blocker Usage[2]	225	83%	93%	93%
Controlled Postoperative Blood Glucose[2]	0	-	93%	93%
Prophylactic Antibiotic Timing[2]	597	98%	97%	97%
Prophylactic Antibiotic Timing (Outpatient)	95	85%	92%	92%
Prophylactic Antibiotic Selection[2]	597	98%	98%	97%
Prophylactic Antibiotic Select. (Outpatient)	89	94%	95%	94%
Prophylactic Antibiotic Stopped[2]	593	95%	95%	94%
Recommended VTP Ordered[2]	203	99%	92%	94%
Urinary Catheter Removal[2]	400	99%	92%	90%
Children's Asthma Care				
Received Systemic Corticosteroids	-	-	-	100%
Received Home Management Plan	-	-	-	71%
Received Reliever Medication	-	-	-	100%
Use of Medical Imaging				
Combination Abdominal CT Scan	313	0.118	0.237	0.191
Combination Chest CT Scan	184	0.120	0.120	0.054
Follow-up Mammogram/Ultrasound	627	6.7%	8.3%	8.4%
MRI for Low Back Pain	79	39.2%	35.2%	32.7%
Survey of Patients' Hospital Experiences				
Area Around Room 'Always' Quiet at Night	300+	65%	-	58%
Doctors 'Always' Communicated Well	300+	83%	-	80%
Home Recovery Information Given	300+	87%	-	82%
Hospital Given 9 or 10 on 10 Point Scale	300+	79%	-	67%
Meds 'Always' Explained Before Given	300+	65%	-	60%
Nurses 'Always' Communicated Well	300+	80%	-	76%
Pain 'Always' Well Controlled	300+	73%	-	69%
Room and Bathroom 'Always' Clean	300+	79%	-	71%
Timely Help 'Always' Received	300+	64%	-	64%
Would Definitely Recommend Hospital	300+	84%	-	69%

Ball Memorial Hospital

2401 University Avenue Phone: 765-747-3111
Muncie, IN 47303 Fax: 765-747-3404
URL: www.accesschs.org/baal-memorial-l
Type: Acute Care Hospitals Emergency Services: Yes
Ownership: Voluntary Non-Profit - Private Beds: 350

Key Personnel:

CEO/President. . . . . Michael Haley
Cardiac Laboratory. . . . . Marian Kritcer
Infection Control. . . . . Michael Langona
Operating Room. . . . . Shirley Foster
Quality Assurance . . . . Mike Hawkins
Radiology. . . . . Charles Leiphart, MD
Emergency Room . . . . John Nahre, MD
Intensive Care Unit. . . . . Alexis Neal

Measure	Cases	This Hosp.	State Avg.	U.S. Avg.
Heart Attack Care				
ACE Inhibitor or ARB for LVSD	74	97%	96%	96%
Aspirin at Arrival	241	99%	98%	99%
Aspirin at Discharge	335	99%	99%	98%
Beta Blocker at Discharge	323	99%	98%	98%
Fibrinolytic Medication Timing	0	-	37%	55%
PCI Within 90 Minutes of Arrival	60	92%	93%	90%
Smoking Cessation Advice	142	99%	99%	99%
Chest Pain/Possible Heart Attack Care				
Aspirin at Arrival[1]	10	100%	95%	95%
Median Time to ECG (minutes)[1]	15	3	6	8
Median Time to Transfer (minutes)[5]	0	-	49	61
Fibrinolytic Medication Timing[3]	0	-	63%	54%
Heart Failure Care				
ACE Inhibitor or ARB for LVSD[2]	104	96%	92%	94%
Discharge Instructions[2]	214	99%	84%	88%
Evaluation of LVS Function[2]	301	99%	98%	98%
Smoking Cessation Advice[2]	52	100%	99%	98%
Pneumonia Care				
Appropriate Initial Antibiotic	203	99%	90%	92%
Blood Culture Timing	328	98%	95%	96%
Influenza Vaccine	279	94%	93%	91%
Initial Antibiotic Timing	299	97%	96%	95%
Pneumococcal Vaccine	363	96%	94%	93%
Smoking Cessation Advice	177	98%	98%	97%
Surgical Care Improvement Project				
Appropriate VTP Within 24 Hours[2]	288	94%	90%	92%
Appropriate Hair Removal[2]	822	100%	100%	99%
Appropriate Beta Blocker Usage[2]	261	100%	93%	93%
Controlled Postoperative Blood Glucose[2]	132	99%	93%	93%
Prophylactic Antibiotic Timing[2]	606	97%	97%	97%
Prophylactic Antibiotic Timing (Outpatient)	504	95%	92%	92%
Prophylactic Antibiotic Selection[2]	613	100%	98%	97%
Prophylactic Antibiotic Select. (Outpatient)	525	98%	95%	94%
Prophylactic Antibiotic Stopped[2]	564	98%	95%	94%
Recommended VTP Ordered[2]	288	95%	92%	94%
Urinary Catheter Removal[2]	228	94%	92%	90%
Children's Asthma Care				
Received Systemic Corticosteroids	-	-	-	100%
Received Home Management Plan	-	-	-	71%
Received Reliever Medication	-	-	-	100%
Use of Medical Imaging				
Combination Abdominal CT Scan	1,127	0.051	0.237	0.191
Combination Chest CT Scan	584	0.053	0.120	0.054
Follow-up Mammogram/Ultrasound	2,460	8.3%	8.3%	8.4%
MRI for Low Back Pain	186	38.2%	35.2%	32.7%
Survey of Patients' Hospital Experiences				
Area Around Room 'Always' Quiet at Night	300+	54%	-	58%
Doctors 'Always' Communicated Well	300+	80%	-	80%
Home Recovery Information Given	300+	84%	-	82%
Hospital Given 9 or 10 on 10 Point Scale	300+	68%	-	67%
Meds 'Always' Explained Before Given	300+	61%	-	60%
Nurses 'Always' Communicated Well	300+	78%	-	76%
Pain 'Always' Well Controlled	300+	74%	-	69%
Room and Bathroom 'Always' Clean	300+	70%	-	71%
Timely Help 'Always' Received	300+	61%	-	64%
Would Definitely Recommend Hospital	300+	65%	-	69%

Community Hospital

901 Mac Arthur Boulevard Phone: 219-836-1600
Munster, IN 46321 Fax: 219-836-6380
URL: www.comhs.org/community
Type: Acute Care Hospitals Emergency Services: Yes
Ownership: Voluntary Non-Profit - Private Beds: 354

Key Personnel:

Quality Assurance . . . . Patricia Baldwin
Emergency Room . . . . Robert L Cavens, MD

Measure	Cases	This Hosp.	State Avg.	U.S. Avg.
Heart Attack Care				
ACE Inhibitor or ARB for LVSD[1]	18	100%	96%	96%
Aspirin at Arrival	164	96%	98%	99%
Aspirin at Discharge	153	98%	99%	98%
Beta Blocker at Discharge	132	96%	98%	98%
Fibrinolytic Medication Timing	0	-	37%	55%
PCI Within 90 Minutes of Arrival	28	93%	93%	90%
Smoking Cessation Advice	51	100%	99%	99%
Chest Pain/Possible Heart Attack Care				
Aspirin at Arrival[1,3]	9	56%	95%	95%
Median Time to ECG (minutes)[1,3]	9	15	6	8
Median Time to Transfer (minutes)[5]	0	-	49	61
Fibrinolytic Medication Timing[5]	0	-	63%	54%
Heart Failure Care				
ACE Inhibitor or ARB for LVSD[2]	67	94%	92%	94%
Discharge Instructions[2]	232	73%	84%	88%
Evaluation of LVS Function[2]	295	96%	98%	98%
Smoking Cessation Advice[2]	38	100%	99%	98%
Pneumonia Care				
Appropriate Initial Antibiotic[2]	81	91%	90%	92%
Blood Culture Timing[2]	147	93%	95%	96%
Influenza Vaccine[2]	90	94%	93%	91%
Initial Antibiotic Timing[2]	156	96%	96%	95%
Pneumococcal Vaccine[2]	138	93%	94%	93%
Smoking Cessation Advice[2]	40	100%	98%	97%
Surgical Care Improvement Project				
Appropriate VTP Within 24 Hours[2]	226	78%	90%	92%
Appropriate Hair Removal[2]	703	100%	100%	99%
Appropriate Beta Blocker Usage[2]	230	90%	93%	93%
Controlled Postoperative Blood Glucose[2]	151	98%	93%	93%
Prophylactic Antibiotic Timing[2]	495	93%	97%	97%
Prophylactic Antibiotic Timing (Outpatient)	589	94%	92%	92%
Prophylactic Antibiotic Selection[2]	502	97%	98%	97%
Prophylactic Antibiotic Select. (Outpatient)	615	96%	95%	94%
Prophylactic Antibiotic Stopped[2]	465	92%	95%	94%
Recommended VTP Ordered[2]	226	84%	92%	94%
Urinary Catheter Removal[2]	138	86%	92%	90%
Children's Asthma Care				
Received Systemic Corticosteroids	-	-	-	100%
Received Home Management Plan	-	-	-	71%
Received Reliever Medication	-	-	-	100%
Use of Medical Imaging				
Combination Abdominal CT Scan	1,973	0.333	0.237	0.191
Combination Chest CT Scan	1,384	0.300	0.120	0.054
Follow-up Mammogram/Ultrasound	2,396	4.3%	8.3%	8.4%
MRI for Low Back Pain	341	35.5%	35.2%	32.7%
Survey of Patients' Hospital Experiences				
Area Around Room 'Always' Quiet at Night	300+	55%	-	58%
Doctors 'Always' Communicated Well	300+	82%	-	80%
Home Recovery Information Given	300+	83%	-	82%
Hospital Given 9 or 10 on 10 Point Scale	300+	77%	-	67%
Meds 'Always' Explained Before Given	300+	65%	-	60%
Nurses 'Always' Communicated Well	300+	82%	-	76%
Pain 'Always' Well Controlled	300+	74%	-	69%
Room and Bathroom 'Always' Clean	300+	78%	-	71%
Timely Help 'Always' Received	300+	69%	-	64%
Would Definitely Recommend Hospital	300+	80%	-	69%

NOTE: Hospital profiles are in alphabetical order by state, then city, then hospital within the city; Rankings exclude hospitals with less than 25 cases except for patient surveys which excludes hospitals with less than 100 cases; (a) 100–299 cases; (1) The number of cases is too small to be sure how well a hospital is performing; (2) The hospital indicated that the data submitted for this measure were based on a sample of cases; (3) Data was collected during a shorter time period (fewer quarters) than the maximum possible time for this measure; (4) Suppressed for one or more quarters by CMS; (5) No data is available from the hospital for this measure; (6) Fewer than 100 patients completed the HCAHPS survey. Use these rates with caution, as the number of surveys may be too low to reliably assess hospital performance; (7) Survey results are based on less than 12 months of data; (8) Survey results are not available for this reporting period; (9) No or very few patients were eligible for the HCAHPS survey. The scores shown, if any, reflect a very small number of surveys; (10) A state average was not calculated because too few hospitals in the state submitted data; (11) There were discrepancies in the data collection process; Please refer to the User's Guide for a full explanation of data.

Franciscan Physicians Hospital

701 Superior Avenue Phone: 219-922-4200
Munster, IN 46321
Type: Acute Care Hospitals Emergency Services: No
Ownership: Voluntary Non-Profit - Private Beds: 63

Measure	Cases	This Hosp.	State Avg.	U.S. Avg.
Heart Attack Care				
ACE Inhibitor or ARB for LVSD[1]	1	100%	96%	96%
Aspirin at Arrival[1]	12	100%	98%	99%
Aspirin at Discharge[1]	8	100%	99%	98%
Beta Blocker at Discharge[1]	10	100%	98%	98%
Fibrinolytic Medication Timing	0	-	37%	55%
PCI Within 90 Minutes of Arrival[1]	1	100%	93%	90%
Smoking Cessation Advice[1]	2	100%	99%	99%
Chest Pain/Possible Heart Attack Care				
Aspirin at Arrival[5]	0	-	95%	95%
Median Time to ECG (minutes)[5]	0	-	6	8
Median Time to Transfer (minutes)[5]	0	-	49	61
Fibrinolytic Medication Timing[5]	0	-	63%	54%
Heart Failure Care				
ACE Inhibitor or ARB for LVSD[1]	17	88%	92%	94%
Discharge Instructions	43	72%	84%	88%
Evaluation of LVS Function	44	98%	98%	98%
Smoking Cessation Advice[1]	5	80%	99%	98%
Pneumonia Care				
Appropriate Initial Antibiotic[1,3]	18	89%	90%	92%
Blood Culture Timing[3]	0	-	95%	96%
Influenza Vaccine[1]	20	85%	93%	91%
Initial Antibiotic Timing[1,3]	22	100%	96%	95%
Pneumococcal Vaccine[1,3]	16	88%	94%	93%
Smoking Cessation Advice[1,3]	5	100%	98%	97%
Surgical Care Improvement Project				
Appropriate VTP Within 24 Hours	40	88%	90%	92%
Appropriate Hair Removal	84	99%	100%	99%
Appropriate Beta Blocker Usage	30	100%	93%	93%
Controlled Postoperative Blood Glucose	26	85%	93%	93%
Prophylactic Antibiotic Timing	52	98%	97%	97%
Prophylactic Antibiotic Timing (Outpatient)	76	95%	92%	92%
Prophylactic Antibiotic Selection	53	98%	98%	97%
Prophylactic Antibiotic Select. (Outpatient)	75	99%	95%	94%
Prophylactic Antibiotic Stopped	48	92%	95%	94%
Recommended VTP Ordered	40	92%	92%	94%
Urinary Catheter Removal[1]	16	69%	92%	90%
Children's Asthma Care				
Received Systemic Corticosteroids	-	-	-	100%
Received Home Management Plan	-	-	-	71%
Received Reliever Medication	-	-	-	100%
Use of Medical Imaging				
Combination Abdominal CT Scan[1]	26	0.808	0.237	0.191
Combination Chest CT Scan[1]	24	0.250	0.120	0.054
Follow-up Mammogram/Ultrasound	60	6.7%	8.3%	8.4%
MRI for Low Back Pain[1]	13	38.5%	35.2%	32.7%
Survey of Patients' Hospital Experiences				
Area Around Room 'Always' Quiet at Night	300+	66%	-	58%
Doctors 'Always' Communicated Well	300+	81%	-	80%
Home Recovery Information Given	300+	83%	-	82%
Hospital Given 9 or 10 on 10 Point Scale	300+	76%	-	67%
Meds 'Always' Explained Before Given	300+	63%	-	60%
Nurses 'Always' Communicated Well	300+	82%	-	76%
Pain 'Always' Well Controlled	300+	73%	-	69%
Room and Bathroom 'Always' Clean	300+	82%	-	71%
Timely Help 'Always' Received	300+	76%	-	64%
Would Definitely Recommend Hospital	300+	74%	-	69%

Surgical Hospital of Munster

7847 Calumet Ave Phone: 219-836-5102
Munster, IN 46321
URL: www.surgicalhospitalmunster.com
Type: Acute Care Hospitals Emergency Services: No
Ownership: Proprietary

Measure	Cases	This Hosp.	State Avg.	U.S. Avg.
Heart Attack Care				
ACE Inhibitor or ARB for LVSD[5]	0	-	96%	96%
Aspirin at Arrival[5]	0	-	98%	99%
Aspirin at Discharge[5]	0	-	99%	98%
Beta Blocker at Discharge[5]	0	-	98%	98%
Fibrinolytic Medication Timing[5]	0	-	37%	55%
PCI Within 90 Minutes of Arrival[5]	0	-	93%	90%
Smoking Cessation Advice[5]	0	-	99%	99%
Chest Pain/Possible Heart Attack Care				
Aspirin at Arrival[5]	0	-	95%	95%
Median Time to ECG (minutes)[5]	0	-	6	8
Median Time to Transfer (minutes)[5]	0	-	49	61
Fibrinolytic Medication Timing[5]	0	-	63%	54%
Heart Failure Care				
ACE Inhibitor or ARB for LVSD[5]	0	-	92%	94%
Discharge Instructions[5]	0	-	84%	88%
Evaluation of LVS Function[5]	0	-	98%	98%
Smoking Cessation Advice[5]	0	-	99%	98%
Pneumonia Care				
Appropriate Initial Antibiotic[5]	0	-	90%	92%
Blood Culture Timing[5]	0	-	95%	96%
Influenza Vaccine[5]	0	-	93%	91%
Initial Antibiotic Timing[5]	0	-	96%	95%
Pneumococcal Vaccine[5]	0	-	94%	93%
Smoking Cessation Advice[5]	0	-	98%	97%
Surgical Care Improvement Project				
Appropriate VTP Within 24 Hours[1,2]	5	100%	90%	92%
Appropriate Hair Removal[2]	80	100%	100%	99%
Appropriate Beta Blocker Usage[1,2]	9	100%	93%	93%
Controlled Postoperative Blood Glucose[2]	0	-	93%	93%
Prophylactic Antibiotic Timing[2]	69	83%	97%	97%
Prophylactic Antibiotic Timing (Outpatient)	30	80%	92%	92%
Prophylactic Antibiotic Selection[2]	69	72%	98%	97%
Prophylactic Antibiotic Select. (Outpatient)	27	96%	95%	94%
Prophylactic Antibiotic Stopped[2]	69	100%	95%	94%
Recommended VTP Ordered[1,2]	5	100%	92%	94%
Urinary Catheter Removal[1,2]	17	94%	92%	90%
Children's Asthma Care				
Received Systemic Corticosteroids	-	-	-	100%
Received Home Management Plan	-	-	-	71%
Received Reliever Medication	-	-	-	100%
Use of Medical Imaging				
Combination Abdominal CT Scan[5]	0	-	0.237	0.191
Combination Chest CT Scan[5]	0	-	0.120	0.054
Follow-up Mammogram/Ultrasound[5]	0	-	8.3%	8.4%
MRI for Low Back Pain[5]	0	-	35.2%	32.7%
Survey of Patients' Hospital Experiences				
Area Around Room 'Always' Quiet at Night[6]	<100	90%	-	58%
Doctors 'Always' Communicated Well[6]	<100	89%	-	80%
Home Recovery Information Given[6]	<100	92%	-	82%
Hospital Given 9 or 10 on 10 Point Scale[6]	<100	90%	-	67%
Meds 'Always' Explained Before Given[6]	<100	82%	-	60%
Nurses 'Always' Communicated Well[6]	<100	92%	-	76%
Pain 'Always' Well Controlled[6]	<100	86%	-	69%
Room and Bathroom 'Always' Clean[6]	<100	87%	-	71%
Timely Help 'Always' Received[6]	<100	92%	-	64%
Would Definitely Recommend Hospital	<100	91%	-	69%

Floyd Memorial Hospital and Health Services

1850 State Street Phone: 812-949-5500
New Albany, IN 47150 Fax: 812-949-5607
URL: www.floydmedical.org
Type: Acute Care Hospitals Emergency Services: Yes
Ownership: Government - Local Beds: 245

Key Personnel:
CEO/President. . . . . Bryant R Hanson
Operating Room. . . . . Paul Bennett Brock
Pediatric Ambulatory Care . . . . . . Stuart Eldridge, MD
Pediatric In-Patient Care . . . . Stuart Eldridge, MD
Quality Assurance . . . . Carol Mullen, RN
Radiology. . . . . Damon Andrew Black, MD
Emergency Room . . . . Ruth Heideman

Measure	Cases	This Hosp.	State Avg.	U.S. Avg.
Heart Attack Care				
ACE Inhibitor or ARB for LVSD	83	96%	96%	96%
Aspirin at Arrival	257	100%	98%	99%
Aspirin at Discharge	298	98%	99%	98%
Beta Blocker at Discharge	273	98%	98%	98%
Fibrinolytic Medication Timing	0	-	37%	55%
PCI Within 90 Minutes of Arrival	51	94%	93%	90%
Smoking Cessation Advice	113	100%	99%	99%
Chest Pain/Possible Heart Attack Care				
Aspirin at Arrival[1,3]	1	100%	95%	95%
Median Time to ECG (minutes)[1,3]	1	39	6	8
Median Time to Transfer (minutes)[5]	0	-	49	61
Fibrinolytic Medication Timing[5]	0	-	63%	54%
Heart Failure Care				
ACE Inhibitor or ARB for LVSD	95	89%	92%	94%
Discharge Instructions	286	90%	84%	88%
Evaluation of LVS Function	388	97%	98%	98%
Smoking Cessation Advice	63	100%	99%	98%
Pneumonia Care				
Appropriate Initial Antibiotic	216	93%	90%	92%
Blood Culture Timing	424	97%	95%	96%
Influenza Vaccine	325	85%	93%	91%
Initial Antibiotic Timing	376	97%	96%	95%
Pneumococcal Vaccine	386	95%	94%	93%
Smoking Cessation Advice	186	99%	98%	97%
Surgical Care Improvement Project				
Appropriate VTP Within 24 Hours	234	79%	90%	92%
Appropriate Hair Removal	741	100%	100%	99%
Appropriate Beta Blocker Usage	242	100%	93%	93%
Controlled Postoperative Blood Glucose	144	94%	93%	93%
Prophylactic Antibiotic Timing	441	96%	97%	97%
Prophylactic Antibiotic Timing (Outpatient)	327	97%	92%	92%
Prophylactic Antibiotic Selection	444	98%	98%	97%
Prophylactic Antibiotic Select. (Outpatient)	317	89%	95%	94%
Prophylactic Antibiotic Stopped	407	90%	95%	94%
Recommended VTP Ordered	235	81%	92%	94%
Urinary Catheter Removal	178	96%	92%	90%
Children's Asthma Care				
Received Systemic Corticosteroids	-	-	-	100%
Received Home Management Plan	-	-	-	71%
Received Reliever Medication	-	-	-	100%
Use of Medical Imaging				
Combination Abdominal CT Scan	1,127	0.648	0.237	0.191
Combination Chest CT Scan	889	0.043	0.120	0.054
Follow-up Mammogram/Ultrasound	1,540	8.5%	8.3%	8.4%
MRI for Low Back Pain	188	31.9%	35.2%	32.7%
Survey of Patients' Hospital Experiences				
Area Around Room 'Always' Quiet at Night	300+	65%	-	58%
Doctors 'Always' Communicated Well	300+	83%	-	80%
Home Recovery Information Given	300+	82%	-	82%
Hospital Given 9 or 10 on 10 Point Scale	300+	80%	-	67%
Meds 'Always' Explained Before Given	300+	59%	-	60%
Nurses 'Always' Communicated Well	300+	79%	-	76%
Pain 'Always' Well Controlled	300+	68%	-	69%
Room and Bathroom 'Always' Clean	300+	71%	-	71%
Timely Help 'Always' Received	300+	69%	-	64%
Would Definitely Recommend Hospital	300+	82%	-	69%

NOTE: Hospital profiles are in alphabetical order by state, then city, then hospital within the city; Rankings exclude hospitals with less than 25 cases except for patient surveys which excludes hospitals with less than 100 cases; (a) 100–299 cases; (1) The number of cases is too small to be sure how well a hospital is performing; (2) The hospital indicated that the data submitted for this measure were based on a sample of cases; (3) Data was collected during a shorter time period (fewer quarters) than the maximum possible time for this measure; (4) Suppressed for one or more quarters by CMS; (5) No data is available from the hospital for this measure; (6) Fewer than 100 patients completed the HCAHPS survey. Use these rates with caution, as the number of surveys may be too low to reliably assess hospital performance; (7) Survey results are based on less than 12 months of data; (8) Survey results are not available for this reporting period; (9) No or very few patients were eligible for the HCAHPS survey. The scores shown, if any, reflect a very small number of surveys; (10) A state average was not calculated because too few hospitals in the state submitted data; (11) There were discrepancies in the data collection process; Please refer to the User's Guide for a full explanation of data.

Physicians' Medical Center

4023 Reas Lane
New Albany, IN 47150
Phone: 812-206-7660
URL: pmcdev.interactivemedialab.com
Type: Acute Care Hospitals
Emergency Services: No
Ownership: Proprietary

Measure	Cases	This Hosp.	State Avg.	U.S. Avg.
Heart Attack Care				
ACE Inhibitor or ARB for LVSD[5]	0	-	96%	96%
Aspirin at Arrival[5]	0	-	98%	99%
Aspirin at Discharge[5]	0	-	99%	98%
Beta Blocker at Discharge[5]	0	-	98%	98%
Fibrinolytic Medication Timing[5]	0	-	37%	55%
PCI Within 90 Minutes of Arrival[5]	0	-	93%	90%
Smoking Cessation Advice[5]	0	-	99%	99%
Chest Pain/Possible Heart Attack Care				
Aspirin at Arrival[5]	0	-	95%	95%
Median Time to ECG (minutes)[5]	0	-	6	8
Median Time to Transfer (minutes)[5]	0	-	49	61
Fibrinolytic Medication Timing[5]	0	-	63%	54%
Heart Failure Care				
ACE Inhibitor or ARB for LVSD[5]	0	-	92%	94%
Discharge Instructions[5]	0	-	84%	88%
Evaluation of LVS Function[5]	0	-	98%	98%
Smoking Cessation Advice[5]	0	-	99%	98%
Pneumonia Care				
Appropriate Initial Antibiotic[5]	0	-	90%	92%
Blood Culture Timing[5]	0	-	95%	96%
Influenza Vaccine[5]	0	-	93%	91%
Initial Antibiotic Timing[5]	0	-	96%	95%
Pneumococcal Vaccine[5]	0	-	94%	93%
Smoking Cessation Advice[5]	0	-	98%	97%
Surgical Care Improvement Project				
Appropriate VTP Within 24 Hours[1,2]	8	100%	90%	92%
Appropriate Hair Removal[2]	152	99%	100%	99%
Appropriate Beta Blocker Usage[2]	28	79%	93%	93%
Controlled Postoperative Blood Glucose[2]	0	-	93%	93%
Prophylactic Antibiotic Timing[2]	143	97%	97%	97%
Prophylactic Antibiotic Timing (Outpatient)	187	91%	92%	92%
Prophylactic Antibiotic Selection[2]	143	87%	98%	97%
Prophylactic Antibiotic Select. (Outpatient)	194	79%	95%	94%
Prophylactic Antibiotic Stopped[2]	143	99%	95%	94%
Recommended VTP Ordered[1,2]	8	100%	92%	94%
Urinary Catheter Removal[2]	41	90%	92%	90%
Children's Asthma Care				
Received Systemic Corticosteroids	-	-	-	100%
Received Home Management Plan	-	-	-	71%
Received Reliever Medication	-	-	-	100%
Use of Medical Imaging				
Combination Abdominal CT Scan[5]	0	-	0.237	0.191
Combination Chest CT Scan[5]	0	-	0.120	0.054
Follow-up Mammogram/Ultrasound[5]	0	-	8.3%	8.4%
MRI for Low Back Pain[5]	0	-	35.2%	32.7%
Survey of Patients' Hospital Experiences				
Area Around Room 'Always' Quiet at Night	(a)	84%	-	58%
Doctors 'Always' Communicated Well	(a)	91%	-	80%
Home Recovery Information Given	(a)	85%	-	82%
Hospital Given 9 or 10 on 10 Point Scale	(a)	83%	-	67%
Meds 'Always' Explained Before Given	(a)	75%	-	60%
Nurses 'Always' Communicated Well	(a)	84%	-	76%
Pain 'Always' Well Controlled	(a)	77%	-	69%
Room and Bathroom 'Always' Clean	(a)	75%	-	71%
Timely Help 'Always' Received	(a)	83%	-	64%
Would Definitely Recommend Hospital	(a)	83%	-	69%

Henry County Memorial Hospital

1000 N 16th St
New Castle, IN 47362
Phone: 765-521-0890
Fax: 765-521-1555
URL: www.hcmhcares.org
Type: Acute Care Hospitals
Emergency Services: Yes
Ownership: Government - Local
Beds: 107

Key Personnel:
CEO/President. . . . . Blake Dye
Operating Room. . . . . Sandy Campbell, RN
Quality Assurance . . . . Chuck Butler
Radiology. . . . . Randall Fields
Emergency Room . . . . Mark Doyle

Measure	Cases	This Hosp.	State Avg.	U.S. Avg.
Heart Attack Care				
ACE Inhibitor or ARB for LVSD[1]	1	100%	96%	96%
Aspirin at Arrival[1]	10	100%	98%	99%
Aspirin at Discharge[1]	5	100%	99%	98%
Beta Blocker at Discharge[1]	5	100%	98%	98%
Fibrinolytic Medication Timing	0	-	37%	55%
PCI Within 90 Minutes of Arrival	0	-	93%	90%
Smoking Cessation Advice[1]	1	100%	99%	99%
Chest Pain/Possible Heart Attack Care				
Aspirin at Arrival	240	97%	95%	95%
Median Time to ECG (minutes)	268	4	6	8
Median Time to Transfer (minutes)[1]	4	22	49	61
Fibrinolytic Medication Timing[1]	1	100%	63%	54%
Heart Failure Care				
ACE Inhibitor or ARB for LVSD	38	100%	92%	94%
Discharge Instructions	80	95%	84%	88%
Evaluation of LVS Function	111	100%	98%	98%
Smoking Cessation Advice[1]	24	100%	99%	98%
Pneumonia Care				
Appropriate Initial Antibiotic	106	93%	90%	92%
Blood Culture Timing	112	96%	95%	96%
Influenza Vaccine	78	100%	93%	91%
Initial Antibiotic Timing	157	99%	96%	95%
Pneumococcal Vaccine	121	100%	94%	93%
Smoking Cessation Advice	57	100%	98%	97%
Surgical Care Improvement Project				
Appropriate VTP Within 24 Hours	111	95%	90%	92%
Appropriate Hair Removal	359	100%	100%	99%
Appropriate Beta Blocker Usage	177	97%	93%	93%
Controlled Postoperative Blood Glucose	0	-	93%	93%
Prophylactic Antibiotic Timing	276	99%	97%	97%
Prophylactic Antibiotic Timing (Outpatient)	157	95%	92%	92%
Prophylactic Antibiotic Selection	279	100%	98%	97%
Prophylactic Antibiotic Select. (Outpatient)	151	95%	95%	94%
Prophylactic Antibiotic Stopped	266	98%	95%	94%
Recommended VTP Ordered	111	95%	92%	94%
Urinary Catheter Removal	45	98%	92%	90%
Children's Asthma Care				
Received Systemic Corticosteroids	-	-	-	100%
Received Home Management Plan	-	-	-	71%
Received Reliever Medication	-	-	-	100%
Use of Medical Imaging				
Combination Abdominal CT Scan	629	0.060	0.237	0.191
Combination Chest CT Scan	299	0.027	0.120	0.054
Follow-up Mammogram/Ultrasound	1,010	4.1%	8.3%	8.4%
MRI for Low Back Pain	136	35.3%	35.2%	32.7%
Survey of Patients' Hospital Experiences				
Area Around Room 'Always' Quiet at Night	300+	58%	-	58%
Doctors 'Always' Communicated Well	300+	83%	-	80%
Home Recovery Information Given	300+	85%	-	82%
Hospital Given 9 or 10 on 10 Point Scale	300+	71%	-	67%
Meds 'Always' Explained Before Given	300+	64%	-	60%
Nurses 'Always' Communicated Well	300+	81%	-	76%
Pain 'Always' Well Controlled	300+	74%	-	69%
Room and Bathroom 'Always' Clean	300+	75%	-	71%
Timely Help 'Always' Received	300+	66%	-	64%
Would Definitely Recommend Hospital	300+	70%	-	69%

The Heart Hospital at Deaconess Gateway

4007 Gateway Blvd
Newburgh, IN 47630
Phone: 812-842-4784
URL: www.deaconess.com
Type: Acute Care Hospitals
Emergency Services: No
Ownership: Proprietary
Beds: 145

Measure	Cases	This Hosp.	State Avg.	U.S. Avg.
Heart Attack Care				
ACE Inhibitor or ARB for LVSD[3]	27	89%	96%	96%
Aspirin at Arrival[1,3]	2	100%	98%	99%
Aspirin at Discharge[3]	136	99%	99%	98%
Beta Blocker at Discharge[3]	139	96%	98%	98%
Fibrinolytic Medication Timing[3]	0	-	37%	55%
PCI Within 90 Minutes of Arrival[3]	0	-	93%	90%
Smoking Cessation Advice[3]	54	91%	99%	99%
Chest Pain/Possible Heart Attack Care				
Aspirin at Arrival[5]	0	-	95%	95%
Median Time to ECG (minutes)[5]	0	-	6	8
Median Time to Transfer (minutes)[5]	0	-	49	61
Fibrinolytic Medication Timing[5]	0	-	63%	54%
Heart Failure Care				
ACE Inhibitor or ARB for LVSD[1,3]	24	67%	92%	94%
Discharge Instructions[3]	54	69%	84%	88%
Evaluation of LVS Function[3]	70	94%	98%	98%
Smoking Cessation Advice[1,3]	21	90%	99%	98%
Pneumonia Care				
Appropriate Initial Antibiotic[3]	0	-	90%	92%
Blood Culture Timing[3]	0	-	95%	96%
Influenza Vaccine[1]	3	100%	93%	91%
Initial Antibiotic Timing[3]	0	-	96%	95%
Pneumococcal Vaccine[1,3]	2	50%	94%	93%
Smoking Cessation Advice[1,3]	2	100%	98%	97%
Surgical Care Improvement Project				
Appropriate VTP Within 24 Hours[1,2,3]	4	100%	90%	92%
Appropriate Hair Removal[2,3]	171	99%	100%	99%
Appropriate Beta Blocker Usage[2,3]	95	87%	93%	93%
Controlled Postoperative Blood Glucose[2,3]	163	95%	93%	93%
Prophylactic Antibiotic Timing[2,3]	102	90%	97%	97%
Prophylactic Antibiotic Timing (Outpatient)[3]	128	70%	92%	92%
Prophylactic Antibiotic Selection[2,3]	106	100%	98%	97%
Prophylactic Antibiotic Select. (Outpatient)[3]	128	98%	95%	94%
Prophylactic Antibiotic Stopped[2,3]	100	87%	95%	94%
Recommended VTP Ordered[1,2,3]	4	100%	92%	94%
Urinary Catheter Removal[2]	99	98%	92%	90%
Children's Asthma Care				
Received Systemic Corticosteroids	-	-	-	100%
Received Home Management Plan	-	-	-	71%
Received Reliever Medication	-	-	-	100%
Use of Medical Imaging				
Combination Abdominal CT Scan[5]	0	-	0.237	0.191
Combination Chest CT Scan[5]	0	-	0.120	0.054
Follow-up Mammogram/Ultrasound[5]	0	-	8.3%	8.4%
MRI for Low Back Pain[5]	0	-	35.2%	32.7%
Survey of Patients' Hospital Experiences				
Area Around Room 'Always' Quiet at Night[8]	-	-	-	58%
Doctors 'Always' Communicated Well[8]	-	-	-	80%
Home Recovery Information Given[8]	-	-	-	82%
Hospital Given 9 or 10 on 10 Point Scale[8]	-	-	-	67%
Meds 'Always' Explained Before Given[8]	-	-	-	60%
Nurses 'Always' Communicated Well[8]	-	-	-	76%
Pain 'Always' Well Controlled[8]	-	-	-	69%
Room and Bathroom 'Always' Clean[8]	-	-	-	71%
Timely Help 'Always' Received[8]	-	-	-	64%
Would Definitely Recommend Hospital[8]	-	-	-	69%

NOTE: Hospital profiles are in alphabetical order by state, then city, then hospital within the city; Rankings exclude hospitals with less than 25 cases except for patient surveys which excludes hospitals with less than 100 cases; (a) 100–299 cases; (1) The number of cases is too small to be sure how well a hospital is performing; (2) The hospital indicated that the data submitted for this measure were based on a sample of cases; (3) Data was collected during a shorter time period (fewer quarters) than the maximum possible time for this measure; (4) Suppressed for one or more quarters by CMS; (5) No data is available from the hospital for this measure; (6) Fewer than 100 patients completed the HCAHPS survey. Use these rates with caution, as the number of surveys may be too low to reliably assess hospital performance; (7) Survey results are based on less than 12 months of data; (8) Survey results are not available for this reporting period; (9) No or very few patients were eligible for the HCAHPS survey. The scores shown, if any, reflect a very small number of surveys; (10) A state average was not calculated because too few hospitals in the state submitted data; (11) There were discrepancies in the data collection process; Please refer to the User's Guide for a full explanation of data.

The Women's Hospital

4199 Gateway Blvd
Newburgh, IN 47630
Phone: 812-842-4200
URL: www.deaconess.com
Type: Acute Care Hospitals
Emergency Services: No
Ownership: Proprietary
Key Personnel:
CEO/President. . . . . Christina Ryan

Measure	Cases	This Hosp.	State Avg.	U.S. Avg.
Heart Attack Care				
ACE Inhibitor or ARB for LVSD[5]	0	-	96%	96%
Aspirin at Arrival[5]	0	-	98%	99%
Aspirin at Discharge[5]	0	-	99%	98%
Beta Blocker at Discharge[5]	0	-	98%	98%
Fibrinolytic Medication Timing[5]	0	-	37%	55%
PCI Within 90 Minutes of Arrival[5]	0	-	93%	90%
Smoking Cessation Advice[5]	0	-	99%	99%
Chest Pain/Possible Heart Attack Care				
Aspirin at Arrival[5]	0	-	95%	95%
Median Time to ECG (minutes)[5]	0	-	6	8
Median Time to Transfer (minutes)[5]	0	-	49	61
Fibrinolytic Medication Timing[5]	0	-	63%	54%
Heart Failure Care				
ACE Inhibitor or ARB for LVSD[5]	0	-	92%	94%
Discharge Instructions[5]	0	-	84%	88%
Evaluation of LVS Function[5]	0	-	98%	98%
Smoking Cessation Advice[5]	0	-	99%	98%
Pneumonia Care				
Appropriate Initial Antibiotic[5]	0	-	90%	92%
Blood Culture Timing[5]	0	-	95%	96%
Influenza Vaccine[5]	0	-	93%	91%
Initial Antibiotic Timing[5]	0	-	96%	95%
Pneumococcal Vaccine[5]	0	-	94%	93%
Smoking Cessation Advice[5]	0	-	98%	97%
Surgical Care Improvement Project				
Appropriate VTP Within 24 Hours[1]	19	95%	90%	92%
Appropriate Hair Removal	189	100%	100%	99%
Appropriate Beta Blocker Usage[1]	20	100%	93%	93%
Controlled Postoperative Blood Glucose	0	-	93%	93%
Prophylactic Antibiotic Timing	141	94%	97%	97%
Prophylactic Antibiotic Timing (Outpatient)	474	98%	92%	92%
Prophylactic Antibiotic Selection	141	99%	98%	97%
Prophylactic Antibiotic Select. (Outpatient)	473	97%	95%	94%
Prophylactic Antibiotic Stopped	133	97%	95%	94%
Recommended VTP Ordered[1]	19	95%	92%	94%
Urinary Catheter Removal[1]	2	100%	92%	90%
Children's Asthma Care				
Received Systemic Corticosteroids	-	-	-	100%
Received Home Management Plan	-	-	-	71%
Received Reliever Medication	-	-	-	100%
Use of Medical Imaging				
Combination Abdominal CT Scan[5]	0	-	0.237	0.191
Combination Chest CT Scan[5]	0	-	0.120	0.054
Follow-up Mammogram/Ultrasound[5]	0	-	8.3%	8.4%
MRI for Low Back Pain[5]	0	-	35.2%	32.7%
Survey of Patients' Hospital Experiences				
Area Around Room 'Always' Quiet at Night	300+	69%	-	58%
Doctors 'Always' Communicated Well	300+	84%	-	80%
Home Recovery Information Given	300+	88%	-	82%
Hospital Given 9 or 10 on 10 Point Scale	300+	86%	-	67%
Meds 'Always' Explained Before Given	300+	57%	-	60%
Nurses 'Always' Communicated Well	300+	79%	-	76%
Pain 'Always' Well Controlled	300+	72%	-	69%
Room and Bathroom 'Always' Clean	300+	82%	-	71%
Timely Help 'Always' Received	300+	67%	-	64%
Would Definitely Recommend Hospital	300+	86%	-	69%

Riverview Hospital

395 Westfield Rd
Noblesville, IN 46060
Phone: 317-776-7108
Fax: 317-776-7134
URL: www.riverviewhospital.org
Type: Acute Care Hospitals
Emergency Services: Yes
Ownership: Government - Local
Beds: 161
Key Personnel:
CEO/President. . . . . Patricia K Fox
Radiology. Eric Beltz
Patient Relations . . . . Jared Stark

Measure	Cases	This Hosp.	State Avg.	U.S. Avg.
Heart Attack Care				
ACE Inhibitor or ARB for LVSD[1]	21	100%	96%	96%
Aspirin at Arrival	101	100%	98%	99%
Aspirin at Discharge	97	100%	99%	98%
Beta Blocker at Discharge	97	100%	98%	98%
Fibrinolytic Medication Timing	0	-	37%	55%
PCI Within 90 Minutes of Arrival	28	93%	93%	90%
Smoking Cessation Advice	35	100%	99%	99%
Chest Pain/Possible Heart Attack Care				
Aspirin at Arrival[1,3]	2	100%	95%	95%
Median Time to ECG (minutes)[1,3]	2	2	6	8
Median Time to Transfer (minutes)[5]	0	-	49	61
Fibrinolytic Medication Timing[5]	0	-	63%	54%
Heart Failure Care				
ACE Inhibitor or ARB for LVSD	34	97%	92%	94%
Discharge Instructions	66	92%	84%	88%
Evaluation of LVS Function	110	99%	98%	98%
Smoking Cessation Advice[1]	15	100%	99%	98%
Pneumonia Care				
Appropriate Initial Antibiotic	86	84%	90%	92%
Blood Culture Timing	114	96%	95%	96%
Influenza Vaccine	99	98%	93%	91%
Initial Antibiotic Timing	125	95%	96%	95%
Pneumococcal Vaccine	123	96%	94%	93%
Smoking Cessation Advice	35	97%	98%	97%
Surgical Care Improvement Project				
Appropriate VTP Within 24 Hours	140	97%	90%	92%
Appropriate Hair Removal	569	100%	100%	99%
Appropriate Beta Blocker Usage	178	98%	93%	93%
Controlled Postoperative Blood Glucose	46	89%	93%	93%
Prophylactic Antibiotic Timing	403	99%	97%	97%
Prophylactic Antibiotic Timing (Outpatient)	177	99%	92%	92%
Prophylactic Antibiotic Selection	402	98%	98%	97%
Prophylactic Antibiotic Select. (Outpatient)	176	94%	95%	94%
Prophylactic Antibiotic Stopped	390	93%	95%	94%
Recommended VTP Ordered	140	97%	92%	94%
Urinary Catheter Removal	167	98%	92%	90%
Children's Asthma Care				
Received Systemic Corticosteroids	-	-	-	100%
Received Home Management Plan	-	-	-	71%
Received Reliever Medication	-	-	-	100%
Use of Medical Imaging				
Combination Abdominal CT Scan	544	0.059	0.237	0.191
Combination Chest CT Scan	435	0.016	0.120	0.054
Follow-up Mammogram/Ultrasound	1,032	9.7%	8.3%	8.4%
MRI for Low Back Pain	126	31.0%	35.2%	32.7%
Survey of Patients' Hospital Experiences				
Area Around Room 'Always' Quiet at Night	300+	57%	-	58%
Doctors 'Always' Communicated Well	300+	82%	-	80%
Home Recovery Information Given	300+	86%	-	82%
Hospital Given 9 or 10 on 10 Point Scale	300+	72%	-	67%
Meds 'Always' Explained Before Given	300+	64%	-	60%
Nurses 'Always' Communicated Well	300+	76%	-	76%
Pain 'Always' Well Controlled	300+	71%	-	69%
Room and Bathroom 'Always' Clean	300+	76%	-	71%
Timely Help 'Always' Received	300+	62%	-	64%
Would Definitely Recommend Hospital	300+	72%	-	69%

Saint Vincent Jennings Hospital

301 Henry St
North Vernon, IN 47265
Phone: 812-352-4200
Fax: 812-352-4201
URL: www.stvincent.org/faccen/jennings
Type: Critical Access Hospitals
Emergency Services: Yes
Ownership: Voluntary Non-Profit - Church
Beds: 25
Key Personnel:
CEO/President. . . . . Anthony R Tersigni, EdD
Chief of Medical Staff . . . . Rashid Alsabeh, MD
Quality Assurance . . . . John D Doyle
Radiology. Thomas M Ralston, MD

Measure	Cases	This Hosp.	State Avg.	U.S. Avg.
Heart Attack Care				
ACE Inhibitor or ARB for LVSD[3]	0	-	96%	96%
Aspirin at Arrival[3]	0	-	98%	99%
Aspirin at Discharge[3]	0	-	99%	98%
Beta Blocker at Discharge[3]	0	-	98%	98%
Fibrinolytic Medication Timing[3]	0	-	37%	55%
PCI Within 90 Minutes of Arrival[5]	0	-	93%	90%
Smoking Cessation Advice[3]	0	-	99%	99%
Chest Pain/Possible Heart Attack Care				
Aspirin at Arrival	-	-	95%	95%
Median Time to ECG (minutes)	-	-	6	8
Median Time to Transfer (minutes)	-	-	49	61
Fibrinolytic Medication Timing	-	-	63%	54%
Heart Failure Care				
ACE Inhibitor or ARB for LVSD[1]	8	100%	92%	94%
Discharge Instructions[1]	7	43%	84%	88%
Evaluation of LVS Function[1]	8	100%	98%	98%
Smoking Cessation Advice[1]	4	100%	99%	98%
Pneumonia Care				
Appropriate Initial Antibiotic[3]	30	83%	90%	92%
Blood Culture Timing[1,3]	13	69%	95%	96%
Influenza Vaccine[1,3]	8	100%	93%	91%
Initial Antibiotic Timing[1,3]	23	83%	96%	95%
Pneumococcal Vaccine[1,3]	23	91%	94%	93%
Smoking Cessation Advice[1,3]	9	100%	98%	97%
Surgical Care Improvement Project				
Appropriate VTP Within 24 Hours[5]	0	-	90%	92%
Appropriate Hair Removal[5]	0	-	100%	99%
Appropriate Beta Blocker Usage[5]	0	-	93%	93%
Controlled Postoperative Blood Glucose[5]	0	-	93%	93%
Prophylactic Antibiotic Timing[5]	0	-	97%	97%
Prophylactic Antibiotic Timing (Outpatient)	-	-	92%	92%
Prophylactic Antibiotic Selection[5]	0	-	98%	97%
Prophylactic Antibiotic Select. (Outpatient)	-	-	95%	94%
Prophylactic Antibiotic Stopped[5]	0	-	95%	94%
Recommended VTP Ordered[5]	0	-	92%	94%
Urinary Catheter Removal[5]	0	-	92%	90%
Children's Asthma Care				
Received Systemic Corticosteroids	-	-	-	100%
Received Home Management Plan	-	-	-	71%
Received Reliever Medication	-	-	-	100%
Use of Medical Imaging				
Combination Abdominal CT Scan	-	-	0.237	0.191
Combination Chest CT Scan	-	-	0.120	0.054
Follow-up Mammogram/Ultrasound	-	-	8.3%	8.4%
MRI for Low Back Pain	-	-	35.2%	32.7%
Survey of Patients' Hospital Experiences				
Area Around Room 'Always' Quiet at Night[6]	<100	63%	-	58%
Doctors 'Always' Communicated Well[6]	<100	85%	-	80%
Home Recovery Information Given[6]	<100	77%	-	82%
Hospital Given 9 or 10 on 10 Point Scale[6]	<100	64%	-	67%
Meds 'Always' Explained Before Given[6]	<100	66%	-	60%
Nurses 'Always' Communicated Well[6]	<100	86%	-	76%
Pain 'Always' Well Controlled[6]	<100	75%	-	69%
Room and Bathroom 'Always' Clean[6]	<100	94%	-	71%
Timely Help 'Always' Received[6]	<100	80%	-	64%
Would Definitely Recommend Hospital	<100	70%	-	69%

NOTE: Hospital profiles are in alphabetical order by state, then city, then hospital within the city; Rankings exclude hospitals with less than 25 cases except for patient surveys which excludes hospitals with less than 100 cases; (a) 100–299 cases; (1) The number of cases is too small to be sure how well a hospital is performing; (2) The hospital indicated that the data submitted for this measure were based on a sample of cases; (3) Data was collected during a shorter time period (fewer quarters) than the maximum possible time for this measure; (4) Suppressed for one or more quarters by CMS; (5) No data is available from the hospital for this measure; (6) Fewer than 100 patients completed the HCAHPS survey. Use these rates with caution, as the number of surveys may be too low to reliably assess hospital performance; (7) Survey results are based on less than 12 months of data; (8) Survey results are not available for this reporting period; (9) No or very few patients were eligible for the HCAHPS survey. The scores shown, if any, reflect a very small number of surveys; (10) A state average was not calculated because too few hospitals in the state submitted data; (11) There were discrepancies in the data collection process; Please refer to the User's Guide for a full explanation of data.

Dukes Memorial Hospital

275 W 12th Street
Peru, IN 46970
Phone: 765-472-8000
Fax: 765-473-8244
URL: www.dukesmemorialhosp.com
Type: Critical Access Hospitals
Emergency Services: Yes
Ownership: Voluntary Non-Profit - Private
Beds: 158

Key Personnel:
CEO/President. . . . . Mike Funk
Chief of Medical Staff . . . . Neil J Stalker
Infection Control. . . . . Gail Berkheiser
Emergency Room . . . . Fran Owens
Intensive Care Unit. . . . . Sally Piper

Measure	Cases	This Hosp.	State Avg.	U.S. Avg.
Heart Attack Care				
ACE Inhibitor or ARB for LVSD	0	-	96%	96%
Aspirin at Arrival[1]	5	80%	98%	99%
Aspirin at Discharge[1]	3	100%	99%	98%
Beta Blocker at Discharge[1]	3	67%	98%	98%
Fibrinolytic Medication Timing	0	-	37%	55%
PCI Within 90 Minutes of Arrival	0	-	93%	90%
Smoking Cessation Advice	0	-	99%	99%
Chest Pain/Possible Heart Attack Care				
Aspirin at Arrival	172	98%	95%	95%
Median Time to ECG (minutes)	181	7	6	8
Median Time to Transfer (minutes)[1]	18	50	49	61
Fibrinolytic Medication Timing	0	-	63%	54%
Heart Failure Care				
ACE Inhibitor or ARB for LVSD[1]	9	100%	92%	94%
Discharge Instructions[1]	20	95%	84%	88%
Evaluation of LVS Function	31	94%	98%	98%
Smoking Cessation Advice[1]	3	100%	99%	98%
Pneumonia Care				
Appropriate Initial Antibiotic	36	97%	90%	92%
Blood Culture Timing	36	97%	95%	96%
Influenza Vaccine	37	86%	93%	91%
Initial Antibiotic Timing	54	100%	96%	95%
Pneumococcal Vaccine	51	94%	94%	93%
Smoking Cessation Advice[1]	19	100%	98%	97%
Surgical Care Improvement Project				
Appropriate VTP Within 24 Hours[1]	11	64%	90%	92%
Appropriate Hair Removal[1]	22	100%	100%	99%
Appropriate Beta Blocker Usage[1]	4	100%	93%	93%
Controlled Postoperative Blood Glucose	0	-	93%	93%
Prophylactic Antibiotic Timing[1]	12	92%	97%	97%
Prophylactic Antibiotic Timing (Outpatient)	46	100%	92%	92%
Prophylactic Antibiotic Selection[1]	11	91%	98%	97%
Prophylactic Antibiotic Select. (Outpatient)	46	98%	95%	94%
Prophylactic Antibiotic Stopped[1]	11	91%	95%	94%
Recommended VTP Ordered[1]	11	82%	92%	94%
Urinary Catheter Removal[1]	2	100%	92%	90%
Children's Asthma Care				
Received Systemic Corticosteroids	-	-	-	100%
Received Home Management Plan	-	-	-	71%
Received Reliever Medication	-	-	-	100%
Use of Medical Imaging				
Combination Abdominal CT Scan	249	0.032	0.237	0.191
Combination Chest CT Scan	208	0.019	0.120	0.054
Follow-up Mammogram/Ultrasound	299	6.4%	8.3%	8.4%
MRI for Low Back Pain	54	31.5%	35.2%	32.7%
Survey of Patients' Hospital Experiences				
Area Around Room 'Always' Quiet at Night	(a)	65%	-	58%
Doctors 'Always' Communicated Well	(a)	83%	-	80%
Home Recovery Information Given	(a)	88%	-	82%
Hospital Given 9 or 10 on 10 Point Scale	(a)	64%	-	67%
Meds 'Always' Explained Before Given	(a)	65%	-	60%
Nurses 'Always' Communicated Well	(a)	77%	-	76%
Pain 'Always' Well Controlled	(a)	75%	-	69%
Room and Bathroom 'Always' Clean	(a)	67%	-	71%
Timely Help 'Always' Received	(a)	70%	-	64%
Would Definitely Recommend Hospital	(a)	66%	-	69%

Saint Joseph's Regional Medical Center - Plymouth

1915 Lake Avenue
Plymouth, IN 46563
Phone: 574-936-3181
Fax: 574-935-2250
URL: www.sjmed.com
Type: Acute Care Hospitals
Emergency Services: No
Ownership: Voluntary Non-Profit - Church
Beds: 58

Key Personnel:
CEO/President. . . . . Lori Price
Chief of Medical Staff . . . . Todd Stillson, MD
Quality Assurance . . . . Tammy Awland
Emergency Room . . . . Joan Hum

Measure	Cases	This Hosp.	State Avg.	U.S. Avg.
Heart Attack Care				
ACE Inhibitor or ARB for LVSD[1]	6	100%	96%	96%
Aspirin at Arrival	34	100%	98%	99%
Aspirin at Discharge[1]	22	95%	99%	98%
Beta Blocker at Discharge[1]	24	96%	98%	98%
Fibrinolytic Medication Timing	0	-	37%	55%
PCI Within 90 Minutes of Arrival	0	-	93%	90%
Smoking Cessation Advice[1]	6	100%	99%	99%
Chest Pain/Possible Heart Attack Care				
Aspirin at Arrival	44	100%	95%	95%
Median Time to ECG (minutes)	45	7	6	8
Median Time to Transfer (minutes)[3]	0	-	49	61
Fibrinolytic Medication Timing[1]	15	67%	63%	54%
Heart Failure Care				
ACE Inhibitor or ARB for LVSD[1]	23	96%	92%	94%
Discharge Instructions	60	92%	84%	88%
Evaluation of LVS Function	90	100%	98%	98%
Smoking Cessation Advice[1]	22	100%	99%	98%
Pneumonia Care				
Appropriate Initial Antibiotic	67	90%	90%	92%
Blood Culture Timing	72	99%	95%	96%
Influenza Vaccine	65	98%	93%	91%
Initial Antibiotic Timing	103	100%	96%	95%
Pneumococcal Vaccine	88	99%	94%	93%
Smoking Cessation Advice	36	100%	98%	97%
Surgical Care Improvement Project				
Appropriate VTP Within 24 Hours	38	95%	90%	92%
Appropriate Hair Removal	196	100%	100%	99%
Appropriate Beta Blocker Usage	42	95%	93%	93%
Controlled Postoperative Blood Glucose	0	-	93%	93%
Prophylactic Antibiotic Timing	164	100%	97%	97%
Prophylactic Antibiotic Timing (Outpatient)	40	98%	92%	92%
Prophylactic Antibiotic Selection	165	99%	98%	97%
Prophylactic Antibiotic Select. (Outpatient)	40	100%	95%	94%
Prophylactic Antibiotic Stopped	159	97%	95%	94%
Recommended VTP Ordered	38	100%	92%	94%
Urinary Catheter Removal[1]	5	100%	92%	90%
Children's Asthma Care				
Received Systemic Corticosteroids	-	-	-	100%
Received Home Management Plan	-	-	-	71%
Received Reliever Medication	-	-	-	100%
Use of Medical Imaging				
Combination Abdominal CT Scan	432	0.023	0.237	0.191
Combination Chest CT Scan	292	0.000	0.120	0.054
Follow-up Mammogram/Ultrasound	543	13.4%	8.3%	8.4%
MRI for Low Back Pain[5]	0	-	35.2%	32.7%
Survey of Patients' Hospital Experiences				
Area Around Room 'Always' Quiet at Night	300+	58%	-	58%
Doctors 'Always' Communicated Well	300+	83%	-	80%
Home Recovery Information Given	300+	87%	-	82%
Hospital Given 9 or 10 on 10 Point Scale	300+	79%	-	67%
Meds 'Always' Explained Before Given	300+	64%	-	60%
Nurses 'Always' Communicated Well	300+	82%	-	76%
Pain 'Always' Well Controlled	300+	74%	-	69%
Room and Bathroom 'Always' Clean	300+	72%	-	71%
Timely Help 'Always' Received	300+	74%	-	64%
Would Definitely Recommend Hospital	300+	77%	-	69%

Jay County Hospital

500 W Votaw St
Portland, IN 47371
Phone: 260-726-7131
Fax: 260-726-1986
URL: www.jaycountyhospital.com
Type: Critical Access Hospitals
Emergency Services: Yes
Ownership: Government - Local
Beds: 65

Key Personnel:
CEO/President. . . . . R Joe Johnston
Chief of Medical Staff . . . . Ellen Countryman
Infection Control. . . . . Emma Gayle Collins
Operating Room. . . . . Herman Burgermeister
Radiology. . . . . Rose
Anesthesiology. . . . . John F Martig
Emergency Room . . . . Charles Carroll, MD
Intensive Care Unit. . . . . Jane Jobe

Measure	Cases	This Hosp.	State Avg.	U.S. Avg.
Heart Attack Care				
ACE Inhibitor or ARB for LVSD[3]	0	-	96%	96%
Aspirin at Arrival[1,3]	1	0%	98%	99%
Aspirin at Discharge[1,3]	1	100%	99%	98%
Beta Blocker at Discharge[1,3]	2	100%	98%	98%
Fibrinolytic Medication Timing[5]	0	-	37%	55%
PCI Within 90 Minutes of Arrival[5]	0	-	93%	90%
Smoking Cessation Advice[1,3]	1	100%	99%	99%
Chest Pain/Possible Heart Attack Care				
Aspirin at Arrival	106	87%	95%	95%
Median Time to ECG (minutes)	112	6	6	8
Median Time to Transfer (minutes)[3]	0	-	49	61
Fibrinolytic Medication Timing	0	-	63%	54%
Heart Failure Care				
ACE Inhibitor or ARB for LVSD[1,3]	7	100%	92%	94%
Discharge Instructions[1,3]	9	56%	84%	88%
Evaluation of LVS Function[1,3]	15	67%	98%	98%
Smoking Cessation Advice[1,3]	1	100%	99%	98%
Pneumonia Care				
Appropriate Initial Antibiotic	34	91%	90%	92%
Blood Culture Timing	47	89%	95%	96%
Influenza Vaccine	38	95%	93%	91%
Initial Antibiotic Timing	62	90%	96%	95%
Pneumococcal Vaccine	47	89%	94%	93%
Smoking Cessation Advice[1]	16	69%	98%	97%
Surgical Care Improvement Project				
Appropriate VTP Within 24 Hours[1,3]	16	38%	90%	92%
Appropriate Hair Removal[3]	31	100%	100%	99%
Appropriate Beta Blocker Usage[1,3]	1	0%	93%	93%
Controlled Postoperative Blood Glucose[5]	0	-	93%	93%
Prophylactic Antibiotic Timing[1,3]	11	64%	97%	97%
Prophylactic Antibiotic Timing (Outpatient)[5]	0	-	92%	92%
Prophylactic Antibiotic Selection[1,3]	16	100%	98%	97%
Prophylactic Antibiotic Select. (Outpatient)[5]	0	-	95%	94%
Prophylactic Antibiotic Stopped[1,3]	11	100%	95%	94%
Recommended VTP Ordered[1,3]	16	38%	92%	94%
Urinary Catheter Removal[1,3]	3	100%	92%	90%
Children's Asthma Care				
Received Systemic Corticosteroids	-	-	-	100%
Received Home Management Plan	-	-	-	71%
Received Reliever Medication	-	-	-	100%
Use of Medical Imaging				
Combination Abdominal CT Scan	268	0.183	0.237	0.191
Combination Chest CT Scan	104	0.115	0.120	0.054
Follow-up Mammogram/Ultrasound	345	14.8%	8.3%	8.4%
MRI for Low Back Pain	51	43.1%	35.2%	32.7%
Survey of Patients' Hospital Experiences				
Area Around Room 'Always' Quiet at Night	(a)	71%	-	58%
Doctors 'Always' Communicated Well	(a)	85%	-	80%
Home Recovery Information Given	(a)	88%	-	82%
Hospital Given 9 or 10 on 10 Point Scale	(a)	75%	-	67%
Meds 'Always' Explained Before Given	(a)	68%	-	60%
Nurses 'Always' Communicated Well	(a)	80%	-	76%
Pain 'Always' Well Controlled	(a)	75%	-	69%
Room and Bathroom 'Always' Clean	(a)	71%	-	71%
Timely Help 'Always' Received	(a)	74%	-	64%
Would Definitely Recommend Hospital	(a)	74%	-	69%

NOTE: Hospital profiles are in alphabetical order by state, then city, then hospital within the city; Rankings exclude hospitals with less than 25 cases except for patient surveys which excludes hospitals with less than 100 cases; (a) 100–299 cases; (1) The number of cases is too small to be sure how well a hospital is performing; (2) The hospital indicated that the data submitted for this measure were based on a sample of cases; (3) Data was collected during a shorter time period (fewer quarters) than the maximum possible time for this measure; (4) Suppressed for one or more quarters by CMS; (5) No data is available from the hospital for this measure; (6) Fewer than 100 patients completed the HCAHPS survey. Use these rates with caution, as the number of surveys may be too low to reliably assess hospital performance; (7) Survey results are based on less than 12 months of data; (8) Survey results are not available for this reporting period; (9) No or very few patients were eligible for the HCAHPS survey. The scores shown, if any, reflect a very small number of surveys; (10) A state average was not calculated because too few hospitals in the state submitted data; (11) There were discrepancies in the data collection process; Please refer to the User's Guide for a full explanation of data.

Gibson General Hospital

1808 Sherman Drive
Princeton, IN 47670
Phone: 812-385-3401
Fax: 812-385-9323
Type: Critical Access Hospitals
Emergency Services: Yes
Ownership: Voluntary Non-Profit - Private
Beds: 109

Key Personnel:

CEO/President . . . . Emmett Schuster
Chief of Medical Staff . . . . Krishna Murthy, MD
Quality Assurance . . . . Lynette Klostermann
Emergency Room . . . . Richard Griffin, Dir

Measure	Cases	This Hosp.	State Avg.	U.S. Avg.
Heart Attack Care				
ACE Inhibitor or ARB for LVSD[5]	0	-	96%	96%
Aspirin at Arrival[5]	0	-	98%	99%
Aspirin at Discharge[5]	0	-	99%	98%
Beta Blocker at Discharge[5]	0	-	98%	98%
Fibrinolytic Medication Timing[5]	0	-	37%	55%
PCI Within 90 Minutes of Arrival[5]	0	-	93%	90%
Smoking Cessation Advice[5]	0	-	99%	99%
Chest Pain/Possible Heart Attack Care				
Aspirin at Arrival	-	-	95%	95%
Median Time to ECG (minutes)	-	-	6	8
Median Time to Transfer (minutes)	-	-	49	61
Fibrinolytic Medication Timing	-	-	63%	54%
Heart Failure Care				
ACE Inhibitor or ARB for LVSD[1]	6	100%	92%	94%
Discharge Instructions[1]	6	83%	84%	88%
Evaluation of LVS Function[1]	19	95%	98%	98%
Smoking Cessation Advice[1]	1	100%	99%	98%
Pneumonia Care				
Appropriate Initial Antibiotic	29	93%	90%	92%
Blood Culture Timing	47	91%	95%	96%
Influenza Vaccine[1]	21	95%	93%	91%
Initial Antibiotic Timing	45	96%	96%	95%
Pneumococcal Vaccine	30	97%	94%	93%
Smoking Cessation Advice[1]	24	96%	98%	97%
Surgical Care Improvement Project				
Appropriate VTP Within 24 Hours[5]	0	-	90%	92%
Appropriate Hair Removal[5]	0	-	100%	99%
Appropriate Beta Blocker Usage[5]	0	-	93%	93%
Controlled Postoperative Blood Glucose[5]	0	-	93%	93%
Prophylactic Antibiotic Timing[5]	0	-	97%	97%
Prophylactic Antibiotic Timing (Outpatient)	-	-	92%	92%
Prophylactic Antibiotic Selection[5]	0	-	98%	97%
Prophylactic Antibiotic Select. (Outpatient)	-	-	95%	94%
Prophylactic Antibiotic Stopped[5]	0	-	95%	94%
Recommended VTP Ordered[5]	0	-	92%	94%
Urinary Catheter Removal[5]	0	-	92%	90%
Children's Asthma Care				
Received Systemic Corticosteroids	-	-	-	100%
Received Home Management Plan	-	-	-	71%
Received Reliever Medication	-	-	-	100%
Use of Medical Imaging				
Combination Abdominal CT Scan	-	-	0.237	0.191
Combination Chest CT Scan	-	-	0.120	0.054
Follow-up Mammogram/Ultrasound	-	-	8.3%	8.4%
MRI for Low Back Pain	-	-	35.2%	32.7%
Survey of Patients' Hospital Experiences				
Area Around Room 'Always' Quiet at Night	(a)	64%	-	58%
Doctors 'Always' Communicated Well	(a)	85%	-	80%
Home Recovery Information Given	(a)	82%	-	82%
Hospital Given 9 or 10 on 10 Point Scale	(a)	73%	-	67%
Meds 'Always' Explained Before Given	(a)	58%	-	60%
Nurses 'Always' Communicated Well	(a)	82%	-	76%
Pain 'Always' Well Controlled	(a)	71%	-	69%
Room and Bathroom 'Always' Clean	(a)	75%	-	71%
Timely Help 'Always' Received	(a)	73%	-	64%
Would Definitely Recommend Hospital	(a)	68%	-	69%

Jasper County Hospital

1104 E Grace Street
Rensselaer, IN 47978
Phone: 219-866-5141
Fax: 219-866-3234
URL: www.jchh.com
Type: Critical Access Hospitals
Emergency Services: Yes
Ownership: Voluntary Non-Profit - Other
Beds: 86

Key Personnel:

CEO/President . . . . Tim Schreeg
Chief of Medical Staff . . . . Robert Darnady
Quality Assurance . . . . Bill Hollerman
Emergency Room . . . . Debra Ellis

Measure	Cases	This Hosp.	State Avg.	U.S. Avg.
Heart Attack Care				
ACE Inhibitor or ARB for LVSD	0	-	96%	96%
Aspirin at Arrival[1]	4	100%	98%	99%
Aspirin at Discharge[1]	3	100%	99%	98%
Beta Blocker at Discharge[1]	3	100%	98%	98%
Fibrinolytic Medication Timing	0	-	37%	55%
PCI Within 90 Minutes of Arrival[5]	0	-	93%	90%
Smoking Cessation Advice	0	-	99%	99%
Chest Pain/Possible Heart Attack Care				
Aspirin at Arrival	-	-	95%	95%
Median Time to ECG (minutes)	-	-	6	8
Median Time to Transfer (minutes)	-	-	49	61
Fibrinolytic Medication Timing	-	-	63%	54%
Heart Failure Care				
ACE Inhibitor or ARB for LVSD[1]	9	67%	92%	94%
Discharge Instructions[1]	22	91%	84%	88%
Evaluation of LVS Function	41	98%	98%	98%
Smoking Cessation Advice[1]	5	80%	99%	98%
Pneumonia Care				
Appropriate Initial Antibiotic	39	82%	90%	92%
Blood Culture Timing	44	77%	95%	96%
Influenza Vaccine	37	73%	93%	91%
Initial Antibiotic Timing	54	93%	96%	95%
Pneumococcal Vaccine	53	87%	94%	93%
Smoking Cessation Advice[1]	13	92%	98%	97%
Surgical Care Improvement Project				
Appropriate VTP Within 24 Hours[5]	0	-	90%	92%
Appropriate Hair Removal[1]	20	100%	100%	99%
Appropriate Beta Blocker Usage[5]	0	-	93%	93%
Controlled Postoperative Blood Glucose[5]	0	-	93%	93%
Prophylactic Antibiotic Timing[1]	20	95%	97%	97%
Prophylactic Antibiotic Timing (Outpatient)	-	-	92%	92%
Prophylactic Antibiotic Selection[1]	20	80%	98%	97%
Prophylactic Antibiotic Select. (Outpatient)	-	-	95%	94%
Prophylactic Antibiotic Stopped[1]	19	89%	95%	94%
Recommended VTP Ordered[5]	0	-	92%	94%
Urinary Catheter Removal[5]	0	-	92%	90%
Children's Asthma Care				
Received Systemic Corticosteroids	-	-	-	100%
Received Home Management Plan	-	-	-	71%
Received Reliever Medication	-	-	-	100%
Use of Medical Imaging				
Combination Abdominal CT Scan	-	-	0.237	0.191
Combination Chest CT Scan	-	-	0.120	0.054
Follow-up Mammogram/Ultrasound	-	-	8.3%	8.4%
MRI for Low Back Pain	-	-	35.2%	32.7%
Survey of Patients' Hospital Experiences				
Area Around Room 'Always' Quiet at Night[8]	-	-	-	58%
Doctors 'Always' Communicated Well[8]	-	-	-	80%
Home Recovery Information Given[8]	-	-	-	82%
Hospital Given 9 or 10 on 10 Point Scale[8]	-	-	-	67%
Meds 'Always' Explained Before Given[8]	-	-	-	60%
Nurses 'Always' Communicated Well[8]	-	-	-	76%
Pain 'Always' Well Controlled[8]	-	-	-	69%
Room and Bathroom 'Always' Clean[8]	-	-	-	71%
Timely Help 'Always' Received[8]	-	-	-	64%
Would Definitely Recommend Hospital[8]	-	-	-	69%

Reid Hospital & Health Care Services

1100 Reid Parkway
Richmond, IN 47374
Phone: 765-983-3000
Fax: 765-983-3219
URL: www.reidhosp.com
Type: Acute Care Hospitals
Emergency Services: Yes
Ownership: Voluntary Non-Profit - Other
Beds: 233

Key Personnel:

CEO/President . . . . Craig Kinyon
Cardiac Laboratory . . . . Jeanette Sullivan
Chief of Medical Staff . . . . Rohit Barva, MD
Coronary Care . . . . Alyson Harrell
Operating Room . . . . Christy Brewer
Quality Assurance . . . . Marilee Crosby
Radiology . . . . Eugene Ditullio

Measure	Cases	This Hosp.	State Avg.	U.S. Avg.
Heart Attack Care				
ACE Inhibitor or ARB for LVSD	57	100%	96%	96%
Aspirin at Arrival	286	100%	98%	99%
Aspirin at Discharge	350	100%	99%	98%
Beta Blocker at Discharge	338	100%	98%	98%
Fibrinolytic Medication Timing	0	-	37%	55%
PCI Within 90 Minutes of Arrival	62	97%	93%	90%
Smoking Cessation Advice	114	100%	99%	99%
Chest Pain/Possible Heart Attack Care				
Aspirin at Arrival[1,3]	5	80%	95%	95%
Median Time to ECG (minutes)[1,3]	5	1	6	8
Median Time to Transfer (minutes)[5]	0	-	49	61
Fibrinolytic Medication Timing[3]	0	-	63%	54%
Heart Failure Care				
ACE Inhibitor or ARB for LVSD	97	99%	92%	94%
Discharge Instructions	277	94%	84%	88%
Evaluation of LVS Function	383	99%	98%	98%
Smoking Cessation Advice	67	100%	99%	98%
Pneumonia Care				
Appropriate Initial Antibiotic	291	98%	90%	92%
Blood Culture Timing	483	100%	95%	96%
Influenza Vaccine	396	99%	93%	91%
Initial Antibiotic Timing	452	99%	96%	95%
Pneumococcal Vaccine	527	100%	94%	93%
Smoking Cessation Advice	210	100%	98%	97%
Surgical Care Improvement Project				
Appropriate VTP Within 24 Hours	230	98%	90%	92%
Appropriate Hair Removal	819	100%	100%	99%
Appropriate Beta Blocker Usage	296	93%	93%	93%
Controlled Postoperative Blood Glucose	165	95%	93%	93%
Prophylactic Antibiotic Timing	571	99%	97%	97%
Prophylactic Antibiotic Timing (Outpatient)	382	93%	92%	92%
Prophylactic Antibiotic Selection	584	99%	98%	97%
Prophylactic Antibiotic Select. (Outpatient)	385	97%	95%	94%
Prophylactic Antibiotic Stopped	526	99%	95%	94%
Recommended VTP Ordered	230	98%	92%	94%
Urinary Catheter Removal	146	95%	92%	90%
Children's Asthma Care				
Received Systemic Corticosteroids	-	-	-	100%
Received Home Management Plan	-	-	-	71%
Received Reliever Medication	-	-	-	100%
Use of Medical Imaging				
Combination Abdominal CT Scan	1,288	0.110	0.237	0.191
Combination Chest CT Scan	806	0.006	0.120	0.054
Follow-up Mammogram/Ultrasound	2,179	5.6%	8.3%	8.4%
MRI for Low Back Pain	348	35.9%	35.2%	32.7%
Survey of Patients' Hospital Experiences				
Area Around Room 'Always' Quiet at Night	300+	54%	-	58%
Doctors 'Always' Communicated Well	300+	79%	-	80%
Home Recovery Information Given	300+	84%	-	82%
Hospital Given 9 or 10 on 10 Point Scale	300+	71%	-	67%
Meds 'Always' Explained Before Given	300+	57%	-	60%
Nurses 'Always' Communicated Well	300+	76%	-	76%
Pain 'Always' Well Controlled	300+	68%	-	69%
Room and Bathroom 'Always' Clean	300+	84%	-	71%
Timely Help 'Always' Received	300+	59%	-	64%
Would Definitely Recommend Hospital	300+	73%	-	69%

NOTE: Hospital profiles are in alphabetical order by state, then city, then hospital within the city; Rankings exclude hospitals with less than 25 cases except for patient surveys which excludes hospitals with less than 100 cases; (a) 100–299 cases; (1) The number of cases is too small to be sure how well a hospital is performing; (2) The hospital indicated that the data submitted for this measure were based on a sample of cases; (3) Data was collected during a shorter time period (fewer quarters) than the maximum possible time for this measure; (4) Suppressed for one or more quarters by CMS; (5) No data is available from the hospital for this measure; (6) Fewer than 100 patients completed the HCAHPS survey. Use these rates with caution, as the number of surveys may be too low to reliably assess hospital performance; (7) Survey results are based on less than 12 months of data; (8) Survey results are not available for this reporting period; (9) No or very few patients were eligible for the HCAHPS survey. The scores shown, if any, reflect a very small number of surveys; (10) A state average was not calculated because too few hospitals in the state submitted data; (11) There were discrepancies in the data collection process; Please refer to the User's Guide for a full explanation of data.

Rush Memorial Hospital

1300 N Main St
Rushville, IN 46173
Phone: 765-932-7513
Fax: 765-932-7523
E-mail: info@rushmemorial.com
URL: www.rushmemorial.com
Type: Critical Access Hospitals
Emergency Services: Yes
Ownership: Government - Local
Beds: 25

Key Personnel:

CEO/President. . . . . Brad Smith
Chief of Medical Staff . . . . Ava Moore
Infection Control. . . . . Carol Tulley MT ASCP
Operating Room. . . . . Kathy Newkirk
Quality Assurance . . . . Linda Noble
Radiology. . . . . Terry Aker

Measure	Cases	This Hosp.	State Avg.	U.S. Avg.
Heart Attack Care				
ACE Inhibitor or ARB for LVSD	-	-	96%	96%
Aspirin at Arrival	-	-	98%	99%
Aspirin at Discharge	-	-	99%	98%
Beta Blocker at Discharge	-	-	98%	98%
Fibrinolytic Medication Timing	-	-	37%	55%
PCI Within 90 Minutes of Arrival	-	-	93%	90%
Smoking Cessation Advice	-	-	99%	99%
Chest Pain/Possible Heart Attack Care				
Aspirin at Arrival[5]	0	-	95%	95%
Median Time to ECG (minutes)[5]	0	-	6	8
Median Time to Transfer (minutes)[5]	0	-	49	61
Fibrinolytic Medication Timing[5]	0	-	63%	54%
Heart Failure Care				
ACE Inhibitor or ARB for LVSD	-	-	92%	94%
Discharge Instructions	-	-	84%	88%
Evaluation of LVS Function	-	-	98%	98%
Smoking Cessation Advice	-	-	99%	98%
Pneumonia Care				
Appropriate Initial Antibiotic	-	-	90%	92%
Blood Culture Timing	-	-	95%	96%
Influenza Vaccine	-	-	93%	91%
Initial Antibiotic Timing	-	-	96%	95%
Pneumococcal Vaccine	-	-	94%	93%
Smoking Cessation Advice	-	-	98%	97%
Surgical Care Improvement Project				
Appropriate VTP Within 24 Hours	-	-	90%	92%
Appropriate Hair Removal	-	-	100%	99%
Appropriate Beta Blocker Usage	-	-	93%	93%
Controlled Postoperative Blood Glucose	-	-	93%	93%
Prophylactic Antibiotic Timing	-	-	97%	97%
Prophylactic Antibiotic Timing (Outpatient)[5]	0	-	92%	92%
Prophylactic Antibiotic Selection	-	-	98%	97%
Prophylactic Antibiotic Select. (Outpatient)[5]	0	-	95%	94%
Prophylactic Antibiotic Stopped	-	-	95%	94%
Recommended VTP Ordered	-	-	92%	94%
Urinary Catheter Removal	-	-	92%	90%
Children's Asthma Care				
Received Systemic Corticosteroids	-	-	-	100%
Received Home Management Plan	-	-	-	71%
Received Reliever Medication	-	-	-	100%
Use of Medical Imaging				
Combination Abdominal CT Scan	191	0.068	0.237	0.191
Combination Chest CT Scan	92	0.000	0.120	0.054
Follow-up Mammogram/Ultrasound	188	7.4%	8.3%	8.4%
MRI for Low Back Pain[1]	27	48.1%	35.2%	32.7%
Survey of Patients' Hospital Experiences				
Area Around Room 'Always' Quiet at Night	-	-	-	58%
Doctors 'Always' Communicated Well	-	-	-	80%
Home Recovery Information Given	-	-	-	82%
Hospital Given 9 or 10 on 10 Point Scale	-	-	-	67%
Meds 'Always' Explained Before Given	-	-	-	60%
Nurses 'Always' Communicated Well	-	-	-	76%
Pain 'Always' Well Controlled	-	-	-	69%
Room and Bathroom 'Always' Clean	-	-	-	71%
Timely Help 'Always' Received	-	-	-	64%
Would Definitely Recommend Hospital	-	-	-	69%

Saint Vincent Salem Hospital

911 N Shelby St
Salem, IN 47167
Phone: 812-883-5881
Fax: 812-883-8563
Type: Critical Access Hospitals
Emergency Services: Yes
Ownership: Voluntary Non-Profit - Other
Beds: 70

Key Personnel:

CEO/President. . . . . Randy Lindauer
Chief of Medical Staff . . . . Rizwan Khan, MD
Infection Control. . . . . Lisa Woodward
Operating Room. . . . . Doris Biddle
Quality Assurance . . . . Jim Steggeman
Radiology. . . . . Abdelrahman Abdalla
Intensive Care Unit. . . . . Patty Saxton

Measure	Cases	This Hosp.	State Avg.	U.S. Avg.
Heart Attack Care				
ACE Inhibitor or ARB for LVSD	-	-	96%	96%
Aspirin at Arrival	-	-	98%	99%
Aspirin at Discharge	-	-	99%	98%
Beta Blocker at Discharge	-	-	98%	98%
Fibrinolytic Medication Timing	-	-	37%	55%
PCI Within 90 Minutes of Arrival	-	-	93%	90%
Smoking Cessation Advice	-	-	99%	99%
Chest Pain/Possible Heart Attack Care				
Aspirin at Arrival[5]	0	-	95%	95%
Median Time to ECG (minutes)[5]	0	-	6	8
Median Time to Transfer (minutes)[5]	0	-	49	61
Fibrinolytic Medication Timing[5]	0	-	63%	54%
Heart Failure Care				
ACE Inhibitor or ARB for LVSD	-	-	92%	94%
Discharge Instructions	-	-	84%	88%
Evaluation of LVS Function	-	-	98%	98%
Smoking Cessation Advice	-	-	99%	98%
Pneumonia Care				
Appropriate Initial Antibiotic	-	-	90%	92%
Blood Culture Timing	-	-	95%	96%
Influenza Vaccine	-	-	93%	91%
Initial Antibiotic Timing	-	-	96%	95%
Pneumococcal Vaccine	-	-	94%	93%
Smoking Cessation Advice	-	-	98%	97%
Surgical Care Improvement Project				
Appropriate VTP Within 24 Hours	-	-	90%	92%
Appropriate Hair Removal	-	-	100%	99%
Appropriate Beta Blocker Usage	-	-	93%	93%
Controlled Postoperative Blood Glucose	-	-	93%	93%
Prophylactic Antibiotic Timing	-	-	97%	97%
Prophylactic Antibiotic Timing (Outpatient)[5]	0	-	92%	92%
Prophylactic Antibiotic Selection	-	-	98%	97%
Prophylactic Antibiotic Select. (Outpatient)[5]	0	-	95%	94%
Prophylactic Antibiotic Stopped	-	-	95%	94%
Recommended VTP Ordered	-	-	92%	94%
Urinary Catheter Removal	-	-	92%	90%
Children's Asthma Care				
Received Systemic Corticosteroids	-	-	-	100%
Received Home Management Plan	-	-	-	71%
Received Reliever Medication	-	-	-	100%
Use of Medical Imaging				
Combination Abdominal CT Scan	166	0.801	0.237	0.191
Combination Chest CT Scan	108	0.315	0.120	0.054
Follow-up Mammogram/Ultrasound	198	16.7%	8.3%	8.4%
MRI for Low Back Pain	43	39.5%	35.2%	32.7%
Survey of Patients' Hospital Experiences				
Area Around Room 'Always' Quiet at Night	-	-	-	58%
Doctors 'Always' Communicated Well	-	-	-	80%
Home Recovery Information Given	-	-	-	82%
Hospital Given 9 or 10 on 10 Point Scale	-	-	-	67%
Meds 'Always' Explained Before Given	-	-	-	60%
Nurses 'Always' Communicated Well	-	-	-	76%
Pain 'Always' Well Controlled	-	-	-	69%
Room and Bathroom 'Always' Clean	-	-	-	71%
Timely Help 'Always' Received	-	-	-	64%
Would Definitely Recommend Hospital	-	-	-	69%

Scott Memorial Hospital

1451 N Gardner St
Scottsburg, IN 47170
Phone: 812-752-3456
Fax: 812-752-5884
E-mail: jwells@hsonline.net
URL: www.scottmemorial.com
Type: Critical Access Hospitals
Emergency Services: Yes
Ownership: Government - Local
Beds: 90

Key Personnel:

CEO/President. . . . . Cliff Nay
Cardiac Laboratory. . . . . Zaka Rahman
Chief of Medical Staff . . . . Shane Avery
Quality Assurance . . . . Cheryl Stultz, RN
Emergency Room . . . . John Croasdell, MD
Patient Relations . . . . Cindy Bush

Measure	Cases	This Hosp.	State Avg.	U.S. Avg.
Heart Attack Care				
ACE Inhibitor or ARB for LVSD	0	-	96%	96%
Aspirin at Arrival[1]	7	57%	98%	99%
Aspirin at Discharge	0	-	99%	98%
Beta Blocker at Discharge[1]	1	100%	98%	98%
Fibrinolytic Medication Timing	0	-	37%	55%
PCI Within 90 Minutes of Arrival[5]	0	-	93%	90%
Smoking Cessation Advice	0	-	99%	99%
Chest Pain/Possible Heart Attack Care				
Aspirin at Arrival	-	-	95%	95%
Median Time to ECG (minutes)	-	-	6	8
Median Time to Transfer (minutes)	-	-	49	61
Fibrinolytic Medication Timing	-	-	63%	54%
Heart Failure Care				
ACE Inhibitor or ARB for LVSD[1]	14	100%	92%	94%
Discharge Instructions	31	90%	84%	88%
Evaluation of LVS Function	29	83%	98%	98%
Smoking Cessation Advice[1]	9	100%	99%	98%
Pneumonia Care				
Appropriate Initial Antibiotic	54	91%	90%	92%
Blood Culture Timing	55	85%	95%	96%
Influenza Vaccine	30	100%	93%	91%
Initial Antibiotic Timing	63	94%	96%	95%
Pneumococcal Vaccine	45	96%	94%	93%
Smoking Cessation Advice	25	96%	98%	97%
Surgical Care Improvement Project				
Appropriate VTP Within 24 Hours[1,3]	2	0%	90%	92%
Appropriate Hair Removal[1,3]	14	93%	100%	99%
Appropriate Beta Blocker Usage[1,3]	1	100%	93%	93%
Controlled Postoperative Blood Glucose[5]	0	-	93%	93%
Prophylactic Antibiotic Timing[1,3]	5	60%	97%	97%
Prophylactic Antibiotic Timing (Outpatient)	-	-	92%	92%
Prophylactic Antibiotic Selection[1,3]	4	0%	98%	97%
Prophylactic Antibiotic Select. (Outpatient)	-	-	95%	94%
Prophylactic Antibiotic Stopped[1,3]	4	100%	95%	94%
Recommended VTP Ordered[1,3]	3	0%	92%	94%
Urinary Catheter Removal[3]	0	-	92%	90%
Children's Asthma Care				
Received Systemic Corticosteroids	-	-	-	100%
Received Home Management Plan	-	-	-	71%
Received Reliever Medication	-	-	-	100%
Use of Medical Imaging				
Combination Abdominal CT Scan	-	-	0.237	0.191
Combination Chest CT Scan	-	-	0.120	0.054
Follow-up Mammogram/Ultrasound	-	-	8.3%	8.4%
MRI for Low Back Pain	-	-	35.2%	32.7%
Survey of Patients' Hospital Experiences				
Area Around Room 'Always' Quiet at Night	(a)	63%	-	58%
Doctors 'Always' Communicated Well	(a)	85%	-	80%
Home Recovery Information Given	(a)	81%	-	82%
Hospital Given 9 or 10 on 10 Point Scale	(a)	73%	-	67%
Meds 'Always' Explained Before Given	(a)	73%	-	60%
Nurses 'Always' Communicated Well	(a)	87%	-	76%
Pain 'Always' Well Controlled	(a)	79%	-	69%
Room and Bathroom 'Always' Clean	(a)	82%	-	71%
Timely Help 'Always' Received	(a)	79%	-	64%
Would Definitely Recommend Hospital	(a)	72%	-	69%

NOTE: Hospital profiles are in alphabetical order by state, then city, then hospital within the city; Rankings exclude hospitals with less than 25 cases except for patient surveys which excludes hospitals with less than 100 cases; (a) 100–299 cases; (1) The number of cases is too small to be sure how well a hospital is performing; (2) The hospital indicated that the data submitted for this measure were based on a sample of cases; (3) Data was collected during a shorter time period (fewer quarters) than the maximum possible time for this measure; (4) Suppressed for one or more quarters by CMS; (5) No data is available from the hospital for this measure; (6) Fewer than 100 patients completed the HCAHPS survey. Use these rates with caution, as the number of surveys may be too low to reliably assess hospital performance; (7) Survey results are based on less than 12 months of data; (8) Survey results are not available for this reporting period; (9) No or very few patients were eligible for the HCAHPS survey. The scores shown, if any, reflect a very small number of surveys; (10) A state average was not calculated because too few hospitals in the state submitted data; (11) There were discrepancies in the data collection process; Please refer to the User's Guide for a full explanation of data.

Schneck Medical Center

411 W Tipton Street
Seymour, IN 47274
Phone: 812-522-2349
Fax: 812-522-0544
E-mail: info@schneckmed.org
URL: www.schneckmed.org
Type: Acute Care Hospitals
Emergency Services: Yes
Ownership: Government - Local
Beds: 166

Key Personnel:
CEO/President. . . . . Gary A Meyer, MHA
Infection Control. . . . . Judy Tape

Measure	Cases	This Hosp.	State Avg.	U.S. Avg.
Heart Attack Care				
ACE Inhibitor or ARB for LVSD	0	-	96%	96%
Aspirin at Arrival[1]	12	100%	98%	99%
Aspirin at Discharge[1]	8	100%	99%	98%
Beta Blocker at Discharge[1]	10	90%	98%	98%
Fibrinolytic Medication Timing	0	-	37%	55%
PCI Within 90 Minutes of Arrival	0	-	93%	90%
Smoking Cessation Advice[1]	2	100%	99%	99%
Chest Pain/Possible Heart Attack Care				
Aspirin at Arrival	170	95%	95%	95%
Median Time to ECG (minutes)	183	8	6	8
Median Time to Transfer (minutes)[1]	11	53	49	61
Fibrinolytic Medication Timing	0	-	63%	54%
Heart Failure Care				
ACE Inhibitor or ARB for LVSD[1]	19	84%	92%	94%
Discharge Instructions	56	88%	84%	88%
Evaluation of LVS Function	73	97%	98%	98%
Smoking Cessation Advice[1]	16	94%	99%	98%
Pneumonia Care				
Appropriate Initial Antibiotic	64	97%	90%	92%
Blood Culture Timing	99	99%	95%	96%
Influenza Vaccine	78	100%	93%	91%
Initial Antibiotic Timing	118	98%	96%	95%
Pneumococcal Vaccine	125	100%	94%	93%
Smoking Cessation Advice	53	94%	98%	97%
Surgical Care Improvement Project				
Appropriate VTP Within 24 Hours	76	91%	90%	92%
Appropriate Hair Removal	247	100%	100%	99%
Appropriate Beta Blocker Usage	65	97%	93%	93%
Controlled Postoperative Blood Glucose	0	-	93%	93%
Prophylactic Antibiotic Timing	170	99%	97%	97%
Prophylactic Antibiotic Timing (Outpatient)	114	97%	92%	92%
Prophylactic Antibiotic Selection	171	99%	98%	97%
Prophylactic Antibiotic Select. (Outpatient)	113	96%	95%	94%
Prophylactic Antibiotic Stopped	163	96%	95%	94%
Recommended VTP Ordered	76	93%	92%	94%
Urinary Catheter Removal[1]	4	75%	92%	90%
Children's Asthma Care				
Received Systemic Corticosteroids	-	-	-	100%
Received Home Management Plan	-	-	-	71%
Received Reliever Medication	-	-	-	100%
Use of Medical Imaging				
Combination Abdominal CT Scan	589	0.041	0.237	0.191
Combination Chest CT Scan	365	0.005	0.120	0.054
Follow-up Mammogram/Ultrasound	704	10.1%	8.3%	8.4%
MRI for Low Back Pain	104	40.4%	35.2%	32.7%
Survey of Patients' Hospital Experiences				
Area Around Room 'Always' Quiet at Night	300+	67%	-	58%
Doctors 'Always' Communicated Well	300+	85%	-	80%
Home Recovery Information Given	300+	84%	-	82%
Hospital Given 9 or 10 on 10 Point Scale	300+	75%	-	67%
Meds 'Always' Explained Before Given	300+	64%	-	60%
Nurses 'Always' Communicated Well	300+	82%	-	76%
Pain 'Always' Well Controlled	300+	76%	-	69%
Room and Bathroom 'Always' Clean	300+	78%	-	71%
Timely Help 'Always' Received	300+	72%	-	64%
Would Definitely Recommend Hospital	300+	78%	-	69%

Major Hospital

150 W Washington St
Shelbyville, IN 46176
Phone: 317-392-3211
Fax: 317-398-5253
E-mail: info@majorhospital.org
URL: www.majorhospital.org
Type: Acute Care Hospitals
Emergency Services: Yes
Ownership: Government - Local
Beds: 89

Key Personnel:
CEO/President. . . . . Anthony B Lennen
Chief of Medical Staff. . . . . Ed Stone, MD
Infection Control. . . . . Candy Oliger
Operating Room. . . . . Carlos A Vieira, RN
Quality Assurance . . . . Candice Oliger
Radiology. . . . . Jonathan R Bielefeld
Anesthesiology. . . . . Jay DeVore, MD
Emergency Room . . . . David Moser, MD

Measure	Cases	This Hosp.	State Avg.	U.S. Avg.
Heart Attack Care				
ACE Inhibitor or ARB for LVSD	0	-	96%	96%
Aspirin at Arrival[1]	6	100%	98%	99%
Aspirin at Discharge[1]	4	100%	99%	98%
Beta Blocker at Discharge[1]	4	100%	98%	98%
Fibrinolytic Medication Timing	0	-	37%	55%
PCI Within 90 Minutes of Arrival	0	-	93%	90%
Smoking Cessation Advice[1]	1	100%	99%	99%
Chest Pain/Possible Heart Attack Care				
Aspirin at Arrival	100	96%	95%	95%
Median Time to ECG (minutes)	105	4	6	8
Median Time to Transfer (minutes)[1]	18	44	49	61
Fibrinolytic Medication Timing	0	-	63%	54%
Heart Failure Care				
ACE Inhibitor or ARB for LVSD	28	93%	92%	94%
Discharge Instructions	51	76%	84%	88%
Evaluation of LVS Function	72	100%	98%	98%
Smoking Cessation Advice[1]	10	100%	99%	98%
Pneumonia Care				
Appropriate Initial Antibiotic	89	97%	90%	92%
Blood Culture Timing	150	99%	95%	96%
Influenza Vaccine	89	100%	93%	91%
Initial Antibiotic Timing	135	100%	96%	95%
Pneumococcal Vaccine	142	100%	94%	93%
Smoking Cessation Advice	59	100%	98%	97%
Surgical Care Improvement Project				
Appropriate VTP Within 24 Hours	57	96%	90%	92%
Appropriate Hair Removal	148	100%	100%	99%
Appropriate Beta Blocker Usage	46	91%	93%	93%
Controlled Postoperative Blood Glucose	0	-	93%	93%
Prophylactic Antibiotic Timing	95	93%	97%	97%
Prophylactic Antibiotic Timing (Outpatient)	45	96%	92%	92%
Prophylactic Antibiotic Selection	95	100%	98%	97%
Prophylactic Antibiotic Select. (Outpatient)	45	100%	95%	94%
Prophylactic Antibiotic Stopped	90	93%	95%	94%
Recommended VTP Ordered	57	96%	92%	94%
Urinary Catheter Removal	44	91%	92%	90%
Children's Asthma Care				
Received Systemic Corticosteroids	-	-	-	100%
Received Home Management Plan	-	-	-	71%
Received Reliever Medication	-	-	-	100%
Use of Medical Imaging				
Combination Abdominal CT Scan	393	0.328	0.237	0.191
Combination Chest CT Scan	300	0.143	0.120	0.054
Follow-up Mammogram/Ultrasound	716	4.9%	8.3%	8.4%
MRI for Low Back Pain	145	27.6%	35.2%	32.7%
Survey of Patients' Hospital Experiences				
Area Around Room 'Always' Quiet at Night	300+	57%	-	58%
Doctors 'Always' Communicated Well	300+	83%	-	80%
Home Recovery Information Given	300+	84%	-	82%
Hospital Given 9 or 10 on 10 Point Scale	300+	72%	-	67%
Meds 'Always' Explained Before Given	300+	65%	-	60%
Nurses 'Always' Communicated Well	300+	83%	-	76%
Pain 'Always' Well Controlled	300+	73%	-	69%
Room and Bathroom 'Always' Clean	300+	82%	-	71%
Timely Help 'Always' Received	300+	75%	-	64%
Would Definitely Recommend Hospital	300+	72%	-	69%

Memorial Hospital of South Bend

615 N Michigan Street
South Bend, IN 46601
Phone: 574-647-3632
Fax: 574-647-3670
E-mail: ltatum@memorialsb.org
URL: www.qualityoflife.org
Type: Acute Care Hospitals
Emergency Services: Yes
Ownership: Voluntary Non-Profit - Other
Beds: 526

Key Personnel:
Chief of Medical Staff. . . . . John Mathis, MD
Infection Control. . . . . Susan Kraska
Operating Room. . . . . Charlotte Zircher
Pediatric Ambulatory Care . . . . . . Michael Hudson, MD
Pediatric In-Patient Care . . . . Michael Hudson, MD
Quality Assurance . . . . Becky Starzynski
Radiology. . . . . Gerard DuPrat, MD

Measure	Cases	This Hosp.	State Avg.	U.S. Avg.
Heart Attack Care				
ACE Inhibitor or ARB for LVSD	27	100%	96%	96%
Aspirin at Arrival	252	98%	98%	99%
Aspirin at Discharge	266	99%	99%	98%
Beta Blocker at Discharge	252	100%	98%	98%
Fibrinolytic Medication Timing	0	-	37%	55%
PCI Within 90 Minutes of Arrival	55	100%	93%	90%
Smoking Cessation Advice	96	98%	99%	99%
Chest Pain/Possible Heart Attack Care				
Aspirin at Arrival[3]	0	-	95%	95%
Median Time to ECG (minutes)[3]	0	-	6	8
Median Time to Transfer (minutes)[5]	0	-	49	61
Fibrinolytic Medication Timing[5]	0	-	63%	54%
Heart Failure Care				
ACE Inhibitor or ARB for LVSD	113	99%	92%	94%
Discharge Instructions	318	94%	84%	88%
Evaluation of LVS Function	403	100%	98%	98%
Smoking Cessation Advice	103	100%	99%	98%
Pneumonia Care				
Appropriate Initial Antibiotic	167	85%	90%	92%
Blood Culture Timing	172	99%	95%	96%
Influenza Vaccine	157	93%	93%	91%
Initial Antibiotic Timing	236	94%	96%	95%
Pneumococcal Vaccine	216	98%	94%	93%
Smoking Cessation Advice	94	98%	98%	97%
Surgical Care Improvement Project				
Appropriate VTP Within 24 Hours[2]	217	79%	90%	92%
Appropriate Hair Removal[2]	815	99%	100%	99%
Appropriate Beta Blocker Usage[2]	227	79%	93%	93%
Controlled Postoperative Blood Glucose[2]	164	87%	93%	93%
Prophylactic Antibiotic Timing[2]	591	92%	97%	97%
Prophylactic Antibiotic Timing (Outpatient)	677	87%	92%	92%
Prophylactic Antibiotic Selection[2]	598	94%	98%	97%
Prophylactic Antibiotic Select. (Outpatient)	654	75%	95%	94%
Prophylactic Antibiotic Stopped[2]	573	95%	95%	94%
Recommended VTP Ordered[2]	218	81%	92%	94%
Urinary Catheter Removal[2]	115	80%	92%	90%
Children's Asthma Care				
Received Systemic Corticosteroids	-	-	-	100%
Received Home Management Plan	-	-	-	71%
Received Reliever Medication	-	-	-	100%
Use of Medical Imaging				
Combination Abdominal CT Scan	757	0.103	0.237	0.191
Combination Chest CT Scan	623	0.026	0.120	0.054
Follow-up Mammogram/Ultrasound	1,224	6.5%	8.3%	8.4%
MRI for Low Back Pain[1]	1	0.0%	35.2%	32.7%
Survey of Patients' Hospital Experiences				
Area Around Room 'Always' Quiet at Night	300+	43%	-	58%
Doctors 'Always' Communicated Well	300+	80%	-	80%
Home Recovery Information Given	300+	84%	-	82%
Hospital Given 9 or 10 on 10 Point Scale	300+	74%	-	67%
Meds 'Always' Explained Before Given	300+	57%	-	60%
Nurses 'Always' Communicated Well	300+	76%	-	76%
Pain 'Always' Well Controlled	300+	72%	-	69%
Room and Bathroom 'Always' Clean	300+	68%	-	71%
Timely Help 'Always' Received	300+	66%	-	64%
Would Definitely Recommend Hospital	300+	76%	-	69%

NOTE: Hospital profiles are in alphabetical order by state, then city, then hospital within the city; Rankings exclude hospitals with less than 25 cases except for patient surveys which excludes hospitals with less than 100 cases; (a) 100–299 cases; (1) The number of cases is too small to be sure how well a hospital is performing; (2) The hospital indicated that the data submitted for this measure were based on a sample of cases; (3) Data was collected during a shorter time period (fewer quarters) than the maximum possible time for this measure; (4) Suppressed for one or more quarters by CMS; (5) No data is available from the hospital for this measure; (6) Fewer than 100 patients completed the HCAHPS survey. Use these rates with caution, as the number of surveys may be too low to reliably assess hospital performance; (7) Survey results are based on less than 12 months of data; (8) Survey results are not available for this reporting period; (9) No or very few patients were eligible for the HCAHPS survey. The scores shown, if any, reflect a very small number of surveys; (10) A state average was not calculated because too few hospitals in the state submitted data; (11) There were discrepancies in the data collection process; Please refer to the User's Guide for a full explanation of data.

Sullivan County Community Hospital

2200 N Section Street Phone: 812-268-4311
Sullivan, IN 47882 Fax: 812-268-2570
E-mail: denisebrashear@schosp.com
URL: www.schosp.com
Type: Critical Access Hospitals Emergency Services: Yes
Ownership: Government - Local Beds: 34

Key Personnel:
CEO/President. . . . . Michelle Sly-Smith
Chief of Medical Staff. . . . . Gene Bourgasser, MD
Infection Control. . . . . Marti Bradbury, RN
Operating Room. . . . . Marilyn Fuson
Quality Assurance . . . . Susan Pershing
Radiology. . . . . Stan Hobbs
Intensive Care Unit. . . . . Marian Bynum, RN
Patient Relations . . . . Michelle Smith

Measure	Cases	This Hosp.	State Avg.	U.S. Avg.
Heart Attack Care				
ACE Inhibitor or ARB for LVSD	0	-	96%	96%
Aspirin at Arrival[1]	8	100%	98%	99%
Aspirin at Discharge[1]	5	100%	99%	98%
Beta Blocker at Discharge[1]	5	100%	98%	98%
Fibrinolytic Medication Timing	0	-	37%	55%
PCI Within 90 Minutes of Arrival	0	-	93%	90%
Smoking Cessation Advice[1]	1	100%	99%	99%
Chest Pain/Possible Heart Attack Care				
Aspirin at Arrival	132	97%	95%	95%
Median Time to ECG (minutes)	142	4	6	8
Median Time to Transfer (minutes)[1]	15	32	49	61
Fibrinolytic Medication Timing[1]	1	100%	63%	54%
Heart Failure Care				
ACE Inhibitor or ARB for LVSD[1]	13	38%	92%	94%
Discharge Instructions[1]	23	78%	84%	88%
Evaluation of LVS Function	42	74%	98%	98%
Smoking Cessation Advice[1]	6	67%	99%	98%
Pneumonia Care				
Appropriate Initial Antibiotic	44	93%	90%	92%
Blood Culture Timing	50	88%	95%	96%
Influenza Vaccine	29	69%	93%	91%
Initial Antibiotic Timing	62	98%	96%	95%
Pneumococcal Vaccine	44	86%	94%	93%
Smoking Cessation Advice	27	81%	98%	97%
Surgical Care Improvement Project				
Appropriate VTP Within 24 Hours[1]	18	89%	90%	92%
Appropriate Hair Removal	30	100%	100%	99%
Appropriate Beta Blocker Usage[1]	9	78%	93%	93%
Controlled Postoperative Blood Glucose[5]	0	-	93%	93%
Prophylactic Antibiotic Timing[1]	19	89%	97%	97%
Prophylactic Antibiotic Timing (Outpatient)[1,3]	3	33%	92%	92%
Prophylactic Antibiotic Selection[1]	19	84%	98%	97%
Prophylactic Antibiotic Select. (Outpatient)[1,3]	1	0%	95%	94%
Prophylactic Antibiotic Stopped[1]	17	71%	95%	94%
Recommended VTP Ordered[1]	19	95%	92%	94%
Urinary Catheter Removal[1]	4	75%	92%	90%
Children's Asthma Care				
Received Systemic Corticosteroids	-	-	-	100%
Received Home Management Plan	-	-	-	71%
Received Reliever Medication	-	-	-	100%
Use of Medical Imaging				
Combination Abdominal CT Scan	284	0.394	0.237	0.191
Combination Chest CT Scan	215	0.042	0.120	0.054
Follow-up Mammogram/Ultrasound	211	2.8%	8.3%	8.4%
MRI for Low Back Pain	43	51.2%	35.2%	32.7%
Survey of Patients' Hospital Experiences				
Area Around Room 'Always' Quiet at Night	(a)	64%	-	58%
Doctors 'Always' Communicated Well	(a)	78%	-	80%
Home Recovery Information Given	(a)	80%	-	82%
Hospital Given 9 or 10 on 10 Point Scale	(a)	67%	-	67%
Meds 'Always' Explained Before Given	(a)	59%	-	60%
Nurses 'Always' Communicated Well	(a)	77%	-	76%
Pain 'Always' Well Controlled	(a)	69%	-	69%
Room and Bathroom 'Always' Clean	(a)	83%	-	71%
Timely Help 'Always' Received	(a)	75%	-	64%
Would Definitely Recommend Hospital	(a)	72%	-	69%

Perry County Memorial Hospital

One Hospital Road Phone: 812-547-7011
Tell City, IN 47586 Fax: 573-547-3776
URL: www.pchospital.org
Type: Critical Access Hospitals Emergency Services: Yes
Ownership: Government - Local Beds: 38

Key Personnel:
CEO/President. . . . . Joseph S Stuber
Coronary Care . . . . Carolyn Hawkns
Infection Control. . . . . Connie Simpson
Operating Room. . . . . Earla Williams
Quality Assurance . . . . Sandra Calvert
Radiology. . . . . Janice Aaron

Measure	Cases	This Hosp.	State Avg.	U.S. Avg.
Heart Attack Care				
ACE Inhibitor or ARB for LVSD[1]	3	67%	96%	96%
Aspirin at Arrival[1]	6	83%	98%	99%
Aspirin at Discharge[1]	4	100%	99%	98%
Beta Blocker at Discharge[1]	3	100%	98%	98%
Fibrinolytic Medication Timing	0	-	37%	55%
PCI Within 90 Minutes of Arrival	0	-	93%	90%
Smoking Cessation Advice	0	-	99%	99%
Chest Pain/Possible Heart Attack Care				
Aspirin at Arrival	-	-	95%	95%
Median Time to ECG (minutes)	-	-	6	8
Median Time to Transfer (minutes)	-	-	49	61
Fibrinolytic Medication Timing	-	-	63%	54%
Heart Failure Care				
ACE Inhibitor or ARB for LVSD[1]	13	69%	92%	94%
Discharge Instructions[1]	23	74%	84%	88%
Evaluation of LVS Function	33	79%	98%	98%
Smoking Cessation Advice[1]	5	80%	99%	98%
Pneumonia Care				
Appropriate Initial Antibiotic	36	72%	90%	92%
Blood Culture Timing	45	98%	95%	96%
Influenza Vaccine	46	98%	93%	91%
Initial Antibiotic Timing	58	91%	96%	95%
Pneumococcal Vaccine	60	95%	94%	93%
Smoking Cessation Advice[1]	23	83%	98%	97%
Surgical Care Improvement Project				
Appropriate VTP Within 24 Hours[5]	0	-	90%	92%
Appropriate Hair Removal[5]	0	-	100%	99%
Appropriate Beta Blocker Usage[5]	0	-	93%	93%
Controlled Postoperative Blood Glucose[5]	0	-	93%	93%
Prophylactic Antibiotic Timing[5]	0	-	97%	97%
Prophylactic Antibiotic Timing (Outpatient)	-	-	92%	92%
Prophylactic Antibiotic Selection[5]	0	-	98%	97%
Prophylactic Antibiotic Select. (Outpatient)	-	-	95%	94%
Prophylactic Antibiotic Stopped[5]	0	-	95%	94%
Recommended VTP Ordered[5]	0	-	92%	94%
Urinary Catheter Removal[5]	0	-	92%	90%
Children's Asthma Care				
Received Systemic Corticosteroids	-	-	-	100%
Received Home Management Plan	-	-	-	71%
Received Reliever Medication	-	-	-	100%
Use of Medical Imaging				
Combination Abdominal CT Scan	-	-	0.237	0.191
Combination Chest CT Scan	-	-	0.120	0.054
Follow-up Mammogram/Ultrasound	-	-	8.3%	8.4%
MRI for Low Back Pain	-	-	35.2%	32.7%
Survey of Patients' Hospital Experiences				
Area Around Room 'Always' Quiet at Night[8]	-	-	-	58%
Doctors 'Always' Communicated Well[8]	-	-	-	80%
Home Recovery Information Given[8]	-	-	-	82%
Hospital Given 9 or 10 on 10 Point Scale[8]	-	-	-	67%
Meds 'Always' Explained Before Given[8]	-	-	-	60%
Nurses 'Always' Communicated Well[8]	-	-	-	76%
Pain 'Always' Well Controlled[8]	-	-	-	69%
Room and Bathroom 'Always' Clean[8]	-	-	-	71%
Timely Help 'Always' Received[8]	-	-	-	64%
Would Definitely Recommend Hospital[8]	-	-	-	69%

Terre Haute Regional Hospital

3901 S Seventh St Phone: 812-232-0021
Terre Haute, IN 47802 Fax: 812-237-9514
Type: Acute Care Hospitals Emergency Services: Yes
Ownership: Proprietary Beds: 278

Key Personnel:
CEO/President. . . . . Chris Hill
Coronary Care . . . . Deb Girton
Infection Control. . . . . Diana Bowden
Operating Room. . . . . Kim Vester
Quality Assurance . . . . Marsha Ciolli
Radiology. . . . . Bruce Adamson
Emergency Room . . . . Julie VanOven

Measure	Cases	This Hosp.	State Avg.	U.S. Avg.
Heart Attack Care				
ACE Inhibitor or ARB for LVSD	30	100%	96%	96%
Aspirin at Arrival	76	99%	98%	99%
Aspirin at Discharge	125	99%	99%	98%
Beta Blocker at Discharge	129	99%	98%	98%
Fibrinolytic Medication Timing	0	-	37%	55%
PCI Within 90 Minutes of Arrival[1]	13	100%	93%	90%
Smoking Cessation Advice	65	100%	99%	99%
Chest Pain/Possible Heart Attack Care				
Aspirin at Arrival[1]	2	100%	95%	95%
Median Time to ECG (minutes)[1]	3	5	6	8
Median Time to Transfer (minutes)[5]	0	-	49	61
Fibrinolytic Medication Timing[5]	0	-	63%	54%
Heart Failure Care				
ACE Inhibitor or ARB for LVSD	56	100%	92%	94%
Discharge Instructions	173	91%	84%	88%
Evaluation of LVS Function	212	100%	98%	98%
Smoking Cessation Advice	59	100%	99%	98%
Pneumonia Care				
Appropriate Initial Antibiotic	78	94%	90%	92%
Blood Culture Timing	111	100%	95%	96%
Influenza Vaccine	103	100%	93%	91%
Initial Antibiotic Timing	112	99%	96%	95%
Pneumococcal Vaccine	95	100%	94%	93%
Smoking Cessation Advice	82	100%	98%	97%
Surgical Care Improvement Project				
Appropriate VTP Within 24 Hours	119	100%	90%	92%
Appropriate Hair Removal	381	100%	100%	99%
Appropriate Beta Blocker Usage	146	99%	93%	93%
Controlled Postoperative Blood Glucose	72	94%	93%	93%
Prophylactic Antibiotic Timing	274	100%	97%	97%
Prophylactic Antibiotic Timing (Outpatient)	223	100%	92%	92%
Prophylactic Antibiotic Selection	276	98%	98%	97%
Prophylactic Antibiotic Select. (Outpatient)	223	98%	95%	94%
Prophylactic Antibiotic Stopped	232	98%	95%	94%
Recommended VTP Ordered	119	100%	92%	94%
Urinary Catheter Removal	50	100%	92%	90%
Children's Asthma Care				
Received Systemic Corticosteroids[1]	11	100%	-	100%
Received Home Management Plan[1]	11	82%	-	71%
Received Reliever Medication[1]	11	100%	-	100%
Use of Medical Imaging				
Combination Abdominal CT Scan	361	0.216	0.237	0.191
Combination Chest CT Scan	256	0.133	0.120	0.054
Follow-up Mammogram/Ultrasound	578	12.1%	8.3%	8.4%
MRI for Low Back Pain[1]	19	21.1%	35.2%	32.7%
Survey of Patients' Hospital Experiences				
Area Around Room 'Always' Quiet at Night	300+	55%	-	58%
Doctors 'Always' Communicated Well	300+	82%	-	80%
Home Recovery Information Given	300+	88%	-	82%
Hospital Given 9 or 10 on 10 Point Scale	300+	71%	-	67%
Meds 'Always' Explained Before Given	300+	62%	-	60%
Nurses 'Always' Communicated Well	300+	78%	-	76%
Pain 'Always' Well Controlled	300+	72%	-	69%
Room and Bathroom 'Always' Clean	300+	74%	-	71%
Timely Help 'Always' Received	300+	67%	-	64%
Would Definitely Recommend Hospital	300+	74%	-	69%

NOTE: Hospital profiles are in alphabetical order by state, then city, then hospital within the city; Rankings exclude hospitals with less than 25 cases except for patient surveys which excludes hospitals with less than 100 cases; (a) 100–299 cases; (1) The number of cases is too small to be sure how well a hospital is performing; (2) The hospital indicated that the data submitted for this measure were based on a sample of cases; (3) Data was collected during a shorter time period (fewer quarters) than the maximum possible time for this measure; (4) Suppressed for one or more quarters by CMS; (5) No data is available from the hospital for this measure; (6) Fewer than 100 patients completed the HCAHPS survey. Use these rates with caution, as the number of surveys may be too low to reliably assess hospital performance; (7) Survey results are based on less than 12 months of data; (8) Survey results are not available for this reporting period; (9) No or very few patients were eligible for the HCAHPS survey. The scores shown, if any, reflect a very small number of surveys; (10) A state average was not calculated because too few hospitals in the state submitted data; (11) There were discrepancies in the data collection process; Please refer to the User's Guide for a full explanation of data.

Union Hospital

1606 N Seventh St
Terre Haute, IN 47804
URL: www.uhhg.org
Phone: 812-238-7601
Type: Acute Care Hospitals
Emergency Services: Yes
Ownership: Voluntary Non-Profit - Other

Key Personnel:
CEO/President. . . . . David Doerr

Measure	Cases	This Hosp.	State Avg.	U.S. Avg.
Heart Attack Care				
ACE Inhibitor or ARB for LVSD	81	96%	96%	96%
Aspirin at Arrival	245	98%	98%	99%
Aspirin at Discharge	321	100%	99%	98%
Beta Blocker at Discharge	314	99%	98%	98%
Fibrinolytic Medication Timing	0	-	37%	55%
PCI Within 90 Minutes of Arrival	46	87%	93%	90%
Smoking Cessation Advice	115	100%	99%	99%
Chest Pain/Possible Heart Attack Care				
Aspirin at Arrival[1]	14	86%	95%	95%
Median Time to ECG (minutes)[1]	14	8	6	8
Median Time to Transfer (minutes)[5]	0	-	49	61
Fibrinolytic Medication Timing[5]	0	-	63%	54%
Heart Failure Care				
ACE Inhibitor or ARB for LVSD	185	96%	92%	94%
Discharge Instructions	470	84%	84%	88%
Evaluation of LVS Function	570	100%	98%	98%
Smoking Cessation Advice	67	100%	99%	98%
Pneumonia Care				
Appropriate Initial Antibiotic	238	90%	90%	92%
Blood Culture Timing	139	94%	95%	96%
Influenza Vaccine	288	94%	93%	91%
Initial Antibiotic Timing	368	93%	96%	95%
Pneumococcal Vaccine	351	98%	94%	93%
Smoking Cessation Advice	188	100%	98%	97%
Surgical Care Improvement Project				
Appropriate VTP Within 24 Hours	413	92%	90%	92%
Appropriate Hair Removal	1,188	99%	100%	99%
Appropriate Beta Blocker Usage	453	89%	93%	93%
Controlled Postoperative Blood Glucose	194	95%	93%	93%
Prophylactic Antibiotic Timing	732	97%	97%	97%
Prophylactic Antibiotic Timing (Outpatient)	850	95%	92%	92%
Prophylactic Antibiotic Selection	731	96%	98%	97%
Prophylactic Antibiotic Select. (Outpatient)	840	95%	95%	94%
Prophylactic Antibiotic Stopped	674	92%	95%	94%
Recommended VTP Ordered	415	95%	92%	94%
Urinary Catheter Removal	267	88%	92%	90%
Children's Asthma Care				
Received Systemic Corticosteroids	-	-	-	100%
Received Home Management Plan	-	-	-	71%
Received Reliever Medication	-	-	-	100%
Use of Medical Imaging				
Combination Abdominal CT Scan	845	0.050	0.237	0.191
Combination Chest CT Scan	421	0.005	0.120	0.054
Follow-up Mammogram/Ultrasound	2,073	11.4%	8.3%	8.4%
MRI for Low Back Pain	215	30.7%	35.2%	32.7%
Survey of Patients' Hospital Experiences				
Area Around Room 'Always' Quiet at Night	300+	49%	-	58%
Doctors 'Always' Communicated Well	300+	75%	-	80%
Home Recovery Information Given	300+	84%	-	82%
Hospital Given 9 or 10 on 10 Point Scale	300+	66%	-	67%
Meds 'Always' Explained Before Given	300+	54%	-	60%
Nurses 'Always' Communicated Well	300+	73%	-	76%
Pain 'Always' Well Controlled	300+	65%	-	69%
Room and Bathroom 'Always' Clean	300+	72%	-	71%
Timely Help 'Always' Received	300+	63%	-	64%
Would Definitely Recommend Hospital	300+	71%	-	69%

Tipton Hospital

1000 S Main St
Tipton, IN 46072
URL: tiptonhospital.org
Phone: 765-675-8500
Fax: 765-675-8222
Type: Critical Access Hospitals
Emergency Services: Yes
Ownership: Government - Local
Beds: 102

Key Personnel:
CEO/President. . . . . Michael L Harlowe, CHE
Chief of Medical Staff . . . . Vincent Delumpa, MD
Infection Control. . . . . Trina Delph
Operating Room. . . . . Vincent Delumpa
Quality Assurance . . . . Trina Delph
Radiology. . . . . Shamim Babchuk
Intensive Care Unit. . . . . JoEllen Scott
Patient Relations . . . . JoEllen Scott, RN

Measure	Cases	This Hosp.	State Avg.	U.S. Avg.
Heart Attack Care				
ACE Inhibitor or ARB for LVSD[1]	1	100%	96%	96%
Aspirin at Arrival[1]	1	100%	98%	99%
Aspirin at Discharge[1]	1	100%	99%	98%
Beta Blocker at Discharge[1]	1	100%	98%	98%
Fibrinolytic Medication Timing	0	-	37%	55%
PCI Within 90 Minutes of Arrival	0	-	93%	90%
Smoking Cessation Advice	0	-	99%	99%
Chest Pain/Possible Heart Attack Care				
Aspirin at Arrival	-	-	95%	95%
Median Time to ECG (minutes)	-	-	6	8
Median Time to Transfer (minutes)	-	-	49	61
Fibrinolytic Medication Timing	-	-	63%	54%
Heart Failure Care				
ACE Inhibitor or ARB for LVSD[1]	14	100%	92%	94%
Discharge Instructions	26	100%	84%	88%
Evaluation of LVS Function	48	100%	98%	98%
Smoking Cessation Advice[1]	5	100%	99%	98%
Pneumonia Care				
Appropriate Initial Antibiotic	35	86%	90%	92%
Blood Culture Timing	39	97%	95%	96%
Influenza Vaccine	37	92%	93%	91%
Initial Antibiotic Timing	49	92%	96%	95%
Pneumococcal Vaccine	50	98%	94%	93%
Smoking Cessation Advice[1]	11	100%	98%	97%
Surgical Care Improvement Project				
Appropriate VTP Within 24 Hours	47	98%	90%	92%
Appropriate Hair Removal	130	100%	100%	99%
Appropriate Beta Blocker Usage	36	97%	93%	93%
Controlled Postoperative Blood Glucose[5]	0	-	93%	93%
Prophylactic Antibiotic Timing	91	100%	97%	97%
Prophylactic Antibiotic Timing (Outpatient)	-	-	92%	92%
Prophylactic Antibiotic Selection	90	98%	98%	97%
Prophylactic Antibiotic Select. (Outpatient)	-	-	95%	94%
Prophylactic Antibiotic Stopped	90	96%	95%	94%
Recommended VTP Ordered	47	98%	92%	94%
Urinary Catheter Removal	44	100%	92%	90%
Children's Asthma Care				
Received Systemic Corticosteroids	-	-	-	100%
Received Home Management Plan	-	-	-	71%
Received Reliever Medication	-	-	-	100%
Use of Medical Imaging				
Combination Abdominal CT Scan	-	-	0.237	0.191
Combination Chest CT Scan	-	-	0.120	0.054
Follow-up Mammogram/Ultrasound	-	-	8.3%	8.4%
MRI for Low Back Pain	-	-	35.2%	32.7%
Survey of Patients' Hospital Experiences				
Area Around Room 'Always' Quiet at Night	300+	66%	-	58%
Doctors 'Always' Communicated Well	300+	88%	-	80%
Home Recovery Information Given	300+	88%	-	82%
Hospital Given 9 or 10 on 10 Point Scale	300+	81%	-	67%
Meds 'Always' Explained Before Given	300+	59%	-	60%
Nurses 'Always' Communicated Well	300+	82%	-	76%
Pain 'Always' Well Controlled	300+	71%	-	69%
Room and Bathroom 'Always' Clean	300+	81%	-	71%
Timely Help 'Always' Received	300+	68%	-	64%
Would Definitely Recommend Hospital	300+	81%	-	69%

Porter Valparaiso Hospital Campus

814 Laporte Avenue
Valparaiso, IN 46383
URL: www.portermemorial.org
Phone: 219-263-4600
Fax: 219-463-4882
Type: Acute Care Hospitals
Emergency Services: Yes
Ownership: Voluntary Non-Profit - Private
Beds: 402

Key Personnel:
CEO/President. . . . . Johnathan Nalli
Chief of Medical Staff . . . . Doug A Mazurek, MD
Infection Control. . . . . Julie Downey, RN
Operating Room. . . . . Rose Mary Mroz
Pediatric In-Patient Care . . . . Jeffrey Miller, MD
Quality Assurance . . . . Michelle Back, RN
Radiology. . . . . Anil Kothari, MD

Measure	Cases	This Hosp.	State Avg.	U.S. Avg.
Heart Attack Care				
ACE Inhibitor or ARB for LVSD[1]	24	96%	96%	96%
Aspirin at Arrival	155	100%	98%	99%
Aspirin at Discharge	179	100%	99%	98%
Beta Blocker at Discharge	176	100%	98%	98%
Fibrinolytic Medication Timing	0	-	37%	55%
PCI Within 90 Minutes of Arrival	39	90%	93%	90%
Smoking Cessation Advice	70	100%	99%	99%
Chest Pain/Possible Heart Attack Care				
Aspirin at Arrival[1]	19	89%	95%	95%
Median Time to ECG (minutes)[1]	22	7	6	8
Median Time to Transfer (minutes)[5]	0	-	49	61
Fibrinolytic Medication Timing[3]	0	-	63%	54%
Heart Failure Care				
ACE Inhibitor or ARB for LVSD	112	100%	92%	94%
Discharge Instructions	252	100%	84%	88%
Evaluation of LVS Function	323	100%	98%	98%
Smoking Cessation Advice	36	100%	99%	98%
Pneumonia Care				
Appropriate Initial Antibiotic	146	90%	90%	92%
Blood Culture Timing	259	94%	95%	96%
Influenza Vaccine	228	95%	93%	91%
Initial Antibiotic Timing	247	93%	96%	95%
Pneumococcal Vaccine	272	96%	94%	93%
Smoking Cessation Advice	100	100%	98%	97%
Surgical Care Improvement Project				
Appropriate VTP Within 24 Hours	236	81%	90%	92%
Appropriate Hair Removal	1,056	100%	100%	99%
Appropriate Beta Blocker Usage	331	97%	93%	93%
Controlled Postoperative Blood Glucose	118	85%	93%	93%
Prophylactic Antibiotic Timing	764	98%	97%	97%
Prophylactic Antibiotic Timing (Outpatient)	527	91%	92%	92%
Prophylactic Antibiotic Selection	769	98%	98%	97%
Prophylactic Antibiotic Select. (Outpatient)	510	95%	95%	94%
Prophylactic Antibiotic Stopped	745	96%	95%	94%
Recommended VTP Ordered	236	85%	92%	94%
Urinary Catheter Removal	156	85%	92%	90%
Children's Asthma Care				
Received Systemic Corticosteroids	-	-	-	100%
Received Home Management Plan	-	-	-	71%
Received Reliever Medication	-	-	-	100%
Use of Medical Imaging				
Combination Abdominal CT Scan	1,328	0.629	0.237	0.191
Combination Chest CT Scan	911	0.583	0.120	0.054
Follow-up Mammogram/Ultrasound	1,834	8.7%	8.3%	8.4%
MRI for Low Back Pain	350	35.1%	35.2%	32.7%
Survey of Patients' Hospital Experiences				
Area Around Room 'Always' Quiet at Night	300+	49%	-	58%
Doctors 'Always' Communicated Well	300+	77%	-	80%
Home Recovery Information Given	300+	81%	-	82%
Hospital Given 9 or 10 on 10 Point Scale	300+	58%	-	67%
Meds 'Always' Explained Before Given	300+	55%	-	60%
Nurses 'Always' Communicated Well	300+	72%	-	76%
Pain 'Always' Well Controlled	300+	67%	-	69%
Room and Bathroom 'Always' Clean	300+	63%	-	71%
Timely Help 'Always' Received	300+	51%	-	64%
Would Definitely Recommend Hospital	300+	60%	-	69%

NOTE: Hospital profiles are in alphabetical order by state, then city, then hospital within the city; Rankings exclude hospitals with less than 25 cases except for patient surveys which excludes hospitals with less than 100 cases; (a) 100–299 cases; (1) The number of cases is too small to be sure how well a hospital is performing; (2) The hospital indicated that the data submitted for this measure were based on a sample of cases; (3) Data was collected during a shorter time period (fewer quarters) than the maximum possible time for this measure; (4) Suppressed for one or more quarters by CMS; (5) No data is available from the hospital for this measure; (6) Fewer than 100 patients completed the HCAHPS survey. Use these rates with caution, as the number of surveys may be too low to reliably assess hospital performance; (7) Survey results are based on less than 12 months of data; (8) Survey results are not available for this reporting period; (9) No or very few patients were eligible for the HCAHPS survey. The scores shown, if any, reflect a very small number of surveys; (10) A state average was not calculated because too few hospitals in the state submitted data; (11) There were discrepancies in the data collection process; Please refer to the User's Guide for a full explanation of data.

Good Samaritan Hospital

520 S 7th Street Phone: 812-882-5220
Vincennes, IN 47591
URL: gshvin.org
Type: Acute Care Hospitals Emergency Services: Yes
Ownership: Government - Local
Key Personnel:
President/CEO. . . . . Robert McLin
Radiology. Gary Chavis

Measure	Cases	This Hosp.	State Avg.	U.S. Avg.
Heart Attack Care				
ACE Inhibitor or ARB for LVSD	31	97%	96%	96%
Aspirin at Arrival	101	99%	98%	99%
Aspirin at Discharge	131	98%	99%	98%
Beta Blocker at Discharge	135	96%	98%	98%
Fibrinolytic Medication Timing	0	-	37%	55%
PCI Within 90 Minutes of Arrival	31	90%	93%	90%
Smoking Cessation Advice	51	96%	99%	99%
Chest Pain/Possible Heart Attack Care				
Aspirin at Arrival[1]	6	83%	95%	95%
Median Time to ECG (minutes)[1]	7	7	6	8
Median Time to Transfer (minutes)[5]	0	-	49	61
Fibrinolytic Medication Timing[5]	0	-	63%	54%
Heart Failure Care				
ACE Inhibitor or ARB for LVSD	98	86%	92%	94%
Discharge Instructions	200	87%	84%	88%
Evaluation of LVS Function	266	93%	98%	98%
Smoking Cessation Advice	35	97%	99%	98%
Pneumonia Care				
Appropriate Initial Antibiotic	120	88%	90%	92%
Blood Culture Timing	156	99%	95%	96%
Influenza Vaccine	184	99%	93%	91%
Initial Antibiotic Timing	195	97%	96%	95%
Pneumococcal Vaccine	194	98%	94%	93%
Smoking Cessation Advice	76	95%	98%	97%
Surgical Care Improvement Project				
Appropriate VTP Within 24 Hours	168	92%	90%	92%
Appropriate Hair Removal	604	100%	100%	99%
Appropriate Beta Blocker Usage	165	96%	93%	93%
Controlled Postoperative Blood Glucose	51	92%	93%	93%
Prophylactic Antibiotic Timing	405	99%	97%	97%
Prophylactic Antibiotic Timing (Outpatient)	168	97%	92%	92%
Prophylactic Antibiotic Selection	413	99%	98%	97%
Prophylactic Antibiotic Select. (Outpatient)	166	95%	95%	94%
Prophylactic Antibiotic Stopped	384	97%	95%	94%
Recommended VTP Ordered	168	94%	92%	94%
Urinary Catheter Removal	45	91%	92%	90%
Children's Asthma Care				
Received Systemic Corticosteroids	-	-	-	100%
Received Home Management Plan	-	-	-	71%
Received Reliever Medication	-	-	-	100%
Use of Medical Imaging				
Combination Abdominal CT Scan	1,034	0.507	0.237	0.191
Combination Chest CT Scan	603	0.114	0.120	0.054
Follow-up Mammogram/Ultrasound	1,542	4.9%	8.3%	8.4%
MRI for Low Back Pain	171	31.6%	35.2%	32.7%
Survey of Patients' Hospital Experiences				
Area Around Room 'Always' Quiet at Night	300+	55%	-	58%
Doctors 'Always' Communicated Well	300+	83%	-	80%
Home Recovery Information Given	300+	89%	-	82%
Hospital Given 9 or 10 on 10 Point Scale	300+	76%	-	67%
Meds 'Always' Explained Before Given	300+	65%	-	60%
Nurses 'Always' Communicated Well	300+	84%	-	76%
Pain 'Always' Well Controlled	300+	78%	-	69%
Room and Bathroom 'Always' Clean	300+	87%	-	71%
Timely Help 'Always' Received	300+	76%	-	64%
Would Definitely Recommend Hospital	300+	79%	-	69%

Wabash County Hospital

710 N East Street Phone: 260-563-3131
Wabash, IN 46992 Fax: 260-569-2410
URL: www.wchospital.com
Type: Critical Access Hospitals Emergency Services: Yes
Ownership: Government - Local Beds: 25
Key Personnel:
CEO/President. . . . . David C Hunter
Chief of Medical Staff . . . . Joseph Rudolph
Infection Control. . . . . Mike Vogel, RN
Operating Room. . . . . Bill Planck, RN
Quality Assurance . . . . Richard Tucker
Radiology. . . . . James Wehrenber, RT
Emergency Room . . . . Jonathan Grandstaff-Dunp
Intensive Care Unit. . . . . Sandy Wright, RN

Measure	Cases	This Hosp.	State Avg.	U.S. Avg.
Heart Attack Care				
ACE Inhibitor or ARB for LVSD	0	-	96%	96%
Aspirin at Arrival[1]	3	100%	98%	99%
Aspirin at Discharge[1]	2	100%	99%	98%
Beta Blocker at Discharge[1]	1	100%	98%	98%
Fibrinolytic Medication Timing	0	-	37%	55%
PCI Within 90 Minutes of Arrival[5]	0	-	93%	90%
Smoking Cessation Advice	0	-	99%	99%
Chest Pain/Possible Heart Attack Care				
Aspirin at Arrival	-	-	95%	95%
Median Time to ECG (minutes)	-	-	6	8
Median Time to Transfer (minutes)	-	-	49	61
Fibrinolytic Medication Timing	-	-	63%	54%
Heart Failure Care				
ACE Inhibitor or ARB for LVSD[1]	11	73%	92%	94%
Discharge Instructions[1]	21	90%	84%	88%
Evaluation of LVS Function	39	90%	98%	98%
Smoking Cessation Advice[1]	4	100%	99%	98%
Pneumonia Care				
Appropriate Initial Antibiotic	33	82%	90%	92%
Blood Culture Timing	33	100%	95%	96%
Influenza Vaccine	29	93%	93%	91%
Initial Antibiotic Timing	30	100%	96%	95%
Pneumococcal Vaccine	39	82%	94%	93%
Smoking Cessation Advice[1]	9	100%	98%	97%
Surgical Care Improvement Project				
Appropriate VTP Within 24 Hours[1]	15	67%	90%	92%
Appropriate Hair Removal	35	100%	100%	99%
Appropriate Beta Blocker Usage[1]	5	40%	93%	93%
Controlled Postoperative Blood Glucose[5]	0	-	93%	93%
Prophylactic Antibiotic Timing[1]	14	64%	97%	97%
Prophylactic Antibiotic Timing (Outpatient)	-	-	92%	92%
Prophylactic Antibiotic Selection[1]	14	100%	98%	97%
Prophylactic Antibiotic Select. (Outpatient)	-	-	95%	94%
Prophylactic Antibiotic Stopped[1]	14	93%	95%	94%
Recommended VTP Ordered[1]	15	67%	92%	94%
Urinary Catheter Removal[1]	4	75%	92%	90%
Children's Asthma Care				
Received Systemic Corticosteroids	-	-	-	100%
Received Home Management Plan	-	-	-	71%
Received Reliever Medication	-	-	-	100%
Use of Medical Imaging				
Combination Abdominal CT Scan	-	-	0.237	0.191
Combination Chest CT Scan	-	-	0.120	0.054
Follow-up Mammogram/Ultrasound	-	-	8.3%	8.4%
MRI for Low Back Pain	-	-	35.2%	32.7%
Survey of Patients' Hospital Experiences				
Area Around Room 'Always' Quiet at Night	(a)	60%	-	58%
Doctors 'Always' Communicated Well	(a)	79%	-	80%
Home Recovery Information Given	(a)	86%	-	82%
Hospital Given 9 or 10 on 10 Point Scale	(a)	71%	-	67%
Meds 'Always' Explained Before Given	(a)	62%	-	60%
Nurses 'Always' Communicated Well	(a)	86%	-	76%
Pain 'Always' Well Controlled	(a)	78%	-	69%
Room and Bathroom 'Always' Clean	(a)	84%	-	71%
Timely Help 'Always' Received	(a)	81%	-	64%
Would Definitely Recommend Hospital	(a)	66%	-	69%

Kosciusko Community Hospital

2101 E Dubois Dr Phone: 574-372-7611
Warsaw, IN 46580 Fax: 574-372-7816
URL: www.kch.com
Type: Acute Care Hospitals Emergency Services: Yes
Ownership: Proprietary Beds: 72
Key Personnel:
CEO/President. . . . . Steve Miller
Chief of Medical Staff . . . . Gregory Haase, DO
Infection Control. . . . . Thomas Kocoshis, MD
Radiology. . . . . Steph Damon
Anesthesiology. . . . . John Hilgenberg, MD
Emergency Room . . . . Linda Law, MD
Intensive Care Unit. . . . . Gregory Haase, DO

Measure	Cases	This Hosp.	State Avg.	U.S. Avg.
Heart Attack Care				
ACE Inhibitor or ARB for LVSD[1]	6	83%	96%	96%
Aspirin at Arrival	42	98%	98%	99%
Aspirin at Discharge[1]	24	100%	99%	98%
Beta Blocker at Discharge[1]	20	100%	98%	98%
Fibrinolytic Medication Timing	0	-	37%	55%
PCI Within 90 Minutes of Arrival	0	-	93%	90%
Smoking Cessation Advice[1]	3	100%	99%	99%
Chest Pain/Possible Heart Attack Care				
Aspirin at Arrival	228	98%	95%	95%
Median Time to ECG (minutes)	234	4	6	8
Median Time to Transfer (minutes)[1]	19	41	49	61
Fibrinolytic Medication Timing	0	-	63%	54%
Heart Failure Care				
ACE Inhibitor or ARB for LVSD	36	94%	92%	94%
Discharge Instructions	100	96%	84%	88%
Evaluation of LVS Function	150	99%	98%	98%
Smoking Cessation Advice	25	100%	99%	98%
Pneumonia Care				
Appropriate Initial Antibiotic	97	95%	90%	92%
Blood Culture Timing	147	98%	95%	96%
Influenza Vaccine	86	98%	93%	91%
Initial Antibiotic Timing	144	97%	96%	95%
Pneumococcal Vaccine	112	98%	94%	93%
Smoking Cessation Advice	41	100%	98%	97%
Surgical Care Improvement Project				
Appropriate VTP Within 24 Hours	71	97%	90%	92%
Appropriate Hair Removal	321	100%	100%	99%
Appropriate Beta Blocker Usage	75	100%	93%	93%
Controlled Postoperative Blood Glucose	0	-	93%	93%
Prophylactic Antibiotic Timing	244	100%	97%	97%
Prophylactic Antibiotic Timing (Outpatient)	99	97%	92%	92%
Prophylactic Antibiotic Selection	245	97%	98%	97%
Prophylactic Antibiotic Select. (Outpatient)	97	99%	95%	94%
Prophylactic Antibiotic Stopped	237	97%	95%	94%
Recommended VTP Ordered	71	97%	92%	94%
Urinary Catheter Removal[1]	21	100%	92%	90%
Children's Asthma Care				
Received Systemic Corticosteroids	-	-	-	100%
Received Home Management Plan	-	-	-	71%
Received Reliever Medication	-	-	-	100%
Use of Medical Imaging				
Combination Abdominal CT Scan	493	0.497	0.237	0.191
Combination Chest CT Scan	283	0.396	0.120	0.054
Follow-up Mammogram/Ultrasound	660	1.2%	8.3%	8.4%
MRI for Low Back Pain	198	32.3%	35.2%	32.7%
Survey of Patients' Hospital Experiences				
Area Around Room 'Always' Quiet at Night	300+	51%	-	58%
Doctors 'Always' Communicated Well	300+	82%	-	80%
Home Recovery Information Given	300+	83%	-	82%
Hospital Given 9 or 10 on 10 Point Scale	300+	64%	-	67%
Meds 'Always' Explained Before Given	300+	57%	-	60%
Nurses 'Always' Communicated Well	300+	75%	-	76%
Pain 'Always' Well Controlled	300+	70%	-	69%
Room and Bathroom 'Always' Clean	300+	69%	-	71%
Timely Help 'Always' Received	300+	58%	-	64%
Would Definitely Recommend Hospital	300+	59%	-	69%

NOTE: Hospital profiles are in alphabetical order by state, then city, then hospital within the city; Rankings exclude hospitals with less than 25 cases except for patient surveys which excludes hospitals with less than 100 cases; (a) 100–299 cases; (1) The number of cases is too small to be sure how well a hospital is performing; (2) The hospital indicated that the data submitted for this measure were based on a sample of cases; (3) Data was collected during a shorter time period (fewer quarters) than the maximum possible time for this measure; (4) Suppressed for one or more quarters by CMS; (5) No data is available from the hospital for this measure; (6) Fewer than 100 patients completed the HCAHPS survey. Use these rates with caution, as the number of surveys may be too low to reliably assess hospital performance; (7) Survey results are based on less than 12 months of data; (8) Survey results are not available for this reporting period; (9) No or very few patients were eligible for the HCAHPS survey. The scores shown, if any, reflect a very small number of surveys; (10) A state average was not calculated because too few hospitals in the state submitted data; (11) There were discrepancies in the data collection process; Please refer to the User's Guide for a full explanation of data.

Daviess Community Hospital

1314 E Walnut St
Washington, IN 47501
Phone: 812-254-2760
Fax: 812-254-8897
E-mail: msmith@dchosp.org
URL: www.dchosp.org
Type: Acute Care Hospitals
Emergency Services: Yes
Ownership: Government - Local
Beds: 120

Key Personnel:
CEO/President. . . . . Gary G Kendrick
Cardiac Laboratory. . . . . Phillip Dawkins, MD
Chief of Medical Staff . . . . James Filler
Infection Control. . . . . Carol Matteson
Operating Room. . . . . Shirley Yoder
Quality Assurance . . . . Mark Dame
Radiology. . . . . E M Cha, MD

Measure	Cases	This Hosp.	State Avg.	U.S. Avg.
Heart Attack Care				
ACE Inhibitor or ARB for LVSD	0	-	96%	96%
Aspirin at Arrival[1]	8	100%	98%	99%
Aspirin at Discharge[1]	7	100%	99%	98%
Beta Blocker at Discharge[1]	8	88%	98%	98%
Fibrinolytic Medication Timing	0	-	37%	55%
PCI Within 90 Minutes of Arrival	0	-	93%	90%
Smoking Cessation Advice[1]	1	100%	99%	99%
Chest Pain/Possible Heart Attack Care				
Aspirin at Arrival	77	99%	95%	95%
Median Time to ECG (minutes)	83	5	6	8
Median Time to Transfer (minutes)[1]	8	65	49	61
Fibrinolytic Medication Timing[1]	1	0%	63%	54%
Heart Failure Care				
ACE Inhibitor or ARB for LVSD[1]	8	88%	92%	94%
Discharge Instructions	35	46%	84%	88%
Evaluation of LVS Function	49	94%	98%	98%
Smoking Cessation Advice[1]	5	80%	99%	98%
Pneumonia Care				
Appropriate Initial Antibiotic	92	91%	90%	92%
Blood Culture Timing	144	94%	95%	96%
Influenza Vaccine	97	79%	93%	91%
Initial Antibiotic Timing	122	99%	96%	95%
Pneumococcal Vaccine	141	75%	94%	93%
Smoking Cessation Advice	56	82%	98%	97%
Surgical Care Improvement Project				
Appropriate VTP Within 24 Hours	32	56%	90%	92%
Appropriate Hair Removal	54	100%	100%	99%
Appropriate Beta Blocker Usage[1]	7	86%	93%	93%
Controlled Postoperative Blood Glucose	0	-	93%	93%
Prophylactic Antibiotic Timing[1]	24	96%	97%	97%
Prophylactic Antibiotic Timing (Outpatient)[1,3]	18	94%	92%	92%
Prophylactic Antibiotic Selection[1]	24	96%	98%	97%
Prophylactic Antibiotic Select. (Outpatient)[1,3]	17	100%	95%	94%
Prophylactic Antibiotic Stopped[1]	21	71%	95%	94%
Recommended VTP Ordered	32	56%	92%	94%
Urinary Catheter Removal[1]	14	86%	92%	90%
Children's Asthma Care				
Received Systemic Corticosteroids	-	-	-	100%
Received Home Management Plan	-	-	-	71%
Received Reliever Medication	-	-	-	100%
Use of Medical Imaging				
Combination Abdominal CT Scan	229	0.830	0.237	0.191
Combination Chest CT Scan	128	0.500	0.120	0.054
Follow-up Mammogram/Ultrasound	452	9.3%	8.3%	8.4%
MRI for Low Back Pain	69	36.2%	35.2%	32.7%
Survey of Patients' Hospital Experiences				
Area Around Room 'Always' Quiet at Night	300+	57%	-	58%
Doctors 'Always' Communicated Well	300+	80%	-	80%
Home Recovery Information Given	300+	81%	-	82%
Hospital Given 9 or 10 on 10 Point Scale	300+	63%	-	67%
Meds 'Always' Explained Before Given	300+	57%	-	60%
Nurses 'Always' Communicated Well	300+	71%	-	76%
Pain 'Always' Well Controlled	300+	67%	-	69%
Room and Bathroom 'Always' Clean	300+	76%	-	71%
Timely Help 'Always' Received	300+	69%	-	64%
Would Definitely Recommend Hospital	300+	58%	-	69%

Saint Vincent Williamsport Hospital

412 N Monroe Street
Williamsport, IN 47993
Phone: 765-762-4000
Fax: 765-762-4126
URL: www.stvincent.org
Type: Critical Access Hospitals
Emergency Services: Yes
Ownership: Voluntary Non-Profit - Church
Beds: 16

Key Personnel:
CEO/President. . . . . Anthony R Tersigni, EdD
Chief of Medical Staff . . . . Dr. Tahir Hafeez
Operating Room. . . . . Chad J Davis
Quality Assurance . . . . John D Doyle
Emergency Room . . . . H Brenner, MD

Measure	Cases	This Hosp.	State Avg.	U.S. Avg.
Heart Attack Care				
ACE Inhibitor or ARB for LVSD[3]	0	-	96%	96%
Aspirin at Arrival[1,3]	2	100%	98%	99%
Aspirin at Discharge[1,3]	2	100%	99%	98%
Beta Blocker at Discharge[1,3]	2	100%	98%	98%
Fibrinolytic Medication Timing[5]	0	-	37%	55%
PCI Within 90 Minutes of Arrival[5]	0	-	93%	90%
Smoking Cessation Advice[3]	0	-	99%	99%
Chest Pain/Possible Heart Attack Care				
Aspirin at Arrival	-	-	95%	95%
Median Time to ECG (minutes)	-	-	6	8
Median Time to Transfer (minutes)	-	-	49	61
Fibrinolytic Medication Timing	-	-	63%	54%
Heart Failure Care				
ACE Inhibitor or ARB for LVSD[1]	12	83%	92%	94%
Discharge Instructions	26	100%	84%	88%
Evaluation of LVS Function	46	98%	98%	98%
Smoking Cessation Advice[1]	4	100%	99%	98%
Pneumonia Care				
Appropriate Initial Antibiotic	29	90%	90%	92%
Blood Culture Timing	46	93%	95%	96%
Influenza Vaccine	30	97%	93%	91%
Initial Antibiotic Timing	44	95%	96%	95%
Pneumococcal Vaccine	39	100%	94%	93%
Smoking Cessation Advice[1]	12	100%	98%	97%
Surgical Care Improvement Project				
Appropriate VTP Within 24 Hours	0	-	90%	92%
Appropriate Hair Removal[1]	12	100%	100%	99%
Appropriate Beta Blocker Usage[1]	1	100%	93%	93%
Controlled Postoperative Blood Glucose[5]	0	-	93%	93%
Prophylactic Antibiotic Timing[1]	12	100%	97%	97%
Prophylactic Antibiotic Timing (Outpatient)	-	-	92%	92%
Prophylactic Antibiotic Selection[1]	12	100%	98%	97%
Prophylactic Antibiotic Select. (Outpatient)	-	-	95%	94%
Prophylactic Antibiotic Stopped[1]	12	75%	95%	94%
Recommended VTP Ordered	0	-	92%	94%
Urinary Catheter Removal	0	-	92%	90%
Children's Asthma Care				
Received Systemic Corticosteroids	-	-	-	100%
Received Home Management Plan	-	-	-	71%
Received Reliever Medication	-	-	-	100%
Use of Medical Imaging				
Combination Abdominal CT Scan	-	-	0.237	0.191
Combination Chest CT Scan	-	-	0.120	0.054
Follow-up Mammogram/Ultrasound	-	-	8.3%	8.4%
MRI for Low Back Pain	-	-	35.2%	32.7%
Survey of Patients' Hospital Experiences				
Area Around Room 'Always' Quiet at Night	(a)	52%	-	58%
Doctors 'Always' Communicated Well	(a)	82%	-	80%
Home Recovery Information Given	(a)	84%	-	82%
Hospital Given 9 or 10 on 10 Point Scale	(a)	68%	-	67%
Meds 'Always' Explained Before Given	(a)	64%	-	60%
Nurses 'Always' Communicated Well	(a)	83%	-	76%
Pain 'Always' Well Controlled	(a)	69%	-	69%
Room and Bathroom 'Always' Clean	(a)	87%	-	71%
Timely Help 'Always' Received	(a)	78%	-	64%
Would Definitely Recommend Hospital	(a)	68%	-	69%

Saint Vincent Randolph Hospital

473 E Greenville Avenue
Winchester, IN 47394
Phone: 765-584-0004
Fax: 765-584-0066
URL: www.stvincent.org
Type: Critical Access Hospitals
Emergency Services: Yes
Ownership: Voluntary Non-Profit - Private
Beds: 25

Key Personnel:
CEO/President. . . . . Francis Albarano
Chief of Medical Staff . . . . Troy A Abbot
Quality Assurance . . . . John D Doyle
Radiology. . . . . Peter D Arfken
Emergency Room . . . . Harry Moynihan MD

Measure	Cases	This Hosp.	State Avg.	U.S. Avg.
Heart Attack Care				
ACE Inhibitor or ARB for LVSD[3]	0	-	96%	96%
Aspirin at Arrival[1,3]	3	100%	98%	99%
Aspirin at Discharge[1,3]	2	100%	99%	98%
Beta Blocker at Discharge[1,3]	2	100%	98%	98%
Fibrinolytic Medication Timing[5]	0	-	37%	55%
PCI Within 90 Minutes of Arrival[5]	0	-	93%	90%
Smoking Cessation Advice[3]	0	-	99%	99%
Chest Pain/Possible Heart Attack Care				
Aspirin at Arrival[5]	0	-	95%	95%
Median Time to ECG (minutes)[5]	0	-	6	8
Median Time to Transfer (minutes)[5]	0	-	49	61
Fibrinolytic Medication Timing[5]	0	-	63%	54%
Heart Failure Care				
ACE Inhibitor or ARB for LVSD[1]	17	82%	92%	94%
Discharge Instructions	43	74%	84%	88%
Evaluation of LVS Function	44	86%	98%	98%
Smoking Cessation Advice[1]	12	92%	99%	98%
Pneumonia Care				
Appropriate Initial Antibiotic	25	92%	90%	92%
Blood Culture Timing	45	93%	95%	96%
Influenza Vaccine	28	89%	93%	91%
Initial Antibiotic Timing	56	96%	96%	95%
Pneumococcal Vaccine	43	93%	94%	93%
Smoking Cessation Advice[1]	12	92%	98%	97%
Surgical Care Improvement Project				
Appropriate VTP Within 24 Hours	0	-	90%	92%
Appropriate Hair Removal[1]	2	100%	100%	99%
Appropriate Beta Blocker Usage	0	-	93%	93%
Controlled Postoperative Blood Glucose	0	-	93%	93%
Prophylactic Antibiotic Timing[1]	2	100%	97%	97%
Prophylactic Antibiotic Timing (Outpatient)[5]	0	-	92%	92%
Prophylactic Antibiotic Selection[1]	2	100%	98%	97%
Prophylactic Antibiotic Select. (Outpatient)[5]	0	-	95%	94%
Prophylactic Antibiotic Stopped[1]	2	100%	95%	94%
Recommended VTP Ordered	0	-	92%	94%
Urinary Catheter Removal	0	-	92%	90%
Children's Asthma Care				
Received Systemic Corticosteroids	-	-	-	100%
Received Home Management Plan	-	-	-	71%
Received Reliever Medication	-	-	-	100%
Use of Medical Imaging				
Combination Abdominal CT Scan	233	0.112	0.237	0.191
Combination Chest CT Scan	139	0.022	0.120	0.054
Follow-up Mammogram/Ultrasound	311	7.4%	8.3%	8.4%
MRI for Low Back Pain[1]	32	34.4%	35.2%	32.7%
Survey of Patients' Hospital Experiences				
Area Around Room 'Always' Quiet at Night	(a)	55%	-	58%
Doctors 'Always' Communicated Well	(a)	82%	-	80%
Home Recovery Information Given	(a)	82%	-	82%
Hospital Given 9 or 10 on 10 Point Scale	(a)	66%	-	67%
Meds 'Always' Explained Before Given	(a)	63%	-	60%
Nurses 'Always' Communicated Well	(a)	74%	-	76%
Pain 'Always' Well Controlled	(a)	69%	-	69%
Room and Bathroom 'Always' Clean	(a)	72%	-	71%
Timely Help 'Always' Received	(a)	70%	-	64%
Would Definitely Recommend Hospital	(a)	61%	-	69%

NOTE: Hospital profiles are in alphabetical order by state, then city, then hospital within the city; Rankings exclude hospitals with less than 25 cases except for patient surveys which excludes hospitals with less than 100 cases; (a) 100–299 cases; (1) The number of cases is too small to be sure how well a hospital is performing; (2) The hospital indicated that the data submitted for this measure were based on a sample of cases; (3) Data was collected during a shorter time period (fewer quarters) than the maximum possible time for this measure; (4) Suppressed for one or more quarters by CMS; (5) No data is available from the hospital for this measure; (6) Fewer than 100 patients completed the HCAHPS survey. Use these rates with caution, as the number of surveys may be too low to reliably assess hospital performance; (7) Survey results are based on less than 12 months of data; (8) Survey results are not available for this reporting period; (9) No or very few patients were eligible for the HCAHPS survey. The scores shown, if any, reflect a very small number of surveys; (10) A state average was not calculated because too few hospitals in the state submitted data; (11) There were discrepancies in the data collection process; Please refer to the User's Guide for a full explanation of data.

Heart Attack Care

1. ACE Inhibitor or ARB for LVSD

Hospital Name	City	Rate	Cases
Mary Greeley Medical Center	Ames	100%	27
Mercy Medical Center-Cedar Rapids	Cedar Rapids	100%	25
Mercy Medical Center-Dubuque	Dubuque	100%	25
Mercy Medical Center-Sioux City	Sioux City	100%	49
Mercy Medical Center-Des Moines	Des Moines	99%	82
Mercy Medical Center-North Iowa	Mason City	99%	69
Trinity Regional Medical Center	Fort Dodge	98%	41
Genesis Medical Center - Davenport[2]	Davenport	97%	63
Iowa Methodist Medical Center[2]	Des Moines	97%	38
Mercy Hospital	Iowa City	96%	28
Saint Lukes Hospital[2]	Cedar Rapids	96%	27
Allen Memorial Hospital[2]	Waterloo	94%	48
University of Iowa Hospital & Clinics	Iowa City	83%	42

2. Aspirin at Arrival

Hospital Name	City	Rate	Cases
Covenant Medical Center	Waterloo	100%	56
Iowa City VA Medical Center	Iowa City	100%	35
Mary Greeley Medical Center	Ames	100%	114
Mercy Hospital	Iowa City	100%	113
Mercy Medical Center-Cedar Rapids	Cedar Rapids	100%	205
Mercy Medical Center-Dubuque	Dubuque	100%	133
Mercy Medical Center-North Iowa	Mason City	100%	156
Mercy Medical Center-Sioux City	Sioux City	100%	223
Saint Lukes Hospital[2]	Cedar Rapids	100%	214
Saint Lukes Regional Medical Center	Sioux City	100%	30
Trinity Bettendorf	Bettendorf	100%	49
University of Iowa Hospital & Clinics	Iowa City	100%	79
Alegent Health Mercy Hospital	Council Bluffs	99%	115
Allen Memorial Hospital[2]	Waterloo	99%	168
Genesis Medical Center - Davenport[2]	Davenport	99%	147
Mercy Medical Center-Clinton	Clinton	99%	124
Mercy Medical Center-Des Moines	Des Moines	99%	343
Great River Medical Center	West Burlington	98%	139
Iowa Lutheran Hospital[2]	Des Moines	98%	121
Iowa Methodist Medical Center[2]	Des Moines	98%	147
Jennie Edmundson Hospital	Council Bluffs	98%	107
Marshalltown Medical & Surgical Center	Marshalltown	98%	56
Trinity Regional Medical Center	Fort Dodge	97%	104
The Finley Hospital	Dubuque	95%	40

3. Aspirin at Discharge

Hospital Name	City	Rate	Cases
Alegent Health Mercy Hospital	Council Bluffs	100%	103
Allen Memorial Hospital[2]	Waterloo	100%	237
Covenant Medical Center	Waterloo	100%	81
Genesis Medical Center - Davenport[2]	Davenport	100%	297
Iowa Lutheran Hospital[2]	Des Moines	100%	116
Mary Greeley Medical Center	Ames	100%	129
Mercy Hospital	Iowa City	100%	221
Mercy Medical Center-Cedar Rapids	Cedar Rapids	100%	198
Mercy Medical Center-Des Moines	Des Moines	100%	639
Mercy Medical Center-North Iowa	Mason City	100%	252
Saint Lukes Hospital[2]	Cedar Rapids	100%	258
Saint Lukes Regional Medical Center	Sioux City	100%	29
Trinity Bettendorf	Bettendorf	100%	49
Trinity Regional Medical Center	Fort Dodge	100%	189
University of Iowa Hospital & Clinics	Iowa City	100%	245
Iowa Methodist Medical Center[2]	Des Moines	99%	268
Mercy Medical Center-Dubuque	Dubuque	99%	224
Marshalltown Medical & Surgical Center	Marshalltown	98%	52
Mercy Medical Center-Sioux City	Sioux City	98%	364
Great River Medical Center	West Burlington	97%	125
Jennie Edmundson Hospital	Council Bluffs	97%	93
Mercy Medical Center-Clinton	Clinton	97%	102
Iowa City VA Medical Center	Iowa City	96%	26
The Finley Hospital	Dubuque	92%	38

4. Beta Blocker at Discharge

Hospital Name	City	Rate	Cases
Alegent Health Mercy Hospital	Council Bluffs	100%	106
Allen Memorial Hospital[2]	Waterloo	100%	233
Mary Greeley Medical Center	Ames	100%	132
Mercy Medical Center-Cedar Rapids	Cedar Rapids	100%	186
Mercy Medical Center-Des Moines	Des Moines	100%	625
Mercy Medical Center-Dubuque	Dubuque	100%	214
Mercy Medical Center-North Iowa	Mason City	100%	245
Saint Lukes Hospital[2]	Cedar Rapids	100%	252
Saint Lukes Regional Medical Center	Sioux City	100%	30
Trinity Bettendorf	Bettendorf	100%	44
Genesis Medical Center - Davenport[2]	Davenport	99%	282
Iowa Methodist Medical Center[2]	Des Moines	99%	258
Mercy Medical Center-Sioux City	Sioux City	99%	367
Trinity Regional Medical Center	Fort Dodge	99%	187
University of Iowa Hospital & Clinics	Iowa City	99%	240
Iowa Lutheran Hospital[2]	Des Moines	98%	112
Jennie Edmundson Hospital	Council Bluffs	98%	91
Marshalltown Medical & Surgical Center	Marshalltown	98%	52
Mercy Hospital	Iowa City	98%	214
Covenant Medical Center	Waterloo	97%	73
The Finley Hospital	Dubuque	97%	35
Mercy Medical Center-Clinton	Clinton	97%	100
Great River Medical Center	West Burlington	94%	125
Iowa City VA Medical Center	Iowa City	93%	27

6. PCI Within 90 Minutes of Arrival

Hospital Name	City	Rate	Cases
Mercy Medical Center-Cedar Rapids	Cedar Rapids	100%	49
Mercy Medical Center-Des Moines	Des Moines	99%	99
Alegent Health Mercy Hospital	Council Bluffs	97%	39
Allen Memorial Hospital[2]	Waterloo	97%	31
Trinity Regional Medical Center	Fort Dodge	97%	30
Genesis Medical Center - Davenport[2]	Davenport	96%	26
Saint Lukes Hospital[2]	Cedar Rapids	96%	49
Mercy Medical Center-Sioux City	Sioux City	95%	38
Mercy Medical Center-Dubuque	Dubuque	94%	33
Covenant Medical Center	Waterloo	89%	27
Iowa Lutheran Hospital[2]	Des Moines	85%	27
Iowa Methodist Medical Center[2]	Des Moines	85%	33

7. Smoking Cessation Advice

Hospital Name	City	Rate	Cases
Alegent Health Mercy Hospital	Council Bluffs	100%	44
Allen Memorial Hospital[2]	Waterloo	100%	79
Covenant Medical Center	Waterloo	100%	32
Genesis Medical Center - Davenport[2]	Davenport	100%	102
Iowa Methodist Medical Center[2]	Des Moines	100%	65
Mary Greeley Medical Center	Ames	100%	34
Mercy Hospital	Iowa City	100%	61
Mercy Medical Center-Cedar Rapids	Cedar Rapids	100%	67
Mercy Medical Center-Clinton	Clinton	100%	39
Mercy Medical Center-Des Moines	Des Moines	100%	248
Mercy Medical Center-Dubuque	Dubuque	100%	65
Mercy Medical Center-North Iowa	Mason City	100%	76
Mercy Medical Center-Sioux City	Sioux City	100%	116
Trinity Regional Medical Center	Fort Dodge	100%	61
Saint Lukes Hospital[2]	Cedar Rapids	99%	86
Iowa Lutheran Hospital[2]	Des Moines	97%	33
Jennie Edmundson Hospital	Council Bluffs	97%	29
University of Iowa Hospital & Clinics	Iowa City	97%	102
Great River Medical Center	West Burlington	84%	38

Chest Pain/Possible Heart Attack Care

8. Aspirin at Arrival

Hospital Name	City	Rate	Cases
Cass County Memorial Hospital	Atlantic	100%	50
Dallas County Hospital	Perry	100%	29
The Finley Hospital	Dubuque	100%	44
Grundy County Memorial Hospital	Grundy Center	100%	30
Lakes Regional Healthcare	Spirit Lake	100%	69
Mahaska Health Partnership	Oskaloosa	100%	52
Saint Anthony Regional Hospital	Carroll	100%	42
Spencer Municipal Hospital	Spencer	100%	37
Trinity Muscatine	Muscatine	100%	114
Broadlawns Medical Center	Des Moines	98%	52
Waverly Health Center	Waverly	97%	92
Belmond Medical Center	Belmond	96%	25
Clarke County Hospital	Osceola	96%	28
Fort Madison Community Hospital	Fort Madison	96%	52
Genesis Medical Center-Dewitt	Dewitt	96%	49
Skiff Medical Center	Newton	96%	52
Grinnell Regional Medical Center	Grinnell	95%	61
Great River Medical Center	West Burlington	93%	103
Keokuk Area Hospital	Keokuk	91%	66
Allen Memorial Hospital	Waterloo	90%	29
Ottumwa Regional Health Center	Ottumwa	90%	103

9. Median Time to ECG (minutes)

Hospital Name	City	Min.	Cases
Genesis Medical Center-Dewitt	Dewitt	1	51
Dallas County Hospital	Perry	2	28
Fort Madison Community Hospital	Fort Madison	3	53
Belmond Medical Center	Belmond	4	28
Grundy County Memorial Hospital	Grundy Center	4	32
Grinnell Regional Medical Center	Grinnell	5	67
Lakes Regional Healthcare	Spirit Lake	5	68
Skiff Medical Center	Newton	5	52
Waverly Health Center	Waverly	5	95
Cass County Memorial Hospital	Atlantic	6	48
Mahaska Health Partnership	Oskaloosa	6	56
Allen Memorial Hospital	Waterloo	8	29
The Finley Hospital	Dubuque	9	44
Ottumwa Regional Health Center	Ottumwa	9	105
Trinity Muscatine	Muscatine	9	114
Clarke County Hospital	Osceola	11	29
Keokuk Area Hospital	Keokuk	11	69
Saint Anthony Regional Hospital	Carroll	11	44
Broadlawns Medical Center	Des Moines	12	54
Great River Medical Center	West Burlington	12	106
Spencer Municipal Hospital	Spencer	13	38

Heart Failure Care

12. ACE Inhibitor or ARB for LVSD

Hospital Name	City	Rate	Cases
Iowa City VA Medical Center	Iowa City	100%	34
Jennie Edmundson Hospital	Council Bluffs	100%	39
Mary Greeley Medical Center	Ames	100%	50
Mercy Medical Center-Des Moines	Des Moines	100%	126
Saint Lukes Regional Medical Center	Sioux City	100%	26
Mercy Medical Center-North Iowa	Mason City	99%	120
Mercy Medical Center-Sioux City[2]	Sioux City	99%	89
Genesis Medical Center - Davenport[2]	Davenport	98%	103
Iowa Lutheran Hospital[2]	Des Moines	98%	60
Mercy Medical Center-Dubuque	Dubuque	98%	47
Mercy Hospital	Iowa City	97%	70
Saint Lukes Hospital[2]	Cedar Rapids	97%	29
Trinity Regional Medical Center	Fort Dodge	97%	64
Allen Memorial Hospital[2]	Waterloo	95%	104
Mercy Medical Center-Cedar Rapids[2]	Cedar Rapids	93%	29
Mercy Medical Center-Clinton	Clinton	93%	46
University of Iowa Hospital & Clinics[2]	Iowa City	91%	121
Iowa Methodist Medical Center[2]	Des Moines	89%	63
Covenant Medical Center	Waterloo	86%	28
Great River Medical Center	West Burlington	84%	56

13. Discharge Instructions

Hospital Name	City	Rate	Cases
Fort Madison Community Hospital	Fort Madison	100%	37
Iowa City VA Medical Center	Iowa City	100%	101
Jennie Edmundson Hospital	Council Bluffs	100%	113
Pella Regional Health Center	Pella	100%	28
Trinity Bettendorf[2]	Bettendorf	100%	49
Trinity Muscatine	Muscatine	100%	25
Winneshiek Medical Center	Decorah	100%	26
Mercy Medical Center-Sioux City[2]	Sioux City	99%	202
Mercy Medical Center-Des Moines	Des Moines	98%	403
Mercy Hospital	Iowa City	97%	177
Mercy Medical Center-North Iowa	Mason City	97%	207
Saint Lukes Regional Medical Center	Sioux City	97%	72
Saint Lukes Hospital[2]	Cedar Rapids	96%	159
VA Central Iowa Healthcare System	Des Moines	96%	46
Mercy Medical Center-Dubuque	Dubuque	95%	146
Saint Anthony Regional Hospital	Carroll	94%	36
Spencer Municipal Hospital	Spencer	93%	27
Alegent Health Mercy Hospital	Council Bluffs	92%	103
Allen Memorial Hospital[2]	Waterloo	92%	233
Great River Medical Center	West Burlington	92%	122
Covenant Medical Center	Waterloo	91%	89
Genesis Medical Center - Davenport[2]	Davenport	90%	239
Floyd Valley Hospital[2]	Le Mars	88%	32
Keokuk Area Hospital	Keokuk	88%	82
Grinnell Regional Medical Center	Grinnell	86%	28
Skiff Medical Center	Newton	86%	44
Mary Greeley Medical Center	Ames	85%	123
The Finley Hospital	Dubuque	84%	57
Trinity Regional Medical Center	Fort Dodge	84%	133
Ottumwa Regional Health Center	Ottumwa	83%	96
Mercy Medical Center-Cedar Rapids[2]	Cedar Rapids	82%	128
Mercy Medical Center-Clinton	Clinton	78%	134
Marshalltown Medical & Surgical Center	Marshalltown	77%	48
Mahaska Health Partnership[2]	Oskaloosa	75%	32
Van Diest Medical Center	Webster City	72%	43
Broadlawns Medical Center	Des Moines	69%	36
Iowa Methodist Medical Center[2]	Des Moines	69%	198
Iowa Lutheran Hospital[2]	Des Moines	55%	159
University of Iowa Hospital & Clinics[2]	Iowa City	55%	255

14. Evaluation of LVS Function

Hospital Name	City	Rate	Cases
Alegent Health Community Memorial Hospital	Missouri Valley	100%	41
Allen Memorial Hospital[2]	Waterloo	100%	300
Cass County Memorial Hospital	Atlantic	100%	30
Fort Madison Community Hospital	Fort Madison	100%	58
Genesis Medical Center - Davenport[2]	Davenport	100%	305
Grinnell Regional Medical Center	Grinnell	100%	48
Iowa City VA Medical Center	Iowa City	100%	106
Mary Greeley Medical Center	Ames	100%	173
Mercy Hospital	Iowa City	100%	212
Mercy Medical Center-Cedar Rapids[2]	Cedar Rapids	100%	194

NOTE: Hospital profiles are in alphabetical order by state, then city, then hospital within the city; Rankings exclude hospitals with less than 25 cases except for patient surveys which excludes hospitals with less than 100 cases; (a) 100–299 cases; (1) The number of cases is too small to be sure how well a hospital is performing; (2) The hospital indicated that the data submitted for this measure were based on a sample of cases; (3) Data was collected during a shorter time period (fewer quarters) than the maximum possible time for this measure; (4) Suppressed for one or more quarters by CMS; (5) No data is available from the hospital for this measure; (6) Fewer than 100 patients completed the HCAHPS survey. Use these rates with caution, as the number of surveys may be too low to reliably assess hospital performance; (7) Survey results are based on less than 12 months of data; (8) Survey results are not available for this reporting period; (9) No or very few patients were eligible for the HCAHPS survey. The scores shown, if any, reflect a very small number of surveys; (10) A state average was not calculated because too few hospitals in the state submitted data; (11) There were discrepancies in the data collection process; Please refer to the User's Guide for a full explanation of data.

Hospital Name	City	Rate	Cases
Mercy Medical Center-Centerville	Centerville	100%	27
Mercy Medical Center-Des Moines	Des Moines	100%	509
Mercy Medical Center-Dubuque	Dubuque	100%	181
Myrtue Medical Center	Harlan	100%	37
Sartori Memorial Hospital	Cedar Falls	100%	25
Trinity Muscatine	Muscatine	100%	45
VA Central Iowa Healthcare System	Des Moines	100%	47
Winneshiek Medical Center	Decorah	100%	45
Alegent Health Mercy Hospital	Council Bluffs	99%	132
Covenant Medical Center	Waterloo	99%	130
The Finley Hospital	Dubuque	99%	82
Iowa Lutheran Hospital[2]	Des Moines	99%	191
Marshalltown Medical & Surgical Center	Marshalltown	99%	73
Mercy Medical Center-Clinton	Clinton	99%	184
Mercy Medical Center-North Iowa	Mason City	99%	319
Mercy Medical Center-Sioux City[2]	Sioux City	99%	251
Saint Lukes Hospital[2]	Cedar Rapids	99%	185
Saint Lukes Regional Medical Center	Sioux City	99%	94
Broadlawns Medical Center	Des Moines	98%	44
Floyd Valley Hospital[2]	Le Mars	98%	44
Iowa Methodist Medical Center[2]	Des Moines	98%	244
Mahaska Health Partnership[2]	Oskaloosa	98%	55
Pella Regional Health Center	Pella	98%	43
Spencer Municipal Hospital	Spencer	98%	45
Trinity Bettendorf[2]	Bettendorf	98%	65
Trinity Regional Medical Center	Fort Dodge	98%	179
University of Iowa Hospital & Clinics[2]	Iowa City	98%	284
Avera Holy Family Health	Estherville	97%	33
Keokuk Area Hospital	Keokuk	97%	101
Saint Anthony Regional Hospital	Carroll	96%	51
Montgomery County Memorial Hospital	Red Oak	95%	37
Jennie Edmundson Hospital	Council Bluffs	94%	138
Boone County Hospital	Boone	93%	29
Lakes Regional Healthcare	Spirit Lake	91%	32
Great River Medical Center	West Burlington	90%	168
Ottumwa Regional Health Center	Ottumwa	89%	128
Van Diest Medical Center	Webster City	87%	63
Cherokee Regional Medical Center	Cherokee	86%	37
Skiff Medical Center	Newton	78%	64
Ellsworth Municipal Hospital	Iowa Falls	45%	40
Davis County Hospital[2]	Bloomfield	33%	30

15. Smoking Cessation Advice

Hospital Name	City	Rate	Cases
Alegent Health Mercy Hospital	Council Bluffs	100%	35
Genesis Medical Center - Davenport[2]	Davenport	100%	55
Iowa City VA Medical Center	Iowa City	100%	30
Iowa Lutheran Hospital[2]	Des Moines	100%	26
Iowa Methodist Medical Center[2]	Des Moines	100%	34
Mercy Medical Center-Des Moines	Des Moines	100%	70
Mercy Medical Center-Dubuque	Dubuque	100%	25
Mercy Medical Center-North Iowa	Mason City	100%	33
Mercy Medical Center-Sioux City[2]	Sioux City	100%	62
Allen Memorial Hospital[2]	Waterloo	98%	47
University of Iowa Hospital & Clinics[2]	Iowa City	97%	67
Mercy Medical Center-Cedar Rapids[2]	Cedar Rapids	88%	25

Pneumonia Care

16. Appropriate Initial Antibiotic

Hospital Name	City	Rate	Cases
Alegent Health Community Memorial Hospital	Missouri Valley	100%	29
Floyd Valley Hospital	Le Mars	100%	32
Genesis Medical Center - Davenport[2]	Davenport	100%	79
Waverly Health Center	Waverly	100%	30
Alegent Health Mercy Hospital	Council Bluffs	99%	95
Mercy Medical Center-Des Moines	Des Moines	99%	276
The Finley Hospital[2]	Dubuque	98%	65
Trinity Bettendorf[2]	Bettendorf	98%	54
Trinity Muscatine	Muscatine	98%	51
Avera Holy Family Health	Estherville	97%	30
Marshalltown Medical & Surgical Center	Marshalltown	97%	64
Mercy Medical Center-Dubuque	Dubuque	97%	79
Palo Alto County Hospital	Emmetsburg	97%	30
Winneshiek Medical Center	Decorah	97%	33
Crawford County Memorial Hospital	Denison	96%	25
Fort Madison Community Hospital	Fort Madison	96%	48
Mercy Medical Center-Clinton	Clinton	96%	157
Mercy Medical Center-Sioux City[2]	Sioux City	96%	120
Saint Lukes Hospital[2]	Cedar Rapids	96%	55
Iowa Lutheran Hospital[2]	Des Moines	94%	86
Cherokee Regional Medical Center	Cherokee	93%	30
Covenant Medical Center	Waterloo	93%	73
Mercy Medical Center-Centerville	Centerville	93%	28
Ottumwa Regional Health Center	Ottumwa	93%	91
Allen Memorial Hospital[2]	Waterloo	92%	92
Broadlawns Medical Center	Des Moines	92%	62
Grinnell Regional Medical Center	Grinnell	91%	43
Mercy Medical Center-Cedar Rapids[2]	Cedar Rapids	91%	57
Mercy Medical Center-North Iowa	Mason City	91%	143
Myrtue Medical Center[2]	Harlan	91%	32
Saint Anthony Regional Hospital	Carroll	91%	44
Saint Lukes Regional Medical Center	Sioux City	91%	127
Great River Medical Center	West Burlington	90%	115
Jennie Edmundson Hospital	Council Bluffs	90%	88
Mary Greeley Medical Center	Ames	90%	107
Spencer Municipal Hospital[2]	Spencer	90%	50
Keokuk Area Hospital	Keokuk	89%	57
Mercy Hospital	Iowa City	89%	82
Orange City Area Health System	Orange City	89%	37
Trinity Regional Medical Center	Fort Dodge	89%	115
Henry County Health Center	Mount Pleasant	88%	25
University of Iowa Hospital & Clinics[2]	Iowa City	88%	33
Burgess Health Center[2,3]	Onawa	87%	30
Cass County Memorial Hospital	Atlantic	87%	30
Knoxville Hospital & Clinics	Knoxville	87%	31
Lakes Regional Healthcare	Spirit Lake	86%	43
Sanford Sheldon Medical Center	Sheldon	86%	35
Jefferson County Health Center	Fairfield	85%	27
Van Diest Medical Center	Webster City	85%	46
Mahaska Health Partnership	Oskaloosa	82%	33
Buena Vista Regional Medical Center	Storm Lake	81%	32
Montgomery County Memorial Hospital	Red Oak	81%	27
Pella Regional Health Center	Pella	80%	51
Iowa Methodist Medical Center[2]	Des Moines	79%	67
Boone County Hospital	Boone	78%	50

17. Blood Culture Timing

Hospital Name	City	Rate	Cases
Alegent Health Community Memorial Hospital	Missouri Valley	100%	27
Alegent Health Mercy Hospital	Council Bluffs	100%	137
Floyd Valley Hospital	Le Mars	100%	51
Fort Madison Community Hospital	Fort Madison	100%	63
Iowa City VA Medical Center	Iowa City	100%	34
Lakes Regional Healthcare	Spirit Lake	100%	54
Mahaska Health Partnership	Oskaloosa	100%	42
Mercy Medical Center-North Iowa	Mason City	100%	186
Myrtue Medical Center[2]	Harlan	100%	47
Regional Medical Center	Manchester	100%	26
Saint Anthony Regional Hospital	Carroll	100%	29
Sartori Memorial Hospital	Cedar Falls	100%	32
Van Diest Medical Center	Webster City	100%	27
Winneshiek Medical Center	Decorah	100%	59
Genesis Medical Center - Davenport[2]	Davenport	99%	143
Mary Greeley Medical Center	Ames	99%	141
Mercy Hospital	Iowa City	99%	112
Mercy Medical Center-Des Moines	Des Moines	99%	545
Mercy Medical Center-Dubuque	Dubuque	99%	127
Mercy Medical Center-Sioux City[2]	Sioux City	99%	146
Saint Lukes Regional Medical Center	Sioux City	99%	141
Broadlawns Medical Center	Des Moines	98%	57
Grinnell Regional Medical Center	Grinnell	98%	41
Iowa Methodist Medical Center[2]	Des Moines	98%	82
Marshalltown Medical & Surgical Center	Marshalltown	98%	105
Mercy Medical Center-Cedar Rapids[2]	Cedar Rapids	98%	100
Mercy Medical Center-Clinton	Clinton	98%	222
Trinity Bettendorf[2]	Bettendorf	98%	89
Trinity Muscatine	Muscatine	98%	54
Trinity Regional Medical Center	Fort Dodge	98%	219
Waverly Health Center	Waverly	98%	40
Allen Memorial Hospital[2]	Waterloo	97%	147
The Finley Hospital[2]	Dubuque	97%	128
Jennie Edmundson Hospital	Council Bluffs	97%	159
Ottumwa Regional Health Center	Ottumwa	97%	129
Cass County Memorial Hospital	Atlantic	96%	25
Great River Medical Center	West Burlington	96%	121
Mercy Medical Center-Centerville	Centerville	96%	25
Orange City Area Health System	Orange City	96%	28
Pella Regional Health Center	Pella	96%	45
Spencer Municipal Hospital[2]	Spencer	96%	52
Burgess Health Center[2,3]	Onawa	95%	44
Saint Lukes Hospital[2]	Cedar Rapids	95%	81
VA Central Iowa Healthcare System	Des Moines	95%	41
Covenant Medical Center	Waterloo	94%	95
Keokuk Area Hospital	Keokuk	93%	43
University of Iowa Hospital & Clinics[2]	Iowa City	93%	58
Iowa Lutheran Hospital[2]	Des Moines	92%	92
Boone County Hospital	Boone	88%	41
Sanford Sheldon Medical Center	Sheldon	86%	36
Knoxville Hospital & Clinics	Knoxville	81%	27

18. Influenza Vaccine

Hospital Name	City	Rate	Cases
Alegent Health Community Memorial Hospital	Missouri Valley	100%	25
Burgess Health Center[2]	Onawa	100%	46
Cass County Memorial Hospital	Atlantic	100%	30
Floyd Valley Hospital	Le Mars	100%	30
Grinnell Regional Medical Center	Grinnell	100%	30
Jones Regional Medical Center	Anamosa	100%	27
Keokuk Area Hospital	Keokuk	100%	55
Mahaska Health Partnership	Oskaloosa	100%	32
Marshalltown Medical & Surgical Center	Marshalltown	100%	63
Mercy Medical Center-Dubuque	Dubuque	100%	99
Montgomery County Memorial Hospital	Red Oak	100%	38
Stewart Memorial Community Hospital	Lake City	100%	29
Trinity Muscatine	Muscatine	100%	35
Winneshiek Medical Center	Decorah	100%	37
Covenant Medical Center	Waterloo	99%	74
Mercy Medical Center-Sioux City[2]	Sioux City	98%	216
Saint Lukes Regional Medical Center	Sioux City	98%	118
Trinity Bettendorf[2]	Bettendorf	98%	49
Trinity Regional Medical Center	Fort Dodge	98%	124
Alegent Health Mercy Hospital	Council Bluffs	97%	74
Boone County Hospital	Boone	97%	37
Iowa Lutheran Hospital[2]	Des Moines	97%	74
Allen Memorial Hospital	Waterloo	96%	145
Spencer Municipal Hospital[2]	Spencer	96%	72
Genesis Medical Center - Davenport[2]	Davenport	95%	102
Mary Greeley Medical Center	Ames	95%	116
Mercy Medical Center-Cedar Rapids[2]	Cedar Rapids	95%	74
Mercy Medical Center-Des Moines	Des Moines	95%	364
Buena Vista Regional Medical Center	Storm Lake	94%	32
Cherokee Regional Medical Center	Cherokee	94%	31
The Finley Hospital[2]	Dubuque	93%	82
Great River Medical Center	West Burlington	93%	115
Iowa Methodist Medical Center[2]	Des Moines	93%	75
Mercy Medical Center-Clinton	Clinton	93%	172
Saint Anthony Regional Hospital	Carroll	93%	42
Fort Madison Community Hospital	Fort Madison	92%	51
Lakes Regional Healthcare	Spirit Lake	92%	39
Mercy Medical Center-North Iowa	Mason City	92%	142
Myrtue Medical Center	Harlan	92%	26
Saint Lukes Hospital[2]	Cedar Rapids	92%	74
Ottumwa Regional Health Center	Ottumwa	91%	89
Van Diest Medical Center	Webster City	90%	40
Clarinda Regional Health Center	Clarinda	89%	28
Iowa City VA Medical Center	Iowa City	89%	36
Sanford Sheldon Medical Center	Sheldon	89%	35
Mercy Hospital	Iowa City	86%	76
Pella Regional Health Center	Pella	85%	48
Skiff Medical Center	Newton	82%	28
Broadlawns Medical Center	Des Moines	81%	27
Veterans Memorial Hospital	Waukon	81%	26
Jennie Edmundson Hospital	Council Bluffs	80%	111
Mercy Medical Center-Centerville	Centerville	70%	30
VA Central Iowa Healthcare System	Des Moines	70%	27
University of Iowa Hospital & Clinics[2]	Iowa City	67%	69

19. Initial Antibiotic Timing

Hospital Name	City	Rate	Cases
Alegent Health Community Memorial Hospital	Missouri Valley	100%	27
Alegent Health Mercy Hospital	Council Bluffs	100%	142
Avera Holy Family Health	Estherville	100%	39
Burgess Health Center[2,3]	Onawa	100%	49
Cass County Memorial Hospital	Atlantic	100%	40
Grinnell Regional Medical Center	Grinnell	100%	57
Henry County Health Center	Mount Pleasant	100%	30
Iowa Lutheran Hospital[2]	Des Moines	100%	115
Madison County Memorial Hospital	Winterset	100%	43
Marshalltown Medical & Surgical Center	Marshalltown	100%	95
Mercy Medical Center-Centerville	Centerville	100%	38
Myrtue Medical Center[2]	Harlan	100%	53
Regional Medical Center	Manchester	100%	25
Spencer Municipal Hospital[2]	Spencer	100%	75
Stewart Memorial Community Hospital	Lake City	100%	34
Winneshiek Medical Center	Decorah	100%	67
The Finley Hospital[2]	Dubuque	99%	98
Great River Medical Center	West Burlington	99%	147
Mary Greeley Medical Center	Ames	99%	166
Saint Lukes Hospital[2]	Cedar Rapids	99%	86
Saint Lukes Regional Medical Center	Sioux City	99%	171
Trinity Bettendorf[2]	Bettendorf	99%	76
Trinity Regional Medical Center	Fort Dodge	99%	201
Floyd Valley Hospital	Le Mars	98%	53
Fort Madison Community Hospital	Fort Madison	98%	66
Mahaska Health Partnership	Oskaloosa	98%	44
Mercy Medical Center-Des Moines	Des Moines	98%	501
Mercy Medical Center-Dubuque	Dubuque	98%	113
Orange City Area Health System	Orange City	98%	42
Saint Anthony Regional Hospital	Carroll	98%	63
Trinity Muscatine	Muscatine	98%	59
Van Diest Medical Center	Webster City	98%	60
Crawford County Memorial Hospital	Denison	97%	37
Lakes Regional Healthcare	Spirit Lake	97%	70
Mercy Hosp of Franciscan Sisters-Oelwein	Oelwein	97%	33
Mercy Medical Center-North Iowa	Mason City	97%	190
Mercy Medical Center-Sioux City[2]	Sioux City	97%	210
Montgomery County Memorial Hospital	Red Oak	97%	34
Sartori Memorial Hospital	Cedar Falls	97%	34
Waverly Health Center	Waverly	97%	39

NOTE: Hospital profiles are in alphabetical order by state, then city, then hospital within the city; Rankings exclude hospitals with less than 25 cases except for patient surveys which excludes hospitals with less than 100 cases; (a) 100–299 cases; (1) The number of cases is too small to be sure how well a hospital is performing; (2) The hospital indicated that the data submitted for this measure were based on a sample of cases; (3) Data was collected during a shorter time period (fewer quarters) than the maximum possible time for this measure; (4) Suppressed for one or more quarters by CMS; (5) No data is available from the hospital for this measure; (6) Fewer than 100 patients completed the HCAHPS survey. Use these rates with caution, as the number of surveys may be too low to reliably assess hospital performance; (7) Survey results are based on less than 12 months of data; (8) Survey results are not available for this reporting period; (9) No or very few patients were eligible for the HCAHPS survey. The scores shown, if any, reflect a very small number of surveys; (10) A state average was not calculated because too few hospitals in the state submitted data; (11) There were discrepancies in the data collection process; Please refer to the User's Guide for a full explanation of data.

Hospital Name	City	Rate	Cases
Genesis Medical Center - Davenport[2]	Davenport	96%	160
Jackson County Regional Health Center	Maquoketa	96%	27
Jones Regional Medical Center	Anamosa	96%	28
Keokuk Area Hospital	Keokuk	96%	77
Mercy Medical Center-Cedar Rapids[2]	Cedar Rapids	96%	101
Mercy Medical Center-Clinton	Clinton	96%	239
Palo Alto County Hospital	Emmetsburg	96%	45
University of Iowa Hospital & Clinics[2]	Iowa City	96%	54
Boone County Hospital	Boone	95%	64
Iowa Methodist Medical Center[2]	Des Moines	95%	106
Jennie Edmundson Hospital	Council Bluffs	95%	197
Ottumwa Regional Health Center	Ottumwa	95%	129
Pella Regional Health Center	Pella	95%	55
Skiff Medical Center	Newton	95%	41
VA Central Iowa Healthcare System	Des Moines	95%	37
Allen Memorial Hospital[2]	Waterloo	94%	142
Broadlawns Medical Center	Des Moines	94%	72
Clarinda Regional Health Center	Clarinda	94%	35
Hancock County Memorial Hospital	Britt	94%	32
Mercy Hospital	Iowa City	94%	109
Cherokee Regional Medical Center	Cherokee	93%	41
Covenant Medical Center	Waterloo	93%	107
Greater Regional Medical Center	Creston	93%	29
Sanford Sheldon Medical Center	Sheldon	93%	56
Iowa City VA Medical Center	Iowa City	90%	29
Ellsworth Municipal Hospital	Iowa Falls	89%	27
Knoxville Hospital & Clinics	Knoxville	88%	41
Veterans Memorial Hospital	Waukon	86%	29
Buena Vista Regional Medical Center	Storm Lake	81%	43

20. Pneumococcal Vaccine

Hospital Name	City	Rate	Cases
Alegent Health Community Memorial Hospital	Missouri Valley	100%	39
Alegent Health Mercy Hospital	Council Bluffs	100%	93
Burgess Health Center[2,3]	Onawa	100%	56
Cass County Memorial Hospital	Atlantic	100%	56
Fort Madison Community Hospital	Fort Madison	100%	69
Grinnell Regional Medical Center	Grinnell	100%	49
Iowa City VA Medical Center	Iowa City	100%	38
Mahaska Health Partnership	Oskaloosa	100%	47
Marshalltown Medical & Surgical Center	Marshalltown	100%	111
Mercy Hosp of Franciscan Sisters-Oelwein	Oelwein	100%	32
Montgomery County Memorial Hospital	Red Oak	100%	52
Myrtue Medical Center[2]	Harlan	100%	53
Regional Medical Center	Manchester	100%	26
Sartori Memorial Hospital	Cedar Falls	100%	37
Trinity Muscatine	Muscatine	100%	52
Winneshiek Medical Center	Decorah	100%	68
Covenant Medical Center	Waterloo	99%	101
Mercy Medical Center-Dubuque	Dubuque	99%	150
Trinity Regional Medical Center	Fort Dodge	99%	197
Buena Vista Regional Medical Center	Storm Lake	98%	44
Cherokee Regional Medical Center	Cherokee	98%	52
Floyd Valley Hospital	Le Mars	98%	50
The Finley Hospital[2]	Dubuque	97%	150
Great River Medical Center	West Burlington	97%	153
Knoxville Hospital & Clinics	Knoxville	97%	33
Mercy Medical Center-Des Moines	Des Moines	97%	452
Mercy Medical Center-Sioux City[2]	Sioux City	97%	271
Saint Lukes Hospital[2]	Cedar Rapids	97%	115
Saint Lukes Regional Medical Center	Sioux City	97%	185
Stewart Memorial Community Hospital	Lake City	97%	33
VA Central Iowa Healthcare System	Des Moines	97%	29
Allen Memorial Hospital[2]	Waterloo	96%	206
Keokuk Area Hospital	Keokuk	96%	82
Mary Greeley Medical Center	Ames	96%	181
Mercy Medical Center-Clinton	Clinton	96%	261
Mercy Medical Center-North Iowa	Mason City	96%	225
Spencer Municipal Hospital[2]	Spencer	96%	89
Trinity Bettendorf[2]	Bettendorf	96%	70
Iowa Methodist Medical Center[2]	Des Moines	95%	109
Mercy Medical Center-Cedar Rapids[2]	Cedar Rapids	95%	118
Waverly Health Center	Waverly	95%	41
Avera Holy Family Health	Estherville	94%	34
Genesis Medical Center - Davenport[2]	Davenport	94%	143
Lakes Regional Healthcare	Spirit Lake	94%	70
Mercy Hospital	Iowa City	94%	125
Ottumwa Regional Health Center	Ottumwa	94%	117
Clarinda Regional Health Center	Clarinda	93%	45
Crawford County Memorial Hospital	Denison	93%	27
Iowa Lutheran Hospital[2]	Des Moines	93%	120
Jennie Edmundson Hospital	Council Bluffs	93%	164
Boone County Hospital	Boone	91%	54
Van Diest Medical Center	Webster City	90%	51
Buchanan County Health Center	Independence	89%	28
Saint Anthony Regional Hospital	Carroll	89%	73
Jefferson County Health Center	Fairfield	88%	25
Madison County Memorial Hospital	Winterset	88%	40
Orange City Area Health System	Orange City	88%	42
Veterans Memorial Hospital	Waukon	88%	48

Hospital Name	City	Rate	Cases
Henry County Health Center	Mount Pleasant	87%	30
Mercy Medical Center-Centerville	Centerville	87%	46
Lucas County Health Center	Chariton	86%	28
Palo Alto County Hospital	Emmetsburg	86%	37
Jones Regional Medical Center	Anamosa	85%	40
Pella Regional Health Center	Pella	85%	66
University of Iowa Hospital & Clinics[2]	Iowa City	85%	73
Jackson County Regional Health Center	Maquoketa	83%	29
Sanford Sheldon Medical Center	Sheldon	81%	57
Shenandoah Medical Center	Shenandoah	77%	30
Ellsworth Municipal Hospital	Iowa Falls	76%	41
Skiff Medical Center	Newton	67%	42
Van Buren County Hospital	Keosauqua	65%	26

21. Smoking Cessation Advice

Hospital Name	City	Rate	Cases
Alegent Health Mercy Hospital	Council Bluffs	100%	62
Broadlawns Medical Center	Des Moines	100%	60
Covenant Medical Center	Waterloo	100%	40
The Finley Hospital[2]	Dubuque	100%	32
Fort Madison Community Hospital	Fort Madison	100%	27
Iowa City VA Medical Center	Iowa City	100%	28
Marshalltown Medical & Surgical Center	Marshalltown	100%	28
Mary Greeley Medical Center	Ames	100%	52
Mercy Hospital	Iowa City	100%	31
Mercy Medical Center-Dubuque	Dubuque	100%	35
Mercy Medical Center-Sioux City[2]	Sioux City	100%	111
Ottumwa Regional Health Center	Ottumwa	100%	28
Saint Lukes Hospital[2]	Cedar Rapids	100%	41
Saint Lukes Regional Medical Center	Sioux City	100%	87
Trinity Regional Medical Center	Fort Dodge	100%	79
Genesis Medical Center - Davenport[2]	Davenport	99%	72
Mercy Medical Center-North Iowa	Mason City	99%	75
Allen Memorial Hospital[2]	Waterloo	98%	61
Iowa Methodist Medical Center[2]	Des Moines	97%	32
Mercy Medical Center-Clinton	Clinton	97%	95
Mercy Medical Center-Des Moines	Des Moines	97%	237
Keokuk Area Hospital	Keokuk	96%	28
University of Iowa Hospital & Clinics[2]	Iowa City	92%	60
Great River Medical Center	West Burlington	90%	52
Mercy Medical Center-Cedar Rapids[2]	Cedar Rapids	90%	41
Iowa Lutheran Hospital[2]	Des Moines	89%	47
Jennie Edmundson Hospital	Council Bluffs	88%	57

Surgical Care Improvement Project

22. Appropriate VTP Within 24 Hours

Hospital Name	City	Rate	Cases
Fort Madison Community Hospital	Fort Madison	100%	38
Grinnell Regional Medical Center	Grinnell	100%	44
Lakes Regional Healthcare	Spirit Lake	100%	55
Mahaska Health Partnership	Oskaloosa	100%	27
Saint Anthony Regional Hospital	Carroll	100%	213
Spencer Municipal Hospital[2]	Spencer	100%	92
Trinity Bettendorf[2]	Bettendorf	100%	45
Trinity Muscatine	Muscatine	100%	39
VA Central Iowa Healthcare System[2]	Des Moines	100%	80
Iowa City VA Medical Center[2]	Iowa City	98%	130
Marshalltown Medical & Surgical Center	Marshalltown	98%	62
Mary Greeley Medical Center	Ames	98%	353
Alegent Health Mercy Hospital[2]	Council Bluffs	97%	167
Mercy Medical Center-Des Moines[2]	Des Moines	97%	190
Mercy Medical Center-Sioux City[2]	Sioux City	97%	383
Waverly Health Center	Waverly	97%	29
Allen Memorial Hospital[2]	Waterloo	96%	138
Iowa Methodist Medical Center[2]	Des Moines	96%	168
Mercy Medical Center-Cedar Rapids[2]	Cedar Rapids	95%	115
Mercy Medical Center-North Iowa	Mason City	95%	288
Saint Lukes Regional Medical Center[2]	Sioux City	95%	222
Skiff Medical Center	Newton	95%	41
University of Iowa Hospital & Clinics[2]	Iowa City	95%	204
Great River Medical Center	West Burlington	94%	248
The Finley Hospital[2]	Dubuque	93%	139
Mercy Medical Center-Clinton	Clinton	93%	112
Broadlawns Medical Center	Des Moines	92%	50
Saint Lukes Hospital[2]	Cedar Rapids	92%	109
Sartori Memorial Hospital	Cedar Falls	92%	100
Covenant Medical Center	Waterloo	91%	332
Genesis Medical Center - Davenport[2]	Davenport	91%	177
Mercy Medical Center-Dubuque[2]	Dubuque	89%	134
Trinity Regional Medical Center[2]	Fort Dodge	89%	80
Iowa Lutheran Hospital[2]	Des Moines	82%	125
Ottumwa Regional Health Center	Ottumwa	81%	98
Pella Regional Health Center[2]	Pella	80%	44
Mercy Hospital	Iowa City	78%	411
Jennie Edmundson Hospital	Council Bluffs	76%	146
Buena Vista Regional Medical Center[2]	Storm Lake	71%	45

23. Appropriate Hair Removal

Hospital Name	City	Rate	Cases
Alegent Health Mercy Hospital[2]	Council Bluffs	100%	712
Allen Memorial Hospital[2]	Waterloo	100%	469
Broadlawns Medical Center	Des Moines	100%	74
Covenant Medical Center	Waterloo	100%	564
The Finley Hospital[2]	Dubuque	100%	310
Floyd Valley Hospital	Le Mars	100%	76
Fort Madison Community Hospital	Fort Madison	100%	110
Genesis Medical Center - Davenport[2]	Davenport	100%	666
Grinnell Regional Medical Center	Grinnell	100%	98
Grundy County Memorial Hospital	Grundy Center	100%	41
Iowa City VA Medical Center[2]	Iowa City	100%	252
Iowa Lutheran Hospital[2]	Des Moines	100%	431
Iowa Methodist Medical Center[2]	Des Moines	100%	632
Keokuk Area Hospital	Keokuk	100%	44
Mahaska Health Partnership	Oskaloosa	100%	96
Marshalltown Medical & Surgical Center	Marshalltown	100%	219
Mary Greeley Medical Center	Ames	100%	732
Mercy Medical Center-Cedar Rapids[2]	Cedar Rapids	100%	349
Mercy Medical Center-Centerville	Centerville	100%	43
Mercy Medical Center-Clinton	Clinton	100%	218
Mercy Medical Center-Des Moines[2]	Des Moines	100%	794
Mercy Medical Center-Dubuque[2]	Dubuque	100%	519
Mercy Medical Center-North Iowa	Mason City	100%	1158
Mercy Medical Center-Sioux City[2]	Sioux City	100%	879
Montgomery County Memorial Hospital	Red Oak	100%	29
Ottumwa Regional Health Center	Ottumwa	100%	211
Pella Regional Health Center[2]	Pella	100%	129
Saint Anthony Regional Hospital	Carroll	100%	274
Saint Lukes Regional Medical Center[2]	Sioux City	100%	687
Sartori Memorial Hospital	Cedar Falls	100%	145
Skiff Medical Center	Newton	100%	177
Spencer Municipal Hospital[2]	Spencer	100%	222
Trinity Bettendorf[2]	Bettendorf	100%	253
Trinity Muscatine	Muscatine	100%	89
Trinity Regional Medical Center[2]	Fort Dodge	100%	321
VA Central Iowa Healthcare System[2]	Des Moines	100%	108
Veterans Memorial Hospital	Waukon	100%	25
Waverly Health Center	Waverly	100%	49
Wright Medical Center	Clarion	100%	307
Great River Medical Center	West Burlington	99%	620
Lakes Regional Healthcare	Spirit Lake	99%	102
Mercy Hospital	Iowa City	99%	1241
Saint Lukes Hospital[2]	Cedar Rapids	99%	494
University of Iowa Hospital & Clinics[2]	Iowa City	99%	604
Boone County Hospital	Boone	98%	60
Jennie Edmundson Hospital	Council Bluffs	98%	468
Orange City Area Health System	Orange City	98%	43
Buena Vista Regional Medical Center[2]	Storm Lake	96%	99
Jefferson County Health Center	Fairfield	96%	26
Van Diest Medical Center	Webster City	96%	27
Greater Regional Medical Center	Creston	88%	32

24. Appropriate Beta Blocker Usage

Hospital Name	City	Rate	Cases
Jennie Edmundson Hospital	Council Bluffs	100%	143
VA Central Iowa Healthcare System[2]	Des Moines	100%	48
Alegent Health Mercy Hospital[2]	Council Bluffs	99%	231
Iowa Lutheran Hospital[2]	Des Moines	99%	121
Iowa Methodist Medical Center[2]	Des Moines	99%	180
Marshalltown Medical & Surgical Center	Marshalltown	99%	69
Mary Greeley Medical Center	Ames	99%	192
Mercy Hospital	Iowa City	99%	385
Mercy Medical Center-Dubuque[2]	Dubuque	99%	174
Iowa City VA Medical Center[2]	Iowa City	98%	94
Skiff Medical Center	Newton	98%	53
The Finley Hospital[2]	Dubuque	97%	66
Fort Madison Community Hospital	Fort Madison	97%	39
Saint Anthony Regional Hospital	Carroll	97%	101
Sartori Memorial Hospital	Cedar Falls	97%	38
Allen Memorial Hospital[2]	Waterloo	96%	180
Saint Lukes Regional Medical Center[2]	Sioux City	96%	157
Trinity Bettendorf[2]	Bettendorf	96%	77
Genesis Medical Center - Davenport[2]	Davenport	95%	237
Mercy Medical Center-Des Moines[2]	Des Moines	95%	315
Saint Lukes Hospital[2]	Cedar Rapids	95%	229
Mercy Medical Center-Cedar Rapids[2]	Cedar Rapids	94%	125
Mercy Medical Center-Sioux City[2]	Sioux City	94%	304
Spencer Municipal Hospital[2]	Spencer	94%	51
Covenant Medical Center	Waterloo	93%	160
Trinity Regional Medical Center[2]	Fort Dodge	93%	116
Mercy Medical Center-North Iowa	Mason City	92%	437
Grinnell Regional Medical Center	Grinnell	90%	31
Mercy Medical Center-Clinton	Clinton	89%	66
Great River Medical Center	West Burlington	88%	190
Ottumwa Regional Health Center	Ottumwa	87%	60
Pella Regional Health Center[2]	Pella	73%	33
University of Iowa Hospital & Clinics[2]	Iowa City	63%	167

NOTE: Hospital profiles are in alphabetical order by state, then city, then hospital within the city; Rankings exclude hospitals with less than 25 cases except for patient surveys which excludes hospitals with less than 100 cases; (a) 100–299 cases; (1) The number of cases is too small to be sure how well a hospital is performing; (2) The hospital indicated that the data submitted for this measure were based on a sample of cases; (3) Data was collected during a shorter time period (fewer quarters) than the maximum possible time for this measure; (4) Suppressed for one or more quarters by CMS; (5) No data is available from the hospital for this measure; (6) Fewer than 100 patients completed the HCAHPS survey. Use these rates with caution, as the number of surveys may be too low to reliably assess hospital performance; (7) Survey results are based on less than 12 months of data; (8) Survey results are not available for this reporting period; (9) No or very few patients were eligible for the HCAHPS survey. The scores shown, if any, reflect a very small number of surveys; (10) A state average was not calculated because too few hospitals in the state submitted data; (11) There were discrepancies in the data collection process; Please refer to the User's Guide for a full explanation of data.

25. Controlled Postoperative Blood Glucose

Hospital Name	City	Rate	Cases
Allen Memorial Hospital[2]	Waterloo	97%	94
Trinity Regional Medical Center[2]	Fort Dodge	97%	70
Mercy Medical Center-Dubuque[2]	Dubuque	96%	83
Genesis Medical Center - Davenport[2]	Davenport	94%	159
Mercy Medical Center-North Iowa	Mason City	94%	185
Mercy Medical Center-Sioux City[2]	Sioux City	94%	78
Mercy Hospital	Iowa City	90%	113
Saint Lukes Hospital[2]	Cedar Rapids	89%	134
University of Iowa Hospital & Clinics[2]	Iowa City	88%	115
Iowa Methodist Medical Center[2]	Des Moines	80%	123
Iowa Lutheran Hospital[2]	Des Moines	79%	86
Mercy Medical Center-Des Moines[2]	Des Moines	79%	175

26. Prophylactic Antibiotic Timing

Hospital Name	City	Rate	Cases
Allen Memorial Hospital[2]	Waterloo	100%	310
The Finley Hospital[2]	Dubuque	100%	208
Mary Greeley Medical Center	Ames	100%	526
Mercy Medical Center-Centerville	Centerville	100%	39
Trinity Bettendorf[2]	Bettendorf	100%	169
Alegent Health Mercy Hospital[2]	Council Bluffs	99%	494
Fort Madison Community Hospital	Fort Madison	99%	86
Genesis Medical Center - Davenport[2]	Davenport	99%	493
Mahaska Health Partnership	Oskaloosa	99%	80
Mercy Medical Center-Cedar Rapids[2]	Cedar Rapids	99%	231
Mercy Medical Center-North Iowa	Mason City	99%	798
Mercy Medical Center-Sioux City[2]	Sioux City	99%	406
Saint Anthony Regional Hospital	Carroll	99%	210
Saint Lukes Hospital[2]	Cedar Rapids	99%	361
University of Iowa Hospital & Clinics[2]	Iowa City	99%	391
Wright Medical Center	Clarion	99%	249
Floyd Valley Hospital	Le Mars	98%	60
Great River Medical Center	West Burlington	98%	421
Grundy County Memorial Hospital	Grundy Center	98%	40
Iowa Lutheran Hospital[2]	Des Moines	98%	299
Lakes Regional Healthcare	Spirit Lake	98%	85
Marshalltown Medical & Surgical Center	Marshalltown	98%	180
Mercy Medical Center-Dubuque[2]	Dubuque	98%	394
Saint Lukes Regional Medical Center[2]	Sioux City	98%	500
Sartori Memorial Hospital	Cedar Falls	98%	91
Skiff Medical Center	Newton	98%	144
Trinity Regional Medical Center[2]	Fort Dodge	98%	227
VA Central Iowa Healthcare System	Des Moines	98%	54
Waverly Health Center	Waverly	98%	41
Covenant Medical Center	Waterloo	97%	377
Mercy Hospital	Iowa City	97%	918
Mercy Medical Center-Clinton	Clinton	97%	132
Mercy Medical Center-Des Moines[2]	Des Moines	97%	537
Ottumwa Regional Health Center	Ottumwa	97%	169
Spencer Municipal Hospital[2]	Spencer	97%	147
Iowa City VA Medical Center	Iowa City	96%	175
Jennie Edmundson Hospital	Council Bluffs	96%	369
Grinnell Regional Medical Center	Grinnell	95%	37
Iowa Methodist Medical Center[2]	Des Moines	95%	456
Broadlawns Medical Center	Des Moines	93%	41
Trinity Muscatine	Muscatine	91%	33
Pella Regional Health Center[2]	Pella	90%	94
Buena Vista Regional Medical Center[2]	Storm Lake	89%	76
Boone County Hospital	Boone	84%	50
Orange City Area Health System	Orange City	83%	41

27. Prophylactic Antibiotic Timing (Outpatient)

Hospital Name	City	Rate	Cases
Grinnell Regional Medical Center	Grinnell	100%	35
Alegent Health Mercy Hospital	Council Bluffs	99%	80
Mercy Medical Center-North Iowa	Mason City	99%	809
Marshalltown Medical & Surgical Center	Marshalltown	98%	97
Mercy Medical Center-Cedar Rapids	Cedar Rapids	98%	814
Trinity Muscatine	Muscatine	98%	43
Saint Lukes Hospital	Cedar Rapids	97%	582
Genesis Medical Center - Davenport	Davenport	96%	654
Mary Greeley Medical Center	Ames	96%	334
Mercy Medical Center-Dubuque	Dubuque	96%	278
Trinity Bettendorf	Bettendorf	96%	162
The Finley Hospital	Dubuque	95%	197
Iowa Methodist Medical Center	Des Moines	95%	710
Mercy Medical Center-Clinton	Clinton	95%	87
Saint Anthony Regional Hospital	Carroll	95%	59
Mercy Hospital	Iowa City	94%	198
Waverly Health Center	Waverly	94%	35
Fort Madison Community Hospital	Fort Madison	93%	42
Mercy Medical Center-Des Moines	Des Moines	93%	654
Allen Memorial Hospital	Waterloo	92%	370
Jennie Edmundson Hospital	Council Bluffs	92%	214
Mercy Medical Center-Sioux City	Sioux City	92%	111
Broadlawns Medical Center	Des Moines	90%	59
Great River Medical Center	West Burlington	90%	217
Trinity Regional Medical Center	Fort Dodge	90%	182
Iowa Lutheran Hospital	Des Moines	89%	226
University of Iowa Hospital & Clinics	Iowa City	89%	532
Saint Lukes Regional Medical Center	Sioux City	88%	102
Skiff Medical Center	Newton	88%	32
Spencer Municipal Hospital	Spencer	88%	108
Covenant Medical Center	Waterloo	87%	454
Ottumwa Regional Health Center	Ottumwa	66%	97

28. Prophylactic Antibiotic Selection

Hospital Name	City	Rate	Cases
Floyd Valley Hospital	Le Mars	100%	60
Grundy County Memorial Hospital	Grundy Center	100%	40
Orange City Area Health System	Orange City	100%	39
Spencer Municipal Hospital[2]	Spencer	100%	144
Trinity Bettendorf[2]	Bettendorf	100%	172
Alegent Health Mercy Hospital[2]	Council Bluffs	99%	497
Allen Memorial Hospital[2]	Waterloo	99%	314
Buena Vista Regional Medical Center[2]	Storm Lake	99%	75
The Finley Hospital[2]	Dubuque	99%	208
Iowa City VA Medical Center	Iowa City	99%	174
Mahaska Health Partnership	Oskaloosa	99%	80
Mary Greeley Medical Center	Ames	99%	527
Mercy Hospital	Iowa City	99%	920
Mercy Medical Center-Des Moines[2]	Des Moines	99%	548
Mercy Medical Center-North Iowa	Mason City	99%	805
Pella Regional Health Center[2]	Pella	99%	92
Saint Anthony Regional Hospital	Carroll	99%	213
Saint Lukes Hospital[2]	Cedar Rapids	99%	366
Covenant Medical Center	Waterloo	98%	374
Genesis Medical Center - Davenport[2]	Davenport	98%	503
Iowa Lutheran Hospital[2]	Des Moines	98%	304
Mercy Medical Center-Cedar Rapids[2]	Cedar Rapids	98%	234
Mercy Medical Center-Dubuque[2]	Dubuque	98%	403
Mercy Medical Center-Sioux City[2]	Sioux City	98%	419
Sartori Memorial Hospital	Cedar Falls	98%	91
Wright Medical Center	Clarion	98%	249
Great River Medical Center	West Burlington	97%	423
Iowa Methodist Medical Center[2]	Des Moines	97%	462
Marshalltown Medical & Surgical Center	Marshalltown	97%	179
Ottumwa Regional Health Center	Ottumwa	97%	171
Skiff Medical Center	Newton	97%	146
Trinity Muscatine	Muscatine	97%	35
University of Iowa Hospital & Clinics[2]	Iowa City	97%	399
Boone County Hospital	Boone	96%	48
Lakes Regional Healthcare	Spirit Lake	96%	85
Saint Lukes Regional Medical Center[2]	Sioux City	96%	499
Trinity Regional Medical Center[2]	Fort Dodge	96%	231
VA Central Iowa Healthcare System	Des Moines	96%	54
Grinnell Regional Medical Center	Grinnell	95%	38
Jennie Edmundson Hospital	Council Bluffs	95%	368
Fort Madison Community Hospital	Fort Madison	94%	86
Mercy Medical Center-Clinton	Clinton	94%	132
Broadlawns Medical Center	Des Moines	93%	41
Waverly Health Center	Waverly	93%	41
Van Diest Medical Center	Webster City	88%	25
Mercy Medical Center-Centerville	Centerville	85%	39

29. Prophylactic Antibiotic Selection (Outpatient)

Hospital Name	City	Rate	Cases
Alegent Health Mercy Hospital	Council Bluffs	100%	80
Broadlawns Medical Center	Des Moines	100%	58
Mary Greeley Medical Center	Ames	100%	347
Trinity Muscatine	Muscatine	100%	43
Marshalltown Medical & Surgical Center	Marshalltown	99%	96
Mercy Medical Center-Cedar Rapids	Cedar Rapids	99%	813
Mercy Medical Center-Dubuque	Dubuque	99%	273
Saint Lukes Hospital	Cedar Rapids	99%	581
Trinity Bettendorf	Bettendorf	99%	160
Allen Memorial Hospital	Waterloo	98%	348
Fort Madison Community Hospital	Fort Madison	98%	46
Mercy Hospital	Iowa City	98%	195
Mercy Medical Center-North Iowa	Mason City	98%	806
Saint Anthony Regional Hospital	Carroll	98%	56
Trinity Regional Medical Center	Fort Dodge	98%	179
Genesis Medical Center - Davenport	Davenport	97%	650
Iowa Lutheran Hospital	Des Moines	97%	217
Iowa Methodist Medical Center	Des Moines	97%	705
Mercy Medical Center-Clinton	Clinton	97%	86
Mercy Medical Center-Sioux City	Sioux City	97%	106
Ottumwa Regional Health Center	Ottumwa	97%	68
Saint Lukes Regional Medical Center	Sioux City	97%	97
Spencer Municipal Hospital	Spencer	97%	102
Covenant Medical Center	Waterloo	96%	417
Great River Medical Center	West Burlington	96%	200
Mercy Medical Center-Des Moines	Des Moines	96%	646
Skiff Medical Center	Newton	96%	28
The Finley Hospital	Dubuque	95%	190
University of Iowa Hospital & Clinics	Iowa City	95%	596
Grinnell Regional Medical Center	Grinnell	94%	35
Jennie Edmundson Hospital	Council Bluffs	94%	203
Waverly Health Center	Waverly	88%	34

30. Prophylactic Antibiotic Stopped

Hospital Name	City	Rate	Cases
Trinity Regional Medical Center[2]	Fort Dodge	100%	217
VA Central Iowa Healthcare System	Des Moines	100%	53
Alegent Health Mercy Hospital[2]	Council Bluffs	99%	480
Mary Greeley Medical Center	Ames	99%	505
Allen Memorial Hospital[2]	Waterloo	98%	300
Floyd Valley Hospital	Le Mars	98%	59
Fort Madison Community Hospital	Fort Madison	98%	86
Marshalltown Medical & Surgical Center	Marshalltown	98%	175
Mercy Medical Center-Des Moines[2]	Des Moines	98%	500
Pella Regional Health Center[2]	Pella	98%	90
Trinity Bettendorf[2]	Bettendorf	98%	164
Wright Medical Center	Clarion	98%	246
The Finley Hospital[2]	Dubuque	97%	201
Mercy Medical Center-Dubuque[2]	Dubuque	97%	380
Mercy Medical Center-North Iowa	Mason City	97%	757
Sartori Memorial Hospital	Cedar Falls	97%	88
Trinity Muscatine	Muscatine	97%	32
Iowa Methodist Medical Center[2]	Des Moines	96%	437
Lakes Regional Healthcare	Spirit Lake	96%	83
Saint Anthony Regional Hospital	Carroll	96%	206
Spencer Municipal Hospital[2]	Spencer	96%	142
Broadlawns Medical Center	Des Moines	95%	39
Iowa Lutheran Hospital[2]	Des Moines	95%	271
Mercy Medical Center-Cedar Rapids[2]	Cedar Rapids	95%	186
Mercy Medical Center-Clinton	Clinton	95%	125
Orange City Area Health System	Orange City	95%	39
Saint Lukes Hospital[2]	Cedar Rapids	95%	309
Genesis Medical Center - Davenport[2]	Davenport	94%	470
Great River Medical Center	West Burlington	94%	399
Saint Lukes Regional Medical Center[2]	Sioux City	94%	460
University of Iowa Hospital & Clinics[2]	Iowa City	93%	370
Buena Vista Regional Medical Center[2]	Storm Lake	92%	74
Grundy County Memorial Hospital	Grundy Center	92%	40
Iowa City VA Medical Center	Iowa City	92%	171
Jennie Edmundson Hospital	Council Bluffs	92%	368
Mercy Medical Center-Sioux City[2]	Sioux City	92%	375
Waverly Health Center	Waverly	92%	39
Grinnell Regional Medical Center	Grinnell	91%	35
Boone County Hospital	Boone	89%	47
Covenant Medical Center	Waterloo	89%	357
Mercy Hospital	Iowa City	89%	893
Mahaska Health Partnership	Oskaloosa	88%	73
Ottumwa Regional Health Center	Ottumwa	88%	162
Skiff Medical Center	Newton	88%	143
Mercy Medical Center-Centerville	Centerville	87%	38

31. Recommended VTP Ordered

Hospital Name	City	Rate	Cases
Fort Madison Community Hospital	Fort Madison	100%	38
Grinnell Regional Medical Center	Grinnell	100%	44
Lakes Regional Healthcare	Spirit Lake	100%	55
Mahaska Health Partnership	Oskaloosa	100%	27
Saint Anthony Regional Hospital	Carroll	100%	213
Spencer Municipal Hospital[2]	Spencer	100%	92
Trinity Bettendorf[2]	Bettendorf	100%	45
Trinity Muscatine	Muscatine	100%	39
VA Central Iowa Healthcare System[2]	Des Moines	100%	80
Waverly Health Center	Waverly	100%	29
Mary Greeley Medical Center	Ames	99%	353
Alegent Health Mercy Hospital[2]	Council Bluffs	98%	167
Iowa City VA Medical Center[2]	Iowa City	98%	130
Marshalltown Medical & Surgical Center	Marshalltown	98%	62
Mercy Medical Center-Cedar Rapids[2]	Cedar Rapids	98%	115
Mercy Medical Center-Des Moines[2]	Des Moines	98%	190
Skiff Medical Center	Newton	98%	41
Allen Memorial Hospital[2]	Waterloo	97%	138
Iowa Methodist Medical Center[2]	Des Moines	97%	168
Mercy Medical Center-Sioux City[2]	Sioux City	97%	385
Great River Medical Center	West Burlington	96%	251
Mercy Medical Center-North Iowa	Mason City	95%	288
Saint Lukes Hospital[2]	Cedar Rapids	95%	109
University of Iowa Hospital & Clinics[2]	Iowa City	95%	205
Broadlawns Medical Center	Des Moines	94%	50
The Finley Hospital[2]	Dubuque	94%	139
Saint Lukes Regional Medical Center[2]	Sioux City	94%	224
Mercy Medical Center-Clinton	Clinton	93%	112
Mercy Medical Center-Dubuque[2]	Dubuque	93%	134
Genesis Medical Center - Davenport[2]	Davenport	92%	177
Sartori Memorial Hospital	Cedar Falls	92%	101
Covenant Medical Center	Waterloo	91%	334
Trinity Regional Medical Center[2]	Fort Dodge	89%	80
Iowa Lutheran Hospital[2]	Des Moines	82%	129
Mercy Hospital	Iowa City	82%	411
Pella Regional Health Center[2]	Pella	82%	44
Jennie Edmundson Hospital	Council Bluffs	80%	146

NOTE: Hospital profiles are in alphabetical order by state, then city, then hospital within the city; Rankings exclude hospitals with less than 25 cases except for patient surveys which excludes hospitals with less than 100 cases; (a) 100–299 cases; (1) The number of cases is too small to be sure how well a hospital is performing; (2) The hospital indicated that the data submitted for this measure were based on a sample of cases; (3) Data was collected during a shorter time period (fewer quarters) than the maximum possible time for this measure; (4) Suppressed for one or more quarters by CMS; (5) No data is available from the hospital for this measure; (6) Fewer than 100 patients completed the HCAHPS survey. Use these rates with caution, as the number of surveys may be too low to reliably assess hospital performance; (7) Survey results are based on less than 12 months of data; (8) Survey results are not available for this reporting period; (9) No or very few patients were eligible for the HCAHPS survey. The scores shown, if any, reflect a very small number of surveys; (10) A state average was not calculated because too few hospitals in the state submitted data; (11) There were discrepancies in the data collection process; Please refer to the User's Guide for a full explanation of data.

Hospital Name	City	Rate	Cases
Ottumwa Regional Health Center	Ottumwa	80%	99
Buena Vista Regional Medical Center[2]	Storm Lake	71%	45

32. Urinary Catheter Removal

Hospital Name	City	Rate	Cases
Fort Madison Community Hospital	Fort Madison	100%	34
Lakes Regional Healthcare	Spirit Lake	100%	30
Mary Greeley Medical Center	Ames	100%	71
Iowa City VA Medical Center[2]	Iowa City	99%	142
Allen Memorial Hospital[2]	Waterloo	97%	62
Mercy Medical Center-Dubuque[2]	Dubuque	97%	160
Spencer Municipal Hospital[2]	Spencer	97%	60
VA Central Iowa Healthcare System[2]	Des Moines	97%	35
Great River Medical Center	West Burlington	96%	201
Iowa Lutheran Hospital[2]	Des Moines	96%	82
Mahaska Health Partnership	Oskaloosa	96%	27
Saint Anthony Regional Hospital	Carroll	96%	85
Iowa Methodist Medical Center[2]	Des Moines	95%	169
Jennie Edmundson Hospital	Council Bluffs	94%	128
Sartori Memorial Hospital	Cedar Falls	93%	43
Trinity Regional Medical Center[2]	Fort Dodge	93%	71
Mercy Medical Center-Cedar Rapids[2]	Cedar Rapids	92%	78
Saint Lukes Hospital[2]	Cedar Rapids	92%	144
Genesis Medical Center - Davenport[2]	Davenport	91%	109
Mercy Hospital	Iowa City	91%	375
Mercy Medical Center-Clinton	Clinton	91%	55
The Finley Hospital[2]	Dubuque	90%	81
Mercy Medical Center-North Iowa	Mason City	88%	107
Buena Vista Regional Medical Center[2]	Storm Lake	86%	28
Covenant Medical Center	Waterloo	86%	138
Mercy Medical Center-Des Moines[2]	Des Moines	85%	120
University of Iowa Hospital & Clinics[2]	Iowa City	85%	146
Mercy Medical Center-Sioux City	Sioux City	84%	83
Saint Lukes Regional Medical Center[2]	Sioux City	54%	26

Use of Medical Imaging

36. Combination Abdominal CT Scan

Hospital Name	City	Ratio	Cases
Genesis Medical Center-Dewitt[1]	Dewitt	0.000	38
Sartori Memorial Hospital	Cedar Falls	0.006	168
Mary Greeley Medical Center	Ames	0.010	203
Trinity Regional Medical Center	Fort Dodge	0.011	380
Waverly Health Center	Waverly	0.011	275
Mercy Medical Center-Des Moines	Des Moines	0.017	1496
Palmer Lutheran Health Center	West Union	0.020	98
Marshalltown Medical & Surgical Center	Marshalltown	0.023	302
Trinity Muscatine	Muscatine	0.024	210
Cass County Memorial Hospital	Atlantic	0.029	208
Skiff Medical Center	Newton	0.030	236
Genesis Medical Center - Davenport	Davenport	0.033	1171
Grundy County Memorial Hospital	Grundy Center	0.037	54
Broadlawns Medical Center	Des Moines	0.042	72
Allen Memorial Hospital	Waterloo	0.046	1144
Covenant Medical Center	Waterloo	0.046	585
Saint Anthony Regional Hospital	Carroll	0.055	343
Trinity Bettendorf	Bettendorf	0.055	255
Iowa Lutheran Hospital	Des Moines	0.058	462
Mercy Hospital	Iowa City	0.067	625
Marengo Memorial Hospital[1]	Marengo	0.073	41
The Finley Hospital	Dubuque	0.074	564
Mercy Medical Center-Cedar Rapids	Cedar Rapids	0.075	783
Mercy Medical Center-North Iowa	Mason City	0.081	1032
Guthrie County Hospital	Guthrie Center	0.091	77
University of Iowa Hospital & Clinics	Iowa City	0.091	1602
Iowa Methodist Medical Center	Des Moines	0.094	479
Grinnell Regional Medical Center	Grinnell	0.099	262
Jennie Edmundson Hospital	Council Bluffs	0.110	573
Saint Lukes Hospital	Cedar Rapids	0.112	881
Clarke County Hospital	Osceola	0.117	103
Hegg Memorial Health Center[1]	Rock Valley	0.127	55
Myrtue Medical Center	Harlan	0.133	195
Belmond Medical Center[1]	Belmond	0.143	42
Audubon County Memorial Hospital	Audubon	0.148	115
Alegent Health Mercy Hospital	Council Bluffs	0.149	496
Mercy Medical Center-Dubuque	Dubuque	0.165	393
Sioux Center Community Hospital	Sioux Center	0.197	76
Spencer Municipal Hospital	Spencer	0.223	282
Keokuk Area Hospital	Keokuk	0.250	284
Dallas County Hospital	Perry	0.290	107
Lakes Regional Healthcare	Spirit Lake	0.395	86
Mercy Medical Center-Sioux City	Sioux City	0.422	535
Ottumwa Regional Health Center[1]	Ottumwa	0.433	30
Saint Lukes Regional Medical Center	Sioux City	0.601	258
Mercy Medical Center-Clinton	Clinton	0.625	168
Mahaska Health Partnership	Oskaloosa	0.711	173
Davis County Hospital	Bloomfield	0.724	105
Great River Medical Center	West Burlington	0.741	854
Fort Madison Community Hospital	Fort Madison	0.775	258
Boone County Hospital	Boone	0.783	138

37. Combination Chest CT Scan

Hospital Name	City	Ratio	Cases
Davis County Hospital[1]	Bloomfield	0.000	31
Grundy County Memorial Hospital[1]	Grundy Center	0.000	31
Marshalltown Medical & Surgical Center	Marshalltown	0.000	188
Palmer Lutheran Health Center[1]	West Union	0.000	37
Sartori Memorial Hospital	Cedar Falls	0.000	102
Trinity Muscatine	Muscatine	0.000	125
Waverly Health Center	Waverly	0.000	124
Mercy Hospital	Iowa City	0.002	583
Trinity Regional Medical Center	Fort Dodge	0.002	445
Covenant Medical Center	Waterloo	0.004	679
Allen Memorial Hospital	Waterloo	0.006	715
Mercy Medical Center-Cedar Rapids	Cedar Rapids	0.008	529
Mercy Medical Center-Sioux City	Sioux City	0.010	298
Jennie Edmundson Hospital	Council Bluffs	0.013	396
Saint Anthony Regional Hospital	Carroll	0.014	212
Mercy Medical Center-North Iowa	Mason City	0.015	1156
University of Iowa Hospital & Clinics	Iowa City	0.015	1581
Genesis Medical Center - Davenport	Davenport	0.016	1200
Skiff Medical Center	Newton	0.019	105
Mercy Medical Center-Des Moines	Des Moines	0.021	1214
Alegent Health Mercy Hospital	Council Bluffs	0.025	275
Mahaska Health Partnership	Oskaloosa	0.025	79
Belmond Medical Center[1]	Belmond	0.026	39
The Finley Hospital	Dubuque	0.029	489
Fort Madison Community Hospital	Fort Madison	0.031	162
Clarke County Hospital	Osceola	0.037	54
Genesis Medical Center-Dewitt[1]	Dewitt	0.045	44
Saint Lukes Hospital	Cedar Rapids	0.048	580
Audubon County Memorial Hospital	Audubon	0.051	59
Boone County Hospital	Boone	0.062	97
Grinnell Regional Medical Center	Grinnell	0.063	144
Great River Medical Center	West Burlington	0.078	774
Guthrie County Hospital[1]	Guthrie Center	0.080	50
Trinity Bettendorf	Bettendorf	0.083	132
Myrtue Medical Center	Harlan	0.091	88
Sioux Center Community Hospital[1]	Sioux Center	0.119	42
Mercy Medical Center-Dubuque	Dubuque	0.125	176
Cass County Memorial Hospital	Atlantic	0.135	141
Iowa Methodist Medical Center	Des Moines	0.147	109
Saint Lukes Regional Medical Center	Sioux City	0.156	90
Ottumwa Regional Health Center[1]	Ottumwa	0.160	25
Iowa Lutheran Hospital	Des Moines	0.171	245
Broadlawns Medical Center[1]	Des Moines	0.175	63
Spencer Municipal Hospital	Spencer	0.179	207
Mary Greeley Medical Center	Ames	0.225	129
Lakes Regional Healthcare[1]	Spirit Lake	0.300	50
Mercy Medical Center-Clinton	Clinton	0.315	111
Dallas County Hospital	Perry	0.400	60
Keokuk Area Hospital	Keokuk	0.506	87

38. Follow-up Mammogram/Ultrasound

Hospital Name	City	Rate	Cases
Lakes Regional Healthcare	Spirit Lake	0.9%	327
Mercy Medical Center-Clinton	Clinton	1.0%	392
Mahaska Health Partnership	Oskaloosa	2.1%	421
Clarke County Hospital	Osceola	2.7%	146
Davis County Hospital	Bloomfield	3.2%	189
Ottumwa Regional Health Center	Ottumwa	3.2%	1120
Alegent Health Mercy Hospital	Council Bluffs	3.3%	693
Skiff Medical Center	Newton	3.6%	638
Audubon County Memorial Hospital	Audubon	3.8%	133
Trinity Muscatine	Muscatine	4.0%	570
Keokuk Area Hospital	Keokuk	4.1%	583
Mercy Medical Center-Sioux City	Sioux City	4.6%	393
Waverly Health Center	Waverly	4.8%	540
Grundy County Memorial Hospital	Grundy Center	5.2%	213
Sartori Memorial Hospital	Cedar Falls	5.4%	516
Cass County Memorial Hospital	Atlantic	6.5%	445
Mercy Medical Center-Des Moines	Des Moines	6.5%	3240
Dallas County Hospital	Perry	6.6%	152
Boone County Hospital	Boone	7.0%	499
Covenant Medical Center	Waterloo	7.3%	1275
Mercy Medical Center-Cedar Rapids	Cedar Rapids	7.4%	2686
Mercy Hospital	Iowa City	7.7%	1189
Allen Memorial Hospital	Waterloo	8.0%	2129
Great River Medical Center	West Burlington	8.2%	1411
Saint Lukes Hospital	Cedar Rapids	8.3%	1591
Saint Anthony Regional Hospital	Carroll	8.5%	519
Myrtue Medical Center	Harlan	9.0%	423
Sioux Center Community Hospital	Sioux Center	9.1%	197
University of Iowa Hospital & Clinics	Iowa City	9.4%	1121
Hegg Memorial Health Center	Rock Valley	9.5%	105
Belmond Medical Center	Belmond	10.1%	109
Mercy Medical Center-Dyersville	Dyersville	10.1%	109
Genesis Medical Center - Davenport	Davenport	10.2%	1620
Jennie Edmundson Hospital	Council Bluffs	10.4%	1046
Mary Greeley Medical Center	Ames	10.5%	190
Mercy Medical Center-North Iowa	Mason City	10.7%	2698
Spencer Municipal Hospital	Spencer	10.7%	568
Genesis Medical Center-Dewitt	Dewitt	10.9%	320
Guthrie County Hospital	Guthrie Center	12.2%	123
Fort Madison Community Hospital	Fort Madison	12.6%	564
Marshalltown Medical & Surgical Center	Marshalltown	13.1%	628
Trinity Bettendorf	Bettendorf	14.7%	251
The Finley Hospital	Dubuque	15.7%	217
Grinnell Regional Medical Center	Grinnell	18.3%	449
Mercy Medical Center-Dubuque[1]	Dubuque	23.3%	30
Iowa Lutheran Hospital	Des Moines	26.8%	1043
Broadlawns Medical Center	Des Moines	29.6%	206

39. MRI for Low Back Pain

Hospital Name	City	Rate	Cases
Sioux Center Community Hospital[1]	Sioux Center	11.1%	27
Mary Greeley Medical Center[1]	Ames	14.8%	27
Saint Anthony Regional Hospital	Carroll	19.0%	100
University of Iowa Hospital & Clinics	Iowa City	23.4%	205
Keokuk Area Hospital[1]	Keokuk	24.5%	53
Boone County Hospital	Boone	24.6%	57
Sartori Memorial Hospital[1]	Cedar Falls	25.0%	48
Skiff Medical Center[1]	Newton	26.9%	52
Waverly Health Center	Waverly	27.6%	58
Genesis Medical Center - Davenport	Davenport	28.1%	135
Trinity Muscatine[1]	Muscatine	28.2%	39
Mercy Hospital	Iowa City	28.3%	269
Great River Medical Center	West Burlington	28.4%	201
Iowa Lutheran Hospital	Des Moines	29.4%	102
Mercy Medical Center-Dubuque[1]	Dubuque	29.8%	47
Saint Lukes Hospital	Cedar Rapids	29.8%	312
Allen Memorial Hospital	Waterloo	30.4%	207
Grinnell Regional Medical Center	Grinnell	30.4%	79
The Finley Hospital	Dubuque	31.4%	315
Trinity Regional Medical Center	Fort Dodge	31.4%	159
Covenant Medical Center	Waterloo	31.6%	171
Mercy Medical Center-Cedar Rapids	Cedar Rapids	31.8%	340
Lakes Regional Healthcare	Spirit Lake	32.1%	53
Spencer Municipal Hospital	Spencer	32.1%	112
Jennie Edmundson Hospital	Council Bluffs	32.8%	180
Davis County Hospital[1]	Bloomfield	33.3%	27
Alegent Health Mercy Hospital	Council Bluffs	34.6%	130
Mahaska Health Partnership[1]	Oskaloosa	35.7%	42
Iowa Methodist Medical Center[1]	Des Moines	36.4%	44
Mercy Medical Center-Des Moines	Des Moines	36.5%	304
Mercy Medical Center-Sioux City	Sioux City	37.1%	143
Ottumwa Regional Health Center	Ottumwa	37.1%	97
Cass County Memorial Hospital[1]	Atlantic	37.5%	32
Fort Madison Community Hospital	Fort Madison	37.5%	72
Myrtue Medical Center	Harlan	39.0%	41
Marshalltown Medical & Surgical Center	Marshalltown	44.9%	49

Survey of Patients' Hospital Experiences

40. Area Around Room 'Always' Quiet at Night

Hospital Name	City	Rate	Cases
Waverly Health Center	Waverly	77%	300+
Clarke County Hospital	Osceola	76%	(a)
Floyd Valley Hospital	Le Mars	74%	300+
Jefferson County Health Center	Fairfield	73%	(a)
Mercy Hosp of Franciscan Sisters-Oelwein	Oelwein	72%	(a)
Osceola Community Hospital	Sibley	72%	(a)
Jackson County Regional Health Center	Maquoketa	71%	(a)
Guttenberg Municipal Hospital	Guttenberg	70%	(a)
Sartori Memorial Hospital	Cedar Falls	69%	300+
Wright Medical Center	Clarion	69%	300+
Mercy Medical Center-Cedar Rapids	Cedar Rapids	68%	300+
Saint Anthony Regional Hospital	Carroll	68%	300+
Alegent Health Mercy Hospital	Council Bluffs	67%	300+
Buchanan County Health Center	Independence	67%	(a)
Grinnell Regional Medical Center	Grinnell	67%	300+
Hegg Memorial Health Center	Rock Valley	67%	(a)
Lakes Regional Healthcare	Spirit Lake	67%	300+
Spencer Municipal Hospital	Spencer	67%	300+
Cass County Memorial Hospital	Atlantic	66%	(a)
Pella Regional Health Center	Pella	66%	300+
Henry County Health Center	Mount Pleasant	65%	(a)
Ottumwa Regional Health Center	Ottumwa	65%	300+
Trinity Bettendorf	Bettendorf	65%	300+
Avera Holy Family Health	Estherville	64%	(a)
Boone County Hospital	Boone	63%	300+
Greater Regional Medical Center	Creston	62%	300+
Broadlawns Medical Center	Des Moines	61%	300+
Fort Madison Community Hospital	Fort Madison	61%	300+
Iowa Methodist Medical Center	Des Moines	61%	300+
Saint Lukes Hospital	Cedar Rapids	61%	300+
Stewart Memorial Community Hospital	Lake City	61%	(a)
Washington County Hospital	Washington	61%	(a)
Burgess Health Center	Onawa	60%	(a)
Clarinda Regional Health Center	Clarinda	60%	(a)
Montgomery County Memorial Hospital	Red Oak	60%	(a)

NOTE: Hospital profiles are in alphabetical order by state, then city, then hospital within the city; Rankings exclude hospitals with less than 25 cases except for patient surveys which excludes hospitals with less than 100 cases; (a) 100–299 cases; (1) The number of cases is too small to be sure how well a hospital is performing; (2) The hospital indicated that the data submitted for this measure were based on a sample of cases; (3) Data was collected during a shorter time period (fewer quarters) than the maximum possible time for this measure; (4) Suppressed for one or more quarters by CMS; (5) No data is available from the hospital for this measure; (6) Fewer than 100 patients completed the HCAHPS survey. Use these rates with caution, as the number of surveys may be too low to reliably assess hospital performance; (7) Survey results are based on less than 12 months of data; (8) Survey results are not available for this reporting period; (9) No or very few patients were eligible for the HCAHPS survey. The scores shown, if any, reflect a very small number of surveys; (10) A state average was not calculated because too few hospitals in the state submitted data; (11) There were discrepancies in the data collection process; Please refer to the User's Guide for a full explanation of data.

Hospital Name	City	Rate	Cases
Sioux Center Community Hospital	Sioux Center	60%	(a)
The Finley Hospital	Dubuque	59%	300+
Sanford Hospital Rock Rapids	Rock Rapids	59%	(a)
Mercy Hospital	Iowa City	58%	300+
Mercy Medical Center-Clinton	Clinton	58%	300+
Mercy Medical Center-Dubuque	Dubuque	58%	300+
Jennie Edmundson Hospital	Council Bluffs	57%	300+
Myrtue Medical Center	Harlan	57%	300+
Iowa Lutheran Hospital	Des Moines	56%	300+
Mercy Medical Center-Des Moines	Des Moines	56%	300+
Van Diest Medical Center	Webster City	56%	(a)
Allen Memorial Hospital	Waterloo	55%	300+
Great River Medical Center	West Burlington	55%	300+
Mahaska Health Partnership	Oskaloosa	55%	(a)
Skiff Medical Center	Newton	55%	300+
Covenant Medical Center	Waterloo	54%	300+
Davis County Hospital	Bloomfield	54%	(a)
Genesis Medical Center - Davenport	Davenport	54%	300+
Mercy Medical Center-North Iowa	Mason City	54%	300+
Marshalltown Medical & Surgical Center	Marshalltown	53%	300+
Trinity Regional Medical Center	Fort Dodge	53%	300+
Mercy Medical Center-Sioux City	Sioux City	52%	300+
Knoxville Hospital & Clinics	Knoxville	49%	(a)
Sanford Sheldon Medical Center	Sheldon	49%	(a)
Trinity Muscatine	Muscatine	49%	300+
Mary Greeley Medical Center	Ames	47%	300+
Saint Lukes Regional Medical Center	Sioux City	47%	300+
Keokuk Area Hospital	Keokuk	46%	(a)
University of Iowa Hospital & Clinics	Iowa City	44%	300+

41. Doctors 'Always' Communicated Well

Hospital Name	City	Rate	Cases
Knoxville Hospital & Clinics	Knoxville	91%	(a)
Henry County Health Center	Mount Pleasant	89%	(a)
Montgomery County Memorial Hospital	Red Oak	89%	(a)
Guttenberg Municipal Hospital	Guttenberg	88%	(a)
Mahaska Health Partnership	Oskaloosa	88%	(a)
Pella Regional Health Center	Pella	88%	300+
Waverly Health Center	Waverly	88%	300+
Clarinda Regional Health Center	Clarinda	87%	(a)
Clarke County Hospital	Osceola	87%	(a)
Davis County Hospital	Bloomfield	87%	(a)
Floyd Valley Hospital	Le Mars	87%	300+
Myrtue Medical Center	Harlan	87%	300+
Avera Holy Family Health	Estherville	86%	(a)
Burgess Health Center	Onawa	86%	(a)
Van Diest Medical Center	Webster City	86%	(a)
Washington County Hospital	Washington	86%	(a)
Grinnell Regional Medical Center	Grinnell	85%	300+
Jefferson County Health Center	Fairfield	85%	(a)
Jennie Edmundson Hospital	Council Bluffs	85%	300+
Mercy Hospital	Iowa City	85%	300+
Mercy Hosp of Franciscan Sisters-Oelwein	Oelwein	85%	(a)
Sanford Hospital Rock Rapids	Rock Rapids	85%	(a)
Skiff Medical Center	Newton	85%	300+
Wright Medical Center	Clarion	85%	300+
Greater Regional Medical Center	Creston	84%	300+
Hegg Memorial Health Center	Rock Valley	84%	(a)
Jackson County Regional Health Center	Maquoketa	84%	(a)
Saint Anthony Regional Hospital	Carroll	84%	300+
Trinity Muscatine	Muscatine	84%	300+
Buchanan County Health Center	Independence	83%	(a)
Lakes Regional Healthcare	Spirit Lake	83%	300+
Osceola Community Hospital	Sibley	83%	(a)
Boone County Hospital	Boone	82%	300+
Ottumwa Regional Health Center	Ottumwa	82%	300+
Sanford Sheldon Medical Center	Sheldon	82%	(a)
Sartori Memorial Hospital	Cedar Falls	82%	300+
Trinity Regional Medical Center	Fort Dodge	82%	300+
Mary Greeley Medical Center	Ames	81%	300+
Mercy Medical Center-Dubuque	Dubuque	81%	300+
Sioux Center Community Hospital	Sioux Center	81%	(a)
Broadlawns Medical Center	Des Moines	80%	300+
The Finley Hospital	Dubuque	80%	300+
Fort Madison Community Hospital	Fort Madison	80%	300+
Marshalltown Medical & Surgical Center	Marshalltown	80%	300+
Spencer Municipal Hospital	Spencer	80%	300+
Alegent Health Mercy Hospital	Council Bluffs	79%	300+
Genesis Medical Center - Davenport	Davenport	79%	300+
Great River Medical Center	West Burlington	79%	300+
Mercy Medical Center-Cedar Rapids	Cedar Rapids	79%	300+
Stewart Memorial Community Hospital	Lake City	79%	(a)
Trinity Bettendorf	Bettendorf	79%	300+
Cass County Memorial Hospital	Atlantic	78%	(a)
Mercy Medical Center-Sioux City	Sioux City	78%	300+
Saint Lukes Hospital	Cedar Rapids	78%	300+
Iowa Methodist Medical Center	Des Moines	77%	300+
Keokuk Area Hospital	Keokuk	77%	(a)
Mercy Medical Center-Des Moines	Des Moines	77%	300+
Mercy Medical Center-North Iowa	Mason City	77%	300+
Covenant Medical Center	Waterloo	76%	300+
Iowa Lutheran Hospital	Des Moines	75%	300+
Mercy Medical Center-Clinton	Clinton	75%	300+
University of Iowa Hospital & Clinics	Iowa City	75%	300+
Allen Memorial Hospital	Waterloo	74%	300+
Saint Lukes Regional Medical Center	Sioux City	74%	300+

42. Home Recovery Information Given

Hospital Name	City	Rate	Cases
Mercy Hospital	Iowa City	92%	300+
Mercy Medical Center-Dubuque	Dubuque	90%	300+
Montgomery County Memorial Hospital	Red Oak	90%	(a)
Wright Medical Center	Clarion	90%	300+
The Finley Hospital	Dubuque	89%	300+
Saint Lukes Hospital	Cedar Rapids	89%	300+
Trinity Regional Medical Center	Fort Dodge	89%	300+
Alegent Health Mercy Hospital	Council Bluffs	88%	300+
Clarke County Hospital	Osceola	88%	(a)
Floyd Valley Hospital	Le Mars	88%	300+
Lakes Regional Healthcare	Spirit Lake	88%	300+
Mercy Hosp of Franciscan Sisters-Oelwein	Oelwein	88%	(a)
Waverly Health Center	Waverly	88%	300+
Grinnell Regional Medical Center	Grinnell	87%	300+
Jennie Edmundson Hospital	Council Bluffs	87%	300+
Mercy Medical Center-North Iowa	Mason City	87%	300+
Spencer Municipal Hospital	Spencer	87%	300+
Trinity Bettendorf	Bettendorf	87%	300+
Hegg Memorial Health Center	Rock Valley	86%	(a)
Mercy Medical Center-Clinton	Clinton	86%	300+
Mercy Medical Center-Sioux City	Sioux City	86%	300+
Saint Anthony Regional Hospital	Carroll	86%	300+
Avera Holy Family Health	Estherville	85%	(a)
Boone County Hospital	Boone	85%	300+
Burgess Health Center	Onawa	85%	(a)
Marshalltown Medical & Surgical Center	Marshalltown	85%	300+
Mercy Medical Center-Des Moines	Des Moines	85%	300+
Pella Regional Health Center	Pella	85%	300+
Cass County Memorial Hospital	Atlantic	84%	(a)
Davis County Hospital	Bloomfield	84%	(a)
Great River Medical Center	West Burlington	84%	300+
Guttenberg Municipal Hospital	Guttenberg	84%	(a)
Henry County Health Center	Mount Pleasant	84%	(a)
Iowa Lutheran Hospital	Des Moines	84%	300+
Knoxville Hospital & Clinics	Knoxville	84%	(a)
Mary Greeley Medical Center	Ames	84%	300+
Myrtue Medical Center	Harlan	84%	300+
Ottumwa Regional Health Center	Ottumwa	84%	300+
University of Iowa Hospital & Clinics	Iowa City	84%	300+
Allen Memorial Hospital	Waterloo	83%	300+
Broadlawns Medical Center	Des Moines	83%	300+
Fort Madison Community Hospital	Fort Madison	83%	300+
Mercy Medical Center-Cedar Rapids	Cedar Rapids	83%	300+
Saint Lukes Regional Medical Center	Sioux City	83%	300+
Sartori Memorial Hospital	Cedar Falls	83%	300+
Skiff Medical Center	Newton	83%	300+
Stewart Memorial Community Hospital	Lake City	83%	(a)
Iowa Methodist Medical Center	Des Moines	82%	300+
Sioux Center Community Hospital	Sioux Center	82%	(a)
Trinity Muscatine	Muscatine	82%	300+
Genesis Medical Center - Davenport	Davenport	81%	300+
Mahaska Health Partnership	Oskaloosa	81%	(a)
Van Diest Medical Center	Webster City	81%	(a)
Washington County Hospital	Washington	81%	(a)
Covenant Medical Center	Waterloo	80%	300+
Greater Regional Medical Center	Creston	80%	300+
Jackson County Regional Health Center	Maquoketa	80%	(a)
Jefferson County Health Center	Fairfield	80%	(a)
Keokuk Area Hospital	Keokuk	80%	(a)
Sanford Hospital Rock Rapids	Rock Rapids	80%	(a)
Buchanan County Health Center	Independence	79%	(a)
Osceola Community Hospital	Sibley	78%	(a)
Clarinda Regional Health Center	Clarinda	76%	(a)
Sanford Sheldon Medical Center	Sheldon	76%	(a)

43. Hospital Given 9 or 10 on 10 Point Scale

Hospital Name	City	Rate	Cases
Sanford Hospital Rock Rapids	Rock Rapids	85%	(a)
Pella Regional Health Center	Pella	84%	300+
Waverly Health Center	Waverly	84%	300+
Osceola Community Hospital	Sibley	83%	(a)
Wright Medical Center	Clarion	83%	300+
Saint Anthony Regional Hospital	Carroll	82%	300+
Hegg Memorial Health Center	Rock Valley	81%	(a)
Jefferson County Health Center	Fairfield	81%	(a)
Montgomery County Memorial Hospital	Red Oak	81%	(a)
Burgess Health Center	Onawa	80%	(a)
Stewart Memorial Community Hospital	Lake City	80%	(a)
Floyd Valley Hospital	Le Mars	79%	300+
Sioux Center Community Hospital	Sioux Center	79%	(a)
Clarke County Hospital	Osceola	78%	(a)
Guttenberg Municipal Hospital	Guttenberg	77%	(a)
Mercy Medical Center-Dubuque	Dubuque	77%	300+
Saint Lukes Hospital	Cedar Rapids	77%	300+
Avera Holy Family Health	Estherville	76%	(a)
Mercy Hospital	Iowa City	76%	300+
Spencer Municipal Hospital	Spencer	76%	300+
Henry County Health Center	Mount Pleasant	75%	(a)
Mercy Medical Center-Cedar Rapids	Cedar Rapids	75%	300+
Alegent Health Mercy Hospital	Council Bluffs	74%	300+
Boone County Hospital	Boone	74%	300+
Fort Madison Community Hospital	Fort Madison	74%	300+
Lakes Regional Healthcare	Spirit Lake	74%	300+
Trinity Bettendorf	Bettendorf	74%	300+
Jennie Edmundson Hospital	Council Bluffs	73%	300+
Myrtue Medical Center	Harlan	73%	300+
The Finley Hospital	Dubuque	72%	300+
Grinnell Regional Medical Center	Grinnell	72%	300+
Iowa Methodist Medical Center	Des Moines	72%	300+
Mercy Medical Center-Des Moines	Des Moines	71%	300+
Mercy Medical Center-Sioux City	Sioux City	71%	300+
Sartori Memorial Hospital	Cedar Falls	71%	300+
Greater Regional Medical Center	Creston	70%	300+
Iowa Lutheran Hospital	Des Moines	70%	300+
Mahaska Health Partnership	Oskaloosa	70%	(a)
Mercy Hosp of Franciscan Sisters-Oelwein	Oelwein	70%	(a)
Washington County Hospital	Washington	70%	(a)
Genesis Medical Center - Davenport	Davenport	69%	300+
Trinity Regional Medical Center	Fort Dodge	69%	300+
Clarinda Regional Health Center	Clarinda	68%	(a)
Great River Medical Center	West Burlington	68%	300+
Knoxville Hospital & Clinics	Knoxville	68%	(a)
Mercy Medical Center-North Iowa	Mason City	68%	300+
Saint Lukes Regional Medical Center	Sioux City	68%	300+
Sanford Sheldon Medical Center	Sheldon	68%	(a)
Skiff Medical Center	Newton	68%	300+
Van Diest Medical Center	Webster City	68%	(a)
Allen Memorial Hospital	Waterloo	67%	300+
Davis County Hospital	Bloomfield	67%	(a)
Mary Greeley Medical Center	Ames	67%	300+
Buchanan County Health Center	Independence	66%	(a)
Mercy Medical Center-Clinton	Clinton	66%	300+
University of Iowa Hospital & Clinics	Iowa City	66%	300+
Marshalltown Medical & Surgical Center	Marshalltown	65%	300+
Ottumwa Regional Health Center	Ottumwa	65%	300+
Broadlawns Medical Center	Des Moines	63%	300+
Cass County Memorial Hospital	Atlantic	63%	(a)
Jackson County Regional Health Center	Maquoketa	63%	(a)
Covenant Medical Center	Waterloo	61%	300+
Keokuk Area Hospital	Keokuk	61%	(a)
Trinity Muscatine	Muscatine	58%	300+

44. Meds 'Always' Explained Before Given

Hospital Name	City	Rate	Cases
Hegg Memorial Health Center	Rock Valley	80%	(a)
Waverly Health Center	Waverly	73%	300+
Floyd Valley Hospital	Le Mars	71%	300+
Guttenberg Municipal Hospital	Guttenberg	71%	(a)
Clarke County Hospital	Osceola	69%	(a)
Greater Regional Medical Center	Creston	68%	300+
Pella Regional Health Center	Pella	68%	300+
Burgess Health Center	Onawa	67%	(a)
Clarinda Regional Health Center	Clarinda	67%	(a)
Grinnell Regional Medical Center	Grinnell	67%	300+
Montgomery County Memorial Hospital	Red Oak	67%	(a)
Mercy Hospital	Iowa City	66%	300+
Osceola Community Hospital	Sibley	66%	(a)
Sioux Center Community Hospital	Sioux Center	66%	(a)
Stewart Memorial Community Hospital	Lake City	66%	(a)
Jennie Edmundson Hospital	Council Bluffs	65%	300+
Lakes Regional Healthcare	Spirit Lake	65%	300+
Saint Anthony Regional Hospital	Carroll	65%	300+
Knoxville Hospital & Clinics	Knoxville	64%	(a)
Mercy Hosp of Franciscan Sisters-Oelwein	Oelwein	63%	(a)
Spencer Municipal Hospital	Spencer	63%	300+
Trinity Regional Medical Center	Fort Dodge	63%	300+
Avera Holy Family Health	Estherville	62%	(a)
Great River Medical Center	West Burlington	62%	300+
Jackson County Regional Health Center	Maquoketa	62%	(a)
Mahaska Health Partnership	Oskaloosa	62%	(a)
Mercy Medical Center-Cedar Rapids	Cedar Rapids	62%	300+
Ottumwa Regional Health Center	Ottumwa	62%	300+
Saint Lukes Hospital	Cedar Rapids	62%	300+
Trinity Bettendorf	Bettendorf	62%	300+
Trinity Muscatine	Muscatine	62%	300+
Wright Medical Center	Clarion	62%	300+
Alegent Health Mercy Hospital	Council Bluffs	61%	300+
Boone County Hospital	Boone	61%	300+
Broadlawns Medical Center	Des Moines	61%	300+
The Finley Hospital	Dubuque	61%	300+
Fort Madison Community Hospital	Fort Madison	61%	300+

NOTE: Hospital profiles are in alphabetical order by state, then city, then hospital within the city; Rankings exclude hospitals with less than 25 cases except for patient surveys which excludes hospitals with less than 100 cases; (a) 100–299 cases; (1) The number of cases is too small to be sure how well a hospital is performing; (2) The hospital indicated that the data submitted for this measure were based on a sample of cases; (3) Data was collected during a shorter time period (fewer quarters) than the maximum possible time for this measure; (4) Suppressed for one or more quarters by CMS; (5) No data is available from the hospital for this measure; (6) Fewer than 100 patients completed the HCAHPS survey. Use these rates with caution, as the number of surveys may be too low to reliably assess hospital performance; (7) Survey results are based on less than 12 months of data; (8) Survey results are not available for this reporting period; (9) No or very few patients were eligible for the HCAHPS survey. The scores shown, if any, reflect a very small number of surveys; (10) A state average was not calculated because too few hospitals in the state submitted data; (11) There were discrepancies in the data collection process; Please refer to the User's Guide for a full explanation of data.

Henry County Health Center	Mount Pleasant	61%	(a)
Mercy Medical Center-Clinton	Clinton	61%	300+
Mercy Medical Center-Dubuque	Dubuque	61%	300+
Myrtue Medical Center	Harlan	61%	300+
Sartori Memorial Hospital	Cedar Falls	61%	300+
Van Diest Medical Center	Webster City	61%	(a)
Washington County Hospital	Washington	61%	(a)
Buchanan County Health Center	Independence	60%	(a)
Davis County Hospital	Bloomfield	60%	(a)
Genesis Medical Center - Davenport	Davenport	60%	300+
Marshalltown Medical & Surgical Center	Marshalltown	60%	300+
Sanford Hospital Rock Rapids	Rock Rapids	60%	(a)
Sanford Sheldon Medical Center	Sheldon	60%	(a)
Skiff Medical Center	Newton	60%	300+
Cass County Memorial Hospital	Atlantic	59%	(a)
Iowa Methodist Medical Center	Des Moines	59%	300+
Mercy Medical Center-Des Moines	Des Moines	59%	300+
Mercy Medical Center-Sioux City	Sioux City	59%	300+
Allen Memorial Hospital	Waterloo	58%	300+
Iowa Lutheran Hospital	Des Moines	58%	300+
Jefferson County Health Center	Fairfield	58%	(a)
Mercy Medical Center-North Iowa	Mason City	58%	300+
Saint Lukes Regional Medical Center	Sioux City	58%	300+
Mary Greeley Medical Center	Ames	56%	300+
Keokuk Area Hospital	Keokuk	55%	(a)
University of Iowa Hospital & Clinics	Iowa City	55%	300+
Covenant Medical Center	Waterloo	52%	300+

45. Nurses 'Always' Communicated Well

Hospital Name	City	Rate	Cases
Jefferson County Health Center	Fairfield	89%	(a)
Clarke County Hospital	Osceola	87%	(a)
Mercy Hosp of Franciscan Sisters-Oelwein	Oelwein	86%	(a)
Guttenberg Municipal Hospital	Guttenberg	85%	(a)
Wright Medical Center	Clarion	85%	300+
Avera Holy Family Health	Estherville	84%	(a)
Montgomery County Memorial Hospital	Red Oak	84%	(a)
Waverly Health Center	Waverly	84%	300+
Burgess Health Center	Onawa	83%	(a)
Floyd Valley Hospital	Le Mars	83%	300+
Sioux Center Community Hospital	Sioux Center	83%	(a)
Greater Regional Medical Center	Creston	82%	300+
Hegg Memorial Health Center	Rock Valley	82%	(a)
Henry County Health Center	Mount Pleasant	82%	(a)
Jennie Edmundson Hospital	Council Bluffs	82%	300+
Osceola Community Hospital	Sibley	82%	(a)
Pella Regional Health Center	Pella	82%	300+
Clarinda Regional Health Center	Clarinda	81%	(a)
Davis County Hospital	Bloomfield	81%	(a)
Grinnell Regional Medical Center	Grinnell	81%	300+
Mercy Hospital	Iowa City	81%	300+
Myrtue Medical Center	Harlan	81%	300+
Saint Anthony Regional Hospital	Carroll	81%	300+
Stewart Memorial Community Hospital	Lake City	81%	(a)
Washington County Hospital	Washington	81%	(a)
Alegent Health Mercy Hospital	Council Bluffs	80%	300+
Fort Madison Community Hospital	Fort Madison	80%	300+
Lakes Regional Healthcare	Spirit Lake	80%	300+
Mahaska Health Partnership	Oskaloosa	80%	(a)
Van Diest Medical Center	Webster City	80%	(a)
Knoxville Hospital & Clinics	Knoxville	79%	(a)
Mercy Medical Center-Clinton	Clinton	79%	300+
Saint Lukes Hospital	Cedar Rapids	79%	300+
Sanford Hospital Rock Rapids	Rock Rapids	79%	(a)
Skiff Medical Center	Newton	79%	300+
The Finley Hospital	Dubuque	78%	300+
Genesis Medical Center - Davenport	Davenport	78%	300+
Great River Medical Center	West Burlington	78%	300+
Ottumwa Regional Health Center	Ottumwa	78%	300+
Sartori Memorial Hospital	Cedar Falls	78%	300+
Spencer Municipal Hospital	Spencer	78%	300+
Trinity Regional Medical Center	Fort Dodge	78%	300+
Buchanan County Health Center	Independence	77%	(a)
Cass County Memorial Hospital	Atlantic	77%	(a)
Mercy Medical Center-Dubuque	Dubuque	77%	300+
Mercy Medical Center-North Iowa	Mason City	77%	300+
Mercy Medical Center-Sioux City	Sioux City	77%	300+
Boone County Hospital	Boone	76%	300+
Broadlawns Medical Center	Des Moines	76%	300+
Jackson County Regional Health Center	Maquoketa	76%	(a)
Mercy Medical Center-Cedar Rapids	Cedar Rapids	76%	300+
Mercy Medical Center-Des Moines	Des Moines	76%	300+
Trinity Bettendorf	Bettendorf	76%	300+
Iowa Methodist Medical Center	Des Moines	75%	300+
Marshalltown Medical & Surgical Center	Marshalltown	75%	300+
Mary Greeley Medical Center	Ames	75%	300+
Trinity Muscatine	Muscatine	75%	300+
Allen Memorial Hospital	Waterloo	74%	300+
Iowa Lutheran Hospital	Des Moines	74%	300+
Saint Lukes Regional Medical Center	Sioux City	73%	300+
Sanford Sheldon Medical Center	Sheldon	73%	(a)
University of Iowa Hospital & Clinics	Iowa City	72%	300+
Covenant Medical Center	Waterloo	71%	300+
Keokuk Area Hospital	Keokuk	71%	(a)

46. Pain 'Always' Well Controlled

Hospital Name	City	Rate	Cases
Floyd Valley Hospital	Le Mars	79%	300+
Van Diest Medical Center	Webster City	78%	(a)
Burgess Health Center	Onawa	77%	(a)
Clarinda Regional Health Center	Clarinda	77%	(a)
Mercy Hosp of Franciscan Sisters-Oelwein	Oelwein	77%	(a)
Wright Medical Center	Clarion	77%	300+
Waverly Health Center	Waverly	76%	300+
Montgomery County Memorial Hospital	Red Oak	75%	(a)
Jackson County Regional Health Center	Maquoketa	74%	(a)
Jefferson County Health Center	Fairfield	74%	(a)
Alegent Health Mercy Hospital	Council Bluffs	73%	300+
Buchanan County Health Center	Independence	73%	(a)
Grinnell Regional Medical Center	Grinnell	73%	300+
Hegg Memorial Health Center	Rock Valley	73%	(a)
Mercy Medical Center-Clinton	Clinton	73%	300+
Guttenberg Municipal Hospital	Guttenberg	72%	(a)
Saint Anthony Regional Hospital	Carroll	72%	300+
Sioux Center Community Hospital	Sioux Center	72%	(a)
Trinity Regional Medical Center	Fort Dodge	72%	300+
Broadlawns Medical Center	Des Moines	71%	300+
Clarke County Hospital	Osceola	71%	(a)
Jennie Edmundson Hospital	Council Bluffs	71%	300+
Lakes Regional Healthcare	Spirit Lake	71%	300+
Mercy Medical Center-Dubuque	Dubuque	71%	300+
Mercy Medical Center-Sioux City	Sioux City	71%	300+
Osceola Community Hospital	Sibley	71%	(a)
Ottumwa Regional Health Center	Ottumwa	71%	300+
Saint Lukes Hospital	Cedar Rapids	71%	300+
Sartori Memorial Hospital	Cedar Falls	71%	300+
Spencer Municipal Hospital	Spencer	71%	300+
Genesis Medical Center - Davenport	Davenport	70%	300+
Great River Medical Center	West Burlington	70%	300+
Knoxville Hospital & Clinics	Knoxville	70%	(a)
Mahaska Health Partnership	Oskaloosa	70%	(a)
Sanford Hospital Rock Rapids	Rock Rapids	70%	(a)
Washington County Hospital	Washington	70%	(a)
Cass County Memorial Hospital	Atlantic	69%	(a)
Greater Regional Medical Center	Creston	69%	300+
Henry County Health Center	Mount Pleasant	69%	(a)
Mercy Hospital	Iowa City	69%	300+
Mercy Medical Center-North Iowa	Mason City	69%	300+
Myrtue Medical Center	Harlan	69%	300+
Stewart Memorial Community Hospital	Lake City	69%	(a)
Trinity Bettendorf	Bettendorf	69%	300+
Davis County Hospital	Bloomfield	68%	(a)
The Finley Hospital	Dubuque	68%	300+
Fort Madison Community Hospital	Fort Madison	68%	300+
Pella Regional Health Center	Pella	68%	300+
Skiff Medical Center	Newton	68%	300+
Allen Memorial Hospital	Waterloo	67%	300+
Avera Holy Family Health	Estherville	67%	(a)
Iowa Lutheran Hospital	Des Moines	67%	300+
Iowa Methodist Medical Center	Des Moines	67%	300+
Mercy Medical Center-Des Moines	Des Moines	67%	300+
Sanford Sheldon Medical Center	Sheldon	67%	(a)
Trinity Muscatine	Muscatine	67%	300+
Boone County Hospital	Boone	65%	300+
Marshalltown Medical & Surgical Center	Marshalltown	65%	300+
Mary Greeley Medical Center	Ames	65%	300+
Saint Lukes Regional Medical Center	Sioux City	65%	300+
Mercy Medical Center-Cedar Rapids	Cedar Rapids	64%	300+
Keokuk Area Hospital	Keokuk	62%	(a)
University of Iowa Hospital & Clinics	Iowa City	62%	300+
Covenant Medical Center	Waterloo	59%	300+

47. Room and Bathroom 'Always' Clean

Hospital Name	City	Rate	Cases
Osceola Community Hospital	Sibley	92%	(a)
Clarke County Hospital	Osceola	91%	(a)
Stewart Memorial Community Hospital	Lake City	91%	(a)
Floyd Valley Hospital	Le Mars	89%	300+
Jefferson County Health Center	Fairfield	89%	(a)
Waverly Health Center	Waverly	89%	300+
Guttenberg Municipal Hospital	Guttenberg	87%	(a)
Mercy Hosp of Franciscan Sisters-Oelwein	Oelwein	87%	(a)
Sanford Hospital Rock Rapids	Rock Rapids	87%	(a)
Myrtue Medical Center	Harlan	84%	300+
Davis County Hospital	Bloomfield	83%	(a)
Clarinda Regional Health Center	Clarinda	82%	(a)
Hegg Memorial Health Center	Rock Valley	82%	(a)
Spencer Municipal Hospital	Spencer	82%	300+
Avera Holy Family Health	Estherville	81%	(a)
Burgess Health Center	Onawa	81%	(a)
Grinnell Regional Medical Center	Grinnell	81%	300+
Knoxville Hospital & Clinics	Knoxville	81%	(a)
Saint Anthony Regional Hospital	Carroll	81%	300+
Boone County Hospital	Boone	80%	300+
Ottumwa Regional Health Center	Ottumwa	80%	300+
Pella Regional Health Center	Pella	80%	300+
Van Diest Medical Center	Webster City	80%	(a)
Washington County Hospital	Washington	80%	(a)
Buchanan County Health Center	Independence	79%	(a)
Sartori Memorial Hospital	Cedar Falls	79%	300+
Wright Medical Center	Clarion	79%	300+
Greater Regional Medical Center	Creston	78%	300+
The Finley Hospital	Dubuque	77%	300+
Jackson County Regional Health Center	Maquoketa	77%	(a)
Lakes Regional Healthcare	Spirit Lake	77%	300+
Sioux Center Community Hospital	Sioux Center	77%	(a)
Cass County Memorial Hospital	Atlantic	76%	(a)
Trinity Bettendorf	Bettendorf	76%	300+
Saint Lukes Hospital	Cedar Rapids	75%	300+
Trinity Regional Medical Center	Fort Dodge	75%	300+
Keokuk Area Hospital	Keokuk	74%	(a)
Jennie Edmundson Hospital	Council Bluffs	73%	300+
Mahaska Health Partnership	Oskaloosa	73%	(a)
Montgomery County Memorial Hospital	Red Oak	73%	(a)
Sanford Sheldon Medical Center	Sheldon	73%	(a)
Trinity Muscatine	Muscatine	73%	300+
Alegent Health Mercy Hospital	Council Bluffs	72%	300+
Allen Memorial Hospital	Waterloo	72%	300+
Fort Madison Community Hospital	Fort Madison	72%	300+
Iowa Lutheran Hospital	Des Moines	72%	300+
Covenant Medical Center	Waterloo	71%	300+
Genesis Medical Center - Davenport	Davenport	71%	300+
Great River Medical Center	West Burlington	71%	300+
Mercy Medical Center-Dubuque	Dubuque	71%	300+
Mercy Medical Center-North Iowa	Mason City	71%	300+
Mercy Medical Center-Sioux City	Sioux City	71%	300+
Iowa Methodist Medical Center	Des Moines	70%	300+
Marshalltown Medical & Surgical Center	Marshalltown	70%	300+
Mercy Hospital	Iowa City	70%	300+
Saint Lukes Regional Medical Center	Sioux City	70%	300+
Mary Greeley Medical Center	Ames	69%	300+
Mercy Medical Center-Cedar Rapids	Cedar Rapids	68%	300+
Mercy Medical Center-Des Moines	Des Moines	68%	300+
Skiff Medical Center	Newton	67%	300+
Broadlawns Medical Center	Des Moines	66%	300+
University of Iowa Hospital & Clinics	Iowa City	66%	300+
Mercy Medical Center-Clinton	Clinton	65%	300+
Henry County Health Center	Mount Pleasant	64%	(a)

48. Timely Help 'Always' Received

Hospital Name	City	Rate	Cases
Jefferson County Health Center	Fairfield	81%	(a)
Osceola Community Hospital	Sibley	80%	(a)
Clarinda Regional Health Center	Clarinda	79%	(a)
Guttenberg Municipal Hospital	Guttenberg	79%	(a)
Sanford Hospital Rock Rapids	Rock Rapids	78%	(a)
Wright Medical Center	Clarion	78%	300+
Buchanan County Health Center	Independence	77%	(a)
Clarke County Hospital	Osceola	76%	(a)
Greater Regional Medical Center	Creston	76%	300+
Henry County Health Center	Mount Pleasant	75%	(a)
Sioux Center Community Hospital	Sioux Center	75%	(a)
Grinnell Regional Medical Center	Grinnell	74%	300+
Hegg Memorial Health Center	Rock Valley	74%	(a)
Montgomery County Memorial Hospital	Red Oak	74%	(a)
Van Diest Medical Center	Webster City	74%	(a)
Waverly Health Center	Waverly	74%	300+
Davis County Hospital	Bloomfield	73%	(a)
Floyd Valley Hospital	Le Mars	73%	300+
Mercy Hospital	Iowa City	72%	300+
Stewart Memorial Community Hospital	Lake City	72%	(a)
Cass County Memorial Hospital	Atlantic	71%	(a)
Lakes Regional Healthcare	Spirit Lake	71%	300+
Mercy Hosp of Franciscan Sisters-Oelwein	Oelwein	71%	(a)
Ottumwa Regional Health Center	Ottumwa	71%	300+
Pella Regional Health Center	Pella	71%	300+
Saint Anthony Regional Hospital	Carroll	71%	300+
Avera Holy Family Health	Estherville	70%	(a)
Fort Madison Community Hospital	Fort Madison	70%	300+
Burgess Health Center	Onawa	68%	(a)
Jennie Edmundson Hospital	Council Bluffs	68%	300+
Spencer Municipal Hospital	Spencer	68%	300+
Knoxville Hospital & Clinics	Knoxville	67%	(a)
Mercy Medical Center-North Iowa	Mason City	67%	300+
Trinity Muscatine	Muscatine	67%	300+
Boone County Hospital	Boone	66%	300+
Skiff Medical Center	Newton	66%	300+
Washington County Hospital	Washington	66%	(a)
Jackson County Regional Health Center	Maquoketa	65%	(a)
Mercy Medical Center-Clinton	Clinton	65%	300+

NOTE: Hospital profiles are in alphabetical order by state, then city, then hospital within the city; Rankings exclude hospitals with less than 25 cases except for patient surveys which excludes hospitals with less than 100 cases; (a) 100–299 cases; (1) The number of cases is too small to be sure how well a hospital is performing; (2) The hospital indicated that the data submitted for this measure were based on a sample of cases; (3) Data was collected during a shorter time period (fewer quarters) than the maximum possible time for this measure; (4) Suppressed for one or more quarters by CMS; (5) No data is available from the hospital for this measure; (6) Fewer than 100 patients completed the HCAHPS survey. Use these rates with caution, as the number of surveys may be too low to reliably assess hospital performance; (7) Survey results are based on less than 12 months of data; (8) Survey results are not available for this reporting period; (9) No or very few patients were eligible for the HCAHPS survey. The scores shown, if any, reflect a very small number of surveys; (10) A state average was not calculated because too few hospitals in the state submitted data; (11) There were discrepancies in the data collection process; Please refer to the User's Guide for a full explanation of data.

Myrtue Medical Center	Harlan	65%	300+
The Finley Hospital	Dubuque	64%	300+
Genesis Medical Center - Davenport	Davenport	64%	300+
Great River Medical Center	West Burlington	64%	300+
Mercy Medical Center-Sioux City	Sioux City	64%	300+
Mercy Medical Center-Dubuque	Dubuque	63%	300+
Trinity Bettendorf	Bettendorf	63%	300+
Trinity Regional Medical Center	Fort Dodge	63%	300+
Alegent Health Mercy Hospital	Council Bluffs	61%	300+
Broadlawns Medical Center	Des Moines	61%	300+
Mahaska Health Partnership	Oskaloosa	61%	(a)
Saint Lukes Hospital	Cedar Rapids	61%	300+
Iowa Lutheran Hospital	Des Moines	60%	300+
Sanford Sheldon Medical Center	Sheldon	60%	(a)
Iowa Methodist Medical Center	Des Moines	59%	300+
Mary Greeley Medical Center	Ames	59%	300+
Covenant Medical Center	Waterloo	58%	300+
Mercy Medical Center-Cedar Rapids	Cedar Rapids	58%	300+
Saint Lukes Regional Medical Center	Sioux City	58%	300+
Sartori Memorial Hospital	Cedar Falls	58%	300+
Mercy Medical Center-Des Moines	Des Moines	57%	300+
Marshalltown Medical & Surgical Center	Marshalltown	56%	300+
Allen Memorial Hospital	Waterloo	55%	300+
University of Iowa Hospital & Clinics	Iowa City	55%	300+
Keokuk Area Hospital	Keokuk	54%	(a)

49. Would Definitely Recommend Hospital

Hospital Name	City	Rate	Cases
Hegg Memorial Health Center	Rock Valley	86%	(a)
Mercy Hospital	Iowa City	86%	300+
Waverly Health Center	Waverly	86%	300+
Wright Medical Center	Clarion	85%	300+
Guttenberg Municipal Hospital	Guttenberg	82%	(a)
Pella Regional Health Center	Pella	82%	300+
Saint Anthony Regional Hospital	Carroll	82%	300+
Saint Lukes Hospital	Cedar Rapids	82%	300+
Mercy Medical Center-Cedar Rapids	Cedar Rapids	81%	300+
Mercy Medical Center-Dubuque	Dubuque	81%	300+
Montgomery County Memorial Hospital	Red Oak	81%	(a)
Avera Holy Family Health	Estherville	80%	(a)
Burgess Health Center	Onawa	80%	(a)
Sioux Center Community Hospital	Sioux Center	80%	(a)
Alegent Health Mercy Hospital	Council Bluffs	79%	300+
Osceola Community Hospital	Sibley	79%	(a)
Sanford Hospital Rock Rapids	Rock Rapids	79%	(a)
Stewart Memorial Community Hospital	Lake City	79%	(a)
Jefferson County Health Center	Fairfield	78%	(a)
Trinity Bettendorf	Bettendorf	78%	300+
Floyd Valley Hospital	Le Mars	77%	300+
Iowa Methodist Medical Center	Des Moines	77%	300+
University of Iowa Hospital & Clinics	Iowa City	77%	300+
Clarke County Hospital	Osceola	76%	(a)
Saint Lukes Regional Medical Center	Sioux City	76%	300+
Spencer Municipal Hospital	Spencer	76%	300+
Fort Madison Community Hospital	Fort Madison	75%	300+
Genesis Medical Center - Davenport	Davenport	75%	300+
Iowa Lutheran Hospital	Des Moines	75%	300+
Mercy Medical Center-Sioux City	Sioux City	75%	300+
The Finley Hospital	Dubuque	74%	300+
Grinnell Regional Medical Center	Grinnell	74%	300+
Jennie Edmundson Hospital	Council Bluffs	74%	300+
Lakes Regional Healthcare	Spirit Lake	74%	300+
Mary Greeley Medical Center	Ames	74%	300+
Mercy Medical Center-Des Moines	Des Moines	74%	300+
Sartori Memorial Hospital	Cedar Falls	74%	300+
Boone County Hospital	Boone	73%	300+
Myrtue Medical Center	Harlan	72%	300+
Sanford Sheldon Medical Center	Sheldon	72%	(a)
Knoxville Hospital & Clinics	Knoxville	71%	(a)
Mercy Medical Center-North Iowa	Mason City	71%	300+
Davis County Hospital	Bloomfield	70%	(a)
Allen Memorial Hospital	Waterloo	69%	300+
Great River Medical Center	West Burlington	69%	300+
Skiff Medical Center	Newton	69%	300+
Washington County Hospital	Washington	69%	(a)
Broadlawns Medical Center	Des Moines	68%	300+
Buchanan County Health Center	Independence	68%	(a)
Henry County Health Center	Mount Pleasant	68%	(a)
Clarinda Regional Health Center	Clarinda	67%	(a)
Greater Regional Medical Center	Creston	67%	300+
Mahaska Health Partnership	Oskaloosa	67%	(a)
Mercy Hosp of Franciscan Sisters-Oelwein	Oelwein	67%	(a)
Trinity Regional Medical Center	Fort Dodge	67%	300+
Covenant Medical Center	Waterloo	65%	300+
Ottumwa Regional Health Center	Ottumwa	64%	300+
Van Diest Medical Center	Webster City	64%	(a)
Mercy Medical Center-Clinton	Clinton	61%	300+
Cass County Memorial Hospital	Atlantic	60%	(a)
Marshalltown Medical & Surgical Center	Marshalltown	60%	300+
Trinity Muscatine	Muscatine	60%	300+
Jackson County Regional Health Center	Maquoketa	59%	(a)
Keokuk Area Hospital	Keokuk	55%	(a)

NOTE: Hospital profiles are in alphabetical order by state, then city, then hospital within the city; Rankings exclude hospitals with less than 25 cases except for patient surveys which excludes hospitals with less than 100 cases; (a) 100–299 cases; (1) The number of cases is too small to be sure how well a hospital is performing; (2) The hospital indicated that the data submitted for this measure were based on a sample of cases; (3) Data was collected during a shorter time period (fewer quarters) than the maximum possible time for this measure; (4) Suppressed for one or more quarters by CMS; (5) No data is available from the hospital for this measure; (6) Fewer than 100 patients completed the HCAHPS survey. Use these rates with caution, as the number of surveys may be too low to reliably assess hospital performance; (7) Survey results are based on less than 12 months of data; (8) Survey results are not available for this reporting period; (9) No or very few patients were eligible for the HCAHPS survey. The scores shown, if any, reflect a very small number of surveys; (10) A state average was not calculated because too few hospitals in the state submitted data; (11) There were discrepancies in the data collection process; Please refer to the User's Guide for a full explanation of data.

Monroe County Hospital

6580 165th Street
Albia, IA 52531
Phone: 641-932-2134
Fax: 641-932-1671
URL: www.mchalbia.com
Type: Critical Access Hospitals
Emergency Services: Yes
Ownership: Voluntary Non-Profit - Other
Beds: 46

Key Personnel:

CEO/President. . . . . Greg Paris
Chief of Medical Staff . . . . Gerald Itaasll, DO
Infection Control. . . . . Jane Koffman, RN
Operating Room. . . . . Wanda Campbell, RN
Quality Assurance . . . . Jane Koffman, RN
Radiology. . . . . Jenny Klyn, MD
Ambulatory Care . . . . Brad Leedom
Emergency Room . . . . Jaime Beaumont

Measure	Cases	This Hosp.	State Avg.	U.S. Avg.
Heart Attack Care				
ACE Inhibitor or ARB for LVSD[5]	0	-	96%	96%
Aspirin at Arrival[5]	0	-	99%	99%
Aspirin at Discharge[5]	0	-	99%	98%
Beta Blocker at Discharge[5]	0	-	99%	98%
Fibrinolytic Medication Timing[5]	0	-	67%	55%
PCI Within 90 Minutes of Arrival[5]	0	-	94%	90%
Smoking Cessation Advice[5]	0	-	99%	99%
Chest Pain/Possible Heart Attack Care				
Aspirin at Arrival	-	-	96%	95%
Median Time to ECG (minutes)	-	-	7	8
Median Time to Transfer (minutes)	-	-	64	61
Fibrinolytic Medication Timing	-	-	45%	54%
Heart Failure Care				
ACE Inhibitor or ARB for LVSD[1]	5	40%	94%	94%
Discharge Instructions[1]	9	89%	86%	88%
Evaluation of LVS Function[1]	18	56%	95%	98%
Smoking Cessation Advice[1]	2	100%	96%	98%
Pneumonia Care				
Appropriate Initial Antibiotic[1]	4	75%	92%	92%
Blood Culture Timing[1]	5	80%	97%	96%
Influenza Vaccine[1]	8	50%	92%	91%
Initial Antibiotic Timing[1]	4	75%	97%	95%
Pneumococcal Vaccine[1]	15	67%	94%	93%
Smoking Cessation Advice[1]	2	0%	95%	97%
Surgical Care Improvement Project				
Appropriate VTP Within 24 Hours[1,3]	1	0%	92%	92%
Appropriate Hair Removal[1,3]	1	100%	100%	99%
Appropriate Beta Blocker Usage[5]	0	-	94%	93%
Controlled Postoperative Blood Glucose[3]	0	-	89%	93%
Prophylactic Antibiotic Timing[1,3]	1	100%	98%	97%
Prophylactic Antibiotic Timing (Outpatient)	-	-	94%	92%
Prophylactic Antibiotic Selection[1,3]	1	0%	98%	97%
Prophylactic Antibiotic Select. (Outpatient)	-	-	97%	94%
Prophylactic Antibiotic Stopped[1,3]	1	100%	95%	94%
Recommended VTP Ordered[1,3]	1	0%	93%	94%
Urinary Catheter Removal[5]	0	-	91%	90%
Children's Asthma Care				
Received Systemic Corticosteroids	-	-	-	100%
Received Home Management Plan	-	-	-	71%
Received Reliever Medication	-	-	-	100%
Use of Medical Imaging				
Combination Abdominal CT Scan	-	-	0.163	0.191
Combination Chest CT Scan	-	-	0.060	0.054
Follow-up Mammogram/Ultrasound	-	-	8.1%	8.4%
MRI for Low Back Pain	-	-	30.2%	32.7%
Survey of Patients' Hospital Experiences				
Area Around Room 'Always' Quiet at Night[8]	-	-	-	58%
Doctors 'Always' Communicated Well[8]	-	-	-	80%
Home Recovery Information Given[8]	-	-	-	82%
Hospital Given 9 or 10 on 10 Point Scale[8]	-	-	-	67%
Meds 'Always' Explained Before Given[8]	-	-	-	60%
Nurses 'Always' Communicated Well[8]	-	-	-	76%
Pain 'Always' Well Controlled[8]	-	-	-	69%
Room and Bathroom 'Always' Clean[8]	-	-	-	71%
Timely Help 'Always' Received[8]	-	-	-	64%
Would Definitely Recommend Hospital[8]	-	-	-	69%

Kossuth Regional Health Center

1515 South Phillips Street
Algona, IA 50511
Phone: 515-295-2451
Fax: 515-295-7089
URL: www.krhc.com
Type: Critical Access Hospitals
Emergency Services: Yes
Ownership: Government - Local
Beds: 24

Key Personnel:

CEO/President. . . . . Scott Curtis
Chief of Medical Staff . . . . Burt J. Bottsen
Infection Control. . . . . Martha Hoffman
Operating Room. . . . . Lori Reding
Radiology. . . . . Kate Mayer
Anesthesiology. . . . . Joe Miller

Measure	Cases	This Hosp.	State Avg.	U.S. Avg.
Heart Attack Care				
ACE Inhibitor or ARB for LVSD[5]	0	-	96%	96%
Aspirin at Arrival[5]	0	-	99%	99%
Aspirin at Discharge[5]	0	-	99%	98%
Beta Blocker at Discharge[5]	0	-	99%	98%
Fibrinolytic Medication Timing[5]	0	-	67%	55%
PCI Within 90 Minutes of Arrival[5]	0	-	94%	90%
Smoking Cessation Advice[5]	0	-	99%	99%
Chest Pain/Possible Heart Attack Care				
Aspirin at Arrival	-	-	96%	95%
Median Time to ECG (minutes)	-	-	7	8
Median Time to Transfer (minutes)	-	-	64	61
Fibrinolytic Medication Timing	-	-	45%	54%
Heart Failure Care				
ACE Inhibitor or ARB for LVSD[1]	9	89%	94%	94%
Discharge Instructions[1]	11	91%	86%	88%
Evaluation of LVS Function[1]	24	83%	95%	98%
Smoking Cessation Advice	0	-	96%	98%
Pneumonia Care				
Appropriate Initial Antibiotic[5]	0	-	92%	92%
Blood Culture Timing[1]	7	86%	97%	96%
Influenza Vaccine[1]	15	73%	92%	91%
Initial Antibiotic Timing[5]	0	-	97%	95%
Pneumococcal Vaccine[1]	20	80%	94%	93%
Smoking Cessation Advice[1]	11	82%	95%	97%
Surgical Care Improvement Project				
Appropriate VTP Within 24 Hours[1,3]	5	40%	92%	92%
Appropriate Hair Removal[1,3]	5	100%	100%	99%
Appropriate Beta Blocker Usage[5]	0	-	94%	93%
Controlled Postoperative Blood Glucose[3]	0	-	89%	93%
Prophylactic Antibiotic Timing[1,3]	2	100%	98%	97%
Prophylactic Antibiotic Timing (Outpatient)	-	-	94%	92%
Prophylactic Antibiotic Selection[1,3]	2	100%	98%	97%
Prophylactic Antibiotic Select. (Outpatient)	-	-	97%	94%
Prophylactic Antibiotic Stopped[1,3]	2	100%	95%	94%
Recommended VTP Ordered[1,3]	5	40%	93%	94%
Urinary Catheter Removal[1]	2	0%	91%	90%
Children's Asthma Care				
Received Systemic Corticosteroids	-	-	-	100%
Received Home Management Plan	-	-	-	71%
Received Reliever Medication	-	-	-	100%
Use of Medical Imaging				
Combination Abdominal CT Scan	-	-	0.163	0.191
Combination Chest CT Scan	-	-	0.060	0.054
Follow-up Mammogram/Ultrasound	-	-	8.1%	8.4%
MRI for Low Back Pain	-	-	30.2%	32.7%
Survey of Patients' Hospital Experiences				
Area Around Room 'Always' Quiet at Night[8]	-	-	-	58%
Doctors 'Always' Communicated Well[8]	-	-	-	80%
Home Recovery Information Given[8]	-	-	-	82%
Hospital Given 9 or 10 on 10 Point Scale[8]	-	-	-	67%
Meds 'Always' Explained Before Given[8]	-	-	-	60%
Nurses 'Always' Communicated Well[8]	-	-	-	76%
Pain 'Always' Well Controlled[8]	-	-	-	69%
Room and Bathroom 'Always' Clean[8]	-	-	-	71%
Timely Help 'Always' Received[8]	-	-	-	64%
Would Definitely Recommend Hospital[8]	-	-	-	69%

Mary Greeley Medical Center

1111 Duff Avenue
Ames, IA 50010
Phone: 515-239-2011
Fax: 515-239-2007
E-mail: yourhealth.mgmc@mgmc.com
URL: www.mgmc.org
Type: Acute Care Hospitals
Emergency Services: Yes
Ownership: Government - Local
Beds: 220

Key Personnel:

CEO/President. . . . . Brian Dieter
Chief of Medical Staff . . . . John Paschen, MD
Infection Control. . . . . Betty Fosse
Operating Room. . . . . Christine Holcomb
Quality Assurance . . . . Darla Handsaker
Radiology. . . . . Sue Scoles
Emergency Room . . . . Leslie Miller

Measure	Cases	This Hosp.	State Avg.	U.S. Avg.
Heart Attack Care				
ACE Inhibitor or ARB for LVSD	27	100%	96%	96%
Aspirin at Arrival	114	100%	99%	99%
Aspirin at Discharge	129	100%	99%	98%
Beta Blocker at Discharge	132	100%	99%	98%
Fibrinolytic Medication Timing	0	-	67%	55%
PCI Within 90 Minutes of Arrival[1]	15	100%	94%	90%
Smoking Cessation Advice	34	100%	99%	99%
Chest Pain/Possible Heart Attack Care				
Aspirin at Arrival[1,3]	3	100%	96%	95%
Median Time to ECG (minutes)[1,3]	3	2	7	8
Median Time to Transfer (minutes)[5]	0	-	64	61
Fibrinolytic Medication Timing[3]	0	-	45%	54%
Heart Failure Care				
ACE Inhibitor or ARB for LVSD	50	100%	94%	94%
Discharge Instructions	123	85%	86%	88%
Evaluation of LVS Function	173	100%	95%	98%
Smoking Cessation Advice[1]	15	100%	96%	98%
Pneumonia Care				
Appropriate Initial Antibiotic	107	90%	92%	92%
Blood Culture Timing	141	99%	97%	96%
Influenza Vaccine	116	95%	92%	91%
Initial Antibiotic Timing	166	99%	97%	95%
Pneumococcal Vaccine	181	96%	94%	93%
Smoking Cessation Advice	52	100%	95%	97%
Surgical Care Improvement Project				
Appropriate VTP Within 24 Hours	353	98%	92%	92%
Appropriate Hair Removal	732	100%	100%	99%
Appropriate Beta Blocker Usage	192	99%	94%	93%
Controlled Postoperative Blood Glucose	0	-	89%	93%
Prophylactic Antibiotic Timing	526	100%	98%	97%
Prophylactic Antibiotic Timing (Outpatient)	334	96%	94%	92%
Prophylactic Antibiotic Selection	527	99%	98%	97%
Prophylactic Antibiotic Select. (Outpatient)	347	100%	97%	94%
Prophylactic Antibiotic Stopped	505	99%	95%	94%
Recommended VTP Ordered	353	99%	93%	94%
Urinary Catheter Removal	71	100%	91%	90%
Children's Asthma Care				
Received Systemic Corticosteroids	-	-	-	100%
Received Home Management Plan	-	-	-	71%
Received Reliever Medication	-	-	-	100%
Use of Medical Imaging				
Combination Abdominal CT Scan	203	0.010	0.163	0.191
Combination Chest CT Scan	129	0.225	0.060	0.054
Follow-up Mammogram/Ultrasound	190	10.5%	8.1%	8.4%
MRI for Low Back Pain[1]	27	14.8%	30.2%	32.7%
Survey of Patients' Hospital Experiences				
Area Around Room 'Always' Quiet at Night	300+	47%	-	58%
Doctors 'Always' Communicated Well	300+	81%	-	80%
Home Recovery Information Given	300+	84%	-	82%
Hospital Given 9 or 10 on 10 Point Scale	300+	67%	-	67%
Meds 'Always' Explained Before Given	300+	56%	-	60%
Nurses 'Always' Communicated Well	300+	75%	-	76%
Pain 'Always' Well Controlled	300+	65%	-	69%
Room and Bathroom 'Always' Clean	300+	69%	-	71%
Timely Help 'Always' Received	300+	59%	-	64%
Would Definitely Recommend Hospital	300+	74%	-	69%

NOTE: Hospital profiles are in alphabetical order by state, then city, then hospital within the city; Rankings exclude hospitals with less than 25 cases except for patient surveys which excludes hospitals with less than 100 cases; (a) 100–299 cases; (1) The number of cases is too small to be sure how well a hospital is performing; (2) The hospital indicated that the data submitted for this measure were based on a sample of cases; (3) Data was collected during a shorter time period (fewer quarters) than the maximum possible time for this measure; (4) Suppressed for one or more quarters by CMS; (5) No data is available from the hospital for this measure; (6) Fewer than 100 patients completed the HCAHPS survey. Use these rates with caution, as the number of surveys may be too low to reliably assess hospital performance; (7) Survey results are based on less than 12 months of data; (8) Survey results are not available for this reporting period; (9) No or very few patients were eligible for the HCAHPS survey. The scores shown, if any, reflect a very small number of surveys; (10) A state average was not calculated because too few hospitals in the state submitted data; (11) There were discrepancies in the data collection process; Please refer to the User's Guide for a full explanation of data.

Jones Regional Medical Center

1795 Highway 64 East Phone: 319-462-6131
Anamosa, IA 52205 Fax: 319-462-4689
E-mail: secrisdr@castlukes.com
URL: www.jonesregional.org
Type: Critical Access Hospitals Emergency Services: Yes
Ownership: Voluntary Non-Profit - Private Beds: 25
Key Personnel:
CEO/President. . . . . Eric Briesemeister
Quality Assurance . . . . Carla Huber
Radiology. . . . . Cara Forbes
Emergency Room . . . . M Weston

Measure	Cases	This Hosp.	State Avg.	U.S. Avg.
Heart Attack Care				
ACE Inhibitor or ARB for LVSD[5]	0	-	96%	96%
Aspirin at Arrival[5]	0	-	99%	99%
Aspirin at Discharge[5]	0	-	99%	98%
Beta Blocker at Discharge[5]	0	-	99%	98%
Fibrinolytic Medication Timing[5]	0	-	67%	55%
PCI Within 90 Minutes of Arrival[5]	0	-	94%	90%
Smoking Cessation Advice[5]	0	-	99%	99%
Chest Pain/Possible Heart Attack Care				
Aspirin at Arrival	-	-	96%	95%
Median Time to ECG (minutes)	-	-	7	8
Median Time to Transfer (minutes)	-	-	64	61
Fibrinolytic Medication Timing	-	-	45%	54%
Heart Failure Care				
ACE Inhibitor or ARB for LVSD[3]	0	-	94%	94%
Discharge Instructions[1,3]	11	91%	86%	88%
Evaluation of LVS Function[1,3]	15	87%	95%	98%
Smoking Cessation Advice[3]	0	-	96%	98%
Pneumonia Care				
Appropriate Initial Antibiotic[1]	24	96%	92%	92%
Blood Culture Timing[1]	23	96%	97%	96%
Influenza Vaccine	27	100%	92%	91%
Initial Antibiotic Timing	28	96%	97%	95%
Pneumococcal Vaccine	40	85%	94%	93%
Smoking Cessation Advice[1]	5	100%	95%	97%
Surgical Care Improvement Project				
Appropriate VTP Within 24 Hours[5]	0	-	92%	92%
Appropriate Hair Removal[5]	0	-	100%	99%
Appropriate Beta Blocker Usage[5]	0	-	94%	93%
Controlled Postoperative Blood Glucose[5]	0	-	89%	93%
Prophylactic Antibiotic Timing[5]	0	-	98%	97%
Prophylactic Antibiotic Timing (Outpatient)	-	-	94%	92%
Prophylactic Antibiotic Selection[5]	0	-	98%	97%
Prophylactic Antibiotic Select. (Outpatient)	-	-	97%	94%
Prophylactic Antibiotic Stopped[5]	0	-	95%	94%
Recommended VTP Ordered[5]	0	-	93%	94%
Urinary Catheter Removal[5]	0	-	91%	90%
Children's Asthma Care				
Received Systemic Corticosteroids	-	-	-	100%
Received Home Management Plan	-	-	-	71%
Received Reliever Medication	-	-	-	100%
Use of Medical Imaging				
Combination Abdominal CT Scan	-	-	0.163	0.191
Combination Chest CT Scan	-	-	0.060	0.054
Follow-up Mammogram/Ultrasound	-	-	8.1%	8.4%
MRI for Low Back Pain	-	-	30.2%	32.7%
Survey of Patients' Hospital Experiences				
Area Around Room 'Always' Quiet at Night[8]	-	-	-	58%
Doctors 'Always' Communicated Well[8]	-	-	-	80%
Home Recovery Information Given[8]	-	-	-	82%
Hospital Given 9 or 10 on 10 Point Scale[8]	-	-	-	67%
Meds 'Always' Explained Before Given[8]	-	-	-	60%
Nurses 'Always' Communicated Well[8]	-	-	-	76%
Pain 'Always' Well Controlled[8]	-	-	-	69%
Room and Bathroom 'Always' Clean[8]	-	-	-	71%
Timely Help 'Always' Received[8]	-	-	-	64%
Would Definitely Recommend Hospital[8]	-	-	-	69%

Cass County Memorial Hospital

1501 East Tenth Street Phone: 712-243-3250
Atlantic, IA 50022
Type: Critical Access Hospitals Emergency Services: Yes
Ownership: Government - Local
Key Personnel:
CEO/President. . . . . Dave Chase

Measure	Cases	This Hosp.	State Avg.	U.S. Avg.
Heart Attack Care				
ACE Inhibitor or ARB for LVSD[1]	1	100%	96%	96%
Aspirin at Arrival[1]	3	100%	99%	99%
Aspirin at Discharge[1]	4	100%	99%	98%
Beta Blocker at Discharge[1]	4	100%	99%	98%
Fibrinolytic Medication Timing	0	-	67%	55%
PCI Within 90 Minutes of Arrival	0	-	94%	90%
Smoking Cessation Advice	0	-	99%	99%
Chest Pain/Possible Heart Attack Care				
Aspirin at Arrival	50	100%	96%	95%
Median Time to ECG (minutes)	48	6	7	8
Median Time to Transfer (minutes)[1]	11	72	64	61
Fibrinolytic Medication Timing	0	-	45%	54%
Heart Failure Care				
ACE Inhibitor or ARB for LVSD[1]	14	100%	94%	94%
Discharge Instructions[1]	9	89%	86%	88%
Evaluation of LVS Function	30	100%	95%	98%
Smoking Cessation Advice[1]	1	100%	96%	98%
Pneumonia Care				
Appropriate Initial Antibiotic	30	87%	92%	92%
Blood Culture Timing	25	96%	97%	96%
Influenza Vaccine	30	100%	92%	91%
Initial Antibiotic Timing	40	100%	97%	95%
Pneumococcal Vaccine	56	100%	94%	93%
Smoking Cessation Advice[1]	12	83%	95%	97%
Surgical Care Improvement Project				
Appropriate VTP Within 24 Hours[1]	13	54%	92%	92%
Appropriate Hair Removal[1]	21	100%	100%	99%
Appropriate Beta Blocker Usage[5]	0	-	94%	93%
Controlled Postoperative Blood Glucose	0	-	89%	93%
Prophylactic Antibiotic Timing[1]	6	83%	98%	97%
Prophylactic Antibiotic Timing (Outpatient)[5]	0	-	94%	92%
Prophylactic Antibiotic Selection[1]	7	100%	98%	97%
Prophylactic Antibiotic Select. (Outpatient)[5]	0	-	97%	94%
Prophylactic Antibiotic Stopped[1]	5	40%	95%	94%
Recommended VTP Ordered[1]	13	54%	93%	94%
Urinary Catheter Removal[1]	7	71%	91%	90%
Children's Asthma Care				
Received Systemic Corticosteroids	-	-	-	100%
Received Home Management Plan	-	-	-	71%
Received Reliever Medication	-	-	-	100%
Use of Medical Imaging				
Combination Abdominal CT Scan	208	0.029	0.163	0.191
Combination Chest CT Scan	141	0.135	0.060	0.054
Follow-up Mammogram/Ultrasound	445	6.5%	8.1%	8.4%
MRI for Low Back Pain[1]	32	37.5%	30.2%	32.7%
Survey of Patients' Hospital Experiences				
Area Around Room 'Always' Quiet at Night	(a)	66%	-	58%
Doctors 'Always' Communicated Well	(a)	78%	-	80%
Home Recovery Information Given	(a)	84%	-	82%
Hospital Given 9 or 10 on 10 Point Scale	(a)	63%	-	67%
Meds 'Always' Explained Before Given	(a)	59%	-	60%
Nurses 'Always' Communicated Well	(a)	77%	-	76%
Pain 'Always' Well Controlled	(a)	69%	-	69%
Room and Bathroom 'Always' Clean	(a)	76%	-	71%
Timely Help 'Always' Received	(a)	71%	-	64%
Would Definitely Recommend Hospital	(a)	60%	-	69%

Audubon County Memorial Hospital

515 Pacific Street Phone: 712-563-2611
Audubon, IA 50025 Fax: 712-563-5277
E-mail: acmhhosp@netins.net
URL: www.acmhhosp.org
Type: Critical Access Hospitals Emergency Services: Yes
Ownership: Voluntary Non-Profit - Other Beds: 25
Key Personnel:
CEO/President. . . . . Thomas Smith
Chief of Medical Staff . . . . James M Cunningham, DO
Infection Control. . . . . Holly Kjergaard, RN
Operating Room. . . . . Ronald Cheney, RN
Quality Assurance . . . . Melissa Christensen
Ambulatory Care . . . . Julie Hoffman, RN
Anesthesiology. . . . . David Moffitt, CRNA
Emergency Room . . . . Bonnie Tigges, RN

Measure	Cases	This Hosp.	State Avg.	U.S. Avg.
Heart Attack Care				
ACE Inhibitor or ARB for LVSD[5]	0	-	96%	96%
Aspirin at Arrival[5]	0	-	99%	99%
Aspirin at Discharge[5]	0	-	99%	98%
Beta Blocker at Discharge[5]	0	-	99%	98%
Fibrinolytic Medication Timing[5]	0	-	67%	55%
PCI Within 90 Minutes of Arrival[5]	0	-	94%	90%
Smoking Cessation Advice[5]	0	-	99%	99%
Chest Pain/Possible Heart Attack Care				
Aspirin at Arrival[1,3]	5	100%	96%	95%
Median Time to ECG (minutes)[1,3]	5	1	7	8
Median Time to Transfer (minutes)[5]	0	-	64	61
Fibrinolytic Medication Timing[1,3]	2	0%	45%	54%
Heart Failure Care				
ACE Inhibitor or ARB for LVSD[1]	2	100%	94%	94%
Discharge Instructions[1]	8	88%	86%	88%
Evaluation of LVS Function[1]	11	55%	95%	98%
Smoking Cessation Advice[1]	2	0%	96%	98%
Pneumonia Care				
Appropriate Initial Antibiotic[1]	8	100%	92%	92%
Blood Culture Timing[1]	14	100%	97%	96%
Influenza Vaccine[1]	9	100%	92%	91%
Initial Antibiotic Timing[1]	14	93%	97%	95%
Pneumococcal Vaccine[1]	14	100%	94%	93%
Smoking Cessation Advice[1]	3	100%	95%	97%
Surgical Care Improvement Project				
Appropriate VTP Within 24 Hours[1,3]	4	75%	92%	92%
Appropriate Hair Removal[1,3]	5	100%	100%	99%
Appropriate Beta Blocker Usage[3]	0	-	94%	93%
Controlled Postoperative Blood Glucose[3]	0	-	89%	93%
Prophylactic Antibiotic Timing[1,3]	4	100%	98%	97%
Prophylactic Antibiotic Timing (Outpatient)[1,3]	13	100%	94%	92%
Prophylactic Antibiotic Selection[1,3]	4	100%	98%	97%
Prophylactic Antibiotic Select. (Outpatient)[1,3]	15	93%	97%	94%
Prophylactic Antibiotic Stopped[1,3]	4	75%	95%	94%
Recommended VTP Ordered[1,3]	4	75%	93%	94%
Urinary Catheter Removal[1]	2	100%	91%	90%
Children's Asthma Care				
Received Systemic Corticosteroids	-	-	-	100%
Received Home Management Plan	-	-	-	71%
Received Reliever Medication	-	-	-	100%
Use of Medical Imaging				
Combination Abdominal CT Scan	115	0.148	0.163	0.191
Combination Chest CT Scan	59	0.051	0.060	0.054
Follow-up Mammogram/Ultrasound	133	3.8%	8.1%	8.4%
MRI for Low Back Pain[1]	18	22.2%	30.2%	32.7%
Survey of Patients' Hospital Experiences				
Area Around Room 'Always' Quiet at Night[6]	<100	63%	-	58%
Doctors 'Always' Communicated Well[6]	<100	90%	-	80%
Home Recovery Information Given[6]	<100	78%	-	82%
Hospital Given 9 or 10 on 10 Point Scale[6]	<100	84%	-	67%
Meds 'Always' Explained Before Given[6]	<100	65%	-	60%
Nurses 'Always' Communicated Well[6]	<100	77%	-	76%
Pain 'Always' Well Controlled[6]	<100	79%	-	69%
Room and Bathroom 'Always' Clean[6]	<100	92%	-	71%
Timely Help 'Always' Received[6]	<100	78%	-	64%
Would Definitely Recommend Hospital	<100	78%	-	69%

NOTE: Hospital profiles are in alphabetical order by state, then city, then hospital within the city; Rankings exclude hospitals with less than 25 cases except for patient surveys which excludes hospitals with less than 100 cases; (a) 100–299 cases; (1) The number of cases is too small to be sure how well a hospital is performing; (2) The hospital indicated that the data submitted for this measure were based on a sample of cases; (3) Data was collected during a shorter time period (fewer quarters) than the maximum possible time for this measure; (4) Suppressed for one or more quarters by CMS; (5) No data is available from the hospital for this measure; (6) Fewer than 100 patients completed the HCAHPS survey. Use these rates with caution, as the number of surveys may be too low to reliably assess hospital performance; (7) Survey results are based on less than 12 months of data; (8) Survey results are not available for this reporting period; (9) No or very few patients were eligible for the HCAHPS survey. The scores shown, if any, reflect a very small number of surveys; (10) A state average was not calculated because too few hospitals in the state submitted data; (11) There were discrepancies in the data collection process; Please refer to the User's Guide for a full explanation of data.

Belmond Medical Center

403 First Street SE
Belmond, IA 50421
Phone: 641-444-3223
Fax: 641-444-4895
URL: www.belmondmedicalcenter.com
Type: Critical Access Hospitals
Emergency Services: Yes
Ownership: Government - Local
Beds: 22

Key Personnel:

CEO/President. . . . . Nancy Gabrielson
Cardiac Laboratory. . . . . Monica Christensen
Chief of Medical Staff . . . . Lindy C Estwell
Infection Control. . . . . Stacey Ritter
Operating Room. . . . . Stacey Ritter
Quality Assurance . . . . Denise Hiscocks
Ambulatory Care . . . . Janet Rockow

Measure	Cases	This Hosp.	State Avg.	U.S. Avg.
Heart Attack Care				
ACE Inhibitor or ARB for LVSD[3]	0	-	96%	96%
Aspirin at Arrival[1,3]	1	100%	99%	99%
Aspirin at Discharge[3]	0	-	99%	98%
Beta Blocker at Discharge[3]	0	-	99%	98%
Fibrinolytic Medication Timing[3]	0	-	67%	55%
PCI Within 90 Minutes of Arrival[3]	0	-	94%	90%
Smoking Cessation Advice[3]	0	-	99%	99%
Chest Pain/Possible Heart Attack Care				
Aspirin at Arrival	25	96%	96%	95%
Median Time to ECG (minutes)	28	4	7	8
Median Time to Transfer (minutes)[5]	0	-	64	61
Fibrinolytic Medication Timing[1,3]	2	0%	45%	54%
Heart Failure Care				
ACE Inhibitor or ARB for LVSD[2,3]	0	-	94%	94%
Discharge Instructions[1,2,3]	1	0%	86%	88%
Evaluation of LVS Function[1,2,3]	1	100%	95%	98%
Smoking Cessation Advice[2,3]	0	-	96%	98%
Pneumonia Care				
Appropriate Initial Antibiotic[1,2]	18	67%	92%	92%
Blood Culture Timing[1,2]	5	60%	97%	96%
Influenza Vaccine[1]	13	85%	92%	91%
Initial Antibiotic Timing[1,2]	21	95%	97%	95%
Pneumococcal Vaccine[1,2]	19	68%	94%	93%
Smoking Cessation Advice[1,2]	7	86%	95%	97%
Surgical Care Improvement Project				
Appropriate VTP Within 24 Hours[3]	0	-	92%	92%
Appropriate Hair Removal[1,3]	4	100%	100%	99%
Appropriate Beta Blocker Usage[5]	0	-	94%	93%
Controlled Postoperative Blood Glucose[3]	0	-	89%	93%
Prophylactic Antibiotic Timing[1,3]	3	67%	98%	97%
Prophylactic Antibiotic Timing (Outpatient)[1,3]	1	100%	94%	92%
Prophylactic Antibiotic Selection[1,3]	3	100%	98%	97%
Prophylactic Antibiotic Select. (Outpatient)[1,3]	1	100%	97%	94%
Prophylactic Antibiotic Stopped[1,3]	3	100%	95%	94%
Recommended VTP Ordered[3]	0	-	93%	94%
Urinary Catheter Removal	0	-	91%	90%
Children's Asthma Care				
Received Systemic Corticosteroids	-	-	-	100%
Received Home Management Plan	-	-	-	71%
Received Reliever Medication	-	-	-	100%
Use of Medical Imaging				
Combination Abdominal CT Scan[1]	42	0.143	0.163	0.191
Combination Chest CT Scan[1]	39	0.026	0.060	0.054
Follow-up Mammogram/Ultrasound	109	10.1%	8.1%	8.4%
MRI for Low Back Pain[1]	7	28.6%	30.2%	32.7%
Survey of Patients' Hospital Experiences				
Area Around Room 'Always' Quiet at Night[6]	<100	75%	-	58%
Doctors 'Always' Communicated Well[6]	<100	96%	-	80%
Home Recovery Information Given[6]	<100	84%	-	82%
Hospital Given 9 or 10 on 10 Point Scale[6]	<100	89%	-	67%
Meds 'Always' Explained Before Given[6]	<100	79%	-	60%
Nurses 'Always' Communicated Well[6]	<100	91%	-	76%
Pain 'Always' Well Controlled[6]	<100	79%	-	69%
Room and Bathroom 'Always' Clean[6]	<100	80%	-	71%
Timely Help 'Always' Received[6]	<100	89%	-	64%
Would Definitely Recommend Hospital	<100	86%	-	69%

Trinity Bettendorf

4500 Utica Ridge Road
Bettendorf, IA 52722
Phone: 563-742-5000
Fax: 563-779-2260
URL: www.trinityqc.com
Type: Acute Care Hospitals
Emergency Services: Yes
Ownership: Voluntary Non-Profit - Private
Beds: 150

Key Personnel:

CEO/President. . . . . Jon S Honesy
Cardiac Laboratory. . . . . Mike Dessert
Quality Assurance . . . . Diana Zogg
Radiology. . . . . Kent S Quinn
Emergency Room . . . . Julie Anderson-Sudda
Patient Relations . . . . Liza Kline

Measure	Cases	This Hosp.	State Avg.	U.S. Avg.
Heart Attack Care				
ACE Inhibitor or ARB for LVSD[1]	8	75%	96%	96%
Aspirin at Arrival	49	100%	99%	99%
Aspirin at Discharge	49	100%	99%	98%
Beta Blocker at Discharge	44	100%	99%	98%
Fibrinolytic Medication Timing	0	-	67%	55%
PCI Within 90 Minutes of Arrival[1]	10	70%	94%	90%
Smoking Cessation Advice[1]	16	100%	99%	99%
Chest Pain/Possible Heart Attack Care				
Aspirin at Arrival[1]	16	100%	96%	95%
Median Time to ECG (minutes)[1]	17	8	7	8
Median Time to Transfer (minutes)[1,3]	1	50	64	61
Fibrinolytic Medication Timing[3]	0	-	45%	54%
Heart Failure Care				
ACE Inhibitor or ARB for LVSD[1,2]	23	100%	94%	94%
Discharge Instructions[2]	49	100%	86%	88%
Evaluation of LVS Function[2]	65	98%	95%	98%
Smoking Cessation Advice[1,2]	10	100%	96%	98%
Pneumonia Care				
Appropriate Initial Antibiotic[2]	54	98%	92%	92%
Blood Culture Timing[2]	89	98%	97%	96%
Influenza Vaccine[2]	49	98%	92%	91%
Initial Antibiotic Timing[2]	76	99%	97%	95%
Pneumococcal Vaccine[2]	70	96%	94%	93%
Smoking Cessation Advice[1,2]	20	100%	95%	97%
Surgical Care Improvement Project				
Appropriate VTP Within 24 Hours[2]	45	100%	92%	92%
Appropriate Hair Removal[2]	253	100%	100%	99%
Appropriate Beta Blocker Usage[2]	77	96%	94%	93%
Controlled Postoperative Blood Glucose[2]	0	-	89%	93%
Prophylactic Antibiotic Timing[2]	169	100%	98%	97%
Prophylactic Antibiotic Timing (Outpatient)	162	96%	94%	92%
Prophylactic Antibiotic Selection[2]	172	100%	98%	97%
Prophylactic Antibiotic Select. (Outpatient)	160	99%	97%	94%
Prophylactic Antibiotic Stopped[2]	164	98%	95%	94%
Recommended VTP Ordered[2]	45	100%	93%	94%
Urinary Catheter Removal[1,2]	24	96%	91%	90%
Children's Asthma Care				
Received Systemic Corticosteroids	-	-	-	100%
Received Home Management Plan	-	-	-	71%
Received Reliever Medication	-	-	-	100%
Use of Medical Imaging				
Combination Abdominal CT Scan	255	0.055	0.163	0.191
Combination Chest CT Scan	132	0.083	0.060	0.054
Follow-up Mammogram/Ultrasound	251	14.7%	8.1%	8.4%
MRI for Low Back Pain[5]	0	-	30.2%	32.7%
Survey of Patients' Hospital Experiences				
Area Around Room 'Always' Quiet at Night	300+	65%	-	58%
Doctors 'Always' Communicated Well	300+	79%	-	80%
Home Recovery Information Given	300+	87%	-	82%
Hospital Given 9 or 10 on 10 Point Scale	300+	74%	-	67%
Meds 'Always' Explained Before Given	300+	62%	-	60%
Nurses 'Always' Communicated Well	300+	76%	-	76%
Pain 'Always' Well Controlled	300+	69%	-	69%
Room and Bathroom 'Always' Clean	300+	76%	-	71%
Timely Help 'Always' Received	300+	63%	-	64%
Would Definitely Recommend Hospital	300+	78%	-	69%

Davis County Hospital

509 North Madison Street
Bloomfield, IA 52537
Phone: 641-664-2145
Fax: 641-664-1669
E-mail: webmaster@daviscountyhospital.org
URL: www.daviscountyhospital.org
Type: Critical Access Hospitals
Emergency Services: Yes
Ownership: Govt - Hospital Dist/Auth
Beds: 57

Key Personnel:

CEO/President. . . . . Deborah Herzberg
Chief of Medical Staff . . . . Donald R Wirtanen, DO
Infection Control. . . . . Joan Morris
Operating Room. . . . . Jake Settles
Quality Assurance . . . . Shelly Bassett
Emergency Room . . . . Theresa Tuvera

Measure	Cases	This Hosp.	State Avg.	U.S. Avg.
Heart Attack Care				
ACE Inhibitor or ARB for LVSD[3]	0	-	96%	96%
Aspirin at Arrival[1,3]	1	0%	99%	99%
Aspirin at Discharge[1,3]	1	0%	99%	98%
Beta Blocker at Discharge[1,3]	1	0%	99%	98%
Fibrinolytic Medication Timing[3]	0	-	67%	55%
PCI Within 90 Minutes of Arrival[3]	0	-	94%	90%
Smoking Cessation Advice[3]	0	-	99%	99%
Chest Pain/Possible Heart Attack Care				
Aspirin at Arrival[1,3]	8	62%	96%	95%
Median Time to ECG (minutes)[1,3]	10	9	7	8
Median Time to Transfer (minutes)[5]	0	-	64	61
Fibrinolytic Medication Timing[3]	0	-	45%	54%
Heart Failure Care				
ACE Inhibitor or ARB for LVSD[1,2]	1	100%	94%	94%
Discharge Instructions[1,2]	24	42%	86%	88%
Evaluation of LVS Function[2]	30	33%	95%	98%
Smoking Cessation Advice[2]	0	-	96%	98%
Pneumonia Care				
Appropriate Initial Antibiotic[1,2]	7	71%	92%	92%
Blood Culture Timing[1,2]	5	40%	97%	96%
Influenza Vaccine[1]	1	100%	92%	91%
Initial Antibiotic Timing[1,2]	6	100%	97%	95%
Pneumococcal Vaccine[1,2]	10	90%	94%	93%
Smoking Cessation Advice[1,2]	4	25%	95%	97%
Surgical Care Improvement Project				
Appropriate VTP Within 24 Hours[3]	0	-	92%	92%
Appropriate Hair Removal[1,3]	1	100%	100%	99%
Appropriate Beta Blocker Usage[5]	0	-	94%	93%
Controlled Postoperative Blood Glucose[3]	0	-	89%	93%
Prophylactic Antibiotic Timing[1,3]	1	100%	98%	97%
Prophylactic Antibiotic Timing (Outpatient)[5]	0	-	94%	92%
Prophylactic Antibiotic Selection[1,3]	1	100%	98%	97%
Prophylactic Antibiotic Select. (Outpatient)[5]	0	-	97%	94%
Prophylactic Antibiotic Stopped[1,3]	1	100%	95%	94%
Recommended VTP Ordered[3]	0	-	93%	94%
Urinary Catheter Removal[5]	0	-	91%	90%
Children's Asthma Care				
Received Systemic Corticosteroids	-	-	-	100%
Received Home Management Plan	-	-	-	71%
Received Reliever Medication	-	-	-	100%
Use of Medical Imaging				
Combination Abdominal CT Scan	105	0.724	0.163	0.191
Combination Chest CT Scan[1]	31	0.000	0.060	0.054
Follow-up Mammogram/Ultrasound	189	3.2%	8.1%	8.4%
MRI for Low Back Pain[1]	27	33.3%	30.2%	32.7%
Survey of Patients' Hospital Experiences				
Area Around Room 'Always' Quiet at Night	(a)	54%	-	58%
Doctors 'Always' Communicated Well	(a)	87%	-	80%
Home Recovery Information Given	(a)	84%	-	82%
Hospital Given 9 or 10 on 10 Point Scale	(a)	67%	-	67%
Meds 'Always' Explained Before Given	(a)	60%	-	60%
Nurses 'Always' Communicated Well	(a)	81%	-	76%
Pain 'Always' Well Controlled	(a)	68%	-	69%
Room and Bathroom 'Always' Clean	(a)	83%	-	71%
Timely Help 'Always' Received	(a)	73%	-	64%
Would Definitely Recommend Hospital	(a)	70%	-	69%

NOTE: Hospital profiles are in alphabetical order by state, then city, then hospital within the city; Rankings exclude hospitals with less than 25 cases except for patient surveys which excludes hospitals with less than 100 cases; (a) 100–299 cases; (1) The number of cases is too small to be sure how well a hospital is performing; (2) The hospital indicated that the data submitted for this measure were based on a sample of cases; (3) Data was collected during a shorter time period (fewer quarters) than the maximum possible time for this measure; (4) Suppressed for one or more quarters by CMS; (5) No data is available from the hospital for this measure; (6) Fewer than 100 patients completed the HCAHPS survey. Use these rates with caution, as the number of surveys may be too low to reliably assess hospital performance; (7) Survey results are based on less than 12 months of data; (8) Survey results are not available for this reporting period; (9) No or very few patients were eligible for the HCAHPS survey. The scores shown, if any, reflect a very small number of surveys; (10) A state average was not calculated because too few hospitals in the state submitted data; (11) There were discrepancies in the data collection process; Please refer to the User's Guide for a full explanation of data.

Boone County Hospital

1015 Union Street Phone: 515-432-3140
Boone, IA 50036 Fax: 515-433-8926
E-mail: dibaltimore@boonecountyhospital.com.
URL: www.boonehospital.com
Type: Critical Access Hospitals Emergency Services: Yes
Ownership: Voluntary Non-Profit - Other Beds: 57

Key Personnel:
CEO/President. . . . . Joe Smith
Chief of Medical Staff. . . . . Scott L Thiel, MD
Infection Control. . . . . Karlene Millang
Operating Room. . . . . Laura Krieger
Quality Assurance . . . . Jackie Reutter
Radiology. . . . . Craig Freeman
Emergency Room . . . . Deana Purdy
Patient Relations . . . . Jackie Reutter

Measure	Cases	This Hosp.	State Avg.	U.S. Avg.
Heart Attack Care				
ACE Inhibitor or ARB for LVSD	0	-	96%	96%
Aspirin at Arrival[1]	9	89%	99%	99%
Aspirin at Discharge[1]	8	75%	99%	98%
Beta Blocker at Discharge[1]	7	100%	99%	98%
Fibrinolytic Medication Timing	0	-	67%	55%
PCI Within 90 Minutes of Arrival	0	-	94%	90%
Smoking Cessation Advice	0	-	99%	99%
Chest Pain/Possible Heart Attack Care				
Aspirin at Arrival[5]	0	-	96%	95%
Median Time to ECG (minutes)[5]	0	-	7	8
Median Time to Transfer (minutes)[5]	0	-	64	61
Fibrinolytic Medication Timing[5]	0	-	45%	54%
Heart Failure Care				
ACE Inhibitor or ARB for LVSD[1]	4	100%	94%	94%
Discharge Instructions[1]	14	86%	86%	88%
Evaluation of LVS Function	29	93%	95%	98%
Smoking Cessation Advice[1]	2	100%	96%	98%
Pneumonia Care				
Appropriate Initial Antibiotic	50	78%	92%	92%
Blood Culture Timing	41	88%	97%	96%
Influenza Vaccine	37	97%	92%	91%
Initial Antibiotic Timing	64	95%	97%	95%
Pneumococcal Vaccine	54	91%	94%	93%
Smoking Cessation Advice[1]	15	87%	95%	97%
Surgical Care Improvement Project				
Appropriate VTP Within 24 Hours[1]	15	87%	92%	92%
Appropriate Hair Removal	60	98%	100%	99%
Appropriate Beta Blocker Usage[1]	12	83%	94%	93%
Controlled Postoperative Blood Glucose	0	-	89%	93%
Prophylactic Antibiotic Timing	50	84%	98%	97%
Prophylactic Antibiotic Timing (Outpatient)[5]	0	-	94%	92%
Prophylactic Antibiotic Selection	48	96%	98%	97%
Prophylactic Antibiotic Select. (Outpatient)[5]	0	-	97%	94%
Prophylactic Antibiotic Stopped	47	89%	95%	94%
Recommended VTP Ordered[1]	15	87%	93%	94%
Urinary Catheter Removal	0	-	91%	90%
Children's Asthma Care				
Received Systemic Corticosteroids	-	-	-	100%
Received Home Management Plan	-	-	-	71%
Received Reliever Medication	-	-	-	100%
Use of Medical Imaging				
Combination Abdominal CT Scan	138	0.783	0.163	0.191
Combination Chest CT Scan	97	0.062	0.060	0.054
Follow-up Mammogram/Ultrasound	499	7.0%	8.1%	8.4%
MRI for Low Back Pain	57	24.6%	30.2%	32.7%
Survey of Patients' Hospital Experiences				
Area Around Room 'Always' Quiet at Night	300+	63%	-	58%
Doctors 'Always' Communicated Well	300+	82%	-	80%
Home Recovery Information Given	300+	85%	-	82%
Hospital Given 9 or 10 on 10 Point Scale	300+	74%	-	67%
Meds 'Always' Explained Before Given	300+	61%	-	60%
Nurses 'Always' Communicated Well	300+	76%	-	76%
Pain 'Always' Well Controlled	300+	65%	-	69%
Room and Bathroom 'Always' Clean	300+	80%	-	71%
Timely Help 'Always' Received	300+	66%	-	64%
Would Definitely Recommend Hospital	300+	73%	-	69%

Hancock County Memorial Hospital

532 1st St NW Phone: 641-843-5000
Britt, IA 50423 Fax: 641-843-5100
URL: www.hancockmemhospital.com
Type: Critical Access Hospitals Emergency Services: Yes
Ownership: Voluntary Non-Profit - Other Beds: 25

Key Personnel:
CEO/President. . . . . Vance Jackson
Chief of Medical Staff . . . . Lyle Fuller, MD
Infection Control. . . . . Robin Bartlett
Operating Room. . . . . Bonnie Wilhite
Quality Assurance . . . . Laura Zwiefel, DON
Radiology. . . . . Jami Hagen
Emergency Room . . . . Bonnie Wilhite
Patient Relations . . . . Andrea Wilson

Measure	Cases	This Hosp.	State Avg.	U.S. Avg.
Heart Attack Care				
ACE Inhibitor or ARB for LVSD[5]	0	-	96%	96%
Aspirin at Arrival[5]	0	-	99%	99%
Aspirin at Discharge[5]	0	-	99%	98%
Beta Blocker at Discharge[5]	0	-	99%	98%
Fibrinolytic Medication Timing[5]	0	-	67%	55%
PCI Within 90 Minutes of Arrival[5]	0	-	94%	90%
Smoking Cessation Advice[5]	0	-	99%	99%
Chest Pain/Possible Heart Attack Care				
Aspirin at Arrival	-	-	96%	95%
Median Time to ECG (minutes)	-	-	7	8
Median Time to Transfer (minutes)	-	-	64	61
Fibrinolytic Medication Timing	-	-	45%	54%
Heart Failure Care				
ACE Inhibitor or ARB for LVSD[1]	5	100%	94%	94%
Discharge Instructions[1]	10	90%	86%	88%
Evaluation of LVS Function[1]	19	89%	95%	98%
Smoking Cessation Advice	0	-	96%	98%
Pneumonia Care				
Appropriate Initial Antibiotic[1]	12	92%	92%	92%
Blood Culture Timing[1]	23	100%	97%	96%
Influenza Vaccine[1]	22	77%	92%	91%
Initial Antibiotic Timing	32	94%	97%	95%
Pneumococcal Vaccine[1]	24	88%	94%	93%
Smoking Cessation Advice[1]	11	100%	95%	97%
Surgical Care Improvement Project				
Appropriate VTP Within 24 Hours[5]	0	-	92%	92%
Appropriate Hair Removal[5]	0	-	100%	99%
Appropriate Beta Blocker Usage[5]	0	-	94%	93%
Controlled Postoperative Blood Glucose[5]	0	-	89%	93%
Prophylactic Antibiotic Timing[5]	0	-	98%	97%
Prophylactic Antibiotic Timing (Outpatient)	-	-	94%	92%
Prophylactic Antibiotic Selection[5]	0	-	98%	97%
Prophylactic Antibiotic Select. (Outpatient)	-	-	97%	94%
Prophylactic Antibiotic Stopped[5]	0	-	95%	94%
Recommended VTP Ordered[5]	0	-	93%	94%
Urinary Catheter Removal[5]	0	-	91%	90%
Children's Asthma Care				
Received Systemic Corticosteroids	-	-	-	100%
Received Home Management Plan	-	-	-	71%
Received Reliever Medication	-	-	-	100%
Use of Medical Imaging				
Combination Abdominal CT Scan	-	-	0.163	0.191
Combination Chest CT Scan	-	-	0.060	0.054
Follow-up Mammogram/Ultrasound	-	-	8.1%	8.4%
MRI for Low Back Pain	-	-	30.2%	32.7%
Survey of Patients' Hospital Experiences				
Area Around Room 'Always' Quiet at Night[8]	-	-	-	58%
Doctors 'Always' Communicated Well[8]	-	-	-	80%
Home Recovery Information Given[8]	-	-	-	82%
Hospital Given 9 or 10 on 10 Point Scale[8]	-	-	-	67%
Meds 'Always' Explained Before Given[8]	-	-	-	60%
Nurses 'Always' Communicated Well[8]	-	-	-	76%
Pain 'Always' Well Controlled[8]	-	-	-	69%
Room and Bathroom 'Always' Clean[8]	-	-	-	71%
Timely Help 'Always' Received[8]	-	-	-	64%
Would Definitely Recommend Hospital[8]	-	-	-	69%

Saint Anthony Regional Hospital

311 South Clark Street Phone: 712-792-3581
Carroll, IA 51401 Fax: 712-792-2124
URL: www.stanthonyhospital.org
Type: Acute Care Hospitals Emergency Services: Yes
Ownership: Voluntary Non-Profit - Church Beds: 178

Key Personnel:
CEO/President. . . . . Gary P Riedmann
Chief of Medical Staff . . . . Lou Ann Lease
Operating Room. . . . . Cindy Erickson
Quality Assurance . . . . Lynda Dorweiler
Radiology. . . . . Robert McCleeary
Emergency Room . . . . Sheryll Stolman
Patient Relations . . . . Cheri Pheulen

Measure	Cases	This Hosp.	State Avg.	U.S. Avg.
Heart Attack Care				
ACE Inhibitor or ARB for LVSD[1,3]	1	100%	96%	96%
Aspirin at Arrival[1,3]	5	100%	99%	99%
Aspirin at Discharge[1,3]	3	100%	99%	98%
Beta Blocker at Discharge[1,3]	3	100%	99%	98%
Fibrinolytic Medication Timing[3]	0	-	67%	55%
PCI Within 90 Minutes of Arrival[3]	0	-	94%	90%
Smoking Cessation Advice[3]	0	-	99%	99%
Chest Pain/Possible Heart Attack Care				
Aspirin at Arrival	42	100%	96%	95%
Median Time to ECG (minutes)	44	11	7	8
Median Time to Transfer (minutes)[1,3]	1	148	64	61
Fibrinolytic Medication Timing[1]	7	57%	45%	54%
Heart Failure Care				
ACE Inhibitor or ARB for LVSD[1]	11	100%	94%	94%
Discharge Instructions	36	94%	86%	88%
Evaluation of LVS Function	51	96%	95%	98%
Smoking Cessation Advice[1]	4	100%	96%	98%
Pneumonia Care				
Appropriate Initial Antibiotic	44	91%	92%	92%
Blood Culture Timing	29	100%	97%	96%
Influenza Vaccine	42	93%	92%	91%
Initial Antibiotic Timing	63	98%	97%	95%
Pneumococcal Vaccine	73	89%	94%	93%
Smoking Cessation Advice[1]	20	95%	95%	97%
Surgical Care Improvement Project				
Appropriate VTP Within 24 Hours	213	100%	92%	92%
Appropriate Hair Removal	274	100%	100%	99%
Appropriate Beta Blocker Usage	101	97%	94%	93%
Controlled Postoperative Blood Glucose	0	-	89%	93%
Prophylactic Antibiotic Timing	210	99%	98%	97%
Prophylactic Antibiotic Timing (Outpatient)	59	95%	94%	92%
Prophylactic Antibiotic Selection	213	99%	98%	97%
Prophylactic Antibiotic Select. (Outpatient)	56	98%	97%	94%
Prophylactic Antibiotic Stopped	206	96%	95%	94%
Recommended VTP Ordered	213	100%	93%	94%
Urinary Catheter Removal	85	96%	91%	90%
Children's Asthma Care				
Received Systemic Corticosteroids	-	-	-	100%
Received Home Management Plan	-	-	-	71%
Received Reliever Medication	-	-	-	100%
Use of Medical Imaging				
Combination Abdominal CT Scan	343	0.055	0.163	0.191
Combination Chest CT Scan	212	0.014	0.060	0.054
Follow-up Mammogram/Ultrasound	519	8.5%	8.1%	8.4%
MRI for Low Back Pain	100	19.0%	30.2%	32.7%
Survey of Patients' Hospital Experiences				
Area Around Room 'Always' Quiet at Night	300+	68%	-	58%
Doctors 'Always' Communicated Well	300+	84%	-	80%
Home Recovery Information Given	300+	86%	-	82%
Hospital Given 9 or 10 on 10 Point Scale	300+	82%	-	67%
Meds 'Always' Explained Before Given	300+	65%	-	60%
Nurses 'Always' Communicated Well	300+	81%	-	76%
Pain 'Always' Well Controlled	300+	72%	-	69%
Room and Bathroom 'Always' Clean	300+	81%	-	71%
Timely Help 'Always' Received	300+	71%	-	64%
Would Definitely Recommend Hospital	300+	82%	-	69%

NOTE: Hospital profiles are in alphabetical order by state, then city, then hospital within the city; Rankings exclude hospitals with less than 25 cases except for patient surveys which excludes hospitals with less than 100 cases; (a) 100–299 cases; (1) The number of cases is too small to be sure how well a hospital is performing; (2) The hospital indicated that the data submitted for this measure were based on a sample of cases; (3) Data was collected during a shorter time period (fewer quarters) than the maximum possible time for this measure; (4) Suppressed for one or more quarters by CMS; (5) No data is available from the hospital for this measure; (6) Fewer than 100 patients completed the HCAHPS survey. Use these rates with caution, as the number of surveys may be too low to reliably assess hospital performance; (7) Survey results are based on less than 12 months of data; (8) Survey results are not available for this reporting period; (9) No or very few patients were eligible for the HCAHPS survey. The scores shown, if any, reflect a very small number of surveys; (10) A state average was not calculated because too few hospitals in the state submitted data; (11) There were discrepancies in the data collection process; Please refer to the User's Guide for a full explanation of data.

Sartori Memorial Hospital

515 College Street
Cedar Falls, IA 50613
Phone: 319-268-3000
Fax: 319-268-3270
E-mail: schaeferk@covhealth.com
URL: www.covhealth.com/sartori.asp
Type: Acute Care Hospitals
Emergency Services: Yes
Ownership: Voluntary Non-Profit - Church
Beds: 100

Key Personnel:

CEO/President. . . . . Sherri Greenwood
Chief of Medical Staff. . . . . Carl Vanderkooi
Infection Control. . . . . Nancy Kiehne, RN
Operating Room. . . . . Linda Meier, RN
Quality Assurance . . . . Kari Kemmer
Emergency Room . . . . Maureen Beckman, RN
Intensive Care Unit. . . . . Denise Lampman, RN

Measure	Cases	This Hosp.	State Avg.	U.S. Avg.
Heart Attack Care				
ACE Inhibitor or ARB for LVSD[1]	2	100%	96%	96%
Aspirin at Arrival[1]	8	88%	99%	99%
Aspirin at Discharge[1]	5	80%	99%	98%
Beta Blocker at Discharge[1]	5	100%	99%	98%
Fibrinolytic Medication Timing	0	-	67%	55%
PCI Within 90 Minutes of Arrival	0	-	94%	90%
Smoking Cessation Advice	0	-	99%	99%
Chest Pain/Possible Heart Attack Care				
Aspirin at Arrival[1,3]	8	100%	96%	95%
Median Time to ECG (minutes)[1,3]	8	5	7	8
Median Time to Transfer (minutes)[1,3]	2	50	64	61
Fibrinolytic Medication Timing[3]	0	-	45%	54%
Heart Failure Care				
ACE Inhibitor or ARB for LVSD[1]	2	50%	94%	94%
Discharge Instructions[1]	12	75%	86%	88%
Evaluation of LVS Function	25	100%	95%	98%
Smoking Cessation Advice[1]	2	100%	96%	98%
Pneumonia Care				
Appropriate Initial Antibiotic[1]	19	100%	92%	92%
Blood Culture Timing	32	100%	97%	96%
Influenza Vaccine[1]	19	100%	92%	91%
Initial Antibiotic Timing	34	97%	97%	95%
Pneumococcal Vaccine	37	100%	94%	93%
Smoking Cessation Advice[1]	5	100%	95%	97%
Surgical Care Improvement Project				
Appropriate VTP Within 24 Hours	100	92%	92%	92%
Appropriate Hair Removal	145	100%	100%	99%
Appropriate Beta Blocker Usage	38	97%	94%	93%
Controlled Postoperative Blood Glucose	0	-	89%	93%
Prophylactic Antibiotic Timing	91	98%	98%	97%
Prophylactic Antibiotic Timing (Outpatient)[1]	21	67%	94%	92%
Prophylactic Antibiotic Selection	91	98%	98%	97%
Prophylactic Antibiotic Select. (Outpatient)[1]	17	88%	97%	94%
Prophylactic Antibiotic Stopped	88	97%	95%	94%
Recommended VTP Ordered	101	92%	93%	94%
Urinary Catheter Removal	43	93%	91%	90%
Children's Asthma Care				
Received Systemic Corticosteroids	-	-	-	100%
Received Home Management Plan	-	-	-	71%
Received Reliever Medication	-	-	-	100%
Use of Medical Imaging				
Combination Abdominal CT Scan	168	0.006	0.163	0.191
Combination Chest CT Scan	102	0.000	0.060	0.054
Follow-up Mammogram/Ultrasound	516	5.4%	8.1%	8.4%
MRI for Low Back Pain[1]	48	25.0%	30.2%	32.7%
Survey of Patients' Hospital Experiences				
Area Around Room 'Always' Quiet at Night	300+	69%	-	58%
Doctors 'Always' Communicated Well	300+	82%	-	80%
Home Recovery Information Given	300+	83%	-	82%
Hospital Given 9 or 10 on 10 Point Scale	300+	71%	-	67%
Meds 'Always' Explained Before Given	300+	61%	-	60%
Nurses 'Always' Communicated Well	300+	78%	-	76%
Pain 'Always' Well Controlled	300+	71%	-	69%
Room and Bathroom 'Always' Clean	300+	79%	-	71%
Timely Help 'Always' Received	300+	58%	-	64%
Would Definitely Recommend Hospital	300+	74%	-	69%

Mercy Medical Center-Cedar Rapids

701 10th Street SE
Cedar Rapids, IA 52403
Phone: 319-398-6011
Fax: 319-398-6912
URL: www.mercycare.org
Type: Acute Care Hospitals
Emergency Services: Yes
Ownership: Voluntary Non-Profit - Church
Beds: 430

Key Personnel:

CEO/President. . . . . A James Tinker
Chief of Medical Staff. . . . . Margie Ebel
Infection Control. . . . . Jolene Utt
Operating Room. . . . . Betty DeBrower
Quality Assurance . . . . Kathy Krusie
Emergency Room . . . . Sue Courts
Intensive Care Unit. . . . . Rose Hutchcroft, RN

Measure	Cases	This Hosp.	State Avg.	U.S. Avg.
Heart Attack Care				
ACE Inhibitor or ARB for LVSD	25	100%	96%	96%
Aspirin at Arrival	205	100%	99%	99%
Aspirin at Discharge	198	100%	99%	98%
Beta Blocker at Discharge	186	100%	99%	98%
Fibrinolytic Medication Timing	0	-	67%	55%
PCI Within 90 Minutes of Arrival	49	100%	94%	90%
Smoking Cessation Advice	67	100%	99%	99%
Chest Pain/Possible Heart Attack Care				
Aspirin at Arrival[1]	6	100%	96%	95%
Median Time to ECG (minutes)[1]	6	2	7	8
Median Time to Transfer (minutes)[5]	0	-	64	61
Fibrinolytic Medication Timing[5]	0	-	45%	54%
Heart Failure Care				
ACE Inhibitor or ARB for LVSD[2]	29	93%	94%	94%
Discharge Instructions[2]	128	82%	86%	88%
Evaluation of LVS Function[2]	194	100%	95%	98%
Smoking Cessation Advice[2]	25	88%	96%	98%
Pneumonia Care				
Appropriate Initial Antibiotic[2]	57	91%	92%	92%
Blood Culture Timing[2]	100	98%	97%	96%
Influenza Vaccine[2]	74	95%	92%	91%
Initial Antibiotic Timing[2]	101	96%	97%	95%
Pneumococcal Vaccine[2]	118	95%	94%	93%
Smoking Cessation Advice[2]	41	90%	95%	97%
Surgical Care Improvement Project				
Appropriate VTP Within 24 Hours[2]	115	95%	92%	92%
Appropriate Hair Removal[2]	349	100%	100%	99%
Appropriate Beta Blocker Usage[2]	125	94%	94%	93%
Controlled Postoperative Blood Glucose[2]	0	-	89%	93%
Prophylactic Antibiotic Timing[2]	231	99%	98%	97%
Prophylactic Antibiotic Timing (Outpatient)	814	98%	94%	92%
Prophylactic Antibiotic Selection[2]	234	98%	98%	97%
Prophylactic Antibiotic Select. (Outpatient)	813	99%	97%	94%
Prophylactic Antibiotic Stopped[2]	186	95%	95%	94%
Recommended VTP Ordered[2]	115	98%	93%	94%
Urinary Catheter Removal[2]	78	92%	91%	90%
Children's Asthma Care				
Received Systemic Corticosteroids	-	-	-	100%
Received Home Management Plan	-	-	-	71%
Received Reliever Medication	-	-	-	100%
Use of Medical Imaging				
Combination Abdominal CT Scan	783	0.075	0.163	0.191
Combination Chest CT Scan	529	0.008	0.060	0.054
Follow-up Mammogram/Ultrasound	2,686	7.4%	8.1%	8.4%
MRI for Low Back Pain	340	31.8%	30.2%	32.7%
Survey of Patients' Hospital Experiences				
Area Around Room 'Always' Quiet at Night	300+	68%	-	58%
Doctors 'Always' Communicated Well	300+	79%	-	80%
Home Recovery Information Given	300+	83%	-	82%
Hospital Given 9 or 10 on 10 Point Scale	300+	75%	-	67%
Meds 'Always' Explained Before Given	300+	62%	-	60%
Nurses 'Always' Communicated Well	300+	76%	-	76%
Pain 'Always' Well Controlled	300+	64%	-	69%
Room and Bathroom 'Always' Clean	300+	68%	-	71%
Timely Help 'Always' Received	300+	58%	-	64%
Would Definitely Recommend Hospital	300+	81%	-	69%

Saint Lukes Hospital

1026 A Ave NE
Cedar Rapids, IA 52402
Phone: 319-369-7211
Fax: 319-369-8036
URL: www.crstlukes.com
Type: Acute Care Hospitals
Emergency Services: Yes
Ownership: Voluntary Non-Profit - Private
Beds: 560

Key Personnel:

CEO/President. . . . . Theodore Townsend
Chief of Medical Staff. . . . . James R. LaMorgese, MD
Infection Control. . . . . Brenda Depue
Operating Room. . . . . Janna Petersen
Pediatric Ambulatory Care . . . . . . Stephen Roth
Pediatric In-Patient Care . . . . Stephen Roth
Quality Assurance . . . . Sherrie Justice
Radiology. . . . . Michael Harleman

Measure	Cases	This Hosp.	State Avg.	U.S. Avg.
Heart Attack Care				
ACE Inhibitor or ARB for LVSD[2]	27	96%	96%	96%
Aspirin at Arrival[2]	214	100%	99%	99%
Aspirin at Discharge[2]	258	100%	99%	98%
Beta Blocker at Discharge[2]	252	100%	99%	98%
Fibrinolytic Medication Timing[1,2]	1	100%	67%	55%
PCI Within 90 Minutes of Arrival[2]	49	96%	94%	90%
Smoking Cessation Advice[2]	86	99%	99%	99%
Chest Pain/Possible Heart Attack Care				
Aspirin at Arrival[1]	21	95%	96%	95%
Median Time to ECG (minutes)[1]	22	12	7	8
Median Time to Transfer (minutes)[5]	0	-	64	61
Fibrinolytic Medication Timing[3]	0	-	45%	54%
Heart Failure Care				
ACE Inhibitor or ARB for LVSD[2]	29	97%	94%	94%
Discharge Instructions[2]	159	96%	86%	88%
Evaluation of LVS Function[2]	185	99%	95%	98%
Smoking Cessation Advice[1,2]	19	100%	96%	98%
Pneumonia Care				
Appropriate Initial Antibiotic[2]	55	96%	92%	92%
Blood Culture Timing[2]	81	95%	97%	96%
Influenza Vaccine[2]	74	92%	92%	91%
Initial Antibiotic Timing[2]	86	99%	97%	95%
Pneumococcal Vaccine[2]	115	97%	94%	93%
Smoking Cessation Advice[2]	41	100%	95%	97%
Surgical Care Improvement Project				
Appropriate VTP Within 24 Hours[2]	109	92%	92%	92%
Appropriate Hair Removal[2]	494	99%	100%	99%
Appropriate Beta Blocker Usage[2]	229	95%	94%	93%
Controlled Postoperative Blood Glucose[2]	134	89%	89%	93%
Prophylactic Antibiotic Timing[2]	361	99%	98%	97%
Prophylactic Antibiotic Timing (Outpatient)	582	97%	94%	92%
Prophylactic Antibiotic Selection[2]	366	99%	98%	97%
Prophylactic Antibiotic Select. (Outpatient)	581	99%	97%	94%
Prophylactic Antibiotic Stopped[2]	309	95%	95%	94%
Recommended VTP Ordered[2]	109	95%	93%	94%
Urinary Catheter Removal[2]	144	92%	91%	90%
Children's Asthma Care				
Received Systemic Corticosteroids	-	-	-	100%
Received Home Management Plan	-	-	-	71%
Received Reliever Medication	-	-	-	100%
Use of Medical Imaging				
Combination Abdominal CT Scan	881	0.112	0.163	0.191
Combination Chest CT Scan	580	0.048	0.060	0.054
Follow-up Mammogram/Ultrasound	1,591	8.3%	8.1%	8.4%
MRI for Low Back Pain	312	29.8%	30.2%	32.7%
Survey of Patients' Hospital Experiences				
Area Around Room 'Always' Quiet at Night	300+	61%	-	58%
Doctors 'Always' Communicated Well	300+	78%	-	80%
Home Recovery Information Given	300+	89%	-	82%
Hospital Given 9 or 10 on 10 Point Scale	300+	77%	-	67%
Meds 'Always' Explained Before Given	300+	62%	-	60%
Nurses 'Always' Communicated Well	300+	79%	-	76%
Pain 'Always' Well Controlled	300+	71%	-	69%
Room and Bathroom 'Always' Clean	300+	75%	-	71%
Timely Help 'Always' Received	300+	61%	-	64%
Would Definitely Recommend Hospital	300+	82%	-	69%

NOTE: Hospital profiles are in alphabetical order by state, then city, then hospital within the city; Rankings exclude hospitals with less than 25 cases except for patient surveys which excludes hospitals with less than 100 cases; (a) 100–299 cases; (1) The number of cases is too small to be sure how well a hospital is performing; (2) The hospital indicated that the data submitted for this measure were based on a sample of cases; (3) Data was collected during a shorter time period (fewer quarters) than the maximum possible time for this measure; (4) Suppressed for one or more quarters by CMS; (5) No data is available from the hospital for this measure; (6) Fewer than 100 patients completed the HCAHPS survey. Use these rates with caution, as the number of surveys may be too low to reliably assess hospital performance; (7) Survey results are based on less than 12 months of data; (8) Survey results are not available for this reporting period; (9) No or very few patients were eligible for the HCAHPS survey. The scores shown, if any, reflect a very small number of surveys; (10) A state average was not calculated because too few hospitals in the state submitted data; (11) There were discrepancies in the data collection process; Please refer to the User's Guide for a full explanation of data.

Mercy Medical Center-Centerville

One St Joseph's Drive — Phone: 641-437-4111
Centerville, IA 52544 — Fax: 641-437-3422
URL: www.mercycenterville.org
Type: Critical Access Hospitals — Emergency Services: Yes
Ownership: Voluntary Non-Profit - Church — Beds: 54

Key Personnel:
CEO/President. . . . . Scott Grodsky
Cardiac Laboratory. . . . . Thomas Brown
Chief of Medical Staff. . . . . Carl Rouse
Operating Room. . . . . Kathy Woolums, RN
Quality Assurance . . . . Tonya Clawson
Radiology. . . . . Don Breit
Emergency Room . . . . Mary Lou Sales, RN

Measure	Cases	This Hosp.	State Avg.	U.S. Avg.
Heart Attack Care				
ACE Inhibitor or ARB for LVSD[1,3]	1	100%	96%	96%
Aspirin at Arrival[1,3]	1	100%	99%	99%
Aspirin at Discharge[1,3]	3	67%	99%	98%
Beta Blocker at Discharge[1,3]	3	100%	99%	98%
Fibrinolytic Medication Timing[3]	0	-	67%	55%
PCI Within 90 Minutes of Arrival[3]	0	-	94%	90%
Smoking Cessation Advice[1,3]	1	100%	99%	99%
Chest Pain/Possible Heart Attack Care				
Aspirin at Arrival	-	-	96%	95%
Median Time to ECG (minutes)	-	-	7	8
Median Time to Transfer (minutes)	-	-	64	61
Fibrinolytic Medication Timing	-	-	45%	54%
Heart Failure Care				
ACE Inhibitor or ARB for LVSD[1]	3	100%	94%	94%
Discharge Instructions[1]	15	80%	86%	88%
Evaluation of LVS Function	27	100%	95%	98%
Smoking Cessation Advice[1]	2	100%	96%	98%
Pneumonia Care				
Appropriate Initial Antibiotic	28	93%	92%	92%
Blood Culture Timing	25	96%	97%	96%
Influenza Vaccine	30	70%	92%	91%
Initial Antibiotic Timing	38	100%	97%	95%
Pneumococcal Vaccine	46	87%	94%	93%
Smoking Cessation Advice[1]	18	100%	95%	97%
Surgical Care Improvement Project				
Appropriate VTP Within 24 Hours[1]	12	75%	92%	92%
Appropriate Hair Removal	43	100%	100%	99%
Appropriate Beta Blocker Usage[1]	10	60%	94%	93%
Controlled Postoperative Blood Glucose	0	-	89%	93%
Prophylactic Antibiotic Timing	39	100%	98%	97%
Prophylactic Antibiotic Timing (Outpatient)	-	-	94%	92%
Prophylactic Antibiotic Selection	39	85%	98%	97%
Prophylactic Antibiotic Select. (Outpatient)	-	-	97%	94%
Prophylactic Antibiotic Stopped	38	87%	95%	94%
Recommended VTP Ordered[1]	12	92%	93%	94%
Urinary Catheter Removal[1]	2	100%	91%	90%
Children's Asthma Care				
Received Systemic Corticosteroids	-	-	-	100%
Received Home Management Plan	-	-	-	71%
Received Reliever Medication	-	-	-	100%
Use of Medical Imaging				
Combination Abdominal CT Scan	-	-	0.163	0.191
Combination Chest CT Scan	-	-	0.060	0.054
Follow-up Mammogram/Ultrasound	-	-	8.1%	8.4%
MRI for Low Back Pain	-	-	30.2%	32.7%
Survey of Patients' Hospital Experiences				
Area Around Room 'Always' Quiet at Night[8]	-	-	-	58%
Doctors 'Always' Communicated Well[8]	-	-	-	80%
Home Recovery Information Given[8]	-	-	-	82%
Hospital Given 9 or 10 on 10 Point Scale[8]	-	-	-	67%
Meds 'Always' Explained Before Given[8]	-	-	-	60%
Nurses 'Always' Communicated Well[8]	-	-	-	76%
Pain 'Always' Well Controlled[8]	-	-	-	69%
Room and Bathroom 'Always' Clean[8]	-	-	-	71%
Timely Help 'Always' Received[8]	-	-	-	64%
Would Definitely Recommend Hospital[8]	-	-	-	69%

Lucas County Health Center

1200 North 7th Street — Phone: 641-774-3000
Chariton, IA 50049 — Fax: 641-774-3296
Type: Critical Access Hospitals — Emergency Services: Yes
Ownership: Voluntary Non-Profit - Other — Beds: 56

Key Personnel:
CEO/President. . . . . Veronica Fuhs
Chief of Medical Staff . . . . Neal R Sokol
Operating Room. . . . . Becky McCorkle
Quality Assurance . . . . Veronica Fuhs
Radiology. . . . . Robert V. Filippone
Emergency Room . . . . Michael Gorski

Measure	Cases	This Hosp.	State Avg.	U.S. Avg.
Heart Attack Care				
ACE Inhibitor or ARB for LVSD[3]	0	-	96%	96%
Aspirin at Arrival[1,3]	2	100%	99%	99%
Aspirin at Discharge[1,3]	1	100%	99%	98%
Beta Blocker at Discharge[1,3]	1	0%	99%	98%
Fibrinolytic Medication Timing[3]	0	-	67%	55%
PCI Within 90 Minutes of Arrival[3]	0	-	94%	90%
Smoking Cessation Advice[3]	0	-	99%	99%
Chest Pain/Possible Heart Attack Care				
Aspirin at Arrival	-	-	96%	95%
Median Time to ECG (minutes)	-	-	7	8
Median Time to Transfer (minutes)	-	-	64	61
Fibrinolytic Medication Timing	-	-	45%	54%
Heart Failure Care				
ACE Inhibitor or ARB for LVSD[1]	2	100%	94%	94%
Discharge Instructions[1]	11	27%	86%	88%
Evaluation of LVS Function[1]	19	58%	95%	98%
Smoking Cessation Advice[1]	1	0%	96%	98%
Pneumonia Care				
Appropriate Initial Antibiotic[1]	15	93%	92%	92%
Blood Culture Timing[1]	17	100%	97%	96%
Influenza Vaccine[1]	23	78%	92%	91%
Initial Antibiotic Timing[1]	23	96%	97%	95%
Pneumococcal Vaccine	28	86%	94%	93%
Smoking Cessation Advice[1]	2	0%	95%	97%
Surgical Care Improvement Project				
Appropriate VTP Within 24 Hours[1]	10	10%	92%	92%
Appropriate Hair Removal[1]	19	89%	100%	99%
Appropriate Beta Blocker Usage[1]	4	50%	94%	93%
Controlled Postoperative Blood Glucose	0	-	89%	93%
Prophylactic Antibiotic Timing[1]	10	80%	98%	97%
Prophylactic Antibiotic Timing (Outpatient)	-	-	94%	92%
Prophylactic Antibiotic Selection[1]	10	100%	98%	97%
Prophylactic Antibiotic Select. (Outpatient)	-	-	97%	94%
Prophylactic Antibiotic Stopped[1]	9	67%	95%	94%
Recommended VTP Ordered[1]	10	10%	93%	94%
Urinary Catheter Removal[1]	7	86%	91%	90%
Children's Asthma Care				
Received Systemic Corticosteroids	-	-	-	100%
Received Home Management Plan	-	-	-	71%
Received Reliever Medication	-	-	-	100%
Use of Medical Imaging				
Combination Abdominal CT Scan	-	-	0.163	0.191
Combination Chest CT Scan	-	-	0.060	0.054
Follow-up Mammogram/Ultrasound	-	-	8.1%	8.4%
MRI for Low Back Pain	-	-	30.2%	32.7%
Survey of Patients' Hospital Experiences				
Area Around Room 'Always' Quiet at Night[8]	-	-	-	58%
Doctors 'Always' Communicated Well[8]	-	-	-	80%
Home Recovery Information Given[8]	-	-	-	82%
Hospital Given 9 or 10 on 10 Point Scale[8]	-	-	-	67%
Meds 'Always' Explained Before Given[8]	-	-	-	60%
Nurses 'Always' Communicated Well[8]	-	-	-	76%
Pain 'Always' Well Controlled[8]	-	-	-	69%
Room and Bathroom 'Always' Clean[8]	-	-	-	71%
Timely Help 'Always' Received[8]	-	-	-	64%
Would Definitely Recommend Hospital[8]	-	-	-	69%

Cherokee Regional Medical Center

300 Sioux Valley Drive — Phone: 712-225-5101
Cherokee, IA 51012 — Fax: 712-225-6870
E-mail: webmaster@cherokeermc.org
URL: www.cherokeermc.org
Type: Critical Access Hospitals — Emergency Services: Yes
Ownership: Voluntary Non-Profit - Private — Beds: 25

Key Personnel:
CEO/President. . . . . John M Comstock
Chief of Medical Staff. . . . . Timothy G Rice
Coronary Care . . . . Wesley Parker MD
Infection Control. . . . . Susie Haselhoff
Operating Room. . . . . Dondee Halverson
Quality Assurance . . . . Susie Hasolhoff
Radiology. . . . . Jeanna Bergendahl

Measure	Cases	This Hosp.	State Avg.	U.S. Avg.
Heart Attack Care				
ACE Inhibitor or ARB for LVSD[5]	0	-	96%	96%
Aspirin at Arrival[5]	0	-	99%	99%
Aspirin at Discharge[5]	0	-	99%	98%
Beta Blocker at Discharge[5]	0	-	99%	98%
Fibrinolytic Medication Timing[5]	0	-	67%	55%
PCI Within 90 Minutes of Arrival[5]	0	-	94%	90%
Smoking Cessation Advice[5]	0	-	99%	99%
Chest Pain/Possible Heart Attack Care				
Aspirin at Arrival	-	-	96%	95%
Median Time to ECG (minutes)	-	-	7	8
Median Time to Transfer (minutes)	-	-	64	61
Fibrinolytic Medication Timing	-	-	45%	54%
Heart Failure Care				
ACE Inhibitor or ARB for LVSD[1]	12	42%	94%	94%
Discharge Instructions[1]	14	71%	86%	88%
Evaluation of LVS Function	37	86%	95%	98%
Smoking Cessation Advice[1]	6	100%	96%	98%
Pneumonia Care				
Appropriate Initial Antibiotic	30	93%	92%	92%
Blood Culture Timing[1]	12	92%	97%	96%
Influenza Vaccine	31	94%	92%	91%
Initial Antibiotic Timing	41	93%	97%	95%
Pneumococcal Vaccine	52	98%	94%	93%
Smoking Cessation Advice[1]	9	56%	95%	97%
Surgical Care Improvement Project				
Appropriate VTP Within 24 Hours[5]	0	-	92%	92%
Appropriate Hair Removal[5]	0	-	100%	99%
Appropriate Beta Blocker Usage[5]	0	-	94%	93%
Controlled Postoperative Blood Glucose[5]	0	-	89%	93%
Prophylactic Antibiotic Timing[5]	0	-	98%	97%
Prophylactic Antibiotic Timing (Outpatient)	-	-	94%	92%
Prophylactic Antibiotic Selection[5]	0	-	98%	97%
Prophylactic Antibiotic Select. (Outpatient)	-	-	97%	94%
Prophylactic Antibiotic Stopped[5]	0	-	95%	94%
Recommended VTP Ordered[5]	0	-	93%	94%
Urinary Catheter Removal[5]	0	-	91%	90%
Children's Asthma Care				
Received Systemic Corticosteroids	-	-	-	100%
Received Home Management Plan	-	-	-	71%
Received Reliever Medication	-	-	-	100%
Use of Medical Imaging				
Combination Abdominal CT Scan	-	-	0.163	0.191
Combination Chest CT Scan	-	-	0.060	0.054
Follow-up Mammogram/Ultrasound	-	-	8.1%	8.4%
MRI for Low Back Pain	-	-	30.2%	32.7%
Survey of Patients' Hospital Experiences				
Area Around Room 'Always' Quiet at Night[8]	-	-	-	58%
Doctors 'Always' Communicated Well[8]	-	-	-	80%
Home Recovery Information Given[8]	-	-	-	82%
Hospital Given 9 or 10 on 10 Point Scale[8]	-	-	-	67%
Meds 'Always' Explained Before Given[8]	-	-	-	60%
Nurses 'Always' Communicated Well[8]	-	-	-	76%
Pain 'Always' Well Controlled[8]	-	-	-	69%
Room and Bathroom 'Always' Clean[8]	-	-	-	71%
Timely Help 'Always' Received[8]	-	-	-	64%
Would Definitely Recommend Hospital[8]	-	-	-	69%

NOTE: Hospital profiles are in alphabetical order by state, then city, then hospital within the city; Rankings exclude hospitals with less than 25 cases except for patient surveys which excludes hospitals with less than 100 cases; (a) 100–299 cases; (1) The number of cases is too small to be sure how well a hospital is performing; (2) The hospital indicated that the data submitted for this measure were based on a sample of cases; (3) Data was collected during a shorter time period (fewer quarters) than the maximum possible time for this measure; (4) Suppressed for one or more quarters by CMS; (5) No data is available from the hospital for this measure; (6) Fewer than 100 patients completed the HCAHPS survey. Use these rates with caution, as the number of surveys may be too low to reliably assess hospital performance; (7) Survey results are based on less than 12 months of data; (8) Survey results are not available for this reporting period; (9) No or very few patients were eligible for the HCAHPS survey. The scores shown, if any, reflect a very small number of surveys; (10) A state average was not calculated because too few hospitals in the state submitted data; (11) There were discrepancies in the data collection process; Please refer to the User's Guide for a full explanation of data.

Clarinda Regional Health Center

823 South 17th		Phone: 712-542-2176
Clarinda, IA 51632		Fax: 712-542-3380
E-mail: rudys@clarinda.heartland.net
URL: www.clarindahealth.com
Type: Critical Access Hospitals		Emergency Services: Yes
Ownership: Government - Local		Beds: 47

Key Personnel:
CEO/President. . . . . Chris Stipe
Chief of Medical Staff . . . . Robert Clemons
Operating Room. . . . . Jan Weakly
Quality Assurance . . . . Janice Brown
Radiology. . . . . Greg Jones
Emergency Room . . . . Cris Meacham

Measure	Cases	This Hosp.	State Avg.	U.S. Avg.
Heart Attack Care				
ACE Inhibitor or ARB for LVSD[3]	0	-	96%	96%
Aspirin at Arrival[3]	0	-	99%	99%
Aspirin at Discharge[3]	0	-	99%	98%
Beta Blocker at Discharge[3]	0	-	99%	98%
Fibrinolytic Medication Timing[3]	0	-	67%	55%
PCI Within 90 Minutes of Arrival[5]	0	-	94%	90%
Smoking Cessation Advice[3]	0	-	99%	99%
Chest Pain/Possible Heart Attack Care				
Aspirin at Arrival	-	-	96%	95%
Median Time to ECG (minutes)	-	-	7	8
Median Time to Transfer (minutes)	-	-	64	61
Fibrinolytic Medication Timing	-	-	45%	54%
Heart Failure Care				
ACE Inhibitor or ARB for LVSD[1]	3	100%	94%	94%
Discharge Instructions[1]	4	75%	86%	88%
Evaluation of LVS Function[1]	7	71%	95%	98%
Smoking Cessation Advice[1]	1	100%	96%	98%
Pneumonia Care				
Appropriate Initial Antibiotic[1]	20	100%	92%	92%
Blood Culture Timing[1]	18	94%	97%	96%
Influenza Vaccine	28	89%	92%	91%
Initial Antibiotic Timing	35	94%	97%	95%
Pneumococcal Vaccine	45	93%	94%	93%
Smoking Cessation Advice[1]	9	100%	95%	97%
Surgical Care Improvement Project				
Appropriate VTP Within 24 Hours[5]	0	-	92%	92%
Appropriate Hair Removal[5]	0	-	100%	99%
Appropriate Beta Blocker Usage[5]	0	-	94%	93%
Controlled Postoperative Blood Glucose[5]	0	-	89%	93%
Prophylactic Antibiotic Timing[5]	0	-	98%	97%
Prophylactic Antibiotic Timing (Outpatient)	-	-	94%	92%
Prophylactic Antibiotic Selection[5]	0	-	98%	97%
Prophylactic Antibiotic Select. (Outpatient)	-	-	97%	94%
Prophylactic Antibiotic Stopped[5]	0	-	95%	94%
Recommended VTP Ordered[5]	0	-	93%	94%
Urinary Catheter Removal[5]	0	-	91%	90%
Children's Asthma Care				
Received Systemic Corticosteroids	-	-	-	100%
Received Home Management Plan	-	-	-	71%
Received Reliever Medication	-	-	-	100%
Use of Medical Imaging				
Combination Abdominal CT Scan	-	-	0.163	0.191
Combination Chest CT Scan	-	-	0.060	0.054
Follow-up Mammogram/Ultrasound	-	-	8.1%	8.4%
MRI for Low Back Pain	-	-	30.2%	32.7%
Survey of Patients' Hospital Experiences				
Area Around Room 'Always' Quiet at Night	(a)	60%	-	58%
Doctors 'Always' Communicated Well	(a)	87%	-	80%
Home Recovery Information Given	(a)	76%	-	82%
Hospital Given 9 or 10 on 10 Point Scale	(a)	68%	-	67%
Meds 'Always' Explained Before Given	(a)	67%	-	60%
Nurses 'Always' Communicated Well	(a)	81%	-	76%
Pain 'Always' Well Controlled	(a)	77%	-	69%
Room and Bathroom 'Always' Clean	(a)	82%	-	71%
Timely Help 'Always' Received	(a)	79%	-	64%
Would Definitely Recommend Hospital	(a)	67%	-	69%

Wright Medical Center

1316 South Main Street		Phone: 515-532-2811
Clarion, IA 50525		Fax: 515-532-3443
E-mail: wmc@wrightmed.com
URL: www.wrightmed.com
Type: Critical Access Hospitals		Emergency Services: Yes
Ownership: Government - Local		Beds: 25

Key Personnel:
CEO/President. . . . . Steve Simonin
Chief of Medical Staff . . . . Dustin Smith, MD
Infection Control. . . . . Tara Wagner, RN
Operating Room. . . . . Robin Meyer, RN
Quality Assurance . . . . Nancy Bakker, RN
Radiology. . . . . Abby Kirstein
Emergency Room . . . . Vinnette PA-C, PA-C
Patient Relations . . . . Annette Odlando

Measure	Cases	This Hosp.	State Avg.	U.S. Avg.
Heart Attack Care				
ACE Inhibitor or ARB for LVSD[5]	0	-	96%	96%
Aspirin at Arrival[5]	0	-	99%	99%
Aspirin at Discharge[5]	0	-	99%	98%
Beta Blocker at Discharge[5]	0	-	99%	98%
Fibrinolytic Medication Timing[5]	0	-	67%	55%
PCI Within 90 Minutes of Arrival[5]	0	-	94%	90%
Smoking Cessation Advice[5]	0	-	99%	99%
Chest Pain/Possible Heart Attack Care				
Aspirin at Arrival	-	-	96%	95%
Median Time to ECG (minutes)	-	-	7	8
Median Time to Transfer (minutes)	-	-	64	61
Fibrinolytic Medication Timing	-	-	45%	54%
Heart Failure Care				
ACE Inhibitor or ARB for LVSD[5]	0	-	94%	94%
Discharge Instructions[5]	0	-	86%	88%
Evaluation of LVS Function[5]	0	-	95%	98%
Smoking Cessation Advice[5]	0	-	96%	98%
Pneumonia Care				
Appropriate Initial Antibiotic[1]	21	86%	92%	92%
Blood Culture Timing[1]	24	96%	97%	96%
Influenza Vaccine[1]	14	64%	92%	91%
Initial Antibiotic Timing[1]	1	0%	97%	95%
Pneumococcal Vaccine[1]	22	50%	94%	93%
Smoking Cessation Advice[1]	2	50%	95%	97%
Surgical Care Improvement Project				
Appropriate VTP Within 24 Hours[1]	22	100%	92%	92%
Appropriate Hair Removal	307	100%	100%	99%
Appropriate Beta Blocker Usage[5]	0	-	94%	93%
Controlled Postoperative Blood Glucose	0	-	89%	93%
Prophylactic Antibiotic Timing	249	99%	98%	97%
Prophylactic Antibiotic Timing (Outpatient)	-	-	94%	92%
Prophylactic Antibiotic Selection	249	98%	98%	97%
Prophylactic Antibiotic Select. (Outpatient)	-	-	97%	94%
Prophylactic Antibiotic Stopped	246	98%	95%	94%
Recommended VTP Ordered[1]	22	100%	93%	94%
Urinary Catheter Removal[1]	3	33%	91%	90%
Children's Asthma Care				
Received Systemic Corticosteroids	-	-	-	100%
Received Home Management Plan	-	-	-	71%
Received Reliever Medication	-	-	-	100%
Use of Medical Imaging				
Combination Abdominal CT Scan	-	-	0.163	0.191
Combination Chest CT Scan	-	-	0.060	0.054
Follow-up Mammogram/Ultrasound	-	-	8.1%	8.4%
MRI for Low Back Pain	-	-	30.2%	32.7%
Survey of Patients' Hospital Experiences				
Area Around Room 'Always' Quiet at Night	300+	69%	-	58%
Doctors 'Always' Communicated Well	300+	85%	-	80%
Home Recovery Information Given	300+	90%	-	82%
Hospital Given 9 or 10 on 10 Point Scale	300+	83%	-	67%
Meds 'Always' Explained Before Given	300+	62%	-	60%
Nurses 'Always' Communicated Well	300+	85%	-	76%
Pain 'Always' Well Controlled	300+	77%	-	69%
Room and Bathroom 'Always' Clean	300+	79%	-	71%
Timely Help 'Always' Received	300+	78%	-	64%
Would Definitely Recommend Hospital	300+	85%	-	69%

Mercy Medical Center-Clinton

1410 North 4th Street		Phone: 563-244-5555
Clinton, IA 52732		Fax: 563-244-5592
Type: Acute Care Hospitals		Emergency Services: Yes
Ownership: Voluntary Non-Profit - Church		Beds: 359

Key Personnel:
CEO/President. . . . . Donna Oliver
Operating Room. . . . . Kim Bush
Quality Assurance . . . . Lisa Hoppe
Radiology. . . . . Juergen Holl, MD

Measure	Cases	This Hosp.	State Avg.	U.S. Avg.
Heart Attack Care				
ACE Inhibitor or ARB for LVSD[1]	7	86%	96%	96%
Aspirin at Arrival	124	99%	99%	99%
Aspirin at Discharge	102	97%	99%	98%
Beta Blocker at Discharge	100	97%	99%	98%
Fibrinolytic Medication Timing[1]	2	50%	67%	55%
PCI Within 90 Minutes of Arrival[1]	16	81%	94%	90%
Smoking Cessation Advice	39	100%	99%	99%
Chest Pain/Possible Heart Attack Care				
Aspirin at Arrival[1]	23	96%	96%	95%
Median Time to ECG (minutes)[1]	23	5	7	8
Median Time to Transfer (minutes)[1,3]	1	97	64	61
Fibrinolytic Medication Timing[3]	0	-	45%	54%
Heart Failure Care				
ACE Inhibitor or ARB for LVSD	46	93%	94%	94%
Discharge Instructions	134	78%	86%	88%
Evaluation of LVS Function	184	99%	95%	98%
Smoking Cessation Advice[1]	22	100%	96%	98%
Pneumonia Care				
Appropriate Initial Antibiotic	157	96%	92%	92%
Blood Culture Timing	222	98%	97%	96%
Influenza Vaccine	172	93%	92%	91%
Initial Antibiotic Timing	239	96%	97%	95%
Pneumococcal Vaccine	261	96%	94%	93%
Smoking Cessation Advice	95	97%	95%	97%
Surgical Care Improvement Project				
Appropriate VTP Within 24 Hours	112	93%	92%	92%
Appropriate Hair Removal	218	100%	100%	99%
Appropriate Beta Blocker Usage	66	89%	94%	93%
Controlled Postoperative Blood Glucose	0	-	89%	93%
Prophylactic Antibiotic Timing	132	97%	98%	97%
Prophylactic Antibiotic Timing (Outpatient)	87	95%	94%	92%
Prophylactic Antibiotic Selection	132	94%	98%	97%
Prophylactic Antibiotic Select. (Outpatient)	86	97%	97%	94%
Prophylactic Antibiotic Stopped	125	95%	95%	94%
Recommended VTP Ordered	112	93%	93%	94%
Urinary Catheter Removal	55	91%	91%	90%
Children's Asthma Care				
Received Systemic Corticosteroids	-	-	-	100%
Received Home Management Plan	-	-	-	71%
Received Reliever Medication	-	-	-	100%
Use of Medical Imaging				
Combination Abdominal CT Scan	168	0.625	0.163	0.191
Combination Chest CT Scan	111	0.315	0.060	0.054
Follow-up Mammogram/Ultrasound	392	1.0%	8.1%	8.4%
MRI for Low Back Pain[1]	2	0.0%	30.2%	32.7%
Survey of Patients' Hospital Experiences				
Area Around Room 'Always' Quiet at Night	300+	58%	-	58%
Doctors 'Always' Communicated Well	300+	75%	-	80%
Home Recovery Information Given	300+	86%	-	82%
Hospital Given 9 or 10 on 10 Point Scale	300+	66%	-	67%
Meds 'Always' Explained Before Given	300+	61%	-	60%
Nurses 'Always' Communicated Well	300+	79%	-	76%
Pain 'Always' Well Controlled	300+	73%	-	69%
Room and Bathroom 'Always' Clean	300+	65%	-	71%
Timely Help 'Always' Received	300+	65%	-	64%
Would Definitely Recommend Hospital	300+	61%	-	69%

NOTE: Hospital profiles are in alphabetical order by state, then city, then hospital within the city; Rankings exclude hospitals with less than 25 cases except for patient surveys which excludes hospitals with less than 100 cases; (a) 100–299 cases; (1) The number of cases is too small to be sure how well a hospital is performing; (2) The hospital indicated that the data submitted for this measure were based on a sample of cases; (3) Data was collected during a shorter time period (fewer quarters) than the maximum possible time for this measure; (4) Suppressed for one or more quarters by CMS; (5) No data is available from the hospital for this measure; (6) Fewer than 100 patients completed the HCAHPS survey. Use these rates with caution, as the number of surveys may be too low to reliably assess hospital performance; (7) Survey results are based on less than 12 months of data; (8) Survey results are not available for this reporting period; (9) No or very few patients were eligible for the HCAHPS survey. The scores shown, if any, reflect a very small number of surveys; (10) A state average was not calculated because too few hospitals in the state submitted data; (11) There were discrepancies in the data collection process; Please refer to the User's Guide for a full explanation of data.

Alegent Health Mercy Hospital

603 Rosary Drive
Corning, IA 50841
Phone: 641-322-3121
Fax: 641-322-3616
URL: www.alegent.com
Type: Critical Access Hospitals
Emergency Services: Yes
Ownership: Voluntary Non-Profit - Other
Beds: 22

Key Personnel:
Cardiac Laboratory. . . . . Rosy Bissell
Emergency Room . . . . Richard Alarid

Measure	Cases	This Hosp.	State Avg.	U.S. Avg.
Heart Attack Care				
ACE Inhibitor or ARB for LVSD[3]	0	-	96%	96%
Aspirin at Arrival[1,3]	1	100%	99%	99%
Aspirin at Discharge[1,3]	1	100%	99%	98%
Beta Blocker at Discharge[1,3]	1	100%	99%	98%
Fibrinolytic Medication Timing[3]	0	-	67%	55%
PCI Within 90 Minutes of Arrival[3]	0	-	94%	90%
Smoking Cessation Advice[3]	0	-	99%	99%
Chest Pain/Possible Heart Attack Care				
Aspirin at Arrival	-	-	96%	95%
Median Time to ECG (minutes)	-	-	7	8
Median Time to Transfer (minutes)	-	-	64	61
Fibrinolytic Medication Timing	-	-	45%	54%
Heart Failure Care				
ACE Inhibitor or ARB for LVSD[1]	4	100%	94%	94%
Discharge Instructions[1]	14	100%	86%	88%
Evaluation of LVS Function[1]	16	100%	95%	98%
Smoking Cessation Advice[1]	1	100%	96%	98%
Pneumonia Care				
Appropriate Initial Antibiotic[1,3]	8	100%	92%	92%
Blood Culture Timing[1,3]	3	100%	97%	96%
Influenza Vaccine[1,3]	2	100%	92%	91%
Initial Antibiotic Timing[1,3]	9	100%	97%	95%
Pneumococcal Vaccine[1,3]	8	100%	94%	93%
Smoking Cessation Advice[1,3]	4	100%	95%	97%
Surgical Care Improvement Project				
Appropriate VTP Within 24 Hours[1,3]	2	100%	92%	92%
Appropriate Hair Removal[1,3]	7	100%	100%	99%
Appropriate Beta Blocker Usage[5]	0	-	94%	93%
Controlled Postoperative Blood Glucose[3]	0	-	89%	93%
Prophylactic Antibiotic Timing[1,3]	6	100%	98%	97%
Prophylactic Antibiotic Timing (Outpatient)	-	-	94%	92%
Prophylactic Antibiotic Selection[1,3]	6	100%	98%	97%
Prophylactic Antibiotic Select. (Outpatient)	-	-	97%	94%
Prophylactic Antibiotic Stopped[1,3]	6	100%	95%	94%
Recommended VTP Ordered[1,3]	2	100%	93%	94%
Urinary Catheter Removal[1]	1	100%	91%	90%
Children's Asthma Care				
Received Systemic Corticosteroids	-	-	-	100%
Received Home Management Plan	-	-	-	71%
Received Reliever Medication	-	-	-	100%
Use of Medical Imaging				
Combination Abdominal CT Scan	-	-	0.163	0.191
Combination Chest CT Scan	-	-	0.060	0.054
Follow-up Mammogram/Ultrasound	-	-	8.1%	8.4%
MRI for Low Back Pain	-	-	30.2%	32.7%
Survey of Patients' Hospital Experiences				
Area Around Room 'Always' Quiet at Night[6]	<100	70%	-	58%
Doctors 'Always' Communicated Well[6]	<100	86%	-	80%
Home Recovery Information Given[6]	<100	84%	-	82%
Hospital Given 9 or 10 on 10 Point Scale[6]	<100	86%	-	67%
Meds 'Always' Explained Before Given[6]	<100	64%	-	60%
Nurses 'Always' Communicated Well[6]	<100	81%	-	76%
Pain 'Always' Well Controlled[6]	<100	76%	-	69%
Room and Bathroom 'Always' Clean[6]	<100	80%	-	71%
Timely Help 'Always' Received[6]	<100	77%	-	64%
Would Definitely Recommend Hospital	<100	83%	-	69%

Wayne County Hospital

417 South East Street
Corydon, IA 50060
Phone: 641-872-2260
Fax: 641-872-3116
Type: Critical Access Hospitals
Emergency Services: Yes
Ownership: Voluntary Non-Profit - Other
Beds: 28

Key Personnel:
CEO/President. . . . . Brian D Burnside
Chief of Medical Staff. . . . . Joel Baker
Coronary Care . . . . Martin Aronow
Operating Room. . . . . Carol Brown
Quality Assurance . . . . Kelli McCarty
Radiology. . . . . Louis K Madison
Emergency Room . . . . Daren PS

Measure	Cases	This Hosp.	State Avg.	U.S. Avg.
Heart Attack Care				
ACE Inhibitor or ARB for LVSD[3]	0	-	96%	96%
Aspirin at Arrival[1,3]	4	100%	99%	99%
Aspirin at Discharge[1,3]	3	100%	99%	98%
Beta Blocker at Discharge[1,3]	3	67%	99%	98%
Fibrinolytic Medication Timing[3]	0	-	67%	55%
PCI Within 90 Minutes of Arrival[3]	0	-	94%	90%
Smoking Cessation Advice[3]	0	-	99%	99%
Chest Pain/Possible Heart Attack Care				
Aspirin at Arrival	-	-	96%	95%
Median Time to ECG (minutes)	-	-	7	8
Median Time to Transfer (minutes)	-	-	64	61
Fibrinolytic Medication Timing	-	-	45%	54%
Heart Failure Care				
ACE Inhibitor or ARB for LVSD[1]	1	0%	94%	94%
Discharge Instructions[1]	12	92%	86%	88%
Evaluation of LVS Function[1]	13	77%	95%	98%
Smoking Cessation Advice	0	-	96%	98%
Pneumonia Care				
Appropriate Initial Antibiotic[1]	21	86%	92%	92%
Blood Culture Timing[1]	6	67%	97%	96%
Influenza Vaccine[1]	11	100%	92%	91%
Initial Antibiotic Timing[1]	23	91%	97%	95%
Pneumococcal Vaccine[1]	17	82%	94%	93%
Smoking Cessation Advice[1]	7	86%	95%	97%
Surgical Care Improvement Project				
Appropriate VTP Within 24 Hours[1,3]	12	100%	92%	92%
Appropriate Hair Removal[1,3]	18	100%	100%	99%
Appropriate Beta Blocker Usage[1,3]	5	100%	94%	93%
Controlled Postoperative Blood Glucose[5]	0	-	89%	93%
Prophylactic Antibiotic Timing[1,3]	16	88%	98%	97%
Prophylactic Antibiotic Timing (Outpatient)	-	-	94%	92%
Prophylactic Antibiotic Selection[1,3]	16	100%	98%	97%
Prophylactic Antibiotic Select. (Outpatient)	-	-	97%	94%
Prophylactic Antibiotic Stopped[1,3]	16	19%	95%	94%
Recommended VTP Ordered[1,3]	12	100%	93%	94%
Urinary Catheter Removal[1]	6	83%	91%	90%
Children's Asthma Care				
Received Systemic Corticosteroids	-	-	-	100%
Received Home Management Plan	-	-	-	71%
Received Reliever Medication	-	-	-	100%
Use of Medical Imaging				
Combination Abdominal CT Scan	-	-	0.163	0.191
Combination Chest CT Scan	-	-	0.060	0.054
Follow-up Mammogram/Ultrasound	-	-	8.1%	8.4%
MRI for Low Back Pain	-	-	30.2%	32.7%
Survey of Patients' Hospital Experiences				
Area Around Room 'Always' Quiet at Night[8]	-	-	-	58%
Doctors 'Always' Communicated Well[8]	-	-	-	80%
Home Recovery Information Given[8]	-	-	-	82%
Hospital Given 9 or 10 on 10 Point Scale[8]	-	-	-	67%
Meds 'Always' Explained Before Given[8]	-	-	-	60%
Nurses 'Always' Communicated Well[8]	-	-	-	76%
Pain 'Always' Well Controlled[8]	-	-	-	69%
Room and Bathroom 'Always' Clean[8]	-	-	-	71%
Timely Help 'Always' Received[8]	-	-	-	64%
Would Definitely Recommend Hospital[8]	-	-	-	69%

Alegent Health Mercy Hospital

800 Mercy Drive
Council Bluffs, IA 51503
Phone: 712-328-5000
Fax: 712-328-5088
URL: www.alegent.com/mercy
Type: Acute Care Hospitals
Emergency Services: Yes
Ownership: Voluntary Non-Profit - Church
Beds: 324

Key Personnel:
CEO/President. . . . . Wayne Sensor
Chief of Medical Staff. . . . . David Hanks, MD
Operating Room. . . . . Robin Allen
Quality Assurance . . . . Connie Blietz
Radiology. . . . . Matthew M Jaksha
Emergency Room . . . . Joe Hoagbin, MD

Measure	Cases	This Hosp.	State Avg.	U.S. Avg.
Heart Attack Care				
ACE Inhibitor or ARB for LVSD[1]	11	100%	96%	96%
Aspirin at Arrival	115	99%	99%	99%
Aspirin at Discharge	103	100%	99%	98%
Beta Blocker at Discharge	106	100%	99%	98%
Fibrinolytic Medication Timing	0	-	67%	55%
PCI Within 90 Minutes of Arrival	39	97%	94%	90%
Smoking Cessation Advice	44	100%	99%	99%
Chest Pain/Possible Heart Attack Care				
Aspirin at Arrival[1,3]	3	100%	96%	95%
Median Time to ECG (minutes)[1,3]	3	48	7	8
Median Time to Transfer (minutes)[5]	0	-	64	61
Fibrinolytic Medication Timing[3]	0	-	45%	54%
Heart Failure Care				
ACE Inhibitor or ARB for LVSD[1]	23	100%	94%	94%
Discharge Instructions	103	92%	86%	88%
Evaluation of LVS Function	132	99%	95%	98%
Smoking Cessation Advice	35	100%	96%	98%
Pneumonia Care				
Appropriate Initial Antibiotic	95	99%	92%	92%
Blood Culture Timing	137	100%	97%	96%
Influenza Vaccine	74	97%	92%	91%
Initial Antibiotic Timing	142	100%	97%	95%
Pneumococcal Vaccine	93	100%	94%	93%
Smoking Cessation Advice	62	100%	95%	97%
Surgical Care Improvement Project				
Appropriate VTP Within 24 Hours[2]	167	97%	92%	92%
Appropriate Hair Removal[2]	712	100%	100%	99%
Appropriate Beta Blocker Usage[2]	231	99%	94%	93%
Controlled Postoperative Blood Glucose[2]	0	-	89%	93%
Prophylactic Antibiotic Timing[2]	494	99%	98%	97%
Prophylactic Antibiotic Timing (Outpatient)	80	99%	94%	92%
Prophylactic Antibiotic Selection[2]	497	99%	98%	97%
Prophylactic Antibiotic Select. (Outpatient)	80	100%	97%	94%
Prophylactic Antibiotic Stopped[2]	480	99%	95%	94%
Recommended VTP Ordered[2]	167	98%	93%	94%
Urinary Catheter Removal[1,2]	8	100%	91%	90%
Children's Asthma Care				
Received Systemic Corticosteroids	-	-	-	100%
Received Home Management Plan	-	-	-	71%
Received Reliever Medication	-	-	-	100%
Use of Medical Imaging				
Combination Abdominal CT Scan	496	0.149	0.163	0.191
Combination Chest CT Scan	275	0.025	0.060	0.054
Follow-up Mammogram/Ultrasound	693	3.3%	8.1%	8.4%
MRI for Low Back Pain	130	34.6%	30.2%	32.7%
Survey of Patients' Hospital Experiences				
Area Around Room 'Always' Quiet at Night	300+	67%	-	58%
Doctors 'Always' Communicated Well	300+	79%	-	80%
Home Recovery Information Given	300+	88%	-	82%
Hospital Given 9 or 10 on 10 Point Scale	300+	74%	-	67%
Meds 'Always' Explained Before Given	300+	61%	-	60%
Nurses 'Always' Communicated Well	300+	80%	-	76%
Pain 'Always' Well Controlled	300+	73%	-	69%
Room and Bathroom 'Always' Clean	300+	72%	-	71%
Timely Help 'Always' Received	300+	61%	-	64%
Would Definitely Recommend Hospital	300+	79%	-	69%

NOTE: Hospital profiles are in alphabetical order by state, then city, then hospital within the city; Rankings exclude hospitals with less than 25 cases except for patient surveys which excludes hospitals with less than 100 cases; (a) 100–299 cases; (1) The number of cases is too small to be sure how well a hospital is performing; (2) The hospital indicated that the data submitted for this measure were based on a sample of cases; (3) Data was collected during a shorter time period (fewer quarters) than the maximum possible time for this measure; (4) Suppressed for one or more quarters by CMS; (5) No data is available from the hospital for this measure; (6) Fewer than 100 patients completed the HCAHPS survey. Use these rates with caution, as the number of surveys may be too low to reliably assess hospital performance; (7) Survey results are based on less than 12 months of data; (8) Survey results are not available for this reporting period; (9) No or very few patients were eligible for the HCAHPS survey. The scores shown, if any, reflect a very small number of surveys; (10) A state average was not calculated because too few hospitals in the state submitted data; (11) There were discrepancies in the data collection process; Please refer to the User's Guide for a full explanation of data.

Jennie Edmundson Hospital

933 East Pierce Street Phone: 712-396-6000
Council Bluffs, IA 51503 Fax: 712-396-7617
URL: www.bestcare.org
Type: Acute Care Hospitals Emergency Services: Yes
Ownership: Voluntary Non-Profit - Private Beds: 118

Key Personnel:
CEO/President. . . . . Steven P Baumert
Chief of Medical Staff . . . . John A Okerbloom, MD
Operating Room. . . . . Patrick Ahrens, RN
Quality Assurance . . . . Kathy Mashanic
Radiology. . . . . Jason A Arthur

Measure	Cases	This Hosp.	State Avg.	U.S. Avg.
Heart Attack Care				
ACE Inhibitor or ARB for LVSD[1]	20	100%	96%	96%
Aspirin at Arrival	107	98%	99%	99%
Aspirin at Discharge	93	97%	99%	98%
Beta Blocker at Discharge	91	98%	99%	98%
Fibrinolytic Medication Timing	0	-	67%	55%
PCI Within 90 Minutes of Arrival[1]	21	86%	94%	90%
Smoking Cessation Advice	29	97%	99%	99%
Chest Pain/Possible Heart Attack Care				
Aspirin at Arrival[5]	0	-	96%	95%
Median Time to ECG (minutes)[5]	0	-	7	8
Median Time to Transfer (minutes)[5]	0	-	64	61
Fibrinolytic Medication Timing[5]	0	-	45%	54%
Heart Failure Care				
ACE Inhibitor or ARB for LVSD	39	100%	94%	94%
Discharge Instructions	113	100%	86%	88%
Evaluation of LVS Function	138	94%	95%	98%
Smoking Cessation Advice[1]	23	87%	96%	98%
Pneumonia Care				
Appropriate Initial Antibiotic	88	90%	92%	92%
Blood Culture Timing	159	97%	97%	96%
Influenza Vaccine	111	80%	92%	91%
Initial Antibiotic Timing	197	95%	97%	95%
Pneumococcal Vaccine	164	93%	94%	93%
Smoking Cessation Advice	57	88%	95%	97%
Surgical Care Improvement Project				
Appropriate VTP Within 24 Hours	146	76%	92%	92%
Appropriate Hair Removal	468	98%	100%	99%
Appropriate Beta Blocker Usage	143	100%	94%	93%
Controlled Postoperative Blood Glucose	0	-	89%	93%
Prophylactic Antibiotic Timing	369	96%	98%	97%
Prophylactic Antibiotic Timing (Outpatient)	214	92%	94%	92%
Prophylactic Antibiotic Selection	368	95%	98%	97%
Prophylactic Antibiotic Select. (Outpatient)	203	94%	97%	94%
Prophylactic Antibiotic Stopped	368	92%	95%	94%
Recommended VTP Ordered	146	80%	93%	94%
Urinary Catheter Removal	128	94%	91%	90%
Children's Asthma Care				
Received Systemic Corticosteroids	-	-	-	100%
Received Home Management Plan	-	-	-	71%
Received Reliever Medication	-	-	-	100%
Use of Medical Imaging				
Combination Abdominal CT Scan	573	0.110	0.163	0.191
Combination Chest CT Scan	396	0.013	0.060	0.054
Follow-up Mammogram/Ultrasound	1,046	10.4%	8.1%	8.4%
MRI for Low Back Pain	180	32.8%	30.2%	32.7%
Survey of Patients' Hospital Experiences				
Area Around Room 'Always' Quiet at Night	300+	57%	-	58%
Doctors 'Always' Communicated Well	300+	85%	-	80%
Home Recovery Information Given	300+	87%	-	82%
Hospital Given 9 or 10 on 10 Point Scale	300+	73%	-	67%
Meds 'Always' Explained Before Given	300+	65%	-	60%
Nurses 'Always' Communicated Well	300+	82%	-	76%
Pain 'Always' Well Controlled	300+	71%	-	69%
Room and Bathroom 'Always' Clean	300+	73%	-	71%
Timely Help 'Always' Received	300+	68%	-	64%
Would Definitely Recommend Hospital	300+	74%	-	69%

Regional Health Services of Howard County

235 8th Avenue West Phone: 563-547-2101
Cresco, IA 52136 Fax: 563-547-4223
URL: www.rhshc.com
Type: Critical Access Hospitals Emergency Services: Yes
Ownership: Government - Local Beds: 32

Key Personnel:
CEO/President. . . . . David J Hartberg
Chief of Medical Staff . . . . Kathy Strike
Operating Room. . . . . Julie Andera
Quality Assurance . . . . Lois Reinhart

Measure	Cases	This Hosp.	State Avg.	U.S. Avg.
Heart Attack Care				
ACE Inhibitor or ARB for LVSD[5]	0	-	96%	96%
Aspirin at Arrival[5]	0	-	99%	99%
Aspirin at Discharge[5]	0	-	99%	98%
Beta Blocker at Discharge[5]	0	-	99%	98%
Fibrinolytic Medication Timing[5]	0	-	67%	55%
PCI Within 90 Minutes of Arrival[5]	0	-	94%	90%
Smoking Cessation Advice[5]	0	-	99%	99%
Chest Pain/Possible Heart Attack Care				
Aspirin at Arrival	-	-	96%	95%
Median Time to ECG (minutes)	-	-	7	8
Median Time to Transfer (minutes)	-	-	64	61
Fibrinolytic Medication Timing	-	-	45%	54%
Heart Failure Care				
ACE Inhibitor or ARB for LVSD[1,3]	2	100%	94%	94%
Discharge Instructions[1,3]	5	20%	86%	88%
Evaluation of LVS Function[1,3]	11	45%	95%	98%
Smoking Cessation Advice[1,3]	1	100%	96%	98%
Pneumonia Care				
Appropriate Initial Antibiotic[1,3]	2	100%	92%	92%
Blood Culture Timing[1,3]	1	100%	97%	96%
Influenza Vaccine[1,3]	2	100%	92%	91%
Initial Antibiotic Timing[1,3]	5	100%	97%	95%
Pneumococcal Vaccine[1,3]	6	50%	94%	93%
Smoking Cessation Advice[3]	0	-	95%	97%
Surgical Care Improvement Project				
Appropriate VTP Within 24 Hours[5]	0	-	92%	92%
Appropriate Hair Removal[5]	0	-	100%	99%
Appropriate Beta Blocker Usage[5]	0	-	94%	93%
Controlled Postoperative Blood Glucose[5]	0	-	89%	93%
Prophylactic Antibiotic Timing[5]	0	-	98%	97%
Prophylactic Antibiotic Timing (Outpatient)	-	-	94%	92%
Prophylactic Antibiotic Selection[5]	0	-	98%	97%
Prophylactic Antibiotic Select. (Outpatient)	-	-	97%	94%
Prophylactic Antibiotic Stopped[5]	0	-	95%	94%
Recommended VTP Ordered[5]	0	-	93%	94%
Urinary Catheter Removal[5]	0	-	91%	90%
Children's Asthma Care				
Received Systemic Corticosteroids	-	-	-	100%
Received Home Management Plan	-	-	-	71%
Received Reliever Medication	-	-	-	100%
Use of Medical Imaging				
Combination Abdominal CT Scan	-	-	0.163	0.191
Combination Chest CT Scan	-	-	0.060	0.054
Follow-up Mammogram/Ultrasound	-	-	8.1%	8.4%
MRI for Low Back Pain	-	-	30.2%	32.7%
Survey of Patients' Hospital Experiences				
Area Around Room 'Always' Quiet at Night[8]	-	-	-	58%
Doctors 'Always' Communicated Well[8]	-	-	-	80%
Home Recovery Information Given[8]	-	-	-	82%
Hospital Given 9 or 10 on 10 Point Scale[8]	-	-	-	67%
Meds 'Always' Explained Before Given[8]	-	-	-	60%
Nurses 'Always' Communicated Well[8]	-	-	-	76%
Pain 'Always' Well Controlled[8]	-	-	-	69%
Room and Bathroom 'Always' Clean[8]	-	-	-	71%
Timely Help 'Always' Received[8]	-	-	-	64%
Would Definitely Recommend Hospital[8]	-	-	-	69%

Greater Regional Medical Center

1700 West Townline Road Phone: 641-782-7091
Creston, IA 50801 Fax: 641-782-3866
Type: Critical Access Hospitals Emergency Services: Yes
Ownership: Voluntary Non-Profit - Other Beds: 25

Key Personnel:
CEO/President. . . . . Monte Neitzel
Chief of Medical Staff . . . . Steve Reeves, MD
Infection Control. . . . . Nancy Anthony
Quality Assurance . . . . Kenya Heffner
Radiology. . . . . Todd Kucera, MD

Measure	Cases	This Hosp.	State Avg.	U.S. Avg.
Heart Attack Care				
ACE Inhibitor or ARB for LVSD[3]	0	-	96%	96%
Aspirin at Arrival[1,3]	6	100%	99%	99%
Aspirin at Discharge[1,3]	4	100%	99%	98%
Beta Blocker at Discharge[1,3]	4	100%	99%	98%
Fibrinolytic Medication Timing[3]	0	-	67%	55%
PCI Within 90 Minutes of Arrival[3]	0	-	94%	90%
Smoking Cessation Advice[3]	0	-	99%	99%
Chest Pain/Possible Heart Attack Care				
Aspirin at Arrival	-	-	96%	95%
Median Time to ECG (minutes)	-	-	7	8
Median Time to Transfer (minutes)	-	-	64	61
Fibrinolytic Medication Timing	-	-	45%	54%
Heart Failure Care				
ACE Inhibitor or ARB for LVSD[1,2]	5	100%	94%	94%
Discharge Instructions[1,2]	15	87%	86%	88%
Evaluation of LVS Function[1,2]	16	69%	95%	98%
Smoking Cessation Advice[1,2]	1	100%	96%	98%
Pneumonia Care				
Appropriate Initial Antibiotic[1]	20	85%	92%	92%
Blood Culture Timing[1]	9	100%	97%	96%
Influenza Vaccine[1]	16	62%	92%	91%
Initial Antibiotic Timing	29	93%	97%	95%
Pneumococcal Vaccine[1]	23	70%	94%	93%
Smoking Cessation Advice[1]	6	100%	95%	97%
Surgical Care Improvement Project				
Appropriate VTP Within 24 Hours[1]	15	93%	92%	92%
Appropriate Hair Removal	32	88%	100%	99%
Appropriate Beta Blocker Usage[5]	0	-	94%	93%
Controlled Postoperative Blood Glucose	0	-	89%	93%
Prophylactic Antibiotic Timing[1]	17	94%	98%	97%
Prophylactic Antibiotic Timing (Outpatient)	-	-	94%	92%
Prophylactic Antibiotic Selection[1]	18	83%	98%	97%
Prophylactic Antibiotic Select. (Outpatient)	-	-	97%	94%
Prophylactic Antibiotic Stopped[1]	17	100%	95%	94%
Recommended VTP Ordered[1]	16	88%	93%	94%
Urinary Catheter Removal[1]	1	100%	91%	90%
Children's Asthma Care				
Received Systemic Corticosteroids	-	-	-	100%
Received Home Management Plan	-	-	-	71%
Received Reliever Medication	-	-	-	100%
Use of Medical Imaging				
Combination Abdominal CT Scan	-	-	0.163	0.191
Combination Chest CT Scan	-	-	0.060	0.054
Follow-up Mammogram/Ultrasound	-	-	8.1%	8.4%
MRI for Low Back Pain	-	-	30.2%	32.7%
Survey of Patients' Hospital Experiences				
Area Around Room 'Always' Quiet at Night	300+	62%	-	58%
Doctors 'Always' Communicated Well	300+	84%	-	80%
Home Recovery Information Given	300+	80%	-	82%
Hospital Given 9 or 10 on 10 Point Scale	300+	70%	-	67%
Meds 'Always' Explained Before Given	300+	68%	-	60%
Nurses 'Always' Communicated Well	300+	82%	-	76%
Pain 'Always' Well Controlled	300+	69%	-	69%
Room and Bathroom 'Always' Clean	300+	78%	-	71%
Timely Help 'Always' Received	300+	76%	-	64%
Would Definitely Recommend Hospital	300+	67%	-	69%

NOTE: Hospital profiles are in alphabetical order by state, then city, then hospital within the city; Rankings exclude hospitals with less than 25 cases except for patient surveys which excludes hospitals with less than 100 cases; (a) 100–299 cases; (1) The number of cases is too small to be sure how well a hospital is performing; (2) The hospital indicated that the data submitted for this measure were based on a sample of cases; (3) Data was collected during a shorter time period (fewer quarters) than the maximum possible time for this measure; (4) Suppressed for one or more quarters by CMS; (5) No data is available from the hospital for this measure; (6) Fewer than 100 patients completed the HCAHPS survey. Use these rates with caution, as the number of surveys may be too low to reliably assess hospital performance; (7) Survey results are based on less than 12 months of data; (8) Survey results are not available for this reporting period; (9) No or very few patients were eligible for the HCAHPS survey. The scores shown, if any, reflect a very small number of surveys; (10) A state average was not calculated because too few hospitals in the state submitted data; (11) There were discrepancies in the data collection process; Please refer to the User's Guide for a full explanation of data.

Genesis Medical Center - Davenport

1227 East Rusholme Street — Phone: 563-421-1000
Davenport, IA 52803 — Fax: 563-421-6279
URL: www.genesishealth.com
Type: Acute Care Hospitals — Emergency Services: Yes
Ownership: Voluntary Non-Profit - Other — Beds: 502

Key Personnel:
CEO/President. . . . . Doug Cropper
Chief of Medical Staff . . . . Frank Claudy MD
Infection Control. . . . . Lisa Caffery
Operating Room. . . . . Rob Nelson MD
Pediatric Ambulatory Care . . . . . . Cindy Chapman
Quality Assurance . . . . Lori Crane
Radiology. . . . . Janet Stensrud

Measure	Cases	This Hosp.	State Avg.	U.S. Avg.
Heart Attack Care				
ACE Inhibitor or ARB for LVSD[2]	63	97%	96%	96%
Aspirin at Arrival[2]	147	99%	99%	99%
Aspirin at Discharge[2]	297	100%	99%	98%
Beta Blocker at Discharge[2]	282	99%	99%	98%
Fibrinolytic Medication Timing[2]	0	-	67%	55%
PCI Within 90 Minutes of Arrival[2]	26	96%	94%	90%
Smoking Cessation Advice[2]	102	100%	99%	99%
Chest Pain/Possible Heart Attack Care				
Aspirin at Arrival[1]	20	85%	96%	95%
Median Time to ECG (minutes)[1]	20	4	7	8
Median Time to Transfer (minutes)[5]	0	-	64	61
Fibrinolytic Medication Timing[5]	0	-	45%	54%
Heart Failure Care				
ACE Inhibitor or ARB for LVSD[2]	103	98%	94%	94%
Discharge Instructions[2]	239	90%	86%	88%
Evaluation of LVS Function[2]	305	100%	95%	98%
Smoking Cessation Advice[2]	55	100%	96%	98%
Pneumonia Care				
Appropriate Initial Antibiotic[2]	79	100%	92%	92%
Blood Culture Timing[2]	143	99%	97%	96%
Influenza Vaccine[2]	102	95%	92%	91%
Initial Antibiotic Timing[2]	160	96%	97%	95%
Pneumococcal Vaccine[2]	143	94%	94%	93%
Smoking Cessation Advice[2]	72	99%	95%	97%
Surgical Care Improvement Project				
Appropriate VTP Within 24 Hours[2]	177	91%	92%	92%
Appropriate Hair Removal[2]	666	100%	100%	99%
Appropriate Beta Blocker Usage[2]	237	95%	94%	93%
Controlled Postoperative Blood Glucose[2]	159	94%	89%	93%
Prophylactic Antibiotic Timing[2]	493	99%	98%	97%
Prophylactic Antibiotic Timing (Outpatient)	654	96%	94%	92%
Prophylactic Antibiotic Selection[2]	503	98%	98%	97%
Prophylactic Antibiotic Select. (Outpatient)	650	97%	97%	94%
Prophylactic Antibiotic Stopped[2]	470	94%	95%	94%
Recommended VTP Ordered[2]	177	92%	93%	94%
Urinary Catheter Removal[2]	109	91%	91%	90%
Children's Asthma Care				
Received Systemic Corticosteroids	-	-	-	100%
Received Home Management Plan	-	-	-	71%
Received Reliever Medication	-	-	-	100%
Use of Medical Imaging				
Combination Abdominal CT Scan	1,171	0.033	0.163	0.191
Combination Chest CT Scan	1,200	0.016	0.060	0.054
Follow-up Mammogram/Ultrasound	1,620	10.2%	8.1%	8.4%
MRI for Low Back Pain	135	28.1%	30.2%	32.7%
Survey of Patients' Hospital Experiences				
Area Around Room 'Always' Quiet at Night	300+	54%	-	58%
Doctors 'Always' Communicated Well	300+	79%	-	80%
Home Recovery Information Given	300+	81%	-	82%
Hospital Given 9 or 10 on 10 Point Scale	300+	69%	-	67%
Meds 'Always' Explained Before Given	300+	60%	-	60%
Nurses 'Always' Communicated Well	300+	78%	-	76%
Pain 'Always' Well Controlled	300+	70%	-	69%
Room and Bathroom 'Always' Clean	300+	71%	-	71%
Timely Help 'Always' Received	300+	64%	-	64%
Would Definitely Recommend Hospital	300+	75%	-	69%

Winneshiek Medical Center

901 Montgomery Street — Phone: 563-382-2911
Decorah, IA 52101 — Fax: 563-387-3102
URL: www.winmedical.org
Type: Critical Access Hospitals — Emergency Services: Yes
Ownership: Voluntary Non-Profit - Other — Beds: 83

Key Personnel:
CEO/President. . . . . Ben Grimstad
Chief of Medical Staff . . . . Kurt A Swanson, MD
Infection Control. . . . . Brenda Schwan, RN
Operating Room. . . . . Mary Sender
Quality Assurance . . . . Linda Klimesh
Radiology. . . . . David Jensen
Emergency Room . . . . Tudy Belay

Measure	Cases	This Hosp.	State Avg.	U.S. Avg.
Heart Attack Care				
ACE Inhibitor or ARB for LVSD[1]	1	100%	96%	96%
Aspirin at Arrival[1]	5	100%	99%	99%
Aspirin at Discharge[1]	1	100%	99%	98%
Beta Blocker at Discharge[1]	2	100%	99%	98%
Fibrinolytic Medication Timing	0	-	67%	55%
PCI Within 90 Minutes of Arrival	0	-	94%	90%
Smoking Cessation Advice	0	-	99%	99%
Chest Pain/Possible Heart Attack Care				
Aspirin at Arrival	-	-	96%	95%
Median Time to ECG (minutes)	-	-	7	8
Median Time to Transfer (minutes)	-	-	64	61
Fibrinolytic Medication Timing	-	-	45%	54%
Heart Failure Care				
ACE Inhibitor or ARB for LVSD[1]	12	100%	94%	94%
Discharge Instructions	26	100%	86%	88%
Evaluation of LVS Function	45	100%	95%	98%
Smoking Cessation Advice[1]	2	100%	96%	98%
Pneumonia Care				
Appropriate Initial Antibiotic	33	97%	92%	92%
Blood Culture Timing	59	100%	97%	96%
Influenza Vaccine	37	100%	92%	91%
Initial Antibiotic Timing	67	100%	97%	95%
Pneumococcal Vaccine	68	100%	94%	93%
Smoking Cessation Advice[1]	4	100%	95%	97%
Surgical Care Improvement Project				
Appropriate VTP Within 24 Hours[1,3]	3	67%	92%	92%
Appropriate Hair Removal[1,3]	4	100%	100%	99%
Appropriate Beta Blocker Usage[5]	0	-	94%	93%
Controlled Postoperative Blood Glucose[3]	0	-	89%	93%
Prophylactic Antibiotic Timing[1,3]	3	67%	98%	97%
Prophylactic Antibiotic Timing (Outpatient)	-	-	94%	92%
Prophylactic Antibiotic Selection[1,3]	3	67%	98%	97%
Prophylactic Antibiotic Select. (Outpatient)	-	-	97%	94%
Prophylactic Antibiotic Stopped[1,3]	3	67%	95%	94%
Recommended VTP Ordered[1,3]	3	67%	93%	94%
Urinary Catheter Removal[1,3]	1	100%	91%	90%
Children's Asthma Care				
Received Systemic Corticosteroids	-	-	-	100%
Received Home Management Plan	-	-	-	71%
Received Reliever Medication	-	-	-	100%
Use of Medical Imaging				
Combination Abdominal CT Scan	-	-	0.163	0.191
Combination Chest CT Scan	-	-	0.060	0.054
Follow-up Mammogram/Ultrasound	-	-	8.1%	8.4%
MRI for Low Back Pain	-	-	30.2%	32.7%
Survey of Patients' Hospital Experiences				
Area Around Room 'Always' Quiet at Night[8]	-	-	-	58%
Doctors 'Always' Communicated Well[8]	-	-	-	80%
Home Recovery Information Given[8]	-	-	-	82%
Hospital Given 9 or 10 on 10 Point Scale[8]	-	-	-	67%
Meds 'Always' Explained Before Given[8]	-	-	-	60%
Nurses 'Always' Communicated Well[8]	-	-	-	76%
Pain 'Always' Well Controlled[8]	-	-	-	69%
Room and Bathroom 'Always' Clean[8]	-	-	-	71%
Timely Help 'Always' Received[8]	-	-	-	64%
Would Definitely Recommend Hospital[8]	-	-	-	69%

Crawford County Memorial Hospital

2020 First Avenue South — Phone: 712-263-5021
Denison, IA 51442 — Fax: 712-263-1711
E-mail: edgast@ccmhia.com
URL: www.ccmhia.com
Type: Critical Access Hospitals — Emergency Services: Yes
Ownership: Voluntary Non-Profit - Other — Beds: 72

Key Personnel:
CEO/President. . . . . Mark Rinehardt
Chief of Medical Staff . . . . John Ingram
Operating Room. . . . . Linda Christensen
Quality Assurance . . . . Nancy Bielenberg
Radiology. . . . . Kari Boyens
Emergency Room . . . . Laurie Powers

Measure	Cases	This Hosp.	State Avg.	U.S. Avg.
Heart Attack Care				
ACE Inhibitor or ARB for LVSD[1,3]	2	50%	96%	96%
Aspirin at Arrival[1,3]	1	100%	99%	99%
Aspirin at Discharge[1,3]	1	100%	99%	98%
Beta Blocker at Discharge[1,3]	3	100%	99%	98%
Fibrinolytic Medication Timing[5]	0	-	67%	55%
PCI Within 90 Minutes of Arrival[5]	0	-	94%	90%
Smoking Cessation Advice[3]	0	-	99%	99%
Chest Pain/Possible Heart Attack Care				
Aspirin at Arrival	-	-	96%	95%
Median Time to ECG (minutes)	-	-	7	8
Median Time to Transfer (minutes)	-	-	64	61
Fibrinolytic Medication Timing	-	-	45%	54%
Heart Failure Care				
ACE Inhibitor or ARB for LVSD[1]	4	75%	94%	94%
Discharge Instructions[1]	11	64%	86%	88%
Evaluation of LVS Function[1]	22	68%	95%	98%
Smoking Cessation Advice	0	-	96%	98%
Pneumonia Care				
Appropriate Initial Antibiotic	25	96%	92%	92%
Blood Culture Timing[1]	21	100%	97%	96%
Influenza Vaccine[1]	20	85%	92%	91%
Initial Antibiotic Timing	37	97%	97%	95%
Pneumococcal Vaccine	27	93%	94%	93%
Smoking Cessation Advice[1]	8	100%	95%	97%
Surgical Care Improvement Project				
Appropriate VTP Within 24 Hours[5]	0	-	92%	92%
Appropriate Hair Removal[5]	0	-	100%	99%
Appropriate Beta Blocker Usage[5]	0	-	94%	93%
Controlled Postoperative Blood Glucose[5]	0	-	89%	93%
Prophylactic Antibiotic Timing[5]	0	-	98%	97%
Prophylactic Antibiotic Timing (Outpatient)	-	-	94%	92%
Prophylactic Antibiotic Selection[5]	0	-	98%	97%
Prophylactic Antibiotic Select. (Outpatient)	-	-	97%	94%
Prophylactic Antibiotic Stopped[5]	0	-	95%	94%
Recommended VTP Ordered[5]	0	-	93%	94%
Urinary Catheter Removal[5]	0	-	91%	90%
Children's Asthma Care				
Received Systemic Corticosteroids	-	-	-	100%
Received Home Management Plan	-	-	-	71%
Received Reliever Medication	-	-	-	100%
Use of Medical Imaging				
Combination Abdominal CT Scan	-	-	0.163	0.191
Combination Chest CT Scan	-	-	0.060	0.054
Follow-up Mammogram/Ultrasound	-	-	8.1%	8.4%
MRI for Low Back Pain	-	-	30.2%	32.7%
Survey of Patients' Hospital Experiences				
Area Around Room 'Always' Quiet at Night[8]	-	-	-	58%
Doctors 'Always' Communicated Well[8]	-	-	-	80%
Home Recovery Information Given[8]	-	-	-	82%
Hospital Given 9 or 10 on 10 Point Scale[8]	-	-	-	67%
Meds 'Always' Explained Before Given[8]	-	-	-	60%
Nurses 'Always' Communicated Well[8]	-	-	-	76%
Pain 'Always' Well Controlled[8]	-	-	-	69%
Room and Bathroom 'Always' Clean[8]	-	-	-	71%
Timely Help 'Always' Received[8]	-	-	-	64%
Would Definitely Recommend Hospital[8]	-	-	-	69%

NOTE: Hospital profiles are in alphabetical order by state, then city, then hospital within the city; Rankings exclude hospitals with less than 25 cases except for patient surveys which excludes hospitals with less than 100 cases; (a) 100–299 cases; (1) The number of cases is too small to be sure how well a hospital is performing; (2) The hospital indicated that the data submitted for this measure were based on a sample of cases; (3) Data was collected during a shorter time period (fewer quarters) than the maximum possible time for this measure; (4) Suppressed for one or more quarters by CMS; (5) No data is available from the hospital for this measure; (6) Fewer than 100 patients completed the HCAHPS survey. Use these rates with caution, as the number of surveys may be too low to reliably assess hospital performance; (7) Survey results are based on less than 12 months of data; (8) Survey results are not available for this reporting period; (9) No or very few patients were eligible for the HCAHPS survey. The scores shown, if any, reflect a very small number of surveys; (10) A state average was not calculated because too few hospitals in the state submitted data; (11) There were discrepancies in the data collection process; Please refer to the User's Guide for a full explanation of data.

Broadlawns Medical Center

1801 Hickman Road, Des Moines, IA 50314
Phone: 515-282-2200
Fax: 515-282-5785
E-mail: externalrelations@broadlawns.org
URL: www.broadlawns.org
Type: Acute Care Hospitals
Emergency Services: Yes
Ownership: Voluntary Non-Profit - Other
Beds: 200

Key Personnel:

CEO/President. . . . . Jody Jenner, II
Chief of Medical Staff . . . . Vincent Mandracchia, MD
Operating Room. . . . . Dapka Baccam
Pediatric Ambulatory Care . . . . . . Scott Barron, DO
Quality Assurance . . . . Kay Brom
Radiology. . . . . Dwight Rafferty, MD
Anesthesiology. . . . . Stephen Stefani, MD
Emergency Room . . . . Jim Cummings, MD

Measure	Cases	This Hosp.	State Avg.	U.S. Avg.
Heart Attack Care				
ACE Inhibitor or ARB for LVSD[1]	1	100%	96%	96%
Aspirin at Arrival[1]	3	100%	99%	99%
Aspirin at Discharge[1]	4	100%	99%	98%
Beta Blocker at Discharge[1]	4	100%	99%	98%
Fibrinolytic Medication Timing	0	-	67%	55%
PCI Within 90 Minutes of Arrival	0	-	94%	90%
Smoking Cessation Advice[1]	3	100%	99%	99%
Chest Pain/Possible Heart Attack Care				
Aspirin at Arrival	52	98%	96%	95%
Median Time to ECG (minutes)	54	12	7	8
Median Time to Transfer (minutes)[1]	5	46	64	61
Fibrinolytic Medication Timing	0	-	45%	54%
Heart Failure Care				
ACE Inhibitor or ARB for LVSD[1]	16	100%	94%	94%
Discharge Instructions	36	69%	86%	88%
Evaluation of LVS Function	44	98%	95%	98%
Smoking Cessation Advice[1]	20	95%	96%	98%
Pneumonia Care				
Appropriate Initial Antibiotic	62	92%	92%	92%
Blood Culture Timing	57	98%	97%	96%
Influenza Vaccine	27	81%	92%	91%
Initial Antibiotic Timing	72	94%	97%	95%
Pneumococcal Vaccine[1]	16	75%	94%	93%
Smoking Cessation Advice	60	100%	95%	97%
Surgical Care Improvement Project				
Appropriate VTP Within 24 Hours	50	92%	92%	92%
Appropriate Hair Removal	74	100%	100%	99%
Appropriate Beta Blocker Usage[1]	12	58%	94%	93%
Controlled Postoperative Blood Glucose	0	-	89%	93%
Prophylactic Antibiotic Timing	41	93%	98%	97%
Prophylactic Antibiotic Timing (Outpatient)	59	90%	94%	92%
Prophylactic Antibiotic Selection	41	93%	98%	97%
Prophylactic Antibiotic Select. (Outpatient)	58	100%	97%	94%
Prophylactic Antibiotic Stopped	39	95%	95%	94%
Recommended VTP Ordered	50	94%	93%	94%
Urinary Catheter Removal[1]	22	95%	91%	90%
Children's Asthma Care				
Received Systemic Corticosteroids	-	-	-	100%
Received Home Management Plan	-	-	-	71%
Received Reliever Medication	-	-	-	100%
Use of Medical Imaging				
Combination Abdominal CT Scan	72	0.042	0.163	0.191
Combination Chest CT Scan[1]	63	0.175	0.060	0.054
Follow-up Mammogram/Ultrasound	206	29.6%	8.1%	8.4%
MRI for Low Back Pain[1]	5	20.0%	30.2%	32.7%
Survey of Patients' Hospital Experiences				
Area Around Room 'Always' Quiet at Night	300+	61%	-	58%
Doctors 'Always' Communicated Well	300+	80%	-	80%
Home Recovery Information Given	300+	83%	-	82%
Hospital Given 9 or 10 on 10 Point Scale	300+	63%	-	67%
Meds 'Always' Explained Before Given	300+	61%	-	60%
Nurses 'Always' Communicated Well	300+	76%	-	76%
Pain 'Always' Well Controlled	300+	71%	-	69%
Room and Bathroom 'Always' Clean	300+	66%	-	71%
Timely Help 'Always' Received	300+	61%	-	64%
Would Definitely Recommend Hospital	300+	68%	-	69%

Iowa Lutheran Hospital

700 East University Avenue, Des Moines, IA 50316
Phone: 515-263-5612
Fax: 515-241-5994
URL: ihsdesmoines.org
Type: Acute Care Hospitals
Emergency Services: No
Ownership: Voluntary Non-Profit - Private
Beds: 465

Key Personnel:

CEO/President. . . . . Eric Crowell
Chief of Medical Staff . . . . Steve Stephenson, DO
Operating Room. . . . . Karen Powell
Quality Assurance . . . . Deb Moyer
Radiology. . . . . Kent S Quinn, MD
Emergency Room . . . . Pam Ballard
Patient Relations . . . . Vicki Berberich

Measure	Cases	This Hosp.	State Avg.	U.S. Avg.
Heart Attack Care				
ACE Inhibitor or ARB for LVSD[1,2]	16	94%	96%	96%
Aspirin at Arrival[2]	121	98%	99%	99%
Aspirin at Discharge[2]	116	100%	99%	98%
Beta Blocker at Discharge[2]	112	98%	99%	98%
Fibrinolytic Medication Timing[2]	0	-	67%	55%
PCI Within 90 Minutes of Arrival[2]	27	85%	94%	90%
Smoking Cessation Advice[2]	33	97%	99%	99%
Chest Pain/Possible Heart Attack Care				
Aspirin at Arrival[1]	3	100%	96%	95%
Median Time to ECG (minutes)[1]	3	24	7	8
Median Time to Transfer (minutes)[5]	0	-	64	61
Fibrinolytic Medication Timing[5]	0	-	45%	54%
Heart Failure Care				
ACE Inhibitor or ARB for LVSD[2]	60	98%	94%	94%
Discharge Instructions[2]	159	55%	86%	88%
Evaluation of LVS Function[2]	191	99%	95%	98%
Smoking Cessation Advice[2]	26	100%	96%	98%
Pneumonia Care				
Appropriate Initial Antibiotic[2]	86	94%	92%	92%
Blood Culture Timing[2]	92	92%	97%	96%
Influenza Vaccine[2]	74	97%	92%	91%
Initial Antibiotic Timing[2]	115	100%	97%	95%
Pneumococcal Vaccine[2]	120	93%	94%	93%
Smoking Cessation Advice[2]	47	89%	95%	97%
Surgical Care Improvement Project				
Appropriate VTP Within 24 Hours[2]	125	82%	92%	92%
Appropriate Hair Removal[2]	431	100%	100%	99%
Appropriate Beta Blocker Usage[2]	121	99%	94%	93%
Controlled Postoperative Blood Glucose[2]	86	79%	89%	93%
Prophylactic Antibiotic Timing[2]	299	98%	98%	97%
Prophylactic Antibiotic Timing (Outpatient)	226	89%	94%	92%
Prophylactic Antibiotic Selection[2]	304	98%	98%	97%
Prophylactic Antibiotic Select. (Outpatient)	217	97%	97%	94%
Prophylactic Antibiotic Stopped[2]	271	95%	95%	94%
Recommended VTP Ordered[2]	129	82%	93%	94%
Urinary Catheter Removal[2]	82	96%	91%	90%
Children's Asthma Care				
Received Systemic Corticosteroids	-	-	-	100%
Received Home Management Plan	-	-	-	71%
Received Reliever Medication	-	-	-	100%
Use of Medical Imaging				
Combination Abdominal CT Scan	462	0.058	0.163	0.191
Combination Chest CT Scan	245	0.171	0.060	0.054
Follow-up Mammogram/Ultrasound	1,043	26.8%	8.1%	8.4%
MRI for Low Back Pain	102	29.4%	30.2%	32.7%
Survey of Patients' Hospital Experiences				
Area Around Room 'Always' Quiet at Night	300+	56%	-	58%
Doctors 'Always' Communicated Well	300+	75%	-	80%
Home Recovery Information Given	300+	84%	-	82%
Hospital Given 9 or 10 on 10 Point Scale	300+	70%	-	67%
Meds 'Always' Explained Before Given	300+	58%	-	60%
Nurses 'Always' Communicated Well	300+	74%	-	76%
Pain 'Always' Well Controlled	300+	67%	-	69%
Room and Bathroom 'Always' Clean	300+	72%	-	71%
Timely Help 'Always' Received	300+	60%	-	64%
Would Definitely Recommend Hospital	300+	75%	-	69%

Iowa Methodist Medical Center

1200 Pleasant Street, Des Moines, IA 50309
Phone: 515-241-6212
Fax: 515-241-8580
URL: www.iowahealth.org
Type: Acute Care Hospitals
Emergency Services: Yes
Ownership: Voluntary Non-Profit - Private
Beds: 373

Key Personnel:

CEO/President. . . . . Eric Crowell
Cardiac Laboratory. . . . . Steve House
Chief of Medical Staff . . . . Dr Josephson
Emergency Room . . . . Lynda Schumaker

Measure	Cases	This Hosp.	State Avg.	U.S. Avg.
Heart Attack Care				
ACE Inhibitor or ARB for LVSD[2]	38	97%	96%	96%
Aspirin at Arrival[2]	147	98%	99%	99%
Aspirin at Discharge[2]	268	99%	99%	98%
Beta Blocker at Discharge[2]	258	99%	99%	98%
Fibrinolytic Medication Timing[2]	0	-	67%	55%
PCI Within 90 Minutes of Arrival[2]	33	85%	94%	90%
Smoking Cessation Advice[2]	65	100%	99%	99%
Chest Pain/Possible Heart Attack Care				
Aspirin at Arrival[1]	7	86%	96%	95%
Median Time to ECG (minutes)[1]	7	11	7	8
Median Time to Transfer (minutes)[5]	0	-	64	61
Fibrinolytic Medication Timing[5]	0	-	45%	54%
Heart Failure Care				
ACE Inhibitor or ARB for LVSD[2]	63	89%	94%	94%
Discharge Instructions[2]	198	69%	86%	88%
Evaluation of LVS Function[2]	244	98%	95%	98%
Smoking Cessation Advice[2]	34	100%	96%	98%
Pneumonia Care				
Appropriate Initial Antibiotic[2]	67	79%	92%	92%
Blood Culture Timing[2]	82	98%	97%	96%
Influenza Vaccine[2]	75	93%	92%	91%
Initial Antibiotic Timing[2]	106	95%	97%	95%
Pneumococcal Vaccine[2]	109	95%	94%	93%
Smoking Cessation Advice[2]	32	97%	95%	97%
Surgical Care Improvement Project				
Appropriate VTP Within 24 Hours[2]	168	96%	92%	92%
Appropriate Hair Removal[2]	632	100%	100%	99%
Appropriate Beta Blocker Usage[2]	180	99%	94%	93%
Controlled Postoperative Blood Glucose[2]	123	80%	89%	93%
Prophylactic Antibiotic Timing[2]	456	95%	98%	97%
Prophylactic Antibiotic Timing (Outpatient)	710	95%	94%	92%
Prophylactic Antibiotic Selection[2]	462	97%	98%	97%
Prophylactic Antibiotic Select. (Outpatient)	705	97%	97%	94%
Prophylactic Antibiotic Stopped[2]	437	96%	95%	94%
Recommended VTP Ordered[2]	168	97%	93%	94%
Urinary Catheter Removal[2]	169	95%	91%	90%
Children's Asthma Care				
Received Systemic Corticosteroids	-	-	-	100%
Received Home Management Plan	-	-	-	71%
Received Reliever Medication	-	-	-	100%
Use of Medical Imaging				
Combination Abdominal CT Scan	479	0.094	0.163	0.191
Combination Chest CT Scan	109	0.147	0.060	0.054
Follow-up Mammogram/Ultrasound[5]	0	-	8.1%	8.4%
MRI for Low Back Pain[1]	44	36.4%	30.2%	32.7%
Survey of Patients' Hospital Experiences				
Area Around Room 'Always' Quiet at Night	300+	61%	-	58%
Doctors 'Always' Communicated Well	300+	77%	-	80%
Home Recovery Information Given	300+	82%	-	82%
Hospital Given 9 or 10 on 10 Point Scale	300+	72%	-	67%
Meds 'Always' Explained Before Given	300+	59%	-	60%
Nurses 'Always' Communicated Well	300+	75%	-	76%
Pain 'Always' Well Controlled	300+	67%	-	69%
Room and Bathroom 'Always' Clean	300+	70%	-	71%
Timely Help 'Always' Received	300+	59%	-	64%
Would Definitely Recommend Hospital	300+	77%	-	69%

NOTE: Hospital profiles are in alphabetical order by state, then city, then hospital within the city; Rankings exclude hospitals with less than 25 cases except for patient surveys which excludes hospitals with less than 100 cases; (a) 100–299 cases; (1) The number of cases is too small to be sure how well a hospital is performing; (2) The hospital indicated that the data submitted for this measure were based on a sample of cases; (3) Data was collected during a shorter time period (fewer quarters) than the maximum possible time for this measure; (4) Suppressed for one or more quarters by CMS; (5) No data is available from the hospital for this measure; (6) Fewer than 100 patients completed the HCAHPS survey. Use these rates with caution, as the number of surveys may be too low to reliably assess hospital performance; (7) Survey results are based on less than 12 months of data; (8) Survey results are not available for this reporting period; (9) No or very few patients were eligible for the HCAHPS survey. The scores shown, if any, reflect a very small number of surveys; (10) A state average was not calculated because too few hospitals in the state submitted data; (11) There were discrepancies in the data collection process; Please refer to the User's Guide for a full explanation of data.

Mercy Medical Center-Des Moines

1111 6th Ave Phone: 515-247-3121
Des Moines, IA 50314 Fax: 515-643-8498
URL: www.mercydesmoines.org
Type: Acute Care Hospitals Emergency Services: Yes
Ownership: Voluntary Non-Profit - Church Beds: 673
Key Personnel:
CEO/President. . . . . David Vellinga
Chief of Medical Staff. . . . . RoseMary Mullin
Infection Control. . . . . Connie Grout
Operating Room. . . . . Sharon Meadowcroft
Pediatric Ambulatory Care . . . . . . Sayeed Hussain, MD
Pediatric In-Patient Care . . . . Sayeed Hussain, MD
Quality Assurance . . . . Jeff Sutting
Radiology. . . . . Ruben Koehler, MD

Measure	Cases	This Hosp.	State Avg.	U.S. Avg.
Heart Attack Care				
ACE Inhibitor or ARB for LVSD	82	99%	96%	96%
Aspirin at Arrival	343	99%	99%	99%
Aspirin at Discharge	639	100%	99%	98%
Beta Blocker at Discharge	625	100%	99%	98%
Fibrinolytic Medication Timing	0	-	67%	55%
PCI Within 90 Minutes of Arrival	99	99%	94%	90%
Smoking Cessation Advice	248	100%	99%	99%
Chest Pain/Possible Heart Attack Care				
Aspirin at Arrival[1,3]	3	100%	96%	95%
Median Time to ECG (minutes)[1,3]	3	7	7	8
Median Time to Transfer (minutes)[5]	0	-	64	61
Fibrinolytic Medication Timing[5]	0	-	45%	54%
Heart Failure Care				
ACE Inhibitor or ARB for LVSD	126	100%	94%	94%
Discharge Instructions	403	98%	86%	88%
Evaluation of LVS Function	509	100%	95%	98%
Smoking Cessation Advice	70	100%	96%	98%
Pneumonia Care				
Appropriate Initial Antibiotic	276	99%	92%	92%
Blood Culture Timing	545	99%	97%	96%
Influenza Vaccine	364	95%	92%	91%
Initial Antibiotic Timing	501	98%	97%	95%
Pneumococcal Vaccine	452	97%	94%	93%
Smoking Cessation Advice	237	97%	95%	97%
Surgical Care Improvement Project				
Appropriate VTP Within 24 Hours[2]	190	97%	92%	92%
Appropriate Hair Removal[2]	794	100%	100%	99%
Appropriate Beta Blocker Usage[2]	315	95%	94%	93%
Controlled Postoperative Blood Glucose[2]	175	79%	89%	93%
Prophylactic Antibiotic Timing[2]	537	97%	98%	97%
Prophylactic Antibiotic Timing (Outpatient)	654	93%	94%	92%
Prophylactic Antibiotic Selection[2]	548	99%	98%	97%
Prophylactic Antibiotic Select. (Outpatient)	646	96%	97%	94%
Prophylactic Antibiotic Stopped[2]	500	98%	95%	94%
Recommended VTP Ordered[2]	190	98%	93%	94%
Urinary Catheter Removal[2]	120	85%	91%	90%
Children's Asthma Care				
Received Systemic Corticosteroids	-	-	-	100%
Received Home Management Plan	-	-	-	71%
Received Reliever Medication	-	-	-	100%
Use of Medical Imaging				
Combination Abdominal CT Scan	1,496	0.017	0.163	0.191
Combination Chest CT Scan	1,214	0.021	0.060	0.054
Follow-up Mammogram/Ultrasound	3,240	6.5%	8.1%	8.4%
MRI for Low Back Pain	304	36.5%	30.2%	32.7%
Survey of Patients' Hospital Experiences				
Area Around Room 'Always' Quiet at Night	300+	56%	-	58%
Doctors 'Always' Communicated Well	300+	77%	-	80%
Home Recovery Information Given	300+	85%	-	82%
Hospital Given 9 or 10 on 10 Point Scale	300+	71%	-	67%
Meds 'Always' Explained Before Given	300+	59%	-	60%
Nurses 'Always' Communicated Well	300+	76%	-	76%
Pain 'Always' Well Controlled	300+	67%	-	69%
Room and Bathroom 'Always' Clean	300+	68%	-	71%
Timely Help 'Always' Received	300+	57%	-	64%
Would Definitely Recommend Hospital	300+	74%	-	69%

VA Central Iowa Healthcare System

3600 30th Street Phone: 515-699-5999
Des Moines, IA 50310 Fax: 515-699-5862
URL: www.va.gov/sta/guide/home.asp
Type: Acute Care-Veterans Administration Emergency Services: No
Ownership: Government - Federal Beds: 327
Key Personnel:
CEO/President. . . . . Donald Cooper
Chief of Medical Staff. . . . . Russell Glynn, MD
Infection Control. . . . . Barbara Livingston
Operating Room. . . . . Jeanne Knight
Quality Assurance . . . . Janelle Runearson
Radiology. . . . . Nita Shirodkar, MD

Measure	Cases	This Hosp.	State Avg.	U.S. Avg.
Heart Attack Care				
ACE Inhibitor or ARB for LVSD[5]	0	-	96%	96%
Aspirin at Arrival[5]	0	-	99%	99%
Aspirin at Discharge[5]	0	-	99%	98%
Beta Blocker at Discharge[5]	0	-	99%	98%
Fibrinolytic Medication Timing[5]	0	-	67%	55%
PCI Within 90 Minutes of Arrival[5]	0	-	94%	90%
Smoking Cessation Advice[5]	0	-	99%	99%
Chest Pain/Possible Heart Attack Care				
Aspirin at Arrival	-	-	96%	95%
Median Time to ECG (minutes)	-	-	7	8
Median Time to Transfer (minutes)	-	-	64	61
Fibrinolytic Medication Timing	-	-	45%	54%
Heart Failure Care				
ACE Inhibitor or ARB for LVSD[1]	17	94%	94%	94%
Discharge Instructions	46	96%	86%	88%
Evaluation of LVS Function	47	100%	95%	98%
Smoking Cessation Advice[1]	9	100%	96%	98%
Pneumonia Care				
Appropriate Initial Antibiotic[1]	21	100%	92%	92%
Blood Culture Timing	41	95%	97%	96%
Influenza Vaccine	27	70%	92%	91%
Initial Antibiotic Timing	37	95%	97%	95%
Pneumococcal Vaccine	29	97%	94%	93%
Smoking Cessation Advice[1]	16	94%	95%	97%
Surgical Care Improvement Project				
Appropriate VTP Within 24 Hours[2]	80	100%	92%	92%
Appropriate Hair Removal[2]	108	100%	100%	99%
Appropriate Beta Blocker Usage[2]	48	100%	94%	93%
Controlled Postoperative Blood Glucose[2,5]	0	-	89%	93%
Prophylactic Antibiotic Timing	54	98%	98%	97%
Prophylactic Antibiotic Timing (Outpatient)	-	-	94%	92%
Prophylactic Antibiotic Selection	54	96%	98%	97%
Prophylactic Antibiotic Select. (Outpatient)	-	-	97%	94%
Prophylactic Antibiotic Stopped	53	100%	95%	94%
Recommended VTP Ordered[2]	80	100%	93%	94%
Urinary Catheter Removal[2]	35	97%	91%	90%
Children's Asthma Care				
Received Systemic Corticosteroids	-	-	-	100%
Received Home Management Plan	-	-	-	71%
Received Reliever Medication	-	-	-	100%
Use of Medical Imaging				
Combination Abdominal CT Scan	-	-	0.163	0.191
Combination Chest CT Scan	-	-	0.060	0.054
Follow-up Mammogram/Ultrasound	-	-	8.1%	8.4%
MRI for Low Back Pain	-	-	30.2%	32.7%
Survey of Patients' Hospital Experiences				
Area Around Room 'Always' Quiet at Night	-	-	-	58%
Doctors 'Always' Communicated Well	-	-	-	80%
Home Recovery Information Given	-	-	-	82%
Hospital Given 9 or 10 on 10 Point Scale	-	-	-	67%
Meds 'Always' Explained Before Given	-	-	-	60%
Nurses 'Always' Communicated Well	-	-	-	76%
Pain 'Always' Well Controlled	-	-	-	69%
Room and Bathroom 'Always' Clean	-	-	-	71%
Timely Help 'Always' Received	-	-	-	64%
Would Definitely Recommend Hospital	-	-	-	69%

Genesis Medical Center-Dewitt

1118 11th Street Phone: 563-659-4200
Dewitt, IA 52742
URL: www.genesishealth.com
Type: Critical Access Hospitals Emergency Services: Yes
Ownership: Voluntary Non-Profit - Private
Key Personnel:
President/CEO. . . . . Jeffrey M Cooper

Measure	Cases	This Hosp.	State Avg.	U.S. Avg.
Heart Attack Care				
ACE Inhibitor or ARB for LVSD[3]	0	-	96%	96%
Aspirin at Arrival[3]	0	-	99%	99%
Aspirin at Discharge[3]	0	-	99%	98%
Beta Blocker at Discharge[3]	0	-	99%	98%
Fibrinolytic Medication Timing[3]	0	-	67%	55%
PCI Within 90 Minutes of Arrival[3]	0	-	94%	90%
Smoking Cessation Advice[3]	0	-	99%	99%
Chest Pain/Possible Heart Attack Care				
Aspirin at Arrival	49	96%	96%	95%
Median Time to ECG (minutes)	51	1	7	8
Median Time to Transfer (minutes)[1,3]	7	30	64	61
Fibrinolytic Medication Timing[1,3]	1	100%	45%	54%
Heart Failure Care				
ACE Inhibitor or ARB for LVSD[1]	2	100%	94%	94%
Discharge Instructions[1]	8	100%	86%	88%
Evaluation of LVS Function[1]	10	100%	95%	98%
Smoking Cessation Advice[1]	1	100%	96%	98%
Pneumonia Care				
Appropriate Initial Antibiotic[1]	5	100%	92%	92%
Blood Culture Timing[1]	6	100%	97%	96%
Influenza Vaccine[1]	11	100%	92%	91%
Initial Antibiotic Timing[1]	13	92%	97%	95%
Pneumococcal Vaccine[1]	15	100%	94%	93%
Smoking Cessation Advice[1]	2	100%	95%	97%
Surgical Care Improvement Project				
Appropriate VTP Within 24 Hours[5]	0	-	92%	92%
Appropriate Hair Removal[5]	0	-	100%	99%
Appropriate Beta Blocker Usage[5]	0	-	94%	93%
Controlled Postoperative Blood Glucose[5]	0	-	89%	93%
Prophylactic Antibiotic Timing[5]	0	-	98%	97%
Prophylactic Antibiotic Timing (Outpatient)[1,3]	5	100%	94%	92%
Prophylactic Antibiotic Selection[5]	0	-	98%	97%
Prophylactic Antibiotic Select. (Outpatient)[1,3]	5	100%	97%	94%
Prophylactic Antibiotic Stopped[5]	0	-	95%	94%
Recommended VTP Ordered[5]	0	-	93%	94%
Urinary Catheter Removal[5]	0	-	91%	90%
Children's Asthma Care				
Received Systemic Corticosteroids	-	-	-	100%
Received Home Management Plan	-	-	-	71%
Received Reliever Medication	-	-	-	100%
Use of Medical Imaging				
Combination Abdominal CT Scan[1]	38	0.000	0.163	0.191
Combination Chest CT Scan[1]	44	0.045	0.060	0.054
Follow-up Mammogram/Ultrasound	320	10.9%	8.1%	8.4%
MRI for Low Back Pain[1]	9	33.3%	30.2%	32.7%
Survey of Patients' Hospital Experiences				
Area Around Room 'Always' Quiet at Night[8]	-	-	-	58%
Doctors 'Always' Communicated Well[8]	-	-	-	80%
Home Recovery Information Given[8]	-	-	-	82%
Hospital Given 9 or 10 on 10 Point Scale[8]	-	-	-	67%
Meds 'Always' Explained Before Given[8]	-	-	-	60%
Nurses 'Always' Communicated Well[8]	-	-	-	76%
Pain 'Always' Well Controlled[8]	-	-	-	69%
Room and Bathroom 'Always' Clean[8]	-	-	-	71%
Timely Help 'Always' Received[8]	-	-	-	64%
Would Definitely Recommend Hospital[8]	-	-	-	69%

NOTE: Hospital profiles are in alphabetical order by state, then city, then hospital within the city; Rankings exclude hospitals with less than 25 cases except for patient surveys which excludes hospitals with less than 100 cases; (a) 100–299 cases; (1) The number of cases is too small to be sure how well a hospital is performing; (2) The hospital indicated that the data submitted for this measure were based on a sample of cases; (3) Data was collected during a shorter time period (fewer quarters) than the maximum possible time for this measure; (4) Suppressed for one or more quarters by CMS; (5) No data is available from the hospital for this measure; (6) Fewer than 100 patients completed the HCAHPS survey. Use these rates with caution, as the number of surveys may be too low to reliably assess hospital performance; (7) Survey results are based on less than 12 months of data; (8) Survey results are not available for this reporting period; (9) No or very few patients were eligible for the HCAHPS survey. The scores shown, if any, reflect a very small number of surveys; (10) A state average was not calculated because too few hospitals in the state submitted data; (11) There were discrepancies in the data collection process; Please refer to the User's Guide for a full explanation of data.

The Finley Hospital

350 North Grandview Avenue
Dubuque, IA 52001
Phone: 563-582-1881
Fax: 563-589-2620
E-mail: cr@finleyhospital.org
URL: www.finleyhospital.org
Type: Acute Care Hospitals
Emergency Services: Yes
Ownership: Government - Local
Beds: 158

Key Personnel:
CEO/President. . . . . John E Knox
Cardiac Laboratory. . . . . Patty Dissell
Chief of Medical Staff. . . . . Thomas J Benda, Jr, MD
Operating Room. . . . . Lavern Bird
Pediatric Ambulatory Care . . . . . R Michael McGill, MD
Pediatric In-Patient Care . . . . . . R Michael McGill, MD
Quality Assurance . . . . Ronda Kirkeguard
Radiology. . . . . Gregory R Grotz, MD

Measure	Cases	This Hosp.	State Avg.	U.S. Avg.
Heart Attack Care				
ACE Inhibitor or ARB for LVSD[1]	10	100%	96%	96%
Aspirin at Arrival	40	95%	99%	99%
Aspirin at Discharge	38	92%	99%	98%
Beta Blocker at Discharge	35	97%	99%	98%
Fibrinolytic Medication Timing	0	-	67%	55%
PCI Within 90 Minutes of Arrival	0	-	94%	90%
Smoking Cessation Advice[1]	5	100%	99%	99%
Chest Pain/Possible Heart Attack Care				
Aspirin at Arrival	44	100%	96%	95%
Median Time to ECG (minutes)	44	9	7	8
Median Time to Transfer (minutes)[1]	5	28	64	61
Fibrinolytic Medication Timing	0	-	45%	54%
Heart Failure Care				
ACE Inhibitor or ARB for LVSD[1]	24	100%	94%	94%
Discharge Instructions	57	84%	86%	88%
Evaluation of LVS Function	82	99%	95%	98%
Smoking Cessation Advice[1]	12	92%	96%	98%
Pneumonia Care				
Appropriate Initial Antibiotic[2]	65	98%	92%	92%
Blood Culture Timing[2]	128	97%	97%	96%
Influenza Vaccine[2]	82	93%	92%	91%
Initial Antibiotic Timing[2]	98	99%	97%	95%
Pneumococcal Vaccine[2]	150	97%	94%	93%
Smoking Cessation Advice[2]	32	100%	95%	97%
Surgical Care Improvement Project				
Appropriate VTP Within 24 Hours[2]	139	93%	92%	92%
Appropriate Hair Removal[2]	310	100%	100%	99%
Appropriate Beta Blocker Usage[2]	66	97%	94%	93%
Controlled Postoperative Blood Glucose[2]	0	-	89%	93%
Prophylactic Antibiotic Timing[2]	208	100%	98%	97%
Prophylactic Antibiotic Timing (Outpatient)	197	95%	94%	92%
Prophylactic Antibiotic Selection[2]	208	99%	98%	97%
Prophylactic Antibiotic Select. (Outpatient)	190	95%	97%	94%
Prophylactic Antibiotic Stopped[2]	201	97%	95%	94%
Recommended VTP Ordered[2]	139	94%	93%	94%
Urinary Catheter Removal[2]	81	90%	91%	90%
Children's Asthma Care				
Received Systemic Corticosteroids	-	-	-	100%
Received Home Management Plan	-	-	-	71%
Received Reliever Medication	-	-	-	100%
Use of Medical Imaging				
Combination Abdominal CT Scan	564	0.074	0.163	0.191
Combination Chest CT Scan	489	0.029	0.060	0.054
Follow-up Mammogram/Ultrasound	217	15.7%	8.1%	8.4%
MRI for Low Back Pain	315	31.4%	30.2%	32.7%
Survey of Patients' Hospital Experiences				
Area Around Room 'Always' Quiet at Night	300+	59%	-	58%
Doctors 'Always' Communicated Well	300+	80%	-	80%
Home Recovery Information Given	300+	89%	-	82%
Hospital Given 9 or 10 on 10 Point Scale	300+	72%	-	67%
Meds 'Always' Explained Before Given	300+	61%	-	60%
Nurses 'Always' Communicated Well	300+	78%	-	76%
Pain 'Always' Well Controlled	300+	68%	-	69%
Room and Bathroom 'Always' Clean	300+	77%	-	71%
Timely Help 'Always' Received	300+	64%	-	64%
Would Definitely Recommend Hospital	300+	74%	-	69%

Mercy Medical Center-Dubuque

250 Mercy Drive
Dubuque, IA 52001
Phone: 563-589-8000
Type: Acute Care Hospitals
Emergency Services: Yes
Ownership: Voluntary Non-Profit - Church

Measure	Cases	This Hosp.	State Avg.	U.S. Avg.
Heart Attack Care				
ACE Inhibitor or ARB for LVSD	25	100%	96%	96%
Aspirin at Arrival	133	100%	99%	99%
Aspirin at Discharge	224	99%	99%	98%
Beta Blocker at Discharge	214	100%	99%	98%
Fibrinolytic Medication Timing	0	-	67%	55%
PCI Within 90 Minutes of Arrival	33	94%	94%	90%
Smoking Cessation Advice	65	100%	99%	99%
Chest Pain/Possible Heart Attack Care				
Aspirin at Arrival[1,3]	5	100%	96%	95%
Median Time to ECG (minutes)[1,3]	5	9	7	8
Median Time to Transfer (minutes)[5]	0	-	64	61
Fibrinolytic Medication Timing[3]	0	-	45%	54%
Heart Failure Care				
ACE Inhibitor or ARB for LVSD	47	98%	94%	94%
Discharge Instructions	146	95%	86%	88%
Evaluation of LVS Function	181	100%	95%	98%
Smoking Cessation Advice	25	100%	96%	98%
Pneumonia Care				
Appropriate Initial Antibiotic	79	97%	92%	92%
Blood Culture Timing	127	99%	97%	96%
Influenza Vaccine	99	100%	92%	91%
Initial Antibiotic Timing	113	98%	97%	95%
Pneumococcal Vaccine	150	99%	94%	93%
Smoking Cessation Advice	35	100%	95%	97%
Surgical Care Improvement Project				
Appropriate VTP Within 24 Hours[2]	134	89%	92%	92%
Appropriate Hair Removal[2]	519	100%	100%	99%
Appropriate Beta Blocker Usage[2]	174	99%	94%	93%
Controlled Postoperative Blood Glucose[2]	83	96%	89%	93%
Prophylactic Antibiotic Timing[2]	394	98%	98%	97%
Prophylactic Antibiotic Timing (Outpatient)	278	96%	94%	92%
Prophylactic Antibiotic Selection[2]	403	98%	98%	97%
Prophylactic Antibiotic Select. (Outpatient)	273	99%	97%	94%
Prophylactic Antibiotic Stopped[2]	380	97%	95%	94%
Recommended VTP Ordered[2]	134	93%	93%	94%
Urinary Catheter Removal[2]	160	97%	91%	90%
Children's Asthma Care				
Received Systemic Corticosteroids	-	-	-	100%
Received Home Management Plan	-	-	-	71%
Received Reliever Medication	-	-	-	100%
Use of Medical Imaging				
Combination Abdominal CT Scan	393	0.165	0.163	0.191
Combination Chest CT Scan	176	0.125	0.060	0.054
Follow-up Mammogram/Ultrasound[1]	30	23.3%	8.1%	8.4%
MRI for Low Back Pain[1]	47	29.8%	30.2%	32.7%
Survey of Patients' Hospital Experiences				
Area Around Room 'Always' Quiet at Night	300+	58%	-	58%
Doctors 'Always' Communicated Well	300+	81%	-	80%
Home Recovery Information Given	300+	90%	-	82%
Hospital Given 9 or 10 on 10 Point Scale	300+	77%	-	67%
Meds 'Always' Explained Before Given	300+	61%	-	60%
Nurses 'Always' Communicated Well	300+	77%	-	76%
Pain 'Always' Well Controlled	300+	71%	-	69%
Room and Bathroom 'Always' Clean	300+	71%	-	71%
Timely Help 'Always' Received	300+	63%	-	64%
Would Definitely Recommend Hospital	300+	81%	-	69%

Mercy Medical Center-Dyersville

1111 3rd Street SW
Dyersville, IA 52040
Phone: 563-875-7101
Fax: 563-875-2904
Type: Critical Access Hospitals
Emergency Services: Yes
Ownership: Voluntary Non-Profit - Other
Beds: 95

Key Personnel:
CEO/President. . . . . Rusty Knight
Operating Room. . . . . Diane Schroeder

Measure	Cases	This Hosp.	State Avg.	U.S. Avg.
Heart Attack Care				
ACE Inhibitor or ARB for LVSD[3]	0	-	96%	96%
Aspirin at Arrival[3]	0	-	99%	99%
Aspirin at Discharge[3]	0	-	99%	98%
Beta Blocker at Discharge[3]	0	-	99%	98%
Fibrinolytic Medication Timing[3]	0	-	67%	55%
PCI Within 90 Minutes of Arrival[3]	0	-	94%	90%
Smoking Cessation Advice[3]	0	-	99%	99%
Chest Pain/Possible Heart Attack Care				
Aspirin at Arrival[5]	0	-	96%	95%
Median Time to ECG (minutes)[5]	0	-	7	8
Median Time to Transfer (minutes)[5]	0	-	64	61
Fibrinolytic Medication Timing[5]	0	-	45%	54%
Heart Failure Care				
ACE Inhibitor or ARB for LVSD[1]	1	100%	94%	94%
Discharge Instructions[1]	4	50%	86%	88%
Evaluation of LVS Function[1]	6	50%	95%	98%
Smoking Cessation Advice	0	-	96%	98%
Pneumonia Care				
Appropriate Initial Antibiotic[1]	5	80%	92%	92%
Blood Culture Timing[1]	3	100%	97%	96%
Influenza Vaccine[1]	3	100%	92%	91%
Initial Antibiotic Timing[1]	4	100%	97%	95%
Pneumococcal Vaccine[1]	4	100%	94%	93%
Smoking Cessation Advice	0	-	95%	97%
Surgical Care Improvement Project				
Appropriate VTP Within 24 Hours[5]	0	-	92%	92%
Appropriate Hair Removal[5]	0	-	100%	99%
Appropriate Beta Blocker Usage[5]	0	-	94%	93%
Controlled Postoperative Blood Glucose[5]	0	-	89%	93%
Prophylactic Antibiotic Timing[5]	0	-	98%	97%
Prophylactic Antibiotic Timing (Outpatient)[5]	0	-	94%	92%
Prophylactic Antibiotic Selection[5]	0	-	98%	97%
Prophylactic Antibiotic Select. (Outpatient)[5]	0	-	97%	94%
Prophylactic Antibiotic Stopped[5]	0	-	95%	94%
Recommended VTP Ordered[5]	0	-	93%	94%
Urinary Catheter Removal[5]	0	-	91%	90%
Children's Asthma Care				
Received Systemic Corticosteroids	-	-	-	100%
Received Home Management Plan	-	-	-	71%
Received Reliever Medication	-	-	-	100%
Use of Medical Imaging				
Combination Abdominal CT Scan[5]	0	-	0.163	0.191
Combination Chest CT Scan[5]	0	-	0.060	0.054
Follow-up Mammogram/Ultrasound	109	10.1%	8.1%	8.4%
MRI for Low Back Pain[5]	0	-	30.2%	32.7%
Survey of Patients' Hospital Experiences				
Area Around Room 'Always' Quiet at Night[8]	-	-	-	58%
Doctors 'Always' Communicated Well[8]	-	-	-	80%
Home Recovery Information Given[8]	-	-	-	82%
Hospital Given 9 or 10 on 10 Point Scale[8]	-	-	-	67%
Meds 'Always' Explained Before Given[8]	-	-	-	60%
Nurses 'Always' Communicated Well[8]	-	-	-	76%
Pain 'Always' Well Controlled[8]	-	-	-	69%
Room and Bathroom 'Always' Clean[8]	-	-	-	71%
Timely Help 'Always' Received[8]	-	-	-	64%
Would Definitely Recommend Hospital[8]	-	-	-	69%

NOTE: Hospital profiles are in alphabetical order by state, then city, then hospital within the city; Rankings exclude hospitals with less than 25 cases except for patient surveys which excludes hospitals with less than 100 cases; (a) 100–299 cases; (1) The number of cases is too small to be sure how well a hospital is performing; (2) The hospital indicated that the data submitted for this measure were based on a sample of cases; (3) Data was collected during a shorter time period (fewer quarters) than the maximum possible time for this measure; (4) Suppressed for one or more quarters by CMS; (5) No data is available from the hospital for this measure; (6) Fewer than 100 patients completed the HCAHPS survey. Use these rates with caution, as the number of surveys may be too low to reliably assess hospital performance; (7) Survey results are based on less than 12 months of data; (8) Survey results are not available for this reporting period; (9) No or very few patients were eligible for the HCAHPS survey. The scores shown, if any, reflect a very small number of surveys; (10) A state average was not calculated because too few hospitals in the state submitted data; (11) There were discrepancies in the data collection process; Please refer to the User's Guide for a full explanation of data.

Central Community Hospital

901 Davidson Street NW
Elkader, IA 52043
Phone: 563-245-7000
Fax: 563-245-7080
Type: Critical Access Hospitals
Emergency Services: Yes
Ownership: Voluntary Non-Profit - Private
Beds: 25

Key Personnel:

CEO/President. . . . . Fran Zichal
Chief of Medical Staff . . . . Kenneth Zichal, MD
Infection Control. . . . . Ann Burds
Operating Room. . . . . Lori Vlazny, RN
Quality Assurance . . . . Lisa Marson
Radiology. . . . . Ken Dettburn
Emergency Room . . . . Natalie Shea

Measure	Cases	This Hosp.	State Avg.	U.S. Avg.
Heart Attack Care				
ACE Inhibitor or ARB for LVSD[3]	0	-	96%	96%
Aspirin at Arrival[1,3]	1	100%	99%	99%
Aspirin at Discharge[1,3]	1	100%	99%	98%
Beta Blocker at Discharge[1,3]	1	100%	99%	98%
Fibrinolytic Medication Timing[5]	0	-	67%	55%
PCI Within 90 Minutes of Arrival[5]	0	-	94%	90%
Smoking Cessation Advice[1,3]	1	100%	99%	99%
Chest Pain/Possible Heart Attack Care				
Aspirin at Arrival	-	-	96%	95%
Median Time to ECG (minutes)	-	-	7	8
Median Time to Transfer (minutes)	-	-	64	61
Fibrinolytic Medication Timing	-	-	45%	54%
Heart Failure Care				
ACE Inhibitor or ARB for LVSD[3]	0	-	94%	94%
Discharge Instructions[1,3]	2	50%	86%	88%
Evaluation of LVS Function[1,3]	9	67%	95%	98%
Smoking Cessation Advice[3]	0	-	96%	98%
Pneumonia Care				
Appropriate Initial Antibiotic[1,3]	4	75%	92%	92%
Blood Culture Timing[1,3]	6	100%	97%	96%
Influenza Vaccine[1]	6	100%	92%	91%
Initial Antibiotic Timing[1,3]	8	88%	97%	95%
Pneumococcal Vaccine[1,3]	8	100%	94%	93%
Smoking Cessation Advice[3]	0	-	95%	97%
Surgical Care Improvement Project				
Appropriate VTP Within 24 Hours[3]	0	-	92%	92%
Appropriate Hair Removal[1,3]	2	100%	100%	99%
Appropriate Beta Blocker Usage[5]	0	-	94%	93%
Controlled Postoperative Blood Glucose[3]	0	-	89%	93%
Prophylactic Antibiotic Timing[1,3]	1	0%	98%	97%
Prophylactic Antibiotic Timing (Outpatient)	-	-	94%	92%
Prophylactic Antibiotic Selection[1,3]	1	100%	98%	97%
Prophylactic Antibiotic Select. (Outpatient)	-	-	97%	94%
Prophylactic Antibiotic Stopped[1,3]	1	100%	95%	94%
Recommended VTP Ordered[1,3]	1	0%	93%	94%
Urinary Catheter Removal[3]	0	-	91%	90%
Children's Asthma Care				
Received Systemic Corticosteroids	-	-	-	100%
Received Home Management Plan	-	-	-	71%
Received Reliever Medication	-	-	-	100%
Use of Medical Imaging				
Combination Abdominal CT Scan	-	-	0.163	0.191
Combination Chest CT Scan	-	-	0.060	0.054
Follow-up Mammogram/Ultrasound	-	-	8.1%	8.4%
MRI for Low Back Pain	-	-	30.2%	32.7%
Survey of Patients' Hospital Experiences				
Area Around Room 'Always' Quiet at Night[8]	-	-	-	58%
Doctors 'Always' Communicated Well[8]	-	-	-	80%
Home Recovery Information Given[8]	-	-	-	82%
Hospital Given 9 or 10 on 10 Point Scale[8]	-	-	-	67%
Meds 'Always' Explained Before Given[8]	-	-	-	60%
Nurses 'Always' Communicated Well[8]	-	-	-	76%
Pain 'Always' Well Controlled[8]	-	-	-	69%
Room and Bathroom 'Always' Clean[8]	-	-	-	71%
Timely Help 'Always' Received[8]	-	-	-	64%
Would Definitely Recommend Hospital[8]	-	-	-	69%

Palo Alto County Hospital

3201 1st Street
Emmetsburg, IA 50536
Phone: 712-852-5500
Fax: 712-852-5508
URL: www.pachs.com
Type: Critical Access Hospitals
Emergency Services: Yes
Ownership: Voluntary Non-Profit - Other
Beds: 47

Key Personnel:

CEO/President. . . . . Thomas J Lee
Chief of Medical Staff . . . . Patricia A Banwart
Operating Room. . . . . Melanie Flynn
Quality Assurance . . . . Kathey Mehan
Radiology. . . . . Melissa Hospelhorn
Ambulatory Care . . . . Sheryl Darling, EMS
Emergency Room . . . . Kim Kerr

Measure	Cases	This Hosp.	State Avg.	U.S. Avg.
Heart Attack Care				
ACE Inhibitor or ARB for LVSD[5]	0	-	96%	96%
Aspirin at Arrival[5]	0	-	99%	99%
Aspirin at Discharge[5]	0	-	99%	98%
Beta Blocker at Discharge[5]	0	-	99%	98%
Fibrinolytic Medication Timing[5]	0	-	67%	55%
PCI Within 90 Minutes of Arrival[5]	0	-	94%	90%
Smoking Cessation Advice[5]	0	-	99%	99%
Chest Pain/Possible Heart Attack Care				
Aspirin at Arrival	-	-	96%	95%
Median Time to ECG (minutes)	-	-	7	8
Median Time to Transfer (minutes)	-	-	64	61
Fibrinolytic Medication Timing	-	-	45%	54%
Heart Failure Care				
ACE Inhibitor or ARB for LVSD[5]	0	-	94%	94%
Discharge Instructions[5]	0	-	86%	88%
Evaluation of LVS Function[5]	0	-	95%	98%
Smoking Cessation Advice[5]	0	-	96%	98%
Pneumonia Care				
Appropriate Initial Antibiotic	30	97%	92%	92%
Blood Culture Timing[1]	9	100%	97%	96%
Influenza Vaccine[1]	19	84%	92%	91%
Initial Antibiotic Timing	45	96%	97%	95%
Pneumococcal Vaccine	37	86%	94%	93%
Smoking Cessation Advice[1]	3	67%	95%	97%
Surgical Care Improvement Project				
Appropriate VTP Within 24 Hours[5]	0	-	92%	92%
Appropriate Hair Removal[5]	0	-	100%	99%
Appropriate Beta Blocker Usage[5]	0	-	94%	93%
Controlled Postoperative Blood Glucose[5]	0	-	89%	93%
Prophylactic Antibiotic Timing[5]	0	-	98%	97%
Prophylactic Antibiotic Timing (Outpatient)	-	-	94%	92%
Prophylactic Antibiotic Selection[5]	0	-	98%	97%
Prophylactic Antibiotic Select. (Outpatient)	-	-	97%	94%
Prophylactic Antibiotic Stopped[5]	0	-	95%	94%
Recommended VTP Ordered[5]	0	-	93%	94%
Urinary Catheter Removal[5]	0	-	91%	90%
Children's Asthma Care				
Received Systemic Corticosteroids	-	-	-	100%
Received Home Management Plan	-	-	-	71%
Received Reliever Medication	-	-	-	100%
Use of Medical Imaging				
Combination Abdominal CT Scan	-	-	0.163	0.191
Combination Chest CT Scan	-	-	0.060	0.054
Follow-up Mammogram/Ultrasound	-	-	8.1%	8.4%
MRI for Low Back Pain	-	-	30.2%	32.7%
Survey of Patients' Hospital Experiences				
Area Around Room 'Always' Quiet at Night[8]	-	-	-	58%
Doctors 'Always' Communicated Well[8]	-	-	-	80%
Home Recovery Information Given[8]	-	-	-	82%
Hospital Given 9 or 10 on 10 Point Scale[8]	-	-	-	67%
Meds 'Always' Explained Before Given[8]	-	-	-	60%
Nurses 'Always' Communicated Well[8]	-	-	-	76%
Pain 'Always' Well Controlled[8]	-	-	-	69%
Room and Bathroom 'Always' Clean[8]	-	-	-	71%
Timely Help 'Always' Received[8]	-	-	-	64%
Would Definitely Recommend Hospital[8]	-	-	-	69%

Avera Holy Family Health

826 North 8th Street
Estherville, IA 51334
Phone: 712-362-2631
Fax: 712-362-2636
URL: www.averaholyfamily.org
Type: Critical Access Hospitals
Emergency Services: Yes
Ownership: Voluntary Non-Profit - Church
Beds: 25

Key Personnel:

CEO/President. . . . . Bill Bumgarner
Chief of Medical Staff . . . . Randy Asman
Infection Control. . . . . Annesley Gunderson
Operating Room. . . . . Joyce Graettinger
Quality Assurance . . . . Cathi Scharnberg
Radiology. . . . . Robert P DeClark
Intensive Care Unit. . . . . Nancy Diekmann
Patient Relations . . . . John Belk

Measure	Cases	This Hosp.	State Avg.	U.S. Avg.
Heart Attack Care				
ACE Inhibitor or ARB for LVSD[3]	0	-	96%	96%
Aspirin at Arrival[3]	0	-	99%	99%
Aspirin at Discharge[1,3]	1	0%	99%	98%
Beta Blocker at Discharge[1,3]	1	100%	99%	98%
Fibrinolytic Medication Timing[3]	0	-	67%	55%
PCI Within 90 Minutes of Arrival[3]	0	-	94%	90%
Smoking Cessation Advice[3]	0	-	99%	99%
Chest Pain/Possible Heart Attack Care				
Aspirin at Arrival	-	-	96%	95%
Median Time to ECG (minutes)	-	-	7	8
Median Time to Transfer (minutes)	-	-	64	61
Fibrinolytic Medication Timing	-	-	45%	54%
Heart Failure Care				
ACE Inhibitor or ARB for LVSD[1]	8	75%	94%	94%
Discharge Instructions[1]	16	100%	86%	88%
Evaluation of LVS Function	33	97%	95%	98%
Smoking Cessation Advice[1]	1	100%	96%	98%
Pneumonia Care				
Appropriate Initial Antibiotic	30	97%	92%	92%
Blood Culture Timing[1]	12	92%	97%	96%
Influenza Vaccine[1]	23	74%	92%	91%
Initial Antibiotic Timing	39	100%	97%	95%
Pneumococcal Vaccine	34	94%	94%	93%
Smoking Cessation Advice[1]	12	100%	95%	97%
Surgical Care Improvement Project				
Appropriate VTP Within 24 Hours[5]	0	-	92%	92%
Appropriate Hair Removal[5]	0	-	100%	99%
Appropriate Beta Blocker Usage[5]	0	-	94%	93%
Controlled Postoperative Blood Glucose[5]	0	-	89%	93%
Prophylactic Antibiotic Timing[5]	0	-	98%	97%
Prophylactic Antibiotic Timing (Outpatient)	-	-	94%	92%
Prophylactic Antibiotic Selection[5]	0	-	98%	97%
Prophylactic Antibiotic Select. (Outpatient)	-	-	97%	94%
Prophylactic Antibiotic Stopped[5]	0	-	95%	94%
Recommended VTP Ordered[5]	0	-	93%	94%
Urinary Catheter Removal[5]	0	-	91%	90%
Children's Asthma Care				
Received Systemic Corticosteroids	-	-	-	100%
Received Home Management Plan	-	-	-	71%
Received Reliever Medication	-	-	-	100%
Use of Medical Imaging				
Combination Abdominal CT Scan	-	-	0.163	0.191
Combination Chest CT Scan	-	-	0.060	0.054
Follow-up Mammogram/Ultrasound	-	-	8.1%	8.4%
MRI for Low Back Pain	-	-	30.2%	32.7%
Survey of Patients' Hospital Experiences				
Area Around Room 'Always' Quiet at Night	(a)	64%	-	58%
Doctors 'Always' Communicated Well	(a)	86%	-	80%
Home Recovery Information Given	(a)	85%	-	82%
Hospital Given 9 or 10 on 10 Point Scale	(a)	76%	-	67%
Meds 'Always' Explained Before Given	(a)	62%	-	60%
Nurses 'Always' Communicated Well	(a)	84%	-	76%
Pain 'Always' Well Controlled	(a)	67%	-	69%
Room and Bathroom 'Always' Clean	(a)	81%	-	71%
Timely Help 'Always' Received	(a)	70%	-	64%
Would Definitely Recommend Hospital	(a)	80%	-	69%

NOTE: Hospital profiles are in alphabetical order by state, then city, then hospital within the city; Rankings exclude hospitals with less than 25 cases except for patient surveys which excludes hospitals with less than 100 cases; (a) 100–299 cases; (1) The number of cases is too small to be sure how well a hospital is performing; (2) The hospital indicated that the data submitted for this measure were based on a sample of cases; (3) Data was collected during a shorter time period (fewer quarters) than the maximum possible time for this measure; (4) Suppressed for one or more quarters by CMS; (5) No data is available from the hospital for this measure; (6) Fewer than 100 patients completed the HCAHPS survey. Use these rates with caution, as the number of surveys may be too low to reliably assess hospital performance; (7) Survey results are based on less than 12 months of data; (8) Survey results are not available for this reporting period; (9) No or very few patients were eligible for the HCAHPS survey. The scores shown, if any, reflect a very small number of surveys; (10) A state average was not calculated because too few hospitals in the state submitted data; (11) There were discrepancies in the data collection process; Please refer to the User's Guide for a full explanation of data.

Jefferson County Health Center

2000 S Main
Fairfield, IA 52556
URL: www.jchospital.org
Type: Critical Access Hospitals
Ownership: Government - Local
Phone: 641-472-4111
Fax: 641-469-4375
Emergency Services: Yes
Beds: 67

Key Personnel:
CEO/President. . . . . Deb Cardin
Chief of Medical Staff . . . . Deb Cardin
Quality Assurance . . . . Kim Woods, RN
Emergency Room . . . . Michael Eisner

Measure	Cases	This Hosp.	State Avg.	U.S. Avg.
Heart Attack Care				
ACE Inhibitor or ARB for LVSD[3]	0	-	96%	96%
Aspirin at Arrival[1,3]	1	100%	99%	99%
Aspirin at Discharge[1,3]	2	100%	99%	98%
Beta Blocker at Discharge[1,3]	2	100%	99%	98%
Fibrinolytic Medication Timing[3]	0	-	67%	55%
PCI Within 90 Minutes of Arrival[3]	0	-	94%	90%
Smoking Cessation Advice[1,3]	1	100%	99%	99%
Chest Pain/Possible Heart Attack Care				
Aspirin at Arrival	-	-	96%	95%
Median Time to ECG (minutes)	-	-	7	8
Median Time to Transfer (minutes)	-	-	64	61
Fibrinolytic Medication Timing	-	-	45%	54%
Heart Failure Care				
ACE Inhibitor or ARB for LVSD[1,3]	1	100%	94%	94%
Discharge Instructions[1,3]	4	100%	86%	88%
Evaluation of LVS Function[1,3]	9	100%	95%	98%
Smoking Cessation Advice[1,3]	1	100%	96%	98%
Pneumonia Care				
Appropriate Initial Antibiotic	27	85%	92%	92%
Blood Culture Timing[1]	18	89%	97%	96%
Influenza Vaccine[1]	20	75%	92%	91%
Initial Antibiotic Timing[1]	5	80%	97%	95%
Pneumococcal Vaccine	25	88%	94%	93%
Smoking Cessation Advice[1]	4	100%	95%	97%
Surgical Care Improvement Project				
Appropriate VTP Within 24 Hours[1]	17	82%	92%	92%
Appropriate Hair Removal	26	96%	100%	99%
Appropriate Beta Blocker Usage[5]	0	-	94%	93%
Controlled Postoperative Blood Glucose	0	-	89%	93%
Prophylactic Antibiotic Timing[1]	16	81%	98%	97%
Prophylactic Antibiotic Timing (Outpatient)	-	-	94%	92%
Prophylactic Antibiotic Selection[1]	16	94%	98%	97%
Prophylactic Antibiotic Select. (Outpatient)	-	-	97%	94%
Prophylactic Antibiotic Stopped[1]	15	73%	95%	94%
Recommended VTP Ordered[1]	17	94%	93%	94%
Urinary Catheter Removal[1]	3	33%	91%	90%
Children's Asthma Care				
Received Systemic Corticosteroids	-	-	-	100%
Received Home Management Plan	-	-	-	71%
Received Reliever Medication	-	-	-	100%
Use of Medical Imaging				
Combination Abdominal CT Scan	-	-	0.163	0.191
Combination Chest CT Scan	-	-	0.060	0.054
Follow-up Mammogram/Ultrasound	-	-	8.1%	8.4%
MRI for Low Back Pain	-	-	30.2%	32.7%
Survey of Patients' Hospital Experiences				
Area Around Room 'Always' Quiet at Night	(a)	73%	-	58%
Doctors 'Always' Communicated Well	(a)	85%	-	80%
Home Recovery Information Given	(a)	80%	-	82%
Hospital Given 9 or 10 on 10 Point Scale	(a)	81%	-	67%
Meds 'Always' Explained Before Given	(a)	58%	-	60%
Nurses 'Always' Communicated Well	(a)	89%	-	76%
Pain 'Always' Well Controlled	(a)	74%	-	69%
Room and Bathroom 'Always' Clean	(a)	89%	-	71%
Timely Help 'Always' Received	(a)	81%	-	64%
Would Definitely Recommend Hospital	(a)	78%	-	69%

Trinity Regional Medical Center

802 Kenyon Rd
Fort Dodge, IA 50501
URL: www.trmc.org
Type: Acute Care Hospitals
Ownership: Voluntary Non-Profit - Private
Phone: 515-573-8710
Fax: 515-573-8710
Emergency Services: Yes
Beds: 200

Key Personnel:
CEO/President. . . . . Tom Tibbits
Chief of Medical Staff . . . . Kenneth Adams, DO
Coronary Care . . . . Sheryl Rogers
Infection Control. . . . . Linda Opheim
Pediatric Ambulatory Care . . . . . . Joan Hisler
Pediatric In-Patient Care . . . . Joan Hisler
Quality Assurance . . . . Steve Gibson
Radiology. . . . . Keith Lacey

Measure	Cases	This Hosp.	State Avg.	U.S. Avg.
Heart Attack Care				
ACE Inhibitor or ARB for LVSD	41	98%	96%	96%
Aspirin at Arrival	104	97%	99%	99%
Aspirin at Discharge	189	100%	99%	98%
Beta Blocker at Discharge	187	99%	99%	98%
Fibrinolytic Medication Timing	0	-	67%	55%
PCI Within 90 Minutes of Arrival	30	97%	94%	90%
Smoking Cessation Advice	61	100%	99%	99%
Chest Pain/Possible Heart Attack Care				
Aspirin at Arrival[1]	11	100%	96%	95%
Median Time to ECG (minutes)[1]	11	6	7	8
Median Time to Transfer (minutes)[5]	0	-	64	61
Fibrinolytic Medication Timing[3]	0	-	45%	54%
Heart Failure Care				
ACE Inhibitor or ARB for LVSD	64	97%	94%	94%
Discharge Instructions	133	84%	86%	88%
Evaluation of LVS Function	179	98%	95%	98%
Smoking Cessation Advice[1]	22	100%	96%	98%
Pneumonia Care				
Appropriate Initial Antibiotic	115	89%	92%	92%
Blood Culture Timing	219	98%	97%	96%
Influenza Vaccine	124	98%	92%	91%
Initial Antibiotic Timing	201	99%	97%	95%
Pneumococcal Vaccine	197	99%	94%	93%
Smoking Cessation Advice	79	100%	95%	97%
Surgical Care Improvement Project				
Appropriate VTP Within 24 Hours[2]	80	89%	92%	92%
Appropriate Hair Removal[2]	321	100%	100%	99%
Appropriate Beta Blocker Usage[2]	116	93%	94%	93%
Controlled Postoperative Blood Glucose[2]	70	97%	89%	93%
Prophylactic Antibiotic Timing[2]	227	98%	98%	97%
Prophylactic Antibiotic Timing (Outpatient)	182	90%	94%	92%
Prophylactic Antibiotic Selection[2]	231	96%	98%	97%
Prophylactic Antibiotic Select. (Outpatient)	179	98%	97%	94%
Prophylactic Antibiotic Stopped[2]	217	100%	95%	94%
Recommended VTP Ordered[2]	80	89%	93%	94%
Urinary Catheter Removal[2]	71	93%	91%	90%
Children's Asthma Care				
Received Systemic Corticosteroids	-	-	-	100%
Received Home Management Plan	-	-	-	71%
Received Reliever Medication	-	-	-	100%
Use of Medical Imaging				
Combination Abdominal CT Scan	380	0.011	0.163	0.191
Combination Chest CT Scan	445	0.002	0.060	0.054
Follow-up Mammogram/Ultrasound[5]	0	-	8.1%	8.4%
MRI for Low Back Pain	159	31.4%	30.2%	32.7%
Survey of Patients' Hospital Experiences				
Area Around Room 'Always' Quiet at Night	300+	53%	-	58%
Doctors 'Always' Communicated Well	300+	82%	-	80%
Home Recovery Information Given	300+	89%	-	82%
Hospital Given 9 or 10 on 10 Point Scale	300+	69%	-	67%
Meds 'Always' Explained Before Given	300+	63%	-	60%
Nurses 'Always' Communicated Well	300+	78%	-	76%
Pain 'Always' Well Controlled	300+	72%	-	69%
Room and Bathroom 'Always' Clean	300+	75%	-	71%
Timely Help 'Always' Received	300+	63%	-	64%
Would Definitely Recommend Hospital	300+	67%	-	69%

Fort Madison Community Hospital

5445 Ave O
Fort Madison, IA 52627
E-mail: jplatt@fmchosp.com
URL: www.fmchosp.com
Type: Acute Care Hospitals
Ownership: Voluntary Non-Profit - Private
Phone: 319-372-6530
Fax: 319-372-9119
Emergency Services: No
Beds: 50

Key Personnel:
CEO/President. . . . . C James Platt
Chief of Medical Staff . . . . David Wenger Keller, MD
Quality Assurance . . . . Meredith Griffith
Radiology. . . . . Steven Davis, MD
Emergency Room . . . . Christina Goebel

Measure	Cases	This Hosp.	State Avg.	U.S. Avg.
Heart Attack Care				
ACE Inhibitor or ARB for LVSD[1]	2	100%	96%	96%
Aspirin at Arrival[1]	17	100%	99%	99%
Aspirin at Discharge[1]	13	100%	99%	98%
Beta Blocker at Discharge[1]	13	92%	99%	98%
Fibrinolytic Medication Timing	0	-	67%	55%
PCI Within 90 Minutes of Arrival	0	-	94%	90%
Smoking Cessation Advice[1]	4	100%	99%	99%
Chest Pain/Possible Heart Attack Care				
Aspirin at Arrival	52	96%	96%	95%
Median Time to ECG (minutes)	53	3	7	8
Median Time to Transfer (minutes)[1,3]	8	102	64	61
Fibrinolytic Medication Timing[1]	4	75%	45%	54%
Heart Failure Care				
ACE Inhibitor or ARB for LVSD[1]	18	100%	94%	94%
Discharge Instructions	37	100%	86%	88%
Evaluation of LVS Function	58	100%	95%	98%
Smoking Cessation Advice[1]	11	100%	96%	98%
Pneumonia Care				
Appropriate Initial Antibiotic	48	96%	92%	92%
Blood Culture Timing	63	100%	97%	96%
Influenza Vaccine	51	92%	92%	91%
Initial Antibiotic Timing	66	98%	97%	95%
Pneumococcal Vaccine	69	100%	94%	93%
Smoking Cessation Advice	27	100%	95%	97%
Surgical Care Improvement Project				
Appropriate VTP Within 24 Hours	38	100%	92%	92%
Appropriate Hair Removal	110	100%	100%	99%
Appropriate Beta Blocker Usage	39	97%	94%	93%
Controlled Postoperative Blood Glucose	0	-	89%	93%
Prophylactic Antibiotic Timing	86	99%	98%	97%
Prophylactic Antibiotic Timing (Outpatient)	42	93%	94%	92%
Prophylactic Antibiotic Selection	86	94%	98%	97%
Prophylactic Antibiotic Select. (Outpatient)	46	98%	97%	94%
Prophylactic Antibiotic Stopped	86	98%	95%	94%
Recommended VTP Ordered	38	100%	93%	94%
Urinary Catheter Removal	34	100%	91%	90%
Children's Asthma Care				
Received Systemic Corticosteroids	-	-	-	100%
Received Home Management Plan	-	-	-	71%
Received Reliever Medication	-	-	-	100%
Use of Medical Imaging				
Combination Abdominal CT Scan	258	0.775	0.163	0.191
Combination Chest CT Scan	162	0.031	0.060	0.054
Follow-up Mammogram/Ultrasound	564	12.6%	8.1%	8.4%
MRI for Low Back Pain	72	37.5%	30.2%	32.7%
Survey of Patients' Hospital Experiences				
Area Around Room 'Always' Quiet at Night	300+	61%	-	58%
Doctors 'Always' Communicated Well	300+	80%	-	80%
Home Recovery Information Given	300+	83%	-	82%
Hospital Given 9 or 10 on 10 Point Scale	300+	74%	-	67%
Meds 'Always' Explained Before Given	300+	61%	-	60%
Nurses 'Always' Communicated Well	300+	80%	-	76%
Pain 'Always' Well Controlled	300+	68%	-	69%
Room and Bathroom 'Always' Clean	300+	72%	-	71%
Timely Help 'Always' Received	300+	70%	-	64%
Would Definitely Recommend Hospital	300+	75%	-	69%

NOTE: Hospital profiles are in alphabetical order by state, then city, then hospital within the city; Rankings exclude hospitals with less than 25 cases except for patient surveys which excludes hospitals with less than 100 cases; (a) 100–299 cases; (1) The number of cases is too small to be sure how well a hospital is performing; (2) The hospital indicated that the data submitted for this measure were based on a sample of cases; (3) Data was collected during a shorter time period (fewer quarters) than the maximum possible time for this measure; (4) Suppressed for one or more quarters by CMS; (5) No data is available from the hospital for this measure; (6) Fewer than 100 patients completed the HCAHPS survey. Use these rates with caution, as the number of surveys may be too low to reliably assess hospital performance; (7) Survey results are based on less than 12 months of data; (8) Survey results are not available for this reporting period; (9) No or very few patients were eligible for the HCAHPS survey. The scores shown, if any, reflect a very small number of surveys; (10) A state average was not calculated because too few hospitals in the state submitted data; (11) There were discrepancies in the data collection process; Please refer to the User's Guide for a full explanation of data.

Adair County Memorial Hospital

609 SE Kent
Greenfield, IA 50849
Phone: 641-743-2123
Fax: 641-743-2610
URL: www.adaircountyhealthsystem.org
Type: Critical Access Hospitals
Emergency Services: Yes
Ownership: Voluntary Non-Profit - Other
Beds: 31

Key Personnel:

CEO/President. . . . . Myrna Erb-Gundel
Chief of Medical Staff. . . . . Troy Renaud
Infection Control. . . . . Deb Tindle, RN
Operating Room. . . . . Marvel Blazer, RN
Quality Assurance . . . . Jan Livingston

Measure	Cases	This Hosp.	State Avg.	U.S. Avg.
Heart Attack Care				
ACE Inhibitor or ARB for LVSD[5]	0	-	96%	96%
Aspirin at Arrival[5]	0	-	99%	99%
Aspirin at Discharge[5]	0	-	99%	98%
Beta Blocker at Discharge[5]	0	-	99%	98%
Fibrinolytic Medication Timing[5]	0	-	67%	55%
PCI Within 90 Minutes of Arrival[5]	0	-	94%	90%
Smoking Cessation Advice[5]	0	-	99%	99%
Chest Pain/Possible Heart Attack Care				
Aspirin at Arrival	-	-	96%	95%
Median Time to ECG (minutes)	-	-	7	8
Median Time to Transfer (minutes)	-	-	64	61
Fibrinolytic Medication Timing	-	-	45%	54%
Heart Failure Care				
ACE Inhibitor or ARB for LVSD[5]	0	-	94%	94%
Discharge Instructions[5]	0	-	86%	88%
Evaluation of LVS Function[5]	0	-	95%	98%
Smoking Cessation Advice[5]	0	-	96%	98%
Pneumonia Care				
Appropriate Initial Antibiotic[5]	0	-	92%	92%
Blood Culture Timing[5]	0	-	97%	96%
Influenza Vaccine[5]	0	-	92%	91%
Initial Antibiotic Timing[5]	0	-	97%	95%
Pneumococcal Vaccine[5]	0	-	94%	93%
Smoking Cessation Advice[5]	0	-	95%	97%
Surgical Care Improvement Project				
Appropriate VTP Within 24 Hours[5]	0	-	92%	92%
Appropriate Hair Removal[5]	0	-	100%	99%
Appropriate Beta Blocker Usage[5]	0	-	94%	93%
Controlled Postoperative Blood Glucose[5]	0	-	89%	93%
Prophylactic Antibiotic Timing[5]	0	-	98%	97%
Prophylactic Antibiotic Timing (Outpatient)	-	-	94%	92%
Prophylactic Antibiotic Selection[5]	0	-	98%	97%
Prophylactic Antibiotic Select. (Outpatient)	-	-	97%	94%
Prophylactic Antibiotic Stopped[5]	0	-	95%	94%
Recommended VTP Ordered[5]	0	-	93%	94%
Urinary Catheter Removal[5]	0	-	91%	90%
Children's Asthma Care				
Received Systemic Corticosteroids	-	-	-	100%
Received Home Management Plan	-	-	-	71%
Received Reliever Medication	-	-	-	100%
Use of Medical Imaging				
Combination Abdominal CT Scan	-	-	0.163	0.191
Combination Chest CT Scan	-	-	0.060	0.054
Follow-up Mammogram/Ultrasound	-	-	8.1%	8.4%
MRI for Low Back Pain	-	-	30.2%	32.7%
Survey of Patients' Hospital Experiences				
Area Around Room 'Always' Quiet at Night[8]	-	-	-	58%
Doctors 'Always' Communicated Well[8]	-	-	-	80%
Home Recovery Information Given[8]	-	-	-	82%
Hospital Given 9 or 10 on 10 Point Scale[8]	-	-	-	67%
Meds 'Always' Explained Before Given[8]	-	-	-	60%
Nurses 'Always' Communicated Well[8]	-	-	-	76%
Pain 'Always' Well Controlled[8]	-	-	-	69%
Room and Bathroom 'Always' Clean[8]	-	-	-	71%
Timely Help 'Always' Received[8]	-	-	-	64%
Would Definitely Recommend Hospital[8]	-	-	-	69%

Grinnell Regional Medical Center

210 Fourth Avenue
Grinnell, IA 50112
Phone: 641-236-7511
Fax: 641-236-2995
URL: www.grmc.us
Type: Acute Care Hospitals
Emergency Services: Yes
Ownership: Voluntary Non-Profit - Private
Beds: 81

Key Personnel:

CEO/President. . . . . Todd C Linden
Chief of Medical Staff. . . . . Roy Doorebos, MD
Operating Room. . . . . Deb Reding
Radiology. . . . . William D Heggen
Anesthesiology. . . . . James Schuh, MD

Measure	Cases	This Hosp.	State Avg.	U.S. Avg.
Heart Attack Care				
ACE Inhibitor or ARB for LVSD[1]	4	50%	96%	96%
Aspirin at Arrival[1]	14	100%	99%	99%
Aspirin at Discharge[1]	8	88%	99%	98%
Beta Blocker at Discharge[1]	8	100%	99%	98%
Fibrinolytic Medication Timing	0	-	67%	55%
PCI Within 90 Minutes of Arrival	0	-	94%	90%
Smoking Cessation Advice[1]	1	100%	99%	99%
Chest Pain/Possible Heart Attack Care				
Aspirin at Arrival	61	95%	96%	95%
Median Time to ECG (minutes)	67	5	7	8
Median Time to Transfer (minutes)[1,3]	4	68	64	61
Fibrinolytic Medication Timing[1]	1	100%	45%	54%
Heart Failure Care				
ACE Inhibitor or ARB for LVSD[1]	8	75%	94%	94%
Discharge Instructions	28	86%	86%	88%
Evaluation of LVS Function	48	100%	95%	98%
Smoking Cessation Advice[1]	5	100%	96%	98%
Pneumonia Care				
Appropriate Initial Antibiotic	43	91%	92%	92%
Blood Culture Timing	41	98%	97%	96%
Influenza Vaccine	30	100%	92%	91%
Initial Antibiotic Timing	57	100%	97%	95%
Pneumococcal Vaccine	49	100%	94%	93%
Smoking Cessation Advice[1]	20	100%	95%	97%
Surgical Care Improvement Project				
Appropriate VTP Within 24 Hours	44	100%	92%	92%
Appropriate Hair Removal	98	100%	100%	99%
Appropriate Beta Blocker Usage	31	90%	94%	93%
Controlled Postoperative Blood Glucose	0	-	89%	93%
Prophylactic Antibiotic Timing	37	95%	98%	97%
Prophylactic Antibiotic Timing (Outpatient)	35	100%	94%	92%
Prophylactic Antibiotic Selection	38	95%	98%	97%
Prophylactic Antibiotic Select. (Outpatient)	35	94%	97%	94%
Prophylactic Antibiotic Stopped	35	91%	95%	94%
Recommended VTP Ordered	44	100%	93%	94%
Urinary Catheter Removal[1]	12	92%	91%	90%
Children's Asthma Care				
Received Systemic Corticosteroids	-	-	-	100%
Received Home Management Plan	-	-	-	71%
Received Reliever Medication	-	-	-	100%
Use of Medical Imaging				
Combination Abdominal CT Scan	262	0.099	0.163	0.191
Combination Chest CT Scan	144	0.063	0.060	0.054
Follow-up Mammogram/Ultrasound	449	18.3%	8.1%	8.4%
MRI for Low Back Pain	79	30.4%	30.2%	32.7%
Survey of Patients' Hospital Experiences				
Area Around Room 'Always' Quiet at Night	300+	67%	-	58%
Doctors 'Always' Communicated Well	300+	85%	-	80%
Home Recovery Information Given	300+	87%	-	82%
Hospital Given 9 or 10 on 10 Point Scale	300+	72%	-	67%
Meds 'Always' Explained Before Given	300+	67%	-	60%
Nurses 'Always' Communicated Well	300+	81%	-	76%
Pain 'Always' Well Controlled	300+	73%	-	69%
Room and Bathroom 'Always' Clean	300+	81%	-	71%
Timely Help 'Always' Received	300+	74%	-	64%
Would Definitely Recommend Hospital	300+	74%	-	69%

Grundy County Memorial Hospital

201 East J Avenue
Grundy Center, IA 50638
Phone: 319-824-5421
Fax: 319-824-3337
E-mail: janicem@gcmuni.net
URL: www.grundyhospital.com
Type: Critical Access Hospitals
Emergency Services: Yes
Ownership: Voluntary Non-Profit - Other
Beds: 80

Key Personnel:

CEO/President. . . . . Pamela K Delagardelle
Chief of Medical Staff . . . . Ryan Bingman, MD
Operating Room. . . . . Elizabeth Ash
Emergency Room . . . . Elizabeth Ash, RN

Measure	Cases	This Hosp.	State Avg.	U.S. Avg.
Heart Attack Care				
ACE Inhibitor or ARB for LVSD[5]	0	-	96%	96%
Aspirin at Arrival[5]	0	-	99%	99%
Aspirin at Discharge[5]	0	-	99%	98%
Beta Blocker at Discharge[5]	0	-	99%	98%
Fibrinolytic Medication Timing[5]	0	-	67%	55%
PCI Within 90 Minutes of Arrival[5]	0	-	94%	90%
Smoking Cessation Advice[5]	0	-	99%	99%
Chest Pain/Possible Heart Attack Care				
Aspirin at Arrival	30	100%	96%	95%
Median Time to ECG (minutes)	32	4	7	8
Median Time to Transfer (minutes)[1,3]	1	39	64	61
Fibrinolytic Medication Timing[3]	0	-	45%	54%
Heart Failure Care				
ACE Inhibitor or ARB for LVSD[1]	1	100%	94%	94%
Discharge Instructions[1]	13	100%	86%	88%
Evaluation of LVS Function[1]	17	100%	95%	98%
Smoking Cessation Advice	0	-	96%	98%
Pneumonia Care				
Appropriate Initial Antibiotic[1]	11	100%	92%	92%
Blood Culture Timing[1]	9	100%	97%	96%
Influenza Vaccine[1]	6	100%	92%	91%
Initial Antibiotic Timing[1]	12	100%	97%	95%
Pneumococcal Vaccine[1]	13	100%	94%	93%
Smoking Cessation Advice[1]	1	100%	95%	97%
Surgical Care Improvement Project				
Appropriate VTP Within 24 Hours[1]	19	89%	92%	92%
Appropriate Hair Removal	41	100%	100%	99%
Appropriate Beta Blocker Usage[5]	0	-	94%	93%
Controlled Postoperative Blood Glucose	0	-	89%	93%
Prophylactic Antibiotic Timing	40	98%	98%	97%
Prophylactic Antibiotic Timing (Outpatient)[5]	0	-	94%	92%
Prophylactic Antibiotic Selection	40	100%	98%	97%
Prophylactic Antibiotic Select. (Outpatient)[5]	0	-	97%	94%
Prophylactic Antibiotic Stopped	40	92%	95%	94%
Recommended VTP Ordered[1]	19	89%	93%	94%
Urinary Catheter Removal[1]	1	0%	91%	90%
Children's Asthma Care				
Received Systemic Corticosteroids	-	-	-	100%
Received Home Management Plan	-	-	-	71%
Received Reliever Medication	-	-	-	100%
Use of Medical Imaging				
Combination Abdominal CT Scan	54	0.037	0.163	0.191
Combination Chest CT Scan[1]	31	0.000	0.060	0.054
Follow-up Mammogram/Ultrasound	213	5.2%	8.1%	8.4%
MRI for Low Back Pain[1]	8	37.5%	30.2%	32.7%
Survey of Patients' Hospital Experiences				
Area Around Room 'Always' Quiet at Night[6]	<100	72%	-	58%
Doctors 'Always' Communicated Well[6]	<100	81%	-	80%
Home Recovery Information Given[6]	<100	89%	-	82%
Hospital Given 9 or 10 on 10 Point Scale[6]	<100	80%	-	67%
Meds 'Always' Explained Before Given[6]	<100	64%	-	60%
Nurses 'Always' Communicated Well[6]	<100	77%	-	76%
Pain 'Always' Well Controlled[6]	<100	72%	-	69%
Room and Bathroom 'Always' Clean[6]	<100	80%	-	71%
Timely Help 'Always' Received[6]	<100	67%	-	64%
Would Definitely Recommend Hospital	<100	87%	-	69%

NOTE: Hospital profiles are in alphabetical order by state, then city, then hospital within the city; Rankings exclude hospitals with less than 25 cases except for patient surveys which excludes hospitals with less than 100 cases; (a) 100–299 cases; (1) The number of cases is too small to be sure how well a hospital is performing; (2) The hospital indicated that the data submitted for this measure were based on a sample of cases; (3) Data was collected during a shorter time period (fewer quarters) than the maximum possible time for this measure; (4) Suppressed for one or more quarters by CMS; (5) No data is available from the hospital for this measure; (6) Fewer than 100 patients completed the HCAHPS survey. Use these rates with caution, as the number of surveys may be too low to reliably assess hospital performance; (7) Survey results are based on less than 12 months of data; (8) Survey results are not available for this reporting period; (9) No or very few patients were eligible for the HCAHPS survey. The scores shown, if any, reflect a very small number of surveys; (10) A state average was not calculated because too few hospitals in the state submitted data; (11) There were discrepancies in the data collection process; Please refer to the User's Guide for a full explanation of data.

Guthrie County Hospital

710 North 12th Street
Guthrie Center, IA 50115
URL: www.gcho.org
Type: Critical Access Hospitals
Ownership: Voluntary Non-Profit - Other
Phone: 641-332-2201
Fax: 641-332-2702
Emergency Services: Yes
Beds: 25

Key Personnel:
CEO/President. . . . . Gerald Neal
Chief of Medical Staff. . . . . Steven Bascom
Infection Control. . . . . Christine Drake
Operating Room. . . . . Nancy Coffman
Quality Assurance . . . . Kristi Carper
Radiology. . . . . Sarah Madsen
Anesthesiology. . . . . Steve Navarro

Measure	Cases	This Hosp.	State Avg.	U.S. Avg.
Heart Attack Care				
ACE Inhibitor or ARB for LVSD	-	-	96%	96%
Aspirin at Arrival	-	-	99%	99%
Aspirin at Discharge	-	-	99%	98%
Beta Blocker at Discharge	-	-	99%	98%
Fibrinolytic Medication Timing	-	-	67%	55%
PCI Within 90 Minutes of Arrival	-	-	94%	90%
Smoking Cessation Advice	-	-	99%	99%
Chest Pain/Possible Heart Attack Care				
Aspirin at Arrival[5]	0	-	96%	95%
Median Time to ECG (minutes)[5]	0	-	7	8
Median Time to Transfer (minutes)[5]	0	-	64	61
Fibrinolytic Medication Timing[5]	0	-	45%	54%
Heart Failure Care				
ACE Inhibitor or ARB for LVSD	-	-	94%	94%
Discharge Instructions	-	-	86%	88%
Evaluation of LVS Function	-	-	95%	98%
Smoking Cessation Advice	-	-	96%	98%
Pneumonia Care				
Appropriate Initial Antibiotic	-	-	92%	92%
Blood Culture Timing	-	-	97%	96%
Influenza Vaccine	-	-	92%	91%
Initial Antibiotic Timing	-	-	97%	95%
Pneumococcal Vaccine	-	-	94%	93%
Smoking Cessation Advice	-	-	95%	97%
Surgical Care Improvement Project				
Appropriate VTP Within 24 Hours	-	-	92%	92%
Appropriate Hair Removal	-	-	100%	99%
Appropriate Beta Blocker Usage	-	-	94%	93%
Controlled Postoperative Blood Glucose	-	-	89%	93%
Prophylactic Antibiotic Timing	-	-	98%	97%
Prophylactic Antibiotic Timing (Outpatient)[5]	0	-	94%	92%
Prophylactic Antibiotic Selection	-	-	98%	97%
Prophylactic Antibiotic Select. (Outpatient)[5]	0	-	97%	94%
Prophylactic Antibiotic Stopped	-	-	95%	94%
Recommended VTP Ordered	-	-	93%	94%
Urinary Catheter Removal	-	-	91%	90%
Children's Asthma Care				
Received Systemic Corticosteroids	-	-	-	100%
Received Home Management Plan	-	-	-	71%
Received Reliever Medication	-	-	-	100%
Use of Medical Imaging				
Combination Abdominal CT Scan	77	0.091	0.163	0.191
Combination Chest CT Scan[1]	50	0.080	0.060	0.054
Follow-up Mammogram/Ultrasound	123	12.2%	8.1%	8.4%
MRI for Low Back Pain[1]	19	26.3%	30.2%	32.7%
Survey of Patients' Hospital Experiences				
Area Around Room 'Always' Quiet at Night	-	-	-	58%
Doctors 'Always' Communicated Well	-	-	-	80%
Home Recovery Information Given	-	-	-	82%
Hospital Given 9 or 10 on 10 Point Scale	-	-	-	67%
Meds 'Always' Explained Before Given	-	-	-	60%
Nurses 'Always' Communicated Well	-	-	-	76%
Pain 'Always' Well Controlled	-	-	-	69%
Room and Bathroom 'Always' Clean	-	-	-	71%
Timely Help 'Always' Received	-	-	-	64%
Would Definitely Recommend Hospital	-	-	-	69%

Guttenberg Municipal Hospital

200 Main Street
Guttenberg, IA 52052
URL: www.guttenberghospital.org
Type: Critical Access Hospitals
Ownership: Government - Local
Phone: 563-252-1121
Fax: 563-252-3120
Emergency Services: Yes
Beds: 25

Key Personnel:
CEO/President. . . . . Kim Gau
Cardiac Laboratory. . . . . Danelle Krapfl
Chief of Medical Staff. . . . . Will Chance, DO
Infection Control. . . . . Robin Esmann
Operating Room. . . . . Deb Preston
Radiology. . . . . Lori Kann
Emergency Room . . . . Jeff Ashline, PA-C

Measure	Cases	This Hosp.	State Avg.	U.S. Avg.
Heart Attack Care				
ACE Inhibitor or ARB for LVSD[3]	0	-	96%	96%
Aspirin at Arrival[1,3]	2	100%	99%	99%
Aspirin at Discharge[3]	0	-	99%	98%
Beta Blocker at Discharge[3]	0	-	99%	98%
Fibrinolytic Medication Timing[3]	0	-	67%	55%
PCI Within 90 Minutes of Arrival[3]	0	-	94%	90%
Smoking Cessation Advice[3]	0	-	99%	99%
Chest Pain/Possible Heart Attack Care				
Aspirin at Arrival	-	-	96%	95%
Median Time to ECG (minutes)	-	-	7	8
Median Time to Transfer (minutes)	-	-	64	61
Fibrinolytic Medication Timing	-	-	45%	54%
Heart Failure Care				
ACE Inhibitor or ARB for LVSD	0	-	94%	94%
Discharge Instructions[1]	6	50%	86%	88%
Evaluation of LVS Function[1]	15	87%	95%	98%
Smoking Cessation Advice[1]	2	50%	96%	98%
Pneumonia Care				
Appropriate Initial Antibiotic[1]	22	86%	92%	92%
Blood Culture Timing[1]	12	100%	97%	96%
Influenza Vaccine[1]	16	69%	92%	91%
Initial Antibiotic Timing[1]	21	95%	97%	95%
Pneumococcal Vaccine[1]	19	89%	94%	93%
Smoking Cessation Advice[1]	7	71%	95%	97%
Surgical Care Improvement Project				
Appropriate VTP Within 24 Hours[5]	0	-	92%	92%
Appropriate Hair Removal[5]	0	-	100%	99%
Appropriate Beta Blocker Usage[5]	0	-	94%	93%
Controlled Postoperative Blood Glucose[5]	0	-	89%	93%
Prophylactic Antibiotic Timing[5]	0	-	98%	97%
Prophylactic Antibiotic Timing (Outpatient)	-	-	94%	92%
Prophylactic Antibiotic Selection[5]	0	-	98%	97%
Prophylactic Antibiotic Select. (Outpatient)	-	-	97%	94%
Prophylactic Antibiotic Stopped[5]	0	-	95%	94%
Recommended VTP Ordered[5]	0	-	93%	94%
Urinary Catheter Removal[5]	0	-	91%	90%
Children's Asthma Care				
Received Systemic Corticosteroids	-	-	-	100%
Received Home Management Plan	-	-	-	71%
Received Reliever Medication	-	-	-	100%
Use of Medical Imaging				
Combination Abdominal CT Scan	-	-	0.163	0.191
Combination Chest CT Scan	-	-	0.060	0.054
Follow-up Mammogram/Ultrasound	-	-	8.1%	8.4%
MRI for Low Back Pain	-	-	30.2%	32.7%
Survey of Patients' Hospital Experiences				
Area Around Room 'Always' Quiet at Night	(a)	70%	-	58%
Doctors 'Always' Communicated Well	(a)	88%	-	80%
Home Recovery Information Given	(a)	84%	-	82%
Hospital Given 9 or 10 on 10 Point Scale	(a)	77%	-	67%
Meds 'Always' Explained Before Given	(a)	71%	-	60%
Nurses 'Always' Communicated Well	(a)	85%	-	76%
Pain 'Always' Well Controlled	(a)	72%	-	69%
Room and Bathroom 'Always' Clean	(a)	87%	-	71%
Timely Help 'Always' Received	(a)	79%	-	64%
Would Definitely Recommend Hospital	(a)	82%	-	69%

Franklin General Hospital

1720 Central Avenue East
Hampton, IA 50441
URL: www.franklingeneral.com
Type: Critical Access Hospitals
Ownership: Government - Local
Phone: 641-456-5000
Fax: 641-456-5020
Emergency Services: Yes
Beds: 77

Key Personnel:
Chief of Medical Staff. . . . . Brian J Hansen
Infection Control. . . . . Lori West, RN
Operating Room. . . . . Karen Miller, RN
Radiology. . . . . Meggan M Cearley
Emergency Room . . . . Dawn Craighton, RN

Measure	Cases	This Hosp.	State Avg.	U.S. Avg.
Heart Attack Care				
ACE Inhibitor or ARB for LVSD[3]	0	-	96%	96%
Aspirin at Arrival[1,3]	1	100%	99%	99%
Aspirin at Discharge[3]	0	-	99%	98%
Beta Blocker at Discharge[3]	0	-	99%	98%
Fibrinolytic Medication Timing[3]	0	-	67%	55%
PCI Within 90 Minutes of Arrival[3]	0	-	94%	90%
Smoking Cessation Advice[3]	0	-	99%	99%
Chest Pain/Possible Heart Attack Care				
Aspirin at Arrival	-	-	96%	95%
Median Time to ECG (minutes)	-	-	7	8
Median Time to Transfer (minutes)	-	-	64	61
Fibrinolytic Medication Timing	-	-	45%	54%
Heart Failure Care				
ACE Inhibitor or ARB for LVSD[1]	2	0%	94%	94%
Discharge Instructions[1]	9	56%	86%	88%
Evaluation of LVS Function[1]	12	75%	95%	98%
Smoking Cessation Advice[1]	3	33%	96%	98%
Pneumonia Care				
Appropriate Initial Antibiotic[1]	8	88%	92%	92%
Blood Culture Timing[1]	4	75%	97%	96%
Influenza Vaccine[1]	7	86%	92%	91%
Initial Antibiotic Timing[1]	9	89%	97%	95%
Pneumococcal Vaccine[1]	11	82%	94%	93%
Smoking Cessation Advice[1]	4	75%	95%	97%
Surgical Care Improvement Project				
Appropriate VTP Within 24 Hours[5]	0	-	92%	92%
Appropriate Hair Removal[5]	0	-	100%	99%
Appropriate Beta Blocker Usage[5]	0	-	94%	93%
Controlled Postoperative Blood Glucose[5]	0	-	89%	93%
Prophylactic Antibiotic Timing[5]	0	-	98%	97%
Prophylactic Antibiotic Timing (Outpatient)	-	-	94%	92%
Prophylactic Antibiotic Selection[5]	0	-	98%	97%
Prophylactic Antibiotic Select. (Outpatient)	-	-	97%	94%
Prophylactic Antibiotic Stopped[5]	0	-	95%	94%
Recommended VTP Ordered[5]	0	-	93%	94%
Urinary Catheter Removal[5]	0	-	91%	90%
Children's Asthma Care				
Received Systemic Corticosteroids	-	-	-	100%
Received Home Management Plan	-	-	-	71%
Received Reliever Medication	-	-	-	100%
Use of Medical Imaging				
Combination Abdominal CT Scan	-	-	0.163	0.191
Combination Chest CT Scan	-	-	0.060	0.054
Follow-up Mammogram/Ultrasound	-	-	8.1%	8.4%
MRI for Low Back Pain	-	-	30.2%	32.7%
Survey of Patients' Hospital Experiences				
Area Around Room 'Always' Quiet at Night[8]	-	-	-	58%
Doctors 'Always' Communicated Well[8]	-	-	-	80%
Home Recovery Information Given[8]	-	-	-	82%
Hospital Given 9 or 10 on 10 Point Scale[8]	-	-	-	67%
Meds 'Always' Explained Before Given[8]	-	-	-	60%
Nurses 'Always' Communicated Well[8]	-	-	-	76%
Pain 'Always' Well Controlled[8]	-	-	-	69%
Room and Bathroom 'Always' Clean[8]	-	-	-	71%
Timely Help 'Always' Received[8]	-	-	-	64%
Would Definitely Recommend Hospital[8]	-	-	-	69%

NOTE: Hospital profiles are in alphabetical order by state, then city, then hospital within the city; Rankings exclude hospitals with less than 25 cases except for patient surveys which excludes hospitals with less than 100 cases; (a) 100–299 cases; (1) The number of cases is too small to be sure how well a hospital is performing; (2) The hospital indicated that the data submitted for this measure were based on a sample of cases; (3) Data was collected during a shorter time period (fewer quarters) than the maximum possible time for this measure; (4) Suppressed for one or more quarters by CMS; (5) No data is available from the hospital for this measure; (6) Fewer than 100 patients completed the HCAHPS survey. Use these rates with caution, as the number of surveys may be too low to reliably assess hospital performance; (7) Survey results are based on less than 12 months of data; (8) Survey results are not available for this reporting period; (9) No or very few patients were eligible for the HCAHPS survey. The scores shown, if any, reflect a very small number of surveys; (10) A state average was not calculated because too few hospitals in the state submitted data; (11) There were discrepancies in the data collection process; Please refer to the User's Guide for a full explanation of data.

Myrtue Medical Center

1213 Garfield Avenue Phone: 712-755-5161
Harlan, IA 51537 Fax: 712-755-2640
URL: www.shelbycohealth.com
Type: Critical Access Hospitals Emergency Services: Yes
Ownership: Voluntary Non-Profit - Other Beds: 52

Key Personnel:
CEO/President. . . . . Mark Woodring
Chief of Medical Staff . . . . Don Klilgaard
Operating Room. . . . . Pat Boettger
Quality Assurance . . . . Judy Zea
Emergency Room . . . . Scott Markham

Measure	Cases	This Hosp.	State Avg.	U.S. Avg.
Heart Attack Care				
ACE Inhibitor or ARB for LVSD[5]	0	-	96%	96%
Aspirin at Arrival[5]	0	-	99%	99%
Aspirin at Discharge[5]	0	-	99%	98%
Beta Blocker at Discharge[5]	0	-	99%	98%
Fibrinolytic Medication Timing[5]	0	-	67%	55%
PCI Within 90 Minutes of Arrival[5]	0	-	94%	90%
Smoking Cessation Advice[5]	0	-	99%	99%
Chest Pain/Possible Heart Attack Care				
Aspirin at Arrival[5]	0	-	96%	95%
Median Time to ECG (minutes)[5]	0	-	7	8
Median Time to Transfer (minutes)[5]	0	-	64	61
Fibrinolytic Medication Timing[5]	0	-	45%	54%
Heart Failure Care				
ACE Inhibitor or ARB for LVSD[1]	12	100%	94%	94%
Discharge Instructions[1]	15	87%	86%	88%
Evaluation of LVS Function	37	100%	95%	98%
Smoking Cessation Advice[1]	4	75%	96%	98%
Pneumonia Care				
Appropriate Initial Antibiotic[2]	32	91%	92%	92%
Blood Culture Timing[2]	47	100%	97%	96%
Influenza Vaccine	26	92%	92%	91%
Initial Antibiotic Timing[2]	53	100%	97%	95%
Pneumococcal Vaccine[2]	53	100%	94%	93%
Smoking Cessation Advice[1,2]	13	85%	95%	97%
Surgical Care Improvement Project				
Appropriate VTP Within 24 Hours[5]	0	-	92%	92%
Appropriate Hair Removal[5]	0	-	100%	99%
Appropriate Beta Blocker Usage[5]	0	-	94%	93%
Controlled Postoperative Blood Glucose[5]	0	-	89%	93%
Prophylactic Antibiotic Timing[5]	0	-	98%	97%
Prophylactic Antibiotic Timing (Outpatient)[5]	0	-	94%	92%
Prophylactic Antibiotic Selection[5]	0	-	98%	97%
Prophylactic Antibiotic Select. (Outpatient)[5]	0	-	97%	94%
Prophylactic Antibiotic Stopped[5]	0	-	95%	94%
Recommended VTP Ordered[5]	0	-	93%	94%
Urinary Catheter Removal[5]	0	-	91%	90%
Children's Asthma Care				
Received Systemic Corticosteroids	-	-	-	100%
Received Home Management Plan	-	-	-	71%
Received Reliever Medication	-	-	-	100%
Use of Medical Imaging				
Combination Abdominal CT Scan	195	0.133	0.163	0.191
Combination Chest CT Scan	88	0.091	0.060	0.054
Follow-up Mammogram/Ultrasound	423	9.0%	8.1%	8.4%
MRI for Low Back Pain	41	39.0%	30.2%	32.7%
Survey of Patients' Hospital Experiences				
Area Around Room 'Always' Quiet at Night	300+	57%	-	58%
Doctors 'Always' Communicated Well	300+	87%	-	80%
Home Recovery Information Given	300+	84%	-	82%
Hospital Given 9 or 10 on 10 Point Scale	300+	73%	-	67%
Meds 'Always' Explained Before Given	300+	61%	-	60%
Nurses 'Always' Communicated Well	300+	81%	-	76%
Pain 'Always' Well Controlled	300+	69%	-	69%
Room and Bathroom 'Always' Clean	300+	84%	-	71%
Timely Help 'Always' Received	300+	65%	-	64%
Would Definitely Recommend Hospital	300+	72%	-	69%

Hawarden Community Hospital

1111 11th Street Phone: 712-551-3100
Hawarden, IA 51023 Fax: 712-551-3106
E-mail: commhosp@acsnet.com
URL: www.acsnet.com
Type: Critical Access Hospitals Emergency Services: Yes
Ownership: Voluntary Non-Profit - Other Beds: 18

Key Personnel:
CEO/President. . . . . Chad Markham
Chief of Medical Staff . . . . Dale Nystrom
Coronary Care . . . . Jeanna Negaard
Quality Assurance . . . . Ruth Dickmann
Emergency Room . . . . Lorna Westra

Measure	Cases	This Hosp.	State Avg.	U.S. Avg.
Heart Attack Care				
ACE Inhibitor or ARB for LVSD[5]	0	-	96%	96%
Aspirin at Arrival[5]	0	-	99%	99%
Aspirin at Discharge[5]	0	-	99%	98%
Beta Blocker at Discharge[5]	0	-	99%	98%
Fibrinolytic Medication Timing[5]	0	-	67%	55%
PCI Within 90 Minutes of Arrival[5]	0	-	94%	90%
Smoking Cessation Advice[5]	0	-	99%	99%
Chest Pain/Possible Heart Attack Care				
Aspirin at Arrival	-	-	96%	95%
Median Time to ECG (minutes)	-	-	7	8
Median Time to Transfer (minutes)	-	-	64	61
Fibrinolytic Medication Timing	-	-	45%	54%
Heart Failure Care				
ACE Inhibitor or ARB for LVSD[3]	0	-	94%	94%
Discharge Instructions[3]	0	-	86%	88%
Evaluation of LVS Function[3]	0	-	95%	98%
Smoking Cessation Advice[3]	0	-	96%	98%
Pneumonia Care				
Appropriate Initial Antibiotic[1]	4	100%	92%	92%
Blood Culture Timing[1]	5	100%	97%	96%
Influenza Vaccine[1]	5	100%	92%	91%
Initial Antibiotic Timing[1]	7	100%	97%	95%
Pneumococcal Vaccine[1]	9	100%	94%	93%
Smoking Cessation Advice[1]	2	0%	95%	97%
Surgical Care Improvement Project				
Appropriate VTP Within 24 Hours[5]	0	-	92%	92%
Appropriate Hair Removal[5]	0	-	100%	99%
Appropriate Beta Blocker Usage[5]	0	-	94%	93%
Controlled Postoperative Blood Glucose[5]	0	-	89%	93%
Prophylactic Antibiotic Timing[5]	0	-	98%	97%
Prophylactic Antibiotic Timing (Outpatient)	-	-	94%	92%
Prophylactic Antibiotic Selection[5]	0	-	98%	97%
Prophylactic Antibiotic Select. (Outpatient)	-	-	97%	94%
Prophylactic Antibiotic Stopped[5]	0	-	95%	94%
Recommended VTP Ordered[5]	0	-	93%	94%
Urinary Catheter Removal[5]	0	-	91%	90%
Children's Asthma Care				
Received Systemic Corticosteroids	-	-	-	100%
Received Home Management Plan	-	-	-	71%
Received Reliever Medication	-	-	-	100%
Use of Medical Imaging				
Combination Abdominal CT Scan	-	-	0.163	0.191
Combination Chest CT Scan	-	-	0.060	0.054
Follow-up Mammogram/Ultrasound	-	-	8.1%	8.4%
MRI for Low Back Pain	-	-	30.2%	32.7%
Survey of Patients' Hospital Experiences				
Area Around Room 'Always' Quiet at Night[6]	<100	88%	-	58%
Doctors 'Always' Communicated Well[6]	<100	84%	-	80%
Home Recovery Information Given[6]	<100	69%	-	82%
Hospital Given 9 or 10 on 10 Point Scale[6]	<100	77%	-	67%
Meds 'Always' Explained Before Given[6]	<100	80%	-	60%
Nurses 'Always' Communicated Well[6]	<100	83%	-	76%
Pain 'Always' Well Controlled[6]	<100	62%	-	69%
Room and Bathroom 'Always' Clean[6]	<100	87%	-	71%
Timely Help 'Always' Received[6]	<100	88%	-	64%
Would Definitely Recommend Hospital	<100	78%	-	69%

Horn Memorial Hospital

701 East 2nd Street Phone: 712-364-3311
Ida Grove, IA 51445 Fax: 712-364-3363
E-mail: maugsburger@hornmemorialhospital.org
URL: www.hornmemorialhospital.org
Type: Critical Access Hospitals Emergency Services: Yes
Ownership: Voluntary Non-Profit - Private Beds: 25

Key Personnel:
CEO/President. . . . . Marc Augsburger
Cardiac Laboratory. . . . . Jean Cipperley
Chief of Medical Staff . . . . Albert Veltri
Infection Control. . . . . Robin Lorenzen
Operating Room. . . . . Jill Webb
Quality Assurance . . . . Haether Gann
Radiology. . . . . Jerri Downs

Measure	Cases	This Hosp.	State Avg.	U.S. Avg.
Heart Attack Care				
ACE Inhibitor or ARB for LVSD[5]	0	-	96%	96%
Aspirin at Arrival[5]	0	-	99%	99%
Aspirin at Discharge[5]	0	-	99%	98%
Beta Blocker at Discharge[5]	0	-	99%	98%
Fibrinolytic Medication Timing[5]	0	-	67%	55%
PCI Within 90 Minutes of Arrival[5]	0	-	94%	90%
Smoking Cessation Advice[5]	0	-	99%	99%
Chest Pain/Possible Heart Attack Care				
Aspirin at Arrival	-	-	96%	95%
Median Time to ECG (minutes)	-	-	7	8
Median Time to Transfer (minutes)	-	-	64	61
Fibrinolytic Medication Timing	-	-	45%	54%
Heart Failure Care				
ACE Inhibitor or ARB for LVSD[1]	1	0%	94%	94%
Discharge Instructions[1]	13	15%	86%	88%
Evaluation of LVS Function[1]	21	24%	95%	98%
Smoking Cessation Advice[1]	5	40%	96%	98%
Pneumonia Care				
Appropriate Initial Antibiotic[5]	0	-	92%	92%
Blood Culture Timing[5]	0	-	97%	96%
Influenza Vaccine[5]	0	-	92%	91%
Initial Antibiotic Timing[5]	0	-	97%	95%
Pneumococcal Vaccine[5]	0	-	94%	93%
Smoking Cessation Advice[5]	0	-	95%	97%
Surgical Care Improvement Project				
Appropriate VTP Within 24 Hours[5]	0	-	92%	92%
Appropriate Hair Removal[5]	0	-	100%	99%
Appropriate Beta Blocker Usage[5]	0	-	94%	93%
Controlled Postoperative Blood Glucose[5]	0	-	89%	93%
Prophylactic Antibiotic Timing[5]	0	-	98%	97%
Prophylactic Antibiotic Timing (Outpatient)	-	-	94%	92%
Prophylactic Antibiotic Selection[5]	0	-	98%	97%
Prophylactic Antibiotic Select. (Outpatient)	-	-	97%	94%
Prophylactic Antibiotic Stopped[5]	0	-	95%	94%
Recommended VTP Ordered[5]	0	-	93%	94%
Urinary Catheter Removal[5]	0	-	91%	90%
Children's Asthma Care				
Received Systemic Corticosteroids	-	-	-	100%
Received Home Management Plan	-	-	-	71%
Received Reliever Medication	-	-	-	100%
Use of Medical Imaging				
Combination Abdominal CT Scan	-	-	0.163	0.191
Combination Chest CT Scan	-	-	0.060	0.054
Follow-up Mammogram/Ultrasound	-	-	8.1%	8.4%
MRI for Low Back Pain	-	-	30.2%	32.7%
Survey of Patients' Hospital Experiences				
Area Around Room 'Always' Quiet at Night[8]	-	-	-	58%
Doctors 'Always' Communicated Well[8]	-	-	-	80%
Home Recovery Information Given[8]	-	-	-	82%
Hospital Given 9 or 10 on 10 Point Scale[8]	-	-	-	67%
Meds 'Always' Explained Before Given[8]	-	-	-	60%
Nurses 'Always' Communicated Well[8]	-	-	-	76%
Pain 'Always' Well Controlled[8]	-	-	-	69%
Room and Bathroom 'Always' Clean[8]	-	-	-	71%
Timely Help 'Always' Received[8]	-	-	-	64%
Would Definitely Recommend Hospital[8]	-	-	-	69%

NOTE: Hospital profiles are in alphabetical order by state, then city, then hospital within the city; Rankings exclude hospitals with less than 25 cases except for patient surveys which excludes hospitals with less than 100 cases; (a) 100–299 cases; (1) The number of cases is too small to be sure how well a hospital is performing; (2) The hospital indicated that the data submitted for this measure were based on a sample of cases; (3) Data was collected during a shorter time period (fewer quarters) than the maximum possible time for this measure; (4) Suppressed for one or more quarters by CMS; (5) No data is available from the hospital for this measure; (6) Fewer than 100 patients completed the HCAHPS survey. Use these rates with caution, as the number of surveys may be too low to reliably assess hospital performance; (7) Survey results are based on less than 12 months of data; (8) Survey results are not available for this reporting period; (9) No or very few patients were eligible for the HCAHPS survey. The scores shown, if any, reflect a very small number of surveys; (10) A state average was not calculated because too few hospitals in the state submitted data; (11) There were discrepancies in the data collection process; Please refer to the User's Guide for a full explanation of data.

Buchanan County Health Center

1600 First St East
Independence, IA 50644
Phone: 319-332-0999
Fax: 319-334-6149
URL: www.bchealth.info
Type: Critical Access Hospitals
Emergency Services: Yes
Ownership: Voluntary Non-Profit - Other
Beds: 84

Key Personnel:

CEO/President. . . . . Bob Richard
Cardiac Laboratory. . . . . Deb Recker
Chief of Medical Staff . . . . Dr Julie Sandell
Infection Control. . . . . Mary Schmitt
Operating Room. . . . . Rosalind Gibbs
Quality Assurance . . . . Kathy Post
Emergency Room . . . . Roslind Gibbs

Measure	Cases	This Hosp.	State Avg.	U.S. Avg.
Heart Attack Care				
ACE Inhibitor or ARB for LVSD[5]	0	-	96%	96%
Aspirin at Arrival[5]	0	-	99%	99%
Aspirin at Discharge[5]	0	-	99%	98%
Beta Blocker at Discharge[5]	0	-	99%	98%
Fibrinolytic Medication Timing[5]	0	-	67%	55%
PCI Within 90 Minutes of Arrival[5]	0	-	94%	90%
Smoking Cessation Advice[5]	0	-	99%	99%
Chest Pain/Possible Heart Attack Care				
Aspirin at Arrival	-	-	96%	95%
Median Time to ECG (minutes)	-	-	7	8
Median Time to Transfer (minutes)	-	-	64	61
Fibrinolytic Medication Timing	-	-	45%	54%
Heart Failure Care				
ACE Inhibitor or ARB for LVSD[1]	1	100%	94%	94%
Discharge Instructions[1]	5	100%	86%	88%
Evaluation of LVS Function[1]	7	57%	95%	98%
Smoking Cessation Advice	0	-	96%	98%
Pneumonia Care				
Appropriate Initial Antibiotic[1]	16	94%	92%	92%
Blood Culture Timing[1]	23	96%	97%	96%
Influenza Vaccine[1]	8	100%	92%	91%
Initial Antibiotic Timing[1]	20	95%	97%	95%
Pneumococcal Vaccine	28	89%	94%	93%
Smoking Cessation Advice[1]	3	67%	95%	97%
Surgical Care Improvement Project				
Appropriate VTP Within 24 Hours[5]	0	-	92%	92%
Appropriate Hair Removal[5]	0	-	100%	99%
Appropriate Beta Blocker Usage[5]	0	-	94%	93%
Controlled Postoperative Blood Glucose[5]	0	-	89%	93%
Prophylactic Antibiotic Timing[5]	0	-	98%	97%
Prophylactic Antibiotic Timing (Outpatient)	-	-	94%	92%
Prophylactic Antibiotic Selection[5]	0	-	98%	97%
Prophylactic Antibiotic Select. (Outpatient)	-	-	97%	94%
Prophylactic Antibiotic Stopped[5]	0	-	95%	94%
Recommended VTP Ordered[5]	0	-	93%	94%
Urinary Catheter Removal[5]	0	-	91%	90%
Children's Asthma Care				
Received Systemic Corticosteroids	-	-	-	100%
Received Home Management Plan	-	-	-	71%
Received Reliever Medication	-	-	-	100%
Use of Medical Imaging				
Combination Abdominal CT Scan	-	-	0.163	0.191
Combination Chest CT Scan	-	-	0.060	0.054
Follow-up Mammogram/Ultrasound	-	-	8.1%	8.4%
MRI for Low Back Pain	-	-	30.2%	32.7%
Survey of Patients' Hospital Experiences				
Area Around Room 'Always' Quiet at Night	(a)	67%	-	58%
Doctors 'Always' Communicated Well	(a)	83%	-	80%
Home Recovery Information Given	(a)	79%	-	82%
Hospital Given 9 or 10 on 10 Point Scale	(a)	66%	-	67%
Meds 'Always' Explained Before Given	(a)	60%	-	60%
Nurses 'Always' Communicated Well	(a)	77%	-	76%
Pain 'Always' Well Controlled	(a)	73%	-	69%
Room and Bathroom 'Always' Clean	(a)	79%	-	71%
Timely Help 'Always' Received	(a)	77%	-	64%
Would Definitely Recommend Hospital	(a)	68%	-	69%

Iowa City VA Medical Center

601 Highway 6 West
Iowa City, IA 52246
Phone: 319-338-0581
Fax: 319-339-7171
URL: www.va.gov/sta/guide/home.asp
Type: Acute Care-Veterans Administration
Emergency Services: No
Ownership: Government - Federal
Beds: 93

Key Personnel:

CEO/President. . . . . Barry Sharp, RN
Chief of Medical Staff . . . . John Cowdery, MD
Infection Control. . . . . Mary Fredrickson, RN
Operating Room. . . . . Betty Bream, RN
Quality Assurance . . . . Natalie Good
Radiology. . . . . David Bushnell, MD
Emergency Room . . . . Rodney Zeitler, MD
Intensive Care Unit. . . . . Kevin Dellsperger, MD

Measure	Cases	This Hosp.	State Avg.	U.S. Avg.
Heart Attack Care				
ACE Inhibitor or ARB for LVSD[1]	6	100%	96%	96%
Aspirin at Arrival	35	100%	99%	99%
Aspirin at Discharge	26	96%	99%	98%
Beta Blocker at Discharge	27	93%	99%	98%
Fibrinolytic Medication Timing[5]	0	-	67%	55%
PCI Within 90 Minutes of Arrival[1]	2	50%	94%	90%
Smoking Cessation Advice[1]	7	86%	99%	99%
Chest Pain/Possible Heart Attack Care				
Aspirin at Arrival	-	-	96%	95%
Median Time to ECG (minutes)	-	-	7	8
Median Time to Transfer (minutes)	-	-	64	61
Fibrinolytic Medication Timing	-	-	45%	54%
Heart Failure Care				
ACE Inhibitor or ARB for LVSD	34	100%	94%	94%
Discharge Instructions	101	100%	86%	88%
Evaluation of LVS Function	106	100%	95%	98%
Smoking Cessation Advice	30	100%	96%	98%
Pneumonia Care				
Appropriate Initial Antibiotic[1]	23	91%	92%	92%
Blood Culture Timing	34	100%	97%	96%
Influenza Vaccine	36	89%	92%	91%
Initial Antibiotic Timing	29	90%	97%	95%
Pneumococcal Vaccine	38	100%	94%	93%
Smoking Cessation Advice	28	100%	95%	97%
Surgical Care Improvement Project				
Appropriate VTP Within 24 Hours[2]	130	98%	92%	92%
Appropriate Hair Removal[2]	252	100%	100%	99%
Appropriate Beta Blocker Usage[2]	94	98%	94%	93%
Controlled Postoperative Blood Glucose[2,5]	0	-	89%	93%
Prophylactic Antibiotic Timing	175	96%	98%	97%
Prophylactic Antibiotic Timing (Outpatient)	-	-	94%	92%
Prophylactic Antibiotic Selection	174	99%	98%	97%
Prophylactic Antibiotic Select. (Outpatient)	-	-	97%	94%
Prophylactic Antibiotic Stopped	171	92%	95%	94%
Recommended VTP Ordered[2]	130	98%	93%	94%
Urinary Catheter Removal[2]	142	99%	91%	90%
Children's Asthma Care				
Received Systemic Corticosteroids	-	-	-	100%
Received Home Management Plan	-	-	-	71%
Received Reliever Medication	-	-	-	100%
Use of Medical Imaging				
Combination Abdominal CT Scan	-	-	0.163	0.191
Combination Chest CT Scan	-	-	0.060	0.054
Follow-up Mammogram/Ultrasound	-	-	8.1%	8.4%
MRI for Low Back Pain	-	-	30.2%	32.7%
Survey of Patients' Hospital Experiences				
Area Around Room 'Always' Quiet at Night	-	-	-	58%
Doctors 'Always' Communicated Well	-	-	-	80%
Home Recovery Information Given	-	-	-	82%
Hospital Given 9 or 10 on 10 Point Scale	-	-	-	67%
Meds 'Always' Explained Before Given	-	-	-	60%
Nurses 'Always' Communicated Well	-	-	-	76%
Pain 'Always' Well Controlled	-	-	-	69%
Room and Bathroom 'Always' Clean	-	-	-	71%
Timely Help 'Always' Received	-	-	-	64%
Would Definitely Recommend Hospital	-	-	-	69%

Mercy Hospital

500 E Market Street
Iowa City, IA 52245
Phone: 319-339-0300
Fax: 319-339-3788
URL: www.mercyiowacity.org
Type: Acute Care Hospitals
Emergency Services: Yes
Ownership: Voluntary Non-Profit - Church
Beds: 240

Key Personnel:

CEO/President. . . . . Ronald R Reed
Chief of Medical Staff . . . . Pete Wallace
Coronary Care . . . . Mike Lebsack
Operating Room. . . . . Sid Mills
Quality Assurance . . . . Barb Griswold
Radiology. . . . . Heidi Berns

Measure	Cases	This Hosp.	State Avg.	U.S. Avg.
Heart Attack Care				
ACE Inhibitor or ARB for LVSD	28	96%	96%	96%
Aspirin at Arrival	113	100%	99%	99%
Aspirin at Discharge	221	100%	99%	98%
Beta Blocker at Discharge	214	98%	99%	98%
Fibrinolytic Medication Timing	0	-	67%	55%
PCI Within 90 Minutes of Arrival[1]	23	91%	94%	90%
Smoking Cessation Advice	61	100%	99%	99%
Chest Pain/Possible Heart Attack Care				
Aspirin at Arrival[1,3]	2	100%	96%	95%
Median Time to ECG (minutes)[1,3]	2	14	7	8
Median Time to Transfer (minutes)[5]	0	-	64	61
Fibrinolytic Medication Timing[5]	0	-	45%	54%
Heart Failure Care				
ACE Inhibitor or ARB for LVSD	70	97%	94%	94%
Discharge Instructions	177	97%	86%	88%
Evaluation of LVS Function	212	100%	95%	98%
Smoking Cessation Advice[1]	17	100%	96%	98%
Pneumonia Care				
Appropriate Initial Antibiotic	82	89%	92%	92%
Blood Culture Timing	112	99%	97%	96%
Influenza Vaccine	76	86%	92%	91%
Initial Antibiotic Timing	109	94%	97%	95%
Pneumococcal Vaccine	125	94%	94%	93%
Smoking Cessation Advice	31	100%	95%	97%
Surgical Care Improvement Project				
Appropriate VTP Within 24 Hours	411	78%	92%	92%
Appropriate Hair Removal	1,241	99%	100%	99%
Appropriate Beta Blocker Usage	385	99%	94%	93%
Controlled Postoperative Blood Glucose	113	90%	89%	93%
Prophylactic Antibiotic Timing	918	97%	98%	97%
Prophylactic Antibiotic Timing (Outpatient)	198	94%	94%	92%
Prophylactic Antibiotic Selection	920	99%	98%	97%
Prophylactic Antibiotic Select. (Outpatient)	195	98%	97%	94%
Prophylactic Antibiotic Stopped	893	89%	95%	94%
Recommended VTP Ordered	411	82%	93%	94%
Urinary Catheter Removal	375	91%	91%	90%
Children's Asthma Care				
Received Systemic Corticosteroids	-	-	-	100%
Received Home Management Plan	-	-	-	71%
Received Reliever Medication	-	-	-	100%
Use of Medical Imaging				
Combination Abdominal CT Scan	625	0.067	0.163	0.191
Combination Chest CT Scan	583	0.002	0.060	0.054
Follow-up Mammogram/Ultrasound	1,189	7.7%	8.1%	8.4%
MRI for Low Back Pain	269	28.3%	30.2%	32.7%
Survey of Patients' Hospital Experiences				
Area Around Room 'Always' Quiet at Night	300+	58%	-	58%
Doctors 'Always' Communicated Well	300+	85%	-	80%
Home Recovery Information Given	300+	92%	-	82%
Hospital Given 9 or 10 on 10 Point Scale	300+	76%	-	67%
Meds 'Always' Explained Before Given	300+	66%	-	60%
Nurses 'Always' Communicated Well	300+	81%	-	76%
Pain 'Always' Well Controlled	300+	69%	-	69%
Room and Bathroom 'Always' Clean	300+	70%	-	71%
Timely Help 'Always' Received	300+	72%	-	64%
Would Definitely Recommend Hospital	300+	86%	-	69%

NOTE: Hospital profiles are in alphabetical order by state, then city, then hospital within the city; Rankings exclude hospitals with less than 25 cases except for patient surveys which excludes hospitals with less than 100 cases; (a) 100–299 cases; (1) The number of cases is too small to be sure how well a hospital is performing; (2) The hospital indicated that the data submitted for this measure were based on a sample of cases; (3) Data was collected during a shorter time period (fewer quarters) than the maximum possible time for this measure; (4) Suppressed for one or more quarters by CMS; (5) No data is available from the hospital for this measure; (6) Fewer than 100 patients completed the HCAHPS survey. Use these rates with caution, as the number of surveys may be too low to reliably assess hospital performance; (7) Survey results are based on less than 12 months of data; (8) Survey results are not available for this reporting period; (9) No or very few patients were eligible for the HCAHPS survey. The scores shown, if any, reflect a very small number of surveys; (10) A state average was not calculated because too few hospitals in the state submitted data; (11) There were discrepancies in the data collection process; Please refer to the User's Guide for a full explanation of data.

University of Iowa Hospital & Clinics

200 Hawkins Drive
Iowa City, IA 52242
Phone: 319-356-1616
Fax: 319-356-3862
URL: www.uihealthcare.com
Type: Acute Care Hospitals
Emergency Services: Yes
Ownership: Government - State
Beds: 729

Key Personnel:
CEO/President. . . . . Ken Kates
Chief of Medical Staff . . . . Eva Tsalikian MD
Infection Control. . . . . Loreen Herwaldt MD
Operating Room. . . . . Toni Mueller RN, MSN CCRN
Pediatric Ambulatory Care . . . . . . Michael Artman MD
Radiology. . . . . Laurie Fajardo MD

Measure	Cases	This Hosp.	State Avg.	U.S. Avg.
Heart Attack Care				
ACE Inhibitor or ARB for LVSD	42	83%	96%	96%
Aspirin at Arrival	79	100%	99%	99%
Aspirin at Discharge	245	100%	99%	98%
Beta Blocker at Discharge	240	99%	99%	98%
Fibrinolytic Medication Timing	0	-	67%	55%
PCI Within 90 Minutes of Arrival[1]	16	81%	94%	90%
Smoking Cessation Advice	102	97%	99%	99%
Chest Pain/Possible Heart Attack Care				
Aspirin at Arrival[1]	4	75%	96%	95%
Median Time to ECG (minutes)[1]	4	9	7	8
Median Time to Transfer (minutes)[5]	0	-	64	61
Fibrinolytic Medication Timing[5]	0	-	45%	54%
Heart Failure Care				
ACE Inhibitor or ARB for LVSD[2]	121	91%	94%	94%
Discharge Instructions[2]	255	55%	86%	88%
Evaluation of LVS Function[2]	284	98%	95%	98%
Smoking Cessation Advice[2]	67	97%	96%	98%
Pneumonia Care				
Appropriate Initial Antibiotic[2]	33	88%	92%	92%
Blood Culture Timing[2]	58	93%	97%	96%
Influenza Vaccine[2]	69	67%	92%	91%
Initial Antibiotic Timing[2]	54	96%	97%	95%
Pneumococcal Vaccine[2]	73	85%	94%	93%
Smoking Cessation Advice[2]	60	92%	95%	97%
Surgical Care Improvement Project				
Appropriate VTP Within 24 Hours[2]	204	95%	92%	92%
Appropriate Hair Removal[2]	604	99%	100%	99%
Appropriate Beta Blocker Usage[2]	167	63%	94%	93%
Controlled Postoperative Blood Glucose[2]	115	88%	89%	93%
Prophylactic Antibiotic Timing[2]	391	99%	98%	97%
Prophylactic Antibiotic Timing (Outpatient)	532	89%	94%	92%
Prophylactic Antibiotic Selection[2]	399	97%	98%	97%
Prophylactic Antibiotic Select. (Outpatient)	596	95%	97%	94%
Prophylactic Antibiotic Stopped[2]	370	93%	95%	94%
Recommended VTP Ordered[2]	205	95%	93%	94%
Urinary Catheter Removal[2]	146	85%	91%	90%
Children's Asthma Care				
Received Systemic Corticosteroids	-	-	-	100%
Received Home Management Plan	-	-	-	71%
Received Reliever Medication	-	-	-	100%
Use of Medical Imaging				
Combination Abdominal CT Scan	1,602	0.091	0.163	0.191
Combination Chest CT Scan	1,581	0.015	0.060	0.054
Follow-up Mammogram/Ultrasound	1,121	9.4%	8.1%	8.4%
MRI for Low Back Pain	205	23.4%	30.2%	32.7%
Survey of Patients' Hospital Experiences				
Area Around Room 'Always' Quiet at Night	300+	44%	-	58%
Doctors 'Always' Communicated Well	300+	75%	-	80%
Home Recovery Information Given	300+	84%	-	82%
Hospital Given 9 or 10 on 10 Point Scale	300+	66%	-	67%
Meds 'Always' Explained Before Given	300+	55%	-	60%
Nurses 'Always' Communicated Well	300+	72%	-	76%
Pain 'Always' Well Controlled	300+	62%	-	69%
Room and Bathroom 'Always' Clean	300+	66%	-	71%
Timely Help 'Always' Received	300+	55%	-	64%
Would Definitely Recommend Hospital	300+	77%	-	69%

Ellsworth Municipal Hospital

110 Rocksylvania Avenue
Iowa Falls, IA 50126
Phone: 641-648-4631
Fax: 641-648-2850
URL: www.emhia.com
Type: Critical Access Hospitals
Emergency Services: Yes
Ownership: Government - Local
Beds: 40

Key Personnel:
CEO/President. . . . . Cherelle Montanya
Chief of Medical Staff . . . . Joseph Brunkhorst MD
Infection Control. . . . . Ann Holmguard
Quality Assurance . . . . Katie Ricks
Anesthesiology. . . . . Barb Roby
Intensive Care Unit. . . . . Susan Copp

Measure	Cases	This Hosp.	State Avg.	U.S. Avg.
Heart Attack Care				
ACE Inhibitor or ARB for LVSD[3]	0	-	96%	96%
Aspirin at Arrival[1,3]	1	100%	99%	99%
Aspirin at Discharge[1,3]	2	100%	99%	98%
Beta Blocker at Discharge[1,3]	2	50%	99%	98%
Fibrinolytic Medication Timing[3]	0	-	67%	55%
PCI Within 90 Minutes of Arrival[3]	0	-	94%	90%
Smoking Cessation Advice[3]	0	-	99%	99%
Chest Pain/Possible Heart Attack Care				
Aspirin at Arrival	-	-	96%	95%
Median Time to ECG (minutes)	-	-	7	8
Median Time to Transfer (minutes)	-	-	64	61
Fibrinolytic Medication Timing	-	-	45%	54%
Heart Failure Care				
ACE Inhibitor or ARB for LVSD[1]	3	100%	94%	94%
Discharge Instructions[1]	21	100%	86%	88%
Evaluation of LVS Function	40	45%	95%	98%
Smoking Cessation Advice[1]	3	67%	96%	98%
Pneumonia Care				
Appropriate Initial Antibiotic[1]	18	89%	92%	92%
Blood Culture Timing[1]	10	100%	97%	96%
Influenza Vaccine[1]	21	86%	92%	91%
Initial Antibiotic Timing	27	89%	97%	95%
Pneumococcal Vaccine	41	76%	94%	93%
Smoking Cessation Advice[1]	6	83%	95%	97%
Surgical Care Improvement Project				
Appropriate VTP Within 24 Hours[5]	0	-	92%	92%
Appropriate Hair Removal[5]	0	-	100%	99%
Appropriate Beta Blocker Usage[5]	0	-	94%	93%
Controlled Postoperative Blood Glucose[5]	0	-	89%	93%
Prophylactic Antibiotic Timing[5]	0	-	98%	97%
Prophylactic Antibiotic Timing (Outpatient)	-	-	94%	92%
Prophylactic Antibiotic Selection[5]	0	-	98%	97%
Prophylactic Antibiotic Select. (Outpatient)	-	-	97%	94%
Prophylactic Antibiotic Stopped[5]	0	-	95%	94%
Recommended VTP Ordered[5]	0	-	93%	94%
Urinary Catheter Removal[5]	0	-	91%	90%
Children's Asthma Care				
Received Systemic Corticosteroids	-	-	-	100%
Received Home Management Plan	-	-	-	71%
Received Reliever Medication	-	-	-	100%
Use of Medical Imaging				
Combination Abdominal CT Scan	-	-	0.163	0.191
Combination Chest CT Scan	-	-	0.060	0.054
Follow-up Mammogram/Ultrasound	-	-	8.1%	8.4%
MRI for Low Back Pain	-	-	30.2%	32.7%
Survey of Patients' Hospital Experiences				
Area Around Room 'Always' Quiet at Night[8]	-	-	-	58%
Doctors 'Always' Communicated Well[8]	-	-	-	80%
Home Recovery Information Given[8]	-	-	-	82%
Hospital Given 9 or 10 on 10 Point Scale[8]	-	-	-	67%
Meds 'Always' Explained Before Given[8]	-	-	-	60%
Nurses 'Always' Communicated Well[8]	-	-	-	76%
Pain 'Always' Well Controlled[8]	-	-	-	69%
Room and Bathroom 'Always' Clean[8]	-	-	-	71%
Timely Help 'Always' Received[8]	-	-	-	64%
Would Definitely Recommend Hospital[8]	-	-	-	69%

Greene County Medical Center

1000 West Lincolnway
Jefferson, IA 50129
Phone: 515-386-2114
Fax: 515-386-3695
URL: www.gcmchealth.com
Type: Critical Access Hospitals
Emergency Services: Yes
Ownership: Government - Local
Beds: 127

Key Personnel:
CEO/President. . . . . Karen Bossard
Chief of Medical Staff . . . . Monica L Burgett, MD
Infection Control. . . . . Amy Love
Operating Room. . . . . Kraig Tweed
Quality Assurance . . . . Amy Love
Emergency Room . . . . Jeri Reese, RN
Patient Relations . . . . Jacque Andrew

Measure	Cases	This Hosp.	State Avg.	U.S. Avg.
Heart Attack Care				
ACE Inhibitor or ARB for LVSD[3]	0	-	96%	96%
Aspirin at Arrival[1,3]	1	100%	99%	99%
Aspirin at Discharge[1,3]	1	100%	99%	98%
Beta Blocker at Discharge[1,3]	1	100%	99%	98%
Fibrinolytic Medication Timing[3]	0	-	67%	55%
PCI Within 90 Minutes of Arrival[3]	0	-	94%	90%
Smoking Cessation Advice[3]	0	-	99%	99%
Chest Pain/Possible Heart Attack Care				
Aspirin at Arrival	-	-	96%	95%
Median Time to ECG (minutes)	-	-	7	8
Median Time to Transfer (minutes)	-	-	64	61
Fibrinolytic Medication Timing	-	-	45%	54%
Heart Failure Care				
ACE Inhibitor or ARB for LVSD	0	-	94%	94%
Discharge Instructions[1]	8	88%	86%	88%
Evaluation of LVS Function[1]	17	53%	95%	98%
Smoking Cessation Advice[1]	2	50%	96%	98%
Pneumonia Care				
Appropriate Initial Antibiotic[1]	19	68%	92%	92%
Blood Culture Timing[1]	11	91%	97%	96%
Influenza Vaccine[1]	17	71%	92%	91%
Initial Antibiotic Timing[1]	15	87%	97%	95%
Pneumococcal Vaccine[1]	23	65%	94%	93%
Smoking Cessation Advice[1]	3	0%	95%	97%
Surgical Care Improvement Project				
Appropriate VTP Within 24 Hours[1]	10	40%	92%	92%
Appropriate Hair Removal[1]	16	100%	100%	99%
Appropriate Beta Blocker Usage[5]	0	-	94%	93%
Controlled Postoperative Blood Glucose	0	-	89%	93%
Prophylactic Antibiotic Timing[1]	9	89%	98%	97%
Prophylactic Antibiotic Timing (Outpatient)	-	-	94%	92%
Prophylactic Antibiotic Selection[1]	9	89%	98%	97%
Prophylactic Antibiotic Select. (Outpatient)	-	-	97%	94%
Prophylactic Antibiotic Stopped[1]	9	89%	95%	94%
Recommended VTP Ordered[1]	10	40%	93%	94%
Urinary Catheter Removal[1]	3	67%	91%	90%
Children's Asthma Care				
Received Systemic Corticosteroids	-	-	-	100%
Received Home Management Plan	-	-	-	71%
Received Reliever Medication	-	-	-	100%
Use of Medical Imaging				
Combination Abdominal CT Scan	-	-	0.163	0.191
Combination Chest CT Scan	-	-	0.060	0.054
Follow-up Mammogram/Ultrasound	-	-	8.1%	8.4%
MRI for Low Back Pain	-	-	30.2%	32.7%
Survey of Patients' Hospital Experiences				
Area Around Room 'Always' Quiet at Night[8]	-	-	-	58%
Doctors 'Always' Communicated Well[8]	-	-	-	80%
Home Recovery Information Given[8]	-	-	-	82%
Hospital Given 9 or 10 on 10 Point Scale[8]	-	-	-	67%
Meds 'Always' Explained Before Given[8]	-	-	-	60%
Nurses 'Always' Communicated Well[8]	-	-	-	76%
Pain 'Always' Well Controlled[8]	-	-	-	69%
Room and Bathroom 'Always' Clean[8]	-	-	-	71%
Timely Help 'Always' Received[8]	-	-	-	64%
Would Definitely Recommend Hospital[8]	-	-	-	69%

NOTE: Hospital profiles are in alphabetical order by state, then city, then hospital within the city; Rankings exclude hospitals with less than 25 cases except for patient surveys which excludes hospitals with less than 100 cases; (a) 100–299 cases; (1) The number of cases is too small to be sure how well a hospital is performing; (2) The hospital indicated that the data submitted for this measure were based on a sample of cases; (3) Data was collected during a shorter time period (fewer quarters) than the maximum possible time for this measure; (4) Suppressed for one or more quarters by CMS; (5) No data is available from the hospital for this measure; (6) Fewer than 100 patients completed the HCAHPS survey. Use these rates with caution, as the number of surveys may be too low to reliably assess hospital performance; (7) Survey results are based on less than 12 months of data; (8) Survey results are not available for this reporting period; (9) No or very few patients were eligible for the HCAHPS survey. The scores shown, if any, reflect a very small number of surveys; (10) A state average was not calculated because too few hospitals in the state submitted data; (11) There were discrepancies in the data collection process; Please refer to the User's Guide for a full explanation of data.

Keokuk Area Hospital

1600 Morgan Street Phone: 319-524-7150
Keokuk, IA 52632 Fax: 319-524-5317
URL: www.keokukhealthsystems.org
Type: Acute Care Hospitals Emergency Services: Yes
Ownership: Voluntary Non-Profit - Private Beds: 120

Key Personnel:
CEO/President. . . . . Allan W Zastrow
Chief of Medical Staff . . . . Brigitte Cormier, MD
Infection Control. . . . . Ardath Tweedy, RN
Operating Room. . . . . Dwain Stone
Pediatric Ambulatory Care . . . . . . Barbara Clark
Pediatric In-Patient Care . . . . Barbara Clark
Quality Assurance . . . . Susie Lowe, RN
Radiology. . . . . William Fulcher

Measure	Cases	This Hosp.	State Avg.	U.S. Avg.
Heart Attack Care				
ACE Inhibitor or ARB for LVSD[1]	2	100%	96%	96%
Aspirin at Arrival[1]	20	100%	99%	99%
Aspirin at Discharge[1]	12	92%	99%	98%
Beta Blocker at Discharge[1]	12	92%	99%	98%
Fibrinolytic Medication Timing	0	-	67%	55%
PCI Within 90 Minutes of Arrival	0	-	94%	90%
Smoking Cessation Advice[1]	1	100%	99%	99%
Chest Pain/Possible Heart Attack Care				
Aspirin at Arrival	66	91%	96%	95%
Median Time to ECG (minutes)	69	11	7	8
Median Time to Transfer (minutes)[1,3]	1	44	64	61
Fibrinolytic Medication Timing[1]	7	71%	45%	54%
Heart Failure Care				
ACE Inhibitor or ARB for LVSD[1]	19	68%	94%	94%
Discharge Instructions	82	88%	86%	88%
Evaluation of LVS Function	101	97%	95%	98%
Smoking Cessation Advice[1]	20	100%	96%	98%
Pneumonia Care				
Appropriate Initial Antibiotic	57	89%	92%	92%
Blood Culture Timing	43	93%	97%	96%
Influenza Vaccine	55	100%	92%	91%
Initial Antibiotic Timing	77	96%	97%	95%
Pneumococcal Vaccine	82	96%	94%	93%
Smoking Cessation Advice	28	96%	95%	97%
Surgical Care Improvement Project				
Appropriate VTP Within 24 Hours[1]	23	87%	92%	92%
Appropriate Hair Removal	44	100%	100%	99%
Appropriate Beta Blocker Usage[1]	12	92%	94%	93%
Controlled Postoperative Blood Glucose	0	-	89%	93%
Prophylactic Antibiotic Timing[1]	24	92%	98%	97%
Prophylactic Antibiotic Timing (Outpatient)[1,3]	24	88%	94%	92%
Prophylactic Antibiotic Selection[1]	24	92%	98%	97%
Prophylactic Antibiotic Select. (Outpatient)[3,1]	22	100%	97%	94%
Prophylactic Antibiotic Stopped[1]	22	91%	95%	94%
Recommended VTP Ordered[1]	23	100%	93%	94%
Urinary Catheter Removal[1]	5	80%	91%	90%
Children's Asthma Care				
Received Systemic Corticosteroids	-	-	-	100%
Received Home Management Plan	-	-	-	71%
Received Reliever Medication	-	-	-	100%
Use of Medical Imaging				
Combination Abdominal CT Scan	284	0.250	0.163	0.191
Combination Chest CT Scan	87	0.506	0.060	0.054
Follow-up Mammogram/Ultrasound	583	4.1%	8.1%	8.4%
MRI for Low Back Pain[1]	53	24.5%	30.2%	32.7%
Survey of Patients' Hospital Experiences				
Area Around Room 'Always' Quiet at Night	(a)	46%	-	58%
Doctors 'Always' Communicated Well	(a)	77%	-	80%
Home Recovery Information Given	(a)	80%	-	82%
Hospital Given 9 or 10 on 10 Point Scale	(a)	61%	-	67%
Meds 'Always' Explained Before Given	(a)	55%	-	60%
Nurses 'Always' Communicated Well	(a)	71%	-	76%
Pain 'Always' Well Controlled	(a)	62%	-	69%
Room and Bathroom 'Always' Clean	(a)	74%	-	71%
Timely Help 'Always' Received	(a)	54%	-	64%
Would Definitely Recommend Hospital	(a)	55%	-	69%

Van Buren County Hospital

304 Franklin Street Phone: 319-293-3171
Keosauqua, IA 52565 Fax: 319-293-3142
URL: www.netins.net/showcase/forhealth
Type: Critical Access Hospitals Emergency Services: Yes
Ownership: Government - Local Beds: 25

Key Personnel:
CEO/President. . . . . Lisa Schnedler
Operating Room. . . . . Barbara Hirschler, RN
Radiology. . . . . Betsy Caviness
Emergency Room . . . . Vicki L Robertson, RN, DON

Measure	Cases	This Hosp.	State Avg.	U.S. Avg.
Heart Attack Care				
ACE Inhibitor or ARB for LVSD[1,3]	1	100%	96%	96%
Aspirin at Arrival[1,3]	3	67%	99%	99%
Aspirin at Discharge[1,3]	3	67%	99%	98%
Beta Blocker at Discharge[1,3]	3	33%	99%	98%
Fibrinolytic Medication Timing[3]	0	-	67%	55%
PCI Within 90 Minutes of Arrival[3]	0	-	94%	90%
Smoking Cessation Advice[3]	0	-	99%	99%
Chest Pain/Possible Heart Attack Care				
Aspirin at Arrival	-	-	96%	95%
Median Time to ECG (minutes)	-	-	7	8
Median Time to Transfer (minutes)	-	-	64	61
Fibrinolytic Medication Timing	-	-	45%	54%
Heart Failure Care				
ACE Inhibitor or ARB for LVSD[1]	7	71%	94%	94%
Discharge Instructions[1]	6	83%	86%	88%
Evaluation of LVS Function[1]	23	91%	95%	98%
Smoking Cessation Advice	0	-	96%	98%
Pneumonia Care				
Appropriate Initial Antibiotic[1]	19	79%	92%	92%
Blood Culture Timing[1]	17	94%	97%	96%
Influenza Vaccine[1]	22	59%	92%	91%
Initial Antibiotic Timing[1]	1	0%	97%	95%
Pneumococcal Vaccine	26	65%	94%	93%
Smoking Cessation Advice[1]	8	100%	95%	97%
Surgical Care Improvement Project				
Appropriate VTP Within 24 Hours[5]	0	-	92%	92%
Appropriate Hair Removal[5]	0	-	100%	99%
Appropriate Beta Blocker Usage[5]	0	-	94%	93%
Controlled Postoperative Blood Glucose[5]	0	-	89%	93%
Prophylactic Antibiotic Timing[5]	0	-	98%	97%
Prophylactic Antibiotic Timing (Outpatient)	-	-	94%	92%
Prophylactic Antibiotic Selection[5]	0	-	98%	97%
Prophylactic Antibiotic Select. (Outpatient)	-	-	97%	94%
Prophylactic Antibiotic Stopped[5]	0	-	95%	94%
Recommended VTP Ordered[5]	0	-	93%	94%
Urinary Catheter Removal[5]	0	-	91%	90%
Children's Asthma Care				
Received Systemic Corticosteroids	-	-	-	100%
Received Home Management Plan	-	-	-	71%
Received Reliever Medication	-	-	-	100%
Use of Medical Imaging				
Combination Abdominal CT Scan	-	-	0.163	0.191
Combination Chest CT Scan	-	-	0.060	0.054
Follow-up Mammogram/Ultrasound	-	-	8.1%	8.4%
MRI for Low Back Pain	-	-	30.2%	32.7%
Survey of Patients' Hospital Experiences				
Area Around Room 'Always' Quiet at Night[8]	-	-	-	58%
Doctors 'Always' Communicated Well[8]	-	-	-	80%
Home Recovery Information Given[8]	-	-	-	82%
Hospital Given 9 or 10 on 10 Point Scale[8]	-	-	-	67%
Meds 'Always' Explained Before Given[8]	-	-	-	60%
Nurses 'Always' Communicated Well[8]	-	-	-	76%
Pain 'Always' Well Controlled[8]	-	-	-	69%
Room and Bathroom 'Always' Clean[8]	-	-	-	71%
Timely Help 'Always' Received[8]	-	-	-	64%
Would Definitely Recommend Hospital[8]	-	-	-	69%

Knoxville Hospital & Clinics

1002 South Lincoln Street Phone: 641-842-2151
Knoxville, IA 50138
URL: www.kach.org
Type: Critical Access Hospitals Emergency Services: Yes
Ownership: Voluntary Non-Profit - Private Beds: 25

Key Personnel:
CEO/President. . . . . Ann Helwig
Operating Room. . . . . Amy Zoutte, RN
Radiology. . . . . Amy Heimbaugh
Emergency Room . . . . Melody Abell

Measure	Cases	This Hosp.	State Avg.	U.S. Avg.
Heart Attack Care				
ACE Inhibitor or ARB for LVSD[5]	0	-	96%	96%
Aspirin at Arrival[5]	0	-	99%	99%
Aspirin at Discharge[5]	0	-	99%	98%
Beta Blocker at Discharge[5]	0	-	99%	98%
Fibrinolytic Medication Timing[5]	0	-	67%	55%
PCI Within 90 Minutes of Arrival[5]	0	-	94%	90%
Smoking Cessation Advice[5]	0	-	99%	99%
Chest Pain/Possible Heart Attack Care				
Aspirin at Arrival	-	-	96%	95%
Median Time to ECG (minutes)	-	-	7	8
Median Time to Transfer (minutes)	-	-	64	61
Fibrinolytic Medication Timing	-	-	45%	54%
Heart Failure Care				
ACE Inhibitor or ARB for LVSD[1]	4	75%	94%	94%
Discharge Instructions[1]	18	94%	86%	88%
Evaluation of LVS Function[1]	22	82%	95%	98%
Smoking Cessation Advice[1]	6	83%	96%	98%
Pneumonia Care				
Appropriate Initial Antibiotic	31	87%	92%	92%
Blood Culture Timing	27	81%	97%	96%
Influenza Vaccine[1]	16	100%	92%	91%
Initial Antibiotic Timing	41	88%	97%	95%
Pneumococcal Vaccine	33	97%	94%	93%
Smoking Cessation Advice[1]	9	67%	95%	97%
Surgical Care Improvement Project				
Appropriate VTP Within 24 Hours[3]	0	-	92%	92%
Appropriate Hair Removal[1]	8	100%	100%	99%
Appropriate Beta Blocker Usage[3]	0	-	94%	93%
Controlled Postoperative Blood Glucose[5]	0	-	89%	93%
Prophylactic Antibiotic Timing[1]	1	100%	98%	97%
Prophylactic Antibiotic Timing (Outpatient)	-	-	94%	92%
Prophylactic Antibiotic Selection[1]	2	50%	98%	97%
Prophylactic Antibiotic Select. (Outpatient)	-	-	97%	94%
Prophylactic Antibiotic Stopped[1]	1	100%	95%	94%
Recommended VTP Ordered[1]	4	75%	93%	94%
Urinary Catheter Removal	0	-	91%	90%
Children's Asthma Care				
Received Systemic Corticosteroids	-	-	-	100%
Received Home Management Plan	-	-	-	71%
Received Reliever Medication	-	-	-	100%
Use of Medical Imaging				
Combination Abdominal CT Scan	-	-	0.163	0.191
Combination Chest CT Scan	-	-	0.060	0.054
Follow-up Mammogram/Ultrasound	-	-	8.1%	8.4%
MRI for Low Back Pain	-	-	30.2%	32.7%
Survey of Patients' Hospital Experiences				
Area Around Room 'Always' Quiet at Night	(a)	49%	-	58%
Doctors 'Always' Communicated Well	(a)	91%	-	80%
Home Recovery Information Given	(a)	84%	-	82%
Hospital Given 9 or 10 on 10 Point Scale	(a)	68%	-	67%
Meds 'Always' Explained Before Given	(a)	64%	-	60%
Nurses 'Always' Communicated Well	(a)	79%	-	76%
Pain 'Always' Well Controlled	(a)	70%	-	69%
Room and Bathroom 'Always' Clean	(a)	81%	-	71%
Timely Help 'Always' Received	(a)	67%	-	64%
Would Definitely Recommend Hospital	(a)	71%	-	69%

NOTE: Hospital profiles are in alphabetical order by state, then city, then hospital within the city; Rankings exclude hospitals with less than 25 cases except for patient surveys which excludes hospitals with less than 100 cases; (a) 100–299 cases; (1) The number of cases is too small to be sure how well a hospital is performing; (2) The hospital indicated that the data submitted for this measure were based on a sample of cases; (3) Data was collected during a shorter time period (fewer quarters) than the maximum possible time for this measure; (4) Suppressed for one or more quarters by CMS; (5) No data is available from the hospital for this measure; (6) Fewer than 100 patients completed the HCAHPS survey. Use these rates with caution, as the number of surveys may be too low to reliably assess hospital performance; (7) Survey results are based on less than 12 months of data; (8) Survey results are not available for this reporting period; (9) No or very few patients were eligible for the HCAHPS survey. The scores shown, if any, reflect a very small number of surveys; (10) A state average was not calculated because too few hospitals in the state submitted data; (11) There were discrepancies in the data collection process; Please refer to the User's Guide for a full explanation of data.

Stewart Memorial Community Hospital

1301 West Main Street Phone: 712-464-3171
Lake City, IA 51449 Fax: 712-464-3269
URL: www.stewartmemorial.org
Type: Critical Access Hospitals Emergency Services: Yes
Ownership: Voluntary Non-Profit - Private Beds: 56

Key Personnel:
CEO/President. . . . . Leah Marxen
Chief of Medical Staff . . . . Elsie Verbik
Operating Room. . . . . Kevin Hibbett
Radiology. . . . . Mary Reiter
Anesthesiology. . . . . Perry Henley
Emergency Room . . . . Obediah Kahn

Measure	Cases	This Hosp.	State Avg.	U.S. Avg.
Heart Attack Care				
ACE Inhibitor or ARB for LVSD[3]	0	-	96%	96%
Aspirin at Arrival[1,3]	2	100%	99%	99%
Aspirin at Discharge[1,3]	1	100%	99%	98%
Beta Blocker at Discharge[1,3]	1	100%	99%	98%
Fibrinolytic Medication Timing[3]	0	-	67%	55%
PCI Within 90 Minutes of Arrival[3]	0	-	94%	90%
Smoking Cessation Advice[3]	0	-	99%	99%
Chest Pain/Possible Heart Attack Care				
Aspirin at Arrival	-	-	96%	95%
Median Time to ECG (minutes)	-	-	7	8
Median Time to Transfer (minutes)	-	-	64	61
Fibrinolytic Medication Timing	-	-	45%	54%
Heart Failure Care				
ACE Inhibitor or ARB for LVSD[1]	5	100%	94%	94%
Discharge Instructions[1]	17	71%	86%	88%
Evaluation of LVS Function[1]	23	83%	95%	98%
Smoking Cessation Advice[1]	1	0%	96%	98%
Pneumonia Care				
Appropriate Initial Antibiotic[1]	18	100%	92%	92%
Blood Culture Timing[1]	13	100%	97%	96%
Influenza Vaccine	29	100%	92%	91%
Initial Antibiotic Timing	34	100%	97%	95%
Pneumococcal Vaccine	33	97%	94%	93%
Smoking Cessation Advice[1]	5	100%	95%	97%
Surgical Care Improvement Project				
Appropriate VTP Within 24 Hours[1]	2	100%	92%	92%
Appropriate Hair Removal[1]	5	100%	100%	99%
Appropriate Beta Blocker Usage[5]	0	-	94%	93%
Controlled Postoperative Blood Glucose	0	-	89%	93%
Prophylactic Antibiotic Timing[1]	6	83%	98%	97%
Prophylactic Antibiotic Timing (Outpatient)	-	-	94%	92%
Prophylactic Antibiotic Selection[1]	6	100%	98%	97%
Prophylactic Antibiotic Select. (Outpatient)	-	-	97%	94%
Prophylactic Antibiotic Stopped[1]	6	100%	95%	94%
Recommended VTP Ordered[1]	2	100%	93%	94%
Urinary Catheter Removal	0	-	91%	90%
Children's Asthma Care				
Received Systemic Corticosteroids	-	-	-	100%
Received Home Management Plan	-	-	-	71%
Received Reliever Medication	-	-	-	100%
Use of Medical Imaging				
Combination Abdominal CT Scan	-	-	0.163	0.191
Combination Chest CT Scan	-	-	0.060	0.054
Follow-up Mammogram/Ultrasound	-	-	8.1%	8.4%
MRI for Low Back Pain	-	-	30.2%	32.7%
Survey of Patients' Hospital Experiences				
Area Around Room 'Always' Quiet at Night	(a)	61%	-	58%
Doctors 'Always' Communicated Well	(a)	79%	-	80%
Home Recovery Information Given	(a)	83%	-	82%
Hospital Given 9 or 10 on 10 Point Scale	(a)	80%	-	67%
Meds 'Always' Explained Before Given	(a)	66%	-	60%
Nurses 'Always' Communicated Well	(a)	81%	-	76%
Pain 'Always' Well Controlled	(a)	69%	-	69%
Room and Bathroom 'Always' Clean	(a)	91%	-	71%
Timely Help 'Always' Received	(a)	72%	-	64%
Would Definitely Recommend Hospital	(a)	79%	-	69%

Floyd Valley Hospital

714 Lincoln St NE Phone: 712-546-7871
Le Mars, IA 51031 Fax: 712-546-3352
URL: www.floydvalleyhospital.org
Type: Critical Access Hospitals Emergency Services: Yes
Ownership: Voluntary Non-Profit - Other Beds: 44

Key Personnel:
Cardiac Laboratory. . . . . Lavonne Galles
Chief of Medical Staff . . . . Paul Parmelee, DO
Infection Control. . . . . Robert Norfolk
Operating Room. . . . . Gina Vacuna
Quality Assurance . . . . Renge Detrick
Anesthesiology. . . . . Gary Tillman
Hemotology Center . . . . Liz Kurth, RN
Patient Relations . . . . Lisa Wiese

Measure	Cases	This Hosp.	State Avg.	U.S. Avg.
Heart Attack Care				
ACE Inhibitor or ARB for LVSD[5]	0	-	96%	96%
Aspirin at Arrival[5]	0	-	99%	99%
Aspirin at Discharge[5]	0	-	99%	98%
Beta Blocker at Discharge[5]	0	-	99%	98%
Fibrinolytic Medication Timing[5]	0	-	67%	55%
PCI Within 90 Minutes of Arrival[5]	0	-	94%	90%
Smoking Cessation Advice[5]	0	-	99%	99%
Chest Pain/Possible Heart Attack Care				
Aspirin at Arrival	-	-	96%	95%
Median Time to ECG (minutes)	-	-	7	8
Median Time to Transfer (minutes)	-	-	64	61
Fibrinolytic Medication Timing	-	-	45%	54%
Heart Failure Care				
ACE Inhibitor or ARB for LVSD[1,2]	7	71%	94%	94%
Discharge Instructions[2]	32	88%	86%	88%
Evaluation of LVS Function[2]	44	98%	95%	98%
Smoking Cessation Advice[1,2]	2	100%	96%	98%
Pneumonia Care				
Appropriate Initial Antibiotic	32	100%	92%	92%
Blood Culture Timing	51	100%	97%	96%
Influenza Vaccine	30	100%	92%	91%
Initial Antibiotic Timing	53	98%	97%	95%
Pneumococcal Vaccine	50	98%	94%	93%
Smoking Cessation Advice[1]	4	100%	95%	97%
Surgical Care Improvement Project				
Appropriate VTP Within 24 Hours[1]	23	100%	92%	92%
Appropriate Hair Removal	76	100%	100%	99%
Appropriate Beta Blocker Usage[5]	0	-	94%	93%
Controlled Postoperative Blood Glucose[3]	0	-	89%	93%
Prophylactic Antibiotic Timing	60	98%	98%	97%
Prophylactic Antibiotic Timing (Outpatient)	-	-	94%	92%
Prophylactic Antibiotic Selection	60	100%	98%	97%
Prophylactic Antibiotic Select. (Outpatient)	-	-	97%	94%
Prophylactic Antibiotic Stopped	59	98%	95%	94%
Recommended VTP Ordered[1]	23	100%	93%	94%
Urinary Catheter Removal[1]	4	100%	91%	90%
Children's Asthma Care				
Received Systemic Corticosteroids	-	-	-	100%
Received Home Management Plan	-	-	-	71%
Received Reliever Medication	-	-	-	100%
Use of Medical Imaging				
Combination Abdominal CT Scan	-	-	0.163	0.191
Combination Chest CT Scan	-	-	0.060	0.054
Follow-up Mammogram/Ultrasound	-	-	8.1%	8.4%
MRI for Low Back Pain	-	-	30.2%	32.7%
Survey of Patients' Hospital Experiences				
Area Around Room 'Always' Quiet at Night	300+	74%	-	58%
Doctors 'Always' Communicated Well	300+	87%	-	80%
Home Recovery Information Given	300+	88%	-	82%
Hospital Given 9 or 10 on 10 Point Scale	300+	79%	-	67%
Meds 'Always' Explained Before Given	300+	71%	-	60%
Nurses 'Always' Communicated Well	300+	83%	-	76%
Pain 'Always' Well Controlled	300+	79%	-	69%
Room and Bathroom 'Always' Clean	300+	89%	-	71%
Timely Help 'Always' Received	300+	73%	-	64%
Would Definitely Recommend Hospital	300+	77%	-	69%

Decatur County Hospital

1405 NW Church Street Phone: 641-446-4871
Leon, IA 50144 Fax: 641-446-2201
URL: www.decaturcountyhospital.org
Type: Critical Access Hospitals Emergency Services: Yes
Ownership: Voluntary Non-Profit - Other Beds: 60

Key Personnel:
CEO/President. . . . . Lynn Milnes

Measure	Cases	This Hosp.	State Avg.	U.S. Avg.
Heart Attack Care				
ACE Inhibitor or ARB for LVSD[5]	0	-	96%	96%
Aspirin at Arrival[5]	0	-	99%	99%
Aspirin at Discharge[5]	0	-	99%	98%
Beta Blocker at Discharge[5]	0	-	99%	98%
Fibrinolytic Medication Timing[5]	0	-	67%	55%
PCI Within 90 Minutes of Arrival[5]	0	-	94%	90%
Smoking Cessation Advice[5]	0	-	99%	99%
Chest Pain/Possible Heart Attack Care				
Aspirin at Arrival	-	-	96%	95%
Median Time to ECG (minutes)	-	-	7	8
Median Time to Transfer (minutes)	-	-	64	61
Fibrinolytic Medication Timing	-	-	45%	54%
Heart Failure Care				
ACE Inhibitor or ARB for LVSD[1]	2	100%	94%	94%
Discharge Instructions[1]	9	22%	86%	88%
Evaluation of LVS Function[1]	14	29%	95%	98%
Smoking Cessation Advice[1]	1	100%	96%	98%
Pneumonia Care				
Appropriate Initial Antibiotic[1]	3	100%	92%	92%
Blood Culture Timing[1]	3	100%	97%	96%
Influenza Vaccine[1]	3	67%	92%	91%
Initial Antibiotic Timing[1]	10	100%	97%	95%
Pneumococcal Vaccine[1]	7	71%	94%	93%
Smoking Cessation Advice[1]	3	100%	95%	97%
Surgical Care Improvement Project				
Appropriate VTP Within 24 Hours[5]	0	-	92%	92%
Appropriate Hair Removal[5]	0	-	100%	99%
Appropriate Beta Blocker Usage[5]	0	-	94%	93%
Controlled Postoperative Blood Glucose[5]	0	-	89%	93%
Prophylactic Antibiotic Timing[5]	0	-	98%	97%
Prophylactic Antibiotic Timing (Outpatient)	-	-	94%	92%
Prophylactic Antibiotic Selection[5]	0	-	98%	97%
Prophylactic Antibiotic Select. (Outpatient)	-	-	97%	94%
Prophylactic Antibiotic Stopped[5]	0	-	95%	94%
Recommended VTP Ordered[5]	0	-	93%	94%
Urinary Catheter Removal[5]	0	-	91%	90%
Children's Asthma Care				
Received Systemic Corticosteroids	-	-	-	100%
Received Home Management Plan	-	-	-	71%
Received Reliever Medication	-	-	-	100%
Use of Medical Imaging				
Combination Abdominal CT Scan	-	-	0.163	0.191
Combination Chest CT Scan	-	-	0.060	0.054
Follow-up Mammogram/Ultrasound	-	-	8.1%	8.4%
MRI for Low Back Pain	-	-	30.2%	32.7%
Survey of Patients' Hospital Experiences				
Area Around Room 'Always' Quiet at Night[8]	-	-	-	58%
Doctors 'Always' Communicated Well[8]	-	-	-	80%
Home Recovery Information Given[8]	-	-	-	82%
Hospital Given 9 or 10 on 10 Point Scale[8]	-	-	-	67%
Meds 'Always' Explained Before Given[8]	-	-	-	60%
Nurses 'Always' Communicated Well[8]	-	-	-	76%
Pain 'Always' Well Controlled[8]	-	-	-	69%
Room and Bathroom 'Always' Clean[8]	-	-	-	71%
Timely Help 'Always' Received[8]	-	-	-	64%
Would Definitely Recommend Hospital[8]	-	-	-	69%

NOTE: Hospital profiles are in alphabetical order by state, then city, then hospital within the city; Rankings exclude hospitals with less than 25 cases except for patient surveys which excludes hospitals with less than 100 cases; (a) 100–299 cases; (1) The number of cases is too small to be sure how well a hospital is performing; (2) The hospital indicated that the data submitted for this measure were based on a sample of cases; (3) Data was collected during a shorter time period (fewer quarters) than the maximum possible time for this measure; (4) Suppressed for one or more quarters by CMS; (5) No data is available from the hospital for this measure; (6) Fewer than 100 patients completed the HCAHPS survey. Use these rates with caution, as the number of surveys may be too low to reliably assess hospital performance; (7) Survey results are based on less than 12 months of data; (8) Survey results are not available for this reporting period; (9) No or very few patients were eligible for the HCAHPS survey. The scores shown, if any, reflect a very small number of surveys; (10) A state average was not calculated because too few hospitals in the state submitted data; (11) There were discrepancies in the data collection process; Please refer to the User's Guide for a full explanation of data.

Regional Medical Center

709 W Main
Manchester, IA 52057
Phone: 563-927-3232
Fax: 563-927-7444
E-mail: information@regmedctr.org
URL: www.regmedctr.org
Type: Critical Access Hospitals
Emergency Services: Yes
Ownership: Government - Local

Key Personnel:
CEO/President. . . . . Lon Butikofer, RN
Chief of Medical Staff . . . . R Ried Boom
Operating Room. . . . . Carol Jebens, RN
Quality Assurance . . . . Joan Wessels, RN

Measure	Cases	This Hosp.	State Avg.	U.S. Avg.
Heart Attack Care				
ACE Inhibitor or ARB for LVSD[5]	0	-	96%	96%
Aspirin at Arrival[5]	0	-	99%	99%
Aspirin at Discharge[5]	0	-	99%	98%
Beta Blocker at Discharge[5]	0	-	99%	98%
Fibrinolytic Medication Timing[5]	0	-	67%	55%
PCI Within 90 Minutes of Arrival[5]	0	-	94%	90%
Smoking Cessation Advice[5]	0	-	99%	99%
Chest Pain/Possible Heart Attack Care				
Aspirin at Arrival	-	-	96%	95%
Median Time to ECG (minutes)	-	-	7	8
Median Time to Transfer (minutes)	-	-	64	61
Fibrinolytic Medication Timing	-	-	45%	54%
Heart Failure Care				
ACE Inhibitor or ARB for LVSD[1]	5	100%	94%	94%
Discharge Instructions[1]	10	100%	86%	88%
Evaluation of LVS Function[1]	17	100%	95%	98%
Smoking Cessation Advice[1]	3	100%	96%	98%
Pneumonia Care				
Appropriate Initial Antibiotic[1]	18	100%	92%	92%
Blood Culture Timing	26	100%	97%	96%
Influenza Vaccine[1]	11	100%	92%	91%
Initial Antibiotic Timing	25	100%	97%	95%
Pneumococcal Vaccine	26	100%	94%	93%
Smoking Cessation Advice[1]	5	80%	95%	97%
Surgical Care Improvement Project				
Appropriate VTP Within 24 Hours[5]	0	-	92%	92%
Appropriate Hair Removal[5]	0	-	100%	99%
Appropriate Beta Blocker Usage[5]	0	-	94%	93%
Controlled Postoperative Blood Glucose[5]	0	-	89%	93%
Prophylactic Antibiotic Timing[5]	0	-	98%	97%
Prophylactic Antibiotic Timing (Outpatient)	-	-	94%	92%
Prophylactic Antibiotic Selection[5]	0	-	98%	97%
Prophylactic Antibiotic Select. (Outpatient)	-	-	97%	94%
Prophylactic Antibiotic Stopped[5]	0	-	95%	94%
Recommended VTP Ordered[5]	0	-	93%	94%
Urinary Catheter Removal[5]	0	-	91%	90%
Children's Asthma Care				
Received Systemic Corticosteroids	-	-	-	100%
Received Home Management Plan	-	-	-	71%
Received Reliever Medication	-	-	-	100%
Use of Medical Imaging				
Combination Abdominal CT Scan	-	-	0.163	0.191
Combination Chest CT Scan	-	-	0.060	0.054
Follow-up Mammogram/Ultrasound	-	-	8.1%	8.4%
MRI for Low Back Pain	-	-	30.2%	32.7%
Survey of Patients' Hospital Experiences				
Area Around Room 'Always' Quiet at Night[8]	-	-	-	58%
Doctors 'Always' Communicated Well[8]	-	-	-	80%
Home Recovery Information Given[8]	-	-	-	82%
Hospital Given 9 or 10 on 10 Point Scale[8]	-	-	-	67%
Meds 'Always' Explained Before Given[8]	-	-	-	60%
Nurses 'Always' Communicated Well[8]	-	-	-	76%
Pain 'Always' Well Controlled[8]	-	-	-	69%
Room and Bathroom 'Always' Clean[8]	-	-	-	71%
Timely Help 'Always' Received[8]	-	-	-	64%
Would Definitely Recommend Hospital[8]	-	-	-	69%

Manning Regional Healthcare Center

410 Main Street
Manning, IA 51455
Phone: 712-655-2072
Fax: 712-655-2216
URL: www.mrhcia.com
Type: Critical Access Hospitals
Emergency Services: Yes
Ownership: Voluntary Non-Profit - Private
Beds: 73

Key Personnel:
CEO/President. . . . . Jeanne Goche
Chief of Medical Staff . . . . Tracy Kahl
Operating Room. . . . . Josh A Smith
Quality Assurance . . . . Kim Jahn
Emergency Room . . . . Cynthia Genzen

Measure	Cases	This Hosp.	State Avg.	U.S. Avg.
Heart Attack Care				
ACE Inhibitor or ARB for LVSD[3]	0	-	96%	96%
Aspirin at Arrival[3]	0	-	99%	99%
Aspirin at Discharge[3]	0	-	99%	98%
Beta Blocker at Discharge[3]	0	-	99%	98%
Fibrinolytic Medication Timing[3]	0	-	67%	55%
PCI Within 90 Minutes of Arrival[3]	0	-	94%	90%
Smoking Cessation Advice[3]	0	-	99%	99%
Chest Pain/Possible Heart Attack Care				
Aspirin at Arrival	-	-	96%	95%
Median Time to ECG (minutes)	-	-	7	8
Median Time to Transfer (minutes)	-	-	64	61
Fibrinolytic Medication Timing	-	-	45%	54%
Heart Failure Care				
ACE Inhibitor or ARB for LVSD[1]	1	0%	94%	94%
Discharge Instructions[1]	3	33%	86%	88%
Evaluation of LVS Function[1]	5	60%	95%	98%
Smoking Cessation Advice[1]	1	0%	96%	98%
Pneumonia Care				
Appropriate Initial Antibiotic[1]	9	78%	92%	92%
Blood Culture Timing[1]	10	90%	97%	96%
Influenza Vaccine[1]	13	85%	92%	91%
Initial Antibiotic Timing[1]	8	88%	97%	95%
Pneumococcal Vaccine[1]	23	83%	94%	93%
Smoking Cessation Advice[1]	1	100%	95%	97%
Surgical Care Improvement Project				
Appropriate VTP Within 24 Hours[1,3]	3	100%	92%	92%
Appropriate Hair Removal[1,3]	4	100%	100%	99%
Appropriate Beta Blocker Usage[5]	0	-	94%	93%
Controlled Postoperative Blood Glucose[3]	0	-	89%	93%
Prophylactic Antibiotic Timing[1]	1	0%	98%	97%
Prophylactic Antibiotic Timing (Outpatient)	-	-	94%	92%
Prophylactic Antibiotic Selection[1,3]	1	100%	98%	97%
Prophylactic Antibiotic Select. (Outpatient)	-	-	97%	94%
Prophylactic Antibiotic Stopped[1,3]	1	100%	95%	94%
Recommended VTP Ordered[1,3]	3	100%	93%	94%
Urinary Catheter Removal[1]	1	0%	91%	90%
Children's Asthma Care				
Received Systemic Corticosteroids	-	-	-	100%
Received Home Management Plan	-	-	-	71%
Received Reliever Medication	-	-	-	100%
Use of Medical Imaging				
Combination Abdominal CT Scan	-	-	0.163	0.191
Combination Chest CT Scan	-	-	0.060	0.054
Follow-up Mammogram/Ultrasound	-	-	8.1%	8.4%
MRI for Low Back Pain	-	-	30.2%	32.7%
Survey of Patients' Hospital Experiences				
Area Around Room 'Always' Quiet at Night[8]	-	-	-	58%
Doctors 'Always' Communicated Well[8]	-	-	-	80%
Home Recovery Information Given[8]	-	-	-	82%
Hospital Given 9 or 10 on 10 Point Scale[8]	-	-	-	67%
Meds 'Always' Explained Before Given[8]	-	-	-	60%
Nurses 'Always' Communicated Well[8]	-	-	-	76%
Pain 'Always' Well Controlled[8]	-	-	-	69%
Room and Bathroom 'Always' Clean[8]	-	-	-	71%
Timely Help 'Always' Received[8]	-	-	-	64%
Would Definitely Recommend Hospital[8]	-	-	-	69%

Jackson County Regional Health Center

700 W Grove St
Maquoketa, IA 52060
Phone: 563-652-2474
Fax: 563-652-4018
Type: Critical Access Hospitals
Emergency Services: Yes
Ownership: Proprietary
Beds: 61

Key Personnel:
CEO/President. . . . . Curt Coleman
Chief of Medical Staff . . . . Curt Giswein, MD
Infection Control. . . . . Sandra Rockwell
Operating Room. . . . . Chris Johnson
Emergency Room . . . . Cheryl Wagner

Measure	Cases	This Hosp.	State Avg.	U.S. Avg.
Heart Attack Care				
ACE Inhibitor or ARB for LVSD[5]	0	-	96%	96%
Aspirin at Arrival[5]	0	-	99%	99%
Aspirin at Discharge[5]	0	-	99%	98%
Beta Blocker at Discharge[5]	0	-	99%	98%
Fibrinolytic Medication Timing[5]	0	-	67%	55%
PCI Within 90 Minutes of Arrival[5]	0	-	94%	90%
Smoking Cessation Advice[5]	0	-	99%	99%
Chest Pain/Possible Heart Attack Care				
Aspirin at Arrival	-	-	96%	95%
Median Time to ECG (minutes)	-	-	7	8
Median Time to Transfer (minutes)	-	-	64	61
Fibrinolytic Medication Timing	-	-	45%	54%
Heart Failure Care				
ACE Inhibitor or ARB for LVSD[1,3]	1	0%	94%	94%
Discharge Instructions[1,3]	4	25%	86%	88%
Evaluation of LVS Function[1,3]	5	60%	95%	98%
Smoking Cessation Advice[3]	0	-	96%	98%
Pneumonia Care				
Appropriate Initial Antibiotic[1]	18	89%	92%	92%
Blood Culture Timing[1]	19	100%	97%	96%
Influenza Vaccine[1]	17	88%	92%	91%
Initial Antibiotic Timing	27	96%	97%	95%
Pneumococcal Vaccine	29	83%	94%	93%
Smoking Cessation Advice[1]	4	50%	95%	97%
Surgical Care Improvement Project				
Appropriate VTP Within 24 Hours[1,3]	2	50%	92%	92%
Appropriate Hair Removal[1,3]	4	100%	100%	99%
Appropriate Beta Blocker Usage[5]	0	-	94%	93%
Controlled Postoperative Blood Glucose[3]	0	-	89%	93%
Prophylactic Antibiotic Timing[3]	0	-	98%	97%
Prophylactic Antibiotic Timing (Outpatient)	-	-	94%	92%
Prophylactic Antibiotic Selection[3]	0	-	98%	97%
Prophylactic Antibiotic Select. (Outpatient)	-	-	97%	94%
Prophylactic Antibiotic Stopped[3]	0	-	95%	94%
Recommended VTP Ordered[1,3]	2	50%	93%	94%
Urinary Catheter Removal	0	-	91%	90%
Children's Asthma Care				
Received Systemic Corticosteroids	-	-	-	100%
Received Home Management Plan	-	-	-	71%
Received Reliever Medication	-	-	-	100%
Use of Medical Imaging				
Combination Abdominal CT Scan	-	-	0.163	0.191
Combination Chest CT Scan	-	-	0.060	0.054
Follow-up Mammogram/Ultrasound	-	-	8.1%	8.4%
MRI for Low Back Pain	-	-	30.2%	32.7%
Survey of Patients' Hospital Experiences				
Area Around Room 'Always' Quiet at Night	(a)	71%	-	58%
Doctors 'Always' Communicated Well	(a)	84%	-	80%
Home Recovery Information Given	(a)	80%	-	82%
Hospital Given 9 or 10 on 10 Point Scale	(a)	63%	-	67%
Meds 'Always' Explained Before Given	(a)	62%	-	60%
Nurses 'Always' Communicated Well	(a)	76%	-	76%
Pain 'Always' Well Controlled	(a)	74%	-	69%
Room and Bathroom 'Always' Clean	(a)	77%	-	71%
Timely Help 'Always' Received	(a)	65%	-	64%
Would Definitely Recommend Hospital	(a)	59%	-	69%

NOTE: Hospital profiles are in alphabetical order by state, then city, then hospital within the city; Rankings exclude hospitals with less than 25 cases except for patient surveys which excludes hospitals with less than 100 cases; (a) 100–299 cases; (1) The number of cases is too small to be sure how well a hospital is performing; (2) The hospital indicated that the data submitted for this measure were based on a sample of cases; (3) Data was collected during a shorter time period (fewer quarters) than the maximum possible time for this measure; (4) Suppressed for one or more quarters by CMS; (5) No data is available from the hospital for this measure; (6) Fewer than 100 patients completed the HCAHPS survey. Use these rates with caution, as the number of surveys may be too low to reliably assess hospital performance; (7) Survey results are based on less than 12 months of data; (8) Survey results are not available for this reporting period; (9) No or very few patients were eligible for the HCAHPS survey. The scores shown, if any, reflect a very small number of surveys; (10) A state average was not calculated because too few hospitals in the state submitted data; (11) There were discrepancies in the data collection process; Please refer to the User's Guide for a full explanation of data.

Marengo Memorial Hospital

300 W May St
Marengo, IA 52301
URL: www.marengohospital.org
Type: Critical Access Hospitals
Ownership: Government - Local

Phone: 319-642-5543
Fax: 319-642-8007
Emergency Services: Yes
Beds: 25

Key Personnel:
CEO/President. . . . . Genny Maroc
Chief of Medical Staff. . . . . Endriss Estime
Infection Control. . . . . Sharon Schulte, RN
Emergency Room . . . . Lisa Eckholm

Measure	Cases	This Hosp.	State Avg.	U.S. Avg.
Heart Attack Care				
ACE Inhibitor or ARB for LVSD[5]	0	-	96%	96%
Aspirin at Arrival[5]	0	-	99%	99%
Aspirin at Discharge[5]	0	-	99%	98%
Beta Blocker at Discharge[5]	0	-	99%	98%
Fibrinolytic Medication Timing[5]	0	-	67%	55%
PCI Within 90 Minutes of Arrival[5]	0	-	94%	90%
Smoking Cessation Advice[5]	0	-	99%	99%
Chest Pain/Possible Heart Attack Care				
Aspirin at Arrival[1,3]	3	100%	96%	95%
Median Time to ECG (minutes)[1,3]	3	2	7	8
Median Time to Transfer (minutes)[5]	0	-	64	61
Fibrinolytic Medication Timing[5]	0	-	45%	54%
Heart Failure Care				
ACE Inhibitor or ARB for LVSD[5]	0	-	94%	94%
Discharge Instructions[5]	0	-	86%	88%
Evaluation of LVS Function[5]	0	-	95%	98%
Smoking Cessation Advice[5]	0	-	96%	98%
Pneumonia Care				
Appropriate Initial Antibiotic[1]	10	40%	92%	92%
Blood Culture Timing[1]	11	73%	97%	96%
Influenza Vaccine[1]	3	67%	92%	91%
Initial Antibiotic Timing[1]	8	62%	97%	95%
Pneumococcal Vaccine[1]	10	60%	94%	93%
Smoking Cessation Advice[1]	1	100%	95%	97%
Surgical Care Improvement Project				
Appropriate VTP Within 24 Hours[5]	0	-	92%	92%
Appropriate Hair Removal[5]	0	-	100%	99%
Appropriate Beta Blocker Usage[5]	0	-	94%	93%
Controlled Postoperative Blood Glucose[5]	0	-	89%	93%
Prophylactic Antibiotic Timing[5]	0	-	98%	97%
Prophylactic Antibiotic Timing (Outpatient)[5]	0	-	94%	92%
Prophylactic Antibiotic Selection[5]	0	-	98%	97%
Prophylactic Antibiotic Select. (Outpatient)[5]	0	-	97%	94%
Prophylactic Antibiotic Stopped[5]	0	-	95%	94%
Recommended VTP Ordered[5]	0	-	93%	94%
Urinary Catheter Removal[5]	0	-	91%	90%
Children's Asthma Care				
Received Systemic Corticosteroids	-	-	-	100%
Received Home Management Plan	-	-	-	71%
Received Reliever Medication	-	-	-	100%
Use of Medical Imaging				
Combination Abdominal CT Scan[1]	41	0.073	0.163	0.191
Combination Chest CT Scan[1]	19	0.053	0.060	0.054
Follow-up Mammogram/Ultrasound[5]	0	-	8.1%	8.4%
MRI for Low Back Pain[1]	10	20.0%	30.2%	32.7%
Survey of Patients' Hospital Experiences				
Area Around Room 'Always' Quiet at Night[8]	-	-	-	58%
Doctors 'Always' Communicated Well[8]	-	-	-	80%
Home Recovery Information Given[8]	-	-	-	82%
Hospital Given 9 or 10 on 10 Point Scale[8]	-	-	-	67%
Meds 'Always' Explained Before Given[8]	-	-	-	60%
Nurses 'Always' Communicated Well[8]	-	-	-	76%
Pain 'Always' Well Controlled[8]	-	-	-	69%
Room and Bathroom 'Always' Clean[8]	-	-	-	71%
Timely Help 'Always' Received[8]	-	-	-	64%
Would Definitely Recommend Hospital[8]	-	-	-	69%

Marshalltown Medical & Surgical Center

3 South 4th Avenue
Marshalltown, IA 50158
URL: www.everydaychampions.org
Type: Acute Care Hospitals
Ownership: Voluntary Non-Profit - Private

Phone: 641-754-5151
Fax: 641-753-2570
Emergency Services: Yes
Beds: 176

Key Personnel:
CEO/President. . . . . Rob Cooper
Chief of Medical Staff. . . . . Gary Peasley
Operating Room. . . . . Thomas Foley
Pediatric Ambulatory Care . . . . . . Chris Schill
Pediatric In-Patient Care . . . . Chris Schill
Quality Assurance . . . . Larae Schelling
Radiology. . . . . Richard Bedont
Emergency Room . . . . Donna Schuster

Measure	Cases	This Hosp.	State Avg.	U.S. Avg.
Heart Attack Care				
ACE Inhibitor or ARB for LVSD[1]	8	88%	96%	96%
Aspirin at Arrival	56	98%	99%	99%
Aspirin at Discharge	52	98%	99%	98%
Beta Blocker at Discharge	52	98%	99%	98%
Fibrinolytic Medication Timing	0	-	67%	55%
PCI Within 90 Minutes of Arrival[1]	19	100%	94%	90%
Smoking Cessation Advice[1]	16	100%	99%	99%
Chest Pain/Possible Heart Attack Care				
Aspirin at Arrival[1]	19	100%	96%	95%
Median Time to ECG (minutes)[1]	18	7	7	8
Median Time to Transfer (minutes)[5]	0	-	64	61
Fibrinolytic Medication Timing[3]	0	-	45%	54%
Heart Failure Care				
ACE Inhibitor or ARB for LVSD[1]	22	100%	94%	94%
Discharge Instructions	48	77%	86%	88%
Evaluation of LVS Function	73	99%	95%	98%
Smoking Cessation Advice[1]	12	100%	96%	98%
Pneumonia Care				
Appropriate Initial Antibiotic	64	97%	92%	92%
Blood Culture Timing	105	98%	97%	96%
Influenza Vaccine	63	100%	92%	91%
Initial Antibiotic Timing	95	100%	97%	95%
Pneumococcal Vaccine	111	100%	94%	93%
Smoking Cessation Advice	28	100%	95%	97%
Surgical Care Improvement Project				
Appropriate VTP Within 24 Hours	62	98%	92%	92%
Appropriate Hair Removal	219	100%	100%	99%
Appropriate Beta Blocker Usage	69	99%	94%	93%
Controlled Postoperative Blood Glucose	0	-	89%	93%
Prophylactic Antibiotic Timing	180	98%	98%	97%
Prophylactic Antibiotic Timing (Outpatient)	97	98%	94%	92%
Prophylactic Antibiotic Selection	179	97%	98%	97%
Prophylactic Antibiotic Select. (Outpatient)	96	99%	97%	94%
Prophylactic Antibiotic Stopped	175	98%	95%	94%
Recommended VTP Ordered	62	98%	93%	94%
Urinary Catheter Removal[1]	13	92%	91%	90%
Children's Asthma Care				
Received Systemic Corticosteroids	-	-	-	100%
Received Home Management Plan	-	-	-	71%
Received Reliever Medication	-	-	-	100%
Use of Medical Imaging				
Combination Abdominal CT Scan	302	0.023	0.163	0.191
Combination Chest CT Scan	188	0.000	0.060	0.054
Follow-up Mammogram/Ultrasound	628	13.1%	8.1%	8.4%
MRI for Low Back Pain	49	44.9%	30.2%	32.7%
Survey of Patients' Hospital Experiences				
Area Around Room 'Always' Quiet at Night	300+	53%	-	58%
Doctors 'Always' Communicated Well	300+	80%	-	80%
Home Recovery Information Given	300+	85%	-	82%
Hospital Given 9 or 10 on 10 Point Scale	300+	65%	-	67%
Meds 'Always' Explained Before Given	300+	60%	-	60%
Nurses 'Always' Communicated Well	300+	75%	-	76%
Pain 'Always' Well Controlled	300+	65%	-	69%
Room and Bathroom 'Always' Clean	300+	70%	-	71%
Timely Help 'Always' Received	300+	56%	-	64%
Would Definitely Recommend Hospital	300+	60%	-	69%

Mercy Medical Center-North Iowa

1000 Fourth Street SW
Mason City, IA 50401
URL: www.mercynorthiowa.com
Type: Acute Care Hospitals
Ownership: Voluntary Non-Profit - Church

Phone: 641-422-7000
Fax: 641-422-7827
Emergency Services: Yes
Beds: 346

Key Personnel:
CEO/President. . . . . James G Fitzpatrick
Chief of Medical Staff. . . . . Ron Moeller, MD
Emergency Room . . . . Paul Leavens

Measure	Cases	This Hosp.	State Avg.	U.S. Avg.
Heart Attack Care				
ACE Inhibitor or ARB for LVSD	69	99%	96%	96%
Aspirin at Arrival	156	100%	99%	99%
Aspirin at Discharge	252	100%	99%	98%
Beta Blocker at Discharge	245	100%	99%	98%
Fibrinolytic Medication Timing	0	-	67%	55%
PCI Within 90 Minutes of Arrival[1]	17	94%	94%	90%
Smoking Cessation Advice	76	100%	99%	99%
Chest Pain/Possible Heart Attack Care				
Aspirin at Arrival[1]	6	83%	96%	95%
Median Time to ECG (minutes)[1]	6	25	7	8
Median Time to Transfer (minutes)[5]	0	-	64	61
Fibrinolytic Medication Timing[5]	0	-	45%	54%
Heart Failure Care				
ACE Inhibitor or ARB for LVSD	120	99%	94%	94%
Discharge Instructions	207	97%	86%	88%
Evaluation of LVS Function	319	99%	95%	98%
Smoking Cessation Advice	33	100%	96%	98%
Pneumonia Care				
Appropriate Initial Antibiotic	143	91%	92%	92%
Blood Culture Timing	186	100%	97%	96%
Influenza Vaccine	142	92%	92%	91%
Initial Antibiotic Timing	190	97%	97%	95%
Pneumococcal Vaccine	225	96%	94%	93%
Smoking Cessation Advice	75	99%	95%	97%
Surgical Care Improvement Project				
Appropriate VTP Within 24 Hours	288	95%	92%	92%
Appropriate Hair Removal	1,158	100%	100%	99%
Appropriate Beta Blocker Usage	437	92%	94%	93%
Controlled Postoperative Blood Glucose	185	94%	89%	93%
Prophylactic Antibiotic Timing	798	99%	98%	97%
Prophylactic Antibiotic Timing (Outpatient)	809	99%	94%	92%
Prophylactic Antibiotic Selection	805	99%	98%	97%
Prophylactic Antibiotic Select. (Outpatient)	806	98%	97%	94%
Prophylactic Antibiotic Stopped	757	97%	95%	94%
Recommended VTP Ordered	288	95%	93%	94%
Urinary Catheter Removal	107	88%	91%	90%
Children's Asthma Care				
Received Systemic Corticosteroids	-	-	-	100%
Received Home Management Plan	-	-	-	71%
Received Reliever Medication	-	-	-	100%
Use of Medical Imaging				
Combination Abdominal CT Scan	1,032	0.081	0.163	0.191
Combination Chest CT Scan	1,156	0.015	0.060	0.054
Follow-up Mammogram/Ultrasound	2,698	10.7%	8.1%	8.4%
MRI for Low Back Pain[1]	2	0.0%	30.2%	32.7%
Survey of Patients' Hospital Experiences				
Area Around Room 'Always' Quiet at Night	300+	54%	-	58%
Doctors 'Always' Communicated Well	300+	77%	-	80%
Home Recovery Information Given	300+	87%	-	82%
Hospital Given 9 or 10 on 10 Point Scale	300+	68%	-	67%
Meds 'Always' Explained Before Given	300+	58%	-	60%
Nurses 'Always' Communicated Well	300+	77%	-	76%
Pain 'Always' Well Controlled	300+	69%	-	69%
Room and Bathroom 'Always' Clean	300+	71%	-	71%
Timely Help 'Always' Received	300+	67%	-	64%
Would Definitely Recommend Hospital	300+	71%	-	69%

NOTE: Hospital profiles are in alphabetical order by state, then city, then hospital within the city; Rankings exclude hospitals with less than 25 cases except for patient surveys which excludes hospitals with less than 100 cases; (a) 100–299 cases; (1) The number of cases is too small to be sure how well a hospital is performing; (2) The hospital indicated that the data submitted for this measure were based on a sample of cases; (3) Data was collected during a shorter time period (fewer quarters) than the maximum possible time for this measure; (4) Suppressed for one or more quarters by CMS; (5) No data is available from the hospital for this measure; (6) Fewer than 100 patients completed the HCAHPS survey. Use these rates with caution, as the number of surveys may be too low to reliably assess hospital performance; (7) Survey results are based on less than 12 months of data; (8) Survey results are not available for this reporting period; (9) No or very few patients were eligible for the HCAHPS survey. The scores shown, if any, reflect a very small number of surveys; (10) A state average was not calculated because too few hospitals in the state submitted data; (11) There were discrepancies in the data collection process; Please refer to the User's Guide for a full explanation of data.

Alegent Health Community Memorial Hospital

631 N 8th St
Missouri Valley, IA 51555
Phone: 712-642-2784
Fax: 712-642-2760
URL: www.alegent.org
Type: Critical Access Hospitals
Emergency Services: Yes
Ownership: Voluntary Non-Profit - Private
Beds: 25

Key Personnel:
CEO/President. . . . . Richard A Hachten II
Chief of Medical Staff . . . . Jeffrey Jacobs, MD
Infection Control. . . . . Sue Peschel, RN
Quality Assurance . . . . Anne Hansen, RN
Radiology. . . . . Kimberly Apker
Anesthesiology. . . . . Tom Rice, CRNA
Emergency Room . . . . Joseph T Piccolo, MD
Patient Relations . . . . Marjorie Clark

Measure	Cases	This Hosp.	State Avg.	U.S. Avg.
Heart Attack Care				
ACE Inhibitor or ARB for LVSD	0	-	96%	96%
Aspirin at Arrival[1]	1	100%	99%	99%
Aspirin at Discharge[1]	1	100%	99%	98%
Beta Blocker at Discharge[1]	1	100%	99%	98%
Fibrinolytic Medication Timing	0	-	67%	55%
PCI Within 90 Minutes of Arrival	0	-	94%	90%
Smoking Cessation Advice	0	-	99%	99%
Chest Pain/Possible Heart Attack Care				
Aspirin at Arrival	-	-	96%	95%
Median Time to ECG (minutes)	-	-	7	8
Median Time to Transfer (minutes)	-	-	64	61
Fibrinolytic Medication Timing	-	-	45%	54%
Heart Failure Care				
ACE Inhibitor or ARB for LVSD[1]	6	100%	94%	94%
Discharge Instructions[1]	17	100%	86%	88%
Evaluation of LVS Function	41	100%	95%	98%
Smoking Cessation Advice[1]	2	100%	96%	98%
Pneumonia Care				
Appropriate Initial Antibiotic	29	100%	92%	92%
Blood Culture Timing	27	100%	97%	96%
Influenza Vaccine	25	100%	92%	91%
Initial Antibiotic Timing	27	100%	97%	95%
Pneumococcal Vaccine	39	100%	94%	93%
Smoking Cessation Advice[1]	5	100%	95%	97%
Surgical Care Improvement Project				
Appropriate VTP Within 24 Hours[1,3]	2	100%	92%	92%
Appropriate Hair Removal[1,3]	3	100%	100%	99%
Appropriate Beta Blocker Usage[5]	0	-	94%	93%
Controlled Postoperative Blood Glucose[3]	0	-	89%	93%
Prophylactic Antibiotic Timing[1,3]	1	100%	98%	97%
Prophylactic Antibiotic Timing (Outpatient)	-	-	94%	92%
Prophylactic Antibiotic Selection[1,3]	1	100%	98%	97%
Prophylactic Antibiotic Select. (Outpatient)	-	-	97%	94%
Prophylactic Antibiotic Stopped[1,3]	1	100%	95%	94%
Recommended VTP Ordered[1,3]	2	100%	93%	94%
Urinary Catheter Removal[5]	0	-	91%	90%
Children's Asthma Care				
Received Systemic Corticosteroids	-	-	-	100%
Received Home Management Plan	-	-	-	71%
Received Reliever Medication	-	-	-	100%
Use of Medical Imaging				
Combination Abdominal CT Scan	-	-	0.163	0.191
Combination Chest CT Scan	-	-	0.060	0.054
Follow-up Mammogram/Ultrasound	-	-	8.1%	8.4%
MRI for Low Back Pain	-	-	30.2%	32.7%
Survey of Patients' Hospital Experiences				
Area Around Room 'Always' Quiet at Night[6]	<100	65%	-	58%
Doctors 'Always' Communicated Well[6]	<100	87%	-	80%
Home Recovery Information Given[6]	<100	89%	-	82%
Hospital Given 9 or 10 on 10 Point Scale[6]	<100	74%	-	67%
Meds 'Always' Explained Before Given[6]	<100	70%	-	60%
Nurses 'Always' Communicated Well[6]	<100	80%	-	76%
Pain 'Always' Well Controlled[6]	<100	73%	-	69%
Room and Bathroom 'Always' Clean[6]	<100	83%	-	71%
Timely Help 'Always' Received[6]	<100	71%	-	64%
Would Definitely Recommend Hospital	<100	61%	-	69%

Ringgold County Hospital

504 North Cleveland
Mount Ayr, IA 50854
Phone: 641-464-3226
Fax: 641-464-4420
Type: Critical Access Hospitals
Emergency Services: Yes
Ownership: Government - Local
Beds: 46

Key Personnel:
CEO/President. . . . . Gordon W Winkler
Chief of Medical Staff . . . . Dane Johnson, DO
Operating Room. . . . . Dane Johnson, RN
Ambulatory Care . . . . Joe Dukes

Measure	Cases	This Hosp.	State Avg.	U.S. Avg.
Heart Attack Care				
ACE Inhibitor or ARB for LVSD[5]	0	-	96%	96%
Aspirin at Arrival[5]	0	-	99%	99%
Aspirin at Discharge[5]	0	-	99%	98%
Beta Blocker at Discharge[5]	0	-	99%	98%
Fibrinolytic Medication Timing[5]	0	-	67%	55%
PCI Within 90 Minutes of Arrival[5]	0	-	94%	90%
Smoking Cessation Advice[5]	0	-	99%	99%
Chest Pain/Possible Heart Attack Care				
Aspirin at Arrival	-	-	96%	95%
Median Time to ECG (minutes)	-	-	7	8
Median Time to Transfer (minutes)	-	-	64	61
Fibrinolytic Medication Timing	-	-	45%	54%
Heart Failure Care				
ACE Inhibitor or ARB for LVSD[1]	2	100%	94%	94%
Discharge Instructions[1]	9	0%	86%	88%
Evaluation of LVS Function[1]	11	82%	95%	98%
Smoking Cessation Advice	0	-	96%	98%
Pneumonia Care				
Appropriate Initial Antibiotic[1]	7	71%	92%	92%
Blood Culture Timing	0	-	97%	96%
Influenza Vaccine[1]	7	86%	92%	91%
Initial Antibiotic Timing[1]	9	78%	97%	95%
Pneumococcal Vaccine[1]	14	93%	94%	93%
Smoking Cessation Advice[1]	1	0%	95%	97%
Surgical Care Improvement Project				
Appropriate VTP Within 24 Hours[5]	0	-	92%	92%
Appropriate Hair Removal[5]	0	-	100%	99%
Appropriate Beta Blocker Usage[5]	0	-	94%	93%
Controlled Postoperative Blood Glucose[5]	0	-	89%	93%
Prophylactic Antibiotic Timing[5]	0	-	98%	97%
Prophylactic Antibiotic Timing (Outpatient)	-	-	94%	92%
Prophylactic Antibiotic Selection[5]	0	-	98%	97%
Prophylactic Antibiotic Select. (Outpatient)	-	-	97%	94%
Prophylactic Antibiotic Stopped[5]	0	-	95%	94%
Recommended VTP Ordered[5]	0	-	93%	94%
Urinary Catheter Removal[5]	0	-	91%	90%
Children's Asthma Care				
Received Systemic Corticosteroids	-	-	-	100%
Received Home Management Plan	-	-	-	71%
Received Reliever Medication	-	-	-	100%
Use of Medical Imaging				
Combination Abdominal CT Scan	-	-	0.163	0.191
Combination Chest CT Scan	-	-	0.060	0.054
Follow-up Mammogram/Ultrasound	-	-	8.1%	8.4%
MRI for Low Back Pain	-	-	30.2%	32.7%
Survey of Patients' Hospital Experiences				
Area Around Room 'Always' Quiet at Night[8]	-	-	-	58%
Doctors 'Always' Communicated Well[8]	-	-	-	80%
Home Recovery Information Given[8]	-	-	-	82%
Hospital Given 9 or 10 on 10 Point Scale[8]	-	-	-	67%
Meds 'Always' Explained Before Given[8]	-	-	-	60%
Nurses 'Always' Communicated Well[8]	-	-	-	76%
Pain 'Always' Well Controlled[8]	-	-	-	69%
Room and Bathroom 'Always' Clean[8]	-	-	-	71%
Timely Help 'Always' Received[8]	-	-	-	64%
Would Definitely Recommend Hospital[8]	-	-	-	69%

Henry County Health Center

407 S White St
Mount Pleasant, IA 52641
Phone: 319-385-3141
Fax: 319-385-6731
E-mail: miller@hchc.org
URL: www.hchc.org
Type: Critical Access Hospitals
Emergency Services: Yes
Ownership: Government - Local
Beds: 99

Key Personnel:
CEO/President. . . . . Robert Miller
Chief of Medical Staff . . . . Cheryl Christensen
Operating Room. . . . . Becky Johnson, RN
Quality Assurance . . . . Lois Roth, RN
Emergency Room . . . . Vicky Oge, RN

Measure	Cases	This Hosp.	State Avg.	U.S. Avg.
Heart Attack Care				
ACE Inhibitor or ARB for LVSD[3]	0	-	96%	96%
Aspirin at Arrival[1,3]	4	100%	99%	99%
Aspirin at Discharge[1,3]	2	50%	99%	98%
Beta Blocker at Discharge[1,3]	2	50%	99%	98%
Fibrinolytic Medication Timing[5]	0	-	67%	55%
PCI Within 90 Minutes of Arrival[5]	0	-	94%	90%
Smoking Cessation Advice[3]	0	-	99%	99%
Chest Pain/Possible Heart Attack Care				
Aspirin at Arrival	-	-	96%	95%
Median Time to ECG (minutes)	-	-	7	8
Median Time to Transfer (minutes)	-	-	64	61
Fibrinolytic Medication Timing	-	-	45%	54%
Heart Failure Care				
ACE Inhibitor or ARB for LVSD[1]	2	100%	94%	94%
Discharge Instructions[1]	9	44%	86%	88%
Evaluation of LVS Function[1]	18	72%	95%	98%
Smoking Cessation Advice[1]	2	100%	96%	98%
Pneumonia Care				
Appropriate Initial Antibiotic	25	88%	92%	92%
Blood Culture Timing[1]	24	92%	97%	96%
Influenza Vaccine[1]	20	95%	92%	91%
Initial Antibiotic Timing	30	100%	97%	95%
Pneumococcal Vaccine	30	87%	94%	93%
Smoking Cessation Advice[1]	7	100%	95%	97%
Surgical Care Improvement Project				
Appropriate VTP Within 24 Hours[5]	0	-	92%	92%
Appropriate Hair Removal[1,3]	7	100%	100%	99%
Appropriate Beta Blocker Usage[5]	0	-	94%	93%
Controlled Postoperative Blood Glucose[3]	0	-	89%	93%
Prophylactic Antibiotic Timing[1,3]	5	60%	98%	97%
Prophylactic Antibiotic Timing (Outpatient)	-	-	94%	92%
Prophylactic Antibiotic Selection[1,3]	6	50%	98%	97%
Prophylactic Antibiotic Select. (Outpatient)	-	-	97%	94%
Prophylactic Antibiotic Stopped[1,3]	5	60%	95%	94%
Recommended VTP Ordered[5]	0	-	93%	94%
Urinary Catheter Removal[1,3]	1	100%	91%	90%
Children's Asthma Care				
Received Systemic Corticosteroids	-	-	-	100%
Received Home Management Plan	-	-	-	71%
Received Reliever Medication	-	-	-	100%
Use of Medical Imaging				
Combination Abdominal CT Scan	-	-	0.163	0.191
Combination Chest CT Scan	-	-	0.060	0.054
Follow-up Mammogram/Ultrasound	-	-	8.1%	8.4%
MRI for Low Back Pain	-	-	30.2%	32.7%
Survey of Patients' Hospital Experiences				
Area Around Room 'Always' Quiet at Night	(a)	65%	-	58%
Doctors 'Always' Communicated Well	(a)	89%	-	80%
Home Recovery Information Given	(a)	84%	-	82%
Hospital Given 9 or 10 on 10 Point Scale	(a)	75%	-	67%
Meds 'Always' Explained Before Given	(a)	61%	-	60%
Nurses 'Always' Communicated Well	(a)	82%	-	76%
Pain 'Always' Well Controlled	(a)	69%	-	69%
Room and Bathroom 'Always' Clean	(a)	64%	-	71%
Timely Help 'Always' Received	(a)	75%	-	64%
Would Definitely Recommend Hospital	(a)	68%	-	69%

NOTE: Hospital profiles are in alphabetical order by state, then city, then hospital within the city; Rankings exclude hospitals with less than 25 cases except for patient surveys which excludes hospitals with less than 100 cases; (a) 100–299 cases; (1) The number of cases is too small to be sure how well a hospital is performing; (2) The hospital indicated that the data submitted for this measure were based on a sample of cases; (3) Data was collected during a shorter time period (fewer quarters) than the maximum possible time for this measure; (4) Suppressed for one or more quarters by CMS; (5) No data is available from the hospital for this measure; (6) Fewer than 100 patients completed the HCAHPS survey. Use these rates with caution, as the number of surveys may be too low to reliably assess hospital performance; (7) Survey results are based on less than 12 months of data; (8) Survey results are not available for this reporting period; (9) No or very few patients were eligible for the HCAHPS survey. The scores shown, if any, reflect a very small number of surveys; (10) A state average was not calculated because too few hospitals in the state submitted data; (11) There were discrepancies in the data collection process; Please refer to the User's Guide for a full explanation of data.

Trinity Muscatine

1518 Mulberry Avenue Phone: 563-264-9100
Muscatine, IA 52761 Fax: 563-264-9463
E-mail: tvanwey@unityiowa.org
URL: www.unityiowa.com
Type: Acute Care Hospitals Emergency Services: Yes
Ownership: Voluntary Non-Profit - Private Beds: 80

Key Personnel:
CEO/President. . . . . Vincent A Keane
Chief of Medical Staff. . . . . Janelle Goetcheus, DO
Infection Control. . . . . Teresa Coder, RN
Operating Room. . . . . Lynn Volkyl
Pediatric In-Patient Care . . . . Pam Askew, RN
Quality Assurance . . . . Toni Booker
Intensive Care Unit. . . . . Pam Askew, RN
Patient Relations . . . . Zerita Hadden-Hudson

Measure	Cases	This Hosp.	State Avg.	U.S. Avg.
Heart Attack Care				
ACE Inhibitor or ARB for LVSD[1]	2	100%	96%	96%
Aspirin at Arrival[1]	5	100%	99%	99%
Aspirin at Discharge[1]	5	100%	99%	98%
Beta Blocker at Discharge[1]	5	100%	99%	98%
Fibrinolytic Medication Timing	0	-	67%	55%
PCI Within 90 Minutes of Arrival	0	-	94%	90%
Smoking Cessation Advice	0	-	99%	99%
Chest Pain/Possible Heart Attack Care				
Aspirin at Arrival	114	100%	96%	95%
Median Time to ECG (minutes)	114	9	7	8
Median Time to Transfer (minutes)[1,3]	5	65	64	61
Fibrinolytic Medication Timing[1]	2	50%	45%	54%
Heart Failure Care				
ACE Inhibitor or ARB for LVSD[1]	16	100%	94%	94%
Discharge Instructions	25	100%	86%	88%
Evaluation of LVS Function	45	100%	95%	98%
Smoking Cessation Advice[1]	5	100%	96%	98%
Pneumonia Care				
Appropriate Initial Antibiotic	51	98%	92%	92%
Blood Culture Timing	54	98%	97%	96%
Influenza Vaccine	35	100%	92%	91%
Initial Antibiotic Timing	59	98%	97%	95%
Pneumococcal Vaccine	52	100%	94%	93%
Smoking Cessation Advice[1]	21	100%	95%	97%
Surgical Care Improvement Project				
Appropriate VTP Within 24 Hours	39	100%	92%	92%
Appropriate Hair Removal	89	100%	100%	99%
Appropriate Beta Blocker Usage[1]	24	100%	94%	93%
Controlled Postoperative Blood Glucose	0	-	89%	93%
Prophylactic Antibiotic Timing	33	91%	98%	97%
Prophylactic Antibiotic Timing (Outpatient)	43	98%	94%	92%
Prophylactic Antibiotic Selection	35	97%	98%	97%
Prophylactic Antibiotic Select. (Outpatient)	43	100%	97%	94%
Prophylactic Antibiotic Stopped	32	97%	95%	94%
Recommended VTP Ordered	39	100%	93%	94%
Urinary Catheter Removal[1]	9	100%	91%	90%
Children's Asthma Care				
Received Systemic Corticosteroids	-	-	-	100%
Received Home Management Plan	-	-	-	71%
Received Reliever Medication	-	-	-	100%
Use of Medical Imaging				
Combination Abdominal CT Scan	210	0.024	0.163	0.191
Combination Chest CT Scan	125	0.000	0.060	0.054
Follow-up Mammogram/Ultrasound	570	4.0%	8.1%	8.4%
MRI for Low Back Pain[1]	39	28.2%	30.2%	32.7%
Survey of Patients' Hospital Experiences				
Area Around Room 'Always' Quiet at Night	300+	49%	-	58%
Doctors 'Always' Communicated Well	300+	84%	-	80%
Home Recovery Information Given	300+	82%	-	82%
Hospital Given 9 or 10 on 10 Point Scale	300+	58%	-	67%
Meds 'Always' Explained Before Given	300+	62%	-	60%
Nurses 'Always' Communicated Well	300+	75%	-	76%
Pain 'Always' Well Controlled	300+	67%	-	69%
Room and Bathroom 'Always' Clean	300+	73%	-	71%
Timely Help 'Always' Received	300+	67%	-	64%
Would Definitely Recommend Hospital	300+	60%	-	69%

Story County Hospital

640 South 19th Street Phone: 515-382-2111
Nevada, IA 50201 Fax: 515-382-6617
URL: www.scmcnevada.org
Type: Critical Access Hospitals Emergency Services: Yes
Ownership: Government - Local Beds: 122

Key Personnel:
CEO/President. . . . . Todd M Willert
Chief of Medical Staff. . . . . Alison Carleton
Operating Room. . . . . Marcia Engler
Quality Assurance . . . . Julie Schreitmueller
Radiology. . . . . Cindy White
Emergency Room . . . . Lisa Whitaker

Measure	Cases	This Hosp.	State Avg.	U.S. Avg.
Heart Attack Care				
ACE Inhibitor or ARB for LVSD[5]	0	-	96%	96%
Aspirin at Arrival[5]	0	-	99%	99%
Aspirin at Discharge[5]	0	-	99%	98%
Beta Blocker at Discharge[5]	0	-	99%	98%
Fibrinolytic Medication Timing[5]	0	-	67%	55%
PCI Within 90 Minutes of Arrival[5]	0	-	94%	90%
Smoking Cessation Advice[5]	0	-	99%	99%
Chest Pain/Possible Heart Attack Care				
Aspirin at Arrival	-	-	96%	95%
Median Time to ECG (minutes)	-	-	7	8
Median Time to Transfer (minutes)	-	-	64	61
Fibrinolytic Medication Timing	-	-	45%	54%
Heart Failure Care				
ACE Inhibitor or ARB for LVSD[1,3]	1	100%	94%	94%
Discharge Instructions[1,3]	1	0%	86%	88%
Evaluation of LVS Function[1,3]	2	50%	95%	98%
Smoking Cessation Advice[3]	0	-	96%	98%
Pneumonia Care				
Appropriate Initial Antibiotic[1]	11	73%	92%	92%
Blood Culture Timing[1]	4	75%	97%	96%
Influenza Vaccine[1]	12	42%	92%	91%
Initial Antibiotic Timing[1]	15	100%	97%	95%
Pneumococcal Vaccine[1]	16	56%	94%	93%
Smoking Cessation Advice[1]	3	100%	95%	97%
Surgical Care Improvement Project				
Appropriate VTP Within 24 Hours[5]	0	-	92%	92%
Appropriate Hair Removal[5]	0	-	100%	99%
Appropriate Beta Blocker Usage[5]	0	-	94%	93%
Controlled Postoperative Blood Glucose[5]	0	-	89%	93%
Prophylactic Antibiotic Timing[5]	0	-	98%	97%
Prophylactic Antibiotic Timing (Outpatient)	-	-	94%	92%
Prophylactic Antibiotic Selection[5]	0	-	98%	97%
Prophylactic Antibiotic Select. (Outpatient)	-	-	97%	94%
Prophylactic Antibiotic Stopped[5]	0	-	95%	94%
Recommended VTP Ordered[5]	0	-	93%	94%
Urinary Catheter Removal[5]	0	-	91%	90%
Children's Asthma Care				
Received Systemic Corticosteroids	-	-	-	100%
Received Home Management Plan	-	-	-	71%
Received Reliever Medication	-	-	-	100%
Use of Medical Imaging				
Combination Abdominal CT Scan	-	-	0.163	0.191
Combination Chest CT Scan	-	-	0.060	0.054
Follow-up Mammogram/Ultrasound	-	-	8.1%	8.4%
MRI for Low Back Pain	-	-	30.2%	32.7%
Survey of Patients' Hospital Experiences				
Area Around Room 'Always' Quiet at Night[8]	-	-	-	58%
Doctors 'Always' Communicated Well[8]	-	-	-	80%
Home Recovery Information Given[8]	-	-	-	82%
Hospital Given 9 or 10 on 10 Point Scale[8]	-	-	-	67%
Meds 'Always' Explained Before Given[8]	-	-	-	60%
Nurses 'Always' Communicated Well[8]	-	-	-	76%
Pain 'Always' Well Controlled[8]	-	-	-	69%
Room and Bathroom 'Always' Clean[8]	-	-	-	71%
Timely Help 'Always' Received[8]	-	-	-	64%
Would Definitely Recommend Hospital[8]	-	-	-	69%

Mercy Medical Center-New Hampton

308 North Maple Avenue Phone: 641-394-4121
New Hampton, IA 50659 Fax: 641-394-2328
URL: www.mercynewhampton.com
Type: Critical Access Hospitals Emergency Services: Yes
Ownership: Voluntary Non-Profit - Church Beds: 18

Key Personnel:
CEO/President. . . . . Bruce Roesler
Chief of Medical Staff. . . . . Luke Brinkman, DO
Infection Control. . . . . Sharon Heiring, RN
Emergency Room . . . . Jessie Durnan

Measure	Cases	This Hosp.	State Avg.	U.S. Avg.
Heart Attack Care				
ACE Inhibitor or ARB for LVSD[1]	4	75%	96%	96%
Aspirin at Arrival[1]	6	100%	99%	99%
Aspirin at Discharge[1]	6	100%	99%	98%
Beta Blocker at Discharge[1]	6	83%	99%	98%
Fibrinolytic Medication Timing	0	-	67%	55%
PCI Within 90 Minutes of Arrival	0	-	94%	90%
Smoking Cessation Advice[1]	1	100%	99%	99%
Chest Pain/Possible Heart Attack Care				
Aspirin at Arrival	-	-	96%	95%
Median Time to ECG (minutes)	-	-	7	8
Median Time to Transfer (minutes)	-	-	64	61
Fibrinolytic Medication Timing	-	-	45%	54%
Heart Failure Care				
ACE Inhibitor or ARB for LVSD[1]	6	100%	94%	94%
Discharge Instructions[1]	6	83%	86%	88%
Evaluation of LVS Function[1]	13	69%	95%	98%
Smoking Cessation Advice[1]	2	50%	96%	98%
Pneumonia Care				
Appropriate Initial Antibiotic[1]	8	100%	92%	92%
Blood Culture Timing[1]	15	100%	97%	96%
Influenza Vaccine[1]	11	100%	92%	91%
Initial Antibiotic Timing[1]	17	100%	97%	95%
Pneumococcal Vaccine[1]	20	80%	94%	93%
Smoking Cessation Advice[1]	4	50%	95%	97%
Surgical Care Improvement Project				
Appropriate VTP Within 24 Hours[5]	0	-	92%	92%
Appropriate Hair Removal[5]	0	-	100%	99%
Appropriate Beta Blocker Usage[5]	0	-	94%	93%
Controlled Postoperative Blood Glucose[5]	0	-	89%	93%
Prophylactic Antibiotic Timing[5]	0	-	98%	97%
Prophylactic Antibiotic Timing (Outpatient)	-	-	94%	92%
Prophylactic Antibiotic Selection[5]	0	-	98%	97%
Prophylactic Antibiotic Select. (Outpatient)	-	-	97%	94%
Prophylactic Antibiotic Stopped[5]	0	-	95%	94%
Recommended VTP Ordered[5]	0	-	93%	94%
Urinary Catheter Removal[5]	0	-	91%	90%
Children's Asthma Care				
Received Systemic Corticosteroids	-	-	-	100%
Received Home Management Plan	-	-	-	71%
Received Reliever Medication	-	-	-	100%
Use of Medical Imaging				
Combination Abdominal CT Scan	-	-	0.163	0.191
Combination Chest CT Scan	-	-	0.060	0.054
Follow-up Mammogram/Ultrasound	-	-	8.1%	8.4%
MRI for Low Back Pain	-	-	30.2%	32.7%
Survey of Patients' Hospital Experiences				
Area Around Room 'Always' Quiet at Night[8]	-	-	-	58%
Doctors 'Always' Communicated Well[8]	-	-	-	80%
Home Recovery Information Given[8]	-	-	-	82%
Hospital Given 9 or 10 on 10 Point Scale[8]	-	-	-	67%
Meds 'Always' Explained Before Given[8]	-	-	-	60%
Nurses 'Always' Communicated Well[8]	-	-	-	76%
Pain 'Always' Well Controlled[8]	-	-	-	69%
Room and Bathroom 'Always' Clean[8]	-	-	-	71%
Timely Help 'Always' Received[8]	-	-	-	64%
Would Definitely Recommend Hospital[8]	-	-	-	69%

NOTE: Hospital profiles are in alphabetical order by state, then city, then hospital within the city; Rankings exclude hospitals with less than 25 cases except for patient surveys which excludes hospitals with less than 100 cases; (a) 100–299 cases; (1) The number of cases is too small to be sure how well a hospital is performing; (2) The hospital indicated that the data submitted for this measure were based on a sample of cases; (3) Data was collected during a shorter time period (fewer quarters) than the maximum possible time for this measure; (4) Suppressed for one or more quarters by CMS; (5) No data is available from the hospital for this measure; (6) Fewer than 100 patients completed the HCAHPS survey. Use these rates with caution, as the number of surveys may be too low to reliably assess hospital performance; (7) Survey results are based on less than 12 months of data; (8) Survey results are not available for this reporting period; (9) No or very few patients were eligible for the HCAHPS survey. The scores shown, if any, reflect a very small number of surveys; (10) A state average was not calculated because too few hospitals in the state submitted data; (11) There were discrepancies in the data collection process; Please refer to the User's Guide for a full explanation of data.

Skiff Medical Center

204 North 4th Avenue East
Newton, IA 50208
Phone: 641-792-1273
Fax: 641-792-4603
E-mail: info@skiffmed.com
URL: www.skiffmed.com
Type: Acute Care Hospitals
Emergency Services: Yes
Ownership: Government - Local
Beds: 68

Key Personnel:

CEO/President.................. Francie Jahn
Chief of Medical Staff.......... Tammy Chance, DO
Infection Control............... Lisa Guldberg, RN BSN
Operating Room.............. Ann Polking, RN
Quality Assurance .... Robert Campbell
Radiology.................... Jane Hettinger
Emergency Room .... Susan Carzoli, RN
Patient Relations .... Steve Wilbur

Measure	Cases	This Hosp.	State Avg.	U.S. Avg.
Heart Attack Care				
ACE Inhibitor or ARB for LVSD[1]	1	100%	96%	96%
Aspirin at Arrival[1]	10	80%	99%	99%
Aspirin at Discharge[1]	8	75%	99%	98%
Beta Blocker at Discharge[1]	8	75%	99%	98%
Fibrinolytic Medication Timing	0	-	67%	55%
PCI Within 90 Minutes of Arrival	0	-	94%	90%
Smoking Cessation Advice[1]	1	100%	99%	99%
Chest Pain/Possible Heart Attack Care				
Aspirin at Arrival	52	96%	96%	95%
Median Time to ECG (minutes)	52	5	7	8
Median Time to Transfer (minutes)[1]	8	54	64	61
Fibrinolytic Medication Timing	0	-	45%	54%
Heart Failure Care				
ACE Inhibitor or ARB for LVSD[1]	14	79%	94%	94%
Discharge Instructions	44	86%	86%	88%
Evaluation of LVS Function	64	78%	95%	98%
Smoking Cessation Advice[1]	10	90%	96%	98%
Pneumonia Care				
Appropriate Initial Antibiotic[1]	24	83%	92%	92%
Blood Culture Timing[1]	15	100%	97%	96%
Influenza Vaccine	28	82%	92%	91%
Initial Antibiotic Timing	41	95%	97%	95%
Pneumococcal Vaccine	42	67%	94%	93%
Smoking Cessation Advice[1]	12	92%	95%	97%
Surgical Care Improvement Project				
Appropriate VTP Within 24 Hours	41	95%	92%	92%
Appropriate Hair Removal	177	100%	100%	99%
Appropriate Beta Blocker Usage	53	98%	94%	93%
Controlled Postoperative Blood Glucose	0	-	89%	93%
Prophylactic Antibiotic Timing	144	98%	98%	97%
Prophylactic Antibiotic Timing (Outpatient)	32	88%	94%	92%
Prophylactic Antibiotic Selection	146	97%	98%	97%
Prophylactic Antibiotic Select. (Outpatient)	28	96%	97%	94%
Prophylactic Antibiotic Stopped	143	88%	95%	94%
Recommended VTP Ordered	41	98%	93%	94%
Urinary Catheter Removal[1]	5	100%	91%	90%
Children's Asthma Care				
Received Systemic Corticosteroids	-	-	-	100%
Received Home Management Plan	-	-	-	71%
Received Reliever Medication	-	-	-	100%
Use of Medical Imaging				
Combination Abdominal CT Scan	236	0.030	0.163	0.191
Combination Chest CT Scan	105	0.019	0.060	0.054
Follow-up Mammogram/Ultrasound	638	3.6%	8.1%	8.4%
MRI for Low Back Pain[1]	52	26.9%	30.2%	32.7%
Survey of Patients' Hospital Experiences				
Area Around Room 'Always' Quiet at Night	300+	55%	-	58%
Doctors 'Always' Communicated Well	300+	85%	-	80%
Home Recovery Information Given	300+	83%	-	82%
Hospital Given 9 or 10 on 10 Point Scale	300+	68%	-	67%
Meds 'Always' Explained Before Given	300+	60%	-	60%
Nurses 'Always' Communicated Well	300+	79%	-	76%
Pain 'Always' Well Controlled	300+	68%	-	69%
Room and Bathroom 'Always' Clean	300+	67%	-	71%
Timely Help 'Always' Received	300+	66%	-	64%
Would Definitely Recommend Hospital	300+	69%	-	69%

Mercy Hospital of Franciscan Sisters-Oelwein

201 Eighth Avenue SE
Oelwein, IA 50662
Phone: 319-283-6000
Fax: 319-283-6004
URL: www.covhealth.com
Type: Critical Access Hospitals
Emergency Services: Yes
Ownership: Voluntary Non-Profit - Other
Beds: 64

Key Personnel:

CEO/President.................. Katherine Hintz
Chief of Medical Staff.......... Michael Atherley
Operating Room.............. Anthony Leo, RN
Quality Assurance .... DeAnne Fox, RN
Emergency Room .... Judy Malget, RN

Measure	Cases	This Hosp.	State Avg.	U.S. Avg.
Heart Attack Care				
ACE Inhibitor or ARB for LVSD[3]	0	-	96%	96%
Aspirin at Arrival[3]	0	-	99%	99%
Aspirin at Discharge[3]	0	-	99%	98%
Beta Blocker at Discharge[3]	0	-	99%	98%
Fibrinolytic Medication Timing[3]	0	-	67%	55%
PCI Within 90 Minutes of Arrival[3]	0	-	94%	90%
Smoking Cessation Advice[3]	0	-	99%	99%
Chest Pain/Possible Heart Attack Care				
Aspirin at Arrival	-	-	96%	95%
Median Time to ECG (minutes)	-	-	7	8
Median Time to Transfer (minutes)	-	-	64	61
Fibrinolytic Medication Timing	-	-	45%	54%
Heart Failure Care				
ACE Inhibitor or ARB for LVSD[1]	1	100%	94%	94%
Discharge Instructions[1]	11	82%	86%	88%
Evaluation of LVS Function[1]	22	91%	95%	98%
Smoking Cessation Advice[1]	3	100%	96%	98%
Pneumonia Care				
Appropriate Initial Antibiotic[1]	18	100%	92%	92%
Blood Culture Timing[1]	21	95%	97%	96%
Influenza Vaccine[1]	15	93%	92%	91%
Initial Antibiotic Timing	33	97%	97%	95%
Pneumococcal Vaccine	32	100%	94%	93%
Smoking Cessation Advice[1]	7	86%	95%	97%
Surgical Care Improvement Project				
Appropriate VTP Within 24 Hours[1]	14	86%	92%	92%
Appropriate Hair Removal[1]	17	100%	100%	99%
Appropriate Beta Blocker Usage[1]	4	100%	94%	93%
Controlled Postoperative Blood Glucose[5]	0	-	89%	93%
Prophylactic Antibiotic Timing[1]	5	60%	98%	97%
Prophylactic Antibiotic Timing (Outpatient)	-	-	94%	92%
Prophylactic Antibiotic Selection[1]	4	100%	98%	97%
Prophylactic Antibiotic Select. (Outpatient)	-	-	97%	94%
Prophylactic Antibiotic Stopped[1]	3	100%	95%	94%
Recommended VTP Ordered[1]	14	86%	93%	94%
Urinary Catheter Removal[1]	1	100%	91%	90%
Children's Asthma Care				
Received Systemic Corticosteroids	-	-	-	100%
Received Home Management Plan	-	-	-	71%
Received Reliever Medication	-	-	-	100%
Use of Medical Imaging				
Combination Abdominal CT Scan	-	-	0.163	0.191
Combination Chest CT Scan	-	-	0.060	0.054
Follow-up Mammogram/Ultrasound	-	-	8.1%	8.4%
MRI for Low Back Pain	-	-	30.2%	32.7%
Survey of Patients' Hospital Experiences				
Area Around Room 'Always' Quiet at Night	(a)	72%	-	58%
Doctors 'Always' Communicated Well	(a)	85%	-	80%
Home Recovery Information Given	(a)	88%	-	82%
Hospital Given 9 or 10 on 10 Point Scale	(a)	70%	-	67%
Meds 'Always' Explained Before Given	(a)	63%	-	60%
Nurses 'Always' Communicated Well	(a)	86%	-	76%
Pain 'Always' Well Controlled	(a)	77%	-	69%
Room and Bathroom 'Always' Clean	(a)	87%	-	71%
Timely Help 'Always' Received	(a)	71%	-	64%
Would Definitely Recommend Hospital	(a)	67%	-	69%

Burgess Health Center

1600 Diamond Street
Onawa, IA 51040
Phone: 712-423-2311
Fax: 712-423-3500
URL: www.burgesshc.org
Type: Critical Access Hospitals
Emergency Services: Yes
Ownership: Voluntary Non-Profit - Private
Beds: 48

Key Personnel:

Chief of Medical Staff.......... John L Garred Sr, Sr MD
Infection Control............... Rose Bunstead, RN
Pediatric In-Patient Care .... Anne Hansen
Quality Assurance .... Kim Leif
Radiology.................... Robert Faulk
Emergency Room .... John L Garred, Jr, MD

Measure	Cases	This Hosp.	State Avg.	U.S. Avg.
Heart Attack Care				
ACE Inhibitor or ARB for LVSD[3]	0	-	96%	96%
Aspirin at Arrival[1,3]	1	100%	99%	99%
Aspirin at Discharge[3]	0	-	99%	98%
Beta Blocker at Discharge[3]	0	-	99%	98%
Fibrinolytic Medication Timing[3]	0	-	67%	55%
PCI Within 90 Minutes of Arrival[3]	0	-	94%	90%
Smoking Cessation Advice[3]	0	-	99%	99%
Chest Pain/Possible Heart Attack Care				
Aspirin at Arrival	-	-	96%	95%
Median Time to ECG (minutes)	-	-	7	8
Median Time to Transfer (minutes)	-	-	64	61
Fibrinolytic Medication Timing	-	-	45%	54%
Heart Failure Care				
ACE Inhibitor or ARB for LVSD[1,3]	4	100%	94%	94%
Discharge Instructions[1,3]	15	93%	86%	88%
Evaluation of LVS Function[1,3]	20	100%	95%	98%
Smoking Cessation Advice[1,3]	6	100%	96%	98%
Pneumonia Care				
Appropriate Initial Antibiotic[2,3]	30	87%	92%	92%
Blood Culture Timing[2,3]	44	95%	97%	96%
Influenza Vaccine[2]	46	100%	92%	91%
Initial Antibiotic Timing[2,3]	49	100%	97%	95%
Pneumococcal Vaccine[2,3]	56	100%	94%	93%
Smoking Cessation Advice[1,2,3]	18	100%	95%	97%
Surgical Care Improvement Project				
Appropriate VTP Within 24 Hours[1,3]	1	100%	92%	92%
Appropriate Hair Removal[1,3]	1	100%	100%	99%
Appropriate Beta Blocker Usage[5]	0	-	94%	93%
Controlled Postoperative Blood Glucose[3]	0	-	89%	93%
Prophylactic Antibiotic Timing[3]	0	-	98%	97%
Prophylactic Antibiotic Timing (Outpatient)	-	-	94%	92%
Prophylactic Antibiotic Selection[3]	0	-	98%	97%
Prophylactic Antibiotic Select. (Outpatient)	-	-	97%	94%
Prophylactic Antibiotic Stopped[3]	0	-	95%	94%
Recommended VTP Ordered[1,3]	1	100%	93%	94%
Urinary Catheter Removal[5]	0	-	91%	90%
Children's Asthma Care				
Received Systemic Corticosteroids	-	-	-	100%
Received Home Management Plan	-	-	-	71%
Received Reliever Medication	-	-	-	100%
Use of Medical Imaging				
Combination Abdominal CT Scan	-	-	0.163	0.191
Combination Chest CT Scan	-	-	0.060	0.054
Follow-up Mammogram/Ultrasound	-	-	8.1%	8.4%
MRI for Low Back Pain	-	-	30.2%	32.7%
Survey of Patients' Hospital Experiences				
Area Around Room 'Always' Quiet at Night	(a)	60%	-	58%
Doctors 'Always' Communicated Well	(a)	86%	-	80%
Home Recovery Information Given	(a)	85%	-	82%
Hospital Given 9 or 10 on 10 Point Scale	(a)	80%	-	67%
Meds 'Always' Explained Before Given	(a)	67%	-	60%
Nurses 'Always' Communicated Well	(a)	83%	-	76%
Pain 'Always' Well Controlled	(a)	77%	-	69%
Room and Bathroom 'Always' Clean	(a)	81%	-	71%
Timely Help 'Always' Received	(a)	68%	-	64%
Would Definitely Recommend Hospital	(a)	80%	-	69%

NOTE: Hospital profiles are in alphabetical order by state, then city, then hospital within the city; Rankings exclude hospitals with less than 25 cases except for patient surveys which excludes hospitals with less than 100 cases; (a) 100–299 cases; (1) The number of cases is too small to be sure how well a hospital is performing; (2) The hospital indicated that the data submitted for this measure were based on a sample of cases; (3) Data was collected during a shorter time period (fewer quarters) than the maximum possible time for this measure; (4) Suppressed for one or more quarters by CMS; (5) No data is available from the hospital for this measure; (6) Fewer than 100 patients completed the HCAHPS survey. Use these rates with caution, as the number of surveys may be too low to reliably assess hospital performance; (7) Survey results are based on less than 12 months of data; (8) Survey results are not available for this reporting period; (9) No or very few patients were eligible for the HCAHPS survey. The scores shown, if any, reflect a very small number of surveys; (10) A state average was not calculated because too few hospitals in the state submitted data; (11) There were discrepancies in the data collection process; Please refer to the User's Guide for a full explanation of data.

Orange City Area Health System

1000 Lincoln Circle SE Phone: 712-737-4984
Orange City, IA 51041 Fax: 712-737-5252
URL: www.ochealthsystem.org
Type: Critical Access Hospitals Emergency Services: Yes
Ownership: Government - Local Beds: 68

Key Personnel:
CEO/President. . . . . Martin W Guthmiller
Chief of Medical Staff . . . . John Weber, MD
Infection Control. . . . . Val Droog
Operating Room. . . . . Steven C Locker
Quality Assurance . . . . Val Droog
Radiology. . . . . Nicholas de Vries
Emergency Room . . . . Amy Van Beck
Patient Relations . . . . Melinda Kentfield

Measure	Cases	This Hosp.	State Avg.	U.S. Avg.
Heart Attack Care				
ACE Inhibitor or ARB for LVSD[1]	2	100%	96%	96%
Aspirin at Arrival[1]	9	100%	99%	99%
Aspirin at Discharge[1]	7	100%	99%	98%
Beta Blocker at Discharge[1]	6	100%	99%	98%
Fibrinolytic Medication Timing[5]	0	-	67%	55%
PCI Within 90 Minutes of Arrival[5]	0	-	94%	90%
Smoking Cessation Advice	0	-	99%	99%
Chest Pain/Possible Heart Attack Care				
Aspirin at Arrival	-	-	96%	95%
Median Time to ECG (minutes)	-	-	7	8
Median Time to Transfer (minutes)	-	-	64	61
Fibrinolytic Medication Timing	-	-	45%	54%
Heart Failure Care				
ACE Inhibitor or ARB for LVSD[1]	4	100%	94%	94%
Discharge Instructions[1]	12	92%	86%	88%
Evaluation of LVS Function[1]	13	85%	95%	98%
Smoking Cessation Advice[1]	1	100%	96%	98%
Pneumonia Care				
Appropriate Initial Antibiotic	37	89%	92%	92%
Blood Culture Timing	28	96%	97%	96%
Influenza Vaccine[1]	23	91%	92%	91%
Initial Antibiotic Timing	42	98%	97%	95%
Pneumococcal Vaccine	42	88%	94%	93%
Smoking Cessation Advice[1]	2	50%	95%	97%
Surgical Care Improvement Project				
Appropriate VTP Within 24 Hours[1,3]	4	100%	92%	92%
Appropriate Hair Removal	43	98%	100%	99%
Appropriate Beta Blocker Usage[5]	0	-	94%	93%
Controlled Postoperative Blood Glucose[3]	0	-	89%	93%
Prophylactic Antibiotic Timing	41	83%	98%	97%
Prophylactic Antibiotic Timing (Outpatient)	-	-	94%	92%
Prophylactic Antibiotic Selection	39	100%	98%	97%
Prophylactic Antibiotic Select. (Outpatient)	-	-	97%	94%
Prophylactic Antibiotic Stopped	39	95%	95%	94%
Recommended VTP Ordered[1]	15	67%	93%	94%
Urinary Catheter Removal[5]	0	-	91%	90%
Children's Asthma Care				
Received Systemic Corticosteroids	-	-	-	100%
Received Home Management Plan	-	-	-	71%
Received Reliever Medication	-	-	-	100%
Use of Medical Imaging				
Combination Abdominal CT Scan	-	-	0.163	0.191
Combination Chest CT Scan	-	-	0.060	0.054
Follow-up Mammogram/Ultrasound	-	-	8.1%	8.4%
MRI for Low Back Pain	-	-	30.2%	32.7%
Survey of Patients' Hospital Experiences				
Area Around Room 'Always' Quiet at Night[8]	-	-	-	58%
Doctors 'Always' Communicated Well[8]	-	-	-	80%
Home Recovery Information Given[8]	-	-	-	82%
Hospital Given 9 or 10 on 10 Point Scale[8]	-	-	-	67%
Meds 'Always' Explained Before Given[8]	-	-	-	60%
Nurses 'Always' Communicated Well[8]	-	-	-	76%
Pain 'Always' Well Controlled[8]	-	-	-	69%
Room and Bathroom 'Always' Clean[8]	-	-	-	71%
Timely Help 'Always' Received[8]	-	-	-	64%
Would Definitely Recommend Hospital[8]	-	-	-	69%

Clarke County Hospital

800 S Fillmore St Phone: 641-342-2184
Osceola, IA 50213 Fax: 641-342-5378
URL: www.clarkehosp.org
Type: Critical Access Hospitals Emergency Services: Yes
Ownership: Government - Local Beds: 55

Key Personnel:
CEO/President. . . . . Brian Evans
Cardiac Laboratory. . . . . Peggie Dumber
Chief of Medical Staff . . . . Vicki Irvin
Infection Control. . . . . Cindy Johnson
Quality Assurance . . . . Deb Lundquist
Radiology. . . . . Robert Filippone
Emergency Room . . . . Neline Halls

Measure	Cases	This Hosp.	State Avg.	U.S. Avg.
Heart Attack Care				
ACE Inhibitor or ARB for LVSD[5]	0	-	96%	96%
Aspirin at Arrival[5]	0	-	99%	99%
Aspirin at Discharge[5]	0	-	99%	98%
Beta Blocker at Discharge[5]	0	-	99%	98%
Fibrinolytic Medication Timing[5]	0	-	67%	55%
PCI Within 90 Minutes of Arrival[5]	0	-	94%	90%
Smoking Cessation Advice[5]	0	-	99%	99%
Chest Pain/Possible Heart Attack Care				
Aspirin at Arrival	28	96%	96%	95%
Median Time to ECG (minutes)	29	11	7	8
Median Time to Transfer (minutes)[1]	4	62	64	61
Fibrinolytic Medication Timing	0	-	45%	54%
Heart Failure Care				
ACE Inhibitor or ARB for LVSD[1]	1	0%	94%	94%
Discharge Instructions[1]	4	75%	86%	88%
Evaluation of LVS Function[1]	7	86%	95%	98%
Smoking Cessation Advice[1]	1	100%	96%	98%
Pneumonia Care				
Appropriate Initial Antibiotic[1]	14	100%	92%	92%
Blood Culture Timing[1]	15	93%	97%	96%
Influenza Vaccine[1]	12	92%	92%	91%
Initial Antibiotic Timing[1]	15	93%	97%	95%
Pneumococcal Vaccine[1]	16	100%	94%	93%
Smoking Cessation Advice	0	-	95%	97%
Surgical Care Improvement Project				
Appropriate VTP Within 24 Hours[5]	0	-	92%	92%
Appropriate Hair Removal[5]	0	-	100%	99%
Appropriate Beta Blocker Usage[5]	0	-	94%	93%
Controlled Postoperative Blood Glucose[5]	0	-	89%	93%
Prophylactic Antibiotic Timing[5]	0	-	98%	97%
Prophylactic Antibiotic Timing (Outpatient)[5]	0	-	94%	92%
Prophylactic Antibiotic Selection[5]	0	-	98%	97%
Prophylactic Antibiotic Select. (Outpatient)[5]	0	-	97%	94%
Prophylactic Antibiotic Stopped[5]	0	-	95%	94%
Recommended VTP Ordered[5]	0	-	93%	94%
Urinary Catheter Removal[5]	0	-	91%	90%
Children's Asthma Care				
Received Systemic Corticosteroids	-	-	-	100%
Received Home Management Plan	-	-	-	71%
Received Reliever Medication	-	-	-	100%
Use of Medical Imaging				
Combination Abdominal CT Scan	103	0.117	0.163	0.191
Combination Chest CT Scan	54	0.037	0.060	0.054
Follow-up Mammogram/Ultrasound	146	2.7%	8.1%	8.4%
MRI for Low Back Pain[1]	16	43.8%	30.2%	32.7%
Survey of Patients' Hospital Experiences				
Area Around Room 'Always' Quiet at Night	(a)	76%	-	58%
Doctors 'Always' Communicated Well	(a)	87%	-	80%
Home Recovery Information Given	(a)	88%	-	82%
Hospital Given 9 or 10 on 10 Point Scale	(a)	78%	-	67%
Meds 'Always' Explained Before Given	(a)	69%	-	60%
Nurses 'Always' Communicated Well	(a)	87%	-	76%
Pain 'Always' Well Controlled	(a)	71%	-	69%
Room and Bathroom 'Always' Clean	(a)	91%	-	71%
Timely Help 'Always' Received	(a)	76%	-	64%
Would Definitely Recommend Hospital	(a)	76%	-	69%

Mahaska Health Partnership

1229 C Avenue East Phone: 641-672-3100
Oskaloosa, IA 52577 Fax: 641-672-3153
URL: www.mahaskahospital.com
Type: Critical Access Hospitals Emergency Services: Yes
Ownership: Voluntary Non-Profit - Other Beds: 69

Key Personnel:
Cardiac Laboratory. . . . . Faye Drosg
Chief of Medical Staff . . . . Shawn Dawson
Infection Control. . . . . Julie Gibbons
Operating Room. . . . . Timothy Breon
Quality Assurance . . . . Steve Conner
Radiology. . . . . Akhtar Ashraf
Emergency Room . . . . Matt Whitis

Measure	Cases	This Hosp.	State Avg.	U.S. Avg.
Heart Attack Care				
ACE Inhibitor or ARB for LVSD[5]	0	-	96%	96%
Aspirin at Arrival[5]	0	-	99%	99%
Aspirin at Discharge[5]	0	-	99%	98%
Beta Blocker at Discharge[5]	0	-	99%	98%
Fibrinolytic Medication Timing[5]	0	-	67%	55%
PCI Within 90 Minutes of Arrival[5]	0	-	94%	90%
Smoking Cessation Advice[5]	0	-	99%	99%
Chest Pain/Possible Heart Attack Care				
Aspirin at Arrival	52	100%	96%	95%
Median Time to ECG (minutes)	56	6	7	8
Median Time to Transfer (minutes)[1]	5	86	64	61
Fibrinolytic Medication Timing[1]	1	0%	45%	54%
Heart Failure Care				
ACE Inhibitor or ARB for LVSD[1,2]	13	77%	94%	94%
Discharge Instructions[2]	32	75%	86%	88%
Evaluation of LVS Function[2]	55	98%	95%	98%
Smoking Cessation Advice[1,2]	7	86%	96%	98%
Pneumonia Care				
Appropriate Initial Antibiotic	33	82%	92%	92%
Blood Culture Timing	42	100%	97%	96%
Influenza Vaccine	32	100%	92%	91%
Initial Antibiotic Timing	44	98%	97%	95%
Pneumococcal Vaccine	47	100%	94%	93%
Smoking Cessation Advice[1]	12	50%	95%	97%
Surgical Care Improvement Project				
Appropriate VTP Within 24 Hours	27	100%	92%	92%
Appropriate Hair Removal	96	100%	100%	99%
Appropriate Beta Blocker Usage[1]	24	100%	94%	93%
Controlled Postoperative Blood Glucose	0	-	89%	93%
Prophylactic Antibiotic Timing	80	99%	98%	97%
Prophylactic Antibiotic Timing (Outpatient)[1,3]	5	100%	94%	92%
Prophylactic Antibiotic Selection	80	99%	98%	97%
Prophylactic Antibiotic Select. (Outpatient)[1,3]	5	100%	97%	94%
Prophylactic Antibiotic Stopped	73	88%	95%	94%
Recommended VTP Ordered	27	100%	93%	94%
Urinary Catheter Removal	27	96%	91%	90%
Children's Asthma Care				
Received Systemic Corticosteroids	-	-	-	100%
Received Home Management Plan	-	-	-	71%
Received Reliever Medication	-	-	-	100%
Use of Medical Imaging				
Combination Abdominal CT Scan	173	0.711	0.163	0.191
Combination Chest CT Scan	79	0.025	0.060	0.054
Follow-up Mammogram/Ultrasound	421	2.1%	8.1%	8.4%
MRI for Low Back Pain[1]	42	35.7%	30.2%	32.7%
Survey of Patients' Hospital Experiences				
Area Around Room 'Always' Quiet at Night	(a)	55%	-	58%
Doctors 'Always' Communicated Well	(a)	88%	-	80%
Home Recovery Information Given	(a)	81%	-	82%
Hospital Given 9 or 10 on 10 Point Scale	(a)	70%	-	67%
Meds 'Always' Explained Before Given	(a)	62%	-	60%
Nurses 'Always' Communicated Well	(a)	80%	-	76%
Pain 'Always' Well Controlled	(a)	70%	-	69%
Room and Bathroom 'Always' Clean	(a)	73%	-	71%
Timely Help 'Always' Received	(a)	61%	-	64%
Would Definitely Recommend Hospital	(a)	67%	-	69%

NOTE: Hospital profiles are in alphabetical order by state, then city, then hospital within the city; Rankings exclude hospitals with less than 25 cases except for patient surveys which excludes hospitals with less than 100 cases; (a) 100–299 cases; (1) The number of cases is too small to be sure how well a hospital is performing; (2) The hospital indicated that the data submitted for this measure were based on a sample of cases; (3) Data was collected during a shorter time period (fewer quarters) than the maximum possible time for this measure; (4) Suppressed for one or more quarters by CMS; (5) No data is available from the hospital for this measure; (6) Fewer than 100 patients completed the HCAHPS survey. Use these rates with caution, as the number of surveys may be too low to reliably assess hospital performance; (7) Survey results are based on less than 12 months of data; (8) Survey results are not available for this reporting period; (9) No or very few patients were eligible for the HCAHPS survey. The scores shown, if any, reflect a very small number of surveys; (10) A state average was not calculated because too few hospitals in the state submitted data; (11) There were discrepancies in the data collection process; Please refer to the User's Guide for a full explanation of data.

Ottumwa Regional Health Center

1001 E Pennsylvania
Ottumwa, IA 52501
E-mail: webmaster@orhc.com
URL: www.orhc.com
Phone: 641-684-2300
Fax: 641-684-3154

Type: Acute Care Hospitals
Ownership: Voluntary Non-Profit - Private
Emergency Services: Yes
Beds: 250

Key Personnel:

CEO/President. . . . . Tom Siemers
Chief of Medical Staff . . . . Kenneth Wayne
Infection Control. . . . . Paula Simplot
Operating Room. . . . . Brenda Jeffers
Quality Assurance . . . . Curt Mecks
Radiology. . . . . Lynn Manning

Measure	Cases	This Hosp.	State Avg.	U.S. Avg.
Heart Attack Care				
ACE Inhibitor or ARB for LVSD[1]	3	100%	96%	96%
Aspirin at Arrival[1]	22	95%	99%	99%
Aspirin at Discharge[1]	18	100%	99%	98%
Beta Blocker at Discharge[1]	21	95%	99%	98%
Fibrinolytic Medication Timing	0	-	67%	55%
PCI Within 90 Minutes of Arrival	0	-	94%	90%
Smoking Cessation Advice[1]	4	75%	99%	99%
Chest Pain/Possible Heart Attack Care				
Aspirin at Arrival	103	90%	96%	95%
Median Time to ECG (minutes)	105	9	7	8
Median Time to Transfer (minutes)[1]	22	94	64	61
Fibrinolytic Medication Timing[1]	7	0%	45%	54%
Heart Failure Care				
ACE Inhibitor or ARB for LVSD[1]	24	96%	94%	94%
Discharge Instructions	96	83%	86%	88%
Evaluation of LVS Function	128	89%	95%	98%
Smoking Cessation Advice[1]	18	100%	96%	98%
Pneumonia Care				
Appropriate Initial Antibiotic	91	93%	92%	92%
Blood Culture Timing	129	97%	97%	96%
Influenza Vaccine	89	91%	92%	91%
Initial Antibiotic Timing	129	95%	97%	95%
Pneumococcal Vaccine	117	94%	94%	93%
Smoking Cessation Advice	28	100%	95%	97%
Surgical Care Improvement Project				
Appropriate VTP Within 24 Hours	98	81%	92%	92%
Appropriate Hair Removal	211	100%	100%	99%
Appropriate Beta Blocker Usage	60	87%	94%	93%
Controlled Postoperative Blood Glucose	0	-	89%	93%
Prophylactic Antibiotic Timing	169	97%	98%	97%
Prophylactic Antibiotic Timing (Outpatient)	97	66%	94%	92%
Prophylactic Antibiotic Selection	171	97%	98%	97%
Prophylactic Antibiotic Select. (Outpatient)	68	97%	97%	94%
Prophylactic Antibiotic Stopped	162	88%	95%	94%
Recommended VTP Ordered	99	80%	93%	94%
Urinary Catheter Removal[1]	4	25%	91%	90%
Children's Asthma Care				
Received Systemic Corticosteroids	-	-	-	100%
Received Home Management Plan	-	-	-	71%
Received Reliever Medication	-	-	-	100%
Use of Medical Imaging				
Combination Abdominal CT Scan[1]	30	0.433	0.163	0.191
Combination Chest CT Scan[1]	25	0.160	0.060	0.054
Follow-up Mammogram/Ultrasound	1,120	3.2%	8.1%	8.4%
MRI for Low Back Pain	97	37.1%	30.2%	32.7%
Survey of Patients' Hospital Experiences				
Area Around Room 'Always' Quiet at Night	300+	65%	-	58%
Doctors 'Always' Communicated Well	300+	82%	-	80%
Home Recovery Information Given	300+	84%	-	82%
Hospital Given 9 or 10 on 10 Point Scale	300+	65%	-	67%
Meds 'Always' Explained Before Given	300+	62%	-	60%
Nurses 'Always' Communicated Well	300+	78%	-	76%
Pain 'Always' Well Controlled	300+	71%	-	69%
Room and Bathroom 'Always' Clean	300+	80%	-	71%
Timely Help 'Always' Received	300+	71%	-	64%
Would Definitely Recommend Hospital	300+	64%	-	69%

Pella Regional Health Center

404 Jefferson Street
Pella, IA 50219
E-mail: info@pellahealth.org
URL: www.pellahealth.org
Phone: 641-628-3150
Fax: 641-628-8901

Type: Critical Access Hospitals
Ownership: Voluntary Non-Profit - Other
Emergency Services: Yes
Beds: 47

Key Personnel:

CEO/President. . . . . Bob Kroese
Cardiac Laboratory. . . . . Sherilyn Nickel
Chief of Medical Staff . . . . Jeffrey Hartung, MD
Infection Control. . . . . Cheryl Thomson, RN
Operating Room. . . . . Matt Morgan, RN
Quality Assurance . . . . Barb Braafhart
Radiology. . . . . Lee Henry, DO

Measure	Cases	This Hosp.	State Avg.	U.S. Avg.
Heart Attack Care				
ACE Inhibitor or ARB for LVSD[1,3]	1	100%	96%	96%
Aspirin at Arrival[1,3]	2	100%	99%	99%
Aspirin at Discharge[1,3]	2	100%	99%	98%
Beta Blocker at Discharge[1,3]	2	50%	99%	98%
Fibrinolytic Medication Timing[3]	0	-	67%	55%
PCI Within 90 Minutes of Arrival[5]	0	-	94%	90%
Smoking Cessation Advice[3]	0	-	99%	99%
Chest Pain/Possible Heart Attack Care				
Aspirin at Arrival	-	-	96%	95%
Median Time to ECG (minutes)	-	-	7	8
Median Time to Transfer (minutes)	-	-	64	61
Fibrinolytic Medication Timing	-	-	45%	54%
Heart Failure Care				
ACE Inhibitor or ARB for LVSD[1]	15	93%	94%	94%
Discharge Instructions	28	100%	86%	88%
Evaluation of LVS Function	43	98%	95%	98%
Smoking Cessation Advice[1]	3	100%	96%	98%
Pneumonia Care				
Appropriate Initial Antibiotic	51	80%	92%	92%
Blood Culture Timing	45	96%	97%	96%
Influenza Vaccine	48	85%	92%	91%
Initial Antibiotic Timing	55	95%	97%	95%
Pneumococcal Vaccine	66	85%	94%	93%
Smoking Cessation Advice[1]	12	75%	95%	97%
Surgical Care Improvement Project				
Appropriate VTP Within 24 Hours[2]	44	80%	92%	92%
Appropriate Hair Removal[2]	129	100%	100%	99%
Appropriate Beta Blocker Usage[2]	33	73%	94%	93%
Controlled Postoperative Blood Glucose[5]	0	-	89%	93%
Prophylactic Antibiotic Timing[2]	94	90%	98%	97%
Prophylactic Antibiotic Timing (Outpatient)	-	-	94%	92%
Prophylactic Antibiotic Selection[2]	92	99%	98%	97%
Prophylactic Antibiotic Select. (Outpatient)	-	-	97%	94%
Prophylactic Antibiotic Stopped[2]	90	98%	95%	94%
Recommended VTP Ordered[2]	44	82%	93%	94%
Urinary Catheter Removal[1]	7	86%	91%	90%
Children's Asthma Care				
Received Systemic Corticosteroids	-	-	-	100%
Received Home Management Plan	-	-	-	71%
Received Reliever Medication	-	-	-	100%
Use of Medical Imaging				
Combination Abdominal CT Scan	-	-	0.163	0.191
Combination Chest CT Scan	-	-	0.060	0.054
Follow-up Mammogram/Ultrasound	-	-	8.1%	8.4%
MRI for Low Back Pain	-	-	30.2%	32.7%
Survey of Patients' Hospital Experiences				
Area Around Room 'Always' Quiet at Night	300+	66%	-	58%
Doctors 'Always' Communicated Well	300+	88%	-	80%
Home Recovery Information Given	300+	85%	-	82%
Hospital Given 9 or 10 on 10 Point Scale	300+	84%	-	67%
Meds 'Always' Explained Before Given	300+	68%	-	60%
Nurses 'Always' Communicated Well	300+	82%	-	76%
Pain 'Always' Well Controlled	300+	68%	-	69%
Room and Bathroom 'Always' Clean	300+	80%	-	71%
Timely Help 'Always' Received	300+	71%	-	64%
Would Definitely Recommend Hospital	300+	82%	-	69%

Dallas County Hospital

610 Tenth Street
Perry, IA 50220
URL: www.dallascohospital.org
Phone: 515-465-3547
Fax: 515-465-2922

Type: Critical Access Hospitals
Ownership: Voluntary Non-Profit - Other
Emergency Services: Yes
Beds: 25

Key Personnel:

CEO/President. . . . . Laurie Conner
Chief of Medical Staff . . . . Steven C Johnson, MD
Infection Control. . . . . Candace Jackson
Operating Room. . . . . Katie Heldt, RN
Quality Assurance . . . . Candace Jackson
Emergency Room . . . . Katie Heldt, RN

Measure	Cases	This Hosp.	State Avg.	U.S. Avg.
Heart Attack Care				
ACE Inhibitor or ARB for LVSD[5]	0	-	96%	96%
Aspirin at Arrival[5]	0	-	99%	99%
Aspirin at Discharge[5]	0	-	99%	98%
Beta Blocker at Discharge[5]	0	-	99%	98%
Fibrinolytic Medication Timing[5]	0	-	67%	55%
PCI Within 90 Minutes of Arrival[5]	0	-	94%	90%
Smoking Cessation Advice[5]	0	-	99%	99%
Chest Pain/Possible Heart Attack Care				
Aspirin at Arrival	29	100%	96%	95%
Median Time to ECG (minutes)	28	2	7	8
Median Time to Transfer (minutes)[1,3]	1	25	64	61
Fibrinolytic Medication Timing[3]	0	-	45%	54%
Heart Failure Care				
ACE Inhibitor or ARB for LVSD[1]	1	100%	94%	94%
Discharge Instructions[1]	5	80%	86%	88%
Evaluation of LVS Function[1]	8	100%	95%	98%
Smoking Cessation Advice[1]	1	100%	96%	98%
Pneumonia Care				
Appropriate Initial Antibiotic[1]	11	91%	92%	92%
Blood Culture Timing[1]	13	92%	97%	96%
Influenza Vaccine[1]	9	89%	92%	91%
Initial Antibiotic Timing[1]	18	94%	97%	95%
Pneumococcal Vaccine[1]	20	90%	94%	93%
Smoking Cessation Advice	0	-	95%	97%
Surgical Care Improvement Project				
Appropriate VTP Within 24 Hours[5]	0	-	92%	92%
Appropriate Hair Removal[5]	0	-	100%	99%
Appropriate Beta Blocker Usage[5]	0	-	94%	93%
Controlled Postoperative Blood Glucose[5]	0	-	89%	93%
Prophylactic Antibiotic Timing[5]	0	-	98%	97%
Prophylactic Antibiotic Timing (Outpatient)[5]	0	-	94%	92%
Prophylactic Antibiotic Selection[5]	0	-	98%	97%
Prophylactic Antibiotic Select. (Outpatient)[5]	0	-	97%	94%
Prophylactic Antibiotic Stopped[5]	0	-	95%	94%
Recommended VTP Ordered[5]	0	-	93%	94%
Urinary Catheter Removal[5]	0	-	91%	90%
Children's Asthma Care				
Received Systemic Corticosteroids	-	-	-	100%
Received Home Management Plan	-	-	-	71%
Received Reliever Medication	-	-	-	100%
Use of Medical Imaging				
Combination Abdominal CT Scan	107	0.290	0.163	0.191
Combination Chest CT Scan	60	0.400	0.060	0.054
Follow-up Mammogram/Ultrasound	152	6.6%	8.1%	8.4%
MRI for Low Back Pain[1]	21	33.3%	30.2%	32.7%
Survey of Patients' Hospital Experiences				
Area Around Room 'Always' Quiet at Night[6]	<100	74%	-	58%
Doctors 'Always' Communicated Well[6]	<100	83%	-	80%
Home Recovery Information Given[6]	<100	84%	-	82%
Hospital Given 9 or 10 on 10 Point Scale[6]	<100	81%	-	67%
Meds 'Always' Explained Before Given[6]	<100	77%	-	60%
Nurses 'Always' Communicated Well[6]	<100	88%	-	76%
Pain 'Always' Well Controlled[6]	<100	81%	-	69%
Room and Bathroom 'Always' Clean[6]	<100	84%	-	71%
Timely Help 'Always' Received[6]	<100	83%	-	64%
Would Definitely Recommend Hospital	<100	86%	-	69%

NOTE: Hospital profiles are in alphabetical order by state, then city, then hospital within the city; Rankings exclude hospitals with less than 25 cases except for patient surveys which excludes hospitals with less than 100 cases; (a) 100–299 cases; (1) The number of cases is too small to be sure how well a hospital is performing; (2) The hospital indicated that the data submitted for this measure were based on a sample of cases; (3) Data was collected during a shorter time period (fewer quarters) than the maximum possible time for this measure; (4) Suppressed for one or more quarters by CMS; (5) No data is available from the hospital for this measure; (6) Fewer than 100 patients completed the HCAHPS survey. Use these rates with caution, as the number of surveys may be too low to reliably assess hospital performance; (7) Survey results are based on less than 12 months of data; (8) Survey results are not available for this reporting period; (9) No or very few patients were eligible for the HCAHPS survey. The scores shown, if any, reflect a very small number of surveys; (10) A state average was not calculated because too few hospitals in the state submitted data; (11) There were discrepancies in the data collection process; Please refer to the User's Guide for a full explanation of data.

Baum Harmon Mercy Hospital

255 N Welch Avenue Phone: 712-957-2300
Primghar, IA 51245 Fax: 712-757-0300
URL: www.baumharmon.org
Type: Critical Access Hospitals Emergency Services: Yes
Ownership: Voluntary Non-Profit - Church Beds: 14

Key Personnel:
CEO/President. . . . . Rob Monical
Chief of Medical Staff . . . . Shailosh Desai, MD
Infection Control . . . . Tracy Lenz
Operating Room. . . . . Linda Bindner
Quality Assurance . . . . Allyson Thomas
Radiology. . . . . Amy Halverson
Ambulatory Care . . . . Shirley Lenhart
Emergency Room . . . . Linda Bindner

Measure	Cases	This Hosp.	State Avg.	U.S. Avg.
Heart Attack Care				
ACE Inhibitor or ARB for LVSD[5]	0	-	96%	96%
Aspirin at Arrival[5]	0	-	99%	99%
Aspirin at Discharge[5]	0	-	99%	98%
Beta Blocker at Discharge[5]	0	-	99%	98%
Fibrinolytic Medication Timing[5]	0	-	67%	55%
PCI Within 90 Minutes of Arrival[5]	0	-	94%	90%
Smoking Cessation Advice[5]	0	-	99%	99%
Chest Pain/Possible Heart Attack Care				
Aspirin at Arrival	-	-	96%	95%
Median Time to ECG (minutes)	-	-	7	8
Median Time to Transfer (minutes)	-	-	64	61
Fibrinolytic Medication Timing	-	-	45%	54%
Heart Failure Care				
ACE Inhibitor or ARB for LVSD[3]	0	-	94%	94%
Discharge Instructions[1,3]	2	0%	86%	88%
Evaluation of LVS Function[1,3]	6	0%	95%	98%
Smoking Cessation Advice[1,3]	1	0%	96%	98%
Pneumonia Care				
Appropriate Initial Antibiotic[3]	0	-	92%	92%
Blood Culture Timing[3]	0	-	97%	96%
Influenza Vaccine[5]	0	-	92%	91%
Initial Antibiotic Timing[3]	0	-	97%	95%
Pneumococcal Vaccine[1,3]	1	100%	94%	93%
Smoking Cessation Advice[3]	0	-	95%	97%
Surgical Care Improvement Project				
Appropriate VTP Within 24 Hours[5]	0	-	92%	92%
Appropriate Hair Removal[5]	0	-	100%	99%
Appropriate Beta Blocker Usage[5]	0	-	94%	93%
Controlled Postoperative Blood Glucose[5]	0	-	89%	93%
Prophylactic Antibiotic Timing[5]	0	-	98%	97%
Prophylactic Antibiotic Timing (Outpatient)	0	-	94%	92%
Prophylactic Antibiotic Selection[5]	0	-	98%	97%
Prophylactic Antibiotic Select. (Outpatient)	0	-	97%	94%
Prophylactic Antibiotic Stopped[5]	0	-	95%	94%
Recommended VTP Ordered[5]	0	-	93%	94%
Urinary Catheter Removal[5]	0	-	91%	90%
Children's Asthma Care				
Received Systemic Corticosteroids	-	-	-	100%
Received Home Management Plan	-	-	-	71%
Received Reliever Medication	-	-	-	100%
Use of Medical Imaging				
Combination Abdominal CT Scan	-	-	0.163	0.191
Combination Chest CT Scan	-	-	0.060	0.054
Follow-up Mammogram/Ultrasound	-	-	8.1%	8.4%
MRI for Low Back Pain	-	-	30.2%	32.7%
Survey of Patients' Hospital Experiences				
Area Around Room 'Always' Quiet at Night[8]	-	-	-	58%
Doctors 'Always' Communicated Well[8]	-	-	-	80%
Home Recovery Information Given[8]	-	-	-	82%
Hospital Given 9 or 10 on 10 Point Scale[8]	-	-	-	67%
Meds 'Always' Explained Before Given[8]	-	-	-	60%
Nurses 'Always' Communicated Well[8]	-	-	-	76%
Pain 'Always' Well Controlled[8]	-	-	-	69%
Room and Bathroom 'Always' Clean[8]	-	-	-	71%
Timely Help 'Always' Received[8]	-	-	-	64%
Would Definitely Recommend Hospital[8]	-	-	-	69%

Montgomery County Memorial Hospital

2301 Eastern Avenue Phone: 712-623-7000
Red Oak, IA 51566 Fax: 712-623-7180
URL: www.mcmh.org
Type: Critical Access Hospitals Emergency Services: Yes
Ownership: Government - Local Beds: 40

Key Personnel:
CEO/President. . . . . Allen E Pohren
Chief of Medical Staff . . . . Edward Piller
Operating Room. . . . . Jane King
Quality Assurance . . . . Ron Kloewer
Radiology. . . . . Peggy Reed

Measure	Cases	This Hosp.	State Avg.	U.S. Avg.
Heart Attack Care				
ACE Inhibitor or ARB for LVSD	0	-	96%	96%
Aspirin at Arrival[1]	8	100%	99%	99%
Aspirin at Discharge[1]	9	100%	99%	98%
Beta Blocker at Discharge[1]	8	75%	99%	98%
Fibrinolytic Medication Timing	0	-	67%	55%
PCI Within 90 Minutes of Arrival	0	-	94%	90%
Smoking Cessation Advice[1]	1	100%	99%	99%
Chest Pain/Possible Heart Attack Care				
Aspirin at Arrival	-	-	96%	95%
Median Time to ECG (minutes)	-	-	7	8
Median Time to Transfer (minutes)	-	-	64	61
Fibrinolytic Medication Timing	-	-	45%	54%
Heart Failure Care				
ACE Inhibitor or ARB for LVSD[1]	5	80%	94%	94%
Discharge Instructions[1]	16	88%	86%	88%
Evaluation of LVS Function	37	95%	95%	98%
Smoking Cessation Advice[1]	2	100%	96%	98%
Pneumonia Care				
Appropriate Initial Antibiotic	27	81%	92%	92%
Blood Culture Timing[1]	18	94%	97%	96%
Influenza Vaccine	38	100%	92%	91%
Initial Antibiotic Timing	34	97%	97%	95%
Pneumococcal Vaccine	52	100%	94%	93%
Smoking Cessation Advice[1]	9	100%	95%	97%
Surgical Care Improvement Project				
Appropriate VTP Within 24 Hours[1]	18	100%	92%	92%
Appropriate Hair Removal	29	100%	100%	99%
Appropriate Beta Blocker Usage[5]	0	-	94%	93%
Controlled Postoperative Blood Glucose	0	-	89%	93%
Prophylactic Antibiotic Timing[1]	11	100%	98%	97%
Prophylactic Antibiotic Timing (Outpatient)	-	-	94%	92%
Prophylactic Antibiotic Selection[1]	11	91%	98%	97%
Prophylactic Antibiotic Select. (Outpatient)	-	-	97%	94%
Prophylactic Antibiotic Stopped[1]	11	100%	95%	94%
Recommended VTP Ordered[1]	18	100%	93%	94%
Urinary Catheter Removal[1]	5	60%	91%	90%
Children's Asthma Care				
Received Systemic Corticosteroids	-	-	-	100%
Received Home Management Plan	-	-	-	71%
Received Reliever Medication	-	-	-	100%
Use of Medical Imaging				
Combination Abdominal CT Scan	-	-	0.163	0.191
Combination Chest CT Scan	-	-	0.060	0.054
Follow-up Mammogram/Ultrasound	-	-	8.1%	8.4%
MRI for Low Back Pain	-	-	30.2%	32.7%
Survey of Patients' Hospital Experiences				
Area Around Room 'Always' Quiet at Night	(a)	60%	-	58%
Doctors 'Always' Communicated Well	(a)	89%	-	80%
Home Recovery Information Given	(a)	90%	-	82%
Hospital Given 9 or 10 on 10 Point Scale	(a)	81%	-	67%
Meds 'Always' Explained Before Given	(a)	67%	-	60%
Nurses 'Always' Communicated Well	(a)	84%	-	76%
Pain 'Always' Well Controlled	(a)	75%	-	69%
Room and Bathroom 'Always' Clean	(a)	73%	-	71%
Timely Help 'Always' Received	(a)	74%	-	64%
Would Definitely Recommend Hospital	(a)	81%	-	69%

Sanford Hospital Rock Rapids

801 South Greene Street Phone: 712-472-2591
Rock Rapids, IA 51246 Fax: 712-472-2552
URL: www.merrillpioneer.org
Type: Critical Access Hospitals Emergency Services: Yes
Ownership: Voluntary Non-Profit - Private Beds: 25

Key Personnel:
CEO/President. . . . . Gordy Smith
Chief of Medical Staff . . . . David Springer, MD
Infection Control . . . . Linda Brinkhous
Operating Room. . . . . William Jongewaard
Radiology. . . . . Robert Thorbrogger
Emergency Room . . . . Cathy Huff

Measure	Cases	This Hosp.	State Avg.	U.S. Avg.
Heart Attack Care				
ACE Inhibitor or ARB for LVSD[5]	0	-	96%	96%
Aspirin at Arrival[5]	0	-	99%	99%
Aspirin at Discharge[5]	0	-	99%	98%
Beta Blocker at Discharge[5]	0	-	99%	98%
Fibrinolytic Medication Timing[5]	0	-	67%	55%
PCI Within 90 Minutes of Arrival[5]	0	-	94%	90%
Smoking Cessation Advice[5]	0	-	99%	99%
Chest Pain/Possible Heart Attack Care				
Aspirin at Arrival	-	-	96%	95%
Median Time to ECG (minutes)	-	-	7	8
Median Time to Transfer (minutes)	-	-	64	61
Fibrinolytic Medication Timing	-	-	45%	54%
Heart Failure Care				
ACE Inhibitor or ARB for LVSD	0	-	94%	94%
Discharge Instructions[1]	3	67%	86%	88%
Evaluation of LVS Function[1]	5	40%	95%	98%
Smoking Cessation Advice	0	-	96%	98%
Pneumonia Care				
Appropriate Initial Antibiotic[1]	9	78%	92%	92%
Blood Culture Timing[1]	3	100%	97%	96%
Influenza Vaccine[1]	9	100%	92%	91%
Initial Antibiotic Timing[1]	13	100%	97%	95%
Pneumococcal Vaccine[1]	17	94%	94%	93%
Smoking Cessation Advice[1]	2	50%	95%	97%
Surgical Care Improvement Project				
Appropriate VTP Within 24 Hours[1,3]	2	100%	92%	92%
Appropriate Hair Removal[1,3]	2	100%	100%	99%
Appropriate Beta Blocker Usage[5]	0	-	94%	93%
Controlled Postoperative Blood Glucose[3]	0	-	89%	93%
Prophylactic Antibiotic Timing[3]	0	-	98%	97%
Prophylactic Antibiotic Timing (Outpatient)	-	-	94%	92%
Prophylactic Antibiotic Selection[3]	0	-	98%	97%
Prophylactic Antibiotic Select. (Outpatient)	-	-	97%	94%
Prophylactic Antibiotic Stopped[3]	0	-	95%	94%
Recommended VTP Ordered[1,3]	2	100%	93%	94%
Urinary Catheter Removal[1,3]	1	0%	91%	90%
Children's Asthma Care				
Received Systemic Corticosteroids	-	-	-	100%
Received Home Management Plan	-	-	-	71%
Received Reliever Medication	-	-	-	100%
Use of Medical Imaging				
Combination Abdominal CT Scan	-	-	0.163	0.191
Combination Chest CT Scan	-	-	0.060	0.054
Follow-up Mammogram/Ultrasound	-	-	8.1%	8.4%
MRI for Low Back Pain	-	-	30.2%	32.7%
Survey of Patients' Hospital Experiences				
Area Around Room 'Always' Quiet at Night	(a)	59%	-	58%
Doctors 'Always' Communicated Well	(a)	85%	-	80%
Home Recovery Information Given	(a)	80%	-	82%
Hospital Given 9 or 10 on 10 Point Scale	(a)	85%	-	67%
Meds 'Always' Explained Before Given	(a)	60%	-	60%
Nurses 'Always' Communicated Well	(a)	79%	-	76%
Pain 'Always' Well Controlled	(a)	70%	-	69%
Room and Bathroom 'Always' Clean	(a)	87%	-	71%
Timely Help 'Always' Received	(a)	78%	-	64%
Would Definitely Recommend Hospital	(a)	79%	-	69%

NOTE: Hospital profiles are in alphabetical order by state, then city, then hospital within the city; Rankings exclude hospitals with less than 25 cases except for patient surveys which excludes hospitals with less than 100 cases; (a) 100–299 cases; (1) The number of cases is too small to be sure how well a hospital is performing; (2) The hospital indicated that the data submitted for this measure were based on a sample of cases; (3) Data was collected during a shorter time period (fewer quarters) than the maximum possible time for this measure; (4) Suppressed for one or more quarters by CMS; (5) No data is available from the hospital for this measure; (6) Fewer than 100 patients completed the HCAHPS survey. Use these rates with caution, as the number of surveys may be too low to reliably assess hospital performance; (7) Survey results are based on less than 12 months of data; (8) Survey results are not available for this reporting period; (9) No or very few patients were eligible for the HCAHPS survey. The scores shown, if any, reflect a very small number of surveys; (10) A state average was not calculated because too few hospitals in the state submitted data; (11) There were discrepancies in the data collection process; Please refer to the User's Guide for a full explanation of data.

Hegg Memorial Health Center

1202 21st Avenue Phone: 712-476-8000
Rock Valley, IA 51247 Fax: 712-476-8090
URL: www.heggmemorialhealthcenter.org
Type: Critical Access Hospitals Emergency Services: Yes
Ownership: Voluntary Non-Profit - Private Beds: 123

Key Personnel:
CEO/President............... Glenn Zevenbergen
Chief of Medical Staff.......... Brad Kamstra
Operating Room.............. Alma Post
Quality Assurance .... Stacey Jumbeck
Radiology.................. Tami Berkenpas

Measure	Cases	This Hosp.	State Avg.	U.S. Avg.
Heart Attack Care				
ACE Inhibitor or ARB for LVSD[5]	0	-	96%	96%
Aspirin at Arrival[5]	0	-	99%	99%
Aspirin at Discharge[5]	0	-	99%	98%
Beta Blocker at Discharge[5]	0	-	99%	98%
Fibrinolytic Medication Timing[5]	0	-	67%	55%
PCI Within 90 Minutes of Arrival[5]	0	-	94%	90%
Smoking Cessation Advice[5]	0	-	99%	99%
Chest Pain/Possible Heart Attack Care				
Aspirin at Arrival[5]	0	-	96%	95%
Median Time to ECG (minutes)[5]	0	-	7	8
Median Time to Transfer (minutes)[5]	0	-	64	61
Fibrinolytic Medication Timing[5]	0	-	45%	54%
Heart Failure Care				
ACE Inhibitor or ARB for LVSD[1,3]	2	100%	94%	94%
Discharge Instructions[1,3]	2	50%	86%	88%
Evaluation of LVS Function[1,3]	6	83%	95%	98%
Smoking Cessation Advice[3]	0	-	96%	98%
Pneumonia Care				
Appropriate Initial Antibiotic[1]	4	100%	92%	92%
Blood Culture Timing[1]	2	100%	97%	96%
Influenza Vaccine[1]	7	100%	92%	91%
Initial Antibiotic Timing[1]	9	100%	97%	95%
Pneumococcal Vaccine[1]	13	100%	94%	93%
Smoking Cessation Advice	0	-	95%	97%
Surgical Care Improvement Project				
Appropriate VTP Within 24 Hours[5]	0	-	92%	92%
Appropriate Hair Removal[5]	0	-	100%	99%
Appropriate Beta Blocker Usage[5]	0	-	94%	93%
Controlled Postoperative Blood Glucose[5]	0	-	89%	93%
Prophylactic Antibiotic Timing[5]	0	-	98%	97%
Prophylactic Antibiotic Timing (Outpatient)[5]	0	-	94%	92%
Prophylactic Antibiotic Selection[5]	0	-	98%	97%
Prophylactic Antibiotic Select. (Outpatient)[5]	0	-	97%	94%
Prophylactic Antibiotic Stopped[5]	0	-	95%	94%
Recommended VTP Ordered[5]	0	-	93%	94%
Urinary Catheter Removal[5]	0	-	91%	90%
Children's Asthma Care				
Received Systemic Corticosteroids	-	-	-	100%
Received Home Management Plan	-	-	-	71%
Received Reliever Medication	-	-	-	100%
Use of Medical Imaging				
Combination Abdominal CT Scan[1]	55	0.127	0.163	0.191
Combination Chest CT Scan[1]	22	0.182	0.060	0.054
Follow-up Mammogram/Ultrasound	105	9.5%	8.1%	8.4%
MRI for Low Back Pain[1]	11	18.2%	30.2%	32.7%
Survey of Patients' Hospital Experiences				
Area Around Room 'Always' Quiet at Night	(a)	67%	-	58%
Doctors 'Always' Communicated Well	(a)	84%	-	80%
Home Recovery Information Given	(a)	86%	-	82%
Hospital Given 9 or 10 on 10 Point Scale	(a)	81%	-	67%
Meds 'Always' Explained Before Given	(a)	80%	-	60%
Nurses 'Always' Communicated Well	(a)	82%	-	76%
Pain 'Always' Well Controlled	(a)	73%	-	69%
Room and Bathroom 'Always' Clean	(a)	82%	-	71%
Timely Help 'Always' Received	(a)	74%	-	64%
Would Definitely Recommend Hospital	(a)	86%	-	69%

Sanford Sheldon Medical Center

118 North 7th Avenue Phone: 712-324-5041
Sheldon, IA 51201 Fax: 712-324-6015
URL: www.nwiowahealthcenter.org
Type: Critical Access Hospitals Emergency Services: Yes
Ownership: Voluntary Non-Profit - Private Beds: 28

Key Personnel:
CEO/President............... Charles R Miller
Chief of Medical Staff.......... Amy M Badberg
Operating Room.............. William Jongewaard
Quality Assurance .... Beverly Scholten
Emergency Room .... Kathy Altena, RN

Measure	Cases	This Hosp.	State Avg.	U.S. Avg.
Heart Attack Care				
ACE Inhibitor or ARB for LVSD[5]	0	-	96%	96%
Aspirin at Arrival[5]	0	-	99%	99%
Aspirin at Discharge[5]	0	-	99%	98%
Beta Blocker at Discharge[5]	0	-	99%	98%
Fibrinolytic Medication Timing[5]	0	-	67%	55%
PCI Within 90 Minutes of Arrival[5]	0	-	94%	90%
Smoking Cessation Advice[5]	0	-	99%	99%
Chest Pain/Possible Heart Attack Care				
Aspirin at Arrival	-	-	96%	95%
Median Time to ECG (minutes)	-	-	7	8
Median Time to Transfer (minutes)	-	-	64	61
Fibrinolytic Medication Timing	-	-	45%	54%
Heart Failure Care				
ACE Inhibitor or ARB for LVSD[1]	2	50%	94%	94%
Discharge Instructions[1]	9	78%	86%	88%
Evaluation of LVS Function[1]	14	71%	95%	98%
Smoking Cessation Advice	0	-	96%	98%
Pneumonia Care				
Appropriate Initial Antibiotic	35	86%	92%	92%
Blood Culture Timing	36	86%	97%	96%
Influenza Vaccine	35	89%	92%	91%
Initial Antibiotic Timing	56	93%	97%	95%
Pneumococcal Vaccine	57	81%	94%	93%
Smoking Cessation Advice[1]	5	100%	95%	97%
Surgical Care Improvement Project				
Appropriate VTP Within 24 Hours[5]	0	-	92%	92%
Appropriate Hair Removal[5]	0	-	100%	99%
Appropriate Beta Blocker Usage[5]	0	-	94%	93%
Controlled Postoperative Blood Glucose[5]	0	-	89%	93%
Prophylactic Antibiotic Timing[5]	0	-	98%	97%
Prophylactic Antibiotic Timing (Outpatient)	-	-	94%	92%
Prophylactic Antibiotic Selection[5]	0	-	98%	97%
Prophylactic Antibiotic Select. (Outpatient)	-	-	97%	94%
Prophylactic Antibiotic Stopped[5]	0	-	95%	94%
Recommended VTP Ordered[5]	0	-	93%	94%
Urinary Catheter Removal[5]	0	-	91%	90%
Children's Asthma Care				
Received Systemic Corticosteroids	-	-	-	100%
Received Home Management Plan	-	-	-	71%
Received Reliever Medication	-	-	-	100%
Use of Medical Imaging				
Combination Abdominal CT Scan	-	-	0.163	0.191
Combination Chest CT Scan	-	-	0.060	0.054
Follow-up Mammogram/Ultrasound	-	-	8.1%	8.4%
MRI for Low Back Pain	-	-	30.2%	32.7%
Survey of Patients' Hospital Experiences				
Area Around Room 'Always' Quiet at Night	(a)	49%	-	58%
Doctors 'Always' Communicated Well	(a)	82%	-	80%
Home Recovery Information Given	(a)	76%	-	82%
Hospital Given 9 or 10 on 10 Point Scale	(a)	68%	-	67%
Meds 'Always' Explained Before Given	(a)	60%	-	60%
Nurses 'Always' Communicated Well	(a)	73%	-	76%
Pain 'Always' Well Controlled	(a)	67%	-	69%
Room and Bathroom 'Always' Clean	(a)	73%	-	71%
Timely Help 'Always' Received	(a)	60%	-	64%
Would Definitely Recommend Hospital	(a)	72%	-	69%

Shenandoah Medical Center

300 Pershing Avenue Phone: 712-246-1230
Shenandoah, IA 51601 Fax: 712-246-4737
URL: www.shenandoahmedcenter.com
Type: Critical Access Hospitals Emergency Services: Yes
Ownership: Voluntary Non-Profit - Private Beds: 88

Key Personnel:
CEO/President............... Susan McGough
Chief of Medical Staff.......... John Bowery
Operating Room.............. Hamid Kakavandi
Quality Assurance .... Jo McKeown
Radiology.................. Linda Head
Emergency Room .... Tammy Franks
Intensive Care Unit........... Dana Grady

Measure	Cases	This Hosp.	State Avg.	U.S. Avg.
Heart Attack Care				
ACE Inhibitor or ARB for LVSD[5]	0	-	96%	96%
Aspirin at Arrival[5]	0	-	99%	99%
Aspirin at Discharge[5]	0	-	99%	98%
Beta Blocker at Discharge[5]	0	-	99%	98%
Fibrinolytic Medication Timing[5]	0	-	67%	55%
PCI Within 90 Minutes of Arrival[5]	0	-	94%	90%
Smoking Cessation Advice[5]	0	-	99%	99%
Chest Pain/Possible Heart Attack Care				
Aspirin at Arrival	-	-	96%	95%
Median Time to ECG (minutes)	-	-	7	8
Median Time to Transfer (minutes)	-	-	64	61
Fibrinolytic Medication Timing	-	-	45%	54%
Heart Failure Care				
ACE Inhibitor or ARB for LVSD	0	-	94%	94%
Discharge Instructions[1]	5	100%	86%	88%
Evaluation of LVS Function[1]	9	44%	95%	98%
Smoking Cessation Advice[1]	2	100%	96%	98%
Pneumonia Care				
Appropriate Initial Antibiotic[1]	12	100%	92%	92%
Blood Culture Timing[1]	20	100%	97%	96%
Influenza Vaccine[1]	16	69%	92%	91%
Initial Antibiotic Timing[1]	19	95%	97%	95%
Pneumococcal Vaccine	30	77%	94%	93%
Smoking Cessation Advice[1]	6	100%	95%	97%
Surgical Care Improvement Project				
Appropriate VTP Within 24 Hours[1]	2	50%	92%	92%
Appropriate Hair Removal[1]	15	93%	100%	99%
Appropriate Beta Blocker Usage[1]	3	67%	94%	93%
Controlled Postoperative Blood Glucose	0	-	89%	93%
Prophylactic Antibiotic Timing[1]	14	71%	98%	97%
Prophylactic Antibiotic Timing (Outpatient)	-	-	94%	92%
Prophylactic Antibiotic Selection[1]	14	64%	98%	97%
Prophylactic Antibiotic Select. (Outpatient)	-	-	97%	94%
Prophylactic Antibiotic Stopped[1]	14	93%	95%	94%
Recommended VTP Ordered[1]	2	100%	93%	94%
Urinary Catheter Removal[1]	2	50%	91%	90%
Children's Asthma Care				
Received Systemic Corticosteroids	-	-	-	100%
Received Home Management Plan	-	-	-	71%
Received Reliever Medication	-	-	-	100%
Use of Medical Imaging				
Combination Abdominal CT Scan	-	-	0.163	0.191
Combination Chest CT Scan	-	-	0.060	0.054
Follow-up Mammogram/Ultrasound	-	-	8.1%	8.4%
MRI for Low Back Pain	-	-	30.2%	32.7%
Survey of Patients' Hospital Experiences				
Area Around Room 'Always' Quiet at Night[6]	<100	47%	-	58%
Doctors 'Always' Communicated Well[6]	<100	89%	-	80%
Home Recovery Information Given[6]	<100	83%	-	82%
Hospital Given 9 or 10 on 10 Point Scale[6]	<100	68%	-	67%
Meds 'Always' Explained Before Given[6]	<100	70%	-	60%
Nurses 'Always' Communicated Well[6]	<100	76%	-	76%
Pain 'Always' Well Controlled[6]	<100	67%	-	69%
Room and Bathroom 'Always' Clean[6]	<100	65%	-	71%
Timely Help 'Always' Received[6]	<100	69%	-	64%
Would Definitely Recommend Hospital	<100	69%	-	69%

NOTE: Hospital profiles are in alphabetical order by state, then city, then hospital within the city; Rankings exclude hospitals with less than 25 cases except for patient surveys which excludes hospitals with less than 100 cases; (a) 100–299 cases; (1) The number of cases is too small to be sure how well a hospital is performing; (2) The hospital indicated that the data submitted for this measure were based on a sample of cases; (3) Data was collected during a shorter time period (fewer quarters) than the maximum possible time for this measure; (4) Suppressed for one or more quarters by CMS; (5) No data is available from the hospital for this measure; (6) Fewer than 100 patients completed the HCAHPS survey. Use these rates with caution, as the number of surveys may be too low to reliably assess hospital performance; (7) Survey results are based on less than 12 months of data; (8) Survey results are not available for this reporting period; (9) No or very few patients were eligible for the HCAHPS survey. The scores shown, if any, reflect a very small number of surveys; (10) A state average was not calculated because too few hospitals in the state submitted data; (11) There were discrepancies in the data collection process; Please refer to the User's Guide for a full explanation of data.

Osceola Community Hospital

600 9th Avenue North Phone: 712-754-2574
Sibley, IA 51249 Fax: 712-754-3782
URL: www.osceolacommunityhospital.org
Type: Critical Access Hospitals Emergency Services: Yes
Ownership: Voluntary Non-Profit - Private Beds: 32

Key Personnel:
CEO/President. . . . . Janet Dykstra
Chief of Medical Staff . . . . William Hicks
Operating Room. . . . . Pauline Van Engen
Quality Assurance . . . . Sherry McElroy
Radiology. . . . . R W Thorbrogger

Measure	Cases	This Hosp.	State Avg.	U.S. Avg.
Heart Attack Care				
ACE Inhibitor or ARB for LVSD[5]	0	-	96%	96%
Aspirin at Arrival[5]	0	-	99%	99%
Aspirin at Discharge[5]	0	-	99%	98%
Beta Blocker at Discharge[5]	0	-	99%	98%
Fibrinolytic Medication Timing[5]	0	-	67%	55%
PCI Within 90 Minutes of Arrival[5]	0	-	94%	90%
Smoking Cessation Advice[5]	0	-	99%	99%
Chest Pain/Possible Heart Attack Care				
Aspirin at Arrival	-	-	96%	95%
Median Time to ECG (minutes)	-	-	7	8
Median Time to Transfer (minutes)	-	-	64	61
Fibrinolytic Medication Timing	-	-	45%	54%
Heart Failure Care				
ACE Inhibitor or ARB for LVSD[1,3]	4	25%	94%	94%
Discharge Instructions[1,3]	3	100%	86%	88%
Evaluation of LVS Function[1,3]	7	100%	95%	98%
Smoking Cessation Advice[3]	0	-	96%	98%
Pneumonia Care				
Appropriate Initial Antibiotic[1,3]	2	50%	92%	92%
Blood Culture Timing[1,3]	1	100%	97%	96%
Influenza Vaccine[3]	0	-	92%	91%
Initial Antibiotic Timing[1,3]	4	75%	97%	95%
Pneumococcal Vaccine[1,3]	3	100%	94%	93%
Smoking Cessation Advice[3]	0	-	95%	97%
Surgical Care Improvement Project				
Appropriate VTP Within 24 Hours[1,3]	1	100%	92%	92%
Appropriate Hair Removal[1,3]	5	100%	100%	99%
Appropriate Beta Blocker Usage[5]	0	-	94%	93%
Controlled Postoperative Blood Glucose[3]	0	-	89%	93%
Prophylactic Antibiotic Timing[1,3]	5	100%	98%	97%
Prophylactic Antibiotic Timing (Outpatient)	-	-	94%	92%
Prophylactic Antibiotic Selection[1,3]	5	100%	98%	97%
Prophylactic Antibiotic Select. (Outpatient)	-	-	97%	94%
Prophylactic Antibiotic Stopped[1,3]	5	100%	95%	94%
Recommended VTP Ordered[1,3]	1	100%	93%	94%
Urinary Catheter Removal[3]	0	-	91%	90%
Children's Asthma Care				
Received Systemic Corticosteroids	-	-	-	100%
Received Home Management Plan	-	-	-	71%
Received Reliever Medication	-	-	-	100%
Use of Medical Imaging				
Combination Abdominal CT Scan	-	-	0.163	0.191
Combination Chest CT Scan	-	-	0.060	0.054
Follow-up Mammogram/Ultrasound	-	-	8.1%	8.4%
MRI for Low Back Pain	-	-	30.2%	32.7%
Survey of Patients' Hospital Experiences				
Area Around Room 'Always' Quiet at Night	(a)	72%	-	58%
Doctors 'Always' Communicated Well	(a)	83%	-	80%
Home Recovery Information Given	(a)	78%	-	82%
Hospital Given 9 or 10 on 10 Point Scale	(a)	83%	-	67%
Meds 'Always' Explained Before Given	(a)	66%	-	60%
Nurses 'Always' Communicated Well	(a)	82%	-	76%
Pain 'Always' Well Controlled	(a)	71%	-	69%
Room and Bathroom 'Always' Clean	(a)	92%	-	71%
Timely Help 'Always' Received	(a)	80%	-	64%
Would Definitely Recommend Hospital	(a)	79%	-	69%

Sioux Center Community Hospital & Health Center

605 South Main Avenue Phone: 712-722-1271
Sioux Center, IA 51250 Fax: 712-722-0787
URL: www.schospital.org
Type: Critical Access Hospitals Emergency Services: Yes
Ownership: Voluntary Non-Profit - Private Beds: 90

Key Personnel:
CEO/President. . . . . Kayleen Lee
Chief of Medical Staff . . . . Mary McClung
Quality Assurance . . . . Sheryl Hulstein
Radiology. . . . . Robert P DeClark

Measure	Cases	This Hosp.	State Avg.	U.S. Avg.
Heart Attack Care				
ACE Inhibitor or ARB for LVSD[5]	0	-	96%	96%
Aspirin at Arrival[5]	0	-	99%	99%
Aspirin at Discharge[5]	0	-	99%	98%
Beta Blocker at Discharge[5]	0	-	99%	98%
Fibrinolytic Medication Timing[5]	0	-	67%	55%
PCI Within 90 Minutes of Arrival[5]	0	-	94%	90%
Smoking Cessation Advice[5]	0	-	99%	99%
Chest Pain/Possible Heart Attack Care				
Aspirin at Arrival[5]	0	-	96%	95%
Median Time to ECG (minutes)[5]	0	-	7	8
Median Time to Transfer (minutes)[5]	0	-	64	61
Fibrinolytic Medication Timing[5]	0	-	45%	54%
Heart Failure Care				
ACE Inhibitor or ARB for LVSD[1,3]	1	100%	94%	94%
Discharge Instructions[1,3]	2	100%	86%	88%
Evaluation of LVS Function[1,3]	6	100%	95%	98%
Smoking Cessation Advice[3]	0	-	96%	98%
Pneumonia Care				
Appropriate Initial Antibiotic[1]	14	100%	92%	92%
Blood Culture Timing[1]	10	100%	97%	96%
Influenza Vaccine[1]	11	100%	92%	91%
Initial Antibiotic Timing[1]	16	94%	97%	95%
Pneumococcal Vaccine[1]	14	100%	94%	93%
Smoking Cessation Advice[1]	4	75%	95%	97%
Surgical Care Improvement Project				
Appropriate VTP Within 24 Hours[1]	4	75%	92%	92%
Appropriate Hair Removal[1]	10	100%	100%	99%
Appropriate Beta Blocker Usage[1]	2	100%	94%	93%
Controlled Postoperative Blood Glucose	0	-	89%	93%
Prophylactic Antibiotic Timing[1]	9	100%	98%	97%
Prophylactic Antibiotic Timing (Outpatient)[5]	0	-	94%	92%
Prophylactic Antibiotic Selection[1]	9	100%	98%	97%
Prophylactic Antibiotic Select. (Outpatient)[5]	0	-	97%	94%
Prophylactic Antibiotic Stopped[1]	9	100%	95%	94%
Recommended VTP Ordered[1]	4	75%	93%	94%
Urinary Catheter Removal[1]	1	0%	91%	90%
Children's Asthma Care				
Received Systemic Corticosteroids	-	-	-	100%
Received Home Management Plan	-	-	-	71%
Received Reliever Medication	-	-	-	100%
Use of Medical Imaging				
Combination Abdominal CT Scan	76	0.197	0.163	0.191
Combination Chest CT Scan[1]	42	0.119	0.060	0.054
Follow-up Mammogram/Ultrasound	197	9.1%	8.1%	8.4%
MRI for Low Back Pain[1]	27	11.1%	30.2%	32.7%
Survey of Patients' Hospital Experiences				
Area Around Room 'Always' Quiet at Night	(a)	60%	-	58%
Doctors 'Always' Communicated Well	(a)	81%	-	80%
Home Recovery Information Given	(a)	82%	-	82%
Hospital Given 9 or 10 on 10 Point Scale	(a)	79%	-	67%
Meds 'Always' Explained Before Given	(a)	66%	-	60%
Nurses 'Always' Communicated Well	(a)	83%	-	76%
Pain 'Always' Well Controlled	(a)	72%	-	69%
Room and Bathroom 'Always' Clean	(a)	77%	-	71%
Timely Help 'Always' Received	(a)	75%	-	64%
Would Definitely Recommend Hospital	(a)	80%	-	69%

Mercy Medical Center-Sioux City

801 5th St Box #316b Phone: 712-279-2010
Sioux City, IA 51101 Fax: 712-279-5624
URL: www.mercysiouxcity.com
Type: Acute Care Hospitals Emergency Services: Yes
Ownership: Voluntary Non-Profit - Private Beds: 483

Key Personnel:
CEO/President. . . . . Mari Kaptain-Dahlen
Chief of Medical Staff . . . . Bruce Miller, MD
Coronary Care . . . . Mitchell Horowitz, MD
Infection Control. . . . . Diane Priekfat
Pediatric Ambulatory Care . . . . . . Vijay Chawala, MD
Pediatric In-Patient Care . . . . Vijay Chawala, MD
Quality Assurance . . . . Chris Kelly
Radiology. . . . . Jonathan C Beeler, MD

Measure	Cases	This Hosp.	State Avg.	U.S. Avg.
Heart Attack Care				
ACE Inhibitor or ARB for LVSD	49	100%	96%	96%
Aspirin at Arrival	223	100%	99%	99%
Aspirin at Discharge	364	98%	99%	98%
Beta Blocker at Discharge	367	99%	99%	98%
Fibrinolytic Medication Timing	0	-	67%	55%
PCI Within 90 Minutes of Arrival	38	95%	94%	90%
Smoking Cessation Advice	116	100%	99%	99%
Chest Pain/Possible Heart Attack Care				
Aspirin at Arrival[5]	0	-	96%	95%
Median Time to ECG (minutes)[5]	0	-	7	8
Median Time to Transfer (minutes)[5]	0	-	64	61
Fibrinolytic Medication Timing[5]	0	-	45%	54%
Heart Failure Care				
ACE Inhibitor or ARB for LVSD[2]	89	99%	94%	94%
Discharge Instructions[2]	202	99%	86%	88%
Evaluation of LVS Function[2]	251	99%	95%	98%
Smoking Cessation Advice[2]	62	100%	96%	98%
Pneumonia Care				
Appropriate Initial Antibiotic[2]	120	96%	92%	92%
Blood Culture Timing[2]	146	99%	97%	96%
Influenza Vaccine[2]	216	98%	92%	91%
Initial Antibiotic Timing[2]	210	97%	97%	95%
Pneumococcal Vaccine[2]	271	97%	94%	93%
Smoking Cessation Advice[2]	111	100%	95%	97%
Surgical Care Improvement Project				
Appropriate VTP Within 24 Hours[2]	383	97%	92%	92%
Appropriate Hair Removal[2]	879	100%	100%	99%
Appropriate Beta Blocker Usage[2]	304	94%	94%	93%
Controlled Postoperative Blood Glucose[2]	78	94%	89%	93%
Prophylactic Antibiotic Timing[2]	406	99%	98%	97%
Prophylactic Antibiotic Timing (Outpatient)	111	92%	94%	92%
Prophylactic Antibiotic Selection[2]	419	98%	98%	97%
Prophylactic Antibiotic Select. (Outpatient)	106	97%	97%	94%
Prophylactic Antibiotic Stopped[2]	375	92%	95%	94%
Recommended VTP Ordered[2]	385	97%	93%	94%
Urinary Catheter Removal	83	84%	91%	90%
Children's Asthma Care				
Received Systemic Corticosteroids	-	-	-	100%
Received Home Management Plan	-	-	-	71%
Received Reliever Medication	-	-	-	100%
Use of Medical Imaging				
Combination Abdominal CT Scan	535	0.422	0.163	0.191
Combination Chest CT Scan	298	0.010	0.060	0.054
Follow-up Mammogram/Ultrasound	393	4.6%	8.1%	8.4%
MRI for Low Back Pain	143	37.1%	30.2%	32.7%
Survey of Patients' Hospital Experiences				
Area Around Room 'Always' Quiet at Night	300+	52%	-	58%
Doctors 'Always' Communicated Well	300+	78%	-	80%
Home Recovery Information Given	300+	86%	-	82%
Hospital Given 9 or 10 on 10 Point Scale	300+	71%	-	67%
Meds 'Always' Explained Before Given	300+	59%	-	60%
Nurses 'Always' Communicated Well	300+	77%	-	76%
Pain 'Always' Well Controlled	300+	71%	-	69%
Room and Bathroom 'Always' Clean	300+	71%	-	71%
Timely Help 'Always' Received	300+	64%	-	64%
Would Definitely Recommend Hospital	300+	75%	-	69%

NOTE: Hospital profiles are in alphabetical order by state, then city, then hospital within the city; Rankings exclude hospitals with less than 25 cases except for patient surveys which excludes hospitals with less than 100 cases; (a) 100–299 cases; (1) The number of cases is too small to be sure how well a hospital is performing; (2) The hospital indicated that the data submitted for this measure were based on a sample of cases; (3) Data was collected during a shorter time period (fewer quarters) than the maximum possible time for this measure; (4) Suppressed for one or more quarters by CMS; (5) No data is available from the hospital for this measure; (6) Fewer than 100 patients completed the HCAHPS survey. Use these rates with caution, as the number of surveys may be too low to reliably assess hospital performance; (7) Survey results are based on less than 12 months of data; (8) Survey results are not available for this reporting period; (9) No or very few patients were eligible for the HCAHPS survey. The scores shown, if any, reflect a very small number of surveys; (10) A state average was not calculated because too few hospitals in the state submitted data; (11) There were discrepancies in the data collection process; Please refer to the User's Guide for a full explanation of data.

Saint Lukes Regional Medical Center

2720 Stone Park Boulevard
Sioux City, IA 51104
URL: www.stlukes.org
Type: Acute Care Hospitals
Ownership: Voluntary Non-Profit - Private
Phone: 712-279-3500
Fax: 712-279-7958
Emergency Services: Yes
Beds: 353

Key Personnel:
Chief of Medical Staff.......... Richard Hildebrand, DO
Infection Control.............. Dee Pedersen, RN
Operating Room.............. Becky Arnburg, RN
Pediatric Ambulatory Care ...... Colleen Johnson, RN
Pediatric In-Patient Care .... Colleen Johnson, RN
Quality Assurance .... Raeann Isaacson
Anesthesiology............... Paul Burke, DO
Emergency Room .... Paul Berger, MD

Measure	Cases	This Hosp.	State Avg.	U.S. Avg.
Heart Attack Care				
ACE Inhibitor or ARB for LVSD[1]	5	100%	96%	96%
Aspirin at Arrival	30	100%	99%	99%
Aspirin at Discharge	29	100%	99%	98%
Beta Blocker at Discharge	30	100%	99%	98%
Fibrinolytic Medication Timing	0	-	67%	55%
PCI Within 90 Minutes of Arrival[1]	5	100%	94%	90%
Smoking Cessation Advice[1]	8	100%	99%	99%
Chest Pain/Possible Heart Attack Care				
Aspirin at Arrival[1]	17	100%	96%	95%
Median Time to ECG (minutes)[1]	17	4	7	8
Median Time to Transfer (minutes)[1]	13	37	64	61
Fibrinolytic Medication Timing	0	-	45%	54%
Heart Failure Care				
ACE Inhibitor or ARB for LVSD	26	100%	94%	94%
Discharge Instructions	72	97%	86%	88%
Evaluation of LVS Function	94	99%	95%	98%
Smoking Cessation Advice[1]	10	100%	96%	98%
Pneumonia Care				
Appropriate Initial Antibiotic	127	91%	92%	92%
Blood Culture Timing	141	99%	97%	96%
Influenza Vaccine	118	98%	92%	91%
Initial Antibiotic Timing	171	99%	97%	95%
Pneumococcal Vaccine	185	97%	94%	93%
Smoking Cessation Advice	87	100%	95%	97%
Surgical Care Improvement Project				
Appropriate VTP Within 24 Hours[2]	222	95%	92%	92%
Appropriate Hair Removal[2]	687	100%	100%	99%
Appropriate Beta Blocker Usage[2]	157	96%	94%	93%
Controlled Postoperative Blood Glucose[2]	0	-	89%	93%
Prophylactic Antibiotic Timing[2]	500	98%	98%	97%
Prophylactic Antibiotic Timing (Outpatient)	102	88%	94%	92%
Prophylactic Antibiotic Selection[2]	499	96%	98%	97%
Prophylactic Antibiotic Select. (Outpatient)	97	97%	97%	94%
Prophylactic Antibiotic Stopped[2]	460	94%	95%	94%
Recommended VTP Ordered[2]	224	94%	93%	94%
Urinary Catheter Removal[2]	26	54%	91%	90%
Children's Asthma Care				
Received Systemic Corticosteroids	-	-	-	100%
Received Home Management Plan	-	-	-	71%
Received Reliever Medication	-	-	-	100%
Use of Medical Imaging				
Combination Abdominal CT Scan	258	0.601	0.163	0.191
Combination Chest CT Scan	90	0.156	0.060	0.054
Follow-up Mammogram/Ultrasound[5]	0	-	8.1%	8.4%
MRI for Low Back Pain[1]	12	33.3%	30.2%	32.7%
Survey of Patients' Hospital Experiences				
Area Around Room 'Always' Quiet at Night	300+	47%	-	58%
Doctors 'Always' Communicated Well	300+	74%	-	80%
Home Recovery Information Given	300+	83%	-	82%
Hospital Given 9 or 10 on 10 Point Scale	300+	68%	-	67%
Meds 'Always' Explained Before Given	300+	58%	-	60%
Nurses 'Always' Communicated Well	300+	73%	-	76%
Pain 'Always' Well Controlled	300+	65%	-	69%
Room and Bathroom 'Always' Clean	300+	70%	-	71%
Timely Help 'Always' Received	300+	58%	-	64%
Would Definitely Recommend Hospital	300+	76%	-	69%

Spencer Municipal Hospital

1200 1st Avenue East
Spencer, IA 51301
E-mail: ddoorn@spencerhospital.org
URL: www.spencerhospital.org
Type: Acute Care Hospitals
Ownership: Government - Local
Phone: 712-264-8300
Fax: 712-264-6404
Emergency Services: Yes
Beds: 99

Key Personnel:
CEO/President............... Jason Harrington
Chief of Medical Staff.......... John Hill
Operating Room.............. Jeffre Helmink
Radiology.................. Charles Crouch
Emergency Room .... Deb Brodersen

Measure	Cases	This Hosp.	State Avg.	U.S. Avg.
Heart Attack Care				
ACE Inhibitor or ARB for LVSD[5]	0	-	96%	96%
Aspirin at Arrival[5]	0	-	99%	99%
Aspirin at Discharge[5]	0	-	99%	98%
Beta Blocker at Discharge[5]	0	-	99%	98%
Fibrinolytic Medication Timing[5]	0	-	67%	55%
PCI Within 90 Minutes of Arrival[5]	0	-	94%	90%
Smoking Cessation Advice[5]	0	-	99%	99%
Chest Pain/Possible Heart Attack Care				
Aspirin at Arrival	37	100%	96%	95%
Median Time to ECG (minutes)	38	13	7	8
Median Time to Transfer (minutes)[1,3]	1	115	64	61
Fibrinolytic Medication Timing[1,3]	2	0%	45%	54%
Heart Failure Care				
ACE Inhibitor or ARB for LVSD[1]	15	87%	94%	94%
Discharge Instructions	27	93%	86%	88%
Evaluation of LVS Function	45	98%	95%	98%
Smoking Cessation Advice[1]	8	100%	96%	98%
Pneumonia Care				
Appropriate Initial Antibiotic[2]	50	90%	92%	92%
Blood Culture Timing[2]	52	96%	97%	96%
Influenza Vaccine[2]	72	96%	92%	91%
Initial Antibiotic Timing[2]	75	100%	97%	95%
Pneumococcal Vaccine[2]	89	96%	94%	93%
Smoking Cessation Advice[1,2]	16	100%	95%	97%
Surgical Care Improvement Project				
Appropriate VTP Within 24 Hours[2]	92	100%	92%	92%
Appropriate Hair Removal[2]	222	100%	100%	99%
Appropriate Beta Blocker Usage[2]	51	94%	94%	93%
Controlled Postoperative Blood Glucose[2]	0	-	89%	93%
Prophylactic Antibiotic Timing[2]	147	97%	98%	97%
Prophylactic Antibiotic Timing (Outpatient)	108	88%	94%	92%
Prophylactic Antibiotic Selection[2]	144	100%	98%	97%
Prophylactic Antibiotic Select. (Outpatient)	102	97%	97%	94%
Prophylactic Antibiotic Stopped[2]	142	96%	95%	94%
Recommended VTP Ordered[2]	92	100%	93%	94%
Urinary Catheter Removal[2]	60	97%	91%	90%
Children's Asthma Care				
Received Systemic Corticosteroids	-	-	-	100%
Received Home Management Plan	-	-	-	71%
Received Reliever Medication	-	-	-	100%
Use of Medical Imaging				
Combination Abdominal CT Scan	282	0.223	0.163	0.191
Combination Chest CT Scan	207	0.179	0.060	0.054
Follow-up Mammogram/Ultrasound	568	10.7%	8.1%	8.4%
MRI for Low Back Pain	112	32.1%	30.2%	32.7%
Survey of Patients' Hospital Experiences				
Area Around Room 'Always' Quiet at Night	300+	67%	-	58%
Doctors 'Always' Communicated Well	300+	80%	-	80%
Home Recovery Information Given	300+	87%	-	82%
Hospital Given 9 or 10 on 10 Point Scale	300+	76%	-	67%
Meds 'Always' Explained Before Given	300+	63%	-	60%
Nurses 'Always' Communicated Well	300+	78%	-	76%
Pain 'Always' Well Controlled	300+	71%	-	69%
Room and Bathroom 'Always' Clean	300+	82%	-	71%
Timely Help 'Always' Received	300+	68%	-	64%
Would Definitely Recommend Hospital	300+	76%	-	69%

Lakes Regional Healthcare

2301 Highway 71
Spirit Lake, IA 51360
URL: www.lakeshealth.org
Type: Acute Care Hospitals
Ownership: Government - Local
Phone: 712-336-1230
Fax: 712-336-8626
Emergency Services: Yes
Beds: 49

Key Personnel:
CEO/President............... Richard C Kielman
Chief of Medical Staff.......... Andrew Brevik
Operating Room.............. Jeffre Helmink
Radiology.................. Jim Myerly
Emergency Room .... Geoff Messerole

Measure	Cases	This Hosp.	State Avg.	U.S. Avg.
Heart Attack Care				
ACE Inhibitor or ARB for LVSD	0	-	96%	96%
Aspirin at Arrival[1]	5	100%	99%	99%
Aspirin at Discharge[1]	4	100%	99%	98%
Beta Blocker at Discharge[1]	4	100%	99%	98%
Fibrinolytic Medication Timing	0	-	67%	55%
PCI Within 90 Minutes of Arrival	0	-	94%	90%
Smoking Cessation Advice	0	-	99%	99%
Chest Pain/Possible Heart Attack Care				
Aspirin at Arrival	69	100%	96%	95%
Median Time to ECG (minutes)	68	5	7	8
Median Time to Transfer (minutes)[3]	0	-	64	61
Fibrinolytic Medication Timing[1]	8	62%	45%	54%
Heart Failure Care				
ACE Inhibitor or ARB for LVSD[1]	1	100%	94%	94%
Discharge Instructions[1]	23	91%	86%	88%
Evaluation of LVS Function	32	91%	95%	98%
Smoking Cessation Advice[1]	3	100%	96%	98%
Pneumonia Care				
Appropriate Initial Antibiotic	43	86%	92%	92%
Blood Culture Timing	54	100%	97%	96%
Influenza Vaccine	39	92%	92%	91%
Initial Antibiotic Timing	70	97%	97%	95%
Pneumococcal Vaccine	70	94%	94%	93%
Smoking Cessation Advice[1]	13	100%	95%	97%
Surgical Care Improvement Project				
Appropriate VTP Within 24 Hours	55	100%	92%	92%
Appropriate Hair Removal	102	99%	100%	99%
Appropriate Beta Blocker Usage[1]	21	100%	94%	93%
Controlled Postoperative Blood Glucose	0	-	89%	93%
Prophylactic Antibiotic Timing	85	98%	98%	97%
Prophylactic Antibiotic Timing (Outpatient)[1]	23	83%	94%	92%
Prophylactic Antibiotic Selection	85	96%	98%	97%
Prophylactic Antibiotic Select. (Outpatient)[1]	22	95%	97%	94%
Prophylactic Antibiotic Stopped	83	96%	95%	94%
Recommended VTP Ordered	55	100%	93%	94%
Urinary Catheter Removal	30	100%	91%	90%
Children's Asthma Care				
Received Systemic Corticosteroids	-	-	-	100%
Received Home Management Plan	-	-	-	71%
Received Reliever Medication	-	-	-	100%
Use of Medical Imaging				
Combination Abdominal CT Scan	86	0.395	0.163	0.191
Combination Chest CT Scan[1]	50	0.300	0.060	0.054
Follow-up Mammogram/Ultrasound	327	0.9%	8.1%	8.4%
MRI for Low Back Pain	53	32.1%	30.2%	32.7%
Survey of Patients' Hospital Experiences				
Area Around Room 'Always' Quiet at Night	300+	67%	-	58%
Doctors 'Always' Communicated Well	300+	83%	-	80%
Home Recovery Information Given	300+	88%	-	82%
Hospital Given 9 or 10 on 10 Point Scale	300+	74%	-	67%
Meds 'Always' Explained Before Given	300+	65%	-	60%
Nurses 'Always' Communicated Well	300+	80%	-	76%
Pain 'Always' Well Controlled	300+	71%	-	69%
Room and Bathroom 'Always' Clean	300+	77%	-	71%
Timely Help 'Always' Received	300+	71%	-	64%
Would Definitely Recommend Hospital	300+	74%	-	69%

NOTE: Hospital profiles are in alphabetical order by state, then city, then hospital within the city; Rankings exclude hospitals with less than 25 cases except for patient surveys which excludes hospitals with less than 100 cases; (a) 100–299 cases; (1) The number of cases is too small to be sure how well a hospital is performing; (2) The hospital indicated that the data submitted for this measure were based on a sample of cases; (3) Data was collected during a shorter time period (fewer quarters) than the maximum possible time for this measure; (4) Suppressed for one or more quarters by CMS; (5) No data is available from the hospital for this measure; (6) Fewer than 100 patients completed the HCAHPS survey. Use these rates with caution, as the number of surveys may be too low to reliably assess hospital performance; (7) Survey results are based on less than 12 months of data; (8) Survey results are not available for this reporting period; (9) No or very few patients were eligible for the HCAHPS survey. The scores shown, if any, reflect a very small number of surveys; (10) A state average was not calculated because too few hospitals in the state submitted data; (11) There were discrepancies in the data collection process; Please refer to the User's Guide for a full explanation of data.

Buena Vista Regional Medical Center

1525 West 5th Street
Storm Lake, IA 50588
Phone: 712-732-4030
Fax: 712-213-1233
E-mail: marketing-info@bvrmc.org
URL: www.bvrmc.org
Type: Critical Access Hospitals
Emergency Services: Yes
Ownership: Government - Local
Beds: 54

Key Personnel:

CEO/President . . . . Todd Hudspeth
Chief of Medical Staff . . . . David Archer
Infection Control . . . . Judy Kropf
Operating Room . . . . Jason Dierking
Quality Assurance . . . . Kathy Collins
Radiology . . . . Ingrid Franze
Emergency Room . . . . Denise Haisch

Measure	Cases	This Hosp.	State Avg.	U.S. Avg.
Heart Attack Care				
ACE Inhibitor or ARB for LVSD[1]	1	100%	96%	96%
Aspirin at Arrival[1]	8	100%	99%	99%
Aspirin at Discharge[1]	6	100%	99%	98%
Beta Blocker at Discharge[1]	5	100%	99%	98%
Fibrinolytic Medication Timing[5]	0	-	67%	55%
PCI Within 90 Minutes of Arrival[5]	0	-	94%	90%
Smoking Cessation Advice	0	-	99%	99%
Chest Pain/Possible Heart Attack Care				
Aspirin at Arrival	-	-	96%	95%
Median Time to ECG (minutes)	-	-	7	8
Median Time to Transfer (minutes)	-	-	64	61
Fibrinolytic Medication Timing	-	-	45%	54%
Heart Failure Care				
ACE Inhibitor or ARB for LVSD[1]	6	100%	94%	94%
Discharge Instructions[1]	10	60%	86%	88%
Evaluation of LVS Function[1]	18	100%	95%	98%
Smoking Cessation Advice	0	-	96%	98%
Pneumonia Care				
Appropriate Initial Antibiotic	32	81%	92%	92%
Blood Culture Timing[1]	23	74%	97%	96%
Influenza Vaccine	32	94%	92%	91%
Initial Antibiotic Timing	43	81%	97%	95%
Pneumococcal Vaccine	44	98%	94%	93%
Smoking Cessation Advice[1]	16	50%	95%	97%
Surgical Care Improvement Project				
Appropriate VTP Within 24 Hours[2]	45	71%	92%	92%
Appropriate Hair Removal[2]	99	96%	100%	99%
Appropriate Beta Blocker Usage[5]	0	-	94%	93%
Controlled Postoperative Blood Glucose[2]	0	-	89%	93%
Prophylactic Antibiotic Timing[2]	76	89%	98%	97%
Prophylactic Antibiotic Timing (Outpatient)	-	-	94%	92%
Prophylactic Antibiotic Selection[2]	75	99%	98%	97%
Prophylactic Antibiotic Select. (Outpatient)	-	-	97%	94%
Prophylactic Antibiotic Stopped[2]	74	92%	95%	94%
Recommended VTP Ordered[2]	45	71%	93%	94%
Urinary Catheter Removal[2]	28	86%	91%	90%
Children's Asthma Care				
Received Systemic Corticosteroids	-	-	-	100%
Received Home Management Plan	-	-	-	71%
Received Reliever Medication	-	-	-	100%
Use of Medical Imaging				
Combination Abdominal CT Scan	-	-	0.163	0.191
Combination Chest CT Scan	-	-	0.060	0.054
Follow-up Mammogram/Ultrasound	-	-	8.1%	8.4%
MRI for Low Back Pain	-	-	30.2%	32.7%
Survey of Patients' Hospital Experiences				
Area Around Room 'Always' Quiet at Night[8]	-	-	-	58%
Doctors 'Always' Communicated Well[8]	-	-	-	80%
Home Recovery Information Given[8]	-	-	-	82%
Hospital Given 9 or 10 on 10 Point Scale[8]	-	-	-	67%
Meds 'Always' Explained Before Given[8]	-	-	-	60%
Nurses 'Always' Communicated Well[8]	-	-	-	76%
Pain 'Always' Well Controlled[8]	-	-	-	69%
Room and Bathroom 'Always' Clean[8]	-	-	-	71%
Timely Help 'Always' Received[8]	-	-	-	64%
Would Definitely Recommend Hospital[8]	-	-	-	69%

Washington County Hospital

400 East Polk Street
Washington, IA 52353
Phone: 319-653-5481
Fax: 319-653-3401
URL: www.wchc.org
Type: Critical Access Hospitals
Emergency Services: Yes
Ownership: Voluntary Non-Profit - Other
Beds: 91

Key Personnel:

CEO/President . . . . Don Patterson
Chief of Medical Staff . . . . Robin Plattenberger-
Operating Room . . . . Frank Sanfiel
Quality Assurance . . . . Kathy Richardson
Radiology . . . . Douglas Boatman
Emergency Room . . . . Cathy Buffington

Measure	Cases	This Hosp.	State Avg.	U.S. Avg.
Heart Attack Care				
ACE Inhibitor or ARB for LVSD[5]	0	-	96%	96%
Aspirin at Arrival[5]	0	-	99%	99%
Aspirin at Discharge[5]	0	-	99%	98%
Beta Blocker at Discharge[5]	0	-	99%	98%
Fibrinolytic Medication Timing[5]	0	-	67%	55%
PCI Within 90 Minutes of Arrival[5]	0	-	94%	90%
Smoking Cessation Advice[5]	0	-	99%	99%
Chest Pain/Possible Heart Attack Care				
Aspirin at Arrival	-	-	96%	95%
Median Time to ECG (minutes)	-	-	7	8
Median Time to Transfer (minutes)	-	-	64	61
Fibrinolytic Medication Timing	-	-	45%	54%
Heart Failure Care				
ACE Inhibitor or ARB for LVSD[1,3]	6	100%	94%	94%
Discharge Instructions[1,3]	6	50%	86%	88%
Evaluation of LVS Function[1,3]	15	67%	95%	98%
Smoking Cessation Advice[1,3]	1	100%	96%	98%
Pneumonia Care				
Appropriate Initial Antibiotic[1,2,3]	11	64%	92%	92%
Blood Culture Timing[1,2,3]	6	100%	97%	96%
Influenza Vaccine[1,2]	23	48%	92%	91%
Initial Antibiotic Timing[1,2,3]	23	91%	97%	95%
Pneumococcal Vaccine[1,2,3]	18	33%	94%	93%
Smoking Cessation Advice[1,2,3]	3	67%	95%	97%
Surgical Care Improvement Project				
Appropriate VTP Within 24 Hours[3]	0	-	92%	92%
Appropriate Hair Removal[1,3]	10	100%	100%	99%
Appropriate Beta Blocker Usage[5]	0	-	94%	93%
Controlled Postoperative Blood Glucose[3]	0	-	89%	93%
Prophylactic Antibiotic Timing[1,3]	10	100%	98%	97%
Prophylactic Antibiotic Timing (Outpatient)	-	-	94%	92%
Prophylactic Antibiotic Selection[1,3]	10	60%	98%	97%
Prophylactic Antibiotic Select. (Outpatient)	-	-	97%	94%
Prophylactic Antibiotic Stopped[1,3]	10	100%	95%	94%
Recommended VTP Ordered[3]	0	-	93%	94%
Urinary Catheter Removal[3]	0	-	91%	90%
Children's Asthma Care				
Received Systemic Corticosteroids	-	-	-	100%
Received Home Management Plan	-	-	-	71%
Received Reliever Medication	-	-	-	100%
Use of Medical Imaging				
Combination Abdominal CT Scan	-	-	0.163	0.191
Combination Chest CT Scan	-	-	0.060	0.054
Follow-up Mammogram/Ultrasound	-	-	8.1%	8.4%
MRI for Low Back Pain	-	-	30.2%	32.7%
Survey of Patients' Hospital Experiences				
Area Around Room 'Always' Quiet at Night	(a)	61%	-	58%
Doctors 'Always' Communicated Well	(a)	86%	-	80%
Home Recovery Information Given	(a)	81%	-	82%
Hospital Given 9 or 10 on 10 Point Scale	(a)	70%	-	67%
Meds 'Always' Explained Before Given	(a)	61%	-	60%
Nurses 'Always' Communicated Well	(a)	81%	-	76%
Pain 'Always' Well Controlled	(a)	70%	-	69%
Room and Bathroom 'Always' Clean	(a)	80%	-	71%
Timely Help 'Always' Received	(a)	66%	-	64%
Would Definitely Recommend Hospital	(a)	69%	-	69%

Allen Memorial Hospital

1825 Logan Avenue
Waterloo, IA 50703
Phone: 319-235-3941
Fax: 319-235-3461
URL: www.allenhospital.org
Type: Acute Care Hospitals
Emergency Services: Yes
Ownership: Voluntary Non-Profit - Private
Beds: 234

Key Personnel:

CEO/President . . . . Richard A Seidler
Chief of Medical Staff . . . . Thomas S Gorsche, MD
Coronary Care . . . . Deb Gingrich
Infection Control . . . . Bill Farmer
Pediatric Ambulatory Care . . . . . . Vonice Hoffman
Pediatric In-Patient Care . . . . Dee Van Beiser
Quality Assurance . . . . Bill Farmer
Radiology . . . . Kent S Quinn

Measure	Cases	This Hosp.	State Avg.	U.S. Avg.
Heart Attack Care				
ACE Inhibitor or ARB for LVSD[2]	48	94%	96%	96%
Aspirin at Arrival[2]	168	99%	99%	99%
Aspirin at Discharge[2]	237	100%	99%	98%
Beta Blocker at Discharge[2]	233	100%	99%	98%
Fibrinolytic Medication Timing[2]	0	-	67%	55%
PCI Within 90 Minutes of Arrival[2]	31	97%	94%	90%
Smoking Cessation Advice[2]	79	100%	99%	99%
Chest Pain/Possible Heart Attack Care				
Aspirin at Arrival	29	90%	96%	95%
Median Time to ECG (minutes)	29	8	7	8
Median Time to Transfer (minutes)[5]	0	-	64	61
Fibrinolytic Medication Timing[3]	0	-	45%	54%
Heart Failure Care				
ACE Inhibitor or ARB for LVSD[2]	104	95%	94%	94%
Discharge Instructions[2]	233	92%	86%	88%
Evaluation of LVS Function[2]	300	100%	95%	98%
Smoking Cessation Advice[2]	47	98%	96%	98%
Pneumonia Care				
Appropriate Initial Antibiotic[2]	92	92%	92%	92%
Blood Culture Timing[2]	147	97%	97%	96%
Influenza Vaccine	145	96%	92%	91%
Initial Antibiotic Timing[2]	142	94%	97%	95%
Pneumococcal Vaccine[2]	206	96%	94%	93%
Smoking Cessation Advice[2]	61	98%	95%	97%
Surgical Care Improvement Project				
Appropriate VTP Within 24 Hours[2]	138	96%	92%	92%
Appropriate Hair Removal[2]	469	100%	100%	99%
Appropriate Beta Blocker Usage[2]	180	96%	94%	93%
Controlled Postoperative Blood Glucose[2]	94	97%	89%	93%
Prophylactic Antibiotic Timing[2]	310	100%	98%	97%
Prophylactic Antibiotic Timing (Outpatient)	370	92%	94%	92%
Prophylactic Antibiotic Selection[2]	314	99%	98%	97%
Prophylactic Antibiotic Select. (Outpatient)	348	98%	97%	94%
Prophylactic Antibiotic Stopped[2]	300	98%	95%	94%
Recommended VTP Ordered[2]	138	97%	93%	94%
Urinary Catheter Removal[2]	62	97%	91%	90%
Children's Asthma Care				
Received Systemic Corticosteroids	-	-	-	100%
Received Home Management Plan	-	-	-	71%
Received Reliever Medication	-	-	-	100%
Use of Medical Imaging				
Combination Abdominal CT Scan	1,144	0.046	0.163	0.191
Combination Chest CT Scan	715	0.006	0.060	0.054
Follow-up Mammogram/Ultrasound	2,129	8.0%	8.1%	8.4%
MRI for Low Back Pain	207	30.4%	30.2%	32.7%
Survey of Patients' Hospital Experiences				
Area Around Room 'Always' Quiet at Night	300+	55%	-	58%
Doctors 'Always' Communicated Well	300+	74%	-	80%
Home Recovery Information Given	300+	83%	-	82%
Hospital Given 9 or 10 on 10 Point Scale	300+	67%	-	67%
Meds 'Always' Explained Before Given	300+	58%	-	60%
Nurses 'Always' Communicated Well	300+	74%	-	76%
Pain 'Always' Well Controlled	300+	67%	-	69%
Room and Bathroom 'Always' Clean	300+	72%	-	71%
Timely Help 'Always' Received	300+	55%	-	64%
Would Definitely Recommend Hospital	300+	69%	-	69%

NOTE: Hospital profiles are in alphabetical order by state, then city, then hospital within the city; Rankings exclude hospitals with less than 25 cases except for patient surveys which excludes hospitals with less than 100 cases; (a) 100–299 cases; (1) The number of cases is too small to be sure how well a hospital is performing; (2) The hospital indicated that the data submitted for this measure were based on a sample of cases; (3) Data was collected during a shorter time period (fewer quarters) than the maximum possible time for this measure; (4) Suppressed for one or more quarters by CMS; (5) No data is available from the hospital for this measure; (6) Fewer than 100 patients completed the HCAHPS survey. Use these rates with caution, as the number of surveys may be too low to reliably assess hospital performance; (7) Survey results are based on less than 12 months of data; (8) Survey results are not available for this reporting period; (9) No or very few patients were eligible for the HCAHPS survey. The scores shown, if any, reflect a very small number of surveys; (10) A state average was not calculated because too few hospitals in the state submitted data; (11) There were discrepancies in the data collection process; Please refer to the User's Guide for a full explanation of data.

Covenant Medical Center

3421 West Ninth Street
Waterloo, IA 50702
URL: www.covhealth.com
Type: Acute Care Hospitals
Ownership: Voluntary Non-Profit - Church
Phone: 319-272-8000
Fax: 319-272-7313
Emergency Services: Yes
Beds: 346

Key Personnel:
Chief of Medical Staff . . . . Cassandra Foensr, MD
Infection Control . . . . Nancy Schuler
Operating Room. . . . . Niki Maas
Pediatric Ambulatory Care . . . . . . Stephen Riggs, MD
Pediatric In-Patient Care . . . . Siddiq Arab, MD
Quality Assurance . . . . Nancy Schuler, RN
Radiology. . . . . Lawrence Furlong, MD
Intensive Care Unit. . . . . Denise Lampman, RN

Measure	Cases	This Hosp.	State Avg.	U.S. Avg.
Heart Attack Care				
ACE Inhibitor or ARB for LVSD[1]	7	86%	96%	96%
Aspirin at Arrival	56	100%	99%	99%
Aspirin at Discharge	81	100%	99%	98%
Beta Blocker at Discharge	73	97%	99%	98%
Fibrinolytic Medication Timing	0	-	67%	55%
PCI Within 90 Minutes of Arrival	27	89%	94%	90%
Smoking Cessation Advice	32	100%	99%	99%
Chest Pain/Possible Heart Attack Care				
Aspirin at Arrival[1,3]	5	100%	96%	95%
Median Time to ECG (minutes)[1,3]	5	4	7	8
Median Time to Transfer (minutes)[1,3]	1	102	64	61
Fibrinolytic Medication Timing[3]	0	-	45%	54%
Heart Failure Care				
ACE Inhibitor or ARB for LVSD	28	86%	94%	94%
Discharge Instructions	89	91%	86%	88%
Evaluation of LVS Function	130	99%	95%	98%
Smoking Cessation Advice[1]	14	100%	96%	98%
Pneumonia Care				
Appropriate Initial Antibiotic	73	93%	92%	92%
Blood Culture Timing	95	94%	97%	96%
Influenza Vaccine	74	99%	92%	91%
Initial Antibiotic Timing	107	93%	97%	95%
Pneumococcal Vaccine	101	99%	94%	93%
Smoking Cessation Advice	40	100%	95%	97%
Surgical Care Improvement Project				
Appropriate VTP Within 24 Hours	332	91%	92%	92%
Appropriate Hair Removal	564	100%	100%	99%
Appropriate Beta Blocker Usage	160	93%	94%	93%
Controlled Postoperative Blood Glucose	0	-	89%	93%
Prophylactic Antibiotic Timing	377	97%	98%	97%
Prophylactic Antibiotic Timing (Outpatient)	454	87%	94%	92%
Prophylactic Antibiotic Selection	374	98%	98%	97%
Prophylactic Antibiotic Select. (Outpatient)	417	96%	97%	94%
Prophylactic Antibiotic Stopped	357	89%	95%	94%
Recommended VTP Ordered	334	91%	93%	94%
Urinary Catheter Removal	138	86%	91%	90%
Children's Asthma Care				
Received Systemic Corticosteroids	-	-	-	100%
Received Home Management Plan	-	-	-	71%
Received Reliever Medication	-	-	-	100%
Use of Medical Imaging				
Combination Abdominal CT Scan	585	0.046	0.163	0.191
Combination Chest CT Scan	679	0.004	0.060	0.054
Follow-up Mammogram/Ultrasound	1,275	7.3%	8.1%	8.4%
MRI for Low Back Pain	171	31.6%	30.2%	32.7%
Survey of Patients' Hospital Experiences				
Area Around Room 'Always' Quiet at Night	300+	54%	-	58%
Doctors 'Always' Communicated Well	300+	76%	-	80%
Home Recovery Information Given	300+	80%	-	82%
Hospital Given 9 or 10 on 10 Point Scale	300+	61%	-	67%
Meds 'Always' Explained Before Given	300+	52%	-	60%
Nurses 'Always' Communicated Well	300+	71%	-	76%
Pain 'Always' Well Controlled	300+	59%	-	69%
Room and Bathroom 'Always' Clean	300+	71%	-	71%
Timely Help 'Always' Received	300+	58%	-	64%
Would Definitely Recommend Hospital	300+	65%	-	69%

Veterans Memorial Hospital

40 1st Street SE
Waukon, IA 52172
URL: www.vmhospital.com
Type: Critical Access Hospitals
Ownership: Government - Local
Phone: 563-568-3411
Fax: 563-568-5550
Emergency Services: Yes
Beds: 25

Key Personnel:
CEO/President. . . . . Michael D Myers
Cardiac Laboratory. . . . . Lynn Ohara
Chief of Medical Staff . . . . Larry Bartel
Operating Room. . . . . Barb Wilkes, RN
Quality Assurance . . . . Fred Mathews
Emergency Room . . . . Diane Butikofer

Measure	Cases	This Hosp.	State Avg.	U.S. Avg.
Heart Attack Care				
ACE Inhibitor or ARB for LVSD[3]	0	-	96%	96%
Aspirin at Arrival[3]	0	-	99%	99%
Aspirin at Discharge[3]	0	-	99%	98%
Beta Blocker at Discharge[3]	0	-	99%	98%
Fibrinolytic Medication Timing[3]	0	-	67%	55%
PCI Within 90 Minutes of Arrival[3]	0	-	94%	90%
Smoking Cessation Advice[3]	0	-	99%	99%
Chest Pain/Possible Heart Attack Care				
Aspirin at Arrival	-	-	96%	95%
Median Time to ECG (minutes)	-	-	7	8
Median Time to Transfer (minutes)	-	-	64	61
Fibrinolytic Medication Timing	-	-	45%	54%
Heart Failure Care				
ACE Inhibitor or ARB for LVSD[1]	8	50%	94%	94%
Discharge Instructions[1]	12	100%	86%	88%
Evaluation of LVS Function[1]	21	76%	95%	98%
Smoking Cessation Advice[1]	1	100%	96%	98%
Pneumonia Care				
Appropriate Initial Antibiotic[1]	23	91%	92%	92%
Blood Culture Timing[1]	23	91%	97%	96%
Influenza Vaccine	26	81%	92%	91%
Initial Antibiotic Timing	29	86%	97%	95%
Pneumococcal Vaccine	48	88%	94%	93%
Smoking Cessation Advice[1]	8	50%	95%	97%
Surgical Care Improvement Project				
Appropriate VTP Within 24 Hours[1]	4	100%	92%	92%
Appropriate Hair Removal	25	100%	100%	99%
Appropriate Beta Blocker Usage[5]	0	-	94%	93%
Controlled Postoperative Blood Glucose	0	-	89%	93%
Prophylactic Antibiotic Timing[1]	24	96%	98%	97%
Prophylactic Antibiotic Timing (Outpatient)	-	-	94%	92%
Prophylactic Antibiotic Selection[1]	24	100%	98%	97%
Prophylactic Antibiotic Select. (Outpatient)	-	-	97%	94%
Prophylactic Antibiotic Stopped[1]	24	96%	95%	94%
Recommended VTP Ordered[1]	4	100%	93%	94%
Urinary Catheter Removal	0	-	91%	90%
Children's Asthma Care				
Received Systemic Corticosteroids	-	-	-	100%
Received Home Management Plan	-	-	-	71%
Received Reliever Medication	-	-	-	100%
Use of Medical Imaging				
Combination Abdominal CT Scan	-	-	0.163	0.191
Combination Chest CT Scan	-	-	0.060	0.054
Follow-up Mammogram/Ultrasound	-	-	8.1%	8.4%
MRI for Low Back Pain	-	-	30.2%	32.7%
Survey of Patients' Hospital Experiences				
Area Around Room 'Always' Quiet at Night[8]	-	-	-	58%
Doctors 'Always' Communicated Well[8]	-	-	-	80%
Home Recovery Information Given[8]	-	-	-	82%
Hospital Given 9 or 10 on 10 Point Scale[8]	-	-	-	67%
Meds 'Always' Explained Before Given[8]	-	-	-	60%
Nurses 'Always' Communicated Well[8]	-	-	-	76%
Pain 'Always' Well Controlled[8]	-	-	-	69%
Room and Bathroom 'Always' Clean[8]	-	-	-	71%
Timely Help 'Always' Received[8]	-	-	-	64%
Would Definitely Recommend Hospital[8]	-	-	-	69%

Waverly Health Center

312 9th Street SW
Waverly, IA 50677
E-mail: aflessner@wavhosp.org
URL: www.waverlyhealthcenter.org
Type: Critical Access Hospitals
Ownership: Government - Local
Phone: 319-352-4120
Fax: 319-352-3992
Emergency Services: Yes
Beds: 45

Key Personnel:
CEO/President. . . . . Michael Trachta
Chief of Medical Staff . . . . Terrie Thurm
Infection Control. . . . . Dixie Kramer
Operating Room. . . . . Lisa Warne
Pediatric Ambulatory Care . . . . . . David Rathe, DO
Pediatric In-Patient Care . . . . David Rathe, DO
Quality Assurance . . . . Carol Stone
Radiology. . . . . Rajeev Anugu

Measure	Cases	This Hosp.	State Avg.	U.S. Avg.
Heart Attack Care				
ACE Inhibitor or ARB for LVSD[1,3]	1	100%	96%	96%
Aspirin at Arrival[1,3]	1	100%	99%	99%
Aspirin at Discharge[1,3]	1	100%	99%	98%
Beta Blocker at Discharge[1,3]	1	100%	99%	98%
Fibrinolytic Medication Timing[3]	0	-	67%	55%
PCI Within 90 Minutes of Arrival[3]	0	-	94%	90%
Smoking Cessation Advice[3]	0	-	99%	99%
Chest Pain/Possible Heart Attack Care				
Aspirin at Arrival	92	97%	96%	95%
Median Time to ECG (minutes)	95	5	7	8
Median Time to Transfer (minutes)[1,3]	2	96	64	61
Fibrinolytic Medication Timing	0	-	45%	54%
Heart Failure Care				
ACE Inhibitor or ARB for LVSD[1]	4	100%	94%	94%
Discharge Instructions[1]	16	62%	86%	88%
Evaluation of LVS Function[1]	22	68%	95%	98%
Smoking Cessation Advice	0	-	96%	98%
Pneumonia Care				
Appropriate Initial Antibiotic	30	100%	92%	92%
Blood Culture Timing	40	98%	97%	96%
Influenza Vaccine[1]	21	90%	92%	91%
Initial Antibiotic Timing	39	97%	97%	95%
Pneumococcal Vaccine	41	95%	94%	93%
Smoking Cessation Advice[1]	4	100%	95%	97%
Surgical Care Improvement Project				
Appropriate VTP Within 24 Hours	29	97%	92%	92%
Appropriate Hair Removal	49	100%	100%	99%
Appropriate Beta Blocker Usage[5]	0	-	94%	93%
Controlled Postoperative Blood Glucose	0	-	89%	93%
Prophylactic Antibiotic Timing	41	98%	98%	97%
Prophylactic Antibiotic Timing (Outpatient)	35	94%	94%	92%
Prophylactic Antibiotic Selection	41	93%	98%	97%
Prophylactic Antibiotic Select. (Outpatient)	34	88%	97%	94%
Prophylactic Antibiotic Stopped	39	92%	95%	94%
Recommended VTP Ordered	29	100%	93%	94%
Urinary Catheter Removal[1]	6	100%	91%	90%
Children's Asthma Care				
Received Systemic Corticosteroids	-	-	-	100%
Received Home Management Plan	-	-	-	71%
Received Reliever Medication	-	-	-	100%
Use of Medical Imaging				
Combination Abdominal CT Scan	275	0.011	0.163	0.191
Combination Chest CT Scan	124	0.000	0.060	0.054
Follow-up Mammogram/Ultrasound	540	4.8%	8.1%	8.4%
MRI for Low Back Pain	58	27.6%	30.2%	32.7%
Survey of Patients' Hospital Experiences				
Area Around Room 'Always' Quiet at Night	300+	77%	-	58%
Doctors 'Always' Communicated Well	300+	88%	-	80%
Home Recovery Information Given	300+	88%	-	82%
Hospital Given 9 or 10 on 10 Point Scale	300+	84%	-	67%
Meds 'Always' Explained Before Given	300+	73%	-	60%
Nurses 'Always' Communicated Well	300+	84%	-	76%
Pain 'Always' Well Controlled	300+	76%	-	69%
Room and Bathroom 'Always' Clean	300+	89%	-	71%
Timely Help 'Always' Received	300+	74%	-	64%
Would Definitely Recommend Hospital	300+	86%	-	69%

NOTE: Hospital profiles are in alphabetical order by state, then city, then hospital within the city; Rankings exclude hospitals with less than 25 cases except for patient surveys which excludes hospitals with less than 100 cases; (a) 100–299 cases; (1) The number of cases is too small to be sure how well a hospital is performing; (2) The hospital indicated that the data submitted for this measure were based on a sample of cases; (3) Data was collected during a shorter time period (fewer quarters) than the maximum possible time for this measure; (4) Suppressed for one or more quarters by CMS; (5) No data is available from the hospital for this measure; (6) Fewer than 100 patients completed the HCAHPS survey. Use these rates with caution, as the number of surveys may be too low to reliably assess hospital performance; (7) Survey results are based on less than 12 months of data; (8) Survey results are not available for this reporting period; (9) No or very few patients were eligible for the HCAHPS survey. The scores shown, if any, reflect a very small number of surveys; (10) A state average was not calculated because too few hospitals in the state submitted data; (11) There were discrepancies in the data collection process; Please refer to the User's Guide for a full explanation of data.

Van Diest Medical Center

2350 Hospital Drive
Webster City, IA 50595
URL: www.hamiltonhospital.com
Type: Critical Access Hospitals
Ownership: Government - Local

Phone: 515-832-9400
Emergency Services: Yes
Beds: 25

Measure	Cases	This Hosp.	State Avg.	U.S. Avg.
Heart Attack Care				
ACE Inhibitor or ARB for LVSD	0	-	96%	96%
Aspirin at Arrival[1]	6	100%	99%	99%
Aspirin at Discharge[1]	6	83%	99%	98%
Beta Blocker at Discharge[1]	7	57%	99%	98%
Fibrinolytic Medication Timing	0	-	67%	55%
PCI Within 90 Minutes of Arrival	0	-	94%	90%
Smoking Cessation Advice[1]	1	100%	99%	99%
Chest Pain/Possible Heart Attack Care				
Aspirin at Arrival	-	-	96%	95%
Median Time to ECG (minutes)	-	-	7	8
Median Time to Transfer (minutes)	-	-	64	61
Fibrinolytic Medication Timing	-	-	45%	54%
Heart Failure Care				
ACE Inhibitor or ARB for LVSD[1]	8	62%	94%	94%
Discharge Instructions	43	72%	86%	88%
Evaluation of LVS Function	63	87%	95%	98%
Smoking Cessation Advice[1]	3	100%	96%	98%
Pneumonia Care				
Appropriate Initial Antibiotic	46	85%	92%	92%
Blood Culture Timing	27	100%	97%	96%
Influenza Vaccine	40	90%	92%	91%
Initial Antibiotic Timing	60	98%	97%	95%
Pneumococcal Vaccine	51	90%	94%	93%
Smoking Cessation Advice[1]	10	100%	95%	97%
Surgical Care Improvement Project				
Appropriate VTP Within 24 Hours[1]	5	100%	92%	92%
Appropriate Hair Removal	27	96%	100%	99%
Appropriate Beta Blocker Usage[5]	0	-	94%	93%
Controlled Postoperative Blood Glucose	0	-	89%	93%
Prophylactic Antibiotic Timing[1]	24	100%	98%	97%
Prophylactic Antibiotic Timing (Outpatient)	-	-	94%	92%
Prophylactic Antibiotic Selection	25	88%	98%	97%
Prophylactic Antibiotic Select. (Outpatient)	-	-	97%	94%
Prophylactic Antibiotic Stopped[1]	23	96%	95%	94%
Recommended VTP Ordered[1]	5	100%	93%	94%
Urinary Catheter Removal	0	-	91%	90%
Children's Asthma Care				
Received Systemic Corticosteroids	-	-	-	100%
Received Home Management Plan	-	-	-	71%
Received Reliever Medication	-	-	-	100%
Use of Medical Imaging				
Combination Abdominal CT Scan	-	-	0.163	0.191
Combination Chest CT Scan	-	-	0.060	0.054
Follow-up Mammogram/Ultrasound	-	-	8.1%	8.4%
MRI for Low Back Pain	-	-	30.2%	32.7%
Survey of Patients' Hospital Experiences				
Area Around Room 'Always' Quiet at Night	(a)	56%	-	58%
Doctors 'Always' Communicated Well	(a)	86%	-	80%
Home Recovery Information Given	(a)	81%	-	82%
Hospital Given 9 or 10 on 10 Point Scale	(a)	68%	-	67%
Meds 'Always' Explained Before Given	(a)	61%	-	60%
Nurses 'Always' Communicated Well	(a)	80%	-	76%
Pain 'Always' Well Controlled	(a)	78%	-	69%
Room and Bathroom 'Always' Clean	(a)	80%	-	71%
Timely Help 'Always' Received	(a)	74%	-	64%
Would Definitely Recommend Hospital	(a)	64%	-	69%

Great River Medical Center

1221 South Gear Avenue
West Burlington, IA 52655
URL: www.greatrivermedical.org
Type: Acute Care Hospitals
Ownership: Voluntary Non-Profit - Private

Phone: 319-768-1000
Fax: 319-768-3306
Emergency Services: Yes
Beds: 378

Key Personnel:
CEO/President. . . . . Mark Richardson
Chief of Medical Staff. . . . . Doug Peters, MD
Operating Room. . . . . Ann Hannum, RN
Quality Assurance . . . . Tom Zimmerman
Radiology. . . . . Donald Gale, MD
Emergency Room . . . . James Vandenberg, MD
Intensive Care Unit. . . . . Edna Smull, MD

Measure	Cases	This Hosp.	State Avg.	U.S. Avg.
Heart Attack Care				
ACE Inhibitor or ARB for LVSD[1]	18	89%	96%	96%
Aspirin at Arrival	139	98%	99%	99%
Aspirin at Discharge	125	97%	99%	98%
Beta Blocker at Discharge	125	94%	99%	98%
Fibrinolytic Medication Timing	0	-	67%	55%
PCI Within 90 Minutes of Arrival[1]	16	81%	94%	90%
Smoking Cessation Advice	38	84%	99%	99%
Chest Pain/Possible Heart Attack Care				
Aspirin at Arrival	103	93%	96%	95%
Median Time to ECG (minutes)	106	12	7	8
Median Time to Transfer (minutes)[1,3]	4	66	64	61
Fibrinolytic Medication Timing[1]	5	40%	45%	54%
Heart Failure Care				
ACE Inhibitor or ARB for LVSD	56	84%	94%	94%
Discharge Instructions	122	92%	86%	88%
Evaluation of LVS Function	168	90%	95%	98%
Smoking Cessation Advice[1]	19	95%	96%	98%
Pneumonia Care				
Appropriate Initial Antibiotic	115	90%	92%	92%
Blood Culture Timing	121	96%	97%	96%
Influenza Vaccine	115	93%	92%	91%
Initial Antibiotic Timing	147	99%	97%	95%
Pneumococcal Vaccine	153	97%	94%	93%
Smoking Cessation Advice	52	90%	95%	97%
Surgical Care Improvement Project				
Appropriate VTP Within 24 Hours	248	94%	92%	92%
Appropriate Hair Removal	620	99%	100%	99%
Appropriate Beta Blocker Usage	190	88%	94%	93%
Controlled Postoperative Blood Glucose	0	-	89%	93%
Prophylactic Antibiotic Timing	421	98%	98%	97%
Prophylactic Antibiotic Timing (Outpatient)	217	90%	94%	92%
Prophylactic Antibiotic Selection	423	97%	98%	97%
Prophylactic Antibiotic Select. (Outpatient)	200	96%	97%	94%
Prophylactic Antibiotic Stopped	399	94%	95%	94%
Recommended VTP Ordered	251	96%	93%	94%
Urinary Catheter Removal	201	96%	91%	90%
Children's Asthma Care				
Received Systemic Corticosteroids	-	-	-	100%
Received Home Management Plan	-	-	-	71%
Received Reliever Medication	-	-	-	100%
Use of Medical Imaging				
Combination Abdominal CT Scan	854	0.741	0.163	0.191
Combination Chest CT Scan	774	0.078	0.060	0.054
Follow-up Mammogram/Ultrasound	1,411	8.2%	8.1%	8.4%
MRI for Low Back Pain	201	28.4%	30.2%	32.7%
Survey of Patients' Hospital Experiences				
Area Around Room 'Always' Quiet at Night	300+	55%	-	58%
Doctors 'Always' Communicated Well	300+	79%	-	80%
Home Recovery Information Given	300+	84%	-	82%
Hospital Given 9 or 10 on 10 Point Scale	300+	68%	-	67%
Meds 'Always' Explained Before Given	300+	62%	-	60%
Nurses 'Always' Communicated Well	300+	78%	-	76%
Pain 'Always' Well Controlled	300+	70%	-	69%
Room and Bathroom 'Always' Clean	300+	71%	-	71%
Timely Help 'Always' Received	300+	64%	-	64%
Would Definitely Recommend Hospital	300+	69%	-	69%

Palmer Lutheran Health Center

112 Jefferson Street
West Union, IA 52175
Type: Critical Access Hospitals
Ownership: Voluntary Non-Profit - Private

Phone: 563-422-3811
Fax: 563-422-3664
Emergency Services: Yes
Beds: 25

Key Personnel:
CEO/President. . . . . Debrah Chensvold
Chief of Medical Staff . . . . Chaudri Rasool
Operating Room. . . . . Sue Schneider, RN
Quality Assurance . . . . Julie Ball
Emergency Room . . . . Jon Suddarth, RN

Measure	Cases	This Hosp.	State Avg.	U.S. Avg.
Heart Attack Care				
ACE Inhibitor or ARB for LVSD[5]	0	-	96%	96%
Aspirin at Arrival[5]	0	-	99%	99%
Aspirin at Discharge[5]	0	-	99%	98%
Beta Blocker at Discharge[5]	0	-	99%	98%
Fibrinolytic Medication Timing[5]	0	-	67%	55%
PCI Within 90 Minutes of Arrival[5]	0	-	94%	90%
Smoking Cessation Advice[5]	0	-	99%	99%
Chest Pain/Possible Heart Attack Care				
Aspirin at Arrival[5]	0	-	96%	95%
Median Time to ECG (minutes)[5]	0	-	7	8
Median Time to Transfer (minutes)[5]	0	-	64	61
Fibrinolytic Medication Timing[5]	0	-	45%	54%
Heart Failure Care				
ACE Inhibitor or ARB for LVSD[1,3]	4	100%	94%	94%
Discharge Instructions[1,3]	6	100%	86%	88%
Evaluation of LVS Function[1,3]	15	73%	95%	98%
Smoking Cessation Advice[1,3]	1	100%	96%	98%
Pneumonia Care				
Appropriate Initial Antibiotic[1,2]	6	100%	92%	92%
Blood Culture Timing[1,2]	10	90%	97%	96%
Influenza Vaccine[1,2]	8	75%	92%	91%
Initial Antibiotic Timing[1,2]	9	89%	97%	95%
Pneumococcal Vaccine[1,2]	12	92%	94%	93%
Smoking Cessation Advice[2]	0	-	95%	97%
Surgical Care Improvement Project				
Appropriate VTP Within 24 Hours[5]	0	-	92%	92%
Appropriate Hair Removal[5]	0	-	100%	99%
Appropriate Beta Blocker Usage[5]	0	-	94%	93%
Controlled Postoperative Blood Glucose[5]	0	-	89%	93%
Prophylactic Antibiotic Timing[5]	0	-	98%	97%
Prophylactic Antibiotic Timing (Outpatient)[5]	0	-	94%	92%
Prophylactic Antibiotic Selection[5]	0	-	98%	97%
Prophylactic Antibiotic Select. (Outpatient)[5]	0	-	97%	94%
Prophylactic Antibiotic Stopped[5]	0	-	95%	94%
Recommended VTP Ordered[5]	0	-	93%	94%
Urinary Catheter Removal[5]	0	-	91%	90%
Children's Asthma Care				
Received Systemic Corticosteroids	-	-	-	100%
Received Home Management Plan	-	-	-	71%
Received Reliever Medication	-	-	-	100%
Use of Medical Imaging				
Combination Abdominal CT Scan	98	0.020	0.163	0.191
Combination Chest CT Scan[1]	37	0.000	0.060	0.054
Follow-up Mammogram/Ultrasound[5]	0	-	8.1%	8.4%
MRI for Low Back Pain[1]	18	33.3%	30.2%	32.7%
Survey of Patients' Hospital Experiences				
Area Around Room 'Always' Quiet at Night[8]	-	-	-	58%
Doctors 'Always' Communicated Well[8]	-	-	-	80%
Home Recovery Information Given[8]	-	-	-	82%
Hospital Given 9 or 10 on 10 Point Scale[8]	-	-	-	67%
Meds 'Always' Explained Before Given[8]	-	-	-	60%
Nurses 'Always' Communicated Well[8]	-	-	-	76%
Pain 'Always' Well Controlled[8]	-	-	-	69%
Room and Bathroom 'Always' Clean[8]	-	-	-	71%
Timely Help 'Always' Received[8]	-	-	-	64%
Would Definitely Recommend Hospital[8]	-	-	-	69%

NOTE: Hospital profiles are in alphabetical order by state, then city, then hospital within the city; Rankings exclude hospitals with less than 25 cases except for patient surveys which excludes hospitals with less than 100 cases; (a) 100–299 cases; (1) The number of cases is too small to be sure how well a hospital is performing; (2) The hospital indicated that the data submitted for this measure were based on a sample of cases; (3) Data was collected during a shorter time period (fewer quarters) than the maximum possible time for this measure; (4) Suppressed for one or more quarters by CMS; (5) No data is available from the hospital for this measure; (6) Fewer than 100 patients completed the HCAHPS survey. Use these rates with caution, as the number of surveys may be too low to reliably assess hospital performance; (7) Survey results are based on less than 12 months of data; (8) Survey results are not available for this reporting period; (9) No or very few patients were eligible for the HCAHPS survey. The scores shown, if any, reflect a very small number of surveys; (10) A state average was not calculated because too few hospitals in the state submitted data; (11) There were discrepancies in the data collection process; Please refer to the User's Guide for a full explanation of data.

Madison County Memorial Hospital

300 West Hutchings Street Phone: 515-462-2373
Winterset, IA 50273 Fax: 515-462-5008
URL: www.madisonhealth.com
Type: Critical Access Hospitals Emergency Services: Yes
Ownership: Voluntary Non-Profit - Other Beds: 31

Key Personnel:

CEO/President. . . . . Marcia Harris
Chief of Medical Staff . . . . Sherrie Broadbent
Operating Room. . . . . Janet Loomis
Quality Assurance . . . . Terri Simmons
Emergency Room . . . . Cindy Frank

Measure	Cases	This Hosp.	State Avg.	U.S. Avg.
Heart Attack Care				
ACE Inhibitor or ARB for LVSD[3]	0	-	96%	96%
Aspirin at Arrival[1,3]	3	100%	99%	99%
Aspirin at Discharge[1,3]	3	100%	99%	98%
Beta Blocker at Discharge[1,3]	4	75%	99%	98%
Fibrinolytic Medication Timing[3]	0	-	67%	55%
PCI Within 90 Minutes of Arrival[3]	0	-	94%	90%
Smoking Cessation Advice[1,3]	1	100%	99%	99%
Chest Pain/Possible Heart Attack Care				
Aspirin at Arrival	-	-	96%	95%
Median Time to ECG (minutes)	-	-	7	8
Median Time to Transfer (minutes)	-	-	64	61
Fibrinolytic Medication Timing	-	-	45%	54%
Heart Failure Care				
ACE Inhibitor or ARB for LVSD[1]	2	50%	94%	94%
Discharge Instructions[1]	10	100%	86%	88%
Evaluation of LVS Function[1]	18	72%	95%	98%
Smoking Cessation Advice[1]	1	100%	96%	98%
Pneumonia Care				
Appropriate Initial Antibiotic[1]	22	91%	92%	92%
Blood Culture Timing[1]	6	67%	97%	96%
Influenza Vaccine[1]	21	86%	92%	91%
Initial Antibiotic Timing	43	100%	97%	95%
Pneumococcal Vaccine	40	88%	94%	93%
Smoking Cessation Advice[1]	7	100%	95%	97%
Surgical Care Improvement Project				
Appropriate VTP Within 24 Hours[3]	0	-	92%	92%
Appropriate Hair Removal[1,3]	1	0%	100%	99%
Appropriate Beta Blocker Usage[5]	0	-	94%	93%
Controlled Postoperative Blood Glucose[3]	0	-	89%	93%
Prophylactic Antibiotic Timing[3]	0	-	98%	97%
Prophylactic Antibiotic Timing (Outpatient)	-	-	94%	92%
Prophylactic Antibiotic Selection[3]	0	-	98%	97%
Prophylactic Antibiotic Select. (Outpatient)	-	-	97%	94%
Prophylactic Antibiotic Stopped[3]	0	-	95%	94%
Recommended VTP Ordered[3]	0	-	93%	94%
Urinary Catheter Removal[1,3]	1	100%	91%	90%
Children's Asthma Care				
Received Systemic Corticosteroids	-	-	-	100%
Received Home Management Plan	-	-	-	71%
Received Reliever Medication	-	-	-	100%
Use of Medical Imaging				
Combination Abdominal CT Scan	-	-	0.163	0.191
Combination Chest CT Scan	-	-	0.060	0.054
Follow-up Mammogram/Ultrasound	-	-	8.1%	8.4%
MRI for Low Back Pain	-	-	30.2%	32.7%
Survey of Patients' Hospital Experiences				
Area Around Room 'Always' Quiet at Night[8]	-	-	-	58%
Doctors 'Always' Communicated Well[8]	-	-	-	80%
Home Recovery Information Given[8]	-	-	-	82%
Hospital Given 9 or 10 on 10 Point Scale[8]	-	-	-	67%
Meds 'Always' Explained Before Given[8]	-	-	-	60%
Nurses 'Always' Communicated Well[8]	-	-	-	76%
Pain 'Always' Well Controlled[8]	-	-	-	69%
Room and Bathroom 'Always' Clean[8]	-	-	-	71%
Timely Help 'Always' Received[8]	-	-	-	64%
Would Definitely Recommend Hospital[8]	-	-	-	69%

NOTE: Hospital profiles are in alphabetical order by state, then city, then hospital within the city; Rankings exclude hospitals with less than 25 cases except for patient surveys which excludes hospitals with less than 100 cases; (a) 100–299 cases; (1) The number of cases is too small to be sure how well a hospital is performing; (2) The hospital indicated that the data submitted for this measure were based on a sample of cases; (3) Data was collected during a shorter time period (fewer quarters) than the maximum possible time for this measure; (4) Suppressed for one or more quarters by CMS; (5) No data is available from the hospital for this measure; (6) Fewer than 100 patients completed the HCAHPS survey. Use these rates with caution, as the number of surveys may be too low to reliably assess hospital performance; (7) Survey results are based on less than 12 months of data; (8) Survey results are not available for this reporting period; (9) No or very few patients were eligible for the HCAHPS survey. The scores shown, if any, reflect a very small number of surveys; (10) A state average was not calculated because too few hospitals in the state submitted data; (11) There were discrepancies in the data collection process; Please refer to the User's Guide for a full explanation of data.

Heart Attack Care

1. ACE Inhibitor or ARB for LVSD

Hospital Name	City	Rate	Cases
Hays Medical Center[2]	Hays	100%	27
Olathe Medical Center	Olathe	100%	39
Saint Francis Health Center	Topeka	100%	28
Stormont-Vail Healthcare	Topeka	100%	45
Wesley Medical Center	Wichita	100%	43
Via Christi Hospitals Wichita[2]	Wichita	96%	50
Providence Medical Center	Kansas City	94%	33
University of Kansas Hospital	Kansas City	94%	36
Kansas Heart Hospital	Wichita	93%	27
Salina Regional Health Center[2]	Salina	93%	28
Promise Regional Medical Center Hutchinson	Hutchinson	92%	25
Shawnee Mission Medical Center	Shawnee Miss.	92%	38

2. Aspirin at Arrival

Hospital Name	City	Rate	Cases
Lawrence Memorial Hospital	Lawrence	100%	89
Mercy Regional Health Center	Manhattan	100%	71
Overland Park Regional Medical Center	Overland Park	100%	106
Promise Regional Medical Center Hutchinson	Hutchinson	100%	135
Saint Catherine Hospital	Garden City	100%	29
Saint Luke's South Hospital	Overland Park	100%	80
University of Kansas Hospital	Kansas City	100%	109
Hays Medical Center[2]	Hays	99%	81
Olathe Medical Center	Olathe	99%	189
Providence Medical Center	Kansas City	99%	148
Salina Regional Health Center[2]	Salina	99%	96
Shawnee Mission Medical Center	Shawnee Miss.	99%	185
Stormont-Vail Healthcare	Topeka	99%	190
Via Christi Hospitals Wichita[2]	Wichita	99%	272
Wesley Medical Center	Wichita	99%	252
Galichia Heart Hospital	Wichita	98%	66
Saint Francis Health Center	Topeka	98%	112
Via Christi Hospital Pittsburg	Pittsburg	98%	58
Menorah Medical Center	Overland Park	97%	35
Newton Medical Center	Newton	92%	25
Kansas Heart Hospital	Wichita	89%	35

3. Aspirin at Discharge

Hospital Name	City	Rate	Cases
Hays Medical Center[2]	Hays	100%	220
Kansas Heart Hospital	Wichita	100%	221
Lawrence Memorial Hospital	Lawrence	100%	80
Menorah Medical Center	Overland Park	100%	39
Overland Park Regional Medical Center	Overland Park	100%	106
Saint Catherine Hospital	Garden City	100%	36
Shawnee Mission Medical Center	Shawnee Miss.	100%	208
University of Kansas Hospital	Kansas City	100%	187
Wesley Medical Center	Wichita	100%	355
Western Plains Medical Complex	Dodge City	100%	31
Galichia Heart Hospital	Wichita	99%	110
Olathe Medical Center	Olathe	99%	221
Providence Medical Center	Kansas City	99%	154
Saint Francis Health Center	Topeka	99%	168
Salina Regional Health Center[2]	Salina	99%	142
Stormont-Vail Healthcare	Topeka	99%	283
Via Christi Hospitals Wichita[2]	Wichita	99%	298
Promise Regional Medical Center Hutchinson	Hutchinson	98%	170
Mercy Regional Health Center	Manhattan	97%	76
Saint Luke's South Hospital	Overland Park	97%	79
Kansas Medical Center	Andover	95%	88
Via Christi Hospital Pittsburg	Pittsburg	85%	54

4. Beta Blocker at Discharge

Hospital Name	City	Rate	Cases
Galichia Heart Hospital	Wichita	100%	97
Lawrence Memorial Hospital	Lawrence	100%	72
Menorah Medical Center	Overland Park	100%	36
Overland Park Regional Medical Center	Overland Park	100%	96
Saint Catherine Hospital	Garden City	100%	35
Saint Luke's South Hospital	Overland Park	100%	77
Shawnee Mission Medical Center	Shawnee Miss.	100%	201
Stormont-Vail Healthcare	Topeka	100%	285
University of Kansas Hospital	Kansas City	100%	176
Wesley Medical Center	Wichita	100%	337
Hays Medical Center[2]	Hays	99%	208
Salina Regional Health Center[2]	Salina	99%	134
Kansas Heart Hospital	Wichita	98%	208
Providence Medical Center	Kansas City	98%	151
Saint Francis Health Center	Topeka	98%	159
Via Christi Hospitals Wichita[2]	Wichita	98%	280
Olathe Medical Center	Olathe	97%	211
Kansas Medical Center	Andover	92%	77
Mercy Regional Health Center	Manhattan	92%	73
Promise Regional Medical Center Hutchinson	Hutchinson	92%	145
Via Christi Hospital Pittsburg	Pittsburg	92%	50

6. PCI Within 90 Minutes of Arrival

Hospital Name	City	Rate	Cases
Lawrence Memorial Hospital	Lawrence	100%	25
Saint Francis Health Center	Topeka	100%	32
Stormont-Vail Healthcare	Topeka	100%	49
Shawnee Mission Medical Center	Shawnee Miss.	97%	38
Overland Park Regional Medical Center	Overland Park	96%	27
Wesley Medical Center	Wichita	94%	63
Olathe Medical Center	Olathe	93%	41
Providence Medical Center	Kansas City	92%	36
Via Christi Hospitals Wichita[2]	Wichita	81%	53
Promise Regional Medical Center Hutchinson	Hutchinson	77%	31

7. Smoking Cessation Advice

Hospital Name	City	Rate	Cases
Galichia Heart Hospital	Wichita	100%	42
Hays Medical Center[2]	Hays	100%	68
Kansas Medical Center	Andover	100%	27
Lawrence Memorial Hospital	Lawrence	100%	28
Mercy Regional Health Center	Manhattan	100%	26
Olathe Medical Center	Olathe	100%	78
Overland Park Regional Medical Center	Overland Park	100%	28
Promise Regional Medical Center Hutchinson	Hutchinson	100%	55
Providence Medical Center	Kansas City	100%	67
Saint Francis Health Center	Topeka	100%	64
Salina Regional Health Center[2]	Salina	100%	47
Shawnee Mission Medical Center	Shawnee Miss.	100%	61
Stormont-Vail Healthcare	Topeka	100%	101
University of Kansas Hospital	Kansas City	100%	85
Via Christi Hospitals Wichita[2]	Wichita	100%	124
Wesley Medical Center	Wichita	100%	134
Kansas Heart Hospital	Wichita	94%	66

Chest Pain/Possible Heart Attack Care

8. Aspirin at Arrival

Hospital Name	City	Rate	Cases
Anderson County Hospital	Garnett	100%	33
Lawrence Memorial Hospital	Lawrence	100%	27
Neosho Memorial Regional Medical Center	Chanute	100%	43
Allen County Hospital	Iola	97%	87
Cushing Memorial Hospital	Leavenworth	97%	29
Labette Health	Parsons	96%	68
Memorial Hospital	Mcpherson	96%	110
Southwest Medical Center	Liberal	96%	45
Susan B Allen Memorial Hospital	El Dorado	95%	150
William Newton Hospital	Winfield	95%	82
Ransom Memorial Hospital	Ottawa	94%	49
Central Kansas Medical Center	Great Bend	93%	70
Geary Community Hospital	Junction City	93%	29
Newman Regional Health	Emporia	93%	128
Mercy Health Center	Fort Scott	92%	63
Sumner Regional Medical Center	Wellington	92%	87
Pratt Regional Medical Center	Pratt	91%	70
Mercy Hospital of Kansas Independence	Independence	89%	56
South Central Ks Regional Medical Center	Arkansas City	89%	47
Miami County Medical Center	Paola	86%	69
Newton Medical Center	Newton	85%	82
Coffey County Hospital	Burlington	84%	31
Great Bend Regional Hospital[3]	Great Bend	80%	35
Mercy Regional Health Center	Manhattan	74%	27

9. Median Time to ECG (minutes)

Hospital Name	City	Min.	Cases
Newman Regional Health	Emporia	3	135
Lawrence Memorial Hospital	Lawrence	4	27
William Newton Hospital	Winfield	4	84
Ransom Memorial Hospital	Ottawa	5	48
Labette Health	Parsons	6	68
Mercy Hospital of Kansas Independence	Independence	6	56
Neosho Memorial Regional Medical Center	Chanute	8	45
Susan B Allen Memorial Hospital	El Dorado	8	153
Coffey County Hospital	Burlington	9	32
Sumner Regional Medical Center	Wellington	10	88
Anderson County Hospital	Garnett	11	34
Mercy Health Center	Fort Scott	12	64
Pratt Regional Medical Center	Pratt	12	70
South Central Ks Regional Medical Center	Arkansas City	12	47
Southwest Medical Center	Liberal	12	46
Geary Community Hospital	Junction City	13	25
Mercy Regional Health Center	Manhattan	13	27
Cushing Memorial Hospital	Leavenworth	14	30
Memorial Hospital	Mcpherson	14	112
Newton Medical Center	Newton	15	88
Miami County Medical Center	Paola	16	70
Great Bend Regional Hospital[3]	Great Bend	17	35
Allen County Hospital	Iola	18	94
Central Kansas Medical Center	Great Bend	18	72

Heart Failure Care

12. ACE Inhibitor or ARB for LVSD

Hospital Name	City	Rate	Cases
Lawrence Memorial Hospital	Lawrence	100%	32
Menorah Medical Center	Overland Park	100%	25
Overland Park Regional Medical Center	Overland Park	100%	47
Salina Regional Health Center	Salina	100%	26
VA Eastern Kansas Healthcare System	Leavenworth	100%	41
Wesley Medical Center	Wichita	100%	94
Wichita VA Medical Center	Wichita	100%	32
University of Kansas Hospital	Kansas City	99%	136
Hays Medical Center	Hays	98%	57
Saint Luke's South Hospital	Overland Park	98%	44
Kansas Heart Hospital	Wichita	97%	39
Shawnee Mission Medical Center	Shawnee Miss.	97%	112
Kansas Medical Center	Andover	96%	25
Galichia Heart Hospital[2]	Wichita	95%	58
Saint Francis Health Center	Topeka	94%	80
Stormont-Vail Healthcare	Topeka	94%	88
Promise Regional Medical Center Hutchinson	Hutchinson	93%	46
Olathe Medical Center	Olathe	91%	67
Via Christi Hospitals Wichita[2]	Wichita	90%	99
Providence Medical Center	Kansas City	89%	130
Via Christi Hospital Pittsburg	Pittsburg	80%	44
Newman Regional Health	Emporia	79%	29
Coffeyville Regional Medical Center	Coffeyville	62%	42

13. Discharge Instructions

Hospital Name	City	Rate	Cases
Galichia Heart Hospital[2]	Wichita	100%	213
Lawrence Memorial Hospital	Lawrence	100%	91
Neosho Memorial Regional Medical Center	Chanute	100%	43
Wichita VA Medical Center	Wichita	100%	74
Menorah Medical Center	Overland Park	98%	95
Saint John Hospital	Leavenworth	98%	45
Salina Regional Health Center	Salina	98%	63
University of Kansas Hospital	Kansas City	97%	376
Susan B Allen Memorial Hospital	El Dorado	96%	26
Wesley Medical Center	Wichita	96%	216
Via Christi Hospitals Wichita[2]	Wichita	95%	265
Overland Park Regional Medical Center	Overland Park	94%	123
Saint Catherine Hospital	Garden City	94%	34
VA Eastern Kansas Healthcare System	Leavenworth	93%	102
Kansas Heart Hospital	Wichita	91%	104
Mercy Health Center	Fort Scott	91%	44
Promise Regional Medical Center Hutchinson	Hutchinson	91%	94
Saint Francis Health Center	Topeka	90%	174
Stormont-Vail Healthcare	Topeka	90%	234
Western Plains Medical Complex	Dodge City	89%	37
Mercy Hospital of Kansas Independence	Independence	86%	29
Hays Medical Center	Hays	84%	133
Shawnee Mission Medical Center	Shawnee Miss.	84%	292
Olathe Medical Center	Olathe	82%	182
Kansas Medical Center	Andover	81%	54
Cloud County Health Center	Concordia	79%	33
Via Christi Hospital Pittsburg	Pittsburg	79%	67
Providence Medical Center	Kansas City	78%	263
Saint Luke's South Hospital	Overland Park	76%	118
Newman Regional Health	Emporia	72%	53
Coffeyville Regional Medical Center	Coffeyville	69%	91
Mercy Regional Health Center[2]	Manhattan	69%	59
Labette Health	Parsons	60%	25
Geary Community Hospital	Junction City	57%	30
Pratt Regional Medical Center	Pratt	54%	26
Newton Medical Center	Newton	37%	57
Coffey County Hospital	Burlington	27%	37
Morris County Hospital	Council Grove	25%	28

14. Evaluation of LVS Function

Hospital Name	City	Rate	Cases
Kansas Heart Hospital	Wichita	100%	118
Lawrence Memorial Hospital	Lawrence	100%	125
Menorah Medical Center	Overland Park	100%	138
Mercy Health Center	Fort Scott	100%	77
Mercy Hospital of Kansas Independence	Independence	100%	41
Neosho Memorial Regional Medical Center	Chanute	100%	69
Overland Park Regional Medical Center	Overland Park	100%	162
Stormont-Vail Healthcare	Topeka	100%	334
Susan B Allen Memorial Hospital	El Dorado	100%	50
University of Kansas Hospital	Kansas City	100%	420
VA Eastern Kansas Healthcare System	Leavenworth	100%	113
Wesley Medical Center	Wichita	100%	302
Wichita VA Medical Center	Wichita	100%	81
Galichia Heart Hospital[2]	Wichita	99%	251
Hays Medical Center	Hays	99%	170

NOTE: Hospital profiles are in alphabetical order by state, then city, then hospital within the city; Rankings exclude hospitals with less than 25 cases except for patient surveys which excludes hospitals with less than 100 cases; (a) 100–299 cases; (1) The number of cases is too small to be sure how well a hospital is performing; (2) The hospital indicated that the data submitted for this measure were based on a sample of cases; (3) Data was collected during a shorter time period (fewer quarters) than the maximum possible time for this measure; (4) Suppressed for one or more quarters by CMS; (5) No data is available from the hospital for this measure; (6) Fewer than 100 patients completed the HCAHPS survey. Use these rates with caution, as the number of surveys may be too low to reliably assess hospital performance; (7) Survey results are based on less than 12 months of data; (8) Survey results are not available for this reporting period; (9) No or very few patients were eligible for the HCAHPS survey. The scores shown, if any, reflect a very small number of surveys; (10) A state average was not calculated because too few hospitals in the state submitted data; (11) There were discrepancies in the data collection process; Please refer to the User's Guide for a full explanation of data.

Providence Medical Center	Kansas City	99%	319
Saint Francis Health Center	Topeka	99%	229
Saint John Hospital	Leavenworth	99%	72
Saint Luke's South Hospital	Overland Park	99%	137
Shawnee Mission Medical Center	Shawnee Miss.	99%	375
Via Christi Hospitals Wichita[2]	Wichita	99%	329
Olathe Medical Center	Olathe	98%	260
Via Christi Hospital Pittsburg	Pittsburg	98%	102
Western Plains Medical Complex	Dodge City	98%	50
Kansas Medical Center	Andover	97%	63
Labette Health	Parsons	97%	32
Mitchell County Hospital Health Systems	Beloit	97%	33
Promise Regional Medical Center Hutchinson	Hutchinson	96%	140
Saint Catherine Hospital	Garden City	95%	40
Coffeyville Regional Medical Center	Coffeyville	93%	131
Mercy Regional Health Center[2]	Manhattan	92%	76
Allen County Hospital	Iola	89%	28
Southwest Medical Center	Liberal	89%	27
Cushing Memorial Hospital	Leavenworth	88%	33
Salina Regional Health Center	Salina	88%	86
Memorial Hospital	Mcpherson	87%	30
Girard Medical Center	Girard	86%	29
Newman Regional Health	Emporia	86%	93
Newton Medical Center	Newton	86%	125
Ellsworth County Medical Center[2]	Ellsworth	82%	34
Memorial Hospital	Abilene	79%	33
Geary Community Hospital	Junction City	77%	39
South Central Ks Regional Medical Center	Arkansas City	75%	28
Community Hosp-Onaga & St Marys Campus	Onaga	73%	30
Trego County Lemke Memorial Hospital	Wa Keeney	63%	38
Morton County Hospital[2]	Elkhart	57%	42
Cloud County Health Center	Concordia	48%	50
Graham County Hospital	Hill City	47%	38
Coffey County Hospital	Burlington	38%	61
Morris County Hospital	Council Grove	33%	57
Pratt Regional Medical Center	Pratt	33%	30

15. Smoking Cessation Advice

Hospital Name	City	Rate	Cases
Galichia Heart Hospital[2]	Wichita	100%	39
Olathe Medical Center	Olathe	100%	32
Providence Medical Center	Kansas City	100%	72
Shawnee Mission Medical Center	Shawnee Miss.	100%	47
Stormont-Vail Healthcare	Topeka	100%	56
University of Kansas Hospital	Kansas City	100%	98
Via Christi Hospitals Wichita[2]	Wichita	100%	79
Wesley Medical Center	Wichita	100%	43
Saint Francis Health Center	Topeka	98%	50

Pneumonia Care

16. Appropriate Initial Antibiotic

Hospital Name	City	Rate	Cases
Allen County Hospital	Iola	100%	30
Mercy Health Center[2]	Fort Scott	100%	40
Overland Park Regional Medical Center	Overland Park	100%	72
Coffey County Hospital	Burlington	97%	39
Lawrence Memorial Hospital	Lawrence	97%	89
Memorial Hospital	Mcpherson	97%	35
Wesley Medical Center[2]	Wichita	97%	75
University of Kansas Hospital	Kansas City	96%	112
Western Plains Medical Complex	Dodge City	96%	47
Ransom Memorial Hospital	Ottawa	95%	42
Saint Francis Health Center	Topeka	95%	159
Menorah Medical Center	Overland Park	94%	88
Mercy Regional Health Center[2]	Manhattan	94%	67
Neosho Memorial Regional Medical Center	Chanute	94%	50
Saint Luke's South Hospital	Overland Park	94%	62
Susan B Allen Memorial Hospital	El Dorado	94%	53
Saint Catherine Hospital	Garden City	93%	58
Shawnee Mission Medical Center	Shawnee Miss.	93%	268
Wichita VA Medical Center	Wichita	93%	46
Providence Medical Center	Kansas City	92%	109
VA Eastern Kansas Healthcare System	Leavenworth	92%	65
Labette Health	Parsons	91%	43
Newman Regional Health	Emporia	91%	57
Saint John Hospital	Leavenworth	91%	46
Salina Regional Health Center	Salina	91%	91
Cushing Memorial Hospital	Leavenworth	89%	47
Newton Medical Center	Newton	88%	78
Stormont-Vail Healthcare	Topeka	88%	147
Via Christi Hospital Pittsburg	Pittsburg	87%	79
Via Christi Hospitals Wichita[2]	Wichita	86%	72
Olathe Medical Center	Olathe	83%	122
Promise Regional Medical Center Hutchinson	Hutchinson	83%	123
Central Kansas Medical Center	Great Bend	81%	32
Trego County Lemke Memorial Hospital	Wa Keeney	81%	31
Pratt Regional Medical Center	Pratt	79%	38
Geary Community Hospital	Junction City	77%	30
Coffeyville Regional Medical Center	Coffeyville	75%	59
Hays Medical Center[2]	Hays	73%	56
Galichia Heart Hospital	Wichita	71%	59
Meade District Hospital	Meade	59%	27
Mitchell County Hospital Health Systems	Beloit	59%	29
Morton County Hospital[2]	Elkhart	29%	28

17. Blood Culture Timing

Hospital Name	City	Rate	Cases
Allen County Hospital	Iola	100%	25
Central Kansas Medical Center	Great Bend	100%	36
Memorial Hospital	Mcpherson	100%	31
Mercy Health Center[2]	Fort Scott	100%	53
Neosho Memorial Regional Medical Center	Chanute	100%	85
Ransom Memorial Hospital	Ottawa	100%	57
Saint Francis Health Center	Topeka	100%	208
Saint John Hospital	Leavenworth	100%	46
Susan B Allen Memorial Hospital	El Dorado	100%	42
Via Christi Hospital Pittsburg	Pittsburg	100%	120
Wichita VA Medical Center	Wichita	100%	70
Labette Health	Parsons	99%	68
Overland Park Regional Medical Center	Overland Park	99%	148
Saint Luke's South Hospital	Overland Park	99%	77
Coffeyville Regional Medical Center	Coffeyville	98%	55
Cushing Memorial Hospital	Leavenworth	98%	48
Girard Medical Center	Girard	98%	41
Olathe Medical Center	Olathe	98%	172
Providence Medical Center	Kansas City	98%	170
Salina Regional Health Center	Salina	98%	130
Shawnee Mission Medical Center	Shawnee Miss.	98%	257
VA Eastern Kansas Healthcare System	Leavenworth	98%	116
Wesley Medical Center[2]	Wichita	98%	95
Menorah Medical Center	Overland Park	97%	135
Saint Catherine Hospital	Garden City	97%	71
Western Plains Medical Complex	Dodge City	97%	72
Mercy Regional Health Center[2]	Manhattan	96%	74
Newman Regional Health	Emporia	96%	50
Promise Regional Medical Center Hutchinson	Hutchinson	96%	120
Stormont-Vail Healthcare	Topeka	96%	235
University of Kansas Hospital	Kansas City	95%	275
Lawrence Memorial Hospital	Lawrence	94%	109
Via Christi Hospitals Wichita[2]	Wichita	94%	175
William Newton Hospital	Winfield	94%	32
Mercy Hospital of Kansas Independence[2]	Independence	93%	27
Newton Medical Center	Newton	92%	78
Hays Medical Center[2]	Hays	91%	81
Mitchell County Hospital Health Systems	Beloit	88%	26
Galichia Heart Hospital	Wichita	77%	73

18. Influenza Vaccine

Hospital Name	City	Rate	Cases
Allen County Hospital	Iola	100%	33
Cushing Memorial Hospital	Leavenworth	100%	26
Menorah Medical Center	Overland Park	100%	95
Salina Regional Health Center	Salina	100%	107
Wesley Medical Center[2]	Wichita	100%	97
Saint Francis Health Center	Topeka	99%	178
Lawrence Memorial Hospital	Lawrence	98%	87
Saint Catherine Hospital	Garden City	98%	50
Saint John Hospital	Leavenworth	98%	43
Stormont-Vail Healthcare	Topeka	98%	207
University of Kansas Hospital	Kansas City	98%	181
Wichita VA Medical Center	Wichita	98%	54
Overland Park Regional Medical Center	Overland Park	97%	105
VA Eastern Kansas Healthcare System	Leavenworth	97%	87
Mercy Health Center[2]	Fort Scott	96%	52
Neosho Memorial Regional Medical Center	Chanute	95%	64
Promise Regional Medical Center Hutchinson	Hutchinson	95%	151
Ransom Memorial Hospital	Ottawa	95%	41
Western Plains Medical Complex	Dodge City	95%	55
Saint Luke's South Hospital	Overland Park	94%	64
Coffeyville Regional Medical Center	Coffeyville	93%	82
Providence Medical Center	Kansas City	93%	111
Galichia Heart Hospital	Wichita	92%	63
Labette Health	Parsons	90%	59
Shawnee Mission Medical Center	Shawnee Miss.	90%	234
South Central Ks Regional Medical Center	Arkansas City	89%	27
William Newton Hospital	Winfield	89%	35
Susan B Allen Memorial Hospital	El Dorado	88%	51
Olathe Medical Center	Olathe	87%	173
Meade District Hospital	Meade	85%	33
Memorial Hospital	Mcpherson	84%	43
Mercy Regional Health Center[2]	Manhattan	80%	64
Via Christi Hospitals Wichita[2]	Wichita	80%	89
Hays Medical Center[2]	Hays	78%	94
Newman Regional Health	Emporia	78%	45
Mitchell County Hospital Health Systems	Beloit	77%	31
Newton Medical Center	Newton	77%	78
Memorial Hospital	Abilene	76%	29
Pratt Regional Medical Center	Pratt	74%	31
Central Kansas Medical Center	Great Bend	73%	30
Community Hosp-Onaga & St Marys Campus	Onaga	72%	32
Ellsworth County Medical Center[2]	Ellsworth	72%	25
Geary Community Hospital	Junction City	72%	36
Via Christi Hospital Pittsburg	Pittsburg	71%	86
Coffey County Hospital	Burlington	68%	47
Trego County Lemke Memorial Hospital	Wa Keeney	68%	25

19. Initial Antibiotic Timing

Hospital Name	City	Rate	Cases
Allen County Hospital	Iola	100%	50
Community Hosp-Onaga & St Marys Campus	Onaga	100%	32
Kingman Community Hospital	Kingman	100%	28
Mercy Health Center[2]	Fort Scott	100%	61
Mercy Hospital of Kansas Independence[2]	Independence	100%	37
Neosho Memorial Regional Medical Center	Chanute	100%	113
Southwest Medical Center	Liberal	100%	33
Lawrence Memorial Hospital	Lawrence	99%	120
Menorah Medical Center	Overland Park	99%	118
Overland Park Regional Medical Center	Overland Park	99%	133
Coffey County Hospital	Burlington	98%	56
Cushing Memorial Hospital	Leavenworth	98%	52
Meade District Hospital	Meade	98%	41
Memorial Hospital	Mcpherson	98%	65
Olathe Medical Center	Olathe	98%	197
Pratt Regional Medical Center	Pratt	98%	46
Providence Medical Center	Kansas City	98%	181
Saint Francis Health Center	Topeka	98%	250
Via Christi Hospital Pittsburg	Pittsburg	98%	122
William Newton Hospital	Winfield	98%	51
Central Kansas Medical Center	Great Bend	97%	38
Cloud County Health Center	Concordia	97%	34
Ransom Memorial Hospital	Ottawa	97%	67
Salina Regional Health Center	Salina	97%	144
Stormont-Vail Healthcare	Topeka	97%	267
Susan B Allen Memorial Hospital	El Dorado	97%	60
Labette Health	Parsons	96%	69
Memorial Hospital	Abilene	96%	25
Miami County Medical Center	Paola	96%	27
Newman Regional Health	Emporia	96%	71
Saint John Hospital	Leavenworth	96%	56
Saint Luke's South Hospital	Overland Park	96%	85
Western Plains Medical Complex	Dodge City	96%	83
Wichita VA Medical Center	Wichita	96%	57
Shawnee Mission Medical Center	Shawnee Miss.	95%	336
VA Eastern Kansas Healthcare System	Leavenworth	95%	117
Wesley Medical Center[2]	Wichita	95%	108
Hays Medical Center[2]	Hays	94%	78
Mercy Regional Health Center[2]	Manhattan	94%	96
South Central Ks Regional Medical Center	Arkansas City	94%	36
Greenwood County Hospital	Eureka	93%	42
Promise Regional Medical Center Hutchinson	Hutchinson	93%	179
University of Kansas Hospital	Kansas City	93%	241
Via Christi Hospitals Wichita[2]	Wichita	93%	168
Mitchell County Hospital Health Systems	Beloit	92%	53
Saint Catherine Hospital	Garden City	92%	97
Sumner Regional Medical Center	Wellington	92%	26
Newton Medical Center	Newton	91%	117
Coffeyville Regional Medical Center	Coffeyville	90%	40
Ellsworth County Medical Center[2]	Ellsworth	89%	36
Trego County Lemke Memorial Hospital	Wa Keeney	89%	38
Hodgeman County Health Center	Jetmore	88%	25
Geary Community Hospital	Junction City	87%	52
Galichia Heart Hospital	Wichita	84%	79

20. Pneumococcal Vaccine

Hospital Name	City	Rate	Cases
Clay County Medical Center[2]	Clay Center	100%	35
Kingman Community Hospital	Kingman	100%	36
Menorah Medical Center	Overland Park	100%	132
Mercy Health Center[2]	Fort Scott	100%	79
Stormont-Vail Healthcare	Topeka	100%	253
VA Eastern Kansas Healthcare System	Leavenworth	100%	80
Wichita VA Medical Center	Wichita	100%	48
Lawrence Memorial Hospital	Lawrence	99%	123
Overland Park Regional Medical Center	Overland Park	99%	137
Saint Francis Health Center	Topeka	99%	238
Salina Regional Health Center	Salina	99%	157
Wesley Medical Center[2]	Wichita	99%	144
Providence Medical Center	Kansas City	98%	152
Mercy Hospital of Kansas Independence[2]	Independence	97%	31
Neosho Memorial Regional Medical Center	Chanute	97%	86
Saint Catherine Hospital	Garden City	97%	60
Saint Luke's South Hospital	Overland Park	97%	101
University of Kansas Hospital	Kansas City	97%	189
Allen County Hospital	Iola	96%	47
Olathe Medical Center	Olathe	96%	200
Ransom Memorial Hospital	Ottawa	96%	69
Western Plains Medical Complex	Dodge City	96%	81
Shawnee Mission Medical Center	Shawnee Miss.	95%	295
Promise Regional Medical Center Hutchinson	Hutchinson	94%	219

NOTE: Hospital profiles are in alphabetical order by state, then city, then hospital within the city; Rankings exclude hospitals with less than 25 cases except for patient surveys which excludes hospitals with less than 100 cases; (a) 100–299 cases; (1) The number of cases is too small to be sure how well a hospital is performing; (2) The hospital indicated that the data submitted for this measure were based on a sample of cases; (3) Data was collected during a shorter time period (fewer quarters) than the maximum possible time for this measure; (4) Suppressed for one or more quarters by CMS; (5) No data is available from the hospital for this measure; (6) Fewer than 100 patients completed the HCAHPS survey. Use these rates with caution, as the number of surveys may be too low to reliably assess hospital performance; (7) Survey results are based on less than 12 months of data; (8) Survey results are not available for this reporting period; (9) No or very few patients were eligible for the HCAHPS survey. The scores shown, if any, reflect a very small number of surveys; (10) A state average was not calculated because too few hospitals in the state submitted data; (11) There were discrepancies in the data collection process; Please refer to the User's Guide for a full explanation of data.

Hospital Name	City	Rate	Cases
Newton Medical Center	Newton	92%	127
Saint John Hospital	Leavenworth	92%	40
Cushing Memorial Hospital	Leavenworth	91%	46
Mercy Regional Health Center[2]	Manhattan	90%	88
Sumner Regional Medical Center	Wellington	90%	31
Galichia Heart Hospital	Wichita	89%	101
Geary Community Hospital	Junction City	89%	53
Girard Medical Center	Girard	89%	45
Via Christi Hospital Pittsburg	Pittsburg	89%	120
Newman Regional Health	Emporia	88%	68
South Central Ks Regional Medical Center	Arkansas City	87%	31
William Newton Hospital	Winfield	87%	46
Coffeyville Regional Medical Center	Coffeyville	83%	128
Central Kansas Medical Center	Great Bend	82%	38
Labette Health	Parsons	82%	72
Memorial Hospital	Mcpherson	82%	61
Mitchell County Hospital Health Systems	Beloit	82%	50
Hays Medical Center[2]	Hays	81%	144
Susan B Allen Memorial Hospital	El Dorado	81%	69
Via Christi Hospitals Wichita[2]	Wichita	79%	142
Meade District Hospital	Meade	77%	53
Kansas Medical Center	Andover	74%	27
Southwest Medical Center	Liberal	72%	29
Ellsworth County Medical Center[2]	Ellsworth	70%	43
Coffey County Hospital	Burlington	65%	57
Community Hosp-Onaga & St Marys Campus	Onaga	64%	36
Pratt Regional Medical Center	Pratt	63%	54
Greenwood County Hospital	Eureka	61%	38
Cloud County Health Center	Concordia	59%	32
Republic County Hospital[2,3]	Belleville	59%	27
Memorial Hospital	Abilene	58%	36
Gove County Medical Center[3]	Quinter	49%	35
Morton County Hospital[2]	Elkhart	48%	31
Trego County Lemke Memorial Hospital	Wa Keeney	32%	56
Morris County Hospital	Council Grove	15%	26

21. Smoking Cessation Advice

Hospital Name	City	Rate	Cases
Galichia Heart Hospital	Wichita	100%	26
Hays Medical Center[2]	Hays	100%	47
Lawrence Memorial Hospital	Lawrence	100%	53
Menorah Medical Center	Overland Park	100%	35
Olathe Medical Center	Olathe	100%	94
Promise Regional Medical Center Hutchinson	Hutchinson	100%	71
Providence Medical Center	Kansas City	100%	94
Saint Catherine Hospital	Garden City	100%	36
Salina Regional Health Center	Salina	100%	50
Stormont-Vail Healthcare	Topeka	100%	121
Susan B Allen Memorial Hospital	El Dorado	100%	35
University of Kansas Hospital	Kansas City	100%	147
VA Eastern Kansas Healthcare System	Leavenworth	100%	65
Wesley Medical Center[2]	Wichita	100%	64
Wichita VA Medical Center	Wichita	100%	37
Saint Francis Health Center	Topeka	99%	111
Shawnee Mission Medical Center	Shawnee Miss.	99%	99
Mercy Regional Health Center[2]	Manhattan	98%	42
Neosho Memorial Regional Medical Center	Chanute	98%	47
Overland Park Regional Medical Center	Overland Park	98%	49
Labette Health	Parsons	97%	32
Newman Regional Health	Emporia	97%	31
Saint John Hospital	Leavenworth	97%	33
Cushing Memorial Hospital	Leavenworth	96%	25
Ransom Memorial Hospital	Ottawa	96%	28
Via Christi Hospital Pittsburg	Pittsburg	96%	53
Via Christi Hospitals Wichita[2]	Wichita	96%	90
Newton Medical Center	Newton	91%	33
Saint Luke's South Hospital	Overland Park	88%	25
Coffeyville Regional Medical Center	Coffeyville	73%	44

Surgical Care Improvement Project

22. Appropriate VTP Within 24 Hours

Hospital Name	City	Rate	Cases
Miami County Medical Center	Paola	100%	30
Wesley Medical Center[2]	Wichita	99%	296
Wichita VA Medical Center[2]	Wichita	99%	69
Kansas Spine Hospital	Wichita	98%	42
Pratt Regional Medical Center[2]	Pratt	98%	107
Ransom Memorial Hospital	Ottawa	97%	35
Cushing Memorial Hospital	Leavenworth	96%	26
Overland Park Regional Medical Center[2]	Overland Park	96%	189
Saint Francis Health Center[2]	Topeka	96%	180
Susan B Allen Memorial Hospital	El Dorado	96%	25
Kansas Heart Hospital[2]	Wichita	95%	44
Shawnee Mission Medical Center[2]	Shawnee Miss.	95%	398
Kansas Medical Center[2]	Andover	94%	49
Saint Catherine Hospital	Garden City	94%	158
Salina Surgical Hospital	Salina	94%	77
Central Kansas Medical Center	Great Bend	93%	28
Menorah Medical Center[2]	Overland Park	93%	178
Olathe Medical Center[2]	Olathe	93%	307
University of Kansas Hospital[2]	Kansas City	93%	246
Western Plains Medical Complex	Dodge City	93%	76
Great Bend Regional Hospital[2]	Great Bend	92%	157
Salina Regional Health Center	Salina	92%	352
Lawrence Memorial Hospital	Lawrence	90%	222
Via Christi Hospital Pittsburg	Pittsburg	90%	109
Southwest Medical Center	Liberal	89%	80
Stormont-Vail Healthcare[2]	Topeka	89%	262
Hays Medical Center[2]	Hays	88%	203
Saint Luke's South Hospital	Overland Park	87%	134
Mercy Regional Health Center	Manhattan	86%	125
Mercy Hospital of Kansas Independence[2]	Independence	85%	33
Providence Medical Center[2]	Kansas City	85%	155
Via Christi Hospitals Wichita[2]	Wichita	85%	292
Labette Health	Parsons	84%	115
Mercy Health Center[2]	Fort Scott	83%	30
Coffeyville Regional Medical Center	Coffeyville	81%	57
Newton Medical Center	Newton	80%	172
Geary Community Hospital	Junction City	73%	52
Promise Regional Medical Center Hutchinson	Hutchinson	71%	253
Galichia Heart Hospital	Wichita	69%	52
South Central Ks Regional Medical Center	Arkansas City	67%	42
Saint John Hospital	Leavenworth	56%	25
Newman Regional Health	Emporia	55%	102

23. Appropriate Hair Removal

Hospital Name	City	Rate	Cases
Allen County Hospital	Iola	100%	25
Central Kansas Medical Center	Great Bend	100%	61
Coffeyville Regional Medical Center	Coffeyville	100%	113
Cushing Memorial Hospital	Leavenworth	100%	74
Hays Medical Center[2]	Hays	100%	555
Kansas City Orthopaedic Institute[2]	Leawood	100%	184
Kansas Spine Hospital	Wichita	100%	66
Kansas Surgery & Recovery Center[2]	Wichita	100%	361
Labette Health	Parsons	100%	601
Lawrence Memorial Hospital	Lawrence	100%	626
Meade District Hospital	Meade	100%	57
Memorial Hospital	Mcpherson	100%	31
Menorah Medical Center[2]	Overland Park	100%	526
Mercy Health Center[2]	Fort Scott	100%	102
Mercy Hospital of Kansas Independence[2]	Independence	100%	66
Miami County Medical Center	Paola	100%	139
Neosho Memorial Regional Medical Center	Chanute	100%	48
Newton Medical Center	Newton	100%	509
Olathe Medical Center[2]	Olathe	100%	1069
Overland Park Regional Medical Center[2]	Overland Park	100%	562
Promise Regional Medical Center Hutchinson	Hutchinson	100%	844
Ransom Memorial Hospital	Ottawa	100%	111
Saint Catherine Hospital	Garden City	100%	321
Saint Francis Health Center[2]	Topeka	100%	910
Saint John Hospital	Leavenworth	100%	44
Saint Luke's South Hospital	Overland Park	100%	757
Salina Regional Health Center	Salina	100%	776
Salina Surgical Hospital	Salina	100%	623
Shawnee Mission Medical Center[2]	Shawnee Miss.	100%	1366
South Central Ks Regional Medical Center	Arkansas City	100%	70
Southwest Medical Center	Liberal	100%	104
Stormont-Vail Healthcare[2]	Topeka	100%	1228
Summit Surgical	Hutchinson	100%	293
Susan B Allen Memorial Hospital	El Dorado	100%	116
Via Christi Hospitals Wichita[2]	Wichita	100%	841
Wesley Medical Center[2]	Wichita	100%	823
Wichita VA Medical Center[2]	Wichita	100%	106
William Newton Hospital	Winfield	100%	74
Geary Community Hospital	Junction City	99%	178
Great Bend Regional Hospital[2]	Great Bend	99%	351
Heartland Surgical Spec Hospital	Overland Park	99%	102
Kansas Heart Hospital[2]	Wichita	99%	450
Mercy Regional Health Center	Manhattan	99%	625
Pratt Regional Medical Center[2]	Pratt	99%	198
Providence Medical Center[2]	Kansas City	99%	608
University of Kansas Hospital[2]	Kansas City	99%	588
Via Christi Hospital Pittsburg	Pittsburg	99%	293
Western Plains Medical Complex	Dodge City	99%	240
Kansas Medical Center[2]	Andover	98%	389
Manhattan Surgical Hospital	Manhattan	98%	233
Newman Regional Health	Emporia	98%	219
Galichia Heart Hospital	Wichita	97%	310
Coffey County Hospital	Burlington	77%	30

24. Appropriate Beta Blocker Usage

Hospital Name	City	Rate	Cases
Saint Francis Health Center[2]	Topeka	100%	293
Wichita VA Medical Center[2]	Wichita	100%	31
Overland Park Regional Medical Center[2]	Overland Park	99%	166
Saint Catherine Hospital	Garden City	99%	73
Salina Surgical Hospital	Salina	99%	145
Summit Surgical	Hutchinson	98%	42
Stormont-Vail Healthcare[2]	Topeka	97%	424
Hays Medical Center[2]	Hays	96%	179
Wesley Medical Center[2]	Wichita	96%	226
Olathe Medical Center[2]	Olathe	95%	357
Menorah Medical Center[2]	Overland Park	94%	127
Providence Medical Center[2]	Kansas City	94%	190
Saint Luke's South Hospital	Overland Park	94%	208
Salina Regional Health Center	Salina	93%	260
Western Plains Medical Complex	Dodge City	93%	55
Coffeyville Regional Medical Center	Coffeyville	92%	26
Galichia Heart Hospital	Wichita	92%	120
Lawrence Memorial Hospital	Lawrence	91%	128
Newton Medical Center	Newton	91%	141
Kansas Heart Hospital[2]	Wichita	90%	201
Mercy Regional Health Center	Manhattan	90%	142
University of Kansas Hospital[2]	Kansas City	89%	178
Miami County Medical Center	Paola	88%	25
Shawnee Mission Medical Center[2]	Shawnee Miss.	86%	417
Kansas Surgery & Recovery Center[2]	Wichita	85%	66
Kansas Medical Center[2]	Andover	84%	158
Labette Health	Parsons	84%	173
Great Bend Regional Hospital[2]	Great Bend	82%	88
Via Christi Hospitals Wichita[2]	Wichita	82%	237
Via Christi Hospital Pittsburg	Pittsburg	80%	71
Newman Regional Health	Emporia	78%	54
Geary Community Hospital	Junction City	73%	41
Heartland Surgical Spec Hospital	Overland Park	72%	32
Kansas Spine Hospital	Wichita	69%	26
Promise Regional Medical Center Hutchinson	Hutchinson	69%	229
Pratt Regional Medical Center[2]	Pratt	63%	52

25. Controlled Postoperative Blood Glucose

Hospital Name	City	Rate	Cases
Shawnee Mission Medical Center[2]	Shawnee Miss.	99%	169
University of Kansas Hospital[2]	Kansas City	99%	126
Providence Medical Center[2]	Kansas City	98%	65
Saint Francis Health Center[2]	Topeka	98%	118
Via Christi Hospitals Wichita[2]	Wichita	97%	151
Salina Regional Health Center	Salina	96%	82
Olathe Medical Center[2]	Olathe	94%	108
Kansas Heart Hospital[2]	Wichita	93%	287
Overland Park Regional Medical Center[2]	Overland Park	93%	61
Hays Medical Center[2]	Hays	90%	81
Stormont-Vail Healthcare[2]	Topeka	89%	187
Wesley Medical Center[2]	Wichita	89%	168
Kansas Medical Center[2]	Andover	87%	164
Promise Regional Medical Center Hutchinson	Hutchinson	83%	143
Galichia Heart Hospital	Wichita	82%	183
Menorah Medical Center[2]	Overland Park	78%	36

26. Prophylactic Antibiotic Timing

Hospital Name	City	Rate	Cases
Meade District Hospital	Meade	100%	53
Mercy Health Center[2]	Fort Scott	100%	68
Saint Luke's South Hospital	Overland Park	100%	589
Wesley Medical Center[2]	Wichita	100%	540
Heartland Surgical Spec Hospital	Overland Park	99%	84
Kansas Surgery & Recovery Center[2]	Wichita	99%	361
Lawrence Memorial Hospital	Lawrence	99%	451
Providence Medical Center[2]	Kansas City	99%	457
Saint Catherine Hospital	Garden City	99%	241
Salina Surgical Hospital	Salina	99%	568
Stormont-Vail Healthcare[2]	Topeka	99%	962
Summit Surgical	Hutchinson	99%	279
Wichita VA Medical Center	Wichita	99%	67
Labette Health	Parsons	98%	485
Manhattan Surgical Hospital	Manhattan	98%	229
Menorah Medical Center[2]	Overland Park	98%	352
Miami County Medical Center	Paola	98%	90
Overland Park Regional Medical Center[2]	Overland Park	98%	379
Pratt Regional Medical Center[2]	Pratt	98%	147
Salina Regional Health Center	Salina	98%	447
South Central Ks Regional Medical Center	Arkansas City	98%	44
Susan B Allen Memorial Hospital	El Dorado	98%	93
Via Christi Hospital Pittsburg	Pittsburg	98%	192
Kansas City Orthopaedic Institute[2]	Leawood	97%	158
Kansas Heart Hospital[2]	Wichita	97%	343
Saint Francis Health Center[2]	Topeka	97%	730
Shawnee Mission Medical Center[2]	Shawnee Miss.	97%	1083
University of Kansas Hospital[2]	Kansas City	97%	381
Via Christi Hospitals Wichita[2]	Wichita	97%	557
Kansas Spine Hospital	Wichita	96%	49
Olathe Medical Center[2]	Olathe	96%	778
Mercy Regional Health Center	Manhattan	95%	444
Western Plains Medical Complex	Dodge City	95%	178
Cushing Memorial Hospital	Leavenworth	94%	53
Mercy Hospital of Kansas Independence[2]	Independence	94%	49
Central Kansas Medical Center	Great Bend	93%	44
Kansas Medical Center[2]	Andover	93%	274
Galichia Heart Hospital	Wichita	91%	221

NOTE: Hospital profiles are in alphabetical order by state, then city, then hospital within the city; Rankings exclude hospitals with less than 25 cases except for patient surveys which excludes hospitals with less than 100 cases; (a) 100–299 cases; (1) The number of cases is too small to be sure how well a hospital is performing; (2) The hospital indicated that the data submitted for this measure were based on a sample of cases; (3) Data was collected during a shorter time period (fewer quarters) than the maximum possible time for this measure; (4) Suppressed for one or more quarters by CMS; (5) No data is available from the hospital for this measure; (6) Fewer than 100 patients completed the HCAHPS survey. Use these rates with caution, as the number of surveys may be too low to reliably assess hospital performance; (7) Survey results are based on less than 12 months of data; (8) Survey results are not available for this reporting period; (9) No or very few patients were eligible for the HCAHPS survey. The scores shown, if any, reflect a very small number of surveys; (10) A state average was not calculated because too few hospitals in the state submitted data; (11) There were discrepancies in the data collection process; Please refer to the User's Guide for a full explanation of data.

Ransom Memorial Hospital	Ottawa	91%	95
Southwest Medical Center	Liberal	91%	55
Newton Medical Center	Newton	90%	370
Coffeyville Regional Medical Center	Coffeyville	89%	38
Hays Medical Center[2]	Hays	89%	363
Newman Regional Health	Emporia	89%	149
William Newton Hospital	Winfield	88%	50
Great Bend Regional Hospital[2]	Great Bend	87%	311
Promise Regional Medical Center Hutchinson	Hutchinson	86%	559
Geary Community Hospital	Junction City	74%	133
Coffey County Hospital	Burlington	62%	26

27. Prophylactic Antibiotic Timing (Outpatient)

Hospital Name	City	Rate	Cases
Kansas Surgery & Recovery Center	Wichita	100%	109
Neosho Memorial Regional Medical Center	Chanute	100%	77
Pratt Regional Medical Center[3]	Pratt	100%	35
Saint Catherine Hospital	Garden City	100%	71
Kansas Medical Center	Andover	99%	181
Kansas Spine Hospital	Wichita	99%	315
Manhattan Surgical Hospital	Manhattan	98%	148
Menorah Medical Center	Overland Park	98%	333
Susan B Allen Memorial Hospital	El Dorado	98%	46
Heartland Surgical Spec Hospital	Overland Park	97%	352
Kansas Heart Hospital	Wichita	97%	263
Overland Park Regional Medical Center	Overland Park	97%	642
Via Christi Hospitals Wichita	Wichita	97%	598
Wesley Medical Center	Wichita	97%	704
Lawrence Memorial Hospital	Lawrence	96%	161
Saint John Hospital	Leavenworth	96%	27
Olathe Medical Center	Olathe	95%	653
Providence Medical Center	Kansas City	95%	336
Southwest Medical Center	Liberal	95%	213
Stormont-Vail Healthcare	Topeka	95%	806
Galichia Heart Hospital	Wichita	94%	170
Via Christi Hospital Pittsburg	Pittsburg	94%	67
Western Plains Medical Complex	Dodge City	94%	79
Newman Regional Health	Emporia	93%	60
Saint Francis Health Center	Topeka	93%	581
Saint Luke's South Hospital	Overland Park	93%	140
Central Kansas Medical Center	Great Bend	92%	74
Labette Health	Parsons	91%	76
Mercy Hospital of Kansas Independence	Independence	89%	28
University of Kansas Hospital	Kansas City	89%	452
Coffeyville Regional Medical Center	Coffeyville	88%	50
Salina Surgical Hospital	Salina	88%	75
Cushing Memorial Hospital	Leavenworth	86%	36
Mercy Regional Health Center	Manhattan	83%	120
Shawnee Mission Medical Center	Shawnee Miss.	83%	676
Salina Regional Health Center	Salina	82%	164
Hays Medical Center	Hays	80%	241
Doctors Hospital[3]	Leawood	77%	39
Promise Regional Medical Center Hutchinson	Hutchinson	77%	285
Newton Medical Center	Newton	73%	90
Great Bend Regional Hospital[3]	Great Bend	71%	28

28. Prophylactic Antibiotic Selection

Hospital Name	City	Rate	Cases
Coffey County Hospital	Burlington	100%	26
Coffeyville Regional Medical Center	Coffeyville	100%	40
Heartland Surgical Spec Hospital	Overland Park	100%	84
Kansas City Orthopaedic Institute[2]	Leawood	100%	158
Kansas Heart Hospital[2]	Wichita	100%	352
Kansas Medical Center[2]	Andover	100%	277
Kansas Spine Hospital	Wichita	100%	49
Kansas Surgery & Recovery Center[2]	Wichita	100%	361
Miami County Medical Center	Paola	100%	90
Saint Francis Health Center[2]	Topeka	100%	740
Saint Luke's South Hospital	Overland Park	100%	594
Wichita VA Medical Center	Wichita	100%	66
Labette Health	Parsons	99%	486
Overland Park Regional Medical Center[2]	Overland Park	99%	384
Providence Medical Center[2]	Kansas City	99%	467
Salina Surgical Hospital	Salina	99%	568
Summit Surgical	Hutchinson	99%	279
Wesley Medical Center[2]	Wichita	99%	551
Lawrence Memorial Hospital	Lawrence	98%	452
Menorah Medical Center[2]	Overland Park	98%	355
Mercy Regional Health Center	Manhattan	98%	442
Salina Regional Health Center	Salina	98%	457
Shawnee Mission Medical Center[2]	Shawnee Miss.	98%	1088
Southwest Medical Center	Liberal	98%	53
Western Plains Medical Complex	Dodge City	98%	178
Galichia Heart Hospital	Wichita	97%	220
Olathe Medical Center[2]	Olathe	97%	786
Stormont-Vail Healthcare[2]	Topeka	97%	974
Via Christi Hospitals Wichita[2]	Wichita	97%	558
Cushing Memorial Hospital	Leavenworth	96%	53
Great Bend Regional Hospital[2]	Great Bend	96%	311
Saint Catherine Hospital	Garden City	96%	241
South Central Ks Regional Medical Center	Arkansas City	96%	45
University of Kansas Hospital[2]	Kansas City	96%	386
Via Christi Hospital Pittsburg	Pittsburg	96%	196
Central Kansas Medical Center	Great Bend	95%	44
Manhattan Surgical Hospital	Manhattan	95%	228
Newman Regional Health	Emporia	95%	149
Pratt Regional Medical Center[2]	Pratt	95%	148
Promise Regional Medical Center Hutchinson	Hutchinson	95%	558
Meade District Hospital	Meade	94%	53
Mercy Hospital of Kansas Independence[2]	Independence	94%	48
Susan B Allen Memorial Hospital	El Dorado	94%	96
William Newton Hospital	Winfield	94%	51
Geary Community Hospital	Junction City	92%	132
Mercy Health Center[2]	Fort Scott	91%	69
Ransom Memorial Hospital	Ottawa	91%	94
Hays Medical Center[2]	Hays	90%	369
Newton Medical Center	Newton	86%	363

29. Prophylactic Antibiotic Selection (Outpatient)

Hospital Name	City	Rate	Cases
Kansas Spine Hospital	Wichita	100%	315
Kansas Surgery & Recovery Center	Wichita	100%	109
Mercy Hospital of Kansas Independence	Independence	100%	25
Susan B Allen Memorial Hospital	El Dorado	100%	45
Heartland Surgical Spec Hospital	Overland Park	99%	349
Kansas Medical Center	Andover	99%	181
Menorah Medical Center	Overland Park	99%	332
Mercy Regional Health Center	Manhattan	99%	107
Western Plains Medical Complex	Dodge City	99%	77
Galichia Heart Hospital	Wichita	98%	168
Olathe Medical Center	Olathe	98%	643
Overland Park Regional Medical Center	Overland Park	98%	628
Providence Medical Center	Kansas City	98%	327
Ransom Memorial Hospital	Ottawa	98%	61
University of Kansas Hospital	Kansas City	98%	445
Wesley Medical Center	Wichita	98%	701
Kansas Heart Hospital	Wichita	97%	265
Lawrence Memorial Hospital	Lawrence	97%	255
Pratt Regional Medical Center[3]	Pratt	97%	35
Saint Francis Health Center	Topeka	97%	567
Southwest Medical Center	Liberal	97%	210
Via Christi Hospitals Wichita	Wichita	97%	592
Central Kansas Medical Center	Great Bend	96%	72
Manhattan Surgical Hospital	Manhattan	96%	149
Newton Medical Center	Newton	96%	117
Saint Catherine Hospital	Garden City	96%	71
Labette Health	Parsons	95%	73
Shawnee Mission Medical Center	Shawnee Miss.	95%	609
Coffeyville Regional Medical Center	Coffeyville	94%	69
Salina Surgical Hospital	Salina	94%	68
Stormont-Vail Healthcare	Topeka	94%	800
Via Christi Hospital Pittsburg	Pittsburg	94%	67
Saint John Hospital	Leavenworth	93%	28
Doctors Hospital[3]	Leawood	92%	36
Hays Medical Center	Hays	92%	212
Neosho Memorial Regional Medical Center	Chanute	92%	80
Newman Regional Health	Emporia	91%	58
Saint Luke's South Hospital	Overland Park	90%	135
Salina Regional Health Center	Salina	87%	144
Promise Regional Medical Center Hutchinson	Hutchinson	84%	274
Cushing Memorial Hospital	Leavenworth	63%	35

30. Prophylactic Antibiotic Stopped

Hospital Name	City	Rate	Cases
Meade District Hospital	Meade	100%	53
South Central Ks Regional Medical Center	Arkansas City	100%	44
Summit Surgical	Hutchinson	100%	278
Labette Health	Parsons	99%	460
Mercy Health Center[2]	Fort Scott	99%	67
Pratt Regional Medical Center[2]	Pratt	99%	146
Providence Medical Center[2]	Kansas City	99%	432
Saint Francis Health Center[2]	Topeka	99%	700
Cushing Memorial Hospital	Leavenworth	98%	52
Lawrence Memorial Hospital	Lawrence	98%	442
Mercy Hospital of Kansas Independence[2]	Independence	98%	47
Ransom Memorial Hospital	Ottawa	98%	88
Wesley Medical Center[2]	Wichita	98%	503
William Newton Hospital	Winfield	98%	49
Coffeyville Regional Medical Center	Coffeyville	97%	32
Mercy Regional Health Center	Manhattan	97%	436
Overland Park Regional Medical Center[2]	Overland Park	97%	351
Kansas Heart Hospital[2]	Wichita	96%	337
Kansas Surgery & Recovery Center[2]	Wichita	96%	361
Menorah Medical Center[2]	Overland Park	96%	340
Saint Luke's South Hospital	Overland Park	96%	575
Central Kansas Medical Center	Great Bend	95%	44
Heartland Surgical Spec Hospital	Overland Park	95%	80
Kansas City Orthopaedic Institute[2]	Leawood	95%	158
Salina Regional Health Center	Salina	95%	421
Shawnee Mission Medical Center[2]	Shawnee Miss.	95%	1041
Stormont-Vail Healthcare[2]	Topeka	95%	925
University of Kansas Hospital[2]	Kansas City	95%	365
Olathe Medical Center[2]	Olathe	94%	746
Southwest Medical Center	Liberal	94%	48
Susan B Allen Memorial Hospital	El Dorado	93%	91
Wichita VA Medical Center	Wichita	93%	60
Manhattan Surgical Hospital	Manhattan	92%	228
Newton Medical Center	Newton	92%	347
Salina Surgical Hospital	Salina	92%	562
Galichia Heart Hospital	Wichita	91%	209
Miami County Medical Center	Paola	91%	88
Via Christi Hospitals Wichita[2]	Wichita	91%	533
Western Plains Medical Complex	Dodge City	91%	170
Geary Community Hospital	Junction City	90%	130
Newman Regional Health	Emporia	90%	146
Kansas Medical Center[2]	Andover	89%	270
Hays Medical Center[2]	Hays	86%	340
Via Christi Hospital Pittsburg	Pittsburg	86%	177
Great Bend Regional Hospital[2]	Great Bend	81%	306
Promise Regional Medical Center Hutchinson	Hutchinson	81%	542
Coffey County Hospital	Burlington	80%	25
Saint Catherine Hospital	Garden City	69%	240
Kansas Spine Hospital	Wichita	0%	49

31. Recommended VTP Ordered

Hospital Name	City	Rate	Cases
Miami County Medical Center	Paola	100%	30
Ransom Memorial Hospital	Ottawa	100%	35
Wesley Medical Center[2]	Wichita	99%	296
Wichita VA Medical Center[2]	Wichita	99%	69
Kansas Heart Hospital[2]	Wichita	98%	44
Kansas Spine Hospital	Wichita	98%	42
Pratt Regional Medical Center[2]	Pratt	98%	107
Menorah Medical Center[2]	Overland Park	97%	179
Mercy Hospital of Kansas Independence[2]	Independence	97%	33
Overland Park Regional Medical Center[2]	Overland Park	97%	190
Saint Francis Health Center[2]	Topeka	97%	180
Cushing Memorial Hospital	Leavenworth	96%	26
Olathe Medical Center[2]	Olathe	96%	307
Shawnee Mission Medical Center[2]	Shawnee Miss.	96%	400
Susan B Allen Memorial Hospital	El Dorado	96%	25
Salina Regional Health Center	Salina	95%	352
Salina Surgical Hospital	Salina	95%	77
University of Kansas Hospital[2]	Kansas City	95%	246
Western Plains Medical Complex	Dodge City	95%	76
Kansas Medical Center[2]	Andover	94%	50
Lawrence Memorial Hospital	Lawrence	94%	223
Saint Catherine Hospital	Garden City	94%	158
Stormont-Vail Healthcare[2]	Topeka	94%	264
Via Christi Hospital Pittsburg	Pittsburg	94%	109
Central Kansas Medical Center	Great Bend	93%	28
Labette Health	Parsons	92%	115
Saint Luke's South Hospital	Overland Park	92%	134
Great Bend Regional Hospital[2]	Great Bend	90%	161
Hays Medical Center[2]	Hays	90%	203
Providence Medical Center[2]	Kansas City	90%	155
Via Christi Hospitals Wichita[2]	Wichita	90%	294
Southwest Medical Center	Liberal	89%	80
Mercy Regional Health Center	Manhattan	87%	127
Newton Medical Center	Newton	87%	175
Mercy Health Center[2]	Fort Scott	83%	30
Coffeyville Regional Medical Center	Coffeyville	79%	58
Geary Community Hospital	Junction City	74%	54
Promise Regional Medical Center Hutchinson	Hutchinson	72%	255
Galichia Heart Hospital	Wichita	70%	54
Newman Regional Health	Emporia	70%	102
South Central Ks Regional Medical Center	Arkansas City	69%	42
Saint John Hospital	Leavenworth	60%	25

32. Urinary Catheter Removal

Hospital Name	City	Rate	Cases
Summit Surgical	Hutchinson	100%	79
Saint Francis Health Center[2]	Topeka	99%	265
Overland Park Regional Medical Center[2]	Overland Park	97%	61
Wesley Medical Center[2]	Wichita	97%	89
Kansas Heart Hospital[2]	Wichita	96%	68
Mercy Regional Health Center	Manhattan	96%	135
Lawrence Memorial Hospital	Lawrence	95%	172
Galichia Heart Hospital	Wichita	94%	78
Heartland Surgical Spec Hospital	Overland Park	93%	44
Kansas Spine Hospital	Wichita	93%	29
Menorah Medical Center[2]	Overland Park	92%	73
Providence Medical Center[2]	Kansas City	92%	133
Olathe Medical Center[2]	Olathe	91%	316
Labette Health	Parsons	90%	62
Pratt Regional Medical Center[2]	Pratt	90%	63
University of Kansas Hospital[2]	Kansas City	90%	132
Kansas Medical Center[2]	Andover	89%	134
Miami County Medical Center	Paola	89%	44
Saint Luke's South Hospital	Overland Park	85%	26

NOTE: Hospital profiles are in alphabetical order by state, then city, then hospital within the city; Rankings exclude hospitals with less than 25 cases except for patient surveys which excludes hospitals with less than 100 cases; (a) 100–299 cases; (1) The number of cases is too small to be sure how well a hospital is performing; (2) The hospital indicated that the data submitted for this measure were based on a sample of cases; (3) Data was collected during a shorter time period (fewer quarters) than the maximum possible time for this measure; (4) Suppressed for one or more quarters by CMS; (5) No data is available from the hospital for this measure; (6) Fewer than 100 patients completed the HCAHPS survey. Use these rates with caution, as the number of surveys may be too low to reliably assess hospital performance; (7) Survey results are based on less than 12 months of data; (8) Survey results are not available for this reporting period; (9) No or very few patients were eligible for the HCAHPS survey. The scores shown, if any, reflect a very small number of surveys; (10) A state average was not calculated because too few hospitals in the state submitted data; (11) There were discrepancies in the data collection process; Please refer to the User's Guide for a full explanation of data.

Hospital Name	City	Rate	Cases
Stormont-Vail Healthcare[2]	Topeka	85%	155
Promise Regional Medical Center Hutchinson	Hutchinson	84%	217
Saint Catherine Hospital	Garden City	83%	76
Newton Medical Center	Newton	82%	139
Shawnee Mission Medical Center[2]	Shawnee Miss.	79%	173
Geary Community Hospital	Junction City	78%	59
Newman Regional Health	Emporia	78%	64
Via Christi Hospitals Wichita[2]	Wichita	78%	126
Salina Regional Health Center	Salina	76%	88
Hays Medical Center[2]	Hays	75%	116
Southwest Medical Center	Liberal	74%	31
South Central Ks Regional Medical Center	Arkansas City	63%	30
Great Bend Regional Hospital	Great Bend	59%	137
Via Christi Hospital Pittsburg	Pittsburg	56%	39

Children's Asthma Care

33. Received Systemic Corticosteroids

Hospital Name	City	Rate	Cases
Wesley Medical Center	Wichita	99%	112

34. Received Home Management Plan of Care

Hospital Name	City	Rate	Cases
Wesley Medical Center	Wichita	85%	111

35. Received Reliever Medication

Hospital Name	City	Rate	Cases
Wesley Medical Center	Wichita	100%	112

Use of Medical Imaging

36. Combination Abdominal CT Scan

Hospital Name	City	Ratio	Cases
Susan B Allen Memorial Hospital	El Dorado	0.014	420
Miami County Medical Center	Paola	0.015	202
Promise Regional Medical Center Hutchinson	Hutchinson	0.019	320
Providence Medical Center	Kansas City	0.023	385
Olathe Medical Center	Olathe	0.024	706
Geary Community Hospital	Junction City	0.036	247
Central Kansas Medical Center	Great Bend	0.039	727
Saint John Hospital	Leavenworth	0.046	151
Ransom Memorial Hospital	Ottawa	0.057	244
Wamego City Hospital[1]	Wamego	0.057	53
Neosho Memorial Regional Medical Center	Chanute	0.062	306
Stormont-Vail Healthcare	Topeka	0.072	1314
Coffeyville Regional Medical Center	Coffeyville	0.082	389
Overland Park Regional Medical Center	Overland Park	0.084	275
Mercy Regional Health Center	Manhattan	0.088	273
Bob Wilson Memorial Grant County Hospital[1]	Ulysses	0.089	56
Menorah Medical Center	Overland Park	0.102	392
Mercy Health Center	Fort Scott	0.111	216
Saint Francis Health Center	Topeka	0.111	1053
Anderson County Hospital	Garnett	0.131	107
Lawrence Memorial Hospital	Lawrence	0.133	976
Shawnee Mission Medical Center	Shawnee Miss.	0.138	821
Smith County Memorial Hospital[1]	Smith Center	0.143	63
Saint Luke's South Hospital	Overland Park	0.224	361
Holton Community Hospital	Holton	0.247	93
Salina Regional Health Center	Salina	0.275	516
Hillsboro Community Hospital[1]	Hillsboro	0.296	27
Cushing Memorial Hospital	Leavenworth	0.302	106
Kansas Medical Center	Andover	0.355	110
Heartland Surgical Spec Hospital[1]	Overland Park	0.375	32
Via Christi Hospital Pittsburg	Pittsburg	0.383	439
Clara Barton Hospital	Hoisington	0.392	189
Galichia Heart Hospital	Wichita	0.401	167
Ellsworth County Medical Center	Ellsworth	0.402	107
Western Plains Medical Complex	Dodge City	0.406	133
Saint Catherine Hospital	Garden City	0.457	341
Wesley Medical Center	Wichita	0.575	1064
Hays Medical Center	Hays	0.586	630
Morton County Hospital[1]	Elkhart	0.600	35
Via Christi Hospitals Wichita	Wichita	0.634	1437
Sumner Regional Medical Center	Wellington	0.647	139
Graham County Hospital	Hill City	0.648	88
Memorial Hospital	Mcpherson	0.656	320
Southwest Medical Center	Liberal	0.683	221
Mercy Hospital of Kansas Independence	Independence	0.730	148
Allen County Hospital	Iola	0.758	182
Newton Medical Center	Newton	0.760	288
Pratt Regional Medical Center	Pratt	0.761	255
University of Kansas Hospital	Kansas City	0.764	1617
Labette Health	Parsons	0.829	439
South Central Ks Regional Medical Center	Arkansas City	0.834	145
William Newton Hospital	Winfield	0.838	247
Newman Regional Health	Emporia	0.849	370
Coffey County Hospital	Burlington	0.902	112

37. Combination Chest CT Scan

Hospital Name	City	Ratio	Cases
Lawrence Memorial Hospital	Lawrence	0.000	660
Mercy Regional Health Center	Manhattan	0.000	194
Miami County Medical Center	Paola	0.000	105
Newton Medical Center	Newton	0.000	193
Promise Regional Medical Center Hutchinson	Hutchinson	0.000	139
Ransom Memorial Hospital	Ottawa	0.000	177
Saint Catherine Hospital	Garden City	0.000	143
Salina Regional Health Center	Salina	0.002	540
Olathe Medical Center	Olathe	0.003	684
Susan B Allen Memorial Hospital	El Dorado	0.003	342
Coffeyville Regional Medical Center	Coffeyville	0.004	236
Newman Regional Health	Emporia	0.004	251
William Newton Hospital	Winfield	0.004	249
University of Kansas Hospital	Kansas City	0.005	1980
Hays Medical Center	Hays	0.006	710
Stormont-Vail Healthcare	Topeka	0.008	660
Geary Community Hospital	Junction City	0.011	185
Cushing Memorial Hospital	Leavenworth	0.012	81
Menorah Medical Center	Overland Park	0.014	437
Allen County Hospital	Iola	0.015	66
Central Kansas Medical Center	Great Bend	0.015	710
Saint Francis Health Center	Topeka	0.018	554
South Central Ks Regional Medical Center	Arkansas City	0.023	130
Memorial Hospital	Mcpherson	0.028	283
Saint John Hospital	Leavenworth	0.029	137
Graham County Hospital	Hill City	0.035	85
Neosho Memorial Regional Medical Center	Chanute	0.038	211
Ellsworth County Medical Center	Ellsworth	0.044	68
Providence Medical Center	Kansas City	0.049	425
Holton Community Hospital[1]	Holton	0.050	40
Saint Luke's South Hospital	Overland Park	0.052	230
Overland Park Regional Medical Center	Overland Park	0.055	217
Mercy Hospital of Kansas Independence	Independence	0.056	90
Sumner Regional Medical Center	Wellington	0.067	75
Mercy Health Center	Fort Scott	0.069	131
Bob Wilson Memorial Grant County Hospital[1]	Ulysses	0.071	28
Clara Barton Hospital	Hoisington	0.079	139
Shawnee Mission Medical Center	Shawnee Miss.	0.081	431
Western Plains Medical Complex	Dodge City	0.086	70
Via Christi Hospitals Wichita	Wichita	0.097	781
Smith County Memorial Hospital[1]	Smith Center	0.100	60
Via Christi Hospital Pittsburg	Pittsburg	0.105	285
Wesley Medical Center	Wichita	0.109	477
Wamego City Hospital[1]	Wamego	0.121	33
Kansas Medical Center	Andover	0.131	84
Coffey County Hospital	Burlington	0.288	59
Anderson County Hospital[1]	Garnett	0.294	34
Pratt Regional Medical Center	Pratt	0.299	204
Labette Health	Parsons	0.483	298
Galichia Heart Hospital	Wichita	0.504	133
Southwest Medical Center	Liberal	0.719	139

38. Follow-up Mammogram/Ultrasound

Hospital Name	City	Rate	Cases
Allen County Hospital	Iola	0.8%	260
Saint Catherine Hospital	Garden City	0.9%	423
Anderson County Hospital	Garnett	1.9%	162
Clara Barton Hospital	Hoisington	2.5%	163
Coffey County Hospital	Burlington	2.5%	243
Saint John Hospital	Leavenworth	2.7%	377
Labette Health	Parsons	3.2%	409
Neosho Memorial Regional Medical Center	Chanute	3.5%	425
Holton Community Hospital	Holton	4.0%	201
Geary Community Hospital	Junction City	4.2%	647
Ellsworth County Medical Center	Ellsworth	4.7%	128
Saint Francis Health Center	Topeka	5.1%	2599
Central Kansas Medical Center	Great Bend	5.3%	437
Southwest Medical Center	Liberal	5.3%	303
Hays Medical Center	Hays	5.5%	1025
Via Christi Hospital Pittsburg	Pittsburg	5.7%	757
Western Plains Medical Complex	Dodge City	5.9%	119
Wesley Medical Center	Wichita	6.0%	265
Wamego City Hospital	Wamego	6.1%	165
Mercy Hospital of Kansas Independence	Independence	6.3%	384
Shawnee Mission Medical Center	Shawnee Miss.	6.9%	2262
Bob Wilson Memorial Grant County Hospital	Ulysses	7.0%	114
Lawrence Memorial Hospital	Lawrence	7.0%	2133
Newton Medical Center	Newton	7.2%	947
Salina Regional Health Center	Salina	7.3%	232
Providence Medical Center	Kansas City	7.4%	488
Sumner Regional Medical Center	Wellington	7.4%	282
Mercy Regional Health Center	Manhattan	7.5%	1442
Cushing Memorial Hospital	Leavenworth	7.6%	341
Miami County Medical Center	Paola	8.5%	496
Overland Park Regional Medical Center	Overland Park	8.5%	376
Saint Luke's South Hospital	Overland Park	8.5%	672
Via Christi Hospitals Wichita	Wichita	8.7%	1022
South Central Ks Regional Medical Center	Arkansas City	8.8%	240
Mercy Health Center	Fort Scott	9.2%	469
Pratt Regional Medical Center	Pratt	9.2%	609
Morton County Hospital[1]	Elkhart	9.5%	42
Graham County Hospital	Hill City	9.8%	92
Ransom Memorial Hospital	Ottawa	9.8%	439
William Newton Hospital	Winfield	9.8%	579
Memorial Hospital	Mcpherson	9.9%	514
Olathe Medical Center	Olathe	9.9%	1292
Smith County Memorial Hospital	Smith Center	10.1%	169
University of Kansas Hospital	Kansas City	10.2%	1327
Coffeyville Regional Medical Center	Coffeyville	11.1%	497
Menorah Medical Center	Overland Park	11.2%	824
Susan B Allen Memorial Hospital	El Dorado	22.0%	554

39. MRI for Low Back Pain

Hospital Name	City	Rate	Cases
Providence Medical Center[1]	Kansas City	23.5%	51
South Central Ks Regional Medical Center[1]	Arkansas City	23.8%	42
Susan B Allen Memorial Hospital	El Dorado	23.9%	159
Newton Medical Center	Newton	25.6%	78
Mercy Regional Health Center[1]	Manhattan	25.7%	35
Kansas Spine Hospital	Wichita	26.7%	161
Kansas Surgery & Recovery Center	Wichita	26.7%	217
University of Kansas Hospital	Kansas City	27.4%	146
Ransom Memorial Hospital	Ottawa	27.5%	80
Via Christi Hospital Pittsburg	Pittsburg	28.8%	73
Promise Regional Medical Center Hutchinson	Hutchinson	29.2%	72
Kansas City Orthopaedic Institute	Leawood	29.3%	150
Shawnee Mission Medical Center	Shawnee Miss.	29.5%	315
Heartland Surgical Spec Hospital	Overland Park	30.2%	169
Saint Luke's South Hospital	Overland Park	30.5%	131
Memorial Hospital	Mcpherson	30.6%	62
Newman Regional Health	Emporia	30.6%	180
Coffey County Hospital	Burlington	30.8%	52
Coffeyville Regional Medical Center[1]	Coffeyville	31.1%	45
Wesley Medical Center	Wichita	31.5%	130
Overland Park Regional Medical Center[1]	Overland Park	31.7%	41
Graham County Hospital[1]	Hill City	32.0%	25
Salina Regional Health Center	Salina	32.1%	187
Pratt Regional Medical Center	Pratt	33.9%	121
Miami County Medical Center	Paola	34.5%	58
Geary Community Hospital	Junction City	34.6%	52
Saint Francis Health Center	Topeka	35.5%	394
Central Kansas Medical Center	Great Bend	35.7%	70
Clara Barton Hospital[1]	Hoisington	36.0%	25
Mercy Health Center	Fort Scott	36.7%	49
Stormont-Vail Healthcare	Topeka	37.2%	527
Lawrence Memorial Hospital	Lawrence	37.7%	316
Saint Catherine Hospital	Garden City	37.7%	77
William Newton Hospital	Winfield	37.7%	69
Olathe Medical Center	Olathe	37.8%	283
Southwest Medical Center	Liberal	38.6%	70
Labette Health	Parsons	40.6%	165
Hays Medical Center	Hays	41.3%	160
Menorah Medical Center	Overland Park	41.9%	86
Mercy Hospital of Kansas Independence	Independence	42.9%	42
Neosho Memorial Regional Medical Center	Chanute	43.4%	53
Holton Community Hospital	Holton	44.7%	38
Sumner Regional Medical Center	Wellington	52.6%	57
Allen County Hospital	Iola	53.7%	41
Smith County Memorial Hospital[1]	Smith Center	58.8%	34

Survey of Patients' Hospital Experiences

40. Area Around Room 'Always' Quiet at Night

Hospital Name	City	Rate	Cases
Manhattan Surgical Hospital	Manhattan	93%	(a)
Doctors Hospital	Leawood	91%	(a)
Heartland Surgical Spec Hospital	Overland Park	82%	300+
Summit Surgical	Hutchinson	81%	(a)
Salina Surgical Hospital	Salina	80%	300+
Kansas Spine Hospital	Wichita	76%	300+
Miami County Medical Center	Paola	76%	(a)
Mercy Hospital	Moundridge	73%	(a)
Bob Wilson Memorial Grant County Hospital	Ulysses	71%	(a)
Neosho Memorial Regional Medical Center	Chanute	71%	300+
Kansas Medical Center	Andover	70%	300+
South Central Ks Regional Medical Center	Arkansas City	69%	(a)
Great Bend Regional Hospital	Great Bend	68%	300+
Kansas City Orthopaedic Institute	Leawood	68%	300+
Mercy Health Center	Fort Scott	68%	300+
Coffey County Hospital	Burlington	66%	300+
Pratt Regional Medical Center	Pratt	66%	300+
Stormont-Vail Healthcare	Topeka	66%	300+
Geary Community Hospital[11]	Junction City	65%	300+
Kansas Surgery & Recovery Center	Wichita	64%	300+
Hays Medical Center	Hays	63%	300+
William Newton Hospital	Winfield	63%	(a)
Central Kansas Medical Center	Great Bend	62%	(a)
Mercy Regional Health Center	Manhattan	62%	300+

NOTE: Hospital profiles are in alphabetical order by state, then city, then hospital within the city; Rankings exclude hospitals with less than 25 cases except for patient surveys which excludes hospitals with less than 100 cases; (a) 100–299 cases; (1) The number of cases is too small to be sure how well a hospital is performing; (2) The hospital indicated that the data submitted for this measure were based on a sample of cases; (3) Data was collected during a shorter time period (fewer quarters) than the maximum possible time for this measure; (4) Suppressed for one or more quarters by CMS; (5) No data is available from the hospital for this measure; (6) Fewer than 100 patients completed the HCAHPS survey. Use these rates with caution, as the number of surveys may be too low to reliably assess hospital performance; (7) Survey results are based on less than 12 months of data; (8) Survey results are not available for this reporting period; (9) No or very few patients were eligible for the HCAHPS survey. The scores shown, if any, reflect a very small number of surveys; (10) A state average was not calculated because too few hospitals in the state submitted data; (11) There were discrepancies in the data collection process; Please refer to the User's Guide for a full explanation of data.

Hospital Name	City	Rate	Cases
Galichia Heart Hospital	Wichita	61%	300+
Saint Luke's South Hospital	Overland Park	61%	300+
Cushing Memorial Hospital	Leavenworth	60%	(a)
Ellsworth County Medical Center	Ellsworth	60%	(a)
Menorah Medical Center	Overland Park	60%	300+
Mercy Hospital of Kansas Independence	Independence	60%	(a)
University of Kansas Hospital	Kansas City	60%	300+
Via Christi Hospital Pittsburg	Pittsburg	60%	300+
Kansas Heart Hospital	Wichita	59%	300+
Labette Health	Parsons	58%	300+
Susan B Allen Memorial Hospital	El Dorado	58%	300+
Memorial Hospital	Mcpherson	57%	300+
Newman Regional Health	Emporia	57%	300+
Lawrence Memorial Hospital	Lawrence	56%	300+
Newton Medical Center	Newton	56%	300+
Olathe Medical Center	Olathe	56%	300+
Ransom Memorial Hospital	Ottawa	55%	300+
Shawnee Mission Medical Center	Shawnee Miss.	55%	300+
Kingman Community Hospital	Kingman	54%	(a)
Overland Park Regional Medical Center	Overland Park	54%	300+
Salina Regional Health Center	Salina	54%	300+
Wesley Medical Center	Wichita	54%	300+
Saint Catherine Hospital	Garden City	53%	300+
Southwest Medical Center	Liberal	53%	300+
Providence Medical Center	Kansas City	52%	300+
Saint Francis Health Center	Topeka	51%	300+
Western Plains Medical Complex	Dodge City	50%	300+
Coffeyville Regional Medical Center	Coffeyville	49%	300+
Promise Regional Medical Center Hutchinson	Hutchinson	47%	300+
Via Christi Hospitals Wichita	Wichita	46%	300+
Saint John Hospital	Leavenworth	44%	(a)
Morton County Hospital	Elkhart	43%	(a)

41. Doctors 'Always' Communicated Well

Hospital Name	City	Rate	Cases
Manhattan Surgical Hospital	Manhattan	95%	(a)
Kansas City Orthopaedic Institute	Leawood	91%	300+
South Central Ks Regional Medical Center	Arkansas City	90%	(a)
Salina Surgical Hospital	Salina	89%	300+
Kansas Surgery & Recovery Center	Wichita	88%	300+
Mercy Hospital	Moundridge	88%	(a)
Neosho Memorial Regional Medical Center	Chanute	88%	300+
Summit Surgical	Hutchinson	88%	(a)
Kingman Community Hospital	Kingman	87%	(a)
Mercy Hospital of Kansas Independence	Independence	87%	(a)
Miami County Medical Center	Paola	87%	(a)
Ransom Memorial Hospital	Ottawa	87%	300+
Great Bend Regional Hospital	Great Bend	86%	300+
Kansas Heart Hospital	Wichita	86%	300+
Via Christi Hospital Pittsburg	Pittsburg	86%	300+
Geary Community Hospital[11]	Junction City	85%	300+
Heartland Surgical Spec Hospital	Overland Park	85%	300+
Mercy Health Center	Fort Scott	85%	300+
Morton County Hospital	Elkhart	85%	(a)
Pratt Regional Medical Center	Pratt	85%	300+
Susan B Allen Memorial Hospital	El Dorado	85%	300+
Coffey County Hospital	Burlington	84%	300+
Doctors Hospital	Leawood	84%	(a)
Kansas Medical Center	Andover	84%	300+
Kansas Spine Hospital	Wichita	84%	300+
William Newton Hospital	Winfield	84%	(a)
Bob Wilson Memorial Grant County Hospital	Ulysses	83%	(a)
Ellsworth County Medical Center	Ellsworth	83%	(a)
Lawrence Memorial Hospital	Lawrence	83%	300+
Mercy Regional Health Center	Manhattan	83%	300+
Newton Medical Center	Newton	83%	300+
Memorial Hospital	Mcpherson	82%	300+
Stormont-Vail Healthcare	Topeka	82%	300+
Central Kansas Medical Center	Great Bend	81%	(a)
Labette Health	Parsons	81%	300+
Salina Regional Health Center	Salina	81%	300+
Coffeyville Regional Medical Center	Coffeyville	80%	300+
Olathe Medical Center	Olathe	80%	300+
Overland Park Regional Medical Center	Overland Park	80%	300+
Saint Catherine Hospital	Garden City	80%	300+
Southwest Medical Center	Liberal	80%	300+
University of Kansas Hospital	Kansas City	80%	300+
Menorah Medical Center	Overland Park	79%	300+
Newman Regional Health	Emporia	79%	300+
Western Plains Medical Complex	Dodge City	79%	300+
Cushing Memorial Hospital	Leavenworth	78%	(a)
Hays Medical Center	Hays	78%	300+
Wesley Medical Center	Wichita	78%	300+
Saint Luke's South Hospital	Overland Park	77%	300+
Saint Francis Health Center	Topeka	76%	300+
Shawnee Mission Medical Center	Shawnee Miss.	76%	300+
Promise Regional Medical Center Hutchinson	Hutchinson	75%	300+
Galichia Heart Hospital	Wichita	74%	300+
Saint John Hospital	Leavenworth	74%	(a)
Via Christi Hospitals Wichita	Wichita	74%	300+

Hospital Name	City	Rate	Cases
Providence Medical Center	Kansas City	72%	300+

42. Home Recovery Information Given

Hospital Name	City	Rate	Cases
Kansas City Orthopaedic Institute	Leawood	93%	300+
Summit Surgical	Hutchinson	90%	(a)
Central Kansas Medical Center	Great Bend	89%	(a)
Labette Health	Parsons	89%	300+
Manhattan Surgical Hospital	Manhattan	89%	(a)
Salina Surgical Hospital	Salina	89%	300+
Lawrence Memorial Hospital	Lawrence	88%	300+
University of Kansas Hospital	Kansas City	88%	300+
Doctors Hospital	Leawood	87%	(a)
Heartland Surgical Spec Hospital	Overland Park	87%	300+
Kansas Spine Hospital	Wichita	87%	300+
Kansas Surgery & Recovery Center	Wichita	87%	300+
Miami County Medical Center	Paola	87%	(a)
Neosho Memorial Regional Medical Center	Chanute	87%	300+
Olathe Medical Center	Olathe	87%	300+
Geary Community Hospital[11]	Junction City	86%	300+
Hays Medical Center	Hays	86%	300+
Kansas Medical Center	Andover	86%	300+
Menorah Medical Center	Overland Park	86%	300+
Mercy Hospital of Kansas Independence	Independence	86%	(a)
Mercy Regional Health Center	Manhattan	86%	300+
Overland Park Regional Medical Center	Overland Park	86%	300+
Shawnee Mission Medical Center	Shawnee Miss.	86%	300+
Ransom Memorial Hospital	Ottawa	85%	300+
Saint Luke's South Hospital	Overland Park	85%	300+
South Central Ks Regional Medical Center	Arkansas City	85%	(a)
Stormont-Vail Healthcare	Topeka	85%	300+
Via Christi Hospital Pittsburg	Pittsburg	85%	300+
Saint Catherine Hospital	Garden City	84%	300+
Coffey County Hospital	Burlington	83%	300+
Mercy Health Center	Fort Scott	83%	300+
Southwest Medical Center	Liberal	83%	300+
William Newton Hospital	Winfield	83%	(a)
Cushing Memorial Hospital	Leavenworth	82%	(a)
Kingman Community Hospital	Kingman	82%	(a)
Newton Medical Center	Newton	82%	300+
Pratt Regional Medical Center	Pratt	82%	300+
Saint Francis Health Center	Topeka	82%	300+
Susan B Allen Memorial Hospital	El Dorado	81%	300+
Wesley Medical Center	Wichita	81%	300+
Galichia Heart Hospital	Wichita	80%	300+
Great Bend Regional Hospital	Great Bend	80%	300+
Memorial Hospital	Mcpherson	80%	300+
Mercy Hospital	Moundridge	80%	(a)
Salina Regional Health Center	Salina	80%	300+
Kansas Heart Hospital	Wichita	79%	300+
Promise Regional Medical Center Hutchinson	Hutchinson	79%	300+
Providence Medical Center	Kansas City	79%	300+
Via Christi Hospitals Wichita	Wichita	78%	300+
Coffeyville Regional Medical Center	Coffeyville	77%	300+
Newman Regional Health	Emporia	77%	300+
Western Plains Medical Complex	Dodge City	77%	300+
Bob Wilson Memorial Grant County Hospital	Ulysses	76%	(a)
Saint John Hospital	Leavenworth	75%	(a)
Ellsworth County Medical Center	Ellsworth	71%	(a)
Morton County Hospital	Elkhart	67%	(a)

43. Hospital Given 9 or 10 on 10 Point Scale

Hospital Name	City	Rate	Cases
Manhattan Surgical Hospital	Manhattan	95%	(a)
Salina Surgical Hospital	Salina	95%	300+
Heartland Surgical Spec Hospital	Overland Park	91%	300+
Kansas City Orthopaedic Institute	Leawood	89%	300+
Summit Surgical	Hutchinson	88%	(a)
Kansas Heart Hospital	Wichita	87%	300+
Mercy Hospital	Moundridge	85%	(a)
Miami County Medical Center	Paola	84%	(a)
Kansas Medical Center	Andover	83%	300+
Kansas Spine Hospital	Wichita	83%	300+
Neosho Memorial Regional Medical Center	Chanute	81%	300+
Doctors Hospital	Leawood	80%	(a)
Kansas Surgery & Recovery Center	Wichita	80%	300+
Newton Medical Center	Newton	79%	300+
Saint Luke's South Hospital	Overland Park	79%	300+
Kingman Community Hospital	Kingman	78%	(a)
Ellsworth County Medical Center	Ellsworth	77%	(a)
Coffey County Hospital	Burlington	76%	300+
Great Bend Regional Hospital	Great Bend	76%	300+
Stormont-Vail Healthcare	Topeka	75%	300+
University of Kansas Hospital	Kansas City	75%	300+
Galichia Heart Hospital	Wichita	73%	300+
Lawrence Memorial Hospital	Lawrence	73%	300+
Olathe Medical Center	Olathe	73%	300+
Pratt Regional Medical Center	Pratt	73%	300+
Susan B Allen Memorial Hospital	El Dorado	72%	300+
Via Christi Hospital Pittsburg	Pittsburg	72%	300+

Hospital Name	City	Rate	Cases
Central Kansas Medical Center	Great Bend	70%	(a)
Hays Medical Center	Hays	70%	300+
Labette Health	Parsons	70%	300+
Ransom Memorial Hospital	Ottawa	70%	300+
Mercy Health Center	Fort Scott	69%	300+
Mercy Hospital of Kansas Independence	Independence	69%	(a)
Mercy Regional Health Center	Manhattan	69%	300+
Salina Regional Health Center	Salina	69%	300+
Shawnee Mission Medical Center	Shawnee Miss.	69%	300+
Geary Community Hospital[11]	Junction City	68%	300+
Saint Francis Health Center	Topeka	68%	300+
William Newton Hospital	Winfield	68%	(a)
Menorah Medical Center	Overland Park	67%	300+
Memorial Hospital	Mcpherson	66%	300+
Overland Park Regional Medical Center	Overland Park	66%	300+
South Central Ks Regional Medical Center	Arkansas City	66%	(a)
Southwest Medical Center	Liberal	66%	300+
Bob Wilson Memorial Grant County Hospital	Ulysses	64%	(a)
Via Christi Hospitals Wichita	Wichita	64%	300+
Saint Catherine Hospital	Garden City	63%	300+
Cushing Memorial Hospital	Leavenworth	62%	(a)
Wesley Medical Center	Wichita	62%	300+
Western Plains Medical Complex	Dodge City	62%	300+
Coffeyville Regional Medical Center	Coffeyville	61%	300+
Newman Regional Health	Emporia	61%	300+
Promise Regional Medical Center Hutchinson	Hutchinson	61%	300+
Providence Medical Center	Kansas City	60%	300+
Morton County Hospital	Elkhart	59%	(a)
Saint John Hospital	Leavenworth	57%	(a)

44. Meds 'Always' Explained Before Given

Hospital Name	City	Rate	Cases
Salina Surgical Hospital	Salina	80%	300+
Kansas City Orthopaedic Institute	Leawood	74%	300+
Miami County Medical Center	Paola	74%	(a)
Manhattan Surgical Hospital	Manhattan	72%	(a)
William Newton Hospital	Winfield	71%	(a)
Heartland Surgical Spec Hospital	Overland Park	69%	300+
Via Christi Hospital Pittsburg	Pittsburg	69%	300+
Kansas Heart Hospital	Wichita	67%	300+
Neosho Memorial Regional Medical Center	Chanute	67%	300+
South Central Ks Regional Medical Center	Arkansas City	67%	(a)
Ellsworth County Medical Center	Ellsworth	66%	(a)
Kansas Spine Hospital	Wichita	66%	300+
Kansas Surgery & Recovery Center	Wichita	66%	300+
University of Kansas Hospital	Kansas City	66%	300+
Geary Community Hospital[11]	Junction City	65%	300+
Kansas Medical Center	Andover	65%	300+
Lawrence Memorial Hospital	Lawrence	65%	300+
Pratt Regional Medical Center	Pratt	65%	300+
Cushing Memorial Hospital	Leavenworth	64%	(a)
Mercy Hospital of Kansas Independence	Independence	64%	(a)
Southwest Medical Center	Liberal	64%	300+
Coffey County Hospital	Burlington	63%	300+
Great Bend Regional Hospital	Great Bend	63%	300+
Summit Surgical	Hutchinson	63%	(a)
Doctors Hospital	Leawood	62%	(a)
Kingman Community Hospital	Kingman	62%	(a)
Mercy Health Center	Fort Scott	62%	300+
Mercy Hospital	Moundridge	62%	(a)
Saint Francis Health Center	Topeka	62%	300+
Saint Luke's South Hospital	Overland Park	62%	300+
Hays Medical Center	Hays	61%	300+
Olathe Medical Center	Olathe	61%	300+
Susan B Allen Memorial Hospital	El Dorado	61%	300+
Central Kansas Medical Center	Great Bend	60%	(a)
Newman Regional Health	Emporia	60%	300+
Ransom Memorial Hospital	Ottawa	60%	300+
Shawnee Mission Medical Center	Shawnee Miss.	60%	300+
Stormont-Vail Healthcare	Topeka	60%	300+
Memorial Hospital	Mcpherson	59%	300+
Newton Medical Center	Newton	59%	300+
Coffeyville Regional Medical Center	Coffeyville	58%	300+
Menorah Medical Center	Overland Park	58%	300+
Mercy Regional Health Center	Manhattan	58%	300+
Providence Medical Center	Kansas City	57%	300+
Salina Regional Health Center	Salina	57%	300+
Bob Wilson Memorial Grant County Hospital	Ulysses	56%	(a)
Overland Park Regional Medical Center	Overland Park	56%	300+
Saint Catherine Hospital	Garden City	56%	300+
Western Plains Medical Complex	Dodge City	55%	300+
Labette Health	Parsons	54%	300+
Saint John Hospital	Leavenworth	53%	(a)
Via Christi Hospitals Wichita	Wichita	53%	300+
Wesley Medical Center	Wichita	53%	300+
Promise Regional Medical Center Hutchinson	Hutchinson	52%	300+
Galichia Heart Hospital	Wichita	50%	300+
Morton County Hospital	Elkhart	46%	(a)

NOTE: Hospital profiles are in alphabetical order by state, then city, then hospital within the city; Rankings exclude hospitals with less than 25 cases except for patient surveys which excludes hospitals with less than 100 cases; (a) 100–299 cases; (1) The number of cases is too small to be sure how well a hospital is performing; (2) The hospital indicated that the data submitted for this measure were based on a sample of cases; (3) Data was collected during a shorter time period (fewer quarters) than the maximum possible time for this measure; (4) Suppressed for one or more quarters by CMS; (5) No data is available from the hospital for this measure; (6) Fewer than 100 patients completed the HCAHPS survey. Use these rates with caution, as the number of surveys may be too low to reliably assess hospital performance; (7) Survey results are based on less than 12 months of data; (8) Survey results are not available for this reporting period; (9) No or very few patients were eligible for the HCAHPS survey. The scores shown, if any, reflect a very small number of surveys; (10) A state average was not calculated because too few hospitals in the state submitted data; (11) There were discrepancies in the data collection process; Please refer to the User's Guide for a full explanation of data.

45. Nurses 'Always' Communicated Well

Hospital Name	City	Rate	Cases
Salina Surgical Hospital	Salina	92%	300+
Manhattan Surgical Hospital	Manhattan	90%	(a)
Summit Surgical	Hutchinson	88%	(a)
Doctors Hospital	Leawood	86%	(a)
Kansas Heart Hospital	Wichita	86%	300+
Kingman Community Hospital	Kingman	86%	(a)
Neosho Memorial Regional Medical Center	Chanute	86%	300+
Heartland Surgical Spec Hospital	Overland Park	85%	300+
Kansas City Orthopaedic Institute	Leawood	85%	300+
Mercy Hospital	Moundridge	84%	(a)
Miami County Medical Center	Paola	83%	(a)
Pratt Regional Medical Center	Pratt	83%	300+
Kansas Medical Center	Andover	82%	300+
Mercy Health Center	Fort Scott	82%	300+
Kansas Spine Hospital	Wichita	81%	300+
William Newton Hospital	Winfield	81%	(a)
Kansas Surgery & Recovery Center	Wichita	80%	300+
Ransom Memorial Hospital	Ottawa	80%	300+
Via Christi Hospital Pittsburg	Pittsburg	80%	300+
South Central Ks Regional Medical Center	Arkansas City	79%	(a)
University of Kansas Hospital	Kansas City	79%	300+
Coffey County Hospital	Burlington	78%	300+
Great Bend Regional Hospital	Great Bend	78%	300+
Lawrence Memorial Hospital	Lawrence	78%	300+
Mercy Hospital of Kansas Independence	Independence	78%	(a)
Mercy Regional Health Center	Manhattan	78%	300+
Newton Medical Center	Newton	78%	300+
Central Kansas Medical Center	Great Bend	77%	(a)
Galichia Heart Hospital	Wichita	77%	300+
Geary Community Hospital[11]	Junction City	77%	300+
Labette Health	Parsons	77%	300+
Stormont-Vail Healthcare	Topeka	77%	300+
Bob Wilson Memorial Grant County Hospital	Ulysses	76%	(a)
Cushing Memorial Hospital	Leavenworth	76%	(a)
Ellsworth County Medical Center	Ellsworth	76%	(a)
Hays Medical Center	Hays	76%	300+
Saint Francis Health Center	Topeka	76%	300+
Olathe Medical Center	Olathe	75%	300+
Saint Luke's South Hospital	Overland Park	75%	300+
Susan B Allen Memorial Hospital	El Dorado	75%	300+
Memorial Hospital	Mcpherson	74%	300+
Salina Regional Health Center	Salina	74%	300+
Coffeyville Regional Medical Center	Coffeyville	73%	300+
Newman Regional Health	Emporia	73%	300+
Overland Park Regional Medical Center	Overland Park	73%	300+
Shawnee Mission Medical Center	Shawnee Miss.	73%	300+
Southwest Medical Center	Liberal	73%	300+
Western Plains Medical Complex	Dodge City	73%	300+
Menorah Medical Center	Overland Park	72%	300+
Saint John Hospital	Leavenworth	72%	(a)
Promise Regional Medical Center Hutchinson	Hutchinson	70%	300+
Providence Medical Center	Kansas City	70%	300+
Saint Catherine Hospital	Garden City	70%	300+
Via Christi Hospitals Wichita	Wichita	69%	300+
Wesley Medical Center	Wichita	69%	300+
Morton County Hospital	Elkhart	68%	(a)

46. Pain 'Always' Well Controlled

Hospital Name	City	Rate	Cases
Manhattan Surgical Hospital	Manhattan	83%	(a)
Kansas City Orthopaedic Institute	Leawood	79%	300+
Salina Surgical Hospital	Salina	79%	300+
Miami County Medical Center	Paola	77%	(a)
Neosho Memorial Regional Medical Center	Chanute	77%	300+
Heartland Surgical Spec Hospital	Overland Park	76%	300+
Pratt Regional Medical Center	Pratt	76%	300+
Doctors Hospital	Leawood	75%	(a)
Kansas Heart Hospital	Wichita	75%	300+
Mercy Hospital	Moundridge	75%	(a)
Mercy Hospital of Kansas Independence	Independence	75%	(a)
Summit Surgical	Hutchinson	75%	(a)
Kingman Community Hospital	Kingman	74%	(a)
William Newton Hospital	Winfield	74%	(a)
Kansas Spine Hospital	Wichita	73%	300+
Kansas Surgery & Recovery Center	Wichita	73%	300+
Mercy Regional Health Center	Manhattan	73%	300+
South Central Ks Regional Medical Center	Arkansas City	73%	(a)
Via Christi Hospital Pittsburg	Pittsburg	73%	300+
Great Bend Regional Hospital	Great Bend	72%	300+
Mercy Health Center	Fort Scott	72%	300+
Newton Medical Center	Newton	72%	300+
Saint Francis Health Center	Topeka	72%	300+
Saint Luke's South Hospital	Overland Park	72%	300+
Ransom Memorial Hospital	Ottawa	71%	300+
Bob Wilson Memorial Grant County Hospital	Ulysses	70%	(a)
Coffey County Hospital	Burlington	70%	300+
Cushing Memorial Hospital	Leavenworth	70%	(a)
Galichia Heart Hospital	Wichita	70%	300+
Kansas Medical Center	Andover	70%	300+
Memorial Hospital	Mcpherson	69%	300+
Olathe Medical Center	Olathe	69%	300+
Overland Park Regional Medical Center	Overland Park	69%	300+
Shawnee Mission Medical Center	Shawnee Miss.	69%	300+
Southwest Medical Center	Liberal	69%	300+
Stormont-Vail Healthcare	Topeka	69%	300+
University of Kansas Hospital	Kansas City	69%	300+
Geary Community Hospital[11]	Junction City	68%	300+
Hays Medical Center	Hays	68%	300+
Labette Health	Parsons	68%	300+
Lawrence Memorial Hospital	Lawrence	68%	300+
Menorah Medical Center	Overland Park	68%	300+
Newman Regional Health	Emporia	68%	300+
Saint Catherine Hospital	Garden City	68%	300+
Susan B Allen Memorial Hospital	El Dorado	68%	300+
Western Plains Medical Complex	Dodge City	68%	300+
Central Kansas Medical Center	Great Bend	67%	(a)
Coffeyville Regional Medical Center	Coffeyville	65%	300+
Saint John Hospital	Leavenworth	65%	(a)
Wesley Medical Center	Wichita	65%	300+
Ellsworth County Medical Center	Ellsworth	64%	(a)
Promise Regional Medical Center Hutchinson	Hutchinson	63%	300+
Salina Regional Health Center	Salina	63%	300+
Via Christi Hospitals Wichita	Wichita	62%	300+
Morton County Hospital	Elkhart	61%	(a)
Providence Medical Center	Kansas City	61%	300+

47. Room and Bathroom 'Always' Clean

Hospital Name	City	Rate	Cases
Kansas Heart Hospital	Wichita	90%	300+
Manhattan Surgical Hospital	Manhattan	90%	(a)
Salina Surgical Hospital	Salina	89%	300+
Mercy Hospital	Moundridge	86%	(a)
Doctors Hospital	Leawood	85%	(a)
Neosho Memorial Regional Medical Center	Chanute	85%	300+
Ellsworth County Medical Center	Ellsworth	82%	(a)
Summit Surgical	Hutchinson	82%	(a)
Heartland Surgical Spec Hospital	Overland Park	81%	300+
Coffey County Hospital	Burlington	80%	300+
Kansas City Orthopaedic Institute	Leawood	80%	300+
Kansas Medical Center	Andover	80%	300+
Kansas Surgery & Recovery Center	Wichita	80%	300+
Bob Wilson Memorial Grant County Hospital	Ulysses	77%	(a)
Kansas Spine Hospital	Wichita	77%	300+
Mercy Health Center	Fort Scott	77%	300+
Pratt Regional Medical Center	Pratt	77%	300+
Miami County Medical Center	Paola	76%	(a)
Newton Medical Center	Newton	76%	300+
William Newton Hospital	Winfield	76%	(a)
Cushing Memorial Hospital	Leavenworth	75%	(a)
Great Bend Regional Hospital	Great Bend	75%	300+
Mercy Hospital of Kansas Independence	Independence	75%	(a)
South Central Ks Regional Medical Center	Arkansas City	75%	(a)
Southwest Medical Center	Liberal	75%	300+
Hays Medical Center	Hays	74%	300+
Labette Health	Parsons	74%	300+
Newman Regional Health	Emporia	74%	300+
Via Christi Hospital Pittsburg	Pittsburg	74%	300+
Salina Regional Health Center	Salina	73%	300+
Geary Community Hospital[11]	Junction City	72%	300+
Lawrence Memorial Hospital	Lawrence	72%	300+
Galichia Heart Hospital	Wichita	71%	300+
Memorial Hospital	Mcpherson	71%	300+
Saint Luke's South Hospital	Overland Park	71%	300+
Kingman Community Hospital	Kingman	70%	(a)
Ransom Memorial Hospital	Ottawa	69%	300+
Stormont-Vail Healthcare	Topeka	69%	300+
Susan B Allen Memorial Hospital	El Dorado	69%	300+
Mercy Regional Health Center	Manhattan	68%	300+
Saint Catherine Hospital	Garden City	68%	300+
University of Kansas Hospital	Kansas City	68%	300+
Central Kansas Medical Center	Great Bend	67%	(a)
Morton County Hospital	Elkhart	67%	(a)
Coffeyville Regional Medical Center	Coffeyville	66%	300+
Promise Regional Medical Center Hutchinson	Hutchinson	66%	300+
Saint John Hospital	Leavenworth	66%	(a)
Shawnee Mission Medical Center	Shawnee Miss.	66%	300+
Via Christi Hospitals Wichita	Wichita	66%	300+
Olathe Medical Center	Olathe	63%	300+
Overland Park Regional Medical Center	Overland Park	63%	300+
Saint Francis Health Center	Topeka	63%	300+
Providence Medical Center	Kansas City	61%	300+
Wesley Medical Center	Wichita	61%	300+
Western Plains Medical Complex	Dodge City	60%	300+
Menorah Medical Center	Overland Park	57%	300+

48. Timely Help 'Always' Received

Hospital Name	City	Rate	Cases
Kansas City Orthopaedic Institute	Leawood	89%	300+
Manhattan Surgical Hospital	Manhattan	89%	(a)
Salina Surgical Hospital	Salina	89%	300+
Heartland Surgical Spec Hospital	Overland Park	85%	300+
Summit Surgical	Hutchinson	84%	(a)
Kansas Heart Hospital	Wichita	83%	300+
Mercy Hospital	Moundridge	80%	(a)
Doctors Hospital	Leawood	77%	(a)
Neosho Memorial Regional Medical Center	Chanute	77%	300+
Mercy Health Center	Fort Scott	75%	300+
Mercy Hospital of Kansas Independence	Independence	75%	(a)
Kansas Medical Center	Andover	74%	300+
Pratt Regional Medical Center	Pratt	74%	300+
Central Kansas Medical Center	Great Bend	73%	(a)
Kansas Spine Hospital	Wichita	73%	300+
Miami County Medical Center	Paola	73%	(a)
Cushing Memorial Hospital	Leavenworth	72%	(a)
Great Bend Regional Hospital	Great Bend	72%	300+
Kingman Community Hospital	Kingman	72%	(a)
Saint Luke's South Hospital	Overland Park	72%	300+
Ellsworth County Medical Center	Ellsworth	71%	(a)
South Central Ks Regional Medical Center	Arkansas City	71%	(a)
Ransom Memorial Hospital	Ottawa	70%	300+
William Newton Hospital	Winfield	70%	(a)
Kansas Surgery & Recovery Center	Wichita	69%	300+
Bob Wilson Memorial Grant County Hospital	Ulysses	68%	(a)
Coffey County Hospital	Burlington	68%	300+
Labette Health	Parsons	67%	300+
Memorial Hospital	Mcpherson	67%	300+
Newton Medical Center	Newton	67%	300+
Via Christi Hospital Pittsburg	Pittsburg	67%	300+
Lawrence Memorial Hospital	Lawrence	66%	300+
Susan B Allen Memorial Hospital	El Dorado	66%	300+
Mercy Regional Health Center	Manhattan	65%	300+
Saint John Hospital	Leavenworth	65%	(a)
Stormont-Vail Healthcare	Topeka	65%	300+
Geary Community Hospital[11]	Junction City	64%	300+
Galichia Heart Hospital	Wichita	63%	300+
University of Kansas Hospital	Kansas City	63%	300+
Newman Regional Health	Emporia	62%	300+
Saint Francis Health Center	Topeka	62%	300+
Southwest Medical Center	Liberal	62%	300+
Olathe Medical Center	Olathe	61%	300+
Coffeyville Regional Medical Center	Coffeyville	60%	300+
Hays Medical Center	Hays	60%	300+
Providence Medical Center	Kansas City	59%	300+
Salina Regional Health Center	Salina	58%	300+
Shawnee Mission Medical Center	Shawnee Miss.	57%	300+
Menorah Medical Center	Overland Park	56%	300+
Overland Park Regional Medical Center	Overland Park	56%	300+
Promise Regional Medical Center Hutchinson	Hutchinson	56%	300+
Saint Catherine Hospital	Garden City	56%	300+
Western Plains Medical Complex	Dodge City	55%	300+
Morton County Hospital	Elkhart	53%	(a)
Wesley Medical Center	Wichita	53%	300+
Via Christi Hospitals Wichita	Wichita	50%	300+

49. Would Definitely Recommend Hospital

Hospital Name	City	Rate	Cases
Manhattan Surgical Hospital	Manhattan	94%	(a)
Salina Surgical Hospital	Salina	94%	300+
Kansas City Orthopaedic Institute	Leawood	93%	300+
Heartland Surgical Spec Hospital	Overland Park	91%	300+
Kansas Heart Hospital	Wichita	91%	300+
Summit Surgical	Hutchinson	90%	(a)
Mercy Hospital	Moundridge	87%	(a)
Kansas Spine Hospital	Wichita	84%	300+
Kansas Surgery & Recovery Center	Wichita	84%	300+
Doctors Hospital	Leawood	83%	(a)
Newton Medical Center	Newton	82%	300+
Great Bend Regional Hospital	Great Bend	80%	300+
Kansas Medical Center	Andover	79%	300+
Miami County Medical Center	Paola	79%	(a)
Neosho Memorial Regional Medical Center	Chanute	79%	300+
Saint Luke's South Hospital	Overland Park	79%	300+
University of Kansas Hospital	Kansas City	79%	300+
Coffey County Hospital	Burlington	78%	300+
Galichia Heart Hospital	Wichita	78%	300+
Pratt Regional Medical Center	Pratt	78%	300+
Stormont-Vail Healthcare	Topeka	78%	300+
Kingman Community Hospital	Kingman	76%	(a)
Lawrence Memorial Hospital	Lawrence	76%	300+
Olathe Medical Center	Olathe	76%	300+
Saint Francis Health Center	Topeka	74%	300+
Mercy Regional Health Center	Manhattan	73%	300+
Salina Regional Health Center	Salina	73%	300+
Menorah Medical Center	Overland Park	72%	300+
Ransom Memorial Hospital	Ottawa	72%	300+
Shawnee Mission Medical Center	Shawnee Miss.	72%	300+
William Newton Hospital	Winfield	72%	(a)
Ellsworth County Medical Center	Ellsworth	71%	(a)

NOTE: Hospital profiles are in alphabetical order by state, then city, then hospital within the city; Rankings exclude hospitals with less than 25 cases except for patient surveys which excludes hospitals with less than 100 cases; (a) 100–299 cases; (1) The number of cases is too small to be sure how well a hospital is performing; (2) The hospital indicated that the data submitted for this measure were based on a sample of cases; (3) Data was collected during a shorter time period (fewer quarters) than the maximum possible time for this measure; (4) Suppressed for one or more quarters by CMS; (5) No data is available from the hospital for this measure; (6) Fewer than 100 patients completed the HCAHPS survey. Use these rates with caution, as the number of surveys may be too low to reliably assess hospital performance; (7) Survey results are based on less than 12 months of data; (8) Survey results are not available for this reporting period; (9) No or very few patients were eligible for the HCAHPS survey. The scores shown, if any, reflect a very small number of surveys; (10) A state average was not calculated because too few hospitals in the state submitted data; (11) There were discrepancies in the data collection process; Please refer to the User's Guide for a full explanation of data.

Hays Medical Center	Hays	71%	300+
Susan B Allen Memorial Hospital	El Dorado	71%	300+
Geary Community Hospital[11]	Junction City	70%	300+
Morton County Hospital	Elkhart	69%	(a)
Via Christi Hospitals Wichita	Wichita	69%	300+
Central Kansas Medical Center	Great Bend	68%	(a)
Labette Health	Parsons	68%	300+
Overland Park Regional Medical Center	Overland Park	68%	300+
Via Christi Hospital Pittsburg	Pittsburg	68%	300+
Cushing Memorial Hospital	Leavenworth	67%	(a)
Southwest Medical Center	Liberal	67%	300+
Mercy Hospital of Kansas Independence	Independence	66%	(a)
Memorial Hospital	Mcpherson	65%	300+
South Central Ks Regional Medical Center	Arkansas City	65%	(a)
Saint John Hospital	Leavenworth	63%	(a)
Wesley Medical Center	Wichita	63%	300+
Bob Wilson Memorial Grant County Hospital	Ulysses	62%	(a)
Promise Regional Medical Center Hutchinson	Hutchinson	62%	300+
Saint Catherine Hospital	Garden City	62%	300+
Mercy Health Center	Fort Scott	61%	300+
Coffeyville Regional Medical Center	Coffeyville	59%	300+
Providence Medical Center	Kansas City	58%	300+
Western Plains Medical Complex	Dodge City	55%	300+
Newman Regional Health	Emporia	54%	300+

NOTE: Hospital profiles are in alphabetical order by state, then city, then hospital within the city; Rankings exclude hospitals with less than 25 cases except for patient surveys which excludes hospitals with less than 100 cases; (a) 100–299 cases; (1) The number of cases is too small to be sure how well a hospital is performing; (2) The hospital indicated that the data submitted for this measure were based on a sample of cases; (3) Data was collected during a shorter time period (fewer quarters) than the maximum possible time for this measure; (4) Suppressed for one or more quarters by CMS; (5) No data is available from the hospital for this measure; (6) Fewer than 100 patients completed the HCAHPS survey. Use these rates with caution, as the number of surveys may be too low to reliably assess hospital performance; (7) Survey results are based on less than 12 months of data; (8) Survey results are not available for this reporting period; (9) No or very few patients were eligible for the HCAHPS survey. The scores shown, if any, reflect a very small number of surveys; (10) A state average was not calculated because too few hospitals in the state submitted data; (11) There were discrepancies in the data collection process; Please refer to the User's Guide for a full explanation of data.

Memorial Hospital

511 NE 10th St
Abilene, KS 67410
Phone: 620-263-6610
Fax: 785-263-6622
URL: www.mhsks.org
Type: Critical Access Hospitals
Emergency Services: Yes
Ownership: Govt - Hospital Dist/Auth
Beds: 25

Key Personnel:
CEO/President . . . . Mark A Miller
Chief of Medical Staff . . . . Chantel Long, MD
Infection Control . . . . Carol Landis, RN
Operating Room . . . . Marcus Gann, MD
Quality Assurance . . . . Sara Rosebrook
Radiology . . . . Jim Bartin
Emergency Room . . . . Carol Ross

Measure	Cases	This Hosp.	State Avg.	U.S. Avg.
Heart Attack Care				
ACE Inhibitor or ARB for LVSD	0	-	95%	96%
Aspirin at Arrival[1]	4	100%	98%	99%
Aspirin at Discharge[1]	2	100%	98%	98%
Beta Blocker at Discharge[1]	3	100%	98%	98%
Fibrinolytic Medication Timing	0	-	44%	55%
PCI Within 90 Minutes of Arrival	0	-	91%	90%
Smoking Cessation Advice	0	-	99%	99%
Chest Pain/Possible Heart Attack Care				
Aspirin at Arrival	-	-	92%	95%
Median Time to ECG (minutes)	-	-	10	8
Median Time to Transfer (minutes)	-	-	60	61
Fibrinolytic Medication Timing	-	-	42%	54%
Heart Failure Care				
ACE Inhibitor or ARB for LVSD[1]	2	50%	91%	94%
Discharge Instructions[1]	11	9%	83%	88%
Evaluation of LVS Function	33	79%	92%	98%
Smoking Cessation Advice[1]	1	0%	94%	98%
Pneumonia Care				
Appropriate Initial Antibiotic[1]	22	64%	87%	92%
Blood Culture Timing[1]	18	83%	96%	96%
Influenza Vaccine	29	76%	87%	91%
Initial Antibiotic Timing	25	96%	95%	95%
Pneumococcal Vaccine	36	58%	88%	93%
Smoking Cessation Advice[1]	4	50%	93%	97%
Surgical Care Improvement Project				
Appropriate VTP Within 24 Hours[5]	0	-	89%	92%
Appropriate Hair Removal[5]	0	-	100%	99%
Appropriate Beta Blocker Usage[5]	0	-	90%	93%
Controlled Postoperative Blood Glucose[5]	0	-	92%	93%
Prophylactic Antibiotic Timing[5]	0	-	96%	97%
Prophylactic Antibiotic Timing (Outpatient)	-	-	93%	92%
Prophylactic Antibiotic Selection[5]	0	-	97%	97%
Prophylactic Antibiotic Select. (Outpatient)	-	-	96%	94%
Prophylactic Antibiotic Stopped[5]	0	-	93%	94%
Recommended VTP Ordered[5]	0	-	91%	94%
Urinary Catheter Removal[5]	0	-	86%	90%
Children's Asthma Care				
Received Systemic Corticosteroids	-	-	-	100%
Received Home Management Plan	-	-	-	71%
Received Reliever Medication	-	-	-	100%
Use of Medical Imaging				
Combination Abdominal CT Scan	-	-	0.365	0.191
Combination Chest CT Scan	-	-	0.065	0.054
Follow-up Mammogram/Ultrasound	-	-	7.3%	8.4%
MRI for Low Back Pain	-	-	34.5%	32.7%
Survey of Patients' Hospital Experiences				
Area Around Room 'Always' Quiet at Night[8]	-	-	-	58%
Doctors 'Always' Communicated Well[8]	-	-	-	80%
Home Recovery Information Given[8]	-	-	-	82%
Hospital Given 9 or 10 on 10 Point Scale[8]	-	-	-	67%
Meds 'Always' Explained Before Given[8]	-	-	-	60%
Nurses 'Always' Communicated Well[8]	-	-	-	76%
Pain 'Always' Well Controlled[8]	-	-	-	69%
Room and Bathroom 'Always' Clean[8]	-	-	-	71%
Timely Help 'Always' Received[8]	-	-	-	64%
Would Definitely Recommend Hospital[8]	-	-	-	69%

Kansas Medical Center

1124 West 21st Street
Andover, KS 67002
Phone: 316-300-4000
URL: www.ksmedcenter.com
Type: Acute Care Hospitals
Emergency Services: No
Ownership: Proprietary
Beds: 60

Measure	Cases	This Hosp.	State Avg.	U.S. Avg.
Heart Attack Care				
ACE Inhibitor or ARB for LVSD[1]	15	93%	95%	96%
Aspirin at Arrival[1]	24	96%	98%	99%
Aspirin at Discharge	88	95%	98%	98%
Beta Blocker at Discharge	77	92%	98%	98%
Fibrinolytic Medication Timing	0	-	44%	55%
PCI Within 90 Minutes of Arrival[1]	5	100%	91%	90%
Smoking Cessation Advice	27	100%	99%	99%
Chest Pain/Possible Heart Attack Care				
Aspirin at Arrival[1,3]	3	67%	92%	95%
Median Time to ECG (minutes)[1,3]	3	17	10	8
Median Time to Transfer (minutes)[5]	0	-	60	61
Fibrinolytic Medication Timing[5]	0	-	42%	54%
Heart Failure Care				
ACE Inhibitor or ARB for LVSD	25	96%	91%	94%
Discharge Instructions	54	81%	83%	88%
Evaluation of LVS Function	63	97%	92%	98%
Smoking Cessation Advice[1]	10	90%	94%	98%
Pneumonia Care				
Appropriate Initial Antibiotic[1]	11	82%	87%	92%
Blood Culture Timing[1]	16	94%	96%	96%
Influenza Vaccine[1]	13	85%	87%	91%
Initial Antibiotic Timing[1]	13	92%	95%	95%
Pneumococcal Vaccine	27	74%	88%	93%
Smoking Cessation Advice[1]	5	100%	93%	97%
Surgical Care Improvement Project				
Appropriate VTP Within 24 Hours[2]	49	94%	89%	92%
Appropriate Hair Removal[2]	389	98%	100%	99%
Appropriate Beta Blocker Usage[2]	158	84%	90%	93%
Controlled Postoperative Blood Glucose[2]	164	87%	92%	93%
Prophylactic Antibiotic Timing[2]	274	93%	96%	97%
Prophylactic Antibiotic Timing (Outpatient)	181	99%	93%	92%
Prophylactic Antibiotic Selection[2]	277	100%	97%	97%
Prophylactic Antibiotic Select. (Outpatient)	181	99%	96%	94%
Prophylactic Antibiotic Stopped[2]	270	89%	93%	94%
Recommended VTP Ordered[2]	50	94%	91%	94%
Urinary Catheter Removal[2]	134	89%	86%	90%
Children's Asthma Care				
Received Systemic Corticosteroids	-	-	-	100%
Received Home Management Plan	-	-	-	71%
Received Reliever Medication	-	-	-	100%
Use of Medical Imaging				
Combination Abdominal CT Scan	110	0.355	0.365	0.191
Combination Chest CT Scan	84	0.131	0.065	0.054
Follow-up Mammogram/Ultrasound[5]	0	-	7.3%	8.4%
MRI for Low Back Pain[5]	0	-	34.5%	32.7%
Survey of Patients' Hospital Experiences				
Area Around Room 'Always' Quiet at Night	300+	70%	-	58%
Doctors 'Always' Communicated Well	300+	84%	-	80%
Home Recovery Information Given	300+	86%	-	82%
Hospital Given 9 or 10 on 10 Point Scale	300+	83%	-	67%
Meds 'Always' Explained Before Given	300+	65%	-	60%
Nurses 'Always' Communicated Well	300+	82%	-	76%
Pain 'Always' Well Controlled	300+	70%	-	69%
Room and Bathroom 'Always' Clean	300+	80%	-	71%
Timely Help 'Always' Received	300+	74%	-	64%
Would Definitely Recommend Hospital	300+	79%	-	69%

South Central Ks Regional Medical Center

216 West Birch Avenue
Arkansas City, KS 67005
Phone: 620-442-2500
Fax: 620-441-5966
E-mail: ceo@sckrmc.com
URL: www.sckrmc.com
Type: Acute Care Hospitals
Emergency Services: Yes
Ownership: Voluntary Non-Profit - Other
Beds: 85

Key Personnel:
CEO/President . . . . Phyllis Macy-Mills
Chief of Medical Staff . . . . Kamran Shahzada, MD

Measure	Cases	This Hosp.	State Avg.	U.S. Avg.
Heart Attack Care				
ACE Inhibitor or ARB for LVSD[1,3]	1	100%	95%	96%
Aspirin at Arrival[1,3]	3	100%	98%	99%
Aspirin at Discharge[1,3]	3	100%	98%	98%
Beta Blocker at Discharge[1,3]	4	50%	98%	98%
Fibrinolytic Medication Timing[1,3]	1	0%	44%	55%
PCI Within 90 Minutes of Arrival[3]	0	-	91%	90%
Smoking Cessation Advice[1,3]	1	100%	99%	99%
Chest Pain/Possible Heart Attack Care				
Aspirin at Arrival	47	89%	92%	95%
Median Time to ECG (minutes)	47	12	10	8
Median Time to Transfer (minutes)[1,3]	2	156	60	61
Fibrinolytic Medication Timing[1]	4	25%	42%	54%
Heart Failure Care				
ACE Inhibitor or ARB for LVSD[1]	4	100%	91%	94%
Discharge Instructions[1]	21	33%	83%	88%
Evaluation of LVS Function	28	75%	92%	98%
Smoking Cessation Advice[1]	2	100%	94%	98%
Pneumonia Care				
Appropriate Initial Antibiotic[1]	19	79%	87%	92%
Blood Culture Timing[1]	6	100%	96%	96%
Influenza Vaccine	27	89%	87%	91%
Initial Antibiotic Timing	36	94%	95%	95%
Pneumococcal Vaccine	31	87%	88%	93%
Smoking Cessation Advice[1]	11	91%	93%	97%
Surgical Care Improvement Project				
Appropriate VTP Within 24 Hours	42	67%	89%	92%
Appropriate Hair Removal	70	100%	100%	99%
Appropriate Beta Blocker Usage[1]	18	94%	90%	93%
Controlled Postoperative Blood Glucose	0	-	92%	93%
Prophylactic Antibiotic Timing	44	98%	96%	97%
Prophylactic Antibiotic Timing (Outpatient)[1,3]	2	100%	93%	92%
Prophylactic Antibiotic Selection	45	96%	97%	97%
Prophylactic Antibiotic Select. (Outpatient)[1,3]	2	0%	96%	94%
Prophylactic Antibiotic Stopped	44	100%	93%	94%
Recommended VTP Ordered	42	69%	91%	94%
Urinary Catheter Removal	30	63%	86%	90%
Children's Asthma Care				
Received Systemic Corticosteroids	-	-	-	100%
Received Home Management Plan	-	-	-	71%
Received Reliever Medication	-	-	-	100%
Use of Medical Imaging				
Combination Abdominal CT Scan	145	0.834	0.365	0.191
Combination Chest CT Scan	130	0.023	0.065	0.054
Follow-up Mammogram/Ultrasound	240	8.8%	7.3%	8.4%
MRI for Low Back Pain[1]	42	23.8%	34.5%	32.7%
Survey of Patients' Hospital Experiences				
Area Around Room 'Always' Quiet at Night	(a)	69%	-	58%
Doctors 'Always' Communicated Well	(a)	90%	-	80%
Home Recovery Information Given	(a)	85%	-	82%
Hospital Given 9 or 10 on 10 Point Scale	(a)	66%	-	67%
Meds 'Always' Explained Before Given	(a)	67%	-	60%
Nurses 'Always' Communicated Well	(a)	79%	-	76%
Pain 'Always' Well Controlled	(a)	73%	-	69%
Room and Bathroom 'Always' Clean	(a)	75%	-	71%
Timely Help 'Always' Received	(a)	71%	-	64%
Would Definitely Recommend Hospital	(a)	65%	-	69%

NOTE: Hospital profiles are in alphabetical order by state, then city, then hospital within the city; Rankings exclude hospitals with less than 25 cases except for patient surveys which excludes hospitals with less than 100 cases; (a) 100–299 cases; (1) The number of cases is too small to be sure how well a hospital is performing; (2) The hospital indicated that the data submitted for this measure were based on a sample of cases; (3) Data was collected during a shorter time period (fewer quarters) than the maximum possible time for this measure; (4) Suppressed for one or more quarters by CMS; (5) No data is available from the hospital for this measure; (6) Fewer than 100 patients completed the HCAHPS survey. Use these rates with caution, as the number of surveys may be too low to reliably assess hospital performance; (7) Survey results are based on less than 12 months of data; (8) Survey results are not available for this reporting period; (9) No or very few patients were eligible for the HCAHPS survey. The scores shown, if any, reflect a very small number of surveys; (10) A state average was not calculated because too few hospitals in the state submitted data; (11) There were discrepancies in the data collection process; Please refer to the User's Guide for a full explanation of data.

Ashland Health Center

709 Oak Street
Ashland, KS 67831
URL: www.phn.org
Type: Critical Access Hospitals
Ownership: Govt - Hospital Dist/Auth
Phone: 620-635-2241
Fax: 620-635-2229
Emergency Services: Yes
Beds: 47

Key Personnel:
CEO/President............... Daryl Marshall
Cardiac Laboratory............ Samuel Todd Stephens, MD
Chief of Medical Staff........ Samuel Todd Stephens
Quality Assurance .... Michelle Moore
Emergency Room .... Michelle Moore

Measure	Cases	This Hosp.	State Avg.	U.S. Avg.
Heart Attack Care				
ACE Inhibitor or ARB for LVSD[3]	0	-	95%	96%
Aspirin at Arrival[3]	0	-	98%	99%
Aspirin at Discharge[3]	0	-	98%	98%
Beta Blocker at Discharge[3]	0	-	98%	98%
Fibrinolytic Medication Timing[3]	0	-	44%	55%
PCI Within 90 Minutes of Arrival[3]	0	-	91%	90%
Smoking Cessation Advice[3]	0	-	99%	99%
Chest Pain/Possible Heart Attack Care				
Aspirin at Arrival	-	-	92%	95%
Median Time to ECG (minutes)	-	-	10	8
Median Time to Transfer (minutes)	-	-	60	61
Fibrinolytic Medication Timing	-	-	42%	54%
Heart Failure Care				
ACE Inhibitor or ARB for LVSD[1,3]	1	100%	91%	94%
Discharge Instructions[1,3]	1	100%	83%	88%
Evaluation of LVS Function[1,3]	4	75%	92%	98%
Smoking Cessation Advice[3]	0	-	94%	98%
Pneumonia Care				
Appropriate Initial Antibiotic[1,3]	6	83%	87%	92%
Blood Culture Timing[3]	0	-	96%	96%
Influenza Vaccine[1,3]	1	100%	87%	91%
Initial Antibiotic Timing[1,3]	5	100%	95%	95%
Pneumococcal Vaccine[1,3]	9	100%	88%	93%
Smoking Cessation Advice[1,3]	2	0%	93%	97%
Surgical Care Improvement Project				
Appropriate VTP Within 24 Hours[5]	0	-	89%	92%
Appropriate Hair Removal[5]	0	-	100%	99%
Appropriate Beta Blocker Usage[5]	0	-	90%	93%
Controlled Postoperative Blood Glucose[5]	0	-	92%	93%
Prophylactic Antibiotic Timing[5]	0	-	96%	97%
Prophylactic Antibiotic Timing (Outpatient)	-	-	93%	92%
Prophylactic Antibiotic Selection[5]	0	-	97%	97%
Prophylactic Antibiotic Select. (Outpatient)	-	-	96%	94%
Prophylactic Antibiotic Stopped[5]	0	-	93%	94%
Recommended VTP Ordered[5]	0	-	91%	94%
Urinary Catheter Removal[5]	0	-	86%	90%
Children's Asthma Care				
Received Systemic Corticosteroids	-	-	-	100%
Received Home Management Plan	-	-	-	71%
Received Reliever Medication	-	-	-	100%
Use of Medical Imaging				
Combination Abdominal CT Scan	-	-	0.365	0.191
Combination Chest CT Scan	-	-	0.065	0.054
Follow-up Mammogram/Ultrasound	-	-	7.3%	8.4%
MRI for Low Back Pain	-	-	34.5%	32.7%
Survey of Patients' Hospital Experiences				
Area Around Room 'Always' Quiet at Night[8]	-	-	-	58%
Doctors 'Always' Communicated Well[8]	-	-	-	80%
Home Recovery Information Given[8]	-	-	-	82%
Hospital Given 9 or 10 on 10 Point Scale[8]	-	-	-	67%
Meds 'Always' Explained Before Given[8]	-	-	-	60%
Nurses 'Always' Communicated Well[8]	-	-	-	76%
Pain 'Always' Well Controlled[8]	-	-	-	69%
Room and Bathroom 'Always' Clean[8]	-	-	-	71%
Timely Help 'Always' Received[8]	-	-	-	64%
Would Definitely Recommend Hospital[8]	-	-	-	69%

Atchison Hospital

800 Ravin Hill Drive
Atchison, KS 66002
Type: Critical Access Hospitals
Ownership: Voluntary Non-Profit - Private
Phone: 913-367-2131
Fax: 913-367-2913
Emergency Services: Yes
Beds: 115

Key Personnel:
CEO/President............... John Jacobson
Chief of Medical Staff.......... Ryan Thomas, MD
Infection Control............. Jim Brown
Operating Room............... Jean Ober
Quality Assurance .... Kathy Butler
Radiology.................... Maryann Scholz
Intensive Care Unit........... Lora Willming
Patient Relations .... Susan Gilkison

Measure	Cases	This Hosp.	State Avg.	U.S. Avg.
Heart Attack Care				
ACE Inhibitor or ARB for LVSD[5]	0	-	95%	96%
Aspirin at Arrival[5]	0	-	98%	99%
Aspirin at Discharge[5]	0	-	98%	98%
Beta Blocker at Discharge[5]	0	-	98%	98%
Fibrinolytic Medication Timing[5]	0	-	44%	55%
PCI Within 90 Minutes of Arrival[5]	0	-	91%	90%
Smoking Cessation Advice[5]	0	-	99%	99%
Chest Pain/Possible Heart Attack Care				
Aspirin at Arrival	-	-	92%	95%
Median Time to ECG (minutes)	-	-	10	8
Median Time to Transfer (minutes)	-	-	60	61
Fibrinolytic Medication Timing	-	-	42%	54%
Heart Failure Care				
ACE Inhibitor or ARB for LVSD[5]	0	-	91%	94%
Discharge Instructions[5]	0	-	83%	88%
Evaluation of LVS Function[5]	0	-	92%	98%
Smoking Cessation Advice[5]	0	-	94%	98%
Pneumonia Care				
Appropriate Initial Antibiotic[5]	0	-	87%	92%
Blood Culture Timing[5]	0	-	96%	96%
Influenza Vaccine[5]	0	-	87%	91%
Initial Antibiotic Timing[5]	0	-	95%	95%
Pneumococcal Vaccine[5]	0	-	88%	93%
Smoking Cessation Advice[5]	0	-	93%	97%
Surgical Care Improvement Project				
Appropriate VTP Within 24 Hours[5]	0	-	89%	92%
Appropriate Hair Removal[5]	0	-	100%	99%
Appropriate Beta Blocker Usage[5]	0	-	90%	93%
Controlled Postoperative Blood Glucose[5]	0	-	92%	93%
Prophylactic Antibiotic Timing[5]	0	-	96%	97%
Prophylactic Antibiotic Timing (Outpatient)	-	-	93%	92%
Prophylactic Antibiotic Selection[5]	0	-	97%	97%
Prophylactic Antibiotic Select. (Outpatient)	-	-	96%	94%
Prophylactic Antibiotic Stopped[5]	0	-	93%	94%
Recommended VTP Ordered[5]	0	-	91%	94%
Urinary Catheter Removal[5]	0	-	86%	90%
Children's Asthma Care				
Received Systemic Corticosteroids	-	-	-	100%
Received Home Management Plan	-	-	-	71%
Received Reliever Medication	-	-	-	100%
Use of Medical Imaging				
Combination Abdominal CT Scan	-	-	0.365	0.191
Combination Chest CT Scan	-	-	0.065	0.054
Follow-up Mammogram/Ultrasound	-	-	7.3%	8.4%
MRI for Low Back Pain	-	-	34.5%	32.7%
Survey of Patients' Hospital Experiences				
Area Around Room 'Always' Quiet at Night[8]	-	-	-	58%
Doctors 'Always' Communicated Well[8]	-	-	-	80%
Home Recovery Information Given[8]	-	-	-	82%
Hospital Given 9 or 10 on 10 Point Scale[8]	-	-	-	67%
Meds 'Always' Explained Before Given[8]	-	-	-	60%
Nurses 'Always' Communicated Well[8]	-	-	-	76%
Pain 'Always' Well Controlled[8]	-	-	-	69%
Room and Bathroom 'Always' Clean[8]	-	-	-	71%
Timely Help 'Always' Received[8]	-	-	-	64%
Would Definitely Recommend Hospital[8]	-	-	-	69%

Republic County Hospital

2420 G Street
Belleville, KS 66935
E-mail: rchospital1@nckcn.com
URL: www.republiccountyhospital.org
Type: Critical Access Hospitals
Ownership: Voluntary Non-Profit - Other
Phone: 785-527-2254
Fax: 785-527-2324
Emergency Services: Yes
Beds: 63

Key Personnel:
CEO/President............... Blaine Miller
Chief of Medical Staff.......... Robert Holt
Radiology.................... Linda Elliott

Measure	Cases	This Hosp.	State Avg.	U.S. Avg.
Heart Attack Care				
ACE Inhibitor or ARB for LVSD[5]	0	-	95%	96%
Aspirin at Arrival[1,3]	6	100%	98%	99%
Aspirin at Discharge[1,3]	5	80%	98%	98%
Beta Blocker at Discharge[1,3]	5	100%	98%	98%
Fibrinolytic Medication Timing[3]	0	-	44%	55%
PCI Within 90 Minutes of Arrival[5]	0	-	91%	90%
Smoking Cessation Advice[3]	0	-	99%	99%
Chest Pain/Possible Heart Attack Care				
Aspirin at Arrival	-	-	92%	95%
Median Time to ECG (minutes)	-	-	10	8
Median Time to Transfer (minutes)	-	-	60	61
Fibrinolytic Medication Timing	-	-	42%	54%
Heart Failure Care				
ACE Inhibitor or ARB for LVSD[5]	0	-	91%	94%
Discharge Instructions[5]	0	-	83%	88%
Evaluation of LVS Function[5]	0	-	92%	98%
Smoking Cessation Advice[5]	0	-	94%	98%
Pneumonia Care				
Appropriate Initial Antibiotic[1,2,3]	15	73%	87%	92%
Blood Culture Timing[2,3]	0	-	96%	96%
Influenza Vaccine[1,3]	13	62%	87%	91%
Initial Antibiotic Timing[1,2,3]	21	95%	95%	95%
Pneumococcal Vaccine[2,3]	27	59%	88%	93%
Smoking Cessation Advice[1,2,3]	4	100%	93%	97%
Surgical Care Improvement Project				
Appropriate VTP Within 24 Hours[1,3]	9	89%	89%	92%
Appropriate Hair Removal[1,3]	15	100%	100%	99%
Appropriate Beta Blocker Usage[5]	0	-	90%	93%
Controlled Postoperative Blood Glucose[3]	0	-	92%	93%
Prophylactic Antibiotic Timing[1,3]	15	80%	96%	97%
Prophylactic Antibiotic Timing (Outpatient)	-	-	93%	92%
Prophylactic Antibiotic Selection[1,3]	15	100%	97%	97%
Prophylactic Antibiotic Select. (Outpatient)	-	-	96%	94%
Prophylactic Antibiotic Stopped[1,3]	15	93%	93%	94%
Recommended VTP Ordered[1,3]	9	89%	91%	94%
Urinary Catheter Removal[1]	5	40%	86%	90%
Children's Asthma Care				
Received Systemic Corticosteroids	-	-	-	100%
Received Home Management Plan	-	-	-	71%
Received Reliever Medication	-	-	-	100%
Use of Medical Imaging				
Combination Abdominal CT Scan	-	-	0.365	0.191
Combination Chest CT Scan	-	-	0.065	0.054
Follow-up Mammogram/Ultrasound	-	-	7.3%	8.4%
MRI for Low Back Pain	-	-	34.5%	32.7%
Survey of Patients' Hospital Experiences				
Area Around Room 'Always' Quiet at Night[8]	-	-	-	58%
Doctors 'Always' Communicated Well[8]	-	-	-	80%
Home Recovery Information Given[8]	-	-	-	82%
Hospital Given 9 or 10 on 10 Point Scale[8]	-	-	-	67%
Meds 'Always' Explained Before Given[8]	-	-	-	60%
Nurses 'Always' Communicated Well[8]	-	-	-	76%
Pain 'Always' Well Controlled[8]	-	-	-	69%
Room and Bathroom 'Always' Clean[8]	-	-	-	71%
Timely Help 'Always' Received[8]	-	-	-	64%
Would Definitely Recommend Hospital[8]	-	-	-	69%

NOTE: Hospital profiles are in alphabetical order by state, then city, then hospital within the city; Rankings exclude hospitals with less than 25 cases except for patient surveys which excludes hospitals with less than 100 cases; (a) 100–299 cases; (1) The number of cases is too small to be sure how well a hospital is performing; (2) The hospital indicated that the data submitted for this measure were based on a sample of cases; (3) Data was collected during a shorter time period (fewer quarters) than the maximum possible time for this measure; (4) Suppressed for one or more quarters by CMS; (5) No data is available from the hospital for this measure; (6) Fewer than 100 patients completed the HCAHPS survey. Use these rates with caution, as the number of surveys may be too low to reliably assess hospital performance; (7) Survey results are based on less than 12 months of data; (8) Survey results are not available for this reporting period; (9) No or very few patients were eligible for the HCAHPS survey. The scores shown, if any, reflect a very small number of surveys; (10) A state average was not calculated because too few hospitals in the state submitted data; (11) There were discrepancies in the data collection process; Please refer to the User's Guide for a full explanation of data.

Mitchell County Hospital Health Systems

400 W 8th Street Phone: 785-738-2266
Beloit, KS 67420 Fax: 785-738-9503
URL: www.gpha.com
Type: Critical Access Hospitals Emergency Services: Yes
Ownership: Government - Local Beds: 99

Key Personnel:
CEO/President. . . . . David Dick
Chief of Medical Staff . . . . Douglas J Drake
Radiology. . . . . Richard J Kueker
Emergency Room . . . . Mary Grey

Measure	Cases	This Hosp.	State Avg.	U.S. Avg.
Heart Attack Care				
ACE Inhibitor or ARB for LVSD[1]	2	100%	95%	96%
Aspirin at Arrival[1]	7	100%	98%	99%
Aspirin at Discharge[1]	5	100%	98%	98%
Beta Blocker at Discharge[1]	6	100%	98%	98%
Fibrinolytic Medication Timing	0	-	44%	55%
PCI Within 90 Minutes of Arrival	0	-	91%	90%
Smoking Cessation Advice[1]	1	0%	99%	99%
Chest Pain/Possible Heart Attack Care				
Aspirin at Arrival	-	-	92%	95%
Median Time to ECG (minutes)	-	-	10	8
Median Time to Transfer (minutes)	-	-	60	61
Fibrinolytic Medication Timing	-	-	42%	54%
Heart Failure Care				
ACE Inhibitor or ARB for LVSD[1]	8	88%	91%	94%
Discharge Instructions[1]	17	59%	83%	88%
Evaluation of LVS Function	33	97%	92%	98%
Smoking Cessation Advice[1]	1	100%	94%	98%
Pneumonia Care				
Appropriate Initial Antibiotic	29	59%	87%	92%
Blood Culture Timing	26	88%	96%	96%
Influenza Vaccine	31	77%	87%	91%
Initial Antibiotic Timing	53	92%	95%	95%
Pneumococcal Vaccine	50	82%	88%	93%
Smoking Cessation Advice[1]	5	100%	93%	97%
Surgical Care Improvement Project				
Appropriate VTP Within 24 Hours[1]	10	80%	89%	92%
Appropriate Hair Removal[1]	18	100%	100%	99%
Appropriate Beta Blocker Usage[1]	6	100%	90%	93%
Controlled Postoperative Blood Glucose	0	-	92%	93%
Prophylactic Antibiotic Timing[1]	11	91%	96%	97%
Prophylactic Antibiotic Timing (Outpatient)	-	-	93%	92%
Prophylactic Antibiotic Selection[1]	11	91%	97%	97%
Prophylactic Antibiotic Select. (Outpatient)	-	-	96%	94%
Prophylactic Antibiotic Stopped[1]	9	100%	93%	94%
Recommended VTP Ordered[1]	10	80%	91%	94%
Urinary Catheter Removal[1]	5	100%	86%	90%
Children's Asthma Care				
Received Systemic Corticosteroids	-	-	-	100%
Received Home Management Plan	-	-	-	71%
Received Reliever Medication	-	-	-	100%
Use of Medical Imaging				
Combination Abdominal CT Scan	-	-	0.365	0.191
Combination Chest CT Scan	-	-	0.065	0.054
Follow-up Mammogram/Ultrasound	-	-	7.3%	8.4%
MRI for Low Back Pain	-	-	34.5%	32.7%
Survey of Patients' Hospital Experiences				
Area Around Room 'Always' Quiet at Night[8]	-	-	-	58%
Doctors 'Always' Communicated Well[8]	-	-	-	80%
Home Recovery Information Given[8]	-	-	-	82%
Hospital Given 9 or 10 on 10 Point Scale[8]	-	-	-	67%
Meds 'Always' Explained Before Given[8]	-	-	-	60%
Nurses 'Always' Communicated Well[8]	-	-	-	76%
Pain 'Always' Well Controlled[8]	-	-	-	69%
Room and Bathroom 'Always' Clean[8]	-	-	-	71%
Timely Help 'Always' Received[8]	-	-	-	64%
Would Definitely Recommend Hospital[8]	-	-	-	69%

Coffey County Hospital

801 N 4th St Phone: 620-364-2121
Burlington, KS 66839 Fax: 620-364-2605
URL: www.coffeyhealth.org
Type: Acute Care Hospitals Emergency Services: Yes
Ownership: Government - Local Beds: 78

Key Personnel:
CEO/President. . . . . Dennis George
Chief of Medical Staff . . . . John Shell, MD
Infection Control. . . . . Elaine Weston, RN
Operating Room. . . . . Sherry Young
Quality Assurance . . . . Rebecca Thurman
Radiology. . . . . Kevin Hughes
Emergency Room . . . . John Shell
Patient Relations . . . . Krystal Nicholson

Measure	Cases	This Hosp.	State Avg.	U.S. Avg.
Heart Attack Care				
ACE Inhibitor or ARB for LVSD[3]	0	-	95%	96%
Aspirin at Arrival[1,3]	2	100%	98%	99%
Aspirin at Discharge[3]	0	-	98%	98%
Beta Blocker at Discharge[3]	0	-	98%	98%
Fibrinolytic Medication Timing[3]	0	-	44%	55%
PCI Within 90 Minutes of Arrival[3]	0	-	91%	90%
Smoking Cessation Advice[3]	0	-	99%	99%
Chest Pain/Possible Heart Attack Care				
Aspirin at Arrival	31	84%	92%	95%
Median Time to ECG (minutes)	32	9	10	8
Median Time to Transfer (minutes)[5]	0	-	60	61
Fibrinolytic Medication Timing[1,3]	1	0%	42%	54%
Heart Failure Care				
ACE Inhibitor or ARB for LVSD[1]	8	62%	91%	94%
Discharge Instructions	37	27%	83%	88%
Evaluation of LVS Function	61	38%	92%	98%
Smoking Cessation Advice[1]	1	100%	94%	98%
Pneumonia Care				
Appropriate Initial Antibiotic	39	97%	87%	92%
Blood Culture Timing[1]	7	100%	96%	96%
Influenza Vaccine	47	68%	87%	91%
Initial Antibiotic Timing	56	98%	95%	95%
Pneumococcal Vaccine	57	65%	88%	93%
Smoking Cessation Advice[1]	20	50%	93%	97%
Surgical Care Improvement Project				
Appropriate VTP Within 24 Hours[1]	3	67%	89%	92%
Appropriate Hair Removal	30	77%	100%	99%
Appropriate Beta Blocker Usage[1]	5	40%	90%	93%
Controlled Postoperative Blood Glucose	0	-	92%	93%
Prophylactic Antibiotic Timing	26	62%	96%	97%
Prophylactic Antibiotic Timing (Outpatient)[1]	13	46%	93%	92%
Prophylactic Antibiotic Selection	26	100%	97%	97%
Prophylactic Antibiotic Select. (Outpatient)[1]	12	67%	96%	94%
Prophylactic Antibiotic Stopped	25	80%	93%	94%
Recommended VTP Ordered[1]	3	67%	91%	94%
Urinary Catheter Removal[1]	11	100%	86%	90%
Children's Asthma Care				
Received Systemic Corticosteroids	-	-	-	100%
Received Home Management Plan	-	-	-	71%
Received Reliever Medication	-	-	-	100%
Use of Medical Imaging				
Combination Abdominal CT Scan	112	0.902	0.365	0.191
Combination Chest CT Scan	59	0.288	0.065	0.054
Follow-up Mammogram/Ultrasound	243	2.5%	7.3%	8.4%
MRI for Low Back Pain	52	30.8%	34.5%	32.7%
Survey of Patients' Hospital Experiences				
Area Around Room 'Always' Quiet at Night	300+	66%	-	58%
Doctors 'Always' Communicated Well	300+	84%	-	80%
Home Recovery Information Given	300+	83%	-	82%
Hospital Given 9 or 10 on 10 Point Scale	300+	76%	-	67%
Meds 'Always' Explained Before Given	300+	63%	-	60%
Nurses 'Always' Communicated Well	300+	78%	-	76%
Pain 'Always' Well Controlled	300+	70%	-	69%
Room and Bathroom 'Always' Clean	300+	80%	-	71%
Timely Help 'Always' Received	300+	68%	-	64%
Would Definitely Recommend Hospital	300+	78%	-	69%

Neosho Memorial Regional Medical Center

629 South Plummer Phone: 620-431-4000
Chanute, KS 66720 Fax: 620-431-7556
URL: www.nmrmc.com
Type: Critical Access Hospitals Emergency Services: Yes
Ownership: Government - Local Beds: 97

Key Personnel:
CEO/President. . . . . Murray L Brown
Chief of Medical Staff . . . . DeAnna Vaugh, MD
Infection Control. . . . . Kathy Wicker, RN
Operating Room. . . . . Billy Browne, RN
Quality Assurance . . . . Sandy Froemming, RN
Radiology. . . . . Mark Witaczack
Emergency Room . . . . Pat Lucke, RN
Intensive Care Unit. . . . . Sandy Froemming, RN

Measure	Cases	This Hosp.	State Avg.	U.S. Avg.
Heart Attack Care				
ACE Inhibitor or ARB for LVSD[1,2]	1	100%	95%	96%
Aspirin at Arrival[1,2]	7	100%	98%	99%
Aspirin at Discharge[1,2]	5	100%	98%	98%
Beta Blocker at Discharge[1,2]	4	75%	98%	98%
Fibrinolytic Medication Timing[5]	0	-	44%	55%
PCI Within 90 Minutes of Arrival[5]	0	-	91%	90%
Smoking Cessation Advice[1,2]	2	100%	99%	99%
Chest Pain/Possible Heart Attack Care				
Aspirin at Arrival	43	100%	92%	95%
Median Time to ECG (minutes)	45	8	10	8
Median Time to Transfer (minutes)[1,3]	2	162	60	61
Fibrinolytic Medication Timing[3]	0	-	42%	54%
Heart Failure Care				
ACE Inhibitor or ARB for LVSD[1]	15	100%	91%	94%
Discharge Instructions	43	100%	83%	88%
Evaluation of LVS Function	69	100%	92%	98%
Smoking Cessation Advice[1]	7	86%	94%	98%
Pneumonia Care				
Appropriate Initial Antibiotic	50	94%	87%	92%
Blood Culture Timing	85	100%	96%	96%
Influenza Vaccine	64	95%	87%	91%
Initial Antibiotic Timing	113	100%	95%	95%
Pneumococcal Vaccine	86	97%	88%	93%
Smoking Cessation Advice	47	98%	93%	97%
Surgical Care Improvement Project				
Appropriate VTP Within 24 Hours[1]	24	92%	89%	92%
Appropriate Hair Removal	48	100%	100%	99%
Appropriate Beta Blocker Usage[1]	9	89%	90%	93%
Controlled Postoperative Blood Glucose[5]	0	-	92%	93%
Prophylactic Antibiotic Timing[1]	21	100%	96%	97%
Prophylactic Antibiotic Timing (Outpatient)	77	100%	93%	92%
Prophylactic Antibiotic Selection[1]	21	100%	97%	97%
Prophylactic Antibiotic Select. (Outpatient)	80	92%	96%	94%
Prophylactic Antibiotic Stopped[1]	20	90%	93%	94%
Recommended VTP Ordered[1]	24	92%	91%	94%
Urinary Catheter Removal[1]	9	100%	86%	90%
Children's Asthma Care				
Received Systemic Corticosteroids	-	-	-	100%
Received Home Management Plan	-	-	-	71%
Received Reliever Medication	-	-	-	100%
Use of Medical Imaging				
Combination Abdominal CT Scan	306	0.062	0.365	0.191
Combination Chest CT Scan	211	0.038	0.065	0.054
Follow-up Mammogram/Ultrasound	425	3.5%	7.3%	8.4%
MRI for Low Back Pain	53	43.4%	34.5%	32.7%
Survey of Patients' Hospital Experiences				
Area Around Room 'Always' Quiet at Night	300+	71%	-	58%
Doctors 'Always' Communicated Well	300+	88%	-	80%
Home Recovery Information Given	300+	87%	-	82%
Hospital Given 9 or 10 on 10 Point Scale	300+	81%	-	67%
Meds 'Always' Explained Before Given	300+	67%	-	60%
Nurses 'Always' Communicated Well	300+	86%	-	76%
Pain 'Always' Well Controlled	300+	77%	-	69%
Room and Bathroom 'Always' Clean	300+	85%	-	71%
Timely Help 'Always' Received	300+	77%	-	64%
Would Definitely Recommend Hospital	300+	79%	-	69%

NOTE: Hospital profiles are in alphabetical order by state, then city, then hospital within the city; Rankings exclude hospitals with less than 25 cases except for patient surveys which excludes hospitals with less than 100 cases; (a) 100–299 cases; (1) The number of cases is too small to be sure how well a hospital is performing; (2) The hospital indicated that the data submitted for this measure were based on a sample of cases; (3) Data was collected during a shorter time period (fewer quarters) than the maximum possible time for this measure; (4) Suppressed for one or more quarters by CMS; (5) No data is available from the hospital for this measure; (6) Fewer than 100 patients completed the HCAHPS survey. Use these rates with caution, as the number of surveys may be too low to reliably assess hospital performance; (7) Survey results are based on less than 12 months of data; (8) Survey results are not available for this reporting period; (9) No or very few patients were eligible for the HCAHPS survey. The scores shown, if any, reflect a very small number of surveys; (10) A state average was not calculated because too few hospitals in the state submitted data; (11) There were discrepancies in the data collection process; Please refer to the User's Guide for a full explanation of data.

Clay County Medical Center

617 Liberty
Clay Center, KS 67432
Phone: 785-632-2144
Type: Critical Access Hospitals
Emergency Services: Yes
Ownership: Voluntary Non-Profit - Other

Key Personnel:
CEO/President. . . . . Ron Bender
Radiology. . . . . James Peterson
Anesthesiology. . . . . Scott Husted

Measure	Cases	This Hosp.	State Avg.	U.S. Avg.
Heart Attack Care				
ACE Inhibitor or ARB for LVSD[5]	0	-	95%	96%
Aspirin at Arrival[5]	0	-	98%	99%
Aspirin at Discharge[5]	0	-	98%	98%
Beta Blocker at Discharge[5]	0	-	98%	98%
Fibrinolytic Medication Timing[5]	0	-	44%	55%
PCI Within 90 Minutes of Arrival[5]	0	-	91%	90%
Smoking Cessation Advice[5]	0	-	99%	99%
Chest Pain/Possible Heart Attack Care				
Aspirin at Arrival	-	-	92%	95%
Median Time to ECG (minutes)	-	-	10	8
Median Time to Transfer (minutes)	-	-	60	61
Fibrinolytic Medication Timing	-	-	42%	54%
Heart Failure Care				
ACE Inhibitor or ARB for LVSD	0	-	91%	94%
Discharge Instructions[1]	7	57%	83%	88%
Evaluation of LVS Function[1]	14	21%	92%	98%
Smoking Cessation Advice[1]	1	0%	94%	98%
Pneumonia Care				
Appropriate Initial Antibiotic[1,2]	17	71%	87%	92%
Blood Culture Timing[1,2]	12	75%	96%	96%
Influenza Vaccine[1]	20	80%	87%	91%
Initial Antibiotic Timing[1,2]	17	71%	95%	95%
Pneumococcal Vaccine[2]	35	100%	88%	93%
Smoking Cessation Advice[1,2]	4	50%	93%	97%
Surgical Care Improvement Project				
Appropriate VTP Within 24 Hours[5]	0	-	89%	92%
Appropriate Hair Removal[5]	0	-	100%	99%
Appropriate Beta Blocker Usage[5]	0	-	90%	93%
Controlled Postoperative Blood Glucose[5]	0	-	92%	93%
Prophylactic Antibiotic Timing[5]	0	-	96%	97%
Prophylactic Antibiotic Timing (Outpatient)	-	-	93%	92%
Prophylactic Antibiotic Selection[5]	0	-	97%	97%
Prophylactic Antibiotic Select. (Outpatient)	-	-	96%	94%
Prophylactic Antibiotic Stopped[5]	0	-	93%	94%
Recommended VTP Ordered[5]	0	-	91%	94%
Urinary Catheter Removal[5]	0	-	86%	90%
Children's Asthma Care				
Received Systemic Corticosteroids	-	-	-	100%
Received Home Management Plan	-	-	-	71%
Received Reliever Medication	-	-	-	100%
Use of Medical Imaging				
Combination Abdominal CT Scan	-	-	0.365	0.191
Combination Chest CT Scan	-	-	0.065	0.054
Follow-up Mammogram/Ultrasound	-	-	7.3%	8.4%
MRI for Low Back Pain	-	-	34.5%	32.7%
Survey of Patients' Hospital Experiences				
Area Around Room 'Always' Quiet at Night[8]	-	-	-	58%
Doctors 'Always' Communicated Well[8]	-	-	-	80%
Home Recovery Information Given[8]	-	-	-	82%
Hospital Given 9 or 10 on 10 Point Scale[8]	-	-	-	67%
Meds 'Always' Explained Before Given[8]	-	-	-	60%
Nurses 'Always' Communicated Well[8]	-	-	-	76%
Pain 'Always' Well Controlled[8]	-	-	-	69%
Room and Bathroom 'Always' Clean[8]	-	-	-	71%
Timely Help 'Always' Received[8]	-	-	-	64%
Would Definitely Recommend Hospital[8]	-	-	-	69%

Coffeyville Regional Medical Center

1400 W 4th St
Coffeyville, KS 67337
Phone: 620-252-1200
Fax: 620-252-1562
E-mail: humanresources@crmcinc.com
URL: www.crmcinc.com
Type: Acute Care Hospitals
Emergency Services: Yes
Ownership: Government - Local
Beds: 148

Key Personnel:
CEO/President. . . . . Jerry Marquette
Chief of Medical Staff . . . . Tiru M Venkat
Quality Assurance . . . . Laura Robson
Radiology. . . . . Donald White

Measure	Cases	This Hosp.	State Avg.	U.S. Avg.
Heart Attack Care				
ACE Inhibitor or ARB for LVSD[1]	4	75%	95%	96%
Aspirin at Arrival[1]	17	88%	98%	99%
Aspirin at Discharge[1]	11	73%	98%	98%
Beta Blocker at Discharge[1]	11	64%	98%	98%
Fibrinolytic Medication Timing	0	-	44%	55%
PCI Within 90 Minutes of Arrival	0	-	91%	90%
Smoking Cessation Advice[1]	2	50%	99%	99%
Chest Pain/Possible Heart Attack Care				
Aspirin at Arrival[1,3]	8	75%	92%	95%
Median Time to ECG (minutes)[1,3]	9	3	10	8
Median Time to Transfer (minutes)[1,3]	1	90	60	61
Fibrinolytic Medication Timing[3]	0	-	42%	54%
Heart Failure Care				
ACE Inhibitor or ARB for LVSD	42	62%	91%	94%
Discharge Instructions	91	69%	83%	88%
Evaluation of LVS Function	131	93%	92%	98%
Smoking Cessation Advice[1]	17	82%	94%	98%
Pneumonia Care				
Appropriate Initial Antibiotic	59	75%	87%	92%
Blood Culture Timing	55	98%	96%	96%
Influenza Vaccine	82	93%	87%	91%
Initial Antibiotic Timing	40	90%	95%	95%
Pneumococcal Vaccine	128	83%	88%	93%
Smoking Cessation Advice	44	73%	93%	97%
Surgical Care Improvement Project				
Appropriate VTP Within 24 Hours	57	81%	89%	92%
Appropriate Hair Removal	113	100%	100%	99%
Appropriate Beta Blocker Usage	26	92%	90%	93%
Controlled Postoperative Blood Glucose	0	-	92%	93%
Prophylactic Antibiotic Timing	38	89%	96%	97%
Prophylactic Antibiotic Timing (Outpatient)	50	88%	93%	92%
Prophylactic Antibiotic Selection	40	100%	97%	97%
Prophylactic Antibiotic Select. (Outpatient)	69	94%	96%	94%
Prophylactic Antibiotic Stopped	32	97%	93%	94%
Recommended VTP Ordered	58	79%	91%	94%
Urinary Catheter Removal[1]	16	88%	86%	90%
Children's Asthma Care				
Received Systemic Corticosteroids	-	-	-	100%
Received Home Management Plan	-	-	-	71%
Received Reliever Medication	-	-	-	100%
Use of Medical Imaging				
Combination Abdominal CT Scan	389	0.082	0.365	0.191
Combination Chest CT Scan	236	0.004	0.065	0.054
Follow-up Mammogram/Ultrasound	497	11.1%	7.3%	8.4%
MRI for Low Back Pain[1]	45	31.1%	34.5%	32.7%
Survey of Patients' Hospital Experiences				
Area Around Room 'Always' Quiet at Night	300+	49%	-	58%
Doctors 'Always' Communicated Well	300+	80%	-	80%
Home Recovery Information Given	300+	77%	-	82%
Hospital Given 9 or 10 on 10 Point Scale	300+	61%	-	67%
Meds 'Always' Explained Before Given	300+	58%	-	60%
Nurses 'Always' Communicated Well	300+	73%	-	76%
Pain 'Always' Well Controlled	300+	65%	-	69%
Room and Bathroom 'Always' Clean	300+	66%	-	71%
Timely Help 'Always' Received	300+	60%	-	64%
Would Definitely Recommend Hospital	300+	59%	-	69%

Comanche County Hospital

2nd & Frisco Street
Coldwater, KS 67029
Phone: 620-582-2144
Fax: 620-582-2572
URL: www.gpha.com
Type: Critical Access Hospitals
Emergency Services: Yes
Ownership: Government - Local
Beds: 14

Measure	Cases	This Hosp.	State Avg.	U.S. Avg.
Heart Attack Care				
ACE Inhibitor or ARB for LVSD[5]	0	-	95%	96%
Aspirin at Arrival[5]	0	-	98%	99%
Aspirin at Discharge[5]	0	-	98%	98%
Beta Blocker at Discharge[5]	0	-	98%	98%
Fibrinolytic Medication Timing[5]	0	-	44%	55%
PCI Within 90 Minutes of Arrival[5]	0	-	91%	90%
Smoking Cessation Advice[5]	0	-	99%	99%
Chest Pain/Possible Heart Attack Care				
Aspirin at Arrival	-	-	92%	95%
Median Time to ECG (minutes)	-	-	10	8
Median Time to Transfer (minutes)	-	-	60	61
Fibrinolytic Medication Timing	-	-	42%	54%
Heart Failure Care				
ACE Inhibitor or ARB for LVSD[5]	0	-	91%	94%
Discharge Instructions[5]	0	-	83%	88%
Evaluation of LVS Function[5]	0	-	92%	98%
Smoking Cessation Advice[5]	0	-	94%	98%
Pneumonia Care				
Appropriate Initial Antibiotic[3]	0	-	87%	92%
Blood Culture Timing[3]	0	-	96%	96%
Influenza Vaccine[1,3]	4	75%	87%	91%
Initial Antibiotic Timing[1,3]	2	100%	95%	95%
Pneumococcal Vaccine[1,3]	6	83%	88%	93%
Smoking Cessation Advice[3]	0	-	93%	97%
Surgical Care Improvement Project				
Appropriate VTP Within 24 Hours[5]	0	-	89%	92%
Appropriate Hair Removal[5]	0	-	100%	99%
Appropriate Beta Blocker Usage[5]	0	-	90%	93%
Controlled Postoperative Blood Glucose[5]	0	-	92%	93%
Prophylactic Antibiotic Timing[5]	0	-	96%	97%
Prophylactic Antibiotic Timing (Outpatient)	-	-	93%	92%
Prophylactic Antibiotic Selection[5]	0	-	97%	97%
Prophylactic Antibiotic Select. (Outpatient)	-	-	96%	94%
Prophylactic Antibiotic Stopped[5]	0	-	93%	94%
Recommended VTP Ordered[5]	0	-	91%	94%
Urinary Catheter Removal[5]	0	-	86%	90%
Children's Asthma Care				
Received Systemic Corticosteroids	-	-	-	100%
Received Home Management Plan	-	-	-	71%
Received Reliever Medication	-	-	-	100%
Use of Medical Imaging				
Combination Abdominal CT Scan	-	-	0.365	0.191
Combination Chest CT Scan	-	-	0.065	0.054
Follow-up Mammogram/Ultrasound	-	-	7.3%	8.4%
MRI for Low Back Pain	-	-	34.5%	32.7%
Survey of Patients' Hospital Experiences				
Area Around Room 'Always' Quiet at Night[8]	-	-	-	58%
Doctors 'Always' Communicated Well[8]	-	-	-	80%
Home Recovery Information Given[8]	-	-	-	82%
Hospital Given 9 or 10 on 10 Point Scale[8]	-	-	-	67%
Meds 'Always' Explained Before Given[8]	-	-	-	60%
Nurses 'Always' Communicated Well[8]	-	-	-	76%
Pain 'Always' Well Controlled[8]	-	-	-	69%
Room and Bathroom 'Always' Clean[8]	-	-	-	71%
Timely Help 'Always' Received[8]	-	-	-	64%
Would Definitely Recommend Hospital[8]	-	-	-	69%

NOTE: Hospital profiles are in alphabetical order by state, then city, then hospital within the city; Rankings exclude hospitals with less than 25 cases except for patient surveys which excludes hospitals with less than 100 cases; (a) 100–299 cases; (1) The number of cases is too small to be sure how well a hospital is performing; (2) The hospital indicated that the data submitted for this measure were based on a sample of cases; (3) Data was collected during a shorter time period (fewer quarters) than the maximum possible time for this measure; (4) Suppressed for one or more quarters by CMS; (5) No data is available from the hospital for this measure; (6) Fewer than 100 patients completed the HCAHPS survey. Use these rates with caution, as the number of surveys may be too low to reliably assess hospital performance; (7) Survey results are based on less than 12 months of data; (8) Survey results are not available for this reporting period; (9) No or very few patients were eligible for the HCAHPS survey. The scores shown, if any, reflect a very small number of surveys; (10) A state average was not calculated because too few hospitals in the state submitted data; (11) There were discrepancies in the data collection process; Please refer to the User's Guide for a full explanation of data.

Cloud County Health Center

1100 Highland Drive Phone: 785-243-1234
Concordia, KS 66901 Fax: 785-243-8411
URL: www.cchc.com
Type: Critical Access Hospitals Emergency Services: Yes
Ownership: Voluntary Non-Profit - Private Beds: 25

Key Personnel:
CEO/President. . . . . James Wahlmeier
Chief of Medical Staff. . . . . Travis Jordan, DO
Operating Room. . . . . Muhammad Butt, MD
Quality Assurance . . . . Lisa Hasenbank
Radiology. . . . . Richard J Kueker
Emergency Room . . . . Dana Jordan
Intensive Care Unit. . . . . Laura Otte

Measure	Cases	This Hosp.	State Avg.	U.S. Avg.
Heart Attack Care				
ACE Inhibitor or ARB for LVSD[1,3]	1	0%	95%	96%
Aspirin at Arrival[1,3]	2	100%	98%	99%
Aspirin at Discharge[1,3]	2	100%	98%	98%
Beta Blocker at Discharge[1,3]	2	100%	98%	98%
Fibrinolytic Medication Timing[3]	0	-	44%	55%
PCI Within 90 Minutes of Arrival[3]	0	-	91%	90%
Smoking Cessation Advice[1,3]	1	100%	99%	99%
Chest Pain/Possible Heart Attack Care				
Aspirin at Arrival	-	-	92%	95%
Median Time to ECG (minutes)	-	-	10	8
Median Time to Transfer (minutes)	-	-	60	61
Fibrinolytic Medication Timing	-	-	42%	54%
Heart Failure Care				
ACE Inhibitor or ARB for LVSD[1]	6	83%	91%	94%
Discharge Instructions	33	79%	83%	88%
Evaluation of LVS Function	50	48%	92%	98%
Smoking Cessation Advice[1]	9	56%	94%	98%
Pneumonia Care				
Appropriate Initial Antibiotic[1]	17	94%	87%	92%
Blood Culture Timing[1]	10	80%	96%	96%
Influenza Vaccine[1]	19	68%	87%	91%
Initial Antibiotic Timing	34	97%	95%	95%
Pneumococcal Vaccine	32	59%	88%	93%
Smoking Cessation Advice[1]	2	100%	93%	97%
Surgical Care Improvement Project				
Appropriate VTP Within 24 Hours[1,3]	4	0%	89%	92%
Appropriate Hair Removal[1,3]	7	86%	100%	99%
Appropriate Beta Blocker Usage[1,3]	1	100%	90%	93%
Controlled Postoperative Blood Glucose[3]	0	-	92%	93%
Prophylactic Antibiotic Timing[1,3]	4	100%	96%	97%
Prophylactic Antibiotic Timing (Outpatient)	-	-	93%	92%
Prophylactic Antibiotic Selection[1,3]	5	100%	97%	97%
Prophylactic Antibiotic Select. (Outpatient)	-	-	96%	94%
Prophylactic Antibiotic Stopped[1,3]	4	100%	93%	94%
Recommended VTP Ordered[1,3]	4	0%	91%	94%
Urinary Catheter Removal[3]	0	-	86%	90%
Children's Asthma Care				
Received Systemic Corticosteroids	-	-	-	100%
Received Home Management Plan	-	-	-	71%
Received Reliever Medication	-	-	-	100%
Use of Medical Imaging				
Combination Abdominal CT Scan	-	-	0.365	0.191
Combination Chest CT Scan	-	-	0.065	0.054
Follow-up Mammogram/Ultrasound	-	-	7.3%	8.4%
MRI for Low Back Pain	-	-	34.5%	32.7%
Survey of Patients' Hospital Experiences				
Area Around Room 'Always' Quiet at Night[8]	-	-	-	58%
Doctors 'Always' Communicated Well[8]	-	-	-	80%
Home Recovery Information Given[8]	-	-	-	82%
Hospital Given 9 or 10 on 10 Point Scale[8]	-	-	-	67%
Meds 'Always' Explained Before Given[8]	-	-	-	60%
Nurses 'Always' Communicated Well[8]	-	-	-	76%
Pain 'Always' Well Controlled[8]	-	-	-	69%
Room and Bathroom 'Always' Clean[8]	-	-	-	71%
Timely Help 'Always' Received[8]	-	-	-	64%
Would Definitely Recommend Hospital[8]	-	-	-	69%

Morris County Hospital

600 N Washington St Phone: 620-767-6811
Council Grove, KS 66846 Fax: 620-767-5611
URL: www.mrchosp.com
Type: Critical Access Hospitals Emergency Services: Yes
Ownership: Government - Local Beds: 28

Key Personnel:
CEO/President. . . . . James H Reagan Jr, MD
Chief of Medical Staff. . . . . Daniel R Frese
Radiology. . . . . Stephen M Knecht
Emergency Room . . . . Joel Hornung

Measure	Cases	This Hosp.	State Avg.	U.S. Avg.
Heart Attack Care				
ACE Inhibitor or ARB for LVSD[3]	0	-	95%	96%
Aspirin at Arrival[1,3]	2	100%	98%	99%
Aspirin at Discharge[1,3]	2	100%	98%	98%
Beta Blocker at Discharge[1,3]	2	100%	98%	98%
Fibrinolytic Medication Timing[3]	0	-	44%	55%
PCI Within 90 Minutes of Arrival[3]	0	-	91%	90%
Smoking Cessation Advice[3]	0	-	99%	99%
Chest Pain/Possible Heart Attack Care				
Aspirin at Arrival	-	-	92%	95%
Median Time to ECG (minutes)	-	-	10	8
Median Time to Transfer (minutes)	-	-	60	61
Fibrinolytic Medication Timing	-	-	42%	54%
Heart Failure Care				
ACE Inhibitor or ARB for LVSD[1]	6	83%	91%	94%
Discharge Instructions	28	25%	83%	88%
Evaluation of LVS Function	57	33%	92%	98%
Smoking Cessation Advice[1]	7	43%	94%	98%
Pneumonia Care				
Appropriate Initial Antibiotic[1]	14	93%	87%	92%
Blood Culture Timing[1]	1	100%	96%	96%
Influenza Vaccine[1]	11	9%	87%	91%
Initial Antibiotic Timing[1]	18	100%	95%	95%
Pneumococcal Vaccine	26	15%	88%	93%
Smoking Cessation Advice[1]	3	100%	93%	97%
Surgical Care Improvement Project				
Appropriate VTP Within 24 Hours[5]	0	-	89%	92%
Appropriate Hair Removal[5]	0	-	100%	99%
Appropriate Beta Blocker Usage[5]	0	-	90%	93%
Controlled Postoperative Blood Glucose[5]	0	-	92%	93%
Prophylactic Antibiotic Timing[5]	0	-	96%	97%
Prophylactic Antibiotic Timing (Outpatient)	-	-	93%	92%
Prophylactic Antibiotic Selection[5]	0	-	97%	97%
Prophylactic Antibiotic Select. (Outpatient)	-	-	96%	94%
Prophylactic Antibiotic Stopped[5]	0	-	93%	94%
Recommended VTP Ordered[5]	0	-	91%	94%
Urinary Catheter Removal[5]	0	-	86%	90%
Children's Asthma Care				
Received Systemic Corticosteroids	-	-	-	100%
Received Home Management Plan	-	-	-	71%
Received Reliever Medication	-	-	-	100%
Use of Medical Imaging				
Combination Abdominal CT Scan	-	-	0.365	0.191
Combination Chest CT Scan	-	-	0.065	0.054
Follow-up Mammogram/Ultrasound	-	-	7.3%	8.4%
MRI for Low Back Pain	-	-	34.5%	32.7%
Survey of Patients' Hospital Experiences				
Area Around Room 'Always' Quiet at Night[8]	-	-	-	58%
Doctors 'Always' Communicated Well[8]	-	-	-	80%
Home Recovery Information Given[8]	-	-	-	82%
Hospital Given 9 or 10 on 10 Point Scale[8]	-	-	-	67%
Meds 'Always' Explained Before Given[8]	-	-	-	60%
Nurses 'Always' Communicated Well[8]	-	-	-	76%
Pain 'Always' Well Controlled[8]	-	-	-	69%
Room and Bathroom 'Always' Clean[8]	-	-	-	71%
Timely Help 'Always' Received[8]	-	-	-	64%
Would Definitely Recommend Hospital[8]	-	-	-	69%

Western Plains Medical Complex

3001 Avenue A Phone: 620-225-8400
Dodge City, KS 67801 Fax: 620-225-8403
URL: www.westernplainsmc.com
Type: Acute Care Hospitals Emergency Services: No
Ownership: Proprietary Beds: 110

Key Personnel:
CEO/President. . . . . John E Walker
Chief of Medical Staff. . . . . R C Trotter, MD
Radiology. . . . . Carl Fieser
Emergency Room . . . . Phillis Williams

Measure	Cases	This Hosp.	State Avg.	U.S. Avg.
Heart Attack Care				
ACE Inhibitor or ARB for LVSD[1]	4	100%	95%	96%
Aspirin at Arrival[1]	24	100%	98%	99%
Aspirin at Discharge	31	100%	98%	98%
Beta Blocker at Discharge[1]	24	96%	98%	98%
Fibrinolytic Medication Timing	0	-	44%	55%
PCI Within 90 Minutes of Arrival[1]	3	100%	91%	90%
Smoking Cessation Advice[1]	13	100%	99%	99%
Chest Pain/Possible Heart Attack Care				
Aspirin at Arrival[1]	17	100%	92%	95%
Median Time to ECG (minutes)[1]	17	9	10	8
Median Time to Transfer (minutes)[5]	0	-	60	61
Fibrinolytic Medication Timing[3]	0	-	42%	54%
Heart Failure Care				
ACE Inhibitor or ARB for LVSD[1]	20	95%	91%	94%
Discharge Instructions	37	89%	83%	88%
Evaluation of LVS Function	50	98%	92%	98%
Smoking Cessation Advice[1]	3	100%	94%	98%
Pneumonia Care				
Appropriate Initial Antibiotic	47	96%	87%	92%
Blood Culture Timing	72	97%	96%	96%
Influenza Vaccine	55	95%	87%	91%
Initial Antibiotic Timing	83	96%	95%	95%
Pneumococcal Vaccine	81	96%	88%	93%
Smoking Cessation Advice[1]	24	100%	93%	97%
Surgical Care Improvement Project				
Appropriate VTP Within 24 Hours	76	93%	89%	92%
Appropriate Hair Removal	240	99%	100%	99%
Appropriate Beta Blocker Usage	55	93%	90%	93%
Controlled Postoperative Blood Glucose	0	-	92%	93%
Prophylactic Antibiotic Timing	178	95%	96%	97%
Prophylactic Antibiotic Timing (Outpatient)	79	94%	93%	92%
Prophylactic Antibiotic Selection	178	98%	97%	97%
Prophylactic Antibiotic Select. (Outpatient)	77	99%	96%	94%
Prophylactic Antibiotic Stopped	170	91%	93%	94%
Recommended VTP Ordered	76	95%	91%	94%
Urinary Catheter Removal[1]	12	83%	86%	90%
Children's Asthma Care				
Received Systemic Corticosteroids	-	-	-	100%
Received Home Management Plan	-	-	-	71%
Received Reliever Medication	-	-	-	100%
Use of Medical Imaging				
Combination Abdominal CT Scan	133	0.406	0.365	0.191
Combination Chest CT Scan	70	0.086	0.065	0.054
Follow-up Mammogram/Ultrasound	119	5.9%	7.3%	8.4%
MRI for Low Back Pain[1]	15	46.7%	34.5%	32.7%
Survey of Patients' Hospital Experiences				
Area Around Room 'Always' Quiet at Night	300+	50%	-	58%
Doctors 'Always' Communicated Well	300+	79%	-	80%
Home Recovery Information Given	300+	77%	-	82%
Hospital Given 9 or 10 on 10 Point Scale	300+	62%	-	67%
Meds 'Always' Explained Before Given	300+	55%	-	60%
Nurses 'Always' Communicated Well	300+	73%	-	76%
Pain 'Always' Well Controlled	300+	68%	-	69%
Room and Bathroom 'Always' Clean	300+	60%	-	71%
Timely Help 'Always' Received	300+	55%	-	64%
Would Definitely Recommend Hospital	300+	55%	-	69%

NOTE: Hospital profiles are in alphabetical order by state, then city, then hospital within the city; Rankings exclude hospitals with less than 25 cases except for patient surveys which excludes hospitals with less than 100 cases; (a) 100–299 cases; (1) The number of cases is too small to be sure how well a hospital is performing; (2) The hospital indicated that the data submitted for this measure were based on a sample of cases; (3) Data was collected during a shorter time period (fewer quarters) than the maximum possible time for this measure; (4) Suppressed for one or more quarters by CMS; (5) No data is available from the hospital for this measure; (6) Fewer than 100 patients completed the HCAHPS survey. Use these rates with caution, as the number of surveys may be too low to reliably assess hospital performance; (7) Survey results are based on less than 12 months of data; (8) Survey results are not available for this reporting period; (9) No or very few patients were eligible for the HCAHPS survey. The scores shown, if any, reflect a very small number of surveys; (10) A state average was not calculated because too few hospitals in the state submitted data; (11) There were discrepancies in the data collection process; Please refer to the User's Guide for a full explanation of data.

Susan B Allen Memorial Hospital

720 W Central St Phone: 316-322-4557
El Dorado, KS 67042 Fax: 316-321-2916
URL: www.sbamh.com
Type: Acute Care Hospitals Emergency Services: Yes
Ownership: Voluntary Non-Profit - Private Beds: 103

Key Personnel:
CEO/President. . . . . Gayle Arnett
Chief of Medical Staff . . . . Cathy N Cooper
Radiology. . . . . Hilary Zarnow, MD/FACR

Measure	Cases	This Hosp.	State Avg.	U.S. Avg.
Heart Attack Care				
ACE Inhibitor or ARB for LVSD[1,3]	1	100%	95%	96%
Aspirin at Arrival[1,3]	1	100%	98%	99%
Aspirin at Discharge[1,3]	1	100%	98%	98%
Beta Blocker at Discharge[1,3]	1	100%	98%	98%
Fibrinolytic Medication Timing[3]	0	-	44%	55%
PCI Within 90 Minutes of Arrival[3]	0	-	91%	90%
Smoking Cessation Advice[3]	0	-	99%	99%
Chest Pain/Possible Heart Attack Care				
Aspirin at Arrival	150	95%	92%	95%
Median Time to ECG (minutes)	153	8	10	8
Median Time to Transfer (minutes)[1,3]	2	64	60	61
Fibrinolytic Medication Timing[1]	2	50%	42%	54%
Heart Failure Care				
ACE Inhibitor or ARB for LVSD[1]	8	75%	91%	94%
Discharge Instructions	26	96%	83%	88%
Evaluation of LVS Function	50	100%	92%	98%
Smoking Cessation Advice[1]	7	100%	94%	98%
Pneumonia Care				
Appropriate Initial Antibiotic	53	94%	87%	92%
Blood Culture Timing	42	100%	96%	96%
Influenza Vaccine	51	88%	87%	91%
Initial Antibiotic Timing	60	97%	95%	95%
Pneumococcal Vaccine	69	81%	88%	93%
Smoking Cessation Advice	35	100%	93%	97%
Surgical Care Improvement Project				
Appropriate VTP Within 24 Hours	25	96%	89%	92%
Appropriate Hair Removal	116	100%	100%	99%
Appropriate Beta Blocker Usage[1]	14	93%	90%	93%
Controlled Postoperative Blood Glucose	0	-	92%	93%
Prophylactic Antibiotic Timing	93	98%	96%	97%
Prophylactic Antibiotic Timing (Outpatient)	46	98%	93%	92%
Prophylactic Antibiotic Selection	96	94%	97%	97%
Prophylactic Antibiotic Select. (Outpatient)	45	100%	96%	94%
Prophylactic Antibiotic Stopped	91	93%	93%	94%
Recommended VTP Ordered	25	96%	91%	94%
Urinary Catheter Removal[1]	9	100%	86%	90%
Children's Asthma Care				
Received Systemic Corticosteroids	-	-	-	100%
Received Home Management Plan	-	-	-	71%
Received Reliever Medication	-	-	-	100%
Use of Medical Imaging				
Combination Abdominal CT Scan	420	0.014	0.365	0.191
Combination Chest CT Scan	342	0.003	0.065	0.054
Follow-up Mammogram/Ultrasound	554	22.0%	7.3%	8.4%
MRI for Low Back Pain	159	23.9%	34.5%	32.7%
Survey of Patients' Hospital Experiences				
Area Around Room 'Always' Quiet at Night	300+	58%	-	58%
Doctors 'Always' Communicated Well	300+	85%	-	80%
Home Recovery Information Given	300+	81%	-	82%
Hospital Given 9 or 10 on 10 Point Scale	300+	72%	-	67%
Meds 'Always' Explained Before Given	300+	61%	-	60%
Nurses 'Always' Communicated Well	300+	75%	-	76%
Pain 'Always' Well Controlled	300+	68%	-	69%
Room and Bathroom 'Always' Clean	300+	69%	-	71%
Timely Help 'Always' Received	300+	66%	-	64%
Would Definitely Recommend Hospital	300+	71%	-	69%

Morton County Hospital

445 N Hilltop Phone: 620-697-2141
Elkhart, KS 67950 Fax: 620-697-4766
URL: www.mchswecare.com
Type: Acute Care Hospitals Emergency Services: Yes
Ownership: Voluntary Non-Profit - Other Beds: 120

Key Personnel:
CEO/President. . . . . Leonard Hernandez
Chief of Medical Staff . . . . Dominador Perido, MD
Radiology. . . . . Mindano Beltran

Measure	Cases	This Hosp.	State Avg.	U.S. Avg.
Heart Attack Care				
ACE Inhibitor or ARB for LVSD[2,3]	0	-	95%	96%
Aspirin at Arrival[1,2,3]	1	100%	98%	99%
Aspirin at Discharge[2,3]	0	-	98%	98%
Beta Blocker at Discharge[2,3]	0	-	98%	98%
Fibrinolytic Medication Timing[2,3]	0	-	44%	55%
PCI Within 90 Minutes of Arrival[2,3]	0	-	91%	90%
Smoking Cessation Advice[2,3]	0	-	99%	99%
Chest Pain/Possible Heart Attack Care				
Aspirin at Arrival[5]	0	-	92%	95%
Median Time to ECG (minutes)[5]	0	-	10	8
Median Time to Transfer (minutes)[5]	0	-	60	61
Fibrinolytic Medication Timing[5]	0	-	42%	54%
Heart Failure Care				
ACE Inhibitor or ARB for LVSD[1,2]	4	100%	91%	94%
Discharge Instructions[1,2]	16	0%	83%	88%
Evaluation of LVS Function[2]	42	57%	92%	98%
Smoking Cessation Advice[2,1]	5	60%	94%	98%
Pneumonia Care				
Appropriate Initial Antibiotic[2]	28	29%	87%	92%
Blood Culture Timing[1,2]	10	80%	96%	96%
Influenza Vaccine[1,2]	20	35%	87%	91%
Initial Antibiotic Timing[1,2]	14	79%	95%	95%
Pneumococcal Vaccine[2]	31	48%	88%	93%
Smoking Cessation Advice[1,2]	10	70%	93%	97%
Surgical Care Improvement Project				
Appropriate VTP Within 24 Hours[5]	0	-	89%	92%
Appropriate Hair Removal[5]	0	-	100%	99%
Appropriate Beta Blocker Usage[5]	0	-	90%	93%
Controlled Postoperative Blood Glucose[5]	0	-	92%	93%
Prophylactic Antibiotic Timing[5]	0	-	96%	97%
Prophylactic Antibiotic Timing (Outpatient)[1,3]	3	0%	93%	92%
Prophylactic Antibiotic Selection[5]	0	-	97%	97%
Prophylactic Antibiotic Select. (Outpatient)[3]	0	-	96%	94%
Prophylactic Antibiotic Stopped[5]	0	-	93%	94%
Recommended VTP Ordered[5]	0	-	91%	94%
Urinary Catheter Removal[5]	0	-	86%	90%
Children's Asthma Care				
Received Systemic Corticosteroids	-	-	-	100%
Received Home Management Plan	-	-	-	71%
Received Reliever Medication	-	-	-	100%
Use of Medical Imaging				
Combination Abdominal CT Scan[1]	35	0.600	0.365	0.191
Combination Chest CT Scan[1]	15	0.467	0.065	0.054
Follow-up Mammogram/Ultrasound[1]	42	9.5%	7.3%	8.4%
MRI for Low Back Pain[1]	8	37.5%	34.5%	32.7%
Survey of Patients' Hospital Experiences				
Area Around Room 'Always' Quiet at Night	(a)	43%	-	58%
Doctors 'Always' Communicated Well	(a)	85%	-	80%
Home Recovery Information Given	(a)	67%	-	82%
Hospital Given 9 or 10 on 10 Point Scale	(a)	59%	-	67%
Meds 'Always' Explained Before Given	(a)	46%	-	60%
Nurses 'Always' Communicated Well	(a)	68%	-	76%
Pain 'Always' Well Controlled	(a)	61%	-	69%
Room and Bathroom 'Always' Clean	(a)	67%	-	71%
Timely Help 'Always' Received	(a)	53%	-	64%
Would Definitely Recommend Hospital	(a)	69%	-	69%

Ellsworth County Medical Center

1604 Aylward Avenue Phone: 785-472-5028
Ellsworth, KS 67439 Fax: 785-472-5760
URL: www.ewmed.com
Type: Critical Access Hospitals Emergency Services: Yes
Ownership: Government - Local Beds: 20

Key Personnel:
CEO/President. . . . . Roger Masse
Chief of Medical Staff . . . . Ronald Whitmer, DO
Infection Control. . . . . Sue Wolf
Quality Assurance . . . . Teresa Pearson
Radiology. . . . . Randy Packard
Emergency Room . . . . Tammy Stefek

Measure	Cases	This Hosp.	State Avg.	U.S. Avg.
Heart Attack Care				
ACE Inhibitor or ARB for LVSD[1,2]	1	100%	95%	96%
Aspirin at Arrival[1,2]	10	70%	98%	99%
Aspirin at Discharge[1,2]	8	88%	98%	98%
Beta Blocker at Discharge[1,2]	10	90%	98%	98%
Fibrinolytic Medication Timing[5]	0	-	44%	55%
PCI Within 90 Minutes of Arrival[5]	0	-	91%	90%
Smoking Cessation Advice[2]	0	-	99%	99%
Chest Pain/Possible Heart Attack Care				
Aspirin at Arrival[5]	0	-	92%	95%
Median Time to ECG (minutes)[5]	0	-	10	8
Median Time to Transfer (minutes)[5]	0	-	60	61
Fibrinolytic Medication Timing[5]	0	-	42%	54%
Heart Failure Care				
ACE Inhibitor or ARB for LVSD[1,2]	10	60%	91%	94%
Discharge Instructions[1,2]	19	58%	83%	88%
Evaluation of LVS Function[2]	34	82%	92%	98%
Smoking Cessation Advice[1,2]	3	33%	94%	98%
Pneumonia Care				
Appropriate Initial Antibiotic[1,2]	19	47%	87%	92%
Blood Culture Timing[1,2]	14	100%	96%	96%
Influenza Vaccine[2]	25	72%	87%	91%
Initial Antibiotic Timing[2]	36	89%	95%	95%
Pneumococcal Vaccine[2]	43	70%	88%	93%
Smoking Cessation Advice[1,2]	9	89%	93%	97%
Surgical Care Improvement Project				
Appropriate VTP Within 24 Hours[5]	0	-	89%	92%
Appropriate Hair Removal[5]	0	-	100%	99%
Appropriate Beta Blocker Usage[5]	0	-	90%	93%
Controlled Postoperative Blood Glucose[5]	0	-	92%	93%
Prophylactic Antibiotic Timing[5]	0	-	96%	97%
Prophylactic Antibiotic Timing (Outpatient)[5]	0	-	93%	92%
Prophylactic Antibiotic Selection[5]	0	-	97%	97%
Prophylactic Antibiotic Select. (Outpatient)[5]	0	-	96%	94%
Prophylactic Antibiotic Stopped[5]	0	-	93%	94%
Recommended VTP Ordered[5]	0	-	91%	94%
Urinary Catheter Removal[5]	0	-	86%	90%
Children's Asthma Care				
Received Systemic Corticosteroids	-	-	-	100%
Received Home Management Plan	-	-	-	71%
Received Reliever Medication	-	-	-	100%
Use of Medical Imaging				
Combination Abdominal CT Scan	107	0.402	0.365	0.191
Combination Chest CT Scan	68	0.044	0.065	0.054
Follow-up Mammogram/Ultrasound	128	4.7%	7.3%	8.4%
MRI for Low Back Pain[1]	21	47.6%	34.5%	32.7%
Survey of Patients' Hospital Experiences				
Area Around Room 'Always' Quiet at Night	(a)	60%	-	58%
Doctors 'Always' Communicated Well	(a)	83%	-	80%
Home Recovery Information Given	(a)	71%	-	82%
Hospital Given 9 or 10 on 10 Point Scale	(a)	77%	-	67%
Meds 'Always' Explained Before Given	(a)	66%	-	60%
Nurses 'Always' Communicated Well	(a)	76%	-	76%
Pain 'Always' Well Controlled	(a)	64%	-	69%
Room and Bathroom 'Always' Clean	(a)	82%	-	71%
Timely Help 'Always' Received	(a)	71%	-	64%
Would Definitely Recommend Hospital	(a)	71%	-	69%

NOTE: Hospital profiles are in alphabetical order by state, then city, then hospital within the city; Rankings exclude hospitals with less than 25 cases except for patient surveys which excludes hospitals with less than 100 cases; (a) 100–299 cases; (1) The number of cases is too small to be sure how well a hospital is performing; (2) The hospital indicated that the data submitted for this measure were based on a sample of cases; (3) Data was collected during a shorter time period (fewer quarters) than the maximum possible time for this measure; (4) Suppressed for one or more quarters by CMS; (5) No data is available from the hospital for this measure; (6) Fewer than 100 patients completed the HCAHPS survey. Use these rates with caution, as the number of surveys may be too low to reliably assess hospital performance; (7) Survey results are based on less than 12 months of data; (8) Survey results are not available for this reporting period; (9) No or very few patients were eligible for the HCAHPS survey. The scores shown, if any, reflect a very small number of surveys; (10) A state average was not calculated because too few hospitals in the state submitted data; (11) There were discrepancies in the data collection process; Please refer to the User's Guide for a full explanation of data.

Newman Regional Health

1201 West 12th Avenue
Emporia, KS 66801
URL: www.newmanrh.org
Type: Acute Care Hospitals
Ownership: Government - Local
Phone: 620-343-6800
Fax: 620-341-7801
Emergency Services: Yes
Beds: 178

Key Personnel:
CEO/President. . . . . Bob Driewer
Cardiac Laboratory. . . . . Jim Pelch
Chief of Medical Staff . . . . Cy K Anderson, MD
Infection Control. . . . . Jami White
Operating Room. . . . . Robert Dorsey
Pediatric In-Patient Care . . . . Amy Jarvis
Quality Assurance . . . . Kathie Butcher
Radiology. . . . . Stephen M Knecht

Measure	Cases	This Hosp.	State Avg.	U.S. Avg.
Heart Attack Care				
ACE Inhibitor or ARB for LVSD	0	-	95%	96%
Aspirin at Arrival[1]	10	100%	98%	99%
Aspirin at Discharge[1]	8	100%	98%	98%
Beta Blocker at Discharge[1]	7	86%	98%	98%
Fibrinolytic Medication Timing	0	-	44%	55%
PCI Within 90 Minutes of Arrival	0	-	91%	90%
Smoking Cessation Advice[1]	1	100%	99%	99%
Chest Pain/Possible Heart Attack Care				
Aspirin at Arrival	128	93%	92%	95%
Median Time to ECG (minutes)	135	3	10	8
Median Time to Transfer (minutes)[1,3]	6	40	60	61
Fibrinolytic Medication Timing[1]	11	36%	42%	54%
Heart Failure Care				
ACE Inhibitor or ARB for LVSD	29	79%	91%	94%
Discharge Instructions	53	72%	83%	88%
Evaluation of LVS Function	93	86%	92%	98%
Smoking Cessation Advice[1]	12	92%	94%	98%
Pneumonia Care				
Appropriate Initial Antibiotic	57	91%	87%	92%
Blood Culture Timing	50	96%	96%	96%
Influenza Vaccine	45	78%	87%	91%
Initial Antibiotic Timing	71	96%	95%	95%
Pneumococcal Vaccine	68	88%	88%	93%
Smoking Cessation Advice	31	97%	93%	97%
Surgical Care Improvement Project				
Appropriate VTP Within 24 Hours	102	55%	89%	92%
Appropriate Hair Removal	219	98%	100%	99%
Appropriate Beta Blocker Usage	54	78%	90%	93%
Controlled Postoperative Blood Glucose	0	-	92%	93%
Prophylactic Antibiotic Timing	149	89%	96%	97%
Prophylactic Antibiotic Timing (Outpatient)	60	93%	93%	92%
Prophylactic Antibiotic Selection	149	95%	97%	97%
Prophylactic Antibiotic Select. (Outpatient)	58	91%	96%	94%
Prophylactic Antibiotic Stopped	146	90%	93%	94%
Recommended VTP Ordered	102	70%	91%	94%
Urinary Catheter Removal	64	78%	86%	90%
Children's Asthma Care				
Received Systemic Corticosteroids	-	-	-	100%
Received Home Management Plan	-	-	-	71%
Received Reliever Medication	-	-	-	100%
Use of Medical Imaging				
Combination Abdominal CT Scan	370	0.849	0.365	0.191
Combination Chest CT Scan	251	0.004	0.065	0.054
Follow-up Mammogram/Ultrasound[5]	0	-	7.3%	8.4%
MRI for Low Back Pain	180	30.6%	34.5%	32.7%
Survey of Patients' Hospital Experiences				
Area Around Room 'Always' Quiet at Night	300+	57%	-	58%
Doctors 'Always' Communicated Well	300+	79%	-	80%
Home Recovery Information Given	300+	77%	-	82%
Hospital Given 9 or 10 on 10 Point Scale	300+	61%	-	67%
Meds 'Always' Explained Before Given	300+	60%	-	60%
Nurses 'Always' Communicated Well	300+	73%	-	76%
Pain 'Always' Well Controlled	300+	68%	-	69%
Room and Bathroom 'Always' Clean	300+	74%	-	71%
Timely Help 'Always' Received	300+	62%	-	64%
Would Definitely Recommend Hospital	300+	54%	-	69%

Greenwood County Hospital

100 W 16th Street
Eureka, KS 67045
Type: Critical Access Hospitals
Ownership: Government - Local
Phone: 620-583-7451
Fax: 620-583-6884
Emergency Services: Yes
Beds: 25

Key Personnel:
CEO/President. . . . . Bruce Birchell

Measure	Cases	This Hosp.	State Avg.	U.S. Avg.
Heart Attack Care				
ACE Inhibitor or ARB for LVSD[3]	0	-	95%	96%
Aspirin at Arrival[3]	0	-	98%	99%
Aspirin at Discharge[3]	0	-	98%	98%
Beta Blocker at Discharge[3]	0	-	98%	98%
Fibrinolytic Medication Timing[1,3]	1	0%	44%	55%
PCI Within 90 Minutes of Arrival[3]	0	-	91%	90%
Smoking Cessation Advice[3]	0	-	99%	99%
Chest Pain/Possible Heart Attack Care				
Aspirin at Arrival	-	-	92%	95%
Median Time to ECG (minutes)	-	-	10	8
Median Time to Transfer (minutes)	-	-	60	61
Fibrinolytic Medication Timing	-	-	42%	54%
Heart Failure Care				
ACE Inhibitor or ARB for LVSD[1]	1	100%	91%	94%
Discharge Instructions[1]	9	22%	83%	88%
Evaluation of LVS Function[1]	17	12%	92%	98%
Smoking Cessation Advice[1]	1	100%	94%	98%
Pneumonia Care				
Appropriate Initial Antibiotic[1]	22	41%	87%	92%
Blood Culture Timing[1]	5	60%	96%	96%
Influenza Vaccine[1]	24	67%	87%	91%
Initial Antibiotic Timing	42	93%	95%	95%
Pneumococcal Vaccine	38	61%	88%	93%
Smoking Cessation Advice[1]	10	100%	93%	97%
Surgical Care Improvement Project				
Appropriate VTP Within 24 Hours[5]	0	-	89%	92%
Appropriate Hair Removal[5]	0	-	100%	99%
Appropriate Beta Blocker Usage[5]	0	-	90%	93%
Controlled Postoperative Blood Glucose[5]	0	-	92%	93%
Prophylactic Antibiotic Timing[5]	0	-	96%	97%
Prophylactic Antibiotic Timing (Outpatient)	-	-	93%	92%
Prophylactic Antibiotic Selection[5]	0	-	97%	97%
Prophylactic Antibiotic Select. (Outpatient)	-	-	96%	94%
Prophylactic Antibiotic Stopped[5]	0	-	93%	94%
Recommended VTP Ordered[5]	0	-	91%	94%
Urinary Catheter Removal[5]	0	-	86%	90%
Children's Asthma Care				
Received Systemic Corticosteroids	-	-	-	100%
Received Home Management Plan	-	-	-	71%
Received Reliever Medication	-	-	-	100%
Use of Medical Imaging				
Combination Abdominal CT Scan	-	-	0.365	0.191
Combination Chest CT Scan	-	-	0.065	0.054
Follow-up Mammogram/Ultrasound	-	-	7.3%	8.4%
MRI for Low Back Pain	-	-	34.5%	32.7%
Survey of Patients' Hospital Experiences				
Area Around Room 'Always' Quiet at Night[8]	-	-	-	58%
Doctors 'Always' Communicated Well[8]	-	-	-	80%
Home Recovery Information Given[8]	-	-	-	82%
Hospital Given 9 or 10 on 10 Point Scale[8]	-	-	-	67%
Meds 'Always' Explained Before Given[8]	-	-	-	60%
Nurses 'Always' Communicated Well[8]	-	-	-	76%
Pain 'Always' Well Controlled[8]	-	-	-	69%
Room and Bathroom 'Always' Clean[8]	-	-	-	71%
Timely Help 'Always' Received[8]	-	-	-	64%
Would Definitely Recommend Hospital[8]	-	-	-	69%

Mercy Health Center

401 Woodland Hills Blvd
Fort Scott, KS 66701
Type: Acute Care Hospitals
Ownership: Voluntary Non-Profit - Church
Phone: 620-223-7057
Emergency Services: Yes

Key Personnel:
Operating Room. . . . . Ralph Hall
Radiology. . . . . Becky Williams

Measure	Cases	This Hosp.	State Avg.	U.S. Avg.
Heart Attack Care				
ACE Inhibitor or ARB for LVSD[1]	1	100%	95%	96%
Aspirin at Arrival[1]	7	86%	98%	99%
Aspirin at Discharge[1]	3	100%	98%	98%
Beta Blocker at Discharge[1]	5	80%	98%	98%
Fibrinolytic Medication Timing	0	-	44%	55%
PCI Within 90 Minutes of Arrival	0	-	91%	90%
Smoking Cessation Advice	0	-	99%	99%
Chest Pain/Possible Heart Attack Care				
Aspirin at Arrival	63	92%	92%	95%
Median Time to ECG (minutes)	64	12	10	8
Median Time to Transfer (minutes)[1,3]	3	131	60	61
Fibrinolytic Medication Timing[1]	7	0%	42%	54%
Heart Failure Care				
ACE Inhibitor or ARB for LVSD[1]	22	95%	91%	94%
Discharge Instructions	44	91%	83%	88%
Evaluation of LVS Function	77	100%	92%	98%
Smoking Cessation Advice[1]	6	100%	94%	98%
Pneumonia Care				
Appropriate Initial Antibiotic[2]	40	100%	87%	92%
Blood Culture Timing[2]	53	100%	96%	96%
Influenza Vaccine[2]	52	96%	87%	91%
Initial Antibiotic Timing[2]	61	100%	95%	95%
Pneumococcal Vaccine[2]	79	100%	88%	93%
Smoking Cessation Advice[1,2]	23	100%	93%	97%
Surgical Care Improvement Project				
Appropriate VTP Within 24 Hours[2]	30	83%	89%	92%
Appropriate Hair Removal[2]	102	100%	100%	99%
Appropriate Beta Blocker Usage[1,2]	19	79%	90%	93%
Controlled Postoperative Blood Glucose[2]	0	-	92%	93%
Prophylactic Antibiotic Timing[2]	68	100%	96%	97%
Prophylactic Antibiotic Timing (Outpatient)[1]	13	77%	93%	92%
Prophylactic Antibiotic Selection[2]	69	91%	97%	97%
Prophylactic Antibiotic Select. (Outpatient)[1]	13	92%	96%	94%
Prophylactic Antibiotic Stopped[2]	67	99%	93%	94%
Recommended VTP Ordered[2]	30	83%	91%	94%
Urinary Catheter Removal[1,2]	12	75%	86%	90%
Children's Asthma Care				
Received Systemic Corticosteroids	-	-	-	100%
Received Home Management Plan	-	-	-	71%
Received Reliever Medication	-	-	-	100%
Use of Medical Imaging				
Combination Abdominal CT Scan	216	0.111	0.365	0.191
Combination Chest CT Scan	131	0.069	0.065	0.054
Follow-up Mammogram/Ultrasound	469	9.2%	7.3%	8.4%
MRI for Low Back Pain	49	36.7%	34.5%	32.7%
Survey of Patients' Hospital Experiences				
Area Around Room 'Always' Quiet at Night	300+	68%	-	58%
Doctors 'Always' Communicated Well	300+	85%	-	80%
Home Recovery Information Given	300+	83%	-	82%
Hospital Given 9 or 10 on 10 Point Scale	300+	69%	-	67%
Meds 'Always' Explained Before Given	300+	62%	-	60%
Nurses 'Always' Communicated Well	300+	82%	-	76%
Pain 'Always' Well Controlled	300+	72%	-	69%
Room and Bathroom 'Always' Clean	300+	77%	-	71%
Timely Help 'Always' Received	300+	75%	-	64%
Would Definitely Recommend Hospital	300+	61%	-	69%

NOTE: Hospital profiles are in alphabetical order by state, then city, then hospital within the city; Rankings exclude hospitals with less than 25 cases except for patient surveys which excludes hospitals with less than 100 cases; (a) 100–299 cases; (1) The number of cases is too small to be sure how well a hospital is performing; (2) The hospital indicated that the data submitted for this measure were based on a sample of cases; (3) Data was collected during a shorter time period (fewer quarters) than the maximum possible time for this measure; (4) Suppressed for one or more quarters by CMS; (5) No data is available from the hospital for this measure; (6) Fewer than 100 patients completed the HCAHPS survey. Use these rates with caution, as the number of surveys may be too low to reliably assess hospital performance; (7) Survey results are based on less than 12 months of data; (8) Survey results are not available for this reporting period; (9) No or very few patients were eligible for the HCAHPS survey. The scores shown, if any, reflect a very small number of surveys; (10) A state average was not calculated because too few hospitals in the state submitted data; (11) There were discrepancies in the data collection process; Please refer to the User's Guide for a full explanation of data.

Fredonia Regional Hospital

1527 Madison
Fredonia, KS 66736
Phone: 620-378-2121
Fax: 620-378-3169
URL: www.gpha.com
Type: Critical Access Hospitals
Emergency Services: Yes
Ownership: Voluntary Non-Profit - Other
Beds: 25

Key Personnel:
CEO/President. . . . . Terry Deschaine
Chief of Medical Staff . . . . Oswaldo Bacami
Infection Control. . . . . Darrell Odell
Emergency Room . . . . Kim Buttler

Measure	Cases	This Hosp.	State Avg.	U.S. Avg.
Heart Attack Care				
ACE Inhibitor or ARB for LVSD[3]	0	-	95%	96%
Aspirin at Arrival[3]	0	-	98%	99%
Aspirin at Discharge[3]	0	-	98%	98%
Beta Blocker at Discharge[3]	0	-	98%	98%
Fibrinolytic Medication Timing[3]	0	-	44%	55%
PCI Within 90 Minutes of Arrival[3]	0	-	91%	90%
Smoking Cessation Advice[3]	0	-	99%	99%
Chest Pain/Possible Heart Attack Care				
Aspirin at Arrival	-	-	92%	95%
Median Time to ECG (minutes)	-	-	10	8
Median Time to Transfer (minutes)	-	-	60	61
Fibrinolytic Medication Timing	-	-	42%	54%
Heart Failure Care				
ACE Inhibitor or ARB for LVSD[3]	0	-	91%	94%
Discharge Instructions[1,3]	3	33%	83%	88%
Evaluation of LVS Function[1,3]	6	33%	92%	98%
Smoking Cessation Advice[3]	0	-	94%	98%
Pneumonia Care				
Appropriate Initial Antibiotic[1,3]	8	88%	87%	92%
Blood Culture Timing[3]	0	-	96%	96%
Influenza Vaccine[1,3]	6	83%	87%	91%
Initial Antibiotic Timing[1,3]	3	33%	95%	95%
Pneumococcal Vaccine[1,3]	9	89%	88%	93%
Smoking Cessation Advice[1,3]	4	50%	93%	97%
Surgical Care Improvement Project				
Appropriate VTP Within 24 Hours[5]	0	-	89%	92%
Appropriate Hair Removal[5]	0	-	100%	99%
Appropriate Beta Blocker Usage[5]	0	-	90%	93%
Controlled Postoperative Blood Glucose[5]	0	-	92%	93%
Prophylactic Antibiotic Timing[5]	0	-	96%	97%
Prophylactic Antibiotic Timing (Outpatient)	-	-	93%	92%
Prophylactic Antibiotic Selection[5]	0	-	97%	97%
Prophylactic Antibiotic Select. (Outpatient)	-	-	96%	94%
Prophylactic Antibiotic Stopped[5]	0	-	93%	94%
Recommended VTP Ordered[5]	0	-	91%	94%
Urinary Catheter Removal[5]	0	-	86%	90%
Children's Asthma Care				
Received Systemic Corticosteroids	-	-	-	100%
Received Home Management Plan	-	-	-	71%
Received Reliever Medication	-	-	-	100%
Use of Medical Imaging				
Combination Abdominal CT Scan	-	-	0.365	0.191
Combination Chest CT Scan	-	-	0.065	0.054
Follow-up Mammogram/Ultrasound	-	-	7.3%	8.4%
MRI for Low Back Pain	-	-	34.5%	32.7%
Survey of Patients' Hospital Experiences				
Area Around Room 'Always' Quiet at Night[8]	-	-	-	58%
Doctors 'Always' Communicated Well[8]	-	-	-	80%
Home Recovery Information Given[8]	-	-	-	82%
Hospital Given 9 or 10 on 10 Point Scale[8]	-	-	-	67%
Meds 'Always' Explained Before Given[8]	-	-	-	60%
Nurses 'Always' Communicated Well[8]	-	-	-	76%
Pain 'Always' Well Controlled[8]	-	-	-	69%
Room and Bathroom 'Always' Clean[8]	-	-	-	71%
Timely Help 'Always' Received[8]	-	-	-	64%
Would Definitely Recommend Hospital[8]	-	-	-	69%

Saint Catherine Hospital

401 East Spruce
Garden City, KS 67846
Phone: 620-272-2561
Fax: 620-272-2528
URL: www.stcath-hosp.org
Type: Acute Care Hospitals
Emergency Services: No
Ownership: Voluntary Non-Profit - Church

Key Personnel:
CEO/President. . . . . Scott Taylor
Chief of Medical Staff . . . . James Bruno
Radiology. . . . . Soen Liong

Measure	Cases	This Hosp.	State Avg.	U.S. Avg.
Heart Attack Care				
ACE Inhibitor or ARB for LVSD[1]	5	100%	95%	96%
Aspirin at Arrival	29	100%	98%	99%
Aspirin at Discharge	36	100%	98%	98%
Beta Blocker at Discharge	35	100%	98%	98%
Fibrinolytic Medication Timing	0	-	44%	55%
PCI Within 90 Minutes of Arrival[1]	4	100%	91%	90%
Smoking Cessation Advice[1]	15	100%	99%	99%
Chest Pain/Possible Heart Attack Care				
Aspirin at Arrival[1]	20	90%	92%	95%
Median Time to ECG (minutes)[1]	19	11	10	8
Median Time to Transfer (minutes)[1,3]	1	104	60	61
Fibrinolytic Medication Timing[1]	2	0%	42%	54%
Heart Failure Care				
ACE Inhibitor or ARB for LVSD[1]	10	100%	91%	94%
Discharge Instructions	34	94%	83%	88%
Evaluation of LVS Function	40	95%	92%	98%
Smoking Cessation Advice[1]	6	100%	94%	98%
Pneumonia Care				
Appropriate Initial Antibiotic	58	93%	87%	92%
Blood Culture Timing	71	97%	96%	96%
Influenza Vaccine	50	98%	87%	91%
Initial Antibiotic Timing	97	92%	95%	95%
Pneumococcal Vaccine	60	97%	88%	93%
Smoking Cessation Advice	36	100%	93%	97%
Surgical Care Improvement Project				
Appropriate VTP Within 24 Hours	158	94%	89%	92%
Appropriate Hair Removal	321	100%	100%	99%
Appropriate Beta Blocker Usage	73	99%	90%	93%
Controlled Postoperative Blood Glucose	0	-	92%	93%
Prophylactic Antibiotic Timing	241	99%	96%	97%
Prophylactic Antibiotic Timing (Outpatient)	71	100%	93%	92%
Prophylactic Antibiotic Selection	241	96%	97%	97%
Prophylactic Antibiotic Select. (Outpatient)	71	96%	96%	94%
Prophylactic Antibiotic Stopped	240	69%	93%	94%
Recommended VTP Ordered	158	94%	91%	94%
Urinary Catheter Removal	76	83%	86%	90%
Children's Asthma Care				
Received Systemic Corticosteroids	-	-	-	100%
Received Home Management Plan	-	-	-	71%
Received Reliever Medication	-	-	-	100%
Use of Medical Imaging				
Combination Abdominal CT Scan	341	0.457	0.365	0.191
Combination Chest CT Scan	143	0.000	0.065	0.054
Follow-up Mammogram/Ultrasound	423	0.9%	7.3%	8.4%
MRI for Low Back Pain	77	37.7%	34.5%	32.7%
Survey of Patients' Hospital Experiences				
Area Around Room 'Always' Quiet at Night	300+	53%	-	58%
Doctors 'Always' Communicated Well	300+	80%	-	80%
Home Recovery Information Given	300+	84%	-	82%
Hospital Given 9 or 10 on 10 Point Scale	300+	63%	-	67%
Meds 'Always' Explained Before Given	300+	56%	-	60%
Nurses 'Always' Communicated Well	300+	70%	-	76%
Pain 'Always' Well Controlled	300+	68%	-	69%
Room and Bathroom 'Always' Clean	300+	68%	-	71%
Timely Help 'Always' Received	300+	56%	-	64%
Would Definitely Recommend Hospital	300+	62%	-	69%

Anderson County Hospital

421 S Maple
Garnett, KS 66032
Phone: 785-204-4000
Fax: 785-448-3118
URL: www.saintlukeshealthsystem.org
Type: Critical Access Hospitals
Emergency Services: Yes
Ownership: Voluntary Non-Profit - Private
Beds: 57

Key Personnel:
CEO/President. . . . . Dennis A Hachenberg
Pediatric In-Patient Care . . . . Beth Anderson

Measure	Cases	This Hosp.	State Avg.	U.S. Avg.
Heart Attack Care				
ACE Inhibitor or ARB for LVSD[3]	0	-	95%	96%
Aspirin at Arrival[3]	0	-	98%	99%
Aspirin at Discharge[1,3]	1	100%	98%	98%
Beta Blocker at Discharge[3]	0	-	98%	98%
Fibrinolytic Medication Timing[3]	0	-	44%	55%
PCI Within 90 Minutes of Arrival[3]	0	-	91%	90%
Smoking Cessation Advice[3]	0	-	99%	99%
Chest Pain/Possible Heart Attack Care				
Aspirin at Arrival	33	100%	92%	95%
Median Time to ECG (minutes)	34	11	10	8
Median Time to Transfer (minutes)[1,3]	2	88	60	61
Fibrinolytic Medication Timing	0	-	42%	54%
Heart Failure Care				
ACE Inhibitor or ARB for LVSD[1]	3	100%	91%	94%
Discharge Instructions[1]	6	33%	83%	88%
Evaluation of LVS Function[1]	9	100%	92%	98%
Smoking Cessation Advice	0	-	94%	98%
Pneumonia Care				
Appropriate Initial Antibiotic[1]	10	100%	87%	92%
Blood Culture Timing[1]	9	100%	96%	96%
Influenza Vaccine[1]	10	100%	87%	91%
Initial Antibiotic Timing[1]	12	75%	95%	95%
Pneumococcal Vaccine[1]	18	89%	88%	93%
Smoking Cessation Advice[1]	2	50%	93%	97%
Surgical Care Improvement Project				
Appropriate VTP Within 24 Hours[5]	0	-	89%	92%
Appropriate Hair Removal[5]	0	-	100%	99%
Appropriate Beta Blocker Usage[5]	0	-	90%	93%
Controlled Postoperative Blood Glucose[5]	0	-	92%	93%
Prophylactic Antibiotic Timing[5]	0	-	96%	97%
Prophylactic Antibiotic Timing (Outpatient)[5]	0	-	93%	92%
Prophylactic Antibiotic Selection[5]	0	-	97%	97%
Prophylactic Antibiotic Select. (Outpatient)[5]	0	-	96%	94%
Prophylactic Antibiotic Stopped[5]	0	-	93%	94%
Recommended VTP Ordered[5]	0	-	91%	94%
Urinary Catheter Removal[5]	0	-	86%	90%
Children's Asthma Care				
Received Systemic Corticosteroids	-	-	-	100%
Received Home Management Plan	-	-	-	71%
Received Reliever Medication	-	-	-	100%
Use of Medical Imaging				
Combination Abdominal CT Scan	107	0.131	0.365	0.191
Combination Chest CT Scan[1]	34	0.294	0.065	0.054
Follow-up Mammogram/Ultrasound	162	1.9%	7.3%	8.4%
MRI for Low Back Pain[1]	15	26.7%	34.5%	32.7%
Survey of Patients' Hospital Experiences				
Area Around Room 'Always' Quiet at Night[6]	<100	68%	-	58%
Doctors 'Always' Communicated Well[6]	<100	92%	-	80%
Home Recovery Information Given[6]	<100	78%	-	82%
Hospital Given 9 or 10 on 10 Point Scale[6]	<100	80%	-	67%
Meds 'Always' Explained Before Given[6]	<100	76%	-	60%
Nurses 'Always' Communicated Well[6]	<100	85%	-	76%
Pain 'Always' Well Controlled[6]	<100	76%	-	69%
Room and Bathroom 'Always' Clean[6]	<100	86%	-	71%
Timely Help 'Always' Received[6]	<100	78%	-	64%
Would Definitely Recommend Hospital	<100	89%	-	69%

NOTE: Hospital profiles are in alphabetical order by state, then city, then hospital within the city; Rankings exclude hospitals with less than 25 cases except for patient surveys which excludes hospitals with less than 100 cases; (a) 100–299 cases; (1) The number of cases is too small to be sure how well a hospital is performing; (2) The hospital indicated that the data submitted for this measure were based on a sample of cases; (3) Data was collected during a shorter time period (fewer quarters) than the maximum possible time for this measure; (4) Suppressed for one or more quarters by CMS; (5) No data is available from the hospital for this measure; (6) Fewer than 100 patients completed the HCAHPS survey. Use these rates with caution, as the number of surveys may be too low to reliably assess hospital performance; (7) Survey results are based on less than 12 months of data; (8) Survey results are not available for this reporting period; (9) No or very few patients were eligible for the HCAHPS survey. The scores shown, if any, reflect a very small number of surveys; (10) A state average was not calculated because too few hospitals in the state submitted data; (11) There were discrepancies in the data collection process; Please refer to the User's Guide for a full explanation of data.

Girard Medical Center

302 North Hospital Drive
Girard, KS 66743
Phone: 620-724-8291
Fax: 620-724-6332
Type: Critical Access Hospitals
Emergency Services: Yes
Ownership: Govt - Hospital Dist/Auth
Beds: 38

Key Personnel:
CEO/President. . . . . Kenneth Boyd, Jr
Chief of Medical Staff. . . . . Ronald Edwards, MD
Coronary Care . . . . Don Shull
Infection Control. . . . . Karen Brooks
Operating Room. . . . . Carol Diskin, RN
Quality Assurance . . . . Joyce Geier
Intensive Care Unit. . . . . Donald Shull
Patient Relations . . . . Joyce Geier

Measure	Cases	This Hosp.	State Avg.	U.S. Avg.
Heart Attack Care				
ACE Inhibitor or ARB for LVSD[5]	0	-	95%	96%
Aspirin at Arrival[5]	0	-	98%	99%
Aspirin at Discharge[5]	0	-	98%	98%
Beta Blocker at Discharge[5]	0	-	98%	98%
Fibrinolytic Medication Timing[5]	0	-	44%	55%
PCI Within 90 Minutes of Arrival[5]	0	-	91%	90%
Smoking Cessation Advice[5]	0	-	99%	99%
Chest Pain/Possible Heart Attack Care				
Aspirin at Arrival	-	-	92%	95%
Median Time to ECG (minutes)	-	-	10	8
Median Time to Transfer (minutes)	-	-	60	61
Fibrinolytic Medication Timing	-	-	42%	54%
Heart Failure Care				
ACE Inhibitor or ARB for LVSD[1]	6	67%	91%	94%
Discharge Instructions[1]	18	83%	83%	88%
Evaluation of LVS Function	29	86%	92%	98%
Smoking Cessation Advice[1]	6	100%	94%	98%
Pneumonia Care				
Appropriate Initial Antibiotic[1]	15	87%	87%	92%
Blood Culture Timing	41	98%	96%	96%
Influenza Vaccine[1]	23	78%	87%	91%
Initial Antibiotic Timing[5]	0	-	95%	95%
Pneumococcal Vaccine	45	89%	88%	93%
Smoking Cessation Advice[1]	11	91%	93%	97%
Surgical Care Improvement Project				
Appropriate VTP Within 24 Hours[1]	12	67%	89%	92%
Appropriate Hair Removal[1]	17	100%	100%	99%
Appropriate Beta Blocker Usage[1]	4	25%	90%	93%
Controlled Postoperative Blood Glucose	0	-	92%	93%
Prophylactic Antibiotic Timing[1]	9	100%	96%	97%
Prophylactic Antibiotic Timing (Outpatient)	-	-	93%	92%
Prophylactic Antibiotic Selection[1]	10	100%	97%	97%
Prophylactic Antibiotic Select. (Outpatient)	-	-	96%	94%
Prophylactic Antibiotic Stopped[1]	7	86%	93%	94%
Recommended VTP Ordered[1]	12	75%	91%	94%
Urinary Catheter Removal[1]	4	75%	86%	90%
Children's Asthma Care				
Received Systemic Corticosteroids	-	-	-	100%
Received Home Management Plan	-	-	-	71%
Received Reliever Medication	-	-	-	100%
Use of Medical Imaging				
Combination Abdominal CT Scan	-	-	0.365	0.191
Combination Chest CT Scan	-	-	0.065	0.054
Follow-up Mammogram/Ultrasound	-	-	7.3%	8.4%
MRI for Low Back Pain	-	-	34.5%	32.7%
Survey of Patients' Hospital Experiences				
Area Around Room 'Always' Quiet at Night[8]	-	-	-	58%
Doctors 'Always' Communicated Well[8]	-	-	-	80%
Home Recovery Information Given[8]	-	-	-	82%
Hospital Given 9 or 10 on 10 Point Scale[8]	-	-	-	67%
Meds 'Always' Explained Before Given[8]	-	-	-	60%
Nurses 'Always' Communicated Well[8]	-	-	-	76%
Pain 'Always' Well Controlled[8]	-	-	-	69%
Room and Bathroom 'Always' Clean[8]	-	-	-	71%
Timely Help 'Always' Received[8]	-	-	-	64%
Would Definitely Recommend Hospital[8]	-	-	-	69%

Goodland Regional Medical Center

220 West Second Street
Goodland, KS 67735
Phone: 785-890-3625
Fax: 785-890-7209
Type: Critical Access Hospitals
Emergency Services: Yes
Ownership: Government - Local
Beds: 25

Key Personnel:
CEO/President. . . . . Jay Jolly
Chief of Medical Staff. . . . . Travis Daise, MD
Infection Control. . . . . Karen Hooker, RRT
Operating Room. . . . . Florida Cruz, RN
Quality Assurance . . . . Mary Ann Elliott, RN
Radiology. . . . . Carl W Fieser, ARRT
Emergency Room . . . . Kathy Erickson, RN
Patient Relations . . . . Brenda McCants

Measure	Cases	This Hosp.	State Avg.	U.S. Avg.
Heart Attack Care				
ACE Inhibitor or ARB for LVSD[5]	0	-	95%	96%
Aspirin at Arrival[5]	0	-	98%	99%
Aspirin at Discharge[5]	0	-	98%	98%
Beta Blocker at Discharge[5]	0	-	98%	98%
Fibrinolytic Medication Timing[5]	0	-	44%	55%
PCI Within 90 Minutes of Arrival[5]	0	-	91%	90%
Smoking Cessation Advice[5]	0	-	99%	99%
Chest Pain/Possible Heart Attack Care				
Aspirin at Arrival	-	-	92%	95%
Median Time to ECG (minutes)	-	-	10	8
Median Time to Transfer (minutes)	-	-	60	61
Fibrinolytic Medication Timing	-	-	42%	54%
Heart Failure Care				
ACE Inhibitor or ARB for LVSD[5]	0	-	91%	94%
Discharge Instructions[5]	0	-	83%	88%
Evaluation of LVS Function[5]	0	-	92%	98%
Smoking Cessation Advice[5]	0	-	94%	98%
Pneumonia Care				
Appropriate Initial Antibiotic[5]	0	-	87%	92%
Blood Culture Timing[5]	0	-	96%	96%
Influenza Vaccine[5]	0	-	87%	91%
Initial Antibiotic Timing[5]	0	-	95%	95%
Pneumococcal Vaccine[5]	0	-	88%	93%
Smoking Cessation Advice[5]	0	-	93%	97%
Surgical Care Improvement Project				
Appropriate VTP Within 24 Hours[5]	0	-	89%	92%
Appropriate Hair Removal[5]	0	-	100%	99%
Appropriate Beta Blocker Usage[5]	0	-	90%	93%
Controlled Postoperative Blood Glucose[5]	0	-	92%	93%
Prophylactic Antibiotic Timing[5]	0	-	96%	97%
Prophylactic Antibiotic Timing (Outpatient)	-	-	93%	92%
Prophylactic Antibiotic Selection[5]	0	-	97%	97%
Prophylactic Antibiotic Select. (Outpatient)	-	-	96%	94%
Prophylactic Antibiotic Stopped[5]	0	-	93%	94%
Recommended VTP Ordered[5]	0	-	91%	94%
Urinary Catheter Removal[5]	0	-	86%	90%
Children's Asthma Care				
Received Systemic Corticosteroids	-	-	-	100%
Received Home Management Plan	-	-	-	71%
Received Reliever Medication	-	-	-	100%
Use of Medical Imaging				
Combination Abdominal CT Scan	-	-	0.365	0.191
Combination Chest CT Scan	-	-	0.065	0.054
Follow-up Mammogram/Ultrasound	-	-	7.3%	8.4%
MRI for Low Back Pain	-	-	34.5%	32.7%
Survey of Patients' Hospital Experiences				
Area Around Room 'Always' Quiet at Night[8]	-	-	-	58%
Doctors 'Always' Communicated Well[8]	-	-	-	80%
Home Recovery Information Given[8]	-	-	-	82%
Hospital Given 9 or 10 on 10 Point Scale[8]	-	-	-	67%
Meds 'Always' Explained Before Given[8]	-	-	-	60%
Nurses 'Always' Communicated Well[8]	-	-	-	76%
Pain 'Always' Well Controlled[8]	-	-	-	69%
Room and Bathroom 'Always' Clean[8]	-	-	-	71%
Timely Help 'Always' Received[8]	-	-	-	64%
Would Definitely Recommend Hospital[8]	-	-	-	69%

Central Kansas Medical Center

3515 Broadway St
Great Bend, KS 67530
Phone: 620-786-6101
Fax: 620-786-6298
URL: www.ckmc.org
Type: Acute Care Hospitals
Emergency Services: Yes
Ownership: Voluntary Non-Profit - Church
Beds: 367

Key Personnel:
CEO/President. . . . . Chris Thomas
Chief of Medical Staff . . . . William Slater, MD
Operating Room. . . . . Monica Powers
Intensive Care Unit. . . . . Carolyn Mikesell
Patient Relations . . . . Sue Pfeifer

Measure	Cases	This Hosp.	State Avg.	U.S. Avg.
Heart Attack Care				
ACE Inhibitor or ARB for LVSD[2,3]	0	-	95%	96%
Aspirin at Arrival[1,2,3]	2	100%	98%	99%
Aspirin at Discharge[2,3]	0	-	98%	98%
Beta Blocker at Discharge[2,3]	0	-	98%	98%
Fibrinolytic Medication Timing[2,3]	0	-	44%	55%
PCI Within 90 Minutes of Arrival[2,3]	0	-	91%	90%
Smoking Cessation Advice[2,3]	0	-	99%	99%
Chest Pain/Possible Heart Attack Care				
Aspirin at Arrival	70	93%	92%	95%
Median Time to ECG (minutes)	72	18	10	8
Median Time to Transfer (minutes)[1,3]	1	131	60	61
Fibrinolytic Medication Timing[1]	2	0%	42%	54%
Heart Failure Care				
ACE Inhibitor or ARB for LVSD[1,2]	1	100%	91%	94%
Discharge Instructions[1,2]	16	50%	83%	88%
Evaluation of LVS Function[1,2]	24	92%	92%	98%
Smoking Cessation Advice[1,2]	6	100%	94%	98%
Pneumonia Care				
Appropriate Initial Antibiotic	32	81%	87%	92%
Blood Culture Timing	36	100%	96%	96%
Influenza Vaccine	30	73%	87%	91%
Initial Antibiotic Timing	38	97%	95%	95%
Pneumococcal Vaccine	38	82%	88%	93%
Smoking Cessation Advice[1]	8	100%	93%	97%
Surgical Care Improvement Project				
Appropriate VTP Within 24 Hours	28	93%	89%	92%
Appropriate Hair Removal	61	100%	100%	99%
Appropriate Beta Blocker Usage[1]	15	87%	90%	93%
Controlled Postoperative Blood Glucose	0	-	92%	93%
Prophylactic Antibiotic Timing	44	93%	96%	97%
Prophylactic Antibiotic Timing (Outpatient)	74	92%	93%	92%
Prophylactic Antibiotic Selection	44	95%	97%	97%
Prophylactic Antibiotic Select. (Outpatient)	72	96%	96%	94%
Prophylactic Antibiotic Stopped	44	95%	93%	94%
Recommended VTP Ordered	28	93%	91%	94%
Urinary Catheter Removal[1]	11	91%	86%	90%
Children's Asthma Care				
Received Systemic Corticosteroids	-	-	-	100%
Received Home Management Plan	-	-	-	71%
Received Reliever Medication	-	-	-	100%
Use of Medical Imaging				
Combination Abdominal CT Scan	727	0.039	0.365	0.191
Combination Chest CT Scan	710	0.015	0.065	0.054
Follow-up Mammogram/Ultrasound	437	5.3%	7.3%	8.4%
MRI for Low Back Pain	70	35.7%	34.5%	32.7%
Survey of Patients' Hospital Experiences				
Area Around Room 'Always' Quiet at Night	(a)	62%	-	58%
Doctors 'Always' Communicated Well	(a)	81%	-	80%
Home Recovery Information Given	(a)	89%	-	82%
Hospital Given 9 or 10 on 10 Point Scale	(a)	70%	-	67%
Meds 'Always' Explained Before Given	(a)	60%	-	60%
Nurses 'Always' Communicated Well	(a)	77%	-	76%
Pain 'Always' Well Controlled	(a)	67%	-	69%
Room and Bathroom 'Always' Clean	(a)	67%	-	71%
Timely Help 'Always' Received	(a)	73%	-	64%
Would Definitely Recommend Hospital	(a)	68%	-	69%

NOTE: Hospital profiles are in alphabetical order by state, then city, then hospital within the city; Rankings exclude hospitals with less than 25 cases except for patient surveys which excludes hospitals with less than 100 cases; (a) 100–299 cases; (1) The number of cases is too small to be sure how well a hospital is performing; (2) The hospital indicated that the data submitted for this measure were based on a sample of cases; (3) Data was collected during a shorter time period (fewer quarters) than the maximum possible time for this measure; (4) Suppressed for one or more quarters by CMS; (5) No data is available from the hospital for this measure; (6) Fewer than 100 patients completed the HCAHPS survey. Use these rates with caution, as the number of surveys may be too low to reliably assess hospital performance; (7) Survey results are based on less than 12 months of data; (8) Survey results are not available for this reporting period; (9) No or very few patients were eligible for the HCAHPS survey. The scores shown, if any, reflect a very small number of surveys; (10) A state average was not calculated because too few hospitals in the state submitted data; (11) There were discrepancies in the data collection process; Please refer to the User's Guide for a full explanation of data.

Great Bend Regional Hospital

514 Cleveland Street | Phone: 620-792-8833
Great Bend, KS 67530 | Fax: 6207921448
URL: www.greatbendsurgical.com
Type: Acute Care Hospitals | Emergency Services: Yes
Ownership: Voluntary Non-Profit - Other | Beds: 9

Key Personnel:
CEO/President. . . . . Pamela Chambers

Measure	Cases	This Hosp.	State Avg.	U.S. Avg.
Heart Attack Care				
ACE Inhibitor or ARB for LVSD[3]	0	-	95%	96%
Aspirin at Arrival[1,3]	1	100%	98%	99%
Aspirin at Discharge[1,3]	1	100%	98%	98%
Beta Blocker at Discharge[1,3]	1	100%	98%	98%
Fibrinolytic Medication Timing[3]	0	-	44%	55%
PCI Within 90 Minutes of Arrival[3]	0	-	91%	90%
Smoking Cessation Advice[1,3]	1	0%	99%	99%
Chest Pain/Possible Heart Attack Care				
Aspirin at Arrival[3]	35	80%	92%	95%
Median Time to ECG (minutes)[3]	35	17	10	8
Median Time to Transfer (minutes)[5]	0	-	60	61
Fibrinolytic Medication Timing[5]	0	-	42%	54%
Heart Failure Care				
ACE Inhibitor or ARB for LVSD[1,3]	1	0%	91%	94%
Discharge Instructions[1,3]	12	8%	83%	88%
Evaluation of LVS Function[1,3]	13	15%	92%	98%
Smoking Cessation Advice[3]	0	-	94%	98%
Pneumonia Care				
Appropriate Initial Antibiotic[1]	11	55%	87%	92%
Blood Culture Timing[1]	7	86%	96%	96%
Influenza Vaccine[1]	16	25%	87%	91%
Initial Antibiotic Timing[1]	17	100%	95%	95%
Pneumococcal Vaccine[1]	22	45%	88%	93%
Smoking Cessation Advice[1]	3	0%	93%	97%
Surgical Care Improvement Project				
Appropriate VTP Within 24 Hours[2]	157	92%	89%	92%
Appropriate Hair Removal[2]	351	99%	100%	99%
Appropriate Beta Blocker Usage[2]	88	82%	90%	93%
Controlled Postoperative Blood Glucose[2]	0	-	92%	93%
Prophylactic Antibiotic Timing[2]	311	87%	96%	97%
Prophylactic Antibiotic Timing (Outpatient)[3]	28	71%	93%	92%
Prophylactic Antibiotic Selection[2]	311	96%	97%	97%
Prophylactic Antibiotic Select. (Outpatient)[1,3]	20	100%	96%	94%
Prophylactic Antibiotic Stopped[2]	306	81%	93%	94%
Recommended VTP Ordered[2]	161	90%	91%	94%
Urinary Catheter Removal	137	59%	86%	90%
Children's Asthma Care				
Received Systemic Corticosteroids	-	-	-	100%
Received Home Management Plan	-	-	-	71%
Received Reliever Medication	-	-	-	100%
Use of Medical Imaging				
Combination Abdominal CT Scan[5]	0	-	0.365	0.191
Combination Chest CT Scan[5]	0	-	0.065	0.054
Follow-up Mammogram/Ultrasound[5]	0	-	7.3%	8.4%
MRI for Low Back Pain[5]	0	-	34.5%	32.7%
Survey of Patients' Hospital Experiences				
Area Around Room 'Always' Quiet at Night	300+	68%	-	58%
Doctors 'Always' Communicated Well	300+	86%	-	80%
Home Recovery Information Given	300+	80%	-	82%
Hospital Given 9 or 10 on 10 Point Scale	300+	76%	-	67%
Meds 'Always' Explained Before Given	300+	63%	-	60%
Nurses 'Always' Communicated Well	300+	78%	-	76%
Pain 'Always' Well Controlled	300+	72%	-	69%
Room and Bathroom 'Always' Clean	300+	75%	-	71%
Timely Help 'Always' Received	300+	72%	-	64%
Would Definitely Recommend Hospital	300+	80%	-	69%

Harper Hospital District #5

700 West 13th | Phone: 620-896-7324
Harper, KS 67058 | Fax: 620-896-7127
URL: www.harperhosp.com
Type: Critical Access Hospitals | Emergency Services: Yes
Ownership: Govt - Hospital Dist/Auth | Beds: 38

Key Personnel:
CEO/President. . . . . Kim Cinelli
Chief of Medical Staff. . . . . Ralph Bellar
Infection Control. . . . . Nearaj Vasishtha
Operating Room. . . . . Donald Ransom, DO
Emergency Room . . . . Martha Ediger

Measure	Cases	This Hosp.	State Avg.	U.S. Avg.
Heart Attack Care				
ACE Inhibitor or ARB for LVSD[3]	0	-	95%	96%
Aspirin at Arrival[3]	0	-	98%	99%
Aspirin at Discharge[3]	0	-	98%	98%
Beta Blocker at Discharge[3]	0	-	98%	98%
Fibrinolytic Medication Timing[3]	0	-	44%	55%
PCI Within 90 Minutes of Arrival[3]	0	-	91%	90%
Smoking Cessation Advice[3]	0	-	99%	99%
Chest Pain/Possible Heart Attack Care				
Aspirin at Arrival	-	-	92%	95%
Median Time to ECG (minutes)	-	-	10	8
Median Time to Transfer (minutes)	-	-	60	61
Fibrinolytic Medication Timing	-	-	42%	54%
Heart Failure Care				
ACE Inhibitor or ARB for LVSD[3]	0	-	91%	94%
Discharge Instructions[1,3]	3	0%	83%	88%
Evaluation of LVS Function[1,3]	5	0%	92%	98%
Smoking Cessation Advice[3]	0	-	94%	98%
Pneumonia Care				
Appropriate Initial Antibiotic[1,3]	10	70%	87%	92%
Blood Culture Timing[3]	0	-	96%	96%
Influenza Vaccine[1]	12	58%	87%	91%
Initial Antibiotic Timing[1,3]	10	100%	95%	95%
Pneumococcal Vaccine[1,3]	11	64%	88%	93%
Smoking Cessation Advice[1,3]	4	25%	93%	97%
Surgical Care Improvement Project				
Appropriate VTP Within 24 Hours[5]	0	-	89%	92%
Appropriate Hair Removal[5]	0	-	100%	99%
Appropriate Beta Blocker Usage[5]	0	-	90%	93%
Controlled Postoperative Blood Glucose[5]	0	-	92%	93%
Prophylactic Antibiotic Timing[5]	0	-	96%	97%
Prophylactic Antibiotic Timing (Outpatient)	-	-	93%	92%
Prophylactic Antibiotic Selection[5]	0	-	97%	97%
Prophylactic Antibiotic Select. (Outpatient)	-	-	96%	94%
Prophylactic Antibiotic Stopped[5]	0	-	93%	94%
Recommended VTP Ordered[5]	0	-	91%	94%
Urinary Catheter Removal[5]	0	-	86%	90%
Children's Asthma Care				
Received Systemic Corticosteroids	-	-	-	100%
Received Home Management Plan	-	-	-	71%
Received Reliever Medication	-	-	-	100%
Use of Medical Imaging				
Combination Abdominal CT Scan	-	-	0.365	0.191
Combination Chest CT Scan	-	-	0.065	0.054
Follow-up Mammogram/Ultrasound	-	-	7.3%	8.4%
MRI for Low Back Pain	-	-	34.5%	32.7%
Survey of Patients' Hospital Experiences				
Area Around Room 'Always' Quiet at Night[8]	-	-	-	58%
Doctors 'Always' Communicated Well[8]	-	-	-	80%
Home Recovery Information Given[8]	-	-	-	82%
Hospital Given 9 or 10 on 10 Point Scale[8]	-	-	-	67%
Meds 'Always' Explained Before Given[8]	-	-	-	60%
Nurses 'Always' Communicated Well[8]	-	-	-	76%
Pain 'Always' Well Controlled[8]	-	-	-	69%
Room and Bathroom 'Always' Clean[8]	-	-	-	71%
Timely Help 'Always' Received[8]	-	-	-	64%
Would Definitely Recommend Hospital[8]	-	-	-	69%

Hays Medical Center

2220 Canterbury Drive | Phone: 785-623-5000
Hays, KS 67601 | Fax: 785-623-5627
URL: www.haysmed.com
Type: Acute Care Hospitals | Emergency Services: Yes
Ownership: Voluntary Non-Profit - Private | Beds: 158

Key Personnel:
CEO/President. . . . . John H Jeter
Chief of Medical Staff. . . . . Ken Lindsey
Radiology. . . . . Michael Wright

Measure	Cases	This Hosp.	State Avg.	U.S. Avg.
Heart Attack Care				
ACE Inhibitor or ARB for LVSD[2]	27	100%	95%	96%
Aspirin at Arrival[2]	81	99%	98%	99%
Aspirin at Discharge[2]	220	100%	98%	98%
Beta Blocker at Discharge[2]	208	99%	98%	98%
Fibrinolytic Medication Timing[2]	0	-	44%	55%
PCI Within 90 Minutes of Arrival[1,2]	8	50%	91%	90%
Smoking Cessation Advice[2]	68	100%	99%	99%
Chest Pain/Possible Heart Attack Care				
Aspirin at Arrival[1,3]	1	100%	92%	95%
Median Time to ECG (minutes)[1,3]	2	7	10	8
Median Time to Transfer (minutes)[5]	0	-	60	61
Fibrinolytic Medication Timing[3]	0	-	42%	54%
Heart Failure Care				
ACE Inhibitor or ARB for LVSD	57	98%	91%	94%
Discharge Instructions	133	84%	83%	88%
Evaluation of LVS Function	170	99%	92%	98%
Smoking Cessation Advice[1]	19	95%	94%	98%
Pneumonia Care				
Appropriate Initial Antibiotic[2]	56	73%	87%	92%
Blood Culture Timing[2]	81	91%	96%	96%
Influenza Vaccine[2]	94	78%	87%	91%
Initial Antibiotic Timing[2]	78	94%	95%	95%
Pneumococcal Vaccine[2]	144	81%	88%	93%
Smoking Cessation Advice[2]	47	100%	93%	97%
Surgical Care Improvement Project				
Appropriate VTP Within 24 Hours[2]	203	88%	89%	92%
Appropriate Hair Removal[2]	555	100%	100%	99%
Appropriate Beta Blocker Usage[2]	179	96%	90%	93%
Controlled Postoperative Blood Glucose[2]	81	90%	92%	93%
Prophylactic Antibiotic Timing[2]	363	89%	96%	97%
Prophylactic Antibiotic Timing (Outpatient)	241	80%	93%	92%
Prophylactic Antibiotic Selection[2]	369	90%	97%	97%
Prophylactic Antibiotic Select. (Outpatient)	212	92%	96%	94%
Prophylactic Antibiotic Stopped[2]	340	86%	93%	94%
Recommended VTP Ordered[2]	203	90%	91%	94%
Urinary Catheter Removal[2]	116	75%	86%	90%
Children's Asthma Care				
Received Systemic Corticosteroids	-	-	-	100%
Received Home Management Plan	-	-	-	71%
Received Reliever Medication	-	-	-	100%
Use of Medical Imaging				
Combination Abdominal CT Scan	630	0.586	0.365	0.191
Combination Chest CT Scan	710	0.006	0.065	0.054
Follow-up Mammogram/Ultrasound	1,025	5.5%	7.3%	8.4%
MRI for Low Back Pain	160	41.3%	34.5%	32.7%
Survey of Patients' Hospital Experiences				
Area Around Room 'Always' Quiet at Night	300+	63%	-	58%
Doctors 'Always' Communicated Well	300+	78%	-	80%
Home Recovery Information Given	300+	86%	-	82%
Hospital Given 9 or 10 on 10 Point Scale	300+	70%	-	67%
Meds 'Always' Explained Before Given	300+	61%	-	60%
Nurses 'Always' Communicated Well	300+	76%	-	76%
Pain 'Always' Well Controlled	300+	68%	-	69%
Room and Bathroom 'Always' Clean	300+	74%	-	71%
Timely Help 'Always' Received	300+	60%	-	64%
Would Definitely Recommend Hospital	300+	71%	-	69%

NOTE: Hospital profiles are in alphabetical order by state, then city, then hospital within the city; Rankings exclude hospitals with less than 25 cases except for patient surveys which excludes hospitals with less than 100 cases; (a) 100–299 cases; (1) The number of cases is too small to be sure how well a hospital is performing; (2) The hospital indicated that the data submitted for this measure were based on a sample of cases; (3) Data was collected during a shorter time period (fewer quarters) than the maximum possible time for this measure; (4) Suppressed for one or more quarters by CMS; (5) No data is available from the hospital for this measure; (6) Fewer than 100 patients completed the HCAHPS survey. Use these rates with caution, as the number of surveys may be too low to reliably assess hospital performance; (7) Survey results are based on less than 12 months of data; (8) Survey results are not available for this reporting period; (9) No or very few patients were eligible for the HCAHPS survey. The scores shown, if any, reflect a very small number of surveys; (10) A state average was not calculated because too few hospitals in the state submitted data; (11) There were discrepancies in the data collection process; Please refer to the User's Guide for a full explanation of data.

Herington Municipal Hospital

100 E Helen Street
Herington, KS 67449
Type: Critical Access Hospitals
Ownership: Voluntary Non-Profit - Other
Phone: 785-258-2207
Fax: 785-258-5127
Emergency Services: Yes
Beds: 25

Key Personnel:
Chief of Medical Staff . . . . John Mosier
Infection Control . . . . Marge Bergstrom, RN
Operating Room . . . . Rose Stimac, RN
Quality Assurance . . . . Mary Steiner, RN
Emergency Room . . . . Rose Stimac, RN

Measure	Cases	This Hosp.	State Avg.	U.S. Avg.
Heart Attack Care				
ACE Inhibitor or ARB for LVSD[5]	0	-	95%	96%
Aspirin at Arrival[5]	0	-	98%	99%
Aspirin at Discharge[5]	0	-	98%	98%
Beta Blocker at Discharge[5]	0	-	98%	98%
Fibrinolytic Medication Timing[5]	0	-	44%	55%
PCI Within 90 Minutes of Arrival[5]	0	-	91%	90%
Smoking Cessation Advice[5]	0	-	99%	99%
Chest Pain/Possible Heart Attack Care				
Aspirin at Arrival	-	-	92%	95%
Median Time to ECG (minutes)	-	-	10	8
Median Time to Transfer (minutes)	-	-	60	61
Fibrinolytic Medication Timing	-	-	42%	54%
Heart Failure Care				
ACE Inhibitor or ARB for LVSD[5]	0	-	91%	94%
Discharge Instructions[5]	0	-	83%	88%
Evaluation of LVS Function[5]	0	-	92%	98%
Smoking Cessation Advice[5]	0	-	94%	98%
Pneumonia Care				
Appropriate Initial Antibiotic[3]	0	-	87%	92%
Blood Culture Timing[3]	0	-	96%	96%
Influenza Vaccine[5]	0	-	87%	91%
Initial Antibiotic Timing[3]	0	-	95%	95%
Pneumococcal Vaccine[3]	0	-	88%	93%
Smoking Cessation Advice[1,3]	1	0%	93%	97%
Surgical Care Improvement Project				
Appropriate VTP Within 24 Hours[5]	0	-	89%	92%
Appropriate Hair Removal[5]	0	-	100%	99%
Appropriate Beta Blocker Usage[5]	0	-	90%	93%
Controlled Postoperative Blood Glucose[5]	0	-	92%	93%
Prophylactic Antibiotic Timing[5]	0	-	96%	97%
Prophylactic Antibiotic Timing (Outpatient)	-	-	93%	92%
Prophylactic Antibiotic Selection[5]	0	-	97%	97%
Prophylactic Antibiotic Select. (Outpatient)	-	-	96%	94%
Prophylactic Antibiotic Stopped[5]	0	-	93%	94%
Recommended VTP Ordered[5]	0	-	91%	94%
Urinary Catheter Removal[5]	0	-	86%	90%
Children's Asthma Care				
Received Systemic Corticosteroids	-	-	-	100%
Received Home Management Plan	-	-	-	71%
Received Reliever Medication	-	-	-	100%
Use of Medical Imaging				
Combination Abdominal CT Scan	-	-	0.365	0.191
Combination Chest CT Scan	-	-	0.065	0.054
Follow-up Mammogram/Ultrasound	-	-	7.3%	8.4%
MRI for Low Back Pain	-	-	34.5%	32.7%
Survey of Patients' Hospital Experiences				
Area Around Room 'Always' Quiet at Night[8]	-	-	-	58%
Doctors 'Always' Communicated Well[8]	-	-	-	80%
Home Recovery Information Given[8]	-	-	-	82%
Hospital Given 9 or 10 on 10 Point Scale[8]	-	-	-	67%
Meds 'Always' Explained Before Given[8]	-	-	-	60%
Nurses 'Always' Communicated Well[8]	-	-	-	76%
Pain 'Always' Well Controlled[8]	-	-	-	69%
Room and Bathroom 'Always' Clean[8]	-	-	-	71%
Timely Help 'Always' Received[8]	-	-	-	64%
Would Definitely Recommend Hospital[8]	-	-	-	69%

Hiawatha Community Hospital

300 Utah Street
Hiawatha, KS 66434
Type: Critical Access Hospitals
Ownership: Voluntary Non-Profit - Private
Phone: 785-742-2131
Emergency Services: Yes

Measure	Cases	This Hosp.	State Avg.	U.S. Avg.
Heart Attack Care				
ACE Inhibitor or ARB for LVSD[3,1]	1	0%	95%	96%
Aspirin at Arrival[1,3]	2	100%	98%	99%
Aspirin at Discharge[1,3]	2	100%	98%	98%
Beta Blocker at Discharge[1,3]	1	100%	98%	98%
Fibrinolytic Medication Timing[3]	0	-	44%	55%
PCI Within 90 Minutes of Arrival[3]	0	-	91%	90%
Smoking Cessation Advice[3]	0	-	99%	99%
Chest Pain/Possible Heart Attack Care				
Aspirin at Arrival	-	-	92%	95%
Median Time to ECG (minutes)	-	-	10	8
Median Time to Transfer (minutes)	-	-	60	61
Fibrinolytic Medication Timing	-	-	42%	54%
Heart Failure Care				
ACE Inhibitor or ARB for LVSD[1,3]	3	67%	91%	94%
Discharge Instructions[1,3]	9	89%	83%	88%
Evaluation of LVS Function[1,3]	18	56%	92%	98%
Smoking Cessation Advice[1,3]	2	100%	94%	98%
Pneumonia Care				
Appropriate Initial Antibiotic[1,3]	7	71%	87%	92%
Blood Culture Timing[1,3]	13	77%	96%	96%
Influenza Vaccine[1]	23	70%	87%	91%
Initial Antibiotic Timing[1,3]	3	0%	95%	95%
Pneumococcal Vaccine[1,3]	22	73%	88%	93%
Smoking Cessation Advice[1,3]	6	100%	93%	97%
Surgical Care Improvement Project				
Appropriate VTP Within 24 Hours[1,3]	4	100%	89%	92%
Appropriate Hair Removal[1,3]	19	100%	100%	99%
Appropriate Beta Blocker Usage[5]	0	-	90%	93%
Controlled Postoperative Blood Glucose[3]	0	-	92%	93%
Prophylactic Antibiotic Timing[1,3]	13	38%	96%	97%
Prophylactic Antibiotic Timing (Outpatient)	-	-	93%	92%
Prophylactic Antibiotic Selection[1,3]	12	100%	97%	97%
Prophylactic Antibiotic Select. (Outpatient)	-	-	96%	94%
Prophylactic Antibiotic Stopped[1,3]	12	92%	93%	94%
Recommended VTP Ordered[1,3]	11	36%	91%	94%
Urinary Catheter Removal[1,3]	2	100%	86%	90%
Children's Asthma Care				
Received Systemic Corticosteroids	-	-	-	100%
Received Home Management Plan	-	-	-	71%
Received Reliever Medication	-	-	-	100%
Use of Medical Imaging				
Combination Abdominal CT Scan	-	-	0.365	0.191
Combination Chest CT Scan	-	-	0.065	0.054
Follow-up Mammogram/Ultrasound	-	-	7.3%	8.4%
MRI for Low Back Pain	-	-	34.5%	32.7%
Survey of Patients' Hospital Experiences				
Area Around Room 'Always' Quiet at Night[8]	-	-	-	58%
Doctors 'Always' Communicated Well[8]	-	-	-	80%
Home Recovery Information Given[8]	-	-	-	82%
Hospital Given 9 or 10 on 10 Point Scale[8]	-	-	-	67%
Meds 'Always' Explained Before Given[8]	-	-	-	60%
Nurses 'Always' Communicated Well[8]	-	-	-	76%
Pain 'Always' Well Controlled[8]	-	-	-	69%
Room and Bathroom 'Always' Clean[8]	-	-	-	71%
Timely Help 'Always' Received[8]	-	-	-	64%
Would Definitely Recommend Hospital[8]	-	-	-	69%

Graham County Hospital

304 West Prout Street
Hill City, KS 67642
Type: Critical Access Hospitals
Ownership: Government - Local
Phone: 785-421-2121
Fax: 785-421-2034
Emergency Services: Yes
Beds: 25

Key Personnel:
CEO/President. . . . . Doug Newman
Quality Assurance . . . . Kathy Richmeier

Measure	Cases	This Hosp.	State Avg.	U.S. Avg.
Heart Attack Care				
ACE Inhibitor or ARB for LVSD[5]	0	-	95%	96%
Aspirin at Arrival[5]	0	-	98%	99%
Aspirin at Discharge[5]	0	-	98%	98%
Beta Blocker at Discharge[5]	0	-	98%	98%
Fibrinolytic Medication Timing[5]	0	-	44%	55%
PCI Within 90 Minutes of Arrival[5]	0	-	91%	90%
Smoking Cessation Advice[5]	0	-	99%	99%
Chest Pain/Possible Heart Attack Care				
Aspirin at Arrival[1]	16	100%	92%	95%
Median Time to ECG (minutes)[1]	17	10	10	8
Median Time to Transfer (minutes)[5]	0	-	60	61
Fibrinolytic Medication Timing[1,3]	1	0%	42%	54%
Heart Failure Care				
ACE Inhibitor or ARB for LVSD[1]	5	100%	91%	94%
Discharge Instructions[1]	12	25%	83%	88%
Evaluation of LVS Function	38	47%	92%	98%
Smoking Cessation Advice[1]	11	0%	94%	98%
Pneumonia Care				
Appropriate Initial Antibiotic[1]	11	100%	87%	92%
Blood Culture Timing[1]	3	100%	96%	96%
Influenza Vaccine[1]	11	27%	87%	91%
Initial Antibiotic Timing[1]	13	85%	95%	95%
Pneumococcal Vaccine[1]	11	64%	88%	93%
Smoking Cessation Advice[1]	6	0%	93%	97%
Surgical Care Improvement Project				
Appropriate VTP Within 24 Hours[5]	0	-	89%	92%
Appropriate Hair Removal[5]	0	-	100%	99%
Appropriate Beta Blocker Usage[5]	0	-	90%	93%
Controlled Postoperative Blood Glucose[5]	0	-	92%	93%
Prophylactic Antibiotic Timing[5]	0	-	96%	97%
Prophylactic Antibiotic Timing (Outpatient)[5]	0	-	93%	92%
Prophylactic Antibiotic Selection[5]	0	-	97%	97%
Prophylactic Antibiotic Select. (Outpatient)[5]	0	-	96%	94%
Prophylactic Antibiotic Stopped[5]	0	-	93%	94%
Recommended VTP Ordered[5]	0	-	91%	94%
Urinary Catheter Removal[5]	0	-	86%	90%
Children's Asthma Care				
Received Systemic Corticosteroids	-	-	-	100%
Received Home Management Plan	-	-	-	71%
Received Reliever Medication	-	-	-	100%
Use of Medical Imaging				
Combination Abdominal CT Scan	88	0.648	0.365	0.191
Combination Chest CT Scan	85	0.035	0.065	0.054
Follow-up Mammogram/Ultrasound	92	9.8%	7.3%	8.4%
MRI for Low Back Pain[1]	25	32.0%	34.5%	32.7%
Survey of Patients' Hospital Experiences				
Area Around Room 'Always' Quiet at Night[8]	-	-	-	58%
Doctors 'Always' Communicated Well[8]	-	-	-	80%
Home Recovery Information Given[8]	-	-	-	82%
Hospital Given 9 or 10 on 10 Point Scale[8]	-	-	-	67%
Meds 'Always' Explained Before Given[8]	-	-	-	60%
Nurses 'Always' Communicated Well[8]	-	-	-	76%
Pain 'Always' Well Controlled[8]	-	-	-	69%
Room and Bathroom 'Always' Clean[8]	-	-	-	71%
Timely Help 'Always' Received[8]	-	-	-	64%
Would Definitely Recommend Hospital[8]	-	-	-	69%

NOTE: Hospital profiles are in alphabetical order by state, then city, then hospital within the city; Rankings exclude hospitals with less than 25 cases except for patient surveys which excludes hospitals with less than 100 cases; (a) 100–299 cases; (1) The number of cases is too small to be sure how well a hospital is performing; (2) The hospital indicated that the data submitted for this measure were based on a sample of cases; (3) Data was collected during a shorter time period (fewer quarters) than the maximum possible time for this measure; (4) Suppressed for one or more quarters by CMS; (5) No data is available from the hospital for this measure; (6) Fewer than 100 patients completed the HCAHPS survey. Use these rates with caution, as the number of surveys may be too low to reliably assess hospital performance; (7) Survey results are based on less than 12 months of data; (8) Survey results are not available for this reporting period; (9) No or very few patients were eligible for the HCAHPS survey. The scores shown, if any, reflect a very small number of surveys; (10) A state average was not calculated because too few hospitals in the state submitted data; (11) There were discrepancies in the data collection process; Please refer to the User's Guide for a full explanation of data.

Hillsboro Community Hospital

701 S Main Street Phone: 620-947-3114
Hillsboro, KS 67063 Fax: 620-947-5690
E-mail: comf@southwind.net
URL: www.hillsboromedicalcenter.org
Type: Critical Access Hospitals Emergency Services: Yes
Ownership: Proprietary Beds: 79

Key Personnel:
CEO/President............... Michael Ryan
Chief of Medical Staff.......... A Randal Claassen
Infection Control............. Cayle Goertzen, MT
Quality Assurance .... Ken Johnson, RT
Radiology.................. Billie Kueser
Anesthesiology.............. Bob Reese, CRNA
Emergency Room .... Jan Fenske, RN

Measure	Cases	This Hosp.	State Avg.	U.S. Avg.
Heart Attack Care				
ACE Inhibitor or ARB for LVSD[3]	0	-	95%	96%
Aspirin at Arrival[1,3]	1	100%	98%	99%
Aspirin at Discharge[1,3]	1	100%	98%	98%
Beta Blocker at Discharge[1,3]	1	100%	98%	98%
Fibrinolytic Medication Timing[3]	0	-	44%	55%
PCI Within 90 Minutes of Arrival[3]	0	-	91%	90%
Smoking Cessation Advice[3]	0	-	99%	99%
Chest Pain/Possible Heart Attack Care				
Aspirin at Arrival[1,3]	8	62%	92%	95%
Median Time to ECG (minutes)[1,3]	8	10	10	8
Median Time to Transfer (minutes)[5]	0	-	60	61
Fibrinolytic Medication Timing[5]	0	-	42%	54%
Heart Failure Care				
ACE Inhibitor or ARB for LVSD[1]	1	100%	91%	94%
Discharge Instructions[1]	5	40%	83%	88%
Evaluation of LVS Function[1]	8	75%	92%	98%
Smoking Cessation Advice[1]	2	0%	94%	98%
Pneumonia Care				
Appropriate Initial Antibiotic[1,3]	4	25%	87%	92%
Blood Culture Timing[1,3]	1	100%	96%	96%
Influenza Vaccine[1]	4	75%	87%	91%
Initial Antibiotic Timing[1,3]	2	100%	95%	95%
Pneumococcal Vaccine[1,3]	4	75%	88%	93%
Smoking Cessation Advice[3]	0	-	93%	97%
Surgical Care Improvement Project				
Appropriate VTP Within 24 Hours[5]	0	-	89%	92%
Appropriate Hair Removal[5]	0	-	100%	99%
Appropriate Beta Blocker Usage[5]	0	-	90%	93%
Controlled Postoperative Blood Glucose[5]	0	-	92%	93%
Prophylactic Antibiotic Timing[5]	0	-	96%	97%
Prophylactic Antibiotic Timing (Outpatient)[5]	0	-	93%	92%
Prophylactic Antibiotic Selection[5]	0	-	97%	97%
Prophylactic Antibiotic Select. (Outpatient)[5]	0	-	96%	94%
Prophylactic Antibiotic Stopped[5]	0	-	93%	94%
Recommended VTP Ordered[5]	0	-	91%	94%
Urinary Catheter Removal[5]	0	-	86%	90%
Children's Asthma Care				
Received Systemic Corticosteroids	-	-	-	100%
Received Home Management Plan	-	-	-	71%
Received Reliever Medication	-	-	-	100%
Use of Medical Imaging				
Combination Abdominal CT Scan[1]	27	0.296	0.365	0.191
Combination Chest CT Scan[1]	14	0.000	0.065	0.054
Follow-up Mammogram/Ultrasound[5]	0	-	7.3%	8.4%
MRI for Low Back Pain[1]	10	30.0%	34.5%	32.7%
Survey of Patients' Hospital Experiences				
Area Around Room 'Always' Quiet at Night[8]	-	-	-	58%
Doctors 'Always' Communicated Well[8]	-	-	-	80%
Home Recovery Information Given[8]	-	-	-	82%
Hospital Given 9 or 10 on 10 Point Scale[8]	-	-	-	67%
Meds 'Always' Explained Before Given[8]	-	-	-	60%
Nurses 'Always' Communicated Well[8]	-	-	-	76%
Pain 'Always' Well Controlled[8]	-	-	-	69%
Room and Bathroom 'Always' Clean[8]	-	-	-	71%
Timely Help 'Always' Received[8]	-	-	-	64%
Would Definitely Recommend Hospital[8]	-	-	-	69%

Clara Barton Hospital

250 W 9th Street Phone: 620-653-2114
Hoisington, KS 67544 Fax: 620-653-2350
URL: www.clarabartonhospital.org
Type: Critical Access Hospitals Emergency Services: Yes
Ownership: Voluntary Non-Profit - Private Beds: 48

Key Personnel:
CEO/President............... W Charles Waters, CHE
Chief of Medical Staff.......... Cameron Knacksedt, DO
Infection Control............. Stacey Dolechek
Operating Room............. Robert Arnold, RN
Quality Assurance .... Colletta Debes, RN
Radiology.................. Robert Bowerman

Measure	Cases	This Hosp.	State Avg.	U.S. Avg.
Heart Attack Care				
ACE Inhibitor or ARB for LVSD[5]	0	-	95%	96%
Aspirin at Arrival[5]	0	-	98%	99%
Aspirin at Discharge[5]	0	-	98%	98%
Beta Blocker at Discharge[5]	0	-	98%	98%
Fibrinolytic Medication Timing[5]	0	-	44%	55%
PCI Within 90 Minutes of Arrival[5]	0	-	91%	90%
Smoking Cessation Advice[5]	0	-	99%	99%
Chest Pain/Possible Heart Attack Care				
Aspirin at Arrival[5]	0	-	92%	95%
Median Time to ECG (minutes)[5]	0	-	10	8
Median Time to Transfer (minutes)[5]	0	-	60	61
Fibrinolytic Medication Timing[5]	0	-	42%	54%
Heart Failure Care				
ACE Inhibitor or ARB for LVSD[1,3]	1	0%	91%	94%
Discharge Instructions[1,3]	4	0%	83%	88%
Evaluation of LVS Function[1,3]	9	33%	92%	98%
Smoking Cessation Advice[3]	0	-	94%	98%
Pneumonia Care				
Appropriate Initial Antibiotic[1]	14	79%	87%	92%
Blood Culture Timing[1]	6	100%	96%	96%
Influenza Vaccine[1]	9	56%	87%	91%
Initial Antibiotic Timing[1]	16	94%	95%	95%
Pneumococcal Vaccine[1]	14	50%	88%	93%
Smoking Cessation Advice[1]	3	67%	93%	97%
Surgical Care Improvement Project				
Appropriate VTP Within 24 Hours[1]	5	60%	89%	92%
Appropriate Hair Removal[1]	14	93%	100%	99%
Appropriate Beta Blocker Usage[5]	0	-	90%	93%
Controlled Postoperative Blood Glucose	0	-	92%	93%
Prophylactic Antibiotic Timing[1]	11	91%	96%	97%
Prophylactic Antibiotic Timing (Outpatient)[5]	0	-	93%	92%
Prophylactic Antibiotic Selection[1]	11	73%	97%	97%
Prophylactic Antibiotic Select. (Outpatient)[5]	0	-	96%	94%
Prophylactic Antibiotic Stopped[1]	11	91%	93%	94%
Recommended VTP Ordered[1]	5	60%	91%	94%
Urinary Catheter Removal[1]	3	100%	86%	90%
Children's Asthma Care				
Received Systemic Corticosteroids	-	-	-	100%
Received Home Management Plan	-	-	-	71%
Received Reliever Medication	-	-	-	100%
Use of Medical Imaging				
Combination Abdominal CT Scan	189	0.392	0.365	0.191
Combination Chest CT Scan	139	0.079	0.065	0.054
Follow-up Mammogram/Ultrasound	163	2.5%	7.3%	8.4%
MRI for Low Back Pain[1]	25	36.0%	34.5%	32.7%
Survey of Patients' Hospital Experiences				
Area Around Room 'Always' Quiet at Night[8]	-	-	-	58%
Doctors 'Always' Communicated Well[8]	-	-	-	80%
Home Recovery Information Given[8]	-	-	-	82%
Hospital Given 9 or 10 on 10 Point Scale[8]	-	-	-	67%
Meds 'Always' Explained Before Given[8]	-	-	-	60%
Nurses 'Always' Communicated Well[8]	-	-	-	76%
Pain 'Always' Well Controlled[8]	-	-	-	69%
Room and Bathroom 'Always' Clean[8]	-	-	-	71%
Timely Help 'Always' Received[8]	-	-	-	64%
Would Definitely Recommend Hospital[8]	-	-	-	69%

Holton Community Hospital

1110 Columbine Dr Phone: 785-364-2116
Holton, KS 66436
Type: Critical Access Hospitals Emergency Services: Yes
Ownership: Voluntary Non-Profit - Other

Key Personnel:
CEO/President............... Ron Marshall
Cardiac Laboratory........... Beth Nelson
Operating Room............. April Zeller
Radiology.................. Deb Davies

Measure	Cases	This Hosp.	State Avg.	U.S. Avg.
Heart Attack Care				
ACE Inhibitor or ARB for LVSD[5]	0	-	95%	96%
Aspirin at Arrival[5]	0	-	98%	99%
Aspirin at Discharge[5]	0	-	98%	98%
Beta Blocker at Discharge[5]	0	-	98%	98%
Fibrinolytic Medication Timing[5]	0	-	44%	55%
PCI Within 90 Minutes of Arrival[5]	0	-	91%	90%
Smoking Cessation Advice[5]	0	-	99%	99%
Chest Pain/Possible Heart Attack Care				
Aspirin at Arrival[5]	0	-	92%	95%
Median Time to ECG (minutes)[5]	0	-	10	8
Median Time to Transfer (minutes)[5]	0	-	60	61
Fibrinolytic Medication Timing[5]	0	-	42%	54%
Heart Failure Care				
ACE Inhibitor or ARB for LVSD[1]	2	0%	91%	94%
Discharge Instructions[1]	4	50%	83%	88%
Evaluation of LVS Function[1]	8	62%	92%	98%
Smoking Cessation Advice	0	-	94%	98%
Pneumonia Care				
Appropriate Initial Antibiotic[1]	15	87%	87%	92%
Blood Culture Timing[1]	1	100%	96%	96%
Influenza Vaccine[1]	7	100%	87%	91%
Initial Antibiotic Timing[1]	15	100%	95%	95%
Pneumococcal Vaccine[1]	19	84%	88%	93%
Smoking Cessation Advice[1]	5	60%	93%	97%
Surgical Care Improvement Project				
Appropriate VTP Within 24 Hours[5]	0	-	89%	92%
Appropriate Hair Removal[5]	0	-	100%	99%
Appropriate Beta Blocker Usage[5]	0	-	90%	93%
Controlled Postoperative Blood Glucose[5]	0	-	92%	93%
Prophylactic Antibiotic Timing[5]	0	-	96%	97%
Prophylactic Antibiotic Timing (Outpatient)[5]	0	-	93%	92%
Prophylactic Antibiotic Selection[5]	0	-	97%	97%
Prophylactic Antibiotic Select. (Outpatient)[5]	0	-	96%	94%
Prophylactic Antibiotic Stopped[5]	0	-	93%	94%
Recommended VTP Ordered[5]	0	-	91%	94%
Urinary Catheter Removal[5]	0	-	86%	90%
Children's Asthma Care				
Received Systemic Corticosteroids	-	-	-	100%
Received Home Management Plan	-	-	-	71%
Received Reliever Medication	-	-	-	100%
Use of Medical Imaging				
Combination Abdominal CT Scan	93	0.247	0.365	0.191
Combination Chest CT Scan[1]	40	0.050	0.065	0.054
Follow-up Mammogram/Ultrasound	201	4.0%	7.3%	8.4%
MRI for Low Back Pain	38	44.7%	34.5%	32.7%
Survey of Patients' Hospital Experiences				
Area Around Room 'Always' Quiet at Night[8]	-	-	-	58%
Doctors 'Always' Communicated Well[8]	-	-	-	80%
Home Recovery Information Given[8]	-	-	-	82%
Hospital Given 9 or 10 on 10 Point Scale[8]	-	-	-	67%
Meds 'Always' Explained Before Given[8]	-	-	-	60%
Nurses 'Always' Communicated Well[8]	-	-	-	76%
Pain 'Always' Well Controlled[8]	-	-	-	69%
Room and Bathroom 'Always' Clean[8]	-	-	-	71%
Timely Help 'Always' Received[8]	-	-	-	64%
Would Definitely Recommend Hospital[8]	-	-	-	69%

NOTE: Hospital profiles are in alphabetical order by state, then city, then hospital within the city; Rankings exclude hospitals with less than 25 cases except for patient surveys which excludes hospitals with less than 100 cases; (a) 100–299 cases; (1) The number of cases is too small to be sure how well a hospital is performing; (2) The hospital indicated that the data submitted for this measure were based on a sample of cases; (3) Data was collected during a shorter time period (fewer quarters) than the maximum possible time for this measure; (4) Suppressed for one or more quarters by CMS; (5) No data is available from the hospital for this measure; (6) Fewer than 100 patients completed the HCAHPS survey. Use these rates with caution, as the number of surveys may be too low to reliably assess hospital performance; (7) Survey results are based on less than 12 months of data; (8) Survey results are not available for this reporting period; (9) No or very few patients were eligible for the HCAHPS survey. The scores shown, if any, reflect a very small number of surveys; (10) A state average was not calculated because too few hospitals in the state submitted data; (11) There were discrepancies in the data collection process; Please refer to the User's Guide for a full explanation of data.

Sheridan County Hospital

826 18th Street Phone: 785-675-3281
Hoxie, KS 67740
URL: www.sheridanhospital.org
Type: Critical Access Hospitals Emergency Services: Yes
Ownership: Government - Local
Key Personnel:
CEO . . . . Mike McCafferty

Measure	Cases	This Hosp.	State Avg.	U.S. Avg.
Heart Attack Care				
ACE Inhibitor or ARB for LVSD[5]	0	-	95%	96%
Aspirin at Arrival[5]	0	-	98%	99%
Aspirin at Discharge[5]	0	-	98%	98%
Beta Blocker at Discharge[5]	0	-	98%	98%
Fibrinolytic Medication Timing[5]	0	-	44%	55%
PCI Within 90 Minutes of Arrival[5]	0	-	91%	90%
Smoking Cessation Advice[5]	0	-	99%	99%
Chest Pain/Possible Heart Attack Care				
Aspirin at Arrival	-	-	92%	95%
Median Time to ECG (minutes)	-	-	10	8
Median Time to Transfer (minutes)	-	-	60	61
Fibrinolytic Medication Timing	-	-	42%	54%
Heart Failure Care				
ACE Inhibitor or ARB for LVSD[5]	0	-	91%	94%
Discharge Instructions[5]	0	-	83%	88%
Evaluation of LVS Function[5]	0	-	92%	98%
Smoking Cessation Advice[5]	0	-	94%	98%
Pneumonia Care				
Appropriate Initial Antibiotic[1]	4	25%	87%	92%
Blood Culture Timing[1]	2	100%	96%	96%
Influenza Vaccine[1]	11	82%	87%	91%
Initial Antibiotic Timing[1]	12	83%	95%	95%
Pneumococcal Vaccine[1]	20	75%	88%	93%
Smoking Cessation Advice[1]	3	67%	93%	97%
Surgical Care Improvement Project				
Appropriate VTP Within 24 Hours[5]	0	-	89%	92%
Appropriate Hair Removal[5]	0	-	100%	99%
Appropriate Beta Blocker Usage[5]	0	-	90%	93%
Controlled Postoperative Blood Glucose[5]	0	-	92%	93%
Prophylactic Antibiotic Timing[5]	0	-	96%	97%
Prophylactic Antibiotic Timing (Outpatient)	-	-	93%	92%
Prophylactic Antibiotic Selection[5]	0	-	97%	97%
Prophylactic Antibiotic Select. (Outpatient)	-	-	96%	94%
Prophylactic Antibiotic Stopped[5]	0	-	93%	94%
Recommended VTP Ordered[5]	0	-	91%	94%
Urinary Catheter Removal[5]	0	-	86%	90%
Children's Asthma Care				
Received Systemic Corticosteroids	-	-	-	100%
Received Home Management Plan	-	-	-	71%
Received Reliever Medication	-	-	-	100%
Use of Medical Imaging				
Combination Abdominal CT Scan	-	-	0.365	0.191
Combination Chest CT Scan	-	-	0.065	0.054
Follow-up Mammogram/Ultrasound	-	-	7.3%	8.4%
MRI for Low Back Pain	-	-	34.5%	32.7%
Survey of Patients' Hospital Experiences				
Area Around Room 'Always' Quiet at Night[8]	-	-	-	58%
Doctors 'Always' Communicated Well[8]	-	-	-	80%
Home Recovery Information Given[8]	-	-	-	82%
Hospital Given 9 or 10 on 10 Point Scale[8]	-	-	-	67%
Meds 'Always' Explained Before Given[8]	-	-	-	60%
Nurses 'Always' Communicated Well[8]	-	-	-	76%
Pain 'Always' Well Controlled[8]	-	-	-	69%
Room and Bathroom 'Always' Clean[8]	-	-	-	71%
Timely Help 'Always' Received[8]	-	-	-	64%
Would Definitely Recommend Hospital[8]	-	-	-	69%

Promise Regional Medical Center Hutchinson

1701 E 23rd Avenue Phone: 620-665-2001
Hutchinson, KS 67502 Fax: 620-513-3811
E-mail: info@hhosp.com
URL: hutchinsonhospital.com
Type: Acute Care Hospitals Emergency Services: Yes
Ownership: Proprietary Beds: 200
Key Personnel:
CEO/President. . . . . Mark Norrell

Measure	Cases	This Hosp.	State Avg.	U.S. Avg.
Heart Attack Care				
ACE Inhibitor or ARB for LVSD	25	92%	95%	96%
Aspirin at Arrival	135	100%	98%	99%
Aspirin at Discharge	170	98%	98%	98%
Beta Blocker at Discharge	145	92%	98%	98%
Fibrinolytic Medication Timing	0	-	44%	55%
PCI Within 90 Minutes of Arrival	31	77%	91%	90%
Smoking Cessation Advice	55	100%	99%	99%
Chest Pain/Possible Heart Attack Care				
Aspirin at Arrival[1]	12	100%	92%	95%
Median Time to ECG (minutes)[1]	12	10	10	8
Median Time to Transfer (minutes)[5]	0	-	60	61
Fibrinolytic Medication Timing[5]	0	-	42%	54%
Heart Failure Care				
ACE Inhibitor or ARB for LVSD	46	93%	91%	94%
Discharge Instructions	94	91%	83%	88%
Evaluation of LVS Function	140	96%	92%	98%
Smoking Cessation Advice[1]	17	100%	94%	98%
Pneumonia Care				
Appropriate Initial Antibiotic	123	83%	87%	92%
Blood Culture Timing	120	96%	96%	96%
Influenza Vaccine	151	95%	87%	91%
Initial Antibiotic Timing	179	93%	95%	95%
Pneumococcal Vaccine	219	94%	88%	93%
Smoking Cessation Advice	71	100%	93%	97%
Surgical Care Improvement Project				
Appropriate VTP Within 24 Hours	253	71%	89%	92%
Appropriate Hair Removal	844	100%	100%	99%
Appropriate Beta Blocker Usage	229	69%	90%	93%
Controlled Postoperative Blood Glucose	143	83%	92%	93%
Prophylactic Antibiotic Timing	559	86%	96%	97%
Prophylactic Antibiotic Timing (Outpatient)	285	77%	93%	92%
Prophylactic Antibiotic Selection	558	95%	97%	97%
Prophylactic Antibiotic Select. (Outpatient)	274	84%	96%	94%
Prophylactic Antibiotic Stopped	542	81%	93%	94%
Recommended VTP Ordered	255	72%	91%	94%
Urinary Catheter Removal	217	84%	86%	90%
Children's Asthma Care				
Received Systemic Corticosteroids	-	-	-	100%
Received Home Management Plan	-	-	-	71%
Received Reliever Medication	-	-	-	100%
Use of Medical Imaging				
Combination Abdominal CT Scan	320	0.019	0.365	0.191
Combination Chest CT Scan	139	0.000	0.065	0.054
Follow-up Mammogram/Ultrasound[5]	0	-	7.3%	8.4%
MRI for Low Back Pain	72	29.2%	34.5%	32.7%
Survey of Patients' Hospital Experiences				
Area Around Room 'Always' Quiet at Night	300+	47%	-	58%
Doctors 'Always' Communicated Well	300+	75%	-	80%
Home Recovery Information Given	300+	79%	-	82%
Hospital Given 9 or 10 on 10 Point Scale	300+	61%	-	67%
Meds 'Always' Explained Before Given	300+	52%	-	60%
Nurses 'Always' Communicated Well	300+	70%	-	76%
Pain 'Always' Well Controlled	300+	63%	-	69%
Room and Bathroom 'Always' Clean	300+	66%	-	71%
Timely Help 'Always' Received	300+	56%	-	64%
Would Definitely Recommend Hospital	300+	62%	-	69%

Summit Surgical

1818 East 23rd Avenue Phone: 620-663-4800
Hutchinson, KS 67502
URL: www.summitks.com
Type: Acute Care Hospitals Emergency Services: No
Ownership: Voluntary Non-Profit - Private Beds: 6

Measure	Cases	This Hosp.	State Avg.	U.S. Avg.
Heart Attack Care				
ACE Inhibitor or ARB for LVSD[5]	0	-	95%	96%
Aspirin at Arrival[5]	0	-	98%	99%
Aspirin at Discharge[5]	0	-	98%	98%
Beta Blocker at Discharge[5]	0	-	98%	98%
Fibrinolytic Medication Timing[5]	0	-	44%	55%
PCI Within 90 Minutes of Arrival[5]	0	-	91%	90%
Smoking Cessation Advice[5]	0	-	99%	99%
Chest Pain/Possible Heart Attack Care				
Aspirin at Arrival[5]	0	-	92%	95%
Median Time to ECG (minutes)[5]	0	-	10	8
Median Time to Transfer (minutes)[5]	0	-	60	61
Fibrinolytic Medication Timing[5]	0	-	42%	54%
Heart Failure Care				
ACE Inhibitor or ARB for LVSD[5]	0	-	91%	94%
Discharge Instructions[5]	0	-	83%	88%
Evaluation of LVS Function[5]	0	-	92%	98%
Smoking Cessation Advice[5]	0	-	94%	98%
Pneumonia Care				
Appropriate Initial Antibiotic[5]	0	-	87%	92%
Blood Culture Timing[5]	0	-	96%	96%
Influenza Vaccine[5]	0	-	87%	91%
Initial Antibiotic Timing[5]	0	-	95%	95%
Pneumococcal Vaccine[5]	0	-	88%	93%
Smoking Cessation Advice[5]	0	-	93%	97%
Surgical Care Improvement Project				
Appropriate VTP Within 24 Hours[1]	2	100%	89%	92%
Appropriate Hair Removal	293	100%	100%	99%
Appropriate Beta Blocker Usage	42	98%	90%	93%
Controlled Postoperative Blood Glucose	0	-	92%	93%
Prophylactic Antibiotic Timing	279	99%	96%	97%
Prophylactic Antibiotic Timing (Outpatient)[1]	11	100%	93%	92%
Prophylactic Antibiotic Selection	279	99%	97%	97%
Prophylactic Antibiotic Select. (Outpatient)[1]	11	100%	96%	94%
Prophylactic Antibiotic Stopped	278	100%	93%	94%
Recommended VTP Ordered[1]	2	100%	91%	94%
Urinary Catheter Removal	79	100%	86%	90%
Children's Asthma Care				
Received Systemic Corticosteroids	-	-	-	100%
Received Home Management Plan	-	-	-	71%
Received Reliever Medication	-	-	-	100%
Use of Medical Imaging				
Combination Abdominal CT Scan[5]	0	-	0.365	0.191
Combination Chest CT Scan[5]	0	-	0.065	0.054
Follow-up Mammogram/Ultrasound[5]	0	-	7.3%	8.4%
MRI for Low Back Pain[5]	0	-	34.5%	32.7%
Survey of Patients' Hospital Experiences				
Area Around Room 'Always' Quiet at Night	(a)	81%	-	58%
Doctors 'Always' Communicated Well	(a)	88%	-	80%
Home Recovery Information Given	(a)	90%	-	82%
Hospital Given 9 or 10 on 10 Point Scale	(a)	88%	-	67%
Meds 'Always' Explained Before Given	(a)	63%	-	60%
Nurses 'Always' Communicated Well	(a)	88%	-	76%
Pain 'Always' Well Controlled	(a)	75%	-	69%
Room and Bathroom 'Always' Clean	(a)	82%	-	71%
Timely Help 'Always' Received	(a)	84%	-	64%
Would Definitely Recommend Hospital	(a)	90%	-	69%

NOTE: Hospital profiles are in alphabetical order by state, then city, then hospital within the city; Rankings exclude hospitals with less than 25 cases except for patient surveys which excludes hospitals with less than 100 cases; (a) 100–299 cases; (1) The number of cases is too small to be sure how well a hospital is performing; (2) The hospital indicated that the data submitted for this measure were based on a sample of cases; (3) Data was collected during a shorter time period (fewer quarters) than the maximum possible time for this measure; (4) Suppressed for one or more quarters by CMS; (5) No data is available from the hospital for this measure; (6) Fewer than 100 patients completed the HCAHPS survey. Use these rates with caution, as the number of surveys may be too low to reliably assess hospital performance; (7) Survey results are based on less than 12 months of data; (8) Survey results are not available for this reporting period; (9) No or very few patients were eligible for the HCAHPS survey. The scores shown, if any, reflect a very small number of surveys; (10) A state average was not calculated because too few hospitals in the state submitted data; (11) There were discrepancies in the data collection process; Please refer to the User's Guide for a full explanation of data.

Mercy Hospital of Kansas Independence

800 W Myrtle Street   Phone: 620-331-2200
Independence, KS 67301   Fax: 620-332-3270
Type: Acute Care Hospitals   Emergency Services: No
Ownership: Voluntary Non-Profit - Church   Beds: 93

Key Personnel:

CEO/President. . . . . John Woodrich
Chief of Medical Staff . . . . Cathey Henisey
Infection Control. . . . . Michelle Foreman
Operating Room. . . . . Ralph Hall
Quality Assurance . . . . Eric Asmussen
Radiology. . . . . Kevin Hamm, MD
Emergency Room . . . . Charles Empson, MD
Intensive Care Unit. . . . . Michelle Foreman

Measure	Cases	This Hosp.	State Avg.	U.S. Avg.
Heart Attack Care				
ACE Inhibitor or ARB for LVSD[1,3]	1	100%	95%	96%
Aspirin at Arrival[1,3]	4	100%	98%	99%
Aspirin at Discharge[1,3]	4	100%	98%	98%
Beta Blocker at Discharge[1,3]	3	67%	98%	98%
Fibrinolytic Medication Timing[3]	0	-	44%	55%
PCI Within 90 Minutes of Arrival[3]	0	-	91%	90%
Smoking Cessation Advice[1,3]	1	100%	99%	99%
Chest Pain/Possible Heart Attack Care				
Aspirin at Arrival	56	89%	92%	95%
Median Time to ECG (minutes)	56	6	10	8
Median Time to Transfer (minutes)[1,3]	2	79	60	61
Fibrinolytic Medication Timing[1,3]	1	0%	42%	54%
Heart Failure Care				
ACE Inhibitor or ARB for LVSD[1]	8	88%	91%	94%
Discharge Instructions	29	86%	83%	88%
Evaluation of LVS Function	41	100%	92%	98%
Smoking Cessation Advice[1]	6	100%	94%	98%
Pneumonia Care				
Appropriate Initial Antibiotic[1,2]	16	81%	87%	92%
Blood Culture Timing[2]	27	93%	96%	96%
Influenza Vaccine[1,2]	23	100%	87%	91%
Initial Antibiotic Timing[2]	37	100%	95%	95%
Pneumococcal Vaccine[2]	31	97%	88%	93%
Smoking Cessation Advice[1,2]	12	100%	93%	97%
Surgical Care Improvement Project				
Appropriate VTP Within 24 Hours[2]	33	85%	89%	92%
Appropriate Hair Removal[2]	66	100%	100%	99%
Appropriate Beta Blocker Usage[1,2]	15	67%	90%	93%
Controlled Postoperative Blood Glucose[2]	0	-	92%	93%
Prophylactic Antibiotic Timing[2]	49	94%	96%	97%
Prophylactic Antibiotic Timing (Outpatient)	28	89%	93%	92%
Prophylactic Antibiotic Selection[2]	48	94%	97%	97%
Prophylactic Antibiotic Select. (Outpatient)	25	100%	96%	94%
Prophylactic Antibiotic Stopped[2]	47	98%	93%	94%
Recommended VTP Ordered[2]	33	97%	91%	94%
Urinary Catheter Removal[1,2]	9	33%	86%	90%
Children's Asthma Care				
Received Systemic Corticosteroids	-	-	-	100%
Received Home Management Plan	-	-	-	71%
Received Reliever Medication	-	-	-	100%
Use of Medical Imaging				
Combination Abdominal CT Scan	148	0.730	0.365	0.191
Combination Chest CT Scan	90	0.056	0.065	0.054
Follow-up Mammogram/Ultrasound	384	6.3%	7.3%	8.4%
MRI for Low Back Pain	42	42.9%	34.5%	32.7%
Survey of Patients' Hospital Experiences				
Area Around Room 'Always' Quiet at Night	(a)	60%	-	58%
Doctors 'Always' Communicated Well	(a)	87%	-	80%
Home Recovery Information Given	(a)	86%	-	82%
Hospital Given 9 or 10 on 10 Point Scale	(a)	69%	-	67%
Meds 'Always' Explained Before Given	(a)	64%	-	60%
Nurses 'Always' Communicated Well	(a)	78%	-	76%
Pain 'Always' Well Controlled	(a)	75%	-	69%
Room and Bathroom 'Always' Clean	(a)	75%	-	71%
Timely Help 'Always' Received	(a)	75%	-	64%
Would Definitely Recommend Hospital	(a)	66%	-	69%

Allen County Hospital

101 South 1st Street   Phone: 620-365-1021
Iola, KS 66749   Fax: 620-365-1140
URL: www.allencountyhospital.com
Type: Critical Access Hospitals   Emergency Services: Yes
Ownership: Proprietary   Beds: 25

Key Personnel:

CEO/President. . . . . Jennifer Jackman

Measure	Cases	This Hosp.	State Avg.	U.S. Avg.
Heart Attack Care				
ACE Inhibitor or ARB for LVSD[3]	0	-	95%	96%
Aspirin at Arrival[1,3]	1	100%	98%	99%
Aspirin at Discharge[1,3]	1	100%	98%	98%
Beta Blocker at Discharge[1,3]	4	50%	98%	98%
Fibrinolytic Medication Timing[3]	0	-	44%	55%
PCI Within 90 Minutes of Arrival[3]	0	-	91%	90%
Smoking Cessation Advice[1,3]	1	100%	99%	99%
Chest Pain/Possible Heart Attack Care				
Aspirin at Arrival	87	97%	92%	95%
Median Time to ECG (minutes)	94	18	10	8
Median Time to Transfer (minutes)[3]	0	-	60	61
Fibrinolytic Medication Timing[1]	3	100%	42%	54%
Heart Failure Care				
ACE Inhibitor or ARB for LVSD[1]	5	60%	91%	94%
Discharge Instructions[1]	13	92%	83%	88%
Evaluation of LVS Function	28	89%	92%	98%
Smoking Cessation Advice[1]	4	100%	94%	98%
Pneumonia Care				
Appropriate Initial Antibiotic	30	100%	87%	92%
Blood Culture Timing	25	100%	96%	96%
Influenza Vaccine	33	100%	87%	91%
Initial Antibiotic Timing	50	100%	95%	95%
Pneumococcal Vaccine	47	96%	88%	93%
Smoking Cessation Advice[1]	13	100%	93%	97%
Surgical Care Improvement Project				
Appropriate VTP Within 24 Hours[1]	12	83%	89%	92%
Appropriate Hair Removal	25	100%	100%	99%
Appropriate Beta Blocker Usage[1]	2	100%	90%	93%
Controlled Postoperative Blood Glucose	0	-	92%	93%
Prophylactic Antibiotic Timing[1]	11	91%	96%	97%
Prophylactic Antibiotic Timing (Outpatient)[1,3]	1	100%	93%	92%
Prophylactic Antibiotic Selection[1]	11	91%	97%	97%
Prophylactic Antibiotic Select. (Outpatient)[1,3]	1	100%	96%	94%
Prophylactic Antibiotic Stopped[1]	10	100%	93%	94%
Recommended VTP Ordered[1]	12	92%	91%	94%
Urinary Catheter Removal[1]	1	0%	86%	90%
Children's Asthma Care				
Received Systemic Corticosteroids	-	-	-	100%
Received Home Management Plan	-	-	-	71%
Received Reliever Medication	-	-	-	100%
Use of Medical Imaging				
Combination Abdominal CT Scan	182	0.758	0.365	0.191
Combination Chest CT Scan	66	0.015	0.065	0.054
Follow-up Mammogram/Ultrasound	260	0.8%	7.3%	8.4%
MRI for Low Back Pain	41	53.7%	34.5%	32.7%
Survey of Patients' Hospital Experiences				
Area Around Room 'Always' Quiet at Night[8]	-	-	-	58%
Doctors 'Always' Communicated Well[8]	-	-	-	80%
Home Recovery Information Given[8]	-	-	-	82%
Hospital Given 9 or 10 on 10 Point Scale[8]	-	-	-	67%
Meds 'Always' Explained Before Given[8]	-	-	-	60%
Nurses 'Always' Communicated Well[8]	-	-	-	76%
Pain 'Always' Well Controlled[8]	-	-	-	69%
Room and Bathroom 'Always' Clean[8]	-	-	-	71%
Timely Help 'Always' Received[8]	-	-	-	64%
Would Definitely Recommend Hospital[8]	-	-	-	69%

Hodgeman County Health Center

809 Bramley   Phone: 620-357-8361
Jetmore, KS 67854   Fax: 620-357-6120
E-mail: vbamberger@hchconline.org
URL: www.hchconline.org
Type: Critical Access Hospitals   Emergency Services: Yes
Ownership: Government - Local   Beds: 52

Key Personnel:

Chief of Medical Staff . . . . Richard Alan Snodgrass
Infection Control. . . . . Nancy Ferguson, RN
Operating Room. . . . . Julie Schraeder
Quality Assurance . . . . Nancy Ferguson, RN
Emergency Room . . . . Gail Tucker
Intensive Care Unit. . . . . Gail Tucker

Measure	Cases	This Hosp.	State Avg.	U.S. Avg.
Heart Attack Care				
ACE Inhibitor or ARB for LVSD[5]	0	-	95%	96%
Aspirin at Arrival[5]	0	-	98%	99%
Aspirin at Discharge[5]	0	-	98%	98%
Beta Blocker at Discharge[5]	0	-	98%	98%
Fibrinolytic Medication Timing[5]	0	-	44%	55%
PCI Within 90 Minutes of Arrival[5]	0	-	91%	90%
Smoking Cessation Advice[5]	0	-	99%	99%
Chest Pain/Possible Heart Attack Care				
Aspirin at Arrival	-	-	92%	95%
Median Time to ECG (minutes)	-	-	10	8
Median Time to Transfer (minutes)	-	-	60	61
Fibrinolytic Medication Timing	-	-	42%	54%
Heart Failure Care				
ACE Inhibitor or ARB for LVSD[5]	0	-	91%	94%
Discharge Instructions[5]	0	-	83%	88%
Evaluation of LVS Function[5]	0	-	92%	98%
Smoking Cessation Advice[5]	0	-	94%	98%
Pneumonia Care				
Appropriate Initial Antibiotic[1]	21	33%	87%	92%
Blood Culture Timing[1]	3	0%	96%	96%
Influenza Vaccine[1]	11	91%	87%	91%
Initial Antibiotic Timing	25	88%	95%	95%
Pneumococcal Vaccine[1]	21	95%	88%	93%
Smoking Cessation Advice[1]	3	67%	93%	97%
Surgical Care Improvement Project				
Appropriate VTP Within 24 Hours[5]	0	-	89%	92%
Appropriate Hair Removal[5]	0	-	100%	99%
Appropriate Beta Blocker Usage[5]	0	-	90%	93%
Controlled Postoperative Blood Glucose[5]	0	-	92%	93%
Prophylactic Antibiotic Timing[5]	0	-	96%	97%
Prophylactic Antibiotic Timing (Outpatient)	-	-	93%	92%
Prophylactic Antibiotic Selection[5]	0	-	97%	97%
Prophylactic Antibiotic Select. (Outpatient)	-	-	96%	94%
Prophylactic Antibiotic Stopped[5]	0	-	93%	94%
Recommended VTP Ordered[5]	0	-	91%	94%
Urinary Catheter Removal[5]	0	-	86%	90%
Children's Asthma Care				
Received Systemic Corticosteroids	-	-	-	100%
Received Home Management Plan	-	-	-	71%
Received Reliever Medication	-	-	-	100%
Use of Medical Imaging				
Combination Abdominal CT Scan	-	-	0.365	0.191
Combination Chest CT Scan	-	-	0.065	0.054
Follow-up Mammogram/Ultrasound	-	-	7.3%	8.4%
MRI for Low Back Pain	-	-	34.5%	32.7%
Survey of Patients' Hospital Experiences				
Area Around Room 'Always' Quiet at Night[8]	-	-	-	58%
Doctors 'Always' Communicated Well[8]	-	-	-	80%
Home Recovery Information Given[8]	-	-	-	82%
Hospital Given 9 or 10 on 10 Point Scale[8]	-	-	-	67%
Meds 'Always' Explained Before Given[8]	-	-	-	60%
Nurses 'Always' Communicated Well[8]	-	-	-	76%
Pain 'Always' Well Controlled[8]	-	-	-	69%
Room and Bathroom 'Always' Clean[8]	-	-	-	71%
Timely Help 'Always' Received[8]	-	-	-	64%
Would Definitely Recommend Hospital[8]	-	-	-	69%

NOTE: Hospital profiles are in alphabetical order by state, then city, then hospital within the city; Rankings exclude hospitals with less than 25 cases except for patient surveys which excludes hospitals with less than 100 cases; (a) 100–299 cases; (1) The number of cases is too small to be sure how well a hospital is performing; (2) The hospital indicated that the data submitted for this measure were based on a sample of cases; (3) Data was collected during a shorter time period (fewer quarters) than the maximum possible time for this measure; (4) Suppressed for one or more quarters by CMS; (5) No data is available from the hospital for this measure; (6) Fewer than 100 patients completed the HCAHPS survey. Use these rates with caution, as the number of surveys may be too low to reliably assess hospital performance; (7) Survey results are based on less than 12 months of data; (8) Survey results are not available for this reporting period; (9) No or very few patients were eligible for the HCAHPS survey. The scores shown, if any, reflect a very small number of surveys; (10) A state average was not calculated because too few hospitals in the state submitted data; (11) There were discrepancies in the data collection process; Please refer to the User's Guide for a full explanation of data.

Geary Community Hospital

1102 St Mary's Road
Junction City, KS 66441
E-mail: ceo@gchks.org
URL: www.gchks.org
Type: Acute Care Hospitals
Ownership: Government - Local
Phone: 913-238-4131
Fax: 785-238-5278
Emergency Services: Yes
Beds: 92

Key Personnel:
CEO/President. . . . . David K Bradley, CHE
Chief of Medical Staff . . . . Charles Bollman, MD
Infection Control. . . . . Sandy Grant, RN
Operating Room. . . . . Karen Roles, RN
Pediatric Ambulatory Care . . . . . Monika Strauhal, MD
Quality Assurance . . . . Elaine Becker, RN
Radiology. . . . . Pat Small

Measure	Cases	This Hosp.	State Avg.	U.S. Avg.
Heart Attack Care				
ACE Inhibitor or ARB for LVSD[1]	2	100%	95%	96%
Aspirin at Arrival[1]	6	83%	98%	99%
Aspirin at Discharge[1]	4	75%	98%	98%
Beta Blocker at Discharge[1]	4	100%	98%	98%
Fibrinolytic Medication Timing	0	-	44%	55%
PCI Within 90 Minutes of Arrival	0	-	91%	90%
Smoking Cessation Advice	0	-	99%	99%
Chest Pain/Possible Heart Attack Care				
Aspirin at Arrival	29	93%	92%	95%
Median Time to ECG (minutes)	25	13	10	8
Median Time to Transfer (minutes)[1,3]	3	109	60	61
Fibrinolytic Medication Timing[1]	2	100%	42%	54%
Heart Failure Care				
ACE Inhibitor or ARB for LVSD[1]	11	91%	91%	94%
Discharge Instructions	30	57%	83%	88%
Evaluation of LVS Function	39	77%	92%	98%
Smoking Cessation Advice[1]	5	80%	94%	98%
Pneumonia Care				
Appropriate Initial Antibiotic	30	77%	87%	92%
Blood Culture Timing[1]	17	88%	96%	96%
Influenza Vaccine	36	72%	87%	91%
Initial Antibiotic Timing	52	87%	95%	95%
Pneumococcal Vaccine	53	89%	88%	93%
Smoking Cessation Advice[1]	20	95%	93%	97%
Surgical Care Improvement Project				
Appropriate VTP Within 24 Hours	52	73%	89%	92%
Appropriate Hair Removal	178	99%	100%	99%
Appropriate Beta Blocker Usage	41	73%	90%	93%
Controlled Postoperative Blood Glucose	0	-	92%	93%
Prophylactic Antibiotic Timing	133	74%	96%	97%
Prophylactic Antibiotic Timing (Outpatient)[1]	19	84%	93%	92%
Prophylactic Antibiotic Selection	132	92%	97%	97%
Prophylactic Antibiotic Select. (Outpatient)[1]	20	90%	96%	94%
Prophylactic Antibiotic Stopped	130	90%	93%	94%
Recommended VTP Ordered	54	74%	91%	94%
Urinary Catheter Removal	59	78%	86%	90%
Children's Asthma Care				
Received Systemic Corticosteroids	-	-	-	100%
Received Home Management Plan	-	-	-	71%
Received Reliever Medication	-	-	-	100%
Use of Medical Imaging				
Combination Abdominal CT Scan	247	0.036	0.365	0.191
Combination Chest CT Scan	185	0.011	0.065	0.054
Follow-up Mammogram/Ultrasound	647	4.2%	7.3%	8.4%
MRI for Low Back Pain	52	34.6%	34.5%	32.7%
Survey of Patients' Hospital Experiences				
Area Around Room 'Always' Quiet at Night[11]	300+	65%	-	58%
Doctors 'Always' Communicated Well[11]	300+	85%	-	80%
Home Recovery Information Given[11]	300+	86%	-	82%
Hospital Given 9 or 10 on 10 Point Scale[11]	300+	68%	-	67%
Meds 'Always' Explained Before Given[11]	300+	65%	-	60%
Nurses 'Always' Communicated Well[11]	300+	77%	-	76%
Pain 'Always' Well Controlled[11]	300+	68%	-	69%
Room and Bathroom 'Always' Clean[11]	300+	72%	-	71%
Timely Help 'Always' Received[11]	300+	64%	-	64%
Would Definitely Recommend Hospital[11]	300+	70%	-	69%

Providence Medical Center

8929 Parallel Parkway
Kansas City, KS 66112
URL: www.providence-health.org
Type: Acute Care Hospitals
Ownership: Voluntary Non-Profit - Church
Phone: 913-596-3930
Fax: 913-596-4324
Emergency Services: Yes
Beds: 400

Key Personnel:
CEO/President. . . . . Juanita Roy
Operating Room. . . . . Scott D Ellison
Quality Assurance . . . . Julie Bogart
Radiology. . . . . William H Brooks
Emergency Room . . . . Victoria C Allison, MD
Intensive Care Unit. . . . . Patty Geiger
Patient Relations . . . . Vicki Short

Measure	Cases	This Hosp.	State Avg.	U.S. Avg.
Heart Attack Care				
ACE Inhibitor or ARB for LVSD	33	94%	95%	96%
Aspirin at Arrival	148	99%	98%	99%
Aspirin at Discharge	154	99%	98%	98%
Beta Blocker at Discharge	151	98%	98%	98%
Fibrinolytic Medication Timing	0	-	44%	55%
PCI Within 90 Minutes of Arrival	36	92%	91%	90%
Smoking Cessation Advice	67	100%	99%	99%
Chest Pain/Possible Heart Attack Care				
Aspirin at Arrival[5]	0	-	92%	95%
Median Time to ECG (minutes)[5]	0	-	10	8
Median Time to Transfer (minutes)[5]	0	-	60	61
Fibrinolytic Medication Timing[5]	0	-	42%	54%
Heart Failure Care				
ACE Inhibitor or ARB for LVSD	130	89%	91%	94%
Discharge Instructions	263	78%	83%	88%
Evaluation of LVS Function	319	99%	92%	98%
Smoking Cessation Advice	72	100%	94%	98%
Pneumonia Care				
Appropriate Initial Antibiotic	109	92%	87%	92%
Blood Culture Timing	170	98%	96%	96%
Influenza Vaccine	111	93%	87%	91%
Initial Antibiotic Timing	181	98%	95%	95%
Pneumococcal Vaccine	152	98%	88%	93%
Smoking Cessation Advice	94	100%	93%	97%
Surgical Care Improvement Project				
Appropriate VTP Within 24 Hours[2]	155	85%	89%	92%
Appropriate Hair Removal[2]	608	99%	100%	99%
Appropriate Beta Blocker Usage[2]	190	94%	90%	93%
Controlled Postoperative Blood Glucose[2]	65	98%	92%	93%
Prophylactic Antibiotic Timing[2]	457	99%	96%	97%
Prophylactic Antibiotic Timing (Outpatient)	336	95%	93%	92%
Prophylactic Antibiotic Selection[2]	467	99%	97%	97%
Prophylactic Antibiotic Select. (Outpatient)	327	98%	96%	94%
Prophylactic Antibiotic Stopped[2]	432	99%	93%	94%
Recommended VTP Ordered[2]	155	90%	91%	94%
Urinary Catheter Removal[2]	133	92%	86%	90%
Children's Asthma Care				
Received Systemic Corticosteroids	-	-	-	100%
Received Home Management Plan	-	-	-	71%
Received Reliever Medication	-	-	-	100%
Use of Medical Imaging				
Combination Abdominal CT Scan	385	0.023	0.365	0.191
Combination Chest CT Scan	425	0.049	0.065	0.054
Follow-up Mammogram/Ultrasound	488	7.4%	7.3%	8.4%
MRI for Low Back Pain[1]	51	23.5%	34.5%	32.7%
Survey of Patients' Hospital Experiences				
Area Around Room 'Always' Quiet at Night	300+	52%	-	58%
Doctors 'Always' Communicated Well	300+	72%	-	80%
Home Recovery Information Given	300+	79%	-	82%
Hospital Given 9 or 10 on 10 Point Scale	300+	60%	-	67%
Meds 'Always' Explained Before Given	300+	57%	-	60%
Nurses 'Always' Communicated Well	300+	70%	-	76%
Pain 'Always' Well Controlled	300+	61%	-	69%
Room and Bathroom 'Always' Clean	300+	61%	-	71%
Timely Help 'Always' Received	300+	59%	-	64%
Would Definitely Recommend Hospital	300+	58%	-	69%

University of Kansas Hospital

3901 Rainbow Blvd
Kansas City, KS 66160
URL: www.kumc.edu
Type: Acute Care Hospitals
Ownership: Govt - Hospital Dist/Auth
Phone: 913-588-7332
Fax: 913-588-5863
Emergency Services: Yes
Beds: 620

Key Personnel:
CEO/President. . . . . Irene Cumming
Infection Control. . . . . Daivd Woods
Operating Room. . . . . Laurie Wood
Pediatric Ambulatory Care . . . . . Cynthia Sparks
Pediatric In-Patient Care . . . . . . Cynthia Sparks
Quality Assurance . . . . Robin Heckelbeck
Radiology. . . . . Mary Monroe

Measure	Cases	This Hosp.	State Avg.	U.S. Avg.
Heart Attack Care				
ACE Inhibitor or ARB for LVSD	36	94%	95%	96%
Aspirin at Arrival	109	100%	98%	99%
Aspirin at Discharge	187	100%	98%	98%
Beta Blocker at Discharge	176	100%	98%	98%
Fibrinolytic Medication Timing	0	-	44%	55%
PCI Within 90 Minutes of Arrival[1]	23	96%	91%	90%
Smoking Cessation Advice	85	100%	99%	99%
Chest Pain/Possible Heart Attack Care				
Aspirin at Arrival[5]	0	-	92%	95%
Median Time to ECG (minutes)[5]	0	-	10	8
Median Time to Transfer (minutes)[5]	0	-	60	61
Fibrinolytic Medication Timing[5]	0	-	42%	54%
Heart Failure Care				
ACE Inhibitor or ARB for LVSD	136	99%	91%	94%
Discharge Instructions	376	97%	83%	88%
Evaluation of LVS Function	420	100%	92%	98%
Smoking Cessation Advice	98	100%	94%	98%
Pneumonia Care				
Appropriate Initial Antibiotic	112	96%	87%	92%
Blood Culture Timing	275	95%	96%	96%
Influenza Vaccine	181	98%	87%	91%
Initial Antibiotic Timing	241	93%	95%	95%
Pneumococcal Vaccine	189	97%	88%	93%
Smoking Cessation Advice	147	100%	93%	97%
Surgical Care Improvement Project				
Appropriate VTP Within 24 Hours[2]	246	93%	89%	92%
Appropriate Hair Removal[2]	588	99%	100%	99%
Appropriate Beta Blocker Usage[2]	178	89%	90%	93%
Controlled Postoperative Blood Glucose[2]	126	99%	92%	93%
Prophylactic Antibiotic Timing[2]	381	97%	96%	97%
Prophylactic Antibiotic Timing (Outpatient)	452	89%	93%	92%
Prophylactic Antibiotic Selection[2]	386	96%	97%	97%
Prophylactic Antibiotic Select. (Outpatient)	445	98%	96%	94%
Prophylactic Antibiotic Stopped[2]	365	95%	93%	94%
Recommended VTP Ordered[2]	246	95%	91%	94%
Urinary Catheter Removal[2]	132	90%	86%	90%
Children's Asthma Care				
Received Systemic Corticosteroids	-	-	-	100%
Received Home Management Plan	-	-	-	71%
Received Reliever Medication	-	-	-	100%
Use of Medical Imaging				
Combination Abdominal CT Scan	1,617	0.764	0.365	0.191
Combination Chest CT Scan	1,980	0.005	0.065	0.054
Follow-up Mammogram/Ultrasound	1,327	10.2%	7.3%	8.4%
MRI for Low Back Pain	146	27.4%	34.5%	32.7%
Survey of Patients' Hospital Experiences				
Area Around Room 'Always' Quiet at Night	300+	60%	-	58%
Doctors 'Always' Communicated Well	300+	80%	-	80%
Home Recovery Information Given	300+	88%	-	82%
Hospital Given 9 or 10 on 10 Point Scale	300+	75%	-	67%
Meds 'Always' Explained Before Given	300+	66%	-	60%
Nurses 'Always' Communicated Well	300+	79%	-	76%
Pain 'Always' Well Controlled	300+	69%	-	69%
Room and Bathroom 'Always' Clean	300+	68%	-	71%
Timely Help 'Always' Received	300+	63%	-	64%
Would Definitely Recommend Hospital	300+	79%	-	69%

NOTE: Hospital profiles are in alphabetical order by state, then city, then hospital within the city; Rankings exclude hospitals with less than 25 cases except for patient surveys which excludes hospitals with less than 100 cases; (a) 100–299 cases; (1) The number of cases is too small to be sure how well a hospital is performing; (2) The hospital indicated that the data submitted for this measure were based on a sample of cases; (3) Data was collected during a shorter time period (fewer quarters) than the maximum possible time for this measure; (4) Suppressed for one or more quarters by CMS; (5) No data is available from the hospital for this measure; (6) Fewer than 100 patients completed the HCAHPS survey. Use these rates with caution, as the number of surveys may be too low to reliably assess hospital performance; (7) Survey results are based on less than 12 months of data; (8) Survey results are not available for this reporting period; (9) No or very few patients were eligible for the HCAHPS survey. The scores shown, if any, reflect a very small number of surveys; (10) A state average was not calculated because too few hospitals in the state submitted data; (11) There were discrepancies in the data collection process; Please refer to the User's Guide for a full explanation of data.

Kingman Community Hospital

750 W Ave D
Kingman, KS 67068
Phone: 620-532-3147
Fax: 620-532-5221
E-mail: nvhs@ink.org
URL: www.nvhsinc.com
Type: Critical Access Hospitals
Emergency Services: Yes
Ownership: Voluntary Non-Profit - Private
Beds: 50

Key Personnel:

CEO/President............... Gary Tiller
Chief of Medical Staff.......... Victoria Moots, DO
Infection Control.............. Nancy Wilson, RN
Quality Assurance .... Gayle Easley, BSN
Radiology.................... Connie Johnson
Emergency Room .... Nita McFarland

Measure	Cases	This Hosp.	State Avg.	U.S. Avg.
Heart Attack Care				
ACE Inhibitor or ARB for LVSD[5]	0	-	95%	96%
Aspirin at Arrival[5]	0	-	98%	99%
Aspirin at Discharge[5]	0	-	98%	98%
Beta Blocker at Discharge[5]	0	-	98%	98%
Fibrinolytic Medication Timing[5]	0	-	44%	55%
PCI Within 90 Minutes of Arrival[5]	0	-	91%	90%
Smoking Cessation Advice[5]	0	-	99%	99%
Chest Pain/Possible Heart Attack Care				
Aspirin at Arrival	-	-	92%	95%
Median Time to ECG (minutes)	-	-	10	8
Median Time to Transfer (minutes)	-	-	60	61
Fibrinolytic Medication Timing	-	-	42%	54%
Heart Failure Care				
ACE Inhibitor or ARB for LVSD[1,3]	2	100%	91%	94%
Discharge Instructions[1,3]	2	50%	83%	88%
Evaluation of LVS Function[1,3]	10	90%	92%	98%
Smoking Cessation Advice[1,3]	1	100%	94%	98%
Pneumonia Care				
Appropriate Initial Antibiotic[1]	24	92%	87%	92%
Blood Culture Timing[1]	6	83%	96%	96%
Influenza Vaccine[1]	20	100%	87%	91%
Initial Antibiotic Timing	28	100%	95%	95%
Pneumococcal Vaccine	36	100%	88%	93%
Smoking Cessation Advice[1]	6	100%	93%	97%
Surgical Care Improvement Project				
Appropriate VTP Within 24 Hours[1]	5	40%	89%	92%
Appropriate Hair Removal[1]	7	100%	100%	99%
Appropriate Beta Blocker Usage[1]	2	50%	90%	93%
Controlled Postoperative Blood Glucose[5]	0	-	92%	93%
Prophylactic Antibiotic Timing[1]	7	29%	96%	97%
Prophylactic Antibiotic Timing (Outpatient)	-	-	93%	92%
Prophylactic Antibiotic Selection[1]	7	57%	97%	97%
Prophylactic Antibiotic Select. (Outpatient)	-	-	96%	94%
Prophylactic Antibiotic Stopped[1]	7	57%	93%	94%
Recommended VTP Ordered[1]	5	40%	91%	94%
Urinary Catheter Removal[1]	3	100%	86%	90%
Children's Asthma Care				
Received Systemic Corticosteroids	-	-	-	100%
Received Home Management Plan	-	-	-	71%
Received Reliever Medication	-	-	-	100%
Use of Medical Imaging				
Combination Abdominal CT Scan	-	-	0.365	0.191
Combination Chest CT Scan	-	-	0.065	0.054
Follow-up Mammogram/Ultrasound	-	-	7.3%	8.4%
MRI for Low Back Pain	-	-	34.5%	32.7%
Survey of Patients' Hospital Experiences				
Area Around Room 'Always' Quiet at Night	(a)	54%	-	58%
Doctors 'Always' Communicated Well	(a)	87%	-	80%
Home Recovery Information Given	(a)	82%	-	82%
Hospital Given 9 or 10 on 10 Point Scale	(a)	78%	-	67%
Meds 'Always' Explained Before Given	(a)	62%	-	60%
Nurses 'Always' Communicated Well	(a)	86%	-	76%
Pain 'Always' Well Controlled	(a)	74%	-	69%
Room and Bathroom 'Always' Clean	(a)	70%	-	71%
Timely Help 'Always' Received	(a)	72%	-	64%
Would Definitely Recommend Hospital	(a)	76%	-	69%

Edwards County Hospital

620 West Eighth Street
Kinsley, KS 67547
Phone: 620-659-3621
URL: www.edwardscohospital.com
Type: Critical Access Hospitals
Emergency Services: Yes
Ownership: Government - Local

Key Personnel:

CEO .... Bob Krickbaum
Radiology.................. Janna Simmons

Measure	Cases	This Hosp.	State Avg.	U.S. Avg.
Heart Attack Care				
ACE Inhibitor or ARB for LVSD[5]	0	-	95%	96%
Aspirin at Arrival[5]	0	-	98%	99%
Aspirin at Discharge[5]	0	-	98%	98%
Beta Blocker at Discharge[5]	0	-	98%	98%
Fibrinolytic Medication Timing[5]	0	-	44%	55%
PCI Within 90 Minutes of Arrival[5]	0	-	91%	90%
Smoking Cessation Advice[5]	0	-	99%	99%
Chest Pain/Possible Heart Attack Care				
Aspirin at Arrival	-	-	92%	95%
Median Time to ECG (minutes)	-	-	10	8
Median Time to Transfer (minutes)	-	-	60	61
Fibrinolytic Medication Timing	-	-	42%	54%
Heart Failure Care				
ACE Inhibitor or ARB for LVSD[3]	0	-	91%	94%
Discharge Instructions[1,3]	1	100%	83%	88%
Evaluation of LVS Function[1,3]	2	50%	92%	98%
Smoking Cessation Advice[3]	0	-	94%	98%
Pneumonia Care				
Appropriate Initial Antibiotic[1,3]	8	88%	87%	92%
Blood Culture Timing[1,3]	1	100%	96%	96%
Influenza Vaccine[1]	4	75%	87%	91%
Initial Antibiotic Timing[1,3]	7	86%	95%	95%
Pneumococcal Vaccine[1,3]	6	83%	88%	93%
Smoking Cessation Advice[1,3]	2	50%	93%	97%
Surgical Care Improvement Project				
Appropriate VTP Within 24 Hours[5]	0	-	89%	92%
Appropriate Hair Removal[5]	0	-	100%	99%
Appropriate Beta Blocker Usage[5]	0	-	90%	93%
Controlled Postoperative Blood Glucose[5]	0	-	92%	93%
Prophylactic Antibiotic Timing[5]	0	-	96%	97%
Prophylactic Antibiotic Timing (Outpatient)	-	-	93%	92%
Prophylactic Antibiotic Selection[5]	0	-	97%	97%
Prophylactic Antibiotic Select. (Outpatient)	-	-	96%	94%
Prophylactic Antibiotic Stopped[5]	0	-	93%	94%
Recommended VTP Ordered[5]	0	-	91%	94%
Urinary Catheter Removal[5]	0	-	86%	90%
Children's Asthma Care				
Received Systemic Corticosteroids	-	-	-	100%
Received Home Management Plan	-	-	-	71%
Received Reliever Medication	-	-	-	100%
Use of Medical Imaging				
Combination Abdominal CT Scan	-	-	0.365	0.191
Combination Chest CT Scan	-	-	0.065	0.054
Follow-up Mammogram/Ultrasound	-	-	7.3%	8.4%
MRI for Low Back Pain	-	-	34.5%	32.7%
Survey of Patients' Hospital Experiences				
Area Around Room 'Always' Quiet at Night[8]	-	-	-	58%
Doctors 'Always' Communicated Well[8]	-	-	-	80%
Home Recovery Information Given[8]	-	-	-	82%
Hospital Given 9 or 10 on 10 Point Scale[8]	-	-	-	67%
Meds 'Always' Explained Before Given[8]	-	-	-	60%
Nurses 'Always' Communicated Well[8]	-	-	-	76%
Pain 'Always' Well Controlled[8]	-	-	-	69%
Room and Bathroom 'Always' Clean[8]	-	-	-	71%
Timely Help 'Always' Received[8]	-	-	-	64%
Would Definitely Recommend Hospital[8]	-	-	-	69%

Kiowa District Hospital

810 Drumm Street
Kiowa, KS 67070
Phone: 620-825-4131
Fax: 620-825-4667
Type: Critical Access Hospitals
Emergency Services: Yes
Ownership: Govt - Hospital Dist/Auth
Beds: 24

Key Personnel:

CEO/President............... Brian Stacey
Chief of Medical Staff.......... Paul Wilhelm, MD
Infection Control.............. Patty McNamar
Quality Assurance .... Kathy Winters
Anesthesiology............... Jerry Darger
Emergency Room .... Patty McNamar

Measure	Cases	This Hosp.	State Avg.	U.S. Avg.
Heart Attack Care				
ACE Inhibitor or ARB for LVSD[5]	0	-	95%	96%
Aspirin at Arrival[5]	0	-	98%	99%
Aspirin at Discharge[5]	0	-	98%	98%
Beta Blocker at Discharge[5]	0	-	98%	98%
Fibrinolytic Medication Timing[5]	0	-	44%	55%
PCI Within 90 Minutes of Arrival[5]	0	-	91%	90%
Smoking Cessation Advice[5]	0	-	99%	99%
Chest Pain/Possible Heart Attack Care				
Aspirin at Arrival[1]	12	92%	92%	95%
Median Time to ECG (minutes)[1]	12	10	10	8
Median Time to Transfer (minutes)[1,3]	1	100	60	61
Fibrinolytic Medication Timing[1,3]	2	50%	42%	54%
Heart Failure Care				
ACE Inhibitor or ARB for LVSD[5]	0	-	91%	94%
Discharge Instructions[5]	0	-	83%	88%
Evaluation of LVS Function[5]	0	-	92%	98%
Smoking Cessation Advice[5]	0	-	94%	98%
Pneumonia Care				
Appropriate Initial Antibiotic[1]	9	78%	87%	92%
Blood Culture Timing	0	-	96%	96%
Influenza Vaccine[1]	9	22%	87%	91%
Initial Antibiotic Timing[1]	10	90%	95%	95%
Pneumococcal Vaccine[1]	11	18%	88%	93%
Smoking Cessation Advice[1]	3	33%	93%	97%
Surgical Care Improvement Project				
Appropriate VTP Within 24 Hours[5]	0	-	89%	92%
Appropriate Hair Removal[5]	0	-	100%	99%
Appropriate Beta Blocker Usage[5]	0	-	90%	93%
Controlled Postoperative Blood Glucose[5]	0	-	92%	93%
Prophylactic Antibiotic Timing[5]	0	-	96%	97%
Prophylactic Antibiotic Timing (Outpatient)[5]	0	-	93%	92%
Prophylactic Antibiotic Selection[5]	0	-	97%	97%
Prophylactic Antibiotic Select. (Outpatient)[5]	0	-	96%	94%
Prophylactic Antibiotic Stopped[5]	0	-	93%	94%
Recommended VTP Ordered[5]	0	-	91%	94%
Urinary Catheter Removal[5]	0	-	86%	90%
Children's Asthma Care				
Received Systemic Corticosteroids	-	-	-	100%
Received Home Management Plan	-	-	-	71%
Received Reliever Medication	-	-	-	100%
Use of Medical Imaging				
Combination Abdominal CT Scan[1]	17	0.647	0.365	0.191
Combination Chest CT Scan[1]	13	0.769	0.065	0.054
Follow-up Mammogram/Ultrasound[5]	0	-	7.3%	8.4%
MRI for Low Back Pain[1]	4	50.0%	34.5%	32.7%
Survey of Patients' Hospital Experiences				
Area Around Room 'Always' Quiet at Night[8]	-	-	-	58%
Doctors 'Always' Communicated Well[8]	-	-	-	80%
Home Recovery Information Given[8]	-	-	-	82%
Hospital Given 9 or 10 on 10 Point Scale[8]	-	-	-	67%
Meds 'Always' Explained Before Given[8]	-	-	-	60%
Nurses 'Always' Communicated Well[8]	-	-	-	76%
Pain 'Always' Well Controlled[8]	-	-	-	69%
Room and Bathroom 'Always' Clean[8]	-	-	-	71%
Timely Help 'Always' Received[8]	-	-	-	64%
Would Definitely Recommend Hospital[8]	-	-	-	69%

NOTE: Hospital profiles are in alphabetical order by state, then city, then hospital within the city; Rankings exclude hospitals with less than 25 cases except for patient surveys which excludes hospitals with less than 100 cases; (a) 100–299 cases; (1) The number of cases is too small to be sure how well a hospital is performing; (2) The hospital indicated that the data submitted for this measure were based on a sample of cases; (3) Data was collected during a shorter time period (fewer quarters) than the maximum possible time for this measure; (4) Suppressed for one or more quarters by CMS; (5) No data is available from the hospital for this measure; (6) Fewer than 100 patients completed the HCAHPS survey. Use these rates with caution, as the number of surveys may be too low to reliably assess hospital performance; (7) Survey results are based on less than 12 months of data; (8) Survey results are not available for this reporting period; (9) No or very few patients were eligible for the HCAHPS survey. The scores shown, if any, reflect a very small number of surveys; (10) A state average was not calculated because too few hospitals in the state submitted data; (11) There were discrepancies in the data collection process; Please refer to the User's Guide for a full explanation of data.

Kearny County Hospital

500 Thorpe Street
Lakin, KS 67860
URL: www.kearnycountyhospital.com
Type: Critical Access Hospitals
Ownership: Government - Local
Phone: 620-355-7111
Fax: 620-355-1527
Emergency Services: Yes
Beds: 90

Key Personnel:
Infection Control. . . . . Ken Barnett, RN

Measure	Cases	This Hosp.	State Avg.	U.S. Avg.
Heart Attack Care				
ACE Inhibitor or ARB for LVSD[3]	0	-	95%	96%
Aspirin at Arrival[3]	0	-	98%	99%
Aspirin at Discharge[3]	0	-	98%	98%
Beta Blocker at Discharge[3]	0	-	98%	98%
Fibrinolytic Medication Timing[3]	0	-	44%	55%
PCI Within 90 Minutes of Arrival[3]	0	-	91%	90%
Smoking Cessation Advice[3]	0	-	99%	99%
Chest Pain/Possible Heart Attack Care				
Aspirin at Arrival	-	-	92%	95%
Median Time to ECG (minutes)	-	-	10	8
Median Time to Transfer (minutes)	-	-	60	61
Fibrinolytic Medication Timing	-	-	42%	54%
Heart Failure Care				
ACE Inhibitor or ARB for LVSD[1]	4	50%	91%	94%
Discharge Instructions[1]	13	92%	83%	88%
Evaluation of LVS Function[1]	15	73%	92%	98%
Smoking Cessation Advice[1]	3	100%	94%	98%
Pneumonia Care				
Appropriate Initial Antibiotic[1]	5	100%	87%	92%
Blood Culture Timing[1]	1	100%	96%	96%
Influenza Vaccine[1]	5	80%	87%	91%
Initial Antibiotic Timing[1]	7	71%	95%	95%
Pneumococcal Vaccine[1]	8	88%	88%	93%
Smoking Cessation Advice[1]	1	100%	93%	97%
Surgical Care Improvement Project				
Appropriate VTP Within 24 Hours[5]	0	-	89%	92%
Appropriate Hair Removal[5]	0	-	100%	99%
Appropriate Beta Blocker Usage[5]	0	-	90%	93%
Controlled Postoperative Blood Glucose[5]	0	-	92%	93%
Prophylactic Antibiotic Timing[5]	0	-	96%	97%
Prophylactic Antibiotic Timing (Outpatient)	-	-	93%	92%
Prophylactic Antibiotic Selection[5]	0	-	97%	97%
Prophylactic Antibiotic Select. (Outpatient)	-	-	96%	94%
Prophylactic Antibiotic Stopped[5]	0	-	93%	94%
Recommended VTP Ordered[5]	0	-	91%	94%
Urinary Catheter Removal[5]	0	-	86%	90%
Children's Asthma Care				
Received Systemic Corticosteroids	-	-	-	100%
Received Home Management Plan	-	-	-	71%
Received Reliever Medication	-	-	-	100%
Use of Medical Imaging				
Combination Abdominal CT Scan	-	-	0.365	0.191
Combination Chest CT Scan	-	-	0.065	0.054
Follow-up Mammogram/Ultrasound	-	-	7.3%	8.4%
MRI for Low Back Pain	-	-	34.5%	32.7%
Survey of Patients' Hospital Experiences				
Area Around Room 'Always' Quiet at Night[8]	-	-	-	58%
Doctors 'Always' Communicated Well[8]	-	-	-	80%
Home Recovery Information Given[8]	-	-	-	82%
Hospital Given 9 or 10 on 10 Point Scale[8]	-	-	-	67%
Meds 'Always' Explained Before Given[8]	-	-	-	60%
Nurses 'Always' Communicated Well[8]	-	-	-	76%
Pain 'Always' Well Controlled[8]	-	-	-	69%
Room and Bathroom 'Always' Clean[8]	-	-	-	71%
Timely Help 'Always' Received[8]	-	-	-	64%
Would Definitely Recommend Hospital[8]	-	-	-	69%

Lawrence Memorial Hospital

325 Maine St
Lawrence, KS 66044
URL: www.lmh.org
Type: Acute Care Hospitals
Ownership: Government - Local
Phone: 913-749-6100
Fax: 785-749-6126
Emergency Services: Yes
Beds: 173

Key Personnel:
CEO/President. . . . . Gene Meyer
Chief of Medical Staff . . . . Sherri Vaughn, MD
Infection Control. . . . . Janet Wehrle
Operating Room. . . . . Dale Denning
Anesthesiology. . . . . Christopher Malikfs, MD
Emergency Room . . . . Darin Elo, RN, BSN
Intensive Care Unit. . . . . Carol Cockrett

Measure	Cases	This Hosp.	State Avg.	U.S. Avg.
Heart Attack Care				
ACE Inhibitor or ARB for LVSD[1]	17	100%	95%	96%
Aspirin at Arrival	89	100%	98%	99%
Aspirin at Discharge	80	100%	98%	98%
Beta Blocker at Discharge	72	100%	98%	98%
Fibrinolytic Medication Timing	0	-	44%	55%
PCI Within 90 Minutes of Arrival	25	100%	91%	90%
Smoking Cessation Advice	28	100%	99%	99%
Chest Pain/Possible Heart Attack Care				
Aspirin at Arrival	27	100%	92%	95%
Median Time to ECG (minutes)	27	4	10	8
Median Time to Transfer (minutes)[1,3]	5	17	60	61
Fibrinolytic Medication Timing[3]	0	-	42%	54%
Heart Failure Care				
ACE Inhibitor or ARB for LVSD	32	100%	91%	94%
Discharge Instructions	91	100%	83%	88%
Evaluation of LVS Function	125	100%	92%	98%
Smoking Cessation Advice[1]	20	100%	94%	98%
Pneumonia Care				
Appropriate Initial Antibiotic	89	97%	87%	92%
Blood Culture Timing	109	94%	96%	96%
Influenza Vaccine	87	98%	87%	91%
Initial Antibiotic Timing	120	99%	95%	95%
Pneumococcal Vaccine	123	99%	88%	93%
Smoking Cessation Advice	53	100%	93%	97%
Surgical Care Improvement Project				
Appropriate VTP Within 24 Hours	222	90%	89%	92%
Appropriate Hair Removal	626	100%	100%	99%
Appropriate Beta Blocker Usage	128	91%	90%	93%
Controlled Postoperative Blood Glucose	0	-	92%	93%
Prophylactic Antibiotic Timing	451	99%	96%	97%
Prophylactic Antibiotic Timing (Outpatient)	161	96%	93%	92%
Prophylactic Antibiotic Selection	452	98%	97%	97%
Prophylactic Antibiotic Select. (Outpatient)	255	97%	96%	94%
Prophylactic Antibiotic Stopped	442	98%	93%	94%
Recommended VTP Ordered	223	94%	91%	94%
Urinary Catheter Removal	172	95%	86%	90%
Children's Asthma Care				
Received Systemic Corticosteroids	-	-	-	100%
Received Home Management Plan	-	-	-	71%
Received Reliever Medication	-	-	-	100%
Use of Medical Imaging				
Combination Abdominal CT Scan	976	0.133	0.365	0.191
Combination Chest CT Scan	660	0.000	0.065	0.054
Follow-up Mammogram/Ultrasound	2,133	7.0%	7.3%	8.4%
MRI for Low Back Pain	316	37.7%	34.5%	32.7%
Survey of Patients' Hospital Experiences				
Area Around Room 'Always' Quiet at Night	300+	56%	-	58%
Doctors 'Always' Communicated Well	300+	83%	-	80%
Home Recovery Information Given	300+	88%	-	82%
Hospital Given 9 or 10 on 10 Point Scale	300+	73%	-	67%
Meds 'Always' Explained Before Given	300+	65%	-	60%
Nurses 'Always' Communicated Well	300+	78%	-	76%
Pain 'Always' Well Controlled	300+	68%	-	69%
Room and Bathroom 'Always' Clean	300+	72%	-	71%
Timely Help 'Always' Received	300+	66%	-	64%
Would Definitely Recommend Hospital	300+	76%	-	69%

Cushing Memorial Hospital

711 Marshall Street
Leavenworth, KS 66048
URL: www.saintlukeshealthsystem.org
Type: Acute Care Hospitals
Ownership: Voluntary Non-Profit - Private
Phone: 913-684-1102
Fax: 913-684-1390
Emergency Services: Yes
Beds: 74

Key Personnel:
CEO/President. . . . . Ron Baker
Chief of Medical Staff . . . . Dr Habib
Radiology. . . . . John H MacMillan
Emergency Room . . . . Jonathan Finks

Measure	Cases	This Hosp.	State Avg.	U.S. Avg.
Heart Attack Care				
ACE Inhibitor or ARB for LVSD	0	-	95%	96%
Aspirin at Arrival[1]	3	67%	98%	99%
Aspirin at Discharge[1]	2	100%	98%	98%
Beta Blocker at Discharge	0	-	98%	98%
Fibrinolytic Medication Timing	0	-	44%	55%
PCI Within 90 Minutes of Arrival	0	-	91%	90%
Smoking Cessation Advice	0	-	99%	99%
Chest Pain/Possible Heart Attack Care				
Aspirin at Arrival	29	97%	92%	95%
Median Time to ECG (minutes)	30	14	10	8
Median Time to Transfer (minutes)[1,3]	2	1067	60	61
Fibrinolytic Medication Timing[3]	0	-	42%	54%
Heart Failure Care				
ACE Inhibitor or ARB for LVSD[1]	13	100%	91%	94%
Discharge Instructions[1]	24	54%	83%	88%
Evaluation of LVS Function	33	88%	92%	98%
Smoking Cessation Advice[1]	5	100%	94%	98%
Pneumonia Care				
Appropriate Initial Antibiotic	47	89%	87%	92%
Blood Culture Timing	48	98%	96%	96%
Influenza Vaccine	26	100%	87%	91%
Initial Antibiotic Timing	52	98%	95%	95%
Pneumococcal Vaccine	46	91%	88%	93%
Smoking Cessation Advice	25	96%	93%	97%
Surgical Care Improvement Project				
Appropriate VTP Within 24 Hours	26	96%	89%	92%
Appropriate Hair Removal	74	100%	100%	99%
Appropriate Beta Blocker Usage[1]	16	88%	90%	93%
Controlled Postoperative Blood Glucose	0	-	92%	93%
Prophylactic Antibiotic Timing	53	94%	96%	97%
Prophylactic Antibiotic Timing (Outpatient)	36	86%	93%	92%
Prophylactic Antibiotic Selection	53	96%	97%	97%
Prophylactic Antibiotic Select. (Outpatient)	35	63%	96%	94%
Prophylactic Antibiotic Stopped	52	98%	93%	94%
Recommended VTP Ordered	26	96%	91%	94%
Urinary Catheter Removal[1]	14	86%	86%	90%
Children's Asthma Care				
Received Systemic Corticosteroids	-	-	-	100%
Received Home Management Plan	-	-	-	71%
Received Reliever Medication	-	-	-	100%
Use of Medical Imaging				
Combination Abdominal CT Scan	106	0.302	0.365	0.191
Combination Chest CT Scan	81	0.012	0.065	0.054
Follow-up Mammogram/Ultrasound	341	7.6%	7.3%	8.4%
MRI for Low Back Pain[5]	0	-	34.5%	32.7%
Survey of Patients' Hospital Experiences				
Area Around Room 'Always' Quiet at Night	(a)	60%	-	58%
Doctors 'Always' Communicated Well	(a)	78%	-	80%
Home Recovery Information Given	(a)	82%	-	82%
Hospital Given 9 or 10 on 10 Point Scale	(a)	62%	-	67%
Meds 'Always' Explained Before Given	(a)	64%	-	60%
Nurses 'Always' Communicated Well	(a)	76%	-	76%
Pain 'Always' Well Controlled	(a)	70%	-	69%
Room and Bathroom 'Always' Clean	(a)	75%	-	71%
Timely Help 'Always' Received	(a)	72%	-	64%
Would Definitely Recommend Hospital	(a)	67%	-	69%

NOTE: Hospital profiles are in alphabetical order by state, then city, then hospital within the city; Rankings exclude hospitals with less than 25 cases except for patient surveys which excludes hospitals with less than 100 cases; (a) 100–299 cases; (1) The number of cases is too small to be sure how well a hospital is performing; (2) The hospital indicated that the data submitted for this measure were based on a sample of cases; (3) Data was collected during a shorter time period (fewer quarters) than the maximum possible time for this measure; (4) Suppressed for one or more quarters by CMS; (5) No data is available from the hospital for this measure; (6) Fewer than 100 patients completed the HCAHPS survey. Use these rates with caution, as the number of surveys may be too low to reliably assess hospital performance; (7) Survey results are based on less than 12 months of data; (8) Survey results are not available for this reporting period; (9) No or very few patients were eligible for the HCAHPS survey. The scores shown, if any, reflect a very small number of surveys; (10) A state average was not calculated because too few hospitals in the state submitted data; (11) There were discrepancies in the data collection process; Please refer to the User's Guide for a full explanation of data.

Saint John Hospital

3500 South 4th Street — Phone: 913-596-5031
Leavenworth, KS 66048 — Fax: 913-680-6013
URL: www.providence-health.org
Type: Acute Care Hospitals — Emergency Services: Yes
Ownership: Voluntary Non-Profit - Other — Beds: 76

Key Personnel:
CEO/President.............. Michael A Dorsey
Chief of Medical Staff.......... Greg Madsen
Infection Control.............. Barbara McNett, RN
Operating Room............. Brenda Johnson
Pediatric Ambulatory Care...... Jeffrey Lawhead, MD
Pediatric In-Patient Care....... Jeffrey Lawhead, MD
Quality Assurance............ Lynda Grimm
Intensive Care Unit........... Donna Steward, MD

Measure	Cases	This Hosp.	State Avg.	U.S. Avg.
Heart Attack Care				
ACE Inhibitor or ARB for LVSD	0	-	95%	96%
Aspirin at Arrival[1]	10	100%	98%	99%
Aspirin at Discharge[1]	5	80%	98%	98%
Beta Blocker at Discharge[1]	5	100%	98%	98%
Fibrinolytic Medication Timing	0	-	44%	55%
PCI Within 90 Minutes of Arrival	0	-	91%	90%
Smoking Cessation Advice	0	-	99%	99%
Chest Pain/Possible Heart Attack Care				
Aspirin at Arrival[1]	16	100%	92%	95%
Median Time to ECG (minutes)[1]	16	12	10	8
Median Time to Transfer (minutes)[1,3]	1	175	60	61
Fibrinolytic Medication Timing	0	-	42%	54%
Heart Failure Care				
ACE Inhibitor or ARB for LVSD[1]	21	95%	91%	94%
Discharge Instructions	45	98%	83%	88%
Evaluation of LVS Function	72	99%	92%	98%
Smoking Cessation Advice[1]	11	91%	94%	98%
Pneumonia Care				
Appropriate Initial Antibiotic	46	91%	87%	92%
Blood Culture Timing	46	100%	96%	96%
Influenza Vaccine	43	98%	87%	91%
Initial Antibiotic Timing	56	96%	95%	95%
Pneumococcal Vaccine	40	92%	88%	93%
Smoking Cessation Advice	33	97%	93%	97%
Surgical Care Improvement Project				
Appropriate VTP Within 24 Hours	25	56%	89%	92%
Appropriate Hair Removal	44	100%	100%	99%
Appropriate Beta Blocker Usage[1]	15	100%	90%	93%
Controlled Postoperative Blood Glucose	0	-	92%	93%
Prophylactic Antibiotic Timing[1]	21	90%	96%	97%
Prophylactic Antibiotic Timing (Outpatient)	27	96%	93%	92%
Prophylactic Antibiotic Selection[1]	21	81%	97%	97%
Prophylactic Antibiotic Select. (Outpatient)	28	93%	96%	94%
Prophylactic Antibiotic Stopped[1]	21	86%	93%	94%
Recommended VTP Ordered	25	60%	91%	94%
Urinary Catheter Removal[1]	7	57%	86%	90%
Children's Asthma Care				
Received Systemic Corticosteroids	-	-	-	100%
Received Home Management Plan	-	-	-	71%
Received Reliever Medication	-	-	-	100%
Use of Medical Imaging				
Combination Abdominal CT Scan	151	0.046	0.365	0.191
Combination Chest CT Scan	137	0.029	0.065	0.054
Follow-up Mammogram/Ultrasound	377	2.7%	7.3%	8.4%
MRI for Low Back Pain[5]	0	-	34.5%	32.7%
Survey of Patients' Hospital Experiences				
Area Around Room 'Always' Quiet at Night	(a)	44%	-	58%
Doctors 'Always' Communicated Well	(a)	74%	-	80%
Home Recovery Information Given	(a)	75%	-	82%
Hospital Given 9 or 10 on 10 Point Scale	(a)	57%	-	67%
Meds 'Always' Explained Before Given	(a)	53%	-	60%
Nurses 'Always' Communicated Well	(a)	72%	-	76%
Pain 'Always' Well Controlled	(a)	65%	-	69%
Room and Bathroom 'Always' Clean	(a)	66%	-	71%
Timely Help 'Always' Received	(a)	65%	-	64%
Would Definitely Recommend Hospital	(a)	63%	-	69%

VA Eastern Kansas Healthcare System

4101 S. 4th Street — Phone: 913-682-2000
Leavenworth, KS 66048 — Fax: 785-350-4474
URL: www.leavenworth.va.gov
Type: Acute Care-Veterans Administration — Emergency Services: No
Ownership: Government - Federal — Beds: 197

Key Personnel:
CEO/President.............. Judy K McKee, FACHE
Chief of Medical Staff.......... Rajeev Trehan, MD/MBBS
Operating Room............. Chris Haller, MD
Radiology.................. M G Rao, MD
Patient Relations............ Rebecca M Garcia, RN/MSN

Measure	Cases	This Hosp.	State Avg.	U.S. Avg.
Heart Attack Care				
ACE Inhibitor or ARB for LVSD[1]	1	100%	95%	96%
Aspirin at Arrival[1]	13	100%	98%	99%
Aspirin at Discharge[1]	4	100%	98%	98%
Beta Blocker at Discharge[1]	5	100%	98%	98%
Fibrinolytic Medication Timing[5]	0	-	44%	55%
PCI Within 90 Minutes of Arrival[5]	0	-	91%	90%
Smoking Cessation Advice[1]	2	100%	99%	99%
Chest Pain/Possible Heart Attack Care				
Aspirin at Arrival	-	-	92%	95%
Median Time to ECG (minutes)	-	-	10	8
Median Time to Transfer (minutes)	-	-	60	61
Fibrinolytic Medication Timing	-	-	42%	54%
Heart Failure Care				
ACE Inhibitor or ARB for LVSD	41	100%	91%	94%
Discharge Instructions	102	93%	83%	88%
Evaluation of LVS Function	113	100%	92%	98%
Smoking Cessation Advice[1]	23	96%	94%	98%
Pneumonia Care				
Appropriate Initial Antibiotic	65	92%	87%	92%
Blood Culture Timing	116	98%	96%	96%
Influenza Vaccine	87	97%	87%	91%
Initial Antibiotic Timing	117	95%	95%	95%
Pneumococcal Vaccine	80	100%	88%	93%
Smoking Cessation Advice	65	100%	93%	97%
Surgical Care Improvement Project				
Appropriate VTP Within 24 Hours[1,2]	6	100%	89%	92%
Appropriate Hair Removal[1,2]	8	100%	100%	99%
Appropriate Beta Blocker Usage[1,2]	2	100%	90%	93%
Controlled Postoperative Blood Glucose[2,5]	0	-	92%	93%
Prophylactic Antibiotic Timing[5]	0	-	96%	97%
Prophylactic Antibiotic Timing (Outpatient)	-	-	93%	92%
Prophylactic Antibiotic Selection[5]	0	-	97%	97%
Prophylactic Antibiotic Select. (Outpatient)	-	-	96%	94%
Prophylactic Antibiotic Stopped[5]	0	-	93%	94%
Recommended VTP Ordered[1,2]	6	100%	91%	94%
Urinary Catheter Removal[1,2]	4	100%	86%	90%
Children's Asthma Care				
Received Systemic Corticosteroids	-	-	-	100%
Received Home Management Plan	-	-	-	71%
Received Reliever Medication	-	-	-	100%
Use of Medical Imaging				
Combination Abdominal CT Scan	-	-	0.365	0.191
Combination Chest CT Scan	-	-	0.065	0.054
Follow-up Mammogram/Ultrasound	-	-	7.3%	8.4%
MRI for Low Back Pain	-	-	34.5%	32.7%
Survey of Patients' Hospital Experiences				
Area Around Room 'Always' Quiet at Night	-	-	-	58%
Doctors 'Always' Communicated Well	-	-	-	80%
Home Recovery Information Given	-	-	-	82%
Hospital Given 9 or 10 on 10 Point Scale	-	-	-	67%
Meds 'Always' Explained Before Given	-	-	-	60%
Nurses 'Always' Communicated Well	-	-	-	76%
Pain 'Always' Well Controlled	-	-	-	69%
Room and Bathroom 'Always' Clean	-	-	-	71%
Timely Help 'Always' Received	-	-	-	64%
Would Definitely Recommend Hospital	-	-	-	69%

Doctors Hospital

4901 College Blvd — Phone: 913-529-1801
Leawood, KS 66211
Type: Acute Care Hospitals — Emergency Services: Yes
Ownership: Proprietary

Measure	Cases	This Hosp.	State Avg.	U.S. Avg.
Heart Attack Care				
ACE Inhibitor or ARB for LVSD[5]	0	-	95%	96%
Aspirin at Arrival[5]	0	-	98%	99%
Aspirin at Discharge[5]	0	-	98%	98%
Beta Blocker at Discharge[5]	0	-	98%	98%
Fibrinolytic Medication Timing[5]	0	-	44%	55%
PCI Within 90 Minutes of Arrival[5]	0	-	91%	90%
Smoking Cessation Advice[5]	0	-	99%	99%
Chest Pain/Possible Heart Attack Care				
Aspirin at Arrival[5]	0	-	92%	95%
Median Time to ECG (minutes)[5]	0	-	10	8
Median Time to Transfer (minutes)[5]	0	-	60	61
Fibrinolytic Medication Timing[5]	0	-	42%	54%
Heart Failure Care				
ACE Inhibitor or ARB for LVSD[5]	0	-	91%	94%
Discharge Instructions[5]	0	-	83%	88%
Evaluation of LVS Function[5]	0	-	92%	98%
Smoking Cessation Advice[5]	0	-	94%	98%
Pneumonia Care				
Appropriate Initial Antibiotic[5]	0	-	87%	92%
Blood Culture Timing[5]	0	-	96%	96%
Influenza Vaccine[5]	0	-	87%	91%
Initial Antibiotic Timing[5]	0	-	95%	95%
Pneumococcal Vaccine[5]	0	-	88%	93%
Smoking Cessation Advice[5]	0	-	93%	97%
Surgical Care Improvement Project				
Appropriate VTP Within 24 Hours[3]	0	-	89%	92%
Appropriate Hair Removal[1,3]	12	100%	100%	99%
Appropriate Beta Blocker Usage[1,3]	8	88%	90%	93%
Controlled Postoperative Blood Glucose[3]	0	-	92%	93%
Prophylactic Antibiotic Timing[1,3]	11	73%	96%	97%
Prophylactic Antibiotic Timing (Outpatient)[3]	39	77%	93%	92%
Prophylactic Antibiotic Selection[1,3]	11	91%	97%	97%
Prophylactic Antibiotic Select. (Outpatient)[3]	36	92%	96%	94%
Prophylactic Antibiotic Stopped[1,3]	11	100%	93%	94%
Recommended VTP Ordered[3]	0	-	91%	94%
Urinary Catheter Removal[3,1]	1	0%	86%	90%
Children's Asthma Care				
Received Systemic Corticosteroids	-	-	-	100%
Received Home Management Plan	-	-	-	71%
Received Reliever Medication	-	-	-	100%
Use of Medical Imaging				
Combination Abdominal CT Scan[1]	2	0.000	0.365	0.191
Combination Chest CT Scan[5]	0	-	0.065	0.054
Follow-up Mammogram/Ultrasound[5]	0	-	7.3%	8.4%
MRI for Low Back Pain[1]	9	33.3%	34.5%	32.7%
Survey of Patients' Hospital Experiences				
Area Around Room 'Always' Quiet at Night	(a)	91%	-	58%
Doctors 'Always' Communicated Well	(a)	84%	-	80%
Home Recovery Information Given	(a)	87%	-	82%
Hospital Given 9 or 10 on 10 Point Scale	(a)	80%	-	67%
Meds 'Always' Explained Before Given	(a)	62%	-	60%
Nurses 'Always' Communicated Well	(a)	86%	-	76%
Pain 'Always' Well Controlled	(a)	75%	-	69%
Room and Bathroom 'Always' Clean	(a)	85%	-	71%
Timely Help 'Always' Received	(a)	77%	-	64%
Would Definitely Recommend Hospital	(a)	83%	-	69%

NOTE: Hospital profiles are in alphabetical order by state, then city, then hospital within the city; Rankings exclude hospitals with less than 25 cases except for patient surveys which excludes hospitals with less than 100 cases; (a) 100–299 cases; (1) The number of cases is too small to be sure how well a hospital is performing; (2) The hospital indicated that the data submitted for this measure were based on a sample of cases; (3) Data was collected during a shorter time period (fewer quarters) than the maximum possible time for this measure; (4) Suppressed for one or more quarters by CMS; (5) No data is available from the hospital for this measure; (6) Fewer than 100 patients completed the HCAHPS survey. Use these rates with caution, as the number of surveys may be too low to reliably assess hospital performance; (7) Survey results are based on less than 12 months of data; (8) Survey results are not available for this reporting period; (9) No or very few patients were eligible for the HCAHPS survey. The scores shown, if any, reflect a very small number of surveys; (10) A state average was not calculated because too few hospitals in the state submitted data; (11) There were discrepancies in the data collection process; Please refer to the User's Guide for a full explanation of data.

Kansas City Orthopaedic Institute

3651 College Blvd
Leawood, KS 66211
URL: www.kcoi.com
Type: Acute Care Hospitals
Ownership: Voluntary Non-Profit - Private

Phone: 913-319-7633
Fax: 816-531-5313
Emergency Services: No
Beds: 9

Measure	Cases	This Hosp.	State Avg.	U.S. Avg.
Heart Attack Care				
ACE Inhibitor or ARB for LVSD[5]	0	-	95%	96%
Aspirin at Arrival[5]	0	-	98%	99%
Aspirin at Discharge[5]	0	-	98%	98%
Beta Blocker at Discharge[5]	0	-	98%	98%
Fibrinolytic Medication Timing[5]	0	-	44%	55%
PCI Within 90 Minutes of Arrival[5]	0	-	91%	90%
Smoking Cessation Advice[5]	0	-	99%	99%
Chest Pain/Possible Heart Attack Care				
Aspirin at Arrival[5]	0	-	92%	95%
Median Time to ECG (minutes)[5]	0	-	10	8
Median Time to Transfer (minutes)[5]	0	-	60	61
Fibrinolytic Medication Timing[5]	0	-	42%	54%
Heart Failure Care				
ACE Inhibitor or ARB for LVSD[5]	0	-	91%	94%
Discharge Instructions[5]	0	-	83%	88%
Evaluation of LVS Function[5]	0	-	92%	98%
Smoking Cessation Advice[5]	0	-	94%	98%
Pneumonia Care				
Appropriate Initial Antibiotic[5]	0	-	87%	92%
Blood Culture Timing[5]	0	-	96%	96%
Influenza Vaccine[5]	0	-	87%	91%
Initial Antibiotic Timing[5]	0	-	95%	95%
Pneumococcal Vaccine[5]	0	-	88%	93%
Smoking Cessation Advice[5]	0	-	93%	97%
Surgical Care Improvement Project				
Appropriate VTP Within 24 Hours[1,2]	11	100%	89%	92%
Appropriate Hair Removal[2]	184	100%	100%	99%
Appropriate Beta Blocker Usage[1,2]	15	100%	90%	93%
Controlled Postoperative Blood Glucose[2]	0	-	92%	93%
Prophylactic Antibiotic Timing[2]	158	97%	96%	97%
Prophylactic Antibiotic Timing (Outpatient)[1]	21	100%	93%	92%
Prophylactic Antibiotic Selection[2]	158	100%	97%	97%
Prophylactic Antibiotic Select. (Outpatient)[1]	21	100%	96%	94%
Prophylactic Antibiotic Stopped[2]	158	95%	93%	94%
Recommended VTP Ordered[1,2]	11	100%	91%	94%
Urinary Catheter Removal[2]	0	-	86%	90%
Children's Asthma Care				
Received Systemic Corticosteroids	-	-	-	100%
Received Home Management Plan	-	-	-	71%
Received Reliever Medication	-	-	-	100%
Use of Medical Imaging				
Combination Abdominal CT Scan[5]	0	-	0.365	0.191
Combination Chest CT Scan[5]	0	-	0.065	0.054
Follow-up Mammogram/Ultrasound[5]	0	-	7.3%	8.4%
MRI for Low Back Pain	150	29.3%	34.5%	32.7%
Survey of Patients' Hospital Experiences				
Area Around Room 'Always' Quiet at Night	300+	68%	-	58%
Doctors 'Always' Communicated Well	300+	91%	-	80%
Home Recovery Information Given	300+	93%	-	82%
Hospital Given 9 or 10 on 10 Point Scale	300+	89%	-	67%
Meds 'Always' Explained Before Given	300+	74%	-	60%
Nurses 'Always' Communicated Well	300+	85%	-	76%
Pain 'Always' Well Controlled	300+	79%	-	69%
Room and Bathroom 'Always' Clean	300+	80%	-	71%
Timely Help 'Always' Received	300+	89%	-	64%
Would Definitely Recommend Hospital	300+	93%	-	69%

Wichita County Health Center

211 E Earl Street
Leoti, KS 67861
Type: Critical Access Hospitals
Ownership: Government - Local

Phone: 620-375-2233
Fax: 620-375-2248
Emergency Services: Yes
Beds: 39

Key Personnel:
Infection Control. . . . . Beverly White, RN
Quality Assurance . . . . Beverly White, RN

Measure	Cases	This Hosp.	State Avg.	U.S. Avg.
Heart Attack Care				
ACE Inhibitor or ARB for LVSD[5]	0	-	95%	96%
Aspirin at Arrival[5]	0	-	98%	99%
Aspirin at Discharge[5]	0	-	98%	98%
Beta Blocker at Discharge[5]	0	-	98%	98%
Fibrinolytic Medication Timing[5]	0	-	44%	55%
PCI Within 90 Minutes of Arrival[5]	0	-	91%	90%
Smoking Cessation Advice[5]	0	-	99%	99%
Chest Pain/Possible Heart Attack Care				
Aspirin at Arrival	-	-	92%	95%
Median Time to ECG (minutes)	-	-	10	8
Median Time to Transfer (minutes)	-	-	60	61
Fibrinolytic Medication Timing	-	-	42%	54%
Heart Failure Care				
ACE Inhibitor or ARB for LVSD[5]	0	-	91%	94%
Discharge Instructions[5]	0	-	83%	88%
Evaluation of LVS Function[5]	0	-	92%	98%
Smoking Cessation Advice[5]	0	-	94%	98%
Pneumonia Care				
Appropriate Initial Antibiotic[5]	0	-	87%	92%
Blood Culture Timing[5]	0	-	96%	96%
Influenza Vaccine[5]	0	-	87%	91%
Initial Antibiotic Timing[5]	0	-	95%	95%
Pneumococcal Vaccine[5]	0	-	88%	93%
Smoking Cessation Advice[5]	0	-	93%	97%
Surgical Care Improvement Project				
Appropriate VTP Within 24 Hours[5]	0	-	89%	92%
Appropriate Hair Removal[5]	0	-	100%	99%
Appropriate Beta Blocker Usage[5]	0	-	90%	93%
Controlled Postoperative Blood Glucose[5]	0	-	92%	93%
Prophylactic Antibiotic Timing[5]	0	-	96%	97%
Prophylactic Antibiotic Timing (Outpatient)	-	-	93%	92%
Prophylactic Antibiotic Selection[5]	0	-	97%	97%
Prophylactic Antibiotic Select. (Outpatient)	-	-	96%	94%
Prophylactic Antibiotic Stopped[5]	0	-	93%	94%
Recommended VTP Ordered[5]	0	-	91%	94%
Urinary Catheter Removal[5]	0	-	86%	90%
Children's Asthma Care				
Received Systemic Corticosteroids	-	-	-	100%
Received Home Management Plan	-	-	-	71%
Received Reliever Medication	-	-	-	100%
Use of Medical Imaging				
Combination Abdominal CT Scan	-	-	0.365	0.191
Combination Chest CT Scan	-	-	0.065	0.054
Follow-up Mammogram/Ultrasound	-	-	7.3%	8.4%
MRI for Low Back Pain	-	-	34.5%	32.7%
Survey of Patients' Hospital Experiences				
Area Around Room 'Always' Quiet at Night[8]	-	-	-	58%
Doctors 'Always' Communicated Well[8]	-	-	-	80%
Home Recovery Information Given[8]	-	-	-	82%
Hospital Given 9 or 10 on 10 Point Scale[8]	-	-	-	67%
Meds 'Always' Explained Before Given[8]	-	-	-	60%
Nurses 'Always' Communicated Well[8]	-	-	-	76%
Pain 'Always' Well Controlled[8]	-	-	-	69%
Room and Bathroom 'Always' Clean[8]	-	-	-	71%
Timely Help 'Always' Received[8]	-	-	-	64%
Would Definitely Recommend Hospital[8]	-	-	-	69%

Southwest Medical Center

315 West 15th Street
Liberal, KS 67901
URL: www.swmedcenter.com
Type: Acute Care Hospitals
Ownership: Government - Local

Phone: 620-629-6291
Emergency Services: Yes
Beds: 80

Key Personnel:
President/CEO. . . . . Norman T Lambert

Measure	Cases	This Hosp.	State Avg.	U.S. Avg.
Heart Attack Care				
ACE Inhibitor or ARB for LVSD	0	-	95%	96%
Aspirin at Arrival[1]	2	100%	98%	99%
Aspirin at Discharge[1]	2	100%	98%	98%
Beta Blocker at Discharge[1]	2	50%	98%	98%
Fibrinolytic Medication Timing	0	-	44%	55%
PCI Within 90 Minutes of Arrival	0	-	91%	90%
Smoking Cessation Advice	0	-	99%	99%
Chest Pain/Possible Heart Attack Care				
Aspirin at Arrival	45	96%	92%	95%
Median Time to ECG (minutes)	46	12	10	8
Median Time to Transfer (minutes)[1,3]	1	140	60	61
Fibrinolytic Medication Timing[1]	5	60%	42%	54%
Heart Failure Care				
ACE Inhibitor or ARB for LVSD[1]	13	69%	91%	94%
Discharge Instructions[1]	24	79%	83%	88%
Evaluation of LVS Function	27	89%	92%	98%
Smoking Cessation Advice[1]	2	100%	94%	98%
Pneumonia Care				
Appropriate Initial Antibiotic[1]	22	95%	87%	92%
Blood Culture Timing[1]	19	84%	96%	96%
Influenza Vaccine[1]	20	55%	87%	91%
Initial Antibiotic Timing	33	100%	95%	95%
Pneumococcal Vaccine	29	72%	88%	93%
Smoking Cessation Advice[1]	7	71%	93%	97%
Surgical Care Improvement Project				
Appropriate VTP Within 24 Hours	80	89%	89%	92%
Appropriate Hair Removal	104	100%	100%	99%
Appropriate Beta Blocker Usage[1]	18	94%	90%	93%
Controlled Postoperative Blood Glucose	0	-	92%	93%
Prophylactic Antibiotic Timing	55	91%	96%	97%
Prophylactic Antibiotic Timing (Outpatient)	213	95%	93%	92%
Prophylactic Antibiotic Selection	53	98%	97%	97%
Prophylactic Antibiotic Select. (Outpatient)	210	97%	96%	94%
Prophylactic Antibiotic Stopped	48	94%	93%	94%
Recommended VTP Ordered	80	89%	91%	94%
Urinary Catheter Removal	31	74%	86%	90%
Children's Asthma Care				
Received Systemic Corticosteroids	-	-	-	100%
Received Home Management Plan	-	-	-	71%
Received Reliever Medication	-	-	-	100%
Use of Medical Imaging				
Combination Abdominal CT Scan	221	0.683	0.365	0.191
Combination Chest CT Scan	139	0.719	0.065	0.054
Follow-up Mammogram/Ultrasound	303	5.3%	7.3%	8.4%
MRI for Low Back Pain	70	38.6%	34.5%	32.7%
Survey of Patients' Hospital Experiences				
Area Around Room 'Always' Quiet at Night	300+	53%	-	58%
Doctors 'Always' Communicated Well	300+	80%	-	80%
Home Recovery Information Given	300+	83%	-	82%
Hospital Given 9 or 10 on 10 Point Scale	300+	66%	-	67%
Meds 'Always' Explained Before Given	300+	64%	-	60%
Nurses 'Always' Communicated Well	300+	73%	-	76%
Pain 'Always' Well Controlled	300+	69%	-	69%
Room and Bathroom 'Always' Clean	300+	75%	-	71%
Timely Help 'Always' Received	300+	62%	-	64%
Would Definitely Recommend Hospital	300+	67%	-	69%

NOTE: Hospital profiles are in alphabetical order by state, then city, then hospital within the city; Rankings exclude hospitals with less than 25 cases except for patient surveys which excludes hospitals with less than 100 cases; (a) 100–299 cases; (1) The number of cases is too small to be sure how well a hospital is performing; (2) The hospital indicated that the data submitted for this measure were based on a sample of cases; (3) Data was collected during a shorter time period (fewer quarters) than the maximum possible time for this measure; (4) Suppressed for one or more quarters by CMS; (5) No data is available from the hospital for this measure; (6) Fewer than 100 patients completed the HCAHPS survey. Use these rates with caution, as the number of surveys may be too low to reliably assess hospital performance; (7) Survey results are based on less than 12 months of data; (8) Survey results are not available for this reporting period; (9) No or very few patients were eligible for the HCAHPS survey. The scores shown, if any, reflect a very small number of surveys; (10) A state average was not calculated because too few hospitals in the state submitted data; (11) There were discrepancies in the data collection process; Please refer to the User's Guide for a full explanation of data.

Lindsborg Community Hospital

605 W Lincoln Street
Lindsborg, KS 67456
E-mail: lch@lindsborghospital.org
URL: www.lindsborghospital.org
Type: Critical Access Hospitals
Ownership: Voluntary Non-Profit - Private
Phone: 785-227-3308
Fax: 785-227-4130
Emergency Services: Yes
Beds: 25

Key Personnel:
CEO/President. . . . . Larry VanDerWege
Chief of Medical Staff . . . . Susan Chrislip
Infection Control. . . . . Beth Hedberg, RN
Operating Room. . . . . Joanie Worthen, RN, B
Quality Assurance . . . . Joanie Worthen, RN, B
Emergency Room . . . . Beth Hedberg, RN

Measure	Cases	This Hosp.	State Avg.	U.S. Avg.
Heart Attack Care				
ACE Inhibitor or ARB for LVSD[1,3]	1	100%	95%	96%
Aspirin at Arrival[1,3]	1	100%	98%	99%
Aspirin at Discharge[1,3]	1	100%	98%	98%
Beta Blocker at Discharge[1,3]	1	100%	98%	98%
Fibrinolytic Medication Timing[3]	0	-	44%	55%
PCI Within 90 Minutes of Arrival[3]	0	-	91%	90%
Smoking Cessation Advice[3]	0	-	99%	99%
Chest Pain/Possible Heart Attack Care				
Aspirin at Arrival	-	-	92%	95%
Median Time to ECG (minutes)	-	-	10	8
Median Time to Transfer (minutes)	-	-	60	61
Fibrinolytic Medication Timing	-	-	42%	54%
Heart Failure Care				
ACE Inhibitor or ARB for LVSD[3]	0	-	91%	94%
Discharge Instructions[1,3]	3	33%	83%	88%
Evaluation of LVS Function[1,3]	9	89%	92%	98%
Smoking Cessation Advice[1,3]	1	100%	94%	98%
Pneumonia Care				
Appropriate Initial Antibiotic[1]	7	57%	87%	92%
Blood Culture Timing	0	-	96%	96%
Influenza Vaccine[1]	13	92%	87%	91%
Initial Antibiotic Timing[1]	12	100%	95%	95%
Pneumococcal Vaccine[1]	19	58%	88%	93%
Smoking Cessation Advice	0	-	93%	97%
Surgical Care Improvement Project				
Appropriate VTP Within 24 Hours[5]	0	-	89%	92%
Appropriate Hair Removal[5]	0	-	100%	99%
Appropriate Beta Blocker Usage[5]	0	-	90%	93%
Controlled Postoperative Blood Glucose[5]	0	-	92%	93%
Prophylactic Antibiotic Timing[5]	0	-	96%	97%
Prophylactic Antibiotic Timing (Outpatient)	-	-	93%	92%
Prophylactic Antibiotic Selection[5]	0	-	97%	97%
Prophylactic Antibiotic Select. (Outpatient)	-	-	96%	94%
Prophylactic Antibiotic Stopped[5]	0	-	93%	94%
Recommended VTP Ordered[5]	0	-	91%	94%
Urinary Catheter Removal[5]	0	-	86%	90%
Children's Asthma Care				
Received Systemic Corticosteroids	-	-	-	100%
Received Home Management Plan	-	-	-	71%
Received Reliever Medication	-	-	-	100%
Use of Medical Imaging				
Combination Abdominal CT Scan	-	-	0.365	0.191
Combination Chest CT Scan	-	-	0.065	0.054
Follow-up Mammogram/Ultrasound	-	-	7.3%	8.4%
MRI for Low Back Pain	-	-	34.5%	32.7%
Survey of Patients' Hospital Experiences				
Area Around Room 'Always' Quiet at Night[8]	-	-	-	58%
Doctors 'Always' Communicated Well[8]	-	-	-	80%
Home Recovery Information Given[8]	-	-	-	82%
Hospital Given 9 or 10 on 10 Point Scale[8]	-	-	-	67%
Meds 'Always' Explained Before Given[8]	-	-	-	60%
Nurses 'Always' Communicated Well[8]	-	-	-	76%
Pain 'Always' Well Controlled[8]	-	-	-	69%
Room and Bathroom 'Always' Clean[8]	-	-	-	71%
Timely Help 'Always' Received[8]	-	-	-	64%
Would Definitely Recommend Hospital[8]	-	-	-	69%

Manhattan Surgical Hospital

1829 College Avenue
Manhattan, KS 66502
URL: www.manhattansurgical.com
Type: Acute Care Hospitals
Ownership: Proprietary
Phone: 785-776-5100
Emergency Services: Yes

Measure	Cases	This Hosp.	State Avg.	U.S. Avg.
Heart Attack Care				
ACE Inhibitor or ARB for LVSD[5]	0	-	95%	96%
Aspirin at Arrival[5]	0	-	98%	99%
Aspirin at Discharge[5]	0	-	98%	98%
Beta Blocker at Discharge[5]	0	-	98%	98%
Fibrinolytic Medication Timing[5]	0	-	44%	55%
PCI Within 90 Minutes of Arrival[5]	0	-	91%	90%
Smoking Cessation Advice[5]	0	-	99%	99%
Chest Pain/Possible Heart Attack Care				
Aspirin at Arrival[5]	0	-	92%	95%
Median Time to ECG (minutes)[5]	0	-	10	8
Median Time to Transfer (minutes)[5]	0	-	60	61
Fibrinolytic Medication Timing[5]	0	-	42%	54%
Heart Failure Care				
ACE Inhibitor or ARB for LVSD[5]	0	-	91%	94%
Discharge Instructions[5]	0	-	83%	88%
Evaluation of LVS Function[5]	0	-	92%	98%
Smoking Cessation Advice[5]	0	-	94%	98%
Pneumonia Care				
Appropriate Initial Antibiotic[5]	0	-	87%	92%
Blood Culture Timing[5]	0	-	96%	96%
Influenza Vaccine[5]	0	-	87%	91%
Initial Antibiotic Timing[5]	0	-	95%	95%
Pneumococcal Vaccine[5]	0	-	88%	93%
Smoking Cessation Advice[5]	0	-	93%	97%
Surgical Care Improvement Project				
Appropriate VTP Within 24 Hours[1]	1	100%	89%	92%
Appropriate Hair Removal	233	98%	100%	99%
Appropriate Beta Blocker Usage[1]	16	56%	90%	93%
Controlled Postoperative Blood Glucose	0	-	92%	93%
Prophylactic Antibiotic Timing	229	98%	96%	97%
Prophylactic Antibiotic Timing (Outpatient)	148	98%	93%	92%
Prophylactic Antibiotic Selection	228	95%	97%	97%
Prophylactic Antibiotic Select. (Outpatient)	149	96%	96%	94%
Prophylactic Antibiotic Stopped	228	92%	93%	94%
Recommended VTP Ordered[1]	1	100%	91%	94%
Urinary Catheter Removal	0	-	86%	90%
Children's Asthma Care				
Received Systemic Corticosteroids	-	-	-	100%
Received Home Management Plan	-	-	-	71%
Received Reliever Medication	-	-	-	100%
Use of Medical Imaging				
Combination Abdominal CT Scan[5]	0	-	0.365	0.191
Combination Chest CT Scan[5]	0	-	0.065	0.054
Follow-up Mammogram/Ultrasound[5]	0	-	7.3%	8.4%
MRI for Low Back Pain[5]	0	-	34.5%	32.7%
Survey of Patients' Hospital Experiences				
Area Around Room 'Always' Quiet at Night	(a)	93%	-	58%
Doctors 'Always' Communicated Well	(a)	95%	-	80%
Home Recovery Information Given	(a)	89%	-	82%
Hospital Given 9 or 10 on 10 Point Scale	(a)	95%	-	67%
Meds 'Always' Explained Before Given	(a)	72%	-	60%
Nurses 'Always' Communicated Well	(a)	90%	-	76%
Pain 'Always' Well Controlled	(a)	83%	-	69%
Room and Bathroom 'Always' Clean	(a)	90%	-	71%
Timely Help 'Always' Received	(a)	89%	-	64%
Would Definitely Recommend Hospital	(a)	94%	-	69%

Mercy Regional Health Center

1823 College Ave
Manhattan, KS 66502
URL: www.mercyregional.org
Type: Acute Care Hospitals
Ownership: Voluntary Non-Profit - Church
Phone: 913-776-2831
Fax: 785-776-2804
Emergency Services: Yes
Beds: 150

Key Personnel:
CEO/President. . . . . John Broberg
Cardiac Laboratory. . . . . Don Hedden
Chief of Medical Staff. . . . . Joe Philipp
Infection Control. . . . . Vivian Nutsch
Operating Room. . . . . Dante Wheat
Pediatric In-Patient Care . . . . . . Dawn Julian
Quality Assurance . . . . Denise Klimek
Radiology. . . . . Gary Whitlock

Measure	Cases	This Hosp.	State Avg.	U.S. Avg.
Heart Attack Care				
ACE Inhibitor or ARB for LVSD[1]	8	100%	95%	96%
Aspirin at Arrival	71	100%	98%	99%
Aspirin at Discharge	76	97%	98%	98%
Beta Blocker at Discharge	73	92%	98%	98%
Fibrinolytic Medication Timing[1]	1	0%	44%	55%
PCI Within 90 Minutes of Arrival[1]	18	83%	91%	90%
Smoking Cessation Advice	26	100%	99%	99%
Chest Pain/Possible Heart Attack Care				
Aspirin at Arrival	27	74%	92%	95%
Median Time to ECG (minutes)	27	13	10	8
Median Time to Transfer (minutes)[5]	0	-	60	61
Fibrinolytic Medication Timing[1,3]	2	50%	42%	54%
Heart Failure Care				
ACE Inhibitor or ARB for LVSD[1,2]	24	83%	91%	94%
Discharge Instructions[2]	59	69%	83%	88%
Evaluation of LVS Function[2]	76	92%	92%	98%
Smoking Cessation Advice[1,2]	15	100%	94%	98%
Pneumonia Care				
Appropriate Initial Antibiotic[2]	67	94%	87%	92%
Blood Culture Timing[2]	74	96%	96%	96%
Influenza Vaccine[2]	64	80%	87%	91%
Initial Antibiotic Timing[2]	96	94%	95%	95%
Pneumococcal Vaccine[2]	88	90%	88%	93%
Smoking Cessation Advice[2]	42	98%	93%	97%
Surgical Care Improvement Project				
Appropriate VTP Within 24 Hours	125	86%	89%	92%
Appropriate Hair Removal	625	99%	100%	99%
Appropriate Beta Blocker Usage	142	90%	90%	93%
Controlled Postoperative Blood Glucose	0	-	92%	93%
Prophylactic Antibiotic Timing	444	95%	96%	97%
Prophylactic Antibiotic Timing (Outpatient)	120	83%	93%	92%
Prophylactic Antibiotic Selection	442	98%	97%	97%
Prophylactic Antibiotic Select. (Outpatient)	107	99%	96%	94%
Prophylactic Antibiotic Stopped	436	97%	93%	94%
Recommended VTP Ordered	127	87%	91%	94%
Urinary Catheter Removal	135	96%	86%	90%
Children's Asthma Care				
Received Systemic Corticosteroids	-	-	-	100%
Received Home Management Plan	-	-	-	71%
Received Reliever Medication	-	-	-	100%
Use of Medical Imaging				
Combination Abdominal CT Scan	273	0.088	0.365	0.191
Combination Chest CT Scan	194	0.000	0.065	0.054
Follow-up Mammogram/Ultrasound	1,442	7.5%	7.3%	8.4%
MRI for Low Back Pain[1]	35	25.7%	34.5%	32.7%
Survey of Patients' Hospital Experiences				
Area Around Room 'Always' Quiet at Night	300+	62%	-	58%
Doctors 'Always' Communicated Well	300+	83%	-	80%
Home Recovery Information Given	300+	86%	-	82%
Hospital Given 9 or 10 on 10 Point Scale	300+	69%	-	67%
Meds 'Always' Explained Before Given	300+	58%	-	60%
Nurses 'Always' Communicated Well	300+	78%	-	76%
Pain 'Always' Well Controlled	300+	73%	-	69%
Room and Bathroom 'Always' Clean	300+	68%	-	71%
Timely Help 'Always' Received	300+	65%	-	64%
Would Definitely Recommend Hospital	300+	73%	-	69%

NOTE: Hospital profiles are in alphabetical order by state, then city, then hospital within the city; Rankings exclude hospitals with less than 25 cases except for patient surveys which excludes hospitals with less than 100 cases; (a) 100–299 cases; (1) The number of cases is too small to be sure how well a hospital is performing; (2) The hospital indicated that the data submitted for this measure were based on a sample of cases; (3) Data was collected during a shorter time period (fewer quarters) than the maximum possible time for this measure; (4) Suppressed for one or more quarters by CMS; (5) No data is available from the hospital for this measure; (6) Fewer than 100 patients completed the HCAHPS survey. Use these rates with caution, as the number of surveys may be too low to reliably assess hospital performance; (7) Survey results are based on less than 12 months of data; (8) Survey results are not available for this reporting period; (9) No or very few patients were eligible for the HCAHPS survey. The scores shown, if any, reflect a very small number of surveys; (10) A state average was not calculated because too few hospitals in the state submitted data; (11) There were discrepancies in the data collection process; Please refer to the User's Guide for a full explanation of data.

Jewell County Hospital

100 Crestvue Ave
Mankato, KS 66956
E-mail: jchosp@ruraltel.net
Type: Critical Access Hospitals
Ownership: Government - Local
Phone: 785-378-3137
Fax: 785-378-3450
Emergency Services: Yes
Beds: 37

Key Personnel:
CEO/President. . . . . Aloha Kier
Chief of Medical Staff . . . . Farhat Mehmood, MD
Infection Control. . . . . Lynette Engelbert
Quality Assurance . . . . Susan Newell
Emergency Room . . . . Farhat Mehmood, MD

Measure	Cases	This Hosp.	State Avg.	U.S. Avg.
Heart Attack Care				
ACE Inhibitor or ARB for LVSD[5]	0	-	95%	96%
Aspirin at Arrival[5]	0	-	98%	99%
Aspirin at Discharge[5]	0	-	98%	98%
Beta Blocker at Discharge[5]	0	-	98%	98%
Fibrinolytic Medication Timing[5]	0	-	44%	55%
PCI Within 90 Minutes of Arrival[5]	0	-	91%	90%
Smoking Cessation Advice[5]	0	-	99%	99%
Chest Pain/Possible Heart Attack Care				
Aspirin at Arrival	-	-	92%	95%
Median Time to ECG (minutes)	-	-	10	8
Median Time to Transfer (minutes)	-	-	60	61
Fibrinolytic Medication Timing	-	-	42%	54%
Heart Failure Care				
ACE Inhibitor or ARB for LVSD[5]	0	-	91%	94%
Discharge Instructions[5]	0	-	83%	88%
Evaluation of LVS Function[5]	0	-	92%	98%
Smoking Cessation Advice[5]	0	-	94%	98%
Pneumonia Care				
Appropriate Initial Antibiotic[5]	0	-	87%	92%
Blood Culture Timing[5]	0	-	96%	96%
Influenza Vaccine[5]	0	-	87%	91%
Initial Antibiotic Timing[5]	0	-	95%	95%
Pneumococcal Vaccine[5]	0	-	88%	93%
Smoking Cessation Advice[5]	0	-	93%	97%
Surgical Care Improvement Project				
Appropriate VTP Within 24 Hours[5]	0	-	89%	92%
Appropriate Hair Removal[5]	0	-	100%	99%
Appropriate Beta Blocker Usage[5]	0	-	90%	93%
Controlled Postoperative Blood Glucose[5]	0	-	92%	93%
Prophylactic Antibiotic Timing[5]	0	-	96%	97%
Prophylactic Antibiotic Timing (Outpatient)	-	-	93%	92%
Prophylactic Antibiotic Selection[5]	0	-	97%	97%
Prophylactic Antibiotic Select. (Outpatient)	-	-	96%	94%
Prophylactic Antibiotic Stopped[5]	0	-	93%	94%
Recommended VTP Ordered[5]	0	-	91%	94%
Urinary Catheter Removal[5]	0	-	86%	90%
Children's Asthma Care				
Received Systemic Corticosteroids	-	-	-	100%
Received Home Management Plan	-	-	-	71%
Received Reliever Medication	-	-	-	100%
Use of Medical Imaging				
Combination Abdominal CT Scan	-	-	0.365	0.191
Combination Chest CT Scan	-	-	0.065	0.054
Follow-up Mammogram/Ultrasound	-	-	7.3%	8.4%
MRI for Low Back Pain	-	-	34.5%	32.7%
Survey of Patients' Hospital Experiences				
Area Around Room 'Always' Quiet at Night[8]	-	-	-	58%
Doctors 'Always' Communicated Well[8]	-	-	-	80%
Home Recovery Information Given[8]	-	-	-	82%
Hospital Given 9 or 10 on 10 Point Scale[8]	-	-	-	67%
Meds 'Always' Explained Before Given[8]	-	-	-	60%
Nurses 'Always' Communicated Well[8]	-	-	-	76%
Pain 'Always' Well Controlled[8]	-	-	-	69%
Room and Bathroom 'Always' Clean[8]	-	-	-	71%
Timely Help 'Always' Received[8]	-	-	-	64%
Would Definitely Recommend Hospital[8]	-	-	-	69%

Saint Luke Hospital & Living Center

535 South Freebron
Marion, KS 66861
URL: www.slhmarion.org
Type: Critical Access Hospitals
Ownership: Govt - Hospital Dist/Auth
Phone: 620-382-2177
Fax: 620-382-9104
Emergency Services: Yes
Beds: 54

Key Personnel:
CEO/President. . . . . Jeremy Armstrong
Chief of Medical Staff . . . . Don Hudson
Operating Room. . . . . Clayton Fetsch
Quality Assurance . . . . Vickie Guetersloh
Anesthesiology. . . . . Bruce Skiles CRNA
Emergency Room . . . . Linda Kennedy

Measure	Cases	This Hosp.	State Avg.	U.S. Avg.
Heart Attack Care				
ACE Inhibitor or ARB for LVSD[5]	0	-	95%	96%
Aspirin at Arrival[5]	0	-	98%	99%
Aspirin at Discharge[5]	0	-	98%	98%
Beta Blocker at Discharge[5]	0	-	98%	98%
Fibrinolytic Medication Timing[5]	0	-	44%	55%
PCI Within 90 Minutes of Arrival[5]	0	-	91%	90%
Smoking Cessation Advice[5]	0	-	99%	99%
Chest Pain/Possible Heart Attack Care				
Aspirin at Arrival	-	-	92%	95%
Median Time to ECG (minutes)	-	-	10	8
Median Time to Transfer (minutes)	-	-	60	61
Fibrinolytic Medication Timing	-	-	42%	54%
Heart Failure Care				
ACE Inhibitor or ARB for LVSD	0	-	91%	94%
Discharge Instructions[1]	6	33%	83%	88%
Evaluation of LVS Function[1]	8	62%	92%	98%
Smoking Cessation Advice[1]	1	100%	94%	98%
Pneumonia Care				
Appropriate Initial Antibiotic[1]	7	86%	87%	92%
Blood Culture Timing	0	-	96%	96%
Influenza Vaccine[1]	3	33%	87%	91%
Initial Antibiotic Timing[1]	6	100%	95%	95%
Pneumococcal Vaccine[1]	3	100%	88%	93%
Smoking Cessation Advice[1]	2	50%	93%	97%
Surgical Care Improvement Project				
Appropriate VTP Within 24 Hours[5]	0	-	89%	92%
Appropriate Hair Removal[5]	0	-	100%	99%
Appropriate Beta Blocker Usage[5]	0	-	90%	93%
Controlled Postoperative Blood Glucose[5]	0	-	92%	93%
Prophylactic Antibiotic Timing[5]	0	-	96%	97%
Prophylactic Antibiotic Timing (Outpatient)	-	-	93%	92%
Prophylactic Antibiotic Selection[5]	0	-	97%	97%
Prophylactic Antibiotic Select. (Outpatient)	-	-	96%	94%
Prophylactic Antibiotic Stopped[5]	0	-	93%	94%
Recommended VTP Ordered[5]	0	-	91%	94%
Urinary Catheter Removal[5]	0	-	86%	90%
Children's Asthma Care				
Received Systemic Corticosteroids	-	-	-	100%
Received Home Management Plan	-	-	-	71%
Received Reliever Medication	-	-	-	100%
Use of Medical Imaging				
Combination Abdominal CT Scan	-	-	0.365	0.191
Combination Chest CT Scan	-	-	0.065	0.054
Follow-up Mammogram/Ultrasound	-	-	7.3%	8.4%
MRI for Low Back Pain	-	-	34.5%	32.7%
Survey of Patients' Hospital Experiences				
Area Around Room 'Always' Quiet at Night[8]	-	-	-	58%
Doctors 'Always' Communicated Well[8]	-	-	-	80%
Home Recovery Information Given[8]	-	-	-	82%
Hospital Given 9 or 10 on 10 Point Scale[8]	-	-	-	67%
Meds 'Always' Explained Before Given[8]	-	-	-	60%
Nurses 'Always' Communicated Well[8]	-	-	-	76%
Pain 'Always' Well Controlled[8]	-	-	-	69%
Room and Bathroom 'Always' Clean[8]	-	-	-	71%
Timely Help 'Always' Received[8]	-	-	-	64%
Would Definitely Recommend Hospital[8]	-	-	-	69%

Memorial Hospital

1000 Hospital Drive
Mcpherson, KS 67460
Type: Acute Care Hospitals
Ownership: Voluntary Non-Profit - Private
Phone: 620-241-2250
Fax: 620-245-9153
Emergency Services: Yes
Beds: 70

Key Personnel:
CEO/President. . . . . Rex Walk
Chief of Medical Staff . . . . Trish Goad
Infection Control. . . . . Kathy Rishel
Quality Assurance . . . . Terri Gehring
Emergency Room . . . . Richard L Watson
Intensive Care Unit. . . . . Cheryl Vincent, RN

Measure	Cases	This Hosp.	State Avg.	U.S. Avg.
Heart Attack Care				
ACE Inhibitor or ARB for LVSD[3]	0	-	95%	96%
Aspirin at Arrival[1,3]	4	25%	98%	99%
Aspirin at Discharge[1,3]	4	25%	98%	98%
Beta Blocker at Discharge[1,3]	4	100%	98%	98%
Fibrinolytic Medication Timing[3]	0	-	44%	55%
PCI Within 90 Minutes of Arrival[3]	0	-	91%	90%
Smoking Cessation Advice[3]	0	-	99%	99%
Chest Pain/Possible Heart Attack Care				
Aspirin at Arrival	110	96%	92%	95%
Median Time to ECG (minutes)	112	14	10	8
Median Time to Transfer (minutes)[5]	0	-	60	61
Fibrinolytic Medication Timing[3]	0	-	42%	54%
Heart Failure Care				
ACE Inhibitor or ARB for LVSD[1]	7	86%	91%	94%
Discharge Instructions[1]	21	57%	83%	88%
Evaluation of LVS Function	30	87%	92%	98%
Smoking Cessation Advice[1]	1	100%	94%	98%
Pneumonia Care				
Appropriate Initial Antibiotic	35	97%	87%	92%
Blood Culture Timing	31	100%	96%	96%
Influenza Vaccine	43	84%	87%	91%
Initial Antibiotic Timing	65	98%	95%	95%
Pneumococcal Vaccine	61	82%	88%	93%
Smoking Cessation Advice[1]	8	88%	93%	97%
Surgical Care Improvement Project				
Appropriate VTP Within 24 Hours[1]	20	90%	89%	92%
Appropriate Hair Removal	31	100%	100%	99%
Appropriate Beta Blocker Usage[1]	6	100%	90%	93%
Controlled Postoperative Blood Glucose	0	-	92%	93%
Prophylactic Antibiotic Timing[1]	11	73%	96%	97%
Prophylactic Antibiotic Timing (Outpatient)[1,3]	2	50%	93%	92%
Prophylactic Antibiotic Selection[1]	10	90%	97%	97%
Prophylactic Antibiotic Select. (Outpatient)[1,3]	2	100%	96%	94%
Prophylactic Antibiotic Stopped[1]	10	100%	93%	94%
Recommended VTP Ordered[1]	20	90%	91%	94%
Urinary Catheter Removal[1]	4	75%	86%	90%
Children's Asthma Care				
Received Systemic Corticosteroids	-	-	-	100%
Received Home Management Plan	-	-	-	71%
Received Reliever Medication	-	-	-	100%
Use of Medical Imaging				
Combination Abdominal CT Scan	320	0.656	0.365	0.191
Combination Chest CT Scan	283	0.028	0.065	0.054
Follow-up Mammogram/Ultrasound	514	9.9%	7.3%	8.4%
MRI for Low Back Pain	62	30.6%	34.5%	32.7%
Survey of Patients' Hospital Experiences				
Area Around Room 'Always' Quiet at Night	300+	57%	-	58%
Doctors 'Always' Communicated Well	300+	82%	-	80%
Home Recovery Information Given	300+	80%	-	82%
Hospital Given 9 or 10 on 10 Point Scale	300+	66%	-	67%
Meds 'Always' Explained Before Given	300+	59%	-	60%
Nurses 'Always' Communicated Well	300+	74%	-	76%
Pain 'Always' Well Controlled	300+	69%	-	69%
Room and Bathroom 'Always' Clean	300+	71%	-	71%
Timely Help 'Always' Received	300+	67%	-	64%
Would Definitely Recommend Hospital	300+	65%	-	69%

NOTE: Hospital profiles are in alphabetical order by state, then city, then hospital within the city; Rankings exclude hospitals with less than 25 cases except for patient surveys which excludes hospitals with less than 100 cases; (a) 100–299 cases; (1) The number of cases is too small to be sure how well a hospital is performing; (2) The hospital indicated that the data submitted for this measure were based on a sample of cases; (3) Data was collected during a shorter time period (fewer quarters) than the maximum possible time for this measure; (4) Suppressed for one or more quarters by CMS; (5) No data is available from the hospital for this measure; (6) Fewer than 100 patients completed the HCAHPS survey. Use these rates with caution, as the number of surveys may be too low to reliably assess hospital performance; (7) Survey results are based on less than 12 months of data; (8) Survey results are not available for this reporting period; (9) No or very few patients were eligible for the HCAHPS survey. The scores shown, if any, reflect a very small number of surveys; (10) A state average was not calculated because too few hospitals in the state submitted data; (11) There were discrepancies in the data collection process; Please refer to the User's Guide for a full explanation of data.

Meade District Hospital

510 E Carthage
Meade, KS 67864
URL: www.meadehospital.com
Type: Critical Access Hospitals
Ownership: Govt - Hospital Dist/Auth
Phone: 620-873-5500
Fax: 620-873-2576
Emergency Services: Yes

Key Personnel:
CEO/President. . . . . Mickey Thomas
Operating Room. . . . . Jane Chance RN
Radiology. . . . . Brad Bird ARRT

Measure	Cases	This Hosp.	State Avg.	U.S. Avg.
Heart Attack Care				
ACE Inhibitor or ARB for LVSD[3]	0	-	95%	96%
Aspirin at Arrival[1,3]	2	100%	98%	99%
Aspirin at Discharge[1,3]	2	100%	98%	98%
Beta Blocker at Discharge[1,3]	2	100%	98%	98%
Fibrinolytic Medication Timing[3]	0	-	44%	55%
PCI Within 90 Minutes of Arrival[3]	0	-	91%	90%
Smoking Cessation Advice[3]	0	-	99%	99%
Chest Pain/Possible Heart Attack Care				
Aspirin at Arrival	-	-	92%	95%
Median Time to ECG (minutes)	-	-	10	8
Median Time to Transfer (minutes)	-	-	60	61
Fibrinolytic Medication Timing	-	-	42%	54%
Heart Failure Care				
ACE Inhibitor or ARB for LVSD[1]	4	50%	91%	94%
Discharge Instructions[1]	15	27%	83%	88%
Evaluation of LVS Function[1]	17	82%	92%	98%
Smoking Cessation Advice	0	-	94%	98%
Pneumonia Care				
Appropriate Initial Antibiotic	27	59%	87%	92%
Blood Culture Timing[1]	4	100%	96%	96%
Influenza Vaccine	33	85%	87%	91%
Initial Antibiotic Timing	41	98%	95%	95%
Pneumococcal Vaccine	53	77%	88%	93%
Smoking Cessation Advice[1]	2	0%	93%	97%
Surgical Care Improvement Project				
Appropriate VTP Within 24 Hours[1]	15	100%	89%	92%
Appropriate Hair Removal	57	100%	100%	99%
Appropriate Beta Blocker Usage[5]	0	-	90%	93%
Controlled Postoperative Blood Glucose	0	-	92%	93%
Prophylactic Antibiotic Timing	53	100%	96%	97%
Prophylactic Antibiotic Timing (Outpatient)	-	-	93%	92%
Prophylactic Antibiotic Selection	53	94%	97%	97%
Prophylactic Antibiotic Select. (Outpatient)	-	-	96%	94%
Prophylactic Antibiotic Stopped	53	100%	93%	94%
Recommended VTP Ordered[1]	15	100%	91%	94%
Urinary Catheter Removal	0	-	86%	90%
Children's Asthma Care				
Received Systemic Corticosteroids	-	-	-	100%
Received Home Management Plan	-	-	-	71%
Received Reliever Medication	-	-	-	100%
Use of Medical Imaging				
Combination Abdominal CT Scan	-	-	0.365	0.191
Combination Chest CT Scan	-	-	0.065	0.054
Follow-up Mammogram/Ultrasound	-	-	7.3%	8.4%
MRI for Low Back Pain	-	-	34.5%	32.7%
Survey of Patients' Hospital Experiences				
Area Around Room 'Always' Quiet at Night[8]	-	-	-	58%
Doctors 'Always' Communicated Well[8]	-	-	-	80%
Home Recovery Information Given[8]	-	-	-	82%
Hospital Given 9 or 10 on 10 Point Scale[8]	-	-	-	67%
Meds 'Always' Explained Before Given[8]	-	-	-	60%
Nurses 'Always' Communicated Well[8]	-	-	-	76%
Pain 'Always' Well Controlled[8]	-	-	-	69%
Room and Bathroom 'Always' Clean[8]	-	-	-	71%
Timely Help 'Always' Received[8]	-	-	-	64%
Would Definitely Recommend Hospital[8]	-	-	-	69%

Ottawa County Health Center

215 E 8th Street
Minneapolis, KS 67467
Type: Critical Access Hospitals
Ownership: Government - Local
Phone: 785-392-2122
Fax: 785-392-2852
Emergency Services: Yes
Beds: 25

Key Personnel:
CEO/President. . . . . Joy Reed
Quality Assurance . . . . Debbie Comfort

Measure	Cases	This Hosp.	State Avg.	U.S. Avg.
Heart Attack Care				
ACE Inhibitor or ARB for LVSD[5]	0	-	95%	96%
Aspirin at Arrival[5]	0	-	98%	99%
Aspirin at Discharge[5]	0	-	98%	98%
Beta Blocker at Discharge[5]	0	-	98%	98%
Fibrinolytic Medication Timing[5]	0	-	44%	55%
PCI Within 90 Minutes of Arrival[5]	0	-	91%	90%
Smoking Cessation Advice[5]	0	-	99%	99%
Chest Pain/Possible Heart Attack Care				
Aspirin at Arrival[1]	13	77%	92%	95%
Median Time to ECG (minutes)[1]	13	15	10	8
Median Time to Transfer (minutes)[5]	0	-	60	61
Fibrinolytic Medication Timing[5]	0	-	42%	54%
Heart Failure Care				
ACE Inhibitor or ARB for LVSD[5]	0	-	91%	94%
Discharge Instructions[5]	0	-	83%	88%
Evaluation of LVS Function[5]	0	-	92%	98%
Smoking Cessation Advice[5]	0	-	94%	98%
Pneumonia Care				
Appropriate Initial Antibiotic[1,2]	7	86%	87%	92%
Blood Culture Timing[1,2]	1	100%	96%	96%
Influenza Vaccine[1]	7	57%	87%	91%
Initial Antibiotic Timing[1,2]	9	100%	95%	95%
Pneumococcal Vaccine[1,2]	10	70%	88%	93%
Smoking Cessation Advice[1,2]	1	0%	93%	97%
Surgical Care Improvement Project				
Appropriate VTP Within 24 Hours[5]	0	-	89%	92%
Appropriate Hair Removal[5]	0	-	100%	99%
Appropriate Beta Blocker Usage[5]	0	-	90%	93%
Controlled Postoperative Blood Glucose[5]	0	-	92%	93%
Prophylactic Antibiotic Timing[5]	0	-	96%	97%
Prophylactic Antibiotic Timing (Outpatient)[5]	0	-	93%	92%
Prophylactic Antibiotic Selection[5]	0	-	97%	97%
Prophylactic Antibiotic Select. (Outpatient)[5]	0	-	96%	94%
Prophylactic Antibiotic Stopped[5]	0	-	93%	94%
Recommended VTP Ordered[5]	0	-	91%	94%
Urinary Catheter Removal[5]	0	-	86%	90%
Children's Asthma Care				
Received Systemic Corticosteroids	-	-	-	100%
Received Home Management Plan	-	-	-	71%
Received Reliever Medication	-	-	-	100%
Use of Medical Imaging				
Combination Abdominal CT Scan[1]	4	1.000	0.365	0.191
Combination Chest CT Scan[1]	4	0.250	0.065	0.054
Follow-up Mammogram/Ultrasound[5]	0	-	7.3%	8.4%
MRI for Low Back Pain[5]	0	-	34.5%	32.7%
Survey of Patients' Hospital Experiences				
Area Around Room 'Always' Quiet at Night[8]	-	-	-	58%
Doctors 'Always' Communicated Well[8]	-	-	-	80%
Home Recovery Information Given[8]	-	-	-	82%
Hospital Given 9 or 10 on 10 Point Scale[8]	-	-	-	67%
Meds 'Always' Explained Before Given[8]	-	-	-	60%
Nurses 'Always' Communicated Well[8]	-	-	-	76%
Pain 'Always' Well Controlled[8]	-	-	-	69%
Room and Bathroom 'Always' Clean[8]	-	-	-	71%
Timely Help 'Always' Received[8]	-	-	-	64%
Would Definitely Recommend Hospital[8]	-	-	-	69%

Mercy Hospital

218 E Pack St
Moundridge, KS 67107
Type: Acute Care Hospitals
Ownership: Voluntary Non-Profit - Church
Phone: 620-345-6391
Fax: 620-345-6344
Emergency Services: No
Beds: 21

Key Personnel:
Coronary Care . . . . Karen Ratzlaff
Quality Assurance . . . . Verla Friesen, RN RM
Emergency Room . . . . Donnella Unruh, RN

Measure	Cases	This Hosp.	State Avg.	U.S. Avg.
Heart Attack Care				
ACE Inhibitor or ARB for LVSD[1]	2	0%	95%	96%
Aspirin at Arrival[1]	3	100%	98%	99%
Aspirin at Discharge[1]	3	0%	98%	98%
Beta Blocker at Discharge[1]	3	0%	98%	98%
Fibrinolytic Medication Timing	0	-	44%	55%
PCI Within 90 Minutes of Arrival	0	-	91%	90%
Smoking Cessation Advice	0	-	99%	99%
Chest Pain/Possible Heart Attack Care				
Aspirin at Arrival[5]	0	-	92%	95%
Median Time to ECG (minutes)[5]	0	-	10	8
Median Time to Transfer (minutes)[5]	0	-	60	61
Fibrinolytic Medication Timing[5]	0	-	42%	54%
Heart Failure Care				
ACE Inhibitor or ARB for LVSD[1]	10	80%	91%	94%
Discharge Instructions[1]	9	67%	83%	88%
Evaluation of LVS Function[1]	16	88%	92%	98%
Smoking Cessation Advice	0	-	94%	98%
Pneumonia Care				
Appropriate Initial Antibiotic[1]	7	100%	87%	92%
Blood Culture Timing	0	-	96%	96%
Influenza Vaccine[1]	7	57%	87%	91%
Initial Antibiotic Timing[1]	16	88%	95%	95%
Pneumococcal Vaccine[1]	20	80%	88%	93%
Smoking Cessation Advice	0	-	93%	97%
Surgical Care Improvement Project				
Appropriate VTP Within 24 Hours[5]	0	-	89%	92%
Appropriate Hair Removal[5]	0	-	100%	99%
Appropriate Beta Blocker Usage[5]	0	-	90%	93%
Controlled Postoperative Blood Glucose[5]	0	-	92%	93%
Prophylactic Antibiotic Timing[5]	0	-	96%	97%
Prophylactic Antibiotic Timing (Outpatient)[5]	0	-	93%	92%
Prophylactic Antibiotic Selection[5]	0	-	97%	97%
Prophylactic Antibiotic Select. (Outpatient)[5]	0	-	96%	94%
Prophylactic Antibiotic Stopped[5]	0	-	93%	94%
Recommended VTP Ordered[5]	0	-	91%	94%
Urinary Catheter Removal[5]	0	-	86%	90%
Children's Asthma Care				
Received Systemic Corticosteroids	-	-	-	100%
Received Home Management Plan	-	-	-	71%
Received Reliever Medication	-	-	-	100%
Use of Medical Imaging				
Combination Abdominal CT Scan[5]	0	-	0.365	0.191
Combination Chest CT Scan[5]	0	-	0.065	0.054
Follow-up Mammogram/Ultrasound[5]	0	-	7.3%	8.4%
MRI for Low Back Pain[5]	0	-	34.5%	32.7%
Survey of Patients' Hospital Experiences				
Area Around Room 'Always' Quiet at Night	(a)	73%	-	58%
Doctors 'Always' Communicated Well	(a)	88%	-	80%
Home Recovery Information Given	(a)	80%	-	82%
Hospital Given 9 or 10 on 10 Point Scale	(a)	85%	-	67%
Meds 'Always' Explained Before Given	(a)	62%	-	60%
Nurses 'Always' Communicated Well	(a)	84%	-	76%
Pain 'Always' Well Controlled	(a)	75%	-	69%
Room and Bathroom 'Always' Clean	(a)	86%	-	71%
Timely Help 'Always' Received	(a)	80%	-	64%
Would Definitely Recommend Hospital	(a)	87%	-	69%

NOTE: Hospital profiles are in alphabetical order by state, then city, then hospital within the city; Rankings exclude hospitals with less than 25 cases except for patient surveys which excludes hospitals with less than 100 cases; (a) 100–299 cases; (1) The number of cases is too small to be sure how well a hospital is performing; (2) The hospital indicated that the data submitted for this measure were based on a sample of cases; (3) Data was collected during a shorter time period (fewer quarters) than the maximum possible time for this measure; (4) Suppressed for one or more quarters by CMS; (5) No data is available from the hospital for this measure; (6) Fewer than 100 patients completed the HCAHPS survey. Use these rates with caution, as the number of surveys may be too low to reliably assess hospital performance; (7) Survey results are based on less than 12 months of data; (8) Survey results are not available for this reporting period; (9) No or very few patients were eligible for the HCAHPS survey. The scores shown, if any, reflect a very small number of surveys; (10) A state average was not calculated because too few hospitals in the state submitted data; (11) There were discrepancies in the data collection process; Please refer to the User's Guide for a full explanation of data.

Wilson Medical Center

Reece Campus 2600 Ottawa Road
Neodesha, KS 66757
Phone: 620-325-8369
Fax: 620-325-2907
URL: www.wilsoncountyhospital.org
Type: Critical Access Hospitals
Emergency Services: Yes
Ownership: Voluntary Non-Profit - Other
Beds: 38

Key Personnel:
CEO/President. . . . . John Gutschenritter
Chief of Medical Staff . . . . Amy Cunningham

Measure	Cases	This Hosp.	State Avg.	U.S. Avg.
Heart Attack Care				
ACE Inhibitor or ARB for LVSD[5]	0	-	95%	96%
Aspirin at Arrival[5]	0	-	98%	99%
Aspirin at Discharge[5]	0	-	98%	98%
Beta Blocker at Discharge[5]	0	-	98%	98%
Fibrinolytic Medication Timing[5]	0	-	44%	55%
PCI Within 90 Minutes of Arrival[5]	0	-	91%	90%
Smoking Cessation Advice[5]	0	-	99%	99%
Chest Pain/Possible Heart Attack Care				
Aspirin at Arrival	-	-	92%	95%
Median Time to ECG (minutes)	-	-	10	8
Median Time to Transfer (minutes)	-	-	60	61
Fibrinolytic Medication Timing	-	-	42%	54%
Heart Failure Care				
ACE Inhibitor or ARB for LVSD[3]	0	-	91%	94%
Discharge Instructions[1,3]	3	0%	83%	88%
Evaluation of LVS Function[1,3]	3	0%	92%	98%
Smoking Cessation Advice[3]	0	-	94%	98%
Pneumonia Care				
Appropriate Initial Antibiotic[1]	6	33%	87%	92%
Blood Culture Timing[1]	8	88%	96%	96%
Influenza Vaccine[1]	4	25%	87%	91%
Initial Antibiotic Timing[1]	8	88%	95%	95%
Pneumococcal Vaccine[1]	6	33%	88%	93%
Smoking Cessation Advice[1]	5	40%	93%	97%
Surgical Care Improvement Project				
Appropriate VTP Within 24 Hours[5]	0	-	89%	92%
Appropriate Hair Removal[5]	0	-	100%	99%
Appropriate Beta Blocker Usage[5]	0	-	90%	93%
Controlled Postoperative Blood Glucose[5]	0	-	92%	93%
Prophylactic Antibiotic Timing[5]	0	-	96%	97%
Prophylactic Antibiotic Timing (Outpatient)	-	-	93%	92%
Prophylactic Antibiotic Selection[5]	0	-	97%	97%
Prophylactic Antibiotic Select. (Outpatient)	-	-	96%	94%
Prophylactic Antibiotic Stopped[5]	0	-	93%	94%
Recommended VTP Ordered[5]	0	-	91%	94%
Urinary Catheter Removal[5]	0	-	86%	90%
Children's Asthma Care				
Received Systemic Corticosteroids	-	-	-	100%
Received Home Management Plan	-	-	-	71%
Received Reliever Medication	-	-	-	100%
Use of Medical Imaging				
Combination Abdominal CT Scan	-	-	0.365	0.191
Combination Chest CT Scan	-	-	0.065	0.054
Follow-up Mammogram/Ultrasound	-	-	7.3%	8.4%
MRI for Low Back Pain	-	-	34.5%	32.7%
Survey of Patients' Hospital Experiences				
Area Around Room 'Always' Quiet at Night[8]	-	-	-	58%
Doctors 'Always' Communicated Well[8]	-	-	-	80%
Home Recovery Information Given[8]	-	-	-	82%
Hospital Given 9 or 10 on 10 Point Scale[8]	-	-	-	67%
Meds 'Always' Explained Before Given[8]	-	-	-	60%
Nurses 'Always' Communicated Well[8]	-	-	-	76%
Pain 'Always' Well Controlled[8]	-	-	-	69%
Room and Bathroom 'Always' Clean[8]	-	-	-	71%
Timely Help 'Always' Received[8]	-	-	-	64%
Would Definitely Recommend Hospital[8]	-	-	-	69%

Ness County Hospital District #2

312 Custer Street
Ness City, KS 67560
Phone: 785-798-2291
Fax: 785-798-3435
E-mail: nesshosp@gbta.net
Type: Critical Access Hospitals
Emergency Services: Yes
Ownership: Govt - Hospital Dist/Auth
Beds: 20

Key Personnel:
Infection Control. . . . . Brenda Sutton, RN
Quality Assurance . . . . Susan Kuehn
Emergency Room . . . . Brenda Wassinger

Measure	Cases	This Hosp.	State Avg.	U.S. Avg.
Heart Attack Care				
ACE Inhibitor or ARB for LVSD[5]	0	-	95%	96%
Aspirin at Arrival[5]	0	-	98%	99%
Aspirin at Discharge[5]	0	-	98%	98%
Beta Blocker at Discharge[5]	0	-	98%	98%
Fibrinolytic Medication Timing[5]	0	-	44%	55%
PCI Within 90 Minutes of Arrival[5]	0	-	91%	90%
Smoking Cessation Advice[5]	0	-	99%	99%
Chest Pain/Possible Heart Attack Care				
Aspirin at Arrival	-	-	92%	95%
Median Time to ECG (minutes)	-	-	10	8
Median Time to Transfer (minutes)	-	-	60	61
Fibrinolytic Medication Timing	-	-	42%	54%
Heart Failure Care				
ACE Inhibitor or ARB for LVSD[5]	0	-	91%	94%
Discharge Instructions[5]	0	-	83%	88%
Evaluation of LVS Function[5]	0	-	92%	98%
Smoking Cessation Advice[5]	0	-	94%	98%
Pneumonia Care				
Appropriate Initial Antibiotic[1]	8	100%	87%	92%
Blood Culture Timing[1]	6	100%	96%	96%
Influenza Vaccine[1]	18	72%	87%	91%
Initial Antibiotic Timing[1]	11	100%	95%	95%
Pneumococcal Vaccine[1]	18	67%	88%	93%
Smoking Cessation Advice[1]	1	0%	93%	97%
Surgical Care Improvement Project				
Appropriate VTP Within 24 Hours[5]	0	-	89%	92%
Appropriate Hair Removal[5]	0	-	100%	99%
Appropriate Beta Blocker Usage[5]	0	-	90%	93%
Controlled Postoperative Blood Glucose[5]	0	-	92%	93%
Prophylactic Antibiotic Timing[5]	0	-	96%	97%
Prophylactic Antibiotic Timing (Outpatient)	-	-	93%	92%
Prophylactic Antibiotic Selection[5]	0	-	97%	97%
Prophylactic Antibiotic Select. (Outpatient)	-	-	96%	94%
Prophylactic Antibiotic Stopped[5]	0	-	93%	94%
Recommended VTP Ordered[5]	0	-	91%	94%
Urinary Catheter Removal[5]	0	-	86%	90%
Children's Asthma Care				
Received Systemic Corticosteroids	-	-	-	100%
Received Home Management Plan	-	-	-	71%
Received Reliever Medication	-	-	-	100%
Use of Medical Imaging				
Combination Abdominal CT Scan	-	-	0.365	0.191
Combination Chest CT Scan	-	-	0.065	0.054
Follow-up Mammogram/Ultrasound	-	-	7.3%	8.4%
MRI for Low Back Pain	-	-	34.5%	32.7%
Survey of Patients' Hospital Experiences				
Area Around Room 'Always' Quiet at Night[8]	-	-	-	58%
Doctors 'Always' Communicated Well[8]	-	-	-	80%
Home Recovery Information Given[8]	-	-	-	82%
Hospital Given 9 or 10 on 10 Point Scale[8]	-	-	-	67%
Meds 'Always' Explained Before Given[8]	-	-	-	60%
Nurses 'Always' Communicated Well[8]	-	-	-	76%
Pain 'Always' Well Controlled[8]	-	-	-	69%
Room and Bathroom 'Always' Clean[8]	-	-	-	71%
Timely Help 'Always' Received[8]	-	-	-	64%
Would Definitely Recommend Hospital[8]	-	-	-	69%

Newton Medical Center

800 Medical Center Dr
Newton, KS 67114
Phone: 316-804-6001
Fax: 316-804-6260
E-mail: nmcinfor@newmedctr.org
URL: www.newtonmedicalcenter.com
Type: Acute Care Hospitals
Emergency Services: Yes
Ownership: Voluntary Non-Profit - Private
Beds: 103

Key Personnel:
CEO/President. . . . . Steven G Kelly, FACHE
Chief of Medical Staff . . . . Joseph Aiyenowo
Radiology. . . . . Maj-Beth Biernacki

Measure	Cases	This Hosp.	State Avg.	U.S. Avg.
Heart Attack Care				
ACE Inhibitor or ARB for LVSD[1]	2	100%	95%	96%
Aspirin at Arrival	25	92%	98%	99%
Aspirin at Discharge[1]	20	95%	98%	98%
Beta Blocker at Discharge[1]	20	100%	98%	98%
Fibrinolytic Medication Timing	0	-	44%	55%
PCI Within 90 Minutes of Arrival	0	-	91%	90%
Smoking Cessation Advice[1]	3	100%	99%	99%
Chest Pain/Possible Heart Attack Care				
Aspirin at Arrival	82	85%	92%	95%
Median Time to ECG (minutes)	88	15	10	8
Median Time to Transfer (minutes)[1,3]	3	76	60	61
Fibrinolytic Medication Timing[1]	2	50%	42%	54%
Heart Failure Care				
ACE Inhibitor or ARB for LVSD[1]	22	77%	91%	94%
Discharge Instructions	57	37%	83%	88%
Evaluation of LVS Function	125	86%	92%	98%
Smoking Cessation Advice[1]	20	85%	94%	98%
Pneumonia Care				
Appropriate Initial Antibiotic	78	88%	87%	92%
Blood Culture Timing	78	92%	96%	96%
Influenza Vaccine	78	77%	87%	91%
Initial Antibiotic Timing	117	91%	95%	95%
Pneumococcal Vaccine	127	92%	88%	93%
Smoking Cessation Advice	33	91%	93%	97%
Surgical Care Improvement Project				
Appropriate VTP Within 24 Hours	172	80%	89%	92%
Appropriate Hair Removal	509	100%	100%	99%
Appropriate Beta Blocker Usage	141	91%	90%	93%
Controlled Postoperative Blood Glucose	0	-	92%	93%
Prophylactic Antibiotic Timing	370	90%	96%	97%
Prophylactic Antibiotic Timing (Outpatient)	90	73%	93%	92%
Prophylactic Antibiotic Selection	363	86%	97%	97%
Prophylactic Antibiotic Select. (Outpatient)	117	96%	96%	94%
Prophylactic Antibiotic Stopped	347	92%	93%	94%
Recommended VTP Ordered	175	87%	91%	94%
Urinary Catheter Removal	139	82%	86%	90%
Children's Asthma Care				
Received Systemic Corticosteroids	-	-	-	100%
Received Home Management Plan	-	-	-	71%
Received Reliever Medication	-	-	-	100%
Use of Medical Imaging				
Combination Abdominal CT Scan	288	0.760	0.365	0.191
Combination Chest CT Scan	193	0.000	0.065	0.054
Follow-up Mammogram/Ultrasound	947	7.2%	7.3%	8.4%
MRI for Low Back Pain	78	25.6%	34.5%	32.7%
Survey of Patients' Hospital Experiences				
Area Around Room 'Always' Quiet at Night	300+	56%	-	58%
Doctors 'Always' Communicated Well	300+	83%	-	80%
Home Recovery Information Given	300+	82%	-	82%
Hospital Given 9 or 10 on 10 Point Scale	300+	79%	-	67%
Meds 'Always' Explained Before Given	300+	59%	-	60%
Nurses 'Always' Communicated Well	300+	78%	-	76%
Pain 'Always' Well Controlled	300+	72%	-	69%
Room and Bathroom 'Always' Clean	300+	76%	-	71%
Timely Help 'Always' Received	300+	67%	-	64%
Would Definitely Recommend Hospital	300+	82%	-	69%

NOTE: Hospital profiles are in alphabetical order by state, then city, then hospital within the city; Rankings exclude hospitals with less than 25 cases except for patient surveys which excludes hospitals with less than 100 cases; (a) 100–299 cases; (1) The number of cases is too small to be sure how well a hospital is performing; (2) The hospital indicated that the data submitted for this measure were based on a sample of cases; (3) Data was collected during a shorter time period (fewer quarters) than the maximum possible time for this measure; (4) Suppressed for one or more quarters by CMS; (5) No data is available from the hospital for this measure; (6) Fewer than 100 patients completed the HCAHPS survey. Use these rates with caution, as the number of surveys may be too low to reliably assess hospital performance; (7) Survey results are based on less than 12 months of data; (8) Survey results are not available for this reporting period; (9) No or very few patients were eligible for the HCAHPS survey. The scores shown, if any, reflect a very small number of surveys; (10) A state average was not calculated because too few hospitals in the state submitted data; (11) There were discrepancies in the data collection process; Please refer to the User's Guide for a full explanation of data.

Norton County Hospital

102 E Holme Street
Norton, KS 67654
Phone: 785-877-3351
Fax: 785-877-2841
E-mail: ntcohoso@ruraltel.net
Type: Critical Access Hospitals
Emergency Services: Yes
Ownership: Government - Local
Beds: 43

Key Personnel:

CEO/President. . . . . Richard Miller
Chief of Medical Staff . . . . Glenda Maurer, MD
Quality Assurance . . . . Lyn Thiele
Emergency Room . . . . Georgia Brier

Measure	Cases	This Hosp.	State Avg.	U.S. Avg.
Heart Attack Care				
ACE Inhibitor or ARB for LVSD[5]	0	-	95%	96%
Aspirin at Arrival[5]	0	-	98%	99%
Aspirin at Discharge[5]	0	-	98%	98%
Beta Blocker at Discharge[5]	0	-	98%	98%
Fibrinolytic Medication Timing[5]	0	-	44%	55%
PCI Within 90 Minutes of Arrival[5]	0	-	91%	90%
Smoking Cessation Advice[5]	0	-	99%	99%
Chest Pain/Possible Heart Attack Care				
Aspirin at Arrival	-	-	92%	95%
Median Time to ECG (minutes)	-	-	10	8
Median Time to Transfer (minutes)	-	-	60	61
Fibrinolytic Medication Timing	-	-	42%	54%
Heart Failure Care				
ACE Inhibitor or ARB for LVSD[5]	0	-	91%	94%
Discharge Instructions[5]	0	-	83%	88%
Evaluation of LVS Function[5]	0	-	92%	98%
Smoking Cessation Advice[5]	0	-	94%	98%
Pneumonia Care				
Appropriate Initial Antibiotic[1]	7	29%	87%	92%
Blood Culture Timing	0	-	96%	96%
Influenza Vaccine[1]	10	80%	87%	91%
Initial Antibiotic Timing[1]	10	90%	95%	95%
Pneumococcal Vaccine[1]	17	53%	88%	93%
Smoking Cessation Advice	0	-	93%	97%
Surgical Care Improvement Project				
Appropriate VTP Within 24 Hours[5]	0	-	89%	92%
Appropriate Hair Removal[5]	0	-	100%	99%
Appropriate Beta Blocker Usage[5]	0	-	90%	93%
Controlled Postoperative Blood Glucose[5]	0	-	92%	93%
Prophylactic Antibiotic Timing[5]	0	-	96%	97%
Prophylactic Antibiotic Timing (Outpatient)	-	-	93%	92%
Prophylactic Antibiotic Selection[5]	0	-	97%	97%
Prophylactic Antibiotic Select. (Outpatient)	-	-	96%	94%
Prophylactic Antibiotic Stopped[5]	0	-	93%	94%
Recommended VTP Ordered[5]	0	-	91%	94%
Urinary Catheter Removal[5]	0	-	86%	90%
Children's Asthma Care				
Received Systemic Corticosteroids	-	-	-	100%
Received Home Management Plan	-	-	-	71%
Received Reliever Medication	-	-	-	100%
Use of Medical Imaging				
Combination Abdominal CT Scan	-	-	0.365	0.191
Combination Chest CT Scan	-	-	0.065	0.054
Follow-up Mammogram/Ultrasound	-	-	7.3%	8.4%
MRI for Low Back Pain	-	-	34.5%	32.7%
Survey of Patients' Hospital Experiences				
Area Around Room 'Always' Quiet at Night[8]	-	-	-	58%
Doctors 'Always' Communicated Well[8]	-	-	-	80%
Home Recovery Information Given[8]	-	-	-	82%
Hospital Given 9 or 10 on 10 Point Scale[8]	-	-	-	67%
Meds 'Always' Explained Before Given[8]	-	-	-	60%
Nurses 'Always' Communicated Well[8]	-	-	-	76%
Pain 'Always' Well Controlled[8]	-	-	-	69%
Room and Bathroom 'Always' Clean[8]	-	-	-	71%
Timely Help 'Always' Received[8]	-	-	-	64%
Would Definitely Recommend Hospital[8]	-	-	-	69%

Olathe Medical Center

20375 W 151st St #303
Olathe, KS 66061
Phone: 913-791-4200
Fax: 913-791-4393
URL: www.ohsi.com
Type: Acute Care Hospitals
Emergency Services: Yes
Ownership: Voluntary Non-Profit - Other
Beds: 200

Key Personnel:

Cardiac Laboratory. . . . . Kit Power
Chief of Medical Staff . . . . Bruce Snider, MD
Infection Control. . . . . Elaine Fitzmaurice
Operating Room. . . . . Dave Wayatt
Quality Assurance . . . . Nancy Schnegelberger
Radiology. . . . . Donald J Boss
Emergency Room . . . . Cindy Kolich
Intensive Care Unit. . . . . Carol Cleek

Measure	Cases	This Hosp.	State Avg.	U.S. Avg.
Heart Attack Care				
ACE Inhibitor or ARB for LVSD	39	100%	95%	96%
Aspirin at Arrival	189	99%	98%	99%
Aspirin at Discharge	221	99%	98%	98%
Beta Blocker at Discharge	211	97%	98%	98%
Fibrinolytic Medication Timing	0	-	44%	55%
PCI Within 90 Minutes of Arrival	41	93%	91%	90%
Smoking Cessation Advice	78	100%	99%	99%
Chest Pain/Possible Heart Attack Care				
Aspirin at Arrival[3]	0	-	92%	95%
Median Time to ECG (minutes)[3]	0	-	10	8
Median Time to Transfer (minutes)[5]	0	-	60	61
Fibrinolytic Medication Timing[5]	0	-	42%	54%
Heart Failure Care				
ACE Inhibitor or ARB for LVSD	67	91%	91%	94%
Discharge Instructions	182	82%	83%	88%
Evaluation of LVS Function	260	98%	92%	98%
Smoking Cessation Advice	32	100%	94%	98%
Pneumonia Care				
Appropriate Initial Antibiotic	122	83%	87%	92%
Blood Culture Timing	172	98%	96%	96%
Influenza Vaccine	173	87%	87%	91%
Initial Antibiotic Timing	197	98%	95%	95%
Pneumococcal Vaccine	200	96%	88%	93%
Smoking Cessation Advice	94	100%	93%	97%
Surgical Care Improvement Project				
Appropriate VTP Within 24 Hours[2]	307	93%	89%	92%
Appropriate Hair Removal[2]	1,069	100%	100%	99%
Appropriate Beta Blocker Usage[2]	357	95%	90%	93%
Controlled Postoperative Blood Glucose[2]	108	94%	92%	93%
Prophylactic Antibiotic Timing[2]	778	96%	96%	97%
Prophylactic Antibiotic Timing (Outpatient)	653	95%	93%	92%
Prophylactic Antibiotic Selection[2]	786	97%	97%	97%
Prophylactic Antibiotic Select. (Outpatient)	643	98%	96%	94%
Prophylactic Antibiotic Stopped[2]	746	94%	93%	94%
Recommended VTP Ordered[2]	307	96%	91%	94%
Urinary Catheter Removal[2]	316	91%	86%	90%
Children's Asthma Care				
Received Systemic Corticosteroids	-	-	-	100%
Received Home Management Plan	-	-	-	71%
Received Reliever Medication	-	-	-	100%
Use of Medical Imaging				
Combination Abdominal CT Scan	706	0.024	0.365	0.191
Combination Chest CT Scan	684	0.003	0.065	0.054
Follow-up Mammogram/Ultrasound	1,292	9.9%	7.3%	8.4%
MRI for Low Back Pain	283	37.8%	34.5%	32.7%
Survey of Patients' Hospital Experiences				
Area Around Room 'Always' Quiet at Night	300+	56%	-	58%
Doctors 'Always' Communicated Well	300+	80%	-	80%
Home Recovery Information Given	300+	87%	-	82%
Hospital Given 9 or 10 on 10 Point Scale	300+	73%	-	67%
Meds 'Always' Explained Before Given	300+	61%	-	60%
Nurses 'Always' Communicated Well	300+	75%	-	76%
Pain 'Always' Well Controlled	300+	69%	-	69%
Room and Bathroom 'Always' Clean	300+	63%	-	71%
Timely Help 'Always' Received	300+	61%	-	64%
Would Definitely Recommend Hospital	300+	76%	-	69%

Community Hospital - Onaga and St Marys Campus

120 West 8th Street
Onaga, KS 66521
Phone: 785-889-4272
Fax: 785-889-7163
URL: www.chcs-ks.org
Type: Critical Access Hospitals
Emergency Services: Yes
Ownership: Voluntary Non-Profit - Private
Beds: 30

Key Personnel:

CEO/President. . . . . Greg Unruh
Chief of Medical Staff . . . . Nancy J Zidek
Infection Control. . . . . Cathy VanDonge
Pediatric Ambulatory Care . . . . . . Elaine Becker
Pediatric In-Patient Care . . . . Elaine Becker
Quality Assurance . . . . Pam Wilkie
Emergency Room . . . . Mary Matzke
Patient Relations . . . . Melinda May, RN

Measure	Cases	This Hosp.	State Avg.	U.S. Avg.
Heart Attack Care				
ACE Inhibitor or ARB for LVSD[5]	0	-	95%	96%
Aspirin at Arrival[5]	0	-	98%	99%
Aspirin at Discharge[5]	0	-	98%	98%
Beta Blocker at Discharge[5]	0	-	98%	98%
Fibrinolytic Medication Timing[5]	0	-	44%	55%
PCI Within 90 Minutes of Arrival[5]	0	-	91%	90%
Smoking Cessation Advice[5]	0	-	99%	99%
Chest Pain/Possible Heart Attack Care				
Aspirin at Arrival	-	-	92%	95%
Median Time to ECG (minutes)	-	-	10	8
Median Time to Transfer (minutes)	-	-	60	61
Fibrinolytic Medication Timing	-	-	42%	54%
Heart Failure Care				
ACE Inhibitor or ARB for LVSD[1]	6	50%	91%	94%
Discharge Instructions[1]	11	45%	83%	88%
Evaluation of LVS Function	30	73%	92%	98%
Smoking Cessation Advice	0	-	94%	98%
Pneumonia Care				
Appropriate Initial Antibiotic[1]	19	95%	87%	92%
Blood Culture Timing[1]	2	100%	96%	96%
Influenza Vaccine	32	72%	87%	91%
Initial Antibiotic Timing	32	100%	95%	95%
Pneumococcal Vaccine	36	64%	88%	93%
Smoking Cessation Advice[1]	8	38%	93%	97%
Surgical Care Improvement Project				
Appropriate VTP Within 24 Hours[5]	0	-	89%	92%
Appropriate Hair Removal[5]	0	-	100%	99%
Appropriate Beta Blocker Usage[5]	0	-	90%	93%
Controlled Postoperative Blood Glucose[5]	0	-	92%	93%
Prophylactic Antibiotic Timing[5]	0	-	96%	97%
Prophylactic Antibiotic Timing (Outpatient)	-	-	93%	92%
Prophylactic Antibiotic Selection[5]	0	-	97%	97%
Prophylactic Antibiotic Select. (Outpatient)	-	-	96%	94%
Prophylactic Antibiotic Stopped[5]	0	-	93%	94%
Recommended VTP Ordered[5]	0	-	91%	94%
Urinary Catheter Removal[5]	0	-	86%	90%
Children's Asthma Care				
Received Systemic Corticosteroids	-	-	-	100%
Received Home Management Plan	-	-	-	71%
Received Reliever Medication	-	-	-	100%
Use of Medical Imaging				
Combination Abdominal CT Scan	-	-	0.365	0.191
Combination Chest CT Scan	-	-	0.065	0.054
Follow-up Mammogram/Ultrasound	-	-	7.3%	8.4%
MRI for Low Back Pain	-	-	34.5%	32.7%
Survey of Patients' Hospital Experiences				
Area Around Room 'Always' Quiet at Night[8]	-	-	-	58%
Doctors 'Always' Communicated Well[8]	-	-	-	80%
Home Recovery Information Given[8]	-	-	-	82%
Hospital Given 9 or 10 on 10 Point Scale[8]	-	-	-	67%
Meds 'Always' Explained Before Given[8]	-	-	-	60%
Nurses 'Always' Communicated Well[8]	-	-	-	76%
Pain 'Always' Well Controlled[8]	-	-	-	69%
Room and Bathroom 'Always' Clean[8]	-	-	-	71%
Timely Help 'Always' Received[8]	-	-	-	64%
Would Definitely Recommend Hospital[8]	-	-	-	69%

NOTE: Hospital profiles are in alphabetical order by state, then city, then hospital within the city; Rankings exclude hospitals with less than 25 cases except for patient surveys which excludes hospitals with less than 100 cases; (a) 100–299 cases; (1) The number of cases is too small to be sure how well a hospital is performing; (2) The hospital indicated that the data submitted for this measure were based on a sample of cases; (3) Data was collected during a shorter time period (fewer quarters) than the maximum possible time for this measure; (4) Suppressed for one or more quarters by CMS; (5) No data is available from the hospital for this measure; (6) Fewer than 100 patients completed the HCAHPS survey. Use these rates with caution, as the number of surveys may be too low to reliably assess hospital performance; (7) Survey results are based on less than 12 months of data; (8) Survey results are not available for this reporting period; (9) No or very few patients were eligible for the HCAHPS survey. The scores shown, if any, reflect a very small number of surveys; (10) A state average was not calculated because too few hospitals in the state submitted data; (11) There were discrepancies in the data collection process; Please refer to the User's Guide for a full explanation of data.

Osborne County Memorial Hospital

424 W New Hampshire
Osborne, KS 67473
URL: www.ocmh.org
Type: Critical Access Hospitals
Ownership: Voluntary Non-Profit - Other
Phone: 785-346-2121
Fax: 785-346-5498
Emergency Services: Yes
Beds: 25

Key Personnel:
CEO/President . . . . Roger John
Chief of Medical Staff . . . . Barbara Brown

Measure	Cases	This Hosp.	State Avg.	U.S. Avg.
Heart Attack Care				
ACE Inhibitor or ARB for LVSD[5]	0	-	95%	96%
Aspirin at Arrival[5]	0	-	98%	99%
Aspirin at Discharge[5]	0	-	98%	98%
Beta Blocker at Discharge[5]	0	-	98%	98%
Fibrinolytic Medication Timing[5]	0	-	44%	55%
PCI Within 90 Minutes of Arrival[5]	0	-	91%	90%
Smoking Cessation Advice[5]	0	-	99%	99%
Chest Pain/Possible Heart Attack Care				
Aspirin at Arrival	-	-	92%	95%
Median Time to ECG (minutes)	-	-	10	8
Median Time to Transfer (minutes)	-	-	60	61
Fibrinolytic Medication Timing	-	-	42%	54%
Heart Failure Care				
ACE Inhibitor or ARB for LVSD[5]	0	-	91%	94%
Discharge Instructions[5]	0	-	83%	88%
Evaluation of LVS Function[5]	0	-	92%	98%
Smoking Cessation Advice[5]	0	-	94%	98%
Pneumonia Care				
Appropriate Initial Antibiotic[5]	0	-	87%	92%
Blood Culture Timing[5]	0	-	96%	96%
Influenza Vaccine[5]	0	-	87%	91%
Initial Antibiotic Timing[5]	0	-	95%	95%
Pneumococcal Vaccine[5]	0	-	88%	93%
Smoking Cessation Advice[5]	0	-	93%	97%
Surgical Care Improvement Project				
Appropriate VTP Within 24 Hours[5]	0	-	89%	92%
Appropriate Hair Removal[5]	0	-	100%	99%
Appropriate Beta Blocker Usage[5]	0	-	90%	93%
Controlled Postoperative Blood Glucose[5]	0	-	92%	93%
Prophylactic Antibiotic Timing[5]	0	-	96%	97%
Prophylactic Antibiotic Timing (Outpatient)	-	-	93%	92%
Prophylactic Antibiotic Selection[5]	0	-	97%	97%
Prophylactic Antibiotic Select. (Outpatient)	-	-	96%	94%
Prophylactic Antibiotic Stopped[5]	0	-	93%	94%
Recommended VTP Ordered[5]	0	-	91%	94%
Urinary Catheter Removal[5]	0	-	86%	90%
Children's Asthma Care				
Received Systemic Corticosteroids	-	-	-	100%
Received Home Management Plan	-	-	-	71%
Received Reliever Medication	-	-	-	100%
Use of Medical Imaging				
Combination Abdominal CT Scan	-	-	0.365	0.191
Combination Chest CT Scan	-	-	0.065	0.054
Follow-up Mammogram/Ultrasound	-	-	7.3%	8.4%
MRI for Low Back Pain	-	-	34.5%	32.7%
Survey of Patients' Hospital Experiences				
Area Around Room 'Always' Quiet at Night[8]	-	-	-	58%
Doctors 'Always' Communicated Well[8]	-	-	-	80%
Home Recovery Information Given[8]	-	-	-	82%
Hospital Given 9 or 10 on 10 Point Scale[8]	-	-	-	67%
Meds 'Always' Explained Before Given[8]	-	-	-	60%
Nurses 'Always' Communicated Well[8]	-	-	-	76%
Pain 'Always' Well Controlled[8]	-	-	-	69%
Room and Bathroom 'Always' Clean[8]	-	-	-	71%
Timely Help 'Always' Received[8]	-	-	-	64%
Would Definitely Recommend Hospital[8]	-	-	-	69%

Oswego Community Hospital

800 Barker Drive
Oswego, KS 67356
Type: Critical Access Hospitals
Ownership: Voluntary Non-Profit - Private
Phone: 620-795-2921
Fax: 620-795-3094
Emergency Services: Yes
Beds: 12

Key Personnel:
Chief of Medical Staff . . . . Stanley Haag, MD

Measure	Cases	This Hosp.	State Avg.	U.S. Avg.
Heart Attack Care				
ACE Inhibitor or ARB for LVSD[5]	0	-	95%	96%
Aspirin at Arrival[5]	0	-	98%	99%
Aspirin at Discharge[5]	0	-	98%	98%
Beta Blocker at Discharge[5]	0	-	98%	98%
Fibrinolytic Medication Timing[5]	0	-	44%	55%
PCI Within 90 Minutes of Arrival[5]	0	-	91%	90%
Smoking Cessation Advice[5]	0	-	99%	99%
Chest Pain/Possible Heart Attack Care				
Aspirin at Arrival	-	-	92%	95%
Median Time to ECG (minutes)	-	-	10	8
Median Time to Transfer (minutes)	-	-	60	61
Fibrinolytic Medication Timing	-	-	42%	54%
Heart Failure Care				
ACE Inhibitor or ARB for LVSD[5]	0	-	91%	94%
Discharge Instructions[5]	0	-	83%	88%
Evaluation of LVS Function[5]	0	-	92%	98%
Smoking Cessation Advice[5]	0	-	94%	98%
Pneumonia Care				
Appropriate Initial Antibiotic[5]	0	-	87%	92%
Blood Culture Timing[5]	0	-	96%	96%
Influenza Vaccine[5]	0	-	87%	91%
Initial Antibiotic Timing[5]	0	-	95%	95%
Pneumococcal Vaccine[5]	0	-	88%	93%
Smoking Cessation Advice[5]	0	-	93%	97%
Surgical Care Improvement Project				
Appropriate VTP Within 24 Hours[5]	0	-	89%	92%
Appropriate Hair Removal[5]	0	-	100%	99%
Appropriate Beta Blocker Usage[5]	0	-	90%	93%
Controlled Postoperative Blood Glucose[5]	0	-	92%	93%
Prophylactic Antibiotic Timing[5]	0	-	96%	97%
Prophylactic Antibiotic Timing (Outpatient)	-	-	93%	92%
Prophylactic Antibiotic Selection[5]	0	-	97%	97%
Prophylactic Antibiotic Select. (Outpatient)	-	-	96%	94%
Prophylactic Antibiotic Stopped[5]	0	-	93%	94%
Recommended VTP Ordered[5]	0	-	91%	94%
Urinary Catheter Removal[5]	0	-	86%	90%
Children's Asthma Care				
Received Systemic Corticosteroids	-	-	-	100%
Received Home Management Plan	-	-	-	71%
Received Reliever Medication	-	-	-	100%
Use of Medical Imaging				
Combination Abdominal CT Scan	-	-	0.365	0.191
Combination Chest CT Scan	-	-	0.065	0.054
Follow-up Mammogram/Ultrasound	-	-	7.3%	8.4%
MRI for Low Back Pain	-	-	34.5%	32.7%
Survey of Patients' Hospital Experiences				
Area Around Room 'Always' Quiet at Night[8]	-	-	-	58%
Doctors 'Always' Communicated Well[8]	-	-	-	80%
Home Recovery Information Given[8]	-	-	-	82%
Hospital Given 9 or 10 on 10 Point Scale[8]	-	-	-	67%
Meds 'Always' Explained Before Given[8]	-	-	-	60%
Nurses 'Always' Communicated Well[8]	-	-	-	76%
Pain 'Always' Well Controlled[8]	-	-	-	69%
Room and Bathroom 'Always' Clean[8]	-	-	-	71%
Timely Help 'Always' Received[8]	-	-	-	64%
Would Definitely Recommend Hospital[8]	-	-	-	69%

Ransom Memorial Hospital

1301 S Main Street
Ottawa, KS 66067
URL: www.ransom.org
Type: Acute Care Hospitals
Ownership: Government - Local
Phone: 785-229-8308
Fax: 785-242-8339
Emergency Services: Yes
Beds: 55

Key Personnel:
CEO/President . . . . Larry Felix
Infection Control . . . . Linda Reed
Operating Room . . . . Rick Coffman
Quality Assurance . . . . Susan Ward
Radiology . . . . Roger Lawrence
Emergency Room . . . . Marilyn Holland
Patient Relations . . . . Susan Ward

Measure	Cases	This Hosp.	State Avg.	U.S. Avg.
Heart Attack Care				
ACE Inhibitor or ARB for LVSD[1]	1	100%	95%	96%
Aspirin at Arrival[1]	4	50%	98%	99%
Aspirin at Discharge[1]	3	33%	98%	98%
Beta Blocker at Discharge[1]	2	100%	98%	98%
Fibrinolytic Medication Timing	0	-	44%	55%
PCI Within 90 Minutes of Arrival	0	-	91%	90%
Smoking Cessation Advice[1]	2	100%	99%	99%
Chest Pain/Possible Heart Attack Care				
Aspirin at Arrival	49	94%	92%	95%
Median Time to ECG (minutes)	48	5	10	8
Median Time to Transfer (minutes)[1,3]	4	36	60	61
Fibrinolytic Medication Timing[3]	0	-	42%	54%
Heart Failure Care				
ACE Inhibitor or ARB for LVSD[1]	2	100%	91%	94%
Discharge Instructions[1]	15	87%	83%	88%
Evaluation of LVS Function[1]	23	100%	92%	98%
Smoking Cessation Advice[1]	4	100%	94%	98%
Pneumonia Care				
Appropriate Initial Antibiotic	42	95%	87%	92%
Blood Culture Timing	57	100%	96%	96%
Influenza Vaccine	41	95%	87%	91%
Initial Antibiotic Timing	67	97%	95%	95%
Pneumococcal Vaccine	69	96%	88%	93%
Smoking Cessation Advice	28	96%	93%	97%
Surgical Care Improvement Project				
Appropriate VTP Within 24 Hours	35	97%	89%	92%
Appropriate Hair Removal	111	100%	100%	99%
Appropriate Beta Blocker Usage[1]	17	88%	90%	93%
Controlled Postoperative Blood Glucose	0	-	92%	93%
Prophylactic Antibiotic Timing	95	91%	96%	97%
Prophylactic Antibiotic Timing (Outpatient)[1]	20	75%	93%	92%
Prophylactic Antibiotic Selection	94	91%	97%	97%
Prophylactic Antibiotic Select. (Outpatient)	61	98%	96%	94%
Prophylactic Antibiotic Stopped	88	98%	93%	94%
Recommended VTP Ordered	35	100%	91%	94%
Urinary Catheter Removal[1]	16	94%	86%	90%
Children's Asthma Care				
Received Systemic Corticosteroids	-	-	-	100%
Received Home Management Plan	-	-	-	71%
Received Reliever Medication	-	-	-	100%
Use of Medical Imaging				
Combination Abdominal CT Scan	244	0.057	0.365	0.191
Combination Chest CT Scan	177	0.000	0.065	0.054
Follow-up Mammogram/Ultrasound	439	9.8%	7.3%	8.4%
MRI for Low Back Pain	80	27.5%	34.5%	32.7%
Survey of Patients' Hospital Experiences				
Area Around Room 'Always' Quiet at Night	300+	55%	-	58%
Doctors 'Always' Communicated Well	300+	87%	-	80%
Home Recovery Information Given	300+	85%	-	82%
Hospital Given 9 or 10 on 10 Point Scale	300+	70%	-	67%
Meds 'Always' Explained Before Given	300+	60%	-	60%
Nurses 'Always' Communicated Well	300+	80%	-	76%
Pain 'Always' Well Controlled	300+	71%	-	69%
Room and Bathroom 'Always' Clean	300+	69%	-	71%
Timely Help 'Always' Received	300+	70%	-	64%
Would Definitely Recommend Hospital	300+	72%	-	69%

NOTE: Hospital profiles are in alphabetical order by state, then city, then hospital within the city; Rankings exclude hospitals with less than 25 cases except for patient surveys which excludes hospitals with less than 100 cases; (a) 100–299 cases; (1) The number of cases is too small to be sure how well a hospital is performing; (2) The hospital indicated that the data submitted for this measure were based on a sample of cases; (3) Data was collected during a shorter time period (fewer quarters) than the maximum possible time for this measure; (4) Suppressed for one or more quarters by CMS; (5) No data is available from the hospital for this measure; (6) Fewer than 100 patients completed the HCAHPS survey. Use these rates with caution, as the number of surveys may be too low to reliably assess hospital performance; (7) Survey results are based on less than 12 months of data; (8) Survey results are not available for this reporting period; (9) No or very few patients were eligible for the HCAHPS survey. The scores shown, if any, reflect a very small number of surveys; (10) A state average was not calculated because too few hospitals in the state submitted data; (11) There were discrepancies in the data collection process; Please refer to the User's Guide for a full explanation of data.

Heartland Surgical Spec Hospital

10720 Nall Avenue Phone: 913-754-4505
Overland Park, KS 66211
Type: Acute Care Hospitals Emergency Services: No
Ownership: Proprietary

Measure	Cases	This Hosp.	State Avg.	U.S. Avg.
Heart Attack Care				
ACE Inhibitor or ARB for LVSD[5]	0	-	95%	96%
Aspirin at Arrival[5]	0	-	98%	99%
Aspirin at Discharge[5]	0	-	98%	98%
Beta Blocker at Discharge[5]	0	-	98%	98%
Fibrinolytic Medication Timing[5]	0	-	44%	55%
PCI Within 90 Minutes of Arrival[5]	0	-	91%	90%
Smoking Cessation Advice[5]	0	-	99%	99%
Chest Pain/Possible Heart Attack Care				
Aspirin at Arrival[5]	0	-	92%	95%
Median Time to ECG (minutes)[5]	0	-	10	8
Median Time to Transfer (minutes)[5]	0	-	60	61
Fibrinolytic Medication Timing[5]	0	-	42%	54%
Heart Failure Care				
ACE Inhibitor or ARB for LVSD[5]	0	-	91%	94%
Discharge Instructions[5]	0	-	83%	88%
Evaluation of LVS Function[5]	0	-	92%	98%
Smoking Cessation Advice[5]	0	-	94%	98%
Pneumonia Care				
Appropriate Initial Antibiotic[5]	0	-	87%	92%
Blood Culture Timing[5]	0	-	96%	96%
Influenza Vaccine[5]	0	-	87%	91%
Initial Antibiotic Timing[5]	0	-	95%	95%
Pneumococcal Vaccine[5]	0	-	88%	93%
Smoking Cessation Advice[5]	0	-	93%	97%
Surgical Care Improvement Project				
Appropriate VTP Within 24 Hours[1]	12	100%	89%	92%
Appropriate Hair Removal	102	99%	100%	99%
Appropriate Beta Blocker Usage	32	72%	90%	93%
Controlled Postoperative Blood Glucose	0	-	92%	93%
Prophylactic Antibiotic Timing	84	99%	96%	97%
Prophylactic Antibiotic Timing (Outpatient)	352	97%	93%	92%
Prophylactic Antibiotic Selection	84	100%	97%	97%
Prophylactic Antibiotic Select. (Outpatient)	349	99%	96%	94%
Prophylactic Antibiotic Stopped	80	95%	93%	94%
Recommended VTP Ordered[1]	12	100%	91%	94%
Urinary Catheter Removal	44	93%	86%	90%
Children's Asthma Care				
Received Systemic Corticosteroids	-	-	-	100%
Received Home Management Plan	-	-	-	71%
Received Reliever Medication	-	-	-	100%
Use of Medical Imaging				
Combination Abdominal CT Scan[1]	32	0.375	0.365	0.191
Combination Chest CT Scan[1]	5	0.400	0.065	0.054
Follow-up Mammogram/Ultrasound[5]	0	-	7.3%	8.4%
MRI for Low Back Pain	169	30.2%	34.5%	32.7%
Survey of Patients' Hospital Experiences				
Area Around Room 'Always' Quiet at Night	300+	82%	-	58%
Doctors 'Always' Communicated Well	300+	85%	-	80%
Home Recovery Information Given	300+	87%	-	82%
Hospital Given 9 or 10 on 10 Point Scale	300+	91%	-	67%
Meds 'Always' Explained Before Given	300+	69%	-	60%
Nurses 'Always' Communicated Well	300+	85%	-	76%
Pain 'Always' Well Controlled	300+	76%	-	69%
Room and Bathroom 'Always' Clean	300+	81%	-	71%
Timely Help 'Always' Received	300+	85%	-	64%
Would Definitely Recommend Hospital	300+	91%	-	69%

Menorah Medical Center

5721 West 119th Street Phone: 913-498-6773
Overland Park, KS 66209 Fax: 913-498-7106
URL: www.menorahmedicalcenter.com
Type: Acute Care Hospitals Emergency Services: Yes
Ownership: Voluntary Non-Profit - Other Beds: 158
Key Personnel:
CEO/President. . . . . Steven Wilkinson

Measure	Cases	This Hosp.	State Avg.	U.S. Avg.
Heart Attack Care				
ACE Inhibitor or ARB for LVSD[1]	8	100%	95%	96%
Aspirin at Arrival	35	97%	98%	99%
Aspirin at Discharge	39	100%	98%	98%
Beta Blocker at Discharge	36	100%	98%	98%
Fibrinolytic Medication Timing	0	-	44%	55%
PCI Within 90 Minutes of Arrival[1]	12	92%	91%	90%
Smoking Cessation Advice[1]	9	100%	99%	99%
Chest Pain/Possible Heart Attack Care				
Aspirin at Arrival[5]	0	-	92%	95%
Median Time to ECG (minutes)[5]	0	-	10	8
Median Time to Transfer (minutes)[5]	0	-	60	61
Fibrinolytic Medication Timing[5]	0	-	42%	54%
Heart Failure Care				
ACE Inhibitor or ARB for LVSD	25	100%	91%	94%
Discharge Instructions	95	98%	83%	88%
Evaluation of LVS Function	138	100%	92%	98%
Smoking Cessation Advice[1]	7	100%	94%	98%
Pneumonia Care				
Appropriate Initial Antibiotic	88	94%	87%	92%
Blood Culture Timing	135	97%	96%	96%
Influenza Vaccine	95	100%	87%	91%
Initial Antibiotic Timing	118	99%	95%	95%
Pneumococcal Vaccine	132	100%	88%	93%
Smoking Cessation Advice	35	100%	93%	97%
Surgical Care Improvement Project				
Appropriate VTP Within 24 Hours[2]	178	93%	89%	92%
Appropriate Hair Removal[2]	526	100%	100%	99%
Appropriate Beta Blocker Usage[2]	127	94%	90%	93%
Controlled Postoperative Blood Glucose[2]	36	78%	92%	93%
Prophylactic Antibiotic Timing[2]	352	98%	96%	97%
Prophylactic Antibiotic Timing (Outpatient)	333	98%	93%	92%
Prophylactic Antibiotic Selection[2]	355	98%	97%	97%
Prophylactic Antibiotic Select. (Outpatient)	332	99%	96%	94%
Prophylactic Antibiotic Stopped[2]	340	96%	93%	94%
Recommended VTP Ordered[2]	179	97%	91%	94%
Urinary Catheter Removal[2]	73	92%	86%	90%
Children's Asthma Care				
Received Systemic Corticosteroids	-	-	-	100%
Received Home Management Plan	-	-	-	71%
Received Reliever Medication	-	-	-	100%
Use of Medical Imaging				
Combination Abdominal CT Scan	392	0.102	0.365	0.191
Combination Chest CT Scan	437	0.014	0.065	0.054
Follow-up Mammogram/Ultrasound	824	11.2%	7.3%	8.4%
MRI for Low Back Pain	86	41.9%	34.5%	32.7%
Survey of Patients' Hospital Experiences				
Area Around Room 'Always' Quiet at Night	300+	60%	-	58%
Doctors 'Always' Communicated Well	300+	79%	-	80%
Home Recovery Information Given	300+	86%	-	82%
Hospital Given 9 or 10 on 10 Point Scale	300+	67%	-	67%
Meds 'Always' Explained Before Given	300+	58%	-	60%
Nurses 'Always' Communicated Well	300+	72%	-	76%
Pain 'Always' Well Controlled	300+	68%	-	69%
Room and Bathroom 'Always' Clean	300+	57%	-	71%
Timely Help 'Always' Received	300+	56%	-	64%
Would Definitely Recommend Hospital	300+	72%	-	69%

Overland Park Regional Medical Center

10500 Quivira Road Phone: 913-541-5301
Overland Park, KS 66215 Fax: 913-541-5790
URL: www.oprmc.com
Type: Acute Care Hospitals Emergency Services: Yes
Ownership: Proprietary Beds: 236
Key Personnel:
CEO/President. . . . . Kevin J Hicks
Radiology. . . . . James R Bergh

Measure	Cases	This Hosp.	State Avg.	U.S. Avg.
Heart Attack Care				
ACE Inhibitor or ARB for LVSD[1]	16	100%	95%	96%
Aspirin at Arrival	106	100%	98%	99%
Aspirin at Discharge	106	100%	98%	98%
Beta Blocker at Discharge	96	100%	98%	98%
Fibrinolytic Medication Timing	0	-	44%	55%
PCI Within 90 Minutes of Arrival	27	96%	91%	90%
Smoking Cessation Advice	28	100%	99%	99%
Chest Pain/Possible Heart Attack Care				
Aspirin at Arrival[5]	0	-	92%	95%
Median Time to ECG (minutes)[5]	0	-	10	8
Median Time to Transfer (minutes)[5]	0	-	60	61
Fibrinolytic Medication Timing[5]	0	-	42%	54%
Heart Failure Care				
ACE Inhibitor or ARB for LVSD	47	100%	91%	94%
Discharge Instructions	123	94%	83%	88%
Evaluation of LVS Function	162	100%	92%	98%
Smoking Cessation Advice[1]	12	100%	94%	98%
Pneumonia Care				
Appropriate Initial Antibiotic	72	100%	87%	92%
Blood Culture Timing	148	99%	96%	96%
Influenza Vaccine	105	97%	87%	91%
Initial Antibiotic Timing	133	99%	95%	95%
Pneumococcal Vaccine	137	99%	88%	93%
Smoking Cessation Advice	49	98%	93%	97%
Surgical Care Improvement Project				
Appropriate VTP Within 24 Hours[2]	189	96%	89%	92%
Appropriate Hair Removal[2]	562	100%	100%	99%
Appropriate Beta Blocker Usage[2]	166	99%	90%	93%
Controlled Postoperative Blood Glucose[2]	61	93%	92%	93%
Prophylactic Antibiotic Timing[2]	379	98%	96%	97%
Prophylactic Antibiotic Timing (Outpatient)	642	97%	93%	92%
Prophylactic Antibiotic Selection[2]	384	99%	97%	97%
Prophylactic Antibiotic Select. (Outpatient)	628	98%	96%	94%
Prophylactic Antibiotic Stopped[2]	351	97%	93%	94%
Recommended VTP Ordered[2]	190	97%	91%	94%
Urinary Catheter Removal[2]	61	97%	86%	90%
Children's Asthma Care				
Received Systemic Corticosteroids	-	-	-	100%
Received Home Management Plan	-	-	-	71%
Received Reliever Medication	-	-	-	100%
Use of Medical Imaging				
Combination Abdominal CT Scan	275	0.084	0.365	0.191
Combination Chest CT Scan	217	0.055	0.065	0.054
Follow-up Mammogram/Ultrasound	376	8.5%	7.3%	8.4%
MRI for Low Back Pain[1]	41	31.7%	34.5%	32.7%
Survey of Patients' Hospital Experiences				
Area Around Room 'Always' Quiet at Night	300+	54%	-	58%
Doctors 'Always' Communicated Well	300+	80%	-	80%
Home Recovery Information Given	300+	86%	-	82%
Hospital Given 9 or 10 on 10 Point Scale	300+	66%	-	67%
Meds 'Always' Explained Before Given	300+	56%	-	60%
Nurses 'Always' Communicated Well	300+	73%	-	76%
Pain 'Always' Well Controlled	300+	69%	-	69%
Room and Bathroom 'Always' Clean	300+	63%	-	71%
Timely Help 'Always' Received	300+	56%	-	64%
Would Definitely Recommend Hospital	300+	68%	-	69%

NOTE: Hospital profiles are in alphabetical order by state, then city, then hospital within the city; Rankings exclude hospitals with less than 25 cases except for patient surveys which excludes hospitals with less than 100 cases; (a) 100–299 cases; (1) The number of cases is too small to be sure how well a hospital is performing; (2) The hospital indicated that the data submitted for this measure were based on a sample of cases; (3) Data was collected during a shorter time period (fewer quarters) than the maximum possible time for this measure; (4) Suppressed for one or more quarters by CMS; (5) No data is available from the hospital for this measure; (6) Fewer than 100 patients completed the HCAHPS survey. Use these rates with caution, as the number of surveys may be too low to reliably assess hospital performance; (7) Survey results are based on less than 12 months of data; (8) Survey results are not available for this reporting period; (9) No or very few patients were eligible for the HCAHPS survey. The scores shown, if any, reflect a very small number of surveys; (10) A state average was not calculated because too few hospitals in the state submitted data; (11) There were discrepancies in the data collection process; Please refer to the User's Guide for a full explanation of data.

Saint Luke's South Hospital

12300 Metcalf Avenue
Overland Park, KS 66213
URL: www.saintlukeshealthsystem.org
Type: Acute Care Hospitals
Ownership: Voluntary Non-Profit - Other

Phone: 913-317-7904
Fax: 913-317-7672
Emergency Services: Yes
Beds: 89

Key Personnel:
CEO/President. . . . . Julie Quirin
Radiology. . . . . David Marcus

Measure	Cases	This Hosp.	State Avg.	U.S. Avg.
Heart Attack Care				
ACE Inhibitor or ARB for LVSD[1]	8	100%	95%	96%
Aspirin at Arrival	80	100%	98%	99%
Aspirin at Discharge	79	97%	98%	98%
Beta Blocker at Discharge	77	100%	98%	98%
Fibrinolytic Medication Timing	0	-	44%	55%
PCI Within 90 Minutes of Arrival[1]	13	85%	91%	90%
Smoking Cessation Advice[1]	18	100%	99%	99%
Chest Pain/Possible Heart Attack Care				
Aspirin at Arrival[1]	9	100%	92%	95%
Median Time to ECG (minutes)[1]	9	9	10	8
Median Time to Transfer (minutes)[5]	0	-	60	61
Fibrinolytic Medication Timing[3]	0	-	42%	54%
Heart Failure Care				
ACE Inhibitor or ARB for LVSD	44	98%	91%	94%
Discharge Instructions	118	76%	83%	88%
Evaluation of LVS Function	137	99%	92%	98%
Smoking Cessation Advice[1]	10	100%	94%	98%
Pneumonia Care				
Appropriate Initial Antibiotic	62	94%	87%	92%
Blood Culture Timing	77	99%	96%	96%
Influenza Vaccine	64	94%	87%	91%
Initial Antibiotic Timing	85	96%	95%	95%
Pneumococcal Vaccine	101	97%	88%	93%
Smoking Cessation Advice	25	88%	93%	97%
Surgical Care Improvement Project				
Appropriate VTP Within 24 Hours	134	87%	89%	92%
Appropriate Hair Removal	757	100%	100%	99%
Appropriate Beta Blocker Usage	208	94%	90%	93%
Controlled Postoperative Blood Glucose	0	-	92%	93%
Prophylactic Antibiotic Timing	589	100%	96%	97%
Prophylactic Antibiotic Timing (Outpatient)	140	93%	93%	92%
Prophylactic Antibiotic Selection	594	100%	97%	97%
Prophylactic Antibiotic Select. (Outpatient)	135	90%	96%	94%
Prophylactic Antibiotic Stopped	575	96%	93%	94%
Recommended VTP Ordered	134	92%	91%	94%
Urinary Catheter Removal	26	85%	86%	90%
Children's Asthma Care				
Received Systemic Corticosteroids	-	-	-	100%
Received Home Management Plan	-	-	-	71%
Received Reliever Medication	-	-	-	100%
Use of Medical Imaging				
Combination Abdominal CT Scan	361	0.224	0.365	0.191
Combination Chest CT Scan	230	0.052	0.065	0.054
Follow-up Mammogram/Ultrasound	672	8.5%	7.3%	8.4%
MRI for Low Back Pain	131	30.5%	34.5%	32.7%
Survey of Patients' Hospital Experiences				
Area Around Room 'Always' Quiet at Night	300+	61%	-	58%
Doctors 'Always' Communicated Well	300+	77%	-	80%
Home Recovery Information Given	300+	85%	-	82%
Hospital Given 9 or 10 on 10 Point Scale	300+	79%	-	67%
Meds 'Always' Explained Before Given	300+	62%	-	60%
Nurses 'Always' Communicated Well	300+	75%	-	76%
Pain 'Always' Well Controlled	300+	72%	-	69%
Room and Bathroom 'Always' Clean	300+	71%	-	71%
Timely Help 'Always' Received	300+	72%	-	64%
Would Definitely Recommend Hospital	300+	79%	-	69%

Miami County Medical Center

2100 Baptiste Drive
Paola, KS 66071
URL: www.olathehealth.org
Type: Acute Care Hospitals
Ownership: Govt - Hospital Dist/Auth

Phone: 913-557-4385
Fax: 913-294-5919
Emergency Services: Yes
Beds: 39

Key Personnel:
CEO/President. . . . . Frank H Devocelle
Chief of Medical Staff. . . . . Jack Campbell
Infection Control. . . . . Kathy Auten
Operating Room. . . . . Sharon Bell
Quality Assurance . . . . Jerry Wiesner
Emergency Room . . . . Stacy Steiner

Measure	Cases	This Hosp.	State Avg.	U.S. Avg.
Heart Attack Care				
ACE Inhibitor or ARB for LVSD[1,3]	1	100%	95%	96%
Aspirin at Arrival[1,3]	2	100%	98%	99%
Aspirin at Discharge[1,3]	1	100%	98%	98%
Beta Blocker at Discharge[1,3]	1	100%	98%	98%
Fibrinolytic Medication Timing[3]	0	-	44%	55%
PCI Within 90 Minutes of Arrival[3]	0	-	91%	90%
Smoking Cessation Advice[3]	0	-	99%	99%
Chest Pain/Possible Heart Attack Care				
Aspirin at Arrival	69	86%	92%	95%
Median Time to ECG (minutes)	70	16	10	8
Median Time to Transfer (minutes)[1,3]	9	28	60	61
Fibrinolytic Medication Timing	0	-	42%	54%
Heart Failure Care				
ACE Inhibitor or ARB for LVSD[1]	3	100%	91%	94%
Discharge Instructions[1]	3	100%	83%	88%
Evaluation of LVS Function[1]	8	100%	92%	98%
Smoking Cessation Advice	0	-	94%	98%
Pneumonia Care				
Appropriate Initial Antibiotic[1]	19	95%	87%	92%
Blood Culture Timing[1]	23	100%	96%	96%
Influenza Vaccine[1]	20	100%	87%	91%
Initial Antibiotic Timing	27	96%	95%	95%
Pneumococcal Vaccine[1]	14	93%	88%	93%
Smoking Cessation Advice[1]	15	100%	93%	97%
Surgical Care Improvement Project				
Appropriate VTP Within 24 Hours	30	100%	89%	92%
Appropriate Hair Removal	139	100%	100%	99%
Appropriate Beta Blocker Usage	25	88%	90%	93%
Controlled Postoperative Blood Glucose	0	-	92%	93%
Prophylactic Antibiotic Timing	90	98%	96%	97%
Prophylactic Antibiotic Timing (Outpatient)[1]	20	90%	93%	92%
Prophylactic Antibiotic Selection	90	100%	97%	97%
Prophylactic Antibiotic Select. (Outpatient)[1]	19	95%	96%	94%
Prophylactic Antibiotic Stopped	88	91%	93%	94%
Recommended VTP Ordered	30	100%	91%	94%
Urinary Catheter Removal	44	89%	86%	90%
Children's Asthma Care				
Received Systemic Corticosteroids	-	-	-	100%
Received Home Management Plan	-	-	-	71%
Received Reliever Medication	-	-	-	100%
Use of Medical Imaging				
Combination Abdominal CT Scan	202	0.015	0.365	0.191
Combination Chest CT Scan	105	0.000	0.065	0.054
Follow-up Mammogram/Ultrasound	496	8.5%	7.3%	8.4%
MRI for Low Back Pain	58	34.5%	34.5%	32.7%
Survey of Patients' Hospital Experiences				
Area Around Room 'Always' Quiet at Night	(a)	76%	-	58%
Doctors 'Always' Communicated Well	(a)	87%	-	80%
Home Recovery Information Given	(a)	87%	-	82%
Hospital Given 9 or 10 on 10 Point Scale	(a)	84%	-	67%
Meds 'Always' Explained Before Given	(a)	74%	-	60%
Nurses 'Always' Communicated Well	(a)	83%	-	76%
Pain 'Always' Well Controlled	(a)	77%	-	69%
Room and Bathroom 'Always' Clean	(a)	76%	-	71%
Timely Help 'Always' Received	(a)	73%	-	64%
Would Definitely Recommend Hospital	(a)	79%	-	69%

Labette Health

1902 South Us Hwy 59
Parsons, KS 67357
URL: www.lcmc.com
Type: Acute Care Hospitals
Ownership: Government - Local

Phone: 620-820-5371
Fax: 620-421-5042
Emergency Services: Yes
Beds: 109

Key Personnel:
CEO/President. . . . . William Mahoney
Chief of Medical Staff. . . . . Dr Rothstein
Infection Control. . . . . Carol Hale
Operating Room. . . . . JoDee Witty
Quality Assurance . . . . Debra Herrman
Radiology. . . . . Robert Gibbs
Intensive Care Unit. . . . . Kathy McKinney
Patient Relations . . . . Janet Ball

Measure	Cases	This Hosp.	State Avg.	U.S. Avg.
Heart Attack Care				
ACE Inhibitor or ARB for LVSD	0	-	95%	96%
Aspirin at Arrival[1]	8	88%	98%	99%
Aspirin at Discharge[1]	4	100%	98%	98%
Beta Blocker at Discharge[1]	4	50%	98%	98%
Fibrinolytic Medication Timing	0	-	44%	55%
PCI Within 90 Minutes of Arrival	0	-	91%	90%
Smoking Cessation Advice[1]	1	100%	99%	99%
Chest Pain/Possible Heart Attack Care				
Aspirin at Arrival	68	96%	92%	95%
Median Time to ECG (minutes)	68	6	10	8
Median Time to Transfer (minutes)[1]	6	50	60	61
Fibrinolytic Medication Timing[1]	3	100%	42%	54%
Heart Failure Care				
ACE Inhibitor or ARB for LVSD[1]	10	80%	91%	94%
Discharge Instructions	25	60%	83%	88%
Evaluation of LVS Function	32	97%	92%	98%
Smoking Cessation Advice[1]	4	100%	94%	98%
Pneumonia Care				
Appropriate Initial Antibiotic	43	91%	87%	92%
Blood Culture Timing	68	99%	96%	96%
Influenza Vaccine	59	90%	87%	91%
Initial Antibiotic Timing	69	96%	95%	95%
Pneumococcal Vaccine	72	82%	88%	93%
Smoking Cessation Advice	32	97%	93%	97%
Surgical Care Improvement Project				
Appropriate VTP Within 24 Hours	115	84%	89%	92%
Appropriate Hair Removal	601	100%	100%	99%
Appropriate Beta Blocker Usage	173	84%	90%	93%
Controlled Postoperative Blood Glucose	0	-	92%	93%
Prophylactic Antibiotic Timing	485	98%	96%	97%
Prophylactic Antibiotic Timing (Outpatient)	76	91%	93%	92%
Prophylactic Antibiotic Selection	486	99%	97%	97%
Prophylactic Antibiotic Select. (Outpatient)	73	95%	96%	94%
Prophylactic Antibiotic Stopped	460	99%	93%	94%
Recommended VTP Ordered	115	92%	91%	94%
Urinary Catheter Removal	62	90%	86%	90%
Children's Asthma Care				
Received Systemic Corticosteroids	-	-	-	100%
Received Home Management Plan	-	-	-	71%
Received Reliever Medication	-	-	-	100%
Use of Medical Imaging				
Combination Abdominal CT Scan	439	0.829	0.365	0.191
Combination Chest CT Scan	298	0.483	0.065	0.054
Follow-up Mammogram/Ultrasound	409	3.2%	7.3%	8.4%
MRI for Low Back Pain	165	40.6%	34.5%	32.7%
Survey of Patients' Hospital Experiences				
Area Around Room 'Always' Quiet at Night	300+	58%	-	58%
Doctors 'Always' Communicated Well	300+	81%	-	80%
Home Recovery Information Given	300+	89%	-	82%
Hospital Given 9 or 10 on 10 Point Scale	300+	70%	-	67%
Meds 'Always' Explained Before Given	300+	54%	-	60%
Nurses 'Always' Communicated Well	300+	77%	-	76%
Pain 'Always' Well Controlled	300+	68%	-	69%
Room and Bathroom 'Always' Clean	300+	74%	-	71%
Timely Help 'Always' Received	300+	67%	-	64%
Would Definitely Recommend Hospital	300+	68%	-	69%

NOTE: Hospital profiles are in alphabetical order by state, then city, then hospital within the city; Rankings exclude hospitals with less than 25 cases except for patient surveys which excludes hospitals with less than 100 cases; (a) 100–299 cases; (1) The number of cases is too small to be sure how well a hospital is performing; (2) The hospital indicated that the data submitted for this measure were based on a sample of cases; (3) Data was collected during a shorter time period (fewer quarters) than the maximum possible time for this measure; (4) Suppressed for one or more quarters by CMS; (5) No data is available from the hospital for this measure; (6) Fewer than 100 patients completed the HCAHPS survey. Use these rates with caution, as the number of surveys may be too low to reliably assess hospital performance; (7) Survey results are based on less than 12 months of data; (8) Survey results are not available for this reporting period; (9) No or very few patients were eligible for the HCAHPS survey. The scores shown, if any, reflect a very small number of surveys; (10) A state average was not calculated because too few hospitals in the state submitted data; (11) There were discrepancies in the data collection process; Please refer to the User's Guide for a full explanation of data.

Phillips County Hospital

1150 State Street
Phillipsburg, KS 67661
Phone: 785-543-5226
Fax: 785-543-6272
Type: Critical Access Hospitals
Emergency Services: Yes
Ownership: Government - Local
Beds: 62

Key Personnel:

CEO/President. . . . . Heather Harper
Operating Room. . . . . Hazel Ames
Quality Assurance . . . . Hazel Ames

Measure	Cases	This Hosp.	State Avg.	U.S. Avg.
Heart Attack Care				
ACE Inhibitor or ARB for LVSD[5]	0	-	95%	96%
Aspirin at Arrival[5]	0	-	98%	99%
Aspirin at Discharge[5]	0	-	98%	98%
Beta Blocker at Discharge[5]	0	-	98%	98%
Fibrinolytic Medication Timing[5]	0	-	44%	55%
PCI Within 90 Minutes of Arrival[5]	0	-	91%	90%
Smoking Cessation Advice[5]	0	-	99%	99%
Chest Pain/Possible Heart Attack Care				
Aspirin at Arrival	-	-	92%	95%
Median Time to ECG (minutes)	-	-	10	8
Median Time to Transfer (minutes)	-	-	60	61
Fibrinolytic Medication Timing	-	-	42%	54%
Heart Failure Care				
ACE Inhibitor or ARB for LVSD[3]	0	-	91%	94%
Discharge Instructions[3]	0	-	83%	88%
Evaluation of LVS Function[1,3]	1	0%	92%	98%
Smoking Cessation Advice[3]	0	-	94%	98%
Pneumonia Care				
Appropriate Initial Antibiotic[1,3]	2	100%	87%	92%
Blood Culture Timing[3]	0	-	96%	96%
Influenza Vaccine[1]	8	62%	87%	91%
Initial Antibiotic Timing[1,3]	8	88%	95%	95%
Pneumococcal Vaccine[1,3]	8	75%	88%	93%
Smoking Cessation Advice[3]	0	-	93%	97%
Surgical Care Improvement Project				
Appropriate VTP Within 24 Hours[5]	0	-	89%	92%
Appropriate Hair Removal[5]	0	-	100%	99%
Appropriate Beta Blocker Usage[5]	0	-	90%	93%
Controlled Postoperative Blood Glucose[5]	0	-	92%	93%
Prophylactic Antibiotic Timing[5]	0	-	96%	97%
Prophylactic Antibiotic Timing (Outpatient)	-	-	93%	92%
Prophylactic Antibiotic Selection[5]	0	-	97%	97%
Prophylactic Antibiotic Select. (Outpatient)	-	-	96%	94%
Prophylactic Antibiotic Stopped[5]	0	-	93%	94%
Recommended VTP Ordered[5]	0	-	91%	94%
Urinary Catheter Removal[5]	0	-	86%	90%
Children's Asthma Care				
Received Systemic Corticosteroids	-	-	-	100%
Received Home Management Plan	-	-	-	71%
Received Reliever Medication	-	-	-	100%
Use of Medical Imaging				
Combination Abdominal CT Scan	-	-	0.365	0.191
Combination Chest CT Scan	-	-	0.065	0.054
Follow-up Mammogram/Ultrasound	-	-	7.3%	8.4%
MRI for Low Back Pain	-	-	34.5%	32.7%
Survey of Patients' Hospital Experiences				
Area Around Room 'Always' Quiet at Night[8]	-	-	-	58%
Doctors 'Always' Communicated Well[8]	-	-	-	80%
Home Recovery Information Given[8]	-	-	-	82%
Hospital Given 9 or 10 on 10 Point Scale[8]	-	-	-	67%
Meds 'Always' Explained Before Given[8]	-	-	-	60%
Nurses 'Always' Communicated Well[8]	-	-	-	76%
Pain 'Always' Well Controlled[8]	-	-	-	69%
Room and Bathroom 'Always' Clean[8]	-	-	-	71%
Timely Help 'Always' Received[8]	-	-	-	64%
Would Definitely Recommend Hospital[8]	-	-	-	69%

Via Christi Hospital Pittsburg

1 Mt Carmel Way
Pittsburg, KS 66762
Phone: 620-232-0109
URL: www.via-christi.org
Type: Acute Care Hospitals
Emergency Services: No
Ownership: Voluntary Non-Profit - Private
Beds: 188

Measure	Cases	This Hosp.	State Avg.	U.S. Avg.
Heart Attack Care				
ACE Inhibitor or ARB for LVSD[1]	9	78%	95%	96%
Aspirin at Arrival	58	98%	98%	99%
Aspirin at Discharge	54	85%	98%	98%
Beta Blocker at Discharge	50	92%	98%	98%
Fibrinolytic Medication Timing[1]	2	100%	44%	55%
PCI Within 90 Minutes of Arrival[1]	7	86%	91%	90%
Smoking Cessation Advice[1]	11	100%	99%	99%
Chest Pain/Possible Heart Attack Care				
Aspirin at Arrival[1,3]	21	100%	92%	95%
Median Time to ECG (minutes)[1,3]	21	7	10	8
Median Time to Transfer (minutes)[1,3]	1	98	60	61
Fibrinolytic Medication Timing[1,3]	5	100%	42%	54%
Heart Failure Care				
ACE Inhibitor or ARB for LVSD	44	80%	91%	94%
Discharge Instructions	67	79%	83%	88%
Evaluation of LVS Function	102	98%	92%	98%
Smoking Cessation Advice[1]	18	100%	94%	98%
Pneumonia Care				
Appropriate Initial Antibiotic	79	87%	87%	92%
Blood Culture Timing	120	100%	96%	96%
Influenza Vaccine	86	71%	87%	91%
Initial Antibiotic Timing	122	98%	95%	95%
Pneumococcal Vaccine	120	89%	88%	93%
Smoking Cessation Advice	53	96%	93%	97%
Surgical Care Improvement Project				
Appropriate VTP Within 24 Hours	109	90%	89%	92%
Appropriate Hair Removal	293	99%	100%	99%
Appropriate Beta Blocker Usage	71	80%	90%	93%
Controlled Postoperative Blood Glucose	0	-	92%	93%
Prophylactic Antibiotic Timing	192	98%	96%	97%
Prophylactic Antibiotic Timing (Outpatient)	67	94%	93%	92%
Prophylactic Antibiotic Selection	196	96%	97%	97%
Prophylactic Antibiotic Select. (Outpatient)	67	94%	96%	94%
Prophylactic Antibiotic Stopped	177	86%	93%	94%
Recommended VTP Ordered	109	94%	91%	94%
Urinary Catheter Removal	39	56%	86%	90%
Children's Asthma Care				
Received Systemic Corticosteroids	-	-	-	100%
Received Home Management Plan	-	-	-	71%
Received Reliever Medication	-	-	-	100%
Use of Medical Imaging				
Combination Abdominal CT Scan	439	0.383	0.365	0.191
Combination Chest CT Scan	285	0.105	0.065	0.054
Follow-up Mammogram/Ultrasound	757	5.7%	7.3%	8.4%
MRI for Low Back Pain	73	28.8%	34.5%	32.7%
Survey of Patients' Hospital Experiences				
Area Around Room 'Always' Quiet at Night	300+	60%	-	58%
Doctors 'Always' Communicated Well	300+	86%	-	80%
Home Recovery Information Given	300+	85%	-	82%
Hospital Given 9 or 10 on 10 Point Scale	300+	72%	-	67%
Meds 'Always' Explained Before Given	300+	69%	-	60%
Nurses 'Always' Communicated Well	300+	80%	-	76%
Pain 'Always' Well Controlled	300+	73%	-	69%
Room and Bathroom 'Always' Clean	300+	74%	-	71%
Timely Help 'Always' Received	300+	67%	-	64%
Would Definitely Recommend Hospital	300+	68%	-	69%

Pratt Regional Medical Center

200 Commodore St
Pratt, KS 67124
Phone: 620-450-1160
Fax: 620-672-2113
E-mail: spage@prmc.org
URL: www.prmc.org
Type: Acute Care Hospitals
Emergency Services: Yes
Ownership: Voluntary Non-Profit - Private
Beds: 84

Key Personnel:

CEO/President. . . . . Susan Page
Chief of Medical Staff . . . . Barbara Cudney, MD
Infection Control. . . . . Cecile Pearce, RN
Operating Room. . . . . Brandi Graf
Quality Assurance . . . . Marla Rose
Radiology. . . . . Connie Adelhardt
Intensive Care Unit. . . . . Brandi Graf

Measure	Cases	This Hosp.	State Avg.	U.S. Avg.
Heart Attack Care				
ACE Inhibitor or ARB for LVSD[3]	0	-	95%	96%
Aspirin at Arrival[1,3]	1	100%	98%	99%
Aspirin at Discharge[1,3]	1	100%	98%	98%
Beta Blocker at Discharge[1,3]	1	100%	98%	98%
Fibrinolytic Medication Timing[3]	0	-	44%	55%
PCI Within 90 Minutes of Arrival[3]	0	-	91%	90%
Smoking Cessation Advice[3]	0	-	99%	99%
Chest Pain/Possible Heart Attack Care				
Aspirin at Arrival	70	91%	92%	95%
Median Time to ECG (minutes)	70	12	10	8
Median Time to Transfer (minutes)[5]	0	-	60	61
Fibrinolytic Medication Timing[3]	0	-	42%	54%
Heart Failure Care				
ACE Inhibitor or ARB for LVSD[1]	2	100%	91%	94%
Discharge Instructions	26	54%	83%	88%
Evaluation of LVS Function	30	33%	92%	98%
Smoking Cessation Advice[1]	3	33%	94%	98%
Pneumonia Care				
Appropriate Initial Antibiotic	38	79%	87%	92%
Blood Culture Timing[1]	16	100%	96%	96%
Influenza Vaccine	31	74%	87%	91%
Initial Antibiotic Timing	46	98%	95%	95%
Pneumococcal Vaccine	54	63%	88%	93%
Smoking Cessation Advice[1]	10	50%	93%	97%
Surgical Care Improvement Project				
Appropriate VTP Within 24 Hours[2]	107	98%	89%	92%
Appropriate Hair Removal[2]	198	99%	100%	99%
Appropriate Beta Blocker Usage[2]	52	63%	90%	93%
Controlled Postoperative Blood Glucose[2]	0	-	92%	93%
Prophylactic Antibiotic Timing[2]	147	98%	96%	97%
Prophylactic Antibiotic Timing (Outpatient)[3]	35	100%	93%	92%
Prophylactic Antibiotic Selection[2]	148	95%	97%	97%
Prophylactic Antibiotic Select. (Outpatient)[3]	35	97%	96%	94%
Prophylactic Antibiotic Stopped[2]	146	99%	93%	94%
Recommended VTP Ordered[2]	107	98%	91%	94%
Urinary Catheter Removal[2]	63	90%	86%	90%
Children's Asthma Care				
Received Systemic Corticosteroids	-	-	-	100%
Received Home Management Plan	-	-	-	71%
Received Reliever Medication	-	-	-	100%
Use of Medical Imaging				
Combination Abdominal CT Scan	255	0.761	0.365	0.191
Combination Chest CT Scan	204	0.299	0.065	0.054
Follow-up Mammogram/Ultrasound	609	9.2%	7.3%	8.4%
MRI for Low Back Pain	121	33.9%	34.5%	32.7%
Survey of Patients' Hospital Experiences				
Area Around Room 'Always' Quiet at Night	300+	66%	-	58%
Doctors 'Always' Communicated Well	300+	85%	-	80%
Home Recovery Information Given	300+	82%	-	82%
Hospital Given 9 or 10 on 10 Point Scale	300+	73%	-	67%
Meds 'Always' Explained Before Given	300+	65%	-	60%
Nurses 'Always' Communicated Well	300+	83%	-	76%
Pain 'Always' Well Controlled	300+	76%	-	69%
Room and Bathroom 'Always' Clean	300+	77%	-	71%
Timely Help 'Always' Received	300+	74%	-	64%
Would Definitely Recommend Hospital	300+	78%	-	69%

NOTE: Hospital profiles are in alphabetical order by state, then city, then hospital within the city; Rankings exclude hospitals with less than 25 cases except for patient surveys which excludes hospitals with less than 100 cases; (a) 100–299 cases; (1) The number of cases is too small to be sure how well a hospital is performing; (2) The hospital indicated that the data submitted for this measure were based on a sample of cases; (3) Data was collected during a shorter time period (fewer quarters) than the maximum possible time for this measure; (4) Suppressed for one or more quarters by CMS; (5) No data is available from the hospital for this measure; (6) Fewer than 100 patients completed the HCAHPS survey. Use these rates with caution, as the number of surveys may be too low to reliably assess hospital performance; (7) Survey results are based on less than 12 months of data; (8) Survey results are not available for this reporting period; (9) No or very few patients were eligible for the HCAHPS survey. The scores shown, if any, reflect a very small number of surveys; (10) A state average was not calculated because too few hospitals in the state submitted data; (11) There were discrepancies in the data collection process; Please refer to the User's Guide for a full explanation of data.

Gove County Medical Center

520 West 5th Street — Phone: 785-754-3341
Quinter, KS 67752 — Fax: 785-754-3329
Type: Critical Access Hospitals — Emergency Services: Yes
Ownership: Voluntary Non-Profit - Other — Beds: 21

Key Personnel:
CEO/President. . . . . Paul Davis

Measure	Cases	This Hosp.	State Avg.	U.S. Avg.
Heart Attack Care				
ACE Inhibitor or ARB for LVSD[5]	0	-	95%	96%
Aspirin at Arrival[5]	0	-	98%	99%
Aspirin at Discharge[5]	0	-	98%	98%
Beta Blocker at Discharge[5]	0	-	98%	98%
Fibrinolytic Medication Timing[5]	0	-	44%	55%
PCI Within 90 Minutes of Arrival[5]	0	-	91%	90%
Smoking Cessation Advice[5]	0	-	99%	99%
Chest Pain/Possible Heart Attack Care				
Aspirin at Arrival	-	-	92%	95%
Median Time to ECG (minutes)	-	-	10	8
Median Time to Transfer (minutes)	-	-	60	61
Fibrinolytic Medication Timing	-	-	42%	54%
Heart Failure Care				
ACE Inhibitor or ARB for LVSD[5]	0	-	91%	94%
Discharge Instructions[5]	0	-	83%	88%
Evaluation of LVS Function[5]	0	-	92%	98%
Smoking Cessation Advice[5]	0	-	94%	98%
Pneumonia Care				
Appropriate Initial Antibiotic[1,3]	16	38%	87%	92%
Blood Culture Timing[3]	0	-	96%	96%
Influenza Vaccine[1]	23	74%	87%	91%
Initial Antibiotic Timing[1,3]	24	100%	95%	95%
Pneumococcal Vaccine[3]	35	49%	88%	93%
Smoking Cessation Advice[1,3]	1	0%	93%	97%
Surgical Care Improvement Project				
Appropriate VTP Within 24 Hours[5]	0	-	89%	92%
Appropriate Hair Removal[5]	0	-	100%	99%
Appropriate Beta Blocker Usage[5]	0	-	90%	93%
Controlled Postoperative Blood Glucose[5]	0	-	92%	93%
Prophylactic Antibiotic Timing[5]	0	-	96%	97%
Prophylactic Antibiotic Timing (Outpatient)	-	-	93%	92%
Prophylactic Antibiotic Selection[5]	0	-	97%	97%
Prophylactic Antibiotic Select. (Outpatient)	-	-	96%	94%
Prophylactic Antibiotic Stopped[5]	0	-	93%	94%
Recommended VTP Ordered[5]	0	-	91%	94%
Urinary Catheter Removal[5]	0	-	86%	90%
Children's Asthma Care				
Received Systemic Corticosteroids	-	-	-	100%
Received Home Management Plan	-	-	-	71%
Received Reliever Medication	-	-	-	100%
Use of Medical Imaging				
Combination Abdominal CT Scan	-	-	0.365	0.191
Combination Chest CT Scan	-	-	0.065	0.054
Follow-up Mammogram/Ultrasound	-	-	7.3%	8.4%
MRI for Low Back Pain	-	-	34.5%	32.7%
Survey of Patients' Hospital Experiences				
Area Around Room 'Always' Quiet at Night[8]	-	-	-	58%
Doctors 'Always' Communicated Well[8]	-	-	-	80%
Home Recovery Information Given[8]	-	-	-	82%
Hospital Given 9 or 10 on 10 Point Scale[8]	-	-	-	67%
Meds 'Always' Explained Before Given[8]	-	-	-	60%
Nurses 'Always' Communicated Well[8]	-	-	-	76%
Pain 'Always' Well Controlled[8]	-	-	-	69%
Room and Bathroom 'Always' Clean[8]	-	-	-	71%
Timely Help 'Always' Received[8]	-	-	-	64%
Would Definitely Recommend Hospital[8]	-	-	-	69%

Grisell Memorial Hospital District #1

210 South Vermont Avenue — Phone: 785-731-2231
Ransom, KS 67572 — Fax: 785-731-2895
Type: Critical Access Hospitals — Emergency Services: Yes
Ownership: Govt - Hospital Dist/Auth — Beds: 46

Key Personnel:
CEO/President. . . . . Kris Ochs
Chief of Medical Staff . . . . Allen McLean, MD
Emergency Room . . . . Allen McLean, MD

Measure	Cases	This Hosp.	State Avg.	U.S. Avg.
Heart Attack Care				
ACE Inhibitor or ARB for LVSD[5]	0	-	95%	96%
Aspirin at Arrival[5]	0	-	98%	99%
Aspirin at Discharge[5]	0	-	98%	98%
Beta Blocker at Discharge[5]	0	-	98%	98%
Fibrinolytic Medication Timing[5]	0	-	44%	55%
PCI Within 90 Minutes of Arrival[5]	0	-	91%	90%
Smoking Cessation Advice[5]	0	-	99%	99%
Chest Pain/Possible Heart Attack Care				
Aspirin at Arrival	-	-	92%	95%
Median Time to ECG (minutes)	-	-	10	8
Median Time to Transfer (minutes)	-	-	60	61
Fibrinolytic Medication Timing	-	-	42%	54%
Heart Failure Care				
ACE Inhibitor or ARB for LVSD[5]	0	-	91%	94%
Discharge Instructions[5]	0	-	83%	88%
Evaluation of LVS Function[5]	0	-	92%	98%
Smoking Cessation Advice[5]	0	-	94%	98%
Pneumonia Care				
Appropriate Initial Antibiotic[1]	7	100%	87%	92%
Blood Culture Timing[1]	1	100%	96%	96%
Influenza Vaccine[1]	7	86%	87%	91%
Initial Antibiotic Timing[1]	7	100%	95%	95%
Pneumococcal Vaccine[1]	9	100%	88%	93%
Smoking Cessation Advice[1]	1	100%	93%	97%
Surgical Care Improvement Project				
Appropriate VTP Within 24 Hours[5]	0	-	89%	92%
Appropriate Hair Removal[5]	0	-	100%	99%
Appropriate Beta Blocker Usage[5]	0	-	90%	93%
Controlled Postoperative Blood Glucose[5]	0	-	92%	93%
Prophylactic Antibiotic Timing[5]	0	-	96%	97%
Prophylactic Antibiotic Timing (Outpatient)	-	-	93%	92%
Prophylactic Antibiotic Selection[5]	0	-	97%	97%
Prophylactic Antibiotic Select. (Outpatient)	-	-	96%	94%
Prophylactic Antibiotic Stopped[5]	0	-	93%	94%
Recommended VTP Ordered[5]	0	-	91%	94%
Urinary Catheter Removal[5]	0	-	86%	90%
Children's Asthma Care				
Received Systemic Corticosteroids	-	-	-	100%
Received Home Management Plan	-	-	-	71%
Received Reliever Medication	-	-	-	100%
Use of Medical Imaging				
Combination Abdominal CT Scan	-	-	0.365	0.191
Combination Chest CT Scan	-	-	0.065	0.054
Follow-up Mammogram/Ultrasound	-	-	7.3%	8.4%
MRI for Low Back Pain	-	-	34.5%	32.7%
Survey of Patients' Hospital Experiences				
Area Around Room 'Always' Quiet at Night[8]	-	-	-	58%
Doctors 'Always' Communicated Well[8]	-	-	-	80%
Home Recovery Information Given[8]	-	-	-	82%
Hospital Given 9 or 10 on 10 Point Scale[8]	-	-	-	67%
Meds 'Always' Explained Before Given[8]	-	-	-	60%
Nurses 'Always' Communicated Well[8]	-	-	-	76%
Pain 'Always' Well Controlled[8]	-	-	-	69%
Room and Bathroom 'Always' Clean[8]	-	-	-	71%
Timely Help 'Always' Received[8]	-	-	-	64%
Would Definitely Recommend Hospital[8]	-	-	-	69%

Russell Regional Hospital

200 S Main Street — Phone: 785-483-3131
Russell, KS 67665 — Fax: 785-483-2037
URL: www.russellhospital.org
Type: Critical Access Hospitals — Emergency Services: Yes
Ownership: Govt - Hospital Dist/Auth — Beds: 25

Key Personnel:
Chief of Medical Staff . . . . Earl Merkel, MD
Infection Control. . . . . Kay Haywood, RN
Operating Room. . . . . Janet Cable, RN
Quality Assurance . . . . Kay Haywood, RN
Anesthesiology. . . . . Darrell Millon
Emergency Room . . . . Kay Steinert, RN

Measure	Cases	This Hosp.	State Avg.	U.S. Avg.
Heart Attack Care				
ACE Inhibitor or ARB for LVSD[5]	0	-	95%	96%
Aspirin at Arrival[5]	0	-	98%	99%
Aspirin at Discharge[5]	0	-	98%	98%
Beta Blocker at Discharge[5]	0	-	98%	98%
Fibrinolytic Medication Timing[5]	0	-	44%	55%
PCI Within 90 Minutes of Arrival[5]	0	-	91%	90%
Smoking Cessation Advice[5]	0	-	99%	99%
Chest Pain/Possible Heart Attack Care				
Aspirin at Arrival	-	-	92%	95%
Median Time to ECG (minutes)	-	-	10	8
Median Time to Transfer (minutes)	-	-	60	61
Fibrinolytic Medication Timing	-	-	42%	54%
Heart Failure Care				
ACE Inhibitor or ARB for LVSD[5]	0	-	91%	94%
Discharge Instructions[5]	0	-	83%	88%
Evaluation of LVS Function[5]	0	-	92%	98%
Smoking Cessation Advice[5]	0	-	94%	98%
Pneumonia Care				
Appropriate Initial Antibiotic[1]	9	56%	87%	92%
Blood Culture Timing[1]	5	60%	96%	96%
Influenza Vaccine[1]	8	75%	87%	91%
Initial Antibiotic Timing[1]	15	87%	95%	95%
Pneumococcal Vaccine[1]	16	31%	88%	93%
Smoking Cessation Advice[1]	8	25%	93%	97%
Surgical Care Improvement Project				
Appropriate VTP Within 24 Hours[5]	0	-	89%	92%
Appropriate Hair Removal[5]	0	-	100%	99%
Appropriate Beta Blocker Usage[5]	0	-	90%	93%
Controlled Postoperative Blood Glucose[5]	0	-	92%	93%
Prophylactic Antibiotic Timing[5]	0	-	96%	97%
Prophylactic Antibiotic Timing (Outpatient)	-	-	93%	92%
Prophylactic Antibiotic Selection[5]	0	-	97%	97%
Prophylactic Antibiotic Select. (Outpatient)	-	-	96%	94%
Prophylactic Antibiotic Stopped[5]	0	-	93%	94%
Recommended VTP Ordered[5]	0	-	91%	94%
Urinary Catheter Removal[5]	0	-	86%	90%
Children's Asthma Care				
Received Systemic Corticosteroids	-	-	-	100%
Received Home Management Plan	-	-	-	71%
Received Reliever Medication	-	-	-	100%
Use of Medical Imaging				
Combination Abdominal CT Scan	-	-	0.365	0.191
Combination Chest CT Scan	-	-	0.065	0.054
Follow-up Mammogram/Ultrasound	-	-	7.3%	8.4%
MRI for Low Back Pain	-	-	34.5%	32.7%
Survey of Patients' Hospital Experiences				
Area Around Room 'Always' Quiet at Night[8]	-	-	-	58%
Doctors 'Always' Communicated Well[8]	-	-	-	80%
Home Recovery Information Given[8]	-	-	-	82%
Hospital Given 9 or 10 on 10 Point Scale[8]	-	-	-	67%
Meds 'Always' Explained Before Given[8]	-	-	-	60%
Nurses 'Always' Communicated Well[8]	-	-	-	76%
Pain 'Always' Well Controlled[8]	-	-	-	69%
Room and Bathroom 'Always' Clean[8]	-	-	-	71%
Timely Help 'Always' Received[8]	-	-	-	64%
Would Definitely Recommend Hospital[8]	-	-	-	69%

NOTE: Hospital profiles are in alphabetical order by state, then city, then hospital within the city; Rankings exclude hospitals with less than 25 cases except for patient surveys which excludes hospitals with less than 100 cases; (a) 100–299 cases; (1) The number of cases is too small to be sure how well a hospital is performing; (2) The hospital indicated that the data submitted for this measure were based on a sample of cases; (3) Data was collected during a shorter time period (fewer quarters) than the maximum possible time for this measure; (4) Suppressed for one or more quarters by CMS; (5) No data is available from the hospital for this measure; (6) Fewer than 100 patients completed the HCAHPS survey. Use these rates with caution, as the number of surveys may be too low to reliably assess hospital performance; (7) Survey results are based on less than 12 months of data; (8) Survey results are not available for this reporting period; (9) No or very few patients were eligible for the HCAHPS survey. The scores shown, if any, reflect a very small number of surveys; (10) A state average was not calculated because too few hospitals in the state submitted data; (11) There were discrepancies in the data collection process; Please refer to the User's Guide for a full explanation of data.

Sabetha Community Hospital

14th & Oregon
Sabetha, KS 66534
Type: Critical Access Hospitals
Ownership: Government - Local
Phone: 785-284-2121
Fax: 785-284-2516
Emergency Services: Yes
Beds: 27

Key Personnel:
CEO/President. . . . . Rita Buurman
Patient Relations . . . . Linnae Coker

Measure	Cases	This Hosp.	State Avg.	U.S. Avg.
Heart Attack Care				
ACE Inhibitor or ARB for LVSD[5]	0	-	95%	96%
Aspirin at Arrival[5]	0	-	98%	99%
Aspirin at Discharge[5]	0	-	98%	98%
Beta Blocker at Discharge[5]	0	-	98%	98%
Fibrinolytic Medication Timing[5]	0	-	44%	55%
PCI Within 90 Minutes of Arrival[5]	0	-	91%	90%
Smoking Cessation Advice[5]	0	-	99%	99%
Chest Pain/Possible Heart Attack Care				
Aspirin at Arrival	-	-	92%	95%
Median Time to ECG (minutes)	-	-	10	8
Median Time to Transfer (minutes)	-	-	60	61
Fibrinolytic Medication Timing	-	-	42%	54%
Heart Failure Care				
ACE Inhibitor or ARB for LVSD[1]	3	100%	91%	94%
Discharge Instructions[1]	4	25%	83%	88%
Evaluation of LVS Function[1]	8	100%	92%	98%
Smoking Cessation Advice[1]	1	0%	94%	98%
Pneumonia Care				
Appropriate Initial Antibiotic[1]	14	100%	87%	92%
Blood Culture Timing[1]	2	100%	96%	96%
Influenza Vaccine[1]	8	75%	87%	91%
Initial Antibiotic Timing[1]	13	100%	95%	95%
Pneumococcal Vaccine[1]	11	73%	88%	93%
Smoking Cessation Advice[1]	3	0%	93%	97%
Surgical Care Improvement Project				
Appropriate VTP Within 24 Hours[1,3]	2	50%	89%	92%
Appropriate Hair Removal[1,3]	2	100%	100%	99%
Appropriate Beta Blocker Usage[3]	0	-	90%	93%
Controlled Postoperative Blood Glucose[3]	0	-	92%	93%
Prophylactic Antibiotic Timing[1,3]	1	100%	96%	97%
Prophylactic Antibiotic Timing (Outpatient)	-	-	93%	92%
Prophylactic Antibiotic Selection[1,3]	1	100%	97%	97%
Prophylactic Antibiotic Select. (Outpatient)	-	-	96%	94%
Prophylactic Antibiotic Stopped[1,3]	1	100%	93%	94%
Recommended VTP Ordered[1,3]	2	50%	91%	94%
Urinary Catheter Removal[3]	0	-	86%	90%
Children's Asthma Care				
Received Systemic Corticosteroids	-	-	-	100%
Received Home Management Plan	-	-	-	71%
Received Reliever Medication	-	-	-	100%
Use of Medical Imaging				
Combination Abdominal CT Scan	-	-	0.365	0.191
Combination Chest CT Scan	-	-	0.065	0.054
Follow-up Mammogram/Ultrasound	-	-	7.3%	8.4%
MRI for Low Back Pain	-	-	34.5%	32.7%
Survey of Patients' Hospital Experiences				
Area Around Room 'Always' Quiet at Night[6]	<100	59%	-	58%
Doctors 'Always' Communicated Well[6]	<100	92%	-	80%
Home Recovery Information Given[6]	<100	80%	-	82%
Hospital Given 9 or 10 on 10 Point Scale[6]	<100	84%	-	67%
Meds 'Always' Explained Before Given[6]	<100	70%	-	60%
Nurses 'Always' Communicated Well[6]	<100	88%	-	76%
Pain 'Always' Well Controlled[6]	<100	80%	-	69%
Room and Bathroom 'Always' Clean[6]	<100	84%	-	71%
Timely Help 'Always' Received[6]	<100	81%	-	64%
Would Definitely Recommend Hospital	<100	92%	-	69%

Cheyenne County Hospital

210 West 1st Street
Saint Francis, KS 67756
E-mail: llacy@cheyennecountyhospital.com
URL: cheyennecountyhospital.com
Type: Critical Access Hospitals
Ownership: Government - Local
Phone: 785-332-2104
Fax: 785-332-3255
Emergency Services: Yes
Beds: 16

Key Personnel:
CEO/President. . . . . Leslie Lacey
Operating Room. . . . . Amelia Zuege
Quality Assurance . . . . JoAnn Klre
Anesthesiology. . . . . Kim Zweygardt, CRNA
Emergency Room . . . . Tenille Lee, RN

Measure	Cases	This Hosp.	State Avg.	U.S. Avg.
Heart Attack Care				
ACE Inhibitor or ARB for LVSD[3]	0	-	95%	96%
Aspirin at Arrival[3]	0	-	98%	99%
Aspirin at Discharge[3]	0	-	98%	98%
Beta Blocker at Discharge[3]	0	-	98%	98%
Fibrinolytic Medication Timing[3]	0	-	44%	55%
PCI Within 90 Minutes of Arrival[3]	0	-	91%	90%
Smoking Cessation Advice[3]	0	-	99%	99%
Chest Pain/Possible Heart Attack Care				
Aspirin at Arrival	-	-	92%	95%
Median Time to ECG (minutes)	-	-	10	8
Median Time to Transfer (minutes)	-	-	60	61
Fibrinolytic Medication Timing	-	-	42%	54%
Heart Failure Care				
ACE Inhibitor or ARB for LVSD[1,3]	5	20%	91%	94%
Discharge Instructions[1,3]	2	0%	83%	88%
Evaluation of LVS Function[1,3]	8	100%	92%	98%
Smoking Cessation Advice[3]	0	-	94%	98%
Pneumonia Care				
Appropriate Initial Antibiotic[1,3]	2	0%	87%	92%
Blood Culture Timing[1,3]	1	0%	96%	96%
Influenza Vaccine[3]	0	-	87%	91%
Initial Antibiotic Timing[1,3]	2	0%	95%	95%
Pneumococcal Vaccine[1,3]	5	60%	88%	93%
Smoking Cessation Advice[3]	0	-	93%	97%
Surgical Care Improvement Project				
Appropriate VTP Within 24 Hours[5]	0	-	89%	92%
Appropriate Hair Removal[5]	0	-	100%	99%
Appropriate Beta Blocker Usage[5]	0	-	90%	93%
Controlled Postoperative Blood Glucose[5]	0	-	92%	93%
Prophylactic Antibiotic Timing[5]	0	-	96%	97%
Prophylactic Antibiotic Timing (Outpatient)	-	-	93%	92%
Prophylactic Antibiotic Selection[5]	0	-	97%	97%
Prophylactic Antibiotic Select. (Outpatient)	-	-	96%	94%
Prophylactic Antibiotic Stopped[5]	0	-	93%	94%
Recommended VTP Ordered[5]	0	-	91%	94%
Urinary Catheter Removal[5]	0	-	86%	90%
Children's Asthma Care				
Received Systemic Corticosteroids	-	-	-	100%
Received Home Management Plan	-	-	-	71%
Received Reliever Medication	-	-	-	100%
Use of Medical Imaging				
Combination Abdominal CT Scan	-	-	0.365	0.191
Combination Chest CT Scan	-	-	0.065	0.054
Follow-up Mammogram/Ultrasound	-	-	7.3%	8.4%
MRI for Low Back Pain	-	-	34.5%	32.7%
Survey of Patients' Hospital Experiences				
Area Around Room 'Always' Quiet at Night[8]	-	-	-	58%
Doctors 'Always' Communicated Well[8]	-	-	-	80%
Home Recovery Information Given[8]	-	-	-	82%
Hospital Given 9 or 10 on 10 Point Scale[8]	-	-	-	67%
Meds 'Always' Explained Before Given[8]	-	-	-	60%
Nurses 'Always' Communicated Well[8]	-	-	-	76%
Pain 'Always' Well Controlled[8]	-	-	-	69%
Room and Bathroom 'Always' Clean[8]	-	-	-	71%
Timely Help 'Always' Received[8]	-	-	-	64%
Would Definitely Recommend Hospital[8]	-	-	-	69%

Salina Regional Health Center

400 South Santa Fe Avenue
Salina, KS 67401
E-mail: srhc@midusa.net
URL: www.srhc.com
Type: Acute Care Hospitals
Ownership: Voluntary Non-Profit - Private
Phone: 785-452-7000
Fax: 785-452-6963
Emergency Services: Yes
Beds: 385

Key Personnel:
CEO/President. . . . . Randy Peterson
Chief of Medical Staff . . . . Mark Mikinski, MD
Infection Control. . . . . Kelli Olson
Operating Room. . . . . David E Smith
Pediatric Ambulatory Care . . . . . . Deb Hyman
Pediatric In-Patient Care . . . . Deb Hyman
Quality Assurance . . . . Melda Allen
Radiology. . . . . Andrew M Brittan

Measure	Cases	This Hosp.	State Avg.	U.S. Avg.
Heart Attack Care				
ACE Inhibitor or ARB for LVSD[2]	28	93%	95%	96%
Aspirin at Arrival[2]	96	99%	98%	99%
Aspirin at Discharge[2]	142	99%	98%	98%
Beta Blocker at Discharge[2]	134	99%	98%	98%
Fibrinolytic Medication Timing[1,2]	17	53%	44%	55%
PCI Within 90 Minutes of Arrival[1,2]	4	0%	91%	90%
Smoking Cessation Advice[2]	47	100%	99%	99%
Chest Pain/Possible Heart Attack Care				
Aspirin at Arrival[1]	6	100%	92%	95%
Median Time to ECG (minutes)[1]	6	6	10	8
Median Time to Transfer (minutes)[5]	0	-	60	61
Fibrinolytic Medication Timing[3]	0	-	42%	54%
Heart Failure Care				
ACE Inhibitor or ARB for LVSD	26	100%	91%	94%
Discharge Instructions	63	98%	83%	88%
Evaluation of LVS Function	86	88%	92%	98%
Smoking Cessation Advice[1]	11	100%	94%	98%
Pneumonia Care				
Appropriate Initial Antibiotic	91	91%	87%	92%
Blood Culture Timing	130	98%	96%	96%
Influenza Vaccine	107	100%	87%	91%
Initial Antibiotic Timing	144	97%	95%	95%
Pneumococcal Vaccine	157	99%	88%	93%
Smoking Cessation Advice	50	100%	93%	97%
Surgical Care Improvement Project				
Appropriate VTP Within 24 Hours	352	92%	89%	92%
Appropriate Hair Removal	776	100%	100%	99%
Appropriate Beta Blocker Usage	260	93%	90%	93%
Controlled Postoperative Blood Glucose	82	96%	92%	93%
Prophylactic Antibiotic Timing	447	98%	96%	97%
Prophylactic Antibiotic Timing (Outpatient)	164	82%	93%	92%
Prophylactic Antibiotic Selection	457	98%	97%	97%
Prophylactic Antibiotic Select. (Outpatient)	144	87%	96%	94%
Prophylactic Antibiotic Stopped	421	95%	93%	94%
Recommended VTP Ordered	352	95%	91%	94%
Urinary Catheter Removal	88	76%	86%	90%
Children's Asthma Care				
Received Systemic Corticosteroids	-	-	-	100%
Received Home Management Plan	-	-	-	71%
Received Reliever Medication	-	-	-	100%
Use of Medical Imaging				
Combination Abdominal CT Scan	516	0.275	0.365	0.191
Combination Chest CT Scan	540	0.002	0.065	0.054
Follow-up Mammogram/Ultrasound	232	7.3%	7.3%	8.4%
MRI for Low Back Pain	187	32.1%	34.5%	32.7%
Survey of Patients' Hospital Experiences				
Area Around Room 'Always' Quiet at Night	300+	54%	-	58%
Doctors 'Always' Communicated Well	300+	81%	-	80%
Home Recovery Information Given	300+	80%	-	82%
Hospital Given 9 or 10 on 10 Point Scale	300+	69%	-	67%
Meds 'Always' Explained Before Given	300+	57%	-	60%
Nurses 'Always' Communicated Well	300+	74%	-	76%
Pain 'Always' Well Controlled	300+	63%	-	69%
Room and Bathroom 'Always' Clean	300+	73%	-	71%
Timely Help 'Always' Received	300+	58%	-	64%
Would Definitely Recommend Hospital	300+	73%	-	69%

NOTE: Hospital profiles are in alphabetical order by state, then city, then hospital within the city; Rankings exclude hospitals with less than 25 cases except for patient surveys which excludes hospitals with less than 100 cases; (a) 100–299 cases; (1) The number of cases is too small to be sure how well a hospital is performing; (2) The hospital indicated that the data submitted for this measure were based on a sample of cases; (3) Data was collected during a shorter time period (fewer quarters) than the maximum possible time for this measure; (4) Suppressed for one or more quarters by CMS; (5) No data is available from the hospital for this measure; (6) Fewer than 100 patients completed the HCAHPS survey. Use these rates with caution, as the number of surveys may be too low to reliably assess hospital performance; (7) Survey results are based on less than 12 months of data; (8) Survey results are not available for this reporting period; (9) No or very few patients were eligible for the HCAHPS survey. The scores shown, if any, reflect a very small number of surveys; (10) A state average was not calculated because too few hospitals in the state submitted data; (11) There were discrepancies in the data collection process; Please refer to the User's Guide for a full explanation of data.

Salina Surgical Hospital

401 South Santa Fe Avenue
Salina, KS 67401
URL: www.salinasurgical.com
Type: Acute Care Hospitals
Ownership: Voluntary Non-Profit - Private

Phone: 785-493-0685
Emergency Services: No
Beds: 16

Key Personnel:
CEO/President. . . . . James Sergeant

Measure	Cases	This Hosp.	State Avg.	U.S. Avg.
Heart Attack Care				
ACE Inhibitor or ARB for LVSD[5]	0	-	95%	96%
Aspirin at Arrival[5]	0	-	98%	99%
Aspirin at Discharge[5]	0	-	98%	98%
Beta Blocker at Discharge[5]	0	-	98%	98%
Fibrinolytic Medication Timing[5]	0	-	44%	55%
PCI Within 90 Minutes of Arrival[5]	0	-	91%	90%
Smoking Cessation Advice[5]	0	-	99%	99%
Chest Pain/Possible Heart Attack Care				
Aspirin at Arrival[5]	0	-	92%	95%
Median Time to ECG (minutes)[5]	0	-	10	8
Median Time to Transfer (minutes)[5]	0	-	60	61
Fibrinolytic Medication Timing[5]	0	-	42%	54%
Heart Failure Care				
ACE Inhibitor or ARB for LVSD[5]	0	-	91%	94%
Discharge Instructions[5]	0	-	83%	88%
Evaluation of LVS Function[5]	0	-	92%	98%
Smoking Cessation Advice[5]	0	-	94%	98%
Pneumonia Care				
Appropriate Initial Antibiotic[5]	0	-	87%	92%
Blood Culture Timing[5]	0	-	96%	96%
Influenza Vaccine[5]	0	-	87%	91%
Initial Antibiotic Timing[5]	0	-	95%	95%
Pneumococcal Vaccine[5]	0	-	88%	93%
Smoking Cessation Advice[5]	0	-	93%	97%
Surgical Care Improvement Project				
Appropriate VTP Within 24 Hours	77	94%	89%	92%
Appropriate Hair Removal	623	100%	100%	99%
Appropriate Beta Blocker Usage	145	99%	90%	93%
Controlled Postoperative Blood Glucose	0	-	92%	93%
Prophylactic Antibiotic Timing	568	99%	96%	97%
Prophylactic Antibiotic Timing (Outpatient)	75	88%	93%	92%
Prophylactic Antibiotic Selection	568	99%	97%	97%
Prophylactic Antibiotic Select. (Outpatient)	68	94%	96%	94%
Prophylactic Antibiotic Stopped	562	92%	93%	94%
Recommended VTP Ordered	77	95%	91%	94%
Urinary Catheter Removal[1]	16	81%	86%	90%
Children's Asthma Care				
Received Systemic Corticosteroids	-	-	-	100%
Received Home Management Plan	-	-	-	71%
Received Reliever Medication	-	-	-	100%
Use of Medical Imaging				
Combination Abdominal CT Scan[5]	0	-	0.365	0.191
Combination Chest CT Scan[5]	0	-	0.065	0.054
Follow-up Mammogram/Ultrasound[5]	0	-	7.3%	8.4%
MRI for Low Back Pain[5]	0	-	34.5%	32.7%
Survey of Patients' Hospital Experiences				
Area Around Room 'Always' Quiet at Night	300+	80%	-	58%
Doctors 'Always' Communicated Well	300+	89%	-	80%
Home Recovery Information Given	300+	89%	-	82%
Hospital Given 9 or 10 on 10 Point Scale	300+	95%	-	67%
Meds 'Always' Explained Before Given	300+	80%	-	60%
Nurses 'Always' Communicated Well	300+	92%	-	76%
Pain 'Always' Well Controlled	300+	79%	-	69%
Room and Bathroom 'Always' Clean	300+	89%	-	71%
Timely Help 'Always' Received	300+	89%	-	64%
Would Definitely Recommend Hospital	300+	94%	-	69%

Scott County Hospital

310 E 3rd Street
Scott City, KS 67871
URL: www.scotthospital.net
Type: Critical Access Hospitals
Ownership: Government - Local

Phone: 620-872-5811
Fax: 620-872-7193
Emergency Services: Yes
Beds: 27

Key Personnel:
CEO/President. . . . . Mark Burnett
Chief of Medical Staff. . . . . Christian Cupp
Infection Control. . . . . Thea Beckman
Operating Room. . . . . Deanna Kennedy
Intensive Care Unit. . . . . Jenie Griswold

Measure	Cases	This Hosp.	State Avg.	U.S. Avg.
Heart Attack Care				
ACE Inhibitor or ARB for LVSD[5]	0	-	95%	96%
Aspirin at Arrival[5]	0	-	98%	99%
Aspirin at Discharge[5]	0	-	98%	98%
Beta Blocker at Discharge[5]	0	-	98%	98%
Fibrinolytic Medication Timing[5]	0	-	44%	55%
PCI Within 90 Minutes of Arrival[5]	0	-	91%	90%
Smoking Cessation Advice[5]	0	-	99%	99%
Chest Pain/Possible Heart Attack Care				
Aspirin at Arrival	-	-	92%	95%
Median Time to ECG (minutes)	-	-	10	8
Median Time to Transfer (minutes)	-	-	60	61
Fibrinolytic Medication Timing	-	-	42%	54%
Heart Failure Care				
ACE Inhibitor or ARB for LVSD[1,3]	3	67%	91%	94%
Discharge Instructions[1,3]	9	11%	83%	88%
Evaluation of LVS Function[1,3]	21	24%	92%	98%
Smoking Cessation Advice[1,3]	1	0%	94%	98%
Pneumonia Care				
Appropriate Initial Antibiotic[1,3]	7	57%	87%	92%
Blood Culture Timing[1,3]	3	33%	96%	96%
Influenza Vaccine[1]	7	71%	87%	91%
Initial Antibiotic Timing[1,3]	1	0%	95%	95%
Pneumococcal Vaccine[1,3]	10	40%	88%	93%
Smoking Cessation Advice[1,3]	2	50%	93%	97%
Surgical Care Improvement Project				
Appropriate VTP Within 24 Hours[5]	0	-	89%	92%
Appropriate Hair Removal[5]	0	-	100%	99%
Appropriate Beta Blocker Usage[5]	0	-	90%	93%
Controlled Postoperative Blood Glucose[5]	0	-	92%	93%
Prophylactic Antibiotic Timing[5]	0	-	96%	97%
Prophylactic Antibiotic Timing (Outpatient)	-	-	93%	92%
Prophylactic Antibiotic Selection[5]	0	-	97%	97%
Prophylactic Antibiotic Select. (Outpatient)	-	-	96%	94%
Prophylactic Antibiotic Stopped[5]	0	-	93%	94%
Recommended VTP Ordered[5]	0	-	91%	94%
Urinary Catheter Removal[5]	0	-	86%	90%
Children's Asthma Care				
Received Systemic Corticosteroids	-	-	-	100%
Received Home Management Plan	-	-	-	71%
Received Reliever Medication	-	-	-	100%
Use of Medical Imaging				
Combination Abdominal CT Scan	-	-	0.365	0.191
Combination Chest CT Scan	-	-	0.065	0.054
Follow-up Mammogram/Ultrasound	-	-	7.3%	8.4%
MRI for Low Back Pain	-	-	34.5%	32.7%
Survey of Patients' Hospital Experiences				
Area Around Room 'Always' Quiet at Night[8]	-	-	-	58%
Doctors 'Always' Communicated Well[8]	-	-	-	80%
Home Recovery Information Given[8]	-	-	-	82%
Hospital Given 9 or 10 on 10 Point Scale[8]	-	-	-	67%
Meds 'Always' Explained Before Given[8]	-	-	-	60%
Nurses 'Always' Communicated Well[8]	-	-	-	76%
Pain 'Always' Well Controlled[8]	-	-	-	69%
Room and Bathroom 'Always' Clean[8]	-	-	-	71%
Timely Help 'Always' Received[8]	-	-	-	64%
Would Definitely Recommend Hospital[8]	-	-	-	69%

Sedan City Hospital

300 North Street
Sedan, KS 67361
Type: Critical Access Hospitals
Ownership: Government - Local

Phone: 620-725-3115
Fax: 620-725-3297
Emergency Services: Yes
Beds: 25

Key Personnel:
Chief of Medical Staff. . . . . James McDermott, DO
Quality Assurance . . . . Candy Kairchmer
Emergency Room . . . . James Mcdermott, DO

Measure	Cases	This Hosp.	State Avg.	U.S. Avg.
Heart Attack Care				
ACE Inhibitor or ARB for LVSD[5]	0	-	95%	96%
Aspirin at Arrival[5]	0	-	98%	99%
Aspirin at Discharge[5]	0	-	98%	98%
Beta Blocker at Discharge[5]	0	-	98%	98%
Fibrinolytic Medication Timing[5]	0	-	44%	55%
PCI Within 90 Minutes of Arrival[5]	0	-	91%	90%
Smoking Cessation Advice[5]	0	-	99%	99%
Chest Pain/Possible Heart Attack Care				
Aspirin at Arrival	-	-	92%	95%
Median Time to ECG (minutes)	-	-	10	8
Median Time to Transfer (minutes)	-	-	60	61
Fibrinolytic Medication Timing	-	-	42%	54%
Heart Failure Care				
ACE Inhibitor or ARB for LVSD[5]	0	-	91%	94%
Discharge Instructions[5]	0	-	83%	88%
Evaluation of LVS Function[5]	0	-	92%	98%
Smoking Cessation Advice[5]	0	-	94%	98%
Pneumonia Care				
Appropriate Initial Antibiotic[5]	0	-	87%	92%
Blood Culture Timing[5]	0	-	96%	96%
Influenza Vaccine[5]	0	-	87%	91%
Initial Antibiotic Timing[5]	0	-	95%	95%
Pneumococcal Vaccine[5]	0	-	88%	93%
Smoking Cessation Advice[5]	0	-	93%	97%
Surgical Care Improvement Project				
Appropriate VTP Within 24 Hours[5]	0	-	89%	92%
Appropriate Hair Removal[5]	0	-	100%	99%
Appropriate Beta Blocker Usage[5]	0	-	90%	93%
Controlled Postoperative Blood Glucose[5]	0	-	92%	93%
Prophylactic Antibiotic Timing[5]	0	-	96%	97%
Prophylactic Antibiotic Timing (Outpatient)	-	-	93%	92%
Prophylactic Antibiotic Selection[5]	0	-	97%	97%
Prophylactic Antibiotic Select. (Outpatient)	-	-	96%	94%
Prophylactic Antibiotic Stopped[5]	0	-	93%	94%
Recommended VTP Ordered[5]	0	-	91%	94%
Urinary Catheter Removal[5]	0	-	86%	90%
Children's Asthma Care				
Received Systemic Corticosteroids	-	-	-	100%
Received Home Management Plan	-	-	-	71%
Received Reliever Medication	-	-	-	100%
Use of Medical Imaging				
Combination Abdominal CT Scan	-	-	0.365	0.191
Combination Chest CT Scan	-	-	0.065	0.054
Follow-up Mammogram/Ultrasound	-	-	7.3%	8.4%
MRI for Low Back Pain	-	-	34.5%	32.7%
Survey of Patients' Hospital Experiences				
Area Around Room 'Always' Quiet at Night[8]	-	-	-	58%
Doctors 'Always' Communicated Well[8]	-	-	-	80%
Home Recovery Information Given[8]	-	-	-	82%
Hospital Given 9 or 10 on 10 Point Scale[8]	-	-	-	67%
Meds 'Always' Explained Before Given[8]	-	-	-	60%
Nurses 'Always' Communicated Well[8]	-	-	-	76%
Pain 'Always' Well Controlled[8]	-	-	-	69%
Room and Bathroom 'Always' Clean[8]	-	-	-	71%
Timely Help 'Always' Received[8]	-	-	-	64%
Would Definitely Recommend Hospital[8]	-	-	-	69%

NOTE: Hospital profiles are in alphabetical order by state, then city, then hospital within the city; Rankings exclude hospitals with less than 25 cases except for patient surveys which excludes hospitals with less than 100 cases; (a) 100–299 cases; (1) The number of cases is too small to be sure how well a hospital is performing; (2) The hospital indicated that the data submitted for this measure were based on a sample of cases; (3) Data was collected during a shorter time period (fewer quarters) than the maximum possible time for this measure; (4) Suppressed for one or more quarters by CMS; (5) No data is available from the hospital for this measure; (6) Fewer than 100 patients completed the HCAHPS survey. Use these rates with caution, as the number of surveys may be too low to reliably assess hospital performance; (7) Survey results are based on less than 12 months of data; (8) Survey results are not available for this reporting period; (9) No or very few patients were eligible for the HCAHPS survey. The scores shown, if any, reflect a very small number of surveys; (10) A state average was not calculated because too few hospitals in the state submitted data; (11) There were discrepancies in the data collection process; Please refer to the User's Guide for a full explanation of data.

Nemaha Valley Community Hospital

1600 Community Dr Phone: 785-336-6181
Seneca, KS 66538 Fax: 785-336-3052
Type: Critical Access Hospitals Emergency Services: Yes
Ownership: Voluntary Non-Profit - Private Beds: 24

Key Personnel:
CEO/President.............. Stan Regehr
Infection Control............. Donna Stallbuam

Measure	Cases	This Hosp.	State Avg.	U.S. Avg.
Heart Attack Care				
ACE Inhibitor or ARB for LVSD[3]	0	-	95%	96%
Aspirin at Arrival[3]	0	-	98%	99%
Aspirin at Discharge[3]	0	-	98%	98%
Beta Blocker at Discharge[3]	0	-	98%	98%
Fibrinolytic Medication Timing[3]	0	-	44%	55%
PCI Within 90 Minutes of Arrival[3]	0	-	91%	90%
Smoking Cessation Advice[3]	0	-	99%	99%
Chest Pain/Possible Heart Attack Care				
Aspirin at Arrival	-	-	92%	95%
Median Time to ECG (minutes)	-	-	10	8
Median Time to Transfer (minutes)	-	-	60	61
Fibrinolytic Medication Timing	-	-	42%	54%
Heart Failure Care				
ACE Inhibitor or ARB for LVSD	0	-	91%	94%
Discharge Instructions[1]	6	50%	83%	88%
Evaluation of LVS Function[1]	16	6%	92%	98%
Smoking Cessation Advice	0	-	94%	98%
Pneumonia Care				
Appropriate Initial Antibiotic[1]	17	94%	87%	92%
Blood Culture Timing[1]	1	0%	96%	96%
Influenza Vaccine[1]	8	88%	87%	91%
Initial Antibiotic Timing[1]	11	91%	95%	95%
Pneumococcal Vaccine[1]	22	68%	88%	93%
Smoking Cessation Advice[1]	5	20%	93%	97%
Surgical Care Improvement Project				
Appropriate VTP Within 24 Hours[1,3]	3	0%	89%	92%
Appropriate Hair Removal[1,3]	3	100%	100%	99%
Appropriate Beta Blocker Usage[5]	0	-	90%	93%
Controlled Postoperative Blood Glucose[3]	0	-	92%	93%
Prophylactic Antibiotic Timing[1,3]	1	0%	96%	97%
Prophylactic Antibiotic Timing (Outpatient)	-	-	93%	92%
Prophylactic Antibiotic Selection[1,3]	1	100%	97%	97%
Prophylactic Antibiotic Select. (Outpatient)	-	-	96%	94%
Prophylactic Antibiotic Stopped[1,3]	1	100%	93%	94%
Recommended VTP Ordered[1,3]	3	0%	91%	94%
Urinary Catheter Removal[1,3]	1	100%	86%	90%
Children's Asthma Care				
Received Systemic Corticosteroids	-	-	-	100%
Received Home Management Plan	-	-	-	71%
Received Reliever Medication	-	-	-	100%
Use of Medical Imaging				
Combination Abdominal CT Scan	-	-	0.365	0.191
Combination Chest CT Scan	-	-	0.065	0.054
Follow-up Mammogram/Ultrasound	-	-	7.3%	8.4%
MRI for Low Back Pain	-	-	34.5%	32.7%
Survey of Patients' Hospital Experiences				
Area Around Room 'Always' Quiet at Night[8]	-	-	-	58%
Doctors 'Always' Communicated Well[8]	-	-	-	80%
Home Recovery Information Given[8]	-	-	-	82%
Hospital Given 9 or 10 on 10 Point Scale[8]	-	-	-	67%
Meds 'Always' Explained Before Given[8]	-	-	-	60%
Nurses 'Always' Communicated Well[8]	-	-	-	76%
Pain 'Always' Well Controlled[8]	-	-	-	69%
Room and Bathroom 'Always' Clean[8]	-	-	-	71%
Timely Help 'Always' Received[8]	-	-	-	64%
Would Definitely Recommend Hospital[8]	-	-	-	69%

Shawnee Mission Medical Center

9100 W 74th Street Phone: 913-676-2151
Shawnee Mission, KS 66204 Fax: 913-676-7724
E-mail: webmaster@shawneemission.org
URL: www.shawneemission.org
Type: Acute Care Hospitals Emergency Services: Yes
Ownership: Voluntary Non-Profit - Church Beds: 383

Key Personnel:
CEO/President............... Samuel H Turner, Sr
Chief of Medical Staff........ Robin Harrold
Coronary Care............... Louise Rada

Measure	Cases	This Hosp.	State Avg.	U.S. Avg.
Heart Attack Care				
ACE Inhibitor or ARB for LVSD	38	92%	95%	96%
Aspirin at Arrival	185	99%	98%	99%
Aspirin at Discharge	208	100%	98%	98%
Beta Blocker at Discharge	201	100%	98%	98%
Fibrinolytic Medication Timing	0	-	44%	55%
PCI Within 90 Minutes of Arrival	38	97%	91%	90%
Smoking Cessation Advice	61	100%	99%	99%
Chest Pain/Possible Heart Attack Care				
Aspirin at Arrival[1,3]	8	88%	92%	95%
Median Time to ECG (minutes)[1,3]	9	8	10	8
Median Time to Transfer (minutes)[5]	0	-	60	61
Fibrinolytic Medication Timing[5]	0	-	42%	54%
Heart Failure Care				
ACE Inhibitor or ARB for LVSD	112	97%	91%	94%
Discharge Instructions	292	84%	83%	88%
Evaluation of LVS Function	375	99%	92%	98%
Smoking Cessation Advice	47	100%	94%	98%
Pneumonia Care				
Appropriate Initial Antibiotic	268	93%	87%	92%
Blood Culture Timing	257	98%	96%	96%
Influenza Vaccine	234	90%	87%	91%
Initial Antibiotic Timing	336	95%	95%	95%
Pneumococcal Vaccine	295	95%	88%	93%
Smoking Cessation Advice	99	99%	93%	97%
Surgical Care Improvement Project				
Appropriate VTP Within 24 Hours[2]	398	95%	89%	92%
Appropriate Hair Removal[2]	1,366	100%	100%	99%
Appropriate Beta Blocker Usage[2]	417	86%	90%	93%
Controlled Postoperative Blood Glucose[2]	169	99%	92%	93%
Prophylactic Antibiotic Timing[2]	1,083	97%	96%	97%
Prophylactic Antibiotic Timing (Outpatient)	676	83%	93%	92%
Prophylactic Antibiotic Selection[2]	1,088	98%	97%	97%
Prophylactic Antibiotic Select. (Outpatient)	609	95%	96%	94%
Prophylactic Antibiotic Stopped[2]	1,041	95%	93%	94%
Recommended VTP Ordered[2]	400	96%	91%	94%
Urinary Catheter Removal[2]	173	79%	86%	90%
Children's Asthma Care				
Received Systemic Corticosteroids	-	-	-	100%
Received Home Management Plan	-	-	-	71%
Received Reliever Medication	-	-	-	100%
Use of Medical Imaging				
Combination Abdominal CT Scan	821	0.138	0.365	0.191
Combination Chest CT Scan	431	0.081	0.065	0.054
Follow-up Mammogram/Ultrasound	2,262	6.9%	7.3%	8.4%
MRI for Low Back Pain	315	29.5%	34.5%	32.7%
Survey of Patients' Hospital Experiences				
Area Around Room 'Always' Quiet at Night	300+	55%	-	58%
Doctors 'Always' Communicated Well	300+	76%	-	80%
Home Recovery Information Given	300+	86%	-	82%
Hospital Given 9 or 10 on 10 Point Scale	300+	69%	-	67%
Meds 'Always' Explained Before Given	300+	60%	-	60%
Nurses 'Always' Communicated Well	300+	73%	-	76%
Pain 'Always' Well Controlled	300+	69%	-	69%
Room and Bathroom 'Always' Clean	300+	66%	-	71%
Timely Help 'Always' Received	300+	57%	-	64%
Would Definitely Recommend Hospital	300+	72%	-	69%

Smith County Memorial Hospital

614 S Main Street Phone: 785-282-6845
Smith Center, KS 66967 Fax: 785-282-6331
URL: www.smithcohosp.org
Type: Critical Access Hospitals Emergency Services: Yes
Ownership: Voluntary Non-Profit - Other Beds: 25

Key Personnel:
CEO/President................ Carolyn Hess, RN
Cardiac Laboratory............ Paula Hayes, RN
Chief of Medical Staff......... Joe Barnes
Infection Control............. Karen Herndon
Operating Room.............. Chris Horn, RN
Quality Assurance .... Julie Haresnape
Radiology................... Kayla Wolf
Emergency Room .... Laura Kingsbury, RN

Measure	Cases	This Hosp.	State Avg.	U.S. Avg.
Heart Attack Care				
ACE Inhibitor or ARB for LVSD[3]	0	-	95%	96%
Aspirin at Arrival[1,3]	1	100%	98%	99%
Aspirin at Discharge[1,3]	1	100%	98%	98%
Beta Blocker at Discharge[1,3]	1	100%	98%	98%
Fibrinolytic Medication Timing[3]	0	-	44%	55%
PCI Within 90 Minutes of Arrival[3]	0	-	91%	90%
Smoking Cessation Advice[3]	0	-	99%	99%
Chest Pain/Possible Heart Attack Care				
Aspirin at Arrival[1,3]	1	100%	92%	95%
Median Time to ECG (minutes)[1,3]	1	22	10	8
Median Time to Transfer (minutes)[5]	0	-	60	61
Fibrinolytic Medication Timing[5]	0	-	42%	54%
Heart Failure Care				
ACE Inhibitor or ARB for LVSD	0	-	91%	94%
Discharge Instructions[1]	7	14%	83%	88%
Evaluation of LVS Function[1]	12	50%	92%	98%
Smoking Cessation Advice[1]	1	0%	94%	98%
Pneumonia Care				
Appropriate Initial Antibiotic[1]	6	83%	87%	92%
Blood Culture Timing[1]	5	80%	96%	96%
Influenza Vaccine[1]	9	22%	87%	91%
Initial Antibiotic Timing[1]	15	100%	95%	95%
Pneumococcal Vaccine[1]	13	92%	88%	93%
Smoking Cessation Advice[1]	3	0%	93%	97%
Surgical Care Improvement Project				
Appropriate VTP Within 24 Hours[3]	0	-	89%	92%
Appropriate Hair Removal[1,3]	1	100%	100%	99%
Appropriate Beta Blocker Usage[5]	0	-	90%	93%
Controlled Postoperative Blood Glucose[3]	0	-	92%	93%
Prophylactic Antibiotic Timing[1,3]	1	0%	96%	97%
Prophylactic Antibiotic Timing (Outpatient)[5]	0	-	93%	92%
Prophylactic Antibiotic Selection[3]	0	-	97%	97%
Prophylactic Antibiotic Select. (Outpatient)[5]	0	-	96%	94%
Prophylactic Antibiotic Stopped[3]	0	-	93%	94%
Recommended VTP Ordered[3]	0	-	91%	94%
Urinary Catheter Removal[3]	0	-	86%	90%
Children's Asthma Care				
Received Systemic Corticosteroids	-	-	-	100%
Received Home Management Plan	-	-	-	71%
Received Reliever Medication	-	-	-	100%
Use of Medical Imaging				
Combination Abdominal CT Scan[1]	63	0.143	0.365	0.191
Combination Chest CT Scan[1]	60	0.100	0.065	0.054
Follow-up Mammogram/Ultrasound	169	10.1%	7.3%	8.4%
MRI for Low Back Pain[1]	34	58.8%	34.5%	32.7%
Survey of Patients' Hospital Experiences				
Area Around Room 'Always' Quiet at Night[8]	-	-	-	58%
Doctors 'Always' Communicated Well[8]	-	-	-	80%
Home Recovery Information Given[8]	-	-	-	82%
Hospital Given 9 or 10 on 10 Point Scale[8]	-	-	-	67%
Meds 'Always' Explained Before Given[8]	-	-	-	60%
Nurses 'Always' Communicated Well[8]	-	-	-	76%
Pain 'Always' Well Controlled[8]	-	-	-	69%
Room and Bathroom 'Always' Clean[8]	-	-	-	71%
Timely Help 'Always' Received[8]	-	-	-	64%
Would Definitely Recommend Hospital[8]	-	-	-	69%

NOTE: Hospital profiles are in alphabetical order by state, then city, then hospital within the city; Rankings exclude hospitals with less than 25 cases except for patient surveys which excludes hospitals with less than 100 cases; (a) 100–299 cases; (1) The number of cases is too small to be sure how well a hospital is performing; (2) The hospital indicated that the data submitted for this measure were based on a sample of cases; (3) Data was collected during a shorter time period (fewer quarters) than the maximum possible time for this measure; (4) Suppressed for one or more quarters by CMS; (5) No data is available from the hospital for this measure; (6) Fewer than 100 patients completed the HCAHPS survey. Use these rates with caution, as the number of surveys may be too low to reliably assess hospital performance; (7) Survey results are based on less than 12 months of data; (8) Survey results are not available for this reporting period; (9) No or very few patients were eligible for the HCAHPS survey. The scores shown, if any, reflect a very small number of surveys; (10) A state average was not calculated because too few hospitals in the state submitted data; (11) There were discrepancies in the data collection process; Please refer to the User's Guide for a full explanation of data.

Hamilton County Hospital

700 North Huser
Syracuse, KS 67878
URL: www.hamiltoncountyhospital.net
Type: Critical Access Hospitals
Ownership: Government - Local
Phone: 620-384-7461
Fax: 620-384-5500
Emergency Services: Yes
Beds: 29

Key Personnel:

CEO/President. . . . . Todd Burch
Operating Room. . . . . Loraine Durler, RN
Quality Assurance . . . . Loraine Durler, RN
Radiology. . . . . Fred Nichols
Emergency Room . . . . Joseph Rehal, MD

Measure	Cases	This Hosp.	State Avg.	U.S. Avg.
Heart Attack Care				
ACE Inhibitor or ARB for LVSD[5]	0	-	95%	96%
Aspirin at Arrival[5]	0	-	98%	99%
Aspirin at Discharge[5]	0	-	98%	98%
Beta Blocker at Discharge[5]	0	-	98%	98%
Fibrinolytic Medication Timing[5]	0	-	44%	55%
PCI Within 90 Minutes of Arrival[5]	0	-	91%	90%
Smoking Cessation Advice[5]	0	-	99%	99%
Chest Pain/Possible Heart Attack Care				
Aspirin at Arrival	-	-	92%	95%
Median Time to ECG (minutes)	-	-	10	8
Median Time to Transfer (minutes)	-	-	60	61
Fibrinolytic Medication Timing	-	-	42%	54%
Heart Failure Care				
ACE Inhibitor or ARB for LVSD	0	-	91%	94%
Discharge Instructions[1]	1	0%	83%	88%
Evaluation of LVS Function[1]	3	0%	92%	98%
Smoking Cessation Advice	0	-	94%	98%
Pneumonia Care				
Appropriate Initial Antibiotic[1]	7	71%	87%	92%
Blood Culture Timing[1]	5	40%	96%	96%
Influenza Vaccine[1]	4	0%	87%	91%
Initial Antibiotic Timing[1]	11	73%	95%	95%
Pneumococcal Vaccine[1]	4	25%	88%	93%
Smoking Cessation Advice[1]	2	50%	93%	97%
Surgical Care Improvement Project				
Appropriate VTP Within 24 Hours[5]	0	-	89%	92%
Appropriate Hair Removal[5]	0	-	100%	99%
Appropriate Beta Blocker Usage[5]	0	-	90%	93%
Controlled Postoperative Blood Glucose[5]	0	-	92%	93%
Prophylactic Antibiotic Timing[5]	0	-	96%	97%
Prophylactic Antibiotic Timing (Outpatient)	-	-	93%	92%
Prophylactic Antibiotic Selection[5]	0	-	97%	97%
Prophylactic Antibiotic Select. (Outpatient)	-	-	96%	94%
Prophylactic Antibiotic Stopped[5]	0	-	93%	94%
Recommended VTP Ordered[5]	0	-	91%	94%
Urinary Catheter Removal[5]	0	-	86%	90%
Children's Asthma Care				
Received Systemic Corticosteroids	-	-	-	100%
Received Home Management Plan	-	-	-	71%
Received Reliever Medication	-	-	-	100%
Use of Medical Imaging				
Combination Abdominal CT Scan	-	-	0.365	0.191
Combination Chest CT Scan	-	-	0.065	0.054
Follow-up Mammogram/Ultrasound	-	-	7.3%	8.4%
MRI for Low Back Pain	-	-	34.5%	32.7%
Survey of Patients' Hospital Experiences				
Area Around Room 'Always' Quiet at Night[8]	-	-	-	58%
Doctors 'Always' Communicated Well[8]	-	-	-	80%
Home Recovery Information Given[8]	-	-	-	82%
Hospital Given 9 or 10 on 10 Point Scale[8]	-	-	-	67%
Meds 'Always' Explained Before Given[8]	-	-	-	60%
Nurses 'Always' Communicated Well[8]	-	-	-	76%
Pain 'Always' Well Controlled[8]	-	-	-	69%
Room and Bathroom 'Always' Clean[8]	-	-	-	71%
Timely Help 'Always' Received[8]	-	-	-	64%
Would Definitely Recommend Hospital[8]	-	-	-	69%

Saint Francis Health Center

1700 SW 7th Street
Topeka, KS 66606
E-mail: cr@stfrancistopeka.org
URL: www.stfrancistopeka.org
Type: Acute Care Hospitals
Ownership: Voluntary Non-Profit - Church
Phone: 785-295-8000
Fax: 785-295-7854
Emergency Services: Yes
Beds: 378

Key Personnel:

CEO/President. . . . . Loretto Marie Colwell
Chief of Medical Staff . . . . John Kleinholz, MD
Coronary Care . . . . Moussa Elbayoumy
Infection Control. . . . . Nancy Krohe
Operating Room. . . . . Bernita Berntsen, RN

Measure	Cases	This Hosp.	State Avg.	U.S. Avg.
Heart Attack Care				
ACE Inhibitor or ARB for LVSD	28	100%	95%	96%
Aspirin at Arrival	112	98%	98%	99%
Aspirin at Discharge	168	99%	98%	98%
Beta Blocker at Discharge	159	98%	98%	98%
Fibrinolytic Medication Timing	0	-	44%	55%
PCI Within 90 Minutes of Arrival	32	100%	91%	90%
Smoking Cessation Advice	64	100%	99%	99%
Chest Pain/Possible Heart Attack Care				
Aspirin at Arrival[5]	0	-	92%	95%
Median Time to ECG (minutes)[5]	0	-	10	8
Median Time to Transfer (minutes)[5]	0	-	60	61
Fibrinolytic Medication Timing[5]	0	-	42%	54%
Heart Failure Care				
ACE Inhibitor or ARB for LVSD	80	94%	91%	94%
Discharge Instructions	174	90%	83%	88%
Evaluation of LVS Function	229	99%	92%	98%
Smoking Cessation Advice	50	98%	94%	98%
Pneumonia Care				
Appropriate Initial Antibiotic	159	95%	87%	92%
Blood Culture Timing	208	100%	96%	96%
Influenza Vaccine	178	99%	87%	91%
Initial Antibiotic Timing	250	98%	95%	95%
Pneumococcal Vaccine	238	99%	88%	93%
Smoking Cessation Advice	111	99%	93%	97%
Surgical Care Improvement Project				
Appropriate VTP Within 24 Hours[2]	180	96%	89%	92%
Appropriate Hair Removal[2]	910	100%	100%	99%
Appropriate Beta Blocker Usage[2]	293	100%	90%	93%
Controlled Postoperative Blood Glucose[2]	118	98%	92%	93%
Prophylactic Antibiotic Timing[2]	730	97%	96%	97%
Prophylactic Antibiotic Timing (Outpatient)	581	93%	93%	92%
Prophylactic Antibiotic Selection[2]	740	100%	97%	97%
Prophylactic Antibiotic Select. (Outpatient)	567	97%	96%	94%
Prophylactic Antibiotic Stopped[2]	700	99%	93%	94%
Recommended VTP Ordered[2]	180	97%	91%	94%
Urinary Catheter Removal[2]	265	99%	86%	90%
Children's Asthma Care				
Received Systemic Corticosteroids	-	-	-	100%
Received Home Management Plan	-	-	-	71%
Received Reliever Medication	-	-	-	100%
Use of Medical Imaging				
Combination Abdominal CT Scan	1,053	0.111	0.365	0.191
Combination Chest CT Scan	554	0.018	0.065	0.054
Follow-up Mammogram/Ultrasound	2,599	5.1%	7.3%	8.4%
MRI for Low Back Pain	394	35.5%	34.5%	32.7%
Survey of Patients' Hospital Experiences				
Area Around Room 'Always' Quiet at Night	300+	51%	-	58%
Doctors 'Always' Communicated Well	300+	76%	-	80%
Home Recovery Information Given	300+	82%	-	82%
Hospital Given 9 or 10 on 10 Point Scale	300+	68%	-	67%
Meds 'Always' Explained Before Given	300+	62%	-	60%
Nurses 'Always' Communicated Well	300+	76%	-	76%
Pain 'Always' Well Controlled	300+	72%	-	69%
Room and Bathroom 'Always' Clean	300+	63%	-	71%
Timely Help 'Always' Received	300+	62%	-	64%
Would Definitely Recommend Hospital	300+	74%	-	69%

Stormont-Vail Healthcare

1500 SW 10th St
Topeka, KS 66604
URL: www.stormontvail.org
Type: Acute Care Hospitals
Ownership: Voluntary Non-Profit - Private
Phone: 785-354-6121
Fax: 785-354-5123
Emergency Services: Yes
Beds: 586

Key Personnel:

CEO/President. . . . . Maynard Ohverius
Chief of Medical Staff. . . . . Kent Palmberg, MD
Operating Room. . . . . Jane Asher, RN
Quality Assurance . . . . Mike Lummis
Radiology. . . . . James Kilmartin, MD
Emergency Room . . . . Dorothy Rice, RN
Patient Relations . . . . Carol Perry, RN

Measure	Cases	This Hosp.	State Avg.	U.S. Avg.
Heart Attack Care				
ACE Inhibitor or ARB for LVSD	45	100%	95%	96%
Aspirin at Arrival	190	99%	98%	99%
Aspirin at Discharge	283	99%	98%	98%
Beta Blocker at Discharge	285	100%	98%	98%
Fibrinolytic Medication Timing	0	-	44%	55%
PCI Within 90 Minutes of Arrival	49	100%	91%	90%
Smoking Cessation Advice	101	100%	99%	99%
Chest Pain/Possible Heart Attack Care				
Aspirin at Arrival[3]	0	-	92%	95%
Median Time to ECG (minutes)[3]	0	-	10	8
Median Time to Transfer (minutes)[5]	0	-	60	61
Fibrinolytic Medication Timing[5]	0	-	42%	54%
Heart Failure Care				
ACE Inhibitor or ARB for LVSD	88	94%	91%	94%
Discharge Instructions	234	90%	83%	88%
Evaluation of LVS Function	334	100%	92%	98%
Smoking Cessation Advice	56	100%	94%	98%
Pneumonia Care				
Appropriate Initial Antibiotic	147	88%	87%	92%
Blood Culture Timing	235	96%	96%	96%
Influenza Vaccine	207	98%	87%	91%
Initial Antibiotic Timing	267	97%	95%	95%
Pneumococcal Vaccine	253	100%	88%	93%
Smoking Cessation Advice	121	100%	93%	97%
Surgical Care Improvement Project				
Appropriate VTP Within 24 Hours[2]	262	89%	89%	92%
Appropriate Hair Removal[2]	1,228	100%	100%	99%
Appropriate Beta Blocker Usage[2]	424	97%	90%	93%
Controlled Postoperative Blood Glucose[2]	187	89%	92%	93%
Prophylactic Antibiotic Timing[2]	962	99%	96%	97%
Prophylactic Antibiotic Timing (Outpatient)	806	95%	93%	92%
Prophylactic Antibiotic Selection[2]	974	97%	97%	97%
Prophylactic Antibiotic Select. (Outpatient)	800	94%	96%	94%
Prophylactic Antibiotic Stopped[2]	925	95%	93%	94%
Recommended VTP Ordered[2]	264	94%	91%	94%
Urinary Catheter Removal[2]	155	85%	86%	90%
Children's Asthma Care				
Received Systemic Corticosteroids	-	-	-	100%
Received Home Management Plan	-	-	-	71%
Received Reliever Medication	-	-	-	100%
Use of Medical Imaging				
Combination Abdominal CT Scan	1,314	0.072	0.365	0.191
Combination Chest CT Scan	660	0.008	0.065	0.054
Follow-up Mammogram/Ultrasound[5]	0	-	7.3%	8.4%
MRI for Low Back Pain	527	37.2%	34.5%	32.7%
Survey of Patients' Hospital Experiences				
Area Around Room 'Always' Quiet at Night	300+	66%	-	58%
Doctors 'Always' Communicated Well	300+	82%	-	80%
Home Recovery Information Given	300+	85%	-	82%
Hospital Given 9 or 10 on 10 Point Scale	300+	75%	-	67%
Meds 'Always' Explained Before Given	300+	60%	-	60%
Nurses 'Always' Communicated Well	300+	77%	-	76%
Pain 'Always' Well Controlled	300+	69%	-	69%
Room and Bathroom 'Always' Clean	300+	69%	-	71%
Timely Help 'Always' Received	300+	65%	-	64%
Would Definitely Recommend Hospital	300+	78%	-	69%

NOTE: Hospital profiles are in alphabetical order by state, then city, then hospital within the city; Rankings exclude hospitals with less than 25 cases except for patient surveys which excludes hospitals with less than 100 cases; (a) 100–299 cases; (1) The number of cases is too small to be sure how well a hospital is performing; (2) The hospital indicated that the data submitted for this measure were based on a sample of cases; (3) Data was collected during a shorter time period (fewer quarters) than the maximum possible time for this measure; (4) Suppressed for one or more quarters by CMS; (5) No data is available from the hospital for this measure; (6) Fewer than 100 patients completed the HCAHPS survey. Use these rates with caution, as the number of surveys may be too low to reliably assess hospital performance; (7) Survey results are based on less than 12 months of data; (8) Survey results are not available for this reporting period; (9) No or very few patients were eligible for the HCAHPS survey. The scores shown, if any, reflect a very small number of surveys; (10) A state average was not calculated because too few hospitals in the state submitted data; (11) There were discrepancies in the data collection process; Please refer to the User's Guide for a full explanation of data.

Greeley County Health Services

506 3rd Street Phone: 620-376-4221
Tribune, KS 67879 Fax: 620-376-2406
Type: Critical Access Hospitals Emergency Services: Yes
Ownership: Government - Local Beds: 18

Key Personnel:
CEO/President.............. Todd Burch
Chief of Medical Staff.......... Robert P Moser MD
Infection Control.............. Linda Peterson RN
Quality Assurance............ Lisa Larkin RN
Emergency Room............ Robert P Moser MD

Measure	Cases	This Hosp.	State Avg.	U.S. Avg.
Heart Attack Care				
ACE Inhibitor or ARB for LVSD[5]	0	-	95%	96%
Aspirin at Arrival[5]	0	-	98%	99%
Aspirin at Discharge[5]	0	-	98%	98%
Beta Blocker at Discharge[5]	0	-	98%	98%
Fibrinolytic Medication Timing[5]	0	-	44%	55%
PCI Within 90 Minutes of Arrival[5]	0	-	91%	90%
Smoking Cessation Advice[5]	0	-	99%	99%
Chest Pain/Possible Heart Attack Care				
Aspirin at Arrival	-	-	92%	95%
Median Time to ECG (minutes)	-	-	10	8
Median Time to Transfer (minutes)	-	-	60	61
Fibrinolytic Medication Timing	-	-	42%	54%
Heart Failure Care				
ACE Inhibitor or ARB for LVSD[3]	0	-	91%	94%
Discharge Instructions[1,3]	2	0%	83%	88%
Evaluation of LVS Function[1,3]	3	0%	92%	98%
Smoking Cessation Advice[3]	0	-	94%	98%
Pneumonia Care				
Appropriate Initial Antibiotic[1,2,3]	1	100%	87%	92%
Blood Culture Timing[2,3]	0	-	96%	96%
Influenza Vaccine[1,2,3]	3	0%	87%	91%
Initial Antibiotic Timing[1,2,3]	1	0%	95%	95%
Pneumococcal Vaccine[1,2,3]	3	0%	88%	93%
Smoking Cessation Advice[2,3]	0	-	93%	97%
Surgical Care Improvement Project				
Appropriate VTP Within 24 Hours[5]	0	-	89%	92%
Appropriate Hair Removal[5]	0	-	100%	99%
Appropriate Beta Blocker Usage[5]	0	-	90%	93%
Controlled Postoperative Blood Glucose[5]	0	-	92%	93%
Prophylactic Antibiotic Timing[5]	0	-	96%	97%
Prophylactic Antibiotic Timing (Outpatient)	-	-	93%	92%
Prophylactic Antibiotic Selection[5]	0	-	97%	97%
Prophylactic Antibiotic Select. (Outpatient)	-	-	96%	94%
Prophylactic Antibiotic Stopped[5]	0	-	93%	94%
Recommended VTP Ordered[5]	0	-	91%	94%
Urinary Catheter Removal[5]	0	-	86%	90%
Children's Asthma Care				
Received Systemic Corticosteroids	-	-	-	100%
Received Home Management Plan	-	-	-	71%
Received Reliever Medication	-	-	-	100%
Use of Medical Imaging				
Combination Abdominal CT Scan	-	-	0.365	0.191
Combination Chest CT Scan	-	-	0.065	0.054
Follow-up Mammogram/Ultrasound	-	-	7.3%	8.4%
MRI for Low Back Pain	-	-	34.5%	32.7%
Survey of Patients' Hospital Experiences				
Area Around Room 'Always' Quiet at Night[8]	-	-	-	58%
Doctors 'Always' Communicated Well[8]	-	-	-	80%
Home Recovery Information Given[8]	-	-	-	82%
Hospital Given 9 or 10 on 10 Point Scale[8]	-	-	-	67%
Meds 'Always' Explained Before Given[8]	-	-	-	60%
Nurses 'Always' Communicated Well[8]	-	-	-	76%
Pain 'Always' Well Controlled[8]	-	-	-	69%
Room and Bathroom 'Always' Clean[8]	-	-	-	71%
Timely Help 'Always' Received[8]	-	-	-	64%
Would Definitely Recommend Hospital[8]	-	-	-	69%

Bob Wilson Memorial Grant County Hospital

415 N Main Street Phone: 620-356-1266
Ulysses, KS 67880 Fax: 620-356-2302
URL: bwmgch.com
Type: Acute Care Hospitals Emergency Services: Yes
Ownership: Government - Local Beds: 46

Key Personnel:
CEO/President.............. Steve Daniel
Quality Assurance............ Karoala Nicholas

Measure	Cases	This Hosp.	State Avg.	U.S. Avg.
Heart Attack Care				
ACE Inhibitor or ARB for LVSD[3]	0	-	95%	96%
Aspirin at Arrival[1,3]	1	0%	98%	99%
Aspirin at Discharge[1,3]	1	0%	98%	98%
Beta Blocker at Discharge[1,3]	1	0%	98%	98%
Fibrinolytic Medication Timing[3]	0	-	44%	55%
PCI Within 90 Minutes of Arrival[3]	0	-	91%	90%
Smoking Cessation Advice[3]	0	-	99%	99%
Chest Pain/Possible Heart Attack Care				
Aspirin at Arrival[1]	23	87%	92%	95%
Median Time to ECG (minutes)[1]	22	8	10	8
Median Time to Transfer (minutes)[5]	0	-	60	61
Fibrinolytic Medication Timing	0	-	42%	54%
Heart Failure Care				
ACE Inhibitor or ARB for LVSD[1]	3	100%	91%	94%
Discharge Instructions[1]	13	23%	83%	88%
Evaluation of LVS Function[1]	17	82%	92%	98%
Smoking Cessation Advice[1]	2	0%	94%	98%
Pneumonia Care				
Appropriate Initial Antibiotic[1]	12	83%	87%	92%
Blood Culture Timing[1]	8	88%	96%	96%
Influenza Vaccine[1]	15	67%	87%	91%
Initial Antibiotic Timing[1]	18	94%	95%	95%
Pneumococcal Vaccine[1]	24	54%	88%	93%
Smoking Cessation Advice[1]	5	60%	93%	97%
Surgical Care Improvement Project				
Appropriate VTP Within 24 Hours[1]	9	89%	89%	92%
Appropriate Hair Removal[1]	21	95%	100%	99%
Appropriate Beta Blocker Usage[1]	5	60%	90%	93%
Controlled Postoperative Blood Glucose	0	-	92%	93%
Prophylactic Antibiotic Timing[1]	13	92%	96%	97%
Prophylactic Antibiotic Timing (Outpatient)[5]	0	-	93%	92%
Prophylactic Antibiotic Selection[1]	13	46%	97%	97%
Prophylactic Antibiotic Select. (Outpatient)[5]	0	-	96%	94%
Prophylactic Antibiotic Stopped[1]	13	100%	93%	94%
Recommended VTP Ordered[1]	9	89%	91%	94%
Urinary Catheter Removal[1]	6	50%	86%	90%
Children's Asthma Care				
Received Systemic Corticosteroids	-	-	-	100%
Received Home Management Plan	-	-	-	71%
Received Reliever Medication	-	-	-	100%
Use of Medical Imaging				
Combination Abdominal CT Scan[1]	56	0.089	0.365	0.191
Combination Chest CT Scan[1]	28	0.071	0.065	0.054
Follow-up Mammogram/Ultrasound	114	7.0%	7.3%	8.4%
MRI for Low Back Pain[1]	9	55.6%	34.5%	32.7%
Survey of Patients' Hospital Experiences				
Area Around Room 'Always' Quiet at Night	(a)	71%	-	58%
Doctors 'Always' Communicated Well	(a)	83%	-	80%
Home Recovery Information Given	(a)	76%	-	82%
Hospital Given 9 or 10 on 10 Point Scale	(a)	64%	-	67%
Meds 'Always' Explained Before Given	(a)	56%	-	60%
Nurses 'Always' Communicated Well	(a)	76%	-	76%
Pain 'Always' Well Controlled	(a)	70%	-	69%
Room and Bathroom 'Always' Clean	(a)	77%	-	71%
Timely Help 'Always' Received	(a)	68%	-	64%
Would Definitely Recommend Hospital	(a)	62%	-	69%

Trego County Lemke Memorial Hospital

320 Thirteenth St Phone: 785-743-2182
Wa Keeney, KS 67672 Fax: 785-743-6317
Type: Critical Access Hospitals Emergency Services: Yes
Ownership: Government - Local Beds: 25

Key Personnel:
CEO/President.............. Stacey Malson
Infection Control.............. Mary Jo McClannahan
Operating Room.............. Judy Hearting
Quality Assurance............ Lavonne Finck
Radiology.................. Brian Shaw
Emergency Room............ Judy Hearting

Measure	Cases	This Hosp.	State Avg.	U.S. Avg.
Heart Attack Care				
ACE Inhibitor or ARB for LVSD[5]	0	-	95%	96%
Aspirin at Arrival[5]	0	-	98%	99%
Aspirin at Discharge[5]	0	-	98%	98%
Beta Blocker at Discharge[5]	0	-	98%	98%
Fibrinolytic Medication Timing[5]	0	-	44%	55%
PCI Within 90 Minutes of Arrival[5]	0	-	91%	90%
Smoking Cessation Advice[5]	0	-	99%	99%
Chest Pain/Possible Heart Attack Care				
Aspirin at Arrival	-	-	92%	95%
Median Time to ECG (minutes)	-	-	10	8
Median Time to Transfer (minutes)	-	-	60	61
Fibrinolytic Medication Timing	-	-	42%	54%
Heart Failure Care				
ACE Inhibitor or ARB for LVSD[1]	5	100%	91%	94%
Discharge Instructions[1]	12	8%	83%	88%
Evaluation of LVS Function	38	63%	92%	98%
Smoking Cessation Advice[1]	1	0%	94%	98%
Pneumonia Care				
Appropriate Initial Antibiotic	31	81%	87%	92%
Blood Culture Timing[1]	10	80%	96%	96%
Influenza Vaccine	25	68%	87%	91%
Initial Antibiotic Timing	38	89%	95%	95%
Pneumococcal Vaccine	56	32%	88%	93%
Smoking Cessation Advice[1]	6	0%	93%	97%
Surgical Care Improvement Project				
Appropriate VTP Within 24 Hours[5]	0	-	89%	92%
Appropriate Hair Removal[5]	0	-	100%	99%
Appropriate Beta Blocker Usage[5]	0	-	90%	93%
Controlled Postoperative Blood Glucose[5]	0	-	92%	93%
Prophylactic Antibiotic Timing[5]	0	-	96%	97%
Prophylactic Antibiotic Timing (Outpatient)	-	-	93%	92%
Prophylactic Antibiotic Selection[5]	0	-	97%	97%
Prophylactic Antibiotic Select. (Outpatient)	-	-	96%	94%
Prophylactic Antibiotic Stopped[5]	0	-	93%	94%
Recommended VTP Ordered[5]	0	-	91%	94%
Urinary Catheter Removal[5]	0	-	86%	90%
Children's Asthma Care				
Received Systemic Corticosteroids	-	-	-	100%
Received Home Management Plan	-	-	-	71%
Received Reliever Medication	-	-	-	100%
Use of Medical Imaging				
Combination Abdominal CT Scan	-	-	0.365	0.191
Combination Chest CT Scan	-	-	0.065	0.054
Follow-up Mammogram/Ultrasound	-	-	7.3%	8.4%
MRI for Low Back Pain	-	-	34.5%	32.7%
Survey of Patients' Hospital Experiences				
Area Around Room 'Always' Quiet at Night[8]	-	-	-	58%
Doctors 'Always' Communicated Well[8]	-	-	-	80%
Home Recovery Information Given[8]	-	-	-	82%
Hospital Given 9 or 10 on 10 Point Scale[8]	-	-	-	67%
Meds 'Always' Explained Before Given[8]	-	-	-	60%
Nurses 'Always' Communicated Well[8]	-	-	-	76%
Pain 'Always' Well Controlled[8]	-	-	-	69%
Room and Bathroom 'Always' Clean[8]	-	-	-	71%
Timely Help 'Always' Received[8]	-	-	-	64%
Would Definitely Recommend Hospital[8]	-	-	-	69%

NOTE: Hospital profiles are in alphabetical order by state, then city, then hospital within the city; Rankings exclude hospitals with less than 25 cases except for patient surveys which excludes hospitals with less than 100 cases; (a) 100–299 cases; (1) The number of cases is too small to be sure how well a hospital is performing; (2) The hospital indicated that the data submitted for this measure were based on a sample of cases; (3) Data was collected during a shorter time period (fewer quarters) than the maximum possible time for this measure; (4) Suppressed for one or more quarters by CMS; (5) No data is available from the hospital for this measure; (6) Fewer than 100 patients completed the HCAHPS survey. Use these rates with caution, as the number of surveys may be too low to reliably assess hospital performance; (7) Survey results are based on less than 12 months of data; (8) Survey results are not available for this reporting period; (9) No or very few patients were eligible for the HCAHPS survey. The scores shown, if any, reflect a very small number of surveys; (10) A state average was not calculated because too few hospitals in the state submitted data; (11) There were discrepancies in the data collection process; Please refer to the User's Guide for a full explanation of data.

Wamego City Hospital

711 Genn Drive
Wamego, KS 66547
URL: www.wamegocityhospital.com
Type: Critical Access Hospitals
Ownership: Voluntary Non-Profit - Other

Phone: 785-458-7201
Fax: 785-456-6916
Emergency Services: Yes
Beds: 26

Measure	Cases	This Hosp.	State Avg.	U.S. Avg.
Heart Attack Care				
ACE Inhibitor or ARB for LVSD[3]	0	-	95%	96%
Aspirin at Arrival[1,3]	3	100%	98%	99%
Aspirin at Discharge[1,3]	2	100%	98%	98%
Beta Blocker at Discharge[1,3]	2	100%	98%	98%
Fibrinolytic Medication Timing[3]	0	-	44%	55%
PCI Within 90 Minutes of Arrival[3]	0	-	91%	90%
Smoking Cessation Advice[3]	0	-	99%	99%
Chest Pain/Possible Heart Attack Care				
Aspirin at Arrival[5]	0	-	92%	95%
Median Time to ECG (minutes)[5]	0	-	10	8
Median Time to Transfer (minutes)[5]	0	-	60	61
Fibrinolytic Medication Timing[5]	0	-	42%	54%
Heart Failure Care				
ACE Inhibitor or ARB for LVSD[1]	2	100%	91%	94%
Discharge Instructions[1]	9	100%	83%	88%
Evaluation of LVS Function[1]	18	78%	92%	98%
Smoking Cessation Advice[1]	4	100%	94%	98%
Pneumonia Care				
Appropriate Initial Antibiotic[1]	3	67%	87%	92%
Blood Culture Timing	0	-	96%	96%
Influenza Vaccine[1]	5	80%	87%	.91%
Initial Antibiotic Timing[1]	4	100%	95%	95%
Pneumococcal Vaccine[1]	9	67%	88%	93%
Smoking Cessation Advice[1]	3	100%	93%	97%
Surgical Care Improvement Project				
Appropriate VTP Within 24 Hours[5]	0	-	89%	92%
Appropriate Hair Removal[5]	0	-	100%	99%
Appropriate Beta Blocker Usage[5]	0	-	90%	93%
Controlled Postoperative Blood Glucose[5]	0	-	92%	93%
Prophylactic Antibiotic Timing[5]	0	-	96%	97%
Prophylactic Antibiotic Timing (Outpatient)[5]	0	-	93%	92%
Prophylactic Antibiotic Selection[5]	0	-	97%	97%
Prophylactic Antibiotic Select. (Outpatient)[5]	0	-	96%	94%
Prophylactic Antibiotic Stopped[5]	0	-	93%	94%
Recommended VTP Ordered[5]	0	-	91%	94%
Urinary Catheter Removal[5]	0	-	86%	90%
Children's Asthma Care				
Received Systemic Corticosteroids	-	-	-	100%
Received Home Management Plan	-	-	-	71%
Received Reliever Medication	-	-	-	100%
Use of Medical Imaging				
Combination Abdominal CT Scan[1]	53	0.057	0.365	0.191
Combination Chest CT Scan[1]	33	0.121	0.065	0.054
Follow-up Mammogram/Ultrasound	165	6.1%	7.3%	8.4%
MRI for Low Back Pain[1]	18	38.9%	34.5%	32.7%
Survey of Patients' Hospital Experiences				
Area Around Room 'Always' Quiet at Night[6]	<100	56%	-	58%
Doctors 'Always' Communicated Well[6]	<100	80%	-	80%
Home Recovery Information Given[6]	<100	76%	-	82%
Hospital Given 9 or 10 on 10 Point Scale[6]	<100	78%	-	67%
Meds 'Always' Explained Before Given[6]	<100	59%	-	60%
Nurses 'Always' Communicated Well[6]	<100	74%	-	76%
Pain 'Always' Well Controlled[6]	<100	57%	-	69%
Room and Bathroom 'Always' Clean[6]	<100	80%	-	71%
Timely Help 'Always' Received[6]	<100	74%	-	64%
Would Definitely Recommend Hospital	<100	80%	-	69%

Washington County Hospital

304 E 3rd Street
Washington, KS 66968
Type: Critical Access Hospitals
Ownership: Government - Local

Phone: 785-325-2211
Fax: 785-325-3224
Emergency Services: Yes
Beds: 27

Key Personnel:
CEO/President. . . . . Everett Lutjemeier
Chief of Medical Staff . . . . David Hodgson
Quality Assurance . . . . Clifford Steward
Emergency Room . . . . Marry Walter

Measure	Cases	This Hosp.	State Avg.	U.S. Avg.
Heart Attack Care				
ACE Inhibitor or ARB for LVSD[3]	0	-	95%	96%
Aspirin at Arrival[1,3]	2	100%	98%	99%
Aspirin at Discharge[1,3]	2	100%	98%	98%
Beta Blocker at Discharge[1,3]	1	100%	98%	98%
Fibrinolytic Medication Timing[3]	0	-	44%	55%
PCI Within 90 Minutes of Arrival[3]	0	-	91%	90%
Smoking Cessation Advice[1,3]	1	0%	99%	99%
Chest Pain/Possible Heart Attack Care				
Aspirin at Arrival	-	-	92%	95%
Median Time to ECG (minutes)	-	-	10	8
Median Time to Transfer (minutes)	-	-	60	61
Fibrinolytic Medication Timing	-	-	42%	54%
Heart Failure Care				
ACE Inhibitor or ARB for LVSD[1,3]	1	100%	91%	94%
Discharge Instructions[1,3]	2	0%	83%	88%
Evaluation of LVS Function[1,3]	3	67%	92%	98%
Smoking Cessation Advice[3]	0	-	94%	98%
Pneumonia Care				
Appropriate Initial Antibiotic[1]	3	100%	87%	92%
Blood Culture Timing	0	-	96%	96%
Influenza Vaccine[1]	12	83%	87%	91%
Initial Antibiotic Timing[1]	15	73%	95%	95%
Pneumococcal Vaccine[1]	15	93%	88%	93%
Smoking Cessation Advice	0	-	93%	97%
Surgical Care Improvement Project				
Appropriate VTP Within 24 Hours[5]	0	-	89%	92%
Appropriate Hair Removal[5]	0	-	100%	99%
Appropriate Beta Blocker Usage[5]	0	-	90%	93%
Controlled Postoperative Blood Glucose[5]	0	-	92%	93%
Prophylactic Antibiotic Timing[5]	0	-	96%	97%
Prophylactic Antibiotic Timing (Outpatient)	-	-	93%	92%
Prophylactic Antibiotic Selection[5]	0	-	97%	97%
Prophylactic Antibiotic Select. (Outpatient)	-	-	96%	94%
Prophylactic Antibiotic Stopped[5]	0	-	93%	94%
Recommended VTP Ordered[5]	0	-	91%	94%
Urinary Catheter Removal[5]	0	-	86%	90%
Children's Asthma Care				
Received Systemic Corticosteroids	-	-	-	100%
Received Home Management Plan	-	-	-	71%
Received Reliever Medication	-	-	-	100%
Use of Medical Imaging				
Combination Abdominal CT Scan	-	-	0.365	0.191
Combination Chest CT Scan	-	-	0.065	0.054
Follow-up Mammogram/Ultrasound	-	-	7.3%	8.4%
MRI for Low Back Pain	-	-	34.5%	32.7%
Survey of Patients' Hospital Experiences				
Area Around Room 'Always' Quiet at Night[8]	-	-	-	58%
Doctors 'Always' Communicated Well[8]	-	-	-	80%
Home Recovery Information Given[8]	-	-	-	82%
Hospital Given 9 or 10 on 10 Point Scale[8]	-	-	-	67%
Meds 'Always' Explained Before Given[8]	-	-	-	60%
Nurses 'Always' Communicated Well[8]	-	-	-	76%
Pain 'Always' Well Controlled[8]	-	-	-	69%
Room and Bathroom 'Always' Clean[8]	-	-	-	71%
Timely Help 'Always' Received[8]	-	-	-	64%
Would Definitely Recommend Hospital[8]	-	-	-	69%

Sumner Regional Medical Center

1323 North A St
Wellington, KS 67152
URL: www.srmcks.org
Type: Acute Care Hospitals
Ownership: Government - Local

Phone: 620-399-1299
Fax: 620-326-2225
Emergency Services: Yes
Beds: 80

Key Personnel:
CEO/President. . . . . Robert H Bean, PhD
Chief of Medical Staff . . . . Larry Anderson
Quality Assurance . . . . Susan Runyan
Radiology. . . . . Neil Rosenquist

Measure	Cases	This Hosp.	State Avg.	U.S. Avg.
Heart Attack Care				
ACE Inhibitor or ARB for LVSD[5]	0	-	95%	96%
Aspirin at Arrival[5]	0	-	98%	99%
Aspirin at Discharge[5]	0	-	98%	98%
Beta Blocker at Discharge[5]	0	-	98%	98%
Fibrinolytic Medication Timing[5]	0	-	44%	55%
PCI Within 90 Minutes of Arrival[5]	0	-	91%	90%
Smoking Cessation Advice[5]	0	-	99%	99%
Chest Pain/Possible Heart Attack Care				
Aspirin at Arrival	87	92%	92%	95%
Median Time to ECG (minutes)	88	10	10	8
Median Time to Transfer (minutes)[3]	0	-	60	61
Fibrinolytic Medication Timing[1,3]	1	0%	42%	54%
Heart Failure Care				
ACE Inhibitor or ARB for LVSD[1,3]	2	0%	91%	94%
Discharge Instructions[1,3]	9	78%	83%	88%
Evaluation of LVS Function[1,3]	17	41%	92%	98%
Smoking Cessation Advice[1,3]	1	100%	94%	98%
Pneumonia Care				
Appropriate Initial Antibiotic[1]	22	73%	87%	92%
Blood Culture Timing[1]	3	100%	96%	96%
Influenza Vaccine[1]	24	83%	87%	91%
Initial Antibiotic Timing	26	92%	95%	95%
Pneumococcal Vaccine	31	90%	88%	93%
Smoking Cessation Advice[1]	11	73%	93%	97%
Surgical Care Improvement Project				
Appropriate VTP Within 24 Hours[1,2,3]	6	100%	89%	92%
Appropriate Hair Removal[1,2,3]	12	100%	100%	99%
Appropriate Beta Blocker Usage[1,2,3]	4	25%	90%	93%
Controlled Postoperative Blood Glucose[2,3]	0	-	92%	93%
Prophylactic Antibiotic Timing[1,2,3]	6	67%	96%	97%
Prophylactic Antibiotic Timing (Outpatient)[1,3]	6	100%	93%	92%
Prophylactic Antibiotic Selection[1,2,3]	6	100%	97%	97%
Prophylactic Antibiotic Select. (Outpatient)[1,3]	6	100%	96%	94%
Prophylactic Antibiotic Stopped[1,2,3]	6	67%	93%	94%
Recommended VTP Ordered[1,2,3]	6	100%	91%	94%
Urinary Catheter Removal[3]	0	-	86%	90%
Children's Asthma Care				
Received Systemic Corticosteroids	-	-	-	100%
Received Home Management Plan	-	-	-	71%
Received Reliever Medication	-	-	-	100%
Use of Medical Imaging				
Combination Abdominal CT Scan	139	0.647	0.365	0.191
Combination Chest CT Scan	75	0.067	0.065	0.054
Follow-up Mammogram/Ultrasound	282	7.4%	7.3%	8.4%
MRI for Low Back Pain	57	52.6%	34.5%	32.7%
Survey of Patients' Hospital Experiences				
Area Around Room 'Always' Quiet at Night[6]	<100	61%	-	58%
Doctors 'Always' Communicated Well[6]	<100	90%	-	80%
Home Recovery Information Given[6]	<100	76%	-	82%
Hospital Given 9 or 10 on 10 Point Scale[6]	<100	72%	-	67%
Meds 'Always' Explained Before Given[6]	<100	65%	-	60%
Nurses 'Always' Communicated Well[6]	<100	77%	-	76%
Pain 'Always' Well Controlled[6]	<100	69%	-	69%
Room and Bathroom 'Always' Clean[6]	<100	84%	-	71%
Timely Help 'Always' Received[6]	<100	66%	-	64%
Would Definitely Recommend Hospital	<100	78%	-	69%

NOTE: Hospital profiles are in alphabetical order by state, then city, then hospital within the city; Rankings exclude hospitals with less than 25 cases except for patient surveys which excludes hospitals with less than 100 cases; (a) 100–299 cases; (1) The number of cases is too small to be sure how well a hospital is performing; (2) The hospital indicated that the data submitted for this measure were based on a sample of cases; (3) Data was collected during a shorter time period (fewer quarters) than the maximum possible time for this measure; (4) Suppressed for one or more quarters by CMS; (5) No data is available from the hospital for this measure; (6) Fewer than 100 patients completed the HCAHPS survey. Use these rates with caution, as the number of surveys may be too low to reliably assess hospital performance; (7) Survey results are based on less than 12 months of data; (8) Survey results are not available for this reporting period; (9) No or very few patients were eligible for the HCAHPS survey. The scores shown, if any, reflect a very small number of surveys; (10) A state average was not calculated because too few hospitals in the state submitted data; (11) There were discrepancies in the data collection process; Please refer to the User's Guide for a full explanation of data.

Galichia Heart Hospital

2610 N Woodlawn
Wichita, KS 67220
URL: www.ghhospital.com
Type: Acute Care Hospitals
Ownership: Proprietary
Phone: 316-858-2610
Fax: 316-858-2790
Emergency Services: Yes
Beds: 82

Key Personnel:
CEO/President. . . . . Tom Nester

Measure	Cases	This Hosp.	State Avg.	U.S. Avg.
Heart Attack Care				
ACE Inhibitor or ARB for LVSD[1]	18	94%	95%	96%
Aspirin at Arrival	66	98%	98%	99%
Aspirin at Discharge	110	99%	98%	98%
Beta Blocker at Discharge	97	100%	98%	98%
Fibrinolytic Medication Timing[1]	3	0%	44%	55%
PCI Within 90 Minutes of Arrival[1]	8	88%	91%	90%
Smoking Cessation Advice	42	100%	99%	99%
Chest Pain/Possible Heart Attack Care				
Aspirin at Arrival[1,3]	2	100%	92%	95%
Median Time to ECG (minutes)[1,3]	2	5051	10	8
Median Time to Transfer (minutes)[5]	0	-	60	61
Fibrinolytic Medication Timing[5]	0	-	42%	54%
Heart Failure Care				
ACE Inhibitor or ARB for LVSD[2]	58	95%	91%	94%
Discharge Instructions[2]	213	100%	83%	88%
Evaluation of LVS Function[2]	251	99%	92%	98%
Smoking Cessation Advice[2]	39	100%	94%	98%
Pneumonia Care				
Appropriate Initial Antibiotic	59	71%	87%	92%
Blood Culture Timing	73	77%	96%	96%
Influenza Vaccine	63	92%	87%	91%
Initial Antibiotic Timing	79	84%	95%	95%
Pneumococcal Vaccine	101	89%	88%	93%
Smoking Cessation Advice	26	100%	93%	97%
Surgical Care Improvement Project				
Appropriate VTP Within 24 Hours	52	69%	89%	92%
Appropriate Hair Removal	310	97%	100%	99%
Appropriate Beta Blocker Usage	120	92%	90%	93%
Controlled Postoperative Blood Glucose	183	82%	92%	93%
Prophylactic Antibiotic Timing	221	91%	96%	97%
Prophylactic Antibiotic Timing (Outpatient)	170	94%	93%	92%
Prophylactic Antibiotic Selection	220	97%	97%	97%
Prophylactic Antibiotic Select. (Outpatient)	168	98%	96%	94%
Prophylactic Antibiotic Stopped	209	91%	93%	94%
Recommended VTP Ordered	54	70%	91%	94%
Urinary Catheter Removal	78	94%	86%	90%
Children's Asthma Care				
Received Systemic Corticosteroids	-	-	-	100%
Received Home Management Plan	-	-	-	71%
Received Reliever Medication	-	-	-	100%
Use of Medical Imaging				
Combination Abdominal CT Scan	167	0.401	0.365	0.191
Combination Chest CT Scan	133	0.504	0.065	0.054
Follow-up Mammogram/Ultrasound[5]	0	-	7.3%	8.4%
MRI for Low Back Pain[5]	0	-	34.5%	32.7%
Survey of Patients' Hospital Experiences				
Area Around Room 'Always' Quiet at Night	300+	61%	-	58%
Doctors 'Always' Communicated Well	300+	74%	-	80%
Home Recovery Information Given	300+	80%	-	82%
Hospital Given 9 or 10 on 10 Point Scale	300+	73%	-	67%
Meds 'Always' Explained Before Given	300+	50%	-	60%
Nurses 'Always' Communicated Well	300+	77%	-	76%
Pain 'Always' Well Controlled	300+	70%	-	69%
Room and Bathroom 'Always' Clean	300+	71%	-	71%
Timely Help 'Always' Received	300+	63%	-	64%
Would Definitely Recommend Hospital	300+	78%	-	69%

Kansas Heart Hospital

3601 North Webb Road
Wichita, KS 67226
URL: www.kansasheart.com
Type: Acute Care Hospitals
Ownership: Proprietary
Phone: 316-630-5000
Fax: 316-630-5050
Emergency Services: No
Beds: 54

Key Personnel:
CEO/President. . . . . Thomas L Aschom, MD

Measure	Cases	This Hosp.	State Avg.	U.S. Avg.
Heart Attack Care				
ACE Inhibitor or ARB for LVSD	27	93%	95%	96%
Aspirin at Arrival	35	89%	98%	99%
Aspirin at Discharge	221	100%	98%	98%
Beta Blocker at Discharge	208	98%	98%	98%
Fibrinolytic Medication Timing	0	-	44%	55%
PCI Within 90 Minutes of Arrival[1]	1	100%	91%	90%
Smoking Cessation Advice	66	94%	99%	99%
Chest Pain/Possible Heart Attack Care				
Aspirin at Arrival[5]	0	-	92%	95%
Median Time to ECG (minutes)[5]	0	-	10	8
Median Time to Transfer (minutes)[5]	0	-	60	61
Fibrinolytic Medication Timing[5]	0	-	42%	54%
Heart Failure Care				
ACE Inhibitor or ARB for LVSD	39	97%	91%	94%
Discharge Instructions	104	91%	83%	88%
Evaluation of LVS Function	118	100%	92%	98%
Smoking Cessation Advice[1]	22	100%	94%	98%
Pneumonia Care				
Appropriate Initial Antibiotic[3]	0	-	87%	92%
Blood Culture Timing[3]	0	-	96%	96%
Influenza Vaccine[1]	5	100%	87%	91%
Initial Antibiotic Timing[3]	0	-	95%	95%
Pneumococcal Vaccine[1,3]	5	100%	88%	93%
Smoking Cessation Advice[1,3]	4	100%	93%	97%
Surgical Care Improvement Project				
Appropriate VTP Within 24 Hours[2]	44	95%	89%	92%
Appropriate Hair Removal[2]	450	99%	100%	99%
Appropriate Beta Blocker Usage[2]	201	90%	90%	93%
Controlled Postoperative Blood Glucose[2]	287	93%	92%	93%
Prophylactic Antibiotic Timing[2]	343	97%	96%	97%
Prophylactic Antibiotic Timing (Outpatient)	263	97%	93%	92%
Prophylactic Antibiotic Selection[2]	352	100%	97%	97%
Prophylactic Antibiotic Select. (Outpatient)	265	97%	96%	94%
Prophylactic Antibiotic Stopped[2]	337	96%	93%	94%
Recommended VTP Ordered[2]	44	98%	91%	94%
Urinary Catheter Removal[2]	68	96%	86%	90%
Children's Asthma Care				
Received Systemic Corticosteroids	-	-	-	100%
Received Home Management Plan	-	-	-	71%
Received Reliever Medication	-	-	-	100%
Use of Medical Imaging				
Combination Abdominal CT Scan[1]	1	1.000	0.365	0.191
Combination Chest CT Scan[1]	1	1.000	0.065	0.054
Follow-up Mammogram/Ultrasound[5]	0	-	7.3%	8.4%
MRI for Low Back Pain[5]	0	-	34.5%	32.7%
Survey of Patients' Hospital Experiences				
Area Around Room 'Always' Quiet at Night	300+	59%	-	58%
Doctors 'Always' Communicated Well	300+	86%	-	80%
Home Recovery Information Given	300+	79%	-	82%
Hospital Given 9 or 10 on 10 Point Scale	300+	87%	-	67%
Meds 'Always' Explained Before Given	300+	67%	-	60%
Nurses 'Always' Communicated Well	300+	86%	-	76%
Pain 'Always' Well Controlled	300+	75%	-	69%
Room and Bathroom 'Always' Clean	300+	90%	-	71%
Timely Help 'Always' Received	300+	83%	-	64%
Would Definitely Recommend Hospital	300+	91%	-	69%

Kansas Spine Hospital

3333 North Webb Road
Wichita, KS 67226
Type: Acute Care Hospitals
Ownership: Voluntary Non-Profit - Private
Phone: 316-462-5326
Emergency Services: No
Beds: 22

Key Personnel:
CEO/President. . . . . Thomas M. Schmitt

Measure	Cases	This Hosp.	State Avg.	U.S. Avg.
Heart Attack Care				
ACE Inhibitor or ARB for LVSD[5]	0	-	95%	96%
Aspirin at Arrival[5]	0	-	98%	99%
Aspirin at Discharge[5]	0	-	98%	98%
Beta Blocker at Discharge[5]	0	-	98%	98%
Fibrinolytic Medication Timing[5]	0	-	44%	55%
PCI Within 90 Minutes of Arrival[5]	0	-	91%	90%
Smoking Cessation Advice[5]	0	-	99%	99%
Chest Pain/Possible Heart Attack Care				
Aspirin at Arrival[5]	0	-	92%	95%
Median Time to ECG (minutes)[5]	0	-	10	8
Median Time to Transfer (minutes)[5]	0	-	60	61
Fibrinolytic Medication Timing[5]	0	-	42%	54%
Heart Failure Care				
ACE Inhibitor or ARB for LVSD[5]	0	-	91%	94%
Discharge Instructions[5]	0	-	83%	88%
Evaluation of LVS Function[5]	0	-	92%	98%
Smoking Cessation Advice[5]	0	-	94%	98%
Pneumonia Care				
Appropriate Initial Antibiotic[5]	0	-	87%	92%
Blood Culture Timing[5]	0	-	96%	96%
Influenza Vaccine[5]	0	-	87%	91%
Initial Antibiotic Timing[5]	0	-	95%	95%
Pneumococcal Vaccine[5]	0	-	88%	93%
Smoking Cessation Advice[5]	0	-	93%	97%
Surgical Care Improvement Project				
Appropriate VTP Within 24 Hours	42	98%	89%	92%
Appropriate Hair Removal	66	100%	100%	99%
Appropriate Beta Blocker Usage	26	69%	90%	93%
Controlled Postoperative Blood Glucose	0	-	92%	93%
Prophylactic Antibiotic Timing	49	96%	96%	97%
Prophylactic Antibiotic Timing (Outpatient)	315	99%	93%	92%
Prophylactic Antibiotic Selection	49	100%	97%	97%
Prophylactic Antibiotic Select. (Outpatient)	315	100%	96%	94%
Prophylactic Antibiotic Stopped	49	0%	93%	94%
Recommended VTP Ordered	42	98%	91%	94%
Urinary Catheter Removal	29	93%	86%	90%
Children's Asthma Care				
Received Systemic Corticosteroids	-	-	-	100%
Received Home Management Plan	-	-	-	71%
Received Reliever Medication	-	-	-	100%
Use of Medical Imaging				
Combination Abdominal CT Scan[1]	6	0.833	0.365	0.191
Combination Chest CT Scan[1]	7	1.000	0.065	0.054
Follow-up Mammogram/Ultrasound[5]	0	-	7.3%	8.4%
MRI for Low Back Pain	161	26.7%	34.5%	32.7%
Survey of Patients' Hospital Experiences				
Area Around Room 'Always' Quiet at Night	300+	76%	-	58%
Doctors 'Always' Communicated Well	300+	84%	-	80%
Home Recovery Information Given	300+	87%	-	82%
Hospital Given 9 or 10 on 10 Point Scale	300+	83%	-	67%
Meds 'Always' Explained Before Given	300+	66%	-	60%
Nurses 'Always' Communicated Well	300+	81%	-	76%
Pain 'Always' Well Controlled	300+	73%	-	69%
Room and Bathroom 'Always' Clean	300+	77%	-	71%
Timely Help 'Always' Received	300+	73%	-	64%
Would Definitely Recommend Hospital	300+	84%	-	69%

NOTE: Hospital profiles are in alphabetical order by state, then city, then hospital within the city; Rankings exclude hospitals with less than 25 cases except for patient surveys which excludes hospitals with less than 100 cases; (a) 100–299 cases; (1) The number of cases is too small to be sure how well a hospital is performing; (2) The hospital indicated that the data submitted for this measure were based on a sample of cases; (3) Data was collected during a shorter time period (fewer quarters) than the maximum possible time for this measure; (4) Suppressed for one or more quarters by CMS; (5) No data is available from the hospital for this measure; (6) Fewer than 100 patients completed the HCAHPS survey. Use these rates with caution, as the number of surveys may be too low to reliably assess hospital performance; (7) Survey results are based on less than 12 months of data; (8) Survey results are not available for this reporting period; (9) No or very few patients were eligible for the HCAHPS survey. The scores shown, if any, reflect a very small number of surveys; (10) A state average was not calculated because too few hospitals in the state submitted data; (11) There were discrepancies in the data collection process; Please refer to the User's Guide for a full explanation of data.

Kansas Surgery & Recovery Center

2770 N Webb Road
Wichita, KS 67226
Phone: 316-634-0090
Fax: 316-634-0005
URL: www.ksrc.org
Type: Acute Care Hospitals
Emergency Services: No
Ownership: Proprietary
Beds: 24

Key Personnel:

Radiology. . . . . Amanda Zernickow

Measure	Cases	This Hosp.	State Avg.	U.S. Avg.
Heart Attack Care				
ACE Inhibitor or ARB for LVSD[5]	0	-	95%	96%
Aspirin at Arrival[5]	0	-	98%	99%
Aspirin at Discharge[5]	0	-	98%	98%
Beta Blocker at Discharge[5]	0	-	98%	98%
Fibrinolytic Medication Timing[5]	0	-	44%	55%
PCI Within 90 Minutes of Arrival[5]	0	-	91%	90%
Smoking Cessation Advice[5]	0	-	99%	99%
Chest Pain/Possible Heart Attack Care				
Aspirin at Arrival[5]	0	-	92%	95%
Median Time to ECG (minutes)[5]	0	-	10	8
Median Time to Transfer (minutes)[5]	0	-	60	61
Fibrinolytic Medication Timing[5]	0	-	42%	54%
Heart Failure Care				
ACE Inhibitor or ARB for LVSD[5]	0	-	91%	94%
Discharge Instructions[5]	0	-	83%	88%
Evaluation of LVS Function[5]	0	-	92%	98%
Smoking Cessation Advice[5]	0	-	94%	98%
Pneumonia Care				
Appropriate Initial Antibiotic[5]	0	-	87%	92%
Blood Culture Timing[5]	0	-	96%	96%
Influenza Vaccine[5]	0	-	87%	91%
Initial Antibiotic Timing[5]	0	-	95%	95%
Pneumococcal Vaccine[5]	0	-	88%	93%
Smoking Cessation Advice[5]	0	-	93%	97%
Surgical Care Improvement Project				
Appropriate VTP Within 24 Hours[1,2]	22	100%	89%	92%
Appropriate Hair Removal[2]	361	100%	100%	99%
Appropriate Beta Blocker Usage[2]	66	85%	90%	93%
Controlled Postoperative Blood Glucose[2]	0	-	92%	93%
Prophylactic Antibiotic Timing[2]	361	99%	96%	97%
Prophylactic Antibiotic Timing (Outpatient)	109	100%	93%	92%
Prophylactic Antibiotic Selection[2]	361	100%	97%	97%
Prophylactic Antibiotic Select. (Outpatient)	109	100%	96%	94%
Prophylactic Antibiotic Stopped[2]	361	96%	93%	94%
Recommended VTP Ordered[1,2]	22	100%	91%	94%
Urinary Catheter Removal[1,2]	4	100%	86%	90%
Children's Asthma Care				
Received Systemic Corticosteroids	-	-	-	100%
Received Home Management Plan	-	-	-	71%
Received Reliever Medication	-	-	-	100%
Use of Medical Imaging				
Combination Abdominal CT Scan[1]	10	0.500	0.365	0.191
Combination Chest CT Scan[1]	11	0.545	0.065	0.054
Follow-up Mammogram/Ultrasound[5]	0	-	7.3%	8.4%
MRI for Low Back Pain	217	26.7%	34.5%	32.7%
Survey of Patients' Hospital Experiences				
Area Around Room 'Always' Quiet at Night	300+	64%	-	58%
Doctors 'Always' Communicated Well	300+	88%	-	80%
Home Recovery Information Given	300+	87%	-	82%
Hospital Given 9 or 10 on 10 Point Scale	300+	80%	-	67%
Meds 'Always' Explained Before Given	300+	66%	-	60%
Nurses 'Always' Communicated Well	300+	80%	-	76%
Pain 'Always' Well Controlled	300+	73%	-	69%
Room and Bathroom 'Always' Clean	300+	80%	-	71%
Timely Help 'Always' Received	300+	69%	-	64%
Would Definitely Recommend Hospital	300+	84%	-	69%

Via Christi Hospital Wichita - Saint Teresa

14800 West St Teresa
Wichita, KS 67235
Phone: 316-796-7000
URL: www.via-christi.org
Type: Acute Care Hospitals
Emergency Services: No
Ownership: Voluntary Non-Profit - Church
Beds: 68

Measure	Cases	This Hosp.	State Avg.	U.S. Avg.
Heart Attack Care				
ACE Inhibitor or ARB for LVSD[5]	0	-	95%	96%
Aspirin at Arrival[5]	0	-	98%	99%
Aspirin at Discharge[5]	0	-	98%	98%
Beta Blocker at Discharge[5]	0	-	98%	98%
Fibrinolytic Medication Timing[5]	0	-	44%	55%
PCI Within 90 Minutes of Arrival[5]	0	-	91%	90%
Smoking Cessation Advice[5]	0	-	99%	99%
Chest Pain/Possible Heart Attack Care				
Aspirin at Arrival	-	-	92%	95%
Median Time to ECG (minutes)	-	-	10	8
Median Time to Transfer (minutes)	-	-	60	61
Fibrinolytic Medication Timing	-	-	42%	54%
Heart Failure Care				
ACE Inhibitor or ARB for LVSD[5]	0	-	91%	94%
Discharge Instructions[5]	0	-	83%	88%
Evaluation of LVS Function[5]	0	-	92%	98%
Smoking Cessation Advice[5]	0	-	94%	98%
Pneumonia Care				
Appropriate Initial Antibiotic[5]	0	-	87%	92%
Blood Culture Timing[5]	0	-	96%	96%
Influenza Vaccine[5]	0	-	87%	91%
Initial Antibiotic Timing[5]	0	-	95%	95%
Pneumococcal Vaccine[5]	0	-	88%	93%
Smoking Cessation Advice[5]	0	-	93%	97%
Surgical Care Improvement Project				
Appropriate VTP Within 24 Hours[5]	0	-	89%	92%
Appropriate Hair Removal[5]	0	-	100%	99%
Appropriate Beta Blocker Usage[5]	0	-	90%	93%
Controlled Postoperative Blood Glucose[5]	0	-	92%	93%
Prophylactic Antibiotic Timing[5]	0	-	96%	97%
Prophylactic Antibiotic Timing (Outpatient)	-	-	93%	92%
Prophylactic Antibiotic Selection[5]	0	-	97%	97%
Prophylactic Antibiotic Select. (Outpatient)	-	-	96%	94%
Prophylactic Antibiotic Stopped[5]	0	-	93%	94%
Recommended VTP Ordered[5]	0	-	91%	94%
Urinary Catheter Removal[5]	0	-	86%	90%
Children's Asthma Care				
Received Systemic Corticosteroids	-	-	-	100%
Received Home Management Plan	-	-	-	71%
Received Reliever Medication	-	-	-	100%
Use of Medical Imaging				
Combination Abdominal CT Scan	-	-	0.365	0.191
Combination Chest CT Scan	-	-	0.065	0.054
Follow-up Mammogram/Ultrasound	-	-	7.3%	8.4%
MRI for Low Back Pain	-	-	34.5%	32.7%
Survey of Patients' Hospital Experiences				
Area Around Room 'Always' Quiet at Night[8]	-	-	-	58%
Doctors 'Always' Communicated Well[8]	-	-	-	80%
Home Recovery Information Given[8]	-	-	-	82%
Hospital Given 9 or 10 on 10 Point Scale[8]	-	-	-	67%
Meds 'Always' Explained Before Given[8]	-	-	-	60%
Nurses 'Always' Communicated Well[8]	-	-	-	76%
Pain 'Always' Well Controlled[8]	-	-	-	69%
Room and Bathroom 'Always' Clean[8]	-	-	-	71%
Timely Help 'Always' Received[8]	-	-	-	64%
Would Definitely Recommend Hospital[8]	-	-	-	69%

Via Christi Hospitals Wichita

929 N St Francis St
Wichita, KS 67214
Phone: 316-268-5000
Fax: 316-291-4570
URL: www.via-christi.org
Type: Acute Care Hospitals
Emergency Services: Yes
Ownership: Voluntary Non-Profit - Church
Beds: 840

Key Personnel:

CEO/President. . . . . Michalene Maringer
Infection Control. . . . . Susan Hendrickson
Pediatric In-Patient Care . . . . Dimitrios E Stephanopoulos, MD, FAAP
Radiology. . . . . Jon Anders MD
Anesthesiology. . . . . Bryan Black, MD
Emergency Room . . . . Cindy Prine
Hemotology Center . . . . Shaker R Dakhil MD, FACP
Patient Relations . . . . Susan Hendriskson

Measure	Cases	This Hosp.	State Avg.	U.S. Avg.
Heart Attack Care				
ACE Inhibitor or ARB for LVSD[2]	50	96%	95%	96%
Aspirin at Arrival[2]	272	99%	98%	99%
Aspirin at Discharge[2]	298	99%	98%	98%
Beta Blocker at Discharge[2]	280	98%	98%	98%
Fibrinolytic Medication Timing[2]	0	-	44%	55%
PCI Within 90 Minutes of Arrival[2]	53	81%	91%	90%
Smoking Cessation Advice[2]	124	100%	99%	99%
Chest Pain/Possible Heart Attack Care				
Aspirin at Arrival[1,3]	6	100%	92%	95%
Median Time to ECG (minutes)[1,3]	6	14	10	8
Median Time to Transfer (minutes)[5]	0	-	60	61
Fibrinolytic Medication Timing[5]	0	-	42%	54%
Heart Failure Care				
ACE Inhibitor or ARB for LVSD[2]	99	90%	91%	94%
Discharge Instructions[2]	265	95%	83%	88%
Evaluation of LVS Function[2]	329	99%	92%	98%
Smoking Cessation Advice[2]	79	100%	94%	98%
Pneumonia Care				
Appropriate Initial Antibiotic[2]	72	86%	87%	92%
Blood Culture Timing[2]	175	94%	96%	96%
Influenza Vaccine[2]	89	80%	87%	91%
Initial Antibiotic Timing[2]	168	93%	95%	95%
Pneumococcal Vaccine[2]	142	79%	88%	93%
Smoking Cessation Advice[2]	90	96%	93%	97%
Surgical Care Improvement Project				
Appropriate VTP Within 24 Hours[2]	292	85%	89%	92%
Appropriate Hair Removal[2]	841	100%	100%	99%
Appropriate Beta Blocker Usage[2]	237	82%	90%	93%
Controlled Postoperative Blood Glucose[2]	151	97%	92%	93%
Prophylactic Antibiotic Timing[2]	557	97%	96%	97%
Prophylactic Antibiotic Timing (Outpatient)	598	97%	93%	92%
Prophylactic Antibiotic Selection[2]	558	97%	97%	97%
Prophylactic Antibiotic Select. (Outpatient)	592	97%	96%	94%
Prophylactic Antibiotic Stopped[2]	533	91%	93%	94%
Recommended VTP Ordered[2]	294	90%	91%	94%
Urinary Catheter Removal[2]	126	78%	86%	90%
Children's Asthma Care				
Received Systemic Corticosteroids	-	-	-	100%
Received Home Management Plan	-	-	-	71%
Received Reliever Medication	-	-	-	100%
Use of Medical Imaging				
Combination Abdominal CT Scan	1,437	0.634	0.365	0.191
Combination Chest CT Scan	781	0.097	0.065	0.054
Follow-up Mammogram/Ultrasound	1,022	8.7%	7.3%	8.4%
MRI for Low Back Pain[1]	2	50.0%	34.5%	32.7%
Survey of Patients' Hospital Experiences				
Area Around Room 'Always' Quiet at Night	300+	46%	-	58%
Doctors 'Always' Communicated Well	300+	74%	-	80%
Home Recovery Information Given	300+	78%	-	82%
Hospital Given 9 or 10 on 10 Point Scale	300+	64%	-	67%
Meds 'Always' Explained Before Given	300+	53%	-	60%
Nurses 'Always' Communicated Well	300+	69%	-	76%
Pain 'Always' Well Controlled	300+	62%	-	69%
Room and Bathroom 'Always' Clean	300+	66%	-	71%
Timely Help 'Always' Received	300+	50%	-	64%
Would Definitely Recommend Hospital	300+	69%	-	69%

NOTE: Hospital profiles are in alphabetical order by state, then city, then hospital within the city; Rankings exclude hospitals with less than 25 cases except for patient surveys which excludes hospitals with less than 100 cases; (a) 100–299 cases; (1) The number of cases is too small to be sure how well a hospital is performing; (2) The hospital indicated that the data submitted for this measure were based on a sample of cases; (3) Data was collected during a shorter time period (fewer quarters) than the maximum possible time for this measure; (4) Suppressed for one or more quarters by CMS; (5) No data is available from the hospital for this measure; (6) Fewer than 100 patients completed the HCAHPS survey. Use these rates with caution, as the number of surveys may be too low to reliably assess hospital performance; (7) Survey results are based on less than 12 months of data; (8) Survey results are not available for this reporting period; (9) No or very few patients were eligible for the HCAHPS survey. The scores shown, if any, reflect a very small number of surveys; (10) A state average was not calculated because too few hospitals in the state submitted data; (11) There were discrepancies in the data collection process; Please refer to the User's Guide for a full explanation of data.

Wesley Medical Center

550 N Hillside St
Wichita, KS 67214
URL: www.wesleymc.com
Type: Acute Care Hospitals
Ownership: Proprietary
Phone: 316-962-2000
Fax: 316-962-7076
Emergency Services: Yes
Beds: 760

Key Personnel:
CEO/President. . . . . David Nevill
Chief of Medical Staff. . . . . Francie Ekengren
Operating Room. . . . . Sue Ebertowski, RN
Pediatric In-Patient Care . . . . Curt Pickert, MD
Radiology. . . . . Richard Ahlstrand, MD
Anesthesiology. . . . . Robert McKay, MD
Emergency Room . . . . Diane Lippolt

Measure	Cases	This Hosp.	State Avg.	U.S. Avg.
Heart Attack Care				
ACE Inhibitor or ARB for LVSD	43	100%	95%	96%
Aspirin at Arrival	252	99%	98%	99%
Aspirin at Discharge	355	100%	98%	98%
Beta Blocker at Discharge	337	100%	98%	98%
Fibrinolytic Medication Timing	0	-	44%	55%
PCI Within 90 Minutes of Arrival	63	94%	91%	90%
Smoking Cessation Advice	134	100%	99%	99%
Chest Pain/Possible Heart Attack Care				
Aspirin at Arrival[3]	0	-	92%	95%
Median Time to ECG (minutes)[3]	0	-	10	8
Median Time to Transfer (minutes)[5]	0	-	60	61
Fibrinolytic Medication Timing[5]	0	-	42%	54%
Heart Failure Care				
ACE Inhibitor or ARB for LVSD	94	100%	91%	94%
Discharge Instructions	216	96%	83%	88%
Evaluation of LVS Function	302	100%	92%	98%
Smoking Cessation Advice	43	100%	94%	98%
Pneumonia Care				
Appropriate Initial Antibiotic[2]	75	97%	87%	92%
Blood Culture Timing[2]	95	98%	96%	96%
Influenza Vaccine[2]	97	100%	87%	91%
Initial Antibiotic Timing[2]	108	95%	95%	95%
Pneumococcal Vaccine[2]	144	99%	88%	93%
Smoking Cessation Advice[2]	64	100%	93%	97%
Surgical Care Improvement Project				
Appropriate VTP Within 24 Hours[2]	296	99%	89%	92%
Appropriate Hair Removal[2]	823	100%	100%	99%
Appropriate Beta Blocker Usage[2]	226	96%	90%	93%
Controlled Postoperative Blood Glucose[2]	168	89%	92%	93%
Prophylactic Antibiotic Timing[2]	540	100%	96%	97%
Prophylactic Antibiotic Timing (Outpatient)	704	97%	93%	92%
Prophylactic Antibiotic Selection[2]	551	99%	97%	97%
Prophylactic Antibiotic Select. (Outpatient)	701	98%	96%	94%
Prophylactic Antibiotic Stopped[2]	503	98%	93%	94%
Recommended VTP Ordered[2]	296	99%	91%	94%
Urinary Catheter Removal[2]	89	97%	86%	90%
Children's Asthma Care				
Received Systemic Corticosteroids	112	99%	-	100%
Received Home Management Plan	111	85%	-	71%
Received Reliever Medication	112	100%	-	100%
Use of Medical Imaging				
Combination Abdominal CT Scan	1,064	0.575	0.365	0.191
Combination Chest CT Scan	477	0.109	0.065	0.054
Follow-up Mammogram/Ultrasound	265	6.0%	7.3%	8.4%
MRI for Low Back Pain	130	31.5%	34.5%	32.7%
Survey of Patients' Hospital Experiences				
Area Around Room 'Always' Quiet at Night	300+	54%	-	58%
Doctors 'Always' Communicated Well	300+	78%	-	80%
Home Recovery Information Given	300+	81%	-	82%
Hospital Given 9 or 10 on 10 Point Scale	300+	62%	-	67%
Meds 'Always' Explained Before Given	300+	53%	-	60%
Nurses 'Always' Communicated Well	300+	69%	-	76%
Pain 'Always' Well Controlled	300+	65%	-	69%
Room and Bathroom 'Always' Clean	300+	61%	-	71%
Timely Help 'Always' Received	300+	53%	-	64%
Would Definitely Recommend Hospital	300+	63%	-	69%

Wichita VA Medical Center

5500 E. Kellog
Wichita, KS 67218
Type: Acute Care-Veterans Administration
Ownership: Government - Federal
Phone: 316-685-2221
Fax: 316-651-3666
Emergency Services: No
Beds: 72

Key Personnel:
CEO/President. . . . . Thomas Sanders, FACHE
Chief of Medical Staff. . . . . Kent Murray, MD
Intensive Care Unit. . . . . Zubair Hassan, MD
Patient Relations . . . . Linda Guhr

Measure	Cases	This Hosp.	State Avg.	U.S. Avg.
Heart Attack Care				
ACE Inhibitor or ARB for LVSD[5]	0	-	95%	96%
Aspirin at Arrival[5]	0	-	98%	99%
Aspirin at Discharge[5]	0	-	98%	98%
Beta Blocker at Discharge[5]	0	-	98%	98%
Fibrinolytic Medication Timing[5]	0	-	44%	55%
PCI Within 90 Minutes of Arrival[5]	0	-	91%	90%
Smoking Cessation Advice[5]	0	-	99%	99%
Chest Pain/Possible Heart Attack Care				
Aspirin at Arrival	-	-	92%	95%
Median Time to ECG (minutes)	-	-	10	8
Median Time to Transfer (minutes)	-	-	60	61
Fibrinolytic Medication Timing	-	-	42%	54%
Heart Failure Care				
ACE Inhibitor or ARB for LVSD	32	100%	91%	94%
Discharge Instructions	74	100%	83%	88%
Evaluation of LVS Function	81	100%	92%	98%
Smoking Cessation Advice[1]	24	100%	94%	98%
Pneumonia Care				
Appropriate Initial Antibiotic	46	93%	87%	92%
Blood Culture Timing	70	100%	96%	96%
Influenza Vaccine	54	98%	87%	91%
Initial Antibiotic Timing	57	96%	95%	95%
Pneumococcal Vaccine	48	100%	88%	93%
Smoking Cessation Advice	37	100%	93%	97%
Surgical Care Improvement Project				
Appropriate VTP Within 24 Hours[2]	69	99%	89%	92%
Appropriate Hair Removal[2]	106	100%	100%	99%
Appropriate Beta Blocker Usage[2]	31	100%	90%	93%
Controlled Postoperative Blood Glucose[2,5]	0	-	92%	93%
Prophylactic Antibiotic Timing	67	99%	96%	97%
Prophylactic Antibiotic Timing (Outpatient)	-	-	93%	92%
Prophylactic Antibiotic Selection	66	100%	97%	97%
Prophylactic Antibiotic Select. (Outpatient)	-	-	96%	94%
Prophylactic Antibiotic Stopped	60	93%	93%	94%
Recommended VTP Ordered[2]	69	99%	91%	94%
Urinary Catheter Removal[1,2]	8	88%	86%	90%
Children's Asthma Care				
Received Systemic Corticosteroids	-	-	-	100%
Received Home Management Plan	-	-	-	71%
Received Reliever Medication	-	-	-	100%
Use of Medical Imaging				
Combination Abdominal CT Scan	-	-	0.365	0.191
Combination Chest CT Scan	-	-	0.065	0.054
Follow-up Mammogram/Ultrasound	-	-	7.3%	8.4%
MRI for Low Back Pain	-	-	34.5%	32.7%
Survey of Patients' Hospital Experiences				
Area Around Room 'Always' Quiet at Night	-	-	-	58%
Doctors 'Always' Communicated Well	-	-	-	80%
Home Recovery Information Given	-	-	-	82%
Hospital Given 9 or 10 on 10 Point Scale	-	-	-	67%
Meds 'Always' Explained Before Given	-	-	-	60%
Nurses 'Always' Communicated Well	-	-	-	76%
Pain 'Always' Well Controlled	-	-	-	69%
Room and Bathroom 'Always' Clean	-	-	-	71%
Timely Help 'Always' Received	-	-	-	64%
Would Definitely Recommend Hospital	-	-	-	69%

Jefferson County Memorial Hospital

408 Delaware St
Winchester, KS 66097
URL: www.jcmhospital.org
Type: Critical Access Hospitals
Ownership: Voluntary Non-Profit - Private
Phone: 913-774-4340
Fax: 913-774-8605
Emergency Services: Yes
Beds: 25

Key Personnel:
CEO/President. . . . . Joye H Huston, RN, M
Chief of Medical Staff. . . . . Larry Campbell

Measure	Cases	This Hosp.	State Avg.	U.S. Avg.
Heart Attack Care				
ACE Inhibitor or ARB for LVSD[5]	0	-	95%	96%
Aspirin at Arrival[5]	0	-	98%	99%
Aspirin at Discharge[5]	0	-	98%	98%
Beta Blocker at Discharge[5]	0	-	98%	98%
Fibrinolytic Medication Timing[5]	0	-	44%	55%
PCI Within 90 Minutes of Arrival[5]	0	-	91%	90%
Smoking Cessation Advice[5]	0	-	99%	99%
Chest Pain/Possible Heart Attack Care				
Aspirin at Arrival	-	-	92%	95%
Median Time to ECG (minutes)	-	-	10	8
Median Time to Transfer (minutes)	-	-	60	61
Fibrinolytic Medication Timing	-	-	42%	54%
Heart Failure Care				
ACE Inhibitor or ARB for LVSD[5]	0	-	91%	94%
Discharge Instructions[5]	0	-	83%	88%
Evaluation of LVS Function[5]	0	-	92%	98%
Smoking Cessation Advice[5]	0	-	94%	98%
Pneumonia Care				
Appropriate Initial Antibiotic[5]	0	-	87%	92%
Blood Culture Timing[5]	0	-	96%	96%
Influenza Vaccine[5]	0	-	87%	91%
Initial Antibiotic Timing[5]	0	-	95%	95%
Pneumococcal Vaccine[5]	0	-	88%	93%
Smoking Cessation Advice[5]	0	-	93%	97%
Surgical Care Improvement Project				
Appropriate VTP Within 24 Hours[5]	0	-	89%	92%
Appropriate Hair Removal[5]	0	-	100%	99%
Appropriate Beta Blocker Usage[5]	0	-	90%	93%
Controlled Postoperative Blood Glucose[5]	0	-	92%	93%
Prophylactic Antibiotic Timing[5]	0	-	96%	97%
Prophylactic Antibiotic Timing (Outpatient)	-	-	93%	92%
Prophylactic Antibiotic Selection[5]	0	-	97%	97%
Prophylactic Antibiotic Select. (Outpatient)	-	-	96%	94%
Prophylactic Antibiotic Stopped[5]	0	-	93%	94%
Recommended VTP Ordered[5]	0	-	91%	94%
Urinary Catheter Removal[5]	0	-	86%	90%
Children's Asthma Care				
Received Systemic Corticosteroids	-	-	-	100%
Received Home Management Plan	-	-	-	71%
Received Reliever Medication	-	-	-	100%
Use of Medical Imaging				
Combination Abdominal CT Scan	-	-	0.365	0.191
Combination Chest CT Scan	-	-	0.065	0.054
Follow-up Mammogram/Ultrasound	-	-	7.3%	8.4%
MRI for Low Back Pain	-	-	34.5%	32.7%
Survey of Patients' Hospital Experiences				
Area Around Room 'Always' Quiet at Night[8]	-	-	-	58%
Doctors 'Always' Communicated Well[8]	-	-	-	80%
Home Recovery Information Given[8]	-	-	-	82%
Hospital Given 9 or 10 on 10 Point Scale[8]	-	-	-	67%
Meds 'Always' Explained Before Given[8]	-	-	-	60%
Nurses 'Always' Communicated Well[8]	-	-	-	76%
Pain 'Always' Well Controlled[8]	-	-	-	69%
Room and Bathroom 'Always' Clean[8]	-	-	-	71%
Timely Help 'Always' Received[8]	-	-	-	64%
Would Definitely Recommend Hospital[8]	-	-	-	69%

NOTE: Hospital profiles are in alphabetical order by state, then city, then hospital within the city; Rankings exclude hospitals with less than 25 cases except for patient surveys which excludes hospitals with less than 100 cases; (a) 100–299 cases; (1) The number of cases is too small to be sure how well a hospital is performing; (2) The hospital indicated that the data submitted for this measure were based on a sample of cases; (3) Data was collected during a shorter time period (fewer quarters) than the maximum possible time for this measure; (4) Suppressed for one or more quarters by CMS; (5) No data is available from the hospital for this measure; (6) Fewer than 100 patients completed the HCAHPS survey. Use these rates with caution, as the number of surveys may be too low to reliably assess hospital performance; (7) Survey results are based on less than 12 months of data; (8) Survey results are not available for this reporting period; (9) No or very few patients were eligible for the HCAHPS survey. The scores shown, if any, reflect a very small number of surveys; (10) A state average was not calculated because too few hospitals in the state submitted data; (11) There were discrepancies in the data collection process; Please refer to the User's Guide for a full explanation of data.

William Newton Hospital

1300 East Fifth Avenue
Winfield, KS 67156
URL: www.wnmh.org
Type: Critical Access Hospitals
Ownership: Government - Local
Phone: 620-221-2300
Fax: 620-221-3594
Emergency Services: Yes
Beds: 25

Key Personnel:
Chief of Medical Staff.......... Tom Embers
Infection Control.............. Linda King, RN
Operating Room.............. Amy Soto, RN
Quality Assurance.............. Jamie Kaiser, RN
Emergency Room .... Greg Faimon, MD
Intensive Care Unit............ Barbara Humpert, RN

Measure	Cases	This Hosp.	State Avg.	U.S. Avg.
Heart Attack Care				
ACE Inhibitor or ARB for LVSD[1]	2	50%	95%	96%
Aspirin at Arrival[1]	6	100%	98%	99%
Aspirin at Discharge[1]	5	100%	98%	98%
Beta Blocker at Discharge[1]	6	100%	98%	98%
Fibrinolytic Medication Timing	0	-	44%	55%
PCI Within 90 Minutes of Arrival	0	-	91%	90%
Smoking Cessation Advice[1]	1	0%	99%	99%
Chest Pain/Possible Heart Attack Care				
Aspirin at Arrival	82	95%	92%	95%
Median Time to ECG (minutes)	84	4	10	8
Median Time to Transfer (minutes)[1]	1	132	60	61
Fibrinolytic Medication Timing[1]	6	17%	42%	54%
Heart Failure Care				
ACE Inhibitor or ARB for LVSD[1]	2	100%	91%	94%
Discharge Instructions[1]	5	60%	83%	88%
Evaluation of LVS Function[1]	15	80%	92%	98%
Smoking Cessation Advice[1]	1	100%	94%	98%
Pneumonia Care				
Appropriate Initial Antibiotic[1]	24	88%	87%	92%
Blood Culture Timing	32	94%	96%	96%
Influenza Vaccine	35	89%	87%	91%
Initial Antibiotic Timing	51	98%	95%	95%
Pneumococcal Vaccine	46	87%	88%	93%
Smoking Cessation Advice[1]	10	90%	93%	97%
Surgical Care Improvement Project				
Appropriate VTP Within 24 Hours[1]	11	73%	89%	92%
Appropriate Hair Removal	74	100%	100%	99%
Appropriate Beta Blocker Usage[5]	0	-	90%	93%
Controlled Postoperative Blood Glucose	0	-	92%	93%
Prophylactic Antibiotic Timing	50	88%	96%	97%
Prophylactic Antibiotic Timing (Outpatient)[1]	21	86%	93%	92%
Prophylactic Antibiotic Selection	51	94%	97%	97%
Prophylactic Antibiotic Select. (Outpatient)[1]	20	95%	96%	94%
Prophylactic Antibiotic Stopped	49	98%	93%	94%
Recommended VTP Ordered[1]	14	71%	91%	94%
Urinary Catheter Removal[1]	3	67%	86%	90%
Children's Asthma Care				
Received Systemic Corticosteroids	-	-	-	100%
Received Home Management Plan	-	-	-	71%
Received Reliever Medication	-	-	-	100%
Use of Medical Imaging				
Combination Abdominal CT Scan	247	0.838	0.365	0.191
Combination Chest CT Scan	249	0.004	0.065	0.054
Follow-up Mammogram/Ultrasound	579	9.8%	7.3%	8.4%
MRI for Low Back Pain	69	37.7%	34.5%	32.7%
Survey of Patients' Hospital Experiences				
Area Around Room 'Always' Quiet at Night	(a)	63%	-	58%
Doctors 'Always' Communicated Well	(a)	84%	-	80%
Home Recovery Information Given	(a)	83%	-	82%
Hospital Given 9 or 10 on 10 Point Scale	(a)	68%	-	67%
Meds 'Always' Explained Before Given	(a)	71%	-	60%
Nurses 'Always' Communicated Well	(a)	81%	-	76%
Pain 'Always' Well Controlled	(a)	74%	-	69%
Room and Bathroom 'Always' Clean	(a)	76%	-	71%
Timely Help 'Always' Received	(a)	70%	-	64%
Would Definitely Recommend Hospital	(a)	72%	-	69%

NOTE: Hospital profiles are in alphabetical order by state, then city, then hospital within the city; Rankings exclude hospitals with less than 25 cases except for patient surveys which excludes hospitals with less than 100 cases; (a) 100–299 cases; (1) The number of cases is too small to be sure how well a hospital is performing; (2) The hospital indicated that the data submitted for this measure were based on a sample of cases; (3) Data was collected during a shorter time period (fewer quarters) than the maximum possible time for this measure; (4) Suppressed for one or more quarters by CMS; (5) No data is available from the hospital for this measure; (6) Fewer than 100 patients completed the HCAHPS survey. Use these rates with caution, as the number of surveys may be too low to reliably assess hospital performance; (7) Survey results are based on less than 12 months of data; (8) Survey results are not available for this reporting period; (9) No or very few patients were eligible for the HCAHPS survey. The scores shown, if any, reflect a very small number of surveys; (10) A state average was not calculated because too few hospitals in the state submitted data; (11) There were discrepancies in the data collection process; Please refer to the User's Guide for a full explanation of data.

Heart Attack Care

1. ACE Inhibitor or ARB for LVSD

Hospital Name	City	Rate	Cases
Crittenton Hospital Medical Center	Rochester	100%	25
Harper University Hospital	Detroit	100%	76
Henry Ford Macomb Hospital	Clinton Twp	100%	85
Mclaren Regional Medical Center[2]	Flint	100%	72
Providence Hospital and Medical Centers	Southfield	100%	83
Saint Joseph Mercy Oakland[2]	Pontiac	100%	69
Sinai-Grace Hospital	Detroit	100%	68
Spectrum Health - Butterworth Campus	Grand Rapids	100%	130
University of Michigan Health System	Ann Arbor	100%	68
William Beaumont Hospital[2]	Royal Oak	100%	107
William Beaumont Hospital-Troy	Troy	100%	84
Edward W Sparrow Hospital	Lansing	99%	70
Oakwood Hospital and Medical Center	Dearborn	99%	240
Mercy Health Partners - Mercy Campus	Muskegon	98%	59
Northern Michigan Regional Hospital	Petoskey	98%	57
Saint Joseph Mercy Hospital	Ann Arbor	98%	104
Henry Ford Hospital	Detroit	97%	158
Munson Medical Center	Traverse City	97%	154
St John Macomb-Oakland Hosp-Macomb Ctr	Warren	97%	66
Bay Regional Medical Center	Bay City	96%	74
Covenant Medical Center	Saginaw	96%	83
Botsford Hospital	Farmington Hills	95%	40
Midmichigan Medical Center-Midland[2]	Midland	95%	57
Saint Mary Mercy Hospital	Livonia	95%	43
Allegiance Health	Jackson	94%	53
Bronson Methodist Hospital	Kalamazoo	94%	69
Mount Clemens Regional Medical Center	Mount Clemens	93%	30
Saint John Hospital and Medical Center	Detroit	93%	101
Battle Creek Health System	Battle Creek	92%	25
Borgess Medical Center[2]	Kalamazoo	92%	53
Port Huron Hospital	Port Huron	92%	76
Saint Mary's of Michigan Medical Center[2]	Saginaw	92%	51
Genesys Regional Med Ctr-Health Park[2]	Grand Blanc	91%	68
Hurley Medical Center	Flint	90%	31
Marquette General Hospital	Marquette	90%	59
Henry Ford Wyandotte Hospital	Wyandotte	88%	33
Ingham Regional Medical Center	Lansing	87%	86
Lakeland Hospital - St Joseph	Saint Joseph	87%	71
Huron Valley-Sinai Hospital	Commerce Twp	86%	29

2. Aspirin at Arrival

Hospital Name	City	Rate	Cases
Battle Creek Health System	Battle Creek	100%	134
Beaumont Hospital - Grosse Pointe	Grosse Pointe	100%	63
Borgess Medical Center[2]	Kalamazoo	100%	98
Botsford Hospital	Farmington Hills	100%	241
Central Michigan Community Hospital	Mount Pleasant	100%	27
Detroit Receiving Hosp & Univ Health Ctr	Detroit	100%	68
Dickinson County Memorial Hospital	Iron Mountain	100%	33
Genesys Regional Med Ctr-Health Park[2]	Grand Blanc	100%	424
Henry Ford Macomb Hospital	Clinton Twp	100%	476
Holland Community Hospital	Holland	100%	105
Marquette General Hospital	Marquette	100%	86
Mercy Health Partners - Mercy Campus	Muskegon	100%	243
Mercy Hospital - Cadillac	Cadillac	100%	51
Metro Health Hospital	Wyoming	100%	140
Midmichigan Medical Center-Midland[2]	Midland	100%	128
Munson Medical Center	Traverse City	100%	430
Northern Michigan Regional Hospital	Petoskey	100%	129
Oakwood Annapolis Hospital	Wayne	100%	116
Oakwood Heritage Hospital	Taylor	100%	32
Oakwood Hospital and Medical Center	Dearborn	100%	581
Port Huron Hospital	Port Huron	100%	239
Saint Joseph Mercy Oakland[2]	Pontiac	100%	253
Saint Joseph Mercy Port Huron	Port Huron	100%	31
University of Michigan Health System	Ann Arbor	100%	246
VA Ann Arbor Healthcare System	Ann Arbor	100%	45
William Beaumont Hospital[2]	Royal Oak	100%	601
William Beaumont Hospital-Troy	Troy	100%	438
Allegiance Health	Jackson	99%	354
Bronson Methodist Hospital	Kalamazoo	99%	278
Edward W Sparrow Hospital	Lansing	99%	266
Harper University Hospital	Detroit	99%	149
Henry Ford Hospital	Detroit	99%	581
Hurley Medical Center	Flint	99%	175
Huron Valley-Sinai Hospital	Commerce Twp	99%	157
Lakeland Hospital - St Joseph	Saint Joseph	99%	332
Mclaren Regional Medical Center[2]	Flint	99%	344
Mount Clemens Regional Medical Center	Mount Clemens	99%	253
Oakwood Southshore Medical Center	Trenton	99%	112
Providence Hospital and Medical Centers	Southfield	99%	254
Saint John Hospital and Medical Center	Detroit	99%	347
St John Macomb-Oakland Hosp-Macomb Ctr	Warren	99%	318
Saint Joseph Mercy Hospital	Ann Arbor	99%	508
Saint Mary Mercy Hospital	Livonia	99%	253
Sinai-Grace Hospital	Detroit	99%	323
Spectrum Health - Butterworth Campus	Grand Rapids	99%	424
Alpena Regional Medical Center	Alpena	98%	47
Covenant Medical Center	Saginaw	98%	369
Crittenton Hospital Medical Center	Rochester	98%	141
Emma L Bixby Medical Center	Adrian	98%	54
Henry Ford West Bloomfield Hospital	West Bloomfield	98%	90
Henry Ford Wyandotte Hospital	Wyandotte	98%	235
Mercy Memorial Hospital System	Monroe	98%	144
Saint Mary's Health Care	Grand Rapids	98%	111
Saint Mary's of Michigan Medical Center[2]	Saginaw	98%	120
Bay Regional Medical Center	Bay City	97%	204
Chippewa County War Memorial Hospital	Sault Ste Marie	97%	37
Garden City Hospital	Garden City	97%	204
Ingham Regional Medical Center	Lansing	97%	226
Mercy Hospital - Grayling	Grayling	97%	34
Poh Medical Center	Pontiac	95%	38
Gratiot Medical Center	Alma	94%	34
Lapeer Regional Medical Center	Lapeer	88%	59

3. Aspirin at Discharge

Hospital Name	City	Rate	Cases
Beaumont Hospital - Grosse Pointe	Grosse Pointe	100%	39
Edward W Sparrow Hospital	Lansing	100%	410
Genesys Regional Med Ctr-Health Park[2]	Grand Blanc	100%	424
Henry Ford Macomb Hospital	Clinton Twp	100%	451
Holland Community Hospital	Holland	100%	73
Lakeland Hospital - St Joseph	Saint Joseph	100%	340
Marquette General Hospital	Marquette	100%	351
Mercy Health Partners - Mercy Campus	Muskegon	100%	365
Munson Medical Center	Traverse City	100%	892
Oakwood Annapolis Hospital	Wayne	100%	85
Oakwood Hospital and Medical Center	Dearborn	100%	939
Saint Mary's Health Care	Grand Rapids	100%	75
Spectrum Health - Butterworth Campus	Grand Rapids	100%	855
University of Michigan Health System	Ann Arbor	100%	351
VA Ann Arbor Healthcare System	Ann Arbor	100%	50
William Beaumont Hospital[2]	Royal Oak	100%	619
William Beaumont Hospital-Troy	Troy	100%	414
Allegiance Health	Jackson	99%	333
Battle Creek Health System	Battle Creek	99%	90
Bay Regional Medical Center	Bay City	99%	318
Borgess Medical Center[2]	Kalamazoo	99%	276
Bronson Methodist Hospital	Kalamazoo	99%	413
Harper University Hospital	Detroit	99%	355
Henry Ford Hospital	Detroit	99%	898
Mclaren Regional Medical Center[2]	Flint	99%	407
Midmichigan Medical Center-Midland[2]	Midland	99%	267
Mount Clemens Regional Medical Center	Mount Clemens	99%	240
Northern Michigan Regional Hospital	Petoskey	99%	356
Providence Hospital and Medical Centers	Southfield	99%	421
Saint Joseph Mercy Oakland[2]	Pontiac	99%	305
Sinai-Grace Hospital	Detroit	99%	285
Covenant Medical Center	Saginaw	98%	452
Crittenton Hospital Medical Center	Rochester	98%	128
Detroit Receiving Hosp & Univ Health Ctr	Detroit	98%	58
Hurley Medical Center	Flint	98%	117
Ingham Regional Medical Center	Lansing	98%	321
Mercy Memorial Hospital System	Monroe	98%	60
Port Huron Hospital	Port Huron	98%	313
Saint John Hospital and Medical Center	Detroit	98%	426
St John Macomb-Oakland Hosp-Macomb Ctr	Warren	98%	301
Saint Joseph Mercy Hospital	Ann Arbor	98%	732
Alpena Regional Medical Center	Alpena	97%	29
Emma L Bixby Medical Center	Adrian	97%	38
Henry Ford Wyandotte Hospital	Wyandotte	97%	170
Metro Health Hospital	Wyoming	97%	116
Oakwood Southshore Medical Center	Trenton	97%	70
Poh Medical Center	Pontiac	97%	33
Huron Valley-Sinai Hospital	Commerce Twp	95%	111
Mercy Hospital - Cadillac	Cadillac	95%	39
Saint Mary Mercy Hospital	Livonia	95%	170
Saint Mary's of Michigan Medical Center[2]	Saginaw	95%	282
Henry Ford West Bloomfield Hospital	West Bloomfield	94%	65
Botsford Hospital	Farmington Hills	90%	157
Garden City Hospital	Garden City	90%	140
Lapeer Regional Medical Center	Lapeer	84%	32

4. Beta Blocker at Discharge

Hospital Name	City	Rate	Cases
Beaumont Hospital - Grosse Pointe	Grosse Pointe	100%	38
Edward W Sparrow Hospital	Lansing	100%	403
Henry Ford Macomb Hospital	Clinton Twp	100%	450
Holland Community Hospital	Holland	100%	77
Mercy Health Partners - Mercy Campus	Muskegon	100%	359
Mercy Memorial Hospital System	Monroe	100%	61
Midmichigan Medical Center-Midland[2]	Midland	100%	268
Mount Clemens Regional Medical Center	Mount Clemens	100%	227
Oakwood Annapolis Hospital	Wayne	100%	83
Oakwood Southshore Medical Center	Trenton	100%	71
Poh Medical Center	Pontiac	100%	35
Saint Joseph Mercy Port Huron	Port Huron	100%	25
Saint Mary's Health Care	Grand Rapids	100%	75
Spectrum Health - Butterworth Campus	Grand Rapids	100%	830
University of Michigan Health System	Ann Arbor	100%	322
VA Ann Arbor Healthcare System	Ann Arbor	100%	48
William Beaumont Hospital[2]	Royal Oak	100%	590
William Beaumont Hospital-Troy	Troy	100%	417
Allegiance Health	Jackson	99%	329
Battle Creek Health System	Battle Creek	99%	94
Borgess Medical Center[2]	Kalamazoo	99%	267
Bronson Methodist Hospital	Kalamazoo	99%	413
Covenant Medical Center	Saginaw	99%	436
Crittenton Hospital Medical Center	Rochester	99%	122
Genesys Regional Med Ctr-Health Park[2]	Grand Blanc	99%	394
Harper University Hospital	Detroit	99%	351
Ingham Regional Medical Center	Lansing	99%	313
Mclaren Regional Medical Center[2]	Flint	99%	408
Metro Health Hospital	Wyoming	99%	110
Munson Medical Center	Traverse City	99%	816
Northern Michigan Regional Hospital	Petoskey	99%	335
Oakwood Hospital and Medical Center	Dearborn	99%	965
Providence Hospital and Medical Centers	Southfield	99%	404
St John Macomb-Oakland Hosp-Macomb Ctr	Warren	99%	291
Saint Joseph Mercy Hospital	Ann Arbor	99%	690
Saint Joseph Mercy Oakland[2]	Pontiac	99%	290
Saint Mary Mercy Hospital	Livonia	99%	188
Detroit Receiving Hosp & Univ Health Ctr	Detroit	98%	61
Emma L Bixby Medical Center	Adrian	98%	42
Henry Ford Hospital	Detroit	98%	884
Lakeland Hospital - St Joseph	Saint Joseph	98%	322
Saint John Hospital and Medical Center	Detroit	98%	430
Saint Mary's of Michigan Medical Center[2]	Saginaw	98%	270
Sinai-Grace Hospital	Detroit	98%	278
Henry Ford West Bloomfield Hospital	West Bloomfield	97%	60
Henry Ford Wyandotte Hospital	Wyandotte	97%	163
Marquette General Hospital	Marquette	97%	337
Port Huron Hospital	Port Huron	97%	312
Alpena Regional Medical Center	Alpena	96%	27
Bay Regional Medical Center	Bay City	96%	310
Garden City Hospital	Garden City	96%	135
Hurley Medical Center	Flint	96%	117
Mercy Hospital - Cadillac	Cadillac	95%	39
Huron Valley-Sinai Hospital	Commerce Twp	94%	113
Lapeer Regional Medical Center	Lapeer	94%	33
Botsford Hospital	Farmington Hills	93%	153

6. PCI Within 90 Minutes of Arrival

Hospital Name	City	Rate	Cases
Henry Ford Hospital	Detroit	100%	36
Henry Ford Macomb Hospital	Clinton Twp	100%	77
Allegiance Health	Jackson	99%	77
William Beaumont Hospital-Troy	Troy	99%	71
Huron Valley-Sinai Hospital	Commerce Twp	98%	45
Mount Clemens Regional Medical Center	Mount Clemens	97%	67
William Beaumont Hospital[2]	Royal Oak	97%	69
Garden City Hospital	Garden City	96%	54
Holland Community Hospital	Holland	96%	26
Providence Hospital and Medical Centers	Southfield	95%	37
Spectrum Health - Butterworth Campus	Grand Rapids	94%	108
University of Michigan Health System	Ann Arbor	94%	64
Mclaren Regional Medical Center[2]	Flint	92%	76
Bay Regional Medical Center	Bay City	91%	53
Saint Joseph Mercy Hospital	Ann Arbor	91%	103
Saint John Hospital and Medical Center	Detroit	90%	72
Saint Joseph Mercy Oakland[2]	Pontiac	90%	48
Ingham Regional Medical Center	Lansing	89%	37
Oakwood Annapolis Hospital	Wayne	89%	28
Oakwood Hospital and Medical Center	Dearborn	89%	84
Saint Mary Mercy Hospital	Livonia	89%	64
Covenant Medical Center	Saginaw	88%	33
Metro Health Hospital	Wyoming	88%	43
Midmichigan Medical Center-Midland[2]	Midland	88%	26
Botsford Hospital	Farmington Hills	86%	29
Oakwood Southshore Medical Center	Trenton	86%	29
Bronson Methodist Hospital	Kalamazoo	85%	72
St John Macomb-Oakland Hosp-Macomb Ctr	Warren	85%	54
Saint Mary's Health Care	Grand Rapids	85%	26
Munson Medical Center	Traverse City	83%	71
Northern Michigan Regional Hospital	Petoskey	83%	29
Genesys Regional Med Ctr-Health Park[2]	Grand Blanc	82%	62
Lakeland Hospital - St Joseph	Saint Joseph	82%	40
Edward W Sparrow Hospital	Lansing	81%	36
Mercy Health Partners - Mercy Campus	Muskegon	80%	54
Port Huron Hospital	Port Huron	76%	50
Sinai-Grace Hospital	Detroit	76%	33
Henry Ford Wyandotte Hospital	Wyandotte	73%	44
Hurley Medical Center	Flint	72%	29

NOTE: Hospital profiles are in alphabetical order by state, then city, then hospital within the city; Rankings exclude hospitals with less than 25 cases except for patient surveys which excludes hospitals with less than 100 cases; (a) 100–299 cases; (1) The number of cases is too small to be sure how well a hospital is performing; (2) The hospital indicated that the data submitted for this measure were based on a sample of cases; (3) Data was collected during a shorter time period (fewer quarters) than the maximum possible time for this measure; (4) Suppressed for one or more quarters by CMS; (5) No data is available from the hospital for this measure; (6) Fewer than 100 patients completed the HCAHPS survey. Use these rates with caution, as the number of surveys may be too low to reliably assess hospital performance; (7) Survey results are based on less than 12 months of data; (8) Survey results are not available for this reporting period; (9) No or very few patients were eligible for the HCAHPS survey. The scores shown, if any, reflect a very small number of surveys; (10) A state average was not calculated because too few hospitals in the state submitted data; (11) There were discrepancies in the data collection process; Please refer to the User's Guide for a full explanation of data.

7. Smoking Cessation Advice

Hospital Name	City	Rate	Cases
Battle Creek Health System	Battle Creek	100%	25
Bay Regional Medical Center	Bay City	100%	132
Borgess Medical Center[2]	Kalamazoo	100%	119
Botsford Hospital	Farmington Hills	100%	34
Bronson Methodist Hospital	Kalamazoo	100%	151
Covenant Medical Center	Saginaw	100%	151
Crittenton Hospital Medical Center	Rochester	100%	38
Edward W Sparrow Hospital	Lansing	100%	146
Garden City Hospital	Garden City	100%	46
Genesys Regional Med Ctr-Health Park[2]	Grand Blanc	100%	154
Harper University Hospital	Detroit	100%	144
Henry Ford Hospital	Detroit	100%	310
Henry Ford Macomb Hospital	Clinton Twp	100%	137
Henry Ford Wyandotte Hospital	Wyandotte	100%	69
Hurley Medical Center	Flint	100%	65
Huron Valley-Sinai Hospital	Commerce Twp	100%	34
Lakeland Hospital - St Joseph	Saint Joseph	100%	119
Mclaren Regional Medical Center[2]	Flint	100%	144
Mercy Health Partners - Mercy Campus	Muskegon	100%	147
Metro Health Hospital	Wyoming	100%	43
Munson Medical Center	Traverse City	100%	304
Northern Michigan Regional Hospital	Petoskey	100%	126
Oakwood Annapolis Hospital	Wayne	100%	37
Oakwood Hospital and Medical Center	Dearborn	100%	338
Oakwood Southshore Medical Center	Trenton	100%	27
Port Huron Hospital	Port Huron	100%	106
Providence Hospital and Medical Centers	Southfield	100%	120
St John Macomb-Oakland Hosp-Macomb Ctr	Warren	100%	108
Saint Joseph Mercy Hospital	Ann Arbor	100%	200
Saint Joseph Mercy Oakland[2]	Pontiac	100%	96
Saint Mary Mercy Hospital	Livonia	100%	33
Saint Mary's Health Care	Grand Rapids	100%	33
University of Michigan Health System	Ann Arbor	100%	121
William Beaumont Hospital[2]	Royal Oak	100%	143
William Beaumont Hospital-Troy	Troy	100%	120
Allegiance Health	Jackson	99%	108
Saint John Hospital and Medical Center	Detroit	99%	158
Saint Mary's of Michigan Medical Center[2]	Saginaw	99%	103
Spectrum Health - Butterworth Campus	Grand Rapids	99%	310
Ingham Regional Medical Center	Lansing	98%	121
Marquette General Hospital	Marquette	98%	122
Midmichigan Medical Center-Midland[2]	Midland	98%	98
Mount Clemens Regional Medical Center	Mount Clemens	96%	102
Sinai-Grace Hospital	Detroit	96%	113

Chest Pain/Possible Heart Attack Care

8. Aspirin at Arrival

Hospital Name	City	Rate	Cases
Bronson Vicksburg Hospital[3]	Vicksburg	100%	34
Carson City Hospital	Carson City	100%	130
Detroit Receiving Hosp & Univ Health Ctr	Detroit	100%	626
Henry Ford Hospital	Detroit	100%	69
Mercy Hospital - Cadillac	Cadillac	100%	75
North Ottawa Community Hospital	Grand Haven	100%	43
Portage Health Hospital	Hancock	100%	46
Providence Hospital and Medical Centers	Southfield	100%	36
Saint John River District Hospital	East China	100%	46
Saint Joseph Mercy Port Huron	Port Huron	100%	33
Saint Mary's Standish Community Hospital[3]	Standish	100%	49
Spectrum Health - Reed City Campus	Reed City	100%	83
Spectrum Hlth United Mem-Kelsey Campus	Lakeview	100%	68
Zeeland Community Hospital	Zeeland	100%	51
Central Michigan Community Hospital	Mount Pleasant	99%	92
Chippewa County War Memorial Hospital	Sault Ste Marie	99%	105
Memorial Medical Center of West Michigan	Ludington	99%	78
Midmichigan Medical Center-Gladwin[3]	Gladwin	99%	75
South Haven Community Hospital	South Haven	99%	121
Spectrum Health Gerber Memorial	Fremont	99%	126
Spectrum Health United Mem-United Campus	Greenville	99%	110
Alpena Regional Medical Center	Alpena	98%	108
Chelsea Community Hospital	Chelsea	98%	89
Gratiot Medical Center	Alma	98%	95
Henry Ford Macomb Hospital	Clinton Twp	98%	51
Huron Medical Center	Bad Axe	98%	105
Mercy Hospital - Grayling	Grayling	98%	190
Oaklawn Hospital	Marshall	98%	320
Battle Creek Health System	Battle Creek	97%	115
Garden City Hospital	Garden City	97%	86
Holland Community Hospital	Holland	97%	36
Lapeer Regional Medical Center	Lapeer	97%	77
Mecosta County Medical Center	Big Rapids	97%	138
Mercy Memorial Hospital System	Monroe	97%	73
Pennock Hospital	Hastings	97%	60
Saint Francis Hospital	Escanaba	97%	132
Tawas Saint Joseph Hospital	Tawas City	97%	289
Dickinson County Memorial Hospital	Iron Mountain	96%	94
Hillsdale Community Health Center	Hillsdale	96%	50
Marlette Regional Hospital	Marlette	96%	79
Memorial Healthcare	Owosso	96%	150
Otsego Memorial Hospital	Gaylord	96%	157
St John Macomb-Oakland Hosp-Macomb Ctr	Warren	96%	77
Botsford Hospital	Farmington Hills	95%	39
Community Health Center of Branch County	Coldwater	95%	234
Doctor's Hospital of Michigan	Pontiac	95%	38
Midmichigan Medical Center-Clare	Clare	95%	100
Saint John Hospital and Medical Center	Detroit	95%	101
West Shore Medical Center	Manistee	95%	63
Harper University Hospital	Detroit	94%	35
Huron Valley-Sinai Hospital	Commerce Twp	94%	36
Three Rivers Health	Three Rivers	94%	152
West Branch Regional Medical Center	West Branch	94%	153
Community Hospital	Watervliet	93%	112
Hills & Dales General Hospital	Cass City	92%	36
McKenzie Memorial Hospital	Sandusky	92%	75
Oakwood Southshore Medical Center	Trenton	92%	63
Henry Ford Wyandotte Hospital	Wyandotte	91%	225
Oakwood Annapolis Hospital	Wayne	91%	56
Poh Medical Center	Pontiac	91%	91
Beaumont Hospital - Grosse Pointe	Grosse Pointe	89%	27
Mercy Health Partners - Hackley Campus	Muskegon	89%	45
Oakwood Heritage Hospital	Taylor	89%	101
Saint Mary Mercy Hospital	Livonia	89%	124
Eaton Rapids Medical Center	Eaton Rapids	88%	68
Emma L Bixby Medical Center	Adrian	85%	197
Sinai-Grace Hospital	Detroit	85%	27
Oakwood Hospital and Medical Center	Dearborn	84%	90
Saint Joseph Mercy Livingston Hospital	Howell	75%	367
Saint Joseph Mercy Saline Hospital	Saline	75%	272
William Beaumont Hospital-Troy	Troy	54%	26
Saint Joseph Mercy Hospital	Ann Arbor	48%	50

9. Median Time to ECG (minutes)

Hospital Name	City	Min.	Cases
Oakwood Annapolis Hospital	Wayne	0	58
Saint John River District Hospital	East China	2	48
Bronson Vicksburg Hospital[3]	Vicksburg	3	37
Lapeer Regional Medical Center	Lapeer	3	78
Oakwood Hospital and Medical Center	Dearborn	4	94
Garden City Hospital	Garden City	5	87
Gratiot Medical Center	Alma	5	100
Mercy Hospital - Grayling	Grayling	5	194
Poh Medical Center	Pontiac	5	95
Spectrum Health - Reed City Campus	Reed City	5	83
Botsford Hospital	Farmington Hills	6	40
Huron Valley-Sinai Hospital	Commerce Twp	6	37
Mercy Health Partners - Hackley Campus	Muskegon	6	47
Mercy Memorial Hospital System	Monroe	6	78
North Ottawa Community Hospital	Grand Haven	6	45
Oakwood Southshore Medical Center	Trenton	6	66
Portage Health Hospital	Hancock	6	46
Spectrum Health United Mem-United Campus	Greenville	6	113
Central Michigan Community Hospital	Mount Pleasant	7	95
McKenzie Memorial Hospital	Sandusky	7	77
Saint John Hospital and Medical Center	Detroit	7	107
Henry Ford Wyandotte Hospital	Wyandotte	8	236
Memorial Medical Center of West Michigan	Ludington	8	80
Otsego Memorial Hospital	Gaylord	8	162
Providence Hospital and Medical Centers	Southfield	8	37
William Beaumont Hospital-Troy	Troy	8	28
Alpena Regional Medical Center	Alpena	9	113
Chelsea Community Hospital	Chelsea	9	95
Holland Community Hospital	Holland	9	38
Midmichigan Medical Center-Gladwin[3]	Gladwin	9	76
Oaklawn Hospital	Marshall	9	333
Oakwood Heritage Hospital	Taylor	9	108
Saint Joseph Mercy Livingston Hospital	Howell	9	369
South Haven Community Hospital	South Haven	9	128
Spectrum Hlth United Mem-Kelsey Campus	Lakeview	9	73
Tawas Saint Joseph Hospital	Tawas City	9	298
West Branch Regional Medical Center	West Branch	9	166
Beaumont Hospital - Grosse Pointe	Grosse Pointe	10	26
Community Health Center of Branch County	Coldwater	10	243
Dickinson County Memorial Hospital	Iron Mountain	10	97
Hillsdale Community Health Center	Hillsdale	10	54
Huron Medical Center	Bad Axe	10	113
Mecosta County Medical Center	Big Rapids	10	146
Mercy Hospital - Cadillac	Cadillac	10	74
Pennock Hospital	Hastings	10	61
Saint Joseph Mercy Saline Hospital	Saline	10	275
Saint Mary Mercy Hospital	Livonia	10	129
Sinai-Grace Hospital	Detroit	10	29
Spectrum Health Gerber Memorial	Fremont	10	130
West Shore Medical Center	Manistee	10	66
Community Hospital	Watervliet	11	117
Emma L Bixby Medical Center	Adrian	11	202
Henry Ford Hospital	Detroit	11	71
Marlette Regional Hospital	Marlette	11	82
Zeeland Community Hospital	Zeeland	11	53
Doctor's Hospital of Michigan	Pontiac	12	38
Memorial Healthcare	Owosso	12	154
Saint Joseph Mercy Hospital	Ann Arbor	12	43
Carson City Hospital	Carson City	13	131
Chippewa County War Memorial Hospital	Sault Ste Marie	13	107
Saint Joseph Mercy Port Huron	Port Huron	13	32
Harper University Hospital	Detroit	14	34
Saint Francis Hospital	Escanaba	14	144
St John Macomb-Oakland Hosp-Macomb Ctr	Warren	14	79
Detroit Receiving Hosp & Univ Health Ctr	Detroit	15	663
Hills & Dales General Hospital	Cass City	15	38
Midmichigan Medical Center-Clare	Clare	15	104
Battle Creek Health System	Battle Creek	16	118
Eaton Rapids Medical Center	Eaton Rapids	16	78
Henry Ford Macomb Hospital	Clinton Twp	16	57
Saint Mary's Standish Community Hospital[3]	Standish	16	52
Three Rivers Health	Three Rivers	18	164

10. Median Time to Transfer (minutes)

Hospital Name	City	Min.	Cases
Detroit Receiving Hosp & Univ Health Ctr	Detroit	28	78
Lapeer Regional Medical Center	Lapeer	35	32

Heart Failure Care

12. ACE Inhibitor or ARB for LVSD

Hospital Name	City	Rate	Cases
Henry Ford Macomb Hospital[2]	Clinton Twp	100%	78
Holland Community Hospital	Holland	100%	36
Mercy Health Partners - Hackley Campus	Muskegon	100%	42
Mercy Memorial Hospital System	Monroe	100%	81
Oakwood Heritage Hospital	Taylor	100%	51
Pennock Hospital	Hastings	100%	28
William Beaumont Hospital-Troy[2]	Troy	100%	156
Battle Creek Health System	Battle Creek	99%	117
Genesys Regional Med Ctr-Health Park[2]	Grand Blanc	99%	137
Hurley Medical Center[2]	Flint	99%	133
Providence Hospital and Medical Centers	Southfield	99%	422
Saint Mary's Health Care	Grand Rapids	99%	83
University of Michigan Health System	Ann Arbor	99%	289
Bronson Methodist Hospital	Kalamazoo	98%	149
Covenant Medical Center	Saginaw	98%	228
Crittenton Hospital Medical Center	Rochester	98%	130
Emma L Bixby Medical Center	Adrian	98%	48
Marquette General Hospital	Marquette	98%	41
Mercy Health Partners - Mercy Campus	Muskegon	98%	94
Oakwood Hospital and Medical Center	Dearborn	98%	475
Saint John Hospital and Medical Center[2]	Detroit	98%	288
Spectrum Health - Butterworth Campus	Grand Rapids	98%	350
William Beaumont Hospital[2]	Royal Oak	98%	369
Beaumont Hospital - Grosse Pointe	Grosse Pointe	97%	135
Central Michigan Community Hospital	Mount Pleasant	97%	31
Lakeland Hospital - St Joseph	Saint Joseph	97%	179
Northern Michigan Regional Hospital	Petoskey	97%	119
Port Huron Hospital	Port Huron	97%	103
St John Macomb-Oakland Hosp-Macomb Ctr	Warren	97%	320
Saint Joseph Mercy Livingston Hospital	Howell	97%	31
Saint Joseph Mercy Port Huron	Port Huron	97%	31
West Branch Regional Medical Center	West Branch	97%	35
Detroit (John D. Dingell) VA Medical Center	Detroit	96%	82
Harper University Hospital	Detroit	96%	257
Midmichigan Medical Center-Midland[2]	Midland	96%	69
Saint Francis Hospital	Escanaba	96%	28
Saint Joseph Mercy Oakland[2]	Pontiac	96%	109
Detroit Receiving Hosp & Univ Health Ctr	Detroit	95%	277
Edward W Sparrow Hospital	Lansing	95%	191
Metro Health Hospital	Wyoming	95%	61
Poh Medical Center[2]	Pontiac	95%	80
VA Ann Arbor Healthcare System	Ann Arbor	95%	57
Allegiance Health	Jackson	94%	124
Chippewa County War Memorial Hospital	Sault Ste Marie	94%	33
Mercy Hospital - Cadillac	Cadillac	94%	33
Munson Medical Center	Traverse City	94%	145
Oakwood Southshore Medical Center	Trenton	94%	95
Saint Joseph Mercy Hospital	Ann Arbor	94%	276
Henry Ford Wyandotte Hospital	Wyandotte	93%	199
Huron Valley-Sinai Hospital	Commerce Twp	93%	100
Lapeer Regional Medical Center	Lapeer	93%	45
Mclaren Regional Medical Center[2]	Flint	93%	262
Botsford Hospital	Farmington Hills	92%	170
Garden City Hospital	Garden City	92%	85
Oakwood Annapolis Hospital	Wayne	92%	109
Saint Mary Mercy Hospital	Livonia	92%	146
Saint Mary's of Michigan Medical Center[2]	Saginaw	92%	102
Henry Ford Hospital[2]	Detroit	91%	172
Sinai-Grace Hospital	Detroit	91%	440
Alpena Regional Medical Center	Alpena	90%	61
Borgess Medical Center[2]	Kalamazoo	90%	71
Bay Regional Medical Center	Bay City	88%	174

NOTE: Hospital profiles are in alphabetical order by state, then city, then hospital within the city; Rankings exclude hospitals with less than 25 cases except for patient surveys which excludes hospitals with less than 100 cases; (a) 100–299 cases; (1) The number of cases is too small to be sure how well a hospital is performing; (2) The hospital indicated that the data submitted for this measure were based on a sample of cases; (3) Data was collected during a shorter time period (fewer quarters) than the maximum possible time for this measure; (4) Suppressed for one or more quarters by CMS; (5) No data is available from the hospital for this measure; (6) Fewer than 100 patients completed the HCAHPS survey. Use these rates with caution, as the number of surveys may be too low to reliably assess hospital performance; (7) Survey results are based on less than 12 months of data; (8) Survey results are not available for this reporting period; (9) No or very few patients were eligible for the HCAHPS survey. The scores shown, if any, reflect a very small number of surveys; (10) A state average was not calculated because too few hospitals in the state submitted data; (11) There were discrepancies in the data collection process; Please refer to the User's Guide for a full explanation of data.

Hospital Name	City	Rate	Cases
Mercy Hospital - Grayling	Grayling	87%	38
Ingham Regional Medical Center	Lansing	83%	190
Gratiot Medical Center	Alma	82%	38
Hillsdale Community Health Center	Hillsdale	82%	38
Henry Ford West Bloomfield Hospital	West Bloomfield	81%	97
Mount Clemens Regional Medical Center	Mount Clemens	81%	167
Midmichigan Medical Center-Clare	Clare	80%	41

13. Discharge Instructions

Hospital Name	City	Rate	Cases
Bronson Lakeview Hospital	Paw Paw	100%	37
Community Health Center of Branch County	Coldwater	100%	82
Detroit Receiving Hosp & Univ Health Ctr	Detroit	100%	521
Huron Medical Center	Bad Axe	100%	29
Saginaw VA Medical Center	Saginaw	100%	33
Saint John River District Hospital	East China	100%	61
Bay Regional Medical Center	Bay City	99%	502
Botsford Hospital	Farmington Hills	99%	462
Spectrum Health United Mem-United Campus	Greenville	99%	68
Tawas Saint Joseph Hospital	Tawas City	99%	73
University of Michigan Health System	Ann Arbor	99%	710
William Beaumont Hospital-Troy[2]	Troy	99%	506
Allegan General Hospital	Allegan	98%	59
Central Michigan Community Hospital	Mount Pleasant	98%	84
Genesys Regional Med Ctr-Health Park[2]	Grand Blanc	98%	394
Midmichigan Medical Center-Gladwin	Gladwin	98%	47
Pennock Hospital	Hastings	98%	97
VA Ann Arbor Healthcare System	Ann Arbor	98%	140
Beaumont Hospital - Grosse Pointe	Grosse Pointe	97%	326
Iron Mountain VA Medical Center	Iron Mountain	97%	39
Mercy Health Partners - Mercy Campus	Muskegon	97%	212
Oakwood Heritage Hospital	Taylor	97%	99
Zeeland Community Hospital	Zeeland	97%	60
Chelsea Community Hospital	Chelsea	96%	49
Dickinson County Memorial Hospital	Iron Mountain	96%	67
Mercy Health Partners - Hackley Campus	Muskegon	96%	79
Mercy Hospital - Grayling	Grayling	96%	81
Portage Health Hospital	Hancock	96%	47
Saint Mary Mercy Hospital	Livonia	96%	353
Spectrum Health Gerber Memorial	Fremont	96%	51
Oakwood Southshore Medical Center	Trenton	95%	230
Otsego Memorial Hospital	Gaylord	95%	56
St John Macomb-Oakland Hosp-Macomb Ctr	Warren	95%	850
Saint Joseph Mercy Hospital	Ann Arbor	95%	654
Saint Joseph Mercy Livingston Hospital	Howell	95%	96
Bronson Methodist Hospital	Kalamazoo	94%	497
Chippewa County War Memorial Hospital	Sault Ste Marie	94%	82
Clinton Memorial Hospital	Saint Johns	94%	36
Eaton Rapids Medical Center	Eaton Rapids	94%	31
Henry Ford Macomb Hospital[2]	Clinton Twp	94%	271
Mercy Hospital - Cadillac	Cadillac	94%	102
Mercy Memorial Hospital System	Monroe	94%	191
Oaklawn Hospital	Marshall	94%	69
Saint Joseph Mercy Oakland[2]	Pontiac	94%	255
West Branch Regional Medical Center	West Branch	94%	128
Lakeland Hospital - St Joseph	Saint Joseph	93%	403
Munson Medical Center	Traverse City	93%	482
Saint John Hospital and Medical Center[2]	Detroit	93%	662
Saint Mary's Health Care	Grand Rapids	93%	258
Three Rivers Health	Three Rivers	93%	58
William Beaumont Hospital[2]	Royal Oak	93%	1063
Carson City Hospital	Carson City	92%	26
Herrick Memorial Hospital	Tecumseh	92%	36
Holland Community Hospital	Holland	92%	88
Ingham Regional Medical Center	Lansing	92%	463
Oakwood Annapolis Hospital	Wayne	92%	270
Oakwood Hospital and Medical Center	Dearborn	92%	1053
Saint Francis Hospital	Escanaba	92%	86
Spectrum Health - Reed City Campus	Reed City	92%	26
Sturgis Hospital	Sturgis	92%	50
Crittenton Hospital Medical Center	Rochester	91%	287
Saint Joseph Mercy Port Huron	Port Huron	91%	108
South Haven Community Hospital	South Haven	91%	44
Garden City Hospital	Garden City	90%	321
Memorial Medical Center of West Michigan	Ludington	90%	48
Emma L Bixby Medical Center	Adrian	89%	90
Mecosta County Medical Center	Big Rapids	89%	55
Spectrum Health - Butterworth Campus	Grand Rapids	89%	904
Harper University Hospital	Detroit	88%	676
Hurley Medical Center[2]	Flint	88%	336
North Ottawa Community Hospital	Grand Haven	88%	34
Port Huron Hospital	Port Huron	88%	265
Providence Hospital and Medical Centers	Southfield	88%	1022
Sinai-Grace Hospital	Detroit	88%	887
Allegiance Health	Jackson	87%	341
Northern Michigan Regional Hospital	Petoskey	87%	244
Huron Valley-Sinai Hospital	Commerce Twp	86%	276
Henry Ford Hospital[2]	Detroit	85%	354
Marquette General Hospital	Marquette	85%	140
Memorial Healthcare	Owosso	85%	53
Alpena Regional Medical Center	Alpena	84%	152
Battle Creek Health System	Battle Creek	84%	381
Borgess Medical Center[2]	Kalamazoo	83%	228
Borgess-Lee Memorial Hospital	Dowagiac	83%	47
Covenant Medical Center	Saginaw	83%	573
Mclaren Regional Medical Center[2]	Flint	83%	655
Community Hospital	Watervliet	82%	38
Henry Ford Wyandotte Hospital	Wyandotte	82%	560
Midmichigan Medical Center-Midland[2]	Midland	82%	218
Lapeer Regional Medical Center	Lapeer	81%	155
Edward W Sparrow Hospital	Lansing	80%	467
Doctor's Hospital of Michigan	Pontiac	78%	89
Saint Mary's of Michigan Medical Center[2]	Saginaw	77%	249
Midmichigan Medical Center-Clare	Clare	76%	131
Detroit (John D. Dingell) VA Medical Center	Detroit	75%	148
Metro Health Hospital	Wyoming	72%	159
Gratiot Medical Center	Alma	71%	155
Marlette Regional Hospital	Marlette	65%	31
Hillsdale Community Health Center	Hillsdale	64%	66
Henry Ford West Bloomfield Hospital	West Bloomfield	62%	225
Mount Clemens Regional Medical Center	Mount Clemens	50%	406
Northstar Health System	Iron River	50%	32
West Shore Medical Center	Manistee	42%	38
Poh Medical Center[2]	Pontiac	39%	192

14. Evaluation of LVS Function

Hospital Name	City	Rate	Cases
Allegan General Hospital	Allegan	100%	75
Allegiance Health	Jackson	100%	430
Aspirus Grand View Hospital	Ironwood	100%	40
Battle Creek Health System	Battle Creek	100%	449
Beaumont Hospital - Grosse Pointe	Grosse Pointe	100%	375
Bronson Lakeview Hospital	Paw Paw	100%	38
Central Michigan Community Hospital	Mount Pleasant	100%	112
Chelsea Community Hospital	Chelsea	100%	63
Chippewa County War Memorial Hospital	Sault Ste Marie	100%	96
Clinton Memorial Hospital	Saint Johns	100%	46
Community Health Center of Branch County	Coldwater	100%	98
Detroit (John D. Dingell) VA Medical Center	Detroit	100%	155
Detroit Receiving Hosp & Univ Health Ctr	Detroit	100%	578
Genesys Regional Med Ctr-Health Park[2]	Grand Blanc	100%	464
Gratiot Medical Center	Alma	100%	224
Harper University Hospital	Detroit	100%	786
Hayes Green Beach Memorial Hospital	Charlotte	100%	27
Henry Ford Macomb Hospital[2]	Clinton Twp	100%	338
Holland Community Hospital	Holland	100%	120
Mercy Health Partners - Hackley Campus	Muskegon	100%	101
Mercy Hospital - Cadillac	Cadillac	100%	120
Mercy Hospital - Grayling	Grayling	100%	98
Mercy Memorial Hospital System	Monroe	100%	280
Metro Health Hospital	Wyoming	100%	195
Midmichigan Medical Center-Gladwin	Gladwin	100%	66
Munson Medical Center	Traverse City	100%	536
North Ottawa Community Hospital	Grand Haven	100%	49
Oaklawn Hospital	Marshall	100%	85
Oakwood Heritage Hospital	Taylor	100%	167
Oakwood Hospital and Medical Center	Dearborn	100%	1263
Pennock Hospital	Hastings	100%	107
Poh Medical Center[2]	Pontiac	100%	221
Providence Hospital and Medical Centers	Southfield	100%	1248
Saginaw VA Medical Center	Saginaw	100%	41
Saint Joseph Mercy Livingston Hospital	Howell	100%	131
Saint Joseph Mercy Port Huron	Port Huron	100%	146
Saint Joseph Mercy Saline Hospital	Saline	100%	34
Saint Mary Mercy Hospital	Livonia	100%	517
Saint Mary's Health Care	Grand Rapids	100%	310
Saint Mary's of Michigan Medical Center[2]	Saginaw	100%	301
Spectrum Health - Butterworth Campus	Grand Rapids	100%	1066
Spectrum Health - Reed City Campus	Reed City	100%	35
Spectrum Health Gerber Memorial	Fremont	100%	61
Spectrum Health United Mem-United Campus	Greenville	100%	96
University of Michigan Health System	Ann Arbor	100%	800
VA Ann Arbor Healthcare System	Ann Arbor	100%	151
West Shore Medical Center	Manistee	100%	49
William Beaumont Hospital[2]	Royal Oak	100%	1306
William Beaumont Hospital-Troy[2]	Troy	100%	616
Zeeland Community Hospital	Zeeland	100%	70
Borgess Medical Center[2]	Kalamazoo	99%	279
Bronson Methodist Hospital	Kalamazoo	99%	579
Covenant Medical Center	Saginaw	99%	701
Crittenton Hospital Medical Center	Rochester	99%	368
Dickinson County Memorial Hospital	Iron Mountain	99%	100
Emma L Bixby Medical Center	Adrian	99%	117
Henry Ford Hospital[2]	Detroit	99%	396
Henry Ford Wyandotte Hospital	Wyandotte	99%	672
Lakeland Hospital - St Joseph	Saint Joseph	99%	498
Memorial Healthcare	Owosso	99%	82
Mercy Health Partners - Mercy Campus	Muskegon	99%	246
Midmichigan Medical Center-Midland[2]	Midland	99%	262
Northern Michigan Regional Hospital	Petoskey	99%	274
Oakwood Annapolis Hospital	Wayne	99%	337
Oakwood Southshore Medical Center	Trenton	99%	287
Saint John Hospital and Medical Center[2]	Detroit	99%	763
St John Macomb-Oakland Hosp-Macomb Ctr	Warren	99%	1048
Saint John River District Hospital	East China	99%	93
Saint Joseph Mercy Hospital	Ann Arbor	99%	791
Saint Joseph Mercy Oakland[2]	Pontiac	99%	298
Sinai-Grace Hospital	Detroit	99%	1042
Tawas Saint Joseph Hospital	Tawas City	99%	88
Borgess-Lee Memorial Hospital	Dowagiac	98%	52
Edward W Sparrow Hospital	Lansing	98%	559
Henry Ford West Bloomfield Hospital	West Bloomfield	98%	281
Herrick Memorial Hospital	Tecumseh	98%	42
Huron Medical Center	Bad Axe	98%	46
Huron Valley-Sinai Hospital	Commerce Twp	98%	350
Iron Mountain VA Medical Center	Iron Mountain	98%	53
Lapeer Regional Medical Center	Lapeer	98%	193
Mount Clemens Regional Medical Center	Mount Clemens	98%	494
Port Huron Hospital	Port Huron	98%	325
Portage Health Hospital	Hancock	98%	62
Alpena Regional Medical Center	Alpena	97%	197
Botsford Hospital	Farmington Hills	97%	612
Eaton Rapids Medical Center	Eaton Rapids	97%	29
Ingham Regional Medical Center	Lansing	97%	516
Sturgis Hospital	Sturgis	97%	60
West Branch Regional Medical Center	West Branch	97%	152
Bay Regional Medical Center	Bay City	96%	601
Garden City Hospital	Garden City	96%	401
Hurley Medical Center[2]	Flint	96%	362
Mclaren Regional Medical Center[2]	Flint	96%	770
Midmichigan Medical Center-Clare	Clare	96%	151
Carson City Hospital	Carson City	95%	37
Otsego Memorial Hospital	Gaylord	95%	66
Saint Francis Hospital	Escanaba	95%	106
Three Rivers Health	Three Rivers	95%	80
Marquette General Hospital	Marquette	94%	171
South Haven Community Hospital	South Haven	94%	50
Memorial Medical Center of West Michigan	Ludington	93%	57
Mecosta County Medical Center	Big Rapids	92%	63
Hillsdale Community Health Center	Hillsdale	90%	88
Marlette Regional Hospital	Marlette	85%	33
Doctor's Hospital of Michigan	Pontiac	83%	103
Saint Mary's Standish Community Hospital[3]	Standish	81%	32
Northstar Health System	Iron River	80%	45
Community Hospital	Watervliet	68%	41

15. Smoking Cessation Advice

Hospital Name	City	Rate	Cases
Allegiance Health	Jackson	100%	84
Alpena Regional Medical Center	Alpena	100%	26
Battle Creek Health System	Battle Creek	100%	118
Beaumont Hospital - Grosse Pointe	Grosse Pointe	100%	70
Bronson Methodist Hospital	Kalamazoo	100%	103
Covenant Medical Center	Saginaw	100%	124
Crittenton Hospital Medical Center	Rochester	100%	43
Detroit (John D. Dingell) VA Medical Center	Detroit	100%	31
Detroit Receiving Hosp & Univ Health Ctr	Detroit	100%	237
Edward W Sparrow Hospital	Lansing	100%	120
Garden City Hospital	Garden City	100%	71
Genesys Regional Med Ctr-Health Park[2]	Grand Blanc	100%	88
Gratiot Medical Center	Alma	100%	25
Harper University Hospital	Detroit	100%	193
Henry Ford Macomb Hospital[2]	Clinton Twp	100%	37
Henry Ford Wyandotte Hospital	Wyandotte	100%	115
Huron Valley-Sinai Hospital	Commerce Twp	100%	57
Ingham Regional Medical Center	Lansing	100%	79
Lakeland Hospital - St Joseph	Saint Joseph	100%	110
Marquette General Hospital	Marquette	100%	31
Mercy Health Partners - Hackley Campus	Muskegon	100%	30
Mercy Health Partners - Mercy Campus	Muskegon	100%	51
Mercy Memorial Hospital System	Monroe	100%	54
Metro Health Hospital	Wyoming	100%	36
Northern Michigan Regional Hospital	Petoskey	100%	40
Oakwood Annapolis Hospital	Wayne	100%	83
Oakwood Heritage Hospital	Taylor	100%	33
Oakwood Hospital and Medical Center	Dearborn	100%	292
Oakwood Southshore Medical Center	Trenton	100%	38
Saint Joseph Mercy Hospital	Ann Arbor	100%	90
Saint Joseph Mercy Oakland[2]	Pontiac	100%	53
Saint Joseph Mercy Port Huron	Port Huron	100%	30
Saint Mary Mercy Hospital	Livonia	100%	44
Saint Mary's Health Care	Grand Rapids	100%	67
Spectrum Health - Butterworth Campus	Grand Rapids	100%	160
University of Michigan Health System	Ann Arbor	100%	104
West Branch Regional Medical Center	West Branch	100%	26
William Beaumont Hospital[2]	Royal Oak	100%	177
William Beaumont Hospital-Troy[2]	Troy	100%	70
Bay Regional Medical Center	Bay City	99%	81
Henry Ford Hospital[2]	Detroit	99%	102
Hurley Medical Center[2]	Flint	99%	132

NOTE: Hospital profiles are in alphabetical order by state, then city, then hospital within the city; Rankings exclude hospitals with less than 25 cases except for patient surveys which excludes hospitals with less than 100 cases; (a) 100–299 cases; (1) The number of cases is too small to be sure how well a hospital is performing; (2) The hospital indicated that the data submitted for this measure were based on a sample of cases; (3) Data was collected during a shorter time period (fewer quarters) than the maximum possible time for this measure; (4) Suppressed for one or more quarters by CMS; (5) No data is available from the hospital for this measure; (6) Fewer than 100 patients completed the HCAHPS survey. Use these rates with caution, as the number of surveys may be too low to reliably assess hospital performance; (7) Survey results are based on less than 12 months of data; (8) Survey results are not available for this reporting period; (9) No or very few patients were eligible for the HCAHPS survey. The scores shown, if any, reflect a very small number of surveys; (10) A state average was not calculated because too few hospitals in the state submitted data; (11) There were discrepancies in the data collection process; Please refer to the User's Guide for a full explanation of data.

Hospital Name	City	Rate	Cases
Mclaren Regional Medical Center[2]	Flint	99%	118
Munson Medical Center	Traverse City	99%	73
Providence Hospital and Medical Centers	Southfield	99%	159
Saint John Hospital and Medical Center[2]	Detroit	99%	162
St John Macomb-Oakland Hosp-Macomb Ctr	Warren	99%	177
Borgess Medical Center[2]	Kalamazoo	98%	46
Botsford Hospital	Farmington Hills	98%	112
Sinai-Grace Hospital	Detroit	98%	396
Midmichigan Medical Center-Clare	Clare	97%	36
Saint Mary's of Michigan Medical Center[2]	Saginaw	97%	63
Mount Clemens Regional Medical Center	Mount Clemens	96%	77
VA Ann Arbor Healthcare System	Ann Arbor	96%	26
Midmichigan Medical Center-Midland[2]	Midland	94%	49
Port Huron Hospital	Port Huron	91%	55
Poh Medical Center[2]	Pontiac	77%	77

Pneumonia Care

16. Appropriate Initial Antibiotic

Hospital Name	City	Rate	Cases
Hayes Green Beach Memorial Hospital	Charlotte	100%	42
Munson Medical Center	Traverse City	100%	228
Otsego Memorial Hospital	Gaylord	100%	59
Saint Joseph Mercy Saline Hospital	Saline	100%	51
Spectrum Hlth United Mem-Kelsey Campus	Lakeview	100%	26
Zeeland Community Hospital	Zeeland	100%	44
Central Michigan Community Hospital	Mount Pleasant	99%	131
Chippewa County War Memorial Hospital	Sault Ste Marie	99%	86
Harper University Hospital	Detroit	99%	71
Holland Community Hospital	Holland	99%	138
Aspirus Grand View Hospital	Ironwood	98%	54
Bronson Lakeview Hospital	Paw Paw	98%	60
Detroit Receiving Hosp & Univ Health Ctr	Detroit	98%	98
Metro Health Hospital[2]	Wyoming	98%	90
Oaklawn Hospital	Marshall	98%	80
Pennock Hospital	Hastings	98%	86
Providence Hospital and Medical Centers	Southfield	98%	409
South Haven Community Hospital	South Haven	98%	44
Spectrum Health - Reed City Campus	Reed City	98%	52
West Shore Medical Center	Manistee	98%	43
Clinton Memorial Hospital	Saint Johns	97%	33
Dickinson County Memorial Hospital	Iron Mountain	97%	73
Huron Valley-Sinai Hospital	Commerce Twp	97%	117
Mclaren Regional Medical Center[2]	Flint	97%	215
Mercy Health Partners - Hackley Campus	Muskegon	97%	133
Oakwood Heritage Hospital	Taylor	97%	144
Oakwood Southshore Medical Center	Trenton	97%	209
Saint Mary's Health Care	Grand Rapids	97%	195
Sinai-Grace Hospital	Detroit	97%	183
Spectrum Health - Butterworth Campus	Grand Rapids	97%	600
Herrick Memorial Hospital	Tecumseh	96%	45
Mercy Hospital - Grayling[2]	Grayling	96%	93
Oakwood Hospital and Medical Center[2]	Dearborn	96%	370
Port Huron Hospital	Port Huron	96%	189
Saginaw VA Medical Center	Saginaw	96%	28
Saint John Hospital and Medical Center	Detroit	96%	267
St John Macomb-Oakland Hosp-Macomb Ctr	Warren	96%	387
Spectrum Health Gerber Memorial	Fremont	96%	92
Alpena Regional Medical Center	Alpena	95%	95
Battle Creek Health System	Battle Creek	95%	223
Henry Ford Macomb Hospital	Clinton Twp	95%	315
Lakeland Hospital - St Joseph	Saint Joseph	95%	234
Mercy Memorial Hospital System	Monroe	95%	162
Midmichigan Medical Center-Gladwin	Gladwin	95%	38
Saint John River District Hospital	East China	95%	78
Saint Joseph Mercy Oakland[2]	Pontiac	95%	84
Spectrum Health United Mem-United Campus	Greenville	95%	107
Tawas Saint Joseph Hospital	Tawas City	95%	95
William Beaumont Hospital-Troy[2]	Troy	95%	147
Beaumont Hospital - Grosse Pointe	Grosse Pointe	94%	177
Bronson Methodist Hospital	Kalamazoo	94%	260
Community Hospital	Watervliet	94%	66
Gratiot Medical Center	Alma	94%	109
Mercy Hospital - Cadillac[2]	Cadillac	94%	97
Oakwood Annapolis Hospital	Wayne	94%	163
William Beaumont Hospital[2]	Royal Oak	94%	86
Allegiance Health[2]	Jackson	93%	99
Community Health Center of Branch County	Coldwater	93%	105
Edward W Sparrow Hospital	Lansing	93%	305
Henry Ford Wyandotte Hospital	Wyandotte	93%	292
Memorial Medical Center of West Michigan	Ludington	93%	57
Mercy Health Partners - Mercy Campus	Muskegon	93%	119
Midmichigan Medical Center-Midland[2]	Midland	93%	87
Northern Michigan Regional Hospital	Petoskey	93%	83
Northstar Health System	Iron River	93%	28
Saint Mary's of Michigan Medical Center[2]	Saginaw	93%	46
University of Michigan Health System	Ann Arbor	93%	203
Borgess Medical Center[2]	Kalamazoo	92%	53
Botsford Hospital	Farmington Hills	92%	115
Chelsea Community Hospital	Chelsea	92%	72
Detroit (John D. Dingell) VA Medical Center	Detroit	92%	52
Lapeer Regional Medical Center	Lapeer	92%	190
Carson City Hospital	Carson City	91%	45
Garden City Hospital	Garden City	91%	170
Henry Ford Hospital[2]	Detroit	91%	64
Huron Medical Center	Bad Axe	91%	33
Saint Mary Mercy Hospital	Livonia	91%	205
Three Rivers Health	Three Rivers	91%	46
West Branch Regional Medical Center	West Branch	91%	81
Bay Regional Medical Center	Bay City	90%	136
Covenant Medical Center	Saginaw	90%	224
Emma L Bixby Medical Center[2]	Adrian	90%	62
Genesys Regional Med Ctr-Health Park[2]	Grand Blanc	90%	96
Ingham Regional Medical Center	Lansing	90%	233
Marlette Regional Hospital	Marlette	90%	68
North Ottawa Community Hospital	Grand Haven	90%	50
Hillsdale Community Health Center	Hillsdale	89%	114
Memorial Healthcare	Owosso	89%	91
Midmichigan Medical Center-Clare	Clare	89%	76
Mount Clemens Regional Medical Center	Mount Clemens	89%	184
Portage Health Hospital	Hancock	89%	28
Saint Joseph Mercy Livingston Hospital	Howell	89%	103
Crittenton Hospital Medical Center	Rochester	88%	121
Mecosta County Medical Center	Big Rapids	88%	72
Poh Medical Center[2]	Pontiac	88%	88
Saint Francis Hospital	Escanaba	88%	81
Saint Joseph Mercy Hospital	Ann Arbor	88%	285
Sturgis Hospital	Sturgis	88%	50
Ionia County Memorial Hospital	Ionia	87%	31
Saint Joseph Mercy Port Huron	Port Huron	87%	78
VA Ann Arbor Healthcare System	Ann Arbor	87%	47
Henry Ford West Bloomfield Hospital	West Bloomfield	83%	119
Marquette General Hospital	Marquette	82%	57
Hurley Medical Center[2]	Flint	81%	121
Allegan General Hospital	Allegan	79%	43
Doctor's Hospital of Michigan	Pontiac	79%	33
Borgess-Lee Memorial Hospital	Dowagiac	78%	36

17. Blood Culture Timing

Hospital Name	City	Rate	Cases
Gratiot Medical Center	Alma	100%	91
Huron Medical Center	Bad Axe	100%	60
Lapeer Regional Medical Center	Lapeer	100%	252
Mercy Hospital - Grayling[2]	Grayling	100%	132
Saint John River District Hospital	East China	100%	85
Saint Joseph Mercy Oakland[2]	Pontiac	100%	77
Saint Mary's Health Care	Grand Rapids	100%	330
Spectrum Hlth United Mem-Kelsey Campus	Lakeview	100%	27
Zeeland Community Hospital	Zeeland	100%	112
Aspirus Grand View Hospital	Ironwood	99%	87
Battle Creek Health System	Battle Creek	99%	367
Detroit (John D. Dingell) VA Medical Center	Detroit	99%	74
Dickinson County Memorial Hospital	Iron Mountain	99%	86
Hayes Green Beach Memorial Hospital	Charlotte	99%	67
Holland Community Hospital	Holland	99%	250
Marquette General Hospital	Marquette	99%	99
Mercy Memorial Hospital System	Monroe	99%	278
North Ottawa Community Hospital	Grand Haven	99%	88
Oakwood Heritage Hospital	Taylor	99%	297
Saint Joseph Mercy Port Huron	Port Huron	99%	125
Allegiance Health[2]	Jackson	98%	124
Alpena Regional Medical Center	Alpena	98%	129
Beaumont Hospital - Grosse Pointe	Grosse Pointe	98%	202
Community Health Center of Branch County	Coldwater	98%	121
Detroit Receiving Hosp & Univ Health Ctr	Detroit	98%	333
Harper University Hospital	Detroit	98%	177
Herrick Memorial Hospital	Tecumseh	98%	62
Lakeland Hospital - St Joseph	Saint Joseph	98%	296
Mecosta County Medical Center	Big Rapids	98%	93
Munson Medical Center	Traverse City	98%	386
Oaklawn Hospital	Marshall	98%	93
Oakwood Annapolis Hospital	Wayne	98%	268
St John Macomb-Oakland Hosp-Macomb Ctr	Warren	98%	454
Saint Mary Mercy Hospital	Livonia	98%	313
Spectrum Health Gerber Memorial	Fremont	98%	132
Spectrum Health United Mem-United Campus	Greenville	98%	186
University of Michigan Health System	Ann Arbor	98%	324
Bay Regional Medical Center	Bay City	97%	159
Central Michigan Community Hospital	Mount Pleasant	97%	179
Chelsea Community Hospital	Chelsea	97%	99
Henry Ford Macomb Hospital	Clinton Twp	97%	476
Henry Ford Wyandotte Hospital	Wyandotte	97%	419
Hurley Medical Center[2]	Flint	97%	109
Memorial Medical Center of West Michigan	Ludington	97%	120
Mercy Health Partners - Hackley Campus	Muskegon	97%	214
Mercy Health Partners - Mercy Campus	Muskegon	97%	193
Midmichigan Medical Center-Midland[2]	Midland	97%	145
Northern Michigan Regional Hospital	Petoskey	97%	129
Oakwood Southshore Medical Center	Trenton	97%	269
Pennock Hospital	Hastings	97%	104
Spectrum Health - Butterworth Campus	Grand Rapids	97%	1062
Sturgis Hospital	Sturgis	97%	59
Allegan General Hospital	Allegan	96%	56
Borgess Medical Center[2]	Kalamazoo	96%	91
Borgess-Lee Memorial Hospital	Dowagiac	96%	28
Chippewa County War Memorial Hospital	Sault Ste Marie	96%	114
Doctor's Hospital of Michigan	Pontiac	96%	46
Garden City Hospital	Garden City	96%	260
Huron Valley-Sinai Hospital	Commerce Twp	96%	212
Iron Mountain VA Medical Center	Iron Mountain	96%	27
Mclaren Regional Medical Center[2]	Flint	96%	103
Metro Health Hospital[2]	Wyoming	96%	194
Midmichigan Medical Center-Gladwin	Gladwin	96%	45
Oakwood Hospital and Medical Center[2]	Dearborn	96%	285
Providence Hospital and Medical Centers	Southfield	96%	526
Saint Mary's Standish Community Hospital	Standish	96%	49
South Haven Community Hospital	South Haven	96%	50
William Beaumont Hospital[2]	Royal Oak	96%	121
William Beaumont Hospital-Troy[2]	Troy	96%	165
Botsford Hospital	Farmington Hills	95%	294
Otsego Memorial Hospital	Gaylord	95%	80
Poh Medical Center[2]	Pontiac	95%	84
Port Huron Hospital	Port Huron	95%	261
Portage Health Hospital	Hancock	95%	37
Saint John Hospital and Medical Center	Detroit	95%	205
Saint Joseph Mercy Livingston Hospital	Howell	95%	110
VA Ann Arbor Healthcare System	Ann Arbor	95%	78
Edward W Sparrow Hospital	Lansing	94%	404
Genesys Regional Med Ctr-Health Park[2]	Grand Blanc	94%	171
Mercy Hospital - Cadillac[2]	Cadillac	94%	151
Mount Clemens Regional Medical Center	Mount Clemens	94%	277
West Branch Regional Medical Center	West Branch	94%	118
Bronson Lakeview Hospital	Paw Paw	93%	61
Henry Ford Hospital[2]	Detroit	93%	188
Midmichigan Medical Center-Clare	Clare	93%	59
Saint Francis Hospital	Escanaba	93%	139
Saint Mary's of Michigan Medical Center[2]	Saginaw	93%	99
Spectrum Health - Reed City Campus	Reed City	93%	85
Tawas Saint Joseph Hospital	Tawas City	93%	144
Three Rivers Health	Three Rivers	93%	58
Bronson Methodist Hospital	Kalamazoo	92%	349
Carson City Hospital	Carson City	92%	37
Emma L Bixby Medical Center[2]	Adrian	92%	96
Saint Joseph Mercy Hospital	Ann Arbor	92%	137
Covenant Medical Center	Saginaw	91%	400
West Shore Medical Center	Manistee	90%	31
Clinton Memorial Hospital	Saint Johns	89%	37
Hillsdale Community Health Center	Hillsdale	89%	111
Sinai-Grace Hospital	Detroit	89%	446
Northstar Health System	Iron River	87%	77
Memorial Healthcare	Owosso	86%	127
Henry Ford West Bloomfield Hospital	West Bloomfield	84%	219
Ingham Regional Medical Center	Lansing	84%	196
Crittenton Hospital Medical Center	Rochester	83%	165
Community Hospital	Watervliet	82%	61
Marlette Regional Hospital	Marlette	78%	59

18. Influenza Vaccine

Hospital Name	City	Rate	Cases
Aspirus Grand View Hospital	Ironwood	100%	36
Bronson Lakeview Hospital	Paw Paw	100%	44
Chelsea Community Hospital	Chelsea	100%	59
Mercy Hospital - Cadillac[2]	Cadillac	100%	82
Munson Medical Center	Traverse City	100%	219
Oaklawn Hospital	Marshall	100%	59
Oakwood Annapolis Hospital	Wayne	100%	154
Oakwood Heritage Hospital	Taylor	100%	168
Saint Mary's Standish Community Hospital	Standish	100%	32
Spectrum Health Gerber Memorial	Fremont	100%	69
Spectrum Health United Mem-United Campus	Greenville	100%	114
Holland Community Hospital	Holland	99%	163
Mercy Hospital - Grayling[2]	Grayling	99%	72
Metro Health Hospital[2]	Wyoming	99%	77
Dickinson County Memorial Hospital	Iron Mountain	98%	62
Harper University Hospital	Detroit	98%	100
Lapeer Regional Medical Center	Lapeer	98%	127
Mercy Memorial Hospital System	Monroe	98%	160
Pennock Hospital	Hastings	98%	56
St John Macomb-Oakland Hosp-Macomb Ctr	Warren	98%	442
Saint John River District Hospital	East China	98%	80
Saint Joseph Mercy Port Huron	Port Huron	98%	83
Battle Creek Health System	Battle Creek	97%	235
Hayes Green Beach Memorial Hospital	Charlotte	97%	32
Henry Ford Wyandotte Hospital	Wyandotte	97%	307
Oakwood Southshore Medical Center	Trenton	97%	188
Saint Francis Hospital	Escanaba	97%	104
Sturgis Hospital	Sturgis	97%	37
Tawas Saint Joseph Hospital	Tawas City	97%	74
William Beaumont Hospital[2]	Royal Oak	97%	116
William Beaumont Hospital-Troy[2]	Troy	97%	154

NOTE: Hospital profiles are in alphabetical order by state, then city, then hospital within the city; Rankings exclude hospitals with less than 25 cases except for patient surveys which excludes hospitals with less than 100 cases; (a) 100–299 cases; (1) The number of cases is too small to be sure how well a hospital is performing; (2) The hospital indicated that the data submitted for this measure were based on a sample of cases; (3) Data was collected during a shorter time period (fewer quarters) than the maximum possible time for this measure; (4) Suppressed for one or more quarters by CMS; (5) No data is available from the hospital for this measure; (6) Fewer than 100 patients completed the HCAHPS survey. Use these rates with caution, as the number of surveys may be too low to reliably assess hospital performance; (7) Survey results are based on less than 12 months of data; (8) Survey results are not available for this reporting period; (9) No or very few patients were eligible for the HCAHPS survey. The scores shown, if any, reflect a very small number of surveys; (10) A state average was not calculated because too few hospitals in the state submitted data; (11) There were discrepancies in the data collection process; Please refer to the User's Guide for a full explanation of data.

Clinton Memorial Hospital	Saint Johns	96%	27
Detroit (John D. Dingell) VA Medical Center	Detroit	96%	47
Otsego Memorial Hospital	Gaylord	96%	46
Spectrum Health - Butterworth Campus	Grand Rapids	96%	631
Spectrum Health - Reed City Campus	Reed City	96%	27
Zeeland Community Hospital	Zeeland	96%	57
Allegiance Health[2]	Jackson	95%	87
Bronson Methodist Hospital	Kalamazoo	95%	148
Central Michigan Community Hospital	Mount Pleasant	95%	116
Detroit Receiving Hosp & Univ Health Ctr	Detroit	95%	142
Mercy Health Partners - Mercy Campus	Muskegon	95%	113
Providence Hospital and Medical Centers	Southfield	95%	386
Saint Mary's Health Care	Grand Rapids	95%	209
Community Health Center of Branch County	Coldwater	94%	67
Community Hospital	Watervliet	94%	36
Lakeland Hospital - St Joseph	Saint Joseph	94%	247
North Ottawa Community Hospital	Grand Haven	94%	50
Saint John Hospital and Medical Center	Detroit	94%	271
Saint Mary Mercy Hospital	Livonia	94%	266
South Haven Community Hospital	South Haven	94%	31
Beaumont Hospital - Grosse Pointe	Grosse Pointe	93%	168
Emma L Bixby Medical Center[2]	Adrian	93%	75
Genesys Regional Med Ctr-Health Park[2]	Grand Blanc	93%	164
Memorial Healthcare	Owosso	93%	76
Mercy Health Partners - Hackley Campus	Muskegon	93%	86
Midmichigan Medical Center-Clare	Clare	93%	55
Port Huron Hospital	Port Huron	93%	169
Chippewa County War Memorial Hospital	Sault Ste Marie	92%	53
Memorial Medical Center of West Michigan	Ludington	92%	50
Northern Michigan Regional Hospital	Petoskey	92%	106
Poh Medical Center[2]	Pontiac	92%	64
Sinai-Grace Hospital	Detroit	92%	212
Covenant Medical Center	Saginaw	91%	369
Crittenton Hospital Medical Center	Rochester	91%	129
Henry Ford Macomb Hospital	Clinton Twp	91%	293
Saint Joseph Mercy Livingston Hospital	Howell	91%	81
West Branch Regional Medical Center	West Branch	90%	58
Botsford Hospital	Farmington Hills	89%	124
Doctor's Hospital of Michigan	Pontiac	89%	28
Huron Valley-Sinai Hospital	Commerce Twp	89%	124
Saint Joseph Mercy Saline Hospital	Saline	89%	46
Gratiot Medical Center	Alma	88%	105
Mclaren Regional Medical Center[2]	Flint	88%	225
Saint Joseph Mercy Oakland[2]	Pontiac	88%	83
University of Michigan Health System	Ann Arbor	88%	268
Alpena Regional Medical Center	Alpena	87%	101
Carson City Hospital	Carson City	87%	31
Ingham Regional Medical Center	Lansing	87%	166
Mecosta County Medical Center	Big Rapids	87%	62
Midmichigan Medical Center-Midland[2]	Midland	87%	78
Borgess Medical Center[2]	Kalamazoo	86%	72
Garden City Hospital	Garden City	86%	139
Herrick Memorial Hospital	Tecumseh	86%	42
Hurley Medical Center[2]	Flint	86%	80
Edward W Sparrow Hospital	Lansing	85%	366
Marquette General Hospital	Marquette	85%	94
VA Ann Arbor Healthcare System	Ann Arbor	85%	54
Mount Clemens Regional Medical Center	Mount Clemens	82%	202
Oakwood Hospital and Medical Center	Dearborn	82%	347
West Shore Medical Center	Manistee	82%	38
Allegan General Hospital	Allegan	81%	47
Bay Regional Medical Center	Bay City	81%	140
Huron Medical Center	Bad Axe	81%	27
Saint Mary's of Michigan Medical Center[2]	Saginaw	81%	81
Henry Ford Hospital[2]	Detroit	79%	101
Saint Joseph Mercy Hospital	Ann Arbor	78%	412
Northstar Health System	Iron River	74%	68
Three Rivers Health	Three Rivers	71%	28
Henry Ford West Bloomfield Hospital	West Bloomfield	62%	123
Marlette Regional Hospital	Marlette	61%	38
Hillsdale Community Health Center	Hillsdale	52%	90

19. Initial Antibiotic Timing

Hospital Name	City	Rate	Cases
Aspirus Grand View Hospital	Ironwood	100%	79
Hayes Green Beach Memorial Hospital	Charlotte	100%	59
Holland Community Hospital	Holland	100%	232
Huron Medical Center	Bad Axe	100%	52
Mercy Health Partners - Hackley Campus	Muskegon	100%	203
North Ottawa Community Hospital	Grand Haven	100%	80
Portage Health Hospital	Hancock	100%	44
Saint John River District Hospital	East China	100%	96
Saint Mary's Standish Community Hospital	Standish	100%	46
Spectrum Health United Mem-United Campus	Greenville	100%	165
Beaumont Hospital - Grosse Pointe	Grosse Pointe	99%	243
Bronson Lakeview Hospital	Paw Paw	99%	79
Huron Valley-Sinai Hospital	Commerce Twp	99%	192
Mecosta County Medical Center	Big Rapids	99%	75
Metro Health Hospital[2]	Wyoming	99%	159
Munson Medical Center	Traverse City	99%	318
Otsego Memorial Hospital	Gaylord	99%	76
Saint Joseph Mercy Port Huron	Port Huron	99%	133
Saint Mary's Health Care	Grand Rapids	99%	362
Spectrum Health Gerber Memorial	Fremont	99%	118
Battle Creek Health System	Battle Creek	98%	337
Central Michigan Community Hospital	Mount Pleasant	98%	181
Chippewa County War Memorial Hospital	Sault Ste Marie	98%	126
Clinton Memorial Hospital	Saint Johns	98%	40
Detroit Receiving Hosp & Univ Health Ctr	Detroit	98%	315
Dickinson County Memorial Hospital	Iron Mountain	98%	90
Gratiot Medical Center	Alma	98%	160
Mercy Health Partners - Mercy Campus	Muskegon	98%	176
Mercy Hospital - Cadillac[2]	Cadillac	98%	128
Mercy Memorial Hospital System	Monroe	98%	257
Saint Joseph Mercy Saline Hospital	Saline	98%	66
Tawas Saint Joseph Hospital	Tawas City	98%	133
Zeeland Community Hospital	Zeeland	98%	100
Allegan General Hospital	Allegan	97%	64
Alpena Regional Medical Center	Alpena	97%	126
Bay Regional Medical Center	Bay City	97%	241
Covenant Medical Center	Saginaw	97%	448
Henry Ford Wyandotte Hospital	Wyandotte	97%	519
Lapeer Regional Medical Center	Lapeer	97%	231
Marquette General Hospital	Marquette	97%	97
Memorial Medical Center of West Michigan	Ludington	97%	97
Mercy Hospital - Grayling[2]	Grayling	97%	132
Oaklawn Hospital	Marshall	97%	118
Oakwood Heritage Hospital	Taylor	97%	286
Oakwood Southshore Medical Center	Trenton	97%	325
Providence Hospital and Medical Centers	Southfield	97%	656
Saginaw VA Medical Center	Saginaw	97%	36
Saint Francis Hospital	Escanaba	97%	119
Saint Mary Mercy Hospital	Livonia	97%	433
Sinai-Grace Hospital	Detroit	97%	396
Spectrum Health - Butterworth Campus	Grand Rapids	97%	948
Spectrum Health - Reed City Campus	Reed City	97%	73
West Shore Medical Center	Manistee	97%	63
Borgess-Lee Memorial Hospital	Dowagiac	96%	45
Botsford Hospital	Farmington Hills	96%	250
Chelsea Community Hospital	Chelsea	96%	83
Community Health Center of Branch County	Coldwater	96%	128
Crittenton Hospital Medical Center	Rochester	96%	191
Detroit (John D. Dingell) VA Medical Center	Detroit	96%	67
Emma L Bixby Medical Center[2]	Adrian	96%	96
Garden City Hospital	Garden City	96%	258
Memorial Healthcare	Owosso	96%	122
Northstar Health System	Iron River	96%	78
St John Macomb-Oakland Hosp-Macomb Ctr	Warren	96%	634
Saint Joseph Mercy Livingston Hospital	Howell	96%	142
Saint Mary's of Michigan Medical Center[2]	Saginaw	96%	83
South Haven Community Hospital	South Haven	96%	54
Three Rivers Health	Three Rivers	96%	56
University of Michigan Health System	Ann Arbor	96%	403
Allegiance Health[2]	Jackson	95%	140
Bronson Methodist Hospital	Kalamazoo	95%	384
Henry Ford Macomb Hospital	Clinton Twp	95%	497
Mount Clemens Regional Medical Center	Mount Clemens	95%	288
Oakwood Annapolis Hospital	Wayne	95%	294
Pennock Hospital	Hastings	95%	115
Saint John Hospital and Medical Center	Detroit	95%	449
Sturgis Hospital	Sturgis	95%	77
VA Ann Arbor Healthcare System	Ann Arbor	95%	81
West Branch Regional Medical Center	West Branch	95%	106
William Beaumont Hospital[2]	Royal Oak	95%	177
Genesys Regional Med Ctr-Health Park[2]	Grand Blanc	94%	211
Henry Ford West Bloomfield Hospital	West Bloomfield	94%	213
Midmichigan Medical Center-Clare	Clare	94%	109
Midmichigan Medical Center-Gladwin	Gladwin	94%	53
Midmichigan Medical Center-Midland[2]	Midland	94%	121
Oakwood Hospital and Medical Center	Dearborn	94%	572
Poh Medical Center[2]	Pontiac	94%	113
Saint Joseph Mercy Hospital	Ann Arbor	94%	512
Saint Joseph Mercy Oakland[2]	Pontiac	94%	126
Borgess Medical Center[2]	Kalamazoo	93%	116
Carson City Hospital	Carson City	93%	46
Edward W Sparrow Hospital	Lansing	93%	500
William Beaumont Hospital-Troy[2]	Troy	93%	230
Harper University Hospital	Detroit	92%	169
Henry Ford Hospital[2]	Detroit	92%	135
Herrick Memorial Hospital	Tecumseh	92%	64
Ingham Regional Medical Center	Lansing	92%	274
Lakeland Hospital - St Joseph	Saint Joseph	92%	373
Community Hospital	Watervliet	91%	66
Port Huron Hospital	Port Huron	91%	279
Hurley Medical Center[2]	Flint	90%	179
Ionia County Memorial Hospital	Ionia	90%	29
Mclaren Regional Medical Center[2]	Flint	90%	346
Northern Michigan Regional Hospital	Petoskey	90%	125
Marlette Regional Hospital	Marlette	89%	79
Schoolcraft Memorial Hospital	Manistique	89%	27
Doctor's Hospital of Michigan	Pontiac	86%	50
Hillsdale Community Health Center	Hillsdale	85%	134

20. Pneumococcal Vaccine

Hospital Name	City	Rate	Cases
Aspirus Grand View Hospital	Ironwood	100%	68
Chelsea Community Hospital	Chelsea	100%	82
Harper University Hospital	Detroit	100%	109
Holland Community Hospital	Holland	100%	228
Iron Mountain VA Medical Center	Iron Mountain	100%	30
Midmichigan Medical Center-Gladwin	Gladwin	100%	41
Munson Medical Center	Traverse City	100%	342
Oakwood Annapolis Hospital	Wayne	100%	186
Oakwood Heritage Hospital	Taylor	100%	207
Pennock Hospital	Hastings	100%	93
Saint Mary's Standish Community Hospital	Standish	100%	40
Spectrum Health United Mem-United Campus	Greenville	100%	149
Zeeland Community Hospital	Zeeland	100%	100
Battle Creek Health System	Battle Creek	99%	275
Central Michigan Community Hospital	Mount Pleasant	99%	165
Chippewa County War Memorial Hospital	Sault Ste Marie	99%	105
Memorial Healthcare	Owosso	99%	92
Mercy Memorial Hospital System	Monroe	99%	217
Metro Health Hospital[2]	Wyoming	99%	101
St John Macomb-Oakland Hosp-Macomb Ctr	Warren	99%	600
Saint John River District Hospital	East China	99%	95
Spectrum Health - Butterworth Campus	Grand Rapids	99%	822
William Beaumont Hospital[2]	Royal Oak	99%	154
Bronson Lakeview Hospital	Paw Paw	98%	59
Community Health Center of Branch County	Coldwater	98%	93
Genesys Regional Med Ctr-Health Park[2]	Grand Blanc	98%	200
Hayes Green Beach Memorial Hospital	Charlotte	98%	50
Lapeer Regional Medical Center	Lapeer	98%	206
Mercy Hospital - Cadillac[2]	Cadillac	98%	117
North Ottawa Community Hospital	Grand Haven	98%	63
Oaklawn Hospital	Marshall	98%	90
South Haven Community Hospital	South Haven	98%	45
Spectrum Health - Reed City Campus	Reed City	98%	60
Spectrum Health Gerber Memorial	Fremont	98%	100
William Beaumont Hospital-Troy[2]	Troy	98%	219
Allegiance Health[2]	Jackson	97%	125
Detroit (John D. Dingell) VA Medical Center	Detroit	97%	36
Detroit Receiving Hosp & Univ Health Ctr	Detroit	97%	115
Herrick Memorial Hospital	Tecumseh	97%	58
Huron Valley-Sinai Hospital	Commerce Twp	97%	156
Oakwood Southshore Medical Center	Trenton	97%	257
Saint John Hospital and Medical Center	Detroit	97%	300
Saint Joseph Mercy Port Huron	Port Huron	97%	95
Saint Mary's Health Care	Grand Rapids	97%	257
Tawas Saint Joseph Hospital	Tawas City	97%	113
Beaumont Hospital - Grosse Pointe	Grosse Pointe	96%	211
Botsford Hospital	Farmington Hills	96%	189
Dickinson County Memorial Hospital	Iron Mountain	96%	90
Henry Ford Wyandotte Hospital	Wyandotte	96%	432
Lakeland Hospital - St Joseph	Saint Joseph	96%	332
Memorial Medical Center of West Michigan	Ludington	96%	82
Mercy Health Partners - Hackley Campus	Muskegon	96%	124
Mercy Hospital - Grayling[2]	Grayling	96%	112
Midmichigan Medical Center-Clare	Clare	96%	77
Northern Michigan Regional Hospital	Petoskey	96%	137
Saint Francis Hospital	Escanaba	96%	141
Borgess Medical Center[2]	Kalamazoo	95%	101
Clinton Memorial Hospital	Saint Johns	95%	41
Emma L Bixby Medical Center[2]	Adrian	95%	96
Mercy Health Partners - Mercy Campus	Muskegon	95%	159
Saint Mary Mercy Hospital	Livonia	95%	439
Sturgis Hospital	Sturgis	95%	65
Crittenton Hospital Medical Center	Rochester	94%	214
Gratiot Medical Center	Alma	94%	125
Henry Ford Macomb Hospital	Clinton Twp	94%	472
Port Huron Hospital	Port Huron	94%	239
Sinai-Grace Hospital	Detroit	94%	256
Covenant Medical Center	Saginaw	93%	488
Providence Hospital and Medical Centers	Southfield	93%	495
Saint Joseph Mercy Oakland[2]	Pontiac	93%	116
University of Michigan Health System	Ann Arbor	93%	296
VA Ann Arbor Healthcare System	Ann Arbor	93%	60
Bay Regional Medical Center	Bay City	92%	201
Ingham Regional Medical Center	Lansing	92%	238
Mecosta County Medical Center	Big Rapids	92%	74
Otsego Memorial Hospital	Gaylord	92%	78
Portage Health Hospital	Hancock	92%	37
West Branch Regional Medical Center	West Branch	92%	101
Community Hospital	Watervliet	91%	53
Mclaren Regional Medical Center[2]	Flint	91%	301
Midmichigan Medical Center-Midland[2]	Midland	91%	125
Poh Medical Center[2]	Pontiac	91%	79
Bronson Methodist Hospital	Kalamazoo	90%	332
Carson City Hospital	Carson City	89%	35
Garden City Hospital	Garden City	89%	178
Oakwood Hospital and Medical Center[2]	Dearborn	89%	475

NOTE: Hospital profiles are in alphabetical order by state, then city, then hospital within the city; Rankings exclude hospitals with less than 25 cases except for patient surveys which excludes hospitals with less than 100 cases; (a) 100–299 cases; (1) The number of cases is too small to be sure how well a hospital is performing; (2) The hospital indicated that the data submitted for this measure were based on a sample of cases; (3) Data was collected during a shorter time period (fewer quarters) than the maximum possible time for this measure; (4) Suppressed for one or more quarters by CMS; (5) No data is available from the hospital for this measure; (6) Fewer than 100 patients completed the HCAHPS survey. Use these rates with caution, as the number of surveys may be too low to reliably assess hospital performance; (7) Survey results are based on less than 12 months of data; (8) Survey results are not available for this reporting period; (9) No or very few patients were eligible for the HCAHPS survey. The scores shown, if any, reflect a very small number of surveys; (10) A state average was not calculated because too few hospitals in the state submitted data; (11) There were discrepancies in the data collection process; Please refer to the User's Guide for a full explanation of data.

Hospital Name	City	Rate	Cases
Saint Joseph Mercy Livingston Hospital	Howell	89%	132
Alpena Regional Medical Center	Alpena	88%	138
Huron Medical Center	Bad Axe	88%	52
West Shore Medical Center	Manistee	88%	59
Allegan General Hospital	Allegan	87%	52
Doctor's Hospital of Michigan	Pontiac	87%	30
Edward W Sparrow Hospital	Lansing	87%	436
Borgess-Lee Memorial Hospital	Dowagiac	85%	34
Saint Joseph Mercy Saline Hospital	Saline	84%	64
Marquette General Hospital	Marquette	83%	128
Saint Mary's of Michigan Medical Center[2]	Saginaw	81%	104
Three Rivers Health	Three Rivers	81%	47
Hurley Medical Center[2]	Flint	79%	102
Saint Joseph Mercy Hospital	Ann Arbor	79%	496
Henry Ford Hospital[2]	Detroit	76%	116
Mount Clemens Regional Medical Center	Mount Clemens	76%	234
Northstar Health System	Iron River	72%	93
Henry Ford West Bloomfield Hospital	West Bloomfield	62%	196
Marlette Regional Hospital	Marlette	49%	53
Hillsdale Community Health Center	Hillsdale	42%	128

21. Smoking Cessation Advice

Hospital Name	City	Rate	Cases
Battle Creek Health System	Battle Creek	100%	163
Bronson Lakeview Hospital	Paw Paw	100%	36
Central Michigan Community Hospital	Mount Pleasant	100%	62
Community Health Center of Branch County	Coldwater	100%	50
Community Hospital	Watervliet	100%	27
Covenant Medical Center	Saginaw	100%	226
Detroit (John D. Dingell) VA Medical Center	Detroit	100%	38
Dickinson County Memorial Hospital	Iron Mountain	100%	33
Edward W Sparrow Hospital	Lansing	100%	222
Emma L Bixby Medical Center[2]	Adrian	100%	42
Garden City Hospital	Garden City	100%	80
Genesys Regional Med Ctr-Health Park[2]	Grand Blanc	100%	90
Gratiot Medical Center	Alma	100%	44
Harper University Hospital	Detroit	100%	47
Henry Ford Hospital[2]	Detroit	100%	80
Henry Ford Macomb Hospital	Clinton Twp	100%	160
Henry Ford Wyandotte Hospital	Wyandotte	100%	237
Holland Community Hospital	Holland	100%	66
Marquette General Hospital	Marquette	100%	52
Mclaren Regional Medical Center[2]	Flint	100%	115
Mecosta County Medical Center	Big Rapids	100%	30
Memorial Healthcare	Owosso	100%	47
Mercy Hospital - Cadillac[2]	Cadillac	100%	42
Mercy Memorial Hospital System	Monroe	100%	120
Metro Health Hospital[2]	Wyoming	100%	47
Oakwood Annapolis Hospital	Wayne	100%	104
Oakwood Heritage Hospital	Taylor	100%	105
Oakwood Hospital and Medical Center[2]	Dearborn	100%	224
Oakwood Southshore Medical Center	Trenton	100%	101
Pennock Hospital	Hastings	100%	28
Saint Francis Hospital	Escanaba	100%	42
Saint Joseph Mercy Hospital	Ann Arbor	100%	180
Saint Joseph Mercy Livingston Hospital	Howell	100%	28
Saint Joseph Mercy Oakland[2]	Pontiac	100%	58
Saint Joseph Mercy Port Huron	Port Huron	100%	56
Saint Mary Mercy Hospital	Livonia	100%	75
Sinai-Grace Hospital	Detroit	100%	153
Spectrum Health Gerber Memorial	Fremont	100%	41
Spectrum Health United Mem-United Campus	Greenville	100%	50
Tawas Saint Joseph Hospital	Tawas City	100%	54
University of Michigan Health System	Ann Arbor	100%	155
West Branch Regional Medical Center	West Branch	100%	33
Zeeland Community Hospital	Zeeland	100%	27
Botsford Hospital	Farmington Hills	99%	79
Hurley Medical Center[2]	Flint	99%	100
Ingham Regional Medical Center	Lansing	99%	122
Lakeland Hospital - St Joseph	Saint Joseph	99%	169
Munson Medical Center	Traverse City	99%	160
Providence Hospital and Medical Centers	Southfield	99%	157
Saint John Hospital and Medical Center	Detroit	99%	187
Saint Mary's Health Care	Grand Rapids	99%	123
William Beaumont Hospital-Troy[2]	Troy	99%	76
Alpena Regional Medical Center	Alpena	98%	53
Bay Regional Medical Center	Bay City	98%	85
Borgess Medical Center[2]	Kalamazoo	98%	41
Bronson Methodist Hospital	Kalamazoo	98%	188
Detroit Receiving Hosp & Univ Health Ctr	Detroit	98%	165
Lapeer Regional Medical Center	Lapeer	98%	65
Mercy Health Partners - Mercy Campus	Muskegon	98%	88
Mercy Hospital - Grayling[2]	Grayling	98%	48
Midmichigan Medical Center-Clare	Clare	98%	45
Mount Clemens Regional Medical Center	Mount Clemens	98%	135
Northern Michigan Regional Hospital	Petoskey	98%	63
St John Macomb-Oakland Hosp-Macomb Ctr	Warren	98%	251
Saint Mary's of Michigan Medical Center[2]	Saginaw	98%	51
VA Ann Arbor Healthcare System	Ann Arbor	98%	45
William Beaumont Hospital[2]	Royal Oak	98%	51

Hospital Name	City	Rate	Cases
Allegiance Health[2]	Jackson	97%	76
Chelsea Community Hospital	Chelsea	97%	30
Huron Valley-Sinai Hospital	Commerce Twp	97%	69
Oaklawn Hospital	Marshall	97%	33
Port Huron Hospital	Port Huron	97%	97
Spectrum Health - Butterworth Campus	Grand Rapids	97%	282
Crittenton Hospital Medical Center	Rochester	96%	48
Henry Ford West Bloomfield Hospital	West Bloomfield	96%	25
Midmichigan Medical Center-Midland[2]	Midland	96%	57
Beaumont Hospital - Grosse Pointe	Grosse Pointe	95%	88
Mercy Health Partners - Hackley Campus	Muskegon	95%	76
Hillsdale Community Health Center	Hillsdale	91%	65
Chippewa County War Memorial Hospital	Sault Ste Marie	90%	42
Memorial Medical Center of West Michigan	Ludington	89%	28
Poh Medical Center[2]	Pontiac	73%	67
Doctor's Hospital of Michigan	Pontiac	72%	29

Surgical Care Improvement Project

22. Appropriate VTP Within 24 Hours

Hospital Name	City	Rate	Cases
Chelsea Community Hospital[2]	Chelsea	100%	281
Clinton Memorial Hospital	Saint Johns	100%	27
Otsego Memorial Hospital[2]	Gaylord	100%	45
Tawas Saint Joseph Hospital[2]	Tawas City	100%	45
Botsford Hospital[2]	Farmington Hills	99%	267
Henry Ford Wyandotte Hospital[2]	Wyandotte	99%	208
Holland Community Hospital[2]	Holland	99%	156
Oakwood Heritage Hospital[2]	Taylor	99%	90
Oakwood Southshore Medical Center[2]	Trenton	99%	149
Port Huron Hospital[2]	Port Huron	99%	280
St John Macomb-Oakland Hosp-Macomb Ctr[2]	Warren	99%	406
Saint Joseph Mercy Oakland[2]	Pontiac	99%	161
Saint Joseph Mercy Port Huron[2]	Port Huron	99%	165
Spectrum Health - Butterworth Campus[2]	Grand Rapids	99%	262
University of Michigan Health System[2]	Ann Arbor	99%	699
Carson City Hospital	Carson City	98%	66
Chippewa County War Memorial Hospital	Sault Ste Marie	98%	89
Dickinson County Memorial Hospital	Iron Mountain	98%	149
Henry Ford Hospital[2]	Detroit	98%	300
Henry Ford Macomb Hospital[2]	Clinton Twp	98%	379
Lakeland Hospital - St Joseph[2]	Saint Joseph	98%	294
Oakwood Hospital and Medical Center[2]	Dearborn	98%	516
Saint John Hospital and Medical Center[2]	Detroit	98%	394
Saint Mary's Health Care[2]	Grand Rapids	98%	162
Sinai-Grace Hospital[2]	Detroit	98%	280
Alpena Regional Medical Center[2]	Alpena	97%	115
Henry Ford West Bloomfield Hospital	West Bloomfield	97%	240
Lapeer Regional Medical Center[2]	Lapeer	97%	128
Mercy Health Partners - Hackley Campus	Muskegon	97%	278
Munson Medical Center[2]	Traverse City	97%	254
North Ottawa Community Hospital	Grand Haven	97%	65
Oaklawn Hospital[2]	Marshall	97%	116
William Beaumont Hospital[2]	Royal Oak	97%	309
Beaumont Hospital - Grosse Pointe[2]	Grosse Pointe	96%	225
Detroit (John D. Dingell) VA Medical Center[2]	Detroit	96%	161
Mount Clemens Regional Medical Center[2]	Mount Clemens	96%	298
Providence Hospital and Medical Centers[2]	Southfield	96%	785
Saint John River District Hospital	East China	96%	45
Sturgis Hospital	Sturgis	96%	49
West Branch Regional Medical Center[2]	West Branch	96%	175
Zeeland Community Hospital	Zeeland	96%	50
Allegiance Health[2]	Jackson	95%	164
Hurley Medical Center[2]	Flint	95%	175
Portage Health Hospital	Hancock	95%	64
Saint Joseph Mercy Hospital[2]	Ann Arbor	95%	242
Battle Creek Health System[2]	Battle Creek	94%	179
Mercy Hospital - Grayling[2]	Grayling	94%	63
Mercy Memorial Hospital System	Monroe	94%	244
Midmichigan Medical Center-Midland[2]	Midland	94%	154
VA Ann Arbor Healthcare System[2]	Ann Arbor	94%	163
Borgess Medical Center[2]	Kalamazoo	93%	116
Huron Valley-Sinai Hospital[2]	Commerce Twp	93%	179
Karmanos Cancer Center[2]	Detroit	93%	227
Mclaren Regional Medical Center[2]	Flint	93%	291
Mercy Hospital - Cadillac	Cadillac	93%	86
Northern Michigan Regional Hospital[2]	Petoskey	93%	145
Saint Francis Hospital	Escanaba	93%	57
Saint Mary's of Michigan Medical Center[2]	Saginaw	93%	188
Genesys Regional Med Ctr-Health Park[2]	Grand Blanc	92%	410
Mercy Health Partners - Mercy Campus	Muskegon	92%	298
Poh Medical Center[2]	Pontiac	92%	105
Community Hospital	Watervliet	91%	45
Crittenton Hospital Medical Center[2]	Rochester	91%	148
Detroit Receiving Hosp & Univ Health Ctr	Detroit	91%	362
Garden City Hospital	Garden City	91%	306
Harper University Hospital[2]	Detroit	91%	155
Metro Health Hospital[2]	Wyoming	91%	144
Oakwood Annapolis Hospital[2]	Wayne	91%	180
Spectrum Health United Mem-United Campus	Greenville	91%	70
Bronson Methodist Hospital[2]	Kalamazoo	90%	384
Central Michigan Community Hospital	Mount Pleasant	90%	41
Saint Mary Mercy Hospital	Livonia	90%	364
Spectrum Health Gerber Memorial	Fremont	90%	73
Doctor's Hospital of Michigan[2]	Pontiac	89%	89
Emma L Bixby Medical Center[2]	Adrian	89%	112
William Beaumont Hospital-Troy[2]	Troy	89%	162
Covenant Medical Center[2]	Saginaw	88%	226
Ingham Regional Medical Center[2]	Lansing	88%	190
Edward W Sparrow Hospital[2]	Lansing	87%	442
Memorial Healthcare	Owosso	87%	138
Bay Regional Medical Center	Bay City	86%	394
Marquette General Hospital[2]	Marquette	86%	126
Mecosta County Medical Center	Big Rapids	86%	28
Saint Joseph Mercy Livingston Hospital[2]	Howell	86%	93
Community Health Center of Branch County	Coldwater	85%	117
Pennock Hospital[2]	Hastings	85%	73
Midmichigan Medical Center-Clare	Clare	83%	54
Hillsdale Community Health Center	Hillsdale	80%	59
Gratiot Medical Center	Alma	79%	154
Memorial Medical Center of West Michigan	Ludington	79%	126
West Shore Medical Center	Manistee	79%	76
Allegan General Hospital[2]	Allegan	73%	73
Marlette Regional Hospital	Marlette	68%	25

23. Appropriate Hair Removal

Hospital Name	City	Rate	Cases
Allegan General Hospital[2]	Allegan	100%	157
Allegiance Health[2]	Jackson	100%	619
Aspirus Grand View Hospital	Ironwood	100%	81
Battle Creek Health System[2]	Battle Creek	100%	986
Bay Regional Medical Center	Bay City	100%	1514
Beaumont Hospital - Grosse Pointe[2]	Grosse Pointe	100%	693
Borgess Medical Center[2]	Kalamazoo	100%	567
Botsford Hospital[2]	Farmington Hills	100%	666
Bronson Methodist Hospital[2]	Kalamazoo	100%	1477
Central Michigan Community Hospital	Mount Pleasant	100%	276
Chelsea Community Hospital[2]	Chelsea	100%	887
Chippewa County War Memorial Hospital	Sault Ste Marie	100%	248
Clinton Memorial Hospital	Saint Johns	100%	59
Community Health Center of Branch County	Coldwater	100%	275
Community Hospital	Watervliet	100%	137
Crittenton Hospital Medical Center[2]	Rochester	100%	546
Detroit (John D. Dingell) VA Medical Center[2]	Detroit	100%	281
Detroit Receiving Hosp & Univ Health Ctr	Detroit	100%	608
Dickinson County Memorial Hospital	Iron Mountain	100%	320
Emma L Bixby Medical Center[2]	Adrian	100%	274
Gratiot Medical Center	Alma	100%	345
Harper University Hospital[2]	Detroit	100%	615
Hayes Green Beach Memorial Hospital	Charlotte	100%	46
Henry Ford Hospital[2]	Detroit	100%	842
Henry Ford Macomb Hospital[2]	Clinton Twp	100%	1559
Henry Ford Wyandotte Hospital[2]	Wyandotte	100%	482
Holland Community Hospital[2]	Holland	100%	654
Huron Medical Center[2]	Bad Axe	100%	178
Huron Valley-Sinai Hospital[2]	Commerce Twp	100%	657
Ingham Regional Medical Center[2]	Lansing	100%	1240
Karmanos Cancer Center[2]	Detroit	100%	355
Lapeer Regional Medical Center[2]	Lapeer	100%	517
Mclaren Regional Medical Center[2]	Flint	100%	1345
Mecosta County Medical Center	Big Rapids	100%	227
Memorial Healthcare	Owosso	100%	333
Mercy Health Partners - Mercy Campus	Muskegon	100%	1450
Mercy Hospital - Cadillac	Cadillac	100%	422
Mercy Hospital - Grayling[2]	Grayling	100%	209
Mercy Memorial Hospital System	Monroe	100%	728
Metro Health Hospital[2]	Wyoming	100%	458
Midmichigan Medical Center-Clare	Clare	100%	109
Midmichigan Medical Center-Midland[2]	Midland	100%	710
Munson Medical Center[2]	Traverse City	100%	920
North Ottawa Community Hospital	Grand Haven	100%	257
Oaklawn Hospital[2]	Marshall	100%	568
Oakwood Annapolis Hospital[2]	Wayne	100%	448
Oakwood Heritage Hospital[2]	Taylor	100%	314
Oakwood Hospital and Medical Center[2]	Dearborn	100%	1665
Oakwood Southshore Medical Center[2]	Trenton	100%	549
Otsego Memorial Hospital[2]	Gaylord	100%	217
Pennock Hospital[2]	Hastings	100%	266
Poh Medical Center[2]	Pontiac	100%	291
Portage Health Hospital	Hancock	100%	200
Providence Hospital and Medical Centers[2]	Southfield	100%	2310
Saint Francis Hospital	Escanaba	100%	139
Saint John Hospital and Medical Center[2]	Detroit	100%	1512
St John Macomb-Oakland Hosp-Macomb Ctr[2]	Warren	100%	1366
Saint John River District Hospital	East China	100%	105
Saint Joseph Mercy Hospital[2]	Ann Arbor	100%	827
Saint Joseph Mercy Livingston Hospital[2]	Howell	100%	310
Saint Joseph Mercy Oakland[2]	Pontiac	100%	630
Saint Joseph Mercy Port Huron[2]	Port Huron	100%	415
Saint Joseph Mercy Saline Hospital	Saline	100%	56

NOTE: Hospital profiles are in alphabetical order by state, then city, then hospital within the city; Rankings exclude hospitals with less than 25 cases except for patient surveys which excludes hospitals with less than 100 cases; (a) 100–299 cases; (1) The number of cases is too small to be sure how well a hospital is performing; (2) The hospital indicated that the data submitted for this measure were based on a sample of cases; (3) Data was collected during a shorter time period (fewer quarters) than the maximum possible time for this measure; (4) Suppressed for one or more quarters by CMS; (5) No data is available from the hospital for this measure; (6) Fewer than 100 patients completed the HCAHPS survey. Use these rates with caution, as the number of surveys may be too low to reliably assess hospital performance; (7) Survey results are based on less than 12 months of data; (8) Survey results are not available for this reporting period; (9) No or very few patients were eligible for the HCAHPS survey. The scores shown, if any, reflect a very small number of surveys; (10) A state average was not calculated because too few hospitals in the state submitted data; (11) There were discrepancies in the data collection process; Please refer to the User's Guide for a full explanation of data.

Saint Mary Mercy Hospital	Livonia	100%	898
Saint Mary's Health Care[2]	Grand Rapids	100%	596
Saint Mary's of Michigan Medical Center[2]	Saginaw	100%	566
Sinai-Grace Hospital[2]	Detroit	100%	862
South Haven Community Hospital	South Haven	100%	101
Spectrum Health - Butterworth Campus[2]	Grand Rapids	100%	1143
Spectrum Health Gerber Memorial	Fremont	100%	330
Spectrum Health United Mem-United Campus	Greenville	100%	202
Tawas Saint Joseph Hospital[2]	Tawas City	100%	223
VA Ann Arbor Healthcare System[2]	Ann Arbor	100%	488
William Beaumont Hospital[2]	Royal Oak	100%	977
William Beaumont Hospital-Troy[2]	Troy	100%	688
Zeeland Community Hospital	Zeeland	100%	251
Alpena Regional Medical Center[2]	Alpena	99%	415
Doctor's Hospital of Michigan[2]	Pontiac	99%	132
Garden City Hospital	Garden City	99%	634
Henry Ford West Bloomfield Hospital	West Bloomfield	99%	661
Hillsdale Community Health Center	Hillsdale	99%	246
Hurley Medical Center[2]	Flint	99%	443
Lakeland Hospital - St Joseph[2]	Saint Joseph	99%	964
Memorial Medical Center of West Michigan	Ludington	99%	299
Mount Clemens Regional Medical Center[2]	Mount Clemens	99%	1177
Northern Michigan Regional Hospital[2]	Petoskey	99%	615
Sturgis Hospital	Sturgis	99%	127
West Shore Medical Center	Manistee	99%	185
Edward W Sparrow Hospital[2]	Lansing	98%	1697
Mercy Health Partners - Hackley Campus	Muskegon	98%	992
Port Huron Hospital[2]	Port Huron	98%	836
Three Rivers Health	Three Rivers	98%	94
University of Michigan Health System[2]	Ann Arbor	98%	2332
West Branch Regional Medical Center[2]	West Branch	98%	335
Covenant Medical Center[2]	Saginaw	97%	824
Oakland Regional Hospital[3]	Southfield	97%	33
Carson City Hospital	Carson City	95%	219
Genesys Regional Med Ctr-Health Park[2]	Grand Blanc	94%	1555
Borgess-Lee Memorial Hospital	Dowagiac	93%	29
Marquette General Hospital[2]	Marquette	91%	517
Marlette Regional Hospital	Marlette	68%	37

24. Appropriate Beta Blocker Usage

Hospital Name	City	Rate	Cases
Chelsea Community Hospital[2]	Chelsea	100%	197
Holland Community Hospital[2]	Holland	100%	160
Huron Medical Center[2]	Bad Axe	100%	44
VA Ann Arbor Healthcare System[2]	Ann Arbor	100%	291
West Branch Regional Medical Center[2]	West Branch	100%	112
Community Health Center of Branch County	Coldwater	99%	76
Harper University Hospital[2]	Detroit	99%	167
Karmanos Cancer Center[2]	Detroit	99%	96
Mercy Memorial Hospital System	Monroe	99%	193
Sinai-Grace Hospital[2]	Detroit	99%	210
Borgess Medical Center[2]	Kalamazoo	98%	206
Botsford Hospital[2]	Farmington Hills	98%	189
Bronson Methodist Hospital[2]	Kalamazoo	98%	455
Detroit Receiving Hosp & Univ Health Ctr	Detroit	98%	119
Dickinson County Memorial Hospital	Iron Mountain	98%	84
Munson Medical Center[2]	Traverse City	98%	269
Pennock Hospital[2]	Hastings	98%	59
Saint John Hospital and Medical Center[2]	Detroit	98%	515
Central Michigan Community Hospital	Mount Pleasant	97%	76
Crittenton Hospital Medical Center[2]	Rochester	97%	186
Emma L Bixby Medical Center[2]	Adrian	97%	60
Lapeer Regional Medical Center[2]	Lapeer	97%	158
Oaklawn Hospital[2]	Marshall	97%	148
Otsego Memorial Hospital[2]	Gaylord	97%	63
St John Macomb-Oakland Hosp-Macomb Ctr[2]	Warren	97%	460
Spectrum Health United Mem-United Campus	Greenville	97%	34
William Beaumont Hospital-Troy[2]	Troy	97%	277
Zeeland Community Hospital	Zeeland	97%	64
Allegiance Health[2]	Jackson	96%	267
Detroit (John D. Dingell) VA Medical Center[2]	Detroit	96%	109
Garden City Hospital	Garden City	96%	193
Genesys Regional Med Ctr-Health Park[2]	Grand Blanc	96%	562
Mercy Hospital - Grayling[2]	Grayling	96%	53
Midmichigan Medical Center-Midland[2]	Midland	96%	213
Oakwood Heritage Hospital[2]	Taylor	96%	93
Saint Joseph Mercy Oakland[2]	Pontiac	96%	201
Saint Mary's Health Care[2]	Grand Rapids	96%	179
Sturgis Hospital	Sturgis	96%	27
William Beaumont Hospital[2]	Royal Oak	96%	363
Beaumont Hospital - Grosse Pointe[2]	Grosse Pointe	95%	214
Chippewa County War Memorial Hospital	Sault Ste Marie	95%	77
Henry Ford Macomb Hospital[2]	Clinton Twp	95%	534
Memorial Healthcare	Owosso	95%	79
Memorial Medical Center of West Michigan	Ludington	95%	91
Saint Joseph Mercy Port Huron[2]	Port Huron	95%	142
Spectrum Health - Butterworth Campus[2]	Grand Rapids	95%	383
Tawas Saint Joseph Hospital[2]	Tawas City	95%	76
West Shore Medical Center	Manistee	95%	60
Huron Valley-Sinai Hospital[2]	Commerce Twp	94%	161
Midmichigan Medical Center-Clare	Clare	94%	36
Saint Mary's of Michigan Medical Center[2]	Saginaw	94%	230
Spectrum Health Gerber Memorial	Fremont	94%	68
Battle Creek Health System[2]	Battle Creek	93%	264
Bay Regional Medical Center	Bay City	93%	522
Oakwood Annapolis Hospital[2]	Wayne	93%	136
Oakwood Hospital and Medical Center[2]	Dearborn	93%	657
Oakwood Southshore Medical Center[2]	Trenton	93%	181
Providence Hospital and Medical Centers[2]	Southfield	93%	709
Henry Ford Wyandotte Hospital[2]	Wyandotte	92%	158
Lakeland Hospital - St Joseph[2]	Saint Joseph	92%	292
Northern Michigan Regional Hospital[2]	Petoskey	92%	223
Portage Health Hospital	Hancock	92%	51
Edward W Sparrow Hospital[2]	Lansing	91%	416
Hurley Medical Center[2]	Flint	91%	98
Ingham Regional Medical Center[2]	Lansing	91%	380
Mclaren Regional Medical Center[2]	Flint	91%	426
Saint Mary Mercy Hospital	Livonia	91%	264
Mercy Health Partners - Hackley Campus	Muskegon	90%	221
Mercy Hospital - Cadillac	Cadillac	90%	102
North Ottawa Community Hospital	Grand Haven	90%	67
Covenant Medical Center[2]	Saginaw	89%	291
Gratiot Medical Center	Alma	89%	112
Mercy Health Partners - Mercy Campus	Muskegon	89%	440
Saint Joseph Mercy Hospital[2]	Ann Arbor	88%	279
Marquette General Hospital[2]	Marquette	87%	170
Metro Health Hospital[2]	Wyoming	86%	99
Alpena Regional Medical Center[2]	Alpena	84%	125
Doctor's Hospital of Michigan[2]	Pontiac	84%	25
Mecosta County Medical Center	Big Rapids	83%	54
Port Huron Hospital[2]	Port Huron	81%	260
University of Michigan Health System[2]	Ann Arbor	80%	887
Hillsdale Community Health Center	Hillsdale	79%	73
Henry Ford West Bloomfield Hospital	West Bloomfield	78%	158
Poh Medical Center[2]	Pontiac	78%	64
Saint Joseph Mercy Livingston Hospital[2]	Howell	78%	67
Carson City Hospital	Carson City	77%	31
Community Hospital	Watervliet	77%	39
Henry Ford Hospital[2]	Detroit	70%	320
Mount Clemens Regional Medical Center[2]	Mount Clemens	68%	405

25. Controlled Postoperative Blood Glucose

Hospital Name	City	Rate	Cases
Bronson Methodist Hospital[2]	Kalamazoo	100%	201
Port Huron Hospital[2]	Port Huron	99%	150
Lakeland Hospital - St Joseph[2]	Saint Joseph	98%	126
Spectrum Health - Butterworth Campus[2]	Grand Rapids	98%	187
University of Michigan Health System[2]	Ann Arbor	98%	651
Crittenton Hospital Medical Center[2]	Rochester	97%	77
Providence Hospital and Medical Centers[2]	Southfield	97%	218
Saint Joseph Mercy Hospital[2]	Ann Arbor	97%	175
Borgess Medical Center[2]	Kalamazoo	96%	132
Henry Ford Hospital[2]	Detroit	96%	181
Henry Ford Macomb Hospital[2]	Clinton Twp	96%	168
Marquette General Hospital[2]	Marquette	96%	125
Sinai-Grace Hospital[2]	Detroit	96%	82
Mercy Health Partners - Mercy Campus	Muskegon	95%	217
Midmichigan Medical Center-Midland[2]	Midland	95%	126
Munson Medical Center[2]	Traverse City	95%	169
Saint John Hospital and Medical Center[2]	Detroit	95%	260
Allegiance Health[2]	Jackson	94%	107
Genesys Regional Med Ctr-Health Park[2]	Grand Blanc	94%	160
St John Macomb-Oakland Hosp-Macomb Ctr[2]	Warren	94%	192
Saint Joseph Mercy Oakland[2]	Pontiac	94%	130
VA Ann Arbor Healthcare System[2]	Ann Arbor	94%	163
William Beaumont Hospital[2]	Royal Oak	94%	176
Northern Michigan Regional Hospital[2]	Petoskey	93%	125
Oakwood Hospital and Medical Center[2]	Dearborn	93%	387
Bay Regional Medical Center	Bay City	92%	387
William Beaumont Hospital-Troy[2]	Troy	92%	153
Saint Mary's of Michigan Medical Center[2]	Saginaw	90%	124
Edward W Sparrow Hospital[2]	Lansing	89%	187
Covenant Medical Center[2]	Saginaw	86%	132
Ingham Regional Medical Center[2]	Lansing	85%	240
Mount Clemens Regional Medical Center[2]	Mount Clemens	85%	119
Mclaren Regional Medical Center[2]	Flint	84%	252
Harper University Hospital[2]	Detroit	78%	99

26. Prophylactic Antibiotic Timing

Hospital Name	City	Rate	Cases
Aspirus Grand View Hospital	Ironwood	100%	43
Chelsea Community Hospital[2]	Chelsea	100%	741
Detroit Receiving Hosp & Univ Health Ctr	Detroit	100%	277
Harper University Hospital[2]	Detroit	100%	414
Holland Community Hospital[2]	Holland	100%	500
North Ottawa Community Hospital	Grand Haven	100%	203
Oakwood Heritage Hospital[2]	Taylor	100%	234
Pennock Hospital[2]	Hastings	100%	202
Saint Francis Hospital	Escanaba	100%	74
Saint John River District Hospital	East China	100%	45
Battle Creek Health System[2]	Battle Creek	99%	800
Beaumont Hospital - Grosse Pointe[2]	Grosse Pointe	99%	513
Chippewa County War Memorial Hospital	Sault Ste Marie	99%	197
Dickinson County Memorial Hospital	Iron Mountain	99%	236
Hurley Medical Center[2]	Flint	99%	286
Huron Medical Center[2]	Bad Axe	99%	148
Lakeland Hospital - St Joseph[2]	Saint Joseph	99%	632
Lapeer Regional Medical Center[2]	Lapeer	99%	396
Mercy Hospital - Grayling[2]	Grayling	99%	138
Oaklawn Hospital[2]	Marshall	99%	426
Oakwood Southshore Medical Center[2]	Trenton	99%	403
Poh Medical Center[2]	Pontiac	99%	178
Portage Health Hospital	Hancock	99%	171
Saint Joseph Mercy Oakland[2]	Pontiac	99%	459
Saint Mary's of Michigan Medical Center[2]	Saginaw	99%	388
South Haven Community Hospital	South Haven	99%	82
Spectrum Health Gerber Memorial	Fremont	99%	266
Spectrum Health United Mem-United Campus	Greenville	99%	145
West Shore Medical Center	Manistee	99%	116
Zeeland Community Hospital	Zeeland	99%	196
Bay Regional Medical Center	Bay City	98%	995
Central Michigan Community Hospital	Mount Pleasant	98%	229
Clinton Memorial Hospital	Saint Johns	98%	40
Community Health Center of Branch County	Coldwater	98%	165
Crittenton Hospital Medical Center[2]	Rochester	98%	400
Emma L Bixby Medical Center[2]	Adrian	98%	195
Genesys Regional Med Ctr-Health Park[2]	Grand Blanc	98%	1320
Henry Ford Macomb Hospital[2]	Clinton Twp	98%	1264
Huron Valley-Sinai Hospital[2]	Commerce Twp	98%	489
Karmanos Cancer Center[2]	Detroit	98%	130
Mclaren Regional Medical Center[2]	Flint	98%	1069
Memorial Medical Center of West Michigan	Ludington	98%	242
Mercy Memorial Hospital System	Monroe	98%	522
Oakwood Annapolis Hospital[2]	Wayne	98%	312
Oakwood Hospital and Medical Center[2]	Dearborn	98%	1267
Providence Hospital and Medical Centers[2]	Southfield	98%	1577
Saint John Hospital and Medical Center[2]	Detroit	98%	1213
Saint Joseph Mercy Hospital[2]	Ann Arbor	98%	577
Saint Joseph Mercy Port Huron[2]	Port Huron	98%	316
Sinai-Grace Hospital[2]	Detroit	98%	555
Three Rivers Health	Three Rivers	98%	57
University of Michigan Health System[2]	Ann Arbor	98%	1735
Allegiance Health[2]	Jackson	97%	433
Borgess Medical Center[2]	Kalamazoo	97%	418
Botsford Hospital[2]	Farmington Hills	97%	502
Bronson Methodist Hospital[2]	Kalamazoo	97%	1198
Detroit (John D. Dingell) VA Medical Center	Detroit	97%	191
Henry Ford Hospital[2]	Detroit	97%	571
Ingham Regional Medical Center[2]	Lansing	97%	957
Marquette General Hospital[2]	Marquette	97%	373
Metro Health Hospital[2]	Wyoming	97%	322
Northern Michigan Regional Hospital[2]	Petoskey	97%	447
Port Huron Hospital[2]	Port Huron	97%	613
St John Macomb-Oakland Hosp-Macomb Ctr[2]	Warren	97%	1068
Saint Joseph Mercy Livingston Hospital[2]	Howell	97%	227
Tawas Saint Joseph Hospital[2]	Tawas City	97%	151
Allegan General Hospital[2]	Allegan	96%	126
Alpena Regional Medical Center[2]	Alpena	96%	299
Covenant Medical Center[2]	Saginaw	96%	535
Henry Ford West Bloomfield Hospital	West Bloomfield	96%	445
Memorial Healthcare	Owosso	96%	222
Mercy Hospital - Cadillac	Cadillac	96%	322
Mount Clemens Regional Medical Center[2]	Mount Clemens	96%	847
Munson Medical Center[2]	Traverse City	96%	586
Saint Mary Mercy Hospital	Livonia	96%	520
Saint Mary's Health Care[2]	Grand Rapids	96%	397
VA Ann Arbor Healthcare System	Ann Arbor	96%	363
William Beaumont Hospital[2]	Royal Oak	96%	645
William Beaumont Hospital-Troy[2]	Troy	96%	456
Gratiot Medical Center	Alma	95%	219
Mercy Health Partners - Mercy Campus	Muskegon	95%	1088
Spectrum Health - Butterworth Campus[2]	Grand Rapids	95%	750
Hayes Green Beach Memorial Hospital	Charlotte	94%	31
Henry Ford Wyandotte Hospital[2]	Wyandotte	94%	308
Saint Joseph Mercy Saline Hospital	Saline	94%	47
Mecosta County Medical Center	Big Rapids	93%	199
Mercy Health Partners - Hackley Campus	Muskegon	93%	646
Midmichigan Medical Center-Midland[2]	Midland	93%	486
Edward W Sparrow Hospital[2]	Lansing	92%	1370
Midmichigan Medical Center-Clare	Clare	92%	60
Garden City Hospital	Garden City	91%	391
Carson City Hospital	Carson City	90%	197
Otsego Memorial Hospital[2]	Gaylord	90%	169
Sturgis Hospital	Sturgis	90%	89
Community Hospital	Watervliet	89%	122
West Branch Regional Medical Center[2]	West Branch	89%	270
Marlette Regional Hospital	Marlette	88%	25
Oakland Regional Hospital[3]	Southfield	84%	32
Hillsdale Community Health Center	Hillsdale	79%	184
Doctor's Hospital of Michigan[2]	Pontiac	42%	57

NOTE: Hospital profiles are in alphabetical order by state, then city, then hospital within the city; Rankings exclude hospitals with less than 25 cases except for patient surveys which excludes hospitals with less than 100 cases; (a) 100–299 cases; (1) The number of cases is too small to be sure how well a hospital is performing; (2) The hospital indicated that the data submitted for this measure were based on a sample of cases; (3) Data was collected during a shorter time period (fewer quarters) than the maximum possible time for this measure; (4) Suppressed for one or more quarters by CMS; (5) No data is available from the hospital for this measure; (6) Fewer than 100 patients completed the HCAHPS survey. Use these rates with caution, as the number of surveys may be too low to reliably assess hospital performance; (7) Survey results are based on less than 12 months of data; (8) Survey results are not available for this reporting period; (9) No or very few patients were eligible for the HCAHPS survey. The scores shown, if any, reflect a very small number of surveys; (10) A state average was not calculated because too few hospitals in the state submitted data; (11) There were discrepancies in the data collection process; Please refer to the User's Guide for a full explanation of data.

27. Prophylactic Antibiotic Timing (Outpatient)

Hospital Name	City	Rate	Cases
Holland Community Hospital	Holland	100%	301
West Branch Regional Medical Center	West Branch	100%	63
Chelsea Community Hospital	Chelsea	99%	136
North Ottawa Community Hospital	Grand Haven	99%	80
Saint Joseph Mercy Oakland	Pontiac	99%	421
Battle Creek Health System	Battle Creek	98%	248
Oakland Regional Hospital	Southfield	98%	49
Saint Joseph Mercy Saline Hospital	Saline	98%	50
Saint Mary's of Michigan Medical Center	Saginaw	98%	430
Mercy Hospital - Grayling	Grayling	97%	99
Saint Joseph Mercy Hospital	Ann Arbor	97%	921
Lapeer Regional Medical Center	Lapeer	96%	81
Oakwood Hospital and Medical Center	Dearborn	96%	320
Saint John River District Hospital	East China	96%	47
Spectrum Health - Butterworth Campus	Grand Rapids	96%	1225
Detroit Receiving Hosp & Univ Health Ctr	Detroit	95%	73
Providence Hospital and Medical Centers	Southfield	95%	884
Saint Mary's Health Care	Grand Rapids	95%	314
Zeeland Community Hospital	Zeeland	95%	57
Emma L Bixby Medical Center	Adrian	94%	87
Henry Ford Macomb Hospital	Clinton Twp	94%	352
Memorial Healthcare	Owosso	94%	126
Metro Health Hospital	Wyoming	94%	258
Saint John Hospital and Medical Center	Detroit	94%	642
Tawas Saint Joseph Hospital	Tawas City	94%	63
William Beaumont Hospital	Royal Oak	94%	727
Chippewa County War Memorial Hospital	Sault Ste Marie	93%	27
Lakeland Hospital - St Joseph	Saint Joseph	93%	391
Mclaren Regional Medical Center	Flint	93%	428
Mercy Health Partners - Mercy Campus	Muskegon	93%	482
Mercy Hospital - Cadillac	Cadillac	93%	153
Oaklawn Hospital	Marshall	93%	67
Spectrum Health United Mem-United Campus	Greenville	93%	55
Allegiance Health	Jackson	92%	420
Saint Mary Mercy Hospital	Livonia	92%	253
Botsford Hospital	Farmington Hills	91%	240
Mercy Health Partners - Hackley Campus	Muskegon	91%	320
Midmichigan Medical Center-Midland	Midland	91%	391
Oakwood Annapolis Hospital	Wayne	91%	284
St John Macomb-Oakland Hosp-Macomb Ctr	Warren	91%	446
Saint Joseph Mercy Port Huron	Port Huron	91%	32
William Beaumont Hospital-Troy	Troy	91%	471
Beaumont Hospital - Grosse Pointe	Grosse Pointe	90%	230
Bronson Methodist Hospital	Kalamazoo	90%	396
Mount Clemens Regional Medical Center	Mount Clemens	90%	244
Munson Medical Center	Traverse City	90%	339
Port Huron Hospital	Port Huron	90%	142
Covenant Medical Center	Saginaw	89%	625
Eaton Rapids Medical Center	Eaton Rapids	89%	64
Southeast Michigan Surgical Hospital	Warren	89%	108
Alpena Regional Medical Center	Alpena	88%	166
Henry Ford Wyandotte Hospital	Wyandotte	88%	334
Pennock Hospital	Hastings	88%	68
Edward W Sparrow Hospital	Lansing	87%	599
Central Michigan Community Hospital	Mount Pleasant	86%	65
Saint Joseph Mercy Livingston Hospital	Howell	86%	96
Crittenton Hospital Medical Center	Rochester	85%	247
Mercy Memorial Hospital System	Monroe	85%	117
Spectrum Health Gerber Memorial	Fremont	85%	27
Garden City Hospital	Garden City	84%	257
Northern Michigan Regional Hospital	Petoskey	84%	362
Oakwood Southshore Medical Center	Trenton	83%	133
Genesys Regional Med Ctr-Health Park	Grand Blanc	81%	479
Community Health Center of Branch County	Coldwater	80%	82
Henry Ford Hospital	Detroit	79%	476
Ingham Regional Medical Center	Lansing	79%	574
Poh Medical Center	Pontiac	79%	100
Otsego Memorial Hospital	Gaylord	78%	27
Borgess Medical Center	Kalamazoo	77%	620
Carson City Hospital	Carson City	77%	39
Henry Ford West Bloomfield Hospital	West Bloomfield	77%	140
Marquette General Hospital	Marquette	76%	640
Sturgis Hospital	Sturgis	75%	75
Huron Valley-Sinai Hospital	Commerce Twp	74%	196
University of Michigan Health System	Ann Arbor	74%	541
Bay Regional Medical Center	Bay City	73%	460
Memorial Medical Center of West Michigan	Ludington	73%	26
Sinai-Grace Hospital	Detroit	73%	487
Gratiot Medical Center	Alma	71%	156
Saint Francis Hospital	Escanaba	71%	42
Hurley Medical Center	Flint	70%	172
Portage Health Hospital	Hancock	69%	29
Hillsdale Community Health Center	Hillsdale	66%	38
Dickinson County Memorial Hospital	Iron Mountain	64%	39
Harper University Hospital	Detroit	61%	590
Karmanos Cancer Center	Detroit	53%	95
Doctor's Hospital of Michigan	Pontiac	52%	94
Mecosta County Medical Center	Big Rapids	27%	83

28. Prophylactic Antibiotic Selection

Hospital Name	City	Rate	Cases
Chelsea Community Hospital[2]	Chelsea	100%	743
Detroit Receiving Hosp & Univ Health Ctr	Detroit	100%	279
Lapeer Regional Medical Center[2]	Lapeer	100%	398
Oakland Regional Hospital[3]	Southfield	100%	32
Saint John River District Hospital	East China	100%	45
Saint Joseph Mercy Saline Hospital	Saline	100%	47
Spectrum Health United Mem-United Campus	Greenville	100%	146
Battle Creek Health System[2]	Battle Creek	99%	806
Beaumont Hospital - Grosse Pointe[2]	Grosse Pointe	99%	516
Botsford Hospital[2]	Farmington Hills	99%	504
Chippewa County War Memorial Hospital	Sault Ste Marie	99%	197
Crittenton Hospital Medical Center[2]	Rochester	99%	405
Henry Ford Hospital[2]	Detroit	99%	583
Henry Ford Macomb Hospital[2]	Clinton Twp	99%	1271
Holland Community Hospital[2]	Holland	99%	504
Huron Valley-Sinai Hospital[2]	Commerce Twp	99%	502
Mercy Health Partners - Mercy Campus	Muskegon	99%	1087
Mercy Memorial Hospital System	Monroe	99%	524
Munson Medical Center[2]	Traverse City	99%	596
Northern Michigan Regional Hospital[2]	Petoskey	99%	458
Oakwood Heritage Hospital[2]	Taylor	99%	235
Oakwood Hospital and Medical Center[2]	Dearborn	99%	1281
Oakwood Southshore Medical Center[2]	Trenton	99%	403
Portage Health Hospital	Hancock	99%	173
Providence Hospital and Medical Centers[2]	Southfield	99%	1597
St John Macomb-Oakland Hosp-Macomb Ctr[2]	Warren	99%	1079
Saint Joseph Mercy Oakland[2]	Pontiac	99%	473
Saint Joseph Mercy Port Huron[2]	Port Huron	99%	318
Saint Mary Mercy Hospital	Livonia	99%	524
Sinai-Grace Hospital[2]	Detroit	99%	563
Spectrum Health Gerber Memorial	Fremont	99%	267
Sturgis Hospital	Sturgis	99%	89
Tawas Saint Joseph Hospital[2]	Tawas City	99%	154
University of Michigan Health System[2]	Ann Arbor	99%	1766
VA Ann Arbor Healthcare System	Ann Arbor	99%	363
William Beaumont Hospital[2]	Royal Oak	99%	663
William Beaumont Hospital-Troy[2]	Troy	99%	457
Allegiance Health[2]	Jackson	98%	434
Aspirus Grand View Hospital	Ironwood	98%	43
Bronson Methodist Hospital[2]	Kalamazoo	98%	1201
Community Hospital	Watervliet	98%	123
Emma L Bixby Medical Center[2]	Adrian	98%	195
Henry Ford West Bloomfield Hospital	West Bloomfield	98%	443
Henry Ford Wyandotte Hospital[2]	Wyandotte	98%	310
Marquette General Hospital[2]	Marquette	98%	376
Memorial Medical Center of West Michigan	Ludington	98%	244
Mercy Health Partners - Hackley Campus	Muskegon	98%	637
Mercy Hospital - Grayling[2]	Grayling	98%	142
Midmichigan Medical Center-Midland[2]	Midland	98%	491
North Ottawa Community Hospital	Grand Haven	98%	205
Oaklawn Hospital[2]	Marshall	98%	427
Oakwood Annapolis Hospital[2]	Wayne	98%	313
Otsego Memorial Hospital[2]	Gaylord	98%	168
Saint John Hospital and Medical Center[2]	Detroit	98%	1228
Saint Mary's Health Care[2]	Grand Rapids	98%	389
Saint Mary's of Michigan Medical Center[2]	Saginaw	98%	391
Spectrum Health - Butterworth Campus[2]	Grand Rapids	98%	761
West Branch Regional Medical Center[2]	West Branch	98%	269
Borgess Medical Center[2]	Kalamazoo	97%	426
Central Michigan Community Hospital	Mount Pleasant	97%	228
Detroit (John D. Dingell) VA Medical Center	Detroit	97%	192
Dickinson County Memorial Hospital	Iron Mountain	97%	236
Edward W Sparrow Hospital[2]	Lansing	97%	1383
Hurley Medical Center[2]	Flint	97%	287
Huron Medical Center[2]	Bad Axe	97%	149
Mclaren Regional Medical Center[2]	Flint	97%	1091
Mercy Hospital - Cadillac	Cadillac	97%	322
Metro Health Hospital[2]	Wyoming	97%	323
Mount Clemens Regional Medical Center[2]	Mount Clemens	97%	856
Pennock Hospital[2]	Hastings	97%	202
Port Huron Hospital[2]	Port Huron	97%	616
Saint Joseph Mercy Hospital[2]	Ann Arbor	97%	584
Saint Joseph Mercy Livingston Hospital[2]	Howell	97%	227
West Shore Medical Center	Manistee	97%	117
Zeeland Community Hospital	Zeeland	97%	198
Allegan General Hospital[2]	Allegan	96%	127
Bay Regional Medical Center	Bay City	96%	1013
Covenant Medical Center[2]	Saginaw	96%	545
Genesys Regional Med Ctr-Health Park[2]	Grand Blanc	96%	1333
Lakeland Hospital - St Joseph[2]	Saint Joseph	96%	643
Community Health Center of Branch County	Coldwater	95%	164
Garden City Hospital	Garden City	95%	394
Harper University Hospital[2]	Detroit	95%	428
Mecosta County Medical Center	Big Rapids	95%	199
Memorial Healthcare	Owosso	95%	220
Poh Medical Center[2]	Pontiac	95%	184
South Haven Community Hospital	South Haven	95%	82
Carson City Hospital	Carson City	93%	200
Ingham Regional Medical Center[2]	Lansing	93%	969
Saint Francis Hospital	Escanaba	93%	74
Three Rivers Health	Three Rivers	93%	58
Alpena Regional Medical Center[2]	Alpena	92%	300
Clinton Memorial Hospital	Saint Johns	92%	39
Karmanos Cancer Center[2]	Detroit	89%	130
Gratiot Medical Center	Alma	88%	219
Hayes Green Beach Memorial Hospital	Charlotte	87%	30
Midmichigan Medical Center-Clare	Clare	87%	60
Doctor's Hospital of Michigan[2]	Pontiac	80%	51
Hillsdale Community Health Center	Hillsdale	79%	176

29. Prophylactic Antibiotic Selection (Outpatient)

Hospital Name	City	Rate	Cases
Saint Francis Hospital	Escanaba	100%	30
Saint John River District Hospital	East China	100%	46
Zeeland Community Hospital	Zeeland	100%	54
Beaumont Hospital - Grosse Pointe	Grosse Pointe	99%	218
Chelsea Community Hospital	Chelsea	99%	151
Port Huron Hospital	Port Huron	99%	136
Providence Hospital and Medical Centers	Southfield	99%	866
Southeast Michigan Surgical Hospital	Warren	99%	106
Battle Creek Health System	Battle Creek	98%	251
Eaton Rapids Medical Center	Eaton Rapids	98%	63
Holland Community Hospital	Holland	98%	300
Mercy Health Partners - Hackley Campus	Muskegon	98%	328
Mercy Hospital - Grayling	Grayling	98%	96
Mercy Memorial Hospital System	Monroe	98%	107
Oakland Regional Hospital	Southfield	98%	49
Saint Joseph Mercy Oakland	Pontiac	98%	438
Saint Joseph Mercy Saline Hospital	Saline	98%	50
Spectrum Health United Mem-United Campus	Greenville	98%	53
Bronson Methodist Hospital	Kalamazoo	97%	376
Lapeer Regional Medical Center	Lapeer	97%	79
Mercy Health Partners - Mercy Campus	Muskegon	97%	595
Metro Health Hospital	Wyoming	97%	298
Munson Medical Center	Traverse City	97%	390
Saint John Hospital and Medical Center	Detroit	97%	622
St John Macomb-Oakland Hosp-Macomb Ctr	Warren	97%	422
Saint Joseph Mercy Hospital	Ann Arbor	97%	936
Saint Mary's of Michigan Medical Center	Saginaw	97%	438
Tawas Saint Joseph Hospital	Tawas City	97%	62
Botsford Hospital	Farmington Hills	96%	224
Community Health Center of Branch County	Coldwater	96%	71
Mclaren Regional Medical Center	Flint	96%	419
Memorial Medical Center of West Michigan	Ludington	96%	26
Oaklawn Hospital	Marshall	96%	70
Oakwood Hospital and Medical Center	Dearborn	96%	344
Spectrum Health - Butterworth Campus	Grand Rapids	96%	1197
Borgess Medical Center	Kalamazoo	95%	598
Henry Ford Macomb Hospital	Clinton Twp	95%	344
Mount Clemens Regional Medical Center	Mount Clemens	95%	235
North Ottawa Community Hospital	Grand Haven	95%	87
Northern Michigan Regional Hospital	Petoskey	95%	334
Saint Joseph Mercy Livingston Hospital	Howell	95%	113
Saint Mary Mercy Hospital	Livonia	95%	243
Sturgis Hospital	Sturgis	95%	58
Bay Regional Medical Center	Bay City	94%	450
Covenant Medical Center	Saginaw	94%	591
Huron Valley-Sinai Hospital	Commerce Twp	94%	158
Saint Joseph Mercy Port Huron	Port Huron	94%	32
William Beaumont Hospital-Troy	Troy	94%	464
Alpena Regional Medical Center	Alpena	93%	155
Detroit Receiving Hosp & Univ Health Ctr	Detroit	93%	71
Dickinson County Memorial Hospital	Iron Mountain	93%	27
Oakwood Southshore Medical Center	Trenton	93%	126
Allegiance Health	Jackson	92%	408
Central Michigan Community Hospital	Mount Pleasant	92%	60
Huron Medical Center	Bad Axe	92%	26
Lakeland Hospital - St Joseph	Saint Joseph	92%	381
Memorial Healthcare	Owosso	92%	122
Oakwood Annapolis Hospital	Wayne	92%	318
West Branch Regional Medical Center	West Branch	92%	63
Crittenton Hospital Medical Center	Rochester	91%	227
Gratiot Medical Center	Alma	91%	117
Midmichigan Medical Center-Midland	Midland	91%	378
William Beaumont Hospital	Royal Oak	91%	732
Ingham Regional Medical Center	Lansing	90%	547
Saint Mary's Health Care	Grand Rapids	90%	307
Chippewa County War Memorial Hospital	Sault Ste Marie	89%	57
Carson City Hospital	Carson City	88%	34
Edward W Sparrow Hospital	Lansing	88%	581
Henry Ford Wyandotte Hospital	Wyandotte	88%	325
Hurley Medical Center	Flint	88%	153
Portage Health Hospital	Hancock	88%	52
University of Michigan Health System	Ann Arbor	88%	694
Genesys Regional Med Ctr-Health Park	Grand Blanc	87%	488
Henry Ford Hospital	Detroit	86%	907
Marquette General Hospital	Marquette	86%	593
Harper University Hospital	Detroit	85%	476

NOTE: Hospital profiles are in alphabetical order by state, then city, then hospital within the city; Rankings exclude hospitals with less than 25 cases except for patient surveys which excludes hospitals with less than 100 cases; (a) 100–299 cases; (1) The number of cases is too small to be sure how well a hospital is performing; (2) The hospital indicated that the data submitted for this measure were based on a sample of cases; (3) Data was collected during a shorter time period (fewer quarters) than the maximum possible time for this measure; (4) Suppressed for one or more quarters by CMS; (5) No data is available from the hospital for this measure; (6) Fewer than 100 patients completed the HCAHPS survey. Use these rates with caution, as the number of surveys may be too low to reliably assess hospital performance; (7) Survey results are based on less than 12 months of data; (8) Survey results are not available for this reporting period; (9) No or very few patients were eligible for the HCAHPS survey. The scores shown, if any, reflect a very small number of surveys; (10) A state average was not calculated because too few hospitals in the state submitted data; (11) There were discrepancies in the data collection process; Please refer to the User's Guide for a full explanation of data.

Pennock Hospital	Hastings	83%	60
Mercy Hospital - Cadillac	Cadillac	82%	151
Sinai-Grace Hospital	Detroit	82%	379
Hillsdale Community Health Center	Hillsdale	81%	32
Karmanos Cancer Center	Detroit	78%	67
Poh Medical Center	Pontiac	76%	88
Henry Ford West Bloomfield Hospital	West Bloomfield	73%	273
Doctor's Hospital of Michigan	Pontiac	61%	75
Garden City Hospital	Garden City	61%	244
Emma L Bixby Medical Center	Adrian	58%	84

30. Prophylactic Antibiotic Stopped

Hospital Name	City	Rate	Cases
Holland Community Hospital[2]	Holland	100%	490
Huron Medical Center[2]	Bad Axe	100%	146
Oakland Regional Hospital[3]	Southfield	100%	31
Oakwood Heritage Hospital[2]	Taylor	100%	224
Saint John River District Hospital	East China	100%	45
South Haven Community Hospital	South Haven	100%	81
Spectrum Health United Mem-United Campus	Greenville	100%	137
Three Rivers Health	Three Rivers	100%	57
Chelsea Community Hospital[2]	Chelsea	99%	732
Lakeland Hospital - St Joseph[2]	Saint Joseph	99%	610
Mercy Health Partners - Hackley Campus	Muskegon	99%	631
North Ottawa Community Hospital	Grand Haven	99%	201
Saint Francis Hospital	Escanaba	99%	73
Tawas Saint Joseph Hospital[2]	Tawas City	99%	148
Allegiance Health[2]	Jackson	98%	410
Bronson Methodist Hospital[2]	Kalamazoo	98%	1169
Chippewa County War Memorial Hospital	Sault Ste Marie	98%	192
Munson Medical Center[2]	Traverse City	98%	568
Oaklawn Hospital[2]	Marshall	98%	422
Oakwood Southshore Medical Center[2]	Trenton	98%	392
Port Huron Hospital[2]	Port Huron	98%	587
Saint Joseph Mercy Oakland[2]	Pontiac	98%	426
Saint Joseph Mercy Saline Hospital	Saline	98%	45
Sinai-Grace Hospital[2]	Detroit	98%	529
Spectrum Health - Butterworth Campus[2]	Grand Rapids	98%	715
William Beaumont Hospital-Troy[2]	Troy	98%	388
Zeeland Community Hospital	Zeeland	98%	188
Battle Creek Health System[2]	Battle Creek	97%	741
Beaumont Hospital - Grosse Pointe[2]	Grosse Pointe	97%	497
Borgess Medical Center[2]	Kalamazoo	97%	402
Botsford Hospital[2]	Farmington Hills	97%	480
Community Hospital	Watervliet	97%	122
Dickinson County Memorial Hospital	Iron Mountain	97%	230
Hayes Green Beach Memorial Hospital	Charlotte	97%	30
Henry Ford Macomb Hospital[2]	Clinton Twp	97%	1216
Lapeer Regional Medical Center[2]	Lapeer	97%	386
Otsego Memorial Hospital[2]	Gaylord	97%	167
Pennock Hospital[2]	Hastings	97%	201
St John Macomb-Oakland Hosp-Macomb Ctr[2]	Warren	97%	971
Saint Joseph Mercy Hospital[2]	Ann Arbor	97%	560
Saint Joseph Mercy Port Huron[2]	Port Huron	97%	272
Saint Mary's Health Care[2]	Grand Rapids	97%	373
West Shore Medical Center	Manistee	97%	113
William Beaumont Hospital[2]	Royal Oak	97%	609
Bay Regional Medical Center	Bay City	96%	975
Detroit Receiving Hosp & Univ Health Ctr	Detroit	96%	274
Edward W Sparrow Hospital[2]	Lansing	96%	1333
Emma L Bixby Medical Center[2]	Adrian	96%	189
Huron Valley-Sinai Hospital[2]	Commerce Twp	96%	486
Mercy Hospital - Cadillac	Cadillac	96%	318
Mercy Memorial Hospital System	Monroe	96%	493
Metro Health Hospital[2]	Wyoming	96%	308
Midmichigan Medical Center-Midland[2]	Midland	96%	471
Providence Hospital and Medical Centers[2]	Southfield	96%	1431
Saint John Hospital and Medical Center[2]	Detroit	96%	1155
Saint Mary's of Michigan Medical Center[2]	Saginaw	96%	376
Spectrum Health Gerber Memorial	Fremont	96%	260
Alpena Regional Medical Center[2]	Alpena	95%	284
Crittenton Hospital Medical Center[2]	Rochester	95%	370
Detroit (John D. Dingell) VA Medical Center	Detroit	95%	188
Mclaren Regional Medical Center[2]	Flint	95%	1018
Mercy Health Partners - Mercy Campus	Muskegon	95%	1051
Midmichigan Medical Center-Clare	Clare	95%	56
Saint Joseph Mercy Livingston Hospital[2]	Howell	95%	223
Saint Mary Mercy Hospital	Livonia	95%	504
Central Michigan Community Hospital	Mount Pleasant	94%	219
Garden City Hospital	Garden City	94%	370
Genesys Regional Med Ctr-Health Park[2]	Grand Blanc	94%	1251
Henry Ford West Bloomfield Hospital	West Bloomfield	94%	435
Henry Ford Wyandotte Hospital[2]	Wyandotte	94%	285
Hurley Medical Center[2]	Flint	94%	272
Mecosta County Medical Center	Big Rapids	94%	195
Memorial Healthcare	Owosso	94%	216
Memorial Medical Center of West Michigan	Ludington	94%	239
Mount Clemens Regional Medical Center[2]	Mount Clemens	94%	762
Oakwood Annapolis Hospital[2]	Wayne	94%	299
Oakwood Hospital and Medical Center[2]	Dearborn	94%	1197
Harper University Hospital[2]	Detroit	93%	383
Henry Ford Hospital[2]	Detroit	93%	561
Ingham Regional Medical Center[2]	Lansing	93%	944
Mercy Hospital - Grayling[2]	Grayling	93%	133
Portage Health Hospital	Hancock	93%	162
University of Michigan Health System[2]	Ann Arbor	93%	1625
Carson City Hospital	Carson City	92%	193
Clinton Memorial Hospital	Saint Johns	92%	39
Doctor's Hospital of Michigan[2]	Pontiac	92%	50
Karmanos Cancer Center[2]	Detroit	92%	129
Allegan General Hospital[2]	Allegan	91%	126
Northern Michigan Regional Hospital[2]	Petoskey	91%	427
Community Health Center of Branch County	Coldwater	90%	159
Marquette General Hospital[2]	Marquette	89%	366
Aspirus Grand View Hospital	Ironwood	87%	39
Sturgis Hospital	Sturgis	87%	87
VA Ann Arbor Healthcare System	Ann Arbor	87%	350
Poh Medical Center[2]	Pontiac	86%	170
West Branch Regional Medical Center[2]	West Branch	86%	259
Hillsdale Community Health Center	Hillsdale	83%	173
Gratiot Medical Center	Alma	82%	211
Covenant Medical Center[2]	Saginaw	70%	518

31. Recommended VTP Ordered

Hospital Name	City	Rate	Cases
Carson City Hospital	Carson City	100%	66
Chelsea Community Hospital[2]	Chelsea	100%	281
Henry Ford Wyandotte Hospital[2]	Wyandotte	100%	208
Otsego Memorial Hospital[2]	Gaylord	100%	45
Saint Joseph Mercy Port Huron[2]	Port Huron	100%	165
Spectrum Health - Butterworth Campus[2]	Grand Rapids	100%	262
Tawas Saint Joseph Hospital[2]	Tawas City	100%	45
Botsford Hospital[2]	Farmington Hills	99%	267
Henry Ford Hospital[2]	Detroit	99%	300
Henry Ford Macomb Hospital[2]	Clinton Twp	99%	379
Holland Community Hospital[2]	Holland	99%	156
Oakwood Heritage Hospital[2]	Taylor	99%	90
Oakwood Hospital and Medical Center[2]	Dearborn	99%	518
Oakwood Southshore Medical Center[2]	Trenton	99%	149
Port Huron Hospital[2]	Port Huron	99%	280
Saint John Hospital and Medical Center[2]	Detroit	99%	394
St John Macomb-Oakland Hosp-Macomb Ctr[2]	Warren	99%	407
Saint Joseph Mercy Oakland[2]	Pontiac	99%	161
Saint Mary's Health Care[2]	Grand Rapids	99%	162
Spectrum Health United Mem-United Campus	Greenville	99%	70
University of Michigan Health System[2]	Ann Arbor	99%	700
William Beaumont Hospital[2]	Royal Oak	99%	309
Detroit (John D. Dingell) VA Medical Center[2]	Detroit	98%	161
Dickinson County Memorial Hospital	Iron Mountain	98%	149
Genesys Regional Med Ctr-Health Park[2]	Grand Blanc	98%	411
Henry Ford West Bloomfield Hospital	West Bloomfield	98%	241
Lakeland Hospital - St Joseph[2]	Saint Joseph	98%	294
Lapeer Regional Medical Center[2]	Lapeer	98%	128
Mount Clemens Regional Medical Center[2]	Mount Clemens	98%	298
Munson Medical Center[2]	Traverse City	98%	255
Portage Health Hospital	Hancock	98%	64
Saint Joseph Mercy Hospital[2]	Ann Arbor	98%	243
Sinai-Grace Hospital[2]	Detroit	98%	281
Sturgis Hospital	Sturgis	98%	49
Alpena Regional Medical Center[2]	Alpena	97%	115
Beaumont Hospital - Grosse Pointe[2]	Grosse Pointe	97%	225
Chippewa County War Memorial Hospital	Sault Ste Marie	97%	90
Garden City Hospital	Garden City	97%	306
Hurley Medical Center[2]	Flint	97%	176
Mclaren Regional Medical Center[2]	Flint	97%	291
North Ottawa Community Hospital	Grand Haven	97%	65
Oaklawn Hospital[2]	Marshall	97%	116
Providence Hospital and Medical Centers[2]	Southfield	97%	785
VA Ann Arbor Healthcare System[2]	Ann Arbor	97%	163
West Branch Regional Medical Center[2]	West Branch	97%	175
Allegiance Health[2]	Jackson	96%	164
Bronson Methodist Hospital[2]	Kalamazoo	96%	384
Clinton Memorial Hospital	Saint Johns	96%	28
Karmanos Cancer Center[2]	Detroit	96%	230
Mercy Health Partners - Hackley Campus	Muskegon	96%	281
Saint John River District Hospital	East China	96%	45
Zeeland Community Hospital	Zeeland	96%	50
Battle Creek Health System[2]	Battle Creek	95%	179
Borgess Medical Center[2]	Kalamazoo	95%	116
Mercy Memorial Hospital System	Monroe	95%	244
Edward W Sparrow Hospital[2]	Lansing	94%	442
Mercy Hospital - Cadillac	Cadillac	94%	86
Mercy Hospital - Grayling[2]	Grayling	94%	63
Metro Health Hospital[2]	Wyoming	94%	144
Midmichigan Medical Center-Midland[2]	Midland	94%	154
Oakwood Annapolis Hospital[2]	Wayne	94%	184
Poh Medical Center[2]	Pontiac	94%	106
Saint Mary's of Michigan Medical Center[2]	Saginaw	94%	188
Central Michigan Community Hospital	Mount Pleasant	93%	41
Huron Valley-Sinai Hospital[2]	Commerce Twp	93%	179
Mercy Health Partners - Mercy Campus	Muskegon	93%	299
Saint Francis Hospital	Escanaba	93%	57
William Beaumont Hospital-Troy[2]	Troy	93%	162
Detroit Receiving Hosp & Univ Health Ctr	Detroit	92%	362
Ingham Regional Medical Center[2]	Lansing	92%	190
Memorial Healthcare	Owosso	92%	140
Saint Mary Mercy Hospital	Livonia	92%	365
Crittenton Hospital Medical Center[2]	Rochester	91%	148
Doctor's Hospital of Michigan[2]	Pontiac	91%	90
Northern Michigan Regional Hospital[2]	Petoskey	90%	155
Bay Regional Medical Center	Bay City	89%	394
Community Hospital	Watervliet	89%	46
Covenant Medical Center[2]	Saginaw	89%	228
Emma L Bixby Medical Center[2]	Adrian	89%	114
Marquette General Hospital[2]	Marquette	89%	126
Pennock Hospital[2]	Hastings	89%	74
Spectrum Health Gerber Memorial	Fremont	89%	74
Harper University Hospital[2]	Detroit	88%	162
West Shore Medical Center	Manistee	88%	76
Saint Joseph Mercy Livingston Hospital[2]	Howell	87%	93
Community Health Center of Branch County	Coldwater	86%	117
Midmichigan Medical Center-Clare	Clare	85%	54
Mecosta County Medical Center	Big Rapids	83%	29
Memorial Medical Center of West Michigan	Ludington	80%	126
Gratiot Medical Center	Alma	79%	156
Hillsdale Community Health Center	Hillsdale	78%	60
Allegan General Hospital[2]	Allegan	72%	74
Marlette Regional Hospital	Marlette	68%	25

32. Urinary Catheter Removal

Hospital Name	City	Rate	Cases
Battle Creek Health System[2]	Battle Creek	100%	279
North Ottawa Community Hospital	Grand Haven	100%	94
Oakwood Heritage Hospital[2]	Taylor	100%	37
Otsego Memorial Hospital[2]	Gaylord	100%	62
South Haven Community Hospital	South Haven	100%	29
Tawas Saint Joseph Hospital	Tawas City	100%	41
Beaumont Hospital - Grosse Pointe[2]	Grosse Pointe	98%	172
Central Michigan Community Hospital	Mount Pleasant	98%	43
Saint Joseph Mercy Port Huron[2]	Port Huron	98%	177
Emma L Bixby Medical Center[2]	Adrian	97%	70
Henry Ford Macomb Hospital[2]	Clinton Twp	97%	461
Holland Community Hospital[2]	Holland	97%	33
Huron Medical Center[2]	Bad Axe	97%	33
Mercy Hospital - Cadillac	Cadillac	97%	102
St John Macomb-Oakland Hosp-Macomb Ctr[2]	Warren	97%	310
Sinai-Grace Hospital[2]	Detroit	97%	223
Allegiance Health[2]	Jackson	96%	69
Chelsea Community Hospital[2]	Chelsea	96%	246
Genesys Regional Med Ctr-Health Park[2]	Grand Blanc	96%	391
Saint John Hospital and Medical Center[2]	Detroit	96%	198
Saint Mary's Health Care[2]	Grand Rapids	96%	135
VA Ann Arbor Healthcare System[2]	Ann Arbor	96%	199
West Branch Regional Medical Center[2]	West Branch	96%	57
Alpena Regional Medical Center[2]	Alpena	95%	95
Chippewa County War Memorial Hospital	Sault Ste Marie	95%	97
Lakeland Hospital - St Joseph[2]	Saint Joseph	95%	215
Memorial Healthcare	Owosso	95%	100
Mercy Health Partners - Hackley Campus	Muskegon	95%	64
Mercy Health Partners - Mercy Campus	Muskegon	95%	382
Oaklawn Hospital[2]	Marshall	95%	117
Spectrum Health United Mem-United Campus	Greenville	95%	37
Botsford Hospital[2]	Farmington Hills	94%	199
Midmichigan Medical Center-Midland[2]	Midland	94%	170
Mount Clemens Regional Medical Center[2]	Mount Clemens	94%	294
Munson Medical Center[2]	Traverse City	94%	113
Providence Hospital and Medical Centers[2]	Southfield	94%	564
Borgess Medical Center[2]	Kalamazoo	93%	106
Bronson Methodist Hospital[2]	Kalamazoo	93%	336
Detroit Receiving Hosp & Univ Health Ctr	Detroit	93%	204
Henry Ford West Bloomfield Hospital	West Bloomfield	93%	214
William Beaumont Hospital-Troy[2]	Troy	93%	148
Community Hospital	Watervliet	92%	61
Hurley Medical Center[2]	Flint	92%	75
Midmichigan Medical Center-Clare	Clare	92%	26
Saint Joseph Mercy Oakland[2]	Pontiac	92%	143
West Shore Medical Center	Manistee	92%	53
Detroit (John D. Dingell) VA Medical Center[2]	Detroit	91%	32
Huron Valley-Sinai Hospital[2]	Commerce Twp	91%	185
Mecosta County Medical Center	Big Rapids	91%	56
Hillsdale Community Health Center	Hillsdale	90%	62
Metro Health Hospital[2]	Wyoming	90%	97
Spectrum Health - Butterworth Campus[2]	Grand Rapids	90%	323
Henry Ford Hospital[2]	Detroit	89%	198
Northern Michigan Regional Hospital[2]	Petoskey	89%	105
University of Michigan Health System[2]	Ann Arbor	89%	683
Garden City Hospital	Garden City	88%	153
Gratiot Medical Center	Alma	88%	72
Saint Mary Mercy Hospital	Livonia	88%	221
Covenant Medical Center[2]	Saginaw	87%	100

NOTE: Hospital profiles are in alphabetical order by state, then city, then hospital within the city; Rankings exclude hospitals with less than 25 cases except for patient surveys which excludes hospitals with less than 100 cases; (a) 100–299 cases; (1) The number of cases is too small to be sure how well a hospital is performing; (2) The hospital indicated that the data submitted for this measure were based on a sample of cases; (3) Data was collected during a shorter time period (fewer quarters) than the maximum possible time for this measure; (4) Suppressed for one or more quarters by CMS; (5) No data is available from the hospital for this measure; (6) Fewer than 100 patients completed the HCAHPS survey. Use these rates with caution, as the number of surveys may be too low to reliably assess hospital performance; (7) Survey results are based on less than 12 months of data; (8) Survey results are not available for this reporting period; (9) No or very few patients were eligible for the HCAHPS survey. The scores shown, if any, reflect a very small number of surveys; (10) A state average was not calculated because too few hospitals in the state submitted data; (11) There were discrepancies in the data collection process; Please refer to the User's Guide for a full explanation of data.

William Beaumont Hospital[2]	Royal Oak	87%	236
Poh Medical Center[2]	Pontiac	86%	88
Pennock Hospital[2]	Hastings	84%	25
Bay Regional Medical Center	Bay City	81%	267
Edward W Sparrow Hospital[2]	Lansing	81%	204
Ingham Regional Medical Center[2]	Lansing	80%	171
Portage Health Hospital	Hancock	80%	40
Marquette General Hospital[2]	Marquette	79%	94
Mclaren Regional Medical Center[2]	Flint	79%	152
Saint Mary's of Michigan Medical Center[2]	Saginaw	79%	94
Carson City Hospital	Carson City	78%	54
Crittenton Hospital Medical Center[2]	Rochester	78%	69
Doctor's Hospital of Michigan	Pontiac	78%	41
Harper University Hospital[2]	Detroit	78%	87
Saint Joseph Mercy Livingston Hospital[2]	Howell	78%	108
Oakwood Hospital and Medical Center[2]	Dearborn	77%	266
Saint Joseph Mercy Hospital[2]	Ann Arbor	75%	202
Oakwood Southshore Medical Center[2]	Trenton	74%	35
Port Huron Hospital[2]	Port Huron	74%	246
Community Health Center of Branch County	Coldwater	73%	77
Henry Ford Wyandotte Hospital[2]	Wyandotte	69%	42
Karmanos Cancer Center[2]	Detroit	50%	48

Children's Asthma Care

33. Received Systemic Corticosteroids

Hospital Name	City	Rate	Cases
Children's Hospital of Michigan[2]	Detroit	100%	401
Bronson Methodist Hospital	Kalamazoo	99%	87
Spectrum Health - Butterworth Campus	Grand Rapids	98%	185

34. Received Home Management Plan of Care

Hospital Name	City	Rate	Cases
Children's Hospital of Michigan[2]	Detroit	84%	401
Bronson Methodist Hospital	Kalamazoo	83%	87
Spectrum Health - Butterworth Campus	Grand Rapids	78%	185

35. Received Reliever Medication

Hospital Name	City	Rate	Cases
Children's Hospital of Michigan[2]	Detroit	100%	401
Spectrum Health - Butterworth Campus	Grand Rapids	100%	185
Bronson Methodist Hospital	Kalamazoo	99%	87

Use of Medical Imaging

36. Combination Abdominal CT Scan

Hospital Name	City	Ratio	Cases
Spectrum Health Gerber Memorial	Fremont	0.010	415
Mercy Health Partners - Mercy Campus	Muskegon	0.016	903
Oaklawn Hospital	Marshall	0.017	526
Saint Joseph Mercy Port Huron	Port Huron	0.020	345
Mercy Hospital - Cadillac	Cadillac	0.024	638
Memorial Healthcare	Owosso	0.029	655
Henry Ford Wyandotte Hospital	Wyandotte	0.030	1215
Port Huron Hospital	Port Huron	0.030	897
Deckerville Community Hospital[1]	Deckerville	0.031	32
Battle Creek Health System	Battle Creek	0.034	1160
Munson Medical Center	Traverse City	0.034	1305
Oakwood Heritage Hospital	Taylor	0.035	254
Paul Oliver Memorial Hospital	Frankfort	0.035	141
Central Michigan Community Hospital	Mount Pleasant	0.036	388
Community Hospital	Watervliet	0.038	212
Saint John River District Hospital	East China	0.040	272
Saint Joseph Mercy Livingston Hospital	Howell	0.042	552
Spectrum Health - Reed City Campus	Reed City	0.042	479
Spectrum Hlth United Mem-Kelsey Campus	Lakeview	0.044	91
Spectrum Health - Butterworth Campus	Grand Rapids	0.045	2656
Genesys Regional Med Ctr-Health Park	Grand Blanc	0.047	916
North Ottawa Community Hospital	Grand Haven	0.049	185
Emma L Bixby Medical Center	Adrian	0.051	585
Otsego Memorial Hospital	Gaylord	0.052	383
Northern Michigan Regional Hospital	Petoskey	0.053	837
Spectrum Health United Mem-United Campus	Greenville	0.053	543
Midmichigan Medical Center-Gladwin	Gladwin	0.054	331
Beaumont Hospital - Grosse Pointe	Grosse Pointe	0.057	703
Mercy Memorial Hospital System	Monroe	0.057	840
McKenzie Memorial Hospital	Sandusky	0.058	138
Allegiance Health	Jackson	0.060	1644
Henry Ford Hospital	Detroit	0.061	3298
Midmichigan Medical Center-Midland	Midland	0.061	1238
Three Rivers Health	Three Rivers	0.062	341
Oakwood Hospital and Medical Center	Dearborn	0.063	1724
Clinton Memorial Hospital	Saint Johns	0.064	311
Pennock Hospital	Hastings	0.064	342
Gratiot Medical Center	Alma	0.065	480
Zeeland Community Hospital	Zeeland	0.065	186
Midmichigan Medical Center-Clare	Clare	0.072	362
William Beaumont Hospital	Royal Oak	0.072	3843
Bronson Methodist Hospital	Kalamazoo	0.073	1162
Ionia County Memorial Hospital	Ionia	0.073	164
Providence Hospital and Medical Centers	Southfield	0.073	2330
South Haven Community Hospital	South Haven	0.073	218
Saint Mary's Health Care	Grand Rapids	0.078	1051
Edward W Sparrow Hospital	Lansing	0.079	1265
Holland Community Hospital	Holland	0.079	726
Portage Health Hospital	Hancock	0.087	196
Bay Regional Medical Center	Bay City	0.089	1135
Botsford Hospital	Farmington Hills	0.090	1124
Mercy Health Partners - Hackley Campus	Muskegon	0.091	789
Saint Joseph Mercy Saline Hospital	Saline	0.092	380
Lakeland Hospital - St Joseph	Saint Joseph	0.093	1890
Carson City Hospital	Carson City	0.094	235
Dickinson County Memorial Hospital	Iron Mountain	0.097	464
Lapeer Regional Medical Center	Lapeer	0.097	454
Saint Mary's Standish Community Hospital	Standish	0.097	331
Chelsea Community Hospital	Chelsea	0.098	356
Metro Health Hospital	Wyoming	0.098	945
Huron Valley-Sinai Hospital	Commerce Twp	0.099	547
Huron Medical Center	Bad Axe	0.102	354
University of Michigan Health System	Ann Arbor	0.102	2805
Saint Joseph Mercy Hospital	Ann Arbor	0.103	2089
Oakwood Annapolis Hospital	Wayne	0.104	548
Harper University Hospital	Detroit	0.108	636
Mercy Hospital - Grayling	Grayling	0.115	460
Garden City Hospital	Garden City	0.116	782
Oakwood Southshore Medical Center	Trenton	0.124	704
Karmanos Cancer Center	Detroit	0.125	1164
Tawas Saint Joseph Hospital	Tawas City	0.125	654
Hurley Medical Center	Flint	0.137	489
William Beaumont Hospital-Troy	Troy	0.137	2371
Saint Mary's of Michigan Medical Center	Saginaw	0.143	1205
Poh Medical Center	Pontiac	0.147	395
Crittenton Hospital Medical Center	Rochester	0.151	820
Saint Joseph Mercy Oakland	Pontiac	0.152	999
Saint John Hospital and Medical Center	Detroit	0.155	1107
Borgess Medical Center	Kalamazoo	0.157	1205
Ingham Regional Medical Center	Lansing	0.157	904
West Branch Regional Medical Center	West Branch	0.157	762
Alpena Regional Medical Center	Alpena	0.164	1011
Sinai-Grace Hospital	Detroit	0.182	939
Marlette Regional Hospital	Marlette	0.187	252
Covenant Medical Center	Saginaw	0.196	1615
Henry Ford Macomb Hospital	Clinton Twp	0.210	1019
Doctor's Hospital of Michigan	Pontiac	0.214	262
Detroit Receiving Hosp & Univ Health Ctr	Detroit	0.221	421
Community Health Center of Branch County	Coldwater	0.251	351
Hillsdale Community Health Center	Hillsdale	0.273	326
Eaton Rapids Medical Center	Eaton Rapids	0.286	161
Hills & Dales General Hospital	Cass City	0.325	160
Mount Clemens Regional Medical Center	Mount Clemens	0.328	1212
St John Macomb-Oakland Hosp-Macomb Ctr	Warren	0.348	1539
Mclaren Regional Medical Center	Flint	0.429	1408
Saint Mary Mercy Hospital	Livonia	0.463	1108
Mecosta County Medical Center	Big Rapids	0.488	330
Memorial Medical Center of West Michigan	Ludington	0.664	580
Marquette General Hospital	Marquette	0.724	638
Chippewa County War Memorial Hospital	Sault Ste Marie	0.785	330
Saint Francis Hospital	Escanaba	0.847	472
Sturgis Hospital	Sturgis	0.931	218

37. Combination Chest CT Scan

Hospital Name	City	Ratio	Cases
Clinton Memorial Hospital	Saint Johns	0.000	213
Northern Michigan Regional Hospital	Petoskey	0.000	827
Oaklawn Hospital	Marshall	0.000	361
Otsego Memorial Hospital	Gaylord	0.000	305
Saint Joseph Mercy Port Huron	Port Huron	0.000	383
Allegiance Health	Jackson	0.001	1117
Mclaren Regional Medical Center	Flint	0.001	1214
Edward W Sparrow Hospital	Lansing	0.002	979
Huron Valley-Sinai Hospital	Commerce Twp	0.002	582
Port Huron Hospital	Port Huron	0.002	833
Bronson Methodist Hospital	Kalamazoo	0.003	657
Munson Medical Center	Traverse City	0.003	901
Spectrum Health United Mem-United Campus	Greenville	0.003	350
Beaumont Hospital - Grosse Pointe	Grosse Pointe	0.004	550
University of Michigan Health System	Ann Arbor	0.004	3659
Harper University Hospital	Detroit	0.005	558
Memorial Healthcare	Owosso	0.005	576
Mercy Hospital - Cadillac	Cadillac	0.005	440
Saint Joseph Mercy Saline Hospital	Saline	0.005	204
Garden City Hospital	Garden City	0.006	668
Lapeer Regional Medical Center	Lapeer	0.006	358
Mercy Memorial Hospital System	Monroe	0.006	708
St John Macomb-Oakland Hosp-Macomb Ctr	Warren	0.007	992
Battle Creek Health System	Battle Creek	0.009	694
Lakeland Hospital - St Joseph	Saint Joseph	0.011	1229
Saint Joseph Mercy Hospital	Ann Arbor	0.011	1498
Providence Hospital and Medical Centers	Southfield	0.012	1788
Dickinson County Memorial Hospital	Iron Mountain	0.013	399
Oakwood Southshore Medical Center	Trenton	0.013	533
Paul Oliver Memorial Hospital	Frankfort	0.013	76
Portage Health Hospital	Hancock	0.013	153
Three Rivers Health	Three Rivers	0.013	149
Crittenton Hospital Medical Center	Rochester	0.014	698
Saint John River District Hospital	East China	0.014	218
Spectrum Health Gerber Memorial	Fremont	0.014	367
Gratiot Medical Center	Alma	0.015	539
Pennock Hospital	Hastings	0.015	200
Community Hospital	Watervliet	0.016	128
McKenzie Memorial Hospital	Sandusky	0.018	112
William Beaumont Hospital-Troy	Troy	0.018	2328
Saint Joseph Mercy Livingston Hospital	Howell	0.021	233
Oakwood Heritage Hospital	Taylor	0.022	268
Sinai-Grace Hospital	Detroit	0.022	912
Henry Ford Hospital	Detroit	0.023	3061
William Beaumont Hospital	Royal Oak	0.023	3829
Karmanos Cancer Center	Detroit	0.024	2088
Midmichigan Medical Center-Midland	Midland	0.026	956
Doctor's Hospital of Michigan	Pontiac	0.027	188
Bay Regional Medical Center	Bay City	0.029	864
Emma L Bixby Medical Center	Adrian	0.031	356
Botsford Hospital	Farmington Hills	0.032	816
Carson City Hospital	Carson City	0.032	187
Ingham Regional Medical Center	Lansing	0.032	555
Mecosta County Medical Center	Big Rapids	0.032	310
Saint Mary's Health Care	Grand Rapids	0.032	875
Henry Ford Wyandotte Hospital	Wyandotte	0.033	1120
Spectrum Hlth United Mem-Kelsey Campus	Lakeview	0.034	58
Central Michigan Community Hospital	Mount Pleasant	0.036	338
Oakwood Hospital and Medical Center	Dearborn	0.036	1438
Mercy Hospital - Grayling	Grayling	0.039	409
Chelsea Community Hospital	Chelsea	0.040	200
West Branch Regional Medical Center	West Branch	0.041	955
Holland Community Hospital	Holland	0.044	454
Spectrum Health - Butterworth Campus	Grand Rapids	0.045	1622
Saint Mary's Standish Community Hospital	Standish	0.053	281
Hillsdale Community Health Center	Hillsdale	0.055	256
Spectrum Health - Reed City Campus	Reed City	0.056	321
South Haven Community Hospital	South Haven	0.058	103
Poh Medical Center	Pontiac	0.059	272
Mercy Health Partners - Mercy Campus	Muskegon	0.061	821
Oakwood Annapolis Hospital	Wayne	0.062	308
Midmichigan Medical Center-Gladwin	Gladwin	0.065	399
Huron Medical Center	Bad Axe	0.083	133
Saint Joseph Mercy Oakland	Pontiac	0.084	818
Tawas Saint Joseph Hospital	Tawas City	0.093	377
Borgess Medical Center	Kalamazoo	0.095	1005
Alpena Regional Medical Center	Alpena	0.102	777
Zeeland Community Hospital	Zeeland	0.104	67
Mercy Health Partners - Hackley Campus	Muskegon	0.108	471
Metro Health Hospital	Wyoming	0.120	581
Mount Clemens Regional Medical Center	Mount Clemens	0.124	964
Marlette Regional Hospital	Marlette	0.125	200
Hurley Medical Center	Flint	0.127	307
Midmichigan Medical Center-Clare	Clare	0.145	249
Chippewa County War Memorial Hospital	Sault Ste Marie	0.168	262
North Ottawa Community Hospital	Grand Haven	0.170	159
Saint John Hospital and Medical Center	Detroit	0.170	778
Henry Ford Macomb Hospital	Clinton Twp	0.174	745
Community Health Center of Branch County	Coldwater	0.176	261
Detroit Receiving Hosp & Univ Health Ctr	Detroit	0.201	309
Saint Mary's of Michigan Medical Center	Saginaw	0.202	889
Ionia County Memorial Hospital	Ionia	0.204	98
Covenant Medical Center	Saginaw	0.238	1086
Saint Mary Mercy Hospital	Livonia	0.370	1222
Marquette General Hospital	Marquette	0.387	553
Genesys Regional Med Ctr-Health Park	Grand Blanc	0.393	580
Eaton Rapids Medical Center	Eaton Rapids	0.424	59
Hills & Dales General Hospital	Cass City	0.536	84
Sturgis Hospital	Sturgis	0.835	182
Saint Francis Hospital	Escanaba	0.847	405
Memorial Medical Center of West Michigan	Ludington	0.893	506

38. Follow-up Mammogram/Ultrasound

Hospital Name	City	Rate	Cases
South Haven Community Hospital	South Haven	1.6%	305
Gratiot Medical Center	Alma	2.1%	811
Saint John Hospital and Medical Center	Detroit	2.5%	2562
Ingham Regional Medical Center	Lansing	2.7%	911
Huron Medical Center	Bad Axe	3.0%	428
Spectrum Hlth United Mem-Kelsey Campus	Lakeview	3.1%	194
Doctor's Hospital of Michigan	Pontiac	3.2%	818
Allegiance Health	Jackson	3.6%	2442
Oaklawn Hospital	Marshall	3.6%	913
West Branch Regional Medical Center	West Branch	3.6%	505
Midmichigan Medical Center-Gladwin	Gladwin	3.8%	636
Northern Michigan Regional Hospital	Petoskey	4.0%	1214

NOTE: Hospital profiles are in alphabetical order by state, then city, then hospital within the city; Rankings exclude hospitals with less than 25 cases except for patient surveys which excludes hospitals with less than 100 cases; (a) 100–299 cases; (1) The number of cases is too small to be sure how well a hospital is performing; (2) The hospital indicated that the data submitted for this measure were based on a sample of cases; (3) Data was collected during a shorter time period (fewer quarters) than the maximum possible time for this measure; (4) Suppressed for one or more quarters by CMS; (5) No data is available from the hospital for this measure; (6) Fewer than 100 patients completed the HCAHPS survey. Use these rates with caution, as the number of surveys may be too low to reliably assess hospital performance; (7) Survey results are based on less than 12 months of data; (8) Survey results are not available for this reporting period; (9) No or very few patients were eligible for the HCAHPS survey. The scores shown, if any, reflect a very small number of surveys; (10) A state average was not calculated because too few hospitals in the state submitted data; (11) There were discrepancies in the data collection process; Please refer to the User's Guide for a full explanation of data.

Battle Creek Health System	Battle Creek	4.3%	1745
Bay Regional Medical Center	Bay City	4.3%	2019
Holland Community Hospital	Holland	4.3%	1383
Bronson Vicksburg Hospital	Vicksburg	4.4%	272
St John Macomb-Oakland Hosp-Macomb Ctr	Warren	4.4%	2133
Beaumont Hospital - Grosse Pointe	Grosse Pointe	4.5%	819
Covenant Medical Center	Saginaw	4.6%	2883
Karmanos Cancer Center	Detroit	4.7%	2378
Mercy Health Partners - Mercy Campus	Muskegon	4.7%	1547
Providence Hospital and Medical Centers	Southfield	4.7%	4175
Edward W Sparrow Hospital	Lansing	4.8%	1194
Clinton Memorial Hospital	Saint Johns	4.9%	243
Saint Francis Hospital	Escanaba	4.9%	667
Sturgis Hospital	Sturgis	5.1%	534
Spectrum Health United Mem-United Campus	Greenville	5.2%	601
Community Health Center of Branch County	Coldwater	5.6%	622
Marlette Regional Hospital	Marlette	5.7%	283
Memorial Medical Center of West Michigan	Ludington	5.7%	1037
Saint Mary's Health Care	Grand Rapids	5.7%	1769
Oakwood Hospital and Medical Center	Dearborn	5.8%	2597
Midmichigan Medical Center-Midland	Midland	5.9%	2207
North Ottawa Community Hospital	Grand Haven	6.0%	662
Bronson Methodist Hospital	Kalamazoo	6.1%	1020
Central Michigan Community Hospital	Mount Pleasant	6.3%	492
Huron Valley-Sinai Hospital	Commerce Twp	6.4%	815
Mclaren Regional Medical Center	Flint	6.4%	1642
Saint Joseph Mercy Oakland	Pontiac	6.4%	1613
Three Rivers Health	Three Rivers	6.4%	344
Mercy Health Partners - Hackley Campus	Muskegon	6.5%	1745
Mercy Hospital - Cadillac	Cadillac	6.5%	842
Dickinson County Memorial Hospital	Iron Mountain	6.7%	765
Lakeland Hospital - St Joseph	Saint Joseph	6.7%	2810
Saint Joseph Mercy Saline Hospital	Saline	6.7%	525
Mercy Memorial Hospital System	Monroe	6.9%	1229
Tawas Saint Joseph Hospital	Tawas City	6.9%	1172
Community Hospital	Watervliet	7.0%	342
Zeeland Community Hospital	Zeeland	7.0%	372
Oakwood Heritage Hospital	Taylor	7.1%	1012
Saint Mary's of Michigan Medical Center	Saginaw	7.1%	1558
Spectrum Health Gerber Memorial	Fremont	7.1%	709
Saint Joseph Mercy Livingston Hospital	Howell	7.2%	585
William Beaumont Hospital-Troy	Troy	7.2%	3408
Memorial Healthcare	Owosso	7.3%	1438
Saint Mary's Standish Community Hospital	Standish	7.3%	262
Saint Joseph Mercy Hospital	Ann Arbor	7.4%	3075
William Beaumont Hospital	Royal Oak	7.4%	6797
Alpena Regional Medical Center	Alpena	7.5%	1631
Midmichigan Medical Center-Clare	Clare	7.7%	794
Crittenton Hospital Medical Center	Rochester	7.9%	1401
Paul Oliver Memorial Hospital	Frankfort	8.2%	403
Botsford Hospital	Farmington Hills	8.3%	1044
Eaton Rapids Medical Center	Eaton Rapids	8.3%	205
Henry Ford Wyandotte Hospital	Wyandotte	8.3%	1228
University of Michigan Health System	Ann Arbor	8.5%	2433
Mecosta County Medical Center	Big Rapids	8.6%	571
Munson Medical Center	Traverse City	8.8%	2443
Garden City Hospital	Garden City	8.9%	415
Spectrum Health - Butterworth Campus	Grand Rapids	9.0%	4174
Henry Ford Macomb Hospital	Clinton Twp	9.9%	1851
Hurley Medical Center	Flint	9.9%	142
Hillsdale Community Health Center	Hillsdale	10.0%	653
Hills & Dales General Hospital	Cass City	10.1%	158
Ionia County Memorial Hospital	Ionia	10.2%	187
Pennock Hospital	Hastings	10.2%	695
Chippewa County War Memorial Hospital	Sault Ste Marie	10.5%	599
Henry Ford Hospital	Detroit	10.7%	5254
Borgess Medical Center	Kalamazoo	10.8%	1607
Emma L Bixby Medical Center	Adrian	10.8%	945
Chelsea Community Hospital	Chelsea	10.9%	847
Oakwood Annapolis Hospital	Wayne	10.9%	742
Spectrum Health - Reed City Campus	Reed City	10.9%	366
Mercy Hospital - Grayling	Grayling	11.2%	1083
Oakwood Southshore Medical Center	Trenton	11.2%	519
Otsego Memorial Hospital	Gaylord	11.4%	431
Metro Health Hospital	Wyoming	11.9%	1050
McKenzie Memorial Hospital	Sandusky	12.0%	167
Portage Health Hospital	Hancock	12.2%	353
Port Huron Hospital	Port Huron	12.4%	1448
Saint Mary Mercy Hospital	Livonia	12.4%	1401
Sinai-Grace Hospital	Detroit	12.8%	1235
Carson City Hospital	Carson City	12.9%	294
Deckerville Community Hospital	Deckerville	15.4%	117
Marquette General Hospital	Marquette	15.6%	909
Poh Medical Center	Pontiac	16.4%	341
Saint Joseph Mercy Port Huron	Port Huron	16.7%	701
Saint John River District Hospital	East China	18.7%	504
Genesys Regional Med Ctr-Health Park	Grand Blanc	31.8%	374

39. MRI for Low Back Pain

Hospital Name	City	Rate	Cases
Oakwood Annapolis Hospital	Wayne	20.4%	152
Harper University Hospital	Detroit	21.4%	350
University of Michigan Health System	Ann Arbor	22.7%	396
St John Macomb-Oakland Hosp-Macomb Ctr	Warren	23.9%	205
Saint Joseph Mercy Oakland	Pontiac	24.5%	282
Chelsea Community Hospital	Chelsea	24.8%	161
Oakwood Hospital and Medical Center	Dearborn	24.8%	202
Saint Mary Mercy Hospital	Livonia	24.8%	258
Sinai-Grace Hospital	Detroit	25.2%	222
Mercy Memorial Hospital System	Monroe	25.6%	129
Oakland Regional Hospital[1]	Southfield	25.9%	27
Allegiance Health	Jackson	26.0%	423
William Beaumont Hospital	Royal Oak	26.0%	781
Henry Ford Macomb Hospital	Clinton Twp	26.1%	161
Henry Ford Wyandotte Hospital	Wyandotte	26.3%	319
Huron Valley-Sinai Hospital	Commerce Twp	26.4%	174
Spectrum Health United Mem-United Campus	Greenville	26.4%	239
William Beaumont Hospital-Troy	Troy	26.4%	606
Beaumont Hospital - Grosse Pointe	Grosse Pointe	26.7%	116
Garden City Hospital	Garden City	26.7%	120
Providence Hospital and Medical Centers	Southfield	26.7%	424
Clinton Memorial Hospital	Saint Johns	26.8%	82
Oakwood Southshore Medical Center	Trenton	27.7%	130
Community Health Center of Branch County	Coldwater	28.2%	85
Oakwood Heritage Hospital	Taylor	28.2%	110
Saint Joseph Mercy Livingston Hospital	Howell	28.2%	110
Community Hospital	Watervliet	28.6%	63
Metro Health Hospital	Wyoming	29.4%	282
Bronson Methodist Hospital	Kalamazoo	29.6%	324
Saint John Hospital and Medical Center	Detroit	29.6%	294
Lakeland Hospital - St Joseph	Saint Joseph	29.8%	275
Ingham Regional Medical Center	Lansing	30.0%	170
Botsford Hospital	Farmington Hills	30.1%	93
Midmichigan Medical Center-Midland	Midland	30.1%	489
Portage Health Hospital	Hancock	30.2%	96
Doctor's Hospital of Michigan[1]	Pontiac	30.8%	39
Emma L Bixby Medical Center	Adrian	30.8%	130
Saint Joseph Mercy Hospital	Ann Arbor	30.8%	370
Zeeland Community Hospital[1]	Zeeland	31.0%	29
Memorial Medical Center of West Michigan	Ludington	31.2%	154
Dickinson County Memorial Hospital	Iron Mountain	31.9%	204
Munson Medical Center	Traverse City	32.3%	542
Memorial Healthcare	Owosso	32.4%	207
Mercy Health Partners - Mercy Campus	Muskegon	32.4%	552
Henry Ford Hospital	Detroit	32.7%	447
Borgess Medical Center	Kalamazoo	33.0%	469
Battle Creek Health System	Battle Creek	33.2%	220
Central Michigan Community Hospital	Mount Pleasant	34.0%	103
Sturgis Hospital	Sturgis	34.0%	50
Mercy Health Partners - Hackley Campus	Muskegon	34.1%	264
Pennock Hospital	Hastings	34.1%	123
Lapeer Regional Medical Center	Lapeer	34.7%	193
Saint Mary's Health Care	Grand Rapids	34.8%	244
Mecosta County Medical Center	Big Rapids	35.1%	154
Hillsdale Community Health Center	Hillsdale	35.2%	142
Midmichigan Medical Center-Gladwin	Gladwin	35.2%	88
Gratiot Medical Center	Alma	35.3%	190
Spectrum Health - Butterworth Campus	Grand Rapids	36.0%	702
West Branch Regional Medical Center	West Branch	36.3%	237
Oaklawn Hospital[1]	Marshall	36.4%	44
Saint Joseph Mercy Saline Hospital	Saline	36.8%	223
Northern Michigan Regional Hospital	Petoskey	36.9%	206
Covenant Medical Center	Saginaw	37.2%	401
Bay Regional Medical Center	Bay City	37.3%	415
North Ottawa Community Hospital	Grand Haven	37.3%	59
Saint Mary's of Michigan Medical Center	Saginaw	37.3%	576
Ionia County Memorial Hospital[1]	Ionia	37.5%	32
Midmichigan Medical Center-Clare	Clare	37.5%	128
Mercy Hospital - Cadillac	Cadillac	38.5%	262
South Haven Community Hospital	South Haven	39.1%	46
Spectrum Health - Reed City Campus	Reed City	39.1%	64
Alpena Regional Medical Center	Alpena	39.3%	257
Holland Community Hospital	Holland	40.6%	229
Chippewa County War Memorial Hospital	Sault Ste Marie	41.2%	165
Three Rivers Health	Three Rivers	41.4%	70
Marquette General Hospital	Marquette	41.5%	207
Otsego Memorial Hospital	Gaylord	41.5%	135
Tawas Saint Joseph Hospital	Tawas City	41.7%	223
Carson City Hospital	Carson City	42.9%	133
Saint Francis Hospital	Escanaba	43.8%	112
Spectrum Health Gerber Memorial	Fremont	43.9%	82
Saint Mary's Standish Community Hospital	Standish	45.5%	66
Mercy Hospital - Grayling	Grayling	54.5%	220

Survey of Patients' Hospital Experiences

40. Area Around Room 'Always' Quiet at Night

Hospital Name	City	Rate	Cases
Henry Ford West Bloomfield Hospital	West Bloomfield	75%	300+
Midmichigan Medical Center-Gladwin	Gladwin	72%	(a)
Saint Joseph Mercy Saline Hospital	Saline	71%	(a)
North Ottawa Community Hospital	Grand Haven	70%	300+
Hills & Dales General Hospital	Cass City	69%	(a)
Oaklawn Hospital	Marshall	67%	300+
Allegan General Hospital	Allegan	66%	(a)
Chelsea Community Hospital	Chelsea	66%	300+
Community Hospital	Watervliet	64%	(a)
Gratiot Medical Center	Alma	64%	300+
Metro Health Hospital	Wyoming	64%	300+
Zeeland Community Hospital	Zeeland	64%	300+
Midmichigan Medical Center-Clare	Clare	63%	300+
Saint Joseph Mercy Port Huron	Port Huron	63%	300+
West Shore Medical Center	Manistee	63%	300+
Saint Mary's Health Care	Grand Rapids	62%	300+
Dickinson County Memorial Hospital	Iron Mountain	61%	300+
Karmanos Cancer Center	Detroit	61%	300+
Mecosta County Medical Center	Big Rapids	61%	300+
Mercy Hospital - Cadillac	Cadillac	61%	300+
Oakwood Southshore Medical Center	Trenton	61%	300+
Sturgis Hospital	Sturgis	61%	300+
Bronson Lakeview Hospital	Paw Paw	60%	(a)
Portage Health Hospital	Hancock	60%	300+
Sinai-Grace Hospital	Detroit	60%	300+
Spectrum Hlth United Mem-Kelsey Campus	Lakeview	60%	(a)
Spectrum Health United Mem-United Campus	Greenville	60%	300+
Carson City Hospital	Carson City	59%	300+
Harper University Hospital	Detroit	59%	300+
Hayes Green Beach Memorial Hospital	Charlotte	59%	(a)
Huron Medical Center	Bad Axe	59%	300+
Marlette Regional Hospital	Marlette	59%	(a)
Saint Joseph Mercy Livingston Hospital	Howell	59%	300+
Spectrum Health - Reed City Campus	Reed City	59%	(a)
Allegiance Health	Jackson	58%	300+
Borgess-Lee Memorial Hospital	Dowagiac	58%	(a)
Bronson Methodist Hospital	Kalamazoo	58%	300+
Crittenton Hospital Medical Center	Rochester	58%	300+
Doctor's Hospital of Michigan	Pontiac	58%	300+
Herrick Memorial Hospital	Tecumseh	58%	300+
Mercy Hospital - Grayling	Grayling	58%	300+
Tawas Saint Joseph Hospital	Tawas City	58%	300+
Clinton Memorial Hospital	Saint Johns	57%	300+
Otsego Memorial Hospital	Gaylord	57%	300+
Pennock Hospital	Hastings	57%	300+
Saint Joseph Mercy Hospital	Ann Arbor	57%	300+
Spectrum Health Gerber Memorial	Fremont	57%	300+
Detroit Receiving Hosp & Univ Health Ctr	Detroit	56%	300+
Lakeland Hospital - St Joseph	Saint Joseph	56%	300+
Memorial Medical Center of West Michigan	Ludington	56%	300+
Providence Hospital and Medical Centers	Southfield	56%	300+
Emma L Bixby Medical Center	Adrian	55%	300+
Holland Community Hospital	Holland	55%	300+
Battle Creek Health System	Battle Creek	54%	300+
Central Michigan Community Hospital	Mount Pleasant	54%	300+
Henry Ford Hospital	Detroit	54%	300+
Saint John Hospital and Medical Center	Detroit	54%	300+
West Branch Regional Medical Center	West Branch	54%	300+
Chippewa County War Memorial Hospital	Sault Ste Marie	53%	300+
Huron Valley-Sinai Hospital	Commerce Twp	53%	300+
South Haven Community Hospital	South Haven	53%	(a)
Borgess Medical Center	Kalamazoo	52%	300+
Mercy Health Partners - Mercy Campus	Muskegon	52%	300+
Midmichigan Medical Center-Midland	Midland	52%	300+
Munson Medical Center	Traverse City	52%	300+
Oakwood Annapolis Hospital	Wayne	52%	300+
Saint John River District Hospital	East China	52%	300+
Beaumont Hospital - Grosse Pointe	Grosse Pointe	51%	300+
Community Health Center of Branch County	Coldwater	51%	300+
Hillsdale Community Health Center	Hillsdale	51%	300+
Memorial Healthcare	Owosso	51%	300+
Northern Michigan Regional Hospital	Petoskey	51%	300+
Oakwood Heritage Hospital	Taylor	51%	300+
Port Huron Hospital	Port Huron	51%	300+
Saint Joseph Mercy Oakland	Pontiac	51%	300+
Mercy Health Partners - Hackley Campus	Muskegon	50%	300+
Spectrum Health - Butterworth Campus	Grand Rapids	50%	300+
Ingham Regional Medical Center	Lansing	49%	300+
Edward W Sparrow Hospital	Lansing	48%	300+
Henry Ford Macomb Hospital	Clinton Twp	48%	300+
Henry Ford Wyandotte Hospital	Wyandotte	48%	300+
Hurley Medical Center	Flint	48%	300+
Marquette General Hospital	Marquette	48%	300+
Oakwood Hospital and Medical Center	Dearborn	48%	300+
Poh Medical Center	Pontiac	48%	300+
Lapeer Regional Medical Center	Lapeer	47%	300+
Mercy Memorial Hospital System	Monroe	47%	300+

NOTE: Hospital profiles are in alphabetical order by state, then city, then hospital within the city; Rankings exclude hospitals with less than 25 cases except for patient surveys which excludes hospitals with less than 100 cases; (a) 100–299 cases; (1) The number of cases is too small to be sure how well a hospital is performing; (2) The hospital indicated that the data submitted for this measure were based on a sample of cases; (3) Data was collected during a shorter time period (fewer quarters) than the maximum possible time for this measure; (4) Suppressed for one or more quarters by CMS; (5) No data is available from the hospital for this measure; (6) Fewer than 100 patients completed the HCAHPS survey. Use these rates with caution, as the number of surveys may be too low to reliably assess hospital performance; (7) Survey results are based on less than 12 months of data; (8) Survey results are not available for this reporting period; (9) No or very few patients were eligible for the HCAHPS survey. The scores shown, if any, reflect a very small number of surveys; (10) A state average was not calculated because too few hospitals in the state submitted data; (11) There were discrepancies in the data collection process; Please refer to the User's Guide for a full explanation of data.

Saint Francis Hospital	Escanaba	47%	300+
Bay Regional Medical Center	Bay City	45%	300+
Genesys Regional Med Ctr-Health Park	Grand Blanc	45%	300+
Botsford Hospital	Farmington Hills	44%	300+
Covenant Medical Center	Saginaw	44%	300+
Mclaren Regional Medical Center	Flint	44%	300+
Mount Clemens Regional Medical Center	Mount Clemens	44%	300+
Saint Mary's of Michigan Medical Center	Saginaw	44%	300+
William Beaumont Hospital-Troy	Troy	44%	300+
Garden City Hospital	Garden City	43%	300+
Three Rivers Health	Three Rivers	43%	(a)
Saint Mary Mercy Hospital	Livonia	42%	300+
University of Michigan Health System	Ann Arbor	42%	300+
William Beaumont Hospital	Royal Oak	42%	300+
St John Macomb-Oakland Hosp-Macomb Ctr	Warren	41%	300+
Alpena Regional Medical Center	Alpena	37%	(a)

41. Doctors 'Always' Communicated Well

Hospital Name	City	Rate	Cases
Clinton Memorial Hospital	Saint Johns	87%	300+
Midmichigan Medical Center-Gladwin	Gladwin	87%	(a)
Otsego Memorial Hospital	Gaylord	86%	300+
West Shore Medical Center	Manistee	86%	300+
Bronson Lakeview Hospital	Paw Paw	85%	(a)
Marlette Regional Hospital	Marlette	85%	(a)
Spectrum Health - Reed City Campus	Reed City	84%	(a)
Spectrum Health United Mem-United Campus	Greenville	84%	300+
Carson City Hospital	Carson City	83%	300+
Chelsea Community Hospital	Chelsea	83%	300+
Chippewa County War Memorial Hospital	Sault Ste Marie	83%	300+
Community Hospital	Watervliet	83%	(a)
Dickinson County Memorial Hospital	Iron Mountain	83%	300+
Holland Community Hospital	Holland	83%	300+
Huron Medical Center	Bad Axe	83%	300+
Pennock Hospital	Hastings	83%	300+
Saint Francis Hospital	Escanaba	83%	300+
South Haven Community Hospital	South Haven	83%	(a)
Spectrum Health Gerber Memorial	Fremont	83%	300+
Zeeland Community Hospital	Zeeland	83%	300+
Emma L Bixby Medical Center	Adrian	82%	300+
Gratiot Medical Center	Alma	82%	300+
Hills & Dales General Hospital	Cass City	82%	(a)
Midmichigan Medical Center-Clare	Clare	82%	300+
Northern Michigan Regional Hospital	Petoskey	82%	300+
Sturgis Hospital	Sturgis	82%	300+
Allegan General Hospital	Allegan	81%	(a)
Central Michigan Community Hospital	Mount Pleasant	81%	300+
Memorial Medical Center of West Michigan	Ludington	81%	300+
Mercy Hospital - Cadillac	Cadillac	81%	300+
Midmichigan Medical Center-Midland	Midland	81%	300+
Munson Medical Center	Traverse City	81%	300+
Oaklawn Hospital	Marshall	81%	300+
Oakwood Southshore Medical Center	Trenton	81%	300+
Portage Health Hospital	Hancock	81%	300+
West Branch Regional Medical Center	West Branch	81%	300+
Bronson Methodist Hospital	Kalamazoo	80%	300+
Henry Ford West Bloomfield Hospital	West Bloomfield	80%	300+
Mercy Hospital - Grayling	Grayling	80%	300+
Metro Health Hospital	Wyoming	80%	300+
North Ottawa Community Hospital	Grand Haven	80%	300+
Saint Joseph Mercy Saline Hospital	Saline	80%	(a)
Saint Mary's Health Care	Grand Rapids	80%	300+
Tawas Saint Joseph Hospital	Tawas City	80%	300+
Crittenton Hospital Medical Center	Rochester	79%	300+
Huron Valley-Sinai Hospital	Commerce Twp	79%	300+
Lakeland Hospital - St Joseph	Saint Joseph	79%	300+
Mecosta County Medical Center	Big Rapids	79%	300+
Mercy Health Partners - Hackley Campus	Muskegon	79%	300+
Oakwood Hospital and Medical Center	Dearborn	79%	300+
Saint John River District Hospital	East China	79%	300+
William Beaumont Hospital-Troy	Troy	79%	300+
Beaumont Hospital - Grosse Pointe	Grosse Pointe	78%	300+
Marquette General Hospital	Marquette	78%	300+
Mercy Health Partners - Mercy Campus	Muskegon	78%	300+
Oakwood Annapolis Hospital	Wayne	78%	300+
Saint Joseph Mercy Hospital	Ann Arbor	78%	300+
Saint Joseph Mercy Livingston Hospital	Howell	78%	300+
Saint Joseph Mercy Port Huron	Port Huron	78%	300+
Spectrum Hlth United Mem-Kelsey Campus	Lakeview	78%	(a)
University of Michigan Health System	Ann Arbor	78%	300+
William Beaumont Hospital	Royal Oak	78%	300+
Covenant Medical Center	Saginaw	77%	300+
Garden City Hospital	Garden City	77%	300+
Harper University Hospital	Detroit	77%	300+
Hayes Green Beach Memorial Hospital	Charlotte	77%	(a)
Henry Ford Macomb Hospital	Clinton Twp	77%	300+
Hillsdale Community Health Center	Hillsdale	77%	300+
Ingham Regional Medical Center	Lansing	77%	300+
Karmanos Cancer Center	Detroit	77%	300+
Port Huron Hospital	Port Huron	77%	300+
Providence Hospital and Medical Centers	Southfield	77%	300+
Spectrum Health - Butterworth Campus	Grand Rapids	77%	300+
Allegiance Health	Jackson	76%	300+
Battle Creek Health System	Battle Creek	76%	300+
Bay Regional Medical Center	Bay City	76%	300+
Botsford Hospital	Farmington Hills	76%	300+
Community Health Center of Branch County	Coldwater	76%	300+
Henry Ford Wyandotte Hospital	Wyandotte	76%	300+
Mercy Memorial Hospital System	Monroe	76%	300+
Mount Clemens Regional Medical Center	Mount Clemens	76%	300+
Oakwood Heritage Hospital	Taylor	76%	300+
Saint Joseph Mercy Oakland	Pontiac	76%	300+
Saint Mary Mercy Hospital	Livonia	76%	300+
Borgess Medical Center	Kalamazoo	75%	300+
Detroit Receiving Hosp & Univ Health Ctr	Detroit	75%	300+
Genesys Regional Med Ctr-Health Park	Grand Blanc	75%	300+
Henry Ford Hospital	Detroit	75%	300+
Herrick Memorial Hospital	Tecumseh	75%	300+
Doctor's Hospital of Michigan	Pontiac	74%	300+
Edward W Sparrow Hospital	Lansing	74%	300+
Saint Mary's of Michigan Medical Center	Saginaw	74%	300+
Sinai-Grace Hospital	Detroit	74%	300+
Alpena Regional Medical Center	Alpena	73%	(a)
Hurley Medical Center	Flint	73%	300+
Lapeer Regional Medical Center	Lapeer	73%	300+
Saint John Hospital and Medical Center	Detroit	73%	300+
Mclaren Regional Medical Center	Flint	72%	300+
Memorial Healthcare	Owosso	71%	300+
Poh Medical Center	Pontiac	70%	300+
St John Macomb-Oakland Hosp-Macomb Ctr	Warren	70%	300+
Three Rivers Health	Three Rivers	70%	(a)
Borgess-Lee Memorial Hospital	Dowagiac	68%	(a)

42. Home Recovery Information Given

Hospital Name	City	Rate	Cases
Central Michigan Community Hospital	Mount Pleasant	90%	300+
Holland Community Hospital	Holland	90%	300+
Northern Michigan Regional Hospital	Petoskey	90%	300+
Saint Joseph Mercy Saline Hospital	Saline	90%	(a)
Zeeland Community Hospital	Zeeland	90%	300+
Allegan General Hospital	Allegan	89%	(a)
Huron Medical Center	Bad Axe	89%	300+
Mercy Hospital - Grayling	Grayling	89%	300+
Saint Joseph Mercy Livingston Hospital	Howell	89%	300+
Spectrum Health Gerber Memorial	Fremont	89%	300+
Battle Creek Health System	Battle Creek	88%	300+
Chelsea Community Hospital	Chelsea	88%	300+
Community Hospital	Watervliet	88%	(a)
Gratiot Medical Center	Alma	88%	300+
Karmanos Cancer Center	Detroit	88%	300+
Mercy Hospital - Cadillac	Cadillac	88%	300+
Metro Health Hospital	Wyoming	88%	300+
North Ottawa Community Hospital	Grand Haven	88%	300+
Oaklawn Hospital	Marshall	88%	300+
Saint Mary's Health Care	Grand Rapids	88%	300+
Spectrum Health - Reed City Campus	Reed City	88%	(a)
University of Michigan Health System	Ann Arbor	88%	300+
Bronson Lakeview Hospital	Paw Paw	87%	(a)
Midmichigan Medical Center-Gladwin	Gladwin	87%	(a)
West Branch Regional Medical Center	West Branch	87%	300+
Clinton Memorial Hospital	Saint Johns	86%	300+
Community Health Center of Branch County	Coldwater	86%	300+
Covenant Medical Center	Saginaw	86%	300+
Edward W Sparrow Hospital	Lansing	86%	300+
Marquette General Hospital	Marquette	86%	300+
Mercy Health Partners - Mercy Campus	Muskegon	86%	300+
Midmichigan Medical Center-Clare	Clare	86%	300+
Munson Medical Center	Traverse City	86%	300+
Pennock Hospital	Hastings	86%	300+
Saint Joseph Mercy Hospital	Ann Arbor	86%	300+
South Haven Community Hospital	South Haven	86%	(a)
Borgess Medical Center	Kalamazoo	85%	300+
Bronson Methodist Hospital	Kalamazoo	85%	300+
Carson City Hospital	Carson City	85%	300+
Hayes Green Beach Memorial Hospital	Charlotte	85%	(a)
Mecosta County Medical Center	Big Rapids	85%	300+
Memorial Medical Center of West Michigan	Ludington	85%	300+
Saint Joseph Mercy Port Huron	Port Huron	85%	300+
Spectrum Health - Butterworth Campus	Grand Rapids	85%	300+
Spectrum Health United Mem-United Campus	Greenville	85%	300+
Tawas Saint Joseph Hospital	Tawas City	85%	300+
West Shore Medical Center	Manistee	85%	300+
Allegiance Health	Jackson	84%	300+
Ingham Regional Medical Center	Lansing	84%	300+
Marlette Regional Hospital	Marlette	84%	(a)
Mercy Health Partners - Hackley Campus	Muskegon	84%	300+
Saint Francis Hospital	Escanaba	84%	300+
Saint Mary's of Michigan Medical Center	Saginaw	84%	300+
Three Rivers Health	Three Rivers	84%	(a)
William Beaumont Hospital	Royal Oak	84%	300+
Bay Regional Medical Center	Bay City	83%	300+
Botsford Hospital	Farmington Hills	83%	300+
Chippewa County War Memorial Hospital	Sault Ste Marie	83%	300+
Dickinson County Memorial Hospital	Iron Mountain	83%	300+
Emma L Bixby Medical Center	Adrian	83%	300+
Midmichigan Medical Center-Midland	Midland	83%	300+
Otsego Memorial Hospital	Gaylord	83%	300+
Portage Health Hospital	Hancock	83%	300+
Saint Joseph Mercy Oakland	Pontiac	83%	300+
Sturgis Hospital	Sturgis	83%	300+
Crittenton Hospital Medical Center	Rochester	82%	300+
Henry Ford Hospital	Detroit	82%	300+
Henry Ford Macomb Hospital	Clinton Twp	82%	300+
Henry Ford West Bloomfield Hospital	West Bloomfield	82%	300+
Herrick Memorial Hospital	Tecumseh	82%	300+
Hurley Medical Center	Flint	82%	300+
Saint John River District Hospital	East China	82%	300+
Saint Mary Mercy Hospital	Livonia	82%	300+
Spectrum Hlth United Mem-Kelsey Campus	Lakeview	82%	(a)
Genesys Regional Med Ctr-Health Park	Grand Blanc	81%	300+
Memorial Healthcare	Owosso	81%	300+
Oakwood Southshore Medical Center	Trenton	81%	300+
Port Huron Hospital	Port Huron	81%	300+
Beaumont Hospital - Grosse Pointe	Grosse Pointe	80%	300+
Huron Valley-Sinai Hospital	Commerce Twp	80%	300+
Lakeland Hospital - St Joseph	Saint Joseph	80%	300+
Lapeer Regional Medical Center	Lapeer	80%	300+
Mount Clemens Regional Medical Center	Mount Clemens	80%	300+
William Beaumont Hospital-Troy	Troy	80%	300+
Detroit Receiving Hosp & Univ Health Ctr	Detroit	79%	300+
Doctor's Hospital of Michigan	Pontiac	79%	300+
Garden City Hospital	Garden City	79%	300+
Hills & Dales General Hospital	Cass City	79%	(a)
Oakwood Heritage Hospital	Taylor	79%	300+
Saint John Hospital and Medical Center	Detroit	79%	300+
Alpena Regional Medical Center	Alpena	78%	(a)
Hillsdale Community Health Center	Hillsdale	78%	300+
Harper University Hospital	Detroit	77%	300+
Henry Ford Wyandotte Hospital	Wyandotte	77%	300+
Mclaren Regional Medical Center	Flint	77%	300+
Oakwood Hospital and Medical Center	Dearborn	77%	300+
Providence Hospital and Medical Centers	Southfield	77%	300+
Sinai-Grace Hospital	Detroit	76%	300+
Mercy Memorial Hospital System	Monroe	75%	300+
Poh Medical Center	Pontiac	75%	300+
Oakwood Annapolis Hospital	Wayne	74%	300+
St John Macomb-Oakland Hosp-Macomb Ctr	Warren	74%	300+
Borgess-Lee Memorial Hospital	Dowagiac	73%	(a)

43. Hospital Given 9 or 10 on 10 Point Scale

Hospital Name	City	Rate	Cases
Munson Medical Center	Traverse City	83%	300+
Zeeland Community Hospital	Zeeland	83%	300+
Chelsea Community Hospital	Chelsea	82%	300+
Clinton Memorial Hospital	Saint Johns	82%	300+
Henry Ford West Bloomfield Hospital	West Bloomfield	81%	300+
Spectrum Hlth United Mem-Kelsey Campus	Lakeview	80%	(a)
Holland Community Hospital	Holland	79%	300+
Metro Health Hospital	Wyoming	79%	300+
Oaklawn Hospital	Marshall	79%	300+
Allegan General Hospital	Allegan	78%	(a)
Bronson Methodist Hospital	Kalamazoo	78%	300+
Karmanos Cancer Center	Detroit	78%	300+
Huron Medical Center	Bad Axe	77%	300+
Gratiot Medical Center	Alma	76%	300+
Mercy Hospital - Cadillac	Cadillac	76%	300+
Spectrum Health - Reed City Campus	Reed City	76%	(a)
Central Michigan Community Hospital	Mount Pleasant	75%	300+
North Ottawa Community Hospital	Grand Haven	75%	300+
Northern Michigan Regional Hospital	Petoskey	75%	300+
Community Hospital	Watervliet	74%	(a)
Hills & Dales General Hospital	Cass City	74%	(a)
Saint Joseph Mercy Hospital	Ann Arbor	74%	300+
Saint Joseph Mercy Saline Hospital	Saline	74%	(a)
University of Michigan Health System	Ann Arbor	74%	300+
West Shore Medical Center	Manistee	74%	300+
Carson City Hospital	Carson City	73%	300+
Midmichigan Medical Center-Midland	Midland	73%	300+
Oakwood Southshore Medical Center	Trenton	73%	300+
Saint Mary's Health Care	Grand Rapids	73%	300+
Spectrum Health Gerber Memorial	Fremont	73%	300+
Sturgis Hospital	Sturgis	73%	300+
Tawas Saint Joseph Hospital	Tawas City	73%	300+
Hayes Green Beach Memorial Hospital	Charlotte	72%	(a)
Pennock Hospital	Hastings	72%	300+
Spectrum Health - Butterworth Campus	Grand Rapids	72%	300+
West Branch Regional Medical Center	West Branch	72%	300+
Crittenton Hospital Medical Center	Rochester	71%	300+
Marlette Regional Hospital	Marlette	71%	(a)
Mercy Hospital - Grayling	Grayling	71%	300+

NOTE: Hospital profiles are in alphabetical order by state, then city, then hospital within the city; Rankings exclude hospitals with less than 25 cases except for patient surveys which excludes hospitals with less than 100 cases; (a) 100–299 cases; (1) The number of cases is too small to be sure how well a hospital is performing; (2) The hospital indicated that the data submitted for this measure were based on a sample of cases; (3) Data was collected during a shorter time period (fewer quarters) than the maximum possible time for this measure; (4) Suppressed for one or more quarters by CMS; (5) No data is available from the hospital for this measure; (6) Fewer than 100 patients completed the HCAHPS survey. Use these rates with caution, as the number of surveys may be too low to reliably assess hospital performance; (7) Survey results are based on less than 12 months of data; (8) Survey results are not available for this reporting period; (9) No or very few patients were eligible for the HCAHPS survey. The scores shown, if any, reflect a very small number of surveys; (10) A state average was not calculated because too few hospitals in the state submitted data; (11) There were discrepancies in the data collection process; Please refer to the User's Guide for a full explanation of data.

Midmichigan Medical Center-Gladwin	Gladwin	71%	(a)
Spectrum Health United Mem-United Campus	Greenville	71%	300+
Saint Joseph Mercy Livingston Hospital	Howell	70%	300+
Beaumont Hospital - Grosse Pointe	Grosse Pointe	69%	300+
Bronson Lakeview Hospital	Paw Paw	69%	(a)
Mecosta County Medical Center	Big Rapids	69%	300+
Portage Health Hospital	Hancock	69%	300+
South Haven Community Hospital	South Haven	69%	(a)
William Beaumont Hospital	Royal Oak	69%	300+
William Beaumont Hospital-Troy	Troy	69%	300+
Chippewa County War Memorial Hospital	Sault Ste Marie	68%	300+
Huron Valley-Sinai Hospital	Commerce Twp	68%	300+
Mercy Health Partners - Hackley Campus	Muskegon	68%	300+
Mercy Health Partners - Mercy Campus	Muskegon	68%	300+
Otsego Memorial Hospital	Gaylord	68%	300+
Providence Hospital and Medical Centers	Southfield	68%	300+
Saint Francis Hospital	Escanaba	68%	300+
Saint John River District Hospital	East China	68%	300+
Saint Joseph Mercy Port Huron	Port Huron	68%	300+
Borgess Medical Center	Kalamazoo	67%	300+
Community Health Center of Branch County	Coldwater	67%	300+
Covenant Medical Center	Saginaw	67%	300+
Edward W Sparrow Hospital	Lansing	67%	300+
Emma L Bixby Medical Center	Adrian	67%	300+
Henry Ford Hospital	Detroit	67%	300+
Memorial Medical Center of West Michigan	Ludington	67%	300+
Port Huron Hospital	Port Huron	67%	300+
Allegiance Health	Jackson	66%	300+
Genesys Regional Med Ctr-Health Park	Grand Blanc	66%	300+
Midmichigan Medical Center-Clare	Clare	66%	300+
Oakwood Hospital and Medical Center	Dearborn	66%	300+
Saint Joseph Mercy Oakland	Pontiac	66%	300+
Harper University Hospital	Detroit	65%	300+
Battle Creek Health System	Battle Creek	64%	300+
Dickinson County Memorial Hospital	Iron Mountain	64%	300+
Henry Ford Wyandotte Hospital	Wyandotte	64%	300+
Herrick Memorial Hospital	Tecumseh	64%	300+
Lakeland Hospital - St Joseph	Saint Joseph	64%	300+
Marquette General Hospital	Marquette	64%	300+
Bay Regional Medical Center	Bay City	63%	300+
Borgess-Lee Memorial Hospital	Dowagiac	63%	(a)
Ingham Regional Medical Center	Lansing	63%	300+
Detroit Receiving Hosp & Univ Health Ctr	Detroit	62%	300+
Henry Ford Macomb Hospital	Clinton Twp	62%	300+
Saint John Hospital and Medical Center	Detroit	62%	300+
Saint Mary Mercy Hospital	Livonia	62%	300+
Hurley Medical Center	Flint	61%	300+
Alpena Regional Medical Center	Alpena	60%	(a)
Botsford Hospital	Farmington Hills	60%	300+
Garden City Hospital	Garden City	60%	300+
Oakwood Heritage Hospital	Taylor	60%	300+
Poh Medical Center	Pontiac	60%	300+
Three Rivers Health	Three Rivers	60%	(a)
Lapeer Regional Medical Center	Lapeer	59%	300+
Mclaren Regional Medical Center	Flint	59%	300+
Oakwood Annapolis Hospital	Wayne	59%	300+
Doctor's Hospital of Michigan	Pontiac	58%	300+
Hillsdale Community Health Center	Hillsdale	58%	300+
Mount Clemens Regional Medical Center	Mount Clemens	58%	300+
St John Macomb-Oakland Hosp-Macomb Ctr	Warren	57%	300+
Saint Mary's of Michigan Medical Center	Saginaw	57%	300+
Sinai-Grace Hospital	Detroit	56%	300+
Memorial Healthcare	Owosso	54%	300+
Mercy Memorial Hospital System	Monroe	54%	300+

44. Meds 'Always' Explained Before Given

Hospital Name	City	Rate	Cases
Northern Michigan Regional Hospital	Petoskey	70%	300+
Spectrum Health - Reed City Campus	Reed City	70%	(a)
Chelsea Community Hospital	Chelsea	69%	300+
Spectrum Health Gerber Memorial	Fremont	69%	300+
Spectrum Hlth United Mem-Kelsey Campus	Lakeview	69%	(a)
Hills & Dales General Hospital	Cass City	68%	(a)
Karmanos Cancer Center	Detroit	68%	300+
West Shore Medical Center	Manistee	68%	300+
Clinton Memorial Hospital	Saint Johns	66%	300+
Otsego Memorial Hospital	Gaylord	66%	300+
Portage Health Hospital	Hancock	66%	300+
Spectrum Health United Mem-United Campus	Greenville	66%	300+
Gratiot Medical Center	Alma	65%	300+
Mercy Hospital - Cadillac	Cadillac	65%	300+
Munson Medical Center	Traverse City	65%	300+
Community Health Center of Branch County	Coldwater	64%	300+
Emma L Bixby Medical Center	Adrian	64%	300+
Henry Ford West Bloomfield Hospital	West Bloomfield	64%	300+
Holland Community Hospital	Holland	64%	300+
Mercy Hospital - Grayling	Grayling	64%	300+
Saint Joseph Mercy Livingston Hospital	Howell	64%	300+
Huron Medical Center	Bad Axe	63%	300+
Metro Health Hospital	Wyoming	63%	300+
Oakwood Annapolis Hospital	Wayne	63%	300+
Oakwood Southshore Medical Center	Trenton	63%	300+
Saint Joseph Mercy Saline Hospital	Saline	63%	(a)
Saint Mary's Health Care	Grand Rapids	63%	300+
South Haven Community Hospital	South Haven	63%	(a)
Zeeland Community Hospital	Zeeland	63%	300+
Carson City Hospital	Carson City	62%	300+
Dickinson County Memorial Hospital	Iron Mountain	62%	300+
Marlette Regional Hospital	Marlette	62%	(a)
Mercy Health Partners - Hackley Campus	Muskegon	62%	300+
Bronson Methodist Hospital	Kalamazoo	61%	300+
Central Michigan Community Hospital	Mount Pleasant	61%	300+
Edward W Sparrow Hospital	Lansing	61%	300+
Huron Valley-Sinai Hospital	Commerce Twp	61%	300+
Mecosta County Medical Center	Big Rapids	61%	300+
Memorial Medical Center of West Michigan	Ludington	61%	300+
North Ottawa Community Hospital	Grand Haven	61%	300+
Oaklawn Hospital	Marshall	61%	300+
Oakwood Hospital and Medical Center	Dearborn	61%	300+
Saint Francis Hospital	Escanaba	61%	300+
Saint Joseph Mercy Hospital	Ann Arbor	61%	300+
Allegiance Health	Jackson	60%	300+
Beaumont Hospital - Grosse Pointe	Grosse Pointe	60%	300+
Community Hospital	Watervliet	60%	(a)
Henry Ford Wyandotte Hospital	Wyandotte	60%	300+
Lapeer Regional Medical Center	Lapeer	60%	300+
Midmichigan Medical Center-Midland	Midland	60%	300+
Tawas Saint Joseph Hospital	Tawas City	60%	300+
University of Michigan Health System	Ann Arbor	60%	300+
Battle Creek Health System	Battle Creek	59%	300+
Bay Regional Medical Center	Bay City	59%	300+
Bronson Lakeview Hospital	Paw Paw	59%	(a)
Covenant Medical Center	Saginaw	59%	300+
Garden City Hospital	Garden City	59%	300+
Harper University Hospital	Detroit	59%	300+
Henry Ford Hospital	Detroit	59%	300+
Midmichigan Medical Center-Clare	Clare	59%	300+
Midmichigan Medical Center-Gladwin	Gladwin	59%	(a)
Spectrum Health - Butterworth Campus	Grand Rapids	59%	300+
Three Rivers Health	Three Rivers	59%	(a)
Allegan General Hospital	Allegan	58%	(a)
Chippewa County War Memorial Hospital	Sault Ste Marie	58%	300+
Doctor's Hospital of Michigan	Pontiac	58%	300+
Henry Ford Macomb Hospital	Clinton Twp	58%	300+
Herrick Memorial Hospital	Tecumseh	58%	300+
Marquette General Hospital	Marquette	58%	300+
Oakwood Heritage Hospital	Taylor	58%	300+
Port Huron Hospital	Port Huron	58%	300+
Sturgis Hospital	Sturgis	58%	300+
Genesys Regional Med Ctr-Health Park	Grand Blanc	57%	300+
Hillsdale Community Health Center	Hillsdale	57%	300+
Lakeland Hospital - St Joseph	Saint Joseph	57%	300+
Mercy Health Partners - Mercy Campus	Muskegon	57%	300+
Saint John Hospital and Medical Center	Detroit	57%	300+
Saint John River District Hospital	East China	57%	300+
Saint Joseph Mercy Oakland	Pontiac	57%	300+
Saint Joseph Mercy Port Huron	Port Huron	57%	300+
Borgess Medical Center	Kalamazoo	56%	300+
Detroit Receiving Hosp & Univ Health Ctr	Detroit	56%	300+
Hurley Medical Center	Flint	56%	300+
Mercy Memorial Hospital System	Monroe	56%	300+
West Branch Regional Medical Center	West Branch	56%	300+
William Beaumont Hospital	Royal Oak	56%	300+
William Beaumont Hospital-Troy	Troy	56%	300+
Mount Clemens Regional Medical Center	Mount Clemens	55%	300+
Pennock Hospital	Hastings	55%	300+
Borgess-Lee Memorial Hospital	Dowagiac	54%	(a)
Crittenton Hospital Medical Center	Rochester	54%	300+
Hayes Green Beach Memorial Hospital	Charlotte	54%	(a)
Ingham Regional Medical Center	Lansing	54%	300+
Mclaren Regional Medical Center	Flint	54%	300+
Memorial Healthcare	Owosso	54%	300+
Poh Medical Center	Pontiac	54%	300+
Providence Hospital and Medical Centers	Southfield	54%	300+
St John Macomb-Oakland Hosp-Macomb Ctr	Warren	54%	300+
Sinai-Grace Hospital	Detroit	54%	300+
Saint Mary Mercy Hospital	Livonia	53%	300+
Saint Mary's of Michigan Medical Center	Saginaw	52%	300+
Alpena Regional Medical Center	Alpena	48%	(a)
Botsford Hospital	Farmington Hills	48%	300+

45. Nurses 'Always' Communicated Well

Hospital Name	City	Rate	Cases
Spectrum Hlth United Mem-Kelsey Campus	Lakeview	88%	(a)
Spectrum Health - Reed City Campus	Reed City	84%	(a)
Chelsea Community Hospital	Chelsea	83%	300+
Clinton Memorial Hospital	Saint Johns	83%	300+
Karmanos Cancer Center	Detroit	83%	300+
Munson Medical Center	Traverse City	83%	300+
Saint Francis Hospital	Escanaba	83%	300+
Allegan General Hospital	Allegan	82%	(a)
Chippewa County War Memorial Hospital	Sault Ste Marie	82%	300+
Gratiot Medical Center	Alma	82%	300+
Hills & Dales General Hospital	Cass City	82%	(a)
Midmichigan Medical Center-Gladwin	Gladwin	82%	(a)
Spectrum Health Gerber Memorial	Fremont	82%	300+
Zeeland Community Hospital	Zeeland	82%	300+
Bronson Lakeview Hospital	Paw Paw	81%	(a)
Central Michigan Community Hospital	Mount Pleasant	81%	300+
West Shore Medical Center	Manistee	81%	300+
Huron Medical Center	Bad Axe	80%	300+
Mercy Hospital - Cadillac	Cadillac	80%	300+
Mercy Hospital - Grayling	Grayling	80%	300+
Northern Michigan Regional Hospital	Petoskey	80%	300+
Oakwood Hospital and Medical Center	Dearborn	80%	300+
Saint Joseph Mercy Livingston Hospital	Howell	80%	300+
Saint Joseph Mercy Saline Hospital	Saline	80%	(a)
Tawas Saint Joseph Hospital	Tawas City	80%	300+
Bronson Methodist Hospital	Kalamazoo	79%	300+
Community Hospital	Watervliet	79%	(a)
Covenant Medical Center	Saginaw	79%	300+
Holland Community Hospital	Holland	79%	300+
Oaklawn Hospital	Marshall	79%	300+
Port Huron Hospital	Port Huron	79%	300+
Portage Health Hospital	Hancock	79%	300+
Spectrum Health - Butterworth Campus	Grand Rapids	79%	300+
Crittenton Hospital Medical Center	Rochester	78%	300+
Dickinson County Memorial Hospital	Iron Mountain	78%	300+
Hayes Green Beach Memorial Hospital	Charlotte	78%	(a)
Henry Ford West Bloomfield Hospital	West Bloomfield	78%	300+
North Ottawa Community Hospital	Grand Haven	78%	300+
Oakwood Southshore Medical Center	Trenton	78%	300+
Otsego Memorial Hospital	Gaylord	78%	300+
South Haven Community Hospital	South Haven	78%	(a)
Spectrum Health United Mem-United Campus	Greenville	78%	300+
West Branch Regional Medical Center	West Branch	78%	300+
Allegiance Health	Jackson	77%	300+
Carson City Hospital	Carson City	77%	300+
Community Health Center of Branch County	Coldwater	77%	300+
Edward W Sparrow Hospital	Lansing	77%	300+
Huron Valley-Sinai Hospital	Commerce Twp	77%	300+
Metro Health Hospital	Wyoming	77%	300+
Saint Mary's Health Care	Grand Rapids	77%	300+
Sturgis Hospital	Sturgis	77%	300+
University of Michigan Health System	Ann Arbor	77%	300+
Battle Creek Health System	Battle Creek	76%	300+
Bay Regional Medical Center	Bay City	76%	300+
Emma L Bixby Medical Center	Adrian	76%	300+
Harper University Hospital	Detroit	76%	300+
Henry Ford Macomb Hospital	Clinton Twp	76%	300+
Memorial Medical Center of West Michigan	Ludington	76%	300+
Midmichigan Medical Center-Midland	Midland	76%	300+
Oakwood Annapolis Hospital	Wayne	76%	300+
Saint John River District Hospital	East China	76%	300+
Saint Joseph Mercy Hospital	Ann Arbor	76%	300+
Beaumont Hospital - Grosse Pointe	Grosse Pointe	75%	300+
Doctor's Hospital of Michigan	Pontiac	75%	300+
Henry Ford Hospital	Detroit	75%	300+
Henry Ford Wyandotte Hospital	Wyandotte	75%	300+
Marlette Regional Hospital	Marlette	75%	(a)
Mercy Health Partners - Hackley Campus	Muskegon	75%	300+
Midmichigan Medical Center-Clare	Clare	75%	300+
Oakwood Heritage Hospital	Taylor	75%	300+
Pennock Hospital	Hastings	75%	300+
Saint John Hospital and Medical Center	Detroit	75%	300+
Saint Joseph Mercy Port Huron	Port Huron	75%	300+
William Beaumont Hospital	Royal Oak	75%	300+
William Beaumont Hospital-Troy	Troy	75%	300+
Hillsdale Community Health Center	Hillsdale	74%	300+
Ingham Regional Medical Center	Lansing	74%	300+
Lakeland Hospital - St Joseph	Saint Joseph	74%	300+
Providence Hospital and Medical Centers	Southfield	74%	300+
Saint Mary Mercy Hospital	Livonia	74%	300+
Genesys Regional Med Ctr-Health Park	Grand Blanc	73%	300+
Herrick Memorial Hospital	Tecumseh	73%	300+
Hurley Medical Center	Flint	73%	300+
Mecosta County Medical Center	Big Rapids	73%	300+
Mercy Health Partners - Mercy Campus	Muskegon	73%	300+
Mercy Memorial Hospital System	Monroe	73%	300+
Saint Joseph Mercy Oakland	Pontiac	73%	300+
Sinai-Grace Hospital	Detroit	73%	300+
Borgess-Lee Memorial Hospital	Dowagiac	72%	(a)
Detroit Receiving Hosp & Univ Health Ctr	Detroit	72%	300+
Lapeer Regional Medical Center	Lapeer	72%	300+
Marquette General Hospital	Marquette	72%	300+
Three Rivers Health	Three Rivers	72%	(a)
Borgess Medical Center	Kalamazoo	71%	300+
Botsford Hospital	Farmington Hills	71%	300+
Garden City Hospital	Garden City	71%	300+
Memorial Healthcare	Owosso	71%	300+
Mount Clemens Regional Medical Center	Mount Clemens	71%	300+

NOTE: Hospital profiles are in alphabetical order by state, then city, then hospital within the city; Rankings exclude hospitals with less than 25 cases except for patient surveys which excludes hospitals with less than 100 cases; (a) 100–299 cases; (1) The number of cases is too small to be sure how well a hospital is performing; (2) The hospital indicated that the data submitted for this measure were based on a sample of cases; (3) Data was collected during a shorter time period (fewer quarters) than the maximum possible time for this measure; (4) Suppressed for one or more quarters by CMS; (5) No data is available from the hospital for this measure; (6) Fewer than 100 patients completed the HCAHPS survey. Use these rates with caution, as the number of surveys may be too low to reliably assess hospital performance; (7) Survey results are based on less than 12 months of data; (8) Survey results are not available for this reporting period; (9) No or very few patients were eligible for the HCAHPS survey. The scores shown, if any, reflect a very small number of surveys; (10) A state average was not calculated because too few hospitals in the state submitted data; (11) There were discrepancies in the data collection process; Please refer to the User's Guide for a full explanation of data.

Poh Medical Center	Pontiac	71%	300+
St John Macomb-Oakland Hosp-Macomb Ctr	Warren	70%	300+
Mclaren Regional Medical Center	Flint	69%	300+
Saint Mary's of Michigan Medical Center	Saginaw	67%	300+
Alpena Regional Medical Center	Alpena	63%	(a)

46. Pain 'Always' Well Controlled

Hospital Name	City	Rate	Cases
Spectrum Health - Reed City Campus	Reed City	78%	(a)
Spectrum Hlth United Mem-Kelsey Campus	Lakeview	78%	(a)
Clinton Memorial Hospital	Saint Johns	77%	300+
Community Hospital	Watervliet	77%	(a)
Midmichigan Medical Center-Gladwin	Gladwin	77%	(a)
Tawas Saint Joseph Hospital	Tawas City	76%	300+
Allegan General Hospital	Allegan	75%	(a)
Huron Medical Center	Bad Axe	75%	300+
Midmichigan Medical Center-Clare	Clare	75%	300+
Midmichigan Medical Center-Midland	Midland	75%	300+
Northern Michigan Regional Hospital	Petoskey	75%	300+
Bronson Lakeview Hospital	Paw Paw	74%	(a)
Karmanos Cancer Center	Detroit	74%	300+
Oaklawn Hospital	Marshall	74%	300+
Saint Francis Hospital	Escanaba	74%	300+
Saint John River District Hospital	East China	74%	300+
Spectrum Health Gerber Memorial	Fremont	74%	300+
West Shore Medical Center	Manistee	74%	300+
Bronson Methodist Hospital	Kalamazoo	73%	300+
Central Michigan Community Hospital	Mount Pleasant	73%	300+
Covenant Medical Center	Saginaw	73%	300+
Dickinson County Memorial Hospital	Iron Mountain	73%	300+
Emma L Bixby Medical Center	Adrian	73%	300+
Hayes Green Beach Memorial Hospital	Charlotte	73%	(a)
Marlette Regional Hospital	Marlette	73%	(a)
Mercy Hospital - Cadillac	Cadillac	73%	300+
Mercy Hospital - Grayling	Grayling	73%	300+
Munson Medical Center	Traverse City	73%	300+
Oakwood Southshore Medical Center	Trenton	73%	300+
Saint Joseph Mercy Livingston Hospital	Howell	73%	300+
Saint Joseph Mercy Saline Hospital	Saline	73%	(a)
West Branch Regional Medical Center	West Branch	73%	300+
Zeeland Community Hospital	Zeeland	73%	300+
Chelsea Community Hospital	Chelsea	72%	300+
Metro Health Hospital	Wyoming	72%	300+
Spectrum Health United Mem-United Campus	Greenville	72%	300+
Chippewa County War Memorial Hospital	Sault Ste Marie	71%	300+
Edward W Sparrow Hospital	Lansing	71%	300+
Memorial Medical Center of West Michigan	Ludington	71%	300+
North Ottawa Community Hospital	Grand Haven	71%	300+
Oakwood Heritage Hospital	Taylor	71%	300+
Oakwood Hospital and Medical Center	Dearborn	71%	300+
Otsego Memorial Hospital	Gaylord	71%	300+
Port Huron Hospital	Port Huron	71%	300+
South Haven Community Hospital	South Haven	71%	(a)
Sturgis Hospital	Sturgis	71%	300+
Crittenton Hospital Medical Center	Rochester	70%	300+
Henry Ford West Bloomfield Hospital	West Bloomfield	70%	300+
Holland Community Hospital	Holland	70%	300+
Lakeland Hospital - St Joseph	Saint Joseph	70%	300+
Mercy Health Partners - Hackley Campus	Muskegon	70%	300+
Oakwood Annapolis Hospital	Wayne	70%	300+
Portage Health Hospital	Hancock	70%	300+
Saint Mary's Health Care	Grand Rapids	70%	300+
Spectrum Health - Butterworth Campus	Grand Rapids	70%	300+
William Beaumont Hospital	Royal Oak	70%	300+
Battle Creek Health System	Battle Creek	69%	300+
Bay Regional Medical Center	Bay City	69%	300+
Beaumont Hospital - Grosse Pointe	Grosse Pointe	69%	300+
Mecosta County Medical Center	Big Rapids	69%	300+
William Beaumont Hospital-Troy	Troy	69%	300+
Carson City Hospital	Carson City	68%	300+
Genesys Regional Med Ctr-Health Park	Grand Blanc	68%	300+
Henry Ford Macomb Hospital	Clinton Twp	68%	300+
Mercy Health Partners - Mercy Campus	Muskegon	68%	300+
Poh Medical Center	Pontiac	68%	300+
Saint Joseph Mercy Port Huron	Port Huron	68%	300+
Saint Mary Mercy Hospital	Livonia	68%	300+
University of Michigan Health System	Ann Arbor	68%	300+
Allegiance Health	Jackson	67%	300+
Borgess Medical Center	Kalamazoo	67%	300+
Doctor's Hospital of Michigan	Pontiac	67%	300+
Garden City Hospital	Garden City	67%	300+
Gratiot Medical Center	Alma	67%	300+
Harper University Hospital	Detroit	67%	300+
Henry Ford Hospital	Detroit	67%	300+
Hurley Medical Center	Flint	67%	300+
Huron Valley-Sinai Hospital	Commerce Twp	67%	300+
Lapeer Regional Medical Center	Lapeer	67%	300+
Pennock Hospital	Hastings	67%	300+
Saint John Hospital and Medical Center	Detroit	67%	300+
Saint Joseph Mercy Hospital	Ann Arbor	67%	300+
Sinai-Grace Hospital	Detroit	67%	300+
Community Health Center of Branch County	Coldwater	66%	300+
Henry Ford Wyandotte Hospital	Wyandotte	66%	300+
Herrick Memorial Hospital	Tecumseh	66%	300+
Hills & Dales General Hospital	Cass City	66%	(a)
Hillsdale Community Health Center	Hillsdale	66%	300+
Saint Joseph Mercy Oakland	Pontiac	66%	300+
Mclaren Regional Medical Center	Flint	65%	300+
Memorial Healthcare	Owosso	65%	300+
Mercy Memorial Hospital System	Monroe	65%	300+
Mount Clemens Regional Medical Center	Mount Clemens	65%	300+
Providence Hospital and Medical Centers	Southfield	65%	300+
St John Macomb-Oakland Hosp-Macomb Ctr	Warren	65%	300+
Botsford Hospital	Farmington Hills	64%	300+
Ingham Regional Medical Center	Lansing	64%	300+
Detroit Receiving Hosp & Univ Health Ctr	Detroit	63%	300+
Saint Mary's of Michigan Medical Center	Saginaw	63%	300+
Marquette General Hospital	Marquette	62%	300+
Three Rivers Health	Three Rivers	60%	(a)
Borgess-Lee Memorial Hospital	Dowagiac	59%	(a)
Alpena Regional Medical Center	Alpena	57%	(a)

47. Room and Bathroom 'Always' Clean

Hospital Name	City	Rate	Cases
Spectrum Hlth United Mem-Kelsey Campus	Lakeview	92%	(a)
Clinton Memorial Hospital	Saint Johns	84%	300+
Dickinson County Memorial Hospital	Iron Mountain	84%	300+
Allegan General Hospital	Allegan	81%	(a)
Spectrum Health - Reed City Campus	Reed City	81%	(a)
Borgess-Lee Memorial Hospital	Dowagiac	80%	(a)
Hayes Green Beach Memorial Hospital	Charlotte	80%	(a)
Holland Community Hospital	Holland	80%	300+
Zeeland Community Hospital	Zeeland	80%	300+
Chelsea Community Hospital	Chelsea	79%	300+
Portage Health Hospital	Hancock	79%	300+
Spectrum Health United Mem-United Campus	Greenville	79%	300+
Carson City Hospital	Carson City	78%	300+
Gratiot Medical Center	Alma	78%	300+
Herrick Memorial Hospital	Tecumseh	78%	300+
Hills & Dales General Hospital	Cass City	78%	(a)
Lakeland Hospital - St Joseph	Saint Joseph	78%	300+
Saint John River District Hospital	East China	78%	300+
Marlette Regional Hospital	Marlette	77%	(a)
Chippewa County War Memorial Hospital	Sault Ste Marie	76%	300+
Huron Medical Center	Bad Axe	76%	300+
Saint Francis Hospital	Escanaba	76%	300+
West Shore Medical Center	Manistee	76%	300+
Emma L Bixby Medical Center	Adrian	75%	300+
Metro Health Hospital	Wyoming	75%	300+
Oakwood Southshore Medical Center	Trenton	75%	300+
Bronson Methodist Hospital	Kalamazoo	74%	300+
Community Hospital	Watervliet	74%	(a)
Memorial Healthcare	Owosso	74%	300+
Poh Medical Center	Pontiac	74%	300+
Bronson Lakeview Hospital	Paw Paw	73%	(a)
Hillsdale Community Health Center	Hillsdale	73%	300+
Lapeer Regional Medical Center	Lapeer	73%	300+
Marquette General Hospital	Marquette	73%	300+
Saint Joseph Mercy Port Huron	Port Huron	73%	300+
Central Michigan Community Hospital	Mount Pleasant	72%	300+
Doctor's Hospital of Michigan	Pontiac	72%	300+
Midmichigan Medical Center-Clare	Clare	72%	300+
Oaklawn Hospital	Marshall	72%	300+
Saint Joseph Mercy Hospital	Ann Arbor	72%	300+
Mercy Hospital - Grayling	Grayling	71%	300+
Munson Medical Center	Traverse City	71%	300+
North Ottawa Community Hospital	Grand Haven	71%	300+
Otsego Memorial Hospital	Gaylord	71%	300+
Port Huron Hospital	Port Huron	71%	300+
Spectrum Health - Butterworth Campus	Grand Rapids	71%	300+
Spectrum Health Gerber Memorial	Fremont	71%	300+
West Branch Regional Medical Center	West Branch	71%	300+
Henry Ford Macomb Hospital	Clinton Twp	70%	300+
Tawas Saint Joseph Hospital	Tawas City	70%	300+
Allegiance Health	Jackson	69%	300+
Battle Creek Health System	Battle Creek	69%	300+
Garden City Hospital	Garden City	69%	300+
Midmichigan Medical Center-Gladwin	Gladwin	69%	(a)
Saint Joseph Mercy Livingston Hospital	Howell	69%	300+
Saint Mary's Health Care	Grand Rapids	69%	300+
Sturgis Hospital	Sturgis	69%	300+
Three Rivers Health	Three Rivers	69%	(a)
Henry Ford Hospital	Detroit	68%	300+
Henry Ford West Bloomfield Hospital	West Bloomfield	68%	300+
Henry Ford Wyandotte Hospital	Wyandotte	68%	300+
Ingham Regional Medical Center	Lansing	68%	300+
Memorial Medical Center of West Michigan	Ludington	68%	300+
Mercy Hospital - Cadillac	Cadillac	68%	300+
Oakwood Annapolis Hospital	Wayne	68%	300+
Saint Joseph Mercy Saline Hospital	Saline	68%	(a)
South Haven Community Hospital	South Haven	68%	(a)
William Beaumont Hospital-Troy	Troy	68%	300+
Beaumont Hospital - Grosse Pointe	Grosse Pointe	67%	300+
Borgess Medical Center	Kalamazoo	67%	300+
Community Health Center of Branch County	Coldwater	67%	300+
Crittenton Hospital Medical Center	Rochester	67%	300+
Harper University Hospital	Detroit	67%	300+
Midmichigan Medical Center-Midland	Midland	67%	300+
Oakwood Hospital and Medical Center	Dearborn	67%	300+
Sinai-Grace Hospital	Detroit	67%	300+
Covenant Medical Center	Saginaw	66%	300+
Huron Valley-Sinai Hospital	Commerce Twp	66%	300+
Karmanos Cancer Center	Detroit	66%	300+
Mercy Health Partners - Mercy Campus	Muskegon	66%	300+
Northern Michigan Regional Hospital	Petoskey	66%	300+
Oakwood Heritage Hospital	Taylor	66%	300+
Bay Regional Medical Center	Bay City	65%	300+
Edward W Sparrow Hospital	Lansing	65%	300+
Providence Hospital and Medical Centers	Southfield	64%	300+
William Beaumont Hospital	Royal Oak	64%	300+
Mercy Memorial Hospital System	Monroe	63%	300+
Mount Clemens Regional Medical Center	Mount Clemens	63%	300+
Botsford Hospital	Farmington Hills	62%	300+
Mecosta County Medical Center	Big Rapids	62%	300+
Saint Mary's of Michigan Medical Center	Saginaw	62%	300+
Genesys Regional Med Ctr-Health Park	Grand Blanc	61%	300+
Mercy Health Partners - Hackley Campus	Muskegon	61%	300+
Pennock Hospital	Hastings	61%	300+
University of Michigan Health System	Ann Arbor	61%	300+
Detroit Receiving Hosp & Univ Health Ctr	Detroit	60%	300+
Hurley Medical Center	Flint	60%	300+
Alpena Regional Medical Center	Alpena	59%	(a)
St John Macomb-Oakland Hosp-Macomb Ctr	Warren	59%	300+
Saint John Hospital and Medical Center	Detroit	58%	300+
Saint Joseph Mercy Oakland	Pontiac	58%	300+
Saint Mary Mercy Hospital	Livonia	57%	300+
Mclaren Regional Medical Center	Flint	56%	300+

48. Timely Help 'Always' Received

Hospital Name	City	Rate	Cases
Hills & Dales General Hospital	Cass City	86%	(a)
Spectrum Hlth United Mem-Kelsey Campus	Lakeview	83%	(a)
Community Hospital	Watervliet	79%	(a)
Chippewa County War Memorial Hospital	Sault Ste Marie	77%	300+
Allegan General Hospital	Allegan	76%	(a)
Bronson Lakeview Hospital	Paw Paw	76%	(a)
Huron Medical Center	Bad Axe	75%	300+
Midmichigan Medical Center-Gladwin	Gladwin	75%	(a)
Saint Joseph Mercy Livingston Hospital	Howell	75%	300+
West Shore Medical Center	Manistee	75%	300+
Central Michigan Community Hospital	Mount Pleasant	74%	300+
Chelsea Community Hospital	Chelsea	74%	300+
Mercy Hospital - Cadillac	Cadillac	74%	300+
Portage Health Hospital	Hancock	74%	300+
Saint Francis Hospital	Escanaba	74%	300+
Saint Joseph Mercy Saline Hospital	Saline	74%	(a)
Spectrum Health - Reed City Campus	Reed City	74%	(a)
Oaklawn Hospital	Marshall	73%	300+
Carson City Hospital	Carson City	72%	300+
Memorial Medical Center of West Michigan	Ludington	72%	300+
North Ottawa Community Hospital	Grand Haven	72%	300+
Spectrum Health Gerber Memorial	Fremont	72%	300+
Mercy Hospital - Grayling	Grayling	71%	300+
Midmichigan Medical Center-Clare	Clare	71%	300+
Munson Medical Center	Traverse City	71%	300+
Tawas Saint Joseph Hospital	Tawas City	71%	300+
Sturgis Hospital	Sturgis	70%	300+
Zeeland Community Hospital	Zeeland	70%	300+
Clinton Memorial Hospital	Saint Johns	69%	300+
Dickinson County Memorial Hospital	Iron Mountain	69%	300+
Emma L Bixby Medical Center	Adrian	69%	300+
Northern Michigan Regional Hospital	Petoskey	69%	300+
Otsego Memorial Hospital	Gaylord	69%	300+
Saint John River District Hospital	East China	69%	300+
South Haven Community Hospital	South Haven	69%	(a)
West Branch Regional Medical Center	West Branch	69%	300+
Gratiot Medical Center	Alma	68%	300+
Henry Ford West Bloomfield Hospital	West Bloomfield	68%	300+
Holland Community Hospital	Holland	68%	300+
Karmanos Cancer Center	Detroit	68%	300+
Allegiance Health	Jackson	67%	300+
Battle Creek Health System	Battle Creek	67%	300+
Bay Regional Medical Center	Bay City	67%	300+
Covenant Medical Center	Saginaw	67%	300+
Hayes Green Beach Memorial Hospital	Charlotte	67%	(a)
Midmichigan Medical Center-Midland	Midland	67%	300+
Borgess-Lee Memorial Hospital	Dowagiac	66%	(a)
Genesys Regional Med Ctr-Health Park	Grand Blanc	66%	300+
Mecosta County Medical Center	Big Rapids	66%	300+
Huron Valley-Sinai Hospital	Commerce Twp	65%	300+

NOTE: Hospital profiles are in alphabetical order by state, then city, then hospital within the city; Rankings exclude hospitals with less than 25 cases except for patient surveys which excludes hospitals with less than 100 cases; (a) 100–299 cases; (1) The number of cases is too small to be sure how well a hospital is performing; (2) The hospital indicated that the data submitted for this measure were based on a sample of cases; (3) Data was collected during a shorter time period (fewer quarters) than the maximum possible time for this measure; (4) Suppressed for one or more quarters by CMS; (5) No data is available from the hospital for this measure; (6) Fewer than 100 patients completed the HCAHPS survey. Use these rates with caution, as the number of surveys may be too low to reliably assess hospital performance; (7) Survey results are based on less than 12 months of data; (8) Survey results are not available for this reporting period; (9) No or very few patients were eligible for the HCAHPS survey. The scores shown, if any, reflect a very small number of surveys; (10) A state average was not calculated because too few hospitals in the state submitted data; (11) There were discrepancies in the data collection process; Please refer to the User's Guide for a full explanation of data.

Oakwood Southshore Medical Center	Trenton	65%	300+
Crittenton Hospital Medical Center	Rochester	64%	300+
Harper University Hospital	Detroit	64%	300+
Mercy Health Partners - Hackley Campus	Muskegon	64%	300+
Oakwood Hospital and Medical Center	Dearborn	64%	300+
Port Huron Hospital	Port Huron	64%	300+
Saint Joseph Mercy Hospital	Ann Arbor	64%	300+
Spectrum Health - Butterworth Campus	Grand Rapids	64%	300+
Bronson Methodist Hospital	Kalamazoo	63%	300+
Detroit Receiving Hosp & Univ Health Ctr	Detroit	63%	300+
Mercy Health Partners - Mercy Campus	Muskegon	63%	300+
Saint Joseph Mercy Port Huron	Port Huron	63%	300+
Saint Mary's Health Care	Grand Rapids	63%	300+
William Beaumont Hospital-Troy	Troy	63%	300+
Doctor's Hospital of Michigan	Pontiac	62%	300+
Garden City Hospital	Garden City	62%	300+
Henry Ford Macomb Hospital	Clinton Twp	62%	300+
Henry Ford Wyandotte Hospital	Wyandotte	62%	300+
Herrick Memorial Hospital	Tecumseh	62%	300+
Hillsdale Community Health Center	Hillsdale	62%	300+
Lakeland Hospital - St Joseph	Saint Joseph	62%	300+
Marquette General Hospital	Marquette	62%	300+
Sinai-Grace Hospital	Detroit	62%	300+
Spectrum Health United Mem-United Campus	Greenville	62%	300+
University of Michigan Health System	Ann Arbor	62%	300+
Community Health Center of Branch County	Coldwater	61%	300+
Metro Health Hospital	Wyoming	61%	300+
Pennock Hospital	Hastings	61%	300+
Beaumont Hospital - Grosse Pointe	Grosse Pointe	60%	300+
Edward W Sparrow Hospital	Lansing	60%	300+
Henry Ford Hospital	Detroit	60%	300+
Hurley Medical Center	Flint	60%	300+
Marlette Regional Hospital	Marlette	60%	(a)
Memorial Healthcare	Owosso	60%	300+
Mercy Memorial Hospital System	Monroe	60%	300+
Poh Medical Center	Pontiac	60%	300+
Providence Hospital and Medical Centers	Southfield	60%	300+
Saint Mary's of Michigan Medical Center	Saginaw	60%	300+
Three Rivers Health	Three Rivers	60%	(a)
Botsford Hospital	Farmington Hills	59%	300+
Oakwood Annapolis Hospital	Wayne	59%	300+
Oakwood Heritage Hospital	Taylor	59%	300+
Ingham Regional Medical Center	Lansing	58%	300+
Lapeer Regional Medical Center	Lapeer	57%	300+
Mount Clemens Regional Medical Center	Mount Clemens	57%	300+
Saint Mary Mercy Hospital	Livonia	57%	300+
Saint Joseph Mercy Oakland	Pontiac	56%	300+
William Beaumont Hospital	Royal Oak	56%	300+
Alpena Regional Medical Center	Alpena	55%	(a)
St John Macomb-Oakland Hosp-Macomb Ctr	Warren	55%	300+
Saint John Hospital and Medical Center	Detroit	54%	300+
Mclaren Regional Medical Center	Flint	53%	300+
Borgess Medical Center	Kalamazoo	52%	300+

49. Would Definitely Recommend Hospital

Hospital Name	City	Rate	Cases
Zeeland Community Hospital	Zeeland	87%	300+
Chelsea Community Hospital	Chelsea	85%	300+
Munson Medical Center	Traverse City	85%	300+
Oaklawn Hospital	Marshall	83%	300+
University of Michigan Health System	Ann Arbor	83%	300+
Bronson Methodist Hospital	Kalamazoo	82%	300+
Henry Ford West Bloomfield Hospital	West Bloomfield	82%	300+
Holland Community Hospital	Holland	80%	300+
Karmanos Cancer Center	Detroit	80%	300+
Metro Health Hospital	Wyoming	80%	300+
Saint Joseph Mercy Hospital	Ann Arbor	80%	300+
Spectrum Hlth United Mem-Kelsey Campus	Lakeview	80%	(a)
Clinton Memorial Hospital	Saint Johns	79%	300+
Marlette Regional Hospital	Marlette	79%	(a)
Northern Michigan Regional Hospital	Petoskey	78%	300+
Spectrum Health - Butterworth Campus	Grand Rapids	78%	300+
Allegan General Hospital	Allegan	77%	(a)
Central Michigan Community Hospital	Mount Pleasant	77%	300+
Saint Joseph Mercy Saline Hospital	Saline	77%	(a)
William Beaumont Hospital-Troy	Troy	77%	300+
Portage Health Hospital	Hancock	76%	300+
Community Hospital	Watervliet	75%	(a)
Gratiot Medical Center	Alma	75%	300+
Huron Medical Center	Bad Axe	75%	300+
Midmichigan Medical Center-Midland	Midland	75%	300+
North Ottawa Community Hospital	Grand Haven	75%	300+
Saint Mary's Health Care	Grand Rapids	75%	300+
Spectrum Health - Reed City Campus	Reed City	75%	(a)
West Branch Regional Medical Center	West Branch	75%	300+
Edward W Sparrow Hospital	Lansing	74%	300+
Oakwood Southshore Medical Center	Trenton	74%	300+
Covenant Medical Center	Saginaw	73%	300+
Crittenton Hospital Medical Center	Rochester	73%	300+
Mercy Hospital - Cadillac	Cadillac	73%	300+
Pennock Hospital	Hastings	73%	300+
Hayes Green Beach Memorial Hospital	Charlotte	72%	(a)
Mercy Health Partners - Hackley Campus	Muskegon	72%	300+
Providence Hospital and Medical Centers	Southfield	72%	300+
Saint Joseph Mercy Livingston Hospital	Howell	72%	300+
Spectrum Health United Mem-United Campus	Greenville	72%	300+
William Beaumont Hospital	Royal Oak	72%	300+
Beaumont Hospital - Grosse Pointe	Grosse Pointe	71%	300+
Borgess Medical Center	Kalamazoo	71%	300+
Huron Valley-Sinai Hospital	Commerce Twp	71%	300+
Mercy Hospital - Grayling	Grayling	71%	300+
Carson City Hospital	Carson City	70%	300+
Ingham Regional Medical Center	Lansing	70%	300+
Mercy Health Partners - Mercy Campus	Muskegon	70%	300+
Port Huron Hospital	Port Huron	70%	300+
Saint Joseph Mercy Oakland	Pontiac	70%	300+
Tawas Saint Joseph Hospital	Tawas City	70%	300+
Bronson Lakeview Hospital	Paw Paw	69%	(a)
Genesys Regional Med Ctr-Health Park	Grand Blanc	69%	300+
Hills & Dales General Hospital	Cass City	69%	(a)
Marquette General Hospital	Marquette	69%	300+
Spectrum Health Gerber Memorial	Fremont	69%	300+
West Shore Medical Center	Manistee	69%	300+
Chippewa County War Memorial Hospital	Sault Ste Marie	68%	300+
Henry Ford Hospital	Detroit	68%	300+
Mecosta County Medical Center	Big Rapids	68%	300+
Oakwood Hospital and Medical Center	Dearborn	68%	300+
Otsego Memorial Hospital	Gaylord	68%	300+
Saint Joseph Mercy Port Huron	Port Huron	68%	300+
Saint John Hospital and Medical Center	Detroit	67%	300+
Sturgis Hospital	Sturgis	67%	300+
Bay Regional Medical Center	Bay City	66%	300+
Dickinson County Memorial Hospital	Iron Mountain	66%	300+
Henry Ford Macomb Hospital	Clinton Twp	66%	300+
Midmichigan Medical Center-Gladwin	Gladwin	66%	(a)
South Haven Community Hospital	South Haven	66%	(a)
Botsford Hospital	Farmington Hills	65%	300+
Detroit Receiving Hosp & Univ Health Ctr	Detroit	65%	300+
Harper University Hospital	Detroit	65%	300+
Saint Francis Hospital	Escanaba	65%	300+
Saint John River District Hospital	East China	65%	300+
Allegiance Health	Jackson	64%	300+
Borgess-Lee Memorial Hospital	Dowagiac	64%	(a)
Herrick Memorial Hospital	Tecumseh	64%	300+
Hurley Medical Center	Flint	64%	300+
Memorial Medical Center of West Michigan	Ludington	64%	300+
Saint Mary Mercy Hospital	Livonia	64%	300+
Emma L Bixby Medical Center	Adrian	63%	300+
Garden City Hospital	Garden City	63%	300+
Henry Ford Wyandotte Hospital	Wyandotte	63%	300+
Saint Mary's of Michigan Medical Center	Saginaw	63%	300+
Mclaren Regional Medical Center	Flint	62%	300+
Oakwood Heritage Hospital	Taylor	62%	300+
Community Health Center of Branch County	Coldwater	61%	300+
Doctor's Hospital of Michigan	Pontiac	61%	300+
Lakeland Hospital - St Joseph	Saint Joseph	60%	300+
Midmichigan Medical Center-Clare	Clare	60%	300+
Oakwood Annapolis Hospital	Wayne	60%	300+
Battle Creek Health System	Battle Creek	59%	300+
Mount Clemens Regional Medical Center	Mount Clemens	59%	300+
Poh Medical Center	Pontiac	59%	300+
Lapeer Regional Medical Center	Lapeer	58%	300+
Three Rivers Health	Three Rivers	58%	(a)
Memorial Healthcare	Owosso	57%	300+
St John Macomb-Oakland Hosp-Macomb Ctr	Warren	55%	300+
Hillsdale Community Health Center	Hillsdale	54%	300+
Alpena Regional Medical Center	Alpena	52%	(a)
Sinai-Grace Hospital	Detroit	51%	300+
Mercy Memorial Hospital System	Monroe	46%	300+

NOTE: Hospital profiles are in alphabetical order by state, then city, then hospital within the city; Rankings exclude hospitals with less than 25 cases except for patient surveys which excludes hospitals with less than 100 cases; (a) 100–299 cases; (1) The number of cases is too small to be sure how well a hospital is performing; (2) The hospital indicated that the data submitted for this measure were based on a sample of cases; (3) Data was collected during a shorter time period (fewer quarters) than the maximum possible time for this measure; (4) Suppressed for one or more quarters by CMS; (5) No data is available from the hospital for this measure; (6) Fewer than 100 patients completed the HCAHPS survey. Use these rates with caution, as the number of surveys may be too low to reliably assess hospital performance; (7) Survey results are based on less than 12 months of data; (8) Survey results are not available for this reporting period; (9) No or very few patients were eligible for the HCAHPS survey. The scores shown, if any, reflect a very small number of surveys; (10) A state average was not calculated because too few hospitals in the state submitted data; (11) There were discrepancies in the data collection process; Please refer to the User's Guide for a full explanation of data.

Emma L Bixby Medical Center

818 Riverside Avenue
Adrian, MI 49221
URL: www.promedica.org
Type: Acute Care Hospitals
Ownership: Voluntary Non-Profit - Other
Phone: 517-265-0900
Fax: 517-265-0918
Emergency Services: Yes
Beds: 88

Key Personnel:
CEO/President. . . . . Randy Oostra
Operating Room. . . . . Abdul Arshad
Quality Assurance . . . . Linda Yielding
Patient Relations . . . . Sheila Schwartz

Measure	Cases	This Hosp.	State Avg.	U.S. Avg.
Heart Attack Care				
ACE Inhibitor or ARB for LVSD[1]	14	100%	96%	96%
Aspirin at Arrival	54	98%	99%	99%
Aspirin at Discharge	38	97%	99%	98%
Beta Blocker at Discharge	42	98%	99%	98%
Fibrinolytic Medication Timing	0	-	55%	55%
PCI Within 90 Minutes of Arrival	0	-	89%	90%
Smoking Cessation Advice[1]	4	75%	100%	99%
Chest Pain/Possible Heart Attack Care				
Aspirin at Arrival	197	85%	94%	95%
Median Time to ECG (minutes)	202	11	10	8
Median Time to Transfer (minutes)	0	-	54	61
Fibrinolytic Medication Timing[1]	2	0%	60%	54%
Heart Failure Care				
ACE Inhibitor or ARB for LVSD	48	98%	95%	94%
Discharge Instructions	90	89%	89%	88%
Evaluation of LVS Function	117	99%	99%	98%
Smoking Cessation Advice[1]	13	100%	99%	98%
Pneumonia Care				
Appropriate Initial Antibiotic[2]	62	90%	94%	92%
Blood Culture Timing[2]	96	92%	96%	96%
Influenza Vaccine[2]	75	93%	91%	91%
Initial Antibiotic Timing[2]	96	96%	96%	95%
Pneumococcal Vaccine[2]	96	95%	93%	93%
Smoking Cessation Advice[2]	42	100%	98%	97%
Surgical Care Improvement Project				
Appropriate VTP Within 24 Hours[2]	112	89%	94%	92%
Appropriate Hair Removal[2]	274	100%	99%	99%
Appropriate Beta Blocker Usage[2]	60	97%	92%	93%
Controlled Postoperative Blood Glucose[2]	0	-	94%	93%
Prophylactic Antibiotic Timing[2]	195	98%	97%	97%
Prophylactic Antibiotic Timing (Outpatient)	87	94%	87%	92%
Prophylactic Antibiotic Selection[2]	195	98%	98%	97%
Prophylactic Antibiotic Select. (Outpatient)	84	58%	92%	94%
Prophylactic Antibiotic Stopped[2]	189	96%	95%	94%
Recommended VTP Ordered[2]	114	89%	95%	94%
Urinary Catheter Removal[2]	70	97%	91%	90%
Children's Asthma Care				
Received Systemic Corticosteroids	-	-	-	100%
Received Home Management Plan	-	-	-	71%
Received Reliever Medication	-	-	-	100%
Use of Medical Imaging				
Combination Abdominal CT Scan	585	0.051	0.135	0.191
Combination Chest CT Scan	356	0.031	0.068	0.054
Follow-up Mammogram/Ultrasound	945	10.8%	7.4%	8.4%
MRI for Low Back Pain	130	30.8%	32%	32.7%
Survey of Patients' Hospital Experiences				
Area Around Room 'Always' Quiet at Night	300+	55%	-	58%
Doctors 'Always' Communicated Well	300+	82%	-	80%
Home Recovery Information Given	300+	83%	-	82%
Hospital Given 9 or 10 on 10 Point Scale	300+	67%	-	67%
Meds 'Always' Explained Before Given	300+	64%	-	60%
Nurses 'Always' Communicated Well	300+	76%	-	76%
Pain 'Always' Well Controlled	300+	73%	-	69%
Room and Bathroom 'Always' Clean	300+	75%	-	71%
Timely Help 'Always' Received	300+	69%	-	64%
Would Definitely Recommend Hospital	300+	63%	-	69%

Allegan General Hospital

555 Linn Street
Allegan, MI 49010
Type: Critical Access Hospitals
Ownership: Voluntary Non-Profit - Other
Phone: 269-686-4101
Fax: 269-673-4344
Emergency Services: Yes
Beds: 63

Key Personnel:
CEO/President. . . . . Gerald Barbins
Infection Control. . . . . Sandra Brenner
Operating Room. . . . . Phyllis Wilson
Quality Assurance . . . . Linda Curry
Anesthesiology. . . . . Kenneth Whitcomb
Emergency Room . . . . Timothy Hall
Intensive Care Unit. . . . . Timothy Hall
Patient Relations . . . . Grace Gant

Measure	Cases	This Hosp.	State Avg.	U.S. Avg.
Heart Attack Care				
ACE Inhibitor or ARB for LVSD[1,2]	1	100%	96%	96%
Aspirin at Arrival[1,2]	6	100%	99%	99%
Aspirin at Discharge[1,2]	5	80%	99%	98%
Beta Blocker at Discharge[1,2]	4	75%	99%	98%
Fibrinolytic Medication Timing[2]	0	-	55%	55%
PCI Within 90 Minutes of Arrival[2]	0	-	89%	90%
Smoking Cessation Advice[1,2]	3	100%	100%	99%
Chest Pain/Possible Heart Attack Care				
Aspirin at Arrival	-	-	94%	95%
Median Time to ECG (minutes)	-	-	10	8
Median Time to Transfer (minutes)	-	-	54	61
Fibrinolytic Medication Timing	-	-	60%	54%
Heart Failure Care				
ACE Inhibitor or ARB for LVSD[1]	22	68%	95%	94%
Discharge Instructions	59	98%	89%	88%
Evaluation of LVS Function	75	100%	99%	98%
Smoking Cessation Advice[1]	18	100%	99%	98%
Pneumonia Care				
Appropriate Initial Antibiotic	43	79%	94%	92%
Blood Culture Timing	56	96%	96%	96%
Influenza Vaccine	47	81%	91%	91%
Initial Antibiotic Timing	64	97%	96%	95%
Pneumococcal Vaccine	52	87%	93%	93%
Smoking Cessation Advice[1]	19	89%	98%	97%
Surgical Care Improvement Project				
Appropriate VTP Within 24 Hours[2]	73	73%	94%	92%
Appropriate Hair Removal[2]	157	100%	99%	99%
Appropriate Beta Blocker Usage[5]	0	-	92%	93%
Controlled Postoperative Blood Glucose[2]	0	-	94%	93%
Prophylactic Antibiotic Timing[2]	126	96%	97%	97%
Prophylactic Antibiotic Timing (Outpatient)	-	-	87%	92%
Prophylactic Antibiotic Selection[2]	127	96%	98%	97%
Prophylactic Antibiotic Select. (Outpatient)	-	-	92%	94%
Prophylactic Antibiotic Stopped[2]	126	91%	95%	94%
Recommended VTP Ordered[2]	74	72%	95%	94%
Urinary Catheter Removal[1,2]	16	81%	91%	90%
Children's Asthma Care				
Received Systemic Corticosteroids	-	-	-	100%
Received Home Management Plan	-	-	-	71%
Received Reliever Medication	-	-	-	100%
Use of Medical Imaging				
Combination Abdominal CT Scan	-	-	0.135	0.191
Combination Chest CT Scan	-	-	0.068	0.054
Follow-up Mammogram/Ultrasound	-	-	7.4%	8.4%
MRI for Low Back Pain	-	-	32%	32.7%
Survey of Patients' Hospital Experiences				
Area Around Room 'Always' Quiet at Night	(a)	66%	-	58%
Doctors 'Always' Communicated Well	(a)	81%	-	80%
Home Recovery Information Given	(a)	89%	-	82%
Hospital Given 9 or 10 on 10 Point Scale	(a)	78%	-	67%
Meds 'Always' Explained Before Given	(a)	58%	-	60%
Nurses 'Always' Communicated Well	(a)	82%	-	76%
Pain 'Always' Well Controlled	(a)	75%	-	69%
Room and Bathroom 'Always' Clean	(a)	81%	-	71%
Timely Help 'Always' Received	(a)	76%	-	64%
Would Definitely Recommend Hospital	(a)	77%	-	69%

Gratiot Medical Center

300 E Warwick Dr
Alma, MI 48801
URL: www.midmichigan.org
Type: Acute Care Hospitals
Ownership: Voluntary Non-Profit - Private
Phone: 989-463-1101
Fax: 989-463-6948
Emergency Services: Yes
Beds: 142

Key Personnel:
CEO/President. . . . . Tom Desauw
Infection Control. . . . . Janet Davis, RN
Operating Room. . . . . Tammy Terrell, RN
Quality Assurance . . . . Jill Goodell
Radiology. . . . . Johannes Buiteweg
Emergency Room . . . . Kim Noreen, RN
Intensive Care Unit. . . . . Glenn King, RN
Patient Relations . . . . Penny Daniels

Measure	Cases	This Hosp.	State Avg.	U.S. Avg.
Heart Attack Care				
ACE Inhibitor or ARB for LVSD[1]	4	50%	96%	96%
Aspirin at Arrival	34	94%	99%	99%
Aspirin at Discharge[1]	23	87%	99%	98%
Beta Blocker at Discharge[1]	23	100%	99%	98%
Fibrinolytic Medication Timing[1]	1	0%	55%	55%
PCI Within 90 Minutes of Arrival	0	-	89%	90%
Smoking Cessation Advice[1]	5	100%	100%	99%
Chest Pain/Possible Heart Attack Care				
Aspirin at Arrival	95	98%	94%	95%
Median Time to ECG (minutes)	100	5	10	8
Median Time to Transfer (minutes)[1]	7	160	54	61
Fibrinolytic Medication Timing[1]	13	38%	60%	54%
Heart Failure Care				
ACE Inhibitor or ARB for LVSD	38	82%	95%	94%
Discharge Instructions	155	71%	89%	88%
Evaluation of LVS Function	224	100%	99%	98%
Smoking Cessation Advice	25	100%	99%	98%
Pneumonia Care				
Appropriate Initial Antibiotic	109	94%	94%	92%
Blood Culture Timing	91	100%	96%	96%
Influenza Vaccine	105	88%	91%	91%
Initial Antibiotic Timing	160	98%	96%	95%
Pneumococcal Vaccine	125	94%	93%	93%
Smoking Cessation Advice	44	100%	98%	97%
Surgical Care Improvement Project				
Appropriate VTP Within 24 Hours	154	79%	94%	92%
Appropriate Hair Removal	345	100%	99%	99%
Appropriate Beta Blocker Usage	112	89%	92%	93%
Controlled Postoperative Blood Glucose	0	-	94%	93%
Prophylactic Antibiotic Timing	219	95%	97%	97%
Prophylactic Antibiotic Timing (Outpatient)	156	71%	87%	92%
Prophylactic Antibiotic Selection	219	88%	98%	97%
Prophylactic Antibiotic Select. (Outpatient)	117	91%	92%	94%
Prophylactic Antibiotic Stopped	211	82%	95%	94%
Recommended VTP Ordered	156	79%	95%	94%
Urinary Catheter Removal	72	88%	91%	90%
Children's Asthma Care				
Received Systemic Corticosteroids[1]	11	100%	-	100%
Received Home Management Plan[1]	11	0%	-	71%
Received Reliever Medication[1]	11	100%	-	100%
Use of Medical Imaging				
Combination Abdominal CT Scan	480	0.065	0.135	0.191
Combination Chest CT Scan	539	0.015	0.068	0.054
Follow-up Mammogram/Ultrasound	811	2.1%	7.4%	8.4%
MRI for Low Back Pain	190	35.3%	32%	32.7%
Survey of Patients' Hospital Experiences				
Area Around Room 'Always' Quiet at Night	300+	64%	-	58%
Doctors 'Always' Communicated Well	300+	82%	-	80%
Home Recovery Information Given	300+	88%	-	82%
Hospital Given 9 or 10 on 10 Point Scale	300+	76%	-	67%
Meds 'Always' Explained Before Given	300+	65%	-	60%
Nurses 'Always' Communicated Well	300+	82%	-	76%
Pain 'Always' Well Controlled	300+	67%	-	69%
Room and Bathroom 'Always' Clean	300+	78%	-	71%
Timely Help 'Always' Received	300+	68%	-	64%
Would Definitely Recommend Hospital	300+	75%	-	69%

NOTE: Hospital profiles are in alphabetical order by state, then city, then hospital within the city; Rankings exclude hospitals with less than 25 cases except for patient surveys which excludes hospitals with less than 100 cases; (a) 100–299 cases; (1) The number of cases is too small to be sure how well a hospital is performing; (2) The hospital indicated that the data submitted for this measure were based on a sample of cases; (3) Data was collected during a shorter time period (fewer quarters) than the maximum possible time for this measure; (4) Suppressed for one or more quarters by CMS; (5) No data is available from the hospital for this measure; (6) Fewer than 100 patients completed the HCAHPS survey. Use these rates with caution, as the number of surveys may be too low to reliably assess hospital performance; (7) Survey results are based on less than 12 months of data; (8) Survey results are not available for this reporting period; (9) No or very few patients were eligible for the HCAHPS survey. The scores shown, if any, reflect a very small number of surveys; (10) A state average was not calculated because too few hospitals in the state submitted data; (11) There were discrepancies in the data collection process; Please refer to the User's Guide for a full explanation of data.

Alpena Regional Medical Center

1501 W Chisholm St | Phone: 989-356-7390
Alpena, MI 49707 | Fax: 989-356-7773
E-mail: info@agh.org
URL: www.agh.org
Type: Acute Care Hospitals | Emergency Services: Yes
Ownership: Proprietary | Beds: 146

Key Personnel:
CEO/President. . . . . John McVeety
Pediatric Ambulatory Care . . . . . . Richard F Willis, MD
Anesthesiology. . . . . John Banish, MD

Measure	Cases	This Hosp.	State Avg.	U.S. Avg.
Heart Attack Care				
ACE Inhibitor or ARB for LVSD[1]	5	100%	96%	96%
Aspirin at Arrival	47	98%	99%	99%
Aspirin at Discharge	29	97%	99%	98%
Beta Blocker at Discharge	27	96%	99%	98%
Fibrinolytic Medication Timing[1]	1	100%	55%	55%
PCI Within 90 Minutes of Arrival	0	-	89%	90%
Smoking Cessation Advice[1]	7	100%	100%	99%
Chest Pain/Possible Heart Attack Care				
Aspirin at Arrival	108	98%	94%	95%
Median Time to ECG (minutes)	113	9	10	8
Median Time to Transfer (minutes)[1,3]	1	233	54	61
Fibrinolytic Medication Timing[1]	15	67%	60%	54%
Heart Failure Care				
ACE Inhibitor or ARB for LVSD	61	90%	95%	94%
Discharge Instructions	152	84%	89%	88%
Evaluation of LVS Function	197	97%	99%	98%
Smoking Cessation Advice	26	100%	99%	98%
Pneumonia Care				
Appropriate Initial Antibiotic	95	95%	94%	92%
Blood Culture Timing	129	98%	96%	96%
Influenza Vaccine	101	87%	91%	91%
Initial Antibiotic Timing	126	97%	96%	95%
Pneumococcal Vaccine	138	88%	93%	93%
Smoking Cessation Advice	53	98%	98%	97%
Surgical Care Improvement Project				
Appropriate VTP Within 24 Hours[2]	115	97%	94%	92%
Appropriate Hair Removal[2]	415	99%	99%	99%
Appropriate Beta Blocker Usage[2]	125	84%	92%	93%
Controlled Postoperative Blood Glucose[2]	0	-	94%	93%
Prophylactic Antibiotic Timing[2]	299	96%	97%	97%
Prophylactic Antibiotic Timing (Outpatient)	166	88%	87%	92%
Prophylactic Antibiotic Selection[2]	300	92%	98%	97%
Prophylactic Antibiotic Select. (Outpatient)	155	93%	92%	94%
Prophylactic Antibiotic Stopped[2]	284	95%	95%	94%
Recommended VTP Ordered[2]	115	97%	95%	94%
Urinary Catheter Removal[2]	95	95%	91%	90%
Children's Asthma Care				
Received Systemic Corticosteroids	-	-	-	100%
Received Home Management Plan	-	-	-	71%
Received Reliever Medication	-	-	-	100%
Use of Medical Imaging				
Combination Abdominal CT Scan	1,011	0.164	0.135	0.191
Combination Chest CT Scan	777	0.102	0.068	0.054
Follow-up Mammogram/Ultrasound	1,631	7.5%	7.4%	8.4%
MRI for Low Back Pain	257	39.3%	32%	32.7%
Survey of Patients' Hospital Experiences				
Area Around Room 'Always' Quiet at Night	(a)	37%	-	58%
Doctors 'Always' Communicated Well	(a)	73%	-	80%
Home Recovery Information Given	(a)	78%	-	82%
Hospital Given 9 or 10 on 10 Point Scale	(a)	60%	-	67%
Meds 'Always' Explained Before Given	(a)	48%	-	60%
Nurses 'Always' Communicated Well	(a)	63%	-	76%
Pain 'Always' Well Controlled	(a)	57%	-	69%
Room and Bathroom 'Always' Clean	(a)	59%	-	71%
Timely Help 'Always' Received	(a)	55%	-	64%
Would Definitely Recommend Hospital	(a)	52%	-	69%

Saint Joseph Mercy Hospital

5301 E Huron River Dr | Phone: 734-712-3791
Ann Arbor, MI 48106 | Fax: 734-712-7133
Type: Acute Care Hospitals | Emergency Services: Yes
Ownership: Voluntary Non-Profit - Church | Beds: 581

Key Personnel:
Cardiac Laboratory. . . . . Mary Poskie
Chief of Medical Staff. . . . . Rossana DGrood
Operating Room. . . . . Harriet Hnis
Quality Assurance . . . . Dolores Adroiune
Emergency Room . . . . John McCabe, MD

Measure	Cases	This Hosp.	State Avg.	U.S. Avg.
Heart Attack Care				
ACE Inhibitor or ARB for LVSD	104	98%	96%	96%
Aspirin at Arrival	508	99%	99%	99%
Aspirin at Discharge	732	98%	99%	98%
Beta Blocker at Discharge	690	99%	99%	98%
Fibrinolytic Medication Timing	0	-	55%	55%
PCI Within 90 Minutes of Arrival	103	91%	89%	90%
Smoking Cessation Advice	200	100%	100%	99%
Chest Pain/Possible Heart Attack Care				
Aspirin at Arrival	50	48%	94%	95%
Median Time to ECG (minutes)	43	12	10	8
Median Time to Transfer (minutes)[5]	0	-	54	61
Fibrinolytic Medication Timing[5]	0	-	60%	54%
Heart Failure Care				
ACE Inhibitor or ARB for LVSD	276	94%	95%	94%
Discharge Instructions	654	95%	89%	88%
Evaluation of LVS Function	791	99%	99%	98%
Smoking Cessation Advice	90	100%	99%	98%
Pneumonia Care				
Appropriate Initial Antibiotic	285	88%	94%	92%
Blood Culture Timing	137	92%	96%	96%
Influenza Vaccine	412	78%	91%	91%
Initial Antibiotic Timing	512	94%	96%	95%
Pneumococcal Vaccine	496	79%	93%	93%
Smoking Cessation Advice	180	100%	98%	97%
Surgical Care Improvement Project				
Appropriate VTP Within 24 Hours[2]	242	95%	94%	92%
Appropriate Hair Removal[2]	827	100%	99%	99%
Appropriate Beta Blocker Usage[2]	279	88%	92%	93%
Controlled Postoperative Blood Glucose[2]	175	97%	94%	93%
Prophylactic Antibiotic Timing[2]	577	98%	97%	97%
Prophylactic Antibiotic Timing (Outpatient)	921	97%	87%	92%
Prophylactic Antibiotic Selection[2]	584	97%	98%	97%
Prophylactic Antibiotic Select. (Outpatient)	936	97%	92%	94%
Prophylactic Antibiotic Stopped[2]	560	97%	95%	94%
Recommended VTP Ordered[2]	243	98%	95%	94%
Urinary Catheter Removal[2]	202	75%	91%	90%
Children's Asthma Care				
Received Systemic Corticosteroids	-	-	-	100%
Received Home Management Plan	-	-	-	71%
Received Reliever Medication	-	-	-	100%
Use of Medical Imaging				
Combination Abdominal CT Scan	2,089	0.103	0.135	0.191
Combination Chest CT Scan	1,498	0.011	0.068	0.054
Follow-up Mammogram/Ultrasound	3,075	7.4%	7.4%	8.4%
MRI for Low Back Pain	370	30.8%	32%	32.7%
Survey of Patients' Hospital Experiences				
Area Around Room 'Always' Quiet at Night	300+	57%	-	58%
Doctors 'Always' Communicated Well	300+	78%	-	80%
Home Recovery Information Given	300+	86%	-	82%
Hospital Given 9 or 10 on 10 Point Scale	300+	74%	-	67%
Meds 'Always' Explained Before Given	300+	61%	-	60%
Nurses 'Always' Communicated Well	300+	76%	-	76%
Pain 'Always' Well Controlled	300+	67%	-	69%
Room and Bathroom 'Always' Clean	300+	72%	-	71%
Timely Help 'Always' Received	300+	64%	-	64%
Would Definitely Recommend Hospital	300+	80%	-	69%

University of Michigan Health System

1500 E Medical Center Drive | Phone: 734-764-1505
Ann Arbor, MI 48109
URL: www.med.umich.edu
Type: Acute Care Hospitals | Emergency Services: Yes
Ownership: Voluntary Non-Profit - Private | Beds: 930

Key Personnel:
CEO/President. . . . . Ora Hirsch Pescovitz, MD
Chief of Medical Staff . . . . D Campbell, MD
Infection Control. . . . . Candace Friedman, MPH
Operating Room. . . . . Sheri Dufek
Pediatric Ambulatory Care . . . . . . Valerie Castle, MD
Quality Assurance . . . . S Anderson
Radiology. . . . . N Reed Dunnick, MD

Measure	Cases	This Hosp.	State Avg.	U.S. Avg.
Heart Attack Care				
ACE Inhibitor or ARB for LVSD	68	100%	96%	96%
Aspirin at Arrival	246	100%	99%	99%
Aspirin at Discharge	351	100%	99%	98%
Beta Blocker at Discharge	322	100%	99%	98%
Fibrinolytic Medication Timing	0	-	55%	55%
PCI Within 90 Minutes of Arrival	64	94%	89%	90%
Smoking Cessation Advice	121	100%	100%	99%
Chest Pain/Possible Heart Attack Care				
Aspirin at Arrival[5]	0	-	94%	95%
Median Time to ECG (minutes)[5]	0	-	10	8
Median Time to Transfer (minutes)[5]	0	-	54	61
Fibrinolytic Medication Timing[5]	0	-	60%	54%
Heart Failure Care				
ACE Inhibitor or ARB for LVSD	289	99%	95%	94%
Discharge Instructions	710	99%	89%	88%
Evaluation of LVS Function	800	100%	99%	98%
Smoking Cessation Advice	104	100%	99%	98%
Pneumonia Care				
Appropriate Initial Antibiotic	203	93%	94%	92%
Blood Culture Timing	324	98%	96%	96%
Influenza Vaccine	268	88%	91%	91%
Initial Antibiotic Timing	403	96%	96%	95%
Pneumococcal Vaccine	296	93%	93%	93%
Smoking Cessation Advice	155	100%	98%	97%
Surgical Care Improvement Project				
Appropriate VTP Within 24 Hours[2]	699	99%	94%	92%
Appropriate Hair Removal[2]	2,332	98%	99%	99%
Appropriate Beta Blocker Usage[2]	887	80%	92%	93%
Controlled Postoperative Blood Glucose[2]	651	98%	94%	93%
Prophylactic Antibiotic Timing[2]	1,735	98%	97%	97%
Prophylactic Antibiotic Timing (Outpatient)	541	74%	87%	92%
Prophylactic Antibiotic Selection[2]	1,766	99%	98%	97%
Prophylactic Antibiotic Select. (Outpatient)	694	88%	92%	94%
Prophylactic Antibiotic Stopped[2]	1,625	93%	95%	94%
Recommended VTP Ordered[2]	700	99%	95%	94%
Urinary Catheter Removal[2]	683	89%	91%	90%
Children's Asthma Care				
Received Systemic Corticosteroids	-	-	-	100%
Received Home Management Plan	-	-	-	71%
Received Reliever Medication	-	-	-	100%
Use of Medical Imaging				
Combination Abdominal CT Scan	2,805	0.102	0.135	0.191
Combination Chest CT Scan	3,659	0.004	0.068	0.054
Follow-up Mammogram/Ultrasound	2,433	8.5%	7.4%	8.4%
MRI for Low Back Pain	396	22.7%	32%	32.7%
Survey of Patients' Hospital Experiences				
Area Around Room 'Always' Quiet at Night	300+	42%	-	58%
Doctors 'Always' Communicated Well	300+	78%	-	80%
Home Recovery Information Given	300+	88%	-	82%
Hospital Given 9 or 10 on 10 Point Scale	300+	74%	-	67%
Meds 'Always' Explained Before Given	300+	60%	-	60%
Nurses 'Always' Communicated Well	300+	77%	-	76%
Pain 'Always' Well Controlled	300+	68%	-	69%
Room and Bathroom 'Always' Clean	300+	61%	-	71%
Timely Help 'Always' Received	300+	62%	-	64%
Would Definitely Recommend Hospital	300+	83%	-	69%

NOTE: Hospital profiles are in alphabetical order by state, then city, then hospital within the city; Rankings exclude hospitals with less than 25 cases except for patient surveys which excludes hospitals with less than 100 cases; (a) 100–299 cases; (1) The number of cases is too small to be sure how well a hospital is performing; (2) The hospital indicated that the data submitted for this measure were based on a sample of cases; (3) Data was collected during a shorter time period (fewer quarters) than the maximum possible time for this measure; (4) Suppressed for one or more quarters by CMS; (5) No data is available from the hospital for this measure; (6) Fewer than 100 patients completed the HCAHPS survey. Use these rates with caution, as the number of surveys may be too low to reliably assess hospital performance; (7) Survey results are based on less than 12 months of data; (8) Survey results are not available for this reporting period; (9) No or very few patients were eligible for the HCAHPS survey. The scores shown, if any, reflect a very small number of surveys; (10) A state average was not calculated because too few hospitals in the state submitted data; (11) There were discrepancies in the data collection process; Please refer to the User's Guide for a full explanation of data.

VA Ann Arbor Healthcare System

2215 Fuller Road — Phone: 734-769-7100
Ann Arbor, MI 48105 — Fax: 734-761-7870
Type: Acute Care-Veterans Administration — Emergency Services: No
Ownership: Government - Federal — Beds: 132

Key Personnel:
CEO/President. . . . . Lou Ann Atkins
Chief of Medical Staff . . . . Eric W Young

Measure	Cases	This Hosp.	State Avg.	U.S. Avg.
Heart Attack Care				
ACE Inhibitor or ARB for LVSD[1]	7	86%	96%	96%
Aspirin at Arrival	45	100%	99%	99%
Aspirin at Discharge	50	100%	99%	98%
Beta Blocker at Discharge	48	100%	99%	98%
Fibrinolytic Medication Timing[5]	0	-	55%	55%
PCI Within 90 Minutes of Arrival[1]	1	100%	89%	90%
Smoking Cessation Advice[1]	15	100%	100%	99%
Chest Pain/Possible Heart Attack Care				
Aspirin at Arrival	-	-	94%	95%
Median Time to ECG (minutes)	-	-	10	8
Median Time to Transfer (minutes)	-	-	54	61
Fibrinolytic Medication Timing	-	-	60%	54%
Heart Failure Care				
ACE Inhibitor or ARB for LVSD	57	95%	95%	94%
Discharge Instructions	140	98%	89%	88%
Evaluation of LVS Function	151	100%	99%	98%
Smoking Cessation Advice	26	96%	99%	98%
Pneumonia Care				
Appropriate Initial Antibiotic	47	87%	94%	92%
Blood Culture Timing	78	95%	96%	96%
Influenza Vaccine	54	85%	91%	91%
Initial Antibiotic Timing	81	95%	96%	95%
Pneumococcal Vaccine	60	93%	93%	93%
Smoking Cessation Advice	45	98%	98%	97%
Surgical Care Improvement Project				
Appropriate VTP Within 24 Hours[2]	163	94%	94%	92%
Appropriate Hair Removal[2]	488	100%	99%	99%
Appropriate Beta Blocker Usage[2]	291	100%	92%	93%
Controlled Postoperative Blood Glucose[2]	163	94%	94%	93%
Prophylactic Antibiotic Timing	363	96%	97%	97%
Prophylactic Antibiotic Timing (Outpatient)	-	-	87%	92%
Prophylactic Antibiotic Selection	363	99%	98%	97%
Prophylactic Antibiotic Select. (Outpatient)	-	-	92%	94%
Prophylactic Antibiotic Stopped	350	87%	95%	94%
Recommended VTP Ordered[2]	163	97%	95%	94%
Urinary Catheter Removal[2]	199	96%	91%	90%
Children's Asthma Care				
Received Systemic Corticosteroids	-	-	-	100%
Received Home Management Plan	-	-	-	71%
Received Reliever Medication	-	-	-	100%
Use of Medical Imaging				
Combination Abdominal CT Scan	-	-	0.135	0.191
Combination Chest CT Scan	-	-	0.068	0.054
Follow-up Mammogram/Ultrasound	-	-	7.4%	8.4%
MRI for Low Back Pain	-	-	32%	32.7%
Survey of Patients' Hospital Experiences				
Area Around Room 'Always' Quiet at Night	-	-	-	58%
Doctors 'Always' Communicated Well	-	-	-	80%
Home Recovery Information Given	-	-	-	82%
Hospital Given 9 or 10 on 10 Point Scale	-	-	-	67%
Meds 'Always' Explained Before Given	-	-	-	60%
Nurses 'Always' Communicated Well	-	-	-	76%
Pain 'Always' Well Controlled	-	-	-	69%
Room and Bathroom 'Always' Clean	-	-	-	71%
Timely Help 'Always' Received	-	-	-	64%
Would Definitely Recommend Hospital	-	-	-	69%

Huron Medical Center

1100 South Van Dyke Road — Phone: 989-269-9521
Bad Axe, MI 48413 — Fax: 989-269-7948
URL: www.huronmedicalcenter.org
Type: Acute Care Hospitals — Emergency Services: Yes
Ownership: Voluntary Non-Profit - Private — Beds: 64

Key Personnel:
CEO/President. . . . . Jan Sternberg
Chief of Medical Staff . . . . Jerome Yaklic
Operating Room. . . . . Linda Dumaw
Quality Assurance . . . . Laura Abraham-Acker
Radiology. . . . . David Carter
Emergency Room . . . . Bryon Beck
Patient Relations . . . . Len Matestic

Measure	Cases	This Hosp.	State Avg.	U.S. Avg.
Heart Attack Care				
ACE Inhibitor or ARB for LVSD[1]	2	100%	96%	96%
Aspirin at Arrival[1]	6	100%	99%	99%
Aspirin at Discharge[1]	3	100%	99%	98%
Beta Blocker at Discharge[1]	6	83%	99%	98%
Fibrinolytic Medication Timing	0	-	55%	55%
PCI Within 90 Minutes of Arrival	0	-	89%	90%
Smoking Cessation Advice	0	-	100%	99%
Chest Pain/Possible Heart Attack Care				
Aspirin at Arrival	105	98%	94%	95%
Median Time to ECG (minutes)	113	10	10	8
Median Time to Transfer (minutes)[3]	0	-	54	61
Fibrinolytic Medication Timing[1]	3	33%	60%	54%
Heart Failure Care				
ACE Inhibitor or ARB for LVSD[1]	5	100%	95%	94%
Discharge Instructions	29	100%	89%	88%
Evaluation of LVS Function	46	98%	99%	98%
Smoking Cessation Advice[1]	5	100%	99%	98%
Pneumonia Care				
Appropriate Initial Antibiotic	33	91%	94%	92%
Blood Culture Timing	60	100%	96%	96%
Influenza Vaccine	27	81%	91%	91%
Initial Antibiotic Timing	52	100%	96%	95%
Pneumococcal Vaccine	52	88%	93%	93%
Smoking Cessation Advice[1]	7	100%	98%	97%
Surgical Care Improvement Project				
Appropriate VTP Within 24 Hours[1,2]	23	91%	94%	92%
Appropriate Hair Removal[2]	178	100%	99%	99%
Appropriate Beta Blocker Usage[2]	44	100%	92%	93%
Controlled Postoperative Blood Glucose[2]	0	-	94%	93%
Prophylactic Antibiotic Timing[2]	148	99%	97%	97%
Prophylactic Antibiotic Timing (Outpatient)[1]	11	73%	87%	92%
Prophylactic Antibiotic Selection[2]	149	97%	98%	97%
Prophylactic Antibiotic Select. (Outpatient)	26	92%	92%	94%
Prophylactic Antibiotic Stopped[2]	146	100%	95%	94%
Recommended VTP Ordered[1,2]	23	91%	95%	94%
Urinary Catheter Removal[2]	33	97%	91%	90%
Children's Asthma Care				
Received Systemic Corticosteroids	-	-	-	100%
Received Home Management Plan	-	-	-	71%
Received Reliever Medication	-	-	-	100%
Use of Medical Imaging				
Combination Abdominal CT Scan	354	0.102	0.135	0.191
Combination Chest CT Scan	133	0.083	0.068	0.054
Follow-up Mammogram/Ultrasound	428	3.0%	7.4%	8.4%
MRI for Low Back Pain[5]	0	-	32%	32.7%
Survey of Patients' Hospital Experiences				
Area Around Room 'Always' Quiet at Night	300+	59%	-	58%
Doctors 'Always' Communicated Well	300+	83%	-	80%
Home Recovery Information Given	300+	89%	-	82%
Hospital Given 9 or 10 on 10 Point Scale	300+	77%	-	67%
Meds 'Always' Explained Before Given	300+	63%	-	60%
Nurses 'Always' Communicated Well	300+	80%	-	76%
Pain 'Always' Well Controlled	300+	75%	-	69%
Room and Bathroom 'Always' Clean	300+	76%	-	71%
Timely Help 'Always' Received	300+	75%	-	64%
Would Definitely Recommend Hospital	300+	75%	-	69%

Battle Creek Health System

300 North Avenue — Phone: 269-966-8000
Battle Creek, MI 49017 — Fax: 269-966-8366
URL: www.bchealth.com
Type: Acute Care Hospitals — Emergency Services: Yes
Ownership: Proprietary — Beds: 315

Key Personnel:
CEO/President. . . . . Pat Garrett
Pediatric Ambulatory Care . . . . . . Samuel Grossman, DO
Pediatric In-Patient Care . . . . Shohreh Moazami, MD
Radiology. . . . . Steven Miltz-Miller, MD
Intensive Care Unit. . . . . Annette Berning

Measure	Cases	This Hosp.	State Avg.	U.S. Avg.
Heart Attack Care				
ACE Inhibitor or ARB for LVSD	25	92%	96%	96%
Aspirin at Arrival	134	100%	99%	99%
Aspirin at Discharge	90	99%	99%	98%
Beta Blocker at Discharge	94	99%	99%	98%
Fibrinolytic Medication Timing	0	-	55%	55%
PCI Within 90 Minutes of Arrival	0	-	89%	90%
Smoking Cessation Advice	25	100%	100%	99%
Chest Pain/Possible Heart Attack Care				
Aspirin at Arrival	115	97%	94%	95%
Median Time to ECG (minutes)	118	16	10	8
Median Time to Transfer (minutes)[1]	12	56	54	61
Fibrinolytic Medication Timing	0	-	60%	54%
Heart Failure Care				
ACE Inhibitor or ARB for LVSD	117	99%	95%	94%
Discharge Instructions	381	84%	89%	88%
Evaluation of LVS Function	449	100%	99%	98%
Smoking Cessation Advice	118	100%	99%	98%
Pneumonia Care				
Appropriate Initial Antibiotic	223	95%	94%	92%
Blood Culture Timing	367	99%	96%	96%
Influenza Vaccine	235	97%	91%	91%
Initial Antibiotic Timing	337	98%	96%	95%
Pneumococcal Vaccine	275	99%	93%	93%
Smoking Cessation Advice	163	100%	98%	97%
Surgical Care Improvement Project				
Appropriate VTP Within 24 Hours[2]	179	94%	94%	92%
Appropriate Hair Removal[2]	986	100%	99%	99%
Appropriate Beta Blocker Usage[2]	264	93%	92%	93%
Controlled Postoperative Blood Glucose[1,2]	1	0%	94%	93%
Prophylactic Antibiotic Timing[2]	800	99%	97%	97%
Prophylactic Antibiotic Timing (Outpatient)	248	98%	87%	92%
Prophylactic Antibiotic Selection[2]	806	99%	98%	97%
Prophylactic Antibiotic Select. (Outpatient)	251	98%	92%	94%
Prophylactic Antibiotic Stopped[2]	741	97%	95%	94%
Recommended VTP Ordered[2]	179	95%	95%	94%
Urinary Catheter Removal[2]	279	100%	91%	90%
Children's Asthma Care				
Received Systemic Corticosteroids	-	-	-	100%
Received Home Management Plan	-	-	-	71%
Received Reliever Medication	-	-	-	100%
Use of Medical Imaging				
Combination Abdominal CT Scan	1,160	0.034	0.135	0.191
Combination Chest CT Scan	694	0.009	0.068	0.054
Follow-up Mammogram/Ultrasound	1,745	4.3%	7.4%	8.4%
MRI for Low Back Pain	220	33.2%	32%	32.7%
Survey of Patients' Hospital Experiences				
Area Around Room 'Always' Quiet at Night	300+	54%	-	58%
Doctors 'Always' Communicated Well	300+	76%	-	80%
Home Recovery Information Given	300+	88%	-	82%
Hospital Given 9 or 10 on 10 Point Scale	300+	64%	-	67%
Meds 'Always' Explained Before Given	300+	59%	-	60%
Nurses 'Always' Communicated Well	300+	76%	-	76%
Pain 'Always' Well Controlled	300+	69%	-	69%
Room and Bathroom 'Always' Clean	300+	69%	-	71%
Timely Help 'Always' Received	300+	67%	-	64%
Would Definitely Recommend Hospital	300+	59%	-	69%

NOTE: Hospital profiles are in alphabetical order by state, then city, then hospital within the city; Rankings exclude hospitals with less than 25 cases except for patient surveys which excludes hospitals with less than 100 cases; (a) 100–299 cases; (1) The number of cases is too small to be sure how well a hospital is performing; (2) The hospital indicated that the data submitted for this measure were based on a sample of cases; (3) Data was collected during a shorter time period (fewer quarters) than the maximum possible time for this measure; (4) Suppressed for one or more quarters by CMS; (5) No data is available from the hospital for this measure; (6) Fewer than 100 patients completed the HCAHPS survey. Use these rates with caution, as the number of surveys may be too low to reliably assess hospital performance; (7) Survey results are based on less than 12 months of data; (8) Survey results are not available for this reporting period; (9) No or very few patients were eligible for the HCAHPS survey. The scores shown, if any, reflect a very small number of surveys; (10) A state average was not calculated because too few hospitals in the state submitted data; (11) There were discrepancies in the data collection process; Please refer to the User's Guide for a full explanation of data.

Battle Creek VA Medical Center

5500 Armstrong Rd. Phone: 269-966-5600
Battle Creek, MI 49015
URL: www.battlecreek.va.gov
Type: Acute Care-Veterans Administration Emergency Services: No
Ownership: Government - Federal

Key Personnel:
CEO/President. . . . . Suzanne Klinker
Chief of Medical Staff . . . . Ketan Shah, MD
Coronary Care . . . . Helen Parkis, RN
Infection Control. . . . . Daniel Allen
Quality Assurance . . . . Gail M O'Dwyer
Radiology. . . . . Jeff Brewster
Emergency Room . . . . Donna Sumrall, RN
Intensive Care Unit. . . . . Nina Santos, RN

Measure	Cases	This Hosp.	State Avg.	U.S. Avg.
Heart Attack Care				
ACE Inhibitor or ARB for LVSD[5]	0	-	96%	96%
Aspirin at Arrival[5]	0	-	99%	99%
Aspirin at Discharge[5]	0	-	99%	98%
Beta Blocker at Discharge[5]	0	-	99%	98%
Fibrinolytic Medication Timing[5]	0	-	55%	55%
PCI Within 90 Minutes of Arrival[5]	0	-	89%	90%
Smoking Cessation Advice[5]	0	-	100%	99%
Chest Pain/Possible Heart Attack Care				
Aspirin at Arrival	-	-	94%	95%
Median Time to ECG (minutes)	-	-	10	8
Median Time to Transfer (minutes)	-	-	54	61
Fibrinolytic Medication Timing	-	-	60%	54%
Heart Failure Care				
ACE Inhibitor or ARB for LVSD[1]	5	60%	95%	94%
Discharge Instructions[1]	14	100%	89%	88%
Evaluation of LVS Function[1]	15	100%	99%	98%
Smoking Cessation Advice[1]	5	100%	99%	98%
Pneumonia Care				
Appropriate Initial Antibiotic[1]	12	67%	94%	92%
Blood Culture Timing[5]	0	-	96%	96%
Influenza Vaccine[1]	14	86%	91%	91%
Initial Antibiotic Timing[1]	21	90%	96%	95%
Pneumococcal Vaccine[1]	14	100%	93%	93%
Smoking Cessation Advice[1]	14	100%	98%	97%
Surgical Care Improvement Project				
Appropriate VTP Within 24 Hours[2,5]	0	-	94%	92%
Appropriate Hair Removal[2,5]	0	-	99%	99%
Appropriate Beta Blocker Usage[2,5]	0	-	92%	93%
Controlled Postoperative Blood Glucose[2,5]	0	-	94%	93%
Prophylactic Antibiotic Timing[5]	0	-	97%	97%
Prophylactic Antibiotic Timing (Outpatient)	-	-	87%	92%
Prophylactic Antibiotic Selection[5]	0	-	98%	97%
Prophylactic Antibiotic Select. (Outpatient)	-	-	92%	94%
Prophylactic Antibiotic Stopped[5]	0	-	95%	94%
Recommended VTP Ordered[2,5]	0	-	95%	94%
Urinary Catheter Removal[2,5]	0	-	91%	90%
Children's Asthma Care				
Received Systemic Corticosteroids	-	-	-	100%
Received Home Management Plan	-	-	-	71%
Received Reliever Medication	-	-	-	100%
Use of Medical Imaging				
Combination Abdominal CT Scan	-	-	0.135	0.191
Combination Chest CT Scan	-	-	0.068	0.054
Follow-up Mammogram/Ultrasound	-	-	7.4%	8.4%
MRI for Low Back Pain	-	-	32%	32.7%
Survey of Patients' Hospital Experiences				
Area Around Room 'Always' Quiet at Night	-	-	-	58%
Doctors 'Always' Communicated Well	-	-	-	80%
Home Recovery Information Given	-	-	-	82%
Hospital Given 9 or 10 on 10 Point Scale	-	-	-	67%
Meds 'Always' Explained Before Given	-	-	-	60%
Nurses 'Always' Communicated Well	-	-	-	76%
Pain 'Always' Well Controlled	-	-	-	69%
Room and Bathroom 'Always' Clean	-	-	-	71%
Timely Help 'Always' Received	-	-	-	64%
Would Definitely Recommend Hospital	-	-	-	69%

Bay Regional Medical Center

1900 Columbus Ave Phone: 989-894-3000
Bay City, MI 48708 Fax: 989-894-4464
URL: www.baymed.org
Type: Acute Care Hospitals Emergency Services: Yes
Ownership: Voluntary Non-Profit - Other Beds: 415

Key Personnel:
CEO/President. . . . . Robert Wright
Chief of Medical Staff . . . . Christopher Brueck, MD
Coronary Care . . . . Willa Rousseau
Infection Control. . . . . Karen Frahm, RN
Pediatric Ambulatory Care . . . . . . RE Bickham, MD
Pediatric In-Patient Care . . . . Carol Jones
Quality Assurance . . . . Jack Miller
Radiology. . . . . Dave Nall

Measure	Cases	This Hosp.	State Avg.	U.S. Avg.
Heart Attack Care				
ACE Inhibitor or ARB for LVSD	74	96%	96%	96%
Aspirin at Arrival	204	97%	99%	99%
Aspirin at Discharge	318	99%	99%	98%
Beta Blocker at Discharge	310	96%	99%	98%
Fibrinolytic Medication Timing	0	-	55%	55%
PCI Within 90 Minutes of Arrival	53	91%	89%	90%
Smoking Cessation Advice	132	100%	100%	99%
Chest Pain/Possible Heart Attack Care				
Aspirin at Arrival[1,3]	1	100%	94%	95%
Median Time to ECG (minutes)[1,3]	1	23	10	8
Median Time to Transfer (minutes)[5]	0	-	54	61
Fibrinolytic Medication Timing[5]	0	-	60%	54%
Heart Failure Care				
ACE Inhibitor or ARB for LVSD	174	88%	95%	94%
Discharge Instructions	502	99%	89%	88%
Evaluation of LVS Function	601	96%	99%	98%
Smoking Cessation Advice	81	99%	99%	98%
Pneumonia Care				
Appropriate Initial Antibiotic	136	90%	94%	92%
Blood Culture Timing	159	97%	96%	96%
Influenza Vaccine	140	81%	91%	91%
Initial Antibiotic Timing	241	97%	96%	95%
Pneumococcal Vaccine	201	92%	93%	93%
Smoking Cessation Advice	85	98%	98%	97%
Surgical Care Improvement Project				
Appropriate VTP Within 24 Hours	394	86%	94%	92%
Appropriate Hair Removal	1,514	100%	99%	99%
Appropriate Beta Blocker Usage	522	93%	92%	93%
Controlled Postoperative Blood Glucose	387	92%	94%	93%
Prophylactic Antibiotic Timing	995	98%	97%	97%
Prophylactic Antibiotic Timing (Outpatient)	460	73%	87%	92%
Prophylactic Antibiotic Selection	1,013	96%	98%	97%
Prophylactic Antibiotic Select. (Outpatient)	450	94%	92%	94%
Prophylactic Antibiotic Stopped	975	96%	95%	94%
Recommended VTP Ordered	394	89%	95%	94%
Urinary Catheter Removal	267	81%	91%	90%
Children's Asthma Care				
Received Systemic Corticosteroids	-	-	-	100%
Received Home Management Plan	-	-	-	71%
Received Reliever Medication	-	-	-	100%
Use of Medical Imaging				
Combination Abdominal CT Scan	1,135	0.089	0.135	0.191
Combination Chest CT Scan	864	0.029	0.068	0.054
Follow-up Mammogram/Ultrasound	2,019	4.3%	7.4%	8.4%
MRI for Low Back Pain	415	37.3%	32%	32.7%
Survey of Patients' Hospital Experiences				
Area Around Room 'Always' Quiet at Night	300+	45%	-	58%
Doctors 'Always' Communicated Well	300+	76%	-	80%
Home Recovery Information Given	300+	83%	-	82%
Hospital Given 9 or 10 on 10 Point Scale	300+	63%	-	67%
Meds 'Always' Explained Before Given	300+	59%	-	60%
Nurses 'Always' Communicated Well	300+	76%	-	76%
Pain 'Always' Well Controlled	300+	69%	-	69%
Room and Bathroom 'Always' Clean	300+	65%	-	71%
Timely Help 'Always' Received	300+	67%	-	64%
Would Definitely Recommend Hospital	300+	66%	-	69%

Mecosta County Medical Center

605 Oak Street Phone: 231-796-8691
Big Rapids, MI 49307 Fax: 231-592-4462
URL: www.mcmc.br.com
Type: Acute Care Hospitals Emergency Services: Yes
Ownership: Government - Local Beds: 74

Key Personnel:
CEO/President. . . . . Sam Daugherty
Chief of Medical Staff . . . . Charles Brummeler
Quality Assurance . . . . Amanda Jensen
Radiology. . . . . Blase Vitello
Emergency Room . . . . Virginia Keusch, RN

Measure	Cases	This Hosp.	State Avg.	U.S. Avg.
Heart Attack Care				
ACE Inhibitor or ARB for LVSD	0	-	96%	96%
Aspirin at Arrival[1]	12	92%	99%	99%
Aspirin at Discharge[1]	9	100%	99%	98%
Beta Blocker at Discharge[1]	9	89%	99%	98%
Fibrinolytic Medication Timing	0	-	55%	55%
PCI Within 90 Minutes of Arrival	0	-	89%	90%
Smoking Cessation Advice[1]	1	100%	100%	99%
Chest Pain/Possible Heart Attack Care				
Aspirin at Arrival	138	97%	94%	95%
Median Time to ECG (minutes)	146	10	10	8
Median Time to Transfer (minutes)	0	-	54	61
Fibrinolytic Medication Timing[1]	8	75%	60%	54%
Heart Failure Care				
ACE Inhibitor or ARB for LVSD[1]	20	90%	95%	94%
Discharge Instructions	55	89%	89%	88%
Evaluation of LVS Function	63	92%	99%	98%
Smoking Cessation Advice[1]	11	100%	99%	98%
Pneumonia Care				
Appropriate Initial Antibiotic	72	88%	94%	92%
Blood Culture Timing	93	98%	96%	96%
Influenza Vaccine	62	87%	91%	91%
Initial Antibiotic Timing	75	99%	96%	95%
Pneumococcal Vaccine	74	92%	93%	93%
Smoking Cessation Advice	30	100%	98%	97%
Surgical Care Improvement Project				
Appropriate VTP Within 24 Hours	28	86%	94%	92%
Appropriate Hair Removal	227	100%	99%	99%
Appropriate Beta Blocker Usage	54	83%	92%	93%
Controlled Postoperative Blood Glucose	0	-	94%	93%
Prophylactic Antibiotic Timing	199	93%	97%	97%
Prophylactic Antibiotic Timing (Outpatient)	83	27%	87%	92%
Prophylactic Antibiotic Selection	199	95%	98%	97%
Prophylactic Antibiotic Select. (Outpatient)[1]	23	91%	92%	94%
Prophylactic Antibiotic Stopped	195	94%	95%	94%
Recommended VTP Ordered	29	83%	95%	94%
Urinary Catheter Removal	56	91%	91%	90%
Children's Asthma Care				
Received Systemic Corticosteroids	-	-	-	100%
Received Home Management Plan	-	-	-	71%
Received Reliever Medication	-	-	-	100%
Use of Medical Imaging				
Combination Abdominal CT Scan	330	0.488	0.135	0.191
Combination Chest CT Scan	310	0.032	0.068	0.054
Follow-up Mammogram/Ultrasound	571	8.6%	7.4%	8.4%
MRI for Low Back Pain	154	35.1%	32%	32.7%
Survey of Patients' Hospital Experiences				
Area Around Room 'Always' Quiet at Night	300+	61%	-	58%
Doctors 'Always' Communicated Well	300+	79%	-	80%
Home Recovery Information Given	300+	85%	-	82%
Hospital Given 9 or 10 on 10 Point Scale	300+	69%	-	67%
Meds 'Always' Explained Before Given	300+	61%	-	60%
Nurses 'Always' Communicated Well	300+	73%	-	76%
Pain 'Always' Well Controlled	300+	69%	-	69%
Room and Bathroom 'Always' Clean	300+	62%	-	71%
Timely Help 'Always' Received	300+	66%	-	64%
Would Definitely Recommend Hospital	300+	68%	-	69%

NOTE: Hospital profiles are in alphabetical order by state, then city, then hospital within the city; Rankings exclude hospitals with less than 25 cases except for patient surveys which excludes hospitals with less than 100 cases; (a) 100–299 cases; (1) The number of cases is too small to be sure how well a hospital is performing; (2) The hospital indicated that the data submitted for this measure were based on a sample of cases; (3) Data was collected during a shorter time period (fewer quarters) than the maximum possible time for this measure; (4) Suppressed for one or more quarters by CMS; (5) No data is available from the hospital for this measure; (6) Fewer than 100 patients completed the HCAHPS survey. Use these rates with caution, as the number of surveys may be too low to reliably assess hospital performance; (7) Survey results are based on less than 12 months of data; (8) Survey results are not available for this reporting period; (9) No or very few patients were eligible for the HCAHPS survey. The scores shown, if any, reflect a very small number of surveys; (10) A state average was not calculated because too few hospitals in the state submitted data; (11) There were discrepancies in the data collection process; Please refer to the User's Guide for a full explanation of data.

Brighton Hospital

12851 E Grand River
Brighton, MI 48116
Phone: 810-227-1211
Fax: 810-227-1869
E-mail: info@brightonhospital.org
URL: www.stjohn.org/brighton
Type: Acute Care Hospitals
Emergency Services: No
Ownership: Voluntary Non-Profit - Private
Beds: 63

Key Personnel:
CEO/President. . . . . Denise Bertin-Epp
Chief of Medical Staff . . . . Michael Brooks, MD

Measure	Cases	This Hosp.	State Avg.	U.S. Avg.
Heart Attack Care				
ACE Inhibitor or ARB for LVSD[5]	0	-	96%	96%
Aspirin at Arrival[5]	0	-	99%	99%
Aspirin at Discharge[5]	0	-	99%	98%
Beta Blocker at Discharge[5]	0	-	99%	98%
Fibrinolytic Medication Timing[5]	0	-	55%	55%
PCI Within 90 Minutes of Arrival[5]	0	-	89%	90%
Smoking Cessation Advice[5]	0	-	100%	99%
Chest Pain/Possible Heart Attack Care				
Aspirin at Arrival[5]	0	-	94%	95%
Median Time to ECG (minutes)[5]	0	-	10	8
Median Time to Transfer (minutes)[5]	0	-	54	61
Fibrinolytic Medication Timing[5]	0	-	60%	54%
Heart Failure Care				
ACE Inhibitor or ARB for LVSD[5]	0	-	95%	94%
Discharge Instructions[5]	0	-	89%	88%
Evaluation of LVS Function[5]	0	-	99%	98%
Smoking Cessation Advice[5]	0	-	99%	98%
Pneumonia Care				
Appropriate Initial Antibiotic[5]	0	-	94%	92%
Blood Culture Timing[5]	0	-	96%	96%
Influenza Vaccine[5]	0	-	91%	91%
Initial Antibiotic Timing[5]	0	-	96%	95%
Pneumococcal Vaccine[5]	0	-	93%	93%
Smoking Cessation Advice[5]	0	-	98%	97%
Surgical Care Improvement Project				
Appropriate VTP Within 24 Hours[5]	0	-	94%	92%
Appropriate Hair Removal[5]	0	-	99%	99%
Appropriate Beta Blocker Usage[5]	0	-	92%	93%
Controlled Postoperative Blood Glucose[5]	0	-	94%	93%
Prophylactic Antibiotic Timing[5]	0	-	97%	97%
Prophylactic Antibiotic Timing (Outpatient)[5]	0	-	87%	92%
Prophylactic Antibiotic Selection[5]	0	-	98%	97%
Prophylactic Antibiotic Select. (Outpatient)[5]	0	-	92%	94%
Prophylactic Antibiotic Stopped[5]	0	-	95%	94%
Recommended VTP Ordered[5]	0	-	95%	94%
Urinary Catheter Removal[5]	0	-	91%	90%
Children's Asthma Care				
Received Systemic Corticosteroids	-	-	-	100%
Received Home Management Plan	-	-	-	71%
Received Reliever Medication	-	-	-	100%
Use of Medical Imaging				
Combination Abdominal CT Scan[5]	0	-	0.135	0.191
Combination Chest CT Scan[5]	0	-	0.068	0.054
Follow-up Mammogram/Ultrasound[5]	0	-	7.4%	8.4%
MRI for Low Back Pain[5]	0	-	32%	32.7%
Survey of Patients' Hospital Experiences				
Area Around Room 'Always' Quiet at Night[9]	-	-	-	58%
Doctors 'Always' Communicated Well[9]	-	-	-	80%
Home Recovery Information Given[9]	-	-	-	82%
Hospital Given 9 or 10 on 10 Point Scale[9]	-	-	-	67%
Meds 'Always' Explained Before Given[9]	-	-	-	60%
Nurses 'Always' Communicated Well[9]	-	-	-	76%
Pain 'Always' Well Controlled[9]	-	-	-	69%
Room and Bathroom 'Always' Clean[9]	-	-	-	71%
Timely Help 'Always' Received[9]	-	-	-	64%
Would Definitely Recommend Hospital[9]	-	-	-	69%

Mercy Hospital - Cadillac

400 Hobart St
Cadillac, MI 49601
Phone: 231-876-7200
Fax: 231-876-7439
E-mail: mercycadillac@trinity-health.org
URL: www.mercycadillac.munsonhealthcare.org
Type: Acute Care Hospitals
Emergency Services: Yes
Ownership: Voluntary Non-Profit - Church
Beds: 174

Key Personnel:
CEO/President. . . . . John H Macleod
Emergency Room . . . . Janet Eng

Measure	Cases	This Hosp.	State Avg.	U.S. Avg.
Heart Attack Care				
ACE Inhibitor or ARB for LVSD[1]	10	100%	96%	96%
Aspirin at Arrival	51	100%	99%	99%
Aspirin at Discharge	39	95%	99%	98%
Beta Blocker at Discharge	39	95%	99%	98%
Fibrinolytic Medication Timing	0	-	55%	55%
PCI Within 90 Minutes of Arrival	0	-	89%	90%
Smoking Cessation Advice[1]	8	100%	100%	99%
Chest Pain/Possible Heart Attack Care				
Aspirin at Arrival	75	100%	94%	95%
Median Time to ECG (minutes)	74	10	10	8
Median Time to Transfer (minutes)[1]	6	153	54	61
Fibrinolytic Medication Timing[1]	5	80%	60%	54%
Heart Failure Care				
ACE Inhibitor or ARB for LVSD	33	94%	95%	94%
Discharge Instructions	102	94%	89%	88%
Evaluation of LVS Function	120	100%	99%	98%
Smoking Cessation Advice[1]	22	100%	99%	98%
Pneumonia Care				
Appropriate Initial Antibiotic[2]	97	94%	94%	92%
Blood Culture Timing[2]	151	94%	96%	96%
Influenza Vaccine[2]	82	100%	91%	91%
Initial Antibiotic Timing[2]	128	98%	96%	95%
Pneumococcal Vaccine[2]	117	98%	93%	93%
Smoking Cessation Advice[2]	42	100%	98%	97%
Surgical Care Improvement Project				
Appropriate VTP Within 24 Hours	86	93%	94%	92%
Appropriate Hair Removal	422	100%	99%	99%
Appropriate Beta Blocker Usage	102	90%	92%	93%
Controlled Postoperative Blood Glucose	0	-	94%	93%
Prophylactic Antibiotic Timing	322	96%	97%	97%
Prophylactic Antibiotic Timing (Outpatient)	153	93%	87%	92%
Prophylactic Antibiotic Selection	322	97%	98%	97%
Prophylactic Antibiotic Select. (Outpatient)	151	82%	92%	94%
Prophylactic Antibiotic Stopped	318	96%	95%	94%
Recommended VTP Ordered	86	94%	95%	94%
Urinary Catheter Removal	102	97%	91%	90%
Children's Asthma Care				
Received Systemic Corticosteroids	-	-	-	100%
Received Home Management Plan	-	-	-	71%
Received Reliever Medication	-	-	-	100%
Use of Medical Imaging				
Combination Abdominal CT Scan	638	0.024	0.135	0.191
Combination Chest CT Scan	440	0.005	0.068	0.054
Follow-up Mammogram/Ultrasound	842	6.5%	7.4%	8.4%
MRI for Low Back Pain	262	38.5%	32%	32.7%
Survey of Patients' Hospital Experiences				
Area Around Room 'Always' Quiet at Night	300+	61%	-	58%
Doctors 'Always' Communicated Well	300+	81%	-	80%
Home Recovery Information Given	300+	88%	-	82%
Hospital Given 9 or 10 on 10 Point Scale	300+	76%	-	67%
Meds 'Always' Explained Before Given	300+	65%	-	60%
Nurses 'Always' Communicated Well	300+	80%	-	76%
Pain 'Always' Well Controlled	300+	73%	-	69%
Room and Bathroom 'Always' Clean	300+	68%	-	71%
Timely Help 'Always' Received	300+	74%	-	64%
Would Definitely Recommend Hospital	300+	73%	-	69%

Caro Community Hospital

401 N Hooper Street
Caro, MI 48723
Phone: 989-673-3141
Fax: 989-673-8471
Type: Critical Access Hospitals
Emergency Services: Yes
Ownership: Voluntary Non-Profit - Private
Beds: 25

Key Personnel:
CEO/President. . . . . William P Miller
Chief of Medical Staff . . . . A Ferreira, MD
Infection Control. . . . . Tammy Gugel
Quality Assurance . . . . Sue Morris, RN

Measure	Cases	This Hosp.	State Avg.	U.S. Avg.
Heart Attack Care				
ACE Inhibitor or ARB for LVSD[5]	0	-	96%	96%
Aspirin at Arrival[5]	0	-	99%	99%
Aspirin at Discharge[5]	0	-	99%	98%
Beta Blocker at Discharge[5]	0	-	99%	98%
Fibrinolytic Medication Timing[5]	0	-	55%	55%
PCI Within 90 Minutes of Arrival[5]	0	-	89%	90%
Smoking Cessation Advice[5]	0	-	100%	99%
Chest Pain/Possible Heart Attack Care				
Aspirin at Arrival	-	-	94%	95%
Median Time to ECG (minutes)	-	-	10	8
Median Time to Transfer (minutes)	-	-	54	61
Fibrinolytic Medication Timing	-	-	60%	54%
Heart Failure Care				
ACE Inhibitor or ARB for LVSD[1]	3	67%	95%	94%
Discharge Instructions[1]	6	83%	89%	88%
Evaluation of LVS Function[1]	10	100%	99%	98%
Smoking Cessation Advice[1]	2	50%	99%	98%
Pneumonia Care				
Appropriate Initial Antibiotic[1]	12	100%	94%	92%
Blood Culture Timing[1]	13	100%	96%	96%
Influenza Vaccine[1]	12	58%	91%	91%
Initial Antibiotic Timing[1]	9	89%	96%	95%
Pneumococcal Vaccine[1]	11	73%	93%	93%
Smoking Cessation Advice[1]	2	50%	98%	97%
Surgical Care Improvement Project				
Appropriate VTP Within 24 Hours[3]	0	-	94%	92%
Appropriate Hair Removal[1,3]	6	83%	99%	99%
Appropriate Beta Blocker Usage[5]	0	-	92%	93%
Controlled Postoperative Blood Glucose[3]	0	-	94%	93%
Prophylactic Antibiotic Timing[1,3]	6	83%	97%	97%
Prophylactic Antibiotic Timing (Outpatient)	-	-	87%	92%
Prophylactic Antibiotic Selection[1,3]	6	100%	98%	97%
Prophylactic Antibiotic Select. (Outpatient)	-	-	92%	94%
Prophylactic Antibiotic Stopped[1,3]	6	100%	95%	94%
Recommended VTP Ordered[3]	0	-	95%	94%
Urinary Catheter Removal[1,3]	3	100%	91%	90%
Children's Asthma Care				
Received Systemic Corticosteroids	-	-	-	100%
Received Home Management Plan	-	-	-	71%
Received Reliever Medication	-	-	-	100%
Use of Medical Imaging				
Combination Abdominal CT Scan	-	-	0.135	0.191
Combination Chest CT Scan	-	-	0.068	0.054
Follow-up Mammogram/Ultrasound	-	-	7.4%	8.4%
MRI for Low Back Pain	-	-	32%	32.7%
Survey of Patients' Hospital Experiences				
Area Around Room 'Always' Quiet at Night[6]	<100	55%	-	58%
Doctors 'Always' Communicated Well[6]	<100	80%	-	80%
Home Recovery Information Given[6]	<100	83%	-	82%
Hospital Given 9 or 10 on 10 Point Scale[6]	<100	72%	-	67%
Meds 'Always' Explained Before Given[6]	<100	42%	-	60%
Nurses 'Always' Communicated Well[6]	<100	74%	-	76%
Pain 'Always' Well Controlled[6]	<100	69%	-	69%
Room and Bathroom 'Always' Clean[6]	<100	72%	-	71%
Timely Help 'Always' Received[6]	<100	78%	-	64%
Would Definitely Recommend Hospital	<100	64%	-	69%

NOTE: Hospital profiles are in alphabetical order by state, then city, then hospital within the city; Rankings exclude hospitals with less than 25 cases except for patient surveys which excludes hospitals with less than 100 cases; (a) 100–299 cases; (1) The number of cases is too small to be sure how well a hospital is performing; (2) The hospital indicated that the data submitted for this measure were based on a sample of cases; (3) Data was collected during a shorter time period (fewer quarters) than the maximum possible time for this measure; (4) Suppressed for one or more quarters by CMS; (5) No data is available from the hospital for this measure; (6) Fewer than 100 patients completed the HCAHPS survey. Use these rates with caution, as the number of surveys may be too low to reliably assess hospital performance; (7) Survey results are based on less than 12 months of data; (8) Survey results are not available for this reporting period; (9) No or very few patients were eligible for the HCAHPS survey. The scores shown, if any, reflect a very small number of surveys; (10) A state average was not calculated because too few hospitals in the state submitted data; (11) There were discrepancies in the data collection process; Please refer to the User's Guide for a full explanation of data.

Carson City Hospital

406 East Elm St
Carson City, MI 48811
Phone: 989-584-3131
Fax: 989-584-6165
E-mail: bruce@carsoncityhospital.com
URL: www.carsoncityhospital.com
Type: Acute Care Hospitals
Emergency Services: Yes
Ownership: Voluntary Non-Profit - Other
Beds: 77

Key Personnel:
CEO/President. . . . . Bruce L Traverse
Chief of Medical Staff . . . . H Chuck Wakefield, DO
Infection Control. . . . . Judy Brown, RN
Operating Room. . . . . Cheryl Young, RN
Pediatric Ambulatory Care . . . . . . Alberto Betancourt, MD
Pediatric In-Patient Care . . . . Alberto Betancourt, MD
Quality Assurance . . . . Shawn Smith

Measure	Cases	This Hosp.	State Avg.	U.S. Avg.
Heart Attack Care				
ACE Inhibitor or ARB for LVSD[1]	2	100%	96%	96%
Aspirin at Arrival[1]	7	100%	99%	99%
Aspirin at Discharge[1]	5	100%	99%	98%
Beta Blocker at Discharge[1]	5	100%	99%	98%
Fibrinolytic Medication Timing	0	-	55%	55%
PCI Within 90 Minutes of Arrival	0	-	89%	90%
Smoking Cessation Advice	0	-	100%	99%
Chest Pain/Possible Heart Attack Care				
Aspirin at Arrival	130	100%	94%	95%
Median Time to ECG (minutes)	131	13	10	8
Median Time to Transfer (minutes)[1,3]	4	108	54	61
Fibrinolytic Medication Timing[1]	3	100%	60%	54%
Heart Failure Care				
ACE Inhibitor or ARB for LVSD[1]	11	82%	95%	94%
Discharge Instructions	26	92%	89%	88%
Evaluation of LVS Function	37	95%	99%	98%
Smoking Cessation Advice[1]	4	100%	99%	98%
Pneumonia Care				
Appropriate Initial Antibiotic	45	91%	94%	92%
Blood Culture Timing	37	92%	96%	96%
Influenza Vaccine	31	87%	91%	91%
Initial Antibiotic Timing	46	93%	96%	95%
Pneumococcal Vaccine	35	89%	93%	93%
Smoking Cessation Advice[1]	14	100%	98%	97%
Surgical Care Improvement Project				
Appropriate VTP Within 24 Hours	66	98%	94%	92%
Appropriate Hair Removal	219	95%	99%	99%
Appropriate Beta Blocker Usage	31	77%	92%	93%
Controlled Postoperative Blood Glucose	0	-	94%	93%
Prophylactic Antibiotic Timing	197	90%	97%	97%
Prophylactic Antibiotic Timing (Outpatient)	39	77%	87%	92%
Prophylactic Antibiotic Selection	200	93%	98%	97%
Prophylactic Antibiotic Select. (Outpatient)	34	88%	92%	94%
Prophylactic Antibiotic Stopped	193	92%	95%	94%
Recommended VTP Ordered	66	100%	95%	94%
Urinary Catheter Removal	54	78%	91%	90%
Children's Asthma Care				
Received Systemic Corticosteroids	-	-	-	100%
Received Home Management Plan	-	-	-	71%
Received Reliever Medication	-	-	-	100%
Use of Medical Imaging				
Combination Abdominal CT Scan	235	0.094	0.135	0.191
Combination Chest CT Scan	187	0.032	0.068	0.054
Follow-up Mammogram/Ultrasound	294	12.9%	7.4%	8.4%
MRI for Low Back Pain	133	42.9%	32%	32.7%
Survey of Patients' Hospital Experiences				
Area Around Room 'Always' Quiet at Night	300+	59%	-	58%
Doctors 'Always' Communicated Well	300+	83%	-	80%
Home Recovery Information Given	300+	85%	-	82%
Hospital Given 9 or 10 on 10 Point Scale	300+	73%	-	67%
Meds 'Always' Explained Before Given	300+	62%	-	60%
Nurses 'Always' Communicated Well	300+	77%	-	76%
Pain 'Always' Well Controlled	300+	68%	-	69%
Room and Bathroom 'Always' Clean	300+	78%	-	71%
Timely Help 'Always' Received	300+	72%	-	64%
Would Definitely Recommend Hospital	300+	70%	-	69%

Hills & Dales General Hospital

4675 Hill Street
Cass City, MI 48726
Phone: 989-872-2121
Fax: 989-872-5376
E-mail: publicinfo@hillsanddales.com
URL: www.hillsanddales.com
Type: Critical Access Hospitals
Emergency Services: Yes
Ownership: Voluntary Non-Profit - Private
Beds: 65

Key Personnel:
CEO/President. . . . . Dee McKrow
Cardiac Laboratory. . . . . Jeffrey Carney, MD
Operating Room. . . . . Francis Ozim, MD
Hemotology Center . . . . John Bartnik, MD

Measure	Cases	This Hosp.	State Avg.	U.S. Avg.
Heart Attack Care				
ACE Inhibitor or ARB for LVSD[3]	0	-	96%	96%
Aspirin at Arrival[3]	0	-	99%	99%
Aspirin at Discharge[3]	0	-	99%	98%
Beta Blocker at Discharge[3]	0	-	99%	98%
Fibrinolytic Medication Timing[3]	0	-	55%	55%
PCI Within 90 Minutes of Arrival[3]	0	-	89%	90%
Smoking Cessation Advice[3]	0	-	100%	99%
Chest Pain/Possible Heart Attack Care				
Aspirin at Arrival	36	92%	94%	95%
Median Time to ECG (minutes)	38	15	10	8
Median Time to Transfer (minutes)[1,3]	1	83	54	61
Fibrinolytic Medication Timing[1,3]	3	67%	60%	54%
Heart Failure Care				
ACE Inhibitor or ARB for LVSD[1]	3	0%	95%	94%
Discharge Instructions[1]	12	50%	89%	88%
Evaluation of LVS Function[1]	15	60%	99%	98%
Smoking Cessation Advice	0	-	99%	98%
Pneumonia Care				
Appropriate Initial Antibiotic[1]	18	83%	94%	92%
Blood Culture Timing[1]	15	80%	96%	96%
Influenza Vaccine[1]	9	67%	91%	91%
Initial Antibiotic Timing[1]	8	100%	96%	95%
Pneumococcal Vaccine[1]	16	38%	93%	93%
Smoking Cessation Advice[1]	3	67%	98%	97%
Surgical Care Improvement Project				
Appropriate VTP Within 24 Hours[1,3]	6	50%	94%	92%
Appropriate Hair Removal[1,3]	9	56%	99%	99%
Appropriate Beta Blocker Usage[5]	0	-	92%	93%
Controlled Postoperative Blood Glucose[3]	0	-	94%	93%
Prophylactic Antibiotic Timing[1,3]	2	100%	97%	97%
Prophylactic Antibiotic Timing (Outpatient)[1]	4	75%	87%	92%
Prophylactic Antibiotic Selection[1,3]	2	100%	98%	97%
Prophylactic Antibiotic Select. (Outpatient)[1]	3	100%	92%	94%
Prophylactic Antibiotic Stopped[1,3]	2	50%	95%	94%
Recommended VTP Ordered[1,3]	6	50%	95%	94%
Urinary Catheter Removal[1,3]	1	100%	91%	90%
Children's Asthma Care				
Received Systemic Corticosteroids	-	-	-	100%
Received Home Management Plan	-	-	-	71%
Received Reliever Medication	-	-	-	100%
Use of Medical Imaging				
Combination Abdominal CT Scan	160	0.325	0.135	0.191
Combination Chest CT Scan	84	0.536	0.068	0.054
Follow-up Mammogram/Ultrasound	158	10.1%	7.4%	8.4%
MRI for Low Back Pain[5]	0	-	32%	32.7%
Survey of Patients' Hospital Experiences				
Area Around Room 'Always' Quiet at Night	(a)	69%	-	58%
Doctors 'Always' Communicated Well	(a)	82%	-	80%
Home Recovery Information Given	(a)	79%	-	82%
Hospital Given 9 or 10 on 10 Point Scale	(a)	74%	-	67%
Meds 'Always' Explained Before Given	(a)	68%	-	60%
Nurses 'Always' Communicated Well	(a)	82%	-	76%
Pain 'Always' Well Controlled	(a)	66%	-	69%
Room and Bathroom 'Always' Clean	(a)	78%	-	71%
Timely Help 'Always' Received	(a)	86%	-	64%
Would Definitely Recommend Hospital	(a)	69%	-	69%

Charlevoix Area Hospital

14700 Lakeshore Drive
Charlevoix, MI 49720
Phone: 231-547-4024
Fax: 231-547-8080
Type: Critical Access Hospitals
Emergency Services: Yes
Ownership: Voluntary Non-Profit - Other
Beds: 50

Key Personnel:
CEO/President. . . . . William Jackson
Chief of Medical Staff . . . . Dennis M Joy, MD
Infection Control. . . . . Karen Withers
Operating Room. . . . . Chris Good, RN
Quality Assurance . . . . Chris Wilhelm
Radiology. . . . . Ralph J Duman
Emergency Room . . . . Dennis Joy
Intensive Care Unit. . . . . James Gels, MD

Measure	Cases	This Hosp.	State Avg.	U.S. Avg.
Heart Attack Care				
ACE Inhibitor or ARB for LVSD[3]	0	-	96%	96%
Aspirin at Arrival[3]	0	-	99%	99%
Aspirin at Discharge[1,3]	1	100%	99%	98%
Beta Blocker at Discharge[1,3]	1	100%	99%	98%
Fibrinolytic Medication Timing[3]	0	-	55%	55%
PCI Within 90 Minutes of Arrival[3]	0	-	89%	90%
Smoking Cessation Advice[3]	0	-	100%	99%
Chest Pain/Possible Heart Attack Care				
Aspirin at Arrival	-	-	94%	95%
Median Time to ECG (minutes)	-	-	10	8
Median Time to Transfer (minutes)	-	-	54	61
Fibrinolytic Medication Timing	-	-	60%	54%
Heart Failure Care				
ACE Inhibitor or ARB for LVSD[3]	0	-	95%	94%
Discharge Instructions[1,3]	1	100%	89%	88%
Evaluation of LVS Function[1,3]	1	100%	99%	98%
Smoking Cessation Advice[1,3]	1	100%	99%	98%
Pneumonia Care				
Appropriate Initial Antibiotic[1,3]	9	100%	94%	92%
Blood Culture Timing[1,3]	9	67%	96%	96%
Influenza Vaccine[5]	0	-	91%	91%
Initial Antibiotic Timing[1,3]	12	100%	96%	95%
Pneumococcal Vaccine[1,3]	9	44%	93%	93%
Smoking Cessation Advice[3]	0	-	98%	97%
Surgical Care Improvement Project				
Appropriate VTP Within 24 Hours[5]	0	-	94%	92%
Appropriate Hair Removal[5]	0	-	99%	99%
Appropriate Beta Blocker Usage[5]	0	-	92%	93%
Controlled Postoperative Blood Glucose[5]	0	-	94%	93%
Prophylactic Antibiotic Timing[5]	0	-	97%	97%
Prophylactic Antibiotic Timing (Outpatient)	-	-	87%	92%
Prophylactic Antibiotic Selection[5]	0	-	98%	97%
Prophylactic Antibiotic Select. (Outpatient)	-	-	92%	94%
Prophylactic Antibiotic Stopped[5]	0	-	95%	94%
Recommended VTP Ordered[5]	0	-	95%	94%
Urinary Catheter Removal[5]	0	-	91%	90%
Children's Asthma Care				
Received Systemic Corticosteroids	-	-	-	100%
Received Home Management Plan	-	-	-	71%
Received Reliever Medication	-	-	-	100%
Use of Medical Imaging				
Combination Abdominal CT Scan	-	-	0.135	0.191
Combination Chest CT Scan	-	-	0.068	0.054
Follow-up Mammogram/Ultrasound	-	-	7.4%	8.4%
MRI for Low Back Pain	-	-	32%	32.7%
Survey of Patients' Hospital Experiences				
Area Around Room 'Always' Quiet at Night[8]	-	-	-	58%
Doctors 'Always' Communicated Well[8]	-	-	-	80%
Home Recovery Information Given[8]	-	-	-	82%
Hospital Given 9 or 10 on 10 Point Scale[8]	-	-	-	67%
Meds 'Always' Explained Before Given[8]	-	-	-	60%
Nurses 'Always' Communicated Well[8]	-	-	-	76%
Pain 'Always' Well Controlled[8]	-	-	-	69%
Room and Bathroom 'Always' Clean[8]	-	-	-	71%
Timely Help 'Always' Received[8]	-	-	-	64%
Would Definitely Recommend Hospital[8]	-	-	-	69%

NOTE: Hospital profiles are in alphabetical order by state, then city, then hospital within the city; Rankings exclude hospitals with less than 25 cases except for patient surveys which excludes hospitals with less than 100 cases; (a) 100–299 cases; (1) The number of cases is too small to be sure how well a hospital is performing; (2) The hospital indicated that the data submitted for this measure were based on a sample of cases; (3) Data was collected during a shorter time period (fewer quarters) than the maximum possible time for this measure; (4) Suppressed for one or more quarters by CMS; (5) No data is available from the hospital for this measure; (6) Fewer than 100 patients completed the HCAHPS survey. Use these rates with caution, as the number of surveys may be too low to reliably assess hospital performance; (7) Survey results are based on less than 12 months of data; (8) Survey results are not available for this reporting period; (9) No or very few patients were eligible for the HCAHPS survey. The scores shown, if any, reflect a very small number of surveys; (10) A state average was not calculated because too few hospitals in the state submitted data; (11) There were discrepancies in the data collection process; Please refer to the User's Guide for a full explanation of data.

Hayes Green Beach Memorial Hospital

321 E Harris Street
Charlotte, MI 48813
Phone: 517-543-1050
Fax: 517-543-0875
E-mail: mrush@hgbhealth.com
URL: www.hgbhealth.com

Type: Critical Access Hospitals
Emergency Services: Yes
Ownership: Voluntary Non-Profit - Other
Beds: 45

Key Personnel:

CEO/President. . . . . Matthew W Rush, CHE
Chief of Medical Staff . . . . Debbie Hallak, DO
Radiology. . . . . Bing Tai
Anesthesiology. . . . . Douglas Wolford
Emergency Room . . . . Sherman Horn

Measure	Cases	This Hosp.	State Avg.	U.S. Avg.
Heart Attack Care				
ACE Inhibitor or ARB for LVSD	0	-	96%	96%
Aspirin at Arrival[1]	3	100%	99%	99%
Aspirin at Discharge[1]	2	100%	99%	98%
Beta Blocker at Discharge[1]	2	100%	99%	98%
Fibrinolytic Medication Timing	0	-	55%	55%
PCI Within 90 Minutes of Arrival	0	-	89%	90%
Smoking Cessation Advice	0	-	100%	99%
Chest Pain/Possible Heart Attack Care				
Aspirin at Arrival	-	-	94%	95%
Median Time to ECG (minutes)	-	-	10	8
Median Time to Transfer (minutes)	-	-	54	61
Fibrinolytic Medication Timing	-	-	60%	54%
Heart Failure Care				
ACE Inhibitor or ARB for LVSD[1]	8	100%	95%	94%
Discharge Instructions[1]	24	100%	89%	88%
Evaluation of LVS Function	27	100%	99%	98%
Smoking Cessation Advice[1]	4	100%	99%	98%
Pneumonia Care				
Appropriate Initial Antibiotic	42	100%	94%	92%
Blood Culture Timing	67	99%	96%	96%
Influenza Vaccine	32	97%	91%	91%
Initial Antibiotic Timing	59	100%	96%	95%
Pneumococcal Vaccine	50	98%	93%	93%
Smoking Cessation Advice[1]	23	100%	98%	97%
Surgical Care Improvement Project				
Appropriate VTP Within 24 Hours[1]	20	95%	94%	92%
Appropriate Hair Removal	46	100%	99%	99%
Appropriate Beta Blocker Usage[1,3]	2	100%	92%	93%
Controlled Postoperative Blood Glucose	0	-	94%	93%
Prophylactic Antibiotic Timing	31	94%	97%	97%
Prophylactic Antibiotic Timing (Outpatient)	-	-	87%	92%
Prophylactic Antibiotic Selection	30	87%	98%	97%
Prophylactic Antibiotic Select. (Outpatient)	-	-	92%	94%
Prophylactic Antibiotic Stopped	30	97%	95%	94%
Recommended VTP Ordered[1]	20	95%	95%	94%
Urinary Catheter Removal[1]	5	60%	91%	90%
Children's Asthma Care				
Received Systemic Corticosteroids	-	-	-	100%
Received Home Management Plan	-	-	-	71%
Received Reliever Medication	-	-	-	100%
Use of Medical Imaging				
Combination Abdominal CT Scan	-	-	0.135	0.191
Combination Chest CT Scan	-	-	0.068	0.054
Follow-up Mammogram/Ultrasound	-	-	7.4%	8.4%
MRI for Low Back Pain	-	-	32%	32.7%
Survey of Patients' Hospital Experiences				
Area Around Room 'Always' Quiet at Night	(a)	59%	-	58%
Doctors 'Always' Communicated Well	(a)	77%	-	80%
Home Recovery Information Given	(a)	85%	-	82%
Hospital Given 9 or 10 on 10 Point Scale	(a)	72%	-	67%
Meds 'Always' Explained Before Given	(a)	54%	-	60%
Nurses 'Always' Communicated Well	(a)	78%	-	76%
Pain 'Always' Well Controlled	(a)	73%	-	69%
Room and Bathroom 'Always' Clean	(a)	80%	-	71%
Timely Help 'Always' Received	(a)	67%	-	64%
Would Definitely Recommend Hospital	(a)	72%	-	69%

Cheboygan Memorial Hospital

748 S Main
Cheboygan, MI 49721
Phone: 231-627-5601
Fax: 231-627-1471
URL: www.cheboyganhospital.org

Type: Acute Care Hospitals
Emergency Services: Yes
Ownership: Voluntary Non-Profit - Private
Beds: 92

Key Personnel:

CEO/President. . . . . Barbara J Cliff
Chief of Medical Staff . . . . Donald Watson
Radiology. . . . . Linda Ciarkowski

Measure	Cases	This Hosp.	State Avg.	U.S. Avg.
Heart Attack Care				
ACE Inhibitor or ARB for LVSD	-	-	96%	96%
Aspirin at Arrival	-	-	99%	99%
Aspirin at Discharge	-	-	99%	98%
Beta Blocker at Discharge	-	-	99%	98%
Fibrinolytic Medication Timing	-	-	55%	55%
PCI Within 90 Minutes of Arrival	-	-	89%	90%
Smoking Cessation Advice	-	-	100%	99%
Chest Pain/Possible Heart Attack Care				
Aspirin at Arrival	-	-	94%	95%
Median Time to ECG (minutes)	-	-	10	8
Median Time to Transfer (minutes)	-	-	54	61
Fibrinolytic Medication Timing	-	-	60%	54%
Heart Failure Care				
ACE Inhibitor or ARB for LVSD	-	-	95%	94%
Discharge Instructions	-	-	89%	88%
Evaluation of LVS Function	-	-	99%	98%
Smoking Cessation Advice	-	-	99%	98%
Pneumonia Care				
Appropriate Initial Antibiotic	-	-	94%	92%
Blood Culture Timing	-	-	96%	96%
Influenza Vaccine	-	-	91%	91%
Initial Antibiotic Timing	-	-	96%	95%
Pneumococcal Vaccine	-	-	93%	93%
Smoking Cessation Advice	-	-	98%	97%
Surgical Care Improvement Project				
Appropriate VTP Within 24 Hours	-	-	94%	92%
Appropriate Hair Removal	-	-	99%	99%
Appropriate Beta Blocker Usage	-	-	92%	93%
Controlled Postoperative Blood Glucose	-	-	94%	93%
Prophylactic Antibiotic Timing	-	-	97%	97%
Prophylactic Antibiotic Timing (Outpatient)	-	-	87%	92%
Prophylactic Antibiotic Selection	-	-	98%	97%
Prophylactic Antibiotic Select. (Outpatient)	-	-	92%	94%
Prophylactic Antibiotic Stopped	-	-	95%	94%
Recommended VTP Ordered	-	-	95%	94%
Urinary Catheter Removal	-	-	91%	90%
Children's Asthma Care				
Received Systemic Corticosteroids	-	-	-	100%
Received Home Management Plan	-	-	-	71%
Received Reliever Medication	-	-	-	100%
Use of Medical Imaging				
Combination Abdominal CT Scan	-	-	0.135	0.191
Combination Chest CT Scan	-	-	0.068	0.054
Follow-up Mammogram/Ultrasound	-	-	7.4%	8.4%
MRI for Low Back Pain	-	-	32%	32.7%
Survey of Patients' Hospital Experiences				
Area Around Room 'Always' Quiet at Night	-	-	-	58%
Doctors 'Always' Communicated Well	-	-	-	80%
Home Recovery Information Given	-	-	-	82%
Hospital Given 9 or 10 on 10 Point Scale	-	-	-	67%
Meds 'Always' Explained Before Given	-	-	-	60%
Nurses 'Always' Communicated Well	-	-	-	76%
Pain 'Always' Well Controlled	-	-	-	69%
Room and Bathroom 'Always' Clean	-	-	-	71%
Timely Help 'Always' Received	-	-	-	64%
Would Definitely Recommend Hospital	-	-	-	69%

Chelsea Community Hospital

775 S Main St
Chelsea, MI 48118
Phone: 734-475-3911
Fax: 734-475-4066
URL: www.cch.org

Type: Acute Care Hospitals
Emergency Services: Yes
Ownership: Voluntary Non-Profit - Private
Beds: 113

Key Personnel:

CEO/President. . . . . Kathleen Griffiths
Chief of Medical Staff . . . . Lawrence Handelsman
Emergency Room . . . . Nancy Fields

Measure	Cases	This Hosp.	State Avg.	U.S. Avg.
Heart Attack Care				
ACE Inhibitor or ARB for LVSD[1]	3	100%	96%	96%
Aspirin at Arrival[1]	8	100%	99%	99%
Aspirin at Discharge[1]	7	100%	99%	98%
Beta Blocker at Discharge[1]	7	100%	99%	98%
Fibrinolytic Medication Timing	0	-	55%	55%
PCI Within 90 Minutes of Arrival	0	-	89%	90%
Smoking Cessation Advice	0	-	100%	99%
Chest Pain/Possible Heart Attack Care				
Aspirin at Arrival	89	98%	94%	95%
Median Time to ECG (minutes)	95	9	10	8
Median Time to Transfer (minutes)[1]	12	52	54	61
Fibrinolytic Medication Timing	0	-	60%	54%
Heart Failure Care				
ACE Inhibitor or ARB for LVSD[1]	13	92%	95%	94%
Discharge Instructions	49	96%	89%	88%
Evaluation of LVS Function	63	100%	99%	98%
Smoking Cessation Advice[1]	8	100%	99%	98%
Pneumonia Care				
Appropriate Initial Antibiotic	72	92%	94%	92%
Blood Culture Timing	99	97%	96%	96%
Influenza Vaccine	59	100%	91%	91%
Initial Antibiotic Timing	83	96%	96%	95%
Pneumococcal Vaccine	82	100%	93%	93%
Smoking Cessation Advice	30	97%	98%	97%
Surgical Care Improvement Project				
Appropriate VTP Within 24 Hours[2]	281	100%	94%	92%
Appropriate Hair Removal[2]	887	100%	99%	99%
Appropriate Beta Blocker Usage[2]	197	100%	92%	93%
Controlled Postoperative Blood Glucose[2]	0	-	94%	93%
Prophylactic Antibiotic Timing[2]	741	100%	97%	97%
Prophylactic Antibiotic Timing (Outpatient)	136	99%	87%	92%
Prophylactic Antibiotic Selection[2]	743	100%	98%	97%
Prophylactic Antibiotic Select. (Outpatient)	151	99%	92%	94%
Prophylactic Antibiotic Stopped[2]	732	99%	95%	94%
Recommended VTP Ordered[2]	281	100%	95%	94%
Urinary Catheter Removal[2]	246	96%	91%	90%
Children's Asthma Care				
Received Systemic Corticosteroids	-	-	-	100%
Received Home Management Plan	-	-	-	71%
Received Reliever Medication	-	-	-	100%
Use of Medical Imaging				
Combination Abdominal CT Scan	356	0.098	0.135	0.191
Combination Chest CT Scan	200	0.040	0.068	0.054
Follow-up Mammogram/Ultrasound	847	10.9%	7.4%	8.4%
MRI for Low Back Pain	161	24.8%	32%	32.7%
Survey of Patients' Hospital Experiences				
Area Around Room 'Always' Quiet at Night	300+	66%	-	58%
Doctors 'Always' Communicated Well	300+	83%	-	80%
Home Recovery Information Given	300+	88%	-	82%
Hospital Given 9 or 10 on 10 Point Scale	300+	82%	-	67%
Meds 'Always' Explained Before Given	300+	69%	-	60%
Nurses 'Always' Communicated Well	300+	83%	-	76%
Pain 'Always' Well Controlled	300+	72%	-	69%
Room and Bathroom 'Always' Clean	300+	79%	-	71%
Timely Help 'Always' Received	300+	74%	-	64%
Would Definitely Recommend Hospital	300+	85%	-	69%

NOTE: Hospital profiles are in alphabetical order by state, then city, then hospital within the city; Rankings exclude hospitals with less than 25 cases except for patient surveys which excludes hospitals with less than 100 cases; (a) 100–299 cases; (1) The number of cases is too small to be sure how well a hospital is performing; (2) The hospital indicated that the data submitted for this measure were based on a sample of cases; (3) Data was collected during a shorter time period (fewer quarters) than the maximum possible time for this measure; (4) Suppressed for one or more quarters by CMS; (5) No data is available from the hospital for this measure; (6) Fewer than 100 patients completed the HCAHPS survey. Use these rates with caution, as the number of surveys may be too low to reliably assess hospital performance; (7) Survey results are based on less than 12 months of data; (8) Survey results are not available for this reporting period; (9) No or very few patients were eligible for the HCAHPS survey. The scores shown, if any, reflect a very small number of surveys; (10) A state average was not calculated because too few hospitals in the state submitted data; (11) There were discrepancies in the data collection process; Please refer to the User's Guide for a full explanation of data.

Midmichigan Medical Center-Clare

703 N Mcewan St Phone: 989-802-5000
Clare, MI 48617 Fax: 989-802-8895
URL: www.midmichigan.org
Type: Acute Care Hospitals Emergency Services: Yes
Ownership: Voluntary Non-Profit - Other Beds: 64

Key Personnel:
Chief of Medical Staff.......... Rajani Mallick
Coronary Care............... Robert Briggs, RN
Infection Control............... Bea Van Buskirk, RN
Operating Room.............. Mary Eppert, RN
Pediatric In-Patient Care .... Bette Shepard, MD
Quality Assurance .... Penny Parsons
Emergency Room .... Gregory Endres-Bercher, MD

Measure	Cases	This Hosp.	State Avg.	U.S. Avg.
Heart Attack Care				
ACE Inhibitor or ARB for LVSD[1]	1	100%	96%	96%
Aspirin at Arrival[1]	15	100%	99%	99%
Aspirin at Discharge[1]	13	77%	99%	98%
Beta Blocker at Discharge[1]	14	93%	99%	98%
Fibrinolytic Medication Timing	0	-	55%	55%
PCI Within 90 Minutes of Arrival	0	-	89%	90%
Smoking Cessation Advice[1]	2	100%	100%	99%
Chest Pain/Possible Heart Attack Care				
Aspirin at Arrival	100	95%	94%	95%
Median Time to ECG (minutes)	104	15	10	8
Median Time to Transfer (minutes)[1,3]	2	120	54	61
Fibrinolytic Medication Timing[1]	13	54%	60%	54%
Heart Failure Care				
ACE Inhibitor or ARB for LVSD	41	80%	95%	94%
Discharge Instructions	131	76%	89%	88%
Evaluation of LVS Function	151	96%	99%	98%
Smoking Cessation Advice	36	97%	99%	98%
Pneumonia Care				
Appropriate Initial Antibiotic	76	89%	94%	92%
Blood Culture Timing	59	93%	96%	96%
Influenza Vaccine	55	93%	91%	91%
Initial Antibiotic Timing	109	94%	96%	95%
Pneumococcal Vaccine	77	96%	93%	93%
Smoking Cessation Advice	45	98%	98%	97%
Surgical Care Improvement Project				
Appropriate VTP Within 24 Hours	54	83%	94%	92%
Appropriate Hair Removal	109	100%	99%	99%
Appropriate Beta Blocker Usage	36	94%	92%	93%
Controlled Postoperative Blood Glucose	0	-	94%	93%
Prophylactic Antibiotic Timing	60	92%	97%	97%
Prophylactic Antibiotic Timing (Outpatient)[1,3]	15	93%	87%	92%
Prophylactic Antibiotic Selection	60	87%	98%	97%
Prophylactic Antibiotic Select. (Outpatient)[1,3]	18	89%	92%	94%
Prophylactic Antibiotic Stopped	56	95%	95%	94%
Recommended VTP Ordered	54	85%	95%	94%
Urinary Catheter Removal	26	92%	91%	90%
Children's Asthma Care				
Received Systemic Corticosteroids	-	-	-	100%
Received Home Management Plan	-	-	-	71%
Received Reliever Medication	-	-	-	100%
Use of Medical Imaging				
Combination Abdominal CT Scan	362	0.072	0.135	0.191
Combination Chest CT Scan	249	0.145	0.068	0.054
Follow-up Mammogram/Ultrasound	794	7.7%	7.4%	8.4%
MRI for Low Back Pain	128	37.5%	32%	32.7%
Survey of Patients' Hospital Experiences				
Area Around Room 'Always' Quiet at Night	300+	63%	-	58%
Doctors 'Always' Communicated Well	300+	82%	-	80%
Home Recovery Information Given	300+	86%	-	82%
Hospital Given 9 or 10 on 10 Point Scale	300+	66%	-	67%
Meds 'Always' Explained Before Given	300+	59%	-	60%
Nurses 'Always' Communicated Well	300+	75%	-	76%
Pain 'Always' Well Controlled	300+	75%	-	69%
Room and Bathroom 'Always' Clean	300+	72%	-	71%
Timely Help 'Always' Received	300+	71%	-	64%
Would Definitely Recommend Hospital	300+	60%	-	69%

Henry Ford Macomb Hospital

15855 Nineteen Mile Rd Phone: 586-263-2300
Clinton Township, MI 48038 Fax: 586-263-2859
URL: www.stjoe-macomb.com
Type: Acute Care Hospitals Emergency Services: Yes
Ownership: Proprietary Beds: 435

Key Personnel:
CEO/President............... Joseph R Swedish
Chief of Medical Staff.......... Richard Stone, MD
Infection Control.............. Sharon Ritter
Operating Room.............. Susan Assaf
Pediatric In-Patient Care .... Allen Balinski, MD
Quality Assurance .... Jane Goldfarb
Radiology.................... Donna Moir

Measure	Cases	This Hosp.	State Avg.	U.S. Avg.
Heart Attack Care				
ACE Inhibitor or ARB for LVSD	85	100%	96%	96%
Aspirin at Arrival	476	100%	99%	99%
Aspirin at Discharge	451	100%	99%	98%
Beta Blocker at Discharge	450	100%	99%	98%
Fibrinolytic Medication Timing	0	-	55%	55%
PCI Within 90 Minutes of Arrival	77	100%	89%	90%
Smoking Cessation Advice	137	100%	100%	99%
Chest Pain/Possible Heart Attack Care				
Aspirin at Arrival	51	98%	94%	95%
Median Time to ECG (minutes)	57	16	10	8
Median Time to Transfer (minutes)[3]	0	-	54	61
Fibrinolytic Medication Timing[3]	0	-	60%	54%
Heart Failure Care				
ACE Inhibitor or ARB for LVSD[2]	78	100%	95%	94%
Discharge Instructions[2]	271	94%	89%	88%
Evaluation of LVS Function[2]	338	100%	99%	98%
Smoking Cessation Advice[2]	37	100%	99%	98%
Pneumonia Care				
Appropriate Initial Antibiotic	315	95%	94%	92%
Blood Culture Timing	476	97%	96%	96%
Influenza Vaccine	293	91%	91%	91%
Initial Antibiotic Timing	497	95%	96%	95%
Pneumococcal Vaccine	472	94%	93%	93%
Smoking Cessation Advice	160	100%	98%	97%
Surgical Care Improvement Project				
Appropriate VTP Within 24 Hours[2]	379	98%	94%	92%
Appropriate Hair Removal[2]	1,559	100%	99%	99%
Appropriate Beta Blocker Usage[2]	534	95%	92%	93%
Controlled Postoperative Blood Glucose[2]	168	96%	94%	93%
Prophylactic Antibiotic Timing[2]	1,264	98%	97%	97%
Prophylactic Antibiotic Timing (Outpatient)	352	94%	87%	92%
Prophylactic Antibiotic Selection[2]	1,271	99%	98%	97%
Prophylactic Antibiotic Select. (Outpatient)	344	95%	92%	94%
Prophylactic Antibiotic Stopped[2]	1,216	97%	95%	94%
Recommended VTP Ordered[2]	379	99%	95%	94%
Urinary Catheter Removal[2]	461	97%	91%	90%
Children's Asthma Care				
Received Systemic Corticosteroids	-	-	-	100%
Received Home Management Plan	-	-	-	71%
Received Reliever Medication	-	-	-	100%
Use of Medical Imaging				
Combination Abdominal CT Scan	1,019	0.210	0.135	0.191
Combination Chest CT Scan	745	0.174	0.068	0.054
Follow-up Mammogram/Ultrasound	1,851	9.9%	7.4%	8.4%
MRI for Low Back Pain	161	26.1%	32%	32.7%
Survey of Patients' Hospital Experiences				
Area Around Room 'Always' Quiet at Night	300+	48%	-	58%
Doctors 'Always' Communicated Well	300+	77%	-	80%
Home Recovery Information Given	300+	82%	-	82%
Hospital Given 9 or 10 on 10 Point Scale	300+	62%	-	67%
Meds 'Always' Explained Before Given	300+	58%	-	60%
Nurses 'Always' Communicated Well	300+	76%	-	76%
Pain 'Always' Well Controlled	300+	68%	-	69%
Room and Bathroom 'Always' Clean	300+	70%	-	71%
Timely Help 'Always' Received	300+	62%	-	64%
Would Definitely Recommend Hospital	300+	66%	-	69%

Community Health Center of Branch County

274 E Chicago St Phone: 517-279-5400
Coldwater, MI 49036 Fax: 517-279-5499
URL: www.chcbc.com
Type: Acute Care Hospitals Emergency Services: Yes
Ownership: Government - Local Beds: 96

Key Personnel:
CEO/President................ Randy DeGroot
Chief of Medical Staff.......... John Sennish
Coronary Care............... Jane Obrochta
Infection Control.............. Connie Meyer
Pediatric Ambulatory Care ...... Edelwina Dy, MD
Pediatric In-Patient Care .... Connie Meyer, MD
Quality Assurance .... Connie Mayers
Radiology................... John Kirkpatrick, MD

Measure	Cases	This Hosp.	State Avg.	U.S. Avg.
Heart Attack Care				
ACE Inhibitor or ARB for LVSD	0	-	96%	96%
Aspirin at Arrival[1]	9	100%	99%	99%
Aspirin at Discharge[1]	6	100%	99%	98%
Beta Blocker at Discharge[1]	7	100%	99%	98%
Fibrinolytic Medication Timing	0	-	55%	55%
PCI Within 90 Minutes of Arrival	0	-	89%	90%
Smoking Cessation Advice[1]	1	100%	100%	99%
Chest Pain/Possible Heart Attack Care				
Aspirin at Arrival	234	95%	94%	95%
Median Time to ECG (minutes)	243	10	10	8
Median Time to Transfer (minutes)[1]	13	65	54	61
Fibrinolytic Medication Timing[1]	2	0%	60%	54%
Heart Failure Care				
ACE Inhibitor or ARB for LVSD[1]	16	100%	95%	94%
Discharge Instructions	82	100%	89%	88%
Evaluation of LVS Function	98	100%	99%	98%
Smoking Cessation Advice[1]	17	100%	99%	98%
Pneumonia Care				
Appropriate Initial Antibiotic	105	93%	94%	92%
Blood Culture Timing	121	98%	96%	96%
Influenza Vaccine	67	94%	91%	91%
Initial Antibiotic Timing	128	96%	96%	95%
Pneumococcal Vaccine	93	98%	93%	93%
Smoking Cessation Advice	50	100%	98%	97%
Surgical Care Improvement Project				
Appropriate VTP Within 24 Hours	117	85%	94%	92%
Appropriate Hair Removal	275	100%	99%	99%
Appropriate Beta Blocker Usage	76	99%	92%	93%
Controlled Postoperative Blood Glucose	0	-	94%	93%
Prophylactic Antibiotic Timing	165	98%	97%	97%
Prophylactic Antibiotic Timing (Outpatient)	82	80%	87%	92%
Prophylactic Antibiotic Selection	164	95%	98%	97%
Prophylactic Antibiotic Select. (Outpatient)	71	96%	92%	94%
Prophylactic Antibiotic Stopped	159	90%	95%	94%
Recommended VTP Ordered	117	86%	95%	94%
Urinary Catheter Removal	77	73%	91%	90%
Children's Asthma Care				
Received Systemic Corticosteroids	-	-	-	100%
Received Home Management Plan	-	-	-	71%
Received Reliever Medication	-	-	-	100%
Use of Medical Imaging				
Combination Abdominal CT Scan	351	0.251	0.135	0.191
Combination Chest CT Scan	261	0.176	0.068	0.054
Follow-up Mammogram/Ultrasound	622	5.6%	7.4%	8.4%
MRI for Low Back Pain	85	28.2%	32%	32.7%
Survey of Patients' Hospital Experiences				
Area Around Room 'Always' Quiet at Night	300+	51%	-	58%
Doctors 'Always' Communicated Well	300+	76%	-	80%
Home Recovery Information Given	300+	86%	-	82%
Hospital Given 9 or 10 on 10 Point Scale	300+	67%	-	67%
Meds 'Always' Explained Before Given	300+	64%	-	60%
Nurses 'Always' Communicated Well	300+	77%	-	76%
Pain 'Always' Well Controlled	300+	66%	-	69%
Room and Bathroom 'Always' Clean	300+	67%	-	71%
Timely Help 'Always' Received	300+	61%	-	64%
Would Definitely Recommend Hospital	300+	61%	-	69%

NOTE: Hospital profiles are in alphabetical order by state, then city, then hospital within the city; Rankings exclude hospitals with less than 25 cases except for patient surveys which excludes hospitals with less than 100 cases; (a) 100–299 cases; (1) The number of cases is too small to be sure how well a hospital is performing; (2) The hospital indicated that the data submitted for this measure were based on a sample of cases; (3) Data was collected during a shorter time period (fewer quarters) than the maximum possible time for this measure; (4) Suppressed for one or more quarters by CMS; (5) No data is available from the hospital for this measure; (6) Fewer than 100 patients completed the HCAHPS survey. Use these rates with caution, as the number of surveys may be too low to reliably assess hospital performance; (7) Survey results are based on less than 12 months of data; (8) Survey results are not available for this reporting period; (9) No or very few patients were eligible for the HCAHPS survey. The scores shown, if any, reflect a very small number of surveys; (10) A state average was not calculated because too few hospitals in the state submitted data; (11) There were discrepancies in the data collection process; Please refer to the User's Guide for a full explanation of data.

Huron Valley-Sinai Hospital

One William Carls Drive
Commerce Township, MI 48382
URL: www.hvsh.org
Type: Acute Care Hospitals
Ownership: Voluntary Non-Profit - Other
Phone: 248-937-3370
Fax: 248-937-5074
Emergency Services: Yes
Beds: 153

Key Personnel:
CEO/President. . . . . Robert J Yellan
Chief of Medical Staff . . . . Marc P Bocknek
Radiology. . . . . John Kelly, DO

Measure	Cases	This Hosp.	State Avg.	U.S. Avg.
Heart Attack Care				
ACE Inhibitor or ARB for LVSD	29	86%	96%	96%
Aspirin at Arrival	157	99%	99%	99%
Aspirin at Discharge	111	95%	99%	98%
Beta Blocker at Discharge	113	94%	99%	98%
Fibrinolytic Medication Timing	0	-	55%	55%
PCI Within 90 Minutes of Arrival	45	98%	89%	90%
Smoking Cessation Advice	34	100%	100%	99%
Chest Pain/Possible Heart Attack Care				
Aspirin at Arrival	36	94%	94%	95%
Median Time to ECG (minutes)	37	6	10	8
Median Time to Transfer (minutes)[5]	0		54	61
Fibrinolytic Medication Timing[3]	0	-	60%	54%
Heart Failure Care				
ACE Inhibitor or ARB for LVSD	100	93%	95%	94%
Discharge Instructions	276	86%	89%	88%
Evaluation of LVS Function	350	98%	99%	98%
Smoking Cessation Advice	57	100%	99%	98%
Pneumonia Care				
Appropriate Initial Antibiotic	117	97%	94%	92%
Blood Culture Timing	212	96%	96%	96%
Influenza Vaccine	124	89%	91%	91%
Initial Antibiotic Timing	192	99%	96%	95%
Pneumococcal Vaccine	156	97%	93%	93%
Smoking Cessation Advice	69	97%	98%	97%
Surgical Care Improvement Project				
Appropriate VTP Within 24 Hours[2]	179	93%	94%	92%
Appropriate Hair Removal[2]	657	100%	99%	99%
Appropriate Beta Blocker Usage[2]	161	94%	92%	93%
Controlled Postoperative Blood Glucose[2]	0	-	94%	93%
Prophylactic Antibiotic Timing[2]	489	98%	97%	97%
Prophylactic Antibiotic Timing (Outpatient)	196	74%	87%	92%
Prophylactic Antibiotic Selection[2]	502	99%	98%	97%
Prophylactic Antibiotic Select. (Outpatient)	158	94%	92%	94%
Prophylactic Antibiotic Stopped[2]	486	96%	95%	94%
Recommended VTP Ordered[2]	179	93%	95%	94%
Urinary Catheter Removal[2]	185	91%	91%	90%
Children's Asthma Care				
Received Systemic Corticosteroids	-	-	-	100%
Received Home Management Plan	-	-	-	71%
Received Reliever Medication	-	-	-	100%
Use of Medical Imaging				
Combination Abdominal CT Scan	547	0.099	0.135	0.191
Combination Chest CT Scan	582	0.002	0.068	0.054
Follow-up Mammogram/Ultrasound	815	6.4%	7.4%	8.4%
MRI for Low Back Pain	174	26.4%	32%	32.7%
Survey of Patients' Hospital Experiences				
Area Around Room 'Always' Quiet at Night	300+	53%	-	58%
Doctors 'Always' Communicated Well	300+	79%	-	80%
Home Recovery Information Given	300+	80%	-	82%
Hospital Given 9 or 10 on 10 Point Scale	300+	68%	-	67%
Meds 'Always' Explained Before Given	300+	61%	-	60%
Nurses 'Always' Communicated Well	300+	77%	-	76%
Pain 'Always' Well Controlled	300+	67%	-	69%
Room and Bathroom 'Always' Clean	300+	66%	-	71%
Timely Help 'Always' Received	300+	65%	-	64%
Would Definitely Recommend Hospital	300+	71%	-	69%

Oakwood Hospital and Medical Center

18101 Oakwood Blvd
Dearborn, MI 48124
E-mail: GUESTREL@oakwood.org
URL: www.oakwood.org
Type: Acute Care Hospitals
Ownership: Proprietary
Phone: 313-593-7125
Fax: 313-436-2038
Emergency Services: Yes
Beds: 632

Key Personnel:
CEO/President. . . . . Jerry Fitzgerald

Measure	Cases	This Hosp.	State Avg.	U.S. Avg.
Heart Attack Care				
ACE Inhibitor or ARB for LVSD	240	99%	96%	96%
Aspirin at Arrival	581	100%	99%	99%
Aspirin at Discharge	939	100%	99%	98%
Beta Blocker at Discharge	965	99%	99%	98%
Fibrinolytic Medication Timing	0	-	55%	55%
PCI Within 90 Minutes of Arrival	84	89%	89%	90%
Smoking Cessation Advice	338	100%	100%	99%
Chest Pain/Possible Heart Attack Care				
Aspirin at Arrival	90	84%	94%	95%
Median Time to ECG (minutes)	94	4	10	8
Median Time to Transfer (minutes)[1,3]	2	56	54	61
Fibrinolytic Medication Timing	0	-	60%	54%
Heart Failure Care				
ACE Inhibitor or ARB for LVSD	475	98%	95%	94%
Discharge Instructions	1,053	92%	89%	88%
Evaluation of LVS Function	1,263	100%	99%	98%
Smoking Cessation Advice	292	100%	99%	98%
Pneumonia Care				
Appropriate Initial Antibiotic[2]	370	96%	94%	92%
Blood Culture Timing[2]	285	96%	96%	96%
Influenza Vaccine	347	82%	91%	91%
Initial Antibiotic Timing[2]	572	94%	96%	95%
Pneumococcal Vaccine[2]	475	89%	93%	93%
Smoking Cessation Advice[2]	224	100%	98%	97%
Surgical Care Improvement Project				
Appropriate VTP Within 24 Hours[2]	516	98%	94%	92%
Appropriate Hair Removal[2]	1,665	100%	99%	99%
Appropriate Beta Blocker Usage[2]	657	93%	92%	93%
Controlled Postoperative Blood Glucose[2]	387	93%	94%	93%
Prophylactic Antibiotic Timing[2]	1,267	98%	97%	97%
Prophylactic Antibiotic Timing (Outpatient)	320	96%	87%	92%
Prophylactic Antibiotic Selection[2]	1,281	99%	98%	97%
Prophylactic Antibiotic Select. (Outpatient)	344	96%	92%	94%
Prophylactic Antibiotic Stopped[2]	1,197	94%	95%	94%
Recommended VTP Ordered[2]	518	99%	95%	94%
Urinary Catheter Removal[2]	266	77%	91%	90%
Children's Asthma Care				
Received Systemic Corticosteroids	-	-	-	100%
Received Home Management Plan	-	-	-	71%
Received Reliever Medication	-	-	-	100%
Use of Medical Imaging				
Combination Abdominal CT Scan	1,724	0.063	0.135	0.191
Combination Chest CT Scan	1,438	0.036	0.068	0.054
Follow-up Mammogram/Ultrasound	2,597	5.8%	7.4%	8.4%
MRI for Low Back Pain	202	24.8%	32%	32.7%
Survey of Patients' Hospital Experiences				
Area Around Room 'Always' Quiet at Night	300+	48%	-	58%
Doctors 'Always' Communicated Well	300+	79%	-	80%
Home Recovery Information Given	300+	77%	-	82%
Hospital Given 9 or 10 on 10 Point Scale	300+	66%	-	67%
Meds 'Always' Explained Before Given	300+	61%	-	60%
Nurses 'Always' Communicated Well	300+	80%	-	76%
Pain 'Always' Well Controlled	300+	71%	-	69%
Room and Bathroom 'Always' Clean	300+	67%	-	71%
Timely Help 'Always' Received	300+	64%	-	64%
Would Definitely Recommend Hospital	300+	68%	-	69%

Deckerville Community Hospital

3559 Pine St
Deckerville, MI 48427
URL: www.deckervillehosp.org
Type: Critical Access Hospitals
Ownership: Voluntary Non-Profit - Other
Phone: 810-376-2835
Emergency Services: Yes

Key Personnel:
CEO . . . . Edward Gamache
Cardiology . . . . Suresh Tumma
Radiology. . . . . App Arao Mukkamala
Emergency . . . . Angie M Connachie

Measure	Cases	This Hosp.	State Avg.	U.S. Avg.
Heart Attack Care				
ACE Inhibitor or ARB for LVSD[5]	0	-	96%	96%
Aspirin at Arrival[5]	0	-	99%	99%
Aspirin at Discharge[5]	0	-	99%	98%
Beta Blocker at Discharge[5]	0	-	99%	98%
Fibrinolytic Medication Timing[5]	0	-	55%	55%
PCI Within 90 Minutes of Arrival[5]	0	-	89%	90%
Smoking Cessation Advice[5]	0	-	100%	99%
Chest Pain/Possible Heart Attack Care				
Aspirin at Arrival[5]	0	-	94%	95%
Median Time to ECG (minutes)[5]	0	-	10	8
Median Time to Transfer (minutes)[5]	0	-	54	61
Fibrinolytic Medication Timing[5]	0	-	60%	54%
Heart Failure Care				
ACE Inhibitor or ARB for LVSD[5]	0	-	95%	94%
Discharge Instructions[5]	0	-	89%	88%
Evaluation of LVS Function[5]	0	-	99%	98%
Smoking Cessation Advice[5]	0	-	99%	98%
Pneumonia Care				
Appropriate Initial Antibiotic[1]	8	100%	94%	92%
Blood Culture Timing[1]	6	100%	96%	96%
Influenza Vaccine[1]	5	60%	91%	91%
Initial Antibiotic Timing[1]	11	91%	96%	95%
Pneumococcal Vaccine[1]	8	75%	93%	93%
Smoking Cessation Advice[1]	2	0%	98%	97%
Surgical Care Improvement Project				
Appropriate VTP Within 24 Hours[5]	0	-	94%	92%
Appropriate Hair Removal[5]	0	-	99%	99%
Appropriate Beta Blocker Usage[5]	0	-	92%	93%
Controlled Postoperative Blood Glucose[5]	0	-	94%	93%
Prophylactic Antibiotic Timing[5]	0	-	97%	97%
Prophylactic Antibiotic Timing (Outpatient)[5]	0	-	87%	92%
Prophylactic Antibiotic Selection[5]	0	-	98%	97%
Prophylactic Antibiotic Select. (Outpatient)[5]	0	-	92%	94%
Prophylactic Antibiotic Stopped[5]	0	-	95%	94%
Recommended VTP Ordered[5]	0	-	95%	94%
Urinary Catheter Removal[5]	0	-	91%	90%
Children's Asthma Care				
Received Systemic Corticosteroids	-	-	-	100%
Received Home Management Plan	-	-	-	71%
Received Reliever Medication	-	-	-	100%
Use of Medical Imaging				
Combination Abdominal CT Scan[1]	32	0.031	0.135	0.191
Combination Chest CT Scan[1]	22	0.000	0.068	0.054
Follow-up Mammogram/Ultrasound	117	15.4%	7.4%	8.4%
MRI for Low Back Pain[5]	0	-	32%	32.7%
Survey of Patients' Hospital Experiences				
Area Around Room 'Always' Quiet at Night[6]	<100	61%	-	58%
Doctors 'Always' Communicated Well[6]	<100	79%	-	80%
Home Recovery Information Given[6]	<100	81%	-	82%
Hospital Given 9 or 10 on 10 Point Scale[6]	<100	68%	-	67%
Meds 'Always' Explained Before Given[6]	<100	65%	-	60%
Nurses 'Always' Communicated Well[6]	<100	83%	-	76%
Pain 'Always' Well Controlled[6]	<100	62%	-	69%
Room and Bathroom 'Always' Clean[6]	<100	71%	-	71%
Timely Help 'Always' Received[6]	<100	69%	-	64%
Would Definitely Recommend Hospital	<100	60%	-	69%

NOTE: Hospital profiles are in alphabetical order by state, then city, then hospital within the city; Rankings exclude hospitals with less than 25 cases except for patient surveys which excludes hospitals with less than 100 cases; (a) 100–299 cases; (1) The number of cases is too small to be sure how well a hospital is performing; (2) The hospital indicated that the data submitted for this measure were based on a sample of cases; (3) Data was collected during a shorter time period (fewer quarters) than the maximum possible time for this measure; (4) Suppressed for one or more quarters by CMS; (5) No data is available from the hospital for this measure; (6) Fewer than 100 patients completed the HCAHPS survey. Use these rates with caution, as the number of surveys may be too low to reliably assess hospital performance; (7) Survey results are based on less than 12 months of data; (8) Survey results are not available for this reporting period; (9) No or very few patients were eligible for the HCAHPS survey. The scores shown, if any, reflect a very small number of surveys; (10) A state average was not calculated because too few hospitals in the state submitted data; (11) There were discrepancies in the data collection process; Please refer to the User's Guide for a full explanation of data.

Children's Hospital of Michigan

3901 Beaubien | Phone: 313-745-5437
Detroit, MI 48201 | Fax: 313-887-5211
URL: www.childrensdmc.org
Type: Childrens | Emergency Services: No
Ownership: Voluntary Non-Profit - Private | Beds: 240

Key Personnel:
CEO/President. . . . . Michael E Duggan, MD
Chief of Medical Staff . . . . M Safwan Badr
Infection Control. . . . . Basim Asmar, MD
Quality Assurance . . . . Marlene Ercolani
Radiology. . . . . Steven Batipps

Measure	Cases	This Hosp.	State Avg.	U.S. Avg.
Heart Attack Care				
ACE Inhibitor or ARB for LVSD	-	-	96%	96%
Aspirin at Arrival	-	-	99%	99%
Aspirin at Discharge	-	-	99%	98%
Beta Blocker at Discharge	-	-	99%	98%
Fibrinolytic Medication Timing	-	-	55%	55%
PCI Within 90 Minutes of Arrival	-	-	89%	90%
Smoking Cessation Advice	-	-	100%	99%
Chest Pain/Possible Heart Attack Care				
Aspirin at Arrival	-	-	94%	95%
Median Time to ECG (minutes)	-	-	10	8
Median Time to Transfer (minutes)	-	-	54	61
Fibrinolytic Medication Timing	-	-	60%	54%
Heart Failure Care				
ACE Inhibitor or ARB for LVSD	-	-	95%	94%
Discharge Instructions	-	-	89%	88%
Evaluation of LVS Function	-	-	99%	98%
Smoking Cessation Advice	-	-	99%	98%
Pneumonia Care				
Appropriate Initial Antibiotic	-	-	94%	92%
Blood Culture Timing	-	-	96%	96%
Influenza Vaccine	-	-	91%	91%
Initial Antibiotic Timing	-	-	96%	95%
Pneumococcal Vaccine	-	-	93%	93%
Smoking Cessation Advice	-	-	98%	97%
Surgical Care Improvement Project				
Appropriate VTP Within 24 Hours	-	-	94%	92%
Appropriate Hair Removal	-	-	99%	99%
Appropriate Beta Blocker Usage	-	-	92%	93%
Controlled Postoperative Blood Glucose	-	-	94%	93%
Prophylactic Antibiotic Timing	-	-	97%	97%
Prophylactic Antibiotic Timing (Outpatient)	-	-	87%	92%
Prophylactic Antibiotic Selection	-	-	98%	97%
Prophylactic Antibiotic Select. (Outpatient)	-	-	92%	94%
Prophylactic Antibiotic Stopped	-	-	95%	94%
Recommended VTP Ordered	-	-	95%	94%
Urinary Catheter Removal	-	-	91%	90%
Children's Asthma Care				
Received Systemic Corticosteroids[2]	401	100%	-	100%
Received Home Management Plan[2]	401	84%	-	71%
Received Reliever Medication[2]	401	100%	-	100%
Use of Medical Imaging				
Combination Abdominal CT Scan	-	-	0.135	0.191
Combination Chest CT Scan	-	-	0.068	0.054
Follow-up Mammogram/Ultrasound	-	-	7.4%	8.4%
MRI for Low Back Pain	-	-	32%	32.7%
Survey of Patients' Hospital Experiences				
Area Around Room 'Always' Quiet at Night	-	-	-	58%
Doctors 'Always' Communicated Well	-	-	-	80%
Home Recovery Information Given	-	-	-	82%
Hospital Given 9 or 10 on 10 Point Scale	-	-	-	67%
Meds 'Always' Explained Before Given	-	-	-	60%
Nurses 'Always' Communicated Well	-	-	-	76%
Pain 'Always' Well Controlled	-	-	-	69%
Room and Bathroom 'Always' Clean	-	-	-	71%
Timely Help 'Always' Received	-	-	-	64%
Would Definitely Recommend Hospital	-	-	-	69%

Detroit (John D. Dingell) VA Medical Center

4646 John R. | Phone: 313-576-1000
Detroit, MI 48201 | Fax: 313-576-1991
Type: Acute Care-Veterans Administration | Emergency Services: No
Ownership: Government - Federal | Beds: 372

Key Personnel:
Chief of Medical Staff . . . . Mark Edelstein, MD
Infection Control. . . . . Ronaldo Supena, MD
Quality Assurance . . . . Marvin Dick
Radiology. . . . . Sue Han, MD
Anesthesiology. . . . . Robert Kozol, MD
Emergency Room . . . . Boaz I Milner, MD
Intensive Care Unit. . . . . Basim Bubaybo, MD

Measure	Cases	This Hosp.	State Avg.	U.S. Avg.
Heart Attack Care				
ACE Inhibitor or ARB for LVSD[1]	3	100%	96%	96%
Aspirin at Arrival[1]	18	94%	99%	99%
Aspirin at Discharge[1]	12	100%	99%	98%
Beta Blocker at Discharge[1]	12	100%	99%	98%
Fibrinolytic Medication Timing[5]	0	-	55%	55%
PCI Within 90 Minutes of Arrival[5]	0	-	89%	90%
Smoking Cessation Advice[1]	4	100%	100%	99%
Chest Pain/Possible Heart Attack Care				
Aspirin at Arrival	-	-	94%	95%
Median Time to ECG (minutes)	-	-	10	8
Median Time to Transfer (minutes)	-	-	54	61
Fibrinolytic Medication Timing	-	-	60%	54%
Heart Failure Care				
ACE Inhibitor or ARB for LVSD	82	96%	95%	94%
Discharge Instructions	148	75%	89%	88%
Evaluation of LVS Function	155	100%	99%	98%
Smoking Cessation Advice	31	100%	99%	98%
Pneumonia Care				
Appropriate Initial Antibiotic	52	92%	94%	92%
Blood Culture Timing	74	99%	96%	96%
Influenza Vaccine	47	96%	91%	91%
Initial Antibiotic Timing	67	96%	96%	95%
Pneumococcal Vaccine	36	97%	93%	93%
Smoking Cessation Advice	38	100%	98%	97%
Surgical Care Improvement Project				
Appropriate VTP Within 24 Hours[2]	161	96%	94%	92%
Appropriate Hair Removal[2]	281	100%	99%	99%
Appropriate Beta Blocker Usage[2]	109	96%	92%	93%
Controlled Postoperative Blood Glucose[2,5]	0	-	94%	93%
Prophylactic Antibiotic Timing	191	97%	97%	97%
Prophylactic Antibiotic Timing (Outpatient)	-	-	87%	92%
Prophylactic Antibiotic Selection	192	97%	98%	97%
Prophylactic Antibiotic Select. (Outpatient)	-	-	92%	94%
Prophylactic Antibiotic Stopped	188	95%	95%	94%
Recommended VTP Ordered[2]	161	98%	95%	94%
Urinary Catheter Removal[2]	32	91%	91%	90%
Children's Asthma Care				
Received Systemic Corticosteroids	-	-	-	100%
Received Home Management Plan	-	-	-	71%
Received Reliever Medication	-	-	-	100%
Use of Medical Imaging				
Combination Abdominal CT Scan	-	-	0.135	0.191
Combination Chest CT Scan	-	-	0.068	0.054
Follow-up Mammogram/Ultrasound	-	-	7.4%	8.4%
MRI for Low Back Pain	-	-	32%	32.7%
Survey of Patients' Hospital Experiences				
Area Around Room 'Always' Quiet at Night	-	-	-	58%
Doctors 'Always' Communicated Well	-	-	-	80%
Home Recovery Information Given	-	-	-	82%
Hospital Given 9 or 10 on 10 Point Scale	-	-	-	67%
Meds 'Always' Explained Before Given	-	-	-	60%
Nurses 'Always' Communicated Well	-	-	-	76%
Pain 'Always' Well Controlled	-	-	-	69%
Room and Bathroom 'Always' Clean	-	-	-	71%
Timely Help 'Always' Received	-	-	-	64%
Would Definitely Recommend Hospital	-	-	-	69%

Detroit Receiving Hospital & Univ Health Center

4201 St Antoine St - 3m | Phone: 313-745-3104
Detroit, MI 48201 | Fax: 313-966-7206
E-mail: lbowman@dmc.org
URL: www.drhuhc.org
Type: Acute Care Hospitals | Emergency Services: Yes
Ownership: Government - Federal | Beds: 258

Key Personnel:
CEO/President. . . . . Iris A Taylor, PhD RN
Chief of Medical Staff . . . . Robert Wilson, MD
Infection Control. . . . . Beth Dziekan
Quality Assurance . . . . Margaret Rand
Radiology. . . . . Gail Alexander
Emergency Room . . . . Padraic J Sweeny, MD
Intensive Care Unit. . . . . Sue Ellen Bennett, RN
Patient Relations . . . . Patricia E Natale

Measure	Cases	This Hosp.	State Avg.	U.S. Avg.
Heart Attack Care				
ACE Inhibitor or ARB for LVSD[1]	21	100%	96%	96%
Aspirin at Arrival	68	100%	99%	99%
Aspirin at Discharge	58	98%	99%	98%
Beta Blocker at Discharge	61	98%	99%	98%
Fibrinolytic Medication Timing	0	-	55%	55%
PCI Within 90 Minutes of Arrival	0	-	89%	90%
Smoking Cessation Advice[1]	17	94%	100%	99%
Chest Pain/Possible Heart Attack Care				
Aspirin at Arrival	626	100%	94%	95%
Median Time to ECG (minutes)	663	15	10	8
Median Time to Transfer (minutes)	78	28	54	61
Fibrinolytic Medication Timing[1]	1	100%	60%	54%
Heart Failure Care				
ACE Inhibitor or ARB for LVSD	277	95%	95%	94%
Discharge Instructions	521	100%	89%	88%
Evaluation of LVS Function	578	100%	99%	98%
Smoking Cessation Advice	237	100%	99%	98%
Pneumonia Care				
Appropriate Initial Antibiotic	98	98%	94%	92%
Blood Culture Timing	333	98%	96%	96%
Influenza Vaccine	142	95%	91%	91%
Initial Antibiotic Timing	315	98%	96%	95%
Pneumococcal Vaccine	115	97%	93%	93%
Smoking Cessation Advice	165	98%	98%	97%
Surgical Care Improvement Project				
Appropriate VTP Within 24 Hours	362	91%	94%	92%
Appropriate Hair Removal	608	100%	99%	99%
Appropriate Beta Blocker Usage	119	98%	92%	93%
Controlled Postoperative Blood Glucose[1]	1	0%	94%	93%
Prophylactic Antibiotic Timing	277	100%	97%	97%
Prophylactic Antibiotic Timing (Outpatient)	73	95%	87%	92%
Prophylactic Antibiotic Selection	279	100%	98%	97%
Prophylactic Antibiotic Select. (Outpatient)	71	93%	92%	94%
Prophylactic Antibiotic Stopped	274	96%	95%	94%
Recommended VTP Ordered	362	92%	95%	94%
Urinary Catheter Removal	204	93%	91%	90%
Children's Asthma Care				
Received Systemic Corticosteroids	-	-	-	100%
Received Home Management Plan	-	-	-	71%
Received Reliever Medication	-	-	-	100%
Use of Medical Imaging				
Combination Abdominal CT Scan	421	0.221	0.135	0.191
Combination Chest CT Scan	309	0.201	0.068	0.054
Follow-up Mammogram/Ultrasound[5]	0	-	7.4%	8.4%
MRI for Low Back Pain[5]	0	-	32%	32.7%
Survey of Patients' Hospital Experiences				
Area Around Room 'Always' Quiet at Night	300+	56%	-	58%
Doctors 'Always' Communicated Well	300+	75%	-	80%
Home Recovery Information Given	300+	79%	-	82%
Hospital Given 9 or 10 on 10 Point Scale	300+	62%	-	67%
Meds 'Always' Explained Before Given	300+	56%	-	60%
Nurses 'Always' Communicated Well	300+	72%	-	76%
Pain 'Always' Well Controlled	300+	63%	-	69%
Room and Bathroom 'Always' Clean	300+	60%	-	71%
Timely Help 'Always' Received	300+	63%	-	64%
Would Definitely Recommend Hospital	300+	65%	-	69%

NOTE: Hospital profiles are in alphabetical order by state, then city, then hospital within the city; Rankings exclude hospitals with less than 25 cases except for patient surveys which excludes hospitals with less than 100 cases; (a) 100–299 cases; (1) The number of cases is too small to be sure how well a hospital is performing; (2) The hospital indicated that the data submitted for this measure were based on a sample of cases; (3) Data was collected during a shorter time period (fewer quarters) than the maximum possible time for this measure; (4) Suppressed for one or more quarters by CMS; (5) No data is available from the hospital for this measure; (6) Fewer than 100 patients completed the HCAHPS survey. Use these rates with caution, as the number of surveys may be too low to reliably assess hospital performance; (7) Survey results are based on less than 12 months of data; (8) Survey results are not available for this reporting period; (9) No or very few patients were eligible for the HCAHPS survey. The scores shown, if any, reflect a very small number of surveys; (10) A state average was not calculated because too few hospitals in the state submitted data; (11) There were discrepancies in the data collection process; Please refer to the User's Guide for a full explanation of data.

Harper University Hospital

3990 John R Street
Detroit, MI 48201
URL: www.harperhospital.org
Type: Acute Care Hospitals
Ownership: Voluntary Non-Profit - Private
Phone: 313-745-6211
Fax: 313-745-1520
Emergency Services: Yes
Beds: 658

Key Personnel:
CEO/President. . . . . Micheal Duggan
Chief of Medical Staff . . . . M Safwan Badr, MD
Radiology. . . . . Mehendra Shah
Emergency Room . . . . Patrick Sweeney

Measure	Cases	This Hosp.	State Avg.	U.S. Avg.
Heart Attack Care				
ACE Inhibitor or ARB for LVSD	76	100%	96%	96%
Aspirin at Arrival	149	99%	99%	99%
Aspirin at Discharge	355	99%	99%	98%
Beta Blocker at Discharge	351	99%	99%	98%
Fibrinolytic Medication Timing	0	-	55%	55%
PCI Within 90 Minutes of Arrival[1]	16	94%	89%	90%
Smoking Cessation Advice	144	100%	100%	99%
Chest Pain/Possible Heart Attack Care				
Aspirin at Arrival	35	94%	94%	95%
Median Time to ECG (minutes)	34	14	10	8
Median Time to Transfer (minutes)[5]	0	-	54	61
Fibrinolytic Medication Timing[3]	0	-	60%	54%
Heart Failure Care				
ACE Inhibitor or ARB for LVSD	257	96%	95%	94%
Discharge Instructions	676	88%	89%	88%
Evaluation of LVS Function	786	100%	99%	98%
Smoking Cessation Advice	193	100%	99%	98%
Pneumonia Care				
Appropriate Initial Antibiotic	71	99%	94%	92%
Blood Culture Timing	177	98%	96%	96%
Influenza Vaccine	100	98%	91%	91%
Initial Antibiotic Timing	169	92%	96%	95%
Pneumococcal Vaccine	109	100%	93%	93%
Smoking Cessation Advice	47	100%	98%	97%
Surgical Care Improvement Project				
Appropriate VTP Within 24 Hours[2]	155	91%	94%	92%
Appropriate Hair Removal[2]	615	100%	99%	99%
Appropriate Beta Blocker Usage[2]	167	99%	92%	93%
Controlled Postoperative Blood Glucose[2]	99	78%	94%	93%
Prophylactic Antibiotic Timing[2]	414	100%	97%	97%
Prophylactic Antibiotic Timing (Outpatient)	590	61%	87%	92%
Prophylactic Antibiotic Selection[2]	428	95%	98%	97%
Prophylactic Antibiotic Select. (Outpatient)	476	85%	92%	94%
Prophylactic Antibiotic Stopped[2]	383	93%	95%	94%
Recommended VTP Ordered[2]	162	88%	95%	94%
Urinary Catheter Removal[2]	87	78%	91%	90%
Children's Asthma Care				
Received Systemic Corticosteroids	-	-	-	100%
Received Home Management Plan	-	-	-	71%
Received Reliever Medication	-	-	-	100%
Use of Medical Imaging				
Combination Abdominal CT Scan	636	0.108	0.135	0.191
Combination Chest CT Scan	558	0.005	0.068	0.054
Follow-up Mammogram/Ultrasound[5]	0	-	7.4%	8.4%
MRI for Low Back Pain	350	21.4%	32%	32.7%
Survey of Patients' Hospital Experiences				
Area Around Room 'Always' Quiet at Night	300+	59%	-	58%
Doctors 'Always' Communicated Well	300+	77%	-	80%
Home Recovery Information Given	300+	77%	-	82%
Hospital Given 9 or 10 on 10 Point Scale	300+	65%	-	67%
Meds 'Always' Explained Before Given	300+	59%	-	60%
Nurses 'Always' Communicated Well	300+	76%	-	76%
Pain 'Always' Well Controlled	300+	67%	-	69%
Room and Bathroom 'Always' Clean	300+	67%	-	71%
Timely Help 'Always' Received	300+	64%	-	64%
Would Definitely Recommend Hospital	300+	65%	-	69%

Henry Ford Hospital

2799 W Grand Blvd
Detroit, MI 48202
URL: www.henryfordhospital.com
Type: Acute Care Hospitals
Ownership: Voluntary Non-Profit - Private
Phone: 313-916-2600
Fax: 313-916-7236
Emergency Services: Yes
Beds: 903

Key Personnel:
CEO/President. . . . . Nancy Schlichting
Cardiac Laboratory. . . . . Hani N. Sabbah, PhD
Chief of Medical Staff . . . . William Conway, MD
Coronary Care . . . . Michael P. Hudson, MD
Operating Room. . . . . Gaylord D. Alexander, MD
Quality Assurance . . . . Irene Turkewycz
Radiology. . . . . Michael Sandler, MD

Measure	Cases	This Hosp.	State Avg.	U.S. Avg.
Heart Attack Care				
ACE Inhibitor or ARB for LVSD	158	97%	96%	96%
Aspirin at Arrival	581	99%	99%	99%
Aspirin at Discharge	898	99%	99%	98%
Beta Blocker at Discharge	884	98%	99%	98%
Fibrinolytic Medication Timing	0	-	55%	55%
PCI Within 90 Minutes of Arrival	36	100%	89%	90%
Smoking Cessation Advice	310	100%	100%	99%
Chest Pain/Possible Heart Attack Care				
Aspirin at Arrival	69	100%	94%	95%
Median Time to ECG (minutes)	71	11	10	8
Median Time to Transfer (minutes)[5]	0	-	54	61
Fibrinolytic Medication Timing	0	-	60%	54%
Heart Failure Care				
ACE Inhibitor or ARB for LVSD[2]	172	91%	95%	94%
Discharge Instructions[2]	354	85%	89%	88%
Evaluation of LVS Function[2]	396	99%	99%	98%
Smoking Cessation Advice[2]	102	99%	99%	98%
Pneumonia Care				
Appropriate Initial Antibiotic[2]	64	91%	94%	92%
Blood Culture Timing[2]	188	93%	96%	96%
Influenza Vaccine[2]	101	79%	91%	91%
Initial Antibiotic Timing[2]	135	92%	96%	95%
Pneumococcal Vaccine[2]	116	76%	93%	93%
Smoking Cessation Advice[2]	80	100%	98%	97%
Surgical Care Improvement Project				
Appropriate VTP Within 24 Hours[2]	300	98%	94%	92%
Appropriate Hair Removal[2]	842	100%	99%	99%
Appropriate Beta Blocker Usage[2]	320	70%	92%	93%
Controlled Postoperative Blood Glucose[2]	181	96%	94%	93%
Prophylactic Antibiotic Timing[2]	571	97%	97%	97%
Prophylactic Antibiotic Timing (Outpatient)	476	79%	87%	92%
Prophylactic Antibiotic Selection[2]	583	99%	98%	97%
Prophylactic Antibiotic Select. (Outpatient)	907	86%	92%	94%
Prophylactic Antibiotic Stopped[2]	561	93%	95%	94%
Recommended VTP Ordered[2]	300	99%	95%	94%
Urinary Catheter Removal[2]	198	89%	91%	90%
Children's Asthma Care				
Received Systemic Corticosteroids	-	-	-	100%
Received Home Management Plan	-	-	-	71%
Received Reliever Medication	-	-	-	100%
Use of Medical Imaging				
Combination Abdominal CT Scan	3,298	0.061	0.135	0.191
Combination Chest CT Scan	3,061	0.023	0.068	0.054
Follow-up Mammogram/Ultrasound	5,254	10.7%	7.4%	8.4%
MRI for Low Back Pain	447	32.7%	32%	32.7%
Survey of Patients' Hospital Experiences				
Area Around Room 'Always' Quiet at Night	300+	54%	-	58%
Doctors 'Always' Communicated Well	300+	75%	-	80%
Home Recovery Information Given	300+	82%	-	82%
Hospital Given 9 or 10 on 10 Point Scale	300+	67%	-	67%
Meds 'Always' Explained Before Given	300+	59%	-	60%
Nurses 'Always' Communicated Well	300+	75%	-	76%
Pain 'Always' Well Controlled	300+	67%	-	69%
Room and Bathroom 'Always' Clean	300+	68%	-	71%
Timely Help 'Always' Received	300+	60%	-	64%
Would Definitely Recommend Hospital	300+	68%	-	69%

Karmanos Cancer Center

4100 John R
Detroit, MI 48201
E-mail: info@karmanos.org
URL: www.karmanos.org
Type: Acute Care Hospitals
Ownership: Proprietary
Phone: 800-576-6266
Emergency Services: No
Beds: 123

Key Personnel:
CEO/President. . . . . John C. Ruckdeschel

Measure	Cases	This Hosp.	State Avg.	U.S. Avg.
Heart Attack Care				
ACE Inhibitor or ARB for LVSD[5]	0	-	96%	96%
Aspirin at Arrival[5]	0	-	99%	99%
Aspirin at Discharge[5]	0	-	99%	98%
Beta Blocker at Discharge[5]	0	-	99%	98%
Fibrinolytic Medication Timing[5]	0	-	55%	55%
PCI Within 90 Minutes of Arrival[5]	0	-	89%	90%
Smoking Cessation Advice[5]	0	-	100%	99%
Chest Pain/Possible Heart Attack Care				
Aspirin at Arrival[5]	0	-	94%	95%
Median Time to ECG (minutes)[5]	0	-	10	8
Median Time to Transfer (minutes)[5]	0	-	54	61
Fibrinolytic Medication Timing[5]	0	-	60%	54%
Heart Failure Care				
ACE Inhibitor or ARB for LVSD[1,3]	2	50%	95%	94%
Discharge Instructions[1,3]	7	29%	89%	88%
Evaluation of LVS Function[1,3]	7	86%	99%	98%
Smoking Cessation Advice[1,3]	1	0%	99%	98%
Pneumonia Care				
Appropriate Initial Antibiotic[1]	1	0%	94%	92%
Blood Culture Timing[1]	1	0%	96%	96%
Influenza Vaccine[1]	24	67%	91%	91%
Initial Antibiotic Timing[1]	10	50%	96%	95%
Pneumococcal Vaccine[1]	17	94%	93%	93%
Smoking Cessation Advice[1]	11	91%	98%	97%
Surgical Care Improvement Project				
Appropriate VTP Within 24 Hours[2]	227	93%	94%	92%
Appropriate Hair Removal[2]	355	100%	99%	99%
Appropriate Beta Blocker Usage[2]	96	99%	92%	93%
Controlled Postoperative Blood Glucose[2]	0	-	94%	93%
Prophylactic Antibiotic Timing[2]	130	98%	97%	97%
Prophylactic Antibiotic Timing (Outpatient)	95	53%	87%	92%
Prophylactic Antibiotic Selection[2]	130	89%	98%	97%
Prophylactic Antibiotic Select. (Outpatient)	67	78%	92%	94%
Prophylactic Antibiotic Stopped[2]	129	92%	95%	94%
Recommended VTP Ordered[2]	230	96%	95%	94%
Urinary Catheter Removal[2]	48	50%	91%	90%
Children's Asthma Care				
Received Systemic Corticosteroids	-	-	-	100%
Received Home Management Plan	-	-	-	71%
Received Reliever Medication	-	-	-	100%
Use of Medical Imaging				
Combination Abdominal CT Scan	1,164	0.125	0.135	0.191
Combination Chest CT Scan	2,088	0.024	0.068	0.054
Follow-up Mammogram/Ultrasound	2,378	4.7%	7.4%	8.4%
MRI for Low Back Pain[1]	22	22.7%	32%	32.7%
Survey of Patients' Hospital Experiences				
Area Around Room 'Always' Quiet at Night	300+	61%	-	58%
Doctors 'Always' Communicated Well	300+	77%	-	80%
Home Recovery Information Given	300+	88%	-	82%
Hospital Given 9 or 10 on 10 Point Scale	300+	78%	-	67%
Meds 'Always' Explained Before Given	300+	68%	-	60%
Nurses 'Always' Communicated Well	300+	83%	-	76%
Pain 'Always' Well Controlled	300+	74%	-	69%
Room and Bathroom 'Always' Clean	300+	66%	-	71%
Timely Help 'Always' Received	300+	68%	-	64%
Would Definitely Recommend Hospital	300+	80%	-	69%

NOTE: Hospital profiles are in alphabetical order by state, then city, then hospital within the city; Rankings exclude hospitals with less than 25 cases except for patient surveys which excludes hospitals with less than 100 cases; (a) 100–299 cases; (1) The number of cases is too small to be sure how well a hospital is performing; (2) The hospital indicated that the data submitted for this measure were based on a sample of cases; (3) Data was collected during a shorter time period (fewer quarters) than the maximum possible time for this measure; (4) Suppressed for one or more quarters by CMS; (5) No data is available from the hospital for this measure; (6) Fewer than 100 patients completed the HCAHPS survey. Use these rates with caution, as the number of surveys may be too low to reliably assess hospital performance; (7) Survey results are based on less than 12 months of data; (8) Survey results are not available for this reporting period; (9) No or very few patients were eligible for the HCAHPS survey. The scores shown, if any, reflect a very small number of surveys; (10) A state average was not calculated because too few hospitals in the state submitted data; (11) There were discrepancies in the data collection process; Please refer to the User's Guide for a full explanation of data.

Saint John Hospital and Medical Center

22101 Moross Rd Phone: 313-343-4000
Detroit, MI 48236
URL: www.stjohnprovidence.org
Type: Acute Care Hospitals Emergency Services: Yes
Ownership: Voluntary Non-Profit - Church Beds: 772

Key Personnel:
President . . . . Diane Radloff

Measure	Cases	This Hosp.	State Avg.	U.S. Avg.
Heart Attack Care				
ACE Inhibitor or ARB for LVSD	101	93%	96%	96%
Aspirin at Arrival	347	99%	99%	99%
Aspirin at Discharge	426	98%	99%	98%
Beta Blocker at Discharge	430	98%	99%	98%
Fibrinolytic Medication Timing	0	-	55%	55%
PCI Within 90 Minutes of Arrival	72	90%	89%	90%
Smoking Cessation Advice	158	99%	100%	99%
Chest Pain/Possible Heart Attack Care				
Aspirin at Arrival	101	95%	94%	95%
Median Time to ECG (minutes)	107	7	10	8
Median Time to Transfer (minutes)[1,3]	2	50	54	61
Fibrinolytic Medication Timing[3]	0	-	60%	54%
Heart Failure Care				
ACE Inhibitor or ARB for LVSD[2]	288	98%	95%	94%
Discharge Instructions[2]	662	93%	89%	88%
Evaluation of LVS Function[2]	763	99%	99%	98%
Smoking Cessation Advice[2]	162	99%	99%	98%
Pneumonia Care				
Appropriate Initial Antibiotic	267	96%	94%	92%
Blood Culture Timing	205	95%	96%	96%
Influenza Vaccine	271	94%	91%	91%
Initial Antibiotic Timing	449	95%	96%	95%
Pneumococcal Vaccine	300	97%	93%	93%
Smoking Cessation Advice	187	99%	98%	97%
Surgical Care Improvement Project				
Appropriate VTP Within 24 Hours[2]	394	98%	94%	92%
Appropriate Hair Removal[2]	1,512	100%	99%	99%
Appropriate Beta Blocker Usage[2]	515	98%	92%	93%
Controlled Postoperative Blood Glucose[2]	260	95%	94%	93%
Prophylactic Antibiotic Timing[2]	1,213	98%	97%	97%
Prophylactic Antibiotic Timing (Outpatient)	642	94%	87%	92%
Prophylactic Antibiotic Selection[2]	1,228	98%	98%	97%
Prophylactic Antibiotic Select. (Outpatient)	622	97%	92%	94%
Prophylactic Antibiotic Stopped[2]	1,155	96%	95%	94%
Recommended VTP Ordered[2]	394	99%	95%	94%
Urinary Catheter Removal[2]	198	96%	91%	90%
Children's Asthma Care				
Received Systemic Corticosteroids	-	-	-	100%
Received Home Management Plan	-	-	-	71%
Received Reliever Medication	-	-	-	100%
Use of Medical Imaging				
Combination Abdominal CT Scan	1,107	0.155	0.135	0.191
Combination Chest CT Scan	778	0.170	0.068	0.054
Follow-up Mammogram/Ultrasound	2,562	2.5%	7.4%	8.4%
MRI for Low Back Pain	294	29.6%	32%	32.7%
Survey of Patients' Hospital Experiences				
Area Around Room 'Always' Quiet at Night	300+	54%	-	58%
Doctors 'Always' Communicated Well	300+	73%	-	80%
Home Recovery Information Given	300+	79%	-	82%
Hospital Given 9 or 10 on 10 Point Scale	300+	62%	-	67%
Meds 'Always' Explained Before Given	300+	57%	-	60%
Nurses 'Always' Communicated Well	300+	75%	-	76%
Pain 'Always' Well Controlled	300+	67%	-	69%
Room and Bathroom 'Always' Clean	300+	58%	-	71%
Timely Help 'Always' Received	300+	54%	-	64%
Would Definitely Recommend Hospital	300+	67%	-	69%

Sinai-Grace Hospital

6071 W Outer Drive Phone: 313-966-3300
Detroit, MI 48235 Fax: 313-966-3546
URL: www.sinaigrace.org
Type: Acute Care Hospitals Emergency Services: Yes
Ownership: Voluntary Non-Profit - Other Beds: 404

Key Personnel:
CEO/President . . . . Conrad Mallett Jr.
Cardiac Laboratory . . . . Diane Wehby
Chief of Medical Staff . . . . John Haapaniemi, DO
Infection Control . . . . Sheila Finch
Operating Room . . . . Deidra Brown-Cobb
Pediatric Ambulatory Care . . . . . . Anne-Mare Ice, MD
Quality Assurance . . . . Michelle Bellmore
Radiology . . . . Terry Posa

Measure	Cases	This Hosp.	State Avg.	U.S. Avg.
Heart Attack Care				
ACE Inhibitor or ARB for LVSD	68	100%	96%	96%
Aspirin at Arrival	323	99%	99%	99%
Aspirin at Discharge	285	99%	99%	98%
Beta Blocker at Discharge	278	98%	99%	98%
Fibrinolytic Medication Timing	0	-	55%	55%
PCI Within 90 Minutes of Arrival	33	76%	89%	90%
Smoking Cessation Advice	113	96%	100%	99%
Chest Pain/Possible Heart Attack Care				
Aspirin at Arrival	27	85%	94%	95%
Median Time to ECG (minutes)	29	10	10	8
Median Time to Transfer (minutes)[5]	0	-	54	61
Fibrinolytic Medication Timing[3]	0	-	60%	54%
Heart Failure Care				
ACE Inhibitor or ARB for LVSD	440	91%	95%	94%
Discharge Instructions	887	88%	89%	88%
Evaluation of LVS Function	1,042	99%	99%	98%
Smoking Cessation Advice	396	98%	99%	98%
Pneumonia Care				
Appropriate Initial Antibiotic	183	97%	94%	92%
Blood Culture Timing	446	89%	96%	96%
Influenza Vaccine	212	92%	91%	91%
Initial Antibiotic Timing	396	97%	96%	95%
Pneumococcal Vaccine	256	94%	93%	93%
Smoking Cessation Advice	153	100%	98%	97%
Surgical Care Improvement Project				
Appropriate VTP Within 24 Hours[2]	280	98%	94%	92%
Appropriate Hair Removal[2]	862	100%	99%	99%
Appropriate Beta Blocker Usage[2]	210	99%	92%	93%
Controlled Postoperative Blood Glucose[2]	82	96%	94%	93%
Prophylactic Antibiotic Timing[2]	555	98%	97%	97%
Prophylactic Antibiotic Timing (Outpatient)	487	73%	87%	92%
Prophylactic Antibiotic Selection[2]	563	99%	98%	97%
Prophylactic Antibiotic Select. (Outpatient)	379	82%	92%	94%
Prophylactic Antibiotic Stopped[2]	529	98%	95%	94%
Recommended VTP Ordered[2]	281	98%	95%	94%
Urinary Catheter Removal[2]	223	97%	91%	90%
Children's Asthma Care				
Received Systemic Corticosteroids	-	-	-	100%
Received Home Management Plan	-	-	-	71%
Received Reliever Medication	-	-	-	100%
Use of Medical Imaging				
Combination Abdominal CT Scan	939	0.182	0.135	0.191
Combination Chest CT Scan	912	0.022	0.068	0.054
Follow-up Mammogram/Ultrasound	1,235	12.8%	7.4%	8.4%
MRI for Low Back Pain	222	25.2%	32%	32.7%
Survey of Patients' Hospital Experiences				
Area Around Room 'Always' Quiet at Night	300+	60%	-	58%
Doctors 'Always' Communicated Well	300+	74%	-	80%
Home Recovery Information Given	300+	76%	-	82%
Hospital Given 9 or 10 on 10 Point Scale	300+	56%	-	67%
Meds 'Always' Explained Before Given	300+	54%	-	60%
Nurses 'Always' Communicated Well	300+	73%	-	76%
Pain 'Always' Well Controlled	300+	67%	-	69%
Room and Bathroom 'Always' Clean	300+	67%	-	71%
Timely Help 'Always' Received	300+	62%	-	64%
Would Definitely Recommend Hospital	300+	51%	-	69%

Borgess-Lee Memorial Hospital

420 W High Street Phone: 269-782-8681
Dowagiac, MI 49047 Fax: 269-783-3044
Type: Critical Access Hospitals Emergency Services: Yes
Ownership: Voluntary Non-Profit - Private Beds: 74

Key Personnel:
Chief of Medical Staff . . . . Mohammad Taqi
Infection Control . . . . Sandy Claborn
Operating Room . . . . Sandy Claborn
Pediatric Ambulatory Care . . . . . . Jaime Rodriguez, MD
Quality Assurance . . . . Marilyn White, RN
Radiology . . . . Marcio S Curvelo, MD
Emergency Room . . . . Paul Rehkepf, MD
Intensive Care Unit . . . . Boonchoo Chang, MD

Measure	Cases	This Hosp.	State Avg.	U.S. Avg.
Heart Attack Care				
ACE Inhibitor or ARB for LVSD[1]	3	67%	96%	96%
Aspirin at Arrival[1]	16	100%	99%	99%
Aspirin at Discharge[1]	9	100%	99%	98%
Beta Blocker at Discharge[1]	8	100%	99%	98%
Fibrinolytic Medication Timing[1]	2	0%	55%	55%
PCI Within 90 Minutes of Arrival[5]	0	-	89%	90%
Smoking Cessation Advice[1]	1	100%	100%	99%
Chest Pain/Possible Heart Attack Care				
Aspirin at Arrival	-	-	94%	95%
Median Time to ECG (minutes)	-	-	10	8
Median Time to Transfer (minutes)	-	-	54	61
Fibrinolytic Medication Timing	-	-	60%	54%
Heart Failure Care				
ACE Inhibitor or ARB for LVSD[1]	10	90%	95%	94%
Discharge Instructions	47	83%	89%	88%
Evaluation of LVS Function	52	98%	99%	98%
Smoking Cessation Advice[1]	7	100%	99%	98%
Pneumonia Care				
Appropriate Initial Antibiotic	36	78%	94%	92%
Blood Culture Timing	28	96%	96%	96%
Influenza Vaccine[1]	20	65%	91%	91%
Initial Antibiotic Timing	45	96%	96%	95%
Pneumococcal Vaccine	34	85%	93%	93%
Smoking Cessation Advice[1]	15	87%	98%	97%
Surgical Care Improvement Project				
Appropriate VTP Within 24 Hours[1]	23	74%	94%	92%
Appropriate Hair Removal	29	93%	99%	99%
Appropriate Beta Blocker Usage[5]	0	-	92%	93%
Controlled Postoperative Blood Glucose	0	-	94%	93%
Prophylactic Antibiotic Timing[1]	11	82%	97%	97%
Prophylactic Antibiotic Timing (Outpatient)	-	-	87%	92%
Prophylactic Antibiotic Selection[1]	11	73%	98%	97%
Prophylactic Antibiotic Select. (Outpatient)	-	-	92%	94%
Prophylactic Antibiotic Stopped[1]	11	64%	95%	94%
Recommended VTP Ordered[1]	23	74%	95%	94%
Urinary Catheter Removal[1]	8	100%	91%	90%
Children's Asthma Care				
Received Systemic Corticosteroids	-	-	-	100%
Received Home Management Plan	-	-	-	71%
Received Reliever Medication	-	-	-	100%
Use of Medical Imaging				
Combination Abdominal CT Scan	-	-	0.135	0.191
Combination Chest CT Scan	-	-	0.068	0.054
Follow-up Mammogram/Ultrasound	-	-	7.4%	8.4%
MRI for Low Back Pain	-	-	32%	32.7%
Survey of Patients' Hospital Experiences				
Area Around Room 'Always' Quiet at Night	(a)	58%	-	58%
Doctors 'Always' Communicated Well	(a)	68%	-	80%
Home Recovery Information Given	(a)	73%	-	82%
Hospital Given 9 or 10 on 10 Point Scale	(a)	63%	-	67%
Meds 'Always' Explained Before Given	(a)	54%	-	60%
Nurses 'Always' Communicated Well	(a)	72%	-	76%
Pain 'Always' Well Controlled	(a)	59%	-	69%
Room and Bathroom 'Always' Clean	(a)	80%	-	71%
Timely Help 'Always' Received	(a)	66%	-	64%
Would Definitely Recommend Hospital	(a)	64%	-	69%

NOTE: Hospital profiles are in alphabetical order by state, then city, then hospital within the city; Rankings exclude hospitals with less than 25 cases except for patient surveys which excludes hospitals with less than 100 cases; (a) 100–299 cases; (1) The number of cases is too small to be sure how well a hospital is performing; (2) The hospital indicated that the data submitted for this measure were based on a sample of cases; (3) Data was collected during a shorter time period (fewer quarters) than the maximum possible time for this measure; (4) Suppressed for one or more quarters by CMS; (5) No data is available from the hospital for this measure; (6) Fewer than 100 patients completed the HCAHPS survey. Use these rates with caution, as the number of surveys may be too low to reliably assess hospital performance; (7) Survey results are based on less than 12 months of data; (8) Survey results are not available for this reporting period; (9) No or very few patients were eligible for the HCAHPS survey. The scores shown, if any, reflect a very small number of surveys; (10) A state average was not calculated because too few hospitals in the state submitted data; (11) There were discrepancies in the data collection process; Please refer to the User's Guide for a full explanation of data.

Saint John River District Hospital

4100 River Rd
East China, MI 48054
URL: www.stjohn.org
Type: Acute Care Hospitals
Ownership: Govt - Hospital Dist/Auth
Phone: 810-329-7111
Fax: 810-329-8920
Emergency Services: Yes
Beds: 68

Key Personnel:
CEO/President. . . . . Patricia Maryland, EdD
Chief of Medical Staff . . . . Michael C Wiemann, DO
Infection Control. . . . . Heidi Boadway, RN
Operating Room. . . . . Andrew K Gavagan, RN
Pediatric Ambulatory Care . . . . . . John Zmieiko, MD
Quality Assurance . . . . John D Doyle
Radiology. . . . . Herminio C Calderon, MD

Measure	Cases	This Hosp.	State Avg.	U.S. Avg.
Heart Attack Care				
ACE Inhibitor or ARB for LVSD	0	-	96%	96%
Aspirin at Arrival[1]	5	100%	99%	99%
Aspirin at Discharge[1]	1	100%	99%	98%
Beta Blocker at Discharge[1]	2	100%	99%	98%
Fibrinolytic Medication Timing	0	-	55%	55%
PCI Within 90 Minutes of Arrival	0	-	89%	90%
Smoking Cessation Advice	0	-	100%	99%
Chest Pain/Possible Heart Attack Care				
Aspirin at Arrival	46	100%	94%	95%
Median Time to ECG (minutes)	48	2	10	8
Median Time to Transfer (minutes)[1]	2	142	54	61
Fibrinolytic Medication Timing	0	-	60%	54%
Heart Failure Care				
ACE Inhibitor or ARB for LVSD[1]	23	100%	95%	94%
Discharge Instructions	61	100%	89%	88%
Evaluation of LVS Function	93	99%	99%	98%
Smoking Cessation Advice[1]	13	100%	99%	98%
Pneumonia Care				
Appropriate Initial Antibiotic	78	95%	94%	92%
Blood Culture Timing	85	100%	96%	96%
Influenza Vaccine	80	98%	91%	91%
Initial Antibiotic Timing	96	100%	96%	95%
Pneumococcal Vaccine	95	99%	93%	93%
Smoking Cessation Advice[1]	23	96%	98%	97%
Surgical Care Improvement Project				
Appropriate VTP Within 24 Hours	45	96%	94%	92%
Appropriate Hair Removal	105	100%	99%	99%
Appropriate Beta Blocker Usage[1]	24	100%	92%	93%
Controlled Postoperative Blood Glucose	0	-	94%	93%
Prophylactic Antibiotic Timing	45	100%	97%	97%
Prophylactic Antibiotic Timing (Outpatient)	47	96%	87%	92%
Prophylactic Antibiotic Selection	45	100%	98%	97%
Prophylactic Antibiotic Select. (Outpatient)	46	100%	92%	94%
Prophylactic Antibiotic Stopped	45	100%	95%	94%
Recommended VTP Ordered	45	96%	95%	94%
Urinary Catheter Removal[1]	20	100%	91%	90%
Children's Asthma Care				
Received Systemic Corticosteroids	-	-	-	100%
Received Home Management Plan	-	-	-	71%
Received Reliever Medication	-	-	-	100%
Use of Medical Imaging				
Combination Abdominal CT Scan	272	0.040	0.135	0.191
Combination Chest CT Scan	218	0.014	0.068	0.054
Follow-up Mammogram/Ultrasound	504	18.7%	7.4%	8.4%
MRI for Low Back Pain[5]	0	-	32%	32.7%
Survey of Patients' Hospital Experiences				
Area Around Room 'Always' Quiet at Night	300+	52%	-	58%
Doctors 'Always' Communicated Well	300+	79%	-	80%
Home Recovery Information Given	300+	82%	-	82%
Hospital Given 9 or 10 on 10 Point Scale	300+	68%	-	67%
Meds 'Always' Explained Before Given	300+	57%	-	60%
Nurses 'Always' Communicated Well	300+	76%	-	76%
Pain 'Always' Well Controlled	300+	74%	-	69%
Room and Bathroom 'Always' Clean	300+	78%	-	71%
Timely Help 'Always' Received	300+	69%	-	64%
Would Definitely Recommend Hospital	300+	65%	-	69%

Eaton Rapids Medical Center

1500 S Main Street
Eaton Rapids, MI 48827
URL: www.eatonrapidsmedicalcenter.org
Type: Critical Access Hospitals
Ownership: Voluntary Non-Profit - Private
Phone: 517-663-2671
Fax: 517-663-4920
Emergency Services: Yes
Beds: 20

Key Personnel:
CEO/President. . . . . Jack Denton
Chief of Medical Staff . . . . Ashok Gupta
Operating Room. . . . . Jeffrey Deppen
Radiology. . . . . Pauline Chee

Measure	Cases	This Hosp.	State Avg.	U.S. Avg.
Heart Attack Care				
ACE Inhibitor or ARB for LVSD	0	-	96%	96%
Aspirin at Arrival[1]	3	100%	99%	99%
Aspirin at Discharge[1]	1	100%	99%	98%
Beta Blocker at Discharge[1]	1	100%	99%	98%
Fibrinolytic Medication Timing	0	-	55%	55%
PCI Within 90 Minutes of Arrival	0	-	89%	90%
Smoking Cessation Advice	0	-	100%	99%
Chest Pain/Possible Heart Attack Care				
Aspirin at Arrival	68	88%	94%	95%
Median Time to ECG (minutes)	78	16	10	8
Median Time to Transfer (minutes)[1,3]	3	105	54	61
Fibrinolytic Medication Timing[1]	4	25%	60%	54%
Heart Failure Care				
ACE Inhibitor or ARB for LVSD[1]	6	100%	95%	94%
Discharge Instructions	31	94%	89%	88%
Evaluation of LVS Function	29	97%	99%	98%
Smoking Cessation Advice[1]	3	100%	99%	98%
Pneumonia Care				
Appropriate Initial Antibiotic[1]	22	95%	94%	92%
Blood Culture Timing[1]	19	95%	96%	96%
Influenza Vaccine[1]	15	80%	91%	91%
Initial Antibiotic Timing[1]	21	95%	96%	95%
Pneumococcal Vaccine[1]	13	69%	93%	93%
Smoking Cessation Advice[1]	5	100%	98%	97%
Surgical Care Improvement Project				
Appropriate VTP Within 24 Hours[5]	0	-	94%	92%
Appropriate Hair Removal[5]	0	-	99%	99%
Appropriate Beta Blocker Usage[5]	0	-	92%	93%
Controlled Postoperative Blood Glucose[5]	0	-	94%	93%
Prophylactic Antibiotic Timing[5]	0	-	97%	97%
Prophylactic Antibiotic Timing (Outpatient)	64	89%	87%	92%
Prophylactic Antibiotic Selection[5]	0	-	98%	97%
Prophylactic Antibiotic Select. (Outpatient)	63	98%	92%	94%
Prophylactic Antibiotic Stopped[5]	0	-	95%	94%
Recommended VTP Ordered[5]	0	-	95%	94%
Urinary Catheter Removal[5]	0	-	91%	90%
Children's Asthma Care				
Received Systemic Corticosteroids	-	-	-	100%
Received Home Management Plan	-	-	-	71%
Received Reliever Medication	-	-	-	100%
Use of Medical Imaging				
Combination Abdominal CT Scan	161	0.286	0.135	0.191
Combination Chest CT Scan	59	0.424	0.068	0.054
Follow-up Mammogram/Ultrasound	205	8.3%	7.4%	8.4%
MRI for Low Back Pain[1]	18	22.2%	32%	32.7%
Survey of Patients' Hospital Experiences				
Area Around Room 'Always' Quiet at Night[8]	-	-	-	58%
Doctors 'Always' Communicated Well[8]	-	-	-	80%
Home Recovery Information Given[8]	-	-	-	82%
Hospital Given 9 or 10 on 10 Point Scale[8]	-	-	-	67%
Meds 'Always' Explained Before Given[8]	-	-	-	60%
Nurses 'Always' Communicated Well[8]	-	-	-	76%
Pain 'Always' Well Controlled[8]	-	-	-	69%
Room and Bathroom 'Always' Clean[8]	-	-	-	71%
Timely Help 'Always' Received[8]	-	-	-	64%
Would Definitely Recommend Hospital[8]	-	-	-	69%

Saint Francis Hospital

3401 Ludington St
Escanaba, MI 49829
Type: Acute Care Hospitals
Ownership: Voluntary Non-Profit - Church
Phone: 906-786-3311
Fax: 906-786-4004
Emergency Services: Yes
Beds: 110

Key Personnel:
CEO/President. . . . . Peter Jennings
Chief of Medical Staff . . . . Ronald Bissett
Quality Assurance . . . . Pat Savitski
Radiology. . . . . Leon E Kinasiewicz
Emergency Room . . . . Shirley Parr

Measure	Cases	This Hosp.	State Avg.	U.S. Avg.
Heart Attack Care				
ACE Inhibitor or ARB for LVSD[1]	4	75%	96%	96%
Aspirin at Arrival[1]	20	100%	99%	99%
Aspirin at Discharge[1]	15	100%	99%	98%
Beta Blocker at Discharge[1]	16	100%	99%	98%
Fibrinolytic Medication Timing	0	-	55%	55%
PCI Within 90 Minutes of Arrival	0	-	89%	90%
Smoking Cessation Advice[1]	2	100%	100%	99%
Chest Pain/Possible Heart Attack Care				
Aspirin at Arrival	132	97%	94%	95%
Median Time to ECG (minutes)	144	14	10	8
Median Time to Transfer (minutes)[1,3]	1	165	54	61
Fibrinolytic Medication Timing[1]	15	67%	60%	54%
Heart Failure Care				
ACE Inhibitor or ARB for LVSD	28	96%	95%	94%
Discharge Instructions	86	92%	89%	88%
Evaluation of LVS Function	106	95%	99%	98%
Smoking Cessation Advice[1]	6	100%	99%	98%
Pneumonia Care				
Appropriate Initial Antibiotic	81	88%	94%	92%
Blood Culture Timing	139	93%	96%	96%
Influenza Vaccine	104	97%	91%	91%
Initial Antibiotic Timing	119	97%	96%	95%
Pneumococcal Vaccine	141	96%	93%	93%
Smoking Cessation Advice	42	100%	98%	97%
Surgical Care Improvement Project				
Appropriate VTP Within 24 Hours	57	93%	94%	92%
Appropriate Hair Removal	139	100%	99%	99%
Appropriate Beta Blocker Usage[1]	20	95%	92%	93%
Controlled Postoperative Blood Glucose	0	-	94%	93%
Prophylactic Antibiotic Timing	74	100%	97%	97%
Prophylactic Antibiotic Timing (Outpatient)	42	71%	87%	92%
Prophylactic Antibiotic Selection	74	93%	98%	97%
Prophylactic Antibiotic Select. (Outpatient)	30	100%	92%	94%
Prophylactic Antibiotic Stopped	73	99%	95%	94%
Recommended VTP Ordered	57	93%	95%	94%
Urinary Catheter Removal[1]	15	100%	91%	90%
Children's Asthma Care				
Received Systemic Corticosteroids	-	-	-	100%
Received Home Management Plan	-	-	-	71%
Received Reliever Medication	-	-	-	100%
Use of Medical Imaging				
Combination Abdominal CT Scan	472	0.847	0.135	0.191
Combination Chest CT Scan	405	0.847	0.068	0.054
Follow-up Mammogram/Ultrasound	667	4.9%	7.4%	8.4%
MRI for Low Back Pain	112	43.8%	32%	32.7%
Survey of Patients' Hospital Experiences				
Area Around Room 'Always' Quiet at Night	300+	47%	-	58%
Doctors 'Always' Communicated Well	300+	83%	-	80%
Home Recovery Information Given	300+	84%	-	82%
Hospital Given 9 or 10 on 10 Point Scale	300+	68%	-	67%
Meds 'Always' Explained Before Given	300+	61%	-	60%
Nurses 'Always' Communicated Well	300+	83%	-	76%
Pain 'Always' Well Controlled	300+	74%	-	69%
Room and Bathroom 'Always' Clean	300+	76%	-	71%
Timely Help 'Always' Received	300+	74%	-	64%
Would Definitely Recommend Hospital	300+	65%	-	69%

NOTE: Hospital profiles are in alphabetical order by state, then city, then hospital within the city; Rankings exclude hospitals with less than 25 cases except for patient surveys which excludes hospitals with less than 100 cases; (a) 100–299 cases; (1) The number of cases is too small to be sure how well a hospital is performing; (2) The hospital indicated that the data submitted for this measure were based on a sample of cases; (3) Data was collected during a shorter time period (fewer quarters) than the maximum possible time for this measure; (4) Suppressed for one or more quarters by CMS; (5) No data is available from the hospital for this measure; (6) Fewer than 100 patients completed the HCAHPS survey. Use these rates with caution, as the number of surveys may be too low to reliably assess hospital performance; (7) Survey results are based on less than 12 months of data; (8) Survey results are not available for this reporting period; (9) No or very few patients were eligible for the HCAHPS survey. The scores shown, if any, reflect a very small number of surveys; (10) A state average was not calculated because too few hospitals in the state submitted data; (11) There were discrepancies in the data collection process; Please refer to the User's Guide for a full explanation of data.

Botsford Hospital

28050 Grand River Avenue Phone: 248-471-8000
Farmington Hills, MI 48336 Fax: 248-615-1125
URL: www.botsfordsystem.org
Type: Acute Care Hospitals Emergency Services: Yes
Ownership: Voluntary Non-Profit - Private Beds: 330

Key Personnel:
CEO/President. . . . . Dr Paul LaCasse
Chief of Medical Staff . . . . David Susser, DO
Operating Room. . . . . Rita Julius, RN
Pediatric In-Patient Care . . . . Harold Margolis, DO
Quality Assurance . . . . Judy O'Connor
Radiology. . . . . Stephan Morse, DO

Measure	Cases	This Hosp.	State Avg.	U.S. Avg.
Heart Attack Care				
ACE Inhibitor or ARB for LVSD	40	95%	96%	96%
Aspirin at Arrival	241	100%	99%	99%
Aspirin at Discharge	157	90%	99%	98%
Beta Blocker at Discharge	153	93%	99%	98%
Fibrinolytic Medication Timing	0	-	55%	55%
PCI Within 90 Minutes of Arrival	29	86%	89%	90%
Smoking Cessation Advice	34	100%	100%	99%
Chest Pain/Possible Heart Attack Care				
Aspirin at Arrival	39	95%	94%	95%
Median Time to ECG (minutes)	40	6	10	8
Median Time to Transfer (minutes)[1]	7	73	54	61
Fibrinolytic Medication Timing	0	-	60%	54%
Heart Failure Care				
ACE Inhibitor or ARB for LVSD	170	92%	95%	94%
Discharge Instructions	462	99%	89%	88%
Evaluation of LVS Function	612	97%	99%	98%
Smoking Cessation Advice	112	98%	99%	98%
Pneumonia Care				
Appropriate Initial Antibiotic	115	92%	94%	92%
Blood Culture Timing	294	95%	96%	96%
Influenza Vaccine	124	89%	91%	91%
Initial Antibiotic Timing	250	96%	96%	95%
Pneumococcal Vaccine	189	96%	93%	93%
Smoking Cessation Advice	79	99%	98%	97%
Surgical Care Improvement Project				
Appropriate VTP Within 24 Hours[2]	267	99%	94%	92%
Appropriate Hair Removal[2]	666	100%	99%	99%
Appropriate Beta Blocker Usage[2]	189	98%	92%	93%
Controlled Postoperative Blood Glucose[2]	0	-	94%	93%
Prophylactic Antibiotic Timing[2]	502	97%	97%	97%
Prophylactic Antibiotic Timing (Outpatient)	240	91%	87%	92%
Prophylactic Antibiotic Selection[2]	504	99%	98%	97%
Prophylactic Antibiotic Select. (Outpatient)	224	96%	92%	94%
Prophylactic Antibiotic Stopped[2]	480	97%	95%	94%
Recommended VTP Ordered[2]	267	99%	95%	94%
Urinary Catheter Removal[2]	199	94%	91%	90%
Children's Asthma Care				
Received Systemic Corticosteroids	-	-	-	100%
Received Home Management Plan	-	-	-	71%
Received Reliever Medication	-	-	-	100%
Use of Medical Imaging				
Combination Abdominal CT Scan	1,124	0.090	0.135	0.191
Combination Chest CT Scan	816	0.032	0.068	0.054
Follow-up Mammogram/Ultrasound	1,044	8.3%	7.4%	8.4%
MRI for Low Back Pain	93	30.1%	32%	32.7%
Survey of Patients' Hospital Experiences				
Area Around Room 'Always' Quiet at Night	300+	44%	-	58%
Doctors 'Always' Communicated Well	300+	76%	-	80%
Home Recovery Information Given	300+	83%	-	82%
Hospital Given 9 or 10 on 10 Point Scale	300+	60%	-	67%
Meds 'Always' Explained Before Given	300+	48%	-	60%
Nurses 'Always' Communicated Well	300+	71%	-	76%
Pain 'Always' Well Controlled	300+	64%	-	69%
Room and Bathroom 'Always' Clean	300+	62%	-	71%
Timely Help 'Always' Received	300+	59%	-	64%
Would Definitely Recommend Hospital	300+	65%	-	69%

Hurley Medical Center

One Hurley Plaza Phone: 810-257-9000
Flint, MI 48503 Fax: 810-257-9111
URL: www.hurleymc.com
Type: Acute Care Hospitals Emergency Services: No
Ownership: Voluntary Non-Profit - Other Beds: 443

Key Personnel:
CEO/President. . . . . Patrick Wardell
Quality Assurance . . . . William Smith

Measure	Cases	This Hosp.	State Avg.	U.S. Avg.
Heart Attack Care				
ACE Inhibitor or ARB for LVSD	31	90%	96%	96%
Aspirin at Arrival	175	99%	99%	99%
Aspirin at Discharge	117	98%	99%	98%
Beta Blocker at Discharge	117	96%	99%	98%
Fibrinolytic Medication Timing[1]	1	0%	55%	55%
PCI Within 90 Minutes of Arrival	29	72%	89%	90%
Smoking Cessation Advice	65	100%	100%	99%
Chest Pain/Possible Heart Attack Care				
Aspirin at Arrival[1]	12	83%	94%	95%
Median Time to ECG (minutes)[1]	12	8	10	8
Median Time to Transfer (minutes)[1,3]	1	130	54	61
Fibrinolytic Medication Timing[3]	0	-	60%	54%
Heart Failure Care				
ACE Inhibitor or ARB for LVSD[2]	133	99%	95%	94%
Discharge Instructions[2]	336	88%	89%	88%
Evaluation of LVS Function[2]	362	96%	99%	98%
Smoking Cessation Advice[2]	132	99%	99%	98%
Pneumonia Care				
Appropriate Initial Antibiotic[2]	121	81%	94%	92%
Blood Culture Timing[2]	109	97%	96%	96%
Influenza Vaccine[2]	80	86%	91%	91%
Initial Antibiotic Timing[2]	179	90%	96%	95%
Pneumococcal Vaccine[2]	102	79%	93%	93%
Smoking Cessation Advice[2]	100	99%	98%	97%
Surgical Care Improvement Project				
Appropriate VTP Within 24 Hours[2]	175	95%	94%	92%
Appropriate Hair Removal[2]	443	99%	99%	99%
Appropriate Beta Blocker Usage[2]	98	91%	92%	93%
Controlled Postoperative Blood Glucose[2]	0	-	94%	93%
Prophylactic Antibiotic Timing[2]	286	99%	97%	97%
Prophylactic Antibiotic Timing (Outpatient)	172	70%	87%	92%
Prophylactic Antibiotic Selection[2]	287	97%	98%	97%
Prophylactic Antibiotic Select. (Outpatient)	153	88%	92%	94%
Prophylactic Antibiotic Stopped[2]	272	94%	95%	94%
Recommended VTP Ordered[2]	176	97%	95%	94%
Urinary Catheter Removal[2]	75	92%	91%	90%
Children's Asthma Care				
Received Systemic Corticosteroids	-	-	-	100%
Received Home Management Plan	-	-	-	71%
Received Reliever Medication	-	-	-	100%
Use of Medical Imaging				
Combination Abdominal CT Scan	489	0.137	0.135	0.191
Combination Chest CT Scan	307	0.127	0.068	0.054
Follow-up Mammogram/Ultrasound	142	9.9%	7.4%	8.4%
MRI for Low Back Pain[5]	0	-	32%	32.7%
Survey of Patients' Hospital Experiences				
Area Around Room 'Always' Quiet at Night	300+	48%	-	58%
Doctors 'Always' Communicated Well	300+	73%	-	80%
Home Recovery Information Given	300+	82%	-	82%
Hospital Given 9 or 10 on 10 Point Scale	300+	61%	-	67%
Meds 'Always' Explained Before Given	300+	56%	-	60%
Nurses 'Always' Communicated Well	300+	73%	-	76%
Pain 'Always' Well Controlled	300+	67%	-	69%
Room and Bathroom 'Always' Clean	300+	60%	-	71%
Timely Help 'Always' Received	300+	60%	-	64%
Would Definitely Recommend Hospital	300+	64%	-	69%

Mclaren Regional Medical Center

401 S Ballenger Highway Phone: 810-342-2000
Flint, MI 48532 Fax: 810-342-2428
URL: www.mclaren.org
Type: Acute Care Hospitals Emergency Services: Yes
Ownership: Voluntary Non-Profit - Other Beds: 452

Key Personnel:
CEO/President. . . . . Donald C Kooy
Chief of Medical Staff . . . . Jagdish Bhagat, MD
Infection Control . . . . Janee Macklin
Operating Room. . . . . Debra Stephenson
Pediatric Ambulatory Care . . . . . . KE Vobach, MD
Quality Assurance . . . . Richard Sardelli
Radiology. . . . . ML Kahn, MD
Patient Relations . . . . Annetta Wilbon

Measure	Cases	This Hosp.	State Avg.	U.S. Avg.
Heart Attack Care				
ACE Inhibitor or ARB for LVSD[2]	72	100%	96%	96%
Aspirin at Arrival[2]	344	99%	99%	99%
Aspirin at Discharge[2]	407	99%	99%	98%
Beta Blocker at Discharge[2]	408	99%	99%	98%
Fibrinolytic Medication Timing[1,2]	1	0%	55%	55%
PCI Within 90 Minutes of Arrival[2]	76	92%	89%	90%
Smoking Cessation Advice[2]	144	100%	100%	99%
Chest Pain/Possible Heart Attack Care				
Aspirin at Arrival[1]	5	100%	94%	95%
Median Time to ECG (minutes)[1]	6	4	10	8
Median Time to Transfer (minutes)[5]	0	-	54	61
Fibrinolytic Medication Timing[5]	0	-	60%	54%
Heart Failure Care				
ACE Inhibitor or ARB for LVSD[2]	262	93%	95%	94%
Discharge Instructions[2]	655	83%	89%	88%
Evaluation of LVS Function[2]	770	96%	99%	98%
Smoking Cessation Advice[2]	118	99%	99%	98%
Pneumonia Care				
Appropriate Initial Antibiotic[2]	215	97%	94%	92%
Blood Culture Timing[2]	103	96%	96%	96%
Influenza Vaccine[2]	225	88%	91%	91%
Initial Antibiotic Timing[2]	346	90%	96%	95%
Pneumococcal Vaccine[2]	301	91%	93%	93%
Smoking Cessation Advice[2]	115	100%	98%	97%
Surgical Care Improvement Project				
Appropriate VTP Within 24 Hours[2]	291	93%	94%	92%
Appropriate Hair Removal[2]	1,345	100%	99%	99%
Appropriate Beta Blocker Usage[2]	426	91%	92%	93%
Controlled Postoperative Blood Glucose[2]	252	84%	94%	93%
Prophylactic Antibiotic Timing[2]	1,069	98%	97%	97%
Prophylactic Antibiotic Timing (Outpatient)	428	93%	87%	92%
Prophylactic Antibiotic Selection[2]	1,091	97%	98%	97%
Prophylactic Antibiotic Select. (Outpatient)	419	96%	92%	94%
Prophylactic Antibiotic Stopped[2]	1,018	95%	95%	94%
Recommended VTP Ordered[2]	291	97%	95%	94%
Urinary Catheter Removal[2]	152	79%	91%	90%
Children's Asthma Care				
Received Systemic Corticosteroids	-	-	-	100%
Received Home Management Plan	-	-	-	71%
Received Reliever Medication	-	-	-	100%
Use of Medical Imaging				
Combination Abdominal CT Scan	1,408	0.429	0.135	0.191
Combination Chest CT Scan	1,214	0.001	0.068	0.054
Follow-up Mammogram/Ultrasound	1,642	6.4%	7.4%	8.4%
MRI for Low Back Pain[1]	4	25.0%	32%	32.7%
Survey of Patients' Hospital Experiences				
Area Around Room 'Always' Quiet at Night	300+	44%	-	58%
Doctors 'Always' Communicated Well	300+	72%	-	80%
Home Recovery Information Given	300+	77%	-	82%
Hospital Given 9 or 10 on 10 Point Scale	300+	59%	-	67%
Meds 'Always' Explained Before Given	300+	54%	-	60%
Nurses 'Always' Communicated Well	300+	69%	-	76%
Pain 'Always' Well Controlled	300+	65%	-	69%
Room and Bathroom 'Always' Clean	300+	56%	-	71%
Timely Help 'Always' Received	300+	53%	-	64%
Would Definitely Recommend Hospital	300+	62%	-	69%

NOTE: Hospital profiles are in alphabetical order by state, then city, then hospital within the city; Rankings exclude hospitals with less than 25 cases except for patient surveys which excludes hospitals with less than 100 cases; (a) 100–299 cases; (1) The number of cases is too small to be sure how well a hospital is performing; (2) The hospital indicated that the data submitted for this measure were based on a sample of cases; (3) Data was collected during a shorter time period (fewer quarters) than the maximum possible time for this measure; (4) Suppressed for one or more quarters by CMS; (5) No data is available from the hospital for this measure; (6) Fewer than 100 patients completed the HCAHPS survey. Use these rates with caution, as the number of surveys may be too low to reliably assess hospital performance; (7) Survey results are based on less than 12 months of data; (8) Survey results are not available for this reporting period; (9) No or very few patients were eligible for the HCAHPS survey. The scores shown, if any, reflect a very small number of surveys; (10) A state average was not calculated because too few hospitals in the state submitted data; (11) There were discrepancies in the data collection process; Please refer to the User's Guide for a full explanation of data.

Paul Oliver Memorial Hospital

224 Park Avenue
Frankfort, MI 49635
Phone: 231-352-2200
Fax: 231-352-9621
E-mail: pomh@mhc.net
URL: www.munsonhealthcare.org
Type: Critical Access Hospitals
Emergency Services: Yes
Ownership: Government - Local
Beds: 48

Key Personnel:
Chief of Medical Staff.......... Gerard Mahoney
Infection Control.............. Sandra Honigfort
Operating Room............... Angela Anderson, RN
Quality Assurance .... Debra Link
Emergency Room .... Donna Clarke, RN
Patient Relations .... Debbie Link

Measure	Cases	This Hosp.	State Avg.	U.S. Avg.
Heart Attack Care				
ACE Inhibitor or ARB for LVSD	-	-	96%	96%
Aspirin at Arrival	-	-	99%	99%
Aspirin at Discharge	-	-	99%	98%
Beta Blocker at Discharge	-	-	99%	98%
Fibrinolytic Medication Timing	-	-	55%	55%
PCI Within 90 Minutes of Arrival	-	-	89%	90%
Smoking Cessation Advice	-	-	100%	99%
Chest Pain/Possible Heart Attack Care				
Aspirin at Arrival[5]	0	-	94%	95%
Median Time to ECG (minutes)[5]	0	-	10	8
Median Time to Transfer (minutes)[5]	0	-	54	61
Fibrinolytic Medication Timing[5]	0	-	60%	54%
Heart Failure Care				
ACE Inhibitor or ARB for LVSD	-	-	95%	94%
Discharge Instructions	-	-	89%	88%
Evaluation of LVS Function	-	-	99%	98%
Smoking Cessation Advice	-	-	99%	98%
Pneumonia Care				
Appropriate Initial Antibiotic	-	-	94%	92%
Blood Culture Timing	-	-	96%	96%
Influenza Vaccine	-	-	91%	91%
Initial Antibiotic Timing	-	-	96%	95%
Pneumococcal Vaccine	-	-	93%	93%
Smoking Cessation Advice	-	-	98%	97%
Surgical Care Improvement Project				
Appropriate VTP Within 24 Hours	-	-	94%	92%
Appropriate Hair Removal	-	-	99%	99%
Appropriate Beta Blocker Usage	-	-	92%	93%
Controlled Postoperative Blood Glucose	-	-	94%	93%
Prophylactic Antibiotic Timing	-	-	97%	97%
Prophylactic Antibiotic Timing (Outpatient)[5]	0	-	87%	92%
Prophylactic Antibiotic Selection	-	-	98%	97%
Prophylactic Antibiotic Select. (Outpatient)[5]	0	-	92%	94%
Prophylactic Antibiotic Stopped	-	-	95%	94%
Recommended VTP Ordered	-	-	95%	94%
Urinary Catheter Removal	-	-	91%	90%
Children's Asthma Care				
Received Systemic Corticosteroids	-	-	-	100%
Received Home Management Plan	-	-	-	71%
Received Reliever Medication	-	-	-	100%
Use of Medical Imaging				
Combination Abdominal CT Scan	141	0.035	0.135	0.191
Combination Chest CT Scan	76	0.013	0.068	0.054
Follow-up Mammogram/Ultrasound	403	8.2%	7.4%	8.4%
MRI for Low Back Pain[5]	0	-	32%	32.7%
Survey of Patients' Hospital Experiences				
Area Around Room 'Always' Quiet at Night	-	-	-	58%
Doctors 'Always' Communicated Well	-	-	-	80%
Home Recovery Information Given	-	-	-	82%
Hospital Given 9 or 10 on 10 Point Scale	-	-	-	67%
Meds 'Always' Explained Before Given	-	-	-	60%
Nurses 'Always' Communicated Well	-	-	-	76%
Pain 'Always' Well Controlled	-	-	-	69%
Room and Bathroom 'Always' Clean	-	-	-	71%
Timely Help 'Always' Received	-	-	-	64%
Would Definitely Recommend Hospital	-	-	-	69%

Spectrum Health Gerber Memorial

212 S Sullivan St
Fremont, MI 49412
Phone: 231-924-3300
Fax: 231-924-1320
E-mail: hr@gmhs.org
URL: www.gmhs.org
Type: Acute Care Hospitals
Emergency Services: Yes
Ownership: Voluntary Non-Profit - Private
Beds: 77

Key Personnel:
CEO/President................ Randal Stasik
Chief of Medical Staff.......... Douglas Johnson
Infection Control.............. Gretchen Farinosi
Operating Room............... Marianne Patton
Radiology.................... Joseph Marous
Hemotology Center .... Kathy Evans
Intensive Care Unit............ Patti Wethington
Patient Relations .... Sharon Boczkaja

Measure	Cases	This Hosp.	State Avg.	U.S. Avg.
Heart Attack Care				
ACE Inhibitor or ARB for LVSD[1]	1	100%	96%	96%
Aspirin at Arrival[1]	5	100%	99%	99%
Aspirin at Discharge[1]	4	100%	99%	98%
Beta Blocker at Discharge[1]	4	100%	99%	98%
Fibrinolytic Medication Timing	0	-	55%	55%
PCI Within 90 Minutes of Arrival	0	-	89%	90%
Smoking Cessation Advice	0	-	100%	99%
Chest Pain/Possible Heart Attack Care				
Aspirin at Arrival	126	99%	94%	95%
Median Time to ECG (minutes)	130	10	10	8
Median Time to Transfer (minutes)[1]	15	55	54	61
Fibrinolytic Medication Timing[1]	5	60%	60%	54%
Heart Failure Care				
ACE Inhibitor or ARB for LVSD[1]	19	100%	95%	94%
Discharge Instructions	51	96%	89%	88%
Evaluation of LVS Function	61	100%	99%	98%
Smoking Cessation Advice[1]	13	100%	99%	98%
Pneumonia Care				
Appropriate Initial Antibiotic	92	96%	94%	92%
Blood Culture Timing	132	98%	96%	96%
Influenza Vaccine	69	100%	91%	91%
Initial Antibiotic Timing	118	99%	96%	95%
Pneumococcal Vaccine	100	98%	93%	93%
Smoking Cessation Advice	41	100%	98%	97%
Surgical Care Improvement Project				
Appropriate VTP Within 24 Hours	73	90%	94%	92%
Appropriate Hair Removal	330	100%	99%	99%
Appropriate Beta Blocker Usage	68	94%	92%	93%
Controlled Postoperative Blood Glucose	0	-	94%	93%
Prophylactic Antibiotic Timing	266	99%	97%	97%
Prophylactic Antibiotic Timing (Outpatient)	27	85%	87%	92%
Prophylactic Antibiotic Selection	267	99%	98%	97%
Prophylactic Antibiotic Select. (Outpatient)[1]	23	91%	92%	94%
Prophylactic Antibiotic Stopped	260	96%	95%	94%
Recommended VTP Ordered	74	89%	95%	94%
Urinary Catheter Removal[1]	15	87%	91%	90%
Children's Asthma Care				
Received Systemic Corticosteroids	-	-	-	100%
Received Home Management Plan	-	-	-	71%
Received Reliever Medication	-	-	-	100%
Use of Medical Imaging				
Combination Abdominal CT Scan	415	0.010	0.135	0.191
Combination Chest CT Scan	367	0.014	0.068	0.054
Follow-up Mammogram/Ultrasound	709	7.1%	7.4%	8.4%
MRI for Low Back Pain	82	43.9%	32%	32.7%
Survey of Patients' Hospital Experiences				
Area Around Room 'Always' Quiet at Night	300+	57%	-	58%
Doctors 'Always' Communicated Well	300+	83%	-	80%
Home Recovery Information Given	300+	89%	-	82%
Hospital Given 9 or 10 on 10 Point Scale	300+	73%	-	67%
Meds 'Always' Explained Before Given	300+	69%	-	60%
Nurses 'Always' Communicated Well	300+	82%	-	76%
Pain 'Always' Well Controlled	300+	74%	-	69%
Room and Bathroom 'Always' Clean	300+	71%	-	71%
Timely Help 'Always' Received	300+	72%	-	64%
Would Definitely Recommend Hospital	300+	69%	-	69%

Garden City Hospital

6245 Inkster Rd
Garden City, MI 48135
Phone: 734-421-3300
Fax: 734-421-0593
URL: www.gchosp.org
Type: Acute Care Hospitals
Emergency Services: Yes
Ownership: Voluntary Non-Profit - Private
Beds: 323

Key Personnel:
CEO/President................ Gary R Ley
Cardiac Laboratory............ Debbie DeMatteis
Operating Room............... Annette Krupa
Quality Assurance .... Lisa Sielski
Radiology.................... Jim Williamson
Patient Relations .... Malissa Stringer

Measure	Cases	This Hosp.	State Avg.	U.S. Avg.
Heart Attack Care				
ACE Inhibitor or ARB for LVSD[1]	24	96%	96%	96%
Aspirin at Arrival	204	97%	99%	99%
Aspirin at Discharge	140	90%	99%	98%
Beta Blocker at Discharge	135	96%	99%	98%
Fibrinolytic Medication Timing	0	-	55%	55%
PCI Within 90 Minutes of Arrival	54	96%	89%	90%
Smoking Cessation Advice	46	100%	100%	99%
Chest Pain/Possible Heart Attack Care				
Aspirin at Arrival	86	97%	94%	95%
Median Time to ECG (minutes)	87	5	10	8
Median Time to Transfer (minutes)[1,3]	4	118	54	61
Fibrinolytic Medication Timing	0	-	60%	54%
Heart Failure Care				
ACE Inhibitor or ARB for LVSD	85	92%	95%	94%
Discharge Instructions	321	90%	89%	88%
Evaluation of LVS Function	401	96%	99%	98%
Smoking Cessation Advice	71	100%	99%	98%
Pneumonia Care				
Appropriate Initial Antibiotic	170	91%	94%	92%
Blood Culture Timing	260	96%	96%	96%
Influenza Vaccine	139	86%	91%	91%
Initial Antibiotic Timing	258	96%	96%	95%
Pneumococcal Vaccine	178	89%	93%	93%
Smoking Cessation Advice	80	100%	98%	97%
Surgical Care Improvement Project				
Appropriate VTP Within 24 Hours	306	91%	94%	92%
Appropriate Hair Removal	634	99%	99%	99%
Appropriate Beta Blocker Usage	193	96%	92%	93%
Controlled Postoperative Blood Glucose	0	-	94%	93%
Prophylactic Antibiotic Timing	391	91%	97%	97%
Prophylactic Antibiotic Timing (Outpatient)	257	84%	87%	92%
Prophylactic Antibiotic Selection	394	95%	98%	97%
Prophylactic Antibiotic Select. (Outpatient)	244	61%	92%	94%
Prophylactic Antibiotic Stopped	370	94%	95%	94%
Recommended VTP Ordered	306	97%	95%	94%
Urinary Catheter Removal	153	88%	91%	90%
Children's Asthma Care				
Received Systemic Corticosteroids	-	-	-	100%
Received Home Management Plan	-	-	-	71%
Received Reliever Medication	-	-	-	100%
Use of Medical Imaging				
Combination Abdominal CT Scan	782	0.116	0.135	0.191
Combination Chest CT Scan	668	0.006	0.068	0.054
Follow-up Mammogram/Ultrasound	415	8.9%	7.4%	8.4%
MRI for Low Back Pain	120	26.7%	32%	32.7%
Survey of Patients' Hospital Experiences				
Area Around Room 'Always' Quiet at Night	300+	43%	-	58%
Doctors 'Always' Communicated Well	300+	77%	-	80%
Home Recovery Information Given	300+	79%	-	82%
Hospital Given 9 or 10 on 10 Point Scale	300+	60%	-	67%
Meds 'Always' Explained Before Given	300+	59%	-	60%
Nurses 'Always' Communicated Well	300+	71%	-	76%
Pain 'Always' Well Controlled	300+	67%	-	69%
Room and Bathroom 'Always' Clean	300+	69%	-	71%
Timely Help 'Always' Received	300+	62%	-	64%
Would Definitely Recommend Hospital	300+	63%	-	69%

NOTE: Hospital profiles are in alphabetical order by state, then city, then hospital within the city; Rankings exclude hospitals with less than 25 cases except for patient surveys which excludes hospitals with less than 100 cases; (a) 100–299 cases; (1) The number of cases is too small to be sure how well a hospital is performing; (2) The hospital indicated that the data submitted for this measure were based on a sample of cases; (3) Data was collected during a shorter time period (fewer quarters) than the maximum possible time for this measure; (4) Suppressed for one or more quarters by CMS; (5) No data is available from the hospital for this measure; (6) Fewer than 100 patients completed the HCAHPS survey. Use these rates with caution, as the number of surveys may be too low to reliably assess hospital performance; (7) Survey results are based on less than 12 months of data; (8) Survey results are not available for this reporting period; (9) No or very few patients were eligible for the HCAHPS survey. The scores shown, if any, reflect a very small number of surveys; (10) A state average was not calculated because too few hospitals in the state submitted data; (11) There were discrepancies in the data collection process; Please refer to the User's Guide for a full explanation of data.

Otsego Memorial Hospital

825 N Center Ave Phone: 989-731-2100
Gaylord, MI 49735 Fax: 989-731-7792
E-mail: omh@otsegomemorialhospital.org
URL: otsegomemorialhospital.org
Type: Acute Care Hospitals Emergency Services: Yes
Ownership: Voluntary Non-Profit - Private Beds: 53

Key Personnel:
CEO/President. . . . . David Schuster
Chief of Medical Staff . . . . David Miner, MD
Infection Control. . . . . Lisa Stier, RN
Operating Room. . . . . Wendy Frye
Pediatric Ambulatory Care . . . . . . Alida Asencio, MD
Pediatric In-Patient Care . . . . Alida Asencio, MD
Quality Assurance . . . . Maryann Hoffmann
Radiology. . . . . Michael Angileri

Measure	Cases	This Hosp.	State Avg.	U.S. Avg.
Heart Attack Care				
ACE Inhibitor or ARB for LVSD[1]	2	100%	96%	96%
Aspirin at Arrival[1]	5	100%	99%	99%
Aspirin at Discharge[1]	4	100%	99%	98%
Beta Blocker at Discharge[1]	6	100%	99%	98%
Fibrinolytic Medication Timing	0	-	55%	55%
PCI Within 90 Minutes of Arrival	0	-	89%	90%
Smoking Cessation Advice	0	-	100%	99%
Chest Pain/Possible Heart Attack Care				
Aspirin at Arrival	157	96%	94%	95%
Median Time to ECG (minutes)	162	8	10	8
Median Time to Transfer (minutes)[1]	10	48	54	61
Fibrinolytic Medication Timing[1]	10	40%	60%	54%
Heart Failure Care				
ACE Inhibitor or ARB for LVSD[1]	15	100%	95%	94%
Discharge Instructions	56	95%	89%	88%
Evaluation of LVS Function	66	95%	99%	98%
Smoking Cessation Advice[1]	9	100%	99%	98%
Pneumonia Care				
Appropriate Initial Antibiotic	59	100%	94%	92%
Blood Culture Timing	80	95%	96%	96%
Influenza Vaccine	46	96%	91%	91%
Initial Antibiotic Timing	76	99%	96%	95%
Pneumococcal Vaccine	78	92%	93%	93%
Smoking Cessation Advice[1]	18	100%	98%	97%
Surgical Care Improvement Project				
Appropriate VTP Within 24 Hours[2]	45	100%	94%	92%
Appropriate Hair Removal[2]	217	100%	99%	99%
Appropriate Beta Blocker Usage[2]	63	97%	92%	93%
Controlled Postoperative Blood Glucose[2]	0	-	94%	93%
Prophylactic Antibiotic Timing[2]	169	90%	97%	97%
Prophylactic Antibiotic Timing (Outpatient)	27	78%	87%	92%
Prophylactic Antibiotic Selection[2]	168	98%	98%	97%
Prophylactic Antibiotic Select. (Outpatient)[1]	23	100%	92%	94%
Prophylactic Antibiotic Stopped[2]	167	97%	95%	94%
Recommended VTP Ordered[2]	45	100%	95%	94%
Urinary Catheter Removal[2]	62	100%	91%	90%
Children's Asthma Care				
Received Systemic Corticosteroids	-	-	-	100%
Received Home Management Plan	-	-	-	71%
Received Reliever Medication	-	-	-	100%
Use of Medical Imaging				
Combination Abdominal CT Scan	383	0.052	0.135	0.191
Combination Chest CT Scan	305	0.000	0.068	0.054
Follow-up Mammogram/Ultrasound	431	11.4%	7.4%	8.4%
MRI for Low Back Pain	135	41.5%	32%	32.7%
Survey of Patients' Hospital Experiences				
Area Around Room 'Always' Quiet at Night	300+	57%	-	58%
Doctors 'Always' Communicated Well	300+	86%	-	80%
Home Recovery Information Given	300+	83%	-	82%
Hospital Given 9 or 10 on 10 Point Scale	300+	68%	-	67%
Meds 'Always' Explained Before Given	300+	66%	-	60%
Nurses 'Always' Communicated Well	300+	78%	-	76%
Pain 'Always' Well Controlled	300+	71%	-	69%
Room and Bathroom 'Always' Clean	300+	71%	-	71%
Timely Help 'Always' Received	300+	69%	-	64%
Would Definitely Recommend Hospital	300+	68%	-	69%

Midmichigan Medical Center-Gladwin

515 Quarter Street Phone: 989-426-9286
Gladwin, MI 48624 Fax: 989-246-6400
URL: www.midmichigan.org
Type: Critical Access Hospitals Emergency Services: Yes
Ownership: Voluntary Non-Profit - Private Beds: 25

Key Personnel:
CEO/President. . . . . Raymond H Stover
Infection Control. . . . . Dana Garafalo
Operating Room. . . . . Christy Gary
Emergency Room . . . . Donald Willman

Measure	Cases	This Hosp.	State Avg.	U.S. Avg.
Heart Attack Care				
ACE Inhibitor or ARB for LVSD[3]	0	-	96%	96%
Aspirin at Arrival[1,3]	2	100%	99%	99%
Aspirin at Discharge[1,3]	1	100%	99%	98%
Beta Blocker at Discharge[3]	0	-	99%	98%
Fibrinolytic Medication Timing[3]	0	-	55%	55%
PCI Within 90 Minutes of Arrival[3]	0	-	89%	90%
Smoking Cessation Advice[3]	0	-	100%	99%
Chest Pain/Possible Heart Attack Care				
Aspirin at Arrival[3]	75	99%	94%	95%
Median Time to ECG (minutes)[3]	76	9	10	8
Median Time to Transfer (minutes)[1,3]	2	86	54	61
Fibrinolytic Medication Timing[1,3]	8	25%	60%	54%
Heart Failure Care				
ACE Inhibitor or ARB for LVSD[1]	11	91%	95%	94%
Discharge Instructions	47	98%	89%	88%
Evaluation of LVS Function	66	100%	99%	98%
Smoking Cessation Advice[1]	11	100%	99%	98%
Pneumonia Care				
Appropriate Initial Antibiotic	38	95%	94%	92%
Blood Culture Timing	45	96%	96%	96%
Influenza Vaccine[1]	22	95%	91%	91%
Initial Antibiotic Timing	53	94%	96%	95%
Pneumococcal Vaccine	41	100%	93%	93%
Smoking Cessation Advice[1]	15	100%	98%	97%
Surgical Care Improvement Project				
Appropriate VTP Within 24 Hours[5]	0	-	94%	92%
Appropriate Hair Removal[5]	0	-	99%	99%
Appropriate Beta Blocker Usage[5]	0	-	92%	93%
Controlled Postoperative Blood Glucose[5]	0	-	94%	93%
Prophylactic Antibiotic Timing[5]	0	-	97%	97%
Prophylactic Antibiotic Timing (Outpatient)[5]	0	-	87%	92%
Prophylactic Antibiotic Selection[5]	0	-	98%	97%
Prophylactic Antibiotic Select. (Outpatient)[5]	0	-	92%	94%
Prophylactic Antibiotic Stopped[5]	0	-	95%	94%
Recommended VTP Ordered[5]	0	-	95%	94%
Urinary Catheter Removal[5]	0	-	91%	90%
Children's Asthma Care				
Received Systemic Corticosteroids	-	-	-	100%
Received Home Management Plan	-	-	-	71%
Received Reliever Medication	-	-	-	100%
Use of Medical Imaging				
Combination Abdominal CT Scan	331	0.054	0.135	0.191
Combination Chest CT Scan	399	0.065	0.068	0.054
Follow-up Mammogram/Ultrasound	636	3.8%	7.4%	8.4%
MRI for Low Back Pain	88	35.2%	32%	32.7%
Survey of Patients' Hospital Experiences				
Area Around Room 'Always' Quiet at Night	(a)	72%	-	58%
Doctors 'Always' Communicated Well	(a)	87%	-	80%
Home Recovery Information Given	(a)	87%	-	82%
Hospital Given 9 or 10 on 10 Point Scale	(a)	71%	-	67%
Meds 'Always' Explained Before Given	(a)	59%	-	60%
Nurses 'Always' Communicated Well	(a)	82%	-	76%
Pain 'Always' Well Controlled	(a)	77%	-	69%
Room and Bathroom 'Always' Clean	(a)	69%	-	71%
Timely Help 'Always' Received	(a)	75%	-	64%
Would Definitely Recommend Hospital	(a)	66%	-	69%

Genesys Regional Medical Center - Health Park

One Genesys Parkway Phone: 810-606-5000
Grand Blanc, MI 48439 Fax: 810-606-6279
URL: www.genesys.org
Type: Acute Care Hospitals Emergency Services: Yes
Ownership: Voluntary Non-Profit - Church Beds: 410

Key Personnel:
CEO/President. . . . . Elizabeth Aderholdt
Cardiac Laboratory. . . . . Paul Brown
Chief of Medical Staff . . . . Kenneth Steibel, MD
Infection Control. . . . . Pamela Goran
Operating Room. . . . . Karen Ferrara
Pediatric Ambulatory Care . . . . . . Kamale Hasan, MD
Quality Assurance . . . . Greg Knuth
Radiology. . . . . Michael Gedwill

Measure	Cases	This Hosp.	State Avg.	U.S. Avg.
Heart Attack Care				
ACE Inhibitor or ARB for LVSD[2]	68	91%	96%	96%
Aspirin at Arrival[2]	424	100%	99%	99%
Aspirin at Discharge[2]	424	100%	99%	98%
Beta Blocker at Discharge[2]	394	99%	99%	98%
Fibrinolytic Medication Timing[2]	0	-	55%	55%
PCI Within 90 Minutes of Arrival[2]	62	82%	89%	90%
Smoking Cessation Advice[2]	154	100%	100%	99%
Chest Pain/Possible Heart Attack Care				
Aspirin at Arrival[5]	0	-	94%	95%
Median Time to ECG (minutes)[5]	0	-	10	8
Median Time to Transfer (minutes)[5]	0	-	54	61
Fibrinolytic Medication Timing[5]	0	-	60%	54%
Heart Failure Care				
ACE Inhibitor or ARB for LVSD[2]	137	99%	95%	94%
Discharge Instructions[2]	394	98%	89%	88%
Evaluation of LVS Function[2]	464	100%	99%	98%
Smoking Cessation Advice[2]	88	100%	99%	98%
Pneumonia Care				
Appropriate Initial Antibiotic[2]	96	90%	94%	92%
Blood Culture Timing[2]	171	94%	96%	96%
Influenza Vaccine[2]	164	93%	91%	91%
Initial Antibiotic Timing[2]	211	94%	96%	95%
Pneumococcal Vaccine[2]	200	98%	93%	93%
Smoking Cessation Advice[2]	90	100%	98%	97%
Surgical Care Improvement Project				
Appropriate VTP Within 24 Hours[2]	410	92%	94%	92%
Appropriate Hair Removal[2]	1,555	94%	99%	99%
Appropriate Beta Blocker Usage[2]	562	96%	92%	93%
Controlled Postoperative Blood Glucose[2]	160	94%	94%	93%
Prophylactic Antibiotic Timing[2]	1,320	98%	97%	97%
Prophylactic Antibiotic Timing (Outpatient)	479	81%	87%	92%
Prophylactic Antibiotic Selection[2]	1,333	96%	98%	97%
Prophylactic Antibiotic Select. (Outpatient)	488	87%	92%	94%
Prophylactic Antibiotic Stopped[2]	1,251	94%	95%	94%
Recommended VTP Ordered[2]	411	98%	95%	94%
Urinary Catheter Removal[2]	391	96%	91%	90%
Children's Asthma Care				
Received Systemic Corticosteroids	-	-	-	100%
Received Home Management Plan	-	-	-	71%
Received Reliever Medication	-	-	-	100%
Use of Medical Imaging				
Combination Abdominal CT Scan	916	0.047	0.135	0.191
Combination Chest CT Scan	580	0.393	0.068	0.054
Follow-up Mammogram/Ultrasound	374	31.8%	7.4%	8.4%
MRI for Low Back Pain[5]	0	-	32%	32.7%
Survey of Patients' Hospital Experiences				
Area Around Room 'Always' Quiet at Night	300+	45%	-	58%
Doctors 'Always' Communicated Well	300+	75%	-	80%
Home Recovery Information Given	300+	81%	-	82%
Hospital Given 9 or 10 on 10 Point Scale	300+	66%	-	67%
Meds 'Always' Explained Before Given	300+	57%	-	60%
Nurses 'Always' Communicated Well	300+	73%	-	76%
Pain 'Always' Well Controlled	300+	68%	-	69%
Room and Bathroom 'Always' Clean	300+	61%	-	71%
Timely Help 'Always' Received	300+	66%	-	64%
Would Definitely Recommend Hospital	300+	69%	-	69%

NOTE: Hospital profiles are in alphabetical order by state, then city, then hospital within the city; Rankings exclude hospitals with less than 25 cases except for patient surveys which excludes hospitals with less than 100 cases; (a) 100–299 cases; (1) The number of cases is too small to be sure how well a hospital is performing; (2) The hospital indicated that the data submitted for this measure were based on a sample of cases; (3) Data was collected during a shorter time period (fewer quarters) than the maximum possible time for this measure; (4) Suppressed for one or more quarters by CMS; (5) No data is available from the hospital for this measure; (6) Fewer than 100 patients completed the HCAHPS survey. Use these rates with caution, as the number of surveys may be too low to reliably assess hospital performance; (7) Survey results are based on less than 12 months of data; (8) Survey results are not available for this reporting period; (9) No or very few patients were eligible for the HCAHPS survey. The scores shown, if any, reflect a very small number of surveys; (10) A state average was not calculated because too few hospitals in the state submitted data; (11) There were discrepancies in the data collection process; Please refer to the User's Guide for a full explanation of data.

North Ottawa Community Hospital

1309 Sheldon Rd Phone: 616-842-3600
Grand Haven, MI 49417 Fax: 616-847-5621
URL: www.noch.org
Type: Acute Care Hospitals Emergency Services: Yes
Ownership: Govt - Hospital Dist/Auth Beds: 81

Key Personnel:
CEO/President. . . . . Michael Payne
Chief of Medical Staff . . . . M Gary Robertson, MD
Pediatric In-Patient Care . . . . Linda Bouman
Radiology. . . . . Lynn S McCurdy

Measure	Cases	This Hosp.	State Avg.	U.S. Avg.
Heart Attack Care				
ACE Inhibitor or ARB for LVSD[1]	1	100%	96%	96%
Aspirin at Arrival[1]	6	100%	99%	99%
Aspirin at Discharge[1]	5	100%	99%	98%
Beta Blocker at Discharge[1]	6	100%	99%	98%
Fibrinolytic Medication Timing	0	-	55%	55%
PCI Within 90 Minutes of Arrival	0	-	89%	90%
Smoking Cessation Advice[1]	1	100%	100%	99%
Chest Pain/Possible Heart Attack Care				
Aspirin at Arrival	43	100%	94%	95%
Median Time to ECG (minutes)	45	6	10	8
Median Time to Transfer (minutes)[1]	14	56	54	61
Fibrinolytic Medication Timing	0	-	60%	54%
Heart Failure Care				
ACE Inhibitor or ARB for LVSD[1]	12	92%	95%	94%
Discharge Instructions	34	88%	89%	88%
Evaluation of LVS Function	49	100%	99%	98%
Smoking Cessation Advice[1]	4	100%	99%	98%
Pneumonia Care				
Appropriate Initial Antibiotic	50	90%	94%	92%
Blood Culture Timing	88	99%	96%	96%
Influenza Vaccine	50	94%	91%	91%
Initial Antibiotic Timing	80	100%	96%	95%
Pneumococcal Vaccine	63	98%	93%	93%
Smoking Cessation Advice[1]	17	100%	98%	97%
Surgical Care Improvement Project				
Appropriate VTP Within 24 Hours	65	97%	94%	92%
Appropriate Hair Removal	257	100%	99%	99%
Appropriate Beta Blocker Usage	67	90%	92%	93%
Controlled Postoperative Blood Glucose	0	-	94%	93%
Prophylactic Antibiotic Timing	203	100%	97%	97%
Prophylactic Antibiotic Timing (Outpatient)	80	99%	87%	92%
Prophylactic Antibiotic Selection	205	98%	98%	97%
Prophylactic Antibiotic Select. (Outpatient)	87	95%	92%	94%
Prophylactic Antibiotic Stopped	201	99%	95%	94%
Recommended VTP Ordered	65	97%	95%	94%
Urinary Catheter Removal	94	100%	91%	90%
Children's Asthma Care				
Received Systemic Corticosteroids	-	-	-	100%
Received Home Management Plan	-	-	-	71%
Received Reliever Medication	-	-	-	100%
Use of Medical Imaging				
Combination Abdominal CT Scan	185	0.049	0.135	0.191
Combination Chest CT Scan	159	0.170	0.068	0.054
Follow-up Mammogram/Ultrasound	662	6.0%	7.4%	8.4%
MRI for Low Back Pain	59	37.3%	32%	32.7%
Survey of Patients' Hospital Experiences				
Area Around Room 'Always' Quiet at Night	300+	70%	-	58%
Doctors 'Always' Communicated Well	300+	80%	-	80%
Home Recovery Information Given	300+	88%	-	82%
Hospital Given 9 or 10 on 10 Point Scale	300+	75%	-	67%
Meds 'Always' Explained Before Given	300+	61%	-	60%
Nurses 'Always' Communicated Well	300+	78%	-	76%
Pain 'Always' Well Controlled	300+	71%	-	69%
Room and Bathroom 'Always' Clean	300+	71%	-	71%
Timely Help 'Always' Received	300+	72%	-	64%
Would Definitely Recommend Hospital	300+	75%	-	69%

Saint Mary's Health Care

200 Jefferson Avenue SE Phone: 616-685-5000
Grand Rapids, MI 49503 Fax: 616-732-3035
URL: www.smhealthcare.org
Type: Acute Care Hospitals Emergency Services: Yes
Ownership: Voluntary Non-Profit - Church Beds: 324

Key Personnel:
CEO/President. . . . . David Blair MD
Chief of Medical Staff . . . . Terrance Wright MD
Infection Control. . . . . Mary Neuman, RN
Quality Assurance . . . . Barb Vanpattan
Radiology. . . . . Earl Monks
Emergency Room . . . . Michael Olgren MD
Patient Relations . . . . Vicki Garrett, RN

Measure	Cases	This Hosp.	State Avg.	U.S. Avg.
Heart Attack Care				
ACE Inhibitor or ARB for LVSD[1]	14	100%	96%	96%
Aspirin at Arrival	111	98%	99%	99%
Aspirin at Discharge	75	100%	99%	98%
Beta Blocker at Discharge	75	100%	99%	98%
Fibrinolytic Medication Timing	0	-	55%	55%
PCI Within 90 Minutes of Arrival	26	85%	89%	90%
Smoking Cessation Advice	33	100%	100%	99%
Chest Pain/Possible Heart Attack Care				
Aspirin at Arrival[1]	14	100%	94%	95%
Median Time to ECG (minutes)[1]	13	6	10	8
Median Time to Transfer (minutes)[1,3]	1	40	54	61
Fibrinolytic Medication Timing	0	-	60%	54%
Heart Failure Care				
ACE Inhibitor or ARB for LVSD	83	99%	95%	94%
Discharge Instructions	258	93%	89%	88%
Evaluation of LVS Function	310	100%	99%	98%
Smoking Cessation Advice	67	100%	99%	98%
Pneumonia Care				
Appropriate Initial Antibiotic	195	97%	94%	92%
Blood Culture Timing	330	100%	96%	96%
Influenza Vaccine	209	95%	91%	91%
Initial Antibiotic Timing	362	99%	96%	95%
Pneumococcal Vaccine	257	97%	93%	93%
Smoking Cessation Advice	123	99%	98%	97%
Surgical Care Improvement Project				
Appropriate VTP Within 24 Hours[2]	162	98%	94%	92%
Appropriate Hair Removal[2]	596	100%	99%	99%
Appropriate Beta Blocker Usage[2]	179	96%	92%	93%
Controlled Postoperative Blood Glucose[2]	0	-	94%	93%
Prophylactic Antibiotic Timing[2]	397	96%	97%	97%
Prophylactic Antibiotic Timing (Outpatient)	314	95%	87%	92%
Prophylactic Antibiotic Selection[2]	389	98%	98%	97%
Prophylactic Antibiotic Select. (Outpatient)	307	90%	92%	94%
Prophylactic Antibiotic Stopped[2]	373	97%	95%	94%
Recommended VTP Ordered[2]	162	99%	95%	94%
Urinary Catheter Removal[2]	135	96%	91%	90%
Children's Asthma Care				
Received Systemic Corticosteroids	-	-	-	100%
Received Home Management Plan	-	-	-	71%
Received Reliever Medication	-	-	-	100%
Use of Medical Imaging				
Combination Abdominal CT Scan	1,051	0.078	0.135	0.191
Combination Chest CT Scan	875	0.032	0.068	0.054
Follow-up Mammogram/Ultrasound	1,769	5.7%	7.4%	8.4%
MRI for Low Back Pain	244	34.8%	32%	32.7%
Survey of Patients' Hospital Experiences				
Area Around Room 'Always' Quiet at Night	300+	62%	-	58%
Doctors 'Always' Communicated Well	300+	80%	-	80%
Home Recovery Information Given	300+	88%	-	82%
Hospital Given 9 or 10 on 10 Point Scale	300+	73%	-	67%
Meds 'Always' Explained Before Given	300+	63%	-	60%
Nurses 'Always' Communicated Well	300+	77%	-	76%
Pain 'Always' Well Controlled	300+	70%	-	69%
Room and Bathroom 'Always' Clean	300+	69%	-	71%
Timely Help 'Always' Received	300+	63%	-	64%
Would Definitely Recommend Hospital	300+	75%	-	69%

Spectrum Health - Butterworth Campus

100 Michigan St NE Phone: 616-391-1774
Grand Rapids, MI 49503 Fax: 616-391-2780
URL: www.spectrum-health.org
Type: Acute Care Hospitals Emergency Services: Yes
Ownership: Voluntary Non-Profit - Private Beds: 986

Key Personnel:
CEO/President. . . . . Richard C Breon
Cardiac Laboratory. . . . . Marla Niedzwiecki
Chief of Medical Staff . . . . Brian Roelof
Infection Control. . . . . Deb Paul
Operating Room. . . . . Kathy Shaneberger
Pediatric In-Patient Care . . . . Ronald Hofmann
Quality Assurance . . . . Nancy Hansen
Radiology. . . . . Charles Luhenton

Measure	Cases	This Hosp.	State Avg.	U.S. Avg.
Heart Attack Care				
ACE Inhibitor or ARB for LVSD	130	100%	96%	96%
Aspirin at Arrival	424	99%	99%	99%
Aspirin at Discharge	855	100%	99%	98%
Beta Blocker at Discharge	830	100%	99%	98%
Fibrinolytic Medication Timing	0	-	55%	55%
PCI Within 90 Minutes of Arrival	108	94%	89%	90%
Smoking Cessation Advice	310	99%	100%	99%
Chest Pain/Possible Heart Attack Care				
Aspirin at Arrival[5]	0	-	94%	95%
Median Time to ECG (minutes)[5]	0	-	10	8
Median Time to Transfer (minutes)[5]	0	-	54	61
Fibrinolytic Medication Timing[5]	0	-	60%	54%
Heart Failure Care				
ACE Inhibitor or ARB for LVSD	350	98%	95%	94%
Discharge Instructions	904	89%	89%	88%
Evaluation of LVS Function	1,066	100%	99%	98%
Smoking Cessation Advice	160	100%	99%	98%
Pneumonia Care				
Appropriate Initial Antibiotic	600	97%	94%	92%
Blood Culture Timing	1,062	97%	96%	96%
Influenza Vaccine	631	96%	91%	91%
Initial Antibiotic Timing	948	97%	96%	95%
Pneumococcal Vaccine	822	99%	93%	93%
Smoking Cessation Advice	282	97%	98%	97%
Surgical Care Improvement Project				
Appropriate VTP Within 24 Hours[2]	262	99%	94%	92%
Appropriate Hair Removal[2]	1,143	100%	99%	99%
Appropriate Beta Blocker Usage[2]	383	95%	92%	93%
Controlled Postoperative Blood Glucose[2]	187	98%	94%	93%
Prophylactic Antibiotic Timing[2]	750	95%	97%	97%
Prophylactic Antibiotic Timing (Outpatient)	1,225	96%	87%	92%
Prophylactic Antibiotic Selection[2]	761	98%	98%	97%
Prophylactic Antibiotic Select. (Outpatient)	1,197	96%	92%	94%
Prophylactic Antibiotic Stopped[2]	715	98%	95%	94%
Recommended VTP Ordered[2]	262	100%	95%	94%
Urinary Catheter Removal[2]	323	90%	91%	90%
Children's Asthma Care				
Received Systemic Corticosteroids	185	98%	-	100%
Received Home Management Plan	185	78%	-	71%
Received Reliever Medication	185	100%	-	100%
Use of Medical Imaging				
Combination Abdominal CT Scan	2,656	0.045	0.135	0.191
Combination Chest CT Scan	1,622	0.045	0.068	0.054
Follow-up Mammogram/Ultrasound	4,174	9.0%	7.4%	8.4%
MRI for Low Back Pain	702	36.0%	32%	32.7%
Survey of Patients' Hospital Experiences				
Area Around Room 'Always' Quiet at Night	300+	50%	-	58%
Doctors 'Always' Communicated Well	300+	77%	-	80%
Home Recovery Information Given	300+	85%	-	82%
Hospital Given 9 or 10 on 10 Point Scale	300+	72%	-	67%
Meds 'Always' Explained Before Given	300+	59%	-	60%
Nurses 'Always' Communicated Well	300+	79%	-	76%
Pain 'Always' Well Controlled	300+	70%	-	69%
Room and Bathroom 'Always' Clean	300+	71%	-	71%
Timely Help 'Always' Received	300+	64%	-	64%
Would Definitely Recommend Hospital	300+	78%	-	69%

NOTE: Hospital profiles are in alphabetical order by state, then city, then hospital within the city; Rankings exclude hospitals with less than 25 cases except for patient surveys which excludes hospitals with less than 100 cases; (a) 100–299 cases; (1) The number of cases is too small to be sure how well a hospital is performing; (2) The hospital indicated that the data submitted for this measure were based on a sample of cases; (3) Data was collected during a shorter time period (fewer quarters) than the maximum possible time for this measure; (4) Suppressed for one or more quarters by CMS; (5) No data is available from the hospital for this measure; (6) Fewer than 100 patients completed the HCAHPS survey. Use these rates with caution, as the number of surveys may be too low to reliably assess hospital performance; (7) Survey results are based on less than 12 months of data; (8) Survey results are not available for this reporting period; (9) No or very few patients were eligible for the HCAHPS survey. The scores shown, if any, reflect a very small number of surveys; (10) A state average was not calculated because too few hospitals in the state submitted data; (11) There were discrepancies in the data collection process; Please refer to the User's Guide for a full explanation of data.

Mercy Hospital - Grayling

1100 E Michigan Ave Phone: 989-348-5461
Grayling, MI 49738 Fax: 989-348-0485
URL: www.mercygrayling.munsonhealthcare.org
Type: Acute Care Hospitals Emergency Services: Yes
Ownership: Voluntary Non-Profit - Church Beds: 130

Key Personnel:
CEO/President. . . . . Stephen Reimer-Matuzsak
Cardiac Laboratory. . . . . Sue Boardman
Chief of Medical Staff . . . . David Hunter
Emergency Room . . . . D Gulow, MD

Measure	Cases	This Hosp.	State Avg.	U.S. Avg.
Heart Attack Care				
ACE Inhibitor or ARB for LVSD[1]	5	80%	96%	96%
Aspirin at Arrival	34	97%	99%	99%
Aspirin at Discharge[1]	20	90%	99%	98%
Beta Blocker at Discharge[1]	23	91%	99%	98%
Fibrinolytic Medication Timing	0	-	55%	55%
PCI Within 90 Minutes of Arrival	0	-	89%	90%
Smoking Cessation Advice[1]	4	100%	100%	99%
Chest Pain/Possible Heart Attack Care				
Aspirin at Arrival	190	98%	94%	95%
Median Time to ECG (minutes)	194	5	10	8
Median Time to Transfer (minutes)[1]	3	35	54	61
Fibrinolytic Medication Timing[1]	21	81%	60%	54%
Heart Failure Care				
ACE Inhibitor or ARB for LVSD	38	87%	95%	94%
Discharge Instructions	81	96%	89%	88%
Evaluation of LVS Function	98	100%	99%	98%
Smoking Cessation Advice[1]	23	100%	99%	98%
Pneumonia Care				
Appropriate Initial Antibiotic[2]	93	96%	94%	92%
Blood Culture Timing[2]	132	100%	96%	96%
Influenza Vaccine[2]	72	99%	91%	91%
Initial Antibiotic Timing[2]	132	97%	96%	95%
Pneumococcal Vaccine[2]	112	96%	93%	93%
Smoking Cessation Advice[2]	48	98%	98%	97%
Surgical Care Improvement Project				
Appropriate VTP Within 24 Hours[2]	63	94%	94%	92%
Appropriate Hair Removal[2]	209	100%	99%	99%
Appropriate Beta Blocker Usage[2]	53	96%	92%	93%
Controlled Postoperative Blood Glucose[2]	0	-	94%	93%
Prophylactic Antibiotic Timing[2]	138	99%	97%	97%
Prophylactic Antibiotic Timing (Outpatient)	99	97%	87%	92%
Prophylactic Antibiotic Selection[2]	142	98%	98%	97%
Prophylactic Antibiotic Select. (Outpatient)	96	98%	92%	94%
Prophylactic Antibiotic Stopped[2]	133	93%	95%	94%
Recommended VTP Ordered[2]	63	94%	95%	94%
Urinary Catheter Removal[1,2]	16	100%	91%	90%
Children's Asthma Care				
Received Systemic Corticosteroids	-	-	-	100%
Received Home Management Plan	-	-	-	71%
Received Reliever Medication	-	-	-	100%
Use of Medical Imaging				
Combination Abdominal CT Scan	460	0.115	0.135	0.191
Combination Chest CT Scan	409	0.039	0.068	0.054
Follow-up Mammogram/Ultrasound	1,083	11.2%	7.4%	8.4%
MRI for Low Back Pain	220	54.5%	32%	32.7%
Survey of Patients' Hospital Experiences				
Area Around Room 'Always' Quiet at Night	300+	58%	-	58%
Doctors 'Always' Communicated Well	300+	80%	-	80%
Home Recovery Information Given	300+	89%	-	82%
Hospital Given 9 or 10 on 10 Point Scale	300+	71%	-	67%
Meds 'Always' Explained Before Given	300+	64%	-	60%
Nurses 'Always' Communicated Well	300+	80%	-	76%
Pain 'Always' Well Controlled	300+	73%	-	69%
Room and Bathroom 'Always' Clean	300+	71%	-	71%
Timely Help 'Always' Received	300+	71%	-	64%
Would Definitely Recommend Hospital	300+	71%	-	69%

Spectrum Health United Memorial - United Campus

615 S Bower Street Phone: 616-754-4691
Greenville, MI 48838 Fax: 616-754-5054
E-mail: contactus@umha.org
URL: www.umha.org
Type: Acute Care Hospitals Emergency Services: Yes
Ownership: Voluntary Non-Profit - Other Beds: 105

Key Personnel:
CEO/President. . . . . Paul Donir
Quality Assurance . . . . Etta Barrera
Ambulatory Care . . . . Stephen Romanella

Measure	Cases	This Hosp.	State Avg.	U.S. Avg.
Heart Attack Care				
ACE Inhibitor or ARB for LVSD	0	-	96%	96%
Aspirin at Arrival[1]	12	92%	99%	99%
Aspirin at Discharge[1]	7	100%	99%	98%
Beta Blocker at Discharge[1]	5	100%	99%	98%
Fibrinolytic Medication Timing	0	-	55%	55%
PCI Within 90 Minutes of Arrival	0	-	89%	90%
Smoking Cessation Advice[1]	1	100%	100%	99%
Chest Pain/Possible Heart Attack Care				
Aspirin at Arrival	110	99%	94%	95%
Median Time to ECG (minutes)	113	6	10	8
Median Time to Transfer (minutes)[1]	10	57	54	61
Fibrinolytic Medication Timing	0	-	60%	54%
Heart Failure Care				
ACE Inhibitor or ARB for LVSD[1]	15	100%	95%	94%
Discharge Instructions	68	99%	89%	88%
Evaluation of LVS Function	96	100%	99%	98%
Smoking Cessation Advice[1]	12	100%	99%	98%
Pneumonia Care				
Appropriate Initial Antibiotic	107	95%	94%	92%
Blood Culture Timing	186	98%	96%	96%
Influenza Vaccine	114	100%	91%	91%
Initial Antibiotic Timing	165	100%	96%	95%
Pneumococcal Vaccine	149	100%	93%	93%
Smoking Cessation Advice	50	100%	98%	97%
Surgical Care Improvement Project				
Appropriate VTP Within 24 Hours	70	91%	94%	92%
Appropriate Hair Removal	202	100%	99%	99%
Appropriate Beta Blocker Usage	34	97%	92%	93%
Controlled Postoperative Blood Glucose	0	-	94%	93%
Prophylactic Antibiotic Timing	145	99%	97%	97%
Prophylactic Antibiotic Timing (Outpatient)	55	93%	87%	92%
Prophylactic Antibiotic Selection	146	100%	98%	97%
Prophylactic Antibiotic Select. (Outpatient)	53	98%	92%	94%
Prophylactic Antibiotic Stopped	137	100%	95%	94%
Recommended VTP Ordered	70	99%	95%	94%
Urinary Catheter Removal	37	95%	91%	90%
Children's Asthma Care				
Received Systemic Corticosteroids	-	-	-	100%
Received Home Management Plan	-	-	-	71%
Received Reliever Medication	-	-	-	100%
Use of Medical Imaging				
Combination Abdominal CT Scan	543	0.053	0.135	0.191
Combination Chest CT Scan	350	0.003	0.068	0.054
Follow-up Mammogram/Ultrasound	601	5.2%	7.4%	8.4%
MRI for Low Back Pain	239	26.4%	32%	32.7%
Survey of Patients' Hospital Experiences				
Area Around Room 'Always' Quiet at Night	300+	60%	-	58%
Doctors 'Always' Communicated Well	300+	84%	-	80%
Home Recovery Information Given	300+	85%	-	82%
Hospital Given 9 or 10 on 10 Point Scale	300+	71%	-	67%
Meds 'Always' Explained Before Given	300+	66%	-	60%
Nurses 'Always' Communicated Well	300+	78%	-	76%
Pain 'Always' Well Controlled	300+	72%	-	69%
Room and Bathroom 'Always' Clean	300+	79%	-	71%
Timely Help 'Always' Received	300+	62%	-	64%
Would Definitely Recommend Hospital	300+	72%	-	69%

Beaumont Hospital - Grosse Pointe

468 Cadieux Rd Phone: 313-343-1000
Grosse Pointe, MI 48230 Fax: 313-343-1327
URL: www.beaumonthospitals.com
Type: Acute Care Hospitals Emergency Services: Yes
Ownership: Voluntary Non-Profit - Private Beds: 289

Key Personnel:
CEO/President. . . . . Kenneth Matzick
Infection Control. . . . . Suzanne Gardner
Operating Room. . . . . Gail Pietrzyk
Quality Assurance . . . . Barb Stemmer
Hemotology Center . . . . Jackie Fisher

Measure	Cases	This Hosp.	State Avg.	U.S. Avg.
Heart Attack Care				
ACE Inhibitor or ARB for LVSD[1]	7	100%	96%	96%
Aspirin at Arrival	63	100%	99%	99%
Aspirin at Discharge	39	100%	99%	98%
Beta Blocker at Discharge	38	100%	99%	98%
Fibrinolytic Medication Timing	0	-	55%	55%
PCI Within 90 Minutes of Arrival	0	-	89%	90%
Smoking Cessation Advice[1]	4	100%	100%	99%
Chest Pain/Possible Heart Attack Care				
Aspirin at Arrival	27	89%	94%	95%
Median Time to ECG (minutes)	26	10	10	8
Median Time to Transfer (minutes)[1]	9	56	54	61
Fibrinolytic Medication Timing	0	-	60%	54%
Heart Failure Care				
ACE Inhibitor or ARB for LVSD	135	97%	95%	94%
Discharge Instructions	326	97%	89%	88%
Evaluation of LVS Function	375	100%	99%	98%
Smoking Cessation Advice	70	100%	99%	98%
Pneumonia Care				
Appropriate Initial Antibiotic	177	94%	94%	92%
Blood Culture Timing	202	98%	96%	96%
Influenza Vaccine	168	93%	91%	91%
Initial Antibiotic Timing	243	99%	96%	95%
Pneumococcal Vaccine	211	96%	93%	93%
Smoking Cessation Advice	88	95%	98%	97%
Surgical Care Improvement Project				
Appropriate VTP Within 24 Hours[2]	225	96%	94%	92%
Appropriate Hair Removal[2]	693	100%	99%	99%
Appropriate Beta Blocker Usage[2]	214	95%	92%	93%
Controlled Postoperative Blood Glucose[2]	0	-	94%	93%
Prophylactic Antibiotic Timing[2]	513	99%	97%	97%
Prophylactic Antibiotic Timing (Outpatient)	230	90%	87%	92%
Prophylactic Antibiotic Selection[2]	516	99%	98%	97%
Prophylactic Antibiotic Select. (Outpatient)	218	99%	92%	94%
Prophylactic Antibiotic Stopped[2]	497	97%	95%	94%
Recommended VTP Ordered[2]	225	97%	95%	94%
Urinary Catheter Removal[2]	172	98%	91%	90%
Children's Asthma Care				
Received Systemic Corticosteroids	-	-	-	100%
Received Home Management Plan	-	-	-	71%
Received Reliever Medication	-	-	-	100%
Use of Medical Imaging				
Combination Abdominal CT Scan	703	0.057	0.135	0.191
Combination Chest CT Scan	550	0.004	0.068	0.054
Follow-up Mammogram/Ultrasound	819	4.5%	7.4%	8.4%
MRI for Low Back Pain	116	26.7%	32%	32.7%
Survey of Patients' Hospital Experiences				
Area Around Room 'Always' Quiet at Night	300+	51%	-	58%
Doctors 'Always' Communicated Well	300+	78%	-	80%
Home Recovery Information Given	300+	80%	-	82%
Hospital Given 9 or 10 on 10 Point Scale	300+	69%	-	67%
Meds 'Always' Explained Before Given	300+	60%	-	60%
Nurses 'Always' Communicated Well	300+	75%	-	76%
Pain 'Always' Well Controlled	300+	69%	-	69%
Room and Bathroom 'Always' Clean	300+	67%	-	71%
Timely Help 'Always' Received	300+	60%	-	64%
Would Definitely Recommend Hospital	300+	71%	-	69%

NOTE: Hospital profiles are in alphabetical order by state, then city, then hospital within the city; Rankings exclude hospitals with less than 25 cases except for patient surveys which excludes hospitals with less than 100 cases; (a) 100–299 cases; (1) The number of cases is too small to be sure how well a hospital is performing; (2) The hospital indicated that the data submitted for this measure were based on a sample of cases; (3) Data was collected during a shorter time period (fewer quarters) than the maximum possible time for this measure; (4) Suppressed for one or more quarters by CMS; (5) No data is available from the hospital for this measure; (6) Fewer than 100 patients completed the HCAHPS survey. Use these rates with caution, as the number of surveys may be too low to reliably assess hospital performance; (7) Survey results are based on less than 12 months of data; (8) Survey results are not available for this reporting period; (9) No or very few patients were eligible for the HCAHPS survey. The scores shown, if any, reflect a very small number of surveys; (10) A state average was not calculated because too few hospitals in the state submitted data; (11) There were discrepancies in the data collection process; Please refer to the User's Guide for a full explanation of data.

Portage Health Hospital

500 Campus Drive Phone: 906-483-1000
Hancock, MI 49930 Fax: 906-483-1521
E-mail: jsbigan@phsys.org
URL: www.portagehealth.org
Type: Acute Care Hospitals Emergency Services: Yes
Ownership: Voluntary Non-Profit - Other Beds: 74

Key Personnel:

CEO/President. . . . . James Bogan
Chief of Medical Staff . . . . David Kass, MD
Pediatric In-Patient Care . . . . Sarah Campbell, MD
Radiology. . . . . Ethelbert Lara, MD
Anesthesiology. . . . . Kirk R Klemme, MD
Emergency Room . . . . Mary Beth Hines
Hemotology Center . . . . Savitri Padmanabhan, MD

Measure	Cases	This Hosp.	State Avg.	U.S. Avg.
Heart Attack Care				
ACE Inhibitor or ARB for LVSD[1]	3	100%	96%	96%
Aspirin at Arrival[1]	12	100%	99%	99%
Aspirin at Discharge[1]	8	100%	99%	98%
Beta Blocker at Discharge[1]	9	100%	99%	98%
Fibrinolytic Medication Timing	0	-	55%	55%
PCI Within 90 Minutes of Arrival	0	-	89%	90%
Smoking Cessation Advice	0	-	100%	99%
Chest Pain/Possible Heart Attack Care				
Aspirin at Arrival	46	100%	94%	95%
Median Time to ECG (minutes)	46	6	10	8
Median Time to Transfer (minutes)[3]	0	-	54	61
Fibrinolytic Medication Timing[1]	4	25%	60%	54%
Heart Failure Care				
ACE Inhibitor or ARB for LVSD[1]	15	100%	95%	94%
Discharge Instructions	47	96%	89%	88%
Evaluation of LVS Function	62	98%	99%	98%
Smoking Cessation Advice[1]	7	86%	99%	98%
Pneumonia Care				
Appropriate Initial Antibiotic	28	89%	94%	92%
Blood Culture Timing	37	95%	96%	96%
Influenza Vaccine[1]	22	86%	91%	91%
Initial Antibiotic Timing	44	100%	96%	95%
Pneumococcal Vaccine	37	92%	93%	93%
Smoking Cessation Advice[1]	15	93%	98%	97%
Surgical Care Improvement Project				
Appropriate VTP Within 24 Hours	64	95%	94%	92%
Appropriate Hair Removal	200	100%	99%	99%
Appropriate Beta Blocker Usage	51	92%	92%	93%
Controlled Postoperative Blood Glucose	0	-	94%	93%
Prophylactic Antibiotic Timing	171	99%	97%	97%
Prophylactic Antibiotic Timing (Outpatient)	29	69%	87%	92%
Prophylactic Antibiotic Selection	173	99%	98%	97%
Prophylactic Antibiotic Select. (Outpatient)	52	88%	92%	94%
Prophylactic Antibiotic Stopped	162	93%	95%	94%
Recommended VTP Ordered	64	98%	95%	94%
Urinary Catheter Removal	40	80%	91%	90%
Children's Asthma Care				
Received Systemic Corticosteroids	-	-	-	100%
Received Home Management Plan	-	-	-	71%
Received Reliever Medication	-	-	-	100%
Use of Medical Imaging				
Combination Abdominal CT Scan	196	0.087	0.135	0.191
Combination Chest CT Scan	153	0.013	0.068	0.054
Follow-up Mammogram/Ultrasound	353	12.2%	7.4%	8.4%
MRI for Low Back Pain	96	30.2%	32%	32.7%
Survey of Patients' Hospital Experiences				
Area Around Room 'Always' Quiet at Night	300+	60%	-	58%
Doctors 'Always' Communicated Well	300+	81%	-	80%
Home Recovery Information Given	300+	83%	-	82%
Hospital Given 9 or 10 on 10 Point Scale	300+	69%	-	67%
Meds 'Always' Explained Before Given	300+	66%	-	60%
Nurses 'Always' Communicated Well	300+	79%	-	76%
Pain 'Always' Well Controlled	300+	70%	-	69%
Room and Bathroom 'Always' Clean	300+	79%	-	71%
Timely Help 'Always' Received	300+	74%	-	64%
Would Definitely Recommend Hospital	300+	76%	-	69%

Harbor Beach Community Hospital

210 S First St Phone: 989-479-3201
Harbor Beach, MI 48441 Fax: 989-479-5000
E-mail: admin@hbch.com
URL: www.hbch.org
Type: Critical Access Hospitals Emergency Services: Yes
Ownership: Voluntary Non-Profit - Private Beds: 61

Key Personnel:

CEO/President. . . . . Edward Gamache
Chief of Medical Staff . . . . Jaime Tan MD

Measure	Cases	This Hosp.	State Avg.	U.S. Avg.
Heart Attack Care				
ACE Inhibitor or ARB for LVSD[5]	0	-	96%	96%
Aspirin at Arrival[5]	0	-	99%	99%
Aspirin at Discharge[5]	0	-	99%	98%
Beta Blocker at Discharge[5]	0	-	99%	98%
Fibrinolytic Medication Timing[5]	0	-	55%	55%
PCI Within 90 Minutes of Arrival[5]	0	-	89%	90%
Smoking Cessation Advice[5]	0	-	100%	99%
Chest Pain/Possible Heart Attack Care				
Aspirin at Arrival	-	-	94%	95%
Median Time to ECG (minutes)	-	-	10	8
Median Time to Transfer (minutes)	-	-	54	61
Fibrinolytic Medication Timing	-	-	60%	54%
Heart Failure Care				
ACE Inhibitor or ARB for LVSD[5]	0	-	95%	94%
Discharge Instructions[5]	0	-	89%	88%
Evaluation of LVS Function[5]	0	-	99%	98%
Smoking Cessation Advice[5]	0	-	99%	98%
Pneumonia Care				
Appropriate Initial Antibiotic[1]	8	75%	94%	92%
Blood Culture Timing[1]	8	62%	96%	96%
Influenza Vaccine[1]	4	100%	91%	91%
Initial Antibiotic Timing[1]	8	88%	96%	95%
Pneumococcal Vaccine[1]	6	83%	93%	93%
Smoking Cessation Advice[1]	2	0%	98%	97%
Surgical Care Improvement Project				
Appropriate VTP Within 24 Hours[5]	0	-	94%	92%
Appropriate Hair Removal[5]	0	-	99%	99%
Appropriate Beta Blocker Usage[5]	0	-	92%	93%
Controlled Postoperative Blood Glucose[5]	0	-	94%	93%
Prophylactic Antibiotic Timing[5]	0	-	97%	97%
Prophylactic Antibiotic Timing (Outpatient)	-	-	87%	92%
Prophylactic Antibiotic Selection[5]	0	-	98%	97%
Prophylactic Antibiotic Select. (Outpatient)	-	-	92%	94%
Prophylactic Antibiotic Stopped[5]	0	-	95%	94%
Recommended VTP Ordered[5]	0	-	95%	94%
Urinary Catheter Removal[5]	0	-	91%	90%
Children's Asthma Care				
Received Systemic Corticosteroids	-	-	-	100%
Received Home Management Plan	-	-	-	71%
Received Reliever Medication	-	-	-	100%
Use of Medical Imaging				
Combination Abdominal CT Scan	-	-	0.135	0.191
Combination Chest CT Scan	-	-	0.068	0.054
Follow-up Mammogram/Ultrasound	-	-	7.4%	8.4%
MRI for Low Back Pain	-	-	32%	32.7%
Survey of Patients' Hospital Experiences				
Area Around Room 'Always' Quiet at Night[6]	<100	61%	-	58%
Doctors 'Always' Communicated Well[6]	<100	89%	-	80%
Home Recovery Information Given[6]	<100	89%	-	82%
Hospital Given 9 or 10 on 10 Point Scale[6]	<100	86%	-	67%
Meds 'Always' Explained Before Given[6]	<100	70%	-	60%
Nurses 'Always' Communicated Well[6]	<100	87%	-	76%
Pain 'Always' Well Controlled[6]	<100	77%	-	69%
Room and Bathroom 'Always' Clean[6]	<100	88%	-	71%
Timely Help 'Always' Received[6]	<100	76%	-	64%
Would Definitely Recommend Hospital	<100	89%	-	69%

Pennock Hospital

1009 W Green St Phone: 269-945-3451
Hastings, MI 49058
E-mail: info@pennockhealth.com
URL: www.pennockhealth.com
Type: Acute Care Hospitals Emergency Services: Yes
Ownership: Voluntary Non-Profit - Other Beds: 88

Key Personnel:

CEO/President. . . . . Sheryl Lewis Blake
Chief of Medical Staff . . . . Matt Garber MD
Infection Control. . . . . Jeanne Pugh
Operating Room. . . . . Diana Overmire
Quality Assurance . . . . Carla Neil
Radiology. . . . . Dennis Bruce
Emergency Room . . . . Natalie Goran
Intensive Care Unit. . . . . Diana Overmire

Measure	Cases	This Hosp.	State Avg.	U.S. Avg.
Heart Attack Care				
ACE Inhibitor or ARB for LVSD[1]	2	100%	96%	96%
Aspirin at Arrival[1]	14	100%	99%	99%
Aspirin at Discharge[1]	6	100%	99%	98%
Beta Blocker at Discharge[1]	8	100%	99%	98%
Fibrinolytic Medication Timing	0	-	55%	55%
PCI Within 90 Minutes of Arrival	0	-	89%	90%
Smoking Cessation Advice[1]	1	100%	100%	99%
Chest Pain/Possible Heart Attack Care				
Aspirin at Arrival	60	97%	94%	95%
Median Time to ECG (minutes)	61	10	10	8
Median Time to Transfer (minutes)[1,3]	5	28	54	61
Fibrinolytic Medication Timing	0	-	60%	54%
Heart Failure Care				
ACE Inhibitor or ARB for LVSD	28	100%	95%	94%
Discharge Instructions	97	98%	89%	88%
Evaluation of LVS Function	107	100%	99%	98%
Smoking Cessation Advice[1]	8	100%	99%	98%
Pneumonia Care				
Appropriate Initial Antibiotic	86	98%	94%	92%
Blood Culture Timing	104	97%	96%	96%
Influenza Vaccine	56	98%	91%	91%
Initial Antibiotic Timing	115	95%	96%	95%
Pneumococcal Vaccine	93	100%	93%	93%
Smoking Cessation Advice	28	100%	98%	97%
Surgical Care Improvement Project				
Appropriate VTP Within 24 Hours[2]	73	85%	94%	92%
Appropriate Hair Removal[2]	266	100%	99%	99%
Appropriate Beta Blocker Usage[2]	59	98%	92%	93%
Controlled Postoperative Blood Glucose[2]	0	-	94%	93%
Prophylactic Antibiotic Timing[2]	202	100%	97%	97%
Prophylactic Antibiotic Timing (Outpatient)	68	88%	87%	92%
Prophylactic Antibiotic Selection[2]	202	97%	98%	97%
Prophylactic Antibiotic Select. (Outpatient)	60	83%	92%	94%
Prophylactic Antibiotic Stopped[2]	201	97%	95%	94%
Recommended VTP Ordered[2]	74	89%	95%	94%
Urinary Catheter Removal[2]	25	84%	91%	90%
Children's Asthma Care				
Received Systemic Corticosteroids	-	-	-	100%
Received Home Management Plan	-	-	-	71%
Received Reliever Medication	-	-	-	100%
Use of Medical Imaging				
Combination Abdominal CT Scan	342	0.064	0.135	0.191
Combination Chest CT Scan	200	0.015	0.068	0.054
Follow-up Mammogram/Ultrasound	695	10.2%	7.4%	8.4%
MRI for Low Back Pain	123	34.1%	32%	32.7%
Survey of Patients' Hospital Experiences				
Area Around Room 'Always' Quiet at Night	300+	57%	-	58%
Doctors 'Always' Communicated Well	300+	83%	-	80%
Home Recovery Information Given	300+	86%	-	82%
Hospital Given 9 or 10 on 10 Point Scale	300+	72%	-	67%
Meds 'Always' Explained Before Given	300+	55%	-	60%
Nurses 'Always' Communicated Well	300+	75%	-	76%
Pain 'Always' Well Controlled	300+	67%	-	69%
Room and Bathroom 'Always' Clean	300+	61%	-	71%
Timely Help 'Always' Received	300+	61%	-	64%
Would Definitely Recommend Hospital	300+	73%	-	69%

NOTE: Hospital profiles are in alphabetical order by state, then city, then hospital within the city; Rankings exclude hospitals with less than 25 cases except for patient surveys which excludes hospitals with less than 100 cases; (a) 100–299 cases; (1) The number of cases is too small to be sure how well a hospital is performing; (2) The hospital indicated that the data submitted for this measure were based on a sample of cases; (3) Data was collected during a shorter time period (fewer quarters) than the maximum possible time for this measure; (4) Suppressed for one or more quarters by CMS; (5) No data is available from the hospital for this measure; (6) Fewer than 100 patients completed the HCAHPS survey. Use these rates with caution, as the number of surveys may be too low to reliably assess hospital performance; (7) Survey results are based on less than 12 months of data; (8) Survey results are not available for this reporting period; (9) No or very few patients were eligible for the HCAHPS survey. The scores shown, if any, reflect a very small number of surveys; (10) A state average was not calculated because too few hospitals in the state submitted data; (11) There were discrepancies in the data collection process; Please refer to the User's Guide for a full explanation of data.

Hillsdale Community Health Center

168 S Howell Street Phone: 517-437-4451
Hillsdale, MI 49242
URL: www.hchc.com
Type: Acute Care Hospitals Emergency Services: Yes
Ownership: Government - Federal Beds: 65

Key Personnel:
Chief of Medical Staff.......... Pat Sudds
Coronary Care.............. Doris Whorley
Infection Control.............. Debra Shatelrow RN
Operating Room............. Denise Baker
Quality Assurance........... Doris Whorley RN
Radiology................... Rocky Saenz
Emergency Room............ Keith Baron MD
Intensive Care Unit........... Janice Gutowski

Measure	Cases	This Hosp.	State Avg.	U.S. Avg.
Heart Attack Care				
ACE Inhibitor or ARB for LVSD[1]	6	33%	96%	96%
Aspirin at Arrival[1]	21	95%	99%	99%
Aspirin at Discharge[1]	14	79%	99%	98%
Beta Blocker at Discharge[1]	17	82%	99%	98%
Fibrinolytic Medication Timing	0	-	55%	55%
PCI Within 90 Minutes of Arrival	0	-	89%	90%
Smoking Cessation Advice[1]	4	100%	100%	99%
Chest Pain/Possible Heart Attack Care				
Aspirin at Arrival	50	96%	94%	95%
Median Time to ECG (minutes)	54	10	10	8
Median Time to Transfer (minutes)[1]	7	60	54	61
Fibrinolytic Medication Timing	0	-	60%	54%
Heart Failure Care				
ACE Inhibitor or ARB for LVSD	38	82%	95%	94%
Discharge Instructions	66	64%	89%	88%
Evaluation of LVS Function	88	90%	99%	98%
Smoking Cessation Advice[1]	12	83%	99%	98%
Pneumonia Care				
Appropriate Initial Antibiotic	114	89%	94%	92%
Blood Culture Timing	111	89%	96%	96%
Influenza Vaccine	90	52%	91%	91%
Initial Antibiotic Timing	134	85%	96%	95%
Pneumococcal Vaccine	128	42%	93%	93%
Smoking Cessation Advice	65	91%	98%	97%
Surgical Care Improvement Project				
Appropriate VTP Within 24 Hours	59	80%	94%	92%
Appropriate Hair Removal	246	99%	99%	99%
Appropriate Beta Blocker Usage	73	79%	92%	93%
Controlled Postoperative Blood Glucose	0	-	94%	93%
Prophylactic Antibiotic Timing	184	79%	97%	97%
Prophylactic Antibiotic Timing (Outpatient)	38	66%	87%	92%
Prophylactic Antibiotic Selection	176	79%	98%	97%
Prophylactic Antibiotic Select. (Outpatient)	32	81%	92%	94%
Prophylactic Antibiotic Stopped	173	83%	95%	94%
Recommended VTP Ordered	60	78%	95%	94%
Urinary Catheter Removal	62	90%	91%	90%
Children's Asthma Care				
Received Systemic Corticosteroids	-	-	-	100%
Received Home Management Plan	-	-	-	71%
Received Reliever Medication	-	-	-	100%
Use of Medical Imaging				
Combination Abdominal CT Scan	326	0.273	0.135	0.191
Combination Chest CT Scan	256	0.055	0.068	0.054
Follow-up Mammogram/Ultrasound	653	10.0%	7.4%	8.4%
MRI for Low Back Pain	142	35.2%	32%	32.7%
Survey of Patients' Hospital Experiences				
Area Around Room 'Always' Quiet at Night	300+	51%	-	58%
Doctors 'Always' Communicated Well	300+	77%	-	80%
Home Recovery Information Given	300+	78%	-	82%
Hospital Given 9 or 10 on 10 Point Scale	300+	58%	-	67%
Meds 'Always' Explained Before Given	300+	57%	-	60%
Nurses 'Always' Communicated Well	300+	74%	-	76%
Pain 'Always' Well Controlled	300+	66%	-	69%
Room and Bathroom 'Always' Clean	300+	73%	-	71%
Timely Help 'Always' Received	300+	62%	-	64%
Would Definitely Recommend Hospital	300+	54%	-	69%

Holland Community Hospital

602 Michigan Ave Phone: 616-392-5141
Holland, MI 49423 Fax: 616-394-3572
E-mail: info@hollandhospital.org
URL: www.hoho.org
Type: Acute Care Hospitals Emergency Services: Yes
Ownership: Voluntary Non-Profit - Private Beds: 205

Key Personnel:
CEO/President............... Dale Sowders
Chief of Medical Staff.......... Anthony Yasick, MD
Infection Control.............. Theresa Ellis, RN
Operating Room............. James S Ceton, RN
Pediatric Ambulatory Care...... Kathy Austin
Quality Assurance............ Laurel Barens
Radiology................... Anthony D Barclay
Patient Relations............ Kathy Henry

Measure	Cases	This Hosp.	State Avg.	U.S. Avg.
Heart Attack Care				
ACE Inhibitor or ARB for LVSD[1]	9	100%	96%	96%
Aspirin at Arrival	105	100%	99%	99%
Aspirin at Discharge	73	100%	99%	98%
Beta Blocker at Discharge	77	100%	99%	98%
Fibrinolytic Medication Timing	0	-	55%	55%
PCI Within 90 Minutes of Arrival	26	96%	89%	90%
Smoking Cessation Advice[1]	19	100%	100%	99%
Chest Pain/Possible Heart Attack Care				
Aspirin at Arrival	36	97%	94%	95%
Median Time to ECG (minutes)	38	9	10	8
Median Time to Transfer (minutes)[3]	0	-	54	61
Fibrinolytic Medication Timing[3]	0	-	60%	54%
Heart Failure Care				
ACE Inhibitor or ARB for LVSD	36	100%	95%	94%
Discharge Instructions	88	92%	89%	88%
Evaluation of LVS Function	120	100%	99%	98%
Smoking Cessation Advice[1]	8	100%	99%	98%
Pneumonia Care				
Appropriate Initial Antibiotic	138	99%	94%	92%
Blood Culture Timing	250	99%	96%	96%
Influenza Vaccine	163	99%	91%	91%
Initial Antibiotic Timing	232	100%	96%	95%
Pneumococcal Vaccine	228	100%	93%	93%
Smoking Cessation Advice	66	100%	98%	97%
Surgical Care Improvement Project				
Appropriate VTP Within 24 Hours[2]	156	99%	94%	92%
Appropriate Hair Removal[2]	654	100%	99%	99%
Appropriate Beta Blocker Usage[2]	160	100%	92%	93%
Controlled Postoperative Blood Glucose[2]	0	-	94%	93%
Prophylactic Antibiotic Timing[2]	500	100%	97%	97%
Prophylactic Antibiotic Timing (Outpatient)	301	100%	87%	92%
Prophylactic Antibiotic Selection[2]	504	99%	98%	97%
Prophylactic Antibiotic Select. (Outpatient)	300	98%	92%	94%
Prophylactic Antibiotic Stopped[2]	490	100%	95%	94%
Recommended VTP Ordered[2]	156	99%	95%	94%
Urinary Catheter Removal[2]	33	97%	91%	90%
Children's Asthma Care				
Received Systemic Corticosteroids	-	-	-	100%
Received Home Management Plan	-	-	-	71%
Received Reliever Medication	-	-	-	100%
Use of Medical Imaging				
Combination Abdominal CT Scan	726	0.079	0.135	0.191
Combination Chest CT Scan	454	0.044	0.068	0.054
Follow-up Mammogram/Ultrasound	1,383	4.3%	7.4%	8.4%
MRI for Low Back Pain	229	40.6%	32%	32.7%
Survey of Patients' Hospital Experiences				
Area Around Room 'Always' Quiet at Night	300+	55%	-	58%
Doctors 'Always' Communicated Well	300+	83%	-	80%
Home Recovery Information Given	300+	90%	-	82%
Hospital Given 9 or 10 on 10 Point Scale	300+	79%	-	67%
Meds 'Always' Explained Before Given	300+	64%	-	60%
Nurses 'Always' Communicated Well	300+	79%	-	76%
Pain 'Always' Well Controlled	300+	70%	-	69%
Room and Bathroom 'Always' Clean	300+	80%	-	71%
Timely Help 'Always' Received	300+	68%	-	64%
Would Definitely Recommend Hospital	300+	80%	-	69%

Saint Joseph Mercy Livingston Hospital

620 Byron Rd Phone: 517-545-6000
Howell, MI 48843 Fax: 517-545-6192
URL: www.sjmh.com
Type: Acute Care Hospitals Emergency Services: Yes
Ownership: Voluntary Non-Profit - Other Beds: 136

Key Personnel:
CEO/President............... Garry Faja
Chief of Medical Staff.......... Charles Kelly, DO
Infection Control.............. Charles Craig, MD
Operating Room............. Joyce Kessler
Quality Assurance............ Peggy Casper
Radiology................... Cheryl Rusk, DO
Emergency Room............ Pat Claffey, RN
Intensive Care Unit........... Fran Rocheleau, RN

Measure	Cases	This Hosp.	State Avg.	U.S. Avg.
Heart Attack Care				
ACE Inhibitor or ARB for LVSD[1]	1	100%	96%	96%
Aspirin at Arrival[1]	13	100%	99%	99%
Aspirin at Discharge[1]	10	90%	99%	98%
Beta Blocker at Discharge[1]	10	90%	99%	98%
Fibrinolytic Medication Timing	0	-	55%	55%
PCI Within 90 Minutes of Arrival	0	-	89%	90%
Smoking Cessation Advice	0	-	100%	99%
Chest Pain/Possible Heart Attack Care				
Aspirin at Arrival	367	75%	94%	95%
Median Time to ECG (minutes)	369	9	10	8
Median Time to Transfer (minutes)[1]	12	66	54	61
Fibrinolytic Medication Timing[1]	1	0%	60%	54%
Heart Failure Care				
ACE Inhibitor or ARB for LVSD	31	97%	95%	94%
Discharge Instructions	96	95%	89%	88%
Evaluation of LVS Function	131	100%	99%	98%
Smoking Cessation Advice[1]	8	100%	99%	98%
Pneumonia Care				
Appropriate Initial Antibiotic	103	89%	94%	92%
Blood Culture Timing	110	95%	96%	96%
Influenza Vaccine	81	91%	91%	91%
Initial Antibiotic Timing	142	96%	96%	95%
Pneumococcal Vaccine	132	89%	93%	93%
Smoking Cessation Advice	28	100%	98%	97%
Surgical Care Improvement Project				
Appropriate VTP Within 24 Hours[2]	93	86%	94%	92%
Appropriate Hair Removal[2]	310	100%	99%	99%
Appropriate Beta Blocker Usage[2]	67	78%	92%	93%
Controlled Postoperative Blood Glucose[2]	0	-	94%	93%
Prophylactic Antibiotic Timing[2]	227	97%	97%	97%
Prophylactic Antibiotic Timing (Outpatient)	96	86%	87%	92%
Prophylactic Antibiotic Selection[2]	227	97%	98%	97%
Prophylactic Antibiotic Select. (Outpatient)	113	95%	92%	94%
Prophylactic Antibiotic Stopped[2]	223	95%	95%	94%
Recommended VTP Ordered[2]	93	87%	95%	94%
Urinary Catheter Removal[2]	108	78%	91%	90%
Children's Asthma Care				
Received Systemic Corticosteroids	-	-	-	100%
Received Home Management Plan	-	-	-	71%
Received Reliever Medication	-	-	-	100%
Use of Medical Imaging				
Combination Abdominal CT Scan	552	0.042	0.135	0.191
Combination Chest CT Scan	233	0.021	0.068	0.054
Follow-up Mammogram/Ultrasound	585	7.2%	7.4%	8.4%
MRI for Low Back Pain	110	28.2%	32%	32.7%
Survey of Patients' Hospital Experiences				
Area Around Room 'Always' Quiet at Night	300+	59%	-	58%
Doctors 'Always' Communicated Well	300+	78%	-	80%
Home Recovery Information Given	300+	89%	-	82%
Hospital Given 9 or 10 on 10 Point Scale	300+	70%	-	67%
Meds 'Always' Explained Before Given	300+	64%	-	60%
Nurses 'Always' Communicated Well	300+	80%	-	76%
Pain 'Always' Well Controlled	300+	73%	-	69%
Room and Bathroom 'Always' Clean	300+	69%	-	71%
Timely Help 'Always' Received	300+	75%	-	64%
Would Definitely Recommend Hospital	300+	72%	-	69%

NOTE: Hospital profiles are in alphabetical order by state, then city, then hospital within the city; Rankings exclude hospitals with less than 25 cases except for patient surveys which excludes hospitals with less than 100 cases; (a) 100–299 cases; (1) The number of cases is too small to be sure how well a hospital is performing; (2) The hospital indicated that the data submitted for this measure were based on a sample of cases; (3) Data was collected during a shorter time period (fewer quarters) than the maximum possible time for this measure; (4) Suppressed for one or more quarters by CMS; (5) No data is available from the hospital for this measure; (6) Fewer than 100 patients completed the HCAHPS survey. Use these rates with caution, as the number of surveys may be too low to reliably assess hospital performance; (7) Survey results are based on less than 12 months of data; (8) Survey results are not available for this reporting period; (9) No or very few patients were eligible for the HCAHPS survey. The scores shown, if any, reflect a very small number of surveys; (10) A state average was not calculated because too few hospitals in the state submitted data; (11) There were discrepancies in the data collection process; Please refer to the User's Guide for a full explanation of data.

Ionia County Memorial Hospital

479 Lafayette Street Phone: 616-527-4200
Ionia, MI 48846 Fax: 616-527-5731
E-mail: ltjalsma@ioniahoapitl.org
URL: www.ioniahospital.org
Type: Critical Access Hospitals Emergency Services: Yes
Ownership: Voluntary Non-Profit - Private Beds: 25

Key Personnel:
CEO/President. . . . . William Roeser
Chief of Medical Staff . . . . Barb Dora, MD
Infection Control. . . . . Cheryl Koon, RN
Operating Room. . . . . Amy B Jentz
Quality Assurance . . . . Barb Dora
Radiology. . . . . Robert Hills
Emergency Room . . . . Dr. Doyle Calley
Patient Relations . . . . Ricki Burk, BS, RN

Measure	Cases	This Hosp.	State Avg.	U.S. Avg.
Heart Attack Care				
ACE Inhibitor or ARB for LVSD[5]	0	-	96%	96%
Aspirin at Arrival[5]	0	-	99%	99%
Aspirin at Discharge[5]	0	-	99%	98%
Beta Blocker at Discharge[5]	0	-	99%	98%
Fibrinolytic Medication Timing[5]	0	-	55%	55%
PCI Within 90 Minutes of Arrival[5]	0	-	89%	90%
Smoking Cessation Advice[5]	0	-	100%	99%
Chest Pain/Possible Heart Attack Care				
Aspirin at Arrival[5]	0	-	94%	95%
Median Time to ECG (minutes)[5]	0	-	10	8
Median Time to Transfer (minutes)[5]	0	-	54	61
Fibrinolytic Medication Timing[5]	0	-	60%	54%
Heart Failure Care				
ACE Inhibitor or ARB for LVSD[1]	4	100%	95%	94%
Discharge Instructions[1]	22	77%	89%	88%
Evaluation of LVS Function[1]	24	96%	99%	98%
Smoking Cessation Advice[1]	5	100%	99%	98%
Pneumonia Care				
Appropriate Initial Antibiotic	31	87%	94%	92%
Blood Culture Timing[1]	23	91%	96%	96%
Influenza Vaccine[1]	12	92%	91%	91%
Initial Antibiotic Timing	29	90%	96%	95%
Pneumococcal Vaccine[1]	23	78%	93%	93%
Smoking Cessation Advice[1]	14	79%	98%	97%
Surgical Care Improvement Project				
Appropriate VTP Within 24 Hours[1]	4	75%	94%	92%
Appropriate Hair Removal[1]	7	86%	99%	99%
Appropriate Beta Blocker Usage[5]	0	-	92%	93%
Controlled Postoperative Blood Glucose	0	-	94%	93%
Prophylactic Antibiotic Timing[1]	1	100%	97%	97%
Prophylactic Antibiotic Timing (Outpatient)[5]	0	-	87%	92%
Prophylactic Antibiotic Selection[1]	1	0%	98%	97%
Prophylactic Antibiotic Select. (Outpatient)[5]	0	-	92%	94%
Prophylactic Antibiotic Stopped[1]	1	100%	95%	94%
Recommended VTP Ordered[1]	4	100%	95%	94%
Urinary Catheter Removal[1]	1	100%	91%	90%
Children's Asthma Care				
Received Systemic Corticosteroids	-	-	-	100%
Received Home Management Plan	-	-	-	71%
Received Reliever Medication	-	-	-	100%
Use of Medical Imaging				
Combination Abdominal CT Scan	164	0.073	0.135	0.191
Combination Chest CT Scan	98	0.204	0.068	0.054
Follow-up Mammogram/Ultrasound	187	10.2%	7.4%	8.4%
MRI for Low Back Pain[1]	32	37.5%	32%	32.7%
Survey of Patients' Hospital Experiences				
Area Around Room 'Always' Quiet at Night[8]	-	-	-	58%
Doctors 'Always' Communicated Well[8]	-	-	-	80%
Home Recovery Information Given[8]	-	-	-	82%
Hospital Given 9 or 10 on 10 Point Scale[8]	-	-	-	67%
Meds 'Always' Explained Before Given[8]	-	-	-	60%
Nurses 'Always' Communicated Well[8]	-	-	-	76%
Pain 'Always' Well Controlled[8]	-	-	-	69%
Room and Bathroom 'Always' Clean[8]	-	-	-	71%
Timely Help 'Always' Received[8]	-	-	-	64%
Would Definitely Recommend Hospital[8]	-	-	-	69%

Dickinson County Memorial Hospital

1721 S Stephenson Ave Phone: 906-774-1313
Iron Mountain, MI 49801 Fax: 906-776-5791
URL: www.dchs.org
Type: Acute Care Hospitals Emergency Services: Yes
Ownership: Government - Local Beds: 96

Key Personnel:
Chief of Medical Staff . . . . Daniel Benishek
Quality Assurance . . . . Mark Rossato

Measure	Cases	This Hosp.	State Avg.	U.S. Avg.
Heart Attack Care				
ACE Inhibitor or ARB for LVSD[1]	2	100%	96%	96%
Aspirin at Arrival	33	100%	99%	99%
Aspirin at Discharge[1]	18	100%	99%	98%
Beta Blocker at Discharge[1]	19	100%	99%	98%
Fibrinolytic Medication Timing	0	-	55%	55%
PCI Within 90 Minutes of Arrival	0	-	89%	90%
Smoking Cessation Advice[1]	3	100%	100%	99%
Chest Pain/Possible Heart Attack Care				
Aspirin at Arrival	94	96%	94%	95%
Median Time to ECG (minutes)	97	10	10	8
Median Time to Transfer (minutes)[1]	1	225	54	61
Fibrinolytic Medication Timing[1]	9	67%	60%	54%
Heart Failure Care				
ACE Inhibitor or ARB for LVSD[1]	13	100%	95%	94%
Discharge Instructions	67	96%	89%	88%
Evaluation of LVS Function	100	99%	99%	98%
Smoking Cessation Advice[1]	14	100%	99%	98%
Pneumonia Care				
Appropriate Initial Antibiotic	73	97%	94%	92%
Blood Culture Timing	86	99%	96%	96%
Influenza Vaccine	62	98%	91%	91%
Initial Antibiotic Timing	90	98%	96%	95%
Pneumococcal Vaccine	90	96%	93%	93%
Smoking Cessation Advice	33	100%	98%	97%
Surgical Care Improvement Project				
Appropriate VTP Within 24 Hours	149	98%	94%	92%
Appropriate Hair Removal	320	100%	99%	99%
Appropriate Beta Blocker Usage	84	98%	92%	93%
Controlled Postoperative Blood Glucose	0	-	94%	93%
Prophylactic Antibiotic Timing	236	99%	97%	97%
Prophylactic Antibiotic Timing (Outpatient)	39	64%	87%	92%
Prophylactic Antibiotic Selection	236	97%	98%	97%
Prophylactic Antibiotic Select. (Outpatient)	27	93%	92%	94%
Prophylactic Antibiotic Stopped	230	97%	95%	94%
Recommended VTP Ordered	149	98%	95%	94%
Urinary Catheter Removal[1]	20	90%	91%	90%
Children's Asthma Care				
Received Systemic Corticosteroids	-	-	-	100%
Received Home Management Plan	-	-	-	71%
Received Reliever Medication	-	-	-	100%
Use of Medical Imaging				
Combination Abdominal CT Scan	464	0.097	0.135	0.191
Combination Chest CT Scan	399	0.013	0.068	0.054
Follow-up Mammogram/Ultrasound	765	6.7%	7.4%	8.4%
MRI for Low Back Pain	204	31.9%	32%	32.7%
Survey of Patients' Hospital Experiences				
Area Around Room 'Always' Quiet at Night	300+	61%	-	58%
Doctors 'Always' Communicated Well	300+	83%	-	80%
Home Recovery Information Given	300+	83%	-	82%
Hospital Given 9 or 10 on 10 Point Scale	300+	64%	-	67%
Meds 'Always' Explained Before Given	300+	62%	-	60%
Nurses 'Always' Communicated Well	300+	78%	-	76%
Pain 'Always' Well Controlled	300+	73%	-	69%
Room and Bathroom 'Always' Clean	300+	84%	-	71%
Timely Help 'Always' Received	300+	69%	-	64%
Would Definitely Recommend Hospital	300+	66%	-	69%

Iron Mountain VA Medical Center

325 East H Street Phone: 906-774-3300
Iron Mountain, MI 49801 Fax: 906-779-3114
Type: Acute Care-Veterans Administration Emergency Services: No
Ownership: Government - Federal Beds: 61

Key Personnel:
Chief of Medical Staff . . . . John Frahm, DO
Operating Room. . . . . Mary L Limback, MD
Quality Assurance . . . . Mary Gagala, RN

Measure	Cases	This Hosp.	State Avg.	U.S. Avg.
Heart Attack Care				
ACE Inhibitor or ARB for LVSD[1]	1	100%	96%	96%
Aspirin at Arrival[1]	3	100%	99%	99%
Aspirin at Discharge[1]	2	100%	99%	98%
Beta Blocker at Discharge[1]	2	100%	99%	98%
Fibrinolytic Medication Timing[1]	1	0%	55%	55%
PCI Within 90 Minutes of Arrival[5]	0	-	89%	90%
Smoking Cessation Advice[5]	0	-	100%	99%
Chest Pain/Possible Heart Attack Care				
Aspirin at Arrival	-	-	94%	95%
Median Time to ECG (minutes)	-	-	10	8
Median Time to Transfer (minutes)	-	-	54	61
Fibrinolytic Medication Timing	-	-	60%	54%
Heart Failure Care				
ACE Inhibitor or ARB for LVSD[1]	19	100%	95%	94%
Discharge Instructions	39	97%	89%	88%
Evaluation of LVS Function	53	98%	99%	98%
Smoking Cessation Advice[1]	7	86%	99%	98%
Pneumonia Care				
Appropriate Initial Antibiotic[1]	20	95%	94%	92%
Blood Culture Timing	27	96%	96%	96%
Influenza Vaccine[1]	14	100%	91%	91%
Initial Antibiotic Timing[1]	2	100%	96%	95%
Pneumococcal Vaccine	30	100%	93%	93%
Smoking Cessation Advice[1]	14	100%	98%	97%
Surgical Care Improvement Project				
Appropriate VTP Within 24 Hours[2,5]	0	-	94%	92%
Appropriate Hair Removal[2,5]	0	-	99%	99%
Appropriate Beta Blocker Usage[2,5]	0	-	92%	93%
Controlled Postoperative Blood Glucose[2,5]	0	-	94%	93%
Prophylactic Antibiotic Timing[5]	0	-	97%	97%
Prophylactic Antibiotic Timing (Outpatient)	-	-	87%	92%
Prophylactic Antibiotic Selection[5]	0	-	98%	97%
Prophylactic Antibiotic Select. (Outpatient)	-	-	92%	94%
Prophylactic Antibiotic Stopped[5]	0	-	95%	94%
Recommended VTP Ordered[2,5]	0	-	95%	94%
Urinary Catheter Removal[2,5]	0	-	91%	90%
Children's Asthma Care				
Received Systemic Corticosteroids	-	-	-	100%
Received Home Management Plan	-	-	-	71%
Received Reliever Medication	-	-	-	100%
Use of Medical Imaging				
Combination Abdominal CT Scan	-	-	0.135	0.191
Combination Chest CT Scan	-	-	0.068	0.054
Follow-up Mammogram/Ultrasound	-	-	7.4%	8.4%
MRI for Low Back Pain	-	-	32%	32.7%
Survey of Patients' Hospital Experiences				
Area Around Room 'Always' Quiet at Night	-	-	-	58%
Doctors 'Always' Communicated Well	-	-	-	80%
Home Recovery Information Given	-	-	-	82%
Hospital Given 9 or 10 on 10 Point Scale	-	-	-	67%
Meds 'Always' Explained Before Given	-	-	-	60%
Nurses 'Always' Communicated Well	-	-	-	76%
Pain 'Always' Well Controlled	-	-	-	69%
Room and Bathroom 'Always' Clean	-	-	-	71%
Timely Help 'Always' Received	-	-	-	64%
Would Definitely Recommend Hospital	-	-	-	69%

NOTE: Hospital profiles are in alphabetical order by state, then city, then hospital name within the city; Rankings exclude hospitals with less than 25 cases except for patient surveys which excludes hospitals with less than 100 cases; (a) 100–299 cases; (1) The number of cases is too small to be sure how well a hospital is performing; (2) The hospital indicated that the data submitted for this measure were based on a sample of cases; (3) Data was collected during a shorter time period (fewer quarters) than the maximum possible time for this measure; (4) Suppressed for one or more quarters by CMS; (5) No data is available from the hospital for this measure; (6) Fewer than 100 patients completed the HCAHPS survey. Use these rates with caution, as the number of surveys may be too low to reliably assess hospital performance; (7) Survey results are based on less than 12 months of data; (8) Survey results are not available for this reporting period; (9) No or very few patients were eligible for the HCAHPS survey. The scores shown, if any, reflect a very small number of surveys; (10) A state average was not calculated because too few hospitals in the state submitted data; (11) There were discrepancies in the data collection process; Please refer to the User's Guide for a full explanation of data.

Northstar Health System

1400 W Ice Lake Road
Iron River, MI 49935
Phone: 906-265-6121
Fax: 906-265-9793
URL: www.icch.org
Type: Critical Access Hospitals
Emergency Services: Yes
Ownership: Voluntary Non-Profit - Other
Beds: 67

Key Personnel:
CEO/President. . . . . David Huff
Chief of Medical Staff . . . . Nase Rizkalla
Infection Control. . . . . Carolyn Dunlap
Operating Room. . . . . Jean Stroud
Quality Assurance . . . . Carolyn Dunlap
Radiology. . . . . Jane Cook
Emergency Room . . . . James Grebner, MD
Intensive Care Unit. . . . . Mary Larson

Measure	Cases	This Hosp.	State Avg.	U.S. Avg.
Heart Attack Care				
ACE Inhibitor or ARB for LVSD[3]	0	-	96%	96%
Aspirin at Arrival[3]	0	-	99%	99%
Aspirin at Discharge[3]	0	-	99%	98%
Beta Blocker at Discharge[3]	0	-	99%	98%
Fibrinolytic Medication Timing[3]	0	-	55%	55%
PCI Within 90 Minutes of Arrival[3]	0	-	89%	90%
Smoking Cessation Advice[3]	0	-	100%	99%
Chest Pain/Possible Heart Attack Care				
Aspirin at Arrival	-	-	94%	95%
Median Time to ECG (minutes)	-	-	10	8
Median Time to Transfer (minutes)	-	-	54	61
Fibrinolytic Medication Timing	-	-	60%	54%
Heart Failure Care				
ACE Inhibitor or ARB for LVSD[1]	10	70%	95%	94%
Discharge Instructions	32	50%	89%	88%
Evaluation of LVS Function	45	80%	99%	98%
Smoking Cessation Advice[1]	6	83%	99%	98%
Pneumonia Care				
Appropriate Initial Antibiotic	28	93%	94%	92%
Blood Culture Timing	77	87%	96%	96%
Influenza Vaccine	68	74%	91%	91%
Initial Antibiotic Timing	78	96%	96%	95%
Pneumococcal Vaccine	93	72%	93%	93%
Smoking Cessation Advice[1]	23	96%	98%	97%
Surgical Care Improvement Project				
Appropriate VTP Within 24 Hours[5]	0	-	94%	92%
Appropriate Hair Removal[5]	0	-	99%	99%
Appropriate Beta Blocker Usage[5]	0	-	92%	93%
Controlled Postoperative Blood Glucose[5]	0	-	94%	93%
Prophylactic Antibiotic Timing[5]	0	-	97%	97%
Prophylactic Antibiotic Timing (Outpatient)	-	-	87%	92%
Prophylactic Antibiotic Selection[5]	0	-	98%	97%
Prophylactic Antibiotic Select. (Outpatient)	-	-	92%	94%
Prophylactic Antibiotic Stopped[5]	0	-	95%	94%
Recommended VTP Ordered[5]	0	-	95%	94%
Urinary Catheter Removal[5]	0	-	91%	90%
Children's Asthma Care				
Received Systemic Corticosteroids	-	-	-	100%
Received Home Management Plan	-	-	-	71%
Received Reliever Medication	-	-	-	100%
Use of Medical Imaging				
Combination Abdominal CT Scan	-	-	0.135	0.191
Combination Chest CT Scan	-	-	0.068	0.054
Follow-up Mammogram/Ultrasound	-	-	7.4%	8.4%
MRI for Low Back Pain	-	-	32%	32.7%
Survey of Patients' Hospital Experiences				
Area Around Room 'Always' Quiet at Night[8]	-	-	-	58%
Doctors 'Always' Communicated Well[8]	-	-	-	80%
Home Recovery Information Given[8]	-	-	-	82%
Hospital Given 9 or 10 on 10 Point Scale[8]	-	-	-	67%
Meds 'Always' Explained Before Given[8]	-	-	-	60%
Nurses 'Always' Communicated Well[8]	-	-	-	76%
Pain 'Always' Well Controlled[8]	-	-	-	69%
Room and Bathroom 'Always' Clean[8]	-	-	-	71%
Timely Help 'Always' Received[8]	-	-	-	64%
Would Definitely Recommend Hospital[8]	-	-	-	69%

Aspirus Grand View Hospital

N10561 Grand View Lane
Ironwood, MI 49938
Phone: 906-932-2525
Fax: 906-932-1921
E-mail: rkimmes@gvhs.org
URL: www.gvhs.org
Type: Critical Access Hospitals
Emergency Services: Yes
Ownership: Voluntary Non-Profit - Other
Beds: 25

Key Personnel:
CEO/President. . . . . David Hartberg
Chief of Medical Staff . . . . Jeffrey Edwards, MD
Infection Control. . . . . Jean Peterson, RN
Operating Room. . . . . Sandra Case, RN
Quality Assurance . . . . Judith Holst
Radiology. . . . . Jorge E Arsuaga
Emergency Room . . . . Curtis Buchheit, RN
Intensive Care Unit. . . . . Julie Monville, RN

Measure	Cases	This Hosp.	State Avg.	U.S. Avg.
Heart Attack Care				
ACE Inhibitor or ARB for LVSD[1]	1	100%	96%	96%
Aspirin at Arrival[1]	9	100%	99%	99%
Aspirin at Discharge[1]	5	100%	99%	98%
Beta Blocker at Discharge[1]	6	100%	99%	98%
Fibrinolytic Medication Timing	0	-	55%	55%
PCI Within 90 Minutes of Arrival	0	-	89%	90%
Smoking Cessation Advice	0	-	100%	99%
Chest Pain/Possible Heart Attack Care				
Aspirin at Arrival	-	-	94%	95%
Median Time to ECG (minutes)	-	-	10	8
Median Time to Transfer (minutes)	-	-	54	61
Fibrinolytic Medication Timing	-	-	60%	54%
Heart Failure Care				
ACE Inhibitor or ARB for LVSD[1]	15	100%	95%	94%
Discharge Instructions[1]	24	100%	89%	88%
Evaluation of LVS Function	40	100%	99%	98%
Smoking Cessation Advice[1]	4	100%	99%	98%
Pneumonia Care				
Appropriate Initial Antibiotic	54	98%	94%	92%
Blood Culture Timing	87	99%	96%	96%
Influenza Vaccine	36	100%	91%	91%
Initial Antibiotic Timing	79	100%	96%	95%
Pneumococcal Vaccine	68	100%	93%	93%
Smoking Cessation Advice[1]	12	100%	98%	97%
Surgical Care Improvement Project				
Appropriate VTP Within 24 Hours[5]	0	-	94%	92%
Appropriate Hair Removal	81	100%	99%	99%
Appropriate Beta Blocker Usage[5]	0	-	92%	93%
Controlled Postoperative Blood Glucose	0	-	94%	93%
Prophylactic Antibiotic Timing	43	100%	97%	97%
Prophylactic Antibiotic Timing (Outpatient)	-	-	87%	92%
Prophylactic Antibiotic Selection	43	98%	98%	97%
Prophylactic Antibiotic Select. (Outpatient)	-	-	92%	94%
Prophylactic Antibiotic Stopped	39	87%	95%	94%
Recommended VTP Ordered[5]	0	-	95%	94%
Urinary Catheter Removal[1]	10	100%	91%	90%
Children's Asthma Care				
Received Systemic Corticosteroids	-	-	-	100%
Received Home Management Plan	-	-	-	71%
Received Reliever Medication	-	-	-	100%
Use of Medical Imaging				
Combination Abdominal CT Scan	-	-	0.135	0.191
Combination Chest CT Scan	-	-	0.068	0.054
Follow-up Mammogram/Ultrasound	-	-	7.4%	8.4%
MRI for Low Back Pain	-	-	32%	32.7%
Survey of Patients' Hospital Experiences				
Area Around Room 'Always' Quiet at Night[8]	-	-	-	58%
Doctors 'Always' Communicated Well[8]	-	-	-	80%
Home Recovery Information Given[8]	-	-	-	82%
Hospital Given 9 or 10 on 10 Point Scale[8]	-	-	-	67%
Meds 'Always' Explained Before Given[8]	-	-	-	60%
Nurses 'Always' Communicated Well[8]	-	-	-	76%
Pain 'Always' Well Controlled[8]	-	-	-	69%
Room and Bathroom 'Always' Clean[8]	-	-	-	71%
Timely Help 'Always' Received[8]	-	-	-	64%
Would Definitely Recommend Hospital[8]	-	-	-	69%

Bell Memorial Hospital

901 Lakeshore Drive
Ishpeming, MI 49849
Phone: 906-486-4431
Fax: 906-485-2136
E-mail: dedwards@bellmi.org
URL: www.bellhospital.org
Type: Critical Access Hospitals
Emergency Services: Yes
Ownership: Voluntary Non-Profit - Private
Beds: 69

Key Personnel:
CEO/President. . . . . Rick Ament
Chief of Medical Staff . . . . Marie Syrjala
Operating Room. . . . . Kim Dunlap
Pediatric In-Patient Care . . . . Dr Kurt Lehmann
Quality Assurance . . . . Teresa Howell RN
Radiology. . . . . Paul Lyle
Hemotology Center . . . . Cathleen Chen MD
Patient Relations . . . . Peg Strickle

Measure	Cases	This Hosp.	State Avg.	U.S. Avg.
Heart Attack Care				
ACE Inhibitor or ARB for LVSD[3]	0	-	96%	96%
Aspirin at Arrival[1,3]	4	100%	99%	99%
Aspirin at Discharge[1,3]	3	67%	99%	98%
Beta Blocker at Discharge[1,3]	3	100%	99%	98%
Fibrinolytic Medication Timing[3]	0	-	55%	55%
PCI Within 90 Minutes of Arrival[3]	0	-	89%	90%
Smoking Cessation Advice[3]	0	-	100%	99%
Chest Pain/Possible Heart Attack Care				
Aspirin at Arrival	-	-	94%	95%
Median Time to ECG (minutes)	-	-	10	8
Median Time to Transfer (minutes)	-	-	54	61
Fibrinolytic Medication Timing	-	-	60%	54%
Heart Failure Care				
ACE Inhibitor or ARB for LVSD[3]	0	-	95%	94%
Discharge Instructions[1,3]	3	0%	89%	88%
Evaluation of LVS Function[1,3]	3	100%	99%	98%
Smoking Cessation Advice[3]	0	-	99%	98%
Pneumonia Care				
Appropriate Initial Antibiotic[1,3]	13	92%	94%	92%
Blood Culture Timing[1,3]	16	88%	96%	96%
Influenza Vaccine[5]	0	-	91%	91%
Initial Antibiotic Timing[1,3]	15	100%	96%	95%
Pneumococcal Vaccine[1,3]	16	69%	93%	93%
Smoking Cessation Advice[1,3]	6	67%	98%	97%
Surgical Care Improvement Project				
Appropriate VTP Within 24 Hours[5]	0	-	94%	92%
Appropriate Hair Removal[5]	0	-	99%	99%
Appropriate Beta Blocker Usage[5]	0	-	92%	93%
Controlled Postoperative Blood Glucose[5]	0	-	94%	93%
Prophylactic Antibiotic Timing[5]	0	-	97%	97%
Prophylactic Antibiotic Timing (Outpatient)	-	-	87%	92%
Prophylactic Antibiotic Selection[5]	0	-	98%	97%
Prophylactic Antibiotic Select. (Outpatient)	-	-	92%	94%
Prophylactic Antibiotic Stopped[5]	0	-	95%	94%
Recommended VTP Ordered[5]	0	-	95%	94%
Urinary Catheter Removal[5]	0	-	91%	90%
Children's Asthma Care				
Received Systemic Corticosteroids	-	-	-	100%
Received Home Management Plan	-	-	-	71%
Received Reliever Medication	-	-	-	100%
Use of Medical Imaging				
Combination Abdominal CT Scan	-	-	0.135	0.191
Combination Chest CT Scan	-	-	0.068	0.054
Follow-up Mammogram/Ultrasound	-	-	7.4%	8.4%
MRI for Low Back Pain	-	-	32%	32.7%
Survey of Patients' Hospital Experiences				
Area Around Room 'Always' Quiet at Night[8]	-	-	-	58%
Doctors 'Always' Communicated Well[8]	-	-	-	80%
Home Recovery Information Given[8]	-	-	-	82%
Hospital Given 9 or 10 on 10 Point Scale[8]	-	-	-	67%
Meds 'Always' Explained Before Given[8]	-	-	-	60%
Nurses 'Always' Communicated Well[8]	-	-	-	76%
Pain 'Always' Well Controlled[8]	-	-	-	69%
Room and Bathroom 'Always' Clean[8]	-	-	-	71%
Timely Help 'Always' Received[8]	-	-	-	64%
Would Definitely Recommend Hospital[8]	-	-	-	69%

NOTE: Hospital profiles are in alphabetical order by state, then city, then hospital within the city; Rankings exclude hospitals with less than 25 cases except for patient surveys which excludes hospitals with less than 100 cases; (a) 100–299 cases; (1) The number of cases is too small to be sure how well a hospital is performing; (2) The hospital indicated that the data submitted for this measure were based on a sample of cases; (3) Data was collected during a shorter time period (fewer quarters) than the maximum possible time for this measure; (4) Suppressed for one or more quarters by CMS; (5) No data is available from the hospital for this measure; (6) Fewer than 100 patients completed the HCAHPS survey. Use these rates with caution, as the number of surveys may be too low to reliably assess hospital performance; (7) Survey results are based on less than 12 months of data; (8) Survey results are not available for this reporting period; (9) No or very few patients were eligible for the HCAHPS survey. The scores shown, if any, reflect a very small number of surveys; (10) A state average was not calculated because too few hospitals in the state submitted data; (11) There were discrepancies in the data collection process; Please refer to the User's Guide for a full explanation of data.

Allegiance Health

205 N East Ave
Jackson, MI 49201
Phone: 517-788-4800
Fax: 517-788-4829
URL: www.footehealth.org
Type: Acute Care Hospitals
Emergency Services: Yes
Ownership: Voluntary Non-Profit - Other
Beds: 411

Key Personnel:
Chief of Medical Staff .... Ray King, MD
Patient Relations .... Jacalyn Liebowitz, RN

Measure	Cases	This Hosp.	State Avg.	U.S. Avg.
Heart Attack Care				
ACE Inhibitor or ARB for LVSD	53	94%	96%	96%
Aspirin at Arrival	354	99%	99%	99%
Aspirin at Discharge	333	99%	99%	98%
Beta Blocker at Discharge	329	99%	99%	98%
Fibrinolytic Medication Timing	0	-	55%	55%
PCI Within 90 Minutes of Arrival	77	99%	89%	90%
Smoking Cessation Advice	108	99%	100%	99%
Chest Pain/Possible Heart Attack Care				
Aspirin at Arrival[1]	8	100%	94%	95%
Median Time to ECG (minutes)[1]	11	6	10	8
Median Time to Transfer (minutes)[5]	0	-	54	61
Fibrinolytic Medication Timing	0	-	60%	54%
Heart Failure Care				
ACE Inhibitor or ARB for LVSD	124	94%	95%	94%
Discharge Instructions	341	87%	89%	88%
Evaluation of LVS Function	430	100%	99%	98%
Smoking Cessation Advice	84	100%	99%	98%
Pneumonia Care				
Appropriate Initial Antibiotic[2]	99	93%	94%	92%
Blood Culture Timing[2]	124	98%	96%	96%
Influenza Vaccine[2]	87	95%	91%	91%
Initial Antibiotic Timing[2]	140	95%	96%	95%
Pneumococcal Vaccine[2]	125	97%	93%	93%
Smoking Cessation Advice[2]	76	97%	98%	97%
Surgical Care Improvement Project				
Appropriate VTP Within 24 Hours[2]	164	95%	94%	92%
Appropriate Hair Removal[2]	619	100%	99%	99%
Appropriate Beta Blocker Usage[2]	267	96%	92%	93%
Controlled Postoperative Blood Glucose[2]	107	94%	94%	93%
Prophylactic Antibiotic Timing[2]	433	97%	97%	97%
Prophylactic Antibiotic Timing (Outpatient)	420	92%	87%	92%
Prophylactic Antibiotic Selection[2]	434	98%	98%	97%
Prophylactic Antibiotic Select. (Outpatient)	408	92%	92%	94%
Prophylactic Antibiotic Stopped[2]	410	98%	95%	94%
Recommended VTP Ordered[2]	164	96%	95%	94%
Urinary Catheter Removal[2]	69	96%	91%	90%
Children's Asthma Care				
Received Systemic Corticosteroids	-	-	-	100%
Received Home Management Plan	-	-	-	71%
Received Reliever Medication	-	-	-	100%
Use of Medical Imaging				
Combination Abdominal CT Scan	1,644	0.060	0.135	0.191
Combination Chest CT Scan	1,117	0.001	0.068	0.054
Follow-up Mammogram/Ultrasound	2,442	3.6%	7.4%	8.4%
MRI for Low Back Pain	423	26.0%	32%	32.7%
Survey of Patients' Hospital Experiences				
Area Around Room 'Always' Quiet at Night	300+	58%	-	58%
Doctors 'Always' Communicated Well	300+	76%	-	80%
Home Recovery Information Given	300+	84%	-	82%
Hospital Given 9 or 10 on 10 Point Scale	300+	66%	-	67%
Meds 'Always' Explained Before Given	300+	60%	-	60%
Nurses 'Always' Communicated Well	300+	77%	-	76%
Pain 'Always' Well Controlled	300+	67%	-	69%
Room and Bathroom 'Always' Clean	300+	69%	-	71%
Timely Help 'Always' Received	300+	67%	-	64%
Would Definitely Recommend Hospital	300+	64%	-	69%

Borgess Medical Center

1521 Gull Road
Kalamazoo, MI 49048
Phone: 269-226-7000
Fax: 269-226-5966
URL: www.borgess.com
Type: Acute Care Hospitals
Emergency Services: Yes
Ownership: Voluntary Non-Profit - Other
Beds: 424

Key Personnel:
CEO/President .... Paul Spaude
Cardiac Laboratory .... Sharon Bedecsll, MD
Chief of Medical Staff .... Dale Rowe, MD
Coronary Care .... Steve Marzloff
Infection Control .... Karen Miller
Operating Room .... Rand O'Leary
Pediatric In-Patient Care .... Kathy Hornbeck, RN
Quality Assurance .... Jan Anderson

Measure	Cases	This Hosp.	State Avg.	U.S. Avg.
Heart Attack Care				
ACE Inhibitor or ARB for LVSD[2]	53	92%	96%	96%
Aspirin at Arrival[2]	98	100%	99%	99%
Aspirin at Discharge[2]	276	99%	99%	98%
Beta Blocker at Discharge[2]	267	99%	99%	98%
Fibrinolytic Medication Timing[2]	0	-	55%	55%
PCI Within 90 Minutes of Arrival[1,2]	17	88%	89%	90%
Smoking Cessation Advice[2]	119	100%	100%	99%
Chest Pain/Possible Heart Attack Care				
Aspirin at Arrival[1,3]	1	100%	94%	95%
Median Time to ECG (minutes)[1,3]	1	10	10	8
Median Time to Transfer (minutes)[5]	0	-	54	61
Fibrinolytic Medication Timing[5]	0	-	60%	54%
Heart Failure Care				
ACE Inhibitor or ARB for LVSD[2]	71	90%	95%	94%
Discharge Instructions[2]	228	83%	89%	88%
Evaluation of LVS Function[2]	279	99%	99%	98%
Smoking Cessation Advice[2]	46	98%	99%	98%
Pneumonia Care				
Appropriate Initial Antibiotic[2]	53	92%	94%	92%
Blood Culture Timing[2]	91	96%	96%	96%
Influenza Vaccine[2]	72	86%	91%	91%
Initial Antibiotic Timing[2]	116	93%	96%	95%
Pneumococcal Vaccine[2]	101	95%	93%	93%
Smoking Cessation Advice[2]	41	98%	98%	97%
Surgical Care Improvement Project				
Appropriate VTP Within 24 Hours[2]	116	93%	94%	92%
Appropriate Hair Removal[2]	567	100%	99%	99%
Appropriate Beta Blocker Usage[2]	206	98%	92%	93%
Controlled Postoperative Blood Glucose[2]	132	96%	94%	93%
Prophylactic Antibiotic Timing[2]	418	97%	97%	97%
Prophylactic Antibiotic Timing (Outpatient)	620	77%	87%	92%
Prophylactic Antibiotic Selection[2]	426	97%	98%	97%
Prophylactic Antibiotic Select. (Outpatient)	598	95%	92%	94%
Prophylactic Antibiotic Stopped[2]	402	97%	95%	94%
Recommended VTP Ordered[2]	116	95%	95%	94%
Urinary Catheter Removal[2]	106	93%	91%	90%
Children's Asthma Care				
Received Systemic Corticosteroids	-	-	-	100%
Received Home Management Plan	-	-	-	71%
Received Reliever Medication	-	-	-	100%
Use of Medical Imaging				
Combination Abdominal CT Scan	1,205	0.157	0.135	0.191
Combination Chest CT Scan	1,005	0.095	0.068	0.054
Follow-up Mammogram/Ultrasound	1,607	10.8%	7.4%	8.4%
MRI for Low Back Pain	469	33.0%	32%	32.7%
Survey of Patients' Hospital Experiences				
Area Around Room 'Always' Quiet at Night	300+	52%	-	58%
Doctors 'Always' Communicated Well	300+	75%	-	80%
Home Recovery Information Given	300+	85%	-	82%
Hospital Given 9 or 10 on 10 Point Scale	300+	67%	-	67%
Meds 'Always' Explained Before Given	300+	56%	-	60%
Nurses 'Always' Communicated Well	300+	71%	-	76%
Pain 'Always' Well Controlled	300+	67%	-	69%
Room and Bathroom 'Always' Clean	300+	67%	-	71%
Timely Help 'Always' Received	300+	52%	-	64%
Would Definitely Recommend Hospital	300+	71%	-	69%

Bronson Methodist Hospital

601 John Street
Kalamazoo, MI 49007
Phone: 269-341-6000
Fax: 269-341-8696
E-mail: bennettk@bronsonhg.org
URL: www.bronsonhealth.com
Type: Acute Care Hospitals
Emergency Services: Yes
Ownership: Voluntary Non-Profit - Private
Beds: 343

Key Personnel:
CEO/President .... Frank J Sardone
Chief of Medical Staff .... Marijo Snyder, MD
Quality Assurance .... Cheryl L Knapp
Ambulatory Care .... Brook Ward
Patient Relations .... Katie Harrelson, RN MSA

Measure	Cases	This Hosp.	State Avg.	U.S. Avg.
Heart Attack Care				
ACE Inhibitor or ARB for LVSD	69	94%	96%	96%
Aspirin at Arrival	278	99%	99%	99%
Aspirin at Discharge	413	99%	99%	98%
Beta Blocker at Discharge	413	99%	99%	98%
Fibrinolytic Medication Timing[1]	1	0%	55%	55%
PCI Within 90 Minutes of Arrival	72	85%	89%	90%
Smoking Cessation Advice	151	100%	100%	99%
Chest Pain/Possible Heart Attack Care				
Aspirin at Arrival[1,3]	4	75%	94%	95%
Median Time to ECG (minutes)[1,3]	4	36	10	8
Median Time to Transfer (minutes)[5]	0	-	54	61
Fibrinolytic Medication Timing[5]	0	-	60%	54%
Heart Failure Care				
ACE Inhibitor or ARB for LVSD	149	98%	95%	94%
Discharge Instructions	497	94%	89%	88%
Evaluation of LVS Function	579	99%	99%	98%
Smoking Cessation Advice	103	100%	99%	98%
Pneumonia Care				
Appropriate Initial Antibiotic	260	94%	94%	92%
Blood Culture Timing	349	92%	96%	96%
Influenza Vaccine	148	95%	91%	91%
Initial Antibiotic Timing	384	95%	96%	95%
Pneumococcal Vaccine	332	90%	93%	93%
Smoking Cessation Advice	188	98%	98%	97%
Surgical Care Improvement Project				
Appropriate VTP Within 24 Hours[2]	384	90%	94%	92%
Appropriate Hair Removal[2]	1,477	100%	99%	99%
Appropriate Beta Blocker Usage[2]	455	98%	92%	93%
Controlled Postoperative Blood Glucose[2]	201	100%	94%	93%
Prophylactic Antibiotic Timing[2]	1,198	97%	97%	97%
Prophylactic Antibiotic Timing (Outpatient)	396	90%	87%	92%
Prophylactic Antibiotic Selection[2]	1,201	98%	98%	97%
Prophylactic Antibiotic Select. (Outpatient)	376	97%	92%	94%
Prophylactic Antibiotic Stopped[2]	1,169	98%	95%	94%
Recommended VTP Ordered[2]	384	96%	95%	94%
Urinary Catheter Removal[2]	336	93%	91%	90%
Children's Asthma Care				
Received Systemic Corticosteroids	87	99%	-	100%
Received Home Management Plan	87	83%	-	71%
Received Reliever Medication	87	99%	-	100%
Use of Medical Imaging				
Combination Abdominal CT Scan	1,162	0.073	0.135	0.191
Combination Chest CT Scan	657	0.003	0.068	0.054
Follow-up Mammogram/Ultrasound	1,020	6.1%	7.4%	8.4%
MRI for Low Back Pain	324	29.6%	32%	32.7%
Survey of Patients' Hospital Experiences				
Area Around Room 'Always' Quiet at Night	300+	58%	-	58%
Doctors 'Always' Communicated Well	300+	80%	-	80%
Home Recovery Information Given	300+	85%	-	82%
Hospital Given 9 or 10 on 10 Point Scale	300+	78%	-	67%
Meds 'Always' Explained Before Given	300+	61%	-	60%
Nurses 'Always' Communicated Well	300+	79%	-	76%
Pain 'Always' Well Controlled	300+	73%	-	69%
Room and Bathroom 'Always' Clean	300+	74%	-	71%
Timely Help 'Always' Received	300+	63%	-	64%
Would Definitely Recommend Hospital	300+	82%	-	69%

NOTE: Hospital profiles are in alphabetical order by state, then city, then hospital within the city; Rankings exclude hospitals with less than 25 cases except for patient surveys which excludes hospitals with less than 100 cases; (a) 100–299 cases; (1) The number of cases is too small to be sure how well a hospital is performing; (2) The hospital indicated that the data submitted for this measure were based on a sample of cases; (3) Data was collected during a shorter time period (fewer quarters) than the maximum possible time for this measure; (4) Suppressed for one or more quarters by CMS; (5) No data is available from the hospital for this measure; (6) Fewer than 100 patients completed the HCAHPS survey. Use these rates with caution, as the number of surveys may be too low to reliably assess hospital performance; (7) Survey results are based on less than 12 months of data; (8) Survey results are not available for this reporting period; (9) No or very few patients were eligible for the HCAHPS survey. The scores shown, if any, reflect a very small number of surveys; (10) A state average was not calculated because too few hospitals in the state submitted data; (11) There were discrepancies in the data collection process; Please refer to the User's Guide for a full explanation of data.

Baraga County Memorial Hospital

770 N Main St — Phone: 906-524-3300
L'Anse, MI 49946 — Fax: 906-524-5466
E-mail: flozier@bcmh.org
URL: www.bcmh.org
Type: Critical Access Hospitals — Emergency Services: Yes
Ownership: Government - Local — Beds: 44

Key Personnel:

CEO/President. . . . . John Tembreull
Chief of Medical Staff . . . . Craig Vickstrom, MD
Infection Control. . . . . Andrea Uren, RN
Operating Room. . . . . Mary Grondin, RN
Radiology. . . . . Dean Jackson, RT
Ambulatory Care . . . . Mary Grondin, RN
Anesthesiology. . . . . Jerry Hill, CRNA

Measure	Cases	This Hosp.	State Avg.	U.S. Avg.
Heart Attack Care				
ACE Inhibitor or ARB for LVSD[5]	0	-	96%	96%
Aspirin at Arrival[5]	0	-	99%	99%
Aspirin at Discharge[5]	0	-	99%	98%
Beta Blocker at Discharge[5]	0	-	99%	98%
Fibrinolytic Medication Timing[5]	0	-	55%	55%
PCI Within 90 Minutes of Arrival[5]	0	-	89%	90%
Smoking Cessation Advice[5]	0	-	100%	99%
Chest Pain/Possible Heart Attack Care				
Aspirin at Arrival	-	-	94%	95%
Median Time to ECG (minutes)	-	-	10	8
Median Time to Transfer (minutes)	-	-	54	61
Fibrinolytic Medication Timing	-	-	60%	54%
Heart Failure Care				
ACE Inhibitor or ARB for LVSD[5]	0	-	95%	94%
Discharge Instructions[5]	0	-	89%	88%
Evaluation of LVS Function[5]	0	-	99%	98%
Smoking Cessation Advice[5]	0	-	99%	98%
Pneumonia Care				
Appropriate Initial Antibiotic[5]	0	-	94%	92%
Blood Culture Timing[5]	0	-	96%	96%
Influenza Vaccine[5]	0	-	91%	91%
Initial Antibiotic Timing[5]	0	-	96%	95%
Pneumococcal Vaccine[5]	0	-	93%	93%
Smoking Cessation Advice[5]	0	-	98%	97%
Surgical Care Improvement Project				
Appropriate VTP Within 24 Hours[5]	0	-	94%	92%
Appropriate Hair Removal[5]	0	-	99%	99%
Appropriate Beta Blocker Usage[5]	0	-	92%	93%
Controlled Postoperative Blood Glucose[5]	0	-	94%	93%
Prophylactic Antibiotic Timing[5]	0	-	97%	97%
Prophylactic Antibiotic Timing (Outpatient)	-	-	87%	92%
Prophylactic Antibiotic Selection[5]	0	-	98%	97%
Prophylactic Antibiotic Select. (Outpatient)	-	-	92%	94%
Prophylactic Antibiotic Stopped[5]	0	-	95%	94%
Recommended VTP Ordered[5]	0	-	95%	94%
Urinary Catheter Removal[5]	0	-	91%	90%
Children's Asthma Care				
Received Systemic Corticosteroids	-	-	-	100%
Received Home Management Plan	-	-	-	71%
Received Reliever Medication	-	-	-	100%
Use of Medical Imaging				
Combination Abdominal CT Scan	-	-	0.135	0.191
Combination Chest CT Scan	-	-	0.068	0.054
Follow-up Mammogram/Ultrasound	-	-	7.4%	8.4%
MRI for Low Back Pain	-	-	32%	32.7%
Survey of Patients' Hospital Experiences				
Area Around Room 'Always' Quiet at Night[8]	-	-	-	58%
Doctors 'Always' Communicated Well[8]	-	-	-	80%
Home Recovery Information Given[8]	-	-	-	82%
Hospital Given 9 or 10 on 10 Point Scale[8]	-	-	-	67%
Meds 'Always' Explained Before Given[8]	-	-	-	60%
Nurses 'Always' Communicated Well[8]	-	-	-	76%
Pain 'Always' Well Controlled[8]	-	-	-	69%
Room and Bathroom 'Always' Clean[8]	-	-	-	71%
Timely Help 'Always' Received[8]	-	-	-	64%
Would Definitely Recommend Hospital[8]	-	-	-	69%

Spectrum Health United Memorial - Kelsey Campus

418 Washington — Phone: 989-352-7211
Lakeview, MI 48850 — Fax: 616-754-5054
Type: Critical Access Hospitals — Emergency Services: Yes
Ownership: Voluntary Non-Profit - Other — Beds: 94

Key Personnel:

CEO/President. . . . . Ken Cegner
Chief of Medical Staff . . . . M Dewys
Quality Assurance . . . . Etta Barrera

Measure	Cases	This Hosp.	State Avg.	U.S. Avg.
Heart Attack Care				
ACE Inhibitor or ARB for LVSD[3]	0	-	96%	96%
Aspirin at Arrival[1,3]	1	100%	99%	99%
Aspirin at Discharge[3]	0	-	99%	98%
Beta Blocker at Discharge[1,3]	1	100%	99%	98%
Fibrinolytic Medication Timing[3]	0	-	55%	55%
PCI Within 90 Minutes of Arrival[3]	0	-	89%	90%
Smoking Cessation Advice[3]	0	-	100%	99%
Chest Pain/Possible Heart Attack Care				
Aspirin at Arrival	68	100%	94%	95%
Median Time to ECG (minutes)	73	9	10	8
Median Time to Transfer (minutes)[1,3]	4	28	54	61
Fibrinolytic Medication Timing[1]	1	0%	60%	54%
Heart Failure Care				
ACE Inhibitor or ARB for LVSD[1]	5	60%	95%	94%
Discharge Instructions[1]	12	92%	89%	88%
Evaluation of LVS Function[1]	17	100%	99%	98%
Smoking Cessation Advice[1]	4	100%	99%	98%
Pneumonia Care				
Appropriate Initial Antibiotic	26	100%	94%	92%
Blood Culture Timing	27	100%	96%	96%
Influenza Vaccine[1]	11	100%	91%	91%
Initial Antibiotic Timing[1]	24	100%	96%	95%
Pneumococcal Vaccine[1]	24	100%	93%	93%
Smoking Cessation Advice[1]	11	100%	98%	97%
Surgical Care Improvement Project				
Appropriate VTP Within 24 Hours[5]	0	-	94%	92%
Appropriate Hair Removal[5]	0	-	99%	99%
Appropriate Beta Blocker Usage[5]	0	-	92%	93%
Controlled Postoperative Blood Glucose[5]	0	-	94%	93%
Prophylactic Antibiotic Timing[5]	0	-	97%	97%
Prophylactic Antibiotic Timing (Outpatient)	0	-	87%	92%
Prophylactic Antibiotic Selection[5]	0	-	98%	97%
Prophylactic Antibiotic Select. (Outpatient)[1]	9	100%	92%	94%
Prophylactic Antibiotic Stopped[5]	0	-	95%	94%
Recommended VTP Ordered[5]	0	-	95%	94%
Urinary Catheter Removal[5]	0	-	91%	90%
Children's Asthma Care				
Received Systemic Corticosteroids	-	-	-	100%
Received Home Management Plan	-	-	-	71%
Received Reliever Medication	-	-	-	100%
Use of Medical Imaging				
Combination Abdominal CT Scan	91	0.044	0.135	0.191
Combination Chest CT Scan	58	0.034	0.068	0.054
Follow-up Mammogram/Ultrasound	194	3.1%	7.4%	8.4%
MRI for Low Back Pain[5]	0	-	32%	32.7%
Survey of Patients' Hospital Experiences				
Area Around Room 'Always' Quiet at Night	(a)	60%	-	58%
Doctors 'Always' Communicated Well	(a)	78%	-	80%
Home Recovery Information Given	(a)	82%	-	82%
Hospital Given 9 or 10 on 10 Point Scale	(a)	80%	-	67%
Meds 'Always' Explained Before Given	(a)	69%	-	60%
Nurses 'Always' Communicated Well	(a)	88%	-	76%
Pain 'Always' Well Controlled	(a)	78%	-	69%
Room and Bathroom 'Always' Clean	(a)	92%	-	71%
Timely Help 'Always' Received	(a)	83%	-	64%
Would Definitely Recommend Hospital	(a)	80%	-	69%

Edward W Sparrow Hospital

1215 E Michigan Avenue — Phone: 517-364-5000
Lansing, MI 48912 — Fax: 517-364-5050
URL: www.sparrow.org
Type: Acute Care Hospitals — Emergency Services: Yes
Ownership: Voluntary Non-Profit - Other — Beds: 535

Key Personnel:

CEO/President. . . . . Joe Damore
Infection Control. . . . . John Dyke, MD
Operating Room. . . . . Phyllis Kik, RN
Quality Assurance . . . . John Dyke

Measure	Cases	This Hosp.	State Avg.	U.S. Avg.
Heart Attack Care				
ACE Inhibitor or ARB for LVSD	70	99%	96%	96%
Aspirin at Arrival	266	99%	99%	99%
Aspirin at Discharge	410	100%	99%	98%
Beta Blocker at Discharge	403	100%	99%	98%
Fibrinolytic Medication Timing	0	-	55%	55%
PCI Within 90 Minutes of Arrival	36	81%	89%	90%
Smoking Cessation Advice	146	100%	100%	99%
Chest Pain/Possible Heart Attack Care				
Aspirin at Arrival[1,3]	3	67%	94%	95%
Median Time to ECG (minutes)[1,3]	3	18	10	8
Median Time to Transfer (minutes)[5]	0	-	54	61
Fibrinolytic Medication Timing[5]	0	-	60%	54%
Heart Failure Care				
ACE Inhibitor or ARB for LVSD	191	95%	95%	94%
Discharge Instructions	467	80%	89%	88%
Evaluation of LVS Function	559	98%	99%	98%
Smoking Cessation Advice	120	100%	99%	98%
Pneumonia Care				
Appropriate Initial Antibiotic	305	93%	94%	92%
Blood Culture Timing	404	94%	96%	96%
Influenza Vaccine	366	85%	91%	91%
Initial Antibiotic Timing	500	93%	96%	95%
Pneumococcal Vaccine	436	87%	93%	93%
Smoking Cessation Advice	222	100%	98%	97%
Surgical Care Improvement Project				
Appropriate VTP Within 24 Hours[2]	442	87%	94%	92%
Appropriate Hair Removal[2]	1,697	98%	99%	99%
Appropriate Beta Blocker Usage[2]	416	91%	92%	93%
Controlled Postoperative Blood Glucose[2]	187	89%	94%	93%
Prophylactic Antibiotic Timing[2]	1,370	92%	97%	97%
Prophylactic Antibiotic Timing (Outpatient)	599	87%	87%	92%
Prophylactic Antibiotic Selection[2]	1,383	97%	98%	97%
Prophylactic Antibiotic Select. (Outpatient)	581	88%	92%	94%
Prophylactic Antibiotic Stopped[2]	1,333	96%	95%	94%
Recommended VTP Ordered[2]	442	94%	95%	94%
Urinary Catheter Removal[2]	204	81%	91%	90%
Children's Asthma Care				
Received Systemic Corticosteroids	-	-	-	100%
Received Home Management Plan	-	-	-	71%
Received Reliever Medication	-	-	-	100%
Use of Medical Imaging				
Combination Abdominal CT Scan	1,265	0.079	0.135	0.191
Combination Chest CT Scan	979	0.002	0.068	0.054
Follow-up Mammogram/Ultrasound	1,194	4.8%	7.4%	8.4%
MRI for Low Back Pain[5]	0	-	32%	32.7%
Survey of Patients' Hospital Experiences				
Area Around Room 'Always' Quiet at Night	300+	48%	-	58%
Doctors 'Always' Communicated Well	300+	74%	-	80%
Home Recovery Information Given	300+	86%	-	82%
Hospital Given 9 or 10 on 10 Point Scale	300+	67%	-	67%
Meds 'Always' Explained Before Given	300+	61%	-	60%
Nurses 'Always' Communicated Well	300+	77%	-	76%
Pain 'Always' Well Controlled	300+	71%	-	69%
Room and Bathroom 'Always' Clean	300+	65%	-	71%
Timely Help 'Always' Received	300+	60%	-	64%
Would Definitely Recommend Hospital	300+	74%	-	69%

NOTE: Hospital profiles are in alphabetical order by state, then city, then hospital within the city; Rankings exclude hospitals with less than 25 cases except for patient surveys which excludes hospitals with less than 100 cases; (a) 100–299 cases; (1) The number of cases is too small to be sure how well a hospital is performing; (2) The hospital indicated that the data submitted for this measure were based on a sample of cases; (3) Data was collected during a shorter time period (fewer quarters) than the maximum possible time for this measure; (4) Suppressed for one or more quarters by CMS; (5) No data is available from the hospital for this measure; (6) Fewer than 100 patients completed the HCAHPS survey. Use these rates with caution, as the number of surveys may be too low to reliably assess hospital performance; (7) Survey results are based on less than 12 months of data; (8) Survey results are not available for this reporting period; (9) No or very few patients were eligible for the HCAHPS survey. The scores shown, if any, reflect a very small number of surveys; (10) A state average was not calculated because too few hospitals in the state submitted data; (11) There were discrepancies in the data collection process; Please refer to the User's Guide for a full explanation of data.

Ingham Regional Medical Center

401 W Greenlawn Ave Phone: 517-975-6000
Lansing, MI 48910
Type: Acute Care Hospitals Emergency Services: Yes
Ownership: Voluntary Non-Profit - Private
Key Personnel:
Infection Control. . . . . Theresa Larsen
Quality Assurance . . . . Theresa Larsen

Measure	Cases	This Hosp.	State Avg.	U.S. Avg.
Heart Attack Care				
ACE Inhibitor or ARB for LVSD	86	87%	96%	96%
Aspirin at Arrival	226	97%	99%	99%
Aspirin at Discharge	321	98%	99%	98%
Beta Blocker at Discharge	313	99%	99%	98%
Fibrinolytic Medication Timing	0	-	55%	55%
PCI Within 90 Minutes of Arrival	37	89%	89%	90%
Smoking Cessation Advice	121	98%	100%	99%
Chest Pain/Possible Heart Attack Care				
Aspirin at Arrival[1]	2	100%	94%	95%
Median Time to ECG (minutes)[1]	2	23	10	8
Median Time to Transfer (minutes)[5]	0	-	54	61
Fibrinolytic Medication Timing[5]	0	-	60%	54%
Heart Failure Care				
ACE Inhibitor or ARB for LVSD	190	83%	95%	94%
Discharge Instructions	463	92%	89%	88%
Evaluation of LVS Function	516	97%	99%	98%
Smoking Cessation Advice	79	100%	99%	98%
Pneumonia Care				
Appropriate Initial Antibiotic	233	90%	94%	92%
Blood Culture Timing	196	84%	96%	96%
Influenza Vaccine	166	87%	91%	91%
Initial Antibiotic Timing	274	92%	96%	95%
Pneumococcal Vaccine	238	92%	93%	93%
Smoking Cessation Advice	122	99%	98%	97%
Surgical Care Improvement Project				
Appropriate VTP Within 24 Hours[2]	190	88%	94%	92%
Appropriate Hair Removal[2]	1,240	100%	99%	99%
Appropriate Beta Blocker Usage[2]	380	91%	92%	93%
Controlled Postoperative Blood Glucose[2]	240	85%	94%	93%
Prophylactic Antibiotic Timing[2]	957	97%	97%	97%
Prophylactic Antibiotic Timing (Outpatient)	574	79%	87%	92%
Prophylactic Antibiotic Selection[2]	969	93%	98%	97%
Prophylactic Antibiotic Select. (Outpatient)	547	90%	92%	94%
Prophylactic Antibiotic Stopped[2]	944	93%	95%	94%
Recommended VTP Ordered[2]	190	92%	95%	94%
Urinary Catheter Removal[2]	171	80%	91%	90%
Children's Asthma Care				
Received Systemic Corticosteroids	-	-	-	100%
Received Home Management Plan	-	-	-	71%
Received Reliever Medication	-	-	-	100%
Use of Medical Imaging				
Combination Abdominal CT Scan	904	0.157	0.135	0.191
Combination Chest CT Scan	555	0.032	0.068	0.054
Follow-up Mammogram/Ultrasound	911	2.7%	7.4%	8.4%
MRI for Low Back Pain	170	30.0%	32%	32.7%
Survey of Patients' Hospital Experiences				
Area Around Room 'Always' Quiet at Night	300+	49%	-	58%
Doctors 'Always' Communicated Well	300+	77%	-	80%
Home Recovery Information Given	300+	84%	-	82%
Hospital Given 9 or 10 on 10 Point Scale	300+	63%	-	67%
Meds 'Always' Explained Before Given	300+	54%	-	60%
Nurses 'Always' Communicated Well	300+	74%	-	76%
Pain 'Always' Well Controlled	300+	64%	-	69%
Room and Bathroom 'Always' Clean	300+	68%	-	71%
Timely Help 'Always' Received	300+	58%	-	64%
Would Definitely Recommend Hospital	300+	70%	-	69%

Lapeer Regional Medical Center

1375 N Main St Phone: 810-667-5500
Lapeer, MI 48446 Fax: 810-667-5582
URL: www.lapeerregional.org
Type: Acute Care Hospitals Emergency Services: No
Ownership: Voluntary Non-Profit - Private Beds: 185
Key Personnel:
CEO/President. . . . . Barton Buxton, EdD
Chief of Medical Staff. . . . . Darlin David, MD
Infection Control. . . . . Florence Elston, RN
Operating Room. . . . . Robert M Stenz, RN
Pediatric Ambulatory Care . . . . . . Mark Braniecki, DO
Pediatric In-Patient Care . . . . . . Mark Braniecki, DO
Quality Assurance . . . . Terri Capdeville
Radiology. . . . . Richard F Grzybowski, DO

Measure	Cases	This Hosp.	State Avg.	U.S. Avg.
Heart Attack Care				
ACE Inhibitor or ARB for LVSD[1]	9	56%	96%	96%
Aspirin at Arrival	59	88%	99%	99%
Aspirin at Discharge	32	84%	99%	98%
Beta Blocker at Discharge	33	94%	99%	98%
Fibrinolytic Medication Timing	0	-	55%	55%
PCI Within 90 Minutes of Arrival	0	-	89%	90%
Smoking Cessation Advice[1]	4	100%	100%	99%
Chest Pain/Possible Heart Attack Care				
Aspirin at Arrival	77	97%	94%	95%
Median Time to ECG (minutes)	78	3	10	8
Median Time to Transfer (minutes)	32	35	54	61
Fibrinolytic Medication Timing	0	-	60%	54%
Heart Failure Care				
ACE Inhibitor or ARB for LVSD	45	93%	95%	94%
Discharge Instructions	155	81%	89%	88%
Evaluation of LVS Function	193	98%	99%	98%
Smoking Cessation Advice[1]	18	100%	99%	98%
Pneumonia Care				
Appropriate Initial Antibiotic	190	92%	94%	92%
Blood Culture Timing	252	100%	96%	96%
Influenza Vaccine	127	98%	91%	91%
Initial Antibiotic Timing	231	97%	96%	95%
Pneumococcal Vaccine	206	98%	93%	93%
Smoking Cessation Advice	65	98%	98%	97%
Surgical Care Improvement Project				
Appropriate VTP Within 24 Hours[2]	128	97%	94%	92%
Appropriate Hair Removal[2]	517	100%	99%	99%
Appropriate Beta Blocker Usage[2]	158	97%	92%	93%
Controlled Postoperative Blood Glucose[2]	0	-	94%	93%
Prophylactic Antibiotic Timing[2]	396	99%	97%	97%
Prophylactic Antibiotic Timing (Outpatient)	81	96%	87%	92%
Prophylactic Antibiotic Selection[2]	398	100%	98%	97%
Prophylactic Antibiotic Select. (Outpatient)	79	97%	92%	94%
Prophylactic Antibiotic Stopped[2]	386	97%	95%	94%
Recommended VTP Ordered[2]	128	98%	95%	94%
Urinary Catheter Removal[1,2]	1	100%	91%	90%
Children's Asthma Care				
Received Systemic Corticosteroids	-	-	-	100%
Received Home Management Plan	-	-	-	71%
Received Reliever Medication	-	-	-	100%
Use of Medical Imaging				
Combination Abdominal CT Scan	454	0.097	0.135	0.191
Combination Chest CT Scan	358	0.006	0.068	0.054
Follow-up Mammogram/Ultrasound[5]	0	-	7.4%	8.4%
MRI for Low Back Pain	193	34.7%	32%	32.7%
Survey of Patients' Hospital Experiences				
Area Around Room 'Always' Quiet at Night	300+	47%	-	58%
Doctors 'Always' Communicated Well	300+	73%	-	80%
Home Recovery Information Given	300+	80%	-	82%
Hospital Given 9 or 10 on 10 Point Scale	300+	59%	-	67%
Meds 'Always' Explained Before Given	300+	60%	-	60%
Nurses 'Always' Communicated Well	300+	72%	-	76%
Pain 'Always' Well Controlled	300+	67%	-	69%
Room and Bathroom 'Always' Clean	300+	73%	-	71%
Timely Help 'Always' Received	300+	57%	-	64%
Would Definitely Recommend Hospital	300+	58%	-	69%

Saint Mary Mercy Hospital

36475 Five Mile Road Phone: 734-655-4800
Livonia, MI 48154 Fax: 734-591-3854
URL: www.stmarymercy.org
Type: Acute Care Hospitals Emergency Services: Yes
Ownership: Voluntary Non-Profit - Church Beds: 304
Key Personnel:
CEO/President. . . . . David Spivey
Chief of Medical Staff. . . . . Prasad Mikkilineni, MD
Coronary Care . . . . Butchi B Paidipaty
Infection Control. . . . . Jennifer L Furman
Quality Assurance . . . . Lucy Caramanna
Radiology. . . . . Christopher Ess, MD

Measure	Cases	This Hosp.	State Avg.	U.S. Avg.
Heart Attack Care				
ACE Inhibitor or ARB for LVSD	43	95%	96%	96%
Aspirin at Arrival	253	99%	99%	99%
Aspirin at Discharge	170	95%	99%	98%
Beta Blocker at Discharge	188	99%	99%	98%
Fibrinolytic Medication Timing	0	-	55%	55%
PCI Within 90 Minutes of Arrival	64	89%	89%	90%
Smoking Cessation Advice	33	100%	100%	99%
Chest Pain/Possible Heart Attack Care				
Aspirin at Arrival	124	89%	94%	95%
Median Time to ECG (minutes)	129	10	10	8
Median Time to Transfer (minutes)[5]	0	-	54	61
Fibrinolytic Medication Timing	0	-	60%	54%
Heart Failure Care				
ACE Inhibitor or ARB for LVSD	146	92%	95%	94%
Discharge Instructions	353	96%	89%	88%
Evaluation of LVS Function	517	100%	99%	98%
Smoking Cessation Advice	44	100%	99%	98%
Pneumonia Care				
Appropriate Initial Antibiotic	205	91%	94%	92%
Blood Culture Timing	313	98%	96%	96%
Influenza Vaccine	266	94%	91%	91%
Initial Antibiotic Timing	433	97%	96%	95%
Pneumococcal Vaccine	439	95%	93%	93%
Smoking Cessation Advice	75	100%	98%	97%
Surgical Care Improvement Project				
Appropriate VTP Within 24 Hours	364	90%	94%	92%
Appropriate Hair Removal	898	100%	99%	99%
Appropriate Beta Blocker Usage	264	91%	92%	93%
Controlled Postoperative Blood Glucose[1]	2	100%	94%	93%
Prophylactic Antibiotic Timing	520	96%	97%	97%
Prophylactic Antibiotic Timing (Outpatient)	253	92%	87%	92%
Prophylactic Antibiotic Selection	524	99%	98%	97%
Prophylactic Antibiotic Select. (Outpatient)	243	95%	92%	94%
Prophylactic Antibiotic Stopped	504	95%	95%	94%
Recommended VTP Ordered	365	92%	95%	94%
Urinary Catheter Removal	221	88%	91%	90%
Children's Asthma Care				
Received Systemic Corticosteroids	-	-	-	100%
Received Home Management Plan	-	-	-	71%
Received Reliever Medication	-	-	-	100%
Use of Medical Imaging				
Combination Abdominal CT Scan	1,108	0.463	0.135	0.191
Combination Chest CT Scan	1,222	0.370	0.068	0.054
Follow-up Mammogram/Ultrasound	1,401	12.4%	7.4%	8.4%
MRI for Low Back Pain	258	24.8%	32%	32.7%
Survey of Patients' Hospital Experiences				
Area Around Room 'Always' Quiet at Night	300+	42%	-	58%
Doctors 'Always' Communicated Well	300+	76%	-	80%
Home Recovery Information Given	300+	82%	-	82%
Hospital Given 9 or 10 on 10 Point Scale	300+	62%	-	67%
Meds 'Always' Explained Before Given	300+	53%	-	60%
Nurses 'Always' Communicated Well	300+	74%	-	76%
Pain 'Always' Well Controlled	300+	68%	-	69%
Room and Bathroom 'Always' Clean	300+	57%	-	71%
Timely Help 'Always' Received	300+	57%	-	64%
Would Definitely Recommend Hospital	300+	64%	-	69%

NOTE: Hospital profiles are in alphabetical order by state, then city, then hospital within the city; Rankings exclude hospitals with less than 25 cases except for patient surveys which excludes hospitals with less than 100 cases; (a) 100–299 cases; (1) The number of cases is too small to be sure how well a hospital is performing; (2) The hospital indicated that the data submitted for this measure were based on a sample of cases; (3) Data was collected during a shorter time period (fewer quarters) than the maximum possible time for this measure; (4) Suppressed for one or more quarters by CMS; (5) No data is available from the hospital for this measure; (6) Fewer than 100 patients completed the HCAHPS survey. Use these rates with caution, as the number of surveys may be too low to reliably assess hospital performance; (7) Survey results are based on less than 12 months of data; (8) Survey results are not available for this reporting period; (9) No or very few patients were eligible for the HCAHPS survey. The scores shown, if any, reflect a very small number of surveys; (10) A state average was not calculated because too few hospitals in the state submitted data; (11) There were discrepancies in the data collection process; Please refer to the User's Guide for a full explanation of data.

Memorial Medical Center of West Michigan

1 N Atkinson Drive — Phone: 231-843-2591
Ludington, MI 49431 — Fax: 231-845-1732
E-mail: bobm@mmcwm.com
URL: www.mmcwm.com
Type: Acute Care Hospitals — Emergency Services: Yes
Ownership: Voluntary Non-Profit - Other

Key Personnel:
CEO/President. . . . . Mark Vipperman, FACHE
Chief of Medical Staff. . . . . Allan Nelson, MD
Emergency Room . . . . Steven Strbick, DO
Patient Relations . . . . Helen Johnson, RN MSN

Measure	Cases	This Hosp.	State Avg.	U.S. Avg.
Heart Attack Care				
ACE Inhibitor or ARB for LVSD[1]	2	100%	96%	96%
Aspirin at Arrival[1]	12	100%	99%	99%
Aspirin at Discharge[1]	5	100%	99%	98%
Beta Blocker at Discharge[1]	5	100%	99%	98%
Fibrinolytic Medication Timing	0	-	55%	55%
PCI Within 90 Minutes of Arrival	0	-	89%	90%
Smoking Cessation Advice	0	-	100%	99%
Chest Pain/Possible Heart Attack Care				
Aspirin at Arrival	78	99%	94%	95%
Median Time to ECG (minutes)	80	8	10	8
Median Time to Transfer (minutes)[1]	4	54	54	61
Fibrinolytic Medication Timing[1]	9	56%	60%	54%
Heart Failure Care				
ACE Inhibitor or ARB for LVSD[1]	16	88%	95%	94%
Discharge Instructions	48	90%	89%	88%
Evaluation of LVS Function	57	93%	99%	98%
Smoking Cessation Advice[1]	4	100%	99%	98%
Pneumonia Care				
Appropriate Initial Antibiotic	57	93%	94%	92%
Blood Culture Timing	120	97%	96%	96%
Influenza Vaccine	50	92%	91%	91%
Initial Antibiotic Timing	97	97%	96%	95%
Pneumococcal Vaccine	82	96%	93%	93%
Smoking Cessation Advice	28	89%	98%	97%
Surgical Care Improvement Project				
Appropriate VTP Within 24 Hours	126	79%	94%	92%
Appropriate Hair Removal	299	99%	99%	99%
Appropriate Beta Blocker Usage	91	95%	92%	93%
Controlled Postoperative Blood Glucose	0	-	94%	93%
Prophylactic Antibiotic Timing	242	98%	97%	97%
Prophylactic Antibiotic Timing (Outpatient)	26	73%	87%	92%
Prophylactic Antibiotic Selection	244	98%	98%	97%
Prophylactic Antibiotic Select. (Outpatient)	26	96%	92%	94%
Prophylactic Antibiotic Stopped	239	94%	95%	94%
Recommended VTP Ordered	126	80%	95%	94%
Urinary Catheter Removal[1]	15	100%	91%	90%
Children's Asthma Care				
Received Systemic Corticosteroids	-	-	-	100%
Received Home Management Plan	-	-	-	71%
Received Reliever Medication	-	-	-	100%
Use of Medical Imaging				
Combination Abdominal CT Scan	580	0.664	0.135	0.191
Combination Chest CT Scan	506	0.893	0.068	0.054
Follow-up Mammogram/Ultrasound	1,037	5.7%	7.4%	8.4%
MRI for Low Back Pain	154	31.2%	32%	32.7%
Survey of Patients' Hospital Experiences				
Area Around Room 'Always' Quiet at Night	300+	56%	-	58%
Doctors 'Always' Communicated Well	300+	81%	-	80%
Home Recovery Information Given	300+	85%	-	82%
Hospital Given 9 or 10 on 10 Point Scale	300+	67%	-	67%
Meds 'Always' Explained Before Given	300+	61%	-	60%
Nurses 'Always' Communicated Well	300+	76%	-	76%
Pain 'Always' Well Controlled	300+	71%	-	69%
Room and Bathroom 'Always' Clean	300+	68%	-	71%
Timely Help 'Always' Received	300+	72%	-	64%
Would Definitely Recommend Hospital	300+	64%	-	69%

West Shore Medical Center

1465 E Parkdale Avenue — Phone: 231-398-1000
Manistee, MI 49660 — Fax: 231-398-1098
URL: www.westshoremedcenter.org
Type: Critical Access Hospitals — Emergency Services: Yes
Ownership: Proprietary

Key Personnel:
CEO/President. . . . . Burton Parks
Chief of Medical Staff. . . . . Glenn Griffiths
Operating Room. . . . . Eduardo Barlan
Quality Assurance . . . . Sandy Arnold
Radiology. . . . . John Raymond
Emergency Room . . . . Donald Albrecht
Intensive Care Unit. . . . . Joyce Miler

Measure	Cases	This Hosp.	State Avg.	U.S. Avg.
Heart Attack Care				
ACE Inhibitor or ARB for LVSD[1]	1	100%	96%	96%
Aspirin at Arrival[1]	8	88%	99%	99%
Aspirin at Discharge[1]	5	60%	99%	98%
Beta Blocker at Discharge[1]	5	80%	99%	98%
Fibrinolytic Medication Timing	0	-	55%	55%
PCI Within 90 Minutes of Arrival	0	-	89%	90%
Smoking Cessation Advice	0	-	100%	99%
Chest Pain/Possible Heart Attack Care				
Aspirin at Arrival	63	95%	94%	95%
Median Time to ECG (minutes)	66	10	10	8
Median Time to Transfer (minutes)[1]	3	26	54	61
Fibrinolytic Medication Timing[1]	1	100%	60%	54%
Heart Failure Care				
ACE Inhibitor or ARB for LVSD[1]	14	100%	95%	94%
Discharge Instructions	38	42%	89%	88%
Evaluation of LVS Function	49	100%	99%	98%
Smoking Cessation Advice[1]	2	100%	99%	98%
Pneumonia Care				
Appropriate Initial Antibiotic	43	98%	94%	92%
Blood Culture Timing	31	90%	96%	96%
Influenza Vaccine	38	82%	91%	91%
Initial Antibiotic Timing	63	97%	96%	95%
Pneumococcal Vaccine	59	88%	93%	93%
Smoking Cessation Advice[1]	18	89%	98%	97%
Surgical Care Improvement Project				
Appropriate VTP Within 24 Hours	76	79%	94%	92%
Appropriate Hair Removal	185	99%	99%	99%
Appropriate Beta Blocker Usage	60	95%	92%	93%
Controlled Postoperative Blood Glucose	0	-	94%	93%
Prophylactic Antibiotic Timing	116	99%	97%	97%
Prophylactic Antibiotic Timing (Outpatient)[1,3]	18	83%	87%	92%
Prophylactic Antibiotic Selection	117	97%	98%	97%
Prophylactic Antibiotic Select. (Outpatient)[1,3]	16	94%	92%	94%
Prophylactic Antibiotic Stopped	113	97%	95%	94%
Recommended VTP Ordered	76	88%	95%	94%
Urinary Catheter Removal	53	92%	91%	90%
Children's Asthma Care				
Received Systemic Corticosteroids	-	-	-	100%
Received Home Management Plan	-	-	-	71%
Received Reliever Medication	-	-	-	100%
Use of Medical Imaging				
Combination Abdominal CT Scan[5]	0	-	0.135	0.191
Combination Chest CT Scan[5]	0	-	0.068	0.054
Follow-up Mammogram/Ultrasound[5]	0	-	7.4%	8.4%
MRI for Low Back Pain[5]	0	-	32%	32.7%
Survey of Patients' Hospital Experiences				
Area Around Room 'Always' Quiet at Night	300+	63%	-	58%
Doctors 'Always' Communicated Well	300+	86%	-	80%
Home Recovery Information Given	300+	85%	-	82%
Hospital Given 9 or 10 on 10 Point Scale	300+	74%	-	67%
Meds 'Always' Explained Before Given	300+	68%	-	60%
Nurses 'Always' Communicated Well	300+	81%	-	76%
Pain 'Always' Well Controlled	300+	74%	-	69%
Room and Bathroom 'Always' Clean	300+	76%	-	71%
Timely Help 'Always' Received	300+	75%	-	64%
Would Definitely Recommend Hospital	300+	69%	-	69%

Schoolcraft Memorial Hospital

500 Main St — Phone: 906-341-3200
Manistique, MI 49854 — Fax: 906-341-3297
E-mail: ajones@scmh.org
URL: www.scmh.org
Type: Critical Access Hospitals — Emergency Services: Yes
Ownership: Government - Local — Beds: 25

Key Personnel:
CEO/President. . . . . David B Jahn

Measure	Cases	This Hosp.	State Avg.	U.S. Avg.
Heart Attack Care				
ACE Inhibitor or ARB for LVSD[3]	0	-	96%	96%
Aspirin at Arrival[3]	0	-	99%	99%
Aspirin at Discharge[3]	0	-	99%	98%
Beta Blocker at Discharge[3]	0	-	99%	98%
Fibrinolytic Medication Timing[1,3]	1	100%	55%	55%
PCI Within 90 Minutes of Arrival[3]	0	-	89%	90%
Smoking Cessation Advice[3]	0	-	100%	99%
Chest Pain/Possible Heart Attack Care				
Aspirin at Arrival	-	-	94%	95%
Median Time to ECG (minutes)	-	-	10	8
Median Time to Transfer (minutes)	-	-	54	61
Fibrinolytic Medication Timing	-	-	60%	54%
Heart Failure Care				
ACE Inhibitor or ARB for LVSD[5]	0	-	95%	94%
Discharge Instructions[5]	0	-	89%	88%
Evaluation of LVS Function[5]	0	-	99%	98%
Smoking Cessation Advice[5]	0	-	99%	98%
Pneumonia Care				
Appropriate Initial Antibiotic[1]	19	100%	94%	92%
Blood Culture Timing[1]	19	79%	96%	96%
Influenza Vaccine[1]	10	80%	91%	91%
Initial Antibiotic Timing	27	89%	96%	95%
Pneumococcal Vaccine[1]	20	80%	93%	93%
Smoking Cessation Advice[1]	7	43%	98%	97%
Surgical Care Improvement Project				
Appropriate VTP Within 24 Hours[5]	0	-	94%	92%
Appropriate Hair Removal[5]	0	-	99%	99%
Appropriate Beta Blocker Usage[5]	0	-	92%	93%
Controlled Postoperative Blood Glucose[5]	0	-	94%	93%
Prophylactic Antibiotic Timing[5]	0	-	97%	97%
Prophylactic Antibiotic Timing (Outpatient)	-	-	87%	92%
Prophylactic Antibiotic Selection[5]	0	-	98%	97%
Prophylactic Antibiotic Select. (Outpatient)	-	-	92%	94%
Prophylactic Antibiotic Stopped[5]	0	-	95%	94%
Recommended VTP Ordered[5]	0	-	95%	94%
Urinary Catheter Removal[5]	0	-	91%	90%
Children's Asthma Care				
Received Systemic Corticosteroids	-	-	-	100%
Received Home Management Plan	-	-	-	71%
Received Reliever Medication	-	-	-	100%
Use of Medical Imaging				
Combination Abdominal CT Scan	-	-	0.135	0.191
Combination Chest CT Scan	-	-	0.068	0.054
Follow-up Mammogram/Ultrasound	-	-	7.4%	8.4%
MRI for Low Back Pain	-	-	32%	32.7%
Survey of Patients' Hospital Experiences				
Area Around Room 'Always' Quiet at Night[8]	-	-	-	58%
Doctors 'Always' Communicated Well[8]	-	-	-	80%
Home Recovery Information Given[8]	-	-	-	82%
Hospital Given 9 or 10 on 10 Point Scale[8]	-	-	-	67%
Meds 'Always' Explained Before Given[8]	-	-	-	60%
Nurses 'Always' Communicated Well[8]	-	-	-	76%
Pain 'Always' Well Controlled[8]	-	-	-	69%
Room and Bathroom 'Always' Clean[8]	-	-	-	71%
Timely Help 'Always' Received[8]	-	-	-	64%
Would Definitely Recommend Hospital[8]	-	-	-	69%

NOTE: Hospital profiles are in alphabetical order by state, then city, then hospital within the city; Rankings exclude hospitals with less than 25 cases except for patient surveys which excludes hospitals with less than 100 cases; (a) 100–299 cases; (1) The number of cases is too small to be sure how well a hospital is performing; (2) The hospital indicated that the data submitted for this measure were based on a sample of cases; (3) Data was collected during a shorter time period (fewer quarters) than the maximum possible time for this measure; (4) Suppressed for one or more quarters by CMS; (5) No data is available from the hospital for this measure; (6) Fewer than 100 patients completed the HCAHPS survey. Use these rates with caution, as the number of surveys may be too low to reliably assess hospital performance; (7) Survey results are based on less than 12 months of data; (8) Survey results are not available for this reporting period; (9) No or very few patients were eligible for the HCAHPS survey. The scores shown, if any, reflect a very small number of surveys; (10) A state average was not calculated because too few hospitals in the state submitted data; (11) There were discrepancies in the data collection process; Please refer to the User's Guide for a full explanation of data.

Marlette Regional Hospital

2770 Main Street | Phone: 989-635-4000
Marlette, MI 48453 | Fax: 989-635-4027
URL: www.marlettecommunityhospital.com
Type: Critical Access Hospitals | Emergency Services: Yes
Ownership: Voluntary Non-Profit - Private | Beds: 97

Key Personnel:
CEO/President. . . . . David S McEwen
Chief of Medical Staff. . . . . William Starbird, MD
Infection Control. . . . . Sharon Kasprzyk, RN
Operating Room. . . . . Mohan Dass Macha
Quality Assurance . . . . Bobbi Jones
Anesthesiology. . . . . Jody Bovenschen
Emergency Room . . . . Susan Brzezinski
Patient Relations . . . . Molly Disteirath

Measure	Cases	This Hosp.	State Avg.	U.S. Avg.
Heart Attack Care				
ACE Inhibitor or ARB for LVSD[1]	1	100%	96%	96%
Aspirin at Arrival[1]	8	88%	99%	99%
Aspirin at Discharge[1]	6	83%	99%	98%
Beta Blocker at Discharge[1]	6	100%	99%	98%
Fibrinolytic Medication Timing	0	-	55%	55%
PCI Within 90 Minutes of Arrival	0	-	89%	90%
Smoking Cessation Advice[1]	1	100%	100%	99%
Chest Pain/Possible Heart Attack Care				
Aspirin at Arrival	79	96%	94%	95%
Median Time to ECG (minutes)	82	11	10	8
Median Time to Transfer (minutes)[1]	8	139	54	61
Fibrinolytic Medication Timing[1]	5	40%	60%	54%
Heart Failure Care				
ACE Inhibitor or ARB for LVSD[1]	13	62%	95%	94%
Discharge Instructions	31	65%	89%	88%
Evaluation of LVS Function	33	85%	99%	98%
Smoking Cessation Advice[1]	4	25%	99%	98%
Pneumonia Care				
Appropriate Initial Antibiotic	68	90%	94%	92%
Blood Culture Timing	59	78%	96%	96%
Influenza Vaccine	38	61%	91%	91%
Initial Antibiotic Timing	79	89%	96%	95%
Pneumococcal Vaccine	53	49%	93%	93%
Smoking Cessation Advice[1]	20	60%	98%	97%
Surgical Care Improvement Project				
Appropriate VTP Within 24 Hours	25	68%	94%	92%
Appropriate Hair Removal	37	68%	99%	99%
Appropriate Beta Blocker Usage[5]	0	-	92%	93%
Controlled Postoperative Blood Glucose	0	-	94%	93%
Prophylactic Antibiotic Timing	25	88%	97%	97%
Prophylactic Antibiotic Timing (Outpatient)[1]	19	68%	87%	92%
Prophylactic Antibiotic Selection[1]	23	87%	98%	97%
Prophylactic Antibiotic Select. (Outpatient)[1]	15	100%	92%	94%
Prophylactic Antibiotic Stopped[1]	22	100%	95%	94%
Recommended VTP Ordered	25	68%	95%	94%
Urinary Catheter Removal[1]	11	91%	91%	90%
Children's Asthma Care				
Received Systemic Corticosteroids	-	-	-	100%
Received Home Management Plan	-	-	-	71%
Received Reliever Medication	-	-	-	100%
Use of Medical Imaging				
Combination Abdominal CT Scan	252	0.187	0.135	0.191
Combination Chest CT Scan	200	0.125	0.068	0.054
Follow-up Mammogram/Ultrasound	283	5.7%	7.4%	8.4%
MRI for Low Back Pain[5]	0	-	32%	32.7%
Survey of Patients' Hospital Experiences				
Area Around Room 'Always' Quiet at Night	(a)	59%	-	58%
Doctors 'Always' Communicated Well	(a)	85%	-	80%
Home Recovery Information Given	(a)	84%	-	82%
Hospital Given 9 or 10 on 10 Point Scale	(a)	71%	-	67%
Meds 'Always' Explained Before Given	(a)	62%	-	60%
Nurses 'Always' Communicated Well	(a)	75%	-	76%
Pain 'Always' Well Controlled	(a)	73%	-	69%
Room and Bathroom 'Always' Clean	(a)	77%	-	71%
Timely Help 'Always' Received	(a)	60%	-	64%
Would Definitely Recommend Hospital	(a)	79%	-	69%

Marquette General Hospital

420 West Magnetic Street | Phone: 906-228-9440
Marquette, MI 49855 | Fax: 906-225-3098
URL: www.mgh.org
Type: Acute Care Hospitals | Emergency Services: Yes
Ownership: Government - Local | Beds: 352

Key Personnel:
CEO/President. . . . . Bill Nemacheck
Chief of Medical Staff . . . . Deb Morley, MD

Measure	Cases	This Hosp.	State Avg.	U.S. Avg.
Heart Attack Care				
ACE Inhibitor or ARB for LVSD	59	90%	96%	96%
Aspirin at Arrival	86	100%	99%	99%
Aspirin at Discharge	351	100%	99%	98%
Beta Blocker at Discharge	337	97%	99%	98%
Fibrinolytic Medication Timing	0	-	55%	55%
PCI Within 90 Minutes of Arrival[1]	19	63%	89%	90%
Smoking Cessation Advice	122	98%	100%	99%
Chest Pain/Possible Heart Attack Care				
Aspirin at Arrival[1,3]	1	100%	94%	95%
Median Time to ECG (minutes)[1,3]	1	7	10	8
Median Time to Transfer (minutes)[5]	0	-	54	61
Fibrinolytic Medication Timing[5]	0	-	60%	54%
Heart Failure Care				
ACE Inhibitor or ARB for LVSD	41	98%	95%	94%
Discharge Instructions	140	85%	89%	88%
Evaluation of LVS Function	171	94%	99%	98%
Smoking Cessation Advice	31	100%	99%	98%
Pneumonia Care				
Appropriate Initial Antibiotic	57	82%	94%	92%
Blood Culture Timing	99	99%	96%	96%
Influenza Vaccine	94	85%	91%	91%
Initial Antibiotic Timing	97	97%	96%	95%
Pneumococcal Vaccine	128	83%	93%	93%
Smoking Cessation Advice	52	100%	98%	97%
Surgical Care Improvement Project				
Appropriate VTP Within 24 Hours[2]	126	86%	94%	92%
Appropriate Hair Removal[2]	517	91%	99%	99%
Appropriate Beta Blocker Usage[2]	170	87%	92%	93%
Controlled Postoperative Blood Glucose[2]	125	96%	94%	93%
Prophylactic Antibiotic Timing[2]	373	97%	97%	97%
Prophylactic Antibiotic Timing (Outpatient)	640	76%	87%	92%
Prophylactic Antibiotic Selection[2]	376	98%	98%	97%
Prophylactic Antibiotic Select. (Outpatient)	593	86%	92%	94%
Prophylactic Antibiotic Stopped[2]	366	89%	95%	94%
Recommended VTP Ordered[2]	126	89%	95%	94%
Urinary Catheter Removal[2]	94	79%	91%	90%
Children's Asthma Care				
Received Systemic Corticosteroids	-	-	-	100%
Received Home Management Plan	-	-	-	71%
Received Reliever Medication	-	-	-	100%
Use of Medical Imaging				
Combination Abdominal CT Scan	638	0.724	0.135	0.191
Combination Chest CT Scan	553	0.387	0.068	0.054
Follow-up Mammogram/Ultrasound	909	15.6%	7.4%	8.4%
MRI for Low Back Pain	207	41.5%	32%	32.7%
Survey of Patients' Hospital Experiences				
Area Around Room 'Always' Quiet at Night	300+	48%	-	58%
Doctors 'Always' Communicated Well	300+	78%	-	80%
Home Recovery Information Given	300+	86%	-	82%
Hospital Given 9 or 10 on 10 Point Scale	300+	64%	-	67%
Meds 'Always' Explained Before Given	300+	58%	-	60%
Nurses 'Always' Communicated Well	300+	72%	-	76%
Pain 'Always' Well Controlled	300+	62%	-	69%
Room and Bathroom 'Always' Clean	300+	73%	-	71%
Timely Help 'Always' Received	300+	62%	-	64%
Would Definitely Recommend Hospital	300+	69%	-	69%

Oaklawn Hospital

200 N Madison | Phone: 269-781-4271
Marshall, MI 49068 | Fax: 269-781-7117
URL: www.oaklawnhospital.org
Type: Acute Care Hospitals | Emergency Services: Yes
Ownership: Voluntary Non-Profit - Other | Beds: 94

Key Personnel:
Chief of Medical Staff. . . . . George Seifert, MD
Infection Control. . . . . Pat Jendryka, RN
Operating Room. . . . . Thomas Casale, RN
Radiology. . . . . Indraneel Baner, RRT
Anesthesiology. . . . . Rick Gorham
Emergency Room . . . . Dr David Komasara
Intensive Care Unit. . . . . Dr Alcides Gil-Acosta

Measure	Cases	This Hosp.	State Avg.	U.S. Avg.
Heart Attack Care				
ACE Inhibitor or ARB for LVSD[1]	1	100%	96%	96%
Aspirin at Arrival[1]	9	100%	99%	99%
Aspirin at Discharge[1]	6	100%	99%	98%
Beta Blocker at Discharge[1]	7	100%	99%	98%
Fibrinolytic Medication Timing	0	-	55%	55%
PCI Within 90 Minutes of Arrival	0	-	89%	90%
Smoking Cessation Advice[1]	1	100%	100%	99%
Chest Pain/Possible Heart Attack Care				
Aspirin at Arrival	320	98%	94%	95%
Median Time to ECG (minutes)	333	9	10	8
Median Time to Transfer (minutes)[1]	9	40	54	61
Fibrinolytic Medication Timing	0	-	60%	54%
Heart Failure Care				
ACE Inhibitor or ARB for LVSD[1]	14	86%	95%	94%
Discharge Instructions	69	94%	89%	88%
Evaluation of LVS Function	85	100%	99%	98%
Smoking Cessation Advice[1]	15	93%	99%	98%
Pneumonia Care				
Appropriate Initial Antibiotic	80	98%	94%	92%
Blood Culture Timing	93	98%	96%	96%
Influenza Vaccine	59	100%	91%	91%
Initial Antibiotic Timing	118	97%	96%	95%
Pneumococcal Vaccine	90	98%	93%	93%
Smoking Cessation Advice	33	97%	98%	97%
Surgical Care Improvement Project				
Appropriate VTP Within 24 Hours[2]	116	97%	94%	92%
Appropriate Hair Removal[2]	568	100%	99%	99%
Appropriate Beta Blocker Usage[2]	148	97%	92%	93%
Controlled Postoperative Blood Glucose[2]	0	-	94%	93%
Prophylactic Antibiotic Timing[2]	426	99%	97%	97%
Prophylactic Antibiotic Timing (Outpatient)	67	93%	87%	92%
Prophylactic Antibiotic Selection[2]	427	98%	98%	97%
Prophylactic Antibiotic Select. (Outpatient)	70	96%	92%	94%
Prophylactic Antibiotic Stopped[2]	422	98%	95%	94%
Recommended VTP Ordered[2]	116	97%	95%	94%
Urinary Catheter Removal[2]	117	95%	91%	90%
Children's Asthma Care				
Received Systemic Corticosteroids	-	-	-	100%
Received Home Management Plan	-	-	-	71%
Received Reliever Medication	-	-	-	100%
Use of Medical Imaging				
Combination Abdominal CT Scan	526	0.017	0.135	0.191
Combination Chest CT Scan	361	0.000	0.068	0.054
Follow-up Mammogram/Ultrasound	913	3.6%	7.4%	8.4%
MRI for Low Back Pain[1]	44	36.4%	32%	32.7%
Survey of Patients' Hospital Experiences				
Area Around Room 'Always' Quiet at Night	300+	67%	-	58%
Doctors 'Always' Communicated Well	300+	81%	-	80%
Home Recovery Information Given	300+	88%	-	82%
Hospital Given 9 or 10 on 10 Point Scale	300+	79%	-	67%
Meds 'Always' Explained Before Given	300+	61%	-	60%
Nurses 'Always' Communicated Well	300+	79%	-	76%
Pain 'Always' Well Controlled	300+	74%	-	69%
Room and Bathroom 'Always' Clean	300+	72%	-	71%
Timely Help 'Always' Received	300+	73%	-	64%
Would Definitely Recommend Hospital	300+	83%	-	69%

NOTE: Hospital profiles are in alphabetical order by state, then city, then hospital within the city; Rankings exclude hospitals with less than 25 cases except for patient surveys which excludes hospitals with less than 100 cases; (a) 100–299 cases; (1) The number of cases is too small to be sure how well a hospital is performing; (2) The hospital indicated that the data submitted for this measure were based on a sample of cases; (3) Data was collected during a shorter time period (fewer quarters) than the maximum possible time for this measure; (4) Suppressed for one or more quarters by CMS; (5) No data is available from the hospital for this measure; (6) Fewer than 100 patients completed the HCAHPS survey. Use these rates with caution, as the number of surveys may be too low to reliably assess hospital performance; (7) Survey results are based on less than 12 months of data; (8) Survey results are not available for this reporting period; (9) No or very few patients were eligible for the HCAHPS survey. The scores shown, if any, reflect a very small number of surveys; (10) A state average was not calculated because too few hospitals in the state submitted data; (11) There were discrepancies in the data collection process; Please refer to the User's Guide for a full explanation of data.

Midmichigan Medical Center-Midland

4005 Orchard Drive | Phone: 989-839-3000
Midland, MI 48670 | Fax: 989-839-3307
URL: www.midmichigan.org
Type: Acute Care Hospitals | Emergency Services: Yes
Ownership: Voluntary Non-Profit - Other | Beds: 250

Key Personnel:
CEO/President. . . . . Rick Reynolds
Cardiac Laboratory. . . . . Karen Colkins
Chief of Medical Staff. . . . . Mark Goethe, MD
Infection Control. . . . . Brenda Dauer, RN
Operating Room. . . . . Cindy Ferdrich
Pediatric In-Patient Care . . . . Denise Schaffert, MD
Quality Assurance . . . . Chandra Morse
Radiology. . . . . Rajnikant Mehta, MD

Measure	Cases	This Hosp.	State Avg.	U.S. Avg.
Heart Attack Care				
ACE Inhibitor or ARB for LVSD[2]	57	95%	96%	96%
Aspirin at Arrival[2]	128	100%	99%	99%
Aspirin at Discharge[2]	267	99%	99%	98%
Beta Blocker at Discharge[2]	268	100%	99%	98%
Fibrinolytic Medication Timing[2]	0	-	55%	55%
PCI Within 90 Minutes of Arrival[2]	26	88%	89%	90%
Smoking Cessation Advice[2]	98	98%	100%	99%
Chest Pain/Possible Heart Attack Care				
Aspirin at Arrival[1]	11	100%	94%	95%
Median Time to ECG (minutes)[1]	11	9	10	8
Median Time to Transfer (minutes)[5]	0	-	54	61
Fibrinolytic Medication Timing[5]	0	-	60%	54%
Heart Failure Care				
ACE Inhibitor or ARB for LVSD[2]	69	96%	95%	94%
Discharge Instructions[2]	218	82%	89%	88%
Evaluation of LVS Function[2]	262	99%	99%	98%
Smoking Cessation Advice[2]	49	94%	99%	98%
Pneumonia Care				
Appropriate Initial Antibiotic[2]	87	93%	94%	92%
Blood Culture Timing[2]	145	97%	96%	96%
Influenza Vaccine[2]	78	87%	91%	91%
Initial Antibiotic Timing[2]	121	94%	96%	95%
Pneumococcal Vaccine[2]	125	91%	93%	93%
Smoking Cessation Advice[2]	57	96%	98%	97%
Surgical Care Improvement Project				
Appropriate VTP Within 24 Hours[2]	154	94%	94%	92%
Appropriate Hair Removal[2]	710	100%	99%	99%
Appropriate Beta Blocker Usage[2]	213	96%	92%	93%
Controlled Postoperative Blood Glucose[2]	126	95%	94%	93%
Prophylactic Antibiotic Timing[2]	486	93%	97%	97%
Prophylactic Antibiotic Timing (Outpatient)	391	91%	87%	92%
Prophylactic Antibiotic Selection[2]	491	98%	98%	97%
Prophylactic Antibiotic Select. (Outpatient)	378	91%	92%	94%
Prophylactic Antibiotic Stopped[2]	471	96%	95%	94%
Recommended VTP Ordered[2]	154	94%	95%	94%
Urinary Catheter Removal[2]	170	94%	91%	90%
Children's Asthma Care				
Received Systemic Corticosteroids	-	-	-	100%
Received Home Management Plan	-	-	-	71%
Received Reliever Medication	-	-	-	100%
Use of Medical Imaging				
Combination Abdominal CT Scan	1,238	0.061	0.135	0.191
Combination Chest CT Scan	956	0.026	0.068	0.054
Follow-up Mammogram/Ultrasound	2,207	5.9%	7.4%	8.4%
MRI for Low Back Pain	489	30.1%	32%	32.7%
Survey of Patients' Hospital Experiences				
Area Around Room 'Always' Quiet at Night	300+	52%	-	58%
Doctors 'Always' Communicated Well	300+	81%	-	80%
Home Recovery Information Given	300+	83%	-	82%
Hospital Given 9 or 10 on 10 Point Scale	300+	73%	-	67%
Meds 'Always' Explained Before Given	300+	60%	-	60%
Nurses 'Always' Communicated Well	300+	76%	-	76%
Pain 'Always' Well Controlled	300+	75%	-	69%
Room and Bathroom 'Always' Clean	300+	67%	-	71%
Timely Help 'Always' Received	300+	67%	-	64%
Would Definitely Recommend Hospital	300+	75%	-	69%

Mercy Memorial Hospital System

718 N Macomb St | Phone: 734-240-8400
Monroe, MI 48162 | Fax: 734-241-0032
URL: www.mercymemorial.org
Type: Acute Care Hospitals | Emergency Services: Yes
Ownership: Voluntary Non-Profit - Other | Beds: 238

Key Personnel:
CEO/President. . . . . Annette Phillips
Cardiac Laboratory. . . . . David Rhodes
Chief of Medical Staff . . . . Danilo Dona
Operating Room. . . . . Pam Haddix
Emergency Room . . . . Lynn Lohner

Measure	Cases	This Hosp.	State Avg.	U.S. Avg.
Heart Attack Care				
ACE Inhibitor or ARB for LVSD[1]	17	100%	96%	96%
Aspirin at Arrival	144	98%	99%	99%
Aspirin at Discharge	60	98%	99%	98%
Beta Blocker at Discharge	61	100%	99%	98%
Fibrinolytic Medication Timing[1]	9	67%	55%	55%
PCI Within 90 Minutes of Arrival	0	-	89%	90%
Smoking Cessation Advice[1]	3	100%	100%	99%
Chest Pain/Possible Heart Attack Care				
Aspirin at Arrival	73	97%	94%	95%
Median Time to ECG (minutes)	78	6	10	8
Median Time to Transfer (minutes)[1]	4	68	54	61
Fibrinolytic Medication Timing[1]	8	62%	60%	54%
Heart Failure Care				
ACE Inhibitor or ARB for LVSD	81	100%	95%	94%
Discharge Instructions	191	94%	89%	88%
Evaluation of LVS Function	280	100%	99%	98%
Smoking Cessation Advice	54	100%	99%	98%
Pneumonia Care				
Appropriate Initial Antibiotic	162	95%	94%	92%
Blood Culture Timing	278	99%	96%	96%
Influenza Vaccine	160	98%	91%	91%
Initial Antibiotic Timing	257	98%	96%	95%
Pneumococcal Vaccine	217	99%	93%	93%
Smoking Cessation Advice	120	100%	98%	97%
Surgical Care Improvement Project				
Appropriate VTP Within 24 Hours	244	94%	94%	92%
Appropriate Hair Removal	728	100%	99%	99%
Appropriate Beta Blocker Usage	193	99%	92%	93%
Controlled Postoperative Blood Glucose	0	-	94%	93%
Prophylactic Antibiotic Timing	522	98%	97%	97%
Prophylactic Antibiotic Timing (Outpatient)	117	85%	87%	92%
Prophylactic Antibiotic Selection	524	99%	98%	97%
Prophylactic Antibiotic Select. (Outpatient)	107	98%	92%	94%
Prophylactic Antibiotic Stopped	493	96%	95%	94%
Recommended VTP Ordered	244	95%	95%	94%
Urinary Catheter Removal[1]	19	100%	91%	90%
Children's Asthma Care				
Received Systemic Corticosteroids	-	-	-	100%
Received Home Management Plan	-	-	-	71%
Received Reliever Medication	-	-	-	100%
Use of Medical Imaging				
Combination Abdominal CT Scan	840	0.057	0.135	0.191
Combination Chest CT Scan	708	0.006	0.068	0.054
Follow-up Mammogram/Ultrasound	1,229	6.9%	7.4%	8.4%
MRI for Low Back Pain	129	25.6%	32%	32.7%
Survey of Patients' Hospital Experiences				
Area Around Room 'Always' Quiet at Night	300+	47%	-	58%
Doctors 'Always' Communicated Well	300+	76%	-	80%
Home Recovery Information Given	300+	75%	-	82%
Hospital Given 9 or 10 on 10 Point Scale	300+	54%	-	67%
Meds 'Always' Explained Before Given	300+	56%	-	60%
Nurses 'Always' Communicated Well	300+	73%	-	76%
Pain 'Always' Well Controlled	300+	65%	-	69%
Room and Bathroom 'Always' Clean	300+	63%	-	71%
Timely Help 'Always' Received	300+	60%	-	64%
Would Definitely Recommend Hospital	300+	46%	-	69%

Mount Clemens Regional Medical Center

1000 Harrington Blvd | Phone: 586-493-8000
Mount Clemens, MI 48043 | Fax: 586-741-4179
URL: www.mcrmc.org
Type: Acute Care Hospitals | Emergency Services: Yes
Ownership: Proprietary | Beds: 288

Key Personnel:
CEO/President. . . . . Mark O;Halla
Chief of Medical Staff. . . . . Michael Tawney, DO
Pediatric Ambulatory Care . . . . . . Bahman Mehdizadeh, MD
Pediatric In-Patient Care . . . . Bahman Mehdizadeh, MD
Quality Assurance . . . . Heather Tweed
Radiology. . . . . Michele Blair, DO
Emergency Room . . . . Sue Durst, RN

Measure	Cases	This Hosp.	State Avg.	U.S. Avg.
Heart Attack Care				
ACE Inhibitor or ARB for LVSD	30	93%	96%	96%
Aspirin at Arrival	253	99%	99%	99%
Aspirin at Discharge	240	99%	99%	98%
Beta Blocker at Discharge	227	100%	99%	98%
Fibrinolytic Medication Timing	0	-	55%	55%
PCI Within 90 Minutes of Arrival	67	97%	89%	90%
Smoking Cessation Advice	102	96%	100%	99%
Chest Pain/Possible Heart Attack Care				
Aspirin at Arrival[1]	16	94%	94%	95%
Median Time to ECG (minutes)[1]	16	4	10	8
Median Time to Transfer (minutes)[5]	0	-	54	61
Fibrinolytic Medication Timing[5]	0	-	60%	54%
Heart Failure Care				
ACE Inhibitor or ARB for LVSD	167	81%	95%	94%
Discharge Instructions	406	50%	89%	88%
Evaluation of LVS Function	494	98%	99%	98%
Smoking Cessation Advice	77	96%	99%	98%
Pneumonia Care				
Appropriate Initial Antibiotic	184	89%	94%	92%
Blood Culture Timing	277	94%	96%	96%
Influenza Vaccine	202	82%	91%	91%
Initial Antibiotic Timing	288	95%	96%	95%
Pneumococcal Vaccine	234	76%	93%	93%
Smoking Cessation Advice	135	98%	98%	97%
Surgical Care Improvement Project				
Appropriate VTP Within 24 Hours[2]	298	96%	94%	92%
Appropriate Hair Removal[2]	1,177	99%	99%	99%
Appropriate Beta Blocker Usage[2]	405	68%	92%	93%
Controlled Postoperative Blood Glucose[2]	119	85%	94%	93%
Prophylactic Antibiotic Timing[2]	847	96%	97%	97%
Prophylactic Antibiotic Timing (Outpatient)	244	90%	87%	92%
Prophylactic Antibiotic Selection[2]	856	97%	98%	97%
Prophylactic Antibiotic Select. (Outpatient)	235	95%	92%	94%
Prophylactic Antibiotic Stopped[2]	762	94%	95%	94%
Recommended VTP Ordered[2]	298	98%	95%	94%
Urinary Catheter Removal[2]	294	94%	91%	90%
Children's Asthma Care				
Received Systemic Corticosteroids	-	-	-	100%
Received Home Management Plan	-	-	-	71%
Received Reliever Medication	-	-	-	100%
Use of Medical Imaging				
Combination Abdominal CT Scan	1,212	0.328	0.135	0.191
Combination Chest CT Scan	964	0.124	0.068	0.054
Follow-up Mammogram/Ultrasound[5]	0	-	7.4%	8.4%
MRI for Low Back Pain[1]	1	0.0%	32%	32.7%
Survey of Patients' Hospital Experiences				
Area Around Room 'Always' Quiet at Night	300+	44%	-	58%
Doctors 'Always' Communicated Well	300+	76%	-	80%
Home Recovery Information Given	300+	80%	-	82%
Hospital Given 9 or 10 on 10 Point Scale	300+	58%	-	67%
Meds 'Always' Explained Before Given	300+	55%	-	60%
Nurses 'Always' Communicated Well	300+	71%	-	76%
Pain 'Always' Well Controlled	300+	65%	-	69%
Room and Bathroom 'Always' Clean	300+	63%	-	71%
Timely Help 'Always' Received	300+	57%	-	64%
Would Definitely Recommend Hospital	300+	59%	-	69%

NOTE: Hospital profiles are in alphabetical order by state, then city, then hospital within the city; Rankings exclude hospitals with less than 25 cases except for patient surveys which excludes hospitals with less than 100 cases; (a) 100–299 cases; (1) The number of cases is too small to be sure how well a hospital is performing; (2) The hospital indicated that the data submitted for this measure were based on a sample of cases; (3) Data was collected during a shorter time period (fewer quarters) than the maximum possible time for this measure; (4) Suppressed for one or more quarters by CMS; (5) No data is available from the hospital for this measure; (6) Fewer than 100 patients completed the HCAHPS survey. Use these rates with caution, as the number of surveys may be too low to reliably assess hospital performance; (7) Survey results are based on less than 12 months of data; (8) Survey results are not available for this reporting period; (9) No or very few patients were eligible for the HCAHPS survey. The scores shown, if any, reflect a very small number of surveys; (10) A state average was not calculated because too few hospitals in the state submitted data; (11) There were discrepancies in the data collection process; Please refer to the User's Guide for a full explanation of data.

Central Michigan Community Hospital

1221 South Drive Phone: 989-772-6700
Mount Pleasant, MI 48858 Fax: 989-772-1150
E-mail: mbousley@voyager.net
URL: www.cmch.org
Type: Acute Care Hospitals Emergency Services: Yes
Ownership: Voluntary Non-Profit - Private Beds: 137

Key Personnel:
CEO/President. . . . . Bill Lawrence
Chief of Medical Staff . . . . Ashok Vashishta, MD
Radiology. . . . . David Dubriwny

Measure	Cases	This Hosp.	State Avg.	U.S. Avg.
Heart Attack Care				
ACE Inhibitor or ARB for LVSD[1]	2	100%	96%	96%
Aspirin at Arrival	27	100%	99%	99%
Aspirin at Discharge[1]	18	100%	99%	98%
Beta Blocker at Discharge[1]	17	94%	99%	98%
Fibrinolytic Medication Timing	0	-	55%	55%
PCI Within 90 Minutes of Arrival	0	-	89%	90%
Smoking Cessation Advice[1]	6	100%	100%	99%
Chest Pain/Possible Heart Attack Care				
Aspirin at Arrival	92	99%	94%	95%
Median Time to ECG (minutes)	95	7	10	8
Median Time to Transfer (minutes)[1,3]	1	61	54	61
Fibrinolytic Medication Timing[1]	11	82%	60%	54%
Heart Failure Care				
ACE Inhibitor or ARB for LVSD	31	97%	95%	94%
Discharge Instructions	84	98%	89%	88%
Evaluation of LVS Function	112	100%	99%	98%
Smoking Cessation Advice[1]	7	100%	99%	98%
Pneumonia Care				
Appropriate Initial Antibiotic	131	99%	94%	92%
Blood Culture Timing	179	97%	96%	96%
Influenza Vaccine	116	95%	91%	91%
Initial Antibiotic Timing	181	98%	96%	95%
Pneumococcal Vaccine	165	99%	93%	93%
Smoking Cessation Advice	62	100%	98%	97%
Surgical Care Improvement Project				
Appropriate VTP Within 24 Hours	41	90%	94%	92%
Appropriate Hair Removal	276	100%	99%	99%
Appropriate Beta Blocker Usage	76	97%	92%	93%
Controlled Postoperative Blood Glucose	0	-	94%	93%
Prophylactic Antibiotic Timing	229	98%	97%	97%
Prophylactic Antibiotic Timing (Outpatient)	65	86%	87%	92%
Prophylactic Antibiotic Selection	228	97%	98%	97%
Prophylactic Antibiotic Select. (Outpatient)	60	92%	92%	94%
Prophylactic Antibiotic Stopped	219	94%	95%	94%
Recommended VTP Ordered	41	93%	95%	94%
Urinary Catheter Removal	43	98%	91%	90%
Children's Asthma Care				
Received Systemic Corticosteroids	-	-	-	100%
Received Home Management Plan	-	-	-	71%
Received Reliever Medication	-	-	-	100%
Use of Medical Imaging				
Combination Abdominal CT Scan	388	0.036	0.135	0.191
Combination Chest CT Scan	338	0.036	0.068	0.054
Follow-up Mammogram/Ultrasound	492	6.3%	7.4%	8.4%
MRI for Low Back Pain	103	34.0%	32%	32.7%
Survey of Patients' Hospital Experiences				
Area Around Room 'Always' Quiet at Night	300+	54%	-	58%
Doctors 'Always' Communicated Well	300+	81%	-	80%
Home Recovery Information Given	300+	90%	-	82%
Hospital Given 9 or 10 on 10 Point Scale	300+	75%	-	67%
Meds 'Always' Explained Before Given	300+	61%	-	60%
Nurses 'Always' Communicated Well	300+	81%	-	76%
Pain 'Always' Well Controlled	300+	73%	-	69%
Room and Bathroom 'Always' Clean	300+	72%	-	71%
Timely Help 'Always' Received	300+	74%	-	64%
Would Definitely Recommend Hospital	300+	77%	-	69%

Mercy Health Partners - Hackley Campus

1700 Clinton Street Phone: 231-726-3511
Muskegon, MI 49442 Fax: 231-726-2232
URL: www.hackley.org
Type: Acute Care Hospitals Emergency Services: No
Ownership: Voluntary Non-Profit - Private Beds: 181

Key Personnel:
CEO/President. . . . . Gordon A Mudler
Chief of Medical Staff . . . . Herbert Miller, MD
Operating Room. . . . . Brian Gluck
Quality Assurance . . . . Eileen Howe

Measure	Cases	This Hosp.	State Avg.	U.S. Avg.
Heart Attack Care				
ACE Inhibitor or ARB for LVSD[1]	4	100%	96%	96%
Aspirin at Arrival[1]	19	100%	99%	99%
Aspirin at Discharge[1]	11	100%	99%	98%
Beta Blocker at Discharge[1]	13	100%	99%	98%
Fibrinolytic Medication Timing	0	-	55%	55%
PCI Within 90 Minutes of Arrival	0	-	89%	90%
Smoking Cessation Advice[1]	1	100%	100%	99%
Chest Pain/Possible Heart Attack Care				
Aspirin at Arrival	45	89%	94%	95%
Median Time to ECG (minutes)	47	6	10	8
Median Time to Transfer (minutes)[1]	19	41	54	61
Fibrinolytic Medication Timing	0	-	60%	54%
Heart Failure Care				
ACE Inhibitor or ARB for LVSD	42	100%	95%	94%
Discharge Instructions	79	96%	89%	88%
Evaluation of LVS Function	101	100%	99%	98%
Smoking Cessation Advice	30	100%	99%	98%
Pneumonia Care				
Appropriate Initial Antibiotic	133	97%	94%	92%
Blood Culture Timing	214	97%	96%	96%
Influenza Vaccine	86	93%	91%	91%
Initial Antibiotic Timing	203	100%	96%	95%
Pneumococcal Vaccine	124	96%	93%	93%
Smoking Cessation Advice	76	95%	98%	97%
Surgical Care Improvement Project				
Appropriate VTP Within 24 Hours	278	97%	94%	92%
Appropriate Hair Removal	992	98%	99%	99%
Appropriate Beta Blocker Usage	221	90%	92%	93%
Controlled Postoperative Blood Glucose	0	-	94%	93%
Prophylactic Antibiotic Timing	646	93%	97%	97%
Prophylactic Antibiotic Timing (Outpatient)	320	91%	87%	92%
Prophylactic Antibiotic Selection	637	98%	98%	97%
Prophylactic Antibiotic Select. (Outpatient)	328	98%	92%	94%
Prophylactic Antibiotic Stopped	631	99%	95%	94%
Recommended VTP Ordered	281	96%	95%	94%
Urinary Catheter Removal	64	95%	91%	90%
Children's Asthma Care				
Received Systemic Corticosteroids	-	-	-	100%
Received Home Management Plan	-	-	-	71%
Received Reliever Medication	-	-	-	100%
Use of Medical Imaging				
Combination Abdominal CT Scan	789	0.091	0.135	0.191
Combination Chest CT Scan	471	0.108	0.068	0.054
Follow-up Mammogram/Ultrasound	1,745	6.5%	7.4%	8.4%
MRI for Low Back Pain	264	34.1%	32%	32.7%
Survey of Patients' Hospital Experiences				
Area Around Room 'Always' Quiet at Night	300+	50%	-	58%
Doctors 'Always' Communicated Well	300+	79%	-	80%
Home Recovery Information Given	300+	84%	-	82%
Hospital Given 9 or 10 on 10 Point Scale	300+	68%	-	67%
Meds 'Always' Explained Before Given	300+	62%	-	60%
Nurses 'Always' Communicated Well	300+	75%	-	76%
Pain 'Always' Well Controlled	300+	70%	-	69%
Room and Bathroom 'Always' Clean	300+	61%	-	71%
Timely Help 'Always' Received	300+	64%	-	64%
Would Definitely Recommend Hospital	300+	72%	-	69%

Mercy Health Partners - Mercy Campus

1500 E Sherman Boulevard Phone: 231-672-3901
Muskegon, MI 49444 Fax: 231-672-3854
URL: www.mghp.com
Type: Acute Care Hospitals Emergency Services: Yes
Ownership: Voluntary Non-Profit - Church Beds: 282

Key Personnel:
CEO/President. . . . . Glenn Goldberg
Chief of Medical Staff . . . . F Remington Sprague, MD
Coronary Care . . . . Rick Denaie
Infection Control. . . . . Kurt Atton
Operating Room. . . . . Kathy Shoneberger
Pediatric Ambulatory Care . . . . Kathy Halfpap
Quality Assurance . . . . Julie Erickson
Radiology. . . . . Ken Uganski

Measure	Cases	This Hosp.	State Avg.	U.S. Avg.
Heart Attack Care				
ACE Inhibitor or ARB for LVSD	59	98%	96%	96%
Aspirin at Arrival	243	100%	99%	99%
Aspirin at Discharge	365	100%	99%	98%
Beta Blocker at Discharge	359	100%	99%	98%
Fibrinolytic Medication Timing[1]	1	100%	55%	55%
PCI Within 90 Minutes of Arrival	54	80%	89%	90%
Smoking Cessation Advice	147	100%	100%	99%
Chest Pain/Possible Heart Attack Care				
Aspirin at Arrival[1,3]	6	83%	94%	95%
Median Time to ECG (minutes)[1,3]	5	6	10	8
Median Time to Transfer (minutes)[5]	0	-	54	61
Fibrinolytic Medication Timing[5]	0	-	60%	54%
Heart Failure Care				
ACE Inhibitor or ARB for LVSD	94	98%	95%	94%
Discharge Instructions	212	97%	89%	88%
Evaluation of LVS Function	246	99%	99%	98%
Smoking Cessation Advice	51	100%	99%	98%
Pneumonia Care				
Appropriate Initial Antibiotic	119	93%	94%	92%
Blood Culture Timing	193	97%	96%	96%
Influenza Vaccine	113	95%	91%	91%
Initial Antibiotic Timing	176	98%	96%	95%
Pneumococcal Vaccine	159	95%	93%	93%
Smoking Cessation Advice	88	98%	98%	97%
Surgical Care Improvement Project				
Appropriate VTP Within 24 Hours	298	92%	94%	92%
Appropriate Hair Removal	1,450	100%	99%	99%
Appropriate Beta Blocker Usage	440	89%	92%	93%
Controlled Postoperative Blood Glucose	217	95%	94%	93%
Prophylactic Antibiotic Timing	1,088	95%	97%	97%
Prophylactic Antibiotic Timing (Outpatient)	482	93%	87%	92%
Prophylactic Antibiotic Selection	1,087	99%	98%	97%
Prophylactic Antibiotic Select. (Outpatient)	595	97%	92%	94%
Prophylactic Antibiotic Stopped	1,051	95%	95%	94%
Recommended VTP Ordered	299	93%	95%	94%
Urinary Catheter Removal	382	95%	91%	90%
Children's Asthma Care				
Received Systemic Corticosteroids	-	-	-	100%
Received Home Management Plan	-	-	-	71%
Received Reliever Medication	-	-	-	100%
Use of Medical Imaging				
Combination Abdominal CT Scan	903	0.016	0.135	0.191
Combination Chest CT Scan	821	0.061	0.068	0.054
Follow-up Mammogram/Ultrasound	1,547	4.7%	7.4%	8.4%
MRI for Low Back Pain	552	32.4%	32%	32.7%
Survey of Patients' Hospital Experiences				
Area Around Room 'Always' Quiet at Night	300+	52%	-	58%
Doctors 'Always' Communicated Well	300+	78%	-	80%
Home Recovery Information Given	300+	86%	-	82%
Hospital Given 9 or 10 on 10 Point Scale	300+	68%	-	67%
Meds 'Always' Explained Before Given	300+	57%	-	60%
Nurses 'Always' Communicated Well	300+	73%	-	76%
Pain 'Always' Well Controlled	300+	68%	-	69%
Room and Bathroom 'Always' Clean	300+	66%	-	71%
Timely Help 'Always' Received	300+	63%	-	64%
Would Definitely Recommend Hospital	300+	70%	-	69%

NOTE: Hospital profiles are in alphabetical order by state, then city, then hospital within the city; Rankings exclude hospitals with less than 25 cases except for patient surveys which excludes hospitals with less than 100 cases; (a) 100–299 cases; (1) The number of cases is too small to be sure how well a hospital is performing; (2) The hospital indicated that the data submitted for this measure were based on a sample of cases; (3) Data was collected during a shorter time period (fewer quarters) than the maximum possible time for this measure; (4) Suppressed for one or more quarters by CMS; (5) No data is available from the hospital for this measure; (6) Fewer than 100 patients completed the HCAHPS survey. Use these rates with caution, as the number of surveys may be too low to reliably assess hospital performance; (7) Survey results are based on less than 12 months of data; (8) Survey results are not available for this reporting period; (9) No or very few patients were eligible for the HCAHPS survey. The scores shown, if any, reflect a very small number of surveys; (10) A state average was not calculated because too few hospitals in the state submitted data; (11) There were discrepancies in the data collection process; Please refer to the User's Guide for a full explanation of data.

Memorial Healthcare

826 West King Street, Owosso, MI 48867
Phone: 989-723-5211
Fax: 989-725-8937
URL: www.memorialhealthcare.org
Type: Acute Care Hospitals
Emergency Services: Yes
Ownership: Voluntary Non-Profit - Other
Beds: 143

Key Personnel:
CEO/President. . . . . Cheryl Peterson
Cardiac Laboratory. . . . . Kathy Whal
Chief of Medical Staff . . . . Michael Schmidt, DO
Infection Control. . . . . Lynn Howes
Operating Room. . . . . Vicki Watkins
Pediatric In-Patient Care . . . . Kathy Roberts
Quality Assurance . . . . Sue Spragg
Radiology. . . . . Keith Morrow

Measure	Cases	This Hosp.	State Avg.	U.S. Avg.
Heart Attack Care				
ACE Inhibitor or ARB for LVSD[1]	7	86%	96%	96%
Aspirin at Arrival[1]	19	95%	99%	99%
Aspirin at Discharge[1]	18	89%	99%	98%
Beta Blocker at Discharge[1]	18	100%	99%	98%
Fibrinolytic Medication Timing	0	-	55%	55%
PCI Within 90 Minutes of Arrival	0	-	89%	90%
Smoking Cessation Advice[1]	2	100%	100%	99%
Chest Pain/Possible Heart Attack Care				
Aspirin at Arrival	150	96%	94%	95%
Median Time to ECG (minutes)	154	12	10	8
Median Time to Transfer (minutes)[1,3]	2	245	54	61
Fibrinolytic Medication Timing[1]	11	55%	60%	54%
Heart Failure Care				
ACE Inhibitor or ARB for LVSD[1]	22	91%	95%	94%
Discharge Instructions	53	85%	89%	88%
Evaluation of LVS Function	82	99%	99%	98%
Smoking Cessation Advice[1]	13	100%	99%	98%
Pneumonia Care				
Appropriate Initial Antibiotic	91	89%	94%	92%
Blood Culture Timing	127	86%	96%	96%
Influenza Vaccine	76	93%	91%	91%
Initial Antibiotic Timing	122	96%	96%	95%
Pneumococcal Vaccine	92	99%	93%	93%
Smoking Cessation Advice	47	100%	98%	97%
Surgical Care Improvement Project				
Appropriate VTP Within 24 Hours	138	87%	94%	92%
Appropriate Hair Removal	333	100%	99%	99%
Appropriate Beta Blocker Usage	79	95%	92%	93%
Controlled Postoperative Blood Glucose	0	-	94%	93%
Prophylactic Antibiotic Timing	222	96%	97%	97%
Prophylactic Antibiotic Timing (Outpatient)	126	94%	87%	92%
Prophylactic Antibiotic Selection	220	95%	98%	97%
Prophylactic Antibiotic Select. (Outpatient)	122	92%	92%	94%
Prophylactic Antibiotic Stopped	216	94%	95%	94%
Recommended VTP Ordered	140	92%	95%	94%
Urinary Catheter Removal	100	95%	91%	90%
Children's Asthma Care				
Received Systemic Corticosteroids	-	-	-	100%
Received Home Management Plan	-	-	-	71%
Received Reliever Medication	-	-	-	100%
Use of Medical Imaging				
Combination Abdominal CT Scan	655	0.029	0.135	0.191
Combination Chest CT Scan	576	0.005	0.068	0.054
Follow-up Mammogram/Ultrasound	1,438	7.3%	7.4%	8.4%
MRI for Low Back Pain	207	32.4%	32%	32.7%
Survey of Patients' Hospital Experiences				
Area Around Room 'Always' Quiet at Night	300+	51%	-	58%
Doctors 'Always' Communicated Well	300+	71%	-	80%
Home Recovery Information Given	300+	81%	-	82%
Hospital Given 9 or 10 on 10 Point Scale	300+	54%	-	67%
Meds 'Always' Explained Before Given	300+	54%	-	60%
Nurses 'Always' Communicated Well	300+	71%	-	76%
Pain 'Always' Well Controlled	300+	65%	-	69%
Room and Bathroom 'Always' Clean	300+	74%	-	71%
Timely Help 'Always' Received	300+	60%	-	64%
Would Definitely Recommend Hospital	300+	57%	-	69%

Bronson Lakeview Hospital

408 Hazen Street, Paw Paw, MI 49079
Phone: 269-657-1400
Fax: 269-657-1339
Type: Critical Access Hospitals
Emergency Services: Yes
Ownership: Govt - Hospital Dist/Auth
Beds: 174

Key Personnel:
CEO/President. . . . . Sue E Johnson-Phillip
Chief of Medical Staff . . . . David B Peirce, MD
Infection Control. . . . . Sandra Oszaniec
Operating Room. . . . . Mary Starkweather
Pediatric Ambulatory Care . . . . . . Jay J Bathani, MD
Pediatric In-Patient Care . . . . Jay J Bathani, MD
Quality Assurance . . . . Sandra Oszaniec
Radiology. . . . . Sue Szakal, MD

Measure	Cases	This Hosp.	State Avg.	U.S. Avg.
Heart Attack Care				
ACE Inhibitor or ARB for LVSD[3]	0	-	96%	96%
Aspirin at Arrival[1,3]	2	100%	99%	99%
Aspirin at Discharge[1,3]	2	100%	99%	98%
Beta Blocker at Discharge[1,3]	2	100%	99%	98%
Fibrinolytic Medication Timing[3]	0	-	55%	55%
PCI Within 90 Minutes of Arrival[3]	0	-	89%	90%
Smoking Cessation Advice[3]	0	-	100%	99%
Chest Pain/Possible Heart Attack Care				
Aspirin at Arrival	-	-	94%	95%
Median Time to ECG (minutes)	-	-	10	8
Median Time to Transfer (minutes)	-	-	54	61
Fibrinolytic Medication Timing	-	-	60%	54%
Heart Failure Care				
ACE Inhibitor or ARB for LVSD[1]	16	94%	95%	94%
Discharge Instructions	37	100%	89%	88%
Evaluation of LVS Function	38	100%	99%	98%
Smoking Cessation Advice[1]	6	100%	99%	98%
Pneumonia Care				
Appropriate Initial Antibiotic	60	98%	94%	92%
Blood Culture Timing	61	93%	96%	96%
Influenza Vaccine	44	100%	91%	91%
Initial Antibiotic Timing	79	99%	96%	95%
Pneumococcal Vaccine	59	98%	93%	93%
Smoking Cessation Advice	36	100%	98%	97%
Surgical Care Improvement Project				
Appropriate VTP Within 24 Hours[5]	0	-	94%	92%
Appropriate Hair Removal[5]	0	-	99%	99%
Appropriate Beta Blocker Usage[5]	0	-	92%	93%
Controlled Postoperative Blood Glucose[5]	0	-	94%	93%
Prophylactic Antibiotic Timing[5]	0	-	97%	97%
Prophylactic Antibiotic Timing (Outpatient)	-	-	87%	92%
Prophylactic Antibiotic Selection[5]	0	-	98%	97%
Prophylactic Antibiotic Select. (Outpatient)	-	-	92%	94%
Prophylactic Antibiotic Stopped[5]	0	-	95%	94%
Recommended VTP Ordered[5]	0	-	95%	94%
Urinary Catheter Removal[5]	0	-	91%	90%
Children's Asthma Care				
Received Systemic Corticosteroids	-	-	-	100%
Received Home Management Plan	-	-	-	71%
Received Reliever Medication	-	-	-	100%
Use of Medical Imaging				
Combination Abdominal CT Scan	-	-	0.135	0.191
Combination Chest CT Scan	-	-	0.068	0.054
Follow-up Mammogram/Ultrasound	-	-	7.4%	8.4%
MRI for Low Back Pain	-	-	32%	32.7%
Survey of Patients' Hospital Experiences				
Area Around Room 'Always' Quiet at Night	(a)	60%	-	58%
Doctors 'Always' Communicated Well	(a)	85%	-	80%
Home Recovery Information Given	(a)	87%	-	82%
Hospital Given 9 or 10 on 10 Point Scale	(a)	69%	-	67%
Meds 'Always' Explained Before Given	(a)	59%	-	60%
Nurses 'Always' Communicated Well	(a)	81%	-	76%
Pain 'Always' Well Controlled	(a)	74%	-	69%
Room and Bathroom 'Always' Clean	(a)	73%	-	71%
Timely Help 'Always' Received	(a)	76%	-	64%
Would Definitely Recommend Hospital	(a)	69%	-	69%

Northern Michigan Regional Hospital

416 Connable Ave, Petoskey, MI 49770
Phone: 231-487-4000
Fax: 231-487-7798
URL: www.northernhealth.org
Type: Acute Care Hospitals
Emergency Services: Yes
Ownership: Voluntary Non-Profit - Other
Beds: 243

Key Personnel:
CEO/President. . . . . Thomas Mroczkowski
Chief of Medical Staff . . . . John Bednar, MD
Quality Assurance . . . . Ingrid Flemming
Radiology. . . . . William E Henry

Measure	Cases	This Hosp.	State Avg.	U.S. Avg.
Heart Attack Care				
ACE Inhibitor or ARB for LVSD	57	98%	96%	96%
Aspirin at Arrival	129	100%	99%	99%
Aspirin at Discharge	356	99%	99%	98%
Beta Blocker at Discharge	335	99%	99%	98%
Fibrinolytic Medication Timing	0	-	55%	55%
PCI Within 90 Minutes of Arrival	29	83%	89%	90%
Smoking Cessation Advice	126	100%	100%	99%
Chest Pain/Possible Heart Attack Care				
Aspirin at Arrival[5]	0	-	94%	95%
Median Time to ECG (minutes)[5]	0	-	10	8
Median Time to Transfer (minutes)[5]	0	-	54	61
Fibrinolytic Medication Timing[5]	0	-	60%	54%
Heart Failure Care				
ACE Inhibitor or ARB for LVSD	119	97%	95%	94%
Discharge Instructions	244	87%	89%	88%
Evaluation of LVS Function	274	99%	99%	98%
Smoking Cessation Advice	40	100%	99%	98%
Pneumonia Care				
Appropriate Initial Antibiotic	83	93%	94%	92%
Blood Culture Timing	129	97%	96%	96%
Influenza Vaccine	106	92%	91%	91%
Initial Antibiotic Timing	125	90%	96%	95%
Pneumococcal Vaccine	137	96%	93%	93%
Smoking Cessation Advice	63	98%	98%	97%
Surgical Care Improvement Project				
Appropriate VTP Within 24 Hours[2]	145	93%	94%	92%
Appropriate Hair Removal[2]	615	99%	99%	99%
Appropriate Beta Blocker Usage[2]	223	92%	92%	93%
Controlled Postoperative Blood Glucose[2]	125	93%	94%	93%
Prophylactic Antibiotic Timing[2]	447	97%	97%	97%
Prophylactic Antibiotic Timing (Outpatient)	362	84%	87%	92%
Prophylactic Antibiotic Selection[2]	458	99%	98%	97%
Prophylactic Antibiotic Select. (Outpatient)	334	95%	92%	94%
Prophylactic Antibiotic Stopped[2]	427	91%	95%	94%
Recommended VTP Ordered[2]	155	90%	95%	94%
Urinary Catheter Removal[2]	105	89%	91%	90%
Children's Asthma Care				
Received Systemic Corticosteroids	-	-	-	100%
Received Home Management Plan	-	-	-	71%
Received Reliever Medication	-	-	-	100%
Use of Medical Imaging				
Combination Abdominal CT Scan	837	0.053	0.135	0.191
Combination Chest CT Scan	827	0.000	0.068	0.054
Follow-up Mammogram/Ultrasound	1,214	4.0%	7.4%	8.4%
MRI for Low Back Pain	206	36.9%	32%	32.7%
Survey of Patients' Hospital Experiences				
Area Around Room 'Always' Quiet at Night	300+	51%	-	58%
Doctors 'Always' Communicated Well	300+	82%	-	80%
Home Recovery Information Given	300+	90%	-	82%
Hospital Given 9 or 10 on 10 Point Scale	300+	75%	-	67%
Meds 'Always' Explained Before Given	300+	70%	-	60%
Nurses 'Always' Communicated Well	300+	80%	-	76%
Pain 'Always' Well Controlled	300+	75%	-	69%
Room and Bathroom 'Always' Clean	300+	66%	-	71%
Timely Help 'Always' Received	300+	69%	-	64%
Would Definitely Recommend Hospital	300+	78%	-	69%

NOTE: Hospital profiles are in alphabetical order by state, then city, then hospital within the city; Rankings exclude hospitals with less than 25 cases except for patient surveys which excludes hospitals with less than 100 cases; (a) 100–299 cases; (1) The number of cases is too small to be sure how well a hospital is performing; (2) The hospital indicated that the data submitted for this measure were based on a sample of cases; (3) Data was collected during a shorter time period (fewer quarters) than the maximum possible time for this measure; (4) Suppressed for one or more quarters by CMS; (5) No data is available from the hospital for this measure; (6) Fewer than 100 patients completed the HCAHPS survey. Use these rates with caution, as the number of surveys may be too low to reliably assess hospital performance; (7) Survey results are based on less than 12 months of data; (8) Survey results are not available for this reporting period; (9) No or very few patients were eligible for the HCAHPS survey. The scores shown, if any, reflect a very small number of surveys; (10) A state average was not calculated because too few hospitals in the state submitted data; (11) There were discrepancies in the data collection process; Please refer to the User's Guide for a full explanation of data.

Doctor's Hospital of Michigan

461 W Huron St
Pontiac, MI 48341
Phone: 248-857-7200
Fax: 248-857-6801
URL: www.nomc.org
Type: Acute Care Hospitals
Emergency Services: Yes
Ownership: Voluntary Non-Profit - Private
Beds: 380

Key Personnel:
CEO/President. . . . . Robert Davis
Chief of Medical Staff . . . . Bruce Lessien
Infection Control. . . . . Luretta Pandya, RN
Quality Assurance . . . . Rodger Chrysler
Radiology. . . . . M Khalid, MD
Anesthesiology. . . . . Y Falick, MD
Emergency Room . . . . Derrek McCallmont, MD

Measure	Cases	This Hosp.	State Avg.	U.S. Avg.
Heart Attack Care				
ACE Inhibitor or ARB for LVSD[1]	2	50%	96%	96%
Aspirin at Arrival[1]	11	100%	99%	99%
Aspirin at Discharge[1]	8	75%	99%	98%
Beta Blocker at Discharge[1]	7	86%	99%	98%
Fibrinolytic Medication Timing	0	-	55%	55%
PCI Within 90 Minutes of Arrival	0	-	89%	90%
Smoking Cessation Advice	0	-	100%	99%
Chest Pain/Possible Heart Attack Care				
Aspirin at Arrival	38	95%	94%	95%
Median Time to ECG (minutes)	38	12	10	8
Median Time to Transfer (minutes)[1,3]	2	130	54	61
Fibrinolytic Medication Timing	0	-	60%	54%
Heart Failure Care				
ACE Inhibitor or ARB for LVSD[1]	20	90%	95%	94%
Discharge Instructions	89	78%	89%	88%
Evaluation of LVS Function	103	83%	99%	98%
Smoking Cessation Advice[1]	21	90%	99%	98%
Pneumonia Care				
Appropriate Initial Antibiotic	33	79%	94%	92%
Blood Culture Timing	46	96%	96%	96%
Influenza Vaccine	28	89%	91%	91%
Initial Antibiotic Timing	50	86%	96%	95%
Pneumococcal Vaccine	30	87%	93%	93%
Smoking Cessation Advice	29	72%	98%	97%
Surgical Care Improvement Project				
Appropriate VTP Within 24 Hours[2]	89	89%	94%	92%
Appropriate Hair Removal[2]	132	99%	99%	99%
Appropriate Beta Blocker Usage[2]	25	84%	92%	93%
Controlled Postoperative Blood Glucose[2]	0	-	94%	93%
Prophylactic Antibiotic Timing[2]	57	42%	97%	97%
Prophylactic Antibiotic Timing (Outpatient)	94	52%	87%	92%
Prophylactic Antibiotic Selection[2]	51	80%	98%	97%
Prophylactic Antibiotic Select. (Outpatient)	75	61%	92%	94%
Prophylactic Antibiotic Stopped[2]	50	92%	95%	94%
Recommended VTP Ordered[2]	90	91%	95%	94%
Urinary Catheter Removal	41	78%	91%	90%
Children's Asthma Care				
Received Systemic Corticosteroids	-	-	-	100%
Received Home Management Plan	-	-	-	71%
Received Reliever Medication	-	-	-	100%
Use of Medical Imaging				
Combination Abdominal CT Scan	262	0.214	0.135	0.191
Combination Chest CT Scan	188	0.027	0.068	0.054
Follow-up Mammogram/Ultrasound	818	3.2%	7.4%	8.4%
MRI for Low Back Pain[1]	39	30.8%	32%	32.7%
Survey of Patients' Hospital Experiences				
Area Around Room 'Always' Quiet at Night	300+	58%	-	58%
Doctors 'Always' Communicated Well	300+	74%	-	80%
Home Recovery Information Given	300+	79%	-	82%
Hospital Given 9 or 10 on 10 Point Scale	300+	58%	-	67%
Meds 'Always' Explained Before Given	300+	58%	-	60%
Nurses 'Always' Communicated Well	300+	75%	-	76%
Pain 'Always' Well Controlled	300+	67%	-	69%
Room and Bathroom 'Always' Clean	300+	72%	-	71%
Timely Help 'Always' Received	300+	62%	-	64%
Would Definitely Recommend Hospital	300+	61%	-	69%

Poh Medical Center

50 North Perry
Pontiac, MI 48342
Phone: 248-338-5000
Fax: 248-338-5667
URL: www.pohmedical.org
Type: Acute Care Hospitals
Emergency Services: Yes
Ownership: Voluntary Non-Profit - Private
Beds: 308

Key Personnel:
CEO/President. . . . . Patrick Lamberti
Chief of Medical Staff . . . . Steve Calkin
Infection Control. . . . . MO Doyle, DO
Operating Room. . . . . Jackie Adams, RN
Pediatric Ambulatory Care . . . . . . ID Kernis, DO
Pediatric In-Patient Care . . . . ID Kernis, DO
Quality Assurance . . . . Lynn Kirby
Radiology. . . . . DA Kellam, DO

Measure	Cases	This Hosp.	State Avg.	U.S. Avg.
Heart Attack Care				
ACE Inhibitor or ARB for LVSD[1]	9	89%	96%	96%
Aspirin at Arrival	38	95%	99%	99%
Aspirin at Discharge	33	97%	99%	98%
Beta Blocker at Discharge	35	100%	99%	98%
Fibrinolytic Medication Timing	0	-	55%	55%
PCI Within 90 Minutes of Arrival	0	-	89%	90%
Smoking Cessation Advice[1]	9	100%	100%	99%
Chest Pain/Possible Heart Attack Care				
Aspirin at Arrival	91	91%	94%	95%
Median Time to ECG (minutes)	95	5	10	8
Median Time to Transfer (minutes)[1]	10	49	54	61
Fibrinolytic Medication Timing	0	-	60%	54%
Heart Failure Care				
ACE Inhibitor or ARB for LVSD[2]	80	95%	95%	94%
Discharge Instructions[2]	192	39%	89%	88%
Evaluation of LVS Function[2]	221	100%	99%	98%
Smoking Cessation Advice[2]	77	77%	99%	98%
Pneumonia Care				
Appropriate Initial Antibiotic[2]	88	88%	94%	92%
Blood Culture Timing[2]	84	95%	96%	96%
Influenza Vaccine[2]	64	92%	91%	91%
Initial Antibiotic Timing[2]	113	94%	96%	95%
Pneumococcal Vaccine[2]	79	91%	93%	93%
Smoking Cessation Advice[2]	67	73%	98%	97%
Surgical Care Improvement Project				
Appropriate VTP Within 24 Hours[2]	105	92%	94%	92%
Appropriate Hair Removal[2]	291	100%	99%	99%
Appropriate Beta Blocker Usage[2]	64	78%	92%	93%
Controlled Postoperative Blood Glucose[2]	0	-	94%	93%
Prophylactic Antibiotic Timing[2]	178	99%	97%	97%
Prophylactic Antibiotic Timing (Outpatient)	100	79%	87%	92%
Prophylactic Antibiotic Selection[2]	184	95%	98%	97%
Prophylactic Antibiotic Select. (Outpatient)	88	76%	92%	94%
Prophylactic Antibiotic Stopped[2]	170	86%	95%	94%
Recommended VTP Ordered[2]	106	94%	95%	94%
Urinary Catheter Removal[2]	88	86%	91%	90%
Children's Asthma Care				
Received Systemic Corticosteroids	-	-	-	100%
Received Home Management Plan	-	-	-	71%
Received Reliever Medication	-	-	-	100%
Use of Medical Imaging				
Combination Abdominal CT Scan	395	0.147	0.135	0.191
Combination Chest CT Scan	272	0.059	0.068	0.054
Follow-up Mammogram/Ultrasound	341	16.4%	7.4%	8.4%
MRI for Low Back Pain[5]	0	-	32%	32.7%
Survey of Patients' Hospital Experiences				
Area Around Room 'Always' Quiet at Night	300+	48%	-	58%
Doctors 'Always' Communicated Well	300+	70%	-	80%
Home Recovery Information Given	300+	75%	-	82%
Hospital Given 9 or 10 on 10 Point Scale	300+	60%	-	67%
Meds 'Always' Explained Before Given	300+	54%	-	60%
Nurses 'Always' Communicated Well	300+	71%	-	76%
Pain 'Always' Well Controlled	300+	68%	-	69%
Room and Bathroom 'Always' Clean	300+	74%	-	71%
Timely Help 'Always' Received	300+	60%	-	64%
Would Definitely Recommend Hospital	300+	59%	-	69%

Saint Joseph Mercy Oakland

44405 Woodward Ave
Pontiac, MI 48341
Phone: 248-858-3000
Fax: 248-858-3155
URL: www.stjoesoakland.org
Type: Acute Care Hospitals
Emergency Services: Yes
Ownership: Voluntary Non-Profit - Private
Beds: 443

Key Personnel:
CEO/President. . . . . Jack Weiner
Chief of Medical Staff . . . . Donald Bignotti MD
Operating Room. . . . . Trudy Lentini
Pediatric Ambulatory Care . . . . . . Rajendra Desai MD
Radiology. . . . . Babu Vemuri MD
Emergency Room . . . . Mary Jo Malafa

Measure	Cases	This Hosp.	State Avg.	U.S. Avg.
Heart Attack Care				
ACE Inhibitor or ARB for LVSD[2]	69	100%	96%	96%
Aspirin at Arrival[2]	253	100%	99%	99%
Aspirin at Discharge[2]	305	99%	99%	98%
Beta Blocker at Discharge[2]	290	99%	99%	98%
Fibrinolytic Medication Timing[2]	0	-	55%	55%
PCI Within 90 Minutes of Arrival[2]	48	90%	89%	90%
Smoking Cessation Advice[2]	96	100%	100%	99%
Chest Pain/Possible Heart Attack Care				
Aspirin at Arrival[1]	12	100%	94%	95%
Median Time to ECG (minutes)[1]	13	12	10	8
Median Time to Transfer (minutes)[5]	0	-	54	61
Fibrinolytic Medication Timing[3]	0	-	60%	54%
Heart Failure Care				
ACE Inhibitor or ARB for LVSD[2]	109	96%	95%	94%
Discharge Instructions[2]	255	94%	89%	88%
Evaluation of LVS Function[2]	298	99%	99%	98%
Smoking Cessation Advice[2]	53	100%	99%	98%
Pneumonia Care				
Appropriate Initial Antibiotic[2]	84	95%	94%	92%
Blood Culture Timing[2]	77	100%	96%	96%
Influenza Vaccine[2]	83	88%	91%	91%
Initial Antibiotic Timing[2]	126	94%	96%	95%
Pneumococcal Vaccine[2]	116	93%	93%	93%
Smoking Cessation Advice[2]	58	100%	98%	97%
Surgical Care Improvement Project				
Appropriate VTP Within 24 Hours[2]	161	99%	94%	92%
Appropriate Hair Removal[2]	630	100%	99%	99%
Appropriate Beta Blocker Usage[2]	201	96%	92%	93%
Controlled Postoperative Blood Glucose[2]	130	94%	94%	93%
Prophylactic Antibiotic Timing[2]	459	99%	97%	97%
Prophylactic Antibiotic Timing (Outpatient)	421	99%	87%	92%
Prophylactic Antibiotic Selection[2]	473	99%	98%	97%
Prophylactic Antibiotic Select. (Outpatient)	438	98%	92%	94%
Prophylactic Antibiotic Stopped[2]	426	98%	95%	94%
Recommended VTP Ordered[2]	161	99%	95%	94%
Urinary Catheter Removal[2]	143	92%	91%	90%
Children's Asthma Care				
Received Systemic Corticosteroids	-	-	-	100%
Received Home Management Plan	-	-	-	71%
Received Reliever Medication	-	-	-	100%
Use of Medical Imaging				
Combination Abdominal CT Scan	999	0.152	0.135	0.191
Combination Chest CT Scan	818	0.084	0.068	0.054
Follow-up Mammogram/Ultrasound	1,613	6.4%	7.4%	8.4%
MRI for Low Back Pain	282	24.5%	32%	32.7%
Survey of Patients' Hospital Experiences				
Area Around Room 'Always' Quiet at Night	300+	51%	-	58%
Doctors 'Always' Communicated Well	300+	76%	-	80%
Home Recovery Information Given	300+	83%	-	82%
Hospital Given 9 or 10 on 10 Point Scale	300+	66%	-	67%
Meds 'Always' Explained Before Given	300+	57%	-	60%
Nurses 'Always' Communicated Well	300+	73%	-	76%
Pain 'Always' Well Controlled	300+	66%	-	69%
Room and Bathroom 'Always' Clean	300+	58%	-	71%
Timely Help 'Always' Received	300+	56%	-	64%
Would Definitely Recommend Hospital	300+	70%	-	69%

NOTE: Hospital profiles are in alphabetical order by state, then city, then hospital within the city; Rankings exclude hospitals with less than 25 cases except for patient surveys which excludes hospitals with less than 100 cases; (a) 100–299 cases; (1) The number of cases is too small to be sure how well a hospital is performing; (2) The hospital indicated that the data submitted for this measure were based on a sample of cases; (3) Data was collected during a shorter time period (fewer quarters) than the maximum possible time for this measure; (4) Suppressed for one or more quarters by CMS; (5) No data is available from the hospital for this measure; (6) Fewer than 100 patients completed the HCAHPS survey. Use these rates with caution, as the number of surveys may be too low to reliably assess hospital performance; (7) Survey results are based on less than 12 months of data; (8) Survey results are not available for this reporting period; (9) No or very few patients were eligible for the HCAHPS survey. The scores shown, if any, reflect a very small number of surveys; (10) A state average was not calculated because too few hospitals in the state submitted data; (11) There were discrepancies in the data collection process; Please refer to the User's Guide for a full explanation of data.

Port Huron Hospital

1221 Pine Grove Ave
Port Huron, MI 48060
Phone: 810-987-5000
Fax: 810-985-2675
E-mail: phhwebmaster@porthuronhosp.org
URL: www.porthuronhospital.org
Type: Acute Care Hospitals
Emergency Services: Yes
Ownership: Voluntary Non-Profit - Other
Beds: 186

Key Personnel:
CEO/President. . . . . Thomas DeFauw
Cardiac Laboratory. . . . . Maryann Barnes
Chief of Medical Staff . . . . Michael Tawney, DO
Operating Room. . . . . Frank Brettschneider, DO
Pediatric Ambulatory Care . . . . . . Kathy Richards
Quality Assurance . . . . Mary Pool
Radiology. . . . . F William Coop

Measure	Cases	This Hosp.	State Avg.	U.S. Avg.
Heart Attack Care				
ACE Inhibitor or ARB for LVSD	76	92%	96%	96%
Aspirin at Arrival	239	100%	99%	99%
Aspirin at Discharge	313	98%	99%	98%
Beta Blocker at Discharge	312	97%	99%	98%
Fibrinolytic Medication Timing	0	-	55%	55%
PCI Within 90 Minutes of Arrival	50	76%	89%	90%
Smoking Cessation Advice	106	100%	100%	99%
Chest Pain/Possible Heart Attack Care				
Aspirin at Arrival[1]	2	50%	94%	95%
Median Time to ECG (minutes)[1]	2	16	10	8
Median Time to Transfer (minutes)[5]	0	-	54	61
Fibrinolytic Medication Timing[5]	0	-	60%	54%
Heart Failure Care				
ACE Inhibitor or ARB for LVSD	103	97%	95%	94%
Discharge Instructions	265	88%	89%	88%
Evaluation of LVS Function	325	98%	99%	98%
Smoking Cessation Advice	55	91%	99%	98%
Pneumonia Care				
Appropriate Initial Antibiotic	189	96%	94%	92%
Blood Culture Timing	261	95%	96%	96%
Influenza Vaccine	169	93%	91%	91%
Initial Antibiotic Timing	279	91%	96%	95%
Pneumococcal Vaccine	239	94%	93%	93%
Smoking Cessation Advice	97	97%	98%	97%
Surgical Care Improvement Project				
Appropriate VTP Within 24 Hours[2]	280	99%	94%	92%
Appropriate Hair Removal[2]	836	98%	99%	99%
Appropriate Beta Blocker Usage[2]	260	81%	92%	93%
Controlled Postoperative Blood Glucose[2]	150	99%	94%	93%
Prophylactic Antibiotic Timing[2]	613	97%	97%	97%
Prophylactic Antibiotic Timing (Outpatient)	142	90%	87%	92%
Prophylactic Antibiotic Selection[2]	616	97%	98%	97%
Prophylactic Antibiotic Select. (Outpatient)	136	99%	92%	94%
Prophylactic Antibiotic Stopped[2]	587	98%	95%	94%
Recommended VTP Ordered[2]	280	99%	95%	94%
Urinary Catheter Removal[2]	246	74%	91%	90%
Children's Asthma Care				
Received Systemic Corticosteroids	-	-	-	100%
Received Home Management Plan	-	-	-	71%
Received Reliever Medication	-	-	-	100%
Use of Medical Imaging				
Combination Abdominal CT Scan	897	0.030	0.135	0.191
Combination Chest CT Scan	833	0.002	0.068	0.054
Follow-up Mammogram/Ultrasound	1,448	12.4%	7.4%	8.4%
MRI for Low Back Pain[5]	0	-	32%	32.7%
Survey of Patients' Hospital Experiences				
Area Around Room 'Always' Quiet at Night	300+	51%	-	58%
Doctors 'Always' Communicated Well	300+	77%	-	80%
Home Recovery Information Given	300+	81%	-	82%
Hospital Given 9 or 10 on 10 Point Scale	300+	67%	-	67%
Meds 'Always' Explained Before Given	300+	58%	-	60%
Nurses 'Always' Communicated Well	300+	79%	-	76%
Pain 'Always' Well Controlled	300+	71%	-	69%
Room and Bathroom 'Always' Clean	300+	71%	-	71%
Timely Help 'Always' Received	300+	64%	-	64%
Would Definitely Recommend Hospital	300+	70%	-	69%

Saint Joseph Mercy Port Huron

2601 Electric Avenue
Port Huron, MI 48060
Phone: 810-985-1510
Fax: 810-985-1508
URL: www.mercyporthuron.com
Type: Acute Care Hospitals
Emergency Services: Yes
Ownership: Voluntary Non-Profit - Church
Beds: 119

Key Personnel:
CEO/President. . . . . Peter Karadjoff
Chief of Medical Staff . . . . Aaron Clark
Infection Control. . . . . D Heide
Operating Room. . . . . Brenda Miller
Quality Assurance . . . . Julie Schieman
Radiology. . . . . Daniel Shogren
Emergency Room . . . . Jere Baldwin, MD
Intensive Care Unit. . . . . Brian Thick

Measure	Cases	This Hosp.	State Avg.	U.S. Avg.
Heart Attack Care				
ACE Inhibitor or ARB for LVSD[1]	7	100%	96%	96%
Aspirin at Arrival	31	100%	99%	99%
Aspirin at Discharge[1]	24	100%	99%	98%
Beta Blocker at Discharge	25	100%	99%	98%
Fibrinolytic Medication Timing	0	-	55%	55%
PCI Within 90 Minutes of Arrival	0	-	89%	90%
Smoking Cessation Advice[1]	6	100%	100%	99%
Chest Pain/Possible Heart Attack Care				
Aspirin at Arrival	33	100%	94%	95%
Median Time to ECG (minutes)	32	13	10	8
Median Time to Transfer (minutes)[1]	9	52	54	61
Fibrinolytic Medication Timing	0	-	60%	54%
Heart Failure Care				
ACE Inhibitor or ARB for LVSD	31	97%	95%	94%
Discharge Instructions	108	91%	89%	88%
Evaluation of LVS Function	146	100%	99%	98%
Smoking Cessation Advice	30	100%	99%	98%
Pneumonia Care				
Appropriate Initial Antibiotic	78	87%	94%	92%
Blood Culture Timing	125	99%	96%	96%
Influenza Vaccine	83	98%	91%	91%
Initial Antibiotic Timing	133	99%	96%	95%
Pneumococcal Vaccine	95	97%	93%	93%
Smoking Cessation Advice	56	100%	98%	97%
Surgical Care Improvement Project				
Appropriate VTP Within 24 Hours[2]	165	99%	94%	92%
Appropriate Hair Removal[2]	415	100%	99%	99%
Appropriate Beta Blocker Usage[2]	142	95%	92%	93%
Controlled Postoperative Blood Glucose[2]	0	-	94%	93%
Prophylactic Antibiotic Timing[2]	316	98%	97%	97%
Prophylactic Antibiotic Timing (Outpatient)	32	91%	87%	92%
Prophylactic Antibiotic Selection[2]	318	99%	98%	97%
Prophylactic Antibiotic Select. (Outpatient)	32	94%	92%	94%
Prophylactic Antibiotic Stopped[2]	272	97%	95%	94%
Recommended VTP Ordered[2]	165	100%	95%	94%
Urinary Catheter Removal[2]	177	98%	91%	90%
Children's Asthma Care				
Received Systemic Corticosteroids	-	-	-	100%
Received Home Management Plan	-	-	-	71%
Received Reliever Medication	-	-	-	100%
Use of Medical Imaging				
Combination Abdominal CT Scan	345	0.020	0.135	0.191
Combination Chest CT Scan	383	0.000	0.068	0.054
Follow-up Mammogram/Ultrasound	701	16.7%	7.4%	8.4%
MRI for Low Back Pain[5]	0	-	32%	32.7%
Survey of Patients' Hospital Experiences				
Area Around Room 'Always' Quiet at Night	300+	63%	-	58%
Doctors 'Always' Communicated Well	300+	78%	-	80%
Home Recovery Information Given	300+	85%	-	82%
Hospital Given 9 or 10 on 10 Point Scale	300+	68%	-	67%
Meds 'Always' Explained Before Given	300+	57%	-	60%
Nurses 'Always' Communicated Well	300+	75%	-	76%
Pain 'Always' Well Controlled	300+	68%	-	69%
Room and Bathroom 'Always' Clean	300+	73%	-	71%
Timely Help 'Always' Received	300+	63%	-	64%
Would Definitely Recommend Hospital	300+	68%	-	69%

Spectrum Health - Reed City Campus

300 N Patterson
Reed City, MI 49677
Phone: 231-832-3271
Fax: 231-832-1817
URL: www.spectrum-health.org
Type: Critical Access Hospitals
Emergency Services: Yes
Ownership: Voluntary Non-Profit - Private
Beds: 106

Key Personnel:
CEO/President. . . . . Tom Kauffman

Measure	Cases	This Hosp.	State Avg.	U.S. Avg.
Heart Attack Care				
ACE Inhibitor or ARB for LVSD[1]	1	0%	96%	96%
Aspirin at Arrival[1]	3	100%	99%	99%
Aspirin at Discharge[1]	3	100%	99%	98%
Beta Blocker at Discharge[1]	3	100%	99%	98%
Fibrinolytic Medication Timing	0	-	55%	55%
PCI Within 90 Minutes of Arrival	0	-	89%	90%
Smoking Cessation Advice	0	-	100%	99%
Chest Pain/Possible Heart Attack Care				
Aspirin at Arrival	83	100%	94%	95%
Median Time to ECG (minutes)	83	5	10	8
Median Time to Transfer (minutes)[1]	10	34	54	61
Fibrinolytic Medication Timing[1]	2	50%	60%	54%
Heart Failure Care				
ACE Inhibitor or ARB for LVSD[1]	11	91%	95%	94%
Discharge Instructions	26	92%	89%	88%
Evaluation of LVS Function	35	100%	99%	98%
Smoking Cessation Advice[1]	5	80%	99%	98%
Pneumonia Care				
Appropriate Initial Antibiotic	52	98%	94%	92%
Blood Culture Timing	85	93%	96%	96%
Influenza Vaccine	27	96%	91%	91%
Initial Antibiotic Timing	73	97%	96%	95%
Pneumococcal Vaccine	60	98%	93%	93%
Smoking Cessation Advice[1]	15	100%	98%	97%
Surgical Care Improvement Project				
Appropriate VTP Within 24 Hours[1]	1	100%	94%	92%
Appropriate Hair Removal[1]	16	100%	99%	99%
Appropriate Beta Blocker Usage[5]	0	-	92%	93%
Controlled Postoperative Blood Glucose	0	-	94%	93%
Prophylactic Antibiotic Timing[1]	14	100%	97%	97%
Prophylactic Antibiotic Timing (Outpatient)[1]	18	94%	87%	92%
Prophylactic Antibiotic Selection[1]	14	100%	98%	97%
Prophylactic Antibiotic Select. (Outpatient)[1]	17	76%	92%	94%
Prophylactic Antibiotic Stopped[1]	14	100%	95%	94%
Recommended VTP Ordered[1]	1	100%	95%	94%
Urinary Catheter Removal	0	-	91%	90%
Children's Asthma Care				
Received Systemic Corticosteroids	-	-	-	100%
Received Home Management Plan	-	-	-	71%
Received Reliever Medication	-	-	-	100%
Use of Medical Imaging				
Combination Abdominal CT Scan	479	0.042	0.135	0.191
Combination Chest CT Scan	321	0.056	0.068	0.054
Follow-up Mammogram/Ultrasound	366	10.9%	7.4%	8.4%
MRI for Low Back Pain	64	39.1%	32%	32.7%
Survey of Patients' Hospital Experiences				
Area Around Room 'Always' Quiet at Night	(a)	59%	-	58%
Doctors 'Always' Communicated Well	(a)	84%	-	80%
Home Recovery Information Given	(a)	88%	-	82%
Hospital Given 9 or 10 on 10 Point Scale	(a)	76%	-	67%
Meds 'Always' Explained Before Given	(a)	70%	-	60%
Nurses 'Always' Communicated Well	(a)	84%	-	76%
Pain 'Always' Well Controlled	(a)	78%	-	69%
Room and Bathroom 'Always' Clean	(a)	81%	-	71%
Timely Help 'Always' Received	(a)	74%	-	64%
Would Definitely Recommend Hospital	(a)	75%	-	69%

NOTE: Hospital profiles are in alphabetical order by state, then city, then hospital within the city; Rankings exclude hospitals with less than 25 cases except for patient surveys which excludes hospitals with less than 100 cases; (a) 100–299 cases; (1) The number of cases is too small to be sure how well a hospital is performing; (2) The hospital indicated that the data submitted for this measure were based on a sample of cases; (3) Data was collected during a shorter time period (fewer quarters) than the maximum possible time for this measure; (4) Suppressed for one or more quarters by CMS; (5) No data is available from the hospital for this measure; (6) Fewer than 100 patients completed the HCAHPS survey. Use these rates with caution, as the number of surveys may be too low to reliably assess hospital performance; (7) Survey results are based on less than 12 months of data; (8) Survey results are not available for this reporting period; (9) No or very few patients were eligible for the HCAHPS survey. The scores shown, if any, reflect a very small number of surveys; (10) A state average was not calculated because too few hospitals in the state submitted data; (11) There were discrepancies in the data collection process; Please refer to the User's Guide for a full explanation of data.

Crittenton Hospital Medical Center

1101 W University Drive — Phone: 248-652-5000
Rochester, MI 48307 — Fax: 248-650-0353
URL: www.crittenton.com
Type: Acute Care Hospitals — Emergency Services: Yes
Ownership: Voluntary Non-Profit - Private — Beds: 290

Key Personnel:
CEO/President. . . . . Lynn C Orfgen
Chief of Medical Staff . . . . Frank D Sottile, MD

Measure	Cases	This Hosp.	State Avg.	U.S. Avg.
Heart Attack Care				
ACE Inhibitor or ARB for LVSD	25	100%	96%	96%
Aspirin at Arrival	141	98%	99%	99%
Aspirin at Discharge	128	98%	99%	98%
Beta Blocker at Discharge	122	99%	99%	98%
Fibrinolytic Medication Timing	0	-	55%	55%
PCI Within 90 Minutes of Arrival[1]	22	91%	89%	90%
Smoking Cessation Advice	38	100%	100%	99%
Chest Pain/Possible Heart Attack Care				
Aspirin at Arrival[1,3]	6	100%	94%	95%
Median Time to ECG (minutes)[1,3]	6	13	10	8
Median Time to Transfer (minutes)[5]	0	-	54	61
Fibrinolytic Medication Timing[3]	0	-	60%	54%
Heart Failure Care				
ACE Inhibitor or ARB for LVSD	130	98%	95%	94%
Discharge Instructions	287	91%	89%	88%
Evaluation of LVS Function	368	99%	99%	98%
Smoking Cessation Advice	43	100%	99%	98%
Pneumonia Care				
Appropriate Initial Antibiotic	121	88%	94%	92%
Blood Culture Timing	165	83%	96%	96%
Influenza Vaccine	129	91%	91%	91%
Initial Antibiotic Timing	191	96%	96%	95%
Pneumococcal Vaccine	214	94%	93%	93%
Smoking Cessation Advice	48	96%	98%	97%
Surgical Care Improvement Project				
Appropriate VTP Within 24 Hours[2]	148	91%	94%	92%
Appropriate Hair Removal[2]	546	100%	99%	99%
Appropriate Beta Blocker Usage[2]	186	97%	92%	93%
Controlled Postoperative Blood Glucose[2]	77	97%	94%	93%
Prophylactic Antibiotic Timing[2]	400	98%	97%	97%
Prophylactic Antibiotic Timing (Outpatient)	247	85%	87%	92%
Prophylactic Antibiotic Selection[2]	405	99%	98%	97%
Prophylactic Antibiotic Select. (Outpatient)	227	91%	92%	94%
Prophylactic Antibiotic Stopped[2]	370	95%	95%	94%
Recommended VTP Ordered[2]	148	91%	95%	94%
Urinary Catheter Removal[2]	69	78%	91%	90%
Children's Asthma Care				
Received Systemic Corticosteroids	-	-	-	100%
Received Home Management Plan	-	-	-	71%
Received Reliever Medication	-	-	-	100%
Use of Medical Imaging				
Combination Abdominal CT Scan	820	0.151	0.135	0.191
Combination Chest CT Scan	698	0.014	0.068	0.054
Follow-up Mammogram/Ultrasound	1,401	7.9%	7.4%	8.4%
MRI for Low Back Pain[1]	2	50.0%	32%	32.7%
Survey of Patients' Hospital Experiences				
Area Around Room 'Always' Quiet at Night	300+	58%	-	58%
Doctors 'Always' Communicated Well	300+	79%	-	80%
Home Recovery Information Given	300+	82%	-	82%
Hospital Given 9 or 10 on 10 Point Scale	300+	71%	-	67%
Meds 'Always' Explained Before Given	300+	54%	-	60%
Nurses 'Always' Communicated Well	300+	78%	-	76%
Pain 'Always' Well Controlled	300+	70%	-	69%
Room and Bathroom 'Always' Clean	300+	67%	-	71%
Timely Help 'Always' Received	300+	64%	-	64%
Would Definitely Recommend Hospital	300+	73%	-	69%

William Beaumont Hospital

3601 W Thirteen Mile Rd — Phone: 248-898-5000
Royal Oak, MI 48073 — Fax: 248-551-0854
URL: www.beaumonthospitals.com
Type: Acute Care Hospitals — Emergency Services: Yes
Ownership: Proprietary — Beds: 1,061

Key Personnel:
CEO/President. . . . . Ted Wasson
Chief of Medical Staff . . . . Ronald B Irwin, MD
Infection Control. . . . . Jeffrey Bond, MD
Quality Assurance . . . . Edward R Grima
Anesthesiology. . . . . N Sean O'Hanian, MD
Emergency Room . . . . Andrew Wilson, MD

Measure	Cases	This Hosp.	State Avg.	U.S. Avg.
Heart Attack Care				
ACE Inhibitor or ARB for LVSD[2]	107	100%	96%	96%
Aspirin at Arrival[2]	601	100%	99%	99%
Aspirin at Discharge[2]	619	100%	99%	98%
Beta Blocker at Discharge[2]	590	100%	99%	98%
Fibrinolytic Medication Timing[2]	0	-	55%	55%
PCI Within 90 Minutes of Arrival[2]	69	97%	89%	90%
Smoking Cessation Advice[2]	143	100%	100%	99%
Chest Pain/Possible Heart Attack Care				
Aspirin at Arrival[1]	6	100%	94%	95%
Median Time to ECG (minutes)[1]	8	0	10	8
Median Time to Transfer (minutes)[5]	0	-	54	61
Fibrinolytic Medication Timing[5]	0	-	60%	54%
Heart Failure Care				
ACE Inhibitor or ARB for LVSD[2]	369	98%	95%	94%
Discharge Instructions[2]	1,063	93%	89%	88%
Evaluation of LVS Function[2]	1,306	100%	99%	98%
Smoking Cessation Advice[2]	177	100%	99%	98%
Pneumonia Care				
Appropriate Initial Antibiotic[2]	86	94%	94%	92%
Blood Culture Timing[2]	121	96%	96%	96%
Influenza Vaccine[2]	116	97%	91%	91%
Initial Antibiotic Timing[2]	177	95%	96%	95%
Pneumococcal Vaccine[2]	154	99%	93%	93%
Smoking Cessation Advice[2]	51	98%	98%	97%
Surgical Care Improvement Project				
Appropriate VTP Within 24 Hours[2]	309	97%	94%	92%
Appropriate Hair Removal[2]	977	100%	99%	99%
Appropriate Beta Blocker Usage[2]	363	96%	92%	93%
Controlled Postoperative Blood Glucose[2]	176	94%	94%	93%
Prophylactic Antibiotic Timing[2]	645	96%	97%	97%
Prophylactic Antibiotic Timing (Outpatient)	727	94%	87%	92%
Prophylactic Antibiotic Selection[2]	663	99%	98%	97%
Prophylactic Antibiotic Select. (Outpatient)	732	91%	92%	94%
Prophylactic Antibiotic Stopped[2]	609	97%	95%	94%
Recommended VTP Ordered[2]	309	99%	95%	94%
Urinary Catheter Removal[2]	236	87%	91%	90%
Children's Asthma Care				
Received Systemic Corticosteroids	-	-	-	100%
Received Home Management Plan	-	-	-	71%
Received Reliever Medication	-	-	-	100%
Use of Medical Imaging				
Combination Abdominal CT Scan	3,843	0.072	0.135	0.191
Combination Chest CT Scan	3,829	0.023	0.068	0.054
Follow-up Mammogram/Ultrasound	6,797	7.4%	7.4%	8.4%
MRI for Low Back Pain	781	26.0%	32%	32.7%
Survey of Patients' Hospital Experiences				
Area Around Room 'Always' Quiet at Night	300+	42%	-	58%
Doctors 'Always' Communicated Well	300+	78%	-	80%
Home Recovery Information Given	300+	84%	-	82%
Hospital Given 9 or 10 on 10 Point Scale	300+	69%	-	67%
Meds 'Always' Explained Before Given	300+	56%	-	60%
Nurses 'Always' Communicated Well	300+	75%	-	76%
Pain 'Always' Well Controlled	300+	70%	-	69%
Room and Bathroom 'Always' Clean	300+	64%	-	71%
Timely Help 'Always' Received	300+	56%	-	64%
Would Definitely Recommend Hospital	300+	72%	-	69%

Covenant Medical Center

1447 N Harrison — Phone: 989-583-4000
Saginaw, MI 48602 — Fax: 989-583-6457
URL: www.covenanthealthcare.com
Type: Acute Care Hospitals — Emergency Services: Yes
Ownership: Voluntary Non-Profit - Other — Beds: 601

Key Personnel:
CEO/President. . . . . Spencer T Maidlow
Chief of Medical Staff . . . . John Kasanovich, MD
Operating Room. . . . . John Germain
Quality Assurance . . . . Sue Paterson
Radiology. . . . . Ginny Latty
Emergency Room . . . . Joesph C Spadafore, MD
Intensive Care Unit. . . . . Jan Penney, RN
Patient Relations . . . . Alison Van Norman

Measure	Cases	This Hosp.	State Avg.	U.S. Avg.
Heart Attack Care				
ACE Inhibitor or ARB for LVSD	83	96%	96%	96%
Aspirin at Arrival	369	98%	99%	99%
Aspirin at Discharge	452	98%	99%	98%
Beta Blocker at Discharge	436	99%	99%	98%
Fibrinolytic Medication Timing	0	-	55%	55%
PCI Within 90 Minutes of Arrival	33	88%	89%	90%
Smoking Cessation Advice	151	100%	100%	99%
Chest Pain/Possible Heart Attack Care				
Aspirin at Arrival[1]	3	100%	94%	95%
Median Time to ECG (minutes)[1]	4	8	10	8
Median Time to Transfer (minutes)[5]	0	-	54	61
Fibrinolytic Medication Timing[5]	0	-	60%	54%
Heart Failure Care				
ACE Inhibitor or ARB for LVSD	228	98%	95%	94%
Discharge Instructions	573	83%	89%	88%
Evaluation of LVS Function	701	99%	99%	98%
Smoking Cessation Advice	124	100%	99%	98%
Pneumonia Care				
Appropriate Initial Antibiotic	224	90%	94%	92%
Blood Culture Timing	400	91%	96%	96%
Influenza Vaccine	369	91%	91%	91%
Initial Antibiotic Timing	448	97%	96%	95%
Pneumococcal Vaccine	488	93%	93%	93%
Smoking Cessation Advice	226	100%	98%	97%
Surgical Care Improvement Project				
Appropriate VTP Within 24 Hours[2]	226	88%	94%	92%
Appropriate Hair Removal[2]	824	97%	99%	99%
Appropriate Beta Blocker Usage[2]	291	89%	92%	93%
Controlled Postoperative Blood Glucose[2]	132	86%	94%	93%
Prophylactic Antibiotic Timing[2]	535	96%	97%	97%
Prophylactic Antibiotic Timing (Outpatient)	625	89%	87%	92%
Prophylactic Antibiotic Selection[2]	545	96%	98%	97%
Prophylactic Antibiotic Select. (Outpatient)	591	94%	92%	94%
Prophylactic Antibiotic Stopped[2]	518	70%	95%	94%
Recommended VTP Ordered[2]	228	89%	95%	94%
Urinary Catheter Removal[2]	100	87%	91%	90%
Children's Asthma Care				
Received Systemic Corticosteroids	-	-	-	100%
Received Home Management Plan	-	-	-	71%
Received Reliever Medication	-	-	-	100%
Use of Medical Imaging				
Combination Abdominal CT Scan	1,615	0.196	0.135	0.191
Combination Chest CT Scan	1,086	0.238	0.068	0.054
Follow-up Mammogram/Ultrasound	2,883	4.6%	7.4%	8.4%
MRI for Low Back Pain	401	37.2%	32%	32.7%
Survey of Patients' Hospital Experiences				
Area Around Room 'Always' Quiet at Night	300+	44%	-	58%
Doctors 'Always' Communicated Well	300+	77%	-	80%
Home Recovery Information Given	300+	86%	-	82%
Hospital Given 9 or 10 on 10 Point Scale	300+	67%	-	67%
Meds 'Always' Explained Before Given	300+	59%	-	60%
Nurses 'Always' Communicated Well	300+	79%	-	76%
Pain 'Always' Well Controlled	300+	73%	-	69%
Room and Bathroom 'Always' Clean	300+	66%	-	71%
Timely Help 'Always' Received	300+	67%	-	64%
Would Definitely Recommend Hospital	300+	73%	-	69%

NOTE: Hospital profiles are in alphabetical order by state, then city, then hospital within the city; Rankings exclude hospitals with less than 25 cases except for patient surveys which excludes hospitals with less than 100 cases; (a) 100–299 cases; (1) The number of cases is too small to be sure how well a hospital is performing; (2) The hospital indicated that the data submitted for this measure were based on a sample of cases; (3) Data was collected during a shorter time period (fewer quarters) than the maximum possible time for this measure; (4) Suppressed for one or more quarters by CMS; (5) No data is available from the hospital for this measure; (6) Fewer than 100 patients completed the HCAHPS survey. Use these rates with caution, as the number of surveys may be too low to reliably assess hospital performance; (7) Survey results are based on less than 12 months of data; (8) Survey results are not available for this reporting period; (9) No or very few patients were eligible for the HCAHPS survey. The scores shown, if any, reflect a very small number of surveys; (10) A state average was not calculated because too few hospitals in the state submitted data; (11) There were discrepancies in the data collection process; Please refer to the User's Guide for a full explanation of data.

Healthsource Saginaw

3340 Hospital Road
Saginaw, MI 48608
Phone: 989-790-7888
Fax: 989-790-9297
Type: Acute Care Hospitals
Emergency Services: Yes
Ownership: Voluntary Non-Profit - Other
Beds: 317

Key Personnel:
CEO/President. . . . . Lester Heybor Jr
Chief of Medical Staff . . . . D Kuligowsky, MD
Infection Control. . . . . Sherry Baker
Quality Assurance . . . . Rich Firebaugh

Measure	Cases	This Hosp.	State Avg.	U.S. Avg.
Heart Attack Care				
ACE Inhibitor or ARB for LVSD[5]	0	-	96%	96%
Aspirin at Arrival[5]	0	-	99%	99%
Aspirin at Discharge[5]	0	-	99%	98%
Beta Blocker at Discharge[5]	0	-	99%	98%
Fibrinolytic Medication Timing[5]	0	-	55%	55%
PCI Within 90 Minutes of Arrival[5]	0	-	89%	90%
Smoking Cessation Advice[5]	0	-	100%	99%
Chest Pain/Possible Heart Attack Care				
Aspirin at Arrival[5]	0	-	94%	95%
Median Time to ECG (minutes)[5]	0	-	10	8
Median Time to Transfer (minutes)[5]	0	-	54	61
Fibrinolytic Medication Timing[5]	0	-	60%	54%
Heart Failure Care				
ACE Inhibitor or ARB for LVSD[5]	0	-	95%	94%
Discharge Instructions[5]	0	-	89%	88%
Evaluation of LVS Function[5]	0	-	99%	98%
Smoking Cessation Advice[5]	0	-	99%	98%
Pneumonia Care				
Appropriate Initial Antibiotic[5]	0	-	94%	92%
Blood Culture Timing[5]	0	-	96%	96%
Influenza Vaccine[5]	0	-	91%	91%
Initial Antibiotic Timing[5]	0	-	96%	95%
Pneumococcal Vaccine[5]	0	-	93%	93%
Smoking Cessation Advice[5]	0	-	98%	97%
Surgical Care Improvement Project				
Appropriate VTP Within 24 Hours[5]	0	-	94%	92%
Appropriate Hair Removal[5]	0	-	99%	99%
Appropriate Beta Blocker Usage[5]	0	-	92%	93%
Controlled Postoperative Blood Glucose[5]	0	-	94%	93%
Prophylactic Antibiotic Timing[5]	0	-	97%	97%
Prophylactic Antibiotic Timing (Outpatient)[5]	0	-	87%	92%
Prophylactic Antibiotic Selection[5]	0	-	98%	97%
Prophylactic Antibiotic Select. (Outpatient)[5]	0	-	92%	94%
Prophylactic Antibiotic Stopped[5]	0	-	95%	94%
Recommended VTP Ordered[5]	0	-	95%	94%
Urinary Catheter Removal[5]	0	-	91%	90%
Children's Asthma Care				
Received Systemic Corticosteroids	-	-	-	100%
Received Home Management Plan	-	-	-	71%
Received Reliever Medication	-	-	-	100%
Use of Medical Imaging				
Combination Abdominal CT Scan[5]	0	-	0.135	0.191
Combination Chest CT Scan[5]	0	-	0.068	0.054
Follow-up Mammogram/Ultrasound[5]	0	-	7.4%	8.4%
MRI for Low Back Pain[5]	0	-	32%	32.7%
Survey of Patients' Hospital Experiences				
Area Around Room 'Always' Quiet at Night[9]	-	-	-	58%
Doctors 'Always' Communicated Well[9]	-	-	-	80%
Home Recovery Information Given[9]	-	-	-	82%
Hospital Given 9 or 10 on 10 Point Scale[9]	-	-	-	67%
Meds 'Always' Explained Before Given[9]	-	-	-	60%
Nurses 'Always' Communicated Well[9]	-	-	-	76%
Pain 'Always' Well Controlled[9]	-	-	-	69%
Room and Bathroom 'Always' Clean[9]	-	-	-	71%
Timely Help 'Always' Received[9]	-	-	-	64%
Would Definitely Recommend Hospital[9]	-	-	-	69%

Saginaw VA Medical Center

1500 Weiss Street
Saginaw, MI 48602
Phone: 989-497-2500
Fax: 989-791-2217
Type: Acute Care-Veterans Administration
Emergency Services: No
Ownership: Government - Federal
Beds: 238

Key Personnel:
Chief of Medical Staff . . . . Menham Lender, MD

Measure	Cases	This Hosp.	State Avg.	U.S. Avg.
Heart Attack Care				
ACE Inhibitor or ARB for LVSD[5]	0	-	96%	96%
Aspirin at Arrival[1]	5	100%	99%	99%
Aspirin at Discharge[1]	2	100%	99%	98%
Beta Blocker at Discharge[1]	2	100%	99%	98%
Fibrinolytic Medication Timing[5]	0	-	55%	55%
PCI Within 90 Minutes of Arrival[5]	0	-	89%	90%
Smoking Cessation Advice[5]	0	-	100%	99%
Chest Pain/Possible Heart Attack Care				
Aspirin at Arrival	-	-	94%	95%
Median Time to ECG (minutes)	-	-	10	8
Median Time to Transfer (minutes)	-	-	54	61
Fibrinolytic Medication Timing	-	-	60%	54%
Heart Failure Care				
ACE Inhibitor or ARB for LVSD[1]	17	100%	95%	94%
Discharge Instructions	33	100%	89%	88%
Evaluation of LVS Function	41	100%	99%	98%
Smoking Cessation Advice[1]	5	100%	99%	98%
Pneumonia Care				
Appropriate Initial Antibiotic	28	96%	94%	92%
Blood Culture Timing[1]	24	100%	96%	96%
Influenza Vaccine[1]	21	95%	91%	91%
Initial Antibiotic Timing	36	97%	96%	95%
Pneumococcal Vaccine[1]	23	100%	93%	93%
Smoking Cessation Advice[1]	18	100%	98%	97%
Surgical Care Improvement Project				
Appropriate VTP Within 24 Hours[2,5]	0	-	94%	92%
Appropriate Hair Removal[2,5]	0	-	99%	99%
Appropriate Beta Blocker Usage[2,5]	0	-	92%	93%
Controlled Postoperative Blood Glucose[2,5]	0	-	94%	93%
Prophylactic Antibiotic Timing[5]	0	-	97%	97%
Prophylactic Antibiotic Timing (Outpatient)	-	-	87%	92%
Prophylactic Antibiotic Selection[5]	0	-	98%	97%
Prophylactic Antibiotic Select. (Outpatient)	-	-	92%	94%
Prophylactic Antibiotic Stopped[5]	0	-	95%	94%
Recommended VTP Ordered[2,5]	0	-	95%	94%
Urinary Catheter Removal[2,5]	0	-	91%	90%
Children's Asthma Care				
Received Systemic Corticosteroids	-	-	-	100%
Received Home Management Plan	-	-	-	71%
Received Reliever Medication	-	-	-	100%
Use of Medical Imaging				
Combination Abdominal CT Scan	-	-	0.135	0.191
Combination Chest CT Scan	-	-	0.068	0.054
Follow-up Mammogram/Ultrasound	-	-	7.4%	8.4%
MRI for Low Back Pain	-	-	32%	32.7%
Survey of Patients' Hospital Experiences				
Area Around Room 'Always' Quiet at Night	-	-	-	58%
Doctors 'Always' Communicated Well	-	-	-	80%
Home Recovery Information Given	-	-	-	82%
Hospital Given 9 or 10 on 10 Point Scale	-	-	-	67%
Meds 'Always' Explained Before Given	-	-	-	60%
Nurses 'Always' Communicated Well	-	-	-	76%
Pain 'Always' Well Controlled	-	-	-	69%
Room and Bathroom 'Always' Clean	-	-	-	71%
Timely Help 'Always' Received	-	-	-	64%
Would Definitely Recommend Hospital	-	-	-	69%

Saint Mary's of Michigan Medical Center

800 S Washington Avenu
Saginaw, MI 48601
Phone: 989-776-8000
Fax: 989-907-8141
URL: www.stmarysofmichigan.org
Type: Acute Care Hospitals
Emergency Services: Yes
Ownership: Voluntary Non-Profit - Church
Beds: 268

Key Personnel:
CEO/President. . . . . John Graham
Chief of Medical Staff . . . . Baghuram Sarvepalli, MD
Quality Assurance . . . . Mary Storm
Radiology. . . . . Gary Stefanko
Emergency Room . . . . Louise Beyerlein

Measure	Cases	This Hosp.	State Avg.	U.S. Avg.
Heart Attack Care				
ACE Inhibitor or ARB for LVSD[2]	51	92%	96%	96%
Aspirin at Arrival[2]	120	98%	99%	99%
Aspirin at Discharge[2]	282	95%	99%	98%
Beta Blocker at Discharge[2]	270	98%	99%	98%
Fibrinolytic Medication Timing[2]	0	-	55%	55%
PCI Within 90 Minutes of Arrival[1,2]	14	64%	89%	90%
Smoking Cessation Advice[2]	103	99%	100%	99%
Chest Pain/Possible Heart Attack Care				
Aspirin at Arrival[1]	17	82%	94%	95%
Median Time to ECG (minutes)[1]	18	11	10	8
Median Time to Transfer (minutes)[5]	0	-	54	61
Fibrinolytic Medication Timing[5]	0	-	60%	54%
Heart Failure Care				
ACE Inhibitor or ARB for LVSD[2]	102	92%	95%	94%
Discharge Instructions[2]	249	77%	89%	88%
Evaluation of LVS Function[2]	301	100%	99%	98%
Smoking Cessation Advice[2]	63	97%	99%	98%
Pneumonia Care				
Appropriate Initial Antibiotic[2]	46	93%	94%	92%
Blood Culture Timing[2]	99	93%	96%	96%
Influenza Vaccine[2]	81	81%	91%	91%
Initial Antibiotic Timing[2]	83	96%	96%	95%
Pneumococcal Vaccine[2]	104	81%	93%	93%
Smoking Cessation Advice[2]	51	98%	98%	97%
Surgical Care Improvement Project				
Appropriate VTP Within 24 Hours[2]	188	93%	94%	92%
Appropriate Hair Removal[2]	566	100%	99%	99%
Appropriate Beta Blocker Usage[2]	230	94%	92%	93%
Controlled Postoperative Blood Glucose[2]	124	90%	94%	93%
Prophylactic Antibiotic Timing[2]	388	99%	97%	97%
Prophylactic Antibiotic Timing (Outpatient)	430	98%	87%	92%
Prophylactic Antibiotic Selection[2]	391	98%	98%	97%
Prophylactic Antibiotic Select. (Outpatient)	438	97%	92%	94%
Prophylactic Antibiotic Stopped[2]	376	96%	95%	94%
Recommended VTP Ordered[2]	188	94%	95%	94%
Urinary Catheter Removal[2]	94	79%	91%	90%
Children's Asthma Care				
Received Systemic Corticosteroids	-	-	-	100%
Received Home Management Plan	-	-	-	71%
Received Reliever Medication	-	-	-	100%
Use of Medical Imaging				
Combination Abdominal CT Scan	1,205	0.143	0.135	0.191
Combination Chest CT Scan	889	0.202	0.068	0.054
Follow-up Mammogram/Ultrasound	1,558	7.1%	7.4%	8.4%
MRI for Low Back Pain	576	37.3%	32%	32.7%
Survey of Patients' Hospital Experiences				
Area Around Room 'Always' Quiet at Night	300+	44%	-	58%
Doctors 'Always' Communicated Well	300+	74%	-	80%
Home Recovery Information Given	300+	84%	-	82%
Hospital Given 9 or 10 on 10 Point Scale	300+	57%	-	67%
Meds 'Always' Explained Before Given	300+	52%	-	60%
Nurses 'Always' Communicated Well	300+	67%	-	76%
Pain 'Always' Well Controlled	300+	63%	-	69%
Room and Bathroom 'Always' Clean	300+	62%	-	71%
Timely Help 'Always' Received	300+	60%	-	64%
Would Definitely Recommend Hospital	300+	63%	-	69%

NOTE: Hospital profiles are in alphabetical order by state, then city, then hospital within the city; Rankings exclude hospitals with less than 25 cases except for patient surveys which excludes hospitals with less than 100 cases; (a) 100–299 cases; (1) The number of cases is too small to be sure how well a hospital is performing; (2) The hospital indicated that the data submitted for this measure were based on a sample of cases; (3) Data was collected during a shorter time period (fewer quarters) than the maximum possible time for this measure; (4) Suppressed for one or more quarters by CMS; (5) No data is available from the hospital for this measure; (6) Fewer than 100 patients completed the HCAHPS survey. Use these rates with caution, as the number of surveys may be too low to reliably assess hospital performance; (7) Survey results are based on less than 12 months of data; (8) Survey results are not available for this reporting period; (9) No or very few patients were eligible for the HCAHPS survey. The scores shown, if any, reflect a very small number of surveys; (10) A state average was not calculated because too few hospitals in the state submitted data; (11) There were discrepancies in the data collection process; Please refer to the User's Guide for a full explanation of data.

Clinton Memorial Hospital

805 S Oakland
Saint Johns, MI 48879
URL: www.clintonmemorial.org
Phone: 989-224-6881
Fax: 989-227-3347
Type: Critical Access Hospitals
Emergency Services: Yes
Ownership: Proprietary
Beds: 28

Key Personnel:
CEO/President. . . . . Ed Brunn
Chief of Medical Staff . . . . Paul David Minnick
Infection Control. . . . . Ricki Burk
Operating Room. . . . . Kathleen McElroy
Quality Assurance . . . . Cathy Hallead
Radiology. . . . . Michael Buetow
Emergency Room . . . . Diane Simon

Measure	Cases	This Hosp.	State Avg.	U.S. Avg.
Heart Attack Care				
ACE Inhibitor or ARB for LVSD[3]	0	-	96%	96%
Aspirin at Arrival[1,3]	1	100%	99%	99%
Aspirin at Discharge[3]	0	-	99%	98%
Beta Blocker at Discharge[1,3]	1	100%	99%	98%
Fibrinolytic Medication Timing[3]	0	-	55%	55%
PCI Within 90 Minutes of Arrival[3]	0	-	89%	90%
Smoking Cessation Advice[3]	0	-	100%	99%
Chest Pain/Possible Heart Attack Care				
Aspirin at Arrival[5]	0	-	94%	95%
Median Time to ECG (minutes)[5]	0	-	10	8
Median Time to Transfer (minutes)[5]	0	-	54	61
Fibrinolytic Medication Timing[5]	0	-	60%	54%
Heart Failure Care				
ACE Inhibitor or ARB for LVSD[1]	13	100%	95%	94%
Discharge Instructions	36	94%	89%	88%
Evaluation of LVS Function	46	100%	99%	98%
Smoking Cessation Advice[1]	2	100%	99%	98%
Pneumonia Care				
Appropriate Initial Antibiotic	33	97%	94%	92%
Blood Culture Timing	37	89%	96%	96%
Influenza Vaccine	27	96%	91%	91%
Initial Antibiotic Timing	40	98%	96%	95%
Pneumococcal Vaccine	41	95%	93%	93%
Smoking Cessation Advice[1]	11	100%	98%	97%
Surgical Care Improvement Project				
Appropriate VTP Within 24 Hours	27	100%	94%	92%
Appropriate Hair Removal	59	100%	99%	99%
Appropriate Beta Blocker Usage[5]	0	-	92%	93%
Controlled Postoperative Blood Glucose	0	-	94%	93%
Prophylactic Antibiotic Timing	40	98%	97%	97%
Prophylactic Antibiotic Timing (Outpatient)[5]	0	-	87%	92%
Prophylactic Antibiotic Selection	39	92%	98%	97%
Prophylactic Antibiotic Select. (Outpatient)[5]	0	-	92%	94%
Prophylactic Antibiotic Stopped	39	92%	95%	94%
Recommended VTP Ordered	28	96%	95%	94%
Urinary Catheter Removal[1]	13	100%	91%	90%
Children's Asthma Care				
Received Systemic Corticosteroids	-	-	-	100%
Received Home Management Plan	-	-	-	71%
Received Reliever Medication	-	-	-	100%
Use of Medical Imaging				
Combination Abdominal CT Scan	311	0.064	0.135	0.191
Combination Chest CT Scan	213	0.000	0.068	0.054
Follow-up Mammogram/Ultrasound	243	4.9%	7.4%	8.4%
MRI for Low Back Pain	82	26.8%	32%	32.7%
Survey of Patients' Hospital Experiences				
Area Around Room 'Always' Quiet at Night	300+	57%	-	58%
Doctors 'Always' Communicated Well	300+	87%	-	80%
Home Recovery Information Given	300+	86%	-	82%
Hospital Given 9 or 10 on 10 Point Scale	300+	82%	-	67%
Meds 'Always' Explained Before Given	300+	66%	-	60%
Nurses 'Always' Communicated Well	300+	83%	-	76%
Pain 'Always' Well Controlled	300+	77%	-	69%
Room and Bathroom 'Always' Clean	300+	84%	-	71%
Timely Help 'Always' Received	300+	69%	-	64%
Would Definitely Recommend Hospital	300+	79%	-	69%

Lakeland Hospital - St Joseph

1234 Napier Avenue
Saint Joseph, MI 49085
URL: www.lakelandhealth.org
Phone: 269-983-8300
Fax: 269-982-4855
Type: Acute Care Hospitals
Emergency Services: Yes
Ownership: Voluntary Non-Profit - Private
Beds: 254

Key Personnel:
CEO/President. . . . . Joseph Wasserman
Cardiac Laboratory. . . . . Bart Btrndt
Chief of Medical Staff . . . . Ken Edwards, MD
Operating Room. . . . . Gayle Beward
Pediatric In-Patient Care . . . . Fred Johansen, MD
Quality Assurance . . . . Mary Ann Pater
Radiology. . . . . William Leahey, MD
Patient Relations . . . . Eileen Willits

Measure	Cases	This Hosp.	State Avg.	U.S. Avg.
Heart Attack Care				
ACE Inhibitor or ARB for LVSD	71	87%	96%	96%
Aspirin at Arrival	332	99%	99%	99%
Aspirin at Discharge	340	100%	99%	98%
Beta Blocker at Discharge	322	98%	99%	98%
Fibrinolytic Medication Timing[1]	4	75%	55%	55%
PCI Within 90 Minutes of Arrival	40	82%	89%	90%
Smoking Cessation Advice	119	100%	100%	99%
Chest Pain/Possible Heart Attack Care				
Aspirin at Arrival[1]	12	100%	94%	95%
Median Time to ECG (minutes)[1]	16	16	10	8
Median Time to Transfer (minutes)[5]	0	-	54	61
Fibrinolytic Medication Timing[3]	0	-	60%	54%
Heart Failure Care				
ACE Inhibitor or ARB for LVSD	179	97%	95%	94%
Discharge Instructions	403	93%	89%	88%
Evaluation of LVS Function	498	99%	99%	98%
Smoking Cessation Advice	110	100%	99%	98%
Pneumonia Care				
Appropriate Initial Antibiotic	234	95%	94%	92%
Blood Culture Timing	296	98%	96%	96%
Influenza Vaccine	247	94%	91%	91%
Initial Antibiotic Timing	373	92%	96%	95%
Pneumococcal Vaccine	332	96%	93%	93%
Smoking Cessation Advice	169	99%	98%	97%
Surgical Care Improvement Project				
Appropriate VTP Within 24 Hours[2]	294	98%	94%	92%
Appropriate Hair Removal[2]	964	99%	99%	99%
Appropriate Beta Blocker Usage[2]	292	92%	92%	93%
Controlled Postoperative Blood Glucose[2]	126	98%	94%	93%
Prophylactic Antibiotic Timing[2]	632	99%	97%	97%
Prophylactic Antibiotic Timing (Outpatient)	391	93%	87%	92%
Prophylactic Antibiotic Selection[2]	643	96%	98%	97%
Prophylactic Antibiotic Select. (Outpatient)	381	92%	92%	94%
Prophylactic Antibiotic Stopped[2]	610	99%	95%	94%
Recommended VTP Ordered[2]	294	98%	95%	94%
Urinary Catheter Removal[2]	215	95%	91%	90%
Children's Asthma Care				
Received Systemic Corticosteroids	-	-	-	100%
Received Home Management Plan	-	-	-	71%
Received Reliever Medication	-	-	-	100%
Use of Medical Imaging				
Combination Abdominal CT Scan	1,890	0.093	0.135	0.191
Combination Chest CT Scan	1,229	0.011	0.068	0.054
Follow-up Mammogram/Ultrasound	2,810	6.7%	7.4%	8.4%
MRI for Low Back Pain	275	29.8%	32%	32.7%
Survey of Patients' Hospital Experiences				
Area Around Room 'Always' Quiet at Night	300+	56%	-	58%
Doctors 'Always' Communicated Well	300+	79%	-	80%
Home Recovery Information Given	300+	80%	-	82%
Hospital Given 9 or 10 on 10 Point Scale	300+	64%	-	67%
Meds 'Always' Explained Before Given	300+	57%	-	60%
Nurses 'Always' Communicated Well	300+	74%	-	76%
Pain 'Always' Well Controlled	300+	70%	-	69%
Room and Bathroom 'Always' Clean	300+	78%	-	71%
Timely Help 'Always' Received	300+	62%	-	64%
Would Definitely Recommend Hospital	300+	60%	-	69%

Saint Joseph Mercy Saline Hospital

400 W Russell St
Saline, MI 48176
URL: www.sjmh.com/who/saline
Phone: 734-429-1500
Fax: 734-429-4662
Type: Acute Care Hospitals
Emergency Services: Yes
Ownership: Voluntary Non-Profit - Church
Beds: 82

Key Personnel:
CEO/President. . . . . Stacey Breedveld
Chief of Medical Staff . . . . Renee Kinch
Operating Room. . . . . Linda Detzler, RN
Quality Assurance . . . . Marlene Mason
Radiology. . . . . Joaquin Uy, MD
Emergency Room . . . . Robert McCurdy, MD

Measure	Cases	This Hosp.	State Avg.	U.S. Avg.
Heart Attack Care				
ACE Inhibitor or ARB for LVSD[3]	0	-	96%	96%
Aspirin at Arrival[1,3]	4	100%	99%	99%
Aspirin at Discharge[1,3]	2	100%	99%	98%
Beta Blocker at Discharge[1,3]	1	100%	99%	98%
Fibrinolytic Medication Timing[3]	0	-	55%	55%
PCI Within 90 Minutes of Arrival[3]	0	-	89%	90%
Smoking Cessation Advice[3]	0	-	100%	99%
Chest Pain/Possible Heart Attack Care				
Aspirin at Arrival	272	75%	94%	95%
Median Time to ECG (minutes)	275	10	10	8
Median Time to Transfer (minutes)[1]	9	69	54	61
Fibrinolytic Medication Timing	0	-	60%	54%
Heart Failure Care				
ACE Inhibitor or ARB for LVSD[1]	4	100%	95%	94%
Discharge Instructions[1]	24	96%	89%	88%
Evaluation of LVS Function	34	100%	99%	98%
Smoking Cessation Advice[1]	2	100%	99%	98%
Pneumonia Care				
Appropriate Initial Antibiotic	51	100%	94%	92%
Blood Culture Timing[1]	16	81%	96%	96%
Influenza Vaccine	46	89%	91%	91%
Initial Antibiotic Timing	66	98%	96%	95%
Pneumococcal Vaccine	64	84%	93%	93%
Smoking Cessation Advice[1]	11	100%	98%	97%
Surgical Care Improvement Project				
Appropriate VTP Within 24 Hours[1]	13	85%	94%	92%
Appropriate Hair Removal	56	100%	99%	99%
Appropriate Beta Blocker Usage[1]	11	91%	92%	93%
Controlled Postoperative Blood Glucose	0	-	94%	93%
Prophylactic Antibiotic Timing	47	94%	97%	97%
Prophylactic Antibiotic Timing (Outpatient)	50	98%	87%	92%
Prophylactic Antibiotic Selection	47	100%	98%	97%
Prophylactic Antibiotic Select. (Outpatient)	50	98%	92%	94%
Prophylactic Antibiotic Stopped	45	98%	95%	94%
Recommended VTP Ordered[1]	13	85%	95%	94%
Urinary Catheter Removal[1]	15	93%	91%	90%
Children's Asthma Care				
Received Systemic Corticosteroids	-	-	-	100%
Received Home Management Plan	-	-	-	71%
Received Reliever Medication	-	-	-	100%
Use of Medical Imaging				
Combination Abdominal CT Scan	380	0.092	0.135	0.191
Combination Chest CT Scan	204	0.005	0.068	0.054
Follow-up Mammogram/Ultrasound	525	6.7%	7.4%	8.4%
MRI for Low Back Pain	223	36.8%	32%	32.7%
Survey of Patients' Hospital Experiences				
Area Around Room 'Always' Quiet at Night	(a)	71%	-	58%
Doctors 'Always' Communicated Well	(a)	80%	-	80%
Home Recovery Information Given	(a)	90%	-	82%
Hospital Given 9 or 10 on 10 Point Scale	(a)	74%	-	67%
Meds 'Always' Explained Before Given	(a)	63%	-	60%
Nurses 'Always' Communicated Well	(a)	80%	-	76%
Pain 'Always' Well Controlled	(a)	73%	-	69%
Room and Bathroom 'Always' Clean	(a)	68%	-	71%
Timely Help 'Always' Received	(a)	74%	-	64%
Would Definitely Recommend Hospital	(a)	77%	-	69%

NOTE: Hospital profiles are in alphabetical order by state, then city, then hospital within the city; Rankings exclude hospitals with less than 25 cases except for patient surveys which excludes hospitals with less than 100 cases; (a) 100–299 cases; (1) The number of cases is too small to be sure how well a hospital is performing; (2) The hospital indicated that the data submitted for this measure were based on a sample of cases; (3) Data was collected during a shorter time period (fewer quarters) than the maximum possible time for this measure; (4) Suppressed for one or more quarters by CMS; (5) No data is available from the hospital for this measure; (6) Fewer than 100 patients completed the HCAHPS survey. Use these rates with caution, as the number of surveys may be too low to reliably assess hospital performance; (7) Survey results are based on less than 12 months of data; (8) Survey results are not available for this reporting period; (9) No or very few patients were eligible for the HCAHPS survey. The scores shown, if any, reflect a very small number of surveys; (10) A state average was not calculated because too few hospitals in the state submitted data; (11) There were discrepancies in the data collection process; Please refer to the User's Guide for a full explanation of data.

McKenzie Memorial Hospital

120 Delaware Street
Sandusky, MI 48471
URL: www.mckenziehospital.com
Phone: 810-648-3770
Fax: 810-648-4204
Type: Critical Access Hospitals
Emergency Services: Yes
Ownership: Voluntary Non-Profit - Private
Beds: 25

Key Personnel:
CEO/President. . . . . Steve Barnett
Chief of Medical Staff . . . . M M Elrahman, MD
Infection Control. . . . . Bonnie Powell, RN
Operating Room. . . . . Sue Abrego, RN
Quality Assurance . . . . Jenny Morzo, RN
Emergency Room . . . . Allen Williams, MD
Patient Relations . . . . Jenny Morzo, RN

Measure	Cases	This Hosp.	State Avg.	U.S. Avg.
Heart Attack Care				
ACE Inhibitor or ARB for LVSD[5]	0	-	96%	96%
Aspirin at Arrival[5]	0	-	99%	99%
Aspirin at Discharge[5]	0	-	99%	98%
Beta Blocker at Discharge[5]	0	-	99%	98%
Fibrinolytic Medication Timing[5]	0	-	55%	55%
PCI Within 90 Minutes of Arrival[5]	0	-	89%	90%
Smoking Cessation Advice[5]	0	-	100%	99%
Chest Pain/Possible Heart Attack Care				
Aspirin at Arrival	75	92%	94%	95%
Median Time to ECG (minutes)	77	7	10	8
Median Time to Transfer (minutes)[1,3]	3	247	54	61
Fibrinolytic Medication Timing[1]	2	0%	60%	54%
Heart Failure Care				
ACE Inhibitor or ARB for LVSD[5]	0	-	95%	94%
Discharge Instructions[5]	0	-	89%	88%
Evaluation of LVS Function[5]	0	-	99%	98%
Smoking Cessation Advice[5]	0	-	99%	98%
Pneumonia Care				
Appropriate Initial Antibiotic[1]	21	100%	94%	92%
Blood Culture Timing[1]	12	83%	96%	96%
Influenza Vaccine[1]	18	78%	91%	91%
Initial Antibiotic Timing[1]	22	95%	96%	95%
Pneumococcal Vaccine[1]	21	95%	93%	93%
Smoking Cessation Advice[1]	3	33%	98%	97%
Surgical Care Improvement Project				
Appropriate VTP Within 24 Hours[1]	10	90%	94%	92%
Appropriate Hair Removal[1]	16	94%	99%	99%
Appropriate Beta Blocker Usage[1]	2	50%	92%	93%
Controlled Postoperative Blood Glucose	0	-	94%	93%
Prophylactic Antibiotic Timing[1]	8	100%	97%	97%
Prophylactic Antibiotic Timing (Outpatient)[1,3]	10	100%	87%	92%
Prophylactic Antibiotic Selection[1]	8	100%	98%	97%
Prophylactic Antibiotic Select. (Outpatient)[1,3]	10	100%	92%	94%
Prophylactic Antibiotic Stopped[1]	8	88%	95%	94%
Recommended VTP Ordered[1]	10	90%	95%	94%
Urinary Catheter Removal[1]	5	40%	91%	90%
Children's Asthma Care				
Received Systemic Corticosteroids	-	-	-	100%
Received Home Management Plan	-	-	-	71%
Received Reliever Medication	-	-	-	100%
Use of Medical Imaging				
Combination Abdominal CT Scan	138	0.058	0.135	0.191
Combination Chest CT Scan	112	0.018	0.068	0.054
Follow-up Mammogram/Ultrasound	167	12.0%	7.4%	8.4%
MRI for Low Back Pain[5]	0	-	32%	32.7%
Survey of Patients' Hospital Experiences				
Area Around Room 'Always' Quiet at Night[6]	<100	54%	-	58%
Doctors 'Always' Communicated Well[6]	<100	80%	-	80%
Home Recovery Information Given[6]	<100	89%	-	82%
Hospital Given 9 or 10 on 10 Point Scale[6]	<100	75%	-	67%
Meds 'Always' Explained Before Given[6]	<100	69%	-	60%
Nurses 'Always' Communicated Well[6]	<100	81%	-	76%
Pain 'Always' Well Controlled[6]	<100	74%	-	69%
Room and Bathroom 'Always' Clean[6]	<100	75%	-	71%
Timely Help 'Always' Received[6]	<100	78%	-	64%
Would Definitely Recommend Hospital	<100	73%	-	69%

Chippewa County War Memorial Hospital

500 Osborn Blvd
Sault Sainte Marie, MI 49783
Phone: 906-635-4460
Fax: 906-635-4467
Type: Acute Care Hospitals
Emergency Services: Yes
Ownership: Voluntary Non-Profit - Other

Key Personnel:
CEO/President. . . . . David Jahn
Chief of Medical Staff . . . . R J Graham
Quality Assurance . . . . Mitch Zaborowski
Radiology. . . . . R J Duman
Emergency Room . . . . Jane McLeod, RN

Measure	Cases	This Hosp.	State Avg.	U.S. Avg.
Heart Attack Care				
ACE Inhibitor or ARB for LVSD[1]	5	80%	96%	96%
Aspirin at Arrival	37	97%	99%	99%
Aspirin at Discharge[1]	21	100%	99%	98%
Beta Blocker at Discharge[1]	20	100%	99%	98%
Fibrinolytic Medication Timing	0	-	55%	55%
PCI Within 90 Minutes of Arrival	0	-	89%	90%
Smoking Cessation Advice[1]	1	100%	100%	99%
Chest Pain/Possible Heart Attack Care				
Aspirin at Arrival	105	99%	94%	95%
Median Time to ECG (minutes)	107	13	10	8
Median Time to Transfer (minutes)[1,3]	1	307	54	61
Fibrinolytic Medication Timing[1]	3	67%	60%	54%
Heart Failure Care				
ACE Inhibitor or ARB for LVSD	33	94%	95%	94%
Discharge Instructions	82	94%	89%	88%
Evaluation of LVS Function	96	100%	99%	98%
Smoking Cessation Advice[1]	13	92%	99%	98%
Pneumonia Care				
Appropriate Initial Antibiotic	86	99%	94%	92%
Blood Culture Timing	114	96%	96%	96%
Influenza Vaccine	53	92%	91%	91%
Initial Antibiotic Timing	126	98%	96%	95%
Pneumococcal Vaccine	105	99%	93%	93%
Smoking Cessation Advice	42	90%	98%	97%
Surgical Care Improvement Project				
Appropriate VTP Within 24 Hours	89	98%	94%	92%
Appropriate Hair Removal	248	100%	99%	99%
Appropriate Beta Blocker Usage	77	95%	92%	93%
Controlled Postoperative Blood Glucose	0	-	94%	93%
Prophylactic Antibiotic Timing	197	99%	97%	97%
Prophylactic Antibiotic Timing (Outpatient)	27	93%	87%	92%
Prophylactic Antibiotic Selection	197	99%	98%	97%
Prophylactic Antibiotic Select. (Outpatient)	57	89%	92%	94%
Prophylactic Antibiotic Stopped	192	98%	95%	94%
Recommended VTP Ordered	90	97%	95%	94%
Urinary Catheter Removal	97	95%	91%	90%
Children's Asthma Care				
Received Systemic Corticosteroids	-	-	-	100%
Received Home Management Plan	-	-	-	71%
Received Reliever Medication	-	-	-	100%
Use of Medical Imaging				
Combination Abdominal CT Scan	330	0.785	0.135	0.191
Combination Chest CT Scan	262	0.168	0.068	0.054
Follow-up Mammogram/Ultrasound	599	10.5%	7.4%	8.4%
MRI for Low Back Pain	165	41.2%	32%	32.7%
Survey of Patients' Hospital Experiences				
Area Around Room 'Always' Quiet at Night	300+	53%	-	58%
Doctors 'Always' Communicated Well	300+	83%	-	80%
Home Recovery Information Given	300+	83%	-	82%
Hospital Given 9 or 10 on 10 Point Scale	300+	68%	-	67%
Meds 'Always' Explained Before Given	300+	58%	-	60%
Nurses 'Always' Communicated Well	300+	82%	-	76%
Pain 'Always' Well Controlled	300+	71%	-	69%
Room and Bathroom 'Always' Clean	300+	76%	-	71%
Timely Help 'Always' Received	300+	77%	-	64%
Would Definitely Recommend Hospital	300+	68%	-	69%

Sheridan Community Hospital

301 N Main St
Sheridan, MI 48884
URL: www.sheridanhospital.com
Phone: 989-291-3261
Fax: 989-291-3062
Type: Critical Access Hospitals
Emergency Services: Yes
Ownership: Voluntary Non-Profit - Other
Beds: 25

Key Personnel:
CEO/President. . . . . Kevin J Cawley
Chief of Medical Staff . . . . Brian Thwaites
Radiology. . . . . Donna R Moyer

Measure	Cases	This Hosp.	State Avg.	U.S. Avg.
Heart Attack Care				
ACE Inhibitor or ARB for LVSD[3]	0	-	96%	96%
Aspirin at Arrival[1,3]	1	0%	99%	99%
Aspirin at Discharge[1,3]	1	0%	99%	98%
Beta Blocker at Discharge[1,3]	1	100%	99%	98%
Fibrinolytic Medication Timing[3]	0	-	55%	55%
PCI Within 90 Minutes of Arrival[3]	0	-	89%	90%
Smoking Cessation Advice[3]	0	-	100%	99%
Chest Pain/Possible Heart Attack Care				
Aspirin at Arrival	-	-	94%	95%
Median Time to ECG (minutes)	-	-	10	8
Median Time to Transfer (minutes)	-	-	54	61
Fibrinolytic Medication Timing	-	-	60%	54%
Heart Failure Care				
ACE Inhibitor or ARB for LVSD[5]	0	-	95%	94%
Discharge Instructions[5]	0	-	89%	88%
Evaluation of LVS Function[5]	0	-	99%	98%
Smoking Cessation Advice[5]	0	-	99%	98%
Pneumonia Care				
Appropriate Initial Antibiotic[1,3]	23	74%	94%	92%
Blood Culture Timing[1,3]	16	75%	96%	96%
Influenza Vaccine[1]	16	94%	91%	91%
Initial Antibiotic Timing[1,3]	20	100%	96%	95%
Pneumococcal Vaccine[1,3]	15	80%	93%	93%
Smoking Cessation Advice[1,3]	4	50%	98%	97%
Surgical Care Improvement Project				
Appropriate VTP Within 24 Hours[1,3]	1	0%	94%	92%
Appropriate Hair Removal[1,3]	1	100%	99%	99%
Appropriate Beta Blocker Usage[5]	0	-	92%	93%
Controlled Postoperative Blood Glucose[3]	0	-	94%	93%
Prophylactic Antibiotic Timing[1,3]	1	100%	97%	97%
Prophylactic Antibiotic Timing (Outpatient)	-	-	87%	92%
Prophylactic Antibiotic Selection[1,3]	1	100%	98%	97%
Prophylactic Antibiotic Select. (Outpatient)	-	-	92%	94%
Prophylactic Antibiotic Stopped[1,3]	1	100%	95%	94%
Recommended VTP Ordered[1,3]	1	0%	95%	94%
Urinary Catheter Removal[1,3]	1	100%	91%	90%
Children's Asthma Care				
Received Systemic Corticosteroids	-	-	-	100%
Received Home Management Plan	-	-	-	71%
Received Reliever Medication	-	-	-	100%
Use of Medical Imaging				
Combination Abdominal CT Scan	-	-	0.135	0.191
Combination Chest CT Scan	-	-	0.068	0.054
Follow-up Mammogram/Ultrasound	-	-	7.4%	8.4%
MRI for Low Back Pain	-	-	32%	32.7%
Survey of Patients' Hospital Experiences				
Area Around Room 'Always' Quiet at Night[8]	-	-	-	58%
Doctors 'Always' Communicated Well[8]	-	-	-	80%
Home Recovery Information Given[8]	-	-	-	82%
Hospital Given 9 or 10 on 10 Point Scale[8]	-	-	-	67%
Meds 'Always' Explained Before Given[8]	-	-	-	60%
Nurses 'Always' Communicated Well[8]	-	-	-	76%
Pain 'Always' Well Controlled[8]	-	-	-	69%
Room and Bathroom 'Always' Clean[8]	-	-	-	71%
Timely Help 'Always' Received[8]	-	-	-	64%
Would Definitely Recommend Hospital[8]	-	-	-	69%

NOTE: Hospital profiles are in alphabetical order by state, then city, then hospital within the city; Rankings exclude hospitals with less than 25 cases except for patient surveys which excludes hospitals with less than 100 cases; (a) 100–299 cases; (1) The number of cases is too small to be sure how well a hospital is performing; (2) The hospital indicated that the data submitted for this measure were based on a sample of cases; (3) Data was collected during a shorter time period (fewer quarters) than the maximum possible time for this measure; (4) Suppressed for one or more quarters by CMS; (5) No data is available from the hospital for this measure; (6) Fewer than 100 patients completed the HCAHPS survey. Use these rates with caution, as the number of surveys may be too low to reliably assess hospital performance; (7) Survey results are based on less than 12 months of data; (8) Survey results are not available for this reporting period; (9) No or very few patients were eligible for the HCAHPS survey. The scores shown, if any, reflect a very small number of surveys; (10) A state average was not calculated because too few hospitals in the state submitted data; (11) There were discrepancies in the data collection process; Please refer to the User's Guide for a full explanation of data.

South Haven Community Hospital

955 S Bailey Ave
South Haven, MI 49090
Phone: 269-637-5271
Fax: 269-639-1208
E-mail: info@shch.org
URL: www.shch.org
Type: Acute Care Hospitals
Emergency Services: Yes
Ownership: Govt - Hospital Dist/Auth
Beds: 82

Key Personnel:

CEO/President. . . . . Joanne Urbanski
Cardiac Laboratory. . . . . Tom Bauer
Chief of Medical Staff . . . . Karen Janson, MD
Infection Control. . . . . Teresa Horan
Pediatric Ambulatory Care . . . . . . Karen Janson, MD
Quality Assurance . . . . Debbie Smith, RN
Radiology. . . . . E Theodore Ostermann, MD
Emergency Room . . . . Paul Wahby, DO

Measure	Cases	This Hosp.	State Avg.	U.S. Avg.
Heart Attack Care				
ACE Inhibitor or ARB for LVSD[1,3]	1	100%	96%	96%
Aspirin at Arrival[1,3]	3	100%	99%	99%
Aspirin at Discharge[1,3]	3	100%	99%	98%
Beta Blocker at Discharge[1,3]	3	100%	99%	98%
Fibrinolytic Medication Timing[3]	0	-	55%	55%
PCI Within 90 Minutes of Arrival[3]	0	-	89%	90%
Smoking Cessation Advice[3]	0	-	100%	99%
Chest Pain/Possible Heart Attack Care				
Aspirin at Arrival	121	99%	94%	95%
Median Time to ECG (minutes)	128	9	10	8
Median Time to Transfer (minutes)[1,3]	4	110	54	61
Fibrinolytic Medication Timing[1]	7	57%	60%	54%
Heart Failure Care				
ACE Inhibitor or ARB for LVSD[1]	16	94%	95%	94%
Discharge Instructions	44	91%	89%	88%
Evaluation of LVS Function	50	94%	99%	98%
Smoking Cessation Advice[1]	11	64%	99%	98%
Pneumonia Care				
Appropriate Initial Antibiotic	44	98%	94%	92%
Blood Culture Timing	50	96%	96%	96%
Influenza Vaccine	31	94%	91%	91%
Initial Antibiotic Timing	54	96%	96%	95%
Pneumococcal Vaccine	45	98%	93%	93%
Smoking Cessation Advice[1]	16	100%	98%	97%
Surgical Care Improvement Project				
Appropriate VTP Within 24 Hours[1]	13	100%	94%	92%
Appropriate Hair Removal	101	100%	99%	99%
Appropriate Beta Blocker Usage[1]	20	95%	92%	93%
Controlled Postoperative Blood Glucose	0	-	94%	93%
Prophylactic Antibiotic Timing	82	99%	97%	97%
Prophylactic Antibiotic Timing (Outpatient)[1]	13	85%	87%	92%
Prophylactic Antibiotic Selection	82	95%	98%	97%
Prophylactic Antibiotic Select. (Outpatient)[1]	11	82%	92%	94%
Prophylactic Antibiotic Stopped	81	100%	95%	94%
Recommended VTP Ordered[1]	13	100%	95%	94%
Urinary Catheter Removal	29	100%	91%	90%
Children's Asthma Care				
Received Systemic Corticosteroids	-	-	-	100%
Received Home Management Plan	-	-	-	71%
Received Reliever Medication	-	-	-	100%
Use of Medical Imaging				
Combination Abdominal CT Scan	218	0.073	0.135	0.191
Combination Chest CT Scan	103	0.058	0.068	0.054
Follow-up Mammogram/Ultrasound	305	1.6%	7.4%	8.4%
MRI for Low Back Pain	46	39.1%	32%	32.7%
Survey of Patients' Hospital Experiences				
Area Around Room 'Always' Quiet at Night	(a)	53%	-	58%
Doctors 'Always' Communicated Well	(a)	83%	-	80%
Home Recovery Information Given	(a)	86%	-	82%
Hospital Given 9 or 10 on 10 Point Scale	(a)	69%	-	67%
Meds 'Always' Explained Before Given	(a)	63%	-	60%
Nurses 'Always' Communicated Well	(a)	78%	-	76%
Pain 'Always' Well Controlled	(a)	71%	-	69%
Room and Bathroom 'Always' Clean	(a)	68%	-	71%
Timely Help 'Always' Received	(a)	69%	-	64%
Would Definitely Recommend Hospital	(a)	66%	-	69%

Oakland Regional Hospital

22401 Foster Winter Drive
Southfield, MI 48075
Phone: 248-423-5100
URL: oaklandregionalhospital.com
Type: Acute Care Hospitals
Emergency Services: No
Ownership: Proprietary

Key Personnel:

CEO . . . . Dan Babb
Chairman/CEO . . . . Edward Burke
Radiology. . . . . Marianne Chrzanowski

Measure	Cases	This Hosp.	State Avg.	U.S. Avg.
Heart Attack Care				
ACE Inhibitor or ARB for LVSD[5]	0	-	96%	96%
Aspirin at Arrival[5]	0	-	99%	99%
Aspirin at Discharge[5]	0	-	99%	98%
Beta Blocker at Discharge[5]	0	-	99%	98%
Fibrinolytic Medication Timing[5]	0	-	55%	55%
PCI Within 90 Minutes of Arrival[5]	0	-	89%	90%
Smoking Cessation Advice[5]	0	-	100%	99%
Chest Pain/Possible Heart Attack Care				
Aspirin at Arrival[5]	0	-	94%	95%
Median Time to ECG (minutes)[5]	0	-	10	8
Median Time to Transfer (minutes)[5]	0	-	54	61
Fibrinolytic Medication Timing[5]	0	-	60%	54%
Heart Failure Care				
ACE Inhibitor or ARB for LVSD[3]	0	-	95%	94%
Discharge Instructions[1,3]	1	0%	89%	88%
Evaluation of LVS Function[1,3]	1	0%	99%	98%
Smoking Cessation Advice[3]	0	-	99%	98%
Pneumonia Care				
Appropriate Initial Antibiotic[5]	0	-	94%	92%
Blood Culture Timing[5]	0	-	96%	96%
Influenza Vaccine[5]	0	-	91%	91%
Initial Antibiotic Timing[5]	0	-	96%	95%
Pneumococcal Vaccine[5]	0	-	93%	93%
Smoking Cessation Advice[5]	0	-	98%	97%
Surgical Care Improvement Project				
Appropriate VTP Within 24 Hours[1,3]	10	100%	94%	92%
Appropriate Hair Removal[3]	33	97%	99%	99%
Appropriate Beta Blocker Usage[1,3]	7	86%	92%	93%
Controlled Postoperative Blood Glucose[3]	0	-	94%	93%
Prophylactic Antibiotic Timing[3]	32	84%	97%	97%
Prophylactic Antibiotic Timing (Outpatient)	49	98%	87%	92%
Prophylactic Antibiotic Selection[3]	32	100%	98%	97%
Prophylactic Antibiotic Select. (Outpatient)	49	98%	92%	94%
Prophylactic Antibiotic Stopped[3]	31	100%	95%	94%
Recommended VTP Ordered[1,3]	10	100%	95%	94%
Urinary Catheter Removal[1,3]	5	80%	91%	90%
Children's Asthma Care				
Received Systemic Corticosteroids	-	-	-	100%
Received Home Management Plan	-	-	-	71%
Received Reliever Medication	-	-	-	100%
Use of Medical Imaging				
Combination Abdominal CT Scan[5]	0	-	0.135	0.191
Combination Chest CT Scan[5]	0	-	0.068	0.054
Follow-up Mammogram/Ultrasound[5]	0	-	7.4%	8.4%
MRI for Low Back Pain[1]	27	25.9%	32%	32.7%
Survey of Patients' Hospital Experiences				
Area Around Room 'Always' Quiet at Night[6]	<100	67%	-	58%
Doctors 'Always' Communicated Well[6]	<100	83%	-	80%
Home Recovery Information Given[6]	<100	84%	-	82%
Hospital Given 9 or 10 on 10 Point Scale[6]	<100	67%	-	67%
Meds 'Always' Explained Before Given[6]	<100	66%	-	60%
Nurses 'Always' Communicated Well[6]	<100	83%	-	76%
Pain 'Always' Well Controlled[6]	<100	81%	-	69%
Room and Bathroom 'Always' Clean[6]	<100	81%	-	71%
Timely Help 'Always' Received[6]	<100	65%	-	64%
Would Definitely Recommend Hospital	<100	74%	-	69%

Providence Hospital and Medical Centers

16001 W Nine Mile Rd
Southfield, MI 48075
Phone: 248-849-3011
Fax: 248-849-3035
URL: www.stjohn.org/Providence
Type: Acute Care Hospitals
Emergency Services: Yes
Ownership: Voluntary Non-Profit - Church
Beds: 459

Key Personnel:

CEO/President. . . . . Michael Wiemann
Infection Control. . . . . Tom Madhaven, MD
Radiology. . . . . James Karo, MD
Anesthesiology. . . . . Gregory Smith
Emergency Room . . . . John McCabe, MD

Measure	Cases	This Hosp.	State Avg.	U.S. Avg.
Heart Attack Care				
ACE Inhibitor or ARB for LVSD	83	100%	96%	96%
Aspirin at Arrival	254	99%	99%	99%
Aspirin at Discharge	421	99%	99%	98%
Beta Blocker at Discharge	404	99%	99%	98%
Fibrinolytic Medication Timing	0	-	55%	55%
PCI Within 90 Minutes of Arrival	37	95%	89%	90%
Smoking Cessation Advice	120	100%	100%	99%
Chest Pain/Possible Heart Attack Care				
Aspirin at Arrival	36	100%	94%	95%
Median Time to ECG (minutes)	37	8	10	8
Median Time to Transfer (minutes)[5]	0	-	54	61
Fibrinolytic Medication Timing[3]	0	-	60%	54%
Heart Failure Care				
ACE Inhibitor or ARB for LVSD	422	99%	95%	94%
Discharge Instructions	1,022	88%	89%	88%
Evaluation of LVS Function	1,248	100%	99%	98%
Smoking Cessation Advice	159	99%	99%	98%
Pneumonia Care				
Appropriate Initial Antibiotic	409	98%	94%	92%
Blood Culture Timing	526	96%	96%	96%
Influenza Vaccine	386	95%	91%	91%
Initial Antibiotic Timing	656	97%	96%	95%
Pneumococcal Vaccine	495	93%	93%	93%
Smoking Cessation Advice	157	99%	98%	97%
Surgical Care Improvement Project				
Appropriate VTP Within 24 Hours[2]	785	96%	94%	92%
Appropriate Hair Removal[2]	2,310	100%	99%	99%
Appropriate Beta Blocker Usage[2]	709	93%	92%	93%
Controlled Postoperative Blood Glucose[2]	218	97%	94%	93%
Prophylactic Antibiotic Timing[2]	1,577	98%	97%	97%
Prophylactic Antibiotic Timing (Outpatient)	884	95%	87%	92%
Prophylactic Antibiotic Selection[2]	1,597	99%	98%	97%
Prophylactic Antibiotic Select. (Outpatient)	866	99%	92%	94%
Prophylactic Antibiotic Stopped[2]	1,431	96%	95%	94%
Recommended VTP Ordered[2]	785	97%	95%	94%
Urinary Catheter Removal[2]	564	94%	91%	90%
Children's Asthma Care				
Received Systemic Corticosteroids	-	-	-	100%
Received Home Management Plan	-	-	-	71%
Received Reliever Medication	-	-	-	100%
Use of Medical Imaging				
Combination Abdominal CT Scan	2,330	0.073	0.135	0.191
Combination Chest CT Scan	1,788	0.012	0.068	0.054
Follow-up Mammogram/Ultrasound	4,175	4.7%	7.4%	8.4%
MRI for Low Back Pain	424	26.7%	32%	32.7%
Survey of Patients' Hospital Experiences				
Area Around Room 'Always' Quiet at Night	300+	56%	-	58%
Doctors 'Always' Communicated Well	300+	77%	-	80%
Home Recovery Information Given	300+	77%	-	82%
Hospital Given 9 or 10 on 10 Point Scale	300+	68%	-	67%
Meds 'Always' Explained Before Given	300+	54%	-	60%
Nurses 'Always' Communicated Well	300+	74%	-	76%
Pain 'Always' Well Controlled	300+	65%	-	69%
Room and Bathroom 'Always' Clean	300+	64%	-	71%
Timely Help 'Always' Received	300+	60%	-	64%
Would Definitely Recommend Hospital	300+	72%	-	69%

NOTE: Hospital profiles are in alphabetical order by state, then city, then hospital within the city; Rankings exclude hospitals with less than 25 cases except for patient surveys which excludes hospitals with less than 100 cases; (a) 100–299 cases; (1) The number of cases is too small to be sure how well a hospital is performing; (2) The hospital indicated that the data submitted for this measure were based on a sample of cases; (3) Data was collected during a shorter time period (fewer quarters) than the maximum possible time for this measure; (4) Suppressed for one or more quarters by CMS; (5) No data is available from the hospital for this measure; (6) Fewer than 100 patients completed the HCAHPS survey. Use these rates with caution, as the number of surveys may be too low to reliably assess hospital performance; (7) Survey results are based on less than 12 months of data; (8) Survey results are not available for this reporting period; (9) No or very few patients were eligible for the HCAHPS survey. The scores shown, if any, reflect a very small number of surveys; (10) A state average was not calculated because too few hospitals in the state submitted data; (11) There were discrepancies in the data collection process; Please refer to the User's Guide for a full explanation of data.

Straith Hospital for Special Surgery

23901 Lahser Phone: 248-357-3360
Southfield, MI 48033
Type: Acute Care Hospitals Emergency Services: No
Ownership: Voluntary Non-Profit - Private Beds: 27
Key Personnel:
CEO/President. . . . . Gregory Hoose

Measure	Cases	This Hosp.	State Avg.	U.S. Avg.
Heart Attack Care				
ACE Inhibitor or ARB for LVSD[5]	0	-	96%	96%
Aspirin at Arrival[5]	0	-	99%	99%
Aspirin at Discharge[5]	0	-	99%	98%
Beta Blocker at Discharge[5]	0	-	99%	98%
Fibrinolytic Medication Timing[5]	0	-	55%	55%
PCI Within 90 Minutes of Arrival[5]	0	-	89%	90%
Smoking Cessation Advice[5]	0	-	100%	99%
Chest Pain/Possible Heart Attack Care				
Aspirin at Arrival[5]	0	-	94%	95%
Median Time to ECG (minutes)[5]	0	-	10	8
Median Time to Transfer (minutes)[5]	0	-	54	61
Fibrinolytic Medication Timing[5]	0	-	60%	54%
Heart Failure Care				
ACE Inhibitor or ARB for LVSD[5]	0	-	95%	94%
Discharge Instructions[5]	0	-	89%	88%
Evaluation of LVS Function[5]	0	-	99%	98%
Smoking Cessation Advice[5]	0	-	99%	98%
Pneumonia Care				
Appropriate Initial Antibiotic[5]	0	-	94%	92%
Blood Culture Timing[5]	0	-	96%	96%
Influenza Vaccine[5]	0	-	91%	91%
Initial Antibiotic Timing[5]	0	-	96%	95%
Pneumococcal Vaccine[5]	0	-	93%	93%
Smoking Cessation Advice[5]	0	-	98%	97%
Surgical Care Improvement Project				
Appropriate VTP Within 24 Hours[5]	0	-	94%	92%
Appropriate Hair Removal[5]	0	-	99%	99%
Appropriate Beta Blocker Usage[5]	0	-	92%	93%
Controlled Postoperative Blood Glucose[5]	0	-	94%	93%
Prophylactic Antibiotic Timing[5]	0	-	97%	97%
Prophylactic Antibiotic Timing (Outpatient)[5]	0	-	87%	92%
Prophylactic Antibiotic Selection[5]	0	-	98%	97%
Prophylactic Antibiotic Select. (Outpatient)[5]	0	-	92%	94%
Prophylactic Antibiotic Stopped[5]	0	-	95%	94%
Recommended VTP Ordered[5]	0	-	95%	94%
Urinary Catheter Removal[5]	0	-	91%	90%
Children's Asthma Care				
Received Systemic Corticosteroids	-	-	-	100%
Received Home Management Plan	-	-	-	71%
Received Reliever Medication	-	-	-	100%
Use of Medical Imaging				
Combination Abdominal CT Scan[5]	0	-	0.135	0.191
Combination Chest CT Scan[5]	0	-	0.068	0.054
Follow-up Mammogram/Ultrasound[5]	0	-	7.4%	8.4%
MRI for Low Back Pain[5]	0	-	32%	32.7%
Survey of Patients' Hospital Experiences				
Area Around Room 'Always' Quiet at Night[9]	-	-	-	58%
Doctors 'Always' Communicated Well[9]	-	-	-	80%
Home Recovery Information Given[9]	-	-	-	82%
Hospital Given 9 or 10 on 10 Point Scale[9]	-	-	-	67%
Meds 'Always' Explained Before Given[9]	-	-	-	60%
Nurses 'Always' Communicated Well[9]	-	-	-	76%
Pain 'Always' Well Controlled[9]	-	-	-	69%
Room and Bathroom 'Always' Clean[9]	-	-	-	71%
Timely Help 'Always' Received[9]	-	-	-	64%
Would Definitely Recommend Hospital[9]	-	-	-	69%

Saint Mary's Standish Community Hospital

805 W Cedar St Phone: 517-846-4521
Standish, MI 48658 Fax: 989-846-3549
Type: Critical Access Hospitals Emergency Services: Yes
Ownership: Voluntary Non-Profit - Private Beds: 68
Key Personnel:
CEO/President. . . . . Jeff Probus
Chief of Medical Staff. . . . . Gordon Page, MD
Coronary Care . . . . Roxanne Lushnat
Infection Control. . . . . Jean Lohr
Operating Room. . . . . Kim Szostak, RN
Pediatric Ambulatory Care . . . . . . I Shamieh, MD
Pediatric In-Patient Care . . . . I Shamieh, MD
Quality Assurance . . . . Joe Nicholl

Measure	Cases	This Hosp.	State Avg.	U.S. Avg.
Heart Attack Care				
ACE Inhibitor or ARB for LVSD	0	-	96%	96%
Aspirin at Arrival[1]	1	100%	99%	99%
Aspirin at Discharge[1]	1	0%	99%	98%
Beta Blocker at Discharge[1]	1	100%	99%	98%
Fibrinolytic Medication Timing	0	-	55%	55%
PCI Within 90 Minutes of Arrival	0	-	89%	90%
Smoking Cessation Advice	0	-	100%	99%
Chest Pain/Possible Heart Attack Care				
Aspirin at Arrival[3]	49	100%	94%	95%
Median Time to ECG (minutes)[3]	52	16	10	8
Median Time to Transfer (minutes)[1,3]	2	32	54	61
Fibrinolytic Medication Timing[1,3]	3	67%	60%	54%
Heart Failure Care				
ACE Inhibitor or ARB for LVSD[1,3]	2	100%	95%	94%
Discharge Instructions[1,3]	19	89%	89%	88%
Evaluation of LVS Function[3]	32	81%	99%	98%
Smoking Cessation Advice[1,3]	3	67%	99%	98%
Pneumonia Care				
Appropriate Initial Antibiotic[1]	22	86%	94%	92%
Blood Culture Timing	49	96%	96%	96%
Influenza Vaccine	32	100%	91%	91%
Initial Antibiotic Timing	46	100%	96%	95%
Pneumococcal Vaccine	40	100%	93%	93%
Smoking Cessation Advice[1]	21	95%	98%	97%
Surgical Care Improvement Project				
Appropriate VTP Within 24 Hours[1]	9	100%	94%	92%
Appropriate Hair Removal[1]	10	100%	99%	99%
Appropriate Beta Blocker Usage[1,3]	1	100%	92%	93%
Controlled Postoperative Blood Glucose	0	-	94%	93%
Prophylactic Antibiotic Timing[1]	3	0%	97%	97%
Prophylactic Antibiotic Timing (Outpatient)[1,3]	3	100%	87%	92%
Prophylactic Antibiotic Selection[1]	3	67%	98%	97%
Prophylactic Antibiotic Select. (Outpatient)[1,3]	3	100%	92%	94%
Prophylactic Antibiotic Stopped[1]	2	100%	95%	94%
Recommended VTP Ordered[1]	9	100%	95%	94%
Urinary Catheter Removal	0	-	91%	90%
Children's Asthma Care				
Received Systemic Corticosteroids	-	-	-	100%
Received Home Management Plan	-	-	-	71%
Received Reliever Medication	-	-	-	100%
Use of Medical Imaging				
Combination Abdominal CT Scan	331	0.097	0.135	0.191
Combination Chest CT Scan	281	0.053	0.068	0.054
Follow-up Mammogram/Ultrasound	262	7.3%	7.4%	8.4%
MRI for Low Back Pain	66	45.5%	32%	32.7%
Survey of Patients' Hospital Experiences				
Area Around Room 'Always' Quiet at Night[8]	-	-	-	58%
Doctors 'Always' Communicated Well[8]	-	-	-	80%
Home Recovery Information Given[8]	-	-	-	82%
Hospital Given 9 or 10 on 10 Point Scale[8]	-	-	-	67%
Meds 'Always' Explained Before Given[8]	-	-	-	60%
Nurses 'Always' Communicated Well[8]	-	-	-	76%
Pain 'Always' Well Controlled[8]	-	-	-	69%
Room and Bathroom 'Always' Clean[8]	-	-	-	71%
Timely Help 'Always' Received[8]	-	-	-	64%
Would Definitely Recommend Hospital[8]	-	-	-	69%

Sturgis Hospital

916 Myrtle Ave Phone: 269-651-7824
Sturgis, MI 49091 Fax: 269-659-6713
URL: www.sturgishospital.com
Type: Acute Care Hospitals Emergency Services: Yes
Ownership: Government - Local Beds: 94
Key Personnel:
CEO/President. . . . . Robert L LaBarge
Cardiac Laboratory. . . . . Shirley Betts
Chief of Medical Staff. . . . . Edward Griffin, MD
Infection Control. . . . . Sarah Hagen
Operating Room. . . . . Martha Gillespie
Quality Assurance . . . . Shari Ransberger, RN
Radiology. . . . . John C Kirkpatrick, MD

Measure	Cases	This Hosp.	State Avg.	U.S. Avg.
Heart Attack Care				
ACE Inhibitor or ARB for LVSD	0	-	96%	96%
Aspirin at Arrival[1]	4	100%	99%	99%
Aspirin at Discharge[1]	4	75%	99%	98%
Beta Blocker at Discharge[1]	3	67%	99%	98%
Fibrinolytic Medication Timing	0	-	55%	55%
PCI Within 90 Minutes of Arrival	0	-	89%	90%
Smoking Cessation Advice	0	-	100%	99%
Chest Pain/Possible Heart Attack Care				
Aspirin at Arrival[1,3]	18	78%	94%	95%
Median Time to ECG (minutes)[1,3]	19	7	10	8
Median Time to Transfer (minutes)[1,3]	1	120	54	61
Fibrinolytic Medication Timing[3]	0	-	60%	54%
Heart Failure Care				
ACE Inhibitor or ARB for LVSD[1]	15	80%	95%	94%
Discharge Instructions	50	92%	89%	88%
Evaluation of LVS Function	60	97%	99%	98%
Smoking Cessation Advice[1]	7	100%	99%	98%
Pneumonia Care				
Appropriate Initial Antibiotic	50	88%	94%	92%
Blood Culture Timing	59	97%	96%	96%
Influenza Vaccine	37	97%	91%	91%
Initial Antibiotic Timing	77	95%	96%	95%
Pneumococcal Vaccine	65	95%	93%	93%
Smoking Cessation Advice[1]	17	71%	98%	97%
Surgical Care Improvement Project				
Appropriate VTP Within 24 Hours	49	96%	94%	92%
Appropriate Hair Removal	127	99%	99%	99%
Appropriate Beta Blocker Usage	27	96%	92%	93%
Controlled Postoperative Blood Glucose	0	-	94%	93%
Prophylactic Antibiotic Timing	89	90%	97%	97%
Prophylactic Antibiotic Timing (Outpatient)	75	75%	87%	92%
Prophylactic Antibiotic Selection	89	99%	98%	97%
Prophylactic Antibiotic Select. (Outpatient)	58	95%	92%	94%
Prophylactic Antibiotic Stopped	87	87%	95%	94%
Recommended VTP Ordered	49	98%	95%	94%
Urinary Catheter Removal[1]	24	100%	91%	90%
Children's Asthma Care				
Received Systemic Corticosteroids	-	-	-	100%
Received Home Management Plan	-	-	-	71%
Received Reliever Medication	-	-	-	100%
Use of Medical Imaging				
Combination Abdominal CT Scan	218	0.931	0.135	0.191
Combination Chest CT Scan	182	0.835	0.068	0.054
Follow-up Mammogram/Ultrasound	534	5.1%	7.4%	8.4%
MRI for Low Back Pain	50	34.0%	32%	32.7%
Survey of Patients' Hospital Experiences				
Area Around Room 'Always' Quiet at Night	300+	61%	-	58%
Doctors 'Always' Communicated Well	300+	82%	-	80%
Home Recovery Information Given	300+	83%	-	82%
Hospital Given 9 or 10 on 10 Point Scale	300+	73%	-	67%
Meds 'Always' Explained Before Given	300+	58%	-	60%
Nurses 'Always' Communicated Well	300+	77%	-	76%
Pain 'Always' Well Controlled	300+	71%	-	69%
Room and Bathroom 'Always' Clean	300+	69%	-	71%
Timely Help 'Always' Received	300+	70%	-	64%
Would Definitely Recommend Hospital	300+	67%	-	69%

NOTE: Hospital profiles are in alphabetical order by state, then city, then hospital within the city; Rankings exclude hospitals with less than 25 cases except for patient surveys which excludes hospitals with less than 100 cases; (a) 100–299 cases; (1) The number of cases is too small to be sure how well a hospital is performing; (2) The hospital indicated that the data submitted for this measure were based on a sample of cases; (3) Data was collected during a shorter time period (fewer quarters) than the maximum possible time for this measure; (4) Suppressed for one or more quarters by CMS; (5) No data is available from the hospital for this measure; (6) Fewer than 100 patients completed the HCAHPS survey. Use these rates with caution, as the number of surveys may be too low to reliably assess hospital performance; (7) Survey results are based on less than 12 months of data; (8) Survey results are not available for this reporting period; (9) No or very few patients were eligible for the HCAHPS survey. The scores shown, if any, reflect a very small number of surveys; (10) A state average was not calculated because too few hospitals in the state submitted data; (11) There were discrepancies in the data collection process; Please refer to the User's Guide for a full explanation of data.

Tawas Saint Joseph Hospital

200 Hemlock M-55
Tawas City, MI 48763
URL: www.sjhsys.org
Type: Acute Care Hospitals
Ownership: Voluntary Non-Profit - Other

Phone: 989-362-9301
Fax: 989-362-9376
Emergency Services: Yes
Beds: 49

Key Personnel:
CEO/President............... Patrick J Murtha
Operating Room.............. Pat Visscher
Anesthesiology.............. Jon Kaliszewski, MD
Patient Relations............ Martie Hang

Measure	Cases	This Hosp.	State Avg.	U.S. Avg.
Heart Attack Care				
ACE Inhibitor or ARB for LVSD[1]	1	100%	96%	96%
Aspirin at Arrival[1]	4	100%	99%	99%
Aspirin at Discharge[1]	2	100%	99%	98%
Beta Blocker at Discharge[1]	2	100%	99%	98%
Fibrinolytic Medication Timing	0	-	55%	55%
PCI Within 90 Minutes of Arrival	0	-	89%	90%
Smoking Cessation Advice	0	-	100%	99%
Chest Pain/Possible Heart Attack Care				
Aspirin at Arrival	289	97%	94%	95%
Median Time to ECG (minutes)	298	9	10	8
Median Time to Transfer (minutes)[1,3]	6	104	54	61
Fibrinolytic Medication Timing[1]	14	36%	60%	54%
Heart Failure Care				
ACE Inhibitor or ARB for LVSD[1]	22	95%	95%	94%
Discharge Instructions	73	99%	89%	88%
Evaluation of LVS Function	88	99%	99%	98%
Smoking Cessation Advice[1]	14	100%	99%	98%
Pneumonia Care				
Appropriate Initial Antibiotic	95	95%	94%	92%
Blood Culture Timing	144	93%	96%	96%
Influenza Vaccine	74	97%	91%	91%
Initial Antibiotic Timing	133	98%	96%	95%
Pneumococcal Vaccine	113	97%	93%	93%
Smoking Cessation Advice	54	100%	98%	97%
Surgical Care Improvement Project				
Appropriate VTP Within 24 Hours[2]	45	100%	94%	92%
Appropriate Hair Removal[2]	223	100%	99%	99%
Appropriate Beta Blocker Usage[2]	76	95%	92%	93%
Controlled Postoperative Blood Glucose[2]	0	-	94%	93%
Prophylactic Antibiotic Timing[2]	151	97%	97%	97%
Prophylactic Antibiotic Timing (Outpatient)	63	94%	87%	92%
Prophylactic Antibiotic Selection[2]	154	99%	98%	97%
Prophylactic Antibiotic Select. (Outpatient)	62	97%	92%	94%
Prophylactic Antibiotic Stopped[2]	148	99%	95%	94%
Recommended VTP Ordered[2]	45	100%	95%	94%
Urinary Catheter Removal	41	100%	91%	90%
Children's Asthma Care				
Received Systemic Corticosteroids	-	-	-	100%
Received Home Management Plan	-	-	-	71%
Received Reliever Medication	-	-	-	100%
Use of Medical Imaging				
Combination Abdominal CT Scan	654	0.125	0.135	0.191
Combination Chest CT Scan	377	0.093	0.068	0.054
Follow-up Mammogram/Ultrasound	1,172	6.9%	7.4%	8.4%
MRI for Low Back Pain	223	41.7%	32%	32.7%
Survey of Patients' Hospital Experiences				
Area Around Room 'Always' Quiet at Night	300+	58%	-	58%
Doctors 'Always' Communicated Well	300+	80%	-	80%
Home Recovery Information Given	300+	85%	-	82%
Hospital Given 9 or 10 on 10 Point Scale	300+	73%	-	67%
Meds 'Always' Explained Before Given	300+	60%	-	60%
Nurses 'Always' Communicated Well	300+	80%	-	76%
Pain 'Always' Well Controlled	300+	76%	-	69%
Room and Bathroom 'Always' Clean	300+	70%	-	71%
Timely Help 'Always' Received	300+	71%	-	64%
Would Definitely Recommend Hospital	300+	70%	-	69%

Oakwood Heritage Hospital

10000 Telegraph Road
Taylor, MI 48180
E-mail: LEIJAS@oakwood.org
URL: www.oakwod.org
Type: Acute Care Hospitals
Ownership: Govt - Hospital Dist/Auth

Phone: 313-295-5253
Fax: 313-295-5085
Emergency Services: Yes
Beds: 248

Key Personnel:
CEO/President............... Rick Hillbom
Chief of Medical Staff.......... Vijay Khanna, MD
Coronary Care............... Abil Karamali
Operating Room.............. Sameeh Kawar
Quality Assurance............ Tina Lowery
Emergency Room............ Deb Vogel, RN

Measure	Cases	This Hosp.	State Avg.	U.S. Avg.
Heart Attack Care				
ACE Inhibitor or ARB for LVSD[1]	8	100%	96%	96%
Aspirin at Arrival	32	100%	99%	99%
Aspirin at Discharge[1]	22	100%	99%	98%
Beta Blocker at Discharge[1]	24	100%	99%	98%
Fibrinolytic Medication Timing	0	-	55%	55%
PCI Within 90 Minutes of Arrival	0	-	89%	90%
Smoking Cessation Advice[1]	4	100%	100%	99%
Chest Pain/Possible Heart Attack Care				
Aspirin at Arrival	101	89%	94%	95%
Median Time to ECG (minutes)	108	9	10	8
Median Time to Transfer (minutes)[1,3]	5	55	54	61
Fibrinolytic Medication Timing	0	-	60%	54%
Heart Failure Care				
ACE Inhibitor or ARB for LVSD	51	100%	95%	94%
Discharge Instructions	99	97%	89%	88%
Evaluation of LVS Function	167	100%	99%	98%
Smoking Cessation Advice	33	100%	99%	98%
Pneumonia Care				
Appropriate Initial Antibiotic	144	97%	94%	92%
Blood Culture Timing	297	99%	96%	96%
Influenza Vaccine	168	100%	91%	91%
Initial Antibiotic Timing	286	97%	96%	95%
Pneumococcal Vaccine	207	100%	93%	93%
Smoking Cessation Advice	105	100%	98%	97%
Surgical Care Improvement Project				
Appropriate VTP Within 24 Hours[2]	90	99%	94%	92%
Appropriate Hair Removal[2]	314	100%	99%	99%
Appropriate Beta Blocker Usage[2]	93	96%	92%	93%
Controlled Postoperative Blood Glucose[2]	0	-	94%	93%
Prophylactic Antibiotic Timing[2]	234	100%	97%	97%
Prophylactic Antibiotic Timing (Outpatient)[1]	16	81%	87%	92%
Prophylactic Antibiotic Selection[2]	235	99%	98%	97%
Prophylactic Antibiotic Select. (Outpatient)[1]	16	88%	92%	94%
Prophylactic Antibiotic Stopped[2]	224	100%	95%	94%
Recommended VTP Ordered[2]	90	99%	95%	94%
Urinary Catheter Removal[2]	37	100%	91%	90%
Children's Asthma Care				
Received Systemic Corticosteroids	-	-	-	100%
Received Home Management Plan	-	-	-	71%
Received Reliever Medication	-	-	-	100%
Use of Medical Imaging				
Combination Abdominal CT Scan	254	0.035	0.135	0.191
Combination Chest CT Scan	268	0.022	0.068	0.054
Follow-up Mammogram/Ultrasound	1,012	7.1%	7.4%	8.4%
MRI for Low Back Pain	110	28.2%	32%	32.7%
Survey of Patients' Hospital Experiences				
Area Around Room 'Always' Quiet at Night	300+	51%	-	58%
Doctors 'Always' Communicated Well	300+	76%	-	80%
Home Recovery Information Given	300+	79%	-	82%
Hospital Given 9 or 10 on 10 Point Scale	300+	60%	-	67%
Meds 'Always' Explained Before Given	300+	58%	-	60%
Nurses 'Always' Communicated Well	300+	75%	-	76%
Pain 'Always' Well Controlled	300+	71%	-	69%
Room and Bathroom 'Always' Clean	300+	66%	-	71%
Timely Help 'Always' Received	300+	59%	-	64%
Would Definitely Recommend Hospital	300+	62%	-	69%

Herrick Memorial Hospital

500 E Pottawatamie Street
Tecumseh, MI 49286
Type: Critical Access Hospitals
Ownership: Government - Federal

Phone: 517-424-3000
Fax: 517-424-3900
Emergency Services: Yes
Beds: 100

Key Personnel:
CEO/President............... John Robertstad
Chief of Medical Staff.......... David Kaisler, MD
Infection Control.............. Claudette Bryan
Operating Room.............. Marcia Olieman
Quality Assurance............ Linda Yielding
Anesthesiology.............. Cathy Cook, D.O.
Emergency Room............ Rosalie Turek, MD
Intensive Care Unit........... Christine Mathis

Measure	Cases	This Hosp.	State Avg.	U.S. Avg.
Heart Attack Care				
ACE Inhibitor or ARB for LVSD[1,3]	3	67%	96%	96%
Aspirin at Arrival[1,3]	9	100%	99%	99%
Aspirin at Discharge[1,3]	7	86%	99%	98%
Beta Blocker at Discharge[1,3]	8	88%	99%	98%
Fibrinolytic Medication Timing[3]	0	-	55%	55%
PCI Within 90 Minutes of Arrival[3]	0	-	89%	90%
Smoking Cessation Advice[3]	0	-	100%	99%
Chest Pain/Possible Heart Attack Care				
Aspirin at Arrival	-	-	94%	95%
Median Time to ECG (minutes)	-	-	10	8
Median Time to Transfer (minutes)	-	-	54	61
Fibrinolytic Medication Timing	-	-	60%	54%
Heart Failure Care				
ACE Inhibitor or ARB for LVSD[1]	14	93%	95%	94%
Discharge Instructions	36	92%	89%	88%
Evaluation of LVS Function	42	98%	99%	98%
Smoking Cessation Advice[1]	4	100%	99%	98%
Pneumonia Care				
Appropriate Initial Antibiotic	45	96%	94%	92%
Blood Culture Timing	62	98%	96%	96%
Influenza Vaccine	42	86%	91%	91%
Initial Antibiotic Timing	64	92%	96%	95%
Pneumococcal Vaccine	58	97%	93%	93%
Smoking Cessation Advice[1]	17	94%	98%	97%
Surgical Care Improvement Project				
Appropriate VTP Within 24 Hours[5]	0	-	94%	92%
Appropriate Hair Removal[5]	0	-	99%	99%
Appropriate Beta Blocker Usage[5]	0	-	92%	93%
Controlled Postoperative Blood Glucose[5]	0	-	94%	93%
Prophylactic Antibiotic Timing[5]	0	-	97%	97%
Prophylactic Antibiotic Timing (Outpatient)	-	-	87%	92%
Prophylactic Antibiotic Selection[5]	0	-	98%	97%
Prophylactic Antibiotic Select. (Outpatient)	-	-	92%	94%
Prophylactic Antibiotic Stopped[5]	0	-	95%	94%
Recommended VTP Ordered[5]	0	-	95%	94%
Urinary Catheter Removal[5]	0	-	91%	90%
Children's Asthma Care				
Received Systemic Corticosteroids	-	-	-	100%
Received Home Management Plan	-	-	-	71%
Received Reliever Medication	-	-	-	100%
Use of Medical Imaging				
Combination Abdominal CT Scan	-	-	0.135	0.191
Combination Chest CT Scan	-	-	0.068	0.054
Follow-up Mammogram/Ultrasound	-	-	7.4%	8.4%
MRI for Low Back Pain	-	-	32%	32.7%
Survey of Patients' Hospital Experiences				
Area Around Room 'Always' Quiet at Night	300+	58%	-	58%
Doctors 'Always' Communicated Well	300+	75%	-	80%
Home Recovery Information Given	300+	82%	-	82%
Hospital Given 9 or 10 on 10 Point Scale	300+	64%	-	67%
Meds 'Always' Explained Before Given	300+	58%	-	60%
Nurses 'Always' Communicated Well	300+	73%	-	76%
Pain 'Always' Well Controlled	300+	66%	-	69%
Room and Bathroom 'Always' Clean	300+	78%	-	71%
Timely Help 'Always' Received	300+	62%	-	64%
Would Definitely Recommend Hospital	300+	64%	-	69%

NOTE: Hospital profiles are in alphabetical order by state, then city, then hospital within the city; Rankings exclude hospitals with less than 25 cases except for patient surveys which excludes hospitals with less than 100 cases; (a) 100–299 cases; (1) The number of cases is too small to be sure how well a hospital is performing; (2) The hospital indicated that the data submitted for this measure were based on a sample of cases; (3) Data was collected during a shorter time period (fewer quarters) than the maximum possible time for this measure; (4) Suppressed for one or more quarters by CMS; (5) No data is available from the hospital for this measure; (6) Fewer than 100 patients completed the HCAHPS survey. Use these rates with caution, as the number of surveys may be too low to reliably assess hospital performance; (7) Survey results are based on less than 12 months of data; (8) Survey results are not available for this reporting period; (9) No or very few patients were eligible for the HCAHPS survey. The scores shown, if any, reflect a very small number of surveys; (10) A state average was not calculated because too few hospitals in the state submitted data; (11) There were discrepancies in the data collection process; Please refer to the User's Guide for a full explanation of data.

Three Rivers Health

701 S Health Parkway | Phone: 269-273-9602
Three Rivers, MI 49093 | Fax: 269-273-9611
E-mail: info@threerivershealth.org
URL: www.threerivershealth.org
Type: Acute Care Hospitals | Emergency Services: Yes
Ownership: Govt - Hospital Dist/Auth | Beds: 60

Key Personnel:
Operating Room.............. Jo Lindsley, RN
Radiology.................... George J Balogh
Anesthesiology............... Lalitha Mutnal, MD
Emergency Room .... Brian Bowdich, MD

Measure	Cases	This Hosp.	State Avg.	U.S. Avg.
Heart Attack Care				
ACE Inhibitor or ARB for LVSD[3]	0	-	96%	96%
Aspirin at Arrival[3]	0	-	99%	99%
Aspirin at Discharge[3]	0	-	99%	98%
Beta Blocker at Discharge[3]	0	-	99%	98%
Fibrinolytic Medication Timing[3]	0	-	55%	55%
PCI Within 90 Minutes of Arrival[3]	0	-	89%	90%
Smoking Cessation Advice[3]	0	-	100%	99%
Chest Pain/Possible Heart Attack Care				
Aspirin at Arrival	152	94%	94%	95%
Median Time to ECG (minutes)	164	18	10	8
Median Time to Transfer (minutes)[1]	23	76	54	61
Fibrinolytic Medication Timing[1]	2	100%	60%	54%
Heart Failure Care				
ACE Inhibitor or ARB for LVSD[1]	17	76%	95%	94%
Discharge Instructions	58	93%	89%	88%
Evaluation of LVS Function	80	95%	99%	98%
Smoking Cessation Advice[1]	12	100%	99%	98%
Pneumonia Care				
Appropriate Initial Antibiotic	46	91%	94%	92%
Blood Culture Timing	58	93%	96%	96%
Influenza Vaccine	28	71%	91%	91%
Initial Antibiotic Timing	56	96%	96%	95%
Pneumococcal Vaccine	47	81%	93%	93%
Smoking Cessation Advice[1]	23	78%	98%	97%
Surgical Care Improvement Project				
Appropriate VTP Within 24 Hours[1]	21	71%	94%	92%
Appropriate Hair Removal	94	98%	99%	99%
Appropriate Beta Blocker Usage[1]	17	94%	92%	93%
Controlled Postoperative Blood Glucose	0	-	94%	93%
Prophylactic Antibiotic Timing	57	98%	97%	97%
Prophylactic Antibiotic Timing (Outpatient)[5]	0	-	87%	92%
Prophylactic Antibiotic Selection	58	93%	98%	97%
Prophylactic Antibiotic Select. (Outpatient)[5]	0	-	92%	94%
Prophylactic Antibiotic Stopped	57	100%	95%	94%
Recommended VTP Ordered[1]	21	71%	95%	94%
Urinary Catheter Removal[1]	18	94%	91%	90%
Children's Asthma Care				
Received Systemic Corticosteroids	-	-	-	100%
Received Home Management Plan	-	-	-	71%
Received Reliever Medication	-	-	-	100%
Use of Medical Imaging				
Combination Abdominal CT Scan	341	0.062	0.135	0.191
Combination Chest CT Scan	149	0.013	0.068	0.054
Follow-up Mammogram/Ultrasound	344	6.4%	7.4%	8.4%
MRI for Low Back Pain	70	41.4%	32%	32.7%
Survey of Patients' Hospital Experiences				
Area Around Room 'Always' Quiet at Night	(a)	43%	-	58%
Doctors 'Always' Communicated Well	(a)	70%	-	80%
Home Recovery Information Given	(a)	84%	-	82%
Hospital Given 9 or 10 on 10 Point Scale	(a)	60%	-	67%
Meds 'Always' Explained Before Given	(a)	59%	-	60%
Nurses 'Always' Communicated Well	(a)	72%	-	76%
Pain 'Always' Well Controlled	(a)	60%	-	69%
Room and Bathroom 'Always' Clean	(a)	69%	-	71%
Timely Help 'Always' Received	(a)	60%	-	64%
Would Definitely Recommend Hospital	(a)	58%	-	69%

Munson Medical Center

1105 Sixth Street | Phone: 231-935-5000
Traverse City, MI 49684 | Fax: 231-935-6548
E-mail: contact@mhc.net
URL: www.munsonhealthcare.org
Type: Acute Care Hospitals | Emergency Services: Yes
Ownership: Voluntary Non-Profit - Other | Beds: 391

Key Personnel:
CEO/President................ K. Douglas Deck
Quality Assurance .... Terry Haslinger
Patient Relations .... Jim P Fischer

Measure	Cases	This Hosp.	State Avg.	U.S. Avg.
Heart Attack Care				
ACE Inhibitor or ARB for LVSD	154	97%	96%	96%
Aspirin at Arrival	430	100%	99%	99%
Aspirin at Discharge	892	100%	99%	98%
Beta Blocker at Discharge	816	99%	99%	98%
Fibrinolytic Medication Timing	0	-	55%	55%
PCI Within 90 Minutes of Arrival	71	83%	89%	90%
Smoking Cessation Advice	304	100%	100%	99%
Chest Pain/Possible Heart Attack Care				
Aspirin at Arrival[5]	0	-	94%	95%
Median Time to ECG (minutes)[5]	0	-	10	8
Median Time to Transfer (minutes)[5]	0	-	54	61
Fibrinolytic Medication Timing[5]	0	-	60%	54%
Heart Failure Care				
ACE Inhibitor or ARB for LVSD	145	94%	95%	94%
Discharge Instructions	482	93%	89%	88%
Evaluation of LVS Function	536	100%	99%	98%
Smoking Cessation Advice	73	99%	99%	98%
Pneumonia Care				
Appropriate Initial Antibiotic	228	100%	94%	92%
Blood Culture Timing	386	98%	96%	96%
Influenza Vaccine	219	100%	91%	91%
Initial Antibiotic Timing	318	99%	96%	95%
Pneumococcal Vaccine	342	100%	93%	93%
Smoking Cessation Advice	160	99%	98%	97%
Surgical Care Improvement Project				
Appropriate VTP Within 24 Hours[2]	254	97%	94%	92%
Appropriate Hair Removal[2]	920	100%	99%	99%
Appropriate Beta Blocker Usage[2]	269	98%	92%	93%
Controlled Postoperative Blood Glucose[2]	169	95%	94%	93%
Prophylactic Antibiotic Timing[2]	586	96%	97%	97%
Prophylactic Antibiotic Timing (Outpatient)	339	90%	87%	92%
Prophylactic Antibiotic Selection[2]	596	99%	98%	97%
Prophylactic Antibiotic Select. (Outpatient)	390	97%	92%	94%
Prophylactic Antibiotic Stopped[2]	568	98%	95%	94%
Recommended VTP Ordered[2]	255	98%	95%	94%
Urinary Catheter Removal[2]	113	94%	91%	90%
Children's Asthma Care				
Received Systemic Corticosteroids	-	-	-	100%
Received Home Management Plan	-	-	-	71%
Received Reliever Medication	-	-	-	100%
Use of Medical Imaging				
Combination Abdominal CT Scan	1,305	0.034	0.135	0.191
Combination Chest CT Scan	901	0.003	0.068	0.054
Follow-up Mammogram/Ultrasound	2,443	8.8%	7.4%	8.4%
MRI for Low Back Pain	542	32.3%	32%	32.7%
Survey of Patients' Hospital Experiences				
Area Around Room 'Always' Quiet at Night	300+	52%	-	58%
Doctors 'Always' Communicated Well	300+	81%	-	80%
Home Recovery Information Given	300+	86%	-	82%
Hospital Given 9 or 10 on 10 Point Scale	300+	83%	-	67%
Meds 'Always' Explained Before Given	300+	65%	-	60%
Nurses 'Always' Communicated Well	300+	83%	-	76%
Pain 'Always' Well Controlled	300+	73%	-	69%
Room and Bathroom 'Always' Clean	300+	71%	-	71%
Timely Help 'Always' Received	300+	71%	-	64%
Would Definitely Recommend Hospital	300+	85%	-	69%

Oakwood Southshore Medical Center

5450 Fort Street | Phone: 734-671-3800
Trenton, MI 48183 | Fax: 734-671-3891
Type: Acute Care Hospitals | Emergency Services: Yes
Ownership: Govt - Hospital Dist/Auth | Beds: 203

Key Personnel:
CEO/President................ Jerry Fitzgerald
Cardiac Laboratory............ D Flood
Chief of Medical Staff.......... Malcolm Henoch
Infection Control.............. Susan Ottosen
Operating Room............... Joanne McKay
Anesthesiology................ Eric Suris, DO
Intensive Care Unit............ Carol Lampe
Patient Relations .... Jan Sladewski

Measure	Cases	This Hosp.	State Avg.	U.S. Avg.
Heart Attack Care				
ACE Inhibitor or ARB for LVSD[1]	17	100%	96%	96%
Aspirin at Arrival	112	99%	99%	99%
Aspirin at Discharge	70	97%	99%	98%
Beta Blocker at Discharge	71	100%	99%	98%
Fibrinolytic Medication Timing	0	-	55%	55%
PCI Within 90 Minutes of Arrival	29	86%	89%	90%
Smoking Cessation Advice	27	100%	100%	99%
Chest Pain/Possible Heart Attack Care				
Aspirin at Arrival	63	92%	94%	95%
Median Time to ECG (minutes)	66	6	10	8
Median Time to Transfer (minutes)[1,3]	1	40	54	61
Fibrinolytic Medication Timing	0	-	60%	54%
Heart Failure Care				
ACE Inhibitor or ARB for LVSD	95	94%	95%	94%
Discharge Instructions	230	95%	89%	88%
Evaluation of LVS Function	287	99%	99%	98%
Smoking Cessation Advice	38	100%	99%	98%
Pneumonia Care				
Appropriate Initial Antibiotic	209	97%	94%	92%
Blood Culture Timing	269	97%	96%	96%
Influenza Vaccine	188	97%	91%	91%
Initial Antibiotic Timing	325	97%	96%	95%
Pneumococcal Vaccine	257	97%	93%	93%
Smoking Cessation Advice	101	100%	98%	97%
Surgical Care Improvement Project				
Appropriate VTP Within 24 Hours[2]	149	99%	94%	92%
Appropriate Hair Removal[2]	549	100%	99%	99%
Appropriate Beta Blocker Usage[2]	181	93%	92%	93%
Controlled Postoperative Blood Glucose[2]	0	-	94%	93%
Prophylactic Antibiotic Timing[2]	403	99%	97%	97%
Prophylactic Antibiotic Timing (Outpatient)	133	83%	87%	92%
Prophylactic Antibiotic Selection[2]	403	99%	98%	97%
Prophylactic Antibiotic Select. (Outpatient)	126	93%	92%	94%
Prophylactic Antibiotic Stopped[2]	392	98%	95%	94%
Recommended VTP Ordered[2]	149	99%	95%	94%
Urinary Catheter Removal[2]	35	74%	91%	90%
Children's Asthma Care				
Received Systemic Corticosteroids	-	-	-	100%
Received Home Management Plan	-	-	-	71%
Received Reliever Medication	-	-	-	100%
Use of Medical Imaging				
Combination Abdominal CT Scan	704	0.124	0.135	0.191
Combination Chest CT Scan	533	0.013	0.068	0.054
Follow-up Mammogram/Ultrasound	519	11.2%	7.4%	8.4%
MRI for Low Back Pain	130	27.7%	32%	32.7%
Survey of Patients' Hospital Experiences				
Area Around Room 'Always' Quiet at Night	300+	61%	-	58%
Doctors 'Always' Communicated Well	300+	81%	-	80%
Home Recovery Information Given	300+	81%	-	82%
Hospital Given 9 or 10 on 10 Point Scale	300+	73%	-	67%
Meds 'Always' Explained Before Given	300+	63%	-	60%
Nurses 'Always' Communicated Well	300+	78%	-	76%
Pain 'Always' Well Controlled	300+	73%	-	69%
Room and Bathroom 'Always' Clean	300+	75%	-	71%
Timely Help 'Always' Received	300+	65%	-	64%
Would Definitely Recommend Hospital	300+	74%	-	69%

NOTE: Hospital profiles are in alphabetical order by state, then city, then hospital within the city; Rankings exclude hospitals with less than 25 cases except for patient surveys which excludes hospitals with less than 100 cases; (a) 100–299 cases; (1) The number of cases is too small to be sure how well a hospital is performing; (2) The hospital indicated that the data submitted for this measure were based on a sample of cases; (3) Data was collected during a shorter time period (fewer quarters) than the maximum possible time for this measure; (4) Suppressed for one or more quarters by CMS; (5) No data is available from the hospital for this measure; (6) Fewer than 100 patients completed the HCAHPS survey. Use these rates with caution, as the number of surveys may be too low to reliably assess hospital performance; (7) Survey results are based on less than 12 months of data; (8) Survey results are not available for this reporting period; (9) No or very few patients were eligible for the HCAHPS survey. The scores shown, if any, reflect a very small number of surveys; (10) A state average was not calculated because too few hospitals in the state submitted data; (11) There were discrepancies in the data collection process; Please refer to the User's Guide for a full explanation of data.

William Beaumont Hospital-Troy

44201 Dequindre Road
Troy, MI 48085
Phone: 248-964-8800
Fax: 248-964-8842
URL: www.beaumonthospitals.com
Type: Acute Care Hospitals
Emergency Services: Yes
Ownership: Voluntary Non-Profit - Other
Beds: 226

Key Personnel:

Cardiac Laboratory. . . . . Terry Wagner
Chief of Medical Staff . . . . Richardpher Herbert, DO
Infection Control. . . . . Doris Neumeyer
Operating Room. . . . . Dee Henderson
Pediatric Ambulatory Care . . . . . . Karen Hufnagle, MD
Pediatric In-Patient Care . . . . Karen Hufnagle, MD
Quality Assurance . . . . Janna Hoff
Radiology. . . . . Thomas Verhelle, MD

Measure	Cases	This Hosp.	State Avg.	U.S. Avg.
Heart Attack Care				
ACE Inhibitor or ARB for LVSD	84	100%	96%	96%
Aspirin at Arrival	438	100%	99%	99%
Aspirin at Discharge	414	100%	99%	98%
Beta Blocker at Discharge	417	100%	99%	98%
Fibrinolytic Medication Timing	0	-	55%	55%
PCI Within 90 Minutes of Arrival	71	99%	89%	90%
Smoking Cessation Advice	120	100%	100%	99%
Chest Pain/Possible Heart Attack Care				
Aspirin at Arrival	26	54%	94%	95%
Median Time to ECG (minutes)	28	8	10	8
Median Time to Transfer (minutes)[1,3]	1	73	54	61
Fibrinolytic Medication Timing[3]	0	-	60%	54%
Heart Failure Care				
ACE Inhibitor or ARB for LVSD[2]	156	100%	95%	94%
Discharge Instructions[2]	506	99%	89%	88%
Evaluation of LVS Function[2]	616	100%	99%	98%
Smoking Cessation Advice[2]	70	100%	99%	98%
Pneumonia Care				
Appropriate Initial Antibiotic[2]	147	95%	94%	92%
Blood Culture Timing[2]	165	96%	96%	96%
Influenza Vaccine[2]	154	97%	91%	91%
Initial Antibiotic Timing[2]	230	93%	96%	95%
Pneumococcal Vaccine[2]	219	98%	93%	93%
Smoking Cessation Advice[2]	76	99%	98%	97%
Surgical Care Improvement Project				
Appropriate VTP Within 24 Hours[2]	162	89%	94%	92%
Appropriate Hair Removal[2]	688	100%	99%	99%
Appropriate Beta Blocker Usage[2]	277	97%	92%	93%
Controlled Postoperative Blood Glucose[2]	153	92%	94%	93%
Prophylactic Antibiotic Timing[2]	456	96%	97%	97%
Prophylactic Antibiotic Timing (Outpatient)	471	91%	87%	92%
Prophylactic Antibiotic Selection[2]	457	99%	98%	97%
Prophylactic Antibiotic Select. (Outpatient)	464	94%	92%	94%
Prophylactic Antibiotic Stopped[2]	388	98%	95%	94%
Recommended VTP Ordered[2]	162	93%	95%	94%
Urinary Catheter Removal[2]	148	93%	91%	90%
Children's Asthma Care				
Received Systemic Corticosteroids	-	-	-	100%
Received Home Management Plan	-	-	-	71%
Received Reliever Medication	-	-	-	100%
Use of Medical Imaging				
Combination Abdominal CT Scan	2,371	0.137	0.135	0.191
Combination Chest CT Scan	2,328	0.018	0.068	0.054
Follow-up Mammogram/Ultrasound	3,408	7.2%	7.4%	8.4%
MRI for Low Back Pain	606	26.4%	32%	32.7%
Survey of Patients' Hospital Experiences				
Area Around Room 'Always' Quiet at Night	300+	44%	-	58%
Doctors 'Always' Communicated Well	300+	79%	-	80%
Home Recovery Information Given	300+	80%	-	82%
Hospital Given 9 or 10 on 10 Point Scale	300+	69%	-	67%
Meds 'Always' Explained Before Given	300+	56%	-	60%
Nurses 'Always' Communicated Well	300+	75%	-	76%
Pain 'Always' Well Controlled	300+	69%	-	69%
Room and Bathroom 'Always' Clean	300+	68%	-	71%
Timely Help 'Always' Received	300+	63%	-	64%
Would Definitely Recommend Hospital	300+	77%	-	69%

Bronson Vicksburg Hospital

13326 North Boulevard
Vicksburg, MI 49097
Phone: 269-649-2321
Fax: 269-649-2905
URL: www.bronsonhealth.com
Type: Acute Care Hospitals
Emergency Services: Yes
Ownership: Voluntary Non-Profit - Other
Beds: 41

Key Personnel:

CEO/President. . . . . Frank Sardone
Emergency Room . . . . Gerald A Friedman, MD

Measure	Cases	This Hosp.	State Avg.	U.S. Avg.
Heart Attack Care				
ACE Inhibitor or ARB for LVSD[5]	0	-	96%	96%
Aspirin at Arrival[5]	0	-	99%	99%
Aspirin at Discharge[5]	0	-	99%	98%
Beta Blocker at Discharge[5]	0	-	99%	98%
Fibrinolytic Medication Timing[5]	0	-	55%	55%
PCI Within 90 Minutes of Arrival[5]	0	-	89%	90%
Smoking Cessation Advice[5]	0	-	100%	99%
Chest Pain/Possible Heart Attack Care				
Aspirin at Arrival[3]	34	100%	94%	95%
Median Time to ECG (minutes)[3]	37	3	10	8
Median Time to Transfer (minutes)[1,3]	4	58	54	61
Fibrinolytic Medication Timing[3]	0	-	60%	54%
Heart Failure Care				
ACE Inhibitor or ARB for LVSD[5]	0	-	95%	94%
Discharge Instructions[5]	0	-	89%	88%
Evaluation of LVS Function[5]	0	-	99%	98%
Smoking Cessation Advice[5]	0	-	99%	98%
Pneumonia Care				
Appropriate Initial Antibiotic[5]	0	-	94%	92%
Blood Culture Timing[5]	0	-	96%	96%
Influenza Vaccine[5]	0	-	91%	91%
Initial Antibiotic Timing[5]	0	-	96%	95%
Pneumococcal Vaccine[5]	0	-	93%	93%
Smoking Cessation Advice[5]	0	-	98%	97%
Surgical Care Improvement Project				
Appropriate VTP Within 24 Hours[5]	0	-	94%	92%
Appropriate Hair Removal[5]	0	-	99%	99%
Appropriate Beta Blocker Usage[5]	0	-	92%	93%
Controlled Postoperative Blood Glucose[5]	0	-	94%	93%
Prophylactic Antibiotic Timing[5]	0	-	97%	97%
Prophylactic Antibiotic Timing (Outpatient)[5]	0	-	87%	92%
Prophylactic Antibiotic Selection[5]	0	-	98%	97%
Prophylactic Antibiotic Select. (Outpatient)[5]	0	-	92%	94%
Prophylactic Antibiotic Stopped[5]	0	-	95%	94%
Recommended VTP Ordered[5]	0	-	95%	94%
Urinary Catheter Removal[5]	0	-	91%	90%
Children's Asthma Care				
Received Systemic Corticosteroids	-	-	-	100%
Received Home Management Plan	-	-	-	71%
Received Reliever Medication	-	-	-	100%
Use of Medical Imaging				
Combination Abdominal CT Scan[5]	0	-	0.135	0.191
Combination Chest CT Scan[5]	0	-	0.068	0.054
Follow-up Mammogram/Ultrasound	272	4.4%	7.4%	8.4%
MRI for Low Back Pain[5]	0	-	32%	32.7%
Survey of Patients' Hospital Experiences				
Area Around Room 'Always' Quiet at Night[9]	-	-	-	58%
Doctors 'Always' Communicated Well[9]	-	-	-	80%
Home Recovery Information Given[9]	-	-	-	82%
Hospital Given 9 or 10 on 10 Point Scale[9]	-	-	-	67%
Meds 'Always' Explained Before Given[9]	-	-	-	60%
Nurses 'Always' Communicated Well[9]	-	-	-	76%
Pain 'Always' Well Controlled[9]	-	-	-	69%
Room and Bathroom 'Always' Clean[9]	-	-	-	71%
Timely Help 'Always' Received[9]	-	-	-	64%
Would Definitely Recommend Hospital[9]	-	-	-	69%

Saint John Macomb-Oakland Hospital-Macomb Center

11800 East Twelve Mile Road
Warren, MI 48093
Phone: 586-573-5000
Fax: 586-573-5199
URL: www.stjohn.org
Type: Acute Care Hospitals
Emergency Services: Yes
Ownership: Government - Federal
Beds: 376

Key Personnel:

CEO/President. . . . . John E Knox
Chief of Medical Staff . . . . Suraj Nighoon, MD
Infection Control. . . . . Richard Pokriefka, D.O.
Operating Room. . . . . Suzanne Wassom
Pediatric In-Patient Care . . . . Mun Kim, MD
Quality Assurance . . . . Sue M Carrier-Winzer
Radiology. . . . . Jay Zeskino, MD

Measure	Cases	This Hosp.	State Avg.	U.S. Avg.
Heart Attack Care				
ACE Inhibitor or ARB for LVSD	66	97%	96%	96%
Aspirin at Arrival	318	99%	99%	99%
Aspirin at Discharge	301	98%	99%	98%
Beta Blocker at Discharge	291	99%	99%	98%
Fibrinolytic Medication Timing	0	-	55%	55%
PCI Within 90 Minutes of Arrival	54	85%	89%	90%
Smoking Cessation Advice	108	100%	100%	99%
Chest Pain/Possible Heart Attack Care				
Aspirin at Arrival	77	96%	94%	95%
Median Time to ECG (minutes)	79	14	10	8
Median Time to Transfer (minutes)[1]	18	54	54	61
Fibrinolytic Medication Timing	0	-	60%	54%
Heart Failure Care				
ACE Inhibitor or ARB for LVSD	320	97%	95%	94%
Discharge Instructions	850	95%	89%	88%
Evaluation of LVS Function	1,048	99%	99%	98%
Smoking Cessation Advice	177	99%	99%	98%
Pneumonia Care				
Appropriate Initial Antibiotic	387	96%	94%	92%
Blood Culture Timing	454	98%	96%	96%
Influenza Vaccine	442	98%	91%	91%
Initial Antibiotic Timing	634	96%	96%	95%
Pneumococcal Vaccine	600	99%	93%	93%
Smoking Cessation Advice	251	98%	98%	97%
Surgical Care Improvement Project				
Appropriate VTP Within 24 Hours[2]	406	99%	94%	92%
Appropriate Hair Removal[2]	1,366	100%	99%	99%
Appropriate Beta Blocker Usage[2]	460	97%	92%	93%
Controlled Postoperative Blood Glucose[2]	192	94%	94%	93%
Prophylactic Antibiotic Timing[2]	1,068	97%	97%	97%
Prophylactic Antibiotic Timing (Outpatient)	446	91%	87%	92%
Prophylactic Antibiotic Selection[2]	1,079	99%	98%	97%
Prophylactic Antibiotic Select. (Outpatient)	422	97%	92%	94%
Prophylactic Antibiotic Stopped[2]	971	97%	95%	94%
Recommended VTP Ordered[2]	407	99%	95%	94%
Urinary Catheter Removal[2]	310	97%	91%	90%
Children's Asthma Care				
Received Systemic Corticosteroids	-	-	-	100%
Received Home Management Plan	-	-	-	71%
Received Reliever Medication	-	-	-	100%
Use of Medical Imaging				
Combination Abdominal CT Scan	1,539	0.348	0.135	0.191
Combination Chest CT Scan	992	0.007	0.068	0.054
Follow-up Mammogram/Ultrasound	2,133	4.4%	7.4%	8.4%
MRI for Low Back Pain	205	23.9%	32%	32.7%
Survey of Patients' Hospital Experiences				
Area Around Room 'Always' Quiet at Night	300+	41%	-	58%
Doctors 'Always' Communicated Well	300+	70%	-	80%
Home Recovery Information Given	300+	74%	-	82%
Hospital Given 9 or 10 on 10 Point Scale	300+	57%	-	67%
Meds 'Always' Explained Before Given	300+	54%	-	60%
Nurses 'Always' Communicated Well	300+	70%	-	76%
Pain 'Always' Well Controlled	300+	65%	-	69%
Room and Bathroom 'Always' Clean	300+	59%	-	71%
Timely Help 'Always' Received	300+	55%	-	64%
Would Definitely Recommend Hospital	300+	55%	-	69%

NOTE: Hospital profiles are in alphabetical order by state, then city, then hospital within the city; Rankings exclude hospitals with less than 25 cases except for patient surveys which excludes hospitals with less than 100 cases; (a) 100–299 cases; (1) The number of cases is too small to be sure how well a hospital is performing; (2) The hospital indicated that the data submitted for this measure were based on a sample of cases; (3) Data was collected during a shorter time period (fewer quarters) than the maximum possible time for this measure; (4) Suppressed for one or more quarters by CMS; (5) No data is available from the hospital for this measure; (6) Fewer than 100 patients completed the HCAHPS survey. Use these rates with caution, as the number of surveys may be too low to reliably assess hospital performance; (7) Survey results are based on less than 12 months of data; (8) Survey results are not available for this reporting period; (9) No or very few patients were eligible for the HCAHPS survey. The scores shown, if any, reflect a very small number of surveys; (10) A state average was not calculated because too few hospitals in the state submitted data; (11) There were discrepancies in the data collection process; Please refer to the User's Guide for a full explanation of data.

Southeast Michigan Surgical Hospital

21230 Dequindre Road | Phone: 586-427-1000
Warren, MI 48091 | Fax: 586-759-0237
Type: Acute Care Hospitals | Emergency Services: No
Ownership: Voluntary Non-Profit - Private | Beds: 20

Key Personnel:
CEO/President. . . . . Larry Belenke
Chief of Medical Staff . . . . John D'Alessandro, DO

Measure	Cases	This Hosp.	State Avg.	U.S. Avg.
Heart Attack Care				
ACE Inhibitor or ARB for LVSD[5]	0	-	96%	96%
Aspirin at Arrival[5]	0	-	99%	99%
Aspirin at Discharge[5]	0	-	99%	98%
Beta Blocker at Discharge[5]	0	-	99%	98%
Fibrinolytic Medication Timing[5]	0	-	55%	55%
PCI Within 90 Minutes of Arrival[5]	0	-	89%	90%
Smoking Cessation Advice[5]	0	-	100%	99%
Chest Pain/Possible Heart Attack Care				
Aspirin at Arrival[5]	0	-	94%	95%
Median Time to ECG (minutes)[5]	0	-	10	8
Median Time to Transfer (minutes)[5]	0	-	54	61
Fibrinolytic Medication Timing[5]	0	-	60%	54%
Heart Failure Care				
ACE Inhibitor or ARB for LVSD[5]	0	-	95%	94%
Discharge Instructions[5]	0	-	89%	88%
Evaluation of LVS Function[5]	0	-	99%	98%
Smoking Cessation Advice[5]	0	-	99%	98%
Pneumonia Care				
Appropriate Initial Antibiotic[5]	0	-	94%	92%
Blood Culture Timing[5]	0	-	96%	96%
Influenza Vaccine[5]	0	-	91%	91%
Initial Antibiotic Timing[5]	0	-	96%	95%
Pneumococcal Vaccine[5]	0	-	93%	93%
Smoking Cessation Advice[5]	0	-	98%	97%
Surgical Care Improvement Project				
Appropriate VTP Within 24 Hours[1,2,3]	2	100%	94%	92%
Appropriate Hair Removal[1,2,3]	8	100%	99%	99%
Appropriate Beta Blocker Usage[1,2,3]	2	100%	92%	93%
Controlled Postoperative Blood Glucose[2,3]	0	-	94%	93%
Prophylactic Antibiotic Timing[1,2,3]	8	38%	97%	97%
Prophylactic Antibiotic Timing (Outpatient)	108	89%	87%	92%
Prophylactic Antibiotic Selection[1,2,3]	8	100%	98%	97%
Prophylactic Antibiotic Select. (Outpatient)	106	99%	92%	94%
Prophylactic Antibiotic Stopped[1,2,3]	8	100%	95%	94%
Recommended VTP Ordered[1,2,3]	2	100%	95%	94%
Urinary Catheter Removal[1,2]	7	100%	91%	90%
Children's Asthma Care				
Received Systemic Corticosteroids	-	-	-	100%
Received Home Management Plan	-	-	-	71%
Received Reliever Medication	-	-	-	100%
Use of Medical Imaging				
Combination Abdominal CT Scan[5]	0	-	0.135	0.191
Combination Chest CT Scan[5]	0	-	0.068	0.054
Follow-up Mammogram/Ultrasound[5]	0	-	7.4%	8.4%
MRI for Low Back Pain[5]	0	-	32%	32.7%
Survey of Patients' Hospital Experiences				
Area Around Room 'Always' Quiet at Night[6]	<100	83%	-	58%
Doctors 'Always' Communicated Well[6]	<100	82%	-	80%
Home Recovery Information Given[6]	<100	88%	-	82%
Hospital Given 9 or 10 on 10 Point Scale[6]	<100	86%	-	67%
Meds 'Always' Explained Before Given[6]	<100	77%	-	60%
Nurses 'Always' Communicated Well[6]	<100	91%	-	76%
Pain 'Always' Well Controlled[6]	<100	74%	-	69%
Room and Bathroom 'Always' Clean[6]	<100	90%	-	71%
Timely Help 'Always' Received[6]	<100	90%	-	64%
Would Definitely Recommend Hospital	<100	84%	-	69%

Community Hospital

400 Medical Park Dr | Phone: 269-463-3111
Watervliet, MI 49098 | Fax: 269-463-3177
URL: www.communityhospitalwatervliet.com
Type: Acute Care Hospitals | Emergency Services: Yes
Ownership: Voluntary Non-Profit - Private | Beds: 70

Key Personnel:
CEO/President. . . . . Fritz Fahrenbacher
Cardiac Laboratory. . . . . Donald Brooks
Infection Control . . . . Theda Koshar
Operating Room. . . . . Edythe Hedman
Radiology. . . . . Craig Davis
Emergency Room . . . . Kathy Davis

Measure	Cases	This Hosp.	State Avg.	U.S. Avg.
Heart Attack Care				
ACE Inhibitor or ARB for LVSD[1]	1	100%	96%	96%
Aspirin at Arrival[1]	3	100%	99%	99%
Aspirin at Discharge[1]	2	100%	99%	98%
Beta Blocker at Discharge[1]	1	0%	99%	98%
Fibrinolytic Medication Timing	0	-	55%	55%
PCI Within 90 Minutes of Arrival	0	-	89%	90%
Smoking Cessation Advice	0	-	100%	99%
Chest Pain/Possible Heart Attack Care				
Aspirin at Arrival	112	93%	94%	95%
Median Time to ECG (minutes)	117	11	10	8
Median Time to Transfer (minutes)	0	-	54	61
Fibrinolytic Medication Timing	0	-	60%	54%
Heart Failure Care				
ACE Inhibitor or ARB for LVSD[1]	6	83%	95%	94%
Discharge Instructions	38	82%	89%	88%
Evaluation of LVS Function	41	68%	99%	98%
Smoking Cessation Advice[1]	7	100%	99%	98%
Pneumonia Care				
Appropriate Initial Antibiotic	66	94%	94%	92%
Blood Culture Timing	61	82%	96%	96%
Influenza Vaccine	36	94%	91%	91%
Initial Antibiotic Timing	66	91%	96%	95%
Pneumococcal Vaccine	53	91%	93%	93%
Smoking Cessation Advice	27	100%	98%	97%
Surgical Care Improvement Project				
Appropriate VTP Within 24 Hours	45	91%	94%	92%
Appropriate Hair Removal	137	100%	99%	99%
Appropriate Beta Blocker Usage	39	77%	92%	93%
Controlled Postoperative Blood Glucose	0	-	94%	93%
Prophylactic Antibiotic Timing	122	89%	97%	97%
Prophylactic Antibiotic Timing (Outpatient)[1,3]	7	71%	87%	92%
Prophylactic Antibiotic Selection	123	98%	98%	97%
Prophylactic Antibiotic Select. (Outpatient)[1,3]	5	100%	92%	94%
Prophylactic Antibiotic Stopped	122	97%	95%	94%
Recommended VTP Ordered	46	89%	95%	94%
Urinary Catheter Removal	61	92%	91%	90%
Children's Asthma Care				
Received Systemic Corticosteroids	-	-	-	100%
Received Home Management Plan	-	-	-	71%
Received Reliever Medication	-	-	-	100%
Use of Medical Imaging				
Combination Abdominal CT Scan	212	0.038	0.135	0.191
Combination Chest CT Scan	128	0.016	0.068	0.054
Follow-up Mammogram/Ultrasound	342	7.0%	7.4%	8.4%
MRI for Low Back Pain	63	28.6%	32%	32.7%
Survey of Patients' Hospital Experiences				
Area Around Room 'Always' Quiet at Night	(a)	64%	-	58%
Doctors 'Always' Communicated Well	(a)	83%	-	80%
Home Recovery Information Given	(a)	88%	-	82%
Hospital Given 9 or 10 on 10 Point Scale	(a)	74%	-	67%
Meds 'Always' Explained Before Given	(a)	60%	-	60%
Nurses 'Always' Communicated Well	(a)	79%	-	76%
Pain 'Always' Well Controlled	(a)	77%	-	69%
Room and Bathroom 'Always' Clean	(a)	74%	-	71%
Timely Help 'Always' Received	(a)	79%	-	64%
Would Definitely Recommend Hospital	(a)	75%	-	69%

Oakwood Annapolis Hospital

33155 Annapolis Ave | Phone: 734-467-4175
Wayne, MI 48184 | Fax: 734-467-4017
E-mail: FILEKM@oakwood.org
URL: www.oakwood.org
Type: Acute Care Hospitals | Emergency Services: Yes
Ownership: Govt - Hospital Dist/Auth | Beds: 247

Key Personnel:
CEO/President. . . . . Tom Kochis
Operating Room. . . . . Muzammil Ahmed
Pediatric In-Patient Care . . . . Ben Raju, MD
Quality Assurance . . . . Marie Daneil
Anesthesiology. . . . . John Rivard
Emergency Room . . . . Charles Ceeter

Measure	Cases	This Hosp.	State Avg.	U.S. Avg.
Heart Attack Care				
ACE Inhibitor or ARB for LVSD[1]	24	100%	96%	96%
Aspirin at Arrival	116	100%	99%	99%
Aspirin at Discharge	85	100%	99%	98%
Beta Blocker at Discharge	83	100%	99%	98%
Fibrinolytic Medication Timing	0	-	55%	55%
PCI Within 90 Minutes of Arrival	28	89%	89%	90%
Smoking Cessation Advice	37	100%	100%	99%
Chest Pain/Possible Heart Attack Care				
Aspirin at Arrival	56	91%	94%	95%
Median Time to ECG (minutes)	58	0	10	8
Median Time to Transfer (minutes)[3]	0	-	54	61
Fibrinolytic Medication Timing	0	-	60%	54%
Heart Failure Care				
ACE Inhibitor or ARB for LVSD	109	92%	95%	94%
Discharge Instructions	270	92%	89%	88%
Evaluation of LVS Function	337	99%	99%	98%
Smoking Cessation Advice	83	100%	99%	98%
Pneumonia Care				
Appropriate Initial Antibiotic	163	94%	94%	92%
Blood Culture Timing	268	98%	96%	96%
Influenza Vaccine	154	100%	91%	91%
Initial Antibiotic Timing	294	95%	96%	95%
Pneumococcal Vaccine	186	100%	93%	93%
Smoking Cessation Advice	104	100%	98%	97%
Surgical Care Improvement Project				
Appropriate VTP Within 24 Hours[2]	180	91%	94%	92%
Appropriate Hair Removal[2]	448	100%	99%	99%
Appropriate Beta Blocker Usage[2]	136	93%	92%	93%
Controlled Postoperative Blood Glucose[2]	0	-	94%	93%
Prophylactic Antibiotic Timing[2]	312	98%	97%	97%
Prophylactic Antibiotic Timing (Outpatient)	284	91%	87%	92%
Prophylactic Antibiotic Selection[2]	313	98%	98%	97%
Prophylactic Antibiotic Select. (Outpatient)	318	92%	92%	94%
Prophylactic Antibiotic Stopped[2]	299	94%	95%	94%
Recommended VTP Ordered[2]	184	94%	95%	94%
Urinary Catheter Removal[1,2]	20	60%	91%	90%
Children's Asthma Care				
Received Systemic Corticosteroids	-	-	-	100%
Received Home Management Plan	-	-	-	71%
Received Reliever Medication	-	-	-	100%
Use of Medical Imaging				
Combination Abdominal CT Scan	548	0.104	0.135	0.191
Combination Chest CT Scan	308	0.062	0.068	0.054
Follow-up Mammogram/Ultrasound	742	10.9%	7.4%	8.4%
MRI for Low Back Pain	152	20.4%	32%	32.7%
Survey of Patients' Hospital Experiences				
Area Around Room 'Always' Quiet at Night	300+	52%	-	58%
Doctors 'Always' Communicated Well	300+	78%	-	80%
Home Recovery Information Given	300+	74%	-	82%
Hospital Given 9 or 10 on 10 Point Scale	300+	59%	-	67%
Meds 'Always' Explained Before Given	300+	63%	-	60%
Nurses 'Always' Communicated Well	300+	76%	-	76%
Pain 'Always' Well Controlled	300+	70%	-	69%
Room and Bathroom 'Always' Clean	300+	68%	-	71%
Timely Help 'Always' Received	300+	59%	-	64%
Would Definitely Recommend Hospital	300+	60%	-	69%

NOTE: Hospital profiles are in alphabetical order by state, then city, then hospital within the city; Rankings exclude hospitals with less than 25 cases except for patient surveys which excludes hospitals with less than 100 cases; (a) 100–299 cases; (1) The number of cases is too small to be sure how well a hospital is performing; (2) The hospital indicated that the data submitted for this measure were based on a sample of cases; (3) Data was collected during a shorter time period (fewer quarters) than the maximum possible time for this measure; (4) Suppressed for one or more quarters by CMS; (5) No data is available from the hospital for this measure; (6) Fewer than 100 patients completed the HCAHPS survey. Use these rates with caution, as the number of surveys may be too low to reliably assess hospital performance; (7) Survey results are based on less than 12 months of data; (8) Survey results are not available for this reporting period; (9) No or very few patients were eligible for the HCAHPS survey. The scores shown, if any, reflect a very small number of surveys; (10) A state average was not calculated because too few hospitals in the state submitted data; (11) There were discrepancies in the data collection process; Please refer to the User's Guide for a full explanation of data.

Henry Ford West Bloomfield Hospital

6777 West Maple Road — Phone: 248-325-1000
West Bloomfield, MI 48322
URL: www.henryford.com
Type: Acute Care Hospitals — Emergency Services: No
Ownership: Govt - Hospital Dist/Auth — Beds: 300

Key Personnel:
CEO . . . . Nancy M Schlichting
President . . . . Robert G Ringley
Emergency . . . . Debbie Spencer

Measure	Cases	This Hosp.	State Avg.	U.S. Avg.
Heart Attack Care				
ACE Inhibitor or ARB for LVSD[1]	16	94%	96%	96%
Aspirin at Arrival	90	98%	99%	99%
Aspirin at Discharge	65	94%	99%	98%
Beta Blocker at Discharge	60	97%	99%	98%
Fibrinolytic Medication Timing	0	-	55%	55%
PCI Within 90 Minutes of Arrival	0	-	89%	90%
Smoking Cessation Advice[1]	9	100%	100%	99%
Chest Pain/Possible Heart Attack Care				
Aspirin at Arrival[5]	0	-	94%	95%
Median Time to ECG (minutes)[5]	0	-	10	8
Median Time to Transfer (minutes)[5]	0	-	54	61
Fibrinolytic Medication Timing[5]	0	-	60%	54%
Heart Failure Care				
ACE Inhibitor or ARB for LVSD	97	81%	95%	94%
Discharge Instructions	225	62%	89%	88%
Evaluation of LVS Function	281	98%	99%	98%
Smoking Cessation Advice[1]	19	100%	99%	98%
Pneumonia Care				
Appropriate Initial Antibiotic	119	83%	94%	92%
Blood Culture Timing	219	84%	96%	96%
Influenza Vaccine	123	62%	91%	91%
Initial Antibiotic Timing	213	94%	96%	95%
Pneumococcal Vaccine	196	62%	93%	93%
Smoking Cessation Advice	25	96%	98%	97%
Surgical Care Improvement Project				
Appropriate VTP Within 24 Hours	240	97%	94%	92%
Appropriate Hair Removal	661	99%	99%	99%
Appropriate Beta Blocker Usage	158	78%	92%	93%
Controlled Postoperative Blood Glucose	0	-	94%	93%
Prophylactic Antibiotic Timing	445	96%	97%	97%
Prophylactic Antibiotic Timing (Outpatient)	140	77%	87%	92%
Prophylactic Antibiotic Selection	443	98%	98%	97%
Prophylactic Antibiotic Select. (Outpatient)	273	73%	92%	94%
Prophylactic Antibiotic Stopped	435	94%	95%	94%
Recommended VTP Ordered	241	98%	95%	94%
Urinary Catheter Removal	214	93%	91%	90%
Children's Asthma Care				
Received Systemic Corticosteroids	-	-	-	100%
Received Home Management Plan	-	-	-	71%
Received Reliever Medication	-	-	-	100%
Use of Medical Imaging				
Combination Abdominal CT Scan[5]	0	-	0.135	0.191
Combination Chest CT Scan[5]	0	-	0.068	0.054
Follow-up Mammogram/Ultrasound[5]	0	-	7.4%	8.4%
MRI for Low Back Pain[5]	0	-	32%	32.7%
Survey of Patients' Hospital Experiences				
Area Around Room 'Always' Quiet at Night	300+	75%	-	58%
Doctors 'Always' Communicated Well	300+	80%	-	80%
Home Recovery Information Given	300+	82%	-	82%
Hospital Given 9 or 10 on 10 Point Scale	300+	81%	-	67%
Meds 'Always' Explained Before Given	300+	64%	-	60%
Nurses 'Always' Communicated Well	300+	78%	-	76%
Pain 'Always' Well Controlled	300+	70%	-	69%
Room and Bathroom 'Always' Clean	300+	68%	-	71%
Timely Help 'Always' Received	300+	68%	-	64%
Would Definitely Recommend Hospital	300+	82%	-	69%

West Branch Regional Medical Center

2463 South M-30 — Phone: 989-345-6366
West Branch, MI 48661 — Fax: 989-343-3113
URL: www.wbrmc.org
Type: Acute Care Hospitals — Emergency Services: Yes
Ownership: Government - Local — Beds: 88

Key Personnel:
CEO/President. . . . . Douglas E Pattullo
Chief of Medical Staff . . . . Wilfredo Abesamis, MD
Infection Control. . . . . Kathleen DeHaan, RN
Operating Room. . . . . Bobbi Simon
Pediatric Ambulatory Care . . . . . . Wilfredo Abesamis, MD
Pediatric In-Patient Care . . . . Wilfredo Abesamis, MD
Quality Assurance . . . . Edward A Napierala
Radiology. . . . . Mathew Waack, MD

Measure	Cases	This Hosp.	State Avg.	U.S. Avg.
Heart Attack Care				
ACE Inhibitor or ARB for LVSD[1]	1	100%	96%	96%
Aspirin at Arrival[1]	18	100%	99%	99%
Aspirin at Discharge[1]	10	100%	99%	98%
Beta Blocker at Discharge[1]	12	100%	99%	98%
Fibrinolytic Medication Timing	0	-	55%	55%
PCI Within 90 Minutes of Arrival	0	-	89%	90%
Smoking Cessation Advice[1]	1	100%	100%	99%
Chest Pain/Possible Heart Attack Care				
Aspirin at Arrival	153	94%	94%	95%
Median Time to ECG (minutes)	166	9	10	8
Median Time to Transfer (minutes)[3]	0	-	54	61
Fibrinolytic Medication Timing[1]	21	95%	60%	54%
Heart Failure Care				
ACE Inhibitor or ARB for LVSD	35	97%	95%	94%
Discharge Instructions	128	94%	89%	88%
Evaluation of LVS Function	152	97%	99%	98%
Smoking Cessation Advice	26	100%	99%	98%
Pneumonia Care				
Appropriate Initial Antibiotic	81	91%	94%	92%
Blood Culture Timing	118	94%	96%	96%
Influenza Vaccine	58	90%	91%	91%
Initial Antibiotic Timing	106	95%	96%	95%
Pneumococcal Vaccine	101	92%	93%	93%
Smoking Cessation Advice	33	100%	98%	97%
Surgical Care Improvement Project				
Appropriate VTP Within 24 Hours[2]	175	96%	94%	92%
Appropriate Hair Removal[2]	335	98%	99%	99%
Appropriate Beta Blocker Usage[2]	112	100%	92%	93%
Controlled Postoperative Blood Glucose[2]	0	-	94%	93%
Prophylactic Antibiotic Timing[2]	270	89%	97%	97%
Prophylactic Antibiotic Timing (Outpatient)	63	100%	87%	92%
Prophylactic Antibiotic Selection[2]	269	98%	98%	97%
Prophylactic Antibiotic Select. (Outpatient)	63	92%	92%	94%
Prophylactic Antibiotic Stopped[2]	259	86%	95%	94%
Recommended VTP Ordered[2]	175	97%	95%	94%
Urinary Catheter Removal[2]	57	96%	91%	90%
Children's Asthma Care				
Received Systemic Corticosteroids	-	-	-	100%
Received Home Management Plan	-	-	-	71%
Received Reliever Medication	-	-	-	100%
Use of Medical Imaging				
Combination Abdominal CT Scan	762	0.157	0.135	0.191
Combination Chest CT Scan	955	0.041	0.068	0.054
Follow-up Mammogram/Ultrasound	505	3.6%	7.4%	8.4%
MRI for Low Back Pain	237	36.3%	32%	32.7%
Survey of Patients' Hospital Experiences				
Area Around Room 'Always' Quiet at Night	300+	54%	-	58%
Doctors 'Always' Communicated Well	300+	81%	-	80%
Home Recovery Information Given	300+	87%	-	82%
Hospital Given 9 or 10 on 10 Point Scale	300+	72%	-	67%
Meds 'Always' Explained Before Given	300+	56%	-	60%
Nurses 'Always' Communicated Well	300+	78%	-	76%
Pain 'Always' Well Controlled	300+	73%	-	69%
Room and Bathroom 'Always' Clean	300+	71%	-	71%
Timely Help 'Always' Received	300+	69%	-	64%
Would Definitely Recommend Hospital	300+	75%	-	69%

Henry Ford Wyandotte Hospital

2333 Biddle Ave — Phone: 734-246-6000
Wyandotte, MI 48192 — Fax: 734-246-8795
URL: www.henryfordwyandotte.com
Type: Acute Care Hospitals — Emergency Services: Yes
Ownership: Voluntary Non-Profit - Private — Beds: 162

Key Personnel:
CEO/President. . . . . Anthony Armada
Chief of Medical Staff . . . . Malcolm E Williamson, DO
Operating Room. . . . . Pat Egbert
Quality Assurance . . . . Cathy Garrett
Radiology. . . . . Manuel Brown
Emergency Room . . . . Paula Lane, RN
Patient Relations . . . . Bridget Schenavar

Measure	Cases	This Hosp.	State Avg.	U.S. Avg.
Heart Attack Care				
ACE Inhibitor or ARB for LVSD	33	88%	96%	96%
Aspirin at Arrival	235	98%	99%	99%
Aspirin at Discharge	170	97%	99%	98%
Beta Blocker at Discharge	163	97%	99%	98%
Fibrinolytic Medication Timing	0	-	55%	55%
PCI Within 90 Minutes of Arrival	44	73%	89%	90%
Smoking Cessation Advice	69	100%	100%	99%
Chest Pain/Possible Heart Attack Care				
Aspirin at Arrival	225	91%	94%	95%
Median Time to ECG (minutes)	236	8	10	8
Median Time to Transfer (minutes)[1,3]	3	54	54	61
Fibrinolytic Medication Timing	0	-	60%	54%
Heart Failure Care				
ACE Inhibitor or ARB for LVSD	199	93%	95%	94%
Discharge Instructions	560	82%	89%	88%
Evaluation of LVS Function	672	99%	99%	98%
Smoking Cessation Advice	115	100%	99%	98%
Pneumonia Care				
Appropriate Initial Antibiotic	292	93%	94%	92%
Blood Culture Timing	419	97%	96%	96%
Influenza Vaccine	307	97%	91%	91%
Initial Antibiotic Timing	519	97%	96%	95%
Pneumococcal Vaccine	432	96%	93%	93%
Smoking Cessation Advice	237	100%	98%	97%
Surgical Care Improvement Project				
Appropriate VTP Within 24 Hours[2]	208	99%	94%	92%
Appropriate Hair Removal[2]	482	100%	99%	99%
Appropriate Beta Blocker Usage[2]	158	92%	92%	93%
Controlled Postoperative Blood Glucose[2]	0	-	94%	93%
Prophylactic Antibiotic Timing[2]	308	94%	97%	97%
Prophylactic Antibiotic Timing (Outpatient)	334	88%	87%	92%
Prophylactic Antibiotic Selection[2]	310	98%	98%	97%
Prophylactic Antibiotic Select. (Outpatient)	325	88%	92%	94%
Prophylactic Antibiotic Stopped[2]	285	94%	95%	94%
Recommended VTP Ordered[2]	208	100%	95%	94%
Urinary Catheter Removal[2]	42	69%	91%	90%
Children's Asthma Care				
Received Systemic Corticosteroids	-	-	-	100%
Received Home Management Plan	-	-	-	71%
Received Reliever Medication	-	-	-	100%
Use of Medical Imaging				
Combination Abdominal CT Scan	1,215	0.030	0.135	0.191
Combination Chest CT Scan	1,120	0.033	0.068	0.054
Follow-up Mammogram/Ultrasound	1,228	8.3%	7.4%	8.4%
MRI for Low Back Pain	319	26.3%	32%	32.7%
Survey of Patients' Hospital Experiences				
Area Around Room 'Always' Quiet at Night	300+	48%	-	58%
Doctors 'Always' Communicated Well	300+	76%	-	80%
Home Recovery Information Given	300+	77%	-	82%
Hospital Given 9 or 10 on 10 Point Scale	300+	64%	-	67%
Meds 'Always' Explained Before Given	300+	60%	-	60%
Nurses 'Always' Communicated Well	300+	75%	-	76%
Pain 'Always' Well Controlled	300+	66%	-	69%
Room and Bathroom 'Always' Clean	300+	68%	-	71%
Timely Help 'Always' Received	300+	62%	-	64%
Would Definitely Recommend Hospital	300+	63%	-	69%

NOTE: Hospital profiles are in alphabetical order by state, then city, then hospital within the city; Rankings exclude hospitals with less than 25 cases except for patient surveys which excludes hospitals with less than 100 cases; (a) 100–299 cases; (1) The number of cases is too small to be sure how well a hospital is performing; (2) The hospital indicated that the data submitted for this measure were based on a sample of cases; (3) Data was collected during a shorter time period (fewer quarters) than the maximum possible time for this measure; (4) Suppressed for one or more quarters by CMS; (5) No data is available from the hospital for this measure; (6) Fewer than 100 patients completed the HCAHPS survey. Use these rates with caution, as the number of surveys may be too low to reliably assess hospital performance; (7) Survey results are based on less than 12 months of data; (8) Survey results are not available for this reporting period; (9) No or very few patients were eligible for the HCAHPS survey. The scores shown, if any, reflect a very small number of surveys; (10) A state average was not calculated because too few hospitals in the state submitted data; (11) There were discrepancies in the data collection process; Please refer to the User's Guide for a full explanation of data.

Metro Health Hospital

5900 Byron Center Avenue, SW
Wyoming, MI 49519
URL: www.metrohealth.net
Type: Acute Care Hospitals
Ownership: Voluntary Non-Profit - Private
Phone: 616-252-7200
Fax: 616-252-7478
Emergency Services: Yes
Beds: 208

Key Personnel:
CEO/President. . . . . Michael Faas
Chief of Medical Staff . . . . William Cunningham, MD
Infection Control. . . . . Deborah Paul-Cheadle
Operating Room. . . . . Robert Cali
Quality Assurance . . . . Christine Lawrence
Radiology. . . . . Farid Aladham
Ambulatory Care . . . . Daryl Lawrence-Fried
Intensive Care Unit. . . . . Ann Glass

Measure	Cases	This Hosp.	State Avg.	U.S. Avg.
Heart Attack Care				
ACE Inhibitor or ARB for LVSD[1]	20	100%	96%	96%
Aspirin at Arrival	140	100%	99%	99%
Aspirin at Discharge	116	97%	99%	98%
Beta Blocker at Discharge	110	99%	99%	98%
Fibrinolytic Medication Timing	0	-	55%	55%
PCI Within 90 Minutes of Arrival	43	88%	89%	90%
Smoking Cessation Advice	43	100%	100%	99%
Chest Pain/Possible Heart Attack Care				
Aspirin at Arrival[1,3]	7	100%	94%	95%
Median Time to ECG (minutes)[1,3]	7	6	10	8
Median Time to Transfer (minutes)[5]	0	-	54	61
Fibrinolytic Medication Timing[3]	0	-	60%	54%
Heart Failure Care				
ACE Inhibitor or ARB for LVSD	61	95%	95%	94%
Discharge Instructions	159	72%	89%	88%
Evaluation of LVS Function	195	100%	99%	98%
Smoking Cessation Advice	36	100%	99%	98%
Pneumonia Care				
Appropriate Initial Antibiotic[2]	90	98%	94%	92%
Blood Culture Timing[2]	194	96%	96%	96%
Influenza Vaccine[2]	77	99%	91%	91%
Initial Antibiotic Timing[2]	159	99%	96%	95%
Pneumococcal Vaccine[2]	101	99%	93%	93%
Smoking Cessation Advice[2]	47	100%	98%	97%
Surgical Care Improvement Project				
Appropriate VTP Within 24 Hours[2]	144	91%	94%	92%
Appropriate Hair Removal[2]	458	100%	99%	99%
Appropriate Beta Blocker Usage[2]	99	86%	92%	93%
Controlled Postoperative Blood Glucose[2]	0	-	94%	93%
Prophylactic Antibiotic Timing[2]	322	97%	97%	97%
Prophylactic Antibiotic Timing (Outpatient)	258	94%	87%	92%
Prophylactic Antibiotic Selection[2]	323	97%	98%	97%
Prophylactic Antibiotic Select. (Outpatient)	298	97%	92%	94%
Prophylactic Antibiotic Stopped[2]	308	96%	95%	94%
Recommended VTP Ordered[2]	144	94%	95%	94%
Urinary Catheter Removal[2]	97	90%	91%	90%
Children's Asthma Care				
Received Systemic Corticosteroids	-	-	-	100%
Received Home Management Plan	-	-	-	71%
Received Reliever Medication	-	-	-	100%
Use of Medical Imaging				
Combination Abdominal CT Scan	945	0.098	0.135	0.191
Combination Chest CT Scan	581	0.120	0.068	0.054
Follow-up Mammogram/Ultrasound	1,050	11.9%	7.4%	8.4%
MRI for Low Back Pain	282	29.4%	32%	32.7%
Survey of Patients' Hospital Experiences				
Area Around Room 'Always' Quiet at Night	300+	64%	-	58%
Doctors 'Always' Communicated Well	300+	80%	-	80%
Home Recovery Information Given	300+	88%	-	82%
Hospital Given 9 or 10 on 10 Point Scale	300+	79%	-	67%
Meds 'Always' Explained Before Given	300+	63%	-	60%
Nurses 'Always' Communicated Well	300+	77%	-	76%
Pain 'Always' Well Controlled	300+	72%	-	69%
Room and Bathroom 'Always' Clean	300+	75%	-	71%
Timely Help 'Always' Received	300+	61%	-	64%
Would Definitely Recommend Hospital	300+	80%	-	69%

Zeeland Community Hospital

8333 Felch St
Zeeland, MI 49464
E-mail: parnoldink@zch.org
URL: www.zch.org
Type: Acute Care Hospitals
Ownership: Voluntary Non-Profit - Private
Phone: 616-772-4644
Fax: 616-748-2828
Emergency Services: Yes
Beds: 57

Key Personnel:
CEO/President. . . . . Henry A Veenstra
Chief of Medical Staff . . . . Michael Byars
Infection Control. . . . . Pat VanOmen, RN
Operating Room. . . . . Marlene Holstine
Pediatric Ambulatory Care . . . . . . Julianne Carey
Pediatric In-Patient Care . . . . . . Julianne Carey
Quality Assurance . . . . Carrie Miedema
Radiology. . . . . Scott Weenum

Measure	Cases	This Hosp.	State Avg.	U.S. Avg.
Heart Attack Care				
ACE Inhibitor or ARB for LVSD[1]	1	100%	96%	96%
Aspirin at Arrival[1]	8	100%	99%	99%
Aspirin at Discharge[1]	5	100%	99%	98%
Beta Blocker at Discharge[1]	4	100%	99%	98%
Fibrinolytic Medication Timing	0	-	55%	55%
PCI Within 90 Minutes of Arrival	0	-	89%	90%
Smoking Cessation Advice	0	-	100%	99%
Chest Pain/Possible Heart Attack Care				
Aspirin at Arrival	51	100%	94%	95%
Median Time to ECG (minutes)	53	11	10	8
Median Time to Transfer (minutes)[1]	9	38	54	61
Fibrinolytic Medication Timing	0	-	60%	54%
Heart Failure Care				
ACE Inhibitor or ARB for LVSD[1]	13	92%	95%	94%
Discharge Instructions	60	97%	89%	88%
Evaluation of LVS Function	70	100%	99%	98%
Smoking Cessation Advice[1]	10	100%	99%	98%
Pneumonia Care				
Appropriate Initial Antibiotic	44	100%	94%	92%
Blood Culture Timing	112	100%	96%	96%
Influenza Vaccine	57	96%	91%	91%
Initial Antibiotic Timing	100	98%	96%	95%
Pneumococcal Vaccine	100	100%	93%	93%
Smoking Cessation Advice	27	100%	98%	97%
Surgical Care Improvement Project				
Appropriate VTP Within 24 Hours	50	96%	94%	92%
Appropriate Hair Removal	251	100%	99%	99%
Appropriate Beta Blocker Usage	64	97%	92%	93%
Controlled Postoperative Blood Glucose	0	-	94%	93%
Prophylactic Antibiotic Timing	196	99%	97%	97%
Prophylactic Antibiotic Timing (Outpatient)	57	95%	87%	92%
Prophylactic Antibiotic Selection	198	97%	98%	97%
Prophylactic Antibiotic Select. (Outpatient)	54	100%	92%	94%
Prophylactic Antibiotic Stopped	188	98%	95%	94%
Recommended VTP Ordered	50	96%	95%	94%
Urinary Catheter Removal[1]	16	100%	91%	90%
Children's Asthma Care				
Received Systemic Corticosteroids	-	-	-	100%
Received Home Management Plan	-	-	-	71%
Received Reliever Medication	-	-	-	100%
Use of Medical Imaging				
Combination Abdominal CT Scan	186	0.065	0.135	0.191
Combination Chest CT Scan	67	0.104	0.068	0.054
Follow-up Mammogram/Ultrasound	372	7.0%	7.4%	8.4%
MRI for Low Back Pain[1]	29	31.0%	32%	32.7%
Survey of Patients' Hospital Experiences				
Area Around Room 'Always' Quiet at Night	300+	64%	-	58%
Doctors 'Always' Communicated Well	300+	83%	-	80%
Home Recovery Information Given	300+	90%	-	82%
Hospital Given 9 or 10 on 10 Point Scale	300+	83%	-	67%
Meds 'Always' Explained Before Given	300+	63%	-	60%
Nurses 'Always' Communicated Well	300+	82%	-	76%
Pain 'Always' Well Controlled	300+	73%	-	69%
Room and Bathroom 'Always' Clean	300+	80%	-	71%
Timely Help 'Always' Received	300+	70%	-	64%
Would Definitely Recommend Hospital	300+	87%	-	69%

NOTE: Hospital profiles are in alphabetical order by state, then city, then hospital within the city; Rankings exclude hospitals with less than 25 cases except for patient surveys which excludes hospitals with less than 100 cases; (a) 100–299 cases; (1) The number of cases is too small to be sure how well a hospital is performing; (2) The hospital indicated that the data submitted for this measure were based on a sample of cases; (3) Data was collected during a shorter time period (fewer quarters) than the maximum possible time for this measure; (4) Suppressed for one or more quarters by CMS; (5) No data is available from the hospital for this measure; (6) Fewer than 100 patients completed the HCAHPS survey. Use these rates with caution, as the number of surveys may be too low to reliably assess hospital performance; (7) Survey results are based on less than 12 months of data; (8) Survey results are not available for this reporting period; (9) No or very few patients were eligible for the HCAHPS survey. The scores shown, if any, reflect a very small number of surveys; (10) A state average was not calculated because too few hospitals in the state submitted data; (11) There were discrepancies in the data collection process; Please refer to the User's Guide for a full explanation of data.

Heart Attack Care

1. ACE Inhibitor or ARB for LVSD

Hospital Name	City	Rate	Cases
Abbott Northwestern Hospital	Minneapolis	100%	113
Hennepin County Medical Center	Minneapolis	100%	43
Immanuel-St Josephs-Mayo Health System[2]	Mankato	100%	39
Mayo Clinic - Saint Marys Hospital[2]	Rochester	100%	45
Mercy Hospital	Coon Rapids	100%	61
North Memorial Medical Center[2]	Robbinsdale	100%	49
Regions Hospital	Saint Paul	100%	65
Saint Joseph's Hospital	Saint Paul	100%	60
Univ of Minnesota Med Ctr-Fairview	Minneapolis	100%	34
Fairview Southdale Hospital	Edina	99%	92
Park Nicollet Methodist Hospital	Saint Louis Park	98%	50
United Hospital	Saint Paul	95%	61
Essentia Health St Mary's Medical Center[2]	Duluth	93%	58
Saint Cloud Hospital	Saint Cloud	93%	92

2. Aspirin at Arrival

Hospital Name	City	Rate	Cases
Abbott Northwestern Hospital	Minneapolis	100%	223
Fairmont Medical Center	Fairmont	100%	25
Fairview Northland Regional Hospital	Princeton	100%	26
Fairview Ridges Hospital	Burnsville	100%	69
Fairview Southdale Hospital	Edina	100%	334
Healtheast St John's Hospital	Maplewood	100%	55
Hennepin County Medical Center	Minneapolis	100%	200
Immanuel-St Josephs-Mayo Health System[2]	Mankato	100%	165
Mayo Clinic - Saint Marys Hospital[2]	Rochester	100%	128
North Memorial Medical Center[2]	Robbinsdale	100%	263
Park Nicollet Methodist Hospital	Saint Louis Park	100%	301
Regions Hospital	Saint Paul	100%	307
Ridgeview Medical Center	Waconia	100%	33
Saint Cloud Hospital	Saint Cloud	100%	213
Saint Joseph's Hospital	Saint Paul	100%	152
Saint Lukes Hospital	Duluth	100%	122
Unity Hospital	Fridley	100%	40
Univ of Minnesota Med Ctr-Fairview	Minneapolis	100%	110
Mercy Hospital	Coon Rapids	99%	326
United Hospital	Saint Paul	99%	296
Essentia Health St Mary's Medical Center[2]	Duluth	98%	99
Minneapolis VA Medical Center	Minneapolis	98%	132
Naeve Hospital	Albert Lea	98%	43
Lake Region Healthcare Corporation	Fergus Falls	97%	30
Essentia Health St Joseph's Medical Center	Brainerd	94%	33
University Med Ctr-Mesabi/Mesaba	Hibbing	93%	27

3. Aspirin at Discharge

Hospital Name	City	Rate	Cases
Abbott Northwestern Hospital	Minneapolis	100%	837
Fairview Southdale Hospital	Edina	100%	439
Healtheast St John's Hospital	Maplewood	100%	25
Hennepin County Medical Center	Minneapolis	100%	198
Immanuel-St Josephs-Mayo Health System[2]	Mankato	100%	226
Mayo Clinic - Saint Marys Hospital[2]	Rochester	100%	302
Mercy Hospital	Coon Rapids	100%	439
Minneapolis VA Medical Center	Minneapolis	100%	143
North Memorial Medical Center[2]	Robbinsdale	100%	271
Park Nicollet Methodist Hospital	Saint Louis Park	100%	337
Saint Cloud Hospital	Saint Cloud	100%	664
United Hospital	Saint Paul	100%	427
Essentia Health St Mary's Medical Center[2]	Duluth	99%	350
Regions Hospital	Saint Paul	99%	417
Saint Joseph's Hospital	Saint Paul	99%	327
Saint Lukes Hospital	Duluth	99%	165
Univ of Minnesota Med Ctr-Fairview	Minneapolis	99%	198
Fairview Ridges Hospital	Burnsville	98%	60
Naeve Hospital	Albert Lea	94%	36

4. Beta Blocker at Discharge

Hospital Name	City	Rate	Cases
Abbott Northwestern Hospital	Minneapolis	100%	806
Fairview Ridges Hospital	Burnsville	100%	59
Fairview Southdale Hospital	Edina	100%	428
Healtheast St John's Hospital	Maplewood	100%	27
Immanuel-St Josephs-Mayo Health System[2]	Mankato	100%	210
Mayo Clinic - Saint Marys Hospital[2]	Rochester	100%	294
Minneapolis VA Medical Center	Minneapolis	100%	139
Essentia Health St Mary's Medical Center[2]	Duluth	99%	338
Mercy Hospital	Coon Rapids	99%	437
North Memorial Medical Center[2]	Robbinsdale	99%	277
Park Nicollet Methodist Hospital	Saint Louis Park	99%	337
Regions Hospital	Saint Paul	99%	419
Saint Cloud Hospital	Saint Cloud	99%	640
Saint Joseph's Hospital	Saint Paul	99%	315
Saint Lukes Hospital	Duluth	99%	164
United Hospital	Saint Paul	99%	399
Univ of Minnesota Med Ctr-Fairview	Minneapolis	99%	188
Hennepin County Medical Center	Minneapolis	98%	188
Naeve Hospital	Albert Lea	94%	36

6. PCI Within 90 Minutes of Arrival

Hospital Name	City	Rate	Cases
North Memorial Medical Center[2]	Robbinsdale	100%	62
Fairview Southdale Hospital	Edina	98%	63
Regions Hospital	Saint Paul	98%	61
Abbott Northwestern Hospital	Minneapolis	96%	51
Park Nicollet Methodist Hospital	Saint Louis Park	94%	53
United Hospital	Saint Paul	94%	80
Immanuel-St Josephs-Mayo Health System[2]	Mankato	93%	29
Mercy Hospital	Coon Rapids	91%	91
Hennepin County Medical Center	Minneapolis	90%	49
Saint Cloud Hospital	Saint Cloud	87%	62

7. Smoking Cessation Advice

Hospital Name	City	Rate	Cases
Abbott Northwestern Hospital	Minneapolis	100%	249
Fairview Southdale Hospital	Edina	100%	115
Hennepin County Medical Center	Minneapolis	100%	83
Immanuel-St Josephs-Mayo Health System[2]	Mankato	100%	57
Mayo Clinic - Saint Marys Hospital[2]	Rochester	100%	75
Mercy Hospital	Coon Rapids	100%	174
Minneapolis VA Medical Center	Minneapolis	100%	33
Park Nicollet Methodist Hospital	Saint Louis Park	100%	82
Regions Hospital	Saint Paul	100%	151
Saint Cloud Hospital	Saint Cloud	100%	218
Saint Joseph's Hospital	Saint Paul	100%	94
Univ of Minnesota Med Ctr-Fairview	Minneapolis	100%	71
Essentia Health St Mary's Medical Center[2]	Duluth	99%	128
United Hospital	Saint Paul	99%	134
Saint Lukes Hospital	Duluth	96%	55
North Memorial Medical Center[2]	Robbinsdale	95%	79

Chest Pain/Possible Heart Attack Care

8. Aspirin at Arrival

Hospital Name	City	Rate	Cases
Buffalo Hospital	Buffalo	100%	94
Cambridge Medical Center	Cambridge	100%	75
Fairview Red Wing Hospital	Red Wing	100%	91
Fairview Ridges Hospital	Burnsville	100%	101
Grand Itasca Clinic and Hospital	Grand Rapids	100%	71
New Ulm Medical Center	New Ulm	100%	48
Queen of Peace Hospital[3]	New Prague	100%	27
Saint Francis Regional Medical Center	Shakopee	100%	98
Saint Gabriels Hospital[3]	Little Falls	100%	32
University Med Ctr-Mesabi/Mesaba	Hibbing	100%	87
Windom Area Hospital	Windom	100%	36
Austin Medical Center	Austin	99%	90
District One Hospital	Faribault	99%	117
Essentia Health St Joseph's Medical Center	Brainerd	99%	159
Hutchinson Area Health Care	Hutchinson	99%	87
Lifecare Medical Center	Roseau	99%	82
Northfield Hospital	Northfield	99%	73
Saint Marys Regional Health Center	Detroit Lakes	99%	77
Unity Hospital	Fridley	99%	88
Winona Health Services	Winona	99%	90
Community Memorial Hospital[3]	Cloquet	98%	55
Douglas County Hospital	Alexandria	98%	127
Fairmont Medical Center	Fairmont	98%	42
Fairview Lakes Health Services	Wyoming	98%	186
Perham Memorial Hospital[3]	Perham	98%	48
Fairview Northland Regional Hospital	Princeton	97%	72
Healtheast St John's Hospital	Maplewood	97%	111
Rice Memorial Hospital	Willmar	97%	75
River's Edge Hospital & Clinic	Saint Peter	97%	76
Sanford Worthington Medical Center	Worthington	97%	61
Healtheast Woodwinds Hospital	Woodbury	96%	81
Virginia Regional Medical Center	Virginia	96%	93
Glencoe Regional Health Services	Glencoe	95%	37
Lake Region Healthcare Corporation	Fergus Falls	95%	57
Saint Josephs Area Health Services[3]	Park Rapids	95%	42
Avera Marshall Regional Medical Center[3]	Marshall	94%	35
Naeve Hospital	Albert Lea	94%	129
North Country Regional Hospital	Bemidji	94%	125
Owatonna Hospital	Owatonna	94%	110
Centracare Health System - Long Prairie	Long Prairie	93%	29
Regina Medical Center	Hastings	93%	185
Essentia Health Sandstone[3]	Sandstone	92%	25
Kanabec Hospital[3]	Mora	92%	40
Lakeview Memorial Hospital	Stillwater	92%	60
Olmsted Medical Center	Rochester	92%	59
Ridgeview Medical Center	Waconia	92%	63

9. Median Time to ECG (minutes)

Hospital Name	City	Min.	Cases
Avera Marshall Regional Medical Center[3]	Marshall	0	35
Centracare Health System - Long Prairie	Long Prairie	0	28
Cambridge Medical Center	Cambridge	2	76
Northfield Hospital	Northfield	2	75
Lakeview Memorial Hospital	Stillwater	3	60
Douglas County Hospital	Alexandria	4	126
Grand Itasca Clinic and Hospital	Grand Rapids	4	68
New Ulm Medical Center	New Ulm	4	46
Unity Hospital	Fridley	4	88
Community Memorial Hospital[3]	Cloquet	5	54
District One Hospital	Faribault	5	123
Fairmont Medical Center	Fairmont	5	42
Fairview Red Wing Hospital	Red Wing	5	92
River's Edge Hospital & Clinic	Saint Peter	5	77
Healtheast Woodwinds Hospital	Woodbury	6	81
Hutchinson Area Health Care	Hutchinson	6	87
Lake Region Healthcare Corporation	Fergus Falls	6	59
Lifecare Medical Center	Roseau	6	85
Saint Francis Regional Medical Center	Shakopee	6	100
Saint Gabriels Hospital[3]	Little Falls	6	33
Winona Health Services	Winona	6	95
Fairview Northland Regional Hospital	Princeton	7	77
Kanabec Hospital[3]	Mora	7	41
Naeve Hospital	Albert Lea	7	130
Olmsted Medical Center	Rochester	7	60
Perham Memorial Hospital[3]	Perham	7	48
Regina Medical Center	Hastings	7	191
Saint Marys Regional Health Center	Detroit Lakes	7	81
Sanford Worthington Medical Center	Worthington	7	62
University Med Ctr-Mesabi/Mesaba	Hibbing	7	90
Austin Medical Center	Austin	8	95
Fairview Lakes Health Services	Wyoming	8	189
Glencoe Regional Health Services	Glencoe	8	38
North Country Regional Hospital	Bemidji	8	127
Owatonna Hospital	Owatonna	8	111
Queen of Peace Hospital[3]	New Prague	8	29
Rice Memorial Hospital	Willmar	8	77
Buffalo Hospital	Buffalo	9	100
Essentia Health St Joseph's Medical Center	Brainerd	9	164
Tri County Hospital[3]	Wadena	9	25
Essentia Health Sandstone[3]	Sandstone	10	26
Ridgeview Medical Center	Waconia	10	59
Virginia Regional Medical Center	Virginia	10	95
Healtheast St John's Hospital	Maplewood	13	110
Saint Josephs Area Health Services[3]	Park Rapids	13	43
Fairview Ridges Hospital	Burnsville	14	109
Windom Area Hospital	Windom	19	37

10. Median Time to Transfer (minutes)

Hospital Name	City	Min.	Cases
Ridgeview Medical Center	Waconia	42	34
Fairview Ridges Hospital	Burnsville	54	29
Healtheast St John's Hospital	Maplewood	62	31

Heart Failure Care

12. ACE Inhibitor or ARB for LVSD

Hospital Name	City	Rate	Cases
Austin Medical Center	Austin	100%	30
Healtheast St John's Hospital	Maplewood	100%	44
Lake Region Healthcare Corporation	Fergus Falls	100%	26
Minneapolis VA Medical Center	Minneapolis	100%	56
Saint Francis Regional Medical Center	Shakopee	100%	25
Saint Joseph's Hospital	Saint Paul	100%	96
Unity Hospital	Fridley	100%	37
Winona Health Services	Winona	100%	25
Abbott Northwestern Hospital	Minneapolis	99%	268
Hennepin County Medical Center[2]	Minneapolis	99%	142
Mayo Clinic - Saint Marys Hospital[2]	Rochester	99%	80
Mercy Hospital	Coon Rapids	99%	89
North Memorial Medical Center[2]	Robbinsdale	99%	77
Regions Hospital	Saint Paul	99%	115
United Hospital	Saint Paul	99%	168
Immanuel-St Josephs-Mayo Health System	Mankato	98%	45
Park Nicollet Methodist Hospital[2]	Saint Louis Park	98%	133
Univ of Minnesota Med Ctr-Fairview	Minneapolis	98%	117
Douglas County Hospital	Alexandria	97%	29
Fairview Southdale Hospital	Edina	97%	120
Saint Cloud Hospital	Saint Cloud	97%	229
University Med Ctr-Mesabi/Mesaba	Hibbing	97%	30
Saint Lukes Hospital	Duluth	96%	75
Fairview Ridges Hospital	Burnsville	95%	40
Fairview Lakes Health Services	Wyoming	92%	26
Essentia Health St Mary's Medical Center[2]	Duluth	91%	100
Ridgeview Medical Center	Waconia	91%	34
North Country Regional Hospital	Bemidji	89%	28
Healtheast Woodwinds Hospital	Woodbury	88%	26

NOTE: Hospital profiles are in alphabetical order by state, then city, then hospital within the city; Rankings exclude hospitals with less than 25 cases except for patient surveys which excludes hospitals with less than 100 cases; (a) 100–299 cases; (1) The number of cases is too small to be sure how well a hospital is performing; (2) The hospital indicated that the data submitted for this measure were based on a sample of cases; (3) Data was collected during a shorter time period (fewer quarters) than the maximum possible time for this measure; (4) Suppressed for one or more quarters by CMS; (5) No data is available from the hospital for this measure; (6) Fewer than 100 patients completed the HCAHPS survey. Use these rates with caution, as the number of surveys may be too low to reliably assess hospital performance; (7) Survey results are based on less than 12 months of data; (8) Survey results are not available for this reporting period; (9) No or very few patients were eligible for the HCAHPS survey. The scores shown, if any, reflect a very small number of surveys; (10) A state average was not calculated because too few hospitals in the state submitted data; (11) There were discrepancies in the data collection process; Please refer to the User's Guide for a full explanation of data.

Hospital Name	City	Rate	Cases
Essentia Health St Joseph's Medical Center	Brainerd	78%	54

13. Discharge Instructions

Hospital Name	City	Rate	Cases
Fairview Northland Regional Hospital	Princeton	100%	44
Fairview Ridges Hospital	Burnsville	99%	122
Unity Hospital	Fridley	99%	141
Austin Medical Center	Austin	97%	77
Fairview Red Wing Hospital	Red Wing	97%	34
Fairview Southdale Hospital	Edina	97%	255
Kanabec Hospital	Mora	97%	30
Lakeview Memorial Hospital	Stillwater	97%	35
New Ulm Medical Center	New Ulm	97%	39
Univ of Minnesota Med Ctr-Fairview	Minneapolis	97%	264
Fairview Lakes Health Services	Wyoming	96%	67
Mille Lacs Health System	Onamia	96%	25
Ridgeview Medical Center	Waconia	96%	68
Saint Francis Regional Medical Center	Shakopee	96%	73
Buffalo Hospital	Buffalo	95%	38
Cambridge Medical Center	Cambridge	95%	38
Mercy Hospital	Coon Rapids	95%	254
Minneapolis VA Medical Center	Minneapolis	95%	175
New River Medical Center	Monticello	95%	38
Regina Medical Center	Hastings	95%	37
Hutchinson Area Health Care	Hutchinson	94%	47
Mayo Clinic - Saint Marys Hospital[2]	Rochester	94%	207
Fairmont Medical Center	Fairmont	93%	44
Regions Hospital	Saint Paul	93%	309
United Hospital	Saint Paul	93%	372
Abbott Northwestern Hospital	Minneapolis	92%	551
Park Nicollet Methodist Hospital[2]	Saint Louis Park	91%	280
Hennepin County Medical Center[2]	Minneapolis	90%	262
Winona Health Services	Winona	90%	49
Immanuel-St Josephs-Mayo Health System	Mankato	89%	144
Owatonna Hospital	Owatonna	89%	35
Saint Cloud Hospital	Saint Cloud	89%	499
District One Hospital	Faribault	86%	29
Saint Francis Healthcare Campus	Breckenridge	86%	36
Lake Region Healthcare Corporation	Fergus Falls	85%	54
Tri County Hospital	Wadena	85%	34
Douglas County Hospital	Alexandria	84%	45
Healtheast St John's Hospital	Maplewood	84%	166
University Med Ctr-Mesabi/Mesaba	Hibbing	84%	69
Rice Memorial Hospital	Willmar	83%	36
Saint Joseph's Hospital	Saint Paul	83%	175
Essentia Health St Mary's Medical Center[2]	Duluth	82%	215
Healtheast Woodwinds Hospital	Woodbury	81%	78
North Memorial Medical Center[2]	Robbinsdale	79%	229
Saint Lukes Hospital	Duluth	78%	147
Grand Itasca Clinic and Hospital	Grand Rapids	77%	43
North Country Regional Hospital	Bemidji	76%	70
Essentia Health St Joseph's Medical Center	Brainerd	73%	126
Northfield Hospital	Northfield	67%	30
Naeve Hospital	Albert Lea	57%	49

14. Evaluation of LVS Function

Hospital Name	City	Rate	Cases
Abbott Northwestern Hospital	Minneapolis	100%	679
Austin Medical Center	Austin	100%	112
Buffalo Hospital	Buffalo	100%	61
Cambridge Medical Center	Cambridge	100%	50
Essentia Health St Mary's Medical Center[2]	Duluth	100%	255
Fairview Lakes Health Services	Wyoming	100%	76
Fairview Northland Regional Hospital	Princeton	100%	63
Fairview Red Wing Hospital	Red Wing	100%	47
Hennepin County Medical Center[2]	Minneapolis	100%	331
Immanuel-St Josephs-Mayo Health System	Mankato	100%	198
Lake Region Healthcare Corporation	Fergus Falls	100%	79
Mayo Clinic - Saint Marys Hospital[2]	Rochester	100%	277
Mercy Hospital	Coon Rapids	100%	306
Minneapolis VA Medical Center	Minneapolis	100%	201
New Ulm Medical Center	New Ulm	100%	62
Owatonna Hospital	Owatonna	100%	55
Regina Medical Center	Hastings	100%	52
Regions Hospital	Saint Paul	100%	381
Ridgeview Medical Center	Waconia	100%	113
Saint Cloud Hospital	Saint Cloud	100%	679
Saint Joseph's Hospital	Saint Paul	100%	234
United Hospital	Saint Paul	100%	478
Unity Hospital	Fridley	100%	160
Univ of Minnesota Med Ctr-Fairview	Minneapolis	100%	322
Winona Health Services	Winona	100%	82
Fairview Ridges Hospital	Burnsville	99%	151
Fairview Southdale Hospital	Edina	99%	359
Healtheast St John's Hospital	Maplewood	99%	212
North Country Regional Hospital	Bemidji	99%	84
North Memorial Medical Center[2]	Robbinsdale	99%	296
Park Nicollet Methodist Hospital[2]	Saint Louis Park	99%	386
Saint Francis Regional Medical Center	Shakopee	99%	93
Saint Lukes Hospital	Duluth	99%	199
Fairmont Medical Center	Fairmont	98%	103
Healtheast Woodwinds Hospital	Woodbury	98%	100
Lakeview Memorial Hospital	Stillwater	98%	50
New River Medical Center	Monticello	98%	48
Northfield Hospital	Northfield	98%	47
Essentia Health Fosston	Fosston	97%	36
Glencoe Regional Health Services	Glencoe	97%	33
Hutchinson Area Health Care	Hutchinson	97%	70
Lifecare Medical Center	Roseau	97%	30
Rice Memorial Hospital	Willmar	97%	58
Essentia Health St Joseph's Medical Center	Brainerd	96%	191
Grand Itasca Clinic and Hospital	Grand Rapids	96%	52
University Med Ctr-Mesabi/Mesaba	Hibbing	96%	90
Virginia Regional Medical Center	Virginia	96%	49
District One Hospital	Faribault	95%	38
Douglas County Hospital	Alexandria	95%	87
Saint Francis Healthcare Campus	Breckenridge	95%	42
Queen of Peace Hospital	New Prague	94%	35
Saint Josephs Area Health Services	Park Rapids	93%	30
Naeve Hospital	Albert Lea	92%	73
Mille Lacs Health System	Onamia	90%	30
Saint Gabriels Hospital	Little Falls	90%	30
Sanford Medical Center Thief River Falls	Thief River Falls	90%	40
Riverview Hospital	Crookston	87%	38
Kanabec Hospital	Mora	85%	48
Glacial Ridge Hospital	Glenwood	80%	25
Tri County Hospital	Wadena	78%	50
Sanford Worthington Medical Center	Worthington	73%	26
Cuyuna Regional Medical Center[3]	Crosby	69%	35
Meeker Memorial Hospital	Litchfield	63%	41
Stevens Community Medical Center	Morris	44%	36

15. Smoking Cessation Advice

Hospital Name	City	Rate	Cases
Abbott Northwestern Hospital	Minneapolis	100%	117
Fairview Ridges Hospital	Burnsville	100%	29
Fairview Southdale Hospital	Edina	100%	45
Healtheast St John's Hospital	Maplewood	100%	25
Hennepin County Medical Center[2]	Minneapolis	100%	132
Mercy Hospital	Coon Rapids	100%	58
Park Nicollet Methodist Hospital[2]	Saint Louis Park	100%	47
Regions Hospital	Saint Paul	100%	95
Saint Cloud Hospital	Saint Cloud	100%	72
Saint Joseph's Hospital	Saint Paul	100%	34
Univ of Minnesota Med Ctr-Fairview	Minneapolis	100%	53
United Hospital	Saint Paul	99%	73
Essentia Health St Mary's Medical Center[2]	Duluth	98%	58
Saint Lukes Hospital	Duluth	97%	35
North Memorial Medical Center[2]	Robbinsdale	93%	43

Pneumonia Care

16. Appropriate Initial Antibiotic

Hospital Name	City	Rate	Cases
Fairview Red Wing Hospital	Red Wing	100%	62
Lakeview Memorial Hospital	Stillwater	100%	25
Regions Hospital	Saint Paul	99%	165
Saint Francis Regional Medical Center	Shakopee	98%	100
Mercy Hospital & Health Care Center	Moose Lake	97%	31
Regina Medical Center	Hastings	97%	33
Unity Hospital	Fridley	97%	138
Fairview Northland Regional Hospital	Princeton	96%	69
Glacial Ridge Hospital	Glenwood	96%	25
Grand Itasca Clinic and Hospital	Grand Rapids	96%	49
Hutchinson Area Health Care	Hutchinson	96%	45
Mercy Hospital	Coon Rapids	96%	170
Minneapolis VA Medical Center	Minneapolis	96%	46
Northfield Hospital	Northfield	96%	46
Buffalo Hospital	Buffalo	95%	40
Fairmont Medical Center	Fairmont	95%	79
Healtheast St John's Hospital[2]	Maplewood	95%	103
Kanabec Hospital	Mora	95%	39
New River Medical Center	Monticello	95%	43
United Hospital	Saint Paul	95%	152
Fairview Ridges Hospital	Burnsville	94%	115
Healtheast Woodwinds Hospital	Woodbury	94%	79
Lake Region Healthcare Corporation	Fergus Falls	94%	63
Abbott Northwestern Hospital	Minneapolis	93%	116
Austin Medical Center	Austin	93%	115
Cuyuna Regional Medical Center[3]	Crosby	92%	25
Park Nicollet Methodist Hospital	Saint Louis Park	92%	217
Saint Cloud Hospital	Saint Cloud	92%	186
Saint Joseph's Hospital[2]	Saint Paul	92%	75
Saint Marys Regional Health Center	Detroit Lakes	92%	59
University Med Ctr-Mesabi/Mesaba	Hibbing	92%	93
Community Memorial Hospital	Cloquet	91%	43
Essentia Health St Mary's Medical Center[2]	Duluth	91%	54
Owatonna Hospital	Owatonna	91%	35
Winona Health Services	Winona	91%	66
Cambridge Medical Center	Cambridge	90%	52
Hennepin County Medical Center[2]	Minneapolis	90%	119
Immanuel-St Josephs-Mayo Health System	Mankato	90%	96
North Country Regional Hospital	Bemidji	90%	63
Univ of Minnesota Med Ctr-Fairview	Minneapolis	90%	83
District One Hospital	Faribault	89%	57
Fairview Southdale Hospital	Edina	89%	206
Perham Memorial Hospital	Perham	89%	27
Ridgeview Medical Center	Waconia	89%	108
Saint Lukes Hospital	Duluth	89%	106
Mayo Clinic - Saint Marys Hospital[2]	Rochester	88%	32
Rice Memorial Hospital	Willmar	88%	69
Fairview Lakes Health Services	Wyoming	87%	67
Tri County Hospital	Wadena	86%	29
Virginia Regional Medical Center	Virginia	86%	36
Douglas County Hospital[2]	Alexandria	85%	72
Essentia Health St Joseph's Medical Center	Brainerd	85%	65
Lakewood Health System	Staples	85%	34
Stevens Community Medical Center	Morris	84%	32
Olmsted Medical Center	Rochester	83%	29
Saint Josephs Area Health Services	Park Rapids	83%	41
North Memorial Medical Center[2]	Robbinsdale	82%	95
Saint Gabriels Hospital	Little Falls	81%	58
Saint Francis Healthcare Campus	Breckenridge	77%	43
Naeve Hospital	Albert Lea	73%	55
Avera Marshall Regional Medical Center	Marshall	60%	48

17. Blood Culture Timing

Hospital Name	City	Rate	Cases
Fairmont Medical Center	Fairmont	100%	94
Fairview Northland Regional Hospital	Princeton	100%	101
Kanabec Hospital	Mora	100%	31
Saint Francis Regional Medical Center	Shakopee	100%	87
Austin Medical Center	Austin	99%	172
Essentia Health St Joseph's Medical Center	Brainerd	99%	108
Fairview Southdale Hospital	Edina	99%	304
Healtheast Woodwinds Hospital	Woodbury	99%	98
Saint Lukes Hospital	Duluth	99%	144
Cambridge Medical Center	Cambridge	98%	81
District One Hospital	Faribault	98%	54
Fairview Red Wing Hospital	Red Wing	98%	63
Healtheast St John's Hospital[2]	Maplewood	98%	131
Minneapolis VA Medical Center	Minneapolis	98%	81
New Ulm Medical Center	New Ulm	98%	42
Queen of Peace Hospital	New Prague	98%	40
Saint Gabriels Hospital	Little Falls	98%	55
Saint Joseph's Hospital[2]	Saint Paul	98%	86
Saint Marys Regional Health Center	Detroit Lakes	98%	44
Winona Health Services	Winona	98%	108
Abbott Northwestern Hospital	Minneapolis	97%	213
Essentia Health St Mary's Medical Center[2]	Duluth	97%	66
Fairview Lakes Health Services	Wyoming	97%	87
New River Medical Center	Monticello	97%	58
Rice Memorial Hospital	Willmar	97%	86
Ridgeview Medical Center	Waconia	97%	154
Tri County Hospital	Wadena	97%	30
University Med Ctr-Mesabi/Mesaba	Hibbing	97%	69
Univ of Minnesota Med Ctr-Fairview	Minneapolis	97%	196
Fairview Ridges Hospital	Burnsville	96%	238
Lake Region Healthcare Corporation	Fergus Falls	96%	96
Mercy Hospital & Health Care Center	Moose Lake	96%	27
Park Nicollet Methodist Hospital	Saint Louis Park	96%	328
Regina Medical Center	Hastings	96%	52
Saint Cloud Hospital	Saint Cloud	96%	243
United Hospital	Saint Paul	96%	196
Unity Hospital	Fridley	95%	226
Community Memorial Hospital	Cloquet	94%	31
Hutchinson Area Health Care	Hutchinson	94%	50
Lakeview Memorial Hospital	Stillwater	94%	31
Lakewood Health System	Staples	94%	35
Mercy Hospital	Coon Rapids	94%	165
Northfield Hospital	Northfield	94%	34
Regions Hospital	Saint Paul	94%	162
Buffalo Hospital	Buffalo	93%	42
Immanuel-St Josephs-Mayo Health System	Mankato	93%	94
North Memorial Medical Center[2]	Robbinsdale	93%	147
Saint Josephs Area Health Services	Park Rapids	93%	42
Avera Marshall Regional Medical Center	Marshall	92%	37
Douglas County Hospital[2]	Alexandria	91%	88
Grand Itasca Clinic and Hospital	Grand Rapids	90%	62
Naeve Hospital	Albert Lea	90%	87
Olmsted Medical Center	Rochester	90%	31
North Country Regional Hospital	Bemidji	89%	102
Mayo Clinic - Saint Marys Hospital[2]	Rochester	88%	78
Hennepin County Medical Center[2]	Minneapolis	77%	242

18. Influenza Vaccine

Hospital Name	City	Rate	Cases
Buffalo Hospital	Buffalo	100%	29
Cambridge Medical Center	Cambridge	100%	40
Community Memorial Hospital	Cloquet	100%	26

NOTE: Hospital profiles are in alphabetical order by state, then city, then hospital within the city; Rankings exclude hospitals with less than 25 cases except for patient surveys which excludes hospitals with less than 100 cases; (a) 100–299 cases; (1) The number of cases is too small to be sure how well a hospital is performing; (2) The hospital indicated that the data submitted for this measure were based on a sample of cases; (3) Data was collected during a shorter time period (fewer quarters) than the maximum possible time for this measure; (4) Suppressed for one or more quarters by CMS; (5) No data is available from the hospital for this measure; (6) Fewer than 100 patients completed the HCAHPS survey. Use these rates with caution, as the number of surveys may be too low to reliably assess hospital performance; (7) Survey results are based on less than 12 months of data; (8) Survey results are not available for this reporting period; (9) No or very few patients were eligible for the HCAHPS survey. The scores shown, if any, reflect a very small number of surveys; (10) A state average was not calculated because too few hospitals in the state submitted data; (11) There were discrepancies in the data collection process; Please refer to the User's Guide for a full explanation of data.

Hospital Name	City	Rate	Cases
Fairview Northland Regional Hospital	Princeton	100%	60
Fairview Red Wing Hospital	Red Wing	100%	36
Grand Itasca Clinic and Hospital	Grand Rapids	100%	52
New River Medical Center	Monticello	100%	27
Regina Medical Center	Hastings	100%	36
Saint Francis Regional Medical Center	Shakopee	99%	89
Unity Hospital	Fridley	99%	142
Winona Health Services	Winona	99%	73
Austin Medical Center	Austin	98%	99
District One Hospital	Faribault	98%	57
Douglas County Hospital	Alexandria	98%	82
Healtheast St John's Hospital[2]	Maplewood	98%	92
Lake Region Healthcare Corporation	Fergus Falls	98%	84
Naeve Hospital	Albert Lea	98%	53
Park Nicollet Methodist Hospital	Saint Louis Park	98%	325
Abbott Northwestern Hospital	Minneapolis	97%	175
Fairmont Medical Center	Fairmont	97%	94
Minneapolis VA Medical Center	Minneapolis	97%	70
Saint Cloud Hospital	Saint Cloud	97%	244
Saint Francis Healthcare Campus	Breckenridge	97%	33
Saint Gabriels Hospital	Little Falls	97%	30
Fairview Lakes Health Services	Wyoming	96%	55
Fairview Ridges Hospital	Burnsville	96%	134
North Country Regional Hospital	Bemidji	96%	72
Owatonna Hospital	Owatonna	96%	26
Ridgeview Medical Center	Waconia	96%	84
Saint Josephs Area Health Services	Park Rapids	96%	27
Hennepin County Medical Center	Minneapolis	95%	151
Regions Hospital	Saint Paul	95%	223
Saint Joseph's Hospital[2]	Saint Paul	95%	93
Saint Lukes Hospital	Duluth	95%	126
United Hospital	Saint Paul	95%	203
Healtheast Woodwinds Hospital	Woodbury	94%	69
Mayo Clinic - Saint Marys Hospital[2]	Rochester	94%	87
Mercy Hospital	Coon Rapids	94%	160
Queen of Peace Hospital	New Prague	94%	32
Rice Memorial Hospital	Willmar	94%	70
Fairview Southdale Hospital	Edina	93%	221
Immanuel-St Josephs-Mayo Health System	Mankato	93%	135
Essentia Health St Mary's Medical Center[2]	Duluth	92%	93
Hutchinson Area Health Care	Hutchinson	92%	36
University Med Ctr-Mesabi/Mesaba	Hibbing	92%	61
Essentia Health St Joseph's Medical Center	Brainerd	91%	70
New Ulm Medical Center	New Ulm	89%	36
Saint Marys Regional Health Center	Detroit Lakes	89%	37
Univ of Minnesota Med Ctr-Fairview	Minneapolis	88%	139
North Memorial Medical Center[2]	Robbinsdale	86%	122
Sanford Medical Center Thief River Falls	Thief River Falls	84%	32
Tri County Hospital	Wadena	78%	41
Mayo Clinic - Methodist Hospital	Rochester	76%	33
Virginia Regional Medical Center	Virginia	76%	29
Stevens Community Medical Center	Morris	74%	38
Lakewood Health System	Staples	43%	28
Cuyuna Regional Medical Center	Crosby	33%	27
Glacial Ridge Hospital	Glenwood	17%	30

19. Initial Antibiotic Timing

Hospital Name	City	Rate	Cases
Austin Medical Center	Austin	100%	168
Cambridge Medical Center	Cambridge	100%	63
Fairview Northland Regional Hospital	Princeton	100%	99
Fairview Red Wing Hospital	Red Wing	100%	74
Healtheast Woodwinds Hospital	Woodbury	100%	99
Lifecare Medical Center	Roseau	100%	33
New River Medical Center	Monticello	100%	60
New Ulm Medical Center	New Ulm	100%	46
Queen of Peace Hospital	New Prague	100%	42
Regina Medical Center	Hastings	100%	58
Saint Francis Regional Medical Center	Shakopee	100%	131
Sanford Worthington Medical Center	Worthington	100%	28
Stevens Community Medical Center	Morris	100%	40
Tri County Hospital	Wadena	100%	74
University Med Ctr-Mesabi/Mesaba	Hibbing	100%	118
Winona Health Services	Winona	100%	106
District One Hospital	Faribault	99%	84
Essentia Health St Joseph's Medical Center	Brainerd	99%	106
Grand Itasca Clinic and Hospital	Grand Rapids	99%	68
Saint Gabriels Hospital	Little Falls	99%	71
Unity Hospital	Fridley	99%	209
Abbott Northwestern Hospital	Minneapolis	98%	216
Buffalo Hospital	Buffalo	98%	52
Douglas County Hospital[2]	Alexandria	98%	122
Fairmont Medical Center	Fairmont	98%	114
Hutchinson Area Health Care	Hutchinson	98%	60
North Memorial Medical Center[2]	Robbinsdale	98%	181
Northfield Hospital	Northfield	98%	45
Owatonna Hospital	Owatonna	98%	40
Rice Memorial Hospital	Willmar	98%	117
Saint Cloud Hospital	Saint Cloud	98%	298
Sanford Medical Center Thief River Falls	Thief River Falls	98%	54
Univ of Minnesota Med Ctr-Fairview	Minneapolis	98%	156
Fairview Ridges Hospital	Burnsville	97%	222
Healtheast St John's Hospital[2]	Maplewood	97%	146
Immanuel-St Josephs-Mayo Health System	Mankato	97%	156
Mercy Hospital & Health Care Center	Moose Lake	97%	38
Mille Lacs Health System	Onamia	97%	32
Park Nicollet Methodist Hospital	Saint Louis Park	97%	350
Perham Memorial Hospital	Perham	97%	34
Ridgeview Medical Center	Waconia	97%	139
Saint Joseph's Hospital[2]	Saint Paul	97%	143
United Hospital	Saint Paul	97%	201
Community Memorial Hospital	Cloquet	96%	57
Fairview Lakes Health Services	Wyoming	96%	98
Fairview Southdale Hospital	Edina	96%	311
Kanabec Hospital	Mora	96%	53
Lakeview Memorial Hospital	Stillwater	96%	45
Regions Hospital	Saint Paul	96%	306
Saint Josephs Area Health Services	Park Rapids	96%	47
Essentia Health St Mary's Medical Center[2]	Duluth	95%	97
Lake Region Healthcare Corporation	Fergus Falls	95%	104
Mercy Hospital	Coon Rapids	95%	245
Minneapolis VA Medical Center	Minneapolis	95%	98
Saint Marys Regional Health Center	Detroit Lakes	95%	66
Riverview Hospital	Crookston	94%	36
Saint Lukes Hospital	Duluth	94%	177
Saint Francis Healthcare Campus	Breckenridge	93%	43
Sanford Luverne Medical Center[2]	Luverne	93%	28
Mayo Clinic - Saint Marys Hospital[2]	Rochester	92%	104
North Country Regional Hospital	Bemidji	92%	114
United Hospital District	Blue Earth	92%	37
Hennepin County Medical Center[2]	Minneapolis	91%	246
Naeve Hospital	Albert Lea	91%	98
Virginia Regional Medical Center	Virginia	89%	54
Lakewood Health System	Staples	88%	59
Glacial Ridge Hospital	Glenwood	86%	37
Cuyuna Regional Medical Center[3]	Crosby	82%	38
Olmsted Medical Center	Rochester	82%	34
Avera Marshall Regional Medical Center	Marshall	76%	54

20. Pneumococcal Vaccine

Hospital Name	City	Rate	Cases
Buffalo Hospital	Buffalo	100%	45
Community Memorial Hospital	Cloquet	100%	41
District One Hospital	Faribault	100%	80
Fairview Northland Regional Hospital	Princeton	100%	84
Fairview Red Wing Hospital	Red Wing	100%	61
Lake Region Healthcare Corporation	Fergus Falls	100%	109
Lifecare Medical Center	Roseau	100%	37
Minneapolis VA Medical Center	Minneapolis	100%	120
New Ulm Medical Center	New Ulm	100%	57
Regina Medical Center	Hastings	100%	50
Saint Francis Regional Medical Center	Shakopee	100%	116
Saint Marys Regional Health Center	Detroit Lakes	100%	57
United Hospital District	Blue Earth	100%	37
Unity Hospital	Fridley	100%	188
Fairview Lakes Health Services	Wyoming	99%	89
Mercy Hospital	Coon Rapids	99%	201
North Country Regional Hospital	Bemidji	99%	107
United Hospital	Saint Paul	99%	245
Winona Health Services	Winona	99%	109
Austin Medical Center	Austin	98%	182
Essentia Health St Mary's Medical Center[2]	Duluth	98%	121
Fairmont Medical Center	Fairmont	98%	129
Naeve Hospital	Albert Lea	98%	100
Regions Hospital	Saint Paul	98%	250
Saint Francis Healthcare Campus	Breckenridge	98%	60
Abbott Northwestern Hospital	Minneapolis	97%	256
Cambridge Medical Center	Cambridge	97%	67
Fairview Ridges Hospital	Burnsville	97%	168
Mercy Hospital & Health Care Center	Moose Lake	97%	34
Park Nicollet Methodist Hospital	Saint Louis Park	97%	457
Saint Cloud Hospital	Saint Cloud	97%	342
Saint Gabriels Hospital	Little Falls	97%	62
Fairview Southdale Hospital	Edina	96%	294
Healtheast St John's Hospital[2]	Maplewood	96%	142
Mayo Clinic - Saint Marys Hospital[2]	Rochester	96%	135
New River Medical Center	Monticello	96%	45
Owatonna Hospital	Owatonna	96%	50
Ridgeview Medical Center	Waconia	96%	136
Douglas County Hospital[2]	Alexandria	95%	151
Hennepin County Medical Center[2]	Minneapolis	95%	118
Hutchinson Area Health Care	Hutchinson	95%	62
University Med Ctr-Mesabi/Mesaba	Hibbing	95%	86
Saint Lukes Hospital	Duluth	94%	194
Avera Marshall Regional Medical Center	Marshall	93%	44
Grand Itasca Clinic and Hospital	Grand Rapids	93%	70
Healtheast Woodwinds Hospital	Woodbury	93%	84
Mayo Clinic - Methodist Hospital	Rochester	92%	36
Redwood Area Hospital	Redwood Falls	92%	25
Immanuel-St Josephs-Mayo Health System	Mankato	91%	173
Rice Memorial Hospital	Willmar	91%	127
Univ of Minnesota Med Ctr-Fairview	Minneapolis	91%	154
Municipal Hospital and Granite Manor	Granite Falls	90%	30
Sanford Luverne Medical Center[2]	Luverne	90%	29
Queen of Peace Hospital	New Prague	89%	47
Saint Joseph's Hospital[2]	Saint Paul	89%	136
Saint Josephs Area Health Services	Park Rapids	88%	56
Essentia Health St Joseph's Medical Center	Brainerd	86%	132
Kanabec Hospital	Mora	86%	50
Riverview Hospital	Crookston	86%	36
Virginia Regional Medical Center	Virginia	86%	50
Lakeview Memorial Hospital	Stillwater	85%	27
Northfield Hospital	Northfield	85%	39
Olmsted Medical Center	Rochester	84%	32
North Memorial Medical Center[2]	Robbinsdale	83%	150
Sanford Medical Center Thief River Falls	Thief River Falls	83%	54
Tri County Hospital	Wadena	82%	57
Perham Memorial Hospital	Perham	79%	42
Sanford Worthington Medical Center	Worthington	71%	31
Stevens Community Medical Center	Morris	70%	53
Cuyuna Regional Medical Center[3]	Crosby	67%	42
Chippewa County Hospital	Montevideo	62%	29
Lakewood Health System	Staples	61%	46
Glacial Ridge Hospital	Glenwood	36%	45

21. Smoking Cessation Advice

Hospital Name	City	Rate	Cases
Douglas County Hospital[2]	Alexandria	100%	29
Fairview Northland Regional Hospital	Princeton	100%	39
Fairview Ridges Hospital	Burnsville	100%	47
Fairview Southdale Hospital	Edina	100%	70
Healtheast St John's Hospital[2]	Maplewood	100%	37
Healtheast Woodwinds Hospital	Woodbury	100%	27
Hennepin County Medical Center[2]	Minneapolis	100%	169
Park Nicollet Methodist Hospital	Saint Louis Park	100%	115
Ridgeview Medical Center	Waconia	100%	31
Saint Cloud Hospital	Saint Cloud	100%	138
Saint Francis Regional Medical Center	Shakopee	100%	47
Saint Joseph's Hospital[2]	Saint Paul	100%	42
Unity Hospital	Fridley	100%	92
Univ of Minnesota Med Ctr-Fairview	Minneapolis	100%	94
Winona Health Services	Winona	100%	32
Abbott Northwestern Hospital	Minneapolis	99%	143
Mercy Hospital	Coon Rapids	99%	107
Regions Hospital	Saint Paul	99%	157
United Hospital	Saint Paul	99%	96
North Country Regional Hospital	Bemidji	98%	43
Essentia Health St Mary's Medical Center[2]	Duluth	97%	74
Mayo Clinic - Saint Marys Hospital[2]	Rochester	97%	31
Fairmont Medical Center	Fairmont	93%	28
Austin Medical Center	Austin	91%	33
Immanuel-St Josephs-Mayo Health System	Mankato	91%	46
Essentia Health St Joseph's Medical Center	Brainerd	90%	40
University Med Ctr-Mesabi/Mesaba	Hibbing	87%	45
North Memorial Medical Center[2]	Robbinsdale	86%	57
Saint Lukes Hospital	Duluth	86%	100

Surgical Care Improvement Project

22. Appropriate VTP Within 24 Hours

Hospital Name	City	Rate	Cases
Buffalo Hospital	Buffalo	100%	51
Fairview Northland Regional Hospital[2]	Princeton	100%	42
Fairview Red Wing Hospital[2]	Red Wing	100%	39
New Ulm Medical Center	New Ulm	100%	49
Ridgeview Medical Center[2]	Waconia	100%	121
Hutchinson Area Health Care	Hutchinson	99%	67
Mayo Clinic - Methodist Hospital[2]	Rochester	99%	202
Unity Hospital[2]	Fridley	99%	166
Essentia Health St Joseph's Medical Center[2]	Brainerd	98%	89
Mayo Clinic - Saint Marys Hospital[2]	Rochester	98%	259
Regina Medical Center[2]	Hastings	98%	64
Cambridge Medical Center	Cambridge	97%	35
Community Memorial Hospital[2]	Cloquet	97%	39
Essentia Health St Mary's Medical Center[2]	Duluth	97%	201
Fairmont Medical Center	Fairmont	97%	71
Mercy Hospital[2]	Coon Rapids	97%	165
Minneapolis VA Medical Center[2]	Minneapolis	97%	206
Naeve Hospital	Albert Lea	97%	144
Saint Josephs Area Health Services	Park Rapids	97%	88
Austin Medical Center	Austin	96%	125
Kanabec Hospital	Mora	96%	46
Saint Elizabeth Medical Center	Wabasha	96%	25
Immanuel-St Josephs-Mayo Health System[2]	Mankato	95%	223
Univ of Minnesota Med Ctr-Fairview[2]	Minneapolis	95%	433
Abbott Northwestern Hospital[2]	Minneapolis	94%	216
Fairview Lakes Health Services[2]	Wyoming	94%	103
Fairview Southdale Hospital[2]	Edina	94%	357
Queen of Peace Hospital	New Prague	94%	33
Grand Itasca Clinic and Hospital	Grand Rapids	93%	58

NOTE: Hospital profiles are in alphabetical order by state, then city, then hospital within the city; Rankings exclude hospitals with less than 25 cases except for patient surveys which excludes hospitals with less than 100 cases; (a) 100–299 cases; (1) The number of cases is too small to be sure how well a hospital is performing; (2) The hospital indicated that the data submitted for this measure were based on a sample of cases; (3) Data was collected during a shorter time period (fewer quarters) than the maximum possible time for this measure; (4) Suppressed for one or more quarters by CMS; (5) No data is available from the hospital for this measure; (6) Fewer than 100 patients completed the HCAHPS survey. Use these rates with caution, as the number of surveys may be too low to reliably assess hospital performance; (7) Survey results are based on less than 12 months of data; (8) Survey results are not available for this reporting period; (9) No or very few patients were eligible for the HCAHPS survey. The scores shown, if any, reflect a very small number of surveys; (10) A state average was not calculated because too few hospitals in the state submitted data; (11) There were discrepancies in the data collection process; Please refer to the User's Guide for a full explanation of data.

Healtheast St John's Hospital[2]	Maplewood	93%	292
Hennepin County Medical Center[2]	Minneapolis	93%	165
United Hospital[2]	Saint Paul	93%	159
Douglas County Hospital[2]	Alexandria	92%	139
Healtheast Woodwinds Hospital[2]	Woodbury	92%	132
Saint Cloud Hospital[2]	Saint Cloud	92%	152
Winona Health Services	Winona	92%	75
Northfield Hospital	Northfield	91%	57
Park Nicollet Methodist Hospital[2]	Saint Louis Park	91%	187
Lake Region Healthcare Corporation	Fergus Falls	90%	115
Rice Memorial Hospital[2]	Willmar	90%	104
Saint Francis Regional Medical Center[2]	Shakopee	90%	115
Saint Joseph's Hospital[2]	Saint Paul	89%	225
University Med Ctr-Mesabi/Mesaba[2]	Hibbing	89%	63
Chippewa County Hospital	Montevideo	88%	25
District One Hospital	Faribault	86%	59
Regions Hospital[2]	Saint Paul	86%	209
North Country Regional Hospital	Bemidji	85%	280
Sanford Medical Center Thief River Falls	Thief River Falls	85%	26
Lakeview Memorial Hospital[2]	Stillwater	84%	69
Riverview Hospital	Crookston	84%	31
Olmsted Medical Center	Rochester	83%	76
Saint Gabriels Hospital[2]	Little Falls	83%	46
Mercy Hospital & Health Care Center	Moose Lake	82%	28
Owatonna Hospital[2]	Owatonna	82%	39
Saint Lukes Hospital[2]	Duluth	82%	164
Virginia Regional Medical Center[2]	Virginia	80%	65
Fairview Ridges Hospital[2]	Burnsville	79%	160
North Memorial Medical Center[2]	Robbinsdale	72%	165
Saint Marys Regional Health Center[2]	Detroit Lakes	72%	50
Saint Francis Healthcare Campus[2]	Breckenridge	60%	30

23. Appropriate Hair Removal

Hospital Name	City	Rate	Cases
Abbott Northwestern Hospital[2]	Minneapolis	100%	814
Austin Medical Center	Austin	100%	241
Avera Marshall Regional Medical Center[3]	Marshall	100%	86
Bigfork Valley Hospital	Bigfork	100%	62
Buffalo Hospital	Buffalo	100%	219
Cannon Falls Medical Center Mayo	Cannon Falls	100%	27
Community Memorial Hospital[2]	Cloquet	100%	121
District One Hospital	Faribault	100%	173
Douglas County Hospital[2]	Alexandria	100%	422
Essentia Health Duluth[2]	Duluth	100%	212
Essentia Health St Joseph's Medical Center[2]	Brainerd	100%	348
Essentia Health St Mary's Medical Center[2]	Duluth	100%	765
Fairmont Medical Center	Fairmont	100%	211
Fairview Lakes Health Services[2]	Wyoming	100%	440
Fairview Northland Regional Hospital[2]	Princeton	100%	217
Fairview Red Wing Hospital[2]	Red Wing	100%	214
Fairview Ridges Hospital[2]	Burnsville	100%	767
Fairview Southdale Hospital[2]	Edina	100%	2200
Glencoe Regional Health Services	Glencoe	100%	74
Healtheast St John's Hospital[2]	Maplewood	100%	899
Healtheast Woodwinds Hospital[2]	Woodbury	100%	1153
Hennepin County Medical Center[2]	Minneapolis	100%	396
Hutchinson Area Health Care	Hutchinson	100%	195
Immanuel-St Josephs-Mayo Health System[2]	Mankato	100%	533
Lake City Medical Center Mayo Health System	Lake City	100%	33
Lake Region Healthcare Corporation	Fergus Falls	100%	260
Lakeview Memorial Hospital[2]	Stillwater	100%	463
Lakewood Health System	Staples	100%	65
Mayo Clinic - Saint Marys Hospital[2]	Rochester	100%	786
Mercy Hospital[2]	Coon Rapids	100%	667
Mercy Hospital & Health Care Center	Moose Lake	100%	68
Minneapolis VA Medical Center[2]	Minneapolis	100%	498
Naeve Hospital	Albert Lea	100%	347
New River Medical Center	Monticello	100%	55
New Ulm Medical Center	New Ulm	100%	155
North Country Regional Hospital	Bemidji	100%	613
North Memorial Medical Center[2]	Robbinsdale	100%	650
Northfield Hospital	Northfield	100%	193
Olmsted Medical Center	Rochester	100%	287
Owatonna Hospital[2]	Owatonna	100%	272
Park Nicollet Methodist Hospital[2]	Saint Louis Park	100%	822
Pipestone County Medical Center	Pipestone	100%	47
Queen of Peace Hospital	New Prague	100%	129
Regina Medical Center[2]	Hastings	100%	245
Regions Hospital[2]	Saint Paul	100%	692
Rice Memorial Hospital[2]	Willmar	100%	274
Ridgeview Medical Center[2]	Waconia	100%	433
Riverview Hospital	Crookston	100%	72
Riverwood Healthcare Center	Aitkin	100%	59
Saint Cloud Hospital[2]	Saint Cloud	100%	665
Saint Elizabeth Medical Center	Wabasha	100%	36
Saint Francis Regional Medical Center[2]	Shakopee	100%	478
Saint Lukes Hospital[2]	Duluth	100%	477
Saint Marys Regional Health Center[2]	Detroit Lakes	100%	245
Sanford Worthington Medical Center	Worthington	100%	89
Tri County Hospital	Wadena	100%	51
United Hospital[2]	Saint Paul	100%	738
United Hospital District	Blue Earth	100%	41
Unity Hospital[2]	Fridley	100%	492
University Med Ctr-Mesabi/Mesaba[2]	Hibbing	100%	125
Univ of Minnesota Med Ctr-Fairview[2]	Minneapolis	100%	1026
Virginia Regional Medical Center[2]	Virginia	100%	171
Winona Health Services	Winona	100%	176
Cambridge Medical Center	Cambridge	99%	257
Mayo Clinic - Methodist Hospital[2]	Rochester	99%	666
Saint Gabriels Hospital[2]	Little Falls	99%	219
Saint Joseph's Hospital[2]	Saint Paul	99%	902
Saint Josephs Area Health Services	Park Rapids	99%	119
Paynesville Area Hospital	Paynesville	98%	47
Sanford Medical Center Thief River Falls	Thief River Falls	98%	114
Kanabec Hospital	Mora	97%	78
Saint Francis Healthcare Campus[2]	Breckenridge	93%	44
Grand Itasca Clinic and Hospital	Grand Rapids	92%	211
Chippewa County Hospital	Montevideo	76%	38
Cuyuna Regional Medical Center[3]	Crosby	76%	96
Meeker Memorial Hospital	Litchfield	74%	27
Stevens Community Medical Center	Morris	74%	50
Swift County Benson Hospital	Benson	14%	35

24. Appropriate Beta Blocker Usage

Hospital Name	City	Rate	Cases
Buffalo Hospital	Buffalo	100%	48
Fairmont Medical Center	Fairmont	100%	82
Fairview Red Wing Hospital[2]	Red Wing	100%	68
Regina Medical Center[2]	Hastings	100%	34
Ridgeview Medical Center[2]	Waconia	100%	76
Winona Health Services	Winona	100%	52
Mayo Clinic - Methodist Hospital[2]	Rochester	99%	164
Olmsted Medical Center	Rochester	99%	90
Owatonna Hospital[2]	Owatonna	99%	88
Cambridge Medical Center	Cambridge	98%	66
Fairview Southdale Hospital[2]	Edina	98%	799
Grand Itasca Clinic and Hospital	Grand Rapids	98%	57
Mayo Clinic - Saint Marys Hospital[2]	Rochester	98%	337
New Ulm Medical Center	New Ulm	98%	60
North Memorial Medical Center[2]	Robbinsdale	98%	247
Austin Medical Center	Austin	97%	96
Fairview Northland Regional Hospital[2]	Princeton	97%	61
Hutchinson Area Health Care	Hutchinson	97%	64
Mercy Hospital[2]	Coon Rapids	97%	279
Minneapolis VA Medical Center[2]	Minneapolis	97%	230
Saint Lukes Hospital[2]	Duluth	97%	152
Univ of Minnesota Med Ctr-Fairview[2]	Minneapolis	97%	298
Abbott Northwestern Hospital[2]	Minneapolis	96%	303
Community Memorial Hospital[2]	Cloquet	96%	28
Douglas County Hospital[2]	Alexandria	96%	130
Healtheast Woodwinds Hospital[2]	Woodbury	96%	272
Naeve Hospital	Albert Lea	96%	94
United Hospital[2]	Saint Paul	96%	257
Saint Cloud Hospital[2]	Saint Cloud	95%	248
District One Hospital	Faribault	94%	50
Hennepin County Medical Center[2]	Minneapolis	94%	111
Immanuel-St Josephs-Mayo Health System[2]	Mankato	94%	152
Saint Francis Regional Medical Center[2]	Shakopee	94%	136
Saint Marys Regional Health Center[2]	Detroit Lakes	94%	64
Essentia Health St Mary's Medical Center[2]	Duluth	93%	321
Fairview Lakes Health Services[2]	Wyoming	93%	161
Lake Region Healthcare Corporation	Fergus Falls	93%	59
Regions Hospital[2]	Saint Paul	93%	254
Saint Joseph's Hospital[2]	Saint Paul	93%	327
Unity Hospital[2]	Fridley	93%	172
Essentia Health St Joseph's Medical Center[2]	Brainerd	92%	99
Park Nicollet Methodist Hospital[2]	Saint Louis Park	91%	328
Northfield Hospital	Northfield	90%	51
Queen of Peace Hospital	New Prague	90%	30
North Country Regional Hospital	Bemidji	89%	177
Cuyuna Regional Medical Center[3]	Crosby	88%	33
Fairview Ridges Hospital[2]	Burnsville	87%	222
Healtheast St John's Hospital[2]	Maplewood	87%	208
Saint Gabriels Hospital[2]	Little Falls	87%	54
Sanford Medical Center Thief River Falls	Thief River Falls	87%	31
Lakeview Memorial Hospital[2]	Stillwater	84%	98
Rice Memorial Hospital[2]	Willmar	84%	63
Virginia Regional Medical Center[2]	Virginia	81%	58
Essentia Health Duluth[2]	Duluth	80%	25
Glencoe Regional Health Services	Glencoe	80%	25
Bigfork Valley Hospital	Bigfork	54%	28

25. Controlled Postoperative Blood Glucose

Hospital Name	City	Rate	Cases
Mercy Hospital[2]	Coon Rapids	98%	141
Abbott Northwestern Hospital[2]	Minneapolis	97%	138
Park Nicollet Methodist Hospital[2]	Saint Louis Park	97%	175
United Hospital[2]	Saint Paul	97%	173
Regions Hospital[2]	Saint Paul	96%	136
Essentia Health St Mary's Medical Center[2]	Duluth	95%	170
Fairview Southdale Hospital[2]	Edina	94%	203
Hennepin County Medical Center[2]	Minneapolis	94%	65
Univ of Minnesota Med Ctr-Fairview[2]	Minneapolis	94%	127
Saint Joseph's Hospital[2]	Saint Paul	93%	191
Saint Lukes Hospital[2]	Duluth	93%	85
Minneapolis VA Medical Center[2]	Minneapolis	91%	181
Saint Cloud Hospital[2]	Saint Cloud	88%	152
Mayo Clinic - Saint Marys Hospital[2]	Rochester	87%	254
North Memorial Medical Center[2]	Robbinsdale	71%	156

26. Prophylactic Antibiotic Timing

Hospital Name	City	Rate	Cases
Austin Medical Center	Austin	100%	208
Healtheast Woodwinds Hospital[2]	Woodbury	100%	1013
Community Memorial Hospital[2]	Cloquet	99%	105
Fairview Northland Regional Hospital[2]	Princeton	99%	176
Fairview Red Wing Hospital[2]	Red Wing	99%	165
Fairview Southdale Hospital[2]	Edina	99%	1882
Immanuel-St Josephs-Mayo Health System[2]	Mankato	99%	307
Minneapolis VA Medical Center	Minneapolis	99%	392
Naeve Hospital	Albert Lea	99%	272
New Ulm Medical Center	New Ulm	99%	107
Park Nicollet Methodist Hospital[2]	Saint Louis Park	99%	602
Saint Joseph's Hospital[2]	Saint Paul	99%	698
Saint Marys Regional Health Center[2]	Detroit Lakes	99%	198
Univ of Minnesota Med Ctr-Fairview[2]	Minneapolis	99%	758
Abbott Northwestern Hospital[2]	Minneapolis	98%	557
Buffalo Hospital	Buffalo	98%	161
Cambridge Medical Center	Cambridge	98%	194
Fairview Ridges Hospital[2]	Burnsville	98%	620
Mayo Clinic - Methodist Hospital[2]	Rochester	98%	412
New River Medical Center	Monticello	98%	49
Paynesville Area Hospital	Paynesville	98%	53
Unity Hospital[2]	Fridley	98%	299
Winona Health Services	Winona	98%	133
Hennepin County Medical Center[2]	Minneapolis	97%	271
Lakeview Memorial Hospital[2]	Stillwater	97%	302
Mercy Hospital[2]	Coon Rapids	97%	434
Northfield Hospital	Northfield	97%	162
Owatonna Hospital[2]	Owatonna	97%	224
Saint Francis Regional Medical Center[2]	Shakopee	97%	327
Saint Lukes Hospital[2]	Duluth	97%	354
United Hospital[2]	Saint Paul	97%	544
University Med Ctr-Mesabi/Mesaba[2]	Hibbing	97%	79
Virginia Regional Medical Center[2]	Virginia	97%	128
Bigfork Valley Hospital	Bigfork	96%	55
District One Hospital	Faribault	96%	154
Essentia Health Duluth[2]	Duluth	96%	188
Essentia Health St Joseph's Medical Center[2]	Brainerd	96%	257
Essentia Health St Mary's Medical Center[2]	Duluth	96%	534
Fairmont Medical Center	Fairmont	96%	163
Fairview Lakes Health Services[2]	Wyoming	96%	347
Healtheast St John's Hospital[2]	Maplewood	96%	760
Mayo Clinic - Saint Marys Hospital[2]	Rochester	96%	408
North Country Regional Hospital	Bemidji	96%	509
Regions Hospital[2]	Saint Paul	96%	465
Saint Cloud Hospital[2]	Saint Cloud	96%	461
North Memorial Medical Center[2]	Robbinsdale	95%	498
Queen of Peace Hospital	New Prague	95%	115
Regina Medical Center[2]	Hastings	95%	182
Ridgeview Medical Center[2]	Waconia	95%	294
Glencoe Regional Health Services	Glencoe	94%	67
Grand Itasca Clinic and Hospital	Grand Rapids	94%	155
Hutchinson Area Health Care	Hutchinson	94%	144
Swift County Benson Hospital	Benson	94%	31
Kanabec Hospital	Mora	93%	75
Douglas County Hospital[2]	Alexandria	91%	306
Saint Gabriels Hospital[2]	Little Falls	91%	186
Sanford Medical Center Thief River Falls	Thief River Falls	91%	110
Sanford Worthington Medical Center	Worthington	91%	76
Stevens Community Medical Center	Morris	91%	46
United Hospital District	Blue Earth	91%	33
Lake City Medical Center Mayo Health System	Lake City	90%	29
Lake Region Healthcare Corporation	Fergus Falls	90%	193
Riverwood Healthcare Center	Aitkin	90%	49
Saint Elizabeth Medical Center	Wabasha	90%	31
Mercy Hospital & Health Care Center	Moose Lake	89%	63
Olmsted Medical Center	Rochester	89%	251
Rice Memorial Hospital[2]	Willmar	89%	201
Meeker Memorial Hospital	Litchfield	85%	26
Riverview Hospital	Crookston	85%	55
Pipestone County Medical Center	Pipestone	81%	37
Avera Marshall Regional Medical Center	Marshall	79%	81
Chippewa County Hospital	Montevideo	73%	33
Saint Francis Healthcare Campus[2]	Breckenridge	62%	26
Lakewood Health System	Staples	40%	65
Cuyuna Regional Medical Center[3]	Crosby	33%	73

NOTE: Hospital profiles are in alphabetical order by state, then city, then hospital within the city; Rankings exclude hospitals with less than 25 cases except for patient surveys which excludes hospitals with less than 100 cases; (a) 100–299 cases; (1) The number of cases is too small to be sure how well a hospital is performing; (2) The hospital indicated that the data submitted for this measure were based on a sample of cases; (3) Data was collected during a shorter time period (fewer quarters) than the maximum possible time for this measure; (4) Suppressed for one or more quarters by CMS; (5) No data is available from the hospital for this measure; (6) Fewer than 100 patients completed the HCAHPS survey. Use these rates with caution, as the number of surveys may be too low to reliably assess hospital performance; (7) Survey results are based on less than 12 months of data; (8) Survey results are not available for this reporting period; (9) No or very few patients were eligible for the HCAHPS survey. The scores shown, if any, reflect a very small number of surveys; (10) A state average was not calculated because too few hospitals in the state submitted data; (11) There were discrepancies in the data collection process; Please refer to the User's Guide for a full explanation of data.

27. Prophylactic Antibiotic Timing (Outpatient)

Hospital Name	City	Rate	Cases
Fairview Red Wing Hospital	Red Wing	100%	52
Saint Marys Regional Health Center	Detroit Lakes	100%	27
Healtheast St John's Hospital	Maplewood	99%	204
Mercy Hospital	Coon Rapids	97%	443
Owatonna Hospital	Owatonna	97%	91
Saint Francis Regional Medical Center	Shakopee	97%	106
Unity Hospital	Fridley	97%	152
Virginia Regional Medical Center	Virginia	97%	32
Regions Hospital	Saint Paul	96%	321
Ridgeview Medical Center	Waconia	96%	152
Buffalo Hospital	Buffalo	95%	82
Essentia Health St Mary's Medical Center	Duluth	95%	521
Fairview Ridges Hospital	Burnsville	95%	253
Hennepin County Medical Center	Minneapolis	95%	172
Immanuel-St Josephs-Mayo Health System	Mankato	95%	100
Lakeview Memorial Hospital	Stillwater	95%	207
Mayo Clinic - Methodist Hospital	Rochester	95%	329
Saint Joseph's Hospital	Saint Paul	95%	264
Univ of Minnesota Med Ctr-Fairview	Minneapolis	95%	377
Healtheast Woodwinds Hospital	Woodbury	94%	200
Regina Medical Center	Hastings	94%	82
Abbott Northwestern Hospital	Minneapolis	93%	524
Park Nicollet Methodist Hospital	Saint Louis Park	93%	570
Saint Lukes Hospital	Duluth	93%	135
Winona Health Services	Winona	92%	71
Douglas County Hospital	Alexandria	91%	179
Essentia Health St Joseph's Medical Center	Brainerd	91%	47
North Memorial Medical Center[3]	Robbinsdale	91%	262
District One Hospital	Faribault	90%	52
Fairview Lakes Health Services	Wyoming	90%	173
Fairview Northland Regional Hospital	Princeton	89%	53
Olmsted Medical Center	Rochester	89%	106
Saint Cloud Hospital	Saint Cloud	89%	412
Austin Medical Center	Austin	88%	32
Sanford Worthington Medical Center	Worthington	87%	30
United Hospital	Saint Paul	86%	469
Northfield Hospital	Northfield	85%	52
Hutchinson Area Health Care	Hutchinson	84%	45
Mayo Clinic - Saint Marys Hospital	Rochester	84%	628
Lake Region Healthcare Corporation	Fergus Falls	83%	72
North Country Regional Hospital	Bemidji	82%	72
Rice Memorial Hospital	Willmar	79%	73
Fairmont Medical Center	Fairmont	77%	39
Naeve Hospital	Albert Lea	76%	38
Essentia Health Duluth	Duluth	74%	293
Fairview Southdale Hospital	Edina	70%	662
Paynesville Area Hospital	Paynesville	56%	36
New Ulm Medical Center	New Ulm	50%	42

28. Prophylactic Antibiotic Selection

Hospital Name	City	Rate	Cases
Bigfork Valley Hospital	Bigfork	100%	55
Community Memorial Hospital[2]	Cloquet	100%	107
Fairview Northland Regional Hospital[2]	Princeton	100%	178
Fairview Ridges Hospital[2]	Burnsville	100%	622
Kanabec Hospital	Mora	100%	75
Lake City Medical Center Mayo Health System	Lake City	100%	29
Mercy Hospital[2]	Coon Rapids	100%	447
Mercy Hospital & Health Care Center	Moose Lake	100%	64
New River Medical Center	Monticello	100%	49
New Ulm Medical Center	New Ulm	100%	107
Regions Hospital[2]	Saint Paul	100%	479
Sanford Worthington Medical Center	Worthington	100%	76
Stevens Community Medical Center	Morris	100%	46
Swift County Benson Hospital	Benson	100%	32
United Hospital District	Blue Earth	100%	33
Avera Marshall Regional Medical Center	Marshall	99%	80
Buffalo Hospital	Buffalo	99%	163
Cuyuna Regional Medical Center[3]	Crosby	99%	70
Fairview Lakes Health Services[2]	Wyoming	99%	350
Fairview Southdale Hospital[2]	Edina	99%	1900
Healtheast Woodwinds Hospital[2]	Woodbury	99%	1015
Lakeview Memorial Hospital[2]	Stillwater	99%	302
Mayo Clinic - Methodist Hospital[2]	Rochester	99%	411
Naeve Hospital	Albert Lea	99%	277
Park Nicollet Methodist Hospital[2]	Saint Louis Park	99%	611
Saint Francis Regional Medical Center[2]	Shakopee	99%	328
Saint Gabriels Hospital[2]	Little Falls	99%	184
Saint Joseph's Hospital[2]	Saint Paul	99%	707
Saint Lukes Hospital[2]	Duluth	99%	354
Abbott Northwestern Hospital[2]	Minneapolis	98%	563
Austin Medical Center	Austin	98%	209
Cambridge Medical Center	Cambridge	98%	196
Essentia Health St Mary's Medical Center[2]	Duluth	98%	556
Fairmont Medical Center	Fairmont	98%	163
Fairview Red Wing Hospital[2]	Red Wing	98%	167
Lakewood Health System	Staples	98%	56
Mayo Clinic - Saint Marys Hospital[2]	Rochester	98%	438
Northfield Hospital	Northfield	98%	163
Paynesville Area Hospital	Paynesville	98%	53
Saint Cloud Hospital[2]	Saint Cloud	98%	476
Saint Marys Regional Health Center[2]	Detroit Lakes	98%	200
United Hospital[2]	Saint Paul	98%	549
Unity Hospital[2]	Fridley	98%	300
Univ of Minnesota Med Ctr-Fairview[2]	Minneapolis	98%	766
District One Hospital	Faribault	97%	152
Essentia Health Duluth[2]	Duluth	97%	191
Grand Itasca Clinic and Hospital	Grand Rapids	97%	147
Healtheast St John's Hospital[2]	Maplewood	97%	766
Hennepin County Medical Center[2]	Minneapolis	97%	276
Immanuel-St Josephs-Mayo Health System[2]	Mankato	97%	305
Minneapolis VA Medical Center	Minneapolis	97%	396
North Memorial Medical Center[2]	Robbinsdale	97%	511
Owatonna Hospital[2]	Owatonna	97%	222
Pipestone County Medical Center	Pipestone	97%	37
Regina Medical Center[2]	Hastings	97%	182
Rice Memorial Hospital[2]	Willmar	97%	199
Ridgeview Medical Center[2]	Waconia	97%	298
Saint Elizabeth Medical Center	Wabasha	97%	32
Douglas County Hospital[2]	Alexandria	96%	306
Essentia Health St Joseph's Medical Center[2]	Brainerd	96%	257
Lake Region Healthcare Corporation	Fergus Falls	96%	193
North Country Regional Hospital	Bemidji	96%	512
Olmsted Medical Center	Rochester	96%	248
University Med Ctr-Mesabi/Mesaba[2]	Hibbing	96%	82
Riverview Hospital	Crookston	95%	55
Virginia Regional Medical Center[2]	Virginia	95%	130
Chippewa County Hospital	Montevideo	94%	31
Glencoe Regional Health Services	Glencoe	94%	67
Queen of Peace Hospital	New Prague	94%	111
Sanford Medical Center Thief River Falls	Thief River Falls	94%	108
Hutchinson Area Health Care	Hutchinson	92%	146
Meeker Memorial Hospital	Litchfield	92%	26
Saint Francis Healthcare Campus[2]	Breckenridge	92%	25
Riverwood Healthcare Center	Aitkin	90%	48
Winona Health Services	Winona	88%	133

29. Prophylactic Antibiotic Selection (Outpatient)

Hospital Name	City	Rate	Cases
Austin Medical Center	Austin	100%	35
Naeve Hospital	Albert Lea	100%	30
Saint Marys Regional Health Center	Detroit Lakes	100%	27
Sanford Worthington Medical Center	Worthington	100%	31
Fairview Lakes Health Services	Wyoming	99%	167
Fairview Ridges Hospital	Burnsville	99%	249
Owatonna Hospital	Owatonna	99%	90
District One Hospital	Faribault	98%	50
Fairview Southdale Hospital	Edina	98%	597
Healtheast Woodwinds Hospital	Woodbury	98%	191
Hutchinson Area Health Care	Hutchinson	98%	40
Mayo Clinic - Saint Marys Hospital	Rochester	98%	581
Mercy Hospital	Coon Rapids	98%	443
Ridgeview Medical Center	Waconia	98%	158
Saint Francis Regional Medical Center	Shakopee	98%	103
Unity Hospital	Fridley	98%	152
Douglas County Hospital	Alexandria	97%	172
Essentia Health St Mary's Medical Center	Duluth	97%	523
Grand Itasca Clinic and Hospital	Grand Rapids	97%	36
Immanuel-St Josephs-Mayo Health System	Mankato	97%	99
Mayo Clinic - Methodist Hospital	Rochester	97%	566
Park Nicollet Methodist Hospital	Saint Louis Park	97%	538
Regions Hospital	Saint Paul	97%	317
Virginia Regional Medical Center	Virginia	97%	31
Buffalo Hospital	Buffalo	96%	79
Northfield Hospital	Northfield	96%	45
Regina Medical Center	Hastings	96%	79
Abbott Northwestern Hospital	Minneapolis	95%	505
Essentia Health Duluth	Duluth	95%	367
Healtheast St John's Hospital	Maplewood	95%	203
North Memorial Medical Center[3]	Robbinsdale	95%	253
Olmsted Medical Center	Rochester	95%	101
Rice Memorial Hospital	Willmar	95%	66
Saint Cloud Hospital	Saint Cloud	95%	411
Saint Joseph's Hospital	Saint Paul	95%	260
Fairview Northland Regional Hospital	Princeton	94%	49
Lakeview Memorial Hospital	Stillwater	94%	207
North Country Regional Hospital	Bemidji	94%	66
Univ of Minnesota Med Ctr-Fairview	Minneapolis	94%	470
Essentia Health St Joseph's Medical Center	Brainerd	93%	45
Lake Region Healthcare Corporation	Fergus Falls	93%	73
Winona Health Services	Winona	93%	92
Fairview Red Wing Hospital	Red Wing	92%	65
Saint Lukes Hospital	Duluth	92%	132
Hennepin County Medical Center	Minneapolis	88%	168
Fairmont Medical Center	Fairmont	86%	56
United Hospital	Saint Paul	73%	434
Paynesville Area Hospital	Paynesville	71%	38

30. Prophylactic Antibiotic Stopped

Hospital Name	City	Rate	Cases
Austin Medical Center	Austin	100%	204
Glencoe Regional Health Services	Glencoe	100%	67
Grand Itasca Clinic and Hospital	Grand Rapids	100%	147
Hutchinson Area Health Care	Hutchinson	100%	136
Lake City Medical Center Mayo Health System	Lake City	100%	29
Lakeview Memorial Hospital[2]	Stillwater	100%	295
Meeker Memorial Hospital	Litchfield	100%	26
New Ulm Medical Center	New Ulm	100%	106
Regina Medical Center[2]	Hastings	100%	181
Ridgeview Medical Center[2]	Waconia	100%	294
Saint Francis Regional Medical Center[2]	Shakopee	100%	318
Sanford Worthington Medical Center	Worthington	100%	75
Stevens Community Medical Center	Morris	100%	46
Swift County Benson Hospital	Benson	100%	31
Cuyuna Regional Medical Center[3]	Crosby	99%	70
Douglas County Hospital[2]	Alexandria	99%	294
Fairmont Medical Center	Fairmont	99%	157
Fairview Lakes Health Services[2]	Wyoming	99%	334
Mayo Clinic - Methodist Hospital[2]	Rochester	99%	403
Mercy Hospital[2]	Coon Rapids	99%	414
Cambridge Medical Center	Cambridge	98%	186
Fairview Northland Regional Hospital[2]	Princeton	98%	173
Fairview Red Wing Hospital[2]	Red Wing	98%	161
Healtheast St John's Hospital[2]	Maplewood	98%	740
Healtheast Woodwinds Hospital[2]	Woodbury	98%	998
Hennepin County Medical Center[2]	Minneapolis	98%	256
Naeve Hospital	Albert Lea	98%	266
Owatonna Hospital[2]	Owatonna	98%	215
Park Nicollet Methodist Hospital[2]	Saint Louis Park	98%	556
Regions Hospital[2]	Saint Paul	98%	447
Buffalo Hospital	Buffalo	97%	151
Community Memorial Hospital[2]	Cloquet	97%	104
Essentia Health St Mary's Medical Center[2]	Duluth	97%	512
Fairview Ridges Hospital[2]	Burnsville	97%	616
Lake Region Healthcare Corporation	Fergus Falls	97%	190
Minneapolis VA Medical Center	Minneapolis	97%	384
Olmsted Medical Center	Rochester	97%	246
Rice Memorial Hospital[2]	Willmar	97%	195
Saint Cloud Hospital[2]	Saint Cloud	97%	431
Saint Joseph's Hospital[2]	Saint Paul	97%	662
Saint Marys Regional Health Center[2]	Detroit Lakes	97%	192
United Hospital District	Blue Earth	97%	33
Univ of Minnesota Med Ctr-Fairview[2]	Minneapolis	97%	725
Abbott Northwestern Hospital[2]	Minneapolis	96%	528
Bigfork Valley Hospital	Bigfork	96%	55
Fairview Southdale Hospital[2]	Edina	96%	1811
Immanuel-St Josephs-Mayo Health System[2]	Mankato	96%	292
Northfield Hospital	Northfield	96%	157
Queen of Peace Hospital	New Prague	96%	107
Saint Gabriels Hospital[2]	Little Falls	96%	178
United Hospital[2]	Saint Paul	96%	514
Unity Hospital[2]	Fridley	96%	281
Mayo Clinic - Saint Marys Hospital[2]	Rochester	95%	392
Saint Lukes Hospital[2]	Duluth	95%	348
Sanford Medical Center Thief River Falls	Thief River Falls	95%	107
University Med Ctr-Mesabi/Mesaba[2]	Hibbing	95%	75
Virginia Regional Medical Center[2]	Virginia	95%	120
Essentia Health St Joseph's Medical Center[2]	Brainerd	94%	247
Mercy Hospital & Health Care Center	Moose Lake	94%	62
North Country Regional Hospital	Bemidji	94%	499
North Memorial Medical Center[2]	Robbinsdale	94%	493
Pipestone County Medical Center	Pipestone	94%	36
District One Hospital	Faribault	93%	151
New River Medical Center	Monticello	93%	46
Winona Health Services	Winona	92%	131
Kanabec Hospital	Mora	91%	75
Lakewood Health System	Staples	91%	55
Riverwood Healthcare Center	Aitkin	90%	48
Essentia Health Duluth[2]	Duluth	89%	187
Riverview Hospital	Crookston	89%	54
Paynesville Area Hospital	Paynesville	87%	52
Saint Elizabeth Medical Center	Wabasha	87%	30
Avera Marshall Regional Medical Center	Marshall	84%	80
Saint Francis Healthcare Campus[2]	Breckenridge	84%	25
Chippewa County Hospital	Montevideo	77%	31

31. Recommended VTP Ordered

Hospital Name	City	Rate	Cases
Buffalo Hospital	Buffalo	100%	51
Cambridge Medical Center	Cambridge	100%	35
Fairview Northland Regional Hospital[2]	Princeton	100%	42
Fairview Red Wing Hospital[2]	Red Wing	100%	39
Hutchinson Area Health Care	Hutchinson	100%	67
Kanabec Hospital	Mora	100%	46
Mayo Clinic - Methodist Hospital[2]	Rochester	100%	202
New Ulm Medical Center	New Ulm	100%	49
Ridgeview Medical Center[2]	Waconia	100%	121
Unity Hospital[2]	Fridley	100%	166

NOTE: Hospital profiles are in alphabetical order by state, then city, then hospital within the city; Rankings exclude hospitals with less than 25 cases except for patient surveys which excludes hospitals with less than 100 cases; (a) 100–299 cases; (1) The number of cases is too small to be sure how well a hospital is performing; (2) The hospital indicated that the data submitted for this measure were based on a sample of cases; (3) Data was collected during a shorter time period (fewer quarters) than the maximum possible time for this measure; (4) Suppressed for one or more quarters by CMS; (5) No data is available from the hospital for this measure; (6) Fewer than 100 patients completed the HCAHPS survey. Use these rates with caution, as the number of surveys may be too low to reliably assess hospital performance; (7) Survey results are based on less than 12 months of data; (8) Survey results are not available for this reporting period; (9) No or very few patients were eligible for the HCAHPS survey. The scores shown, if any, reflect a very small number of surveys; (10) A state average was not calculated because too few hospitals in the state submitted data; (11) There were discrepancies in the data collection process; Please refer to the User's Guide for a full explanation of data.

Hospital Name	City	Rate	Cases
Essentia Health St Mary's Medical Center[2]	Duluth	99%	201
Mayo Clinic - Saint Marys Hospital[2]	Rochester	99%	259
Mercy Hospital[2]	Coon Rapids	99%	165
Austin Medical Center	Austin	98%	125
Essentia Health St Joseph's Medical Center[2]	Brainerd	98%	89
Minneapolis VA Medical Center[2]	Minneapolis	98%	206
Regina Medical Center[2]	Hastings	98%	64
Community Memorial Hospital[2]	Cloquet	97%	39
Fairmont Medical Center	Fairmont	97%	71
Fairview Lakes Health Services[2]	Wyoming	97%	103
Naeve Hospital	Albert Lea	97%	145
Queen of Peace Hospital	New Prague	97%	34
Saint Josephs Area Health Services	Park Rapids	97%	88
Abbott Northwestern Hospital[2]	Minneapolis	96%	216
Fairview Southdale Hospital[2]	Edina	96%	357
Hennepin County Medical Center[2]	Minneapolis	96%	165
Immanuel-St Josephs-Mayo Health System[2]	Mankato	96%	224
Northfield Hospital	Northfield	96%	57
Saint Elizabeth Medical Center	Wabasha	96%	25
Univ of Minnesota Med Ctr-Fairview[2]	Minneapolis	96%	434
Healtheast St John's Hospital[2]	Maplewood	95%	292
United Hospital[2]	Saint Paul	95%	159
Douglas County Hospital[2]	Alexandria	94%	139
Saint Francis Regional Medical Center[2]	Shakopee	94%	115
Grand Itasca Clinic and Hospital	Grand Rapids	93%	58
Lake Region Healthcare Corporation	Fergus Falls	93%	115
Rice Memorial Hospital[2]	Willmar	93%	104
Healtheast Woodwinds Hospital[2]	Woodbury	92%	132
Regions Hospital[2]	Saint Paul	92%	209
Saint Cloud Hospital[2]	Saint Cloud	92%	152
Winona Health Services	Winona	92%	75
Fairview Ridges Hospital[2]	Burnsville	91%	160
Riverview Hospital	Crookston	90%	31
Park Nicollet Methodist Hospital[2]	Saint Louis Park	89%	192
Saint Joseph's Hospital[2]	Saint Paul	89%	225
University Med Ctr-Mesabi/Mesaba[2]	Hibbing	89%	63
Lakeview Memorial Hospital[2]	Stillwater	87%	69
District One Hospital	Faribault	86%	59
Saint Lukes Hospital[2]	Duluth	86%	164
Chippewa County Hospital	Montevideo	85%	26
Owatonna Hospital[2]	Owatonna	85%	39
Saint Gabriels Hospital[2]	Little Falls	85%	46
Sanford Medical Center Thief River Falls	Thief River Falls	85%	26
North Country Regional Hospital	Bemidji	84%	282
Olmsted Medical Center	Rochester	83%	76
Virginia Regional Medical Center[2]	Virginia	83%	65
Mercy Hospital & Health Care Center	Moose Lake	82%	28
Saint Marys Regional Health Center[2]	Detroit Lakes	76%	50
North Memorial Medical Center[2]	Robbinsdale	72%	166
Saint Francis Healthcare Campus[2]	Breckenridge	60%	30

32. Urinary Catheter Removal

Hospital Name	City	Rate	Cases
Bigfork Valley Hospital	Bigfork	100%	33
Buffalo Hospital	Buffalo	100%	58
Fairview Red Wing Hospital[2]	Red Wing	100%	56
Saint Francis Regional Medical Center[2]	Shakopee	100%	46
Saint Gabriels Hospital[2]	Little Falls	100%	40
Owatonna Hospital[2]	Owatonna	99%	71
Lake Region Healthcare Corporation	Fergus Falls	98%	45
Austin Medical Center	Austin	97%	78
District One Hospital	Faribault	97%	33
Fairview Lakes Health Services[2]	Wyoming	97%	32
Minneapolis VA Medical Center[2]	Minneapolis	97%	157
Naeve Hospital	Albert Lea	97%	90
Northfield Hospital	Northfield	97%	36
Regina Medical Center[2]	Hastings	97%	31
Saint Marys Regional Health Center[2]	Detroit Lakes	97%	69
Cambridge Medical Center	Cambridge	96%	53
Fairview Southdale Hospital[2]	Edina	96%	477
Regions Hospital[2]	Saint Paul	96%	180
Avera Marshall Regional Medical Center	Marshall	95%	40
Fairview Ridges Hospital[2]	Burnsville	95%	326
Healtheast Woodwinds Hospital[2]	Woodbury	95%	101
Olmsted Medical Center	Rochester	95%	82
Sanford Medical Center Thief River Falls	Thief River Falls	95%	39
Douglas County Hospital[2]	Alexandria	94%	115
Mayo Clinic - Methodist Hospital[2]	Rochester	94%	78
Abbott Northwestern Hospital[2]	Minneapolis	93%	187
Univ of Minnesota Med Ctr-Fairview[2]	Minneapolis	92%	402
Fairmont Medical Center	Fairmont	91%	45
Community Memorial Hospital[2]	Cloquet	90%	29
United Hospital[2]	Saint Paul	90%	130
Mercy Hospital[2]	Coon Rapids	88%	104
Hennepin County Medical Center[2]	Minneapolis	87%	60
North Country Regional Hospital	Bemidji	87%	128
Saint Cloud Hospital[2]	Saint Cloud	87%	111
Immanuel-St Josephs-Mayo Health System[2]	Mankato	86%	85
Ridgeview Medical Center[2]	Waconia	86%	56
Virginia Regional Medical Center[2]	Virginia	86%	51
Essentia Health St Mary's Medical Center[2]	Duluth	85%	220
Queen of Peace Hospital	New Prague	84%	32
Rice Memorial Hospital[2]	Willmar	84%	85
North Memorial Medical Center[2]	Robbinsdale	83%	191
Saint Joseph's Hospital[2]	Saint Paul	83%	158
Grand Itasca Clinic and Hospital	Grand Rapids	82%	28
Healtheast St John's Hospital[2]	Maplewood	82%	78
Winona Health Services	Winona	80%	40
Mayo Clinic - Saint Marys Hospital[2]	Rochester	79%	158
Park Nicollet Methodist Hospital[2]	Saint Louis Park	79%	211
Saint Lukes Hospital[2]	Duluth	73%	71

Children's Asthma Care

33. Received Systemic Corticosteroids

Hospital Name	City	Rate	Cases
Hennepin County Medical Center	Minneapolis	100%	36
Univ of Minnesota Med Ctr-Fairview	Minneapolis	100%	31
Children's Hospitals & Clinics[2]	Minneapolis	98%	331

34. Received Home Management Plan of Care

Hospital Name	City	Rate	Cases
Hennepin County Medical Center[2]	Minneapolis	89%	36
Children's Hospitals & Clinics[2]	Minneapolis	41%	331
Univ of Minnesota Med Ctr-Fairview	Minneapolis	19%	32

35. Received Reliever Medication

Hospital Name	City	Rate	Cases
Children's Hospitals & Clinics[2]	Minneapolis	100%	331
Hennepin County Medical Center	Minneapolis	100%	36
Univ of Minnesota Med Ctr-Fairview	Minneapolis	100%	32

Use of Medical Imaging

36. Combination Abdominal CT Scan

Hospital Name	City	Ratio	Cases
Bigfork Valley Hospital[1]	Bigfork	0.000	33
Essentia Health Fosston	Fosston	0.000	50
Mahnomen Health Center[1]	Mahnomen	0.000	25
Northern Pines Medical Center[1]	Aurora	0.000	32
United Hospital District	Blue Earth	0.000	104
Lifecare Medical Center	Roseau	0.011	95
Saint Michaels Hospital & Nursing Home	Sauk Centre	0.013	77
Deer River Healthcare Center	Deer River	0.014	73
North Country Regional Hospital	Bemidji	0.023	222
Minnesota Valley Health Center[1]	Le Sueur	0.024	42
Unity Hospital	Fridley	0.024	594
Saint Cloud Hospital	Saint Cloud	0.026	1399
Univ of Minnesota Med Ctr-Fairview	Minneapolis	0.026	1332
Fairview Northland Regional Hospital	Princeton	0.032	281
River's Edge Hospital & Clinic	Saint Peter	0.032	95
Riverview Hospital	Crookston	0.033	91
Buffalo Hospital	Buffalo	0.034	295
Healtheast Woodwinds Hospital	Woodbury	0.037	565
Ridgeview Medical Center	Waconia	0.037	515
Sibley Medical Center	Arlington	0.037	82
Perham Memorial Hospital	Perham	0.039	102
Windom Area Hospital	Windom	0.040	100
Cambridge Medical Center	Cambridge	0.041	366
Redwood Area Hospital	Redwood Falls	0.043	140
St James Med Ctr-Mayo Health System	Saint James	0.043	46
Saint Francis Regional Medical Center	Shakopee	0.044	525
Essentia Health St Joseph's Medical Center	Brainerd	0.046	648
Mercy Hospital	Coon Rapids	0.046	842
Douglas County Hospital	Alexandria	0.047	297
Mayo Clinic - Saint Marys Hospital	Rochester	0.047	576
Fairview Ridges Hospital	Burnsville	0.048	684
Regina Medical Center	Hastings	0.049	284
Saint Elizabeth Medical Center	Wabasha	0.049	61
District One Hospital	Faribault	0.050	240
Lakeview Memorial Hospital	Stillwater	0.050	457
Tri County Hospital	Wadena	0.051	196
Naeve Hospital	Albert Lea	0.053	399
Rice Memorial Hospital	Willmar	0.054	148
Springfield Med Ctr Mayo Health Sys	Springfield	0.054	56
Hutchinson Area Health Care	Hutchinson	0.060	281
Centracare Health System - Melrose Hospital	Melrose	0.062	65
Centracare Health System - Long Prairie	Long Prairie	0.063	80
Glencoe Regional Health Services	Glencoe	0.064	218
Kanabec Hospital	Mora	0.064	220
United Hospital	Saint Paul	0.064	746
Fairmont Medical Center	Fairmont	0.065	306
Northfield Hospital	Northfield	0.065	107
Sleepy Eye Municipal Hospital	Sleepy Eye	0.065	124
Murray County Memorial Hospital	Slayton	0.067	60
Park Nicollet Methodist Hospital	Saint Louis Park	0.067	1318
Paynesville Area Hospital	Paynesville	0.068	148
Saint Gabriels Hospital	Little Falls	0.068	207
Saint Joseph's Hospital	Saint Paul	0.068	399
Swift County Benson Hospital	Benson	0.068	73
Winona Health Services	Winona	0.069	245
Albany Area Hospital[1]	Albany	0.070	43
Immanuel-St Josephs-Mayo Health System	Mankato	0.070	569
New River Medical Center	Monticello	0.071	155
Community Memorial Hospital	Cloquet	0.073	193
Abbott Northwestern Hospital	Minneapolis	0.074	1685
Essentia Health Sandstone[1]	Sandstone	0.074	54
Hennepin County Medical Center	Minneapolis	0.074	435
Fairview Red Wing Hospital	Red Wing	0.076	185
Healtheast St John's Hospital	Maplewood	0.079	903
Municipal Hospital and Granite Manor	Granite Falls	0.080	87
North Memorial Medical Center	Robbinsdale	0.083	1034
New Ulm Medical Center	New Ulm	0.084	263
University Med Ctr-Mesabi/Mesaba	Hibbing	0.085	260
Fairview Southdale Hospital	Edina	0.086	954
Sanford Worthington Medical Center	Worthington	0.087	138
Fairview Lakes Health Services	Wyoming	0.089	493
Mayo Clinic - Methodist Hospital	Rochester	0.101	189
Mercy Hospital & Health Care Center	Moose Lake	0.102	88
Grand Itasca Clinic and Hospital	Grand Rapids	0.106	273
Avera Marshall Regional Medical Center	Marshall	0.108	241
Saint Francis Healthcare Campus	Breckenridge	0.112	170
Lake City Medical Center Mayo Health System[1]	Lake City	0.114	44
Lake Region Healthcare Corporation	Fergus Falls	0.118	373
Saint Marys Regional Health Center	Detroit Lakes	0.122	189
Waseca Med Ctr-Mayo Health System	Waseca	0.127	102
Stevens Community Medical Center	Morris	0.129	170
Queen of Peace Hospital	New Prague	0.131	237
Wheaton Community Hospital[1]	Wheaton	0.141	64
Regions Hospital	Saint Paul	0.148	1491
Hendricks Community Hospital[1]	Hendricks	0.161	56
Sanford Luverne Medical Center	Luverne	0.180	89
Lakewood Health Center[1]	Baudette	0.190	42
Essentia Health St Mary's Medical Center	Duluth	0.215	636
Saint Lukes Hospital	Duluth	0.222	919
Saint Josephs Area Health Services	Park Rapids	0.235	293
Olmsted Medical Center	Rochester	0.344	227
Cannon Falls Medical Center Mayo[1]	Cannon Falls	0.360	25
Austin Medical Center	Austin	0.369	279
Owatonna Hospital	Owatonna	0.373	158
Pipestone County Medical Center	Pipestone	0.375	120
Glacial Ridge Hospital	Glenwood	0.413	92
Virginia Regional Medical Center	Virginia	0.417	424
Tyler Healthcare Center	Tyler	0.431	58
Renville County Hospital and Clinics[1]	Olivia	0.649	37
Sanford Canby Medical Center[1]	Canby	0.761	46
Chippewa County Hospital	Montevideo	0.804	97
Johnson Memorial Hospital[1]	Dawson	0.840	25
Meeker Memorial Hospital	Litchfield	0.864	110
Ortonville Area Health Services	Ortonville	0.924	66

37. Combination Chest CT Scan

Hospital Name	City	Ratio	Cases
Centracare Health System - Melrose Hospital[1]	Melrose	0.000	43
Community Memorial Hospital	Cloquet	0.000	105
Essentia Health Fosston[1]	Fosston	0.000	35
Essentia Health Sandstone[1]	Sandstone	0.000	30
Essentia Health St Joseph's Medical Center	Brainerd	0.000	679
Fairmont Medical Center	Fairmont	0.000	214
Glencoe Regional Health Services	Glencoe	0.000	96
Hutchinson Area Health Care	Hutchinson	0.000	216
Lifecare Medical Center	Roseau	0.000	79
Mercy Hospital & Health Care Center	Moose Lake	0.000	70
Municipal Hospital and Granite Manor	Granite Falls	0.000	64
Murray County Memorial Hospital[1]	Slayton	0.000	27
Naeve Hospital	Albert Lea	0.000	137
New River Medical Center	Monticello	0.000	86
North Country Regional Hospital	Bemidji	0.000	74
Northern Pines Medical Center[1]	Aurora	0.000	25
Perham Memorial Hospital	Perham	0.000	67
Rice Memorial Hospital	Willmar	0.000	77
River's Edge Hospital & Clinic	Saint Peter	0.000	74
Sleepy Eye Municipal Hospital	Sleepy Eye	0.000	49
Tri County Hospital	Wadena	0.000	111
United Hospital District	Blue Earth	0.000	70
University Med Ctr-Mesabi/Mesaba	Hibbing	0.000	220
Hennepin County Medical Center	Minneapolis	0.002	439
Immanuel-St Josephs-Mayo Health System	Mankato	0.002	401
Regions Hospital	Saint Paul	0.002	1324
Ridgeview Medical Center	Waconia	0.002	427
Unity Hospital	Fridley	0.002	614
Healtheast Woodwinds Hospital	Woodbury	0.003	370
Saint Cloud Hospital	Saint Cloud	0.003	1472
Douglas County Hospital	Alexandria	0.004	224
Buffalo Hospital	Buffalo	0.005	220
Fairview Northland Regional Hospital	Princeton	0.005	209
Fairview Ridges Hospital	Burnsville	0.005	651
Regina Medical Center	Hastings	0.005	197

NOTE: Hospital profiles are in alphabetical order by state, then city, then hospital within the city; Rankings exclude hospitals with less than 25 cases except for patient surveys which excludes hospitals with less than 100 cases; (a) 100–299 cases; (1) The number of cases is too small to be sure how well a hospital is performing; (2) The hospital indicated that the data submitted for this measure were based on a sample of cases; (3) Data was collected during a shorter time period (fewer quarters) than the maximum possible time for this measure; (4) Suppressed for one or more quarters by CMS; (5) No data is available from the hospital for this measure; (6) Fewer than 100 patients completed the HCAHPS survey. Use these rates with caution, as the number of surveys may be too low to reliably assess hospital performance; (7) Survey results are based on less than 12 months of data; (8) Survey results are not available for this reporting period; (9) No or very few patients were eligible for the HCAHPS survey. The scores shown, if any, reflect a very small number of surveys; (10) A state average was not calculated because too few hospitals in the state submitted data; (11) There were discrepancies in the data collection process; Please refer to the User's Guide for a full explanation of data.

Hospital Name	City	Rate	Cases
United Hospital	Saint Paul	0.005	412
Fairview Lakes Health Services	Wyoming	0.006	499
Mayo Clinic - Methodist Hospital	Rochester	0.006	155
Queen of Peace Hospital	New Prague	0.006	158
Saint Gabriels Hospital	Little Falls	0.006	162
Fairview Southdale Hospital	Edina	0.007	854
Lakeview Memorial Hospital	Stillwater	0.007	289
Paynesville Area Hospital	Paynesville	0.007	144
Avera Marshall Regional Medical Center	Marshall	0.008	132
Mayo Clinic - Saint Marys Hospital	Rochester	0.008	260
Univ of Minnesota Med Ctr-Fairview	Minneapolis	0.008	1423
Saint Lukes Hospital	Duluth	0.009	814
Grand Itasca Clinic and Hospital	Grand Rapids	0.011	184
Redwood Area Hospital	Redwood Falls	0.011	89
Saint Joseph's Hospital	Saint Paul	0.011	273
Abbott Northwestern Hospital	Minneapolis	0.014	1699
Virginia Regional Medical Center	Virginia	0.014	276
Healtheast St John's Hospital	Maplewood	0.015	523
North Memorial Medical Center	Robbinsdale	0.016	943
Saint Michaels Hospital & Nursing Home	Sauk Centre	0.016	63
Mercy Hospital	Coon Rapids	0.017	823
Deer River Healthcare Center	Deer River	0.018	55
Saint Josephs Area Health Services	Park Rapids	0.018	217
Sanford Worthington Medical Center	Worthington	0.018	56
Cambridge Medical Center	Cambridge	0.019	269
Centracare Health System - Long Prairie	Long Prairie	0.020	49
Northfield Hospital	Northfield	0.020	100
Waseca Med Ctr-Mayo Health System	Waseca	0.021	47
Park Nicollet Methodist Hospital	Saint Louis Park	0.022	959
New Ulm Medical Center	New Ulm	0.025	202
Glacial Ridge Hospital	Glenwood	0.029	70
Essentia Health St Mary's Medical Center	Duluth	0.031	351
Kanabec Hospital	Mora	0.031	131
Renville County Hospital and Clinics[1]	Olivia	0.031	32
Swift County Benson Hospital	Benson	0.031	65
Lake Region Healthcare Corporation	Fergus Falls	0.032	252
Saint Francis Regional Medical Center	Shakopee	0.033	366
Saint Elizabeth Medical Center	Wabasha	0.034	58
Stevens Community Medical Center	Morris	0.036	83
Fairview Red Wing Hospital	Red Wing	0.041	146
Winona Health Services	Winona	0.041	122
Riverview Hospital	Crookston	0.043	69
Windom Area Hospital	Windom	0.043	47
District One Hospital	Faribault	0.048	209
Chippewa County Hospital	Montevideo	0.051	59
Ortonville Area Health Services	Ortonville	0.054	56
Sibley Medical Center	Arlington	0.066	91
Meeker Memorial Hospital[1]	Litchfield	0.081	62
Hendricks Community Hospital[1]	Hendricks	0.088	34
Pipestone County Medical Center[1]	Pipestone	0.094	32
Saint Marys Regional Health Center	Detroit Lakes	0.112	170
Saint Francis Healthcare Campus	Breckenridge	0.136	88
Owatonna Hospital	Owatonna	0.152	99
Sanford Luverne Medical Center[1]	Luverne	0.175	40
Wheaton Community Hospital[1]	Wheaton	0.179	28
Austin Medical Center	Austin	0.240	167
Olmsted Medical Center	Rochester	0.253	146
Sanford Canby Medical Center[1]	Canby	0.385	26

38. Follow-up Mammogram/Ultrasound

Hospital Name	City	Rate	Cases
Buffalo Hospital	Buffalo	1.6%	248
Pipestone County Medical Center	Pipestone	1.7%	293
Sanford Canby Medical Center	Canby	2.1%	191
Hendricks Community Hospital	Hendricks	2.2%	138
Meeker Memorial Hospital	Litchfield	2.5%	275
Rice Memorial Hospital	Willmar	2.7%	222
Swift County Benson Hospital	Benson	2.8%	143
Sibley Medical Center	Arlington	2.9%	104
Sleepy Eye Municipal Hospital	Sleepy Eye	2.9%	104
Saint Francis Healthcare Campus	Breckenridge	3.0%	133
Community Memorial Hospital	Cloquet	3.3%	90
Douglas County Hospital	Alexandria	3.3%	61
Essentia Health Sandstone	Sandstone	3.3%	61
Saint Francis Regional Medical Center	Shakopee	3.4%	533
Ridgeview Medical Center	Waconia	3.5%	462
Winona Health Services	Winona	3.5%	677
Fairview Red Wing Hospital	Red Wing	3.9%	584
Riverview Hospital	Crookston	3.9%	335
Mercy Hospital & Health Care Center	Moose Lake	4.0%	226
Abbott Northwestern Hospital	Minneapolis	4.2%	2250
Healtheast St John's Hospital	Maplewood	4.2%	2809
Lakeview Memorial Hospital	Stillwater	4.2%	991
New Ulm Medical Center	New Ulm	4.2%	622
Queen of Peace Hospital	New Prague	4.3%	418
St James Med Ctr-Mayo Health System	Saint James	4.3%	161
Tri County Hospital	Wadena	4.3%	258
Wheaton Community Hospital	Wheaton	4.3%	162
Springfield Med Ctr Mayo Health Sys	Springfield	4.4%	206
Centracare Health System - Long Prairie	Long Prairie	4.5%	89
Redwood Area Hospital	Redwood Falls	4.5%	67
Kittson Memorial Hospital	Hallock	4.7%	85
Cambridge Medical Center	Cambridge	4.8%	686
Municipal Hospital and Granite Manor	Granite Falls	4.8%	189
Bigfork Valley Hospital	Bigfork	4.9%	122
Chippewa County Hospital	Montevideo	4.9%	267
Fairview Lakes Health Services	Wyoming	4.9%	815
Lake Region Healthcare Corporation	Fergus Falls	5.0%	783
Regina Medical Center	Hastings	5.0%	279
Grand Itasca Clinic and Hospital	Grand Rapids	5.1%	740
Ortonville Area Health Services	Ortonville	5.1%	216
Albany Area Hospital	Albany	5.3%	76
Paynesville Area Hospital	Paynesville	5.3%	264
Essentia Health St Joseph's Medical Center	Brainerd	5.4%	1511
Kanabec Hospital	Mora	5.5%	237
University Med Ctr-Mesabi/Mesaba	Hibbing	5.5%	383
Immanuel-St Josephs-Mayo Health System	Mankato	5.7%	454
Olmsted Medical Center	Rochester	5.7%	1053
Austin Medical Center	Austin	5.8%	1115
Hutchinson Area Health Care	Hutchinson	5.8%	591
Johnson Memorial Hospital	Dawson	5.9%	85
River's Edge Hospital & Clinic	Saint Peter	6.0%	251
Saint Cloud Hospital	Saint Cloud	6.0%	1525
Glencoe Regional Health Services	Glencoe	6.1%	293
Univ of Minnesota Med Ctr-Fairview	Minneapolis	6.1%	604
Fairmont Medical Center	Fairmont	6.3%	649
Sanford Westbrook Medical Center	Westbrook	6.3%	95
Murray County Memorial Hospital	Slayton	6.5%	155
Deer River Healthcare Center	Deer River	6.6%	136
Fairview Southdale Hospital	Edina	6.6%	728
Waseca Med Ctr-Mayo Health System	Waseca	6.8%	221
North Memorial Medical Center	Robbinsdale	6.9%	711
Centracare Health System - Melrose Hospital	Melrose	7.0%	201
Sanford Luverne Medical Center	Luverne	7.1%	367
Cannon Falls Medical Center Mayo	Cannon Falls	7.2%	97
Renville County Hospital and Clinics	Olivia	7.6%	172
Saint Joseph's Hospital	Saint Paul	7.6%	683
Mahnomen Health Center	Mahnomen	7.7%	65
North Country Regional Hospital[1]	Bemidji	7.8%	51
Glacial Ridge Hospital	Glenwood	7.9%	203
Essentia Health Fosston	Fosston	8.0%	88
Perham Memorial Hospital	Perham	8.0%	262
Hennepin County Medical Center	Minneapolis	8.4%	735
Naeve Hospital	Albert Lea	8.4%	857
Fairview Northland Regional Hospital	Princeton	8.6%	617
Saint Michaels Hospital & Nursing Home	Sauk Centre	8.6%	186
United Hospital	Saint Paul	8.6%	1247
Madison Hospital	Madison	9.0%	78
Saint Gabriels Hospital	Little Falls	9.0%	466
United Hospital District	Blue Earth	9.0%	255
Bridges Medical Services[1]	Ada	9.1%	44
Healtheast Woodwinds Hospital	Woodbury	9.1%	1139
Regions Hospital	Saint Paul	9.2%	1265
New River Medical Center	Monticello	9.3%	182
Lifecare Medical Center	Roseau	9.4%	171
Saint Elizabeth Medical Center	Wabasha	9.4%	266
Saint Josephs Area Health Services	Park Rapids	9.4%	551
Sanford Jackson Medical Center	Jackson	10.5%	105
Tyler Healthcare Center	Tyler	10.5%	86
Avera Marshall Regional Medical Center	Marshall	10.7%	112
Fairview Ridges Hospital	Burnsville	10.8%	908
Lakewood Health Center	Baudette	11.0%	91
Saint Lukes Hospital	Duluth	11.0%	1350
Lake City Medical Center Mayo Health System	Lake City	11.3%	247
Northfield Hospital	Northfield	11.3%	133
Virginia Regional Medical Center	Virginia	12.6%	231
Holy Trinity Hospital[1]	Graceville	13.1%	61
District One Hospital[1]	Faribault	13.2%	53
Windom Area Hospital	Windom	13.2%	129
Stevens Community Medical Center	Morris	14.6%	192

39. MRI for Low Back Pain

Hospital Name	City	Rate	Cases
Olmsted Medical Center[1]	Rochester	14.6%	41
Saint Michaels Hospital & Nursing Home[1]	Sauk Centre	16.0%	25
Riverview Hospital[1]	Crookston	17.9%	56
Meeker Memorial Hospital[1]	Litchfield	20.0%	25
Regina Medical Center[1]	Hastings	22.5%	40
Northfield Hospital[1]	Northfield	23.1%	39
Redwood Area Hospital[1]	Redwood Falls	24.2%	33
Immanuel-St Josephs-Mayo Health System	Mankato	25.0%	64
New River Medical Center[1]	Monticello	25.7%	35
Avera Marshall Regional Medical Center[1]	Marshall	26.1%	46
Hennepin County Medical Center[1]	Minneapolis	26.3%	38
New Ulm Medical Center	New Ulm	26.6%	64
Fairmont Medical Center	Fairmont	26.9%	93
Hutchinson Area Health Care	Hutchinson	27.0%	74
Saint Marys Regional Health Center[1]	Detroit Lakes	27.3%	44
Queen of Peace Hospital	New Prague	27.5%	69
Naeve Hospital	Albert Lea	27.8%	72
Saint Francis Healthcare Campus	Breckenridge	28.6%	56
Fairview Northland Regional Hospital	Princeton	32.3%	62
Kanabec Hospital	Mora	32.7%	52
Buffalo Hospital	Buffalo	33.0%	88
Sanford Luverne Medical Center	Luverne	33.3%	57
Fairview Lakes Health Services	Wyoming	33.5%	173
Abbott Northwestern Hospital	Minneapolis	34.8%	302
Douglas County Hospital	Alexandria	35.1%	222
Austin Medical Center	Austin	35.3%	51
Deer River Healthcare Center[1]	Deer River	36.0%	25
Saint Josephs Area Health Services	Park Rapids	36.1%	83
Grand Itasca Clinic and Hospital	Grand Rapids	36.5%	85
Lake Region Healthcare Corporation	Fergus Falls	36.5%	85
Fairview Red Wing Hospital	Red Wing	37.1%	89
Virginia Regional Medical Center	Virginia	37.5%	128
Essentia Health St Joseph's Medical Center	Brainerd	37.6%	210
Glacial Ridge Hospital[1]	Glenwood	38.5%	26
Sanford Worthington Medical Center	Worthington	38.6%	44
Saint Joseph's Hospital	Saint Paul	38.7%	62
Unity Hospital[1]	Fridley	39.3%	28
Saint Francis Regional Medical Center	Shakopee	39.8%	103
Tri County Hospital	Wadena	40.0%	40
Healtheast St John's Hospital	Maplewood	41.0%	166
Fairview Ridges Hospital	Burnsville	41.4%	99
North Country Regional Hospital	Bemidji	41.6%	101
Healtheast Woodwinds Hospital	Woodbury	42.1%	133
Univ of Minnesota Med Ctr-Fairview	Minneapolis	42.3%	104
United Hospital	Saint Paul	43.1%	109
Cambridge Medical Center	Cambridge	43.3%	120
Saint Cloud Hospital	Saint Cloud	43.3%	277
Fairview Southdale Hospital	Edina	44.4%	108
Park Nicollet Methodist Hospital	Saint Louis Park	45.0%	300
Lakeview Memorial Hospital	Stillwater	45.9%	146
Pipestone County Medical Center[1]	Pipestone	46.2%	26
Glencoe Regional Health Services	Glencoe	47.7%	44
Winona Health Services	Winona	47.7%	44
Mercy Hospital	Coon Rapids	48.3%	58
Saint Gabriels Hospital	Little Falls	48.4%	64
District One Hospital	Faribault	49.2%	61
Community Memorial Hospital	Cloquet	50.0%	32
Ridgeview Medical Center	Waconia	51.0%	147
University Med Ctr-Mesabi/Mesaba	Hibbing	51.9%	106
North Memorial Medical Center	Robbinsdale	54.3%	210
Regions Hospital	Saint Paul	56.9%	320

Survey of Patients' Hospital Experiences

40. Area Around Room 'Always' Quiet at Night

Hospital Name	City	Rate	Cases
Phillips Eye Institute	Minneapolis	88%	(a)
Meeker Memorial Hospital	Litchfield	80%	(a)
Redwood Area Hospital[11]	Redwood Falls	77%	(a)
Paynesville Area Hospital	Paynesville	76%	(a)
Saint Gabriels Hospital	Little Falls	74%	(a)
United Hospital District	Blue Earth	74%	(a)
Lakewood Health System	Staples	73%	300+
Springfield Med Ctr Mayo Health Sys	Springfield	73%	(a)
Bigfork Valley Hospital	Bigfork	71%	(a)
Healtheast Woodwinds Hospital	Woodbury	70%	300+
Regina Medical Center	Hastings	70%	300+
Swift County Benson Hospital[11]	Benson	69%	(a)
Saint Josephs Area Health Services	Park Rapids	68%	300+
Saint Francis Regional Medical Center	Shakopee	67%	300+
Lakeview Memorial Hospital	Stillwater	66%	300+
Rice Memorial Hospital	Willmar	66%	300+
Ridgeview Medical Center	Waconia	66%	300+
Lifecare Medical Center	Roseau	65%	(a)
Queen of Peace Hospital	New Prague	65%	300+
Saint Elizabeth Medical Center	Wabasha	65%	(a)
Sanford Luverne Medical Center	Luverne	65%	(a)
Windom Area Hospital	Windom	65%	(a)
District One Hospital	Faribault	64%	300+
Glencoe Regional Health Services	Glencoe	64%	300+
New River Medical Center	Monticello	64%	300+
Chippewa County Hospital[11]	Montevideo	63%	300+
Cuyuna Regional Medical Center	Crosby	63%	300+
Fairview Red Wing Hospital	Red Wing	63%	300+
Hutchinson Area Health Care	Hutchinson	63%	300+
Lake Region Healthcare Corporation	Fergus Falls	63%	(a)
Rainy Lake Medical Center	Int'l Falls	63%	(a)
Sanford Worthington Medical Center	Worthington	63%	300+
Grand Itasca Clinic and Hospital	Grand Rapids	62%	300+
Mayo Clinic - Saint Marys Hospital	Rochester	62%	300+
Pipestone County Medical Center	Pipestone	62%	(a)
Riverview Hospital	Crookston	62%	(a)
Saint Cloud Hospital	Saint Cloud	62%	300+
Saint Marys Regional Health Center	Detroit Lakes	62%	300+
Essentia Health Fosston	Fosston	61%	(a)
Essentia Health St Joseph's Medical Center	Brainerd	61%	300+
Saint Francis Healthcare Campus	Breckenridge	61%	(a)

NOTE: Hospital profiles are in alphabetical order by state, then city, then hospital within the city; Rankings exclude hospitals with less than 25 cases except for patient surveys which excludes hospitals with less than 100 cases; (a) 100–299 cases; (1) The number of cases is too small to be sure how well a hospital is performing; (2) The hospital indicated that the data submitted for this measure were based on a sample of cases; (3) Data was collected during a shorter time period (fewer quarters) than the maximum possible time for this measure; (4) Suppressed for one or more quarters by CMS; (5) No data is available from the hospital for this measure; (6) Fewer than 100 patients completed the HCAHPS survey. Use these rates with caution, as the number of surveys may be too low to reliably assess hospital performance; (7) Survey results are based on less than 12 months of data; (8) Survey results are not available for this reporting period; (9) No or very few patients were eligible for the HCAHPS survey. The scores shown, if any, reflect a very small number of surveys; (10) A state average was not calculated because too few hospitals in the state submitted data; (11) There were discrepancies in the data collection process; Please refer to the User's Guide for a full explanation of data.

Hospital Name	City	Rate	Cases
Sanford Medical Center Thief River Falls	Thief River Falls	61%	300+
Cambridge Medical Center	Cambridge	60%	300+
Lake City Medical Center Mayo Health System	Lake City	60%	(a)
Mille Lacs Health System	Onamia	60%	(a)
Tri County Hospital	Wadena	60%	300+
University Med Ctr-Mesabi/Mesaba[11]	Hibbing	60%	300+
Avera Marshall Regional Medical Center	Marshall	59%	300+
Ortonville Area Health Services	Ortonville	59%	(a)
Riverwood Healthcare Center	Aitkin	59%	300+
Community Memorial Hospital	Cloquet	58%	300+
Ely Bloomenson Community Hospital	Ely	58%	(a)
Mayo Clinic - Methodist Hospital	Rochester	58%	300+
Naeve Hospital	Albert Lea	58%	300+
New Ulm Medical Center	New Ulm	58%	300+
North Country Regional Hospital	Bemidji	58%	300+
Northfield Hospital	Northfield	58%	300+
Buffalo Hospital	Buffalo	57%	300+
Fairview Northland Regional Hospital	Princeton	57%	300+
Olmsted Medical Center	Rochester	57%	300+
Regions Hospital	Saint Paul	57%	300+
Saint Lukes Hospital	Duluth	57%	300+
Douglas County Hospital	Alexandria	56%	300+
Fairview Ridges Hospital	Burnsville	56%	300+
Mercy Hospital	Coon Rapids	56%	300+
Sanford Canby Medical Center	Canby	56%	(a)
Fairmont Medical Center	Fairmont	55%	300+
Kanabec Hospital	Mora	55%	300+
Owatonna Hospital	Owatonna	54%	300+
Virginia Regional Medical Center	Virginia	54%	300+
Winona Health Services	Winona	54%	300+
Abbott Northwestern Hospital	Minneapolis	52%	300+
Austin Medical Center	Austin	52%	300+
Fairview Lakes Health Services	Wyoming	52%	300+
North Memorial Medical Center	Robbinsdale	52%	300+
Saint Joseph's Hospital	Saint Paul	50%	300+
Unity Hospital	Fridley	50%	300+
Fairview Southdale Hospital	Edina	49%	300+
Healtheast St John's Hospital	Maplewood	49%	300+
Hennepin County Medical Center	Minneapolis	48%	300+
United Hospital	Saint Paul	48%	300+
Univ of Minnesota Med Ctr-Fairview	Minneapolis	47%	300+
Essentia Health Duluth	Duluth	46%	300+
Essentia Health St Mary's Medical Center	Duluth	46%	300+
Immanuel-St Josephs-Mayo Health System	Mankato	44%	300+
Park Nicollet Methodist Hospital	Saint Louis Park	44%	300+

41. Doctors 'Always' Communicated Well

Hospital Name	City	Rate	Cases
Phillips Eye Institute	Minneapolis	91%	(a)
Bigfork Valley Hospital	Bigfork	90%	(a)
Essentia Health Fosston	Fosston	89%	(a)
Mille Lacs Health System	Onamia	88%	(a)
United Hospital District	Blue Earth	88%	(a)
Lakewood Health System	Staples	87%	300+
Saint Francis Healthcare Campus	Breckenridge	87%	(a)
University Med Ctr-Mesabi/Mesaba[11]	Hibbing	87%	300+
Lifecare Medical Center	Roseau	86%	(a)
Springfield Med Ctr Mayo Health Sys	Springfield	86%	(a)
Lakeview Memorial Hospital	Stillwater	85%	300+
Saint Gabriels Hospital	Little Falls	85%	(a)
Chippewa County Hospital[11]	Montevideo	84%	300+
Community Memorial Hospital	Cloquet	84%	300+
Cuyuna Regional Medical Center	Crosby	84%	300+
Glencoe Regional Health Services	Glencoe	84%	300+
Queen of Peace Hospital	New Prague	84%	300+
Saint Elizabeth Medical Center	Wabasha	84%	(a)
Tri County Hospital	Wadena	84%	300+
Windom Area Hospital	Windom	84%	(a)
Essentia Health Duluth	Duluth	83%	300+
Grand Itasca Clinic and Hospital	Grand Rapids	83%	300+
Lake City Medical Center Mayo Health System	Lake City	83%	(a)
Mayo Clinic - Methodist Hospital	Rochester	83%	300+
Meeker Memorial Hospital	Litchfield	83%	(a)
Naeve Hospital	Albert Lea	83%	300+
New Ulm Medical Center	New Ulm	83%	300+
Rainy Lake Medical Center	Int'l Falls	83%	(a)
Riverview Hospital	Crookston	83%	(a)
Sanford Luverne Medical Center	Luverne	83%	(a)
Fairmont Medical Center	Fairmont	82%	300+
Fairview Red Wing Hospital	Red Wing	82%	300+
Hutchinson Area Health Care	Hutchinson	82%	300+
Mayo Clinic - Saint Marys Hospital	Rochester	82%	300+
Ortonville Area Health Services	Ortonville	82%	(a)
Paynesville Area Hospital	Paynesville	82%	(a)
Redwood Area Hospital[11]	Redwood Falls	82%	(a)
Regina Medical Center	Hastings	82%	300+
Rice Memorial Hospital	Willmar	82%	300+
Saint Josephs Area Health Services	Park Rapids	82%	300+
Saint Marys Regional Health Center	Detroit Lakes	82%	300+
District One Hospital	Faribault	81%	300+
Fairview Northland Regional Hospital	Princeton	81%	300+
Lake Region Healthcare Corporation	Fergus Falls	81%	(a)
Northfield Hospital	Northfield	81%	300+
Swift County Benson Hospital[11]	Benson	81%	(a)
Cambridge Medical Center	Cambridge	80%	300+
Douglas County Hospital	Alexandria	80%	300+
Ely Bloomenson Community Hospital	Ely	80%	(a)
Essentia Health St Mary's Medical Center	Duluth	80%	300+
Fairview Lakes Health Services	Wyoming	80%	300+
Olmsted Medical Center	Rochester	80%	300+
Ridgeview Medical Center	Waconia	80%	300+
Saint Cloud Hospital	Saint Cloud	80%	300+
Saint Lukes Hospital	Duluth	80%	300+
Virginia Regional Medical Center	Virginia	80%	300+
Austin Medical Center	Austin	79%	300+
Buffalo Hospital	Buffalo	79%	300+
Essentia Health St Joseph's Medical Center	Brainerd	79%	300+
Pipestone County Medical Center	Pipestone	79%	(a)
Riverwood Healthcare Center	Aitkin	79%	300+
Winona Health Services	Winona	79%	300+
Abbott Northwestern Hospital	Minneapolis	78%	300+
North Country Regional Hospital	Bemidji	78%	300+
Owatonna Hospital	Owatonna	78%	300+
Saint Francis Regional Medical Center	Shakopee	78%	300+
Avera Marshall Regional Medical Center	Marshall	77%	300+
New River Medical Center	Monticello	77%	300+
Regions Hospital	Saint Paul	77%	300+
Sanford Canby Medical Center	Canby	77%	(a)
Fairview Ridges Hospital	Burnsville	76%	300+
Fairview Southdale Hospital	Edina	76%	300+
Healtheast Woodwinds Hospital	Woodbury	76%	300+
Kanabec Hospital	Mora	76%	300+
Sanford Medical Center Thief River Falls	Thief River Falls	76%	300+
Unity Hospital	Fridley	76%	300+
Mercy Hospital	Coon Rapids	75%	300+
Park Nicollet Methodist Hospital	Saint Louis Park	75%	300+
United Hospital	Saint Paul	75%	300+
Sanford Worthington Medical Center	Worthington	74%	300+
North Memorial Medical Center	Robbinsdale	73%	300+
Univ of Minnesota Med Ctr-Fairview	Minneapolis	73%	300+
Healtheast St John's Hospital	Maplewood	72%	300+
Hennepin County Medical Center	Minneapolis	72%	300+
Immanuel-St Josephs-Mayo Health System	Mankato	72%	300+
Saint Joseph's Hospital	Saint Paul	70%	300+

42. Home Recovery Information Given

Hospital Name	City	Rate	Cases
Bigfork Valley Hospital	Bigfork	90%	(a)
Lake Region Healthcare Corporation	Fergus Falls	90%	(a)
Olmsted Medical Center	Rochester	90%	300+
Redwood Area Hospital[11]	Redwood Falls	90%	(a)
Essentia Health Fosston	Fosston	89%	(a)
Lakeview Memorial Hospital	Stillwater	89%	300+
Saint Josephs Area Health Services	Park Rapids	89%	300+
Essentia Health Duluth	Duluth	88%	300+
Healtheast Woodwinds Hospital	Woodbury	88%	300+
Mayo Clinic - Methodist Hospital	Rochester	88%	300+
Mille Lacs Health System	Onamia	88%	(a)
Queen of Peace Hospital	New Prague	88%	300+
Rainy Lake Medical Center	Int'l Falls	88%	(a)
United Hospital District	Blue Earth	88%	(a)
Buffalo Hospital	Buffalo	87%	300+
Cambridge Medical Center	Cambridge	87%	300+
Douglas County Hospital	Alexandria	87%	300+
Fairview Ridges Hospital	Burnsville	87%	300+
Healtheast St John's Hospital	Maplewood	87%	300+
Lakewood Health System	Staples	87%	300+
Mercy Hospital	Coon Rapids	87%	300+
New Ulm Medical Center	New Ulm	87%	300+
Saint Gabriels Hospital	Little Falls	87%	(a)
Abbott Northwestern Hospital	Minneapolis	86%	300+
Cuyuna Regional Medical Center	Crosby	86%	300+
Essentia Health St Joseph's Medical Center	Brainerd	86%	300+
Fairview Red Wing Hospital	Red Wing	86%	300+
Hutchinson Area Health Care	Hutchinson	86%	300+
Lifecare Medical Center	Roseau	86%	(a)
Northfield Hospital	Northfield	86%	300+
Phillips Eye Institute	Minneapolis	86%	(a)
Rice Memorial Hospital	Willmar	86%	300+
Saint Francis Regional Medical Center	Shakopee	86%	300+
Unity Hospital	Fridley	86%	300+
University Med Ctr-Mesabi/Mesaba[11]	Hibbing	86%	300+
Essentia Health St Mary's Medical Center	Duluth	85%	300+
Fairview Northland Regional Hospital	Princeton	85%	300+
Owatonna Hospital	Owatonna	85%	300+
Paynesville Area Hospital	Paynesville	85%	(a)
Regions Hospital	Saint Paul	85%	300+
Riverwood Healthcare Center	Aitkin	85%	300+
Saint Elizabeth Medical Center	Wabasha	85%	(a)
Sanford Canby Medical Center	Canby	85%	(a)
Swift County Benson Hospital[11]	Benson	85%	(a)
Chippewa County Hospital[11]	Montevideo	84%	300+
Fairmont Medical Center	Fairmont	84%	300+
Fairview Southdale Hospital	Edina	84%	300+
Hennepin County Medical Center	Minneapolis	84%	300+
Kanabec Hospital	Mora	84%	300+
Mayo Clinic - Saint Marys Hospital	Rochester	84%	300+
Saint Cloud Hospital	Saint Cloud	84%	300+
Saint Lukes Hospital	Duluth	84%	300+
Sanford Worthington Medical Center	Worthington	84%	300+
Univ of Minnesota Med Ctr-Fairview	Minneapolis	84%	300+
Avera Marshall Regional Medical Center	Marshall	83%	300+
District One Hospital	Faribault	83%	300+
Grand Itasca Clinic and Hospital	Grand Rapids	83%	300+
Meeker Memorial Hospital	Litchfield	83%	(a)
New River Medical Center	Monticello	83%	300+
Regina Medical Center	Hastings	83%	300+
Ridgeview Medical Center	Waconia	83%	300+
Riverview Hospital	Crookston	83%	(a)
Saint Francis Healthcare Campus	Breckenridge	83%	(a)
United Hospital	Saint Paul	83%	300+
Fairview Lakes Health Services	Wyoming	82%	300+
Glencoe Regional Health Services	Glencoe	82%	300+
North Country Regional Hospital	Bemidji	82%	300+
Pipestone County Medical Center	Pipestone	82%	(a)
Saint Joseph's Hospital	Saint Paul	82%	300+
Winona Health Services	Winona	82%	300+
Naeve Hospital	Albert Lea	81%	300+
North Memorial Medical Center	Robbinsdale	81%	300+
Saint Marys Regional Health Center	Detroit Lakes	81%	300+
Tri County Hospital	Wadena	81%	300+
Virginia Regional Medical Center	Virginia	81%	300+
Community Memorial Hospital	Cloquet	80%	300+
Lake City Medical Center Mayo Health System	Lake City	80%	(a)
Windom Area Hospital	Windom	80%	(a)
Immanuel-St Josephs-Mayo Health System	Mankato	79%	300+
Austin Medical Center	Austin	78%	300+
Springfield Med Ctr Mayo Health Sys	Springfield	78%	(a)
Sanford Luverne Medical Center	Luverne	77%	(a)
Sanford Medical Center Thief River Falls	Thief River Falls	77%	300+
Park Nicollet Methodist Hospital	Saint Louis Park	76%	300+
Ortonville Area Health Services	Ortonville	75%	(a)
Ely Bloomenson Community Hospital	Ely	73%	(a)

43. Hospital Given 9 or 10 on 10 Point Scale

Hospital Name	City	Rate	Cases
Bigfork Valley Hospital	Bigfork	88%	(a)
Phillips Eye Institute	Minneapolis	86%	(a)
Lakewood Health System	Staples	85%	300+
Saint Elizabeth Medical Center	Wabasha	83%	(a)
Swift County Benson Hospital[11]	Benson	83%	(a)
Lakeview Memorial Hospital	Stillwater	81%	300+
Mayo Clinic - Saint Marys Hospital	Rochester	81%	300+
United Hospital District	Blue Earth	81%	(a)
Mayo Clinic - Methodist Hospital	Rochester	80%	300+
Springfield Med Ctr Mayo Health Sys	Springfield	80%	(a)
Ridgeview Medical Center	Waconia	79%	300+
Cuyuna Regional Medical Center	Crosby	78%	300+
Essentia Health Fosston	Fosston	78%	(a)
Healtheast Woodwinds Hospital	Woodbury	78%	300+
Queen of Peace Hospital	New Prague	78%	300+
Paynesville Area Hospital	Paynesville	77%	(a)
Riverwood Healthcare Center	Aitkin	77%	300+
Saint Gabriels Hospital	Little Falls	77%	(a)
Lake Region Healthcare Corporation	Fergus Falls	76%	(a)
Saint Josephs Area Health Services	Park Rapids	76%	300+
Meeker Memorial Hospital	Litchfield	75%	(a)
Sanford Luverne Medical Center	Luverne	75%	(a)
Douglas County Hospital	Alexandria	74%	300+
Fairview Northland Regional Hospital	Princeton	73%	300+
Lake City Medical Center Mayo Health System	Lake City	73%	(a)
Olmsted Medical Center	Rochester	73%	300+
Saint Cloud Hospital	Saint Cloud	73%	300+
Saint Francis Healthcare Campus	Breckenridge	73%	(a)
Sanford Canby Medical Center	Canby	73%	(a)
Redwood Area Hospital[11]	Redwood Falls	72%	(a)
Regina Medical Center	Hastings	72%	300+
Windom Area Hospital	Windom	72%	(a)
Glencoe Regional Health Services	Glencoe	71%	300+
Rice Memorial Hospital	Willmar	71%	300+
Tri County Hospital	Wadena	71%	300+
Abbott Northwestern Hospital	Minneapolis	70%	300+
Fairview Red Wing Hospital	Red Wing	70%	300+
Hutchinson Area Health Care	Hutchinson	70%	300+
Naeve Hospital	Albert Lea	70%	300+
Northfield Hospital	Northfield	70%	300+
Saint Francis Regional Medical Center	Shakopee	70%	300+
Saint Lukes Hospital	Duluth	70%	300+
District One Hospital	Faribault	69%	300+
Essentia Health St Joseph's Medical Center	Brainerd	69%	300+

NOTE: Hospital profiles are in alphabetical order by state, then city, then hospital within the city; Rankings exclude hospitals with less than 25 cases except for patient surveys which excludes hospitals with less than 100 cases; (a) 100–299 cases; (1) The number of cases is too small to be sure how well a hospital is performing; (2) The hospital indicated that the data submitted for this measure were based on a sample of cases; (3) Data was collected during a shorter time period (fewer quarters) than the maximum possible time for this measure; (4) Suppressed for one or more quarters by CMS; (5) No data is available from the hospital for this measure; (6) Fewer than 100 patients completed the HCAHPS survey. Use these rates with caution, as the number of surveys may be too low to reliably assess hospital performance; (7) Survey results are based on less than 12 months of data; (8) Survey results are not available for this reporting period; (9) No or very few patients were eligible for the HCAHPS survey. The scores shown, if any, reflect a very small number of surveys; (10) A state average was not calculated because too few hospitals in the state submitted data; (11) There were discrepancies in the data collection process; Please refer to the User's Guide for a full explanation of data.

Grand Itasca Clinic and Hospital	Grand Rapids	69%	300+
Lifecare Medical Center	Roseau	69%	(a)
Community Memorial Hospital	Cloquet	68%	300+
Essentia Health Duluth	Duluth	68%	300+
Fairview Lakes Health Services	Wyoming	68%	300+
Fairview Ridges Hospital	Burnsville	68%	300+
Saint Marys Regional Health Center	Detroit Lakes	68%	300+
University Med Ctr-Mesabi/Mesaba[11]	Hibbing	68%	300+
Chippewa County Hospital[11]	Montevideo	67%	300+
Mille Lacs Health System	Onamia	67%	(a)
Ortonville Area Health Services	Ortonville	67%	(a)
Riverview Hospital	Crookston	67%	(a)
Healtheast St John's Hospital	Maplewood	66%	300+
Regions Hospital	Saint Paul	66%	300+
Buffalo Hospital	Buffalo	65%	300+
Cambridge Medical Center	Cambridge	65%	300+
Kanabec Hospital	Mora	65%	300+
Mercy Hospital	Coon Rapids	65%	300+
New Ulm Medical Center	New Ulm	65%	300+
Sanford Worthington Medical Center	Worthington	65%	300+
Virginia Regional Medical Center	Virginia	65%	300+
Austin Medical Center	Austin	64%	300+
Ely Bloomenson Community Hospital	Ely	64%	(a)
Fairmont Medical Center	Fairmont	63%	300+
New River Medical Center	Monticello	63%	300+
North Country Regional Hospital	Bemidji	63%	300+
Rainy Lake Medical Center	Int'l Falls	63%	(a)
Saint Joseph's Hospital	Saint Paul	63%	300+
United Hospital	Saint Paul	63%	300+
Pipestone County Medical Center	Pipestone	62%	(a)
Univ of Minnesota Med Ctr-Fairview	Minneapolis	62%	300+
Avera Marshall Regional Medical Center	Marshall	61%	300+
Essentia Health St Mary's Medical Center	Duluth	61%	300+
Fairview Southdale Hospital	Edina	61%	300+
Winona Health Services	Winona	61%	300+
Hennepin County Medical Center	Minneapolis	60%	300+
Owatonna Hospital	Owatonna	60%	300+
Unity Hospital	Fridley	60%	300+
Immanuel-St Josephs-Mayo Health System	Mankato	58%	300+
North Memorial Medical Center	Robbinsdale	56%	300+
Sanford Medical Center Thief River Falls	Thief River Falls	55%	300+
Park Nicollet Methodist Hospital	Saint Louis Park	54%	300+

44. Meds 'Always' Explained Before Given

Hospital Name	City	Rate	Cases
Bigfork Valley Hospital	Bigfork	80%	(a)
Phillips Eye Institute	Minneapolis	76%	(a)
Lakeview Memorial Hospital	Stillwater	72%	300+
Queen of Peace Hospital	New Prague	72%	300+
Saint Elizabeth Medical Center	Wabasha	72%	(a)
Saint Francis Healthcare Campus	Breckenridge	72%	(a)
Cuyuna Regional Medical Center	Crosby	69%	300+
Lifecare Medical Center	Roseau	68%	(a)
Saint Josephs Area Health Services	Park Rapids	68%	(a)
Tri County Hospital	Wadena	68%	300+
Lake Region Healthcare Corporation	Fergus Falls	67%	(a)
Mayo Clinic - Saint Marys Hospital	Rochester	67%	300+
Naeve Hospital	Albert Lea	67%	300+
Olmsted Medical Center	Rochester	67%	300+
Redwood Area Hospital[11]	Redwood Falls	67%	(a)
United Hospital District	Blue Earth	67%	(a)
University Med Ctr-Mesabi/Mesaba[11]	Hibbing	67%	300+
Community Memorial Hospital	Cloquet	66%	300+
Lakewood Health System	Staples	66%	300+
Mille Lacs Health System	Onamia	66%	(a)
Paynesville Area Hospital	Paynesville	66%	(a)
Essentia Health Fosston	Fosston	65%	(a)
Healtheast Woodwinds Hospital	Woodbury	65%	300+
Kanabec Hospital	Mora	65%	300+
Mayo Clinic - Methodist Hospital	Rochester	65%	300+
Saint Cloud Hospital	Saint Cloud	65%	300+
Saint Gabriels Hospital	Little Falls	65%	(a)
Saint Lukes Hospital	Duluth	65%	300+
Essentia Health Duluth	Duluth	64%	300+
Fairview Northland Regional Hospital	Princeton	64%	300+
Pipestone County Medical Center	Pipestone	64%	(a)
Regina Medical Center	Hastings	64%	300+
Rice Memorial Hospital	Willmar	64%	300+
Ridgeview Medical Center	Waconia	64%	300+
Austin Medical Center	Austin	63%	300+
Douglas County Hospital	Alexandria	63%	300+
Fairview Lakes Health Services	Wyoming	63%	300+
Rainy Lake Medical Center	Int'l Falls	63%	(a)
Riverwood Healthcare Center	Aitkin	63%	300+
Sanford Canby Medical Center	Canby	63%	(a)
Sanford Luverne Medical Center	Luverne	63%	(a)
Springfield Med Ctr Mayo Health Sys	Springfield	63%	(a)
District One Hospital	Faribault	62%	300+
Essentia Health St Joseph's Medical Center	Brainerd	62%	300+
Fairview Red Wing Hospital	Red Wing	62%	300+
Northfield Hospital	Northfield	62%	300+
Buffalo Hospital	Buffalo	61%	300+
Grand Itasca Clinic and Hospital	Grand Rapids	61%	300+
Hutchinson Area Health Care	Hutchinson	61%	300+
Meeker Memorial Hospital	Litchfield	61%	(a)
New Ulm Medical Center	New Ulm	61%	300+
Riverview Hospital	Crookston	61%	(a)
Saint Francis Regional Medical Center	Shakopee	61%	300+
Saint Marys Regional Health Center	Detroit Lakes	61%	300+
Sanford Worthington Medical Center	Worthington	61%	300+
Windom Area Hospital	Windom	61%	(a)
Cambridge Medical Center	Cambridge	60%	300+
Fairview Ridges Hospital	Burnsville	60%	300+
Mercy Hospital	Coon Rapids	60%	300+
New River Medical Center	Monticello	60%	300+
Regions Hospital	Saint Paul	60%	300+
Virginia Regional Medical Center	Virginia	60%	300+
Fairmont Medical Center	Fairmont	59%	300+
Lake City Medical Center Mayo Health System	Lake City	59%	(a)
North Country Regional Hospital	Bemidji	59%	300+
Owatonna Hospital	Owatonna	59%	300+
Univ of Minnesota Med Ctr-Fairview	Minneapolis	59%	300+
Abbott Northwestern Hospital	Minneapolis	58%	300+
Fairview Southdale Hospital	Edina	58%	300+
Glencoe Regional Health Services	Glencoe	58%	300+
Park Nicollet Methodist Hospital	Saint Louis Park	58%	300+
Swift County Benson Hospital[11]	Benson	58%	(a)
Ely Bloomenson Community Hospital	Ely	57%	(a)
Essentia Health St Mary's Medical Center	Duluth	57%	300+
Immanuel-St Josephs-Mayo Health System	Mankato	57%	300+
Sanford Medical Center Thief River Falls	Thief River Falls	57%	300+
United Hospital	Saint Paul	57%	300+
Unity Hospital	Fridley	56%	300+
Avera Marshall Regional Medical Center	Marshall	55%	300+
Healtheast St John's Hospital	Maplewood	55%	300+
Ortonville Area Health Services	Ortonville	55%	(a)
Winona Health Services	Winona	55%	300+
North Memorial Medical Center	Robbinsdale	54%	300+
Chippewa County Hospital[11]	Montevideo	53%	300+
Hennepin County Medical Center	Minneapolis	53%	300+
Saint Joseph's Hospital	Saint Paul	52%	300+

45. Nurses 'Always' Communicated Well

Hospital Name	City	Rate	Cases
Phillips Eye Institute	Minneapolis	92%	(a)
Bigfork Valley Hospital	Bigfork	88%	(a)
United Hospital District	Blue Earth	88%	(a)
Queen of Peace Hospital	New Prague	87%	300+
Lakewood Health System	Staples	85%	300+
Lakeview Memorial Hospital	Stillwater	84%	300+
Paynesville Area Hospital	Paynesville	84%	(a)
Windom Area Hospital	Windom	84%	(a)
Cuyuna Regional Medical Center	Crosby	83%	300+
Essentia Health Fosston	Fosston	83%	(a)
Saint Josephs Area Health Services	Park Rapids	83%	300+
Naeve Hospital	Albert Lea	82%	300+
Springfield Med Ctr Mayo Health Sys	Springfield	82%	(a)
Lake Region Healthcare Corporation	Fergus Falls	81%	(a)
Mayo Clinic - Methodist Hospital	Rochester	81%	300+
Mille Lacs Health System	Onamia	81%	(a)
Redwood Area Hospital[11]	Redwood Falls	81%	(a)
Saint Gabriels Hospital	Little Falls	81%	(a)
Sanford Canby Medical Center	Canby	81%	(a)
Swift County Benson Hospital[11]	Benson	81%	(a)
University Med Ctr-Mesabi/Mesaba[11]	Hibbing	81%	300+
Meeker Memorial Hospital	Litchfield	80%	(a)
Saint Elizabeth Medical Center	Wabasha	80%	(a)
Buffalo Hospital	Buffalo	79%	300+
Grand Itasca Clinic and Hospital	Grand Rapids	79%	300+
Mayo Clinic - Saint Marys Hospital	Rochester	79%	300+
Saint Francis Healthcare Campus	Breckenridge	79%	(a)
Tri County Hospital	Wadena	79%	300+
Community Memorial Hospital	Cloquet	78%	300+
Essentia Health St Joseph's Medical Center	Brainerd	78%	300+
Fairview Northland Regional Hospital	Princeton	78%	300+
Regina Medical Center	Hastings	78%	300+
Saint Cloud Hospital	Saint Cloud	78%	300+
Saint Marys Regional Health Center	Detroit Lakes	78%	300+
Sanford Luverne Medical Center	Luverne	78%	(a)
Virginia Regional Medical Center	Virginia	78%	300+
Cambridge Medical Center	Cambridge	77%	300+
Douglas County Hospital	Alexandria	77%	300+
Essentia Health Duluth	Duluth	77%	300+
Fairview Red Wing Hospital	Red Wing	77%	300+
Lake City Medical Center Mayo Health System	Lake City	77%	(a)
New River Medical Center	Monticello	77%	300+
Ortonville Area Health Services	Ortonville	77%	(a)
Rice Memorial Hospital	Willmar	77%	300+
Riverwood Healthcare Center	Aitkin	77%	300+
Saint Francis Regional Medical Center	Shakopee	77%	300+
Austin Medical Center	Austin	76%	300+
District One Hospital	Faribault	76%	300+
Fairview Lakes Health Services	Wyoming	76%	300+
Healtheast Woodwinds Hospital	Woodbury	76%	300+
Hutchinson Area Health Care	Hutchinson	76%	300+
Mercy Hospital	Coon Rapids	76%	300+
Rainy Lake Medical Center	Int'l Falls	76%	(a)
Riverview Hospital	Crookston	76%	(a)
Sanford Worthington Medical Center	Worthington	76%	300+
Abbott Northwestern Hospital	Minneapolis	75%	300+
Ely Bloomenson Community Hospital	Ely	75%	(a)
Glencoe Regional Health Services	Glencoe	75%	300+
Kanabec Hospital	Mora	75%	300+
Lifecare Medical Center	Roseau	75%	(a)
Olmsted Medical Center	Rochester	75%	300+
Ridgeview Medical Center	Waconia	75%	300+
Saint Lukes Hospital	Duluth	75%	300+
Fairmont Medical Center	Fairmont	74%	300+
New Ulm Medical Center	New Ulm	74%	300+
Pipestone County Medical Center	Pipestone	74%	(a)
Regions Hospital	Saint Paul	74%	300+
Avera Marshall Regional Medical Center	Marshall	73%	300+
Essentia Health St Mary's Medical Center	Duluth	73%	300+
Owatonna Hospital	Owatonna	73%	300+
Sanford Medical Center Thief River Falls	Thief River Falls	73%	300+
United Hospital	Saint Paul	73%	300+
Winona Health Services	Winona	73%	300+
Fairview Ridges Hospital	Burnsville	72%	300+
Healtheast St John's Hospital	Maplewood	72%	300+
North Country Regional Hospital	Bemidji	72%	300+
Northfield Hospital	Northfield	72%	300+
Unity Hospital	Fridley	72%	300+
Chippewa County Hospital[11]	Montevideo	71%	300+
Fairview Southdale Hospital	Edina	71%	300+
Univ of Minnesota Med Ctr-Fairview	Minneapolis	70%	300+
Immanuel-St Josephs-Mayo Health System	Mankato	69%	300+
Saint Joseph's Hospital	Saint Paul	69%	300+
North Memorial Medical Center	Robbinsdale	68%	300+
Hennepin County Medical Center	Minneapolis	65%	300+
Park Nicollet Methodist Hospital	Saint Louis Park	65%	300+

46. Pain 'Always' Well Controlled

Hospital Name	City	Rate	Cases
Bigfork Valley Hospital	Bigfork	83%	(a)
Phillips Eye Institute	Minneapolis	79%	(a)
Ely Bloomenson Community Hospital	Ely	78%	(a)
Essentia Health Fosston	Fosston	77%	(a)
Lakeview Memorial Hospital	Stillwater	77%	300+
Lakewood Health System	Staples	77%	300+
United Hospital District	Blue Earth	77%	(a)
Queen of Peace Hospital	New Prague	76%	300+
Riverwood Healthcare Center	Aitkin	75%	300+
Lake Region Healthcare Corporation	Fergus Falls	74%	(a)
Saint Gabriels Hospital	Little Falls	74%	(a)
Saint Josephs Area Health Services	Park Rapids	74%	300+
Swift County Benson Hospital[11]	Benson	74%	(a)
Fairview Northland Regional Hospital	Princeton	73%	300+
Mayo Clinic - Saint Marys Hospital	Rochester	73%	300+
Meeker Memorial Hospital	Litchfield	73%	(a)
Saint Francis Healthcare Campus	Breckenridge	73%	(a)
Fairview Red Wing Hospital	Red Wing	72%	300+
Sanford Luverne Medical Center	Luverne	72%	(a)
Grand Itasca Clinic and Hospital	Grand Rapids	71%	300+
Paynesville Area Hospital	Paynesville	71%	(a)
Saint Elizabeth Medical Center	Wabasha	71%	(a)
Saint Marys Regional Health Center	Detroit Lakes	71%	300+
Tri County Hospital	Wadena	71%	300+
University Med Ctr-Mesabi/Mesaba[11]	Hibbing	71%	300+
Virginia Regional Medical Center	Virginia	71%	300+
Cuyuna Regional Medical Center	Crosby	70%	300+
District One Hospital	Faribault	70%	300+
Douglas County Hospital	Alexandria	70%	300+
Essentia Health Duluth	Duluth	70%	300+
Essentia Health St Joseph's Medical Center	Brainerd	70%	300+
Fairview Lakes Health Services	Wyoming	70%	300+
Lake City Medical Center Mayo Health System	Lake City	70%	(a)
Lifecare Medical Center	Roseau	70%	(a)
Naeve Hospital	Albert Lea	70%	300+
New River Medical Center	Monticello	70%	300+
Redwood Area Hospital[11]	Redwood Falls	70%	(a)
Regina Medical Center	Hastings	70%	300+
Rice Memorial Hospital	Willmar	70%	300+
Community Memorial Hospital	Cloquet	69%	300+
Fairmont Medical Center	Fairmont	69%	300+
Healtheast Woodwinds Hospital	Woodbury	69%	300+
Hutchinson Area Health Care	Hutchinson	69%	300+
Mayo Clinic - Methodist Hospital	Rochester	69%	300+
Mille Lacs Health System	Onamia	69%	(a)
Olmsted Medical Center	Rochester	69%	300+
Rainy Lake Medical Center	Int'l Falls	69%	(a)

NOTE: Hospital profiles are in alphabetical order by state, then city, then hospital within the city; Rankings exclude hospitals with less than 25 cases except for patient surveys which excludes hospitals with less than 100 cases; (a) 100–299 cases; (1) The number of cases is too small to be sure how well a hospital is performing; (2) The hospital indicated that the data submitted for this measure were based on a sample of cases; (3) Data was collected during a shorter time period (fewer quarters) than the maximum possible time for this measure; (4) Suppressed for one or more quarters by CMS; (5) No data is available from the hospital for this measure; (6) Fewer than 100 patients completed the HCAHPS survey. Use these rates with caution, as the number of surveys may be too low to reliably assess hospital performance; (7) Survey results are based on less than 12 months of data; (8) Survey results are not available for this reporting period; (9) No or very few patients were eligible for the HCAHPS survey. The scores shown, if any, reflect a very small number of surveys; (10) A state average was not calculated because too few hospitals in the state submitted data; (11) There were discrepancies in the data collection process; Please refer to the User's Guide for a full explanation of data.

Hospital Name	City	Rate	Cases
Saint Cloud Hospital	Saint Cloud	69%	300+
Saint Francis Regional Medical Center	Shakopee	69%	300+
Springfield Med Ctr Mayo Health Sys	Springfield	69%	(a)
Windom Area Hospital	Windom	69%	(a)
Buffalo Hospital	Buffalo	68%	300+
Healtheast St John's Hospital	Maplewood	68%	300+
Kanabec Hospital	Mora	68%	300+
Abbott Northwestern Hospital	Minneapolis	67%	300+
Avera Marshall Regional Medical Center	Marshall	67%	300+
Cambridge Medical Center	Cambridge	67%	300+
Essentia Health St Mary's Medical Center	Duluth	67%	300+
Glencoe Regional Health Services	Glencoe	67%	300+
Mercy Hospital	Coon Rapids	67%	300+
Northfield Hospital	Northfield	67%	300+
Owatonna Hospital	Owatonna	67%	300+
Pipestone County Medical Center	Pipestone	67%	(a)
Sanford Medical Center Thief River Falls	Thief River Falls	67%	300+
Austin Medical Center	Austin	66%	300+
North Memorial Medical Center	Robbinsdale	66%	300+
Ridgeview Medical Center	Waconia	66%	300+
Saint Lukes Hospital	Duluth	66%	300+
United Hospital	Saint Paul	66%	300+
Regions Hospital	Saint Paul	65%	300+
Sanford Worthington Medical Center	Worthington	65%	300+
Univ of Minnesota Med Ctr-Fairview	Minneapolis	65%	300+
Fairview Southdale Hospital	Edina	64%	300+
New Ulm Medical Center	New Ulm	64%	300+
North Country Regional Hospital	Bemidji	64%	300+
Ortonville Area Health Services	Ortonville	64%	(a)
Park Nicollet Methodist Hospital	Saint Louis Park	64%	300+
Unity Hospital	Fridley	64%	300+
Winona Health Services	Winona	63%	300+
Chippewa County Hospital[11]	Montevideo	62%	300+
Fairview Ridges Hospital	Burnsville	62%	300+
Immanuel-St Josephs-Mayo Health System	Mankato	62%	300+
Riverview Hospital	Crookston	61%	(a)
Hennepin County Medical Center	Minneapolis	60%	300+
Saint Joseph's Hospital	Saint Paul	59%	300+
Sanford Canby Medical Center	Canby	59%	(a)

47. Room and Bathroom 'Always' Clean

Hospital Name	City	Rate	Cases
Bigfork Valley Hospital	Bigfork	93%	(a)
Springfield Med Ctr Mayo Health Sys	Springfield	93%	(a)
Phillips Eye Institute	Minneapolis	89%	(a)
Queen of Peace Hospital	New Prague	88%	300+
Saint Elizabeth Medical Center	Wabasha	87%	(a)
Swift County Benson Hospital[11]	Benson	87%	(a)
Redwood Area Hospital[11]	Redwood Falls	86%	(a)
United Hospital District	Blue Earth	86%	(a)
Paynesville Area Hospital	Paynesville	84%	(a)
Riverwood Healthcare Center	Aitkin	84%	300+
Windom Area Hospital	Windom	84%	(a)
Lake City Medical Center Mayo Health System	Lake City	83%	(a)
Lake Region Healthcare Corporation	Fergus Falls	83%	(a)
Meeker Memorial Hospital	Litchfield	83%	(a)
Ridgeview Medical Center	Waconia	83%	300+
Sanford Worthington Medical Center	Worthington	83%	300+
Douglas County Hospital	Alexandria	82%	300+
Lakewood Health System	Staples	82%	300+
Lifecare Medical Center	Roseau	82%	(a)
Naeve Hospital	Albert Lea	81%	300+
New River Medical Center	Monticello	81%	300+
Saint Gabriels Hospital	Little Falls	81%	(a)
Sanford Luverne Medical Center	Luverne	81%	(a)
Tri County Hospital	Wadena	81%	300+
Austin Medical Center	Austin	80%	300+
Essentia Health Fosston	Fosston	80%	(a)
Glencoe Regional Health Services	Glencoe	79%	300+
Saint Josephs Area Health Services	Park Rapids	79%	300+
Sanford Canby Medical Center	Canby	79%	(a)
Ely Bloomenson Community Hospital	Ely	78%	(a)
Pipestone County Medical Center	Pipestone	78%	(a)
Saint Francis Healthcare Campus	Breckenridge	78%	(a)
Community Memorial Hospital	Cloquet	77%	300+
Cuyuna Regional Medical Center	Crosby	77%	300+
Essentia Health St Joseph's Medical Center	Brainerd	77%	300+
Fairview Northland Regional Hospital	Princeton	77%	300+
Lakeview Memorial Hospital	Stillwater	77%	300+
Ortonville Area Health Services	Ortonville	77%	(a)
Saint Marys Regional Health Center	Detroit Lakes	77%	300+
Fairview Red Wing Hospital	Red Wing	76%	300+
Mille Lacs Health System	Onamia	76%	(a)
University Med Ctr-Mesabi/Mesaba[11]	Hibbing	76%	300+
Virginia Regional Medical Center	Virginia	76%	300+
Buffalo Hospital	Buffalo	75%	300+
District One Hospital	Faribault	75%	300+
Kanabec Hospital	Mora	75%	300+
New Ulm Medical Center	New Ulm	75%	300+
Rainy Lake Medical Center	Int'l Falls	75%	(a)
Saint Cloud Hospital	Saint Cloud	75%	300+
Saint Francis Regional Medical Center	Shakopee	75%	300+
Sanford Medical Center Thief River Falls	Thief River Falls	75%	300+
Chippewa County Hospital[11]	Montevideo	74%	300+
Hutchinson Area Health Care	Hutchinson	74%	300+
Mayo Clinic - Saint Marys Hospital	Rochester	74%	300+
Fairview Lakes Health Services	Wyoming	73%	300+
Rice Memorial Hospital	Willmar	73%	300+
Grand Itasca Clinic and Hospital	Grand Rapids	72%	300+
Regina Medical Center	Hastings	72%	300+
Avera Marshall Regional Medical Center	Marshall	71%	300+
North Country Regional Hospital	Bemidji	71%	300+
Winona Health Services	Winona	71%	300+
Essentia Health Duluth	Duluth	70%	300+
Fairmont Medical Center	Fairmont	70%	300+
Healtheast St John's Hospital	Maplewood	70%	300+
Healtheast Woodwinds Hospital	Woodbury	70%	300+
Olmsted Medical Center	Rochester	70%	300+
Owatonna Hospital	Owatonna	70%	300+
Regions Hospital	Saint Paul	70%	300+
Riverview Hospital	Crookston	70%	(a)
Cambridge Medical Center	Cambridge	69%	300+
Fairview Ridges Hospital	Burnsville	68%	300+
Mayo Clinic - Methodist Hospital	Rochester	68%	300+
Mercy Hospital	Coon Rapids	68%	300+
Saint Lukes Hospital	Duluth	68%	300+
Immanuel-St Josephs-Mayo Health System	Mankato	67%	300+
Abbott Northwestern Hospital	Minneapolis	65%	300+
Fairview Southdale Hospital	Edina	65%	300+
Northfield Hospital	Northfield	65%	300+
Unity Hospital	Fridley	64%	300+
Hennepin County Medical Center	Minneapolis	63%	300+
Saint Joseph's Hospital	Saint Paul	63%	300+
United Hospital	Saint Paul	63%	300+
Univ of Minnesota Med Ctr-Fairview	Minneapolis	62%	300+
North Memorial Medical Center	Robbinsdale	60%	300+
Essentia Health St Mary's Medical Center	Duluth	59%	300+
Park Nicollet Methodist Hospital	Saint Louis Park	57%	300+

48. Timely Help 'Always' Received

Hospital Name	City	Rate	Cases
Phillips Eye Institute	Minneapolis	94%	(a)
Bigfork Valley Hospital	Bigfork	93%	(a)
Queen of Peace Hospital	New Prague	85%	300+
Saint Elizabeth Medical Center	Wabasha	84%	(a)
Redwood Area Hospital[11]	Redwood Falls	82%	(a)
Springfield Med Ctr Mayo Health Sys	Springfield	82%	(a)
Swift County Benson Hospital[11]	Benson	82%	(a)
Lakeview Memorial Hospital	Stillwater	79%	300+
Paynesville Area Hospital	Paynesville	79%	(a)
United Hospital District	Blue Earth	79%	(a)
Ely Bloomenson Community Hospital	Ely	77%	(a)
Saint Gabriels Hospital	Little Falls	77%	(a)
Essentia Health Fosston	Fosston	76%	(a)
Lakewood Health System	Staples	76%	300+
Riverwood Healthcare Center	Aitkin	76%	300+
Sanford Luverne Medical Center	Luverne	76%	(a)
Community Memorial Hospital	Cloquet	75%	300+
Fairview Red Wing Hospital	Red Wing	75%	300+
Cuyuna Regional Medical Center	Crosby	74%	300+
Lifecare Medical Center	Roseau	74%	(a)
Mille Lacs Health System	Onamia	74%	(a)
Rainy Lake Medical Center	Int'l Falls	74%	(a)
Windom Area Hospital	Windom	74%	(a)
Cambridge Medical Center	Cambridge	73%	300+
Meeker Memorial Hospital	Litchfield	73%	(a)
Regina Medical Center	Hastings	73%	300+
Saint Marys Regional Health Center	Detroit Lakes	73%	300+
Tri County Hospital	Wadena	73%	300+
District One Hospital	Faribault	72%	300+
Lake Region Healthcare Corporation	Fergus Falls	72%	(a)
Saint Francis Healthcare Campus	Breckenridge	72%	(a)
Virginia Regional Medical Center	Virginia	72%	300+
Fairview Lakes Health Services	Wyoming	71%	300+
Fairview Northland Regional Hospital	Princeton	71%	300+
Grand Itasca Clinic and Hospital	Grand Rapids	71%	300+
Kanabec Hospital	Mora	71%	300+
Naeve Hospital	Albert Lea	71%	300+
New Ulm Medical Center	New Ulm	71%	300+
Rice Memorial Hospital	Willmar	71%	300+
Saint Cloud Hospital	Saint Cloud	71%	300+
Saint Josephs Area Health Services	Park Rapids	71%	300+
Essentia Health St Joseph's Medical Center	Brainerd	70%	300+
Lake City Medical Center Mayo Health System	Lake City	70%	(a)
Mayo Clinic - Saint Marys Hospital	Rochester	70%	300+
Olmsted Medical Center	Rochester	70%	300+
Sanford Canby Medical Center	Canby	70%	(a)
Douglas County Hospital	Alexandria	69%	300+
Ortonville Area Health Services	Ortonville	69%	(a)
Ridgeview Medical Center	Waconia	69%	300+
Riverview Hospital	Crookston	69%	(a)
Sanford Worthington Medical Center	Worthington	69%	300+
Essentia Health Duluth	Duluth	68%	300+
Mayo Clinic - Methodist Hospital	Rochester	68%	300+
Saint Francis Regional Medical Center	Shakopee	68%	300+
University Med Ctr-Mesabi/Mesaba[11]	Hibbing	68%	300+
Buffalo Hospital	Buffalo	67%	300+
Healtheast Woodwinds Hospital	Woodbury	67%	300+
Owatonna Hospital	Owatonna	67%	300+
Glencoe Regional Health Services	Glencoe	66%	300+
Hutchinson Area Health Care	Hutchinson	66%	300+
New River Medical Center	Monticello	66%	300+
Abbott Northwestern Hospital	Minneapolis	64%	300+
Chippewa County Hospital[11]	Montevideo	64%	300+
Northfield Hospital	Northfield	64%	300+
Sanford Medical Center Thief River Falls	Thief River Falls	64%	300+
Winona Health Services	Winona	64%	300+
Mercy Hospital	Coon Rapids	63%	300+
Austin Medical Center	Austin	62%	300+
Essentia Health St Mary's Medical Center	Duluth	62%	300+
Fairview Ridges Hospital	Burnsville	62%	300+
Regions Hospital	Saint Paul	62%	300+
Pipestone County Medical Center	Pipestone	61%	(a)
Saint Lukes Hospital	Duluth	61%	300+
United Hospital	Saint Paul	61%	300+
Fairmont Medical Center	Fairmont	60%	300+
Avera Marshall Regional Medical Center	Marshall	57%	300+
Fairview Southdale Hospital	Edina	57%	300+
Healtheast St John's Hospital	Maplewood	57%	300+
Immanuel-St Josephs-Mayo Health System	Mankato	57%	300+
North Country Regional Hospital	Bemidji	57%	300+
Unity Hospital	Fridley	57%	300+
Univ of Minnesota Med Ctr-Fairview	Minneapolis	56%	300+
Saint Joseph's Hospital	Saint Paul	53%	300+
North Memorial Medical Center	Robbinsdale	52%	300+
Park Nicollet Methodist Hospital	Saint Louis Park	51%	300+
Hennepin County Medical Center	Minneapolis	48%	300+

49. Would Definitely Recommend Hospital

Hospital Name	City	Rate	Cases
Bigfork Valley Hospital	Bigfork	93%	(a)
Phillips Eye Institute	Minneapolis	93%	(a)
Lakewood Health System	Staples	88%	300+
Cuyuna Regional Medical Center	Crosby	87%	300+
Mayo Clinic - Saint Marys Hospital	Rochester	85%	300+
Ridgeview Medical Center	Waconia	85%	300+
Lakeview Memorial Hospital	Stillwater	84%	300+
United Hospital District	Blue Earth	84%	(a)
Mayo Clinic - Methodist Hospital	Rochester	83%	300+
Essentia Health Fosston	Fosston	82%	(a)
Olmsted Medical Center	Rochester	82%	300+
Sanford Luverne Medical Center	Luverne	82%	(a)
Springfield Med Ctr Mayo Health Sys	Springfield	82%	(a)
Swift County Benson Hospital[11]	Benson	82%	(a)
Healtheast Woodwinds Hospital	Woodbury	80%	300+
Saint Elizabeth Medical Center	Wabasha	80%	(a)
Queen of Peace Hospital	New Prague	79%	300+
Riverwood Healthcare Center	Aitkin	79%	300+
Abbott Northwestern Hospital	Minneapolis	78%	300+
Saint Josephs Area Health Services	Park Rapids	78%	300+
Lake City Medical Center Mayo Health System	Lake City	77%	(a)
Saint Gabriels Hospital	Little Falls	77%	(a)
Saint Lukes Hospital	Duluth	77%	300+
Meeker Memorial Hospital	Litchfield	76%	(a)
Paynesville Area Hospital	Paynesville	76%	(a)
Riverview Hospital	Crookston	75%	(a)
Saint Cloud Hospital	Saint Cloud	75%	300+
Windom Area Hospital	Windom	75%	(a)
Douglas County Hospital	Alexandria	74%	300+
Glencoe Regional Health Services	Glencoe	74%	300+
Lake Region Healthcare Corporation	Fergus Falls	74%	(a)
Northfield Hospital	Northfield	74%	300+
Regina Medical Center	Hastings	74%	300+
Saint Francis Healthcare Campus	Breckenridge	74%	(a)
Saint Francis Regional Medical Center	Shakopee	74%	300+
Essentia Health St Mary's Medical Center	Duluth	73%	300+
Naeve Hospital	Albert Lea	73%	300+
Fairview Red Wing Hospital	Red Wing	72%	300+
Fairview Ridges Hospital	Burnsville	72%	300+
Hutchinson Area Health Care	Hutchinson	72%	300+
Essentia Health Duluth	Duluth	71%	300+
Fairview Lakes Health Services	Wyoming	71%	300+
Fairview Northland Regional Hospital	Princeton	71%	300+
Mercy Hospital	Coon Rapids	71%	300+
Regions Hospital	Saint Paul	71%	300+
Rice Memorial Hospital	Willmar	71%	300+
Saint Joseph's Hospital	Saint Paul	71%	300+
Tri County Hospital	Wadena	71%	300+
Ortonville Area Health Services	Ortonville	70%	(a)
Redwood Area Hospital[11]	Redwood Falls	70%	(a)

NOTE: Hospital profiles are in alphabetical order by state, then city, then hospital within the city; Rankings exclude hospitals with less than 25 cases except for patient surveys which excludes hospitals with less than 100 cases; (a) 100–299 cases; (1) The number of cases is too small to be sure how well a hospital is performing; (2) The hospital indicated that the data submitted for this measure were based on a sample of cases; (3) Data was collected during a shorter time period (fewer quarters) than the maximum possible time for this measure; (4) Suppressed for one or more quarters by CMS; (5) No data is available from the hospital for this measure; (6) Fewer than 100 patients completed the HCAHPS survey. Use these rates with caution, as the number of surveys may be too low to reliably assess hospital performance; (7) Survey results are based on less than 12 months of data; (8) Survey results are not available for this reporting period; (9) No or very few patients were eligible for the HCAHPS survey. The scores shown, if any, reflect a very small number of surveys; (10) A state average was not calculated because too few hospitals in the state submitted data; (11) There were discrepancies in the data collection process; Please refer to the User's Guide for a full explanation of data.

United Hospital	Saint Paul	70%	300+
Chippewa County Hospital[11]	Montevideo	69%	300+
Community Memorial Hospital	Cloquet	69%	300+
Univ of Minnesota Med Ctr-Fairview	Minneapolis	69%	300+
Essentia Health St Joseph's Medical Center	Brainerd	68%	300+
Fairview Southdale Hospital	Edina	68%	300+
Grand Itasca Clinic and Hospital	Grand Rapids	68%	300+
Healtheast St John's Hospital	Maplewood	68%	300+
Mille Lacs Health System	Onamia	68%	(a)
New River Medical Center	Monticello	68%	300+
New Ulm Medical Center	New Ulm	68%	300+
Saint Marys Regional Health Center	Detroit Lakes	68%	300+
Buffalo Hospital	Buffalo	67%	300+
Cambridge Medical Center	Cambridge	67%	300+
District One Hospital	Faribault	67%	300+
Lifecare Medical Center	Roseau	67%	(a)
Owatonna Hospital	Owatonna	67%	300+
Pipestone County Medical Center	Pipestone	67%	(a)
Avera Marshall Regional Medical Center	Marshall	66%	300+
Kanabec Hospital	Mora	66%	300+
Ely Bloomenson Community Hospital	Ely	65%	(a)
Park Nicollet Methodist Hospital	Saint Louis Park	65%	300+
University Med Ctr-Mesabi/Mesaba[11]	Hibbing	65%	300+
Winona Health Services	Winona	65%	300+
North Memorial Medical Center	Robbinsdale	64%	300+
Sanford Canby Medical Center	Canby	64%	(a)
Sanford Worthington Medical Center	Worthington	64%	300+
Unity Hospital	Fridley	64%	300+
Austin Medical Center	Austin	63%	300+
Fairmont Medical Center	Fairmont	63%	300+
Hennepin County Medical Center	Minneapolis	63%	300+
Rainy Lake Medical Center	Int'l Falls	63%	(a)
North Country Regional Hospital	Bemidji	62%	300+
Virginia Regional Medical Center	Virginia	62%	300+
Immanuel-St Josephs-Mayo Health System	Mankato	59%	300+
Sanford Medical Center Thief River Falls	Thief River Falls	57%	300+

NOTE: Hospital profiles are in alphabetical order by state, then city, then hospital within the city; Rankings exclude hospitals with less than 25 cases except for patient surveys which excludes hospitals with less than 100 cases; (a) 100–299 cases; (1) The number of cases is too small to be sure how well a hospital is performing; (2) The hospital indicated that the data submitted for this measure were based on a sample of cases; (3) Data was collected during a shorter time period (fewer quarters) than the maximum possible time for this measure; (4) Suppressed for one or more quarters by CMS; (5) No data is available from the hospital for this measure; (6) Fewer than 100 patients completed the HCAHPS survey. Use these rates with caution, as the number of surveys may be too low to reliably assess hospital performance; (7) Survey results are based on less than 12 months of data; (8) Survey results are not available for this reporting period; (9) No or very few patients were eligible for the HCAHPS survey. The scores shown, if any, reflect a very small number of surveys; (10) A state average was not calculated because too few hospitals in the state submitted data; (11) There were discrepancies in the data collection process; Please refer to the User's Guide for a full explanation of data.

Bridges Medical Services

201 9th Street West
Ada, MN 56510
Phone: 218-784-5000
Fax: 218-784-3753
Type: Critical Access Hospitals
Emergency Services: Yes
Ownership: Voluntary Non-Profit - Private
Beds: 63

Key Personnel:

CEO/President. . . . . Dan Rohrbach
Chief of Medical Staff . . . . Jeff Peterson

Measure	Cases	This Hosp.	State Avg.	U.S. Avg.
Heart Attack Care				
ACE Inhibitor or ARB for LVSD[5]	0	-	97%	96%
Aspirin at Arrival[5]	0	-	99%	99%
Aspirin at Discharge[5]	0	-	99%	98%
Beta Blocker at Discharge[5]	0	-	99%	98%
Fibrinolytic Medication Timing[5]	0	-	55%	55%
PCI Within 90 Minutes of Arrival[5]	0	-	94%	90%
Smoking Cessation Advice[5]	0	-	99%	99%
Chest Pain/Possible Heart Attack Care				
Aspirin at Arrival[5]	0	-	97%	95%
Median Time to ECG (minutes)[5]	0	-	7	8
Median Time to Transfer (minutes)[5]	0	-	50	61
Fibrinolytic Medication Timing[5]	0	-	58%	54%
Heart Failure Care				
ACE Inhibitor or ARB for LVSD[3]	0	-	96%	94%
Discharge Instructions[1,3]	4	75%	86%	88%
Evaluation of LVS Function[1,3]	2	0%	96%	98%
Smoking Cessation Advice[1,3]	1	0%	96%	98%
Pneumonia Care				
Appropriate Initial Antibiotic[1,3]	9	89%	90%	92%
Blood Culture Timing[3]	0	-	95%	96%
Influenza Vaccine[1]	10	40%	92%	91%
Initial Antibiotic Timing[1,3]	13	85%	96%	95%
Pneumococcal Vaccine[1,3]	11	55%	92%	93%
Smoking Cessation Advice[1,3]	2	0%	95%	97%
Surgical Care Improvement Project				
Appropriate VTP Within 24 Hours[5]	0	-	92%	92%
Appropriate Hair Removal[5]	0	-	99%	99%
Appropriate Beta Blocker Usage[5]	0	-	94%	93%
Controlled Postoperative Blood Glucose[5]	0	-	92%	93%
Prophylactic Antibiotic Timing[5]	0	-	96%	97%
Prophylactic Antibiotic Timing (Outpatient)[5]	0	-	89%	92%
Prophylactic Antibiotic Selection[5]	0	-	98%	97%
Prophylactic Antibiotic Select. (Outpatient)[5]	0	-	95%	94%
Prophylactic Antibiotic Stopped[5]	0	-	97%	94%
Recommended VTP Ordered[5]	0	-	93%	94%
Urinary Catheter Removal[5]	0	-	90%	90%
Children's Asthma Care				
Received Systemic Corticosteroids	-	-	-	100%
Received Home Management Plan	-	-	-	71%
Received Reliever Medication	-	-	-	100%
Use of Medical Imaging				
Combination Abdominal CT Scan[1]	17	0.412	0.100	0.191
Combination Chest CT Scan[1]	11	0.545	0.018	0.054
Follow-up Mammogram/Ultrasound[1]	44	9.1%	6.4%	8.4%
MRI for Low Back Pain[1]	10	20.0%	39.7%	32.7%
Survey of Patients' Hospital Experiences				
Area Around Room 'Always' Quiet at Night[8]	-	-	-	58%
Doctors 'Always' Communicated Well[8]	-	-	-	80%
Home Recovery Information Given[8]	-	-	-	82%
Hospital Given 9 or 10 on 10 Point Scale[8]	-	-	-	67%
Meds 'Always' Explained Before Given[8]	-	-	-	60%
Nurses 'Always' Communicated Well[8]	-	-	-	76%
Pain 'Always' Well Controlled[8]	-	-	-	69%
Room and Bathroom 'Always' Clean[8]	-	-	-	71%
Timely Help 'Always' Received[8]	-	-	-	64%
Would Definitely Recommend Hospital[8]	-	-	-	69%

Riverwood Healthcare Center

200 Bunker Hill Drive
Aitkin, MN 56431
Phone: 218-927-5501
Fax: 218-927-5575
URL: www.riverwoodhealthcare.com
Type: Critical Access Hospitals
Emergency Services: Yes
Ownership: Voluntary Non-Profit - Private
Beds: 36

Key Personnel:

CEO/President. . . . . Michael Hagen
Chief of Medical Staff . . . . James Harris, MD
Infection Control. . . . . Linda Chantland, RN
Quality Assurance . . . . Jayme Anderson
Emergency Room . . . . James Harris

Measure	Cases	This Hosp.	State Avg.	U.S. Avg.
Heart Attack Care				
ACE Inhibitor or ARB for LVSD[1,2,3]	2	100%	97%	96%
Aspirin at Arrival[1,2,3]	3	100%	99%	99%
Aspirin at Discharge[1,2,3]	2	100%	99%	98%
Beta Blocker at Discharge[1,2,3]	2	100%	99%	98%
Fibrinolytic Medication Timing[2,3]	0	-	55%	55%
PCI Within 90 Minutes of Arrival[2,3]	0	-	94%	90%
Smoking Cessation Advice[2,3]	0	-	99%	99%
Chest Pain/Possible Heart Attack Care				
Aspirin at Arrival	-	-	97%	95%
Median Time to ECG (minutes)	-	-	7	8
Median Time to Transfer (minutes)	-	-	50	61
Fibrinolytic Medication Timing	-	-	58%	54%
Heart Failure Care				
ACE Inhibitor or ARB for LVSD[1,2]	5	100%	96%	94%
Discharge Instructions[1,2]	23	70%	86%	88%
Evaluation of LVS Function[1,2]	24	92%	96%	98%
Smoking Cessation Advice[1,2]	1	100%	96%	98%
Pneumonia Care				
Appropriate Initial Antibiotic[1,2]	16	94%	90%	92%
Blood Culture Timing[1,2]	14	79%	95%	96%
Influenza Vaccine[1,2]	14	86%	92%	91%
Initial Antibiotic Timing[1,2]	13	92%	96%	95%
Pneumococcal Vaccine[1,2]	24	88%	92%	93%
Smoking Cessation Advice[1,2]	5	80%	95%	97%
Surgical Care Improvement Project				
Appropriate VTP Within 24 Hours[1]	19	95%	92%	92%
Appropriate Hair Removal	59	100%	99%	99%
Appropriate Beta Blocker Usage[5]	0	-	94%	93%
Controlled Postoperative Blood Glucose	0	-	92%	93%
Prophylactic Antibiotic Timing	49	90%	96%	97%
Prophylactic Antibiotic Timing (Outpatient)	-	-	89%	92%
Prophylactic Antibiotic Selection	48	90%	98%	97%
Prophylactic Antibiotic Select. (Outpatient)	-	-	95%	94%
Prophylactic Antibiotic Stopped	48	90%	97%	94%
Recommended VTP Ordered[1]	19	95%	93%	94%
Urinary Catheter Removal[1]	5	100%	90%	90%
Children's Asthma Care				
Received Systemic Corticosteroids	-	-	-	100%
Received Home Management Plan	-	-	-	71%
Received Reliever Medication	-	-	-	100%
Use of Medical Imaging				
Combination Abdominal CT Scan	-	-	0.100	0.191
Combination Chest CT Scan	-	-	0.018	0.054
Follow-up Mammogram/Ultrasound	-	-	6.4%	8.4%
MRI for Low Back Pain	-	-	39.7%	32.7%
Survey of Patients' Hospital Experiences				
Area Around Room 'Always' Quiet at Night	300+	59%	-	58%
Doctors 'Always' Communicated Well	300+	79%	-	80%
Home Recovery Information Given	300+	85%	-	82%
Hospital Given 9 or 10 on 10 Point Scale	300+	77%	-	67%
Meds 'Always' Explained Before Given	300+	63%	-	60%
Nurses 'Always' Communicated Well	300+	77%	-	76%
Pain 'Always' Well Controlled	300+	75%	-	69%
Room and Bathroom 'Always' Clean	300+	84%	-	71%
Timely Help 'Always' Received	300+	76%	-	64%
Would Definitely Recommend Hospital	300+	79%	-	69%

Albany Area Hospital

300 Third Avenue
Albany, MN 56307
Phone: 320-845-2121
Fax: 320-845-4707
E-mail: mgoebel@means.net
URL: www.albanyareahospital.com
Type: Critical Access Hospitals
Emergency Services: Yes
Ownership: Voluntary Non-Profit - Church
Beds: 17

Key Personnel:

Chief of Medical Staff . . . . Daron Gersch
Infection Control. . . . . Bernita Hinnenkamp
Radiology. . . . . Mohammad Dogar
Emergency Room . . . . Daron Gersch

Measure	Cases	This Hosp.	State Avg.	U.S. Avg.
Heart Attack Care				
ACE Inhibitor or ARB for LVSD[5]	0	-	97%	96%
Aspirin at Arrival[5]	0	-	99%	99%
Aspirin at Discharge[5]	0	-	99%	98%
Beta Blocker at Discharge[5]	0	-	99%	98%
Fibrinolytic Medication Timing[5]	0	-	55%	55%
PCI Within 90 Minutes of Arrival[5]	0	-	94%	90%
Smoking Cessation Advice[5]	0	-	99%	99%
Chest Pain/Possible Heart Attack Care				
Aspirin at Arrival[5]	0	-	97%	95%
Median Time to ECG (minutes)[5]	0	-	7	8
Median Time to Transfer (minutes)[5]	0	-	50	61
Fibrinolytic Medication Timing[5]	0	-	58%	54%
Heart Failure Care				
ACE Inhibitor or ARB for LVSD[1,3]	1	100%	96%	94%
Discharge Instructions[1,3]	6	100%	86%	88%
Evaluation of LVS Function[1,3]	10	10%	96%	98%
Smoking Cessation Advice[1,3]	1	100%	96%	98%
Pneumonia Care				
Appropriate Initial Antibiotic[1,3]	6	67%	90%	92%
Blood Culture Timing[3]	0	-	95%	96%
Influenza Vaccine[1,3]	4	50%	92%	91%
Initial Antibiotic Timing[1,3]	9	89%	96%	95%
Pneumococcal Vaccine[1,3]	13	77%	92%	93%
Smoking Cessation Advice[1,3]	1	0%	95%	97%
Surgical Care Improvement Project				
Appropriate VTP Within 24 Hours[3]	0	-	92%	92%
Appropriate Hair Removal[1,3]	1	100%	99%	99%
Appropriate Beta Blocker Usage[5]	0	-	94%	93%
Controlled Postoperative Blood Glucose[3]	0	-	92%	93%
Prophylactic Antibiotic Timing[1,3]	1	0%	96%	97%
Prophylactic Antibiotic Timing (Outpatient)[5]	0	-	89%	92%
Prophylactic Antibiotic Selection[1,3]	1	100%	98%	97%
Prophylactic Antibiotic Select. (Outpatient)[5]	0	-	95%	94%
Prophylactic Antibiotic Stopped[1,3]	1	100%	97%	94%
Recommended VTP Ordered[3]	0	-	93%	94%
Urinary Catheter Removal[3]	0	-	90%	90%
Children's Asthma Care				
Received Systemic Corticosteroids	-	-	-	100%
Received Home Management Plan	-	-	-	71%
Received Reliever Medication	-	-	-	100%
Use of Medical Imaging				
Combination Abdominal CT Scan[1]	43	0.070	0.100	0.191
Combination Chest CT Scan[1]	18	0.000	0.018	0.054
Follow-up Mammogram/Ultrasound	76	5.3%	6.4%	8.4%
MRI for Low Back Pain[1]	15	60.0%	39.7%	32.7%
Survey of Patients' Hospital Experiences				
Area Around Room 'Always' Quiet at Night[6]	<100	69%	-	58%
Doctors 'Always' Communicated Well[6]	<100	87%	-	80%
Home Recovery Information Given[6]	<100	88%	-	82%
Hospital Given 9 or 10 on 10 Point Scale[6]	<100	82%	-	67%
Meds 'Always' Explained Before Given[6]	<100	66%	-	60%
Nurses 'Always' Communicated Well[6]	<100	83%	-	76%
Pain 'Always' Well Controlled[6]	<100	73%	-	69%
Room and Bathroom 'Always' Clean[6]	<100	77%	-	71%
Timely Help 'Always' Received[6]	<100	85%	-	64%
Would Definitely Recommend Hospital	<100	81%	-	69%

NOTE: Hospital profiles are in alphabetical order by state, then city, then hospital within the city; Rankings exclude hospitals with less than 25 cases except for patient surveys which excludes hospitals with less than 100 cases; (a) 100–299 cases; (1) The number of cases is too small to be sure how well a hospital is performing; (2) The hospital indicated that the data submitted for this measure were based on a sample of cases; (3) Data was collected during a shorter time period (fewer quarters) than the maximum possible time for this measure; (4) Suppressed for one or more quarters by CMS; (5) No data is available from the hospital for this measure; (6) Fewer than 100 patients completed the HCAHPS survey. Use these rates with caution, as the number of surveys may be too low to reliably assess hospital performance; (7) Survey results are based on less than 12 months of data; (8) Survey results are not available for this reporting period; (9) No or very few patients were eligible for the HCAHPS survey. The scores shown, if any, reflect a very small number of surveys; (10) A state average was not calculated because too few hospitals in the state submitted data; (11) There were discrepancies in the data collection process; Please refer to the User's Guide for a full explanation of data.

Naeve Hospital

404 West Fountain Street
Albert Lea, MN 56007
Type: Acute Care Hospitals
Ownership: Voluntary Non-Profit - Private
Phone: 507-373-2384
Fax: 507-377-6248
Emergency Services: Yes
Beds: 119

Key Personnel:

CEO/President. . . . . Mark Ciota, MD
Chief of Medical Staff . . . . John Grzybowski, MD
Infection Control. . . . . Tammy Williams
Operating Room. . . . . Jill Berg
Quality Assurance . . . . Toni Lauer
Radiology. . . . . Lisa Routh
Intensive Care Unit. . . . . Nancy Christensen
Patient Relations . . . . Jane Killpack

Measure	Cases	This Hosp.	State Avg.	U.S. Avg.
Heart Attack Care				
ACE Inhibitor or ARB for LVSD[1]	9	78%	97%	96%
Aspirin at Arrival	43	98%	99%	99%
Aspirin at Discharge	36	94%	99%	98%
Beta Blocker at Discharge	36	94%	99%	98%
Fibrinolytic Medication Timing	0	-	55%	55%
PCI Within 90 Minutes of Arrival	0	-	94%	90%
Smoking Cessation Advice[1]	2	100%	99%	99%
Chest Pain/Possible Heart Attack Care				
Aspirin at Arrival	129	94%	97%	95%
Median Time to ECG (minutes)	130	7	7	8
Median Time to Transfer (minutes)[1,3]	4	80	50	61
Fibrinolytic Medication Timing[1]	4	50%	58%	54%
Heart Failure Care				
ACE Inhibitor or ARB for LVSD[1]	18	100%	96%	94%
Discharge Instructions	49	57%	86%	88%
Evaluation of LVS Function	73	92%	96%	98%
Smoking Cessation Advice[1]	10	100%	96%	98%
Pneumonia Care				
Appropriate Initial Antibiotic	55	73%	90%	92%
Blood Culture Timing	87	90%	95%	96%
Influenza Vaccine	53	98%	92%	91%
Initial Antibiotic Timing	98	91%	96%	95%
Pneumococcal Vaccine	100	98%	92%	93%
Smoking Cessation Advice[1]	10	70%	95%	97%
Surgical Care Improvement Project				
Appropriate VTP Within 24 Hours	144	97%	92%	92%
Appropriate Hair Removal	347	100%	99%	99%
Appropriate Beta Blocker Usage	94	96%	94%	93%
Controlled Postoperative Blood Glucose	0	-	92%	93%
Prophylactic Antibiotic Timing	272	99%	96%	97%
Prophylactic Antibiotic Timing (Outpatient)	38	76%	89%	92%
Prophylactic Antibiotic Selection	277	99%	98%	97%
Prophylactic Antibiotic Select. (Outpatient)	30	100%	95%	94%
Prophylactic Antibiotic Stopped	266	98%	97%	94%
Recommended VTP Ordered	145	97%	93%	94%
Urinary Catheter Removal	90	97%	90%	90%
Children's Asthma Care				
Received Systemic Corticosteroids	-	-	-	100%
Received Home Management Plan	-	-	-	71%
Received Reliever Medication	-	-	-	100%
Use of Medical Imaging				
Combination Abdominal CT Scan	399	0.053	0.100	0.191
Combination Chest CT Scan	137	0.000	0.018	0.054
Follow-up Mammogram/Ultrasound	857	8.4%	6.4%	8.4%
MRI for Low Back Pain	72	27.8%	39.7%	32.7%
Survey of Patients' Hospital Experiences				
Area Around Room 'Always' Quiet at Night	300+	58%	-	58%
Doctors 'Always' Communicated Well	300+	83%	-	80%
Home Recovery Information Given	300+	81%	-	82%
Hospital Given 9 or 10 on 10 Point Scale	300+	70%	-	67%
Meds 'Always' Explained Before Given	300+	67%	-	60%
Nurses 'Always' Communicated Well	300+	82%	-	76%
Pain 'Always' Well Controlled	300+	70%	-	69%
Room and Bathroom 'Always' Clean	300+	81%	-	71%
Timely Help 'Always' Received	300+	71%	-	64%
Would Definitely Recommend Hospital	300+	73%	-	69%

Douglas County Hospital

111 17th Avenue East
Alexandria, MN 56308
E-mail: hr@dchospital.com
URL: www.dchospital.com
Type: Acute Care Hospitals
Ownership: Government - Local
Phone: 320-762-1511
Fax: 320-762-6034
Emergency Services: Yes
Beds: 127

Key Personnel:

Chief of Medical Staff. . . . . Bruce Wymore
Infection Control. . . . . Bonnie Freudenberg
Operating Room. . . . . Billie Glade
Quality Assurance . . . . Doug Leinhart
Radiology. . . . . Richard D Eiser
Emergency Room . . . . Kevin Wedman, RN
Intensive Care Unit. . . . . Lois Nelson, RN

Measure	Cases	This Hosp.	State Avg.	U.S. Avg.
Heart Attack Care				
ACE Inhibitor or ARB for LVSD[1]	1	100%	97%	96%
Aspirin at Arrival[1]	8	100%	99%	99%
Aspirin at Discharge[1]	5	100%	99%	98%
Beta Blocker at Discharge[1]	4	75%	99%	98%
Fibrinolytic Medication Timing	0	-	55%	55%
PCI Within 90 Minutes of Arrival	0	-	94%	90%
Smoking Cessation Advice	0	-	99%	99%
Chest Pain/Possible Heart Attack Care				
Aspirin at Arrival	127	98%	97%	95%
Median Time to ECG (minutes)	126	4	7	8
Median Time to Transfer (minutes)[1]	12	56	50	61
Fibrinolytic Medication Timing	0	-	58%	54%
Heart Failure Care				
ACE Inhibitor or ARB for LVSD	29	97%	96%	94%
Discharge Instructions	45	84%	86%	88%
Evaluation of LVS Function	87	95%	96%	98%
Smoking Cessation Advice[1]	10	100%	96%	98%
Pneumonia Care				
Appropriate Initial Antibiotic[2]	72	85%	90%	92%
Blood Culture Timing[2]	88	91%	95%	96%
Influenza Vaccine	82	98%	92%	91%
Initial Antibiotic Timing[2]	122	98%	96%	95%
Pneumococcal Vaccine[2]	151	95%	92%	93%
Smoking Cessation Advice[2]	29	100%	95%	97%
Surgical Care Improvement Project				
Appropriate VTP Within 24 Hours[2]	139	92%	92%	92%
Appropriate Hair Removal[2]	422	100%	99%	99%
Appropriate Beta Blocker Usage[2]	130	96%	94%	93%
Controlled Postoperative Blood Glucose[2]	0	-	92%	93%
Prophylactic Antibiotic Timing[2]	306	91%	96%	97%
Prophylactic Antibiotic Timing (Outpatient)	179	91%	89%	92%
Prophylactic Antibiotic Selection[2]	306	96%	98%	97%
Prophylactic Antibiotic Select. (Outpatient)	172	97%	95%	94%
Prophylactic Antibiotic Stopped[2]	294	99%	97%	94%
Recommended VTP Ordered[2]	139	94%	93%	94%
Urinary Catheter Removal[2]	115	94%	90%	90%
Children's Asthma Care				
Received Systemic Corticosteroids	-	-	-	100%
Received Home Management Plan	-	-	-	71%
Received Reliever Medication	-	-	-	100%
Use of Medical Imaging				
Combination Abdominal CT Scan	297	0.047	0.100	0.191
Combination Chest CT Scan	224	0.004	0.018	0.054
Follow-up Mammogram/Ultrasound	61	3.3%	6.4%	8.4%
MRI for Low Back Pain	222	35.1%	39.7%	32.7%
Survey of Patients' Hospital Experiences				
Area Around Room 'Always' Quiet at Night	300+	56%	-	58%
Doctors 'Always' Communicated Well	300+	80%	-	80%
Home Recovery Information Given	300+	87%	-	82%
Hospital Given 9 or 10 on 10 Point Scale	300+	74%	-	67%
Meds 'Always' Explained Before Given	300+	63%	-	60%
Nurses 'Always' Communicated Well	300+	77%	-	76%
Pain 'Always' Well Controlled	300+	70%	-	69%
Room and Bathroom 'Always' Clean	300+	82%	-	71%
Timely Help 'Always' Received	300+	69%	-	64%
Would Definitely Recommend Hospital	300+	74%	-	69%

Appleton Municipal Hospital

30 South Behl Street
Appleton, MN 56208
Type: Critical Access Hospitals
Ownership: Government - Local
Phone: 320-289-2422
Fax: 320-289-1797
Emergency Services: Yes
Beds: 131

Key Personnel:

CEO/President. . . . . Daniel Swenson
Emergency Room . . . . Limpi Ado, MD

Measure	Cases	This Hosp.	State Avg.	U.S. Avg.
Heart Attack Care				
ACE Inhibitor or ARB for LVSD[3]	0	-	97%	96%
Aspirin at Arrival[1,3]	1	100%	99%	99%
Aspirin at Discharge[1,3]	1	100%	99%	98%
Beta Blocker at Discharge[1,3]	1	100%	99%	98%
Fibrinolytic Medication Timing[3]	0	-	55%	55%
PCI Within 90 Minutes of Arrival[3]	0	-	94%	90%
Smoking Cessation Advice[3]	0	-	99%	99%
Chest Pain/Possible Heart Attack Care				
Aspirin at Arrival	-	-	97%	95%
Median Time to ECG (minutes)	-	-	7	8
Median Time to Transfer (minutes)	-	-	50	61
Fibrinolytic Medication Timing	-	-	58%	54%
Heart Failure Care				
ACE Inhibitor or ARB for LVSD[3]	0	-	96%	94%
Discharge Instructions[1,3]	1	0%	86%	88%
Evaluation of LVS Function[1,3]	3	100%	96%	98%
Smoking Cessation Advice[3]	0	-	96%	98%
Pneumonia Care				
Appropriate Initial Antibiotic[3]	0	-	90%	92%
Blood Culture Timing[3]	0	-	95%	96%
Influenza Vaccine[5]	0	-	92%	91%
Initial Antibiotic Timing[1,3]	1	100%	96%	95%
Pneumococcal Vaccine[1,3]	1	100%	92%	93%
Smoking Cessation Advice[3]	0	-	95%	97%
Surgical Care Improvement Project				
Appropriate VTP Within 24 Hours[5]	0	-	92%	92%
Appropriate Hair Removal[5]	0	-	99%	99%
Appropriate Beta Blocker Usage[5]	0	-	94%	93%
Controlled Postoperative Blood Glucose[5]	0	-	92%	93%
Prophylactic Antibiotic Timing[5]	0	-	96%	97%
Prophylactic Antibiotic Timing (Outpatient)	-	-	89%	92%
Prophylactic Antibiotic Selection[5]	0	-	98%	97%
Prophylactic Antibiotic Select. (Outpatient)	-	-	95%	94%
Prophylactic Antibiotic Stopped[5]	0	-	97%	94%
Recommended VTP Ordered[5]	0	-	93%	94%
Urinary Catheter Removal[5]	0	-	90%	90%
Children's Asthma Care				
Received Systemic Corticosteroids	-	-	-	100%
Received Home Management Plan	-	-	-	71%
Received Reliever Medication	-	-	-	100%
Use of Medical Imaging				
Combination Abdominal CT Scan	-	-	0.100	0.191
Combination Chest CT Scan	-	-	0.018	0.054
Follow-up Mammogram/Ultrasound	-	-	6.4%	8.4%
MRI for Low Back Pain	-	-	39.7%	32.7%
Survey of Patients' Hospital Experiences				
Area Around Room 'Always' Quiet at Night[8]	-	-	-	58%
Doctors 'Always' Communicated Well[8]	-	-	-	80%
Home Recovery Information Given[8]	-	-	-	82%
Hospital Given 9 or 10 on 10 Point Scale[8]	-	-	-	67%
Meds 'Always' Explained Before Given[8]	-	-	-	60%
Nurses 'Always' Communicated Well[8]	-	-	-	76%
Pain 'Always' Well Controlled[8]	-	-	-	69%
Room and Bathroom 'Always' Clean[8]	-	-	-	71%
Timely Help 'Always' Received[8]	-	-	-	64%
Would Definitely Recommend Hospital[8]	-	-	-	69%

NOTE: Hospital profiles are in alphabetical order by state, then city, then hospital within the city; Rankings exclude hospitals with less than 25 cases except for patient surveys which excludes hospitals with less than 100 cases; (a) 100–299 cases; (1) The number of cases is too small to be sure how well a hospital is performing; (2) The hospital indicated that the data submitted for this measure were based on a sample of cases; (3) Data was collected during a shorter time period (fewer quarters) than the maximum possible time for this measure; (4) Suppressed for one or more quarters by CMS; (5) No data is available from the hospital for this measure; (6) Fewer than 100 patients completed the HCAHPS survey. Use these rates with caution, as the number of surveys may be too low to reliably assess hospital performance; (7) Survey results are based on less than 12 months of data; (8) Survey results are not available for this reporting period; (9) No or very few patients were eligible for the HCAHPS survey. The scores shown, if any, reflect a very small number of surveys; (10) A state average was not calculated because too few hospitals in the state submitted data; (11) There were discrepancies in the data collection process; Please refer to the User's Guide for a full explanation of data.

Sibley Medical Center

601 W Chandler
Arlington, MN 55307
Phone: 507-964-2271
Fax: 507-964-5898
E-mail: anhhosp@frontiernet.net
URL: www.sibleymedical.com
Type: Critical Access Hospitals
Emergency Services: Yes
Ownership: Government - Local
Beds: 20

Key Personnel:

CEO/President. . . . . Rhonda Matz
Chief of Medical Staff. . . . . Dean Bergersen
Operating Room. . . . . Beth Miller, RN

Measure	Cases	This Hosp.	State Avg.	U.S. Avg.
Heart Attack Care				
ACE Inhibitor or ARB for LVSD[5]	0	-	97%	96%
Aspirin at Arrival[5]	0	-	99%	99%
Aspirin at Discharge[5]	0	-	99%	98%
Beta Blocker at Discharge[5]	0	-	99%	98%
Fibrinolytic Medication Timing[5]	0	-	55%	55%
PCI Within 90 Minutes of Arrival[5]	0	-	94%	90%
Smoking Cessation Advice[5]	0	-	99%	99%
Chest Pain/Possible Heart Attack Care				
Aspirin at Arrival[5]	0	-	97%	95%
Median Time to ECG (minutes)[5]	0	-	7	8
Median Time to Transfer (minutes)[5]	0	-	50	61
Fibrinolytic Medication Timing[5]	0	-	58%	54%
Heart Failure Care				
ACE Inhibitor or ARB for LVSD[3]	0	-	96%	94%
Discharge Instructions[3]	0	-	86%	88%
Evaluation of LVS Function[3]	0	-	96%	98%
Smoking Cessation Advice[3]	0	-	96%	98%
Pneumonia Care				
Appropriate Initial Antibiotic[1]	19	84%	90%	92%
Blood Culture Timing[1]	7	71%	95%	96%
Influenza Vaccine[1]	15	87%	92%	91%
Initial Antibiotic Timing[1]	3	100%	96%	95%
Pneumococcal Vaccine[1]	23	83%	92%	93%
Smoking Cessation Advice[1]	5	80%	95%	97%
Surgical Care Improvement Project				
Appropriate VTP Within 24 Hours[5]	0	-	92%	92%
Appropriate Hair Removal[5]	0	-	99%	99%
Appropriate Beta Blocker Usage[5]	0	-	94%	93%
Controlled Postoperative Blood Glucose[5]	0	-	92%	93%
Prophylactic Antibiotic Timing[5]	0	-	96%	97%
Prophylactic Antibiotic Timing (Outpatient)[5]	0	-	89%	92%
Prophylactic Antibiotic Selection[5]	0	-	98%	97%
Prophylactic Antibiotic Select. (Outpatient)[5]	0	-	95%	94%
Prophylactic Antibiotic Stopped[5]	0	-	97%	94%
Recommended VTP Ordered[5]	0	-	93%	94%
Urinary Catheter Removal[5]	0	-	90%	90%
Children's Asthma Care				
Received Systemic Corticosteroids	-	-	-	100%
Received Home Management Plan	-	-	-	71%
Received Reliever Medication	-	-	-	100%
Use of Medical Imaging				
Combination Abdominal CT Scan	82	0.037	0.100	0.191
Combination Chest CT Scan	91	0.066	0.018	0.054
Follow-up Mammogram/Ultrasound	104	2.9%	6.4%	8.4%
MRI for Low Back Pain[1]	11	18.2%	39.7%	32.7%
Survey of Patients' Hospital Experiences				
Area Around Room 'Always' Quiet at Night[8]	-	-	-	58%
Doctors 'Always' Communicated Well[8]	-	-	-	80%
Home Recovery Information Given[8]	-	-	-	82%
Hospital Given 9 or 10 on 10 Point Scale[8]	-	-	-	67%
Meds 'Always' Explained Before Given[8]	-	-	-	60%
Nurses 'Always' Communicated Well[8]	-	-	-	76%
Pain 'Always' Well Controlled[8]	-	-	-	69%
Room and Bathroom 'Always' Clean[8]	-	-	-	71%
Timely Help 'Always' Received[8]	-	-	-	64%
Would Definitely Recommend Hospital[8]	-	-	-	69%

Northern Pines Medical Center

5211 Highway 110
Aurora, MN 55705
Phone: 218-229-2211
Fax: 218-229-2042
E-mail: info@whitetech.org
URL: www.whitetech.org
Type: Critical Access Hospitals
Emergency Services: Yes
Ownership: Voluntary Non-Profit - Private
Beds: 85

Key Personnel:

CEO/President. . . . . Paula Schaefbauer
Chief of Medical Staff. . . . . Christopher Whiting, MD
Infection Control. . . . . Randi Dix, RN
Quality Assurance . . . . Paula Schaefbauer

Measure	Cases	This Hosp.	State Avg.	U.S. Avg.
Heart Attack Care				
ACE Inhibitor or ARB for LVSD[5]	0	-	97%	96%
Aspirin at Arrival[5]	0	-	99%	99%
Aspirin at Discharge[5]	0	-	99%	98%
Beta Blocker at Discharge[5]	0	-	99%	98%
Fibrinolytic Medication Timing[5]	0	-	55%	55%
PCI Within 90 Minutes of Arrival[5]	0	-	94%	90%
Smoking Cessation Advice[5]	0	-	99%	99%
Chest Pain/Possible Heart Attack Care				
Aspirin at Arrival[5]	0	-	97%	95%
Median Time to ECG (minutes)[5]	0	-	7	8
Median Time to Transfer (minutes)[5]	0	-	50	61
Fibrinolytic Medication Timing[5]	0	-	58%	54%
Heart Failure Care				
ACE Inhibitor or ARB for LVSD[1,3]	1	100%	96%	94%
Discharge Instructions[1,3]	6	17%	86%	88%
Evaluation of LVS Function[1,3]	9	33%	96%	98%
Smoking Cessation Advice[1,3]	1	0%	96%	98%
Pneumonia Care				
Appropriate Initial Antibiotic[1,3]	2	50%	90%	92%
Blood Culture Timing[1,3]	2	100%	95%	96%
Influenza Vaccine[1]	2	50%	92%	91%
Initial Antibiotic Timing[1,3]	4	100%	96%	95%
Pneumococcal Vaccine[1,3]	4	75%	92%	93%
Smoking Cessation Advice[3]	0	-	95%	97%
Surgical Care Improvement Project				
Appropriate VTP Within 24 Hours[5]	0	-	92%	92%
Appropriate Hair Removal[5]	0	-	99%	99%
Appropriate Beta Blocker Usage[5]	0	-	94%	93%
Controlled Postoperative Blood Glucose[5]	0	-	92%	93%
Prophylactic Antibiotic Timing[5]	0	-	96%	97%
Prophylactic Antibiotic Timing (Outpatient)[5]	0	-	89%	92%
Prophylactic Antibiotic Selection[5]	0	-	98%	97%
Prophylactic Antibiotic Select. (Outpatient)[5]	0	-	95%	94%
Prophylactic Antibiotic Stopped[5]	0	-	97%	94%
Recommended VTP Ordered[5]	0	-	93%	94%
Urinary Catheter Removal[5]	0	-	90%	90%
Children's Asthma Care				
Received Systemic Corticosteroids	-	-	-	100%
Received Home Management Plan	-	-	-	71%
Received Reliever Medication	-	-	-	100%
Use of Medical Imaging				
Combination Abdominal CT Scan[1]	32	0.000	0.100	0.191
Combination Chest CT Scan[1]	25	0.000	0.018	0.054
Follow-up Mammogram/Ultrasound[5]	0	-	6.4%	8.4%
MRI for Low Back Pain[5]	0	-	39.7%	32.7%
Survey of Patients' Hospital Experiences				
Area Around Room 'Always' Quiet at Night[8]	-	-	-	58%
Doctors 'Always' Communicated Well[8]	-	-	-	80%
Home Recovery Information Given[8]	-	-	-	82%
Hospital Given 9 or 10 on 10 Point Scale[8]	-	-	-	67%
Meds 'Always' Explained Before Given[8]	-	-	-	60%
Nurses 'Always' Communicated Well[8]	-	-	-	76%
Pain 'Always' Well Controlled[8]	-	-	-	69%
Room and Bathroom 'Always' Clean[8]	-	-	-	71%
Timely Help 'Always' Received[8]	-	-	-	64%
Would Definitely Recommend Hospital[8]	-	-	-	69%

Austin Medical Center

1000 First Drive Northwest
Austin, MN 55912
Phone: 507-433-7351
URL: www.mayohealthsystem.org
Type: Acute Care Hospitals
Emergency Services: Yes
Ownership: Voluntary Non-Profit - Other
Beds: 80

Key Personnel:

CEO/President. . . . . David Agerter, M.D.
Chief of Medical Staff. . . . . Cynthia Dube, M.D.
Operating Room. . . . . Aaron Keenan

Measure	Cases	This Hosp.	State Avg.	U.S. Avg.
Heart Attack Care				
ACE Inhibitor or ARB for LVSD[1,3]	1	100%	97%	96%
Aspirin at Arrival[1,3]	5	100%	99%	99%
Aspirin at Discharge[1,3]	4	100%	99%	98%
Beta Blocker at Discharge[1,3]	3	100%	99%	98%
Fibrinolytic Medication Timing[3]	0	-	55%	55%
PCI Within 90 Minutes of Arrival[3]	0	-	94%	90%
Smoking Cessation Advice[3]	0	-	99%	99%
Chest Pain/Possible Heart Attack Care				
Aspirin at Arrival	90	99%	97%	95%
Median Time to ECG (minutes)	95	8	7	8
Median Time to Transfer (minutes)[1,3]	2	126	50	61
Fibrinolytic Medication Timing[1]	5	80%	58%	54%
Heart Failure Care				
ACE Inhibitor or ARB for LVSD	30	100%	96%	94%
Discharge Instructions	77	97%	86%	88%
Evaluation of LVS Function	112	100%	96%	98%
Smoking Cessation Advice[1]	6	100%	96%	98%
Pneumonia Care				
Appropriate Initial Antibiotic	115	93%	90%	92%
Blood Culture Timing	172	99%	95%	96%
Influenza Vaccine	99	98%	92%	91%
Initial Antibiotic Timing	168	100%	96%	95%
Pneumococcal Vaccine	182	98%	92%	93%
Smoking Cessation Advice	33	91%	95%	97%
Surgical Care Improvement Project				
Appropriate VTP Within 24 Hours	125	96%	92%	92%
Appropriate Hair Removal	241	100%	99%	99%
Appropriate Beta Blocker Usage	96	97%	94%	93%
Controlled Postoperative Blood Glucose	0	-	92%	93%
Prophylactic Antibiotic Timing	208	100%	96%	97%
Prophylactic Antibiotic Timing (Outpatient)	32	88%	89%	92%
Prophylactic Antibiotic Selection	209	98%	98%	97%
Prophylactic Antibiotic Select. (Outpatient)	35	100%	95%	94%
Prophylactic Antibiotic Stopped	204	100%	97%	94%
Recommended VTP Ordered	125	98%	93%	94%
Urinary Catheter Removal	78	97%	90%	90%
Children's Asthma Care				
Received Systemic Corticosteroids	-	-	-	100%
Received Home Management Plan	-	-	-	71%
Received Reliever Medication	-	-	-	100%
Use of Medical Imaging				
Combination Abdominal CT Scan	279	0.369	0.100	0.191
Combination Chest CT Scan	167	0.240	0.018	0.054
Follow-up Mammogram/Ultrasound	1,115	5.8%	6.4%	8.4%
MRI for Low Back Pain	51	35.3%	39.7%	32.7%
Survey of Patients' Hospital Experiences				
Area Around Room 'Always' Quiet at Night	300+	52%	-	58%
Doctors 'Always' Communicated Well	300+	79%	-	80%
Home Recovery Information Given	300+	78%	-	82%
Hospital Given 9 or 10 on 10 Point Scale	300+	64%	-	67%
Meds 'Always' Explained Before Given	300+	63%	-	60%
Nurses 'Always' Communicated Well	300+	76%	-	76%
Pain 'Always' Well Controlled	300+	66%	-	69%
Room and Bathroom 'Always' Clean	300+	80%	-	71%
Timely Help 'Always' Received	300+	62%	-	64%
Would Definitely Recommend Hospital	300+	63%	-	69%

NOTE: Hospital profiles are in alphabetical order by state, then city, then hospital within the city; Rankings exclude hospitals with less than 25 cases except for patient surveys which excludes hospitals with less than 100 cases; (a) 100–299 cases; (1) The number of cases is too small to be sure how well a hospital is performing; (2) The hospital indicated that the data submitted for this measure were based on a sample of cases; (3) Data was collected during a shorter time period (fewer quarters) than the maximum possible time for this measure; (4) Suppressed for one or more quarters by CMS; (5) No data is available from the hospital for this measure; (6) Fewer than 100 patients completed the HCAHPS survey. Use these rates with caution, as the number of surveys may be too low to reliably assess hospital performance; (7) Survey results are based on less than 12 months of data; (8) Survey results are not available for this reporting period; (9) No or very few patients were eligible for the HCAHPS survey. The scores shown, if any, reflect a very small number of surveys; (10) A state average was not calculated because too few hospitals in the state submitted data; (11) There were discrepancies in the data collection process; Please refer to the User's Guide for a full explanation of data.

Clearwater Health Services

203 Fourth Street Northwest
Bagley, MN 56621
E-mail: ccmh@bagley.means.net
URL: www.clearwaterhs.com
Type: Critical Access Hospitals
Ownership: Govt - Hospital Dist/Auth
Phone: 218-694-6501
Fax: 218-694-3528
Emergency Services: Yes
Beds: 77

Key Personnel:
Chief of Medical Staff . . . . Francis Abraham, MD
Infection Control . . . . Bruce Muckala
Operating Room. . . . . Rick Ames
Quality Assurance . . . . Bruce Muckala
Emergency Room . . . . Rick Ames

Measure	Cases	This Hosp.	State Avg.	U.S. Avg.
Heart Attack Care				
ACE Inhibitor or ARB for LVSD[5]	0	-	97%	96%
Aspirin at Arrival[5]	0	-	99%	99%
Aspirin at Discharge[5]	0	-	99%	98%
Beta Blocker at Discharge[5]	0	-	99%	98%
Fibrinolytic Medication Timing[5]	0	-	55%	55%
PCI Within 90 Minutes of Arrival[5]	0	-	94%	90%
Smoking Cessation Advice[5]	0	-	99%	99%
Chest Pain/Possible Heart Attack Care				
Aspirin at Arrival	-	-	97%	95%
Median Time to ECG (minutes)	-	-	7	8
Median Time to Transfer (minutes)	-	-	50	61
Fibrinolytic Medication Timing	-	-	58%	54%
Heart Failure Care				
ACE Inhibitor or ARB for LVSD[3]	0	-	96%	94%
Discharge Instructions[1,3]	2	0%	86%	88%
Evaluation of LVS Function[1,3]	2	0%	96%	98%
Smoking Cessation Advice[1,3]	1	0%	96%	98%
Pneumonia Care				
Appropriate Initial Antibiotic[1,3]	3	100%	90%	92%
Blood Culture Timing[3]	0	-	95%	96%
Influenza Vaccine[5]	0	-	92%	91%
Initial Antibiotic Timing[1,3]	7	100%	96%	95%
Pneumococcal Vaccine[1,3]	5	20%	92%	93%
Smoking Cessation Advice[1,3]	1	0%	95%	97%
Surgical Care Improvement Project				
Appropriate VTP Within 24 Hours[5]	0	-	92%	92%
Appropriate Hair Removal[5]	0	-	99%	99%
Appropriate Beta Blocker Usage[5]	0	-	94%	93%
Controlled Postoperative Blood Glucose[5]	0	-	92%	93%
Prophylactic Antibiotic Timing[5]	0	-	96%	97%
Prophylactic Antibiotic Timing (Outpatient)	-	-	89%	92%
Prophylactic Antibiotic Selection[5]	0	-	98%	97%
Prophylactic Antibiotic Select. (Outpatient)	-	-	95%	94%
Prophylactic Antibiotic Stopped[5]	0	-	97%	94%
Recommended VTP Ordered[5]	0	-	93%	94%
Urinary Catheter Removal[5]	0	-	90%	90%
Children's Asthma Care				
Received Systemic Corticosteroids	-	-	-	100%
Received Home Management Plan	-	-	-	71%
Received Reliever Medication	-	-	-	100%
Use of Medical Imaging				
Combination Abdominal CT Scan	-	-	0.100	0.191
Combination Chest CT Scan	-	-	0.018	0.054
Follow-up Mammogram/Ultrasound	-	-	6.4%	8.4%
MRI for Low Back Pain	-	-	39.7%	32.7%
Survey of Patients' Hospital Experiences				
Area Around Room 'Always' Quiet at Night[8]	-	-	-	58%
Doctors 'Always' Communicated Well[8]	-	-	-	80%
Home Recovery Information Given[8]	-	-	-	82%
Hospital Given 9 or 10 on 10 Point Scale[8]	-	-	-	67%
Meds 'Always' Explained Before Given[8]	-	-	-	60%
Nurses 'Always' Communicated Well[8]	-	-	-	76%
Pain 'Always' Well Controlled[8]	-	-	-	69%
Room and Bathroom 'Always' Clean[8]	-	-	-	71%
Timely Help 'Always' Received[8]	-	-	-	64%
Would Definitely Recommend Hospital[8]	-	-	-	69%

Lakewood Health Center

600 Main Ave S
Baudette, MN 56623
Type: Critical Access Hospitals
Ownership: Voluntary Non-Profit - Church
Phone: 218-634-2120
Fax: 218-634-1307
Emergency Services: Yes
Beds: 65

Key Personnel:
CEO/President. . . . . ShaRray Feickert
Chief of Medical Staff . . . . Robert Rayer, MD
Quality Assurance . . . . Tom Mio

Measure	Cases	This Hosp.	State Avg.	U.S. Avg.
Heart Attack Care				
ACE Inhibitor or ARB for LVSD[3]	0	-	97%	96%
Aspirin at Arrival[1,3]	3	100%	99%	99%
Aspirin at Discharge[1,3]	2	100%	99%	98%
Beta Blocker at Discharge[1,3]	2	100%	99%	98%
Fibrinolytic Medication Timing[3]	0	-	55%	55%
PCI Within 90 Minutes of Arrival[3]	0	-	94%	90%
Smoking Cessation Advice[3]	0	-	99%	99%
Chest Pain/Possible Heart Attack Care				
Aspirin at Arrival[5]	0	-	97%	95%
Median Time to ECG (minutes)[5]	0	-	7	8
Median Time to Transfer (minutes)[5]	0	-	50	61
Fibrinolytic Medication Timing[5]	0	-	58%	54%
Heart Failure Care				
ACE Inhibitor or ARB for LVSD[1]	4	100%	96%	94%
Discharge Instructions[1]	6	83%	86%	88%
Evaluation of LVS Function[1]	13	100%	96%	98%
Smoking Cessation Advice[1]	1	100%	96%	98%
Pneumonia Care				
Appropriate Initial Antibiotic[1]	5	80%	90%	92%
Blood Culture Timing[1]	1	100%	95%	96%
Influenza Vaccine[1]	8	100%	92%	91%
Initial Antibiotic Timing[1]	9	100%	96%	95%
Pneumococcal Vaccine[1]	11	82%	92%	93%
Smoking Cessation Advice[1]	2	50%	95%	97%
Surgical Care Improvement Project				
Appropriate VTP Within 24 Hours[5]	0	-	92%	92%
Appropriate Hair Removal[5]	0	-	99%	99%
Appropriate Beta Blocker Usage[5]	0	-	94%	93%
Controlled Postoperative Blood Glucose[5]	0	-	92%	93%
Prophylactic Antibiotic Timing[5]	0	-	96%	97%
Prophylactic Antibiotic Timing (Outpatient)[5]	0	-	89%	92%
Prophylactic Antibiotic Selection[5]	0	-	98%	97%
Prophylactic Antibiotic Select. (Outpatient)[5]	0	-	95%	94%
Prophylactic Antibiotic Stopped[5]	0	-	97%	94%
Recommended VTP Ordered[5]	0	-	93%	94%
Urinary Catheter Removal[5]	0	-	90%	90%
Children's Asthma Care				
Received Systemic Corticosteroids	-	-	-	100%
Received Home Management Plan	-	-	-	71%
Received Reliever Medication	-	-	-	100%
Use of Medical Imaging				
Combination Abdominal CT Scan[1]	42	0.190	0.100	0.191
Combination Chest CT Scan[1]	23	0.087	0.018	0.054
Follow-up Mammogram/Ultrasound	91	11.0%	6.4%	8.4%
MRI for Low Back Pain[1]	13	30.8%	39.7%	32.7%
Survey of Patients' Hospital Experiences				
Area Around Room 'Always' Quiet at Night[6]	<100	62%	-	58%
Doctors 'Always' Communicated Well[6]	<100	84%	-	80%
Home Recovery Information Given[6]	<100	88%	-	82%
Hospital Given 9 or 10 on 10 Point Scale[6]	<100	81%	-	67%
Meds 'Always' Explained Before Given[6]	<100	62%	-	60%
Nurses 'Always' Communicated Well[6]	<100	84%	-	76%
Pain 'Always' Well Controlled[6]	<100	68%	-	69%
Room and Bathroom 'Always' Clean[6]	<100	87%	-	71%
Timely Help 'Always' Received[6]	<100	82%	-	64%
Would Definitely Recommend Hospital	<100	81%	-	69%

North Country Regional Hospital

1300 Anne St NW
Bemidji, MN 56601
URL: www.nchs.com
Type: Acute Care Hospitals
Ownership: Voluntary Non-Profit - Private
Phone: 218-751-5430
Fax: 218-333-5880
Emergency Services: Yes
Beds: 184

Key Personnel:
CEO/President. . . . . James F Hanko
Chief of Medical Staff . . . . Daniel P DeKrey
Coronary Care . . . . Kathryn Edwards-Olson
Infection Control . . . . Wendy Gullicksrad
Pediatric In-Patient Care . . . . Shannon Rankin, RN
Quality Assurance . . . . Wendy Gullicksrad
Radiology. . . . . Ravishankar Konchada

Measure	Cases	This Hosp.	State Avg.	U.S. Avg.
Heart Attack Care				
ACE Inhibitor or ARB for LVSD[1]	3	100%	97%	96%
Aspirin at Arrival[1]	13	100%	99%	99%
Aspirin at Discharge[1]	9	100%	99%	98%
Beta Blocker at Discharge[1]	9	100%	99%	98%
Fibrinolytic Medication Timing	0	-	55%	55%
PCI Within 90 Minutes of Arrival	0	-	94%	90%
Smoking Cessation Advice[1]	1	100%	99%	99%
Chest Pain/Possible Heart Attack Care				
Aspirin at Arrival	125	94%	97%	95%
Median Time to ECG (minutes)	127	8	7	8
Median Time to Transfer (minutes)[1]	2	545	50	61
Fibrinolytic Medication Timing[1]	9	89%	58%	54%
Heart Failure Care				
ACE Inhibitor or ARB for LVSD	28	89%	96%	94%
Discharge Instructions	70	76%	86%	88%
Evaluation of LVS Function	84	99%	96%	98%
Smoking Cessation Advice[1]	23	100%	96%	98%
Pneumonia Care				
Appropriate Initial Antibiotic	63	90%	90%	92%
Blood Culture Timing	102	89%	95%	96%
Influenza Vaccine	72	96%	92%	91%
Initial Antibiotic Timing	114	92%	96%	95%
Pneumococcal Vaccine	107	99%	92%	93%
Smoking Cessation Advice	43	98%	95%	97%
Surgical Care Improvement Project				
Appropriate VTP Within 24 Hours	280	85%	92%	92%
Appropriate Hair Removal	613	100%	99%	99%
Appropriate Beta Blocker Usage	177	89%	94%	93%
Controlled Postoperative Blood Glucose	0	-	92%	93%
Prophylactic Antibiotic Timing	509	96%	96%	97%
Prophylactic Antibiotic Timing (Outpatient)	72	82%	89%	92%
Prophylactic Antibiotic Selection	512	96%	98%	97%
Prophylactic Antibiotic Select. (Outpatient)	66	94%	95%	94%
Prophylactic Antibiotic Stopped	499	94%	97%	94%
Recommended VTP Ordered	282	84%	93%	94%
Urinary Catheter Removal	128	87%	90%	90%
Children's Asthma Care				
Received Systemic Corticosteroids	-	-	-	100%
Received Home Management Plan	-	-	-	71%
Received Reliever Medication	-	-	-	100%
Use of Medical Imaging				
Combination Abdominal CT Scan	222	0.023	0.100	0.191
Combination Chest CT Scan	74	0.000	0.018	0.054
Follow-up Mammogram/Ultrasound[1]	51	7.8%	6.4%	8.4%
MRI for Low Back Pain	101	41.6%	39.7%	32.7%
Survey of Patients' Hospital Experiences				
Area Around Room 'Always' Quiet at Night	300+	58%	-	58%
Doctors 'Always' Communicated Well	300+	78%	-	80%
Home Recovery Information Given	300+	82%	-	82%
Hospital Given 9 or 10 on 10 Point Scale	300+	63%	-	67%
Meds 'Always' Explained Before Given	300+	59%	-	60%
Nurses 'Always' Communicated Well	300+	72%	-	76%
Pain 'Always' Well Controlled	300+	64%	-	69%
Room and Bathroom 'Always' Clean	300+	70%	-	71%
Timely Help 'Always' Received	300+	57%	-	64%
Would Definitely Recommend Hospital	300+	62%	-	69%

NOTE: Hospital profiles are in alphabetical order by state, then city, then hospital within the city; Rankings exclude hospitals with less than 25 cases except for patient surveys which excludes hospitals with less than 100 cases; (a) 100–299 cases; (1) The number of cases is too small to be sure how well a hospital is performing; (2) The hospital indicated that the data submitted for this measure were based on a sample of cases; (3) Data was collected during a shorter time period (fewer quarters) than the maximum possible time for this measure; (4) Suppressed for one or more quarters by CMS; (5) No data is available from the hospital for this measure; (6) Fewer than 100 patients completed the HCAHPS survey. Use these rates with caution, as the number of surveys may be too low to reliably assess hospital performance; (7) Survey results are based on less than 12 months of data; (8) Survey results are not available for this reporting period; (9) No or very few patients were eligible for the HCAHPS survey. The scores shown, if any, reflect a very small number of surveys; (10) A state average was not calculated because too few hospitals in the state submitted data; (11) There were discrepancies in the data collection process; Please refer to the User's Guide for a full explanation of data.

Swift County Benson Hospital

1815 Wisconsin Avenue
Benson, MN 56215
Phone: 320-843-4232
Fax: 320-843-4172
URL: www.scbh.org
Type: Critical Access Hospitals
Emergency Services: Yes
Ownership: Govt - Hospital Dist/Auth
Beds: 31

Key Personnel:

CEO/President. . . . . Frank Lawatsch
Infection Control. . . . . Holly Rodahl, RN
Operating Room. . . . . Helan Clauseen, RN
Quality Assurance . . . . Stella Kalthoff
Emergency Room . . . . Roberta Carter

Measure	Cases	This Hosp.	State Avg.	U.S. Avg.
Heart Attack Care				
ACE Inhibitor or ARB for LVSD[3]	0	-	97%	96%
Aspirin at Arrival[1,3]	2	50%	99%	99%
Aspirin at Discharge[1,3]	1	100%	99%	98%
Beta Blocker at Discharge[1,3]	1	100%	99%	98%
Fibrinolytic Medication Timing[3]	0	-	55%	55%
PCI Within 90 Minutes of Arrival[3]	0	-	94%	90%
Smoking Cessation Advice[3]	0	-	99%	99%
Chest Pain/Possible Heart Attack Care				
Aspirin at Arrival[5]	0	-	97%	95%
Median Time to ECG (minutes)[5]	0	-	7	8
Median Time to Transfer (minutes)[5]	0	-	50	61
Fibrinolytic Medication Timing[5]	0	-	58%	54%
Heart Failure Care				
ACE Inhibitor or ARB for LVSD[1]	1	100%	96%	94%
Discharge Instructions[1]	2	100%	86%	88%
Evaluation of LVS Function[1]	14	50%	96%	98%
Smoking Cessation Advice[1]	1	0%	96%	98%
Pneumonia Care				
Appropriate Initial Antibiotic[1]	7	43%	90%	92%
Blood Culture Timing[1]	1	100%	95%	96%
Influenza Vaccine[1]	7	86%	92%	91%
Initial Antibiotic Timing[1]	15	100%	96%	95%
Pneumococcal Vaccine[1]	16	69%	92%	93%
Smoking Cessation Advice[1]	2	100%	95%	97%
Surgical Care Improvement Project				
Appropriate VTP Within 24 Hours[1]	19	79%	92%	92%
Appropriate Hair Removal	35	14%	99%	99%
Appropriate Beta Blocker Usage[1]	13	31%	94%	93%
Controlled Postoperative Blood Glucose	0	-	92%	93%
Prophylactic Antibiotic Timing	31	94%	96%	97%
Prophylactic Antibiotic Timing (Outpatient)[5]	0	-	89%	92%
Prophylactic Antibiotic Selection	32	100%	98%	97%
Prophylactic Antibiotic Select. (Outpatient)[5]	0	-	95%	94%
Prophylactic Antibiotic Stopped	31	100%	97%	94%
Recommended VTP Ordered[1]	19	79%	93%	94%
Urinary Catheter Removal[1]	15	87%	90%	90%
Children's Asthma Care				
Received Systemic Corticosteroids	-	-	-	100%
Received Home Management Plan	-	-	-	71%
Received Reliever Medication	-	-	-	100%
Use of Medical Imaging				
Combination Abdominal CT Scan	73	0.068	0.100	0.191
Combination Chest CT Scan	65	0.031	0.018	0.054
Follow-up Mammogram/Ultrasound	143	2.8%	6.4%	8.4%
MRI for Low Back Pain[1]	8	62.5%	39.7%	32.7%
Survey of Patients' Hospital Experiences				
Area Around Room 'Always' Quiet at Night[11]	(a)	69%	-	58%
Doctors 'Always' Communicated Well[11]	(a)	81%	-	80%
Home Recovery Information Given[11]	(a)	85%	-	82%
Hospital Given 9 or 10 on 10 Point Scale[11]	(a)	83%	-	67%
Meds 'Always' Explained Before Given[11]	(a)	58%	-	60%
Nurses 'Always' Communicated Well[11]	(a)	81%	-	76%
Pain 'Always' Well Controlled[11]	(a)	74%	-	69%
Room and Bathroom 'Always' Clean[11]	(a)	87%	-	71%
Timely Help 'Always' Received[11]	(a)	82%	-	64%
Would Definitely Recommend Hospital[11]	(a)	82%	-	69%

Bigfork Valley Hospital

258 Pine Tree Drive
Bigfork, MN 56628
Phone: 218-743-3177
Fax: 218-743-3559
E-mail: wecare@bigforkvalley.org
URL: www.bigforkvalley.org
Type: Critical Access Hospitals
Emergency Services: Yes
Ownership: Govt - Hospital Dist/Auth
Beds: 20

Key Personnel:

Chief of Medical Staff . . . . George Rounds

Measure	Cases	This Hosp.	State Avg.	U.S. Avg.
Heart Attack Care				
ACE Inhibitor or ARB for LVSD[5]	0	-	97%	96%
Aspirin at Arrival[5]	0	-	99%	99%
Aspirin at Discharge[5]	0	-	99%	98%
Beta Blocker at Discharge[5]	0	-	99%	98%
Fibrinolytic Medication Timing[5]	0	-	55%	55%
PCI Within 90 Minutes of Arrival[5]	0	-	94%	90%
Smoking Cessation Advice[5]	0	-	99%	99%
Chest Pain/Possible Heart Attack Care				
Aspirin at Arrival[5]	0	-	97%	95%
Median Time to ECG (minutes)[5]	0	-	7	8
Median Time to Transfer (minutes)[5]	0	-	50	61
Fibrinolytic Medication Timing[5]	0	-	58%	54%
Heart Failure Care				
ACE Inhibitor or ARB for LVSD[1]	1	100%	96%	94%
Discharge Instructions[1]	12	42%	86%	88%
Evaluation of LVS Function[1]	13	85%	96%	98%
Smoking Cessation Advice[1]	1	100%	96%	98%
Pneumonia Care				
Appropriate Initial Antibiotic[1]	5	100%	90%	92%
Blood Culture Timing[1]	7	86%	95%	96%
Influenza Vaccine[1]	10	80%	92%	91%
Initial Antibiotic Timing[1]	14	79%	96%	95%
Pneumococcal Vaccine[1]	14	71%	92%	93%
Smoking Cessation Advice[1]	3	100%	95%	97%
Surgical Care Improvement Project				
Appropriate VTP Within 24 Hours[1]	17	100%	92%	92%
Appropriate Hair Removal	62	100%	99%	99%
Appropriate Beta Blocker Usage	28	54%	94%	93%
Controlled Postoperative Blood Glucose[5]	0	-	92%	93%
Prophylactic Antibiotic Timing	55	96%	96%	97%
Prophylactic Antibiotic Timing (Outpatient)[5]	0	-	89%	92%
Prophylactic Antibiotic Selection	55	100%	98%	97%
Prophylactic Antibiotic Select. (Outpatient)[5]	0	-	95%	94%
Prophylactic Antibiotic Stopped	55	96%	97%	94%
Recommended VTP Ordered[1]	17	100%	93%	94%
Urinary Catheter Removal	33	100%	90%	90%
Children's Asthma Care				
Received Systemic Corticosteroids	-	-	-	100%
Received Home Management Plan	-	-	-	71%
Received Reliever Medication	-	-	-	100%
Use of Medical Imaging				
Combination Abdominal CT Scan[1]	33	0.000	0.100	0.191
Combination Chest CT Scan[1]	23	0.043	0.018	0.054
Follow-up Mammogram/Ultrasound	122	4.9%	6.4%	8.4%
MRI for Low Back Pain[1]	11	27.3%	39.7%	32.7%
Survey of Patients' Hospital Experiences				
Area Around Room 'Always' Quiet at Night	(a)	71%	-	58%
Doctors 'Always' Communicated Well	(a)	90%	-	80%
Home Recovery Information Given	(a)	90%	-	82%
Hospital Given 9 or 10 on 10 Point Scale	(a)	88%	-	67%
Meds 'Always' Explained Before Given	(a)	80%	-	60%
Nurses 'Always' Communicated Well	(a)	88%	-	76%
Pain 'Always' Well Controlled	(a)	83%	-	69%
Room and Bathroom 'Always' Clean	(a)	93%	-	71%
Timely Help 'Always' Received	(a)	93%	-	64%
Would Definitely Recommend Hospital	(a)	93%	-	69%

United Hospital District

515 South Moore Street
Blue Earth, MN 56013
Phone: 507-526-3273
Fax: 507-526-3621
URL: www.uhd.org
Type: Critical Access Hospitals
Emergency Services: Yes
Ownership: Govt - Hospital Dist/Auth
Beds: 43

Key Personnel:

Chief of Medical Staff . . . . Kevin Kimm, DO
Infection Control. . . . . Pam Manzke
Operating Room. . . . . Melissa Storbeck
Quality Assurance . . . . Pam Manzle

Measure	Cases	This Hosp.	State Avg.	U.S. Avg.
Heart Attack Care				
ACE Inhibitor or ARB for LVSD[1,3]	2	50%	97%	96%
Aspirin at Arrival[1,3]	4	100%	99%	99%
Aspirin at Discharge[1,3]	4	100%	99%	98%
Beta Blocker at Discharge[1,3]	3	100%	99%	98%
Fibrinolytic Medication Timing[3]	0	-	55%	55%
PCI Within 90 Minutes of Arrival[3]	0	-	94%	90%
Smoking Cessation Advice[3]	0	-	99%	99%
Chest Pain/Possible Heart Attack Care				
Aspirin at Arrival[1,3]	15	93%	97%	95%
Median Time to ECG (minutes)[1,3]	15	4	7	8
Median Time to Transfer (minutes)[1,3]	2	118	50	61
Fibrinolytic Medication Timing[1,3]	2	50%	58%	54%
Heart Failure Care				
ACE Inhibitor or ARB for LVSD[1]	2	100%	96%	94%
Discharge Instructions[1]	13	38%	86%	88%
Evaluation of LVS Function[1]	18	78%	96%	98%
Smoking Cessation Advice[1]	1	0%	96%	98%
Pneumonia Care				
Appropriate Initial Antibiotic[5]	0	-	90%	92%
Blood Culture Timing[1]	24	88%	95%	96%
Influenza Vaccine[1]	17	100%	92%	91%
Initial Antibiotic Timing	37	92%	96%	95%
Pneumococcal Vaccine	37	100%	92%	93%
Smoking Cessation Advice[1]	3	100%	95%	97%
Surgical Care Improvement Project				
Appropriate VTP Within 24 Hours[1]	8	100%	92%	92%
Appropriate Hair Removal	41	100%	99%	99%
Appropriate Beta Blocker Usage[5]	0	-	94%	93%
Controlled Postoperative Blood Glucose	0	-	92%	93%
Prophylactic Antibiotic Timing	33	91%	96%	97%
Prophylactic Antibiotic Timing (Outpatient)[5]	0	-	89%	92%
Prophylactic Antibiotic Selection	33	100%	98%	97%
Prophylactic Antibiotic Select. (Outpatient)[5]	0	-	95%	94%
Prophylactic Antibiotic Stopped	33	97%	97%	94%
Recommended VTP Ordered[1]	8	100%	93%	94%
Urinary Catheter Removal[1]	19	84%	90%	90%
Children's Asthma Care				
Received Systemic Corticosteroids	-	-	-	100%
Received Home Management Plan	-	-	-	71%
Received Reliever Medication	-	-	-	100%
Use of Medical Imaging				
Combination Abdominal CT Scan	104	0.000	0.100	0.191
Combination Chest CT Scan	70	0.000	0.018	0.054
Follow-up Mammogram/Ultrasound	255	9.0%	6.4%	8.4%
MRI for Low Back Pain[1]	23	39.1%	39.7%	32.7%
Survey of Patients' Hospital Experiences				
Area Around Room 'Always' Quiet at Night	(a)	74%	-	58%
Doctors 'Always' Communicated Well	(a)	88%	-	80%
Home Recovery Information Given	(a)	88%	-	82%
Hospital Given 9 or 10 on 10 Point Scale	(a)	81%	-	67%
Meds 'Always' Explained Before Given	(a)	67%	-	60%
Nurses 'Always' Communicated Well	(a)	88%	-	76%
Pain 'Always' Well Controlled	(a)	77%	-	69%
Room and Bathroom 'Always' Clean	(a)	86%	-	71%
Timely Help 'Always' Received	(a)	79%	-	64%
Would Definitely Recommend Hospital	(a)	84%	-	69%

NOTE: Hospital profiles are in alphabetical order by state, then city, then hospital within the city; Rankings exclude hospitals with less than 25 cases except for patient surveys which excludes hospitals with less than 100 cases; (a) 100–299 cases; (1) The number of cases is too small to be sure how well a hospital is performing; (2) The hospital indicated that the data submitted for this measure were based on a sample of cases; (3) Data was collected during a shorter time period (fewer quarters) than the maximum possible time for this measure; (4) Suppressed for one or more quarters by CMS; (5) No data is available from the hospital for this measure; (6) Fewer than 100 patients completed the HCAHPS survey. Use these rates with caution, as the number of surveys may be too low to reliably assess hospital performance; (7) Survey results are based on less than 12 months of data; (8) Survey results are not available for this reporting period; (9) No or very few patients were eligible for the HCAHPS survey. The scores shown, if any, reflect a very small number of surveys; (10) A state average was not calculated because too few hospitals in the state submitted data; (11) There were discrepancies in the data collection process; Please refer to the User's Guide for a full explanation of data.

Essentia Health St Joseph's Medical Center

523 North 3rd Street Phone: 218-829-2861
Brainerd, MN 56401 Fax: 218-828-3103
URL: www.sjmcmn.org
Type: Acute Care Hospitals Emergency Services: Yes
Ownership: Voluntary Non-Profit - Church Beds: 162
Key Personnel:
CEO/President.............. Jani Wiebolt
Chief of Medical Staff.......... Nicholas Bernier
Quality Assurance .... Dennis A Acrea
Radiology................... Charles A Benson

Measure	Cases	This Hosp.	State Avg.	U.S. Avg.
Heart Attack Care				
ACE Inhibitor or ARB for LVSD[1]	4	75%	97%	96%
Aspirin at Arrival	33	94%	99%	99%
Aspirin at Discharge[1]	24	96%	99%	98%
Beta Blocker at Discharge[1]	22	100%	99%	98%
Fibrinolytic Medication Timing	0	-	55%	55%
PCI Within 90 Minutes of Arrival	0	-	94%	90%
Smoking Cessation Advice[1]	3	100%	99%	99%
Chest Pain/Possible Heart Attack Care				
Aspirin at Arrival	159	99%	97%	95%
Median Time to ECG (minutes)	164	9	7	8
Median Time to Transfer (minutes)[1]	21	28	50	61
Fibrinolytic Medication Timing	0	-	58%	54%
Heart Failure Care				
ACE Inhibitor or ARB for LVSD	54	78%	96%	94%
Discharge Instructions	126	73%	86%	88%
Evaluation of LVS Function	191	96%	96%	98%
Smoking Cessation Advice[1]	23	100%	96%	98%
Pneumonia Care				
Appropriate Initial Antibiotic	65	85%	90%	92%
Blood Culture Timing	108	99%	95%	96%
Influenza Vaccine	70	91%	92%	91%
Initial Antibiotic Timing	106	99%	96%	95%
Pneumococcal Vaccine	132	86%	92%	93%
Smoking Cessation Advice	40	90%	95%	97%
Surgical Care Improvement Project				
Appropriate VTP Within 24 Hours[2]	89	98%	92%	92%
Appropriate Hair Removal[2]	348	100%	99%	99%
Appropriate Beta Blocker Usage[2]	99	92%	94%	93%
Controlled Postoperative Blood Glucose[2]	0	-	92%	93%
Prophylactic Antibiotic Timing[2]	257	96%	96%	97%
Prophylactic Antibiotic Timing (Outpatient)	47	91%	89%	92%
Prophylactic Antibiotic Selection[2]	257	96%	98%	97%
Prophylactic Antibiotic Select. (Outpatient)	45	93%	95%	94%
Prophylactic Antibiotic Stopped[2]	247	94%	97%	94%
Recommended VTP Ordered[2]	89	98%	93%	94%
Urinary Catheter Removal[1,2]	21	76%	90%	90%
Children's Asthma Care				
Received Systemic Corticosteroids	-	-	-	100%
Received Home Management Plan	-	-	-	71%
Received Reliever Medication	-	-	-	100%
Use of Medical Imaging				
Combination Abdominal CT Scan	648	0.046	0.100	0.191
Combination Chest CT Scan	679	0.000	0.018	0.054
Follow-up Mammogram/Ultrasound	1,511	5.4%	6.4%	8.4%
MRI for Low Back Pain	210	37.6%	39.7%	32.7%
Survey of Patients' Hospital Experiences				
Area Around Room 'Always' Quiet at Night	300+	61%	-	58%
Doctors 'Always' Communicated Well	300+	79%	-	80%
Home Recovery Information Given	300+	86%	-	82%
Hospital Given 9 or 10 on 10 Point Scale	300+	69%	-	67%
Meds 'Always' Explained Before Given	300+	62%	-	60%
Nurses 'Always' Communicated Well	300+	78%	-	76%
Pain 'Always' Well Controlled	300+	70%	-	69%
Room and Bathroom 'Always' Clean	300+	77%	-	71%
Timely Help 'Always' Received	300+	70%	-	64%
Would Definitely Recommend Hospital	300+	68%	-	69%

Saint Francis Healthcare Campus

2400 St Francis Drive Phone: 218-643-3000
Breckenridge, MN 56520 Fax: 218-643-7502
URL: www.sfcare.org
Type: Critical Access Hospitals Emergency Services: Yes
Ownership: Voluntary Non-Profit - Church Beds: 42
Key Personnel:
CEO/President.............. David Nelson
Quality Assurance .... Mary Helland
Radiology................... Lawrence Licht, MD

Measure	Cases	This Hosp.	State Avg.	U.S. Avg.
Heart Attack Care				
ACE Inhibitor or ARB for LVSD	0	-	97%	96%
Aspirin at Arrival[1]	9	100%	99%	99%
Aspirin at Discharge[1]	8	88%	99%	98%
Beta Blocker at Discharge[1]	6	67%	99%	98%
Fibrinolytic Medication Timing	0	-	55%	55%
PCI Within 90 Minutes of Arrival	0	-	94%	90%
Smoking Cessation Advice	0	-	99%	99%
Chest Pain/Possible Heart Attack Care				
Aspirin at Arrival[5]	0	-	97%	95%
Median Time to ECG (minutes)[5]	0	-	7	8
Median Time to Transfer (minutes)[5]	0	-	50	61
Fibrinolytic Medication Timing[5]	0	-	58%	54%
Heart Failure Care				
ACE Inhibitor or ARB for LVSD[1]	3	100%	96%	94%
Discharge Instructions	36	86%	86%	88%
Evaluation of LVS Function	42	95%	96%	98%
Smoking Cessation Advice[1]	3	67%	96%	98%
Pneumonia Care				
Appropriate Initial Antibiotic	43	77%	90%	92%
Blood Culture Timing[1]	6	100%	95%	96%
Influenza Vaccine	33	97%	92%	91%
Initial Antibiotic Timing	43	93%	96%	95%
Pneumococcal Vaccine	60	98%	92%	93%
Smoking Cessation Advice[1]	20	100%	95%	97%
Surgical Care Improvement Project				
Appropriate VTP Within 24 Hours[2]	30	60%	92%	92%
Appropriate Hair Removal[2]	44	93%	99%	99%
Appropriate Beta Blocker Usage[1,2]	9	56%	94%	93%
Controlled Postoperative Blood Glucose[2]	0	-	92%	93%
Prophylactic Antibiotic Timing[2]	26	62%	96%	97%
Prophylactic Antibiotic Timing (Outpatient)[5]	0	-	89%	92%
Prophylactic Antibiotic Selection[2]	25	92%	98%	97%
Prophylactic Antibiotic Select. (Outpatient)[5]	0	-	95%	94%
Prophylactic Antibiotic Stopped[2]	25	84%	97%	94%
Recommended VTP Ordered[2]	30	60%	93%	94%
Urinary Catheter Removal[1]	4	50%	90%	90%
Children's Asthma Care				
Received Systemic Corticosteroids	-	-	-	100%
Received Home Management Plan	-	-	-	71%
Received Reliever Medication	-	-	-	100%
Use of Medical Imaging				
Combination Abdominal CT Scan	170	0.112	0.100	0.191
Combination Chest CT Scan	88	0.136	0.018	0.054
Follow-up Mammogram/Ultrasound	133	3.0%	6.4%	8.4%
MRI for Low Back Pain	56	28.6%	39.7%	32.7%
Survey of Patients' Hospital Experiences				
Area Around Room 'Always' Quiet at Night	(a)	61%	-	58%
Doctors 'Always' Communicated Well	(a)	87%	-	80%
Home Recovery Information Given	(a)	83%	-	82%
Hospital Given 9 or 10 on 10 Point Scale	(a)	73%	-	67%
Meds 'Always' Explained Before Given	(a)	72%	-	60%
Nurses 'Always' Communicated Well	(a)	79%	-	76%
Pain 'Always' Well Controlled	(a)	73%	-	69%
Room and Bathroom 'Always' Clean	(a)	78%	-	71%
Timely Help 'Always' Received	(a)	72%	-	64%
Would Definitely Recommend Hospital	(a)	74%	-	69%

Buffalo Hospital

303 Catlin St Phone: 763-684-1212
Buffalo, MN 55313 Fax: 763-684-7104
URL: www.buffalohospital.org
Type: Acute Care Hospitals Emergency Services: Yes
Ownership: Voluntary Non-Profit - Other Beds: 65
Key Personnel:
CEO/President.............. Steve Hatkin
Chief of Medical Staff.......... Dr Charles Yancey
Operating Room.............. Julianne Wagner
Quality Assurance .... Gretchen Frederick
Radiology................... Kurt Scheurer, MD
Emergency Room .... Charles Lick
Intensive Care Unit............ Gretchen Frederick
Patient Relations .... Linda Auleciems

Measure	Cases	This Hosp.	State Avg.	U.S. Avg.
Heart Attack Care				
ACE Inhibitor or ARB for LVSD[1]	2	100%	97%	96%
Aspirin at Arrival[1]	5	100%	99%	99%
Aspirin at Discharge[1]	4	100%	99%	98%
Beta Blocker at Discharge[1]	4	100%	99%	98%
Fibrinolytic Medication Timing	0	-	55%	55%
PCI Within 90 Minutes of Arrival	0	-	94%	90%
Smoking Cessation Advice	0	-	99%	99%
Chest Pain/Possible Heart Attack Care				
Aspirin at Arrival	94	100%	97%	95%
Median Time to ECG (minutes)	100	9	7	8
Median Time to Transfer (minutes)[1,3]	11	48	50	61
Fibrinolytic Medication Timing	0	-	58%	54%
Heart Failure Care				
ACE Inhibitor or ARB for LVSD[1]	7	100%	96%	94%
Discharge Instructions	38	95%	86%	88%
Evaluation of LVS Function	61	100%	96%	98%
Smoking Cessation Advice[1]	4	100%	96%	98%
Pneumonia Care				
Appropriate Initial Antibiotic	40	95%	90%	92%
Blood Culture Timing	42	93%	95%	96%
Influenza Vaccine	29	100%	92%	91%
Initial Antibiotic Timing	52	98%	96%	95%
Pneumococcal Vaccine	45	100%	92%	93%
Smoking Cessation Advice[1]	18	100%	95%	97%
Surgical Care Improvement Project				
Appropriate VTP Within 24 Hours	51	100%	92%	92%
Appropriate Hair Removal	219	100%	99%	99%
Appropriate Beta Blocker Usage	48	100%	94%	93%
Controlled Postoperative Blood Glucose	0	-	92%	93%
Prophylactic Antibiotic Timing	161	98%	96%	97%
Prophylactic Antibiotic Timing (Outpatient)	82	95%	89%	92%
Prophylactic Antibiotic Selection	163	99%	98%	97%
Prophylactic Antibiotic Select. (Outpatient)	79	96%	95%	94%
Prophylactic Antibiotic Stopped	151	97%	97%	94%
Recommended VTP Ordered	51	100%	93%	94%
Urinary Catheter Removal	58	100%	90%	90%
Children's Asthma Care				
Received Systemic Corticosteroids	-	-	-	100%
Received Home Management Plan	-	-	-	71%
Received Reliever Medication	-	-	-	100%
Use of Medical Imaging				
Combination Abdominal CT Scan	295	0.034	0.100	0.191
Combination Chest CT Scan	220	0.005	0.018	0.054
Follow-up Mammogram/Ultrasound	248	1.6%	6.4%	8.4%
MRI for Low Back Pain	88	33.0%	39.7%	32.7%
Survey of Patients' Hospital Experiences				
Area Around Room 'Always' Quiet at Night	300+	57%	-	58%
Doctors 'Always' Communicated Well	300+	79%	-	80%
Home Recovery Information Given	300+	87%	-	82%
Hospital Given 9 or 10 on 10 Point Scale	300+	65%	-	67%
Meds 'Always' Explained Before Given	300+	61%	-	60%
Nurses 'Always' Communicated Well	300+	79%	-	76%
Pain 'Always' Well Controlled	300+	68%	-	69%
Room and Bathroom 'Always' Clean	300+	75%	-	71%
Timely Help 'Always' Received	300+	67%	-	64%
Would Definitely Recommend Hospital	300+	67%	-	69%

NOTE: Hospital profiles are in alphabetical order by state, then city, then hospital within the city; Rankings exclude hospitals with less than 25 cases except for patient surveys which excludes hospitals with less than 100 cases; (a) 100–299 cases; (1) The number of cases is too small to be sure how well a hospital is performing; (2) The hospital indicated that the data submitted for this measure were based on a sample of cases; (3) Data was collected during a shorter time period (fewer quarters) than the maximum possible time for this measure; (4) Suppressed for one or more quarters by CMS; (5) No data is available from the hospital for this measure; (6) Fewer than 100 patients completed the HCAHPS survey. Use these rates with caution, as the number of surveys may be too low to reliably assess hospital performance; (7) Survey results are based on less than 12 months of data; (8) Survey results are not available for this reporting period; (9) No or very few patients were eligible for the HCAHPS survey. The scores shown, if any, reflect a very small number of surveys; (10) A state average was not calculated because too few hospitals in the state submitted data; (11) There were discrepancies in the data collection process; Please refer to the User's Guide for a full explanation of data.

Fairview Ridges Hospital

201 East Nicollet Boulevard   Phone: 952-892-2000
Burnsville, MN 55337   Fax: 952-892-2107
URL: www.fairview.org
Type: Acute Care Hospitals   Emergency Services: Yes
Ownership: Voluntary Non-Profit - Church   Beds: 150

Key Personnel:
CEO/President. . . . . Beth Krehbiel
Chief of Medical Staff . . . . Lois A Lenarz
Patient Relations . . . . Helen Strike

Measure	Cases	This Hosp.	State Avg.	U.S. Avg.
Heart Attack Care				
ACE Inhibitor or ARB for LVSD[1]	7	100%	97%	96%
Aspirin at Arrival	69	100%	99%	99%
Aspirin at Discharge	60	98%	99%	98%
Beta Blocker at Discharge	59	100%	99%	98%
Fibrinolytic Medication Timing[1]	1	100%	55%	55%
PCI Within 90 Minutes of Arrival	0	-	94%	90%
Smoking Cessation Advice[1]	21	100%	99%	99%
Chest Pain/Possible Heart Attack Care				
Aspirin at Arrival	101	100%	97%	95%
Median Time to ECG (minutes)	109	14	7	8
Median Time to Transfer (minutes)	29	54	50	61
Fibrinolytic Medication Timing	0	-	58%	54%
Heart Failure Care				
ACE Inhibitor or ARB for LVSD	40	95%	96%	94%
Discharge Instructions	122	99%	86%	88%
Evaluation of LVS Function	151	99%	96%	98%
Smoking Cessation Advice	29	100%	96%	98%
Pneumonia Care				
Appropriate Initial Antibiotic	115	94%	90%	92%
Blood Culture Timing	238	96%	95%	96%
Influenza Vaccine	134	96%	92%	91%
Initial Antibiotic Timing	222	97%	96%	95%
Pneumococcal Vaccine	168	97%	92%	93%
Smoking Cessation Advice	47	100%	95%	97%
Surgical Care Improvement Project				
Appropriate VTP Within 24 Hours[2]	160	79%	92%	92%
Appropriate Hair Removal[2]	767	100%	99%	99%
Appropriate Beta Blocker Usage[2]	222	87%	94%	93%
Controlled Postoperative Blood Glucose[2]	0	-	92%	93%
Prophylactic Antibiotic Timing[2]	620	98%	96%	97%
Prophylactic Antibiotic Timing (Outpatient)	253	95%	89%	92%
Prophylactic Antibiotic Selection[2]	622	100%	98%	97%
Prophylactic Antibiotic Select. (Outpatient)	249	99%	95%	94%
Prophylactic Antibiotic Stopped[2]	616	97%	97%	94%
Recommended VTP Ordered[2]	160	91%	93%	94%
Urinary Catheter Removal[2]	326	95%	90%	90%
Children's Asthma Care				
Received Systemic Corticosteroids	-	-	-	100%
Received Home Management Plan	-	-	-	71%
Received Reliever Medication	-	-	-	100%
Use of Medical Imaging				
Combination Abdominal CT Scan	684	0.048	0.100	0.191
Combination Chest CT Scan	651	0.005	0.018	0.054
Follow-up Mammogram/Ultrasound	908	10.8%	6.4%	8.4%
MRI for Low Back Pain	99	41.4%	39.7%	32.7%
Survey of Patients' Hospital Experiences				
Area Around Room 'Always' Quiet at Night	300+	56%	-	58%
Doctors 'Always' Communicated Well	300+	76%	-	80%
Home Recovery Information Given	300+	87%	-	82%
Hospital Given 9 or 10 on 10 Point Scale	300+	68%	-	67%
Meds 'Always' Explained Before Given	300+	60%	-	60%
Nurses 'Always' Communicated Well	300+	72%	-	76%
Pain 'Always' Well Controlled	300+	62%	-	69%
Room and Bathroom 'Always' Clean	300+	68%	-	71%
Timely Help 'Always' Received	300+	62%	-	64%
Would Definitely Recommend Hospital	300+	72%	-	69%

Cambridge Medical Center

701 South Dellwood   Phone: 763-689-7700
Cambridge, MN 55008
Type: Acute Care Hospitals   Emergency Services: Yes
Ownership: Voluntary Non-Profit - Private

Key Personnel:
CEO/President. . . . . Dennis Doran
Chief of Medical Staff . . . . Robert Callen MD

Measure	Cases	This Hosp.	State Avg.	U.S. Avg.
Heart Attack Care				
ACE Inhibitor or ARB for LVSD[1]	3	100%	97%	96%
Aspirin at Arrival[1]	10	90%	99%	99%
Aspirin at Discharge[1]	6	100%	99%	98%
Beta Blocker at Discharge[1]	8	100%	99%	98%
Fibrinolytic Medication Timing	0	-	55%	55%
PCI Within 90 Minutes of Arrival	0	-	94%	90%
Smoking Cessation Advice[1]	1	100%	99%	99%
Chest Pain/Possible Heart Attack Care				
Aspirin at Arrival	75	100%	97%	95%
Median Time to ECG (minutes)	76	2	7	8
Median Time to Transfer (minutes)[1,3]	5	44	50	61
Fibrinolytic Medication Timing	0	-	58%	54%
Heart Failure Care				
ACE Inhibitor or ARB for LVSD[1]	12	100%	96%	94%
Discharge Instructions	38	95%	86%	88%
Evaluation of LVS Function	50	100%	96%	98%
Smoking Cessation Advice[1]	8	100%	96%	98%
Pneumonia Care				
Appropriate Initial Antibiotic	52	90%	90%	92%
Blood Culture Timing	81	98%	95%	96%
Influenza Vaccine	40	100%	92%	91%
Initial Antibiotic Timing	63	100%	96%	95%
Pneumococcal Vaccine	67	97%	92%	93%
Smoking Cessation Advice[1]	22	100%	95%	97%
Surgical Care Improvement Project				
Appropriate VTP Within 24 Hours	35	97%	92%	92%
Appropriate Hair Removal	257	99%	99%	99%
Appropriate Beta Blocker Usage	66	98%	94%	93%
Controlled Postoperative Blood Glucose	0	-	92%	93%
Prophylactic Antibiotic Timing	194	98%	96%	97%
Prophylactic Antibiotic Timing (Outpatient)[1,3]	19	89%	89%	92%
Prophylactic Antibiotic Selection	196	98%	98%	97%
Prophylactic Antibiotic Select. (Outpatient)[1,3]	20	100%	95%	94%
Prophylactic Antibiotic Stopped	186	98%	97%	94%
Recommended VTP Ordered	35	100%	93%	94%
Urinary Catheter Removal	53	96%	90%	90%
Children's Asthma Care				
Received Systemic Corticosteroids	-	-	-	100%
Received Home Management Plan	-	-	-	71%
Received Reliever Medication	-	-	-	100%
Use of Medical Imaging				
Combination Abdominal CT Scan	366	0.041	0.100	0.191
Combination Chest CT Scan	269	0.019	0.018	0.054
Follow-up Mammogram/Ultrasound	686	4.8%	6.4%	8.4%
MRI for Low Back Pain	120	43.3%	39.7%	32.7%
Survey of Patients' Hospital Experiences				
Area Around Room 'Always' Quiet at Night	300+	60%	-	58%
Doctors 'Always' Communicated Well	300+	80%	-	80%
Home Recovery Information Given	300+	87%	-	82%
Hospital Given 9 or 10 on 10 Point Scale	300+	65%	-	67%
Meds 'Always' Explained Before Given	300+	60%	-	60%
Nurses 'Always' Communicated Well	300+	77%	-	76%
Pain 'Always' Well Controlled	300+	67%	-	69%
Room and Bathroom 'Always' Clean	300+	69%	-	71%
Timely Help 'Always' Received	300+	73%	-	64%
Would Definitely Recommend Hospital	300+	67%	-	69%

Sanford Canby Medical Center

112 St Olaf Avenue South   Phone: 507-223-7277
Canby, MN 56220   Fax: 507-223-7465
E-mail: info@siouxvalleycanbycampus.org
URL: www.siouxvalleycanbycampus.org
Type: Critical Access Hospitals   Emergency Services: Yes
Ownership: Voluntary Non-Profit - Private   Beds: 102

Key Personnel:
CEO/President. . . . . Robert Foreman
Quality Assurance . . . . Sally Vogt

Measure	Cases	This Hosp.	State Avg.	U.S. Avg.
Heart Attack Care				
ACE Inhibitor or ARB for LVSD	0	-	97%	96%
Aspirin at Arrival[1]	2	50%	99%	99%
Aspirin at Discharge[1]	2	50%	99%	98%
Beta Blocker at Discharge[1]	2	100%	99%	98%
Fibrinolytic Medication Timing	0	-	55%	55%
PCI Within 90 Minutes of Arrival	0	-	94%	90%
Smoking Cessation Advice	0	-	99%	99%
Chest Pain/Possible Heart Attack Care				
Aspirin at Arrival[1,3]	5	80%	97%	95%
Median Time to ECG (minutes)[1,3]	6	4	7	8
Median Time to Transfer (minutes)[5]	0	-	50	61
Fibrinolytic Medication Timing[3]	0	-	58%	54%
Heart Failure Care				
ACE Inhibitor or ARB for LVSD[1,3]	1	100%	96%	94%
Discharge Instructions[1,3]	3	33%	86%	88%
Evaluation of LVS Function[1,3]	5	80%	96%	98%
Smoking Cessation Advice[3]	0	-	96%	98%
Pneumonia Care				
Appropriate Initial Antibiotic[1]	8	75%	90%	92%
Blood Culture Timing[1]	1	100%	95%	96%
Influenza Vaccine[1]	9	67%	92%	91%
Initial Antibiotic Timing[1]	15	87%	96%	95%
Pneumococcal Vaccine[1]	20	75%	92%	93%
Smoking Cessation Advice	0	-	95%	97%
Surgical Care Improvement Project				
Appropriate VTP Within 24 Hours[1]	10	70%	92%	92%
Appropriate Hair Removal[1]	14	93%	99%	99%
Appropriate Beta Blocker Usage[1]	5	100%	94%	93%
Controlled Postoperative Blood Glucose	0	-	92%	93%
Prophylactic Antibiotic Timing[1]	11	91%	96%	97%
Prophylactic Antibiotic Timing (Outpatient)[1,3]	2	0%	89%	92%
Prophylactic Antibiotic Selection[1]	11	82%	98%	97%
Prophylactic Antibiotic Select. (Outpatient)[3]	0	-	95%	94%
Prophylactic Antibiotic Stopped[1]	11	100%	97%	94%
Recommended VTP Ordered[1]	10	70%	93%	94%
Urinary Catheter Removal[1]	4	50%	90%	90%
Children's Asthma Care				
Received Systemic Corticosteroids	-	-	-	100%
Received Home Management Plan	-	-	-	71%
Received Reliever Medication	-	-	-	100%
Use of Medical Imaging				
Combination Abdominal CT Scan[1]	46	0.761	0.100	0.191
Combination Chest CT Scan[1]	26	0.385	0.018	0.054
Follow-up Mammogram/Ultrasound	191	2.1%	6.4%	8.4%
MRI for Low Back Pain[1]	20	35.0%	39.7%	32.7%
Survey of Patients' Hospital Experiences				
Area Around Room 'Always' Quiet at Night	(a)	56%	-	58%
Doctors 'Always' Communicated Well	(a)	77%	-	80%
Home Recovery Information Given	(a)	85%	-	82%
Hospital Given 9 or 10 on 10 Point Scale	(a)	73%	-	67%
Meds 'Always' Explained Before Given	(a)	63%	-	60%
Nurses 'Always' Communicated Well	(a)	81%	-	76%
Pain 'Always' Well Controlled	(a)	59%	-	69%
Room and Bathroom 'Always' Clean	(a)	79%	-	71%
Timely Help 'Always' Received	(a)	70%	-	64%
Would Definitely Recommend Hospital	(a)	64%	-	69%

NOTE: Hospital profiles are in alphabetical order by state, then city, then hospital within the city; Rankings exclude hospitals with less than 25 cases except for patient surveys which excludes hospitals with less than 100 cases; (a) 100–299 cases; (1) The number of cases is too small to be sure how well a hospital is performing; (2) The hospital indicated that the data submitted for this measure were based on a sample of cases; (3) Data was collected during a shorter time period (fewer quarters) than the maximum possible time for this measure; (4) Suppressed for one or more quarters by CMS; (5) No data is available from the hospital for this measure; (6) Fewer than 100 patients completed the HCAHPS survey. Use these rates with caution, as the number of surveys may be too low to reliably assess hospital performance; (7) Survey results are based on less than 12 months of data; (8) Survey results are not available for this reporting period; (9) No or very few patients were eligible for the HCAHPS survey. The scores shown, if any, reflect a very small number of surveys; (10) A state average was not calculated because too few hospitals in the state submitted data; (11) There were discrepancies in the data collection process; Please refer to the User's Guide for a full explanation of data.

Cannon Falls Medical Center Mayo

1116 West Mill Street Phone: 507-263-4221
Cannon Falls, MN 55009 Fax: 507-263-0221
Type: Critical Access Hospitals Emergency Services: Yes
Ownership: Voluntary Non-Profit - Private Beds: 21
Key Personnel:
CEO/President. . . . . Glenn Christian

Measure	Cases	This Hosp.	State Avg.	U.S. Avg.
Heart Attack Care				
ACE Inhibitor or ARB for LVSD[5]	0	-	97%	96%
Aspirin at Arrival[5]	0	-	99%	99%
Aspirin at Discharge[5]	0	-	99%	98%
Beta Blocker at Discharge[5]	0	-	99%	98%
Fibrinolytic Medication Timing[5]	0	-	55%	55%
PCI Within 90 Minutes of Arrival[5]	0	-	94%	90%
Smoking Cessation Advice[5]	0	-	99%	99%
Chest Pain/Possible Heart Attack Care				
Aspirin at Arrival[5]	0	-	97%	95%
Median Time to ECG (minutes)[5]	0	-	7	8
Median Time to Transfer (minutes)[5]	0	-	50	61
Fibrinolytic Medication Timing[5]	0	-	58%	54%
Heart Failure Care				
ACE Inhibitor or ARB for LVSD[1]	3	100%	96%	94%
Discharge Instructions[1]	7	86%	86%	88%
Evaluation of LVS Function[1]	16	94%	96%	98%
Smoking Cessation Advice	0	-	96%	98%
Pneumonia Care				
Appropriate Initial Antibiotic[1]	8	100%	90%	92%
Blood Culture Timing[1]	4	75%	95%	96%
Influenza Vaccine[1]	10	100%	92%	91%
Initial Antibiotic Timing[1]	8	100%	96%	95%
Pneumococcal Vaccine[1]	15	93%	92%	93%
Smoking Cessation Advice[1]	5	100%	95%	97%
Surgical Care Improvement Project				
Appropriate VTP Within 24 Hours[1]	11	100%	92%	92%
Appropriate Hair Removal	27	100%	99%	99%
Appropriate Beta Blocker Usage[1]	14	86%	94%	93%
Controlled Postoperative Blood Glucose	0	-	92%	93%
Prophylactic Antibiotic Timing[1]	24	100%	96%	97%
Prophylactic Antibiotic Timing (Outpatient)[5]	0	-	89%	92%
Prophylactic Antibiotic Selection[1]	24	100%	98%	97%
Prophylactic Antibiotic Select. (Outpatient)[5]	0	-	95%	94%
Prophylactic Antibiotic Stopped[1]	24	96%	97%	94%
Recommended VTP Ordered[1]	11	100%	93%	94%
Urinary Catheter Removal[1]	10	100%	90%	90%
Children's Asthma Care				
Received Systemic Corticosteroids	-	-	-	100%
Received Home Management Plan	-	-	-	71%
Received Reliever Medication	-	-	-	100%
Use of Medical Imaging				
Combination Abdominal CT Scan[1]	25	0.360	0.100	0.191
Combination Chest CT Scan[1]	16	0.188	0.018	0.054
Follow-up Mammogram/Ultrasound	97	7.2%	6.4%	8.4%
MRI for Low Back Pain[1]	9	11.1%	39.7%	32.7%
Survey of Patients' Hospital Experiences				
Area Around Room 'Always' Quiet at Night[8]	-	-	-	58%
Doctors 'Always' Communicated Well[8]	-	-	-	80%
Home Recovery Information Given[8]	-	-	-	82%
Hospital Given 9 or 10 on 10 Point Scale[8]	-	-	-	67%
Meds 'Always' Explained Before Given[8]	-	-	-	60%
Nurses 'Always' Communicated Well[8]	-	-	-	76%
Pain 'Always' Well Controlled[8]	-	-	-	69%
Room and Bathroom 'Always' Clean[8]	-	-	-	71%
Timely Help 'Always' Received[8]	-	-	-	64%
Would Definitely Recommend Hospital[8]	-	-	-	69%

Cass Lake Indian Health Services Hospital

425 7th Street NW Phone: 218-335-3200
Cass Lake, MN 56633
Type: Critical Access Hospitals Emergency Services: Yes
Ownership: Government - Federal

Measure	Cases	This Hosp.	State Avg.	U.S. Avg.
Heart Attack Care				
ACE Inhibitor or ARB for LVSD	-	-	97%	96%
Aspirin at Arrival	-	-	99%	99%
Aspirin at Discharge	-	-	99%	98%
Beta Blocker at Discharge	-	-	99%	98%
Fibrinolytic Medication Timing	-	-	55%	55%
PCI Within 90 Minutes of Arrival	-	-	94%	90%
Smoking Cessation Advice	-	-	99%	99%
Chest Pain/Possible Heart Attack Care				
Aspirin at Arrival[5]	0	-	97%	95%
Median Time to ECG (minutes)[5]	0	-	7	8
Median Time to Transfer (minutes)[5]	0	-	50	61
Fibrinolytic Medication Timing[5]	0	-	58%	54%
Heart Failure Care				
ACE Inhibitor or ARB for LVSD	-	-	96%	94%
Discharge Instructions	-	-	86%	88%
Evaluation of LVS Function	-	-	96%	98%
Smoking Cessation Advice	-	-	96%	98%
Pneumonia Care				
Appropriate Initial Antibiotic	-	-	90%	92%
Blood Culture Timing	-	-	95%	96%
Influenza Vaccine	-	-	92%	91%
Initial Antibiotic Timing	-	-	96%	95%
Pneumococcal Vaccine	-	-	92%	93%
Smoking Cessation Advice	-	-	95%	97%
Surgical Care Improvement Project				
Appropriate VTP Within 24 Hours	-	-	92%	92%
Appropriate Hair Removal	-	-	99%	99%
Appropriate Beta Blocker Usage	-	-	94%	93%
Controlled Postoperative Blood Glucose	-	-	92%	93%
Prophylactic Antibiotic Timing	-	-	96%	97%
Prophylactic Antibiotic Timing (Outpatient)[5]	0	-	89%	92%
Prophylactic Antibiotic Selection	-	-	98%	97%
Prophylactic Antibiotic Select. (Outpatient)[5]	0	-	95%	94%
Prophylactic Antibiotic Stopped	-	-	97%	94%
Recommended VTP Ordered	-	-	93%	94%
Urinary Catheter Removal	-	-	90%	90%
Children's Asthma Care				
Received Systemic Corticosteroids	-	-	-	100%
Received Home Management Plan	-	-	-	71%
Received Reliever Medication	-	-	-	100%
Use of Medical Imaging				
Combination Abdominal CT Scan[5]	0	-	0.100	0.191
Combination Chest CT Scan[5]	0	-	0.018	0.054
Follow-up Mammogram/Ultrasound[5]	0	-	6.4%	8.4%
MRI for Low Back Pain[5]	0	-	39.7%	32.7%
Survey of Patients' Hospital Experiences				
Area Around Room 'Always' Quiet at Night	-	-	-	58%
Doctors 'Always' Communicated Well	-	-	-	80%
Home Recovery Information Given	-	-	-	82%
Hospital Given 9 or 10 on 10 Point Scale	-	-	-	67%
Meds 'Always' Explained Before Given	-	-	-	60%
Nurses 'Always' Communicated Well	-	-	-	76%
Pain 'Always' Well Controlled	-	-	-	69%
Room and Bathroom 'Always' Clean	-	-	-	71%
Timely Help 'Always' Received	-	-	-	64%
Would Definitely Recommend Hospital	-	-	-	69%

Community Memorial Hospital

512 Skyline Boulevard Phone: 218-879-4641
Cloquet, MN 55720 Fax: 218-879-9167
URL: www.cloquethospital.com
Type: Critical Access Hospitals Emergency Services: Yes
Ownership: Voluntary Non-Profit - Private Beds: 124
Key Personnel:
Cardiac Laboratory. . . . . Linda Vittperner
Chief of Medical Staff . . . . Vickie L Anderson, MD
Infection Control. . . . . Andrea Peterson
Operating Room. . . . . Steven Vopat, MD
Pediatric Ambulatory Care . . . . . . Lee E Riess, MD
Quality Assurance . . . . Margo Binsfield
Emergency Room . . . . Kenneth Ripp, MD

Measure	Cases	This Hosp.	State Avg.	U.S. Avg.
Heart Attack Care				
ACE Inhibitor or ARB for LVSD[1]	1	100%	97%	96%
Aspirin at Arrival[1]	4	100%	99%	99%
Aspirin at Discharge[1]	3	100%	99%	98%
Beta Blocker at Discharge[1]	4	100%	99%	98%
Fibrinolytic Medication Timing	0	-	55%	55%
PCI Within 90 Minutes of Arrival[5]	0	-	94%	90%
Smoking Cessation Advice[1]	1	100%	99%	99%
Chest Pain/Possible Heart Attack Care				
Aspirin at Arrival[3]	55	98%	97%	95%
Median Time to ECG (minutes)[3]	54	5	7	8
Median Time to Transfer (minutes)[1,3]	7	42	50	61
Fibrinolytic Medication Timing[3]	0	-	58%	54%
Heart Failure Care				
ACE Inhibitor or ARB for LVSD[1]	9	100%	96%	94%
Discharge Instructions[1]	13	85%	86%	88%
Evaluation of LVS Function[1]	19	100%	96%	98%
Smoking Cessation Advice[1]	3	100%	96%	98%
Pneumonia Care				
Appropriate Initial Antibiotic	43	91%	90%	92%
Blood Culture Timing	31	94%	95%	96%
Influenza Vaccine	26	100%	92%	91%
Initial Antibiotic Timing	57	96%	96%	95%
Pneumococcal Vaccine	41	100%	92%	93%
Smoking Cessation Advice[1]	13	100%	95%	97%
Surgical Care Improvement Project				
Appropriate VTP Within 24 Hours[2]	39	97%	92%	92%
Appropriate Hair Removal[2]	121	100%	99%	99%
Appropriate Beta Blocker Usage[2]	28	96%	94%	93%
Controlled Postoperative Blood Glucose[5]	0	-	92%	93%
Prophylactic Antibiotic Timing[2]	105	99%	96%	97%
Prophylactic Antibiotic Timing (Outpatient)[1,3]	12	100%	89%	92%
Prophylactic Antibiotic Selection[2]	107	100%	98%	97%
Prophylactic Antibiotic Select. (Outpatient)[1,3]	12	100%	95%	94%
Prophylactic Antibiotic Stopped[2]	104	97%	97%	94%
Recommended VTP Ordered[2]	39	97%	93%	94%
Urinary Catheter Removal[2]	29	90%	90%	90%
Children's Asthma Care				
Received Systemic Corticosteroids	-	-	-	100%
Received Home Management Plan	-	-	-	71%
Received Reliever Medication	-	-	-	100%
Use of Medical Imaging				
Combination Abdominal CT Scan	193	0.073	0.100	0.191
Combination Chest CT Scan	105	0.000	0.018	0.054
Follow-up Mammogram/Ultrasound	90	3.3%	6.4%	8.4%
MRI for Low Back Pain	32	50.0%	39.7%	32.7%
Survey of Patients' Hospital Experiences				
Area Around Room 'Always' Quiet at Night	300+	58%	-	58%
Doctors 'Always' Communicated Well	300+	84%	-	80%
Home Recovery Information Given	300+	80%	-	82%
Hospital Given 9 or 10 on 10 Point Scale	300+	68%	-	67%
Meds 'Always' Explained Before Given	300+	66%	-	60%
Nurses 'Always' Communicated Well	300+	78%	-	76%
Pain 'Always' Well Controlled	300+	69%	-	69%
Room and Bathroom 'Always' Clean	300+	77%	-	71%
Timely Help 'Always' Received	300+	75%	-	64%
Would Definitely Recommend Hospital	300+	69%	-	69%

NOTE: Hospital profiles are in alphabetical order by state, then city, then hospital within the city; Rankings exclude hospitals with less than 25 cases except for patient surveys which excludes hospitals with less than 100 cases; (a) 100–299 cases; (1) The number of cases is too small to be sure how well a hospital is performing; (2) The hospital indicated that the data submitted for this measure were based on a sample of cases; (3) Data was collected during a shorter time period (fewer quarters) than the maximum possible time for this measure; (4) Suppressed for one or more quarters by CMS; (5) No data is available from the hospital for this measure; (6) Fewer than 100 patients completed the HCAHPS survey. Use these rates with caution, as the number of surveys may be too low to reliably assess hospital performance; (7) Survey results are based on less than 12 months of data; (8) Survey results are not available for this reporting period; (9) No or very few patients were eligible for the HCAHPS survey. The scores shown, if any, reflect a very small number of surveys; (10) A state average was not calculated because too few hospitals in the state submitted data; (11) There were discrepancies in the data collection process; Please refer to the User's Guide for a full explanation of data.

Cook Hospital

10 SE Fifth St
Cook, MN 55723
Phone: 218-666-5945
Fax: 218-666-6239
Type: Critical Access Hospitals
Emergency Services: Yes
Ownership: Govt - Hospital Dist/Auth
Beds: 14

Key Personnel:
Chief of Medical Staff.......... Harold Johnston, MD
Infection Control.............. Teresa Debevecn
Quality Assurance .... Karen Hollanitsch
Radiology................... Dan Courneya

Measure	Cases	This Hosp.	State Avg.	U.S. Avg.
Heart Attack Care				
ACE Inhibitor or ARB for LVSD[3]	0	-	97%	96%
Aspirin at Arrival[1,3]	1	100%	99%	99%
Aspirin at Discharge[1,3]	1	100%	99%	98%
Beta Blocker at Discharge[1,3]	1	100%	99%	98%
Fibrinolytic Medication Timing[3]	0	-	55%	55%
PCI Within 90 Minutes of Arrival[3]	0	-	94%	90%
Smoking Cessation Advice[3]	0	-	99%	99%
Chest Pain/Possible Heart Attack Care				
Aspirin at Arrival	-	-	97%	95%
Median Time to ECG (minutes)	-	-	7	8
Median Time to Transfer (minutes)	-	-	50	61
Fibrinolytic Medication Timing	-	-	58%	54%
Heart Failure Care				
ACE Inhibitor or ARB for LVSD[1]	1	100%	96%	94%
Discharge Instructions[1]	13	8%	86%	88%
Evaluation of LVS Function[1]	16	19%	96%	98%
Smoking Cessation Advice[1]	1	100%	96%	98%
Pneumonia Care				
Appropriate Initial Antibiotic[1]	14	43%	90%	92%
Blood Culture Timing[1]	3	100%	95%	96%
Influenza Vaccine[1]	6	67%	92%	91%
Initial Antibiotic Timing[1]	19	79%	96%	95%
Pneumococcal Vaccine[1]	17	24%	92%	93%
Smoking Cessation Advice[1]	2	0%	95%	97%
Surgical Care Improvement Project				
Appropriate VTP Within 24 Hours[5]	0	-	92%	92%
Appropriate Hair Removal[5]	0	-	99%	99%
Appropriate Beta Blocker Usage[5]	0	-	94%	93%
Controlled Postoperative Blood Glucose[5]	0	-	92%	93%
Prophylactic Antibiotic Timing[5]	0	-	96%	97%
Prophylactic Antibiotic Timing (Outpatient)	-	-	89%	92%
Prophylactic Antibiotic Selection[5]	0	-	98%	97%
Prophylactic Antibiotic Select. (Outpatient)	-	-	95%	94%
Prophylactic Antibiotic Stopped[5]	0	-	97%	94%
Recommended VTP Ordered[5]	0	-	93%	94%
Urinary Catheter Removal[5]	0	-	90%	90%
Children's Asthma Care				
Received Systemic Corticosteroids	-	-	-	100%
Received Home Management Plan	-	-	-	71%
Received Reliever Medication	-	-	-	100%
Use of Medical Imaging				
Combination Abdominal CT Scan	-	-	0.100	0.191
Combination Chest CT Scan	-	-	0.018	0.054
Follow-up Mammogram/Ultrasound	-	-	6.4%	8.4%
MRI for Low Back Pain	-	-	39.7%	32.7%
Survey of Patients' Hospital Experiences				
Area Around Room 'Always' Quiet at Night[8]	-	-	-	58%
Doctors 'Always' Communicated Well[8]	-	-	-	80%
Home Recovery Information Given[8]	-	-	-	82%
Hospital Given 9 or 10 on 10 Point Scale[8]	-	-	-	67%
Meds 'Always' Explained Before Given[8]	-	-	-	60%
Nurses 'Always' Communicated Well[8]	-	-	-	76%
Pain 'Always' Well Controlled[8]	-	-	-	69%
Room and Bathroom 'Always' Clean[8]	-	-	-	71%
Timely Help 'Always' Received[8]	-	-	-	64%
Would Definitely Recommend Hospital[8]	-	-	-	69%

Mercy Hospital

4050 Coon Rapids Blvd
Coon Rapids, MN 55433
Phone: 763-236-6000
Fax: 763-236-8124
URL: www.allinamercy.org
Type: Acute Care Hospitals
Emergency Services: Yes
Ownership: Voluntary Non-Profit - Other
Beds: 271

Key Personnel:
CEO/President............... Tom O'Connor
Cardiac Laboratory............ Steven Remole
Chief of Medical Staff.......... Donald Collins
Emergency Room .... Allen Fuller

Measure	Cases	This Hosp.	State Avg.	U.S. Avg.
Heart Attack Care				
ACE Inhibitor or ARB for LVSD	61	100%	97%	96%
Aspirin at Arrival	326	99%	99%	99%
Aspirin at Discharge	439	100%	99%	98%
Beta Blocker at Discharge	437	99%	99%	98%
Fibrinolytic Medication Timing[1]	1	100%	55%	55%
PCI Within 90 Minutes of Arrival	91	91%	94%	90%
Smoking Cessation Advice	174	100%	99%	99%
Chest Pain/Possible Heart Attack Care				
Aspirin at Arrival[1,3]	6	83%	97%	95%
Median Time to ECG (minutes)[1,3]	7	4	7	8
Median Time to Transfer (minutes)[5]	0	-	50	61
Fibrinolytic Medication Timing[5]	0	-	58%	54%
Heart Failure Care				
ACE Inhibitor or ARB for LVSD	89	99%	96%	94%
Discharge Instructions	254	95%	86%	88%
Evaluation of LVS Function	306	100%	96%	98%
Smoking Cessation Advice	58	100%	96%	98%
Pneumonia Care				
Appropriate Initial Antibiotic	170	96%	90%	92%
Blood Culture Timing	165	94%	95%	96%
Influenza Vaccine	160	94%	92%	91%
Initial Antibiotic Timing	245	95%	96%	95%
Pneumococcal Vaccine	201	99%	92%	93%
Smoking Cessation Advice	107	99%	95%	97%
Surgical Care Improvement Project				
Appropriate VTP Within 24 Hours[2]	165	97%	92%	92%
Appropriate Hair Removal[2]	667	100%	99%	99%
Appropriate Beta Blocker Usage[2]	279	97%	94%	93%
Controlled Postoperative Blood Glucose[2]	141	98%	92%	93%
Prophylactic Antibiotic Timing[2]	434	97%	96%	97%
Prophylactic Antibiotic Timing (Outpatient)	443	97%	89%	92%
Prophylactic Antibiotic Selection[2]	447	100%	98%	97%
Prophylactic Antibiotic Select. (Outpatient)	443	98%	95%	94%
Prophylactic Antibiotic Stopped[2]	414	99%	97%	94%
Recommended VTP Ordered[2]	165	99%	93%	94%
Urinary Catheter Removal[2]	104	88%	90%	90%
Children's Asthma Care				
Received Systemic Corticosteroids	-	-	-	100%
Received Home Management Plan	-	-	-	71%
Received Reliever Medication	-	-	-	100%
Use of Medical Imaging				
Combination Abdominal CT Scan	842	0.046	0.100	0.191
Combination Chest CT Scan	823	0.017	0.018	0.054
Follow-up Mammogram/Ultrasound[5]	0	-	6.4%	8.4%
MRI for Low Back Pain	58	48.3%	39.7%	32.7%
Survey of Patients' Hospital Experiences				
Area Around Room 'Always' Quiet at Night	300+	56%	-	58%
Doctors 'Always' Communicated Well	300+	75%	-	80%
Home Recovery Information Given	300+	87%	-	82%
Hospital Given 9 or 10 on 10 Point Scale	300+	65%	-	67%
Meds 'Always' Explained Before Given	300+	60%	-	60%
Nurses 'Always' Communicated Well	300+	76%	-	76%
Pain 'Always' Well Controlled	300+	67%	-	69%
Room and Bathroom 'Always' Clean	300+	68%	-	71%
Timely Help 'Always' Received	300+	63%	-	64%
Would Definitely Recommend Hospital	300+	71%	-	69%

Riverview Hospital

323 South Minnesota
Crookston, MN 56716
Phone: 218-281-9200
Fax: 218-281-9222
URL: www.riverviewhealth.org
Type: Critical Access Hospitals
Emergency Services: Yes
Ownership: Voluntary Non-Profit - Private
Beds: 49

Key Personnel:
CEO/President............... Debra Boardman
Chief of Medical Staff .... Dr Erik Kanten, MD
Infection Control.............. Dee Dee Wielsma
Operating Room.............. Idatonye Afonya
Quality Assurance .... Robynn Coavette
Radiology.................... Hilton Bakker
Emergency Room .... Mary Pufall
Patient Relations .... Nancy Lankow

Measure	Cases	This Hosp.	State Avg.	U.S. Avg.
Heart Attack Care				
ACE Inhibitor or ARB for LVSD	0	-	97%	96%
Aspirin at Arrival[1]	4	100%	99%	99%
Aspirin at Discharge[1]	4	75%	99%	98%
Beta Blocker at Discharge[1]	2	100%	99%	98%
Fibrinolytic Medication Timing	0	-	55%	55%
PCI Within 90 Minutes of Arrival	0	-	94%	90%
Smoking Cessation Advice	0	-	99%	99%
Chest Pain/Possible Heart Attack Care				
Aspirin at Arrival[1,3]	20	80%	97%	95%
Median Time to ECG (minutes)[1,3]	21	15	7	8
Median Time to Transfer (minutes)[1,3]	3	49	50	61
Fibrinolytic Medication Timing[3]	0	-	58%	54%
Heart Failure Care				
ACE Inhibitor or ARB for LVSD[1]	12	75%	96%	94%
Discharge Instructions[1]	20	45%	86%	88%
Evaluation of LVS Function	38	87%	96%	98%
Smoking Cessation Advice[1]	2	50%	96%	98%
Pneumonia Care				
Appropriate Initial Antibiotic[1]	20	95%	90%	92%
Blood Culture Timing[1]	19	100%	95%	96%
Influenza Vaccine[1]	21	81%	92%	91%
Initial Antibiotic Timing	36	94%	96%	95%
Pneumococcal Vaccine	36	86%	92%	93%
Smoking Cessation Advice[1]	5	60%	95%	97%
Surgical Care Improvement Project				
Appropriate VTP Within 24 Hours	31	84%	92%	92%
Appropriate Hair Removal	72	100%	99%	99%
Appropriate Beta Blocker Usage[1]	16	88%	94%	93%
Controlled Postoperative Blood Glucose	0	-	92%	93%
Prophylactic Antibiotic Timing	55	85%	96%	97%
Prophylactic Antibiotic Timing (Outpatient)[1,3]	8	100%	89%	92%
Prophylactic Antibiotic Selection	55	95%	98%	97%
Prophylactic Antibiotic Select. (Outpatient)[1,3]	8	100%	95%	94%
Prophylactic Antibiotic Stopped	54	89%	97%	94%
Recommended VTP Ordered	31	90%	93%	94%
Urinary Catheter Removal[1]	10	70%	90%	90%
Children's Asthma Care				
Received Systemic Corticosteroids	-	-	-	100%
Received Home Management Plan	-	-	-	71%
Received Reliever Medication	-	-	-	100%
Use of Medical Imaging				
Combination Abdominal CT Scan	91	0.033	0.100	0.191
Combination Chest CT Scan	69	0.043	0.018	0.054
Follow-up Mammogram/Ultrasound	335	3.9%	6.4%	8.4%
MRI for Low Back Pain[1]	56	17.9%	39.7%	32.7%
Survey of Patients' Hospital Experiences				
Area Around Room 'Always' Quiet at Night	(a)	62%	-	58%
Doctors 'Always' Communicated Well	(a)	83%	-	80%
Home Recovery Information Given	(a)	83%	-	82%
Hospital Given 9 or 10 on 10 Point Scale	(a)	67%	-	67%
Meds 'Always' Explained Before Given	(a)	61%	-	60%
Nurses 'Always' Communicated Well	(a)	76%	-	76%
Pain 'Always' Well Controlled	(a)	61%	-	69%
Room and Bathroom 'Always' Clean	(a)	70%	-	71%
Timely Help 'Always' Received	(a)	69%	-	64%
Would Definitely Recommend Hospital	(a)	75%	-	69%

NOTE: Hospital profiles are in alphabetical order by state, then city, then hospital within the city; Rankings exclude hospitals with less than 25 cases except for patient surveys which excludes hospitals with less than 100 cases; (a) 100–299 cases; (1) The number of cases is too small to be sure how well a hospital is performing; (2) The hospital indicated that the data submitted for this measure were based on a sample of cases; (3) Data was collected during a shorter time period (fewer quarters) than the maximum possible time for this measure; (4) Suppressed for one or more quarters by CMS; (5) No data is available from the hospital for this measure; (6) Fewer than 100 patients completed the HCAHPS survey. Use these rates with caution, as the number of surveys may be too low to reliably assess hospital performance; (7) Survey results are based on less than 12 months of data; (8) Survey results are not available for this reporting period; (9) No or very few patients were eligible for the HCAHPS survey. The scores shown, if any, reflect a very small number of surveys; (10) A state average was not calculated because too few hospitals in the state submitted data; (11) There were discrepancies in the data collection process; Please refer to the User's Guide for a full explanation of data.

Cuyuna Regional Medical Center

320 East Main Street | Phone: 218-546-7000
Crosby, MN 56441 | Fax: 218-546-6091
URL: www.cuyunamed.org
Type: Critical Access Hospitals | Emergency Services: Yes
Ownership: Govt - Hospital Dist/Auth | Beds: 42

Key Personnel:
CEO/President. . . . . Thomas F Reek
Chief of Medical Staff . . . . David Goodwin, MD
Infection Control. . . . . Brian Blom
Operating Room. . . . . Dennis Bowles
Quality Assurance . . . . Maxine Ehlers
Radiology. . . . . Bryan Brindley
Emergency Room . . . . Dr. Howard McOllifter
Hemotology Center . . . . Gail Temple, RN

Measure	Cases	This Hosp.	State Avg.	U.S. Avg.
Heart Attack Care				
ACE Inhibitor or ARB for LVSD[3]	0	-	97%	96%
Aspirin at Arrival[1,3]	5	80%	99%	99%
Aspirin at Discharge[1,3]	3	100%	99%	98%
Beta Blocker at Discharge[1,3]	4	100%	99%	98%
Fibrinolytic Medication Timing[5]	0	-	55%	55%
PCI Within 90 Minutes of Arrival[5]	0	-	94%	90%
Smoking Cessation Advice[3]	0	-	99%	99%
Chest Pain/Possible Heart Attack Care				
Aspirin at Arrival	-	-	97%	95%
Median Time to ECG (minutes)	-	-	7	8
Median Time to Transfer (minutes)	-	-	50	61
Fibrinolytic Medication Timing	-	-	58%	54%
Heart Failure Care				
ACE Inhibitor or ARB for LVSD[1,3]	4	75%	96%	94%
Discharge Instructions[1,3]	20	70%	86%	88%
Evaluation of LVS Function[3]	35	69%	96%	98%
Smoking Cessation Advice[1,3]	1	100%	96%	98%
Pneumonia Care				
Appropriate Initial Antibiotic[3]	25	92%	90%	92%
Blood Culture Timing[1,3]	19	95%	95%	96%
Influenza Vaccine	27	33%	92%	91%
Initial Antibiotic Timing[3]	38	82%	96%	95%
Pneumococcal Vaccine[3]	42	67%	92%	93%
Smoking Cessation Advice[1,3]	8	62%	95%	97%
Surgical Care Improvement Project				
Appropriate VTP Within 24 Hours[1,3]	17	100%	92%	92%
Appropriate Hair Removal[3]	96	76%	99%	99%
Appropriate Beta Blocker Usage[3]	33	88%	94%	93%
Controlled Postoperative Blood Glucose[3]	0	-	92%	93%
Prophylactic Antibiotic Timing[3]	73	33%	96%	97%
Prophylactic Antibiotic Timing (Outpatient)	-	-	89%	92%
Prophylactic Antibiotic Selection[3]	70	99%	98%	97%
Prophylactic Antibiotic Select. (Outpatient)	-	-	95%	94%
Prophylactic Antibiotic Stopped[3]	70	99%	97%	94%
Recommended VTP Ordered[1,3]	17	100%	93%	94%
Urinary Catheter Removal[1]	13	100%	90%	90%
Children's Asthma Care				
Received Systemic Corticosteroids	-	-	-	100%
Received Home Management Plan	-	-	-	71%
Received Reliever Medication	-	-	-	100%
Use of Medical Imaging				
Combination Abdominal CT Scan	-	-	0.100	0.191
Combination Chest CT Scan	-	-	0.018	0.054
Follow-up Mammogram/Ultrasound	-	-	6.4%	8.4%
MRI for Low Back Pain	-	-	39.7%	32.7%
Survey of Patients' Hospital Experiences				
Area Around Room 'Always' Quiet at Night	300+	63%	-	58%
Doctors 'Always' Communicated Well	300+	84%	-	80%
Home Recovery Information Given	300+	86%	-	82%
Hospital Given 9 or 10 on 10 Point Scale	300+	78%	-	67%
Meds 'Always' Explained Before Given	300+	69%	-	60%
Nurses 'Always' Communicated Well	300+	83%	-	76%
Pain 'Always' Well Controlled	300+	70%	-	69%
Room and Bathroom 'Always' Clean	300+	77%	-	71%
Timely Help 'Always' Received	300+	74%	-	64%
Would Definitely Recommend Hospital	300+	87%	-	69%

Johnson Memorial Hospital

1282 Walnut Street | Phone: 320-769-4323
Dawson, MN 56232 | Fax: 320-769-4576
URL: www.jmhsdawson.com
Type: Critical Access Hospitals | Emergency Services: Yes
Ownership: Govt - Hospital Dist/Auth | Beds: 94

Key Personnel:
Chief of Medical Staff . . . . Ralph Gerbig, MD
Quality Assurance . . . . Laura Dahl
Emergency Room . . . . Sue Johnson

Measure	Cases	This Hosp.	State Avg.	U.S. Avg.
Heart Attack Care				
ACE Inhibitor or ARB for LVSD[3]	0	-	97%	96%
Aspirin at Arrival[1,3]	2	100%	99%	99%
Aspirin at Discharge[1,3]	2	100%	99%	98%
Beta Blocker at Discharge[1,3]	1	100%	99%	98%
Fibrinolytic Medication Timing[3]	0	-	55%	55%
PCI Within 90 Minutes of Arrival[3]	0	-	94%	90%
Smoking Cessation Advice[3]	0	-	99%	99%
Chest Pain/Possible Heart Attack Care				
Aspirin at Arrival[5]	0	-	97%	95%
Median Time to ECG (minutes)[5]	0	-	7	8
Median Time to Transfer (minutes)[5]	0	-	50	61
Fibrinolytic Medication Timing[5]	0	-	58%	54%
Heart Failure Care				
ACE Inhibitor or ARB for LVSD[1,3]	1	100%	96%	94%
Discharge Instructions[1,3]	4	50%	86%	88%
Evaluation of LVS Function[1,3]	6	100%	96%	98%
Smoking Cessation Advice[3]	0	-	96%	98%
Pneumonia Care				
Appropriate Initial Antibiotic[1]	7	86%	90%	92%
Blood Culture Timing[1]	1	100%	95%	96%
Influenza Vaccine[1]	10	90%	92%	91%
Initial Antibiotic Timing[1]	16	100%	96%	95%
Pneumococcal Vaccine[1]	14	93%	92%	93%
Smoking Cessation Advice[1]	3	67%	95%	97%
Surgical Care Improvement Project				
Appropriate VTP Within 24 Hours[5]	0	-	92%	92%
Appropriate Hair Removal[5]	0	-	99%	99%
Appropriate Beta Blocker Usage[5]	0	-	94%	93%
Controlled Postoperative Blood Glucose[5]	0	-	92%	93%
Prophylactic Antibiotic Timing[5]	0	-	96%	97%
Prophylactic Antibiotic Timing (Outpatient)[5]	0	-	89%	92%
Prophylactic Antibiotic Selection[5]	0	-	98%	97%
Prophylactic Antibiotic Select. (Outpatient)[5]	0	-	95%	94%
Prophylactic Antibiotic Stopped[5]	0	-	97%	94%
Recommended VTP Ordered[5]	0	-	93%	94%
Urinary Catheter Removal[5]	0	-	90%	90%
Children's Asthma Care				
Received Systemic Corticosteroids	-	-	-	100%
Received Home Management Plan	-	-	-	71%
Received Reliever Medication	-	-	-	100%
Use of Medical Imaging				
Combination Abdominal CT Scan[1]	25	0.840	0.100	0.191
Combination Chest CT Scan[1]	10	0.200	0.018	0.054
Follow-up Mammogram/Ultrasound	85	5.9%	6.4%	8.4%
MRI for Low Back Pain[1]	7	0.0%	39.7%	32.7%
Survey of Patients' Hospital Experiences				
Area Around Room 'Always' Quiet at Night[6,11]	<100	80%	-	58%
Doctors 'Always' Communicated Well[11,6]	<100	89%	-	80%
Home Recovery Information Given[6,11]	<100	87%	-	82%
Hospital Given 9 or 10 on 10 Point Scale[6,11]	<100	84%	-	67%
Meds 'Always' Explained Before Given[6,11]	<100	66%	-	60%
Nurses 'Always' Communicated Well[6,11]	<100	90%	-	76%
Pain 'Always' Well Controlled[11,6]	<100	65%	-	69%
Room and Bathroom 'Always' Clean[6,11]	<100	86%	-	71%
Timely Help 'Always' Received[6,11]	<100	81%	-	64%
Would Definitely Recommend Hospital[11]	<100	91%	-	69%

Deer River Healthcare Center

1002 Comstock Drive | Phone: 218-246-2900
Deer River, MN 56636 | Fax: 218-246-3013
URL: www.drhc.org
Type: Critical Access Hospitals | Emergency Services: Yes
Ownership: Voluntary Non-Profit - Private | Beds: 20

Key Personnel:
CEO/President. . . . . Jeffrey Stampohar
Cardiac Laboratory. . . . . Angie Olson, RN
Chief of Medical Staff . . . . David Goodall, MD
Infection Control. . . . . Christine Adams
Radiology. . . . . Abe Latvala
Emergency Room . . . . Kelly Skelly, RN
Patient Relations . . . . Angela Olson

Measure	Cases	This Hosp.	State Avg.	U.S. Avg.
Heart Attack Care				
ACE Inhibitor or ARB for LVSD	0	-	97%	96%
Aspirin at Arrival[1]	5	100%	99%	99%
Aspirin at Discharge[1]	3	100%	99%	98%
Beta Blocker at Discharge[1]	4	100%	99%	98%
Fibrinolytic Medication Timing	0	-	55%	55%
PCI Within 90 Minutes of Arrival	0	-	94%	90%
Smoking Cessation Advice	0	-	99%	99%
Chest Pain/Possible Heart Attack Care				
Aspirin at Arrival[1,3]	20	90%	97%	95%
Median Time to ECG (minutes)[1,3]	20	11	7	8
Median Time to Transfer (minutes)[1,3]	1	122	50	61
Fibrinolytic Medication Timing[3]	0	-	58%	54%
Heart Failure Care				
ACE Inhibitor or ARB for LVSD[1]	3	100%	96%	94%
Discharge Instructions[1]	19	32%	86%	88%
Evaluation of LVS Function[1]	21	67%	96%	98%
Smoking Cessation Advice[1]	6	33%	96%	98%
Pneumonia Care				
Appropriate Initial Antibiotic[1]	19	84%	90%	92%
Blood Culture Timing[1]	11	73%	95%	96%
Influenza Vaccine[1]	11	100%	92%	91%
Initial Antibiotic Timing[1]	17	71%	96%	95%
Pneumococcal Vaccine[1]	20	90%	92%	93%
Smoking Cessation Advice[1]	3	100%	95%	97%
Surgical Care Improvement Project				
Appropriate VTP Within 24 Hours[1,3]	7	43%	92%	92%
Appropriate Hair Removal[1,3]	7	71%	99%	99%
Appropriate Beta Blocker Usage[1,3]	2	100%	94%	93%
Controlled Postoperative Blood Glucose[3]	0	-	92%	93%
Prophylactic Antibiotic Timing[1,3]	5	20%	96%	97%
Prophylactic Antibiotic Timing (Outpatient)[1,3]	8	75%	89%	92%
Prophylactic Antibiotic Selection[1,3]	5	60%	98%	97%
Prophylactic Antibiotic Select. (Outpatient)[1,3]	8	100%	95%	94%
Prophylactic Antibiotic Stopped[1,3]	5	100%	97%	94%
Recommended VTP Ordered[1,3]	7	43%	93%	94%
Urinary Catheter Removal[1,3]	1	100%	90%	90%
Children's Asthma Care				
Received Systemic Corticosteroids	-	-	-	100%
Received Home Management Plan	-	-	-	71%
Received Reliever Medication	-	-	-	100%
Use of Medical Imaging				
Combination Abdominal CT Scan	73	0.014	0.100	0.191
Combination Chest CT Scan	55	0.018	0.018	0.054
Follow-up Mammogram/Ultrasound	136	6.6%	6.4%	8.4%
MRI for Low Back Pain[1]	25	36.0%	39.7%	32.7%
Survey of Patients' Hospital Experiences				
Area Around Room 'Always' Quiet at Night[8]	-	-	-	58%
Doctors 'Always' Communicated Well[8]	-	-	-	80%
Home Recovery Information Given[8]	-	-	-	82%
Hospital Given 9 or 10 on 10 Point Scale[8]	-	-	-	67%
Meds 'Always' Explained Before Given[8]	-	-	-	60%
Nurses 'Always' Communicated Well[8]	-	-	-	76%
Pain 'Always' Well Controlled[8]	-	-	-	69%
Room and Bathroom 'Always' Clean[8]	-	-	-	71%
Timely Help 'Always' Received[8]	-	-	-	64%
Would Definitely Recommend Hospital[8]	-	-	-	69%

NOTE: Hospital profiles are in alphabetical order by state, then city, then hospital within the city; Rankings exclude hospitals with less than 25 cases except for patient surveys which excludes hospitals with less than 100 cases; (a) 100–299 cases; (1) The number of cases is too small to be sure how well a hospital is performing; (2) The hospital indicated that the data submitted for this measure were based on a sample of cases; (3) Data was collected during a shorter time period (fewer quarters) than the maximum possible time for this measure; (4) Suppressed for one or more quarters by CMS; (5) No data is available from the hospital for this measure; (6) Fewer than 100 patients completed the HCAHPS survey. Use these rates with caution, as the number of surveys may be too low to reliably assess hospital performance; (7) Survey results are based on less than 12 months of data; (8) Survey results are not available for this reporting period; (9) No or very few patients were eligible for the HCAHPS survey. The scores shown, if any, reflect a very small number of surveys; (10) A state average was not calculated because too few hospitals in the state submitted data; (11) There were discrepancies in the data collection process; Please refer to the User's Guide for a full explanation of data.

Saint Marys Regional Health Center

1027 Washington Ave Phone: 218-847-5611
Detroit Lakes, MN 56501 Fax: 218-847-7674
URL: www.smrhc.com
Type: Acute Care Hospitals Emergency Services: Yes
Ownership: Voluntary Non-Profit - Church Beds: 187

Key Personnel:
CEO/President. . . . . Thomas R Thompson
Chief of Medical Staff . . . . Knute Thorsgard, MD
Infection Control. . . . . Jackie Nordick
Operating Room. . . . . Marcia Rogers
Quality Assurance . . . . Dennis A Acrea
Radiology. . . . . A Douglas Landers, MD
Intensive Care Unit. . . . . Peg Severson
Patient Relations . . . . Jane Wasvick

Measure	Cases	This Hosp.	State Avg.	U.S. Avg.
Heart Attack Care				
ACE Inhibitor or ARB for LVSD[1]	1	100%	97%	96%
Aspirin at Arrival[1]	12	100%	99%	99%
Aspirin at Discharge[1]	9	100%	99%	98%
Beta Blocker at Discharge[1]	9	100%	99%	98%
Fibrinolytic Medication Timing	0	-	55%	55%
PCI Within 90 Minutes of Arrival	0	-	94%	90%
Smoking Cessation Advice	0	-	99%	99%
Chest Pain/Possible Heart Attack Care				
Aspirin at Arrival	77	99%	97%	95%
Median Time to ECG (minutes)	81	7	7	8
Median Time to Transfer (minutes)[1,3]	5	44	50	61
Fibrinolytic Medication Timing[1]	6	17%	58%	54%
Heart Failure Care				
ACE Inhibitor or ARB for LVSD[1]	2	50%	96%	94%
Discharge Instructions[1]	9	89%	86%	88%
Evaluation of LVS Function[1]	19	100%	96%	98%
Smoking Cessation Advice[1]	4	100%	96%	98%
Pneumonia Care				
Appropriate Initial Antibiotic	59	92%	90%	92%
Blood Culture Timing	44	98%	95%	96%
Influenza Vaccine	37	89%	92%	91%
Initial Antibiotic Timing	66	95%	96%	95%
Pneumococcal Vaccine	57	100%	92%	93%
Smoking Cessation Advice[1]	20	95%	95%	97%
Surgical Care Improvement Project				
Appropriate VTP Within 24 Hours[2]	50	72%	92%	92%
Appropriate Hair Removal[2]	245	100%	99%	99%
Appropriate Beta Blocker Usage[2]	64	94%	94%	93%
Controlled Postoperative Blood Glucose[2]	0	-	92%	93%
Prophylactic Antibiotic Timing[2]	198	99%	96%	97%
Prophylactic Antibiotic Timing (Outpatient)	27	100%	89%	92%
Prophylactic Antibiotic Selection[2]	200	98%	98%	97%
Prophylactic Antibiotic Select. (Outpatient)	27	100%	95%	94%
Prophylactic Antibiotic Stopped[2]	192	97%	97%	94%
Recommended VTP Ordered[2]	50	76%	93%	94%
Urinary Catheter Removal[2]	69	97%	90%	90%
Children's Asthma Care				
Received Systemic Corticosteroids	-	-	-	100%
Received Home Management Plan	-	-	-	71%
Received Reliever Medication	-	-	-	100%
Use of Medical Imaging				
Combination Abdominal CT Scan	189	0.122	0.100	0.191
Combination Chest CT Scan	170	0.112	0.018	0.054
Follow-up Mammogram/Ultrasound[5]	0	-	6.4%	8.4%
MRI for Low Back Pain[1]	44	27.3%	39.7%	32.7%
Survey of Patients' Hospital Experiences				
Area Around Room 'Always' Quiet at Night	300+	62%	-	58%
Doctors 'Always' Communicated Well	300+	82%	-	80%
Home Recovery Information Given	300+	81%	-	82%
Hospital Given 9 or 10 on 10 Point Scale	300+	68%	-	67%
Meds 'Always' Explained Before Given	300+	61%	-	60%
Nurses 'Always' Communicated Well	300+	78%	-	76%
Pain 'Always' Well Controlled	300+	71%	-	69%
Room and Bathroom 'Always' Clean	300+	77%	-	71%
Timely Help 'Always' Received	300+	73%	-	64%
Would Definitely Recommend Hospital	300+	68%	-	69%

Essentia Health Duluth

502 East Second Street Phone: 218-786-2629
Duluth, MN 55805
Type: Acute Care Hospitals Emergency Services: No
Ownership: Voluntary Non-Profit - Private

Key Personnel:
Chief of Medical Staff . . . . Thomas G Patnoe MD
Ambulatory Care . . . . Michael C Metcalf
Patient Relations . . . . Terri Ruberg

Measure	Cases	This Hosp.	State Avg.	U.S. Avg.
Heart Attack Care				
ACE Inhibitor or ARB for LVSD[3]	0	-	97%	96%
Aspirin at Arrival[3]	0	-	99%	99%
Aspirin at Discharge[1,3]	1	100%	99%	98%
Beta Blocker at Discharge[1,3]	1	100%	99%	98%
Fibrinolytic Medication Timing[3]	0	-	55%	55%
PCI Within 90 Minutes of Arrival[3]	0	-	94%	90%
Smoking Cessation Advice[3]	0	-	99%	99%
Chest Pain/Possible Heart Attack Care				
Aspirin at Arrival[5]	0	-	97%	95%
Median Time to ECG (minutes)[5]	0	-	7	8
Median Time to Transfer (minutes)[5]	0	-	50	61
Fibrinolytic Medication Timing[5]	0	-	58%	54%
Heart Failure Care				
ACE Inhibitor or ARB for LVSD[1]	1	100%	96%	94%
Discharge Instructions[1]	11	9%	86%	88%
Evaluation of LVS Function[1]	19	79%	96%	98%
Smoking Cessation Advice[1]	3	67%	96%	98%
Pneumonia Care				
Appropriate Initial Antibiotic	0	-	90%	92%
Blood Culture Timing	0	-	95%	96%
Influenza Vaccine[1]	15	73%	92%	91%
Initial Antibiotic Timing	0	-	96%	95%
Pneumococcal Vaccine[1]	19	89%	92%	93%
Smoking Cessation Advice[1]	16	94%	95%	97%
Surgical Care Improvement Project				
Appropriate VTP Within 24 Hours[1,2]	4	100%	92%	92%
Appropriate Hair Removal[2]	212	100%	99%	99%
Appropriate Beta Blocker Usage[2]	25	80%	94%	93%
Controlled Postoperative Blood Glucose[2]	0	-	92%	93%
Prophylactic Antibiotic Timing[2]	188	96%	96%	97%
Prophylactic Antibiotic Timing (Outpatient)	293	74%	89%	92%
Prophylactic Antibiotic Selection[2]	191	97%	98%	97%
Prophylactic Antibiotic Select. (Outpatient)	367	95%	95%	94%
Prophylactic Antibiotic Stopped[2]	187	89%	97%	94%
Recommended VTP Ordered[1,2]	4	100%	93%	94%
Urinary Catheter Removal[1,2]	1	100%	90%	90%
Children's Asthma Care				
Received Systemic Corticosteroids	-	-	-	100%
Received Home Management Plan	-	-	-	71%
Received Reliever Medication	-	-	-	100%
Use of Medical Imaging				
Combination Abdominal CT Scan[5]	0	-	0.100	0.191
Combination Chest CT Scan[5]	0	-	0.018	0.054
Follow-up Mammogram/Ultrasound[5]	0	-	6.4%	8.4%
MRI for Low Back Pain[5]	0	-	39.7%	32.7%
Survey of Patients' Hospital Experiences				
Area Around Room 'Always' Quiet at Night	300+	46%	-	58%
Doctors 'Always' Communicated Well	300+	83%	-	80%
Home Recovery Information Given	300+	88%	-	82%
Hospital Given 9 or 10 on 10 Point Scale	300+	68%	-	67%
Meds 'Always' Explained Before Given	300+	64%	-	60%
Nurses 'Always' Communicated Well	300+	77%	-	76%
Pain 'Always' Well Controlled	300+	70%	-	69%
Room and Bathroom 'Always' Clean	300+	70%	-	71%
Timely Help 'Always' Received	300+	68%	-	64%
Would Definitely Recommend Hospital	300+	71%	-	69%

Essentia Health St Mary's Medical Center

407 E 3rd St Phone: 218-786-4000
Duluth, MN 55805 Fax: 218-727-7258
URL: www.smdc.org
Type: Acute Care Hospitals Emergency Services: Yes
Ownership: Voluntary Non-Profit - Church Beds: 690

Key Personnel:
CEO/President. . . . . Peter E Pearson
Chief of Medical Staff . . . . Hugh Renierd
Infection Control. . . . . Cindi Welch
Operating Room. . . . . Thurza Bender
Pediatric Ambulatory Care . . . . . . Cindy Sorenson
Quality Assurance . . . . Suzanne Rozinka
Emergency Room . . . . Linda Waigh
Patient Relations . . . . Suzanne Rozinka

Measure	Cases	This Hosp.	State Avg.	U.S. Avg.
Heart Attack Care				
ACE Inhibitor or ARB for LVSD[2]	58	93%	97%	96%
Aspirin at Arrival[2]	99	98%	99%	99%
Aspirin at Discharge[2]	350	99%	99%	98%
Beta Blocker at Discharge[2]	338	99%	99%	98%
Fibrinolytic Medication Timing[2]	0	-	55%	55%
PCI Within 90 Minutes of Arrival[1,2]	13	77%	94%	90%
Smoking Cessation Advice[2]	128	99%	99%	99%
Chest Pain/Possible Heart Attack Care				
Aspirin at Arrival[1]	5	80%	97%	95%
Median Time to ECG (minutes)[1]	6	27	7	8
Median Time to Transfer (minutes)[5]	0	-	50	61
Fibrinolytic Medication Timing[5]	0	-	58%	54%
Heart Failure Care				
ACE Inhibitor or ARB for LVSD[2]	100	91%	96%	94%
Discharge Instructions[2]	215	82%	86%	88%
Evaluation of LVS Function[2]	255	100%	96%	98%
Smoking Cessation Advice[2]	58	98%	96%	98%
Pneumonia Care				
Appropriate Initial Antibiotic[2]	54	91%	90%	92%
Blood Culture Timing[2]	66	97%	95%	96%
Influenza Vaccine[2]	93	92%	92%	91%
Initial Antibiotic Timing[2]	97	95%	96%	95%
Pneumococcal Vaccine[2]	121	98%	92%	93%
Smoking Cessation Advice[2]	74	97%	95%	97%
Surgical Care Improvement Project				
Appropriate VTP Within 24 Hours[2]	201	97%	92%	92%
Appropriate Hair Removal[2]	765	100%	99%	99%
Appropriate Beta Blocker Usage[2]	321	93%	94%	93%
Controlled Postoperative Blood Glucose[2]	170	95%	92%	93%
Prophylactic Antibiotic Timing[2]	534	96%	96%	97%
Prophylactic Antibiotic Timing (Outpatient)	521	95%	89%	92%
Prophylactic Antibiotic Selection[2]	556	98%	98%	97%
Prophylactic Antibiotic Select. (Outpatient)	523	97%	95%	94%
Prophylactic Antibiotic Stopped[2]	512	97%	97%	94%
Recommended VTP Ordered[2]	201	99%	93%	94%
Urinary Catheter Removal[2]	220	85%	90%	90%
Children's Asthma Care				
Received Systemic Corticosteroids	-	-	-	100%
Received Home Management Plan	-	-	-	71%
Received Reliever Medication	-	-	-	100%
Use of Medical Imaging				
Combination Abdominal CT Scan	636	0.215	0.100	0.191
Combination Chest CT Scan	351	0.031	0.018	0.054
Follow-up Mammogram/Ultrasound[5]	0	-	6.4%	8.4%
MRI for Low Back Pain[5]	0	-	39.7%	32.7%
Survey of Patients' Hospital Experiences				
Area Around Room 'Always' Quiet at Night	300+	46%	-	58%
Doctors 'Always' Communicated Well	300+	80%	-	80%
Home Recovery Information Given	300+	85%	-	82%
Hospital Given 9 or 10 on 10 Point Scale	300+	61%	-	67%
Meds 'Always' Explained Before Given	300+	57%	-	60%
Nurses 'Always' Communicated Well	300+	73%	-	76%
Pain 'Always' Well Controlled	300+	67%	-	69%
Room and Bathroom 'Always' Clean	300+	59%	-	71%
Timely Help 'Always' Received	300+	62%	-	64%
Would Definitely Recommend Hospital	300+	73%	-	69%

NOTE: Hospital profiles are in alphabetical order by state, then city, then hospital within the city; Rankings exclude hospitals with less than 25 cases except for patient surveys which excludes hospitals with less than 100 cases; (a) 100–299 cases; (1) The number of cases is too small to be sure how well a hospital is performing; (2) The hospital indicated that the data submitted for this measure were based on a sample of cases; (3) Data was collected during a shorter time period (fewer quarters) than the maximum possible time for this measure; (4) Suppressed for one or more quarters by CMS; (5) No data is available from the hospital for this measure; (6) Fewer than 100 patients completed the HCAHPS survey. Use these rates with caution, as the number of surveys may be too low to reliably assess hospital performance; (7) Survey results are based on less than 12 months of data; (8) Survey results are not available for this reporting period; (9) No or very few patients were eligible for the HCAHPS survey. The scores shown, if any, reflect a very small number of surveys; (10) A state average was not calculated because too few hospitals in the state submitted data; (11) There were discrepancies in the data collection process; Please refer to the User's Guide for a full explanation of data.

Saint Lukes Hospital

915 E 1st St
Duluth, MN 55805
Phone: 218-249-5555
URL: www.slhduluth.com
Type: Acute Care Hospitals
Emergency Services: Yes
Ownership: Voluntary Non-Profit - Private
Beds: 267
Key Personnel:
CEO/President. . . . . John Strange

Measure	Cases	This Hosp.	State Avg.	U.S. Avg.
Heart Attack Care				
ACE Inhibitor or ARB for LVSD[1]	18	100%	97%	96%
Aspirin at Arrival	122	100%	99%	99%
Aspirin at Discharge	165	99%	99%	98%
Beta Blocker at Discharge	164	99%	99%	98%
Fibrinolytic Medication Timing	0	-	55%	55%
PCI Within 90 Minutes of Arrival[1]	24	96%	94%	90%
Smoking Cessation Advice	55	96%	99%	99%
Chest Pain/Possible Heart Attack Care				
Aspirin at Arrival[5]	0	-	97%	95%
Median Time to ECG (minutes)[5]	0	-	7	8
Median Time to Transfer (minutes)[5]	0	-	50	61
Fibrinolytic Medication Timing[5]	0	-	58%	54%
Heart Failure Care				
ACE Inhibitor or ARB for LVSD	75	96%	96%	94%
Discharge Instructions	147	78%	86%	88%
Evaluation of LVS Function	199	99%	96%	98%
Smoking Cessation Advice	35	97%	96%	98%
Pneumonia Care				
Appropriate Initial Antibiotic	106	89%	90%	92%
Blood Culture Timing	144	99%	95%	96%
Influenza Vaccine	126	95%	92%	91%
Initial Antibiotic Timing	177	94%	96%	95%
Pneumococcal Vaccine	194	94%	92%	93%
Smoking Cessation Advice	100	86%	95%	97%
Surgical Care Improvement Project				
Appropriate VTP Within 24 Hours[2]	164	82%	92%	92%
Appropriate Hair Removal[2]	477	100%	99%	99%
Appropriate Beta Blocker Usage[2]	152	97%	94%	93%
Controlled Postoperative Blood Glucose[2]	85	93%	92%	93%
Prophylactic Antibiotic Timing[2]	354	97%	96%	97%
Prophylactic Antibiotic Timing (Outpatient)	135	93%	89%	92%
Prophylactic Antibiotic Selection[2]	354	99%	98%	97%
Prophylactic Antibiotic Select. (Outpatient)	132	92%	95%	94%
Prophylactic Antibiotic Stopped[2]	348	95%	97%	94%
Recommended VTP Ordered[2]	164	86%	93%	94%
Urinary Catheter Removal[2]	71	73%	90%	90%
Children's Asthma Care				
Received Systemic Corticosteroids	-	-	-	100%
Received Home Management Plan	-	-	-	71%
Received Reliever Medication	-	-	-	100%
Use of Medical Imaging				
Combination Abdominal CT Scan	919	0.222	0.100	0.191
Combination Chest CT Scan	814	0.009	0.018	0.054
Follow-up Mammogram/Ultrasound	1,350	11.0%	6.4%	8.4%
MRI for Low Back Pain[5]	0	-	39.7%	32.7%
Survey of Patients' Hospital Experiences				
Area Around Room 'Always' Quiet at Night	300+	57%	-	58%
Doctors 'Always' Communicated Well	300+	80%	-	80%
Home Recovery Information Given	300+	84%	-	82%
Hospital Given 9 or 10 on 10 Point Scale	300+	70%	-	67%
Meds 'Always' Explained Before Given	300+	65%	-	60%
Nurses 'Always' Communicated Well	300+	75%	-	76%
Pain 'Always' Well Controlled	300+	66%	-	69%
Room and Bathroom 'Always' Clean	300+	68%	-	71%
Timely Help 'Always' Received	300+	61%	-	64%
Would Definitely Recommend Hospital	300+	77%	-	69%

Fairview Southdale Hospital

6401 France Avenue South
Edina, MN 55435
Phone: 952-924-5000
Fax: 952-924-5970
URL: www.fairview.org
Type: Acute Care Hospitals
Emergency Services: Yes
Ownership: Voluntary Non-Profit - Private
Beds: 390
Key Personnel:
CEO/President. . . . . Mark A Eustis
Cardiac Laboratory. . . . . Cheri Hammer
Chief of Medical Staff. . . . . James Bishop, MD
Coronary Care. . . . . Joy Wilde, RN
Infection Control. . . . . Janette Blorn
Operating Room. . . . . Bonnie Herda
Quality Assurance . . . . Laura Deneui
Radiology. . . . . Judy Sager

Measure	Cases	This Hosp.	State Avg.	U.S. Avg.
Heart Attack Care				
ACE Inhibitor or ARB for LVSD	92	99%	97%	96%
Aspirin at Arrival	334	100%	99%	99%
Aspirin at Discharge	439	100%	99%	98%
Beta Blocker at Discharge	428	100%	99%	98%
Fibrinolytic Medication Timing	0	-	55%	55%
PCI Within 90 Minutes of Arrival	63	98%	94%	90%
Smoking Cessation Advice	115	100%	99%	99%
Chest Pain/Possible Heart Attack Care				
Aspirin at Arrival[1,3]	5	100%	97%	95%
Median Time to ECG (minutes)[1,3]	5	5	7	8
Median Time to Transfer (minutes)[5]	0	-	50	61
Fibrinolytic Medication Timing[3]	0	-	58%	54%
Heart Failure Care				
ACE Inhibitor or ARB for LVSD	120	97%	96%	94%
Discharge Instructions	255	97%	86%	88%
Evaluation of LVS Function	359	99%	96%	98%
Smoking Cessation Advice	45	100%	96%	98%
Pneumonia Care				
Appropriate Initial Antibiotic	206	89%	90%	92%
Blood Culture Timing	304	99%	95%	96%
Influenza Vaccine	221	93%	92%	91%
Initial Antibiotic Timing	311	96%	96%	95%
Pneumococcal Vaccine	294	96%	92%	93%
Smoking Cessation Advice	70	100%	95%	97%
Surgical Care Improvement Project				
Appropriate VTP Within 24 Hours[2]	357	94%	92%	92%
Appropriate Hair Removal[2]	2,200	100%	99%	99%
Appropriate Beta Blocker Usage[2]	799	98%	94%	93%
Controlled Postoperative Blood Glucose[2]	203	94%	92%	93%
Prophylactic Antibiotic Timing[2]	1,882	99%	96%	97%
Prophylactic Antibiotic Timing (Outpatient)	662	70%	89%	92%
Prophylactic Antibiotic Selection[2]	1,900	99%	98%	97%
Prophylactic Antibiotic Select. (Outpatient)	597	98%	95%	94%
Prophylactic Antibiotic Stopped[2]	1,811	96%	97%	94%
Recommended VTP Ordered[2]	357	96%	93%	94%
Urinary Catheter Removal[2]	477	96%	90%	90%
Children's Asthma Care				
Received Systemic Corticosteroids	-	-	-	100%
Received Home Management Plan	-	-	-	71%
Received Reliever Medication	-	-	-	100%
Use of Medical Imaging				
Combination Abdominal CT Scan	954	0.086	0.100	0.191
Combination Chest CT Scan	854	0.007	0.018	0.054
Follow-up Mammogram/Ultrasound	728	6.6%	6.4%	8.4%
MRI for Low Back Pain	108	44.4%	39.7%	32.7%
Survey of Patients' Hospital Experiences				
Area Around Room 'Always' Quiet at Night	300+	49%	-	58%
Doctors 'Always' Communicated Well	300+	76%	-	80%
Home Recovery Information Given	300+	84%	-	82%
Hospital Given 9 or 10 on 10 Point Scale	300+	61%	-	67%
Meds 'Always' Explained Before Given	300+	58%	-	60%
Nurses 'Always' Communicated Well	300+	71%	-	76%
Pain 'Always' Well Controlled	300+	64%	-	69%
Room and Bathroom 'Always' Clean	300+	65%	-	71%
Timely Help 'Always' Received	300+	57%	-	64%
Would Definitely Recommend Hospital	300+	68%	-	69%

Prairie Ridge Hospital and Health Services

930 First Street Northeast
Elbow Lake, MN 56531
Phone: 218-685-4461
Fax: 218-685-4240
E-mail: nleavitt@eleahmed.org
URL: www.eleahmed.org
Type: Critical Access Hospitals
Emergency Services: Yes
Ownership: Government - Federal
Beds: 20
Key Personnel:
CEO/President. . . . . Larry Rapp

Measure	Cases	This Hosp.	State Avg.	U.S. Avg.
Heart Attack Care				
ACE Inhibitor or ARB for LVSD[5]	0	-	97%	96%
Aspirin at Arrival[5]	0	-	99%	99%
Aspirin at Discharge[5]	0	-	99%	98%
Beta Blocker at Discharge[5]	0	-	99%	98%
Fibrinolytic Medication Timing[5]	0	-	55%	55%
PCI Within 90 Minutes of Arrival[5]	0	-	94%	90%
Smoking Cessation Advice[5]	0	-	99%	99%
Chest Pain/Possible Heart Attack Care				
Aspirin at Arrival	-	-	97%	95%
Median Time to ECG (minutes)	-	-	7	8
Median Time to Transfer (minutes)	-	-	50	61
Fibrinolytic Medication Timing	-	-	58%	54%
Heart Failure Care				
ACE Inhibitor or ARB for LVSD[1,3]	7	86%	96%	94%
Discharge Instructions[1,3]	7	14%	86%	88%
Evaluation of LVS Function[1,3]	10	70%	96%	98%
Smoking Cessation Advice[1,3]	1	0%	96%	98%
Pneumonia Care				
Appropriate Initial Antibiotic[1,3]	6	67%	90%	92%
Blood Culture Timing[1,3]	2	0%	95%	96%
Influenza Vaccine[1,3]	4	0%	92%	91%
Initial Antibiotic Timing[1,3]	7	71%	96%	95%
Pneumococcal Vaccine[1,3]	17	41%	92%	93%
Smoking Cessation Advice[1,3]	6	33%	95%	97%
Surgical Care Improvement Project				
Appropriate VTP Within 24 Hours[5]	0	-	92%	92%
Appropriate Hair Removal[5]	0	-	99%	99%
Appropriate Beta Blocker Usage[5]	0	-	94%	93%
Controlled Postoperative Blood Glucose[5]	0	-	92%	93%
Prophylactic Antibiotic Timing[5]	0	-	96%	97%
Prophylactic Antibiotic Timing (Outpatient)	-	-	89%	92%
Prophylactic Antibiotic Selection[5]	0	-	98%	97%
Prophylactic Antibiotic Select. (Outpatient)	-	-	95%	94%
Prophylactic Antibiotic Stopped[5]	0	-	97%	94%
Recommended VTP Ordered[5]	0	-	93%	94%
Urinary Catheter Removal[5]	0	-	90%	90%
Children's Asthma Care				
Received Systemic Corticosteroids	-	-	-	100%
Received Home Management Plan	-	-	-	71%
Received Reliever Medication	-	-	-	100%
Use of Medical Imaging				
Combination Abdominal CT Scan	-	-	0.100	0.191
Combination Chest CT Scan	-	-	0.018	0.054
Follow-up Mammogram/Ultrasound	-	-	6.4%	8.4%
MRI for Low Back Pain	-	-	39.7%	32.7%
Survey of Patients' Hospital Experiences				
Area Around Room 'Always' Quiet at Night[8]	-	-	-	58%
Doctors 'Always' Communicated Well[8]	-	-	-	80%
Home Recovery Information Given[8]	-	-	-	82%
Hospital Given 9 or 10 on 10 Point Scale[8]	-	-	-	67%
Meds 'Always' Explained Before Given[8]	-	-	-	60%
Nurses 'Always' Communicated Well[8]	-	-	-	76%
Pain 'Always' Well Controlled[8]	-	-	-	69%
Room and Bathroom 'Always' Clean[8]	-	-	-	71%
Timely Help 'Always' Received[8]	-	-	-	64%
Would Definitely Recommend Hospital[8]	-	-	-	69%

NOTE: Hospital profiles are in alphabetical order by state, then city, then hospital within the city; Rankings exclude hospitals with less than 25 cases except for patient surveys which excludes hospitals with less than 100 cases; (a) 100–299 cases; (1) The number of cases is too small to be sure how well a hospital is performing; (2) The hospital indicated that the data submitted for this measure were based on a sample of cases; (3) Data was collected during a shorter time period (fewer quarters) than the maximum possible time for this measure; (4) Suppressed for one or more quarters by CMS; (5) No data is available from the hospital for this measure; (6) Fewer than 100 patients completed the HCAHPS survey. Use these rates with caution, as the number of surveys may be too low to reliably assess hospital performance; (7) Survey results are based on less than 12 months of data; (8) Survey results are not available for this reporting period; (9) No or very few patients were eligible for the HCAHPS survey. The scores shown, if any, reflect a very small number of surveys; (10) A state average was not calculated because too few hospitals in the state submitted data; (11) There were discrepancies in the data collection process; Please refer to the User's Guide for a full explanation of data.

Ely Bloomenson Community Hospital

328 West Conan Street Phone: 218-365-3271
Ely, MN 55731 Fax: 218-365-8777
URL: www.ebch.org
Type: Critical Access Hospitals Emergency Services: Yes
Ownership: Government - Local Beds: 32

Key Personnel:
Chief of Medical Staff.......... Mary Bianco
Infection Control.............. Mary Ann Smith, RN
Operating Room.............. Kyle Westrick, RN
Quality Assurance............ Nancy Andreae
Radiology.................. Mike Pechek
Anesthesiology............... Bruce Kuam

Measure	Cases	This Hosp.	State Avg.	U.S. Avg.
Heart Attack Care				
ACE Inhibitor or ARB for LVSD[3]	0	-	97%	96%
Aspirin at Arrival[1,3]	1	100%	99%	99%
Aspirin at Discharge[1,3]	1	100%	99%	98%
Beta Blocker at Discharge[1,3]	1	100%	99%	98%
Fibrinolytic Medication Timing[3]	0	-	55%	55%
PCI Within 90 Minutes of Arrival[3]	0	-	94%	90%
Smoking Cessation Advice[3]	0	-	99%	99%
Chest Pain/Possible Heart Attack Care				
Aspirin at Arrival	-	-	97%	95%
Median Time to ECG (minutes)	-	-	7	8
Median Time to Transfer (minutes)	-	-	50	61
Fibrinolytic Medication Timing	-	-	58%	54%
Heart Failure Care				
ACE Inhibitor or ARB for LVSD[1,3]	3	100%	96%	94%
Discharge Instructions[1,3]	6	33%	86%	88%
Evaluation of LVS Function[3,1]	8	75%	96%	98%
Smoking Cessation Advice[1,3]	1	100%	96%	98%
Pneumonia Care				
Appropriate Initial Antibiotic[1,3]	9	89%	90%	92%
Blood Culture Timing[1,3]	3	100%	95%	96%
Influenza Vaccine[1,3]	5	80%	92%	91%
Initial Antibiotic Timing[1,3]	10	100%	96%	95%
Pneumococcal Vaccine[1,3]	14	86%	92%	93%
Smoking Cessation Advice[1,3]	1	100%	95%	97%
Surgical Care Improvement Project				
Appropriate VTP Within 24 Hours[5]	0	-	92%	92%
Appropriate Hair Removal[5]	0	-	99%	99%
Appropriate Beta Blocker Usage[5]	0	-	94%	93%
Controlled Postoperative Blood Glucose[5]	0	-	92%	93%
Prophylactic Antibiotic Timing[5]	0	-	96%	97%
Prophylactic Antibiotic Timing (Outpatient)	-	-	89%	92%
Prophylactic Antibiotic Selection[5]	0	-	98%	97%
Prophylactic Antibiotic Select. (Outpatient)	-	-	95%	94%
Prophylactic Antibiotic Stopped[5]	0	-	97%	94%
Recommended VTP Ordered[5]	0	-	93%	94%
Urinary Catheter Removal[5]	0	-	90%	90%
Children's Asthma Care				
Received Systemic Corticosteroids	-	-	-	100%
Received Home Management Plan	-	-	-	71%
Received Reliever Medication	-	-	-	100%
Use of Medical Imaging				
Combination Abdominal CT Scan	-	-	0.100	0.191
Combination Chest CT Scan	-	-	0.018	0.054
Follow-up Mammogram/Ultrasound	-	-	6.4%	8.4%
MRI for Low Back Pain	-	-	39.7%	32.7%
Survey of Patients' Hospital Experiences				
Area Around Room 'Always' Quiet at Night	(a)	58%	-	58%
Doctors 'Always' Communicated Well	(a)	80%	-	80%
Home Recovery Information Given	(a)	73%	-	82%
Hospital Given 9 or 10 on 10 Point Scale	(a)	64%	-	67%
Meds 'Always' Explained Before Given	(a)	57%	-	60%
Nurses 'Always' Communicated Well	(a)	75%	-	76%
Pain 'Always' Well Controlled	(a)	78%	-	69%
Room and Bathroom 'Always' Clean	(a)	78%	-	71%
Timely Help 'Always' Received	(a)	77%	-	64%
Would Definitely Recommend Hospital	(a)	65%	-	69%

Fairmont Medical Center

835 Johnson Street Phone: 507-238-8100
Fairmont, MN 56031 Fax: 507-238-8686
URL: www.fairmontmedicalcenter.org
Type: Acute Care Hospitals Emergency Services: Yes
Ownership: Voluntary Non-Profit - Other Beds: 94

Key Personnel:
CEO/President............... Barbara Allen, MD
Chief of Medical Staff......... Timothy Bachenberg
Infection Control.............. Roger Drahota
Operating Room.............. Marti Walter
Radiology.................. Rufus Rodriguez
Emergency Room............ Carol Shukla
Intensive Care Unit............ Carol Shukla

Measure	Cases	This Hosp.	State Avg.	U.S. Avg.
Heart Attack Care				
ACE Inhibitor or ARB for LVSD[1]	5	80%	97%	96%
Aspirin at Arrival	25	100%	99%	99%
Aspirin at Discharge[1]	16	100%	99%	98%
Beta Blocker at Discharge[1]	14	93%	99%	98%
Fibrinolytic Medication Timing	0	-	55%	55%
PCI Within 90 Minutes of Arrival	0	-	94%	90%
Smoking Cessation Advice[1]	2	100%	99%	99%
Chest Pain/Possible Heart Attack Care				
Aspirin at Arrival	42	98%	97%	95%
Median Time to ECG (minutes)	42	5	7	8
Median Time to Transfer (minutes)[1]	4	66	50	61
Fibrinolytic Medication Timing[1]	5	20%	58%	54%
Heart Failure Care				
ACE Inhibitor or ARB for LVSD[1]	23	96%	96%	94%
Discharge Instructions	44	93%	86%	88%
Evaluation of LVS Function	103	98%	96%	98%
Smoking Cessation Advice[1]	5	100%	96%	98%
Pneumonia Care				
Appropriate Initial Antibiotic	79	95%	90%	92%
Blood Culture Timing	94	100%	95%	96%
Influenza Vaccine	94	97%	92%	91%
Initial Antibiotic Timing	114	98%	96%	95%
Pneumococcal Vaccine	129	98%	92%	93%
Smoking Cessation Advice	28	93%	95%	97%
Surgical Care Improvement Project				
Appropriate VTP Within 24 Hours	71	97%	92%	92%
Appropriate Hair Removal	211	100%	99%	99%
Appropriate Beta Blocker Usage	82	100%	94%	93%
Controlled Postoperative Blood Glucose	0	-	92%	93%
Prophylactic Antibiotic Timing	163	96%	96%	97%
Prophylactic Antibiotic Timing (Outpatient)	39	77%	89%	92%
Prophylactic Antibiotic Selection	163	98%	98%	97%
Prophylactic Antibiotic Select. (Outpatient)	56	86%	95%	94%
Prophylactic Antibiotic Stopped	157	99%	97%	94%
Recommended VTP Ordered	71	97%	93%	94%
Urinary Catheter Removal	45	91%	90%	90%
Children's Asthma Care				
Received Systemic Corticosteroids	-	-	-	100%
Received Home Management Plan	-	-	-	71%
Received Reliever Medication	-	-	-	100%
Use of Medical Imaging				
Combination Abdominal CT Scan	306	0.065	0.100	0.191
Combination Chest CT Scan	214	0.000	0.018	0.054
Follow-up Mammogram/Ultrasound	649	6.3%	6.4%	8.4%
MRI for Low Back Pain	93	26.9%	39.7%	32.7%
Survey of Patients' Hospital Experiences				
Area Around Room 'Always' Quiet at Night	300+	55%	-	58%
Doctors 'Always' Communicated Well	300+	82%	-	80%
Home Recovery Information Given	300+	84%	-	82%
Hospital Given 9 or 10 on 10 Point Scale	300+	63%	-	67%
Meds 'Always' Explained Before Given	300+	59%	-	60%
Nurses 'Always' Communicated Well	300+	74%	-	76%
Pain 'Always' Well Controlled	300+	69%	-	69%
Room and Bathroom 'Always' Clean	300+	70%	-	71%
Timely Help 'Always' Received	300+	60%	-	64%
Would Definitely Recommend Hospital	300+	63%	-	69%

District One Hospital

200 State Avenue Phone: 507-334-6451
Faribault, MN 55021 Fax: 507-332-4848
E-mail: doh@districtonehospital.com
URL: www.districtonehospital.com
Type: Acute Care Hospitals Emergency Services: Yes
Ownership: Govt - Hospital Dist/Auth Beds: 99

Key Personnel:
CEO/President............... James Wolf
Infection Control.............. Rae Ormsby
Operating Room.............. Kris Bauer
Quality Assurance............ Rhonda Mulder
Anesthesiology............... Charles Boyle, CRNA
Emergency Room............ Melissa Appel
Intensive Care Unit........... Mary Campbell
Patient Relations............ Joan Boysen

Measure	Cases	This Hosp.	State Avg.	U.S. Avg.
Heart Attack Care				
ACE Inhibitor or ARB for LVSD[3]	0	-	97%	96%
Aspirin at Arrival[1,3]	2	100%	99%	99%
Aspirin at Discharge[1,3]	2	100%	99%	98%
Beta Blocker at Discharge[1,3]	2	50%	99%	98%
Fibrinolytic Medication Timing[3]	0	-	55%	55%
PCI Within 90 Minutes of Arrival[3]	0	-	94%	90%
Smoking Cessation Advice[3]	0	-	99%	99%
Chest Pain/Possible Heart Attack Care				
Aspirin at Arrival	117	99%	97%	95%
Median Time to ECG (minutes)	123	5	7	8
Median Time to Transfer (minutes)[1]	15	50	50	61
Fibrinolytic Medication Timing[1]	1	0%	58%	54%
Heart Failure Care				
ACE Inhibitor or ARB for LVSD[1]	9	100%	96%	94%
Discharge Instructions	29	86%	86%	88%
Evaluation of LVS Function	38	95%	96%	98%
Smoking Cessation Advice[1]	2	100%	96%	98%
Pneumonia Care				
Appropriate Initial Antibiotic	57	89%	90%	92%
Blood Culture Timing	54	98%	95%	96%
Influenza Vaccine	57	98%	92%	91%
Initial Antibiotic Timing	84	99%	96%	95%
Pneumococcal Vaccine	80	100%	92%	93%
Smoking Cessation Advice[1]	17	88%	95%	97%
Surgical Care Improvement Project				
Appropriate VTP Within 24 Hours	59	86%	92%	92%
Appropriate Hair Removal	173	100%	99%	99%
Appropriate Beta Blocker Usage	50	94%	94%	93%
Controlled Postoperative Blood Glucose	0	-	92%	93%
Prophylactic Antibiotic Timing	154	96%	96%	97%
Prophylactic Antibiotic Timing (Outpatient)	52	90%	89%	92%
Prophylactic Antibiotic Selection	152	97%	98%	97%
Prophylactic Antibiotic Select. (Outpatient)	50	98%	95%	94%
Prophylactic Antibiotic Stopped	151	93%	97%	94%
Recommended VTP Ordered	59	86%	93%	94%
Urinary Catheter Removal	33	97%	90%	90%
Children's Asthma Care				
Received Systemic Corticosteroids	-	-	-	100%
Received Home Management Plan	-	-	-	71%
Received Reliever Medication	-	-	-	100%
Use of Medical Imaging				
Combination Abdominal CT Scan	240	0.050	0.100	0.191
Combination Chest CT Scan	209	0.048	0.018	0.054
Follow-up Mammogram/Ultrasound[1]	53	13.2%	6.4%	8.4%
MRI for Low Back Pain	61	49.2%	39.7%	32.7%
Survey of Patients' Hospital Experiences				
Area Around Room 'Always' Quiet at Night	300+	64%	-	58%
Doctors 'Always' Communicated Well	300+	81%	-	80%
Home Recovery Information Given	300+	83%	-	82%
Hospital Given 9 or 10 on 10 Point Scale	300+	69%	-	67%
Meds 'Always' Explained Before Given	300+	62%	-	60%
Nurses 'Always' Communicated Well	300+	76%	-	76%
Pain 'Always' Well Controlled	300+	70%	-	69%
Room and Bathroom 'Always' Clean	300+	75%	-	71%
Timely Help 'Always' Received	300+	72%	-	64%
Would Definitely Recommend Hospital	300+	67%	-	69%

NOTE: Hospital profiles are in alphabetical order by state, then city, then hospital within the city; Rankings exclude hospitals with less than 25 cases except for patient surveys which excludes hospitals with less than 100 cases; (a) 100–299 cases; (1) The number of cases is too small to be sure how well a hospital is performing; (2) The hospital indicated that the data submitted for this measure were based on a sample of cases; (3) Data was collected during a shorter time period (fewer quarters) than the maximum possible time for this measure; (4) Suppressed for one or more quarters by CMS; (5) No data is available from the hospital for this measure; (6) Fewer than 100 patients completed the HCAHPS survey. Use these rates with caution, as the number of surveys may be too low to reliably assess hospital performance; (7) Survey results are based on less than 12 months of data; (8) Survey results are not available for this reporting period; (9) No or very few patients were eligible for the HCAHPS survey. The scores shown, if any, reflect a very small number of surveys; (10) A state average was not calculated because too few hospitals in the state submitted data; (11) There were discrepancies in the data collection process; Please refer to the User's Guide for a full explanation of data.

Lake Region Healthcare Corporation

712 South Cascade Phone: 218-736-8000
Fergus Falls, MN 56537 Fax: 218-736-8765
URL: www.lrhc.org
Type: Acute Care Hospitals Emergency Services: Yes
Ownership: Voluntary Non-Profit - Private Beds: 108

Key Personnel:
CEO/President. . . . . Ed Mehl
Chief of Medical Staff. . . . . D Traiser, MD
Coronary Care . . . . Rick Dean
Infection Control. . . . . JoAnn Bowman, RN
Operating Room. . . . . Angelo Griego
Radiology. . . . . Tom Larson
Hemotology Center . . . . Paul Etzell
Intensive Care Unit. . . . . Rick Dean

Measure	Cases	This Hosp.	State Avg.	U.S. Avg.
Heart Attack Care				
ACE Inhibitor or ARB for LVSD[1]	3	100%	97%	96%
Aspirin at Arrival	30	97%	99%	99%
Aspirin at Discharge[1]	19	95%	99%	98%
Beta Blocker at Discharge[1]	19	95%	99%	98%
Fibrinolytic Medication Timing	0	-	55%	55%
PCI Within 90 Minutes of Arrival	0	-	94%	90%
Smoking Cessation Advice[1]	2	100%	99%	99%
Chest Pain/Possible Heart Attack Care				
Aspirin at Arrival	57	95%	97%	95%
Median Time to ECG (minutes)	59	6	7	8
Median Time to Transfer (minutes)[1,3]	1	141	50	61
Fibrinolytic Medication Timing[1]	12	83%	58%	54%
Heart Failure Care				
ACE Inhibitor or ARB for LVSD	26	100%	96%	94%
Discharge Instructions	54	85%	86%	88%
Evaluation of LVS Function	79	100%	96%	98%
Smoking Cessation Advice[1]	3	100%	96%	98%
Pneumonia Care				
Appropriate Initial Antibiotic	63	94%	90%	92%
Blood Culture Timing	96	96%	95%	96%
Influenza Vaccine	84	98%	92%	91%
Initial Antibiotic Timing	104	95%	96%	95%
Pneumococcal Vaccine	109	100%	92%	93%
Smoking Cessation Advice[1]	23	100%	95%	97%
Surgical Care Improvement Project				
Appropriate VTP Within 24 Hours	115	90%	92%	92%
Appropriate Hair Removal	260	100%	99%	99%
Appropriate Beta Blocker Usage	59	93%	94%	93%
Controlled Postoperative Blood Glucose	0	-	92%	93%
Prophylactic Antibiotic Timing	193	90%	96%	97%
Prophylactic Antibiotic Timing (Outpatient)	72	83%	89%	92%
Prophylactic Antibiotic Selection	193	96%	98%	97%
Prophylactic Antibiotic Select. (Outpatient)	73	93%	95%	94%
Prophylactic Antibiotic Stopped	190	97%	97%	94%
Recommended VTP Ordered	115	93%	93%	94%
Urinary Catheter Removal	45	98%	90%	90%
Children's Asthma Care				
Received Systemic Corticosteroids	-	-	-	100%
Received Home Management Plan	-	-	-	71%
Received Reliever Medication	-	-	-	100%
Use of Medical Imaging				
Combination Abdominal CT Scan	373	0.118	0.100	0.191
Combination Chest CT Scan	252	0.032	0.018	0.054
Follow-up Mammogram/Ultrasound	783	5.0%	6.4%	8.4%
MRI for Low Back Pain	85	36.5%	39.7%	32.7%
Survey of Patients' Hospital Experiences				
Area Around Room 'Always' Quiet at Night	(a)	63%	-	58%
Doctors 'Always' Communicated Well	(a)	81%	-	80%
Home Recovery Information Given	(a)	90%	-	82%
Hospital Given 9 or 10 on 10 Point Scale	(a)	76%	-	67%
Meds 'Always' Explained Before Given	(a)	67%	-	60%
Nurses 'Always' Communicated Well	(a)	81%	-	76%
Pain 'Always' Well Controlled	(a)	74%	-	69%
Room and Bathroom 'Always' Clean	(a)	83%	-	71%
Timely Help 'Always' Received	(a)	72%	-	64%
Would Definitely Recommend Hospital	(a)	74%	-	69%

Essentia Health Fosston

900 Hilligoss Blvd SE Phone: 218-435-1133
Fosston, MN 56542
URL: www.firstcare.org
Type: Critical Access Hospitals Emergency Services: Yes
Ownership: Voluntary Non-Profit - Private

Key Personnel:
President . . . . Patricia Wangler

Measure	Cases	This Hosp.	State Avg.	U.S. Avg.
Heart Attack Care				
ACE Inhibitor or ARB for LVSD[3]	0	-	97%	96%
Aspirin at Arrival[1,3]	2	100%	99%	99%
Aspirin at Discharge[1,3]	2	100%	99%	98%
Beta Blocker at Discharge[1,3]	1	100%	99%	98%
Fibrinolytic Medication Timing[3]	0	-	55%	55%
PCI Within 90 Minutes of Arrival[3]	0	-	94%	90%
Smoking Cessation Advice[3]	0	-	99%	99%
Chest Pain/Possible Heart Attack Care				
Aspirin at Arrival[1,3]	1	100%	97%	95%
Median Time to ECG (minutes)[1,3]	1	12	7	8
Median Time to Transfer (minutes)[1,3]	1	90	50	61
Fibrinolytic Medication Timing[3]	0	-	58%	54%
Heart Failure Care				
ACE Inhibitor or ARB for LVSD[1]	9	100%	96%	94%
Discharge Instructions[1]	16	100%	86%	88%
Evaluation of LVS Function	36	97%	96%	98%
Smoking Cessation Advice[1]	6	100%	96%	98%
Pneumonia Care				
Appropriate Initial Antibiotic[1]	8	100%	90%	92%
Blood Culture Timing[1]	5	100%	95%	96%
Influenza Vaccine[1]	10	100%	92%	91%
Initial Antibiotic Timing[1]	16	100%	96%	95%
Pneumococcal Vaccine[1]	17	100%	92%	93%
Smoking Cessation Advice[1]	2	100%	95%	97%
Surgical Care Improvement Project				
Appropriate VTP Within 24 Hours[1]	8	100%	92%	92%
Appropriate Hair Removal[1]	18	100%	99%	99%
Appropriate Beta Blocker Usage[5]	0	-	94%	93%
Controlled Postoperative Blood Glucose	0	-	92%	93%
Prophylactic Antibiotic Timing[1]	16	100%	96%	97%
Prophylactic Antibiotic Timing (Outpatient)[5]	0	-	89%	92%
Prophylactic Antibiotic Selection[1]	16	100%	98%	97%
Prophylactic Antibiotic Select. (Outpatient)[5]	0	-	95%	94%
Prophylactic Antibiotic Stopped[1]	16	100%	97%	94%
Recommended VTP Ordered[1]	8	100%	93%	94%
Urinary Catheter Removal[1]	5	100%	90%	90%
Children's Asthma Care				
Received Systemic Corticosteroids	-	-	-	100%
Received Home Management Plan	-	-	-	71%
Received Reliever Medication	-	-	-	100%
Use of Medical Imaging				
Combination Abdominal CT Scan	50	0.000	0.100	0.191
Combination Chest CT Scan[1]	35	0.000	0.018	0.054
Follow-up Mammogram/Ultrasound	88	8.0%	6.4%	8.4%
MRI for Low Back Pain[1]	17	41.2%	39.7%	32.7%
Survey of Patients' Hospital Experiences				
Area Around Room 'Always' Quiet at Night	(a)	61%	-	58%
Doctors 'Always' Communicated Well	(a)	89%	-	80%
Home Recovery Information Given	(a)	89%	-	82%
Hospital Given 9 or 10 on 10 Point Scale	(a)	78%	-	67%
Meds 'Always' Explained Before Given	(a)	65%	-	60%
Nurses 'Always' Communicated Well	(a)	83%	-	76%
Pain 'Always' Well Controlled	(a)	77%	-	69%
Room and Bathroom 'Always' Clean	(a)	80%	-	71%
Timely Help 'Always' Received	(a)	76%	-	64%
Would Definitely Recommend Hospital	(a)	82%	-	69%

Unity Hospital

550 Osborne Road Phone: 763-236-5000
Fridley, MN 55432 Fax: 763-236-3516
URL: www.mercyunity.com
Type: Acute Care Hospitals Emergency Services: Yes
Ownership: Voluntary Non-Profit - Other Beds: 200

Key Personnel:
CEO/President. . . . . Venetia H M Kudrle
Radiology. . . . . Ellen L Abeln

Measure	Cases	This Hosp.	State Avg.	U.S. Avg.
Heart Attack Care				
ACE Inhibitor or ARB for LVSD	0	-	97%	96%
Aspirin at Arrival	40	100%	99%	99%
Aspirin at Discharge[1]	20	100%	99%	98%
Beta Blocker at Discharge[1]	23	100%	99%	98%
Fibrinolytic Medication Timing	0	-	55%	55%
PCI Within 90 Minutes of Arrival	0	-	94%	90%
Smoking Cessation Advice[1]	3	100%	99%	99%
Chest Pain/Possible Heart Attack Care				
Aspirin at Arrival	88	99%	97%	95%
Median Time to ECG (minutes)	88	4	7	8
Median Time to Transfer (minutes)[1]	15	32	50	61
Fibrinolytic Medication Timing	0	-	58%	54%
Heart Failure Care				
ACE Inhibitor or ARB for LVSD	37	100%	96%	94%
Discharge Instructions	141	99%	86%	88%
Evaluation of LVS Function	160	100%	96%	98%
Smoking Cessation Advice[1]	21	95%	96%	98%
Pneumonia Care				
Appropriate Initial Antibiotic	138	97%	90%	92%
Blood Culture Timing	226	95%	95%	96%
Influenza Vaccine	142	99%	92%	91%
Initial Antibiotic Timing	209	99%	96%	95%
Pneumococcal Vaccine	188	100%	92%	93%
Smoking Cessation Advice	92	100%	95%	97%
Surgical Care Improvement Project				
Appropriate VTP Within 24 Hours[2]	166	99%	92%	92%
Appropriate Hair Removal[2]	492	100%	99%	99%
Appropriate Beta Blocker Usage[2]	172	93%	94%	93%
Controlled Postoperative Blood Glucose[2]	0	-	92%	93%
Prophylactic Antibiotic Timing[2]	299	98%	96%	97%
Prophylactic Antibiotic Timing (Outpatient)	152	97%	89%	92%
Prophylactic Antibiotic Selection[2]	300	98%	98%	97%
Prophylactic Antibiotic Select. (Outpatient)	152	98%	95%	94%
Prophylactic Antibiotic Stopped[2]	281	96%	97%	94%
Recommended VTP Ordered[2]	166	100%	93%	94%
Urinary Catheter Removal[1,2]	23	96%	90%	90%
Children's Asthma Care				
Received Systemic Corticosteroids	-	-	-	100%
Received Home Management Plan	-	-	-	71%
Received Reliever Medication	-	-	-	100%
Use of Medical Imaging				
Combination Abdominal CT Scan	594	0.024	0.100	0.191
Combination Chest CT Scan	614	0.002	0.018	0.054
Follow-up Mammogram/Ultrasound[5]	0	-	6.4%	8.4%
MRI for Low Back Pain[1]	28	39.3%	39.7%	32.7%
Survey of Patients' Hospital Experiences				
Area Around Room 'Always' Quiet at Night	300+	50%	-	58%
Doctors 'Always' Communicated Well	300+	76%	-	80%
Home Recovery Information Given	300+	86%	-	82%
Hospital Given 9 or 10 on 10 Point Scale	300+	60%	-	67%
Meds 'Always' Explained Before Given	300+	56%	-	60%
Nurses 'Always' Communicated Well	300+	72%	-	76%
Pain 'Always' Well Controlled	300+	64%	-	69%
Room and Bathroom 'Always' Clean	300+	64%	-	71%
Timely Help 'Always' Received	300+	57%	-	64%
Would Definitely Recommend Hospital	300+	64%	-	69%

NOTE: Hospital profiles are in alphabetical order by state, then city, then hospital within the city; Rankings exclude hospitals with less than 25 cases except for patient surveys which excludes hospitals with less than 100 cases; (a) 100–299 cases; (1) The number of cases is too small to be sure how well a hospital is performing; (2) The hospital indicated that the data submitted for this measure were based on a sample of cases; (3) Data was collected during a shorter time period (fewer quarters) than the maximum possible time for this measure; (4) Suppressed for one or more quarters by CMS; (5) No data is available from the hospital for this measure; (6) Fewer than 100 patients completed the HCAHPS survey. Use these rates with caution, as the number of surveys may be too low to reliably assess hospital performance; (7) Survey results are based on less than 12 months of data; (8) Survey results are not available for this reporting period; (9) No or very few patients were eligible for the HCAHPS survey. The scores shown, if any, reflect a very small number of surveys; (10) A state average was not calculated because too few hospitals in the state submitted data; (11) There were discrepancies in the data collection process; Please refer to the User's Guide for a full explanation of data.

Glencoe Regional Health Services

1805 Hennepin Avenue North Phone: 320-864-3121
Glencoe, MN 55336 Fax: 320-864-7887
URL: www.grhsonline.org
Type: Critical Access Hospitals Emergency Services: Yes
Ownership: Voluntary Non-Profit - Private Beds: 25

Key Personnel:
CEO/President. . . . . John D Braband
Chief of Medical Staff. . . . . Dennis Jacobson, MD
Infection Control. . . . . Rhonda Buerkle
Operating Room. . . . . John Bergseng, RN
Quality Assurance . . . . Ann Ripley
Anesthesiology. . . . . Bob Larter
Emergency Room . . . . Bryan Petersen, RN
Intensive Care Unit. . . . . Barb Magnuson, RN

Measure	Cases	This Hosp.	State Avg.	U.S. Avg.
Heart Attack Care				
ACE Inhibitor or ARB for LVSD[3]	0	-	97%	96%
Aspirin at Arrival[3]	0	-	99%	99%
Aspirin at Discharge[3]	0	-	99%	98%
Beta Blocker at Discharge[3]	0	-	99%	98%
Fibrinolytic Medication Timing[3]	0	-	55%	55%
PCI Within 90 Minutes of Arrival[3]	0	-	94%	90%
Smoking Cessation Advice[3]	0	-	99%	99%
Chest Pain/Possible Heart Attack Care				
Aspirin at Arrival	37	95%	97%	95%
Median Time to ECG (minutes)	38	8	7	8
Median Time to Transfer (minutes)[1,3]	1	79	50	61
Fibrinolytic Medication Timing[3]	0	-	58%	54%
Heart Failure Care				
ACE Inhibitor or ARB for LVSD[1]	6	100%	96%	94%
Discharge Instructions[1]	12	42%	86%	88%
Evaluation of LVS Function	33	97%	96%	98%
Smoking Cessation Advice[1]	4	75%	96%	98%
Pneumonia Care				
Appropriate Initial Antibiotic[1]	15	80%	90%	92%
Blood Culture Timing[1]	4	75%	95%	96%
Influenza Vaccine[1]	11	91%	92%	91%
Initial Antibiotic Timing[1]	18	94%	96%	95%
Pneumococcal Vaccine[1]	16	94%	92%	93%
Smoking Cessation Advice[1]	1	100%	95%	97%
Surgical Care Improvement Project				
Appropriate VTP Within 24 Hours[1]	23	91%	92%	92%
Appropriate Hair Removal	74	100%	99%	99%
Appropriate Beta Blocker Usage	25	80%	94%	93%
Controlled Postoperative Blood Glucose	0	-	92%	93%
Prophylactic Antibiotic Timing	67	94%	96%	97%
Prophylactic Antibiotic Timing (Outpatient)[1]	12	92%	89%	92%
Prophylactic Antibiotic Selection	67	94%	98%	97%
Prophylactic Antibiotic Select. (Outpatient)[1]	12	100%	95%	94%
Prophylactic Antibiotic Stopped	67	100%	97%	94%
Recommended VTP Ordered[1]	23	91%	93%	94%
Urinary Catheter Removal[1]	6	100%	90%	90%
Children's Asthma Care				
Received Systemic Corticosteroids	-	-	-	100%
Received Home Management Plan	-	-	-	71%
Received Reliever Medication	-	-	-	100%
Use of Medical Imaging				
Combination Abdominal CT Scan	218	0.064	0.100	0.191
Combination Chest CT Scan	96	0.000	0.018	0.054
Follow-up Mammogram/Ultrasound	293	6.1%	6.4%	8.4%
MRI for Low Back Pain	44	47.7%	39.7%	32.7%
Survey of Patients' Hospital Experiences				
Area Around Room 'Always' Quiet at Night	300+	64%	-	58%
Doctors 'Always' Communicated Well	300+	84%	-	80%
Home Recovery Information Given	300+	82%	-	82%
Hospital Given 9 or 10 on 10 Point Scale	300+	71%	-	67%
Meds 'Always' Explained Before Given	300+	58%	-	60%
Nurses 'Always' Communicated Well	300+	75%	-	76%
Pain 'Always' Well Controlled	300+	67%	-	69%
Room and Bathroom 'Always' Clean	300+	79%	-	71%
Timely Help 'Always' Received	300+	66%	-	64%
Would Definitely Recommend Hospital	300+	74%	-	69%

Glacial Ridge Hospital

10 4th Avenue Southeast Phone: 320-634-2208
Glenwood, MN 56334 Fax: 320-634-2253
URL: www.glacialridge.org
Type: Critical Access Hospitals Emergency Services: Yes
Ownership: Govt - Hospital Dist/Auth Beds: 19

Key Personnel:
CEO/President. . . . . Kirk Stensrud
Chief of Medical Staff . . . . D Eric Westberg, MD
Infection Control. . . . . Lynn Flesner
Operating Room. . . . . Lynn Flesner
Emergency Room . . . . D Eric Westberg, MD

Measure	Cases	This Hosp.	State Avg.	U.S. Avg.
Heart Attack Care				
ACE Inhibitor or ARB for LVSD	0	-	97%	96%
Aspirin at Arrival[1]	9	89%	99%	99%
Aspirin at Discharge[1]	6	100%	99%	98%
Beta Blocker at Discharge[1]	7	86%	99%	98%
Fibrinolytic Medication Timing[1]	1	0%	55%	55%
PCI Within 90 Minutes of Arrival[5]	0	-	94%	90%
Smoking Cessation Advice	0	-	99%	99%
Chest Pain/Possible Heart Attack Care				
Aspirin at Arrival[5]	0	-	97%	95%
Median Time to ECG (minutes)[5]	0	-	7	8
Median Time to Transfer (minutes)[5]	0	-	50	61
Fibrinolytic Medication Timing[5]	0	-	58%	54%
Heart Failure Care				
ACE Inhibitor or ARB for LVSD[1]	5	60%	96%	94%
Discharge Instructions[1]	14	0%	86%	88%
Evaluation of LVS Function	25	80%	96%	98%
Smoking Cessation Advice	0	-	96%	98%
Pneumonia Care				
Appropriate Initial Antibiotic	25	96%	90%	92%
Blood Culture Timing	0	-	95%	96%
Influenza Vaccine	30	17%	92%	91%
Initial Antibiotic Timing	37	86%	96%	95%
Pneumococcal Vaccine	45	36%	92%	93%
Smoking Cessation Advice[1]	6	50%	95%	97%
Surgical Care Improvement Project				
Appropriate VTP Within 24 Hours[1,3]	7	86%	92%	92%
Appropriate Hair Removal[1]	12	100%	99%	99%
Appropriate Beta Blocker Usage[1,3]	4	25%	94%	93%
Controlled Postoperative Blood Glucose	0	-	92%	93%
Prophylactic Antibiotic Timing[1,3]	5	80%	96%	97%
Prophylactic Antibiotic Timing (Outpatient)[5]	0	-	89%	92%
Prophylactic Antibiotic Selection[1,3]	5	80%	98%	97%
Prophylactic Antibiotic Select. (Outpatient)[5]	0	-	95%	94%
Prophylactic Antibiotic Stopped[1,3]	5	100%	97%	94%
Recommended VTP Ordered[1,3]	7	86%	93%	94%
Urinary Catheter Removal[1]	4	100%	90%	90%
Children's Asthma Care				
Received Systemic Corticosteroids	-	-	-	100%
Received Home Management Plan	-	-	-	71%
Received Reliever Medication	-	-	-	100%
Use of Medical Imaging				
Combination Abdominal CT Scan	92	0.413	0.100	0.191
Combination Chest CT Scan	70	0.029	0.018	0.054
Follow-up Mammogram/Ultrasound	203	7.9%	6.4%	8.4%
MRI for Low Back Pain[1]	26	38.5%	39.7%	32.7%
Survey of Patients' Hospital Experiences				
Area Around Room 'Always' Quiet at Night[8]	-	-	-	58%
Doctors 'Always' Communicated Well[8]	-	-	-	80%
Home Recovery Information Given[8]	-	-	-	82%
Hospital Given 9 or 10 on 10 Point Scale[8]	-	-	-	67%
Meds 'Always' Explained Before Given[8]	-	-	-	60%
Nurses 'Always' Communicated Well[8]	-	-	-	76%
Pain 'Always' Well Controlled[8]	-	-	-	69%
Room and Bathroom 'Always' Clean[8]	-	-	-	71%
Timely Help 'Always' Received[8]	-	-	-	64%
Would Definitely Recommend Hospital[8]	-	-	-	69%

Holy Trinity Hospital

115 West Second Street, Box 157 Phone: 320-748-7223
Graceville, MN 56240 Fax: 320-748-7225
Type: Critical Access Hospitals Emergency Services: Yes
Ownership: Voluntary Non-Profit - Private Beds: 32

Key Personnel:
Chief of Medical Staff. . . . . Stan Gallagher, MD
Infection Control. . . . . Becky Pansch
Operating Room. . . . . Joanne Abel, RN
Quality Assurance . . . . Carol Lee Brinkman

Measure	Cases	This Hosp.	State Avg.	U.S. Avg.
Heart Attack Care				
ACE Inhibitor or ARB for LVSD[3]	0	-	97%	96%
Aspirin at Arrival[1,3]	2	100%	99%	99%
Aspirin at Discharge[1,3]	2	50%	99%	98%
Beta Blocker at Discharge[1,3]	1	100%	99%	98%
Fibrinolytic Medication Timing[3]	0	-	55%	55%
PCI Within 90 Minutes of Arrival[3]	0	-	94%	90%
Smoking Cessation Advice[3]	0	-	99%	99%
Chest Pain/Possible Heart Attack Care				
Aspirin at Arrival[5]	0	-	97%	95%
Median Time to ECG (minutes)[5]	0	-	7	8
Median Time to Transfer (minutes)[5]	0	-	50	61
Fibrinolytic Medication Timing[5]	0	-	58%	54%
Heart Failure Care				
ACE Inhibitor or ARB for LVSD[3]	0	-	96%	94%
Discharge Instructions[1,3]	1	0%	86%	88%
Evaluation of LVS Function[1,3]	2	50%	96%	98%
Smoking Cessation Advice[3]	0	-	96%	98%
Pneumonia Care				
Appropriate Initial Antibiotic[1]	1	100%	90%	92%
Blood Culture Timing[1]	5	100%	95%	96%
Influenza Vaccine[1]	6	100%	92%	91%
Initial Antibiotic Timing[1]	10	100%	96%	95%
Pneumococcal Vaccine[1]	9	100%	92%	93%
Smoking Cessation Advice[1]	1	0%	95%	97%
Surgical Care Improvement Project				
Appropriate VTP Within 24 Hours[5]	0	-	92%	92%
Appropriate Hair Removal[5]	0	-	99%	99%
Appropriate Beta Blocker Usage[5]	0	-	94%	93%
Controlled Postoperative Blood Glucose[5]	0	-	92%	93%
Prophylactic Antibiotic Timing[5]	0	-	96%	97%
Prophylactic Antibiotic Timing (Outpatient)[1,3]	1	0%	89%	92%
Prophylactic Antibiotic Selection[5]	0	-	98%	97%
Prophylactic Antibiotic Select. (Outpatient)[1,3]	1	0%	95%	94%
Prophylactic Antibiotic Stopped[5]	0	-	97%	94%
Recommended VTP Ordered[5]	0	-	93%	94%
Urinary Catheter Removal[5]	0	-	90%	90%
Children's Asthma Care				
Received Systemic Corticosteroids	-	-	-	100%
Received Home Management Plan	-	-	-	71%
Received Reliever Medication	-	-	-	100%
Use of Medical Imaging				
Combination Abdominal CT Scan[1]	23	0.174	0.100	0.191
Combination Chest CT Scan[1]	16	0.063	0.018	0.054
Follow-up Mammogram/Ultrasound[1]	61	13.1%	6.4%	8.4%
MRI for Low Back Pain[1]	4	75.0%	39.7%	32.7%
Survey of Patients' Hospital Experiences				
Area Around Room 'Always' Quiet at Night[8]	-	-	-	58%
Doctors 'Always' Communicated Well[8]	-	-	-	80%
Home Recovery Information Given[8]	-	-	-	82%
Hospital Given 9 or 10 on 10 Point Scale[8]	-	-	-	67%
Meds 'Always' Explained Before Given[8]	-	-	-	60%
Nurses 'Always' Communicated Well[8]	-	-	-	76%
Pain 'Always' Well Controlled[8]	-	-	-	69%
Room and Bathroom 'Always' Clean[8]	-	-	-	71%
Timely Help 'Always' Received[8]	-	-	-	64%
Would Definitely Recommend Hospital[8]	-	-	-	69%

NOTE: Hospital profiles are in alphabetical order by state, then city, then hospital within the city; Rankings exclude hospitals with less than 25 cases except for patient surveys which excludes hospitals with less than 100 cases; (a) 100–299 cases; (1) The number of cases is too small to be sure how well a hospital is performing; (2) The hospital indicated that the data submitted for this measure were based on a sample of cases; (3) Data was collected during a shorter time period (fewer quarters) than the maximum possible time for this measure; (4) Suppressed for one or more quarters by CMS; (5) No data is available from the hospital for this measure; (6) Fewer than 100 patients completed the HCAHPS survey. Use these rates with caution, as the number of surveys may be too low to reliably assess hospital performance; (7) Survey results are based on less than 12 months of data; (8) Survey results are not available for this reporting period; (9) No or very few patients were eligible for the HCAHPS survey. The scores shown, if any, reflect a very small number of surveys; (10) A state average was not calculated because too few hospitals in the state submitted data; (11) There were discrepancies in the data collection process; Please refer to the User's Guide for a full explanation of data.

Cook County Northshore Hospital

515 5th Ave West
Grand Marais, MN 55604
Phone: 218-387-3040
URL: www.nshorehospital.com
Type: Critical Access Hospitals
Emergency Services: Yes
Ownership: Govt - Hospital Dist/Auth
Beds: 16
Key Personnel:
Administrator . . . . Kimber L Wraalstad
Radiology. Caroline Hanford

Measure	Cases	This Hosp.	State Avg.	U.S. Avg.
Heart Attack Care				
ACE Inhibitor or ARB for LVSD[5]	0	-	97%	96%
Aspirin at Arrival[5]	0	-	99%	99%
Aspirin at Discharge[5]	0	-	99%	98%
Beta Blocker at Discharge[5]	0	-	99%	98%
Fibrinolytic Medication Timing[5]	0	-	55%	55%
PCI Within 90 Minutes of Arrival[5]	0	-	94%	90%
Smoking Cessation Advice[5]	0	-	99%	99%
Chest Pain/Possible Heart Attack Care				
Aspirin at Arrival	-	-	97%	95%
Median Time to ECG (minutes)	-	-	7	8
Median Time to Transfer (minutes)	-	-	50	61
Fibrinolytic Medication Timing	-	-	58%	54%
Heart Failure Care				
ACE Inhibitor or ARB for LVSD[3]	0	-	96%	94%
Discharge Instructions[1,3]	3	0%	86%	88%
Evaluation of LVS Function[1,3]	3	67%	96%	98%
Smoking Cessation Advice[3]	0	-	96%	98%
Pneumonia Care				
Appropriate Initial Antibiotic[1,3]	1	100%	90%	92%
Blood Culture Timing[1,3]	2	100%	95%	96%
Influenza Vaccine[1,3]	1	0%	92%	91%
Initial Antibiotic Timing[1,3]	3	67%	96%	95%
Pneumococcal Vaccine[1,3]	3	0%	92%	93%
Smoking Cessation Advice[1,3]	1	100%	95%	97%
Surgical Care Improvement Project				
Appropriate VTP Within 24 Hours[5]	0	-	92%	92%
Appropriate Hair Removal[5]	0	-	99%	99%
Appropriate Beta Blocker Usage[5]	0	-	94%	93%
Controlled Postoperative Blood Glucose[5]	0	-	92%	93%
Prophylactic Antibiotic Timing[5]	0	-	96%	97%
Prophylactic Antibiotic Timing (Outpatient)	-	-	89%	92%
Prophylactic Antibiotic Selection[5]	0	-	98%	97%
Prophylactic Antibiotic Select. (Outpatient)	-	-	95%	94%
Prophylactic Antibiotic Stopped[5]	0	-	97%	94%
Recommended VTP Ordered[5]	0	-	93%	94%
Urinary Catheter Removal[5]	0	-	90%	90%
Children's Asthma Care				
Received Systemic Corticosteroids	-	-	-	100%
Received Home Management Plan	-	-	-	71%
Received Reliever Medication	-	-	-	100%
Use of Medical Imaging				
Combination Abdominal CT Scan	-	-	0.100	0.191
Combination Chest CT Scan	-	-	0.018	0.054
Follow-up Mammogram/Ultrasound	-	-	6.4%	8.4%
MRI for Low Back Pain	-	-	39.7%	32.7%
Survey of Patients' Hospital Experiences				
Area Around Room 'Always' Quiet at Night[8]	-	-	-	58%
Doctors 'Always' Communicated Well[8]	-	-	-	80%
Home Recovery Information Given[8]	-	-	-	82%
Hospital Given 9 or 10 on 10 Point Scale[8]	-	-	-	67%
Meds 'Always' Explained Before Given[8]	-	-	-	60%
Nurses 'Always' Communicated Well[8]	-	-	-	76%
Pain 'Always' Well Controlled[8]	-	-	-	69%
Room and Bathroom 'Always' Clean[8]	-	-	-	71%
Timely Help 'Always' Received[8]	-	-	-	64%
Would Definitely Recommend Hospital[8]	-	-	-	69%

Grand Itasca Clinic and Hospital

1601 Golf Course Road
Grand Rapids, MN 55744
Phone: 218-326-3401
Fax: 218-999-1514
E-mail: info@granditasca.org
URL: www.granditasca.org
Type: Acute Care Hospitals
Emergency Services: Yes
Ownership: Voluntary Non-Profit - Private
Beds: 60
Key Personnel:
CEO/President. . . . . John Kutch
Chief of Medical Staff . . . . Jack Carlisle
Operating Room. . . . . John Kole, MD
Radiology. . . . . Steve Haugen, MD
Anesthesiology. . . . . Jeffrey Lunn, MD
Emergency Room . . . . Michael Johnson, MD

Measure	Cases	This Hosp.	State Avg.	U.S. Avg.
Heart Attack Care				
ACE Inhibitor or ARB for LVSD[1]	3	100%	97%	96%
Aspirin at Arrival[1]	16	100%	99%	99%
Aspirin at Discharge[1]	14	100%	99%	98%
Beta Blocker at Discharge[1]	12	100%	99%	98%
Fibrinolytic Medication Timing	0	-	55%	55%
PCI Within 90 Minutes of Arrival	0	-	94%	90%
Smoking Cessation Advice	0	-	99%	99%
Chest Pain/Possible Heart Attack Care				
Aspirin at Arrival	71	100%	97%	95%
Median Time to ECG (minutes)	68	4	7	8
Median Time to Transfer (minutes)[1,3]	3	70	50	61
Fibrinolytic Medication Timing[1]	6	67%	58%	54%
Heart Failure Care				
ACE Inhibitor or ARB for LVSD[1]	16	100%	96%	94%
Discharge Instructions	43	77%	86%	88%
Evaluation of LVS Function	52	96%	96%	98%
Smoking Cessation Advice[1]	7	57%	96%	98%
Pneumonia Care				
Appropriate Initial Antibiotic	49	96%	90%	92%
Blood Culture Timing	62	90%	95%	96%
Influenza Vaccine	52	100%	92%	91%
Initial Antibiotic Timing	68	99%	96%	95%
Pneumococcal Vaccine	70	93%	92%	93%
Smoking Cessation Advice[1]	21	90%	95%	97%
Surgical Care Improvement Project				
Appropriate VTP Within 24 Hours	58	93%	92%	92%
Appropriate Hair Removal	211	92%	99%	99%
Appropriate Beta Blocker Usage	57	98%	94%	93%
Controlled Postoperative Blood Glucose	0	-	92%	93%
Prophylactic Antibiotic Timing	155	94%	96%	97%
Prophylactic Antibiotic Timing (Outpatient)[1]	14	100%	89%	92%
Prophylactic Antibiotic Selection	147	97%	98%	97%
Prophylactic Antibiotic Select. (Outpatient)	36	97%	95%	94%
Prophylactic Antibiotic Stopped	147	100%	97%	94%
Recommended VTP Ordered	58	93%	93%	94%
Urinary Catheter Removal	28	82%	90%	90%
Children's Asthma Care				
Received Systemic Corticosteroids	-	-	-	100%
Received Home Management Plan	-	-	-	71%
Received Reliever Medication	-	-	-	100%
Use of Medical Imaging				
Combination Abdominal CT Scan	273	0.106	0.100	0.191
Combination Chest CT Scan	184	0.011	0.018	0.054
Follow-up Mammogram/Ultrasound	740	5.1%	6.4%	8.4%
MRI for Low Back Pain	85	36.5%	39.7%	32.7%
Survey of Patients' Hospital Experiences				
Area Around Room 'Always' Quiet at Night	300+	62%	-	58%
Doctors 'Always' Communicated Well	300+	83%	-	80%
Home Recovery Information Given	300+	83%	-	82%
Hospital Given 9 or 10 on 10 Point Scale	300+	69%	-	67%
Meds 'Always' Explained Before Given	300+	61%	-	60%
Nurses 'Always' Communicated Well	300+	79%	-	76%
Pain 'Always' Well Controlled	300+	71%	-	69%
Room and Bathroom 'Always' Clean	300+	72%	-	71%
Timely Help 'Always' Received	300+	71%	-	64%
Would Definitely Recommend Hospital	300+	68%	-	69%

Municipal Hospital and Granite Manor

345 Tenth Avenue
Granite Falls, MN 56241
Phone: 320-564-3111
URL: www.gfmhm.com
Type: Critical Access Hospitals
Emergency Services: Yes
Ownership: Government - Local
Key Personnel:
CEO/President. . . . . George Gerlach
Cardiac Laboratory. . . . . Dennis Baumann
Infection Control. . . . . Patti Anderson
Operating Room. . . . . Lucy Balfany
Radiology. . . . . Shannon Sander
Ambulatory Care . . . . Gene Hughes
Anesthesiology. . . . . Greg Gill

Measure	Cases	This Hosp.	State Avg.	U.S. Avg.
Heart Attack Care				
ACE Inhibitor or ARB for LVSD[3]	0	-	97%	96%
Aspirin at Arrival[1,3]	3	67%	99%	99%
Aspirin at Discharge[1,3]	2	50%	99%	98%
Beta Blocker at Discharge[1,3]	3	100%	99%	98%
Fibrinolytic Medication Timing[3]	0	-	55%	55%
PCI Within 90 Minutes of Arrival[3]	0	-	94%	90%
Smoking Cessation Advice[3]	0	-	99%	99%
Chest Pain/Possible Heart Attack Care				
Aspirin at Arrival[1,3]	19	100%	97%	95%
Median Time to ECG (minutes)[1,3]	18	19	7	8
Median Time to Transfer (minutes)[1,3]	1	143	50	61
Fibrinolytic Medication Timing[1,3]	1	100%	58%	54%
Heart Failure Care				
ACE Inhibitor or ARB for LVSD	0	-	96%	94%
Discharge Instructions[1]	4	100%	86%	88%
Evaluation of LVS Function[1]	11	91%	96%	98%
Smoking Cessation Advice	0	-	96%	98%
Pneumonia Care				
Appropriate Initial Antibiotic[1]	16	94%	90%	92%
Blood Culture Timing[1]	10	90%	95%	96%
Influenza Vaccine[1]	16	94%	92%	91%
Initial Antibiotic Timing[1]	24	96%	96%	95%
Pneumococcal Vaccine	30	90%	92%	93%
Smoking Cessation Advice[1]	3	67%	95%	97%
Surgical Care Improvement Project				
Appropriate VTP Within 24 Hours[5]	0	-	92%	92%
Appropriate Hair Removal[5]	0	-	99%	99%
Appropriate Beta Blocker Usage[5]	0	-	94%	93%
Controlled Postoperative Blood Glucose[5]	0	-	92%	93%
Prophylactic Antibiotic Timing[5]	0	-	96%	97%
Prophylactic Antibiotic Timing (Outpatient)[5]	0	-	89%	92%
Prophylactic Antibiotic Selection[5]	0	-	98%	97%
Prophylactic Antibiotic Select. (Outpatient)[5]	0	-	95%	94%
Prophylactic Antibiotic Stopped[5]	0	-	97%	94%
Recommended VTP Ordered[5]	0	-	93%	94%
Urinary Catheter Removal[5]	0	-	90%	90%
Children's Asthma Care				
Received Systemic Corticosteroids	-	-	-	100%
Received Home Management Plan	-	-	-	71%
Received Reliever Medication	-	-	-	100%
Use of Medical Imaging				
Combination Abdominal CT Scan	87	0.080	0.100	0.191
Combination Chest CT Scan	64	0.000	0.018	0.054
Follow-up Mammogram/Ultrasound	189	4.8%	6.4%	8.4%
MRI for Low Back Pain[1]	14	14.3%	39.7%	32.7%
Survey of Patients' Hospital Experiences				
Area Around Room 'Always' Quiet at Night[8]	-	-	-	58%
Doctors 'Always' Communicated Well[8]	-	-	-	80%
Home Recovery Information Given[8]	-	-	-	82%
Hospital Given 9 or 10 on 10 Point Scale[8]	-	-	-	67%
Meds 'Always' Explained Before Given[8]	-	-	-	60%
Nurses 'Always' Communicated Well[8]	-	-	-	76%
Pain 'Always' Well Controlled[8]	-	-	-	69%
Room and Bathroom 'Always' Clean[8]	-	-	-	71%
Timely Help 'Always' Received[8]	-	-	-	64%
Would Definitely Recommend Hospital[8]	-	-	-	69%

NOTE: Hospital profiles are in alphabetical order by state, then city, then hospital within the city; Rankings exclude hospitals with less than 25 cases except for patient surveys which excludes hospitals with less than 100 cases; (a) 100–299 cases; (1) The number of cases is too small to be sure how well a hospital is performing; (2) The hospital indicated that the data submitted for this measure were based on a sample of cases; (3) Data was collected during a shorter time period (fewer quarters) than the maximum possible time for this measure; (4) Suppressed for one or more quarters by CMS; (5) No data is available from the hospital for this measure; (6) Fewer than 100 patients completed the HCAHPS survey. Use these rates with caution, as the number of surveys may be too low to reliably assess hospital performance; (7) Survey results are based on less than 12 months of data; (8) Survey results are not available for this reporting period; (9) No or very few patients were eligible for the HCAHPS survey. The scores shown, if any, reflect a very small number of surveys; (10) A state average was not calculated because too few hospitals in the state submitted data; (11) There were discrepancies in the data collection process; Please refer to the User's Guide for a full explanation of data.

Kittson Memorial Hospital

1010 South Birch
Hallock, MN 56728
Phone: 218-843-3612
Fax: 218-843-2311
Type: Critical Access Hospitals
Emergency Services: Yes
Ownership: Voluntary Non-Profit - Other
Beds: 20

Key Personnel:
Chief of Medical Staff .... Roland Larter, MD
Quality Assurance .... Joelle Klegstad, RN
Emergency Room .... Ginger Ledoux

Measure	Cases	This Hosp.	State Avg.	U.S. Avg.
Heart Attack Care				
ACE Inhibitor or ARB for LVSD[3]	0	-	97%	96%
Aspirin at Arrival[1,3]	1	100%	99%	99%
Aspirin at Discharge[1,3]	1	100%	99%	98%
Beta Blocker at Discharge[1,3]	1	100%	99%	98%
Fibrinolytic Medication Timing[3]	0	-	55%	55%
PCI Within 90 Minutes of Arrival[3]	0	-	94%	90%
Smoking Cessation Advice[3]	0	-	99%	99%
Chest Pain/Possible Heart Attack Care				
Aspirin at Arrival[5]	0	-	97%	95%
Median Time to ECG (minutes)[5]	0	-	7	8
Median Time to Transfer (minutes)[5]	0	-	50	61
Fibrinolytic Medication Timing[5]	0	-	58%	54%
Heart Failure Care				
ACE Inhibitor or ARB for LVSD	0	-	96%	94%
Discharge Instructions[1]	5	80%	86%	88%
Evaluation of LVS Function[1]	8	0%	96%	98%
Smoking Cessation Advice	0	-	96%	98%
Pneumonia Care				
Appropriate Initial Antibiotic[1]	7	71%	90%	92%
Blood Culture Timing	0	-	95%	96%
Influenza Vaccine[1]	7	14%	92%	91%
Initial Antibiotic Timing[1]	11	91%	96%	95%
Pneumococcal Vaccine[1]	14	14%	92%	93%
Smoking Cessation Advice	0	-	95%	97%
Surgical Care Improvement Project				
Appropriate VTP Within 24 Hours[5]	0	-	92%	92%
Appropriate Hair Removal[5]	0	-	99%	99%
Appropriate Beta Blocker Usage[5]	0	-	94%	93%
Controlled Postoperative Blood Glucose[5]	0	-	92%	93%
Prophylactic Antibiotic Timing[5]	0	-	96%	97%
Prophylactic Antibiotic Timing (Outpatient)[5]	0	-	89%	92%
Prophylactic Antibiotic Selection[5]	0	-	98%	97%
Prophylactic Antibiotic Select. (Outpatient)[5]	0	-	95%	94%
Prophylactic Antibiotic Stopped[5]	0	-	97%	94%
Recommended VTP Ordered[5]	0	-	93%	94%
Urinary Catheter Removal[5]	0	-	90%	90%
Children's Asthma Care				
Received Systemic Corticosteroids	-	-	-	100%
Received Home Management Plan	-	-	-	71%
Received Reliever Medication	-	-	-	100%
Use of Medical Imaging				
Combination Abdominal CT Scan[1]	14	0.429	0.100	0.191
Combination Chest CT Scan[1]	11	0.182	0.018	0.054
Follow-up Mammogram/Ultrasound	85	4.7%	6.4%	8.4%
MRI for Low Back Pain[1]	3	66.7%	39.7%	32.7%
Survey of Patients' Hospital Experiences				
Area Around Room 'Always' Quiet at Night[8]	-	-	-	58%
Doctors 'Always' Communicated Well[8]	-	-	-	80%
Home Recovery Information Given[8]	-	-	-	82%
Hospital Given 9 or 10 on 10 Point Scale[8]	-	-	-	67%
Meds 'Always' Explained Before Given[8]	-	-	-	60%
Nurses 'Always' Communicated Well[8]	-	-	-	76%
Pain 'Always' Well Controlled[8]	-	-	-	69%
Room and Bathroom 'Always' Clean[8]	-	-	-	71%
Timely Help 'Always' Received[8]	-	-	-	64%
Would Definitely Recommend Hospital[8]	-	-	-	69%

Regina Medical Center

1175 Nininger Road
Hastings, MN 55033
Phone: 651-480-4100
Fax: 651-480-4212
URL: www.reginamedical.org
Type: Acute Care Hospitals
Emergency Services: Yes
Ownership: Voluntary Non-Profit - Church
Beds: 57

Key Personnel:
CEO/President.............. Ty Erickson
Chief of Medical Staff............ James Noreen, MD
Operating Room............. Barb Kendall
Emergency Room .... Lawrence Erickson
Patient Relations .... Solveig Dittmann

Measure	Cases	This Hosp.	State Avg.	U.S. Avg.
Heart Attack Care				
ACE Inhibitor or ARB for LVSD	0	-	97%	96%
Aspirin at Arrival[1]	12	100%	99%	99%
Aspirin at Discharge[1]	11	100%	99%	98%
Beta Blocker at Discharge[1]	12	100%	99%	98%
Fibrinolytic Medication Timing	0	-	55%	55%
PCI Within 90 Minutes of Arrival	0	-	94%	90%
Smoking Cessation Advice	0	-	99%	99%
Chest Pain/Possible Heart Attack Care				
Aspirin at Arrival	185	93%	97%	95%
Median Time to ECG (minutes)	191	7	7	8
Median Time to Transfer (minutes)[1]	15	26	50	61
Fibrinolytic Medication Timing	0	-	58%	54%
Heart Failure Care				
ACE Inhibitor or ARB for LVSD[1]	14	100%	96%	94%
Discharge Instructions	37	95%	86%	88%
Evaluation of LVS Function	52	100%	96%	98%
Smoking Cessation Advice[1]	5	100%	96%	98%
Pneumonia Care				
Appropriate Initial Antibiotic	33	97%	90%	92%
Blood Culture Timing	52	96%	95%	96%
Influenza Vaccine	36	100%	92%	91%
Initial Antibiotic Timing	58	100%	96%	95%
Pneumococcal Vaccine	50	100%	92%	93%
Smoking Cessation Advice[1]	12	92%	95%	97%
Surgical Care Improvement Project				
Appropriate VTP Within 24 Hours[2]	64	98%	92%	92%
Appropriate Hair Removal[2]	245	100%	99%	99%
Appropriate Beta Blocker Usage[2]	34	100%	94%	93%
Controlled Postoperative Blood Glucose[2]	0	-	92%	93%
Prophylactic Antibiotic Timing[2]	182	95%	96%	97%
Prophylactic Antibiotic Timing (Outpatient)	82	94%	89%	92%
Prophylactic Antibiotic Selection[2]	182	97%	98%	97%
Prophylactic Antibiotic Select. (Outpatient)	79	96%	95%	94%
Prophylactic Antibiotic Stopped[2]	181	100%	97%	94%
Recommended VTP Ordered[2]	64	98%	93%	94%
Urinary Catheter Removal[2]	31	97%	90%	90%
Children's Asthma Care				
Received Systemic Corticosteroids	-	-	-	100%
Received Home Management Plan	-	-	-	71%
Received Reliever Medication	-	-	-	100%
Use of Medical Imaging				
Combination Abdominal CT Scan	284	0.049	0.100	0.191
Combination Chest CT Scan	197	0.005	0.018	0.054
Follow-up Mammogram/Ultrasound	279	5.0%	6.4%	8.4%
MRI for Low Back Pain[1]	40	22.5%	39.7%	32.7%
Survey of Patients' Hospital Experiences				
Area Around Room 'Always' Quiet at Night	300+	70%	-	58%
Doctors 'Always' Communicated Well	300+	82%	-	80%
Home Recovery Information Given	300+	83%	-	82%
Hospital Given 9 or 10 on 10 Point Scale	300+	72%	-	67%
Meds 'Always' Explained Before Given	300+	64%	-	60%
Nurses 'Always' Communicated Well	300+	78%	-	76%
Pain 'Always' Well Controlled	300+	70%	-	69%
Room and Bathroom 'Always' Clean	300+	72%	-	71%
Timely Help 'Always' Received	300+	73%	-	64%
Would Definitely Recommend Hospital	300+	74%	-	69%

Hendricks Community Hospital

503 E Lincoln Street
Hendricks, MN 56136
Phone: 507-275-3134
Fax: 507-275-3104
URL: www.hendrickshosp.org
Type: Critical Access Hospitals
Emergency Services: Yes
Ownership: Voluntary Non-Profit - Other
Beds: 26

Measure	Cases	This Hosp.	State Avg.	U.S. Avg.
Heart Attack Care				
ACE Inhibitor or ARB for LVSD[3]	0	-	97%	96%
Aspirin at Arrival[1,3]	1	100%	99%	99%
Aspirin at Discharge[1,3]	2	100%	99%	98%
Beta Blocker at Discharge[1,3]	2	100%	99%	98%
Fibrinolytic Medication Timing[3]	0	-	55%	55%
PCI Within 90 Minutes of Arrival[3]	0	-	94%	90%
Smoking Cessation Advice[1,3]	1	0%	99%	99%
Chest Pain/Possible Heart Attack Care				
Aspirin at Arrival[5]	0	-	97%	95%
Median Time to ECG (minutes)[5]	0	-	7	8
Median Time to Transfer (minutes)[5]	0	-	50	61
Fibrinolytic Medication Timing[5]	0	-	58%	54%
Heart Failure Care				
ACE Inhibitor or ARB for LVSD[1]	2	100%	96%	94%
Discharge Instructions[1]	3	0%	86%	88%
Evaluation of LVS Function[1]	9	78%	96%	98%
Smoking Cessation Advice[1]	1	0%	96%	98%
Pneumonia Care				
Appropriate Initial Antibiotic[1]	3	67%	90%	92%
Blood Culture Timing[1]	1	0%	95%	96%
Influenza Vaccine[1]	2	0%	92%	91%
Initial Antibiotic Timing[1]	3	33%	96%	95%
Pneumococcal Vaccine[1]	6	17%	92%	93%
Smoking Cessation Advice	0	-	95%	97%
Surgical Care Improvement Project				
Appropriate VTP Within 24 Hours[1]	3	100%	92%	92%
Appropriate Hair Removal[1]	13	100%	99%	99%
Appropriate Beta Blocker Usage[5]	0	-	94%	93%
Controlled Postoperative Blood Glucose	0	-	92%	93%
Prophylactic Antibiotic Timing[1]	13	62%	96%	97%
Prophylactic Antibiotic Timing (Outpatient)[5]	0	-	89%	92%
Prophylactic Antibiotic Selection[1]	13	100%	98%	97%
Prophylactic Antibiotic Select. (Outpatient)[5]	0	-	95%	94%
Prophylactic Antibiotic Stopped[1]	13	62%	97%	94%
Recommended VTP Ordered[1]	3	100%	93%	94%
Urinary Catheter Removal[1]	4	100%	90%	90%
Children's Asthma Care				
Received Systemic Corticosteroids	-	-	-	100%
Received Home Management Plan	-	-	-	71%
Received Reliever Medication	-	-	-	100%
Use of Medical Imaging				
Combination Abdominal CT Scan[1]	56	0.161	0.100	0.191
Combination Chest CT Scan[1]	34	0.088	0.018	0.054
Follow-up Mammogram/Ultrasound	138	2.2%	6.4%	8.4%
MRI for Low Back Pain[1]	13	38.5%	39.7%	32.7%
Survey of Patients' Hospital Experiences				
Area Around Room 'Always' Quiet at Night[8]	-	-	-	58%
Doctors 'Always' Communicated Well[8]	-	-	-	80%
Home Recovery Information Given[8]	-	-	-	82%
Hospital Given 9 or 10 on 10 Point Scale[8]	-	-	-	67%
Meds 'Always' Explained Before Given[8]	-	-	-	60%
Nurses 'Always' Communicated Well[8]	-	-	-	76%
Pain 'Always' Well Controlled[8]	-	-	-	69%
Room and Bathroom 'Always' Clean[8]	-	-	-	71%
Timely Help 'Always' Received[8]	-	-	-	64%
Would Definitely Recommend Hospital[8]	-	-	-	69%

NOTE: Hospital profiles are in alphabetical order by state, then city, then hospital within the city; Rankings exclude hospitals with less than 25 cases except for patient surveys which excludes hospitals with less than 100 cases; (a) 100–299 cases; (1) The number of cases is too small to be sure how well a hospital is performing; (2) The hospital indicated that the data submitted for this measure were based on a sample of cases; (3) Data was collected during a shorter time period (fewer quarters) than the maximum possible time for this measure; (4) Suppressed for one or more quarters by CMS; (5) No data is available from the hospital for this measure; (6) Fewer than 100 patients completed the HCAHPS survey. Use these rates with caution, as the number of surveys may be too low to reliably assess hospital performance; (7) Survey results are based on less than 12 months of data; (8) Survey results are not available for this reporting period; (9) No or very few patients were eligible for the HCAHPS survey. The scores shown, if any, reflect a very small number of surveys; (10) A state average was not calculated because too few hospitals in the state submitted data; (11) There were discrepancies in the data collection process; Please refer to the User's Guide for a full explanation of data.

University Medical Center - Mesabi/Mesaba Clinics

750 East 34th St
Hibbing, MN 55746
Type: Acute Care Hospitals
Ownership: Voluntary Non-Profit - Other

Phone: 218-362-6659
Fax: 218-362-6619
Emergency Services: Yes
Beds: 175

Key Personnel:

CEO/President. . . . . Larry Pfaff
Chief of Medical Staff . . . . Ann Steciw, MD
Infection Control. . . . . Char Pulling
Operating Room. . . . . Brenda McIntyre
Pediatric Ambulatory Care . . . . . . Joel Cassingham, MD
Pediatric In-Patient Care . . . . Joel Cassingham, MD
Quality Assurance . . . . Carol Beck
Radiology. . . . . Daniel Courneya, MD

Measure	Cases	This Hosp.	State Avg.	U.S. Avg.
Heart Attack Care				
ACE Inhibitor or ARB for LVSD[1]	6	83%	97%	96%
Aspirin at Arrival	27	93%	99%	99%
Aspirin at Discharge[1]	20	95%	99%	98%
Beta Blocker at Discharge[1]	18	89%	99%	98%
Fibrinolytic Medication Timing	0	-	55%	55%
PCI Within 90 Minutes of Arrival	0	-	94%	90%
Smoking Cessation Advice[1]	3	67%	99%	99%
Chest Pain/Possible Heart Attack Care				
Aspirin at Arrival	87	100%	97%	95%
Median Time to ECG (minutes)	90	7	7	8
Median Time to Transfer (minutes)[1]	7	66	50	61
Fibrinolytic Medication Timing[1]	1	100%	58%	54%
Heart Failure Care				
ACE Inhibitor or ARB for LVSD	30	97%	96%	94%
Discharge Instructions	69	84%	86%	88%
Evaluation of LVS Function	90	96%	96%	98%
Smoking Cessation Advice[1]	15	100%	96%	98%
Pneumonia Care				
Appropriate Initial Antibiotic	93	92%	90%	92%
Blood Culture Timing	69	97%	95%	96%
Influenza Vaccine	61	92%	92%	91%
Initial Antibiotic Timing	118	100%	96%	95%
Pneumococcal Vaccine	86	95%	92%	93%
Smoking Cessation Advice	45	87%	95%	97%
Surgical Care Improvement Project				
Appropriate VTP Within 24 Hours[2]	63	89%	92%	92%
Appropriate Hair Removal[2]	125	100%	99%	99%
Appropriate Beta Blocker Usage[1,2]	16	94%	94%	93%
Controlled Postoperative Blood Glucose[2]	0	-	92%	93%
Prophylactic Antibiotic Timing[2]	79	97%	96%	97%
Prophylactic Antibiotic Timing (Outpatient)[1]	14	93%	89%	92%
Prophylactic Antibiotic Selection[2]	82	96%	98%	97%
Prophylactic Antibiotic Select. (Outpatient)[1]	13	100%	95%	94%
Prophylactic Antibiotic Stopped[2]	75	95%	97%	94%
Recommended VTP Ordered[2]	63	89%	93%	94%
Urinary Catheter Removal[1,2]	14	86%	90%	90%
Children's Asthma Care				
Received Systemic Corticosteroids	-	-	-	100%
Received Home Management Plan	-	-	-	71%
Received Reliever Medication	-	-	-	100%
Use of Medical Imaging				
Combination Abdominal CT Scan	260	0.085	0.100	0.191
Combination Chest CT Scan	220	0.000	0.018	0.054
Follow-up Mammogram/Ultrasound	383	5.5%	6.4%	8.4%
MRI for Low Back Pain	106	51.9%	39.7%	32.7%
Survey of Patients' Hospital Experiences				
Area Around Room 'Always' Quiet at Night[11]	300+	60%	-	58%
Doctors 'Always' Communicated Well[11]	300+	87%	-	80%
Home Recovery Information Given[11]	300+	86%	-	82%
Hospital Given 9 or 10 on 10 Point Scale[11]	300+	68%	-	67%
Meds 'Always' Explained Before Given[11]	300+	67%	-	60%
Nurses 'Always' Communicated Well[11]	300+	81%	-	76%
Pain 'Always' Well Controlled[11]	300+	71%	-	69%
Room and Bathroom 'Always' Clean[11]	300+	76%	-	71%
Timely Help 'Always' Received[11]	300+	68%	-	64%
Would Definitely Recommend Hospital[11]	300+	65%	-	69%

Hutchinson Area Health Care

1095 Highway 15 South
Hutchinson, MN 55350
URL: www.hahc-hmc.com
Type: Acute Care Hospitals
Ownership: Voluntary Non-Profit - Private

Phone: 320-234-5000
Fax: 320-587-3340
Emergency Services: Yes
Beds: 66

Key Personnel:

Infection Control. . . . . Linette Wendlandt
Operating Room. . . . . Barb Keller
Quality Assurance . . . . Corrine Almundson
Radiology. . . . . Daniel S Beggs
Emergency Room . . . . George Gordon

Measure	Cases	This Hosp.	State Avg.	U.S. Avg.
Heart Attack Care				
ACE Inhibitor or ARB for LVSD[3]	0	-	97%	96%
Aspirin at Arrival[1,3]	5	100%	99%	99%
Aspirin at Discharge[1,3]	5	100%	99%	98%
Beta Blocker at Discharge[1,3]	5	80%	99%	98%
Fibrinolytic Medication Timing[3]	0	-	55%	55%
PCI Within 90 Minutes of Arrival[3]	0	-	94%	90%
Smoking Cessation Advice[3]	0	-	99%	99%
Chest Pain/Possible Heart Attack Care				
Aspirin at Arrival	87	99%	97%	95%
Median Time to ECG (minutes)	87	6	7	8
Median Time to Transfer (minutes)[3]	0	-	50	61
Fibrinolytic Medication Timing[1]	8	62%	58%	54%
Heart Failure Care				
ACE Inhibitor or ARB for LVSD[1]	17	94%	96%	94%
Discharge Instructions	47	94%	86%	88%
Evaluation of LVS Function	70	97%	96%	98%
Smoking Cessation Advice[1]	4	100%	96%	98%
Pneumonia Care				
Appropriate Initial Antibiotic	45	96%	90%	92%
Blood Culture Timing	50	94%	95%	96%
Influenza Vaccine	36	92%	92%	91%
Initial Antibiotic Timing	60	98%	96%	95%
Pneumococcal Vaccine	62	95%	92%	93%
Smoking Cessation Advice[1]	11	100%	95%	97%
Surgical Care Improvement Project				
Appropriate VTP Within 24 Hours	67	99%	92%	92%
Appropriate Hair Removal	195	100%	99%	99%
Appropriate Beta Blocker Usage	64	97%	94%	93%
Controlled Postoperative Blood Glucose	0	-	92%	93%
Prophylactic Antibiotic Timing	144	94%	96%	97%
Prophylactic Antibiotic Timing (Outpatient)	45	84%	89%	92%
Prophylactic Antibiotic Selection	146	92%	98%	97%
Prophylactic Antibiotic Select. (Outpatient)	40	98%	95%	94%
Prophylactic Antibiotic Stopped	136	100%	97%	94%
Recommended VTP Ordered	67	100%	93%	94%
Urinary Catheter Removal[1]	16	94%	90%	90%
Children's Asthma Care				
Received Systemic Corticosteroids	-	-	-	100%
Received Home Management Plan	-	-	-	71%
Received Reliever Medication	-	-	-	100%
Use of Medical Imaging				
Combination Abdominal CT Scan	281	0.060	0.100	0.191
Combination Chest CT Scan	216	0.000	0.018	0.054
Follow-up Mammogram/Ultrasound	591	5.8%	6.4%	8.4%
MRI for Low Back Pain	74	27.0%	39.7%	32.7%
Survey of Patients' Hospital Experiences				
Area Around Room 'Always' Quiet at Night	300+	63%	-	58%
Doctors 'Always' Communicated Well	300+	82%	-	80%
Home Recovery Information Given	300+	86%	-	82%
Hospital Given 9 or 10 on 10 Point Scale	300+	70%	-	67%
Meds 'Always' Explained Before Given	300+	61%	-	60%
Nurses 'Always' Communicated Well	300+	76%	-	76%
Pain 'Always' Well Controlled	300+	69%	-	69%
Room and Bathroom 'Always' Clean	300+	74%	-	71%
Timely Help 'Always' Received	300+	66%	-	64%
Would Definitely Recommend Hospital	300+	72%	-	69%

Rainy Lake Medical Center

1400 Highway 71
International Falls, MN 56649
URL: www.fmh-mn.com
Type: Critical Access Hospitals
Ownership: Voluntary Non-Profit - Private

Phone: 218-283-5400
Fax: 218-283-2281
Emergency Services: Yes
Beds: 25

Key Personnel:

CEO/President. . . . . Brian Long
Chief of Medical Staff . . . . Anthony Stone, MD
Infection Control. . . . . Douglas Johnson, MD
Operating Room. . . . . Lori Constantine
Quality Assurance . . . . Laurie Whitefield
Radiology. . . . . Daniel Courneya, MD
Emergency Room . . . . Jay Knaak, MD

Measure	Cases	This Hosp.	State Avg.	U.S. Avg.
Heart Attack Care				
ACE Inhibitor or ARB for LVSD[3]	0	-	97%	96%
Aspirin at Arrival[1,3]	1	0%	99%	99%
Aspirin at Discharge[3]	0	-	99%	98%
Beta Blocker at Discharge[3]	0	-	99%	98%
Fibrinolytic Medication Timing[3]	0	-	55%	55%
PCI Within 90 Minutes of Arrival[3]	0	-	94%	90%
Smoking Cessation Advice[3]	0	-	99%	99%
Chest Pain/Possible Heart Attack Care				
Aspirin at Arrival	-	-	97%	95%
Median Time to ECG (minutes)	-	-	7	8
Median Time to Transfer (minutes)	-	-	50	61
Fibrinolytic Medication Timing	-	-	58%	54%
Heart Failure Care				
ACE Inhibitor or ARB for LVSD[3]	0	-	96%	94%
Discharge Instructions[1,3]	6	67%	86%	88%
Evaluation of LVS Function[1,3]	7	14%	96%	98%
Smoking Cessation Advice[3]	0	-	96%	98%
Pneumonia Care				
Appropriate Initial Antibiotic[1,3]	3	67%	90%	92%
Blood Culture Timing[1,3]	2	50%	95%	96%
Influenza Vaccine[1,3]	3	0%	92%	91%
Initial Antibiotic Timing[3]	0	-	96%	95%
Pneumococcal Vaccine[1,3]	2	0%	92%	93%
Smoking Cessation Advice[1,3]	1	100%	95%	97%
Surgical Care Improvement Project				
Appropriate VTP Within 24 Hours[5]	0	-	92%	92%
Appropriate Hair Removal[5]	0	-	99%	99%
Appropriate Beta Blocker Usage[5]	0	-	94%	93%
Controlled Postoperative Blood Glucose[5]	0	-	92%	93%
Prophylactic Antibiotic Timing[5]	0	-	96%	97%
Prophylactic Antibiotic Timing (Outpatient)	-	-	89%	92%
Prophylactic Antibiotic Selection[5]	0	-	98%	97%
Prophylactic Antibiotic Select. (Outpatient)	-	-	95%	94%
Prophylactic Antibiotic Stopped[5]	0	-	97%	94%
Recommended VTP Ordered[5]	0	-	93%	94%
Urinary Catheter Removal[5]	0	-	90%	90%
Children's Asthma Care				
Received Systemic Corticosteroids	-	-	-	100%
Received Home Management Plan	-	-	-	71%
Received Reliever Medication	-	-	-	100%
Use of Medical Imaging				
Combination Abdominal CT Scan	-	-	0.100	0.191
Combination Chest CT Scan	-	-	0.018	0.054
Follow-up Mammogram/Ultrasound	-	-	6.4%	8.4%
MRI for Low Back Pain	-	-	39.7%	32.7%
Survey of Patients' Hospital Experiences				
Area Around Room 'Always' Quiet at Night	(a)	63%	-	58%
Doctors 'Always' Communicated Well	(a)	83%	-	80%
Home Recovery Information Given	(a)	88%	-	82%
Hospital Given 9 or 10 on 10 Point Scale	(a)	63%	-	67%
Meds 'Always' Explained Before Given	(a)	63%	-	60%
Nurses 'Always' Communicated Well	(a)	76%	-	76%
Pain 'Always' Well Controlled	(a)	69%	-	69%
Room and Bathroom 'Always' Clean	(a)	75%	-	71%
Timely Help 'Always' Received	(a)	74%	-	64%
Would Definitely Recommend Hospital	(a)	63%	-	69%

NOTE: Hospital profiles are in alphabetical order by state, then city, then hospital within the city; Rankings exclude hospitals with less than 25 cases except for patient surveys which excludes hospitals with less than 100 cases; (a) 100–299 cases; (1) The number of cases is too small to be sure how well a hospital is performing; (2) The hospital indicated that the data submitted for this measure were based on a sample of cases; (3) Data was collected during a shorter time period (fewer quarters) than the maximum possible time for this measure; (4) Suppressed for one or more quarters by CMS; (5) No data is available from the hospital for this measure; (6) Fewer than 100 patients completed the HCAHPS survey. Use these rates with caution, as the number of surveys may be too low to reliably assess hospital performance; (7) Survey results are based on less than 12 months of data; (8) Survey results are not available for this reporting period; (9) No or very few patients were eligible for the HCAHPS survey. The scores shown, if any, reflect a very small number of surveys; (10) A state average was not calculated because too few hospitals in the state submitted data; (11) There were discrepancies in the data collection process; Please refer to the User's Guide for a full explanation of data.

Sanford Jackson Medical Center

1430 North Highway Phone: 507-847-2420
Jackson, MN 56143 Fax: 507-847-3728
E-mail: pederson@sanfordhealth.org
URL: www.sanfordjackson.org
Type: Critical Access Hospitals Emergency Services: Yes
Ownership: Voluntary Non-Profit - Other Beds: 20
Key Personnel:
CEO/President. . . . . Mary Ruyter
Chief of Medical Staff. . . . . Marie Paul Lockerd, DO
Operating Room. . . . . Leroy Hodge
Quality Assurance . . . . Karen Anderson
Radiology. . . . . Jeffrey Willis
Hemotology Center . . . . Dr Michael McHale

Measure	Cases	This Hosp.	State Avg.	U.S. Avg.
Heart Attack Care				
ACE Inhibitor or ARB for LVSD[3]	0	-	97%	96%
Aspirin at Arrival[1,3]	1	100%	99%	99%
Aspirin at Discharge[1,3]	1	100%	99%	98%
Beta Blocker at Discharge[1,3]	1	100%	99%	98%
Fibrinolytic Medication Timing[3]	0	-	55%	55%
PCI Within 90 Minutes of Arrival[3]	0	-	94%	90%
Smoking Cessation Advice[3]	0	-	99%	99%
Chest Pain/Possible Heart Attack Care				
Aspirin at Arrival[1]	14	100%	97%	95%
Median Time to ECG (minutes)[1]	15	8	7	8
Median Time to Transfer (minutes)[3]	0	-	50	61
Fibrinolytic Medication Timing[1,3]	5	20%	58%	54%
Heart Failure Care				
ACE Inhibitor or ARB for LVSD	0	-	96%	94%
Discharge Instructions[1]	1	100%	86%	88%
Evaluation of LVS Function[1]	4	50%	96%	98%
Smoking Cessation Advice	0	-	96%	98%
Pneumonia Care				
Appropriate Initial Antibiotic[1]	10	90%	90%	92%
Blood Culture Timing[1]	9	100%	95%	96%
Influenza Vaccine[1]	7	100%	92%	91%
Initial Antibiotic Timing[1]	16	100%	96%	95%
Pneumococcal Vaccine[1]	16	94%	92%	93%
Smoking Cessation Advice[1]	1	0%	95%	97%
Surgical Care Improvement Project				
Appropriate VTP Within 24 Hours[5]	0	-	92%	92%
Appropriate Hair Removal[5]	0	-	99%	99%
Appropriate Beta Blocker Usage[5]	0	-	94%	93%
Controlled Postoperative Blood Glucose[5]	0	-	92%	93%
Prophylactic Antibiotic Timing[5]	0	-	96%	97%
Prophylactic Antibiotic Timing (Outpatient)[5]	0	-	89%	92%
Prophylactic Antibiotic Selection[5]	0	-	98%	97%
Prophylactic Antibiotic Select. (Outpatient)[5]	0	-	95%	94%
Prophylactic Antibiotic Stopped[5]	0	-	97%	94%
Recommended VTP Ordered[5]	0	-	93%	94%
Urinary Catheter Removal[5]	0	-	90%	90%
Children's Asthma Care				
Received Systemic Corticosteroids	-	-	-	100%
Received Home Management Plan	-	-	-	71%
Received Reliever Medication	-	-	-	100%
Use of Medical Imaging				
Combination Abdominal CT Scan[1]	23	0.304	0.100	0.191
Combination Chest CT Scan[1]	15	0.133	0.018	0.054
Follow-up Mammogram/Ultrasound	105	10.5%	6.4%	8.4%
MRI for Low Back Pain[1]	10	60.0%	39.7%	32.7%
Survey of Patients' Hospital Experiences				
Area Around Room 'Always' Quiet at Night[6]	<100	63%	-	58%
Doctors 'Always' Communicated Well[6]	<100	69%	-	80%
Home Recovery Information Given[6]	<100	72%	-	82%
Hospital Given 9 or 10 on 10 Point Scale[6]	<100	59%	-	67%
Meds 'Always' Explained Before Given[6]	<100	57%	-	60%
Nurses 'Always' Communicated Well[6]	<100	78%	-	76%
Pain 'Always' Well Controlled[6]	<100	59%	-	69%
Room and Bathroom 'Always' Clean[6]	<100	67%	-	71%
Timely Help 'Always' Received[6]	<100	61%	-	64%
Would Definitely Recommend Hospital	<100	49%	-	69%

Lake City Medical Center Mayo Health System

500 West Grant Street Phone: 651-345-1114
Lake City, MN 55041
Type: Critical Access Hospitals Emergency Services: Yes
Ownership: Voluntary Non-Profit - Private
Key Personnel:
CEO/President. . . . . Thomas Witt

Measure	Cases	This Hosp.	State Avg.	U.S. Avg.
Heart Attack Care				
ACE Inhibitor or ARB for LVSD[1,3]	2	100%	97%	96%
Aspirin at Arrival[1,3]	4	100%	99%	99%
Aspirin at Discharge[1,3]	4	100%	99%	98%
Beta Blocker at Discharge[1,3]	4	100%	99%	98%
Fibrinolytic Medication Timing[3]	0	-	55%	55%
PCI Within 90 Minutes of Arrival[3]	0	-	94%	90%
Smoking Cessation Advice[3]	0	-	99%	99%
Chest Pain/Possible Heart Attack Care				
Aspirin at Arrival[5]	0	-	97%	95%
Median Time to ECG (minutes)[5]	0	-	7	8
Median Time to Transfer (minutes)[5]	0	-	50	61
Fibrinolytic Medication Timing[5]	0	-	58%	54%
Heart Failure Care				
ACE Inhibitor or ARB for LVSD	0	-	96%	94%
Discharge Instructions[1]	8	12%	86%	88%
Evaluation of LVS Function[1]	9	67%	96%	98%
Smoking Cessation Advice	0	-	96%	98%
Pneumonia Care				
Appropriate Initial Antibiotic[1,3]	3	67%	90%	92%
Blood Culture Timing[1,3]	6	67%	95%	96%
Influenza Vaccine[1,3]	4	75%	92%	91%
Initial Antibiotic Timing[1,3]	9	89%	96%	95%
Pneumococcal Vaccine[1,3]	8	38%	92%	93%
Smoking Cessation Advice[1,3]	3	67%	95%	97%
Surgical Care Improvement Project				
Appropriate VTP Within 24 Hours[1]	12	100%	92%	92%
Appropriate Hair Removal	33	100%	99%	99%
Appropriate Beta Blocker Usage[5]	0	-	94%	93%
Controlled Postoperative Blood Glucose	0	-	92%	93%
Prophylactic Antibiotic Timing	29	90%	96%	97%
Prophylactic Antibiotic Timing (Outpatient)[5]	0	-	89%	92%
Prophylactic Antibiotic Selection	29	100%	98%	97%
Prophylactic Antibiotic Select. (Outpatient)[5]	0	-	95%	94%
Prophylactic Antibiotic Stopped	29	100%	97%	94%
Recommended VTP Ordered[1]	12	100%	93%	94%
Urinary Catheter Removal[1]	16	50%	90%	90%
Children's Asthma Care				
Received Systemic Corticosteroids	-	-	-	100%
Received Home Management Plan	-	-	-	71%
Received Reliever Medication	-	-	-	100%
Use of Medical Imaging				
Combination Abdominal CT Scan[1]	44	0.114	0.100	0.191
Combination Chest CT Scan[1]	18	0.000	0.018	0.054
Follow-up Mammogram/Ultrasound	247	11.3%	6.4%	8.4%
MRI for Low Back Pain[1]	11	27.3%	39.7%	32.7%
Survey of Patients' Hospital Experiences				
Area Around Room 'Always' Quiet at Night	(a)	60%	-	58%
Doctors 'Always' Communicated Well	(a)	83%	-	80%
Home Recovery Information Given	(a)	80%	-	82%
Hospital Given 9 or 10 on 10 Point Scale	(a)	73%	-	67%
Meds 'Always' Explained Before Given	(a)	59%	-	60%
Nurses 'Always' Communicated Well	(a)	77%	-	76%
Pain 'Always' Well Controlled	(a)	70%	-	69%
Room and Bathroom 'Always' Clean	(a)	83%	-	71%
Timely Help 'Always' Received	(a)	70%	-	64%
Would Definitely Recommend Hospital	(a)	77%	-	69%

Minnesota Valley Health Center

621 South Fourth Street Phone: 507-665-3375
Le Sueur, MN 56058 Fax: 507-665-2191
E-mail: mvhc@mnic.net
Type: Critical Access Hospitals Emergency Services: Yes
Ownership: Voluntary Non-Profit - Private Beds: 109
Key Personnel:
Cardiac Laboratory. . . . . John Bernhardson
Chief of Medical Staff . . . . John N Taylor
Emergency Room . . . . Pam William

Measure	Cases	This Hosp.	State Avg.	U.S. Avg.
Heart Attack Care				
ACE Inhibitor or ARB for LVSD[3]	0	-	97%	96%
Aspirin at Arrival[1,3]	1	100%	99%	99%
Aspirin at Discharge[1,3]	1	100%	99%	98%
Beta Blocker at Discharge[1,3]	1	100%	99%	98%
Fibrinolytic Medication Timing[3]	0	-	55%	55%
PCI Within 90 Minutes of Arrival[3]	0	-	94%	90%
Smoking Cessation Advice[3]	0	-	99%	99%
Chest Pain/Possible Heart Attack Care				
Aspirin at Arrival[5]	0	-	97%	95%
Median Time to ECG (minutes)[5]	0	-	7	8
Median Time to Transfer (minutes)[5]	0	-	50	61
Fibrinolytic Medication Timing[5]	0	-	58%	54%
Heart Failure Care				
ACE Inhibitor or ARB for LVSD[1,3]	1	100%	96%	94%
Discharge Instructions[1,3]	1	0%	86%	88%
Evaluation of LVS Function[1,3]	2	100%	96%	98%
Smoking Cessation Advice[3]	0	-	96%	98%
Pneumonia Care				
Appropriate Initial Antibiotic[1]	6	83%	90%	92%
Blood Culture Timing[1]	2	100%	95%	96%
Influenza Vaccine[1]	2	100%	92%	91%
Initial Antibiotic Timing[1]	6	100%	96%	95%
Pneumococcal Vaccine[1]	4	100%	92%	93%
Smoking Cessation Advice	0	-	95%	97%
Surgical Care Improvement Project				
Appropriate VTP Within 24 Hours[5]	0	-	92%	92%
Appropriate Hair Removal[5]	0	-	99%	99%
Appropriate Beta Blocker Usage[5]	0	-	94%	93%
Controlled Postoperative Blood Glucose[5]	0	-	92%	93%
Prophylactic Antibiotic Timing[5]	0	-	96%	97%
Prophylactic Antibiotic Timing (Outpatient)[5]	0	-	89%	92%
Prophylactic Antibiotic Selection[5]	0	-	98%	97%
Prophylactic Antibiotic Select. (Outpatient)[5]	0	-	95%	94%
Prophylactic Antibiotic Stopped[5]	0	-	97%	94%
Recommended VTP Ordered[5]	0	-	93%	94%
Urinary Catheter Removal[5]	0	-	90%	90%
Children's Asthma Care				
Received Systemic Corticosteroids	-	-	-	100%
Received Home Management Plan	-	-	-	71%
Received Reliever Medication	-	-	-	100%
Use of Medical Imaging				
Combination Abdominal CT Scan[1]	42	0.024	0.100	0.191
Combination Chest CT Scan[1]	14	0.000	0.018	0.054
Follow-up Mammogram/Ultrasound[5]	0	-	6.4%	8.4%
MRI for Low Back Pain[1]	3	33.3%	39.7%	32.7%
Survey of Patients' Hospital Experiences				
Area Around Room 'Always' Quiet at Night[8]	-	-	-	58%
Doctors 'Always' Communicated Well[8]	-	-	-	80%
Home Recovery Information Given[8]	-	-	-	82%
Hospital Given 9 or 10 on 10 Point Scale[8]	-	-	-	67%
Meds 'Always' Explained Before Given[8]	-	-	-	60%
Nurses 'Always' Communicated Well[8]	-	-	-	76%
Pain 'Always' Well Controlled[8]	-	-	-	69%
Room and Bathroom 'Always' Clean[8]	-	-	-	71%
Timely Help 'Always' Received[8]	-	-	-	64%
Would Definitely Recommend Hospital[8]	-	-	-	69%

NOTE: Hospital profiles are in alphabetical order by state, then city, then hospital within the city; Rankings exclude hospitals with less than 25 cases except for patient surveys which excludes hospitals with less than 100 cases; (a) 100–299 cases; (1) The number of cases is too small to be sure how well a hospital is performing; (2) The hospital indicated that the data submitted for this measure were based on a sample of cases; (3) Data was collected during a shorter time period (fewer quarters) than the maximum possible time for this measure; (4) Suppressed for one or more quarters by CMS; (5) No data is available from the hospital for this measure; (6) Fewer than 100 patients completed the HCAHPS survey. Use these rates with caution, as the number of surveys may be too low to reliably assess hospital performance; (7) Survey results are based on less than 12 months of data; (8) Survey results are not available for this reporting period; (9) No or very few patients were eligible for the HCAHPS survey. The scores shown, if any, reflect a very small number of surveys; (10) A state average was not calculated because too few hospitals in the state submitted data; (11) There were discrepancies in the data collection process; Please refer to the User's Guide for a full explanation of data.

Meeker Memorial Hospital

612 South Sibley Avenue
Litchfield, MN 55355
URL: www.meekermemorial.org
Type: Critical Access Hospitals
Ownership: Government - Local
Phone: 320-693-3242
Fax: 320-693-4567
Emergency Services: Yes
Beds: 40

Key Personnel:
CEO/President. . . . . Michael Schramm
Chief of Medical Staff . . . . David M Ross, MD
Infection Control. . . . . Joyce Carlson, RN
Operating Room. . . . . Tammy Birr, RN
Quality Assurance . . . . Ann Lien, DON
Emergency Room . . . . David Ross
Hemotology Center . . . . Jeanne Westphal, RN
Intensive Care Unit. . . . . Angie Dietel

Measure	Cases	This Hosp.	State Avg.	U.S. Avg.
Heart Attack Care				
ACE Inhibitor or ARB for LVSD[1,3]	1	100%	97%	96%
Aspirin at Arrival[3]	0	-	99%	99%
Aspirin at Discharge[1,3]	1	100%	99%	98%
Beta Blocker at Discharge[1,3]	1	100%	99%	98%
Fibrinolytic Medication Timing[3]	0	-	55%	55%
PCI Within 90 Minutes of Arrival[3]	0	-	94%	90%
Smoking Cessation Advice[3]	0	-	99%	99%
Chest Pain/Possible Heart Attack Care				
Aspirin at Arrival[1,3]	8	75%	97%	95%
Median Time to ECG (minutes)[1,3]	8	14	7	8
Median Time to Transfer (minutes)[3]	0	-	50	61
Fibrinolytic Medication Timing[3]	0	-	58%	54%
Heart Failure Care				
ACE Inhibitor or ARB for LVSD[1]	11	91%	96%	94%
Discharge Instructions[1]	22	36%	86%	88%
Evaluation of LVS Function	41	63%	96%	98%
Smoking Cessation Advice[1]	9	44%	96%	98%
Pneumonia Care				
Appropriate Initial Antibiotic[1]	10	90%	90%	92%
Blood Culture Timing[1]	8	100%	95%	96%
Influenza Vaccine[1]	8	88%	92%	91%
Initial Antibiotic Timing[1]	17	71%	96%	95%
Pneumococcal Vaccine[1]	17	88%	92%	93%
Smoking Cessation Advice[1]	5	80%	95%	97%
Surgical Care Improvement Project				
Appropriate VTP Within 24 Hours[1]	22	86%	92%	92%
Appropriate Hair Removal	27	74%	99%	99%
Appropriate Beta Blocker Usage[5]	0	-	94%	93%
Controlled Postoperative Blood Glucose	0	-	92%	93%
Prophylactic Antibiotic Timing	26	85%	96%	97%
Prophylactic Antibiotic Timing (Outpatient)[1,3]	2	100%	89%	92%
Prophylactic Antibiotic Selection	26	92%	98%	97%
Prophylactic Antibiotic Select. (Outpatient)[1,3]	2	100%	95%	94%
Prophylactic Antibiotic Stopped	26	100%	97%	94%
Recommended VTP Ordered[1]	24	83%	93%	94%
Urinary Catheter Removal[1]	9	100%	90%	90%
Children's Asthma Care				
Received Systemic Corticosteroids	-	-	-	100%
Received Home Management Plan	-	-	-	71%
Received Reliever Medication	-	-	-	100%
Use of Medical Imaging				
Combination Abdominal CT Scan	110	0.864	0.100	0.191
Combination Chest CT Scan[1]	62	0.081	0.018	0.054
Follow-up Mammogram/Ultrasound	275	2.5%	6.4%	8.4%
MRI for Low Back Pain[1]	25	20.0%	39.7%	32.7%
Survey of Patients' Hospital Experiences				
Area Around Room 'Always' Quiet at Night	(a)	80%	-	58%
Doctors 'Always' Communicated Well	(a)	83%	-	80%
Home Recovery Information Given	(a)	83%	-	82%
Hospital Given 9 or 10 on 10 Point Scale	(a)	75%	-	67%
Meds 'Always' Explained Before Given	(a)	61%	-	60%
Nurses 'Always' Communicated Well	(a)	80%	-	76%
Pain 'Always' Well Controlled	(a)	73%	-	69%
Room and Bathroom 'Always' Clean	(a)	83%	-	71%
Timely Help 'Always' Received	(a)	73%	-	64%
Would Definitely Recommend Hospital	(a)	76%	-	69%

Saint Gabriels Hospital

815 Southeast Second Street
Little Falls, MN 56345
URL: www.stgabriels.com
Type: Critical Access Hospitals
Ownership: Voluntary Non-Profit - Private
Phone: 320-632-5441
Fax: 320-632-1190
Emergency Services: Yes
Beds: 49

Key Personnel:
CEO/President. . . . . Carl Vaagenes
Chief of Medical Staff . . . . Heide Gunn
Coronary Care . . . . Jane Smalley
Infection Control. . . . . Susan Newkirk
Operating Room. . . . . Mary Bauer
Quality Assurance . . . . Peggy Martin
Emergency Room . . . . Heide Gunn
Intensive Care Unit. . . . . Jane Smalley

Measure	Cases	This Hosp.	State Avg.	U.S. Avg.
Heart Attack Care				
ACE Inhibitor or ARB for LVSD[1,3]	1	100%	97%	96%
Aspirin at Arrival[1,3]	2	100%	99%	99%
Aspirin at Discharge[1,3]	2	100%	99%	98%
Beta Blocker at Discharge[1,3]	3	100%	99%	98%
Fibrinolytic Medication Timing[3]	0	-	55%	55%
PCI Within 90 Minutes of Arrival[3]	0	-	94%	90%
Smoking Cessation Advice[3]	0	-	99%	99%
Chest Pain/Possible Heart Attack Care				
Aspirin at Arrival[3]	32	100%	97%	95%
Median Time to ECG (minutes)[3]	33	6	7	8
Median Time to Transfer (minutes)[1,3]	10	38	50	61
Fibrinolytic Medication Timing[3]	0	-	58%	54%
Heart Failure Care				
ACE Inhibitor or ARB for LVSD[1]	6	100%	96%	94%
Discharge Instructions[1]	16	100%	86%	88%
Evaluation of LVS Function	30	90%	96%	98%
Smoking Cessation Advice[1]	2	100%	96%	98%
Pneumonia Care				
Appropriate Initial Antibiotic	58	81%	90%	92%
Blood Culture Timing	55	98%	95%	96%
Influenza Vaccine	30	97%	92%	91%
Initial Antibiotic Timing	71	99%	96%	95%
Pneumococcal Vaccine	62	97%	92%	93%
Smoking Cessation Advice[1]	15	100%	95%	97%
Surgical Care Improvement Project				
Appropriate VTP Within 24 Hours[2]	46	83%	92%	92%
Appropriate Hair Removal[2]	219	99%	99%	99%
Appropriate Beta Blocker Usage[2]	54	87%	94%	93%
Controlled Postoperative Blood Glucose[2]	0	-	92%	93%
Prophylactic Antibiotic Timing[2]	186	91%	96%	97%
Prophylactic Antibiotic Timing (Outpatient)[1,3]	10	100%	89%	92%
Prophylactic Antibiotic Selection[2]	184	99%	98%	97%
Prophylactic Antibiotic Select. (Outpatient)[1,3]	10	100%	95%	94%
Prophylactic Antibiotic Stopped[2]	178	96%	97%	94%
Recommended VTP Ordered[2]	46	85%	93%	94%
Urinary Catheter Removal[2]	40	100%	90%	90%
Children's Asthma Care				
Received Systemic Corticosteroids	-	-	-	100%
Received Home Management Plan	-	-	-	71%
Received Reliever Medication	-	-	-	100%
Use of Medical Imaging				
Combination Abdominal CT Scan	207	0.068	0.100	0.191
Combination Chest CT Scan	162	0.006	0.018	0.054
Follow-up Mammogram/Ultrasound	466	9.0%	6.4%	8.4%
MRI for Low Back Pain	64	48.4%	39.7%	32.7%
Survey of Patients' Hospital Experiences				
Area Around Room 'Always' Quiet at Night	(a)	74%	-	58%
Doctors 'Always' Communicated Well	(a)	85%	-	80%
Home Recovery Information Given	(a)	87%	-	82%
Hospital Given 9 or 10 on 10 Point Scale	(a)	77%	-	67%
Meds 'Always' Explained Before Given	(a)	65%	-	60%
Nurses 'Always' Communicated Well	(a)	81%	-	76%
Pain 'Always' Well Controlled	(a)	74%	-	69%
Room and Bathroom 'Always' Clean	(a)	81%	-	71%
Timely Help 'Always' Received	(a)	77%	-	64%
Would Definitely Recommend Hospital	(a)	77%	-	69%

Centracare Health System - Long Prairie

20 Ninth Street Southeast
Long Prairie, MN 56347
E-mail: lpm@centracare.com
URL: www.centracare.com
Type: Critical Access Hospitals
Ownership: Proprietary
Phone: 320-732-7210
Fax: 320-732-3802
Emergency Services: Yes
Beds: 34

Key Personnel:
CEO/President. . . . . Roger Oberg, MD
Chief of Medical Staff . . . . Rene Eldidy Jr
Operating Room. . . . . Marie Katterhagen
Quality Assurance . . . . Kathy Konetzko
Radiology. . . . . Jody A Bolton

Measure	Cases	This Hosp.	State Avg.	U.S. Avg.
Heart Attack Care				
ACE Inhibitor or ARB for LVSD[3]	0	-	97%	96%
Aspirin at Arrival[1,3]	2	100%	99%	99%
Aspirin at Discharge[1,3]	2	100%	99%	98%
Beta Blocker at Discharge[1,3]	2	50%	99%	98%
Fibrinolytic Medication Timing[3]	0	-	55%	55%
PCI Within 90 Minutes of Arrival[3]	0	-	94%	90%
Smoking Cessation Advice[3]	0	-	99%	99%
Chest Pain/Possible Heart Attack Care				
Aspirin at Arrival	29	93%	97%	95%
Median Time to ECG (minutes)	28	0	7	8
Median Time to Transfer (minutes)[1]	5	38	50	61
Fibrinolytic Medication Timing	0	-	58%	54%
Heart Failure Care				
ACE Inhibitor or ARB for LVSD[1]	4	100%	96%	94%
Discharge Instructions[1]	8	0%	86%	88%
Evaluation of LVS Function[1]	13	62%	96%	98%
Smoking Cessation Advice[1]	2	100%	96%	98%
Pneumonia Care				
Appropriate Initial Antibiotic[1]	12	83%	90%	92%
Blood Culture Timing[1]	10	100%	95%	96%
Influenza Vaccine[1]	15	47%	92%	91%
Initial Antibiotic Timing[1]	21	95%	96%	95%
Pneumococcal Vaccine[1]	24	71%	92%	93%
Smoking Cessation Advice[1]	6	17%	95%	97%
Surgical Care Improvement Project				
Appropriate VTP Within 24 Hours[1,3]	3	100%	92%	92%
Appropriate Hair Removal[1,3]	8	100%	99%	99%
Appropriate Beta Blocker Usage[5]	0	-	94%	93%
Controlled Postoperative Blood Glucose[3]	0	-	92%	93%
Prophylactic Antibiotic Timing[1,3]	7	86%	96%	97%
Prophylactic Antibiotic Timing (Outpatient)[1]	10	60%	89%	92%
Prophylactic Antibiotic Selection[1,3]	7	86%	98%	97%
Prophylactic Antibiotic Select. (Outpatient)[1]	7	86%	95%	94%
Prophylactic Antibiotic Stopped[1,3]	7	86%	97%	94%
Recommended VTP Ordered[1,3]	3	100%	93%	94%
Urinary Catheter Removal[3]	0	-	90%	90%
Children's Asthma Care				
Received Systemic Corticosteroids	-	-	-	100%
Received Home Management Plan	-	-	-	71%
Received Reliever Medication	-	-	-	100%
Use of Medical Imaging				
Combination Abdominal CT Scan	80	0.063	0.100	0.191
Combination Chest CT Scan	49	0.020	0.018	0.054
Follow-up Mammogram/Ultrasound	89	4.5%	6.4%	8.4%
MRI for Low Back Pain[1]	19	68.4%	39.7%	32.7%
Survey of Patients' Hospital Experiences				
Area Around Room 'Always' Quiet at Night[8]	-	-	-	58%
Doctors 'Always' Communicated Well[8]	-	-	-	80%
Home Recovery Information Given[8]	-	-	-	82%
Hospital Given 9 or 10 on 10 Point Scale[8]	-	-	-	67%
Meds 'Always' Explained Before Given[8]	-	-	-	60%
Nurses 'Always' Communicated Well[8]	-	-	-	76%
Pain 'Always' Well Controlled[8]	-	-	-	69%
Room and Bathroom 'Always' Clean[8]	-	-	-	71%
Timely Help 'Always' Received[8]	-	-	-	64%
Would Definitely Recommend Hospital[8]	-	-	-	69%

NOTE: Hospital profiles are in alphabetical order by state, then city, then hospital within the city; Rankings exclude hospitals with less than 25 cases except for patient surveys which excludes hospitals with less than 100 cases; (a) 100–299 cases; (1) The number of cases is too small to be sure how well a hospital is performing; (2) The hospital indicated that the data submitted for this measure were based on a sample of cases; (3) Data was collected during a shorter time period (fewer quarters) than the maximum possible time for this measure; (4) Suppressed for one or more quarters by CMS; (5) No data is available from the hospital for this measure; (6) Fewer than 100 patients completed the HCAHPS survey. Use these rates with caution, as the number of surveys may be too low to reliably assess hospital performance; (7) Survey results are based on less than 12 months of data; (8) Survey results are not available for this reporting period; (9) No or very few patients were eligible for the HCAHPS survey. The scores shown, if any, reflect a very small number of surveys; (10) A state average was not calculated because too few hospitals in the state submitted data; (11) There were discrepancies in the data collection process; Please refer to the User's Guide for a full explanation of data.

Sanford Luverne Medical Center

1600 North Kniss Ave Phone: 507-283-2321
Luverne, MN 56156 Fax: 507-283-2091
E-mail: info@sanfordluverne.org
URL: www.sanfordluverne.org
Type: Critical Access Hospitals Emergency Services: Yes
Ownership: Voluntary Non-Profit - Private Beds: 28

Key Personnel:
CEO/President. . . . . Mark A Henke
Chief of Medical Staff . . . . Richard Morgan, MD
Infection Control. . . . . Kristin Peterson
Operating Room. . . . . Tom Rolfs, RN
Quality Assurance . . . . Nancy Drenth, RN
Anesthesiology. . . . . Dave Knips, CRNA
Emergency Room . . . . Lynn DeBerg, RN
Patient Relations . . . . Sue Sandbulte

Measure	Cases	This Hosp.	State Avg.	U.S. Avg.
Heart Attack Care				
ACE Inhibitor or ARB for LVSD[1,3]	3	67%	97%	96%
Aspirin at Arrival[1,3]	7	86%	99%	99%
Aspirin at Discharge[1,3]	6	67%	99%	98%
Beta Blocker at Discharge[1,3]	6	83%	99%	98%
Fibrinolytic Medication Timing[3]	0	-	55%	55%
PCI Within 90 Minutes of Arrival[3]	0	-	94%	90%
Smoking Cessation Advice[3]	0	-	99%	99%
Chest Pain/Possible Heart Attack Care				
Aspirin at Arrival[5]	0	-	97%	95%
Median Time to ECG (minutes)[5]	0	-	7	8
Median Time to Transfer (minutes)[5]	0	-	50	61
Fibrinolytic Medication Timing[5]	0	-	58%	54%
Heart Failure Care				
ACE Inhibitor or ARB for LVSD[1,2]	2	0%	96%	94%
Discharge Instructions[1,2]	6	100%	86%	88%
Evaluation of LVS Function[1,2]	15	73%	96%	98%
Smoking Cessation Advice[2]	0	-	96%	98%
Pneumonia Care				
Appropriate Initial Antibiotic[1,2]	19	100%	90%	92%
Blood Culture Timing[1,2]	4	100%	95%	96%
Influenza Vaccine[1,2]	21	86%	92%	91%
Initial Antibiotic Timing[2]	28	93%	96%	95%
Pneumococcal Vaccine[2]	29	90%	92%	93%
Smoking Cessation Advice[1,2]	2	0%	95%	97%
Surgical Care Improvement Project				
Appropriate VTP Within 24 Hours[1,3]	4	100%	92%	92%
Appropriate Hair Removal[1,3]	9	89%	99%	99%
Appropriate Beta Blocker Usage[1,3]	2	100%	94%	93%
Controlled Postoperative Blood Glucose[3]	0	-	92%	93%
Prophylactic Antibiotic Timing[1,3]	7	100%	96%	97%
Prophylactic Antibiotic Timing (Outpatient)[5]	0	-	89%	92%
Prophylactic Antibiotic Selection[1,3]	7	100%	98%	97%
Prophylactic Antibiotic Select. (Outpatient)[5]	0	-	95%	94%
Prophylactic Antibiotic Stopped[1,3]	6	100%	97%	94%
Recommended VTP Ordered[1,3]	4	100%	93%	94%
Urinary Catheter Removal[3]	0	-	90%	90%
Children's Asthma Care				
Received Systemic Corticosteroids	-	-	-	100%
Received Home Management Plan	-	-	-	71%
Received Reliever Medication	-	-	-	100%
Use of Medical Imaging				
Combination Abdominal CT Scan	89	0.180	0.100	0.191
Combination Chest CT Scan[1]	40	0.175	0.018	0.054
Follow-up Mammogram/Ultrasound	367	7.1%	6.4%	8.4%
MRI for Low Back Pain	57	33.3%	39.7%	32.7%
Survey of Patients' Hospital Experiences				
Area Around Room 'Always' Quiet at Night	(a)	65%	-	58%
Doctors 'Always' Communicated Well	(a)	83%	-	80%
Home Recovery Information Given	(a)	77%	-	82%
Hospital Given 9 or 10 on 10 Point Scale	(a)	75%	-	67%
Meds 'Always' Explained Before Given	(a)	63%	-	60%
Nurses 'Always' Communicated Well	(a)	78%	-	76%
Pain 'Always' Well Controlled	(a)	72%	-	69%
Room and Bathroom 'Always' Clean	(a)	81%	-	71%
Timely Help 'Always' Received	(a)	76%	-	64%
Would Definitely Recommend Hospital	(a)	82%	-	69%

Madelia Community Hospital

121 Drew Avenue Southeast Phone: 507-642-3255
Madelia, MN 56062 Fax: 507-642-8516
URL: www.mchospital.org
Type: Critical Access Hospitals Emergency Services: Yes
Ownership: Voluntary Non-Profit - Other Beds: 25

Key Personnel:
CEO/President. . . . . Candace Fenske
Chief of Medical Staff . . . . Jennifer Longbehn, DO
Coronary Care . . . . Deidre Hruby
Infection Control. . . . . Terri Baumgartner
Operating Room. . . . . Jennifer McLaughlin
Radiology. . . . . Melissa Hunt
Emergency Room . . . . Jennifer McLoughlin
Intensive Care Unit. . . . . Deidre Hruby

Measure	Cases	This Hosp.	State Avg.	U.S. Avg.
Heart Attack Care				
ACE Inhibitor or ARB for LVSD[3]	0	-	97%	96%
Aspirin at Arrival[1,3]	1	100%	99%	99%
Aspirin at Discharge[3]	0	-	99%	98%
Beta Blocker at Discharge[3]	0	-	99%	98%
Fibrinolytic Medication Timing[3]	0	-	55%	55%
PCI Within 90 Minutes of Arrival[3]	0	-	94%	90%
Smoking Cessation Advice[3]	0	-	99%	99%
Chest Pain/Possible Heart Attack Care				
Aspirin at Arrival	-	-	97%	95%
Median Time to ECG (minutes)	-	-	7	8
Median Time to Transfer (minutes)	-	-	50	61
Fibrinolytic Medication Timing	-	-	58%	54%
Heart Failure Care				
ACE Inhibitor or ARB for LVSD[1]	11	82%	96%	94%
Discharge Instructions[1]	13	85%	86%	88%
Evaluation of LVS Function[1]	23	100%	96%	98%
Smoking Cessation Advice	0	-	96%	98%
Pneumonia Care				
Appropriate Initial Antibiotic[1]	14	86%	90%	92%
Blood Culture Timing[1]	4	100%	95%	96%
Influenza Vaccine[1]	12	75%	92%	91%
Initial Antibiotic Timing[1]	19	95%	96%	95%
Pneumococcal Vaccine[1]	16	94%	92%	93%
Smoking Cessation Advice[1]	2	50%	95%	97%
Surgical Care Improvement Project				
Appropriate VTP Within 24 Hours[1,3]	3	100%	92%	92%
Appropriate Hair Removal[1,3]	4	100%	99%	99%
Appropriate Beta Blocker Usage[5]	0	-	94%	93%
Controlled Postoperative Blood Glucose[3]	0	-	92%	93%
Prophylactic Antibiotic Timing[1,3]	1	100%	96%	97%
Prophylactic Antibiotic Timing (Outpatient)	-	-	89%	92%
Prophylactic Antibiotic Selection[1,3]	1	100%	98%	97%
Prophylactic Antibiotic Select. (Outpatient)	-	-	95%	94%
Prophylactic Antibiotic Stopped[1,3]	1	100%	97%	94%
Recommended VTP Ordered[1,3]	3	100%	93%	94%
Urinary Catheter Removal[1,3]	1	100%	90%	90%
Children's Asthma Care				
Received Systemic Corticosteroids	-	-	-	100%
Received Home Management Plan	-	-	-	71%
Received Reliever Medication	-	-	-	100%
Use of Medical Imaging				
Combination Abdominal CT Scan	-	-	0.100	0.191
Combination Chest CT Scan	-	-	0.018	0.054
Follow-up Mammogram/Ultrasound	-	-	6.4%	8.4%
MRI for Low Back Pain	-	-	39.7%	32.7%
Survey of Patients' Hospital Experiences				
Area Around Room 'Always' Quiet at Night[8]	-	-	-	58%
Doctors 'Always' Communicated Well[8]	-	-	-	80%
Home Recovery Information Given[8]	-	-	-	82%
Hospital Given 9 or 10 on 10 Point Scale[8]	-	-	-	67%
Meds 'Always' Explained Before Given[8]	-	-	-	60%
Nurses 'Always' Communicated Well[8]	-	-	-	76%
Pain 'Always' Well Controlled[8]	-	-	-	69%
Room and Bathroom 'Always' Clean[8]	-	-	-	71%
Timely Help 'Always' Received[8]	-	-	-	64%
Would Definitely Recommend Hospital[8]	-	-	-	69%

Madison Hospital

820 Third Avenue Phone: 320-598-7556
Madison, MN 56256 Fax: 320-598-3923
URL: www.madisonlutheranhome.com
Type: Critical Access Hospitals Emergency Services: Yes
Ownership: Voluntary Non-Profit - Private Beds: 21

Key Personnel:
CEO/President. . . . . Scott Larson
Chief of Medical Staff . . . . Larry Grong, MD
Infection Control. . . . . Mary Woodrich

Measure	Cases	This Hosp.	State Avg.	U.S. Avg.
Heart Attack Care				
ACE Inhibitor or ARB for LVSD[3]	0	-	97%	96%
Aspirin at Arrival[3]	0	-	99%	99%
Aspirin at Discharge[3]	0	-	99%	98%
Beta Blocker at Discharge[3]	0	-	99%	98%
Fibrinolytic Medication Timing[3]	0	-	55%	55%
PCI Within 90 Minutes of Arrival[3]	0	-	94%	90%
Smoking Cessation Advice[3]	0	-	99%	99%
Chest Pain/Possible Heart Attack Care				
Aspirin at Arrival[5]	0	-	97%	95%
Median Time to ECG (minutes)[5]	0	-	7	8
Median Time to Transfer (minutes)[5]	0	-	50	61
Fibrinolytic Medication Timing[5]	0	-	58%	54%
Heart Failure Care				
ACE Inhibitor or ARB for LVSD[1,3]	1	0%	96%	94%
Discharge Instructions[1,3]	5	40%	86%	88%
Evaluation of LVS Function[1,3]	9	22%	96%	98%
Smoking Cessation Advice[3]	0	-	96%	98%
Pneumonia Care				
Appropriate Initial Antibiotic[1,3]	5	20%	90%	92%
Blood Culture Timing[3]	0	-	95%	96%
Influenza Vaccine[1,3]	9	44%	92%	91%
Initial Antibiotic Timing[1,3]	9	89%	96%	95%
Pneumococcal Vaccine[1,3]	12	33%	92%	93%
Smoking Cessation Advice[1,3]	2	50%	95%	97%
Surgical Care Improvement Project				
Appropriate VTP Within 24 Hours[5]	0	-	92%	92%
Appropriate Hair Removal[5]	0	-	99%	99%
Appropriate Beta Blocker Usage[5]	0	-	94%	93%
Controlled Postoperative Blood Glucose[5]	0	-	92%	93%
Prophylactic Antibiotic Timing[5]	0	-	96%	97%
Prophylactic Antibiotic Timing (Outpatient)[5]	0	-	89%	92%
Prophylactic Antibiotic Selection[5]	0	-	98%	97%
Prophylactic Antibiotic Select. (Outpatient)[5]	0	-	95%	94%
Prophylactic Antibiotic Stopped[5]	0	-	97%	94%
Recommended VTP Ordered[5]	0	-	93%	94%
Urinary Catheter Removal[5]	0	-	90%	90%
Children's Asthma Care				
Received Systemic Corticosteroids	-	-	-	100%
Received Home Management Plan	-	-	-	71%
Received Reliever Medication	-	-	-	100%
Use of Medical Imaging				
Combination Abdominal CT Scan[1]	24	0.875	0.100	0.191
Combination Chest CT Scan[1]	24	0.167	0.018	0.054
Follow-up Mammogram/Ultrasound	78	9.0%	6.4%	8.4%
MRI for Low Back Pain[1]	5	60.0%	39.7%	32.7%
Survey of Patients' Hospital Experiences				
Area Around Room 'Always' Quiet at Night[8]	-	-	-	58%
Doctors 'Always' Communicated Well[8]	-	-	-	80%
Home Recovery Information Given[8]	-	-	-	82%
Hospital Given 9 or 10 on 10 Point Scale[8]	-	-	-	67%
Meds 'Always' Explained Before Given[8]	-	-	-	60%
Nurses 'Always' Communicated Well[8]	-	-	-	76%
Pain 'Always' Well Controlled[8]	-	-	-	69%
Room and Bathroom 'Always' Clean[8]	-	-	-	71%
Timely Help 'Always' Received[8]	-	-	-	64%
Would Definitely Recommend Hospital[8]	-	-	-	69%

NOTE: Hospital profiles are in alphabetical order by state, then city, then hospital within the city; Rankings exclude hospitals with less than 25 cases except for patient surveys which excludes hospitals with less than 100 cases; (a) 100–299 cases; (1) The number of cases is too small to be sure how well a hospital is performing; (2) The hospital indicated that the data submitted for this measure were based on a sample of cases; (3) Data was collected during a shorter time period (fewer quarters) than the maximum possible time for this measure; (4) Suppressed for one or more quarters by CMS; (5) No data is available from the hospital for this measure; (6) Fewer than 100 patients completed the HCAHPS survey. Use these rates with caution, as the number of surveys may be too low to reliably assess hospital performance; (7) Survey results are based on less than 12 months of data; (8) Survey results are not available for this reporting period; (9) No or very few patients were eligible for the HCAHPS survey. The scores shown, if any, reflect a very small number of surveys; (10) A state average was not calculated because too few hospitals in the state submitted data; (11) There were discrepancies in the data collection process; Please refer to the User's Guide for a full explanation of data.

Mahnomen Health Center

414 W Jefferson
Mahnomen, MN 56557
Phone: 218-935-2511
Fax: 218-935-2370
URL: www.mahnomenhealthcenter.com
Type: Critical Access Hospitals
Emergency Services: Yes
Ownership: Voluntary Non-Profit - Other
Beds: 63

Key Personnel:

CEO/President. . . . . Sue Klabo
Cardiac Laboratory. . . . . Barbara Fluellen
Chief of Medical Staff . . . . Dr Sanjit Dutta
Quality Assurance . . . . Bob Crawford
Radiology. . . . . Richard Marsden
Emergency Room . . . . Mike Bunker

Measure	Cases	This Hosp.	State Avg.	U.S. Avg.
Heart Attack Care				
ACE Inhibitor or ARB for LVSD[5]	0	-	97%	96%
Aspirin at Arrival[5]	0	-	99%	99%
Aspirin at Discharge[5]	0	-	99%	98%
Beta Blocker at Discharge[5]	0	-	99%	98%
Fibrinolytic Medication Timing[5]	0	-	55%	55%
PCI Within 90 Minutes of Arrival[5]	0	-	94%	90%
Smoking Cessation Advice[5]	0	-	99%	99%
Chest Pain/Possible Heart Attack Care				
Aspirin at Arrival[5]	0	-	97%	95%
Median Time to ECG (minutes)[5]	0	-	7	8
Median Time to Transfer (minutes)[5]	0	-	50	61
Fibrinolytic Medication Timing[5]	0	-	58%	54%
Heart Failure Care				
ACE Inhibitor or ARB for LVSD[1,3]	1	0%	96%	94%
Discharge Instructions[1,3]	3	33%	86%	88%
Evaluation of LVS Function[1,3]	3	33%	96%	98%
Smoking Cessation Advice[1,3]	1	100%	96%	98%
Pneumonia Care				
Appropriate Initial Antibiotic[1,3]	5	80%	90%	92%
Blood Culture Timing[3]	0	-	95%	96%
Influenza Vaccine[1,3]	2	50%	92%	91%
Initial Antibiotic Timing[1,3]	10	80%	96%	95%
Pneumococcal Vaccine[1,3]	9	56%	92%	93%
Smoking Cessation Advice[1,3]	1	100%	95%	97%
Surgical Care Improvement Project				
Appropriate VTP Within 24 Hours[5]	0	-	92%	92%
Appropriate Hair Removal[5]	0	-	99%	99%
Appropriate Beta Blocker Usage[5]	0	-	94%	93%
Controlled Postoperative Blood Glucose[5]	0	-	92%	93%
Prophylactic Antibiotic Timing[5]	0	-	96%	97%
Prophylactic Antibiotic Timing (Outpatient)[5]	0	-	89%	92%
Prophylactic Antibiotic Selection[5]	0	-	98%	97%
Prophylactic Antibiotic Select. (Outpatient)[5]	0	-	95%	94%
Prophylactic Antibiotic Stopped[5]	0	-	97%	94%
Recommended VTP Ordered[5]	0	-	93%	94%
Urinary Catheter Removal[5]	0	-	90%	90%
Children's Asthma Care				
Received Systemic Corticosteroids	-	-	-	100%
Received Home Management Plan	-	-	-	71%
Received Reliever Medication	-	-	-	100%
Use of Medical Imaging				
Combination Abdominal CT Scan[1]	25	0.000	0.100	0.191
Combination Chest CT Scan[1]	10	0.000	0.018	0.054
Follow-up Mammogram/Ultrasound	65	7.7%	6.4%	8.4%
MRI for Low Back Pain[1]	7	28.6%	39.7%	32.7%
Survey of Patients' Hospital Experiences				
Area Around Room 'Always' Quiet at Night[8]	-	-	-	58%
Doctors 'Always' Communicated Well[8]	-	-	-	80%
Home Recovery Information Given[8]	-	-	-	82%
Hospital Given 9 or 10 on 10 Point Scale[8]	-	-	-	67%
Meds 'Always' Explained Before Given[8]	-	-	-	60%
Nurses 'Always' Communicated Well[8]	-	-	-	76%
Pain 'Always' Well Controlled[8]	-	-	-	69%
Room and Bathroom 'Always' Clean[8]	-	-	-	71%
Timely Help 'Always' Received[8]	-	-	-	64%
Would Definitely Recommend Hospital[8]	-	-	-	69%

Immanuel-St Josephs-Mayo Health System

1025 Marsh St
Mankato, MN 56002
Phone: 507-625-4031
Fax: 507-385-2908
E-mail: isjinfo@mayo.edu
URL: www.isj-mhs.org
Type: Acute Care Hospitals
Emergency Services: Yes
Ownership: Voluntary Non-Profit - Private
Beds: 272

Key Personnel:

CEO/President. . . . . Greg Kutcher MD
Chief of Medical Staff . . . . Michael Wolf MD
Infection Control. . . . . Judy Webber RN
Operating Room. . . . . Colette Brust
Quality Assurance . . . . Theresa Mees
Radiology. . . . . Anne Chapman
Patient Relations . . . . Theresa Mees

Measure	Cases	This Hosp.	State Avg.	U.S. Avg.
Heart Attack Care				
ACE Inhibitor or ARB for LVSD[2]	39	100%	97%	96%
Aspirin at Arrival[2]	165	100%	99%	99%
Aspirin at Discharge[2]	226	100%	99%	98%
Beta Blocker at Discharge[2]	210	100%	99%	98%
Fibrinolytic Medication Timing[2]	0	-	55%	55%
PCI Within 90 Minutes of Arrival[2]	29	93%	94%	90%
Smoking Cessation Advice[2]	57	100%	99%	99%
Chest Pain/Possible Heart Attack Care				
Aspirin at Arrival[1,3]	1	100%	97%	95%
Median Time to ECG (minutes)[1,3]	1	34	7	8
Median Time to Transfer (minutes)[5]	0	-	50	61
Fibrinolytic Medication Timing[5]	0	-	58%	54%
Heart Failure Care				
ACE Inhibitor or ARB for LVSD	45	98%	96%	94%
Discharge Instructions	144	89%	86%	88%
Evaluation of LVS Function	198	100%	96%	98%
Smoking Cessation Advice[1]	16	100%	96%	98%
Pneumonia Care				
Appropriate Initial Antibiotic	96	90%	90%	92%
Blood Culture Timing	94	93%	95%	96%
Influenza Vaccine	135	93%	92%	91%
Initial Antibiotic Timing	156	97%	96%	95%
Pneumococcal Vaccine	173	91%	92%	93%
Smoking Cessation Advice	46	91%	95%	97%
Surgical Care Improvement Project				
Appropriate VTP Within 24 Hours[2]	223	95%	92%	92%
Appropriate Hair Removal[2]	533	100%	99%	99%
Appropriate Beta Blocker Usage[2]	152	94%	94%	93%
Controlled Postoperative Blood Glucose[2]	0	-	92%	93%
Prophylactic Antibiotic Timing[2]	307	99%	96%	97%
Prophylactic Antibiotic Timing (Outpatient)	100	95%	89%	92%
Prophylactic Antibiotic Selection[2]	305	97%	98%	97%
Prophylactic Antibiotic Select. (Outpatient)	99	97%	95%	94%
Prophylactic Antibiotic Stopped[2]	292	96%	97%	94%
Recommended VTP Ordered[2]	224	96%	93%	94%
Urinary Catheter Removal[2]	85	86%	90%	90%
Children's Asthma Care				
Received Systemic Corticosteroids	-	-	-	100%
Received Home Management Plan	-	-	-	71%
Received Reliever Medication	-	-	-	100%
Use of Medical Imaging				
Combination Abdominal CT Scan	569	0.070	0.100	0.191
Combination Chest CT Scan	401	0.002	0.018	0.054
Follow-up Mammogram/Ultrasound	454	5.7%	6.4%	8.4%
MRI for Low Back Pain	64	25.0%	39.7%	32.7%
Survey of Patients' Hospital Experiences				
Area Around Room 'Always' Quiet at Night	300+	44%	-	58%
Doctors 'Always' Communicated Well	300+	72%	-	80%
Home Recovery Information Given	300+	79%	-	82%
Hospital Given 9 or 10 on 10 Point Scale	300+	58%	-	67%
Meds 'Always' Explained Before Given	300+	57%	-	60%
Nurses 'Always' Communicated Well	300+	69%	-	76%
Pain 'Always' Well Controlled	300+	62%	-	69%
Room and Bathroom 'Always' Clean	300+	67%	-	71%
Timely Help 'Always' Received	300+	57%	-	64%
Would Definitely Recommend Hospital	300+	59%	-	69%

Maple Grove Hospital

9875 Hospital Drive
Maple Grove, MN 55369
Phone: 763-581-1000
URL: www.maplegrove.org
Type: Acute Care Hospitals
Emergency Services: Yes
Ownership: Voluntary Non-Profit - Private
Beds: 119

Key Personnel:

CEO . . . . Andrew S Cochrane

Measure	Cases	This Hosp.	State Avg.	U.S. Avg.
Heart Attack Care				
ACE Inhibitor or ARB for LVSD[5]	0	-	97%	96%
Aspirin at Arrival[5]	0	-	99%	99%
Aspirin at Discharge[5]	0	-	99%	98%
Beta Blocker at Discharge[5]	0	-	99%	98%
Fibrinolytic Medication Timing[5]	0	-	55%	55%
PCI Within 90 Minutes of Arrival[5]	0	-	94%	90%
Smoking Cessation Advice[5]	0	-	99%	99%
Chest Pain/Possible Heart Attack Care				
Aspirin at Arrival	-	-	97%	95%
Median Time to ECG (minutes)	-	-	7	8
Median Time to Transfer (minutes)	-	-	50	61
Fibrinolytic Medication Timing	-	-	58%	54%
Heart Failure Care				
ACE Inhibitor or ARB for LVSD[5]	0	-	96%	94%
Discharge Instructions[5]	0	-	86%	88%
Evaluation of LVS Function[5]	0	-	96%	98%
Smoking Cessation Advice[5]	0	-	96%	98%
Pneumonia Care				
Appropriate Initial Antibiotic[5]	0	-	90%	92%
Blood Culture Timing[5]	0	-	95%	96%
Influenza Vaccine[5]	0	-	92%	91%
Initial Antibiotic Timing[5]	0	-	96%	95%
Pneumococcal Vaccine[5]	0	-	92%	93%
Smoking Cessation Advice[5]	0	-	95%	97%
Surgical Care Improvement Project				
Appropriate VTP Within 24 Hours[5]	0	-	92%	92%
Appropriate Hair Removal[5]	0	-	99%	99%
Appropriate Beta Blocker Usage[5]	0	-	94%	93%
Controlled Postoperative Blood Glucose[5]	0	-	92%	93%
Prophylactic Antibiotic Timing[5]	0	-	96%	97%
Prophylactic Antibiotic Timing (Outpatient)	-	-	89%	92%
Prophylactic Antibiotic Selection[5]	0	-	98%	97%
Prophylactic Antibiotic Select. (Outpatient)	-	-	95%	94%
Prophylactic Antibiotic Stopped[5]	0	-	97%	94%
Recommended VTP Ordered[5]	0	-	93%	94%
Urinary Catheter Removal[5]	0	-	90%	90%
Children's Asthma Care				
Received Systemic Corticosteroids	-	-	-	100%
Received Home Management Plan	-	-	-	71%
Received Reliever Medication	-	-	-	100%
Use of Medical Imaging				
Combination Abdominal CT Scan	-	-	0.100	0.191
Combination Chest CT Scan	-	-	0.018	0.054
Follow-up Mammogram/Ultrasound	-	-	6.4%	8.4%
MRI for Low Back Pain	-	-	39.7%	32.7%
Survey of Patients' Hospital Experiences				
Area Around Room 'Always' Quiet at Night[8]	-	-	-	58%
Doctors 'Always' Communicated Well[8]	-	-	-	80%
Home Recovery Information Given[8]	-	-	-	82%
Hospital Given 9 or 10 on 10 Point Scale[8]	-	-	-	67%
Meds 'Always' Explained Before Given[8]	-	-	-	60%
Nurses 'Always' Communicated Well[8]	-	-	-	76%
Pain 'Always' Well Controlled[8]	-	-	-	69%
Room and Bathroom 'Always' Clean[8]	-	-	-	71%
Timely Help 'Always' Received[8]	-	-	-	64%
Would Definitely Recommend Hospital[8]	-	-	-	69%

NOTE: Hospital profiles are in alphabetical order by state, then city, then hospital within the city; Rankings exclude hospitals with less than 25 cases except for patient surveys which excludes hospitals with less than 100 cases; (a) 100–299 cases; (1) The number of cases is too small to be sure how well a hospital is performing; (2) The hospital indicated that the data submitted for this measure were based on a sample of cases; (3) Data was collected during a shorter time period (fewer quarters) than the maximum possible time for this measure; (4) Suppressed for one or more quarters by CMS; (5) No data is available from the hospital for this measure; (6) Fewer than 100 patients completed the HCAHPS survey. Use these rates with caution, as the number of surveys may be too low to reliably assess hospital performance; (7) Survey results are based on less than 12 months of data; (8) Survey results are not available for this reporting period; (9) No or very few patients were eligible for the HCAHPS survey. The scores shown, if any, reflect a very small number of surveys; (10) A state average was not calculated because too few hospitals in the state submitted data; (11) There were discrepancies in the data collection process; Please refer to the User's Guide for a full explanation of data.

Healtheast St John's Hospital

1575 Beam Avenue Phone: 651-232-7000
Maplewood, MN 55109 Fax: 651-232-7240
URL: www.stjohnshospital-mn.org
Type: Acute Care Hospitals Emergency Services: Yes
Ownership: Voluntary Non-Profit - Private Beds: 184

Key Personnel:
CEO/President. . . . . Robert Gill
Chief of Medical Staff . . . . Tom Lundsten, MD
Infection Control. . . . . Kathy Miller, RN
Operating Room. . . . . Jan Edwards
Pediatric Ambulatory Care . . . . James Prall, MD
Pediatric In-Patient Care . . . . James Prall, MD
Quality Assurance . . . . Jan Weidner

Measure	Cases	This Hosp.	State Avg.	U.S. Avg.
Heart Attack Care				
ACE Inhibitor or ARB for LVSD[1]	8	100%	97%	96%
Aspirin at Arrival	55	100%	99%	99%
Aspirin at Discharge	25	100%	99%	98%
Beta Blocker at Discharge	27	100%	99%	98%
Fibrinolytic Medication Timing	0	-	55%	55%
PCI Within 90 Minutes of Arrival	0	-	94%	90%
Smoking Cessation Advice[1]	2	100%	99%	99%
Chest Pain/Possible Heart Attack Care				
Aspirin at Arrival	111	97%	97%	95%
Median Time to ECG (minutes)	110	13	7	8
Median Time to Transfer (minutes)	31	62	50	61
Fibrinolytic Medication Timing	0	-	58%	54%
Heart Failure Care				
ACE Inhibitor or ARB for LVSD	44	100%	96%	94%
Discharge Instructions	166	84%	86%	88%
Evaluation of LVS Function	212	99%	96%	98%
Smoking Cessation Advice	25	100%	96%	98%
Pneumonia Care				
Appropriate Initial Antibiotic[2]	103	95%	90%	92%
Blood Culture Timing[2]	131	98%	95%	96%
Influenza Vaccine[2]	92	98%	92%	91%
Initial Antibiotic Timing[2]	146	97%	96%	95%
Pneumococcal Vaccine[2]	142	96%	92%	93%
Smoking Cessation Advice[2]	37	100%	95%	97%
Surgical Care Improvement Project				
Appropriate VTP Within 24 Hours[2]	292	93%	92%	92%
Appropriate Hair Removal[2]	899	100%	99%	99%
Appropriate Beta Blocker Usage[2]	208	87%	94%	93%
Controlled Postoperative Blood Glucose[2]	0	-	92%	93%
Prophylactic Antibiotic Timing[2]	760	96%	96%	97%
Prophylactic Antibiotic Timing (Outpatient)	204	99%	89%	92%
Prophylactic Antibiotic Selection[2]	766	97%	98%	97%
Prophylactic Antibiotic Select. (Outpatient)	203	95%	95%	94%
Prophylactic Antibiotic Stopped[2]	740	98%	97%	94%
Recommended VTP Ordered[2]	292	95%	93%	94%
Urinary Catheter Removal[2]	78	82%	90%	90%
Children's Asthma Care				
Received Systemic Corticosteroids	-	-	-	100%
Received Home Management Plan	-	-	-	71%
Received Reliever Medication	-	-	-	100%
Use of Medical Imaging				
Combination Abdominal CT Scan	903	0.079	0.100	0.191
Combination Chest CT Scan	523	0.015	0.018	0.054
Follow-up Mammogram/Ultrasound	2,809	4.2%	6.4%	8.4%
MRI for Low Back Pain	166	41.0%	39.7%	32.7%
Survey of Patients' Hospital Experiences				
Area Around Room 'Always' Quiet at Night	300+	49%	-	58%
Doctors 'Always' Communicated Well	300+	72%	-	80%
Home Recovery Information Given	300+	87%	-	82%
Hospital Given 9 or 10 on 10 Point Scale	300+	66%	-	67%
Meds 'Always' Explained Before Given	300+	55%	-	60%
Nurses 'Always' Communicated Well	300+	72%	-	76%
Pain 'Always' Well Controlled	300+	68%	-	69%
Room and Bathroom 'Always' Clean	300+	70%	-	71%
Timely Help 'Always' Received	300+	57%	-	64%
Would Definitely Recommend Hospital	300+	68%	-	69%

Avera Marshall Regional Medical Center

300 South Bruce Street Phone: 507-537-9661
Marshall, MN 56258 Fax: 507-537-9053
E-mail: info@averamarshall.org
URL: www.averamarshall.org
Type: Critical Access Hospitals Emergency Services: Yes
Ownership: Government - Local Beds: 49

Key Personnel:
CEO/President. . . . . M Burmam
Cardiac Laboratory. . . . . Monica Senden
Chief of Medical Staff . . . . Joe Willett
Infection Control. . . . . Jo Coover
Operating Room. . . . . Donna Erbes
Anesthesiology. . . . . Gene Larson, CRNA
Emergency Room . . . . T Odland, MD

Measure	Cases	This Hosp.	State Avg.	U.S. Avg.
Heart Attack Care				
ACE Inhibitor or ARB for LVSD	0	-	97%	96%
Aspirin at Arrival[1]	4	100%	99%	99%
Aspirin at Discharge[1]	2	100%	99%	98%
Beta Blocker at Discharge[1]	2	100%	99%	98%
Fibrinolytic Medication Timing	0	-	55%	55%
PCI Within 90 Minutes of Arrival[3]	0	-	94%	90%
Smoking Cessation Advice	0	-	99%	99%
Chest Pain/Possible Heart Attack Care				
Aspirin at Arrival[3]	35	94%	97%	95%
Median Time to ECG (minutes)[3]	35	0	7	8
Median Time to Transfer (minutes)[1,3]	2	60	50	61
Fibrinolytic Medication Timing[1,3]	1	100%	58%	54%
Heart Failure Care				
ACE Inhibitor or ARB for LVSD[1]	6	83%	96%	94%
Discharge Instructions[1]	11	82%	86%	88%
Evaluation of LVS Function[1]	18	100%	96%	98%
Smoking Cessation Advice	0	-	96%	98%
Pneumonia Care				
Appropriate Initial Antibiotic	48	60%	90%	92%
Blood Culture Timing	37	92%	95%	96%
Influenza Vaccine[1]	21	76%	92%	91%
Initial Antibiotic Timing	54	76%	96%	95%
Pneumococcal Vaccine	44	93%	92%	93%
Smoking Cessation Advice[1]	8	88%	95%	97%
Surgical Care Improvement Project				
Appropriate VTP Within 24 Hours[1,3]	20	90%	92%	92%
Appropriate Hair Removal[3]	86	100%	99%	99%
Appropriate Beta Blocker Usage[1,3]	13	100%	94%	93%
Controlled Postoperative Blood Glucose[3]	0	-	92%	93%
Prophylactic Antibiotic Timing	81	79%	96%	97%
Prophylactic Antibiotic Timing (Outpatient)[1,3]	16	88%	89%	92%
Prophylactic Antibiotic Selection	80	99%	98%	97%
Prophylactic Antibiotic Select. (Outpatient)[1,3]	16	81%	95%	94%
Prophylactic Antibiotic Stopped	80	84%	97%	94%
Recommended VTP Ordered[1,3]	21	86%	93%	94%
Urinary Catheter Removal	40	95%	90%	90%
Children's Asthma Care				
Received Systemic Corticosteroids	-	-	-	100%
Received Home Management Plan	-	-	-	71%
Received Reliever Medication	-	-	-	100%
Use of Medical Imaging				
Combination Abdominal CT Scan	241	0.108	0.100	0.191
Combination Chest CT Scan	132	0.008	0.018	0.054
Follow-up Mammogram/Ultrasound	112	10.7%	6.4%	8.4%
MRI for Low Back Pain[1]	46	26.1%	39.7%	32.7%
Survey of Patients' Hospital Experiences				
Area Around Room 'Always' Quiet at Night	300+	59%	-	58%
Doctors 'Always' Communicated Well	300+	77%	-	80%
Home Recovery Information Given	300+	83%	-	82%
Hospital Given 9 or 10 on 10 Point Scale	300+	61%	-	67%
Meds 'Always' Explained Before Given	300+	55%	-	60%
Nurses 'Always' Communicated Well	300+	73%	-	76%
Pain 'Always' Well Controlled	300+	67%	-	69%
Room and Bathroom 'Always' Clean	300+	71%	-	71%
Timely Help 'Always' Received	300+	57%	-	64%
Would Definitely Recommend Hospital	300+	66%	-	69%

Centracare Health System - Melrose Hospital

525 West Main Street Phone: 320-256-4231
Melrose, MN 56352 Fax: 320-256-4949
E-mail: melrosehospital@centracare.com
URL: www.centracare.com/melrose
Type: Critical Access Hospitals Emergency Services: Yes
Ownership: Govt - Hospital Dist/Auth Beds: 28

Key Personnel:
CEO/President. . . . . Gerry Gilbertson, CEO
Chief of Medical Staff . . . . Darte C. Beretta, MD
Ambulatory Care . . . . Keri Wimmer, RN

Measure	Cases	This Hosp.	State Avg.	U.S. Avg.
Heart Attack Care				
ACE Inhibitor or ARB for LVSD[3]	0	-	97%	96%
Aspirin at Arrival[1,3]	2	50%	99%	99%
Aspirin at Discharge[1,3]	2	50%	99%	98%
Beta Blocker at Discharge[1,3]	2	100%	99%	98%
Fibrinolytic Medication Timing[3]	0	-	55%	55%
PCI Within 90 Minutes of Arrival[3]	0	-	94%	90%
Smoking Cessation Advice[3]	0	-	99%	99%
Chest Pain/Possible Heart Attack Care				
Aspirin at Arrival[5]	0	-	97%	95%
Median Time to ECG (minutes)[5]	0	-	7	8
Median Time to Transfer (minutes)[5]	0	-	50	61
Fibrinolytic Medication Timing[5]	0	-	58%	54%
Heart Failure Care				
ACE Inhibitor or ARB for LVSD[1,3]	1	100%	96%	94%
Discharge Instructions[1,3]	1	0%	86%	88%
Evaluation of LVS Function[1,3]	1	100%	96%	98%
Smoking Cessation Advice[3]	0	-	96%	98%
Pneumonia Care				
Appropriate Initial Antibiotic[1]	6	50%	90%	92%
Blood Culture Timing[1]	1	0%	95%	96%
Influenza Vaccine[1]	1	0%	92%	91%
Initial Antibiotic Timing	0	-	96%	95%
Pneumococcal Vaccine[1]	8	100%	92%	93%
Smoking Cessation Advice[1]	1	100%	95%	97%
Surgical Care Improvement Project				
Appropriate VTP Within 24 Hours[3]	0	-	92%	92%
Appropriate Hair Removal[1,3]	2	100%	99%	99%
Appropriate Beta Blocker Usage[5]	0	-	94%	93%
Controlled Postoperative Blood Glucose[3]	0	-	92%	93%
Prophylactic Antibiotic Timing[1,3]	2	0%	96%	97%
Prophylactic Antibiotic Timing (Outpatient)[5]	0	-	89%	92%
Prophylactic Antibiotic Selection[1,3]	2	100%	98%	97%
Prophylactic Antibiotic Select. (Outpatient)[5]	0	-	95%	94%
Prophylactic Antibiotic Stopped[1,3]	2	100%	97%	94%
Recommended VTP Ordered[3]	0	-	93%	94%
Urinary Catheter Removal[5]	0	-	90%	90%
Children's Asthma Care				
Received Systemic Corticosteroids	-	-	-	100%
Received Home Management Plan	-	-	-	71%
Received Reliever Medication	-	-	-	100%
Use of Medical Imaging				
Combination Abdominal CT Scan	65	0.062	0.100	0.191
Combination Chest CT Scan[1]	43	0.000	0.018	0.054
Follow-up Mammogram/Ultrasound	201	7.0%	6.4%	8.4%
MRI for Low Back Pain[1]	19	42.1%	39.7%	32.7%
Survey of Patients' Hospital Experiences				
Area Around Room 'Always' Quiet at Night[8]	-	-	-	58%
Doctors 'Always' Communicated Well[8]	-	-	-	80%
Home Recovery Information Given[8]	-	-	-	82%
Hospital Given 9 or 10 on 10 Point Scale[8]	-	-	-	67%
Meds 'Always' Explained Before Given[8]	-	-	-	60%
Nurses 'Always' Communicated Well[8]	-	-	-	76%
Pain 'Always' Well Controlled[8]	-	-	-	69%
Room and Bathroom 'Always' Clean[8]	-	-	-	71%
Timely Help 'Always' Received[8]	-	-	-	64%
Would Definitely Recommend Hospital[8]	-	-	-	69%

NOTE: Hospital profiles are in alphabetical order by state, then city, then hospital within the city; Rankings exclude hospitals with less than 25 cases except for patient surveys which excludes hospitals with less than 100 cases; (a) 100–299 cases; (1) The number of cases is too small to be sure how well a hospital is performing; (2) The hospital indicated that the data submitted for this measure were based on a sample of cases; (3) Data was collected during a shorter time period (fewer quarters) than the maximum possible time for this measure; (4) Suppressed for one or more quarters by CMS; (5) No data is available from the hospital for this measure; (6) Fewer than 100 patients completed the HCAHPS survey. Use these rates with caution, as the number of surveys may be too low to reliably assess hospital performance; (7) Survey results are based on less than 12 months of data; (8) Survey results are not available for this reporting period; (9) No or very few patients were eligible for the HCAHPS survey. The scores shown, if any, reflect a very small number of surveys; (10) A state average was not calculated because too few hospitals in the state submitted data; (11) There were discrepancies in the data collection process; Please refer to the User's Guide for a full explanation of data.

Abbott Northwestern Hospital

800 East 28th Street Phone: 612-863-4000
Minneapolis, MN 55407 Fax: 612-863-5667
URL: www.abbottnorthwestern.com
Type: Acute Care Hospitals Emergency Services: Yes
Ownership: Voluntary Non-Profit - Private Beds: 926
Key Personnel:
CEO/President. . . . . Jeff Peterson
Cardiac Laboratory. . . . . Robert Hauser, MD
Chief of Medical Staff . . . . Michael Tedford, MD
Operating Room. . . . . Mark Migliori, MD
Radiology. . . . . Wendy Nazarian, MD
Emergency Room . . . . Lee Arostegui, MD
Patient Relations . . . . Terry Graner

Measure	Cases	This Hosp.	State Avg.	U.S. Avg.
Heart Attack Care				
ACE Inhibitor or ARB for LVSD	113	100%	97%	96%
Aspirin at Arrival	223	100%	99%	99%
Aspirin at Discharge	837	100%	99%	98%
Beta Blocker at Discharge	806	100%	99%	98%
Fibrinolytic Medication Timing	0	-	55%	55%
PCI Within 90 Minutes of Arrival	51	96%	94%	90%
Smoking Cessation Advice	249	100%	99%	99%
Chest Pain/Possible Heart Attack Care				
Aspirin at Arrival[1,3]	1	100%	97%	95%
Median Time to ECG (minutes)[1,3]	1	0	7	8
Median Time to Transfer (minutes)[5]	0	-	50	61
Fibrinolytic Medication Timing[5]	0	-	58%	54%
Heart Failure Care				
ACE Inhibitor or ARB for LVSD	268	99%	96%	94%
Discharge Instructions	551	92%	86%	88%
Evaluation of LVS Function	679	100%	96%	98%
Smoking Cessation Advice	117	100%	96%	98%
Pneumonia Care				
Appropriate Initial Antibiotic	116	93%	90%	92%
Blood Culture Timing	213	97%	95%	96%
Influenza Vaccine	175	97%	92%	91%
Initial Antibiotic Timing	216	98%	96%	95%
Pneumococcal Vaccine	256	97%	92%	93%
Smoking Cessation Advice	143	99%	95%	97%
Surgical Care Improvement Project				
Appropriate VTP Within 24 Hours[2]	216	94%	92%	92%
Appropriate Hair Removal[2]	814	100%	99%	99%
Appropriate Beta Blocker Usage[2]	303	96%	94%	93%
Controlled Postoperative Blood Glucose[2]	138	97%	92%	93%
Prophylactic Antibiotic Timing[2]	557	98%	96%	97%
Prophylactic Antibiotic Timing (Outpatient)	524	93%	89%	92%
Prophylactic Antibiotic Selection[2]	563	98%	98%	97%
Prophylactic Antibiotic Select. (Outpatient)	505	95%	95%	94%
Prophylactic Antibiotic Stopped[2]	528	96%	97%	94%
Recommended VTP Ordered[2]	216	96%	93%	94%
Urinary Catheter Removal[2]	187	93%	90%	90%
Children's Asthma Care				
Received Systemic Corticosteroids	-	-	-	100%
Received Home Management Plan	-	-	-	71%
Received Reliever Medication	-	-	-	100%
Use of Medical Imaging				
Combination Abdominal CT Scan	1,685	0.074	0.100	0.191
Combination Chest CT Scan	1,699	0.014	0.018	0.054
Follow-up Mammogram/Ultrasound	2,250	4.2%	6.4%	8.4%
MRI for Low Back Pain	302	34.8%	39.7%	32.7%
Survey of Patients' Hospital Experiences				
Area Around Room 'Always' Quiet at Night	300+	52%	-	58%
Doctors 'Always' Communicated Well	300+	78%	-	80%
Home Recovery Information Given	300+	86%	-	82%
Hospital Given 9 or 10 on 10 Point Scale	300+	70%	-	67%
Meds 'Always' Explained Before Given	300+	58%	-	60%
Nurses 'Always' Communicated Well	300+	75%	-	76%
Pain 'Always' Well Controlled	300+	67%	-	69%
Room and Bathroom 'Always' Clean	300+	65%	-	71%
Timely Help 'Always' Received	300+	64%	-	64%
Would Definitely Recommend Hospital	300+	78%	-	69%

Children's Hospitals & Clinics

2525 Chicago Avenue South Phone: 612-813-6112
Minneapolis, MN 55404
URL: www.childrensmn.org
Type: Childrens Emergency Services: Yes
Ownership: Voluntary Non-Profit - Private Beds: 340
Key Personnel:
President/CEO. . . . . Alan L Goldbloom, MD

Measure	Cases	This Hosp.	State Avg.	U.S. Avg.
Heart Attack Care				
ACE Inhibitor or ARB for LVSD	-	-	97%	96%
Aspirin at Arrival	-	-	99%	99%
Aspirin at Discharge	-	-	99%	98%
Beta Blocker at Discharge	-	-	99%	98%
Fibrinolytic Medication Timing	-	-	55%	55%
PCI Within 90 Minutes of Arrival	-	-	94%	90%
Smoking Cessation Advice	-	-	99%	99%
Chest Pain/Possible Heart Attack Care				
Aspirin at Arrival	-	-	97%	95%
Median Time to ECG (minutes)	-	-	7	8
Median Time to Transfer (minutes)	-	-	50	61
Fibrinolytic Medication Timing	-	-	58%	54%
Heart Failure Care				
ACE Inhibitor or ARB for LVSD	-	-	96%	94%
Discharge Instructions	-	-	86%	88%
Evaluation of LVS Function	-	-	96%	98%
Smoking Cessation Advice	-	-	96%	98%
Pneumonia Care				
Appropriate Initial Antibiotic	-	-	90%	92%
Blood Culture Timing	-	-	95%	96%
Influenza Vaccine	-	-	92%	91%
Initial Antibiotic Timing	-	-	96%	95%
Pneumococcal Vaccine	-	-	92%	93%
Smoking Cessation Advice	-	-	95%	97%
Surgical Care Improvement Project				
Appropriate VTP Within 24 Hours	-	-	92%	92%
Appropriate Hair Removal	-	-	99%	99%
Appropriate Beta Blocker Usage	-	-	94%	93%
Controlled Postoperative Blood Glucose	-	-	92%	93%
Prophylactic Antibiotic Timing	-	-	96%	97%
Prophylactic Antibiotic Timing (Outpatient)	-	-	89%	92%
Prophylactic Antibiotic Selection	-	-	98%	97%
Prophylactic Antibiotic Select. (Outpatient)	-	-	95%	94%
Prophylactic Antibiotic Stopped	-	-	97%	94%
Recommended VTP Ordered	-	-	93%	94%
Urinary Catheter Removal	-	-	90%	90%
Children's Asthma Care				
Received Systemic Corticosteroids[2]	331	98%	-	100%
Received Home Management Plan[2]	331	41%	-	71%
Received Reliever Medication[2]	331	100%	-	100%
Use of Medical Imaging				
Combination Abdominal CT Scan	-	-	0.100	0.191
Combination Chest CT Scan	-	-	0.018	0.054
Follow-up Mammogram/Ultrasound	-	-	6.4%	8.4%
MRI for Low Back Pain	-	-	39.7%	32.7%
Survey of Patients' Hospital Experiences				
Area Around Room 'Always' Quiet at Night	-	-	-	58%
Doctors 'Always' Communicated Well	-	-	-	80%
Home Recovery Information Given	-	-	-	82%
Hospital Given 9 or 10 on 10 Point Scale	-	-	-	67%
Meds 'Always' Explained Before Given	-	-	-	60%
Nurses 'Always' Communicated Well	-	-	-	76%
Pain 'Always' Well Controlled	-	-	-	69%
Room and Bathroom 'Always' Clean	-	-	-	71%
Timely Help 'Always' Received	-	-	-	64%
Would Definitely Recommend Hospital	-	-	-	69%

Hennepin County Medical Center

701 Park Avenue Phone: 612-873-3000
Minneapolis, MN 55415 Fax: 612-904-4214
URL: www.hcmc.org
Type: Acute Care Hospitals Emergency Services: Yes
Ownership: Government - Local Beds: 910
Key Personnel:
CEO/President. . . . . Lynn Abrahamsen MHA
Chief of Medical Staff . . . . Michael B Belzer MD

Measure	Cases	This Hosp.	State Avg.	U.S. Avg.
Heart Attack Care				
ACE Inhibitor or ARB for LVSD	43	100%	97%	96%
Aspirin at Arrival	200	100%	99%	99%
Aspirin at Discharge	198	100%	99%	98%
Beta Blocker at Discharge	188	98%	99%	98%
Fibrinolytic Medication Timing[1]	2	100%	55%	55%
PCI Within 90 Minutes of Arrival	49	90%	94%	90%
Smoking Cessation Advice	83	100%	99%	99%
Chest Pain/Possible Heart Attack Care				
Aspirin at Arrival[5]	0	-	97%	95%
Median Time to ECG (minutes)[5]	0	-	7	8
Median Time to Transfer (minutes)[5]	0	-	50	61
Fibrinolytic Medication Timing[5]	0	-	58%	54%
Heart Failure Care				
ACE Inhibitor or ARB for LVSD[2]	142	99%	96%	94%
Discharge Instructions[2]	262	90%	86%	88%
Evaluation of LVS Function[2]	331	100%	96%	98%
Smoking Cessation Advice[2]	132	100%	96%	98%
Pneumonia Care				
Appropriate Initial Antibiotic[2]	119	90%	90%	92%
Blood Culture Timing[2]	242	77%	95%	96%
Influenza Vaccine	151	95%	92%	91%
Initial Antibiotic Timing[2]	246	91%	96%	95%
Pneumococcal Vaccine[2]	118	95%	92%	93%
Smoking Cessation Advice[2]	169	100%	95%	97%
Surgical Care Improvement Project				
Appropriate VTP Within 24 Hours[2]	165	93%	92%	92%
Appropriate Hair Removal[2]	396	100%	99%	99%
Appropriate Beta Blocker Usage[2]	111	94%	94%	93%
Controlled Postoperative Blood Glucose[2]	65	94%	92%	93%
Prophylactic Antibiotic Timing[2]	271	97%	96%	97%
Prophylactic Antibiotic Timing (Outpatient)	172	95%	89%	92%
Prophylactic Antibiotic Selection[2]	276	97%	98%	97%
Prophylactic Antibiotic Select. (Outpatient)	168	88%	95%	94%
Prophylactic Antibiotic Stopped[2]	256	98%	97%	94%
Recommended VTP Ordered[2]	165	96%	93%	94%
Urinary Catheter Removal[2]	60	87%	90%	90%
Children's Asthma Care				
Received Systemic Corticosteroids	36	100%	-	100%
Received Home Management Plan[2]	36	89%	-	71%
Received Reliever Medication	36	100%	-	100%
Use of Medical Imaging				
Combination Abdominal CT Scan	435	0.074	0.100	0.191
Combination Chest CT Scan	439	0.002	0.018	0.054
Follow-up Mammogram/Ultrasound	735	8.4%	6.4%	8.4%
MRI for Low Back Pain[1]	38	26.3%	39.7%	32.7%
Survey of Patients' Hospital Experiences				
Area Around Room 'Always' Quiet at Night	300+	48%	-	58%
Doctors 'Always' Communicated Well	300+	72%	-	80%
Home Recovery Information Given	300+	84%	-	82%
Hospital Given 9 or 10 on 10 Point Scale	300+	60%	-	67%
Meds 'Always' Explained Before Given	300+	53%	-	60%
Nurses 'Always' Communicated Well	300+	65%	-	76%
Pain 'Always' Well Controlled	300+	60%	-	69%
Room and Bathroom 'Always' Clean	300+	63%	-	71%
Timely Help 'Always' Received	300+	48%	-	64%
Would Definitely Recommend Hospital	300+	63%	-	69%

NOTE: Hospital profiles are in alphabetical order by state, then city, then hospital within the city; Rankings exclude hospitals with less than 25 cases except for patient surveys which excludes hospitals with less than 100 cases; (a) 100–299 cases; (1) The number of cases is too small to be sure how well a hospital is performing; (2) The hospital indicated that the data submitted for this measure were based on a sample of cases; (3) Data was collected during a shorter time period (fewer quarters) than the maximum possible time for this measure; (4) Suppressed for one or more quarters by CMS; (5) No data is available from the hospital for this measure; (6) Fewer than 100 patients completed the HCAHPS survey. Use these rates with caution, as the number of surveys may be too low to reliably assess hospital performance; (7) Survey results are based on less than 12 months of data; (8) Survey results are not available for this reporting period; (9) No or very few patients were eligible for the HCAHPS survey. The scores shown, if any, reflect a very small number of surveys; (10) A state average was not calculated because too few hospitals in the state submitted data; (11) There were discrepancies in the data collection process; Please refer to the User's Guide for a full explanation of data.

Minneapolis VA Medical Center

One Veterans Drive Phone: 612-725-2000
Minneapolis, MN 55417 Fax: 612-725-2049
URL: www1.va.gov/minneapolis
Type: Acute Care-Veterans Administration Emergency Services: No
Ownership: Government - Federal Beds: 341

Key Personnel:
Chief of Medical Staff.......... John J Drucker, MD
Infection Control............. Joseph Thurn, MD
Quality Assurance .... Linda Duffy
Radiology................... Howard Ansel, MD
Anesthesiology............... Shep Cohen, MD
Emergency Room .... Dale Berg, MD
Hemotology Center .... Sharon Luikart, MD

Measure	Cases	This Hosp.	State Avg.	U.S. Avg.
Heart Attack Care				
ACE Inhibitor or ARB for LVSD[1]	17	100%	97%	96%
Aspirin at Arrival	132	98%	99%	99%
Aspirin at Discharge	143	100%	99%	98%
Beta Blocker at Discharge	139	100%	99%	98%
Fibrinolytic Medication Timing[5]	0	-	55%	55%
PCI Within 90 Minutes of Arrival[1]	10	50%	94%	90%
Smoking Cessation Advice	33	100%	99%	99%
Chest Pain/Possible Heart Attack Care				
Aspirin at Arrival	-	-	97%	95%
Median Time to ECG (minutes)	-	-	7	8
Median Time to Transfer (minutes)	-	-	50	61
Fibrinolytic Medication Timing	-	-	58%	54%
Heart Failure Care				
ACE Inhibitor or ARB for LVSD	56	100%	96%	94%
Discharge Instructions	175	95%	86%	88%
Evaluation of LVS Function	201	100%	96%	98%
Smoking Cessation Advice[1]	20	100%	96%	98%
Pneumonia Care				
Appropriate Initial Antibiotic	46	96%	90%	92%
Blood Culture Timing	81	98%	95%	96%
Influenza Vaccine	70	97%	92%	91%
Initial Antibiotic Timing	98	95%	96%	95%
Pneumococcal Vaccine	120	100%	92%	93%
Smoking Cessation Advice[1]	24	100%	95%	97%
Surgical Care Improvement Project				
Appropriate VTP Within 24 Hours[2]	206	97%	92%	92%
Appropriate Hair Removal[2]	498	100%	99%	99%
Appropriate Beta Blocker Usage[2]	230	97%	94%	93%
Controlled Postoperative Blood Glucose[2]	181	91%	92%	93%
Prophylactic Antibiotic Timing	392	99%	96%	97%
Prophylactic Antibiotic Timing (Outpatient)	-	-	89%	92%
Prophylactic Antibiotic Selection	396	97%	98%	97%
Prophylactic Antibiotic Select. (Outpatient)	-	-	95%	94%
Prophylactic Antibiotic Stopped	384	97%	97%	94%
Recommended VTP Ordered[2]	206	98%	93%	94%
Urinary Catheter Removal[2]	157	97%	90%	90%
Children's Asthma Care				
Received Systemic Corticosteroids	-	-	-	100%
Received Home Management Plan	-	-	-	71%
Received Reliever Medication	-	-	-	100%
Use of Medical Imaging				
Combination Abdominal CT Scan	-	-	0.100	0.191
Combination Chest CT Scan	-	-	0.018	0.054
Follow-up Mammogram/Ultrasound	-	-	6.4%	8.4%
MRI for Low Back Pain	-	-	39.7%	32.7%
Survey of Patients' Hospital Experiences				
Area Around Room 'Always' Quiet at Night	-	-	-	58%
Doctors 'Always' Communicated Well	-	-	-	80%
Home Recovery Information Given	-	-	-	82%
Hospital Given 9 or 10 on 10 Point Scale	-	-	-	67%
Meds 'Always' Explained Before Given	-	-	-	60%
Nurses 'Always' Communicated Well	-	-	-	76%
Pain 'Always' Well Controlled	-	-	-	69%
Room and Bathroom 'Always' Clean	-	-	-	71%
Timely Help 'Always' Received	-	-	-	64%
Would Definitely Recommend Hospital	-	-	-	69%

Phillips Eye Institute

2215 Park Avenue South Phone: 612-775-8815
Minneapolis, MN 55404
URL: www.allina.com/ahs/pei.nsf
Type: Acute Care Hospitals Emergency Services: No
Ownership: Government - Federal

Measure	Cases	This Hosp.	State Avg.	U.S. Avg.
Heart Attack Care				
ACE Inhibitor or ARB for LVSD[5]	0	-	97%	96%
Aspirin at Arrival[5]	0	-	99%	99%
Aspirin at Discharge[5]	0	-	99%	98%
Beta Blocker at Discharge[5]	0	-	99%	98%
Fibrinolytic Medication Timing[5]	0	-	55%	55%
PCI Within 90 Minutes of Arrival[5]	0	-	94%	90%
Smoking Cessation Advice[5]	0	-	99%	99%
Chest Pain/Possible Heart Attack Care				
Aspirin at Arrival[5]	0	-	97%	95%
Median Time to ECG (minutes)[5]	0	-	7	8
Median Time to Transfer (minutes)[5]	0	-	50	61
Fibrinolytic Medication Timing[5]	0	-	58%	54%
Heart Failure Care				
ACE Inhibitor or ARB for LVSD[5]	0	-	96%	94%
Discharge Instructions[5]	0	-	86%	88%
Evaluation of LVS Function[5]	0	-	96%	98%
Smoking Cessation Advice[5]	0	-	96%	98%
Pneumonia Care				
Appropriate Initial Antibiotic[5]	0	-	90%	92%
Blood Culture Timing[5]	0	-	95%	96%
Influenza Vaccine[5]	0	-	92%	91%
Initial Antibiotic Timing[5]	0	-	96%	95%
Pneumococcal Vaccine[5]	0	-	92%	93%
Smoking Cessation Advice[5]	0	-	95%	97%
Surgical Care Improvement Project				
Appropriate VTP Within 24 Hours[5]	0	-	92%	92%
Appropriate Hair Removal[5]	0	-	99%	99%
Appropriate Beta Blocker Usage[5]	0	-	94%	93%
Controlled Postoperative Blood Glucose[5]	0	-	92%	93%
Prophylactic Antibiotic Timing[5]	0	-	96%	97%
Prophylactic Antibiotic Timing (Outpatient)[5]	0	-	89%	92%
Prophylactic Antibiotic Selection[5]	0	-	98%	97%
Prophylactic Antibiotic Select. (Outpatient)[5]	0	-	95%	94%
Prophylactic Antibiotic Stopped[5]	0	-	97%	94%
Recommended VTP Ordered[5]	0	-	93%	94%
Urinary Catheter Removal[5]	0	-	90%	90%
Children's Asthma Care				
Received Systemic Corticosteroids	-	-	-	100%
Received Home Management Plan	-	-	-	71%
Received Reliever Medication	-	-	-	100%
Use of Medical Imaging				
Combination Abdominal CT Scan[5]	0	-	0.100	0.191
Combination Chest CT Scan[5]	0	-	0.018	0.054
Follow-up Mammogram/Ultrasound[5]	0	-	6.4%	8.4%
MRI for Low Back Pain[5]	0	-	39.7%	32.7%
Survey of Patients' Hospital Experiences				
Area Around Room 'Always' Quiet at Night	(a)	88%	-	58%
Doctors 'Always' Communicated Well	(a)	91%	-	80%
Home Recovery Information Given	(a)	86%	-	82%
Hospital Given 9 or 10 on 10 Point Scale	(a)	86%	-	67%
Meds 'Always' Explained Before Given	(a)	76%	-	60%
Nurses 'Always' Communicated Well	(a)	92%	-	76%
Pain 'Always' Well Controlled	(a)	79%	-	69%
Room and Bathroom 'Always' Clean	(a)	89%	-	71%
Timely Help 'Always' Received	(a)	94%	-	64%
Would Definitely Recommend Hospital	(a)	93%	-	69%

University of Minnesota Medical Center - Fairview

2450 Riverside Avenue Phone: 612-672-6000
Minneapolis, MN 55454 Fax: 612-672-7186
URL: www.uofmmedicalcenter.org
Type: Acute Care Hospitals Emergency Services: Yes
Ownership: Voluntary Non-Profit - Private Beds: 1,868

Key Personnel:
CEO/President............... Mark A. Eustis
Infection Control............. Frank Rhame, MD
Operating Room............... Cheryl Vogel
Pediatric Ambulatory Care ...... Alfred Michael, MD
Pediatric In-Patient Care .... Alfred Michael, MD
Quality Assurance .... Sally Huntington
Radiology................... William Thompson, MD

Measure	Cases	This Hosp.	State Avg.	U.S. Avg.
Heart Attack Care				
ACE Inhibitor or ARB for LVSD	34	100%	97%	96%
Aspirin at Arrival	110	100%	99%	99%
Aspirin at Discharge	198	99%	99%	98%
Beta Blocker at Discharge	188	99%	99%	98%
Fibrinolytic Medication Timing	0	-	55%	55%
PCI Within 90 Minutes of Arrival[1]	11	91%	94%	90%
Smoking Cessation Advice	71	100%	99%	99%
Chest Pain/Possible Heart Attack Care				
Aspirin at Arrival[1,3]	1	100%	97%	95%
Median Time to ECG (minutes)[1,3]	1	10	7	8
Median Time to Transfer (minutes)[5]	0	-	50	61
Fibrinolytic Medication Timing[5]	0	-	58%	54%
Heart Failure Care				
ACE Inhibitor or ARB for LVSD	117	98%	96%	94%
Discharge Instructions	264	97%	86%	88%
Evaluation of LVS Function	322	100%	96%	98%
Smoking Cessation Advice	53	100%	96%	98%
Pneumonia Care				
Appropriate Initial Antibiotic	83	90%	90%	92%
Blood Culture Timing	196	97%	95%	96%
Influenza Vaccine	139	88%	92%	91%
Initial Antibiotic Timing	156	98%	96%	95%
Pneumococcal Vaccine	154	91%	92%	93%
Smoking Cessation Advice	94	100%	95%	97%
Surgical Care Improvement Project				
Appropriate VTP Within 24 Hours[2]	433	95%	92%	92%
Appropriate Hair Removal[2]	1,026	100%	99%	99%
Appropriate Beta Blocker Usage[2]	298	97%	94%	93%
Controlled Postoperative Blood Glucose[2]	127	94%	92%	93%
Prophylactic Antibiotic Timing[2]	758	99%	96%	97%
Prophylactic Antibiotic Timing (Outpatient)	377	95%	89%	92%
Prophylactic Antibiotic Selection[2]	766	98%	98%	97%
Prophylactic Antibiotic Select. (Outpatient)	470	94%	95%	94%
Prophylactic Antibiotic Stopped[2]	725	97%	97%	94%
Recommended VTP Ordered[2]	434	96%	93%	94%
Urinary Catheter Removal[2]	402	92%	90%	90%
Children's Asthma Care				
Received Systemic Corticosteroids	31	100%	-	100%
Received Home Management Plan	32	19%	-	71%
Received Reliever Medication	32	100%	-	100%
Use of Medical Imaging				
Combination Abdominal CT Scan	1,332	0.026	0.100	0.191
Combination Chest CT Scan	1,423	0.008	0.018	0.054
Follow-up Mammogram/Ultrasound	604	6.1%	6.4%	8.4%
MRI for Low Back Pain	104	42.3%	39.7%	32.7%
Survey of Patients' Hospital Experiences				
Area Around Room 'Always' Quiet at Night	300+	47%	-	58%
Doctors 'Always' Communicated Well	300+	73%	-	80%
Home Recovery Information Given	300+	84%	-	82%
Hospital Given 9 or 10 on 10 Point Scale	300+	62%	-	67%
Meds 'Always' Explained Before Given	300+	59%	-	60%
Nurses 'Always' Communicated Well	300+	70%	-	76%
Pain 'Always' Well Controlled	300+	65%	-	69%
Room and Bathroom 'Always' Clean	300+	62%	-	71%
Timely Help 'Always' Received	300+	56%	-	64%
Would Definitely Recommend Hospital	300+	69%	-	69%

NOTE: Hospital profiles are in alphabetical order by state, then city, then hospital within the city; Rankings exclude hospitals with less than 25 cases except for patient surveys which excludes hospitals with less than 100 cases; (a) 100–299 cases; (1) The number of cases is too small to be sure how well a hospital is performing; (2) The hospital indicated that the data submitted for this measure were based on a sample of cases; (3) Data was collected during a shorter time period (fewer quarters) than the maximum possible time for this measure; (4) Suppressed for one or more quarters by CMS; (5) No data is available from the hospital for this measure; (6) Fewer than 100 patients completed the HCAHPS survey. Use these rates with caution, as the number of surveys may be too low to reliably assess hospital performance; (7) Survey results are based on less than 12 months of data; (8) Survey results are not available for this reporting period; (9) No or very few patients were eligible for the HCAHPS survey. The scores shown, if any, reflect a very small number of surveys; (10) A state average was not calculated because too few hospitals in the state submitted data; (11) There were discrepancies in the data collection process; Please refer to the User's Guide for a full explanation of data.

Chippewa County Hospital

824 North 11th Street
Montevideo, MN 56265
Phone: 320-269-8878
Fax: 320-269-8186
Type: Critical Access Hospitals
Emergency Services: Yes
Ownership: Government - Local
Beds: 35

Key Personnel:
CEO/President............... Mark Paulson
Chief of Medical Staff.......... Eleazar Briones, MD
Hemotology Center .... Harold Windschitl, MD

Measure	Cases	This Hosp.	State Avg.	U.S. Avg.
Heart Attack Care				
ACE Inhibitor or ARB for LVSD	0	-	97%	96%
Aspirin at Arrival[1]	3	100%	99%	99%
Aspirin at Discharge[1]	2	100%	99%	98%
Beta Blocker at Discharge[1]	2	100%	99%	98%
Fibrinolytic Medication Timing	0	-	55%	55%
PCI Within 90 Minutes of Arrival	0	-	94%	90%
Smoking Cessation Advice	0	-	99%	99%
Chest Pain/Possible Heart Attack Care				
Aspirin at Arrival[5]	0	-	97%	95%
Median Time to ECG (minutes)[5]	0	-	7	8
Median Time to Transfer (minutes)[5]	0	-	50	61
Fibrinolytic Medication Timing[5]	0	-	58%	54%
Heart Failure Care				
ACE Inhibitor or ARB for LVSD[1]	6	83%	96%	94%
Discharge Instructions[1]	13	31%	86%	88%
Evaluation of LVS Function[1]	23	70%	96%	98%
Smoking Cessation Advice[1]	2	0%	96%	98%
Pneumonia Care				
Appropriate Initial Antibiotic[1]	9	78%	90%	92%
Blood Culture Timing[1]	17	82%	95%	96%
Influenza Vaccine[1]	12	67%	92%	91%
Initial Antibiotic Timing[1]	16	100%	96%	95%
Pneumococcal Vaccine	29	62%	92%	93%
Smoking Cessation Advice[1]	5	60%	95%	97%
Surgical Care Improvement Project				
Appropriate VTP Within 24 Hours	25	88%	92%	92%
Appropriate Hair Removal	38	76%	99%	99%
Appropriate Beta Blocker Usage[1]	9	89%	94%	93%
Controlled Postoperative Blood Glucose	0	-	92%	93%
Prophylactic Antibiotic Timing	33	73%	96%	97%
Prophylactic Antibiotic Timing (Outpatient)[5]	0	-	89%	92%
Prophylactic Antibiotic Selection	31	94%	98%	97%
Prophylactic Antibiotic Select. (Outpatient)[5]	0	-	95%	94%
Prophylactic Antibiotic Stopped	31	77%	97%	94%
Recommended VTP Ordered	26	85%	93%	94%
Urinary Catheter Removal[1]	15	100%	90%	90%
Children's Asthma Care				
Received Systemic Corticosteroids	-	-	-	100%
Received Home Management Plan	-	-	-	71%
Received Reliever Medication	-	-	-	100%
Use of Medical Imaging				
Combination Abdominal CT Scan	97	0.804	0.100	0.191
Combination Chest CT Scan	59	0.051	0.018	0.054
Follow-up Mammogram/Ultrasound	267	4.9%	6.4%	8.4%
MRI for Low Back Pain[1]	21	38.1%	39.7%	32.7%
Survey of Patients' Hospital Experiences				
Area Around Room 'Always' Quiet at Night[11]	300+	63%	-	58%
Doctors 'Always' Communicated Well[11]	300+	84%	-	80%
Home Recovery Information Given[11]	300+	84%	-	82%
Hospital Given 9 or 10 on 10 Point Scale[11]	300+	67%	-	67%
Meds 'Always' Explained Before Given[11]	300+	53%	-	60%
Nurses 'Always' Communicated Well[11]	300+	71%	-	76%
Pain 'Always' Well Controlled[11]	300+	62%	-	69%
Room and Bathroom 'Always' Clean[11]	300+	74%	-	71%
Timely Help 'Always' Received[11]	300+	64%	-	64%
Would Definitely Recommend Hospital[11]	300+	69%	-	69%

New River Medical Center

1013 Hart Boulevard
Monticello, MN 55362
Phone: 763-271-2211
Fax: 763-295-4593
URL: www.mblch.com
Type: Critical Access Hospitals
Emergency Services: Yes
Ownership: Govt - Hospital Dist/Auth
Beds: 39

Key Personnel:
Chief of Medical Staff.......... William Scheig, MD
Radiology................... Robert Pollock

Measure	Cases	This Hosp.	State Avg.	U.S. Avg.
Heart Attack Care				
ACE Inhibitor or ARB for LVSD[3]	0	-	97%	96%
Aspirin at Arrival[1,3]	3	100%	99%	99%
Aspirin at Discharge[1,3]	1	100%	99%	98%
Beta Blocker at Discharge[1,3]	1	100%	99%	98%
Fibrinolytic Medication Timing[3]	0	-	55%	55%
PCI Within 90 Minutes of Arrival[3]	0	-	94%	90%
Smoking Cessation Advice[3]	0	-	99%	99%
Chest Pain/Possible Heart Attack Care				
Aspirin at Arrival[5]	0	-	97%	95%
Median Time to ECG (minutes)[5]	0	-	7	8
Median Time to Transfer (minutes)[5]	0	-	50	61
Fibrinolytic Medication Timing[5]	0	-	58%	54%
Heart Failure Care				
ACE Inhibitor or ARB for LVSD[1]	9	100%	96%	94%
Discharge Instructions	38	95%	86%	88%
Evaluation of LVS Function	48	98%	96%	98%
Smoking Cessation Advice[1]	4	100%	96%	98%
Pneumonia Care				
Appropriate Initial Antibiotic	43	95%	90%	92%
Blood Culture Timing	58	97%	95%	96%
Influenza Vaccine	27	100%	92%	91%
Initial Antibiotic Timing	60	100%	96%	95%
Pneumococcal Vaccine	45	96%	92%	93%
Smoking Cessation Advice[1]	11	100%	95%	97%
Surgical Care Improvement Project				
Appropriate VTP Within 24 Hours[1]	10	100%	92%	92%
Appropriate Hair Removal	55	100%	99%	99%
Appropriate Beta Blocker Usage[1,3]	2	100%	94%	93%
Controlled Postoperative Blood Glucose	0	-	92%	93%
Prophylactic Antibiotic Timing	49	98%	96%	97%
Prophylactic Antibiotic Timing (Outpatient)[5]	0	-	89%	92%
Prophylactic Antibiotic Selection	49	100%	98%	97%
Prophylactic Antibiotic Select. (Outpatient)[5]	0	-	95%	94%
Prophylactic Antibiotic Stopped	46	93%	97%	94%
Recommended VTP Ordered[1]	10	100%	93%	94%
Urinary Catheter Removal[1]	9	67%	90%	90%
Children's Asthma Care				
Received Systemic Corticosteroids	-	-	-	100%
Received Home Management Plan	-	-	-	71%
Received Reliever Medication	-	-	-	100%
Use of Medical Imaging				
Combination Abdominal CT Scan	155	0.071	0.100	0.191
Combination Chest CT Scan	86	0.000	0.018	0.054
Follow-up Mammogram/Ultrasound	182	9.3%	6.4%	8.4%
MRI for Low Back Pain[1]	35	25.7%	39.7%	32.7%
Survey of Patients' Hospital Experiences				
Area Around Room 'Always' Quiet at Night	300+	64%	-	58%
Doctors 'Always' Communicated Well	300+	77%	-	80%
Home Recovery Information Given	300+	83%	-	82%
Hospital Given 9 or 10 on 10 Point Scale	300+	63%	-	67%
Meds 'Always' Explained Before Given	300+	60%	-	60%
Nurses 'Always' Communicated Well	300+	77%	-	76%
Pain 'Always' Well Controlled	300+	70%	-	69%
Room and Bathroom 'Always' Clean	300+	81%	-	71%
Timely Help 'Always' Received	300+	66%	-	64%
Would Definitely Recommend Hospital	300+	68%	-	69%

Mercy Hospital & Health Care Center

710 Kenwood Avenue
Moose Lake, MN 55767
Phone: 218-485-4481
Fax: 218-485-5855
URL: www.mercymooselake.org
Type: Critical Access Hospitals
Emergency Services: Yes
Ownership: Govt - Hospital Dist/Auth
Beds: 25

Key Personnel:
CEO/President............... Jason Douglas
Chief of Medical Staff.......... Barbara Reed
Infection Control.............. Sally Behn
Quality Assurance .... Trina Lower
Patient Relations .... Linda Johnson

Measure	Cases	This Hosp.	State Avg.	U.S. Avg.
Heart Attack Care				
ACE Inhibitor or ARB for LVSD	0	-	97%	96%
Aspirin at Arrival[1]	4	100%	99%	99%
Aspirin at Discharge[1]	1	100%	99%	98%
Beta Blocker at Discharge[1]	1	100%	99%	98%
Fibrinolytic Medication Timing	0	-	55%	55%
PCI Within 90 Minutes of Arrival	0	-	94%	90%
Smoking Cessation Advice	0	-	99%	99%
Chest Pain/Possible Heart Attack Care				
Aspirin at Arrival[5]	0	-	97%	95%
Median Time to ECG (minutes)[5]	0	-	7	8
Median Time to Transfer (minutes)[5]	0	-	50	61
Fibrinolytic Medication Timing[5]	0	-	58%	54%
Heart Failure Care				
ACE Inhibitor or ARB for LVSD	0	-	96%	94%
Discharge Instructions[1]	11	73%	86%	88%
Evaluation of LVS Function[1]	15	93%	96%	98%
Smoking Cessation Advice	0	-	96%	98%
Pneumonia Care				
Appropriate Initial Antibiotic	31	97%	90%	92%
Blood Culture Timing	27	96%	95%	96%
Influenza Vaccine[1]	21	100%	92%	91%
Initial Antibiotic Timing	38	97%	96%	95%
Pneumococcal Vaccine	34	97%	92%	93%
Smoking Cessation Advice[1]	7	100%	95%	97%
Surgical Care Improvement Project				
Appropriate VTP Within 24 Hours	28	82%	92%	92%
Appropriate Hair Removal	68	100%	99%	99%
Appropriate Beta Blocker Usage[5]	0	-	94%	93%
Controlled Postoperative Blood Glucose	0	-	92%	93%
Prophylactic Antibiotic Timing	63	89%	96%	97%
Prophylactic Antibiotic Timing (Outpatient)[5]	0	-	89%	92%
Prophylactic Antibiotic Selection	64	100%	98%	97%
Prophylactic Antibiotic Select. (Outpatient)[5]	0	-	95%	94%
Prophylactic Antibiotic Stopped	62	94%	97%	94%
Recommended VTP Ordered	28	82%	93%	94%
Urinary Catheter Removal[1]	16	50%	90%	90%
Children's Asthma Care				
Received Systemic Corticosteroids	-	-	-	100%
Received Home Management Plan	-	-	-	71%
Received Reliever Medication	-	-	-	100%
Use of Medical Imaging				
Combination Abdominal CT Scan	88	0.102	0.100	0.191
Combination Chest CT Scan	70	0.000	0.018	0.054
Follow-up Mammogram/Ultrasound	226	4.0%	6.4%	8.4%
MRI for Low Back Pain[1]	21	38.1%	39.7%	32.7%
Survey of Patients' Hospital Experiences				
Area Around Room 'Always' Quiet at Night[8]	-	-	-	58%
Doctors 'Always' Communicated Well[8]	-	-	-	80%
Home Recovery Information Given[8]	-	-	-	82%
Hospital Given 9 or 10 on 10 Point Scale[8]	-	-	-	67%
Meds 'Always' Explained Before Given[8]	-	-	-	60%
Nurses 'Always' Communicated Well[8]	-	-	-	76%
Pain 'Always' Well Controlled[8]	-	-	-	69%
Room and Bathroom 'Always' Clean[8]	-	-	-	71%
Timely Help 'Always' Received[8]	-	-	-	64%
Would Definitely Recommend Hospital[8]	-	-	-	69%

NOTE: Hospital profiles are in alphabetical order by state, then city, then hospital within the city; Rankings exclude hospitals with less than 25 cases except for patient surveys which excludes hospitals with less than 100 cases; (a) 100–299 cases; (1) The number of cases is too small to be sure how well a hospital is performing; (2) The hospital indicated that the data submitted for this measure were based on a sample of cases; (3) Data was collected during a shorter time period (fewer quarters) than the maximum possible time for this measure; (4) Suppressed for one or more quarters by CMS; (5) No data is available from the hospital for this measure; (6) Fewer than 100 patients completed the HCAHPS survey. Use these rates with caution, as the number of surveys may be too low to reliably assess hospital performance; (7) Survey results are based on less than 12 months of data; (8) Survey results are not available for this reporting period; (9) No or very few patients were eligible for the HCAHPS survey. The scores shown, if any, reflect a very small number of surveys; (10) A state average was not calculated because too few hospitals in the state submitted data; (11) There were discrepancies in the data collection process; Please refer to the User's Guide for a full explanation of data.

Kanabec Hospital

301 South Highway 65
Mora, MN 55051
Phone: 320-679-1212
Fax: 320-225-3613

Type: Critical Access Hospitals
Emergency Services: Yes
Ownership: Government - Local
Beds: 49

Key Personnel:

- CEO/President.............. Randy Ulseth
- Chief of Medical Staff.......... Randy Bostrom, MD
- Infection Control.............. Barry Vermilyea
- Operating Room.............. Mary Jo Henk-Buckley
- Quality Assurance .... Diane Saari
- Anesthesiology................ Dustin Paulson
- Emergency Room .... Dorothy Kohl, RN
- Patient Relations .... Diane Saari

Measure	Cases	This Hosp.	State Avg.	U.S. Avg.
Heart Attack Care				
ACE Inhibitor or ARB for LVSD[3]	0	-	97%	96%
Aspirin at Arrival[1,3]	2	100%	99%	99%
Aspirin at Discharge[1,3]	2	50%	99%	98%
Beta Blocker at Discharge[1,3]	1	100%	99%	98%
Fibrinolytic Medication Timing[3]	0	-	55%	55%
PCI Within 90 Minutes of Arrival[3]	0	-	94%	90%
Smoking Cessation Advice[3]	0	-	99%	99%
Chest Pain/Possible Heart Attack Care				
Aspirin at Arrival[3]	40	92%	97%	95%
Median Time to ECG (minutes)[3]	41	7	7	8
Median Time to Transfer (minutes)[5]	0	-	50	61
Fibrinolytic Medication Timing[3]	0	-	58%	54%
Heart Failure Care				
ACE Inhibitor or ARB for LVSD[1]	19	74%	96%	94%
Discharge Instructions	30	97%	86%	88%
Evaluation of LVS Function	48	85%	96%	98%
Smoking Cessation Advice[1]	6	100%	96%	98%
Pneumonia Care				
Appropriate Initial Antibiotic	39	95%	90%	92%
Blood Culture Timing	31	100%	95%	96%
Influenza Vaccine[1]	23	96%	92%	91%
Initial Antibiotic Timing	53	96%	96%	95%
Pneumococcal Vaccine	50	86%	92%	93%
Smoking Cessation Advice[1]	7	100%	95%	97%
Surgical Care Improvement Project				
Appropriate VTP Within 24 Hours	46	96%	92%	92%
Appropriate Hair Removal	78	97%	99%	99%
Appropriate Beta Blocker Usage[1]	22	68%	94%	93%
Controlled Postoperative Blood Glucose	0	-	92%	93%
Prophylactic Antibiotic Timing	75	93%	96%	97%
Prophylactic Antibiotic Timing (Outpatient)[1,3]	22	5%	89%	92%
Prophylactic Antibiotic Selection	75	100%	98%	97%
Prophylactic Antibiotic Select. (Outpatient)[1,3]	2	100%	95%	94%
Prophylactic Antibiotic Stopped	75	91%	97%	94%
Recommended VTP Ordered	46	100%	93%	94%
Urinary Catheter Removal[1]	22	100%	90%	90%
Children's Asthma Care				
Received Systemic Corticosteroids	-	-	-	100%
Received Home Management Plan	-	-	-	71%
Received Reliever Medication	-	-	-	100%
Use of Medical Imaging				
Combination Abdominal CT Scan	220	0.064	0.100	0.191
Combination Chest CT Scan	131	0.031	0.018	0.054
Follow-up Mammogram/Ultrasound	237	5.5%	6.4%	8.4%
MRI for Low Back Pain	52	32.7%	39.7%	32.7%
Survey of Patients' Hospital Experiences				
Area Around Room 'Always' Quiet at Night	300+	55%	-	58%
Doctors 'Always' Communicated Well	300+	76%	-	80%
Home Recovery Information Given	300+	84%	-	82%
Hospital Given 9 or 10 on 10 Point Scale	300+	65%	-	67%
Meds 'Always' Explained Before Given	300+	65%	-	60%
Nurses 'Always' Communicated Well	300+	75%	-	76%
Pain 'Always' Well Controlled	300+	68%	-	69%
Room and Bathroom 'Always' Clean	300+	75%	-	71%
Timely Help 'Always' Received	300+	71%	-	64%
Would Definitely Recommend Hospital	300+	66%	-	69%

Stevens Community Medical Center

400 East First Street
Morris, MN 56267
Phone: 320-589-1313
Fax: 320-589-1065
URL: www.scmcmorris.com

Type: Critical Access Hospitals
Emergency Services: Yes
Ownership: Voluntary Non-Profit - Private
Beds: 54

Key Personnel:

- CEO/President................ John Rau
- Chief of Medical Staff.......... Olyn Wernsing, MD
- Infection Control.............. Bev Larson, RN
- Quality Assurance .... Suzie Erlund, RN
- Radiology.................... Andrea Giambi
- Emergency Room .... Gaither Bynum, MD

Measure	Cases	This Hosp.	State Avg.	U.S. Avg.
Heart Attack Care				
ACE Inhibitor or ARB for LVSD[1]	2	50%	97%	96%
Aspirin at Arrival[1]	9	89%	99%	99%
Aspirin at Discharge[1]	7	86%	99%	98%
Beta Blocker at Discharge[1]	6	83%	99%	98%
Fibrinolytic Medication Timing	0	-	55%	55%
PCI Within 90 Minutes of Arrival	0	-	94%	90%
Smoking Cessation Advice	0	-	99%	99%
Chest Pain/Possible Heart Attack Care				
Aspirin at Arrival[5]	0	-	97%	95%
Median Time to ECG (minutes)[5]	0	-	7	8
Median Time to Transfer (minutes)[5]	0	-	50	61
Fibrinolytic Medication Timing[5]	0	-	58%	54%
Heart Failure Care				
ACE Inhibitor or ARB for LVSD[1]	6	67%	96%	94%
Discharge Instructions[1]	21	24%	86%	88%
Evaluation of LVS Function	36	44%	96%	98%
Smoking Cessation Advice	0	-	96%	98%
Pneumonia Care				
Appropriate Initial Antibiotic	32	84%	90%	92%
Blood Culture Timing[1]	17	94%	95%	96%
Influenza Vaccine	38	74%	92%	91%
Initial Antibiotic Timing	40	100%	96%	95%
Pneumococcal Vaccine	53	70%	92%	93%
Smoking Cessation Advice[1]	8	88%	95%	97%
Surgical Care Improvement Project				
Appropriate VTP Within 24 Hours[1]	24	88%	92%	92%
Appropriate Hair Removal	50	74%	99%	99%
Appropriate Beta Blocker Usage[1]	12	67%	94%	93%
Controlled Postoperative Blood Glucose	0	-	92%	93%
Prophylactic Antibiotic Timing	46	91%	96%	97%
Prophylactic Antibiotic Timing (Outpatient)[5]	0	-	89%	92%
Prophylactic Antibiotic Selection	46	100%	98%	97%
Prophylactic Antibiotic Select. (Outpatient)[5]	0	-	95%	94%
Prophylactic Antibiotic Stopped	46	100%	97%	94%
Recommended VTP Ordered[1]	24	88%	93%	94%
Urinary Catheter Removal[1]	11	64%	90%	90%
Children's Asthma Care				
Received Systemic Corticosteroids	-	-	-	100%
Received Home Management Plan	-	-	-	71%
Received Reliever Medication	-	-	-	100%
Use of Medical Imaging				
Combination Abdominal CT Scan	170	0.129	0.100	0.191
Combination Chest CT Scan	83	0.036	0.018	0.054
Follow-up Mammogram/Ultrasound	192	14.6%	6.4%	8.4%
MRI for Low Back Pain[1]	22	27.3%	39.7%	32.7%
Survey of Patients' Hospital Experiences				
Area Around Room 'Always' Quiet at Night[8]	-	-	-	58%
Doctors 'Always' Communicated Well[8]	-	-	-	80%
Home Recovery Information Given[8]	-	-	-	82%
Hospital Given 9 or 10 on 10 Point Scale[8]	-	-	-	67%
Meds 'Always' Explained Before Given[8]	-	-	-	60%
Nurses 'Always' Communicated Well[8]	-	-	-	76%
Pain 'Always' Well Controlled[8]	-	-	-	69%
Room and Bathroom 'Always' Clean[8]	-	-	-	71%
Timely Help 'Always' Received[8]	-	-	-	64%
Would Definitely Recommend Hospital[8]	-	-	-	69%

Queen of Peace Hospital

301 2nd Street Northeast
New Prague, MN 56071
Phone: 952-758-8101
Fax: 952-758-5009
E-mail: info@qofp.org
URL: www.queenofpeacehospital.com

Type: Critical Access Hospitals
Emergency Services: Yes
Ownership: Voluntary Non-Profit - Private
Beds: 25

Key Personnel:

- CEO/President.............. Mary Klimp
- Coronary Care............... Diann Kelly, RN
- Operating Room.............. Karen Neis, RN
- Quality Assurance .... Mark Powell
- Emergency Room .... Kelly Ashley, RN
- Patient Relations .... Peggy Sullivan

Measure	Cases	This Hosp.	State Avg.	U.S. Avg.
Heart Attack Care				
ACE Inhibitor or ARB for LVSD	0	-	97%	96%
Aspirin at Arrival[1]	5	100%	99%	99%
Aspirin at Discharge[1]	1	100%	99%	98%
Beta Blocker at Discharge[1]	2	100%	99%	98%
Fibrinolytic Medication Timing	0	-	55%	55%
PCI Within 90 Minutes of Arrival[5]	0	-	94%	90%
Smoking Cessation Advice	0	-	99%	99%
Chest Pain/Possible Heart Attack Care				
Aspirin at Arrival[3]	27	100%	97%	95%
Median Time to ECG (minutes)[3]	29	8	7	8
Median Time to Transfer (minutes)[1,3]	4	65	50	61
Fibrinolytic Medication Timing[3]	0	-	58%	54%
Heart Failure Care				
ACE Inhibitor or ARB for LVSD[1]	8	88%	96%	94%
Discharge Instructions[1]	20	95%	86%	88%
Evaluation of LVS Function	35	94%	96%	98%
Smoking Cessation Advice[1]	2	100%	96%	98%
Pneumonia Care				
Appropriate Initial Antibiotic[1]	24	92%	90%	92%
Blood Culture Timing	40	98%	95%	96%
Influenza Vaccine	32	94%	92%	91%
Initial Antibiotic Timing	42	100%	96%	95%
Pneumococcal Vaccine	47	89%	92%	93%
Smoking Cessation Advice[1]	6	100%	95%	97%
Surgical Care Improvement Project				
Appropriate VTP Within 24 Hours	33	94%	92%	92%
Appropriate Hair Removal	129	100%	99%	99%
Appropriate Beta Blocker Usage	30	90%	94%	93%
Controlled Postoperative Blood Glucose	0	-	92%	93%
Prophylactic Antibiotic Timing	115	95%	96%	97%
Prophylactic Antibiotic Timing (Outpatient)[1,3]	5	60%	89%	92%
Prophylactic Antibiotic Selection	111	94%	98%	97%
Prophylactic Antibiotic Select. (Outpatient)[1,3]	19	95%	95%	94%
Prophylactic Antibiotic Stopped	107	96%	97%	94%
Recommended VTP Ordered	34	97%	93%	94%
Urinary Catheter Removal	32	84%	90%	90%
Children's Asthma Care				
Received Systemic Corticosteroids	-	-	-	100%
Received Home Management Plan	-	-	-	71%
Received Reliever Medication	-	-	-	100%
Use of Medical Imaging				
Combination Abdominal CT Scan	237	0.131	0.100	0.191
Combination Chest CT Scan	158	0.006	0.018	0.054
Follow-up Mammogram/Ultrasound	418	4.3%	6.4%	8.4%
MRI for Low Back Pain	69	27.5%	39.7%	32.7%
Survey of Patients' Hospital Experiences				
Area Around Room 'Always' Quiet at Night	300+	65%	-	58%
Doctors 'Always' Communicated Well	300+	84%	-	80%
Home Recovery Information Given	300+	88%	-	82%
Hospital Given 9 or 10 on 10 Point Scale	300+	78%	-	67%
Meds 'Always' Explained Before Given	300+	72%	-	60%
Nurses 'Always' Communicated Well	300+	87%	-	76%
Pain 'Always' Well Controlled	300+	76%	-	69%
Room and Bathroom 'Always' Clean	300+	88%	-	71%
Timely Help 'Always' Received	300+	85%	-	64%
Would Definitely Recommend Hospital	300+	79%	-	69%

NOTE: Hospital profiles are in alphabetical order by state, then city, then hospital within the city; Rankings exclude hospitals with less than 25 cases except for patient surveys which excludes hospitals with less than 100 cases; (a) 100–299 cases; (1) The number of cases is too small to be sure how well a hospital is performing; (2) The hospital indicated that the data submitted for this measure were based on a sample of cases; (3) Data was collected during a shorter time period (fewer quarters) than the maximum possible time for this measure; (4) Suppressed for one or more quarters by CMS; (5) No data is available from the hospital for this measure; (6) Fewer than 100 patients completed the HCAHPS survey. Use these rates with caution, as the number of surveys may be too low to reliably assess hospital performance; (7) Survey results are based on less than 12 months of data; (8) Survey results are not available for this reporting period; (9) No or very few patients were eligible for the HCAHPS survey. The scores shown, if any, reflect a very small number of surveys; (10) A state average was not calculated because too few hospitals in the state submitted data; (11) There were discrepancies in the data collection process; Please refer to the User's Guide for a full explanation of data.

New Ulm Medical Center

1324 Fifth North Street
New Ulm, MN 56073
Phone: 507-233-1000
Fax: 507-233-1552
URL: www.newulmmedicalcenter.com
Type: Critical Access Hospitals
Emergency Services: Yes
Ownership: Voluntary Non-Profit - Private
Beds: 62

Key Personnel:
Chief of Medical Staff . . . . John Krikavar, MD
Infection Control . . . . Connie Thompson
Quality Assurance . . . . Kathy Thompson
Radiology . . . . Kathleen Bauer
Emergency Room . . . . Joan Krikava
Hemotology Center . . . . Brenda Nielsen
Intensive Care Unit . . . . Chris Goplin

Measure	Cases	This Hosp.	State Avg.	U.S. Avg.
Heart Attack Care				
ACE Inhibitor or ARB for LVSD[1]	1	100%	97%	96%
Aspirin at Arrival[1]	10	80%	99%	99%
Aspirin at Discharge[1]	5	100%	99%	98%
Beta Blocker at Discharge[1]	4	100%	99%	98%
Fibrinolytic Medication Timing	0	-	55%	55%
PCI Within 90 Minutes of Arrival	0	-	94%	90%
Smoking Cessation Advice	0	-	99%	99%
Chest Pain/Possible Heart Attack Care				
Aspirin at Arrival	48	100%	97%	95%
Median Time to ECG (minutes)	46	4	7	8
Median Time to Transfer (minutes)[1,3]	1	260	50	61
Fibrinolytic Medication Timing[1]	4	75%	58%	54%
Heart Failure Care				
ACE Inhibitor or ARB for LVSD[1]	11	91%	96%	94%
Discharge Instructions	39	97%	86%	88%
Evaluation of LVS Function	62	100%	96%	98%
Smoking Cessation Advice[1]	8	100%	96%	98%
Pneumonia Care				
Appropriate Initial Antibiotic[1]	24	92%	90%	92%
Blood Culture Timing	42	98%	95%	96%
Influenza Vaccine	36	89%	92%	91%
Initial Antibiotic Timing	46	100%	96%	95%
Pneumococcal Vaccine	57	100%	92%	93%
Smoking Cessation Advice[1]	12	100%	95%	97%
Surgical Care Improvement Project				
Appropriate VTP Within 24 Hours	49	100%	92%	92%
Appropriate Hair Removal	155	100%	99%	99%
Appropriate Beta Blocker Usage	60	98%	94%	93%
Controlled Postoperative Blood Glucose	0	-	92%	93%
Prophylactic Antibiotic Timing	107	99%	96%	97%
Prophylactic Antibiotic Timing (Outpatient)	42	50%	89%	92%
Prophylactic Antibiotic Selection	107	100%	98%	97%
Prophylactic Antibiotic Select. (Outpatient)[1]	22	91%	95%	94%
Prophylactic Antibiotic Stopped	106	100%	97%	94%
Recommended VTP Ordered	49	100%	93%	94%
Urinary Catheter Removal[1]	18	100%	90%	90%
Children's Asthma Care				
Received Systemic Corticosteroids	-	-	-	100%
Received Home Management Plan	-	-	-	71%
Received Reliever Medication	-	-	-	100%
Use of Medical Imaging				
Combination Abdominal CT Scan	263	0.084	0.100	0.191
Combination Chest CT Scan	202	0.025	0.018	0.054
Follow-up Mammogram/Ultrasound	622	4.2%	6.4%	8.4%
MRI for Low Back Pain	64	26.6%	39.7%	32.7%
Survey of Patients' Hospital Experiences				
Area Around Room 'Always' Quiet at Night	300+	58%	-	58%
Doctors 'Always' Communicated Well	300+	83%	-	80%
Home Recovery Information Given	300+	87%	-	82%
Hospital Given 9 or 10 on 10 Point Scale	300+	65%	-	67%
Meds 'Always' Explained Before Given	300+	61%	-	60%
Nurses 'Always' Communicated Well	300+	74%	-	76%
Pain 'Always' Well Controlled	300+	64%	-	69%
Room and Bathroom 'Always' Clean	300+	75%	-	71%
Timely Help 'Always' Received	300+	71%	-	64%
Would Definitely Recommend Hospital	300+	68%	-	69%

Northfield Hospital

2000 North Avenue
Northfield, MN 55057
Phone: 507-646-1000
Fax: 507-646-1392
E-mail: richardsons@northfieldhospital.org
URL: www.northfieldhospital.org
Type: Acute Care Hospitals
Emergency Services: Yes
Ownership: Govt - Hospital Dist/Auth
Beds: 37

Key Personnel:
CEO/President . . . . Ken Bank
Coronary Care . . . . Margi Henry
Infection Control . . . . Bernice Pulja
Operating Room . . . . Karen Geiger
Quality Assurance . . . . Laura Peterson
Radiology . . . . Charles Donovan
Anesthesiology . . . . Dan Olson
Emergency Room . . . . Doris Ertekeson

Measure	Cases	This Hosp.	State Avg.	U.S. Avg.
Heart Attack Care				
ACE Inhibitor or ARB for LVSD[1]	1	100%	97%	96%
Aspirin at Arrival[1]	12	92%	99%	99%
Aspirin at Discharge[1]	10	80%	99%	98%
Beta Blocker at Discharge[1]	9	89%	99%	98%
Fibrinolytic Medication Timing	0	-	55%	55%
PCI Within 90 Minutes of Arrival	0	-	94%	90%
Smoking Cessation Advice[1]	1	100%	99%	99%
Chest Pain/Possible Heart Attack Care				
Aspirin at Arrival	73	99%	97%	95%
Median Time to ECG (minutes)	75	2	7	8
Median Time to Transfer (minutes)[1]	9	57	50	61
Fibrinolytic Medication Timing[1]	2	50%	58%	54%
Heart Failure Care				
ACE Inhibitor or ARB for LVSD[1]	11	73%	96%	94%
Discharge Instructions	30	67%	86%	88%
Evaluation of LVS Function	47	98%	96%	98%
Smoking Cessation Advice[1]	8	75%	96%	98%
Pneumonia Care				
Appropriate Initial Antibiotic	46	96%	90%	92%
Blood Culture Timing	34	94%	95%	96%
Influenza Vaccine[1]	24	62%	92%	91%
Initial Antibiotic Timing	45	98%	96%	95%
Pneumococcal Vaccine	39	85%	92%	93%
Smoking Cessation Advice[1]	11	100%	95%	97%
Surgical Care Improvement Project				
Appropriate VTP Within 24 Hours	57	91%	92%	92%
Appropriate Hair Removal	193	100%	99%	99%
Appropriate Beta Blocker Usage	51	90%	94%	93%
Controlled Postoperative Blood Glucose	0	-	92%	93%
Prophylactic Antibiotic Timing	162	97%	96%	97%
Prophylactic Antibiotic Timing (Outpatient)	52	85%	89%	92%
Prophylactic Antibiotic Selection	163	98%	98%	97%
Prophylactic Antibiotic Select. (Outpatient)	45	96%	95%	94%
Prophylactic Antibiotic Stopped	157	96%	97%	94%
Recommended VTP Ordered	57	96%	93%	94%
Urinary Catheter Removal	36	97%	90%	90%
Children's Asthma Care				
Received Systemic Corticosteroids	-	-	-	100%
Received Home Management Plan	-	-	-	71%
Received Reliever Medication	-	-	-	100%
Use of Medical Imaging				
Combination Abdominal CT Scan	107	0.065	0.100	0.191
Combination Chest CT Scan	100	0.020	0.018	0.054
Follow-up Mammogram/Ultrasound	133	11.3%	6.4%	8.4%
MRI for Low Back Pain[1]	39	23.1%	39.7%	32.7%
Survey of Patients' Hospital Experiences				
Area Around Room 'Always' Quiet at Night	300+	58%	-	58%
Doctors 'Always' Communicated Well	300+	81%	-	80%
Home Recovery Information Given	300+	86%	-	82%
Hospital Given 9 or 10 on 10 Point Scale	300+	70%	-	67%
Meds 'Always' Explained Before Given	300+	62%	-	60%
Nurses 'Always' Communicated Well	300+	72%	-	76%
Pain 'Always' Well Controlled	300+	67%	-	69%
Room and Bathroom 'Always' Clean	300+	65%	-	71%
Timely Help 'Always' Received	300+	64%	-	64%
Would Definitely Recommend Hospital	300+	74%	-	69%

Renville County Hospital and Clinics

611 East Fairview
Olivia, MN 56277
Phone: 320-523-1261
Fax: 320-523-3490
E-mail: mahers@rchospital.com
URL: www.renvillecountyhospital.org
Type: Critical Access Hospitals
Emergency Services: Yes
Ownership: Govt - Hospital Dist/Auth
Beds: 41

Key Personnel:
CEO/President . . . . Glenn Haugo
Chief of Medical Staff . . . . Paul E Thompson

Measure	Cases	This Hosp.	State Avg.	U.S. Avg.
Heart Attack Care				
ACE Inhibitor or ARB for LVSD[1]	1	100%	97%	96%
Aspirin at Arrival[1]	2	100%	99%	99%
Aspirin at Discharge[1]	2	50%	99%	98%
Beta Blocker at Discharge[1]	2	50%	99%	98%
Fibrinolytic Medication Timing[1]	1	100%	55%	55%
PCI Within 90 Minutes of Arrival	0	-	94%	90%
Smoking Cessation Advice	0	-	99%	99%
Chest Pain/Possible Heart Attack Care				
Aspirin at Arrival[5]	0	-	97%	95%
Median Time to ECG (minutes)[5]	0	-	7	8
Median Time to Transfer (minutes)[5]	0	-	50	61
Fibrinolytic Medication Timing[5]	0	-	58%	54%
Heart Failure Care				
ACE Inhibitor or ARB for LVSD[1]	2	100%	96%	94%
Discharge Instructions[1]	10	30%	86%	88%
Evaluation of LVS Function[1]	19	58%	96%	98%
Smoking Cessation Advice[1]	2	50%	96%	98%
Pneumonia Care				
Appropriate Initial Antibiotic[1]	10	90%	90%	92%
Blood Culture Timing	0	-	95%	96%
Influenza Vaccine[1]	9	78%	92%	91%
Initial Antibiotic Timing[1]	5	100%	96%	95%
Pneumococcal Vaccine[1]	8	100%	92%	93%
Smoking Cessation Advice[1]	2	100%	95%	97%
Surgical Care Improvement Project				
Appropriate VTP Within 24 Hours[5]	0	-	92%	92%
Appropriate Hair Removal[5]	0	-	99%	99%
Appropriate Beta Blocker Usage[5]	0	-	94%	93%
Controlled Postoperative Blood Glucose[5]	0	-	92%	93%
Prophylactic Antibiotic Timing[5]	0	-	96%	97%
Prophylactic Antibiotic Timing (Outpatient)[5]	0	-	89%	92%
Prophylactic Antibiotic Selection[5]	0	-	98%	97%
Prophylactic Antibiotic Select. (Outpatient)[5]	0	-	95%	94%
Prophylactic Antibiotic Stopped[5]	0	-	97%	94%
Recommended VTP Ordered[5]	0	-	93%	94%
Urinary Catheter Removal[5]	0	-	90%	90%
Children's Asthma Care				
Received Systemic Corticosteroids	-	-	-	100%
Received Home Management Plan	-	-	-	71%
Received Reliever Medication	-	-	-	100%
Use of Medical Imaging				
Combination Abdominal CT Scan[1]	37	0.649	0.100	0.191
Combination Chest CT Scan[1]	32	0.031	0.018	0.054
Follow-up Mammogram/Ultrasound	172	7.6%	6.4%	8.4%
MRI for Low Back Pain[1]	16	31.3%	39.7%	32.7%
Survey of Patients' Hospital Experiences				
Area Around Room 'Always' Quiet at Night[8]	-	-	-	58%
Doctors 'Always' Communicated Well[8]	-	-	-	80%
Home Recovery Information Given[8]	-	-	-	82%
Hospital Given 9 or 10 on 10 Point Scale[8]	-	-	-	67%
Meds 'Always' Explained Before Given[8]	-	-	-	60%
Nurses 'Always' Communicated Well[8]	-	-	-	76%
Pain 'Always' Well Controlled[8]	-	-	-	69%
Room and Bathroom 'Always' Clean[8]	-	-	-	71%
Timely Help 'Always' Received[8]	-	-	-	64%
Would Definitely Recommend Hospital[8]	-	-	-	69%

NOTE: Hospital profiles are in alphabetical order by state, then city, then hospital within the city; Rankings exclude hospitals with less than 25 cases except for patient surveys which excludes hospitals with less than 100 cases; (a) 100–299 cases; (1) The number of cases is too small to be sure how well a hospital is performing; (2) The hospital indicated that the data submitted for this measure were based on a sample of cases; (3) Data was collected during a shorter time period (fewer quarters) than the maximum possible time for this measure; (4) Suppressed for one or more quarters by CMS; (5) No data is available from the hospital for this measure; (6) Fewer than 100 patients completed the HCAHPS survey. Use these rates with caution, as the number of surveys may be too low to reliably assess hospital performance; (7) Survey results are based on less than 12 months of data; (8) Survey results are not available for this reporting period; (9) No or very few patients were eligible for the HCAHPS survey. The scores shown, if any, reflect a very small number of surveys; (10) A state average was not calculated because too few hospitals in the state submitted data; (11) There were discrepancies in the data collection process; Please refer to the User's Guide for a full explanation of data.

Mille Lacs Health System

200 North Elm Street
Onamia, MN 56359
Phone: 320-532-8020
Fax: 320-532-3111
Type: Critical Access Hospitals
Emergency Services: Yes
Ownership: Voluntary Non-Profit - Private
Beds: 108

Key Personnel:
CEO/President. . . . . Daniel J Reiner
Chief of Medical Staff. . . . . Arden Virnig, MD
Operating Room. . . . . Linda Heinrich
Radiology. . . . . Andrew Burnside

Measure	Cases	This Hosp.	State Avg.	U.S. Avg.
Heart Attack Care				
ACE Inhibitor or ARB for LVSD[3]	0	-	97%	96%
Aspirin at Arrival[1,3]	1	100%	99%	99%
Aspirin at Discharge[1,3]	1	100%	99%	98%
Beta Blocker at Discharge[1,3]	1	100%	99%	98%
Fibrinolytic Medication Timing[3]	0	-	55%	55%
PCI Within 90 Minutes of Arrival[3]	0	-	94%	90%
Smoking Cessation Advice[3]	0	-	99%	99%
Chest Pain/Possible Heart Attack Care				
Aspirin at Arrival	-	-	97%	95%
Median Time to ECG (minutes)	-	-	7	8
Median Time to Transfer (minutes)	-	-	50	61
Fibrinolytic Medication Timing	-	-	58%	54%
Heart Failure Care				
ACE Inhibitor or ARB for LVSD[1]	9	89%	96%	94%
Discharge Instructions	25	96%	86%	88%
Evaluation of LVS Function	30	90%	96%	98%
Smoking Cessation Advice[1]	3	67%	96%	98%
Pneumonia Care				
Appropriate Initial Antibiotic[1]	12	100%	90%	92%
Blood Culture Timing[1]	21	95%	95%	96%
Influenza Vaccine[1]	11	55%	92%	91%
Initial Antibiotic Timing	32	97%	96%	95%
Pneumococcal Vaccine[1]	16	88%	92%	93%
Smoking Cessation Advice[1]	15	80%	95%	97%
Surgical Care Improvement Project				
Appropriate VTP Within 24 Hours[1]	6	83%	92%	92%
Appropriate Hair Removal[1]	14	93%	99%	99%
Appropriate Beta Blocker Usage[5]	0	-	94%	93%
Controlled Postoperative Blood Glucose	0	-	92%	93%
Prophylactic Antibiotic Timing[1]	12	100%	96%	97%
Prophylactic Antibiotic Timing (Outpatient)	-	-	89%	92%
Prophylactic Antibiotic Selection[1]	12	100%	98%	97%
Prophylactic Antibiotic Select. (Outpatient)	-	-	95%	94%
Prophylactic Antibiotic Stopped[1]	12	100%	97%	94%
Recommended VTP Ordered[1]	6	83%	93%	94%
Urinary Catheter Removal	0	-	90%	90%
Children's Asthma Care				
Received Systemic Corticosteroids	-	-	-	100%
Received Home Management Plan	-	-	-	71%
Received Reliever Medication	-	-	-	100%
Use of Medical Imaging				
Combination Abdominal CT Scan	-	-	0.100	0.191
Combination Chest CT Scan	-	-	0.018	0.054
Follow-up Mammogram/Ultrasound	-	-	6.4%	8.4%
MRI for Low Back Pain	-	-	39.7%	32.7%
Survey of Patients' Hospital Experiences				
Area Around Room 'Always' Quiet at Night	(a)	60%	-	58%
Doctors 'Always' Communicated Well	(a)	88%	-	80%
Home Recovery Information Given	(a)	88%	-	82%
Hospital Given 9 or 10 on 10 Point Scale	(a)	67%	-	67%
Meds 'Always' Explained Before Given	(a)	66%	-	60%
Nurses 'Always' Communicated Well	(a)	81%	-	76%
Pain 'Always' Well Controlled	(a)	69%	-	69%
Room and Bathroom 'Always' Clean	(a)	76%	-	71%
Timely Help 'Always' Received	(a)	74%	-	64%
Would Definitely Recommend Hospital	(a)	68%	-	69%

Ortonville Area Health Services

450 Eastvold Ave
Ortonville, MN 56278
Phone: 320-839-2502
Fax: 320-839-4107
E-mail: lillehak@oahs.us
URL: www.oahs.us
Type: Critical Access Hospitals
Emergency Services: Yes
Ownership: Government - Local
Beds: 105

Key Personnel:
CEO/President. . . . . Richard Ash
Chief of Medical Staff . . . . Bryan S Delage, MD
Infection Control. . . . . Kristine Meyer
Operating Room. . . . . Ranet Schmeichel
Quality Assurance . . . . Jeanette Felton, RN
Anesthesiology. . . . . John Sovell
Emergency Room . . . . Linda Sis

Measure	Cases	This Hosp.	State Avg.	U.S. Avg.
Heart Attack Care				
ACE Inhibitor or ARB for LVSD[1,3]	1	100%	97%	96%
Aspirin at Arrival[1,3]	4	100%	99%	99%
Aspirin at Discharge[1,3]	3	100%	99%	98%
Beta Blocker at Discharge[1,3]	4	75%	99%	98%
Fibrinolytic Medication Timing[3]	0	-	55%	55%
PCI Within 90 Minutes of Arrival[3]	0	-	94%	90%
Smoking Cessation Advice[3]	0	-	99%	99%
Chest Pain/Possible Heart Attack Care				
Aspirin at Arrival[1,3]	3	100%	97%	95%
Median Time to ECG (minutes)[1,3]	4	4	7	8
Median Time to Transfer (minutes)[3]	0	-	50	61
Fibrinolytic Medication Timing[1,3]	1	100%	58%	54%
Heart Failure Care				
ACE Inhibitor or ARB for LVSD[1]	6	83%	96%	94%
Discharge Instructions[1]	8	88%	86%	88%
Evaluation of LVS Function[1]	14	71%	96%	98%
Smoking Cessation Advice[1]	2	50%	96%	98%
Pneumonia Care				
Appropriate Initial Antibiotic[1]	12	100%	90%	92%
Blood Culture Timing[1]	1	100%	95%	96%
Influenza Vaccine[1]	3	100%	92%	91%
Initial Antibiotic Timing[1]	2	100%	96%	95%
Pneumococcal Vaccine[1]	10	80%	92%	93%
Smoking Cessation Advice[1]	1	100%	95%	97%
Surgical Care Improvement Project				
Appropriate VTP Within 24 Hours[1]	2	0%	92%	92%
Appropriate Hair Removal[1]	10	100%	99%	99%
Appropriate Beta Blocker Usage[5]	0	-	94%	93%
Controlled Postoperative Blood Glucose	0	-	92%	93%
Prophylactic Antibiotic Timing[1]	4	50%	96%	97%
Prophylactic Antibiotic Timing (Outpatient)[5]	0	-	89%	92%
Prophylactic Antibiotic Selection[1]	2	100%	98%	97%
Prophylactic Antibiotic Select. (Outpatient)[5]	0	-	95%	94%
Prophylactic Antibiotic Stopped[1]	2	100%	97%	94%
Recommended VTP Ordered[1]	2	0%	93%	94%
Urinary Catheter Removal	0	-	90%	90%
Children's Asthma Care				
Received Systemic Corticosteroids	-	-	-	100%
Received Home Management Plan	-	-	-	71%
Received Reliever Medication	-	-	-	100%
Use of Medical Imaging				
Combination Abdominal CT Scan	66	0.924	0.100	0.191
Combination Chest CT Scan	56	0.054	0.018	0.054
Follow-up Mammogram/Ultrasound	216	5.1%	6.4%	8.4%
MRI for Low Back Pain[1]	19	42.1%	39.7%	32.7%
Survey of Patients' Hospital Experiences				
Area Around Room 'Always' Quiet at Night	(a)	59%	-	58%
Doctors 'Always' Communicated Well	(a)	82%	-	80%
Home Recovery Information Given	(a)	75%	-	82%
Hospital Given 9 or 10 on 10 Point Scale	(a)	67%	-	67%
Meds 'Always' Explained Before Given	(a)	55%	-	60%
Nurses 'Always' Communicated Well	(a)	77%	-	76%
Pain 'Always' Well Controlled	(a)	64%	-	69%
Room and Bathroom 'Always' Clean	(a)	77%	-	71%
Timely Help 'Always' Received	(a)	69%	-	64%
Would Definitely Recommend Hospital	(a)	70%	-	69%

Owatonna Hospital

2250 26th Street Northwest
Owatonna, MN 55060
Phone: 507-451-3850
Fax: 507-444-6053
URL: www.owatonnahospital.com
Type: Acute Care Hospitals
Emergency Services: Yes
Ownership: Voluntary Non-Profit - Other
Beds: 77

Key Personnel:
CEO/President. . . . . David Albrecht
Chief of Medical Staff . . . . Michael Baker, MD
Coronary Care . . . . Sharon Kopp
Infection Control. . . . . Pam Schultz
Quality Assurance . . . . Becky Christensen
Radiology. . . . . Joseph Accurso

Measure	Cases	This Hosp.	State Avg.	U.S. Avg.
Heart Attack Care				
ACE Inhibitor or ARB for LVSD	0	-	97%	96%
Aspirin at Arrival[1]	10	100%	99%	99%
Aspirin at Discharge[1]	8	100%	99%	98%
Beta Blocker at Discharge[1]	8	100%	99%	98%
Fibrinolytic Medication Timing	0	-	55%	55%
PCI Within 90 Minutes of Arrival	0	-	94%	90%
Smoking Cessation Advice[1]	1	100%	99%	99%
Chest Pain/Possible Heart Attack Care				
Aspirin at Arrival	110	94%	97%	95%
Median Time to ECG (minutes)	111	8	7	8
Median Time to Transfer (minutes)[1]	4	62	50	61
Fibrinolytic Medication Timing[1]	5	80%	58%	54%
Heart Failure Care				
ACE Inhibitor or ARB for LVSD[1]	8	100%	96%	94%
Discharge Instructions	35	89%	86%	88%
Evaluation of LVS Function	55	100%	96%	98%
Smoking Cessation Advice[1]	4	100%	96%	98%
Pneumonia Care				
Appropriate Initial Antibiotic	35	91%	90%	92%
Blood Culture Timing[1]	20	95%	95%	96%
Influenza Vaccine	26	96%	92%	91%
Initial Antibiotic Timing	40	98%	96%	95%
Pneumococcal Vaccine	50	96%	92%	93%
Smoking Cessation Advice[1]	11	100%	95%	97%
Surgical Care Improvement Project				
Appropriate VTP Within 24 Hours[2]	39	82%	92%	92%
Appropriate Hair Removal[2]	272	100%	99%	99%
Appropriate Beta Blocker Usage[2]	88	99%	94%	93%
Controlled Postoperative Blood Glucose[2]	0	-	92%	93%
Prophylactic Antibiotic Timing[2]	224	97%	96%	97%
Prophylactic Antibiotic Timing (Outpatient)	91	97%	89%	92%
Prophylactic Antibiotic Selection[2]	222	97%	98%	97%
Prophylactic Antibiotic Select. (Outpatient)	90	99%	95%	94%
Prophylactic Antibiotic Stopped[2]	215	98%	97%	94%
Recommended VTP Ordered[2]	39	85%	93%	94%
Urinary Catheter Removal[2]	71	99%	90%	90%
Children's Asthma Care				
Received Systemic Corticosteroids	-	-	-	100%
Received Home Management Plan	-	-	-	71%
Received Reliever Medication	-	-	-	100%
Use of Medical Imaging				
Combination Abdominal CT Scan	158	0.373	0.100	0.191
Combination Chest CT Scan	99	0.152	0.018	0.054
Follow-up Mammogram/Ultrasound[1]	15	6.7%	6.4%	8.4%
MRI for Low Back Pain[5]	0	-	39.7%	32.7%
Survey of Patients' Hospital Experiences				
Area Around Room 'Always' Quiet at Night	300+	54%	-	58%
Doctors 'Always' Communicated Well	300+	78%	-	80%
Home Recovery Information Given	300+	85%	-	82%
Hospital Given 9 or 10 on 10 Point Scale	300+	60%	-	67%
Meds 'Always' Explained Before Given	300+	59%	-	60%
Nurses 'Always' Communicated Well	300+	73%	-	76%
Pain 'Always' Well Controlled	300+	67%	-	69%
Room and Bathroom 'Always' Clean	300+	70%	-	71%
Timely Help 'Always' Received	300+	67%	-	64%
Would Definitely Recommend Hospital	300+	67%	-	69%

NOTE: Hospital profiles are in alphabetical order by state, then city, then hospital within the city; Rankings exclude hospitals with less than 25 cases except for patient surveys which excludes hospitals with less than 100 cases; (a) 100–299 cases; (1) The number of cases is too small to be sure how well a hospital is performing; (2) The hospital indicated that the data submitted for this measure were based on a sample of cases; (3) Data was collected during a shorter time period (fewer quarters) than the maximum possible time for this measure; (4) Suppressed for one or more quarters by CMS; (5) No data is available from the hospital for this measure; (6) Fewer than 100 patients completed the HCAHPS survey. Use these rates with caution, as the number of surveys may be too low to reliably assess hospital performance; (7) Survey results are based on less than 12 months of data; (8) Survey results are not available for this reporting period; (9) No or very few patients were eligible for the HCAHPS survey. The scores shown, if any, reflect a very small number of surveys; (10) A state average was not calculated because too few hospitals in the state submitted data; (11) There were discrepancies in the data collection process; Please refer to the User's Guide for a full explanation of data.

Saint Josephs Area Health Services

600 Pleasant Avenue
Park Rapids, MN 56470
URL: www.sjahs.org
Type: Critical Access Hospitals
Ownership: Voluntary Non-Profit - Church
Phone: 218-732-3311
Fax: 218-732-1368
Emergency Services: Yes
Beds: 50

Key Personnel:
CEO/President. . . . . Peter Jacobson
Operating Room. . . . . Paulette Goldammer
Quality Assurance . . . . Laurie Skare
Radiology. . . . . Donald G Douglas
Ambulatory Care . . . . Judy Thompson
Emergency Room . . . . Darryl A Beehler
Intensive Care Unit. . . . . Bob Sauser
Patient Relations . . . . Nancy Hall

Measure	Cases	This Hosp.	State Avg.	U.S. Avg.
Heart Attack Care				
ACE Inhibitor or ARB for LVSD[3]	0	-	97%	96%
Aspirin at Arrival[1,3]	4	75%	99%	99%
Aspirin at Discharge[1,3]	2	50%	99%	98%
Beta Blocker at Discharge[1,3]	1	0%	99%	98%
Fibrinolytic Medication Timing[1,3]	1	0%	55%	55%
PCI Within 90 Minutes of Arrival[3]	0	-	94%	90%
Smoking Cessation Advice[3]	0	-	99%	99%
Chest Pain/Possible Heart Attack Care				
Aspirin at Arrival[3]	42	95%	97%	95%
Median Time to ECG (minutes)[3]	43	13	7	8
Median Time to Transfer (minutes)[1,3]	1	33	50	61
Fibrinolytic Medication Timing[1,3]	2	0%	58%	54%
Heart Failure Care				
ACE Inhibitor or ARB for LVSD[1]	8	100%	96%	94%
Discharge Instructions[1]	23	91%	86%	88%
Evaluation of LVS Function	30	93%	96%	98%
Smoking Cessation Advice[1]	4	100%	96%	98%
Pneumonia Care				
Appropriate Initial Antibiotic	41	83%	90%	92%
Blood Culture Timing	42	93%	95%	96%
Influenza Vaccine	27	96%	92%	91%
Initial Antibiotic Timing	47	96%	96%	95%
Pneumococcal Vaccine	56	88%	92%	93%
Smoking Cessation Advice[1]	12	100%	95%	97%
Surgical Care Improvement Project				
Appropriate VTP Within 24 Hours	88	97%	92%	92%
Appropriate Hair Removal	119	99%	99%	99%
Appropriate Beta Blocker Usage[1]	21	62%	94%	93%
Controlled Postoperative Blood Glucose	0	-	92%	93%
Prophylactic Antibiotic Timing[1]	20	90%	96%	97%
Prophylactic Antibiotic Timing (Outpatient)[1,3]	4	75%	89%	92%
Prophylactic Antibiotic Selection[1]	20	90%	98%	97%
Prophylactic Antibiotic Select. (Outpatient)[1,3]	3	100%	95%	94%
Prophylactic Antibiotic Stopped[1]	19	84%	97%	94%
Recommended VTP Ordered	88	97%	93%	94%
Urinary Catheter Removal[1]	23	87%	90%	90%
Children's Asthma Care				
Received Systemic Corticosteroids	-	-	-	100%
Received Home Management Plan	-	-	-	71%
Received Reliever Medication	-	-	-	100%
Use of Medical Imaging				
Combination Abdominal CT Scan	293	0.235	0.100	0.191
Combination Chest CT Scan	217	0.018	0.018	0.054
Follow-up Mammogram/Ultrasound	551	9.4%	6.4%	8.4%
MRI for Low Back Pain	83	36.1%	39.7%	32.7%
Survey of Patients' Hospital Experiences				
Area Around Room 'Always' Quiet at Night	300+	68%	-	58%
Doctors 'Always' Communicated Well	300+	82%	-	80%
Home Recovery Information Given	300+	89%	-	82%
Hospital Given 9 or 10 on 10 Point Scale	300+	76%	-	67%
Meds 'Always' Explained Before Given	300+	68%	-	60%
Nurses 'Always' Communicated Well	300+	83%	-	76%
Pain 'Always' Well Controlled	300+	74%	-	69%
Room and Bathroom 'Always' Clean	300+	79%	-	71%
Timely Help 'Always' Received	300+	71%	-	64%
Would Definitely Recommend Hospital	300+	78%	-	69%

Paynesville Area Hospital

200 1st Street West
Paynesville, MN 56362
URL: www.pahcs.com
Type: Critical Access Hospitals
Ownership: Govt - Hospital Dist/Auth
Phone: 320-243-3767
Fax: 320-243-6707
Emergency Services: Yes
Beds: 94

Key Personnel:
CEO/President. . . . . Bobbe Teigen
Infection Control. . . . . Tami Stanger
Radiology. . . . . Mark Dingmann

Measure	Cases	This Hosp.	State Avg.	U.S. Avg.
Heart Attack Care				
ACE Inhibitor or ARB for LVSD[3]	0	-	97%	96%
Aspirin at Arrival[1,3]	2	100%	99%	99%
Aspirin at Discharge[1,3]	2	100%	99%	98%
Beta Blocker at Discharge[1,3]	2	100%	99%	98%
Fibrinolytic Medication Timing[3]	0	-	55%	55%
PCI Within 90 Minutes of Arrival[3]	0	-	94%	90%
Smoking Cessation Advice[3]	0	-	99%	99%
Chest Pain/Possible Heart Attack Care				
Aspirin at Arrival[1]	18	100%	97%	95%
Median Time to ECG (minutes)[1]	20	5	7	8
Median Time to Transfer (minutes)[1]	4	32	50	61
Fibrinolytic Medication Timing	0	-	58%	54%
Heart Failure Care				
ACE Inhibitor or ARB for LVSD[1]	6	100%	96%	94%
Discharge Instructions[1]	13	62%	86%	88%
Evaluation of LVS Function[1]	17	100%	96%	98%
Smoking Cessation Advice	0	-	96%	98%
Pneumonia Care				
Appropriate Initial Antibiotic[1]	7	100%	90%	92%
Blood Culture Timing[1]	3	100%	95%	96%
Influenza Vaccine[1]	5	80%	92%	91%
Initial Antibiotic Timing[1]	5	100%	96%	95%
Pneumococcal Vaccine[1]	9	78%	92%	93%
Smoking Cessation Advice[1]	5	80%	95%	97%
Surgical Care Improvement Project				
Appropriate VTP Within 24 Hours[1]	12	100%	92%	92%
Appropriate Hair Removal	47	98%	99%	99%
Appropriate Beta Blocker Usage[1]	13	85%	94%	93%
Controlled Postoperative Blood Glucose	0	-	92%	93%
Prophylactic Antibiotic Timing	53	98%	96%	97%
Prophylactic Antibiotic Timing (Outpatient)	36	56%	89%	92%
Prophylactic Antibiotic Selection	53	98%	98%	97%
Prophylactic Antibiotic Select. (Outpatient)	38	71%	95%	94%
Prophylactic Antibiotic Stopped	52	87%	97%	94%
Recommended VTP Ordered[1]	12	100%	93%	94%
Urinary Catheter Removal[1]	12	92%	90%	90%
Children's Asthma Care				
Received Systemic Corticosteroids	-	-	-	100%
Received Home Management Plan	-	-	-	71%
Received Reliever Medication	-	-	-	100%
Use of Medical Imaging				
Combination Abdominal CT Scan	148	0.068	0.100	0.191
Combination Chest CT Scan	144	0.007	0.018	0.054
Follow-up Mammogram/Ultrasound	264	5.3%	6.4%	8.4%
MRI for Low Back Pain[1]	21	38.1%	39.7%	32.7%
Survey of Patients' Hospital Experiences				
Area Around Room 'Always' Quiet at Night	(a)	76%	-	58%
Doctors 'Always' Communicated Well	(a)	82%	-	80%
Home Recovery Information Given	(a)	85%	-	82%
Hospital Given 9 or 10 on 10 Point Scale	(a)	77%	-	67%
Meds 'Always' Explained Before Given	(a)	66%	-	60%
Nurses 'Always' Communicated Well	(a)	84%	-	76%
Pain 'Always' Well Controlled	(a)	71%	-	69%
Room and Bathroom 'Always' Clean	(a)	84%	-	71%
Timely Help 'Always' Received	(a)	79%	-	64%
Would Definitely Recommend Hospital	(a)	76%	-	69%

Perham Memorial Hospital

665 Third Street Southwest
Perham, MN 56573
E-mail: information@pmhh.com
URL: www.pmhh.com
Type: Critical Access Hospitals
Ownership: Govt - Hospital Dist/Auth
Phone: 218-346-4500
Fax: 218-346-4540
Emergency Services: Yes
Beds: 25

Key Personnel:
CEO/President. . . . . Roger Gilbertson
Chief of Medical Staff. . . . . Timothy J Studer, MD
Infection Control. . . . . Nancy Fehrenbach
Operating Room. . . . . Mary Peeters
Quality Assurance . . . . Nancy Fehrenbach
Radiology. . . . . Richard Marsden

Measure	Cases	This Hosp.	State Avg.	U.S. Avg.
Heart Attack Care				
ACE Inhibitor or ARB for LVSD	0	-	97%	96%
Aspirin at Arrival[1]	11	100%	99%	99%
Aspirin at Discharge[1]	9	100%	99%	98%
Beta Blocker at Discharge[1]	10	100%	99%	98%
Fibrinolytic Medication Timing	0	-	55%	55%
PCI Within 90 Minutes of Arrival	0	-	94%	90%
Smoking Cessation Advice	0	-	99%	99%
Chest Pain/Possible Heart Attack Care				
Aspirin at Arrival[3]	48	98%	97%	95%
Median Time to ECG (minutes)[3]	48	7	7	8
Median Time to Transfer (minutes)[3]	0	-	50	61
Fibrinolytic Medication Timing[1,3]	4	75%	58%	54%
Heart Failure Care				
ACE Inhibitor or ARB for LVSD[1]	2	100%	96%	94%
Discharge Instructions[1]	9	89%	86%	88%
Evaluation of LVS Function[1]	21	62%	96%	98%
Smoking Cessation Advice[1]	2	50%	96%	98%
Pneumonia Care				
Appropriate Initial Antibiotic	27	89%	90%	92%
Blood Culture Timing[1]	9	78%	95%	96%
Influenza Vaccine[1]	23	78%	92%	91%
Initial Antibiotic Timing	34	97%	96%	95%
Pneumococcal Vaccine	42	79%	92%	93%
Smoking Cessation Advice[1]	4	75%	95%	97%
Surgical Care Improvement Project				
Appropriate VTP Within 24 Hours[1]	12	83%	92%	92%
Appropriate Hair Removal[1]	23	100%	99%	99%
Appropriate Beta Blocker Usage[1]	8	100%	94%	93%
Controlled Postoperative Blood Glucose	0	-	92%	93%
Prophylactic Antibiotic Timing[1]	18	72%	96%	97%
Prophylactic Antibiotic Timing (Outpatient)[5]	0	-	89%	92%
Prophylactic Antibiotic Selection[1]	18	78%	98%	97%
Prophylactic Antibiotic Select. (Outpatient)[5]	0	-	95%	94%
Prophylactic Antibiotic Stopped[1]	18	94%	97%	94%
Recommended VTP Ordered[1]	12	83%	93%	94%
Urinary Catheter Removal[1]	4	100%	90%	90%
Children's Asthma Care				
Received Systemic Corticosteroids	-	-	-	100%
Received Home Management Plan	-	-	-	71%
Received Reliever Medication	-	-	-	100%
Use of Medical Imaging				
Combination Abdominal CT Scan	102	0.039	0.100	0.191
Combination Chest CT Scan	67	0.000	0.018	0.054
Follow-up Mammogram/Ultrasound	262	8.0%	6.4%	8.4%
MRI for Low Back Pain[1]	23	34.8%	39.7%	32.7%
Survey of Patients' Hospital Experiences				
Area Around Room 'Always' Quiet at Night[8]	-	-	-	58%
Doctors 'Always' Communicated Well[8]	-	-	-	80%
Home Recovery Information Given[8]	-	-	-	82%
Hospital Given 9 or 10 on 10 Point Scale[8]	-	-	-	67%
Meds 'Always' Explained Before Given[8]	-	-	-	60%
Nurses 'Always' Communicated Well[8]	-	-	-	76%
Pain 'Always' Well Controlled[8]	-	-	-	69%
Room and Bathroom 'Always' Clean[8]	-	-	-	71%
Timely Help 'Always' Received[8]	-	-	-	64%
Would Definitely Recommend Hospital[8]	-	-	-	69%

NOTE: Hospital profiles are in alphabetical order by state, then city, then hospital within the city; Rankings exclude hospitals with less than 25 cases except for patient surveys which excludes hospitals with less than 100 cases; (a) 100–299 cases; (1) The number of cases is too small to be sure how well a hospital is performing; (2) The hospital indicated that the data submitted for this measure were based on a sample of cases; (3) Data was collected during a shorter time period (fewer quarters) than the maximum possible time for this measure; (4) Suppressed for one or more quarters by CMS; (5) No data is available from the hospital for this measure; (6) Fewer than 100 patients completed the HCAHPS survey. Use these rates with caution, as the number of surveys may be too low to reliably assess hospital performance; (7) Survey results are based on less than 12 months of data; (8) Survey results are not available for this reporting period; (9) No or very few patients were eligible for the HCAHPS survey. The scores shown, if any, reflect a very small number of surveys; (10) A state average was not calculated because too few hospitals in the state submitted data; (11) There were discrepancies in the data collection process; Please refer to the User's Guide for a full explanation of data.

Lakeside Medical Center

129 6th Ave SE
Pine City, MN 55063
Phone: 320-629-2542
Type: Acute Care Hospitals
Emergency Services: No
Ownership: Government - Federal
Key Personnel:
CEO/President. . . . . Max Blaufuss

Measure	Cases	This Hosp.	State Avg.	U.S. Avg.
Heart Attack Care				
ACE Inhibitor or ARB for LVSD[5]	0	-	97%	96%
Aspirin at Arrival[5]	0	-	99%	99%
Aspirin at Discharge[5]	0	-	99%	98%
Beta Blocker at Discharge[5]	0	-	99%	98%
Fibrinolytic Medication Timing[5]	0	-	55%	55%
PCI Within 90 Minutes of Arrival[5]	0	-	94%	90%
Smoking Cessation Advice[5]	0	-	99%	99%
Chest Pain/Possible Heart Attack Care				
Aspirin at Arrival[5]	0	-	97%	95%
Median Time to ECG (minutes)[5]	0	-	7	8
Median Time to Transfer (minutes)[5]	0	-	50	61
Fibrinolytic Medication Timing[5]	0	-	58%	54%
Heart Failure Care				
ACE Inhibitor or ARB for LVSD[5]	0	-	96%	94%
Discharge Instructions[5]	0	-	86%	88%
Evaluation of LVS Function[5]	0	-	96%	98%
Smoking Cessation Advice[5]	0	-	96%	98%
Pneumonia Care				
Appropriate Initial Antibiotic[5]	0	-	90%	92%
Blood Culture Timing[5]	0	-	95%	96%
Influenza Vaccine[5]	0	-	92%	91%
Initial Antibiotic Timing[5]	0	-	96%	95%
Pneumococcal Vaccine[5]	0	-	92%	93%
Smoking Cessation Advice[5]	0	-	95%	97%
Surgical Care Improvement Project				
Appropriate VTP Within 24 Hours[5]	0	-	92%	92%
Appropriate Hair Removal[5]	0	-	99%	99%
Appropriate Beta Blocker Usage[5]	0	-	94%	93%
Controlled Postoperative Blood Glucose[5]	0	-	92%	93%
Prophylactic Antibiotic Timing[5]	0	-	96%	97%
Prophylactic Antibiotic Timing (Outpatient)[5]	0	-	89%	92%
Prophylactic Antibiotic Selection[5]	0	-	98%	97%
Prophylactic Antibiotic Select. (Outpatient)[5]	0	-	95%	94%
Prophylactic Antibiotic Stopped[5]	0	-	97%	94%
Recommended VTP Ordered[5]	0	-	93%	94%
Urinary Catheter Removal[5]	0	-	90%	90%
Children's Asthma Care				
Received Systemic Corticosteroids	-	-	-	100%
Received Home Management Plan	-	-	-	71%
Received Reliever Medication	-	-	-	100%
Use of Medical Imaging				
Combination Abdominal CT Scan[1]	20	0.100	0.100	0.191
Combination Chest CT Scan[1]	17	0.059	0.018	0.054
Follow-up Mammogram/Ultrasound[5]	0	-	6.4%	8.4%
MRI for Low Back Pain[1]	6	50.0%	39.7%	32.7%
Survey of Patients' Hospital Experiences				
Area Around Room 'Always' Quiet at Night[9]	-	-	-	58%
Doctors 'Always' Communicated Well[9]	-	-	-	80%
Home Recovery Information Given[9]	-	-	-	82%
Hospital Given 9 or 10 on 10 Point Scale[9]	-	-	-	67%
Meds 'Always' Explained Before Given[9]	-	-	-	60%
Nurses 'Always' Communicated Well[9]	-	-	-	76%
Pain 'Always' Well Controlled[9]	-	-	-	69%
Room and Bathroom 'Always' Clean[9]	-	-	-	71%
Timely Help 'Always' Received[9]	-	-	-	64%
Would Definitely Recommend Hospital[9]	-	-	-	69%

Pipestone County Medical Center

916 4th Avenue Southwest
Pipestone, MN 56164
Phone: 507-825-5811
Fax: 507-825-5733
URL: www.pcmchealth.org
Type: Critical Access Hospitals
Emergency Services: Yes
Ownership: Government - Local
Beds: 84
Key Personnel:
Infection Control. . . . . Nancy Johnson
Operating Room. . . . . Susan Borman
Quality Assurance . . . . Nancy Johnson, RN
Radiology. . . . . Wayne P Panning

Measure	Cases	This Hosp.	State Avg.	U.S. Avg.
Heart Attack Care				
ACE Inhibitor or ARB for LVSD[1]	1	100%	97%	96%
Aspirin at Arrival[1]	4	100%	99%	99%
Aspirin at Discharge[1]	4	75%	99%	98%
Beta Blocker at Discharge[1]	4	100%	99%	98%
Fibrinolytic Medication Timing[1]	1	100%	55%	55%
PCI Within 90 Minutes of Arrival	0	-	94%	90%
Smoking Cessation Advice	0	-	99%	99%
Chest Pain/Possible Heart Attack Care				
Aspirin at Arrival[5]	0	-	97%	95%
Median Time to ECG (minutes)[5]	0	-	7	8
Median Time to Transfer (minutes)[5]	0	-	50	61
Fibrinolytic Medication Timing[5]	0	-	58%	54%
Heart Failure Care				
ACE Inhibitor or ARB for LVSD[1]	8	75%	96%	94%
Discharge Instructions[1]	11	55%	86%	88%
Evaluation of LVS Function[1]	19	89%	96%	98%
Smoking Cessation Advice	0	-	96%	98%
Pneumonia Care				
Appropriate Initial Antibiotic[1]	15	93%	90%	92%
Blood Culture Timing[1]	4	100%	95%	96%
Influenza Vaccine[1]	17	94%	92%	91%
Initial Antibiotic Timing[1]	15	93%	96%	95%
Pneumococcal Vaccine[1]	20	95%	92%	93%
Smoking Cessation Advice[1]	5	100%	95%	97%
Surgical Care Improvement Project				
Appropriate VTP Within 24 Hours[1]	14	100%	92%	92%
Appropriate Hair Removal	47	100%	99%	99%
Appropriate Beta Blocker Usage[1,3]	7	71%	94%	93%
Controlled Postoperative Blood Glucose[3]	0	-	92%	93%
Prophylactic Antibiotic Timing	37	81%	96%	97%
Prophylactic Antibiotic Timing (Outpatient)[5]	0	-	89%	92%
Prophylactic Antibiotic Selection	37	97%	98%	97%
Prophylactic Antibiotic Select. (Outpatient)[5]	0	-	95%	94%
Prophylactic Antibiotic Stopped	36	94%	97%	94%
Recommended VTP Ordered[1]	14	100%	93%	94%
Urinary Catheter Removal[1]	5	100%	90%	90%
Children's Asthma Care				
Received Systemic Corticosteroids	-	-	-	100%
Received Home Management Plan	-	-	-	71%
Received Reliever Medication	-	-	-	100%
Use of Medical Imaging				
Combination Abdominal CT Scan	120	0.375	0.100	0.191
Combination Chest CT Scan[1]	32	0.094	0.018	0.054
Follow-up Mammogram/Ultrasound	293	1.7%	6.4%	8.4%
MRI for Low Back Pain[1]	26	46.2%	39.7%	32.7%
Survey of Patients' Hospital Experiences				
Area Around Room 'Always' Quiet at Night	(a)	62%	-	58%
Doctors 'Always' Communicated Well	(a)	79%	-	80%
Home Recovery Information Given	(a)	82%	-	82%
Hospital Given 9 or 10 on 10 Point Scale	(a)	62%	-	67%
Meds 'Always' Explained Before Given	(a)	64%	-	60%
Nurses 'Always' Communicated Well	(a)	74%	-	76%
Pain 'Always' Well Controlled	(a)	67%	-	69%
Room and Bathroom 'Always' Clean	(a)	78%	-	71%
Timely Help 'Always' Received	(a)	61%	-	64%
Would Definitely Recommend Hospital	(a)	67%	-	69%

Fairview Northland Regional Hospital

911 Northland Dr
Princeton, MN 55371
Phone: 763-389-1313
Fax: 763-389-6306
Type: Acute Care Hospitals
Emergency Services: Yes
Ownership: Voluntary Non-Profit - Other
Beds: 41
Key Personnel:
CEO/President. . . . . Jon R Campbell
Radiology. . . . . Manfred Benson, MD

Measure	Cases	This Hosp.	State Avg.	U.S. Avg.
Heart Attack Care				
ACE Inhibitor or ARB for LVSD[1]	5	100%	97%	96%
Aspirin at Arrival	26	100%	99%	99%
Aspirin at Discharge[1]	19	100%	99%	98%
Beta Blocker at Discharge[1]	20	100%	99%	98%
Fibrinolytic Medication Timing	0	-	55%	55%
PCI Within 90 Minutes of Arrival	0	-	94%	90%
Smoking Cessation Advice[1]	1	100%	99%	99%
Chest Pain/Possible Heart Attack Care				
Aspirin at Arrival	72	97%	97%	95%
Median Time to ECG (minutes)	77	7	7	8
Median Time to Transfer (minutes)[1]	10	56	50	61
Fibrinolytic Medication Timing	0	-	58%	54%
Heart Failure Care				
ACE Inhibitor or ARB for LVSD[1]	16	100%	96%	94%
Discharge Instructions	44	100%	86%	88%
Evaluation of LVS Function	63	100%	96%	98%
Smoking Cessation Advice[1]	6	100%	96%	98%
Pneumonia Care				
Appropriate Initial Antibiotic	69	96%	90%	92%
Blood Culture Timing	101	100%	95%	96%
Influenza Vaccine	60	100%	92%	91%
Initial Antibiotic Timing	99	100%	96%	95%
Pneumococcal Vaccine	84	100%	92%	93%
Smoking Cessation Advice	39	100%	95%	97%
Surgical Care Improvement Project				
Appropriate VTP Within 24 Hours[2]	42	100%	92%	92%
Appropriate Hair Removal[2]	217	100%	99%	99%
Appropriate Beta Blocker Usage[2]	61	97%	94%	93%
Controlled Postoperative Blood Glucose[2]	0	-	92%	93%
Prophylactic Antibiotic Timing[2]	176	99%	96%	97%
Prophylactic Antibiotic Timing (Outpatient)	53	89%	89%	92%
Prophylactic Antibiotic Selection[2]	178	100%	98%	97%
Prophylactic Antibiotic Select. (Outpatient)	49	94%	95%	94%
Prophylactic Antibiotic Stopped[2]	173	98%	97%	94%
Recommended VTP Ordered[2]	42	100%	93%	94%
Urinary Catheter Removal[1,2]	10	100%	90%	90%
Children's Asthma Care				
Received Systemic Corticosteroids	-	-	-	100%
Received Home Management Plan	-	-	-	71%
Received Reliever Medication	-	-	-	100%
Use of Medical Imaging				
Combination Abdominal CT Scan	281	0.032	0.100	0.191
Combination Chest CT Scan	209	0.005	0.018	0.054
Follow-up Mammogram/Ultrasound	617	8.6%	6.4%	8.4%
MRI for Low Back Pain	62	32.3%	39.7%	32.7%
Survey of Patients' Hospital Experiences				
Area Around Room 'Always' Quiet at Night	300+	57%	-	58%
Doctors 'Always' Communicated Well	300+	81%	-	80%
Home Recovery Information Given	300+	85%	-	82%
Hospital Given 9 or 10 on 10 Point Scale	300+	73%	-	67%
Meds 'Always' Explained Before Given	300+	64%	-	60%
Nurses 'Always' Communicated Well	300+	78%	-	76%
Pain 'Always' Well Controlled	300+	73%	-	69%
Room and Bathroom 'Always' Clean	300+	77%	-	71%
Timely Help 'Always' Received	300+	71%	-	64%
Would Definitely Recommend Hospital	300+	71%	-	69%

NOTE: Hospital profiles are in alphabetical order by state, then city, then hospital within the city; Rankings exclude hospitals with less than 25 cases except for patient surveys which excludes hospitals with less than 100 cases; (a) 100–299 cases; (1) The number of cases is too small to be sure how well a hospital is performing; (2) The hospital indicated that the data submitted for this measure were based on a sample of cases; (3) Data was collected during a shorter time period (fewer quarters) than the maximum possible time for this measure; (4) Suppressed for one or more quarters by CMS; (5) No data is available from the hospital for this measure; (6) Fewer than 100 patients completed the HCAHPS survey. Use these rates with caution, as the number of surveys may be too low to reliably assess hospital performance; (7) Survey results are based on less than 12 months of data; (8) Survey results are not available for this reporting period; (9) No or very few patients were eligible for the HCAHPS survey. The scores shown, if any, reflect a very small number of surveys; (10) A state average was not calculated because too few hospitals in the state submitted data; (11) There were discrepancies in the data collection process; Please refer to the User's Guide for a full explanation of data.

Fairview Red Wing Hospital

701 Fairview Boulevard
Red Wing, MN 55066
URL: www.redwing.fairview.org
Type: Acute Care Hospitals
Ownership: Voluntary Non-Profit - Private
Phone: 651-267-5000
Fax: 651-385-3304
Emergency Services: Yes
Beds: 96

Key Personnel:
Chief of Medical Staff.......... Jack Alexander
Operating Room............. Cheryl Luettinger
Quality Assurance .... Dawn Ulveness
Anesthesiology.............. Shelly Bakker
Emergency Room .... Jane Gisslen
Intensive Care Unit........... Helen McKay

Measure	Cases	This Hosp.	State Avg.	U.S. Avg.
Heart Attack Care				
ACE Inhibitor or ARB for LVSD[1]	3	100%	97%	96%
Aspirin at Arrival[1]	12	100%	99%	99%
Aspirin at Discharge[1]	8	100%	99%	98%
Beta Blocker at Discharge[1]	9	100%	99%	98%
Fibrinolytic Medication Timing	0	-	55%	55%
PCI Within 90 Minutes of Arrival	0	-	94%	90%
Smoking Cessation Advice	0	-	99%	99%
Chest Pain/Possible Heart Attack Care				
Aspirin at Arrival	91	100%	97%	95%
Median Time to ECG (minutes)	92	5	7	8
Median Time to Transfer (minutes)[1,3]	5	85	50	61
Fibrinolytic Medication Timing[1]	3	33%	58%	54%
Heart Failure Care				
ACE Inhibitor or ARB for LVSD[1]	2	100%	96%	94%
Discharge Instructions	34	97%	86%	88%
Evaluation of LVS Function	47	100%	96%	98%
Smoking Cessation Advice[1]	4	100%	96%	98%
Pneumonia Care				
Appropriate Initial Antibiotic	62	100%	90%	92%
Blood Culture Timing	63	98%	95%	96%
Influenza Vaccine	36	100%	92%	91%
Initial Antibiotic Timing	74	100%	96%	95%
Pneumococcal Vaccine	61	100%	92%	93%
Smoking Cessation Advice[1]	21	100%	95%	97%
Surgical Care Improvement Project				
Appropriate VTP Within 24 Hours[2]	39	100%	92%	92%
Appropriate Hair Removal[2]	214	100%	99%	99%
Appropriate Beta Blocker Usage[2]	68	100%	94%	93%
Controlled Postoperative Blood Glucose[2]	0	-	92%	93%
Prophylactic Antibiotic Timing[2]	165	99%	96%	97%
Prophylactic Antibiotic Timing (Outpatient)	52	100%	89%	92%
Prophylactic Antibiotic Selection[2]	167	98%	98%	97%
Prophylactic Antibiotic Select. (Outpatient)	65	92%	95%	94%
Prophylactic Antibiotic Stopped[2]	161	98%	97%	94%
Recommended VTP Ordered[2]	39	100%	93%	94%
Urinary Catheter Removal[2]	56	100%	90%	90%
Children's Asthma Care				
Received Systemic Corticosteroids	-	-	-	100%
Received Home Management Plan	-	-	-	71%
Received Reliever Medication	-	-	-	100%
Use of Medical Imaging				
Combination Abdominal CT Scan	185	0.076	0.100	0.191
Combination Chest CT Scan	146	0.041	0.018	0.054
Follow-up Mammogram/Ultrasound	584	3.9%	6.4%	8.4%
MRI for Low Back Pain	89	37.1%	39.7%	32.7%
Survey of Patients' Hospital Experiences				
Area Around Room 'Always' Quiet at Night	300+	63%	-	58%
Doctors 'Always' Communicated Well	300+	82%	-	80%
Home Recovery Information Given	300+	86%	-	82%
Hospital Given 9 or 10 on 10 Point Scale	300+	70%	-	67%
Meds 'Always' Explained Before Given	300+	62%	-	60%
Nurses 'Always' Communicated Well	300+	77%	-	76%
Pain 'Always' Well Controlled	300+	72%	-	69%
Room and Bathroom 'Always' Clean	300+	76%	-	71%
Timely Help 'Always' Received	300+	75%	-	64%
Would Definitely Recommend Hospital	300+	72%	-	69%

Red Lake Hospital

PO Box 497
Redlake, MN 56671
Type: Acute Care Hospitals
Ownership: Government - Federal
Phone: 218-679-3912
Fax: 218-679-3990
Emergency Services: Yes
Beds: 23

Key Personnel:
CEO/President............... Tony James
Chief of Medical Staff.......... John Robinson
Quality Assurance .... Bonnie Smprud
Emergency Room .... Joyce Kennedy

Measure	Cases	This Hosp.	State Avg.	U.S. Avg.
Heart Attack Care				
ACE Inhibitor or ARB for LVSD[2,3]	0	-	97%	96%
Aspirin at Arrival[2,3]	0	-	99%	99%
Aspirin at Discharge[2,3]	0	-	99%	98%
Beta Blocker at Discharge[2,3]	0	-	99%	98%
Fibrinolytic Medication Timing[2,3]	0	-	55%	55%
PCI Within 90 Minutes of Arrival[2,3]	0	-	94%	90%
Smoking Cessation Advice[2,3]	0	-	99%	99%
Chest Pain/Possible Heart Attack Care				
Aspirin at Arrival	-	-	97%	95%
Median Time to ECG (minutes)	-	-	7	8
Median Time to Transfer (minutes)	-	-	50	61
Fibrinolytic Medication Timing	-	-	58%	54%
Heart Failure Care				
ACE Inhibitor or ARB for LVSD[1,2]	3	100%	96%	94%
Discharge Instructions[1,2]	7	100%	86%	88%
Evaluation of LVS Function[1,2]	6	100%	96%	98%
Smoking Cessation Advice[2]	0	-	96%	98%
Pneumonia Care				
Appropriate Initial Antibiotic[1,2]	13	54%	90%	92%
Blood Culture Timing[1,2]	10	70%	95%	96%
Influenza Vaccine[1,2]	5	20%	92%	91%
Initial Antibiotic Timing[1,2]	14	71%	96%	95%
Pneumococcal Vaccine[1,2]	3	33%	92%	93%
Smoking Cessation Advice[1,2]	5	80%	95%	97%
Surgical Care Improvement Project				
Appropriate VTP Within 24 Hours[5]	0	-	92%	92%
Appropriate Hair Removal[5]	0	-	99%	99%
Appropriate Beta Blocker Usage[5]	0	-	94%	93%
Controlled Postoperative Blood Glucose[5]	0	-	92%	93%
Prophylactic Antibiotic Timing[5]	0	-	96%	97%
Prophylactic Antibiotic Timing (Outpatient)	-	-	89%	92%
Prophylactic Antibiotic Selection[5]	0	-	98%	97%
Prophylactic Antibiotic Select. (Outpatient)	-	-	95%	94%
Prophylactic Antibiotic Stopped[5]	0	-	97%	94%
Recommended VTP Ordered[5]	0	-	93%	94%
Urinary Catheter Removal[5]	0	-	90%	90%
Children's Asthma Care				
Received Systemic Corticosteroids	-	-	-	100%
Received Home Management Plan	-	-	-	71%
Received Reliever Medication	-	-	-	100%
Use of Medical Imaging				
Combination Abdominal CT Scan	-	-	0.100	0.191
Combination Chest CT Scan	-	-	0.018	0.054
Follow-up Mammogram/Ultrasound	-	-	6.4%	8.4%
MRI for Low Back Pain	-	-	39.7%	32.7%
Survey of Patients' Hospital Experiences				
Area Around Room 'Always' Quiet at Night[6]	<100	84%	-	58%
Doctors 'Always' Communicated Well[6]	<100	71%	-	80%
Home Recovery Information Given[6]	<100	70%	-	82%
Hospital Given 9 or 10 on 10 Point Scale[6]	<100	65%	-	67%
Meds 'Always' Explained Before Given[6]	<100	66%	-	60%
Nurses 'Always' Communicated Well[6]	<100	82%	-	76%
Pain 'Always' Well Controlled[6]	<100	74%	-	69%
Room and Bathroom 'Always' Clean[6]	<100	65%	-	71%
Timely Help 'Always' Received[6]	<100	23%	-	64%
Would Definitely Recommend Hospital	<100	40%	-	69%

Redwood Area Hospital

100 Fallwood Road
Redwood Falls, MN 56283
URL: www.redwoodareahospital.org
Type: Critical Access Hospitals
Ownership: Government - Local
Phone: 507-637-4511
Fax: 507-697-6000
Emergency Services: Yes
Beds: 25

Key Personnel:
CEO/President............... James E Schulte
Cardiac Laboratory............ Lori Highty
Chief of Medical Staff.......... Cindi Gronan
Infection Control.............. Julie Fiala RN
Operating Room............. Julie Salmon
Quality Assurance .... Gloria Lothert RN
Anesthesiology............. David Lutz
Emergency Room .... Jo Kremin RN

Measure	Cases	This Hosp.	State Avg.	U.S. Avg.
Heart Attack Care				
ACE Inhibitor or ARB for LVSD[1,3]	1	0%	97%	96%
Aspirin at Arrival[1,3]	5	100%	99%	99%
Aspirin at Discharge[1,3]	3	100%	99%	98%
Beta Blocker at Discharge[1,3]	3	67%	99%	98%
Fibrinolytic Medication Timing[3]	0	-	55%	55%
PCI Within 90 Minutes of Arrival[3]	0	-	94%	90%
Smoking Cessation Advice[3]	0	-	99%	99%
Chest Pain/Possible Heart Attack Care				
Aspirin at Arrival[5]	0	-	97%	95%
Median Time to ECG (minutes)[5]	0	-	7	8
Median Time to Transfer (minutes)[5]	0	-	50	61
Fibrinolytic Medication Timing[5]	0	-	58%	54%
Heart Failure Care				
ACE Inhibitor or ARB for LVSD[1]	5	80%	96%	94%
Discharge Instructions[1]	10	90%	86%	88%
Evaluation of LVS Function[1]	20	80%	96%	98%
Smoking Cessation Advice[1]	1	100%	96%	98%
Pneumonia Care				
Appropriate Initial Antibiotic[1]	17	88%	90%	92%
Blood Culture Timing[1]	12	100%	95%	96%
Influenza Vaccine[1]	16	94%	92%	91%
Initial Antibiotic Timing[1]	23	96%	96%	95%
Pneumococcal Vaccine	25	92%	92%	93%
Smoking Cessation Advice[1]	9	78%	95%	97%
Surgical Care Improvement Project				
Appropriate VTP Within 24 Hours[5]	0	-	92%	92%
Appropriate Hair Removal[5]	0	-	99%	99%
Appropriate Beta Blocker Usage[5]	0	-	94%	93%
Controlled Postoperative Blood Glucose[5]	0	-	92%	93%
Prophylactic Antibiotic Timing[5]	0	-	96%	97%
Prophylactic Antibiotic Timing (Outpatient)[5]	0	-	89%	92%
Prophylactic Antibiotic Selection[5]	0	-	98%	97%
Prophylactic Antibiotic Select. (Outpatient)[5]	0	-	95%	94%
Prophylactic Antibiotic Stopped[5]	0	-	97%	94%
Recommended VTP Ordered[5]	0	-	93%	94%
Urinary Catheter Removal[5]	0	-	90%	90%
Children's Asthma Care				
Received Systemic Corticosteroids	-	-	-	100%
Received Home Management Plan	-	-	-	71%
Received Reliever Medication	-	-	-	100%
Use of Medical Imaging				
Combination Abdominal CT Scan	140	0.043	0.100	0.191
Combination Chest CT Scan	89	0.011	0.018	0.054
Follow-up Mammogram/Ultrasound	67	4.5%	6.4%	8.4%
MRI for Low Back Pain[1]	33	24.2%	39.7%	32.7%
Survey of Patients' Hospital Experiences				
Area Around Room 'Always' Quiet at Night[11]	(a)	77%	-	58%
Doctors 'Always' Communicated Well[11]	(a)	82%	-	80%
Home Recovery Information Given[11]	(a)	90%	-	82%
Hospital Given 9 or 10 on 10 Point Scale[11]	(a)	72%	-	67%
Meds 'Always' Explained Before Given[11]	(a)	67%	-	60%
Nurses 'Always' Communicated Well[11]	(a)	81%	-	76%
Pain 'Always' Well Controlled[11]	(a)	70%	-	69%
Room and Bathroom 'Always' Clean[11]	(a)	86%	-	71%
Timely Help 'Always' Received[11]	(a)	82%	-	64%
Would Definitely Recommend Hospital[11]	(a)	70%	-	69%

NOTE: Hospital profiles are in alphabetical order by state, then city, then hospital within the city; Rankings exclude hospitals with less than 25 cases except for patient surveys which excludes hospitals with less than 100 cases; (a) 100–299 cases; (1) The number of cases is too small to be sure how well a hospital is performing; (2) The hospital indicated that the data submitted for this measure were based on a sample of cases; (3) Data was collected during a shorter time period (fewer quarters) than the maximum possible time for this measure; (4) Suppressed for one or more quarters by CMS; (5) No data is available from the hospital for this measure; (6) Fewer than 100 patients completed the HCAHPS survey. Use these rates with caution, as the number of surveys may be too low to reliably assess hospital performance; (7) Survey results are based on less than 12 months of data; (8) Survey results are not available for this reporting period; (9) No or very few patients were eligible for the HCAHPS survey. The scores shown, if any, reflect a very small number of surveys; (10) A state average was not calculated because too few hospitals in the state submitted data; (11) There were discrepancies in the data collection process; Please refer to the User's Guide for a full explanation of data.

North Memorial Medical Center

3300 Oakdale North Phone: 763-520-5200
Robbinsdale, MN 55422 Fax: 763-520-5006
URL: www.northmemorial.com
Type: Acute Care Hospitals Emergency Services: Yes
Ownership: Voluntary Non-Profit - Private Beds: 518

Key Personnel:
CEO/President. . . . . David Cress
Chief of Medical Staff . . . . Bruce Adams, MD
Infection Control. . . . . CG Schrock, MD
Operating Room. . . . . Lois Bergquist
Pediatric Ambulatory Care . . . . . . Diane Meier, MD
Pediatric In-Patient Care . . . . Diane Meier, MD
Quality Assurance . . . . Cathy Riley
Radiology. . . . . Tony Werner

Measure	Cases	This Hosp.	State Avg.	U.S. Avg.
Heart Attack Care				
ACE Inhibitor or ARB for LVSD[2]	49	100%	97%	96%
Aspirin at Arrival[2]	263	100%	99%	99%
Aspirin at Discharge[2]	271	100%	99%	98%
Beta Blocker at Discharge[2]	277	99%	99%	98%
Fibrinolytic Medication Timing[2]	0	-	55%	55%
PCI Within 90 Minutes of Arrival[2]	62	100%	94%	90%
Smoking Cessation Advice[2]	79	95%	99%	99%
Chest Pain/Possible Heart Attack Care				
Aspirin at Arrival[5]	0	-	97%	95%
Median Time to ECG (minutes)[5]	0	-	7	8
Median Time to Transfer (minutes)[5]	0	-	50	61
Fibrinolytic Medication Timing[5]	0	-	58%	54%
Heart Failure Care				
ACE Inhibitor or ARB for LVSD[2]	77	99%	96%	94%
Discharge Instructions[2]	229	79%	86%	88%
Evaluation of LVS Function[2]	296	99%	96%	98%
Smoking Cessation Advice[2]	43	93%	96%	98%
Pneumonia Care				
Appropriate Initial Antibiotic[2]	95	82%	90%	92%
Blood Culture Timing[2]	147	93%	95%	96%
Influenza Vaccine[2]	122	86%	92%	91%
Initial Antibiotic Timing[2]	181	98%	96%	95%
Pneumococcal Vaccine[2]	150	83%	92%	93%
Smoking Cessation Advice[2]	57	86%	95%	97%
Surgical Care Improvement Project				
Appropriate VTP Within 24 Hours[2]	165	72%	92%	92%
Appropriate Hair Removal[2]	650	100%	99%	99%
Appropriate Beta Blocker Usage[2]	247	98%	94%	93%
Controlled Postoperative Blood Glucose[2]	156	71%	92%	93%
Prophylactic Antibiotic Timing[2]	498	95%	96%	97%
Prophylactic Antibiotic Timing (Outpatient)[3]	262	91%	89%	92%
Prophylactic Antibiotic Selection[2]	511	97%	98%	97%
Prophylactic Antibiotic Select. (Outpatient)[3]	253	95%	95%	94%
Prophylactic Antibiotic Stopped[2]	493	94%	97%	94%
Recommended VTP Ordered[2]	166	72%	93%	94%
Urinary Catheter Removal[2]	191	83%	90%	90%
Children's Asthma Care				
Received Systemic Corticosteroids	-	-	-	100%
Received Home Management Plan	-	-	-	71%
Received Reliever Medication	-	-	-	100%
Use of Medical Imaging				
Combination Abdominal CT Scan	1,034	0.083	0.100	0.191
Combination Chest CT Scan	943	0.016	0.018	0.054
Follow-up Mammogram/Ultrasound	711	6.9%	6.4%	8.4%
MRI for Low Back Pain	210	54.3%	39.7%	32.7%
Survey of Patients' Hospital Experiences				
Area Around Room 'Always' Quiet at Night	300+	52%	-	58%
Doctors 'Always' Communicated Well	300+	73%	-	80%
Home Recovery Information Given	300+	81%	-	82%
Hospital Given 9 or 10 on 10 Point Scale	300+	56%	-	67%
Meds 'Always' Explained Before Given	300+	54%	-	60%
Nurses 'Always' Communicated Well	300+	68%	-	76%
Pain 'Always' Well Controlled	300+	66%	-	69%
Room and Bathroom 'Always' Clean	300+	60%	-	71%
Timely Help 'Always' Received	300+	52%	-	64%
Would Definitely Recommend Hospital	300+	64%	-	69%

Mayo Clinic - Methodist Hospital

201 West Center Street Phone: 507-266-7890
Rochester, MN 55902 Fax: 507-284-0161
URL: www.mayoclinic.org/methodisthospital
Type: Acute Care Hospitals Emergency Services: Yes
Ownership: Voluntary Non-Profit - Other Beds: 794

Key Personnel:
CEO/President. . . . . Denis Cortese, MD
Cardiac Laboratory. . . . . Randal J Thomas MD, MS
Infection Control. . . . . Rodney Thompson, MD
Operating Room. . . . . Doreen Frusti
Anesthesiology. . . . . Duane K Rorie, MD
Hemotology Center . . . . Robert B Diasio MD
Intensive Care Unit. . . . . Malcolm R Bell MD

Measure	Cases	This Hosp.	State Avg.	U.S. Avg.
Heart Attack Care				
ACE Inhibitor or ARB for LVSD[3]	0	-	97%	96%
Aspirin at Arrival[3]	0	-	99%	99%
Aspirin at Discharge[3]	0	-	99%	98%
Beta Blocker at Discharge[3]	0	-	99%	98%
Fibrinolytic Medication Timing[3]	0	-	55%	55%
PCI Within 90 Minutes of Arrival[3]	0	-	94%	90%
Smoking Cessation Advice[3]	0	-	99%	99%
Chest Pain/Possible Heart Attack Care				
Aspirin at Arrival[5]	0	-	97%	95%
Median Time to ECG (minutes)[5]	0	-	7	8
Median Time to Transfer (minutes)[5]	0	-	50	61
Fibrinolytic Medication Timing[5]	0	-	58%	54%
Heart Failure Care				
ACE Inhibitor or ARB for LVSD[1]	1	100%	96%	94%
Discharge Instructions[1]	12	50%	86%	88%
Evaluation of LVS Function[1]	12	100%	96%	98%
Smoking Cessation Advice[1]	1	100%	96%	98%
Pneumonia Care				
Appropriate Initial Antibiotic	0	-	90%	92%
Blood Culture Timing	0	-	95%	96%
Influenza Vaccine	33	76%	92%	91%
Initial Antibiotic Timing[1]	7	71%	96%	95%
Pneumococcal Vaccine	36	92%	92%	93%
Smoking Cessation Advice[1]	6	100%	95%	97%
Surgical Care Improvement Project				
Appropriate VTP Within 24 Hours[2]	202	99%	92%	92%
Appropriate Hair Removal[2]	666	99%	99%	99%
Appropriate Beta Blocker Usage[2]	164	99%	94%	93%
Controlled Postoperative Blood Glucose[2]	0	-	92%	93%
Prophylactic Antibiotic Timing[2]	412	98%	96%	97%
Prophylactic Antibiotic Timing (Outpatient)	329	95%	89%	92%
Prophylactic Antibiotic Selection[2]	411	99%	98%	97%
Prophylactic Antibiotic Select. (Outpatient)	566	97%	95%	94%
Prophylactic Antibiotic Stopped[2]	403	99%	97%	94%
Recommended VTP Ordered[2]	202	100%	93%	94%
Urinary Catheter Removal[2]	78	94%	90%	90%
Children's Asthma Care				
Received Systemic Corticosteroids	-	-	-	100%
Received Home Management Plan	-	-	-	71%
Received Reliever Medication	-	-	-	100%
Use of Medical Imaging				
Combination Abdominal CT Scan	189	0.101	0.100	0.191
Combination Chest CT Scan	155	0.006	0.018	0.054
Follow-up Mammogram/Ultrasound[5]	0	-	6.4%	8.4%
MRI for Low Back Pain[1]	17	17.6%	39.7%	32.7%
Survey of Patients' Hospital Experiences				
Area Around Room 'Always' Quiet at Night	300+	58%	-	58%
Doctors 'Always' Communicated Well	300+	83%	-	80%
Home Recovery Information Given	300+	88%	-	82%
Hospital Given 9 or 10 on 10 Point Scale	300+	80%	-	67%
Meds 'Always' Explained Before Given	300+	65%	-	60%
Nurses 'Always' Communicated Well	300+	81%	-	76%
Pain 'Always' Well Controlled	300+	69%	-	69%
Room and Bathroom 'Always' Clean	300+	68%	-	71%
Timely Help 'Always' Received	300+	68%	-	64%
Would Definitely Recommend Hospital	300+	83%	-	69%

Mayo Clinic - Saint Marys Hospital

1216 Second Street West Phone: 507-255-5123
Rochester, MN 55902
URL: www.mayoclinic.org/saintmaryshospital
Type: Acute Care Hospitals Emergency Services: Yes
Ownership: Voluntary Non-Profit - Church Beds: 1,157

Measure	Cases	This Hosp.	State Avg.	U.S. Avg.
Heart Attack Care				
ACE Inhibitor or ARB for LVSD[2]	45	100%	97%	96%
Aspirin at Arrival[2]	128	100%	99%	99%
Aspirin at Discharge[2]	302	100%	99%	98%
Beta Blocker at Discharge[2]	294	100%	99%	98%
Fibrinolytic Medication Timing[2]	0	-	55%	55%
PCI Within 90 Minutes of Arrival[1,2]	22	95%	94%	90%
Smoking Cessation Advice[2]	75	100%	99%	99%
Chest Pain/Possible Heart Attack Care				
Aspirin at Arrival[1]	2	100%	97%	95%
Median Time to ECG (minutes)[1]	2	8	7	8
Median Time to Transfer (minutes)[5]	0	-	50	61
Fibrinolytic Medication Timing[5]	0	-	58%	54%
Heart Failure Care				
ACE Inhibitor or ARB for LVSD[2]	80	99%	96%	94%
Discharge Instructions[2]	207	94%	86%	88%
Evaluation of LVS Function[2]	277	100%	96%	98%
Smoking Cessation Advice[1,2]	24	100%	96%	98%
Pneumonia Care				
Appropriate Initial Antibiotic[2]	32	88%	90%	92%
Blood Culture Timing[2]	78	88%	95%	96%
Influenza Vaccine[2]	87	94%	92%	91%
Initial Antibiotic Timing[2]	104	92%	96%	95%
Pneumococcal Vaccine[2]	135	96%	92%	93%
Smoking Cessation Advice[2]	31	97%	95%	97%
Surgical Care Improvement Project				
Appropriate VTP Within 24 Hours[2]	259	98%	92%	92%
Appropriate Hair Removal[2]	786	100%	99%	99%
Appropriate Beta Blocker Usage[2]	337	98%	94%	93%
Controlled Postoperative Blood Glucose[2]	254	87%	92%	93%
Prophylactic Antibiotic Timing[2]	408	96%	96%	97%
Prophylactic Antibiotic Timing (Outpatient)	628	84%	89%	92%
Prophylactic Antibiotic Selection[2]	438	98%	98%	97%
Prophylactic Antibiotic Select. (Outpatient)	581	98%	95%	94%
Prophylactic Antibiotic Stopped[2]	392	95%	97%	94%
Recommended VTP Ordered[2]	259	99%	93%	94%
Urinary Catheter Removal[2]	158	79%	90%	90%
Children's Asthma Care				
Received Systemic Corticosteroids	-	-	-	100%
Received Home Management Plan	-	-	-	71%
Received Reliever Medication	-	-	-	100%
Use of Medical Imaging				
Combination Abdominal CT Scan	576	0.047	0.100	0.191
Combination Chest CT Scan	260	0.008	0.018	0.054
Follow-up Mammogram/Ultrasound[5]	0	-	6.4%	8.4%
MRI for Low Back Pain[1]	20	20.0%	39.7%	32.7%
Survey of Patients' Hospital Experiences				
Area Around Room 'Always' Quiet at Night	300+	62%	-	58%
Doctors 'Always' Communicated Well	300+	82%	-	80%
Home Recovery Information Given	300+	84%	-	82%
Hospital Given 9 or 10 on 10 Point Scale	300+	81%	-	67%
Meds 'Always' Explained Before Given	300+	67%	-	60%
Nurses 'Always' Communicated Well	300+	79%	-	76%
Pain 'Always' Well Controlled	300+	73%	-	69%
Room and Bathroom 'Always' Clean	300+	74%	-	71%
Timely Help 'Always' Received	300+	70%	-	64%
Would Definitely Recommend Hospital	300+	85%	-	69%

NOTE: Hospital profiles are in alphabetical order by state, then city, then hospital within the city; Rankings exclude hospitals with less than 25 cases except for patient surveys which excludes hospitals with less than 100 cases; (a) 100–299 cases; (1) The number of cases is too small to be sure how well a hospital is performing; (2) The hospital indicated that the data submitted for this measure were based on a sample of cases; (3) Data was collected during a shorter time period (fewer quarters) than the maximum possible time for this measure; (4) Suppressed for one or more quarters by CMS; (5) No data is available from the hospital for this measure; (6) Fewer than 100 patients completed the HCAHPS survey. Use these rates with caution, as the number of surveys may be too low to reliably assess hospital performance; (7) Survey results are based on less than 12 months of data; (8) Survey results are not available for this reporting period; (9) No or very few patients were eligible for the HCAHPS survey. The scores shown, if any, reflect a very small number of surveys; (10) A state average was not calculated because too few hospitals in the state submitted data; (11) There were discrepancies in the data collection process; Please refer to the User's Guide for a full explanation of data.

Olmsted Medical Center

1650 Fourth Street Southeast
Rochester, MN 55904
Phone: 507-529-6600
Fax: 507-529-6622
URL: www.olmsteadmedicalcenter.org
Type: Acute Care Hospitals
Emergency Services: Yes
Ownership: Voluntary Non-Profit - Private
Beds: 61

Key Personnel:
CEO/President. . . . . Kevin Pitzer
Chief of Medical Staff . . . . David Westgard, MD
Infection Control. . . . . Vicky Shultz
Operating Room. . . . . Ben Riker
Quality Assurance . . . . Sue Klenner
Radiology. . . . . Diya Odeh
Emergency Room . . . . Jay Myers

Measure	Cases	This Hosp.	State Avg.	U.S. Avg.
Heart Attack Care				
ACE Inhibitor or ARB for LVSD[3]	0	-	97%	96%
Aspirin at Arrival[3]	0	-	99%	99%
Aspirin at Discharge[3]	0	-	99%	98%
Beta Blocker at Discharge[3]	0	-	99%	98%
Fibrinolytic Medication Timing[3]	0	-	55%	55%
PCI Within 90 Minutes of Arrival[3]	0	-	94%	90%
Smoking Cessation Advice[3]	0	-	99%	99%
Chest Pain/Possible Heart Attack Care				
Aspirin at Arrival	59	92%	97%	95%
Median Time to ECG (minutes)	60	7	7	8
Median Time to Transfer (minutes)[3]	0	-	50	61
Fibrinolytic Medication Timing	0	-	58%	54%
Heart Failure Care				
ACE Inhibitor or ARB for LVSD[1]	6	100%	96%	94%
Discharge Instructions[1]	14	71%	86%	88%
Evaluation of LVS Function[1]	20	95%	96%	98%
Smoking Cessation Advice[1]	3	67%	96%	98%
Pneumonia Care				
Appropriate Initial Antibiotic	29	83%	90%	92%
Blood Culture Timing	31	90%	95%	96%
Influenza Vaccine[1]	17	71%	92%	91%
Initial Antibiotic Timing	34	82%	96%	95%
Pneumococcal Vaccine	32	84%	92%	93%
Smoking Cessation Advice[1]	8	88%	95%	97%
Surgical Care Improvement Project				
Appropriate VTP Within 24 Hours	76	83%	92%	92%
Appropriate Hair Removal	287	100%	99%	99%
Appropriate Beta Blocker Usage	90	99%	94%	93%
Controlled Postoperative Blood Glucose	0	-	92%	93%
Prophylactic Antibiotic Timing	251	89%	96%	97%
Prophylactic Antibiotic Timing (Outpatient)	106	89%	89%	92%
Prophylactic Antibiotic Selection	248	96%	98%	97%
Prophylactic Antibiotic Select. (Outpatient)	101	95%	95%	94%
Prophylactic Antibiotic Stopped	246	97%	97%	94%
Recommended VTP Ordered	76	83%	93%	94%
Urinary Catheter Removal	82	95%	90%	90%
Children's Asthma Care				
Received Systemic Corticosteroids	-	-	-	100%
Received Home Management Plan	-	-	-	71%
Received Reliever Medication	-	-	-	100%
Use of Medical Imaging				
Combination Abdominal CT Scan	227	0.344	0.100	0.191
Combination Chest CT Scan	146	0.253	0.018	0.054
Follow-up Mammogram/Ultrasound	1,053	5.7%	6.4%	8.4%
MRI for Low Back Pain[1]	41	14.6%	39.7%	32.7%
Survey of Patients' Hospital Experiences				
Area Around Room 'Always' Quiet at Night	300+	57%	-	58%
Doctors 'Always' Communicated Well	300+	80%	-	80%
Home Recovery Information Given	300+	90%	-	82%
Hospital Given 9 or 10 on 10 Point Scale	300+	73%	-	67%
Meds 'Always' Explained Before Given	300+	67%	-	60%
Nurses 'Always' Communicated Well	300+	75%	-	76%
Pain 'Always' Well Controlled	300+	69%	-	69%
Room and Bathroom 'Always' Clean	300+	70%	-	71%
Timely Help 'Always' Received	300+	70%	-	64%
Would Definitely Recommend Hospital	300+	82%	-	69%

Lifecare Medical Center

715 Delmore Drive
Roseau, MN 56751
Phone: 218-463-2500
Fax: 218-463-1266
URL: www.lifecaremedicalcenter.org
Type: Critical Access Hospitals
Emergency Services: Yes
Ownership: Voluntary Non-Profit - Private
Beds: 25

Key Personnel:
CEO/President. . . . . Keith Okeson
Chief of Medical Staff . . . . Robert Anderson, MD
Infection Control. . . . . Jane Hirst, RN
Quality Assurance . . . . Milly Prachar
Radiology. . . . . Sharlene Peterson
Emergency Room . . . . Ronald Brummer, MD
Patient Relations . . . . Sue Lisell

Measure	Cases	This Hosp.	State Avg.	U.S. Avg.
Heart Attack Care				
ACE Inhibitor or ARB for LVSD[3]	0	-	97%	96%
Aspirin at Arrival[1,3]	2	100%	99%	99%
Aspirin at Discharge[1,3]	2	100%	99%	98%
Beta Blocker at Discharge[1,3]	2	100%	99%	98%
Fibrinolytic Medication Timing[1,3]	1	0%	55%	55%
PCI Within 90 Minutes of Arrival[3]	0	-	94%	90%
Smoking Cessation Advice[3]	0	-	99%	99%
Chest Pain/Possible Heart Attack Care				
Aspirin at Arrival	82	99%	97%	95%
Median Time to ECG (minutes)	85	6	7	8
Median Time to Transfer (minutes)[5]	0	-	50	61
Fibrinolytic Medication Timing[1,3]	6	33%	58%	54%
Heart Failure Care				
ACE Inhibitor or ARB for LVSD[1]	11	82%	96%	94%
Discharge Instructions[1]	16	100%	86%	88%
Evaluation of LVS Function	30	97%	96%	98%
Smoking Cessation Advice[1]	2	100%	96%	98%
Pneumonia Care				
Appropriate Initial Antibiotic[1]	18	94%	90%	92%
Blood Culture Timing[1]	11	100%	95%	96%
Influenza Vaccine[1]	19	95%	92%	91%
Initial Antibiotic Timing	33	100%	96%	95%
Pneumococcal Vaccine	37	100%	92%	93%
Smoking Cessation Advice[1]	9	100%	95%	97%
Surgical Care Improvement Project				
Appropriate VTP Within 24 Hours[1,3]	2	50%	92%	92%
Appropriate Hair Removal[1,3]	9	100%	99%	99%
Appropriate Beta Blocker Usage[1,3]	1	0%	94%	93%
Controlled Postoperative Blood Glucose[3]	0	-	92%	93%
Prophylactic Antibiotic Timing[1,3]	6	67%	96%	97%
Prophylactic Antibiotic Timing (Outpatient)[5]	0	-	89%	92%
Prophylactic Antibiotic Selection[1,3]	6	100%	98%	97%
Prophylactic Antibiotic Select. (Outpatient)[5]	0	-	95%	94%
Prophylactic Antibiotic Stopped[1,3]	6	83%	97%	94%
Recommended VTP Ordered[1,3]	2	100%	93%	94%
Urinary Catheter Removal[1]	3	67%	90%	90%
Children's Asthma Care				
Received Systemic Corticosteroids	-	-	-	100%
Received Home Management Plan	-	-	-	71%
Received Reliever Medication	-	-	-	100%
Use of Medical Imaging				
Combination Abdominal CT Scan	95	0.011	0.100	0.191
Combination Chest CT Scan	79	0.000	0.018	0.054
Follow-up Mammogram/Ultrasound	171	9.4%	6.4%	8.4%
MRI for Low Back Pain[1]	20	80.0%	39.7%	32.7%
Survey of Patients' Hospital Experiences				
Area Around Room 'Always' Quiet at Night	(a)	65%	-	58%
Doctors 'Always' Communicated Well	(a)	86%	-	80%
Home Recovery Information Given	(a)	86%	-	82%
Hospital Given 9 or 10 on 10 Point Scale	(a)	69%	-	67%
Meds 'Always' Explained Before Given	(a)	68%	-	60%
Nurses 'Always' Communicated Well	(a)	75%	-	76%
Pain 'Always' Well Controlled	(a)	70%	-	69%
Room and Bathroom 'Always' Clean	(a)	82%	-	71%
Timely Help 'Always' Received	(a)	74%	-	64%
Would Definitely Recommend Hospital	(a)	67%	-	69%

Saint Cloud Hospital

1406 6th Ave North
Saint Cloud, MN 56303
Phone: 320-251-2700
Fax: 320-255-5711
URL: www.centracare.com
Type: Acute Care Hospitals
Emergency Services: Yes
Ownership: Voluntary Non-Profit - Church
Beds: 489

Key Personnel:
CEO/President. . . . . Craig Broman
Chief of Medical Staff . . . . Richard Jolkovsky MD
Operating Room. . . . . Larry Asplin
Pediatric Ambulatory Care . . . . . . Tom Schrup MD
Pediatric In-Patient Care . . . . Tom Schrup MD
Radiology. . . . . Mary Super
Emergency Room . . . . Jack Stinolgel DO

Measure	Cases	This Hosp.	State Avg.	U.S. Avg.
Heart Attack Care				
ACE Inhibitor or ARB for LVSD	92	93%	97%	96%
Aspirin at Arrival	213	100%	99%	99%
Aspirin at Discharge	664	100%	99%	98%
Beta Blocker at Discharge	640	99%	99%	98%
Fibrinolytic Medication Timing	0	-	55%	55%
PCI Within 90 Minutes of Arrival	62	87%	94%	90%
Smoking Cessation Advice	218	100%	99%	99%
Chest Pain/Possible Heart Attack Care				
Aspirin at Arrival[1]	12	92%	97%	95%
Median Time to ECG (minutes)[1]	13	11	7	8
Median Time to Transfer (minutes)[5]	0	-	50	61
Fibrinolytic Medication Timing[5]	0	-	58%	54%
Heart Failure Care				
ACE Inhibitor or ARB for LVSD	229	97%	96%	94%
Discharge Instructions	499	89%	86%	88%
Evaluation of LVS Function	679	100%	96%	98%
Smoking Cessation Advice	72	100%	96%	98%
Pneumonia Care				
Appropriate Initial Antibiotic	186	92%	90%	92%
Blood Culture Timing	243	96%	95%	96%
Influenza Vaccine	244	97%	92%	91%
Initial Antibiotic Timing	298	98%	96%	95%
Pneumococcal Vaccine	342	97%	92%	93%
Smoking Cessation Advice	138	100%	95%	97%
Surgical Care Improvement Project				
Appropriate VTP Within 24 Hours[2]	152	92%	92%	92%
Appropriate Hair Removal[2]	665	100%	99%	99%
Appropriate Beta Blocker Usage[2]	248	95%	94%	93%
Controlled Postoperative Blood Glucose[2]	152	88%	92%	93%
Prophylactic Antibiotic Timing[2]	461	96%	96%	97%
Prophylactic Antibiotic Timing (Outpatient)	412	89%	89%	92%
Prophylactic Antibiotic Selection[2]	476	98%	98%	97%
Prophylactic Antibiotic Select. (Outpatient)	411	95%	95%	94%
Prophylactic Antibiotic Stopped[2]	431	97%	97%	94%
Recommended VTP Ordered[2]	152	92%	93%	94%
Urinary Catheter Removal[2]	111	87%	90%	90%
Children's Asthma Care				
Received Systemic Corticosteroids	-	-	-	100%
Received Home Management Plan	-	-	-	71%
Received Reliever Medication	-	-	-	100%
Use of Medical Imaging				
Combination Abdominal CT Scan	1,399	0.026	0.100	0.191
Combination Chest CT Scan	1,472	0.003	0.018	0.054
Follow-up Mammogram/Ultrasound	1,525	6.0%	6.4%	8.4%
MRI for Low Back Pain	277	43.3%	39.7%	32.7%
Survey of Patients' Hospital Experiences				
Area Around Room 'Always' Quiet at Night	300+	62%	-	58%
Doctors 'Always' Communicated Well	300+	80%	-	80%
Home Recovery Information Given	300+	84%	-	82%
Hospital Given 9 or 10 on 10 Point Scale	300+	73%	-	67%
Meds 'Always' Explained Before Given	300+	65%	-	60%
Nurses 'Always' Communicated Well	300+	78%	-	76%
Pain 'Always' Well Controlled	300+	69%	-	69%
Room and Bathroom 'Always' Clean	300+	75%	-	71%
Timely Help 'Always' Received	300+	71%	-	64%
Would Definitely Recommend Hospital	300+	75%	-	69%

NOTE: Hospital profiles are in alphabetical order by state, then city, then hospital within the city; Rankings exclude hospitals with less than 25 cases except for patient surveys which excludes hospitals with less than 100 cases; (a) 100–299 cases; (1) The number of cases is too small to be sure how well a hospital is performing; (2) The hospital indicated that the data submitted for this measure were based on a sample of cases; (3) Data was collected during a shorter time period (fewer quarters) than the maximum possible time for this measure; (4) Suppressed for one or more quarters by CMS; (5) No data is available from the hospital for this measure; (6) Fewer than 100 patients completed the HCAHPS survey. Use these rates with caution, as the number of surveys may be too low to reliably assess hospital performance; (7) Survey results are based on less than 12 months of data; (8) Survey results are not available for this reporting period; (9) No or very few patients were eligible for the HCAHPS survey. The scores shown, if any, reflect a very small number of surveys; (10) A state average was not calculated because too few hospitals in the state submitted data; (11) There were discrepancies in the data collection process; Please refer to the User's Guide for a full explanation of data.

Saint Cloud VA Medical Center

4801 8th Street N.
Saint Cloud, MN 56303
Phone: 320-252-1670
Fax: 320-255-6426
Type: Acute Care-Veterans Administration
Emergency Services: No
Ownership: Government - Federal
Beds: 408

Key Personnel:

Chief of Medical Staff .... Susan Markstrom, MD
Radiology .... Marilyn Crandell
Ambulatory Care .... George Feyda, MD
Patient Relations .... Barry Venable

Measure	Cases	This Hosp.	State Avg.	U.S. Avg.
Heart Attack Care				
ACE Inhibitor or ARB for LVSD[5]	0	-	97%	96%
Aspirin at Arrival[5]	0	-	99%	99%
Aspirin at Discharge[5]	0	-	99%	98%
Beta Blocker at Discharge[5]	0	-	99%	98%
Fibrinolytic Medication Timing[5]	0	-	55%	55%
PCI Within 90 Minutes of Arrival[5]	0	-	94%	90%
Smoking Cessation Advice[5]	0	-	99%	99%
Chest Pain/Possible Heart Attack Care				
Aspirin at Arrival	-	-	97%	95%
Median Time to ECG (minutes)	-	-	7	8
Median Time to Transfer (minutes)	-	-	50	61
Fibrinolytic Medication Timing	-	-	58%	54%
Heart Failure Care				
ACE Inhibitor or ARB for LVSD[5]	0	-	96%	94%
Discharge Instructions[5]	0	-	86%	88%
Evaluation of LVS Function[5]	0	-	96%	98%
Smoking Cessation Advice[5]	0	-	96%	98%
Pneumonia Care				
Appropriate Initial Antibiotic[5]	0	-	90%	92%
Blood Culture Timing[5]	0	-	95%	96%
Influenza Vaccine[5]	0	-	92%	91%
Initial Antibiotic Timing[5]	0	-	96%	95%
Pneumococcal Vaccine[5]	0	-	92%	93%
Smoking Cessation Advice[5]	0	-	95%	97%
Surgical Care Improvement Project				
Appropriate VTP Within 24 Hours[2,5]	0	-	92%	92%
Appropriate Hair Removal[2,5]	0	-	99%	99%
Appropriate Beta Blocker Usage[2,5]	0	-	94%	93%
Controlled Postoperative Blood Glucose[2,5]	0	-	92%	93%
Prophylactic Antibiotic Timing[5]	0	-	96%	97%
Prophylactic Antibiotic Timing (Outpatient)	-	-	89%	92%
Prophylactic Antibiotic Selection[5]	0	-	98%	97%
Prophylactic Antibiotic Select. (Outpatient)	-	-	95%	94%
Prophylactic Antibiotic Stopped[5]	0	-	97%	94%
Recommended VTP Ordered[2,5]	0	-	93%	94%
Urinary Catheter Removal[2,5]	0	-	90%	90%
Children's Asthma Care				
Received Systemic Corticosteroids	-	-	-	100%
Received Home Management Plan	-	-	-	71%
Received Reliever Medication	-	-	-	100%
Use of Medical Imaging				
Combination Abdominal CT Scan	-	-	0.100	0.191
Combination Chest CT Scan	-	-	0.018	0.054
Follow-up Mammogram/Ultrasound	-	-	6.4%	8.4%
MRI for Low Back Pain	-	-	39.7%	32.7%
Survey of Patients' Hospital Experiences				
Area Around Room 'Always' Quiet at Night	-	-	-	58%
Doctors 'Always' Communicated Well	-	-	-	80%
Home Recovery Information Given	-	-	-	82%
Hospital Given 9 or 10 on 10 Point Scale	-	-	-	67%
Meds 'Always' Explained Before Given	-	-	-	60%
Nurses 'Always' Communicated Well	-	-	-	76%
Pain 'Always' Well Controlled	-	-	-	69%
Room and Bathroom 'Always' Clean	-	-	-	71%
Timely Help 'Always' Received	-	-	-	64%
Would Definitely Recommend Hospital	-	-	-	69%

Saint James Medical Center - Mayo Health System

1101 Moulton and Parsons Dr
Saint James, MN 56081
Phone: 507-375-3261
Fax: 507-375-8605
URL: www.stjmc.org
Type: Critical Access Hospitals
Emergency Services: Yes
Ownership: Voluntary Non-Profit - Other
Beds: 31

Key Personnel:

Infection Control .... Sue Piper
Operating Room .... Linda Winkleman
Quality Assurance .... Doug Holz
Emergency Room .... Linda Winkleman

Measure	Cases	This Hosp.	State Avg.	U.S. Avg.
Heart Attack Care				
ACE Inhibitor or ARB for LVSD[5]	0	-	97%	96%
Aspirin at Arrival[5]	0	-	99%	99%
Aspirin at Discharge[5]	0	-	99%	98%
Beta Blocker at Discharge[5]	0	-	99%	98%
Fibrinolytic Medication Timing[5]	0	-	55%	55%
PCI Within 90 Minutes of Arrival[5]	0	-	94%	90%
Smoking Cessation Advice[5]	0	-	99%	99%
Chest Pain/Possible Heart Attack Care				
Aspirin at Arrival[5]	0	-	97%	95%
Median Time to ECG (minutes)[5]	0	-	7	8
Median Time to Transfer (minutes)[5]	0	-	50	61
Fibrinolytic Medication Timing[5]	0	-	58%	54%
Heart Failure Care				
ACE Inhibitor or ARB for LVSD[1,3]	1	100%	96%	94%
Discharge Instructions[1,3]	5	60%	86%	88%
Evaluation of LVS Function[1,3]	8	75%	96%	98%
Smoking Cessation Advice[1,3]	2	50%	96%	98%
Pneumonia Care				
Appropriate Initial Antibiotic[1]	7	71%	90%	92%
Blood Culture Timing[1]	2	100%	95%	96%
Influenza Vaccine[1]	7	100%	92%	91%
Initial Antibiotic Timing[1]	3	67%	96%	95%
Pneumococcal Vaccine[1]	10	100%	92%	93%
Smoking Cessation Advice[1]	1	0%	95%	97%
Surgical Care Improvement Project				
Appropriate VTP Within 24 Hours[5]	0	-	92%	92%
Appropriate Hair Removal[5]	0	-	99%	99%
Appropriate Beta Blocker Usage[5]	0	-	94%	93%
Controlled Postoperative Blood Glucose[5]	0	-	92%	93%
Prophylactic Antibiotic Timing[5]	0	-	96%	97%
Prophylactic Antibiotic Timing (Outpatient)[5]	0	-	89%	92%
Prophylactic Antibiotic Selection[5]	0	-	98%	97%
Prophylactic Antibiotic Select. (Outpatient)[5]	0	-	95%	94%
Prophylactic Antibiotic Stopped[5]	0	-	97%	94%
Recommended VTP Ordered[5]	0	-	93%	94%
Urinary Catheter Removal[5]	0	-	90%	90%
Children's Asthma Care				
Received Systemic Corticosteroids	-	-	-	100%
Received Home Management Plan	-	-	-	71%
Received Reliever Medication	-	-	-	100%
Use of Medical Imaging				
Combination Abdominal CT Scan	46	0.043	0.100	0.191
Combination Chest CT Scan[1]	20	0.100	0.018	0.054
Follow-up Mammogram/Ultrasound	161	4.3%	6.4%	8.4%
MRI for Low Back Pain[1]	11	54.5%	39.7%	32.7%
Survey of Patients' Hospital Experiences				
Area Around Room 'Always' Quiet at Night[6]	<100	73%	-	58%
Doctors 'Always' Communicated Well[6]	<100	76%	-	80%
Home Recovery Information Given[6]	<100	70%	-	82%
Hospital Given 9 or 10 on 10 Point Scale[6]	<100	61%	-	67%
Meds 'Always' Explained Before Given[6]	<100	42%	-	60%
Nurses 'Always' Communicated Well[6]	<100	70%	-	76%
Pain 'Always' Well Controlled[6]	<100	73%	-	69%
Room and Bathroom 'Always' Clean[6]	<100	81%	-	71%
Timely Help 'Always' Received[6]	<100	71%	-	64%
Would Definitely Recommend Hospital	<100	64%	-	69%

Park Nicollet Methodist Hospital

6500 Excelsior Blvd
Saint Louis Park, MN 55426
Phone: 952-993-5000
Fax: 952-993-5936
URL: www.parknicollet.com/methodist
Type: Acute Care Hospitals
Emergency Services: Yes
Ownership: Voluntary Non-Profit - Private
Beds: 426

Key Personnel:

Infection Control .... Linell Santella
Operating Room .... Kevin Ose, MD
Pediatric In-Patient Care .... Anne Edwards, MD
Quality Assurance .... Victoria Wayne
Radiology .... Kurt Simpson, MD
Anesthesiology .... Beverlee Smiley
Emergency Room .... Rebecca Bryson
Hemotology Center .... Mark Wilkowske

Measure	Cases	This Hosp.	State Avg.	U.S. Avg.
Heart Attack Care				
ACE Inhibitor or ARB for LVSD	50	98%	97%	96%
Aspirin at Arrival	301	100%	99%	99%
Aspirin at Discharge	337	100%	99%	98%
Beta Blocker at Discharge	337	99%	99%	98%
Fibrinolytic Medication Timing	0	-	55%	55%
PCI Within 90 Minutes of Arrival	53	94%	94%	90%
Smoking Cessation Advice	82	100%	99%	99%
Chest Pain/Possible Heart Attack Care				
Aspirin at Arrival[1]	5	100%	97%	95%
Median Time to ECG (minutes)[1]	5	16	7	8
Median Time to Transfer (minutes)[5]	0	-	50	61
Fibrinolytic Medication Timing[5]	0	-	58%	54%
Heart Failure Care				
ACE Inhibitor or ARB for LVSD[2]	133	98%	96%	94%
Discharge Instructions[2]	280	91%	86%	88%
Evaluation of LVS Function[2]	386	99%	96%	98%
Smoking Cessation Advice[2]	47	100%	96%	98%
Pneumonia Care				
Appropriate Initial Antibiotic	217	92%	90%	92%
Blood Culture Timing	328	96%	95%	96%
Influenza Vaccine	325	98%	92%	91%
Initial Antibiotic Timing	350	97%	96%	95%
Pneumococcal Vaccine	457	97%	92%	93%
Smoking Cessation Advice	115	100%	95%	97%
Surgical Care Improvement Project				
Appropriate VTP Within 24 Hours[2]	187	91%	92%	92%
Appropriate Hair Removal[2]	822	100%	99%	99%
Appropriate Beta Blocker Usage[2]	328	91%	94%	93%
Controlled Postoperative Blood Glucose[2]	175	97%	92%	93%
Prophylactic Antibiotic Timing[2]	602	99%	96%	97%
Prophylactic Antibiotic Timing (Outpatient)	570	93%	89%	92%
Prophylactic Antibiotic Selection[2]	611	99%	98%	97%
Prophylactic Antibiotic Select. (Outpatient)	538	97%	95%	94%
Prophylactic Antibiotic Stopped[2]	556	98%	97%	94%
Recommended VTP Ordered[2]	192	89%	93%	94%
Urinary Catheter Removal[2]	211	79%	90%	90%
Children's Asthma Care				
Received Systemic Corticosteroids	-	-	-	100%
Received Home Management Plan	-	-	-	71%
Received Reliever Medication	-	-	-	100%
Use of Medical Imaging				
Combination Abdominal CT Scan	1,318	0.067	0.100	0.191
Combination Chest CT Scan	959	0.022	0.018	0.054
Follow-up Mammogram/Ultrasound[5]	0	-	6.4%	8.4%
MRI for Low Back Pain	300	45.0%	39.7%	32.7%
Survey of Patients' Hospital Experiences				
Area Around Room 'Always' Quiet at Night	300+	44%	-	58%
Doctors 'Always' Communicated Well	300+	75%	-	80%
Home Recovery Information Given	300+	76%	-	82%
Hospital Given 9 or 10 on 10 Point Scale	300+	54%	-	67%
Meds 'Always' Explained Before Given	300+	58%	-	60%
Nurses 'Always' Communicated Well	300+	65%	-	76%
Pain 'Always' Well Controlled	300+	64%	-	69%
Room and Bathroom 'Always' Clean	300+	57%	-	71%
Timely Help 'Always' Received	300+	51%	-	64%
Would Definitely Recommend Hospital	300+	65%	-	69%

NOTE: Hospital profiles are in alphabetical order by state, then city, then hospital within the city; Rankings exclude hospitals with less than 25 cases except for patient surveys which excludes hospitals with less than 100 cases; (a) 100–299 cases; (1) The number of cases is too small to be sure how well a hospital is performing; (2) The hospital indicated that the data submitted for this measure were based on a sample of cases; (3) Data was collected during a shorter time period (fewer quarters) than the maximum possible time for this measure; (4) Suppressed for one or more quarters by CMS; (5) No data is available from the hospital for this measure; (6) Fewer than 100 patients completed the HCAHPS survey. Use these rates with caution, as the number of surveys may be too low to reliably assess hospital performance; (7) Survey results are based on less than 12 months of data; (8) Survey results are not available for this reporting period; (9) No or very few patients were eligible for the HCAHPS survey. The scores shown, if any, reflect a very small number of surveys; (10) A state average was not calculated because too few hospitals in the state submitted data; (11) There were discrepancies in the data collection process; Please refer to the User's Guide for a full explanation of data.

Regions Hospital

640 Jackson Street
Saint Paul, MN 55101
Phone: 651-254-0975
Fax: 651-254-2836
URL: www.regionshospital.com
Type: Acute Care Hospitals
Emergency Services: Yes
Ownership: Voluntary Non-Profit - Private
Beds: 427

Key Personnel:
Chief of Medical Staff.......... Sue Freeman, MD
Operating Room.............. Emily Svendsen
Pediatric Ambulatory Care...... Thomas Rolewicz, MD
Pediatric In-Patient Care....... Thomas Rolewicz, MD
Radiology.................. Joseph Tashjiam, MD
Anesthesiology............... Greg Garbim, MD
Emergency Room............ Wayne Hass, MD
Intensive Care Unit............ Shirley Hubenette

Measure	Cases	This Hosp.	State Avg.	U.S. Avg.
Heart Attack Care				
ACE Inhibitor or ARB for LVSD	65	100%	97%	96%
Aspirin at Arrival	307	100%	99%	99%
Aspirin at Discharge	417	99%	99%	98%
Beta Blocker at Discharge	419	99%	99%	98%
Fibrinolytic Medication Timing	0	-	55%	55%
PCI Within 90 Minutes of Arrival	61	98%	94%	90%
Smoking Cessation Advice	151	100%	99%	99%
Chest Pain/Possible Heart Attack Care				
Aspirin at Arrival[1]	5	80%	97%	95%
Median Time to ECG (minutes)[1]	5	9	7	8
Median Time to Transfer (minutes)[5]	0	-	50	61
Fibrinolytic Medication Timing[5]	0	-	58%	54%
Heart Failure Care				
ACE Inhibitor or ARB for LVSD	115	99%	96%	94%
Discharge Instructions	309	93%	86%	88%
Evaluation of LVS Function	381	100%	96%	98%
Smoking Cessation Advice	95	100%	96%	98%
Pneumonia Care				
Appropriate Initial Antibiotic	165	99%	90%	92%
Blood Culture Timing	162	94%	95%	96%
Influenza Vaccine	223	95%	92%	91%
Initial Antibiotic Timing	306	96%	96%	95%
Pneumococcal Vaccine	250	98%	92%	93%
Smoking Cessation Advice	157	99%	95%	97%
Surgical Care Improvement Project				
Appropriate VTP Within 24 Hours[2]	209	86%	92%	92%
Appropriate Hair Removal[2]	692	100%	99%	99%
Appropriate Beta Blocker Usage[2]	254	93%	94%	93%
Controlled Postoperative Blood Glucose[2]	136	96%	92%	93%
Prophylactic Antibiotic Timing[2]	465	96%	96%	97%
Prophylactic Antibiotic Timing (Outpatient)	321	96%	89%	92%
Prophylactic Antibiotic Selection[2]	479	100%	98%	97%
Prophylactic Antibiotic Select. (Outpatient)	317	97%	95%	94%
Prophylactic Antibiotic Stopped[2]	447	98%	97%	94%
Recommended VTP Ordered[2]	209	92%	93%	94%
Urinary Catheter Removal[2]	180	96%	90%	90%
Children's Asthma Care				
Received Systemic Corticosteroids	-	-	-	100%
Received Home Management Plan	-	-	-	71%
Received Reliever Medication	-	-	-	100%
Use of Medical Imaging				
Combination Abdominal CT Scan	1,491	0.148	0.100	0.191
Combination Chest CT Scan	1,324	0.002	0.018	0.054
Follow-up Mammogram/Ultrasound	1,265	9.2%	6.4%	8.4%
MRI for Low Back Pain	320	56.9%	39.7%	32.7%
Survey of Patients' Hospital Experiences				
Area Around Room 'Always' Quiet at Night	300+	57%	-	58%
Doctors 'Always' Communicated Well	300+	77%	-	80%
Home Recovery Information Given	300+	85%	-	82%
Hospital Given 9 or 10 on 10 Point Scale	300+	66%	-	67%
Meds 'Always' Explained Before Given	300+	60%	-	60%
Nurses 'Always' Communicated Well	300+	74%	-	76%
Pain 'Always' Well Controlled	300+	65%	-	69%
Room and Bathroom 'Always' Clean	300+	70%	-	71%
Timely Help 'Always' Received	300+	62%	-	64%
Would Definitely Recommend Hospital	300+	71%	-	69%

Saint Joseph's Hospital

45 West 10th Street
Saint Paul, MN 55102
Phone: 651-232-3000
Fax: 651-232-3601
URL: www.stjosephs-stpaul.org
Type: Acute Care Hospitals
Emergency Services: Yes
Ownership: Voluntary Non-Profit - Private
Beds: 401

Key Personnel:
CEO/President............... Sara Criger
Infection Control.............. Luis Villar, MD
Operating Room............... Mary Jo Harrington, RN
Pediatric In-Patient Care....... James Prall, MD
Quality Assurance............ Bryan Weinzierl
Radiology................... Duane Ytredal, MD

Measure	Cases	This Hosp.	State Avg.	U.S. Avg.
Heart Attack Care				
ACE Inhibitor or ARB for LVSD	60	100%	97%	96%
Aspirin at Arrival	152	100%	99%	99%
Aspirin at Discharge	327	99%	99%	98%
Beta Blocker at Discharge	315	99%	99%	98%
Fibrinolytic Medication Timing	0	-	55%	55%
PCI Within 90 Minutes of Arrival[1]	24	100%	94%	90%
Smoking Cessation Advice	94	100%	99%	99%
Chest Pain/Possible Heart Attack Care				
Aspirin at Arrival[1,3]	2	50%	97%	95%
Median Time to ECG (minutes)[1,3]	3	7	7	8
Median Time to Transfer (minutes)[5]	0	-	50	61
Fibrinolytic Medication Timing[5]	0	-	58%	54%
Heart Failure Care				
ACE Inhibitor or ARB for LVSD	96	100%	96%	94%
Discharge Instructions	175	83%	86%	88%
Evaluation of LVS Function	234	100%	96%	98%
Smoking Cessation Advice	34	100%	96%	98%
Pneumonia Care				
Appropriate Initial Antibiotic[2]	75	92%	90%	92%
Blood Culture Timing[2]	86	98%	95%	96%
Influenza Vaccine[2]	93	95%	92%	91%
Initial Antibiotic Timing[2]	143	97%	96%	95%
Pneumococcal Vaccine[2]	136	89%	92%	93%
Smoking Cessation Advice[2]	42	100%	95%	97%
Surgical Care Improvement Project				
Appropriate VTP Within 24 Hours[2]	225	89%	92%	92%
Appropriate Hair Removal[2]	902	99%	99%	99%
Appropriate Beta Blocker Usage[2]	327	93%	94%	93%
Controlled Postoperative Blood Glucose[2]	191	93%	92%	93%
Prophylactic Antibiotic Timing[2]	698	99%	96%	97%
Prophylactic Antibiotic Timing (Outpatient)	264	95%	89%	92%
Prophylactic Antibiotic Selection[2]	707	99%	98%	97%
Prophylactic Antibiotic Select. (Outpatient)	260	95%	95%	94%
Prophylactic Antibiotic Stopped[2]	662	97%	97%	94%
Recommended VTP Ordered[2]	225	89%	93%	94%
Urinary Catheter Removal[2]	158	83%	90%	90%
Children's Asthma Care				
Received Systemic Corticosteroids	-	-	-	100%
Received Home Management Plan	-	-	-	71%
Received Reliever Medication	-	-	-	100%
Use of Medical Imaging				
Combination Abdominal CT Scan	399	0.068	0.100	0.191
Combination Chest CT Scan	273	0.011	0.018	0.054
Follow-up Mammogram/Ultrasound	683	7.6%	6.4%	8.4%
MRI for Low Back Pain	62	38.7%	39.7%	32.7%
Survey of Patients' Hospital Experiences				
Area Around Room 'Always' Quiet at Night	300+	50%	-	58%
Doctors 'Always' Communicated Well	300+	70%	-	80%
Home Recovery Information Given	300+	82%	-	82%
Hospital Given 9 or 10 on 10 Point Scale	300+	63%	-	67%
Meds 'Always' Explained Before Given	300+	52%	-	60%
Nurses 'Always' Communicated Well	300+	69%	-	76%
Pain 'Always' Well Controlled	300+	59%	-	69%
Room and Bathroom 'Always' Clean	300+	63%	-	71%
Timely Help 'Always' Received	300+	53%	-	64%
Would Definitely Recommend Hospital	300+	71%	-	69%

United Hospital

333 North Smith
Saint Paul, MN 55102
Phone: 612-298-8888
Fax: 651-241-8118
Type: Acute Care Hospitals
Emergency Services: Yes
Ownership: Voluntary Non-Profit - Private
Beds: 572

Key Personnel:
CEO/President................ Mark Mishek
Chief of Medical Staff.......... Daniel Foley, MD
Infection Control.............. Anita Romani
Operating Room............... Marnie Halligan
Quality Assurance............ Laura Rutledge
Hemotology Center........... Carol Wilcox
Intensive Care Unit........... Julianne Deutsch

Measure	Cases	This Hosp.	State Avg.	U.S. Avg.
Heart Attack Care				
ACE Inhibitor or ARB for LVSD	61	95%	97%	96%
Aspirin at Arrival	296	99%	99%	99%
Aspirin at Discharge	427	100%	99%	98%
Beta Blocker at Discharge	399	99%	99%	98%
Fibrinolytic Medication Timing	0	-	55%	55%
PCI Within 90 Minutes of Arrival	80	94%	94%	90%
Smoking Cessation Advice	134	99%	99%	99%
Chest Pain/Possible Heart Attack Care				
Aspirin at Arrival[1,3]	2	100%	97%	95%
Median Time to ECG (minutes)[1,3]	3	22	7	8
Median Time to Transfer (minutes)[5]	0	-	50	61
Fibrinolytic Medication Timing[5]	0	-	58%	54%
Heart Failure Care				
ACE Inhibitor or ARB for LVSD	168	99%	96%	94%
Discharge Instructions	372	93%	86%	88%
Evaluation of LVS Function	478	100%	96%	98%
Smoking Cessation Advice	73	99%	96%	98%
Pneumonia Care				
Appropriate Initial Antibiotic	152	95%	90%	92%
Blood Culture Timing	196	96%	95%	96%
Influenza Vaccine	203	95%	92%	91%
Initial Antibiotic Timing	201	97%	96%	95%
Pneumococcal Vaccine	245	99%	92%	93%
Smoking Cessation Advice	96	99%	95%	97%
Surgical Care Improvement Project				
Appropriate VTP Within 24 Hours[2]	159	93%	92%	92%
Appropriate Hair Removal[2]	738	100%	99%	99%
Appropriate Beta Blocker Usage[2]	257	96%	94%	93%
Controlled Postoperative Blood Glucose[2]	173	97%	92%	93%
Prophylactic Antibiotic Timing[2]	544	97%	96%	97%
Prophylactic Antibiotic Timing (Outpatient)	469	86%	89%	92%
Prophylactic Antibiotic Selection[2]	549	98%	98%	97%
Prophylactic Antibiotic Select. (Outpatient)	434	73%	95%	94%
Prophylactic Antibiotic Stopped[2]	514	96%	97%	94%
Recommended VTP Ordered[2]	159	95%	93%	94%
Urinary Catheter Removal[2]	130	90%	90%	90%
Children's Asthma Care				
Received Systemic Corticosteroids	-	-	-	100%
Received Home Management Plan	-	-	-	71%
Received Reliever Medication	-	-	-	100%
Use of Medical Imaging				
Combination Abdominal CT Scan	746	0.064	0.100	0.191
Combination Chest CT Scan	412	0.005	0.018	0.054
Follow-up Mammogram/Ultrasound	1,247	8.6%	6.4%	8.4%
MRI for Low Back Pain	109	43.1%	39.7%	32.7%
Survey of Patients' Hospital Experiences				
Area Around Room 'Always' Quiet at Night	300+	48%	-	58%
Doctors 'Always' Communicated Well	300+	75%	-	80%
Home Recovery Information Given	300+	83%	-	82%
Hospital Given 9 or 10 on 10 Point Scale	300+	63%	-	67%
Meds 'Always' Explained Before Given	300+	57%	-	60%
Nurses 'Always' Communicated Well	300+	73%	-	76%
Pain 'Always' Well Controlled	300+	66%	-	69%
Room and Bathroom 'Always' Clean	300+	63%	-	71%
Timely Help 'Always' Received	300+	61%	-	64%
Would Definitely Recommend Hospital	300+	70%	-	69%

NOTE: Hospital profiles are in alphabetical order by state, then city, then hospital within the city; Rankings exclude hospitals with less than 25 cases except for patient surveys which excludes hospitals with less than 100 cases; (a) 100–299 cases; (1) The number of cases is too small to be sure how well a hospital is performing; (2) The hospital indicated that the data submitted for this measure were based on a sample of cases; (3) Data was collected during a shorter time period (fewer quarters) than the maximum possible time for this measure; (4) Suppressed for one or more quarters by CMS; (5) No data is available from the hospital for this measure; (6) Fewer than 100 patients completed the HCAHPS survey. Use these rates with caution, as the number of surveys may be too low to reliably assess hospital performance; (7) Survey results are based on less than 12 months of data; (8) Survey results are not available for this reporting period; (9) No or very few patients were eligible for the HCAHPS survey. The scores shown, if any, reflect a very small number of surveys; (10) A state average was not calculated because too few hospitals in the state submitted data; (11) There were discrepancies in the data collection process; Please refer to the User's Guide for a full explanation of data.

River's Edge Hospital & Clinic

1900 North Sunrise Drive
Saint Peter, MN 56082
URL: www.stpeterhealth.org
Type: Critical Access Hospitals
Ownership: Government - Local
Phone: 507-931-2200
Fax: 507-934-7651
Emergency Services: Yes
Beds: 70

Key Personnel:
CEO/President. . . . . Jeanne Johnson
Chief of Medical Staff . . . . Paulette Redman
Infection Control. . . . . Jan Wimpsett
Operating Room. . . . . Joanne Hohenstein
Quality Assurance . . . . Jan Wimpsett
Intensive Care Unit. . . . . Mary Hirn

Measure	Cases	This Hosp.	State Avg.	U.S. Avg.
Heart Attack Care				
ACE Inhibitor or ARB for LVSD	0	-	97%	96%
Aspirin at Arrival[1]	5	100%	99%	99%
Aspirin at Discharge[1]	3	100%	99%	98%
Beta Blocker at Discharge[1]	3	100%	99%	98%
Fibrinolytic Medication Timing	0	-	55%	55%
PCI Within 90 Minutes of Arrival	0	-	94%	90%
Smoking Cessation Advice	0	-	99%	99%
Chest Pain/Possible Heart Attack Care				
Aspirin at Arrival	76	97%	97%	95%
Median Time to ECG (minutes)	77	5	7	8
Median Time to Transfer (minutes)[1,3]	3	36	50	61
Fibrinolytic Medication Timing	0	-	58%	54%
Heart Failure Care				
ACE Inhibitor or ARB for LVSD[1]	3	100%	96%	94%
Discharge Instructions[1]	6	33%	86%	88%
Evaluation of LVS Function[1]	12	83%	96%	98%
Smoking Cessation Advice[1]	1	100%	96%	98%
Pneumonia Care				
Appropriate Initial Antibiotic[1]	19	95%	90%	92%
Blood Culture Timing[1]	18	94%	95%	96%
Influenza Vaccine[1]	17	94%	92%	91%
Initial Antibiotic Timing[1]	22	100%	96%	95%
Pneumococcal Vaccine[1]	17	100%	92%	93%
Smoking Cessation Advice[1]	11	91%	95%	97%
Surgical Care Improvement Project				
Appropriate VTP Within 24 Hours[5]	0	-	92%	92%
Appropriate Hair Removal[5]	0	-	99%	99%
Appropriate Beta Blocker Usage[5]	0	-	94%	93%
Controlled Postoperative Blood Glucose[5]	0	-	92%	93%
Prophylactic Antibiotic Timing[5]	0	-	96%	97%
Prophylactic Antibiotic Timing (Outpatient)[1,3]	1	100%	89%	92%
Prophylactic Antibiotic Selection[5]	0	-	98%	97%
Prophylactic Antibiotic Select. (Outpatient)[1,3]	1	100%	95%	94%
Prophylactic Antibiotic Stopped[5]	0	-	97%	94%
Recommended VTP Ordered[5]	0	-	93%	94%
Urinary Catheter Removal[5]	0	-	90%	90%
Children's Asthma Care				
Received Systemic Corticosteroids	-	-	-	100%
Received Home Management Plan	-	-	-	71%
Received Reliever Medication	-	-	-	100%
Use of Medical Imaging				
Combination Abdominal CT Scan	95	0.032	0.100	0.191
Combination Chest CT Scan	74	0.000	0.018	0.054
Follow-up Mammogram/Ultrasound	251	6.0%	6.4%	8.4%
MRI for Low Back Pain[1]	13	46.2%	39.7%	32.7%
Survey of Patients' Hospital Experiences				
Area Around Room 'Always' Quiet at Night[6]	<100	75%	-	58%
Doctors 'Always' Communicated Well[6]	<100	91%	-	80%
Home Recovery Information Given[6]	<100	90%	-	82%
Hospital Given 9 or 10 on 10 Point Scale[6]	<100	86%	-	67%
Meds 'Always' Explained Before Given[6]	<100	76%	-	60%
Nurses 'Always' Communicated Well[6]	<100	86%	-	76%
Pain 'Always' Well Controlled[6]	<100	77%	-	69%
Room and Bathroom 'Always' Clean[6]	<100	92%	-	71%
Timely Help 'Always' Received[6]	<100	86%	-	64%
Would Definitely Recommend Hospital	<100	91%	-	69%

Essentia Health Sandstone

109 Court Ave South
Sandstone, MN 55072
URL: www.smdc.org
Type: Critical Access Hospitals
Ownership: Voluntary Non-Profit - Private
Phone: 320-245-5601
Fax: 320-245-2359
Emergency Services: Yes
Beds: 30

Key Personnel:
CEO/President. . . . . Michael Hendrix
Chief of Medical Staff . . . . Brian Barstad, MD
Operating Room. . . . . Mike Monzel, CRNA
Quality Assurance . . . . Katie Runquist
Emergency Room . . . . Kathy Barkhardt, RN
Patient Relations . . . . Teresa Fisher, RN

Measure	Cases	This Hosp.	State Avg.	U.S. Avg.
Heart Attack Care				
ACE Inhibitor or ARB for LVSD	0	-	97%	96%
Aspirin at Arrival[1]	3	100%	99%	99%
Aspirin at Discharge[1]	3	100%	99%	98%
Beta Blocker at Discharge[1]	3	100%	99%	98%
Fibrinolytic Medication Timing	0	-	55%	55%
PCI Within 90 Minutes of Arrival	0	-	94%	90%
Smoking Cessation Advice	0	-	99%	99%
Chest Pain/Possible Heart Attack Care				
Aspirin at Arrival[3]	25	92%	97%	95%
Median Time to ECG (minutes)[3]	26	10	7	8
Median Time to Transfer (minutes)[1,3]	3	114	50	61
Fibrinolytic Medication Timing[1,3]	3	0%	58%	54%
Heart Failure Care				
ACE Inhibitor or ARB for LVSD[1]	2	100%	96%	94%
Discharge Instructions[1]	14	36%	86%	88%
Evaluation of LVS Function[1]	22	55%	96%	98%
Smoking Cessation Advice[1]	3	100%	96%	98%
Pneumonia Care				
Appropriate Initial Antibiotic[1]	16	75%	90%	92%
Blood Culture Timing[1]	9	89%	95%	96%
Influenza Vaccine[1]	14	57%	92%	91%
Initial Antibiotic Timing[1]	19	84%	96%	95%
Pneumococcal Vaccine[1]	19	84%	92%	93%
Smoking Cessation Advice[1]	6	100%	95%	97%
Surgical Care Improvement Project				
Appropriate VTP Within 24 Hours[5]	0	-	92%	92%
Appropriate Hair Removal[5]	0	-	99%	99%
Appropriate Beta Blocker Usage[5]	0	-	94%	93%
Controlled Postoperative Blood Glucose[5]	0	-	92%	93%
Prophylactic Antibiotic Timing[5]	0	-	96%	97%
Prophylactic Antibiotic Timing (Outpatient)[1,3]	1	0%	89%	92%
Prophylactic Antibiotic Selection[5]	0	-	98%	97%
Prophylactic Antibiotic Select. (Outpatient)[1,3]	1	100%	95%	94%
Prophylactic Antibiotic Stopped[5]	0	-	97%	94%
Recommended VTP Ordered[5]	0	-	93%	94%
Urinary Catheter Removal[5]	0	-	90%	90%
Children's Asthma Care				
Received Systemic Corticosteroids	-	-	-	100%
Received Home Management Plan	-	-	-	71%
Received Reliever Medication	-	-	-	100%
Use of Medical Imaging				
Combination Abdominal CT Scan[1]	54	0.074	0.100	0.191
Combination Chest CT Scan[1]	30	0.000	0.018	0.054
Follow-up Mammogram/Ultrasound	61	3.3%	6.4%	8.4%
MRI for Low Back Pain[1]	13	46.2%	39.7%	32.7%
Survey of Patients' Hospital Experiences				
Area Around Room 'Always' Quiet at Night[8]	-	-	-	58%
Doctors 'Always' Communicated Well[8]	-	-	-	80%
Home Recovery Information Given[8]	-	-	-	82%
Hospital Given 9 or 10 on 10 Point Scale[8]	-	-	-	67%
Meds 'Always' Explained Before Given[8]	-	-	-	60%
Nurses 'Always' Communicated Well[8]	-	-	-	76%
Pain 'Always' Well Controlled[8]	-	-	-	69%
Room and Bathroom 'Always' Clean[8]	-	-	-	71%
Timely Help 'Always' Received[8]	-	-	-	64%
Would Definitely Recommend Hospital[8]	-	-	-	69%

Saint Michaels Hospital & Nursing Home

425 North Elm Street
Sauk Centre, MN 56378
E-mail: andreaf@stmichaelshospital.org
URL: www.stmichaelshospital.org
Type: Critical Access Hospitals
Ownership: Government - Local
Phone: 320-352-2221
Fax: 320-352-5150
Emergency Services: Yes
Beds: 28

Key Personnel:
CEO/President. . . . . Del Christianson
Chief of Medical Staff . . . . Keith Olson, MD
Radiology. . . . . Marie George

Measure	Cases	This Hosp.	State Avg.	U.S. Avg.
Heart Attack Care				
ACE Inhibitor or ARB for LVSD[5]	0	-	97%	96%
Aspirin at Arrival[5]	0	-	99%	99%
Aspirin at Discharge[5]	0	-	99%	98%
Beta Blocker at Discharge[5]	0	-	99%	98%
Fibrinolytic Medication Timing[5]	0	-	55%	55%
PCI Within 90 Minutes of Arrival[5]	0	-	94%	90%
Smoking Cessation Advice[5]	0	-	99%	99%
Chest Pain/Possible Heart Attack Care				
Aspirin at Arrival[5]	0	-	97%	95%
Median Time to ECG (minutes)[5]	0	-	7	8
Median Time to Transfer (minutes)[5]	0	-	50	61
Fibrinolytic Medication Timing[5]	0	-	58%	54%
Heart Failure Care				
ACE Inhibitor or ARB for LVSD[1]	1	0%	96%	94%
Discharge Instructions[1]	7	43%	86%	88%
Evaluation of LVS Function[1]	9	67%	96%	98%
Smoking Cessation Advice	0	-	96%	98%
Pneumonia Care				
Appropriate Initial Antibiotic[1]	11	73%	90%	92%
Blood Culture Timing	0	-	95%	96%
Influenza Vaccine[1]	6	83%	92%	91%
Initial Antibiotic Timing[1]	16	94%	96%	95%
Pneumococcal Vaccine[1]	17	82%	92%	93%
Smoking Cessation Advice[1]	1	100%	95%	97%
Surgical Care Improvement Project				
Appropriate VTP Within 24 Hours[5]	0	-	92%	92%
Appropriate Hair Removal[5]	0	-	99%	99%
Appropriate Beta Blocker Usage[5]	0	-	94%	93%
Controlled Postoperative Blood Glucose[5]	0	-	92%	93%
Prophylactic Antibiotic Timing[1,3]	7	57%	96%	97%
Prophylactic Antibiotic Timing (Outpatient)[5]	0	-	89%	92%
Prophylactic Antibiotic Selection[1,3]	4	100%	98%	97%
Prophylactic Antibiotic Select. (Outpatient)[5]	0	-	95%	94%
Prophylactic Antibiotic Stopped[1,3]	4	100%	97%	94%
Recommended VTP Ordered[5]	0	-	93%	94%
Urinary Catheter Removal	0	-	90%	90%
Children's Asthma Care				
Received Systemic Corticosteroids	-	-	-	100%
Received Home Management Plan	-	-	-	71%
Received Reliever Medication	-	-	-	100%
Use of Medical Imaging				
Combination Abdominal CT Scan	77	0.013	0.100	0.191
Combination Chest CT Scan	63	0.016	0.018	0.054
Follow-up Mammogram/Ultrasound	186	8.6%	6.4%	8.4%
MRI for Low Back Pain[1]	25	16.0%	39.7%	32.7%
Survey of Patients' Hospital Experiences				
Area Around Room 'Always' Quiet at Night[8]	-	-	-	58%
Doctors 'Always' Communicated Well[8]	-	-	-	80%
Home Recovery Information Given[8]	-	-	-	82%
Hospital Given 9 or 10 on 10 Point Scale[8]	-	-	-	67%
Meds 'Always' Explained Before Given[8]	-	-	-	60%
Nurses 'Always' Communicated Well[8]	-	-	-	76%
Pain 'Always' Well Controlled[8]	-	-	-	69%
Room and Bathroom 'Always' Clean[8]	-	-	-	71%
Timely Help 'Always' Received[8]	-	-	-	64%
Would Definitely Recommend Hospital[8]	-	-	-	69%

NOTE: Hospital profiles are in alphabetical order by state, then city, then hospital within the city; Rankings exclude hospitals with less than 25 cases except for patient surveys which excludes hospitals with less than 100 cases; (a) 100–299 cases; (1) The number of cases is too small to be sure how well a hospital is performing; (2) The hospital indicated that the data submitted for this measure were based on a sample of cases; (3) Data was collected during a shorter time period (fewer quarters) than the maximum possible time for this measure; (4) Suppressed for one or more quarters by CMS; (5) No data is available from the hospital for this measure; (6) Fewer than 100 patients completed the HCAHPS survey. Use these rates with caution, as the number of surveys may be too low to reliably assess hospital performance; (7) Survey results are based on less than 12 months of data; (8) Survey results are not available for this reporting period; (9) No or very few patients were eligible for the HCAHPS survey. The scores shown, if any, reflect a very small number of surveys; (10) A state average was not calculated because too few hospitals in the state submitted data; (11) There were discrepancies in the data collection process; Please refer to the User's Guide for a full explanation of data.

Saint Francis Regional Medical Center

1455 St Francis Ave
Shakopee, MN 55379
Phone: 952-403-3000
Fax: 952-403-2767
Type: Acute Care Hospitals
Emergency Services: Yes
Ownership: Voluntary Non-Profit - Church
Beds: 70

Key Personnel:
CEO/President. . . . . Michael Baumgartner
Chief of Medical Staff . . . . Matt Risken
Radiology. . . . . Norman Arslanlar
Emergency Room . . . . Matt Risken

Measure	Cases	This Hosp.	State Avg.	U.S. Avg.
Heart Attack Care				
ACE Inhibitor or ARB for LVSD	0	-	97%	96%
Aspirin at Arrival[1]	15	100%	99%	99%
Aspirin at Discharge[1]	6	100%	99%	98%
Beta Blocker at Discharge[1]	6	100%	99%	98%
Fibrinolytic Medication Timing	0	-	55%	55%
PCI Within 90 Minutes of Arrival	0	-	94%	90%
Smoking Cessation Advice[1]	2	100%	99%	99%
Chest Pain/Possible Heart Attack Care				
Aspirin at Arrival	98	100%	97%	95%
Median Time to ECG (minutes)	100	6	7	8
Median Time to Transfer (minutes)[1]	2	80	50	61
Fibrinolytic Medication Timing	0	-	58%	54%
Heart Failure Care				
ACE Inhibitor or ARB for LVSD	25	100%	96%	94%
Discharge Instructions	73	96%	86%	88%
Evaluation of LVS Function	93	99%	96%	98%
Smoking Cessation Advice[1]	11	100%	96%	98%
Pneumonia Care				
Appropriate Initial Antibiotic	100	98%	90%	92%
Blood Culture Timing	87	100%	95%	96%
Influenza Vaccine	89	99%	92%	91%
Initial Antibiotic Timing	131	100%	96%	95%
Pneumococcal Vaccine	116	100%	92%	93%
Smoking Cessation Advice	47	100%	95%	97%
Surgical Care Improvement Project				
Appropriate VTP Within 24 Hours[2]	115	90%	92%	92%
Appropriate Hair Removal[2]	478	100%	99%	99%
Appropriate Beta Blocker Usage[2]	136	94%	94%	93%
Controlled Postoperative Blood Glucose[2]	0	-	92%	93%
Prophylactic Antibiotic Timing[2]	327	97%	96%	97%
Prophylactic Antibiotic Timing (Outpatient)	106	97%	89%	92%
Prophylactic Antibiotic Selection[2]	328	99%	98%	97%
Prophylactic Antibiotic Select. (Outpatient)	103	98%	95%	94%
Prophylactic Antibiotic Stopped[2]	318	100%	97%	94%
Recommended VTP Ordered[2]	115	94%	93%	94%
Urinary Catheter Removal[2]	46	100%	90%	90%
Children's Asthma Care				
Received Systemic Corticosteroids	-	-	-	100%
Received Home Management Plan	-	-	-	71%
Received Reliever Medication	-	-	-	100%
Use of Medical Imaging				
Combination Abdominal CT Scan	525	0.044	0.100	0.191
Combination Chest CT Scan	366	0.033	0.018	0.054
Follow-up Mammogram/Ultrasound	533	3.4%	6.4%	8.4%
MRI for Low Back Pain	103	39.8%	39.7%	32.7%
Survey of Patients' Hospital Experiences				
Area Around Room 'Always' Quiet at Night	300+	67%	-	58%
Doctors 'Always' Communicated Well	300+	78%	-	80%
Home Recovery Information Given	300+	86%	-	82%
Hospital Given 9 or 10 on 10 Point Scale	300+	70%	-	67%
Meds 'Always' Explained Before Given	300+	61%	-	60%
Nurses 'Always' Communicated Well	300+	77%	-	76%
Pain 'Always' Well Controlled	300+	69%	-	69%
Room and Bathroom 'Always' Clean	300+	75%	-	71%
Timely Help 'Always' Received	300+	68%	-	64%
Would Definitely Recommend Hospital	300+	74%	-	69%

Murray County Memorial Hospital

2042 Juniper Avenue
Slayton, MN 56172
Phone: 507-836-1277
Fax: 507-836-6700
URL: www.murraycountymed.org
Type: Critical Access Hospitals
Emergency Services: Yes
Ownership: Voluntary Non-Profit - Other
Beds: 25

Key Personnel:
CEO/President. . . . . Mel Snow
Chief of Medical Staff . . . . Carol Lang, DO
Infection Control. . . . . Darlene Mechtenberg
Operating Room. . . . . Ryan Tjeerdsma, RN
Quality Assurance . . . . Karen Honermann
Radiology. . . . . Nicole Johnson
Emergency Room . . . . Barb Bergman, RN, CNO
Intensive Care Unit. . . . . Shari Achterhoff, RN CNO

Measure	Cases	This Hosp.	State Avg.	U.S. Avg.
Heart Attack Care				
ACE Inhibitor or ARB for LVSD[3]	0	-	97%	96%
Aspirin at Arrival[3]	0	-	99%	99%
Aspirin at Discharge[3]	0	-	99%	98%
Beta Blocker at Discharge[3]	0	-	99%	98%
Fibrinolytic Medication Timing[3]	0	-	55%	55%
PCI Within 90 Minutes of Arrival[3]	0	-	94%	90%
Smoking Cessation Advice[3]	0	-	99%	99%
Chest Pain/Possible Heart Attack Care				
Aspirin at Arrival[5]	0	-	97%	95%
Median Time to ECG (minutes)[5]	0	-	7	8
Median Time to Transfer (minutes)[5]	0	-	50	61
Fibrinolytic Medication Timing[5]	0	-	58%	54%
Heart Failure Care				
ACE Inhibitor or ARB for LVSD[3]	0	-	96%	94%
Discharge Instructions[1,3]	2	0%	86%	88%
Evaluation of LVS Function[1,3]	4	50%	96%	98%
Smoking Cessation Advice[3]	0	-	96%	98%
Pneumonia Care				
Appropriate Initial Antibiotic[1,2,3]	10	90%	90%	92%
Blood Culture Timing[2,3]	0	-	95%	96%
Influenza Vaccine[1,2,3]	6	50%	92%	91%
Initial Antibiotic Timing[5]	0	-	96%	95%
Pneumococcal Vaccine[1,2,3]	13	46%	92%	93%
Smoking Cessation Advice[1,2,3]	3	33%	95%	97%
Surgical Care Improvement Project				
Appropriate VTP Within 24 Hours[1,2,3]	3	100%	92%	92%
Appropriate Hair Removal[1,2,3]	18	94%	99%	99%
Appropriate Beta Blocker Usage[5]	0	-	94%	93%
Controlled Postoperative Blood Glucose[2,3]	0	-	92%	93%
Prophylactic Antibiotic Timing[1,2,3]	15	93%	96%	97%
Prophylactic Antibiotic Timing (Outpatient)[5]	0	-	89%	92%
Prophylactic Antibiotic Selection[1,2,3]	15	100%	98%	97%
Prophylactic Antibiotic Select. (Outpatient)[5]	0	-	95%	94%
Prophylactic Antibiotic Stopped[1,2,3]	15	100%	97%	94%
Recommended VTP Ordered[1,2,3]	3	100%	93%	94%
Urinary Catheter Removal[1]	9	100%	90%	90%
Children's Asthma Care				
Received Systemic Corticosteroids	-	-	-	100%
Received Home Management Plan	-	-	-	71%
Received Reliever Medication	-	-	-	100%
Use of Medical Imaging				
Combination Abdominal CT Scan	60	0.067	0.100	0.191
Combination Chest CT Scan[1]	27	0.000	0.018	0.054
Follow-up Mammogram/Ultrasound	155	6.5%	6.4%	8.4%
MRI for Low Back Pain[1]	14	14.3%	39.7%	32.7%
Survey of Patients' Hospital Experiences				
Area Around Room 'Always' Quiet at Night[8]	-	-	-	58%
Doctors 'Always' Communicated Well[8]	-	-	-	80%
Home Recovery Information Given[8]	-	-	-	82%
Hospital Given 9 or 10 on 10 Point Scale[8]	-	-	-	67%
Meds 'Always' Explained Before Given[8]	-	-	-	60%
Nurses 'Always' Communicated Well[8]	-	-	-	76%
Pain 'Always' Well Controlled[8]	-	-	-	69%
Room and Bathroom 'Always' Clean[8]	-	-	-	71%
Timely Help 'Always' Received[8]	-	-	-	64%
Would Definitely Recommend Hospital[8]	-	-	-	69%

Sleepy Eye Municipal Hospital

400 Fourth Avenue Northwest
Sleepy Eye, MN 56085
Phone: 507-794-3571
Fax: 507-794-5460
Type: Critical Access Hospitals
Emergency Services: Yes
Ownership: Government - Local
Beds: 25

Key Personnel:
Infection Control. . . . . Sandy Domeier
Operating Room. . . . . Venkata K Murthy
Quality Assurance . . . . Cheryl Reniger

Measure	Cases	This Hosp.	State Avg.	U.S. Avg.
Heart Attack Care				
ACE Inhibitor or ARB for LVSD[5]	0	-	97%	96%
Aspirin at Arrival[5]	0	-	99%	99%
Aspirin at Discharge[5]	0	-	99%	98%
Beta Blocker at Discharge[5]	0	-	99%	98%
Fibrinolytic Medication Timing[5]	0	-	55%	55%
PCI Within 90 Minutes of Arrival[5]	0	-	94%	90%
Smoking Cessation Advice[5]	0	-	99%	99%
Chest Pain/Possible Heart Attack Care				
Aspirin at Arrival[5]	0	-	97%	95%
Median Time to ECG (minutes)[5]	0	-	7	8
Median Time to Transfer (minutes)[5]	0	-	50	61
Fibrinolytic Medication Timing[5]	0	-	58%	54%
Heart Failure Care				
ACE Inhibitor or ARB for LVSD[1,3]	1	100%	96%	94%
Discharge Instructions[1,3]	11	64%	86%	88%
Evaluation of LVS Function[1,3]	17	41%	96%	98%
Smoking Cessation Advice[1,3]	1	100%	96%	98%
Pneumonia Care				
Appropriate Initial Antibiotic[1,3]	7	100%	90%	92%
Blood Culture Timing[1,3]	2	100%	95%	96%
Influenza Vaccine[1,3]	3	100%	92%	91%
Initial Antibiotic Timing[1,3]	14	93%	96%	95%
Pneumococcal Vaccine[1,3]	10	60%	92%	93%
Smoking Cessation Advice[1,3]	2	50%	95%	97%
Surgical Care Improvement Project				
Appropriate VTP Within 24 Hours[1,3]	1	100%	92%	92%
Appropriate Hair Removal[1,3]	2	100%	99%	99%
Appropriate Beta Blocker Usage[5]	0	-	94%	93%
Controlled Postoperative Blood Glucose[3]	0	-	92%	93%
Prophylactic Antibiotic Timing[1,3]	3	33%	96%	97%
Prophylactic Antibiotic Timing (Outpatient)[5]	0	-	89%	92%
Prophylactic Antibiotic Selection[1,3]	3	67%	98%	97%
Prophylactic Antibiotic Select. (Outpatient)[5]	0	-	95%	94%
Prophylactic Antibiotic Stopped[1,3]	2	100%	97%	94%
Recommended VTP Ordered[1,3]	1	100%	93%	94%
Urinary Catheter Removal	0	-	90%	90%
Children's Asthma Care				
Received Systemic Corticosteroids	-	-	-	100%
Received Home Management Plan	-	-	-	71%
Received Reliever Medication	-	-	-	100%
Use of Medical Imaging				
Combination Abdominal CT Scan	124	0.065	0.100	0.191
Combination Chest CT Scan	49	0.000	0.018	0.054
Follow-up Mammogram/Ultrasound	104	2.9%	6.4%	8.4%
MRI for Low Back Pain[1]	17	23.5%	39.7%	32.7%
Survey of Patients' Hospital Experiences				
Area Around Room 'Always' Quiet at Night[8]	-	-	-	58%
Doctors 'Always' Communicated Well[8]	-	-	-	80%
Home Recovery Information Given[8]	-	-	-	82%
Hospital Given 9 or 10 on 10 Point Scale[8]	-	-	-	67%
Meds 'Always' Explained Before Given[8]	-	-	-	60%
Nurses 'Always' Communicated Well[8]	-	-	-	76%
Pain 'Always' Well Controlled[8]	-	-	-	69%
Room and Bathroom 'Always' Clean[8]	-	-	-	71%
Timely Help 'Always' Received[8]	-	-	-	64%
Would Definitely Recommend Hospital[8]	-	-	-	69%

NOTE: Hospital profiles are in alphabetical order by state, then city, then hospital within the city; Rankings exclude hospitals with less than 25 cases except for patient surveys which excludes hospitals with less than 100 cases; (a) 100–299 cases; (1) The number of cases is too small to be sure how well a hospital is performing; (2) The hospital indicated that the data submitted for this measure were based on a sample of cases; (3) Data was collected during a shorter time period (fewer quarters) than the maximum possible time for this measure; (4) Suppressed for one or more quarters by CMS; (5) No data is available from the hospital for this measure; (6) Fewer than 100 patients completed the HCAHPS survey. Use these rates with caution, as the number of surveys may be too low to reliably assess hospital performance; (7) Survey results are based on less than 12 months of data; (8) Survey results are not available for this reporting period; (9) No or very few patients were eligible for the HCAHPS survey. The scores shown, if any, reflect a very small number of surveys; (10) A state average was not calculated because too few hospitals in the state submitted data; (11) There were discrepancies in the data collection process; Please refer to the User's Guide for a full explanation of data.

Springfield Medical Center Mayo Health System

625 North Jackson Street Phone: 507-723-6201
Springfield, MN 56087 Fax: 507-723-6447
URL: www.mayohealthsystem.org
Type: Critical Access Hospitals Emergency Services: Yes
Ownership: Government - Federal Beds: 24

Key Personnel:
Chief of Medical Staff. . . . . Margo Woodford
Infection Control. . . . . Janet Redman
Operating Room. . . . . Diane Kruse, RN
Quality Assurance . . . . Diane Kruse, RN
Radiology. . . . . David W Johnson
Anesthesiology. . . . . Fred Probe
Emergency Room . . . . Margo Woodford, RN

Measure	Cases	This Hosp.	State Avg.	U.S. Avg.
Heart Attack Care				
ACE Inhibitor or ARB for LVSD[1,3]	2	50%	97%	96%
Aspirin at Arrival[1,3]	3	67%	99%	99%
Aspirin at Discharge[1,3]	3	67%	99%	98%
Beta Blocker at Discharge[1,3]	3	100%	99%	98%
Fibrinolytic Medication Timing[3]	0	-	55%	55%
PCI Within 90 Minutes of Arrival[3]	0	-	94%	90%
Smoking Cessation Advice[3]	0	-	99%	99%
Chest Pain/Possible Heart Attack Care				
Aspirin at Arrival[1,3]	1	100%	97%	95%
Median Time to ECG (minutes)[1,3]	1	5	7	8
Median Time to Transfer (minutes)[5]	0	-	50	61
Fibrinolytic Medication Timing[5]	0	-	58%	54%
Heart Failure Care				
ACE Inhibitor or ARB for LVSD[1]	3	100%	96%	94%
Discharge Instructions[1]	15	40%	86%	88%
Evaluation of LVS Function[1]	22	86%	96%	98%
Smoking Cessation Advice[1]	2	50%	96%	98%
Pneumonia Care				
Appropriate Initial Antibiotic[1]	5	100%	90%	92%
Blood Culture Timing[1]	3	100%	95%	96%
Influenza Vaccine[1]	9	78%	92%	91%
Initial Antibiotic Timing[1]	10	100%	96%	95%
Pneumococcal Vaccine[1]	19	79%	92%	93%
Smoking Cessation Advice[1]	2	50%	95%	97%
Surgical Care Improvement Project				
Appropriate VTP Within 24 Hours[1,3]	1	0%	92%	92%
Appropriate Hair Removal[1,3]	1	100%	99%	99%
Appropriate Beta Blocker Usage[1,3]	1	100%	94%	93%
Controlled Postoperative Blood Glucose[3]	0	-	92%	93%
Prophylactic Antibiotic Timing[3]	0	-	96%	97%
Prophylactic Antibiotic Timing (Outpatient)[1,3]	3	33%	89%	92%
Prophylactic Antibiotic Selection[3]	0	-	98%	97%
Prophylactic Antibiotic Select. (Outpatient)[1,3]	2	100%	95%	94%
Prophylactic Antibiotic Stopped[3]	0	-	97%	94%
Recommended VTP Ordered[1,3]	1	0%	93%	94%
Urinary Catheter Removal[3]	0	-	90%	90%
Children's Asthma Care				
Received Systemic Corticosteroids	-	-	-	100%
Received Home Management Plan	-	-	-	71%
Received Reliever Medication	-	-	-	100%
Use of Medical Imaging				
Combination Abdominal CT Scan	56	0.054	0.100	0.191
Combination Chest CT Scan[1]	23	0.000	0.018	0.054
Follow-up Mammogram/Ultrasound	206	4.4%	6.4%	8.4%
MRI for Low Back Pain[1]	20	40.0%	39.7%	32.7%
Survey of Patients' Hospital Experiences				
Area Around Room 'Always' Quiet at Night	(a)	73%	-	58%
Doctors 'Always' Communicated Well	(a)	86%	-	80%
Home Recovery Information Given	(a)	78%	-	82%
Hospital Given 9 or 10 on 10 Point Scale	(a)	80%	-	67%
Meds 'Always' Explained Before Given	(a)	63%	-	60%
Nurses 'Always' Communicated Well	(a)	82%	-	76%
Pain 'Always' Well Controlled	(a)	69%	-	69%
Room and Bathroom 'Always' Clean	(a)	93%	-	71%
Timely Help 'Always' Received	(a)	82%	-	64%
Would Definitely Recommend Hospital	(a)	82%	-	69%

Lakewood Health System

49725 County Road 83 Phone: 218-894-1515
Staples, MN 56479 Fax: 218-894-8355
URL: www.lakewoodhealthsystem.com
Type: Critical Access Hospitals Emergency Services: Yes
Ownership: Voluntary Non-Profit - Other Beds: 140

Key Personnel:
CEO/President. . . . . Tim Rice
Chief of Medical Staff. . . . . John Halfen, MD
Quality Assurance . . . . Cindy Denning
Emergency Room . . . . Laurie Bach, MD

Measure	Cases	This Hosp.	State Avg.	U.S. Avg.
Heart Attack Care				
ACE Inhibitor or ARB for LVSD[3]	0	-	97%	96%
Aspirin at Arrival[1,3]	2	100%	99%	99%
Aspirin at Discharge[1,3]	1	100%	99%	98%
Beta Blocker at Discharge[1,3]	1	100%	99%	98%
Fibrinolytic Medication Timing[3]	0	-	55%	55%
PCI Within 90 Minutes of Arrival[3]	0	-	94%	90%
Smoking Cessation Advice[3]	0	-	99%	99%
Chest Pain/Possible Heart Attack Care				
Aspirin at Arrival	-	-	97%	95%
Median Time to ECG (minutes)	-	-	7	8
Median Time to Transfer (minutes)	-	-	50	61
Fibrinolytic Medication Timing	-	-	58%	54%
Heart Failure Care				
ACE Inhibitor or ARB for LVSD[1]	3	67%	96%	94%
Discharge Instructions[1]	16	0%	86%	88%
Evaluation of LVS Function[1]	24	54%	96%	98%
Smoking Cessation Advice[1]	3	100%	96%	98%
Pneumonia Care				
Appropriate Initial Antibiotic	34	85%	90%	92%
Blood Culture Timing	35	94%	95%	96%
Influenza Vaccine	28	43%	92%	91%
Initial Antibiotic Timing	59	88%	96%	95%
Pneumococcal Vaccine	46	61%	92%	93%
Smoking Cessation Advice[1]	12	75%	95%	97%
Surgical Care Improvement Project				
Appropriate VTP Within 24 Hours[1]	7	86%	92%	92%
Appropriate Hair Removal	65	100%	99%	99%
Appropriate Beta Blocker Usage[5]	0	-	94%	93%
Controlled Postoperative Blood Glucose	0	-	92%	93%
Prophylactic Antibiotic Timing	65	40%	96%	97%
Prophylactic Antibiotic Timing (Outpatient)	-	-	89%	92%
Prophylactic Antibiotic Selection	56	98%	98%	97%
Prophylactic Antibiotic Select. (Outpatient)	-	-	95%	94%
Prophylactic Antibiotic Stopped	55	91%	97%	94%
Recommended VTP Ordered[1]	7	86%	93%	94%
Urinary Catheter Removal[1]	2	100%	90%	90%
Children's Asthma Care				
Received Systemic Corticosteroids	-	-	-	100%
Received Home Management Plan	-	-	-	71%
Received Reliever Medication	-	-	-	100%
Use of Medical Imaging				
Combination Abdominal CT Scan	-	-	0.100	0.191
Combination Chest CT Scan	-	-	0.018	0.054
Follow-up Mammogram/Ultrasound	-	-	6.4%	8.4%
MRI for Low Back Pain	-	-	39.7%	32.7%
Survey of Patients' Hospital Experiences				
Area Around Room 'Always' Quiet at Night	300+	73%	-	58%
Doctors 'Always' Communicated Well	300+	87%	-	80%
Home Recovery Information Given	300+	87%	-	82%
Hospital Given 9 or 10 on 10 Point Scale	300+	85%	-	67%
Meds 'Always' Explained Before Given	300+	66%	-	60%
Nurses 'Always' Communicated Well	300+	85%	-	76%
Pain 'Always' Well Controlled	300+	77%	-	69%
Room and Bathroom 'Always' Clean	300+	82%	-	71%
Timely Help 'Always' Received	300+	76%	-	64%
Would Definitely Recommend Hospital	300+	88%	-	69%

Lakeview Memorial Hospital

927 West Churchill Street Phone: 651-439-5330
Stillwater, MN 55082 Fax: 651-430-4528
URL: www.lakeview.org
Type: Acute Care Hospitals Emergency Services: Yes
Ownership: Voluntary Non-Profit - Private Beds: 98

Key Personnel:
CEO/President. . . . . Doug Johnson
Chief of Medical Staff . . . . Charles W Bransford, MD
Quality Assurance . . . . Judy Bakke
Radiology. . . . . Steven D Johnson
Emergency Room . . . . Di Anne, RN

Measure	Cases	This Hosp.	State Avg.	U.S. Avg.
Heart Attack Care				
ACE Inhibitor or ARB for LVSD[1,3]	1	100%	97%	96%
Aspirin at Arrival[1,3]	6	100%	99%	99%
Aspirin at Discharge[1,3]	3	100%	99%	98%
Beta Blocker at Discharge[1,3]	4	100%	99%	98%
Fibrinolytic Medication Timing[3]	0	-	55%	55%
PCI Within 90 Minutes of Arrival[3]	0	-	94%	90%
Smoking Cessation Advice[3]	0	-	99%	99%
Chest Pain/Possible Heart Attack Care				
Aspirin at Arrival	60	92%	97%	95%
Median Time to ECG (minutes)	60	3	7	8
Median Time to Transfer (minutes)[1]	14	30	50	61
Fibrinolytic Medication Timing	0	-	58%	54%
Heart Failure Care				
ACE Inhibitor or ARB for LVSD[1]	15	100%	96%	94%
Discharge Instructions	35	97%	86%	88%
Evaluation of LVS Function	50	98%	96%	98%
Smoking Cessation Advice[1]	6	83%	96%	98%
Pneumonia Care				
Appropriate Initial Antibiotic	25	100%	90%	92%
Blood Culture Timing	31	94%	95%	96%
Influenza Vaccine[1]	19	79%	92%	91%
Initial Antibiotic Timing	45	96%	96%	95%
Pneumococcal Vaccine	27	85%	92%	93%
Smoking Cessation Advice[1]	9	89%	95%	97%
Surgical Care Improvement Project				
Appropriate VTP Within 24 Hours[2]	69	84%	92%	92%
Appropriate Hair Removal[2]	463	100%	99%	99%
Appropriate Beta Blocker Usage[2]	98	84%	94%	93%
Controlled Postoperative Blood Glucose[2]	0	-	92%	93%
Prophylactic Antibiotic Timing[2]	302	97%	96%	97%
Prophylactic Antibiotic Timing (Outpatient)	207	95%	89%	92%
Prophylactic Antibiotic Selection[2]	302	99%	98%	97%
Prophylactic Antibiotic Select. (Outpatient)	207	94%	95%	94%
Prophylactic Antibiotic Stopped[2]	295	100%	97%	94%
Recommended VTP Ordered[2]	69	87%	93%	94%
Urinary Catheter Removal[1,2]	16	88%	90%	90%
Children's Asthma Care				
Received Systemic Corticosteroids	-	-	-	100%
Received Home Management Plan	-	-	-	71%
Received Reliever Medication	-	-	-	100%
Use of Medical Imaging				
Combination Abdominal CT Scan	457	0.050	0.100	0.191
Combination Chest CT Scan	289	0.007	0.018	0.054
Follow-up Mammogram/Ultrasound	991	4.2%	6.4%	8.4%
MRI for Low Back Pain	146	45.9%	39.7%	32.7%
Survey of Patients' Hospital Experiences				
Area Around Room 'Always' Quiet at Night	300+	66%	-	58%
Doctors 'Always' Communicated Well	300+	85%	-	80%
Home Recovery Information Given	300+	89%	-	82%
Hospital Given 9 or 10 on 10 Point Scale	300+	81%	-	67%
Meds 'Always' Explained Before Given	300+	72%	-	60%
Nurses 'Always' Communicated Well	300+	84%	-	76%
Pain 'Always' Well Controlled	300+	77%	-	69%
Room and Bathroom 'Always' Clean	300+	77%	-	71%
Timely Help 'Always' Received	300+	79%	-	64%
Would Definitely Recommend Hospital	300+	84%	-	69%

NOTE: Hospital profiles are in alphabetical order by state, then city, then hospital within the city; Rankings exclude hospitals with less than 25 cases except for patient surveys which excludes hospitals with less than 100 cases; (a) 100–299 cases; (1) The number of cases is too small to be sure how well a hospital is performing; (2) The hospital indicated that the data submitted for this measure were based on a sample of cases; (3) Data was collected during a shorter time period (fewer quarters) than the maximum possible time for this measure; (4) Suppressed for one or more quarters by CMS; (5) No data is available from the hospital for this measure; (6) Fewer than 100 patients completed the HCAHPS survey. Use these rates with caution, as the number of surveys may be too low to reliably assess hospital performance; (7) Survey results are based on less than 12 months of data; (8) Survey results are not available for this reporting period; (9) No or very few patients were eligible for the HCAHPS survey. The scores shown, if any, reflect a very small number of surveys; (10) A state average was not calculated because too few hospitals in the state submitted data; (11) There were discrepancies in the data collection process; Please refer to the User's Guide for a full explanation of data.

Sanford Medical Center Thief River Falls

120 Labree Avenue South
Thief River Falls, MN 56701
Phone: 218-681-4240
Fax: 218-681-5614
E-mail: nwmc@nwmc.org
URL: www.nwmc.org
Type: Critical Access Hospitals
Emergency Services: Yes
Ownership: Proprietary
Beds: 99

Key Personnel:
CEO/President. . . . . Christine Harff
Chief of Medical Staff. . . . . Jaward Khan
Infection Control. . . . . Sharon Jorde, RN
Operating Room. . . . . Susie Koland, RN
Quality Assurance . . . . Tracy Spry

Measure	Cases	This Hosp.	State Avg.	U.S. Avg.
Heart Attack Care				
ACE Inhibitor or ARB for LVSD[1,3]	1	100%	97%	96%
Aspirin at Arrival[1,3]	5	80%	99%	99%
Aspirin at Discharge[1,3]	3	67%	99%	98%
Beta Blocker at Discharge[1,3]	4	75%	99%	98%
Fibrinolytic Medication Timing[3]	0	-	55%	55%
PCI Within 90 Minutes of Arrival[3]	0	-	94%	90%
Smoking Cessation Advice[3]	0	-	99%	99%
Chest Pain/Possible Heart Attack Care				
Aspirin at Arrival	-	-	97%	95%
Median Time to ECG (minutes)	-	-	7	8
Median Time to Transfer (minutes)	-	-	50	61
Fibrinolytic Medication Timing	-	-	58%	54%
Heart Failure Care				
ACE Inhibitor or ARB for LVSD[1]	8	88%	96%	94%
Discharge Instructions[1]	18	56%	86%	88%
Evaluation of LVS Function	40	90%	96%	98%
Smoking Cessation Advice[1]	2	100%	96%	98%
Pneumonia Care				
Appropriate Initial Antibiotic[1]	22	86%	90%	92%
Blood Culture Timing[1]	18	89%	95%	96%
Influenza Vaccine	32	84%	92%	91%
Initial Antibiotic Timing	54	98%	96%	95%
Pneumococcal Vaccine	54	83%	92%	93%
Smoking Cessation Advice[1]	8	50%	95%	97%
Surgical Care Improvement Project				
Appropriate VTP Within 24 Hours	26	85%	92%	92%
Appropriate Hair Removal	114	98%	99%	99%
Appropriate Beta Blocker Usage	31	87%	94%	93%
Controlled Postoperative Blood Glucose	0	-	92%	93%
Prophylactic Antibiotic Timing	110	91%	96%	97%
Prophylactic Antibiotic Timing (Outpatient)	-	-	89%	92%
Prophylactic Antibiotic Selection	108	94%	98%	97%
Prophylactic Antibiotic Select. (Outpatient)	-	-	95%	94%
Prophylactic Antibiotic Stopped	107	95%	97%	94%
Recommended VTP Ordered	26	85%	93%	94%
Urinary Catheter Removal	39	95%	90%	90%
Children's Asthma Care				
Received Systemic Corticosteroids	-	-	-	100%
Received Home Management Plan	-	-	-	71%
Received Reliever Medication	-	-	-	100%
Use of Medical Imaging				
Combination Abdominal CT Scan	-	-	0.100	0.191
Combination Chest CT Scan	-	-	0.018	0.054
Follow-up Mammogram/Ultrasound	-	-	6.4%	8.4%
MRI for Low Back Pain	-	-	39.7%	32.7%
Survey of Patients' Hospital Experiences				
Area Around Room 'Always' Quiet at Night	300+	61%	-	58%
Doctors 'Always' Communicated Well	300+	76%	-	80%
Home Recovery Information Given	300+	77%	-	82%
Hospital Given 9 or 10 on 10 Point Scale	300+	55%	-	67%
Meds 'Always' Explained Before Given	300+	57%	-	60%
Nurses 'Always' Communicated Well	300+	73%	-	76%
Pain 'Always' Well Controlled	300+	67%	-	69%
Room and Bathroom 'Always' Clean	300+	75%	-	71%
Timely Help 'Always' Received	300+	64%	-	64%
Would Definitely Recommend Hospital	300+	57%	-	69%

Sanford Tracy

251 Fifth Street East
Tracy, MN 56175
Phone: 507-629-3200
Fax: 507-629-3202
Type: Critical Access Hospitals
Emergency Services: Yes
Ownership: Voluntary Non-Profit - Private
Beds: 37

Key Personnel:
CEO/President. . . . . Rick Nordahl
Chief of Medical Staff. . . . . Jared Fazal, MD
Infection Control. . . . . Sue Swan, RN
Operating Room. . . . . Maggie Harp, RN
Emergency Room . . . . Becky Iverson, RN

Measure	Cases	This Hosp.	State Avg.	U.S. Avg.
Heart Attack Care				
ACE Inhibitor or ARB for LVSD[5]	0	-	97%	96%
Aspirin at Arrival[5]	0	-	99%	99%
Aspirin at Discharge[5]	0	-	99%	98%
Beta Blocker at Discharge[5]	0	-	99%	98%
Fibrinolytic Medication Timing[5]	0	-	55%	55%
PCI Within 90 Minutes of Arrival[5]	0	-	94%	90%
Smoking Cessation Advice[5]	0	-	99%	99%
Chest Pain/Possible Heart Attack Care				
Aspirin at Arrival	-	-	97%	95%
Median Time to ECG (minutes)	-	-	7	8
Median Time to Transfer (minutes)	-	-	50	61
Fibrinolytic Medication Timing	-	-	58%	54%
Heart Failure Care				
ACE Inhibitor or ARB for LVSD[1,3]	2	50%	96%	94%
Discharge Instructions[1,3]	2	50%	86%	88%
Evaluation of LVS Function[1,3]	4	50%	96%	98%
Smoking Cessation Advice[1,3]	1	100%	96%	98%
Pneumonia Care				
Appropriate Initial Antibiotic[1]	8	88%	90%	92%
Blood Culture Timing[1]	2	50%	95%	96%
Influenza Vaccine[1]	7	86%	92%	91%
Initial Antibiotic Timing[1]	16	94%	96%	95%
Pneumococcal Vaccine[1]	13	69%	92%	93%
Smoking Cessation Advice[1]	3	100%	95%	97%
Surgical Care Improvement Project				
Appropriate VTP Within 24 Hours[5]	0	-	92%	92%
Appropriate Hair Removal[5]	0	-	99%	99%
Appropriate Beta Blocker Usage[5]	0	-	94%	93%
Controlled Postoperative Blood Glucose[5]	0	-	92%	93%
Prophylactic Antibiotic Timing[5]	0	-	96%	97%
Prophylactic Antibiotic Timing (Outpatient)	-	-	89%	92%
Prophylactic Antibiotic Selection[5]	0	-	98%	97%
Prophylactic Antibiotic Select. (Outpatient)	-	-	95%	94%
Prophylactic Antibiotic Stopped[5]	0	-	97%	94%
Recommended VTP Ordered[5]	0	-	93%	94%
Urinary Catheter Removal[5]	0	-	90%	90%
Children's Asthma Care				
Received Systemic Corticosteroids	-	-	-	100%
Received Home Management Plan	-	-	-	71%
Received Reliever Medication	-	-	-	100%
Use of Medical Imaging				
Combination Abdominal CT Scan	-	-	0.100	0.191
Combination Chest CT Scan	-	-	0.018	0.054
Follow-up Mammogram/Ultrasound	-	-	6.4%	8.4%
MRI for Low Back Pain	-	-	39.7%	32.7%
Survey of Patients' Hospital Experiences				
Area Around Room 'Always' Quiet at Night[6]	<100	58%	-	58%
Doctors 'Always' Communicated Well[6]	<100	69%	-	80%
Home Recovery Information Given[6]	<100	80%	-	82%
Hospital Given 9 or 10 on 10 Point Scale[6]	<100	72%	-	67%
Meds 'Always' Explained Before Given[6]	<100	53%	-	60%
Nurses 'Always' Communicated Well[6]	<100	81%	-	76%
Pain 'Always' Well Controlled[6]	<100	50%	-	69%
Room and Bathroom 'Always' Clean[6]	<100	87%	-	71%
Timely Help 'Always' Received[6]	<100	79%	-	64%
Would Definitely Recommend Hospital	<100	75%	-	69%

Lake View Memorial Hospital

325 Eleventh Ave
Two Harbors, MN 55616
Phone: 218-834-7300
Fax: 218-834-7388
Type: Critical Access Hospitals
Emergency Services: Yes
Ownership: Voluntary Non-Profit - Private
Beds: 80

Key Personnel:
CEO/President. . . . . Brian Carlson
Chief of Medical Staff. . . . . Howard Josephs
Radiology. . . . . Terri McDannold

Measure	Cases	This Hosp.	State Avg.	U.S. Avg.
Heart Attack Care				
ACE Inhibitor or ARB for LVSD[3]	0	-	97%	96%
Aspirin at Arrival[3]	0	-	99%	99%
Aspirin at Discharge[3]	0	-	99%	98%
Beta Blocker at Discharge[3]	0	-	99%	98%
Fibrinolytic Medication Timing[3]	0	-	55%	55%
PCI Within 90 Minutes of Arrival[3]	0	-	94%	90%
Smoking Cessation Advice[3]	0	-	99%	99%
Chest Pain/Possible Heart Attack Care				
Aspirin at Arrival	-	-	97%	95%
Median Time to ECG (minutes)	-	-	7	8
Median Time to Transfer (minutes)	-	-	50	61
Fibrinolytic Medication Timing	-	-	58%	54%
Heart Failure Care				
ACE Inhibitor or ARB for LVSD[1,3]	3	33%	96%	94%
Discharge Instructions[1,3]	7	57%	86%	88%
Evaluation of LVS Function[1,3]	9	56%	96%	98%
Smoking Cessation Advice[1,3]	3	0%	96%	98%
Pneumonia Care				
Appropriate Initial Antibiotic[1]	9	67%	90%	92%
Blood Culture Timing[1]	6	67%	95%	96%
Influenza Vaccine[1]	9	100%	92%	91%
Initial Antibiotic Timing[1]	12	100%	96%	95%
Pneumococcal Vaccine[1]	11	91%	92%	93%
Smoking Cessation Advice[1]	2	0%	95%	97%
Surgical Care Improvement Project				
Appropriate VTP Within 24 Hours[5]	0	-	92%	92%
Appropriate Hair Removal[5]	0	-	99%	99%
Appropriate Beta Blocker Usage[5]	0	-	94%	93%
Controlled Postoperative Blood Glucose[5]	0	-	92%	93%
Prophylactic Antibiotic Timing[5]	0	-	96%	97%
Prophylactic Antibiotic Timing (Outpatient)	-	-	89%	92%
Prophylactic Antibiotic Selection[5]	0	-	98%	97%
Prophylactic Antibiotic Select. (Outpatient)	-	-	95%	94%
Prophylactic Antibiotic Stopped[5]	0	-	97%	94%
Recommended VTP Ordered[5]	0	-	93%	94%
Urinary Catheter Removal[5]	0	-	90%	90%
Children's Asthma Care				
Received Systemic Corticosteroids	-	-	-	100%
Received Home Management Plan	-	-	-	71%
Received Reliever Medication	-	-	-	100%
Use of Medical Imaging				
Combination Abdominal CT Scan	-	-	0.100	0.191
Combination Chest CT Scan	-	-	0.018	0.054
Follow-up Mammogram/Ultrasound	-	-	6.4%	8.4%
MRI for Low Back Pain	-	-	39.7%	32.7%
Survey of Patients' Hospital Experiences				
Area Around Room 'Always' Quiet at Night[8]	-	-	-	58%
Doctors 'Always' Communicated Well[8]	-	-	-	80%
Home Recovery Information Given[8]	-	-	-	82%
Hospital Given 9 or 10 on 10 Point Scale[8]	-	-	-	67%
Meds 'Always' Explained Before Given[8]	-	-	-	60%
Nurses 'Always' Communicated Well[8]	-	-	-	76%
Pain 'Always' Well Controlled[8]	-	-	-	69%
Room and Bathroom 'Always' Clean[8]	-	-	-	71%
Timely Help 'Always' Received[8]	-	-	-	64%
Would Definitely Recommend Hospital[8]	-	-	-	69%

NOTE: Hospital profiles are in alphabetical order by state, then city, then hospital within the city; Rankings exclude hospitals with less than 25 cases except for patient surveys which excludes hospitals with less than 100 cases; (a) 100–299 cases; (1) The number of cases is too small to be sure how well a hospital is performing; (2) The hospital indicated that the data submitted for this measure were based on a sample of cases; (3) Data was collected during a shorter time period (fewer quarters) than the maximum possible time for this measure; (4) Suppressed for one or more quarters by CMS; (5) No data is available from the hospital for this measure; (6) Fewer than 100 patients completed the HCAHPS survey. Use these rates with caution, as the number of surveys may be too low to reliably assess hospital performance; (7) Survey results are based on less than 12 months of data; (8) Survey results are not available for this reporting period; (9) No or very few patients were eligible for the HCAHPS survey. The scores shown, if any, reflect a very small number of surveys; (10) A state average was not calculated because too few hospitals in the state submitted data; (11) There were discrepancies in the data collection process; Please refer to the User's Guide for a full explanation of data.

Tyler Healthcare Center

240 Willow Street — Phone: 507-247-5521
Tyler, MN 56178 — Fax: 507-247-5972
URL: www.averamckennan.org
Type: Critical Access Hospitals — Emergency Services: Yes
Ownership: Voluntary Non-Profit - Other — Beds: 20

Key Personnel:
CEO/President. . . . . Dale Kruger
Chief of Medical Staff . . . . Ranilo Asuncion, MD
Infection Control. . . . . Stacy Fritz
Quality Assurance . . . . Laurie Johansen, RN
Emergency Room . . . . Ranilo Asuncion, RN
Patient Relations . . . . Kathe Miranowski

Measure	Cases	This Hosp.	State Avg.	U.S. Avg.
Heart Attack Care				
ACE Inhibitor or ARB for LVSD[3]	0	-	97%	96%
Aspirin at Arrival[1,3]	1	100%	99%	99%
Aspirin at Discharge[1,3]	1	100%	99%	98%
Beta Blocker at Discharge[1,3]	1	100%	99%	98%
Fibrinolytic Medication Timing[1,3]	1	0%	55%	55%
PCI Within 90 Minutes of Arrival[3]	0	-	94%	90%
Smoking Cessation Advice[3]	0	-	99%	99%
Chest Pain/Possible Heart Attack Care				
Aspirin at Arrival[1,3]	4	100%	97%	95%
Median Time to ECG (minutes)[1,3]	4	27	7	8
Median Time to Transfer (minutes)[5]	0	-	50	61
Fibrinolytic Medication Timing[5]	0	-	58%	54%
Heart Failure Care				
ACE Inhibitor or ARB for LVSD[1,2,3]	1	0%	96%	94%
Discharge Instructions[1,2,3]	1	0%	86%	88%
Evaluation of LVS Function[1,2,3]	5	60%	96%	98%
Smoking Cessation Advice[2,3]	0	-	96%	98%
Pneumonia Care				
Appropriate Initial Antibiotic[1,2]	5	60%	90%	92%
Blood Culture Timing[1,2]	3	67%	95%	96%
Influenza Vaccine[1,2]	1	100%	92%	91%
Initial Antibiotic Timing[1,2]	5	80%	96%	95%
Pneumococcal Vaccine[1,2]	4	100%	92%	93%
Smoking Cessation Advice[1,2]	3	33%	95%	97%
Surgical Care Improvement Project				
Appropriate VTP Within 24 Hours[5]	0	-	92%	92%
Appropriate Hair Removal[5]	0	-	99%	99%
Appropriate Beta Blocker Usage[5]	0	-	94%	93%
Controlled Postoperative Blood Glucose[5]	0	-	92%	93%
Prophylactic Antibiotic Timing[5]	0	-	96%	97%
Prophylactic Antibiotic Timing (Outpatient)[1,3]	1	100%	89%	92%
Prophylactic Antibiotic Selection[5]	0	-	98%	97%
Prophylactic Antibiotic Select. (Outpatient)[1,3]	1	0%	95%	94%
Prophylactic Antibiotic Stopped[5]	0	-	97%	94%
Recommended VTP Ordered[5]	0	-	93%	94%
Urinary Catheter Removal[5]	0	-	90%	90%
Children's Asthma Care				
Received Systemic Corticosteroids	-	-	-	100%
Received Home Management Plan	-	-	-	71%
Received Reliever Medication	-	-	-	100%
Use of Medical Imaging				
Combination Abdominal CT Scan	58	0.431	0.100	0.191
Combination Chest CT Scan[1]	19	0.368	0.018	0.054
Follow-up Mammogram/Ultrasound	86	10.5%	6.4%	8.4%
MRI for Low Back Pain[1]	13	30.8%	39.7%	32.7%
Survey of Patients' Hospital Experiences				
Area Around Room 'Always' Quiet at Night[6]	<100	63%	-	58%
Doctors 'Always' Communicated Well[6]	<100	79%	-	80%
Home Recovery Information Given[6]	<100	76%	-	82%
Hospital Given 9 or 10 on 10 Point Scale[6]	<100	65%	-	67%
Meds 'Always' Explained Before Given[6]	<100	44%	-	60%
Nurses 'Always' Communicated Well[6]	<100	80%	-	76%
Pain 'Always' Well Controlled[6]	<100	75%	-	69%
Room and Bathroom 'Always' Clean[6]	<100	75%	-	71%
Timely Help 'Always' Received[6]	<100	74%	-	64%
Would Definitely Recommend Hospital	<100	72%	-	69%

Virginia Regional Medical Center

901 9th St N — Phone: 218-741-3340
Virginia, MN 55792 — Fax: 218-749-9448
E-mail: marketing@vrmc.org
URL: www.vrmc.org
Type: Acute Care Hospitals — Emergency Services: Yes
Ownership: Government - Local — Beds: 83

Key Personnel:
Cardiac Laboratory. . . . . Heather Parenteau
Infection Control. . . . . Jan Jonassen
Operating Room. . . . . Linda Pogorelic
Radiology. . . . . William W Chuang
Anesthesiology. . . . . Ken Klos

Measure	Cases	This Hosp.	State Avg.	U.S. Avg.
Heart Attack Care				
ACE Inhibitor or ARB for LVSD[1]	2	100%	97%	96%
Aspirin at Arrival[1]	7	100%	99%	99%
Aspirin at Discharge[1]	6	100%	99%	98%
Beta Blocker at Discharge[1]	6	83%	99%	98%
Fibrinolytic Medication Timing	0	-	55%	55%
PCI Within 90 Minutes of Arrival	0	-	94%	90%
Smoking Cessation Advice	0	-	99%	99%
Chest Pain/Possible Heart Attack Care				
Aspirin at Arrival	93	96%	97%	95%
Median Time to ECG (minutes)	95	10	7	8
Median Time to Transfer (minutes)[1]	9	49	50	61
Fibrinolytic Medication Timing[1]	1	0%	58%	54%
Heart Failure Care				
ACE Inhibitor or ARB for LVSD[1]	11	82%	96%	94%
Discharge Instructions[1]	21	76%	86%	88%
Evaluation of LVS Function	49	96%	96%	98%
Smoking Cessation Advice[1]	3	67%	96%	98%
Pneumonia Care				
Appropriate Initial Antibiotic	36	86%	90%	92%
Blood Culture Timing[1]	22	86%	95%	96%
Influenza Vaccine	29	76%	92%	91%
Initial Antibiotic Timing	54	89%	96%	95%
Pneumococcal Vaccine	50	86%	92%	93%
Smoking Cessation Advice[1]	20	95%	95%	97%
Surgical Care Improvement Project				
Appropriate VTP Within 24 Hours[2]	65	80%	92%	92%
Appropriate Hair Removal[2]	171	100%	99%	99%
Appropriate Beta Blocker Usage[2]	58	81%	94%	93%
Controlled Postoperative Blood Glucose[2]	0	-	92%	93%
Prophylactic Antibiotic Timing[2]	128	97%	96%	97%
Prophylactic Antibiotic Timing (Outpatient)	32	97%	89%	92%
Prophylactic Antibiotic Selection[2]	130	95%	98%	97%
Prophylactic Antibiotic Select. (Outpatient)	31	97%	95%	94%
Prophylactic Antibiotic Stopped[2]	120	95%	97%	94%
Recommended VTP Ordered[2]	65	83%	93%	94%
Urinary Catheter Removal[2]	51	86%	90%	90%
Children's Asthma Care				
Received Systemic Corticosteroids	-	-	-	100%
Received Home Management Plan	-	-	-	71%
Received Reliever Medication	-	-	-	100%
Use of Medical Imaging				
Combination Abdominal CT Scan	424	0.417	0.100	0.191
Combination Chest CT Scan	276	0.014	0.018	0.054
Follow-up Mammogram/Ultrasound	231	12.6%	6.4%	8.4%
MRI for Low Back Pain	128	37.5%	39.7%	32.7%
Survey of Patients' Hospital Experiences				
Area Around Room 'Always' Quiet at Night	300+	54%	-	58%
Doctors 'Always' Communicated Well	300+	80%	-	80%
Home Recovery Information Given	300+	81%	-	82%
Hospital Given 9 or 10 on 10 Point Scale	300+	65%	-	67%
Meds 'Always' Explained Before Given	300+	60%	-	60%
Nurses 'Always' Communicated Well	300+	78%	-	76%
Pain 'Always' Well Controlled	300+	71%	-	69%
Room and Bathroom 'Always' Clean	300+	76%	-	71%
Timely Help 'Always' Received	300+	72%	-	64%
Would Definitely Recommend Hospital	300+	62%	-	69%

Saint Elizabeth Medical Center

1200 Grant Blvd W — Phone: 651-565-4531
Wabasha, MN 55981 — Fax: 651-565-2482
URL: www.stelizabethswabasha.org
Type: Critical Access Hospitals — Emergency Services: Yes
Ownership: Voluntary Non-Profit - Private — Beds: 31

Key Personnel:
CEO/President. . . . . Tom Crowley
Chief of Medical Staff . . . . Rob Taylor, DO
Operating Room. . . . . Jan Wise
Quality Assurance . . . . Tracy Henn
Emergency Room . . . . Meresa Hager

Measure	Cases	This Hosp.	State Avg.	U.S. Avg.
Heart Attack Care				
ACE Inhibitor or ARB for LVSD[1,3]	1	100%	97%	96%
Aspirin at Arrival[1,3]	2	100%	99%	99%
Aspirin at Discharge[1,3]	2	100%	99%	98%
Beta Blocker at Discharge[1,3]	2	100%	99%	98%
Fibrinolytic Medication Timing[3]	0	-	55%	55%
PCI Within 90 Minutes of Arrival[3]	0	-	94%	90%
Smoking Cessation Advice[3]	0	-	99%	99%
Chest Pain/Possible Heart Attack Care				
Aspirin at Arrival[5]	0	-	97%	95%
Median Time to ECG (minutes)[5]	0	-	7	8
Median Time to Transfer (minutes)[5]	0	-	50	61
Fibrinolytic Medication Timing[5]	0	-	58%	54%
Heart Failure Care				
ACE Inhibitor or ARB for LVSD[1]	5	100%	96%	94%
Discharge Instructions[1]	13	85%	86%	88%
Evaluation of LVS Function[1]	13	92%	96%	98%
Smoking Cessation Advice[1]	1	100%	96%	98%
Pneumonia Care				
Appropriate Initial Antibiotic[1]	13	92%	90%	92%
Blood Culture Timing[1]	12	92%	95%	96%
Influenza Vaccine[1]	7	100%	92%	91%
Initial Antibiotic Timing[1]	15	93%	96%	95%
Pneumococcal Vaccine[1]	16	94%	92%	93%
Smoking Cessation Advice[1]	1	100%	95%	97%
Surgical Care Improvement Project				
Appropriate VTP Within 24 Hours	25	96%	92%	92%
Appropriate Hair Removal	36	100%	99%	99%
Appropriate Beta Blocker Usage[5]	0	-	94%	93%
Controlled Postoperative Blood Glucose	0	-	92%	93%
Prophylactic Antibiotic Timing	31	90%	96%	97%
Prophylactic Antibiotic Timing (Outpatient)[5]	0	-	89%	92%
Prophylactic Antibiotic Selection	32	97%	98%	97%
Prophylactic Antibiotic Select. (Outpatient)[5]	0	-	95%	94%
Prophylactic Antibiotic Stopped	30	87%	97%	94%
Recommended VTP Ordered	25	96%	93%	94%
Urinary Catheter Removal[1]	14	100%	90%	90%
Children's Asthma Care				
Received Systemic Corticosteroids	-	-	-	100%
Received Home Management Plan	-	-	-	71%
Received Reliever Medication	-	-	-	100%
Use of Medical Imaging				
Combination Abdominal CT Scan	61	0.049	0.100	0.191
Combination Chest CT Scan	58	0.034	0.018	0.054
Follow-up Mammogram/Ultrasound	266	9.4%	6.4%	8.4%
MRI for Low Back Pain[1]	18	16.7%	39.7%	32.7%
Survey of Patients' Hospital Experiences				
Area Around Room 'Always' Quiet at Night	(a)	65%	-	58%
Doctors 'Always' Communicated Well	(a)	84%	-	80%
Home Recovery Information Given	(a)	85%	-	82%
Hospital Given 9 or 10 on 10 Point Scale	(a)	83%	-	67%
Meds 'Always' Explained Before Given	(a)	72%	-	60%
Nurses 'Always' Communicated Well	(a)	80%	-	76%
Pain 'Always' Well Controlled	(a)	71%	-	69%
Room and Bathroom 'Always' Clean	(a)	87%	-	71%
Timely Help 'Always' Received	(a)	84%	-	64%
Would Definitely Recommend Hospital	(a)	80%	-	69%

NOTE: Hospital profiles are in alphabetical order by state, then city, then hospital within the city; Rankings exclude hospitals with less than 25 cases except for patient surveys which excludes hospitals with less than 100 cases; (a) 100–299 cases; (1) The number of cases is too small to be sure how well a hospital is performing; (2) The hospital indicated that the data submitted for this measure were based on a sample of cases; (3) Data was collected during a shorter time period (fewer quarters) than the maximum possible time for this measure; (4) Suppressed for one or more quarters by CMS; (5) No data is available from the hospital for this measure; (6) Fewer than 100 patients completed the HCAHPS survey. Use these rates with caution, as the number of surveys may be too low to reliably assess hospital performance; (7) Survey results are based on less than 12 months of data; (8) Survey results are not available for this reporting period; (9) No or very few patients were eligible for the HCAHPS survey. The scores shown, if any, reflect a very small number of surveys; (10) A state average was not calculated because too few hospitals in the state submitted data; (11) There were discrepancies in the data collection process; Please refer to the User's Guide for a full explanation of data.

Ridgeview Medical Center

500 S Maple St
Waconia, MN 55387
Phone: 952-442-2191
Fax: 952-442-6529
E-mail: info@ridgeviewmedical.org
URL: www.ridgeviewmedical.org
Type: Acute Care Hospitals
Emergency Services: Yes
Ownership: Voluntary Non-Profit - Private
Beds: 109

Key Personnel:
CEO/President. . . . . Robert Stevens
Chief of Medical Staff . . . . Charles F Barer
Radiology. . . . . Geoffrey D Raile
Emergency Room . . . . Elizabeth Boyum

Measure	Cases	This Hosp.	State Avg.	U.S. Avg.
Heart Attack Care				
ACE Inhibitor or ARB for LVSD[1]	7	100%	97%	96%
Aspirin at Arrival	33	100%	99%	99%
Aspirin at Discharge[1]	24	96%	99%	98%
Beta Blocker at Discharge[1]	24	100%	99%	98%
Fibrinolytic Medication Timing	0	-	55%	55%
PCI Within 90 Minutes of Arrival	0	-	94%	90%
Smoking Cessation Advice[1]	3	100%	99%	99%
Chest Pain/Possible Heart Attack Care				
Aspirin at Arrival	63	92%	97%	95%
Median Time to ECG (minutes)	59	10	7	8
Median Time to Transfer (minutes)	34	42	50	61
Fibrinolytic Medication Timing	0	-	58%	54%
Heart Failure Care				
ACE Inhibitor or ARB for LVSD	34	91%	96%	94%
Discharge Instructions	68	96%	86%	88%
Evaluation of LVS Function	113	100%	96%	98%
Smoking Cessation Advice[1]	15	93%	96%	98%
Pneumonia Care				
Appropriate Initial Antibiotic	108	89%	90%	92%
Blood Culture Timing	154	97%	95%	96%
Influenza Vaccine	84	96%	92%	91%
Initial Antibiotic Timing	139	97%	96%	95%
Pneumococcal Vaccine	136	96%	92%	93%
Smoking Cessation Advice	31	100%	95%	97%
Surgical Care Improvement Project				
Appropriate VTP Within 24 Hours[2]	121	100%	92%	92%
Appropriate Hair Removal[2]	433	100%	99%	99%
Appropriate Beta Blocker Usage[2]	76	100%	94%	93%
Controlled Postoperative Blood Glucose[2]	0	-	92%	93%
Prophylactic Antibiotic Timing[2]	294	95%	96%	97%
Prophylactic Antibiotic Timing (Outpatient)	152	96%	89%	92%
Prophylactic Antibiotic Selection[2]	298	97%	98%	97%
Prophylactic Antibiotic Select. (Outpatient)	158	98%	95%	94%
Prophylactic Antibiotic Stopped[2]	294	100%	97%	94%
Recommended VTP Ordered[2]	121	100%	93%	94%
Urinary Catheter Removal[2]	56	86%	90%	90%
Children's Asthma Care				
Received Systemic Corticosteroids	-	-	-	100%
Received Home Management Plan	-	-	-	71%
Received Reliever Medication	-	-	-	100%
Use of Medical Imaging				
Combination Abdominal CT Scan	515	0.037	0.100	0.191
Combination Chest CT Scan	427	0.002	0.018	0.054
Follow-up Mammogram/Ultrasound	462	3.5%	6.4%	8.4%
MRI for Low Back Pain	147	51.0%	39.7%	32.7%
Survey of Patients' Hospital Experiences				
Area Around Room 'Always' Quiet at Night	300+	66%	-	58%
Doctors 'Always' Communicated Well	300+	80%	-	80%
Home Recovery Information Given	300+	83%	-	82%
Hospital Given 9 or 10 on 10 Point Scale	300+	79%	-	67%
Meds 'Always' Explained Before Given	300+	64%	-	60%
Nurses 'Always' Communicated Well	300+	75%	-	76%
Pain 'Always' Well Controlled	300+	66%	-	69%
Room and Bathroom 'Always' Clean	300+	83%	-	71%
Timely Help 'Always' Received	300+	69%	-	64%
Would Definitely Recommend Hospital	300+	85%	-	69%

Tri County Hospital

415 Jefferson Street North
Wadena, MN 56482
Phone: 218-631-3510
Fax: 218-631-7496
E-mail: contact@tricountyhospital.org
URL: www.tricountyhospital.org
Type: Critical Access Hospitals
Emergency Services: Yes
Ownership: Voluntary Non-Profit - Other
Beds: 49

Key Personnel:
CEO/President. . . . . Dennis Miley
Cardiac Laboratory. . . . . Lois Miller
Chief of Medical Staff . . . . Shaneen Schmidt, MD
Infection Control. . . . . Corrinne Neisess
Operating Room. . . . . Lois Lawson
Quality Assurance . . . . Kris Anderson
Radiology. . . . . Gerald McCullough

Measure	Cases	This Hosp.	State Avg.	U.S. Avg.
Heart Attack Care				
ACE Inhibitor or ARB for LVSD[1,3]	1	100%	97%	96%
Aspirin at Arrival[1,3]	5	100%	99%	99%
Aspirin at Discharge[1,3]	4	100%	99%	98%
Beta Blocker at Discharge[1,3]	5	100%	99%	98%
Fibrinolytic Medication Timing[3]	0	-	55%	55%
PCI Within 90 Minutes of Arrival[5]	0	-	94%	90%
Smoking Cessation Advice[3]	0	-	99%	99%
Chest Pain/Possible Heart Attack Care				
Aspirin at Arrival[1,3]	24	71%	97%	95%
Median Time to ECG (minutes)[3]	25	9	7	8
Median Time to Transfer (minutes)[3]	0	-	50	61
Fibrinolytic Medication Timing[3]	0	-	58%	54%
Heart Failure Care				
ACE Inhibitor or ARB for LVSD[1]	5	60%	96%	94%
Discharge Instructions	34	85%	86%	88%
Evaluation of LVS Function	50	78%	96%	98%
Smoking Cessation Advice[1]	6	83%	96%	98%
Pneumonia Care				
Appropriate Initial Antibiotic	29	86%	90%	92%
Blood Culture Timing	30	97%	95%	96%
Influenza Vaccine	41	78%	92%	91%
Initial Antibiotic Timing	74	100%	96%	95%
Pneumococcal Vaccine	57	82%	92%	93%
Smoking Cessation Advice[1]	11	91%	95%	97%
Surgical Care Improvement Project				
Appropriate VTP Within 24 Hours[1]	24	75%	92%	92%
Appropriate Hair Removal	51	100%	99%	99%
Appropriate Beta Blocker Usage[1]	11	64%	94%	93%
Controlled Postoperative Blood Glucose[5]	0	-	92%	93%
Prophylactic Antibiotic Timing[1]	20	95%	96%	97%
Prophylactic Antibiotic Timing (Outpatient)[1,3]	5	20%	89%	92%
Prophylactic Antibiotic Selection[1]	20	90%	98%	97%
Prophylactic Antibiotic Select. (Outpatient)[1,3]	12	67%	95%	94%
Prophylactic Antibiotic Stopped[1]	19	79%	97%	94%
Recommended VTP Ordered[1]	24	75%	93%	94%
Urinary Catheter Removal[1]	2	50%	90%	90%
Children's Asthma Care				
Received Systemic Corticosteroids	-	-	-	100%
Received Home Management Plan	-	-	-	71%
Received Reliever Medication	-	-	-	100%
Use of Medical Imaging				
Combination Abdominal CT Scan	196	0.051	0.100	0.191
Combination Chest CT Scan	111	0.000	0.018	0.054
Follow-up Mammogram/Ultrasound	258	4.3%	6.4%	8.4%
MRI for Low Back Pain	40	40.0%	39.7%	32.7%
Survey of Patients' Hospital Experiences				
Area Around Room 'Always' Quiet at Night	300+	60%	-	58%
Doctors 'Always' Communicated Well	300+	84%	-	80%
Home Recovery Information Given	300+	81%	-	82%
Hospital Given 9 or 10 on 10 Point Scale	300+	71%	-	67%
Meds 'Always' Explained Before Given	300+	68%	-	60%
Nurses 'Always' Communicated Well	300+	79%	-	76%
Pain 'Always' Well Controlled	300+	71%	-	69%
Room and Bathroom 'Always' Clean	300+	81%	-	71%
Timely Help 'Always' Received	300+	73%	-	64%
Would Definitely Recommend Hospital	300+	71%	-	69%

North Valley Health Center

109 South Minnesota Street
Warren, MN 56762
Phone: 218-745-4211
Fax: 218-745-4215
Type: Critical Access Hospitals
Emergency Services: Yes
Ownership: Voluntary Non-Profit - Private
Beds: 20

Key Personnel:
CEO/President. . . . . Kevin Smith
Chief of Medical Staff . . . . Judith Campbell, MD

Measure	Cases	This Hosp.	State Avg.	U.S. Avg.
Heart Attack Care				
ACE Inhibitor or ARB for LVSD[5]	0	-	97%	96%
Aspirin at Arrival[5]	0	-	99%	99%
Aspirin at Discharge[5]	0	-	99%	98%
Beta Blocker at Discharge[5]	0	-	99%	98%
Fibrinolytic Medication Timing[5]	0	-	55%	55%
PCI Within 90 Minutes of Arrival[5]	0	-	94%	90%
Smoking Cessation Advice[5]	0	-	99%	99%
Chest Pain/Possible Heart Attack Care				
Aspirin at Arrival	-	-	97%	95%
Median Time to ECG (minutes)	-	-	7	8
Median Time to Transfer (minutes)	-	-	50	61
Fibrinolytic Medication Timing	-	-	58%	54%
Heart Failure Care				
ACE Inhibitor or ARB for LVSD[1,3]	2	100%	96%	94%
Discharge Instructions[1,3]	2	50%	86%	88%
Evaluation of LVS Function[1,3]	4	50%	96%	98%
Smoking Cessation Advice[3]	0	-	96%	98%
Pneumonia Care				
Appropriate Initial Antibiotic[1,2,3]	10	90%	90%	92%
Blood Culture Timing[1,2,3]	1	100%	95%	96%
Influenza Vaccine[1,2]	13	62%	92%	91%
Initial Antibiotic Timing[1,2,3]	15	100%	96%	95%
Pneumococcal Vaccine[1,2,3]	15	20%	92%	93%
Smoking Cessation Advice[1,2,3]	2	50%	95%	97%
Surgical Care Improvement Project				
Appropriate VTP Within 24 Hours[5]	0	-	92%	92%
Appropriate Hair Removal[5]	0	-	99%	99%
Appropriate Beta Blocker Usage[5]	0	-	94%	93%
Controlled Postoperative Blood Glucose[5]	0	-	92%	93%
Prophylactic Antibiotic Timing[5]	0	-	96%	97%
Prophylactic Antibiotic Timing (Outpatient)	-	-	89%	92%
Prophylactic Antibiotic Selection[5]	0	-	98%	97%
Prophylactic Antibiotic Select. (Outpatient)	-	-	95%	94%
Prophylactic Antibiotic Stopped[5]	0	-	97%	94%
Recommended VTP Ordered[5]	0	-	93%	94%
Urinary Catheter Removal[5]	0	-	90%	90%
Children's Asthma Care				
Received Systemic Corticosteroids	-	-	-	100%
Received Home Management Plan	-	-	-	71%
Received Reliever Medication	-	-	-	100%
Use of Medical Imaging				
Combination Abdominal CT Scan	-	-	0.100	0.191
Combination Chest CT Scan	-	-	0.018	0.054
Follow-up Mammogram/Ultrasound	-	-	6.4%	8.4%
MRI for Low Back Pain	-	-	39.7%	32.7%
Survey of Patients' Hospital Experiences				
Area Around Room 'Always' Quiet at Night[8]	-	-	-	58%
Doctors 'Always' Communicated Well[8]	-	-	-	80%
Home Recovery Information Given[8]	-	-	-	82%
Hospital Given 9 or 10 on 10 Point Scale[8]	-	-	-	67%
Meds 'Always' Explained Before Given[8]	-	-	-	60%
Nurses 'Always' Communicated Well[8]	-	-	-	76%
Pain 'Always' Well Controlled[8]	-	-	-	69%
Room and Bathroom 'Always' Clean[8]	-	-	-	71%
Timely Help 'Always' Received[8]	-	-	-	64%
Would Definitely Recommend Hospital[8]	-	-	-	69%

NOTE: Hospital profiles are in alphabetical order by state, then city, then hospital within the city; Rankings exclude hospitals with less than 25 cases except for patient surveys which excludes hospitals with less than 100 cases; (a) 100–299 cases; (1) The number of cases is too small to be sure how well a hospital is performing; (2) The hospital indicated that the data submitted for this measure were based on a sample of cases; (3) Data was collected during a shorter time period (fewer quarters) than the maximum possible time for this measure; (4) Suppressed for one or more quarters by CMS; (5) No data is available from the hospital for this measure; (6) Fewer than 100 patients completed the HCAHPS survey. Use these rates with caution, as the number of surveys may be too low to reliably assess hospital performance; (7) Survey results are based on less than 12 months of data; (8) Survey results are not available for this reporting period; (9) No or very few patients were eligible for the HCAHPS survey. The scores shown, if any, reflect a very small number of surveys; (10) A state average was not calculated because too few hospitals in the state submitted data; (11) There were discrepancies in the data collection process; Please refer to the User's Guide for a full explanation of data.

Waseca Medical Center - Mayo Health System

501 North State Street | Phone: 507-835-1210
Waseca, MN 56093 | Fax: 507-837-4280
Type: Critical Access Hospitals | Emergency Services: Yes
Ownership: Voluntary Non-Profit - Private | Beds: 35

Key Personnel:
Operating Room. . . . . Marian Keller

Measure	Cases	This Hosp.	State Avg.	U.S. Avg.
Heart Attack Care				
ACE Inhibitor or ARB for LVSD[5]	0	-	97%	96%
Aspirin at Arrival[5]	0	-	99%	99%
Aspirin at Discharge[5]	0	-	99%	98%
Beta Blocker at Discharge[5]	0	-	99%	98%
Fibrinolytic Medication Timing[5]	0	-	55%	55%
PCI Within 90 Minutes of Arrival[5]	0	-	94%	90%
Smoking Cessation Advice[5]	0	-	99%	99%
Chest Pain/Possible Heart Attack Care				
Aspirin at Arrival[5]	0	-	97%	95%
Median Time to ECG (minutes)[5]	0	-	7	8
Median Time to Transfer (minutes)[5]	0	-	50	61
Fibrinolytic Medication Timing[5]	0	-	58%	54%
Heart Failure Care				
ACE Inhibitor or ARB for LVSD[1]	1	100%	96%	94%
Discharge Instructions[1]	11	73%	86%	88%
Evaluation of LVS Function[1]	12	100%	96%	98%
Smoking Cessation Advice[1]	1	100%	96%	98%
Pneumonia Care				
Appropriate Initial Antibiotic[1]	17	94%	90%	92%
Blood Culture Timing[1]	20	100%	95%	96%
Influenza Vaccine[1]	12	83%	92%	91%
Initial Antibiotic Timing[1]	11	82%	96%	95%
Pneumococcal Vaccine[1]	19	79%	92%	93%
Smoking Cessation Advice[1]	2	50%	95%	97%
Surgical Care Improvement Project				
Appropriate VTP Within 24 Hours[5]	0	-	92%	92%
Appropriate Hair Removal[5]	0	-	99%	99%
Appropriate Beta Blocker Usage[5]	0	-	94%	93%
Controlled Postoperative Blood Glucose[5]	0	-	92%	93%
Prophylactic Antibiotic Timing[5]	0	-	96%	97%
Prophylactic Antibiotic Timing (Outpatient)[5]	0	-	89%	92%
Prophylactic Antibiotic Selection[5]	0	-	98%	97%
Prophylactic Antibiotic Select. (Outpatient)[5]	0	-	95%	94%
Prophylactic Antibiotic Stopped[5]	0	-	97%	94%
Recommended VTP Ordered[5]	0	-	93%	94%
Urinary Catheter Removal[5]	0	-	90%	90%
Children's Asthma Care				
Received Systemic Corticosteroids	-	-	-	100%
Received Home Management Plan	-	-	-	71%
Received Reliever Medication	-	-	-	100%
Use of Medical Imaging				
Combination Abdominal CT Scan	102	0.127	0.100	0.191
Combination Chest CT Scan	47	0.021	0.018	0.054
Follow-up Mammogram/Ultrasound	221	6.8%	6.4%	8.4%
MRI for Low Back Pain[1]	15	26.7%	39.7%	32.7%
Survey of Patients' Hospital Experiences				
Area Around Room 'Always' Quiet at Night[6]	<100	60%	-	58%
Doctors 'Always' Communicated Well[6]	<100	78%	-	80%
Home Recovery Information Given[6]	<100	89%	-	82%
Hospital Given 9 or 10 on 10 Point Scale[6]	<100	62%	-	67%
Meds 'Always' Explained Before Given[6]	<100	69%	-	60%
Nurses 'Always' Communicated Well[6]	<100	78%	-	76%
Pain 'Always' Well Controlled[6]	<100	68%	-	69%
Room and Bathroom 'Always' Clean[6]	<100	77%	-	71%
Timely Help 'Always' Received[6]	<100	66%	-	64%
Would Definitely Recommend Hospital	<100	67%	-	69%

Sanford Westbrook Medical Center

920 Bell Avenue | Phone: 507-274-6121
Westbrook, MN 56183 | Fax: 507-274-5671
Type: Critical Access Hospitals | Emergency Services: Yes
Ownership: Voluntary Non-Profit - Private | Beds: 13

Key Personnel:
CEO/President. . . . . Rick Nordahl
Chief of Medical Staff . . . . JC Cassel, MD
Infection Control . . . . Karen Fay
Operating Room. . . . . Marna Wahl
Quality Assurance . . . . Diana Williams, RN
Emergency Room . . . . Priscilla Comnick

Measure	Cases	This Hosp.	State Avg.	U.S. Avg.
Heart Attack Care				
ACE Inhibitor or ARB for LVSD[3]	0	-	97%	96%
Aspirin at Arrival[3]	0	-	99%	99%
Aspirin at Discharge[3]	0	-	99%	98%
Beta Blocker at Discharge[3]	0	-	99%	98%
Fibrinolytic Medication Timing[3]	0	-	55%	55%
PCI Within 90 Minutes of Arrival[3]	0	-	94%	90%
Smoking Cessation Advice[3]	0	-	99%	99%
Chest Pain/Possible Heart Attack Care				
Aspirin at Arrival[5]	0	-	97%	95%
Median Time to ECG (minutes)[5]	0	-	7	8
Median Time to Transfer (minutes)[5]	0	-	50	61
Fibrinolytic Medication Timing[5]	0	-	58%	54%
Heart Failure Care				
ACE Inhibitor or ARB for LVSD[3]	0	-	96%	94%
Discharge Instructions[1,3]	1	0%	86%	88%
Evaluation of LVS Function[1,3]	4	100%	96%	98%
Smoking Cessation Advice[1,3]	1	0%	96%	98%
Pneumonia Care				
Appropriate Initial Antibiotic[1,3]	2	100%	90%	92%
Blood Culture Timing[3]	0	-	95%	96%
Influenza Vaccine[1]	2	100%	92%	91%
Initial Antibiotic Timing[1,3]	4	100%	96%	95%
Pneumococcal Vaccine[1,3]	2	100%	92%	93%
Smoking Cessation Advice[1,3]	1	100%	95%	97%
Surgical Care Improvement Project				
Appropriate VTP Within 24 Hours[5]	0	-	92%	92%
Appropriate Hair Removal[5]	0	-	99%	99%
Appropriate Beta Blocker Usage[5]	0	-	94%	93%
Controlled Postoperative Blood Glucose[5]	0	-	92%	93%
Prophylactic Antibiotic Timing[5]	0	-	96%	97%
Prophylactic Antibiotic Timing (Outpatient)[5]	0	-	89%	92%
Prophylactic Antibiotic Selection[5]	0	-	98%	97%
Prophylactic Antibiotic Select. (Outpatient)[5]	0	-	95%	94%
Prophylactic Antibiotic Stopped[5]	0	-	97%	94%
Recommended VTP Ordered[5]	0	-	93%	94%
Urinary Catheter Removal[5]	0	-	90%	90%
Children's Asthma Care				
Received Systemic Corticosteroids	-	-	-	100%
Received Home Management Plan	-	-	-	71%
Received Reliever Medication	-	-	-	100%
Use of Medical Imaging				
Combination Abdominal CT Scan[1]	18	0.333	0.100	0.191
Combination Chest CT Scan[1]	13	0.000	0.018	0.054
Follow-up Mammogram/Ultrasound	95	6.3%	6.4%	8.4%
MRI for Low Back Pain[1]	3	33.3%	39.7%	32.7%
Survey of Patients' Hospital Experiences				
Area Around Room 'Always' Quiet at Night[6]	<100	71%	-	58%
Doctors 'Always' Communicated Well[6]	<100	82%	-	80%
Home Recovery Information Given[6]	<100	84%	-	82%
Hospital Given 9 or 10 on 10 Point Scale[6]	<100	86%	-	67%
Meds 'Always' Explained Before Given[6]	<100	74%	-	60%
Nurses 'Always' Communicated Well[6]	<100	95%	-	76%
Pain 'Always' Well Controlled[6]	<100	58%	-	69%
Room and Bathroom 'Always' Clean[6]	<100	82%	-	71%
Timely Help 'Always' Received[6]	<100	87%	-	64%
Would Definitely Recommend Hospital	<100	87%	-	69%

Wheaton Community Hospital

401 12th Street North | Phone: 320-563-8226
Wheaton, MN 56296 | Fax: 320-563-8012
URL: www.wheatonhealthcare.org
Type: Critical Access Hospitals | Emergency Services: Yes
Ownership: Government - Local | Beds: 25

Key Personnel:
CEO/President. . . . . Joann Foltz
Cardiac Laboratory. . . . . Jo Ann Foltz
Chief of Medical Staff . . . . George Kuzma
Infection Control. . . . . Morgan Rinke
Radiology. . . . . Anthony Aukes
Ambulatory Care . . . . Joann Foltz
Emergency Room . . . . Donna Wahl

Measure	Cases	This Hosp.	State Avg.	U.S. Avg.
Heart Attack Care				
ACE Inhibitor or ARB for LVSD[3]	0	-	97%	96%
Aspirin at Arrival[1,3]	1	100%	99%	99%
Aspirin at Discharge[1,3]	1	100%	99%	98%
Beta Blocker at Discharge[1,3]	1	100%	99%	98%
Fibrinolytic Medication Timing[3]	0	-	55%	55%
PCI Within 90 Minutes of Arrival[3]	0	-	94%	90%
Smoking Cessation Advice[3]	0	-	99%	99%
Chest Pain/Possible Heart Attack Care				
Aspirin at Arrival[5]	0	-	97%	95%
Median Time to ECG (minutes)[5]	0	-	7	8
Median Time to Transfer (minutes)[5]	0	-	50	61
Fibrinolytic Medication Timing[5]	0	-	58%	54%
Heart Failure Care				
ACE Inhibitor or ARB for LVSD[3]	0	-	96%	94%
Discharge Instructions[3]	0	-	86%	88%
Evaluation of LVS Function[3]	0	-	96%	98%
Smoking Cessation Advice[3]	0	-	96%	98%
Pneumonia Care				
Appropriate Initial Antibiotic[1,3]	1	100%	90%	92%
Blood Culture Timing[3]	0	-	95%	96%
Influenza Vaccine[1,3]	1	100%	92%	91%
Initial Antibiotic Timing[1,3]	3	100%	96%	95%
Pneumococcal Vaccine[1,3]	5	80%	92%	93%
Smoking Cessation Advice[3]	0	-	95%	97%
Surgical Care Improvement Project				
Appropriate VTP Within 24 Hours[5]	0	-	92%	92%
Appropriate Hair Removal[5]	0	-	99%	99%
Appropriate Beta Blocker Usage[5]	0	-	94%	93%
Controlled Postoperative Blood Glucose[5]	0	-	92%	93%
Prophylactic Antibiotic Timing[5]	0	-	96%	97%
Prophylactic Antibiotic Timing (Outpatient)[5]	0	-	89%	92%
Prophylactic Antibiotic Selection[5]	0	-	98%	97%
Prophylactic Antibiotic Select. (Outpatient)[5]	0	-	95%	94%
Prophylactic Antibiotic Stopped[5]	0	-	97%	94%
Recommended VTP Ordered[5]	0	-	93%	94%
Urinary Catheter Removal[5]	0	-	90%	90%
Children's Asthma Care				
Received Systemic Corticosteroids	-	-	-	100%
Received Home Management Plan	-	-	-	71%
Received Reliever Medication	-	-	-	100%
Use of Medical Imaging				
Combination Abdominal CT Scan[1]	64	0.141	0.100	0.191
Combination Chest CT Scan[1]	28	0.179	0.018	0.054
Follow-up Mammogram/Ultrasound	162	4.3%	6.4%	8.4%
MRI for Low Back Pain[1]	15	33.3%	39.7%	32.7%
Survey of Patients' Hospital Experiences				
Area Around Room 'Always' Quiet at Night[8]	-	-	-	58%
Doctors 'Always' Communicated Well[8]	-	-	-	80%
Home Recovery Information Given[8]	-	-	-	82%
Hospital Given 9 or 10 on 10 Point Scale[8]	-	-	-	67%
Meds 'Always' Explained Before Given[8]	-	-	-	60%
Nurses 'Always' Communicated Well[8]	-	-	-	76%
Pain 'Always' Well Controlled[8]	-	-	-	69%
Room and Bathroom 'Always' Clean[8]	-	-	-	71%
Timely Help 'Always' Received[8]	-	-	-	64%
Would Definitely Recommend Hospital[8]	-	-	-	69%

NOTE: Hospital profiles are in alphabetical order by state, then city, then hospital within the city; Rankings exclude hospitals with less than 25 cases except for patient surveys which excludes hospitals with less than 100 cases; (a) 100–299 cases; (1) The number of cases is too small to be sure how well a hospital is performing; (2) The hospital indicated that the data submitted for this measure were based on a sample of cases; (3) Data was collected during a shorter time period (fewer quarters) than the maximum possible time for this measure; (4) Suppressed for one or more quarters by CMS; (5) No data is available from the hospital for this measure; (6) Fewer than 100 patients completed the HCAHPS survey. Use these rates with caution, as the number of surveys may be too low to reliably assess hospital performance; (7) Survey results are based on less than 12 months of data; (8) Survey results are not available for this reporting period; (9) No or very few patients were eligible for the HCAHPS survey. The scores shown, if any, reflect a very small number of surveys; (10) A state average was not calculated because too few hospitals in the state submitted data; (11) There were discrepancies in the data collection process; Please refer to the User's Guide for a full explanation of data.

Rice Memorial Hospital

301 Becker Ave SW
Willmar, MN 56201
E-mail: nski@rice.willmar.mn.us
URL: www.ricememorial.com
Type: Acute Care Hospitals
Ownership: Government - Local
Phone: 320-231-4227
Fax: 320-231-4869
Emergency Services: Yes
Beds: 136

Key Personnel:
CEO/President. . . . . Lawrence J Massa
Chief of Medical Staff . . . . Janae Bell, MD
Infection Control. . . . . Barb Piasecki
Operating Room. . . . . Ruth Rand
Pediatric Ambulatory Care . . . . MJ Hodapp
Quality Assurance . . . . Peggy Sietsema, RN
Radiology. . . . . DB Nguyen, MD
Intensive Care Unit. . . . . Kathy Dillox, RN

Measure	Cases	This Hosp.	State Avg.	U.S. Avg.
Heart Attack Care				
ACE Inhibitor or ARB for LVSD[1]	1	100%	97%	96%
Aspirin at Arrival[1]	19	100%	99%	99%
Aspirin at Discharge[1]	12	92%	99%	98%
Beta Blocker at Discharge[1]	14	93%	99%	98%
Fibrinolytic Medication Timing	0	-	55%	55%
PCI Within 90 Minutes of Arrival	0	-	94%	90%
Smoking Cessation Advice	0	-	99%	99%
Chest Pain/Possible Heart Attack Care				
Aspirin at Arrival	75	97%	97%	95%
Median Time to ECG (minutes)	77	8	7	8
Median Time to Transfer (minutes)[1]	9	56	50	61
Fibrinolytic Medication Timing	0	-	58%	54%
Heart Failure Care				
ACE Inhibitor or ARB for LVSD[1]	17	82%	96%	94%
Discharge Instructions	36	83%	86%	88%
Evaluation of LVS Function	58	97%	96%	98%
Smoking Cessation Advice[1]	4	75%	96%	98%
Pneumonia Care				
Appropriate Initial Antibiotic	69	88%	90%	92%
Blood Culture Timing	86	97%	95%	96%
Influenza Vaccine	70	94%	92%	91%
Initial Antibiotic Timing	117	98%	96%	95%
Pneumococcal Vaccine	127	91%	92%	93%
Smoking Cessation Advice[1]	19	89%	95%	97%
Surgical Care Improvement Project				
Appropriate VTP Within 24 Hours[2]	104	90%	92%	92%
Appropriate Hair Removal[2]	274	100%	99%	99%
Appropriate Beta Blocker Usage[2]	63	84%	94%	93%
Controlled Postoperative Blood Glucose[2]	0	-	92%	93%
Prophylactic Antibiotic Timing[2]	201	89%	96%	97%
Prophylactic Antibiotic Timing (Outpatient)	73	79%	89%	92%
Prophylactic Antibiotic Selection[2]	199	97%	98%	97%
Prophylactic Antibiotic Select. (Outpatient)	66	95%	95%	94%
Prophylactic Antibiotic Stopped[2]	195	97%	97%	94%
Recommended VTP Ordered[2]	104	93%	93%	94%
Urinary Catheter Removal[2]	85	84%	90%	90%
Children's Asthma Care				
Received Systemic Corticosteroids	-	-	-	100%
Received Home Management Plan	-	-	-	71%
Received Reliever Medication	-	-	-	100%
Use of Medical Imaging				
Combination Abdominal CT Scan	148	0.054	0.100	0.191
Combination Chest CT Scan	77	0.000	0.018	0.054
Follow-up Mammogram/Ultrasound	222	2.7%	6.4%	8.4%
MRI for Low Back Pain[1]	24	45.8%	39.7%	32.7%
Survey of Patients' Hospital Experiences				
Area Around Room 'Always' Quiet at Night	300+	66%	-	58%
Doctors 'Always' Communicated Well	300+	82%	-	80%
Home Recovery Information Given	300+	86%	-	82%
Hospital Given 9 or 10 on 10 Point Scale	300+	71%	-	67%
Meds 'Always' Explained Before Given	300+	64%	-	60%
Nurses 'Always' Communicated Well	300+	77%	-	76%
Pain 'Always' Well Controlled	300+	70%	-	69%
Room and Bathroom 'Always' Clean	300+	73%	-	71%
Timely Help 'Always' Received	300+	71%	-	64%
Would Definitely Recommend Hospital	300+	71%	-	69%

Windom Area Hospital

2150 Hospital Drive
Windom, MN 56101
E-mail: contactus@windomareahospital.com
URL: www.windomareahospital.com
Type: Critical Access Hospitals
Ownership: Voluntary Non-Profit - Other
Phone: 507-831-2400
Fax: 507-831-5749
Emergency Services: Yes
Beds: 35

Key Personnel:
CEO/President. . . . . Gerri Burmeister
Chief of Medical Staff . . . . Rod Dynes, MD
Infection Control. . . . . Marcia Fast, RN
Operating Room. . . . . Nancy Jenson, RN
Quality Assurance . . . . Marcia Fast, RN
Anesthesiology. . . . . Loretta Krahn, CRNA
Emergency Room . . . . Jeffery Taber, RN

Measure	Cases	This Hosp.	State Avg.	U.S. Avg.
Heart Attack Care				
ACE Inhibitor or ARB for LVSD[3]	0	-	97%	96%
Aspirin at Arrival[1,3]	2	100%	99%	99%
Aspirin at Discharge[1,3]	2	100%	99%	98%
Beta Blocker at Discharge[1,3]	2	100%	99%	98%
Fibrinolytic Medication Timing[1,3]	1	0%	55%	55%
PCI Within 90 Minutes of Arrival[3]	0	-	94%	90%
Smoking Cessation Advice[3]	0	-	99%	99%
Chest Pain/Possible Heart Attack Care				
Aspirin at Arrival	36	100%	97%	95%
Median Time to ECG (minutes)	37	19	7	8
Median Time to Transfer (minutes)[5]	0	-	50	61
Fibrinolytic Medication Timing[1]	1	0%	58%	54%
Heart Failure Care				
ACE Inhibitor or ARB for LVSD[1]	8	88%	96%	94%
Discharge Instructions[1]	15	73%	86%	88%
Evaluation of LVS Function[1]	21	52%	96%	98%
Smoking Cessation Advice[1]	3	67%	96%	98%
Pneumonia Care				
Appropriate Initial Antibiotic[1]	5	100%	90%	92%
Blood Culture Timing[1]	5	100%	95%	96%
Influenza Vaccine[1]	5	100%	92%	91%
Initial Antibiotic Timing[1]	7	100%	96%	95%
Pneumococcal Vaccine[1]	7	100%	92%	93%
Smoking Cessation Advice[1]	1	0%	95%	97%
Surgical Care Improvement Project				
Appropriate VTP Within 24 Hours[5]	0	-	92%	92%
Appropriate Hair Removal[5]	0	-	99%	99%
Appropriate Beta Blocker Usage[5]	0	-	94%	93%
Controlled Postoperative Blood Glucose[5]	0	-	92%	93%
Prophylactic Antibiotic Timing[5]	0	-	96%	97%
Prophylactic Antibiotic Timing (Outpatient)[5]	0	-	89%	92%
Prophylactic Antibiotic Selection[5]	0	-	98%	97%
Prophylactic Antibiotic Select. (Outpatient)[5]	0	-	95%	94%
Prophylactic Antibiotic Stopped[5]	0	-	97%	94%
Recommended VTP Ordered[5]	0	-	93%	94%
Urinary Catheter Removal[5]	0	-	90%	90%
Children's Asthma Care				
Received Systemic Corticosteroids	-	-	-	100%
Received Home Management Plan	-	-	-	71%
Received Reliever Medication	-	-	-	100%
Use of Medical Imaging				
Combination Abdominal CT Scan	100	0.040	0.100	0.191
Combination Chest CT Scan	47	0.043	0.018	0.054
Follow-up Mammogram/Ultrasound	129	13.2%	6.4%	8.4%
MRI for Low Back Pain[1]	22	45.5%	39.7%	32.7%
Survey of Patients' Hospital Experiences				
Area Around Room 'Always' Quiet at Night	(a)	65%	-	58%
Doctors 'Always' Communicated Well	(a)	84%	-	80%
Home Recovery Information Given	(a)	80%	-	82%
Hospital Given 9 or 10 on 10 Point Scale	(a)	72%	-	67%
Meds 'Always' Explained Before Given	(a)	61%	-	60%
Nurses 'Always' Communicated Well	(a)	84%	-	76%
Pain 'Always' Well Controlled	(a)	69%	-	69%
Room and Bathroom 'Always' Clean	(a)	84%	-	71%
Timely Help 'Always' Received	(a)	74%	-	64%
Would Definitely Recommend Hospital	(a)	75%	-	69%

Winona Health Services

855 Mankato Avenue
Winona, MN 55987
URL: www.winonahealth.org
Type: Acute Care Hospitals
Ownership: Voluntary Non-Profit - Private
Phone: 507-454-3650
Fax: 507-457-4413
Emergency Services: Yes
Beds: 99

Key Personnel:
CEO/President. . . . . Rachelle Schultz
Chief of Medical Staff . . . . Charles Shepard
Coronary Care . . . . Kathleen Lanik
Infection Control. . . . . Linda Pozanc
Quality Assurance . . . . Kathleen Lanik
Radiology. . . . . Laurel Littrell, MD

Measure	Cases	This Hosp.	State Avg.	U.S. Avg.
Heart Attack Care				
ACE Inhibitor or ARB for LVSD[1]	3	100%	97%	96%
Aspirin at Arrival[1]	20	95%	99%	99%
Aspirin at Discharge[1]	14	93%	99%	98%
Beta Blocker at Discharge[1]	14	100%	99%	98%
Fibrinolytic Medication Timing	0	-	55%	55%
PCI Within 90 Minutes of Arrival	0	-	94%	90%
Smoking Cessation Advice	0	-	99%	99%
Chest Pain/Possible Heart Attack Care				
Aspirin at Arrival	90	99%	97%	95%
Median Time to ECG (minutes)	95	6	7	8
Median Time to Transfer (minutes)[1]	1	40	50	61
Fibrinolytic Medication Timing[1]	3	100%	58%	54%
Heart Failure Care				
ACE Inhibitor or ARB for LVSD	25	100%	96%	94%
Discharge Instructions	49	90%	86%	88%
Evaluation of LVS Function	82	100%	96%	98%
Smoking Cessation Advice[1]	12	100%	96%	98%
Pneumonia Care				
Appropriate Initial Antibiotic	66	91%	90%	92%
Blood Culture Timing	108	98%	95%	96%
Influenza Vaccine	73	99%	92%	91%
Initial Antibiotic Timing	106	100%	96%	95%
Pneumococcal Vaccine	109	99%	92%	93%
Smoking Cessation Advice	32	100%	95%	97%
Surgical Care Improvement Project				
Appropriate VTP Within 24 Hours	75	92%	92%	92%
Appropriate Hair Removal	176	100%	99%	99%
Appropriate Beta Blocker Usage	52	100%	94%	93%
Controlled Postoperative Blood Glucose	0	-	92%	93%
Prophylactic Antibiotic Timing	133	98%	96%	97%
Prophylactic Antibiotic Timing (Outpatient)	71	92%	89%	92%
Prophylactic Antibiotic Selection	133	88%	98%	97%
Prophylactic Antibiotic Select. (Outpatient)	92	93%	95%	94%
Prophylactic Antibiotic Stopped	131	92%	97%	94%
Recommended VTP Ordered	75	92%	93%	94%
Urinary Catheter Removal	40	80%	90%	90%
Children's Asthma Care				
Received Systemic Corticosteroids	-	-	-	100%
Received Home Management Plan	-	-	-	71%
Received Reliever Medication	-	-	-	100%
Use of Medical Imaging				
Combination Abdominal CT Scan	245	0.069	0.100	0.191
Combination Chest CT Scan	122	0.041	0.018	0.054
Follow-up Mammogram/Ultrasound	677	3.5%	6.4%	8.4%
MRI for Low Back Pain	44	47.7%	39.7%	32.7%
Survey of Patients' Hospital Experiences				
Area Around Room 'Always' Quiet at Night	300+	54%	-	58%
Doctors 'Always' Communicated Well	300+	79%	-	80%
Home Recovery Information Given	300+	82%	-	82%
Hospital Given 9 or 10 on 10 Point Scale	300+	61%	-	67%
Meds 'Always' Explained Before Given	300+	55%	-	60%
Nurses 'Always' Communicated Well	300+	73%	-	76%
Pain 'Always' Well Controlled	300+	63%	-	69%
Room and Bathroom 'Always' Clean	300+	71%	-	71%
Timely Help 'Always' Received	300+	64%	-	64%
Would Definitely Recommend Hospital	300+	65%	-	69%

NOTE: Hospital profiles are in alphabetical order by state, then city, then hospital within the city; Rankings exclude hospitals with less than 25 cases except for patient surveys which excludes hospitals with less than 100 cases; (a) 100–299 cases; (1) The number of cases is too small to be sure how well a hospital is performing; (2) The hospital indicated that the data submitted for this measure were based on a sample of cases; (3) Data was collected during a shorter time period (fewer quarters) than the maximum possible time for this measure; (4) Suppressed for one or more quarters by CMS; (5) No data is available from the hospital for this measure; (6) Fewer than 100 patients completed the HCAHPS survey. Use these rates with caution, as the number of surveys may be too low to reliably assess hospital performance; (7) Survey results are based on less than 12 months of data; (8) Survey results are not available for this reporting period; (9) No or very few patients were eligible for the HCAHPS survey. The scores shown, if any, reflect a very small number of surveys; (10) A state average was not calculated because too few hospitals in the state submitted data; (11) There were discrepancies in the data collection process; Please refer to the User's Guide for a full explanation of data.

Healtheast Woodwinds Hospital

1925 Woodwinds Drive Phone: 651-232-6880
Woodbury, MN 55125 Fax: 651-232-2551
URL: www.woodwinds.org
Type: Acute Care Hospitals Emergency Services: Yes
Ownership: Voluntary Non-Profit - Private Beds: 78
Key Personnel:
CEO/President. . . . . Julie Schmidt
Chief of Medical Staff . . . . Lynne Lillie, MD

Measure	Cases	This Hosp.	State Avg.	U.S. Avg.
Heart Attack Care				
ACE Inhibitor or ARB for LVSD[1]	2	100%	97%	96%
Aspirin at Arrival[1]	20	100%	99%	99%
Aspirin at Discharge[1]	8	100%	99%	98%
Beta Blocker at Discharge[1]	6	100%	99%	98%
Fibrinolytic Medication Timing	0	-	55%	55%
PCI Within 90 Minutes of Arrival	0	-	94%	90%
Smoking Cessation Advice[1]	1	100%	99%	99%
Chest Pain/Possible Heart Attack Care				
Aspirin at Arrival	81	96%	97%	95%
Median Time to ECG (minutes)	81	6	7	8
Median Time to Transfer (minutes)[1]	19	55	50	61
Fibrinolytic Medication Timing[1]	1	100%	58%	54%
Heart Failure Care				
ACE Inhibitor or ARB for LVSD	26	88%	96%	94%
Discharge Instructions	78	81%	86%	88%
Evaluation of LVS Function	100	98%	96%	98%
Smoking Cessation Advice[1]	15	100%	96%	98%
Pneumonia Care				
Appropriate Initial Antibiotic	79	94%	90%	92%
Blood Culture Timing	98	99%	95%	96%
Influenza Vaccine	69	94%	92%	91%
Initial Antibiotic Timing	99	100%	96%	95%
Pneumococcal Vaccine	84	93%	92%	93%
Smoking Cessation Advice	27	100%	95%	97%
Surgical Care Improvement Project				
Appropriate VTP Within 24 Hours[2]	132	92%	92%	92%
Appropriate Hair Removal[2]	1,153	100%	99%	99%
Appropriate Beta Blocker Usage[2]	272	96%	94%	93%
Controlled Postoperative Blood Glucose[2]	0	-	92%	93%
Prophylactic Antibiotic Timing[2]	1,013	100%	96%	97%
Prophylactic Antibiotic Timing (Outpatient)	200	94%	89%	92%
Prophylactic Antibiotic Selection[2]	1,015	99%	98%	97%
Prophylactic Antibiotic Select. (Outpatient)	191	98%	95%	94%
Prophylactic Antibiotic Stopped[2]	998	98%	97%	94%
Recommended VTP Ordered[2]	132	92%	93%	94%
Urinary Catheter Removal[2]	101	95%	90%	90%
Children's Asthma Care				
Received Systemic Corticosteroids	-	-	-	100%
Received Home Management Plan	-	-	-	71%
Received Reliever Medication	-	-	-	100%
Use of Medical Imaging				
Combination Abdominal CT Scan	565	0.037	0.100	0.191
Combination Chest CT Scan	370	0.003	0.018	0.054
Follow-up Mammogram/Ultrasound	1,139	9.1%	6.4%	8.4%
MRI for Low Back Pain	133	42.1%	39.7%	32.7%
Survey of Patients' Hospital Experiences				
Area Around Room 'Always' Quiet at Night	300+	70%	-	58%
Doctors 'Always' Communicated Well	300+	76%	-	80%
Home Recovery Information Given	300+	88%	-	82%
Hospital Given 9 or 10 on 10 Point Scale	300+	78%	-	67%
Meds 'Always' Explained Before Given	300+	65%	-	60%
Nurses 'Always' Communicated Well	300+	76%	-	76%
Pain 'Always' Well Controlled	300+	69%	-	69%
Room and Bathroom 'Always' Clean	300+	70%	-	71%
Timely Help 'Always' Received	300+	67%	-	64%
Would Definitely Recommend Hospital	300+	80%	-	69%

Sanford Worthington Medical Center

1018 Sixth Avenue Phone: 507-372-2941
Worthington, MN 56187 Fax: 507-372-7686
URL: www.worthingtonhospital.com
Type: Acute Care Hospitals Emergency Services: No
Ownership: Proprietary Beds: 66
Key Personnel:
Infection Control. . . . . LaVonne Foss
Operating Room. . . . . Paula Ausham
Quality Assurance . . . . LaVonne Foss
Radiology. . . . . Jim I Myerly
Emergency Room . . . . Charles Fitch, MD
Intensive Care Unit. . . . . Diane Zandstra

Measure	Cases	This Hosp.	State Avg.	U.S. Avg.
Heart Attack Care				
ACE Inhibitor or ARB for LVSD	0	-	97%	96%
Aspirin at Arrival[1]	3	100%	99%	99%
Aspirin at Discharge[1]	1	100%	99%	98%
Beta Blocker at Discharge[1]	2	50%	99%	98%
Fibrinolytic Medication Timing	0	-	55%	55%
PCI Within 90 Minutes of Arrival	0	-	94%	90%
Smoking Cessation Advice	0	-	99%	99%
Chest Pain/Possible Heart Attack Care				
Aspirin at Arrival	61	97%	97%	95%
Median Time to ECG (minutes)	62	7	7	8
Median Time to Transfer (minutes)[1,3]	3	100	50	61
Fibrinolytic Medication Timing[1]	3	100%	58%	54%
Heart Failure Care				
ACE Inhibitor or ARB for LVSD[1]	5	100%	96%	94%
Discharge Instructions[1]	19	79%	86%	88%
Evaluation of LVS Function	26	73%	96%	98%
Smoking Cessation Advice[1]	1	0%	96%	98%
Pneumonia Care				
Appropriate Initial Antibiotic[1]	19	84%	90%	92%
Blood Culture Timing[1]	24	96%	95%	96%
Influenza Vaccine[1]	20	90%	92%	91%
Initial Antibiotic Timing	28	100%	96%	95%
Pneumococcal Vaccine	31	71%	92%	93%
Smoking Cessation Advice[1]	6	83%	95%	97%
Surgical Care Improvement Project				
Appropriate VTP Within 24 Hours[1]	23	91%	92%	92%
Appropriate Hair Removal	89	100%	99%	99%
Appropriate Beta Blocker Usage[1]	24	100%	94%	93%
Controlled Postoperative Blood Glucose	0	-	92%	93%
Prophylactic Antibiotic Timing	76	91%	96%	97%
Prophylactic Antibiotic Timing (Outpatient)	30	87%	89%	92%
Prophylactic Antibiotic Selection	76	100%	98%	97%
Prophylactic Antibiotic Select. (Outpatient)	31	100%	95%	94%
Prophylactic Antibiotic Stopped	75	100%	97%	94%
Recommended VTP Ordered[1]	24	92%	93%	94%
Urinary Catheter Removal[1]	20	65%	90%	90%
Children's Asthma Care				
Received Systemic Corticosteroids	-	-	-	100%
Received Home Management Plan	-	-	-	71%
Received Reliever Medication	-	-	-	100%
Use of Medical Imaging				
Combination Abdominal CT Scan	138	0.087	0.100	0.191
Combination Chest CT Scan	56	0.018	0.018	0.054
Follow-up Mammogram/Ultrasound[5]	0	-	6.4%	8.4%
MRI for Low Back Pain	44	38.6%	39.7%	32.7%
Survey of Patients' Hospital Experiences				
Area Around Room 'Always' Quiet at Night	300+	63%	-	58%
Doctors 'Always' Communicated Well	300+	74%	-	80%
Home Recovery Information Given	300+	84%	-	82%
Hospital Given 9 or 10 on 10 Point Scale	300+	65%	-	67%
Meds 'Always' Explained Before Given	300+	61%	-	60%
Nurses 'Always' Communicated Well	300+	76%	-	76%
Pain 'Always' Well Controlled	300+	65%	-	69%
Room and Bathroom 'Always' Clean	300+	83%	-	71%
Timely Help 'Always' Received	300+	69%	-	64%
Would Definitely Recommend Hospital	300+	64%	-	69%

Fairview Lakes Health Services

5200 Fairview Boulevard Phone: 651-982-7000
Wyoming, MN 55092 Fax: 651-982-7298
URL: www.lakes.fairview.org
Type: Acute Care Hospitals Emergency Services: Yes
Ownership: Voluntary Non-Profit - Private Beds: 59
Key Personnel:
CEO/President. . . . . Mark A Eustis
Chief of Medical Staff . . . . Lois A Lenarz MD AAFP

Measure	Cases	This Hosp.	State Avg.	U.S. Avg.
Heart Attack Care				
ACE Inhibitor or ARB for LVSD[1]	4	100%	97%	96%
Aspirin at Arrival[1]	15	100%	99%	99%
Aspirin at Discharge[1]	7	100%	99%	98%
Beta Blocker at Discharge[1]	13	100%	99%	98%
Fibrinolytic Medication Timing	0	-	55%	55%
PCI Within 90 Minutes of Arrival	0	-	94%	90%
Smoking Cessation Advice	0	-	99%	99%
Chest Pain/Possible Heart Attack Care				
Aspirin at Arrival	186	98%	97%	95%
Median Time to ECG (minutes)	189	8	7	8
Median Time to Transfer (minutes)[1]	15	51	50	61
Fibrinolytic Medication Timing	0	-	58%	54%
Heart Failure Care				
ACE Inhibitor or ARB for LVSD	26	92%	96%	94%
Discharge Instructions	67	96%	86%	88%
Evaluation of LVS Function	76	100%	96%	98%
Smoking Cessation Advice[1]	15	100%	96%	98%
Pneumonia Care				
Appropriate Initial Antibiotic	67	87%	90%	92%
Blood Culture Timing	87	97%	95%	96%
Influenza Vaccine	55	96%	92%	91%
Initial Antibiotic Timing	98	96%	96%	95%
Pneumococcal Vaccine	89	99%	92%	93%
Smoking Cessation Advice[1]	24	100%	95%	97%
Surgical Care Improvement Project				
Appropriate VTP Within 24 Hours[2]	103	94%	92%	92%
Appropriate Hair Removal[2]	440	100%	99%	99%
Appropriate Beta Blocker Usage[2]	161	93%	94%	93%
Controlled Postoperative Blood Glucose[2]	0	-	92%	93%
Prophylactic Antibiotic Timing[2]	347	96%	96%	97%
Prophylactic Antibiotic Timing (Outpatient)	173	90%	89%	92%
Prophylactic Antibiotic Selection[2]	350	99%	98%	97%
Prophylactic Antibiotic Select. (Outpatient)	167	99%	95%	94%
Prophylactic Antibiotic Stopped[2]	334	99%	97%	94%
Recommended VTP Ordered[2]	103	97%	93%	94%
Urinary Catheter Removal[2]	32	97%	90%	90%
Children's Asthma Care				
Received Systemic Corticosteroids	-	-	-	100%
Received Home Management Plan	-	-	-	71%
Received Reliever Medication	-	-	-	100%
Use of Medical Imaging				
Combination Abdominal CT Scan	493	0.089	0.100	0.191
Combination Chest CT Scan	499	0.006	0.018	0.054
Follow-up Mammogram/Ultrasound	815	4.9%	6.4%	8.4%
MRI for Low Back Pain	173	33.5%	39.7%	32.7%
Survey of Patients' Hospital Experiences				
Area Around Room 'Always' Quiet at Night	300+	52%	-	58%
Doctors 'Always' Communicated Well	300+	80%	-	80%
Home Recovery Information Given	300+	82%	-	82%
Hospital Given 9 or 10 on 10 Point Scale	300+	68%	-	67%
Meds 'Always' Explained Before Given	300+	63%	-	60%
Nurses 'Always' Communicated Well	300+	76%	-	76%
Pain 'Always' Well Controlled	300+	70%	-	69%
Room and Bathroom 'Always' Clean	300+	73%	-	71%
Timely Help 'Always' Received	300+	71%	-	64%
Would Definitely Recommend Hospital	300+	71%	-	69%

NOTE: Hospital profiles are in alphabetical order by state, then city, then hospital within the city; Rankings exclude hospitals with less than 25 cases except for patient surveys which excludes hospitals with less than 100 cases; (a) 100–299 cases; (1) The number of cases is too small to be sure how well a hospital is performing; (2) The hospital indicated that the data submitted for this measure were based on a sample of cases; (3) Data was collected during a shorter time period (fewer quarters) than the maximum possible time for this measure; (4) Suppressed for one or more quarters by CMS; (5) No data is available from the hospital for this measure; (6) Fewer than 100 patients completed the HCAHPS survey. Use these rates with caution, as the number of surveys may be too low to reliably assess hospital performance; (7) Survey results are based on less than 12 months of data; (8) Survey results are not available for this reporting period; (9) No or very few patients were eligible for the HCAHPS survey. The scores shown, if any, reflect a very small number of surveys; (10) A state average was not calculated because too few hospitals in the state submitted data; (11) There were discrepancies in the data collection process; Please refer to the User's Guide for a full explanation of data.

Heart Attack Care

1. ACE Inhibitor or ARB for LVSD

Hospital Name	City	Rate	Cases
Capital Region Medical Center	Jefferson City	100%	27
Centerpoint Medical Center of Independence	Independence	100%	54
Freeman Health System - Freeman West	Joplin	100%	51
Heartland Regional Medical Center	Saint Joseph	100%	36
Poplar Bluff Regional Medical Center	Poplar Bluff	100%	33
Research Medical Center	Kansas City	100%	44
Saint Francis Medical Center	Cape Girardeau	100%	37
Saint Johns Mercy Medical Center	Saint Louis	100%	49
Saint Louis University Hospital	Saint Louis	100%	35
Saint Lukes Hospital of Kansas City	Kansas City	100%	64
SSM St Marys Health Center	Richmond Hghts	100%	30
Christian Hospital Northeast	Saint Louis	99%	91
Missouri Baptist Medical Center	Town & Country	99%	96
North Kansas City Hospital[2]	N Kansas City	98%	120
Saint Joseph Medical Center	Kansas City	98%	51
Barnes Jewish Hospital	Saint Louis	97%	135
Boone Hospital Center	Columbia	97%	117
Jefferson Regional Medical Center	Crystal City	97%	38
Saint John's Regional Medical Center	Joplin	97%	90
Saint Lukes Hospital	Chesterfield	97%	33
Lake Regional Health System	Osage Beach	96%	28
Saint John's Regional Health Center[2]	Springfield	96%	79
University of Missouri Health Care	Columbia	95%	56
SSM St Clare Health Center	Fenton	94%	47
SSM St Joseph Health Center	Saint Charles	94%	53
Cox Medical Center	Springfield	93%	94
Southeast Missouri Hospital	Cape Girardeau	90%	52
Liberty Hospital	Liberty	89%	27
Skaggs Community Health Center	Branson	88%	34
SSM Depaul Health Center	Bridgeton	88%	100
Saint Anthony's Medical Center[2]	Saint Louis	82%	61

2. Aspirin at Arrival

Hospital Name	City	Rate	Cases
Audrain Medical Center	Mexico	100%	43
Boone Hospital Center	Columbia	100%	219
Capital Region Medical Center	Jefferson City	100%	143
Centerpoint Medical Center of Independence	Independence	100%	313
Columbia Missouri VA Medical Center	Columbia	100%	49
Freeman Health System - Freeman West	Joplin	100%	205
Heartland Regional Medical Center	Saint Joseph	100%	299
Lee's Summit Medical Center	Lee's Summit	100%	104
Moberly Regional Medical Center	Moberly	100%	25
North Kansas City Hospital[2]	N Kansas City	100%	293
Research Medical Center	Kansas City	100%	143
Saint John's Regional Health Center[2]	Springfield	100%	236
Saint Johns Mercy Hospital	Washington	100%	25
Saint Louis-John Cochran VA Medical Center	Saint Louis	100%	91
Saint Luke's East Lee's Summit Hospital	Lees Summit	100%	121
Saint Lukes Hospital	Chesterfield	100%	281
Saint Lukes Hospital of Kansas City	Kansas City	100%	167
Saint Lukes Northland Hospital	Kansas City	100%	79
Saint Marys Health Center	Jefferson City	100%	119
SSM St Clare Health Center	Fenton	100%	219
SSM St Marys Health Center	Richmond Hghts	100%	167
Barnes Jewish Hospital	Saint Louis	99%	408
Christian Hospital Northeast	Saint Louis	99%	302
Cox Medical Center	Springfield	99%	422
Des Peres Hospital	Saint Louis	99%	73
Hannibal Regional Hospital	Hannibal	99%	102
Jefferson Regional Medical Center	Crystal City	99%	200
Missouri Baptist Medical Center	Town & Country	99%	229
Ozarks Medical Center	West Plains	99%	100
Poplar Bluff Regional Medical Center	Poplar Bluff	99%	107
Saint John's Regional Medical Center	Joplin	99%	204
Saint Johns Mercy Medical Center	Saint Louis	99%	280
Saint Joseph Medical Center	Kansas City	99%	184
Skaggs Community Health Center	Branson	99%	188
Southeast Missouri Hospital	Cape Girardeau	99%	155
University of Missouri Health Care	Columbia	99%	127
Barnes-Jewish St Peters Hospital	Saint Peters	98%	179
Lake Regional Health System	Osage Beach	98%	220
Saint Anthony's Medical Center[2]	Saint Louis	98%	317
Saint Francis Medical Center	Cape Girardeau	98%	127
Saint Louis University Hospital	Saint Louis	98%	110
Saint Mary's Medical Center	Blue Springs	98%	106
SSM Depaul Health Center	Bridgeton	98%	313
SSM St Joseph Health Center	Saint Charles	98%	241
Truman Medical Center - Hospital Hill	Kansas City	98%	50
Bothwell Regional Health Center	Sedalia	97%	58
Liberty Hospital	Liberty	96%	111
SSM St Joseph Hospital West	Lake Saint Louis	96%	52
Phelps County Regional Medical Center	Rolla	94%	68
Kansas City VA Medical Center	Kansas City	89%	28
Missouri Delta Medical Center	Sikeston	87%	31
Citizens Memorial Hospital	Bolivar	86%	35

3. Aspirin at Discharge

Hospital Name	City	Rate	Cases
Audrain Medical Center	Mexico	100%	41
Boone Hospital Center	Columbia	100%	469
Bothwell Regional Health Center	Sedalia	100%	34
Centerpoint Medical Center of Independence	Independence	100%	323
Christian Hospital Northeast	Saint Louis	100%	409
Columbia Missouri VA Medical Center	Columbia	100%	48
Hannibal Regional Hospital	Hannibal	100%	97
Heartland Regional Medical Center	Saint Joseph	100%	391
Jefferson Regional Medical Center	Crystal City	100%	260
Lee's Summit Medical Center	Lee's Summit	100%	95
Missouri Baptist Medical Center	Town & Country	100%	466
Poplar Bluff Regional Medical Center	Poplar Bluff	100%	130
Research Medical Center	Kansas City	100%	242
Saint Francis Medical Center	Cape Girardeau	100%	186
Saint Joseph Medical Center	Kansas City	100%	230
Saint Louis University Hospital	Saint Louis	100%	116
Saint Louis-John Cochran VA Medical Center	Saint Louis	100%	98
Saint Lukes Hospital	Chesterfield	100%	301
Saint Lukes Hospital of Kansas City	Kansas City	100%	441
Saint Mary's Medical Center	Blue Springs	100%	92
Saint Marys Health Center	Jefferson City	100%	114
Skaggs Community Health Center	Branson	100%	190
SSM St Marys Health Center	Richmond Hghts	100%	158
Truman Medical Center - Hospital Hill	Kansas City	100%	61
University of Missouri Health Care	Columbia	100%	249
Barnes Jewish Hospital	Saint Louis	99%	629
Capital Region Medical Center	Jefferson City	99%	137
Des Peres Hospital	Saint Louis	99%	178
Freeman Health System - Freeman West	Joplin	99%	371
Lake Regional Health System	Osage Beach	99%	207
North Kansas City Hospital[2]	N Kansas City	99%	369
Saint John's Regional Medical Center	Joplin	99%	311
Saint Johns Mercy Medical Center	Saint Louis	99%	395
Saint Luke's East Lee's Summit Hospital	Lees Summit	99%	113
Saint Lukes Northland Hospital	Kansas City	99%	71
Barnes-Jewish St Peters Hospital	Saint Peters	98%	183
Cox Medical Center	Springfield	98%	519
Liberty Hospital	Liberty	98%	119
Saint John's Regional Health Center[2]	Springfield	98%	369
SSM Depaul Health Center	Bridgeton	98%	327
SSM St Clare Health Center	Fenton	98%	263
SSM St Joseph Health Center	Saint Charles	98%	356
Ozarks Medical Center	West Plains	96%	95
Saint Anthony's Medical Center[2]	Saint Louis	96%	312
Southeast Missouri Hospital	Cape Girardeau	96%	254
Phelps County Regional Medical Center	Rolla	95%	42
Missouri Delta Medical Center	Sikeston	88%	25
Citizens Memorial Hospital	Bolivar	86%	35

4. Beta Blocker at Discharge

Hospital Name	City	Rate	Cases
Christian Hospital Northeast	Saint Louis	100%	393
Citizens Memorial Hospital	Bolivar	100%	34
Heartland Regional Medical Center	Saint Joseph	100%	384
Jefferson Regional Medical Center	Crystal City	100%	252
Lee's Summit Medical Center	Lee's Summit	100%	90
Missouri Baptist Medical Center	Town & Country	100%	453
Poplar Bluff Regional Medical Center	Poplar Bluff	100%	122
Research Medical Center	Kansas City	100%	225
Saint Joseph Medical Center	Kansas City	100%	218
Saint Lukes Hospital	Chesterfield	100%	298
Saint Lukes Hospital of Kansas City	Kansas City	100%	434
Saint Marys Health Center	Jefferson City	100%	115
SSM St Marys Health Center	Richmond Hghts	100%	148
Truman Medical Center - Hospital Hill	Kansas City	100%	62
Barnes Jewish Hospital	Saint Louis	99%	583
Boone Hospital Center	Columbia	99%	453
Centerpoint Medical Center of Independence	Independence	99%	292
Cox Medical Center	Springfield	99%	502
Des Peres Hospital	Saint Louis	99%	176
Hannibal Regional Hospital	Hannibal	99%	96
North Kansas City Hospital[2]	N Kansas City	99%	367
Saint Francis Medical Center	Cape Girardeau	99%	182
Saint John's Regional Health Center[2]	Springfield	99%	338
Saint Johns Mercy Medical Center	Saint Louis	99%	388
Saint Louis University Hospital	Saint Louis	99%	108
Saint Louis-John Cochran VA Medical Center	Saint Louis	99%	91
Saint Luke's East Lee's Summit Hospital	Lees Summit	99%	110
Skaggs Community Health Center	Branson	99%	178
SSM Depaul Health Center	Bridgeton	99%	318
SSM St Joseph Health Center	Saint Charles	99%	356
University of Missouri Health Care	Columbia	99%	241
Barnes-Jewish St Peters Hospital	Saint Peters	98%	186
Capital Region Medical Center	Jefferson City	98%	132
Freeman Health System - Freeman West	Joplin	98%	312
Lake Regional Health System	Osage Beach	98%	208
Saint Lukes Northland Hospital	Kansas City	98%	63
Saint Mary's Medical Center	Blue Springs	98%	89
SSM St Clare Health Center	Fenton	98%	245
Saint Anthony's Medical Center[2]	Saint Louis	97%	309
Saint John's Regional Medical Center	Joplin	97%	307
Columbia Missouri VA Medical Center	Columbia	96%	51
Liberty Hospital	Liberty	96%	112
Southeast Missouri Hospital	Cape Girardeau	96%	251
Audrain Medical Center	Mexico	95%	42
Phelps County Regional Medical Center	Rolla	95%	43
Bothwell Regional Health Center	Sedalia	94%	36
Ozarks Medical Center	West Plains	94%	96
Missouri Delta Medical Center	Sikeston	88%	26

6. PCI Within 90 Minutes of Arrival

Hospital Name	City	Rate	Cases
Capital Region Medical Center	Jefferson City	100%	25
Poplar Bluff Regional Medical Center	Poplar Bluff	100%	29
Research Medical Center	Kansas City	100%	29
Saint Lukes Hospital	Chesterfield	100%	39
Saint Marys Health Center	Jefferson City	100%	27
Skaggs Community Health Center	Branson	100%	35
SSM St Marys Health Center	Richmond Hghts	100%	31
Barnes Jewish Hospital	Saint Louis	98%	57
North Kansas City Hospital[2]	N Kansas City	98%	80
SSM St Clare Health Center	Fenton	98%	45
Lee's Summit Medical Center	Lee's Summit	97%	32
Saint John's Regional Medical Center	Joplin	97%	33
University of Missouri Health Care	Columbia	97%	38
Heartland Regional Medical Center	Saint Joseph	96%	52
Saint Francis Medical Center	Cape Girardeau	96%	27
Jefferson Regional Medical Center	Crystal City	95%	43
Saint John's Regional Health Center[2]	Springfield	95%	75
Christian Hospital Northeast	Saint Louis	94%	33
Missouri Baptist Medical Center	Town & Country	94%	32
Saint Lukes Hospital of Kansas City	Kansas City	94%	31
Boone Hospital Center	Columbia	93%	54
Centerpoint Medical Center of Independence	Independence	93%	68
Cox Medical Center	Springfield	89%	74
Southeast Missouri Hospital	Cape Girardeau	89%	35
Saint Johns Mercy Medical Center	Saint Louis	88%	34
Barnes-Jewish St Peters Hospital	Saint Peters	86%	29
Hannibal Regional Hospital	Hannibal	86%	35
Saint Anthony's Medical Center[2]	Saint Louis	86%	66
Freeman Health System - Freeman West	Joplin	85%	52
Saint Joseph Medical Center	Kansas City	79%	42
SSM Depaul Health Center	Bridgeton	78%	37
SSM St Joseph Health Center	Saint Charles	75%	51
Lake Regional Health System	Osage Beach	74%	43

7. Smoking Cessation Advice

Hospital Name	City	Rate	Cases
Barnes Jewish Hospital	Saint Louis	100%	217
Barnes-Jewish St Peters Hospital	Saint Peters	100%	61
Boone Hospital Center	Columbia	100%	152
Capital Region Medical Center	Jefferson City	100%	41
Centerpoint Medical Center of Independence	Independence	100%	117
Christian Hospital Northeast	Saint Louis	100%	154
Cox Medical Center	Springfield	100%	226
Des Peres Hospital	Saint Louis	100%	64
Hannibal Regional Hospital	Hannibal	100%	33
Heartland Regional Medical Center	Saint Joseph	100%	160
Jefferson Regional Medical Center	Crystal City	100%	110
Lake Regional Health System	Osage Beach	100%	94
Lee's Summit Medical Center	Lee's Summit	100%	32
Liberty Hospital	Liberty	100%	39
Missouri Baptist Medical Center	Town & Country	100%	128
North Kansas City Hospital[2]	N Kansas City	100%	155
Ozarks Medical Center	West Plains	100%	35
Poplar Bluff Regional Medical Center	Poplar Bluff	100%	70
Saint Francis Medical Center	Cape Girardeau	100%	81
Saint John's Regional Medical Center	Joplin	100%	141
Saint Joseph Medical Center	Kansas City	100%	82
Saint Louis University Hospital	Saint Louis	100%	59
Saint Luke's East Lee's Summit Hospital	Lees Summit	100%	29
Saint Lukes Hospital	Chesterfield	100%	66
Saint Lukes Hospital of Kansas City	Kansas City	100%	157
Saint Lukes Northland Hospital	Kansas City	100%	28
Saint Marys Health Center	Jefferson City	100%	38
SSM Depaul Health Center	Bridgeton	100%	131
SSM St Clare Health Center	Fenton	100%	94
SSM St Joseph Health Center	Saint Charles	100%	135
SSM St Marys Health Center	Richmond Hghts	100%	48
Truman Medical Center - Hospital Hill	Kansas City	100%	44
Freeman Health System - Freeman West	Joplin	99%	192
Research Medical Center	Kansas City	99%	97
Saint John's Regional Health Center[2]	Springfield	99%	136
University of Missouri Health Care	Columbia	99%	121
Saint Johns Mercy Medical Center	Saint Louis	98%	95
Saint Mary's Medical Center	Blue Springs	98%	47
Southeast Missouri Hospital	Cape Girardeau	98%	134
Skaggs Community Health Center	Branson	97%	76

NOTE: Hospital profiles are in alphabetical order by state, then city, then hospital within the city; Rankings exclude hospitals with less than 25 cases except for patient surveys which excludes hospitals with less than 100 cases; (a) 100–299 cases; (1) The number of cases is too small to be sure how well a hospital is performing; (2) The hospital indicated that the data submitted for this measure were based on a sample of cases; (3) Data was collected during a shorter time period (fewer quarters) than the maximum possible time for this measure; (4) Suppressed for one or more quarters by CMS; (5) No data is available from the hospital for this measure; (6) Fewer than 100 patients completed the HCAHPS survey. Use these rates with caution, as the number of surveys may be too low to reliably assess hospital performance; (7) Survey results are based on less than 12 months of data; (8) Survey results are not available for this reporting period; (9) No or very few patients were eligible for the HCAHPS survey. The scores shown, if any, reflect a very small number of surveys; (10) A state average was not calculated because too few hospitals in the state submitted data; (11) There were discrepancies in the data collection process; Please refer to the User's Guide for a full explanation of data.

Hospital Name	City	Rate	Cases
Saint Louis-John Cochran VA Medical Center	Saint Louis	94%	48
Saint Anthony's Medical Center[2]	Saint Louis	91%	112

Chest Pain/Possible Heart Attack Care

8. Aspirin at Arrival

Hospital Name	City	Rate	Cases
Jefferson Regional Medical Center	Crystal City	100%	30
Lafayette Regional Health Center	Lexington	100%	43
Northeast Regional Medical Center	Kirksville	100%	42
Research Belton Hospital	Belton	100%	78
Twin Rivers Regional Medical Center	Kennett	100%	63
Mineral Area Regional Medical Center	Farmington	99%	90
Cameron Regional Medical Center	Cameron	98%	99
Citizens Memorial Hospital	Bolivar	98%	86
Saint Johns Mercy Hospital	Washington	98%	217
Wright Memorial Hospital	Trenton	98%	59
Barnes-Jewish West County Hospital	Creve Coeur	97%	64
Moberly Regional Medical Center	Moberly	97%	114
Parkland Health Center	Farmington	97%	256
Saint Johns Hospital-Lebanon	Lebanon	97%	215
Christian Hospital Northwest	Florissant	96%	322
Cooper County Memorial Hospital	Boonville	96%	56
Golden Valley Memorial Hospital	Clinton	96%	135
Hedrick Medical Center	Chillicothe	96%	179
Nevada Regional Medical Center	Nevada	96%	97
Phelps County Regional Medical Center	Rolla	96%	151
Saint Lukes Northland Hospital	Kansas City	96%	45
SSM St Joseph Hospital West	Lake Saint Louis	96%	96
Texas County Memorial Hospital	Houston	96%	106
Bothwell Regional Health Center	Sedalia	95%	85
Missouri Delta Medical Center	Sikeston	95%	100
Western Missouri Medical Center	Warrensburg	95%	261
Missouri Baptist Hospital Sullivan	Sullivan	94%	163
Progress West Healthcare Center	O'Fallon	94%	33
Liberty Hospital	Liberty	93%	58
Ozarks Medical Center	West Plains	93%	74
Saint Francis Hospital	Maryville	93%	71
Callaway Community Hospital	Fulton	92%	75
Bates County Memorial Hospital	Butler	91%	53
Ripley County Memorial Hospital	Doniphan	91%	44
Missouri Southern Healthcare	Dexter	90%	90
Fitzgibbon Memorial Hospital	Marshall	87%	126
Saint Johns Mercy Medical Center	Saint Louis	85%	72
Saint Luke's East Lee's Summit Hospital	Lees Summit	85%	26
Christian Hospital Northeast	Saint Louis	79%	28

9. Median Time to ECG (minutes)

Hospital Name	City	Min.	Cases
Saint Luke's East Lee's Summit Hospital	Lees Summit	2	31
Missouri Baptist Hospital Sullivan	Sullivan	3	163
Northeast Regional Medical Center	Kirksville	3	43
Christian Hospital Northeast	Saint Louis	4	30
Golden Valley Memorial Hospital	Clinton	4	141
Progress West Healthcare Center	O'Fallon	4	33
Research Belton Hospital	Belton	5	81
Twin Rivers Regional Medical Center	Kennett	5	67
Jefferson Regional Medical Center	Crystal City	6	32
Lafayette Regional Health Center	Lexington	6	42
Saint Francis Hospital	Maryville	6	74
Saint Lukes Northland Hospital	Kansas City	6	45
Mineral Area Regional Medical Center	Farmington	7	94
Barnes-Jewish West County Hospital	Creve Coeur	8	64
Callaway Community Hospital	Fulton	8	77
Cooper County Memorial Hospital	Boonville	8	58
Parkland Health Center	Farmington	8	266
SSM St Joseph Hospital West	Lake Saint Louis	8	97
Cameron Regional Medical Center	Cameron	9	105
Christian Hospital Northwest	Florissant	9	333
Hedrick Medical Center	Chillicothe	9	186
Moberly Regional Medical Center	Moberly	9	121
Saint Johns Mercy Hospital	Washington	9	215
Liberty Hospital	Liberty	10	59
Nevada Regional Medical Center	Nevada	10	99
Saint Johns Mercy Medical Center	Saint Louis	10	71
Ozarks Medical Center	West Plains	11	80
Fitzgibbon Memorial Hospital	Marshall	12	132
Missouri Delta Medical Center	Sikeston	12	104
Phelps County Regional Medical Center	Rolla	12	156
Saint Johns Hospital-Lebanon	Lebanon	12	230
Western Missouri Medical Center	Warrensburg	12	278
Missouri Southern Healthcare	Dexter	13	94
Texas County Memorial Hospital	Houston	14	114
Ripley County Memorial Hospital	Doniphan	17	46
Bates County Memorial Hospital	Butler	18	56
Bothwell Regional Health Center	Sedalia	19	86
Wright Memorial Hospital	Trenton	19	65
Forest Park Hospital	Saint Louis	20	25
Ozarks Community Hospital	Springfield	22	26
Citizens Memorial Hospital	Bolivar	24	96

10. Median Time to Transfer (minutes)

Hospital Name	City	Min.	Cases
Parkland Health Center	Farmington	54	25
Saint Johns Mercy Hospital	Washington	76	30

Heart Failure Care

12. ACE Inhibitor or ARB for LVSD

Hospital Name	City	Rate	Cases
Barnes-Jewish St Peters Hospital	Saint Peters	100%	28
Barnes-Jewish West County Hospital	Creve Coeur	100%	25
Capital Region Medical Center	Jefferson City	100%	70
Centerpoint Medical Center of Independence	Independence	100%	122
Columbia Missouri VA Medical Center	Columbia	100%	48
Heartland Regional Medical Center	Saint Joseph	100%	128
Jefferson Regional Medical Center	Crystal City	100%	108
Lee's Summit Medical Center	Lee's Summit	100%	27
Saint Joseph Medical Center	Kansas City	100%	135
Saint Lukes Hospital of Kansas City	Kansas City	100%	210
Saint Marys Health Center	Jefferson City	100%	62
SSM St Joseph Hospital West	Lake Saint Louis	100%	45
Twin Rivers Regional Medical Center	Kennett	100%	26
Poplar Bluff Regional Medical Center	Poplar Bluff	99%	91
Research Medical Center	Kansas City	99%	121
Saint Louis University Hospital	Saint Louis	99%	202
SSM St Marys Health Center[2]	Richmond Hghts	99%	86
Truman Medical Center - Hospital Hill	Kansas City	99%	176
Audrain Medical Center	Mexico	98%	55
Des Peres Hospital	Saint Louis	98%	83
Barnes Jewish Hospital[2]	Saint Louis	97%	382
Christian Hospital Northeast[2]	Saint Louis	97%	214
Parkland Health Center	Farmington	97%	32
Saint Francis Medical Center	Cape Girardeau	97%	97
Saint Johns Mercy Hospital	Washington	97%	36
Saint Johns Mercy Medical Center	Saint Louis	97%	174
Saint Louis-John Cochran VA Medical Center	Saint Louis	97%	158
Saint Luke's East Lee's Summit Hospital	Lees Summit	97%	58
Saint Lukes Hospital	Chesterfield	97%	143
Truman Medical Center Lakewood	Kansas City	97%	34
Phelps County Regional Medical Center	Rolla	96%	81
Boone Hospital Center[2]	Columbia	95%	222
Cox Medical Center	Springfield	95%	171
Freeman Health System - Freeman West	Joplin	95%	81
Kansas City VA Medical Center	Kansas City	95%	74
University of Missouri Health Care	Columbia	95%	105
Golden Valley Memorial Hospital	Clinton	94%	31
North Kansas City Hospital[2]	N Kansas City	94%	132
SSM St Clare Health Center[2]	Fenton	94%	95
Saint John's Regional Health Center[2]	Springfield	93%	135
Saint John's Regional Medical Center	Joplin	93%	151
Lake Regional Health System	Osage Beach	92%	80
Missouri Baptist Medical Center[2]	Town & Country	92%	198
Missouri Delta Medical Center	Sikeston	92%	75
Hannibal Regional Hospital	Hannibal	91%	58
Liberty Hospital	Liberty	90%	98
SSM Depaul Health Center[2]	Bridgeton	90%	114
SSM St Joseph Health Center[2]	Saint Charles	90%	84
Saint Lukes Northland Hospital	Kansas City	89%	35
Saint Alexius Hospital	Saint Louis	88%	40
Bothwell Regional Health Center	Sedalia	87%	52
Saint Mary's Medical Center	Blue Springs	87%	30
Skaggs Community Health Center[2]	Branson	86%	94
Southeast Missouri Hospital	Cape Girardeau	86%	98
Ozarks Medical Center	West Plains	83%	30
Saint Anthony's Medical Center[2]	Saint Louis	79%	126
Mineral Area Regional Medical Center	Farmington	76%	25
Forest Park Hospital[3]	Saint Louis	72%	29

13. Discharge Instructions

Hospital Name	City	Rate	Cases
Columbia Missouri VA Medical Center	Columbia	100%	137
Heartland Regional Medical Center	Saint Joseph	100%	297
Northeast Regional Medical Center	Kirksville	100%	31
Poplar Bluff Regional Medical Center	Poplar Bluff	100%	269
Poplar Bluff VA Medical Center	Poplar Bluff	100%	96
Saint Marys Health Center	Jefferson City	100%	155
Twin Rivers Regional Medical Center	Kennett	100%	72
Saint Joseph Medical Center	Kansas City	99%	305
Saint Louis University Hospital	Saint Louis	99%	296
Hannibal Regional Hospital	Hannibal	98%	129
Research Medical Center	Kansas City	98%	258
Saint Louis-John Cochran VA Medical Center	Saint Louis	98%	382
Cox Medical Center	Springfield	97%	415
Centerpoint Medical Center of Independence	Independence	96%	325
Jefferson Regional Medical Center	Crystal City	96%	297
Missouri Baptist Hospital Sullivan	Sullivan	96%	55
North Kansas City Hospital[2]	N Kansas City	96%	367
Research Belton Hospital	Belton	96%	25
Saint Johns Mercy Hospital	Washington	96%	135
SSM St Marys Health Center[2]	Richmond Hghts	95%	268
Capital Region Medical Center	Jefferson City	94%	176
SSM St Joseph Health Center[2]	Saint Charles	94%	213
Des Peres Hospital	Saint Louis	93%	205
Kansas City VA Medical Center	Kansas City	93%	177
Moberly Regional Medical Center	Moberly	93%	41
Barnes Jewish Hospital[2]	Saint Louis	92%	731
Barnes-Jewish St Peters Hospital	Saint Peters	92%	122
Bates County Memorial Hospital	Butler	92%	49
SSM St Joseph Hospital West	Lake Saint Louis	92%	170
Boone Hospital Center[2]	Columbia	91%	429
Citizens Memorial Hospital	Bolivar	91%	44
Progress West Healthcare Center	O'Fallon	91%	46
Saint Lukes Hospital	Chesterfield	91%	354
Wright Memorial Hospital	Trenton	91%	43
Audrain Medical Center	Mexico	90%	122
Barnes-Jewish West County Hospital	Creve Coeur	90%	96
Ozarks Medical Center	West Plains	90%	79
Phelps County Regional Medical Center	Rolla	90%	141
University of Missouri Health Care	Columbia	89%	177
Saint Francis Medical Center	Cape Girardeau	88%	264
Saint Mary's Medical Center	Blue Springs	88%	52
SSM Depaul Health Center[2]	Bridgeton	88%	252
SSM St Clare Health Center[2]	Fenton	88%	224
Freeman Neosho Hospital	Neosho	87%	30
Missouri Baptist Medical Center[2]	Town & Country	87%	539
Saint Johns Hospital-Lebanon	Lebanon	87%	62
Truman Medical Center Lakewood	Kansas City	87%	67
Saint Lukes Northland Hospital	Kansas City	86%	77
Lake Regional Health System	Osage Beach	85%	208
Saint John's Regional Medical Center	Joplin	85%	296
Cameron Regional Medical Center	Cameron	84%	25
McCune-Brooks Hospital	Carthage	84%	25
Missouri Delta Medical Center	Sikeston	84%	172
Saint John's Regional Health Center[2]	Springfield	84%	298
Saint Johns Mercy Medical Center	Saint Louis	84%	514
Skaggs Community Health Center[2]	Branson	84%	194
Bothwell Regional Health Center	Sedalia	83%	133
Nevada Regional Medical Center	Nevada	83%	35
Christian Hospital Northeast[2]	Saint Louis	81%	556
Parkland Health Center	Farmington	80%	81
Lee's Summit Medical Center	Lee's Summit	79%	58
Truman Medical Center - Hospital Hill	Kansas City	77%	272
Golden Valley Memorial Hospital	Clinton	76%	55
Saint Lukes Hospital of Kansas City	Kansas City	76%	385
Cass Medical Center	Harrisonville	75%	40
Liberty Hospital	Liberty	75%	208
Ripley County Memorial Hospital	Doniphan	74%	27
Saint Luke's East Lee's Summit Hospital	Lees Summit	74%	140
Freeman Health System - Freeman West	Joplin	73%	223
Saint Alexius Hospital	Saint Louis	73%	112
Mineral Area Regional Medical Center	Farmington	71%	82
Saint Anthony's Medical Center[2]	Saint Louis	68%	244
Forest Park Hospital[3]	Saint Louis	67%	63
Southeast Missouri Hospital	Cape Girardeau	67%	232
Fitzgibbon Memorial Hospital	Marshall	58%	38
Missouri Southern Healthcare	Dexter	36%	72
Pemiscot Memorial Hospital	Hayti	16%	115

14. Evaluation of LVS Function

Hospital Name	City	Rate	Cases
Barnes Jewish Hospital[2]	Saint Louis	100%	817
Capital Region Medical Center	Jefferson City	100%	225
Centerpoint Medical Center of Independence	Independence	100%	424
Cox Medical Center	Springfield	100%	496
Des Peres Hospital	Saint Louis	100%	256
Freeman Neosho Hospital	Neosho	100%	49
Heartland Regional Medical Center	Saint Joseph	100%	388
Kansas City VA Medical Center	Kansas City	100%	202
Lake Regional Health System	Osage Beach	100%	248
Missouri Baptist Hospital Sullivan	Sullivan	100%	78
Missouri Baptist Medical Center[2]	Town & Country	100%	716
Parkland Health Center	Farmington	100%	111
Pike County Memorial Hospital	Louisiana	100%	31
Research Belton Hospital	Belton	100%	33
Research Medical Center	Kansas City	100%	310
Saint Alexius Hospital	Saint Louis	100%	146
Saint Francis Hospital	Maryville	100%	42
Saint Johns Mercy Medical Center	Saint Louis	100%	669
Saint Joseph Medical Center	Kansas City	100%	395
Saint Louis-John Cochran VA Medical Center	Saint Louis	100%	389
Saint Lukes Hospital of Kansas City	Kansas City	100%	456
Saint Lukes Northland Hospital	Kansas City	100%	93
Saint Mary's Medical Center	Blue Springs	100%	79
Saint Marys Health Center	Jefferson City	100%	184
SSM St Clare Health Center[2]	Fenton	100%	290
SSM St Joseph Health Center[2]	Saint Charles	100%	267
SSM St Marys Health Center[2]	Richmond Hghts	100%	317
Truman Medical Center - Hospital Hill	Kansas City	100%	306
Twin Rivers Regional Medical Center	Kennett	100%	92

NOTE: Hospital profiles are in alphabetical order by state, then city, then hospital within the city; Rankings exclude hospitals with less than 25 cases except for patient surveys which excludes hospitals with less than 100 cases; (a) 100–299 cases; (1) The number of cases is too small to be sure how well a hospital is performing; (2) The hospital indicated that the data submitted for this measure were based on a sample of cases; (3) Data was collected during a shorter time period (fewer quarters) than the maximum possible time for this measure; (4) Suppressed for one or more quarters by CMS; (5) No data is available from the hospital for this measure; (6) Fewer than 100 patients completed the HCAHPS survey. Use these rates with caution, as the number of surveys may be too low to reliably assess hospital performance; (7) Survey results are based on less than 12 months of data; (8) Survey results are not available for this reporting period; (9) No or very few patients were eligible for the HCAHPS survey. The scores shown, if any, reflect a very small number of surveys; (10) A state average was not calculated because too few hospitals in the state submitted data; (11) There were discrepancies in the data collection process; Please refer to the User's Guide for a full explanation of data.

Hospital Name	City	Rate	Cases
University of Missouri Health Care	Columbia	100%	224
Audrain Medical Center	Mexico	99%	165
Barnes-Jewish West County Hospital	Creve Coeur	99%	109
Boone Hospital Center[2]	Columbia	99%	513
Bothwell Regional Health Center	Sedalia	99%	164
Christian Hospital Northeast[2]	Saint Louis	99%	655
Columbia Missouri VA Medical Center	Columbia	99%	153
Freeman Health System - Freeman West	Joplin	99%	267
Golden Valley Memorial Hospital	Clinton	99%	107
Jefferson Regional Medical Center	Crystal City	99%	419
Lee's Summit Medical Center	Lee's Summit	99%	86
Moberly Regional Medical Center	Moberly	99%	70
Poplar Bluff Regional Medical Center	Poplar Bluff	99%	330
Saint Francis Medical Center	Cape Girardeau	99%	328
Saint John's Regional Health Center[2]	Springfield	99%	366
Saint John's Regional Medical Center	Joplin	99%	353
Saint Johns Mercy Hospital	Washington	99%	197
Saint Louis University Hospital	Saint Louis	99%	356
Saint Lukes Hospital	Chesterfield	99%	471
Skaggs Community Health Center[2]	Branson	99%	224
SSM St Joseph Hospital West	Lake Saint Louis	99%	227
Barnes-Jewish St Peters Hospital	Saint Peters	98%	154
Hannibal Regional Hospital	Hannibal	98%	172
Missouri Delta Medical Center	Sikeston	98%	223
Northeast Regional Medical Center	Kirksville	98%	46
Saint Anthony's Medical Center[2]	Saint Louis	98%	327
Saint Luke's East Lee's Summit Hospital	Lees Summit	98%	162
Southeast Missouri Hospital	Cape Girardeau	98%	294
SSM Depaul Health Center[2]	Bridgeton	98%	316
Liberty Hospital	Liberty	97%	272
North Kansas City Hospital[2]	N Kansas City	97%	411
Phelps County Regional Medical Center	Rolla	97%	193
Poplar Bluff VA Medical Center	Poplar Bluff	97%	107
Progress West Healthcare Center	O'Fallon	97%	58
Truman Medical Center Lakewood	Kansas City	97%	71
Lincoln County Medical Center	Troy	96%	28
Ozarks Medical Center	West Plains	96%	99
Mineral Area Regional Medical Center	Farmington	95%	119
Callaway Community Hospital	Fulton	94%	32
Ste Genevieve County Memorial Hospital	Ste Genevieve	94%	35
Cass Medical Center	Harrisonville	92%	50
Hedrick Medical Center	Chillicothe	92%	26
Wright Memorial Hospital	Trenton	92%	61
Forest Park Hospital[3]	Saint Louis	88%	85
Ozarks Community Hospital	Springfield	88%	26
Ray County Memorial Hospital	Richmond	88%	33
Western Missouri Medical Center	Warrensburg	88%	42
Cooper County Memorial Hospital	Boonville	87%	31
Nevada Regional Medical Center	Nevada	87%	46
Citizens Memorial Hospital	Bolivar	85%	73
Saint Johns Hospital-Lebanon	Lebanon	84%	75
McCune-Brooks Hospital	Carthage	81%	36
Putnam County Memorial Hospital[3]	Unionville	80%	25
Cameron Regional Medical Center	Cameron	79%	52
Texas County Memorial Hospital	Houston	73%	30
Fitzgibbon Memorial Hospital	Marshall	66%	50
Pemiscot Memorial Hospital	Hayti	62%	137
Ripley County Memorial Hospital	Doniphan	57%	30
Missouri Southern Healthcare	Dexter	46%	93
Bates County Memorial Hospital	Butler	45%	91
Salem Memorial District Hospital	Salem	41%	32
Barton County Memorial Hospital	Lamar	39%	33

15. Smoking Cessation Advice

Hospital Name	City	Rate	Cases
Audrain Medical Center	Mexico	100%	25
Barnes Jewish Hospital[2]	Saint Louis	100%	228
Boone Hospital Center[2]	Columbia	100%	68
Capital Region Medical Center	Jefferson City	100%	33
Centerpoint Medical Center of Independence	Independence	100%	93
Cox Medical Center	Springfield	100%	172
Des Peres Hospital	Saint Louis	100%	46
Forest Park Hospital[3]	Saint Louis	100%	26
Hannibal Regional Hospital	Hannibal	100%	40
Heartland Regional Medical Center	Saint Joseph	100%	66
Jefferson Regional Medical Center	Crystal City	100%	91
Kansas City VA Medical Center	Kansas City	100%	55
Liberty Hospital	Liberty	100%	52
Missouri Baptist Medical Center[2]	Town & Country	100%	69
Missouri Delta Medical Center	Sikeston	100%	49
North Kansas City Hospital[2]	N Kansas City	100%	66
Phelps County Regional Medical Center	Rolla	100%	37
Poplar Bluff Regional Medical Center	Poplar Bluff	100%	60
Research Medical Center	Kansas City	100%	93
Saint Alexius Hospital	Saint Louis	100%	41
Saint Francis Medical Center	Cape Girardeau	100%	60
Saint John's Regional Medical Center	Joplin	100%	69
Saint Johns Mercy Medical Center	Saint Louis	100%	75
Saint Joseph Medical Center	Kansas City	100%	52
Saint Louis University Hospital	Saint Louis	100%	97
Saint Lukes Hospital	Chesterfield	100%	39
Saint Lukes Hospital of Kansas City	Kansas City	100%	107
SSM Depaul Health Center[2]	Bridgeton	100%	49
SSM St Clare Health Center[2]	Fenton	100%	51
SSM St Joseph Health Center[2]	Saint Charles	100%	52
SSM St Joseph Hospital West	Lake Saint Louis	100%	48
SSM St Marys Health Center[2]	Richmond Hghts	100%	57
Truman Medical Center Lakewood	Kansas City	100%	29
Christian Hospital Northeast[2]	Saint Louis	99%	144
Truman Medical Center - Hospital Hill	Kansas City	99%	152
University of Missouri Health Care	Columbia	98%	63
Lake Regional Health System	Osage Beach	97%	58
Skaggs Community Health Center[2]	Branson	96%	54
Saint Louis-John Cochran VA Medical Center	Saint Louis	94%	137
Southeast Missouri Hospital	Cape Girardeau	94%	54
Freeman Health System - Freeman West	Joplin	93%	54
Saint John's Regional Health Center[2]	Springfield	93%	58
Saint Anthony's Medical Center[2]	Saint Louis	89%	45
Pemiscot Memorial Hospital	Hayti	61%	36

Pneumonia Care

16. Appropriate Initial Antibiotic

Hospital Name	City	Rate	Cases
Lee's Summit Medical Center	Lee's Summit	100%	59
Progress West Healthcare Center	O'Fallon	100%	88
Saint Johns Hospital - Cassville	Cassville	100%	34
Saint Louis-John Cochran VA Medical Center	Saint Louis	100%	49
Freeman Neosho Hospital	Neosho	98%	47
Saint John's Regional Health Center[2]	Springfield	98%	83
Saint Johns Hospital - Aurora	Aurora	98%	53
Saint Louis University Hospital	Saint Louis	98%	82
Saint Marys Health Center	Jefferson City	98%	66
Twin Rivers Regional Medical Center	Kennett	98%	48
Heartland Regional Medical Center	Saint Joseph	97%	332
Saint Francis Hospital	Maryville	97%	35
SSM St Marys Health Center[2]	Richmond Hghts	97%	74
Barnes-Jewish St Peters Hospital	Saint Peters	96%	184
Golden Valley Memorial Hospital	Clinton	96%	91
Lincoln County Medical Center	Troy	96%	27
SSM St Clare Health Center[2]	Fenton	96%	111
SSM St Joseph Health Center[2]	Saint Charles	96%	70
Wright Memorial Hospital	Trenton	96%	28
Audrain Medical Center	Mexico	95%	56
Barnes-Jewish West County Hospital	Creve Coeur	95%	38
Bothwell Regional Health Center	Sedalia	95%	132
Christian Hospital Northeast	Saint Louis	95%	155
Cox Monett Hospital	Monett	95%	58
Lafayette Regional Health Center	Lexington	95%	55
Missouri Baptist Hospital Sullivan	Sullivan	95%	96
Missouri Baptist Medical Center[2]	Town & Country	95%	234
Moberly Regional Medical Center	Moberly	95%	58
Parkland Health Center	Farmington	95%	102
Saint Johns Mercy Medical Center[2]	Saint Louis	95%	91
SSM Depaul Health Center[2]	Bridgeton	95%	97
SSM St Joseph Hospital West[2]	Lake Saint Louis	95%	92
Cameron Regional Medical Center	Cameron	94%	52
Cox Medical Center[2]	Springfield	94%	190
Kansas City VA Medical Center	Kansas City	94%	80
North Kansas City Hospital[2]	N Kansas City	94%	170
Skaggs Community Health Center[2]	Branson	94%	124
Cooper County Memorial Hospital	Boonville	93%	27
Des Peres Hospital	Saint Louis	93%	134
Mineral Area Regional Medical Center	Farmington	93%	112
Pike County Memorial Hospital	Louisiana	93%	27
Saint Johns Mercy Hospital[2]	Washington	93%	85
Barnes Jewish Hospital[2]	Saint Louis	92%	169
Barton County Memorial Hospital	Lamar	92%	40
Centerpoint Medical Center of Independence	Independence	92%	194
Forest Park Hospital	Saint Louis	92%	50
Lake Regional Health System	Osage Beach	92%	149
Liberty Hospital	Liberty	92%	159
Poplar Bluff VA Medical Center	Poplar Bluff	92%	25
Saint Luke's East Lee's Summit Hospital	Lees Summit	92%	120
Saint Lukes Northland Hospital	Kansas City	92%	93
Southeast Missouri Hospital	Cape Girardeau	92%	126
Truman Medical Center Lakewood	Kansas City	92%	84
Jefferson Regional Medical Center	Crystal City	91%	197
Poplar Bluff Regional Medical Center	Poplar Bluff	91%	137
Saint Francis Medical Center	Cape Girardeau	91%	213
Saint John's Regional Medical Center	Joplin	91%	201
Saint Johns Hospital-Lebanon	Lebanon	91%	107
Columbia Missouri VA Medical Center	Columbia	90%	39
Hannibal Regional Hospital	Hannibal	90%	136
Missouri Delta Medical Center	Sikeston	90%	115
Nevada Regional Medical Center	Nevada	90%	39
Research Belton Hospital	Belton	90%	41
Washington County Memorial Hospital	Potosi	90%	59
Capital Region Medical Center[2]	Jefferson City	89%	89
Freeman Health System - Freeman West[2]	Joplin	89%	64
Cass Medical Center	Harrisonville	88%	59
McCune-Brooks Hospital	Carthage	88%	42
Northeast Regional Medical Center	Kirksville	88%	34
Saint Mary's Medical Center	Blue Springs	88%	119
Fitzgibbon Memorial Hospital	Marshall	87%	68
Phelps County Regional Medical Center	Rolla	87%	164
Research Medical Center	Kansas City	87%	87
Ripley County Memorial Hospital	Doniphan	87%	30
Saint Anthony's Medical Center[2]	Saint Louis	87%	129
Saint Joseph Medical Center	Kansas City	87%	159
Truman Medical Center - Hospital Hill	Kansas City	87%	89
Boone Hospital Center[2]	Columbia	86%	139
Ozarks Community Hospital[2]	Springfield	86%	50
Saint Alexius Hospital	Saint Louis	84%	91
Hedrick Medical Center	Chillicothe	83%	29
Missouri Southern Healthcare	Dexter	83%	65
Ozarks Medical Center	West Plains	83%	136
University of Missouri Health Care	Columbia	83%	64
Saint Francis Hospital	Mountain View	82%	76
Saint Lukes Hospital[2]	Chesterfield	80%	169
Citizens Memorial Hospital	Bolivar	79%	71
Saint Lukes Hospital of Kansas City	Kansas City	79%	89
Western Missouri Medical Center	Warrensburg	79%	71
Bates County Memorial Hospital	Butler	76%	46
Pemiscot Memorial Hospital	Hayti	76%	37
Texas County Memorial Hospital	Houston	76%	76

17. Blood Culture Timing

Hospital Name	City	Rate	Cases
Audrain Medical Center	Mexico	100%	68
Boone Hospital Center[2]	Columbia	100%	179
Freeman Neosho Hospital	Neosho	100%	43
Golden Valley Memorial Hospital	Clinton	100%	77
Heartland Regional Medical Center	Saint Joseph	100%	453
Lafayette Regional Health Center	Lexington	100%	55
Saint Johns Hospital - Aurora	Aurora	100%	46
Saint Marys Health Center	Jefferson City	100%	174
Wright Memorial Hospital	Trenton	100%	47
Barnes-Jewish St Peters Hospital	Saint Peters	99%	269
Bothwell Regional Health Center	Sedalia	99%	84
Capital Region Medical Center[2]	Jefferson City	99%	141
Centerpoint Medical Center of Independence	Independence	99%	329
Cox Medical Center[2]	Springfield	99%	283
Des Peres Hospital	Saint Louis	99%	263
Fitzgibbon Memorial Hospital	Marshall	99%	76
Kansas City VA Medical Center	Kansas City	99%	122
Mineral Area Regional Medical Center	Farmington	99%	125
Missouri Baptist Medical Center[2]	Town & Country	99%	408
Progress West Healthcare Center	O'Fallon	99%	93
Saint Francis Medical Center	Cape Girardeau	99%	355
Saint Louis-John Cochran VA Medical Center	Saint Louis	99%	86
Cass Medical Center	Harrisonville	98%	59
Jefferson Regional Medical Center	Crystal City	98%	321
Lee's Summit Medical Center	Lee's Summit	98%	99
Missouri Baptist Hospital Sullivan	Sullivan	98%	122
Moberly Regional Medical Center	Moberly	98%	84
Ozarks Community Hospital[2]	Springfield	98%	49
Parkland Health Center	Farmington	98%	139
Research Belton Hospital	Belton	98%	64
Saint Johns Hospital-Lebanon	Lebanon	98%	133
Saint Lukes Hospital[2]	Chesterfield	98%	255
Saint Lukes Hospital of Kansas City	Kansas City	98%	146
Saint Lukes Northland Hospital	Kansas City	98%	108
SSM St Joseph Hospital West[2]	Lake Saint Louis	98%	124
Truman Medical Center - Hospital Hill	Kansas City	98%	138
Truman Medical Center Lakewood	Kansas City	98%	94
University of Missouri Health Care	Columbia	98%	125
Christian Hospital Northeast	Saint Louis	97%	278
Columbia Missouri VA Medical Center	Columbia	97%	65
Lake Regional Health System	Osage Beach	97%	185
Perry County Memorial Hospital	Perryville	97%	39
Poplar Bluff Regional Medical Center	Poplar Bluff	97%	233
Research Medical Center	Kansas City	97%	154
Saint Francis Hospital	Maryville	97%	31
Saint John's Regional Medical Center	Joplin	97%	325
Saint Joseph Medical Center	Kansas City	97%	264
Saint Luke's East Lee's Summit Hospital	Lees Summit	97%	155
Saint Mary's Medical Center	Blue Springs	97%	204
Skaggs Community Health Center[2]	Branson	97%	187
Southeast Missouri Hospital	Cape Girardeau	97%	231
SSM Depaul Health Center[2]	Bridgeton	97%	118
Twin Rivers Regional Medical Center	Kennett	97%	110
Callaway Community Hospital	Fulton	96%	26
Citizens Memorial Hospital	Bolivar	96%	117
Freeman Health System - Freeman West[2]	Joplin	96%	138
Liberty Hospital	Liberty	96%	206
North Kansas City Hospital[2]	N Kansas City	96%	189
Northeast Regional Medical Center	Kirksville	96%	113
Ozarks Medical Center	West Plains	96%	171
Saint Alexius Hospital	Saint Louis	96%	108

NOTE: Hospital profiles are in alphabetical order by state, then city, then hospital within the city; Rankings exclude hospitals with less than 25 cases except for patient surveys which excludes hospitals with less than 100 cases; (a) 100–299 cases; (1) The number of cases is too small to be sure how well a hospital is performing; (2) The hospital indicated that the data submitted for this measure were based on a sample of cases; (3) Data was collected during a shorter time period (fewer quarters) than the maximum possible time for this measure; (4) Suppressed for one or more quarters by CMS; (5) No data is available from the hospital for this measure; (6) Fewer than 100 patients completed the HCAHPS survey. Use these rates with caution, as the number of surveys may be too low to reliably assess hospital performance; (7) Survey results are based on less than 12 months of data; (8) Survey results are not available for this reporting period; (9) No or very few patients were eligible for the HCAHPS survey. The scores shown, if any, reflect a very small number of surveys; (10) A state average was not calculated because too few hospitals in the state submitted data; (11) There were discrepancies in the data collection process; Please refer to the User's Guide for a full explanation of data.

Hospital Name	City	Rate	Cases
Saint Anthony's Medical Center[2]	Saint Louis	96%	141
SSM St Clare Health Center[2]	Fenton	96%	122
Texas County Memorial Hospital	Houston	96%	85
Hannibal Regional Hospital	Hannibal	95%	185
Hedrick Medical Center	Chillicothe	95%	41
Missouri Southern Healthcare	Dexter	95%	41
Saint John's Regional Health Center[2]	Springfield	95%	99
SSM St Joseph Health Center[2]	Saint Charles	95%	88
Saint Francis Hospital	Mountain View	94%	65
Saint Johns Mercy Hospital[2]	Washington	94%	81
SSM St Marys Health Center[2]	Richmond Hghts	94%	97
Western Missouri Medical Center	Warrensburg	94%	69
Barnes Jewish Hospital[2]	Saint Louis	93%	103
Cox Monett Hospital	Monett	93%	59
Forest Park Hospital	Saint Louis	93%	56
Lincoln County Medical Center	Troy	93%	44
McCune-Brooks Hospital	Carthage	93%	58
Saint Johns Hospital - Cassville	Cassville	93%	27
Saint Louis University Hospital	Saint Louis	93%	131
Washington County Memorial Hospital	Potosi	93%	82
Cameron Regional Medical Center	Cameron	92%	61
Ripley County Memorial Hospital	Doniphan	92%	37
Saint Johns Mercy Medical Center[2]	Saint Louis	92%	145
Phelps County Regional Medical Center	Rolla	91%	221
Barnes-Jewish West County Hospital	Creve Coeur	90%	39
Missouri Delta Medical Center	Sikeston	90%	128
Salem Memorial District Hospital	Salem	89%	38
Scotland County Hospital[2]	Memphis	89%	27
Bates County Memorial Hospital	Butler	86%	44

18. Influenza Vaccine

Hospital Name	City	Rate	Cases
Capital Region Medical Center[2]	Jefferson City	100%	115
Des Peres Hospital	Saint Louis	100%	162
Lafayette Regional Health Center	Lexington	100%	48
Lee's Summit Medical Center	Lee's Summit	100%	58
Poplar Bluff Regional Medical Center	Poplar Bluff	100%	161
Saint Francis Hospital	Maryville	100%	28
Saint Johns Mercy Hospital[2]	Washington	100%	76
Saint Lukes Northland Hospital	Kansas City	100%	97
Saint Marys Health Center	Jefferson City	100%	133
Twin Rivers Regional Medical Center	Kennett	100%	59
Heartland Regional Medical Center	Saint Joseph	99%	324
Saint Louis University Hospital	Saint Louis	99%	133
Cox Medical Center[2]	Springfield	98%	212
Golden Valley Memorial Hospital	Clinton	98%	62
Ozarks Community Hospital[2]	Springfield	98%	46
Saint Alexius Hospital	Saint Louis	98%	89
Audrain Medical Center	Mexico	97%	67
Centerpoint Medical Center of Independence	Independence	97%	189
Citizens Memorial Hospital	Bolivar	97%	77
Forest Park Hospital	Saint Louis	97%	33
Lake Regional Health System	Osage Beach	97%	107
Missouri Baptist Hospital Sullivan	Sullivan	97%	61
Missouri Baptist Medical Center[2]	Town & Country	97%	356
Parkland Health Center	Farmington	97%	101
Research Belton Hospital	Belton	97%	35
Saint Francis Hospital	Mountain View	97%	65
Truman Medical Center - Hospital Hill	Kansas City	97%	59
Jefferson Regional Medical Center	Crystal City	96%	210
Liberty Hospital	Liberty	96%	180
North Kansas City Hospital[2]	N Kansas City	96%	159
Pike County Memorial Hospital	Louisiana	96%	28
Skaggs Community Health Center[2]	Branson	96%	104
Hedrick Medical Center	Chillicothe	95%	37
Research Medical Center	Kansas City	95%	186
Saint John's Regional Health Center[2]	Springfield	95%	110
Saint Johns Hospital - Aurora	Aurora	95%	38
Saint Luke's East Lee's Summit Hospital	Lees Summit	95%	106
Salem Memorial District Hospital	Salem	95%	44
SSM St Joseph Hospital West[2]	Lake Saint Louis	95%	81
Cooper County Memorial Hospital	Boonville	94%	31
Lincoln County Medical Center	Troy	94%	34
Moberly Regional Medical Center	Moberly	94%	67
Saint John's Regional Medical Center	Joplin	94%	328
Truman Medical Center Lakewood	Kansas City	94%	52
Mineral Area Regional Medical Center	Farmington	93%	94
Saint Johns Hospital-Lebanon	Lebanon	93%	74
University of Missouri Health Care	Columbia	93%	137
Barnes Jewish Hospital[2]	Saint Louis	91%	273
Cameron Regional Medical Center	Cameron	91%	57
Freeman Health System - Freeman West[2]	Joplin	91%	108
Southeast Missouri Hospital	Cape Girardeau	91%	150
SSM St Clare Health Center[2]	Fenton	91%	77
SSM St Joseph Health Center[2]	Saint Charles	91%	82
Columbia Missouri VA Medical Center	Columbia	90%	61
Freeman Neosho Hospital	Neosho	90%	48
Kansas City VA Medical Center	Kansas City	90%	125
Phelps County Regional Medical Center	Rolla	90%	144
Saint Mary's Medical Center	Blue Springs	90%	112
Barnes-Jewish St Peters Hospital	Saint Peters	89%	174
Boone Hospital Center[2]	Columbia	89%	204
Perry County Memorial Hospital	Perryville	89%	36
Saint Louis-John Cochran VA Medical Center	Saint Louis	89%	62
Saint Lukes Hospital of Kansas City	Kansas City	89%	164
Cox Monett Hospital	Monett	88%	50
Northeast Regional Medical Center	Kirksville	88%	91
Saint Joseph Medical Center	Kansas City	88%	199
Nevada Regional Medical Center	Nevada	86%	37
Progress West Healthcare Center	O'Fallon	85%	60
Cass Medical Center	Harrisonville	84%	49
McCune-Brooks Hospital	Carthage	84%	32
SSM St Marys Health Center[2]	Richmond Hghts	83%	78
Texas County Memorial Hospital	Houston	82%	62
Washington County Memorial Hospital	Potosi	82%	28
Barnes-Jewish West County Hospital	Creve Coeur	81%	27
Christian Hospital Northeast	Saint Louis	81%	213
Saint Anthony's Medical Center[2]	Saint Louis	81%	128
Saint Johns Mercy Medical Center[2]	Saint Louis	80%	87
Saint Francis Medical Center	Cape Girardeau	79%	274
Scotland County Hospital[2]	Memphis	79%	29
Missouri Southern Healthcare	Dexter	78%	77
Saint Lukes Hospital[2]	Chesterfield	78%	308
Hannibal Regional Hospital	Hannibal	77%	162
Missouri Delta Medical Center	Sikeston	77%	117
SSM Depaul Health Center[2]	Bridgeton	76%	74
Fitzgibbon Memorial Hospital	Marshall	75%	68
Western Missouri Medical Center	Warrensburg	75%	64
Bothwell Regional Health Center	Sedalia	71%	90
Ozarks Medical Center	West Plains	68%	120
Ripley County Memorial Hospital	Doniphan	67%	33
Bates County Memorial Hospital	Butler	66%	44
Barton County Memorial Hospital	Lamar	53%	43
Pemiscot Memorial Hospital	Hayti	48%	29

19. Initial Antibiotic Timing

Hospital Name	City	Rate	Cases
Audrain Medical Center	Mexico	100%	82
Lee's Summit Medical Center	Lee's Summit	100%	105
Nevada Regional Medical Center	Nevada	100%	54
Research Belton Hospital	Belton	100%	59
Saint Johns Hospital - Cassville	Cassville	100%	38
Saint Marys Health Center	Jefferson City	100%	212
Ste Genevieve County Memorial Hospital[2]	Ste Genevieve	100%	27
Bates County Memorial Hospital	Butler	99%	80
Cass Medical Center	Harrisonville	99%	86
Golden Valley Memorial Hospital	Clinton	99%	121
Heartland Regional Medical Center	Saint Joseph	99%	432
Jefferson Regional Medical Center	Crystal City	99%	328
Lafayette Regional Health Center	Lexington	99%	67
McCune-Brooks Hospital	Carthage	99%	69
Mineral Area Regional Medical Center	Farmington	99%	139
Saint Johns Mercy Hospital[2]	Washington	99%	143
Saint Johns Mercy Medical Center[2]	Saint Louis	99%	151
Twin Rivers Regional Medical Center	Kennett	99%	106
Barnes-Jewish West County Hospital	Creve Coeur	98%	55
Centerpoint Medical Center of Independence	Independence	98%	304
Des Peres Hospital	Saint Louis	98%	260
Hedrick Medical Center	Chillicothe	98%	58
Liberty Hospital	Liberty	98%	264
Lincoln County Medical Center	Troy	98%	54
Perry County Memorial Hospital	Perryville	98%	50
Progress West Healthcare Center	O'Fallon	98%	85
Western Missouri Medical Center	Warrensburg	98%	118
Barnes-Jewish St Peters Hospital	Saint Peters	97%	265
Boone Hospital Center[2]	Columbia	97%	229
Cameron Regional Medical Center	Cameron	97%	112
Cox Medical Center[2]	Springfield	97%	235
Freeman Health System - Freeman West[2]	Joplin	97%	133
Freeman Neosho Hospital	Neosho	97%	66
Ozarks Community Hospital[2]	Springfield	97%	75
Pike County Memorial Hospital	Louisiana	97%	34
Saint Francis Medical Center	Cape Girardeau	97%	315
Saint Johns Hospital - Aurora	Aurora	97%	71
Saint Johns Hospital-Lebanon	Lebanon	97%	150
Scotland County Hospital[2]	Memphis	97%	38
Capital Region Medical Center[2]	Jefferson City	96%	148
Columbia Missouri VA Medical Center	Columbia	96%	51
Cox Monett Hospital	Monett	96%	69
Forest Park Hospital	Saint Louis	96%	67
Lake Regional Health System	Osage Beach	96%	181
Missouri Baptist Hospital Sullivan	Sullivan	96%	127
Missouri Southern Healthcare	Dexter	96%	94
Moberly Regional Medical Center	Moberly	96%	97
North Kansas City Hospital[2]	N Kansas City	96%	281
Phelps County Regional Medical Center	Rolla	96%	216
Research Medical Center	Kansas City	96%	163
Saint Francis Hospital	Maryville	96%	54
Saint John's Regional Health Center[2]	Springfield	96%	104
Saint John's Regional Medical Center	Joplin	96%	427
Saint Luke's East Lee's Summit Hospital	Lees Summit	96%	158
Saint Mary's Medical Center	Blue Springs	96%	203
Skaggs Community Health Center[2]	Branson	96%	159
Washington County Memorial Hospital	Potosi	96%	75
Barton County Memorial Hospital	Lamar	95%	64
Hannibal Regional Hospital	Hannibal	95%	221
Missouri Baptist Medical Center[2]	Town & Country	95%	431
Saint Anthony's Medical Center[2]	Saint Louis	95%	215
Saint Francis Hospital	Mountain View	95%	95
Saint Louis-John Cochran VA Medical Center	Saint Louis	95%	80
Saint Lukes Northland Hospital	Kansas City	95%	138
Texas County Memorial Hospital	Houston	95%	101
Bothwell Regional Health Center	Sedalia	94%	153
Callaway Community Hospital	Fulton	94%	32
Northeast Regional Medical Center	Kirksville	94%	119
Parkland Health Center	Farmington	94%	148
Poplar Bluff Regional Medical Center	Poplar Bluff	94%	216
Saint Lukes Hospital[2]	Chesterfield	94%	346
SSM St Joseph Health Center[2]	Saint Charles	94%	108
SSM St Joseph Hospital West[2]	Lake Saint Louis	94%	125
Wright Memorial Hospital	Trenton	94%	51
Hermann Area District Hospital	Hermann	93%	28
Kansas City VA Medical Center	Kansas City	93%	123
Missouri Delta Medical Center	Sikeston	93%	163
Ripley County Memorial Hospital	Doniphan	93%	44
Saint Joseph Medical Center	Kansas City	93%	275
Saint Lukes Hospital of Kansas City	Kansas City	93%	205
Citizens Memorial Hospital	Bolivar	92%	133
Pershing Memorial Hospital[3]	Brookfield	92%	25
Saint Alexius Hospital	Saint Louis	92%	125
Saint Louis University Hospital	Saint Louis	92%	157
Southeast Missouri Hospital	Cape Girardeau	92%	196
SSM St Clare Health Center[2]	Fenton	92%	143
Barnes Jewish Hospital[2]	Saint Louis	91%	386
Christian Hospital Northeast	Saint Louis	91%	289
Truman Medical Center - Hospital Hill	Kansas City	91%	152
Salem Memorial District Hospital	Salem	90%	59
SSM Depaul Health Center[2]	Bridgeton	90%	148
Fitzgibbon Memorial Hospital	Marshall	89%	87
Ozarks Medical Center	West Plains	88%	207
Truman Medical Center Lakewood	Kansas City	88%	109
SSM St Marys Health Center[2]	Richmond Hghts	85%	136
University of Missouri Health Care	Columbia	79%	118
Pemiscot Memorial Hospital	Hayti	72%	43

20. Pneumococcal Vaccine

Hospital Name	City	Rate	Cases
Des Peres Hospital	Saint Louis	100%	241
Heartland Regional Medical Center	Saint Joseph	100%	462
Lafayette Regional Health Center	Lexington	100%	60
Lee's Summit Medical Center	Lee's Summit	100%	98
Ozarks Community Hospital[2]	Springfield	100%	58
Pike County Memorial Hospital	Louisiana	100%	30
Poplar Bluff Regional Medical Center	Poplar Bluff	100%	219
Saint Francis Hospital	Maryville	100%	42
Saint Johns Hospital - Cassville	Cassville	100%	25
Saint Marys Health Center	Jefferson City	100%	152
Twin Rivers Regional Medical Center	Kennett	100%	76
Capital Region Medical Center[2]	Jefferson City	99%	142
Columbia Missouri VA Medical Center	Columbia	99%	86
Golden Valley Memorial Hospital	Clinton	99%	95
Moberly Regional Medical Center	Moberly	99%	106
Research Medical Center	Kansas City	99%	187
Saint Francis Hospital	Mountain View	99%	91
Saint Johns Mercy Hospital[2]	Washington	99%	120
Centerpoint Medical Center of Independence	Independence	98%	249
Cox Medical Center[2]	Springfield	98%	230
Hedrick Medical Center	Chillicothe	98%	54
Kansas City VA Medical Center	Kansas City	98%	126
Research Belton Hospital	Belton	98%	44
Saint Johns Hospital - Aurora	Aurora	98%	51
Saint Louis University Hospital	Saint Louis	98%	111
Saint Louis-John Cochran VA Medical Center	Saint Louis	98%	45
Salem Memorial District Hospital	Salem	98%	54
SSM St Joseph Health Center[2]	Saint Charles	98%	135
Lake Regional Health System	Osage Beach	97%	168
Liberty Hospital	Liberty	97%	243
Missouri Baptist Hospital Sullivan	Sullivan	97%	95
Missouri Baptist Medical Center[2]	Town & Country	97%	505
Poplar Bluff VA Medical Center	Poplar Bluff	97%	33
Saint John's Regional Medical Center	Joplin	97%	407
Saint Luke's East Lee's Summit Hospital	Lees Summit	97%	151
Saint Lukes Northland Hospital	Kansas City	97%	101
Barnes-Jewish St Peters Hospital	Saint Peters	96%	206
Citizens Memorial Hospital	Bolivar	96%	108
Freeman Health System - Freeman West[2]	Joplin	96%	139
Freeman Neosho Hospital	Neosho	96%	55
Northeast Regional Medical Center	Kirksville	96%	137
Phelps County Regional Medical Center	Rolla	96%	192
Progress West Healthcare Center	O'Fallon	96%	52

NOTE: Hospital profiles are in alphabetical order by state, then city, then hospital within the city; Rankings exclude hospitals with less than 25 cases except for patient surveys which excludes hospitals with less than 100 cases; (a) 100–299 cases; (1) The number of cases is too small to be sure how well a hospital is performing; (2) The hospital indicated that the data submitted for this measure were based on a sample of cases; (3) Data was collected during a shorter time period (fewer quarters) than the maximum possible time for this measure; (4) Suppressed for one or more quarters by CMS; (5) No data is available from the hospital for this measure; (6) Fewer than 100 patients completed the HCAHPS survey. Use these rates with caution, as the number of surveys may be too low to reliably assess hospital performance; (7) Survey results are based on less than 12 months of data; (8) Survey results are not available for this reporting period; (9) No or very few patients were eligible for the HCAHPS survey. The scores shown, if any, reflect a very small number of surveys; (10) A state average was not calculated because too few hospitals in the state submitted data; (11) There were discrepancies in the data collection process; Please refer to the User's Guide for a full explanation of data.

Saint Johns Hospital-Lebanon	Lebanon	96%	118
SSM St Joseph Hospital West[2]	Lake Saint Louis	96%	134
University of Missouri Health Care	Columbia	96%	137
Cass Medical Center	Harrisonville	95%	64
North Kansas City Hospital[2]	N Kansas City	95%	249
Saint John's Regional Health Center[2]	Springfield	95%	125
Skaggs Community Health Center[2]	Branson	95%	150
Southeast Missouri Hospital	Cape Girardeau	95%	198
SSM St Marys Health Center[2]	Richmond Hghts	95%	125
Audrain Medical Center	Mexico	94%	86
Callaway Community Hospital	Fulton	94%	32
Hannibal Regional Hospital	Hannibal	94%	245
Parkland Health Center	Farmington	94%	122
Saint Alexius Hospital	Saint Louis	94%	94
Barnes-Jewish West County Hospital	Creve Coeur	93%	43
Boone Hospital Center[2]	Columbia	93%	291
Cameron Regional Medical Center	Cameron	93%	92
Forest Park Hospital	Saint Louis	93%	27
Harrison County Community Hospital	Bethany	93%	27
Mineral Area Regional Medical Center	Farmington	93%	103
Ray County Memorial Hospital	Richmond	93%	28
Saint Lukes Hospital of Kansas City	Kansas City	93%	215
Jefferson Regional Medical Center	Crystal City	92%	264
Saint Mary's Medical Center	Blue Springs	92%	166
Truman Medical Center - Hospital Hill	Kansas City	92%	38
Truman Medical Center Lakewood	Kansas City	92%	39
Cox Monett Hospital	Monett	91%	57
SSM Depaul Health Center[2]	Bridgeton	91%	136
Barnes Jewish Hospital[2]	Saint Louis	90%	270
Saint Anthony's Medical Center[2]	Saint Louis	90%	186
SSM St Clare Health Center[2]	Fenton	90%	131
Saint Francis Medical Center	Cape Girardeau	89%	354
Saint Johns Mercy Medical Center[2]	Saint Louis	89%	148
Saint Joseph Medical Center	Kansas City	89%	266
Christian Hospital Northeast	Saint Louis	88%	243
Lincoln County Medical Center	Troy	88%	43
Perry County Memorial Hospital	Perryville	88%	48
Bates County Memorial Hospital	Butler	87%	60
Bothwell Regional Health Center	Sedalia	85%	178
Missouri Southern Healthcare	Dexter	85%	105
Saint Lukes Hospital[2]	Chesterfield	85%	434
McCune-Brooks Hospital	Carthage	84%	45
Fitzgibbon Memorial Hospital	Marshall	82%	95
Missouri Delta Medical Center	Sikeston	82%	154
Cooper County Memorial Hospital	Boonville	81%	32
Scotland County Hospital[2]	Memphis	81%	47
Texas County Memorial Hospital	Houston	81%	88
Wright Memorial Hospital	Trenton	80%	41
Ozarks Medical Center	West Plains	79%	166
Washington County Memorial Hospital	Potosi	79%	56
Nevada Regional Medical Center	Nevada	77%	47
Western Missouri Medical Center	Warrensburg	77%	84
Ripley County Memorial Hospital	Doniphan	73%	45
Barton County Memorial Hospital	Lamar	58%	55

21. Smoking Cessation Advice

Hospital Name	City	Rate	Cases
Audrain Medical Center	Mexico	100%	31
Barnes-Jewish St Peters Hospital	Saint Peters	100%	96
Bothwell Regional Health Center	Sedalia	100%	73
Capital Region Medical Center[2]	Jefferson City	100%	60
Centerpoint Medical Center of Independence	Independence	100%	117
Christian Hospital Northeast	Saint Louis	100%	149
Columbia Missouri VA Medical Center	Columbia	100%	31
Des Peres Hospital	Saint Louis	100%	78
Golden Valley Memorial Hospital	Clinton	100%	48
Hannibal Regional Hospital	Hannibal	100%	97
Heartland Regional Medical Center	Saint Joseph	100%	217
Jefferson Regional Medical Center	Crystal City	100%	162
Kansas City VA Medical Center	Kansas City	100%	57
Lafayette Regional Health Center	Lexington	100%	25
Lee's Summit Medical Center	Lee's Summit	100%	28
Missouri Baptist Hospital Sullivan	Sullivan	100%	48
Missouri Baptist Medical Center[2]	Town & Country	100%	120
Missouri Delta Medical Center	Sikeston	100%	108
Moberly Regional Medical Center	Moberly	100%	45
Nevada Regional Medical Center	Nevada	100%	26
Northeast Regional Medical Center	Kirksville	100%	66
Parkland Health Center	Farmington	100%	77
Phelps County Regional Medical Center	Rolla	100%	99
Poplar Bluff Regional Medical Center	Poplar Bluff	100%	116
Progress West Healthcare Center	O'Fallon	100%	38
Saint Alexius Hospital	Saint Louis	100%	88
Saint John's Regional Medical Center	Joplin	100%	239
Saint Johns Hospital - Aurora	Aurora	100%	30
Saint Johns Mercy Hospital[2]	Washington	100%	47
Saint Johns Mercy Medical Center[2]	Saint Louis	100%	53
Saint Lukes Hospital[2]	Chesterfield	100%	109
Saint Lukes Hospital of Kansas City	Kansas City	100%	98
Saint Lukes Northland Hospital	Kansas City	100%	58
Saint Marys Health Center	Jefferson City	100%	85
SSM Depaul Health Center[2]	Bridgeton	100%	90
SSM St Clare Health Center[2]	Fenton	100%	69
SSM St Joseph Health Center[2]	Saint Charles	100%	62
SSM St Joseph Hospital West[2]	Lake Saint Louis	100%	79
Twin Rivers Regional Medical Center	Kennett	100%	48
Boone Hospital Center[2]	Columbia	99%	83
Saint Francis Medical Center	Cape Girardeau	99%	164
Saint Louis University Hospital	Saint Louis	99%	137
Truman Medical Center - Hospital Hill	Kansas City	99%	146
Barnes Jewish Hospital[2]	Saint Louis	98%	198
Freeman Health System - Freeman West[2]	Joplin	98%	111
Liberty Hospital	Liberty	98%	130
North Kansas City Hospital[2]	N Kansas City	98%	123
Research Medical Center	Kansas City	98%	133
Truman Medical Center Lakewood	Kansas City	98%	48
University of Missouri Health Care	Columbia	98%	89
Cass Medical Center	Harrisonville	97%	37
Cox Medical Center[2]	Springfield	97%	137
Forest Park Hospital	Saint Louis	97%	31
Freeman Neosho Hospital	Neosho	97%	37
Lake Regional Health System	Osage Beach	97%	79
Ozarks Medical Center	West Plains	97%	71
Saint Joseph Medical Center	Kansas City	97%	77
Saint Louis-John Cochran VA Medical Center	Saint Louis	97%	63
Mineral Area Regional Medical Center	Farmington	96%	71
SSM St Marys Health Center[2]	Richmond Hghts	96%	74
Texas County Memorial Hospital	Houston	96%	27
Citizens Memorial Hospital	Bolivar	95%	58
Ozarks Community Hospital[2]	Springfield	95%	39
Saint Johns Hospital-Lebanon	Lebanon	95%	42
Saint Luke's East Lee's Summit Hospital	Lees Summit	95%	41
Saint Anthony's Medical Center[2]	Saint Louis	94%	77
Saint John's Regional Health Center[2]	Springfield	94%	79
Saint Mary's Medical Center	Blue Springs	93%	55
Cox Monett Hospital	Monett	92%	26
Fitzgibbon Memorial Hospital	Marshall	92%	36
Cameron Regional Medical Center	Cameron	90%	51
Missouri Southern Healthcare	Dexter	89%	38
Skaggs Community Health Center[2]	Branson	89%	79
Southeast Missouri Hospital	Cape Girardeau	89%	104
Western Missouri Medical Center	Warrensburg	84%	31
Washington County Memorial Hospital	Potosi	76%	38

Surgical Care Improvement Project

22. Appropriate VTP Within 24 Hours

Hospital Name	City	Rate	Cases
Columbia Missouri VA Medical Center[2]	Columbia	100%	93
Parkland Health Center	Farmington	100%	29
Saint Marys Health Center	Jefferson City	100%	186
Saint Johns Hospital-Lebanon	Lebanon	99%	90
SSM St Joseph Hospital West[2]	Lake Saint Louis	99%	227
Women's and Children's Hospital[2]	Columbia	99%	162
Heartland Regional Medical Center[2]	Saint Joseph	98%	250
Lee's Summit Medical Center	Lee's Summit	98%	119
Moberly Regional Medical Center[2]	Moberly	98%	48
Northeast Regional Medical Center[2]	Kirksville	98%	90
Research Belton Hospital[2]	Belton	98%	45
Saint Francis Hospital	Maryville	98%	41
SSM St Joseph Health Center[2]	Saint Charles	98%	249
University of Missouri Health Care	Columbia	98%	501
Barnes-Jewish West County Hospital[2]	Creve Coeur	97%	178
Freeman Health System - Freeman West[2]	Joplin	97%	255
McCune-Brooks Hospital	Carthage	97%	32
Barnes Jewish Hospital[2]	Saint Louis	96%	261
Barnes-Jewish St Peters Hospital	Saint Peters	96%	186
Capital Region Medical Center[2]	Jefferson City	96%	158
Christian Hospital Northeast[2]	Saint Louis	96%	320
Citizens Memorial Hospital	Bolivar	96%	120
Des Peres Hospital[2]	Saint Louis	96%	142
Kansas City VA Medical Center[2]	Kansas City	96%	113
Missouri Baptist Medical Center[2]	Town & Country	96%	214
Poplar Bluff Regional Medical Center[2]	Poplar Bluff	96%	200
Research Medical Center[2]	Kansas City	96%	252
Saint Louis University Hospital[2]	Saint Louis	96%	230
Saint Louis-John Cochran VA Medical Center[2]	Saint Louis	96%	182
Boone Hospital Center[2]	Columbia	95%	182
Cox Medical Center[2]	Springfield	95%	234
Progress West Healthcare Center	O'Fallon	95%	75
Saint Johns Mercy Hospital[2]	Washington	95%	119
Saint Johns Mercy Medical Center[2]	Saint Louis	95%	143
Saint Lukes Hospital[2]	Chesterfield	95%	317
SSM Depaul Health Center[2]	Bridgeton	95%	197
SSM St Clare Health Center[2]	Fenton	95%	244
Jefferson Regional Medical Center[2]	Crystal City	94%	155
Saint John's Regional Medical Center	Joplin	94%	399
SSM St Marys Health Center[2]	Richmond Hghts	94%	289
Audrain Medical Center	Mexico	93%	60
Hannibal Regional Hospital	Hannibal	93%	152
Saint Francis Medical Center	Cape Girardeau	93%	368
Cameron Regional Medical Center	Cameron	92%	48
Centerpoint Medical Center of Independence[2]	Independence	92%	233
Saint Anthony's Medical Center[2]	Saint Louis	92%	324
Skaggs Community Health Center[2]	Branson	92%	100
Truman Medical Center - Hospital Hill[2]	Kansas City	92%	138
Saint Alexius Hospital	Saint Louis	91%	45
Saint Mary's Medical Center[2]	Blue Springs	91%	133
Saint John's Regional Health Center[2]	Springfield	89%	173
Cass Medical Center	Harrisonville	88%	33
Golden Valley Memorial Hospital	Clinton	88%	40
Saint Lukes Hospital of Kansas City[2]	Kansas City	88%	298
Saint Lukes Northland Hospital	Kansas City	88%	110
Liberty Hospital	Liberty	87%	318
Ozarks Medical Center	West Plains	87%	119
Saint Luke's East Lee's Summit Hospital	Lees Summit	87%	145
Truman Medical Center Lakewood	Kansas City	86%	29
Fitzgibbon Memorial Hospital	Marshall	85%	27
Nevada Regional Medical Center	Nevada	85%	27
Phelps County Regional Medical Center	Rolla	85%	197
Southeast Missouri Hospital[2]	Cape Girardeau	84%	164
Missouri Delta Medical Center	Sikeston	83%	72
Saint Joseph Medical Center[2]	Kansas City	83%	157
Western Missouri Medical Center	Warrensburg	82%	73
Bates County Memorial Hospital	Butler	80%	30
Lake Regional Health System	Osage Beach	80%	201
North Kansas City Hospital[2]	N Kansas City	80%	353
Bothwell Regional Health Center	Sedalia	66%	89

23. Appropriate Hair Removal

Hospital Name	City	Rate	Cases
Audrain Medical Center	Mexico	100%	287
Barnes Jewish Hospital[2]	Saint Louis	100%	896
Barnes-Jewish St Peters Hospital	Saint Peters	100%	420
Barnes-Jewish West County Hospital[2]	Creve Coeur	100%	882
Boone Hospital Center[2]	Columbia	100%	911
Capital Region Medical Center[2]	Jefferson City	100%	545
Centerpoint Medical Center of Independence[2]	Independence	100%	621
Christian Hospital Northeast[2]	Saint Louis	100%	828
Citizens Memorial Hospital	Bolivar	100%	231
Columbia Missouri VA Medical Center[2]	Columbia	100%	275
Cox Medical Center[2]	Springfield	100%	685
Des Peres Hospital[2]	Saint Louis	100%	464
Fitzgibbon Memorial Hospital	Marshall	100%	63
Forest Park Hospital[3]	Saint Louis	100%	25
Freeman Health System - Freeman West[2]	Joplin	100%	820
Golden Valley Memorial Hospital	Clinton	100%	109
Hannibal Regional Hospital	Hannibal	100%	632
Heartland Regional Medical Center[2]	Saint Joseph	100%	1141
Jefferson Regional Medical Center[2]	Crystal City	100%	488
Kansas City VA Medical Center[2]	Kansas City	100%	152
Lake Regional Health System	Osage Beach	100%	385
Lee's Summit Medical Center	Lee's Summit	100%	350
Mineral Area Regional Medical Center[2]	Farmington	100%	72
Missouri Baptist Hospital Sullivan	Sullivan	100%	36
Missouri Baptist Medical Center[2]	Town & Country	100%	921
Missouri Delta Medical Center	Sikeston	100%	184
Missouri Southern Healthcare	Dexter	100%	25
Moberly Regional Medical Center[2]	Moberly	100%	115
Nevada Regional Medical Center	Nevada	100%	34
Northeast Regional Medical Center[2]	Kirksville	100%	246
Ozarks Community Hospital	Springfield	100%	62
Ozarks Medical Center	West Plains	100%	261
Parkland Health Center	Farmington	100%	113
Phelps County Regional Medical Center	Rolla	100%	383
Poplar Bluff Regional Medical Center[2]	Poplar Bluff	100%	763
Progress West Healthcare Center	O'Fallon	100%	350
Research Belton Hospital[2]	Belton	100%	223
Research Medical Center[2]	Kansas City	100%	723
Saint Alexius Hospital	Saint Louis	100%	82
Saint Anthony's Medical Center[2]	Saint Louis	100%	1177
Saint Francis Hospital	Maryville	100%	110
Saint Francis Medical Center	Cape Girardeau	100%	1243
Saint John's Regional Health Center[2]	Springfield	100%	689
Saint John's Regional Medical Center	Joplin	100%	1080
Saint Johns Hospital-Lebanon	Lebanon	100%	231
Saint Johns Mercy Hospital[2]	Washington	100%	306
Saint Johns Mercy Medical Center[2]	Saint Louis	100%	609
Saint Joseph Medical Center[2]	Kansas City	100%	491
Saint Louis University Hospital[2]	Saint Louis	100%	442
Saint Louis-John Cochran VA Medical Center[2]	Saint Louis	100%	260
Saint Luke's East Lee's Summit Hospital	Lees Summit	100%	533
Saint Lukes Cancer Institute[2,3]	Kansas City	100%	84
Saint Lukes Northland Hospital	Kansas City	100%	269
Saint Mary's Medical Center[2]	Blue Springs	100%	282
Saint Marys Health Center	Jefferson City	100%	589
Skaggs Community Health Center[2]	Branson	100%	426
Southeast Missouri Hospital[2]	Cape Girardeau	100%	653
SSM St Clare Health Center[2]	Fenton	100%	802
SSM St Joseph Health Center[2]	Saint Charles	100%	781

NOTE: Hospital profiles are in alphabetical order by state, then city, then hospital within the city; Rankings exclude hospitals with less than 25 cases except for patient surveys which excludes hospitals with less than 100 cases; (a) 100–299 cases; (1) The number of cases is too small to be sure how well a hospital is performing; (2) The hospital indicated that the data submitted for this measure were based on a sample of cases; (3) Data was collected during a shorter time period (fewer quarters) than the maximum possible time for this measure; (4) Suppressed for one or more quarters by CMS; (5) No data is available from the hospital for this measure; (6) Fewer than 100 patients completed the HCAHPS survey. Use these rates with caution, as the number of surveys may be too low to reliably assess hospital performance; (7) Survey results are based on less than 12 months of data; (8) Survey results are not available for this reporting period; (9) No or very few patients were eligible for the HCAHPS survey. The scores shown, if any, reflect a very small number of surveys; (10) A state average was not calculated because too few hospitals in the state submitted data; (11) There were discrepancies in the data collection process; Please refer to the User's Guide for a full explanation of data.

Hospital Name	City	Rate	Cases
SSM St Joseph Hospital West[2]	Lake Saint Louis	100%	537
Truman Medical Center Lakewood	Kansas City	100%	232
Twin Rivers Regional Medical Center	Kennett	100%	79
University of Missouri Health Care	Columbia	100%	911
Western Missouri Medical Center	Warrensburg	100%	210
Women's and Children's Hospital[2]	Columbia	100%	562
Bothwell Regional Health Center	Sedalia	99%	389
Cameron Regional Medical Center	Cameron	99%	95
Liberty Hospital	Liberty	99%	827
North Kansas City Hospital[2]	N Kansas City	99%	938
Saint Lukes Hospital of Kansas City[2]	Kansas City	99%	1190
SSM Depaul Health Center[2]	Bridgeton	99%	849
SSM St Marys Health Center[2]	Richmond Hghts	99%	768
Truman Medical Center - Hospital Hill[2]	Kansas City	99%	316
Lincoln County Medical Center	Troy	98%	47
McCune-Brooks Hospital	Carthage	97%	203
Cass Medical Center	Harrisonville	95%	64
Saint Lukes Hospital[2]	Chesterfield	95%	995
Bates County Memorial Hospital	Butler	86%	37

24. Appropriate Beta Blocker Usage

Hospital Name	City	Rate	Cases
Columbia Missouri VA Medical Center[2]	Columbia	100%	131
Heartland Regional Medical Center[2]	Saint Joseph	100%	444
Northeast Regional Medical Center[2]	Kirksville	100%	69
Research Belton Hospital[2]	Belton	100%	59
Saint Francis Hospital	Maryville	100%	27
Saint Marys Health Center	Jefferson City	100%	161
Barnes-Jewish St Peters Hospital	Saint Peters	99%	94
Barnes-Jewish West County Hospital[2]	Creve Coeur	99%	148
Centerpoint Medical Center of Independence[2]	Independence	99%	159
Christian Hospital Northeast[2]	Saint Louis	99%	283
Poplar Bluff Regional Medical Center[2]	Poplar Bluff	99%	218
SSM St Clare Health Center[2]	Fenton	99%	229
Lee's Summit Medical Center	Lee's Summit	98%	85
Saint John's Regional Medical Center	Joplin	98%	346
Saint Lukes Northland Hospital	Kansas City	98%	59
Truman Medical Center Lakewood	Kansas City	98%	42
Capital Region Medical Center[2]	Jefferson City	97%	179
Des Peres Hospital[2]	Saint Louis	97%	179
Missouri Baptist Medical Center[2]	Town & Country	97%	307
Saint Johns Mercy Medical Center[2]	Saint Louis	97%	176
Saint Lukes Hospital of Kansas City[2]	Kansas City	97%	507
SSM Depaul Health Center[2]	Bridgeton	97%	238
SSM St Joseph Hospital West[2]	Lake Saint Louis	97%	105
SSM St Marys Health Center[2]	Richmond Hghts	97%	209
Missouri Delta Medical Center	Sikeston	96%	28
Saint Johns Hospital-Lebanon	Lebanon	96%	79
Saint Luke's East Lee's Summit Hospital	Lees Summit	96%	138
SSM St Joseph Health Center[2]	Saint Charles	96%	281
Boone Hospital Center[2]	Columbia	95%	263
Cox Medical Center[2]	Springfield	95%	231
Hannibal Regional Hospital	Hannibal	95%	224
Saint Joseph Medical Center[2]	Kansas City	95%	138
Saint Louis University Hospital[2]	Saint Louis	95%	138
Liberty Hospital	Liberty	94%	243
Saint Francis Medical Center	Cape Girardeau	94%	401
Kansas City VA Medical Center[2]	Kansas City	93%	41
Lake Regional Health System	Osage Beach	93%	108
Women's and Children's Hospital[2]	Columbia	93%	126
Barnes Jewish Hospital[2]	Saint Louis	92%	240
Moberly Regional Medical Center[2]	Moberly	92%	36
Saint Lukes Hospital[2]	Chesterfield	92%	320
Saint Mary's Medical Center[2]	Blue Springs	92%	53
Skaggs Community Health Center[2]	Branson	92%	125
Truman Medical Center - Hospital Hill[2]	Kansas City	92%	71
University of Missouri Health Care	Columbia	92%	278
Saint Louis-John Cochran VA Medical Center[2]	Saint Louis	91%	80
Jefferson Regional Medical Center[2]	Crystal City	90%	126
North Kansas City Hospital[2]	N Kansas City	90%	316
Saint Anthony's Medical Center[2]	Saint Louis	90%	358
Western Missouri Medical Center	Warrensburg	90%	39
Cameron Regional Medical Center	Cameron	89%	28
Saint John's Regional Health Center[2]	Springfield	89%	231
Southeast Missouri Hospital[2]	Cape Girardeau	89%	241
Audrain Medical Center	Mexico	88%	72
Research Medical Center[2]	Kansas City	88%	239
Saint Johns Mercy Hospital[2]	Washington	85%	85
Citizens Memorial Hospital	Bolivar	84%	61
Freeman Health System - Freeman West[2]	Joplin	84%	259
Phelps County Regional Medical Center	Rolla	84%	96
Bothwell Regional Health Center	Sedalia	82%	97
Progress West Healthcare Center	O'Fallon	82%	97
Ozarks Medical Center	West Plains	80%	81
Parkland Health Center	Farmington	76%	29
Mineral Area Regional Medical Center[2]	Farmington	75%	28

25. Controlled Postoperative Blood Glucose

Hospital Name	City	Rate	Cases
Saint Marys Health Center	Jefferson City	100%	66
Centerpoint Medical Center of Independence[2]	Independence	99%	110
Columbia Missouri VA Medical Center[2]	Columbia	99%	100
Missouri Baptist Medical Center[2]	Town & Country	99%	187
SSM Depaul Health Center[2]	Bridgeton	99%	159
University of Missouri Health Care	Columbia	99%	93
Liberty Hospital	Liberty	98%	58
North Kansas City Hospital[2]	N Kansas City	98%	181
Saint Johns Mercy Medical Center[2]	Saint Louis	98%	127
Christian Hospital Northeast[2]	Saint Louis	97%	182
Cox Medical Center[2]	Springfield	97%	147
Lake Regional Health System	Osage Beach	96%	52
SSM St Clare Health Center[2]	Fenton	96%	204
SSM St Joseph Health Center[2]	Saint Charles	96%	156
SSM St Marys Health Center[2]	Richmond Hghts	96%	103
Saint Francis Medical Center	Cape Girardeau	95%	222
Saint John's Regional Medical Center	Joplin	95%	155
Saint Lukes Hospital[2]	Chesterfield	95%	194
Boone Hospital Center[2]	Columbia	94%	186
Des Peres Hospital[2]	Saint Louis	94%	125
Heartland Regional Medical Center[2]	Saint Joseph	94%	254
Barnes Jewish Hospital[2]	Saint Louis	93%	148
Freeman Health System - Freeman West[2]	Joplin	93%	179
Research Medical Center[2]	Kansas City	93%	147
Capital Region Medical Center[2]	Jefferson City	92%	86
Poplar Bluff Regional Medical Center[2]	Poplar Bluff	92%	115
Saint John's Regional Health Center[2]	Springfield	92%	146
Saint Joseph Medical Center[2]	Kansas City	92%	108
Saint Louis University Hospital[2]	Saint Louis	92%	64
Saint Lukes Hospital of Kansas City[2]	Kansas City	91%	391
Skaggs Community Health Center[2]	Branson	91%	70
Jefferson Regional Medical Center[2]	Crystal City	89%	57
Saint Anthony's Medical Center[2]	Saint Louis	88%	204
Southeast Missouri Hospital[2]	Cape Girardeau	79%	168

26. Prophylactic Antibiotic Timing

Hospital Name	City	Rate	Cases
Centerpoint Medical Center of Independence[2]	Independence	100%	414
Heartland Regional Medical Center[2]	Saint Joseph	100%	941
Kansas City VA Medical Center	Kansas City	100%	79
Lee's Summit Medical Center	Lee's Summit	100%	232
Saint Lukes Northland Hospital	Kansas City	100%	180
Saint Marys Health Center	Jefferson City	100%	384
Truman Medical Center Lakewood	Kansas City	100%	209
Audrain Medical Center	Mexico	99%	220
Golden Valley Memorial Hospital	Clinton	99%	74
Phelps County Regional Medical Center	Rolla	99%	260
Research Belton Hospital[2]	Belton	99%	177
Saint Francis Hospital	Maryville	99%	100
Saint John's Regional Medical Center	Joplin	99%	659
Saint Luke's East Lee's Summit Hospital	Lees Summit	99%	308
Southeast Missouri Hospital[2]	Cape Girardeau	99%	408
Truman Medical Center - Hospital Hill[2]	Kansas City	99%	223
Western Missouri Medical Center	Warrensburg	99%	173
Barnes Jewish Hospital[2]	Saint Louis	98%	570
Capital Region Medical Center[2]	Jefferson City	98%	373
Christian Hospital Northeast[2]	Saint Louis	98%	459
Missouri Baptist Medical Center[2]	Town & Country	98%	606
Moberly Regional Medical Center[2]	Moberly	98%	81
Poplar Bluff Regional Medical Center[2]	Poplar Bluff	98%	531
Progress West Healthcare Center	O'Fallon	98%	286
Research Medical Center[2]	Kansas City	98%	476
Saint Francis Medical Center	Cape Girardeau	98%	757
Saint Johns Mercy Medical Center[2]	Saint Louis	98%	405
Saint Louis University Hospital[2]	Saint Louis	98%	199
Saint Lukes Cancer Institute[2,3]	Kansas City	98%	53
Saint Mary's Medical Center[2]	Blue Springs	98%	184
SSM Depaul Health Center[2]	Bridgeton	98%	595
SSM St Joseph Hospital West[2]	Lake Saint Louis	98%	376
Twin Rivers Regional Medical Center	Kennett	98%	50
University of Missouri Health Care	Columbia	98%	192
Boone Hospital Center[2]	Columbia	97%	674
Bothwell Regional Health Center	Sedalia	97%	280
Citizens Memorial Hospital	Bolivar	97%	156
Cox Medical Center[2]	Springfield	97%	494
Des Peres Hospital[2]	Saint Louis	97%	321
Hannibal Regional Hospital	Hannibal	97%	461
Parkland Health Center	Farmington	97%	76
Saint Anthony's Medical Center[2]	Saint Louis	97%	816
Saint John's Regional Health Center[2]	Springfield	97%	489
Saint Johns Mercy Hospital[2]	Washington	97%	206
SSM St Clare Health Center[2]	Fenton	97%	575
SSM St Joseph Health Center[2]	Saint Charles	97%	577
SSM St Marys Health Center[2]	Richmond Hghts	97%	550
Freeman Health System - Freeman West[2]	Joplin	96%	598
Missouri Delta Medical Center	Sikeston	96%	106
Northeast Regional Medical Center[2]	Kirksville	96%	159
Ozarks Medical Center	West Plains	96%	184
Saint Johns Hospital-Lebanon	Lebanon	96%	190
Saint Joseph Medical Center[2]	Kansas City	96%	358
Saint Louis-John Cochran VA Medical Center	Saint Louis	96%	162
Saint Lukes Hospital of Kansas City[2]	Kansas City	96%	822
Skaggs Community Health Center[2]	Branson	96%	308
Jefferson Regional Medical Center[2]	Crystal City	95%	339
North Kansas City Hospital[2]	N Kansas City	95%	659
Ozarks Community Hospital	Springfield	95%	64
Columbia Missouri VA Medical Center	Columbia	94%	173
Liberty Hospital	Liberty	94%	490
McCune-Brooks Hospital	Carthage	94%	182
Saint Lukes Hospital[2]	Chesterfield	94%	727
Barnes-Jewish St Peters Hospital	Saint Peters	93%	254
Barnes-Jewish West County Hospital[2]	Creve Coeur	93%	636
Women's and Children's Hospital[2]	Columbia	93%	375
Cameron Regional Medical Center	Cameron	92%	65
Cass Medical Center	Harrisonville	92%	50
Fitzgibbon Memorial Hospital	Marshall	90%	40
Lake Regional Health System	Osage Beach	90%	258
Mineral Area Regional Medical Center[2]	Farmington	88%	40
Lincoln County Medical Center	Troy	84%	38

27. Prophylactic Antibiotic Timing (Outpatient)

Hospital Name	City	Rate	Cases
Parkland Health Center	Farmington	100%	43
Research Belton Hospital	Belton	100%	32
Saint Marys Health Center	Jefferson City	100%	314
Truman Medical Center Lakewood	Kansas City	100%	66
Centerpoint Medical Center of Independence	Independence	99%	531
Heartland Regional Medical Center	Saint Joseph	99%	693
Poplar Bluff Regional Medical Center	Poplar Bluff	99%	223
Citizens Memorial Hospital	Bolivar	98%	173
Saint Johns Mercy Medical Center	Saint Louis	98%	698
Boone Hospital Center	Columbia	97%	724
Capital Region Medical Center	Jefferson City	97%	258
Cox Medical Center	Springfield	97%	778
Des Peres Hospital	Saint Louis	97%	537
Missouri Baptist Medical Center	Town & Country	97%	767
Nevada Regional Medical Center	Nevada	97%	39
Phelps County Regional Medical Center	Rolla	97%	208
Saint John's Regional Medical Center	Joplin	97%	235
Saint Lukes Hospital of Kansas City	Kansas City	97%	529
Saint Mary's Medical Center	Blue Springs	97%	66
SSM St Joseph Health Center	Saint Charles	97%	492
Barnes Jewish Hospital	Saint Louis	96%	765
Barnes-Jewish West County Hospital	Creve Coeur	96%	339
Missouri Delta Medical Center	Sikeston	96%	71
Moberly Regional Medical Center	Moberly	96%	83
Research Medical Center	Kansas City	96%	312
Saint Anthony's Medical Center	Saint Louis	96%	434
Saint Francis Medical Center	Cape Girardeau	96%	843
Saint John's Regional Health Center	Springfield	96%	596
Saint Johns Mercy Hospital	Washington	96%	224
SSM St Clare Health Center	Fenton	96%	516
SSM St Marys Health Center	Richmond Hghts	96%	584
Western Missouri Medical Center	Warrensburg	96%	51
Women's and Children's Hospital	Columbia	96%	372
Fitzgibbon Memorial Hospital	Marshall	95%	106
Ozarks Medical Center	West Plains	95%	222
Saint Joseph Medical Center	Kansas City	95%	395
Saint Louis University Hospital	Saint Louis	95%	171
Southeast Missouri Hospital	Cape Girardeau	95%	565
Audrain Medical Center	Mexico	94%	108
Christian Hospital Northeast	Saint Louis	94%	346
Northeast Regional Medical Center	Kirksville	94%	72
Saint Lukes Cancer Institute[3]	Kansas City	94%	51
Barnes-Jewish St Peters Hospital	Saint Peters	93%	255
Freeman Health System - Freeman West	Joplin	93%	554
Liberty Hospital	Liberty	93%	407
Saint Luke's East Lee's Summit Hospital	Lees Summit	93%	170
SSM Depaul Health Center	Bridgeton	93%	395
Saint Lukes Hospital	Chesterfield	92%	1049
Hannibal Regional Hospital	Hannibal	91%	89
Bothwell Regional Health Center	Sedalia	90%	154
Lee's Summit Medical Center	Lee's Summit	90%	79
North Kansas City Hospital	N Kansas City	90%	761
Ozarks Community Hospital	Springfield	90%	70
University of Missouri Health Care	Columbia	90%	344
Progress West Healthcare Center	O'Fallon	89%	46
SSM St Joseph Hospital West	Lake Saint Louis	89%	214
Golden Valley Memorial Hospital	Clinton	88%	34
Lafayette Regional Health Center	Lexington	88%	26
Saint Lukes Northland Hospital	Kansas City	86%	51
Jefferson Regional Medical Center	Crystal City	85%	149
Mineral Area Regional Medical Center	Farmington	83%	89
Lake Regional Health System	Osage Beach	82%	213
Skaggs Community Health Center	Branson	82%	150
Missouri Baptist Hospital Sullivan	Sullivan	80%	54
Saint Johns Hospital-Lebanon	Lebanon	80%	46
Truman Medical Center - Hospital Hill	Kansas City	79%	207

NOTE: Hospital profiles are in alphabetical order by state, then city, then hospital within the city; Rankings exclude hospitals with less than 25 cases except for patient surveys which excludes hospitals with less than 100 cases; (a) 100–299 cases; (1) The number of cases is too small to be sure how well a hospital is performing; (2) The hospital indicated that the data submitted for this measure were based on a sample of cases; (3) Data was collected during a shorter time period (fewer quarters) than the maximum possible time for this measure; (4) Suppressed for one or more quarters by CMS; (5) No data is available from the hospital for this measure; (6) Fewer than 100 patients completed the HCAHPS survey. Use these rates with caution, as the number of surveys may be too low to reliably assess hospital performance; (7) Survey results are based on less than 12 months of data; (8) Survey results are not available for this reporting period; (9) No or very few patients were eligible for the HCAHPS survey. The scores shown, if any, reflect a very small number of surveys; (10) A state average was not calculated because too few hospitals in the state submitted data; (11) There were discrepancies in the data collection process; Please refer to the User's Guide for a full explanation of data.

28. Prophylactic Antibiotic Selection

Hospital Name	City	Rate	Cases
Barnes-Jewish West County Hospital[2]	Creve Coeur	100%	639
Columbia Missouri VA Medical Center	Columbia	100%	172
Heartland Regional Medical Center[2]	Saint Joseph	100%	951
Kansas City VA Medical Center	Kansas City	100%	79
Saint Marys Health Center	Jefferson City	100%	388
Barnes Jewish Hospital[2]	Saint Louis	99%	579
Centerpoint Medical Center of Independence[2]	Independence	99%	421
Freeman Health System - Freeman West[2]	Joplin	99%	610
Lee's Summit Medical Center	Lee's Summit	99%	233
Liberty Hospital	Liberty	99%	494
McCune-Brooks Hospital	Carthage	99%	182
Moberly Regional Medical Center[2]	Moberly	99%	82
Progress West Healthcare Center	O'Fallon	99%	286
Saint Francis Hospital	Maryville	99%	102
Saint John's Regional Medical Center	Joplin	99%	666
Saint Johns Mercy Hospital[2]	Washington	99%	207
Saint Johns Mercy Medical Center[2]	Saint Louis	99%	417
Saint Louis University Hospital[2]	Saint Louis	99%	205
Saint Louis-John Cochran VA Medical Center	Saint Louis	99%	162
SSM Depaul Health Center[2]	Bridgeton	99%	604
SSM St Joseph Health Center[2]	Saint Charles	99%	581
SSM St Joseph Hospital West[2]	Lake Saint Louis	99%	377
Truman Medical Center - Hospital Hill[2]	Kansas City	99%	226
Fitzgibbon Memorial Hospital	Marshall	98%	40
Missouri Baptist Medical Center[2]	Town & Country	98%	627
Ozarks Medical Center	West Plains	98%	184
Phelps County Regional Medical Center	Rolla	98%	261
Research Belton Hospital[2]	Belton	98%	177
Research Medical Center[2]	Kansas City	98%	480
Saint Francis Medical Center	Cape Girardeau	98%	778
Saint John's Regional Health Center[2]	Springfield	98%	495
Saint Luke's East Lee's Summit Hospital	Lees Summit	98%	308
Saint Lukes Hospital[2]	Chesterfield	98%	751
Saint Lukes Hospital of Kansas City[2]	Kansas City	98%	834
Saint Lukes Northland Hospital	Kansas City	98%	182
Saint Mary's Medical Center[2]	Blue Springs	98%	185
SSM St Clare Health Center[2]	Fenton	98%	585
SSM St Marys Health Center[2]	Richmond Hghts	98%	555
Truman Medical Center Lakewood	Kansas City	98%	210
Women's and Children's Hospital[2]	Columbia	98%	376
Audrain Medical Center	Mexico	97%	223
Boone Hospital Center[2]	Columbia	97%	681
Cameron Regional Medical Center	Cameron	97%	65
Capital Region Medical Center[2]	Jefferson City	97%	377
Citizens Memorial Hospital	Bolivar	97%	155
Cox Medical Center[2]	Springfield	97%	502
Des Peres Hospital[2]	Saint Louis	97%	328
Golden Valley Memorial Hospital	Clinton	97%	74
Hannibal Regional Hospital	Hannibal	97%	460
Northeast Regional Medical Center[2]	Kirksville	97%	160
Parkland Health Center	Farmington	97%	77
Saint Anthony's Medical Center[2]	Saint Louis	97%	833
Saint Johns Hospital-Lebanon	Lebanon	97%	189
Western Missouri Medical Center	Warrensburg	97%	176
Barnes-Jewish St Peters Hospital	Saint Peters	96%	254
Bothwell Regional Health Center	Sedalia	96%	279
Cass Medical Center	Harrisonville	96%	50
North Kansas City Hospital[2]	N Kansas City	96%	669
Poplar Bluff Regional Medical Center[2]	Poplar Bluff	96%	539
Saint Joseph Medical Center[2]	Kansas City	96%	362
Skaggs Community Health Center[2]	Branson	96%	308
Southeast Missouri Hospital[2]	Cape Girardeau	96%	418
Jefferson Regional Medical Center[2]	Crystal City	95%	341
Ozarks Community Hospital	Springfield	95%	63
University of Missouri Health Care	Columbia	95%	201
Saint Lukes Cancer Institute[2,3]	Kansas City	94%	54
Twin Rivers Regional Medical Center	Kennett	94%	53
Lake Regional Health System	Osage Beach	92%	259
Mineral Area Regional Medical Center[2]	Farmington	92%	40
Missouri Delta Medical Center	Sikeston	88%	105
Christian Hospital Northeast[2]	Saint Louis	86%	474
Lincoln County Medical Center	Troy	78%	37

29. Prophylactic Antibiotic Selection (Outpatient)

Hospital Name	City	Rate	Cases
Research Belton Hospital	Belton	100%	32
Saint John's Regional Medical Center	Joplin	100%	230
Audrain Medical Center	Mexico	99%	106
Centerpoint Medical Center of Independence	Independence	99%	529
Des Peres Hospital	Saint Louis	99%	532
Moberly Regional Medical Center	Moberly	99%	82
Saint Anthony's Medical Center	Saint Louis	99%	433
Saint Marys Health Center	Jefferson City	99%	314
SSM St Marys Health Center	Richmond Hghts	99%	580
Fitzgibbon Memorial Hospital	Marshall	98%	101
Saint John's Regional Health Center	Springfield	98%	592
Saint Johns Mercy Hospital	Washington	98%	218
Saint Johns Mercy Medical Center	Saint Louis	98%	746
Saint Lukes Cancer Institute[3]	Kansas City	98%	50
Saint Lukes Northland Hospital	Kansas City	98%	50
Saint Mary's Medical Center	Blue Springs	98%	66
Truman Medical Center Lakewood	Kansas City	98%	66
Christian Hospital Northeast	Saint Louis	97%	338
Cox Medical Center	Springfield	97%	776
Heartland Regional Medical Center	Saint Joseph	97%	687
Lee's Summit Medical Center	Lee's Summit	97%	75
Missouri Delta Medical Center	Sikeston	97%	68
Northeast Regional Medical Center	Kirksville	97%	70
Saint Johns Hospital-Lebanon	Lebanon	97%	38
Saint Lukes Hospital of Kansas City	Kansas City	97%	523
SSM St Clare Health Center	Fenton	97%	512
Barnes-Jewish St Peters Hospital	Saint Peters	96%	248
North Kansas City Hospital	N Kansas City	96%	722
Saint Alexius Hospital	Saint Louis	96%	25
Saint Joseph Medical Center	Kansas City	96%	385
Saint Luke's East Lee's Summit Hospital	Lees Summit	96%	169
Saint Lukes Hospital	Chesterfield	96%	1027
SSM Depaul Health Center	Bridgeton	96%	388
SSM St Joseph Health Center	Saint Charles	96%	487
Truman Medical Center - Hospital Hill	Kansas City	96%	189
University of Missouri Health Care	Columbia	96%	402
Women's and Children's Hospital	Columbia	96%	370
Bothwell Regional Health Center	Sedalia	95%	169
Freeman Health System - Freeman West	Joplin	95%	534
Hannibal Regional Hospital	Hannibal	95%	86
Jefferson Regional Medical Center	Crystal City	95%	141
Liberty Hospital	Liberty	95%	398
Mineral Area Regional Medical Center	Farmington	95%	81
Nevada Regional Medical Center	Nevada	95%	39
Phelps County Regional Medical Center	Rolla	95%	202
Poplar Bluff Regional Medical Center	Poplar Bluff	95%	222
Research Medical Center	Kansas City	95%	324
SSM St Joseph Hospital West	Lake Saint Louis	95%	212
Capital Region Medical Center	Jefferson City	94%	254
Citizens Memorial Hospital	Bolivar	94%	175
Missouri Baptist Hospital Sullivan	Sullivan	93%	44
Ozarks Medical Center	West Plains	93%	219
Barnes-Jewish West County Hospital	Creve Coeur	92%	338
Lake Regional Health System	Osage Beach	92%	192
Missouri Baptist Medical Center	Town & Country	92%	756
Barnes Jewish Hospital	Saint Louis	91%	751
Saint Francis Medical Center	Cape Girardeau	91%	832
Boone Hospital Center	Columbia	90%	714
Ozarks Community Hospital	Springfield	90%	70
Saint Louis University Hospital	Saint Louis	90%	163
Southeast Missouri Hospital	Cape Girardeau	90%	553
Parkland Health Center	Farmington	89%	44
Progress West Healthcare Center	O'Fallon	88%	43
Skaggs Community Health Center	Branson	86%	138
Golden Valley Memorial Hospital	Clinton	79%	34
Western Missouri Medical Center	Warrensburg	55%	49

30. Prophylactic Antibiotic Stopped

Hospital Name	City	Rate	Cases
Columbia Missouri VA Medical Center	Columbia	100%	172
Saint Marys Health Center	Jefferson City	100%	370
Truman Medical Center Lakewood	Kansas City	100%	208
Heartland Regional Medical Center[2]	Saint Joseph	99%	888
Research Belton Hospital[2]	Belton	99%	172
Progress West Healthcare Center	O'Fallon	98%	279
Saint Johns Mercy Hospital[2]	Washington	98%	198
Saint Johns Mercy Medical Center[2]	Saint Louis	98%	386
SSM St Joseph Health Center[2]	Saint Charles	98%	565
SSM St Joseph Hospital West[2]	Lake Saint Louis	98%	366
Twin Rivers Regional Medical Center	Kennett	98%	48
Barnes Jewish Hospital[2]	Saint Louis	97%	546
Capital Region Medical Center[2]	Jefferson City	97%	359
Christian Hospital Northeast[2]	Saint Louis	97%	410
Lee's Summit Medical Center	Lee's Summit	97%	224
Saint Francis Hospital	Maryville	97%	91
Saint Louis University Hospital[2]	Saint Louis	97%	177
Saint Lukes Hospital of Kansas City[2]	Kansas City	97%	781
Saint Lukes Northland Hospital	Kansas City	97%	174
Barnes-Jewish St Peters Hospital	Saint Peters	96%	244
Boone Hospital Center[2]	Columbia	96%	668
Hannibal Regional Hospital	Hannibal	96%	457
Missouri Baptist Medical Center[2]	Town & Country	96%	586
Parkland Health Center	Farmington	96%	73
Poplar Bluff Regional Medical Center[2]	Poplar Bluff	96%	473
Research Medical Center[2]	Kansas City	96%	420
Saint Francis Medical Center	Cape Girardeau	96%	744
Saint Joseph Medical Center[2]	Kansas City	96%	346
Saint Lukes Cancer Institute[2,3]	Kansas City	96%	52
SSM Depaul Health Center[2]	Bridgeton	96%	566
Western Missouri Medical Center	Warrensburg	96%	160
Women's and Children's Hospital[2]	Columbia	96%	373
Centerpoint Medical Center of Independence[2]	Independence	95%	398
Mineral Area Regional Medical Center[2]	Farmington	95%	38
Moberly Regional Medical Center[2]	Moberly	95%	77
Northeast Regional Medical Center[2]	Kirksville	95%	145
Saint John's Regional Medical Center	Joplin	95%	626
Saint Johns Hospital-Lebanon	Lebanon	95%	185
Saint Luke's East Lee's Summit Hospital	Lees Summit	95%	300
Saint Mary's Medical Center[2]	Blue Springs	95%	183
Truman Medical Center - Hospital Hill[2]	Kansas City	95%	213
Audrain Medical Center	Mexico	94%	217
Bothwell Regional Health Center	Sedalia	94%	274
North Kansas City Hospital[2]	N Kansas City	94%	633
Phelps County Regional Medical Center	Rolla	94%	255
SSM St Clare Health Center[2]	Fenton	94%	557
Barnes-Jewish West County Hospital[2]	Creve Coeur	93%	632
Kansas City VA Medical Center	Kansas City	93%	76
Liberty Hospital	Liberty	93%	469
Saint Lukes Hospital[2]	Chesterfield	93%	695
Southeast Missouri Hospital[2]	Cape Girardeau	93%	397
SSM St Marys Health Center[2]	Richmond Hghts	93%	516
Jefferson Regional Medical Center[2]	Crystal City	92%	331
Ozarks Community Hospital	Springfield	92%	61
Saint Anthony's Medical Center[2]	Saint Louis	92%	790
Saint Louis-John Cochran VA Medical Center	Saint Louis	92%	158
Citizens Memorial Hospital	Bolivar	91%	152
Des Peres Hospital[2]	Saint Louis	91%	304
Saint John's Regional Health Center[2]	Springfield	91%	476
Missouri Delta Medical Center	Sikeston	90%	93
Skaggs Community Health Center[2]	Branson	90%	251
University of Missouri Health Care	Columbia	90%	136
Cox Medical Center[2]	Springfield	89%	479
Golden Valley Memorial Hospital	Clinton	89%	71
Cass Medical Center	Harrisonville	88%	49
Freeman Health System - Freeman West[2]	Joplin	88%	565
Lake Regional Health System	Osage Beach	87%	250
Cameron Regional Medical Center	Cameron	86%	63
McCune-Brooks Hospital	Carthage	86%	182
Ozarks Medical Center	West Plains	86%	174
Lincoln County Medical Center	Troy	81%	32
Fitzgibbon Memorial Hospital	Marshall	76%	38

31. Recommended VTP Ordered

Hospital Name	City	Rate	Cases
Columbia Missouri VA Medical Center[2]	Columbia	100%	93
Lee's Summit Medical Center	Lee's Summit	100%	119
Moberly Regional Medical Center[2]	Moberly	100%	48
Parkland Health Center	Farmington	100%	29
Saint Marys Health Center	Jefferson City	100%	186
SSM St Joseph Health Center[2]	Saint Charles	100%	249
SSM St Joseph Hospital West[2]	Lake Saint Louis	100%	227
Capital Region Medical Center[2]	Jefferson City	99%	158
Women's and Children's Hospital[2]	Columbia	99%	162
Christian Hospital Northeast[2]	Saint Louis	98%	320
Des Peres Hospital[2]	Saint Louis	98%	142
Golden Valley Memorial Hospital	Clinton	98%	40
Heartland Regional Medical Center[2]	Saint Joseph	98%	251
Northeast Regional Medical Center[2]	Kirksville	98%	90
Poplar Bluff Regional Medical Center[2]	Poplar Bluff	98%	200
Research Belton Hospital[2]	Belton	98%	45
Saint Francis Hospital	Maryville	98%	43
Saint Louis University Hospital[2]	Saint Louis	98%	230
Saint Louis-John Cochran VA Medical Center[2]	Saint Louis	98%	182
Saint Luke's East Lee's Summit Hospital	Lees Summit	98%	145
Saint Lukes Hospital[2]	Chesterfield	98%	318
University of Missouri Health Care	Columbia	98%	502
Freeman Health System - Freeman West[2]	Joplin	97%	258
Hannibal Regional Hospital	Hannibal	97%	152
Kansas City VA Medical Center[2]	Kansas City	97%	113
McCune-Brooks Hospital	Carthage	97%	32
Missouri Baptist Medical Center[2]	Town & Country	97%	214
Saint Johns Hospital-Lebanon	Lebanon	97%	92
Saint Johns Mercy Hospital[2]	Washington	97%	119
Saint Johns Mercy Medical Center[2]	Saint Louis	97%	143
SSM St Clare Health Center[2]	Fenton	97%	244
Barnes Jewish Hospital[2]	Saint Louis	96%	262
Barnes-Jewish St Peters Hospital	Saint Peters	96%	187
Centerpoint Medical Center of Independence[2]	Independence	96%	234
Citizens Memorial Hospital	Bolivar	96%	120
Nevada Regional Medical Center	Nevada	96%	27
Research Medical Center[2]	Kansas City	96%	252
Skaggs Community Health Center[2]	Branson	96%	100
SSM Depaul Health Center[2]	Bridgeton	96%	197
SSM St Marys Health Center[2]	Richmond Hghts	96%	292
Audrain Medical Center	Mexico	95%	60
Barnes-Jewish West County Hospital[2]	Creve Coeur	95%	181
Cox Medical Center[2]	Springfield	95%	234
Progress West Healthcare Center	O'Fallon	95%	75
Saint John's Regional Medical Center	Joplin	95%	404
Saint Mary's Medical Center[2]	Blue Springs	95%	133
Boone Hospital Center[2]	Columbia	94%	183
Jefferson Regional Medical Center[2]	Crystal City	94%	155
Liberty Hospital	Liberty	94%	320

NOTE: Hospital profiles are in alphabetical order by state, then city, then hospital within the city; Rankings exclude hospitals with less than 25 cases except for patient surveys which excludes hospitals with less than 100 cases; (a) 100–299 cases; (1) The number of cases is too small to be sure how well a hospital is performing; (2) The hospital indicated that the data submitted for this measure were based on a sample of cases; (3) Data was collected during a shorter time period (fewer quarters) than the maximum possible time for this measure; (4) Suppressed for one or more quarters by CMS; (5) No data is available from the hospital for this measure; (6) Fewer than 100 patients completed the HCAHPS survey. Use these rates with caution, as the number of surveys may be too low to reliably assess hospital performance; (7) Survey results are based on less than 12 months of data; (8) Survey results are not available for this reporting period; (9) No or very few patients were eligible for the HCAHPS survey. The scores shown, if any, reflect a very small number of surveys; (10) A state average was not calculated because too few hospitals in the state submitted data; (11) There were discrepancies in the data collection process; Please refer to the User's Guide for a full explanation of data.

Saint Alexius Hospital	Saint Louis	94%	47
Saint Anthony's Medical Center[2]	Saint Louis	94%	327
Saint Francis Medical Center	Cape Girardeau	94%	369
Truman Medical Center - Hospital Hill[2]	Kansas City	94%	139
Cameron Regional Medical Center	Cameron	92%	48
Saint Lukes Hospital of Kansas City[2]	Kansas City	92%	298
Saint Lukes Northland Hospital	Kansas City	92%	110
Southeast Missouri Hospital[2]	Cape Girardeau	91%	166
Saint John's Regional Health Center[2]	Springfield	90%	173
Missouri Delta Medical Center	Sikeston	89%	72
Cass Medical Center	Harrisonville	88%	33
North Kansas City Hospital[2]	N Kansas City	87%	353
Ozarks Medical Center	West Plains	87%	121
Phelps County Regional Medical Center	Rolla	87%	197
Truman Medical Center Lakewood	Kansas City	86%	29
Western Missouri Medical Center	Warrensburg	86%	73
Fitzgibbon Memorial Hospital	Marshall	85%	27
Saint Joseph Medical Center[2]	Kansas City	85%	157
Lake Regional Health System	Osage Beach	80%	205
Bates County Memorial Hospital	Butler	77%	31
Bothwell Regional Health Center	Sedalia	71%	89

32. Urinary Catheter Removal

Hospital Name	City	Rate	Cases
Poplar Bluff Regional Medical Center	Poplar Bluff	100%	130
Saint Louis-John Cochran VA Medical Center[2]	Saint Louis	100%	106
Saint Marys Health Center	Jefferson City	100%	73
Columbia Missouri VA Medical Center[2]	Columbia	99%	137
Kansas City VA Medical Center[2]	Kansas City	98%	59
Progress West Healthcare Center	O'Fallon	98%	133
Western Missouri Medical Center	Warrensburg	98%	42
Bothwell Regional Health Center	Sedalia	97%	92
Centerpoint Medical Center of Independence[2]	Independence	97%	75
Heartland Regional Medical Center[2]	Saint Joseph	97%	277
Research Belton Hospital[2]	Belton	97%	66
Women's and Children's Hospital[2]	Columbia	97%	176
Citizens Memorial Hospital	Bolivar	96%	57
Saint Lukes Hospital of Kansas City[2]	Kansas City	96%	228
Barnes-Jewish West County Hospital[2]	Creve Coeur	95%	248
Capital Region Medical Center[2]	Jefferson City	95%	148
SSM St Clare Health Center[2]	Fenton	95%	189
University of Missouri Health Care	Columbia	94%	128
Boone Hospital Center[2]	Columbia	93%	252
Saint Johns Hospital-Lebanon	Lebanon	93%	75
Saint Johns Mercy Hospital[2]	Washington	93%	72
Saint Joseph Medical Center[2]	Kansas City	92%	60
Saint Louis University Hospital[2]	Saint Louis	92%	99
Des Peres Hospital[2]	Saint Louis	91%	105
Lake Regional Health System	Osage Beach	91%	94
Saint Johns Mercy Medical Center[2]	Saint Louis	91%	105
SSM St Joseph Health Center[2]	Saint Charles	91%	159
SSM St Joseph Hospital West[2]	Lake Saint Louis	91%	92
SSM St Marys Health Center[2]	Richmond Hghts	90%	87
North Kansas City Hospital[2]	N Kansas City	89%	195
Northeast Regional Medical Center	Kirksville	89%	45
Skaggs Community Health Center[2]	Branson	89%	94
Lee's Summit Medical Center	Lee's Summit	87%	30
Jefferson Regional Medical Center[2]	Crystal City	86%	42
Saint Francis Medical Center	Cape Girardeau	86%	209
Saint John's Regional Health Center[2]	Springfield	86%	154
Saint Mary's Medical Center[2]	Blue Springs	86%	64
Christian Hospital Northeast	Saint Louis	85%	132
Missouri Baptist Medical Center[2]	Town & Country	85%	198
Saint John's Regional Medical Center	Joplin	85%	152
Saint Lukes Hospital[2]	Chesterfield	85%	117
Barnes Jewish Hospital[2]	Saint Louis	84%	211
Southeast Missouri Hospital[2]	Cape Girardeau	83%	86
Freeman Health System - Freeman West[2]	Joplin	82%	122
Barnes-Jewish St Peters Hospital	Saint Peters	81%	99
SSM Depaul Health Center[2]	Bridgeton	79%	96
Liberty Hospital	Liberty	78%	100
Ozarks Medical Center	West Plains	78%	45
Research Medical Center[2]	Kansas City	74%	108
Saint Lukes Northland Hospital	Kansas City	73%	33
Saint Anthony's Medical Center[2]	Saint Louis	68%	149
Phelps County Regional Medical Center	Rolla	67%	100
Cox Medical Center[2]	Springfield	56%	156
Hannibal Regional Hospital	Hannibal	53%	32

Children's Asthma Care

33. Received Systemic Corticosteroids

Hospital Name	City	Rate	Cases
Childrens Mercy Hospital[2]	Kansas City	100%	446
Poplar Bluff Regional Medical Center	Poplar Bluff	100%	61
Saint Johns Mercy Medical Center	Saint Louis	100%	195
SSM St Marys Health Center	Richmond Hghts	100%	291

34. Received Home Management Plan of Care

Hospital Name	City	Rate	Cases
Poplar Bluff Regional Medical Center	Poplar Bluff	100%	61
SSM St Marys Health Center	Richmond Hghts	90%	291
Saint Johns Mercy Medical Center	Saint Louis	69%	194
Childrens Mercy Hospital[2]	Kansas City	63%	446

35. Received Reliever Medication

Hospital Name	City	Rate	Cases
Childrens Mercy Hospital[2]	Kansas City	100%	449
Poplar Bluff Regional Medical Center	Poplar Bluff	100%	61
Saint Johns Mercy Medical Center	Saint Louis	100%	195
SSM St Marys Health Center	Richmond Hghts	100%	291

Use of Medical Imaging

36. Combination Abdominal CT Scan

Hospital Name	City	Ratio	Cases
Ripley County Memorial Hospital	Doniphan	0.000	55
Fitzgibbon Memorial Hospital	Marshall	0.017	288
Saint John's Regional Health Center	Springfield	0.017	2112
Saint Lukes Hospital of Kansas City	Kansas City	0.018	342
Lafayette Regional Health Center	Lexington	0.020	201
Missouri Baptist Hospital Sullivan	Sullivan	0.025	316
Saint John's Regional Medical Center	Joplin	0.025	1123
Hedrick Medical Center	Chillicothe	0.029	240
Western Missouri Medical Center	Warrensburg	0.033	239
Saint Johns Mercy Hospital	Washington	0.038	529
Saint Johns Hospital-Lebanon	Lebanon	0.040	346
Missouri Baptist Medical Center	Town & Country	0.044	1663
Cox Medical Center	Springfield	0.048	1960
Saint Francis Hospital	Maryville	0.049	285
Centerpoint Medical Center of Independence	Independence	0.050	539
Saint Luke's East Lee's Summit Hospital	Lees Summit	0.050	537
Skaggs Community Health Center	Branson	0.054	829
Bates County Memorial Hospital	Butler	0.056	215
Saint Johns Mercy Medical Center	Saint Louis	0.057	2017
Progress West Healthcare Center	O'Fallon	0.059	119
Cameron Regional Medical Center	Cameron	0.061	310
Saint Mary's Medical Center	Blue Springs	0.063	459
SSM St Joseph Hospital West	Lake Saint Louis	0.070	682
Parkland Health Center	Farmington	0.074	852
Saint Lukes Hospital	Chesterfield	0.076	1482
SSM St Joseph Health Center	Saint Charles	0.079	768
Golden Valley Memorial Hospital	Clinton	0.083	444
Truman Medical Center Lakewood	Kansas City	0.085	82
Saint Alexius Hospital	Saint Louis	0.087	138
Liberty Hospital	Liberty	0.092	1087
North Kansas City Hospital	N Kansas City	0.093	1477
Pemiscot Memorial Hospital	Hayti	0.100	290
Saint Lukes Northland Hospital	Kansas City	0.102	333
Truman Medical Center - Hospital Hill	Kansas City	0.102	283
Barnes-Jewish West County Hospital	Creve Coeur	0.103	846
Poplar Bluff Regional Medical Center	Poplar Bluff	0.115	356
Barnes Jewish Hospital	Saint Louis	0.121	4449
Texas County Memorial Hospital	Houston	0.123	227
Mineral Area Regional Medical Center	Farmington	0.126	277
Wright Memorial Hospital	Trenton	0.127	158
Heartland Regional Medical Center	Saint Joseph	0.135	1438
Barnes-Jewish St Peters Hospital	Saint Peters	0.137	761
Lee's Summit Medical Center	Lee's Summit	0.140	272
Research Belton Hospital	Belton	0.163	196
Saint Marys Health Center	Jefferson City	0.164	317
Boone Hospital Center	Columbia	0.170	1483
Research Medical Center	Kansas City	0.182	752
Ozarks Community Hospital	Springfield	0.198	177
Twin Rivers Regional Medical Center	Kennett	0.204	265
Ozarks Medical Center	West Plains	0.238	480
Saint Joseph Medical Center	Kansas City	0.272	1054
University of Missouri Health Care	Columbia	0.273	1075
Jefferson Regional Medical Center	Crystal City	0.336	836
Citizens Memorial Hospital	Bolivar	0.358	383
Saint Louis University Hospital	Saint Louis	0.373	807
Phelps County Regional Medical Center	Rolla	0.378	526
Saint Francis Medical Center	Cape Girardeau	0.401	1340
Capital Region Medical Center	Jefferson City	0.409	802
Nevada Regional Medical Center	Nevada	0.409	269
Northeast Regional Medical Center	Kirksville	0.425	374
Christian Hospital Northwest	Florissant	0.438	240
Forest Park Hospital	Saint Louis	0.444	117
Missouri Southern Healthcare	Dexter	0.470	217
SSM Depaul Health Center	Bridgeton	0.503	723
Moberly Regional Medical Center	Moberly	0.506	233
Audrain Medical Center	Mexico	0.520	481
Christian Hospital Northeast	Saint Louis	0.522	783
Freeman Health System - Freeman West	Joplin	0.523	1154
Sullivan County Memorial Hospital[1]	Milan	0.536	28
Des Peres Hospital	Saint Louis	0.621	243
Missouri Delta Medical Center	Sikeston	0.627	327
Hannibal Regional Hospital	Hannibal	0.653	245
Southeast Missouri Hospital	Cape Girardeau	0.660	698
Saint Anthony's Medical Center	Saint Louis	0.666	1358
SSM St Marys Health Center	Richmond Hghts	0.677	899
Women's and Children's Hospital	Columbia	0.717	159
Lake Regional Health System	Osage Beach	0.719	556
Bothwell Regional Health Center	Sedalia	0.730	788
SSM St Clare Health Center	Fenton	0.732	347
SAC-Osage Hospital	Osceola	0.735	68
Cooper County Memorial Hospital	Boonville	0.755	94
Callaway Community Hospital	Fulton	0.784	111

37. Combination Chest CT Scan

Hospital Name	City	Ratio	Cases
Bates County Memorial Hospital	Butler	0.000	119
Bothwell Regional Health Center	Sedalia	0.000	649
Des Peres Hospital	Saint Louis	0.000	90
Forest Park Hospital	Saint Louis	0.000	63
Missouri Baptist Medical Center	Town & Country	0.000	2226
Ozarks Medical Center	West Plains	0.000	308
Progress West Healthcare Center	O'Fallon	0.000	91
Ripley County Memorial Hospital	Doniphan	0.000	52
Saint Johns Mercy Hospital	Washington	0.000	412
Truman Medical Center Lakewood	Kansas City	0.000	50
Saint John's Regional Health Center	Springfield	0.001	1712
Saint John's Regional Medical Center	Joplin	0.001	876
Cox Medical Center	Springfield	0.002	1322
Liberty Hospital	Liberty	0.002	593
Missouri Baptist Hospital Sullivan	Sullivan	0.002	423
Saint Francis Medical Center	Cape Girardeau	0.002	872
Christian Hospital Northeast	Saint Louis	0.003	672
Saint Lukes Northland Hospital	Kansas City	0.004	236
Jefferson Regional Medical Center	Crystal City	0.005	624
Phelps County Regional Medical Center	Rolla	0.005	398
Saint Marys Health Center	Jefferson City	0.005	184
SSM St Joseph Hospital West	Lake Saint Louis	0.006	482
Saint Lukes Hospital	Chesterfield	0.007	1364
Nevada Regional Medical Center	Nevada	0.008	118
Saint Anthony's Medical Center	Saint Louis	0.008	828
Saint Johns Mercy Medical Center	Saint Louis	0.009	1514
Western Missouri Medical Center	Warrensburg	0.009	235
Centerpoint Medical Center of Independence	Independence	0.010	288
SSM St Marys Health Center	Richmond Hghts	0.010	493
Boone Hospital Center	Columbia	0.011	1012
Truman Medical Center - Hospital Hill	Kansas City	0.012	242
Barnes-Jewish West County Hospital	Creve Coeur	0.014	814
Callaway Community Hospital	Fulton	0.014	69
Missouri Southern Healthcare	Dexter	0.017	117
Saint Johns Hospital-Lebanon	Lebanon	0.018	164
Missouri Delta Medical Center	Sikeston	0.021	194
Barnes Jewish Hospital	Saint Louis	0.022	4518
Cameron Regional Medical Center	Cameron	0.022	136
Saint Francis Hospital	Maryville	0.023	177
SAC-Osage Hospital[1]	Osceola	0.024	42
Fitzgibbon Memorial Hospital	Marshall	0.025	119
SSM St Joseph Health Center	Saint Charles	0.029	589
North Kansas City Hospital	N Kansas City	0.034	1088
Skaggs Community Health Center	Branson	0.038	714
Saint Luke's East Lee's Summit Hospital	Lees Summit	0.041	197
University of Missouri Health Care	Columbia	0.042	1213
Ozarks Community Hospital	Springfield	0.047	64
Saint Mary's Medical Center	Blue Springs	0.048	270
Hedrick Medical Center	Chillicothe	0.051	197
Lafayette Regional Health Center	Lexington	0.051	137
Barnes-Jewish St Peters Hospital	Saint Peters	0.052	749
Capital Region Medical Center	Jefferson City	0.056	695
Moberly Regional Medical Center	Moberly	0.057	230
Mineral Area Regional Medical Center	Farmington	0.064	110
Texas County Memorial Hospital	Houston	0.066	137
Poplar Bluff Regional Medical Center	Poplar Bluff	0.068	192
Heartland Regional Medical Center	Saint Joseph	0.070	1277
Saint Alexius Hospital[1]	Saint Louis	0.074	54
Saint Louis University Hospital	Saint Louis	0.076	621
SSM Depaul Health Center	Bridgeton	0.081	507
Golden Valley Memorial Hospital	Clinton	0.084	285
Women's and Children's Hospital	Columbia	0.091	121
Lee's Summit Medical Center	Lee's Summit	0.094	160
Northeast Regional Medical Center	Kirksville	0.104	337
Christian Hospital Northwest	Florissant	0.110	191
SSM St Clare Health Center	Fenton	0.113	231
Pemiscot Memorial Hospital	Hayti	0.114	105
Southeast Missouri Hospital	Cape Girardeau	0.119	614
Saint Joseph Medical Center	Kansas City	0.121	696
Research Belton Hospital	Belton	0.125	112
Parkland Health Center	Farmington	0.126	541
Hannibal Regional Hospital	Hannibal	0.133	143
Research Medical Center	Kansas City	0.140	479
Wright Memorial Hospital	Trenton	0.146	151
Audrain Medical Center	Mexico	0.156	333
Saint Lukes Hospital of Kansas City	Kansas City	0.157	83

NOTE: Hospital profiles are in alphabetical order by state, then city, then hospital within the city; Rankings exclude hospitals with less than 25 cases except for patient surveys which excludes hospitals with less than 100 cases; (a) 100–299 cases; (1) The number of cases is too small to be sure how well a hospital is performing; (2) The hospital indicated that the data submitted for this measure were based on a sample of cases; (3) Data was collected during a shorter time period (fewer quarters) than the maximum possible time for this measure; (4) Suppressed for one or more quarters by CMS; (5) No data is available from the hospital for this measure; (6) Fewer than 100 patients completed the HCAHPS survey. Use these rates with caution, as the number of surveys may be too low to assess hospital performance; (7) Survey results are based on less than 12 months of data; (8) Survey results are not available for this reporting period; (9) No or very few patients were eligible for the HCAHPS survey. The scores shown, if any, reflect a very small number of surveys; (10) A state average was not calculated because too few hospitals in the state submitted data; (11) There were discrepancies in the data collection process; Please refer to the User's Guide for a full explanation of data.

Hospital Name	City	Rate	Cases
Twin Rivers Regional Medical Center	Kennett	0.227	176
Citizens Memorial Hospital	Bolivar	0.310	255
Cooper County Memorial Hospital	Boonville	0.607	56
Freeman Health System - Freeman West	Joplin	0.612	842
Lake Regional Health System	Osage Beach	0.706	361

38. Follow-up Mammogram/Ultrasound

Hospital Name	City	Rate	Cases
Bothwell Regional Health Center	Sedalia	1.2%	752
SAC-Osage Hospital	Osceola	2.5%	161
Twin Rivers Regional Medical Center	Kennett	2.5%	356
Pemiscot Memorial Hospital	Hayti	2.8%	251
Forest Park Hospital	Saint Louis	2.9%	380
Phelps County Regional Medical Center	Rolla	2.9%	1595
Boone Hospital Center	Columbia	3.1%	2578
Fitzgibbon Memorial Hospital	Marshall	3.4%	557
Citizens Memorial Hospital	Bolivar	3.6%	583
Liberty Hospital	Liberty	3.7%	2377
Freeman Health System - Freeman West	Joplin	3.8%	2505
Saint Johns Mercy Hospital	Washington	4.2%	686
Mineral Area Regional Medical Center	Farmington	4.3%	444
Texas County Memorial Hospital	Houston	4.3%	396
Cameron Regional Medical Center	Cameron	4.4%	295
Nevada Regional Medical Center	Nevada	4.4%	411
Saint Francis Hospital	Maryville	4.4%	436
Saint Louis University Hospital	Saint Louis	5.0%	340
Golden Valley Memorial Hospital	Clinton	5.1%	830
Saint Johns Mercy Medical Center	Saint Louis	5.2%	3740
Progress West Healthcare Center	O'Fallon	5.4%	93
Parkland Health Center	Farmington	5.5%	947
Western Missouri Medical Center	Warrensburg	5.5%	544
Des Peres Hospital	Saint Louis	6.0%	150
Lake Regional Health System	Osage Beach	6.1%	1094
Audrain Medical Center	Mexico	6.2%	1041
Centerpoint Medical Center of Independence	Independence	6.2%	1273
Barnes-Jewish West County Hospital	Creve Coeur	6.4%	672
Poplar Bluff Regional Medical Center	Poplar Bluff	6.4%	738
SSM St Joseph Hospital West	Lake Saint Louis	6.4%	691
Saint Lukes Hospital	Chesterfield	6.5%	5188
Saint Anthony's Medical Center	Saint Louis	6.6%	2726
SSM St Joseph Health Center	Saint Charles	6.6%	576
Bates County Memorial Hospital	Butler	7.0%	270
Saint Alexius Hospital	Saint Louis	7.0%	327
Barnes Jewish Hospital	Saint Louis	7.1%	4757
Northeast Regional Medical Center	Kirksville	7.3%	740
Research Medical Center	Kansas City	7.3%	1030
Saint Johns Hospital-Lebanon	Lebanon	7.3%	560
Heartland Regional Medical Center	Saint Joseph	7.5%	2395
Missouri Delta Medical Center	Sikeston	7.5%	738
Saint John's Regional Medical Center	Joplin	7.5%	1878
SSM Depaul Health Center	Bridgeton	7.5%	876
Missouri Baptist Medical Center	Town & Country	7.6%	2421
Barnes-Jewish St Peters Hospital	Saint Peters	7.7%	979
Missouri Baptist Hospital Sullivan	Sullivan	7.7%	456
SSM St Clare Health Center	Fenton	7.8%	1108
Missouri Southern Healthcare	Dexter	8.1%	406
Jefferson Regional Medical Center	Crystal City	8.2%	926
University of Missouri Health Care	Columbia	8.3%	2817
Saint Francis Medical Center	Cape Girardeau	8.6%	1799
Saint John's Regional Health Center	Springfield	8.6%	4865
Hedrick Medical Center	Chillicothe	9.1%	274
Cox Medical Center	Springfield	9.2%	2956
Callaway Community Hospital	Fulton	9.5%	264
Saint Lukes Cancer Institute	Kansas City	9.5%	1341
Ozarks Medical Center	West Plains	9.6%	793
Wright Memorial Hospital	Trenton	9.6%	249
Saint Lukes Northland Hospital	Kansas City	9.7%	639
Saint Mary's Medical Center	Blue Springs	10.6%	756
Saint Joseph Medical Center	Kansas City	10.8%	1626
Christian Hospital Northeast	Saint Louis	10.9%	522
Skaggs Community Health Center	Branson	11.2%	1068
Women's and Children's Hospital	Columbia	11.4%	405
Lafayette Regional Health Center	Lexington	11.8%	221
Moberly Regional Medical Center	Moberly	11.8%	288
Saint Luke's East Lee's Summit Hospital	Lees Summit	11.8%	408
Truman Medical Center Lakewood	Kansas City	12.0%	250
Hannibal Regional Hospital	Hannibal	12.1%	174
SSM St Marys Health Center	Richmond Hghts	12.3%	1630
Christian Hospital Northwest	Florissant	12.5%	861
Truman Medical Center - Hospital Hill	Kansas City	12.5%	607
Saint Marys Health Center	Jefferson City	12.6%	910
Capital Region Medical Center	Jefferson City	13.9%	1083
Research Belton Hospital	Belton	14.1%	467
Lee's Summit Medical Center	Lee's Summit	15.6%	572
North Kansas City Hospital	N Kansas City	15.7%	949

39. MRI for Low Back Pain

Hospital Name	City	Rate	Cases
Western Missouri Medical Center	Warrensburg	26.0%	100
Christian Hospital Northwest[1]	Florissant	26.3%	38
Missouri Southern Healthcare[1]	Dexter	26.3%	38
Saint Francis Medical Center	Cape Girardeau	28.3%	378
Bates County Memorial Hospital	Butler	28.6%	63
Saint Francis Hospital	Maryville	28.9%	76
Barnes-Jewish West County Hospital	Creve Coeur	29.0%	155
University of Missouri Health Care	Columbia	29.0%	62
Barnes Jewish Hospital	Saint Louis	30.0%	533
Skaggs Community Health Center	Branson	30.5%	272
Barnes-Jewish St Peters Hospital	Saint Peters	30.6%	72
Saint Lukes Hospital	Chesterfield	31.0%	474
Women's and Children's Hospital	Columbia	31.0%	129
Freeman Health System - Freeman West	Joplin	31.2%	609
Twin Rivers Regional Medical Center	Kennett	31.3%	128
Hannibal Regional Hospital	Hannibal	31.5%	108
Missouri Baptist Medical Center	Town & Country	31.6%	383
Moberly Regional Medical Center[1]	Moberly	31.6%	38
Saint Anthony's Medical Center	Saint Louis	31.6%	275
Centerpoint Medical Center of Independence	Independence	31.7%	104
Golden Valley Memorial Hospital	Clinton	31.9%	191
Hedrick Medical Center	Chillicothe	32.1%	53
Saint Joseph Medical Center	Kansas City	32.1%	355
Saint Louis University Hospital[1]	Saint Louis	32.3%	31
SSM Depaul Health Center	Bridgeton	32.6%	227
Lake Regional Health System	Osage Beach	32.9%	70
Southeast Missouri Hospital	Cape Girardeau	33.2%	226
SSM St Clare Health Center	Fenton	33.8%	68
Parkland Health Center	Farmington	33.9%	174
Mineral Area Regional Medical Center	Farmington	34.7%	98
Cox Medical Center	Springfield	34.9%	601
Pemiscot Memorial Hospital[1]	Hayti	35.0%	40
Audrain Medical Center	Mexico	35.7%	129
Jefferson Regional Medical Center	Crystal City	35.8%	109
Research Medical Center	Kansas City	35.9%	142
North Kansas City Hospital	N Kansas City	36.2%	442
Saint John's Regional Medical Center	Joplin	36.2%	301
Wright Memorial Hospital[1]	Trenton	36.4%	44
Heartland Regional Medical Center	Saint Joseph	36.5%	373
Lee's Summit Medical Center	Lee's Summit	36.5%	63
Boone Hospital Center	Columbia	36.8%	465
Saint Johns Mercy Medical Center	Saint Louis	37.0%	411
SSM St Joseph Health Center	Saint Charles	37.0%	135
Bothwell Regional Health Center	Sedalia	37.1%	237
Liberty Hospital	Liberty	37.4%	281
Saint Luke's East Lee's Summit Hospital	Lees Summit	38.0%	121
Research Belton Hospital	Belton	38.3%	47
Saint Marys Health Center	Jefferson City	38.9%	131
Christian Hospital Northeast	Saint Louis	39.1%	87
Saint Mary's Medical Center	Blue Springs	39.2%	102
Ozarks Community Hospital	Springfield	39.3%	107
Poplar Bluff Regional Medical Center	Poplar Bluff	39.4%	71
Citizens Memorial Hospital	Bolivar	39.6%	139
Des Peres Hospital	Saint Louis	39.6%	111
Saint Johns Mercy Hospital	Washington	40.3%	129
SSM St Marys Health Center	Richmond Hghts	40.4%	104
Truman Medical Center - Hospital Hill	Kansas City	40.5%	42
Saint John's Regional Health Center	Springfield	40.8%	660
Phelps County Regional Medical Center	Rolla	41.5%	205
Ozarks Medical Center	West Plains	41.9%	136
Callaway Community Hospital[1]	Fulton	42.9%	35
SSM St Joseph Hospital West	Lake Saint Louis	42.9%	91
Northeast Regional Medical Center	Kirksville	43.8%	48
Cameron Regional Medical Center	Cameron	45.1%	51
Lafayette Regional Health Center	Lexington	46.0%	63
Fitzgibbon Memorial Hospital	Marshall	46.8%	94
Capital Region Medical Center	Jefferson City	47.5%	297
Missouri Baptist Hospital Sullivan	Sullivan	47.8%	67
Saint Lukes Northland Hospital	Kansas City	48.3%	58
Nevada Regional Medical Center	Nevada	51.7%	58
Missouri Delta Medical Center	Sikeston	60.8%	74
Saint Johns Hospital-Lebanon	Lebanon	67.5%	77

Survey of Patients' Hospital Experiences

40. Area Around Room 'Always' Quiet at Night

Hospital Name	City	Rate	Cases
SSM St Clare Health Center	Fenton	72%	300+
Christian Hospital Northeast	Saint Louis	71%	300+
Cox Monett Hospital	Monett	70%	(a)
Hedrick Medical Center	Chillicothe	69%	(a)
Missouri Baptist Hospital Sullivan	Sullivan	68%	300+
Saint Francis Hospital	Maryville	68%	300+
Saint Luke's East Lee's Summit Hospital	Lees Summit	68%	300+
Progress West Healthcare Center	O'Fallon	67%	300+
Southeast Missouri Hospital	Cape Girardeau	67%	300+
Centerpoint Medical Center of Independence	Independence	66%	300+
Lee's Summit Medical Center	Lee's Summit	66%	300+
Research Belton Hospital	Belton	65%	300+
Barnes-Jewish West County Hospital	Creve Coeur	64%	300+
McCune-Brooks Hospital	Carthage	64%	300+
Research Medical Center	Kansas City	64%	300+
Bothwell Regional Health Center	Sedalia	63%	300+
Ozarks Community Hospital	Springfield	63%	300+
Women's and Children's Hospital	Columbia	63%	300+
Barnes-Jewish St Peters Hospital	Saint Peters	62%	300+
Capital Region Medical Center	Jefferson City	62%	300+
Heartland Regional Medical Center	Saint Joseph	62%	300+
Forest Park Hospital	Saint Louis	61%	(a)
Lincoln County Medical Center	Troy	61%	(a)
Missouri Delta Medical Center	Sikeston	61%	300+
Moberly Regional Medical Center	Moberly	61%	300+
Northeast Regional Medical Center	Kirksville	61%	300+
Saint Lukes Northland Hospital	Kansas City	61%	300+
Boone Hospital Center	Columbia	60%	300+
Parkland Health Center	Farmington	60%	300+
Saint John's Regional Health Center	Springfield	60%	300+
Mineral Area Regional Medical Center	Farmington	59%	300+
Missouri Southern Healthcare	Dexter	59%	300+
Saint Alexius Hospital	Saint Louis	59%	300+
Saint Anthony's Medical Center	Saint Louis	59%	300+
Saint Johns Mercy Medical Center	Saint Louis	59%	300+
Saint Lukes Cancer Institute	Kansas City	59%	(a)
Saint Marys Health Center	Jefferson City	59%	300+
Wright Memorial Hospital	Trenton	59%	(a)
Nevada Regional Medical Center	Nevada	58%	(a)
SAC-Osage Hospital	Osceola	58%	(a)
Saint John's Regional Medical Center	Joplin	58%	300+
Saint Lukes Hospital	Chesterfield	58%	300+
Saint Mary's Medical Center	Blue Springs	58%	300+
SSM Depaul Health Center	Bridgeton	58%	300+
Truman Medical Center Lakewood	Kansas City	58%	300+
Ozarks Medical Center	West Plains	57%	300+
Saint Francis Medical Center	Cape Girardeau	57%	300+
Saint Johns Mercy Hospital	Washington	57%	300+
Saint Louis University Hospital	Saint Louis	57%	300+
Bates County Memorial Hospital	Butler	56%	300+
Citizens Memorial Hospital	Bolivar	56%	300+
Lafayette Regional Health Center	Lexington	56%	(a)
North Kansas City Hospital	N Kansas City	56%	300+
Saint Lukes Hospital of Kansas City	Kansas City	56%	300+
Skaggs Community Health Center	Branson	56%	300+
Audrain Medical Center	Mexico	55%	300+
Barnes Jewish Hospital	Saint Louis	55%	300+
Des Peres Hospital	Saint Louis	55%	300+
Fitzgibbon Memorial Hospital	Marshall	54%	300+
Lake Regional Health System	Osage Beach	54%	300+
SSM St Joseph Health Center	Saint Charles	54%	300+
Western Missouri Medical Center	Warrensburg	54%	300+
Golden Valley Memorial Hospital	Clinton	53%	300+
Hannibal Regional Hospital	Hannibal	53%	300+
Saint Johns Hospital-Lebanon	Lebanon	53%	300+
Saint Joseph Medical Center	Kansas City	53%	300+
SSM St Joseph Hospital West	Lake Saint Louis	53%	300+
SSM St Marys Health Center	Richmond Hghts	53%	300+
Ste Genevieve County Memorial Hospital	Ste Genevieve	53%	300+
Texas County Memorial Hospital	Houston	53%	300+
Truman Medical Center - Hospital Hill	Kansas City	53%	300+
Freeman Health System - Freeman West	Joplin	52%	300+
Freeman Neosho Hospital	Neosho	52%	300+
Phelps County Regional Medical Center	Rolla	52%	300+
Missouri Baptist Medical Center	Town & Country	51%	300+
Liberty Hospital	Liberty	50%	300+
University of Missouri Health Care	Columbia	50%	300+
Cameron Regional Medical Center	Cameron	49%	300+
Callaway Community Hospital	Fulton	48%	(a)
Twin Rivers Regional Medical Center	Kennett	47%	300+
Jefferson Regional Medical Center	Crystal City	46%	300+
Pemiscot Memorial Hospital	Hayti	46%	300+
Cox Medical Center	Springfield	44%	300+
Poplar Bluff Regional Medical Center	Poplar Bluff	44%	300+
Ripley County Memorial Hospital	Doniphan	42%	(a)

41. Doctors 'Always' Communicated Well

Hospital Name	City	Rate	Cases
Cox Monett Hospital	Monett	89%	(a)
McCune-Brooks Hospital	Carthage	88%	300+
Nevada Regional Medical Center	Nevada	88%	(a)
Ozarks Community Hospital	Springfield	88%	300+
Parkland Health Center	Farmington	88%	300+
Boone Hospital Center	Columbia	87%	300+
Missouri Southern Healthcare	Dexter	87%	300+
Missouri Baptist Hospital Sullivan	Sullivan	86%	300+
Saint Lukes Cancer Institute	Kansas City	86%	(a)
Wright Memorial Hospital	Trenton	86%	(a)
Mineral Area Regional Medical Center	Farmington	85%	300+
Saint Francis Hospital	Maryville	85%	300+
Barnes-Jewish St Peters Hospital	Saint Peters	84%	300+
Barnes-Jewish West County Hospital	Creve Coeur	84%	300+
Christian Hospital Northeast	Saint Louis	84%	300+
Missouri Delta Medical Center	Sikeston	84%	300+
Saint Alexius Hospital	Saint Louis	84%	300+

NOTE: Hospital profiles are in alphabetical order by state, then city, then hospital within the city; Rankings exclude hospitals with less than 25 cases except for patient surveys which excludes hospitals with less than 100 cases; (a) 100–299 cases; (1) The number of cases is too small to be sure how well a hospital is performing; (2) The hospital indicated that the data submitted for this measure were based on a sample of cases; (3) Data was collected during a shorter time period (fewer quarters) than the maximum possible time for this measure; (4) Suppressed for one or more quarters by CMS; (5) No data is available from the hospital for this measure; (6) Fewer than 100 patients completed the HCAHPS survey. Use these rates with caution, as the number of surveys may be too low to reliably assess hospital performance; (7) Survey results are based on less than 12 months of data; (8) Survey results are not available for this reporting period; (9) No or very few patients were eligible for the HCAHPS survey. The scores shown, if any, reflect a very small number of surveys; (10) A state average was not calculated because too few hospitals in the state submitted data; (11) There were discrepancies in the data collection process; Please refer to the User's Guide for a full explanation of data.

Saint Marys Health Center	Jefferson City	84%	300+
Ste Genevieve County Memorial Hospital	Ste Genevieve	84%	300+
Bothwell Regional Health Center	Sedalia	83%	300+
Freeman Neosho Hospital	Neosho	83%	300+
Golden Valley Memorial Hospital	Clinton	83%	300+
Hannibal Regional Hospital	Hannibal	83%	300+
Lincoln County Medical Center	Troy	83%	(a)
Missouri Baptist Medical Center	Town & Country	83%	300+
Ozarks Medical Center	West Plains	83%	300+
Progress West Healthcare Center	O'Fallon	83%	300+
Saint Johns Hospital-Lebanon	Lebanon	83%	300+
Saint Johns Mercy Hospital	Washington	83%	300+
Capital Region Medical Center	Jefferson City	82%	300+
Citizens Memorial Hospital	Bolivar	82%	300+
Des Peres Hospital	Saint Louis	82%	300+
Lafayette Regional Health Center	Lexington	82%	(a)
Pemiscot Memorial Hospital	Hayti	82%	300+
SAC-Osage Hospital	Osceola	82%	(a)
Saint Francis Medical Center	Cape Girardeau	82%	300+
Saint John's Regional Health Center	Springfield	82%	300+
Callaway Community Hospital	Fulton	81%	(a)
Heartland Regional Medical Center	Saint Joseph	81%	300+
Moberly Regional Medical Center	Moberly	81%	300+
Phelps County Regional Medical Center	Rolla	81%	300+
Research Medical Center	Kansas City	81%	300+
Saint Joseph Medical Center	Kansas City	81%	300+
Saint Lukes Hospital	Chesterfield	81%	300+
Southeast Missouri Hospital	Cape Girardeau	81%	300+
Western Missouri Medical Center	Warrensburg	81%	300+
North Kansas City Hospital	N Kansas City	80%	300+
Northeast Regional Medical Center	Kirksville	80%	300+
Saint John's Regional Medical Center	Joplin	80%	300+
Saint Luke's East Lee's Summit Hospital	Lees Summit	80%	300+
Saint Lukes Hospital of Kansas City	Kansas City	80%	300+
Skaggs Community Health Center	Branson	80%	300+
SSM St Clare Health Center	Fenton	80%	300+
Twin Rivers Regional Medical Center	Kennett	80%	300+
Audrain Medical Center	Mexico	79%	300+
Barnes Jewish Hospital	Saint Louis	79%	300+
Cox Medical Center	Springfield	79%	300+
Fitzgibbon Memorial Hospital	Marshall	79%	300+
Ripley County Memorial Hospital	Doniphan	79%	(a)
Saint Johns Mercy Medical Center	Saint Louis	79%	300+
Texas County Memorial Hospital	Houston	79%	300+
Centerpoint Medical Center of Independence	Independence	78%	300+
Hedrick Medical Center	Chillicothe	78%	(a)
Lake Regional Health System	Osage Beach	78%	300+
Research Belton Hospital	Belton	78%	300+
Saint Louis University Hospital	Saint Louis	78%	300+
Saint Lukes Northland Hospital	Kansas City	78%	300+
Saint Mary's Medical Center	Blue Springs	78%	300+
SSM Depaul Health Center	Bridgeton	78%	300+
Forest Park Hospital	Saint Louis	77%	(a)
Liberty Hospital	Liberty	77%	300+
Saint Anthony's Medical Center	Saint Louis	77%	300+
SSM St Joseph Hospital West	Lake Saint Louis	77%	300+
Truman Medical Center Lakewood	Kansas City	77%	300+
Bates County Memorial Hospital	Butler	76%	300+
Freeman Health System - Freeman West	Joplin	76%	300+
Lee's Summit Medical Center	Lee's Summit	76%	300+
Poplar Bluff Regional Medical Center	Poplar Bluff	76%	300+
SSM St Joseph Health Center	Saint Charles	76%	300+
SSM St Marys Health Center	Richmond Hghts	76%	300+
Women's and Children's Hospital	Columbia	76%	300+
Jefferson Regional Medical Center	Crystal City	75%	300+
Truman Medical Center - Hospital Hill	Kansas City	72%	300+
University of Missouri Health Care	Columbia	72%	300+
Cameron Regional Medical Center	Cameron	67%	300+

42. Home Recovery Information Given

Hospital Name	City	Rate	Cases
Boone Hospital Center	Columbia	89%	300+
Moberly Regional Medical Center	Moberly	89%	300+
Saint Lukes Cancer Institute	Kansas City	89%	(a)
Centerpoint Medical Center of Independence	Independence	88%	300+
McCune-Brooks Hospital	Carthage	88%	300+
Saint Joseph Medical Center	Kansas City	88%	300+
Saint Mary's Medical Center	Blue Springs	88%	300+
Southeast Missouri Hospital	Cape Girardeau	88%	300+
Audrain Medical Center	Mexico	87%	300+
Barnes Jewish Hospital	Saint Louis	87%	300+
Barnes-Jewish West County Hospital	Creve Coeur	87%	300+
Hannibal Regional Hospital	Hannibal	87%	300+
Research Belton Hospital	Belton	87%	300+
Saint John's Regional Health Center	Springfield	87%	300+
Ste Genevieve County Memorial Hospital	Ste Genevieve	87%	300+
Women's and Children's Hospital	Columbia	87%	300+
Barnes-Jewish St Peters Hospital	Saint Peters	86%	300+
Nevada Regional Medical Center	Nevada	86%	(a)
Saint Johns Hospital-Lebanon	Lebanon	86%	300+
Saint Louis University Hospital	Saint Louis	86%	300+
Saint Luke's East Lee's Summit Hospital	Lees Summit	86%	300+
SSM St Clare Health Center	Fenton	86%	300+
Western Missouri Medical Center	Warrensburg	86%	300+
Bothwell Regional Health Center	Sedalia	85%	300+
Lafayette Regional Health Center	Lexington	85%	(a)
Lake Regional Health System	Osage Beach	85%	300+
Lee's Summit Medical Center	Lee's Summit	85%	300+
Missouri Baptist Hospital Sullivan	Sullivan	85%	300+
Missouri Baptist Medical Center	Town & Country	85%	300+
Northeast Regional Medical Center	Kirksville	85%	300+
Parkland Health Center	Farmington	85%	300+
Progress West Healthcare Center	O'Fallon	85%	300+
Research Medical Center	Kansas City	85%	300+
Saint John's Regional Medical Center	Joplin	85%	300+
Saint Lukes Hospital of Kansas City	Kansas City	85%	300+
SSM St Joseph Health Center	Saint Charles	85%	300+
University of Missouri Health Care	Columbia	85%	300+
Christian Hospital Northeast	Saint Louis	84%	300+
Fitzgibbon Memorial Hospital	Marshall	84%	300+
Freeman Neosho Hospital	Neosho	84%	300+
Lincoln County Medical Center	Troy	84%	(a)
Phelps County Regional Medical Center	Rolla	84%	300+
Saint Lukes Northland Hospital	Kansas City	84%	300+
Saint Marys Health Center	Jefferson City	84%	300+
SSM St Joseph Hospital West	Lake Saint Louis	84%	300+
Bates County Memorial Hospital	Butler	83%	300+
Citizens Memorial Hospital	Bolivar	83%	300+
Des Peres Hospital	Saint Louis	83%	300+
Heartland Regional Medical Center	Saint Joseph	83%	300+
Mineral Area Regional Medical Center	Farmington	83%	300+
Ozarks Medical Center	West Plains	83%	300+
Saint Francis Medical Center	Cape Girardeau	83%	300+
Truman Medical Center Lakewood	Kansas City	83%	300+
Capital Region Medical Center	Jefferson City	82%	300+
Freeman Health System - Freeman West	Joplin	82%	300+
Golden Valley Memorial Hospital	Clinton	82%	300+
Liberty Hospital	Liberty	82%	300+
Ripley County Memorial Hospital	Doniphan	82%	(a)
Saint Francis Hospital	Maryville	82%	300+
Saint Johns Mercy Hospital	Washington	82%	300+
SSM Depaul Health Center	Bridgeton	82%	300+
Cox Monett Hospital	Monett	81%	(a)
Saint Lukes Hospital	Chesterfield	81%	300+
SSM St Marys Health Center	Richmond Hghts	81%	300+
Texas County Memorial Hospital	Houston	81%	300+
Truman Medical Center - Hospital Hill	Kansas City	81%	300+
Callaway Community Hospital	Fulton	80%	(a)
North Kansas City Hospital	N Kansas City	80%	300+
Ozarks Community Hospital	Springfield	80%	300+
Saint Anthony's Medical Center	Saint Louis	80%	300+
Cox Medical Center	Springfield	79%	300+
Hedrick Medical Center	Chillicothe	79%	(a)
Twin Rivers Regional Medical Center	Kennett	79%	300+
Saint Alexius Hospital	Saint Louis	78%	300+
Skaggs Community Health Center	Branson	78%	300+
Cameron Regional Medical Center	Cameron	77%	300+
Missouri Delta Medical Center	Sikeston	77%	300+
Saint Johns Mercy Medical Center	Saint Louis	77%	300+
Missouri Southern Healthcare	Dexter	76%	300+
Jefferson Regional Medical Center	Crystal City	75%	300+
SAC-Osage Hospital	Osceola	75%	(a)
Wright Memorial Hospital	Trenton	75%	(a)
Poplar Bluff Regional Medical Center	Poplar Bluff	73%	300+
Forest Park Hospital	Saint Louis	67%	(a)
Pemiscot Memorial Hospital	Hayti	62%	300+

43. Hospital Given 9 or 10 on 10 Point Scale

Hospital Name	City	Rate	Cases
McCune-Brooks Hospital	Carthage	83%	300+
Saint Luke's East Lee's Summit Hospital	Lees Summit	83%	300+
Progress West Healthcare Center	O'Fallon	80%	300+
Saint John's Regional Health Center	Springfield	80%	300+
Saint Lukes Hospital	Chesterfield	80%	300+
Southeast Missouri Hospital	Cape Girardeau	80%	300+
Missouri Baptist Hospital Sullivan	Sullivan	79%	300+
Barnes-Jewish West County Hospital	Creve Coeur	78%	300+
Boone Hospital Center	Columbia	78%	300+
Parkland Health Center	Farmington	78%	300+
SSM St Clare Health Center	Fenton	78%	300+
Barnes-Jewish St Peters Hospital	Saint Peters	77%	300+
Capital Region Medical Center	Jefferson City	77%	300+
Saint Marys Health Center	Jefferson City	76%	300+
Liberty Hospital	Liberty	75%	300+
Saint Johns Mercy Medical Center	Saint Louis	75%	300+
Cox Monett Hospital	Monett	74%	(a)
Hannibal Regional Hospital	Hannibal	74%	300+
Ozarks Community Hospital	Springfield	74%	300+
Saint Francis Hospital	Maryville	74%	300+
Saint Francis Medical Center	Cape Girardeau	74%	300+
Saint Lukes Cancer Institute	Kansas City	74%	(a)
Freeman Neosho Hospital	Neosho	73%	300+
Missouri Baptist Medical Center	Town & Country	73%	300+
Saint Lukes Northland Hospital	Kansas City	73%	300+
Women's and Children's Hospital	Columbia	73%	300+
Lee's Summit Medical Center	Lee's Summit	72%	300+
North Kansas City Hospital	N Kansas City	72%	300+
Saint John's Regional Medical Center	Joplin	72%	300+
Saint Lukes Hospital of Kansas City	Kansas City	72%	300+
Saint Mary's Medical Center	Blue Springs	71%	300+
Bothwell Regional Health Center	Sedalia	70%	300+
Lafayette Regional Health Center	Lexington	70%	(a)
Research Belton Hospital	Belton	70%	300+
SSM St Joseph Hospital West	Lake Saint Louis	70%	300+
Bates County Memorial Hospital	Butler	69%	300+
Citizens Memorial Hospital	Bolivar	69%	300+
Ste Genevieve County Memorial Hospital	Ste Genevieve	69%	300+
Centerpoint Medical Center of Independence	Independence	68%	300+
Christian Hospital Northeast	Saint Louis	68%	300+
SSM St Joseph Health Center	Saint Charles	68%	300+
Truman Medical Center Lakewood	Kansas City	68%	300+
Barnes Jewish Hospital	Saint Louis	67%	300+
Fitzgibbon Memorial Hospital	Marshall	67%	300+
Heartland Regional Medical Center	Saint Joseph	67%	300+
Lincoln County Medical Center	Troy	67%	(a)
Saint Joseph Medical Center	Kansas City	67%	300+
Saint Louis University Hospital	Saint Louis	67%	300+
Audrain Medical Center	Mexico	66%	300+
Lake Regional Health System	Osage Beach	66%	300+
Missouri Southern Healthcare	Dexter	66%	300+
Moberly Regional Medical Center	Moberly	66%	300+
Northeast Regional Medical Center	Kirksville	66%	300+
Research Medical Center	Kansas City	66%	300+
Saint Johns Hospital-Lebanon	Lebanon	66%	300+
Freeman Health System - Freeman West	Joplin	65%	300+
Hedrick Medical Center	Chillicothe	65%	(a)
Missouri Delta Medical Center	Sikeston	65%	300+
Saint Alexius Hospital	Saint Louis	65%	300+
Des Peres Hospital	Saint Louis	64%	300+
Golden Valley Memorial Hospital	Clinton	64%	300+
Ozarks Medical Center	West Plains	64%	300+
Skaggs Community Health Center	Branson	64%	300+
Saint Johns Mercy Hospital	Washington	63%	300+
SSM Depaul Health Center	Bridgeton	63%	300+
SSM St Marys Health Center	Richmond Hghts	63%	300+
Wright Memorial Hospital	Trenton	63%	(a)
Jefferson Regional Medical Center	Crystal City	62%	300+
Mineral Area Regional Medical Center	Farmington	62%	300+
Phelps County Regional Medical Center	Rolla	62%	300+
Saint Anthony's Medical Center	Saint Louis	62%	300+
Cox Medical Center	Springfield	61%	300+
University of Missouri Health Care	Columbia	60%	300+
Nevada Regional Medical Center	Nevada	59%	(a)
SAC-Osage Hospital	Osceola	59%	(a)
Texas County Memorial Hospital	Houston	59%	300+
Western Missouri Medical Center	Warrensburg	59%	300+
Callaway Community Hospital	Fulton	58%	(a)
Ripley County Memorial Hospital	Doniphan	57%	(a)
Forest Park Hospital	Saint Louis	55%	(a)
Truman Medical Center - Hospital Hill	Kansas City	55%	300+
Cameron Regional Medical Center	Cameron	52%	300+
Twin Rivers Regional Medical Center	Kennett	52%	300+
Poplar Bluff Regional Medical Center	Poplar Bluff	44%	300+
Pemiscot Memorial Hospital	Hayti	40%	300+

44. Meds 'Always' Explained Before Given

Hospital Name	City	Rate	Cases
Parkland Health Center	Farmington	74%	300+
Boone Hospital Center	Columbia	73%	300+
Saint Lukes Cancer Institute	Kansas City	73%	(a)
Cox Monett Hospital	Monett	71%	(a)
Lincoln County Medical Center	Troy	70%	(a)
SAC-Osage Hospital	Osceola	69%	(a)
Christian Hospital Northeast	Saint Louis	67%	300+
Missouri Baptist Hospital Sullivan	Sullivan	67%	300+
Missouri Delta Medical Center	Sikeston	67%	300+
Saint Francis Medical Center	Cape Girardeau	67%	300+
Bothwell Regional Health Center	Sedalia	66%	300+
Ozarks Community Hospital	Springfield	66%	300+
Saint Francis Hospital	Maryville	66%	300+
Wright Memorial Hospital	Trenton	66%	(a)
Barnes-Jewish St Peters Hospital	Saint Peters	65%	300+
Progress West Healthcare Center	O'Fallon	65%	300+
Saint John's Regional Health Center	Springfield	65%	300+
Saint Johns Hospital-Lebanon	Lebanon	65%	300+
Saint Louis University Hospital	Saint Louis	65%	300+
Lafayette Regional Health Center	Lexington	64%	(a)
McCune-Brooks Hospital	Carthage	64%	300+
Saint Lukes Northland Hospital	Kansas City	64%	300+
Southeast Missouri Hospital	Cape Girardeau	64%	300+

NOTE: Hospital profiles are in alphabetical order by state, then city, then hospital within the city; Rankings exclude hospitals with less than 25 cases except for patient surveys which excludes hospitals with less than 100 cases; (a) 100–299 cases; (1) The number of cases is too small to be sure how well a hospital is performing; (2) The hospital indicated that the data submitted for this measure were based on a sample of cases; (3) Data was collected during a shorter time period (fewer quarters) than the maximum possible time for this measure; (4) Suppressed for one or more quarters by CMS; (5) No data is available from the hospital for this measure; (6) Fewer than 100 patients completed the HCAHPS survey. Use these rates with caution, as the number of surveys may be too low to reliably assess hospital performance; (7) Survey results are based on less than 12 months of data; (8) Survey results are not available for this reporting period; (9) No or very few patients were eligible for the HCAHPS survey. The scores shown, if any, reflect a very small number of surveys; (10) A state average was not calculated because too few hospitals in the state submitted data; (11) There were discrepancies in the data collection process; Please refer to the User's Guide for a full explanation of data.

Hospital Name	City	Rate	Cases
Western Missouri Medical Center	Warrensburg	64%	300+
Callaway Community Hospital	Fulton	63%	(a)
Saint Luke's East Lee's Summit Hospital	Lees Summit	63%	300+
Saint Lukes Hospital of Kansas City	Kansas City	63%	300+
Freeman Neosho Hospital	Neosho	62%	300+
Hannibal Regional Hospital	Hannibal	62%	300+
Heartland Regional Medical Center	Saint Joseph	62%	300+
Liberty Hospital	Liberty	62%	300+
Saint Marys Health Center	Jefferson City	62%	300+
Forest Park Hospital	Saint Louis	61%	(a)
Lake Regional Health System	Osage Beach	61%	300+
Missouri Baptist Medical Center	Town & Country	61%	300+
Saint Alexius Hospital	Saint Louis	61%	300+
Saint Johns Mercy Hospital	Washington	61%	300+
Saint Lukes Hospital	Chesterfield	61%	300+
SSM St Joseph Hospital West	Lake Saint Louis	61%	300+
Ste Genevieve County Memorial Hospital	Ste Genevieve	61%	300+
Truman Medical Center Lakewood	Kansas City	61%	300+
Barnes Jewish Hospital	Saint Louis	60%	300+
Barnes-Jewish West County Hospital	Creve Coeur	60%	300+
Citizens Memorial Hospital	Bolivar	60%	300+
Fitzgibbon Memorial Hospital	Marshall	60%	300+
Missouri Southern Healthcare	Dexter	60%	300+
SSM St Clare Health Center	Fenton	60%	300+
SSM St Joseph Health Center	Saint Charles	60%	300+
Capital Region Medical Center	Jefferson City	59%	300+
North Kansas City Hospital	N Kansas City	59%	300+
Research Medical Center	Kansas City	59%	300+
SSM Depaul Health Center	Bridgeton	59%	300+
Texas County Memorial Hospital	Houston	59%	300+
Audrain Medical Center	Mexico	58%	300+
Bates County Memorial Hospital	Butler	58%	300+
Centerpoint Medical Center of Independence	Independence	58%	300+
Des Peres Hospital	Saint Louis	58%	300+
Northeast Regional Medical Center	Kirksville	58%	300+
Ozarks Medical Center	West Plains	58%	300+
Research Belton Hospital	Belton	58%	300+
Saint Mary's Medical Center	Blue Springs	58%	300+
Truman Medical Center - Hospital Hill	Kansas City	58%	300+
Freeman Health System - Freeman West	Joplin	57%	300+
Golden Valley Memorial Hospital	Clinton	57%	300+
Lee's Summit Medical Center	Lee's Summit	57%	300+
Mineral Area Regional Medical Center	Farmington	57%	300+
Jefferson Regional Medical Center	Crystal City	56%	300+
Moberly Regional Medical Center	Moberly	56%	300+
Nevada Regional Medical Center	Nevada	56%	(a)
Phelps County Regional Medical Center	Rolla	56%	300+
Saint John's Regional Medical Center	Joplin	56%	300+
Saint Joseph Medical Center	Kansas City	56%	300+
Hedrick Medical Center	Chillicothe	55%	(a)
Ripley County Memorial Hospital	Doniphan	55%	(a)
Saint Anthony's Medical Center	Saint Louis	55%	300+
Skaggs Community Health Center	Branson	55%	300+
SSM St Marys Health Center	Richmond Hghts	55%	300+
Women's and Children's Hospital	Columbia	55%	300+
University of Missouri Health Care	Columbia	54%	300+
Cox Medical Center	Springfield	53%	300+
Poplar Bluff Regional Medical Center	Poplar Bluff	52%	300+
Saint Johns Mercy Medical Center	Saint Louis	52%	300+
Twin Rivers Regional Medical Center	Kennett	52%	300+
Pemiscot Memorial Hospital	Hayti	47%	300+
Cameron Regional Medical Center	Cameron	46%	300+

45. Nurses 'Always' Communicated Well

Hospital Name	City	Rate	Cases
Parkland Health Center	Farmington	86%	300+
Saint Lukes Cancer Institute	Kansas City	85%	(a)
Southeast Missouri Hospital	Cape Girardeau	85%	300+
Boone Hospital Center	Columbia	84%	300+
McCune-Brooks Hospital	Carthage	84%	300+
Saint Marys Health Center	Jefferson City	84%	300+
Christian Hospital Northeast	Saint Louis	83%	300+
Cox Monett Hospital	Monett	83%	(a)
Missouri Baptist Hospital Sullivan	Sullivan	83%	300+
Barnes-Jewish St Peters Hospital	Saint Peters	82%	300+
Barnes-Jewish West County Hospital	Creve Coeur	82%	300+
Saint Francis Hospital	Maryville	82%	300+
Bothwell Regional Health Center	Sedalia	81%	300+
Hannibal Regional Hospital	Hannibal	81%	300+
Lincoln County Medical Center	Troy	81%	(a)
Missouri Southern Healthcare	Dexter	81%	300+
SAC-Osage Hospital	Osceola	81%	(a)
Saint Francis Medical Center	Cape Girardeau	81%	300+
Capital Region Medical Center	Jefferson City	80%	300+
Heartland Regional Medical Center	Saint Joseph	80%	300+
Ozarks Community Hospital	Springfield	80%	300+
Phelps County Regional Medical Center	Rolla	80%	300+
Progress West Healthcare Center	O'Fallon	80%	300+
Saint John's Regional Health Center	Springfield	80%	300+
Ste Genevieve County Memorial Hospital	Ste Genevieve	80%	300+
Citizens Memorial Hospital	Bolivar	79%	300+
Forest Park Hospital	Saint Louis	79%	(a)
Lafayette Regional Health Center	Lexington	79%	(a)
Ozarks Medical Center	West Plains	79%	300+
Saint Luke's East Lee's Summit Hospital	Lees Summit	79%	300+
Freeman Neosho Hospital	Neosho	78%	300+
Missouri Delta Medical Center	Sikeston	78%	300+
Saint Alexius Hospital	Saint Louis	78%	300+
Saint Johns Mercy Medical Center	Saint Louis	78%	300+
Saint Lukes Hospital of Kansas City	Kansas City	78%	300+
Saint Mary's Medical Center	Blue Springs	78%	300+
SSM St Clare Health Center	Fenton	78%	300+
SSM St Joseph Hospital West	Lake Saint Louis	78%	300+
Wright Memorial Hospital	Trenton	78%	(a)
Research Belton Hospital	Belton	77%	300+
Saint John's Regional Medical Center	Joplin	77%	300+
Saint Lukes Hospital	Chesterfield	77%	300+
Western Missouri Medical Center	Warrensburg	77%	300+
Audrain Medical Center	Mexico	76%	300+
Fitzgibbon Memorial Hospital	Marshall	76%	300+
Golden Valley Memorial Hospital	Clinton	76%	300+
Lake Regional Health System	Osage Beach	76%	300+
Liberty Hospital	Liberty	76%	300+
Research Medical Center	Kansas City	76%	300+
Saint Johns Hospital-Lebanon	Lebanon	76%	300+
Saint Lukes Northland Hospital	Kansas City	76%	300+
SSM St Joseph Health Center	Saint Charles	76%	300+
Truman Medical Center Lakewood	Kansas City	76%	300+
Bates County Memorial Hospital	Butler	75%	300+
Centerpoint Medical Center of Independence	Independence	75%	300+
Hedrick Medical Center	Chillicothe	75%	(a)
Lee's Summit Medical Center	Lee's Summit	75%	300+
Mineral Area Regional Medical Center	Farmington	75%	300+
Missouri Baptist Medical Center	Town & Country	75%	300+
Nevada Regional Medical Center	Nevada	75%	(a)
North Kansas City Hospital	N Kansas City	75%	300+
Northeast Regional Medical Center	Kirksville	75%	300+
Saint Anthony's Medical Center	Saint Louis	75%	300+
Saint Johns Mercy Hospital	Washington	75%	300+
Women's and Children's Hospital	Columbia	75%	300+
Des Peres Hospital	Saint Louis	74%	300+
Freeman Health System - Freeman West	Joplin	74%	300+
Jefferson Regional Medical Center	Crystal City	74%	300+
Moberly Regional Medical Center	Moberly	74%	300+
Skaggs Community Health Center	Branson	74%	300+
SSM Depaul Health Center	Bridgeton	74%	300+
SSM St Marys Health Center	Richmond Hghts	74%	300+
Barnes Jewish Hospital	Saint Louis	73%	300+
Ripley County Memorial Hospital	Doniphan	73%	(a)
Saint Joseph Medical Center	Kansas City	73%	300+
Cox Medical Center	Springfield	72%	300+
Saint Louis University Hospital	Saint Louis	72%	300+
Texas County Memorial Hospital	Houston	72%	300+
University of Missouri Health Care	Columbia	72%	300+
Callaway Community Hospital	Fulton	71%	(a)
Twin Rivers Regional Medical Center	Kennett	69%	300+
Truman Medical Center - Hospital Hill	Kansas City	68%	300+
Poplar Bluff Regional Medical Center	Poplar Bluff	67%	300+
Cameron Regional Medical Center	Cameron	63%	300+
Pemiscot Memorial Hospital	Hayti	60%	300+

46. Pain 'Always' Well Controlled

Hospital Name	City	Rate	Cases
Cox Monett Hospital	Monett	79%	(a)
Parkland Health Center	Farmington	79%	300+
McCune-Brooks Hospital	Carthage	78%	300+
Barnes-Jewish West County Hospital	Creve Coeur	77%	300+
Forest Park Hospital	Saint Louis	76%	(a)
Missouri Baptist Hospital Sullivan	Sullivan	76%	300+
Missouri Delta Medical Center	Sikeston	75%	300+
Saint Marys Health Center	Jefferson City	75%	300+
Bothwell Regional Health Center	Sedalia	74%	300+
Saint Lukes Hospital of Kansas City	Kansas City	74%	300+
Southeast Missouri Hospital	Cape Girardeau	74%	300+
Christian Hospital Northeast	Saint Louis	73%	300+
Ozarks Medical Center	West Plains	73%	300+
Saint John's Regional Health Center	Springfield	73%	300+
Audrain Medical Center	Mexico	72%	300+
Barnes-Jewish St Peters Hospital	Saint Peters	72%	300+
Capital Region Medical Center	Jefferson City	72%	300+
Citizens Memorial Hospital	Bolivar	72%	300+
Progress West Healthcare Center	O'Fallon	72%	300+
Research Belton Hospital	Belton	72%	300+
Saint Francis Hospital	Maryville	72%	300+
Saint John's Regional Medical Center	Joplin	72%	300+
Saint Lukes Hospital	Chesterfield	72%	300+
Boone Hospital Center	Columbia	71%	300+
Fitzgibbon Memorial Hospital	Marshall	71%	300+
Heartland Regional Medical Center	Saint Joseph	71%	300+
Lincoln County Medical Center	Troy	71%	(a)
Missouri Southern Healthcare	Dexter	71%	300+
Ozarks Community Hospital	Springfield	71%	300+
Phelps County Regional Medical Center	Rolla	71%	300+
Saint Alexius Hospital	Saint Louis	71%	300+
Saint Francis Medical Center	Cape Girardeau	71%	300+
Saint Luke's East Lee's Summit Hospital	Lees Summit	71%	300+
SSM St Clare Health Center	Fenton	71%	300+
Barnes Jewish Hospital	Saint Louis	70%	300+
Centerpoint Medical Center of Independence	Independence	70%	300+
Hannibal Regional Hospital	Hannibal	70%	300+
Lee's Summit Medical Center	Lee's Summit	70%	300+
Saint Anthony's Medical Center	Saint Louis	70%	300+
Saint Lukes Cancer Institute	Kansas City	70%	(a)
Saint Lukes Northland Hospital	Kansas City	70%	300+
Saint Mary's Medical Center	Blue Springs	70%	300+
SSM St Joseph Hospital West	Lake Saint Louis	70%	300+
Des Peres Hospital	Saint Louis	69%	300+
Freeman Neosho Hospital	Neosho	69%	300+
Golden Valley Memorial Hospital	Clinton	69%	300+
Lake Regional Health System	Osage Beach	69%	300+
Missouri Baptist Medical Center	Town & Country	69%	300+
Research Medical Center	Kansas City	69%	300+
Saint Johns Mercy Medical Center	Saint Louis	69%	300+
Western Missouri Medical Center	Warrensburg	69%	300+
Women's and Children's Hospital	Columbia	69%	300+
Bates County Memorial Hospital	Butler	68%	300+
Freeman Health System - Freeman West	Joplin	68%	300+
Lafayette Regional Health Center	Lexington	68%	(a)
North Kansas City Hospital	N Kansas City	68%	300+
Saint Johns Mercy Hospital	Washington	68%	300+
Saint Joseph Medical Center	Kansas City	68%	300+
SSM Depaul Health Center	Bridgeton	68%	300+
SSM St Joseph Health Center	Saint Charles	68%	300+
Ste Genevieve County Memorial Hospital	Ste Genevieve	68%	300+
Wright Memorial Hospital	Trenton	68%	(a)
Jefferson Regional Medical Center	Crystal City	67%	300+
Mineral Area Regional Medical Center	Farmington	67%	300+
Moberly Regional Medical Center	Moberly	66%	300+
Northeast Regional Medical Center	Kirksville	66%	300+
Saint Johns Hospital-Lebanon	Lebanon	66%	300+
Saint Louis University Hospital	Saint Louis	66%	300+
SSM St Marys Health Center	Richmond Hghts	66%	300+
Callaway Community Hospital	Fulton	65%	(a)
Poplar Bluff Regional Medical Center	Poplar Bluff	65%	300+
Truman Medical Center Lakewood	Kansas City	65%	300+
University of Missouri Health Care	Columbia	65%	300+
Hedrick Medical Center	Chillicothe	64%	(a)
Liberty Hospital	Liberty	64%	300+
Skaggs Community Health Center	Branson	64%	300+
Cox Medical Center	Springfield	63%	300+
SAC-Osage Hospital	Osceola	63%	(a)
Texas County Memorial Hospital	Houston	62%	300+
Nevada Regional Medical Center	Nevada	61%	(a)
Truman Medical Center - Hospital Hill	Kansas City	61%	300+
Cameron Regional Medical Center	Cameron	58%	300+
Twin Rivers Regional Medical Center	Kennett	58%	300+
Pemiscot Memorial Hospital	Hayti	56%	300+
Ripley County Memorial Hospital	Doniphan	51%	(a)

47. Room and Bathroom 'Always' Clean

Hospital Name	City	Rate	Cases
Saint Francis Hospital	Maryville	88%	300+
Nevada Regional Medical Center	Nevada	84%	(a)
Missouri Delta Medical Center	Sikeston	83%	300+
Ozarks Community Hospital	Springfield	83%	300+
Saint Johns Hospital-Lebanon	Lebanon	83%	300+
Texas County Memorial Hospital	Houston	82%	300+
Bothwell Regional Health Center	Sedalia	81%	300+
Golden Valley Memorial Hospital	Clinton	81%	300+
Missouri Baptist Hospital Sullivan	Sullivan	81%	300+
SAC-Osage Hospital	Osceola	81%	(a)
Hedrick Medical Center	Chillicothe	80%	(a)
Lincoln County Medical Center	Troy	80%	(a)
McCune-Brooks Hospital	Carthage	80%	300+
Citizens Memorial Hospital	Bolivar	79%	300+
Freeman Neosho Hospital	Neosho	79%	300+
Missouri Southern Healthcare	Dexter	79%	300+
Saint John's Regional Health Center	Springfield	79%	300+
Saint Luke's East Lee's Summit Hospital	Lees Summit	79%	300+
Western Missouri Medical Center	Warrensburg	79%	300+
Lake Regional Health System	Osage Beach	78%	300+
SSM St Clare Health Center	Fenton	78%	300+
Audrain Medical Center	Mexico	77%	300+
Cox Monett Hospital	Monett	77%	(a)
Lafayette Regional Health Center	Lexington	77%	(a)
Phelps County Regional Medical Center	Rolla	77%	300+
Ripley County Memorial Hospital	Doniphan	77%	(a)
Saint Marys Health Center	Jefferson City	77%	300+
Ste Genevieve County Memorial Hospital	Ste Genevieve	77%	300+
Women's and Children's Hospital	Columbia	77%	300+

NOTE: Hospital profiles are in alphabetical order by state, then city, then hospital within the city; Rankings exclude hospitals with less than 25 cases except for patient surveys which excludes hospitals with less than 100 cases; (a) 100–299 cases; (1) The number of cases is too small to be sure how well a hospital is performing; (2) The hospital indicated that the data submitted for this measure were based on a sample of cases; (3) Data was collected during a shorter time period (fewer quarters) than the maximum possible time for this measure; (4) Suppressed for one or more quarters by CMS; (5) No data is available from the hospital for this measure; (6) Fewer than 100 patients completed the HCAHPS survey. Use these rates with caution, as the number of surveys may be too low to reliably assess hospital performance; (7) Survey results are based on less than 12 months of data; (8) Survey results are not available for this reporting period; (9) No or very few patients were eligible for the HCAHPS survey. The scores shown, if any, reflect a very small number of surveys; (10) A state average was not calculated because too few hospitals in the state submitted data; (11) There were discrepancies in the data collection process; Please refer to the User's Guide for a full explanation of data.

Wright Memorial Hospital	Trenton	77%	(a)
Capital Region Medical Center	Jefferson City	76%	300+
Southeast Missouri Hospital	Cape Girardeau	76%	300+
Boone Hospital Center	Columbia	75%	300+
Progress West Healthcare Center	O'Fallon	75%	300+
Saint Francis Medical Center	Cape Girardeau	75%	300+
Saint Johns Mercy Hospital	Washington	75%	300+
Parkland Health Center	Farmington	74%	300+
Saint Lukes Northland Hospital	Kansas City	73%	300+
Lee's Summit Medical Center	Lee's Summit	72%	300+
Mineral Area Regional Medical Center	Farmington	72%	300+
Moberly Regional Medical Center	Moberly	72%	300+
Ozarks Medical Center	West Plains	72%	300+
Saint John's Regional Medical Center	Joplin	72%	300+
Saint Lukes Hospital	Chesterfield	72%	300+
Skaggs Community Health Center	Branson	72%	300+
Barnes-Jewish West County Hospital	Creve Coeur	71%	300+
Bates County Memorial Hospital	Butler	71%	300+
Liberty Hospital	Liberty	71%	300+
Saint Lukes Cancer Institute	Kansas City	71%	(a)
Barnes-Jewish St Peters Hospital	Saint Peters	70%	300+
Hannibal Regional Hospital	Hannibal	70%	300+
Heartland Regional Medical Center	Saint Joseph	70%	300+
Northeast Regional Medical Center	Kirksville	70%	300+
Saint Johns Mercy Medical Center	Saint Louis	70%	300+
Truman Medical Center Lakewood	Kansas City	70%	300+
Cameron Regional Medical Center	Cameron	69%	300+
Centerpoint Medical Center of Independence	Independence	69%	300+
Christian Hospital Northeast	Saint Louis	69%	300+
North Kansas City Hospital	N Kansas City	69%	300+
Saint Anthony's Medical Center	Saint Louis	69%	300+
SSM St Joseph Health Center	Saint Charles	69%	300+
Jefferson Regional Medical Center	Crystal City	68%	300+
Saint Lukes Hospital of Kansas City	Kansas City	68%	300+
Des Peres Hospital	Saint Louis	67%	300+
Research Belton Hospital	Belton	67%	300+
Saint Louis University Hospital	Saint Louis	67%	300+
Saint Mary's Medical Center	Blue Springs	67%	300+
Barnes Jewish Hospital	Saint Louis	66%	300+
Callaway Community Hospital	Fulton	66%	(a)
Fitzgibbon Memorial Hospital	Marshall	66%	300+
Freeman Health System - Freeman West	Joplin	66%	300+
University of Missouri Health Care	Columbia	66%	300+
Cox Medical Center	Springfield	65%	300+
SSM St Joseph Hospital West	Lake Saint Louis	65%	300+
Missouri Baptist Medical Center	Town & Country	64%	300+
Saint Alexius Hospital	Saint Louis	64%	300+
Research Medical Center	Kansas City	63%	300+
SSM Depaul Health Center	Bridgeton	62%	300+
Truman Medical Center - Hospital Hill	Kansas City	62%	300+
SSM St Marys Health Center	Richmond Hghts	61%	300+
Saint Joseph Medical Center	Kansas City	60%	300+
Twin Rivers Regional Medical Center	Kennett	58%	300+
Pemiscot Memorial Hospital	Hayti	57%	300+
Poplar Bluff Regional Medical Center	Poplar Bluff	57%	300+
Forest Park Hospital	Saint Louis	55%	(a)

48. Timely Help 'Always' Received

Hospital Name	City	Rate	Cases
McCune-Brooks Hospital	Carthage	85%	300+
Saint Lukes Cancer Institute	Kansas City	81%	(a)
Parkland Health Center	Farmington	78%	300+
Cox Monett Hospital	Monett	77%	(a)
Bothwell Regional Health Center	Sedalia	76%	300+
Saint Francis Hospital	Maryville	76%	300+
Lincoln County Medical Center	Troy	74%	(a)
Missouri Baptist Hospital Sullivan	Sullivan	73%	300+
Missouri Southern Healthcare	Dexter	73%	300+
Ozarks Community Hospital	Springfield	73%	300+
Barnes-Jewish West County Hospital	Creve Coeur	72%	300+
Ozarks Medical Center	West Plains	72%	300+
Southeast Missouri Hospital	Cape Girardeau	72%	300+
Audrain Medical Center	Mexico	71%	300+
Hedrick Medical Center	Chillicothe	71%	(a)
Nevada Regional Medical Center	Nevada	71%	(a)
Freeman Neosho Hospital	Neosho	70%	300+
Lake Regional Health System	Osage Beach	70%	300+
SAC-Osage Hospital	Osceola	70%	(a)
Boone Hospital Center	Columbia	69%	300+
Callaway Community Hospital	Fulton	68%	(a)
Citizens Memorial Hospital	Bolivar	68%	300+
Fitzgibbon Memorial Hospital	Marshall	68%	300+
Hannibal Regional Hospital	Hannibal	68%	300+
Ripley County Memorial Hospital	Doniphan	68%	(a)
Women's and Children's Hospital	Columbia	68%	300+
Wright Memorial Hospital	Trenton	68%	(a)
Golden Valley Memorial Hospital	Clinton	67%	300+
Missouri Delta Medical Center	Sikeston	67%	300+
Saint John's Regional Health Center	Springfield	67%	300+
Saint Marys Health Center	Jefferson City	67%	300+
Ste Genevieve County Memorial Hospital	Ste Genevieve	67%	300+
Capital Region Medical Center	Jefferson City	66%	300+
Lafayette Regional Health Center	Lexington	66%	(a)
Research Belton Hospital	Belton	66%	300+
Saint Johns Hospital-Lebanon	Lebanon	66%	300+
Saint Lukes Hospital of Kansas City	Kansas City	66%	300+
Progress West Healthcare Center	O'Fallon	65%	300+
Saint Luke's East Lee's Summit Hospital	Lees Summit	65%	300+
SSM St Joseph Health Center	Saint Charles	65%	300+
Christian Hospital Northeast	Saint Louis	64%	300+
Phelps County Regional Medical Center	Rolla	64%	300+
Saint Mary's Medical Center	Blue Springs	64%	300+
Barnes-Jewish St Peters Hospital	Saint Peters	63%	300+
Bates County Memorial Hospital	Butler	63%	300+
Jefferson Regional Medical Center	Crystal City	63%	300+
Moberly Regional Medical Center	Moberly	63%	300+
North Kansas City Hospital	N Kansas City	63%	300+
Saint Francis Medical Center	Cape Girardeau	63%	300+
Skaggs Community Health Center	Branson	63%	300+
SSM St Clare Health Center	Fenton	63%	300+
Centerpoint Medical Center of Independence	Independence	62%	300+
Des Peres Hospital	Saint Louis	62%	300+
Mineral Area Regional Medical Center	Farmington	62%	300+
Saint Alexius Hospital	Saint Louis	62%	300+
Saint John's Regional Medical Center	Joplin	62%	300+
Saint Johns Mercy Medical Center	Saint Louis	62%	300+
Saint Lukes Hospital	Chesterfield	62%	300+
SSM St Joseph Hospital West	Lake Saint Louis	62%	300+
Truman Medical Center Lakewood	Kansas City	62%	300+
Lee's Summit Medical Center	Lee's Summit	61%	300+
Liberty Hospital	Liberty	61%	300+
Poplar Bluff Regional Medical Center	Poplar Bluff	61%	300+
Western Missouri Medical Center	Warrensburg	61%	300+
Heartland Regional Medical Center	Saint Joseph	60%	300+
Saint Louis University Hospital	Saint Louis	60%	300+
Saint Lukes Northland Hospital	Kansas City	60%	300+
Missouri Baptist Medical Center	Town & Country	59%	300+
Northeast Regional Medical Center	Kirksville	59%	300+
Research Medical Center	Kansas City	59%	300+
Saint Johns Mercy Hospital	Washington	59%	300+
Texas County Memorial Hospital	Houston	59%	300+
Cox Medical Center	Springfield	58%	300+
SSM St Marys Health Center	Richmond Hghts	58%	300+
University of Missouri Health Care	Columbia	58%	300+
Forest Park Hospital	Saint Louis	57%	(a)
Freeman Health System - Freeman West	Joplin	56%	300+
Saint Anthony's Medical Center	Saint Louis	56%	300+
SSM Depaul Health Center	Bridgeton	56%	300+
Saint Joseph Medical Center	Kansas City	55%	300+
Barnes Jewish Hospital	Saint Louis	53%	300+
Cameron Regional Medical Center	Cameron	52%	300+
Truman Medical Center - Hospital Hill	Kansas City	52%	300+
Twin Rivers Regional Medical Center	Kennett	52%	300+
Pemiscot Memorial Hospital	Hayti	48%	300+

49. Would Definitely Recommend Hospital

Hospital Name	City	Rate	Cases
Saint Lukes Cancer Institute	Kansas City	87%	(a)
Saint Luke's East Lee's Summit Hospital	Lees Summit	86%	300+
McCune-Brooks Hospital	Carthage	85%	300+
Southeast Missouri Hospital	Cape Girardeau	85%	300+
Saint Lukes Hospital	Chesterfield	84%	300+
Boone Hospital Center	Columbia	83%	300+
Saint John's Regional Health Center	Springfield	83%	300+
Progress West Healthcare Center	O'Fallon	82%	300+
Barnes-Jewish St Peters Hospital	Saint Peters	81%	300+
Capital Region Medical Center	Jefferson City	81%	300+
Saint Lukes Hospital of Kansas City	Kansas City	81%	300+
SSM St Clare Health Center	Fenton	81%	300+
Ozarks Community Hospital	Springfield	80%	300+
Saint Francis Medical Center	Cape Girardeau	80%	300+
Saint Marys Health Center	Jefferson City	80%	300+
Barnes-Jewish West County Hospital	Creve Coeur	79%	300+
Saint Johns Mercy Medical Center	Saint Louis	79%	300+
North Kansas City Hospital	N Kansas City	78%	300+
Liberty Hospital	Liberty	77%	300+
Parkland Health Center	Farmington	77%	300+
Saint Lukes Northland Hospital	Kansas City	77%	300+
Missouri Baptist Medical Center	Town & Country	76%	300+
Women's and Children's Hospital	Columbia	76%	300+
Saint John's Regional Medical Center	Joplin	75%	300+
SSM St Joseph Hospital West	Lake Saint Louis	75%	300+
Saint Joseph Medical Center	Kansas City	73%	300+
Saint Mary's Medical Center	Blue Springs	73%	300+
Barnes Jewish Hospital	Saint Louis	72%	300+
Lee's Summit Medical Center	Lee's Summit	72%	300+
Bates County Memorial Hospital	Butler	71%	300+
Cox Monett Hospital	Monett	71%	(a)
Freeman Neosho Hospital	Neosho	71%	300+
Hannibal Regional Hospital	Hannibal	71%	300+
Missouri Baptist Hospital Sullivan	Sullivan	71%	300+
Saint Francis Hospital	Maryville	71%	300+
Saint Louis University Hospital	Saint Louis	71%	300+
Freeman Health System - Freeman West	Joplin	70%	300+
SSM St Joseph Health Center	Saint Charles	70%	300+
Ste Genevieve County Memorial Hospital	Ste Genevieve	70%	300+
Des Peres Hospital	Saint Louis	69%	300+
Skaggs Community Health Center	Branson	69%	300+
Truman Medical Center Lakewood	Kansas City	69%	300+
Centerpoint Medical Center of Independence	Independence	68%	300+
Cox Medical Center	Springfield	68%	300+
University of Missouri Health Care	Columbia	68%	300+
Bothwell Regional Health Center	Sedalia	67%	300+
Christian Hospital Northeast	Saint Louis	67%	300+
Citizens Memorial Hospital	Bolivar	67%	300+
Saint Johns Hospital-Lebanon	Lebanon	67%	300+
Saint Johns Mercy Hospital	Washington	67%	300+
SSM Depaul Health Center	Bridgeton	67%	300+
Heartland Regional Medical Center	Saint Joseph	66%	300+
Lake Regional Health System	Osage Beach	66%	300+
Ozarks Medical Center	West Plains	66%	300+
SSM St Marys Health Center	Richmond Hghts	66%	300+
Lafayette Regional Health Center	Lexington	65%	(a)
Lincoln County Medical Center	Troy	65%	(a)
Missouri Southern Healthcare	Dexter	65%	300+
Research Belton Hospital	Belton	65%	300+
Saint Alexius Hospital	Saint Louis	65%	300+
Audrain Medical Center	Mexico	64%	300+
Research Medical Center	Kansas City	64%	300+
SAC-Osage Hospital	Osceola	64%	(a)
Golden Valley Memorial Hospital	Clinton	63%	300+
Mineral Area Regional Medical Center	Farmington	63%	300+
Phelps County Regional Medical Center	Rolla	63%	300+
Missouri Delta Medical Center	Sikeston	62%	300+
Jefferson Regional Medical Center	Crystal City	61%	300+
Saint Anthony's Medical Center	Saint Louis	61%	300+
Moberly Regional Medical Center	Moberly	60%	300+
Western Missouri Medical Center	Warrensburg	60%	300+
Northeast Regional Medical Center	Kirksville	59%	300+
Fitzgibbon Memorial Hospital	Marshall	58%	300+
Truman Medical Center - Hospital Hill	Kansas City	58%	300+
Hedrick Medical Center	Chillicothe	57%	(a)
Nevada Regional Medical Center	Nevada	56%	(a)
Ripley County Memorial Hospital	Doniphan	55%	(a)
Texas County Memorial Hospital	Houston	55%	300+
Twin Rivers Regional Medical Center	Kennett	55%	300+
Wright Memorial Hospital	Trenton	55%	(a)
Forest Park Hospital	Saint Louis	54%	(a)
Callaway Community Hospital	Fulton	50%	(a)
Cameron Regional Medical Center	Cameron	50%	300+
Poplar Bluff Regional Medical Center	Poplar Bluff	45%	300+
Pemiscot Memorial Hospital	Hayti	40%	300+

NOTE: Hospital profiles are in alphabetical order by state, then city, then hospital within the city; Rankings exclude hospitals with less than 25 cases except for patient surveys which excludes hospitals with less than 100 cases; (a) 100–299 cases; (1) The number of cases is too small to be sure how well a hospital is performing; (2) The hospital indicated that the data submitted for this measure were based on a sample of cases; (3) Data was collected during a shorter time period (fewer quarters) than the maximum possible time for this measure; (4) Suppressed for one or more quarters by CMS; (5) No data is available from the hospital for this measure; (6) Fewer than 100 patients completed the HCAHPS survey. Use these rates with caution, as the number of surveys may be too low to reliably assess hospital performance; (7) Survey results are based on less than 12 months of data; (8) Survey results are not available for this reporting period; (9) No or very few patients were eligible for the HCAHPS survey. The scores shown, if any, reflect a very small number of surveys; (10) A state average was not calculated because too few hospitals in the state submitted data; (11) There were discrepancies in the data collection process; Please refer to the User's Guide for a full explanation of data.

Northwest Medical Center

705 N College Street
Albany, MO 64402
URL: www.gcmh.org
Type: Critical Access Hospitals
Ownership: Voluntary Non-Profit - Other
Phone: 660-726-3941
Fax: 660-726-3647
Emergency Services: Yes
Beds: 45

Key Personnel:
CEO/President. . . . . Angelia Martin, MD
Chief of Medical Staff . . . . Angelia Martin

Measure	Cases	This Hosp.	State Avg.	U.S. Avg.
Heart Attack Care				
ACE Inhibitor or ARB for LVSD[5]	0	-	96%	96%
Aspirin at Arrival[5]	0	-	99%	99%
Aspirin at Discharge[5]	0	-	99%	98%
Beta Blocker at Discharge[5]	0	-	99%	98%
Fibrinolytic Medication Timing[5]	0	-	27%	55%
PCI Within 90 Minutes of Arrival[5]	0	-	92%	90%
Smoking Cessation Advice[5]	0	-	99%	99%
Chest Pain/Possible Heart Attack Care				
Aspirin at Arrival	-	-	95%	95%
Median Time to ECG (minutes)	-	-	9	8
Median Time to Transfer (minutes)	-	-	64	61
Fibrinolytic Medication Timing	-	-	31%	54%
Heart Failure Care				
ACE Inhibitor or ARB for LVSD[5]	0	-	94%	94%
Discharge Instructions[5]	0	-	87%	88%
Evaluation of LVS Function[5]	0	-	97%	98%
Smoking Cessation Advice[5]	0	-	98%	98%
Pneumonia Care				
Appropriate Initial Antibiotic[5]	0	-	91%	92%
Blood Culture Timing[5]	0	-	97%	96%
Influenza Vaccine[5]	0	-	90%	91%
Initial Antibiotic Timing[5]	0	-	95%	95%
Pneumococcal Vaccine[5]	0	-	93%	93%
Smoking Cessation Advice[5]	0	-	97%	97%
Surgical Care Improvement Project				
Appropriate VTP Within 24 Hours[5]	0	-	93%	92%
Appropriate Hair Removal[5]	0	-	100%	99%
Appropriate Beta Blocker Usage[5]	0	-	94%	93%
Controlled Postoperative Blood Glucose[5]	0	-	94%	93%
Prophylactic Antibiotic Timing[5]	0	-	97%	97%
Prophylactic Antibiotic Timing (Outpatient)	-	-	95%	92%
Prophylactic Antibiotic Selection[5]	0	-	97%	97%
Prophylactic Antibiotic Select. (Outpatient)	-	-	95%	94%
Prophylactic Antibiotic Stopped[5]	0	-	95%	94%
Recommended VTP Ordered[5]	0	-	95%	94%
Urinary Catheter Removal[5]	0	-	88%	90%
Children's Asthma Care				
Received Systemic Corticosteroids	-	-	-	100%
Received Home Management Plan	-	-	-	71%
Received Reliever Medication	-	-	-	100%
Use of Medical Imaging				
Combination Abdominal CT Scan	-	-	0.227	0.191
Combination Chest CT Scan	-	-	0.059	0.054
Follow-up Mammogram/Ultrasound	-	-	7.4%	8.4%
MRI for Low Back Pain	-	-	36%	32.7%
Survey of Patients' Hospital Experiences				
Area Around Room 'Always' Quiet at Night[8]	-	-	-	58%
Doctors 'Always' Communicated Well[8]	-	-	-	80%
Home Recovery Information Given[8]	-	-	-	82%
Hospital Given 9 or 10 on 10 Point Scale[8]	-	-	-	67%
Meds 'Always' Explained Before Given[8]	-	-	-	60%
Nurses 'Always' Communicated Well[8]	-	-	-	76%
Pain 'Always' Well Controlled[8]	-	-	-	69%
Room and Bathroom 'Always' Clean[8]	-	-	-	71%
Timely Help 'Always' Received[8]	-	-	-	64%
Would Definitely Recommend Hospital[8]	-	-	-	69%

Saint Johns Hospital - Aurora

500 Porter Avenue
Aurora, MO 65605
E-mail: ach@achmo.com
URL: www.achmo.com
Type: Critical Access Hospitals
Ownership: Voluntary Non-Profit - Private
Phone: 417-678-2122
Fax: 417-678-7877
Emergency Services: Yes
Beds: 59

Key Personnel:
Cardiac Laboratory. . . . . Dave Dickson
Chief of Medical Staff . . . . Joseph Bizek
Infection Control . . . . Debbie Nelson
Operating Room. . . . . Debbie Ehase
Quality Assurance . . . . Cathy Munden
Emergency Room . . . . Kent Stringer

Measure	Cases	This Hosp.	State Avg.	U.S. Avg.
Heart Attack Care				
ACE Inhibitor or ARB for LVSD[5]	0	-	96%	96%
Aspirin at Arrival[5]	0	-	99%	99%
Aspirin at Discharge[5]	0	-	99%	98%
Beta Blocker at Discharge[5]	0	-	99%	98%
Fibrinolytic Medication Timing[5]	0	-	27%	55%
PCI Within 90 Minutes of Arrival[5]	0	-	92%	90%
Smoking Cessation Advice[5]	0	-	99%	99%
Chest Pain/Possible Heart Attack Care				
Aspirin at Arrival	-	-	95%	95%
Median Time to ECG (minutes)	-	-	9	8
Median Time to Transfer (minutes)	-	-	64	61
Fibrinolytic Medication Timing	-	-	31%	54%
Heart Failure Care				
ACE Inhibitor or ARB for LVSD[1]	3	100%	94%	94%
Discharge Instructions[1]	12	100%	87%	88%
Evaluation of LVS Function[1]	16	94%	97%	98%
Smoking Cessation Advice[1]	2	100%	98%	98%
Pneumonia Care				
Appropriate Initial Antibiotic	53	98%	91%	92%
Blood Culture Timing	46	100%	97%	96%
Influenza Vaccine	38	95%	90%	91%
Initial Antibiotic Timing	71	97%	95%	95%
Pneumococcal Vaccine	51	98%	93%	93%
Smoking Cessation Advice	30	100%	97%	97%
Surgical Care Improvement Project				
Appropriate VTP Within 24 Hours[5]	0	-	93%	92%
Appropriate Hair Removal[5]	0	-	100%	99%
Appropriate Beta Blocker Usage[5]	0	-	94%	93%
Controlled Postoperative Blood Glucose[5]	0	-	94%	93%
Prophylactic Antibiotic Timing[5]	0	-	97%	97%
Prophylactic Antibiotic Timing (Outpatient)	-	-	95%	92%
Prophylactic Antibiotic Selection[5]	0	-	97%	97%
Prophylactic Antibiotic Select. (Outpatient)	-	-	95%	94%
Prophylactic Antibiotic Stopped[5]	0	-	95%	94%
Recommended VTP Ordered[5]	0	-	95%	94%
Urinary Catheter Removal[5]	0	-	88%	90%
Children's Asthma Care				
Received Systemic Corticosteroids	-	-	-	100%
Received Home Management Plan	-	-	-	71%
Received Reliever Medication	-	-	-	100%
Use of Medical Imaging				
Combination Abdominal CT Scan	-	-	0.227	0.191
Combination Chest CT Scan	-	-	0.059	0.054
Follow-up Mammogram/Ultrasound	-	-	7.4%	8.4%
MRI for Low Back Pain	-	-	36%	32.7%
Survey of Patients' Hospital Experiences				
Area Around Room 'Always' Quiet at Night[8]	-	-	-	58%
Doctors 'Always' Communicated Well[8]	-	-	-	80%
Home Recovery Information Given[8]	-	-	-	82%
Hospital Given 9 or 10 on 10 Point Scale[8]	-	-	-	67%
Meds 'Always' Explained Before Given[8]	-	-	-	60%
Nurses 'Always' Communicated Well[8]	-	-	-	76%
Pain 'Always' Well Controlled[8]	-	-	-	69%
Room and Bathroom 'Always' Clean[8]	-	-	-	71%
Timely Help 'Always' Received[8]	-	-	-	64%
Would Definitely Recommend Hospital[8]	-	-	-	69%

Research Belton Hospital

17065 S 71 Highway
Belton, MO 64012
Type: Acute Care Hospitals
Ownership: Voluntary Non-Profit - Private
Phone: 816-348-1236
Fax: 816-348-1293
Emergency Services: Yes
Beds: 75

Key Personnel:
CEO/President. . . . . Steve Newton
Chief of Medical Staff . . . . Kirk Barnett
Infection Control . . . . Cheryl Davis
Operating Room. . . . . Carol Creek, RN
Radiology. . . . . Barry A Gubin
Emergency Room . . . . Carol Creek, RN
Intensive Care Unit. . . . . Fran Florea, RN

Measure	Cases	This Hosp.	State Avg.	U.S. Avg.
Heart Attack Care				
ACE Inhibitor or ARB for LVSD	0	-	96%	96%
Aspirin at Arrival[1]	8	100%	99%	99%
Aspirin at Discharge[1]	8	100%	99%	98%
Beta Blocker at Discharge[1]	7	100%	99%	98%
Fibrinolytic Medication Timing	0	-	27%	55%
PCI Within 90 Minutes of Arrival	0	-	92%	90%
Smoking Cessation Advice[1]	1	100%	99%	99%
Chest Pain/Possible Heart Attack Care				
Aspirin at Arrival	78	100%	95%	95%
Median Time to ECG (minutes)	81	5	9	8
Median Time to Transfer (minutes)[1]	5	35	64	61
Fibrinolytic Medication Timing	0	-	31%	54%
Heart Failure Care				
ACE Inhibitor or ARB for LVSD[1]	6	100%	94%	94%
Discharge Instructions	25	96%	87%	88%
Evaluation of LVS Function	33	100%	97%	98%
Smoking Cessation Advice[1]	5	100%	98%	98%
Pneumonia Care				
Appropriate Initial Antibiotic	41	90%	91%	92%
Blood Culture Timing	64	98%	97%	96%
Influenza Vaccine	35	97%	90%	91%
Initial Antibiotic Timing	59	100%	95%	95%
Pneumococcal Vaccine	44	98%	93%	93%
Smoking Cessation Advice[1]	21	95%	97%	97%
Surgical Care Improvement Project				
Appropriate VTP Within 24 Hours[2]	45	98%	93%	92%
Appropriate Hair Removal[2]	223	100%	100%	99%
Appropriate Beta Blocker Usage[2]	59	100%	94%	93%
Controlled Postoperative Blood Glucose[2]	0	-	94%	93%
Prophylactic Antibiotic Timing[2]	177	99%	97%	97%
Prophylactic Antibiotic Timing (Outpatient)	32	100%	95%	92%
Prophylactic Antibiotic Selection[2]	177	98%	97%	97%
Prophylactic Antibiotic Select. (Outpatient)	32	100%	95%	94%
Prophylactic Antibiotic Stopped[2]	172	99%	95%	94%
Recommended VTP Ordered[2]	45	98%	95%	94%
Urinary Catheter Removal[2]	66	97%	88%	90%
Children's Asthma Care				
Received Systemic Corticosteroids	-	-	-	100%
Received Home Management Plan	-	-	-	71%
Received Reliever Medication	-	-	-	100%
Use of Medical Imaging				
Combination Abdominal CT Scan	196	0.163	0.227	0.191
Combination Chest CT Scan	112	0.125	0.059	0.054
Follow-up Mammogram/Ultrasound	467	14.1%	7.4%	8.4%
MRI for Low Back Pain	47	38.3%	36%	32.7%
Survey of Patients' Hospital Experiences				
Area Around Room 'Always' Quiet at Night	300+	65%	-	58%
Doctors 'Always' Communicated Well	300+	78%	-	80%
Home Recovery Information Given	300+	87%	-	82%
Hospital Given 9 or 10 on 10 Point Scale	300+	70%	-	67%
Meds 'Always' Explained Before Given	300+	58%	-	60%
Nurses 'Always' Communicated Well	300+	77%	-	76%
Pain 'Always' Well Controlled	300+	72%	-	69%
Room and Bathroom 'Always' Clean	300+	67%	-	71%
Timely Help 'Always' Received	300+	66%	-	64%
Would Definitely Recommend Hospital	300+	65%	-	69%

NOTE: Hospital profiles are in alphabetical order by state, then city, then hospital within the city; Rankings exclude hospitals with less than 25 cases except for patient surveys which excludes hospitals with less than 100 cases; (a) 100–299 cases; (1) The number of cases is too small to be sure how well a hospital is performing; (2) The hospital indicated that the data submitted for this measure were based on a sample of cases; (3) Data was collected during a shorter time period (fewer quarters) than the maximum possible time for this measure; (4) Suppressed for one or more quarters by CMS; (5) No data is available from the hospital for this measure; (6) Fewer than 100 patients completed the HCAHPS survey. Use these rates with caution, as the number of surveys may be too low to reliably assess hospital performance; (7) Survey results are based on less than 12 months of data; (8) Survey results are not available for this reporting period; (9) No or very few patients were eligible for the HCAHPS survey. The scores shown, if any, reflect a very small number of surveys; (10) A state average was not calculated because too few hospitals in the state submitted data; (11) There were discrepancies in the data collection process; Please refer to the User's Guide for a full explanation of data.

Harrison County Community Hospital

Hwys 69 & 136 Phone: 660-425-0284
Bethany, MO 64424 Fax: 660-425-8535
URL: www.hcchospital.org
Type: Critical Access Hospitals Emergency Services: Yes
Ownership: Govt - Hospital Dist/Auth Beds: 17
Key Personnel:
Cardiac Laboratory. . . . . Kaeitie Smith
Chief of Medical Staff . . . . Natu Patel
Emergency Room . . . . Crystal Hicks

Measure	Cases	This Hosp.	State Avg.	U.S. Avg.
Heart Attack Care				
ACE Inhibitor or ARB for LVSD[5]	0	-	96%	96%
Aspirin at Arrival[5]	0	-	99%	99%
Aspirin at Discharge[5]	0	-	99%	98%
Beta Blocker at Discharge[5]	0	-	99%	98%
Fibrinolytic Medication Timing[5]	0	-	27%	55%
PCI Within 90 Minutes of Arrival[5]	0	-	92%	90%
Smoking Cessation Advice[5]	0	-	99%	99%
Chest Pain/Possible Heart Attack Care				
Aspirin at Arrival	-	-	95%	95%
Median Time to ECG (minutes)	-	-	9	8
Median Time to Transfer (minutes)	-	-	64	61
Fibrinolytic Medication Timing	-	-	31%	54%
Heart Failure Care				
ACE Inhibitor or ARB for LVSD[1,3]	2	0%	94%	94%
Discharge Instructions[1,3]	7	57%	87%	88%
Evaluation of LVS Function[1,3]	8	75%	97%	98%
Smoking Cessation Advice[1,3]	1	100%	98%	98%
Pneumonia Care				
Appropriate Initial Antibiotic[1]	9	67%	91%	92%
Blood Culture Timing[1]	11	91%	97%	96%
Influenza Vaccine[1]	17	76%	90%	91%
Initial Antibiotic Timing[1]	15	100%	95%	95%
Pneumococcal Vaccine	27	93%	93%	93%
Smoking Cessation Advice[1]	6	33%	97%	97%
Surgical Care Improvement Project				
Appropriate VTP Within 24 Hours[5]	0	-	93%	92%
Appropriate Hair Removal[5]	0	-	100%	99%
Appropriate Beta Blocker Usage[5]	0	-	94%	93%
Controlled Postoperative Blood Glucose[5]	0	-	94%	93%
Prophylactic Antibiotic Timing[5]	0	-	97%	97%
Prophylactic Antibiotic Timing (Outpatient)	-	-	95%	92%
Prophylactic Antibiotic Selection[5]	0	-	97%	97%
Prophylactic Antibiotic Select. (Outpatient)	-	-	95%	94%
Prophylactic Antibiotic Stopped[5]	0	-	95%	94%
Recommended VTP Ordered[5]	0	-	95%	94%
Urinary Catheter Removal[5]	0	-	88%	90%
Children's Asthma Care				
Received Systemic Corticosteroids	-	-	-	100%
Received Home Management Plan	-	-	-	71%
Received Reliever Medication	-	-	-	100%
Use of Medical Imaging				
Combination Abdominal CT Scan	-	-	0.227	0.191
Combination Chest CT Scan	-	-	0.059	0.054
Follow-up Mammogram/Ultrasound	-	-	7.4%	8.4%
MRI for Low Back Pain	-	-	36%	32.7%
Survey of Patients' Hospital Experiences				
Area Around Room 'Always' Quiet at Night[8]	-	-	-	58%
Doctors 'Always' Communicated Well[8]	-	-	-	80%
Home Recovery Information Given[8]	-	-	-	82%
Hospital Given 9 or 10 on 10 Point Scale[8]	-	-	-	67%
Meds 'Always' Explained Before Given[8]	-	-	-	60%
Nurses 'Always' Communicated Well[8]	-	-	-	76%
Pain 'Always' Well Controlled[8]	-	-	-	69%
Room and Bathroom 'Always' Clean[8]	-	-	-	71%
Timely Help 'Always' Received[8]	-	-	-	64%
Would Definitely Recommend Hospital[8]	-	-	-	69%

Saint Mary's Medical Center

201 NW R D Mize Rd Phone: 816-228-5900
Blue Springs, MO 64014 Fax: 816-655-5649
Type: Acute Care Hospitals Emergency Services: Yes
Ownership: Voluntary Non-Profit - Church Beds: 143
Key Personnel:
CEO/President. . . . . Gordon Docking
Cardiac Laboratory. . . . . Cynthia Peters
Chief of Medical Staff . . . . Steve Sanders
Emergency Room . . . . Judy Avise

Measure	Cases	This Hosp.	State Avg.	U.S. Avg.
Heart Attack Care				
ACE Inhibitor or ARB for LVSD[1]	16	94%	96%	96%
Aspirin at Arrival	106	98%	99%	99%
Aspirin at Discharge	92	100%	99%	98%
Beta Blocker at Discharge	89	98%	99%	98%
Fibrinolytic Medication Timing	0	-	27%	55%
PCI Within 90 Minutes of Arrival[1]	15	87%	92%	90%
Smoking Cessation Advice	47	98%	99%	99%
Chest Pain/Possible Heart Attack Care				
Aspirin at Arrival[1]	6	100%	95%	95%
Median Time to ECG (minutes)	0	-	9	8
Median Time to Transfer (minutes)[5]	0	-	64	61
Fibrinolytic Medication Timing[5]	0	-	31%	54%
Heart Failure Care				
ACE Inhibitor or ARB for LVSD	30	87%	94%	94%
Discharge Instructions	52	88%	87%	88%
Evaluation of LVS Function	79	100%	97%	98%
Smoking Cessation Advice[1]	19	95%	98%	98%
Pneumonia Care				
Appropriate Initial Antibiotic	119	88%	91%	92%
Blood Culture Timing	204	97%	97%	96%
Influenza Vaccine	112	90%	90%	91%
Initial Antibiotic Timing	203	96%	95%	95%
Pneumococcal Vaccine	166	92%	93%	93%
Smoking Cessation Advice	55	93%	97%	97%
Surgical Care Improvement Project				
Appropriate VTP Within 24 Hours[2]	133	91%	93%	92%
Appropriate Hair Removal[2]	282	100%	100%	99%
Appropriate Beta Blocker Usage[2]	53	92%	94%	93%
Controlled Postoperative Blood Glucose[2]	0	-	94%	93%
Prophylactic Antibiotic Timing[2]	184	98%	97%	97%
Prophylactic Antibiotic Timing (Outpatient)	66	97%	95%	92%
Prophylactic Antibiotic Selection[2]	185	98%	97%	97%
Prophylactic Antibiotic Select. (Outpatient)	66	98%	95%	94%
Prophylactic Antibiotic Stopped[2]	183	95%	95%	94%
Recommended VTP Ordered[2]	133	95%	95%	94%
Urinary Catheter Removal[2]	64	86%	88%	90%
Children's Asthma Care				
Received Systemic Corticosteroids	-	-	-	100%
Received Home Management Plan	-	-	-	71%
Received Reliever Medication	-	-	-	100%
Use of Medical Imaging				
Combination Abdominal CT Scan	459	0.063	0.227	0.191
Combination Chest CT Scan	270	0.048	0.059	0.054
Follow-up Mammogram/Ultrasound	756	10.6%	7.4%	8.4%
MRI for Low Back Pain	102	39.2%	36%	32.7%
Survey of Patients' Hospital Experiences				
Area Around Room 'Always' Quiet at Night	300+	58%	-	58%
Doctors 'Always' Communicated Well	300+	78%	-	80%
Home Recovery Information Given	300+	88%	-	82%
Hospital Given 9 or 10 on 10 Point Scale	300+	71%	-	67%
Meds 'Always' Explained Before Given	300+	58%	-	60%
Nurses 'Always' Communicated Well	300+	78%	-	76%
Pain 'Always' Well Controlled	300+	70%	-	69%
Room and Bathroom 'Always' Clean	300+	67%	-	71%
Timely Help 'Always' Received	300+	64%	-	64%
Would Definitely Recommend Hospital	300+	73%	-	69%

Citizens Memorial Hospital

1500 N Oakland Phone: 417-326-6000
Bolivar, MO 65613 Fax: 417-326-0338
URL: www.citizensmemorial.com
Type: Acute Care Hospitals Emergency Services: Yes
Ownership: Govt - Hospital Dist/Auth Beds: 74
Key Personnel:
CEO/President. . . . . Donald J Babb
Chief of Medical Staff . . . . Dennis Boeke, DO
Infection Control. . . . . Helen Molchan, RN
Operating Room. . . . . Nancy Nickos
Quality Assurance . . . . Karen Keeton
Radiology. . . . . John Gamble III

Measure	Cases	This Hosp.	State Avg.	U.S. Avg.
Heart Attack Care				
ACE Inhibitor or ARB for LVSD[1]	2	100%	96%	96%
Aspirin at Arrival	35	86%	99%	99%
Aspirin at Discharge	35	86%	99%	98%
Beta Blocker at Discharge	34	100%	99%	98%
Fibrinolytic Medication Timing	0	-	27%	55%
PCI Within 90 Minutes of Arrival[1]	3	67%	92%	90%
Smoking Cessation Advice[1]	9	100%	99%	99%
Chest Pain/Possible Heart Attack Care				
Aspirin at Arrival	86	98%	95%	95%
Median Time to ECG (minutes)	96	24	9	8
Median Time to Transfer (minutes)[1,3]	4	94	64	61
Fibrinolytic Medication Timing[1]	2	0%	31%	54%
Heart Failure Care				
ACE Inhibitor or ARB for LVSD[1]	20	95%	94%	94%
Discharge Instructions	44	91%	87%	88%
Evaluation of LVS Function	73	85%	97%	98%
Smoking Cessation Advice[1]	16	100%	98%	98%
Pneumonia Care				
Appropriate Initial Antibiotic	71	79%	91%	92%
Blood Culture Timing	117	96%	97%	96%
Influenza Vaccine	77	97%	90%	91%
Initial Antibiotic Timing	133	92%	95%	95%
Pneumococcal Vaccine	108	96%	93%	93%
Smoking Cessation Advice	58	95%	97%	97%
Surgical Care Improvement Project				
Appropriate VTP Within 24 Hours	120	96%	93%	92%
Appropriate Hair Removal	231	100%	100%	99%
Appropriate Beta Blocker Usage	61	84%	94%	93%
Controlled Postoperative Blood Glucose	0	-	94%	93%
Prophylactic Antibiotic Timing	156	97%	97%	97%
Prophylactic Antibiotic Timing (Outpatient)	173	98%	95%	92%
Prophylactic Antibiotic Selection	155	97%	97%	97%
Prophylactic Antibiotic Select. (Outpatient)	175	94%	95%	94%
Prophylactic Antibiotic Stopped	152	91%	95%	94%
Recommended VTP Ordered	120	96%	95%	94%
Urinary Catheter Removal	57	96%	88%	90%
Children's Asthma Care				
Received Systemic Corticosteroids	-	-	-	100%
Received Home Management Plan	-	-	-	71%
Received Reliever Medication	-	-	-	100%
Use of Medical Imaging				
Combination Abdominal CT Scan	383	0.358	0.227	0.191
Combination Chest CT Scan	255	0.310	0.059	0.054
Follow-up Mammogram/Ultrasound	583	3.6%	7.4%	8.4%
MRI for Low Back Pain	139	39.6%	36%	32.7%
Survey of Patients' Hospital Experiences				
Area Around Room 'Always' Quiet at Night	300+	56%	-	58%
Doctors 'Always' Communicated Well	300+	82%	-	80%
Home Recovery Information Given	300+	83%	-	82%
Hospital Given 9 or 10 on 10 Point Scale	300+	69%	-	67%
Meds 'Always' Explained Before Given	300+	60%	-	60%
Nurses 'Always' Communicated Well	300+	79%	-	76%
Pain 'Always' Well Controlled	300+	72%	-	69%
Room and Bathroom 'Always' Clean	300+	79%	-	71%
Timely Help 'Always' Received	300+	68%	-	64%
Would Definitely Recommend Hospital	300+	67%	-	69%

NOTE: Hospital profiles are in alphabetical order by state, then city, then hospital within the city; Rankings exclude hospitals with less than 25 cases except for patient surveys which excludes hospitals with less than 100 cases; (a) 100–299 cases; (1) The number of cases is too small to be sure how well a hospital is performing; (2) The hospital indicated that the data submitted for this measure were based on a sample of cases; (3) Data was collected during a shorter time period (fewer quarters) than the maximum possible time for this measure; (4) Suppressed for one or more quarters by CMS; (5) No data is available from the hospital for this measure; (6) Fewer than 100 patients completed the HCAHPS survey. Use these rates with caution, as the number of surveys may be too low to reliably assess hospital performance; (7) Survey results are based on less than 12 months of data; (8) Survey results are not available for this reporting period; (9) No or very few patients were eligible for the HCAHPS survey. The scores shown, if any, reflect a very small number of surveys; (10) A state average was not calculated because too few hospitals in the state submitted data; (11) There were discrepancies in the data collection process; Please refer to the User's Guide for a full explanation of data.

Cooper County Memorial Hospital

17651 B Hwy
Boonville, MO 65233
Type: Acute Care Hospitals
Ownership: Government - Local
Phone: 660-882-7461
Fax: 660-882-6093
Emergency Services: Yes
Beds: 70

Key Personnel:

CEO/President. . . . . Matt Waterman

Measure	Cases	This Hosp.	State Avg.	U.S. Avg.
Heart Attack Care				
ACE Inhibitor or ARB for LVSD	0	-	96%	96%
Aspirin at Arrival[1]	5	100%	99%	99%
Aspirin at Discharge[1]	4	75%	99%	98%
Beta Blocker at Discharge[1]	3	100%	99%	98%
Fibrinolytic Medication Timing	0	-	27%	55%
PCI Within 90 Minutes of Arrival	0	-	92%	90%
Smoking Cessation Advice[1]	1	0%	99%	99%
Chest Pain/Possible Heart Attack Care				
Aspirin at Arrival	56	96%	95%	95%
Median Time to ECG (minutes)	58	8	9	8
Median Time to Transfer (minutes)[1]	8	34	64	61
Fibrinolytic Medication Timing	0	-	31%	54%
Heart Failure Care				
ACE Inhibitor or ARB for LVSD[1]	10	100%	94%	94%
Discharge Instructions[1]	13	100%	87%	88%
Evaluation of LVS Function	31	87%	97%	98%
Smoking Cessation Advice[1]	5	80%	98%	98%
Pneumonia Care				
Appropriate Initial Antibiotic	27	93%	91%	92%
Blood Culture Timing[1]	23	96%	97%	96%
Influenza Vaccine	31	94%	90%	91%
Initial Antibiotic Timing[1]	15	87%	95%	95%
Pneumococcal Vaccine	32	81%	93%	93%
Smoking Cessation Advice[1]	13	85%	97%	97%
Surgical Care Improvement Project				
Appropriate VTP Within 24 Hours[5]	0	-	93%	92%
Appropriate Hair Removal[5]	0	-	100%	99%
Appropriate Beta Blocker Usage[5]	0	-	94%	93%
Controlled Postoperative Blood Glucose[5]	0	-	94%	93%
Prophylactic Antibiotic Timing[5]	0	-	97%	97%
Prophylactic Antibiotic Timing (Outpatient)[5]	0	-	95%	92%
Prophylactic Antibiotic Selection[5]	0	-	97%	97%
Prophylactic Antibiotic Select. (Outpatient)[5]	0	-	95%	94%
Prophylactic Antibiotic Stopped[5]	0	-	95%	94%
Recommended VTP Ordered[5]	0	-	95%	94%
Urinary Catheter Removal[5]	0	-	88%	90%
Children's Asthma Care				
Received Systemic Corticosteroids	-	-	-	100%
Received Home Management Plan	-	-	-	71%
Received Reliever Medication	-	-	-	100%
Use of Medical Imaging				
Combination Abdominal CT Scan	94	0.755	0.227	0.191
Combination Chest CT Scan	56	0.607	0.059	0.054
Follow-up Mammogram/Ultrasound[5]	0	-	7.4%	8.4%
MRI for Low Back Pain[1]	11	18.2%	36%	32.7%
Survey of Patients' Hospital Experiences				
Area Around Room 'Always' Quiet at Night[6]	<100	60%	-	58%
Doctors 'Always' Communicated Well[6]	<100	83%	-	80%
Home Recovery Information Given[6]	<100	81%	-	82%
Hospital Given 9 or 10 on 10 Point Scale[6]	<100	60%	-	67%
Meds 'Always' Explained Before Given[6]	<100	51%	-	60%
Nurses 'Always' Communicated Well[6]	<100	72%	-	76%
Pain 'Always' Well Controlled[6]	<100	63%	-	69%
Room and Bathroom 'Always' Clean[6]	<100	62%	-	71%
Timely Help 'Always' Received[6]	<100	61%	-	64%
Would Definitely Recommend Hospital	<100	71%	-	69%

Skaggs Community Health Center

Bus Hwy 65 & Skaggs Rd
Branson, MO 65616
URL: www.skaggs.net
Type: Acute Care Hospitals
Ownership: Voluntary Non-Profit - Private
Phone: 417-335-7000
Fax: 417-334-1505
Emergency Services: Yes
Beds: 177

Key Personnel:

CEO/President. . . . . Stephen M Erixson, MHA
Cardiac Laboratory. . . . . Jon Jenkins
Chief of Medical Staff . . . . Peter Marcellus, MD
Infection Control. . . . . Ann Erving
Operating Room. . . . . Jackie Rozell
Quality Assurance . . . . Cindy Gaddie
Radiology. . . . . Richard S Makuch
Intensive Care Unit. . . . . Angilee McPathe

Measure	Cases	This Hosp.	State Avg.	U.S. Avg.
Heart Attack Care				
ACE Inhibitor or ARB for LVSD	34	88%	96%	96%
Aspirin at Arrival	188	99%	99%	99%
Aspirin at Discharge	190	100%	99%	98%
Beta Blocker at Discharge	178	99%	99%	98%
Fibrinolytic Medication Timing	0	-	27%	55%
PCI Within 90 Minutes of Arrival	35	100%	92%	90%
Smoking Cessation Advice	76	97%	99%	99%
Chest Pain/Possible Heart Attack Care				
Aspirin at Arrival[1,3]	2	100%	95%	95%
Median Time to ECG (minutes)[1,3]	2	12	9	8
Median Time to Transfer (minutes)[5]	0	-	64	61
Fibrinolytic Medication Timing[3]	0	-	31%	54%
Heart Failure Care				
ACE Inhibitor or ARB for LVSD[2]	94	86%	94%	94%
Discharge Instructions[2]	194	84%	87%	88%
Evaluation of LVS Function[2]	224	99%	97%	98%
Smoking Cessation Advice[2]	54	96%	98%	98%
Pneumonia Care				
Appropriate Initial Antibiotic[2]	124	94%	91%	92%
Blood Culture Timing[2]	187	97%	97%	96%
Influenza Vaccine[2]	104	96%	90%	91%
Initial Antibiotic Timing[2]	159	96%	95%	95%
Pneumococcal Vaccine[2]	150	95%	93%	93%
Smoking Cessation Advice[2]	79	89%	97%	97%
Surgical Care Improvement Project				
Appropriate VTP Within 24 Hours[2]	100	92%	93%	92%
Appropriate Hair Removal[2]	426	100%	100%	99%
Appropriate Beta Blocker Usage[2]	125	92%	94%	93%
Controlled Postoperative Blood Glucose[2]	70	91%	94%	93%
Prophylactic Antibiotic Timing[2]	308	96%	97%	97%
Prophylactic Antibiotic Timing (Outpatient)	150	82%	95%	92%
Prophylactic Antibiotic Selection[2]	308	96%	97%	97%
Prophylactic Antibiotic Select. (Outpatient)	138	86%	95%	94%
Prophylactic Antibiotic Stopped[2]	251	90%	95%	94%
Recommended VTP Ordered[2]	100	96%	95%	94%
Urinary Catheter Removal[2]	94	89%	88%	90%
Children's Asthma Care				
Received Systemic Corticosteroids	-	-	-	100%
Received Home Management Plan	-	-	-	71%
Received Reliever Medication	-	-	-	100%
Use of Medical Imaging				
Combination Abdominal CT Scan	829	0.054	0.227	0.191
Combination Chest CT Scan	714	0.038	0.059	0.054
Follow-up Mammogram/Ultrasound	1,068	11.2%	7.4%	8.4%
MRI for Low Back Pain	272	30.5%	36%	32.7%
Survey of Patients' Hospital Experiences				
Area Around Room 'Always' Quiet at Night	300+	56%	-	58%
Doctors 'Always' Communicated Well	300+	80%	-	80%
Home Recovery Information Given	300+	78%	-	82%
Hospital Given 9 or 10 on 10 Point Scale	300+	64%	-	67%
Meds 'Always' Explained Before Given	300+	55%	-	60%
Nurses 'Always' Communicated Well	300+	74%	-	76%
Pain 'Always' Well Controlled	300+	64%	-	69%
Room and Bathroom 'Always' Clean	300+	72%	-	71%
Timely Help 'Always' Received	300+	63%	-	64%
Would Definitely Recommend Hospital	300+	69%	-	69%

SSM Depaul Health Center

12303 Depaul Drive
Bridgeton, MO 63044
URL: www.ssmdepaul.com
Type: Acute Care Hospitals
Ownership: Proprietary
Phone: 314-344-6000
Fax: 314-344-6840
Emergency Services: Yes
Beds: 538

Key Personnel:

CEO/President. . . . . Pat Komoroski
Cardiac Laboratory. . . . . Mindy Manley
Chief of Medical Staff . . . . Jim E Bieser, MD
Quality Assurance . . . . PamAnn McDonald
Emergency Room . . . . Clare Mir

Measure	Cases	This Hosp.	State Avg.	U.S. Avg.
Heart Attack Care				
ACE Inhibitor or ARB for LVSD	100	88%	96%	96%
Aspirin at Arrival	313	98%	99%	99%
Aspirin at Discharge	327	98%	99%	98%
Beta Blocker at Discharge	318	99%	99%	98%
Fibrinolytic Medication Timing	0	-	27%	55%
PCI Within 90 Minutes of Arrival	37	78%	92%	90%
Smoking Cessation Advice	131	100%	99%	99%
Chest Pain/Possible Heart Attack Care				
Aspirin at Arrival[1]	21	67%	95%	95%
Median Time to ECG (minutes)[1]	21	6	9	8
Median Time to Transfer (minutes)[5]	0	-	64	61
Fibrinolytic Medication Timing[3]	0	-	31%	54%
Heart Failure Care				
ACE Inhibitor or ARB for LVSD[2]	114	90%	94%	94%
Discharge Instructions[2]	252	88%	87%	88%
Evaluation of LVS Function[2]	316	98%	97%	98%
Smoking Cessation Advice[2]	49	100%	98%	98%
Pneumonia Care				
Appropriate Initial Antibiotic[2]	97	95%	91%	92%
Blood Culture Timing[2]	118	97%	97%	96%
Influenza Vaccine[2]	74	76%	90%	91%
Initial Antibiotic Timing[2]	148	90%	95%	95%
Pneumococcal Vaccine[2]	136	91%	93%	93%
Smoking Cessation Advice[2]	90	100%	97%	97%
Surgical Care Improvement Project				
Appropriate VTP Within 24 Hours[2]	197	95%	93%	92%
Appropriate Hair Removal[2]	849	99%	100%	99%
Appropriate Beta Blocker Usage[2]	238	97%	94%	93%
Controlled Postoperative Blood Glucose[2]	159	99%	94%	93%
Prophylactic Antibiotic Timing[2]	595	98%	97%	97%
Prophylactic Antibiotic Timing (Outpatient)	395	93%	95%	92%
Prophylactic Antibiotic Selection[2]	604	99%	97%	97%
Prophylactic Antibiotic Select. (Outpatient)	388	96%	95%	94%
Prophylactic Antibiotic Stopped[2]	566	96%	95%	94%
Recommended VTP Ordered[2]	197	96%	95%	94%
Urinary Catheter Removal[2]	96	79%	88%	90%
Children's Asthma Care				
Received Systemic Corticosteroids	-	-	-	100%
Received Home Management Plan	-	-	-	71%
Received Reliever Medication	-	-	-	100%
Use of Medical Imaging				
Combination Abdominal CT Scan	723	0.503	0.227	0.191
Combination Chest CT Scan	507	0.081	0.059	0.054
Follow-up Mammogram/Ultrasound	876	7.5%	7.4%	8.4%
MRI for Low Back Pain	227	32.6%	36%	32.7%
Survey of Patients' Hospital Experiences				
Area Around Room 'Always' Quiet at Night	300+	58%	-	58%
Doctors 'Always' Communicated Well	300+	78%	-	80%
Home Recovery Information Given	300+	82%	-	82%
Hospital Given 9 or 10 on 10 Point Scale	300+	63%	-	67%
Meds 'Always' Explained Before Given	300+	59%	-	60%
Nurses 'Always' Communicated Well	300+	74%	-	76%
Pain 'Always' Well Controlled	300+	68%	-	69%
Room and Bathroom 'Always' Clean	300+	62%	-	71%
Timely Help 'Always' Received	300+	56%	-	64%
Would Definitely Recommend Hospital	300+	67%	-	69%

NOTE: Hospital profiles are in alphabetical order by state, then city, then hospital within the city; Rankings exclude hospitals with less than 25 cases except for patient surveys which excludes hospitals with less than 100 cases; (a) 100–299 cases; (1) The number of cases is too small to be sure how well a hospital is performing; (2) The hospital indicated that the data submitted for this measure were based on a sample of cases; (3) Data was collected during a shorter time period (fewer quarters) than the maximum possible time for this measure; (4) Suppressed for one or more quarters by CMS; (5) No data is available from the hospital for this measure; (6) Fewer than 100 patients completed the HCAHPS survey. Use these rates with caution, as the number of surveys may be too low to reliably assess hospital performance; (7) Survey results are based on less than 12 months of data; (8) Survey results are not available for this reporting period; (9) No or very few patients were eligible for the HCAHPS survey. The scores shown, if any, reflect a very small number of surveys; (10) A state average was not calculated because too few hospitals in the state submitted data; (11) There were discrepancies in the data collection process; Please refer to the User's Guide for a full explanation of data.

Pershing Memorial Hospital

130 East Lockling
Brookfield, MO 64628
Phone: 660-258-2222
Fax: 660-258-5668
Type: Critical Access Hospitals
Emergency Services: Yes
Ownership: Voluntary Non-Profit - Private
Beds: 57

Key Personnel:

CEO/President. . . . . Phil Hamilton
Chief of Medical Staff . . . . BD Howell, MD
Infection Control. . . . . Randy Kieffer
Quality Assurance . . . . Elaine Sutton
Ambulatory Care . . . . Betty Williams, CNE
Emergency Room . . . . PC Rivera, MD

Measure	Cases	This Hosp.	State Avg.	U.S. Avg.
Heart Attack Care				
ACE Inhibitor or ARB for LVSD[5]	0	-	96%	96%
Aspirin at Arrival[5]	0	-	99%	99%
Aspirin at Discharge[5]	0	-	99%	98%
Beta Blocker at Discharge[5]	0	-	99%	98%
Fibrinolytic Medication Timing[5]	0	-	27%	55%
PCI Within 90 Minutes of Arrival[5]	0	-	92%	90%
Smoking Cessation Advice[5]	0	-	99%	99%
Chest Pain/Possible Heart Attack Care				
Aspirin at Arrival	-	-	95%	95%
Median Time to ECG (minutes)	-	-	9	8
Median Time to Transfer (minutes)	-	-	64	61
Fibrinolytic Medication Timing	-	-	31%	54%
Heart Failure Care				
ACE Inhibitor or ARB for LVSD[3]	0	-	94%	94%
Discharge Instructions[1,3]	11	64%	87%	88%
Evaluation of LVS Function[1,3]	19	26%	97%	98%
Smoking Cessation Advice[3]	0	-	98%	98%
Pneumonia Care				
Appropriate Initial Antibiotic[1,3]	16	56%	91%	92%
Blood Culture Timing[1,3]	10	90%	97%	96%
Influenza Vaccine[5]	0	-	90%	91%
Initial Antibiotic Timing[3]	25	92%	95%	95%
Pneumococcal Vaccine[1,3]	20	75%	93%	93%
Smoking Cessation Advice[1,3]	6	100%	97%	97%
Surgical Care Improvement Project				
Appropriate VTP Within 24 Hours[5]	0	-	93%	92%
Appropriate Hair Removal[5]	0	-	100%	99%
Appropriate Beta Blocker Usage[5]	0	-	94%	93%
Controlled Postoperative Blood Glucose[5]	0	-	94%	93%
Prophylactic Antibiotic Timing[5]	0	-	97%	97%
Prophylactic Antibiotic Timing (Outpatient)	-	-	95%	92%
Prophylactic Antibiotic Selection[5]	0	-	97%	97%
Prophylactic Antibiotic Select. (Outpatient)	-	-	95%	94%
Prophylactic Antibiotic Stopped[5]	0	-	95%	94%
Recommended VTP Ordered[5]	0	-	95%	94%
Urinary Catheter Removal[5]	0	-	88%	90%
Children's Asthma Care				
Received Systemic Corticosteroids	-	-	-	100%
Received Home Management Plan	-	-	-	71%
Received Reliever Medication	-	-	-	100%
Use of Medical Imaging				
Combination Abdominal CT Scan	-	-	0.227	0.191
Combination Chest CT Scan	-	-	0.059	0.054
Follow-up Mammogram/Ultrasound	-	-	7.4%	8.4%
MRI for Low Back Pain	-	-	36%	32.7%
Survey of Patients' Hospital Experiences				
Area Around Room 'Always' Quiet at Night[8]	-	-	-	58%
Doctors 'Always' Communicated Well[8]	-	-	-	80%
Home Recovery Information Given[8]	-	-	-	82%
Hospital Given 9 or 10 on 10 Point Scale[8]	-	-	-	67%
Meds 'Always' Explained Before Given[8]	-	-	-	60%
Nurses 'Always' Communicated Well[8]	-	-	-	76%
Pain 'Always' Well Controlled[8]	-	-	-	69%
Room and Bathroom 'Always' Clean[8]	-	-	-	71%
Timely Help 'Always' Received[8]	-	-	-	64%
Would Definitely Recommend Hospital[8]	-	-	-	69%

Bates County Memorial Hospital

615 W Nursery St
Butler, MO 64730
Phone: 660-200-7000
Fax: 660-200-7016
URL: www.bcmhospital.com
Type: Acute Care Hospitals
Emergency Services: Yes
Ownership: Voluntary Non-Profit - Private
Beds: 60

Key Personnel:

CEO/President. . . . . Wendell Harris, FACHE
Chief of Medical Staff . . . . Joseph Brewster, MD
Infection Control. . . . . Carmen Matter, RN
Operating Room. . . . . Kristie McKee, RN
Quality Assurance . . . . Carol Lewis
Radiology. . . . . Chris Pope
Intensive Care Unit. . . . . Donna Short, RN
Patient Relations . . . . Cheryl Mohr

Measure	Cases	This Hosp.	State Avg.	U.S. Avg.
Heart Attack Care				
ACE Inhibitor or ARB for LVSD[3]	0	-	96%	96%
Aspirin at Arrival[1,3]	3	100%	99%	99%
Aspirin at Discharge[1,3]	3	100%	99%	98%
Beta Blocker at Discharge[1,3]	3	0%	99%	98%
Fibrinolytic Medication Timing[3]	0	-	27%	55%
PCI Within 90 Minutes of Arrival[3]	0	-	92%	90%
Smoking Cessation Advice[3]	0	-	99%	99%
Chest Pain/Possible Heart Attack Care				
Aspirin at Arrival	53	91%	95%	95%
Median Time to ECG (minutes)	56	18	9	8
Median Time to Transfer (minutes)[1,3]	1	55	64	61
Fibrinolytic Medication Timing[1,3]	1	0%	31%	54%
Heart Failure Care				
ACE Inhibitor or ARB for LVSD[1]	3	33%	94%	94%
Discharge Instructions	49	92%	87%	88%
Evaluation of LVS Function	91	45%	97%	98%
Smoking Cessation Advice[1]	12	92%	98%	98%
Pneumonia Care				
Appropriate Initial Antibiotic	46	76%	91%	92%
Blood Culture Timing	44	86%	97%	96%
Influenza Vaccine	44	66%	90%	91%
Initial Antibiotic Timing	80	99%	95%	95%
Pneumococcal Vaccine	60	87%	93%	93%
Smoking Cessation Advice[1]	13	100%	97%	97%
Surgical Care Improvement Project				
Appropriate VTP Within 24 Hours	30	80%	93%	92%
Appropriate Hair Removal	37	86%	100%	99%
Appropriate Beta Blocker Usage[1]	4	75%	94%	93%
Controlled Postoperative Blood Glucose	0	-	94%	93%
Prophylactic Antibiotic Timing[1]	23	91%	97%	97%
Prophylactic Antibiotic Timing (Outpatient)[1]	16	81%	95%	92%
Prophylactic Antibiotic Selection[1]	23	100%	97%	97%
Prophylactic Antibiotic Select. (Outpatient)[1]	15	73%	95%	94%
Prophylactic Antibiotic Stopped[1]	22	82%	95%	94%
Recommended VTP Ordered	31	77%	95%	94%
Urinary Catheter Removal[1]	12	75%	88%	90%
Children's Asthma Care				
Received Systemic Corticosteroids	-	-	-	100%
Received Home Management Plan	-	-	-	71%
Received Reliever Medication	-	-	-	100%
Use of Medical Imaging				
Combination Abdominal CT Scan	215	0.056	0.227	0.191
Combination Chest CT Scan	119	0.000	0.059	0.054
Follow-up Mammogram/Ultrasound	270	7.0%	7.4%	8.4%
MRI for Low Back Pain	63	28.6%	36%	32.7%
Survey of Patients' Hospital Experiences				
Area Around Room 'Always' Quiet at Night	300+	56%	-	58%
Doctors 'Always' Communicated Well	300+	76%	-	80%
Home Recovery Information Given	300+	83%	-	82%
Hospital Given 9 or 10 on 10 Point Scale	300+	69%	-	67%
Meds 'Always' Explained Before Given	300+	58%	-	60%
Nurses 'Always' Communicated Well	300+	75%	-	76%
Pain 'Always' Well Controlled	300+	68%	-	69%
Room and Bathroom 'Always' Clean	300+	71%	-	71%
Timely Help 'Always' Received	300+	63%	-	64%
Would Definitely Recommend Hospital	300+	71%	-	69%

Cameron Regional Medical Center

1600 E Evergreen
Cameron, MO 64429
Phone: 816-632-2101
Fax: 816-649-3206
URL: www.cameronregional.org
Type: Acute Care Hospitals
Emergency Services: Yes
Ownership: Voluntary Non-Profit - Church
Beds: 57

Key Personnel:

CEO/President. . . . . Joseph F Abrutz, Jr
Chief of Medical Staff . . . . Fred Kiehl, DO
Infection Control. . . . . Ginger Graham, RN
Operating Room. . . . . Maria Cowell, RN
Quality Assurance . . . . Joseph Abrutz, Jr
Anesthesiology. . . . . Steve Walker, CRNA
Emergency Room . . . . Fred Kiehl, DO
Intensive Care Unit. . . . . Barbara Guernsey, RN

Measure	Cases	This Hosp.	State Avg.	U.S. Avg.
Heart Attack Care				
ACE Inhibitor or ARB for LVSD[1]	1	0%	96%	96%
Aspirin at Arrival[1]	9	89%	99%	99%
Aspirin at Discharge[1]	7	100%	99%	98%
Beta Blocker at Discharge[1]	8	100%	99%	98%
Fibrinolytic Medication Timing	0	-	27%	55%
PCI Within 90 Minutes of Arrival	0	-	92%	90%
Smoking Cessation Advice[1]	2	100%	99%	99%
Chest Pain/Possible Heart Attack Care				
Aspirin at Arrival	99	98%	95%	95%
Median Time to ECG (minutes)	105	9	9	8
Median Time to Transfer (minutes)[1,3]	7	65	64	61
Fibrinolytic Medication Timing	0	-	31%	54%
Heart Failure Care				
ACE Inhibitor or ARB for LVSD[1]	3	67%	94%	94%
Discharge Instructions	25	84%	87%	88%
Evaluation of LVS Function	52	79%	97%	98%
Smoking Cessation Advice[1]	6	83%	98%	98%
Pneumonia Care				
Appropriate Initial Antibiotic	52	94%	91%	92%
Blood Culture Timing	61	92%	97%	96%
Influenza Vaccine	57	91%	90%	91%
Initial Antibiotic Timing	112	97%	95%	95%
Pneumococcal Vaccine	92	93%	93%	93%
Smoking Cessation Advice	51	90%	97%	97%
Surgical Care Improvement Project				
Appropriate VTP Within 24 Hours	48	92%	93%	92%
Appropriate Hair Removal	95	99%	100%	99%
Appropriate Beta Blocker Usage	28	89%	94%	93%
Controlled Postoperative Blood Glucose	0	-	94%	93%
Prophylactic Antibiotic Timing	65	92%	97%	97%
Prophylactic Antibiotic Timing (Outpatient)[1]	17	76%	95%	92%
Prophylactic Antibiotic Selection	65	97%	97%	97%
Prophylactic Antibiotic Select. (Outpatient)[1]	15	93%	95%	94%
Prophylactic Antibiotic Stopped	63	86%	95%	94%
Recommended VTP Ordered	48	92%	95%	94%
Urinary Catheter Removal[1]	17	94%	88%	90%
Children's Asthma Care				
Received Systemic Corticosteroids	-	-	-	100%
Received Home Management Plan	-	-	-	71%
Received Reliever Medication	-	-	-	100%
Use of Medical Imaging				
Combination Abdominal CT Scan	310	0.061	0.227	0.191
Combination Chest CT Scan	136	0.022	0.059	0.054
Follow-up Mammogram/Ultrasound	295	4.4%	7.4%	8.4%
MRI for Low Back Pain	51	45.1%	36%	32.7%
Survey of Patients' Hospital Experiences				
Area Around Room 'Always' Quiet at Night	300+	49%	-	58%
Doctors 'Always' Communicated Well	300+	67%	-	80%
Home Recovery Information Given	300+	77%	-	82%
Hospital Given 9 or 10 on 10 Point Scale	300+	52%	-	67%
Meds 'Always' Explained Before Given	300+	46%	-	60%
Nurses 'Always' Communicated Well	300+	63%	-	76%
Pain 'Always' Well Controlled	300+	58%	-	69%
Room and Bathroom 'Always' Clean	300+	69%	-	71%
Timely Help 'Always' Received	300+	52%	-	64%
Would Definitely Recommend Hospital	300+	50%	-	69%

NOTE: Hospital profiles are in alphabetical order by state, then city, then hospital within the city; Rankings exclude hospitals with less than 25 cases except for patient surveys which excludes hospitals with less than 100 cases; (a) 100–299 cases; (1) The number of cases is too small to be sure how well a hospital is performing; (2) The hospital indicated that the data submitted for this measure were based on a sample of cases; (3) Data was collected during a shorter time period (fewer quarters) than the maximum possible time for this measure; (4) Suppressed for one or more quarters by CMS; (5) No data is available from the hospital for this measure; (6) Fewer than 100 patients completed the HCAHPS survey. Use these rates with caution, as the number of surveys may be too low to reliably assess hospital performance; (7) Survey results are based on less than 12 months of data; (8) Survey results are not available for this reporting period; (9) No or very few patients were eligible for the HCAHPS survey. The scores shown, if any, reflect a very small number of surveys; (10) A state average was not calculated because too few hospitals in the state submitted data; (11) There were discrepancies in the data collection process; Please refer to the User's Guide for a full explanation of data.

Saint Francis Medical Center

211 St Francis Dr
Cape Girardeau, MO 63703
E-mail: sfmc@sfmc.net
URL: www.sfmc.net
Type: Acute Care Hospitals
Ownership: Voluntary Non-Profit - Church
Phone: 573-331-3000
Fax: 573-331-5009
Emergency Services: Yes
Beds: 264

Key Personnel:
CEO/President. . . . . Stephen Bjlich
Cardiac Laboratory. . . . . Savid Stagner
Chief of Medical Staff . . . . Billy Hammond, MD
Pediatric Ambulatory Care . . . . . . John Russell, MD
Pediatric In-Patient Care . . . . John Russell, MD
Quality Assurance . . . . Rick Fehr
Radiology. . . . . WJ Stoecker, MD
Emergency Room . . . . Marcia Abernathy

Measure	Cases	This Hosp.	State Avg.	U.S. Avg.
Heart Attack Care				
ACE Inhibitor or ARB for LVSD	37	100%	96%	96%
Aspirin at Arrival	127	98%	99%	99%
Aspirin at Discharge	186	100%	99%	98%
Beta Blocker at Discharge	182	99%	99%	98%
Fibrinolytic Medication Timing	0	-	27%	55%
PCI Within 90 Minutes of Arrival	27	96%	92%	90%
Smoking Cessation Advice	81	100%	99%	99%
Chest Pain/Possible Heart Attack Care				
Aspirin at Arrival[1,3]	1	0%	95%	95%
Median Time to ECG (minutes)[1,3]	1	5	9	8
Median Time to Transfer (minutes)[5]	0	-	64	61
Fibrinolytic Medication Timing[5]	0	-	31%	54%
Heart Failure Care				
ACE Inhibitor or ARB for LVSD	97	97%	94%	94%
Discharge Instructions	264	88%	87%	88%
Evaluation of LVS Function	328	99%	97%	98%
Smoking Cessation Advice	60	100%	98%	98%
Pneumonia Care				
Appropriate Initial Antibiotic	213	91%	91%	92%
Blood Culture Timing	355	99%	97%	96%
Influenza Vaccine	274	79%	90%	91%
Initial Antibiotic Timing	315	97%	95%	95%
Pneumococcal Vaccine	354	89%	93%	93%
Smoking Cessation Advice	164	99%	97%	97%
Surgical Care Improvement Project				
Appropriate VTP Within 24 Hours	368	93%	93%	92%
Appropriate Hair Removal	1,243	100%	100%	99%
Appropriate Beta Blocker Usage	401	94%	94%	93%
Controlled Postoperative Blood Glucose	222	95%	94%	93%
Prophylactic Antibiotic Timing	757	98%	97%	97%
Prophylactic Antibiotic Timing (Outpatient)	843	96%	95%	92%
Prophylactic Antibiotic Selection	778	98%	97%	97%
Prophylactic Antibiotic Select. (Outpatient)	832	91%	95%	94%
Prophylactic Antibiotic Stopped	744	96%	95%	94%
Recommended VTP Ordered	369	94%	95%	94%
Urinary Catheter Removal	209	86%	88%	90%
Children's Asthma Care				
Received Systemic Corticosteroids	-	-	-	100%
Received Home Management Plan	-	-	-	71%
Received Reliever Medication	-	-	-	100%
Use of Medical Imaging				
Combination Abdominal CT Scan	1,340	0.401	0.227	0.191
Combination Chest CT Scan	872	0.002	0.059	0.054
Follow-up Mammogram/Ultrasound	1,799	8.6%	7.4%	8.4%
MRI for Low Back Pain	378	28.3%	36%	32.7%
Survey of Patients' Hospital Experiences				
Area Around Room 'Always' Quiet at Night	300+	57%	-	58%
Doctors 'Always' Communicated Well	300+	82%	-	80%
Home Recovery Information Given	300+	83%	-	82%
Hospital Given 9 or 10 on 10 Point Scale	300+	74%	-	67%
Meds 'Always' Explained Before Given	300+	67%	-	60%
Nurses 'Always' Communicated Well	300+	81%	-	76%
Pain 'Always' Well Controlled	300+	71%	-	69%
Room and Bathroom 'Always' Clean	300+	75%	-	71%
Timely Help 'Always' Received	300+	63%	-	64%
Would Definitely Recommend Hospital	300+	80%	-	69%

Southeast Missouri Hospital

1701 Lacey St
Cape Girardeau, MO 63701
URL: www.southeastmissourihospital.com
Type: Acute Care Hospitals
Ownership: Voluntary Non-Profit - Private
Phone: 573-334-4822
Fax: 573-651-5850
Emergency Services: Yes
Beds: 269

Key Personnel:
CEO/President. . . . . James W Wente
Chief of Medical Staff . . . . E Lee Taylor
Radiology. . . . . Jagan Ailinani

Measure	Cases	This Hosp.	State Avg.	U.S. Avg.
Heart Attack Care				
ACE Inhibitor or ARB for LVSD	52	90%	96%	96%
Aspirin at Arrival	155	99%	99%	99%
Aspirin at Discharge	254	96%	99%	98%
Beta Blocker at Discharge	251	96%	99%	98%
Fibrinolytic Medication Timing[1]	2	0%	27%	55%
PCI Within 90 Minutes of Arrival	35	89%	92%	90%
Smoking Cessation Advice	134	98%	99%	99%
Chest Pain/Possible Heart Attack Care				
Aspirin at Arrival[1]	3	100%	95%	95%
Median Time to ECG (minutes)[1]	3	7	9	8
Median Time to Transfer (minutes)[5]	0	-	64	61
Fibrinolytic Medication Timing[5]	0	-	31%	54%
Heart Failure Care				
ACE Inhibitor or ARB for LVSD	98	86%	94%	94%
Discharge Instructions	232	67%	87%	88%
Evaluation of LVS Function	294	98%	97%	98%
Smoking Cessation Advice	54	94%	98%	98%
Pneumonia Care				
Appropriate Initial Antibiotic	126	92%	91%	92%
Blood Culture Timing	231	97%	97%	96%
Influenza Vaccine	150	91%	90%	91%
Initial Antibiotic Timing	196	92%	95%	95%
Pneumococcal Vaccine	198	95%	93%	93%
Smoking Cessation Advice	104	89%	97%	97%
Surgical Care Improvement Project				
Appropriate VTP Within 24 Hours[2]	164	84%	93%	92%
Appropriate Hair Removal[2]	653	100%	100%	99%
Appropriate Beta Blocker Usage[2]	241	89%	94%	93%
Controlled Postoperative Blood Glucose[2]	168	79%	94%	93%
Prophylactic Antibiotic Timing[2]	408	99%	97%	97%
Prophylactic Antibiotic Timing (Outpatient)	565	95%	95%	92%
Prophylactic Antibiotic Selection[2]	418	96%	97%	97%
Prophylactic Antibiotic Select. (Outpatient)	553	90%	95%	94%
Prophylactic Antibiotic Stopped[2]	397	93%	95%	94%
Recommended VTP Ordered[2]	166	91%	95%	94%
Urinary Catheter Removal[2]	86	83%	88%	90%
Children's Asthma Care				
Received Systemic Corticosteroids	-	-	-	100%
Received Home Management Plan	-	-	-	71%
Received Reliever Medication	-	-	-	100%
Use of Medical Imaging				
Combination Abdominal CT Scan	698	0.660	0.227	0.191
Combination Chest CT Scan	614	0.119	0.059	0.054
Follow-up Mammogram/Ultrasound[5]	0	-	7.4%	8.4%
MRI for Low Back Pain	226	33.2%	36%	32.7%
Survey of Patients' Hospital Experiences				
Area Around Room 'Always' Quiet at Night	300+	67%	-	58%
Doctors 'Always' Communicated Well	300+	81%	-	80%
Home Recovery Information Given	300+	88%	-	82%
Hospital Given 9 or 10 on 10 Point Scale	300+	80%	-	67%
Meds 'Always' Explained Before Given	300+	64%	-	60%
Nurses 'Always' Communicated Well	300+	85%	-	76%
Pain 'Always' Well Controlled	300+	74%	-	69%
Room and Bathroom 'Always' Clean	300+	76%	-	71%
Timely Help 'Always' Received	300+	72%	-	64%
Would Definitely Recommend Hospital	300+	85%	-	69%

Carroll County Memorial Hospital

1502 North Jefferson
Carrollton, MO 64633
URL: carrollcountyhospital.org
Type: Critical Access Hospitals
Ownership: Voluntary Non-Profit - Private
Phone: 660-542-1695
Fax: 660-542-0363
Emergency Services: Yes
Beds: 63

Key Personnel:
CEO/President. . . . . Jerry Dover
Chief of Medical Staff . . . . Marvin E Ross, DO
Infection Control. . . . . Vicki Lyon, RN
Operating Room. . . . . Dr Mrosak, MD
Pediatric Ambulatory Care . . . . . . Dr Grace Dymek, MD
Quality Assurance . . . . Vicki Lyon, RN
Radiology. . . . . Jamie Ross

Measure	Cases	This Hosp.	State Avg.	U.S. Avg.
Heart Attack Care				
ACE Inhibitor or ARB for LVSD[5]	0	-	96%	96%
Aspirin at Arrival[5]	0	-	99%	99%
Aspirin at Discharge[5]	0	-	99%	98%
Beta Blocker at Discharge[5]	0	-	99%	98%
Fibrinolytic Medication Timing[5]	0	-	27%	55%
PCI Within 90 Minutes of Arrival[5]	0	-	92%	90%
Smoking Cessation Advice[5]	0	-	99%	99%
Chest Pain/Possible Heart Attack Care				
Aspirin at Arrival	-	-	95%	95%
Median Time to ECG (minutes)	-	-	9	8
Median Time to Transfer (minutes)	-	-	64	61
Fibrinolytic Medication Timing	-	-	31%	54%
Heart Failure Care				
ACE Inhibitor or ARB for LVSD[5]	0	-	94%	94%
Discharge Instructions[5]	0	-	87%	88%
Evaluation of LVS Function[5]	0	-	97%	98%
Smoking Cessation Advice[5]	0	-	98%	98%
Pneumonia Care				
Appropriate Initial Antibiotic[5]	0	-	91%	92%
Blood Culture Timing[5]	0	-	97%	96%
Influenza Vaccine[5]	0	-	90%	91%
Initial Antibiotic Timing[5]	0	-	95%	95%
Pneumococcal Vaccine[5]	0	-	93%	93%
Smoking Cessation Advice[5]	0	-	97%	97%
Surgical Care Improvement Project				
Appropriate VTP Within 24 Hours[5]	0	-	93%	92%
Appropriate Hair Removal[5]	0	-	100%	99%
Appropriate Beta Blocker Usage[5]	0	-	94%	93%
Controlled Postoperative Blood Glucose[5]	0	-	94%	93%
Prophylactic Antibiotic Timing[5]	0	-	97%	97%
Prophylactic Antibiotic Timing (Outpatient)	-	-	95%	92%
Prophylactic Antibiotic Selection[5]	0	-	97%	97%
Prophylactic Antibiotic Select. (Outpatient)	-	-	95%	94%
Prophylactic Antibiotic Stopped[5]	0	-	95%	94%
Recommended VTP Ordered[5]	0	-	95%	94%
Urinary Catheter Removal[5]	0	-	88%	90%
Children's Asthma Care				
Received Systemic Corticosteroids	-	-	-	100%
Received Home Management Plan	-	-	-	71%
Received Reliever Medication	-	-	-	100%
Use of Medical Imaging				
Combination Abdominal CT Scan	-	-	0.227	0.191
Combination Chest CT Scan	-	-	0.059	0.054
Follow-up Mammogram/Ultrasound	-	-	7.4%	8.4%
MRI for Low Back Pain	-	-	36%	32.7%
Survey of Patients' Hospital Experiences				
Area Around Room 'Always' Quiet at Night[8]	-	-	-	58%
Doctors 'Always' Communicated Well[8]	-	-	-	80%
Home Recovery Information Given[8]	-	-	-	82%
Hospital Given 9 or 10 on 10 Point Scale[8]	-	-	-	67%
Meds 'Always' Explained Before Given[8]	-	-	-	60%
Nurses 'Always' Communicated Well[8]	-	-	-	76%
Pain 'Always' Well Controlled[8]	-	-	-	69%
Room and Bathroom 'Always' Clean[8]	-	-	-	71%
Timely Help 'Always' Received[8]	-	-	-	64%
Would Definitely Recommend Hospital[8]	-	-	-	69%

NOTE: Hospital profiles are in alphabetical order by state, then city, then hospital within the city; Rankings exclude hospitals with less than 25 cases except for patient surveys which excludes hospitals with less than 100 cases; (a) 100–299 cases; (1) The number of cases is too small to be sure how well a hospital is performing; (2) The hospital indicated that the data submitted for this measure were based on a sample of cases; (3) Data was collected during a shorter time period (fewer quarters) than the maximum possible time for this measure; (4) Suppressed for one or more quarters by CMS; (5) No data is available from the hospital for this measure; (6) Fewer than 100 patients completed the HCAHPS survey. Use these rates with caution, as the number of surveys may be too low to reliably assess hospital performance; (7) Survey results are based on less than 12 months of data; (8) Survey results are not available for this reporting period; (9) No or very few patients were eligible for the HCAHPS survey. The scores shown, if any, reflect a very small number of surveys; (10) A state average was not calculated because too few hospitals in the state submitted data; (11) There were discrepancies in the data collection process; Please refer to the User's Guide for a full explanation of data.

McCune-Brooks Hospital

3125 Dr Russell Smith Way
Carthage, MO 64836
Phone: 417-358-8121
Fax: 417-359-2522
E-mail: mbhhr1@ipa.net
URL: www.mccunebrooks.org
Type: Critical Access Hospitals
Emergency Services: Yes
Ownership: Government - Local
Beds: 54

Key Personnel:

CEO/President . . . . Robert Copeland
Chief of Medical Staff . . . . Keathe Dillird, MD
Infection Control . . . . Pat Bearden
Operating Room . . . . Donnie Harnar, RN
Quality Assurance . . . . Barbara Brightwell, RN
Radiology . . . . Lowell K Pottenger, DO
Emergency Room . . . . Joseph T Quay Jr, DO

Measure	Cases	This Hosp.	State Avg.	U.S. Avg.
Heart Attack Care				
ACE Inhibitor or ARB for LVSD[1]	1	100%	96%	96%
Aspirin at Arrival[1]	7	43%	99%	99%
Aspirin at Discharge[1]	4	100%	99%	98%
Beta Blocker at Discharge[1]	3	100%	99%	98%
Fibrinolytic Medication Timing	0	-	27%	55%
PCI Within 90 Minutes of Arrival	0	-	92%	90%
Smoking Cessation Advice	0	-	99%	99%
Chest Pain/Possible Heart Attack Care				
Aspirin at Arrival	-	-	95%	95%
Median Time to ECG (minutes)	-	-	9	8
Median Time to Transfer (minutes)	-	-	64	61
Fibrinolytic Medication Timing	-	-	31%	54%
Heart Failure Care				
ACE Inhibitor or ARB for LVSD[1]	9	78%	94%	94%
Discharge Instructions	25	84%	87%	88%
Evaluation of LVS Function	36	81%	97%	98%
Smoking Cessation Advice[1]	4	100%	98%	98%
Pneumonia Care				
Appropriate Initial Antibiotic	42	88%	91%	92%
Blood Culture Timing	58	93%	97%	96%
Influenza Vaccine	32	84%	90%	91%
Initial Antibiotic Timing	69	99%	95%	95%
Pneumococcal Vaccine	45	84%	93%	93%
Smoking Cessation Advice[1]	23	74%	97%	97%
Surgical Care Improvement Project				
Appropriate VTP Within 24 Hours	32	97%	93%	92%
Appropriate Hair Removal	203	97%	100%	99%
Appropriate Beta Blocker Usage[5]	0	-	94%	93%
Controlled Postoperative Blood Glucose	0	-	94%	93%
Prophylactic Antibiotic Timing	182	94%	97%	97%
Prophylactic Antibiotic Timing (Outpatient)	-	-	95%	92%
Prophylactic Antibiotic Selection	182	99%	97%	97%
Prophylactic Antibiotic Select. (Outpatient)	-	-	95%	94%
Prophylactic Antibiotic Stopped	182	86%	95%	94%
Recommended VTP Ordered	32	97%	95%	94%
Urinary Catheter Removal[1]	12	100%	88%	90%
Children's Asthma Care				
Received Systemic Corticosteroids	-	-	-	100%
Received Home Management Plan	-	-	-	71%
Received Reliever Medication	-	-	-	100%
Use of Medical Imaging				
Combination Abdominal CT Scan	-	-	0.227	0.191
Combination Chest CT Scan	-	-	0.059	0.054
Follow-up Mammogram/Ultrasound	-	-	7.4%	8.4%
MRI for Low Back Pain	-	-	36%	32.7%
Survey of Patients' Hospital Experiences				
Area Around Room 'Always' Quiet at Night	300+	64%	-	58%
Doctors 'Always' Communicated Well	300+	88%	-	80%
Home Recovery Information Given	300+	88%	-	82%
Hospital Given 9 or 10 on 10 Point Scale	300+	83%	-	67%
Meds 'Always' Explained Before Given	300+	64%	-	60%
Nurses 'Always' Communicated Well	300+	84%	-	76%
Pain 'Always' Well Controlled	300+	78%	-	69%
Room and Bathroom 'Always' Clean	300+	80%	-	71%
Timely Help 'Always' Received	300+	85%	-	64%
Would Definitely Recommend Hospital	300+	85%	-	69%

Saint Johns Hospital - Cassville

94 Main Street
Cassville, MO 65625
Phone: 417-847-6065
Fax: 417-847-6047
URL: southbarrycountyhospital.com
Type: Critical Access Hospitals
Emergency Services: Yes
Ownership: Voluntary Non-Profit - Church
Beds: 18

Key Personnel:

CEO/President . . . . Gary Jordan
Chief of Medical Staff . . . . K Duane Cox, MD
Infection Control . . . . Joyce Noland, RN
Quality Assurance . . . . Joyce Noland
Emergency Room . . . . Jerry Jumper

Measure	Cases	This Hosp.	State Avg.	U.S. Avg.
Heart Attack Care				
ACE Inhibitor or ARB for LVSD[5]	0	-	96%	96%
Aspirin at Arrival[5]	0	-	99%	99%
Aspirin at Discharge[5]	0	-	99%	98%
Beta Blocker at Discharge[5]	0	-	99%	98%
Fibrinolytic Medication Timing[5]	0	-	27%	55%
PCI Within 90 Minutes of Arrival[5]	0	-	92%	90%
Smoking Cessation Advice[5]	0	-	99%	99%
Chest Pain/Possible Heart Attack Care				
Aspirin at Arrival	-	-	95%	95%
Median Time to ECG (minutes)	-	-	9	8
Median Time to Transfer (minutes)	-	-	64	61
Fibrinolytic Medication Timing	-	-	31%	54%
Heart Failure Care				
ACE Inhibitor or ARB for LVSD[1]	7	86%	94%	94%
Discharge Instructions[1]	18	94%	87%	88%
Evaluation of LVS Function[1]	22	91%	97%	98%
Smoking Cessation Advice[1]	5	100%	98%	98%
Pneumonia Care				
Appropriate Initial Antibiotic	34	100%	91%	92%
Blood Culture Timing	27	93%	97%	96%
Influenza Vaccine[1]	21	100%	90%	91%
Initial Antibiotic Timing	38	100%	95%	95%
Pneumococcal Vaccine	25	100%	93%	93%
Smoking Cessation Advice[1]	17	100%	97%	97%
Surgical Care Improvement Project				
Appropriate VTP Within 24 Hours[5]	0	-	93%	92%
Appropriate Hair Removal[5]	0	-	100%	99%
Appropriate Beta Blocker Usage[5]	0	-	94%	93%
Controlled Postoperative Blood Glucose[5]	0	-	94%	93%
Prophylactic Antibiotic Timing[5]	0	-	97%	97%
Prophylactic Antibiotic Timing (Outpatient)	-	-	95%	92%
Prophylactic Antibiotic Selection[5]	0	-	97%	97%
Prophylactic Antibiotic Select. (Outpatient)	-	-	95%	94%
Prophylactic Antibiotic Stopped[5]	0	-	95%	94%
Recommended VTP Ordered[5]	0	-	95%	94%
Urinary Catheter Removal[5]	0	-	88%	90%
Children's Asthma Care				
Received Systemic Corticosteroids	-	-	-	100%
Received Home Management Plan	-	-	-	71%
Received Reliever Medication	-	-	-	100%
Use of Medical Imaging				
Combination Abdominal CT Scan	-	-	0.227	0.191
Combination Chest CT Scan	-	-	0.059	0.054
Follow-up Mammogram/Ultrasound	-	-	7.4%	8.4%
MRI for Low Back Pain	-	-	36%	32.7%
Survey of Patients' Hospital Experiences				
Area Around Room 'Always' Quiet at Night[8]	-	-	-	58%
Doctors 'Always' Communicated Well[8]	-	-	-	80%
Home Recovery Information Given[8]	-	-	-	82%
Hospital Given 9 or 10 on 10 Point Scale[8]	-	-	-	67%
Meds 'Always' Explained Before Given[8]	-	-	-	60%
Nurses 'Always' Communicated Well[8]	-	-	-	76%
Pain 'Always' Well Controlled[8]	-	-	-	69%
Room and Bathroom 'Always' Clean[8]	-	-	-	71%
Timely Help 'Always' Received[8]	-	-	-	64%
Would Definitely Recommend Hospital[8]	-	-	-	69%

Saint Lukes Hospital

232 S Woods Mill Rd
Chesterfield, MO 63017
Phone: 314-434-1500
Fax: 314-205-6865
URL: www.goodhealthmatters.com
Type: Acute Care Hospitals
Emergency Services: Yes
Ownership: Voluntary Non-Profit - Private
Beds: 493

Key Personnel:

CEO/President . . . . Gary Olson, MD
Cardiac Laboratory . . . . John Hilden
Chief of Medical Staff . . . . Paul A Mennes, MD
Infection Control . . . . Leon Robison, MD
Pediatric Ambulatory Care . . . . . . Janet Ruzycler, MD
Pediatric In-Patient Care . . . . Janet Ruzycler, MD
Quality Assurance . . . . Linda Koste, RN
Radiology . . . . Reggie Hicks

Measure	Cases	This Hosp.	State Avg.	U.S. Avg.
Heart Attack Care				
ACE Inhibitor or ARB for LVSD	33	97%	96%	96%
Aspirin at Arrival	281	100%	99%	99%
Aspirin at Discharge	301	100%	99%	98%
Beta Blocker at Discharge	298	100%	99%	98%
Fibrinolytic Medication Timing	0	-	27%	55%
PCI Within 90 Minutes of Arrival	39	100%	92%	90%
Smoking Cessation Advice	66	100%	99%	99%
Chest Pain/Possible Heart Attack Care				
Aspirin at Arrival[1,3]	1	100%	95%	95%
Median Time to ECG (minutes)[1,3]	1	7	9	8
Median Time to Transfer (minutes)[5]	0	-	64	61
Fibrinolytic Medication Timing[3]	0	-	31%	54%
Heart Failure Care				
ACE Inhibitor or ARB for LVSD	143	97%	94%	94%
Discharge Instructions	354	91%	87%	88%
Evaluation of LVS Function	471	99%	97%	98%
Smoking Cessation Advice	39	100%	98%	98%
Pneumonia Care				
Appropriate Initial Antibiotic[2]	169	80%	91%	92%
Blood Culture Timing[2]	255	98%	97%	96%
Influenza Vaccine[2]	308	78%	90%	91%
Initial Antibiotic Timing[2]	346	94%	95%	95%
Pneumococcal Vaccine[2]	434	85%	93%	93%
Smoking Cessation Advice[2]	109	100%	97%	97%
Surgical Care Improvement Project				
Appropriate VTP Within 24 Hours[2]	317	95%	93%	92%
Appropriate Hair Removal[2]	995	95%	100%	99%
Appropriate Beta Blocker Usage[2]	320	92%	94%	93%
Controlled Postoperative Blood Glucose[2]	194	95%	94%	93%
Prophylactic Antibiotic Timing[2]	727	94%	97%	97%
Prophylactic Antibiotic Timing (Outpatient)	1,049	92%	95%	92%
Prophylactic Antibiotic Selection[2]	751	98%	97%	97%
Prophylactic Antibiotic Select. (Outpatient)	1,027	96%	95%	94%
Prophylactic Antibiotic Stopped[2]	695	93%	95%	94%
Recommended VTP Ordered[2]	318	98%	95%	94%
Urinary Catheter Removal[2]	117	85%	88%	90%
Children's Asthma Care				
Received Systemic Corticosteroids	-	-	-	100%
Received Home Management Plan	-	-	-	71%
Received Reliever Medication	-	-	-	100%
Use of Medical Imaging				
Combination Abdominal CT Scan	1,482	0.076	0.227	0.191
Combination Chest CT Scan	1,364	0.007	0.059	0.054
Follow-up Mammogram/Ultrasound	5,188	6.5%	7.4%	8.4%
MRI for Low Back Pain	474	31.0%	36%	32.7%
Survey of Patients' Hospital Experiences				
Area Around Room 'Always' Quiet at Night	300+	58%	-	58%
Doctors 'Always' Communicated Well	300+	81%	-	80%
Home Recovery Information Given	300+	81%	-	82%
Hospital Given 9 or 10 on 10 Point Scale	300+	80%	-	67%
Meds 'Always' Explained Before Given	300+	61%	-	60%
Nurses 'Always' Communicated Well	300+	77%	-	76%
Pain 'Always' Well Controlled	300+	72%	-	69%
Room and Bathroom 'Always' Clean	300+	72%	-	71%
Timely Help 'Always' Received	300+	62%	-	64%
Would Definitely Recommend Hospital	300+	84%	-	69%

NOTE: Hospital profiles are in alphabetical order by state, then city, then hospital within the city; Rankings exclude hospitals with less than 25 cases except for patient surveys which excludes hospitals with less than 100 cases; (a) 100–299 cases; (1) The number of cases is too small to be sure how well a hospital is performing; (2) The hospital indicated that the data submitted for this measure were based on a sample of cases; (3) Data was collected during a shorter time period (fewer quarters) than the maximum possible time for this measure; (4) Suppressed for one or more quarters by CMS; (5) No data is available from the hospital for this measure; (6) Fewer than 100 patients completed the HCAHPS survey. Use these rates with caution, as the number of surveys may be too low to reliably assess hospital performance; (7) Survey results are based on less than 12 months of data; (8) Survey results are not available for this reporting period; (9) No or very few patients were eligible for the HCAHPS survey. The scores shown, if any, reflect a very small number of surveys; (10) A state average was not calculated because too few hospitals in the state submitted data; (11) There were discrepancies in the data collection process; Please refer to the User's Guide for a full explanation of data.

Hedrick Medical Center

100 Central Street
Chillicothe, MO 64601
Phone: 660-646-1480
Fax: 660-646-6024
URL: www.saintlukeshealthsystem.org
Type: Critical Access Hospitals
Emergency Services: Yes
Ownership: Government - Local
Beds: 49

Key Personnel:
CEO/President. . . . . Brian Johnston
Chief of Medical Staff. . . . . Rick A Bonnette

Measure	Cases	This Hosp.	State Avg.	U.S. Avg.
Heart Attack Care				
ACE Inhibitor or ARB for LVSD[3]	0	-	96%	96%
Aspirin at Arrival[1,3]	4	100%	99%	99%
Aspirin at Discharge[1,3]	3	100%	99%	98%
Beta Blocker at Discharge[1,3]	2	100%	99%	98%
Fibrinolytic Medication Timing[3]	0	-	27%	55%
PCI Within 90 Minutes of Arrival[3]	0	-	92%	90%
Smoking Cessation Advice[3]	0	-	99%	99%
Chest Pain/Possible Heart Attack Care				
Aspirin at Arrival	179	96%	95%	95%
Median Time to ECG (minutes)	186	9	9	8
Median Time to Transfer (minutes)[1]	11	70	64	61
Fibrinolytic Medication Timing[1]	2	50%	31%	54%
Heart Failure Care				
ACE Inhibitor or ARB for LVSD[1]	2	100%	94%	94%
Discharge Instructions[1]	16	88%	87%	88%
Evaluation of LVS Function	26	92%	97%	98%
Smoking Cessation Advice[1]	2	100%	98%	98%
Pneumonia Care				
Appropriate Initial Antibiotic	29	83%	91%	92%
Blood Culture Timing	41	95%	97%	96%
Influenza Vaccine	37	95%	90%	91%
Initial Antibiotic Timing	58	98%	95%	95%
Pneumococcal Vaccine	54	98%	93%	93%
Smoking Cessation Advice[1]	8	88%	97%	97%
Surgical Care Improvement Project				
Appropriate VTP Within 24 Hours[1]	5	0%	93%	92%
Appropriate Hair Removal[1]	16	100%	100%	99%
Appropriate Beta Blocker Usage[1]	2	100%	94%	93%
Controlled Postoperative Blood Glucose	0	-	94%	93%
Prophylactic Antibiotic Timing[1]	10	90%	97%	97%
Prophylactic Antibiotic Timing (Outpatient)[1,3]	4	75%	95%	92%
Prophylactic Antibiotic Selection[1]	11	73%	97%	97%
Prophylactic Antibiotic Select. (Outpatient)[1,3]	3	67%	95%	94%
Prophylactic Antibiotic Stopped[1]	10	100%	95%	94%
Recommended VTP Ordered[1]	5	0%	95%	94%
Urinary Catheter Removal[1]	2	50%	88%	90%
Children's Asthma Care				
Received Systemic Corticosteroids	-	-	-	100%
Received Home Management Plan	-	-	-	71%
Received Reliever Medication	-	-	-	100%
Use of Medical Imaging				
Combination Abdominal CT Scan	240	0.029	0.227	0.191
Combination Chest CT Scan	197	0.051	0.059	0.054
Follow-up Mammogram/Ultrasound	274	9.1%	7.4%	8.4%
MRI for Low Back Pain	53	32.1%	36%	32.7%
Survey of Patients' Hospital Experiences				
Area Around Room 'Always' Quiet at Night	(a)	69%	-	58%
Doctors 'Always' Communicated Well	(a)	78%	-	80%
Home Recovery Information Given	(a)	79%	-	82%
Hospital Given 9 or 10 on 10 Point Scale	(a)	65%	-	67%
Meds 'Always' Explained Before Given	(a)	55%	-	60%
Nurses 'Always' Communicated Well	(a)	75%	-	76%
Pain 'Always' Well Controlled	(a)	64%	-	69%
Room and Bathroom 'Always' Clean	(a)	80%	-	71%
Timely Help 'Always' Received	(a)	71%	-	64%
Would Definitely Recommend Hospital	(a)	57%	-	69%

Golden Valley Memorial Hospital

1600 N 2nd St
Clinton, MO 64735
Phone: 660-885-5511
Fax: 660-885-5012
URL: www.gvmh.org
Type: Acute Care Hospitals
Emergency Services: Yes
Ownership: Govt - Hospital Dist/Auth
Beds: 84

Key Personnel:
CEO/President. . . . . Randy S Wertz
Chief of Medical Staff. . . . . Bruce Bellmay, MD
Infection Control. . . . . Claudia Gibson
Operating Room. . . . . Gus S Wetzel II
Radiology. . . . . Douglas Walrath
Emergency Room . . . . Richard F Beamon

Measure	Cases	This Hosp.	State Avg.	U.S. Avg.
Heart Attack Care				
ACE Inhibitor or ARB for LVSD[1]	1	100%	96%	96%
Aspirin at Arrival[1]	9	100%	99%	99%
Aspirin at Discharge[1]	6	67%	99%	98%
Beta Blocker at Discharge[1]	5	80%	99%	98%
Fibrinolytic Medication Timing	0	-	27%	55%
PCI Within 90 Minutes of Arrival	0	-	92%	90%
Smoking Cessation Advice[1]	2	100%	99%	99%
Chest Pain/Possible Heart Attack Care				
Aspirin at Arrival	135	96%	95%	95%
Median Time to ECG (minutes)	141	4	9	8
Median Time to Transfer (minutes)[1,3]	3	42	64	61
Fibrinolytic Medication Timing[1]	3	0%	31%	54%
Heart Failure Care				
ACE Inhibitor or ARB for LVSD	31	94%	94%	94%
Discharge Instructions	55	76%	87%	88%
Evaluation of LVS Function	107	99%	97%	98%
Smoking Cessation Advice[1]	16	100%	98%	98%
Pneumonia Care				
Appropriate Initial Antibiotic	91	96%	91%	92%
Blood Culture Timing	77	100%	97%	96%
Influenza Vaccine	62	98%	90%	91%
Initial Antibiotic Timing	121	99%	95%	95%
Pneumococcal Vaccine	95	99%	93%	93%
Smoking Cessation Advice	48	100%	97%	97%
Surgical Care Improvement Project				
Appropriate VTP Within 24 Hours	40	88%	93%	92%
Appropriate Hair Removal	109	100%	100%	99%
Appropriate Beta Blocker Usage[1]	20	75%	94%	93%
Controlled Postoperative Blood Glucose	0	-	94%	93%
Prophylactic Antibiotic Timing	74	99%	97%	97%
Prophylactic Antibiotic Timing (Outpatient)	34	88%	95%	92%
Prophylactic Antibiotic Selection	74	97%	97%	97%
Prophylactic Antibiotic Select. (Outpatient)	34	79%	95%	94%
Prophylactic Antibiotic Stopped	71	89%	95%	94%
Recommended VTP Ordered	40	98%	95%	94%
Urinary Catheter Removal[1]	19	84%	88%	90%
Children's Asthma Care				
Received Systemic Corticosteroids	-	-	-	100%
Received Home Management Plan	-	-	-	71%
Received Reliever Medication	-	-	-	100%
Use of Medical Imaging				
Combination Abdominal CT Scan	444	0.083	0.227	0.191
Combination Chest CT Scan	285	0.084	0.059	0.054
Follow-up Mammogram/Ultrasound	830	5.1%	7.4%	8.4%
MRI for Low Back Pain	191	31.9%	36%	32.7%
Survey of Patients' Hospital Experiences				
Area Around Room 'Always' Quiet at Night	300+	53%	-	58%
Doctors 'Always' Communicated Well	300+	83%	-	80%
Home Recovery Information Given	300+	82%	-	82%
Hospital Given 9 or 10 on 10 Point Scale	300+	64%	-	67%
Meds 'Always' Explained Before Given	300+	57%	-	60%
Nurses 'Always' Communicated Well	300+	76%	-	76%
Pain 'Always' Well Controlled	300+	69%	-	69%
Room and Bathroom 'Always' Clean	300+	81%	-	71%
Timely Help 'Always' Received	300+	67%	-	64%
Would Definitely Recommend Hospital	300+	63%	-	69%

Boone Hospital Center

1600 E Broadway
Columbia, MO 65201
Phone: 573-815-8000
Type: Acute Care Hospitals
Emergency Services: Yes
Ownership: Voluntary Non-Profit - Other

Key Personnel:
CEO/President. . . . . Dan Rothery
Chief of Medical Staff . . . . Carol B Danuser

Measure	Cases	This Hosp.	State Avg.	U.S. Avg.
Heart Attack Care				
ACE Inhibitor or ARB for LVSD	117	97%	96%	96%
Aspirin at Arrival	219	100%	99%	99%
Aspirin at Discharge	469	100%	99%	98%
Beta Blocker at Discharge	453	99%	99%	98%
Fibrinolytic Medication Timing	0	-	27%	55%
PCI Within 90 Minutes of Arrival	54	93%	92%	90%
Smoking Cessation Advice	152	100%	99%	99%
Chest Pain/Possible Heart Attack Care				
Aspirin at Arrival[1,3]	1	100%	95%	95%
Median Time to ECG (minutes)[1,3]	2	28	9	8
Median Time to Transfer (minutes)[5]	0	-	64	61
Fibrinolytic Medication Timing[5]	0	-	31%	54%
Heart Failure Care				
ACE Inhibitor or ARB for LVSD[2]	222	95%	94%	94%
Discharge Instructions[2]	429	91%	87%	88%
Evaluation of LVS Function[2]	513	99%	97%	98%
Smoking Cessation Advice[2]	68	100%	98%	98%
Pneumonia Care				
Appropriate Initial Antibiotic[2]	139	86%	91%	92%
Blood Culture Timing[2]	179	100%	97%	96%
Influenza Vaccine[2]	204	89%	90%	91%
Initial Antibiotic Timing[2]	229	97%	95%	95%
Pneumococcal Vaccine[2]	291	93%	93%	93%
Smoking Cessation Advice[2]	83	99%	97%	97%
Surgical Care Improvement Project				
Appropriate VTP Within 24 Hours[2]	182	95%	93%	92%
Appropriate Hair Removal[2]	911	100%	100%	99%
Appropriate Beta Blocker Usage[2]	263	95%	94%	93%
Controlled Postoperative Blood Glucose[2]	186	94%	94%	93%
Prophylactic Antibiotic Timing[2]	674	97%	97%	97%
Prophylactic Antibiotic Timing (Outpatient)	724	97%	95%	92%
Prophylactic Antibiotic Selection[2]	681	97%	97%	97%
Prophylactic Antibiotic Select. (Outpatient)	714	90%	95%	94%
Prophylactic Antibiotic Stopped[2]	668	96%	95%	94%
Recommended VTP Ordered[2]	183	94%	95%	94%
Urinary Catheter Removal[2]	252	93%	88%	90%
Children's Asthma Care				
Received Systemic Corticosteroids	-	-	-	100%
Received Home Management Plan	-	-	-	71%
Received Reliever Medication	-	-	-	100%
Use of Medical Imaging				
Combination Abdominal CT Scan	1,483	0.170	0.227	0.191
Combination Chest CT Scan	1,012	0.011	0.059	0.054
Follow-up Mammogram/Ultrasound	2,578	3.1%	7.4%	8.4%
MRI for Low Back Pain	465	36.8%	36%	32.7%
Survey of Patients' Hospital Experiences				
Area Around Room 'Always' Quiet at Night	300+	60%	-	58%
Doctors 'Always' Communicated Well	300+	87%	-	80%
Home Recovery Information Given	300+	89%	-	82%
Hospital Given 9 or 10 on 10 Point Scale	300+	78%	-	67%
Meds 'Always' Explained Before Given	300+	73%	-	60%
Nurses 'Always' Communicated Well	300+	84%	-	76%
Pain 'Always' Well Controlled	300+	71%	-	69%
Room and Bathroom 'Always' Clean	300+	75%	-	71%
Timely Help 'Always' Received	300+	69%	-	64%
Would Definitely Recommend Hospital	300+	83%	-	69%

NOTE: Hospital profiles are in alphabetical order by state, then city, then hospital within the city; Rankings exclude hospitals with less than 25 cases except for patient surveys which excludes hospitals with less than 100 cases; (a) 100–299 cases; (1) The number of cases is too small to be sure how well a hospital is performing; (2) The hospital indicated that the data submitted for this measure were based on a sample of cases; (3) Data was collected during a shorter time period (fewer quarters) than the maximum possible time for this measure; (4) Suppressed for one or more quarters by CMS; (5) No data is available from the hospital for this measure; (6) Fewer than 100 patients completed the HCAHPS survey. Use these rates with caution, as the number of surveys may be too low to reliably assess hospital performance; (7) Survey results are based on less than 12 months of data; (8) Survey results are not available for this reporting period; (9) No or very few patients were eligible for the HCAHPS survey. The scores shown, if any, reflect a very small number of surveys; (10) A state average was not calculated because too few hospitals in the state submitted data; (11) There were discrepancies in the data collection process; Please refer to the User's Guide for a full explanation of data.

Columbia Missouri VA Medical Center

800 Hospital Dr | Phone: 573-814-6000
Columbia, MO 65201 | Fax: 573-814-6600
URL: www.columbiamo.vc.gov
Type: Acute Care-Veterans Administration | Emergency Services: No
Ownership: Government - Federal | Beds: 123

Key Personnel:
CEO/President. . . . . Sallie Houser- Manfelder, FACHE
Cardiac Laboratory. . . . . Kul Aggarwal, MD
Coronary Care . . . . Hunter Hofmann, MD
Quality Assurance . . . . Crystal Aholt, RN
Anesthesiology. . . . . John Turchiano, MD
Emergency Room . . . . Lula Johnson, RN
Intensive Care Unit. . . . . Stephanie Carter, RN
Patient Relations . . . . Debbie Canow, RN

Measure	Cases	This Hosp.	State Avg.	U.S. Avg.
Heart Attack Care				
ACE Inhibitor or ARB for LVSD[1]	5	100%	96%	96%
Aspirin at Arrival	49	100%	99%	99%
Aspirin at Discharge	48	100%	99%	98%
Beta Blocker at Discharge	51	96%	99%	98%
Fibrinolytic Medication Timing[5]	0	-	27%	55%
PCI Within 90 Minutes of Arrival[1]	7	57%	92%	90%
Smoking Cessation Advice[1]	15	100%	99%	99%
Chest Pain/Possible Heart Attack Care				
Aspirin at Arrival	-	-	95%	95%
Median Time to ECG (minutes)	-	-	9	8
Median Time to Transfer (minutes)	-	-	64	61
Fibrinolytic Medication Timing	-	-	31%	54%
Heart Failure Care				
ACE Inhibitor or ARB for LVSD	48	100%	94%	94%
Discharge Instructions	137	100%	87%	88%
Evaluation of LVS Function	153	99%	97%	98%
Smoking Cessation Advice[1]	23	100%	98%	98%
Pneumonia Care				
Appropriate Initial Antibiotic	39	90%	91%	92%
Blood Culture Timing	65	97%	97%	96%
Influenza Vaccine	61	90%	90%	91%
Initial Antibiotic Timing	51	96%	95%	95%
Pneumococcal Vaccine	86	99%	93%	93%
Smoking Cessation Advice	31	100%	97%	97%
Surgical Care Improvement Project				
Appropriate VTP Within 24 Hours[2]	93	100%	93%	92%
Appropriate Hair Removal[2]	275	100%	100%	99%
Appropriate Beta Blocker Usage[2]	131	100%	94%	93%
Controlled Postoperative Blood Glucose[2]	100	99%	94%	93%
Prophylactic Antibiotic Timing	173	94%	97%	97%
Prophylactic Antibiotic Timing (Outpatient)	-	-	95%	92%
Prophylactic Antibiotic Selection	172	100%	97%	97%
Prophylactic Antibiotic Select. (Outpatient)	-	-	95%	94%
Prophylactic Antibiotic Stopped	172	100%	95%	94%
Recommended VTP Ordered[2]	93	100%	95%	94%
Urinary Catheter Removal[2]	137	99%	88%	90%
Children's Asthma Care				
Received Systemic Corticosteroids	-	-	-	100%
Received Home Management Plan	-	-	-	71%
Received Reliever Medication	-	-	-	100%
Use of Medical Imaging				
Combination Abdominal CT Scan	-	-	0.227	0.191
Combination Chest CT Scan	-	-	0.059	0.054
Follow-up Mammogram/Ultrasound	-	-	7.4%	8.4%
MRI for Low Back Pain	-	-	36%	32.7%
Survey of Patients' Hospital Experiences				
Area Around Room 'Always' Quiet at Night	-	-	-	58%
Doctors 'Always' Communicated Well	-	-	-	80%
Home Recovery Information Given	-	-	-	82%
Hospital Given 9 or 10 on 10 Point Scale	-	-	-	67%
Meds 'Always' Explained Before Given	-	-	-	60%
Nurses 'Always' Communicated Well	-	-	-	76%
Pain 'Always' Well Controlled	-	-	-	69%
Room and Bathroom 'Always' Clean	-	-	-	71%
Timely Help 'Always' Received	-	-	-	64%
Would Definitely Recommend Hospital	-	-	-	69%

University of Missouri Health Care

One Hospital Drive | Phone: 573-882-4141
Columbia, MO 65201 | Fax: 573-884-7470
URL: www.missouri.edu
Type: Acute Care Hospitals | Emergency Services: Yes
Ownership: Government - State | Beds: 495

Key Personnel:
CEO/President. . . . . Patsy J Hart
Chief of Medical Staff . . . . Karl Weber, MD
Infection Control. . . . . E Dale Everett
Operating Room. . . . . Amy Tinsley
Quality Assurance . . . . Myra McCoig
Radiology. . . . . Larry Kirschner
Anesthesiology. . . . . Noel Lawson, MD
Emergency Room . . . . Gwen Burley

Measure	Cases	This Hosp.	State Avg.	U.S. Avg.
Heart Attack Care				
ACE Inhibitor or ARB for LVSD	56	95%	96%	96%
Aspirin at Arrival	127	99%	99%	99%
Aspirin at Discharge	249	100%	99%	98%
Beta Blocker at Discharge	241	99%	99%	98%
Fibrinolytic Medication Timing	0	-	27%	55%
PCI Within 90 Minutes of Arrival	38	97%	92%	90%
Smoking Cessation Advice	121	99%	99%	99%
Chest Pain/Possible Heart Attack Care				
Aspirin at Arrival[1,3]	2	100%	95%	95%
Median Time to ECG (minutes)[1,3]	3	3	9	8
Median Time to Transfer (minutes)[5]	0	-	64	61
Fibrinolytic Medication Timing[5]	0	-	31%	54%
Heart Failure Care				
ACE Inhibitor or ARB for LVSD	105	95%	94%	94%
Discharge Instructions	177	89%	87%	88%
Evaluation of LVS Function	224	100%	97%	98%
Smoking Cessation Advice	63	98%	98%	98%
Pneumonia Care				
Appropriate Initial Antibiotic	64	83%	91%	92%
Blood Culture Timing	125	98%	97%	96%
Influenza Vaccine	137	93%	90%	91%
Initial Antibiotic Timing	118	79%	95%	95%
Pneumococcal Vaccine	137	96%	93%	93%
Smoking Cessation Advice	89	98%	97%	97%
Surgical Care Improvement Project				
Appropriate VTP Within 24 Hours	501	98%	93%	92%
Appropriate Hair Removal	911	100%	100%	99%
Appropriate Beta Blocker Usage	278	92%	94%	93%
Controlled Postoperative Blood Glucose	93	99%	94%	93%
Prophylactic Antibiotic Timing	192	98%	97%	97%
Prophylactic Antibiotic Timing (Outpatient)	344	90%	95%	92%
Prophylactic Antibiotic Selection	201	95%	97%	97%
Prophylactic Antibiotic Select. (Outpatient)	402	96%	95%	94%
Prophylactic Antibiotic Stopped	136	90%	95%	94%
Recommended VTP Ordered	502	98%	95%	94%
Urinary Catheter Removal	128	94%	88%	90%
Children's Asthma Care				
Received Systemic Corticosteroids	-	-	-	100%
Received Home Management Plan	-	-	-	71%
Received Reliever Medication	-	-	-	100%
Use of Medical Imaging				
Combination Abdominal CT Scan	1,075	0.273	0.227	0.191
Combination Chest CT Scan	1,213	0.042	0.059	0.054
Follow-up Mammogram/Ultrasound	2,817	8.3%	7.4%	8.4%
MRI for Low Back Pain	62	29.0%	36%	32.7%
Survey of Patients' Hospital Experiences				
Area Around Room 'Always' Quiet at Night	300+	50%	-	58%
Doctors 'Always' Communicated Well	300+	72%	-	80%
Home Recovery Information Given	300+	85%	-	82%
Hospital Given 9 or 10 on 10 Point Scale	300+	60%	-	67%
Meds 'Always' Explained Before Given	300+	54%	-	60%
Nurses 'Always' Communicated Well	300+	72%	-	76%
Pain 'Always' Well Controlled	300+	65%	-	69%
Room and Bathroom 'Always' Clean	300+	66%	-	71%
Timely Help 'Always' Received	300+	58%	-	64%
Would Definitely Recommend Hospital	300+	68%	-	69%

Women's and Children's Hospital

404 Keene St | Phone: 573-875-9200
Columbia, MO 65201 | Fax: 573-875-9869
URL: www.columbiaregional.org
Type: Acute Care Hospitals | Emergency Services: Yes
Ownership: Government - State | Beds: 177

Key Personnel:
CEO/President. . . . . James Ross
Chief of Medical Staff . . . . Richard W Burns
Operating Room. . . . . Debra Koivunen
Quality Assurance . . . . Dennis G Stambaugh
Radiology. . . . . James C Brown

Measure	Cases	This Hosp.	State Avg.	U.S. Avg.
Heart Attack Care				
ACE Inhibitor or ARB for LVSD[3]	0	-	96%	96%
Aspirin at Arrival[1,3]	5	100%	99%	99%
Aspirin at Discharge[1,3]	4	100%	99%	98%
Beta Blocker at Discharge[1,3]	4	100%	99%	98%
Fibrinolytic Medication Timing[3]	0	-	27%	55%
PCI Within 90 Minutes of Arrival[1,3]	1	0%	92%	90%
Smoking Cessation Advice[1,3]	1	100%	99%	99%
Chest Pain/Possible Heart Attack Care				
Aspirin at Arrival[1]	9	100%	95%	95%
Median Time to ECG (minutes)[1]	10	20	9	8
Median Time to Transfer (minutes)[1,3]	1	45	64	61
Fibrinolytic Medication Timing[3]	0	-	31%	54%
Heart Failure Care				
ACE Inhibitor or ARB for LVSD[1,3]	4	75%	94%	94%
Discharge Instructions[1,3]	7	29%	87%	88%
Evaluation of LVS Function[1,3]	9	100%	97%	98%
Smoking Cessation Advice[3]	0	-	98%	98%
Pneumonia Care				
Appropriate Initial Antibiotic[1]	8	88%	91%	92%
Blood Culture Timing[1]	8	100%	97%	96%
Influenza Vaccine[1]	6	67%	90%	91%
Initial Antibiotic Timing[1]	10	90%	95%	95%
Pneumococcal Vaccine[1]	6	50%	93%	93%
Smoking Cessation Advice[1]	6	83%	97%	97%
Surgical Care Improvement Project				
Appropriate VTP Within 24 Hours[2]	162	99%	93%	92%
Appropriate Hair Removal[2]	562	100%	100%	99%
Appropriate Beta Blocker Usage[2]	126	93%	94%	93%
Controlled Postoperative Blood Glucose[2]	0	-	94%	93%
Prophylactic Antibiotic Timing[2]	375	93%	97%	97%
Prophylactic Antibiotic Timing (Outpatient)	372	96%	95%	92%
Prophylactic Antibiotic Selection[2]	376	98%	97%	97%
Prophylactic Antibiotic Select. (Outpatient)	370	96%	95%	94%
Prophylactic Antibiotic Stopped[2]	373	96%	95%	94%
Recommended VTP Ordered[2]	162	99%	95%	94%
Urinary Catheter Removal[2]	176	97%	88%	90%
Children's Asthma Care				
Received Systemic Corticosteroids	-	-	-	100%
Received Home Management Plan	-	-	-	71%
Received Reliever Medication	-	-	-	100%
Use of Medical Imaging				
Combination Abdominal CT Scan	159	0.717	0.227	0.191
Combination Chest CT Scan	121	0.091	0.059	0.054
Follow-up Mammogram/Ultrasound	405	11.4%	7.4%	8.4%
MRI for Low Back Pain	129	31.0%	36%	32.7%
Survey of Patients' Hospital Experiences				
Area Around Room 'Always' Quiet at Night	300+	63%	-	58%
Doctors 'Always' Communicated Well	300+	76%	-	80%
Home Recovery Information Given	300+	87%	-	82%
Hospital Given 9 or 10 on 10 Point Scale	300+	73%	-	67%
Meds 'Always' Explained Before Given	300+	55%	-	60%
Nurses 'Always' Communicated Well	300+	75%	-	76%
Pain 'Always' Well Controlled	300+	69%	-	69%
Room and Bathroom 'Always' Clean	300+	77%	-	71%
Timely Help 'Always' Received	300+	68%	-	64%
Would Definitely Recommend Hospital	300+	76%	-	69%

NOTE: Hospital profiles are in alphabetical order by state, then city, then hospital within the city; Rankings exclude hospitals with less than 25 cases except for patient surveys which excludes hospitals with less than 100 cases; (a) 100–299 cases; (1) The number of cases is too small to be sure how well a hospital is performing; (2) The hospital indicated that the data submitted for this measure were based on a sample of cases; (3) Data was collected during a shorter time period (fewer quarters) than the maximum possible time for this measure; (4) Suppressed for one or more quarters by CMS; (5) No data is available from the hospital for this measure; (6) Fewer than 100 patients completed the HCAHPS survey. Use these rates with caution, as the number of surveys may be too low to reliably assess hospital performance; (7) Survey results are based on less than 12 months of data; (8) Survey results are not available for this reporting period; (9) No or very few patients were eligible for the HCAHPS survey. The scores shown, if any, reflect a very small number of surveys; (10) A state average was not calculated because too few hospitals in the state submitted data; (11) There were discrepancies in the data collection process; Please refer to the User's Guide for a full explanation of data.

Barnes-Jewish West County Hospital

12634 Olive Boulevard Phone: 314-996-8000
Creve Coeur, MO 63141 Fax: 314-286-0305
URL: www.barnesjewishwestcounty.org
Type: Acute Care Hospitals Emergency Services: Yes
Ownership: Voluntary Non-Profit - Private Beds: 113

Key Personnel:
CEO/President............... Pat Mohrman, RN, MSN
Chief of Medical Staff.......... Alan Londe
Quality Assurance .... Mary Mantese
Emergency Room .... Ren Kozikowski

Measure	Cases	This Hosp.	State Avg.	U.S. Avg.
Heart Attack Care				
ACE Inhibitor or ARB for LVSD[1]	1	100%	96%	96%
Aspirin at Arrival[1]	9	100%	99%	99%
Aspirin at Discharge[1]	7	100%	99%	98%
Beta Blocker at Discharge[1]	6	100%	99%	98%
Fibrinolytic Medication Timing	0	-	27%	55%
PCI Within 90 Minutes of Arrival	0	-	92%	90%
Smoking Cessation Advice[1]	1	100%	99%	99%
Chest Pain/Possible Heart Attack Care				
Aspirin at Arrival	64	97%	95%	95%
Median Time to ECG (minutes)	64	8	9	8
Median Time to Transfer (minutes)[1,3]	8	86	64	61
Fibrinolytic Medication Timing	0	-	31%	54%
Heart Failure Care				
ACE Inhibitor or ARB for LVSD	25	100%	94%	94%
Discharge Instructions	96	90%	87%	88%
Evaluation of LVS Function	109	99%	97%	98%
Smoking Cessation Advice[1]	7	100%	98%	98%
Pneumonia Care				
Appropriate Initial Antibiotic	38	95%	91%	92%
Blood Culture Timing	39	90%	97%	96%
Influenza Vaccine	27	81%	90%	91%
Initial Antibiotic Timing	55	98%	95%	95%
Pneumococcal Vaccine	43	93%	93%	93%
Smoking Cessation Advice[1]	7	100%	97%	97%
Surgical Care Improvement Project				
Appropriate VTP Within 24 Hours[2]	178	97%	93%	92%
Appropriate Hair Removal[2]	882	100%	100%	99%
Appropriate Beta Blocker Usage[2]	148	99%	94%	93%
Controlled Postoperative Blood Glucose[2]	0	-	94%	93%
Prophylactic Antibiotic Timing[2]	636	93%	97%	97%
Prophylactic Antibiotic Timing (Outpatient)	339	96%	95%	92%
Prophylactic Antibiotic Selection[2]	639	100%	97%	97%
Prophylactic Antibiotic Select. (Outpatient)	338	92%	95%	94%
Prophylactic Antibiotic Stopped[2]	632	93%	95%	94%
Recommended VTP Ordered[2]	181	95%	95%	94%
Urinary Catheter Removal[2]	248	95%	88%	90%
Children's Asthma Care				
Received Systemic Corticosteroids	-	-	-	100%
Received Home Management Plan	-	-	-	71%
Received Reliever Medication	-	-	-	100%
Use of Medical Imaging				
Combination Abdominal CT Scan	846	0.103	0.227	0.191
Combination Chest CT Scan	814	0.014	0.059	0.054
Follow-up Mammogram/Ultrasound	672	6.4%	7.4%	8.4%
MRI for Low Back Pain	155	29.0%	36%	32.7%
Survey of Patients' Hospital Experiences				
Area Around Room 'Always' Quiet at Night	300+	64%	-	58%
Doctors 'Always' Communicated Well	300+	84%	-	80%
Home Recovery Information Given	300+	87%	-	82%
Hospital Given 9 or 10 on 10 Point Scale	300+	78%	-	67%
Meds 'Always' Explained Before Given	300+	60%	-	60%
Nurses 'Always' Communicated Well	300+	82%	-	76%
Pain 'Always' Well Controlled	300+	77%	-	69%
Room and Bathroom 'Always' Clean	300+	71%	-	71%
Timely Help 'Always' Received	300+	72%	-	64%
Would Definitely Recommend Hospital	300+	79%	-	69%

Jefferson Regional Medical Center

Hwy 61 South Phone: 636-933-1000
Crystal City, MO 63019 Fax: 636-933-1119
E-mail: info@jeffersonmemorial.org
URL: www.jeffersonmemorial.org
Type: Acute Care Hospitals Emergency Services: Yes
Ownership: Voluntary Non-Profit - Private Beds: 240

Key Personnel:
CEO/President............... Lindell Carter
Chief of Medical Staff.......... Indu Patel
Infection Control.............. Linda Ferrara
Operating Room.............. Lana Gladhill
Pediatric Ambulatory Care ...... Sarah Moerschel, MD
Pediatric In-Patient Care .... Linda Blanc
Quality Assurance .... Sarah Johnson
Radiology.................. Jonathan Dehner MD, MD

Measure	Cases	This Hosp.	State Avg.	U.S. Avg.
Heart Attack Care				
ACE Inhibitor or ARB for LVSD	38	97%	96%	96%
Aspirin at Arrival	200	99%	99%	99%
Aspirin at Discharge	260	100%	99%	98%
Beta Blocker at Discharge	252	100%	99%	98%
Fibrinolytic Medication Timing	0	-	27%	55%
PCI Within 90 Minutes of Arrival	43	95%	92%	90%
Smoking Cessation Advice	110	100%	99%	99%
Chest Pain/Possible Heart Attack Care				
Aspirin at Arrival	30	100%	95%	95%
Median Time to ECG (minutes)	32	6	9	8
Median Time to Transfer (minutes)[5]	0	-	64	61
Fibrinolytic Medication Timing[3]	0	-	31%	54%
Heart Failure Care				
ACE Inhibitor or ARB for LVSD	108	100%	94%	94%
Discharge Instructions	297	96%	87%	88%
Evaluation of LVS Function	419	99%	97%	98%
Smoking Cessation Advice	91	100%	98%	98%
Pneumonia Care				
Appropriate Initial Antibiotic	197	91%	91%	92%
Blood Culture Timing	321	98%	97%	96%
Influenza Vaccine	210	96%	90%	91%
Initial Antibiotic Timing	328	99%	95%	95%
Pneumococcal Vaccine	264	92%	93%	93%
Smoking Cessation Advice	162	100%	97%	97%
Surgical Care Improvement Project				
Appropriate VTP Within 24 Hours[2]	155	94%	93%	92%
Appropriate Hair Removal[2]	488	100%	100%	99%
Appropriate Beta Blocker Usage[2]	126	90%	94%	93%
Controlled Postoperative Blood Glucose[2]	57	89%	94%	93%
Prophylactic Antibiotic Timing[2]	339	95%	97%	97%
Prophylactic Antibiotic Timing (Outpatient)	149	85%	95%	92%
Prophylactic Antibiotic Selection[2]	341	95%	97%	97%
Prophylactic Antibiotic Select. (Outpatient)	141	95%	95%	94%
Prophylactic Antibiotic Stopped[2]	331	92%	95%	94%
Recommended VTP Ordered[2]	155	94%	95%	94%
Urinary Catheter Removal[2]	42	86%	88%	90%
Children's Asthma Care				
Received Systemic Corticosteroids	-	-	-	100%
Received Home Management Plan	-	-	-	71%
Received Reliever Medication	-	-	-	100%
Use of Medical Imaging				
Combination Abdominal CT Scan	836	0.336	0.227	0.191
Combination Chest CT Scan	624	0.005	0.059	0.054
Follow-up Mammogram/Ultrasound	926	8.2%	7.4%	8.4%
MRI for Low Back Pain	109	35.8%	36%	32.7%
Survey of Patients' Hospital Experiences				
Area Around Room 'Always' Quiet at Night	300+	46%	-	58%
Doctors 'Always' Communicated Well	300+	75%	-	80%
Home Recovery Information Given	300+	75%	-	82%
Hospital Given 9 or 10 on 10 Point Scale	300+	62%	-	67%
Meds 'Always' Explained Before Given	300+	56%	-	60%
Nurses 'Always' Communicated Well	300+	74%	-	76%
Pain 'Always' Well Controlled	300+	67%	-	69%
Room and Bathroom 'Always' Clean	300+	68%	-	71%
Timely Help 'Always' Received	300+	63%	-	64%
Would Definitely Recommend Hospital	300+	61%	-	69%

Missouri Southern Healthcare

1200 N One Mile Rd Phone: 573-624-5566
Dexter, MO 63841 Fax: 573-624-6265
Type: Acute Care Hospitals Emergency Services: Yes
Ownership: Proprietary Beds: 50

Key Personnel:
CEO/President............... John Graves
Chief of Medical Staff.......... Reza Jalal, MD
Infection Control.............. Christine Neuber
Operating Room.............. Patti Shell
Quality Assurance .... Judy Pedigo
Radiology.................. Christopher Newberry
Emergency Room .... Cathy Hawthorne
Intensive Care Unit............ Christie DeArmen

Measure	Cases	This Hosp.	State Avg.	U.S. Avg.
Heart Attack Care				
ACE Inhibitor or ARB for LVSD	0	-	96%	96%
Aspirin at Arrival[1]	15	93%	99%	99%
Aspirin at Discharge[1]	11	64%	99%	98%
Beta Blocker at Discharge[1]	11	91%	99%	98%
Fibrinolytic Medication Timing	0	-	27%	55%
PCI Within 90 Minutes of Arrival	0	-	92%	90%
Smoking Cessation Advice	0	-	99%	99%
Chest Pain/Possible Heart Attack Care				
Aspirin at Arrival	90	90%	95%	95%
Median Time to ECG (minutes)	94	13	9	8
Median Time to Transfer (minutes)[1,3]	6	119	64	61
Fibrinolytic Medication Timing[1]	4	50%	31%	54%
Heart Failure Care				
ACE Inhibitor or ARB for LVSD[1]	10	90%	94%	94%
Discharge Instructions	72	36%	87%	88%
Evaluation of LVS Function	93	46%	97%	98%
Smoking Cessation Advice[1]	15	93%	98%	98%
Pneumonia Care				
Appropriate Initial Antibiotic	65	83%	91%	92%
Blood Culture Timing	41	95%	97%	96%
Influenza Vaccine	77	78%	90%	91%
Initial Antibiotic Timing	94	96%	95%	95%
Pneumococcal Vaccine	105	85%	93%	93%
Smoking Cessation Advice	38	89%	97%	97%
Surgical Care Improvement Project				
Appropriate VTP Within 24 Hours[1]	22	68%	93%	92%
Appropriate Hair Removal	25	100%	100%	99%
Appropriate Beta Blocker Usage[1]	6	83%	94%	93%
Controlled Postoperative Blood Glucose	0	-	94%	93%
Prophylactic Antibiotic Timing[1]	7	100%	97%	97%
Prophylactic Antibiotic Timing (Outpatient)[1,3]	4	50%	95%	92%
Prophylactic Antibiotic Selection[1]	7	14%	97%	97%
Prophylactic Antibiotic Select. (Outpatient)[1,3]	3	100%	95%	94%
Prophylactic Antibiotic Stopped[1]	6	100%	95%	94%
Recommended VTP Ordered[1]	22	73%	95%	94%
Urinary Catheter Removal[1]	8	88%	88%	90%
Children's Asthma Care				
Received Systemic Corticosteroids	-	-	-	100%
Received Home Management Plan	-	-	-	71%
Received Reliever Medication	-	-	-	100%
Use of Medical Imaging				
Combination Abdominal CT Scan	217	0.470	0.227	0.191
Combination Chest CT Scan	117	0.017	0.059	0.054
Follow-up Mammogram/Ultrasound	406	8.1%	7.4%	8.4%
MRI for Low Back Pain[1]	38	26.3%	36%	32.7%
Survey of Patients' Hospital Experiences				
Area Around Room 'Always' Quiet at Night	300+	59%	-	58%
Doctors 'Always' Communicated Well	300+	87%	-	80%
Home Recovery Information Given	300+	76%	-	82%
Hospital Given 9 or 10 on 10 Point Scale	300+	66%	-	67%
Meds 'Always' Explained Before Given	300+	60%	-	60%
Nurses 'Always' Communicated Well	300+	81%	-	76%
Pain 'Always' Well Controlled	300+	71%	-	69%
Room and Bathroom 'Always' Clean	300+	79%	-	71%
Timely Help 'Always' Received	300+	73%	-	64%
Would Definitely Recommend Hospital	300+	65%	-	69%

NOTE: Hospital profiles are in alphabetical order by state, then city, then hospital within the city; Rankings exclude hospitals with less than 25 cases except for patient surveys which excludes hospitals with less than 100 cases; (a) 100–299 cases; (1) The number of cases is too small to be sure how well a hospital is performing; (2) The hospital indicated that the data submitted for this measure were based on a sample of cases; (3) Data was collected during a shorter time period (fewer quarters) than the maximum possible time for this measure; (4) Suppressed for one or more quarters by CMS; (5) No data is available from the hospital for this measure; (6) Fewer than 100 patients completed the HCAHPS survey. Use these rates with caution, as the number of surveys may be too low to reliably assess hospital performance; (7) Survey results are based on less than 12 months of data; (8) Survey results are not available for this reporting period; (9) No or very few patients were eligible for the HCAHPS survey. The scores shown, if any, reflect a very small number of surveys; (10) A state average was not calculated because too few hospitals in the state submitted data; (11) There were discrepancies in the data collection process; Please refer to the User's Guide for a full explanation of data.

Ripley County Memorial Hospital

109 Plum St Phone: 573-996-2141
Doniphan, MO 63935 Fax: 573-996-3949
Type: Acute Care Hospitals Emergency Services: Yes
Ownership: Voluntary Non-Profit - Other Beds: 30

Key Personnel:
CEO/President. . . . . Ray Freeman
Chief of Medical Staff. . . . . Gary Ward
Operating Room. . . . . Phyllis Featherston
Quality Assurance . . . . Jackie Johnson
Emergency Room . . . . Tamy Ryan

Measure	Cases	This Hosp.	State Avg.	U.S. Avg.
Heart Attack Care				
ACE Inhibitor or ARB for LVSD[1,3]	1	0%	96%	96%
Aspirin at Arrival[1,3]	1	100%	99%	99%
Aspirin at Discharge[1,3]	1	100%	99%	98%
Beta Blocker at Discharge[1,3]	1	100%	99%	98%
Fibrinolytic Medication Timing[3]	0	-	27%	55%
PCI Within 90 Minutes of Arrival[3]	0	-	92%	90%
Smoking Cessation Advice[3]	0	-	99%	99%
Chest Pain/Possible Heart Attack Care				
Aspirin at Arrival	44	91%	95%	95%
Median Time to ECG (minutes)	46	17	9	8
Median Time to Transfer (minutes)[1,3]	2	79	64	61
Fibrinolytic Medication Timing[3]	0	-	31%	54%
Heart Failure Care				
ACE Inhibitor or ARB for LVSD[1]	4	50%	94%	94%
Discharge Instructions	27	74%	87%	88%
Evaluation of LVS Function	30	57%	97%	98%
Smoking Cessation Advice[1]	3	100%	98%	98%
Pneumonia Care				
Appropriate Initial Antibiotic	30	87%	91%	92%
Blood Culture Timing	37	92%	97%	96%
Influenza Vaccine	33	67%	90%	91%
Initial Antibiotic Timing	44	93%	95%	95%
Pneumococcal Vaccine	45	73%	93%	93%
Smoking Cessation Advice[1]	20	95%	97%	97%
Surgical Care Improvement Project				
Appropriate VTP Within 24 Hours[5]	0	-	93%	92%
Appropriate Hair Removal[5]	0	-	100%	99%
Appropriate Beta Blocker Usage[5]	0	-	94%	93%
Controlled Postoperative Blood Glucose[5]	0	-	94%	93%
Prophylactic Antibiotic Timing[5]	0	-	97%	97%
Prophylactic Antibiotic Timing (Outpatient)[5]	0	-	95%	92%
Prophylactic Antibiotic Selection[5]	0	-	97%	97%
Prophylactic Antibiotic Select. (Outpatient)[5]	0	-	95%	94%
Prophylactic Antibiotic Stopped[5]	0	-	95%	94%
Recommended VTP Ordered[5]	0	-	95%	94%
Urinary Catheter Removal[5]	0	-	88%	90%
Children's Asthma Care				
Received Systemic Corticosteroids	-	-	-	100%
Received Home Management Plan	-	-	-	71%
Received Reliever Medication	-	-	-	100%
Use of Medical Imaging				
Combination Abdominal CT Scan	55	0.000	0.227	0.191
Combination Chest CT Scan	52	0.000	0.059	0.054
Follow-up Mammogram/Ultrasound[5]	0	-	7.4%	8.4%
MRI for Low Back Pain[1]	15	20.0%	36%	32.7%
Survey of Patients' Hospital Experiences				
Area Around Room 'Always' Quiet at Night	(a)	42%	-	58%
Doctors 'Always' Communicated Well	(a)	79%	-	80%
Home Recovery Information Given	(a)	82%	-	82%
Hospital Given 9 or 10 on 10 Point Scale	(a)	57%	-	67%
Meds 'Always' Explained Before Given	(a)	55%	-	60%
Nurses 'Always' Communicated Well	(a)	73%	-	76%
Pain 'Always' Well Controlled	(a)	51%	-	69%
Room and Bathroom 'Always' Clean	(a)	77%	-	71%
Timely Help 'Always' Received	(a)	68%	-	64%
Would Definitely Recommend Hospital	(a)	55%	-	69%

Advanced Healthcare Medical Center

Route 4, Box 4269 Phone: 573-663-2511
Ellington, MO 63638 Fax: 573-663-7264
Type: Critical Access Hospitals Emergency Services: Yes
Ownership: Voluntary Non-Profit - Private Beds: 25

Key Personnel:
CEO/President. . . . . Greg Carda
Chief of Medical Staff. . . . . Tual Rains
Emergency Room . . . . Cherri Barton

Measure	Cases	This Hosp.	State Avg.	U.S. Avg.
Heart Attack Care				
ACE Inhibitor or ARB for LVSD[5]	0	-	96%	96%
Aspirin at Arrival[5]	0	-	99%	99%
Aspirin at Discharge[5]	0	-	99%	98%
Beta Blocker at Discharge[5]	0	-	99%	98%
Fibrinolytic Medication Timing[5]	0	-	27%	55%
PCI Within 90 Minutes of Arrival[5]	0	-	92%	90%
Smoking Cessation Advice[5]	0	-	99%	99%
Chest Pain/Possible Heart Attack Care				
Aspirin at Arrival	-	-	95%	95%
Median Time to ECG (minutes)	-	-	9	8
Median Time to Transfer (minutes)	-	-	64	61
Fibrinolytic Medication Timing	-	-	31%	54%
Heart Failure Care				
ACE Inhibitor or ARB for LVSD[1]	1	100%	94%	94%
Discharge Instructions[1]	9	67%	87%	88%
Evaluation of LVS Function[1]	15	27%	97%	98%
Smoking Cessation Advice[1]	1	100%	98%	98%
Pneumonia Care				
Appropriate Initial Antibiotic[1]	9	89%	91%	92%
Blood Culture Timing[1]	1	100%	97%	96%
Influenza Vaccine[1]	6	50%	90%	91%
Initial Antibiotic Timing[1]	11	100%	95%	95%
Pneumococcal Vaccine[1]	6	67%	93%	93%
Smoking Cessation Advice[1]	5	80%	97%	97%
Surgical Care Improvement Project				
Appropriate VTP Within 24 Hours[5]	0	-	93%	92%
Appropriate Hair Removal[5]	0	-	100%	99%
Appropriate Beta Blocker Usage[5]	0	-	94%	93%
Controlled Postoperative Blood Glucose[5]	0	-	94%	93%
Prophylactic Antibiotic Timing[5]	0	-	97%	97%
Prophylactic Antibiotic Timing (Outpatient)	-	-	95%	92%
Prophylactic Antibiotic Selection[5]	0	-	97%	97%
Prophylactic Antibiotic Select. (Outpatient)	-	-	95%	94%
Prophylactic Antibiotic Stopped[5]	0	-	95%	94%
Recommended VTP Ordered[5]	0	-	95%	94%
Urinary Catheter Removal[5]	0	-	88%	90%
Children's Asthma Care				
Received Systemic Corticosteroids	-	-	-	100%
Received Home Management Plan	-	-	-	71%
Received Reliever Medication	-	-	-	100%
Use of Medical Imaging				
Combination Abdominal CT Scan	-	-	0.227	0.191
Combination Chest CT Scan	-	-	0.059	0.054
Follow-up Mammogram/Ultrasound	-	-	7.4%	8.4%
MRI for Low Back Pain	-	-	36%	32.7%
Survey of Patients' Hospital Experiences				
Area Around Room 'Always' Quiet at Night[8]	-	-	-	58%
Doctors 'Always' Communicated Well[8]	-	-	-	80%
Home Recovery Information Given[8]	-	-	-	82%
Hospital Given 9 or 10 on 10 Point Scale[8]	-	-	-	67%
Meds 'Always' Explained Before Given[8]	-	-	-	60%
Nurses 'Always' Communicated Well[8]	-	-	-	76%
Pain 'Always' Well Controlled[8]	-	-	-	69%
Room and Bathroom 'Always' Clean[8]	-	-	-	71%
Timely Help 'Always' Received[8]	-	-	-	64%
Would Definitely Recommend Hospital[8]	-	-	-	69%

Community Hospital Association

26136 US Highway 59 Phone: 660-686-2111
Fairfax, MO 64446 Fax: 660-686-2618
Type: Critical Access Hospitals Emergency Services: Yes
Ownership: Voluntary Non-Profit - Private Beds: 25

Key Personnel:
Chief of Medical Staff. . . . . James Humphrey, MD
Infection Control. . . . . Linda Winkelman, RN
Operating Room. . . . . Betty Goins, RN
Radiology. . . . . Jack Bridges
Ambulatory Care . . . . Betty Goins, RN
Anesthesiology. . . . . Mary Coleman, CRNA
Emergency Room . . . . Teresa Oylear, FNP

Measure	Cases	This Hosp.	State Avg.	U.S. Avg.
Heart Attack Care				
ACE Inhibitor or ARB for LVSD[5]	0	-	96%	96%
Aspirin at Arrival[5]	0	-	99%	99%
Aspirin at Discharge[5]	0	-	99%	98%
Beta Blocker at Discharge[5]	0	-	99%	98%
Fibrinolytic Medication Timing[5]	0	-	27%	55%
PCI Within 90 Minutes of Arrival[5]	0	-	92%	90%
Smoking Cessation Advice[5]	0	-	99%	99%
Chest Pain/Possible Heart Attack Care				
Aspirin at Arrival	-	-	95%	95%
Median Time to ECG (minutes)	-	-	9	8
Median Time to Transfer (minutes)	-	-	64	61
Fibrinolytic Medication Timing	-	-	31%	54%
Heart Failure Care				
ACE Inhibitor or ARB for LVSD[1]	4	25%	94%	94%
Discharge Instructions[1]	7	71%	87%	88%
Evaluation of LVS Function[1]	12	83%	97%	98%
Smoking Cessation Advice	0	-	98%	98%
Pneumonia Care				
Appropriate Initial Antibiotic[1]	16	81%	91%	92%
Blood Culture Timing	0	-	97%	96%
Influenza Vaccine[1]	12	83%	90%	91%
Initial Antibiotic Timing[1]	22	91%	95%	95%
Pneumococcal Vaccine[1]	22	82%	93%	93%
Smoking Cessation Advice[1]	4	75%	97%	97%
Surgical Care Improvement Project				
Appropriate VTP Within 24 Hours[5]	0	-	93%	92%
Appropriate Hair Removal[5]	0	-	100%	99%
Appropriate Beta Blocker Usage[5]	0	-	94%	93%
Controlled Postoperative Blood Glucose[5]	0	-	94%	93%
Prophylactic Antibiotic Timing[5]	0	-	97%	97%
Prophylactic Antibiotic Timing (Outpatient)	-	-	95%	92%
Prophylactic Antibiotic Selection[5]	0	-	97%	97%
Prophylactic Antibiotic Select. (Outpatient)	-	-	95%	94%
Prophylactic Antibiotic Stopped[5]	0	-	95%	94%
Recommended VTP Ordered[5]	0	-	95%	94%
Urinary Catheter Removal[5]	0	-	88%	90%
Children's Asthma Care				
Received Systemic Corticosteroids	-	-	-	100%
Received Home Management Plan	-	-	-	71%
Received Reliever Medication	-	-	-	100%
Use of Medical Imaging				
Combination Abdominal CT Scan	-	-	0.227	0.191
Combination Chest CT Scan	-	-	0.059	0.054
Follow-up Mammogram/Ultrasound	-	-	7.4%	8.4%
MRI for Low Back Pain	-	-	36%	32.7%
Survey of Patients' Hospital Experiences				
Area Around Room 'Always' Quiet at Night[8]	-	-	-	58%
Doctors 'Always' Communicated Well[8]	-	-	-	80%
Home Recovery Information Given[8]	-	-	-	82%
Hospital Given 9 or 10 on 10 Point Scale[8]	-	-	-	67%
Meds 'Always' Explained Before Given[8]	-	-	-	60%
Nurses 'Always' Communicated Well[8]	-	-	-	76%
Pain 'Always' Well Controlled[8]	-	-	-	69%
Room and Bathroom 'Always' Clean[8]	-	-	-	71%
Timely Help 'Always' Received[8]	-	-	-	64%
Would Definitely Recommend Hospital[8]	-	-	-	69%

NOTE: Hospital profiles are in alphabetical order by state, then city, then hospital within the city; Rankings exclude hospitals with less than 25 cases except for patient surveys which excludes hospitals with less than 100 cases; (a) 100–299 cases; (1) The number of cases is too small to be sure how well a hospital is performing; (2) The hospital indicated that the data submitted for this measure were based on a sample of cases; (3) Data was collected during a shorter time period (fewer quarters) than the maximum possible time for this measure; (4) Suppressed for one or more quarters by CMS; (5) No data is available from the hospital for this measure; (6) Fewer than 100 patients completed the HCAHPS survey. Use these rates with caution, as the number of surveys may be too low to reliably assess hospital performance; (7) Survey results are based on less than 12 months of data; (8) Survey results are not available for this reporting period; (9) No or very few patients were eligible for the HCAHPS survey. The scores shown, if any, reflect a very small number of surveys; (10) A state average was not calculated because too few hospitals in the state submitted data; (11) There were discrepancies in the data collection process; Please refer to the User's Guide for a full explanation of data.

Mineral Area Regional Medical Center

1212 Weber Rd
Farmington, MO 63640
URL: www.marmc.org
Phone: 573-756-4581
Fax: 573-756-5834
Type: Acute Care Hospitals
Ownership: Proprietary
Emergency Services: Yes
Beds: 141

Key Personnel:
CEO/President. . . . . Stephen L Crain
Chief of Medical Staff . . . . Henry Steele
Infection Control . . . . Jack Marler
Operating Room . . . . John Spurgin
Quality Assurance . . . . LaDonna Smith
Emergency Room . . . . Beth Skaggs

Measure	Cases	This Hosp.	State Avg.	U.S. Avg.
Heart Attack Care				
ACE Inhibitor or ARB for LVSD	0	-	96%	96%
Aspirin at Arrival[1]	4	100%	99%	99%
Aspirin at Discharge[1]	3	100%	99%	98%
Beta Blocker at Discharge[1]	3	100%	99%	98%
Fibrinolytic Medication Timing	0	-	27%	55%
PCI Within 90 Minutes of Arrival	0	-	92%	90%
Smoking Cessation Advice[1]	1	100%	99%	99%
Chest Pain/Possible Heart Attack Care				
Aspirin at Arrival	90	99%	95%	95%
Median Time to ECG (minutes)	94	7	9	8
Median Time to Transfer (minutes)[1]	6	49	64	61
Fibrinolytic Medication Timing[1]	8	12%	31%	54%
Heart Failure Care				
ACE Inhibitor or ARB for LVSD	25	76%	94%	94%
Discharge Instructions	82	71%	87%	88%
Evaluation of LVS Function	119	95%	97%	98%
Smoking Cessation Advice[1]	23	96%	98%	98%
Pneumonia Care				
Appropriate Initial Antibiotic	112	93%	91%	92%
Blood Culture Timing	125	99%	97%	96%
Influenza Vaccine	94	93%	90%	91%
Initial Antibiotic Timing	139	99%	95%	95%
Pneumococcal Vaccine	103	93%	93%	93%
Smoking Cessation Advice	71	96%	97%	97%
Surgical Care Improvement Project				
Appropriate VTP Within 24 Hours[1,2]	21	95%	93%	92%
Appropriate Hair Removal[2]	72	100%	100%	99%
Appropriate Beta Blocker Usage[2]	28	75%	94%	93%
Controlled Postoperative Blood Glucose[2]	0	-	94%	93%
Prophylactic Antibiotic Timing[2]	40	88%	97%	97%
Prophylactic Antibiotic Timing (Outpatient)	89	83%	95%	92%
Prophylactic Antibiotic Selection[2]	40	92%	97%	97%
Prophylactic Antibiotic Select. (Outpatient)	81	95%	95%	94%
Prophylactic Antibiotic Stopped[2]	38	95%	95%	94%
Recommended VTP Ordered[1,2]	22	91%	95%	94%
Urinary Catheter Removal[1,2]	24	88%	88%	90%
Children's Asthma Care				
Received Systemic Corticosteroids	-	-	-	100%
Received Home Management Plan	-	-	-	71%
Received Reliever Medication	-	-	-	100%
Use of Medical Imaging				
Combination Abdominal CT Scan	277	0.126	0.227	0.191
Combination Chest CT Scan	110	0.064	0.059	0.054
Follow-up Mammogram/Ultrasound	444	4.3%	7.4%	8.4%
MRI for Low Back Pain	98	34.7%	36%	32.7%
Survey of Patients' Hospital Experiences				
Area Around Room 'Always' Quiet at Night	300+	59%	-	58%
Doctors 'Always' Communicated Well	300+	85%	-	80%
Home Recovery Information Given	300+	83%	-	82%
Hospital Given 9 or 10 on 10 Point Scale	300+	62%	-	67%
Meds 'Always' Explained Before Given	300+	57%	-	60%
Nurses 'Always' Communicated Well	300+	75%	-	76%
Pain 'Always' Well Controlled	300+	67%	-	69%
Room and Bathroom 'Always' Clean	300+	72%	-	71%
Timely Help 'Always' Received	300+	62%	-	64%
Would Definitely Recommend Hospital	300+	63%	-	69%

Parkland Health Center

1101 W Liberty
Farmington, MO 63640
E-mail: ssg.2352@bjc.org
URL: www.bjc.org
Phone: 573-431-6005
Fax: 573-760-8171
Type: Acute Care Hospitals
Ownership: Voluntary Non-Profit - Private
Emergency Services: Yes
Beds: 130

Key Personnel:
CEO/President. . . . . Richard Conklin
Chief of Medical Staff . . . . Gary Grix
Quality Assurance . . . . Carol Coulter
Emergency Room . . . . Dana Day
Intensive Care Unit. . . . . Patty Coleman

Measure	Cases	This Hosp.	State Avg.	U.S. Avg.
Heart Attack Care				
ACE Inhibitor or ARB for LVSD[1]	3	100%	96%	96%
Aspirin at Arrival[1]	24	96%	99%	99%
Aspirin at Discharge[1]	13	100%	99%	98%
Beta Blocker at Discharge[1]	12	83%	99%	98%
Fibrinolytic Medication Timing	0	-	27%	55%
PCI Within 90 Minutes of Arrival	0	-	92%	90%
Smoking Cessation Advice[1]	1	100%	99%	99%
Chest Pain/Possible Heart Attack Care				
Aspirin at Arrival	256	97%	95%	95%
Median Time to ECG (minutes)	266	8	9	8
Median Time to Transfer (minutes)	25	54	64	61
Fibrinolytic Medication Timing	0	-	31%	54%
Heart Failure Care				
ACE Inhibitor or ARB for LVSD	32	97%	94%	94%
Discharge Instructions	81	80%	87%	88%
Evaluation of LVS Function	111	100%	97%	98%
Smoking Cessation Advice[1]	23	100%	98%	98%
Pneumonia Care				
Appropriate Initial Antibiotic	102	95%	91%	92%
Blood Culture Timing	139	98%	97%	96%
Influenza Vaccine	101	97%	90%	91%
Initial Antibiotic Timing	148	94%	95%	95%
Pneumococcal Vaccine	122	94%	93%	93%
Smoking Cessation Advice	77	100%	97%	97%
Surgical Care Improvement Project				
Appropriate VTP Within 24 Hours	29	100%	93%	92%
Appropriate Hair Removal	113	100%	100%	99%
Appropriate Beta Blocker Usage	29	76%	94%	93%
Controlled Postoperative Blood Glucose	0	-	94%	93%
Prophylactic Antibiotic Timing	76	97%	97%	97%
Prophylactic Antibiotic Timing (Outpatient)	43	100%	95%	92%
Prophylactic Antibiotic Selection	77	97%	97%	97%
Prophylactic Antibiotic Select. (Outpatient)	44	89%	95%	94%
Prophylactic Antibiotic Stopped	73	96%	95%	94%
Recommended VTP Ordered	29	100%	95%	94%
Urinary Catheter Removal[1]	17	82%	88%	90%
Children's Asthma Care				
Received Systemic Corticosteroids	-	-	-	100%
Received Home Management Plan	-	-	-	71%
Received Reliever Medication	-	-	-	100%
Use of Medical Imaging				
Combination Abdominal CT Scan	852	0.074	0.227	0.191
Combination Chest CT Scan	541	0.126	0.059	0.054
Follow-up Mammogram/Ultrasound	947	5.5%	7.4%	8.4%
MRI for Low Back Pain	174	33.9%	36%	32.7%
Survey of Patients' Hospital Experiences				
Area Around Room 'Always' Quiet at Night	300+	60%	-	58%
Doctors 'Always' Communicated Well	300+	88%	-	80%
Home Recovery Information Given	300+	85%	-	82%
Hospital Given 9 or 10 on 10 Point Scale	300+	78%	-	67%
Meds 'Always' Explained Before Given	300+	74%	-	60%
Nurses 'Always' Communicated Well	300+	86%	-	76%
Pain 'Always' Well Controlled	300+	79%	-	69%
Room and Bathroom 'Always' Clean	300+	74%	-	71%
Timely Help 'Always' Received	300+	78%	-	64%
Would Definitely Recommend Hospital	300+	77%	-	69%

SSM St Clare Health Center

1015 Bowles
Fenton, MO 63026
URL: www.ssmstclare.com
Phone: 636-496-2000
Type: Acute Care Hospitals
Ownership: Voluntary Non-Profit - Church
Emergency Services: Yes
Beds: 180

Key Personnel:
Chair/CEO . . . . Sister Mary Jea Ryan

Measure	Cases	This Hosp.	State Avg.	U.S. Avg.
Heart Attack Care				
ACE Inhibitor or ARB for LVSD	47	94%	96%	96%
Aspirin at Arrival	219	100%	99%	99%
Aspirin at Discharge	263	98%	99%	98%
Beta Blocker at Discharge	245	98%	99%	98%
Fibrinolytic Medication Timing	0	-	27%	55%
PCI Within 90 Minutes of Arrival	45	98%	92%	90%
Smoking Cessation Advice	94	100%	99%	99%
Chest Pain/Possible Heart Attack Care				
Aspirin at Arrival[5]	0	-	95%	95%
Median Time to ECG (minutes)[5]	0	-	9	8
Median Time to Transfer (minutes)[5]	0	-	64	61
Fibrinolytic Medication Timing[5]	0	-	31%	54%
Heart Failure Care				
ACE Inhibitor or ARB for LVSD[2]	95	94%	94%	94%
Discharge Instructions[2]	224	88%	87%	88%
Evaluation of LVS Function[2]	290	100%	97%	98%
Smoking Cessation Advice[2]	51	100%	98%	98%
Pneumonia Care				
Appropriate Initial Antibiotic[2]	111	96%	91%	92%
Blood Culture Timing[2]	122	96%	97%	96%
Influenza Vaccine[2]	77	91%	90%	91%
Initial Antibiotic Timing[2]	143	92%	95%	95%
Pneumococcal Vaccine[2]	131	90%	93%	93%
Smoking Cessation Advice[2]	69	100%	97%	97%
Surgical Care Improvement Project				
Appropriate VTP Within 24 Hours[2]	244	95%	93%	92%
Appropriate Hair Removal[2]	802	100%	100%	99%
Appropriate Beta Blocker Usage[2]	229	99%	94%	93%
Controlled Postoperative Blood Glucose[2]	204	96%	94%	93%
Prophylactic Antibiotic Timing[2]	575	97%	97%	97%
Prophylactic Antibiotic Timing (Outpatient)	516	96%	95%	92%
Prophylactic Antibiotic Selection[2]	585	98%	97%	97%
Prophylactic Antibiotic Select. (Outpatient)	512	97%	95%	94%
Prophylactic Antibiotic Stopped[2]	557	94%	95%	94%
Recommended VTP Ordered[2]	244	97%	95%	94%
Urinary Catheter Removal[2]	189	95%	88%	90%
Children's Asthma Care				
Received Systemic Corticosteroids	-	-	-	100%
Received Home Management Plan	-	-	-	71%
Received Reliever Medication	-	-	-	100%
Use of Medical Imaging				
Combination Abdominal CT Scan	347	0.732	0.227	0.191
Combination Chest CT Scan	231	0.113	0.059	0.054
Follow-up Mammogram/Ultrasound	1,108	7.8%	7.4%	8.4%
MRI for Low Back Pain	68	33.8%	36%	32.7%
Survey of Patients' Hospital Experiences				
Area Around Room 'Always' Quiet at Night	300+	72%	-	58%
Doctors 'Always' Communicated Well	300+	80%	-	80%
Home Recovery Information Given	300+	86%	-	82%
Hospital Given 9 or 10 on 10 Point Scale	300+	78%	-	67%
Meds 'Always' Explained Before Given	300+	60%	-	60%
Nurses 'Always' Communicated Well	300+	78%	-	76%
Pain 'Always' Well Controlled	300+	71%	-	69%
Room and Bathroom 'Always' Clean	300+	78%	-	71%
Timely Help 'Always' Received	300+	63%	-	64%
Would Definitely Recommend Hospital	300+	81%	-	69%

NOTE: Hospital profiles are in alphabetical order by state, then city, then hospital within the city; Rankings exclude hospitals with less than 25 cases except for patient surveys which excludes hospitals with less than 100 cases; (a) 100–299 cases; (1) The number of cases is too small to be sure how well a hospital is performing; (2) The hospital indicated that the data submitted for this measure were based on a sample of cases; (3) Data was collected during a shorter time period (fewer quarters) than the maximum possible time for this measure; (4) Suppressed for one or more quarters by CMS; (5) No data is available from the hospital for this measure; (6) Fewer than 100 patients completed the HCAHPS survey. Use these rates with caution, as the number of surveys may be too low to reliably assess hospital performance; (7) Survey results are based on less than 12 months of data; (8) Survey results are not available for this reporting period; (9) No or very few patients were eligible for the HCAHPS survey. The scores shown, if any, reflect a very small number of surveys; (10) A state average was not calculated because too few hospitals in the state submitted data; (11) There were discrepancies in the data collection process; Please refer to the User's Guide for a full explanation of data.

Christian Hospital Northwest

1225 Graham Road Phone: 314-953-6742
Florissant, MO 63031 Fax: 314-653-4141
URL: www.bjc.org/chnenw.html
Type: Acute Care Hospitals Emergency Services: Yes
Ownership: Voluntary Non-Profit - Private Beds: 223

Key Personnel:
CEO/President. . . . . Paul Macek
Chief of Medical Staff . . . . Steven Hadvina
Operating Room. . . . . Muhammad Yasin
Emergency Room . . . . Sebastian Rueckert
Intensive Care Unit. . . . . John Gloss

Measure	Cases	This Hosp.	State Avg.	U.S. Avg.
Heart Attack Care				
ACE Inhibitor or ARB for LVSD[5]	0	-	96%	96%
Aspirin at Arrival[5]	0	-	99%	99%
Aspirin at Discharge[5]	0	-	99%	98%
Beta Blocker at Discharge[5]	0	-	99%	98%
Fibrinolytic Medication Timing[5]	0	-	27%	55%
PCI Within 90 Minutes of Arrival[5]	0	-	92%	90%
Smoking Cessation Advice[5]	0	-	99%	99%
Chest Pain/Possible Heart Attack Care				
Aspirin at Arrival	322	96%	95%	95%
Median Time to ECG (minutes)	333	9	9	8
Median Time to Transfer (minutes)[1,3]	5	69	64	61
Fibrinolytic Medication Timing	0	-	31%	54%
Heart Failure Care				
ACE Inhibitor or ARB for LVSD[5]	0	-	94%	94%
Discharge Instructions[5]	0	-	87%	88%
Evaluation of LVS Function[5]	0	-	97%	98%
Smoking Cessation Advice[5]	0	-	98%	98%
Pneumonia Care				
Appropriate Initial Antibiotic[5]	0	-	91%	92%
Blood Culture Timing[5]	0	-	97%	96%
Influenza Vaccine[5]	0	-	90%	91%
Initial Antibiotic Timing[5]	0	-	95%	95%
Pneumococcal Vaccine[5]	0	-	93%	93%
Smoking Cessation Advice[5]	0	-	97%	97%
Surgical Care Improvement Project				
Appropriate VTP Within 24 Hours[5]	0	-	93%	92%
Appropriate Hair Removal[5]	0	-	100%	99%
Appropriate Beta Blocker Usage[5]	0	-	94%	93%
Controlled Postoperative Blood Glucose[5]	0	-	94%	93%
Prophylactic Antibiotic Timing[5]	0	-	97%	97%
Prophylactic Antibiotic Timing (Outpatient)[5]	0	-	95%	92%
Prophylactic Antibiotic Selection[5]	0	-	97%	97%
Prophylactic Antibiotic Select. (Outpatient)[5]	0	-	95%	94%
Prophylactic Antibiotic Stopped[5]	0	-	95%	94%
Recommended VTP Ordered[5]	0	-	95%	94%
Urinary Catheter Removal[5]	0	-	88%	90%
Children's Asthma Care				
Received Systemic Corticosteroids	-	-	-	100%
Received Home Management Plan	-	-	-	71%
Received Reliever Medication	-	-	-	100%
Use of Medical Imaging				
Combination Abdominal CT Scan	240	0.438	0.227	0.191
Combination Chest CT Scan	191	0.110	0.059	0.054
Follow-up Mammogram/Ultrasound	861	12.5%	7.4%	8.4%
MRI for Low Back Pain[1]	38	26.3%	36%	32.7%
Survey of Patients' Hospital Experiences				
Area Around Room 'Always' Quiet at Night[9]	-	-	-	58%
Doctors 'Always' Communicated Well[9]	-	-	-	80%
Home Recovery Information Given[9]	-	-	-	82%
Hospital Given 9 or 10 on 10 Point Scale[9]	-	-	-	67%
Meds 'Always' Explained Before Given[9]	-	-	-	60%
Nurses 'Always' Communicated Well[9]	-	-	-	76%
Pain 'Always' Well Controlled[9]	-	-	-	69%
Room and Bathroom 'Always' Clean[9]	-	-	-	71%
Timely Help 'Always' Received[9]	-	-	-	64%
Would Definitely Recommend Hospital[9]	-	-	-	69%

Callaway Community Hospital

10 South Hospital Drive Phone: 573-642-3376
Fulton, MO 65251 Fax: 573-592-6679
URL: www.cchfulton.com
Type: Acute Care Hospitals Emergency Services: Yes
Ownership: Proprietary Beds: 53

Key Personnel:
CEO/President. . . . . John T Graves
Chief of Medical Staff . . . . Michael Wilson, MD
Infection Control. . . . . Terri Herold
Operating Room. . . . . Dilip Parulekar, RN
Quality Assurance . . . . Simone Camp
Radiology. . . . . Alan Hillard
Emergency Room . . . . Riley Selby
Intensive Care Unit. . . . . Martin Parks, RN

Measure	Cases	This Hosp.	State Avg.	U.S. Avg.
Heart Attack Care				
ACE Inhibitor or ARB for LVSD[3]	0	-	96%	96%
Aspirin at Arrival[1,3]	1	100%	99%	99%
Aspirin at Discharge[3]	0	-	99%	98%
Beta Blocker at Discharge[3]	0	-	99%	98%
Fibrinolytic Medication Timing[3]	0	-	27%	55%
PCI Within 90 Minutes of Arrival[3]	0	-	92%	90%
Smoking Cessation Advice[3]	0	-	99%	99%
Chest Pain/Possible Heart Attack Care				
Aspirin at Arrival	75	92%	95%	95%
Median Time to ECG (minutes)	77	8	9	8
Median Time to Transfer (minutes)[1]	5	80	64	61
Fibrinolytic Medication Timing	0	-	31%	54%
Heart Failure Care				
ACE Inhibitor or ARB for LVSD[1]	4	100%	94%	94%
Discharge Instructions[1]	21	86%	87%	88%
Evaluation of LVS Function	32	94%	97%	98%
Smoking Cessation Advice[1]	4	100%	98%	98%
Pneumonia Care				
Appropriate Initial Antibiotic[1]	21	100%	91%	92%
Blood Culture Timing	26	96%	97%	96%
Influenza Vaccine[1]	17	88%	90%	91%
Initial Antibiotic Timing	32	94%	95%	95%
Pneumococcal Vaccine	32	94%	93%	93%
Smoking Cessation Advice[1]	15	100%	97%	97%
Surgical Care Improvement Project				
Appropriate VTP Within 24 Hours[1]	4	75%	93%	92%
Appropriate Hair Removal[1]	10	100%	100%	99%
Appropriate Beta Blocker Usage[1]	5	80%	94%	93%
Controlled Postoperative Blood Glucose	0	-	94%	93%
Prophylactic Antibiotic Timing[1]	5	100%	97%	97%
Prophylactic Antibiotic Timing (Outpatient)[1,3]	2	100%	95%	92%
Prophylactic Antibiotic Selection[1]	5	80%	97%	97%
Prophylactic Antibiotic Select. (Outpatient)[1,3]	2	100%	95%	94%
Prophylactic Antibiotic Stopped[1]	4	75%	95%	94%
Recommended VTP Ordered[1]	4	75%	95%	94%
Urinary Catheter Removal	0	-	88%	90%
Children's Asthma Care				
Received Systemic Corticosteroids	-	-	-	100%
Received Home Management Plan	-	-	-	71%
Received Reliever Medication	-	-	-	100%
Use of Medical Imaging				
Combination Abdominal CT Scan	111	0.784	0.227	0.191
Combination Chest CT Scan	69	0.014	0.059	0.054
Follow-up Mammogram/Ultrasound	264	9.5%	7.4%	8.4%
MRI for Low Back Pain[1]	35	42.9%	36%	32.7%
Survey of Patients' Hospital Experiences				
Area Around Room 'Always' Quiet at Night	(a)	48%	-	58%
Doctors 'Always' Communicated Well	(a)	81%	-	80%
Home Recovery Information Given	(a)	80%	-	82%
Hospital Given 9 or 10 on 10 Point Scale	(a)	58%	-	67%
Meds 'Always' Explained Before Given	(a)	63%	-	60%
Nurses 'Always' Communicated Well	(a)	71%	-	76%
Pain 'Always' Well Controlled	(a)	65%	-	69%
Room and Bathroom 'Always' Clean	(a)	66%	-	71%
Timely Help 'Always' Received	(a)	68%	-	64%
Would Definitely Recommend Hospital	(a)	50%	-	69%

Hannibal Regional Hospital

6000 Hospital Dr Phone: 573-248-1300
Hannibal, MO 63401 Fax: 573-248-5264
E-mail: webmaster@hrhonline.org
URL: www.hrhonline.org
Type: Acute Care Hospitals Emergency Services: Yes
Ownership: Voluntary Non-Profit - Private Beds: 105

Key Personnel:
CEO/President. . . . . John C Grossmeier
Chief of Medical Staff . . . . Sebastian Baginski, MD
Coronary Care . . . . Laura Miller, RN
Infection Control. . . . . Leanna Darnold
Operating Room. . . . . Michael Bukstei, RN
Pediatric Ambulatory Care . . . . . . Patrick Himer, MD
Quality Assurance . . . . David Hevel
Radiology. . . . . Raman Danrad, MD

Measure	Cases	This Hosp.	State Avg.	U.S. Avg.
Heart Attack Care				
ACE Inhibitor or ARB for LVSD[1]	18	89%	96%	96%
Aspirin at Arrival	102	99%	99%	99%
Aspirin at Discharge	97	100%	99%	98%
Beta Blocker at Discharge	96	99%	99%	98%
Fibrinolytic Medication Timing	0	-	27%	55%
PCI Within 90 Minutes of Arrival	35	86%	92%	90%
Smoking Cessation Advice	33	100%	99%	99%
Chest Pain/Possible Heart Attack Care				
Aspirin at Arrival[1]	14	93%	95%	95%
Median Time to ECG (minutes)[1]	15	8	9	8
Median Time to Transfer (minutes)[5]	0	-	64	61
Fibrinolytic Medication Timing[5]	0	-	31%	54%
Heart Failure Care				
ACE Inhibitor or ARB for LVSD	58	91%	94%	94%
Discharge Instructions	129	98%	87%	88%
Evaluation of LVS Function	172	98%	97%	98%
Smoking Cessation Advice	40	100%	98%	98%
Pneumonia Care				
Appropriate Initial Antibiotic	136	90%	91%	92%
Blood Culture Timing	185	95%	97%	96%
Influenza Vaccine	162	77%	90%	91%
Initial Antibiotic Timing	221	95%	95%	95%
Pneumococcal Vaccine	245	94%	93%	93%
Smoking Cessation Advice	97	100%	97%	97%
Surgical Care Improvement Project				
Appropriate VTP Within 24 Hours	152	93%	93%	92%
Appropriate Hair Removal	632	100%	100%	99%
Appropriate Beta Blocker Usage	224	95%	94%	93%
Controlled Postoperative Blood Glucose	0	-	94%	93%
Prophylactic Antibiotic Timing	461	97%	97%	97%
Prophylactic Antibiotic Timing (Outpatient)	89	91%	95%	92%
Prophylactic Antibiotic Selection	460	97%	97%	97%
Prophylactic Antibiotic Select. (Outpatient)	86	95%	95%	94%
Prophylactic Antibiotic Stopped	457	96%	95%	94%
Recommended VTP Ordered	152	97%	95%	94%
Urinary Catheter Removal	32	53%	88%	90%
Children's Asthma Care				
Received Systemic Corticosteroids	-	-	-	100%
Received Home Management Plan	-	-	-	71%
Received Reliever Medication	-	-	-	100%
Use of Medical Imaging				
Combination Abdominal CT Scan	245	0.653	0.227	0.191
Combination Chest CT Scan	143	0.133	0.059	0.054
Follow-up Mammogram/Ultrasound	174	12.1%	7.4%	8.4%
MRI for Low Back Pain	108	31.5%	36%	32.7%
Survey of Patients' Hospital Experiences				
Area Around Room 'Always' Quiet at Night	300+	53%	-	58%
Doctors 'Always' Communicated Well	300+	83%	-	80%
Home Recovery Information Given	300+	87%	-	82%
Hospital Given 9 or 10 on 10 Point Scale	300+	74%	-	67%
Meds 'Always' Explained Before Given	300+	62%	-	60%
Nurses 'Always' Communicated Well	300+	81%	-	76%
Pain 'Always' Well Controlled	300+	70%	-	69%
Room and Bathroom 'Always' Clean	300+	70%	-	71%
Timely Help 'Always' Received	300+	68%	-	64%
Would Definitely Recommend Hospital	300+	71%	-	69%

NOTE: Hospital profiles are in alphabetical order by state, then city, then hospital within the city; Rankings exclude hospitals with less than 25 cases except for patient surveys which excludes hospitals with less than 100 cases; (a) 100–299 cases; (1) The number of cases is too small to be sure how well a hospital is performing; (2) The hospital indicated that the data submitted for this measure were based on a sample of cases; (3) Data was collected during a shorter time period (fewer quarters) than the maximum possible time for this measure; (4) Suppressed for one or more quarters by CMS; (5) No data is available from the hospital for this measure; (6) Fewer than 100 patients completed the HCAHPS survey. Use these rates with caution, as the number of surveys may be too low to reliably assess hospital performance; (7) Survey results are based on less than 12 months of data; (8) Survey results are not available for this reporting period; (9) No or very few patients were eligible for the HCAHPS survey. The scores shown, if any, reflect a very small number of surveys; (10) A state average was not calculated because too few hospitals in the state submitted data; (11) There were discrepancies in the data collection process; Please refer to the User's Guide for a full explanation of data.

Cass Medical Center

2800 E Rock Haven Road
Harrisonville, MO 64701
URL: www.cassregional.org
Type: Critical Access Hospitals
Ownership: Government - Local

Phone: 816-380-5888
Fax: 816-380-4639
Emergency Services: Yes
Beds: 49

Key Personnel:
CEO/President. . . . . Chris Lang
Chief of Medical Staff. . . . . Christopher D Maxwell
Infection Control. . . . . Melinda Flanner
Operating Room. . . . . Linda Dawson, RN
Quality Assurance . . . . Kendra McClellan, RN BSN
Radiology. . . . . Ellen Clements, ARRT
Emergency Room . . . . Violet Warren
Intensive Care Unit. . . . . Jill Slade, RN CCRN

Measure	Cases	This Hosp.	State Avg.	U.S. Avg.
Heart Attack Care				
ACE Inhibitor or ARB for LVSD[1]	1	100%	96%	96%
Aspirin at Arrival[1]	4	75%	99%	99%
Aspirin at Discharge[1]	3	100%	99%	98%
Beta Blocker at Discharge[1]	3	67%	99%	98%
Fibrinolytic Medication Timing	0	-	27%	55%
PCI Within 90 Minutes of Arrival	0	-	92%	90%
Smoking Cessation Advice	0	-	99%	99%
Chest Pain/Possible Heart Attack Care				
Aspirin at Arrival	-	-	95%	95%
Median Time to ECG (minutes)	-	-	9	8
Median Time to Transfer (minutes)	-	-	64	61
Fibrinolytic Medication Timing	-	-	31%	54%
Heart Failure Care				
ACE Inhibitor or ARB for LVSD[1]	16	69%	94%	94%
Discharge Instructions	40	75%	87%	88%
Evaluation of LVS Function	50	92%	97%	98%
Smoking Cessation Advice[1]	6	83%	98%	98%
Pneumonia Care				
Appropriate Initial Antibiotic	59	88%	91%	92%
Blood Culture Timing	59	98%	97%	96%
Influenza Vaccine	49	84%	90%	91%
Initial Antibiotic Timing	86	99%	95%	95%
Pneumococcal Vaccine	64	95%	93%	93%
Smoking Cessation Advice	37	97%	97%	97%
Surgical Care Improvement Project				
Appropriate VTP Within 24 Hours	33	88%	93%	92%
Appropriate Hair Removal	64	95%	100%	99%
Appropriate Beta Blocker Usage[1]	9	78%	94%	93%
Controlled Postoperative Blood Glucose	0	-	94%	93%
Prophylactic Antibiotic Timing	50	92%	97%	97%
Prophylactic Antibiotic Timing (Outpatient)	-	-	95%	92%
Prophylactic Antibiotic Selection	50	96%	97%	97%
Prophylactic Antibiotic Select. (Outpatient)	-	-	95%	94%
Prophylactic Antibiotic Stopped	49	88%	95%	94%
Recommended VTP Ordered	33	88%	95%	94%
Urinary Catheter Removal[1]	22	91%	88%	90%
Children's Asthma Care				
Received Systemic Corticosteroids	-	-	-	100%
Received Home Management Plan	-	-	-	71%
Received Reliever Medication	-	-	-	100%
Use of Medical Imaging				
Combination Abdominal CT Scan	-	-	0.227	0.191
Combination Chest CT Scan	-	-	0.059	0.054
Follow-up Mammogram/Ultrasound	-	-	7.4%	8.4%
MRI for Low Back Pain	-	-	36%	32.7%
Survey of Patients' Hospital Experiences				
Area Around Room 'Always' Quiet at Night[8]	-	-	-	58%
Doctors 'Always' Communicated Well[8]	-	-	-	80%
Home Recovery Information Given[8]	-	-	-	82%
Hospital Given 9 or 10 on 10 Point Scale[8]	-	-	-	67%
Meds 'Always' Explained Before Given[8]	-	-	-	60%
Nurses 'Always' Communicated Well[8]	-	-	-	76%
Pain 'Always' Well Controlled[8]	-	-	-	69%
Room and Bathroom 'Always' Clean[8]	-	-	-	71%
Timely Help 'Always' Received[8]	-	-	-	64%
Would Definitely Recommend Hospital[8]	-	-	-	69%

Pemiscot Memorial Hospital

Hwy 61 and E Reed
Hayti, MO 63851
Type: Acute Care Hospitals
Ownership: Voluntary Non-Profit - Other

Phone: 573-359-1372
Fax: 573-359-3601
Emergency Services: Yes
Beds: 245

Key Personnel:
Chief of Medical Staff. . . . . Jafer Gheraibeh, MD
Infection Control. . . . . Micky Wilkerson, RN
Quality Assurance . . . . Donna Sanders

Measure	Cases	This Hosp.	State Avg.	U.S. Avg.
Heart Attack Care				
ACE Inhibitor or ARB for LVSD[1]	1	0%	96%	96%
Aspirin at Arrival[1]	10	70%	99%	99%
Aspirin at Discharge[1]	7	14%	99%	98%
Beta Blocker at Discharge[1]	7	29%	99%	98%
Fibrinolytic Medication Timing	0	-	27%	55%
PCI Within 90 Minutes of Arrival	0	-	92%	90%
Smoking Cessation Advice[1]	2	0%	99%	99%
Chest Pain/Possible Heart Attack Care				
Aspirin at Arrival[1]	17	100%	95%	95%
Median Time to ECG (minutes)[1]	17	30	9	8
Median Time to Transfer (minutes)[5]	0	-	64	61
Fibrinolytic Medication Timing[1]	6	33%	31%	54%
Heart Failure Care				
ACE Inhibitor or ARB for LVSD[1]	21	48%	94%	94%
Discharge Instructions	115	16%	87%	88%
Evaluation of LVS Function	137	62%	97%	98%
Smoking Cessation Advice	36	61%	98%	98%
Pneumonia Care				
Appropriate Initial Antibiotic	37	76%	91%	92%
Blood Culture Timing[1]	17	94%	97%	96%
Influenza Vaccine	29	48%	90%	91%
Initial Antibiotic Timing	43	72%	95%	95%
Pneumococcal Vaccine[1]	23	43%	93%	93%
Smoking Cessation Advice[1]	22	55%	97%	97%
Surgical Care Improvement Project				
Appropriate VTP Within 24 Hours[1]	18	61%	93%	92%
Appropriate Hair Removal[1]	19	16%	100%	99%
Appropriate Beta Blocker Usage[1]	4	75%	94%	93%
Controlled Postoperative Blood Glucose	0	-	94%	93%
Prophylactic Antibiotic Timing[1]	6	17%	97%	97%
Prophylactic Antibiotic Timing (Outpatient)[1]	10	50%	95%	92%
Prophylactic Antibiotic Selection[1]	4	25%	97%	97%
Prophylactic Antibiotic Select. (Outpatient)[1]	9	67%	95%	94%
Prophylactic Antibiotic Stopped[1]	4	100%	95%	94%
Recommended VTP Ordered[1]	18	67%	95%	94%
Urinary Catheter Removal[1]	2	50%	88%	90%
Children's Asthma Care				
Received Systemic Corticosteroids	-	-	-	100%
Received Home Management Plan	-	-	-	71%
Received Reliever Medication	-	-	-	100%
Use of Medical Imaging				
Combination Abdominal CT Scan	290	0.100	0.227	0.191
Combination Chest CT Scan	105	0.114	0.059	0.054
Follow-up Mammogram/Ultrasound	251	2.8%	7.4%	8.4%
MRI for Low Back Pain[1]	40	35.0%	36%	32.7%
Survey of Patients' Hospital Experiences				
Area Around Room 'Always' Quiet at Night	300+	46%	-	58%
Doctors 'Always' Communicated Well	300+	82%	-	80%
Home Recovery Information Given	300+	62%	-	82%
Hospital Given 9 or 10 on 10 Point Scale	300+	40%	-	67%
Meds 'Always' Explained Before Given	300+	47%	-	60%
Nurses 'Always' Communicated Well	300+	60%	-	76%
Pain 'Always' Well Controlled	300+	56%	-	69%
Room and Bathroom 'Always' Clean	300+	57%	-	71%
Timely Help 'Always' Received	300+	48%	-	64%
Would Definitely Recommend Hospital	300+	40%	-	69%

Hermann Area District Hospital

509 W 18th St
Hermann, MO 65041
E-mail: hadh@ktif.net
URL: www.hadh.org
Type: Critical Access Hospitals
Ownership: Govt - Hospital Dist/Auth

Phone: 573-486-2191
Fax: 573-486-3743
Emergency Services: Yes
Beds: 44

Key Personnel:
Chief of Medical Staff. . . . . Robert E Henson
Infection Control. . . . . James T Shaw, MD
Operating Room. . . . . David Weston, MD
Pediatric In-Patient Care . . . . Michael W Mahoney, DO
Quality Assurance . . . . Holly Bloch, LPN
Radiology. . . . . Matthew Siebert, MD
Anesthesiology. . . . . Robert E Henson, D.O.
Emergency Room . . . . James W Keith, DO

Measure	Cases	This Hosp.	State Avg.	U.S. Avg.
Heart Attack Care				
ACE Inhibitor or ARB for LVSD[5]	0	-	96%	96%
Aspirin at Arrival[5]	0	-	99%	99%
Aspirin at Discharge[5]	0	-	99%	98%
Beta Blocker at Discharge[5]	0	-	99%	98%
Fibrinolytic Medication Timing[5]	0	-	27%	55%
PCI Within 90 Minutes of Arrival[5]	0	-	92%	90%
Smoking Cessation Advice[5]	0	-	99%	99%
Chest Pain/Possible Heart Attack Care				
Aspirin at Arrival	-	-	95%	95%
Median Time to ECG (minutes)	-	-	9	8
Median Time to Transfer (minutes)	-	-	64	61
Fibrinolytic Medication Timing	-	-	31%	54%
Heart Failure Care				
ACE Inhibitor or ARB for LVSD	0	-	94%	94%
Discharge Instructions[1]	7	29%	87%	88%
Evaluation of LVS Function[1]	20	65%	97%	98%
Smoking Cessation Advice	0	-	98%	98%
Pneumonia Care				
Appropriate Initial Antibiotic[1]	17	94%	91%	92%
Blood Culture Timing[1]	10	90%	97%	96%
Influenza Vaccine[1]	17	53%	90%	91%
Initial Antibiotic Timing	28	93%	95%	95%
Pneumococcal Vaccine[1]	24	46%	93%	93%
Smoking Cessation Advice[1]	11	100%	97%	97%
Surgical Care Improvement Project				
Appropriate VTP Within 24 Hours[5]	0	-	93%	92%
Appropriate Hair Removal[5]	0	-	100%	99%
Appropriate Beta Blocker Usage[5]	0	-	94%	93%
Controlled Postoperative Blood Glucose[5]	0	-	94%	93%
Prophylactic Antibiotic Timing[5]	0	-	97%	97%
Prophylactic Antibiotic Timing (Outpatient)	-	-	95%	92%
Prophylactic Antibiotic Selection[5]	0	-	97%	97%
Prophylactic Antibiotic Select. (Outpatient)	-	-	95%	94%
Prophylactic Antibiotic Stopped[5]	0	-	95%	94%
Recommended VTP Ordered[5]	0	-	95%	94%
Urinary Catheter Removal[5]	0	-	88%	90%
Children's Asthma Care				
Received Systemic Corticosteroids	-	-	-	100%
Received Home Management Plan	-	-	-	71%
Received Reliever Medication	-	-	-	100%
Use of Medical Imaging				
Combination Abdominal CT Scan	-	-	0.227	0.191
Combination Chest CT Scan	-	-	0.059	0.054
Follow-up Mammogram/Ultrasound	-	-	7.4%	8.4%
MRI for Low Back Pain	-	-	36%	32.7%
Survey of Patients' Hospital Experiences				
Area Around Room 'Always' Quiet at Night[8]	-	-	-	58%
Doctors 'Always' Communicated Well[8]	-	-	-	80%
Home Recovery Information Given[8]	-	-	-	82%
Hospital Given 9 or 10 on 10 Point Scale[8]	-	-	-	67%
Meds 'Always' Explained Before Given[8]	-	-	-	60%
Nurses 'Always' Communicated Well[8]	-	-	-	76%
Pain 'Always' Well Controlled[8]	-	-	-	69%
Room and Bathroom 'Always' Clean[8]	-	-	-	71%
Timely Help 'Always' Received[8]	-	-	-	64%
Would Definitely Recommend Hospital[8]	-	-	-	69%

NOTE: Hospital profiles are in alphabetical order by state, then city, then hospital within the city; Rankings exclude hospitals with less than 25 cases except for patient surveys which excludes hospitals with less than 100 cases; (a) 100–299 cases; (1) The number of cases is too small to be sure how well a hospital is performing; (2) The hospital indicated that the data submitted for this measure were based on a sample of cases; (3) Data was collected during a shorter time period (fewer quarters) than the maximum possible time for this measure; (4) Suppressed for one or more quarters by CMS; (5) No data is available from the hospital for this measure; (6) Fewer than 100 patients completed the HCAHPS survey. Use these rates with caution, as the number of surveys may be too low to reliably assess hospital performance; (7) Survey results are based on less than 12 months of data; (8) Survey results are not available for this reporting period; (9) No or very few patients were eligible for the HCAHPS survey. The scores shown, if any, reflect a very small number of surveys; (10) A state average was not calculated because too few hospitals in the state submitted data; (11) There were discrepancies in the data collection process; Please refer to the User's Guide for a full explanation of data.

Texas County Memorial Hospital

1333 Sam Houston Boulevard Phone: 417-967-3311
Houston, MO 65483 Fax: 417-967-1234
URL: www.tcmh.org
Type: Acute Care Hospitals Emergency Services: Yes
Ownership: Voluntary Non-Profit - Other Beds: 66

Key Personnel:
CEO/President. . . . . Wes Murray
Chief of Medical Staff. . . . . Charles Mueller, MD
Infection Control. . . . . Tasaduq Fazili, MD
Operating Room. . . . . Charles Mueller, RN
Emergency Room . . . . Mary Barnes

Measure	Cases	This Hosp.	State Avg.	U.S. Avg.
Heart Attack Care				
ACE Inhibitor or ARB for LVSD[1]	2	100%	96%	96%
Aspirin at Arrival[1]	10	90%	99%	99%
Aspirin at Discharge[1]	8	88%	99%	98%
Beta Blocker at Discharge[1]	9	100%	99%	98%
Fibrinolytic Medication Timing	0	-	27%	55%
PCI Within 90 Minutes of Arrival	0	-	92%	90%
Smoking Cessation Advice	0	-	99%	99%
Chest Pain/Possible Heart Attack Care				
Aspirin at Arrival	106	96%	95%	95%
Median Time to ECG (minutes)	114	14	9	8
Median Time to Transfer (minutes)[3]	0	-	64	61
Fibrinolytic Medication Timing[1]	7	43%	31%	54%
Heart Failure Care				
ACE Inhibitor or ARB for LVSD[1]	10	90%	94%	94%
Discharge Instructions[1]	24	75%	87%	88%
Evaluation of LVS Function	30	73%	97%	98%
Smoking Cessation Advice[1]	3	67%	98%	98%
Pneumonia Care				
Appropriate Initial Antibiotic	76	76%	91%	92%
Blood Culture Timing	85	96%	97%	96%
Influenza Vaccine	62	82%	90%	91%
Initial Antibiotic Timing	101	95%	95%	95%
Pneumococcal Vaccine	88	81%	93%	93%
Smoking Cessation Advice	27	96%	97%	97%
Surgical Care Improvement Project				
Appropriate VTP Within 24 Hours[1,3]	3	100%	93%	92%
Appropriate Hair Removal[1,3]	9	100%	100%	99%
Appropriate Beta Blocker Usage[1,3]	3	67%	94%	93%
Controlled Postoperative Blood Glucose[3]	0	-	94%	93%
Prophylactic Antibiotic Timing[1,3]	3	33%	97%	97%
Prophylactic Antibiotic Timing (Outpatient)[5]	0	-	95%	92%
Prophylactic Antibiotic Selection[1,3]	2	100%	97%	97%
Prophylactic Antibiotic Select. (Outpatient)[5]	0	-	95%	94%
Prophylactic Antibiotic Stopped[1,3]	2	0%	95%	94%
Recommended VTP Ordered[1,3]	3	100%	95%	94%
Urinary Catheter Removal[5]	0	-	88%	90%
Children's Asthma Care				
Received Systemic Corticosteroids	-	-	-	100%
Received Home Management Plan	-	-	-	71%
Received Reliever Medication	-	-	-	100%
Use of Medical Imaging				
Combination Abdominal CT Scan	227	0.123	0.227	0.191
Combination Chest CT Scan	137	0.066	0.059	0.054
Follow-up Mammogram/Ultrasound	396	4.3%	7.4%	8.4%
MRI for Low Back Pain[1]	22	45.5%	36%	32.7%
Survey of Patients' Hospital Experiences				
Area Around Room 'Always' Quiet at Night	300+	53%	-	58%
Doctors 'Always' Communicated Well	300+	79%	-	80%
Home Recovery Information Given	300+	81%	-	82%
Hospital Given 9 or 10 on 10 Point Scale	300+	59%	-	67%
Meds 'Always' Explained Before Given	300+	59%	-	60%
Nurses 'Always' Communicated Well	300+	72%	-	76%
Pain 'Always' Well Controlled	300+	62%	-	69%
Room and Bathroom 'Always' Clean	300+	82%	-	71%
Timely Help 'Always' Received	300+	59%	-	64%
Would Definitely Recommend Hospital	300+	55%	-	69%

Centerpoint Medical Center of Independence

19600 East 39th Street Phone: 816-698-7000
Independence, MO 64057
Type: Acute Care Hospitals Emergency Services: Yes
Ownership: Voluntary Non-Profit - Private

Key Personnel:
CEO/President. . . . . Carolyn Caldwell
Operating Room. . . . . Pascal Spehar
Radiology. . . . . Linda Dunaway

Measure	Cases	This Hosp.	State Avg.	U.S. Avg.
Heart Attack Care				
ACE Inhibitor or ARB for LVSD	54	100%	96%	96%
Aspirin at Arrival	313	100%	99%	99%
Aspirin at Discharge	323	100%	99%	98%
Beta Blocker at Discharge	292	99%	99%	98%
Fibrinolytic Medication Timing	0	-	27%	55%
PCI Within 90 Minutes of Arrival	68	93%	92%	90%
Smoking Cessation Advice	117	100%	99%	99%
Chest Pain/Possible Heart Attack Care				
Aspirin at Arrival[1,3]	4	100%	95%	95%
Median Time to ECG (minutes)[1,3]	4	8	9	8
Median Time to Transfer (minutes)[5]	0	-	64	61
Fibrinolytic Medication Timing[5]	0	-	31%	54%
Heart Failure Care				
ACE Inhibitor or ARB for LVSD	122	100%	94%	94%
Discharge Instructions	325	96%	87%	88%
Evaluation of LVS Function	424	100%	97%	98%
Smoking Cessation Advice	93	100%	98%	98%
Pneumonia Care				
Appropriate Initial Antibiotic	194	92%	91%	92%
Blood Culture Timing	329	99%	97%	96%
Influenza Vaccine	189	97%	90%	91%
Initial Antibiotic Timing	304	98%	95%	95%
Pneumococcal Vaccine	249	98%	93%	93%
Smoking Cessation Advice	117	100%	97%	97%
Surgical Care Improvement Project				
Appropriate VTP Within 24 Hours[2]	233	92%	93%	92%
Appropriate Hair Removal[2]	621	100%	100%	99%
Appropriate Beta Blocker Usage[2]	159	99%	94%	93%
Controlled Postoperative Blood Glucose[2]	110	99%	94%	93%
Prophylactic Antibiotic Timing[2]	414	100%	97%	97%
Prophylactic Antibiotic Timing (Outpatient)	531	99%	95%	92%
Prophylactic Antibiotic Selection[2]	421	99%	97%	97%
Prophylactic Antibiotic Select. (Outpatient)	529	99%	95%	94%
Prophylactic Antibiotic Stopped[2]	398	95%	95%	94%
Recommended VTP Ordered[2]	234	96%	95%	94%
Urinary Catheter Removal[2]	75	97%	88%	90%
Children's Asthma Care				
Received Systemic Corticosteroids	-	-	-	100%
Received Home Management Plan	-	-	-	71%
Received Reliever Medication	-	-	-	100%
Use of Medical Imaging				
Combination Abdominal CT Scan	539	0.050	0.227	0.191
Combination Chest CT Scan	288	0.010	0.059	0.054
Follow-up Mammogram/Ultrasound	1,273	6.2%	7.4%	8.4%
MRI for Low Back Pain	104	31.7%	36%	32.7%
Survey of Patients' Hospital Experiences				
Area Around Room 'Always' Quiet at Night	300+	66%	-	58%
Doctors 'Always' Communicated Well	300+	78%	-	80%
Home Recovery Information Given	300+	88%	-	82%
Hospital Given 9 or 10 on 10 Point Scale	300+	68%	-	67%
Meds 'Always' Explained Before Given	300+	58%	-	60%
Nurses 'Always' Communicated Well	300+	75%	-	76%
Pain 'Always' Well Controlled	300+	70%	-	69%
Room and Bathroom 'Always' Clean	300+	69%	-	71%
Timely Help 'Always' Received	300+	62%	-	64%
Would Definitely Recommend Hospital	300+	68%	-	69%

Capital Region Medical Center

1125 Madison St Phone: 573-632-5000
Jefferson City, MO 65102 Fax: 573-632-5880
E-mail: info@mail.crmc.org
URL: www.crmc.org
Type: Acute Care Hospitals Emergency Services: Yes
Ownership: Voluntary Non-Profit - Private Beds: 114

Key Personnel:
CEO/President. . . . . Ed Farnsworth
Chief of Medical Staff. . . . . Jake Tomblinson
Operating Room. . . . . Chris Medlin
Quality Assurance . . . . Janet Weckenborg
Radiology. . . . . Mitchell Godbee
Patient Relations . . . . Joyce Corman

Measure	Cases	This Hosp.	State Avg.	U.S. Avg.
Heart Attack Care				
ACE Inhibitor or ARB for LVSD	27	100%	96%	96%
Aspirin at Arrival	143	100%	99%	99%
Aspirin at Discharge	137	99%	99%	98%
Beta Blocker at Discharge	132	98%	99%	98%
Fibrinolytic Medication Timing	0	-	27%	55%
PCI Within 90 Minutes of Arrival	25	100%	92%	90%
Smoking Cessation Advice	41	100%	99%	99%
Chest Pain/Possible Heart Attack Care				
Aspirin at Arrival[1,3]	11	73%	95%	95%
Median Time to ECG (minutes)[1,3]	11	1	9	8
Median Time to Transfer (minutes)[5]	0	-	64	61
Fibrinolytic Medication Timing[3]	0	-	31%	54%
Heart Failure Care				
ACE Inhibitor or ARB for LVSD	70	100%	94%	94%
Discharge Instructions	176	94%	87%	88%
Evaluation of LVS Function	225	100%	97%	98%
Smoking Cessation Advice	33	100%	98%	98%
Pneumonia Care				
Appropriate Initial Antibiotic[2]	89	89%	91%	92%
Blood Culture Timing[2]	141	99%	97%	96%
Influenza Vaccine[2]	115	100%	90%	91%
Initial Antibiotic Timing[2]	148	96%	95%	95%
Pneumococcal Vaccine[2]	142	99%	93%	93%
Smoking Cessation Advice[2]	60	100%	97%	97%
Surgical Care Improvement Project				
Appropriate VTP Within 24 Hours[2]	158	96%	93%	92%
Appropriate Hair Removal[2]	545	100%	100%	99%
Appropriate Beta Blocker Usage[2]	179	97%	94%	93%
Controlled Postoperative Blood Glucose[2]	86	92%	94%	93%
Prophylactic Antibiotic Timing[2]	373	98%	97%	97%
Prophylactic Antibiotic Timing (Outpatient)	258	97%	95%	92%
Prophylactic Antibiotic Selection[2]	377	97%	97%	97%
Prophylactic Antibiotic Select. (Outpatient)	254	94%	95%	94%
Prophylactic Antibiotic Stopped[2]	359	97%	95%	94%
Recommended VTP Ordered[2]	158	99%	95%	94%
Urinary Catheter Removal[2]	148	95%	88%	90%
Children's Asthma Care				
Received Systemic Corticosteroids	-	-	-	100%
Received Home Management Plan	-	-	-	71%
Received Reliever Medication	-	-	-	100%
Use of Medical Imaging				
Combination Abdominal CT Scan	802	0.409	0.227	0.191
Combination Chest CT Scan	695	0.056	0.059	0.054
Follow-up Mammogram/Ultrasound	1,083	13.9%	7.4%	8.4%
MRI for Low Back Pain	297	47.5%	36%	32.7%
Survey of Patients' Hospital Experiences				
Area Around Room 'Always' Quiet at Night	300+	62%	-	58%
Doctors 'Always' Communicated Well	300+	82%	-	80%
Home Recovery Information Given	300+	82%	-	82%
Hospital Given 9 or 10 on 10 Point Scale	300+	77%	-	67%
Meds 'Always' Explained Before Given	300+	59%	-	60%
Nurses 'Always' Communicated Well	300+	80%	-	76%
Pain 'Always' Well Controlled	300+	72%	-	69%
Room and Bathroom 'Always' Clean	300+	76%	-	71%
Timely Help 'Always' Received	300+	66%	-	64%
Would Definitely Recommend Hospital	300+	81%	-	69%

NOTE: Hospital profiles are in alphabetical order by state, then city, then hospital within the city; Rankings exclude hospitals with less than 25 cases except for patient surveys which excludes hospitals with less than 100 cases; (a) 100–299 cases; (1) The number of cases is too small to be sure how well a hospital is performing; (2) The hospital indicated that the data submitted for this measure were based on a sample of cases; (3) Data was collected during a shorter time period (fewer quarters) than the maximum possible time for this measure; (4) Suppressed for one or more quarters by CMS; (5) No data is available from the hospital for this measure; (6) Fewer than 100 patients completed the HCAHPS survey. Use these rates with caution, as the number of surveys may be too low to reliably assess hospital performance; (7) Survey results are based on less than 12 months of data; (8) Survey results are not available for this reporting period; (9) No or very few patients were eligible for the HCAHPS survey. The scores shown, if any, reflect a very small number of surveys; (10) A state average was not calculated because too few hospitals in the state submitted data; (11) There were discrepancies in the data collection process; Please refer to the User's Guide for a full explanation of data.

Saint Marys Health Center

100 St Marys Medical Plaza — Phone: 573-761-7000
Jefferson City, MO 65101 — Fax: 573-636-5733
URL: www.stmarys-jeffcity.com
Type: Acute Care Hospitals — Emergency Services: Yes
Ownership: Proprietary — Beds: 167

Key Personnel:
CEO/President. . . . . Elizabeth Aderholdt
Chief of Medical Staff. . . . . John Lucia
Coronary Care. . . . . Gwen Douglas
Infection Control. . . . . Kathy Kormann
Pediatric Ambulatory Care . . . . . . Barb Woods
Pediatric In-Patient Care . . . . Chris Brandel
Quality Assurance . . . . Jan Zimmerman
Radiology. . . . . Ralph Buettner

Measure	Cases	This Hosp.	State Avg.	U.S. Avg.
Heart Attack Care				
ACE Inhibitor or ARB for LVSD[1]	20	100%	96%	96%
Aspirin at Arrival	119	100%	99%	99%
Aspirin at Discharge	114	100%	99%	98%
Beta Blocker at Discharge	115	100%	99%	98%
Fibrinolytic Medication Timing	0	-	27%	55%
PCI Within 90 Minutes of Arrival	27	100%	92%	90%
Smoking Cessation Advice	38	100%	99%	99%
Chest Pain/Possible Heart Attack Care				
Aspirin at Arrival[1]	15	100%	95%	95%
Median Time to ECG (minutes)[1]	15	4	9	8
Median Time to Transfer (minutes)[5]	0	-	64	61
Fibrinolytic Medication Timing[5]	0	-	31%	54%
Heart Failure Care				
ACE Inhibitor or ARB for LVSD	62	100%	94%	94%
Discharge Instructions	155	100%	87%	88%
Evaluation of LVS Function	184	100%	97%	98%
Smoking Cessation Advice[1]	23	100%	98%	98%
Pneumonia Care				
Appropriate Initial Antibiotic	66	98%	91%	92%
Blood Culture Timing	174	100%	97%	96%
Influenza Vaccine	133	100%	90%	91%
Initial Antibiotic Timing	212	100%	95%	95%
Pneumococcal Vaccine	152	100%	93%	93%
Smoking Cessation Advice	85	100%	97%	97%
Surgical Care Improvement Project				
Appropriate VTP Within 24 Hours	186	100%	93%	92%
Appropriate Hair Removal	589	100%	100%	99%
Appropriate Beta Blocker Usage	161	100%	94%	93%
Controlled Postoperative Blood Glucose	66	100%	94%	93%
Prophylactic Antibiotic Timing	384	100%	97%	97%
Prophylactic Antibiotic Timing (Outpatient)	314	100%	95%	92%
Prophylactic Antibiotic Selection	388	100%	97%	97%
Prophylactic Antibiotic Select. (Outpatient)	314	99%	95%	94%
Prophylactic Antibiotic Stopped	370	100%	95%	94%
Recommended VTP Ordered	186	100%	95%	94%
Urinary Catheter Removal	73	100%	88%	90%
Children's Asthma Care				
Received Systemic Corticosteroids	-	-	-	100%
Received Home Management Plan	-	-	-	71%
Received Reliever Medication	-	-	-	100%
Use of Medical Imaging				
Combination Abdominal CT Scan	317	0.164	0.227	0.191
Combination Chest CT Scan	184	0.005	0.059	0.054
Follow-up Mammogram/Ultrasound	910	12.6%	7.4%	8.4%
MRI for Low Back Pain	131	38.9%	36%	32.7%
Survey of Patients' Hospital Experiences				
Area Around Room 'Always' Quiet at Night	300+	59%	-	58%
Doctors 'Always' Communicated Well	300+	84%	-	80%
Home Recovery Information Given	300+	84%	-	82%
Hospital Given 9 or 10 on 10 Point Scale	300+	76%	-	67%
Meds 'Always' Explained Before Given	300+	62%	-	60%
Nurses 'Always' Communicated Well	300+	84%	-	76%
Pain 'Always' Well Controlled	300+	75%	-	69%
Room and Bathroom 'Always' Clean	300+	77%	-	71%
Timely Help 'Always' Received	300+	67%	-	64%
Would Definitely Recommend Hospital	300+	80%	-	69%

Freeman Health System - Freeman West

1102 West 32nd Street — Phone: 417-347-1111
Joplin, MO 64804 — Fax: 417-647-3716
Type: Acute Care Hospitals — Emergency Services: Yes
Ownership: Voluntary Non-Profit - Other — Beds: 203

Key Personnel:
Chief of Medical Staff. . . . . Christopher Andrew, MD
Infection Control. . . . . Madonna Briley
Operating Room. . . . . Patti Boman, RN
Pediatric Ambulatory Care . . . . . . Denise Hamar, DO
Pediatric In-Patient Care . . . . Denise Hamar, DO
Quality Assurance . . . . Kathy Schurman
Radiology. . . . . Mark E Franham

Measure	Cases	This Hosp.	State Avg.	U.S. Avg.
Heart Attack Care				
ACE Inhibitor or ARB for LVSD	51	100%	96%	96%
Aspirin at Arrival	205	100%	99%	99%
Aspirin at Discharge	371	99%	99%	98%
Beta Blocker at Discharge	312	98%	99%	98%
Fibrinolytic Medication Timing	0	-	27%	55%
PCI Within 90 Minutes of Arrival	52	85%	92%	90%
Smoking Cessation Advice	192	99%	99%	99%
Chest Pain/Possible Heart Attack Care				
Aspirin at Arrival[1,3]	2	100%	95%	95%
Median Time to ECG (minutes)[1,3]	2	6	9	8
Median Time to Transfer (minutes)[5]	0	-	64	61
Fibrinolytic Medication Timing[5]	0	-	31%	54%
Heart Failure Care				
ACE Inhibitor or ARB for LVSD	81	95%	94%	94%
Discharge Instructions	223	73%	87%	88%
Evaluation of LVS Function	267	99%	97%	98%
Smoking Cessation Advice	54	93%	98%	98%
Pneumonia Care				
Appropriate Initial Antibiotic[2]	64	89%	91%	92%
Blood Culture Timing[2]	138	96%	97%	96%
Influenza Vaccine[2]	108	91%	90%	91%
Initial Antibiotic Timing[2]	133	97%	95%	95%
Pneumococcal Vaccine[2]	139	96%	93%	93%
Smoking Cessation Advice[2]	111	98%	97%	97%
Surgical Care Improvement Project				
Appropriate VTP Within 24 Hours[2]	255	97%	93%	92%
Appropriate Hair Removal[2]	820	100%	100%	99%
Appropriate Beta Blocker Usage[2]	259	84%	94%	93%
Controlled Postoperative Blood Glucose[2]	179	93%	94%	93%
Prophylactic Antibiotic Timing[2]	598	96%	97%	97%
Prophylactic Antibiotic Timing (Outpatient)	554	93%	95%	92%
Prophylactic Antibiotic Selection[2]	610	99%	97%	97%
Prophylactic Antibiotic Select. (Outpatient)	534	95%	95%	94%
Prophylactic Antibiotic Stopped[2]	565	88%	95%	94%
Recommended VTP Ordered[2]	258	97%	95%	94%
Urinary Catheter Removal[2]	122	82%	88%	90%
Children's Asthma Care				
Received Systemic Corticosteroids	-	-	-	100%
Received Home Management Plan	-	-	-	71%
Received Reliever Medication	-	-	-	100%
Use of Medical Imaging				
Combination Abdominal CT Scan	1,154	0.523	0.227	0.191
Combination Chest CT Scan	842	0.612	0.059	0.054
Follow-up Mammogram/Ultrasound	2,505	3.8%	7.4%	8.4%
MRI for Low Back Pain	609	31.2%	36%	32.7%
Survey of Patients' Hospital Experiences				
Area Around Room 'Always' Quiet at Night	300+	52%	-	58%
Doctors 'Always' Communicated Well	300+	76%	-	80%
Home Recovery Information Given	300+	82%	-	82%
Hospital Given 9 or 10 on 10 Point Scale	300+	65%	-	67%
Meds 'Always' Explained Before Given	300+	57%	-	60%
Nurses 'Always' Communicated Well	300+	74%	-	76%
Pain 'Always' Well Controlled	300+	68%	-	69%
Room and Bathroom 'Always' Clean	300+	66%	-	71%
Timely Help 'Always' Received	300+	56%	-	64%
Would Definitely Recommend Hospital	300+	70%	-	69%

Saint John's Regional Medical Center

2727 Mcclelland Blvd — Phone: 417-781-2727
Joplin, MO 64804 — Fax: 417-625-2910
URL: www.stj.com
Type: Acute Care Hospitals — Emergency Services: Yes
Ownership: Voluntary Non-Profit - Church — Beds: 367

Key Personnel:
CEO/President. . . . . Gary Rowe
Chief of Medical Staff. . . . . J Marhnez, MD
Infection Control. . . . . Donna Stokes
Operating Room. . . . . Christie Joyce
Pediatric Ambulatory Care . . . . . . Barbara Chilton, DO
Pediatric In-Patient Care . . . . Barbara Chilton, DO
Quality Assurance . . . . Dennis Manley
Radiology. . . . . Curtis Hammerman, MD

Measure	Cases	This Hosp.	State Avg.	U.S. Avg.
Heart Attack Care				
ACE Inhibitor or ARB for LVSD	90	97%	96%	96%
Aspirin at Arrival	204	99%	99%	99%
Aspirin at Discharge	311	99%	99%	98%
Beta Blocker at Discharge	307	97%	99%	98%
Fibrinolytic Medication Timing[1]	2	100%	27%	55%
PCI Within 90 Minutes of Arrival	33	97%	92%	90%
Smoking Cessation Advice	141	100%	99%	99%
Chest Pain/Possible Heart Attack Care				
Aspirin at Arrival[1,3]	1	100%	95%	95%
Median Time to ECG (minutes)[1,3]	1	7	9	8
Median Time to Transfer (minutes)[5]	0	-	64	61
Fibrinolytic Medication Timing[5]	0	-	31%	54%
Heart Failure Care				
ACE Inhibitor or ARB for LVSD	151	93%	94%	94%
Discharge Instructions	296	85%	87%	88%
Evaluation of LVS Function	353	99%	97%	98%
Smoking Cessation Advice	69	100%	98%	98%
Pneumonia Care				
Appropriate Initial Antibiotic	201	91%	91%	92%
Blood Culture Timing	325	97%	97%	96%
Influenza Vaccine	328	94%	90%	91%
Initial Antibiotic Timing	427	96%	95%	95%
Pneumococcal Vaccine	407	97%	93%	93%
Smoking Cessation Advice	239	100%	97%	97%
Surgical Care Improvement Project				
Appropriate VTP Within 24 Hours	399	94%	93%	92%
Appropriate Hair Removal	1,080	100%	100%	99%
Appropriate Beta Blocker Usage	346	98%	94%	93%
Controlled Postoperative Blood Glucose	155	95%	94%	93%
Prophylactic Antibiotic Timing	659	99%	97%	97%
Prophylactic Antibiotic Timing (Outpatient)	235	97%	95%	92%
Prophylactic Antibiotic Selection	666	99%	97%	97%
Prophylactic Antibiotic Select. (Outpatient)	230	100%	95%	94%
Prophylactic Antibiotic Stopped	626	95%	95%	94%
Recommended VTP Ordered	404	95%	95%	94%
Urinary Catheter Removal	152	85%	88%	90%
Children's Asthma Care				
Received Systemic Corticosteroids	-	-	-	100%
Received Home Management Plan	-	-	-	71%
Received Reliever Medication	-	-	-	100%
Use of Medical Imaging				
Combination Abdominal CT Scan	1,123	0.025	0.227	0.191
Combination Chest CT Scan	876	0.001	0.059	0.054
Follow-up Mammogram/Ultrasound	1,878	7.5%	7.4%	8.4%
MRI for Low Back Pain	301	36.2%	36%	32.7%
Survey of Patients' Hospital Experiences				
Area Around Room 'Always' Quiet at Night	300+	58%	-	58%
Doctors 'Always' Communicated Well	300+	80%	-	80%
Home Recovery Information Given	300+	85%	-	82%
Hospital Given 9 or 10 on 10 Point Scale	300+	72%	-	67%
Meds 'Always' Explained Before Given	300+	56%	-	60%
Nurses 'Always' Communicated Well	300+	77%	-	76%
Pain 'Always' Well Controlled	300+	72%	-	69%
Room and Bathroom 'Always' Clean	300+	72%	-	71%
Timely Help 'Always' Received	300+	62%	-	64%
Would Definitely Recommend Hospital	300+	75%	-	69%

NOTE: Hospital profiles are in alphabetical order by state, then city, then hospital within the city; Rankings exclude hospitals with less than 25 cases except for patient surveys which excludes hospitals with less than 100 cases; (a) 100–299 cases; (1) The number of cases is too small to be sure how well a hospital is performing; (2) The hospital indicated that the data submitted for this measure were based on a sample of cases; (3) Data was collected during a shorter time period (fewer quarters) than the maximum possible time for this measure; (4) Suppressed for one or more quarters by CMS; (5) No data is available from the hospital for this measure; (6) Fewer than 100 patients completed the HCAHPS survey. Use these rates with caution, as the number of surveys may be too low to reliably assess hospital performance; (7) Survey results are based on less than 12 months of data; (8) Survey results are not available for this reporting period; (9) No or very few patients were eligible for the HCAHPS survey. The scores shown, if any, reflect a very small number of surveys; (10) A state average was not calculated because too few hospitals in the state submitted data; (11) There were discrepancies in the data collection process; Please refer to the User's Guide for a full explanation of data.

Childrens Mercy Hospital

2401 Gillham Road Phone: 816-234-3000
Kansas City, MO 64108 Fax: 816-842-6107
URL: www.childrens-mercy.org
Type: Childrens Emergency Services: Yes
Ownership: Voluntary Non-Profit - Private Beds: 241

Key Personnel:
CEO/President. . . . . Randall L O'Donnell, PhD
Chief of Medical Staff . . . . V Fred Burry, MD
Infection Control. . . . . Cindy Olson - Burgess, RN
Radiology. . . . . James C Brown, MD

Measure	Cases	This Hosp.	State Avg.	U.S. Avg.
Heart Attack Care				
ACE Inhibitor or ARB for LVSD	-	-	96%	96%
Aspirin at Arrival	-	-	99%	99%
Aspirin at Discharge	-	-	99%	98%
Beta Blocker at Discharge	-	-	99%	98%
Fibrinolytic Medication Timing	-	-	27%	55%
PCI Within 90 Minutes of Arrival	-	-	92%	90%
Smoking Cessation Advice	-	-	99%	99%
Chest Pain/Possible Heart Attack Care				
Aspirin at Arrival	-	-	95%	95%
Median Time to ECG (minutes)	-	-	9	8
Median Time to Transfer (minutes)	-	-	64	61
Fibrinolytic Medication Timing	-	-	31%	54%
Heart Failure Care				
ACE Inhibitor or ARB for LVSD	-	-	94%	94%
Discharge Instructions	-	-	87%	88%
Evaluation of LVS Function	-	-	97%	98%
Smoking Cessation Advice	-	-	98%	98%
Pneumonia Care				
Appropriate Initial Antibiotic	-	-	91%	92%
Blood Culture Timing	-	-	97%	96%
Influenza Vaccine	-	-	90%	91%
Initial Antibiotic Timing	-	-	95%	95%
Pneumococcal Vaccine	-	-	93%	93%
Smoking Cessation Advice	-	-	97%	97%
Surgical Care Improvement Project				
Appropriate VTP Within 24 Hours	-	-	93%	92%
Appropriate Hair Removal	-	-	100%	99%
Appropriate Beta Blocker Usage	-	-	94%	93%
Controlled Postoperative Blood Glucose	-	-	94%	93%
Prophylactic Antibiotic Timing	-	-	97%	97%
Prophylactic Antibiotic Timing (Outpatient)	-	-	95%	92%
Prophylactic Antibiotic Selection	-	-	97%	97%
Prophylactic Antibiotic Select. (Outpatient)	-	-	95%	94%
Prophylactic Antibiotic Stopped	-	-	95%	94%
Recommended VTP Ordered	-	-	95%	94%
Urinary Catheter Removal	-	-	88%	90%
Children's Asthma Care				
Received Systemic Corticosteroids[2]	446	100%	-	100%
Received Home Management Plan[2]	446	63%	-	71%
Received Reliever Medication[2]	449	100%	-	100%
Use of Medical Imaging				
Combination Abdominal CT Scan	-	-	0.227	0.191
Combination Chest CT Scan	-	-	0.059	0.054
Follow-up Mammogram/Ultrasound	-	-	7.4%	8.4%
MRI for Low Back Pain	-	-	36%	32.7%
Survey of Patients' Hospital Experiences				
Area Around Room 'Always' Quiet at Night	-	-	-	58%
Doctors 'Always' Communicated Well	-	-	-	80%
Home Recovery Information Given	-	-	-	82%
Hospital Given 9 or 10 on 10 Point Scale	-	-	-	67%
Meds 'Always' Explained Before Given	-	-	-	60%
Nurses 'Always' Communicated Well	-	-	-	76%
Pain 'Always' Well Controlled	-	-	-	69%
Room and Bathroom 'Always' Clean	-	-	-	71%
Timely Help 'Always' Received	-	-	-	64%
Would Definitely Recommend Hospital	-	-	-	69%

Kansas City VA Medical Center

4801 Linwood Blvd. Phone: 816-861-4700
Kansas City, MO 64128 Fax: 816-861-1110
Type: Acute Care-Veterans Administration Emergency Services: No
Ownership: Government - Federal Beds: 213

Key Personnel:
CEO/President. . . . . Hugh Doran
Chief of Medical Staff . . . . James Kennedy, MD
Operating Room. . . . . Norman Probst, RN
Quality Assurance . . . . Barbara Shatto, RN
Emergency Room . . . . Robert Talley, MD

Measure	Cases	This Hosp.	State Avg.	U.S. Avg.
Heart Attack Care				
ACE Inhibitor or ARB for LVSD[1]	4	100%	96%	96%
Aspirin at Arrival	28	89%	99%	99%
Aspirin at Discharge[1]	22	100%	99%	98%
Beta Blocker at Discharge[1]	18	100%	99%	98%
Fibrinolytic Medication Timing[5]	0	-	27%	55%
PCI Within 90 Minutes of Arrival[1]	1	0%	92%	90%
Smoking Cessation Advice[1]	8	100%	99%	99%
Chest Pain/Possible Heart Attack Care				
Aspirin at Arrival	-	-	95%	95%
Median Time to ECG (minutes)	-	-	9	8
Median Time to Transfer (minutes)	-	-	64	61
Fibrinolytic Medication Timing	-	-	31%	54%
Heart Failure Care				
ACE Inhibitor or ARB for LVSD	74	95%	94%	94%
Discharge Instructions	177	93%	87%	88%
Evaluation of LVS Function	202	100%	97%	98%
Smoking Cessation Advice	55	100%	98%	98%
Pneumonia Care				
Appropriate Initial Antibiotic	80	94%	91%	92%
Blood Culture Timing	122	99%	97%	96%
Influenza Vaccine	125	90%	90%	91%
Initial Antibiotic Timing	123	93%	95%	95%
Pneumococcal Vaccine	126	98%	93%	93%
Smoking Cessation Advice	57	100%	97%	97%
Surgical Care Improvement Project				
Appropriate VTP Within 24 Hours[2]	113	96%	93%	92%
Appropriate Hair Removal[2]	152	100%	100%	99%
Appropriate Beta Blocker Usage[2]	41	93%	94%	93%
Controlled Postoperative Blood Glucose[2,5]	0	-	94%	93%
Prophylactic Antibiotic Timing	79	100%	97%	97%
Prophylactic Antibiotic Timing (Outpatient)	-	-	95%	92%
Prophylactic Antibiotic Selection	79	100%	97%	97%
Prophylactic Antibiotic Select. (Outpatient)	-	-	95%	94%
Prophylactic Antibiotic Stopped	76	93%	95%	94%
Recommended VTP Ordered[2]	113	97%	95%	94%
Urinary Catheter Removal[2]	59	98%	88%	90%
Children's Asthma Care				
Received Systemic Corticosteroids	-	-	-	100%
Received Home Management Plan	-	-	-	71%
Received Reliever Medication	-	-	-	100%
Use of Medical Imaging				
Combination Abdominal CT Scan	-	-	0.227	0.191
Combination Chest CT Scan	-	-	0.059	0.054
Follow-up Mammogram/Ultrasound	-	-	7.4%	8.4%
MRI for Low Back Pain	-	-	36%	32.7%
Survey of Patients' Hospital Experiences				
Area Around Room 'Always' Quiet at Night	-	-	-	58%
Doctors 'Always' Communicated Well	-	-	-	80%
Home Recovery Information Given	-	-	-	82%
Hospital Given 9 or 10 on 10 Point Scale	-	-	-	67%
Meds 'Always' Explained Before Given	-	-	-	60%
Nurses 'Always' Communicated Well	-	-	-	76%
Pain 'Always' Well Controlled	-	-	-	69%
Room and Bathroom 'Always' Clean	-	-	-	71%
Timely Help 'Always' Received	-	-	-	64%
Would Definitely Recommend Hospital	-	-	-	69%

Research Medical Center

2316 E Meyer Blvd Phone: 816-276-4000
Kansas City, MO 64132
URL: www.researchmedicalcenter.com
Type: Acute Care Hospitals Emergency Services: Yes
Ownership: Proprietary Beds: 511

Measure	Cases	This Hosp.	State Avg.	U.S. Avg.
Heart Attack Care				
ACE Inhibitor or ARB for LVSD	44	100%	96%	96%
Aspirin at Arrival	143	100%	99%	99%
Aspirin at Discharge	242	100%	99%	98%
Beta Blocker at Discharge	225	100%	99%	98%
Fibrinolytic Medication Timing	0	-	27%	55%
PCI Within 90 Minutes of Arrival	29	100%	92%	90%
Smoking Cessation Advice	97	99%	99%	99%
Chest Pain/Possible Heart Attack Care				
Aspirin at Arrival[1,3]	3	100%	95%	95%
Median Time to ECG (minutes)[1,3]	3	5	9	8
Median Time to Transfer (minutes)[5]	0	-	64	61
Fibrinolytic Medication Timing[3]	0	-	31%	54%
Heart Failure Care				
ACE Inhibitor or ARB for LVSD	121	99%	94%	94%
Discharge Instructions	258	98%	87%	88%
Evaluation of LVS Function	310	100%	97%	98%
Smoking Cessation Advice	93	100%	98%	98%
Pneumonia Care				
Appropriate Initial Antibiotic	87	87%	91%	92%
Blood Culture Timing	154	97%	97%	96%
Influenza Vaccine	186	95%	90%	91%
Initial Antibiotic Timing	163	96%	95%	95%
Pneumococcal Vaccine	187	99%	93%	93%
Smoking Cessation Advice	133	98%	97%	97%
Surgical Care Improvement Project				
Appropriate VTP Within 24 Hours[2]	252	96%	93%	92%
Appropriate Hair Removal[2]	723	100%	100%	99%
Appropriate Beta Blocker Usage[2]	239	88%	94%	93%
Controlled Postoperative Blood Glucose[2]	147	93%	94%	93%
Prophylactic Antibiotic Timing[2]	476	98%	97%	97%
Prophylactic Antibiotic Timing (Outpatient)	312	96%	95%	92%
Prophylactic Antibiotic Selection[2]	480	98%	97%	97%
Prophylactic Antibiotic Select. (Outpatient)	324	95%	95%	94%
Prophylactic Antibiotic Stopped[2]	420	96%	95%	94%
Recommended VTP Ordered[2]	252	96%	95%	94%
Urinary Catheter Removal[2]	108	74%	88%	90%
Children's Asthma Care				
Received Systemic Corticosteroids	-	-	-	100%
Received Home Management Plan	-	-	-	71%
Received Reliever Medication	-	-	-	100%
Use of Medical Imaging				
Combination Abdominal CT Scan	752	0.182	0.227	0.191
Combination Chest CT Scan	479	0.140	0.059	0.054
Follow-up Mammogram/Ultrasound	1,030	7.3%	7.4%	8.4%
MRI for Low Back Pain	142	35.9%	36%	32.7%
Survey of Patients' Hospital Experiences				
Area Around Room 'Always' Quiet at Night	300+	64%	-	58%
Doctors 'Always' Communicated Well	300+	81%	-	80%
Home Recovery Information Given	300+	85%	-	82%
Hospital Given 9 or 10 on 10 Point Scale	300+	66%	-	67%
Meds 'Always' Explained Before Given	300+	59%	-	60%
Nurses 'Always' Communicated Well	300+	76%	-	76%
Pain 'Always' Well Controlled	300+	69%	-	69%
Room and Bathroom 'Always' Clean	300+	63%	-	71%
Timely Help 'Always' Received	300+	59%	-	64%
Would Definitely Recommend Hospital	300+	64%	-	69%

NOTE: Hospital profiles are in alphabetical order by state, then city, then hospital within the city; Rankings exclude hospitals with less than 25 cases except for patient surveys which excludes hospitals with less than 100 cases; (a) 100–299 cases; (1) The number of cases is too small to be sure how well a hospital is performing; (2) The hospital indicated that the data submitted for this measure were based on a sample of cases; (3) Data was collected during a shorter time period (fewer quarters) than the maximum possible time for this measure; (4) Suppressed for one or more quarters by CMS; (5) No data is available from the hospital for this measure; (6) Fewer than 100 patients completed the HCAHPS survey. Use these rates with caution, as the number of surveys may be too low to reliably assess hospital performance; (7) Survey results are based on less than 12 months of data; (8) Survey results are not available for this reporting period; (9) No or very few patients were eligible for the HCAHPS survey. The scores shown, if any, reflect a very small number of surveys; (10) A state average was not calculated because too few hospitals in the state submitted data; (11) There were discrepancies in the data collection process; Please refer to the User's Guide for a full explanation of data.

Saint Joseph Medical Center

1000 Carondelet Dr
Kansas City, MO 64114
Phone: 816-942-4000
Fax: 816-943-2840
URL: www.stjosehkc.com
Type: Acute Care Hospitals
Emergency Services: Yes
Ownership: Voluntary Non-Profit - Church
Beds: 300

Key Personnel:
CEO/President. . . . . Scott Kashman
Operating Room. . . . . Bev Carnelia
Quality Assurance . . . . Lisa Thacker
Radiology. . . . . Gord Hesse
Emergency Room . . . . Kara Wineinger

Measure	Cases	This Hosp.	State Avg.	U.S. Avg.
Heart Attack Care				
ACE Inhibitor or ARB for LVSD	51	98%	96%	96%
Aspirin at Arrival	184	99%	99%	99%
Aspirin at Discharge	230	100%	99%	98%
Beta Blocker at Discharge	218	100%	99%	98%
Fibrinolytic Medication Timing	0	-	27%	55%
PCI Within 90 Minutes of Arrival	42	79%	92%	90%
Smoking Cessation Advice	82	100%	99%	99%
Chest Pain/Possible Heart Attack Care				
Aspirin at Arrival[1]	6	83%	95%	95%
Median Time to ECG (minutes)[1]	1	0	9	8
Median Time to Transfer (minutes)[5]	0	-	64	61
Fibrinolytic Medication Timing[5]	0	-	31%	54%
Heart Failure Care				
ACE Inhibitor or ARB for LVSD	135	100%	94%	94%
Discharge Instructions	305	99%	87%	88%
Evaluation of LVS Function	395	100%	97%	98%
Smoking Cessation Advice	52	100%	98%	98%
Pneumonia Care				
Appropriate Initial Antibiotic	159	87%	91%	92%
Blood Culture Timing	264	97%	97%	96%
Influenza Vaccine	199	88%	90%	91%
Initial Antibiotic Timing	275	93%	95%	95%
Pneumococcal Vaccine	266	89%	93%	93%
Smoking Cessation Advice	77	97%	97%	97%
Surgical Care Improvement Project				
Appropriate VTP Within 24 Hours[2]	157	83%	93%	92%
Appropriate Hair Removal[2]	491	100%	100%	99%
Appropriate Beta Blocker Usage[2]	138	95%	94%	93%
Controlled Postoperative Blood Glucose[2]	108	92%	94%	93%
Prophylactic Antibiotic Timing[2]	358	96%	97%	97%
Prophylactic Antibiotic Timing (Outpatient)	395	95%	95%	92%
Prophylactic Antibiotic Selection[2]	362	96%	97%	97%
Prophylactic Antibiotic Select. (Outpatient)	385	96%	95%	94%
Prophylactic Antibiotic Stopped[2]	346	96%	95%	94%
Recommended VTP Ordered[2]	157	85%	95%	94%
Urinary Catheter Removal[2]	60	92%	88%	90%
Children's Asthma Care				
Received Systemic Corticosteroids	-	-	-	100%
Received Home Management Plan	-	-	-	71%
Received Reliever Medication	-	-	-	100%
Use of Medical Imaging				
Combination Abdominal CT Scan	1,054	0.272	0.227	0.191
Combination Chest CT Scan	696	0.121	0.059	0.054
Follow-up Mammogram/Ultrasound	1,626	10.8%	7.4%	8.4%
MRI for Low Back Pain	355	32.1%	36%	32.7%
Survey of Patients' Hospital Experiences				
Area Around Room 'Always' Quiet at Night	300+	53%	-	58%
Doctors 'Always' Communicated Well	300+	81%	-	80%
Home Recovery Information Given	300+	88%	-	82%
Hospital Given 9 or 10 on 10 Point Scale	300+	67%	-	67%
Meds 'Always' Explained Before Given	300+	56%	-	60%
Nurses 'Always' Communicated Well	300+	73%	-	76%
Pain 'Always' Well Controlled	300+	68%	-	69%
Room and Bathroom 'Always' Clean	300+	60%	-	71%
Timely Help 'Always' Received	300+	55%	-	64%
Would Definitely Recommend Hospital	300+	73%	-	69%

Saint Lukes Cancer Institute

4401 Wornall Road
Kansas City, MO 64111
Phone: 816-932-2823
Type: Acute Care Hospitals
Emergency Services: No
Ownership: Voluntary Non-Profit - Private
Beds: 47

Measure	Cases	This Hosp.	State Avg.	U.S. Avg.
Heart Attack Care				
ACE Inhibitor or ARB for LVSD[5]	0	-	96%	96%
Aspirin at Arrival[5]	0	-	99%	99%
Aspirin at Discharge[5]	0	-	99%	98%
Beta Blocker at Discharge[5]	0	-	99%	98%
Fibrinolytic Medication Timing[5]	0	-	27%	55%
PCI Within 90 Minutes of Arrival[5]	0	-	92%	90%
Smoking Cessation Advice[5]	0	-	99%	99%
Chest Pain/Possible Heart Attack Care				
Aspirin at Arrival[5]	0	-	95%	95%
Median Time to ECG (minutes)[5]	0	-	9	8
Median Time to Transfer (minutes)[5]	0	-	64	61
Fibrinolytic Medication Timing[5]	0	-	31%	54%
Heart Failure Care				
ACE Inhibitor or ARB for LVSD[3]	0	-	94%	94%
Discharge Instructions[1,3]	1	0%	87%	88%
Evaluation of LVS Function[1,3]	1	100%	97%	98%
Smoking Cessation Advice[3]	0	-	98%	98%
Pneumonia Care				
Appropriate Initial Antibiotic[3]	0	-	91%	92%
Blood Culture Timing[1,3]	1	100%	97%	96%
Influenza Vaccine[1,3]	2	100%	90%	91%
Initial Antibiotic Timing[1,3]	1	100%	95%	95%
Pneumococcal Vaccine[1,3]	2	100%	93%	93%
Smoking Cessation Advice[1,3]	1	100%	97%	97%
Surgical Care Improvement Project				
Appropriate VTP Within 24 Hours[1,2,3]	15	80%	93%	92%
Appropriate Hair Removal[2,3]	84	100%	100%	99%
Appropriate Beta Blocker Usage[1,2,3]	13	85%	94%	93%
Controlled Postoperative Blood Glucose[2,3]	0	-	94%	93%
Prophylactic Antibiotic Timing[2,3]	53	98%	97%	97%
Prophylactic Antibiotic Timing (Outpatient)[3]	51	94%	95%	92%
Prophylactic Antibiotic Selection[2,3]	54	94%	97%	97%
Prophylactic Antibiotic Select. (Outpatient)[3]	50	98%	95%	94%
Prophylactic Antibiotic Stopped[2,3]	52	96%	95%	94%
Recommended VTP Ordered[1,2,3]	15	100%	95%	94%
Urinary Catheter Removal[1,2,3]	1	100%	88%	90%
Children's Asthma Care				
Received Systemic Corticosteroids	-	-	-	100%
Received Home Management Plan	-	-	-	71%
Received Reliever Medication	-	-	-	100%
Use of Medical Imaging				
Combination Abdominal CT Scan[1]	3	0.000	0.227	0.191
Combination Chest CT Scan[1]	3	0.000	0.059	0.054
Follow-up Mammogram/Ultrasound	1,341	9.5%	7.4%	8.4%
MRI for Low Back Pain[5]	0	-	36%	32.7%
Survey of Patients' Hospital Experiences				
Area Around Room 'Always' Quiet at Night	(a)	59%	-	58%
Doctors 'Always' Communicated Well	(a)	86%	-	80%
Home Recovery Information Given	(a)	89%	-	82%
Hospital Given 9 or 10 on 10 Point Scale	(a)	74%	-	67%
Meds 'Always' Explained Before Given	(a)	73%	-	60%
Nurses 'Always' Communicated Well	(a)	85%	-	76%
Pain 'Always' Well Controlled	(a)	70%	-	69%
Room and Bathroom 'Always' Clean	(a)	71%	-	71%
Timely Help 'Always' Received	(a)	81%	-	64%
Would Definitely Recommend Hospital	(a)	87%	-	69%

Saint Lukes Hospital of Kansas City

4401 Wornall Road
Kansas City, MO 64111
Phone: 816-932-2000
Fax: 816-932-3599
URL: www.staintlukeshealthsystem.org
Type: Acute Care Hospitals
Emergency Services: Yes
Ownership: Govt - Hospital Dist/Auth
Beds: 629

Key Personnel:
CEO/President. . . . . Rich Hastings
Emergency Room . . . . Denise Kintigh

Measure	Cases	This Hosp.	State Avg.	U.S. Avg.
Heart Attack Care				
ACE Inhibitor or ARB for LVSD	64	100%	96%	96%
Aspirin at Arrival	167	100%	99%	99%
Aspirin at Discharge	441	100%	99%	98%
Beta Blocker at Discharge	434	100%	99%	98%
Fibrinolytic Medication Timing	0	-	27%	55%
PCI Within 90 Minutes of Arrival	31	94%	92%	90%
Smoking Cessation Advice	157	100%	99%	99%
Chest Pain/Possible Heart Attack Care				
Aspirin at Arrival[1]	2	100%	95%	95%
Median Time to ECG (minutes)[1]	2	9	9	8
Median Time to Transfer (minutes)[5]	0	-	64	61
Fibrinolytic Medication Timing[5]	0	-	31%	54%
Heart Failure Care				
ACE Inhibitor or ARB for LVSD	210	100%	94%	94%
Discharge Instructions	385	76%	87%	88%
Evaluation of LVS Function	456	100%	97%	98%
Smoking Cessation Advice	107	100%	98%	98%
Pneumonia Care				
Appropriate Initial Antibiotic	89	79%	91%	92%
Blood Culture Timing	146	98%	97%	96%
Influenza Vaccine	164	89%	90%	91%
Initial Antibiotic Timing	205	93%	95%	95%
Pneumococcal Vaccine	215	93%	93%	93%
Smoking Cessation Advice	98	100%	97%	97%
Surgical Care Improvement Project				
Appropriate VTP Within 24 Hours[2]	298	88%	93%	92%
Appropriate Hair Removal[2]	1,190	99%	100%	99%
Appropriate Beta Blocker Usage[2]	507	97%	94%	93%
Controlled Postoperative Blood Glucose[2]	391	91%	94%	93%
Prophylactic Antibiotic Timing[2]	822	96%	97%	97%
Prophylactic Antibiotic Timing (Outpatient)	529	97%	95%	92%
Prophylactic Antibiotic Selection[2]	834	98%	97%	97%
Prophylactic Antibiotic Select. (Outpatient)	523	97%	95%	94%
Prophylactic Antibiotic Stopped[2]	781	97%	95%	94%
Recommended VTP Ordered[2]	298	92%	95%	94%
Urinary Catheter Removal[2]	228	96%	88%	90%
Children's Asthma Care				
Received Systemic Corticosteroids	-	-	-	100%
Received Home Management Plan	-	-	-	71%
Received Reliever Medication	-	-	-	100%
Use of Medical Imaging				
Combination Abdominal CT Scan	342	0.018	0.227	0.191
Combination Chest CT Scan	83	0.157	0.059	0.054
Follow-up Mammogram/Ultrasound[5]	0	-	7.4%	8.4%
MRI for Low Back Pain[1]	23	30.4%	36%	32.7%
Survey of Patients' Hospital Experiences				
Area Around Room 'Always' Quiet at Night	300+	56%	-	58%
Doctors 'Always' Communicated Well	300+	80%	-	80%
Home Recovery Information Given	300+	85%	-	82%
Hospital Given 9 or 10 on 10 Point Scale	300+	72%	-	67%
Meds 'Always' Explained Before Given	300+	63%	-	60%
Nurses 'Always' Communicated Well	300+	78%	-	76%
Pain 'Always' Well Controlled	300+	74%	-	69%
Room and Bathroom 'Always' Clean	300+	68%	-	71%
Timely Help 'Always' Received	300+	66%	-	64%
Would Definitely Recommend Hospital	300+	81%	-	69%

NOTE: Hospital profiles are in alphabetical order by state, then city, then hospital within the city; Rankings exclude hospitals with less than 25 cases except for patient surveys which excludes hospitals with less than 100 cases; (a) 100–299 cases; (1) The number of cases is too small to be sure how well a hospital is performing; (2) The hospital indicated that the data submitted for this measure were based on a sample of cases; (3) Data was collected during a shorter time period (fewer quarters) than the maximum possible time for this measure; (4) Suppressed for one or more quarters by CMS; (5) No data is available from the hospital for this measure; (6) Fewer than 100 patients completed the HCAHPS survey. Use these rates with caution, as the number of surveys may be too low to reliably assess hospital performance; (7) Survey results are based on less than 12 months of data; (8) Survey results are not available for this reporting period; (9) No or very few patients were eligible for the HCAHPS survey. The scores shown, if any, reflect a very small number of surveys; (10) A state average was not calculated because too few hospitals in the state submitted data; (11) There were discrepancies in the data collection process; Please refer to the User's Guide for a full explanation of data.

Saint Lukes Northland Hospital

5830 N W Barry Road
Kansas City, MO 64154
Phone: 816-891-6000
Fax: 816-880-6155
URL: www.saintlukeshealthsystem.org
Type: Acute Care Hospitals
Emergency Services: Yes
Ownership: Voluntary Non-Profit - Other
Beds: 84

Key Personnel:
CEO/President. . . . . Gary Wages
Chief of Medical Staff . . . . Lance B Waldo
Radiology. . . . . Julie F Harthung

Measure	Cases	This Hosp.	State Avg.	U.S. Avg.
Heart Attack Care				
ACE Inhibitor or ARB for LVSD[1]	5	100%	96%	96%
Aspirin at Arrival	79	100%	99%	99%
Aspirin at Discharge	71	99%	99%	98%
Beta Blocker at Discharge	63	98%	99%	98%
Fibrinolytic Medication Timing	0	-	27%	55%
PCI Within 90 Minutes of Arrival[1]	14	79%	92%	90%
Smoking Cessation Advice	28	100%	99%	99%
Chest Pain/Possible Heart Attack Care				
Aspirin at Arrival	45	96%	95%	95%
Median Time to ECG (minutes)	45	6	9	8
Median Time to Transfer (minutes)[1]	7	465	64	61
Fibrinolytic Medication Timing	0	-	31%	54%
Heart Failure Care				
ACE Inhibitor or ARB for LVSD	35	89%	94%	94%
Discharge Instructions	77	86%	87%	88%
Evaluation of LVS Function	93	100%	97%	98%
Smoking Cessation Advice[1]	15	100%	98%	98%
Pneumonia Care				
Appropriate Initial Antibiotic	93	92%	91%	92%
Blood Culture Timing	108	98%	97%	96%
Influenza Vaccine	97	100%	90%	91%
Initial Antibiotic Timing	138	95%	95%	95%
Pneumococcal Vaccine	101	97%	93%	93%
Smoking Cessation Advice	58	100%	97%	97%
Surgical Care Improvement Project				
Appropriate VTP Within 24 Hours	110	88%	93%	92%
Appropriate Hair Removal	269	100%	100%	99%
Appropriate Beta Blocker Usage	59	98%	94%	93%
Controlled Postoperative Blood Glucose	0	-	94%	93%
Prophylactic Antibiotic Timing	180	100%	97%	97%
Prophylactic Antibiotic Timing (Outpatient)	51	86%	95%	92%
Prophylactic Antibiotic Selection	182	98%	97%	97%
Prophylactic Antibiotic Select. (Outpatient)	50	98%	95%	94%
Prophylactic Antibiotic Stopped	174	97%	95%	94%
Recommended VTP Ordered	110	92%	95%	94%
Urinary Catheter Removal	33	73%	88%	90%
Children's Asthma Care				
Received Systemic Corticosteroids	-	-	-	100%
Received Home Management Plan	-	-	-	71%
Received Reliever Medication	-	-	-	100%
Use of Medical Imaging				
Combination Abdominal CT Scan	333	0.102	0.227	0.191
Combination Chest CT Scan	236	0.004	0.059	0.054
Follow-up Mammogram/Ultrasound	639	9.7%	7.4%	8.4%
MRI for Low Back Pain	58	48.3%	36%	32.7%
Survey of Patients' Hospital Experiences				
Area Around Room 'Always' Quiet at Night	300+	61%	-	58%
Doctors 'Always' Communicated Well	300+	78%	-	80%
Home Recovery Information Given	300+	84%	-	82%
Hospital Given 9 or 10 on 10 Point Scale	300+	73%	-	67%
Meds 'Always' Explained Before Given	300+	64%	-	60%
Nurses 'Always' Communicated Well	300+	76%	-	76%
Pain 'Always' Well Controlled	300+	70%	-	69%
Room and Bathroom 'Always' Clean	300+	73%	-	71%
Timely Help 'Always' Received	300+	60%	-	64%
Would Definitely Recommend Hospital	300+	77%	-	69%

Truman Medical Center - Hospital Hill

2301 Holmes Street
Kansas City, MO 64108
Phone: 816-404-1000
Fax: 816-404-3779
URL: www.trumed.org
Type: Acute Care Hospitals
Emergency Services: Yes
Ownership: Voluntary Non-Profit - Private
Beds: 651

Key Personnel:
CEO/President. . . . . John W Bluford III
Chief of Medical Staff . . . . Mark Steele, MD
Coronary Care . . . . Sharon Snow
Infection Control. . . . . Jette Hogenmiller, PhD
Operating Room. . . . . Todd Clayman
Pediatric In-Patient Care . . . . Michael Sheehan, MD
Quality Assurance . . . . Shauna Roberts, MD
Radiology. . . . . Lawrence Ricci, MD

Measure	Cases	This Hosp.	State Avg.	U.S. Avg.
Heart Attack Care				
ACE Inhibitor or ARB for LVSD[1]	12	100%	96%	96%
Aspirin at Arrival	50	98%	99%	99%
Aspirin at Discharge	61	100%	99%	98%
Beta Blocker at Discharge	62	100%	99%	98%
Fibrinolytic Medication Timing	0	-	27%	55%
PCI Within 90 Minutes of Arrival[1]	9	78%	92%	90%
Smoking Cessation Advice	44	100%	99%	99%
Chest Pain/Possible Heart Attack Care				
Aspirin at Arrival[1,3]	1	100%	95%	95%
Median Time to ECG (minutes)[3]	0	-	9	8
Median Time to Transfer (minutes)[5]	0	-	64	61
Fibrinolytic Medication Timing[3]	0	-	31%	54%
Heart Failure Care				
ACE Inhibitor or ARB for LVSD	176	99%	94%	94%
Discharge Instructions	272	77%	87%	88%
Evaluation of LVS Function	306	100%	97%	98%
Smoking Cessation Advice	152	99%	98%	98%
Pneumonia Care				
Appropriate Initial Antibiotic	89	87%	91%	92%
Blood Culture Timing	138	98%	97%	96%
Influenza Vaccine	59	97%	90%	91%
Initial Antibiotic Timing	152	91%	95%	95%
Pneumococcal Vaccine	38	92%	93%	93%
Smoking Cessation Advice	146	99%	97%	97%
Surgical Care Improvement Project				
Appropriate VTP Within 24 Hours[2]	138	92%	93%	92%
Appropriate Hair Removal[2]	316	99%	100%	99%
Appropriate Beta Blocker Usage[2]	71	92%	94%	93%
Controlled Postoperative Blood Glucose[2]	0	-	94%	93%
Prophylactic Antibiotic Timing[2]	223	99%	97%	97%
Prophylactic Antibiotic Timing (Outpatient)	207	79%	95%	92%
Prophylactic Antibiotic Selection[2]	226	99%	97%	97%
Prophylactic Antibiotic Select. (Outpatient)	189	96%	95%	94%
Prophylactic Antibiotic Stopped[2]	213	95%	95%	94%
Recommended VTP Ordered[2]	139	94%	95%	94%
Urinary Catheter Removal[1,2]	24	92%	88%	90%
Children's Asthma Care				
Received Systemic Corticosteroids	-	-	-	100%
Received Home Management Plan	-	-	-	71%
Received Reliever Medication	-	-	-	100%
Use of Medical Imaging				
Combination Abdominal CT Scan	283	0.102	0.227	0.191
Combination Chest CT Scan	242	0.012	0.059	0.054
Follow-up Mammogram/Ultrasound	607	12.5%	7.4%	8.4%
MRI for Low Back Pain	42	40.5%	36%	32.7%
Survey of Patients' Hospital Experiences				
Area Around Room 'Always' Quiet at Night	300+	53%	-	58%
Doctors 'Always' Communicated Well	300+	72%	-	80%
Home Recovery Information Given	300+	81%	-	82%
Hospital Given 9 or 10 on 10 Point Scale	300+	55%	-	67%
Meds 'Always' Explained Before Given	300+	58%	-	60%
Nurses 'Always' Communicated Well	300+	68%	-	76%
Pain 'Always' Well Controlled	300+	61%	-	69%
Room and Bathroom 'Always' Clean	300+	62%	-	71%
Timely Help 'Always' Received	300+	52%	-	64%
Would Definitely Recommend Hospital	300+	58%	-	69%

Truman Medical Center Lakewood

7900 Lee's Summit Rd
Kansas City, MO 64139
Phone: 816-404-7000
Fax: 816-404-8038
URL: www.trumed.org
Type: Acute Care Hospitals
Emergency Services: Yes
Ownership: Voluntary Non-Profit - Private
Beds: 314

Key Personnel:
CEO/President. . . . . John W Bluford, III
Chief of Medical Staff . . . . John Gianino, MD
Coronary Care . . . . Darinda Reberry, RN
Infection Control. . . . . Jette Hogenmiller, PhD
Pediatric Ambulatory Care . . . . . . Mark Woodring
Pediatric In-Patient Care . . . . Mark Woodring
Quality Assurance . . . . Shauna Roberts, MD
Radiology. . . . . Lawrence Ricci, MD

Measure	Cases	This Hosp.	State Avg.	U.S. Avg.
Heart Attack Care				
ACE Inhibitor or ARB for LVSD[3]	0	-	96%	96%
Aspirin at Arrival[1,3]	1	100%	99%	99%
Aspirin at Discharge[3]	0	-	99%	98%
Beta Blocker at Discharge[3]	0	-	99%	98%
Fibrinolytic Medication Timing[3]	0	-	27%	55%
PCI Within 90 Minutes of Arrival[3]	0	-	92%	90%
Smoking Cessation Advice[3]	0	-	99%	99%
Chest Pain/Possible Heart Attack Care				
Aspirin at Arrival[3,1]	2	100%	95%	95%
Median Time to ECG (minutes)[1,3]	2	14	9	8
Median Time to Transfer (minutes)[3]	0	-	64	61
Fibrinolytic Medication Timing[3]	0	-	31%	54%
Heart Failure Care				
ACE Inhibitor or ARB for LVSD	34	97%	94%	94%
Discharge Instructions	67	87%	87%	88%
Evaluation of LVS Function	71	97%	97%	98%
Smoking Cessation Advice	29	100%	98%	98%
Pneumonia Care				
Appropriate Initial Antibiotic	84	92%	91%	92%
Blood Culture Timing	94	98%	97%	96%
Influenza Vaccine	52	94%	90%	91%
Initial Antibiotic Timing	109	88%	95%	95%
Pneumococcal Vaccine	39	92%	93%	93%
Smoking Cessation Advice	48	98%	97%	97%
Surgical Care Improvement Project				
Appropriate VTP Within 24 Hours	29	86%	93%	92%
Appropriate Hair Removal	232	100%	100%	99%
Appropriate Beta Blocker Usage	42	98%	94%	93%
Controlled Postoperative Blood Glucose	0	-	94%	93%
Prophylactic Antibiotic Timing	209	100%	97%	97%
Prophylactic Antibiotic Timing (Outpatient)	66	100%	95%	92%
Prophylactic Antibiotic Selection	210	98%	97%	97%
Prophylactic Antibiotic Select. (Outpatient)	66	98%	95%	94%
Prophylactic Antibiotic Stopped	208	100%	95%	94%
Recommended VTP Ordered	29	86%	95%	94%
Urinary Catheter Removal[1]	4	75%	88%	90%
Children's Asthma Care				
Received Systemic Corticosteroids	-	-	-	100%
Received Home Management Plan	-	-	-	71%
Received Reliever Medication	-	-	-	100%
Use of Medical Imaging				
Combination Abdominal CT Scan	82	0.085	0.227	0.191
Combination Chest CT Scan	50	0.000	0.059	0.054
Follow-up Mammogram/Ultrasound	250	12.0%	7.4%	8.4%
MRI for Low Back Pain[1]	13	46.2%	36%	32.7%
Survey of Patients' Hospital Experiences				
Area Around Room 'Always' Quiet at Night	300+	58%	-	58%
Doctors 'Always' Communicated Well	300+	77%	-	80%
Home Recovery Information Given	300+	83%	-	82%
Hospital Given 9 or 10 on 10 Point Scale	300+	68%	-	67%
Meds 'Always' Explained Before Given	300+	61%	-	60%
Nurses 'Always' Communicated Well	300+	76%	-	76%
Pain 'Always' Well Controlled	300+	65%	-	69%
Room and Bathroom 'Always' Clean	300+	70%	-	71%
Timely Help 'Always' Received	300+	62%	-	64%
Would Definitely Recommend Hospital	300+	69%	-	69%

NOTE: Hospital profiles are in alphabetical order by state, then city, then hospital within the city; Rankings exclude hospitals with less than 25 cases except for patient surveys which excludes hospitals with less than 100 cases; (a) 100–299 cases; (1) The number of cases is too small to be sure how well a hospital is performing; (2) The hospital indicated that the data submitted for this measure were based on a sample of cases; (3) Data was collected during a shorter time period (fewer quarters) than the maximum possible time for this measure; (4) Suppressed for one or more quarters by CMS; (5) No data is available from the hospital for this measure; (6) Fewer than 100 patients completed the HCAHPS survey. Use these rates with caution, as the number of surveys may be too low to reliably assess hospital performance; (7) Survey results are based on less than 12 months of data; (8) Survey results are not available for this reporting period; (9) No or very few patients were eligible for the HCAHPS survey. The scores shown, if any, reflect a very small number of surveys; (10) A state average was not calculated because too few hospitals in the state submitted data; (11) There were discrepancies in the data collection process; Please refer to the User's Guide for a full explanation of data.

Twin Rivers Regional Medical Center

1301 First St
Kennett, MO 63857
Phone: 573-888-4522
Fax: 573-888-5525
URL: www.twinrivermedcenter.com
Type: Acute Care Hospitals
Emergency Services: Yes
Ownership: Voluntary Non-Profit - Private
Beds: 116

Key Personnel:

CEO/President. . . . . John McClellan
Chief of Medical Staff . . . . Maynard Sisler, MD
Infection Control. . . . . Joanne Burton, RN
Operating Room. . . . . Joyce Danels, RN
Quality Assurance . . . . Geraldine Looney, RN
Radiology. . . . . James G Hazel
Emergency Room . . . . Bobby Sibbens, DO
Intensive Care Unit. . . . . Cathy Bradford, RN

Measure	Cases	This Hosp.	State Avg.	U.S. Avg.
Heart Attack Care				
ACE Inhibitor or ARB for LVSD[1]	5	100%	96%	96%
Aspirin at Arrival[1]	14	100%	99%	99%
Aspirin at Discharge[1]	8	100%	99%	98%
Beta Blocker at Discharge[1]	8	100%	99%	98%
Fibrinolytic Medication Timing	0	-	27%	55%
PCI Within 90 Minutes of Arrival	0	-	92%	90%
Smoking Cessation Advice[1]	1	100%	99%	99%
Chest Pain/Possible Heart Attack Care				
Aspirin at Arrival	63	100%	95%	95%
Median Time to ECG (minutes)	67	5	9	8
Median Time to Transfer (minutes)[3]	0	-	64	61
Fibrinolytic Medication Timing[1]	3	67%	31%	54%
Heart Failure Care				
ACE Inhibitor or ARB for LVSD	26	100%	94%	94%
Discharge Instructions	72	100%	87%	88%
Evaluation of LVS Function	92	100%	97%	98%
Smoking Cessation Advice[1]	16	100%	98%	98%
Pneumonia Care				
Appropriate Initial Antibiotic	48	98%	91%	92%
Blood Culture Timing	110	97%	97%	96%
Influenza Vaccine	59	100%	90%	91%
Initial Antibiotic Timing	106	99%	95%	95%
Pneumococcal Vaccine	76	100%	93%	93%
Smoking Cessation Advice	48	100%	97%	97%
Surgical Care Improvement Project				
Appropriate VTP Within 24 Hours[1]	24	100%	93%	92%
Appropriate Hair Removal	79	100%	100%	99%
Appropriate Beta Blocker Usage[1]	16	100%	94%	93%
Controlled Postoperative Blood Glucose	0	-	94%	93%
Prophylactic Antibiotic Timing	50	98%	97%	97%
Prophylactic Antibiotic Timing (Outpatient)[1]	11	100%	95%	92%
Prophylactic Antibiotic Selection	53	94%	97%	97%
Prophylactic Antibiotic Select. (Outpatient)[1]	11	100%	95%	94%
Prophylactic Antibiotic Stopped	48	98%	95%	94%
Recommended VTP Ordered[1]	24	100%	95%	94%
Urinary Catheter Removal[1]	13	100%	88%	90%
Children's Asthma Care				
Received Systemic Corticosteroids[1]	14	100%	-	100%
Received Home Management Plan[1]	15	100%	-	71%
Received Reliever Medication[1]	15	100%	-	100%
Use of Medical Imaging				
Combination Abdominal CT Scan	265	0.204	0.227	0.191
Combination Chest CT Scan	176	0.227	0.059	0.054
Follow-up Mammogram/Ultrasound	356	2.5%	7.4%	8.4%
MRI for Low Back Pain	128	31.3%	36%	32.7%
Survey of Patients' Hospital Experiences				
Area Around Room 'Always' Quiet at Night	300+	47%	-	58%
Doctors 'Always' Communicated Well	300+	80%	-	80%
Home Recovery Information Given	300+	79%	-	82%
Hospital Given 9 or 10 on 10 Point Scale	300+	52%	-	67%
Meds 'Always' Explained Before Given	300+	52%	-	60%
Nurses 'Always' Communicated Well	300+	69%	-	76%
Pain 'Always' Well Controlled	300+	58%	-	69%
Room and Bathroom 'Always' Clean	300+	58%	-	71%
Timely Help 'Always' Received	300+	52%	-	64%
Would Definitely Recommend Hospital	300+	55%	-	69%

Northeast Regional Medical Center

315 S Osteopathy
Kirksville, MO 63501
Phone: 660-785-1000
Fax: 660-785-1110
URL: www.nermc.com
Type: Acute Care Hospitals
Emergency Services: Yes
Ownership: Proprietary
Beds: 109

Key Personnel:

CEO/President. . . . . Robert Moore
Chief of Medical Staff . . . . Ronald Phillips MD
Infection Control. . . . . Nita Coale RN
Operating Room. . . . . Becky Taylor
Pediatric Ambulatory Care . . . . . . Paul Petry DO
Pediatric In-Patient Care . . . . Paul Petry DO
Quality Assurance . . . . Cindy Dixon RN
Radiology. . . . . Thomas Bryce

Measure	Cases	This Hosp.	State Avg.	U.S. Avg.
Heart Attack Care				
ACE Inhibitor or ARB for LVSD	0	-	96%	96%
Aspirin at Arrival[1]	12	100%	99%	99%
Aspirin at Discharge[1]	9	100%	99%	98%
Beta Blocker at Discharge[1]	9	89%	99%	98%
Fibrinolytic Medication Timing	0	-	27%	55%
PCI Within 90 Minutes of Arrival	0	-	92%	90%
Smoking Cessation Advice[1]	3	100%	99%	99%
Chest Pain/Possible Heart Attack Care				
Aspirin at Arrival	42	100%	95%	95%
Median Time to ECG (minutes)	43	3	9	8
Median Time to Transfer (minutes)[3,1]	5	192	64	61
Fibrinolytic Medication Timing[1]	4	75%	31%	54%
Heart Failure Care				
ACE Inhibitor or ARB for LVSD[1]	10	100%	94%	94%
Discharge Instructions	31	100%	87%	88%
Evaluation of LVS Function	46	98%	97%	98%
Smoking Cessation Advice[1]	8	100%	98%	98%
Pneumonia Care				
Appropriate Initial Antibiotic	34	88%	91%	92%
Blood Culture Timing	113	96%	97%	96%
Influenza Vaccine	91	88%	90%	91%
Initial Antibiotic Timing	119	94%	95%	95%
Pneumococcal Vaccine	137	96%	93%	93%
Smoking Cessation Advice	66	100%	97%	97%
Surgical Care Improvement Project				
Appropriate VTP Within 24 Hours[2]	90	98%	93%	92%
Appropriate Hair Removal[2]	246	100%	100%	99%
Appropriate Beta Blocker Usage[2]	69	100%	94%	93%
Controlled Postoperative Blood Glucose[2]	0	-	94%	93%
Prophylactic Antibiotic Timing[2]	159	96%	97%	97%
Prophylactic Antibiotic Timing (Outpatient)	72	94%	95%	92%
Prophylactic Antibiotic Selection[2]	160	97%	97%	97%
Prophylactic Antibiotic Select. (Outpatient)	70	97%	95%	94%
Prophylactic Antibiotic Stopped[2]	145	95%	95%	94%
Recommended VTP Ordered[2]	90	98%	95%	94%
Urinary Catheter Removal	45	89%	88%	90%
Children's Asthma Care				
Received Systemic Corticosteroids	-	-	-	100%
Received Home Management Plan	-	-	-	71%
Received Reliever Medication	-	-	-	100%
Use of Medical Imaging				
Combination Abdominal CT Scan	374	0.425	0.227	0.191
Combination Chest CT Scan	337	0.104	0.059	0.054
Follow-up Mammogram/Ultrasound	740	7.3%	7.4%	8.4%
MRI for Low Back Pain	48	43.8%	36%	32.7%
Survey of Patients' Hospital Experiences				
Area Around Room 'Always' Quiet at Night	300+	61%	-	58%
Doctors 'Always' Communicated Well	300+	80%	-	80%
Home Recovery Information Given	300+	85%	-	82%
Hospital Given 9 or 10 on 10 Point Scale	300+	66%	-	67%
Meds 'Always' Explained Before Given	300+	58%	-	60%
Nurses 'Always' Communicated Well	300+	75%	-	76%
Pain 'Always' Well Controlled	300+	66%	-	69%
Room and Bathroom 'Always' Clean	300+	70%	-	71%
Timely Help 'Always' Received	300+	59%	-	64%
Would Definitely Recommend Hospital	300+	59%	-	69%

SSM St Joseph Hospital West

100 Medical Plaza
Lake Saint Louis, MO 63367
Phone: 636-625-5200
Fax: 636-625-5314
Type: Acute Care Hospitals
Emergency Services: Yes
Ownership: Voluntary Non-Profit - Church
Beds: 100

Key Personnel:

CEO/President. . . . . Kevin Kast
Chief of Medical Staff . . . . James Freeman, MD
Quality Assurance . . . . Pat Smith, RN
Emergency Room . . . . Tim Thompson, MD

Measure	Cases	This Hosp.	State Avg.	U.S. Avg.
Heart Attack Care				
ACE Inhibitor or ARB for LVSD[1]	6	100%	96%	96%
Aspirin at Arrival	52	96%	99%	99%
Aspirin at Discharge[1]	24	100%	99%	98%
Beta Blocker at Discharge[1]	23	100%	99%	98%
Fibrinolytic Medication Timing	0	-	27%	55%
PCI Within 90 Minutes of Arrival	0	-	92%	90%
Smoking Cessation Advice[1]	3	100%	99%	99%
Chest Pain/Possible Heart Attack Care				
Aspirin at Arrival	96	96%	95%	95%
Median Time to ECG (minutes)	97	8	9	8
Median Time to Transfer (minutes)[1,3]	9	41	64	61
Fibrinolytic Medication Timing	0	-	31%	54%
Heart Failure Care				
ACE Inhibitor or ARB for LVSD	45	100%	94%	94%
Discharge Instructions	170	92%	87%	88%
Evaluation of LVS Function	227	99%	97%	98%
Smoking Cessation Advice	48	100%	98%	98%
Pneumonia Care				
Appropriate Initial Antibiotic[2]	92	95%	91%	92%
Blood Culture Timing[2]	124	98%	97%	96%
Influenza Vaccine[2]	81	95%	90%	91%
Initial Antibiotic Timing[2]	125	94%	95%	95%
Pneumococcal Vaccine[2]	134	96%	93%	93%
Smoking Cessation Advice[2]	79	100%	97%	97%
Surgical Care Improvement Project				
Appropriate VTP Within 24 Hours[2]	227	99%	93%	92%
Appropriate Hair Removal[2]	537	100%	100%	99%
Appropriate Beta Blocker Usage[2]	105	97%	94%	93%
Controlled Postoperative Blood Glucose[2]	0	-	94%	93%
Prophylactic Antibiotic Timing[2]	376	98%	97%	97%
Prophylactic Antibiotic Timing (Outpatient)	214	89%	95%	92%
Prophylactic Antibiotic Selection[2]	377	99%	97%	97%
Prophylactic Antibiotic Select. (Outpatient)	212	95%	95%	94%
Prophylactic Antibiotic Stopped[2]	366	98%	95%	94%
Recommended VTP Ordered[2]	227	100%	95%	94%
Urinary Catheter Removal[2]	92	91%	88%	90%
Children's Asthma Care				
Received Systemic Corticosteroids	-	-	-	100%
Received Home Management Plan	-	-	-	71%
Received Reliever Medication	-	-	-	100%
Use of Medical Imaging				
Combination Abdominal CT Scan	682	0.070	0.227	0.191
Combination Chest CT Scan	482	0.006	0.059	0.054
Follow-up Mammogram/Ultrasound	691	6.4%	7.4%	8.4%
MRI for Low Back Pain	91	42.9%	36%	32.7%
Survey of Patients' Hospital Experiences				
Area Around Room 'Always' Quiet at Night	300+	53%	-	58%
Doctors 'Always' Communicated Well	300+	77%	-	80%
Home Recovery Information Given	300+	84%	-	82%
Hospital Given 9 or 10 on 10 Point Scale	300+	70%	-	67%
Meds 'Always' Explained Before Given	300+	61%	-	60%
Nurses 'Always' Communicated Well	300+	78%	-	76%
Pain 'Always' Well Controlled	300+	70%	-	69%
Room and Bathroom 'Always' Clean	300+	65%	-	71%
Timely Help 'Always' Received	300+	62%	-	64%
Would Definitely Recommend Hospital	300+	75%	-	69%

NOTE: Hospital profiles are in alphabetical order by state, then city, then hospital within the city; Rankings exclude hospitals with less than 25 cases except for patient surveys which excludes hospitals with less than 100 cases; (a) 100–299 cases; (1) The number of cases is too small to be sure how well a hospital is performing; (2) The hospital indicated that the data submitted for this measure were based on a sample of cases; (3) Data was collected during a shorter time period (fewer quarters) than the maximum possible time for this measure; (4) Suppressed for one or more quarters by CMS; (5) No data is available from the hospital for this measure; (6) Fewer than 100 patients completed the HCAHPS survey. Use these rates with caution, as the number of surveys may be too low to reliably assess hospital performance; (7) Survey results are based on less than 12 months of data; (8) Survey results are not available for this reporting period; (9) No or very few patients were eligible for the HCAHPS survey. The scores shown, if any, reflect a very small number of surveys; (10) A state average was not calculated because too few hospitals in the state submitted data; (11) There were discrepancies in the data collection process; Please refer to the User's Guide for a full explanation of data.

Barton County Memorial Hospital

29 NW 1st Lane
Lamar, MO 64759
Type: Critical Access Hospitals
Ownership: Government - Local
Phone: 417-682-6081
Fax: 417-682-2138
Emergency Services: Yes
Beds: 49

Key Personnel:
CEO/President. . . . . Rudy Snedigar
Chief of Medical Staff . . . . Joseph Wilson
Quality Assurance . . . . Kathleen Jones
Emergency Room . . . . Kate Mallumian

Measure	Cases	This Hosp.	State Avg.	U.S. Avg.
Heart Attack Care				
ACE Inhibitor or ARB for LVSD[1]	1	100%	96%	96%
Aspirin at Arrival[1]	8	100%	99%	99%
Aspirin at Discharge[1]	6	83%	99%	98%
Beta Blocker at Discharge[1]	6	100%	99%	98%
Fibrinolytic Medication Timing[5]	0	-	27%	55%
PCI Within 90 Minutes of Arrival[5]	0	-	92%	90%
Smoking Cessation Advice	0	-	99%	99%
Chest Pain/Possible Heart Attack Care				
Aspirin at Arrival	-	-	95%	95%
Median Time to ECG (minutes)	-	-	9	8
Median Time to Transfer (minutes)	-	-	64	61
Fibrinolytic Medication Timing	-	-	31%	54%
Heart Failure Care				
ACE Inhibitor or ARB for LVSD	0	-	94%	94%
Discharge Instructions[1]	20	55%	87%	88%
Evaluation of LVS Function	33	39%	97%	98%
Smoking Cessation Advice	0	-	98%	98%
Pneumonia Care				
Appropriate Initial Antibiotic	40	92%	91%	92%
Blood Culture Timing[1]	23	91%	97%	96%
Influenza Vaccine	43	53%	90%	91%
Initial Antibiotic Timing	64	95%	95%	95%
Pneumococcal Vaccine	55	58%	93%	93%
Smoking Cessation Advice[1]	23	100%	97%	97%
Surgical Care Improvement Project				
Appropriate VTP Within 24 Hours[5]	0	-	93%	92%
Appropriate Hair Removal[5]	0	-	100%	99%
Appropriate Beta Blocker Usage[5]	0	-	94%	93%
Controlled Postoperative Blood Glucose[5]	0	-	94%	93%
Prophylactic Antibiotic Timing[5]	0	-	97%	97%
Prophylactic Antibiotic Timing (Outpatient)	-	-	95%	92%
Prophylactic Antibiotic Selection[5]	0	-	97%	97%
Prophylactic Antibiotic Select. (Outpatient)	-	-	95%	94%
Prophylactic Antibiotic Stopped[5]	0	-	95%	94%
Recommended VTP Ordered[5]	0	-	95%	94%
Urinary Catheter Removal[5]	0	-	88%	90%
Children's Asthma Care				
Received Systemic Corticosteroids	-	-	-	100%
Received Home Management Plan	-	-	-	71%
Received Reliever Medication	-	-	-	100%
Use of Medical Imaging				
Combination Abdominal CT Scan	-	-	0.227	0.191
Combination Chest CT Scan	-	-	0.059	0.054
Follow-up Mammogram/Ultrasound	-	-	7.4%	8.4%
MRI for Low Back Pain	-	-	36%	32.7%
Survey of Patients' Hospital Experiences				
Area Around Room 'Always' Quiet at Night[8]	-	-	-	58%
Doctors 'Always' Communicated Well[8]	-	-	-	80%
Home Recovery Information Given[8]	-	-	-	82%
Hospital Given 9 or 10 on 10 Point Scale[8]	-	-	-	67%
Meds 'Always' Explained Before Given[8]	-	-	-	60%
Nurses 'Always' Communicated Well[8]	-	-	-	76%
Pain 'Always' Well Controlled[8]	-	-	-	69%
Room and Bathroom 'Always' Clean[8]	-	-	-	71%
Timely Help 'Always' Received[8]	-	-	-	64%
Would Definitely Recommend Hospital[8]	-	-	-	69%

Saint Johns Hospital-Lebanon

100 Hospital Drive
Lebanon, MO 65536
E-mail: rttinshaw@sprg.smhs.com
Type: Acute Care Hospitals
Ownership: Voluntary Non-Profit - Church
Phone: 417-533-6100
Fax: 417-533-6040
Emergency Services: Yes
Beds: 41

Key Personnel:
CEO/President. . . . . Gary Pulsipher
Radiology. . . . . Barbara Groves
Patient Relations . . . . Sue Sturgill

Measure	Cases	This Hosp.	State Avg.	U.S. Avg.
Heart Attack Care				
ACE Inhibitor or ARB for LVSD[1]	2	100%	96%	96%
Aspirin at Arrival[1]	5	100%	99%	99%
Aspirin at Discharge[1]	3	100%	99%	98%
Beta Blocker at Discharge[1]	4	100%	99%	98%
Fibrinolytic Medication Timing	0	-	27%	55%
PCI Within 90 Minutes of Arrival	0	-	92%	90%
Smoking Cessation Advice	0	-	99%	99%
Chest Pain/Possible Heart Attack Care				
Aspirin at Arrival	215	97%	95%	95%
Median Time to ECG (minutes)	230	12	9	8
Median Time to Transfer (minutes)[1,3]	1	73	64	61
Fibrinolytic Medication Timing[1]	11	27%	31%	54%
Heart Failure Care				
ACE Inhibitor or ARB for LVSD[1]	24	83%	94%	94%
Discharge Instructions	62	87%	87%	88%
Evaluation of LVS Function	75	84%	97%	98%
Smoking Cessation Advice[1]	20	85%	98%	98%
Pneumonia Care				
Appropriate Initial Antibiotic	107	91%	91%	92%
Blood Culture Timing	133	98%	97%	96%
Influenza Vaccine	74	93%	90%	91%
Initial Antibiotic Timing	150	97%	95%	95%
Pneumococcal Vaccine	118	96%	93%	93%
Smoking Cessation Advice	42	95%	97%	97%
Surgical Care Improvement Project				
Appropriate VTP Within 24 Hours	90	99%	93%	92%
Appropriate Hair Removal	231	100%	100%	99%
Appropriate Beta Blocker Usage	79	96%	94%	93%
Controlled Postoperative Blood Glucose	0	-	94%	93%
Prophylactic Antibiotic Timing	190	96%	97%	97%
Prophylactic Antibiotic Timing (Outpatient)	46	80%	95%	92%
Prophylactic Antibiotic Selection	189	97%	97%	97%
Prophylactic Antibiotic Select. (Outpatient)	38	97%	95%	94%
Prophylactic Antibiotic Stopped	185	95%	95%	94%
Recommended VTP Ordered	92	97%	95%	94%
Urinary Catheter Removal	75	93%	88%	90%
Children's Asthma Care				
Received Systemic Corticosteroids	-	-	-	100%
Received Home Management Plan	-	-	-	71%
Received Reliever Medication	-	-	-	100%
Use of Medical Imaging				
Combination Abdominal CT Scan	346	0.040	0.227	0.191
Combination Chest CT Scan	164	0.018	0.059	0.054
Follow-up Mammogram/Ultrasound	560	7.3%	7.4%	8.4%
MRI for Low Back Pain	77	67.5%	36%	32.7%
Survey of Patients' Hospital Experiences				
Area Around Room 'Always' Quiet at Night	300+	53%	-	58%
Doctors 'Always' Communicated Well	300+	83%	-	80%
Home Recovery Information Given	300+	86%	-	82%
Hospital Given 9 or 10 on 10 Point Scale	300+	66%	-	67%
Meds 'Always' Explained Before Given	300+	65%	-	60%
Nurses 'Always' Communicated Well	300+	76%	-	76%
Pain 'Always' Well Controlled	300+	66%	-	69%
Room and Bathroom 'Always' Clean	300+	83%	-	71%
Timely Help 'Always' Received	300+	66%	-	64%
Would Definitely Recommend Hospital	300+	67%	-	69%

Lee's Summit Medical Center

2100 SE Blue Parkway
Lee's Summit, MO 64063
URL: www.leessummithospital.com
Type: Acute Care Hospitals
Ownership: Proprietary
Phone: 816-282-5000
Fax: 816-969-6523
Emergency Services: Yes
Beds: 83

Key Personnel:
CEO/President. . . . . Carolyn W Caldwell
Chief of Medical Staff . . . . Andrew S Pavlovich, MD

Measure	Cases	This Hosp.	State Avg.	U.S. Avg.
Heart Attack Care				
ACE Inhibitor or ARB for LVSD[1]	13	100%	96%	96%
Aspirin at Arrival	104	100%	99%	99%
Aspirin at Discharge	95	100%	99%	98%
Beta Blocker at Discharge	90	100%	99%	98%
Fibrinolytic Medication Timing	0	-	27%	55%
PCI Within 90 Minutes of Arrival	32	97%	92%	90%
Smoking Cessation Advice	32	100%	99%	99%
Chest Pain/Possible Heart Attack Care				
Aspirin at Arrival[3,1]	3	100%	95%	95%
Median Time to ECG (minutes)[1,3]	4	7	9	8
Median Time to Transfer (minutes)[5]	0	-	64	61
Fibrinolytic Medication Timing[5]	0	-	31%	54%
Heart Failure Care				
ACE Inhibitor or ARB for LVSD	27	100%	94%	94%
Discharge Instructions	58	79%	87%	88%
Evaluation of LVS Function	86	99%	97%	98%
Smoking Cessation Advice[1]	15	100%	98%	98%
Pneumonia Care				
Appropriate Initial Antibiotic	59	100%	91%	92%
Blood Culture Timing	99	98%	97%	96%
Influenza Vaccine	58	100%	90%	91%
Initial Antibiotic Timing	105	100%	95%	95%
Pneumococcal Vaccine	98	100%	93%	93%
Smoking Cessation Advice	28	100%	97%	97%
Surgical Care Improvement Project				
Appropriate VTP Within 24 Hours	119	98%	93%	92%
Appropriate Hair Removal	350	100%	100%	99%
Appropriate Beta Blocker Usage	85	98%	94%	93%
Controlled Postoperative Blood Glucose	0	-	94%	93%
Prophylactic Antibiotic Timing	232	100%	97%	97%
Prophylactic Antibiotic Timing (Outpatient)	79	90%	95%	92%
Prophylactic Antibiotic Selection	233	99%	97%	97%
Prophylactic Antibiotic Select. (Outpatient)	75	97%	95%	94%
Prophylactic Antibiotic Stopped	224	97%	95%	94%
Recommended VTP Ordered	119	100%	95%	94%
Urinary Catheter Removal	30	87%	88%	90%
Children's Asthma Care				
Received Systemic Corticosteroids	-	-	-	100%
Received Home Management Plan	-	-	-	71%
Received Reliever Medication	-	-	-	100%
Use of Medical Imaging				
Combination Abdominal CT Scan	272	0.140	0.227	0.191
Combination Chest CT Scan	160	0.094	0.059	0.054
Follow-up Mammogram/Ultrasound	572	15.6%	7.4%	8.4%
MRI for Low Back Pain	63	36.5%	36%	32.7%
Survey of Patients' Hospital Experiences				
Area Around Room 'Always' Quiet at Night	300+	66%	-	58%
Doctors 'Always' Communicated Well	300+	76%	-	80%
Home Recovery Information Given	300+	85%	-	82%
Hospital Given 9 or 10 on 10 Point Scale	300+	72%	-	67%
Meds 'Always' Explained Before Given	300+	57%	-	60%
Nurses 'Always' Communicated Well	300+	75%	-	76%
Pain 'Always' Well Controlled	300+	70%	-	69%
Room and Bathroom 'Always' Clean	300+	72%	-	71%
Timely Help 'Always' Received	300+	61%	-	64%
Would Definitely Recommend Hospital	300+	72%	-	69%

NOTE: Hospital profiles are in alphabetical order by state, then city, then hospital within the city; Rankings exclude hospitals with less than 25 cases except for patient surveys which excludes hospitals with less than 100 cases; (a) 100–299 cases; (1) The number of cases is too small to be sure how well a hospital is performing; (2) The hospital indicated that the data submitted for this measure were based on a sample of cases; (3) Data was collected during a shorter time period (fewer quarters) than the maximum possible time for this measure; (4) Suppressed for one or more quarters by CMS; (5) No data is available from the hospital for this measure; (6) Fewer than 100 patients completed the HCAHPS survey. Use these rates with caution, as the number of surveys may be too low to reliably assess hospital performance; (7) Survey results are based on less than 12 months of data; (8) Survey results are not available for this reporting period; (9) No or very few patients were eligible for the HCAHPS survey. The scores shown, if any, reflect a very small number of surveys; (10) A state average was not calculated because too few hospitals in the state submitted data; (11) There were discrepancies in the data collection process; Please refer to the User's Guide for a full explanation of data.

Saint Luke's East Lee's Summit Hospital

100 NE Saint Luke's Boulevard Phone: 816-347-5000
Lees Summit, MO 64086
Type: Acute Care Hospitals Emergency Services: Yes
Ownership: Voluntary Non-Profit - Private Beds: 57

Key Personnel:
CEO/President. . . . . George A. Pagels, MD

Measure	Cases	This Hosp.	State Avg.	U.S. Avg.
Heart Attack Care				
ACE Inhibitor or ARB for LVSD[1]	12	100%	96%	96%
Aspirin at Arrival	121	100%	99%	99%
Aspirin at Discharge	113	99%	99%	98%
Beta Blocker at Discharge	110	99%	99%	98%
Fibrinolytic Medication Timing	0	-	27%	55%
PCI Within 90 Minutes of Arrival[1]	23	100%	92%	90%
Smoking Cessation Advice	29	100%	99%	99%
Chest Pain/Possible Heart Attack Care				
Aspirin at Arrival	26	85%	95%	95%
Median Time to ECG (minutes)	31	2	9	8
Median Time to Transfer (minutes)[5]	0	-	64	61
Fibrinolytic Medication Timing[3]	0	-	31%	54%
Heart Failure Care				
ACE Inhibitor or ARB for LVSD	58	97%	94%	94%
Discharge Instructions	140	74%	87%	88%
Evaluation of LVS Function	162	98%	97%	98%
Smoking Cessation Advice[1]	21	100%	98%	98%
Pneumonia Care				
Appropriate Initial Antibiotic	120	92%	91%	92%
Blood Culture Timing	155	97%	97%	96%
Influenza Vaccine	106	95%	90%	91%
Initial Antibiotic Timing	158	96%	95%	95%
Pneumococcal Vaccine	151	97%	93%	93%
Smoking Cessation Advice	41	95%	97%	97%
Surgical Care Improvement Project				
Appropriate VTP Within 24 Hours	145	87%	93%	92%
Appropriate Hair Removal	533	100%	100%	99%
Appropriate Beta Blocker Usage	138	96%	94%	93%
Controlled Postoperative Blood Glucose	0	-	94%	93%
Prophylactic Antibiotic Timing	308	99%	97%	97%
Prophylactic Antibiotic Timing (Outpatient)	170	93%	95%	92%
Prophylactic Antibiotic Selection	308	98%	97%	97%
Prophylactic Antibiotic Select. (Outpatient)	169	96%	95%	94%
Prophylactic Antibiotic Stopped	300	95%	95%	94%
Recommended VTP Ordered	145	98%	95%	94%
Urinary Catheter Removal[1]	22	82%	88%	90%
Children's Asthma Care				
Received Systemic Corticosteroids	-	-	-	100%
Received Home Management Plan	-	-	-	71%
Received Reliever Medication	-	-	-	100%
Use of Medical Imaging				
Combination Abdominal CT Scan	537	0.050	0.227	0.191
Combination Chest CT Scan	197	0.041	0.059	0.054
Follow-up Mammogram/Ultrasound	408	11.8%	7.4%	8.4%
MRI for Low Back Pain	121	38.0%	36%	32.7%
Survey of Patients' Hospital Experiences				
Area Around Room 'Always' Quiet at Night	300+	68%	-	58%
Doctors 'Always' Communicated Well	300+	80%	-	80%
Home Recovery Information Given	300+	86%	-	82%
Hospital Given 9 or 10 on 10 Point Scale	300+	83%	-	67%
Meds 'Always' Explained Before Given	300+	63%	-	60%
Nurses 'Always' Communicated Well	300+	79%	-	76%
Pain 'Always' Well Controlled	300+	71%	-	69%
Room and Bathroom 'Always' Clean	300+	79%	-	71%
Timely Help 'Always' Received	300+	65%	-	64%
Would Definitely Recommend Hospital	300+	86%	-	69%

Lafayette Regional Health Center

1500 State Street Phone: 660-259-2203
Lexington, MO 64067 Fax: 660-259-6819
URL: lafayetteregionalhealthcenter.com
Type: Critical Access Hospitals Emergency Services: Yes
Ownership: Proprietary Beds: 49

Key Personnel:
CEO/President. . . . . Bret Kolmant
Chief of Medical Staff. . . . . Clint Pickett, DO
Infection Control. . . . . Jeannette Buckets, RN
Operating Room. . . . . Julie Osman, RN
Quality Assurance . . . . Debbie Green, RN
Radiology. . . . . Teresa Mannick
Emergency Room . . . . Deb Peck, RN
Intensive Care Unit. . . . . Dena Stark, RN

Measure	Cases	This Hosp.	State Avg.	U.S. Avg.
Heart Attack Care				
ACE Inhibitor or ARB for LVSD[1]	1	100%	96%	96%
Aspirin at Arrival[1]	2	100%	99%	99%
Aspirin at Discharge[1]	2	100%	99%	98%
Beta Blocker at Discharge[1]	2	100%	99%	98%
Fibrinolytic Medication Timing	0	-	27%	55%
PCI Within 90 Minutes of Arrival	0	-	92%	90%
Smoking Cessation Advice	0	-	99%	99%
Chest Pain/Possible Heart Attack Care				
Aspirin at Arrival	43	100%	95%	95%
Median Time to ECG (minutes)	42	6	9	8
Median Time to Transfer (minutes)[1,3]	2	46	64	61
Fibrinolytic Medication Timing[3]	0	-	31%	54%
Heart Failure Care				
ACE Inhibitor or ARB for LVSD[1]	2	100%	94%	94%
Discharge Instructions[1]	6	100%	87%	88%
Evaluation of LVS Function[1]	14	100%	97%	98%
Smoking Cessation Advice[1]	2	50%	98%	98%
Pneumonia Care				
Appropriate Initial Antibiotic	55	95%	91%	92%
Blood Culture Timing	55	100%	97%	96%
Influenza Vaccine	48	100%	90%	91%
Initial Antibiotic Timing	67	99%	95%	95%
Pneumococcal Vaccine	60	100%	93%	93%
Smoking Cessation Advice	25	100%	97%	97%
Surgical Care Improvement Project				
Appropriate VTP Within 24 Hours[1]	18	94%	93%	92%
Appropriate Hair Removal[1]	22	100%	100%	99%
Appropriate Beta Blocker Usage[1]	6	83%	94%	93%
Controlled Postoperative Blood Glucose	0	-	94%	93%
Prophylactic Antibiotic Timing[1]	15	100%	97%	97%
Prophylactic Antibiotic Timing (Outpatient)	26	88%	95%	92%
Prophylactic Antibiotic Selection[1]	15	100%	97%	97%
Prophylactic Antibiotic Select. (Outpatient)[1]	23	96%	95%	94%
Prophylactic Antibiotic Stopped[1]	13	100%	95%	94%
Recommended VTP Ordered[1]	18	94%	95%	94%
Urinary Catheter Removal[1]	2	100%	88%	90%
Children's Asthma Care				
Received Systemic Corticosteroids	-	-	-	100%
Received Home Management Plan	-	-	-	71%
Received Reliever Medication	-	-	-	100%
Use of Medical Imaging				
Combination Abdominal CT Scan	201	0.020	0.227	0.191
Combination Chest CT Scan	137	0.051	0.059	0.054
Follow-up Mammogram/Ultrasound	221	11.8%	7.4%	8.4%
MRI for Low Back Pain	63	46.0%	36%	32.7%
Survey of Patients' Hospital Experiences				
Area Around Room 'Always' Quiet at Night	(a)	56%	-	58%
Doctors 'Always' Communicated Well	(a)	82%	-	80%
Home Recovery Information Given	(a)	85%	-	82%
Hospital Given 9 or 10 on 10 Point Scale	(a)	70%	-	67%
Meds 'Always' Explained Before Given	(a)	64%	-	60%
Nurses 'Always' Communicated Well	(a)	79%	-	76%
Pain 'Always' Well Controlled	(a)	68%	-	69%
Room and Bathroom 'Always' Clean	(a)	77%	-	71%
Timely Help 'Always' Received	(a)	66%	-	64%
Would Definitely Recommend Hospital	(a)	65%	-	69%

Liberty Hospital

2525 Glenn Hendren Dr Phone: 816-781-7200
Liberty, MO 64069 Fax: 816-792-7117
URL: www.libertyhospital.org
Type: Acute Care Hospitals Emergency Services: Yes
Ownership: Govt - Hospital Dist/Auth Beds: 202

Key Personnel:
CEO/President. . . . . Joe Crossett
Cardiac Laboratory. . . . . Georgia Solovic
Chief of Medical Staff . . . . Steve Starr, MD
Infection Control. . . . . Maggie Hagan, MD
Operating Room. . . . . Shelly Moore
Quality Assurance . . . . Sharon Sirridge
Radiology. . . . . Joseph Caresio

Measure	Cases	This Hosp.	State Avg.	U.S. Avg.
Heart Attack Care				
ACE Inhibitor or ARB for LVSD	27	89%	96%	96%
Aspirin at Arrival	111	96%	99%	99%
Aspirin at Discharge	119	98%	99%	98%
Beta Blocker at Discharge	112	96%	99%	98%
Fibrinolytic Medication Timing	0	-	27%	55%
PCI Within 90 Minutes of Arrival[1]	15	80%	92%	90%
Smoking Cessation Advice	39	100%	99%	99%
Chest Pain/Possible Heart Attack Care				
Aspirin at Arrival	58	93%	95%	95%
Median Time to ECG (minutes)	59	10	9	8
Median Time to Transfer (minutes)[1,3]	16	40	64	61
Fibrinolytic Medication Timing[3]	0	-	31%	54%
Heart Failure Care				
ACE Inhibitor or ARB for LVSD	98	90%	94%	94%
Discharge Instructions	208	75%	87%	88%
Evaluation of LVS Function	272	97%	97%	98%
Smoking Cessation Advice	52	100%	98%	98%
Pneumonia Care				
Appropriate Initial Antibiotic	159	92%	91%	92%
Blood Culture Timing	206	96%	97%	96%
Influenza Vaccine	180	96%	90%	91%
Initial Antibiotic Timing	264	98%	95%	95%
Pneumococcal Vaccine	243	97%	93%	93%
Smoking Cessation Advice	130	98%	97%	97%
Surgical Care Improvement Project				
Appropriate VTP Within 24 Hours	318	87%	93%	92%
Appropriate Hair Removal	827	99%	100%	99%
Appropriate Beta Blocker Usage	243	94%	94%	93%
Controlled Postoperative Blood Glucose	58	98%	94%	93%
Prophylactic Antibiotic Timing	490	94%	97%	97%
Prophylactic Antibiotic Timing (Outpatient)	407	93%	95%	92%
Prophylactic Antibiotic Selection	494	99%	97%	97%
Prophylactic Antibiotic Select. (Outpatient)	398	95%	95%	94%
Prophylactic Antibiotic Stopped	469	93%	95%	94%
Recommended VTP Ordered	320	94%	95%	94%
Urinary Catheter Removal	100	78%	88%	90%
Children's Asthma Care				
Received Systemic Corticosteroids	-	-	-	100%
Received Home Management Plan	-	-	-	71%
Received Reliever Medication	-	-	-	100%
Use of Medical Imaging				
Combination Abdominal CT Scan	1,087	0.092	0.227	0.191
Combination Chest CT Scan	593	0.002	0.059	0.054
Follow-up Mammogram/Ultrasound	2,377	3.7%	7.4%	8.4%
MRI for Low Back Pain	281	37.4%	36%	32.7%
Survey of Patients' Hospital Experiences				
Area Around Room 'Always' Quiet at Night	300+	50%	-	58%
Doctors 'Always' Communicated Well	300+	77%	-	80%
Home Recovery Information Given	300+	82%	-	82%
Hospital Given 9 or 10 on 10 Point Scale	300+	75%	-	67%
Meds 'Always' Explained Before Given	300+	62%	-	60%
Nurses 'Always' Communicated Well	300+	76%	-	76%
Pain 'Always' Well Controlled	300+	64%	-	69%
Room and Bathroom 'Always' Clean	300+	71%	-	71%
Timely Help 'Always' Received	300+	61%	-	64%
Would Definitely Recommend Hospital	300+	77%	-	69%

NOTE: Hospital profiles are in alphabetical order by state, then city, then hospital within the city; Rankings exclude hospitals with less than 25 cases except for patient surveys which excludes hospitals with less than 100 cases; (a) 100–299 cases; (1) The number of cases is too small to be sure how well a hospital is performing; (2) The hospital indicated that the data submitted for this measure were based on a sample of cases; (3) Data was collected during a shorter time period (fewer quarters) than the maximum possible time for this measure; (4) Suppressed for one or more quarters by CMS; (5) No data is available from the hospital for this measure; (6) Fewer than 100 patients completed the HCAHPS survey. Use these rates with caution, as the number of surveys may be too low to reliably assess hospital performance; (7) Survey results are based on less than 12 months of data; (8) Survey results are not available for this reporting period; (9) No or very few patients were eligible for the HCAHPS survey. The scores shown, if any, reflect a very small number of surveys; (10) A state average was not calculated because too few hospitals in the state submitted data; (11) There were discrepancies in the data collection process; Please refer to the User's Guide for a full explanation of data.

Pike County Memorial Hospital

2305 West Georgia Street
Louisiana, MO 63353
E-mail: djones@pcmhmo.org
URL: www.pcmh-mo.org
Type: Critical Access Hospitals
Ownership: Government - Local
Phone: 573-754-5531
Fax: 573-754-5874
Emergency Services: Yes
Beds: 25

Key Personnel:
CEO/President . . . . Lorraine Harness
Chief of Medical Staff . . . . Casey Jennings, DO
Infection Control . . . . Paulette Powelson, RN
Operating Room . . . . Dianne Oliver
Quality Assurance . . . . Paulette Powelson
Radiology . . . . Rebekka Thornton
Emergency Room . . . . Dolly Giles, RN

Measure	Cases	This Hosp.	State Avg.	U.S. Avg.
Heart Attack Care				
ACE Inhibitor or ARB for LVSD[3]	0	-	96%	96%
Aspirin at Arrival[3]	0	-	99%	99%
Aspirin at Discharge[1,3]	1	100%	99%	98%
Beta Blocker at Discharge[1,3]	1	0%	99%	98%
Fibrinolytic Medication Timing[3]	0	-	27%	55%
PCI Within 90 Minutes of Arrival[3]	0	-	92%	90%
Smoking Cessation Advice[3]	0	-	99%	99%
Chest Pain/Possible Heart Attack Care				
Aspirin at Arrival	-	-	95%	95%
Median Time to ECG (minutes)	-	-	9	8
Median Time to Transfer (minutes)	-	-	64	61
Fibrinolytic Medication Timing	-	-	31%	54%
Heart Failure Care				
ACE Inhibitor or ARB for LVSD[1]	6	100%	94%	94%
Discharge Instructions[1]	21	100%	87%	88%
Evaluation of LVS Function	31	100%	97%	98%
Smoking Cessation Advice[1]	10	100%	98%	98%
Pneumonia Care				
Appropriate Initial Antibiotic	27	93%	91%	92%
Blood Culture Timing[1]	19	89%	97%	96%
Influenza Vaccine	28	96%	90%	91%
Initial Antibiotic Timing	34	97%	95%	95%
Pneumococcal Vaccine	30	100%	93%	93%
Smoking Cessation Advice[1]	9	100%	97%	97%
Surgical Care Improvement Project				
Appropriate VTP Within 24 Hours[5]	0	-	93%	92%
Appropriate Hair Removal[5]	0	-	100%	99%
Appropriate Beta Blocker Usage[5]	0	-	94%	93%
Controlled Postoperative Blood Glucose[5]	0	-	94%	93%
Prophylactic Antibiotic Timing[5]	0	-	97%	97%
Prophylactic Antibiotic Timing (Outpatient)	-	-	95%	92%
Prophylactic Antibiotic Selection[5]	0	-	97%	97%
Prophylactic Antibiotic Select. (Outpatient)	-	-	95%	94%
Prophylactic Antibiotic Stopped[5]	0	-	95%	94%
Recommended VTP Ordered[5]	0	-	95%	94%
Urinary Catheter Removal[5]	0	-	88%	90%
Children's Asthma Care				
Received Systemic Corticosteroids	-	-	-	100%
Received Home Management Plan	-	-	-	71%
Received Reliever Medication	-	-	-	100%
Use of Medical Imaging				
Combination Abdominal CT Scan	-	-	0.227	0.191
Combination Chest CT Scan	-	-	0.059	0.054
Follow-up Mammogram/Ultrasound	-	-	7.4%	8.4%
MRI for Low Back Pain	-	-	36%	32.7%
Survey of Patients' Hospital Experiences				
Area Around Room 'Always' Quiet at Night[8]	-	-	-	58%
Doctors 'Always' Communicated Well[8]	-	-	-	80%
Home Recovery Information Given[8]	-	-	-	82%
Hospital Given 9 or 10 on 10 Point Scale[8]	-	-	-	67%
Meds 'Always' Explained Before Given[8]	-	-	-	60%
Nurses 'Always' Communicated Well[8]	-	-	-	76%
Pain 'Always' Well Controlled[8]	-	-	-	69%
Room and Bathroom 'Always' Clean[8]	-	-	-	71%
Timely Help 'Always' Received[8]	-	-	-	64%
Would Definitely Recommend Hospital[8]	-	-	-	69%

Fitzgibbon Memorial Hospital

2305 S 65 Highway
Marshall, MO 65340
E-mail: snewman@murlin.com
Type: Acute Care Hospitals
Ownership: Voluntary Non-Profit - Private
Phone: 660-886-7431
Fax: 660-886-9001
Emergency Services: Yes
Beds: 60

Key Personnel:
CEO/President . . . . Ronald A Ott
Chief of Medical Staff . . . . Roy Elsrink
Infection Control . . . . Linda Cook, RN
Operating Room . . . . Millie Langan, RN
Pediatric Ambulatory Care . . . . . . C Alan Scott, MD
Pediatric In-Patient Care . . . . . . C Alan Scott, MD
Quality Assurance . . . . R Bruce Blalock
Radiology . . . . H T Lee

Measure	Cases	This Hosp.	State Avg.	U.S. Avg.
Heart Attack Care				
ACE Inhibitor or ARB for LVSD[1,3]	1	100%	96%	96%
Aspirin at Arrival[1,3]	2	100%	99%	99%
Aspirin at Discharge[1,3]	1	100%	99%	98%
Beta Blocker at Discharge[1,3]	3	67%	99%	98%
Fibrinolytic Medication Timing[3]	0	-	27%	55%
PCI Within 90 Minutes of Arrival[3]	0	-	92%	90%
Smoking Cessation Advice[3]	0	-	99%	99%
Chest Pain/Possible Heart Attack Care				
Aspirin at Arrival	126	87%	95%	95%
Median Time to ECG (minutes)	132	12	9	8
Median Time to Transfer (minutes)[1,3]	8	45	64	61
Fibrinolytic Medication Timing[1]	4	50%	31%	54%
Heart Failure Care				
ACE Inhibitor or ARB for LVSD[1]	4	75%	94%	94%
Discharge Instructions	38	58%	87%	88%
Evaluation of LVS Function	50	66%	97%	98%
Smoking Cessation Advice[1]	6	83%	98%	98%
Pneumonia Care				
Appropriate Initial Antibiotic	68	87%	91%	92%
Blood Culture Timing	76	99%	97%	96%
Influenza Vaccine	68	75%	90%	91%
Initial Antibiotic Timing	87	89%	95%	95%
Pneumococcal Vaccine	95	82%	93%	93%
Smoking Cessation Advice	36	92%	97%	97%
Surgical Care Improvement Project				
Appropriate VTP Within 24 Hours	27	85%	93%	92%
Appropriate Hair Removal	63	100%	100%	99%
Appropriate Beta Blocker Usage[1]	7	71%	94%	93%
Controlled Postoperative Blood Glucose	0	-	94%	93%
Prophylactic Antibiotic Timing	40	90%	97%	97%
Prophylactic Antibiotic Timing (Outpatient)	106	95%	95%	92%
Prophylactic Antibiotic Selection	40	98%	97%	97%
Prophylactic Antibiotic Select. (Outpatient)	101	98%	95%	94%
Prophylactic Antibiotic Stopped	38	76%	95%	94%
Recommended VTP Ordered	27	85%	95%	94%
Urinary Catheter Removal[1]	15	87%	88%	90%
Children's Asthma Care				
Received Systemic Corticosteroids	-	-	-	100%
Received Home Management Plan	-	-	-	71%
Received Reliever Medication	-	-	-	100%
Use of Medical Imaging				
Combination Abdominal CT Scan	288	0.017	0.227	0.191
Combination Chest CT Scan	119	0.025	0.059	0.054
Follow-up Mammogram/Ultrasound	557	3.4%	7.4%	8.4%
MRI for Low Back Pain	94	46.8%	36%	32.7%
Survey of Patients' Hospital Experiences				
Area Around Room 'Always' Quiet at Night	300+	54%	-	58%
Doctors 'Always' Communicated Well	300+	79%	-	80%
Home Recovery Information Given	300+	84%	-	82%
Hospital Given 9 or 10 on 10 Point Scale	300+	67%	-	67%
Meds 'Always' Explained Before Given	300+	60%	-	60%
Nurses 'Always' Communicated Well	300+	76%	-	76%
Pain 'Always' Well Controlled	300+	71%	-	69%
Room and Bathroom 'Always' Clean	300+	66%	-	71%
Timely Help 'Always' Received	300+	68%	-	64%
Would Definitely Recommend Hospital	300+	58%	-	69%

Saint Francis Hospital

2016 South Main St
Maryville, MO 64468
URL: www.stfrancismaryville.com
Type: Acute Care Hospitals
Ownership: Voluntary Non-Profit - Church
Phone: 660-562-2600
Fax: 660-562-7911
Emergency Services: Yes
Beds: 81

Key Personnel:
CEO/President . . . . John Yancey, FSM
Chief of Medical Staff . . . . Michael Wurm
Radiology . . . . Edward Stevens

Measure	Cases	This Hosp.	State Avg.	U.S. Avg.
Heart Attack Care				
ACE Inhibitor or ARB for LVSD	0	-	96%	96%
Aspirin at Arrival[1]	4	100%	99%	99%
Aspirin at Discharge[1]	2	100%	99%	98%
Beta Blocker at Discharge[1]	3	100%	99%	98%
Fibrinolytic Medication Timing	0	-	27%	55%
PCI Within 90 Minutes of Arrival	0	-	92%	90%
Smoking Cessation Advice	0	-	99%	99%
Chest Pain/Possible Heart Attack Care				
Aspirin at Arrival	71	93%	95%	95%
Median Time to ECG (minutes)	74	6	9	8
Median Time to Transfer (minutes)[1,3]	2	60	64	61
Fibrinolytic Medication Timing	0	-	31%	54%
Heart Failure Care				
ACE Inhibitor or ARB for LVSD[1]	14	100%	94%	94%
Discharge Instructions[1]	19	100%	87%	88%
Evaluation of LVS Function	42	100%	97%	98%
Smoking Cessation Advice[1]	2	100%	98%	98%
Pneumonia Care				
Appropriate Initial Antibiotic	35	97%	91%	92%
Blood Culture Timing	31	97%	97%	96%
Influenza Vaccine	28	100%	90%	91%
Initial Antibiotic Timing	54	96%	95%	95%
Pneumococcal Vaccine	42	100%	93%	93%
Smoking Cessation Advice[1]	15	100%	97%	97%
Surgical Care Improvement Project				
Appropriate VTP Within 24 Hours	43	98%	93%	92%
Appropriate Hair Removal	110	100%	100%	99%
Appropriate Beta Blocker Usage	27	100%	94%	93%
Controlled Postoperative Blood Glucose	0	-	94%	93%
Prophylactic Antibiotic Timing	100	99%	97%	97%
Prophylactic Antibiotic Timing (Outpatient)[1]	18	100%	95%	92%
Prophylactic Antibiotic Selection	102	99%	97%	97%
Prophylactic Antibiotic Select. (Outpatient)[1]	18	94%	95%	94%
Prophylactic Antibiotic Stopped	91	97%	95%	94%
Recommended VTP Ordered	43	98%	95%	94%
Urinary Catheter Removal[1]	7	100%	88%	90%
Children's Asthma Care				
Received Systemic Corticosteroids	-	-	-	100%
Received Home Management Plan	-	-	-	71%
Received Reliever Medication	-	-	-	100%
Use of Medical Imaging				
Combination Abdominal CT Scan	285	0.049	0.227	0.191
Combination Chest CT Scan	177	0.023	0.059	0.054
Follow-up Mammogram/Ultrasound	436	4.4%	7.4%	8.4%
MRI for Low Back Pain	76	28.9%	36%	32.7%
Survey of Patients' Hospital Experiences				
Area Around Room 'Always' Quiet at Night	300+	68%	-	58%
Doctors 'Always' Communicated Well	300+	85%	-	80%
Home Recovery Information Given	300+	82%	-	82%
Hospital Given 9 or 10 on 10 Point Scale	300+	74%	-	67%
Meds 'Always' Explained Before Given	300+	66%	-	60%
Nurses 'Always' Communicated Well	300+	82%	-	76%
Pain 'Always' Well Controlled	300+	72%	-	69%
Room and Bathroom 'Always' Clean	300+	88%	-	71%
Timely Help 'Always' Received	300+	76%	-	64%
Would Definitely Recommend Hospital	300+	71%	-	69%

NOTE: Hospital profiles are in alphabetical order by state, then city, then hospital within the city; Rankings exclude hospitals with less than 25 cases except for patient surveys which excludes hospitals with less than 100 cases; (a) 100–299 cases; (1) The number of cases is too small to be sure how well a hospital is performing; (2) The hospital indicated that the data submitted for this measure were based on a sample of cases; (3) Data was collected during a shorter time period (fewer quarters) than the maximum possible time for this measure; (4) Suppressed for one or more quarters by CMS; (5) No data is available from the hospital for this measure; (6) Fewer than 100 patients completed the HCAHPS survey. Use these rates with caution, as the number of surveys may be too low to reliably assess hospital performance; (7) Survey results are based on less than 12 months of data; (8) Survey results are not available for this reporting period; (9) No or very few patients were eligible for the HCAHPS survey. The scores shown, if any, reflect a very small number of surveys; (10) A state average was not calculated because too few hospitals in the state submitted data; (11) There were discrepancies in the data collection process; Please refer to the User's Guide for a full explanation of data.

Scotland County Hospital

450 E Sigler Avenue
Memphis, MO 63555
Phone: 660-465-8511
Fax: 660-465-2513
E-mail: dialm@scotlandcountyhospital.com
Type: Critical Access Hospitals
Emergency Services: Yes
Ownership: Govt - Hospital Dist/Auth
Beds: 40

Key Personnel:
CEO/President. . . . . Marcia R Dial
Chief of Medical Staff. . . . . C .Miller Parish
Operating Room. . . . . Debbie Ward
Emergency Room . . . . Elliot Hix

Measure	Cases	This Hosp.	State Avg.	U.S. Avg.
Heart Attack Care				
ACE Inhibitor or ARB for LVSD[3]	0	-	96%	96%
Aspirin at Arrival[3]	0	-	99%	99%
Aspirin at Discharge[3]	0	-	99%	98%
Beta Blocker at Discharge[3]	0	-	99%	98%
Fibrinolytic Medication Timing[3]	0	-	27%	55%
PCI Within 90 Minutes of Arrival[3]	0	-	92%	90%
Smoking Cessation Advice[3]	0	-	99%	99%
Chest Pain/Possible Heart Attack Care				
Aspirin at Arrival	-	-	95%	95%
Median Time to ECG (minutes)	-	-	9	8
Median Time to Transfer (minutes)	-	-	64	61
Fibrinolytic Medication Timing	-	-	31%	54%
Heart Failure Care				
ACE Inhibitor or ARB for LVSD[1]	4	100%	94%	94%
Discharge Instructions[1]	16	12%	87%	88%
Evaluation of LVS Function[1]	23	39%	97%	98%
Smoking Cessation Advice[1]	4	50%	98%	98%
Pneumonia Care				
Appropriate Initial Antibiotic[1,2]	12	67%	91%	92%
Blood Culture Timing[2]	27	89%	97%	96%
Influenza Vaccine[2]	29	79%	90%	91%
Initial Antibiotic Timing[2]	38	97%	95%	95%
Pneumococcal Vaccine[2]	47	81%	93%	93%
Smoking Cessation Advice[1,2]	14	57%	97%	97%
Surgical Care Improvement Project				
Appropriate VTP Within 24 Hours[5]	0	-	93%	92%
Appropriate Hair Removal[5]	0	-	100%	99%
Appropriate Beta Blocker Usage[5]	0	-	94%	93%
Controlled Postoperative Blood Glucose[5]	0	-	94%	93%
Prophylactic Antibiotic Timing[5]	0	-	97%	97%
Prophylactic Antibiotic Timing (Outpatient)	-	-	95%	92%
Prophylactic Antibiotic Selection[5]	0	-	97%	97%
Prophylactic Antibiotic Select. (Outpatient)	-	-	95%	94%
Prophylactic Antibiotic Stopped[5]	0	-	95%	94%
Recommended VTP Ordered[5]	0	-	95%	94%
Urinary Catheter Removal[5]	0	-	88%	90%
Children's Asthma Care				
Received Systemic Corticosteroids	-	-	-	100%
Received Home Management Plan	-	-	-	71%
Received Reliever Medication	-	-	-	100%
Use of Medical Imaging				
Combination Abdominal CT Scan	-	-	0.227	0.191
Combination Chest CT Scan	-	-	0.059	0.054
Follow-up Mammogram/Ultrasound	-	-	7.4%	8.4%
MRI for Low Back Pain	-	-	36%	32.7%
Survey of Patients' Hospital Experiences				
Area Around Room 'Always' Quiet at Night[8]	-	-	-	58%
Doctors 'Always' Communicated Well[8]	-	-	-	80%
Home Recovery Information Given[8]	-	-	-	82%
Hospital Given 9 or 10 on 10 Point Scale[8]	-	-	-	67%
Meds 'Always' Explained Before Given[8]	-	-	-	60%
Nurses 'Always' Communicated Well[8]	-	-	-	76%
Pain 'Always' Well Controlled[8]	-	-	-	69%
Room and Bathroom 'Always' Clean[8]	-	-	-	71%
Timely Help 'Always' Received[8]	-	-	-	64%
Would Definitely Recommend Hospital[8]	-	-	-	69%

Audrain Medical Center

620 E Monroe
Mexico, MO 65265
Phone: 573-582-5000
Fax: 573-582-3700
URL: www.audrainmedicalcenter.com
Type: Acute Care Hospitals
Emergency Services: Yes
Ownership: Voluntary Non-Profit - Private
Beds: 92

Key Personnel:
CEO/President. . . . . David A Neuendorf
Chief of Medical Staff . . . . Justin Jones, MD
Radiology. . . . . George Kutty Cyriac

Measure	Cases	This Hosp.	State Avg.	U.S. Avg.
Heart Attack Care				
ACE Inhibitor or ARB for LVSD[1]	5	100%	96%	96%
Aspirin at Arrival	43	100%	99%	99%
Aspirin at Discharge	41	100%	99%	98%
Beta Blocker at Discharge	42	95%	99%	98%
Fibrinolytic Medication Timing	0	-	27%	55%
PCI Within 90 Minutes of Arrival[1]	14	93%	92%	90%
Smoking Cessation Advice[1]	22	100%	99%	99%
Chest Pain/Possible Heart Attack Care				
Aspirin at Arrival[1,3]	12	100%	95%	95%
Median Time to ECG (minutes)[1,3]	12	8	9	8
Median Time to Transfer (minutes)[1,3]	1	105	64	61
Fibrinolytic Medication Timing[3]	0	-	31%	54%
Heart Failure Care				
ACE Inhibitor or ARB for LVSD	55	98%	94%	94%
Discharge Instructions	122	90%	87%	88%
Evaluation of LVS Function	165	99%	97%	98%
Smoking Cessation Advice	25	100%	98%	98%
Pneumonia Care				
Appropriate Initial Antibiotic	56	95%	91%	92%
Blood Culture Timing	68	100%	97%	96%
Influenza Vaccine	67	97%	90%	91%
Initial Antibiotic Timing	82	100%	95%	95%
Pneumococcal Vaccine	86	94%	93%	93%
Smoking Cessation Advice	31	100%	97%	97%
Surgical Care Improvement Project				
Appropriate VTP Within 24 Hours	60	93%	93%	92%
Appropriate Hair Removal	287	100%	100%	99%
Appropriate Beta Blocker Usage	72	88%	94%	93%
Controlled Postoperative Blood Glucose	0	-	94%	93%
Prophylactic Antibiotic Timing	220	99%	97%	97%
Prophylactic Antibiotic Timing (Outpatient)	108	94%	95%	92%
Prophylactic Antibiotic Selection	223	97%	97%	97%
Prophylactic Antibiotic Select. (Outpatient)	106	99%	95%	94%
Prophylactic Antibiotic Stopped	217	94%	95%	94%
Recommended VTP Ordered	60	95%	95%	94%
Urinary Catheter Removal[1]	13	69%	88%	90%
Children's Asthma Care				
Received Systemic Corticosteroids	-	-	-	100%
Received Home Management Plan	-	-	-	71%
Received Reliever Medication	-	-	-	100%
Use of Medical Imaging				
Combination Abdominal CT Scan	481	0.520	0.227	0.191
Combination Chest CT Scan	333	0.156	0.059	0.054
Follow-up Mammogram/Ultrasound	1,041	6.2%	7.4%	8.4%
MRI for Low Back Pain	129	35.7%	36%	32.7%
Survey of Patients' Hospital Experiences				
Area Around Room 'Always' Quiet at Night	300+	55%	-	58%
Doctors 'Always' Communicated Well	300+	79%	-	80%
Home Recovery Information Given	300+	87%	-	82%
Hospital Given 9 or 10 on 10 Point Scale	300+	66%	-	67%
Meds 'Always' Explained Before Given	300+	58%	-	60%
Nurses 'Always' Communicated Well	300+	76%	-	76%
Pain 'Always' Well Controlled	300+	72%	-	69%
Room and Bathroom 'Always' Clean	300+	77%	-	71%
Timely Help 'Always' Received	300+	71%	-	64%
Would Definitely Recommend Hospital	300+	64%	-	69%

Sullivan County Memorial Hospital

630 West Third Street
Milan, MO 63556
Phone: 660-265-4212
Fax: 660-265-3609
Type: Critical Access Hospitals
Emergency Services: Yes
Ownership: Government - Local
Beds: 39

Key Personnel:
CEO/President. . . . . Martha Gragg
Chief of Medical Staff . . . . Tom Williams
Infection Control. . . . . Kim Ray, RN
Quality Assurance . . . . Kim Ray, RN
Radiology. . . . . Mary Christians
Emergency Room . . . . Thomas Williams, RN

Measure	Cases	This Hosp.	State Avg.	U.S. Avg.
Heart Attack Care				
ACE Inhibitor or ARB for LVSD[5]	0	-	96%	96%
Aspirin at Arrival[5]	0	-	99%	99%
Aspirin at Discharge[5]	0	-	99%	98%
Beta Blocker at Discharge[5]	0	-	99%	98%
Fibrinolytic Medication Timing[5]	0	-	27%	55%
PCI Within 90 Minutes of Arrival[5]	0	-	92%	90%
Smoking Cessation Advice[5]	0	-	99%	99%
Chest Pain/Possible Heart Attack Care				
Aspirin at Arrival[5]	0	-	95%	95%
Median Time to ECG (minutes)[5]	0	-	9	8
Median Time to Transfer (minutes)[5]	0	-	64	61
Fibrinolytic Medication Timing[5]	0	-	31%	54%
Heart Failure Care				
ACE Inhibitor or ARB for LVSD[1,3]	1	0%	94%	94%
Discharge Instructions[1,3]	5	40%	87%	88%
Evaluation of LVS Function[1,3]	11	27%	97%	98%
Smoking Cessation Advice[1,3]	1	100%	98%	98%
Pneumonia Care				
Appropriate Initial Antibiotic[1,3]	4	75%	91%	92%
Blood Culture Timing[1,3]	5	100%	97%	96%
Influenza Vaccine[1]	4	25%	90%	91%
Initial Antibiotic Timing[1,3]	10	80%	95%	95%
Pneumococcal Vaccine[1,3]	7	29%	93%	93%
Smoking Cessation Advice[1,3]	4	100%	97%	97%
Surgical Care Improvement Project				
Appropriate VTP Within 24 Hours[5]	0	-	93%	92%
Appropriate Hair Removal[5]	0	-	100%	99%
Appropriate Beta Blocker Usage[5]	0	-	94%	93%
Controlled Postoperative Blood Glucose[5]	0	-	94%	93%
Prophylactic Antibiotic Timing[5]	0	-	97%	97%
Prophylactic Antibiotic Timing (Outpatient)[5]	0	-	95%	92%
Prophylactic Antibiotic Selection[5]	0	-	97%	97%
Prophylactic Antibiotic Select. (Outpatient)[5]	0	-	95%	94%
Prophylactic Antibiotic Stopped[5]	0	-	95%	94%
Recommended VTP Ordered[5]	0	-	95%	94%
Urinary Catheter Removal[5]	0	-	88%	90%
Children's Asthma Care				
Received Systemic Corticosteroids	-	-	-	100%
Received Home Management Plan	-	-	-	71%
Received Reliever Medication	-	-	-	100%
Use of Medical Imaging				
Combination Abdominal CT Scan[1]	28	0.536	0.227	0.191
Combination Chest CT Scan[1]	6	0.667	0.059	0.054
Follow-up Mammogram/Ultrasound[5]	0	-	7.4%	8.4%
MRI for Low Back Pain[1]	16	43.8%	36%	32.7%
Survey of Patients' Hospital Experiences				
Area Around Room 'Always' Quiet at Night[8]	-	-	-	58%
Doctors 'Always' Communicated Well[8]	-	-	-	80%
Home Recovery Information Given[8]	-	-	-	82%
Hospital Given 9 or 10 on 10 Point Scale[8]	-	-	-	67%
Meds 'Always' Explained Before Given[8]	-	-	-	60%
Nurses 'Always' Communicated Well[8]	-	-	-	76%
Pain 'Always' Well Controlled[8]	-	-	-	69%
Room and Bathroom 'Always' Clean[8]	-	-	-	71%
Timely Help 'Always' Received[8]	-	-	-	64%
Would Definitely Recommend Hospital[8]	-	-	-	69%

NOTE: Hospital profiles are in alphabetical order by state, then city, then hospital within the city; Rankings exclude hospitals with less than 25 cases except for patient surveys which excludes hospitals with less than 100 cases; (a) 100–299 cases; (1) The number of cases is too small to be sure how well a hospital is performing; (2) The hospital indicated that the data submitted for this measure were based on a sample of cases; (3) Data was collected during a shorter time period (fewer quarters) than the maximum possible time for this measure; (4) Suppressed for one or more quarters by CMS; (5) No data is available from the hospital for this measure; (6) Fewer than 100 patients completed the HCAHPS survey. Use these rates with caution, as the number of surveys may be too low to reliably assess hospital performance; (7) Survey results are based on less than 12 months of data; (8) Survey results are not available for this reporting period; (9) No or very few patients were eligible for the HCAHPS survey. The scores shown, if any, reflect a very small number of surveys; (10) A state average was not calculated because too few hospitals in the state submitted data; (11) There were discrepancies in the data collection process; Please refer to the User's Guide for a full explanation of data.

Moberly Regional Medical Center

1515 Union Ave | Phone: 660-263-8400
Moberly, MO 65270 | Fax: 660-269-3091
URL: www.moberlyhospital.com
Type: Acute Care Hospitals | Emergency Services: Yes
Ownership: Proprietary | Beds: 114

Key Personnel:
CEO/President............... Jay Hodges
Cardiac Laboratory........... Ahmed Habib MD
Chief of Medical Staff.......... Ahmed Habib
Infection Control.............. Roanetta Bodgers
Operating Room............... Sonja Nelson
Quality Assurance .... Roanetta Rodgers
Emergency Room .... Eric Bettis
Intensive Care Unit............ Pat Fischer RN

Measure	Cases	This Hosp.	State Avg.	U.S. Avg.
Heart Attack Care				
ACE Inhibitor or ARB for LVSD	0	-	96%	96%
Aspirin at Arrival	25	100%	99%	99%
Aspirin at Discharge[1]	17	100%	99%	98%
Beta Blocker at Discharge[1]	17	100%	99%	98%
Fibrinolytic Medication Timing	0	-	27%	55%
PCI Within 90 Minutes of Arrival	0	-	92%	90%
Smoking Cessation Advice[1]	1	100%	99%	99%
Chest Pain/Possible Heart Attack Care				
Aspirin at Arrival	114	97%	95%	95%
Median Time to ECG (minutes)	121	9	9	8
Median Time to Transfer (minutes)[1,3]	13	64	64	61
Fibrinolytic Medication Timing[1]	5	40%	31%	54%
Heart Failure Care				
ACE Inhibitor or ARB for LVSD[1]	16	100%	94%	94%
Discharge Instructions	41	93%	87%	88%
Evaluation of LVS Function	70	99%	97%	98%
Smoking Cessation Advice[1]	14	100%	98%	98%
Pneumonia Care				
Appropriate Initial Antibiotic	58	95%	91%	92%
Blood Culture Timing	84	98%	97%	96%
Influenza Vaccine	67	94%	90%	91%
Initial Antibiotic Timing	97	96%	95%	95%
Pneumococcal Vaccine	106	99%	93%	93%
Smoking Cessation Advice	45	100%	97%	97%
Surgical Care Improvement Project				
Appropriate VTP Within 24 Hours[2]	48	98%	93%	92%
Appropriate Hair Removal[2]	115	100%	100%	99%
Appropriate Beta Blocker Usage[2]	36	92%	94%	93%
Controlled Postoperative Blood Glucose[2]	0	-	94%	93%
Prophylactic Antibiotic Timing[2]	81	98%	97%	97%
Prophylactic Antibiotic Timing (Outpatient)	83	96%	95%	92%
Prophylactic Antibiotic Selection[2]	82	99%	97%	97%
Prophylactic Antibiotic Select. (Outpatient)	82	99%	95%	94%
Prophylactic Antibiotic Stopped[2]	77	95%	95%	94%
Recommended VTP Ordered[2]	48	100%	95%	94%
Urinary Catheter Removal[1]	16	62%	88%	90%
Children's Asthma Care				
Received Systemic Corticosteroids	-	-	-	100%
Received Home Management Plan	-	-	-	71%
Received Reliever Medication	-	-	-	100%
Use of Medical Imaging				
Combination Abdominal CT Scan	233	0.506	0.227	0.191
Combination Chest CT Scan	230	0.057	0.059	0.054
Follow-up Mammogram/Ultrasound	288	11.8%	7.4%	8.4%
MRI for Low Back Pain[1]	38	31.6%	36%	32.7%
Survey of Patients' Hospital Experiences				
Area Around Room 'Always' Quiet at Night	300+	61%	-	58%
Doctors 'Always' Communicated Well	300+	81%	-	80%
Home Recovery Information Given	300+	89%	-	82%
Hospital Given 9 or 10 on 10 Point Scale	300+	66%	-	67%
Meds 'Always' Explained Before Given	300+	56%	-	60%
Nurses 'Always' Communicated Well	300+	74%	-	76%
Pain 'Always' Well Controlled	300+	66%	-	69%
Room and Bathroom 'Always' Clean	300+	72%	-	71%
Timely Help 'Always' Received	300+	63%	-	64%
Would Definitely Recommend Hospital	300+	60%	-	69%

Cox Monett Hospital

801 North Lincoln Avenue | Phone: 417-354-1400
Monett, MO 65708 | Fax: 417-354-1412
Type: Critical Access Hospitals | Emergency Services: Yes
Ownership: Voluntary Non-Profit - Private | Beds: 25

Key Personnel:
CEO/President............... Gregory Johnson
Chief of Medical Staff.......... Amber Ecomomu, MD
Quality Assurance .... Jana Perall
Emergency Room .... Stephen Dennis, MD

Measure	Cases	This Hosp.	State Avg.	U.S. Avg.
Heart Attack Care				
ACE Inhibitor or ARB for LVSD[1]	1	100%	96%	96%
Aspirin at Arrival[1]	4	100%	99%	99%
Aspirin at Discharge[1]	2	100%	99%	98%
Beta Blocker at Discharge[1]	3	100%	99%	98%
Fibrinolytic Medication Timing	0	-	27%	55%
PCI Within 90 Minutes of Arrival	0	-	92%	90%
Smoking Cessation Advice	0	-	99%	99%
Chest Pain/Possible Heart Attack Care				
Aspirin at Arrival	-	-	95%	95%
Median Time to ECG (minutes)	-	-	9	8
Median Time to Transfer (minutes)	-	-	64	61
Fibrinolytic Medication Timing	-	-	31%	54%
Heart Failure Care				
ACE Inhibitor or ARB for LVSD[1]	8	88%	94%	94%
Discharge Instructions[1]	16	100%	87%	88%
Evaluation of LVS Function[1]	18	100%	97%	98%
Smoking Cessation Advice[1]	1	100%	98%	98%
Pneumonia Care				
Appropriate Initial Antibiotic	58	95%	91%	92%
Blood Culture Timing	59	93%	97%	96%
Influenza Vaccine	50	88%	90%	91%
Initial Antibiotic Timing	69	96%	95%	95%
Pneumococcal Vaccine	57	91%	93%	93%
Smoking Cessation Advice	26	92%	97%	97%
Surgical Care Improvement Project				
Appropriate VTP Within 24 Hours[1]	13	92%	93%	92%
Appropriate Hair Removal[1]	21	95%	100%	99%
Appropriate Beta Blocker Usage[1]	7	100%	94%	93%
Controlled Postoperative Blood Glucose	0	-	94%	93%
Prophylactic Antibiotic Timing[1]	18	67%	97%	97%
Prophylactic Antibiotic Timing (Outpatient)	-	-	95%	92%
Prophylactic Antibiotic Selection[1]	18	94%	97%	97%
Prophylactic Antibiotic Select. (Outpatient)	-	-	95%	94%
Prophylactic Antibiotic Stopped[1]	17	76%	95%	94%
Recommended VTP Ordered[1]	13	100%	95%	94%
Urinary Catheter Removal[1]	7	14%	88%	90%
Children's Asthma Care				
Received Systemic Corticosteroids	-	-	-	100%
Received Home Management Plan	-	-	-	71%
Received Reliever Medication	-	-	-	100%
Use of Medical Imaging				
Combination Abdominal CT Scan	-	-	0.227	0.191
Combination Chest CT Scan	-	-	0.059	0.054
Follow-up Mammogram/Ultrasound	-	-	7.4%	8.4%
MRI for Low Back Pain	-	-	36%	32.7%
Survey of Patients' Hospital Experiences				
Area Around Room 'Always' Quiet at Night	(a)	70%	-	58%
Doctors 'Always' Communicated Well	(a)	89%	-	80%
Home Recovery Information Given	(a)	81%	-	82%
Hospital Given 9 or 10 on 10 Point Scale	(a)	74%	-	67%
Meds 'Always' Explained Before Given	(a)	71%	-	60%
Nurses 'Always' Communicated Well	(a)	83%	-	76%
Pain 'Always' Well Controlled	(a)	79%	-	69%
Room and Bathroom 'Always' Clean	(a)	77%	-	71%
Timely Help 'Always' Received	(a)	77%	-	64%
Would Definitely Recommend Hospital	(a)	71%	-	69%

Saint Francis Hospital

100 West Highway 60 | Phone: 417-934-7000
Mountain View, MO 65548 | Fax: 417-934-6024
Type: Critical Access Hospitals | Emergency Services: Yes
Ownership: Voluntary Non-Profit - Private | Beds: 42

Key Personnel:
CEO/President............... Don Swafford
Chief of Medical Staff.......... Mohammed Tabibi, DO
Infection Control.............. Jill Mundt, MT ASCP
Operating Room............... Janet Kile, RN
Radiology.................... Brian Denton, RT
Anesthesiology............... Cheryl Thurman, CRNA
Emergency Room .... Ernest L Carampatan, MD

Measure	Cases	This Hosp.	State Avg.	U.S. Avg.
Heart Attack Care				
ACE Inhibitor or ARB for LVSD[5]	0	-	96%	96%
Aspirin at Arrival[5]	0	-	99%	99%
Aspirin at Discharge[5]	0	-	99%	98%
Beta Blocker at Discharge[5]	0	-	99%	98%
Fibrinolytic Medication Timing[5]	0	-	27%	55%
PCI Within 90 Minutes of Arrival[5]	0	-	92%	90%
Smoking Cessation Advice[5]	0	-	99%	99%
Chest Pain/Possible Heart Attack Care				
Aspirin at Arrival	-	-	95%	95%
Median Time to ECG (minutes)	-	-	9	8
Median Time to Transfer (minutes)	-	-	64	61
Fibrinolytic Medication Timing	-	-	31%	54%
Heart Failure Care				
ACE Inhibitor or ARB for LVSD	0	-	94%	94%
Discharge Instructions[1]	4	100%	87%	88%
Evaluation of LVS Function[1]	7	100%	97%	98%
Smoking Cessation Advice[1]	2	100%	98%	98%
Pneumonia Care				
Appropriate Initial Antibiotic	76	82%	91%	92%
Blood Culture Timing	65	94%	97%	96%
Influenza Vaccine	65	97%	90%	91%
Initial Antibiotic Timing	95	95%	95%	95%
Pneumococcal Vaccine	91	99%	93%	93%
Smoking Cessation Advice[1]	23	100%	97%	97%
Surgical Care Improvement Project				
Appropriate VTP Within 24 Hours[5]	0	-	93%	92%
Appropriate Hair Removal[5]	0	-	100%	99%
Appropriate Beta Blocker Usage[5]	0	-	94%	93%
Controlled Postoperative Blood Glucose[5]	0	-	94%	93%
Prophylactic Antibiotic Timing[5]	0	-	97%	97%
Prophylactic Antibiotic Timing (Outpatient)	-	-	95%	92%
Prophylactic Antibiotic Selection[5]	0	-	97%	97%
Prophylactic Antibiotic Select. (Outpatient)	-	-	95%	94%
Prophylactic Antibiotic Stopped[5]	0	-	95%	94%
Recommended VTP Ordered[5]	0	-	95%	94%
Urinary Catheter Removal[5]	0	-	88%	90%
Children's Asthma Care				
Received Systemic Corticosteroids	-	-	-	100%
Received Home Management Plan	-	-	-	71%
Received Reliever Medication	-	-	-	100%
Use of Medical Imaging				
Combination Abdominal CT Scan	-	-	0.227	0.191
Combination Chest CT Scan	-	-	0.059	0.054
Follow-up Mammogram/Ultrasound	-	-	7.4%	8.4%
MRI for Low Back Pain	-	-	36%	32.7%
Survey of Patients' Hospital Experiences				
Area Around Room 'Always' Quiet at Night[8]	-	-	-	58%
Doctors 'Always' Communicated Well[8]	-	-	-	80%
Home Recovery Information Given[8]	-	-	-	82%
Hospital Given 9 or 10 on 10 Point Scale[8]	-	-	-	67%
Meds 'Always' Explained Before Given[8]	-	-	-	60%
Nurses 'Always' Communicated Well[8]	-	-	-	76%
Pain 'Always' Well Controlled[8]	-	-	-	69%
Room and Bathroom 'Always' Clean[8]	-	-	-	71%
Timely Help 'Always' Received[8]	-	-	-	64%
Would Definitely Recommend Hospital[8]	-	-	-	69%

NOTE: Hospital profiles are in alphabetical order by state, then city, then hospital within the city; Rankings exclude hospitals with less than 25 cases except for patient surveys which excludes hospitals with less than 100 cases; (a) 100–299 cases; (1) The number of cases is too small to be sure how well a hospital is performing; (2) The hospital indicated that the data submitted for this measure were based on a sample of cases; (3) Data was collected during a shorter time period (fewer quarters) than the maximum possible time for this measure; (4) Suppressed for one or more quarters by CMS; (5) No data is available from the hospital for this measure; (6) Fewer than 100 patients completed the HCAHPS survey. Use these rates with caution, as the number of surveys may be too low to reliably assess hospital performance; (7) Survey results are based on less than 12 months of data; (8) Survey results are not available for this reporting period; (9) No or very few patients were eligible for the HCAHPS survey. The scores shown, if any, reflect a very small number of surveys; (10) A state average was not calculated because too few hospitals in the state submitted data; (11) There were discrepancies in the data collection process; Please refer to the User's Guide for a full explanation of data.

Freeman Neosho Hospital

113 West Hickory Street
Neosho, MO 64850
URL: www.freemanhealth.com
Type: Critical Access Hospitals
Ownership: Proprietary
Phone: 417-451-1234
Fax: 417-347-3716
Emergency Services: Yes
Beds: 67

Key Personnel:
CEO/President. . . . . Steve Graddy
Radiology. . . . . Roger A Francis

Measure	Cases	This Hosp.	State Avg.	U.S. Avg.
Heart Attack Care				
ACE Inhibitor or ARB for LVSD[1,3]	2	100%	96%	96%
Aspirin at Arrival[1,3]	3	100%	99%	99%
Aspirin at Discharge[1,3]	2	100%	99%	98%
Beta Blocker at Discharge[1,3]	2	100%	99%	98%
Fibrinolytic Medication Timing[3]	0	-	27%	55%
PCI Within 90 Minutes of Arrival[3]	0	-	92%	90%
Smoking Cessation Advice[3]	0	-	99%	99%
Chest Pain/Possible Heart Attack Care				
Aspirin at Arrival	-	-	95%	95%
Median Time to ECG (minutes)	-	-	9	8
Median Time to Transfer (minutes)	-	-	64	61
Fibrinolytic Medication Timing	-	-	31%	54%
Heart Failure Care				
ACE Inhibitor or ARB for LVSD[1]	18	94%	94%	94%
Discharge Instructions	30	87%	87%	88%
Evaluation of LVS Function	49	100%	97%	98%
Smoking Cessation Advice[1]	9	100%	98%	98%
Pneumonia Care				
Appropriate Initial Antibiotic	47	98%	91%	92%
Blood Culture Timing	43	100%	97%	96%
Influenza Vaccine	48	90%	90%	91%
Initial Antibiotic Timing	66	97%	95%	95%
Pneumococcal Vaccine	55	96%	93%	93%
Smoking Cessation Advice	37	97%	97%	97%
Surgical Care Improvement Project				
Appropriate VTP Within 24 Hours[5]	0	-	93%	92%
Appropriate Hair Removal[5]	0	-	100%	99%
Appropriate Beta Blocker Usage[5]	0	-	94%	93%
Controlled Postoperative Blood Glucose[5]	0	-	94%	93%
Prophylactic Antibiotic Timing[5]	0	-	97%	97%
Prophylactic Antibiotic Timing (Outpatient)	-	-	95%	92%
Prophylactic Antibiotic Selection[5]	0	-	97%	97%
Prophylactic Antibiotic Select. (Outpatient)	-	-	95%	94%
Prophylactic Antibiotic Stopped[5]	0	-	95%	94%
Recommended VTP Ordered[5]	0	-	95%	94%
Urinary Catheter Removal[5]	0	-	88%	90%
Children's Asthma Care				
Received Systemic Corticosteroids	-	-	-	100%
Received Home Management Plan	-	-	-	71%
Received Reliever Medication	-	-	-	100%
Use of Medical Imaging				
Combination Abdominal CT Scan	-	-	0.227	0.191
Combination Chest CT Scan	-	-	0.059	0.054
Follow-up Mammogram/Ultrasound	-	-	7.4%	8.4%
MRI for Low Back Pain	-	-	36%	32.7%
Survey of Patients' Hospital Experiences				
Area Around Room 'Always' Quiet at Night	300+	52%	-	58%
Doctors 'Always' Communicated Well	300+	83%	-	80%
Home Recovery Information Given	300+	84%	-	82%
Hospital Given 9 or 10 on 10 Point Scale	300+	73%	-	67%
Meds 'Always' Explained Before Given	300+	62%	-	60%
Nurses 'Always' Communicated Well	300+	78%	-	76%
Pain 'Always' Well Controlled	300+	69%	-	69%
Room and Bathroom 'Always' Clean	300+	79%	-	71%
Timely Help 'Always' Received	300+	70%	-	64%
Would Definitely Recommend Hospital	300+	71%	-	69%

Nevada Regional Medical Center

800 S Ash St
Nevada, MO 64772
URL: www.nrmchealth.com
Type: Acute Care Hospitals
Ownership: Government - Local
Phone: 417-667-3355
Fax: 417-448-3848
Emergency Services: Yes
Beds: 53

Key Personnel:
CEO/President. . . . . Judith Feuquay
Chief of Medical Staff. . . . . Michael Crim
Operating Room. . . . . Joy Jefferies
Quality Assurance . . . . Janie Dickey
Radiology. . . . . Roger Francis
Emergency Room . . . . Holly Busher, RN

Measure	Cases	This Hosp.	State Avg.	U.S. Avg.
Heart Attack Care				
ACE Inhibitor or ARB for LVSD[1]	1	100%	96%	96%
Aspirin at Arrival[1]	4	75%	99%	99%
Aspirin at Discharge[1]	3	67%	99%	98%
Beta Blocker at Discharge[1]	3	100%	99%	98%
Fibrinolytic Medication Timing	0	-	27%	55%
PCI Within 90 Minutes of Arrival	0	-	92%	90%
Smoking Cessation Advice	0	-	99%	99%
Chest Pain/Possible Heart Attack Care				
Aspirin at Arrival	97	96%	95%	95%
Median Time to ECG (minutes)	99	10	9	8
Median Time to Transfer (minutes)[1,3]	3	195	64	61
Fibrinolytic Medication Timing[1]	10	10%	31%	54%
Heart Failure Care				
ACE Inhibitor or ARB for LVSD[1]	15	73%	94%	94%
Discharge Instructions	35	83%	87%	88%
Evaluation of LVS Function	46	87%	97%	98%
Smoking Cessation Advice[1]	5	100%	98%	98%
Pneumonia Care				
Appropriate Initial Antibiotic	39	90%	91%	92%
Blood Culture Timing[1]	19	100%	97%	96%
Influenza Vaccine	37	86%	90%	91%
Initial Antibiotic Timing	54	100%	95%	95%
Pneumococcal Vaccine	47	77%	93%	93%
Smoking Cessation Advice	26	100%	97%	97%
Surgical Care Improvement Project				
Appropriate VTP Within 24 Hours	27	85%	93%	92%
Appropriate Hair Removal	34	100%	100%	99%
Appropriate Beta Blocker Usage[1]	11	55%	94%	93%
Controlled Postoperative Blood Glucose	0	-	94%	93%
Prophylactic Antibiotic Timing[1]	21	86%	97%	97%
Prophylactic Antibiotic Timing (Outpatient)	39	97%	95%	92%
Prophylactic Antibiotic Selection[1]	21	100%	97%	97%
Prophylactic Antibiotic Select. (Outpatient)	39	95%	95%	94%
Prophylactic Antibiotic Stopped[1]	18	89%	95%	94%
Recommended VTP Ordered	27	96%	95%	94%
Urinary Catheter Removal[1]	12	83%	88%	90%
Children's Asthma Care				
Received Systemic Corticosteroids	-	-	-	100%
Received Home Management Plan	-	-	-	71%
Received Reliever Medication	-	-	-	100%
Use of Medical Imaging				
Combination Abdominal CT Scan	269	0.409	0.227	0.191
Combination Chest CT Scan	118	0.008	0.059	0.054
Follow-up Mammogram/Ultrasound	411	4.4%	7.4%	8.4%
MRI for Low Back Pain	58	51.7%	36%	32.7%
Survey of Patients' Hospital Experiences				
Area Around Room 'Always' Quiet at Night	(a)	58%	-	58%
Doctors 'Always' Communicated Well	(a)	88%	-	80%
Home Recovery Information Given	(a)	86%	-	82%
Hospital Given 9 or 10 on 10 Point Scale	(a)	59%	-	67%
Meds 'Always' Explained Before Given	(a)	56%	-	60%
Nurses 'Always' Communicated Well	(a)	75%	-	76%
Pain 'Always' Well Controlled	(a)	61%	-	69%
Room and Bathroom 'Always' Clean	(a)	84%	-	71%
Timely Help 'Always' Received	(a)	71%	-	64%
Would Definitely Recommend Hospital	(a)	56%	-	69%

North Kansas City Hospital

2800 Clay Edwards Drive
North Kansas City, MO 64116
URL: www.nkch.org
Type: Acute Care Hospitals
Ownership: Government - Local
Phone: 816-691-2000
Fax: 816-346-7020
Emergency Services: Yes
Beds: 451

Key Personnel:
CEO/President. . . . . David Carpenter
Cardiac Laboratory. . . . . Fran Marencik
Chief of Medical Staff. . . . . Leslie Thomas, MD
Coronary Care . . . . April Patten
Infection Control. . . . . Tina Harvey
Operating Room. . . . . Dewayne Gossett
Quality Assurance . . . . Connie Griffith
Radiology. . . . . Hanamel Rada

Measure	Cases	This Hosp.	State Avg.	U.S. Avg.
Heart Attack Care				
ACE Inhibitor or ARB for LVSD[2]	120	98%	96%	96%
Aspirin at Arrival[2]	293	100%	99%	99%
Aspirin at Discharge[2]	369	99%	99%	98%
Beta Blocker at Discharge[2]	367	99%	99%	98%
Fibrinolytic Medication Timing[2]	0	-	27%	55%
PCI Within 90 Minutes of Arrival[2]	80	98%	92%	90%
Smoking Cessation Advice[2]	155	100%	99%	99%
Chest Pain/Possible Heart Attack Care				
Aspirin at Arrival[5]	0	-	95%	95%
Median Time to ECG (minutes)[5]	0	-	9	8
Median Time to Transfer (minutes)[5]	0	-	64	61
Fibrinolytic Medication Timing[5]	0	-	31%	54%
Heart Failure Care				
ACE Inhibitor or ARB for LVSD[2]	132	94%	94%	94%
Discharge Instructions[2]	367	96%	87%	88%
Evaluation of LVS Function[2]	411	97%	97%	98%
Smoking Cessation Advice[2]	66	100%	98%	98%
Pneumonia Care				
Appropriate Initial Antibiotic[2]	170	94%	91%	92%
Blood Culture Timing[2]	189	96%	97%	96%
Influenza Vaccine[2]	159	96%	90%	91%
Initial Antibiotic Timing[2]	281	96%	95%	95%
Pneumococcal Vaccine[2]	249	95%	93%	93%
Smoking Cessation Advice[2]	123	98%	97%	97%
Surgical Care Improvement Project				
Appropriate VTP Within 24 Hours[2]	353	80%	93%	92%
Appropriate Hair Removal[2]	938	99%	100%	99%
Appropriate Beta Blocker Usage[2]	316	90%	94%	93%
Controlled Postoperative Blood Glucose[2]	181	98%	94%	93%
Prophylactic Antibiotic Timing[2]	659	95%	97%	97%
Prophylactic Antibiotic Timing (Outpatient)	761	90%	95%	92%
Prophylactic Antibiotic Selection[2]	669	96%	97%	97%
Prophylactic Antibiotic Select. (Outpatient)	722	96%	95%	94%
Prophylactic Antibiotic Stopped[2]	633	94%	95%	94%
Recommended VTP Ordered[2]	353	87%	95%	94%
Urinary Catheter Removal[2]	195	89%	88%	90%
Children's Asthma Care				
Received Systemic Corticosteroids	-	-	-	100%
Received Home Management Plan	-	-	-	71%
Received Reliever Medication	-	-	-	100%
Use of Medical Imaging				
Combination Abdominal CT Scan	1,477	0.093	0.227	0.191
Combination Chest CT Scan	1,088	0.034	0.059	0.054
Follow-up Mammogram/Ultrasound	949	15.7%	7.4%	8.4%
MRI for Low Back Pain	442	36.2%	36%	32.7%
Survey of Patients' Hospital Experiences				
Area Around Room 'Always' Quiet at Night	300+	56%	-	58%
Doctors 'Always' Communicated Well	300+	80%	-	80%
Home Recovery Information Given	300+	80%	-	82%
Hospital Given 9 or 10 on 10 Point Scale	300+	72%	-	67%
Meds 'Always' Explained Before Given	300+	59%	-	60%
Nurses 'Always' Communicated Well	300+	75%	-	76%
Pain 'Always' Well Controlled	300+	68%	-	69%
Room and Bathroom 'Always' Clean	300+	69%	-	71%
Timely Help 'Always' Received	300+	63%	-	64%
Would Definitely Recommend Hospital	300+	78%	-	69%

NOTE: Hospital profiles are in alphabetical order by state, then city, then hospital within the city; Rankings exclude hospitals with less than 25 cases except for patient surveys which excludes hospitals with less than 100 cases; (a) 100–299 cases; (1) The number of cases is too small to be sure how well a hospital is performing; (2) The hospital indicated that the data submitted for this measure were based on a sample of cases; (3) Data was collected during a shorter time period (fewer quarters) than the maximum possible time for this measure; (4) Suppressed for one or more quarters by CMS; (5) No data is available from the hospital for this measure; (6) Fewer than 100 patients completed the HCAHPS survey. Use these rates with caution, as the number of surveys may be too low to reliably assess hospital performance; (7) Survey results are based on less than 12 months of data; (8) Survey results are not available for this reporting period; (9) No or very few patients were eligible for the HCAHPS survey. The scores shown, if any, reflect a very small number of surveys; (10) A state average was not calculated because too few hospitals in the state submitted data; (11) There were discrepancies in the data collection process; Please refer to the User's Guide for a full explanation of data.

Progress West Healthcare Center

2 Progress Point Pkwy Phone: 636-344-1000
O'Fallon, MO 63368
URL: www.progresswesthealthcare.org
Type: Acute Care Hospitals Emergency Services: Yes
Ownership: Voluntary Non-Profit - Private
Key Personnel:
Cardiology . . . . Jeff Haile

Measure	Cases	This Hosp.	State Avg.	U.S. Avg.
Heart Attack Care				
ACE Inhibitor or ARB for LVSD[1]	1	100%	96%	96%
Aspirin at Arrival[1]	13	100%	99%	99%
Aspirin at Discharge[1]	6	100%	99%	98%
Beta Blocker at Discharge[1]	6	100%	99%	98%
Fibrinolytic Medication Timing	0	-	27%	55%
PCI Within 90 Minutes of Arrival	0	-	92%	90%
Smoking Cessation Advice	0	-	99%	99%
Chest Pain/Possible Heart Attack Care				
Aspirin at Arrival	33	94%	95%	95%
Median Time to ECG (minutes)	33	4	9	8
Median Time to Transfer (minutes)[1,3]	3	33	64	61
Fibrinolytic Medication Timing	0	-	31%	54%
Heart Failure Care				
ACE Inhibitor or ARB for LVSD[1]	21	100%	94%	94%
Discharge Instructions	46	91%	87%	88%
Evaluation of LVS Function	58	97%	97%	98%
Smoking Cessation Advice[1]	9	100%	98%	98%
Pneumonia Care				
Appropriate Initial Antibiotic	88	100%	91%	92%
Blood Culture Timing	93	99%	97%	96%
Influenza Vaccine	60	85%	90%	91%
Initial Antibiotic Timing	85	98%	95%	95%
Pneumococcal Vaccine	52	96%	93%	93%
Smoking Cessation Advice	38	100%	97%	97%
Surgical Care Improvement Project				
Appropriate VTP Within 24 Hours	75	95%	93%	92%
Appropriate Hair Removal	350	100%	100%	99%
Appropriate Beta Blocker Usage	97	82%	94%	93%
Controlled Postoperative Blood Glucose	0	-	94%	93%
Prophylactic Antibiotic Timing	286	98%	97%	97%
Prophylactic Antibiotic Timing (Outpatient)	46	89%	95%	92%
Prophylactic Antibiotic Selection	286	99%	97%	97%
Prophylactic Antibiotic Select. (Outpatient)	43	88%	95%	94%
Prophylactic Antibiotic Stopped	279	98%	95%	94%
Recommended VTP Ordered	75	95%	95%	94%
Urinary Catheter Removal	133	98%	88%	90%
Children's Asthma Care				
Received Systemic Corticosteroids	-	-	-	100%
Received Home Management Plan	-	-	-	71%
Received Reliever Medication	-	-	-	100%
Use of Medical Imaging				
Combination Abdominal CT Scan	119	0.059	0.227	0.191
Combination Chest CT Scan	91	0.000	0.059	0.054
Follow-up Mammogram/Ultrasound	93	5.4%	7.4%	8.4%
MRI for Low Back Pain[1]	21	23.8%	36%	32.7%
Survey of Patients' Hospital Experiences				
Area Around Room 'Always' Quiet at Night	300+	67%	-	58%
Doctors 'Always' Communicated Well	300+	83%	-	80%
Home Recovery Information Given	300+	85%	-	82%
Hospital Given 9 or 10 on 10 Point Scale	300+	80%	-	67%
Meds 'Always' Explained Before Given	300+	65%	-	60%
Nurses 'Always' Communicated Well	300+	80%	-	76%
Pain 'Always' Well Controlled	300+	72%	-	69%
Room and Bathroom 'Always' Clean	300+	75%	-	71%
Timely Help 'Always' Received	300+	65%	-	64%
Would Definitely Recommend Hospital	300+	82%	-	69%

Lake Regional Health System

54 Hospital Drive Phone: 573-348-8000
Osage Beach, MO 65065 Fax: 573-348-8268
E-mail: dwakeford@socket.net
URL: www.lakeregional.com
Type: Acute Care Hospitals Emergency Services: Yes
Ownership: Voluntary Non-Profit - Other Beds: 140
Key Personnel:
CEO/President. . . . . Michael E Henze
Cardiac Laboratory. . . . . Tonnie Rugen
Chief of Medical Staff . . . . Grant Barnum, MD
Operating Room. . . . . Michael M Duff, RN
Quality Assurance . . . . Sue Fletcher
Anesthesiology. . . . . Alan Meade, MD
Emergency Room . . . . Terry L Berry
Intensive Care Unit. . . . . Cathlene Vybee

Measure	Cases	This Hosp.	State Avg.	U.S. Avg.
Heart Attack Care				
ACE Inhibitor or ARB for LVSD	28	96%	96%	96%
Aspirin at Arrival	220	98%	99%	99%
Aspirin at Discharge	207	99%	99%	98%
Beta Blocker at Discharge	208	98%	99%	98%
Fibrinolytic Medication Timing	0	-	27%	55%
PCI Within 90 Minutes of Arrival	43	74%	92%	90%
Smoking Cessation Advice	94	100%	99%	99%
Chest Pain/Possible Heart Attack Care				
Aspirin at Arrival[1]	14	100%	95%	95%
Median Time to ECG (minutes)[1]	14	8	9	8
Median Time to Transfer (minutes)[5]	0	-	64	61
Fibrinolytic Medication Timing[3]	0	-	31%	54%
Heart Failure Care				
ACE Inhibitor or ARB for LVSD	80	92%	94%	94%
Discharge Instructions	208	85%	87%	88%
Evaluation of LVS Function	248	100%	97%	98%
Smoking Cessation Advice	58	97%	98%	98%
Pneumonia Care				
Appropriate Initial Antibiotic	149	92%	91%	92%
Blood Culture Timing	185	97%	97%	96%
Influenza Vaccine	107	97%	90%	91%
Initial Antibiotic Timing	181	96%	95%	95%
Pneumococcal Vaccine	168	97%	93%	93%
Smoking Cessation Advice	79	97%	97%	97%
Surgical Care Improvement Project				
Appropriate VTP Within 24 Hours	201	80%	93%	92%
Appropriate Hair Removal	385	100%	100%	99%
Appropriate Beta Blocker Usage	108	93%	94%	93%
Controlled Postoperative Blood Glucose	52	96%	94%	93%
Prophylactic Antibiotic Timing	258	90%	97%	97%
Prophylactic Antibiotic Timing (Outpatient)	213	82%	95%	92%
Prophylactic Antibiotic Selection	259	92%	97%	97%
Prophylactic Antibiotic Select. (Outpatient)	192	92%	95%	94%
Prophylactic Antibiotic Stopped	250	87%	95%	94%
Recommended VTP Ordered	205	80%	95%	94%
Urinary Catheter Removal	94	91%	88%	90%
Children's Asthma Care				
Received Systemic Corticosteroids	-	-	-	100%
Received Home Management Plan	-	-	-	71%
Received Reliever Medication	-	-	-	100%
Use of Medical Imaging				
Combination Abdominal CT Scan	556	0.719	0.227	0.191
Combination Chest CT Scan	361	0.706	0.059	0.054
Follow-up Mammogram/Ultrasound	1,094	6.1%	7.4%	8.4%
MRI for Low Back Pain	70	32.9%	36%	32.7%
Survey of Patients' Hospital Experiences				
Area Around Room 'Always' Quiet at Night	300+	54%	-	58%
Doctors 'Always' Communicated Well	300+	78%	-	80%
Home Recovery Information Given	300+	85%	-	82%
Hospital Given 9 or 10 on 10 Point Scale	300+	66%	-	67%
Meds 'Always' Explained Before Given	300+	61%	-	60%
Nurses 'Always' Communicated Well	300+	76%	-	76%
Pain 'Always' Well Controlled	300+	69%	-	69%
Room and Bathroom 'Always' Clean	300+	78%	-	71%
Timely Help 'Always' Received	300+	70%	-	64%
Would Definitely Recommend Hospital	300+	66%	-	69%

SAC-Osage Hospital

700 Giesler Drive Phone: 417-646-8181
Osceola, MO 64776 Fax: 417-646-8416
Type: Acute Care Hospitals Emergency Services: Yes
Ownership: Govt - Hospital Dist/Auth Beds: 47
Key Personnel:
CEO/President. . . . . Harrell Conelly
Chief of Medical Staff . . . . Wayne L. Morton, MD
Operating Room. . . . . Mary Locke, RN

Measure	Cases	This Hosp.	State Avg.	U.S. Avg.
Heart Attack Care				
ACE Inhibitor or ARB for LVSD[5]	0	-	96%	96%
Aspirin at Arrival[5]	0	-	99%	99%
Aspirin at Discharge[5]	0	-	99%	98%
Beta Blocker at Discharge[5]	0	-	99%	98%
Fibrinolytic Medication Timing[5]	0	-	27%	55%
PCI Within 90 Minutes of Arrival[5]	0	-	92%	90%
Smoking Cessation Advice[5]	0	-	99%	99%
Chest Pain/Possible Heart Attack Care				
Aspirin at Arrival[1]	19	47%	95%	95%
Median Time to ECG (minutes)[1]	17	7	9	8
Median Time to Transfer (minutes)[1,3]	3	90	64	61
Fibrinolytic Medication Timing[1,3]	3	33%	31%	54%
Heart Failure Care				
ACE Inhibitor or ARB for LVSD[1,2]	1	100%	94%	94%
Discharge Instructions[1,2]	16	50%	87%	88%
Evaluation of LVS Function[1,2]	24	4%	97%	98%
Smoking Cessation Advice[1,2]	6	67%	98%	98%
Pneumonia Care				
Appropriate Initial Antibiotic[1,2]	12	75%	91%	92%
Blood Culture Timing[1,2]	6	33%	97%	96%
Influenza Vaccine[1,2]	11	18%	90%	91%
Initial Antibiotic Timing[1,2]	14	71%	95%	95%
Pneumococcal Vaccine[1,2]	15	33%	93%	93%
Smoking Cessation Advice[1,2]	7	100%	97%	97%
Surgical Care Improvement Project				
Appropriate VTP Within 24 Hours[5]	0	-	93%	92%
Appropriate Hair Removal[5]	0	-	100%	99%
Appropriate Beta Blocker Usage[5]	0	-	94%	93%
Controlled Postoperative Blood Glucose[5]	0	-	94%	93%
Prophylactic Antibiotic Timing[5]	0	-	97%	97%
Prophylactic Antibiotic Timing (Outpatient)[5]	0	-	95%	92%
Prophylactic Antibiotic Selection[5]	0	-	97%	97%
Prophylactic Antibiotic Select. (Outpatient)[5]	0	-	95%	94%
Prophylactic Antibiotic Stopped[5]	0	-	95%	94%
Recommended VTP Ordered[5]	0	-	95%	94%
Urinary Catheter Removal[5]	0	-	88%	90%
Children's Asthma Care				
Received Systemic Corticosteroids	-	-	-	100%
Received Home Management Plan	-	-	-	71%
Received Reliever Medication	-	-	-	100%
Use of Medical Imaging				
Combination Abdominal CT Scan	68	0.735	0.227	0.191
Combination Chest CT Scan[1]	42	0.024	0.059	0.054
Follow-up Mammogram/Ultrasound	161	2.5%	7.4%	8.4%
MRI for Low Back Pain[1]	23	43.5%	36%	32.7%
Survey of Patients' Hospital Experiences				
Area Around Room 'Always' Quiet at Night	(a)	58%	-	58%
Doctors 'Always' Communicated Well	(a)	82%	-	80%
Home Recovery Information Given	(a)	75%	-	82%
Hospital Given 9 or 10 on 10 Point Scale	(a)	59%	-	67%
Meds 'Always' Explained Before Given	(a)	69%	-	60%
Nurses 'Always' Communicated Well	(a)	81%	-	76%
Pain 'Always' Well Controlled	(a)	63%	-	69%
Room and Bathroom 'Always' Clean	(a)	81%	-	71%
Timely Help 'Always' Received	(a)	70%	-	64%
Would Definitely Recommend Hospital	(a)	64%	-	69%

NOTE: Hospital profiles are in alphabetical order by state, then city, then hospital within the city; Rankings exclude hospitals with less than 25 cases except for patient surveys which excludes hospitals with less than 100 cases; (a) 100–299 cases; (1) The number of cases is too small to be sure how well a hospital is performing; (2) The hospital indicated that the data submitted for this measure were based on a sample of cases; (3) Data was collected during a shorter time period (fewer quarters) than the maximum possible time for this measure; (4) Suppressed for one or more quarters by CMS; (5) No data is available from the hospital for this measure; (6) Fewer than 100 patients completed the HCAHPS survey. Use these rates with caution, as the number of surveys may be too low to reliably assess hospital performance; (7) Survey results are based on less than 12 months of data; (8) Survey results are not available for this reporting period; (9) No or very few patients were eligible for the HCAHPS survey. The scores shown, if any, reflect a very small number of surveys; (10) A state average was not calculated because too few hospitals in the state submitted data; (11) There were discrepancies in the data collection process; Please refer to the User's Guide for a full explanation of data.

Perry County Memorial Hospital

434 North West Street
Perryville, MO 63775
URL: www.pchmo.org
Type: Critical Access Hospitals
Ownership: Government - Local
Phone: 573-547-2530
Fax: 573-547-3776
Emergency Services: Yes
Beds: 51

Key Personnel:

CEO/President. . . . . Patrick Carron
Chief of Medical Staff . . . . Mohammad Moaddabi
Infection Control. . . . . Katie Godsey
Operating Room. . . . . Lois Prost
Quality Assurance . . . . Linda Brown
Radiology. . . . . Christopher Wibbenme
Emergency Room . . . . Melissa Hayden
Patient Relations . . . . Barbara Ernst

Measure	Cases	This Hosp.	State Avg.	U.S. Avg.
Heart Attack Care				
ACE Inhibitor or ARB for LVSD[3]	0	-	96%	96%
Aspirin at Arrival[1,3]	3	100%	99%	99%
Aspirin at Discharge[1,3]	2	100%	99%	98%
Beta Blocker at Discharge[1,3]	2	100%	99%	98%
Fibrinolytic Medication Timing[3]	0	-	27%	55%
PCI Within 90 Minutes of Arrival[3]	0	-	92%	90%
Smoking Cessation Advice[3]	0	-	99%	99%
Chest Pain/Possible Heart Attack Care				
Aspirin at Arrival	-	-	95%	95%
Median Time to ECG (minutes)	-	-	9	8
Median Time to Transfer (minutes)	-	-	64	61
Fibrinolytic Medication Timing	-	-	31%	54%
Heart Failure Care				
ACE Inhibitor or ARB for LVSD[1]	3	100%	94%	94%
Discharge Instructions[1]	14	57%	87%	88%
Evaluation of LVS Function[1]	23	83%	97%	98%
Smoking Cessation Advice[1]	3	100%	98%	98%
Pneumonia Care				
Appropriate Initial Antibiotic[1]	16	94%	91%	92%
Blood Culture Timing	39	97%	97%	96%
Influenza Vaccine	36	89%	90%	91%
Initial Antibiotic Timing	50	98%	95%	95%
Pneumococcal Vaccine	48	88%	93%	93%
Smoking Cessation Advice[1]	11	100%	97%	97%
Surgical Care Improvement Project				
Appropriate VTP Within 24 Hours[1]	11	82%	93%	92%
Appropriate Hair Removal[1]	22	100%	100%	99%
Appropriate Beta Blocker Usage[1]	3	67%	94%	93%
Controlled Postoperative Blood Glucose	0	-	94%	93%
Prophylactic Antibiotic Timing[1]	13	100%	97%	97%
Prophylactic Antibiotic Timing (Outpatient)	-	-	95%	92%
Prophylactic Antibiotic Selection[1]	13	100%	97%	97%
Prophylactic Antibiotic Select. (Outpatient)	-	-	95%	94%
Prophylactic Antibiotic Stopped[1]	12	92%	95%	94%
Recommended VTP Ordered[1]	11	82%	95%	94%
Urinary Catheter Removal[1]	4	75%	88%	90%
Children's Asthma Care				
Received Systemic Corticosteroids	-	-	-	100%
Received Home Management Plan	-	-	-	71%
Received Reliever Medication	-	-	-	100%
Use of Medical Imaging				
Combination Abdominal CT Scan	-	-	0.227	0.191
Combination Chest CT Scan	-	-	0.059	0.054
Follow-up Mammogram/Ultrasound	-	-	7.4%	8.4%
MRI for Low Back Pain	-	-	36%	32.7%
Survey of Patients' Hospital Experiences				
Area Around Room 'Always' Quiet at Night[8]	-	-	-	58%
Doctors 'Always' Communicated Well[8]	-	-	-	80%
Home Recovery Information Given[8]	-	-	-	82%
Hospital Given 9 or 10 on 10 Point Scale[8]	-	-	-	67%
Meds 'Always' Explained Before Given[8]	-	-	-	60%
Nurses 'Always' Communicated Well[8]	-	-	-	76%
Pain 'Always' Well Controlled[8]	-	-	-	69%
Room and Bathroom 'Always' Clean[8]	-	-	-	71%
Timely Help 'Always' Received[8]	-	-	-	64%
Would Definitely Recommend Hospital[8]	-	-	-	69%

Poplar Bluff Regional Medical Center

2620 N Westwood Blvd
Poplar Bluff, MO 63901
E-mail: info@pbrmc.hma-corp.com
URL: www.poplarbluffregional.com
Type: Acute Care Hospitals
Ownership: Proprietary
Phone: 573-686-5313
Fax: 573-686-5388
Emergency Services: Yes
Beds: 423

Key Personnel:

CEO/President. . . . . Bruce Eady

Measure	Cases	This Hosp.	State Avg.	U.S. Avg.
Heart Attack Care				
ACE Inhibitor or ARB for LVSD	33	100%	96%	96%
Aspirin at Arrival	107	99%	99%	99%
Aspirin at Discharge	130	100%	99%	98%
Beta Blocker at Discharge	122	100%	99%	98%
Fibrinolytic Medication Timing	0	-	27%	55%
PCI Within 90 Minutes of Arrival	29	100%	92%	90%
Smoking Cessation Advice	70	100%	99%	99%
Chest Pain/Possible Heart Attack Care				
Aspirin at Arrival[1]	9	89%	95%	95%
Median Time to ECG (minutes)[1]	9	6	9	8
Median Time to Transfer (minutes)[5]	0	-	64	61
Fibrinolytic Medication Timing[5]	0	-	31%	54%
Heart Failure Care				
ACE Inhibitor or ARB for LVSD	91	99%	94%	94%
Discharge Instructions	269	100%	87%	88%
Evaluation of LVS Function	330	99%	97%	98%
Smoking Cessation Advice	60	100%	98%	98%
Pneumonia Care				
Appropriate Initial Antibiotic	137	91%	91%	92%
Blood Culture Timing	233	97%	97%	96%
Influenza Vaccine	161	100%	90%	91%
Initial Antibiotic Timing	216	94%	95%	95%
Pneumococcal Vaccine	219	100%	93%	93%
Smoking Cessation Advice	116	100%	97%	97%
Surgical Care Improvement Project				
Appropriate VTP Within 24 Hours[2]	200	96%	93%	92%
Appropriate Hair Removal[2]	763	100%	100%	99%
Appropriate Beta Blocker Usage[2]	218	99%	94%	93%
Controlled Postoperative Blood Glucose[2]	115	92%	94%	93%
Prophylactic Antibiotic Timing[2]	531	98%	97%	97%
Prophylactic Antibiotic Timing (Outpatient)	223	99%	95%	92%
Prophylactic Antibiotic Selection[2]	539	96%	97%	97%
Prophylactic Antibiotic Select. (Outpatient)	222	95%	95%	94%
Prophylactic Antibiotic Stopped[2]	473	96%	95%	94%
Recommended VTP Ordered[2]	200	98%	95%	94%
Urinary Catheter Removal	130	100%	88%	90%
Children's Asthma Care				
Received Systemic Corticosteroids	61	100%	-	100%
Received Home Management Plan	61	100%	-	71%
Received Reliever Medication	61	100%	-	100%
Use of Medical Imaging				
Combination Abdominal CT Scan	356	0.115	0.227	0.191
Combination Chest CT Scan	192	0.068	0.059	0.054
Follow-up Mammogram/Ultrasound	738	6.4%	7.4%	8.4%
MRI for Low Back Pain	71	39.4%	36%	32.7%
Survey of Patients' Hospital Experiences				
Area Around Room 'Always' Quiet at Night	300+	44%	-	58%
Doctors 'Always' Communicated Well	300+	76%	-	80%
Home Recovery Information Given	300+	73%	-	82%
Hospital Given 9 or 10 on 10 Point Scale	300+	44%	-	67%
Meds 'Always' Explained Before Given	300+	52%	-	60%
Nurses 'Always' Communicated Well	300+	67%	-	76%
Pain 'Always' Well Controlled	300+	65%	-	69%
Room and Bathroom 'Always' Clean	300+	57%	-	71%
Timely Help 'Always' Received	300+	61%	-	64%
Would Definitely Recommend Hospital	300+	45%	-	69%

Poplar Bluff VA Medical Center

1500 N. Westwood Blvd.
Poplar Bluff, MO 63901
Type: Acute Care-Veterans Administration
Ownership: Government - Federal
Phone: 573-686-4151
Fax: 573-778-4699
Emergency Services: No
Beds: 16

Key Personnel:

CEO/President. . . . . Nancy Arnold

Measure	Cases	This Hosp.	State Avg.	U.S. Avg.
Heart Attack Care				
ACE Inhibitor or ARB for LVSD[5]	0	-	96%	96%
Aspirin at Arrival[1]	3	100%	99%	99%
Aspirin at Discharge[1]	2	100%	99%	98%
Beta Blocker at Discharge[1]	3	100%	99%	98%
Fibrinolytic Medication Timing[1]	3	100%	27%	55%
PCI Within 90 Minutes of Arrival[5]	0	-	92%	90%
Smoking Cessation Advice[5]	0	-	99%	99%
Chest Pain/Possible Heart Attack Care				
Aspirin at Arrival	-	-	95%	95%
Median Time to ECG (minutes)	-	-	9	8
Median Time to Transfer (minutes)	-	-	64	61
Fibrinolytic Medication Timing	-	-	31%	54%
Heart Failure Care				
ACE Inhibitor or ARB for LVSD[1]	21	90%	94%	94%
Discharge Instructions	96	100%	87%	88%
Evaluation of LVS Function	107	97%	97%	98%
Smoking Cessation Advice[1]	20	100%	98%	98%
Pneumonia Care				
Appropriate Initial Antibiotic	25	92%	91%	92%
Blood Culture Timing[1]	16	100%	97%	96%
Influenza Vaccine[1]	20	95%	90%	91%
Initial Antibiotic Timing[1]	8	100%	95%	95%
Pneumococcal Vaccine	33	97%	93%	93%
Smoking Cessation Advice[1]	13	100%	97%	97%
Surgical Care Improvement Project				
Appropriate VTP Within 24 Hours[2,5]	0	-	93%	92%
Appropriate Hair Removal[2,5]	0	-	100%	99%
Appropriate Beta Blocker Usage[2,5]	0	-	94%	93%
Controlled Postoperative Blood Glucose[2,5]	0	-	94%	93%
Prophylactic Antibiotic Timing[5]	0	-	97%	97%
Prophylactic Antibiotic Timing (Outpatient)	-	-	95%	92%
Prophylactic Antibiotic Selection[5]	0	-	97%	97%
Prophylactic Antibiotic Select. (Outpatient)	-	-	95%	94%
Prophylactic Antibiotic Stopped[5]	0	-	95%	94%
Recommended VTP Ordered[2,5]	0	-	95%	94%
Urinary Catheter Removal[2,5]	0	-	88%	90%
Children's Asthma Care				
Received Systemic Corticosteroids	-	-	-	100%
Received Home Management Plan	-	-	-	71%
Received Reliever Medication	-	-	-	100%
Use of Medical Imaging				
Combination Abdominal CT Scan	-	-	0.227	0.191
Combination Chest CT Scan	-	-	0.059	0.054
Follow-up Mammogram/Ultrasound	-	-	7.4%	8.4%
MRI for Low Back Pain	-	-	36%	32.7%
Survey of Patients' Hospital Experiences				
Area Around Room 'Always' Quiet at Night	-	-	-	58%
Doctors 'Always' Communicated Well	-	-	-	80%
Home Recovery Information Given	-	-	-	82%
Hospital Given 9 or 10 on 10 Point Scale	-	-	-	67%
Meds 'Always' Explained Before Given	-	-	-	60%
Nurses 'Always' Communicated Well	-	-	-	76%
Pain 'Always' Well Controlled	-	-	-	69%
Room and Bathroom 'Always' Clean	-	-	-	71%
Timely Help 'Always' Received	-	-	-	64%
Would Definitely Recommend Hospital	-	-	-	69%

NOTE: Hospital profiles are in alphabetical order by state, then city, then hospital within the city; Rankings exclude hospitals with less than 25 cases except for patient surveys which excludes hospitals with less than 100 cases; (a) 100–299 cases; (1) The number of cases is too small to be sure how well a hospital is performing; (2) The hospital indicated that the data submitted for this measure were based on a sample of cases; (3) Data was collected during a shorter time period (fewer quarters) than the maximum possible time for this measure; (4) Suppressed for one or more quarters by CMS; (5) No data is available from the hospital for this measure; (6) Fewer than 100 patients completed the HCAHPS survey. Use these rates with caution, as the number of surveys may be too low to reliably assess hospital performance; (7) Survey results are based on less than 12 months of data; (8) Survey results are not available for this reporting period; (9) No or very few patients were eligible for the HCAHPS survey. The scores shown, if any, reflect a very small number of surveys; (10) A state average was not calculated because too few hospitals in the state submitted data; (11) There were discrepancies in the data collection process; Please refer to the User's Guide for a full explanation of data.

Washington County Memorial Hospital

300 Health Way
Potosi, MO 63664
Phone: 573-438-5451
Fax: 573-438-2399
E-mail: wcmhadm@mail.potosi.k12.mo.us
URL: www.wcmhosp.org
Type: Critical Access Hospitals
Emergency Services: Yes
Ownership: Government - Local
Beds: 42

Key Personnel:
CEO/President. . . . . H Clark Duncan
Cardiac Laboratory. . . . . Bobin Delfield
Chief of Medical Staff. . . . . Frezerick Fyat, MD
Radiology. . . . . Aona DeClue
Emergency Room . . . . A Minichuck

Measure	Cases	This Hosp.	State Avg.	U.S. Avg.
Heart Attack Care				
ACE Inhibitor or ARB for LVSD[3]	0	-	96%	96%
Aspirin at Arrival[3]	0	-	99%	99%
Aspirin at Discharge[3]	0	-	99%	98%
Beta Blocker at Discharge[3]	0	-	99%	98%
Fibrinolytic Medication Timing[3]	0	-	27%	55%
PCI Within 90 Minutes of Arrival[3]	0	-	92%	90%
Smoking Cessation Advice[3]	0	-	99%	99%
Chest Pain/Possible Heart Attack Care				
Aspirin at Arrival	-	-	95%	95%
Median Time to ECG (minutes)	-	-	9	8
Median Time to Transfer (minutes)	-	-	64	61
Fibrinolytic Medication Timing	-	-	31%	54%
Heart Failure Care				
ACE Inhibitor or ARB for LVSD[1]	3	67%	94%	94%
Discharge Instructions[1]	15	60%	87%	88%
Evaluation of LVS Function[1]	15	60%	97%	98%
Smoking Cessation Advice[1]	2	50%	98%	98%
Pneumonia Care				
Appropriate Initial Antibiotic	59	90%	91%	92%
Blood Culture Timing	82	93%	97%	96%
Influenza Vaccine	28	82%	90%	91%
Initial Antibiotic Timing	75	96%	95%	95%
Pneumococcal Vaccine	56	79%	93%	93%
Smoking Cessation Advice	38	76%	97%	97%
Surgical Care Improvement Project				
Appropriate VTP Within 24 Hours[5]	0	-	93%	92%
Appropriate Hair Removal[5]	0	-	100%	99%
Appropriate Beta Blocker Usage[5]	0	-	94%	93%
Controlled Postoperative Blood Glucose[5]	0	-	94%	93%
Prophylactic Antibiotic Timing[5]	0	-	97%	97%
Prophylactic Antibiotic Timing (Outpatient)	-	-	95%	92%
Prophylactic Antibiotic Selection[5]	0	-	97%	97%
Prophylactic Antibiotic Select. (Outpatient)	-	-	95%	94%
Prophylactic Antibiotic Stopped[5]	0	-	95%	94%
Recommended VTP Ordered[5]	0	-	95%	94%
Urinary Catheter Removal[5]	0	-	88%	90%
Children's Asthma Care				
Received Systemic Corticosteroids	-	-	-	100%
Received Home Management Plan	-	-	-	71%
Received Reliever Medication	-	-	-	100%
Use of Medical Imaging				
Combination Abdominal CT Scan	-	-	0.227	0.191
Combination Chest CT Scan	-	-	0.059	0.054
Follow-up Mammogram/Ultrasound	-	-	7.4%	8.4%
MRI for Low Back Pain	-	-	36%	32.7%
Survey of Patients' Hospital Experiences				
Area Around Room 'Always' Quiet at Night[8]	-	-	-	58%
Doctors 'Always' Communicated Well[8]	-	-	-	80%
Home Recovery Information Given[8]	-	-	-	82%
Hospital Given 9 or 10 on 10 Point Scale[8]	-	-	-	67%
Meds 'Always' Explained Before Given[8]	-	-	-	60%
Nurses 'Always' Communicated Well[8]	-	-	-	76%
Pain 'Always' Well Controlled[8]	-	-	-	69%
Room and Bathroom 'Always' Clean[8]	-	-	-	71%
Timely Help 'Always' Received[8]	-	-	-	64%
Would Definitely Recommend Hospital[8]	-	-	-	69%

Ray County Memorial Hospital

904 Wollard Boulevard
Richmond, MO 64085
Phone: 816-470-5432
Fax: 816-470-8382
Type: Critical Access Hospitals
Emergency Services: Yes
Ownership: Government - Local
Beds: 63

Key Personnel:
Chief of Medical Staff . . . . Daniel M Rosak, MD
Infection Control. . . . . Jackie Devaul, RN
Operating Room. . . . . Cindy Rogers
Quality Assurance . . . . Donna Lamar

Measure	Cases	This Hosp.	State Avg.	U.S. Avg.
Heart Attack Care				
ACE Inhibitor or ARB for LVSD[3]	0	-	96%	96%
Aspirin at Arrival[1,3]	1	0%	99%	99%
Aspirin at Discharge[1,3]	1	0%	99%	98%
Beta Blocker at Discharge[1,3]	1	0%	99%	98%
Fibrinolytic Medication Timing[3]	0	-	27%	55%
PCI Within 90 Minutes of Arrival[3]	0	-	92%	90%
Smoking Cessation Advice[3]	0	-	99%	99%
Chest Pain/Possible Heart Attack Care				
Aspirin at Arrival	-	-	95%	95%
Median Time to ECG (minutes)	-	-	9	8
Median Time to Transfer (minutes)	-	-	64	61
Fibrinolytic Medication Timing	-	-	31%	54%
Heart Failure Care				
ACE Inhibitor or ARB for LVSD[1]	8	50%	94%	94%
Discharge Instructions[1]	19	79%	87%	88%
Evaluation of LVS Function	33	88%	97%	98%
Smoking Cessation Advice[1]	6	67%	98%	98%
Pneumonia Care				
Appropriate Initial Antibiotic[1]	16	75%	91%	92%
Blood Culture Timing[1]	3	100%	97%	96%
Influenza Vaccine[1]	12	75%	90%	91%
Initial Antibiotic Timing[1]	19	95%	95%	95%
Pneumococcal Vaccine	28	93%	93%	93%
Smoking Cessation Advice[1]	7	71%	97%	97%
Surgical Care Improvement Project				
Appropriate VTP Within 24 Hours[5]	0	-	93%	92%
Appropriate Hair Removal[5]	0	-	100%	99%
Appropriate Beta Blocker Usage[5]	0	-	94%	93%
Controlled Postoperative Blood Glucose[5]	0	-	94%	93%
Prophylactic Antibiotic Timing[5]	0	-	97%	97%
Prophylactic Antibiotic Timing (Outpatient)	-	-	95%	92%
Prophylactic Antibiotic Selection[5]	0	-	97%	97%
Prophylactic Antibiotic Select. (Outpatient)	-	-	95%	94%
Prophylactic Antibiotic Stopped[5]	0	-	95%	94%
Recommended VTP Ordered[5]	0	-	95%	94%
Urinary Catheter Removal[5]	0	-	88%	90%
Children's Asthma Care				
Received Systemic Corticosteroids	-	-	-	100%
Received Home Management Plan	-	-	-	71%
Received Reliever Medication	-	-	-	100%
Use of Medical Imaging				
Combination Abdominal CT Scan	-	-	0.227	0.191
Combination Chest CT Scan	-	-	0.059	0.054
Follow-up Mammogram/Ultrasound	-	-	7.4%	8.4%
MRI for Low Back Pain	-	-	36%	32.7%
Survey of Patients' Hospital Experiences				
Area Around Room 'Always' Quiet at Night[8]	-	-	-	58%
Doctors 'Always' Communicated Well[8]	-	-	-	80%
Home Recovery Information Given[8]	-	-	-	82%
Hospital Given 9 or 10 on 10 Point Scale[8]	-	-	-	67%
Meds 'Always' Explained Before Given[8]	-	-	-	60%
Nurses 'Always' Communicated Well[8]	-	-	-	76%
Pain 'Always' Well Controlled[8]	-	-	-	69%
Room and Bathroom 'Always' Clean[8]	-	-	-	71%
Timely Help 'Always' Received[8]	-	-	-	64%
Would Definitely Recommend Hospital[8]	-	-	-	69%

SSM St Marys Health Center

6420 Clayton Rd
Richmond Heights, MO 63117
Phone: 314-768-8000
Fax: 314-768-7131
Type: Acute Care Hospitals
Emergency Services: Yes
Ownership: Voluntary Non-Profit - Church
Beds: 622

Key Personnel:
CEO/President. . . . . William Jennings
Chief of Medical Staff. . . . . Stephen Kelly
Infection Control. . . . . Theresa Grattan
Quality Assurance . . . . Shelly Pierce

Measure	Cases	This Hosp.	State Avg.	U.S. Avg.
Heart Attack Care				
ACE Inhibitor or ARB for LVSD	30	100%	96%	96%
Aspirin at Arrival	167	100%	99%	99%
Aspirin at Discharge	158	100%	99%	98%
Beta Blocker at Discharge	148	100%	99%	98%
Fibrinolytic Medication Timing	0	-	27%	55%
PCI Within 90 Minutes of Arrival	31	100%	92%	90%
Smoking Cessation Advice	48	100%	99%	99%
Chest Pain/Possible Heart Attack Care				
Aspirin at Arrival[5]	0	-	95%	95%
Median Time to ECG (minutes)[5]	0	-	9	8
Median Time to Transfer (minutes)[5]	0	-	64	61
Fibrinolytic Medication Timing[5]	0	-	31%	54%
Heart Failure Care				
ACE Inhibitor or ARB for LVSD[2]	86	99%	94%	94%
Discharge Instructions[2]	268	95%	87%	88%
Evaluation of LVS Function[2]	317	100%	97%	98%
Smoking Cessation Advice[2]	57	100%	98%	98%
Pneumonia Care				
Appropriate Initial Antibiotic[2]	74	97%	91%	92%
Blood Culture Timing[2]	97	94%	97%	96%
Influenza Vaccine[2]	78	83%	90%	91%
Initial Antibiotic Timing[2]	136	85%	95%	95%
Pneumococcal Vaccine[2]	125	95%	93%	93%
Smoking Cessation Advice[2]	74	96%	97%	97%
Surgical Care Improvement Project				
Appropriate VTP Within 24 Hours[2]	289	94%	93%	92%
Appropriate Hair Removal[2]	768	99%	100%	99%
Appropriate Beta Blocker Usage[2]	209	97%	94%	93%
Controlled Postoperative Blood Glucose[2]	103	96%	94%	93%
Prophylactic Antibiotic Timing[2]	550	97%	97%	97%
Prophylactic Antibiotic Timing (Outpatient)	584	96%	95%	92%
Prophylactic Antibiotic Selection[2]	555	98%	97%	97%
Prophylactic Antibiotic Select. (Outpatient)	580	99%	95%	94%
Prophylactic Antibiotic Stopped[2]	516	93%	95%	94%
Recommended VTP Ordered[2]	292	96%	95%	94%
Urinary Catheter Removal[2]	87	90%	88%	90%
Children's Asthma Care				
Received Systemic Corticosteroids	291	100%	-	100%
Received Home Management Plan	291	90%	-	71%
Received Reliever Medication	291	100%	-	100%
Use of Medical Imaging				
Combination Abdominal CT Scan	899	0.677	0.227	0.191
Combination Chest CT Scan	493	0.010	0.059	0.054
Follow-up Mammogram/Ultrasound	1,630	12.3%	7.4%	8.4%
MRI for Low Back Pain	104	40.4%	36%	32.7%
Survey of Patients' Hospital Experiences				
Area Around Room 'Always' Quiet at Night	300+	53%	-	58%
Doctors 'Always' Communicated Well	300+	76%	-	80%
Home Recovery Information Given	300+	81%	-	82%
Hospital Given 9 or 10 on 10 Point Scale	300+	63%	-	67%
Meds 'Always' Explained Before Given	300+	55%	-	60%
Nurses 'Always' Communicated Well	300+	74%	-	76%
Pain 'Always' Well Controlled	300+	66%	-	69%
Room and Bathroom 'Always' Clean	300+	61%	-	71%
Timely Help 'Always' Received	300+	58%	-	64%
Would Definitely Recommend Hospital	300+	66%	-	69%

NOTE: Hospital profiles are in alphabetical order by state, then city, then hospital within the city; Rankings exclude hospitals with less than 25 cases except for patient surveys which excludes hospitals with less than 100 cases; (a) 100–299 cases; (1) The number of cases is too small to be sure how well a hospital is performing; (2) The hospital indicated that the data submitted for this measure were based on a sample of cases; (3) Data was collected during a shorter time period (fewer quarters) than the maximum possible time for this measure; (4) Suppressed for one or more quarters by CMS; (5) No data is available from the hospital for this measure; (6) Fewer than 100 patients completed the HCAHPS survey. Use these rates with caution, as the number of surveys may be too low to reliably assess hospital performance; (7) Survey results are based on less than 12 months of data; (8) Survey results are not available for this reporting period; (9) No or very few patients were eligible for the HCAHPS survey. The scores shown, if any, reflect a very small number of surveys; (10) A state average was not calculated because too few hospitals in the state submitted data; (11) There were discrepancies in the data collection process; Please refer to the User's Guide for a full explanation of data.

Phelps County Regional Medical Center

1000 W 10th St
Rolla, MO 65401
Phone: 573-458-8899
Fax: 573-458-8413
E-mail: bharvey@rollanet.org
URL: www.rollanet.org/~pcrmc
Type: Acute Care Hospitals
Emergency Services: Yes
Ownership: Government - Local
Beds: 232

Key Personnel:

CEO/President. . . . . David Ross
Chief of Medical Staff . . . . Jay Crump
Operating Room. . . . . Michael Beard
Pediatric Ambulatory Care . . . . . . Katherine Cook, MD
Pediatric In-Patient Care . . . . Katherine Cook, MD
Quality Assurance . . . . Jean Waterman
Radiology. . . . . Edward Downey, MD
Emergency Room . . . . Jeff Folhein

Measure	Cases	This Hosp.	State Avg.	U.S. Avg.
Heart Attack Care				
ACE Inhibitor or ARB for LVSD[1]	10	100%	96%	96%
Aspirin at Arrival	68	94%	99%	99%
Aspirin at Discharge	42	95%	99%	98%
Beta Blocker at Discharge	43	95%	99%	98%
Fibrinolytic Medication Timing	0	-	27%	55%
PCI Within 90 Minutes of Arrival	0	-	92%	90%
Smoking Cessation Advice[1]	9	100%	99%	99%
Chest Pain/Possible Heart Attack Care				
Aspirin at Arrival	151	96%	95%	95%
Median Time to ECG (minutes)	156	12	9	8
Median Time to Transfer (minutes)[1]	11	135	64	61
Fibrinolytic Medication Timing[1]	5	0%	31%	54%
Heart Failure Care				
ACE Inhibitor or ARB for LVSD	81	96%	94%	94%
Discharge Instructions	141	90%	87%	88%
Evaluation of LVS Function	193	97%	97%	98%
Smoking Cessation Advice	37	100%	98%	98%
Pneumonia Care				
Appropriate Initial Antibiotic	164	87%	91%	92%
Blood Culture Timing	221	91%	97%	96%
Influenza Vaccine	144	90%	90%	91%
Initial Antibiotic Timing	216	96%	95%	95%
Pneumococcal Vaccine	192	96%	93%	93%
Smoking Cessation Advice	99	100%	97%	97%
Surgical Care Improvement Project				
Appropriate VTP Within 24 Hours	197	85%	93%	92%
Appropriate Hair Removal	383	100%	100%	99%
Appropriate Beta Blocker Usage	96	84%	94%	93%
Controlled Postoperative Blood Glucose	0	-	94%	93%
Prophylactic Antibiotic Timing	260	99%	97%	97%
Prophylactic Antibiotic Timing (Outpatient)	208	97%	95%	92%
Prophylactic Antibiotic Selection	261	98%	97%	97%
Prophylactic Antibiotic Select. (Outpatient)	202	95%	95%	94%
Prophylactic Antibiotic Stopped	255	94%	95%	94%
Recommended VTP Ordered	197	87%	95%	94%
Urinary Catheter Removal	100	67%	88%	90%
Children's Asthma Care				
Received Systemic Corticosteroids	-	-	-	100%
Received Home Management Plan	-	-	-	71%
Received Reliever Medication	-	-	-	100%
Use of Medical Imaging				
Combination Abdominal CT Scan	526	0.378	0.227	0.191
Combination Chest CT Scan	398	0.005	0.059	0.054
Follow-up Mammogram/Ultrasound	1,595	2.9%	7.4%	8.4%
MRI for Low Back Pain	205	41.5%	36%	32.7%
Survey of Patients' Hospital Experiences				
Area Around Room 'Always' Quiet at Night	300+	52%	-	58%
Doctors 'Always' Communicated Well	300+	81%	-	80%
Home Recovery Information Given	300+	84%	-	82%
Hospital Given 9 or 10 on 10 Point Scale	300+	62%	-	67%
Meds 'Always' Explained Before Given	300+	56%	-	60%
Nurses 'Always' Communicated Well	300+	80%	-	76%
Pain 'Always' Well Controlled	300+	71%	-	69%
Room and Bathroom 'Always' Clean	300+	77%	-	71%
Timely Help 'Always' Received	300+	64%	-	64%
Would Definitely Recommend Hospital	300+	63%	-	69%

SSM St Joseph Health Center

300 1st Capitol Dr
Saint Charles, MO 63301
Phone: 636-947-5000
Fax: 636-947-5609
E-mail: mblamy@ssmhc.com
Type: Acute Care Hospitals
Emergency Services: Yes
Ownership: Voluntary Non-Profit - Private
Beds: 342

Key Personnel:

CEO/President. . . . . Sherlyn Hailstone
Cardiac Laboratory. . . . . Mark Taber
Chief of Medical Staff . . . . Fil Ferrigni, MD
Operating Room. . . . . Joseph Seger
Pediatric Ambulatory Care . . . . . . Nadira Adil
Pediatric In-Patient Care . . . . Nadira Adil
Quality Assurance . . . . Lois Kohler
Radiology. . . . . Lewis Halberson

Measure	Cases	This Hosp.	State Avg.	U.S. Avg.
Heart Attack Care				
ACE Inhibitor or ARB for LVSD	53	94%	96%	96%
Aspirin at Arrival	241	98%	99%	99%
Aspirin at Discharge	356	98%	99%	98%
Beta Blocker at Discharge	356	99%	99%	98%
Fibrinolytic Medication Timing	0	-	27%	55%
PCI Within 90 Minutes of Arrival	51	75%	92%	90%
Smoking Cessation Advice	135	100%	99%	99%
Chest Pain/Possible Heart Attack Care				
Aspirin at Arrival[1]	8	88%	95%	95%
Median Time to ECG (minutes)[1]	9	9	9	8
Median Time to Transfer (minutes)[5]	0	-	64	61
Fibrinolytic Medication Timing[3]	0	-	31%	54%
Heart Failure Care				
ACE Inhibitor or ARB for LVSD[2]	84	90%	94%	94%
Discharge Instructions[2]	213	94%	87%	88%
Evaluation of LVS Function[2]	267	100%	97%	98%
Smoking Cessation Advice[2]	52	100%	98%	98%
Pneumonia Care				
Appropriate Initial Antibiotic[2]	70	96%	91%	92%
Blood Culture Timing[2]	88	95%	97%	96%
Influenza Vaccine[2]	82	91%	90%	91%
Initial Antibiotic Timing[2]	108	94%	95%	95%
Pneumococcal Vaccine[2]	135	98%	93%	93%
Smoking Cessation Advice[2]	62	100%	97%	97%
Surgical Care Improvement Project				
Appropriate VTP Within 24 Hours[2]	249	98%	93%	92%
Appropriate Hair Removal[2]	781	100%	100%	99%
Appropriate Beta Blocker Usage[2]	281	96%	94%	93%
Controlled Postoperative Blood Glucose[2]	156	96%	94%	93%
Prophylactic Antibiotic Timing[2]	577	97%	97%	97%
Prophylactic Antibiotic Timing (Outpatient)	492	97%	95%	92%
Prophylactic Antibiotic Selection[2]	581	99%	97%	97%
Prophylactic Antibiotic Select. (Outpatient)	487	96%	95%	94%
Prophylactic Antibiotic Stopped[2]	565	98%	95%	94%
Recommended VTP Ordered[2]	249	100%	95%	94%
Urinary Catheter Removal[2]	159	91%	88%	90%
Children's Asthma Care				
Received Systemic Corticosteroids	-	-	-	100%
Received Home Management Plan	-	-	-	71%
Received Reliever Medication	-	-	-	100%
Use of Medical Imaging				
Combination Abdominal CT Scan	768	0.079	0.227	0.191
Combination Chest CT Scan	589	0.029	0.059	0.054
Follow-up Mammogram/Ultrasound	576	6.6%	7.4%	8.4%
MRI for Low Back Pain	135	37.0%	36%	32.7%
Survey of Patients' Hospital Experiences				
Area Around Room 'Always' Quiet at Night	300+	54%	-	58%
Doctors 'Always' Communicated Well	300+	76%	-	80%
Home Recovery Information Given	300+	85%	-	82%
Hospital Given 9 or 10 on 10 Point Scale	300+	68%	-	67%
Meds 'Always' Explained Before Given	300+	60%	-	60%
Nurses 'Always' Communicated Well	300+	76%	-	76%
Pain 'Always' Well Controlled	300+	68%	-	69%
Room and Bathroom 'Always' Clean	300+	69%	-	71%
Timely Help 'Always' Received	300+	65%	-	64%
Would Definitely Recommend Hospital	300+	70%	-	69%

Heartland Regional Medical Center

5325 Faraon Street
Saint Joseph, MO 64506
Phone: 816-271-6000
Fax: 816-271-6656
URL: www.heartland-health.com
Type: Acute Care Hospitals
Emergency Services: Yes
Ownership: Voluntary Non-Profit - Private
Beds: 690

Key Personnel:

CEO/President. . . . . Lowell C Kruse
Chief of Medical Staff . . . . Dr Robert Permut MD
Infection Control . . . . Betty Shellenberder
Pediatric Ambulatory Care . . . . . . Robert B Sturdevant DO
Pediatric In-Patient Care . . . . Robert B Sturdevant DO
Quality Assurance . . . . Julie Ryder
Radiology. . . . . Larry Kirschner

Measure	Cases	This Hosp.	State Avg.	U.S. Avg.
Heart Attack Care				
ACE Inhibitor or ARB for LVSD	36	100%	96%	96%
Aspirin at Arrival	299	100%	99%	99%
Aspirin at Discharge	391	100%	99%	98%
Beta Blocker at Discharge	384	100%	99%	98%
Fibrinolytic Medication Timing	0	-	27%	55%
PCI Within 90 Minutes of Arrival	52	96%	92%	90%
Smoking Cessation Advice	160	100%	99%	99%
Chest Pain/Possible Heart Attack Care				
Aspirin at Arrival[1]	8	100%	95%	95%
Median Time to ECG (minutes)[1]	8	6	9	8
Median Time to Transfer (minutes)[5]	0	-	64	61
Fibrinolytic Medication Timing[5]	0	-	31%	54%
Heart Failure Care				
ACE Inhibitor or ARB for LVSD	128	100%	94%	94%
Discharge Instructions	297	100%	87%	88%
Evaluation of LVS Function	388	100%	97%	98%
Smoking Cessation Advice	66	100%	98%	98%
Pneumonia Care				
Appropriate Initial Antibiotic	332	97%	91%	92%
Blood Culture Timing	453	100%	97%	96%
Influenza Vaccine	324	99%	90%	91%
Initial Antibiotic Timing	432	99%	95%	95%
Pneumococcal Vaccine	462	100%	93%	93%
Smoking Cessation Advice	217	100%	97%	97%
Surgical Care Improvement Project				
Appropriate VTP Within 24 Hours[2]	250	98%	93%	92%
Appropriate Hair Removal[2]	1,141	100%	100%	99%
Appropriate Beta Blocker Usage[2]	444	100%	94%	93%
Controlled Postoperative Blood Glucose[2]	254	94%	94%	93%
Prophylactic Antibiotic Timing[2]	941	100%	97%	97%
Prophylactic Antibiotic Timing (Outpatient)	693	99%	95%	92%
Prophylactic Antibiotic Selection[2]	951	100%	97%	97%
Prophylactic Antibiotic Select. (Outpatient)	687	97%	95%	94%
Prophylactic Antibiotic Stopped[2]	888	99%	95%	94%
Recommended VTP Ordered[2]	251	98%	95%	94%
Urinary Catheter Removal[2]	277	97%	88%	90%
Children's Asthma Care				
Received Systemic Corticosteroids	-	-	-	100%
Received Home Management Plan	-	-	-	71%
Received Reliever Medication	-	-	-	100%
Use of Medical Imaging				
Combination Abdominal CT Scan	1,438	0.135	0.227	0.191
Combination Chest CT Scan	1,277	0.070	0.059	0.054
Follow-up Mammogram/Ultrasound	2,395	7.5%	7.4%	8.4%
MRI for Low Back Pain	373	36.5%	36%	32.7%
Survey of Patients' Hospital Experiences				
Area Around Room 'Always' Quiet at Night	300+	62%	-	58%
Doctors 'Always' Communicated Well	300+	81%	-	80%
Home Recovery Information Given	300+	83%	-	82%
Hospital Given 9 or 10 on 10 Point Scale	300+	67%	-	67%
Meds 'Always' Explained Before Given	300+	62%	-	60%
Nurses 'Always' Communicated Well	300+	80%	-	76%
Pain 'Always' Well Controlled	300+	71%	-	69%
Room and Bathroom 'Always' Clean	300+	70%	-	71%
Timely Help 'Always' Received	300+	60%	-	64%
Would Definitely Recommend Hospital	300+	66%	-	69%

NOTE: Hospital profiles are in alphabetical order by state, then city, then hospital within the city; Rankings exclude hospitals with less than 25 cases except for patient surveys which excludes hospitals with less than 100 cases; (a) 100–299 cases; (1) The number of cases is too small to be sure how well a hospital is performing; (2) The hospital indicated that the data submitted for this measure were based on a sample of cases; (3) Data was collected during a shorter time period (fewer quarters) than the maximum possible time for this measure; (4) Suppressed for one or more quarters by CMS; (5) No data is available from the hospital for this measure; (6) Fewer than 100 patients completed the HCAHPS survey. Use these rates with caution, as the number of surveys may be too low to reliably assess hospital performance; (7) Survey results are based on less than 12 months of data; (8) Survey results are not available for this reporting period; (9) No or very few patients were eligible for the HCAHPS survey. The scores shown, if any, reflect a very small number of surveys; (10) A state average was not calculated because too few hospitals in the state submitted data; (11) There were discrepancies in the data collection process; Please refer to the User's Guide for a full explanation of data.

Barnes Jewish Hospital

One Barnes-Jewish Hospital Plaza Phone: 314-747-3000
Saint Louis, MO 63110 Fax: 314-362-3421
URL: www.barnesjewish.org
Type: Acute Care Hospitals Emergency Services: Yes
Ownership: Voluntary Non-Profit - Other Beds: 1,252
Key Personnel:
CEO/President. . . . . Richard Liekweg
Chief of Medical Staff . . . . John Lynch, MD
Operating Room. . . . . David Jaques, MD
Quality Assurance . . . . Denise Murphy
Patient Relations . . . . Coreen Vlodarchyk

Measure	Cases	This Hosp.	State Avg.	U.S. Avg.
Heart Attack Care				
ACE Inhibitor or ARB for LVSD	135	97%	96%	96%
Aspirin at Arrival	408	99%	99%	99%
Aspirin at Discharge	629	99%	99%	98%
Beta Blocker at Discharge	583	99%	99%	98%
Fibrinolytic Medication Timing	0	-	27%	55%
PCI Within 90 Minutes of Arrival	57	98%	92%	90%
Smoking Cessation Advice	217	100%	99%	99%
Chest Pain/Possible Heart Attack Care				
Aspirin at Arrival[1]	3	67%	95%	95%
Median Time to ECG (minutes)[1]	3	8	9	8
Median Time to Transfer (minutes)[5]	0	-	64	61
Fibrinolytic Medication Timing[5]	0	-	31%	54%
Heart Failure Care				
ACE Inhibitor or ARB for LVSD[2]	382	97%	94%	94%
Discharge Instructions[2]	731	92%	87%	88%
Evaluation of LVS Function[2]	817	100%	97%	98%
Smoking Cessation Advice[2]	228	100%	98%	98%
Pneumonia Care				
Appropriate Initial Antibiotic[2]	169	92%	91%	92%
Blood Culture Timing[2]	103	93%	97%	96%
Influenza Vaccine[2]	273	91%	90%	91%
Initial Antibiotic Timing[2]	386	91%	95%	95%
Pneumococcal Vaccine[2]	270	90%	93%	93%
Smoking Cessation Advice[2]	198	98%	97%	97%
Surgical Care Improvement Project				
Appropriate VTP Within 24 Hours[2]	261	96%	93%	92%
Appropriate Hair Removal[2]	896	100%	100%	99%
Appropriate Beta Blocker Usage[2]	240	92%	94%	93%
Controlled Postoperative Blood Glucose[2]	148	93%	94%	93%
Prophylactic Antibiotic Timing[2]	570	98%	97%	97%
Prophylactic Antibiotic Timing (Outpatient)	765	96%	95%	92%
Prophylactic Antibiotic Selection[2]	579	99%	97%	97%
Prophylactic Antibiotic Select. (Outpatient)	751	91%	95%	94%
Prophylactic Antibiotic Stopped[2]	546	97%	95%	94%
Recommended VTP Ordered[2]	262	96%	95%	94%
Urinary Catheter Removal[2]	211	84%	88%	90%
Children's Asthma Care				
Received Systemic Corticosteroids	-	-	-	100%
Received Home Management Plan	-	-	-	71%
Received Reliever Medication	-	-	-	100%
Use of Medical Imaging				
Combination Abdominal CT Scan	4,449	0.121	0.227	0.191
Combination Chest CT Scan	4,518	0.022	0.059	0.054
Follow-up Mammogram/Ultrasound	4,757	7.1%	7.4%	8.4%
MRI for Low Back Pain	533	30.0%	36%	32.7%
Survey of Patients' Hospital Experiences				
Area Around Room 'Always' Quiet at Night	300+	55%	-	58%
Doctors 'Always' Communicated Well	300+	79%	-	80%
Home Recovery Information Given	300+	87%	-	82%
Hospital Given 9 or 10 on 10 Point Scale	300+	67%	-	67%
Meds 'Always' Explained Before Given	300+	60%	-	60%
Nurses 'Always' Communicated Well	300+	73%	-	76%
Pain 'Always' Well Controlled	300+	70%	-	69%
Room and Bathroom 'Always' Clean	300+	66%	-	71%
Timely Help 'Always' Received	300+	53%	-	64%
Would Definitely Recommend Hospital	300+	72%	-	69%

Christian Hospital Northeast

11133 Dunn Road Phone: 314-653-5000
Saint Louis, MO 63136 Fax: 314-653-4130
URL: www.christianhospital.org
Type: Acute Care Hospitals Emergency Services: Yes
Ownership: Voluntary Non-Profit - Private Beds: 493
Key Personnel:
CEO/President. . . . . Ronald B McMullen
Chief of Medical Staff . . . . Stephen Hazama
Anesthesiology. . . . . Stephen Feit, MD
Emergency Room . . . . Sebastian Rueckert, MD

Measure	Cases	This Hosp.	State Avg.	U.S. Avg.
Heart Attack Care				
ACE Inhibitor or ARB for LVSD	91	99%	96%	96%
Aspirin at Arrival	302	99%	99%	99%
Aspirin at Discharge	409	100%	99%	98%
Beta Blocker at Discharge	393	100%	99%	98%
Fibrinolytic Medication Timing	0	-	27%	55%
PCI Within 90 Minutes of Arrival	33	94%	92%	90%
Smoking Cessation Advice	154	100%	99%	99%
Chest Pain/Possible Heart Attack Care				
Aspirin at Arrival	28	79%	95%	95%
Median Time to ECG (minutes)	30	4	9	8
Median Time to Transfer (minutes)[5]	0	-	64	61
Fibrinolytic Medication Timing[5]	0	-	31%	54%
Heart Failure Care				
ACE Inhibitor or ARB for LVSD[2]	214	97%	94%	94%
Discharge Instructions[2]	556	81%	87%	88%
Evaluation of LVS Function[2]	655	99%	97%	98%
Smoking Cessation Advice[2]	144	99%	98%	98%
Pneumonia Care				
Appropriate Initial Antibiotic	155	95%	91%	92%
Blood Culture Timing	278	97%	97%	96%
Influenza Vaccine	213	81%	90%	91%
Initial Antibiotic Timing	289	91%	95%	95%
Pneumococcal Vaccine	243	88%	93%	93%
Smoking Cessation Advice	149	100%	97%	97%
Surgical Care Improvement Project				
Appropriate VTP Within 24 Hours[2]	320	96%	93%	92%
Appropriate Hair Removal[2]	828	100%	100%	99%
Appropriate Beta Blocker Usage[2]	283	99%	94%	93%
Controlled Postoperative Blood Glucose[2]	182	97%	94%	93%
Prophylactic Antibiotic Timing[2]	459	98%	97%	97%
Prophylactic Antibiotic Timing (Outpatient)	346	94%	95%	92%
Prophylactic Antibiotic Selection[2]	474	86%	97%	97%
Prophylactic Antibiotic Select. (Outpatient)	338	97%	95%	94%
Prophylactic Antibiotic Stopped[2]	410	97%	95%	94%
Recommended VTP Ordered[2]	320	98%	95%	94%
Urinary Catheter Removal	132	85%	88%	90%
Children's Asthma Care				
Received Systemic Corticosteroids	-	-	-	100%
Received Home Management Plan	-	-	-	71%
Received Reliever Medication	-	-	-	100%
Use of Medical Imaging				
Combination Abdominal CT Scan	783	0.522	0.227	0.191
Combination Chest CT Scan	672	0.003	0.059	0.054
Follow-up Mammogram/Ultrasound	522	10.9%	7.4%	8.4%
MRI for Low Back Pain	87	39.1%	36%	32.7%
Survey of Patients' Hospital Experiences				
Area Around Room 'Always' Quiet at Night	300+	71%	-	58%
Doctors 'Always' Communicated Well	300+	84%	-	80%
Home Recovery Information Given	300+	84%	-	82%
Hospital Given 9 or 10 on 10 Point Scale	300+	68%	-	67%
Meds 'Always' Explained Before Given	300+	67%	-	60%
Nurses 'Always' Communicated Well	300+	83%	-	76%
Pain 'Always' Well Controlled	300+	73%	-	69%
Room and Bathroom 'Always' Clean	300+	69%	-	71%
Timely Help 'Always' Received	300+	64%	-	64%
Would Definitely Recommend Hospital	300+	67%	-	69%

Des Peres Hospital

2345 Dougherty Ferry Road Phone: 314-966-9100
Saint Louis, MO 63122 Fax: 314-966-9274
Type: Acute Care Hospitals Emergency Services: Yes
Ownership: Proprietary Beds: 167
Key Personnel:
CEO/President. . . . . Michele Meyer
Chief of Medical Staff . . . . Micheal Chablt
Quality Assurance . . . . Maryann Dundon
Radiology. . . . . James Schoen, MD
Emergency Room . . . . Thomas Hartmann

Measure	Cases	This Hosp.	State Avg.	U.S. Avg.
Heart Attack Care				
ACE Inhibitor or ARB for LVSD[1]	21	100%	96%	96%
Aspirin at Arrival	73	99%	99%	99%
Aspirin at Discharge	178	99%	99%	98%
Beta Blocker at Discharge	176	99%	99%	98%
Fibrinolytic Medication Timing	0	-	27%	55%
PCI Within 90 Minutes of Arrival[1]	19	89%	92%	90%
Smoking Cessation Advice	64	100%	99%	99%
Chest Pain/Possible Heart Attack Care				
Aspirin at Arrival[1,3]	1	100%	95%	95%
Median Time to ECG (minutes)[1,3]	1	4	9	8
Median Time to Transfer (minutes)[5]	0	-	64	61
Fibrinolytic Medication Timing[5]	0	-	31%	54%
Heart Failure Care				
ACE Inhibitor or ARB for LVSD	83	98%	94%	94%
Discharge Instructions	205	93%	87%	88%
Evaluation of LVS Function	256	100%	97%	98%
Smoking Cessation Advice	46	100%	98%	98%
Pneumonia Care				
Appropriate Initial Antibiotic	134	93%	91%	92%
Blood Culture Timing	263	99%	97%	96%
Influenza Vaccine	162	100%	90%	91%
Initial Antibiotic Timing	260	98%	95%	95%
Pneumococcal Vaccine	241	100%	93%	93%
Smoking Cessation Advice	78	100%	97%	97%
Surgical Care Improvement Project				
Appropriate VTP Within 24 Hours[2]	142	96%	93%	92%
Appropriate Hair Removal[2]	464	100%	100%	99%
Appropriate Beta Blocker Usage[2]	179	97%	94%	93%
Controlled Postoperative Blood Glucose[2]	125	94%	94%	93%
Prophylactic Antibiotic Timing[2]	321	97%	97%	97%
Prophylactic Antibiotic Timing (Outpatient)	537	97%	95%	92%
Prophylactic Antibiotic Selection[2]	328	97%	97%	97%
Prophylactic Antibiotic Select. (Outpatient)	532	99%	95%	94%
Prophylactic Antibiotic Stopped[2]	304	91%	95%	94%
Recommended VTP Ordered[2]	142	98%	95%	94%
Urinary Catheter Removal[2]	105	91%	88%	90%
Children's Asthma Care				
Received Systemic Corticosteroids	-	-	-	100%
Received Home Management Plan	-	-	-	71%
Received Reliever Medication	-	-	-	100%
Use of Medical Imaging				
Combination Abdominal CT Scan	243	0.621	0.227	0.191
Combination Chest CT Scan	90	0.000	0.059	0.054
Follow-up Mammogram/Ultrasound	150	6.0%	7.4%	8.4%
MRI for Low Back Pain	111	39.6%	36%	32.7%
Survey of Patients' Hospital Experiences				
Area Around Room 'Always' Quiet at Night	300+	55%	-	58%
Doctors 'Always' Communicated Well	300+	82%	-	80%
Home Recovery Information Given	300+	83%	-	82%
Hospital Given 9 or 10 on 10 Point Scale	300+	64%	-	67%
Meds 'Always' Explained Before Given	300+	58%	-	60%
Nurses 'Always' Communicated Well	300+	74%	-	76%
Pain 'Always' Well Controlled	300+	69%	-	69%
Room and Bathroom 'Always' Clean	300+	67%	-	71%
Timely Help 'Always' Received	300+	62%	-	64%
Would Definitely Recommend Hospital	300+	69%	-	69%

NOTE: Hospital profiles are in alphabetical order by state, then city, then hospital within the city; Rankings exclude hospitals with less than 25 cases except for patient surveys which excludes hospitals with less than 100 cases; (a) 100–299 cases; (1) The number of cases is too small to be sure how well a hospital is performing; (2) The hospital indicated that the data submitted for this measure were based on a sample of cases; (3) Data was collected during a shorter time period (fewer quarters) than the maximum possible time for this measure; (4) Suppressed for one or more quarters by CMS; (5) No data is available from the hospital for this measure; (6) Fewer than 100 patients completed the HCAHPS survey. Use these rates with caution, as the number of surveys may be too low to reliably assess hospital performance; (7) Survey results are based on less than 12 months of data; (8) Survey results are not available for this reporting period; (9) No or very few patients were eligible for the HCAHPS survey. The scores shown, if any, reflect a very small number of surveys; (10) A state average was not calculated because too few hospitals in the state submitted data; (11) There were discrepancies in the data collection process; Please refer to the User's Guide for a full explanation of data.

Forest Park Hospital

6150 Oakland Ave Phone: 314-768-3000
Saint Louis, MO 63139 Fax: 314-768-3990
URL: www.forestparkhospital.com
Type: Acute Care Hospitals Emergency Services: Yes
Ownership: Proprietary Beds: 450

Key Personnel:
CEO/President. . . . . Joan G Phillips, PhD RN
Chief of Medical Staff . . . . M Robert Hill, MD
Operating Room. . . . . Robert Morgan, RN
Pediatric In-Patient Care . . . . . . Rajendra C Parikh, MD
Quality Assurance . . . . Dawn Meyer, RN
Emergency Room . . . . Horacio Marafioti, MD

Measure	Cases	This Hosp.	State Avg.	U.S. Avg.
Heart Attack Care				
ACE Inhibitor or ARB for LVSD[1,3]	1	100%	96%	96%
Aspirin at Arrival[1,3]	6	83%	99%	99%
Aspirin at Discharge[1,3]	1	100%	99%	98%
Beta Blocker at Discharge[1,3]	1	100%	99%	98%
Fibrinolytic Medication Timing[3]	0	-	27%	55%
PCI Within 90 Minutes of Arrival[3]	0	-	92%	90%
Smoking Cessation Advice[3]	0	-	99%	99%
Chest Pain/Possible Heart Attack Care				
Aspirin at Arrival[1]	24	96%	95%	95%
Median Time to ECG (minutes)	25	20	9	8
Median Time to Transfer (minutes)[5]	0	-	64	61
Fibrinolytic Medication Timing[3]	0	-	31%	54%
Heart Failure Care				
ACE Inhibitor or ARB for LVSD[3]	29	72%	94%	94%
Discharge Instructions[3]	63	67%	87%	88%
Evaluation of LVS Function[3]	85	88%	97%	98%
Smoking Cessation Advice[3]	26	100%	98%	98%
Pneumonia Care				
Appropriate Initial Antibiotic	50	92%	91%	92%
Blood Culture Timing	56	93%	97%	96%
Influenza Vaccine	33	97%	90%	91%
Initial Antibiotic Timing	67	96%	95%	95%
Pneumococcal Vaccine	27	93%	93%	93%
Smoking Cessation Advice	31	97%	97%	97%
Surgical Care Improvement Project				
Appropriate VTP Within 24 Hours[1,3]	13	69%	93%	92%
Appropriate Hair Removal[3]	25	100%	100%	99%
Appropriate Beta Blocker Usage[1,3]	3	33%	94%	93%
Controlled Postoperative Blood Glucose[3]	0	-	94%	93%
Prophylactic Antibiotic Timing[1,3]	10	80%	97%	97%
Prophylactic Antibiotic Timing (Outpatient)[1,3]	17	65%	95%	92%
Prophylactic Antibiotic Selection[1,3]	10	100%	97%	97%
Prophylactic Antibiotic Select. (Outpatient)[1,3]	14	93%	95%	94%
Prophylactic Antibiotic Stopped[1,3]	9	89%	95%	94%
Recommended VTP Ordered[1,3]	13	69%	95%	94%
Urinary Catheter Removal[1,3]	1	0%	88%	90%
Children's Asthma Care				
Received Systemic Corticosteroids	-	-	-	100%
Received Home Management Plan	-	-	-	71%
Received Reliever Medication	-	-	-	100%
Use of Medical Imaging				
Combination Abdominal CT Scan	117	0.444	0.227	0.191
Combination Chest CT Scan	63	0.000	0.059	0.054
Follow-up Mammogram/Ultrasound	380	2.9%	7.4%	8.4%
MRI for Low Back Pain[1]	19	52.6%	36%	32.7%
Survey of Patients' Hospital Experiences				
Area Around Room 'Always' Quiet at Night	(a)	61%	-	58%
Doctors 'Always' Communicated Well	(a)	77%	-	80%
Home Recovery Information Given	(a)	67%	-	82%
Hospital Given 9 or 10 on 10 Point Scale	(a)	55%	-	67%
Meds 'Always' Explained Before Given	(a)	61%	-	60%
Nurses 'Always' Communicated Well	(a)	79%	-	76%
Pain 'Always' Well Controlled	(a)	76%	-	69%
Room and Bathroom 'Always' Clean	(a)	55%	-	71%
Timely Help 'Always' Received	(a)	57%	-	64%
Would Definitely Recommend Hospital	(a)	54%	-	69%

Saint Alexius Hospital

3933 S Broadway Phone: 314-865-7000
Saint Louis, MO 63118 Fax: 314-865-7938
URL: www.stalexiushospital.com
Type: Acute Care Hospitals Emergency Services: Yes
Ownership: Proprietary Beds: 203

Key Personnel:
CEO/President. . . . . Robert Adcock
Chief of Medical Staff . . . . Patrick Durbin, MD
Operating Room. . . . . Bonnie Henry, RN
Quality Assurance . . . . Karen Salamone
Emergency Room . . . . Dawn Bassett-McLean, RN

Measure	Cases	This Hosp.	State Avg.	U.S. Avg.
Heart Attack Care				
ACE Inhibitor or ARB for LVSD[1]	3	100%	96%	96%
Aspirin at Arrival[1]	21	90%	99%	99%
Aspirin at Discharge[1]	9	100%	99%	98%
Beta Blocker at Discharge[1]	9	89%	99%	98%
Fibrinolytic Medication Timing	0	-	27%	55%
PCI Within 90 Minutes of Arrival	0	-	92%	90%
Smoking Cessation Advice[1]	5	100%	99%	99%
Chest Pain/Possible Heart Attack Care				
Aspirin at Arrival[1,3]	4	75%	95%	95%
Median Time to ECG (minutes)[1,3]	4	23	9	8
Median Time to Transfer (minutes)[1,3]	1	37	64	61
Fibrinolytic Medication Timing[3]	0	-	31%	54%
Heart Failure Care				
ACE Inhibitor or ARB for LVSD	40	88%	94%	94%
Discharge Instructions	112	73%	87%	88%
Evaluation of LVS Function	146	100%	97%	98%
Smoking Cessation Advice	41	100%	98%	98%
Pneumonia Care				
Appropriate Initial Antibiotic	91	84%	91%	92%
Blood Culture Timing	108	96%	97%	96%
Influenza Vaccine	89	98%	90%	91%
Initial Antibiotic Timing	125	92%	95%	95%
Pneumococcal Vaccine	94	94%	93%	93%
Smoking Cessation Advice	88	100%	97%	97%
Surgical Care Improvement Project				
Appropriate VTP Within 24 Hours	45	91%	93%	92%
Appropriate Hair Removal	82	100%	100%	99%
Appropriate Beta Blocker Usage[1]	17	82%	94%	93%
Controlled Postoperative Blood Glucose	0	-	94%	93%
Prophylactic Antibiotic Timing[1]	20	90%	97%	97%
Prophylactic Antibiotic Timing (Outpatient)[1]	16	50%	95%	92%
Prophylactic Antibiotic Selection[1]	20	100%	97%	97%
Prophylactic Antibiotic Select. (Outpatient)	25	96%	95%	94%
Prophylactic Antibiotic Stopped[1]	17	94%	95%	94%
Recommended VTP Ordered	47	94%	95%	94%
Urinary Catheter Removal[1]	8	62%	88%	90%
Children's Asthma Care				
Received Systemic Corticosteroids	-	-	-	100%
Received Home Management Plan	-	-	-	71%
Received Reliever Medication	-	-	-	100%
Use of Medical Imaging				
Combination Abdominal CT Scan	138	0.087	0.227	0.191
Combination Chest CT Scan[1]	54	0.074	0.059	0.054
Follow-up Mammogram/Ultrasound	327	7.0%	7.4%	8.4%
MRI for Low Back Pain[1]	2	50.0%	36%	32.7%
Survey of Patients' Hospital Experiences				
Area Around Room 'Always' Quiet at Night	300+	59%	-	58%
Doctors 'Always' Communicated Well	300+	84%	-	80%
Home Recovery Information Given	300+	78%	-	82%
Hospital Given 9 or 10 on 10 Point Scale	300+	65%	-	67%
Meds 'Always' Explained Before Given	300+	61%	-	60%
Nurses 'Always' Communicated Well	300+	78%	-	76%
Pain 'Always' Well Controlled	300+	71%	-	69%
Room and Bathroom 'Always' Clean	300+	64%	-	71%
Timely Help 'Always' Received	300+	62%	-	64%
Would Definitely Recommend Hospital	300+	65%	-	69%

Saint Anthony's Medical Center

10010 Kennerly Road Phone: 314-525-1000
Saint Louis, MO 63128 Fax: 314-525-4040
E-mail: webmaster@samcstl.org
URL: www.samcstl.org
Type: Acute Care Hospitals Emergency Services: Yes
Ownership: Voluntary Non-Profit - Church Beds: 767

Key Personnel:
CEO/President. . . . . Thomas H. Rockers
Cardiac Laboratory. . . . . David J. Dobmeyer, MD
Chief of Medical Staff . . . . Robert F. Beckman, MD
Operating Room. . . . . David M. Schuval, MD
Radiology. . . . . Paul A. Oberle, MD
Anesthesiology. . . . . Armin Rahimi, DO
Hemotology Center . . . . R. William Morris, MD

Measure	Cases	This Hosp.	State Avg.	U.S. Avg.
Heart Attack Care				
ACE Inhibitor or ARB for LVSD[2]	61	82%	96%	96%
Aspirin at Arrival[2]	317	98%	99%	99%
Aspirin at Discharge[2]	312	96%	99%	98%
Beta Blocker at Discharge[2]	309	97%	99%	98%
Fibrinolytic Medication Timing[2]	0	-	27%	55%
PCI Within 90 Minutes of Arrival[2]	66	86%	92%	90%
Smoking Cessation Advice[2]	112	91%	99%	99%
Chest Pain/Possible Heart Attack Care				
Aspirin at Arrival[1,3]	6	100%	95%	95%
Median Time to ECG (minutes)[1,3]	6	10	9	8
Median Time to Transfer (minutes)[5]	0	-	64	61
Fibrinolytic Medication Timing[5]	0	-	31%	54%
Heart Failure Care				
ACE Inhibitor or ARB for LVSD[2]	126	79%	94%	94%
Discharge Instructions[2]	244	68%	87%	88%
Evaluation of LVS Function[2]	327	98%	97%	98%
Smoking Cessation Advice[2]	45	89%	98%	98%
Pneumonia Care				
Appropriate Initial Antibiotic[2]	129	87%	91%	92%
Blood Culture Timing[2]	141	96%	97%	96%
Influenza Vaccine[2]	128	81%	90%	91%
Initial Antibiotic Timing[2]	215	95%	95%	95%
Pneumococcal Vaccine[2]	186	90%	93%	93%
Smoking Cessation Advice[2]	77	94%	97%	97%
Surgical Care Improvement Project				
Appropriate VTP Within 24 Hours[2]	324	92%	93%	92%
Appropriate Hair Removal[2]	1,177	100%	100%	99%
Appropriate Beta Blocker Usage[2]	358	90%	94%	93%
Controlled Postoperative Blood Glucose[2]	204	88%	94%	93%
Prophylactic Antibiotic Timing[2]	816	97%	97%	97%
Prophylactic Antibiotic Timing (Outpatient)	434	96%	95%	92%
Prophylactic Antibiotic Selection[2]	833	97%	97%	97%
Prophylactic Antibiotic Select. (Outpatient)	433	99%	95%	94%
Prophylactic Antibiotic Stopped[2]	790	92%	95%	94%
Recommended VTP Ordered[2]	327	94%	95%	94%
Urinary Catheter Removal[2]	149	68%	88%	90%
Children's Asthma Care				
Received Systemic Corticosteroids	-	-	-	100%
Received Home Management Plan	-	-	-	71%
Received Reliever Medication	-	-	-	100%
Use of Medical Imaging				
Combination Abdominal CT Scan	1,358	0.666	0.227	0.191
Combination Chest CT Scan	828	0.008	0.059	0.054
Follow-up Mammogram/Ultrasound	2,726	6.6%	7.4%	8.4%
MRI for Low Back Pain	275	31.6%	36%	32.7%
Survey of Patients' Hospital Experiences				
Area Around Room 'Always' Quiet at Night	300+	59%	-	58%
Doctors 'Always' Communicated Well	300+	77%	-	80%
Home Recovery Information Given	300+	80%	-	82%
Hospital Given 9 or 10 on 10 Point Scale	300+	62%	-	67%
Meds 'Always' Explained Before Given	300+	55%	-	60%
Nurses 'Always' Communicated Well	300+	75%	-	76%
Pain 'Always' Well Controlled	300+	70%	-	69%
Room and Bathroom 'Always' Clean	300+	69%	-	71%
Timely Help 'Always' Received	300+	56%	-	64%
Would Definitely Recommend Hospital	300+	61%	-	69%

NOTE: Hospital profiles are in alphabetical order by state, then city, then hospital within the city; Rankings exclude hospitals with less than 25 cases except for patient surveys which excludes hospitals with less than 100 cases; (a) 100–299 cases; (1) The number of cases is too small to be sure how well a hospital is performing; (2) The hospital indicated that the data submitted for this measure were based on a sample of cases; (3) Data was collected during a shorter time period (fewer quarters) than the maximum possible time for this measure; (4) Suppressed for one or more quarters by CMS; (5) No data is available from the hospital for this measure; (6) Fewer than 100 patients completed the HCAHPS survey. Use these rates with caution, as the number of surveys may be too low to reliably assess hospital performance; (7) Survey results are based on less than 12 months of data; (8) Survey results are not available for this reporting period; (9) No or very few patients were eligible for the HCAHPS survey. The scores shown, if any, reflect a very small number of surveys; (10) A state average was not calculated because too few hospitals in the state submitted data; (11) There were discrepancies in the data collection process; Please refer to the User's Guide for a full explanation of data.

Saint Johns Mercy Medical Center

615 New Ballas Road Phone: 314-569-6000
Saint Louis, MO 63141 Fax: 314-251-4719
URL: www.stjohnsmercy.org
Type: Acute Care Hospitals Emergency Services: Yes
Ownership: Voluntary Non-Profit - Church Beds: 979

Key Personnel:
CEO/President. . . . . John Sullivan
Cardiac Laboratory. . . . . John W. Hubert, MD
Chief of Medical Staff . . . . Martin Bell
Coronary Care . . . . James A. Stokes, MD, FACC

Measure	Cases	This Hosp.	State Avg.	U.S. Avg.
Heart Attack Care				
ACE Inhibitor or ARB for LVSD	49	100%	96%	96%
Aspirin at Arrival	280	99%	99%	99%
Aspirin at Discharge	395	99%	99%	98%
Beta Blocker at Discharge	388	99%	99%	98%
Fibrinolytic Medication Timing	0	-	27%	55%
PCI Within 90 Minutes of Arrival	34	88%	92%	90%
Smoking Cessation Advice	95	98%	99%	99%
Chest Pain/Possible Heart Attack Care				
Aspirin at Arrival	72	85%	95%	95%
Median Time to ECG (minutes)	71	10	9	8
Median Time to Transfer (minutes)[5]	0	-	64	61
Fibrinolytic Medication Timing[5]	0	-	31%	54%
Heart Failure Care				
ACE Inhibitor or ARB for LVSD	174	97%	94%	94%
Discharge Instructions	514	84%	87%	88%
Evaluation of LVS Function	669	100%	97%	98%
Smoking Cessation Advice	75	100%	98%	98%
Pneumonia Care				
Appropriate Initial Antibiotic[2]	91	95%	91%	92%
Blood Culture Timing[2]	145	92%	97%	96%
Influenza Vaccine[2]	87	80%	90%	91%
Initial Antibiotic Timing[2]	151	99%	95%	95%
Pneumococcal Vaccine[2]	148	89%	93%	93%
Smoking Cessation Advice[2]	53	100%	97%	97%
Surgical Care Improvement Project				
Appropriate VTP Within 24 Hours[2]	143	95%	93%	92%
Appropriate Hair Removal[2]	609	100%	100%	99%
Appropriate Beta Blocker Usage[2]	176	97%	94%	93%
Controlled Postoperative Blood Glucose[2]	127	98%	94%	93%
Prophylactic Antibiotic Timing[2]	405	98%	97%	97%
Prophylactic Antibiotic Timing (Outpatient)	698	98%	95%	92%
Prophylactic Antibiotic Selection[2]	417	99%	97%	97%
Prophylactic Antibiotic Select. (Outpatient)	746	98%	95%	94%
Prophylactic Antibiotic Stopped[2]	386	98%	95%	94%
Recommended VTP Ordered[2]	143	97%	95%	94%
Urinary Catheter Removal[2]	105	91%	88%	90%
Children's Asthma Care				
Received Systemic Corticosteroids	195	100%	-	100%
Received Home Management Plan	194	69%	-	71%
Received Reliever Medication	195	100%	-	100%
Use of Medical Imaging				
Combination Abdominal CT Scan	2,017	0.057	0.227	0.191
Combination Chest CT Scan	1,514	0.009	0.059	0.054
Follow-up Mammogram/Ultrasound	3,740	5.2%	7.4%	8.4%
MRI for Low Back Pain	411	37.0%	36%	32.7%
Survey of Patients' Hospital Experiences				
Area Around Room 'Always' Quiet at Night	300+	59%	-	58%
Doctors 'Always' Communicated Well	300+	79%	-	80%
Home Recovery Information Given	300+	77%	-	82%
Hospital Given 9 or 10 on 10 Point Scale	300+	75%	-	67%
Meds 'Always' Explained Before Given	300+	52%	-	60%
Nurses 'Always' Communicated Well	300+	78%	-	76%
Pain 'Always' Well Controlled	300+	69%	-	69%
Room and Bathroom 'Always' Clean	300+	70%	-	71%
Timely Help 'Always' Received	300+	62%	-	64%
Would Definitely Recommend Hospital	300+	79%	-	69%

Saint Louis University Hospital

3635 Vista Ave Phone: 314-577-8000
Saint Louis, MO 63110 Fax: 314-577-8825
E-mail: slucare@slu.edu
URL: www.slucare.edu/clinical
Type: Acute Care Hospitals Emergency Services: Yes
Ownership: Proprietary Beds: 356

Key Personnel:
CEO/President. . . . . James Kimmny
Chief of Medical Staff . . . . Coy Fitch, MD
Infection Control. . . . . Donald J Kennedy, MD
Operating Room. . . . . Judy Mai Lombardo, RN
Pediatric Ambulatory Care . . . . . . George Ray, MD
Pediatric In-Patient Care . . . . George Ray, MD
Radiology. . . . . Ben Frey
Anesthesiology. . . . . Larry Baudendistel, MD

Measure	Cases	This Hosp.	State Avg.	U.S. Avg.
Heart Attack Care				
ACE Inhibitor or ARB for LVSD	35	100%	96%	96%
Aspirin at Arrival	110	98%	99%	99%
Aspirin at Discharge	116	100%	99%	98%
Beta Blocker at Discharge	108	99%	99%	98%
Fibrinolytic Medication Timing	0	-	27%	55%
PCI Within 90 Minutes of Arrival[1]	24	96%	92%	90%
Smoking Cessation Advice	59	100%	99%	99%
Chest Pain/Possible Heart Attack Care				
Aspirin at Arrival[1,3]	2	100%	95%	95%
Median Time to ECG (minutes)[1,3]	2	13	9	8
Median Time to Transfer (minutes)[5]	0	-	64	61
Fibrinolytic Medication Timing[5]	0	-	31%	54%
Heart Failure Care				
ACE Inhibitor or ARB for LVSD	202	99%	94%	94%
Discharge Instructions	296	99%	87%	88%
Evaluation of LVS Function	356	99%	97%	98%
Smoking Cessation Advice	97	100%	98%	98%
Pneumonia Care				
Appropriate Initial Antibiotic	82	98%	91%	92%
Blood Culture Timing	131	93%	97%	96%
Influenza Vaccine	133	99%	90%	91%
Initial Antibiotic Timing	157	92%	95%	95%
Pneumococcal Vaccine	111	98%	93%	93%
Smoking Cessation Advice	137	99%	97%	97%
Surgical Care Improvement Project				
Appropriate VTP Within 24 Hours[2]	230	96%	93%	92%
Appropriate Hair Removal[2]	442	100%	100%	99%
Appropriate Beta Blocker Usage[2]	138	95%	94%	93%
Controlled Postoperative Blood Glucose[2]	64	92%	94%	93%
Prophylactic Antibiotic Timing[2]	199	98%	97%	97%
Prophylactic Antibiotic Timing (Outpatient)	171	95%	95%	92%
Prophylactic Antibiotic Selection[2]	205	99%	97%	97%
Prophylactic Antibiotic Select. (Outpatient)	163	90%	95%	94%
Prophylactic Antibiotic Stopped[2]	177	97%	95%	94%
Recommended VTP Ordered[2]	230	98%	95%	94%
Urinary Catheter Removal[2]	99	92%	88%	90%
Children's Asthma Care				
Received Systemic Corticosteroids	-	-	-	100%
Received Home Management Plan	-	-	-	71%
Received Reliever Medication	-	-	-	100%
Use of Medical Imaging				
Combination Abdominal CT Scan	807	0.373	0.227	0.191
Combination Chest CT Scan	621	0.076	0.059	0.054
Follow-up Mammogram/Ultrasound	340	5.0%	7.4%	8.4%
MRI for Low Back Pain[1]	31	32.3%	36%	32.7%
Survey of Patients' Hospital Experiences				
Area Around Room 'Always' Quiet at Night	300+	57%	-	58%
Doctors 'Always' Communicated Well	300+	78%	-	80%
Home Recovery Information Given	300+	86%	-	82%
Hospital Given 9 or 10 on 10 Point Scale	300+	67%	-	67%
Meds 'Always' Explained Before Given	300+	65%	-	60%
Nurses 'Always' Communicated Well	300+	72%	-	76%
Pain 'Always' Well Controlled	300+	66%	-	69%
Room and Bathroom 'Always' Clean	300+	67%	-	71%
Timely Help 'Always' Received	300+	60%	-	64%
Would Definitely Recommend Hospital	300+	71%	-	69%

Saint Louis-John Cochran VA Medical Center

915 North Grand Phone: 314-652-4100
Saint Louis, MO 63106 Fax: 314-894-6682
Type: Acute Care-Veterans Administration Emergency Services: No
Ownership: Government - Federal Beds: 684

Key Personnel:
Chief of Medical Staff . . . . Margarete Hageman, MD
Quality Assurance . . . . Thomas Lewis
Anesthesiology. . . . . Shigemasa Ikeda, MD
Emergency Room . . . . Laura Kroupa, MD
Hemotology Center . . . . Scot Hichman

Measure	Cases	This Hosp.	State Avg.	U.S. Avg.
Heart Attack Care				
ACE Inhibitor or ARB for LVSD[1]	14	100%	96%	96%
Aspirin at Arrival	91	100%	99%	99%
Aspirin at Discharge	98	100%	99%	98%
Beta Blocker at Discharge	91	99%	99%	98%
Fibrinolytic Medication Timing[1]	1	100%	27%	55%
PCI Within 90 Minutes of Arrival[1]	10	90%	92%	90%
Smoking Cessation Advice	48	94%	99%	99%
Chest Pain/Possible Heart Attack Care				
Aspirin at Arrival	-	-	95%	95%
Median Time to ECG (minutes)	-	-	9	8
Median Time to Transfer (minutes)	-	-	64	61
Fibrinolytic Medication Timing	-	-	31%	54%
Heart Failure Care				
ACE Inhibitor or ARB for LVSD	158	97%	94%	94%
Discharge Instructions	382	98%	87%	88%
Evaluation of LVS Function	389	100%	97%	98%
Smoking Cessation Advice	137	94%	98%	98%
Pneumonia Care				
Appropriate Initial Antibiotic	49	100%	91%	92%
Blood Culture Timing	86	99%	97%	96%
Influenza Vaccine	62	89%	90%	91%
Initial Antibiotic Timing	80	95%	95%	95%
Pneumococcal Vaccine	45	98%	93%	93%
Smoking Cessation Advice	63	97%	97%	97%
Surgical Care Improvement Project				
Appropriate VTP Within 24 Hours[2]	182	96%	93%	92%
Appropriate Hair Removal[2]	260	100%	100%	99%
Appropriate Beta Blocker Usage[2]	80	91%	94%	93%
Controlled Postoperative Blood Glucose[2,5]	0	-	94%	93%
Prophylactic Antibiotic Timing	162	96%	97%	97%
Prophylactic Antibiotic Timing (Outpatient)	-	-	95%	92%
Prophylactic Antibiotic Selection	162	99%	97%	97%
Prophylactic Antibiotic Select. (Outpatient)	-	-	95%	94%
Prophylactic Antibiotic Stopped	158	92%	95%	94%
Recommended VTP Ordered[2]	182	98%	95%	94%
Urinary Catheter Removal[2]	106	100%	88%	90%
Children's Asthma Care				
Received Systemic Corticosteroids	-	-	-	100%
Received Home Management Plan	-	-	-	71%
Received Reliever Medication	-	-	-	100%
Use of Medical Imaging				
Combination Abdominal CT Scan	-	-	0.227	0.191
Combination Chest CT Scan	-	-	0.059	0.054
Follow-up Mammogram/Ultrasound	-	-	7.4%	8.4%
MRI for Low Back Pain	-	-	36%	32.7%
Survey of Patients' Hospital Experiences				
Area Around Room 'Always' Quiet at Night	-	-	-	58%
Doctors 'Always' Communicated Well	-	-	-	80%
Home Recovery Information Given	-	-	-	82%
Hospital Given 9 or 10 on 10 Point Scale	-	-	-	67%
Meds 'Always' Explained Before Given	-	-	-	60%
Nurses 'Always' Communicated Well	-	-	-	76%
Pain 'Always' Well Controlled	-	-	-	69%
Room and Bathroom 'Always' Clean	-	-	-	71%
Timely Help 'Always' Received	-	-	-	64%
Would Definitely Recommend Hospital	-	-	-	69%

NOTE: Hospital profiles are in alphabetical order by state, then city, then hospital within the city; Rankings exclude hospitals with less than 25 cases except for patient surveys which excludes hospitals with less than 100 cases; (a) 100–299 cases; (1) The number of cases is too small to be sure how well a hospital is performing; (2) The hospital indicated that the data submitted for this measure were based on a sample of cases; (3) Data was collected during a shorter time period (fewer quarters) than the maximum possible time for this measure; (4) Suppressed for one or more quarters by CMS; (5) No data is available from the hospital for this measure; (6) Fewer than 100 patients completed the HCAHPS survey. Use these rates with caution, as the number of surveys may be too low to reliably assess hospital performance; (7) Survey results are based on less than 12 months of data; (8) Survey results are not available for this reporting period; (9) No or very few patients were eligible for the HCAHPS survey. The scores shown, if any, reflect a very small number of surveys; (10) A state average was not calculated because too few hospitals in the state submitted data; (11) There were discrepancies in the data collection process; Please refer to the User's Guide for a full explanation of data.

Barnes-Jewish St Peters Hospital

10 Hospital Dr
Saint Peters, MO 63376
Phone: 636-916-9000
Fax: 636-916-9127
URL: www.bjsph.org
Type: Acute Care Hospitals
Emergency Services: Yes
Ownership: Voluntary Non-Profit - Other
Beds: 111

Key Personnel:
CEO/President. . . . . David Ross
Chief of Medical Staff. . . . . Phil Brick
Infection Control. . . . . Janice Setzer
Operating Room. . . . . Mindy Manly
Pediatric Ambulatory Care . . . . . . Michael Dauter
Pediatric In-Patient Care . . . . Michael Dauter
Quality Assurance . . . . Lois Koehler

Measure	Cases	This Hosp.	State Avg.	U.S. Avg.
Heart Attack Care				
ACE Inhibitor or ARB for LVSD[1]	24	100%	96%	96%
Aspirin at Arrival	179	98%	99%	99%
Aspirin at Discharge	183	98%	99%	98%
Beta Blocker at Discharge	186	98%	99%	98%
Fibrinolytic Medication Timing	0	-	27%	55%
PCI Within 90 Minutes of Arrival	29	86%	92%	90%
Smoking Cessation Advice	61	100%	99%	99%
Chest Pain/Possible Heart Attack Care				
Aspirin at Arrival[1]	19	95%	95%	95%
Median Time to ECG (minutes)[1]	19	1	9	8
Median Time to Transfer (minutes)[1,3]	1	1646	64	61
Fibrinolytic Medication Timing[3]	0	-	31%	54%
Heart Failure Care				
ACE Inhibitor or ARB for LVSD	28	100%	94%	94%
Discharge Instructions	122	92%	87%	88%
Evaluation of LVS Function	154	98%	97%	98%
Smoking Cessation Advice[1]	15	100%	98%	98%
Pneumonia Care				
Appropriate Initial Antibiotic	184	96%	91%	92%
Blood Culture Timing	269	99%	97%	96%
Influenza Vaccine	174	89%	90%	91%
Initial Antibiotic Timing	265	97%	95%	95%
Pneumococcal Vaccine	206	96%	93%	93%
Smoking Cessation Advice	96	100%	97%	97%
Surgical Care Improvement Project				
Appropriate VTP Within 24 Hours	186	96%	93%	92%
Appropriate Hair Removal	420	100%	100%	99%
Appropriate Beta Blocker Usage	94	99%	94%	93%
Controlled Postoperative Blood Glucose	0	-	94%	93%
Prophylactic Antibiotic Timing	254	93%	97%	97%
Prophylactic Antibiotic Timing (Outpatient)	255	93%	95%	92%
Prophylactic Antibiotic Selection	254	96%	97%	97%
Prophylactic Antibiotic Select. (Outpatient)	248	96%	95%	94%
Prophylactic Antibiotic Stopped	244	96%	95%	94%
Recommended VTP Ordered	187	96%	95%	94%
Urinary Catheter Removal	99	81%	88%	90%
Children's Asthma Care				
Received Systemic Corticosteroids	-	-	-	100%
Received Home Management Plan	-	-	-	71%
Received Reliever Medication	-	-	-	100%
Use of Medical Imaging				
Combination Abdominal CT Scan	761	0.137	0.227	0.191
Combination Chest CT Scan	749	0.052	0.059	0.054
Follow-up Mammogram/Ultrasound	979	7.7%	7.4%	8.4%
MRI for Low Back Pain	72	30.6%	36%	32.7%
Survey of Patients' Hospital Experiences				
Area Around Room 'Always' Quiet at Night	300+	62%	-	58%
Doctors 'Always' Communicated Well	300+	84%	-	80%
Home Recovery Information Given	300+	86%	-	82%
Hospital Given 9 or 10 on 10 Point Scale	300+	77%	-	67%
Meds 'Always' Explained Before Given	300+	65%	-	60%
Nurses 'Always' Communicated Well	300+	82%	-	76%
Pain 'Always' Well Controlled	300+	72%	-	69%
Room and Bathroom 'Always' Clean	300+	70%	-	71%
Timely Help 'Always' Received	300+	63%	-	64%
Would Definitely Recommend Hospital	300+	81%	-	69%

Ste Genevieve County Memorial Hospital

800 Ste Genevieve Drive
Sainte Genevieve, MO 63670
Phone: 573-883-2751
Type: Critical Access Hospitals
Emergency Services: Yes
Ownership: Voluntary Non-Profit - Other

Key Personnel:
CEO/President. . . . . Thomas Keim
Radiology. . . . . Patrick Cabrera

Measure	Cases	This Hosp.	State Avg.	U.S. Avg.
Heart Attack Care				
ACE Inhibitor or ARB for LVSD[3]	0	-	96%	96%
Aspirin at Arrival[1,3]	1	100%	99%	99%
Aspirin at Discharge[1,3]	1	100%	99%	98%
Beta Blocker at Discharge[1,3]	1	100%	99%	98%
Fibrinolytic Medication Timing[3]	0	-	27%	55%
PCI Within 90 Minutes of Arrival[3]	0	-	92%	90%
Smoking Cessation Advice[3]	0	-	99%	99%
Chest Pain/Possible Heart Attack Care				
Aspirin at Arrival	-	-	95%	95%
Median Time to ECG (minutes)	-	-	9	8
Median Time to Transfer (minutes)	-	-	64	61
Fibrinolytic Medication Timing	-	-	31%	54%
Heart Failure Care				
ACE Inhibitor or ARB for LVSD[1]	4	75%	94%	94%
Discharge Instructions[1]	16	100%	87%	88%
Evaluation of LVS Function	35	94%	97%	98%
Smoking Cessation Advice[1]	3	100%	98%	98%
Pneumonia Care				
Appropriate Initial Antibiotic[1,2]	20	100%	91%	92%
Blood Culture Timing[1,2]	23	91%	97%	96%
Influenza Vaccine[1]	13	85%	90%	91%
Initial Antibiotic Timing[2]	27	100%	95%	95%
Pneumococcal Vaccine[1,2]	21	57%	93%	93%
Smoking Cessation Advice[1,2]	16	100%	97%	97%
Surgical Care Improvement Project				
Appropriate VTP Within 24 Hours[5]	0	-	93%	92%
Appropriate Hair Removal[1,3]	8	100%	100%	99%
Appropriate Beta Blocker Usage[5]	0	-	94%	93%
Controlled Postoperative Blood Glucose[5]	0	-	94%	93%
Prophylactic Antibiotic Timing[1,3]	7	100%	97%	97%
Prophylactic Antibiotic Timing (Outpatient)	-	-	95%	92%
Prophylactic Antibiotic Selection[1,3]	7	100%	97%	97%
Prophylactic Antibiotic Select. (Outpatient)	-	-	95%	94%
Prophylactic Antibiotic Stopped[1,3]	7	100%	95%	94%
Recommended VTP Ordered[5]	0	-	95%	94%
Urinary Catheter Removal[5]	0	-	88%	90%
Children's Asthma Care				
Received Systemic Corticosteroids	-	-	-	100%
Received Home Management Plan	-	-	-	71%
Received Reliever Medication	-	-	-	100%
Use of Medical Imaging				
Combination Abdominal CT Scan	-	-	0.227	0.191
Combination Chest CT Scan	-	-	0.059	0.054
Follow-up Mammogram/Ultrasound	-	-	7.4%	8.4%
MRI for Low Back Pain	-	-	36%	32.7%
Survey of Patients' Hospital Experiences				
Area Around Room 'Always' Quiet at Night	300+	53%	-	58%
Doctors 'Always' Communicated Well	300+	84%	-	80%
Home Recovery Information Given	300+	87%	-	82%
Hospital Given 9 or 10 on 10 Point Scale	300+	69%	-	67%
Meds 'Always' Explained Before Given	300+	61%	-	60%
Nurses 'Always' Communicated Well	300+	80%	-	76%
Pain 'Always' Well Controlled	300+	68%	-	69%
Room and Bathroom 'Always' Clean	300+	77%	-	71%
Timely Help 'Always' Received	300+	67%	-	64%
Would Definitely Recommend Hospital	300+	70%	-	69%

Salem Memorial District Hospital

PO Box 774
Salem, MO 65560
Phone: 573-729-6626
Fax: 573-729-4511
Type: Critical Access Hospitals
Emergency Services: Yes
Ownership: Govt - Hospital Dist/Auth
Beds: 59

Key Personnel:
Infection Control. . . . . Cliff Free
Operating Room. . . . . Lowell Fisher
Quality Assurance . . . . Arlene Cornell
Emergency Room . . . . Brenda Gott

Measure	Cases	This Hosp.	State Avg.	U.S. Avg.
Heart Attack Care				
ACE Inhibitor or ARB for LVSD[1,3]	1	100%	96%	96%
Aspirin at Arrival[1,3]	2	50%	99%	99%
Aspirin at Discharge[1,3]	1	100%	99%	98%
Beta Blocker at Discharge[1,3]	1	100%	99%	98%
Fibrinolytic Medication Timing[3]	0	-	27%	55%
PCI Within 90 Minutes of Arrival[3]	0	-	92%	90%
Smoking Cessation Advice[3]	0	-	99%	99%
Chest Pain/Possible Heart Attack Care				
Aspirin at Arrival	-	-	95%	95%
Median Time to ECG (minutes)	-	-	9	8
Median Time to Transfer (minutes)	-	-	64	61
Fibrinolytic Medication Timing	-	-	31%	54%
Heart Failure Care				
ACE Inhibitor or ARB for LVSD[1]	4	100%	94%	94%
Discharge Instructions[1]	24	75%	87%	88%
Evaluation of LVS Function	32	41%	97%	98%
Smoking Cessation Advice[1]	2	100%	98%	98%
Pneumonia Care				
Appropriate Initial Antibiotic[1]	15	87%	91%	92%
Blood Culture Timing	38	89%	97%	96%
Influenza Vaccine	44	95%	90%	91%
Initial Antibiotic Timing	59	90%	95%	95%
Pneumococcal Vaccine	54	98%	93%	93%
Smoking Cessation Advice[1]	21	86%	97%	97%
Surgical Care Improvement Project				
Appropriate VTP Within 24 Hours[5]	0	-	93%	92%
Appropriate Hair Removal[5]	0	-	100%	99%
Appropriate Beta Blocker Usage[5]	0	-	94%	93%
Controlled Postoperative Blood Glucose[5]	0	-	94%	93%
Prophylactic Antibiotic Timing[5]	0	-	97%	97%
Prophylactic Antibiotic Timing (Outpatient)	-	-	95%	92%
Prophylactic Antibiotic Selection[5]	0	-	97%	97%
Prophylactic Antibiotic Select. (Outpatient)	-	-	95%	94%
Prophylactic Antibiotic Stopped[5]	0	-	95%	94%
Recommended VTP Ordered[5]	0	-	95%	94%
Urinary Catheter Removal[5]	0	-	88%	90%
Children's Asthma Care				
Received Systemic Corticosteroids	-	-	-	100%
Received Home Management Plan	-	-	-	71%
Received Reliever Medication	-	-	-	100%
Use of Medical Imaging				
Combination Abdominal CT Scan	-	-	0.227	0.191
Combination Chest CT Scan	-	-	0.059	0.054
Follow-up Mammogram/Ultrasound	-	-	7.4%	8.4%
MRI for Low Back Pain	-	-	36%	32.7%
Survey of Patients' Hospital Experiences				
Area Around Room 'Always' Quiet at Night[8]	-	-	-	58%
Doctors 'Always' Communicated Well[8]	-	-	-	80%
Home Recovery Information Given[8]	-	-	-	82%
Hospital Given 9 or 10 on 10 Point Scale[8]	-	-	-	67%
Meds 'Always' Explained Before Given[8]	-	-	-	60%
Nurses 'Always' Communicated Well[8]	-	-	-	76%
Pain 'Always' Well Controlled[8]	-	-	-	69%
Room and Bathroom 'Always' Clean[8]	-	-	-	71%
Timely Help 'Always' Received[8]	-	-	-	64%
Would Definitely Recommend Hospital[8]	-	-	-	69%

NOTE: Hospital profiles are in alphabetical order by state, then city, then hospital within the city; Rankings exclude hospitals with less than 25 cases except for patient surveys which excludes hospitals with less than 100 cases; (a) 100–299 cases; (1) The number of cases is too small to be sure how well a hospital is performing; (2) The hospital indicated that the data submitted for this measure were based on a sample of cases; (3) Data was collected during a shorter time period (fewer quarters) than the maximum possible time for this measure; (4) Suppressed for one or more quarters by CMS; (5) No data is available from the hospital for this measure; (6) Fewer than 100 patients completed the HCAHPS survey. Use these rates with caution, as the number of surveys may be too low to reliably assess hospital performance; (7) Survey results are based on less than 12 months of data; (8) Survey results are not available for this reporting period; (9) No or very few patients were eligible for the HCAHPS survey. The scores shown, if any, reflect a very small number of surveys; (10) A state average was not calculated because too few hospitals in the state submitted data; (11) There were discrepancies in the data collection process; Please refer to the User's Guide for a full explanation of data.

Bothwell Regional Health Center

601 E 14th St
Sedalia, MO 65302
URL: www.brhc.org
Type: Acute Care Hospitals
Ownership: Government - Local
Phone: 660-826-8833
Fax: 660-827-6784
Emergency Services: Yes
Beds: 170

Key Personnel:
CEO/President. . . . . John Dawes
Chief of Medical Staff . . . . Phillip Horneospel
Operating Room. . . . . Bobbi McNims, RN
Quality Assurance . . . . Connie Chappel
Radiology. . . . . David H Roehrs, MD
Emergency Room . . . . Karen Toy

Measure	Cases	This Hosp.	State Avg.	U.S. Avg.
Heart Attack Care				
ACE Inhibitor or ARB for LVSD[1]	14	93%	96%	96%
Aspirin at Arrival	58	97%	99%	99%
Aspirin at Discharge	34	100%	99%	98%
Beta Blocker at Discharge	36	94%	99%	98%
Fibrinolytic Medication Timing[1]	4	0%	27%	55%
PCI Within 90 Minutes of Arrival	0	-	92%	90%
Smoking Cessation Advice[1]	10	100%	99%	99%
Chest Pain/Possible Heart Attack Care				
Aspirin at Arrival	85	95%	95%	95%
Median Time to ECG (minutes)	86	19	9	8
Median Time to Transfer (minutes)[1]	10	81	64	61
Fibrinolytic Medication Timing	0	-	31%	54%
Heart Failure Care				
ACE Inhibitor or ARB for LVSD	52	87%	94%	94%
Discharge Instructions	133	83%	87%	88%
Evaluation of LVS Function	164	99%	97%	98%
Smoking Cessation Advice[1]	22	100%	98%	98%
Pneumonia Care				
Appropriate Initial Antibiotic	132	95%	91%	92%
Blood Culture Timing	84	99%	97%	96%
Influenza Vaccine	90	71%	90%	91%
Initial Antibiotic Timing	153	94%	95%	95%
Pneumococcal Vaccine	178	85%	93%	93%
Smoking Cessation Advice	73	100%	97%	97%
Surgical Care Improvement Project				
Appropriate VTP Within 24 Hours	89	66%	93%	92%
Appropriate Hair Removal	389	99%	100%	99%
Appropriate Beta Blocker Usage	97	82%	94%	93%
Controlled Postoperative Blood Glucose	0	-	94%	93%
Prophylactic Antibiotic Timing	280	97%	97%	97%
Prophylactic Antibiotic Timing (Outpatient)	154	90%	95%	92%
Prophylactic Antibiotic Selection	279	96%	97%	97%
Prophylactic Antibiotic Select. (Outpatient)	169	95%	95%	94%
Prophylactic Antibiotic Stopped	274	94%	95%	94%
Recommended VTP Ordered	89	71%	95%	94%
Urinary Catheter Removal	92	97%	88%	90%
Children's Asthma Care				
Received Systemic Corticosteroids	-	-	-	100%
Received Home Management Plan	-	-	-	71%
Received Reliever Medication	-	-	-	100%
Use of Medical Imaging				
Combination Abdominal CT Scan	788	0.730	0.227	0.191
Combination Chest CT Scan	649	0.000	0.059	0.054
Follow-up Mammogram/Ultrasound	752	1.2%	7.4%	8.4%
MRI for Low Back Pain	237	37.1%	36%	32.7%
Survey of Patients' Hospital Experiences				
Area Around Room 'Always' Quiet at Night	300+	63%	-	58%
Doctors 'Always' Communicated Well	300+	83%	-	80%
Home Recovery Information Given	300+	85%	-	82%
Hospital Given 9 or 10 on 10 Point Scale	300+	70%	-	67%
Meds 'Always' Explained Before Given	300+	66%	-	60%
Nurses 'Always' Communicated Well	300+	81%	-	76%
Pain 'Always' Well Controlled	300+	74%	-	69%
Room and Bathroom 'Always' Clean	300+	81%	-	71%
Timely Help 'Always' Received	300+	76%	-	64%
Would Definitely Recommend Hospital	300+	67%	-	69%

Missouri Delta Medical Center

1008 North Main St
Sikeston, MO 63801
URL: www.missouridelta.com
Type: Acute Care Hospitals
Ownership: Voluntary Non-Profit - Other
Phone: 573-471-1600
Fax: 573-472-7606
Emergency Services: Yes
Beds: 188

Key Personnel:
Cardiac Laboratory. . . . . Cindy Shands
Chief of Medical Staff . . . . Mowaffaq Said, MD
Infection Control. . . . . Joy Cauthorn
Operating Room. . . . . Libby Kliptel
Pediatric Ambulatory Care . . . . . . Joseph Blanton, MD
Pediatric In-Patient Care . . . . Joseph Blanton, MD
Quality Assurance . . . . Linda Culbertson
Radiology. . . . . Mahmaud Ziaee

Measure	Cases	This Hosp.	State Avg.	U.S. Avg.
Heart Attack Care				
ACE Inhibitor or ARB for LVSD[1]	9	89%	96%	96%
Aspirin at Arrival	31	87%	99%	99%
Aspirin at Discharge	25	88%	99%	98%
Beta Blocker at Discharge	26	88%	99%	98%
Fibrinolytic Medication Timing	0	-	27%	55%
PCI Within 90 Minutes of Arrival	0	-	92%	90%
Smoking Cessation Advice[1]	10	100%	99%	99%
Chest Pain/Possible Heart Attack Care				
Aspirin at Arrival	100	95%	95%	95%
Median Time to ECG (minutes)	104	12	9	8
Median Time to Transfer (minutes)[1]	6	64	64	61
Fibrinolytic Medication Timing[1]	6	50%	31%	54%
Heart Failure Care				
ACE Inhibitor or ARB for LVSD	75	92%	94%	94%
Discharge Instructions	172	84%	87%	88%
Evaluation of LVS Function	223	98%	97%	98%
Smoking Cessation Advice	49	100%	98%	98%
Pneumonia Care				
Appropriate Initial Antibiotic	115	90%	91%	92%
Blood Culture Timing	128	90%	97%	96%
Influenza Vaccine	117	77%	90%	91%
Initial Antibiotic Timing	163	93%	95%	95%
Pneumococcal Vaccine	154	82%	93%	93%
Smoking Cessation Advice	108	100%	97%	97%
Surgical Care Improvement Project				
Appropriate VTP Within 24 Hours	72	83%	93%	92%
Appropriate Hair Removal	184	100%	100%	99%
Appropriate Beta Blocker Usage	28	96%	94%	93%
Controlled Postoperative Blood Glucose	0	-	94%	93%
Prophylactic Antibiotic Timing	106	96%	97%	97%
Prophylactic Antibiotic Timing (Outpatient)	71	96%	95%	92%
Prophylactic Antibiotic Selection	105	88%	97%	97%
Prophylactic Antibiotic Select. (Outpatient)	68	97%	95%	94%
Prophylactic Antibiotic Stopped	93	90%	95%	94%
Recommended VTP Ordered	72	89%	95%	94%
Urinary Catheter Removal[1]	7	100%	88%	90%
Children's Asthma Care				
Received Systemic Corticosteroids	-	-	-	100%
Received Home Management Plan	-	-	-	71%
Received Reliever Medication	-	-	-	100%
Use of Medical Imaging				
Combination Abdominal CT Scan	327	0.627	0.227	0.191
Combination Chest CT Scan	194	0.021	0.059	0.054
Follow-up Mammogram/Ultrasound	738	7.5%	7.4%	8.4%
MRI for Low Back Pain	74	60.8%	36%	32.7%
Survey of Patients' Hospital Experiences				
Area Around Room 'Always' Quiet at Night	300+	61%	-	58%
Doctors 'Always' Communicated Well	300+	84%	-	80%
Home Recovery Information Given	300+	77%	-	82%
Hospital Given 9 or 10 on 10 Point Scale	300+	65%	-	67%
Meds 'Always' Explained Before Given	300+	67%	-	60%
Nurses 'Always' Communicated Well	300+	78%	-	76%
Pain 'Always' Well Controlled	300+	75%	-	69%
Room and Bathroom 'Always' Clean	300+	83%	-	71%
Timely Help 'Always' Received	300+	67%	-	64%
Would Definitely Recommend Hospital	300+	62%	-	69%

Cox Medical Center

3801 South National Avenue
Springfield, MO 65807
URL: www.coxhealth.com
Type: Acute Care Hospitals
Ownership: Voluntary Non-Profit - Private
Phone: 417-269-6000
Emergency Services: Yes
Beds: 754

Key Personnel:
President/CEO. . . . . Robert H Bezanson

Measure	Cases	This Hosp.	State Avg.	U.S. Avg.
Heart Attack Care				
ACE Inhibitor or ARB for LVSD	94	93%	96%	96%
Aspirin at Arrival	422	99%	99%	99%
Aspirin at Discharge	519	98%	99%	98%
Beta Blocker at Discharge	502	99%	99%	98%
Fibrinolytic Medication Timing[1]	2	0%	27%	55%
PCI Within 90 Minutes of Arrival	74	89%	92%	90%
Smoking Cessation Advice	226	100%	99%	99%
Chest Pain/Possible Heart Attack Care				
Aspirin at Arrival[1,3]	5	80%	95%	95%
Median Time to ECG (minutes)[1,3]	5	2	9	8
Median Time to Transfer (minutes)[5]	0	-	64	61
Fibrinolytic Medication Timing[5]	0	-	31%	54%
Heart Failure Care				
ACE Inhibitor or ARB for LVSD	171	95%	94%	94%
Discharge Instructions	415	97%	87%	88%
Evaluation of LVS Function	496	100%	97%	98%
Smoking Cessation Advice	172	100%	98%	98%
Pneumonia Care				
Appropriate Initial Antibiotic[2]	190	94%	91%	92%
Blood Culture Timing[2]	283	99%	97%	96%
Influenza Vaccine[2]	212	98%	90%	91%
Initial Antibiotic Timing[2]	235	97%	95%	95%
Pneumococcal Vaccine[2]	230	98%	93%	93%
Smoking Cessation Advice[2]	137	97%	97%	97%
Surgical Care Improvement Project				
Appropriate VTP Within 24 Hours[2]	234	95%	93%	92%
Appropriate Hair Removal[2]	685	100%	100%	99%
Appropriate Beta Blocker Usage[2]	231	95%	94%	93%
Controlled Postoperative Blood Glucose[2]	147	97%	94%	93%
Prophylactic Antibiotic Timing[2]	494	97%	97%	97%
Prophylactic Antibiotic Timing (Outpatient)	778	97%	95%	92%
Prophylactic Antibiotic Selection[2]	502	97%	97%	97%
Prophylactic Antibiotic Select. (Outpatient)	776	97%	95%	94%
Prophylactic Antibiotic Stopped[2]	479	89%	95%	94%
Recommended VTP Ordered[2]	234	95%	95%	94%
Urinary Catheter Removal[2]	156	56%	88%	90%
Children's Asthma Care				
Received Systemic Corticosteroids	-	-	-	100%
Received Home Management Plan	-	-	-	71%
Received Reliever Medication	-	-	-	100%
Use of Medical Imaging				
Combination Abdominal CT Scan	1,960	0.048	0.227	0.191
Combination Chest CT Scan	1,322	0.002	0.059	0.054
Follow-up Mammogram/Ultrasound	2,956	9.2%	7.4%	8.4%
MRI for Low Back Pain	601	34.9%	36%	32.7%
Survey of Patients' Hospital Experiences				
Area Around Room 'Always' Quiet at Night	300+	44%	-	58%
Doctors 'Always' Communicated Well	300+	79%	-	80%
Home Recovery Information Given	300+	79%	-	82%
Hospital Given 9 or 10 on 10 Point Scale	300+	61%	-	67%
Meds 'Always' Explained Before Given	300+	53%	-	60%
Nurses 'Always' Communicated Well	300+	72%	-	76%
Pain 'Always' Well Controlled	300+	63%	-	69%
Room and Bathroom 'Always' Clean	300+	65%	-	71%
Timely Help 'Always' Received	300+	58%	-	64%
Would Definitely Recommend Hospital	300+	68%	-	69%

NOTE: Hospital profiles are in alphabetical order by state, then city, then hospital within the city; Rankings exclude hospitals with less than 25 cases except for patient surveys which excludes hospitals with less than 100 cases; (a) 100–299 cases; (1) The number of cases is too small to be sure how well a hospital is performing; (2) The hospital indicated that the data submitted for this measure were based on a sample of cases; (3) Data was collected during a shorter time period (fewer quarters) than the maximum possible time for this measure; (4) Suppressed for one or more quarters by CMS; (5) No data is available from the hospital for this measure; (6) Fewer than 100 patients completed the HCAHPS survey. Use these rates with caution, as the number of surveys may be too low to reliably assess hospital performance; (7) Survey results are based on less than 12 months of data; (8) Survey results are not available for this reporting period; (9) No or very few patients were eligible for the HCAHPS survey. The scores shown, if any, reflect a very small number of surveys; (10) A state average was not calculated because too few hospitals in the state submitted data; (11) There were discrepancies in the data collection process; Please refer to the User's Guide for a full explanation of data.

Ozarks Community Hospital

2828 North National
Springfield, MO 65803
Phone: 417-837-4000
E-mail: info@ochonline.com
URL: ochonline.com
Type: Acute Care Hospitals
Emergency Services: Yes
Ownership: Voluntary Non-Profit - Private
Beds: 45

Key Personnel:
CEO/President. . . . . Paul Taylor

Measure	Cases	This Hosp.	State Avg.	U.S. Avg.
Heart Attack Care				
ACE Inhibitor or ARB for LVSD	0	-	96%	96%
Aspirin at Arrival[1]	5	60%	99%	99%
Aspirin at Discharge[1]	3	33%	99%	98%
Beta Blocker at Discharge[1]	3	67%	99%	98%
Fibrinolytic Medication Timing	0	-	27%	55%
PCI Within 90 Minutes of Arrival	0	-	92%	90%
Smoking Cessation Advice	0	-	99%	99%
Chest Pain/Possible Heart Attack Care				
Aspirin at Arrival[1]	24	92%	95%	95%
Median Time to ECG (minutes)	26	22	9	8
Median Time to Transfer (minutes)[1,3]	2	108	64	61
Fibrinolytic Medication Timing[1]	1	0%	31%	54%
Heart Failure Care				
ACE Inhibitor or ARB for LVSD[1]	5	60%	94%	94%
Discharge Instructions[1]	9	22%	87%	88%
Evaluation of LVS Function	26	88%	97%	98%
Smoking Cessation Advice[1]	3	100%	98%	98%
Pneumonia Care				
Appropriate Initial Antibiotic[2]	50	86%	91%	92%
Blood Culture Timing[2]	49	98%	97%	96%
Influenza Vaccine[2]	46	98%	90%	91%
Initial Antibiotic Timing[2]	75	97%	95%	95%
Pneumococcal Vaccine[2]	58	100%	93%	93%
Smoking Cessation Advice[2]	39	95%	97%	97%
Surgical Care Improvement Project				
Appropriate VTP Within 24 Hours[1]	21	90%	93%	92%
Appropriate Hair Removal	62	100%	100%	99%
Appropriate Beta Blocker Usage[1]	12	25%	94%	93%
Controlled Postoperative Blood Glucose	0	-	94%	93%
Prophylactic Antibiotic Timing	64	95%	97%	97%
Prophylactic Antibiotic Timing (Outpatient)	70	90%	95%	92%
Prophylactic Antibiotic Selection	63	95%	97%	97%
Prophylactic Antibiotic Select. (Outpatient)	70	90%	95%	94%
Prophylactic Antibiotic Stopped	61	92%	95%	94%
Recommended VTP Ordered[1]	21	95%	95%	94%
Urinary Catheter Removal[1]	13	92%	88%	90%
Children's Asthma Care				
Received Systemic Corticosteroids	-	-	-	100%
Received Home Management Plan	-	-	-	71%
Received Reliever Medication	-	-	-	100%
Use of Medical Imaging				
Combination Abdominal CT Scan	177	0.198	0.227	0.191
Combination Chest CT Scan	64	0.047	0.059	0.054
Follow-up Mammogram/Ultrasound[5]	0	-	7.4%	8.4%
MRI for Low Back Pain	107	39.3%	36%	32.7%
Survey of Patients' Hospital Experiences				
Area Around Room 'Always' Quiet at Night	300+	63%	-	58%
Doctors 'Always' Communicated Well	300+	88%	-	80%
Home Recovery Information Given	300+	80%	-	82%
Hospital Given 9 or 10 on 10 Point Scale	300+	74%	-	67%
Meds 'Always' Explained Before Given	300+	66%	-	60%
Nurses 'Always' Communicated Well	300+	80%	-	76%
Pain 'Always' Well Controlled	300+	71%	-	69%
Room and Bathroom 'Always' Clean	300+	83%	-	71%
Timely Help 'Always' Received	300+	73%	-	64%
Would Definitely Recommend Hospital	300+	80%	-	69%

Saint John's Regional Health Center

1235 E Cherokee
Springfield, MO 65804
Phone: 417-820-2000
Fax: 417-820-6996
URL: www.stjohns.com
Type: Acute Care Hospitals
Emergency Services: Yes
Ownership: Voluntary Non-Profit - Church
Beds: 866

Key Personnel:
CEO/President. . . . . Allen L Shockley
Chief of Medical Staff . . . . J Kent Dexter, MD
Infection Control. . . . . Patti Reynolds
Operating Room. . . . . Joe A Olivi
Pediatric Ambulatory Care . . . . Bernard Griesemer, MD
Pediatric In-Patient Care . . . . Bernard Griesemer, MD
Quality Assurance . . . . Kathy Coleman
Radiology. . . . . Julie A Alford

Measure	Cases	This Hosp.	State Avg.	U.S. Avg.
Heart Attack Care				
ACE Inhibitor or ARB for LVSD[2]	79	96%	96%	96%
Aspirin at Arrival[2]	236	100%	99%	99%
Aspirin at Discharge[2]	369	98%	99%	98%
Beta Blocker at Discharge[2]	338	99%	99%	98%
Fibrinolytic Medication Timing[2]	0	-	27%	55%
PCI Within 90 Minutes of Arrival[2]	75	95%	92%	90%
Smoking Cessation Advice[2]	136	99%	99%	99%
Chest Pain/Possible Heart Attack Care				
Aspirin at Arrival[1]	12	92%	95%	95%
Median Time to ECG (minutes)[1]	12	11	9	8
Median Time to Transfer (minutes)[5]	0	-	64	61
Fibrinolytic Medication Timing[5]	0	-	31%	54%
Heart Failure Care				
ACE Inhibitor or ARB for LVSD[2]	135	93%	94%	94%
Discharge Instructions[2]	298	84%	87%	88%
Evaluation of LVS Function[2]	366	99%	97%	98%
Smoking Cessation Advice[2]	58	93%	98%	98%
Pneumonia Care				
Appropriate Initial Antibiotic[2]	83	98%	91%	92%
Blood Culture Timing[2]	99	95%	97%	96%
Influenza Vaccine[2]	110	95%	90%	91%
Initial Antibiotic Timing[2]	104	96%	95%	95%
Pneumococcal Vaccine[2]	125	95%	93%	93%
Smoking Cessation Advice[2]	79	94%	97%	97%
Surgical Care Improvement Project				
Appropriate VTP Within 24 Hours[2]	173	89%	93%	92%
Appropriate Hair Removal[2]	689	100%	100%	99%
Appropriate Beta Blocker Usage[2]	231	89%	94%	93%
Controlled Postoperative Blood Glucose[2]	146	92%	94%	93%
Prophylactic Antibiotic Timing[2]	489	97%	97%	97%
Prophylactic Antibiotic Timing (Outpatient)	596	96%	95%	92%
Prophylactic Antibiotic Selection[2]	495	98%	97%	97%
Prophylactic Antibiotic Select. (Outpatient)	592	98%	95%	94%
Prophylactic Antibiotic Stopped[2]	476	91%	95%	94%
Recommended VTP Ordered[2]	173	90%	95%	94%
Urinary Catheter Removal[2]	154	86%	88%	90%
Children's Asthma Care				
Received Systemic Corticosteroids	-	-	-	100%
Received Home Management Plan	-	-	-	71%
Received Reliever Medication	-	-	-	100%
Use of Medical Imaging				
Combination Abdominal CT Scan	2,112	0.017	0.227	0.191
Combination Chest CT Scan	1,712	0.001	0.059	0.054
Follow-up Mammogram/Ultrasound	4,865	8.6%	7.4%	8.4%
MRI for Low Back Pain	660	40.8%	36%	32.7%
Survey of Patients' Hospital Experiences				
Area Around Room 'Always' Quiet at Night	300+	60%	-	58%
Doctors 'Always' Communicated Well	300+	82%	-	80%
Home Recovery Information Given	300+	87%	-	82%
Hospital Given 9 or 10 on 10 Point Scale	300+	80%	-	67%
Meds 'Always' Explained Before Given	300+	65%	-	60%
Nurses 'Always' Communicated Well	300+	80%	-	76%
Pain 'Always' Well Controlled	300+	73%	-	69%
Room and Bathroom 'Always' Clean	300+	79%	-	71%
Timely Help 'Always' Received	300+	67%	-	64%
Would Definitely Recommend Hospital	300+	83%	-	69%

Missouri Baptist Hospital Sullivan

751 Sappington Bridge Rd
Sullivan, MO 63080
Phone: 573-468-4186
Fax: 573-860-2696
URL: www.missouribaptistsullivan.org
Type: Acute Care Hospitals
Emergency Services: Yes
Ownership: Voluntary Non-Profit - Private
Beds: 46

Key Personnel:
CEO/President. . . . . Tony Schwarm
Radiology. . . . . Douglas Carlson
Emergency Room . . . . JJ Starr

Measure	Cases	This Hosp.	State Avg.	U.S. Avg.
Heart Attack Care				
ACE Inhibitor or ARB for LVSD[1]	5	100%	96%	96%
Aspirin at Arrival[1]	15	100%	99%	99%
Aspirin at Discharge[1]	13	92%	99%	98%
Beta Blocker at Discharge[1]	13	100%	99%	98%
Fibrinolytic Medication Timing	0	-	27%	55%
PCI Within 90 Minutes of Arrival	0	-	92%	90%
Smoking Cessation Advice[1]	2	100%	99%	99%
Chest Pain/Possible Heart Attack Care				
Aspirin at Arrival	163	94%	95%	95%
Median Time to ECG (minutes)	163	3	9	8
Median Time to Transfer (minutes)[1,3]	10	49	64	61
Fibrinolytic Medication Timing	0	-	31%	54%
Heart Failure Care				
ACE Inhibitor or ARB for LVSD[1]	17	100%	94%	94%
Discharge Instructions	55	96%	87%	88%
Evaluation of LVS Function	78	100%	97%	98%
Smoking Cessation Advice[1]	12	100%	98%	98%
Pneumonia Care				
Appropriate Initial Antibiotic	96	95%	91%	92%
Blood Culture Timing	122	98%	97%	96%
Influenza Vaccine	61	97%	90%	91%
Initial Antibiotic Timing	127	96%	95%	95%
Pneumococcal Vaccine	95	97%	93%	93%
Smoking Cessation Advice	48	100%	97%	97%
Surgical Care Improvement Project				
Appropriate VTP Within 24 Hours[1]	21	100%	93%	92%
Appropriate Hair Removal	36	100%	100%	99%
Appropriate Beta Blocker Usage[1]	6	100%	94%	93%
Controlled Postoperative Blood Glucose	0	-	94%	93%
Prophylactic Antibiotic Timing[1]	14	93%	97%	97%
Prophylactic Antibiotic Timing (Outpatient)	54	80%	95%	92%
Prophylactic Antibiotic Selection[1]	14	93%	97%	97%
Prophylactic Antibiotic Select. (Outpatient)	44	93%	95%	94%
Prophylactic Antibiotic Stopped[1]	14	93%	95%	94%
Recommended VTP Ordered[1]	21	100%	95%	94%
Urinary Catheter Removal[1]	9	33%	88%	90%
Children's Asthma Care				
Received Systemic Corticosteroids	-	-	-	100%
Received Home Management Plan	-	-	-	71%
Received Reliever Medication	-	-	-	100%
Use of Medical Imaging				
Combination Abdominal CT Scan	316	0.025	0.227	0.191
Combination Chest CT Scan	423	0.002	0.059	0.054
Follow-up Mammogram/Ultrasound	456	7.7%	7.4%	8.4%
MRI for Low Back Pain	67	47.8%	36%	32.7%
Survey of Patients' Hospital Experiences				
Area Around Room 'Always' Quiet at Night	300+	68%	-	58%
Doctors 'Always' Communicated Well	300+	86%	-	80%
Home Recovery Information Given	300+	85%	-	82%
Hospital Given 9 or 10 on 10 Point Scale	300+	79%	-	67%
Meds 'Always' Explained Before Given	300+	67%	-	60%
Nurses 'Always' Communicated Well	300+	83%	-	76%
Pain 'Always' Well Controlled	300+	76%	-	69%
Room and Bathroom 'Always' Clean	300+	81%	-	71%
Timely Help 'Always' Received	300+	73%	-	64%
Would Definitely Recommend Hospital	300+	71%	-	69%

NOTE: Hospital profiles are in alphabetical order by state, then city, then hospital within the city; Rankings exclude hospitals with less than 25 cases except for patient surveys which excludes hospitals with less than 100 cases; (a) 100–299 cases; (1) The number of cases is too small to be sure how well a hospital is performing; (2) The hospital indicated that the data submitted for this measure were based on a sample of cases; (3) Data was collected during a shorter time period (fewer quarters) than the maximum possible time for this measure; (4) Suppressed for one or more quarters by CMS; (5) No data is available from the hospital for this measure; (6) Fewer than 100 patients completed the HCAHPS survey. Use these rates with caution, as the number of surveys may be too low to reliably assess hospital performance; (7) Survey results are based on less than 12 months of data; (8) Survey results are not available for this reporting period; (9) No or very few patients were eligible for the HCAHPS survey. The scores shown, if any, reflect a very small number of surveys; (10) A state average was not calculated because too few hospitals in the state submitted data; (11) There were discrepancies in the data collection process; Please refer to the User's Guide for a full explanation of data.

Missouri Baptist Medical Center

3015 N Ballas Rd Phone: 314-996-5000
Town and Country, MO 63131 Fax: 314-432-1024
URL: www.missouribaptistmedicalcenter.org
Type: Acute Care Hospitals Emergency Services: Yes
Ownership: Voluntary Non-Profit - Private Beds: 489

Key Personnel:
CEO/President.............. Carm Moceri
Cardiac Laboratory............ Douglas Sohn
Chief of Medical Staff.......... Harry Wartsworth, MD
Operating Room.............. Nancy Hesselbach
Pediatric Ambulatory Care...... Renee Fishering
Quality Assurance............ Carolyn Roth
Radiology................... Vivian Prinster

Measure	Cases	This Hosp.	State Avg.	U.S. Avg.
Heart Attack Care				
ACE Inhibitor or ARB for LVSD	96	98%	96%	96%
Aspirin at Arrival	229	99%	99%	99%
Aspirin at Discharge	466	100%	99%	98%
Beta Blocker at Discharge	453	100%	99%	98%
Fibrinolytic Medication Timing	0	-	27%	55%
PCI Within 90 Minutes of Arrival	32	94%	92%	90%
Smoking Cessation Advice	128	100%	99%	99%
Chest Pain/Possible Heart Attack Care				
Aspirin at Arrival[1,3]	2	0%	95%	95%
Median Time to ECG (minutes)[1,3]	2	0	9	8
Median Time to Transfer (minutes)[5]	0	-	64	61
Fibrinolytic Medication Timing[5]	0	-	31%	54%
Heart Failure Care				
ACE Inhibitor or ARB for LVSD[2]	198	92%	94%	94%
Discharge Instructions[2]	539	87%	87%	88%
Evaluation of LVS Function[2]	716	100%	97%	98%
Smoking Cessation Advice[2]	69	100%	98%	98%
Pneumonia Care				
Appropriate Initial Antibiotic[2]	234	95%	91%	92%
Blood Culture Timing[2]	408	99%	97%	96%
Influenza Vaccine[2]	356	97%	90%	91%
Initial Antibiotic Timing[2]	431	95%	95%	95%
Pneumococcal Vaccine[2]	505	97%	93%	93%
Smoking Cessation Advice[2]	120	100%	97%	97%
Surgical Care Improvement Project				
Appropriate VTP Within 24 Hours[2]	214	96%	93%	92%
Appropriate Hair Removal[2]	921	100%	100%	99%
Appropriate Beta Blocker Usage[2]	307	97%	94%	93%
Controlled Postoperative Blood Glucose[2]	187	99%	94%	93%
Prophylactic Antibiotic Timing[2]	606	98%	97%	97%
Prophylactic Antibiotic Timing (Outpatient)	767	97%	95%	92%
Prophylactic Antibiotic Selection[2]	627	98%	97%	97%
Prophylactic Antibiotic Select. (Outpatient)	756	92%	95%	94%
Prophylactic Antibiotic Stopped[2]	586	96%	95%	94%
Recommended VTP Ordered[2]	214	97%	95%	94%
Urinary Catheter Removal[2]	198	85%	88%	90%
Children's Asthma Care				
Received Systemic Corticosteroids	-	-	-	100%
Received Home Management Plan	-	-	-	71%
Received Reliever Medication	-	-	-	100%
Use of Medical Imaging				
Combination Abdominal CT Scan	1,663	0.044	0.227	0.191
Combination Chest CT Scan	2,226	0.000	0.059	0.054
Follow-up Mammogram/Ultrasound	2,421	7.6%	7.4%	8.4%
MRI for Low Back Pain	383	31.6%	36%	32.7%
Survey of Patients' Hospital Experiences				
Area Around Room 'Always' Quiet at Night	300+	51%	-	58%
Doctors 'Always' Communicated Well	300+	83%	-	80%
Home Recovery Information Given	300+	85%	-	82%
Hospital Given 9 or 10 on 10 Point Scale	300+	73%	-	67%
Meds 'Always' Explained Before Given	300+	61%	-	60%
Nurses 'Always' Communicated Well	300+	75%	-	76%
Pain 'Always' Well Controlled	300+	69%	-	69%
Room and Bathroom 'Always' Clean	300+	64%	-	71%
Timely Help 'Always' Received	300+	59%	-	64%
Would Definitely Recommend Hospital	300+	76%	-	69%

Wright Memorial Hospital

701 East First Street Phone: 660-359-5621
Trenton, MO 64683
URL: www.saintlukeshealthsystem.org
Type: Critical Access Hospitals Emergency Services: Yes
Ownership: Voluntary Non-Profit - Other Beds: 78

Key Personnel:
CEO/President.............. Karen Cole
Chief of Medical Staff.......... Ray Shirley

Measure	Cases	This Hosp.	State Avg.	U.S. Avg.
Heart Attack Care				
ACE Inhibitor or ARB for LVSD	0	-	96%	96%
Aspirin at Arrival[1]	4	100%	99%	99%
Aspirin at Discharge[1]	3	100%	99%	98%
Beta Blocker at Discharge[1]	2	100%	99%	98%
Fibrinolytic Medication Timing	0	-	27%	55%
PCI Within 90 Minutes of Arrival	0	-	92%	90%
Smoking Cessation Advice	0	-	99%	99%
Chest Pain/Possible Heart Attack Care				
Aspirin at Arrival	59	98%	95%	95%
Median Time to ECG (minutes)	65	19	9	8
Median Time to Transfer (minutes)[1,3]	2	80	64	61
Fibrinolytic Medication Timing[3]	0	-	31%	54%
Heart Failure Care				
ACE Inhibitor or ARB for LVSD[1]	10	100%	94%	94%
Discharge Instructions	43	91%	87%	88%
Evaluation of LVS Function	61	92%	97%	98%
Smoking Cessation Advice[1]	11	100%	98%	98%
Pneumonia Care				
Appropriate Initial Antibiotic	28	96%	91%	92%
Blood Culture Timing	47	100%	97%	96%
Influenza Vaccine[1]	20	90%	90%	91%
Initial Antibiotic Timing	51	94%	95%	95%
Pneumococcal Vaccine	41	80%	93%	93%
Smoking Cessation Advice[1]	11	100%	97%	97%
Surgical Care Improvement Project				
Appropriate VTP Within 24 Hours[1,3]	1	100%	93%	92%
Appropriate Hair Removal[1,3]	3	100%	100%	99%
Appropriate Beta Blocker Usage[3]	0	-	94%	93%
Controlled Postoperative Blood Glucose[3]	0	-	94%	93%
Prophylactic Antibiotic Timing[3]	0	-	97%	97%
Prophylactic Antibiotic Timing (Outpatient)[5]	0	-	95%	92%
Prophylactic Antibiotic Selection[3]	0	-	97%	97%
Prophylactic Antibiotic Select. (Outpatient)[5]	0	-	95%	94%
Prophylactic Antibiotic Stopped[3]	0	-	95%	94%
Recommended VTP Ordered[1,3]	1	100%	95%	94%
Urinary Catheter Removal[1]	1	100%	88%	90%
Children's Asthma Care				
Received Systemic Corticosteroids	-	-	-	100%
Received Home Management Plan	-	-	-	71%
Received Reliever Medication	-	-	-	100%
Use of Medical Imaging				
Combination Abdominal CT Scan	158	0.127	0.227	0.191
Combination Chest CT Scan	151	0.146	0.059	0.054
Follow-up Mammogram/Ultrasound	249	9.6%	7.4%	8.4%
MRI for Low Back Pain[1]	44	36.4%	36%	32.7%
Survey of Patients' Hospital Experiences				
Area Around Room 'Always' Quiet at Night	(a)	59%	-	58%
Doctors 'Always' Communicated Well	(a)	86%	-	80%
Home Recovery Information Given	(a)	75%	-	82%
Hospital Given 9 or 10 on 10 Point Scale	(a)	63%	-	67%
Meds 'Always' Explained Before Given	(a)	66%	-	60%
Nurses 'Always' Communicated Well	(a)	78%	-	76%
Pain 'Always' Well Controlled	(a)	68%	-	69%
Room and Bathroom 'Always' Clean	(a)	77%	-	71%
Timely Help 'Always' Received	(a)	68%	-	64%
Would Definitely Recommend Hospital	(a)	55%	-	69%

Lincoln County Medical Center

1000 East Cherry Street Phone: 636-528-8551
Troy, MO 63379
Type: Critical Access Hospitals Emergency Services: Yes
Ownership: Government - Local

Key Personnel:
Chief of Medical Staff.......... Dale Reinker DO
Infection Control............. Becky O'Neal
Quality Assurance............ Marie Collinson
Radiology.................. Greg Heidbrier
Anesthesiology............... Lisa Dugan
Emergency Room............. Mike Dach
Intensive Care Unit............ Barb Dallas

Measure	Cases	This Hosp.	State Avg.	U.S. Avg.
Heart Attack Care				
ACE Inhibitor or ARB for LVSD[3]	0	-	96%	96%
Aspirin at Arrival[3]	0	-	99%	99%
Aspirin at Discharge[3]	0	-	99%	98%
Beta Blocker at Discharge[3]	0	-	99%	98%
Fibrinolytic Medication Timing[3]	0	-	27%	55%
PCI Within 90 Minutes of Arrival[3]	0	-	92%	90%
Smoking Cessation Advice[3]	0	-	99%	99%
Chest Pain/Possible Heart Attack Care				
Aspirin at Arrival	-	-	95%	95%
Median Time to ECG (minutes)	-	-	9	8
Median Time to Transfer (minutes)	-	-	64	61
Fibrinolytic Medication Timing	-	-	31%	54%
Heart Failure Care				
ACE Inhibitor or ARB for LVSD[1]	4	100%	94%	94%
Discharge Instructions[1]	18	72%	87%	88%
Evaluation of LVS Function	28	96%	97%	98%
Smoking Cessation Advice[1]	2	100%	98%	98%
Pneumonia Care				
Appropriate Initial Antibiotic	27	96%	91%	92%
Blood Culture Timing	44	93%	97%	96%
Influenza Vaccine	34	94%	90%	91%
Initial Antibiotic Timing	54	98%	95%	95%
Pneumococcal Vaccine	43	88%	93%	93%
Smoking Cessation Advice[1]	24	83%	97%	97%
Surgical Care Improvement Project				
Appropriate VTP Within 24 Hours[1]	24	100%	93%	92%
Appropriate Hair Removal	47	98%	100%	99%
Appropriate Beta Blocker Usage[1]	7	57%	94%	93%
Controlled Postoperative Blood Glucose	0	-	94%	93%
Prophylactic Antibiotic Timing	38	84%	97%	97%
Prophylactic Antibiotic Timing (Outpatient)	-	-	95%	92%
Prophylactic Antibiotic Selection	37	78%	97%	97%
Prophylactic Antibiotic Select. (Outpatient)	-	-	95%	94%
Prophylactic Antibiotic Stopped	32	81%	95%	94%
Recommended VTP Ordered[1]	24	100%	95%	94%
Urinary Catheter Removal[1]	7	29%	88%	90%
Children's Asthma Care				
Received Systemic Corticosteroids	-	-	-	100%
Received Home Management Plan	-	-	-	71%
Received Reliever Medication	-	-	-	100%
Use of Medical Imaging				
Combination Abdominal CT Scan	-	-	0.227	0.191
Combination Chest CT Scan	-	-	0.059	0.054
Follow-up Mammogram/Ultrasound	-	-	7.4%	8.4%
MRI for Low Back Pain	-	-	36%	32.7%
Survey of Patients' Hospital Experiences				
Area Around Room 'Always' Quiet at Night	(a)	61%	-	58%
Doctors 'Always' Communicated Well	(a)	83%	-	80%
Home Recovery Information Given	(a)	84%	-	82%
Hospital Given 9 or 10 on 10 Point Scale	(a)	67%	-	67%
Meds 'Always' Explained Before Given	(a)	70%	-	60%
Nurses 'Always' Communicated Well	(a)	81%	-	76%
Pain 'Always' Well Controlled	(a)	71%	-	69%
Room and Bathroom 'Always' Clean	(a)	80%	-	71%
Timely Help 'Always' Received	(a)	74%	-	64%
Would Definitely Recommend Hospital	(a)	65%	-	69%

NOTE: Hospital profiles are in alphabetical order by state, then city, then hospital within the city; Rankings exclude hospitals with less than 25 cases except for patient surveys which excludes hospitals with less than 100 cases; (a) 100–299 cases; (1) The number of cases is too small to be sure how well a hospital is performing; (2) The hospital indicated that the data submitted for this measure were based on a sample of cases; (3) Data was collected during a shorter time period (fewer quarters) than the maximum possible time for this measure; (4) Suppressed for one or more quarters by CMS; (5) No data is available from the hospital for this measure; (6) Fewer than 100 patients completed the HCAHPS survey. Use these rates with caution, as the number of surveys may be too low to reliably assess hospital performance; (7) Survey results are based on less than 12 months of data; (8) Survey results are not available for this reporting period; (9) No or very few patients were eligible for the HCAHPS survey. The scores shown, if any, reflect a very small number of surveys; (10) A state average was not calculated because too few hospitals in the state submitted data; (11) There were discrepancies in the data collection process; Please refer to the User's Guide for a full explanation of data.

Putnam County Memorial Hospital

1926 Oak Street
Unionville, MO 63565
E-mail: rmagers@istlaplata.net
Type: Critical Access Hospitals
Ownership: Government - Local
Phone: 660-947-2411
Fax: 660-947-3825
Emergency Services: Yes
Beds: 40

Key Personnel:

CEO/President. . . . . Ray Magers
Chief of Medical Staff. . . . . W Stephen Casady
Infection Control. . . . . Deb Smith, RN
Quality Assurance . . . . Ediph Haffner
Emergency Room . . . . James Pigg

Measure	Cases	This Hosp.	State Avg.	U.S. Avg.
Heart Attack Care				
ACE Inhibitor or ARB for LVSD[3]	0	-	96%	96%
Aspirin at Arrival[1,3]	1	0%	99%	99%
Aspirin at Discharge[1,3]	1	0%	99%	98%
Beta Blocker at Discharge[1,3]	1	0%	99%	98%
Fibrinolytic Medication Timing[3]	0	-	27%	55%
PCI Within 90 Minutes of Arrival[3]	0	-	92%	90%
Smoking Cessation Advice[3]	0	-	99%	99%
Chest Pain/Possible Heart Attack Care				
Aspirin at Arrival	-	-	95%	95%
Median Time to ECG (minutes)	-	-	9	8
Median Time to Transfer (minutes)	-	-	64	61
Fibrinolytic Medication Timing	-	-	31%	54%
Heart Failure Care				
ACE Inhibitor or ARB for LVSD[1,3]	9	89%	94%	94%
Discharge Instructions[1,3]	10	90%	87%	88%
Evaluation of LVS Function[3]	25	80%	97%	98%
Smoking Cessation Advice[1,3]	2	50%	98%	98%
Pneumonia Care				
Appropriate Initial Antibiotic[1,3]	18	94%	91%	92%
Blood Culture Timing[1,3]	3	100%	97%	96%
Influenza Vaccine[1]	16	88%	90%	91%
Initial Antibiotic Timing[1,3]	22	95%	95%	95%
Pneumococcal Vaccine[1,3]	22	77%	93%	93%
Smoking Cessation Advice[1,3]	7	71%	97%	97%
Surgical Care Improvement Project				
Appropriate VTP Within 24 Hours[5]	0	-	93%	92%
Appropriate Hair Removal[5]	0	-	100%	99%
Appropriate Beta Blocker Usage[5]	0	-	94%	93%
Controlled Postoperative Blood Glucose[5]	0	-	94%	93%
Prophylactic Antibiotic Timing[5]	0	-	97%	97%
Prophylactic Antibiotic Timing (Outpatient)	-	-	95%	92%
Prophylactic Antibiotic Selection[5]	0	-	97%	97%
Prophylactic Antibiotic Select. (Outpatient)	-	-	95%	94%
Prophylactic Antibiotic Stopped[5]	0	-	95%	94%
Recommended VTP Ordered[5]	0	-	95%	94%
Urinary Catheter Removal[5]	0	-	88%	90%
Children's Asthma Care				
Received Systemic Corticosteroids	-	-	-	100%
Received Home Management Plan	-	-	-	71%
Received Reliever Medication	-	-	-	100%
Use of Medical Imaging				
Combination Abdominal CT Scan	-	-	0.227	0.191
Combination Chest CT Scan	-	-	0.059	0.054
Follow-up Mammogram/Ultrasound	-	-	7.4%	8.4%
MRI for Low Back Pain	-	-	36%	32.7%
Survey of Patients' Hospital Experiences				
Area Around Room 'Always' Quiet at Night[8]	-	-	-	58%
Doctors 'Always' Communicated Well[8]	-	-	-	80%
Home Recovery Information Given[8]	-	-	-	82%
Hospital Given 9 or 10 on 10 Point Scale[8]	-	-	-	67%
Meds 'Always' Explained Before Given[8]	-	-	-	60%
Nurses 'Always' Communicated Well[8]	-	-	-	76%
Pain 'Always' Well Controlled[8]	-	-	-	69%
Room and Bathroom 'Always' Clean[8]	-	-	-	71%
Timely Help 'Always' Received[8]	-	-	-	64%
Would Definitely Recommend Hospital[8]	-	-	-	69%

Western Missouri Medical Center

403 Burkarth Road
Warrensburg, MO 64093
Type: Acute Care Hospitals
Ownership: Govt - Hospital Dist/Auth
Phone: 660-747-2500
Fax: 660-747-8455
Emergency Services: Yes
Beds: 92

Key Personnel:

CEO/President. . . . . Gregory B Vinardi
Chief of Medical Staff . . . . Linda Pal, MD
Infection Control. . . . . Carol Kientzy, RN
Operating Room. . . . . Linda Pai
Quality Assurance . . . . Deborah Haller
Radiology. . . . . John J Wadell
Emergency Room . . . . Laura Pinson, RN
Intensive Care Unit. . . . . Rosemary Zelazek, RN

Measure	Cases	This Hosp.	State Avg.	U.S. Avg.
Heart Attack Care				
ACE Inhibitor or ARB for LVSD[1]	1	100%	96%	96%
Aspirin at Arrival[1]	15	87%	99%	99%
Aspirin at Discharge[1]	6	100%	99%	98%
Beta Blocker at Discharge[1]	7	86%	99%	98%
Fibrinolytic Medication Timing	0	-	27%	55%
PCI Within 90 Minutes of Arrival	0	-	92%	90%
Smoking Cessation Advice	0	-	99%	99%
Chest Pain/Possible Heart Attack Care				
Aspirin at Arrival	261	95%	95%	95%
Median Time to ECG (minutes)	278	12	9	8
Median Time to Transfer (minutes)[5]	0	-	64	61
Fibrinolytic Medication Timing	0	-	31%	54%
Heart Failure Care				
ACE Inhibitor or ARB for LVSD[1]	11	64%	94%	94%
Discharge Instructions[1]	22	59%	87%	88%
Evaluation of LVS Function	42	88%	97%	98%
Smoking Cessation Advice[1]	5	80%	98%	98%
Pneumonia Care				
Appropriate Initial Antibiotic	71	79%	91%	92%
Blood Culture Timing	69	94%	97%	96%
Influenza Vaccine	64	75%	90%	91%
Initial Antibiotic Timing	118	98%	95%	95%
Pneumococcal Vaccine	84	77%	93%	93%
Smoking Cessation Advice	31	84%	97%	97%
Surgical Care Improvement Project				
Appropriate VTP Within 24 Hours	73	82%	93%	92%
Appropriate Hair Removal	210	100%	100%	99%
Appropriate Beta Blocker Usage	39	90%	94%	93%
Controlled Postoperative Blood Glucose	0	-	94%	93%
Prophylactic Antibiotic Timing	173	99%	97%	97%
Prophylactic Antibiotic Timing (Outpatient)	51	96%	95%	92%
Prophylactic Antibiotic Selection	176	97%	97%	97%
Prophylactic Antibiotic Select. (Outpatient)	49	55%	95%	94%
Prophylactic Antibiotic Stopped	160	96%	95%	94%
Recommended VTP Ordered	73	86%	95%	94%
Urinary Catheter Removal	42	98%	88%	90%
Children's Asthma Care				
Received Systemic Corticosteroids	-	-	-	100%
Received Home Management Plan	-	-	-	71%
Received Reliever Medication	-	-	-	100%
Use of Medical Imaging				
Combination Abdominal CT Scan	239	0.033	0.227	0.191
Combination Chest CT Scan	235	0.009	0.059	0.054
Follow-up Mammogram/Ultrasound	544	5.5%	7.4%	8.4%
MRI for Low Back Pain	100	26.0%	36%	32.7%
Survey of Patients' Hospital Experiences				
Area Around Room 'Always' Quiet at Night	300+	54%	-	58%
Doctors 'Always' Communicated Well	300+	81%	-	80%
Home Recovery Information Given	300+	86%	-	82%
Hospital Given 9 or 10 on 10 Point Scale	300+	59%	-	67%
Meds 'Always' Explained Before Given	300+	64%	-	60%
Nurses 'Always' Communicated Well	300+	77%	-	76%
Pain 'Always' Well Controlled	300+	69%	-	69%
Room and Bathroom 'Always' Clean	300+	79%	-	71%
Timely Help 'Always' Received	300+	61%	-	64%
Would Definitely Recommend Hospital	300+	60%	-	69%

Saint Johns Mercy Hospital

901 East 5th Street
Washington, MO 63090
URL: www.stjohnsmercy.org
Type: Acute Care Hospitals
Ownership: Voluntary Non-Profit - Church
Phone: 636-239-8000
Fax: 314-569-6733
Emergency Services: Yes
Beds: 187

Key Personnel:

CEO/President. . . . . Michael Zilm
Chief of Medical Staff. . . . . Thomas B Riechers, MD, FACS
Infection Control. . . . . Phyllis Cassette, RN
Operating Room. . . . . Kathleen Gnavi, RN
Pediatric Ambulatory Care . . . . Andrew Zupan, MD
Pediatric In-Patient Care . . . . Andrew Zupan, MD
Quality Assurance . . . . Phyllis Cassette, RN
Radiology. . . . . Marc F Clemente

Measure	Cases	This Hosp.	State Avg.	U.S. Avg.
Heart Attack Care				
ACE Inhibitor or ARB for LVSD[1]	3	100%	96%	96%
Aspirin at Arrival	25	100%	99%	99%
Aspirin at Discharge[1]	20	100%	99%	98%
Beta Blocker at Discharge[1]	19	95%	99%	98%
Fibrinolytic Medication Timing	0	-	27%	55%
PCI Within 90 Minutes of Arrival	0	-	92%	90%
Smoking Cessation Advice[1]	2	100%	99%	99%
Chest Pain/Possible Heart Attack Care				
Aspirin at Arrival	217	98%	95%	95%
Median Time to ECG (minutes)	215	9	9	8
Median Time to Transfer (minutes)	30	76	64	61
Fibrinolytic Medication Timing[1]	3	33%	31%	54%
Heart Failure Care				
ACE Inhibitor or ARB for LVSD	36	97%	94%	94%
Discharge Instructions	135	96%	87%	88%
Evaluation of LVS Function	197	99%	97%	98%
Smoking Cessation Advice[1]	22	100%	98%	98%
Pneumonia Care				
Appropriate Initial Antibiotic[2]	85	93%	91%	92%
Blood Culture Timing[2]	81	94%	97%	96%
Influenza Vaccine[2]	76	100%	90%	91%
Initial Antibiotic Timing[2]	143	99%	95%	95%
Pneumococcal Vaccine[2]	120	99%	93%	93%
Smoking Cessation Advice[2]	47	100%	97%	97%
Surgical Care Improvement Project				
Appropriate VTP Within 24 Hours[2]	119	95%	93%	92%
Appropriate Hair Removal[2]	306	100%	100%	99%
Appropriate Beta Blocker Usage[2]	85	85%	94%	93%
Controlled Postoperative Blood Glucose[2]	0	-	94%	93%
Prophylactic Antibiotic Timing[2]	206	97%	97%	97%
Prophylactic Antibiotic Timing (Outpatient)	224	96%	95%	92%
Prophylactic Antibiotic Selection[2]	207	99%	97%	97%
Prophylactic Antibiotic Select. (Outpatient)	218	98%	95%	94%
Prophylactic Antibiotic Stopped[2]	198	98%	95%	94%
Recommended VTP Ordered[2]	119	97%	95%	94%
Urinary Catheter Removal[2]	72	93%	88%	90%
Children's Asthma Care				
Received Systemic Corticosteroids	-	-	-	100%
Received Home Management Plan	-	-	-	71%
Received Reliever Medication	-	-	-	100%
Use of Medical Imaging				
Combination Abdominal CT Scan	529	0.038	0.227	0.191
Combination Chest CT Scan	412	0.000	0.059	0.054
Follow-up Mammogram/Ultrasound	686	4.2%	7.4%	8.4%
MRI for Low Back Pain	129	40.3%	36%	32.7%
Survey of Patients' Hospital Experiences				
Area Around Room 'Always' Quiet at Night	300+	57%	-	58%
Doctors 'Always' Communicated Well	300+	83%	-	80%
Home Recovery Information Given	300+	82%	-	82%
Hospital Given 9 or 10 on 10 Point Scale	300+	63%	-	67%
Meds 'Always' Explained Before Given	300+	61%	-	60%
Nurses 'Always' Communicated Well	300+	75%	-	76%
Pain 'Always' Well Controlled	300+	68%	-	69%
Room and Bathroom 'Always' Clean	300+	75%	-	71%
Timely Help 'Always' Received	300+	59%	-	64%
Would Definitely Recommend Hospital	300+	67%	-	69%

NOTE: Hospital profiles are in alphabetical order by state, then city, then hospital within the city; Rankings exclude hospitals with less than 25 cases except for patient surveys which excludes hospitals with less than 100 cases; (a) 100–299 cases; (1) The number of cases is too small to be sure how well a hospital is performing; (2) The hospital indicated that the data submitted for this measure were based on a sample of cases; (3) Data was collected during a shorter time period (fewer quarters) than the maximum possible time for this measure; (4) Suppressed for one or more quarters by CMS; (5) No data is available from the hospital for this measure; (6) Fewer than 100 patients completed the HCAHPS survey. Use these rates with caution, as the number of surveys may be too low to reliably assess hospital performance; (7) Survey results are based on less than 12 months of data; (8) Survey results are not available for this reporting period; (9) No or very few patients were eligible for the HCAHPS survey. The scores shown, if any, reflect a very small number of surveys; (10) A state average was not calculated because too few hospitals in the state submitted data; (11) There were discrepancies in the data collection process; Please refer to the User's Guide for a full explanation of data.

Ozarks Medical Center

1100 Kentucky Ave
West Plains, MO 65775
URL: www.ozarksmedicalcenter.com
Type: Acute Care Hospitals
Ownership: Voluntary Non-Profit - Other
Phone: 417-256-9111
Fax: 417-257-6770
Emergency Services: Yes
Beds: 114

Key Personnel:
CEO/President. . . . . David M Zechman, FACHE
Cardiac Laboratory. . . . . Tim Kimball, RN
Chief of Medical Staff . . . . Edward Henegar, DO
Infection Control. . . . . Torrance Hughes
Operating Room. . . . . Jill Tate, RN
Quality Assurance . . . . Dona Paschall, RN
Emergency Room . . . . Dennise Lawson, RN
Hemotology Center . . . . Susan Kenolow, RN

Measure	Cases	This Hosp.	State Avg.	U.S. Avg.
Heart Attack Care				
ACE Inhibitor or ARB for LVSD[1]	10	70%	96%	96%
Aspirin at Arrival	100	99%	99%	99%
Aspirin at Discharge	95	96%	99%	98%
Beta Blocker at Discharge	96	94%	99%	98%
Fibrinolytic Medication Timing[1]	1	100%	27%	55%
PCI Within 90 Minutes of Arrival[1]	19	84%	92%	90%
Smoking Cessation Advice	35	100%	99%	99%
Chest Pain/Possible Heart Attack Care				
Aspirin at Arrival	74	93%	95%	95%
Median Time to ECG (minutes)	80	11	9	8
Median Time to Transfer (minutes)[1,3]	2	121	64	61
Fibrinolytic Medication Timing[1]	6	33%	31%	54%
Heart Failure Care				
ACE Inhibitor or ARB for LVSD	30	83%	94%	94%
Discharge Instructions	79	90%	87%	88%
Evaluation of LVS Function	99	96%	97%	98%
Smoking Cessation Advice[1]	17	100%	98%	98%
Pneumonia Care				
Appropriate Initial Antibiotic	136	83%	91%	92%
Blood Culture Timing	171	96%	97%	96%
Influenza Vaccine	120	68%	90%	91%
Initial Antibiotic Timing	207	88%	95%	95%
Pneumococcal Vaccine	166	79%	93%	93%
Smoking Cessation Advice	71	97%	97%	97%
Surgical Care Improvement Project				
Appropriate VTP Within 24 Hours	119	87%	93%	92%
Appropriate Hair Removal	261	100%	100%	99%
Appropriate Beta Blocker Usage	81	80%	94%	93%
Controlled Postoperative Blood Glucose[1]	19	95%	94%	93%
Prophylactic Antibiotic Timing	184	96%	97%	97%
Prophylactic Antibiotic Timing (Outpatient)	222	95%	95%	92%
Prophylactic Antibiotic Selection	184	98%	97%	97%
Prophylactic Antibiotic Select. (Outpatient)	219	93%	95%	94%
Prophylactic Antibiotic Stopped	174	86%	95%	94%
Recommended VTP Ordered	121	87%	95%	94%
Urinary Catheter Removal	45	78%	88%	90%
Children's Asthma Care				
Received Systemic Corticosteroids	-	-	-	100%
Received Home Management Plan	-	-	-	71%
Received Reliever Medication	-	-	-	100%
Use of Medical Imaging				
Combination Abdominal CT Scan	480	0.238	0.227	0.191
Combination Chest CT Scan	308	0.000	0.059	0.054
Follow-up Mammogram/Ultrasound	793	9.6%	7.4%	8.4%
MRI for Low Back Pain	136	41.9%	36%	32.7%
Survey of Patients' Hospital Experiences				
Area Around Room 'Always' Quiet at Night	300+	57%	-	58%
Doctors 'Always' Communicated Well	300+	83%	-	80%
Home Recovery Information Given	300+	83%	-	82%
Hospital Given 9 or 10 on 10 Point Scale	300+	64%	-	67%
Meds 'Always' Explained Before Given	300+	58%	-	60%
Nurses 'Always' Communicated Well	300+	79%	-	76%
Pain 'Always' Well Controlled	300+	73%	-	69%
Room and Bathroom 'Always' Clean	300+	72%	-	71%
Timely Help 'Always' Received	300+	72%	-	64%
Would Definitely Recommend Hospital	300+	66%	-	69%

NOTE: Hospital profiles are in alphabetical order by state, then city, then hospital within the city; Rankings exclude hospitals with less than 25 cases except for patient surveys which excludes hospitals with less than 100 cases; (a) 100–299 cases; (1) The number of cases is too small to be sure how well a hospital is performing; (2) The hospital indicated that the data submitted for this measure were based on a sample of cases; (3) Data was collected during a shorter time period (fewer quarters) than the maximum possible time for this measure; (4) Suppressed for one or more quarters by CMS; (5) No data is available from the hospital for this measure; (6) Fewer than 100 patients completed the HCAHPS survey. Use these rates with caution, as the number of surveys may be too low to reliably assess hospital performance; (7) Survey results are based on less than 12 months of data; (8) Survey results are not available for this reporting period; (9) No or very few patients were eligible for the HCAHPS survey. The scores shown, if any, reflect a very small number of surveys; (10) A state average was not calculated because too few hospitals in the state submitted data; (11) There were discrepancies in the data collection process; Please refer to the User's Guide for a full explanation of data.

Heart Attack Care

1. ACE Inhibitor or ARB for LVSD

Hospital Name	City	Rate	Cases
Alegent Health Bergan Mercy Medical Center	Omaha	100%	30
Creighton Univ Med Ctr-St Joseph	Omaha	100%	68
Nebraska Heart Hospital	Lincoln	100%	45
The Nebraska Methodist Hospital	Omaha	100%	42
Bryanlgh Medical Center	Lincoln	97%	75
Good Samaritan Hospital	Kearney	94%	32
The Nebraska Medical Center[2]	Omaha	90%	41

2. Aspirin at Arrival

Hospital Name	City	Rate	Cases
Alegent Health Immanuel Medical Center	Omaha	100%	101
Alegent Health Midlands Hospital	Papillion	100%	79
Bryanlgh Medical Center	Lincoln	100%	208
Fremont Area Medical Center	Fremont	100%	28
Mary Lanning Memorial Hospital	Hastings	100%	32
Nebraska Heart Hospital	Lincoln	100%	29
Saint Elizabeth Regional Medical Center	Lincoln	100%	98
Alegent Health Bergan Mercy Medical Center	Omaha	99%	160
Alegent Health Lakeside Hospital	Omaha	99%	113
Creighton Univ Med Ctr-St Joseph	Omaha	99%	123
Good Samaritan Hospital	Kearney	99%	75
The Nebraska Methodist Hospital	Omaha	99%	136
Saint Francis Medical Center	Grand Island	99%	83
The Nebraska Medical Center[2]	Omaha	98%	210
Faith Regional Health Services	Norfolk	97%	74

3. Aspirin at Discharge

Hospital Name	City	Rate	Cases
Alegent Health Bergan Mercy Medical Center	Omaha	100%	208
Alegent Health Immanuel Medical Center	Omaha	100%	128
Alegent Health Lakeside Hospital	Omaha	100%	99
Alegent Health Midlands Hospital	Papillion	100%	72
Bryanlgh Medical Center	Lincoln	100%	430
Creighton Univ Med Ctr-St Joseph	Omaha	100%	275
Faith Regional Health Services	Norfolk	100%	108
Fremont Area Medical Center	Fremont	100%	27
Nebraska Heart Hospital	Lincoln	100%	371
The Nebraska Methodist Hospital	Omaha	100%	181
Saint Elizabeth Regional Medical Center	Lincoln	100%	112
Good Samaritan Hospital	Kearney	99%	177
Saint Francis Medical Center	Grand Island	99%	81
The Nebraska Medical Center[2]	Omaha	98%	273
Mary Lanning Memorial Hospital	Hastings	93%	27

4. Beta Blocker at Discharge

Hospital Name	City	Rate	Cases
Alegent Health Bergan Mercy Medical Center	Omaha	100%	204
Alegent Health Immanuel Medical Center	Omaha	100%	125
Alegent Health Lakeside Hospital	Omaha	100%	98
Alegent Health Midlands Hospital	Papillion	100%	72
Bryanlgh Medical Center	Lincoln	100%	422
Creighton Univ Med Ctr-St Joseph	Omaha	100%	264
Faith Regional Health Services	Norfolk	100%	106
Nebraska Heart Hospital	Lincoln	100%	343
Saint Francis Medical Center	Grand Island	100%	81
Saint Elizabeth Regional Medical Center	Lincoln	99%	107
Good Samaritan Hospital	Kearney	97%	169
The Nebraska Medical Center[2]	Omaha	97%	267
The Nebraska Methodist Hospital	Omaha	97%	180

6. PCI Within 90 Minutes of Arrival

Hospital Name	City	Rate	Cases
Alegent Health Midlands Hospital	Papillion	100%	37
Bryanlgh Medical Center	Lincoln	97%	36
Alegent Health Lakeside Hospital	Omaha	94%	33
Alegent Health Bergan Mercy Medical Center	Omaha	93%	28
Alegent Health Immanuel Medical Center	Omaha	89%	28
The Nebraska Medical Center[2]	Omaha	85%	34
The Nebraska Methodist Hospital	Omaha	83%	35

7. Smoking Cessation Advice

Hospital Name	City	Rate	Cases
Alegent Health Bergan Mercy Medical Center	Omaha	100%	73
Alegent Health Immanuel Medical Center	Omaha	100%	52
Alegent Health Lakeside Hospital	Omaha	100%	27
Alegent Health Midlands Hospital	Papillion	100%	28
Bryanlgh Medical Center	Lincoln	100%	152
Creighton Univ Med Ctr-St Joseph	Omaha	100%	105
Faith Regional Health Services	Norfolk	100%	31
Nebraska Heart Hospital	Lincoln	100%	113
Saint Elizabeth Regional Medical Center	Lincoln	100%	30
Saint Francis Medical Center	Grand Island	100%	28
Good Samaritan Hospital	Kearney	99%	67
The Nebraska Medical Center[2]	Omaha	99%	111
The Nebraska Methodist Hospital	Omaha	98%	49

Chest Pain/Possible Heart Attack Care

8. Aspirin at Arrival

Hospital Name	City	Rate	Cases
Fremont Area Medical Center	Fremont	100%	38
Great Plains Regional Medical Center	North Platte	100%	55
Jefferson Community Health Center	Fairbury	100%	27
Columbus Community Hospital	Columbus	98%	123
Regional West Medical Center	Scottsbluff	98%	50
Mary Lanning Memorial Hospital	Hastings	97%	30
Saint Francis Medical Center	Grand Island	93%	58
The Nebraska Medical Center	Omaha	91%	33

9. Median Time to ECG (minutes)

Hospital Name	City	Min.	Cases
Saint Francis Medical Center	Grand Island	2	59
Regional West Medical Center	Scottsbluff	5	50
Fremont Area Medical Center	Fremont	6	38
Columbus Community Hospital	Columbus	7	134
Great Plains Regional Medical Center	North Platte	7	56
Mary Lanning Memorial Hospital	Hastings	10	32
The Nebraska Medical Center	Omaha	12	32
Jefferson Community Health Center	Fairbury	23	32

Heart Failure Care

12. ACE Inhibitor or ARB for LVSD

Hospital Name	City	Rate	Cases
Alegent Health Immanuel Medical Center	Omaha	100%	50
Alegent Health Lakeside Hospital	Omaha	100%	32
Alegent Health Midlands Hospital	Papillion	100%	33
Omaha VA Medical Center	Omaha	100%	48
Bryanlgh Medical Center	Lincoln	99%	129
The Nebraska Methodist Hospital	Omaha	99%	114
Creighton Univ Med Ctr-St Joseph	Omaha	98%	116
Saint Francis Medical Center	Grand Island	97%	33
Faith Regional Health Services	Norfolk	96%	28
Nebraska Heart Hospital	Lincoln	96%	137
Alegent Health Bergan Mercy Medical Center	Omaha	95%	81
The Nebraska Medical Center[2]	Omaha	90%	114
Good Samaritan Hospital	Kearney	89%	45
Mary Lanning Memorial Hospital	Hastings	88%	40
Saint Elizabeth Regional Medical Center	Lincoln	86%	59

13. Discharge Instructions

Hospital Name	City	Rate	Cases
Alegent Health Immanuel Medical Center	Omaha	100%	108
Fremont Area Medical Center	Fremont	100%	35
Omaha VA Medical Center	Omaha	99%	125
The Nebraska Methodist Hospital	Omaha	98%	244
Creighton Univ Med Ctr-St Joseph	Omaha	96%	249
Saint Francis Medical Center	Grand Island	96%	89
Alegent Health Midlands Hospital	Papillion	95%	74
Alegent Health Lakeside Hospital	Omaha	94%	93
Bryanlgh Medical Center	Lincoln	94%	304
Alegent Health Bergan Mercy Medical Center	Omaha	92%	215
Jennie M Melham Memorial Medical Center	Broken Bow	92%	26
Mary Lanning Memorial Hospital	Hastings	87%	78
Great Plains Regional Medical Center	North Platte	86%	70
Nebraska Heart Hospital	Lincoln	86%	227
Good Samaritan Hospital	Kearney	82%	111
The Nebraska Medical Center[2]	Omaha	79%	240
Saint Elizabeth Regional Medical Center	Lincoln	77%	167
Faith Regional Health Services	Norfolk	74%	43
Regional West Medical Center	Scottsbluff	61%	41

14. Evaluation of LVS Function

Hospital Name	City	Rate	Cases
Alegent Health Bergan Mercy Medical Center	Omaha	100%	275
Alegent Health Immanuel Medical Center	Omaha	100%	153
Alegent Health Lakeside Hospital	Omaha	100%	153
Alegent Health Midlands Hospital	Papillion	100%	105
Bryanlgh Medical Center	Lincoln	100%	377
Columbus Community Hospital	Columbus	100%	31
Fremont Area Medical Center	Fremont	100%	79
Nebraska Heart Hospital	Lincoln	100%	263
The Nebraska Medical Center[2]	Omaha	100%	287
The Nebraska Methodist Hospital	Omaha	100%	323
Omaha VA Medical Center	Omaha	100%	154
Regional West Medical Center	Scottsbluff	100%	58
Creighton Univ Med Ctr-St Joseph	Omaha	99%	291
Faith Regional Health Services	Norfolk	99%	79
Good Samaritan Hospital	Kearney	99%	150
Great Plains Regional Medical Center	North Platte	98%	102
Beatrice Community Hospital & Health Center	Beatrice	97%	34
Phelps Memorial Health Center	Holdrege	97%	29
Mary Lanning Memorial Hospital	Hastings	96%	109
Saint Elizabeth Regional Medical Center	Lincoln	96%	209
Saint Francis Memorial Hospital	West Point	96%	26
Saint Francis Medical Center	Grand Island	94%	130
Jennie M Melham Memorial Medical Center	Broken Bow	91%	35
Community Hospital	Mccook	81%	31

15. Smoking Cessation Advice

Hospital Name	City	Rate	Cases
Alegent Health Bergan Mercy Medical Center	Omaha	100%	41
Alegent Health Immanuel Medical Center	Omaha	100%	29
Bryanlgh Medical Center	Lincoln	100%	57
Creighton Univ Med Ctr-St Joseph	Omaha	100%	101
Good Samaritan Hospital	Kearney	100%	25
Nebraska Heart Hospital	Lincoln	100%	42
The Nebraska Methodist Hospital	Omaha	100%	37
Saint Elizabeth Regional Medical Center	Lincoln	100%	29
The Nebraska Medical Center[2]	Omaha	98%	55
Omaha VA Medical Center	Omaha	96%	26

Pneumonia Care

16. Appropriate Initial Antibiotic

Hospital Name	City	Rate	Cases
Alegent Health Immanuel Medical Center	Omaha	100%	58
Alegent Health Midlands Hospital	Papillion	100%	63
Faith Regional Health Services	Norfolk	100%	44
Ogallala Community Hospital	Ogallala	100%	25
Tri-County Area Hospital District[2]	Lexington	100%	28
Columbus Community Hospital	Columbus	98%	40
Creighton Univ Med Ctr-St Joseph	Omaha	98%	54
Great Plains Regional Medical Center[2]	North Platte	98%	90
Alegent Health Bergan Mercy Medical Center	Omaha	97%	116
Regional West Medical Center	Scottsbluff	97%	75
Omaha VA Medical Center	Omaha	96%	28
Saint Elizabeth Regional Medical Center[2]	Lincoln	96%	90
Tri Valley Health System	Cambridge	96%	26
Alegent Health Lakeside Hospital	Omaha	95%	85
Bryanlgh Medical Center[2]	Lincoln	95%	139
Boone County Health Center	Albion	94%	32
Fremont Area Medical Center	Fremont	94%	63
Mary Lanning Memorial Hospital	Hastings	94%	83
Memorial Health Care Systems	Seward	93%	27
Avera Creighton Hospital	Creighton	92%	25
Beatrice Community Hospital & Health Center	Beatrice	92%	36
Good Samaritan Hospital	Kearney	90%	97
Jennie M Melham Memorial Medical Center	Broken Bow	90%	42
Saint Francis Medical Center	Grand Island	90%	118
Avera St Anthony's Hospital	O'Neill	89%	54
Phelps Memorial Health Center	Holdrege	88%	26
Box Butte General Hospital	Alliance	85%	48
The Nebraska Medical Center[2]	Omaha	81%	47
Pender Community Hospital	Pender	76%	25
The Nebraska Methodist Hospital	Omaha	72%	204

17. Blood Culture Timing

Hospital Name	City	Rate	Cases
Alegent Health Midlands Hospital	Papillion	100%	97
Columbus Community Hospital	Columbus	100%	54
Faith Regional Health Services	Norfolk	100%	78
Omaha VA Medical Center	Omaha	100%	63
Regional West Medical Center	Scottsbluff	100%	76
Alegent Health Bergan Mercy Medical Center	Omaha	99%	150
Alegent Health Immanuel Medical Center	Omaha	99%	102
Creighton Univ Med Ctr-St Joseph	Omaha	99%	118
Fremont Area Medical Center	Fremont	99%	88
Great Plains Regional Medical Center[2]	North Platte	99%	141
Saint Francis Medical Center	Grand Island	99%	202
Alegent Health Lakeside Hospital	Omaha	98%	118
Good Samaritan Hospital	Kearney	98%	66
Mary Lanning Memorial Hospital	Hastings	98%	101
Bryanlgh Medical Center[2]	Lincoln	97%	186
Box Butte General Hospital	Alliance	96%	26
The Nebraska Medical Center[2]	Omaha	96%	110
Saint Elizabeth Regional Medical Center[2]	Lincoln	96%	152
The Nebraska Methodist Hospital	Omaha	95%	251
Beatrice Community Hospital & Health Center	Beatrice	92%	72

18. Influenza Vaccine

Hospital Name	City	Rate	Cases
Alegent Health Bergan Mercy Medical Center	Omaha	100%	126
Alegent Health Immanuel Medical Center	Omaha	100%	72
Alegent Health Midlands Hospital	Papillion	100%	49
Boone County Health Center	Albion	100%	33
Alegent Health Lakeside Hospital	Omaha	99%	102
Columbus Community Hospital	Columbus	98%	50
Regional West Medical Center	Scottsbluff	98%	86

NOTE: Hospital profiles are in alphabetical order by state, then city, then hospital within the city; Rankings exclude hospitals with less than 25 cases except for patient surveys which excludes hospitals with less than 100 cases; (a) 100–299 cases; (1) The number of cases is too small to be sure how well a hospital is performing; (2) The hospital indicated that the data submitted for this measure were based on a sample of cases; (3) Data was collected during a shorter time period (fewer quarters) than the maximum possible time for this measure; (4) Suppressed for one or more quarters by CMS; (5) No data is available from the hospital for this measure; (6) Fewer than 100 patients completed the HCAHPS survey. Use these rates with caution, as the number of surveys may be too low to reliably assess hospital performance; (7) Survey results are based on less than 12 months of data; (8) Survey results are not available for this reporting period; (9) No or very few patients were eligible for the HCAHPS survey. The scores shown, if any, reflect a very small number of surveys; (10) A state average was not calculated because too few hospitals in the state submitted data; (11) There were discrepancies in the data collection process; Please refer to the User's Guide for a full explanation of data.

Bryanlgh Medical Center[2]	Lincoln	97%	180
Creighton Univ Med Ctr-St Joseph	Omaha	97%	86
Faith Regional Health Services	Norfolk	96%	54
Beatrice Community Hospital & Health Center	Beatrice	95%	42
Mary Lanning Memorial Hospital	Hastings	95%	81
Great Plains Regional Medical Center[2]	North Platte	94%	83
Omaha VA Medical Center	Omaha	94%	67
The Nebraska Methodist Hospital	Omaha	93%	207
Fremont Area Medical Center	Fremont	91%	66
Jennie M Melham Memorial Medical Center	Broken Bow	91%	46
Good Samaritan Hospital	Kearney	90%	105
Avera St Anthony's Hospital	O'Neill	89%	44
Phelps Memorial Health Center	Holdrege	89%	53
Saint Elizabeth Regional Medical Center[2]	Lincoln	88%	82
Community Hospital	Mccook	87%	39
Saint Francis Medical Center	Grand Island	87%	158
The Nebraska Medical Center[2]	Omaha	83%	76
Memorial Health Care Systems	Seward	77%	26
Tri Valley Health System	Cambridge	68%	31
Box Butte General Hospital	Alliance	23%	35

19. Initial Antibiotic Timing

Hospital Name	City	Rate	Cases
Alegent Health Lakeside Hospital	Omaha	100%	149
Alegent Health Midlands Hospital	Papillion	100%	96
Columbus Community Hospital	Columbus	100%	67
Community Hospital	Mccook	100%	51
Litzenberg Memorial County Hospital	Central City	100%	33
Pender Community Hospital	Pender	100%	31
Tri-County Area Hospital District[2]	Lexington	100%	45
Alegent Health Immanuel Medical Center	Omaha	99%	138
Bryanlgh Medical Center[2]	Lincoln	99%	244
Faith Regional Health Services	Norfolk	99%	88
Fremont Area Medical Center	Fremont	99%	98
Great Plains Regional Medical Center[2]	North Platte	99%	136
Regional West Medical Center	Scottsbluff	99%	100
Alegent Health Bergan Mercy Medical Center	Omaha	98%	182
Beatrice Community Hospital & Health Center	Beatrice	98%	65
Mary Lanning Memorial Hospital	Hastings	98%	125
Saint Francis Medical Center	Grand Island	98%	207
Avera St Anthony's Hospital	O'Neill	97%	68
Creighton Univ Med Ctr-St Joseph	Omaha	97%	111
Good Samaritan Hospital	Kearney	97%	134
Howard County Medical Center	Saint Paul	97%	31
Memorial Health Care Systems	Seward	97%	37
Saint Elizabeth Regional Medical Center[2]	Lincoln	97%	162
Saint Mary's Community Hospital	Nebraska City	97%	36
Boone County Health Center	Albion	96%	54
Jennie M Melham Memorial Medical Center	Broken Bow	95%	61
The Nebraska Medical Center[2]	Omaha	94%	83
Omaha VA Medical Center	Omaha	94%	68
York General Hospital[3]	York	93%	27
The Nebraska Methodist Hospital	Omaha	92%	308
Tri Valley Health System	Cambridge	92%	39
Phelps Memorial Health Center	Holdrege	90%	51

20. Pneumococcal Vaccine

Hospital Name	City	Rate	Cases
Alegent Health Immanuel Medical Center	Omaha	100%	111
Alegent Health Midlands Hospital	Papillion	100%	80
Faith Regional Health Services	Norfolk	100%	86
Memorial Community Hospital	Blair	100%	29
Saint Mary's Community Hospital	Nebraska City	100%	32
Alegent Health Bergan Mercy Medical Center	Omaha	99%	154
Columbus Community Hospital	Columbus	99%	78
Creighton Univ Med Ctr-St Joseph	Omaha	99%	96
Fremont Area Medical Center	Fremont	99%	95
Regional West Medical Center	Scottsbluff	99%	105
Alegent Health Lakeside Hospital	Omaha	98%	127
Bryanlgh Medical Center[2]	Lincoln	98%	265
Litzenberg Memorial County Hospital	Central City	98%	40
Omaha VA Medical Center	Omaha	98%	80
Tri-County Area Hospital District[2]	Lexington	98%	40
Avera Creighton Hospital	Creighton	97%	34
Boone County Health Center	Albion	97%	59
Great Plains Regional Medical Center[2]	North Platte	97%	133
Mary Lanning Memorial Hospital	Hastings	97%	121
Saunders Medical Center[2]	Wahoo	97%	31
York General Hospital[3]	York	96%	27
The Nebraska Methodist Hospital	Omaha	95%	356
Community Hospital	Mccook	94%	49
Phelps Memorial Health Center	Holdrege	94%	62
Beatrice Community Hospital & Health Center	Beatrice	93%	57
Good Samaritan Hospital	Kearney	93%	147
Howard County Medical Center	Saint Paul	93%	28
Saint Elizabeth Regional Medical Center[2]	Lincoln	92%	148
Avera St Anthony's Hospital	O'Neill	91%	56
Providence Medical Center	Wayne	91%	32
Saint Francis Medical Center	Grand Island	91%	210
Ogallala Community Hospital	Ogallala	90%	31
The Nebraska Medical Center[2]	Omaha	84%	102
Pender Community Hospital	Pender	83%	29
Jennie M Melham Memorial Medical Center	Broken Bow	82%	74
Antelope Memorial Hospital[2]	Neligh	74%	27
Memorial Health Care Systems	Seward	71%	35
Tri Valley Health System	Cambridge	70%	40
Memorial Health Center	Sidney	57%	28
Box Butte General Hospital	Alliance	20%	41

21. Smoking Cessation Advice

Hospital Name	City	Rate	Cases
Alegent Health Bergan Mercy Medical Center	Omaha	100%	61
Alegent Health Immanuel Medical Center	Omaha	100%	56
Alegent Health Lakeside Hospital	Omaha	100%	37
Creighton Univ Med Ctr-St Joseph	Omaha	100%	64
Omaha VA Medical Center	Omaha	100%	36
Regional West Medical Center	Scottsbluff	100%	61
Saint Elizabeth Regional Medical Center[2]	Lincoln	100%	34
Saint Francis Medical Center	Grand Island	100%	72
Bryanlgh Medical Center[2]	Lincoln	99%	94
Great Plains Regional Medical Center[2]	North Platte	98%	45
Faith Regional Health Services	Norfolk	96%	25
The Nebraska Medical Center[2]	Omaha	92%	65
The Nebraska Methodist Hospital	Omaha	91%	58
Good Samaritan Hospital	Kearney	90%	41
Mary Lanning Memorial Hospital	Hastings	69%	29

Surgical Care Improvement Project

22. Appropriate VTP Within 24 Hours

Hospital Name	City	Rate	Cases
Fremont Area Medical Center[2]	Fremont	100%	96
Lincoln Surgical Hospital[2]	Lincoln	100%	29
Phelps Memorial Health Center	Holdrege	100%	33
Alegent Health Immanuel Medical Center[2]	Omaha	99%	114
Alegent Health Midlands Hospital	Papillion	98%	59
Avera St Anthony's Hospital	O'Neill	98%	42
Columbus Community Hospital	Columbus	98%	122
Community Hospital	Mccook	98%	54
Faith Regional Health Services	Norfolk	98%	194
Omaha VA Medical Center[2]	Omaha	98%	130
Alegent Health Lakeside Hospital[2]	Omaha	96%	151
The Nebraska Methodist Hospital[2]	Omaha	96%	683
Saint Francis Medical Center	Grand Island	95%	198
Alegent Health Bergan Mercy Medical Center[2]	Omaha	94%	244
Regional West Medical Center[2]	Scottsbluff	94%	224
Creighton Univ Med Ctr-St Joseph[2]	Omaha	93%	189
Good Samaritan Hospital	Kearney	93%	404
Great Plains Regional Medical Center	North Platte	93%	115
Mary Lanning Memorial Hospital	Hastings	93%	204
Bryanlgh Medical Center[2]	Lincoln	92%	285
The Nebraska Medical Center[2]	Omaha	88%	196
Saint Elizabeth Regional Medical Center[2]	Lincoln	76%	197

23. Appropriate Hair Removal

Hospital Name	City	Rate	Cases
Alegent Health Bergan Mercy Medical Center[2]	Omaha	100%	1574
Alegent Health Immanuel Medical Center[2]	Omaha	100%	272
Alegent Health Lakeside Hospital[2]	Omaha	100%	423
Alegent Health Midlands Hospital	Papillion	100%	126
Avera St Anthony's Hospital	O'Neill	100%	53
Beatrice Community Hospital & Health Center	Beatrice	100%	46
Bryanlgh Medical Center[2]	Lincoln	100%	1176
Columbus Community Hospital	Columbus	100%	231
Community Hospital	Mccook	100%	99
Creighton Univ Med Ctr-St Joseph[2]	Omaha	100%	607
Faith Regional Health Services	Norfolk	100%	667
Fremont Area Medical Center[2]	Fremont	100%	474
Great Plains Regional Medical Center	North Platte	100%	342
Lincoln Surgical Hospital[2]	Lincoln	100%	484
Midwest Surgical Hospital	Omaha	100%	129
Nebraska Heart Hospital[2]	Lincoln	100%	327
The Nebraska Medical Center[2]	Omaha	100%	580
Ogallala Community Hospital	Ogallala	100%	35
Omaha VA Medical Center[2]	Omaha	100%	298
Phelps Memorial Health Center	Holdrege	100%	81
Regional West Medical Center[2]	Scottsbluff	100%	520
Saint Elizabeth Regional Medical Center[2]	Lincoln	100%	647
Saint Francis Medical Center	Grand Island	100%	694
Tri-County Area Hospital District	Lexington	100%	45
York General Hospital[3]	York	100%	35
Good Samaritan Hospital	Kearney	99%	1167
Mary Lanning Memorial Hospital	Hastings	99%	593
Nebraska Orthopaedic Hospital[2]	Omaha	99%	231
The Nebraska Methodist Hospital[2]	Omaha	97%	2394
Memorial Hospital	Aurora	96%	28
Saint Francis Memorial Hospital	West Point	94%	33

24. Appropriate Beta Blocker Usage

Hospital Name	City	Rate	Cases
Alegent Health Immanuel Medical Center[2]	Omaha	100%	85
Alegent Health Midlands Hospital	Papillion	100%	31
Fremont Area Medical Center[2]	Fremont	100%	126
Lincoln Surgical Hospital[2]	Lincoln	100%	91
Alegent Health Lakeside Hospital[2]	Omaha	99%	149
The Nebraska Methodist Hospital[2]	Omaha	99%	300
Alegent Health Bergan Mercy Medical Center[2]	Omaha	98%	589
Faith Regional Health Services	Norfolk	98%	248
Great Plains Regional Medical Center	North Platte	97%	115
Omaha VA Medical Center[2]	Omaha	97%	117
Mary Lanning Memorial Hospital	Hastings	96%	128
Columbus Community Hospital	Columbus	95%	77
Creighton Univ Med Ctr-St Joseph[2]	Omaha	95%	231
Nebraska Heart Hospital[2]	Lincoln	95%	180
Bryanlgh Medical Center[2]	Lincoln	94%	430
Regional West Medical Center[2]	Scottsbluff	93%	122
Good Samaritan Hospital	Kearney	91%	406
Nebraska Orthopaedic Hospital[2]	Omaha	90%	77
Saint Francis Medical Center	Grand Island	89%	228
The Nebraska Medical Center[2]	Omaha	88%	256
Midwest Surgical Hospital	Omaha	78%	40
Saint Elizabeth Regional Medical Center[2]	Lincoln	75%	183

25. Controlled Postoperative Blood Glucose

Hospital Name	City	Rate	Cases
Good Samaritan Hospital	Kearney	99%	133
Alegent Health Bergan Mercy Medical Center[2]	Omaha	98%	228
The Nebraska Methodist Hospital[2]	Omaha	98%	287
Bryanlgh Medical Center[2]	Lincoln	96%	291
Saint Elizabeth Regional Medical Center[2]	Lincoln	96%	54
Creighton Univ Med Ctr-St Joseph[2]	Omaha	95%	173
Nebraska Heart Hospital[2]	Lincoln	93%	169
The Nebraska Medical Center[2]	Omaha	91%	124
Faith Regional Health Services	Norfolk	82%	55

26. Prophylactic Antibiotic Timing

Hospital Name	City	Rate	Cases
Alegent Health Immanuel Medical Center[2]	Omaha	100%	146
Alegent Health Lakeside Hospital[2]	Omaha	100%	261
Saint Francis Medical Center	Grand Island	100%	448
York General Hospital[3]	York	100%	37
Creighton Univ Med Ctr-St Joseph[2]	Omaha	99%	407
Faith Regional Health Services	Norfolk	99%	489
Great Plains Regional Medical Center	North Platte	99%	240
Nebraska Orthopaedic Hospital[2]	Omaha	99%	164
Regional West Medical Center[2]	Scottsbluff	99%	391
Beatrice Community Hospital & Health Center	Beatrice	98%	42
Bryanlgh Medical Center[2]	Lincoln	98%	810
Columbus Community Hospital	Columbus	98%	169
Fremont Area Medical Center[2]	Fremont	98%	361
Lincoln Surgical Hospital[2]	Lincoln	98%	432
Nebraska Heart Hospital[2]	Lincoln	98%	213
Alegent Health Midlands Hospital	Papillion	97%	66
Good Samaritan Hospital	Kearney	97%	783
Ogallala Community Hospital	Ogallala	97%	30
Omaha VA Medical Center	Omaha	97%	206
Saint Francis Memorial Hospital	West Point	97%	32
Alegent Health Bergan Mercy Medical Center[2]	Omaha	96%	1292
Mary Lanning Memorial Hospital	Hastings	96%	508
The Nebraska Medical Center[2]	Omaha	96%	361
The Nebraska Methodist Hospital[2]	Omaha	95%	1654
Saint Elizabeth Regional Medical Center[2]	Lincoln	95%	354
Tri-County Area Hospital District	Lexington	95%	39
Midwest Surgical Hospital	Omaha	94%	123
Phelps Memorial Health Center	Holdrege	93%	71
Community Hospital	Mccook	91%	82
Avera St Anthony's Hospital	O'Neill	76%	45

27. Prophylactic Antibiotic Timing (Outpatient)

Hospital Name	City	Rate	Cases
Great Plains Regional Medical Center	North Platte	100%	151
Bryanlgh Medical Center	Lincoln	99%	603
Faith Regional Health Services	Norfolk	99%	136
Nebraska Orthopaedic Hospital	Omaha	99%	147
Lincoln Surgical Hospital	Lincoln	98%	372
Nebraska Heart Hospital	Lincoln	98%	398
Regional West Medical Center	Scottsbluff	98%	171
Creighton Univ Med Ctr-St Joseph	Omaha	97%	259
Alegent Health Bergan Mercy Medical Center	Omaha	94%	469
Alegent Health Midlands Hospital	Papillion	94%	90
Midwest Surgical Hospital	Omaha	94%	409
Columbus Community Hospital	Columbus	93%	68
Good Samaritan Hospital	Kearney	93%	517
Saint Elizabeth Regional Medical Center	Lincoln	93%	495
The Nebraska Methodist Hospital	Omaha	92%	450
Alegent Health Lakeside Hospital	Omaha	90%	168

NOTE: Hospital profiles are in alphabetical order by state, then city, then hospital within the city; Rankings exclude hospitals with less than 25 cases except for patient surveys which excludes hospitals with less than 100 cases; (a) 100–299 cases; (1) The number of cases is too small to be sure how well a hospital is performing; (2) The hospital indicated that the data submitted for this measure were based on a sample of cases; (3) Data was collected during a shorter time period (fewer quarters) than the maximum possible time for this measure; (4) Suppressed for one or more quarters by CMS; (5) No data is available from the hospital for this measure; (6) Fewer than 100 patients completed the HCAHPS survey. Use these rates with caution, as the number of surveys may be too low to reliably assess hospital performance; (7) Survey results are based on less than 12 months of data; (8) Survey results are not available for this reporting period; (9) No or very few patients were eligible for the HCAHPS survey. The scores shown, if any, reflect a very small number of surveys; (10) A state average was not calculated because too few hospitals in the state submitted data; (11) There were discrepancies in the data collection process; Please refer to the User's Guide for a full explanation of data.

Alegent Health Immanuel Medical Center	Omaha	89%	362
Saint Francis Medical Center	Grand Island	88%	84
The Nebraska Medical Center	Omaha	86%	382
Fremont Area Medical Center	Fremont	79%	53
Mary Lanning Memorial Hospital	Hastings	46%	116

28. Prophylactic Antibiotic Selection

Hospital Name	City	Rate	Cases
Alegent Health Immanuel Medical Center[2]	Omaha	100%	148
Great Plains Regional Medical Center	North Platte	100%	240
Lincoln Surgical Hospital[2]	Lincoln	100%	433
Nebraska Heart Hospital[2]	Lincoln	100%	218
Nebraska Orthopaedic Hospital[2]	Omaha	100%	164
Ogallala Community Hospital	Ogallala	100%	30
Omaha VA Medical Center	Omaha	100%	207
Tri-County Area Hospital District	Lexington	100%	39
York General Hospital[3]	York	100%	37
Alegent Health Lakeside Hospital[2]	Omaha	99%	262
Creighton Univ Med Ctr-St Joseph[2]	Omaha	99%	408
Faith Regional Health Services	Norfolk	99%	491
Fremont Area Medical Center[2]	Fremont	99%	361
Good Samaritan Hospital	Kearney	99%	789
Midwest Surgical Hospital	Omaha	99%	121
The Nebraska Medical Center[2]	Omaha	99%	371
Saint Francis Medical Center	Grand Island	99%	451
Columbus Community Hospital	Columbus	98%	168
Regional West Medical Center[2]	Scottsbluff	98%	393
Alegent Health Bergan Mercy Medical Center[2]	Omaha	97%	1294
Mary Lanning Memorial Hospital	Hastings	97%	508
The Nebraska Methodist Hospital[2]	Omaha	97%	1675
Saint Elizabeth Regional Medical Center[2]	Lincoln	97%	356
Saint Francis Memorial Hospital	West Point	97%	32
Bryanlgh Medical Center[2]	Lincoln	96%	830
Phelps Memorial Health Center	Holdrege	96%	71
Alegent Health Midlands Hospital	Papillion	95%	66
Beatrice Community Hospital & Health Center	Beatrice	93%	42
Avera St Anthony's Hospital	O'Neill	88%	43
Community Hospital	Mccook	88%	82

29. Prophylactic Antibiotic Selection (Outpatient)

Hospital Name	City	Rate	Cases
Nebraska Orthopaedic Hospital	Omaha	100%	147
Regional West Medical Center	Scottsbluff	100%	172
Alegent Health Midlands Hospital	Papillion	99%	88
Faith Regional Health Services	Norfolk	99%	136
Great Plains Regional Medical Center	North Platte	99%	152
Lincoln Surgical Hospital	Lincoln	99%	367
Nebraska Heart Hospital	Lincoln	99%	397
Alegent Health Lakeside Hospital	Omaha	98%	161
Bryanlgh Medical Center	Lincoln	98%	601
Creighton Univ Med Ctr-St Joseph	Omaha	98%	258
Good Samaritan Hospital	Kearney	98%	502
Midwest Surgical Hospital	Omaha	98%	403
Alegent Health Bergan Mercy Medical Center	Omaha	97%	460
Alegent Health Immanuel Medical Center	Omaha	97%	343
Saint Francis Medical Center	Grand Island	96%	77
The Nebraska Medical Center	Omaha	95%	365
Columbus Community Hospital	Columbus	94%	65
Mary Lanning Memorial Hospital	Hastings	94%	109
Saint Elizabeth Regional Medical Center	Lincoln	94%	487
The Nebraska Methodist Hospital	Omaha	92%	438
Fremont Area Medical Center	Fremont	87%	53

30. Prophylactic Antibiotic Stopped

Hospital Name	City	Rate	Cases
Alegent Health Midlands Hospital	Papillion	100%	64
Lincoln Surgical Hospital[2]	Lincoln	100%	430
Tri-County Area Hospital District	Lexington	100%	39
York General Hospital[3]	York	100%	37
Alegent Health Lakeside Hospital[2]	Omaha	99%	254
Midwest Surgical Hospital	Omaha	99%	121
Alegent Health Bergan Mercy Medical Center[2]	Omaha	98%	1247
Faith Regional Health Services	Norfolk	98%	473
Omaha VA Medical Center	Omaha	98%	200
Beatrice Community Hospital & Health Center	Beatrice	97%	39
Creighton Univ Med Ctr-St Joseph[2]	Omaha	97%	386
Great Plains Regional Medical Center	North Platte	97%	234
The Nebraska Medical Center[2]	Omaha	97%	349
Regional West Medical Center[2]	Scottsbluff	97%	378
Saint Francis Memorial Hospital	West Point	97%	32
Alegent Health Immanuel Medical Center[2]	Omaha	96%	134
Columbus Community Hospital	Columbus	96%	163
Community Hospital	Mccook	96%	81
Nebraska Heart Hospital[2]	Lincoln	96%	205
Saint Elizabeth Regional Medical Center[2]	Lincoln	96%	336
Nebraska Orthopaedic Hospital[2]	Omaha	95%	164
The Nebraska Methodist Hospital[2]	Omaha	94%	1590
Saint Francis Medical Center	Grand Island	94%	423
Avera St Anthony's Hospital	O'Neill	93%	41
Good Samaritan Hospital	Kearney	93%	748
Ogallala Community Hospital	Ogallala	93%	29
Fremont Area Medical Center[2]	Fremont	91%	355
Phelps Memorial Health Center	Holdrege	91%	66
Bryanlgh Medical Center[2]	Lincoln	90%	764
Mary Lanning Memorial Hospital	Hastings	78%	495

31. Recommended VTP Ordered

Hospital Name	City	Rate	Cases
Alegent Health Immanuel Medical Center[2]	Omaha	100%	114
Avera St Anthony's Hospital	O'Neill	100%	42
Fremont Area Medical Center[2]	Fremont	100%	96
Lincoln Surgical Hospital[2]	Lincoln	100%	29
Faith Regional Health Services	Norfolk	99%	194
Alegent Health Midlands Hospital	Papillion	98%	59
Columbus Community Hospital	Columbus	98%	122
Community Hospital	Mccook	98%	54
Omaha VA Medical Center[2]	Omaha	98%	130
Regional West Medical Center[2]	Scottsbluff	98%	224
Alegent Health Lakeside Hospital[2]	Omaha	97%	151
Great Plains Regional Medical Center	North Platte	97%	115
The Nebraska Methodist Hospital[2]	Omaha	97%	684
Phelps Memorial Health Center	Holdrege	97%	34
Saint Francis Medical Center	Grand Island	97%	198
Good Samaritan Hospital	Kearney	96%	404
Alegent Health Bergan Mercy Medical Center[2]	Omaha	95%	245
Creighton Univ Med Ctr-St Joseph[2]	Omaha	95%	189
Bryanlgh Medical Center[2]	Lincoln	94%	288
Mary Lanning Memorial Hospital	Hastings	92%	206
The Nebraska Medical Center[2]	Omaha	91%	198
Saint Elizabeth Regional Medical Center[2]	Lincoln	82%	197

32. Urinary Catheter Removal

Hospital Name	City	Rate	Cases
Great Plains Regional Medical Center	North Platte	100%	25
Lincoln Surgical Hospital	Lincoln	100%	69
Midwest Surgical Hospital	Omaha	100%	59
Alegent Health Immanuel Medical Center[2]	Omaha	98%	65
Alegent Health Lakeside Hospital[2]	Omaha	98%	97
The Nebraska Methodist Hospital	Omaha	98%	531
Nebraska Orthopaedic Hospital[2]	Omaha	97%	64
Omaha VA Medical Center[2]	Omaha	96%	144
Fremont Area Medical Center[2]	Fremont	94%	69
Faith Regional Health Services	Norfolk	93%	30
Alegent Health Bergan Mercy Medical Center[2]	Omaha	91%	448
Saint Francis Medical Center	Grand Island	87%	174
The Nebraska Medical Center[2]	Omaha	85%	162
Creighton Univ Med Ctr-St Joseph[2]	Omaha	83%	95
Saint Elizabeth Regional Medical Center[2]	Lincoln	78%	72
Mary Lanning Memorial Hospital	Hastings	76%	93
Bryanlgh Medical Center[2]	Lincoln	74%	102
Good Samaritan Hospital	Kearney	69%	134

Children's Asthma Care

33. Received Systemic Corticosteroids

Hospital Name	City	Rate	Cases
Children's Hospital & Medical Center	Omaha	100%	59

34. Received Home Management Plan of Care

Hospital Name	City	Rate	Cases
Children's Hospital & Medical Center	Omaha	93%	61

35. Received Reliever Medication

Hospital Name	City	Rate	Cases
Children's Hospital & Medical Center	Omaha	100%	61

Use of Medical Imaging

36. Combination Abdominal CT Scan

Hospital Name	City	Ratio	Cases
Community Hospital	Mccook	0.009	221
Saint Francis Medical Center	Grand Island	0.012	241
Ogallala Community Hospital	Ogallala	0.040	150
Tri-County Area Hospital District	Lexington	0.041	73
Mary Lanning Memorial Hospital	Hastings	0.048	417
Great Plains Regional Medical Center	North Platte	0.052	737
The Nebraska Methodist Hospital	Omaha	0.052	1493
Saint Elizabeth Regional Medical Center	Lincoln	0.054	847
Alegent Health Bergan Mercy Medical Center	Omaha	0.061	1290
Jefferson Community Health Center	Fairbury	0.071	85
Bryanlgh Medical Center	Lincoln	0.072	1336
The Nebraska Medical Center	Omaha	0.072	1644
Alegent Health Lakeside Hospital	Omaha	0.074	353
Good Samaritan Hospital	Kearney	0.077	491
Alegent Health Immanuel Medical Center	Omaha	0.085	658
Beatrice Community Hospital & Health Center	Beatrice	0.087	344
Alegent Health Midlands Hospital	Papillion	0.113	462
Regional West Medical Center	Scottsbluff	0.131	666
Community Medical Center	Falls City	0.155	103
Providence Medical Center	Wayne	0.272	92
Creighton Univ Med Ctr-St Joseph	Omaha	0.368	345
Faith Regional Health Services	Norfolk	0.746	578
Columbus Community Hospital	Columbus	0.771	389
Fremont Area Medical Center	Fremont	0.772	526

37. Combination Chest CT Scan

Hospital Name	City	Ratio	Cases
Alegent Health Bergan Mercy Medical Center	Omaha	0.000	1190
Providence Medical Center	Wayne	0.000	48
Regional West Medical Center	Scottsbluff	0.000	444
The Nebraska Medical Center	Omaha	0.002	1954
Fremont Area Medical Center	Fremont	0.003	613
Saint Elizabeth Regional Medical Center	Lincoln	0.005	563
Columbus Community Hospital	Columbus	0.011	348
Alegent Health Immanuel Medical Center	Omaha	0.013	640
Alegent Health Lakeside Hospital	Omaha	0.013	228
The Nebraska Methodist Hospital	Omaha	0.013	1465
Jefferson Community Health Center	Fairbury	0.016	63
Good Samaritan Hospital	Kearney	0.019	429
Ogallala Community Hospital	Ogallala	0.025	79
Saint Francis Medical Center	Grand Island	0.025	121
Alegent Health Midlands Hospital	Papillion	0.030	329
Great Plains Regional Medical Center	North Platte	0.032	564
Beatrice Community Hospital & Health Center	Beatrice	0.037	214
Faith Regional Health Services	Norfolk	0.037	647
Community Medical Center	Falls City	0.041	73
Community Hospital	Mccook	0.072	195
Creighton Univ Med Ctr-St Joseph	Omaha	0.073	395
Mary Lanning Memorial Hospital	Hastings	0.080	515
Bryanlgh Medical Center	Lincoln	0.085	729
Tri-County Area Hospital District[1]	Lexington	0.130	54

38. Follow-up Mammogram/Ultrasound

Hospital Name	City	Rate	Cases
Columbus Community Hospital	Columbus	1.2%	734
Tri-County Area Hospital District	Lexington	2.2%	185
Fremont Area Medical Center	Fremont	3.5%	1420
Alegent Health Immanuel Medical Center	Omaha	3.8%	681
Community Medical Center	Falls City	4.6%	109
Saint Francis Medical Center	Grand Island	5.3%	1337
Alegent Health Midlands Hospital	Papillion	5.4%	925
Faith Regional Health Services	Norfolk	5.4%	607
Alegent Health Bergan Mercy Medical Center	Omaha	5.7%	751
The Nebraska Methodist Hospital	Omaha	6.3%	1277
Alegent Health Lakeside Hospital	Omaha	6.7%	744
Good Samaritan Hospital	Kearney	7.1%	707
The Nebraska Medical Center	Omaha	7.2%	1888
Providence Medical Center	Wayne	7.8%	103
Creighton Univ Med Ctr-St Joseph	Omaha	8.8%	512
Mary Lanning Memorial Hospital	Hastings	9.2%	607
Bryanlgh Medical Center	Lincoln	9.3%	2860
Regional West Medical Center	Scottsbluff	9.7%	1488
Great Plains Regional Medical Center	North Platte	9.9%	1184
Jefferson Community Health Center	Fairbury	10.0%	221
Ogallala Community Hospital	Ogallala	10.3%	204
Saint Elizabeth Regional Medical Center	Lincoln	12.2%	1693
Beatrice Community Hospital & Health Center	Beatrice	13.3%	660
Community Hospital	Mccook	13.5%	349

39. MRI for Low Back Pain

Hospital Name	City	Rate	Cases
Community Hospital	Mccook	21.5%	65
Faith Regional Health Services	Norfolk	22.5%	129
Mary Lanning Memorial Hospital	Hastings	24.7%	85
Fremont Area Medical Center	Fremont	26.1%	207
Regional West Medical Center	Scottsbluff	26.7%	300
Columbus Community Hospital	Columbus	28.2%	85
Great Plains Regional Medical Center	North Platte	29.7%	256
Good Samaritan Hospital	Kearney	31.5%	200
Alegent Health Lakeside Hospital	Omaha	32.7%	101
The Nebraska Medical Center	Omaha	33.1%	239
Community Medical Center[1]	Falls City	33.3%	36
Bryanlgh Medical Center	Lincoln	34.7%	245
Nebraska Orthopaedic Hospital	Omaha	35.3%	85
The Nebraska Methodist Hospital	Omaha	35.9%	340
Beatrice Community Hospital & Health Center	Beatrice	36.2%	69
Saint Elizabeth Regional Medical Center	Lincoln	37.4%	147
Alegent Health Immanuel Medical Center	Omaha	37.7%	204
Alegent Health Bergan Mercy Medical Center	Omaha	38.0%	326
Alegent Health Midlands Hospital	Papillion	40.6%	101
Creighton Univ Med Ctr-St Joseph	Omaha	41.2%	51

NOTE: Hospital profiles are in alphabetical order by state, then city, then hospital within the city; Rankings exclude hospitals with less than 25 cases except for patient surveys which excludes hospitals with less than 100 cases; (a) 100–299 cases; (1) The number of cases is too small to be sure how well a hospital is performing; (2) The hospital indicated that the data submitted for this measure were based on a sample of cases; (3) Data was collected during a shorter time period (fewer quarters) than the maximum possible time for this measure; (4) Suppressed for one or more quarters by CMS; (5) No data is available from the hospital for this measure; (6) Fewer than 100 patients completed the HCAHPS survey. Use these rates with caution, as the number of surveys may be too low to reliably assess hospital performance; (7) Survey results are based on less than 12 months of data; (8) Survey results are not available for this reporting period; (9) No or very few patients were eligible for the HCAHPS survey. The scores shown, if any, reflect a very small number of surveys; (10) A state average was not calculated because too few hospitals in the state submitted data; (11) There were discrepancies in the data collection process; Please refer to the User's Guide for a full explanation of data.

Survey of Patients' Hospital Experiences

40. Area Around Room 'Always' Quiet at Night

Hospital Name	City	Rate	Cases
Midwest Surgical Hospital	Omaha	91%	300+
Nebraska Orthopaedic Hospital	Omaha	81%	300+
Lincoln Surgical Hospital	Lincoln	80%	300+
Saint Francis Memorial Hospital	West Point	70%	(a)
Brodstone Memorial Hospital	Superior	68%	(a)
Alegent Health Immanuel Medical Center	Omaha	64%	300+
Alegent Health Midlands Hospital	Papillion	63%	300+
Saint Francis Medical Center	Grand Island	63%	300+
Tri-County Area Hospital District	Lexington	62%	(a)
Ogallala Community Hospital	Ogallala	61%	(a)
Pender Community Hospital	Pender	61%	(a)
Bryanlgh Medical Center	Lincoln	60%	300+
Alegent Health Lakeside Hospital	Omaha	59%	300+
Beatrice Community Hospital & Health Center[7]	Beatrice	59%	(a)
Alegent Health Bergan Mercy Medical Center	Omaha	58%	300+
Tri Valley Health System	Cambridge	58%	(a)
Saint Elizabeth Regional Medical Center	Lincoln	57%	300+
Creighton Univ Med Ctr-St Joseph	Omaha	56%	300+
Fremont Area Medical Center	Fremont	56%	300+
Good Samaritan Hospital	Kearney	56%	300+
Memorial Health Center	Sidney	56%	(a)
Regional West Medical Center	Scottsbluff	56%	300+
Mary Lanning Memorial Hospital	Hastings	55%	300+
The Nebraska Medical Center	Omaha	55%	300+
Phelps Memorial Health Center	Holdrege	54%	300+
Columbus Community Hospital	Columbus	51%	300+
Box Butte General Hospital	Alliance	50%	(a)
Community Hospital	Mccook	49%	300+
Nebraska Heart Hospital	Lincoln	49%	300+
Great Plains Regional Medical Center	North Platte	48%	300+
Avera St Anthony's Hospital	O'Neill	47%	300+
The Nebraska Methodist Hospital	Omaha	46%	300+
Faith Regional Health Services	Norfolk	42%	300+

41. Doctors 'Always' Communicated Well

Hospital Name	City	Rate	Cases
Midwest Surgical Hospital	Omaha	93%	300+
Brodstone Memorial Hospital	Superior	91%	(a)
Pender Community Hospital	Pender	91%	(a)
Tri Valley Health System	Cambridge	88%	(a)
Lincoln Surgical Hospital	Lincoln	87%	300+
Ogallala Community Hospital	Ogallala	87%	(a)
Box Butte General Hospital	Alliance	86%	(a)
Memorial Health Center	Sidney	85%	(a)
Community Hospital	Mccook	84%	300+
Nebraska Orthopaedic Hospital	Omaha	84%	300+
Phelps Memorial Health Center	Holdrege	84%	300+
Saint Francis Memorial Hospital	West Point	84%	(a)
Avera St Anthony's Hospital	O'Neill	83%	300+
Columbus Community Hospital	Columbus	83%	300+
Fremont Area Medical Center	Fremont	83%	300+
Alegent Health Lakeside Hospital	Omaha	82%	300+
The Nebraska Methodist Hospital	Omaha	82%	300+
Alegent Health Midlands Hospital	Papillion	81%	300+
Alegent Health Bergan Mercy Medical Center	Omaha	80%	300+
Alegent Health Immanuel Medical Center	Omaha	80%	300+
Mary Lanning Memorial Hospital	Hastings	80%	300+
Regional West Medical Center	Scottsbluff	80%	300+
Creighton Univ Med Ctr-St Joseph	Omaha	79%	300+
Faith Regional Health Services	Norfolk	79%	300+
Good Samaritan Hospital	Kearney	79%	300+
Great Plains Regional Medical Center	North Platte	79%	300+
Tri-County Area Hospital District	Lexington	79%	(a)
Beatrice Community Hospital & Health Center[7]	Beatrice	78%	(a)
Saint Francis Medical Center	Grand Island	78%	300+
Saint Elizabeth Regional Medical Center	Lincoln	77%	300+
Bryanlgh Medical Center	Lincoln	76%	300+
Nebraska Heart Hospital	Lincoln	76%	300+
The Nebraska Medical Center	Omaha	76%	300+

42. Home Recovery Information Given

Hospital Name	City	Rate	Cases
Lincoln Surgical Hospital	Lincoln	96%	300+
Nebraska Orthopaedic Hospital	Omaha	93%	300+
Midwest Surgical Hospital	Omaha	92%	300+
Saint Francis Memorial Hospital	West Point	92%	(a)
Saint Elizabeth Regional Medical Center	Lincoln	90%	300+
Brodstone Memorial Hospital	Superior	89%	(a)
Bryanlgh Medical Center	Lincoln	89%	300+
Columbus Community Hospital	Columbus	89%	300+
Alegent Health Immanuel Medical Center	Omaha	88%	300+
Alegent Health Lakeside Hospital	Omaha	88%	300+
Saint Francis Medical Center	Grand Island	88%	300+
Alegent Health Midlands Hospital	Papillion	87%	300+
Box Butte General Hospital	Alliance	87%	(a)
The Nebraska Methodist Hospital	Omaha	87%	300+
Alegent Health Bergan Mercy Medical Center	Omaha	86%	300+
Faith Regional Health Services	Norfolk	86%	300+
Fremont Area Medical Center	Fremont	86%	300+
Mary Lanning Memorial Hospital	Hastings	86%	300+
Ogallala Community Hospital	Ogallala	86%	(a)
Good Samaritan Hospital	Kearney	84%	300+
The Nebraska Medical Center	Omaha	84%	300+
Creighton Univ Med Ctr-St Joseph	Omaha	83%	300+
Great Plains Regional Medical Center	North Platte	83%	300+
Tri Valley Health System	Cambridge	83%	(a)
Avera St Anthony's Hospital	O'Neill	82%	300+
Nebraska Heart Hospital	Lincoln	82%	300+
Tri-County Area Hospital District	Lexington	82%	(a)
Community Hospital	Mccook	80%	300+
Pender Community Hospital	Pender	80%	(a)
Phelps Memorial Health Center	Holdrege	80%	300+
Regional West Medical Center	Scottsbluff	79%	300+
Beatrice Community Hospital & Health Center[7]	Beatrice	76%	(a)
Memorial Health Center	Sidney	75%	(a)

43. Hospital Given 9 or 10 on 10 Point Scale

Hospital Name	City	Rate	Cases
Midwest Surgical Hospital	Omaha	95%	300+
Lincoln Surgical Hospital	Lincoln	89%	300+
Nebraska Orthopaedic Hospital	Omaha	85%	300+
Brodstone Memorial Hospital	Superior	81%	(a)
Nebraska Heart Hospital	Lincoln	80%	300+
Pender Community Hospital	Pender	75%	(a)
Saint Francis Memorial Hospital	West Point	75%	(a)
Bryanlgh Medical Center	Lincoln	74%	300+
Columbus Community Hospital	Columbus	74%	300+
Ogallala Community Hospital	Ogallala	74%	(a)
Alegent Health Immanuel Medical Center	Omaha	73%	300+
Alegent Health Midlands Hospital	Papillion	73%	300+
Alegent Health Lakeside Hospital	Omaha	72%	300+
Phelps Memorial Health Center	Holdrege	72%	300+
Saint Elizabeth Regional Medical Center	Lincoln	72%	300+
Saint Francis Medical Center	Grand Island	72%	300+
Fremont Area Medical Center	Fremont	71%	300+
The Nebraska Medical Center	Omaha	71%	300+
The Nebraska Methodist Hospital	Omaha	71%	300+
Avera St Anthony's Hospital	O'Neill	70%	300+
Alegent Health Bergan Mercy Medical Center	Omaha	69%	300+
Good Samaritan Hospital	Kearney	67%	300+
Mary Lanning Memorial Hospital	Hastings	67%	300+
Tri Valley Health System	Cambridge	67%	(a)
Creighton Univ Med Ctr-St Joseph	Omaha	66%	300+
Box Butte General Hospital	Alliance	65%	(a)
Community Hospital	Mccook	65%	300+
Memorial Health Center	Sidney	64%	(a)
Tri-County Area Hospital District	Lexington	64%	(a)
Great Plains Regional Medical Center	North Platte	61%	300+
Faith Regional Health Services	Norfolk	60%	300+
Regional West Medical Center	Scottsbluff	58%	300+
Beatrice Community Hospital & Health Center[7]	Beatrice	46%	(a)

44. Meds 'Always' Explained Before Given

Hospital Name	City	Rate	Cases
Midwest Surgical Hospital	Omaha	81%	300+
Lincoln Surgical Hospital	Lincoln	72%	300+
Pender Community Hospital	Pender	70%	(a)
Nebraska Orthopaedic Hospital	Omaha	67%	300+
Brodstone Memorial Hospital	Superior	66%	(a)
Fremont Area Medical Center	Fremont	65%	300+
Ogallala Community Hospital	Ogallala	65%	(a)
Saint Francis Memorial Hospital	West Point	65%	(a)
Mary Lanning Memorial Hospital	Hastings	64%	300+
Columbus Community Hospital	Columbus	63%	300+
Memorial Health Center	Sidney	63%	(a)
Creighton Univ Med Ctr-St Joseph	Omaha	62%	300+
Tri Valley Health System	Cambridge	62%	(a)
Alegent Health Immanuel Medical Center	Omaha	61%	300+
Alegent Health Midlands Hospital	Papillion	61%	300+
Saint Francis Medical Center	Grand Island	61%	300+
Tri-County Area Hospital District	Lexington	61%	(a)
Avera St Anthony's Hospital	O'Neill	60%	300+
Bryanlgh Medical Center	Lincoln	60%	300+
Community Hospital	Mccook	60%	300+
The Nebraska Medical Center	Omaha	60%	300+
The Nebraska Methodist Hospital	Omaha	60%	300+
Phelps Memorial Health Center	Holdrege	60%	300+
Alegent Health Bergan Mercy Medical Center	Omaha	59%	300+
Good Samaritan Hospital	Kearney	59%	300+
Faith Regional Health Services	Norfolk	58%	300+
Great Plains Regional Medical Center	North Platte	58%	300+
Nebraska Heart Hospital	Lincoln	58%	300+
Regional West Medical Center	Scottsbluff	58%	300+
Saint Elizabeth Regional Medical Center	Lincoln	58%	300+
Alegent Health Lakeside Hospital	Omaha	57%	300+
Box Butte General Hospital	Alliance	55%	(a)
Beatrice Community Hospital & Health Center[7]	Beatrice	38%	(a)

45. Nurses 'Always' Communicated Well

Hospital Name	City	Rate	Cases
Midwest Surgical Hospital	Omaha	91%	300+
Lincoln Surgical Hospital	Lincoln	86%	300+
Nebraska Orthopaedic Hospital	Omaha	86%	300+
Brodstone Memorial Hospital	Superior	81%	(a)
Fremont Area Medical Center	Fremont	81%	300+
Avera St Anthony's Hospital	O'Neill	79%	300+
Columbus Community Hospital	Columbus	79%	300+
The Nebraska Methodist Hospital	Omaha	79%	300+
Pender Community Hospital	Pender	79%	(a)
Saint Francis Memorial Hospital	West Point	79%	(a)
Alegent Health Immanuel Medical Center	Omaha	78%	300+
Nebraska Heart Hospital	Lincoln	78%	300+
Ogallala Community Hospital	Ogallala	78%	(a)
Alegent Health Bergan Mercy Medical Center	Omaha	77%	300+
Alegent Health Lakeside Hospital	Omaha	77%	300+
Alegent Health Midlands Hospital	Papillion	77%	300+
Creighton Univ Med Ctr-St Joseph	Omaha	77%	300+
Faith Regional Health Services	Norfolk	77%	300+
Mary Lanning Memorial Hospital	Hastings	77%	300+
The Nebraska Medical Center	Omaha	77%	300+
Tri Valley Health System	Cambridge	77%	(a)
Community Hospital	Mccook	76%	300+
Saint Elizabeth Regional Medical Center	Lincoln	76%	300+
Tri-County Area Hospital District	Lexington	76%	(a)
Box Butte General Hospital	Alliance	75%	(a)
Good Samaritan Hospital	Kearney	75%	300+
Memorial Health Center	Sidney	75%	(a)
Phelps Memorial Health Center	Holdrege	75%	300+
Bryanlgh Medical Center	Lincoln	74%	300+
Saint Francis Medical Center	Grand Island	74%	300+
Regional West Medical Center	Scottsbluff	72%	300+
Great Plains Regional Medical Center	North Platte	71%	300+
Beatrice Community Hospital & Health Center[7]	Beatrice	68%	(a)

46. Pain 'Always' Well Controlled

Hospital Name	City	Rate	Cases
Midwest Surgical Hospital	Omaha	82%	300+
Lincoln Surgical Hospital	Lincoln	75%	300+
Memorial Health Center	Sidney	75%	(a)
Saint Francis Memorial Hospital	West Point	74%	(a)
Alegent Health Midlands Hospital	Papillion	73%	300+
Box Butte General Hospital	Alliance	73%	(a)
Brodstone Memorial Hospital	Superior	73%	(a)
Fremont Area Medical Center	Fremont	73%	300+
Pender Community Hospital	Pender	73%	(a)
The Nebraska Methodist Hospital	Omaha	72%	300+
Nebraska Orthopaedic Hospital	Omaha	72%	300+
Ogallala Community Hospital	Ogallala	72%	(a)
Avera St Anthony's Hospital	O'Neill	71%	300+
Columbus Community Hospital	Columbus	71%	300+
Alegent Health Bergan Mercy Medical Center	Omaha	70%	300+
Alegent Health Immanuel Medical Center	Omaha	70%	300+
Alegent Health Lakeside Hospital	Omaha	70%	300+
Mary Lanning Memorial Hospital	Hastings	70%	300+
Creighton Univ Med Ctr-St Joseph	Omaha	69%	300+
Phelps Memorial Health Center	Holdrege	69%	300+
Community Hospital	Mccook	68%	300+
Saint Elizabeth Regional Medical Center	Lincoln	68%	300+
Tri-County Area Hospital District	Lexington	68%	(a)
Faith Regional Health Services	Norfolk	67%	300+
Good Samaritan Hospital	Kearney	67%	300+
The Nebraska Medical Center	Omaha	67%	300+
Regional West Medical Center	Scottsbluff	67%	300+
Saint Francis Medical Center	Grand Island	67%	300+
Bryanlgh Medical Center	Lincoln	66%	300+
Great Plains Regional Medical Center	North Platte	66%	300+
Nebraska Heart Hospital	Lincoln	66%	300+
Tri Valley Health System	Cambridge	64%	(a)
Beatrice Community Hospital & Health Center[7]	Beatrice	60%	(a)

47. Room and Bathroom 'Always' Clean

Hospital Name	City	Rate	Cases
Midwest Surgical Hospital	Omaha	90%	300+
Lincoln Surgical Hospital	Lincoln	89%	300+
Ogallala Community Hospital	Ogallala	86%	(a)
Box Butte General Hospital	Alliance	84%	(a)
Brodstone Memorial Hospital	Superior	84%	(a)
Phelps Memorial Health Center	Holdrege	84%	300+
Pender Community Hospital	Pender	83%	(a)
Saint Francis Memorial Hospital	West Point	83%	(a)
Nebraska Heart Hospital	Lincoln	82%	300+
Avera St Anthony's Hospital	O'Neill	81%	300+
Alegent Health Midlands Hospital	Papillion	80%	300+
Fremont Area Medical Center	Fremont	80%	300+

NOTE: Hospital profiles are in alphabetical order by state, then city, then hospital within the city; Rankings exclude hospitals with less than 25 cases except for patient surveys which excludes hospitals with less than 100 cases; (a) 100–299 cases; (1) The number of cases is too small to be sure how well a hospital is performing; (2) The hospital indicated that the data submitted for this measure were based on a sample of cases; (3) Data was collected during a shorter time period (fewer quarters) than the maximum possible time for this measure; (4) Suppressed for one or more quarters by CMS; (5) No data is available from the hospital for this measure; (6) Fewer than 100 patients completed the HCAHPS survey. Use these rates with caution, as the number of surveys may be too low to reliably assess hospital performance; (7) Survey results are based on less than 12 months of data; (8) Survey results are not available for this reporting period; (9) No or very few patients were eligible for the HCAHPS survey. The scores shown, if any, reflect a very small number of surveys; (10) A state average was not calculated because too few hospitals in the state submitted data; (11) There were discrepancies in the data collection process; Please refer to the User's Guide for a full explanation of data.

Memorial Health Center	Sidney	79%	(a)
Columbus Community Hospital	Columbus	78%	300+
Mary Lanning Memorial Hospital	Hastings	78%	300+
Faith Regional Health Services	Norfolk	77%	300+
Tri-County Area Hospital District	Lexington	77%	(a)
Community Hospital	Mccook	75%	300+
Nebraska Orthopaedic Hospital	Omaha	75%	300+
Tri Valley Health System	Cambridge	74%	(a)
Alegent Health Immanuel Medical Center	Omaha	73%	300+
Bryanlgh Medical Center	Lincoln	73%	300+
Saint Francis Medical Center	Grand Island	73%	300+
Good Samaritan Hospital	Kearney	72%	300+
Great Plains Regional Medical Center	North Platte	70%	300+
Alegent Health Lakeside Hospital	Omaha	69%	300+
Regional West Medical Center	Scottsbluff	69%	300+
Saint Elizabeth Regional Medical Center	Lincoln	69%	300+
The Nebraska Medical Center	Omaha	68%	300+
Creighton Univ Med Ctr-St Joseph	Omaha	67%	300+
Beatrice Community Hospital & Health Center[7]	Beatrice	64%	(a)
Alegent Health Bergan Mercy Medical Center	Omaha	63%	300+
The Nebraska Methodist Hospital	Omaha	63%	300+

48. Timely Help 'Always' Received

Hospital Name	City	Rate	Cases
Midwest Surgical Hospital	Omaha	92%	300+
Lincoln Surgical Hospital	Lincoln	85%	300+
Box Butte General Hospital	Alliance	81%	(a)
Nebraska Orthopaedic Hospital	Omaha	78%	300+
Pender Community Hospital	Pender	78%	(a)
Saint Francis Memorial Hospital	West Point	75%	(a)
Brodstone Memorial Hospital	Superior	74%	(a)
Ogallala Community Hospital	Ogallala	74%	(a)
Nebraska Heart Hospital	Lincoln	73%	300+
Avera St Anthony's Hospital	O'Neill	72%	300+
Memorial Health Center	Sidney	72%	(a)
Columbus Community Hospital	Columbus	71%	300+
Alegent Health Midlands Hospital	Papillion	70%	300+
Beatrice Community Hospital & Health Center[7]	Beatrice	70%	(a)
Community Hospital	Mccook	70%	300+
Tri Valley Health System	Cambridge	70%	(a)
Fremont Area Medical Center	Fremont	69%	300+
Great Plains Regional Medical Center	North Platte	67%	300+
Creighton Univ Med Ctr-St Joseph	Omaha	65%	300+
Phelps Memorial Health Center	Holdrege	65%	300+
Saint Francis Medical Center	Grand Island	64%	300+
Bryanlgh Medical Center	Lincoln	63%	300+
Faith Regional Health Services	Norfolk	62%	300+
The Nebraska Medical Center	Omaha	62%	300+
The Nebraska Methodist Hospital	Omaha	62%	300+
Tri-County Area Hospital District	Lexington	62%	(a)
Regional West Medical Center	Scottsbluff	61%	300+
Alegent Health Immanuel Medical Center	Omaha	60%	300+
Alegent Health Lakeside Hospital	Omaha	60%	300+
Mary Lanning Memorial Hospital	Hastings	60%	300+
Alegent Health Bergan Mercy Medical Center	Omaha	58%	300+
Good Samaritan Hospital	Kearney	58%	300+
Saint Elizabeth Regional Medical Center	Lincoln	58%	300+

49. Would Definitely Recommend Hospital

Hospital Name	City	Rate	Cases
Midwest Surgical Hospital	Omaha	94%	300+
Lincoln Surgical Hospital	Lincoln	89%	300+
Nebraska Orthopaedic Hospital	Omaha	88%	300+
Nebraska Heart Hospital	Lincoln	84%	300+
Brodstone Memorial Hospital	Superior	80%	(a)
Bryanlgh Medical Center	Lincoln	79%	300+
Saint Elizabeth Regional Medical Center	Lincoln	78%	300+
The Nebraska Medical Center	Omaha	77%	300+
Pender Community Hospital	Pender	77%	(a)
Alegent Health Lakeside Hospital	Omaha	75%	300+
Phelps Memorial Health Center	Holdrege	75%	300+
Columbus Community Hospital	Columbus	74%	300+
The Nebraska Methodist Hospital	Omaha	74%	300+
Saint Francis Memorial Hospital	West Point	74%	(a)
Avera St Anthony's Hospital	O'Neill	73%	300+
Tri Valley Health System	Cambridge	73%	(a)
Alegent Health Immanuel Medical Center	Omaha	72%	300+
Good Samaritan Hospital	Kearney	72%	300+
Ogallala Community Hospital	Ogallala	72%	(a)
Mary Lanning Memorial Hospital	Hastings	71%	300+
Saint Francis Medical Center	Grand Island	71%	300+
Alegent Health Bergan Mercy Medical Center	Omaha	70%	300+
Alegent Health Midlands Hospital	Papillion	70%	300+
Creighton Univ Med Ctr-St Joseph	Omaha	69%	300+
Community Hospital	Mccook	68%	300+
Fremont Area Medical Center	Fremont	68%	300+
Box Butte General Hospital	Alliance	65%	(a)
Faith Regional Health Services	Norfolk	65%	300+
Tri-County Area Hospital District	Lexington	63%	(a)
Great Plains Regional Medical Center	North Platte	62%	300+
Regional West Medical Center	Scottsbluff	62%	300+
Memorial Health Center	Sidney	58%	(a)
Beatrice Community Hospital & Health Center[7]	Beatrice	44%	(a)

NOTE: Hospital profiles are in alphabetical order by state, then city, then hospital within the city; Rankings exclude hospitals with less than 25 cases except for patient surveys which excludes hospitals with less than 100 cases; (a) 100–299 cases; (1) The number of cases is too small to be sure how well a hospital is performing; (2) The hospital indicated that the data submitted for this measure were based on a sample of cases; (3) Data was collected during a shorter time period (fewer quarters) than the maximum possible time for this measure; (4) Suppressed for one or more quarters by CMS; (5) No data is available from the hospital for this measure; (6) Fewer than 100 patients completed the HCAHPS survey. Use these rates with caution, as the number of surveys may be too low to reliably assess hospital performance; (7) Survey results are based on less than 12 months of data; (8) Survey results are not available for this reporting period; (9) No or very few patients were eligible for the HCAHPS survey. The scores shown, if any, reflect a very small number of surveys; (10) A state average was not calculated because too few hospitals in the state submitted data; (11) There were discrepancies in the data collection process; Please refer to the User's Guide for a full explanation of data.

Brown County Hospital

945 East Zero St
Ainsworth, NE 69210
URL: www.brown county hospital.org
Type: Critical Access Hospitals
Ownership: Government - Local
Phone: 402-387-2800
Fax: 402-387-2804
Emergency Services: Yes
Beds: 25

Key Personnel:

CEO/President. . . . . Shannon Sorensen, CEO
Chief of Medical Staff . . . . Annette Miller, MD
Infection Control. . . . . Shelly Doyle
Operating Room. . . . . Jayce Linse
Quality Assurance . . . . Connie Gouchey
Radiology. . . . . Jennifer Krysi

Measure	Cases	This Hosp.	State Avg.	U.S. Avg.
Heart Attack Care				
ACE Inhibitor or ARB for LVSD	0	-	97%	96%
Aspirin at Arrival[1]	4	75%	99%	99%
Aspirin at Discharge[1]	4	50%	99%	98%
Beta Blocker at Discharge[1]	4	75%	99%	98%
Fibrinolytic Medication Timing[1]	1	0%	20%	55%
PCI Within 90 Minutes of Arrival	0	-	91%	90%
Smoking Cessation Advice	0	-	100%	99%
Chest Pain/Possible Heart Attack Care				
Aspirin at Arrival	-	-	96%	95%
Median Time to ECG (minutes)	-	-	7	8
Median Time to Transfer (minutes)	-	-	68	61
Fibrinolytic Medication Timing	-	-	72%	54%
Heart Failure Care				
ACE Inhibitor or ARB for LVSD[1,3]	2	0%	94%	94%
Discharge Instructions[1,3]	2	50%	87%	88%
Evaluation of LVS Function[1,3]	5	40%	96%	98%
Smoking Cessation Advice[1,3]	1	100%	96%	98%
Pneumonia Care				
Appropriate Initial Antibiotic[1]	7	86%	91%	92%
Blood Culture Timing[1]	1	100%	97%	96%
Influenza Vaccine[1]	7	43%	91%	91%
Initial Antibiotic Timing[1]	11	100%	97%	95%
Pneumococcal Vaccine[1]	16	62%	92%	93%
Smoking Cessation Advice[1]	4	25%	90%	97%
Surgical Care Improvement Project				
Appropriate VTP Within 24 Hours[5]	0	-	94%	92%
Appropriate Hair Removal[5]	0	-	99%	99%
Appropriate Beta Blocker Usage[5]	0	-	94%	93%
Controlled Postoperative Blood Glucose[5]	0	-	96%	93%
Prophylactic Antibiotic Timing[5]	0	-	97%	97%
Prophylactic Antibiotic Timing (Outpatient)	-	-	93%	92%
Prophylactic Antibiotic Selection[5]	0	-	98%	97%
Prophylactic Antibiotic Select. (Outpatient)	-	-	97%	94%
Prophylactic Antibiotic Stopped[5]	0	-	94%	94%
Recommended VTP Ordered[5]	0	-	95%	94%
Urinary Catheter Removal[5]	0	-	90%	90%
Children's Asthma Care				
Received Systemic Corticosteroids	-	-	-	100%
Received Home Management Plan	-	-	-	71%
Received Reliever Medication	-	-	-	100%
Use of Medical Imaging				
Combination Abdominal CT Scan	-	-	0.152	0.191
Combination Chest CT Scan	-	-	0.033	0.054
Follow-up Mammogram/Ultrasound	-	-	8.1%	8.4%
MRI for Low Back Pain	-	-	33.8%	32.7%
Survey of Patients' Hospital Experiences				
Area Around Room 'Always' Quiet at Night[8]	-	-	-	58%
Doctors 'Always' Communicated Well[8]	-	-	-	80%
Home Recovery Information Given[8]	-	-	-	82%
Hospital Given 9 or 10 on 10 Point Scale[8]	-	-	-	67%
Meds 'Always' Explained Before Given[8]	-	-	-	60%
Nurses 'Always' Communicated Well[8]	-	-	-	76%
Pain 'Always' Well Controlled[8]	-	-	-	69%
Room and Bathroom 'Always' Clean[8]	-	-	-	71%
Timely Help 'Always' Received[8]	-	-	-	64%
Would Definitely Recommend Hospital[8]	-	-	-	69%

Boone County Health Center

723 West Fairview St
Albion, NE 68620
E-mail: bchc@boonecohealth.org
URL: www.boonecohealth.org
Type: Critical Access Hospitals
Ownership: Government - Local
Phone: 402-395-2191
Fax: 402-395-5165
Emergency Services: Yes
Beds: 30

Key Personnel:

CEO/President. . . . . Vic Lee, FACHE
Chief of Medical Staff . . . . Bradley Hupp, MD
Operating Room. . . . . Marna Ellenwood, RN
Quality Assurance . . . . Jeanne Temme

Measure	Cases	This Hosp.	State Avg.	U.S. Avg.
Heart Attack Care				
ACE Inhibitor or ARB for LVSD[3]	0	-	97%	96%
Aspirin at Arrival[1,3]	5	100%	99%	99%
Aspirin at Discharge[1,3]	3	100%	99%	98%
Beta Blocker at Discharge[1,3]	3	100%	99%	98%
Fibrinolytic Medication Timing[1,3]	1	0%	20%	55%
PCI Within 90 Minutes of Arrival[3]	0	-	91%	90%
Smoking Cessation Advice[3]	0	-	100%	99%
Chest Pain/Possible Heart Attack Care				
Aspirin at Arrival	-	-	96%	95%
Median Time to ECG (minutes)	-	-	7	8
Median Time to Transfer (minutes)	-	-	68	61
Fibrinolytic Medication Timing	-	-	72%	54%
Heart Failure Care				
ACE Inhibitor or ARB for LVSD[1]	6	83%	94%	94%
Discharge Instructions[1]	13	77%	87%	88%
Evaluation of LVS Function[1]	22	68%	96%	98%
Smoking Cessation Advice	0	-	96%	98%
Pneumonia Care				
Appropriate Initial Antibiotic	32	94%	91%	92%
Blood Culture Timing[1]	6	67%	97%	96%
Influenza Vaccine	33	100%	91%	91%
Initial Antibiotic Timing	54	96%	97%	95%
Pneumococcal Vaccine	59	97%	92%	93%
Smoking Cessation Advice[1]	8	75%	90%	97%
Surgical Care Improvement Project				
Appropriate VTP Within 24 Hours[1]	9	100%	94%	92%
Appropriate Hair Removal[1]	18	100%	99%	99%
Appropriate Beta Blocker Usage[5]	0	-	94%	93%
Controlled Postoperative Blood Glucose	0	-	96%	93%
Prophylactic Antibiotic Timing[1]	17	88%	97%	97%
Prophylactic Antibiotic Timing (Outpatient)	-	-	93%	92%
Prophylactic Antibiotic Selection[1]	17	100%	98%	97%
Prophylactic Antibiotic Select. (Outpatient)	-	-	97%	94%
Prophylactic Antibiotic Stopped[1]	16	94%	94%	94%
Recommended VTP Ordered[1]	9	100%	95%	94%
Urinary Catheter Removal	0	-	90%	90%
Children's Asthma Care				
Received Systemic Corticosteroids	-	-	-	100%
Received Home Management Plan	-	-	-	71%
Received Reliever Medication	-	-	-	100%
Use of Medical Imaging				
Combination Abdominal CT Scan	-	-	0.152	0.191
Combination Chest CT Scan	-	-	0.033	0.054
Follow-up Mammogram/Ultrasound	-	-	8.1%	8.4%
MRI for Low Back Pain	-	-	33.8%	32.7%
Survey of Patients' Hospital Experiences				
Area Around Room 'Always' Quiet at Night[8]	-	-	-	58%
Doctors 'Always' Communicated Well[8]	-	-	-	80%
Home Recovery Information Given[8]	-	-	-	82%
Hospital Given 9 or 10 on 10 Point Scale[8]	-	-	-	67%
Meds 'Always' Explained Before Given[8]	-	-	-	60%
Nurses 'Always' Communicated Well[8]	-	-	-	76%
Pain 'Always' Well Controlled[8]	-	-	-	69%
Room and Bathroom 'Always' Clean[8]	-	-	-	71%
Timely Help 'Always' Received[8]	-	-	-	64%
Would Definitely Recommend Hospital[8]	-	-	-	69%

Box Butte General Hospital

2101 Box Butte Ave
Alliance, NE 69301
E-mail: boxbutte@btigate.com
URL: www.bbgh.org
Type: Critical Access Hospitals
Ownership: Government - Local
Phone: 308-762-6660
Fax: 308-762-1923
Emergency Services: Yes
Beds: 44

Key Personnel:

CEO/President. . . . . Dan Griess
Chief of Medical Staff . . . . David Luedke, MD
Infection Control. . . . . Mary Mockerman
Operating Room. . . . . Glen Forney, RN
Quality Assurance . . . . Mary Mockerman
Emergency Room . . . . Nancy Ross, RN
Hemotology Center . . . . Sharon Groskopf, RN
Intensive Care Unit. . . . . Dewitt Shannon, MD

Measure	Cases	This Hosp.	State Avg.	U.S. Avg.
Heart Attack Care				
ACE Inhibitor or ARB for LVSD[3]	0	-	97%	96%
Aspirin at Arrival[1,3]	1	100%	99%	99%
Aspirin at Discharge[1,3]	1	100%	99%	98%
Beta Blocker at Discharge[1,3]	1	100%	99%	98%
Fibrinolytic Medication Timing[3]	0	-	20%	55%
PCI Within 90 Minutes of Arrival[3]	0	-	91%	90%
Smoking Cessation Advice[3]	0	-	100%	99%
Chest Pain/Possible Heart Attack Care				
Aspirin at Arrival	-	-	96%	95%
Median Time to ECG (minutes)	-	-	7	8
Median Time to Transfer (minutes)	-	-	68	61
Fibrinolytic Medication Timing	-	-	72%	54%
Heart Failure Care				
ACE Inhibitor or ARB for LVSD	0	-	94%	94%
Discharge Instructions[1]	13	62%	87%	88%
Evaluation of LVS Function[1]	22	23%	96%	98%
Smoking Cessation Advice[1]	3	100%	96%	98%
Pneumonia Care				
Appropriate Initial Antibiotic	48	85%	91%	92%
Blood Culture Timing	26	96%	97%	96%
Influenza Vaccine	35	23%	91%	91%
Initial Antibiotic Timing[1]	1	0%	97%	95%
Pneumococcal Vaccine	41	20%	92%	93%
Smoking Cessation Advice[1]	19	79%	90%	97%
Surgical Care Improvement Project				
Appropriate VTP Within 24 Hours[5]	0	-	94%	92%
Appropriate Hair Removal[5]	0	-	99%	99%
Appropriate Beta Blocker Usage[5]	0	-	94%	93%
Controlled Postoperative Blood Glucose[5]	0	-	96%	93%
Prophylactic Antibiotic Timing[5]	0	-	97%	97%
Prophylactic Antibiotic Timing (Outpatient)	-	-	93%	92%
Prophylactic Antibiotic Selection[5]	0	-	98%	97%
Prophylactic Antibiotic Select. (Outpatient)	-	-	97%	94%
Prophylactic Antibiotic Stopped[5]	0	-	94%	94%
Recommended VTP Ordered[5]	0	-	95%	94%
Urinary Catheter Removal[5]	0	-	90%	90%
Children's Asthma Care				
Received Systemic Corticosteroids	-	-	-	100%
Received Home Management Plan	-	-	-	71%
Received Reliever Medication	-	-	-	100%
Use of Medical Imaging				
Combination Abdominal CT Scan	-	-	0.152	0.191
Combination Chest CT Scan	-	-	0.033	0.054
Follow-up Mammogram/Ultrasound	-	-	8.1%	8.4%
MRI for Low Back Pain	-	-	33.8%	32.7%
Survey of Patients' Hospital Experiences				
Area Around Room 'Always' Quiet at Night	(a)	50%	-	58%
Doctors 'Always' Communicated Well	(a)	86%	-	80%
Home Recovery Information Given	(a)	87%	-	82%
Hospital Given 9 or 10 on 10 Point Scale	(a)	65%	-	67%
Meds 'Always' Explained Before Given	(a)	55%	-	60%
Nurses 'Always' Communicated Well	(a)	75%	-	76%
Pain 'Always' Well Controlled	(a)	73%	-	69%
Room and Bathroom 'Always' Clean	(a)	84%	-	71%
Timely Help 'Always' Received	(a)	81%	-	64%
Would Definitely Recommend Hospital	(a)	65%	-	69%

NOTE: Hospital profiles are in alphabetical order by state, then city, then hospital within the city; Rankings exclude hospitals with less than 25 cases except for patient surveys which excludes hospitals with less than 100 cases; (a) 100–299 cases; (1) The number of cases is too small to be sure how well a hospital is performing; (2) The hospital indicated that the data submitted for this measure were based on a sample of cases; (3) Data was collected during a shorter time period (fewer quarters) than the maximum possible time for this measure; (4) Suppressed for one or more quarters by CMS; (5) No data is available from the hospital for this measure; (6) Fewer than 100 patients completed the HCAHPS survey. Use these rates with caution, as the number of surveys may be too low to reliably assess hospital performance; (7) Survey results are based on less than 12 months of data; (8) Survey results are not available for this reporting period; (9) No or very few patients were eligible for the HCAHPS survey. The scores shown, if any, reflect a very small number of surveys; (10) A state average was not calculated because too few hospitals in the state submitted data; (11) There were discrepancies in the data collection process; Please refer to the User's Guide for a full explanation of data.

Harlan County Health System

717 North Brown St | Phone: 308-928-2151
Alma, NE 68920 | Fax: 308-928-2774
Type: Critical Access Hospitals | Emergency Services: Yes
Ownership: Voluntary Non-Profit - Other | Beds: 25

Key Personnel:
Infection Control. . . . . Sharee Ring, RN
Operating Room. . . . . Diane Fegter, RN
Quality Assurance . . . . Sharee Ring, RN

Measure	Cases	This Hosp.	State Avg.	U.S. Avg.
Heart Attack Care				
ACE Inhibitor or ARB for LVSD[1,3]	1	100%	97%	96%
Aspirin at Arrival[1,3]	1	0%	99%	99%
Aspirin at Discharge[1,3]	1	100%	99%	98%
Beta Blocker at Discharge[1,3]	1	100%	99%	98%
Fibrinolytic Medication Timing[3]	0	-	20%	55%
PCI Within 90 Minutes of Arrival[3]	0	-	91%	90%
Smoking Cessation Advice[3]	0	-	100%	99%
Chest Pain/Possible Heart Attack Care				
Aspirin at Arrival	-	-	96%	95%
Median Time to ECG (minutes)	-	-	7	8
Median Time to Transfer (minutes)	-	-	68	61
Fibrinolytic Medication Timing	-	-	72%	54%
Heart Failure Care				
ACE Inhibitor or ARB for LVSD[1]	1	100%	94%	94%
Discharge Instructions[1]	3	100%	87%	88%
Evaluation of LVS Function[1]	3	100%	96%	98%
Smoking Cessation Advice	0	-	96%	98%
Pneumonia Care				
Appropriate Initial Antibiotic[1]	7	86%	91%	92%
Blood Culture Timing[1]	1	100%	97%	96%
Influenza Vaccine[1]	7	86%	91%	91%
Initial Antibiotic Timing[1]	3	100%	97%	95%
Pneumococcal Vaccine[1]	7	71%	92%	93%
Smoking Cessation Advice[1]	1	100%	90%	97%
Surgical Care Improvement Project				
Appropriate VTP Within 24 Hours[5]	0	-	94%	92%
Appropriate Hair Removal[5]	0	-	99%	99%
Appropriate Beta Blocker Usage[5]	0	-	94%	93%
Controlled Postoperative Blood Glucose[5]	0	-	96%	93%
Prophylactic Antibiotic Timing[5]	0	-	97%	97%
Prophylactic Antibiotic Timing (Outpatient)	-	-	93%	92%
Prophylactic Antibiotic Selection[5]	0	-	98%	97%
Prophylactic Antibiotic Select. (Outpatient)	-	-	97%	94%
Prophylactic Antibiotic Stopped[5]	0	-	94%	94%
Recommended VTP Ordered[5]	0	-	95%	94%
Urinary Catheter Removal[5]	0	-	90%	90%
Children's Asthma Care				
Received Systemic Corticosteroids	-	-	-	100%
Received Home Management Plan	-	-	-	71%
Received Reliever Medication	-	-	-	100%
Use of Medical Imaging				
Combination Abdominal CT Scan	-	-	0.152	0.191
Combination Chest CT Scan	-	-	0.033	0.054
Follow-up Mammogram/Ultrasound	-	-	8.1%	8.4%
MRI for Low Back Pain	-	-	33.8%	32.7%
Survey of Patients' Hospital Experiences				
Area Around Room 'Always' Quiet at Night[8]	-	-	-	58%
Doctors 'Always' Communicated Well[8]	-	-	-	80%
Home Recovery Information Given[8]	-	-	-	82%
Hospital Given 9 or 10 on 10 Point Scale[8]	-	-	-	67%
Meds 'Always' Explained Before Given[8]	-	-	-	60%
Nurses 'Always' Communicated Well[8]	-	-	-	76%
Pain 'Always' Well Controlled[8]	-	-	-	69%
Room and Bathroom 'Always' Clean[8]	-	-	-	71%
Timely Help 'Always' Received[8]	-	-	-	64%
Would Definitely Recommend Hospital[8]	-	-	-	69%

West Holt Memorial Hospital

406 W Neely St | Phone: 402-925-2811
Atkinson, NE 68713 | Fax: 402-925-2810
URL: www.westholtmed.org
Type: Critical Access Hospitals | Emergency Services: Yes
Ownership: Voluntary Non-Profit - Private | Beds: 18

Key Personnel:
CEO/President. . . . . John Olson
Chief of Medical Staff . . . . Talaha Shamim, MD
Operating Room. . . . . Peggy Tejral
Radiology. . . . . Mari Osborne, RT(R)
Patient Relations . . . . Sandra Schrunk

Measure	Cases	This Hosp.	State Avg.	U.S. Avg.
Heart Attack Care				
ACE Inhibitor or ARB for LVSD[5]	0	-	97%	96%
Aspirin at Arrival[5]	0	-	99%	99%
Aspirin at Discharge[5]	0	-	99%	98%
Beta Blocker at Discharge[5]	0	-	99%	98%
Fibrinolytic Medication Timing[5]	0	-	20%	55%
PCI Within 90 Minutes of Arrival[5]	0	-	91%	90%
Smoking Cessation Advice[5]	0	-	100%	99%
Chest Pain/Possible Heart Attack Care				
Aspirin at Arrival	-	-	96%	95%
Median Time to ECG (minutes)	-	-	7	8
Median Time to Transfer (minutes)	-	-	68	61
Fibrinolytic Medication Timing	-	-	72%	54%
Heart Failure Care				
ACE Inhibitor or ARB for LVSD[5]	0	-	94%	94%
Discharge Instructions[5]	0	-	87%	88%
Evaluation of LVS Function[5]	0	-	96%	98%
Smoking Cessation Advice[5]	0	-	96%	98%
Pneumonia Care				
Appropriate Initial Antibiotic[1,3]	4	50%	91%	92%
Blood Culture Timing[3]	0	-	97%	96%
Influenza Vaccine[1]	5	80%	91%	91%
Initial Antibiotic Timing[1,3]	6	100%	97%	95%
Pneumococcal Vaccine[1,3]	7	86%	92%	93%
Smoking Cessation Advice[1,3]	3	67%	90%	97%
Surgical Care Improvement Project				
Appropriate VTP Within 24 Hours[5]	0	-	94%	92%
Appropriate Hair Removal[5]	0	-	99%	99%
Appropriate Beta Blocker Usage[5]	0	-	94%	93%
Controlled Postoperative Blood Glucose[5]	0	-	96%	93%
Prophylactic Antibiotic Timing[5]	0	-	97%	97%
Prophylactic Antibiotic Timing (Outpatient)	-	-	93%	92%
Prophylactic Antibiotic Selection[5]	0	-	98%	97%
Prophylactic Antibiotic Select. (Outpatient)	-	-	97%	94%
Prophylactic Antibiotic Stopped[5]	0	-	94%	94%
Recommended VTP Ordered[5]	0	-	95%	94%
Urinary Catheter Removal[5]	0	-	90%	90%
Children's Asthma Care				
Received Systemic Corticosteroids	-	-	-	100%
Received Home Management Plan	-	-	-	71%
Received Reliever Medication	-	-	-	100%
Use of Medical Imaging				
Combination Abdominal CT Scan	-	-	0.152	0.191
Combination Chest CT Scan	-	-	0.033	0.054
Follow-up Mammogram/Ultrasound	-	-	8.1%	8.4%
MRI for Low Back Pain	-	-	33.8%	32.7%
Survey of Patients' Hospital Experiences				
Area Around Room 'Always' Quiet at Night[8]	-	-	-	58%
Doctors 'Always' Communicated Well[8]	-	-	-	80%
Home Recovery Information Given[8]	-	-	-	82%
Hospital Given 9 or 10 on 10 Point Scale[8]	-	-	-	67%
Meds 'Always' Explained Before Given[8]	-	-	-	60%
Nurses 'Always' Communicated Well[8]	-	-	-	76%
Pain 'Always' Well Controlled[8]	-	-	-	69%
Room and Bathroom 'Always' Clean[8]	-	-	-	71%
Timely Help 'Always' Received[8]	-	-	-	64%
Would Definitely Recommend Hospital[8]	-	-	-	69%

Nemaha County Hospital

2022 13th St | Phone: 402-274-4366
Auburn, NE 68305 | Fax: 402-274-4399
E-mail: info@nchnet.org
URL: www.nchnet.org
Type: Critical Access Hospitals | Emergency Services: Yes
Ownership: Government - Local | Beds: 20

Key Personnel:
CEO/President. . . . . Martin Fattig
Chief of Medical Staff . . . . Mike Zaruba
Infection Control . . . . Pam John
Operating Room. . . . . Jackie Obermeyer
Quality Assurance . . . . Marilyn Belding
Emergency Room . . . . Barb Ramer
Intensive Care Unit. . . . . Susan Joy

Measure	Cases	This Hosp.	State Avg.	U.S. Avg.
Heart Attack Care				
ACE Inhibitor or ARB for LVSD[5]	0	-	97%	96%
Aspirin at Arrival[5]	0	-	99%	99%
Aspirin at Discharge[5]	0	-	99%	98%
Beta Blocker at Discharge[5]	0	-	99%	98%
Fibrinolytic Medication Timing[5]	0	-	20%	55%
PCI Within 90 Minutes of Arrival[5]	0	-	91%	90%
Smoking Cessation Advice[5]	0	-	100%	99%
Chest Pain/Possible Heart Attack Care				
Aspirin at Arrival	-	-	96%	95%
Median Time to ECG (minutes)	-	-	7	8
Median Time to Transfer (minutes)	-	-	68	61
Fibrinolytic Medication Timing	-	-	72%	54%
Heart Failure Care				
ACE Inhibitor or ARB for LVSD[3]	0	-	94%	94%
Discharge Instructions[1,3]	2	100%	87%	88%
Evaluation of LVS Function[1,3]	4	100%	96%	98%
Smoking Cessation Advice[3]	0	-	96%	98%
Pneumonia Care				
Appropriate Initial Antibiotic[1,3]	5	100%	91%	92%
Blood Culture Timing[1,3]	1	100%	97%	96%
Influenza Vaccine[1,3]	1	100%	91%	91%
Initial Antibiotic Timing[1,3]	8	88%	97%	95%
Pneumococcal Vaccine[1,3]	7	86%	92%	93%
Smoking Cessation Advice[1,3]	2	100%	90%	97%
Surgical Care Improvement Project				
Appropriate VTP Within 24 Hours[3]	0	-	94%	92%
Appropriate Hair Removal[1,3]	1	100%	99%	99%
Appropriate Beta Blocker Usage[5]	0	-	94%	93%
Controlled Postoperative Blood Glucose[3]	0	-	96%	93%
Prophylactic Antibiotic Timing[1,3]	1	100%	97%	97%
Prophylactic Antibiotic Timing (Outpatient)	-	-	93%	92%
Prophylactic Antibiotic Selection[1,3]	1	100%	98%	97%
Prophylactic Antibiotic Select. (Outpatient)	-	-	97%	94%
Prophylactic Antibiotic Stopped[1,3]	1	100%	94%	94%
Recommended VTP Ordered[3]	0	-	95%	94%
Urinary Catheter Removal[5]	0	-	90%	90%
Children's Asthma Care				
Received Systemic Corticosteroids	-	-	-	100%
Received Home Management Plan	-	-	-	71%
Received Reliever Medication	-	-	-	100%
Use of Medical Imaging				
Combination Abdominal CT Scan	-	-	0.152	0.191
Combination Chest CT Scan	-	-	0.033	0.054
Follow-up Mammogram/Ultrasound	-	-	8.1%	8.4%
MRI for Low Back Pain	-	-	33.8%	32.7%
Survey of Patients' Hospital Experiences				
Area Around Room 'Always' Quiet at Night[6]	<100	64%	-	58%
Doctors 'Always' Communicated Well[6]	<100	84%	-	80%
Home Recovery Information Given[6]	<100	88%	-	82%
Hospital Given 9 or 10 on 10 Point Scale[6]	<100	88%	-	67%
Meds 'Always' Explained Before Given[6]	<100	71%	-	60%
Nurses 'Always' Communicated Well[6]	<100	85%	-	76%
Pain 'Always' Well Controlled[6]	<100	79%	-	69%
Room and Bathroom 'Always' Clean[6]	<100	90%	-	71%
Timely Help 'Always' Received[6]	<100	84%	-	64%
Would Definitely Recommend Hospital	<100	79%	-	69%

NOTE: Hospital profiles are in alphabetical order by state, then city, then hospital within the city; Rankings exclude hospitals with less than 25 cases except for patient surveys which excludes hospitals with less than 100 cases; (a) 100–299 cases; (1) The number of cases is too small to be sure how well a hospital is performing; (2) The hospital indicated that the data submitted for this measure were based on a sample of cases; (3) Data was collected during a shorter time period (fewer quarters) than the maximum possible time for this measure; (4) Suppressed for one or more quarters by CMS; (5) No data is available from the hospital for this measure; (6) Fewer than 100 patients completed the HCAHPS survey. Use these rates with caution, as the number of surveys may be too low to reliably assess hospital performance; (7) Survey results are based on less than 12 months of data; (8) Survey results are not available for this reporting period; (9) No or very few patients were eligible for the HCAHPS survey. The scores shown, if any, reflect a very small number of surveys; (10) A state average was not calculated because too few hospitals in the state submitted data; (11) There were discrepancies in the data collection process; Please refer to the User's Guide for a full explanation of data.

Memorial Hospital

1423 Seventh St
Aurora, NE 68818
Phone: 402-694-3171
Fax: 402-694-3177
URL: www.memorialcommunityhealth.net
Type: Critical Access Hospitals
Emergency Services: Yes
Ownership: Voluntary Non-Profit - Private
Beds: 75

Key Personnel:

CEO/President.............. Diane Keller
Chief of Medical Staff.......... John Wilcox, MD
Infection Control............. Laurie Andrews
Operating Room.............. Teresa Wall, RN
Anesthesiology.............. Timothy Arthur, CRNA
Emergency Room .... Chaeryl Ericson

Measure	Cases	This Hosp.	State Avg.	U.S. Avg.
Heart Attack Care				
ACE Inhibitor or ARB for LVSD[3]	0	-	97%	96%
Aspirin at Arrival[1,3]	2	50%	99%	99%
Aspirin at Discharge[1,3]	2	50%	99%	98%
Beta Blocker at Discharge[1,3]	1	100%	99%	98%
Fibrinolytic Medication Timing[3]	0	-	20%	55%
PCI Within 90 Minutes of Arrival[3]	0	-	91%	90%
Smoking Cessation Advice[3]	0	-	100%	99%
Chest Pain/Possible Heart Attack Care				
Aspirin at Arrival	-	-	96%	95%
Median Time to ECG (minutes)	-	-	7	8
Median Time to Transfer (minutes)	-	-	68	61
Fibrinolytic Medication Timing	-	-	72%	54%
Heart Failure Care				
ACE Inhibitor or ARB for LVSD[1]	1	100%	94%	94%
Discharge Instructions[1]	2	50%	87%	88%
Evaluation of LVS Function[1]	6	100%	96%	98%
Smoking Cessation Advice	0	-	96%	98%
Pneumonia Care				
Appropriate Initial Antibiotic[1]	11	100%	91%	92%
Blood Culture Timing	0	-	97%	96%
Influenza Vaccine[1]	10	100%	91%	91%
Initial Antibiotic Timing[1]	13	100%	97%	95%
Pneumococcal Vaccine[1]	18	100%	92%	93%
Smoking Cessation Advice[1]	2	50%	90%	97%
Surgical Care Improvement Project				
Appropriate VTP Within 24 Hours[1]	12	100%	94%	92%
Appropriate Hair Removal	28	96%	99%	99%
Appropriate Beta Blocker Usage[5]	0	-	94%	93%
Controlled Postoperative Blood Glucose	0	-	96%	93%
Prophylactic Antibiotic Timing[1]	24	88%	97%	97%
Prophylactic Antibiotic Timing (Outpatient)	-	-	93%	92%
Prophylactic Antibiotic Selection[1]	24	92%	98%	97%
Prophylactic Antibiotic Select. (Outpatient)	-	-	97%	94%
Prophylactic Antibiotic Stopped[1]	23	100%	94%	94%
Recommended VTP Ordered[1]	12	100%	95%	94%
Urinary Catheter Removal[1]	6	100%	90%	90%
Children's Asthma Care				
Received Systemic Corticosteroids	-	-	-	100%
Received Home Management Plan	-	-	-	71%
Received Reliever Medication	-	-	-	100%
Use of Medical Imaging				
Combination Abdominal CT Scan	-	-	0.152	0.191
Combination Chest CT Scan	-	-	0.033	0.054
Follow-up Mammogram/Ultrasound	-	-	8.1%	8.4%
MRI for Low Back Pain	-	-	33.8%	32.7%
Survey of Patients' Hospital Experiences				
Area Around Room 'Always' Quiet at Night[8]	-	-	-	58%
Doctors 'Always' Communicated Well[8]	-	-	-	80%
Home Recovery Information Given[8]	-	-	-	82%
Hospital Given 9 or 10 on 10 Point Scale[8]	-	-	-	67%
Meds 'Always' Explained Before Given[8]	-	-	-	60%
Nurses 'Always' Communicated Well[8]	-	-	-	76%
Pain 'Always' Well Controlled[8]	-	-	-	69%
Room and Bathroom 'Always' Clean[8]	-	-	-	71%
Timely Help 'Always' Received[8]	-	-	-	64%
Would Definitely Recommend Hospital[8]	-	-	-	69%

Rock County Hospital

102 East South Street
Bassett, NE 68714
Phone: 402-684-3366
Fax: 402-684-3677
E-mail: rch@huntel.net
URL: www.rockcountyhospital.com
Type: Critical Access Hospitals
Emergency Services: Yes
Ownership: Govt - Hospital Dist/Auth
Beds: 17

Key Personnel:

Chief of Medical Staff.......... John Cherry, MD
Infection Control............. Barb Kaup
Operating Room.............. Carolyn Doke, RN
Emergency Room .... Teresa Patrick, RN, MSN

Measure	Cases	This Hosp.	State Avg.	U.S. Avg.
Heart Attack Care				
ACE Inhibitor or ARB for LVSD[5]	0	-	97%	96%
Aspirin at Arrival[5]	0	-	99%	99%
Aspirin at Discharge[5]	0	-	99%	98%
Beta Blocker at Discharge[5]	0	-	99%	98%
Fibrinolytic Medication Timing[5]	0	-	20%	55%
PCI Within 90 Minutes of Arrival[5]	0	-	91%	90%
Smoking Cessation Advice[5]	0	-	100%	99%
Chest Pain/Possible Heart Attack Care				
Aspirin at Arrival	-	-	96%	95%
Median Time to ECG (minutes)	-	-	7	8
Median Time to Transfer (minutes)	-	-	68	61
Fibrinolytic Medication Timing	-	-	72%	54%
Heart Failure Care				
ACE Inhibitor or ARB for LVSD[5]	0	-	94%	94%
Discharge Instructions[5]	0	-	87%	88%
Evaluation of LVS Function[5]	0	-	96%	98%
Smoking Cessation Advice[5]	0	-	96%	98%
Pneumonia Care				
Appropriate Initial Antibiotic[5]	0	-	91%	92%
Blood Culture Timing[5]	0	-	97%	96%
Influenza Vaccine[5]	0	-	91%	91%
Initial Antibiotic Timing[5]	0	-	97%	95%
Pneumococcal Vaccine[5]	0	-	92%	93%
Smoking Cessation Advice[5]	0	-	90%	97%
Surgical Care Improvement Project				
Appropriate VTP Within 24 Hours[5]	0	-	94%	92%
Appropriate Hair Removal[5]	0	-	99%	99%
Appropriate Beta Blocker Usage[5]	0	-	94%	93%
Controlled Postoperative Blood Glucose[5]	0	-	96%	93%
Prophylactic Antibiotic Timing[5]	0	-	97%	97%
Prophylactic Antibiotic Timing (Outpatient)	-	-	93%	92%
Prophylactic Antibiotic Selection[5]	0	-	98%	97%
Prophylactic Antibiotic Select. (Outpatient)	-	-	97%	94%
Prophylactic Antibiotic Stopped[5]	0	-	94%	94%
Recommended VTP Ordered[5]	0	-	95%	94%
Urinary Catheter Removal[5]	0	-	90%	90%
Children's Asthma Care				
Received Systemic Corticosteroids	-	-	-	100%
Received Home Management Plan	-	-	-	71%
Received Reliever Medication	-	-	-	100%
Use of Medical Imaging				
Combination Abdominal CT Scan	-	-	0.152	0.191
Combination Chest CT Scan	-	-	0.033	0.054
Follow-up Mammogram/Ultrasound	-	-	8.1%	8.4%
MRI for Low Back Pain	-	-	33.8%	32.7%
Survey of Patients' Hospital Experiences				
Area Around Room 'Always' Quiet at Night[8]	-	-	-	58%
Doctors 'Always' Communicated Well[8]	-	-	-	80%
Home Recovery Information Given[8]	-	-	-	82%
Hospital Given 9 or 10 on 10 Point Scale[8]	-	-	-	67%
Meds 'Always' Explained Before Given[8]	-	-	-	60%
Nurses 'Always' Communicated Well[8]	-	-	-	76%
Pain 'Always' Well Controlled[8]	-	-	-	69%
Room and Bathroom 'Always' Clean[8]	-	-	-	71%
Timely Help 'Always' Received[8]	-	-	-	64%
Would Definitely Recommend Hospital[8]	-	-	-	69%

Beatrice Community Hospital & Health Center

1110 North 10th St
Beatrice, NE 68310
Phone: 402-228-3344
Fax: 402-223-7299
E-mail: info@bchhc.org
URL: www.beatricecommunityhospital.com
Type: Critical Access Hospitals
Emergency Services: Yes
Ownership: Voluntary Non-Profit - Private
Beds: 47

Key Personnel:

CEO/President.............. Larry Emerson
Chief of Medical Staff.......... Darin Hoffman
Coronary Care.............. Sue Schouboe
Infection Control............. Rose Wischmeir
Operating Room.............. Karen Johnson, RN
Quality Assurance .... Dorothy Zimmerman

Measure	Cases	This Hosp.	State Avg.	U.S. Avg.
Heart Attack Care				
ACE Inhibitor or ARB for LVSD[5]	0	-	97%	96%
Aspirin at Arrival[5]	0	-	99%	99%
Aspirin at Discharge[5]	0	-	99%	98%
Beta Blocker at Discharge[5]	0	-	99%	98%
Fibrinolytic Medication Timing[5]	0	-	20%	55%
PCI Within 90 Minutes of Arrival[5]	0	-	91%	90%
Smoking Cessation Advice[5]	0	-	100%	99%
Chest Pain/Possible Heart Attack Care				
Aspirin at Arrival[5]	0	-	96%	95%
Median Time to ECG (minutes)[5]	0	-	7	8
Median Time to Transfer (minutes)[5]	0	-	68	61
Fibrinolytic Medication Timing[5]	0	-	72%	54%
Heart Failure Care				
ACE Inhibitor or ARB for LVSD[1]	5	100%	94%	94%
Discharge Instructions[1]	19	100%	87%	88%
Evaluation of LVS Function	34	97%	96%	98%
Smoking Cessation Advice[1]	2	100%	96%	98%
Pneumonia Care				
Appropriate Initial Antibiotic	36	92%	91%	92%
Blood Culture Timing	72	92%	97%	96%
Influenza Vaccine	42	95%	91%	91%
Initial Antibiotic Timing	65	98%	97%	95%
Pneumococcal Vaccine	57	93%	92%	93%
Smoking Cessation Advice[1]	15	80%	90%	97%
Surgical Care Improvement Project				
Appropriate VTP Within 24 Hours[1]	18	67%	94%	92%
Appropriate Hair Removal	46	100%	99%	99%
Appropriate Beta Blocker Usage[5]	0	-	94%	93%
Controlled Postoperative Blood Glucose	0	-	96%	93%
Prophylactic Antibiotic Timing	42	98%	97%	97%
Prophylactic Antibiotic Timing (Outpatient)[5]	0	-	93%	92%
Prophylactic Antibiotic Selection	42	93%	98%	97%
Prophylactic Antibiotic Select. (Outpatient)[5]	0	-	97%	94%
Prophylactic Antibiotic Stopped	39	97%	94%	94%
Recommended VTP Ordered[1]	18	83%	95%	94%
Urinary Catheter Removal[1]	4	100%	90%	90%
Children's Asthma Care				
Received Systemic Corticosteroids	-	-	-	100%
Received Home Management Plan	-	-	-	71%
Received Reliever Medication	-	-	-	100%
Use of Medical Imaging				
Combination Abdominal CT Scan	344	0.087	0.152	0.191
Combination Chest CT Scan	214	0.037	0.033	0.054
Follow-up Mammogram/Ultrasound	660	13.3%	8.1%	8.4%
MRI for Low Back Pain	69	36.2%	33.8%	32.7%
Survey of Patients' Hospital Experiences				
Area Around Room 'Always' Quiet at Night[7]	(a)	59%	-	58%
Doctors 'Always' Communicated Well[7]	(a)	78%	-	80%
Home Recovery Information Given[7]	(a)	76%	-	82%
Hospital Given 9 or 10 on 10 Point Scale[7]	(a)	46%	-	67%
Meds 'Always' Explained Before Given[7]	(a)	38%	-	60%
Nurses 'Always' Communicated Well[7]	(a)	68%	-	76%
Pain 'Always' Well Controlled[7]	(a)	60%	-	69%
Room and Bathroom 'Always' Clean[7]	(a)	64%	-	71%
Timely Help 'Always' Received[7]	(a)	70%	-	64%
Would Definitely Recommend Hospital[7]	(a)	44%	-	69%

NOTE: Hospital profiles are in alphabetical order by state, then city, then hospital within the city; Rankings exclude hospitals with less than 25 cases except for patient surveys which excludes hospitals with less than 100 cases; (a) 100–299 cases; (1) The number of cases is too small to be sure how well a hospital is performing; (2) The hospital indicated that the data submitted for this measure were based on a sample of cases; (3) Data was collected during a shorter time period (fewer quarters) than the maximum possible time for this measure; (4) Suppressed for one or more quarters by CMS; (5) No data is available from the hospital for this measure; (6) Fewer than 100 patients completed the HCAHPS survey. Use these rates with caution, as the number of surveys may be too low to reliably assess hospital performance; (7) Survey results are based on less than 12 months of data; (8) Survey results are not available for this reporting period; (9) No or very few patients were eligible for the HCAHPS survey. The scores shown, if any, reflect a very small number of surveys; (10) A state average was not calculated because too few hospitals in the state submitted data; (11) There were discrepancies in the data collection process; Please refer to the User's Guide for a full explanation of data.

Bellevue Medical Center

2500 Bellevue Medical Center Dr
Bellevue, NE 68123
Phone: 402-763-3600
URL: www.bellevuemed.com
Type: Acute Care Hospitals
Emergency Services: No
Ownership: Proprietary

Measure	Cases	This Hosp.	State Avg.	U.S. Avg.
Heart Attack Care				
ACE Inhibitor or ARB for LVSD[5]	0	-	97%	96%
Aspirin at Arrival[5]	0	-	99%	99%
Aspirin at Discharge[5]	0	-	99%	98%
Beta Blocker at Discharge[5]	0	-	99%	98%
Fibrinolytic Medication Timing[5]	0	-	20%	55%
PCI Within 90 Minutes of Arrival[5]	0	-	91%	90%
Smoking Cessation Advice[5]	0	-	100%	99%
Chest Pain/Possible Heart Attack Care				
Aspirin at Arrival	-	-	96%	95%
Median Time to ECG (minutes)	-	-	7	8
Median Time to Transfer (minutes)	-	-	68	61
Fibrinolytic Medication Timing	-	-	72%	54%
Heart Failure Care				
ACE Inhibitor or ARB for LVSD[5]	0	-	94%	94%
Discharge Instructions[5]	0	-	87%	88%
Evaluation of LVS Function[5]	0	-	96%	98%
Smoking Cessation Advice[5]	0	-	96%	98%
Pneumonia Care				
Appropriate Initial Antibiotic[5]	0	-	91%	92%
Blood Culture Timing[5]	0	-	97%	96%
Influenza Vaccine[5]	0	-	91%	91%
Initial Antibiotic Timing[5]	0	-	97%	95%
Pneumococcal Vaccine[5]	0	-	92%	93%
Smoking Cessation Advice[5]	0	-	90%	97%
Surgical Care Improvement Project				
Appropriate VTP Within 24 Hours[5]	0	-	94%	92%
Appropriate Hair Removal[5]	0	-	99%	99%
Appropriate Beta Blocker Usage[5]	0	-	94%	93%
Controlled Postoperative Blood Glucose[5]	0	-	96%	93%
Prophylactic Antibiotic Timing[5]	0	-	97%	97%
Prophylactic Antibiotic Timing (Outpatient)	-	-	93%	92%
Prophylactic Antibiotic Selection[5]	0	-	98%	97%
Prophylactic Antibiotic Select. (Outpatient)	-	-	97%	94%
Prophylactic Antibiotic Stopped[5]	0	-	94%	94%
Recommended VTP Ordered[5]	0	-	95%	94%
Urinary Catheter Removal[5]	0	-	90%	90%
Children's Asthma Care				
Received Systemic Corticosteroids	-	-	-	100%
Received Home Management Plan	-	-	-	71%
Received Reliever Medication	-	-	-	100%
Use of Medical Imaging				
Combination Abdominal CT Scan	-	-	0.152	0.191
Combination Chest CT Scan	-	-	0.033	0.054
Follow-up Mammogram/Ultrasound	-	-	8.1%	8.4%
MRI for Low Back Pain	-	-	33.8%	32.7%
Survey of Patients' Hospital Experiences				
Area Around Room 'Always' Quiet at Night[8]	-	-	-	58%
Doctors 'Always' Communicated Well[8]	-	-	-	80%
Home Recovery Information Given[8]	-	-	-	82%
Hospital Given 9 or 10 on 10 Point Scale[8]	-	-	-	67%
Meds 'Always' Explained Before Given[8]	-	-	-	60%
Nurses 'Always' Communicated Well[8]	-	-	-	76%
Pain 'Always' Well Controlled[8]	-	-	-	69%
Room and Bathroom 'Always' Clean[8]	-	-	-	71%
Timely Help 'Always' Received[8]	-	-	-	64%
Would Definitely Recommend Hospital[8]	-	-	-	69%

Dundy County Hospital

1313 North Cheyenne St
Benkelman, NE 69021
Phone: 308-423-2204
Fax: 308-423-2298
URL: www.bwtelcom.net/dch
Type: Critical Access Hospitals
Emergency Services: Yes
Ownership: Government - Local
Beds: 14

Key Personnel:

Chief of Medical Staff . . . . Shiuvoun Torres, MD
Infection Control. . . . . Jennifer Hansen
Quality Assurance . . . . Jennifer Hansen
Radiology. . . . . Kelly Custer, RT
Anesthesiology. . . . . Kim Zweygardt, CRNA
Emergency Room . . . . Kellie Minor, RN
Hemotology Center . . . . Kathy Walgren, RN
Patient Relations . . . . Nola Pollman, RN

Measure	Cases	This Hosp.	State Avg.	U.S. Avg.
Heart Attack Care				
ACE Inhibitor or ARB for LVSD[1,3]	1	100%	97%	96%
Aspirin at Arrival[1,3]	1	100%	99%	99%
Aspirin at Discharge[1,3]	1	100%	99%	98%
Beta Blocker at Discharge[1,3]	1	100%	99%	98%
Fibrinolytic Medication Timing[3]	0	-	20%	55%
PCI Within 90 Minutes of Arrival[3]	0	-	91%	90%
Smoking Cessation Advice[1,3]	1	0%	100%	99%
Chest Pain/Possible Heart Attack Care				
Aspirin at Arrival	-	-	96%	95%
Median Time to ECG (minutes)	-	-	7	8
Median Time to Transfer (minutes)	-	-	68	61
Fibrinolytic Medication Timing	-	-	72%	54%
Heart Failure Care				
ACE Inhibitor or ARB for LVSD[3]	0	-	94%	94%
Discharge Instructions[3]	0	-	87%	88%
Evaluation of LVS Function[3]	0	-	96%	98%
Smoking Cessation Advice[3]	0	-	96%	98%
Pneumonia Care				
Appropriate Initial Antibiotic[1]	17	82%	91%	92%
Blood Culture Timing[1]	4	75%	97%	96%
Influenza Vaccine[1]	10	100%	91%	91%
Initial Antibiotic Timing[1]	24	92%	97%	95%
Pneumococcal Vaccine[1]	20	70%	92%	93%
Smoking Cessation Advice[1]	8	75%	90%	97%
Surgical Care Improvement Project				
Appropriate VTP Within 24 Hours[3]	0	-	94%	92%
Appropriate Hair Removal[1,3]	1	100%	99%	99%
Appropriate Beta Blocker Usage[5]	0	-	94%	93%
Controlled Postoperative Blood Glucose[3]	0	-	96%	93%
Prophylactic Antibiotic Timing[1,3]	1	100%	97%	97%
Prophylactic Antibiotic Timing (Outpatient)	-	-	93%	92%
Prophylactic Antibiotic Selection[1,3]	1	100%	98%	97%
Prophylactic Antibiotic Select. (Outpatient)	-	-	97%	94%
Prophylactic Antibiotic Stopped[1,3]	1	100%	94%	94%
Recommended VTP Ordered[3]	0	-	95%	94%
Urinary Catheter Removal[5]	0	-	90%	90%
Children's Asthma Care				
Received Systemic Corticosteroids	-	-	-	100%
Received Home Management Plan	-	-	-	71%
Received Reliever Medication	-	-	-	100%
Use of Medical Imaging				
Combination Abdominal CT Scan	-	-	0.152	0.191
Combination Chest CT Scan	-	-	0.033	0.054
Follow-up Mammogram/Ultrasound	-	-	8.1%	8.4%
MRI for Low Back Pain	-	-	33.8%	32.7%
Survey of Patients' Hospital Experiences				
Area Around Room 'Always' Quiet at Night[8]	-	-	-	58%
Doctors 'Always' Communicated Well[8]	-	-	-	80%
Home Recovery Information Given[8]	-	-	-	82%
Hospital Given 9 or 10 on 10 Point Scale[8]	-	-	-	67%
Meds 'Always' Explained Before Given[8]	-	-	-	60%
Nurses 'Always' Communicated Well[8]	-	-	-	76%
Pain 'Always' Well Controlled[8]	-	-	-	69%
Room and Bathroom 'Always' Clean[8]	-	-	-	71%
Timely Help 'Always' Received[8]	-	-	-	64%
Would Definitely Recommend Hospital[8]	-	-	-	69%

Memorial Community Hospital

810 North 22nd St
Blair, NE 68008
Phone: 402-426-2182
Fax: 402-426-1439
E-mail: jtriplett@mchhs.org
URL: www.mchhs.org
Type: Critical Access Hospitals
Emergency Services: Yes
Ownership: Voluntary Non-Profit - Private
Beds: 29

Key Personnel:

CEO/President. . . . . Sally Harvey
Chief of Medical Staff. . . . . Brad Sawtelle, MD
Infection Control. . . . . Annette Spooner
Operating Room. . . . . Michael Bittles

Measure	Cases	This Hosp.	State Avg.	U.S. Avg.
Heart Attack Care				
ACE Inhibitor or ARB for LVSD[3]	0	-	97%	96%
Aspirin at Arrival[1,3]	3	100%	99%	99%
Aspirin at Discharge[1,3]	2	100%	99%	98%
Beta Blocker at Discharge[1,3]	2	100%	99%	98%
Fibrinolytic Medication Timing[3]	0	-	20%	55%
PCI Within 90 Minutes of Arrival[3]	0	-	91%	90%
Smoking Cessation Advice[1,3]	1	100%	100%	99%
Chest Pain/Possible Heart Attack Care				
Aspirin at Arrival	-	-	96%	95%
Median Time to ECG (minutes)	-	-	7	8
Median Time to Transfer (minutes)	-	-	68	61
Fibrinolytic Medication Timing	-	-	72%	54%
Heart Failure Care				
ACE Inhibitor or ARB for LVSD[1]	3	100%	94%	94%
Discharge Instructions[1]	6	100%	87%	88%
Evaluation of LVS Function[1]	16	100%	96%	98%
Smoking Cessation Advice[1]	3	100%	96%	98%
Pneumonia Care				
Appropriate Initial Antibiotic[1]	19	100%	91%	92%
Blood Culture Timing[1]	19	100%	97%	96%
Influenza Vaccine[1]	23	100%	91%	91%
Initial Antibiotic Timing[1]	18	100%	97%	95%
Pneumococcal Vaccine	29	100%	92%	93%
Smoking Cessation Advice[1]	9	100%	90%	97%
Surgical Care Improvement Project				
Appropriate VTP Within 24 Hours[1]	4	100%	94%	92%
Appropriate Hair Removal[1]	13	100%	99%	99%
Appropriate Beta Blocker Usage[5]	0	-	94%	93%
Controlled Postoperative Blood Glucose	0	-	96%	93%
Prophylactic Antibiotic Timing[1]	8	100%	97%	97%
Prophylactic Antibiotic Timing (Outpatient)	-	-	93%	92%
Prophylactic Antibiotic Selection[1]	9	100%	98%	97%
Prophylactic Antibiotic Select. (Outpatient)	-	-	97%	94%
Prophylactic Antibiotic Stopped[1]	8	100%	94%	94%
Recommended VTP Ordered[1]	4	100%	95%	94%
Urinary Catheter Removal	0	-	90%	90%
Children's Asthma Care				
Received Systemic Corticosteroids	-	-	-	100%
Received Home Management Plan	-	-	-	71%
Received Reliever Medication	-	-	-	100%
Use of Medical Imaging				
Combination Abdominal CT Scan	-	-	0.152	0.191
Combination Chest CT Scan	-	-	0.033	0.054
Follow-up Mammogram/Ultrasound	-	-	8.1%	8.4%
MRI for Low Back Pain	-	-	33.8%	32.7%
Survey of Patients' Hospital Experiences				
Area Around Room 'Always' Quiet at Night[6]	<100	74%	-	58%
Doctors 'Always' Communicated Well[6]	<100	86%	-	80%
Home Recovery Information Given[6]	<100	90%	-	82%
Hospital Given 9 or 10 on 10 Point Scale[6]	<100	89%	-	67%
Meds 'Always' Explained Before Given[6]	<100	57%	-	60%
Nurses 'Always' Communicated Well[6]	<100	85%	-	76%
Pain 'Always' Well Controlled[6]	<100	77%	-	69%
Room and Bathroom 'Always' Clean[6]	<100	87%	-	71%
Timely Help 'Always' Received[6]	<100	79%	-	64%
Would Definitely Recommend Hospital	<100	76%	-	69%

NOTE: Hospital profiles are in alphabetical order by state, then city, then hospital within the city; Rankings exclude hospitals with less than 25 cases except for patient surveys which excludes hospitals with less than 100 cases; (a) 100–299 cases; (1) The number of cases is too small to be sure how well a hospital is performing; (2) The hospital indicated that the data submitted for this measure were based on a sample of cases; (3) Data was collected during a shorter time period (fewer quarters) than the maximum possible time for this measure; (4) Suppressed for one or more quarters by CMS; (5) No data is available from the hospital for this measure; (6) Fewer than 100 patients completed the HCAHPS survey. Use these rates with caution, as the number of surveys may be too low to reliably assess hospital performance; (7) Survey results are based on less than 12 months of data; (8) Survey results are not available for this reporting period; (9) No or very few patients were eligible for the HCAHPS survey. The scores shown, if any, reflect a very small number of surveys; (10) A state average was not calculated because too few hospitals in the state submitted data; (11) There were discrepancies in the data collection process; Please refer to the User's Guide for a full explanation of data.

Morrill County Community Hospital

1313 S Street Phone: 308-262-1616
Bridgeport, NE 69336 Fax: 308-262-0843
E-mail: morrow@hamilton.net
URL: www.morrillcountyhospital.org
Type: Critical Access Hospitals Emergency Services: Yes
Ownership: Government - Local Beds: 20

Key Personnel:
CEO/President. . . . . Julie Morrow
Chief of Medical Staff . . . . Dr John Post
Quality Assurance . . . . Craig Krantz

Measure	Cases	This Hosp.	State Avg.	U.S. Avg.
Heart Attack Care				
ACE Inhibitor or ARB for LVSD[5]	0	-	97%	96%
Aspirin at Arrival[5]	0	-	99%	99%
Aspirin at Discharge[5]	0	-	99%	98%
Beta Blocker at Discharge[5]	0	-	99%	98%
Fibrinolytic Medication Timing[5]	0	-	20%	55%
PCI Within 90 Minutes of Arrival[5]	0	-	91%	90%
Smoking Cessation Advice[5]	0	-	100%	99%
Chest Pain/Possible Heart Attack Care				
Aspirin at Arrival	-	-	96%	95%
Median Time to ECG (minutes)	-	-	7	8
Median Time to Transfer (minutes)	-	-	68	61
Fibrinolytic Medication Timing	-	-	72%	54%
Heart Failure Care				
ACE Inhibitor or ARB for LVSD[5]	0	-	94%	94%
Discharge Instructions[5]	0	-	87%	88%
Evaluation of LVS Function[5]	0	-	96%	98%
Smoking Cessation Advice[5]	0	-	96%	98%
Pneumonia Care				
Appropriate Initial Antibiotic[1,2,3]	3	100%	91%	92%
Blood Culture Timing[2,3]	0	-	97%	96%
Influenza Vaccine[5]	0	-	91%	91%
Initial Antibiotic Timing[2,3]	0	-	97%	95%
Pneumococcal Vaccine[1,2,3]	3	33%	92%	93%
Smoking Cessation Advice[1,2,3]	1	0%	90%	97%
Surgical Care Improvement Project				
Appropriate VTP Within 24 Hours[5]	0	-	94%	92%
Appropriate Hair Removal[5]	0	-	99%	99%
Appropriate Beta Blocker Usage[5]	0	-	94%	93%
Controlled Postoperative Blood Glucose[5]	0	-	96%	93%
Prophylactic Antibiotic Timing[5]	0	-	97%	97%
Prophylactic Antibiotic Timing (Outpatient)	-	-	93%	92%
Prophylactic Antibiotic Selection[5]	0	-	98%	97%
Prophylactic Antibiotic Select. (Outpatient)	-	-	97%	94%
Prophylactic Antibiotic Stopped[5]	0	-	94%	94%
Recommended VTP Ordered[5]	0	-	95%	94%
Urinary Catheter Removal[5]	0	-	90%	90%
Children's Asthma Care				
Received Systemic Corticosteroids	-	-	-	100%
Received Home Management Plan	-	-	-	71%
Received Reliever Medication	-	-	-	100%
Use of Medical Imaging				
Combination Abdominal CT Scan	-	-	0.152	0.191
Combination Chest CT Scan	-	-	0.033	0.054
Follow-up Mammogram/Ultrasound	-	-	8.1%	8.4%
MRI for Low Back Pain	-	-	33.8%	32.7%
Survey of Patients' Hospital Experiences				
Area Around Room 'Always' Quiet at Night[8]	-	-	-	58%
Doctors 'Always' Communicated Well[8]	-	-	-	80%
Home Recovery Information Given[8]	-	-	-	82%
Hospital Given 9 or 10 on 10 Point Scale[8]	-	-	-	67%
Meds 'Always' Explained Before Given[8]	-	-	-	60%
Nurses 'Always' Communicated Well[8]	-	-	-	76%
Pain 'Always' Well Controlled[8]	-	-	-	69%
Room and Bathroom 'Always' Clean[8]	-	-	-	71%
Timely Help 'Always' Received[8]	-	-	-	64%
Would Definitely Recommend Hospital[8]	-	-	-	69%

Jennie M Melham Memorial Medical Center

145 Memorial Drive Phone: 308-872-4100
Broken Bow, NE 68822 Fax: 308-872-6116
URL: www.brokenbow-ne.com/community/healthcare/melham.htm
Type: Critical Access Hospitals Emergency Services: Yes
Ownership: Voluntary Non-Profit - Private Beds: 39

Key Personnel:
CEO/President. . . . . Michael Steckler
Infection Control. . . . . Steve Osborn
Anesthesiology. . . . . Tim Johnson

Measure	Cases	This Hosp.	State Avg.	U.S. Avg.
Heart Attack Care				
ACE Inhibitor or ARB for LVSD[1,3]	1	100%	97%	96%
Aspirin at Arrival[1,3]	3	100%	99%	99%
Aspirin at Discharge[1,3]	4	100%	99%	98%
Beta Blocker at Discharge[1,3]	4	100%	99%	98%
Fibrinolytic Medication Timing[3]	0	-	20%	55%
PCI Within 90 Minutes of Arrival[3]	0	-	91%	90%
Smoking Cessation Advice[3]	0	-	100%	99%
Chest Pain/Possible Heart Attack Care				
Aspirin at Arrival	-	-	96%	95%
Median Time to ECG (minutes)	-	-	7	8
Median Time to Transfer (minutes)	-	-	68	61
Fibrinolytic Medication Timing	-	-	72%	54%
Heart Failure Care				
ACE Inhibitor or ARB for LVSD[1]	9	33%	94%	94%
Discharge Instructions	26	92%	87%	88%
Evaluation of LVS Function	35	91%	96%	98%
Smoking Cessation Advice[1]	5	20%	96%	98%
Pneumonia Care				
Appropriate Initial Antibiotic	42	90%	91%	92%
Blood Culture Timing[1]	17	100%	97%	96%
Influenza Vaccine	46	91%	91%	91%
Initial Antibiotic Timing	61	95%	97%	95%
Pneumococcal Vaccine	74	82%	92%	93%
Smoking Cessation Advice[1]	8	12%	90%	97%
Surgical Care Improvement Project				
Appropriate VTP Within 24 Hours[5]	0	-	94%	92%
Appropriate Hair Removal[5]	0	-	99%	99%
Appropriate Beta Blocker Usage[5]	0	-	94%	93%
Controlled Postoperative Blood Glucose[5]	0	-	96%	93%
Prophylactic Antibiotic Timing[5]	0	-	97%	97%
Prophylactic Antibiotic Timing (Outpatient)	-	-	93%	92%
Prophylactic Antibiotic Selection[5]	0	-	98%	97%
Prophylactic Antibiotic Select. (Outpatient)	-	-	97%	94%
Prophylactic Antibiotic Stopped[5]	0	-	94%	94%
Recommended VTP Ordered[5]	0	-	95%	94%
Urinary Catheter Removal[5]	0	-	90%	90%
Children's Asthma Care				
Received Systemic Corticosteroids	-	-	-	100%
Received Home Management Plan	-	-	-	71%
Received Reliever Medication	-	-	-	100%
Use of Medical Imaging				
Combination Abdominal CT Scan	-	-	0.152	0.191
Combination Chest CT Scan	-	-	0.033	0.054
Follow-up Mammogram/Ultrasound	-	-	8.1%	8.4%
MRI for Low Back Pain	-	-	33.8%	32.7%
Survey of Patients' Hospital Experiences				
Area Around Room 'Always' Quiet at Night[8]	-	-	-	58%
Doctors 'Always' Communicated Well[8]	-	-	-	80%
Home Recovery Information Given[8]	-	-	-	82%
Hospital Given 9 or 10 on 10 Point Scale[8]	-	-	-	67%
Meds 'Always' Explained Before Given[8]	-	-	-	60%
Nurses 'Always' Communicated Well[8]	-	-	-	76%
Pain 'Always' Well Controlled[8]	-	-	-	69%
Room and Bathroom 'Always' Clean[8]	-	-	-	71%
Timely Help 'Always' Received[8]	-	-	-	64%
Would Definitely Recommend Hospital[8]	-	-	-	69%

Callaway District Hospital

211 Kimball St Phone: 308-836-2228
Callaway, NE 68825 Fax: 308-836-2733
URL: callaway-ne.com/hospital
Type: Critical Access Hospitals Emergency Services: Yes
Ownership: Govt - Hospital Dist/Auth Beds: 12

Measure	Cases	This Hosp.	State Avg.	U.S. Avg.
Heart Attack Care				
ACE Inhibitor or ARB for LVSD[5]	0	-	97%	96%
Aspirin at Arrival[5]	0	-	99%	99%
Aspirin at Discharge[5]	0	-	99%	98%
Beta Blocker at Discharge[5]	0	-	99%	98%
Fibrinolytic Medication Timing[5]	0	-	20%	55%
PCI Within 90 Minutes of Arrival[5]	0	-	91%	90%
Smoking Cessation Advice[5]	0	-	100%	99%
Chest Pain/Possible Heart Attack Care				
Aspirin at Arrival	-	-	96%	95%
Median Time to ECG (minutes)	-	-	7	8
Median Time to Transfer (minutes)	-	-	68	61
Fibrinolytic Medication Timing	-	-	72%	54%
Heart Failure Care				
ACE Inhibitor or ARB for LVSD[5]	0	-	94%	94%
Discharge Instructions[5]	0	-	87%	88%
Evaluation of LVS Function[5]	0	-	96%	98%
Smoking Cessation Advice[5]	0	-	96%	98%
Pneumonia Care				
Appropriate Initial Antibiotic[5]	0	-	91%	92%
Blood Culture Timing[5]	0	-	97%	96%
Influenza Vaccine[5]	0	-	91%	91%
Initial Antibiotic Timing[5]	0	-	97%	95%
Pneumococcal Vaccine[5]	0	-	92%	93%
Smoking Cessation Advice[5]	0	-	90%	97%
Surgical Care Improvement Project				
Appropriate VTP Within 24 Hours[5]	0	-	94%	92%
Appropriate Hair Removal[5]	0	-	99%	99%
Appropriate Beta Blocker Usage[5]	0	-	94%	93%
Controlled Postoperative Blood Glucose[5]	0	-	96%	93%
Prophylactic Antibiotic Timing[5]	0	-	97%	97%
Prophylactic Antibiotic Timing (Outpatient)	-	-	93%	92%
Prophylactic Antibiotic Selection[5]	0	-	98%	97%
Prophylactic Antibiotic Select. (Outpatient)	-	-	97%	94%
Prophylactic Antibiotic Stopped[5]	0	-	94%	94%
Recommended VTP Ordered[5]	0	-	95%	94%
Urinary Catheter Removal[5]	0	-	90%	90%
Children's Asthma Care				
Received Systemic Corticosteroids	-	-	-	100%
Received Home Management Plan	-	-	-	71%
Received Reliever Medication	-	-	-	100%
Use of Medical Imaging				
Combination Abdominal CT Scan	-	-	0.152	0.191
Combination Chest CT Scan	-	-	0.033	0.054
Follow-up Mammogram/Ultrasound	-	-	8.1%	8.4%
MRI for Low Back Pain	-	-	33.8%	32.7%
Survey of Patients' Hospital Experiences				
Area Around Room 'Always' Quiet at Night[8]	-	-	-	58%
Doctors 'Always' Communicated Well[8]	-	-	-	80%
Home Recovery Information Given[8]	-	-	-	82%
Hospital Given 9 or 10 on 10 Point Scale[8]	-	-	-	67%
Meds 'Always' Explained Before Given[8]	-	-	-	60%
Nurses 'Always' Communicated Well[8]	-	-	-	76%
Pain 'Always' Well Controlled[8]	-	-	-	69%
Room and Bathroom 'Always' Clean[8]	-	-	-	71%
Timely Help 'Always' Received[8]	-	-	-	64%
Would Definitely Recommend Hospital[8]	-	-	-	69%

NOTE: Hospital profiles are in alphabetical order by state, then city, then hospital within the city; Rankings exclude hospitals with less than 25 cases except for patient surveys which excludes hospitals with less than 100 cases; (a) 100–299 cases; (1) The number of cases is too small to be sure how well a hospital is performing; (2) The hospital indicated that the data submitted for this measure were based on a sample of cases; (3) Data was collected during a shorter time period (fewer quarters) than the maximum possible time for this measure; (4) Suppressed for one or more quarters by CMS; (5) No data is available from the hospital for this measure; (6) Fewer than 100 patients completed the HCAHPS survey. Use these rates with caution, as the number of surveys may be too low to reliably assess hospital performance; (7) Survey results are based on less than 12 months of data; (8) Survey results are not available for this reporting period; (9) No or very few patients were eligible for the HCAHPS survey. The scores shown, if any, reflect a very small number of surveys; (10) A state average was not calculated because too few hospitals in the state submitted data; (11) There were discrepancies in the data collection process; Please refer to the User's Guide for a full explanation of data.

Tri Valley Health System

1305 Highway 6/34
Cambridge, NE 69022
Phone: 308-697-3329
Fax: 308-697-4918
URL: www.trivalleyhealth.com
Type: Critical Access Hospitals
Emergency Services: Yes
Ownership: Voluntary Non-Profit - Private
Beds: 25

Key Personnel:

CEO/President. . . . . Lynn Milnes
Chief of Medical Staff. . . . . Lennis Deaver, MD
Infection Control. . . . . Shelly Shellabarger
Operating Room. . . . . Joyce Thompson, RN
Quality Assurance . . . . Shelly Shellabarger
Ambulatory Care . . . . Joyce Thompson, RN
Anesthesiology. . . . . Rachelle Kaspor-Cope
Emergency Room . . . . Rhonda Sherman

Measure	Cases	This Hosp.	State Avg.	U.S. Avg.
Heart Attack Care				
ACE Inhibitor or ARB for LVSD[3]	0	-	97%	96%
Aspirin at Arrival[1,3]	1	100%	99%	99%
Aspirin at Discharge[1,3]	1	100%	99%	98%
Beta Blocker at Discharge[1,3]	1	100%	99%	98%
Fibrinolytic Medication Timing[3]	0	-	20%	55%
PCI Within 90 Minutes of Arrival[3]	0	-	91%	90%
Smoking Cessation Advice[3]	0	-	100%	99%
Chest Pain/Possible Heart Attack Care				
Aspirin at Arrival	-	-	96%	95%
Median Time to ECG (minutes)	-	-	7	8
Median Time to Transfer (minutes)	-	-	68	61
Fibrinolytic Medication Timing	-	-	72%	54%
Heart Failure Care				
ACE Inhibitor or ARB for LVSD[1]	2	100%	94%	94%
Discharge Instructions[1]	9	67%	87%	88%
Evaluation of LVS Function[1]	19	74%	96%	98%
Smoking Cessation Advice[1]	2	100%	96%	98%
Pneumonia Care				
Appropriate Initial Antibiotic	26	96%	91%	92%
Blood Culture Timing[1]	3	100%	97%	96%
Influenza Vaccine	31	68%	91%	91%
Initial Antibiotic Timing	39	92%	97%	95%
Pneumococcal Vaccine	40	70%	92%	93%
Smoking Cessation Advice[1]	6	100%	90%	97%
Surgical Care Improvement Project				
Appropriate VTP Within 24 Hours[1,3]	1	100%	94%	92%
Appropriate Hair Removal[1,3]	2	100%	99%	99%
Appropriate Beta Blocker Usage[5]	0	-	94%	93%
Controlled Postoperative Blood Glucose[3]	0	-	96%	93%
Prophylactic Antibiotic Timing[1,3]	2	100%	97%	97%
Prophylactic Antibiotic Timing (Outpatient)	-	-	93%	92%
Prophylactic Antibiotic Selection[1,3]	2	0%	98%	97%
Prophylactic Antibiotic Select. (Outpatient)	-	-	97%	94%
Prophylactic Antibiotic Stopped[1,3]	2	100%	94%	94%
Recommended VTP Ordered[1,3]	1	100%	95%	94%
Urinary Catheter Removal[5]	0	-	90%	90%
Children's Asthma Care				
Received Systemic Corticosteroids	-	-	-	100%
Received Home Management Plan	-	-	-	71%
Received Reliever Medication	-	-	-	100%
Use of Medical Imaging				
Combination Abdominal CT Scan	-	-	0.152	0.191
Combination Chest CT Scan	-	-	0.033	0.054
Follow-up Mammogram/Ultrasound	-	-	8.1%	8.4%
MRI for Low Back Pain	-	-	33.8%	32.7%
Survey of Patients' Hospital Experiences				
Area Around Room 'Always' Quiet at Night	(a)	58%	-	58%
Doctors 'Always' Communicated Well	(a)	88%	-	80%
Home Recovery Information Given	(a)	83%	-	82%
Hospital Given 9 or 10 on 10 Point Scale	(a)	67%	-	67%
Meds 'Always' Explained Before Given	(a)	62%	-	60%
Nurses 'Always' Communicated Well	(a)	77%	-	76%
Pain 'Always' Well Controlled	(a)	64%	-	69%
Room and Bathroom 'Always' Clean	(a)	74%	-	71%
Timely Help 'Always' Received	(a)	70%	-	64%
Would Definitely Recommend Hospital	(a)	73%	-	69%

Litzenberg Memorial County Hospital

1715 26th St
Central City, NE 68826
Phone: 308-946-3015
Fax: 308-946-2633
E-mail: mbowman@lmchealth.com
URL: www.lmchealth.com
Type: Critical Access Hospitals
Emergency Services: Yes
Ownership: Government - Local
Beds: 25

Key Personnel:

CEO/President. . . . . Michael Bowman
Chief of Medical Staff. . . . . Gerome Dackey
Infection Control. . . . . Lavonne Solomon, LPN
Quality Assurance . . . . Penny Wetovick
Radiology. . . . . John Allen
Emergency Room . . . . Diane Schoch

Measure	Cases	This Hosp.	State Avg.	U.S. Avg.
Heart Attack Care				
ACE Inhibitor or ARB for LVSD[5]	0	-	97%	96%
Aspirin at Arrival[5]	0	-	99%	99%
Aspirin at Discharge[5]	0	-	99%	98%
Beta Blocker at Discharge[5]	0	-	99%	98%
Fibrinolytic Medication Timing[5]	0	-	20%	55%
PCI Within 90 Minutes of Arrival[5]	0	-	91%	90%
Smoking Cessation Advice[5]	0	-	100%	99%
Chest Pain/Possible Heart Attack Care				
Aspirin at Arrival	-	-	96%	95%
Median Time to ECG (minutes)	-	-	7	8
Median Time to Transfer (minutes)	-	-	68	61
Fibrinolytic Medication Timing	-	-	72%	54%
Heart Failure Care				
ACE Inhibitor or ARB for LVSD	0	-	94%	94%
Discharge Instructions[1]	4	100%	87%	88%
Evaluation of LVS Function[1]	10	100%	96%	98%
Smoking Cessation Advice	0	-	96%	98%
Pneumonia Care				
Appropriate Initial Antibiotic[1]	18	100%	91%	92%
Blood Culture Timing[1]	2	100%	97%	96%
Influenza Vaccine[1]	16	100%	91%	91%
Initial Antibiotic Timing	33	100%	97%	95%
Pneumococcal Vaccine	40	98%	92%	93%
Smoking Cessation Advice[1]	11	73%	90%	97%
Surgical Care Improvement Project				
Appropriate VTP Within 24 Hours[5]	0	-	94%	92%
Appropriate Hair Removal[5]	0	-	99%	99%
Appropriate Beta Blocker Usage[5]	0	-	94%	93%
Controlled Postoperative Blood Glucose[5]	0	-	96%	93%
Prophylactic Antibiotic Timing[5]	0	-	97%	97%
Prophylactic Antibiotic Timing (Outpatient)	-	-	93%	92%
Prophylactic Antibiotic Selection[5]	0	-	98%	97%
Prophylactic Antibiotic Select. (Outpatient)	-	-	97%	94%
Prophylactic Antibiotic Stopped[5]	0	-	94%	94%
Recommended VTP Ordered[5]	0	-	95%	94%
Urinary Catheter Removal[5]	0	-	90%	90%
Children's Asthma Care				
Received Systemic Corticosteroids	-	-	-	100%
Received Home Management Plan	-	-	-	71%
Received Reliever Medication	-	-	-	100%
Use of Medical Imaging				
Combination Abdominal CT Scan	-	-	0.152	0.191
Combination Chest CT Scan	-	-	0.033	0.054
Follow-up Mammogram/Ultrasound	-	-	8.1%	8.4%
MRI for Low Back Pain	-	-	33.8%	32.7%
Survey of Patients' Hospital Experiences				
Area Around Room 'Always' Quiet at Night[8]	-	-	-	58%
Doctors 'Always' Communicated Well[8]	-	-	-	80%
Home Recovery Information Given[8]	-	-	-	82%
Hospital Given 9 or 10 on 10 Point Scale[8]	-	-	-	67%
Meds 'Always' Explained Before Given[8]	-	-	-	60%
Nurses 'Always' Communicated Well[8]	-	-	-	76%
Pain 'Always' Well Controlled[8]	-	-	-	69%
Room and Bathroom 'Always' Clean[8]	-	-	-	71%
Timely Help 'Always' Received[8]	-	-	-	64%
Would Definitely Recommend Hospital[8]	-	-	-	69%

Chadron Community Hospital and Health Services

825 Centennial Drive
Chadron, NE 69337
Phone: 308-432-5586
Fax: 308-432-2737
E-mail: ceo@chadronhospital.com
URL: www.chadronhospital.com
Type: Critical Access Hospitals
Emergency Services: Yes
Ownership: Voluntary Non-Profit - Private
Beds: 25

Key Personnel:

CEO/President. . . . . Harold Krueger Jr.
Chief of Medical Staff. . . . . Jeffrey Lias
Infection Control. . . . . Cheryl Cassiday
Operating Room. . . . . Elinrey D Burgess
Quality Assurance . . . . Amy Hindman
Radiology. . . . . Jodi Dannar
Emergency Room . . . . Sandra Ingwersen
Intensive Care Unit. . . . . Cheryl Cassiday

Measure	Cases	This Hosp.	State Avg.	U.S. Avg.
Heart Attack Care				
ACE Inhibitor or ARB for LVSD[5]	0	-	97%	96%
Aspirin at Arrival[1,3]	3	100%	99%	99%
Aspirin at Discharge[5]	0	-	99%	98%
Beta Blocker at Discharge[5]	0	-	99%	98%
Fibrinolytic Medication Timing[3]	0	-	20%	55%
PCI Within 90 Minutes of Arrival[5]	0	-	91%	90%
Smoking Cessation Advice[5]	0	-	100%	99%
Chest Pain/Possible Heart Attack Care				
Aspirin at Arrival	-	-	96%	95%
Median Time to ECG (minutes)	-	-	7	8
Median Time to Transfer (minutes)	-	-	68	61
Fibrinolytic Medication Timing	-	-	72%	54%
Heart Failure Care				
ACE Inhibitor or ARB for LVSD	0	-	94%	94%
Discharge Instructions[1]	7	57%	87%	88%
Evaluation of LVS Function[1]	15	67%	96%	98%
Smoking Cessation Advice[1]	2	50%	96%	98%
Pneumonia Care				
Appropriate Initial Antibiotic[1]	11	91%	91%	92%
Blood Culture Timing[5]	0	-	97%	96%
Influenza Vaccine[1]	9	44%	91%	91%
Initial Antibiotic Timing[1]	13	92%	97%	95%
Pneumococcal Vaccine[1]	20	80%	92%	93%
Smoking Cessation Advice[1]	5	60%	90%	97%
Surgical Care Improvement Project				
Appropriate VTP Within 24 Hours[1,3]	6	33%	94%	92%
Appropriate Hair Removal[1,3]	7	100%	99%	99%
Appropriate Beta Blocker Usage[5]	0	-	94%	93%
Controlled Postoperative Blood Glucose[5]	0	-	96%	93%
Prophylactic Antibiotic Timing[1,3]	3	33%	97%	97%
Prophylactic Antibiotic Timing (Outpatient)	-	-	93%	92%
Prophylactic Antibiotic Selection[1,3]	3	0%	98%	97%
Prophylactic Antibiotic Select. (Outpatient)	-	-	97%	94%
Prophylactic Antibiotic Stopped[1,3]	3	100%	94%	94%
Recommended VTP Ordered[1,3]	7	29%	95%	94%
Urinary Catheter Removal[1]	1	100%	90%	90%
Children's Asthma Care				
Received Systemic Corticosteroids	-	-	-	100%
Received Home Management Plan	-	-	-	71%
Received Reliever Medication	-	-	-	100%
Use of Medical Imaging				
Combination Abdominal CT Scan	-	-	0.152	0.191
Combination Chest CT Scan	-	-	0.033	0.054
Follow-up Mammogram/Ultrasound	-	-	8.1%	8.4%
MRI for Low Back Pain	-	-	33.8%	32.7%
Survey of Patients' Hospital Experiences				
Area Around Room 'Always' Quiet at Night[8]	-	-	-	58%
Doctors 'Always' Communicated Well[8]	-	-	-	80%
Home Recovery Information Given[8]	-	-	-	82%
Hospital Given 9 or 10 on 10 Point Scale[8]	-	-	-	67%
Meds 'Always' Explained Before Given[8]	-	-	-	60%
Nurses 'Always' Communicated Well[8]	-	-	-	76%
Pain 'Always' Well Controlled[8]	-	-	-	69%
Room and Bathroom 'Always' Clean[8]	-	-	-	71%
Timely Help 'Always' Received[8]	-	-	-	64%
Would Definitely Recommend Hospital[8]	-	-	-	69%

NOTE: Hospital profiles are in alphabetical order by state, then city, then hospital within the city; Rankings exclude hospitals with less than 25 cases except for patient surveys which excludes hospitals with less than 100 cases; (a) 100–299 cases; (1) The number of cases is too small to be sure how well a hospital is performing; (2) The hospital indicated that the data submitted for this measure were based on a sample of cases; (3) Data was collected during a shorter time period (fewer quarters) than the maximum possible time for this measure; (4) Suppressed for one or more quarters by CMS; (5) No data is available from the hospital for this measure; (6) Fewer than 100 patients completed the HCAHPS survey. Use these rates with caution, as the number of surveys may be too low to reliably assess hospital performance; (7) Survey results are based on less than 12 months of data; (8) Survey results are not available for this reporting period; (9) No or very few patients were eligible for the HCAHPS survey. The scores shown, if any, reflect a very small number of surveys; (10) A state average was not calculated because too few hospitals in the state submitted data; (11) There were discrepancies in the data collection process; Please refer to the User's Guide for a full explanation of data.

Columbus Community Hospital

4600 38th St
Columbus, NE 68601
Phone: 402-564-7118
Fax: 402-563-3267
E-mail: info@columbushosp.org
URL: www.columbushosp.org
Type: Acute Care Hospitals
Emergency Services: Yes
Ownership: Voluntary Non-Profit - Other
Beds: 81

Key Personnel:

CEO/President. . . . . Donald Zornes
Infection Control. . . . . Cookie Walsh
Operating Room. . . . . Marlene Engel
Quality Assurance . . . . Cookie Walsh
Radiology. . . . . John P Beauvais
Emergency Room . . . . Cathy Hare

Measure	Cases	This Hosp.	State Avg.	U.S. Avg.
Heart Attack Care				
ACE Inhibitor or ARB for LVSD[1]	3	100%	97%	96%
Aspirin at Arrival[1]	9	78%	99%	99%
Aspirin at Discharge[1]	7	100%	99%	98%
Beta Blocker at Discharge[1]	7	100%	99%	98%
Fibrinolytic Medication Timing	0	-	20%	55%
PCI Within 90 Minutes of Arrival	0	-	91%	90%
Smoking Cessation Advice	0	-	100%	99%
Chest Pain/Possible Heart Attack Care				
Aspirin at Arrival	123	98%	96%	95%
Median Time to ECG (minutes)	134	7	7	8
Median Time to Transfer (minutes)[1]	3	50	68	61
Fibrinolytic Medication Timing[1]	7	100%	72%	54%
Heart Failure Care				
ACE Inhibitor or ARB for LVSD[1]	12	75%	94%	94%
Discharge Instructions[1]	21	81%	87%	88%
Evaluation of LVS Function	31	100%	96%	98%
Smoking Cessation Advice[1]	2	100%	96%	98%
Pneumonia Care				
Appropriate Initial Antibiotic	40	98%	91%	92%
Blood Culture Timing	54	100%	97%	96%
Influenza Vaccine	50	98%	91%	91%
Initial Antibiotic Timing	67	100%	97%	95%
Pneumococcal Vaccine	78	99%	92%	93%
Smoking Cessation Advice[1]	12	100%	90%	97%
Surgical Care Improvement Project				
Appropriate VTP Within 24 Hours	122	98%	94%	92%
Appropriate Hair Removal	231	100%	99%	99%
Appropriate Beta Blocker Usage	77	95%	94%	93%
Controlled Postoperative Blood Glucose	0	-	96%	93%
Prophylactic Antibiotic Timing	169	98%	97%	97%
Prophylactic Antibiotic Timing (Outpatient)	68	93%	93%	92%
Prophylactic Antibiotic Selection	168	98%	98%	97%
Prophylactic Antibiotic Select. (Outpatient)	65	94%	97%	94%
Prophylactic Antibiotic Stopped	163	96%	94%	94%
Recommended VTP Ordered	122	98%	95%	94%
Urinary Catheter Removal[1]	11	91%	90%	90%
Children's Asthma Care				
Received Systemic Corticosteroids	-	-	-	100%
Received Home Management Plan	-	-	-	71%
Received Reliever Medication	-	-	-	100%
Use of Medical Imaging				
Combination Abdominal CT Scan	389	0.771	0.152	0.191
Combination Chest CT Scan	348	0.011	0.033	0.054
Follow-up Mammogram/Ultrasound	734	1.2%	8.1%	8.4%
MRI for Low Back Pain	85	28.2%	33.8%	32.7%
Survey of Patients' Hospital Experiences				
Area Around Room 'Always' Quiet at Night	300+	51%	-	58%
Doctors 'Always' Communicated Well	300+	83%	-	80%
Home Recovery Information Given	300+	89%	-	82%
Hospital Given 9 or 10 on 10 Point Scale	300+	74%	-	67%
Meds 'Always' Explained Before Given	300+	63%	-	60%
Nurses 'Always' Communicated Well	300+	79%	-	76%
Pain 'Always' Well Controlled	300+	71%	-	69%
Room and Bathroom 'Always' Clean	300+	78%	-	71%
Timely Help 'Always' Received	300+	71%	-	64%
Would Definitely Recommend Hospital	300+	74%	-	69%

Cozad Community Hospital

300 East 12th St
Cozad, NE 69130
Phone: 308-784-2261
Fax: 308-784-4691
E-mail: info@cozadcommunityhealth.com
URL: www.cozadhealthcare.com
Type: Critical Access Hospitals
Emergency Services: Yes
Ownership: Voluntary Non-Profit - Other
Beds: 23

Key Personnel:

Infection Control. . . . . Jo Griffith
Operating Room. . . . . Cheryl Brooks
Quality Assurance . . . . Shirley Urwiller
Emergency Room . . . . Tammy McMichael

Measure	Cases	This Hosp.	State Avg.	U.S. Avg.
Heart Attack Care				
ACE Inhibitor or ARB for LVSD[5]	0	-	97%	96%
Aspirin at Arrival[5]	0	-	99%	99%
Aspirin at Discharge[5]	0	-	99%	98%
Beta Blocker at Discharge[5]	0	-	99%	98%
Fibrinolytic Medication Timing[5]	0	-	20%	55%
PCI Within 90 Minutes of Arrival[5]	0	-	91%	90%
Smoking Cessation Advice[5]	0	-	100%	99%
Chest Pain/Possible Heart Attack Care				
Aspirin at Arrival	-	-	96%	95%
Median Time to ECG (minutes)	-	-	7	8
Median Time to Transfer (minutes)	-	-	68	61
Fibrinolytic Medication Timing	-	-	72%	54%
Heart Failure Care				
ACE Inhibitor or ARB for LVSD	0	-	94%	94%
Discharge Instructions[1]	3	0%	87%	88%
Evaluation of LVS Function[1]	10	50%	96%	98%
Smoking Cessation Advice[1]	1	0%	96%	98%
Pneumonia Care				
Appropriate Initial Antibiotic[1,3]	5	100%	91%	92%
Blood Culture Timing[3]	0	-	97%	96%
Influenza Vaccine[1]	3	67%	91%	91%
Initial Antibiotic Timing[1,3]	5	100%	97%	95%
Pneumococcal Vaccine[1,3]	4	75%	92%	93%
Smoking Cessation Advice[1,3]	1	0%	90%	97%
Surgical Care Improvement Project				
Appropriate VTP Within 24 Hours[5]	0	-	94%	92%
Appropriate Hair Removal[5]	0	-	99%	99%
Appropriate Beta Blocker Usage[5]	0	-	94%	93%
Controlled Postoperative Blood Glucose[5]	0	-	96%	93%
Prophylactic Antibiotic Timing[5]	0	-	97%	97%
Prophylactic Antibiotic Timing (Outpatient)	-	-	93%	92%
Prophylactic Antibiotic Selection[5]	0	-	98%	97%
Prophylactic Antibiotic Select. (Outpatient)	-	-	97%	94%
Prophylactic Antibiotic Stopped[5]	0	-	94%	94%
Recommended VTP Ordered[5]	0	-	95%	94%
Urinary Catheter Removal[5]	0	-	90%	90%
Children's Asthma Care				
Received Systemic Corticosteroids	-	-	-	100%
Received Home Management Plan	-	-	-	71%
Received Reliever Medication	-	-	-	100%
Use of Medical Imaging				
Combination Abdominal CT Scan	-	-	0.152	0.191
Combination Chest CT Scan	-	-	0.033	0.054
Follow-up Mammogram/Ultrasound	-	-	8.1%	8.4%
MRI for Low Back Pain	-	-	33.8%	32.7%
Survey of Patients' Hospital Experiences				
Area Around Room 'Always' Quiet at Night[8]	-	-	-	58%
Doctors 'Always' Communicated Well[8]	-	-	-	80%
Home Recovery Information Given[8]	-	-	-	82%
Hospital Given 9 or 10 on 10 Point Scale[8]	-	-	-	67%
Meds 'Always' Explained Before Given[8]	-	-	-	60%
Nurses 'Always' Communicated Well[8]	-	-	-	76%
Pain 'Always' Well Controlled[8]	-	-	-	69%
Room and Bathroom 'Always' Clean[8]	-	-	-	71%
Timely Help 'Always' Received[8]	-	-	-	64%
Would Definitely Recommend Hospital[8]	-	-	-	69%

Avera Creighton Hospital

1503 Main St
Creighton, NE 68729
Phone: 402-358-5700
Fax: 402-358-5769
E-mail: marketing@cahs-ne.org
Type: Critical Access Hospitals
Emergency Services: Yes
Ownership: Government - Local
Beds: 69

Key Personnel:

CEO/President. . . . . Jeffrey A Lingerfelt
Chief of Medical Staff . . . . Ron Morris
Infection Control. . . . . Jean Henes
Operating Room. . . . . Barbara Nielsen

Measure	Cases	This Hosp.	State Avg.	U.S. Avg.
Heart Attack Care				
ACE Inhibitor or ARB for LVSD[1,3]	1	100%	97%	96%
Aspirin at Arrival[1,3]	1	0%	99%	99%
Aspirin at Discharge[1,3]	1	0%	99%	98%
Beta Blocker at Discharge[1,3]	1	100%	99%	98%
Fibrinolytic Medication Timing[3]	0	-	20%	55%
PCI Within 90 Minutes of Arrival[3]	0	-	91%	90%
Smoking Cessation Advice[3]	0	-	100%	99%
Chest Pain/Possible Heart Attack Care				
Aspirin at Arrival	-	-	96%	95%
Median Time to ECG (minutes)	-	-	7	8
Median Time to Transfer (minutes)	-	-	68	61
Fibrinolytic Medication Timing	-	-	72%	54%
Heart Failure Care				
ACE Inhibitor or ARB for LVSD[5]	0	-	94%	94%
Discharge Instructions[5]	0	-	87%	88%
Evaluation of LVS Function[5]	0	-	96%	98%
Smoking Cessation Advice[5]	0	-	96%	98%
Pneumonia Care				
Appropriate Initial Antibiotic	25	92%	91%	92%
Blood Culture Timing[1]	1	100%	97%	96%
Influenza Vaccine[1]	16	100%	91%	91%
Initial Antibiotic Timing[1]	20	100%	97%	95%
Pneumococcal Vaccine	34	97%	92%	93%
Smoking Cessation Advice[1]	8	88%	90%	97%
Surgical Care Improvement Project				
Appropriate VTP Within 24 Hours[5]	0	-	94%	92%
Appropriate Hair Removal[5]	0	-	99%	99%
Appropriate Beta Blocker Usage[5]	0	-	94%	93%
Controlled Postoperative Blood Glucose[5]	0	-	96%	93%
Prophylactic Antibiotic Timing[5]	0	-	97%	97%
Prophylactic Antibiotic Timing (Outpatient)	-	-	93%	92%
Prophylactic Antibiotic Selection[5]	0	-	98%	97%
Prophylactic Antibiotic Select. (Outpatient)	-	-	97%	94%
Prophylactic Antibiotic Stopped[5]	0	-	94%	94%
Recommended VTP Ordered[5]	0	-	95%	94%
Urinary Catheter Removal[5]	0	-	90%	90%
Children's Asthma Care				
Received Systemic Corticosteroids	-	-	-	100%
Received Home Management Plan	-	-	-	71%
Received Reliever Medication	-	-	-	100%
Use of Medical Imaging				
Combination Abdominal CT Scan	-	-	0.152	0.191
Combination Chest CT Scan	-	-	0.033	0.054
Follow-up Mammogram/Ultrasound	-	-	8.1%	8.4%
MRI for Low Back Pain	-	-	33.8%	32.7%
Survey of Patients' Hospital Experiences				
Area Around Room 'Always' Quiet at Night[6]	<100	52%	-	58%
Doctors 'Always' Communicated Well[6]	<100	81%	-	80%
Home Recovery Information Given[6]	<100	79%	-	82%
Hospital Given 9 or 10 on 10 Point Scale[6]	<100	71%	-	67%
Meds 'Always' Explained Before Given[6]	<100	51%	-	60%
Nurses 'Always' Communicated Well[6]	<100	78%	-	76%
Pain 'Always' Well Controlled[6]	<100	73%	-	69%
Room and Bathroom 'Always' Clean[6]	<100	84%	-	71%
Timely Help 'Always' Received[6]	<100	70%	-	64%
Would Definitely Recommend Hospital	<100	70%	-	69%

NOTE: Hospital profiles are in alphabetical order by state, then city, then hospital within the city; Rankings exclude hospitals with less than 25 cases except for patient surveys which excludes hospitals with less than 100 cases; (a) 100–299 cases; (1) The number of cases is too small to be sure how well a hospital is performing; (2) The hospital indicated that the data submitted for this measure were based on a sample of cases; (3) Data was collected during a shorter time period (fewer quarters) than the maximum possible time for this measure; (4) Suppressed for one or more quarters by CMS; (5) No data is available from the hospital for this measure; (6) Fewer than 100 patients completed the HCAHPS survey. Use these rates with caution, as the number of surveys may be too low to reliably assess hospital performance; (7) Survey results are based on less than 12 months of data; (8) Survey results are not available for this reporting period; (9) No or very few patients were eligible for the HCAHPS survey. The scores shown, if any, reflect a very small number of surveys; (10) A state average was not calculated because too few hospitals in the state submitted data; (11) There were discrepancies in the data collection process; Please refer to the User's Guide for a full explanation of data.

Crete Area Medical Center

2910 Betten Dr
Crete, NE 68333
Phone: 402-826-7997
Fax: 402-826-7950
URL: www.creteareamedicalcenter.com

Type: Critical Access Hospitals
Emergency Services: Yes
Ownership: Voluntary Non-Profit - Private
Beds: 57

Key Personnel:
CEO/President. . . . . Carol Friesen
Chief of Medical Staff. . . . . Robert Tuma, MD

Measure	Cases	This Hosp.	State Avg.	U.S. Avg.
Heart Attack Care				
ACE Inhibitor or ARB for LVSD[3]	0	-	97%	96%
Aspirin at Arrival[1,3]	1	100%	99%	99%
Aspirin at Discharge[1,3]	1	100%	99%	98%
Beta Blocker at Discharge[1,3]	1	100%	99%	98%
Fibrinolytic Medication Timing[3]	0	-	20%	55%
PCI Within 90 Minutes of Arrival[3]	0	-	91%	90%
Smoking Cessation Advice[3]	0	-	100%	99%
Chest Pain/Possible Heart Attack Care				
Aspirin at Arrival	-	-	96%	95%
Median Time to ECG (minutes)	-	-	7	8
Median Time to Transfer (minutes)	-	-	68	61
Fibrinolytic Medication Timing	-	-	72%	54%
Heart Failure Care				
ACE Inhibitor or ARB for LVSD[1]	2	50%	94%	94%
Discharge Instructions[1]	9	44%	87%	88%
Evaluation of LVS Function[1]	14	86%	96%	98%
Smoking Cessation Advice	0	-	96%	98%
Pneumonia Care				
Appropriate Initial Antibiotic[1]	9	89%	91%	92%
Blood Culture Timing[1]	4	100%	97%	96%
Influenza Vaccine[1]	9	78%	91%	91%
Initial Antibiotic Timing[1]	17	94%	97%	95%
Pneumococcal Vaccine[1]	16	69%	92%	93%
Smoking Cessation Advice[1]	3	100%	90%	97%
Surgical Care Improvement Project				
Appropriate VTP Within 24 Hours[5]	0	-	94%	92%
Appropriate Hair Removal[5]	0	-	99%	99%
Appropriate Beta Blocker Usage[5]	0	-	94%	93%
Controlled Postoperative Blood Glucose[5]	0	-	96%	93%
Prophylactic Antibiotic Timing[5]	0	-	97%	97%
Prophylactic Antibiotic Timing (Outpatient)	-	-	93%	92%
Prophylactic Antibiotic Selection[5]	0	-	98%	97%
Prophylactic Antibiotic Select. (Outpatient)	-	-	97%	94%
Prophylactic Antibiotic Stopped[5]	0	-	94%	94%
Recommended VTP Ordered[5]	0	-	95%	94%
Urinary Catheter Removal[5]	0	-	90%	90%
Children's Asthma Care				
Received Systemic Corticosteroids	-	-	-	100%
Received Home Management Plan	-	-	-	71%
Received Reliever Medication	-	-	-	100%
Use of Medical Imaging				
Combination Abdominal CT Scan	-	-	0.152	0.191
Combination Chest CT Scan	-	-	0.033	0.054
Follow-up Mammogram/Ultrasound	-	-	8.1%	8.4%
MRI for Low Back Pain	-	-	33.8%	32.7%
Survey of Patients' Hospital Experiences				
Area Around Room 'Always' Quiet at Night[6]	<100	68%	-	58%
Doctors 'Always' Communicated Well[6]	<100	86%	-	80%
Home Recovery Information Given[6]	<100	83%	-	82%
Hospital Given 9 or 10 on 10 Point Scale[6]	<100	80%	-	67%
Meds 'Always' Explained Before Given[6]	<100	62%	-	60%
Nurses 'Always' Communicated Well[6]	<100	77%	-	76%
Pain 'Always' Well Controlled[6]	<100	65%	-	69%
Room and Bathroom 'Always' Clean[6]	<100	82%	-	71%
Timely Help 'Always' Received[6]	<100	56%	-	64%
Would Definitely Recommend Hospital	<100	72%	-	69%

Butler County Health Care Center

372 South 9th St
David City, NE 68632
Phone: 402-367-1200
Fax: 402-367-1350
URL: www.bchccnet.org

Type: Critical Access Hospitals
Emergency Services: Yes
Ownership: Government - Local
Beds: 20

Key Personnel:
CEO/President. . . . . Donald T Naiberk
Chief of Medical Staff . . . . Dr. Victor Thoendel, MD
Infection Control. . . . . Connie Janicek, RN
Operating Room. . . . . Joyce Jelinek, RN
Quality Assurance . . . . Lucy Roberts, RN
Radiology. . . . . Allan Steinberg
Anesthesiology. . . . . Corey Kavan, CRNA
Emergency Room . . . . Sue Birkel, RN

Measure	Cases	This Hosp.	State Avg.	U.S. Avg.
Heart Attack Care				
ACE Inhibitor or ARB for LVSD[3]	0	-	97%	96%
Aspirin at Arrival[1,3]	1	100%	99%	99%
Aspirin at Discharge[1,3]	1	0%	99%	98%
Beta Blocker at Discharge[3]	0	-	99%	98%
Fibrinolytic Medication Timing[3]	0	-	20%	55%
PCI Within 90 Minutes of Arrival[3]	0	-	91%	90%
Smoking Cessation Advice[3]	0	-	100%	99%
Chest Pain/Possible Heart Attack Care				
Aspirin at Arrival	-	-	96%	95%
Median Time to ECG (minutes)	-	-	7	8
Median Time to Transfer (minutes)	-	-	68	61
Fibrinolytic Medication Timing	-	-	72%	54%
Heart Failure Care				
ACE Inhibitor or ARB for LVSD[1]	2	100%	94%	94%
Discharge Instructions[1]	9	67%	87%	88%
Evaluation of LVS Function[1]	13	54%	96%	98%
Smoking Cessation Advice[1]	1	0%	96%	98%
Pneumonia Care				
Appropriate Initial Antibiotic[1]	10	90%	91%	92%
Blood Culture Timing	0	-	97%	96%
Influenza Vaccine[1]	12	75%	91%	91%
Initial Antibiotic Timing[1]	11	100%	97%	95%
Pneumococcal Vaccine[1]	14	79%	92%	93%
Smoking Cessation Advice	0	-	90%	97%
Surgical Care Improvement Project				
Appropriate VTP Within 24 Hours[1]	2	100%	94%	92%
Appropriate Hair Removal[1]	18	100%	99%	99%
Appropriate Beta Blocker Usage[5]	0	-	94%	93%
Controlled Postoperative Blood Glucose	0	-	96%	93%
Prophylactic Antibiotic Timing[1]	22	86%	97%	97%
Prophylactic Antibiotic Timing (Outpatient)	-	-	93%	92%
Prophylactic Antibiotic Selection[1]	22	86%	98%	97%
Prophylactic Antibiotic Select. (Outpatient)	-	-	97%	94%
Prophylactic Antibiotic Stopped[1]	22	95%	94%	94%
Recommended VTP Ordered[1]	2	100%	95%	94%
Urinary Catheter Removal	0	-	90%	90%
Children's Asthma Care				
Received Systemic Corticosteroids	-	-	-	100%
Received Home Management Plan	-	-	-	71%
Received Reliever Medication	-	-	-	100%
Use of Medical Imaging				
Combination Abdominal CT Scan	-	-	0.152	0.191
Combination Chest CT Scan	-	-	0.033	0.054
Follow-up Mammogram/Ultrasound	-	-	8.1%	8.4%
MRI for Low Back Pain	-	-	33.8%	32.7%
Survey of Patients' Hospital Experiences				
Area Around Room 'Always' Quiet at Night[8]	-	-	-	58%
Doctors 'Always' Communicated Well[8]	-	-	-	80%
Home Recovery Information Given[8]	-	-	-	82%
Hospital Given 9 or 10 on 10 Point Scale[8]	-	-	-	67%
Meds 'Always' Explained Before Given[8]	-	-	-	60%
Nurses 'Always' Communicated Well[8]	-	-	-	76%
Pain 'Always' Well Controlled[8]	-	-	-	69%
Room and Bathroom 'Always' Clean[8]	-	-	-	71%
Timely Help 'Always' Received[8]	-	-	-	64%
Would Definitely Recommend Hospital[8]	-	-	-	69%

Jefferson Community Health Center

2200 H St
Fairbury, NE 68352
Phone: 402-729-3351
Fax: 402-729-2102
E-mail: lana.likens@jchc.us
URL: www.jchc.us

Type: Critical Access Hospitals
Emergency Services: Yes
Ownership: Voluntary Non-Profit - Private
Beds: 33

Key Personnel:
CEO/President. . . . . Bill Welch
Cardiac Laboratory. . . . . Elsiee Houser
Chief of Medical Staff. . . . . Craig Shumard, MD
Infection Control. . . . . Mary Heidemann
Operating Room. . . . . Ermel Heuer, RN
Quality Assurance . . . . Sharon Vandegrift
Radiology. . . . . Caryn Bales, RT
Emergency Room . . . . Judy McGee, CNE

Measure	Cases	This Hosp.	State Avg.	U.S. Avg.
Heart Attack Care				
ACE Inhibitor or ARB for LVSD[1,3]	1	100%	97%	96%
Aspirin at Arrival[1,3]	1	100%	99%	99%
Aspirin at Discharge[1,3]	1	100%	99%	98%
Beta Blocker at Discharge[1,3]	1	100%	99%	98%
Fibrinolytic Medication Timing[3]	0	-	20%	55%
PCI Within 90 Minutes of Arrival[3]	0	-	91%	90%
Smoking Cessation Advice[3]	0	-	100%	99%
Chest Pain/Possible Heart Attack Care				
Aspirin at Arrival	27	100%	96%	95%
Median Time to ECG (minutes)	32	23	7	8
Median Time to Transfer (minutes)[5]	0	-	68	61
Fibrinolytic Medication Timing[3]	0	-	72%	54%
Heart Failure Care				
ACE Inhibitor or ARB for LVSD[1,2]	1	100%	94%	94%
Discharge Instructions[1,2]	2	100%	87%	88%
Evaluation of LVS Function[1,2]	5	100%	96%	98%
Smoking Cessation Advice[2]	0	-	96%	98%
Pneumonia Care				
Appropriate Initial Antibiotic[1]	14	100%	91%	92%
Blood Culture Timing[1]	2	100%	97%	96%
Influenza Vaccine[1]	11	91%	91%	91%
Initial Antibiotic Timing[1]	17	100%	97%	95%
Pneumococcal Vaccine[1]	17	100%	92%	93%
Smoking Cessation Advice[1]	4	100%	90%	97%
Surgical Care Improvement Project				
Appropriate VTP Within 24 Hours[1]	6	100%	94%	92%
Appropriate Hair Removal[1]	19	100%	99%	99%
Appropriate Beta Blocker Usage[5]	0	-	94%	93%
Controlled Postoperative Blood Glucose	0	-	96%	93%
Prophylactic Antibiotic Timing[1]	14	100%	97%	97%
Prophylactic Antibiotic Timing (Outpatient)[5]	0	-	93%	92%
Prophylactic Antibiotic Selection[1]	14	100%	98%	97%
Prophylactic Antibiotic Select. (Outpatient)[5]	0	-	97%	94%
Prophylactic Antibiotic Stopped[1]	14	93%	94%	94%
Recommended VTP Ordered[1]	6	100%	95%	94%
Urinary Catheter Removal[1]	5	100%	90%	90%
Children's Asthma Care				
Received Systemic Corticosteroids	-	-	-	100%
Received Home Management Plan	-	-	-	71%
Received Reliever Medication	-	-	-	100%
Use of Medical Imaging				
Combination Abdominal CT Scan	85	0.071	0.152	0.191
Combination Chest CT Scan	63	0.016	0.033	0.054
Follow-up Mammogram/Ultrasound	221	10.0%	8.1%	8.4%
MRI for Low Back Pain[1]	15	20.0%	33.8%	32.7%
Survey of Patients' Hospital Experiences				
Area Around Room 'Always' Quiet at Night[8]	-	-	-	58%
Doctors 'Always' Communicated Well[8]	-	-	-	80%
Home Recovery Information Given[8]	-	-	-	82%
Hospital Given 9 or 10 on 10 Point Scale[8]	-	-	-	67%
Meds 'Always' Explained Before Given[8]	-	-	-	60%
Nurses 'Always' Communicated Well[8]	-	-	-	76%
Pain 'Always' Well Controlled[8]	-	-	-	69%
Room and Bathroom 'Always' Clean[8]	-	-	-	71%
Timely Help 'Always' Received[8]	-	-	-	64%
Would Definitely Recommend Hospital[8]	-	-	-	69%

NOTE: Hospital profiles are in alphabetical order by state, then city, then hospital within the city; Rankings exclude hospitals with less than 25 cases except for patient surveys which excludes hospitals with less than 100 cases; (a) 100–299 cases; (1) The number of cases is too small to be sure how well a hospital is performing; (2) The hospital indicated that the data submitted for this measure were based on a sample of cases; (3) Data was collected during a shorter time period (fewer quarters) than the maximum possible time for this measure; (4) Suppressed for one or more quarters by CMS; (5) No data is available from the hospital for this measure; (6) Fewer than 100 patients completed the HCAHPS survey. Use these rates with caution, as the number of surveys may be too low to reliably assess hospital performance; (7) Survey results are based on less than 12 months of data; (8) Survey results are not available for this reporting period; (9) No or very few patients were eligible for the HCAHPS survey. The scores shown, if any, reflect a very small number of surveys; (10) A state average was not calculated because too few hospitals in the state submitted data; (11) There were discrepancies in the data collection process; Please refer to the User's Guide for a full explanation of data.

Community Medical Center

3307 Barada St Phone: 402-245-2428
Falls City, NE 68355 Fax: 402-245-4841
URL: www.hhs.state.ne.us/index.htm
Type: Critical Access Hospitals Emergency Services: Yes
Ownership: Voluntary Non-Profit - Private Beds: 35

Key Personnel:
Chief of Medical Staff.......... Joann Schaefer

Measure	Cases	This Hosp.	State Avg.	U.S. Avg.
Heart Attack Care				
ACE Inhibitor or ARB for LVSD[5]	0	-	97%	96%
Aspirin at Arrival[5]	0	-	99%	99%
Aspirin at Discharge[5]	0	-	99%	98%
Beta Blocker at Discharge[5]	0	-	99%	98%
Fibrinolytic Medication Timing[5]	0	-	20%	55%
PCI Within 90 Minutes of Arrival[5]	0	-	91%	90%
Smoking Cessation Advice[5]	0	-	100%	99%
Chest Pain/Possible Heart Attack Care				
Aspirin at Arrival[1]	17	94%	96%	95%
Median Time to ECG (minutes)[1]	16	17	7	8
Median Time to Transfer (minutes)[5]	0	-	68	61
Fibrinolytic Medication Timing[5]	0	-	72%	54%
Heart Failure Care				
ACE Inhibitor or ARB for LVSD[1]	6	83%	94%	94%
Discharge Instructions[1]	11	73%	87%	88%
Evaluation of LVS Function[1]	17	88%	96%	98%
Smoking Cessation Advice[1]	2	100%	96%	98%
Pneumonia Care				
Appropriate Initial Antibiotic[1]	10	100%	91%	92%
Blood Culture Timing[1]	3	100%	97%	96%
Influenza Vaccine[1]	9	100%	91%	91%
Initial Antibiotic Timing[1]	16	88%	97%	95%
Pneumococcal Vaccine[1]	17	88%	92%	93%
Smoking Cessation Advice[1]	5	100%	90%	97%
Surgical Care Improvement Project				
Appropriate VTP Within 24 Hours[1,3]	2	50%	94%	92%
Appropriate Hair Removal[1,3]	3	100%	99%	99%
Appropriate Beta Blocker Usage[5]	0	-	94%	93%
Controlled Postoperative Blood Glucose[3]	0	-	96%	93%
Prophylactic Antibiotic Timing[1,3]	2	100%	97%	97%
Prophylactic Antibiotic Timing (Outpatient)[5]	0	-	93%	92%
Prophylactic Antibiotic Selection[1,3]	2	50%	98%	97%
Prophylactic Antibiotic Select. (Outpatient)[5]	0	-	97%	94%
Prophylactic Antibiotic Stopped[1,3]	2	50%	94%	94%
Recommended VTP Ordered[1,3]	2	50%	95%	94%
Urinary Catheter Removal[1]	2	0%	90%	90%
Children's Asthma Care				
Received Systemic Corticosteroids	-	-	-	100%
Received Home Management Plan	-	-	-	71%
Received Reliever Medication	-	-	-	100%
Use of Medical Imaging				
Combination Abdominal CT Scan	103	0.155	0.152	0.191
Combination Chest CT Scan	73	0.041	0.033	0.054
Follow-up Mammogram/Ultrasound	109	4.6%	8.1%	8.4%
MRI for Low Back Pain[1]	36	33.3%	33.8%	32.7%
Survey of Patients' Hospital Experiences				
Area Around Room 'Always' Quiet at Night[8]	-	-	-	58%
Doctors 'Always' Communicated Well[8]	-	-	-	80%
Home Recovery Information Given[8]	-	-	-	82%
Hospital Given 9 or 10 on 10 Point Scale[8]	-	-	-	67%
Meds 'Always' Explained Before Given[8]	-	-	-	60%
Nurses 'Always' Communicated Well[8]	-	-	-	76%
Pain 'Always' Well Controlled[8]	-	-	-	69%
Room and Bathroom 'Always' Clean[8]	-	-	-	71%
Timely Help 'Always' Received[8]	-	-	-	64%
Would Definitely Recommend Hospital[8]	-	-	-	69%

Franklin County Memorial Hospital

1406 Q St Phone: 308-425-6221
Franklin, NE 68939 Fax: 308-425-3164
URL: www.franklincountymemorialhospital.org
Type: Critical Access Hospitals Emergency Services: Yes
Ownership: Government - Local Beds: 12

Key Personnel:
CEO/President............... Jerrell F Gerdes, FACHE
Cardiac Laboratory............ Gaylene Wentworth
Chief of Medical Staff.......... Linda Mazour

Measure	Cases	This Hosp.	State Avg.	U.S. Avg.
Heart Attack Care				
ACE Inhibitor or ARB for LVSD[5]	0	-	97%	96%
Aspirin at Arrival[5]	0	-	99%	99%
Aspirin at Discharge[5]	0	-	99%	98%
Beta Blocker at Discharge[5]	0	-	99%	98%
Fibrinolytic Medication Timing[5]	0	-	20%	55%
PCI Within 90 Minutes of Arrival[5]	0	-	91%	90%
Smoking Cessation Advice[5]	0	-	100%	99%
Chest Pain/Possible Heart Attack Care				
Aspirin at Arrival	-	-	96%	95%
Median Time to ECG (minutes)	-	-	7	8
Median Time to Transfer (minutes)	-	-	68	61
Fibrinolytic Medication Timing	-	-	72%	54%
Heart Failure Care				
ACE Inhibitor or ARB for LVSD[3]	0	-	94%	94%
Discharge Instructions[1,3]	4	0%	87%	88%
Evaluation of LVS Function[1,3]	6	50%	96%	98%
Smoking Cessation Advice[3]	0	-	96%	98%
Pneumonia Care				
Appropriate Initial Antibiotic[1,3]	10	100%	91%	92%
Blood Culture Timing[1,3]	1	100%	97%	96%
Influenza Vaccine[1]	9	100%	91%	91%
Initial Antibiotic Timing[1,3]	17	100%	97%	95%
Pneumococcal Vaccine[1,3]	8	100%	92%	93%
Smoking Cessation Advice[1,3]	3	67%	90%	97%
Surgical Care Improvement Project				
Appropriate VTP Within 24 Hours[5]	0	-	94%	92%
Appropriate Hair Removal[5]	0	-	99%	99%
Appropriate Beta Blocker Usage[5]	0	-	94%	93%
Controlled Postoperative Blood Glucose[5]	0	-	96%	93%
Prophylactic Antibiotic Timing[5]	0	-	97%	97%
Prophylactic Antibiotic Timing (Outpatient)	-	-	93%	92%
Prophylactic Antibiotic Selection[5]	0	-	98%	97%
Prophylactic Antibiotic Select. (Outpatient)	-	-	97%	94%
Prophylactic Antibiotic Stopped[5]	0	-	94%	94%
Recommended VTP Ordered[5]	0	-	95%	94%
Urinary Catheter Removal[5]	0	-	90%	90%
Children's Asthma Care				
Received Systemic Corticosteroids	-	-	-	100%
Received Home Management Plan	-	-	-	71%
Received Reliever Medication	-	-	-	100%
Use of Medical Imaging				
Combination Abdominal CT Scan	-	-	0.152	0.191
Combination Chest CT Scan	-	-	0.033	0.054
Follow-up Mammogram/Ultrasound	-	-	8.1%	8.4%
MRI for Low Back Pain	-	-	33.8%	32.7%
Survey of Patients' Hospital Experiences				
Area Around Room 'Always' Quiet at Night[8]	-	-	-	58%
Doctors 'Always' Communicated Well[8]	-	-	-	80%
Home Recovery Information Given[8]	-	-	-	82%
Hospital Given 9 or 10 on 10 Point Scale[8]	-	-	-	67%
Meds 'Always' Explained Before Given[8]	-	-	-	60%
Nurses 'Always' Communicated Well[8]	-	-	-	76%
Pain 'Always' Well Controlled[8]	-	-	-	69%
Room and Bathroom 'Always' Clean[8]	-	-	-	71%
Timely Help 'Always' Received[8]	-	-	-	64%
Would Definitely Recommend Hospital[8]	-	-	-	69%

Fremont Area Medical Center

450 East 23rd St Phone: 402-721-1610
Fremont, NE 68025 Fax: 402-727-3433
Type: Acute Care Hospitals Emergency Services: Yes
Ownership: Government - Local Beds: 262

Key Personnel:
CEO/President............... Michael Leibert
Cardiac Laboratory............ Brian Brodd
Infection Control.............. Gerri Means
Operating Room............. Don Tricarico
Radiology................. Duane Krause, MD
Anesthesiology............. Jeffrey N Hawthorne, MD
Emergency Room............ Brian K Elliott, MD

Measure	Cases	This Hosp.	State Avg.	U.S. Avg.
Heart Attack Care				
ACE Inhibitor or ARB for LVSD[1]	3	100%	97%	96%
Aspirin at Arrival	28	100%	99%	99%
Aspirin at Discharge	27	100%	99%	98%
Beta Blocker at Discharge[1]	24	100%	99%	98%
Fibrinolytic Medication Timing	0	-	20%	55%
PCI Within 90 Minutes of Arrival[1]	3	100%	91%	90%
Smoking Cessation Advice[1]	6	100%	100%	99%
Chest Pain/Possible Heart Attack Care				
Aspirin at Arrival	38	100%	96%	95%
Median Time to ECG (minutes)	38	6	7	8
Median Time to Transfer (minutes)[1,3]	2	56	68	61
Fibrinolytic Medication Timing[1]	1	100%	72%	54%
Heart Failure Care				
ACE Inhibitor or ARB for LVSD[1]	16	100%	94%	94%
Discharge Instructions	35	100%	87%	88%
Evaluation of LVS Function	79	100%	96%	98%
Smoking Cessation Advice[1]	5	100%	96%	98%
Pneumonia Care				
Appropriate Initial Antibiotic	63	94%	91%	92%
Blood Culture Timing	88	99%	97%	96%
Influenza Vaccine	66	91%	91%	91%
Initial Antibiotic Timing	98	99%	97%	95%
Pneumococcal Vaccine	95	99%	92%	93%
Smoking Cessation Advice[1]	20	95%	90%	97%
Surgical Care Improvement Project				
Appropriate VTP Within 24 Hours[2]	96	100%	94%	92%
Appropriate Hair Removal[2]	474	100%	99%	99%
Appropriate Beta Blocker Usage[2]	126	100%	94%	93%
Controlled Postoperative Blood Glucose[2]	0	-	96%	93%
Prophylactic Antibiotic Timing[2]	361	98%	97%	97%
Prophylactic Antibiotic Timing (Outpatient)	53	79%	93%	92%
Prophylactic Antibiotic Selection[2]	361	99%	98%	97%
Prophylactic Antibiotic Select. (Outpatient)	53	87%	97%	94%
Prophylactic Antibiotic Stopped[2]	355	91%	94%	94%
Recommended VTP Ordered[2]	96	100%	95%	94%
Urinary Catheter Removal[2]	69	94%	90%	90%
Children's Asthma Care				
Received Systemic Corticosteroids	-	-	-	100%
Received Home Management Plan	-	-	-	71%
Received Reliever Medication	-	-	-	100%
Use of Medical Imaging				
Combination Abdominal CT Scan	526	0.772	0.152	0.191
Combination Chest CT Scan	613	0.003	0.033	0.054
Follow-up Mammogram/Ultrasound	1,420	3.5%	8.1%	8.4%
MRI for Low Back Pain	207	26.1%	33.8%	32.7%
Survey of Patients' Hospital Experiences				
Area Around Room 'Always' Quiet at Night	300+	56%	-	58%
Doctors 'Always' Communicated Well	300+	83%	-	80%
Home Recovery Information Given	300+	86%	-	82%
Hospital Given 9 or 10 on 10 Point Scale	300+	71%	-	67%
Meds 'Always' Explained Before Given	300+	65%	-	60%
Nurses 'Always' Communicated Well	300+	81%	-	76%
Pain 'Always' Well Controlled	300+	73%	-	69%
Room and Bathroom 'Always' Clean	300+	80%	-	71%
Timely Help 'Always' Received	300+	69%	-	64%
Would Definitely Recommend Hospital	300+	68%	-	69%

NOTE: Hospital profiles are in alphabetical order by state, then city, then hospital within the city; Rankings exclude hospitals with less than 25 cases except for patient surveys which excludes hospitals with less than 100 cases; (a) 100–299 cases; (1) The number of cases is too small to be sure how well a hospital is performing; (2) The hospital indicated that the data submitted for this measure were based on a sample of cases; (3) Data was collected during a shorter time period (fewer quarters) than the maximum possible time for this measure; (4) Suppressed for one or more quarters by CMS; (5) No data is available from the hospital for this measure; (6) Fewer than 100 patients completed the HCAHPS survey. Use these rates with caution, as the number of surveys may be too low to reliably assess hospital performance; (7) Survey results are based on less than 12 months of data; (8) Survey results are not available for this reporting period; (9) No or very few patients were eligible for the HCAHPS survey. The scores shown, if any, reflect a very small number of surveys; (10) A state average was not calculated because too few hospitals in the state submitted data; (11) There were discrepancies in the data collection process; Please refer to the User's Guide for a full explanation of data.

Warren Memorial Hospital

905 Second St
Friend, NE 68359
Phone: 402-947-2541
Fax: 402-947-2881
URL: www.warrenmemorialhospital.org
Type: Critical Access Hospitals
Emergency Services: Yes
Ownership: Government - Local
Beds: 15

Key Personnel:
CEO/President. . . . . John Wilson
Chief of Medical Staff . . . . Dr Roger Meyer
Radiology. . . . . Tiphanie Potter

Measure	Cases	This Hosp.	State Avg.	U.S. Avg.
Heart Attack Care				
ACE Inhibitor or ARB for LVSD[5]	0	-	97%	96%
Aspirin at Arrival[5]	0	-	99%	99%
Aspirin at Discharge[5]	0	-	99%	98%
Beta Blocker at Discharge[5]	0	-	99%	98%
Fibrinolytic Medication Timing[5]	0	-	20%	55%
PCI Within 90 Minutes of Arrival[5]	0	-	91%	90%
Smoking Cessation Advice[5]	0	-	100%	99%
Chest Pain/Possible Heart Attack Care				
Aspirin at Arrival	-	-	96%	95%
Median Time to ECG (minutes)	-	-	7	8
Median Time to Transfer (minutes)	-	-	68	61
Fibrinolytic Medication Timing	-	-	72%	54%
Heart Failure Care				
ACE Inhibitor or ARB for LVSD[3]	0	-	94%	94%
Discharge Instructions[3]	0	-	87%	88%
Evaluation of LVS Function[3]	0	-	96%	98%
Smoking Cessation Advice[3]	0	-	96%	98%
Pneumonia Care				
Appropriate Initial Antibiotic[5]	0	-	91%	92%
Blood Culture Timing[5]	0	-	97%	96%
Influenza Vaccine[5]	0	-	91%	91%
Initial Antibiotic Timing[5]	0	-	97%	95%
Pneumococcal Vaccine[5]	0	-	92%	93%
Smoking Cessation Advice[5]	0	-	90%	97%
Surgical Care Improvement Project				
Appropriate VTP Within 24 Hours[5]	0	-	94%	92%
Appropriate Hair Removal[5]	0	-	99%	99%
Appropriate Beta Blocker Usage[5]	0	-	94%	93%
Controlled Postoperative Blood Glucose[5]	0	-	96%	93%
Prophylactic Antibiotic Timing[5]	0	-	97%	97%
Prophylactic Antibiotic Timing (Outpatient)	-	-	93%	92%
Prophylactic Antibiotic Selection[5]	0	-	98%	97%
Prophylactic Antibiotic Select. (Outpatient)	-	-	97%	94%
Prophylactic Antibiotic Stopped[5]	0	-	94%	94%
Recommended VTP Ordered[5]	0	-	95%	94%
Urinary Catheter Removal[5]	0	-	90%	90%
Children's Asthma Care				
Received Systemic Corticosteroids	-	-	-	100%
Received Home Management Plan	-	-	-	71%
Received Reliever Medication	-	-	-	100%
Use of Medical Imaging				
Combination Abdominal CT Scan	-	-	0.152	0.191
Combination Chest CT Scan	-	-	0.033	0.054
Follow-up Mammogram/Ultrasound	-	-	8.1%	8.4%
MRI for Low Back Pain	-	-	33.8%	32.7%
Survey of Patients' Hospital Experiences				
Area Around Room 'Always' Quiet at Night[8]	-	-	-	58%
Doctors 'Always' Communicated Well[8]	-	-	-	80%
Home Recovery Information Given[8]	-	-	-	82%
Hospital Given 9 or 10 on 10 Point Scale[8]	-	-	-	67%
Meds 'Always' Explained Before Given[8]	-	-	-	60%
Nurses 'Always' Communicated Well[8]	-	-	-	76%
Pain 'Always' Well Controlled[8]	-	-	-	69%
Room and Bathroom 'Always' Clean[8]	-	-	-	71%
Timely Help 'Always' Received[8]	-	-	-	64%
Would Definitely Recommend Hospital[8]	-	-	-	69%

Fillmore County Hospital

1325 H Street
Geneva, NE 68361
Phone: 402-759-3167
Fax: 402-759-3093
URL: www.fhsofgeneva.org
Type: Critical Access Hospitals
Emergency Services: Yes
Ownership: Government - Local
Beds: 25

Key Personnel:
CEO/President. . . . . Paul Utemark
Cardiac Laboratory. . . . . Ron Fleecs

Measure	Cases	This Hosp.	State Avg.	U.S. Avg.
Heart Attack Care				
ACE Inhibitor or ARB for LVSD[3]	0	-	97%	96%
Aspirin at Arrival[1,3]	1	100%	99%	99%
Aspirin at Discharge[1,3]	1	100%	99%	98%
Beta Blocker at Discharge[1,3]	1	100%	99%	98%
Fibrinolytic Medication Timing[3]	0	-	20%	55%
PCI Within 90 Minutes of Arrival[3]	0	-	91%	90%
Smoking Cessation Advice[3]	0	-	100%	99%
Chest Pain/Possible Heart Attack Care				
Aspirin at Arrival	-	-	96%	95%
Median Time to ECG (minutes)	-	-	7	8
Median Time to Transfer (minutes)	-	-	68	61
Fibrinolytic Medication Timing	-	-	72%	54%
Heart Failure Care				
ACE Inhibitor or ARB for LVSD	0	-	94%	94%
Discharge Instructions[1]	7	0%	87%	88%
Evaluation of LVS Function[1]	11	45%	96%	98%
Smoking Cessation Advice	0	-	96%	98%
Pneumonia Care				
Appropriate Initial Antibiotic[1]	6	100%	91%	92%
Blood Culture Timing[1]	2	100%	97%	96%
Influenza Vaccine[1]	8	100%	91%	91%
Initial Antibiotic Timing[1]	9	100%	97%	95%
Pneumococcal Vaccine[1]	12	92%	92%	93%
Smoking Cessation Advice	0	-	90%	97%
Surgical Care Improvement Project				
Appropriate VTP Within 24 Hours[1]	7	71%	94%	92%
Appropriate Hair Removal[1]	10	100%	99%	99%
Appropriate Beta Blocker Usage[5]	0	-	94%	93%
Controlled Postoperative Blood Glucose	0	-	96%	93%
Prophylactic Antibiotic Timing[1]	9	67%	97%	97%
Prophylactic Antibiotic Timing (Outpatient)	-	-	93%	92%
Prophylactic Antibiotic Selection[1]	10	100%	98%	97%
Prophylactic Antibiotic Select. (Outpatient)	-	-	97%	94%
Prophylactic Antibiotic Stopped[1]	9	78%	94%	94%
Recommended VTP Ordered[1]	7	71%	95%	94%
Urinary Catheter Removal[1]	3	67%	90%	90%
Children's Asthma Care				
Received Systemic Corticosteroids	-	-	-	100%
Received Home Management Plan	-	-	-	71%
Received Reliever Medication	-	-	-	100%
Use of Medical Imaging				
Combination Abdominal CT Scan	-	-	0.152	0.191
Combination Chest CT Scan	-	-	0.033	0.054
Follow-up Mammogram/Ultrasound	-	-	8.1%	8.4%
MRI for Low Back Pain	-	-	33.8%	32.7%
Survey of Patients' Hospital Experiences				
Area Around Room 'Always' Quiet at Night[8]	-	-	-	58%
Doctors 'Always' Communicated Well[8]	-	-	-	80%
Home Recovery Information Given[8]	-	-	-	82%
Hospital Given 9 or 10 on 10 Point Scale[8]	-	-	-	67%
Meds 'Always' Explained Before Given[8]	-	-	-	60%
Nurses 'Always' Communicated Well[8]	-	-	-	76%
Pain 'Always' Well Controlled[8]	-	-	-	69%
Room and Bathroom 'Always' Clean[8]	-	-	-	71%
Timely Help 'Always' Received[8]	-	-	-	64%
Would Definitely Recommend Hospital[8]	-	-	-	69%

Gordon Memorial Hospital District

300 East 8th St
Gordon, NE 69343
Phone: 308-282-0401
Fax: 308-282-0431
URL: www.gordonhospital.org
Type: Critical Access Hospitals
Emergency Services: Yes
Ownership: Govt - Hospital Dist/Auth
Beds: 25

Key Personnel:
CEO/President. . . . . Jim Lebrun
Chief of Medical Staff . . . . Anthony Van Bang, MD
Infection Control. . . . . Kathie King, RN BSN
Operating Room. . . . . Andrea Parks, RN
Quality Assurance . . . . Kathy King, RN BSN
Radiology. . . . . Corrinew Larson, RT, ARRT
Anesthesiology. . . . . Marty Lambert

Measure	Cases	This Hosp.	State Avg.	U.S. Avg.
Heart Attack Care				
ACE Inhibitor or ARB for LVSD[5]	0	-	97%	96%
Aspirin at Arrival[5]	0	-	99%	99%
Aspirin at Discharge[5]	0	-	99%	98%
Beta Blocker at Discharge[5]	0	-	99%	98%
Fibrinolytic Medication Timing[5]	0	-	20%	55%
PCI Within 90 Minutes of Arrival[5]	0	-	91%	90%
Smoking Cessation Advice[5]	0	-	100%	99%
Chest Pain/Possible Heart Attack Care				
Aspirin at Arrival	-	-	96%	95%
Median Time to ECG (minutes)	-	-	7	8
Median Time to Transfer (minutes)	-	-	68	61
Fibrinolytic Medication Timing	-	-	72%	54%
Heart Failure Care				
ACE Inhibitor or ARB for LVSD[5]	0	-	94%	94%
Discharge Instructions[5]	0	-	87%	88%
Evaluation of LVS Function[5]	0	-	96%	98%
Smoking Cessation Advice[5]	0	-	96%	98%
Pneumonia Care				
Appropriate Initial Antibiotic[1]	9	78%	91%	92%
Blood Culture Timing[1]	2	100%	97%	96%
Influenza Vaccine[1]	12	92%	91%	91%
Initial Antibiotic Timing[1]	18	94%	97%	95%
Pneumococcal Vaccine[1]	14	93%	92%	93%
Smoking Cessation Advice[1]	6	100%	90%	97%
Surgical Care Improvement Project				
Appropriate VTP Within 24 Hours[5]	0	-	94%	92%
Appropriate Hair Removal[5]	0	-	99%	99%
Appropriate Beta Blocker Usage[5]	0	-	94%	93%
Controlled Postoperative Blood Glucose[5]	0	-	96%	93%
Prophylactic Antibiotic Timing[5]	0	-	97%	97%
Prophylactic Antibiotic Timing (Outpatient)	-	-	93%	92%
Prophylactic Antibiotic Selection[5]	0	-	98%	97%
Prophylactic Antibiotic Select. (Outpatient)	-	-	97%	94%
Prophylactic Antibiotic Stopped[5]	0	-	94%	94%
Recommended VTP Ordered[5]	0	-	95%	94%
Urinary Catheter Removal[5]	0	-	90%	90%
Children's Asthma Care				
Received Systemic Corticosteroids	-	-	-	100%
Received Home Management Plan	-	-	-	71%
Received Reliever Medication	-	-	-	100%
Use of Medical Imaging				
Combination Abdominal CT Scan	-	-	0.152	0.191
Combination Chest CT Scan	-	-	0.033	0.054
Follow-up Mammogram/Ultrasound	-	-	8.1%	8.4%
MRI for Low Back Pain	-	-	33.8%	32.7%
Survey of Patients' Hospital Experiences				
Area Around Room 'Always' Quiet at Night[8]	-	-	-	58%
Doctors 'Always' Communicated Well[8]	-	-	-	80%
Home Recovery Information Given[8]	-	-	-	82%
Hospital Given 9 or 10 on 10 Point Scale[8]	-	-	-	67%
Meds 'Always' Explained Before Given[8]	-	-	-	60%
Nurses 'Always' Communicated Well[8]	-	-	-	76%
Pain 'Always' Well Controlled[8]	-	-	-	69%
Room and Bathroom 'Always' Clean[8]	-	-	-	71%
Timely Help 'Always' Received[8]	-	-	-	64%
Would Definitely Recommend Hospital[8]	-	-	-	69%

NOTE: Hospital profiles are in alphabetical order by state, then city, then hospital within the city; Rankings exclude hospitals with less than 25 cases except for patient surveys which excludes hospitals with less than 100 cases; (a) 100–299 cases; (1) The number of cases is too small to be sure how well a hospital is performing; (2) The hospital indicated that the data submitted for this measure were based on a sample of cases; (3) Data was collected during a shorter time period (fewer quarters) than the maximum possible time for this measure; (4) Suppressed for one or more quarters by CMS; (5) No data is available from the hospital for this measure; (6) Fewer than 100 patients completed the HCAHPS survey. Use these rates with caution, as the number of surveys may be too low to reliably assess hospital performance; (7) Survey results are based on less than 12 months of data; (8) Survey results are not available for this reporting period; (9) No or very few patients were eligible for the HCAHPS survey. The scores shown, if any, reflect a very small number of surveys; (10) A state average was not calculated because too few hospitals in the state submitted data; (11) There were discrepancies in the data collection process; Please refer to the User's Guide for a full explanation of data.

Gothenburg Memorial Hospital

910 20th St Phone: 308-537-3661
Gothenburg, NE 69138 Fax: 308-537-3048
URL: www.ghospital.org
Type: Critical Access Hospitals Emergency Services: Yes
Ownership: Govt - Hospital Dist/Auth Beds: 25

Key Personnel:
CEO/President. . . . . John Johnson
Cardiac Laboratory. . . . . Myra Gronewold
Operating Room. . . . . Carolyn Evenson
Quality Assurance . . . . Jeanine Kline
Radiology. . . . . Julie Koehler
Anesthesiology. . . . . Stanley Roethemeyer

Measure	Cases	This Hosp.	State Avg.	U.S. Avg.
Heart Attack Care				
ACE Inhibitor or ARB for LVSD[5]	0	-	97%	96%
Aspirin at Arrival[5]	0	-	99%	99%
Aspirin at Discharge[5]	0	-	99%	98%
Beta Blocker at Discharge[5]	0	-	99%	98%
Fibrinolytic Medication Timing[5]	0	-	20%	55%
PCI Within 90 Minutes of Arrival[5]	0	-	91%	90%
Smoking Cessation Advice[5]	0	-	100%	99%
Chest Pain/Possible Heart Attack Care				
Aspirin at Arrival	-	-	96%	95%
Median Time to ECG (minutes)	-	-	7	8
Median Time to Transfer (minutes)	-	-	68	61
Fibrinolytic Medication Timing	-	-	72%	54%
Heart Failure Care				
ACE Inhibitor or ARB for LVSD[1]	1	100%	94%	94%
Discharge Instructions[1]	2	50%	87%	88%
Evaluation of LVS Function[1]	6	33%	96%	98%
Smoking Cessation Advice	0	-	96%	98%
Pneumonia Care				
Appropriate Initial Antibiotic[1]	5	100%	91%	92%
Blood Culture Timing	0	-	97%	96%
Influenza Vaccine[1]	5	100%	91%	91%
Initial Antibiotic Timing[1]	5	100%	97%	95%
Pneumococcal Vaccine[1]	10	90%	92%	93%
Smoking Cessation Advice[1]	2	100%	90%	97%
Surgical Care Improvement Project				
Appropriate VTP Within 24 Hours[5]	0	-	94%	92%
Appropriate Hair Removal[5]	0	-	99%	99%
Appropriate Beta Blocker Usage[5]	0	-	94%	93%
Controlled Postoperative Blood Glucose[5]	0	-	96%	93%
Prophylactic Antibiotic Timing[5]	0	-	97%	97%
Prophylactic Antibiotic Timing (Outpatient)	-	-	93%	92%
Prophylactic Antibiotic Selection[5]	0	-	98%	97%
Prophylactic Antibiotic Select. (Outpatient)	-	-	97%	94%
Prophylactic Antibiotic Stopped[5]	0	-	94%	94%
Recommended VTP Ordered[5]	0	-	95%	94%
Urinary Catheter Removal[5]	0	-	90%	90%
Children's Asthma Care				
Received Systemic Corticosteroids	-	-	-	100%
Received Home Management Plan	-	-	-	71%
Received Reliever Medication	-	-	-	100%
Use of Medical Imaging				
Combination Abdominal CT Scan	-	-	0.152	0.191
Combination Chest CT Scan	-	-	0.033	0.054
Follow-up Mammogram/Ultrasound	-	-	8.1%	8.4%
MRI for Low Back Pain	-	-	33.8%	32.7%
Survey of Patients' Hospital Experiences				
Area Around Room 'Always' Quiet at Night[8]	-	-	-	58%
Doctors 'Always' Communicated Well[8]	-	-	-	80%
Home Recovery Information Given[8]	-	-	-	82%
Hospital Given 9 or 10 on 10 Point Scale[8]	-	-	-	67%
Meds 'Always' Explained Before Given[8]	-	-	-	60%
Nurses 'Always' Communicated Well[8]	-	-	-	76%
Pain 'Always' Well Controlled[8]	-	-	-	69%
Room and Bathroom 'Always' Clean[8]	-	-	-	71%
Timely Help 'Always' Received[8]	-	-	-	64%
Would Definitely Recommend Hospital[8]	-	-	-	69%

Saint Francis Medical Center

2620 West Faidley Ave Phone: 308-384-4600
Grand Island, NE 68803 Fax: 308-398-5589
URL: www.saintfrancisgi.org
Type: Acute Care Hospitals Emergency Services: Yes
Ownership: Voluntary Non-Profit - Church Beds: 200

Key Personnel:
CEO/President. . . . . Michael R Gloor, FACHE
Chief of Medical Staff. . . . . Michael Horn, MD
Operating Room. . . . . Dee Donaldson, RN
Pediatric In-Patient Care . . . . . . Jan Spale
Quality Assurance . . . . Charlene L'Heureux
Radiology. . . . . Jackie Huldt
Hemotology Center . . . . Max Norvell
Patient Relations . . . . Joan Jensen

Measure	Cases	This Hosp.	State Avg.	U.S. Avg.
Heart Attack Care				
ACE Inhibitor or ARB for LVSD[1]	12	100%	97%	96%
Aspirin at Arrival	83	99%	99%	99%
Aspirin at Discharge	81	99%	99%	98%
Beta Blocker at Discharge	81	100%	99%	98%
Fibrinolytic Medication Timing	0	-	20%	55%
PCI Within 90 Minutes of Arrival[1]	16	94%	91%	90%
Smoking Cessation Advice	28	100%	100%	99%
Chest Pain/Possible Heart Attack Care				
Aspirin at Arrival	58	93%	96%	95%
Median Time to ECG (minutes)	59	2	7	8
Median Time to Transfer (minutes)[1,3]	2	68	68	61
Fibrinolytic Medication Timing[1,3]	1	100%	72%	54%
Heart Failure Care				
ACE Inhibitor or ARB for LVSD	33	97%	94%	94%
Discharge Instructions	89	96%	87%	88%
Evaluation of LVS Function	130	94%	96%	98%
Smoking Cessation Advice[1]	15	100%	96%	98%
Pneumonia Care				
Appropriate Initial Antibiotic	118	90%	91%	92%
Blood Culture Timing	202	99%	97%	96%
Influenza Vaccine	158	87%	91%	91%
Initial Antibiotic Timing	207	98%	97%	95%
Pneumococcal Vaccine	210	91%	92%	93%
Smoking Cessation Advice	72	100%	90%	97%
Surgical Care Improvement Project				
Appropriate VTP Within 24 Hours	198	95%	94%	92%
Appropriate Hair Removal	694	100%	99%	99%
Appropriate Beta Blocker Usage	228	89%	94%	93%
Controlled Postoperative Blood Glucose	0	-	96%	93%
Prophylactic Antibiotic Timing	448	100%	97%	97%
Prophylactic Antibiotic Timing (Outpatient)	84	88%	93%	92%
Prophylactic Antibiotic Selection	451	99%	98%	97%
Prophylactic Antibiotic Select. (Outpatient)	77	96%	97%	94%
Prophylactic Antibiotic Stopped	423	94%	94%	94%
Recommended VTP Ordered	198	97%	95%	94%
Urinary Catheter Removal	174	87%	90%	90%
Children's Asthma Care				
Received Systemic Corticosteroids	-	-	-	100%
Received Home Management Plan	-	-	-	71%
Received Reliever Medication	-	-	-	100%
Use of Medical Imaging				
Combination Abdominal CT Scan	241	0.012	0.152	0.191
Combination Chest CT Scan	121	0.025	0.033	0.054
Follow-up Mammogram/Ultrasound	1,337	5.3%	8.1%	8.4%
MRI for Low Back Pain[1]	17	17.6%	33.8%	32.7%
Survey of Patients' Hospital Experiences				
Area Around Room 'Always' Quiet at Night	300+	63%	-	58%
Doctors 'Always' Communicated Well	300+	78%	-	80%
Home Recovery Information Given	300+	88%	-	82%
Hospital Given 9 or 10 on 10 Point Scale	300+	72%	-	67%
Meds 'Always' Explained Before Given	300+	61%	-	60%
Nurses 'Always' Communicated Well	300+	74%	-	76%
Pain 'Always' Well Controlled	300+	67%	-	69%
Room and Bathroom 'Always' Clean	300+	73%	-	71%
Timely Help 'Always' Received	300+	64%	-	64%
Would Definitely Recommend Hospital	300+	71%	-	69%

Perkins County Health Services

900 Lincoln Ave Phone: 308-352-7200
Grant, NE 69140 Fax: 308-352-7291
URL: www.pchsgrant.com
Type: Critical Access Hospitals Emergency Services: Yes
Ownership: Govt - Hospital Dist/Auth Beds: 20

Key Personnel:
Radiology. . . . . Dr Tamara Hlavaty

Measure	Cases	This Hosp.	State Avg.	U.S. Avg.
Heart Attack Care				
ACE Inhibitor or ARB for LVSD[3]	0	-	97%	96%
Aspirin at Arrival[3]	0	-	99%	99%
Aspirin at Discharge[3]	0	-	99%	98%
Beta Blocker at Discharge[3]	0	-	99%	98%
Fibrinolytic Medication Timing[3]	0	-	20%	55%
PCI Within 90 Minutes of Arrival[3]	0	-	91%	90%
Smoking Cessation Advice[3]	0	-	100%	99%
Chest Pain/Possible Heart Attack Care				
Aspirin at Arrival	-	-	96%	95%
Median Time to ECG (minutes)	-	-	7	8
Median Time to Transfer (minutes)	-	-	68	61
Fibrinolytic Medication Timing	-	-	72%	54%
Heart Failure Care				
ACE Inhibitor or ARB for LVSD[3]	0	-	94%	94%
Discharge Instructions[1,3]	1	100%	87%	88%
Evaluation of LVS Function[1,3]	3	0%	96%	98%
Smoking Cessation Advice[1,3]	1	0%	96%	98%
Pneumonia Care				
Appropriate Initial Antibiotic[1]	4	50%	91%	92%
Blood Culture Timing[1]	1	0%	97%	96%
Influenza Vaccine[1]	5	80%	91%	91%
Initial Antibiotic Timing[1]	7	57%	97%	95%
Pneumococcal Vaccine[1]	6	83%	92%	93%
Smoking Cessation Advice[1]	4	25%	90%	97%
Surgical Care Improvement Project				
Appropriate VTP Within 24 Hours[5]	0	-	94%	92%
Appropriate Hair Removal[5]	0	-	99%	99%
Appropriate Beta Blocker Usage[5]	0	-	94%	93%
Controlled Postoperative Blood Glucose[5]	0	-	96%	93%
Prophylactic Antibiotic Timing[5]	0	-	97%	97%
Prophylactic Antibiotic Timing (Outpatient)	-	-	93%	92%
Prophylactic Antibiotic Selection[5]	0	-	98%	97%
Prophylactic Antibiotic Select. (Outpatient)	-	-	97%	94%
Prophylactic Antibiotic Stopped[5]	0	-	94%	94%
Recommended VTP Ordered[5]	0	-	95%	94%
Urinary Catheter Removal[5]	0	-	90%	90%
Children's Asthma Care				
Received Systemic Corticosteroids	-	-	-	100%
Received Home Management Plan	-	-	-	71%
Received Reliever Medication	-	-	-	100%
Use of Medical Imaging				
Combination Abdominal CT Scan	-	-	0.152	0.191
Combination Chest CT Scan	-	-	0.033	0.054
Follow-up Mammogram/Ultrasound	-	-	8.1%	8.4%
MRI for Low Back Pain	-	-	33.8%	32.7%
Survey of Patients' Hospital Experiences				
Area Around Room 'Always' Quiet at Night[8]	-	-	-	58%
Doctors 'Always' Communicated Well[8]	-	-	-	80%
Home Recovery Information Given[8]	-	-	-	82%
Hospital Given 9 or 10 on 10 Point Scale[8]	-	-	-	67%
Meds 'Always' Explained Before Given[8]	-	-	-	60%
Nurses 'Always' Communicated Well[8]	-	-	-	76%
Pain 'Always' Well Controlled[8]	-	-	-	69%
Room and Bathroom 'Always' Clean[8]	-	-	-	71%
Timely Help 'Always' Received[8]	-	-	-	64%
Would Definitely Recommend Hospital[8]	-	-	-	69%

NOTE: Hospital profiles are in alphabetical order by state, then city, then hospital within the city; Rankings exclude hospitals with less than 25 cases except for patient surveys which excludes hospitals with less than 100 cases; (a) 100–299 cases; (1) The number of cases is too small to be sure how well a hospital is performing; (2) The hospital indicated that the data submitted for this measure were based on a sample of cases; (3) Data was collected during a shorter time period (fewer quarters) than the maximum possible time for this measure; (4) Suppressed for one or more quarters by CMS; (5) No data is available from the hospital for this measure; (6) Fewer than 100 patients completed the HCAHPS survey. Use these rates with caution, as the number of surveys may be too low to reliably assess hospital performance; (7) Survey results are based on less than 12 months of data; (8) Survey results are not available for this reporting period; (9) No or very few patients were eligible for the HCAHPS survey. The scores shown, if any, reflect a very small number of surveys; (10) A state average was not calculated because too few hospitals in the state submitted data; (11) There were discrepancies in the data collection process; Please refer to the User's Guide for a full explanation of data.

Mary Lanning Memorial Hospital

715 N St Joseph Ave — Phone: 402-463-4521
Hastings, NE 68901 — Fax: 402-461-5321
Type: Acute Care Hospitals — Emergency Services: Yes
Ownership: Voluntary Non-Profit - Private — Beds: 183

Key Personnel:
CEO/President. . . . . W Michael Kearney
Cardiac Laboratory. . . . . Dave Patterson
Chief of Medical Staff . . . . Gary Caingren
Infection Control. . . . . Connie Hyde
Quality Assurance . . . . Leota Roll
Radiology. . . . . Tami Lipker
Emergency Room . . . . Ronda Ehly

Measure	Cases	This Hosp.	State Avg.	U.S. Avg.
Heart Attack Care				
ACE Inhibitor or ARB for LVSD[1]	2	100%	97%	96%
Aspirin at Arrival	32	100%	99%	99%
Aspirin at Discharge	27	93%	99%	98%
Beta Blocker at Discharge[1]	24	79%	99%	98%
Fibrinolytic Medication Timing	0	-	20%	55%
PCI Within 90 Minutes of Arrival	0	-	91%	90%
Smoking Cessation Advice[1]	6	100%	100%	99%
Chest Pain/Possible Heart Attack Care				
Aspirin at Arrival	30	97%	96%	95%
Median Time to ECG (minutes)	32	10	7	8
Median Time to Transfer (minutes)[1,3]	2	84	68	61
Fibrinolytic Medication Timing[1]	6	50%	72%	54%
Heart Failure Care				
ACE Inhibitor or ARB for LVSD	40	88%	94%	94%
Discharge Instructions	78	87%	87%	88%
Evaluation of LVS Function	109	96%	96%	98%
Smoking Cessation Advice[1]	6	67%	96%	98%
Pneumonia Care				
Appropriate Initial Antibiotic	83	94%	91%	92%
Blood Culture Timing	101	98%	97%	96%
Influenza Vaccine	81	95%	91%	91%
Initial Antibiotic Timing	125	98%	97%	95%
Pneumococcal Vaccine	121	97%	92%	93%
Smoking Cessation Advice	29	69%	90%	97%
Surgical Care Improvement Project				
Appropriate VTP Within 24 Hours	204	93%	94%	92%
Appropriate Hair Removal	593	99%	99%	99%
Appropriate Beta Blocker Usage	128	96%	94%	93%
Controlled Postoperative Blood Glucose	0	-	96%	93%
Prophylactic Antibiotic Timing	508	96%	97%	97%
Prophylactic Antibiotic Timing (Outpatient)	116	46%	93%	92%
Prophylactic Antibiotic Selection	508	97%	98%	97%
Prophylactic Antibiotic Select. (Outpatient)	109	94%	97%	94%
Prophylactic Antibiotic Stopped	495	78%	94%	94%
Recommended VTP Ordered	206	92%	95%	94%
Urinary Catheter Removal	93	76%	90%	90%
Children's Asthma Care				
Received Systemic Corticosteroids	-	-	-	100%
Received Home Management Plan	-	-	-	71%
Received Reliever Medication	-	-	-	100%
Use of Medical Imaging				
Combination Abdominal CT Scan	417	0.048	0.152	0.191
Combination Chest CT Scan	515	0.080	0.033	0.054
Follow-up Mammogram/Ultrasound	607	9.2%	8.1%	8.4%
MRI for Low Back Pain	85	24.7%	33.8%	32.7%
Survey of Patients' Hospital Experiences				
Area Around Room 'Always' Quiet at Night	300+	55%	-	58%
Doctors 'Always' Communicated Well	300+	80%	-	80%
Home Recovery Information Given	300+	86%	-	82%
Hospital Given 9 or 10 on 10 Point Scale	300+	67%	-	67%
Meds 'Always' Explained Before Given	300+	64%	-	60%
Nurses 'Always' Communicated Well	300+	77%	-	76%
Pain 'Always' Well Controlled	300+	70%	-	69%
Room and Bathroom 'Always' Clean	300+	78%	-	71%
Timely Help 'Always' Received	300+	60%	-	64%
Would Definitely Recommend Hospital	300+	71%	-	69%

Thayer County Health Services

120 Park Ave — Phone: 402-768-6041
Hebron, NE 68370 — Fax: 402-768-4669
E-mail: info@ThayerCountyHealth.com
URL: www.thayercountyhealth.com
Type: Critical Access Hospitals — Emergency Services: Yes
Ownership: Government - Local — Beds: 14

Key Personnel:
CEO/President. . . . . Joyce Beck
Chief of Medical Staff . . . . Marlin Bauhard, MD
Infection Control. . . . . Marla Heitmann, RN
Radiology. . . . . Audra Hergott
Intensive Care Unit. . . . . Jolynn Hacker, RN

Measure	Cases	This Hosp.	State Avg.	U.S. Avg.
Heart Attack Care				
ACE Inhibitor or ARB for LVSD[1,2,3]	1	100%	97%	96%
Aspirin at Arrival[1,2,3]	3	67%	99%	99%
Aspirin at Discharge[1,2,3]	1	100%	99%	98%
Beta Blocker at Discharge[1,2,3]	3	67%	99%	98%
Fibrinolytic Medication Timing[2,3]	0	-	20%	55%
PCI Within 90 Minutes of Arrival[2,3]	0	-	91%	90%
Smoking Cessation Advice[2,3]	0	-	100%	99%
Chest Pain/Possible Heart Attack Care				
Aspirin at Arrival	-	-	96%	95%
Median Time to ECG (minutes)	-	-	7	8
Median Time to Transfer (minutes)	-	-	68	61
Fibrinolytic Medication Timing	-	-	72%	54%
Heart Failure Care				
ACE Inhibitor or ARB for LVSD[1,2]	4	75%	94%	94%
Discharge Instructions[1,2]	15	87%	87%	88%
Evaluation of LVS Function[1,2]	18	89%	96%	98%
Smoking Cessation Advice[1,2]	1	0%	96%	98%
Pneumonia Care				
Appropriate Initial Antibiotic[1,2]	7	100%	91%	92%
Blood Culture Timing[1,2]	1	100%	97%	96%
Influenza Vaccine[1,2]	13	85%	91%	91%
Initial Antibiotic Timing[1,2]	13	100%	97%	95%
Pneumococcal Vaccine[1,2]	19	89%	92%	93%
Smoking Cessation Advice[1,2]	2	0%	90%	97%
Surgical Care Improvement Project				
Appropriate VTP Within 24 Hours[1,2]	9	89%	94%	92%
Appropriate Hair Removal[1,2]	20	100%	99%	99%
Appropriate Beta Blocker Usage[5]	0	-	94%	93%
Controlled Postoperative Blood Glucose[2]	0	-	96%	93%
Prophylactic Antibiotic Timing[1,2]	18	89%	97%	97%
Prophylactic Antibiotic Timing (Outpatient)	-	-	93%	92%
Prophylactic Antibiotic Selection[1,2]	18	94%	98%	97%
Prophylactic Antibiotic Select. (Outpatient)	-	-	97%	94%
Prophylactic Antibiotic Stopped[1,2]	18	100%	94%	94%
Recommended VTP Ordered[2,1]	9	100%	95%	94%
Urinary Catheter Removal[1,2]	8	50%	90%	90%
Children's Asthma Care				
Received Systemic Corticosteroids	-	-	-	100%
Received Home Management Plan	-	-	-	71%
Received Reliever Medication	-	-	-	100%
Use of Medical Imaging				
Combination Abdominal CT Scan	-	-	0.152	0.191
Combination Chest CT Scan	-	-	0.033	0.054
Follow-up Mammogram/Ultrasound	-	-	8.1%	8.4%
MRI for Low Back Pain	-	-	33.8%	32.7%
Survey of Patients' Hospital Experiences				
Area Around Room 'Always' Quiet at Night[8]	-	-	-	58%
Doctors 'Always' Communicated Well[8]	-	-	-	80%
Home Recovery Information Given[8]	-	-	-	82%
Hospital Given 9 or 10 on 10 Point Scale[8]	-	-	-	67%
Meds 'Always' Explained Before Given[8]	-	-	-	60%
Nurses 'Always' Communicated Well[8]	-	-	-	76%
Pain 'Always' Well Controlled[8]	-	-	-	69%
Room and Bathroom 'Always' Clean[8]	-	-	-	71%
Timely Help 'Always' Received[8]	-	-	-	64%
Would Definitely Recommend Hospital[8]	-	-	-	69%

Henderson Health Care Services

1621 Front Street — Phone: 402-723-4512
Henderson, NE 68371 — Fax: 402-723-4520
Type: Critical Access Hospitals — Emergency Services: Yes
Ownership: Voluntary Non-Profit - Private — Beds: 59

Key Personnel:
Chief of Medical Staff . . . . Robet J Wochner, MD
Operating Room. . . . . Lela Regier
Quality Assurance . . . . Rita Kroeker

Measure	Cases	This Hosp.	State Avg.	U.S. Avg.
Heart Attack Care				
ACE Inhibitor or ARB for LVSD[5]	0	-	97%	96%
Aspirin at Arrival[5]	0	-	99%	99%
Aspirin at Discharge[5]	0	-	99%	98%
Beta Blocker at Discharge[5]	0	-	99%	98%
Fibrinolytic Medication Timing[5]	0	-	20%	55%
PCI Within 90 Minutes of Arrival[5]	0	-	91%	90%
Smoking Cessation Advice[5]	0	-	100%	99%
Chest Pain/Possible Heart Attack Care				
Aspirin at Arrival	-	-	96%	95%
Median Time to ECG (minutes)	-	-	7	8
Median Time to Transfer (minutes)	-	-	68	61
Fibrinolytic Medication Timing	-	-	72%	54%
Heart Failure Care				
ACE Inhibitor or ARB for LVSD[5]	0	-	94%	94%
Discharge Instructions[5]	0	-	87%	88%
Evaluation of LVS Function[5]	0	-	96%	98%
Smoking Cessation Advice[5]	0	-	96%	98%
Pneumonia Care				
Appropriate Initial Antibiotic[3]	0	-	91%	92%
Blood Culture Timing[3]	0	-	97%	96%
Influenza Vaccine[1,3]	3	100%	91%	91%
Initial Antibiotic Timing[1,3]	2	100%	97%	95%
Pneumococcal Vaccine[1,3]	3	100%	92%	93%
Smoking Cessation Advice[3]	0	-	90%	97%
Surgical Care Improvement Project				
Appropriate VTP Within 24 Hours[5]	0	-	94%	92%
Appropriate Hair Removal[5]	0	-	99%	99%
Appropriate Beta Blocker Usage[5]	0	-	94%	93%
Controlled Postoperative Blood Glucose[5]	0	-	96%	93%
Prophylactic Antibiotic Timing[5]	0	-	97%	97%
Prophylactic Antibiotic Timing (Outpatient)	-	-	93%	92%
Prophylactic Antibiotic Selection[5]	0	-	98%	97%
Prophylactic Antibiotic Select. (Outpatient)	-	-	97%	94%
Prophylactic Antibiotic Stopped[5]	0	-	94%	94%
Recommended VTP Ordered[5]	0	-	95%	94%
Urinary Catheter Removal[5]	0	-	90%	90%
Children's Asthma Care				
Received Systemic Corticosteroids	-	-	-	100%
Received Home Management Plan	-	-	-	71%
Received Reliever Medication	-	-	-	100%
Use of Medical Imaging				
Combination Abdominal CT Scan	-	-	0.152	0.191
Combination Chest CT Scan	-	-	0.033	0.054
Follow-up Mammogram/Ultrasound	-	-	8.1%	8.4%
MRI for Low Back Pain	-	-	33.8%	32.7%
Survey of Patients' Hospital Experiences				
Area Around Room 'Always' Quiet at Night[8]	-	-	-	58%
Doctors 'Always' Communicated Well[8]	-	-	-	80%
Home Recovery Information Given[8]	-	-	-	82%
Hospital Given 9 or 10 on 10 Point Scale[8]	-	-	-	67%
Meds 'Always' Explained Before Given[8]	-	-	-	60%
Nurses 'Always' Communicated Well[8]	-	-	-	76%
Pain 'Always' Well Controlled[8]	-	-	-	69%
Room and Bathroom 'Always' Clean[8]	-	-	-	71%
Timely Help 'Always' Received[8]	-	-	-	64%
Would Definitely Recommend Hospital[8]	-	-	-	69%

NOTE: Hospital profiles are in alphabetical order by state, then city, then hospital within the city; Rankings exclude hospitals with less than 25 cases except for patient surveys which excludes hospitals with less than 100 cases; (a) 100–299 cases; (1) The number of cases is too small to be sure how well a hospital is performing; (2) The hospital indicated that the data submitted for this measure were based on a sample of cases; (3) Data was collected during a shorter time period (fewer quarters) than the maximum possible time for this measure; (4) Suppressed for one or more quarters by CMS; (5) No data is available from the hospital for this measure; (6) Fewer than 100 patients completed the HCAHPS survey. Use these rates with caution, as the number of surveys may be too low to reliably assess hospital performance; (7) Survey results are based on less than 12 months of data; (8) Survey results are not available for this reporting period; (9) No or very few patients were eligible for the HCAHPS survey. The scores shown, if any, reflect a very small number of surveys; (10) A state average was not calculated because too few hospitals in the state submitted data; (11) There were discrepancies in the data collection process; Please refer to the User's Guide for a full explanation of data.

Phelps Memorial Health Center

1215 Tibbals St
Holdrege, NE 68949
Phone: 308-995-2211
Fax: 308-995-3333
URL: www.phelpsmemorial.com
Type: Critical Access Hospitals
Emergency Services: Yes
Ownership: Voluntary Non-Profit - Other
Beds: 49

Key Personnel:

CEO/President. . . . . Mark Harrel
Chief of Medical Staff. . . . . Charles Smith, MD
Coronary Care . . . . Susan Rieker
Infection Control. . . . . Laurie Raboin
Operating Room. . . . . Tammy Nelson, RN
Quality Assurance . . . . Bill Redinger
Emergency Room . . . . Susan Rieker
Intensive Care Unit. . . . . Susan Rieker

Measure	Cases	This Hosp.	State Avg.	U.S. Avg.
Heart Attack Care				
ACE Inhibitor or ARB for LVSD[1,3]	1	0%	97%	96%
Aspirin at Arrival[1,3]	5	80%	99%	99%
Aspirin at Discharge[1,3]	1	100%	99%	98%
Beta Blocker at Discharge[1,3]	2	100%	99%	98%
Fibrinolytic Medication Timing[3]	0	-	20%	55%
PCI Within 90 Minutes of Arrival[3]	0	-	91%	90%
Smoking Cessation Advice[3]	0	-	100%	99%
Chest Pain/Possible Heart Attack Care				
Aspirin at Arrival	-	-	96%	95%
Median Time to ECG (minutes)	-	-	7	8
Median Time to Transfer (minutes)	-	-	68	61
Fibrinolytic Medication Timing	-	-	72%	54%
Heart Failure Care				
ACE Inhibitor or ARB for LVSD[1]	5	40%	94%	94%
Discharge Instructions[1]	9	100%	87%	88%
Evaluation of LVS Function	29	97%	96%	98%
Smoking Cessation Advice[1]	1	0%	96%	98%
Pneumonia Care				
Appropriate Initial Antibiotic	26	88%	91%	92%
Blood Culture Timing[1]	6	83%	97%	96%
Influenza Vaccine	53	89%	91%	91%
Initial Antibiotic Timing	51	90%	97%	95%
Pneumococcal Vaccine	62	94%	92%	93%
Smoking Cessation Advice[1]	5	100%	90%	97%
Surgical Care Improvement Project				
Appropriate VTP Within 24 Hours	33	100%	94%	92%
Appropriate Hair Removal	81	100%	99%	99%
Appropriate Beta Blocker Usage[5]	0	-	94%	93%
Controlled Postoperative Blood Glucose	0	-	96%	93%
Prophylactic Antibiotic Timing	71	93%	97%	97%
Prophylactic Antibiotic Timing (Outpatient)	-	-	93%	92%
Prophylactic Antibiotic Selection	71	96%	98%	97%
Prophylactic Antibiotic Select. (Outpatient)	-	-	97%	94%
Prophylactic Antibiotic Stopped	66	91%	94%	94%
Recommended VTP Ordered	34	97%	95%	94%
Urinary Catheter Removal[1]	5	80%	90%	90%
Children's Asthma Care				
Received Systemic Corticosteroids	-	-	-	100%
Received Home Management Plan	-	-	-	71%
Received Reliever Medication	-	-	-	100%
Use of Medical Imaging				
Combination Abdominal CT Scan	-	-	0.152	0.191
Combination Chest CT Scan	-	-	0.033	0.054
Follow-up Mammogram/Ultrasound	-	-	8.1%	8.4%
MRI for Low Back Pain	-	-	33.8%	32.7%
Survey of Patients' Hospital Experiences				
Area Around Room 'Always' Quiet at Night	300+	54%	-	58%
Doctors 'Always' Communicated Well	300+	84%	-	80%
Home Recovery Information Given	300+	80%	-	82%
Hospital Given 9 or 10 on 10 Point Scale	300+	72%	-	67%
Meds 'Always' Explained Before Given	300+	60%	-	60%
Nurses 'Always' Communicated Well	300+	75%	-	76%
Pain 'Always' Well Controlled	300+	69%	-	69%
Room and Bathroom 'Always' Clean	300+	84%	-	71%
Timely Help 'Always' Received	300+	65%	-	64%
Would Definitely Recommend Hospital	300+	75%	-	69%

Chase County Community Hospital

600 W 12th St
Imperial, NE 69033
Phone: 308-882-7111
Fax: 308-882-5950
E-mail: ccch@chasecountyhospital.com
URL: www.chasecountyhospital.com
Type: Critical Access Hospitals
Emergency Services: Yes
Ownership: Government - Local
Beds: 25

Key Personnel:

Radiology. . . . . Doug Douglas

Measure	Cases	This Hosp.	State Avg.	U.S. Avg.
Heart Attack Care				
ACE Inhibitor or ARB for LVSD[5]	0	-	97%	96%
Aspirin at Arrival[5]	0	-	99%	99%
Aspirin at Discharge[5]	0	-	99%	98%
Beta Blocker at Discharge[5]	0	-	99%	98%
Fibrinolytic Medication Timing[5]	0	-	20%	55%
PCI Within 90 Minutes of Arrival[5]	0	-	91%	90%
Smoking Cessation Advice[5]	0	-	100%	99%
Chest Pain/Possible Heart Attack Care				
Aspirin at Arrival	-	-	96%	95%
Median Time to ECG (minutes)	-	-	7	8
Median Time to Transfer (minutes)	-	-	68	61
Fibrinolytic Medication Timing	-	-	72%	54%
Heart Failure Care				
ACE Inhibitor or ARB for LVSD[3]	0	-	94%	94%
Discharge Instructions[1,3]	1	0%	87%	88%
Evaluation of LVS Function[1,3]	3	0%	96%	98%
Smoking Cessation Advice[3]	0	-	96%	98%
Pneumonia Care				
Appropriate Initial Antibiotic[1,2,3]	6	67%	91%	92%
Blood Culture Timing[2,3]	0	-	97%	96%
Influenza Vaccine[1,2,3]	3	67%	91%	91%
Initial Antibiotic Timing[1,2,3]	7	100%	97%	95%
Pneumococcal Vaccine[1,2,3]	7	43%	92%	93%
Smoking Cessation Advice[1,2,3]	1	100%	90%	97%
Surgical Care Improvement Project				
Appropriate VTP Within 24 Hours[1,3]	3	100%	94%	92%
Appropriate Hair Removal[1,3]	4	50%	99%	99%
Appropriate Beta Blocker Usage[5]	0	-	94%	93%
Controlled Postoperative Blood Glucose[3]	0	-	96%	93%
Prophylactic Antibiotic Timing[1,3]	4	50%	97%	97%
Prophylactic Antibiotic Timing (Outpatient)	-	-	93%	92%
Prophylactic Antibiotic Selection[1,3]	4	75%	98%	97%
Prophylactic Antibiotic Select. (Outpatient)	-	-	97%	94%
Prophylactic Antibiotic Stopped[1,3]	4	75%	94%	94%
Recommended VTP Ordered[1,3]	3	100%	95%	94%
Urinary Catheter Removal[1,3]	1	100%	90%	90%
Children's Asthma Care				
Received Systemic Corticosteroids	-	-	-	100%
Received Home Management Plan	-	-	-	71%
Received Reliever Medication	-	-	-	100%
Use of Medical Imaging				
Combination Abdominal CT Scan	-	-	0.152	0.191
Combination Chest CT Scan	-	-	0.033	0.054
Follow-up Mammogram/Ultrasound	-	-	8.1%	8.4%
MRI for Low Back Pain	-	-	33.8%	32.7%
Survey of Patients' Hospital Experiences				
Area Around Room 'Always' Quiet at Night[8]	-	-	-	58%
Doctors 'Always' Communicated Well[8]	-	-	-	80%
Home Recovery Information Given[8]	-	-	-	82%
Hospital Given 9 or 10 on 10 Point Scale[8]	-	-	-	67%
Meds 'Always' Explained Before Given[8]	-	-	-	60%
Nurses 'Always' Communicated Well[8]	-	-	-	76%
Pain 'Always' Well Controlled[8]	-	-	-	69%
Room and Bathroom 'Always' Clean[8]	-	-	-	71%
Timely Help 'Always' Received[8]	-	-	-	64%
Would Definitely Recommend Hospital[8]	-	-	-	69%

Good Samaritan Hospital

10 East 31st St
Kearney, NE 68848
Phone: 308-865-7900
Fax: 308-865-2924
URL: www.gshs.org
Type: Acute Care Hospitals
Emergency Services: Yes
Ownership: Voluntary Non-Profit - Church
Beds: 287

Key Personnel:

CEO/President. . . . . John W Allen
Operating Room. . . . . Ron Langford
Pediatric In-Patient Care . . . . Coni Rinaker
Quality Assurance . . . . Judy Dady
Radiology. . . . . Chuck Day
Emergency Room . . . . Paul O'Connell
Intensive Care Unit. . . . . Valerie Fredericksen
Patient Relations . . . . Carol Wahl

Measure	Cases	This Hosp.	State Avg.	U.S. Avg.
Heart Attack Care				
ACE Inhibitor or ARB for LVSD	32	94%	97%	96%
Aspirin at Arrival	75	99%	99%	99%
Aspirin at Discharge	177	99%	99%	98%
Beta Blocker at Discharge	169	97%	99%	98%
Fibrinolytic Medication Timing	0	-	20%	55%
PCI Within 90 Minutes of Arrival[1]	21	71%	91%	90%
Smoking Cessation Advice	67	99%	100%	99%
Chest Pain/Possible Heart Attack Care				
Aspirin at Arrival[5]	0	-	96%	95%
Median Time to ECG (minutes)[5]	0	-	7	8
Median Time to Transfer (minutes)[5]	0	-	68	61
Fibrinolytic Medication Timing[5]	0	-	72%	54%
Heart Failure Care				
ACE Inhibitor or ARB for LVSD	45	89%	94%	94%
Discharge Instructions	111	82%	87%	88%
Evaluation of LVS Function	150	99%	96%	98%
Smoking Cessation Advice	25	100%	96%	98%
Pneumonia Care				
Appropriate Initial Antibiotic	97	90%	91%	92%
Blood Culture Timing	66	98%	97%	96%
Influenza Vaccine	105	90%	91%	91%
Initial Antibiotic Timing	134	97%	97%	95%
Pneumococcal Vaccine	147	93%	92%	93%
Smoking Cessation Advice	41	90%	90%	97%
Surgical Care Improvement Project				
Appropriate VTP Within 24 Hours	404	93%	94%	92%
Appropriate Hair Removal	1,167	99%	99%	99%
Appropriate Beta Blocker Usage	406	91%	94%	93%
Controlled Postoperative Blood Glucose	133	99%	96%	93%
Prophylactic Antibiotic Timing	783	97%	97%	97%
Prophylactic Antibiotic Timing (Outpatient)	517	93%	93%	92%
Prophylactic Antibiotic Selection	789	99%	98%	97%
Prophylactic Antibiotic Select. (Outpatient)	502	98%	97%	94%
Prophylactic Antibiotic Stopped	748	93%	94%	94%
Recommended VTP Ordered	404	96%	95%	94%
Urinary Catheter Removal	134	69%	90%	90%
Children's Asthma Care				
Received Systemic Corticosteroids	-	-	-	100%
Received Home Management Plan	-	-	-	71%
Received Reliever Medication	-	-	-	100%
Use of Medical Imaging				
Combination Abdominal CT Scan	491	0.077	0.152	0.191
Combination Chest CT Scan	429	0.019	0.033	0.054
Follow-up Mammogram/Ultrasound	707	7.1%	8.1%	8.4%
MRI for Low Back Pain	200	31.5%	33.8%	32.7%
Survey of Patients' Hospital Experiences				
Area Around Room 'Always' Quiet at Night	300+	56%	-	58%
Doctors 'Always' Communicated Well	300+	79%	-	80%
Home Recovery Information Given	300+	84%	-	82%
Hospital Given 9 or 10 on 10 Point Scale	300+	67%	-	67%
Meds 'Always' Explained Before Given	300+	59%	-	60%
Nurses 'Always' Communicated Well	300+	75%	-	76%
Pain 'Always' Well Controlled	300+	67%	-	69%
Room and Bathroom 'Always' Clean	300+	72%	-	71%
Timely Help 'Always' Received	300+	58%	-	64%
Would Definitely Recommend Hospital	300+	72%	-	69%

NOTE: Hospital profiles are in alphabetical order by state, then city, then hospital within the city; Rankings exclude hospitals with less than 25 cases except for patient surveys which excludes hospitals with less than 100 cases; (a) 100–299 cases; (1) The number of cases is too small to be sure how well a hospital is performing; (2) The hospital indicated that the data submitted for this measure were based on a sample of cases; (3) Data was collected during a shorter time period (fewer quarters) than the maximum possible time for this measure; (4) Suppressed for one or more quarters by CMS; (5) No data is available from the hospital for this measure; (6) Fewer than 100 patients completed the HCAHPS survey. Use these rates with caution, as the number of surveys may be too low to reliably assess hospital performance; (7) Survey results are based on less than 12 months of data; (8) Survey results are not available for this reporting period; (9) No or very few patients were eligible for the HCAHPS survey. The scores shown, if any, reflect a very small number of surveys; (10) A state average was not calculated because too few hospitals in the state submitted data; (11) There were discrepancies in the data collection process; Please refer to the User's Guide for a full explanation of data.

Kimball Health Services

505 South Burg St
Kimball, NE 69145
Phone: 308-235-1952
URL: www.kimballhealth.org
Type: Critical Access Hospitals
Emergency Services: Yes
Ownership: Government - Local
Beds: 20
Key Personnel:
CEO . . . . Julie Schnell

Measure	Cases	This Hosp.	State Avg.	U.S. Avg.
Heart Attack Care				
ACE Inhibitor or ARB for LVSD[5]	0	-	97%	96%
Aspirin at Arrival[5]	0	-	99%	99%
Aspirin at Discharge[5]	0	-	99%	98%
Beta Blocker at Discharge[5]	0	-	99%	98%
Fibrinolytic Medication Timing[5]	0	-	20%	55%
PCI Within 90 Minutes of Arrival[5]	0	-	91%	90%
Smoking Cessation Advice[5]	0	-	100%	99%
Chest Pain/Possible Heart Attack Care				
Aspirin at Arrival	-	-	96%	95%
Median Time to ECG (minutes)	-	-	7	8
Median Time to Transfer (minutes)	-	-	68	61
Fibrinolytic Medication Timing	-	-	72%	54%
Heart Failure Care				
ACE Inhibitor or ARB for LVSD[1,3]	1	100%	94%	94%
Discharge Instructions[1,3]	3	33%	87%	88%
Evaluation of LVS Function[1,3]	4	100%	96%	98%
Smoking Cessation Advice[1,3]	2	0%	96%	98%
Pneumonia Care				
Appropriate Initial Antibiotic[1,3]	5	100%	91%	92%
Blood Culture Timing[3]	0	-	97%	96%
Influenza Vaccine[1]	5	40%	91%	91%
Initial Antibiotic Timing[1,3]	5	100%	97%	95%
Pneumococcal Vaccine[1,3]	6	33%	92%	93%
Smoking Cessation Advice[1,3]	1	100%	90%	97%
Surgical Care Improvement Project				
Appropriate VTP Within 24 Hours[5]	0	-	94%	92%
Appropriate Hair Removal[5]	0	-	99%	99%
Appropriate Beta Blocker Usage[5]	0	-	94%	93%
Controlled Postoperative Blood Glucose[5]	0	-	96%	93%
Prophylactic Antibiotic Timing[5]	0	-	97%	97%
Prophylactic Antibiotic Timing (Outpatient)	-	-	93%	92%
Prophylactic Antibiotic Selection[5]	0	-	98%	97%
Prophylactic Antibiotic Select. (Outpatient)	-	-	97%	94%
Prophylactic Antibiotic Stopped[5]	0	-	94%	94%
Recommended VTP Ordered[5]	0	-	95%	94%
Urinary Catheter Removal[5]	0	-	90%	90%
Children's Asthma Care				
Received Systemic Corticosteroids	-	-	-	100%
Received Home Management Plan	-	-	-	71%
Received Reliever Medication	-	-	-	100%
Use of Medical Imaging				
Combination Abdominal CT Scan	-	-	0.152	0.191
Combination Chest CT Scan	-	-	0.033	0.054
Follow-up Mammogram/Ultrasound	-	-	8.1%	8.4%
MRI for Low Back Pain	-	-	33.8%	32.7%
Survey of Patients' Hospital Experiences				
Area Around Room 'Always' Quiet at Night[6]	<100	74%	-	58%
Doctors 'Always' Communicated Well[6]	<100	89%	-	80%
Home Recovery Information Given[6]	<100	73%	-	82%
Hospital Given 9 or 10 on 10 Point Scale[6]	<100	87%	-	67%
Meds 'Always' Explained Before Given[6]	<100	67%	-	60%
Nurses 'Always' Communicated Well[6]	<100	89%	-	76%
Pain 'Always' Well Controlled[6]	<100	81%	-	69%
Room and Bathroom 'Always' Clean[6]	<100	94%	-	71%
Timely Help 'Always' Received[6]	<100	77%	-	64%
Would Definitely Recommend Hospital	<100	68%	-	69%

Tri-County Area Hospital District

1201 North Erie St
Lexington, NE 68850
Phone: 308-324-5651
Fax: 308-324-8359
URL: www.tricountyhospital.com
Type: Critical Access Hospitals
Emergency Services: Yes
Ownership: Govt - Hospital Dist/Auth
Beds: 40
Key Personnel:
CEO/President. . . . . Leslie Marsh
Cardiac Laboratory. . . . . Mary Kay Rhone
Chief of Medical Staff . . . . Fran Acosta-Carlson, MD
Infection Control. . . . . Hawley Lister
Operating Room. . . . . Pam Teten
Quality Assurance . . . . Sandy Nichelson
Radiology. . . . . Jo Swartz

Measure	Cases	This Hosp.	State Avg.	U.S. Avg.
Heart Attack Care				
ACE Inhibitor or ARB for LVSD[1]	3	100%	97%	96%
Aspirin at Arrival[1]	5	100%	99%	99%
Aspirin at Discharge[1]	5	100%	99%	98%
Beta Blocker at Discharge[1]	5	100%	99%	98%
Fibrinolytic Medication Timing	0	-	20%	55%
PCI Within 90 Minutes of Arrival	0	-	91%	90%
Smoking Cessation Advice	0	-	100%	99%
Chest Pain/Possible Heart Attack Care				
Aspirin at Arrival[5]	0	-	96%	95%
Median Time to ECG (minutes)[5]	0	-	7	8
Median Time to Transfer (minutes)[5]	0	-	68	61
Fibrinolytic Medication Timing[5]	0	-	72%	54%
Heart Failure Care				
ACE Inhibitor or ARB for LVSD[1]	8	100%	94%	94%
Discharge Instructions[1]	11	100%	87%	88%
Evaluation of LVS Function[1]	15	93%	96%	98%
Smoking Cessation Advice[1]	1	100%	96%	98%
Pneumonia Care				
Appropriate Initial Antibiotic[2]	28	100%	91%	92%
Blood Culture Timing[1,2]	13	92%	97%	96%
Influenza Vaccine[1]	22	95%	91%	91%
Initial Antibiotic Timing[2]	45	100%	97%	95%
Pneumococcal Vaccine[2]	40	98%	92%	93%
Smoking Cessation Advice[1,2]	9	100%	90%	97%
Surgical Care Improvement Project				
Appropriate VTP Within 24 Hours[1]	16	100%	94%	92%
Appropriate Hair Removal	45	100%	99%	99%
Appropriate Beta Blocker Usage[1]	9	100%	94%	93%
Controlled Postoperative Blood Glucose	0	-	96%	93%
Prophylactic Antibiotic Timing	39	95%	97%	97%
Prophylactic Antibiotic Timing (Outpatient)[5]	0	-	93%	92%
Prophylactic Antibiotic Selection	39	100%	98%	97%
Prophylactic Antibiotic Select. (Outpatient)[5]	0	-	97%	94%
Prophylactic Antibiotic Stopped	39	100%	94%	94%
Recommended VTP Ordered[1]	16	100%	95%	94%
Urinary Catheter Removal[1]	10	100%	90%	90%
Children's Asthma Care				
Received Systemic Corticosteroids	-	-	-	100%
Received Home Management Plan	-	-	-	71%
Received Reliever Medication	-	-	-	100%
Use of Medical Imaging				
Combination Abdominal CT Scan	73	0.041	0.152	0.191
Combination Chest CT Scan[1]	54	0.130	0.033	0.054
Follow-up Mammogram/Ultrasound	185	2.2%	8.1%	8.4%
MRI for Low Back Pain[1]	11	36.4%	33.8%	32.7%
Survey of Patients' Hospital Experiences				
Area Around Room 'Always' Quiet at Night	(a)	62%	-	58%
Doctors 'Always' Communicated Well	(a)	79%	-	80%
Home Recovery Information Given	(a)	82%	-	82%
Hospital Given 9 or 10 on 10 Point Scale	(a)	64%	-	67%
Meds 'Always' Explained Before Given	(a)	61%	-	60%
Nurses 'Always' Communicated Well	(a)	76%	-	76%
Pain 'Always' Well Controlled	(a)	68%	-	69%
Room and Bathroom 'Always' Clean	(a)	77%	-	71%
Timely Help 'Always' Received	(a)	62%	-	64%
Would Definitely Recommend Hospital	(a)	63%	-	69%

Bryanlgh Medical Center

1600 South 48th St
Lincoln, NE 68506
Phone: 402-489-0200
Fax: 402-481-8306
URL: www.bryan.org
Type: Acute Care Hospitals
Emergency Services: Yes
Ownership: Voluntary Non-Profit - Private
Beds: 316
Key Personnel:
CEO/President. . . . . Craig Ames
Chief of Medical Staff . . . . Kevin Mota MD
Infection Control. . . . . Larry Krebsbach
Operating Room. . . . . Charles Meyer
Quality Assurance . . . . Debbie Fisher
Radiology. . . . . Sharon Harms
Anesthesiology. . . . . Elizabeth Lau MD
Emergency Room . . . . Ed Mlinek MD

Measure	Cases	This Hosp.	State Avg.	U.S. Avg.
Heart Attack Care				
ACE Inhibitor or ARB for LVSD	75	97%	97%	96%
Aspirin at Arrival	208	100%	99%	99%
Aspirin at Discharge	430	100%	99%	98%
Beta Blocker at Discharge	422	100%	99%	98%
Fibrinolytic Medication Timing	0	-	20%	55%
PCI Within 90 Minutes of Arrival	36	97%	91%	90%
Smoking Cessation Advice	152	100%	100%	99%
Chest Pain/Possible Heart Attack Care				
Aspirin at Arrival[1,3]	3	100%	96%	95%
Median Time to ECG (minutes)[1,3]	3	4	7	8
Median Time to Transfer (minutes)[5]	0	-	68	61
Fibrinolytic Medication Timing[5]	0	-	72%	54%
Heart Failure Care				
ACE Inhibitor or ARB for LVSD	129	99%	94%	94%
Discharge Instructions	304	94%	87%	88%
Evaluation of LVS Function	377	100%	96%	98%
Smoking Cessation Advice	57	100%	96%	98%
Pneumonia Care				
Appropriate Initial Antibiotic[2]	139	95%	91%	92%
Blood Culture Timing[2]	186	97%	97%	96%
Influenza Vaccine[2]	180	97%	91%	91%
Initial Antibiotic Timing[2]	244	99%	97%	95%
Pneumococcal Vaccine[2]	265	98%	92%	93%
Smoking Cessation Advice[2]	94	99%	90%	97%
Surgical Care Improvement Project				
Appropriate VTP Within 24 Hours[2]	285	92%	94%	92%
Appropriate Hair Removal[2]	1,176	100%	99%	99%
Appropriate Beta Blocker Usage[2]	430	94%	94%	93%
Controlled Postoperative Blood Glucose[2]	291	96%	96%	93%
Prophylactic Antibiotic Timing[2]	810	98%	97%	97%
Prophylactic Antibiotic Timing (Outpatient)	603	99%	93%	92%
Prophylactic Antibiotic Selection[2]	830	96%	98%	97%
Prophylactic Antibiotic Select. (Outpatient)	601	98%	97%	94%
Prophylactic Antibiotic Stopped[2]	764	90%	94%	94%
Recommended VTP Ordered[2]	288	94%	95%	94%
Urinary Catheter Removal[2]	102	74%	90%	90%
Children's Asthma Care				
Received Systemic Corticosteroids	-	-	-	100%
Received Home Management Plan	-	-	-	71%
Received Reliever Medication	-	-	-	100%
Use of Medical Imaging				
Combination Abdominal CT Scan	1,336	0.072	0.152	0.191
Combination Chest CT Scan	729	0.085	0.033	0.054
Follow-up Mammogram/Ultrasound	2,860	9.3%	8.1%	8.4%
MRI for Low Back Pain	245	34.7%	33.8%	32.7%
Survey of Patients' Hospital Experiences				
Area Around Room 'Always' Quiet at Night	300+	60%	-	58%
Doctors 'Always' Communicated Well	300+	76%	-	80%
Home Recovery Information Given	300+	89%	-	82%
Hospital Given 9 or 10 on 10 Point Scale	300+	74%	-	67%
Meds 'Always' Explained Before Given	300+	60%	-	60%
Nurses 'Always' Communicated Well	300+	74%	-	76%
Pain 'Always' Well Controlled	300+	66%	-	69%
Room and Bathroom 'Always' Clean	300+	73%	-	71%
Timely Help 'Always' Received	300+	63%	-	64%
Would Definitely Recommend Hospital	300+	79%	-	69%

NOTE: Hospital profiles are in alphabetical order by state, then city, then hospital within the city; Rankings exclude hospitals with less than 25 cases except for patient surveys which excludes hospitals with less than 100 cases; (a) 100–299 cases; (1) The number of cases is too small to be sure how well a hospital is performing; (2) The hospital indicated that the data submitted for this measure were based on a sample of cases; (3) Data was collected during a shorter time period (fewer quarters) than the maximum possible time for this measure; (4) Suppressed for one or more quarters by CMS; (5) No data is available from the hospital for this measure; (6) Fewer than 100 patients completed the HCAHPS survey. Use these rates with caution, as the number of surveys may be too low to reliably assess hospital performance; (7) Survey results are based on less than 12 months of data; (8) Survey results are not available for this reporting period; (9) No or very few patients were eligible for the HCAHPS survey. The scores shown, if any, reflect a very small number of surveys; (10) A state average was not calculated because too few hospitals in the state submitted data; (11) There were discrepancies in the data collection process; Please refer to the User's Guide for a full explanation of data.

Lincoln Surgical Hospital

1710 South 70th St, Suite 200 Phone: 402-484-9090
Lincoln, NE 68506
Type: Acute Care Hospitals Emergency Services: No
Ownership: Proprietary
Key Personnel:
CEO/President. . . . . Rob Lanafelter

Measure	Cases	This Hosp.	State Avg.	U.S. Avg.
Heart Attack Care				
ACE Inhibitor or ARB for LVSD[5]	0	-	97%	96%
Aspirin at Arrival[5]	0	-	99%	99%
Aspirin at Discharge[5]	0	-	99%	98%
Beta Blocker at Discharge[5]	0	-	99%	98%
Fibrinolytic Medication Timing[5]	0	-	20%	55%
PCI Within 90 Minutes of Arrival[5]	0	-	91%	90%
Smoking Cessation Advice[5]	0	-	100%	99%
Chest Pain/Possible Heart Attack Care				
Aspirin at Arrival[5]	0	-	96%	95%
Median Time to ECG (minutes)[5]	0	-	7	8
Median Time to Transfer (minutes)[5]	0	-	68	61
Fibrinolytic Medication Timing[5]	0	-	72%	54%
Heart Failure Care				
ACE Inhibitor or ARB for LVSD[5]	0	-	94%	94%
Discharge Instructions[5]	0	-	87%	88%
Evaluation of LVS Function[5]	0	-	96%	98%
Smoking Cessation Advice[5]	0	-	96%	98%
Pneumonia Care				
Appropriate Initial Antibiotic[5]	0	-	91%	92%
Blood Culture Timing[5]	0	-	97%	96%
Influenza Vaccine[5]	0	-	91%	91%
Initial Antibiotic Timing[5]	0	-	97%	95%
Pneumococcal Vaccine[5]	0	-	92%	93%
Smoking Cessation Advice[5]	0	-	90%	97%
Surgical Care Improvement Project				
Appropriate VTP Within 24 Hours[2]	29	100%	94%	92%
Appropriate Hair Removal[2]	484	100%	99%	99%
Appropriate Beta Blocker Usage[2]	91	100%	94%	93%
Controlled Postoperative Blood Glucose[2]	0	-	96%	93%
Prophylactic Antibiotic Timing[2]	432	98%	97%	97%
Prophylactic Antibiotic Timing (Outpatient)	372	98%	93%	92%
Prophylactic Antibiotic Selection[2]	433	100%	98%	97%
Prophylactic Antibiotic Select. (Outpatient)	367	99%	97%	94%
Prophylactic Antibiotic Stopped[2]	430	100%	94%	94%
Recommended VTP Ordered[2]	29	100%	95%	94%
Urinary Catheter Removal	69	100%	90%	90%
Children's Asthma Care				
Received Systemic Corticosteroids	-	-	-	100%
Received Home Management Plan	-	-	-	71%
Received Reliever Medication	-	-	-	100%
Use of Medical Imaging				
Combination Abdominal CT Scan[5]	0	-	0.152	0.191
Combination Chest CT Scan[5]	0	-	0.033	0.054
Follow-up Mammogram/Ultrasound[5]	0	-	8.1%	8.4%
MRI for Low Back Pain[5]	0	-	33.8%	32.7%
Survey of Patients' Hospital Experiences				
Area Around Room 'Always' Quiet at Night	300+	80%	-	58%
Doctors 'Always' Communicated Well	300+	87%	-	80%
Home Recovery Information Given	300+	96%	-	82%
Hospital Given 9 or 10 on 10 Point Scale	300+	89%	-	67%
Meds 'Always' Explained Before Given	300+	72%	-	60%
Nurses 'Always' Communicated Well	300+	86%	-	76%
Pain 'Always' Well Controlled	300+	75%	-	69%
Room and Bathroom 'Always' Clean	300+	89%	-	71%
Timely Help 'Always' Received	300+	85%	-	64%
Would Definitely Recommend Hospital	300+	89%	-	69%

Nebraska Heart Hospital

7500 South 91st St Phone: 402-328-3000
Lincoln, NE 68526 Fax: 402-328-3010
URL: www.neheart.com
Type: Acute Care Hospitals Emergency Services: No
Ownership: Proprietary Beds: 54
Key Personnel:
CEO/President. . . . . Sheryl D Dodds

Measure	Cases	This Hosp.	State Avg.	U.S. Avg.
Heart Attack Care				
ACE Inhibitor or ARB for LVSD	45	100%	97%	96%
Aspirin at Arrival	29	100%	99%	99%
Aspirin at Discharge	371	100%	99%	98%
Beta Blocker at Discharge	343	100%	99%	98%
Fibrinolytic Medication Timing	0	-	20%	55%
PCI Within 90 Minutes of Arrival	0	-	91%	90%
Smoking Cessation Advice	113	100%	100%	99%
Chest Pain/Possible Heart Attack Care				
Aspirin at Arrival[5]	0	-	96%	95%
Median Time to ECG (minutes)[5]	0	-	7	8
Median Time to Transfer (minutes)[5]	0	-	68	61
Fibrinolytic Medication Timing[5]	0	-	72%	54%
Heart Failure Care				
ACE Inhibitor or ARB for LVSD	137	96%	94%	94%
Discharge Instructions	227	86%	87%	88%
Evaluation of LVS Function	263	100%	96%	98%
Smoking Cessation Advice	42	100%	96%	98%
Pneumonia Care				
Appropriate Initial Antibiotic[1,3]	2	100%	91%	92%
Blood Culture Timing[3]	0	-	97%	96%
Influenza Vaccine[1,3]	8	88%	91%	91%
Initial Antibiotic Timing[1,3]	3	100%	97%	95%
Pneumococcal Vaccine[1,3]	15	73%	92%	93%
Smoking Cessation Advice[1,3]	2	100%	90%	97%
Surgical Care Improvement Project				
Appropriate VTP Within 24 Hours[1,2]	21	86%	94%	92%
Appropriate Hair Removal[2]	327	100%	99%	99%
Appropriate Beta Blocker Usage[2]	180	95%	94%	93%
Controlled Postoperative Blood Glucose[2]	169	93%	96%	93%
Prophylactic Antibiotic Timing[2]	213	98%	97%	97%
Prophylactic Antibiotic Timing (Outpatient)	398	98%	93%	92%
Prophylactic Antibiotic Selection[2]	218	100%	98%	97%
Prophylactic Antibiotic Select. (Outpatient)	397	99%	97%	94%
Prophylactic Antibiotic Stopped[2]	205	96%	94%	94%
Recommended VTP Ordered[1,2]	21	90%	95%	94%
Urinary Catheter Removal[1,2]	2	100%	90%	90%
Children's Asthma Care				
Received Systemic Corticosteroids	-	-	-	100%
Received Home Management Plan	-	-	-	71%
Received Reliever Medication	-	-	-	100%
Use of Medical Imaging				
Combination Abdominal CT Scan[5]	0	-	0.152	0.191
Combination Chest CT Scan[1]	1	0.000	0.033	0.054
Follow-up Mammogram/Ultrasound[5]	0	-	8.1%	8.4%
MRI for Low Back Pain[5]	0	-	33.8%	32.7%
Survey of Patients' Hospital Experiences				
Area Around Room 'Always' Quiet at Night	300+	49%	-	58%
Doctors 'Always' Communicated Well	300+	76%	-	80%
Home Recovery Information Given	300+	82%	-	82%
Hospital Given 9 or 10 on 10 Point Scale	300+	80%	-	67%
Meds 'Always' Explained Before Given	300+	58%	-	60%
Nurses 'Always' Communicated Well	300+	78%	-	76%
Pain 'Always' Well Controlled	300+	66%	-	69%
Room and Bathroom 'Always' Clean	300+	82%	-	71%
Timely Help 'Always' Received	300+	73%	-	64%
Would Definitely Recommend Hospital	300+	84%	-	69%

Saint Elizabeth Regional Medical Center

555 South 70th St Phone: 402-219-7700
Lincoln, NE 68510 Fax: 402-219-7673
URL: www.stelizabethonline.com
Type: Acute Care Hospitals Emergency Services: Yes
Ownership: Voluntary Non-Profit - Private Beds: 197
Key Personnel:
CEO/President. . . . . Robert J Lanik
Chief of Medical Staff. . . . . Dr. Greg Heidrick
Operating Room. . . . . Nancy Gondringer, RN
Pediatric In-Patient Care . . . . Dr. Kurstin Friesen
Quality Assurance . . . . Lori Burkett, RN

Measure	Cases	This Hosp.	State Avg.	U.S. Avg.
Heart Attack Care				
ACE Inhibitor or ARB for LVSD[1]	20	90%	97%	96%
Aspirin at Arrival	98	100%	99%	99%
Aspirin at Discharge	112	100%	99%	98%
Beta Blocker at Discharge	107	99%	99%	98%
Fibrinolytic Medication Timing	0	-	20%	55%
PCI Within 90 Minutes of Arrival[1]	23	96%	91%	90%
Smoking Cessation Advice	30	100%	100%	99%
Chest Pain/Possible Heart Attack Care				
Aspirin at Arrival[1]	7	100%	96%	95%
Median Time to ECG (minutes)[1]	7	8	7	8
Median Time to Transfer (minutes)[5]	0	-	68	61
Fibrinolytic Medication Timing[5]	0	-	72%	54%
Heart Failure Care				
ACE Inhibitor or ARB for LVSD	59	86%	94%	94%
Discharge Instructions	167	77%	87%	88%
Evaluation of LVS Function	209	96%	96%	98%
Smoking Cessation Advice	29	100%	96%	98%
Pneumonia Care				
Appropriate Initial Antibiotic[2]	90	96%	91%	92%
Blood Culture Timing[2]	152	96%	97%	96%
Influenza Vaccine[2]	82	88%	91%	91%
Initial Antibiotic Timing[2]	162	97%	97%	95%
Pneumococcal Vaccine[2]	148	92%	92%	93%
Smoking Cessation Advice[2]	34	100%	90%	97%
Surgical Care Improvement Project				
Appropriate VTP Within 24 Hours[2]	197	76%	94%	92%
Appropriate Hair Removal[2]	647	100%	99%	99%
Appropriate Beta Blocker Usage[2]	183	75%	94%	93%
Controlled Postoperative Blood Glucose[2]	54	96%	96%	93%
Prophylactic Antibiotic Timing[2]	354	95%	97%	97%
Prophylactic Antibiotic Timing (Outpatient)	495	93%	93%	92%
Prophylactic Antibiotic Selection[2]	356	97%	98%	97%
Prophylactic Antibiotic Select. (Outpatient)	487	94%	97%	94%
Prophylactic Antibiotic Stopped[2]	336	96%	94%	94%
Recommended VTP Ordered[2]	197	82%	95%	94%
Urinary Catheter Removal[2]	72	78%	90%	90%
Children's Asthma Care				
Received Systemic Corticosteroids	-	-	-	100%
Received Home Management Plan	-	-	-	71%
Received Reliever Medication	-	-	-	100%
Use of Medical Imaging				
Combination Abdominal CT Scan	847	0.054	0.152	0.191
Combination Chest CT Scan	563	0.005	0.033	0.054
Follow-up Mammogram/Ultrasound	1,693	12.2%	8.1%	8.4%
MRI for Low Back Pain	147	37.4%	33.8%	32.7%
Survey of Patients' Hospital Experiences				
Area Around Room 'Always' Quiet at Night	300+	57%	-	58%
Doctors 'Always' Communicated Well	300+	77%	-	80%
Home Recovery Information Given	300+	90%	-	82%
Hospital Given 9 or 10 on 10 Point Scale	300+	72%	-	67%
Meds 'Always' Explained Before Given	300+	58%	-	60%
Nurses 'Always' Communicated Well	300+	76%	-	76%
Pain 'Always' Well Controlled	300+	68%	-	69%
Room and Bathroom 'Always' Clean	300+	69%	-	71%
Timely Help 'Always' Received	300+	58%	-	64%
Would Definitely Recommend Hospital	300+	78%	-	69%

NOTE: Hospital profiles are in alphabetical order by state, then city, then hospital within the city; Rankings exclude hospitals with less than 25 cases except for patient surveys which excludes hospitals with less than 100 cases; (a) 100–299 cases; (1) The number of cases is too small to be sure how well a hospital is performing; (2) The hospital indicated that the data submitted for this measure were based on a sample of cases; (3) Data was collected during a shorter time period (fewer quarters) than the maximum possible time for this measure; (4) Suppressed for one or more quarters by CMS; (5) No data is available from the hospital for this measure; (6) Fewer than 100 patients completed the HCAHPS survey. Use these rates with caution, as the number of surveys may be too low to reliably assess hospital performance; (7) Survey results are based on less than 12 months of data; (8) Survey results are not available for this reporting period; (9) No or very few patients were eligible for the HCAHPS survey. The scores shown, if any, reflect a very small number of surveys; (10) A state average was not calculated because too few hospitals in the state submitted data; (11) There were discrepancies in the data collection process; Please refer to the User's Guide for a full explanation of data.

Niobrara Valley Hospital

401 South 5th Street
Lynch, NE 68746
Phone: 402-569-2451
Fax: 402-569-2474

Type: Critical Access Hospitals
Emergency Services: Yes
Ownership: Voluntary Non-Profit - Private
Beds: 20

Key Personnel:
CEO/President. . . . . Kelly Kalkowski
Infection Control. . . . . Barb Hart, RN
Operating Room. . . . . April Micanek, RN
Quality Assurance . . . . Karlene Classen

Measure	Cases	This Hosp.	State Avg.	U.S. Avg.
Heart Attack Care				
ACE Inhibitor or ARB for LVSD[5]	0	-	97%	96%
Aspirin at Arrival[5]	0	-	99%	99%
Aspirin at Discharge[5]	0	-	99%	98%
Beta Blocker at Discharge[5]	0	-	99%	98%
Fibrinolytic Medication Timing[5]	0	-	20%	55%
PCI Within 90 Minutes of Arrival[5]	0	-	91%	90%
Smoking Cessation Advice[5]	0	-	100%	99%
Chest Pain/Possible Heart Attack Care				
Aspirin at Arrival	-	-	96%	95%
Median Time to ECG (minutes)	-	-	7	8
Median Time to Transfer (minutes)	-	-	68	61
Fibrinolytic Medication Timing	-	-	72%	54%
Heart Failure Care				
ACE Inhibitor or ARB for LVSD[5]	0	-	94%	94%
Discharge Instructions[5]	0	-	87%	88%
Evaluation of LVS Function[5]	0	-	96%	98%
Smoking Cessation Advice[5]	0	-	96%	98%
Pneumonia Care				
Appropriate Initial Antibiotic[3]	0	-	91%	92%
Blood Culture Timing[3]	0	-	97%	96%
Influenza Vaccine[3]	0	-	91%	91%
Initial Antibiotic Timing[3,1]	1	100%	97%	95%
Pneumococcal Vaccine[3]	0	-	92%	93%
Smoking Cessation Advice[3]	0	-	90%	97%
Surgical Care Improvement Project				
Appropriate VTP Within 24 Hours[5]	0	-	94%	92%
Appropriate Hair Removal[5]	0	-	99%	99%
Appropriate Beta Blocker Usage[5]	0	-	94%	93%
Controlled Postoperative Blood Glucose[5]	0	-	96%	93%
Prophylactic Antibiotic Timing[5]	0	-	97%	97%
Prophylactic Antibiotic Timing (Outpatient)	-	-	93%	92%
Prophylactic Antibiotic Selection[5]	0	-	98%	97%
Prophylactic Antibiotic Select. (Outpatient)	-	-	97%	94%
Prophylactic Antibiotic Stopped[5]	0	-	94%	94%
Recommended VTP Ordered[5]	0	-	95%	94%
Urinary Catheter Removal[5]	0	-	90%	90%
Children's Asthma Care				
Received Systemic Corticosteroids	-	-	-	100%
Received Home Management Plan	-	-	-	71%
Received Reliever Medication	-	-	-	100%
Use of Medical Imaging				
Combination Abdominal CT Scan	-	-	0.152	0.191
Combination Chest CT Scan	-	-	0.033	0.054
Follow-up Mammogram/Ultrasound	-	-	8.1%	8.4%
MRI for Low Back Pain	-	-	33.8%	32.7%
Survey of Patients' Hospital Experiences				
Area Around Room 'Always' Quiet at Night[8]	-	-	-	58%
Doctors 'Always' Communicated Well[8]	-	-	-	80%
Home Recovery Information Given[8]	-	-	-	82%
Hospital Given 9 or 10 on 10 Point Scale[8]	-	-	-	67%
Meds 'Always' Explained Before Given[8]	-	-	-	60%
Nurses 'Always' Communicated Well[8]	-	-	-	76%
Pain 'Always' Well Controlled[8]	-	-	-	69%
Room and Bathroom 'Always' Clean[8]	-	-	-	71%
Timely Help 'Always' Received[8]	-	-	-	64%
Would Definitely Recommend Hospital[8]	-	-	-	69%

Community Hospital

1301 East H St
Mccook, NE 69001
Phone: 308-344-2650
Fax: 308-344-8358
E-mail: communityhospital@chmccook.org
URL: www.chmccook.orgerson.com

Type: Critical Access Hospitals
Emergency Services: Yes
Ownership: Voluntary Non-Profit - Other
Beds: 25

Key Personnel:
CEO/President. . . . . James P Ulrich Jr.
Coronary Care . . . . Michael Ball
Infection Control. . . . . Linda Robinson
Operating Room. . . . . Joseph C Baer
Pediatric In-Patient Care . . . . Wilfredo Souchet, MD
Quality Assurance . . . . Natalie Webb
Radiology. . . . . Roger E Brockman
Intensive Care Unit. . . . . Evelyn Bertram

Measure	Cases	This Hosp.	State Avg.	U.S. Avg.
Heart Attack Care				
ACE Inhibitor or ARB for LVSD[3]	0	-	97%	96%
Aspirin at Arrival[1,3]	4	100%	99%	99%
Aspirin at Discharge[1,3]	2	100%	99%	98%
Beta Blocker at Discharge[1,3]	1	100%	99%	98%
Fibrinolytic Medication Timing[1,3]	1	0%	20%	55%
PCI Within 90 Minutes of Arrival[3]	0	-	91%	90%
Smoking Cessation Advice[3]	0	-	100%	99%
Chest Pain/Possible Heart Attack Care				
Aspirin at Arrival[1]	21	95%	96%	95%
Median Time to ECG (minutes)[1]	20	11	7	8
Median Time to Transfer (minutes)[1,3]	1	110	68	61
Fibrinolytic Medication Timing[1,3]	1	100%	72%	54%
Heart Failure Care				
ACE Inhibitor or ARB for LVSD[1]	7	71%	94%	94%
Discharge Instructions[1]	22	77%	87%	88%
Evaluation of LVS Function	31	81%	96%	98%
Smoking Cessation Advice[1]	2	100%	96%	98%
Pneumonia Care				
Appropriate Initial Antibiotic[1]	19	100%	91%	92%
Blood Culture Timing[1]	22	100%	97%	96%
Influenza Vaccine	39	87%	91%	91%
Initial Antibiotic Timing	51	100%	97%	95%
Pneumococcal Vaccine	49	94%	92%	93%
Smoking Cessation Advice[1]	11	91%	90%	97%
Surgical Care Improvement Project				
Appropriate VTP Within 24 Hours	54	98%	94%	92%
Appropriate Hair Removal	99	100%	99%	99%
Appropriate Beta Blocker Usage[5]	0	-	94%	93%
Controlled Postoperative Blood Glucose	0	-	96%	93%
Prophylactic Antibiotic Timing	82	91%	97%	97%
Prophylactic Antibiotic Timing (Outpatient)[5]	0	-	93%	92%
Prophylactic Antibiotic Selection	82	88%	98%	97%
Prophylactic Antibiotic Select. (Outpatient)[5]	0	-	97%	94%
Prophylactic Antibiotic Stopped	81	96%	94%	94%
Recommended VTP Ordered	54	98%	95%	94%
Urinary Catheter Removal[1]	20	85%	90%	90%
Children's Asthma Care				
Received Systemic Corticosteroids	-	-	-	100%
Received Home Management Plan	-	-	-	71%
Received Reliever Medication	-	-	-	100%
Use of Medical Imaging				
Combination Abdominal CT Scan	221	0.009	0.152	0.191
Combination Chest CT Scan	195	0.072	0.033	0.054
Follow-up Mammogram/Ultrasound	349	13.5%	8.1%	8.4%
MRI for Low Back Pain	65	21.5%	33.8%	32.7%
Survey of Patients' Hospital Experiences				
Area Around Room 'Always' Quiet at Night	300+	49%	-	58%
Doctors 'Always' Communicated Well	300+	84%	-	80%
Home Recovery Information Given	300+	80%	-	82%
Hospital Given 9 or 10 on 10 Point Scale	300+	65%	-	67%
Meds 'Always' Explained Before Given	300+	60%	-	60%
Nurses 'Always' Communicated Well	300+	76%	-	76%
Pain 'Always' Well Controlled	300+	68%	-	69%
Room and Bathroom 'Always' Clean	300+	75%	-	71%
Timely Help 'Always' Received	300+	70%	-	64%
Would Definitely Recommend Hospital	300+	68%	-	69%

Kearney County Health Services Hospital

727 East 1st St
Minden, NE 68959
Phone: 308-832-3400
Fax: 308-832-3417
URL: www.kchs.org

Type: Critical Access Hospitals
Emergency Services: Yes
Ownership: Government - Local
Beds: 25

Key Personnel:
CEO/President. . . . . Fred Meis
Chief of Medical Staff . . . . Eddie Pierce, MD
Quality Assurance . . . . Connie Jorgensen
Radiology. . . . . Shelly Hawthorne
Emergency Room . . . . Mary Bunger

Measure	Cases	This Hosp.	State Avg.	U.S. Avg.
Heart Attack Care				
ACE Inhibitor or ARB for LVSD[5]	0	-	97%	96%
Aspirin at Arrival[5]	0	-	99%	99%
Aspirin at Discharge[5]	0	-	99%	98%
Beta Blocker at Discharge[5]	0	-	99%	98%
Fibrinolytic Medication Timing[5]	0	-	20%	55%
PCI Within 90 Minutes of Arrival[5]	0	-	91%	90%
Smoking Cessation Advice[5]	0	-	100%	99%
Chest Pain/Possible Heart Attack Care				
Aspirin at Arrival	-	-	96%	95%
Median Time to ECG (minutes)	-	-	7	8
Median Time to Transfer (minutes)	-	-	68	61
Fibrinolytic Medication Timing	-	-	72%	54%
Heart Failure Care				
ACE Inhibitor or ARB for LVSD[3]	0	-	94%	94%
Discharge Instructions[3]	0	-	87%	88%
Evaluation of LVS Function[3]	0	-	96%	98%
Smoking Cessation Advice[3]	0	-	96%	98%
Pneumonia Care				
Appropriate Initial Antibiotic[1]	2	100%	91%	92%
Blood Culture Timing[1]	1	100%	97%	96%
Influenza Vaccine[1]	4	100%	91%	91%
Initial Antibiotic Timing[1]	2	50%	97%	95%
Pneumococcal Vaccine[1]	6	50%	92%	93%
Smoking Cessation Advice	0	-	90%	97%
Surgical Care Improvement Project				
Appropriate VTP Within 24 Hours[5]	0	-	94%	92%
Appropriate Hair Removal[5]	0	-	99%	99%
Appropriate Beta Blocker Usage[5]	0	-	94%	93%
Controlled Postoperative Blood Glucose[5]	0	-	96%	93%
Prophylactic Antibiotic Timing[5]	0	-	97%	97%
Prophylactic Antibiotic Timing (Outpatient)	-	-	93%	92%
Prophylactic Antibiotic Selection[5]	0	-	98%	97%
Prophylactic Antibiotic Select. (Outpatient)	-	-	97%	94%
Prophylactic Antibiotic Stopped[5]	0	-	94%	94%
Recommended VTP Ordered[5]	0	-	95%	94%
Urinary Catheter Removal[5]	0	-	90%	90%
Children's Asthma Care				
Received Systemic Corticosteroids	-	-	-	100%
Received Home Management Plan	-	-	-	71%
Received Reliever Medication	-	-	-	100%
Use of Medical Imaging				
Combination Abdominal CT Scan	-	-	0.152	0.191
Combination Chest CT Scan	-	-	0.033	0.054
Follow-up Mammogram/Ultrasound	-	-	8.1%	8.4%
MRI for Low Back Pain	-	-	33.8%	32.7%
Survey of Patients' Hospital Experiences				
Area Around Room 'Always' Quiet at Night[8]	-	-	-	58%
Doctors 'Always' Communicated Well[8]	-	-	-	80%
Home Recovery Information Given[8]	-	-	-	82%
Hospital Given 9 or 10 on 10 Point Scale[8]	-	-	-	67%
Meds 'Always' Explained Before Given[8]	-	-	-	60%
Nurses 'Always' Communicated Well[8]	-	-	-	76%
Pain 'Always' Well Controlled[8]	-	-	-	69%
Room and Bathroom 'Always' Clean[8]	-	-	-	71%
Timely Help 'Always' Received[8]	-	-	-	64%
Would Definitely Recommend Hospital[8]	-	-	-	69%

NOTE: Hospital profiles are in alphabetical order by state, then city, then hospital within the city; Rankings exclude hospitals with less than 25 cases except for patient surveys which excludes hospitals with less than 100 cases; (a) 100–299 cases; (1) The number of cases is too small to be sure how well a hospital is performing; (2) The hospital indicated that the data submitted for this measure were based on a sample of cases; (3) Data was collected during a shorter time period (fewer quarters) than the maximum possible time for this measure; (4) Suppressed for one or more quarters by CMS; (5) No data is available from the hospital for this measure; (6) Fewer than 100 patients completed the HCAHPS survey. Use these rates with caution, as the number of surveys may be too low to reliably assess hospital performance; (7) Survey results are based on less than 12 months of data; (8) Survey results are not available for this reporting period; (9) No or very few patients were eligible for the HCAHPS survey. The scores shown, if any, reflect a very small number of surveys; (10) A state average was not calculated because too few hospitals in the state submitted data; (11) There were discrepancies in the data collection process; Please refer to the User's Guide for a full explanation of data.

Saint Mary's Community Hospital

1314 3rd Ave
Nebraska City, NE 68410
URL: www.stmaryshospitalnecity.com
Type: Critical Access Hospitals
Ownership: Voluntary Non-Profit - Church
Phone: 402-873-3321
Fax: 402-873-9033
Emergency Services: Yes
Beds: 18

Key Personnel:
CEO/President. . . . . Daniel Kelly
Chief of Medical Staff . . . . Dr Jonathan Stelling
Infection Control. . . . . Charisse Spitzer, RN
Operating Room. . . . . Tamela Osborn, RN
Quality Assurance . . . . Charisse Spitzer, RN
Radiology. . . . . Curtis R Burhoop

Measure	Cases	This Hosp.	State Avg.	U.S. Avg.
Heart Attack Care				
ACE Inhibitor or ARB for LVSD[1,3]	2	100%	97%	96%
Aspirin at Arrival[3,1]	3	67%	99%	99%
Aspirin at Discharge[1,3]	3	67%	99%	98%
Beta Blocker at Discharge[1,3]	4	100%	99%	98%
Fibrinolytic Medication Timing[3]	0	-	20%	55%
PCI Within 90 Minutes of Arrival[3]	0	-	91%	90%
Smoking Cessation Advice[3]	0	-	100%	99%
Chest Pain/Possible Heart Attack Care				
Aspirin at Arrival	-	-	96%	95%
Median Time to ECG (minutes)	-	-	7	8
Median Time to Transfer (minutes)	-	-	68	61
Fibrinolytic Medication Timing	-	-	72%	54%
Heart Failure Care				
ACE Inhibitor or ARB for LVSD[1]	4	100%	94%	94%
Discharge Instructions[1]	6	50%	87%	88%
Evaluation of LVS Function[1]	11	100%	96%	98%
Smoking Cessation Advice[1]	2	50%	96%	98%
Pneumonia Care				
Appropriate Initial Antibiotic[1]	19	89%	91%	92%
Blood Culture Timing[1]	16	100%	97%	96%
Influenza Vaccine[1]	18	94%	91%	91%
Initial Antibiotic Timing	36	97%	97%	95%
Pneumococcal Vaccine	32	100%	92%	93%
Smoking Cessation Advice[1]	7	71%	90%	97%
Surgical Care Improvement Project				
Appropriate VTP Within 24 Hours[1,3]	1	100%	94%	92%
Appropriate Hair Removal[1,3]	13	100%	99%	99%
Appropriate Beta Blocker Usage[5]	0	-	94%	93%
Controlled Postoperative Blood Glucose[3]	0	-	96%	93%
Prophylactic Antibiotic Timing[1,3]	11	82%	97%	97%
Prophylactic Antibiotic Timing (Outpatient)	-	-	93%	92%
Prophylactic Antibiotic Selection[1,3]	12	100%	98%	97%
Prophylactic Antibiotic Select. (Outpatient)	-	-	97%	94%
Prophylactic Antibiotic Stopped[1,3]	10	100%	94%	94%
Recommended VTP Ordered[1,3]	1	100%	95%	94%
Urinary Catheter Removal[3]	0	-	90%	90%
Children's Asthma Care				
Received Systemic Corticosteroids	-	-	-	100%
Received Home Management Plan	-	-	-	71%
Received Reliever Medication	-	-	-	100%
Use of Medical Imaging				
Combination Abdominal CT Scan	-	-	0.152	0.191
Combination Chest CT Scan	-	-	0.033	0.054
Follow-up Mammogram/Ultrasound	-	-	8.1%	8.4%
MRI for Low Back Pain	-	-	33.8%	32.7%
Survey of Patients' Hospital Experiences				
Area Around Room 'Always' Quiet at Night[8]	-	-	-	58%
Doctors 'Always' Communicated Well[8]	-	-	-	80%
Home Recovery Information Given[8]	-	-	-	82%
Hospital Given 9 or 10 on 10 Point Scale[8]	-	-	-	67%
Meds 'Always' Explained Before Given[8]	-	-	-	60%
Nurses 'Always' Communicated Well[8]	-	-	-	76%
Pain 'Always' Well Controlled[8]	-	-	-	69%
Room and Bathroom 'Always' Clean[8]	-	-	-	71%
Timely Help 'Always' Received[8]	-	-	-	64%
Would Definitely Recommend Hospital[8]	-	-	-	69%

Antelope Memorial Hospital

102 West 9th St
Neligh, NE 68756
URL: www.amhne.org
Type: Critical Access Hospitals
Ownership: Voluntary Non-Profit - Private
Phone: 402-887-4151
Fax: 402-887-4092
Emergency Services: Yes
Beds: 20

Key Personnel:
CEO/President. . . . . Jack Greene

Measure	Cases	This Hosp.	State Avg.	U.S. Avg.
Heart Attack Care				
ACE Inhibitor or ARB for LVSD[3]	0	-	97%	96%
Aspirin at Arrival[1,3]	1	100%	99%	99%
Aspirin at Discharge[1,3]	1	100%	99%	98%
Beta Blocker at Discharge[1,3]	2	100%	99%	98%
Fibrinolytic Medication Timing[3]	0	-	20%	55%
PCI Within 90 Minutes of Arrival[3]	0	-	91%	90%
Smoking Cessation Advice[3]	0	-	100%	99%
Chest Pain/Possible Heart Attack Care				
Aspirin at Arrival	-	-	96%	95%
Median Time to ECG (minutes)	-	-	7	8
Median Time to Transfer (minutes)	-	-	68	61
Fibrinolytic Medication Timing	-	-	72%	54%
Heart Failure Care				
ACE Inhibitor or ARB for LVSD[3]	0	-	94%	94%
Discharge Instructions[1,3]	1	100%	87%	88%
Evaluation of LVS Function[1,3]	1	0%	96%	98%
Smoking Cessation Advice[3]	0	-	96%	98%
Pneumonia Care				
Appropriate Initial Antibiotic[1,2]	7	71%	91%	92%
Blood Culture Timing[2]	0	-	97%	96%
Influenza Vaccine[1]	7	71%	91%	91%
Initial Antibiotic Timing[1,2]	8	100%	97%	95%
Pneumococcal Vaccine[2]	27	74%	92%	93%
Smoking Cessation Advice[1,2]	1	100%	90%	97%
Surgical Care Improvement Project				
Appropriate VTP Within 24 Hours[5]	0	-	94%	92%
Appropriate Hair Removal[5]	0	-	99%	99%
Appropriate Beta Blocker Usage[5]	0	-	94%	93%
Controlled Postoperative Blood Glucose[5]	0	-	96%	93%
Prophylactic Antibiotic Timing[5]	0	-	97%	97%
Prophylactic Antibiotic Timing (Outpatient)	-	-	93%	92%
Prophylactic Antibiotic Selection[5]	0	-	98%	97%
Prophylactic Antibiotic Select. (Outpatient)	-	-	97%	94%
Prophylactic Antibiotic Stopped[5]	0	-	94%	94%
Recommended VTP Ordered[5]	0	-	95%	94%
Urinary Catheter Removal[5]	0	-	90%	90%
Children's Asthma Care				
Received Systemic Corticosteroids	-	-	-	100%
Received Home Management Plan	-	-	-	71%
Received Reliever Medication	-	-	-	100%
Use of Medical Imaging				
Combination Abdominal CT Scan	-	-	0.152	0.191
Combination Chest CT Scan	-	-	0.033	0.054
Follow-up Mammogram/Ultrasound	-	-	8.1%	8.4%
MRI for Low Back Pain	-	-	33.8%	32.7%
Survey of Patients' Hospital Experiences				
Area Around Room 'Always' Quiet at Night[8]	-	-	-	58%
Doctors 'Always' Communicated Well[8]	-	-	-	80%
Home Recovery Information Given[8]	-	-	-	82%
Hospital Given 9 or 10 on 10 Point Scale[8]	-	-	-	67%
Meds 'Always' Explained Before Given[8]	-	-	-	60%
Nurses 'Always' Communicated Well[8]	-	-	-	76%
Pain 'Always' Well Controlled[8]	-	-	-	69%
Room and Bathroom 'Always' Clean[8]	-	-	-	71%
Timely Help 'Always' Received[8]	-	-	-	64%
Would Definitely Recommend Hospital[8]	-	-	-	69%

Faith Regional Health Services

2700 West Norfolk Ave
Norfolk, NE 68701
URL: www.frhs.org
Type: Acute Care Hospitals
Ownership: Voluntary Non-Profit - Other
Phone: 402-371-4880
Fax: 402-644-7324
Emergency Services: Yes
Beds: 166

Key Personnel:
CEO/President. . . . . Robert Driewer
Chief of Medical Staff . . . . Tim Davy
Infection Control. . . . . Laura Hoogestradt
Operating Room. . . . . Mick Pick
Quality Assurance . . . . Mary Meyer
Radiology. . . . . Brian Vonk
Hemotology Center . . . . Jan With
Intensive Care Unit. . . . . Brenda Hokamp, RN

Measure	Cases	This Hosp.	State Avg.	U.S. Avg.
Heart Attack Care				
ACE Inhibitor or ARB for LVSD[1]	19	95%	97%	96%
Aspirin at Arrival	74	97%	99%	99%
Aspirin at Discharge	108	100%	99%	98%
Beta Blocker at Discharge	106	100%	99%	98%
Fibrinolytic Medication Timing[1]	1	0%	20%	55%
PCI Within 90 Minutes of Arrival[1]	6	83%	91%	90%
Smoking Cessation Advice	31	100%	100%	99%
Chest Pain/Possible Heart Attack Care				
Aspirin at Arrival[1,3]	2	100%	96%	95%
Median Time to ECG (minutes)[1,3]	2	3	7	8
Median Time to Transfer (minutes)[5]	0	-	68	61
Fibrinolytic Medication Timing[5]	0	-	72%	54%
Heart Failure Care				
ACE Inhibitor or ARB for LVSD	28	96%	94%	94%
Discharge Instructions	43	74%	87%	88%
Evaluation of LVS Function	79	99%	96%	98%
Smoking Cessation Advice[1]	6	100%	96%	98%
Pneumonia Care				
Appropriate Initial Antibiotic	44	100%	91%	92%
Blood Culture Timing	78	100%	97%	96%
Influenza Vaccine	54	96%	91%	91%
Initial Antibiotic Timing	88	99%	97%	95%
Pneumococcal Vaccine	86	100%	92%	93%
Smoking Cessation Advice	25	96%	90%	97%
Surgical Care Improvement Project				
Appropriate VTP Within 24 Hours	194	98%	94%	92%
Appropriate Hair Removal	667	100%	99%	99%
Appropriate Beta Blocker Usage	248	98%	94%	93%
Controlled Postoperative Blood Glucose	55	82%	96%	93%
Prophylactic Antibiotic Timing	489	99%	97%	97%
Prophylactic Antibiotic Timing (Outpatient)	136	99%	93%	92%
Prophylactic Antibiotic Selection	491	99%	98%	97%
Prophylactic Antibiotic Select. (Outpatient)	136	99%	97%	94%
Prophylactic Antibiotic Stopped	473	98%	94%	94%
Recommended VTP Ordered	194	99%	95%	94%
Urinary Catheter Removal	30	93%	90%	90%
Children's Asthma Care				
Received Systemic Corticosteroids	-	-	-	100%
Received Home Management Plan	-	-	-	71%
Received Reliever Medication	-	-	-	100%
Use of Medical Imaging				
Combination Abdominal CT Scan	578	0.746	0.152	0.191
Combination Chest CT Scan	647	0.037	0.033	0.054
Follow-up Mammogram/Ultrasound	607	5.4%	8.1%	8.4%
MRI for Low Back Pain	129	22.5%	33.8%	32.7%
Survey of Patients' Hospital Experiences				
Area Around Room 'Always' Quiet at Night	300+	42%	-	58%
Doctors 'Always' Communicated Well	300+	79%	-	80%
Home Recovery Information Given	300+	86%	-	82%
Hospital Given 9 or 10 on 10 Point Scale	300+	60%	-	67%
Meds 'Always' Explained Before Given	300+	58%	-	60%
Nurses 'Always' Communicated Well	300+	77%	-	76%
Pain 'Always' Well Controlled	300+	67%	-	69%
Room and Bathroom 'Always' Clean	300+	77%	-	71%
Timely Help 'Always' Received	300+	62%	-	64%
Would Definitely Recommend Hospital	300+	65%	-	69%

NOTE: Hospital profiles are in alphabetical order by state, then city, then hospital within the city; Rankings exclude hospitals with less than 25 cases except for patient surveys which excludes hospitals with less than 100 cases; (a) 100–299 cases; (1) The number of cases is too small to be sure how well a hospital is performing; (2) The hospital indicated that the data submitted for this measure were based on a sample of cases; (3) Data was collected during a shorter time period (fewer quarters) than the maximum possible time for this measure; (4) Suppressed for one or more quarters by CMS; (5) No data is available from the hospital for this measure; (6) Fewer than 100 patients completed the HCAHPS survey. Use these rates with caution, as the number of surveys may be too low to reliably assess hospital performance; (7) Survey results are based on less than 12 months of data; (8) Survey results are not available for this reporting period; (9) No or very few patients were eligible for the HCAHPS survey. The scores shown, if any, reflect a very small number of surveys; (10) A state average was not calculated because too few hospitals in the state submitted data; (11) There were discrepancies in the data collection process; Please refer to the User's Guide for a full explanation of data.

Great Plains Regional Medical Center

601 West Leota St
North Platte, NE 69101
Phone: 308-696-8000
Fax: 308-535-3410
Type: Acute Care Hospitals
Emergency Services: Yes
Ownership: Voluntary Non-Profit - Private
Beds: 116

Key Personnel:
CEO/President. . . . . Lucinda A Bradley
Chief of Medical Staff. . . . . Dr. Clint Schafer
Infection Control. . . . . Teresa Mowak
Operating Room. . . . . Margaret Emme
Pediatric In-Patient Care . . . . Lisa Kosmarek
Quality Assurance . . . . Pam Sweeney
Radiology. . . . . Douglas Child

Measure	Cases	This Hosp.	State Avg.	U.S. Avg.
Heart Attack Care				
ACE Inhibitor or ARB for LVSD[1]	2	100%	97%	96%
Aspirin at Arrival[1]	16	100%	99%	99%
Aspirin at Discharge[1]	17	100%	99%	98%
Beta Blocker at Discharge[1]	14	100%	99%	98%
Fibrinolytic Medication Timing	0	-	20%	55%
PCI Within 90 Minutes of Arrival	0	-	91%	90%
Smoking Cessation Advice[1]	3	100%	100%	99%
Chest Pain/Possible Heart Attack Care				
Aspirin at Arrival	55	100%	96%	95%
Median Time to ECG (minutes)	56	7	7	8
Median Time to Transfer (minutes)[3]	0	-	68	61
Fibrinolytic Medication Timing[1]	15	87%	72%	54%
Heart Failure Care				
ACE Inhibitor or ARB for LVSD[1]	20	95%	94%	94%
Discharge Instructions	70	86%	87%	88%
Evaluation of LVS Function	102	98%	96%	98%
Smoking Cessation Advice[1]	14	100%	96%	98%
Pneumonia Care				
Appropriate Initial Antibiotic[2]	90	98%	91%	92%
Blood Culture Timing[2]	141	99%	97%	96%
Influenza Vaccine[2]	83	94%	91%	91%
Initial Antibiotic Timing[2]	136	99%	97%	95%
Pneumococcal Vaccine[2]	133	97%	92%	93%
Smoking Cessation Advice[2]	45	98%	90%	97%
Surgical Care Improvement Project				
Appropriate VTP Within 24 Hours	115	93%	94%	92%
Appropriate Hair Removal	342	100%	99%	99%
Appropriate Beta Blocker Usage	115	97%	94%	93%
Controlled Postoperative Blood Glucose	0	-	96%	93%
Prophylactic Antibiotic Timing	240	99%	97%	97%
Prophylactic Antibiotic Timing (Outpatient)	151	100%	93%	92%
Prophylactic Antibiotic Selection	240	100%	98%	97%
Prophylactic Antibiotic Select. (Outpatient)	152	99%	97%	94%
Prophylactic Antibiotic Stopped	234	97%	94%	94%
Recommended VTP Ordered	115	97%	95%	94%
Urinary Catheter Removal	25	100%	90%	90%
Children's Asthma Care				
Received Systemic Corticosteroids	-	-	-	100%
Received Home Management Plan	-	-	-	71%
Received Reliever Medication	-	-	-	100%
Use of Medical Imaging				
Combination Abdominal CT Scan	737	0.052	0.152	0.191
Combination Chest CT Scan	564	0.032	0.033	0.054
Follow-up Mammogram/Ultrasound	1,184	9.9%	8.1%	8.4%
MRI for Low Back Pain	256	29.7%	33.8%	32.7%
Survey of Patients' Hospital Experiences				
Area Around Room 'Always' Quiet at Night	300+	48%	-	58%
Doctors 'Always' Communicated Well	300+	79%	-	80%
Home Recovery Information Given	300+	83%	-	82%
Hospital Given 9 or 10 on 10 Point Scale	300+	61%	-	67%
Meds 'Always' Explained Before Given	300+	58%	-	60%
Nurses 'Always' Communicated Well	300+	71%	-	76%
Pain 'Always' Well Controlled	300+	66%	-	69%
Room and Bathroom 'Always' Clean	300+	70%	-	71%
Timely Help 'Always' Received	300+	67%	-	64%
Would Definitely Recommend Hospital	300+	62%	-	69%

Avera St Anthony's Hospital

300 North 2nd St
O'Neill, NE 68763
Phone: 402-336-2611
Fax: 402-336-5145
URL: www.avera-sta.org
Type: Critical Access Hospitals
Emergency Services: Yes
Ownership: Voluntary Non-Profit - Church
Beds: 25

Key Personnel:
CEO/President. . . . . Ronald J Cork
Chief of Medical Staff . . . . Robi Singh, MD
Infection Control. . . . . Val Wecker, RN
Operating Room. . . . . Vicky Harvey, RN
Quality Assurance . . . . Maureen Haggerty, RN
Radiology. . . . . Lawrence Leon
Ambulatory Care . . . . Wendell Spencer
Emergency Room . . . . Mark J Ptacek, MD

Measure	Cases	This Hosp.	State Avg.	U.S. Avg.
Heart Attack Care				
ACE Inhibitor or ARB for LVSD[5]	0	-	97%	96%
Aspirin at Arrival[5]	0	-	99%	99%
Aspirin at Discharge[5]	0	-	99%	98%
Beta Blocker at Discharge[5]	0	-	99%	98%
Fibrinolytic Medication Timing[5]	0	-	20%	55%
PCI Within 90 Minutes of Arrival[5]	0	-	91%	90%
Smoking Cessation Advice[5]	0	-	100%	99%
Chest Pain/Possible Heart Attack Care				
Aspirin at Arrival	-	-	96%	95%
Median Time to ECG (minutes)	-	-	7	8
Median Time to Transfer (minutes)	-	-	68	61
Fibrinolytic Medication Timing	-	-	72%	54%
Heart Failure Care				
ACE Inhibitor or ARB for LVSD[1]	5	100%	94%	94%
Discharge Instructions[1]	9	67%	87%	88%
Evaluation of LVS Function[1]	22	55%	96%	98%
Smoking Cessation Advice	0	-	96%	98%
Pneumonia Care				
Appropriate Initial Antibiotic	54	89%	91%	92%
Blood Culture Timing[1]	6	83%	97%	96%
Influenza Vaccine	44	89%	91%	91%
Initial Antibiotic Timing	68	97%	97%	95%
Pneumococcal Vaccine	56	91%	92%	93%
Smoking Cessation Advice[1]	14	50%	90%	97%
Surgical Care Improvement Project				
Appropriate VTP Within 24 Hours	42	98%	94%	92%
Appropriate Hair Removal	53	100%	99%	99%
Appropriate Beta Blocker Usage[5]	0	-	94%	93%
Controlled Postoperative Blood Glucose	0	-	96%	93%
Prophylactic Antibiotic Timing	45	76%	97%	97%
Prophylactic Antibiotic Timing (Outpatient)	-	-	93%	92%
Prophylactic Antibiotic Selection	43	88%	98%	97%
Prophylactic Antibiotic Select. (Outpatient)	-	-	97%	94%
Prophylactic Antibiotic Stopped	41	93%	94%	94%
Recommended VTP Ordered	42	100%	95%	94%
Urinary Catheter Removal[1]	23	100%	90%	90%
Children's Asthma Care				
Received Systemic Corticosteroids	-	-	-	100%
Received Home Management Plan	-	-	-	71%
Received Reliever Medication	-	-	-	100%
Use of Medical Imaging				
Combination Abdominal CT Scan	-	-	0.152	0.191
Combination Chest CT Scan	-	-	0.033	0.054
Follow-up Mammogram/Ultrasound	-	-	8.1%	8.4%
MRI for Low Back Pain	-	-	33.8%	32.7%
Survey of Patients' Hospital Experiences				
Area Around Room 'Always' Quiet at Night	300+	47%	-	58%
Doctors 'Always' Communicated Well	300+	83%	-	80%
Home Recovery Information Given	300+	82%	-	82%
Hospital Given 9 or 10 on 10 Point Scale	300+	70%	-	67%
Meds 'Always' Explained Before Given	300+	60%	-	60%
Nurses 'Always' Communicated Well	300+	79%	-	76%
Pain 'Always' Well Controlled	300+	71%	-	69%
Room and Bathroom 'Always' Clean	300+	81%	-	71%
Timely Help 'Always' Received	300+	72%	-	64%
Would Definitely Recommend Hospital	300+	73%	-	69%

Oakland Mercy Hospital

601 East Second St
Oakland, NE 68045
Phone: 402-685-5601
Fax: 402-685-6223
URL: www.oaklandhospital.org
Type: Critical Access Hospitals
Emergency Services: Yes
Ownership: Voluntary Non-Profit - Other
Beds: 17

Key Personnel:
CEO/President. . . . . Tim Fischer
Chief of Medical Staff. . . . . Tracy Martin
Infection Control. . . . . Mary Fran Bacon
Quality Assurance . . . . Roy Blomquist
Emergency Room . . . . GE Petersons

Measure	Cases	This Hosp.	State Avg.	U.S. Avg.
Heart Attack Care				
ACE Inhibitor or ARB for LVSD[5]	0	-	97%	96%
Aspirin at Arrival[5]	0	-	99%	99%
Aspirin at Discharge[5]	0	-	99%	98%
Beta Blocker at Discharge[5]	0	-	99%	98%
Fibrinolytic Medication Timing[5]	0	-	20%	55%
PCI Within 90 Minutes of Arrival[5]	0	-	91%	90%
Smoking Cessation Advice[5]	0	-	100%	99%
Chest Pain/Possible Heart Attack Care				
Aspirin at Arrival	-	-	96%	95%
Median Time to ECG (minutes)	-	-	7	8
Median Time to Transfer (minutes)	-	-	68	61
Fibrinolytic Medication Timing	-	-	72%	54%
Heart Failure Care				
ACE Inhibitor or ARB for LVSD[1]	3	33%	94%	94%
Discharge Instructions[1]	5	20%	87%	88%
Evaluation of LVS Function[1]	8	62%	96%	98%
Smoking Cessation Advice[1]	4	50%	96%	98%
Pneumonia Care				
Appropriate Initial Antibiotic[1]	5	80%	91%	92%
Blood Culture Timing[1]	10	90%	97%	96%
Influenza Vaccine[1]	9	67%	91%	91%
Initial Antibiotic Timing[1]	16	94%	97%	95%
Pneumococcal Vaccine[1]	13	69%	92%	93%
Smoking Cessation Advice[1]	8	75%	90%	97%
Surgical Care Improvement Project				
Appropriate VTP Within 24 Hours[5]	0	-	94%	92%
Appropriate Hair Removal[5]	0	-	99%	99%
Appropriate Beta Blocker Usage[5]	0	-	94%	93%
Controlled Postoperative Blood Glucose[5]	0	-	96%	93%
Prophylactic Antibiotic Timing[5]	0	-	97%	97%
Prophylactic Antibiotic Timing (Outpatient)	-	-	93%	92%
Prophylactic Antibiotic Selection[5]	0	-	98%	97%
Prophylactic Antibiotic Select. (Outpatient)	-	-	97%	94%
Prophylactic Antibiotic Stopped[5]	0	-	94%	94%
Recommended VTP Ordered[5]	0	-	95%	94%
Urinary Catheter Removal[5]	0	-	90%	90%
Children's Asthma Care				
Received Systemic Corticosteroids	-	-	-	100%
Received Home Management Plan	-	-	-	71%
Received Reliever Medication	-	-	-	100%
Use of Medical Imaging				
Combination Abdominal CT Scan	-	-	0.152	0.191
Combination Chest CT Scan	-	-	0.033	0.054
Follow-up Mammogram/Ultrasound	-	-	8.1%	8.4%
MRI for Low Back Pain	-	-	33.8%	32.7%
Survey of Patients' Hospital Experiences				
Area Around Room 'Always' Quiet at Night[8]	-	-	-	58%
Doctors 'Always' Communicated Well[8]	-	-	-	80%
Home Recovery Information Given[8]	-	-	-	82%
Hospital Given 9 or 10 on 10 Point Scale[8]	-	-	-	67%
Meds 'Always' Explained Before Given[8]	-	-	-	60%
Nurses 'Always' Communicated Well[8]	-	-	-	76%
Pain 'Always' Well Controlled[8]	-	-	-	69%
Room and Bathroom 'Always' Clean[8]	-	-	-	71%
Timely Help 'Always' Received[8]	-	-	-	64%
Would Definitely Recommend Hospital[8]	-	-	-	69%

NOTE: Hospital profiles are in alphabetical order by state, then city, then hospital within the city; Rankings exclude hospitals with less than 25 cases except for patient surveys which excludes hospitals with less than 100 cases; (a) 100–299 cases; (1) The number of cases is too small to be sure how well a hospital is performing; (2) The hospital indicated that the data submitted for this measure were based on a sample of cases; (3) Data was collected during a shorter time period (fewer quarters) than the maximum possible time for this measure; (4) Suppressed for one or more quarters by CMS; (5) No data is available from the hospital for this measure; (6) Fewer than 100 patients completed the HCAHPS survey. Use these rates with caution, as the number of surveys may be too low to reliably assess hospital performance; (7) Survey results are based on less than 12 months of data; (8) Survey results are not available for this reporting period; (9) No or very few patients were eligible for the HCAHPS survey. The scores shown, if any, reflect a very small number of surveys; (10) A state average was not calculated because too few hospitals in the state submitted data; (11) There were discrepancies in the data collection process; Please refer to the User's Guide for a full explanation of data.

Ogallala Community Hospital

2601 North Spruce St Phone: 308-284-4011
Ogallala, NE 69153 Fax: 308-284-7262
Type: Critical Access Hospitals Emergency Services: Yes
Ownership: Voluntary Non-Profit - Private Beds: 18

Key Personnel:
CEO/President. . . . . Margie Molitor
Infection Control. . . . . Stacy Olea
Operating Room. . . . . Kathy Vacura
Quality Assurance . . . . Sue Hordessen
Anesthesiology. . . . . Michael Martinson
Emergency Room . . . . Aric DeYoung

Measure	Cases	This Hosp.	State Avg.	U.S. Avg.
Heart Attack Care				
ACE Inhibitor or ARB for LVSD[3]	0	-	97%	96%
Aspirin at Arrival[1,3]	1	100%	99%	99%
Aspirin at Discharge[3]	0	-	99%	98%
Beta Blocker at Discharge[1,3]	1	100%	99%	98%
Fibrinolytic Medication Timing[3]	0	-	20%	55%
PCI Within 90 Minutes of Arrival[3]	0	-	91%	90%
Smoking Cessation Advice[3]	0	-	100%	99%
Chest Pain/Possible Heart Attack Care				
Aspirin at Arrival[1]	18	83%	96%	95%
Median Time to ECG (minutes)[1]	16	6	7	8
Median Time to Transfer (minutes)[1,3]	1	230	68	61
Fibrinolytic Medication Timing[1,3]	5	20%	72%	54%
Heart Failure Care				
ACE Inhibitor or ARB for LVSD[1]	8	100%	94%	94%
Discharge Instructions[1]	21	100%	87%	88%
Evaluation of LVS Function[1]	24	100%	96%	98%
Smoking Cessation Advice[1]	1	100%	96%	98%
Pneumonia Care				
Appropriate Initial Antibiotic	25	100%	91%	92%
Blood Culture Timing[1]	9	100%	97%	96%
Influenza Vaccine[1]	12	83%	91%	91%
Initial Antibiotic Timing[1]	21	100%	97%	95%
Pneumococcal Vaccine	31	90%	92%	93%
Smoking Cessation Advice[1]	6	100%	90%	97%
Surgical Care Improvement Project				
Appropriate VTP Within 24 Hours[1]	18	100%	94%	92%
Appropriate Hair Removal	35	100%	99%	99%
Appropriate Beta Blocker Usage[5]	0	-	94%	93%
Controlled Postoperative Blood Glucose	0	-	96%	93%
Prophylactic Antibiotic Timing	30	97%	97%	97%
Prophylactic Antibiotic Timing (Outpatient)[1,3]	2	100%	93%	92%
Prophylactic Antibiotic Selection	30	100%	98%	97%
Prophylactic Antibiotic Select. (Outpatient)[1,3]	2	100%	97%	94%
Prophylactic Antibiotic Stopped	29	93%	94%	94%
Recommended VTP Ordered[1]	18	100%	95%	94%
Urinary Catheter Removal	0	-	90%	90%
Children's Asthma Care				
Received Systemic Corticosteroids	-	-	-	100%
Received Home Management Plan	-	-	-	71%
Received Reliever Medication	-	-	-	100%
Use of Medical Imaging				
Combination Abdominal CT Scan	150	0.040	0.152	0.191
Combination Chest CT Scan	79	0.025	0.033	0.054
Follow-up Mammogram/Ultrasound	204	10.3%	8.1%	8.4%
MRI for Low Back Pain[1]	15	40.0%	33.8%	32.7%
Survey of Patients' Hospital Experiences				
Area Around Room 'Always' Quiet at Night	(a)	61%	-	58%
Doctors 'Always' Communicated Well	(a)	87%	-	80%
Home Recovery Information Given	(a)	86%	-	82%
Hospital Given 9 or 10 on 10 Point Scale	(a)	74%	-	67%
Meds 'Always' Explained Before Given	(a)	65%	-	60%
Nurses 'Always' Communicated Well	(a)	78%	-	76%
Pain 'Always' Well Controlled	(a)	72%	-	69%
Room and Bathroom 'Always' Clean	(a)	86%	-	71%
Timely Help 'Always' Received	(a)	74%	-	64%
Would Definitely Recommend Hospital	(a)	72%	-	69%

Alegent Health Bergan Mercy Medical Center

7500 Mercy Rd Phone: 402-398-6060
Omaha, NE 68124 Fax: 402-343-4316
URL: www.alegent.com
Type: Acute Care Hospitals Emergency Services: Yes
Ownership: Voluntary Non-Profit - Private Beds: 400

Key Personnel:
CEO/President. . . . . Charles Brummund
Chief of Medical Staff. . . . . Joseph A Jarzobski
Infection Control. . . . . Peggy Leubbert
Operating Room. . . . . Joanne Kennebeck
Pediatric Ambulatory Care . . . . . . Shahab F Abdessalam, MD
Pediatric In-Patient Care . . . . Charles T Rush, MD
Quality Assurance . . . . David Parks
Radiology. . . . . Kimberly A Apker, MD

Measure	Cases	This Hosp.	State Avg.	U.S. Avg.
Heart Attack Care				
ACE Inhibitor or ARB for LVSD	30	100%	97%	96%
Aspirin at Arrival	160	99%	99%	99%
Aspirin at Discharge	208	100%	99%	98%
Beta Blocker at Discharge	204	100%	99%	98%
Fibrinolytic Medication Timing	0	-	20%	55%
PCI Within 90 Minutes of Arrival	28	93%	91%	90%
Smoking Cessation Advice	73	100%	100%	99%
Chest Pain/Possible Heart Attack Care				
Aspirin at Arrival[1,3]	4	100%	96%	95%
Median Time to ECG (minutes)[1,3]	4	6	7	8
Median Time to Transfer (minutes)[5]	0	-	68	61
Fibrinolytic Medication Timing[3]	0	-	72%	54%
Heart Failure Care				
ACE Inhibitor or ARB for LVSD	81	95%	94%	94%
Discharge Instructions	215	92%	87%	88%
Evaluation of LVS Function	275	100%	96%	98%
Smoking Cessation Advice	41	100%	96%	98%
Pneumonia Care				
Appropriate Initial Antibiotic	116	97%	91%	92%
Blood Culture Timing	150	99%	97%	96%
Influenza Vaccine	126	100%	91%	91%
Initial Antibiotic Timing	182	98%	97%	95%
Pneumococcal Vaccine	154	99%	92%	93%
Smoking Cessation Advice	61	100%	90%	97%
Surgical Care Improvement Project				
Appropriate VTP Within 24 Hours[2]	244	94%	94%	92%
Appropriate Hair Removal[2]	1,574	100%	99%	99%
Appropriate Beta Blocker Usage[2]	589	98%	94%	93%
Controlled Postoperative Blood Glucose[2]	228	98%	96%	93%
Prophylactic Antibiotic Timing[2]	1,292	96%	97%	97%
Prophylactic Antibiotic Timing (Outpatient)	469	94%	93%	92%
Prophylactic Antibiotic Selection[2]	1,294	97%	98%	97%
Prophylactic Antibiotic Select. (Outpatient)	460	97%	97%	94%
Prophylactic Antibiotic Stopped[2]	1,247	98%	94%	94%
Recommended VTP Ordered[2]	245	95%	95%	94%
Urinary Catheter Removal[2]	448	91%	90%	90%
Children's Asthma Care				
Received Systemic Corticosteroids	-	-	-	100%
Received Home Management Plan	-	-	-	71%
Received Reliever Medication	-	-	-	100%
Use of Medical Imaging				
Combination Abdominal CT Scan	1,290	0.061	0.152	0.191
Combination Chest CT Scan	1,190	0.000	0.033	0.054
Follow-up Mammogram/Ultrasound	751	5.7%	8.1%	8.4%
MRI for Low Back Pain	326	38.0%	33.8%	32.7%
Survey of Patients' Hospital Experiences				
Area Around Room 'Always' Quiet at Night	300+	58%	-	58%
Doctors 'Always' Communicated Well	300+	80%	-	80%
Home Recovery Information Given	300+	86%	-	82%
Hospital Given 9 or 10 on 10 Point Scale	300+	69%	-	67%
Meds 'Always' Explained Before Given	300+	59%	-	60%
Nurses 'Always' Communicated Well	300+	77%	-	76%
Pain 'Always' Well Controlled	300+	70%	-	69%
Room and Bathroom 'Always' Clean	300+	63%	-	71%
Timely Help 'Always' Received	300+	58%	-	64%
Would Definitely Recommend Hospital	300+	70%	-	69%

Alegent Health Immanuel Medical Center

6901 North 72nd St Phone: 402-572-2121
Omaha, NE 68122 Fax: 402-572-2268
URL: www.alegent.com
Type: Acute Care Hospitals Emergency Services: Yes
Ownership: Voluntary Non-Profit - Private Beds: 601

Key Personnel:
CEO/President. . . . . Richard A Hachten II
Quality Assurance . . . . David Parks
Radiology. . . . . Kimberly Apker, MD
Emergency Room . . . . Richard Alarid

Measure	Cases	This Hosp.	State Avg.	U.S. Avg.
Heart Attack Care				
ACE Inhibitor or ARB for LVSD[1]	17	100%	97%	96%
Aspirin at Arrival	101	100%	99%	99%
Aspirin at Discharge	128	100%	99%	98%
Beta Blocker at Discharge	125	100%	99%	98%
Fibrinolytic Medication Timing	0	-	20%	55%
PCI Within 90 Minutes of Arrival	28	89%	91%	90%
Smoking Cessation Advice	52	100%	100%	99%
Chest Pain/Possible Heart Attack Care				
Aspirin at Arrival[1,3]	5	100%	96%	95%
Median Time to ECG (minutes)[1,3]	5	5	7	8
Median Time to Transfer (minutes)[5]	0	-	68	61
Fibrinolytic Medication Timing[5]	0	-	72%	54%
Heart Failure Care				
ACE Inhibitor or ARB for LVSD	50	100%	94%	94%
Discharge Instructions	108	100%	87%	88%
Evaluation of LVS Function	153	100%	96%	98%
Smoking Cessation Advice	29	100%	96%	98%
Pneumonia Care				
Appropriate Initial Antibiotic	58	100%	91%	92%
Blood Culture Timing	102	99%	97%	96%
Influenza Vaccine	72	100%	91%	91%
Initial Antibiotic Timing	138	99%	97%	95%
Pneumococcal Vaccine	111	100%	92%	93%
Smoking Cessation Advice	56	100%	90%	97%
Surgical Care Improvement Project				
Appropriate VTP Within 24 Hours[2]	114	99%	94%	92%
Appropriate Hair Removal[2]	272	100%	99%	99%
Appropriate Beta Blocker Usage[2]	85	100%	94%	93%
Controlled Postoperative Blood Glucose[2]	0	-	96%	93%
Prophylactic Antibiotic Timing[2]	146	100%	97%	97%
Prophylactic Antibiotic Timing (Outpatient)	362	89%	93%	92%
Prophylactic Antibiotic Selection[2]	148	100%	98%	97%
Prophylactic Antibiotic Select. (Outpatient)	343	97%	97%	94%
Prophylactic Antibiotic Stopped[2]	134	96%	94%	94%
Recommended VTP Ordered[2]	114	100%	95%	94%
Urinary Catheter Removal[2]	65	98%	90%	90%
Children's Asthma Care				
Received Systemic Corticosteroids	-	-	-	100%
Received Home Management Plan	-	-	-	71%
Received Reliever Medication	-	-	-	100%
Use of Medical Imaging				
Combination Abdominal CT Scan	658	0.085	0.152	0.191
Combination Chest CT Scan	640	0.013	0.033	0.054
Follow-up Mammogram/Ultrasound	681	3.8%	8.1%	8.4%
MRI for Low Back Pain	204	37.7%	33.8%	32.7%
Survey of Patients' Hospital Experiences				
Area Around Room 'Always' Quiet at Night	300+	64%	-	58%
Doctors 'Always' Communicated Well	300+	80%	-	80%
Home Recovery Information Given	300+	88%	-	82%
Hospital Given 9 or 10 on 10 Point Scale	300+	73%	-	67%
Meds 'Always' Explained Before Given	300+	61%	-	60%
Nurses 'Always' Communicated Well	300+	78%	-	76%
Pain 'Always' Well Controlled	300+	70%	-	69%
Room and Bathroom 'Always' Clean	300+	73%	-	71%
Timely Help 'Always' Received	300+	60%	-	64%
Would Definitely Recommend Hospital	300+	72%	-	69%

NOTE: Hospital profiles are in alphabetical order by state, then city, then hospital within the city; Rankings exclude hospitals with less than 25 cases except for patient surveys which excludes hospitals with less than 100 cases; (a) 100–299 cases; (1) The number of cases is too small to be sure how well a hospital is performing; (2) The hospital indicated that the data submitted for this measure were based on a sample of cases; (3) Data was collected during a shorter time period (fewer quarters) than the maximum possible time for this measure; (4) Suppressed for one or more quarters by CMS; (5) No data is available from the hospital for this measure; (6) Fewer than 100 patients completed the HCAHPS survey. Use these rates with caution, as the number of surveys may be too low to reliably assess hospital performance; (7) Survey results are based on less than 12 months of data; (8) Survey results are not available for this reporting period; (9) No or very few patients were eligible for the HCAHPS survey. The scores shown, if any, reflect a very small number of surveys; (10) A state average was not calculated because too few hospitals in the state submitted data; (11) There were discrepancies in the data collection process; Please refer to the User's Guide for a full explanation of data.

Alegent Health Lakeside Hospital

16901 Lakeside Hills Ct — Phone: 402-717-8000
Omaha, NE 68130
URL: www.alegent.com
Type: Acute Care Hospitals — Emergency Services: Yes
Ownership: Voluntary Non-Profit - Church — Beds: 77
Key Personnel:
CEO/President. . . . . Wayne Sensor

Measure	Cases	This Hosp.	State Avg.	U.S. Avg.
Heart Attack Care				
ACE Inhibitor or ARB for LVSD[1]	11	91%	97%	96%
Aspirin at Arrival	113	99%	99%	99%
Aspirin at Discharge	99	100%	99%	98%
Beta Blocker at Discharge	98	100%	99%	98%
Fibrinolytic Medication Timing	0	-	20%	55%
PCI Within 90 Minutes of Arrival	33	94%	91%	90%
Smoking Cessation Advice	27	100%	100%	99%
Chest Pain/Possible Heart Attack Care				
Aspirin at Arrival[1]	10	90%	96%	95%
Median Time to ECG (minutes)[1]	10	3	7	8
Median Time to Transfer (minutes)[1,3]	2	53	68	61
Fibrinolytic Medication Timing[3]	0	-	72%	54%
Heart Failure Care				
ACE Inhibitor or ARB for LVSD	32	100%	94%	94%
Discharge Instructions	93	94%	87%	88%
Evaluation of LVS Function	153	100%	96%	98%
Smoking Cessation Advice[1]	13	100%	96%	98%
Pneumonia Care				
Appropriate Initial Antibiotic	85	95%	91%	92%
Blood Culture Timing	118	98%	97%	96%
Influenza Vaccine	102	99%	91%	91%
Initial Antibiotic Timing	149	100%	97%	95%
Pneumococcal Vaccine	127	98%	92%	93%
Smoking Cessation Advice	37	100%	90%	97%
Surgical Care Improvement Project				
Appropriate VTP Within 24 Hours[2]	151	96%	94%	92%
Appropriate Hair Removal[2]	423	100%	99%	99%
Appropriate Beta Blocker Usage[2]	149	99%	94%	93%
Controlled Postoperative Blood Glucose[2]	0	-	96%	93%
Prophylactic Antibiotic Timing[2]	261	100%	97%	97%
Prophylactic Antibiotic Timing (Outpatient)	168	90%	93%	92%
Prophylactic Antibiotic Selection[2]	262	99%	98%	97%
Prophylactic Antibiotic Select. (Outpatient)	161	98%	97%	94%
Prophylactic Antibiotic Stopped[2]	254	99%	94%	94%
Recommended VTP Ordered[2]	151	97%	95%	94%
Urinary Catheter Removal[2]	97	98%	90%	90%
Children's Asthma Care				
Received Systemic Corticosteroids	-	-	-	100%
Received Home Management Plan	-	-	-	71%
Received Reliever Medication	-	-	-	100%
Use of Medical Imaging				
Combination Abdominal CT Scan	353	0.074	0.152	0.191
Combination Chest CT Scan	228	0.013	0.033	0.054
Follow-up Mammogram/Ultrasound	744	6.7%	8.1%	8.4%
MRI for Low Back Pain	101	32.7%	33.8%	32.7%
Survey of Patients' Hospital Experiences				
Area Around Room 'Always' Quiet at Night	300+	59%	-	58%
Doctors 'Always' Communicated Well	300+	82%	-	80%
Home Recovery Information Given	300+	88%	-	82%
Hospital Given 9 or 10 on 10 Point Scale	300+	72%	-	67%
Meds 'Always' Explained Before Given	300+	57%	-	60%
Nurses 'Always' Communicated Well	300+	77%	-	76%
Pain 'Always' Well Controlled	300+	70%	-	69%
Room and Bathroom 'Always' Clean	300+	69%	-	71%
Timely Help 'Always' Received	300+	60%	-	64%
Would Definitely Recommend Hospital	300+	75%	-	69%

Children's Hospital & Medical Center

8200 Dodge St — Phone: 402-955-5400
Omaha, NE 68114
URL: childrensomaha.org
Type: Childrens — Emergency Services: Yes
Ownership: Voluntary Non-Profit - Private — Beds: 145
Key Personnel:
President/CEO. . . . . Gary A Perkins

Measure	Cases	This Hosp.	State Avg.	U.S. Avg.
Heart Attack Care				
ACE Inhibitor or ARB for LVSD	-	-	97%	96%
Aspirin at Arrival	-	-	99%	99%
Aspirin at Discharge	-	-	99%	98%
Beta Blocker at Discharge	-	-	99%	98%
Fibrinolytic Medication Timing	-	-	20%	55%
PCI Within 90 Minutes of Arrival	-	-	91%	90%
Smoking Cessation Advice	-	-	100%	99%
Chest Pain/Possible Heart Attack Care				
Aspirin at Arrival	-	-	96%	95%
Median Time to ECG (minutes)	-	-	7	8
Median Time to Transfer (minutes)	-	-	68	61
Fibrinolytic Medication Timing	-	-	72%	54%
Heart Failure Care				
ACE Inhibitor or ARB for LVSD	-	-	94%	94%
Discharge Instructions	-	-	87%	88%
Evaluation of LVS Function	-	-	96%	98%
Smoking Cessation Advice	-	-	96%	98%
Pneumonia Care				
Appropriate Initial Antibiotic	-	-	91%	92%
Blood Culture Timing	-	-	97%	96%
Influenza Vaccine	-	-	91%	91%
Initial Antibiotic Timing	-	-	97%	95%
Pneumococcal Vaccine	-	-	92%	93%
Smoking Cessation Advice	-	-	90%	97%
Surgical Care Improvement Project				
Appropriate VTP Within 24 Hours	-	-	94%	92%
Appropriate Hair Removal	-	-	99%	99%
Appropriate Beta Blocker Usage	-	-	94%	93%
Controlled Postoperative Blood Glucose	-	-	96%	93%
Prophylactic Antibiotic Timing	-	-	97%	97%
Prophylactic Antibiotic Timing (Outpatient)	-	-	93%	92%
Prophylactic Antibiotic Selection	-	-	98%	97%
Prophylactic Antibiotic Select. (Outpatient)	-	-	97%	94%
Prophylactic Antibiotic Stopped	-	-	94%	94%
Recommended VTP Ordered	-	-	95%	94%
Urinary Catheter Removal	-	-	90%	90%
Children's Asthma Care				
Received Systemic Corticosteroids	59	100%	-	100%
Received Home Management Plan	61	93%	-	71%
Received Reliever Medication	61	100%	-	100%
Use of Medical Imaging				
Combination Abdominal CT Scan	-	-	0.152	0.191
Combination Chest CT Scan	-	-	0.033	0.054
Follow-up Mammogram/Ultrasound	-	-	8.1%	8.4%
MRI for Low Back Pain	-	-	33.8%	32.7%
Survey of Patients' Hospital Experiences				
Area Around Room 'Always' Quiet at Night	-	-	-	58%
Doctors 'Always' Communicated Well	-	-	-	80%
Home Recovery Information Given	-	-	-	82%
Hospital Given 9 or 10 on 10 Point Scale	-	-	-	67%
Meds 'Always' Explained Before Given	-	-	-	60%
Nurses 'Always' Communicated Well	-	-	-	76%
Pain 'Always' Well Controlled	-	-	-	69%
Room and Bathroom 'Always' Clean	-	-	-	71%
Timely Help 'Always' Received	-	-	-	64%
Would Definitely Recommend Hospital	-	-	-	69%

Creighton University Medical Center - Saint Joseph

601 North 30th St — Phone: 402-449-4040
Omaha, NE 68131 — Fax: 402-449-5020
URL: www.creightonhospital.com
Type: Acute Care Hospitals — Emergency Services: Yes
Ownership: Voluntary Non-Profit - Other — Beds: 404
Key Personnel:
CEO/President. . . . . Matthew A Kurs
Chief of Medical Staff. . . . . Eugene Rich, MD
Infection Control. . . . . Ann Lorenzen
Operating Room. . . . . Gary Welch, RN
Pediatric Ambulatory Care . . . . . . Stephen A Chartrand, MD
Pediatric In-Patient Care . . . . Stephen A Chartrand, MD
Quality Assurance . . . . Dina Belfare
Radiology. . . . . Charles Lerner, MD

Measure	Cases	This Hosp.	State Avg.	U.S. Avg.
Heart Attack Care				
ACE Inhibitor or ARB for LVSD	68	100%	97%	96%
Aspirin at Arrival	123	99%	99%	99%
Aspirin at Discharge	275	100%	99%	98%
Beta Blocker at Discharge	264	100%	99%	98%
Fibrinolytic Medication Timing	0	-	20%	55%
PCI Within 90 Minutes of Arrival[1]	20	100%	91%	90%
Smoking Cessation Advice	105	100%	100%	99%
Chest Pain/Possible Heart Attack Care				
Aspirin at Arrival[1,3]	3	100%	96%	95%
Median Time to ECG (minutes)[1,3]	3	0	7	8
Median Time to Transfer (minutes)[5]	0	-	68	61
Fibrinolytic Medication Timing[5]	0	-	72%	54%
Heart Failure Care				
ACE Inhibitor or ARB for LVSD	116	98%	94%	94%
Discharge Instructions	249	96%	87%	88%
Evaluation of LVS Function	291	99%	96%	98%
Smoking Cessation Advice	101	100%	96%	98%
Pneumonia Care				
Appropriate Initial Antibiotic	54	98%	91%	92%
Blood Culture Timing	118	99%	97%	96%
Influenza Vaccine	86	97%	91%	91%
Initial Antibiotic Timing	111	97%	97%	95%
Pneumococcal Vaccine	96	99%	92%	93%
Smoking Cessation Advice	64	100%	90%	97%
Surgical Care Improvement Project				
Appropriate VTP Within 24 Hours[2]	189	93%	94%	92%
Appropriate Hair Removal[2]	607	100%	99%	99%
Appropriate Beta Blocker Usage[2]	231	95%	94%	93%
Controlled Postoperative Blood Glucose[2]	173	95%	96%	93%
Prophylactic Antibiotic Timing[2]	407	99%	97%	97%
Prophylactic Antibiotic Timing (Outpatient)	259	97%	93%	92%
Prophylactic Antibiotic Selection[2]	408	99%	98%	97%
Prophylactic Antibiotic Select. (Outpatient)	258	98%	97%	94%
Prophylactic Antibiotic Stopped[2]	386	97%	94%	94%
Recommended VTP Ordered[2]	189	95%	95%	94%
Urinary Catheter Removal[2]	95	83%	90%	90%
Children's Asthma Care				
Received Systemic Corticosteroids	-	-	-	100%
Received Home Management Plan	-	-	-	71%
Received Reliever Medication	-	-	-	100%
Use of Medical Imaging				
Combination Abdominal CT Scan	345	0.368	0.152	0.191
Combination Chest CT Scan	395	0.073	0.033	0.054
Follow-up Mammogram/Ultrasound	512	8.8%	8.1%	8.4%
MRI for Low Back Pain	51	41.2%	33.8%	32.7%
Survey of Patients' Hospital Experiences				
Area Around Room 'Always' Quiet at Night	300+	56%	-	58%
Doctors 'Always' Communicated Well	300+	79%	-	80%
Home Recovery Information Given	300+	83%	-	82%
Hospital Given 9 or 10 on 10 Point Scale	300+	66%	-	67%
Meds 'Always' Explained Before Given	300+	62%	-	60%
Nurses 'Always' Communicated Well	300+	77%	-	76%
Pain 'Always' Well Controlled	300+	69%	-	69%
Room and Bathroom 'Always' Clean	300+	67%	-	71%
Timely Help 'Always' Received	300+	65%	-	64%
Would Definitely Recommend Hospital	300+	69%	-	69%

NOTE: Hospital profiles are in alphabetical order by state, then city, then hospital within the city; Rankings exclude hospitals with less than 25 cases except for patient surveys which excludes hospitals with less than 100 cases; (a) 100–299 cases; (1) The number of cases is too small to be sure how well a hospital is performing; (2) The hospital indicated that the data submitted for this measure were based on a sample of cases; (3) Data was collected during a shorter time period (fewer quarters) than the maximum possible time for this measure; (4) Suppressed for one or more quarters by CMS; (5) No data is available from the hospital for this measure; (6) Fewer than 100 patients completed the HCAHPS survey. Use these rates with caution, as the number of surveys may be too low to reliably assess hospital performance; (7) Survey results are based on less than 12 months of data; (8) Survey results are not available for this reporting period; (9) No or very few patients were eligible for the HCAHPS survey. The scores shown, if any, reflect a very small number of surveys; (10) A state average was not calculated because too few hospitals in the state submitted data; (11) There were discrepancies in the data collection process; Please refer to the User's Guide for a full explanation of data.

Midwest Surgical Hospital

7915 Farnam Drive Phone: 402-399-1900
Omaha, NE 68114
URL: www.mwsurgicalhospital.com
Type: Acute Care Hospitals Emergency Services: No
Ownership: Proprietary

Key Personnel:
Administrator . . . . Charles Livingston

Measure	Cases	This Hosp.	State Avg.	U.S. Avg.
Heart Attack Care				
ACE Inhibitor or ARB for LVSD[5]	0	-	97%	96%
Aspirin at Arrival[5]	0	-	99%	99%
Aspirin at Discharge[5]	0	-	99%	98%
Beta Blocker at Discharge[5]	0	-	99%	98%
Fibrinolytic Medication Timing[5]	0	-	20%	55%
PCI Within 90 Minutes of Arrival[5]	0	-	91%	90%
Smoking Cessation Advice[5]	0	-	100%	99%
Chest Pain/Possible Heart Attack Care				
Aspirin at Arrival[5]	0	-	96%	95%
Median Time to ECG (minutes)[5]	0	-	7	8
Median Time to Transfer (minutes)[5]	0	-	68	61
Fibrinolytic Medication Timing[5]	0	-	72%	54%
Heart Failure Care				
ACE Inhibitor or ARB for LVSD[5]	0	-	94%	94%
Discharge Instructions[5]	0	-	87%	88%
Evaluation of LVS Function[5]	0	-	96%	98%
Smoking Cessation Advice[5]	0	-	96%	98%
Pneumonia Care				
Appropriate Initial Antibiotic[5]	0	-	91%	92%
Blood Culture Timing[5]	0	-	97%	96%
Influenza Vaccine[5]	0	-	91%	91%
Initial Antibiotic Timing[5]	0	-	97%	95%
Pneumococcal Vaccine[5]	0	-	92%	93%
Smoking Cessation Advice[5]	0	-	90%	97%
Surgical Care Improvement Project				
Appropriate VTP Within 24 Hours[1]	2	100%	94%	92%
Appropriate Hair Removal	129	100%	99%	99%
Appropriate Beta Blocker Usage	40	78%	94%	93%
Controlled Postoperative Blood Glucose	0	-	96%	93%
Prophylactic Antibiotic Timing	123	94%	97%	97%
Prophylactic Antibiotic Timing (Outpatient)	409	94%	93%	92%
Prophylactic Antibiotic Selection	121	99%	98%	97%
Prophylactic Antibiotic Select. (Outpatient)	403	98%	97%	94%
Prophylactic Antibiotic Stopped	121	99%	94%	94%
Recommended VTP Ordered[1]	2	100%	95%	94%
Urinary Catheter Removal	59	100%	90%	90%
Children's Asthma Care				
Received Systemic Corticosteroids	-	-	-	100%
Received Home Management Plan	-	-	-	71%
Received Reliever Medication	-	-	-	100%
Use of Medical Imaging				
Combination Abdominal CT Scan[5]	0	-	0.152	0.191
Combination Chest CT Scan[5]	0	-	0.033	0.054
Follow-up Mammogram/Ultrasound[5]	0	-	8.1%	8.4%
MRI for Low Back Pain[5]	0	-	33.8%	32.7%
Survey of Patients' Hospital Experiences				
Area Around Room 'Always' Quiet at Night	300+	91%	-	58%
Doctors 'Always' Communicated Well	300+	93%	-	80%
Home Recovery Information Given	300+	92%	-	82%
Hospital Given 9 or 10 on 10 Point Scale	300+	95%	-	67%
Meds 'Always' Explained Before Given	300+	81%	-	60%
Nurses 'Always' Communicated Well	300+	91%	-	76%
Pain 'Always' Well Controlled	300+	82%	-	69%
Room and Bathroom 'Always' Clean	300+	90%	-	71%
Timely Help 'Always' Received	300+	92%	-	64%
Would Definitely Recommend Hospital	300+	94%	-	69%

The Nebraska Medical Center

987400 Nebraska Medical Center Phone: 402-552-2040
Omaha, NE 68198 Fax: 402-595-1091
URL: www.nebraskamed.com
Type: Acute Care Hospitals Emergency Services: Yes
Ownership: Voluntary Non-Profit - Private Beds: 624

Key Personnel:
CEO/President. . . . . Glenn Fosdick
Chief of Medical Staff . . . . Stephen Smith, MD
Coronary Care . . . . Maureen Kelpe
Infection Control. . . . . Theresa Franco
Operating Room. . . . . Shelley Schwedhelm, RN
Pediatric In-Patient Care . . . . Jackie Parmenter, RN
Quality Assurance . . . . Sue Korth
Radiology. . . . . Terri Paulsen

Measure	Cases	This Hosp.	State Avg.	U.S. Avg.
Heart Attack Care				
ACE Inhibitor or ARB for LVSD[2]	41	90%	97%	96%
Aspirin at Arrival[2]	210	98%	99%	99%
Aspirin at Discharge[2]	273	98%	99%	98%
Beta Blocker at Discharge[2]	267	97%	99%	98%
Fibrinolytic Medication Timing[2]	0	-	20%	55%
PCI Within 90 Minutes of Arrival[2]	34	85%	91%	90%
Smoking Cessation Advice[2]	111	99%	100%	99%
Chest Pain/Possible Heart Attack Care				
Aspirin at Arrival	33	91%	96%	95%
Median Time to ECG (minutes)	32	12	7	8
Median Time to Transfer (minutes)[5]	0	-	68	61
Fibrinolytic Medication Timing[3]	0	-	72%	54%
Heart Failure Care				
ACE Inhibitor or ARB for LVSD[2]	114	90%	94%	94%
Discharge Instructions[2]	240	79%	87%	88%
Evaluation of LVS Function[2]	287	100%	96%	98%
Smoking Cessation Advice[2]	55	98%	96%	98%
Pneumonia Care				
Appropriate Initial Antibiotic[2]	47	81%	91%	92%
Blood Culture Timing[2]	110	96%	97%	96%
Influenza Vaccine[2]	76	83%	91%	91%
Initial Antibiotic Timing[2]	83	94%	97%	95%
Pneumococcal Vaccine[2]	102	84%	92%	93%
Smoking Cessation Advice[2]	65	92%	90%	97%
Surgical Care Improvement Project				
Appropriate VTP Within 24 Hours[2]	196	88%	94%	92%
Appropriate Hair Removal[2]	580	100%	99%	99%
Appropriate Beta Blocker Usage[2]	256	88%	94%	93%
Controlled Postoperative Blood Glucose[2]	124	91%	96%	93%
Prophylactic Antibiotic Timing[2]	361	96%	97%	97%
Prophylactic Antibiotic Timing (Outpatient)	382	86%	93%	92%
Prophylactic Antibiotic Selection[2]	371	99%	98%	97%
Prophylactic Antibiotic Select. (Outpatient)	365	95%	97%	94%
Prophylactic Antibiotic Stopped[2]	349	97%	94%	94%
Recommended VTP Ordered[2]	198	91%	95%	94%
Urinary Catheter Removal[2]	162	85%	90%	90%
Children's Asthma Care				
Received Systemic Corticosteroids	-	-	-	100%
Received Home Management Plan	-	-	-	71%
Received Reliever Medication	-	-	-	100%
Use of Medical Imaging				
Combination Abdominal CT Scan	1,644	0.072	0.152	0.191
Combination Chest CT Scan	1,954	0.002	0.033	0.054
Follow-up Mammogram/Ultrasound	1,888	7.2%	8.1%	8.4%
MRI for Low Back Pain	239	33.1%	33.8%	32.7%
Survey of Patients' Hospital Experiences				
Area Around Room 'Always' Quiet at Night	300+	55%	-	58%
Doctors 'Always' Communicated Well	300+	76%	-	80%
Home Recovery Information Given	300+	84%	-	82%
Hospital Given 9 or 10 on 10 Point Scale	300+	71%	-	67%
Meds 'Always' Explained Before Given	300+	60%	-	60%
Nurses 'Always' Communicated Well	300+	77%	-	76%
Pain 'Always' Well Controlled	300+	67%	-	69%
Room and Bathroom 'Always' Clean	300+	68%	-	71%
Timely Help 'Always' Received	300+	62%	-	64%
Would Definitely Recommend Hospital	300+	77%	-	69%

The Nebraska Methodist Hospital

8303 Dodge St Phone: 402-390-4000
Omaha, NE 68114 Fax: 402-354-8735
URL: www.bestcare.org
Type: Acute Care Hospitals Emergency Services: Yes
Ownership: Voluntary Non-Profit - Private Beds: 430

Key Personnel:
CEO/President. . . . . Stephen L Goeser
Chief of Medical Staff . . . . William Shiffermiller
Operating Room. . . . . Diana Whittle
Quality Assurance . . . . Sara Juster
Radiology. . . . . Brad Hansen

Measure	Cases	This Hosp.	State Avg.	U.S. Avg.
Heart Attack Care				
ACE Inhibitor or ARB for LVSD	42	100%	97%	96%
Aspirin at Arrival	136	99%	99%	99%
Aspirin at Discharge	181	100%	99%	98%
Beta Blocker at Discharge	180	97%	99%	98%
Fibrinolytic Medication Timing	0	-	20%	55%
PCI Within 90 Minutes of Arrival	35	83%	91%	90%
Smoking Cessation Advice	49	98%	100%	99%
Chest Pain/Possible Heart Attack Care				
Aspirin at Arrival[3]	0	-	96%	95%
Median Time to ECG (minutes)[3]	0	-	7	8
Median Time to Transfer (minutes)[5]	0	-	68	61
Fibrinolytic Medication Timing[5]	0	-	72%	54%
Heart Failure Care				
ACE Inhibitor or ARB for LVSD	114	99%	94%	94%
Discharge Instructions	244	98%	87%	88%
Evaluation of LVS Function	323	100%	96%	98%
Smoking Cessation Advice	37	100%	96%	98%
Pneumonia Care				
Appropriate Initial Antibiotic	204	72%	91%	92%
Blood Culture Timing	251	95%	97%	96%
Influenza Vaccine	207	93%	91%	91%
Initial Antibiotic Timing	308	92%	97%	95%
Pneumococcal Vaccine	356	95%	92%	93%
Smoking Cessation Advice	58	91%	90%	97%
Surgical Care Improvement Project				
Appropriate VTP Within 24 Hours[2]	683	96%	94%	92%
Appropriate Hair Removal[2]	2,394	97%	99%	99%
Appropriate Beta Blocker Usage[2]	300	99%	94%	93%
Controlled Postoperative Blood Glucose[2]	287	98%	96%	93%
Prophylactic Antibiotic Timing[2]	1,654	95%	97%	97%
Prophylactic Antibiotic Timing (Outpatient)	450	92%	93%	92%
Prophylactic Antibiotic Selection[2]	1,675	97%	98%	97%
Prophylactic Antibiotic Select. (Outpatient)	438	92%	97%	94%
Prophylactic Antibiotic Stopped[2]	1,590	94%	94%	94%
Recommended VTP Ordered[2]	684	97%	95%	94%
Urinary Catheter Removal	531	98%	90%	90%
Children's Asthma Care				
Received Systemic Corticosteroids	-	-	-	100%
Received Home Management Plan	-	-	-	71%
Received Reliever Medication	-	-	-	100%
Use of Medical Imaging				
Combination Abdominal CT Scan	1,493	0.052	0.152	0.191
Combination Chest CT Scan	1,465	0.013	0.033	0.054
Follow-up Mammogram/Ultrasound	1,277	6.3%	8.1%	8.4%
MRI for Low Back Pain	340	35.9%	33.8%	32.7%
Survey of Patients' Hospital Experiences				
Area Around Room 'Always' Quiet at Night	300+	46%	-	58%
Doctors 'Always' Communicated Well	300+	82%	-	80%
Home Recovery Information Given	300+	87%	-	82%
Hospital Given 9 or 10 on 10 Point Scale	300+	71%	-	67%
Meds 'Always' Explained Before Given	300+	60%	-	60%
Nurses 'Always' Communicated Well	300+	79%	-	76%
Pain 'Always' Well Controlled	300+	72%	-	69%
Room and Bathroom 'Always' Clean	300+	63%	-	71%
Timely Help 'Always' Received	300+	62%	-	64%
Would Definitely Recommend Hospital	300+	74%	-	69%

NOTE: Hospital profiles are in alphabetical order by state, then city, then hospital within the city; Rankings exclude hospitals with less than 25 cases except for patient surveys which excludes hospitals with less than 100 cases; (a) 100–299 cases; (1) The number of cases is too small to be sure how well a hospital is performing; (2) The hospital indicated that the data submitted for this measure were based on a sample of cases; (3) Data was collected during a shorter time period (fewer quarters) than the maximum possible time for this measure; (4) Suppressed for one or more quarters by CMS; (5) No data is available from the hospital for this measure; (6) Fewer than 100 patients completed the HCAHPS survey. Use these rates with caution, as the number of surveys may be too low to reliably assess hospital performance; (7) Survey results are based on less than 12 months of data; (8) Survey results are not available for this reporting period; (9) No or very few patients were eligible for the HCAHPS survey. The scores shown, if any, reflect a very small number of surveys; (10) A state average was not calculated because too few hospitals in the state submitted data; (11) There were discrepancies in the data collection process; Please refer to the User's Guide for a full explanation of data.

Nebraska Orthopaedic Hospital

2808 South 143rd Plz | Phone: 402-637-0600
Omaha, NE 68144
Type: Acute Care Hospitals | Emergency Services: Yes
Ownership: Proprietary

Measure	Cases	This Hosp.	State Avg.	U.S. Avg.
Heart Attack Care				
ACE Inhibitor or ARB for LVSD[5]	0	-	97%	96%
Aspirin at Arrival[5]	0	-	99%	99%
Aspirin at Discharge[5]	0	-	99%	98%
Beta Blocker at Discharge[5]	0	-	99%	98%
Fibrinolytic Medication Timing[5]	0	-	20%	55%
PCI Within 90 Minutes of Arrival[5]	0	-	91%	90%
Smoking Cessation Advice[5]	0	-	100%	99%
Chest Pain/Possible Heart Attack Care				
Aspirin at Arrival[5]	0	-	96%	95%
Median Time to ECG (minutes)[5]	0	-	7	8
Median Time to Transfer (minutes)[5]	0	-	68	61
Fibrinolytic Medication Timing[5]	0	-	72%	54%
Heart Failure Care				
ACE Inhibitor or ARB for LVSD[5]	0	-	94%	94%
Discharge Instructions[5]	0	-	87%	88%
Evaluation of LVS Function[5]	0	-	96%	98%
Smoking Cessation Advice[5]	0	-	96%	98%
Pneumonia Care				
Appropriate Initial Antibiotic[5]	0	-	91%	92%
Blood Culture Timing[5]	0	-	97%	96%
Influenza Vaccine[5]	0	-	91%	91%
Initial Antibiotic Timing[5]	0	-	97%	95%
Pneumococcal Vaccine[5]	0	-	92%	93%
Smoking Cessation Advice[5]	0	-	90%	97%
Surgical Care Improvement Project				
Appropriate VTP Within 24 Hours[1,2]	20	100%	94%	92%
Appropriate Hair Removal[2]	231	99%	99%	99%
Appropriate Beta Blocker Usage[2]	77	90%	94%	93%
Controlled Postoperative Blood Glucose[2]	0	-	96%	93%
Prophylactic Antibiotic Timing[2]	164	99%	97%	97%
Prophylactic Antibiotic Timing (Outpatient)	147	99%	93%	92%
Prophylactic Antibiotic Selection[2]	164	100%	98%	97%
Prophylactic Antibiotic Select. (Outpatient)	147	100%	97%	94%
Prophylactic Antibiotic Stopped[2]	164	95%	94%	94%
Recommended VTP Ordered[1,2]	20	100%	95%	94%
Urinary Catheter Removal[2]	64	97%	90%	90%
Children's Asthma Care				
Received Systemic Corticosteroids	-	-	-	100%
Received Home Management Plan	-	-	-	71%
Received Reliever Medication	-	-	-	100%
Use of Medical Imaging				
Combination Abdominal CT Scan[5]	0	-	0.152	0.191
Combination Chest CT Scan[5]	0	-	0.033	0.054
Follow-up Mammogram/Ultrasound[5]	0	-	8.1%	8.4%
MRI for Low Back Pain	85	35.3%	33.8%	32.7%
Survey of Patients' Hospital Experiences				
Area Around Room 'Always' Quiet at Night	300+	81%	-	58%
Doctors 'Always' Communicated Well	300+	84%	-	80%
Home Recovery Information Given	300+	93%	-	82%
Hospital Given 9 or 10 on 10 Point Scale	300+	85%	-	67%
Meds 'Always' Explained Before Given	300+	67%	-	60%
Nurses 'Always' Communicated Well	300+	86%	-	76%
Pain 'Always' Well Controlled	300+	72%	-	69%
Room and Bathroom 'Always' Clean	300+	75%	-	71%
Timely Help 'Always' Received	300+	78%	-	64%
Would Definitely Recommend Hospital	300+	88%	-	69%

Omaha VA Medical Center

4101 Woolworth Avenue | Phone: 402-346-8800
Omaha, NE 68105 | Fax: 402-449-0618
URL: www.va.gov
Type: Acute Care-Veterans Administration | Emergency Services: No
Ownership: Government - Federal | Beds: 100
Key Personnel:
CEO/President. . . . . John J Phillips
Chief of Medical Staff. . . . . Rowen K Zetterman, MD
Quality Assurance . . . . Shirley A Simons

Measure	Cases	This Hosp.	State Avg.	U.S. Avg.
Heart Attack Care				
ACE Inhibitor or ARB for LVSD[5]	0	-	97%	96%
Aspirin at Arrival[5]	0	-	99%	99%
Aspirin at Discharge[5]	0	-	99%	98%
Beta Blocker at Discharge[5]	0	-	99%	98%
Fibrinolytic Medication Timing[5]	0	-	20%	55%
PCI Within 90 Minutes of Arrival[5]	0	-	91%	90%
Smoking Cessation Advice[5]	0	-	100%	99%
Chest Pain/Possible Heart Attack Care				
Aspirin at Arrival	-	-	96%	95%
Median Time to ECG (minutes)	-	-	7	8
Median Time to Transfer (minutes)	-	-	68	61
Fibrinolytic Medication Timing	-	-	72%	54%
Heart Failure Care				
ACE Inhibitor or ARB for LVSD	48	100%	94%	94%
Discharge Instructions	125	99%	87%	88%
Evaluation of LVS Function	154	100%	96%	98%
Smoking Cessation Advice	26	96%	96%	98%
Pneumonia Care				
Appropriate Initial Antibiotic	28	96%	91%	92%
Blood Culture Timing	63	100%	97%	96%
Influenza Vaccine	67	94%	91%	91%
Initial Antibiotic Timing	68	94%	97%	95%
Pneumococcal Vaccine	80	98%	92%	93%
Smoking Cessation Advice	36	100%	90%	97%
Surgical Care Improvement Project				
Appropriate VTP Within 24 Hours[2]	130	98%	94%	92%
Appropriate Hair Removal[2]	298	100%	99%	99%
Appropriate Beta Blocker Usage[2]	117	97%	94%	93%
Controlled Postoperative Blood Glucose[2,5]	0	-	96%	93%
Prophylactic Antibiotic Timing	206	97%	97%	97%
Prophylactic Antibiotic Timing (Outpatient)	-	-	93%	92%
Prophylactic Antibiotic Selection	207	100%	98%	97%
Prophylactic Antibiotic Select. (Outpatient)	-	-	97%	94%
Prophylactic Antibiotic Stopped	200	98%	94%	94%
Recommended VTP Ordered[2]	130	98%	95%	94%
Urinary Catheter Removal[2]	144	96%	90%	90%
Children's Asthma Care				
Received Systemic Corticosteroids	-	-	-	100%
Received Home Management Plan	-	-	-	71%
Received Reliever Medication	-	-	-	100%
Use of Medical Imaging				
Combination Abdominal CT Scan	-	-	0.152	0.191
Combination Chest CT Scan	-	-	0.033	0.054
Follow-up Mammogram/Ultrasound	-	-	8.1%	8.4%
MRI for Low Back Pain	-	-	33.8%	32.7%
Survey of Patients' Hospital Experiences				
Area Around Room 'Always' Quiet at Night	-	-	-	58%
Doctors 'Always' Communicated Well	-	-	-	80%
Home Recovery Information Given	-	-	-	82%
Hospital Given 9 or 10 on 10 Point Scale	-	-	-	67%
Meds 'Always' Explained Before Given	-	-	-	60%
Nurses 'Always' Communicated Well	-	-	-	76%
Pain 'Always' Well Controlled	-	-	-	69%
Room and Bathroom 'Always' Clean	-	-	-	71%
Timely Help 'Always' Received	-	-	-	64%
Would Definitely Recommend Hospital	-	-	-	69%

Valley County Health System

2707 L Street | Phone: 308-728-4200
Ord, NE 68862 | Fax: 308-728-7809
URL: www.valleycountyhospital.org
Type: Critical Access Hospitals | Emergency Services: Yes
Ownership: Government - Local | Beds: 25
Key Personnel:
CEO/President. . . . . Dean Bither
Chief of Medical Staff. . . . . Jennifer Bengston

Measure	Cases	This Hosp.	State Avg.	U.S. Avg.
Heart Attack Care				
ACE Inhibitor or ARB for LVSD[5]	0	-	97%	96%
Aspirin at Arrival[5]	0	-	99%	99%
Aspirin at Discharge[5]	0	-	99%	98%
Beta Blocker at Discharge[5]	0	-	99%	98%
Fibrinolytic Medication Timing[5]	0	-	20%	55%
PCI Within 90 Minutes of Arrival[5]	0	-	91%	90%
Smoking Cessation Advice[5]	0	-	100%	99%
Chest Pain/Possible Heart Attack Care				
Aspirin at Arrival	-	-	96%	95%
Median Time to ECG (minutes)	-	-	7	8
Median Time to Transfer (minutes)	-	-	68	61
Fibrinolytic Medication Timing	-	-	72%	54%
Heart Failure Care				
ACE Inhibitor or ARB for LVSD[1]	2	100%	94%	94%
Discharge Instructions[1]	7	29%	87%	88%
Evaluation of LVS Function[1]	9	89%	96%	98%
Smoking Cessation Advice[1]	1	0%	96%	98%
Pneumonia Care				
Appropriate Initial Antibiotic[1]	15	93%	91%	92%
Blood Culture Timing[1]	13	92%	97%	96%
Influenza Vaccine[1]	10	50%	91%	91%
Initial Antibiotic Timing[1]	18	100%	97%	95%
Pneumococcal Vaccine[1]	22	77%	92%	93%
Smoking Cessation Advice[1]	5	20%	90%	97%
Surgical Care Improvement Project				
Appropriate VTP Within 24 Hours[5]	0	-	94%	92%
Appropriate Hair Removal[5]	0	-	99%	99%
Appropriate Beta Blocker Usage[5]	0	-	94%	93%
Controlled Postoperative Blood Glucose[5]	0	-	96%	93%
Prophylactic Antibiotic Timing[5]	0	-	97%	97%
Prophylactic Antibiotic Timing (Outpatient)	-	-	93%	92%
Prophylactic Antibiotic Selection[5]	0	-	98%	97%
Prophylactic Antibiotic Select. (Outpatient)	-	-	97%	94%
Prophylactic Antibiotic Stopped[5]	0	-	94%	94%
Recommended VTP Ordered[5]	0	-	95%	94%
Urinary Catheter Removal[5]	0	-	90%	90%
Children's Asthma Care				
Received Systemic Corticosteroids	-	-	-	100%
Received Home Management Plan	-	-	-	71%
Received Reliever Medication	-	-	-	100%
Use of Medical Imaging				
Combination Abdominal CT Scan	-	-	0.152	0.191
Combination Chest CT Scan	-	-	0.033	0.054
Follow-up Mammogram/Ultrasound	-	-	8.1%	8.4%
MRI for Low Back Pain	-	-	33.8%	32.7%
Survey of Patients' Hospital Experiences				
Area Around Room 'Always' Quiet at Night[8]	-	-	-	58%
Doctors 'Always' Communicated Well[8]	-	-	-	80%
Home Recovery Information Given[8]	-	-	-	82%
Hospital Given 9 or 10 on 10 Point Scale[8]	-	-	-	67%
Meds 'Always' Explained Before Given[8]	-	-	-	60%
Nurses 'Always' Communicated Well[8]	-	-	-	76%
Pain 'Always' Well Controlled[8]	-	-	-	69%
Room and Bathroom 'Always' Clean[8]	-	-	-	71%
Timely Help 'Always' Received[8]	-	-	-	64%
Would Definitely Recommend Hospital[8]	-	-	-	69%

NOTE: Hospital profiles are in alphabetical order by state, then city, then hospital within the city; Rankings exclude hospitals with less than 25 cases except for patient surveys which excludes hospitals with less than 100 cases; (a) 100–299 cases; (1) The number of cases is too small to be sure how well a hospital is performing; (2) The hospital indicated that the data submitted for this measure were based on a sample of cases; (3) Data was collected during a shorter time period (fewer quarters) than the maximum possible time for this measure; (4) Suppressed for one or more quarters by CMS; (5) No data is available from the hospital for this measure; (6) Fewer than 100 patients completed the HCAHPS survey. Use these rates with caution, as the number of surveys may be too low to reliably assess hospital performance; (7) Survey results are based on less than 12 months of data; (8) Survey results are not available for this reporting period; (9) No or very few patients were eligible for the HCAHPS survey. The scores shown, if any, reflect a very small number of surveys; (10) A state average was not calculated because too few hospitals in the state submitted data; (11) There were discrepancies in the data collection process; Please refer to the User's Guide for a full explanation of data.

Annie Jeffrey Memorial County Health Center

531 Beebe St Phone: 402-747-2031
Osceola, NE 68651 Fax: 402-747-1405
E-mail: smjohnston89@yahoo.com
URL: www.anniejeffreyhospital.org
Type: Critical Access Hospitals Emergency Services: Yes
Ownership: Government - Local Beds: 21

Key Personnel:
CEO/President. . . . . Kevin A Foote
Operating Room. . . . . Stephen Nagengast
Quality Assurance . . . . Carol Jones
Anesthesiology. . . . . Tom McKenny
Emergency Room . . . . Chris Gabel

Measure	Cases	This Hosp.	State Avg.	U.S. Avg.
Heart Attack Care				
ACE Inhibitor or ARB for LVSD[5]	0	-	97%	96%
Aspirin at Arrival[5]	0	-	99%	99%
Aspirin at Discharge[5]	0	-	99%	98%
Beta Blocker at Discharge[5]	0	-	99%	98%
Fibrinolytic Medication Timing[5]	0	-	20%	55%
PCI Within 90 Minutes of Arrival[5]	0	-	91%	90%
Smoking Cessation Advice[5]	0	-	100%	99%
Chest Pain/Possible Heart Attack Care				
Aspirin at Arrival	-	-	96%	95%
Median Time to ECG (minutes)	-	-	7	8
Median Time to Transfer (minutes)	-	-	68	61
Fibrinolytic Medication Timing	-	-	72%	54%
Heart Failure Care				
ACE Inhibitor or ARB for LVSD[5]	0	-	94%	94%
Discharge Instructions[5]	0	-	87%	88%
Evaluation of LVS Function[5]	0	-	96%	98%
Smoking Cessation Advice[5]	0	-	96%	98%
Pneumonia Care				
Appropriate Initial Antibiotic[1]	7	100%	91%	92%
Blood Culture Timing[1]	4	100%	97%	96%
Influenza Vaccine[1]	7	100%	91%	91%
Initial Antibiotic Timing[1]	10	90%	97%	95%
Pneumococcal Vaccine[1]	12	92%	92%	93%
Smoking Cessation Advice	0	-	90%	97%
Surgical Care Improvement Project				
Appropriate VTP Within 24 Hours[5]	0	-	94%	92%
Appropriate Hair Removal[5]	0	-	99%	99%
Appropriate Beta Blocker Usage[5]	0	-	94%	93%
Controlled Postoperative Blood Glucose[5]	0	-	96%	93%
Prophylactic Antibiotic Timing[5]	0	-	97%	97%
Prophylactic Antibiotic Timing (Outpatient)	-	-	93%	92%
Prophylactic Antibiotic Selection[5]	0	-	98%	97%
Prophylactic Antibiotic Select. (Outpatient)	-	-	97%	94%
Prophylactic Antibiotic Stopped[5]	0	-	94%	94%
Recommended VTP Ordered[5]	0	-	95%	94%
Urinary Catheter Removal[5]	0	-	90%	90%
Children's Asthma Care				
Received Systemic Corticosteroids	-	-	-	100%
Received Home Management Plan	-	-	-	71%
Received Reliever Medication	-	-	-	100%
Use of Medical Imaging				
Combination Abdominal CT Scan	-	-	0.152	0.191
Combination Chest CT Scan	-	-	0.033	0.054
Follow-up Mammogram/Ultrasound	-	-	8.1%	8.4%
MRI for Low Back Pain	-	-	33.8%	32.7%
Survey of Patients' Hospital Experiences				
Area Around Room 'Always' Quiet at Night[8]	-	-	-	58%
Doctors 'Always' Communicated Well[8]	-	-	-	80%
Home Recovery Information Given[8]	-	-	-	82%
Hospital Given 9 or 10 on 10 Point Scale[8]	-	-	-	67%
Meds 'Always' Explained Before Given[8]	-	-	-	60%
Nurses 'Always' Communicated Well[8]	-	-	-	76%
Pain 'Always' Well Controlled[8]	-	-	-	69%
Room and Bathroom 'Always' Clean[8]	-	-	-	71%
Timely Help 'Always' Received[8]	-	-	-	64%
Would Definitely Recommend Hospital[8]	-	-	-	69%

Garden County Health Services

1100 West 2nd St Phone: 308-772-3283
Oshkosh, NE 69154 Fax: 308-772-0143
E-mail: ceo@gchealth.org
URL: www.gchealth.org
Type: Critical Access Hospitals Emergency Services: Yes
Ownership: Government - Local Beds: 10

Key Personnel:
CEO/President. . . . . Carol Kraus
Chief of Medical Staff. . . . . Saurabh Sheel
Radiology. . . . . Gloria Goebel

Measure	Cases	This Hosp.	State Avg.	U.S. Avg.
Heart Attack Care				
ACE Inhibitor or ARB for LVSD[5]	0	-	97%	96%
Aspirin at Arrival[5]	0	-	99%	99%
Aspirin at Discharge[5]	0	-	99%	98%
Beta Blocker at Discharge[5]	0	-	99%	98%
Fibrinolytic Medication Timing[5]	0	-	20%	55%
PCI Within 90 Minutes of Arrival[5]	0	-	91%	90%
Smoking Cessation Advice[5]	0	-	100%	99%
Chest Pain/Possible Heart Attack Care				
Aspirin at Arrival	-	-	96%	95%
Median Time to ECG (minutes)	-	-	7	8
Median Time to Transfer (minutes)	-	-	68	61
Fibrinolytic Medication Timing	-	-	72%	54%
Heart Failure Care				
ACE Inhibitor or ARB for LVSD[3]	0	-	94%	94%
Discharge Instructions[1,3]	1	0%	87%	88%
Evaluation of LVS Function[1,3]	1	0%	96%	98%
Smoking Cessation Advice[3]	0	-	96%	98%
Pneumonia Care				
Appropriate Initial Antibiotic[1]	2	50%	91%	92%
Blood Culture Timing[1]	1	100%	97%	96%
Influenza Vaccine[1]	6	83%	91%	91%
Initial Antibiotic Timing[1]	2	100%	97%	95%
Pneumococcal Vaccine[1]	7	29%	92%	93%
Smoking Cessation Advice[1]	2	0%	90%	97%
Surgical Care Improvement Project				
Appropriate VTP Within 24 Hours[5]	0	-	94%	92%
Appropriate Hair Removal[5]	0	-	99%	99%
Appropriate Beta Blocker Usage[5]	0	-	94%	93%
Controlled Postoperative Blood Glucose[5]	0	-	96%	93%
Prophylactic Antibiotic Timing[5]	0	-	97%	97%
Prophylactic Antibiotic Timing (Outpatient)	-	-	93%	92%
Prophylactic Antibiotic Selection[5]	0	-	98%	97%
Prophylactic Antibiotic Select. (Outpatient)	-	-	97%	94%
Prophylactic Antibiotic Stopped[5]	0	-	94%	94%
Recommended VTP Ordered[5]	0	-	95%	94%
Urinary Catheter Removal[5]	0	-	90%	90%
Children's Asthma Care				
Received Systemic Corticosteroids	-	-	-	100%
Received Home Management Plan	-	-	-	71%
Received Reliever Medication	-	-	-	100%
Use of Medical Imaging				
Combination Abdominal CT Scan	-	-	0.152	0.191
Combination Chest CT Scan	-	-	0.033	0.054
Follow-up Mammogram/Ultrasound	-	-	8.1%	8.4%
MRI for Low Back Pain	-	-	33.8%	32.7%
Survey of Patients' Hospital Experiences				
Area Around Room 'Always' Quiet at Night[8]	-	-	-	58%
Doctors 'Always' Communicated Well[8]	-	-	-	80%
Home Recovery Information Given[8]	-	-	-	82%
Hospital Given 9 or 10 on 10 Point Scale[8]	-	-	-	67%
Meds 'Always' Explained Before Given[8]	-	-	-	60%
Nurses 'Always' Communicated Well[8]	-	-	-	76%
Pain 'Always' Well Controlled[8]	-	-	-	69%
Room and Bathroom 'Always' Clean[8]	-	-	-	71%
Timely Help 'Always' Received[8]	-	-	-	64%
Would Definitely Recommend Hospital[8]	-	-	-	69%

Osmond General Hospital

402 North Maple St Phone: 402-748-3393
Osmond, NE 68765 Fax: 402-748-3349
URL: www.osmondhospital.com
Type: Critical Access Hospitals Emergency Services: Yes
Ownership: Voluntary Non-Profit - Private Beds: 37

Key Personnel:
CEO/President. . . . . Celine M Mlady
Infection Control. . . . . Lynn Riedmiller

Measure	Cases	This Hosp.	State Avg.	U.S. Avg.
Heart Attack Care				
ACE Inhibitor or ARB for LVSD[5]	0	-	97%	96%
Aspirin at Arrival[5]	0	-	99%	99%
Aspirin at Discharge[5]	0	-	99%	98%
Beta Blocker at Discharge[5]	0	-	99%	98%
Fibrinolytic Medication Timing[5]	0	-	20%	55%
PCI Within 90 Minutes of Arrival[5]	0	-	91%	90%
Smoking Cessation Advice[5]	0	-	100%	99%
Chest Pain/Possible Heart Attack Care				
Aspirin at Arrival	-	-	96%	95%
Median Time to ECG (minutes)	-	-	7	8
Median Time to Transfer (minutes)	-	-	68	61
Fibrinolytic Medication Timing	-	-	72%	54%
Heart Failure Care				
ACE Inhibitor or ARB for LVSD[5]	0	-	94%	94%
Discharge Instructions[5]	0	-	87%	88%
Evaluation of LVS Function[5]	0	-	96%	98%
Smoking Cessation Advice[5]	0	-	96%	98%
Pneumonia Care				
Appropriate Initial Antibiotic[1,3]	1	0%	91%	92%
Blood Culture Timing[3]	0	-	97%	96%
Influenza Vaccine[5]	0	-	91%	91%
Initial Antibiotic Timing[1,3]	2	50%	97%	95%
Pneumococcal Vaccine[1,3]	5	60%	92%	93%
Smoking Cessation Advice[3]	0	-	90%	97%
Surgical Care Improvement Project				
Appropriate VTP Within 24 Hours[5]	0	-	94%	92%
Appropriate Hair Removal[5]	0	-	99%	99%
Appropriate Beta Blocker Usage[5]	0	-	94%	93%
Controlled Postoperative Blood Glucose[5]	0	-	96%	93%
Prophylactic Antibiotic Timing[5]	0	-	97%	97%
Prophylactic Antibiotic Timing (Outpatient)	-	-	93%	92%
Prophylactic Antibiotic Selection[5]	0	-	98%	97%
Prophylactic Antibiotic Select. (Outpatient)	-	-	97%	94%
Prophylactic Antibiotic Stopped[5]	0	-	94%	94%
Recommended VTP Ordered[5]	0	-	95%	94%
Urinary Catheter Removal[5]	0	-	90%	90%
Children's Asthma Care				
Received Systemic Corticosteroids	-	-	-	100%
Received Home Management Plan	-	-	-	71%
Received Reliever Medication	-	-	-	100%
Use of Medical Imaging				
Combination Abdominal CT Scan	-	-	0.152	0.191
Combination Chest CT Scan	-	-	0.033	0.054
Follow-up Mammogram/Ultrasound	-	-	8.1%	8.4%
MRI for Low Back Pain	-	-	33.8%	32.7%
Survey of Patients' Hospital Experiences				
Area Around Room 'Always' Quiet at Night[6]	<100	57%	-	58%
Doctors 'Always' Communicated Well[6]	<100	79%	-	80%
Home Recovery Information Given[6]	<100	69%	-	82%
Hospital Given 9 or 10 on 10 Point Scale[6]	<100	71%	-	67%
Meds 'Always' Explained Before Given[6]	<100	63%	-	60%
Nurses 'Always' Communicated Well[6]	<100	83%	-	76%
Pain 'Always' Well Controlled[6]	<100	59%	-	69%
Room and Bathroom 'Always' Clean[6]	<100	75%	-	71%
Timely Help 'Always' Received[6]	<100	73%	-	64%
Would Definitely Recommend Hospital	<100	64%	-	69%

NOTE: Hospital profiles are in alphabetical order by state, then city, then hospital within the city; Rankings exclude hospitals with less than 25 cases except for patient surveys which excludes hospitals with less than 100 cases; (a) 100–299 cases; (1) The number of cases is too small to be sure how well a hospital is performing; (2) The hospital indicated that the data submitted for this measure were based on a sample of cases; (3) Data was collected during a shorter time period (fewer quarters) than the maximum possible time for this measure; (4) Suppressed for one or more quarters by CMS; (5) No data is available from the hospital for this measure; (6) Fewer than 100 patients completed the HCAHPS survey. Use these rates with caution, as the number of surveys may be too low to reliably assess hospital performance; (7) Survey results are based on less than 12 months of data; (8) Survey results are not available for this reporting period; (9) No or very few patients were eligible for the HCAHPS survey. The scores shown, if any, reflect a very small number of surveys; (10) A state average was not calculated because too few hospitals in the state submitted data; (11) There were discrepancies in the data collection process; Please refer to the User's Guide for a full explanation of data.

Alegent Health Midlands Hospital

11111 South 84th St Phone: 402-593-3000
Papillion, NE 68046 Fax: 402-593-3117
URL: www.alegent.com
Type: Acute Care Hospitals Emergency Services: Yes
Ownership: Voluntary Non-Profit - Church Beds: 208

Key Personnel:
Cardiac Laboratory. . . . . Georgia Blobaum
Operating Room. . . . . Lisa Campbell
Radiology. . . . . Jon Bleicher
Emergency Room . . . . Maurice Birdwell
Intensive Care Unit. . . . . Tami Field

Measure	Cases	This Hosp.	State Avg.	U.S. Avg.
Heart Attack Care				
ACE Inhibitor or ARB for LVSD[1]	15	100%	97%	96%
Aspirin at Arrival	79	100%	99%	99%
Aspirin at Discharge	72	100%	99%	98%
Beta Blocker at Discharge	72	100%	99%	98%
Fibrinolytic Medication Timing	0	-	20%	55%
PCI Within 90 Minutes of Arrival	37	100%	91%	90%
Smoking Cessation Advice	28	100%	100%	99%
Chest Pain/Possible Heart Attack Care				
Aspirin at Arrival[1]	20	90%	96%	95%
Median Time to ECG (minutes)[1]	23	8	7	8
Median Time to Transfer (minutes)[3]	0	-	68	61
Fibrinolytic Medication Timing[3]	0	-	72%	54%
Heart Failure Care				
ACE Inhibitor or ARB for LVSD	33	100%	94%	94%
Discharge Instructions	74	95%	87%	88%
Evaluation of LVS Function	105	100%	96%	98%
Smoking Cessation Advice[1]	13	100%	96%	98%
Pneumonia Care				
Appropriate Initial Antibiotic	63	100%	91%	92%
Blood Culture Timing	97	100%	97%	96%
Influenza Vaccine	49	100%	91%	91%
Initial Antibiotic Timing	96	100%	97%	95%
Pneumococcal Vaccine	80	100%	92%	93%
Smoking Cessation Advice[1]	21	100%	90%	97%
Surgical Care Improvement Project				
Appropriate VTP Within 24 Hours	59	98%	94%	92%
Appropriate Hair Removal	126	100%	99%	99%
Appropriate Beta Blocker Usage	31	100%	94%	93%
Controlled Postoperative Blood Glucose	0	-	96%	93%
Prophylactic Antibiotic Timing	66	97%	97%	97%
Prophylactic Antibiotic Timing (Outpatient)	90	94%	93%	92%
Prophylactic Antibiotic Selection	66	95%	98%	97%
Prophylactic Antibiotic Select. (Outpatient)	88	99%	97%	94%
Prophylactic Antibiotic Stopped	64	100%	94%	94%
Recommended VTP Ordered	59	98%	95%	94%
Urinary Catheter Removal[1]	17	100%	90%	90%
Children's Asthma Care				
Received Systemic Corticosteroids	-	-	-	100%
Received Home Management Plan	-	-	-	71%
Received Reliever Medication	-	-	-	100%
Use of Medical Imaging				
Combination Abdominal CT Scan	462	0.113	0.152	0.191
Combination Chest CT Scan	329	0.030	0.033	0.054
Follow-up Mammogram/Ultrasound	925	5.4%	8.1%	8.4%
MRI for Low Back Pain	101	40.6%	33.8%	32.7%
Survey of Patients' Hospital Experiences				
Area Around Room 'Always' Quiet at Night	300+	63%	-	58%
Doctors 'Always' Communicated Well	300+	81%	-	80%
Home Recovery Information Given	300+	87%	-	82%
Hospital Given 9 or 10 on 10 Point Scale	300+	73%	-	67%
Meds 'Always' Explained Before Given	300+	61%	-	60%
Nurses 'Always' Communicated Well	300+	77%	-	76%
Pain 'Always' Well Controlled	300+	73%	-	69%
Room and Bathroom 'Always' Clean	300+	80%	-	71%
Timely Help 'Always' Received	300+	70%	-	64%
Would Definitely Recommend Hospital	300+	70%	-	69%

Pawnee County Memorial Hospital

600 I St Phone: 402-852-2231
Pawnee City, NE 68420 Fax: 402-852-2098
Type: Critical Access Hospitals Emergency Services: Yes
Ownership: Government - Local Beds: 17

Key Personnel:
Chief of Medical Staff . . . . Richard Jackson

Measure	Cases	This Hosp.	State Avg.	U.S. Avg.
Heart Attack Care				
ACE Inhibitor or ARB for LVSD[5]	0	-	97%	96%
Aspirin at Arrival[5]	0	-	99%	99%
Aspirin at Discharge[5]	0	-	99%	98%
Beta Blocker at Discharge[5]	0	-	99%	98%
Fibrinolytic Medication Timing[5]	0	-	20%	55%
PCI Within 90 Minutes of Arrival[5]	0	-	91%	90%
Smoking Cessation Advice[5]	0	-	100%	99%
Chest Pain/Possible Heart Attack Care				
Aspirin at Arrival	-	-	96%	95%
Median Time to ECG (minutes)	-	-	7	8
Median Time to Transfer (minutes)	-	-	68	61
Fibrinolytic Medication Timing	-	-	72%	54%
Heart Failure Care				
ACE Inhibitor or ARB for LVSD[3]	0	-	94%	94%
Discharge Instructions[3]	0	-	87%	88%
Evaluation of LVS Function[3]	0	-	96%	98%
Smoking Cessation Advice[3]	0	-	96%	98%
Pneumonia Care				
Appropriate Initial Antibiotic[1]	7	100%	91%	92%
Blood Culture Timing[1]	3	100%	97%	96%
Influenza Vaccine[1]	8	50%	91%	91%
Initial Antibiotic Timing[1]	5	80%	97%	95%
Pneumococcal Vaccine[1]	8	50%	92%	93%
Smoking Cessation Advice[1]	4	25%	90%	97%
Surgical Care Improvement Project				
Appropriate VTP Within 24 Hours[5]	0	-	94%	92%
Appropriate Hair Removal[5]	0	-	99%	99%
Appropriate Beta Blocker Usage[5]	0	-	94%	93%
Controlled Postoperative Blood Glucose[5]	0	-	96%	93%
Prophylactic Antibiotic Timing[5]	0	-	97%	97%
Prophylactic Antibiotic Timing (Outpatient)	-	-	93%	92%
Prophylactic Antibiotic Selection[5]	0	-	98%	97%
Prophylactic Antibiotic Select. (Outpatient)	-	-	97%	94%
Prophylactic Antibiotic Stopped[5]	0	-	94%	94%
Recommended VTP Ordered[5]	0	-	95%	94%
Urinary Catheter Removal[5]	0	-	90%	90%
Children's Asthma Care				
Received Systemic Corticosteroids	-	-	-	100%
Received Home Management Plan	-	-	-	71%
Received Reliever Medication	-	-	-	100%
Use of Medical Imaging				
Combination Abdominal CT Scan	-	-	0.152	0.191
Combination Chest CT Scan	-	-	0.033	0.054
Follow-up Mammogram/Ultrasound	-	-	8.1%	8.4%
MRI for Low Back Pain	-	-	33.8%	32.7%
Survey of Patients' Hospital Experiences				
Area Around Room 'Always' Quiet at Night[8]	-	-	-	58%
Doctors 'Always' Communicated Well[8]	-	-	-	80%
Home Recovery Information Given[8]	-	-	-	82%
Hospital Given 9 or 10 on 10 Point Scale[8]	-	-	-	67%
Meds 'Always' Explained Before Given[8]	-	-	-	60%
Nurses 'Always' Communicated Well[8]	-	-	-	76%
Pain 'Always' Well Controlled[8]	-	-	-	69%
Room and Bathroom 'Always' Clean[8]	-	-	-	71%
Timely Help 'Always' Received[8]	-	-	-	64%
Would Definitely Recommend Hospital[8]	-	-	-	69%

Pender Community Hospital

603 Earl St Phone: 402-385-3083
Pender, NE 68047 Fax: 402-385-2155
URL: www.pendercommunityhospital.com
Type: Critical Access Hospitals Emergency Services: Yes
Ownership: Govt - Hospital Dist/Auth Beds: 47

Key Personnel:
CEO/President. . . . . Michael Hansen, FACHE
Chief of Medical Staff . . . . David Hollting
Operating Room. . . . . Sue Hansen, RN
Quality Assurance . . . . Gail Brondum
Radiology. . . . . Flora Lehmkuhl
Anesthesiology. . . . . Jerry VandeBrug
Emergency Room . . . . Dee Moeller

Measure	Cases	This Hosp.	State Avg.	U.S. Avg.
Heart Attack Care				
ACE Inhibitor or ARB for LVSD[5]	0	-	97%	96%
Aspirin at Arrival[5]	0	-	99%	99%
Aspirin at Discharge[5]	0	-	99%	98%
Beta Blocker at Discharge[5]	0	-	99%	98%
Fibrinolytic Medication Timing[5]	0	-	20%	55%
PCI Within 90 Minutes of Arrival[5]	0	-	91%	90%
Smoking Cessation Advice[5]	0	-	100%	99%
Chest Pain/Possible Heart Attack Care				
Aspirin at Arrival	-	-	96%	95%
Median Time to ECG (minutes)	-	-	7	8
Median Time to Transfer (minutes)	-	-	68	61
Fibrinolytic Medication Timing	-	-	72%	54%
Heart Failure Care				
ACE Inhibitor or ARB for LVSD[1]	2	100%	94%	94%
Discharge Instructions[1]	8	50%	87%	88%
Evaluation of LVS Function[1]	11	45%	96%	98%
Smoking Cessation Advice[1]	2	0%	96%	98%
Pneumonia Care				
Appropriate Initial Antibiotic	25	76%	91%	92%
Blood Culture Timing[1]	4	100%	97%	96%
Influenza Vaccine[1]	20	90%	91%	91%
Initial Antibiotic Timing	31	100%	97%	95%
Pneumococcal Vaccine	29	83%	92%	93%
Smoking Cessation Advice[1]	5	80%	90%	97%
Surgical Care Improvement Project				
Appropriate VTP Within 24 Hours[1,3]	1	100%	94%	92%
Appropriate Hair Removal[1,3]	7	43%	99%	99%
Appropriate Beta Blocker Usage[5]	0	-	94%	93%
Controlled Postoperative Blood Glucose[3]	0	-	96%	93%
Prophylactic Antibiotic Timing[1,3]	6	83%	97%	97%
Prophylactic Antibiotic Timing (Outpatient)	-	-	93%	92%
Prophylactic Antibiotic Selection[1,3]	6	100%	98%	97%
Prophylactic Antibiotic Select. (Outpatient)	-	-	97%	94%
Prophylactic Antibiotic Stopped[1,3]	6	100%	94%	94%
Recommended VTP Ordered[1,3]	1	100%	95%	94%
Urinary Catheter Removal[5]	0	-	90%	90%
Children's Asthma Care				
Received Systemic Corticosteroids	-	-	-	100%
Received Home Management Plan	-	-	-	71%
Received Reliever Medication	-	-	-	100%
Use of Medical Imaging				
Combination Abdominal CT Scan	-	-	0.152	0.191
Combination Chest CT Scan	-	-	0.033	0.054
Follow-up Mammogram/Ultrasound	-	-	8.1%	8.4%
MRI for Low Back Pain	-	-	33.8%	32.7%
Survey of Patients' Hospital Experiences				
Area Around Room 'Always' Quiet at Night	(a)	61%	-	58%
Doctors 'Always' Communicated Well	(a)	91%	-	80%
Home Recovery Information Given	(a)	80%	-	82%
Hospital Given 9 or 10 on 10 Point Scale	(a)	75%	-	67%
Meds 'Always' Explained Before Given	(a)	70%	-	60%
Nurses 'Always' Communicated Well	(a)	79%	-	76%
Pain 'Always' Well Controlled	(a)	73%	-	69%
Room and Bathroom 'Always' Clean	(a)	83%	-	71%
Timely Help 'Always' Received	(a)	78%	-	64%
Would Definitely Recommend Hospital	(a)	77%	-	69%

NOTE: Hospital profiles are in alphabetical order by state, then city, then hospital within the city; Rankings exclude hospitals with less than 25 cases except for patient surveys which excludes hospitals with less than 100 cases; (a) 100–299 cases; (1) The number of cases is too small to be sure how well a hospital is performing; (2) The hospital indicated that the data submitted for this measure were based on a sample of cases; (3) Data was collected during a shorter time period (fewer quarters) than the maximum possible time for this measure; (4) Suppressed for one or more quarters by CMS; (5) No data is available from the hospital for this measure; (6) Fewer than 100 patients completed the HCAHPS survey. Use these rates with caution, as the number of surveys may be too low to reliably assess hospital performance; (7) Survey results are based on less than 12 months of data; (8) Survey results are not available for this reporting period; (9) No or very few patients were eligible for the HCAHPS survey. The scores shown, if any, reflect a very small number of surveys; (10) A state average was not calculated because too few hospitals in the state submitted data; (11) There were discrepancies in the data collection process; Please refer to the User's Guide for a full explanation of data.

Plainview Public Hospital

704 North Third St
Plainview, NE 68769
Type: Critical Access Hospitals
Ownership: Government - Local
Phone: 402-582-4245
Fax: 402-582-3940
Emergency Services: Yes
Beds: 20

Key Personnel:

CEO/President. . . . . Bryan Roby
Cardiac Laboratory. . . . . Jill Anson, RN
Chief of Medical Staff . . . . Edward Botha, MD
Operating Room. . . . . Nancy Green, RD
Emergency Room . . . . Deb Rutledge, RN

Measure	Cases	This Hosp.	State Avg.	U.S. Avg.
Heart Attack Care				
ACE Inhibitor or ARB for LVSD[3]	0	-	97%	96%
Aspirin at Arrival[1,3]	1	100%	99%	99%
Aspirin at Discharge[1,3]	1	100%	99%	98%
Beta Blocker at Discharge[1,3]	1	100%	99%	98%
Fibrinolytic Medication Timing[3]	0	-	20%	55%
PCI Within 90 Minutes of Arrival[3]	0	-	91%	90%
Smoking Cessation Advice[3]	0	-	100%	99%
Chest Pain/Possible Heart Attack Care				
Aspirin at Arrival	-	-	96%	95%
Median Time to ECG (minutes)	-	-	7	8
Median Time to Transfer (minutes)	-	-	68	61
Fibrinolytic Medication Timing	-	-	72%	54%
Heart Failure Care				
ACE Inhibitor or ARB for LVSD[3]	0	-	94%	94%
Discharge Instructions[3]	0	-	87%	88%
Evaluation of LVS Function[1,3]	1	0%	96%	98%
Smoking Cessation Advice[3]	0	-	96%	98%
Pneumonia Care				
Appropriate Initial Antibiotic[1,3]	6	100%	91%	92%
Blood Culture Timing[1,3]	1	100%	97%	96%
Influenza Vaccine[1,3]	4	100%	91%	91%
Initial Antibiotic Timing[1,3]	7	86%	97%	95%
Pneumococcal Vaccine[1,3]	11	91%	92%	93%
Smoking Cessation Advice[1,3]	1	100%	90%	97%
Surgical Care Improvement Project				
Appropriate VTP Within 24 Hours[5]	0	-	94%	92%
Appropriate Hair Removal[5]	0	-	99%	99%
Appropriate Beta Blocker Usage[5]	0	-	94%	93%
Controlled Postoperative Blood Glucose[5]	0	-	96%	93%
Prophylactic Antibiotic Timing[5]	0	-	97%	97%
Prophylactic Antibiotic Timing (Outpatient)	-	-	93%	92%
Prophylactic Antibiotic Selection[5]	0	-	98%	97%
Prophylactic Antibiotic Select. (Outpatient)	-	-	97%	94%
Prophylactic Antibiotic Stopped[5]	0	-	94%	94%
Recommended VTP Ordered[5]	0	-	95%	94%
Urinary Catheter Removal[5]	0	-	90%	90%
Children's Asthma Care				
Received Systemic Corticosteroids	-	-	-	100%
Received Home Management Plan	-	-	-	71%
Received Reliever Medication	-	-	-	100%
Use of Medical Imaging				
Combination Abdominal CT Scan	-	-	0.152	0.191
Combination Chest CT Scan	-	-	0.033	0.054
Follow-up Mammogram/Ultrasound	-	-	8.1%	8.4%
MRI for Low Back Pain	-	-	33.8%	32.7%
Survey of Patients' Hospital Experiences				
Area Around Room 'Always' Quiet at Night[8]	-	-	-	58%
Doctors 'Always' Communicated Well[8]	-	-	-	80%
Home Recovery Information Given[8]	-	-	-	82%
Hospital Given 9 or 10 on 10 Point Scale[8]	-	-	-	67%
Meds 'Always' Explained Before Given[8]	-	-	-	60%
Nurses 'Always' Communicated Well[8]	-	-	-	76%
Pain 'Always' Well Controlled[8]	-	-	-	69%
Room and Bathroom 'Always' Clean[8]	-	-	-	71%
Timely Help 'Always' Received[8]	-	-	-	64%
Would Definitely Recommend Hospital[8]	-	-	-	69%

Webster County Community Hospital

6th and Franklin Sts
Red Cloud, NE 68970
URL: www.websterhospital.org
Type: Critical Access Hospitals
Ownership: Government - Local
Phone: 402-746-5600
Fax: 402-746-2910
Emergency Services: Yes
Beds: 16

Key Personnel:

CEO/President. . . . . Robert Sheckler
Chief of Medical Staff . . . . Della Chan
Operating Room. . . . . Diane Hoffman
Quality Assurance . . . . Terry Hoffart

Measure	Cases	This Hosp.	State Avg.	U.S. Avg.
Heart Attack Care				
ACE Inhibitor or ARB for LVSD[5]	0	-	97%	96%
Aspirin at Arrival[5]	0	-	99%	99%
Aspirin at Discharge[5]	0	-	99%	98%
Beta Blocker at Discharge[5]	0	-	99%	98%
Fibrinolytic Medication Timing[5]	0	-	20%	55%
PCI Within 90 Minutes of Arrival[5]	0	-	91%	90%
Smoking Cessation Advice[5]	0	-	100%	99%
Chest Pain/Possible Heart Attack Care				
Aspirin at Arrival	-	-	96%	95%
Median Time to ECG (minutes)	-	-	7	8
Median Time to Transfer (minutes)	-	-	68	61
Fibrinolytic Medication Timing	-	-	72%	54%
Heart Failure Care				
ACE Inhibitor or ARB for LVSD[1]	6	100%	94%	94%
Discharge Instructions[1]	4	75%	87%	88%
Evaluation of LVS Function[1]	10	90%	96%	98%
Smoking Cessation Advice[1]	1	0%	96%	98%
Pneumonia Care				
Appropriate Initial Antibiotic[1,3]	2	100%	91%	92%
Blood Culture Timing[3]	0	-	97%	96%
Influenza Vaccine[1]	4	100%	91%	91%
Initial Antibiotic Timing[3]	0	-	97%	95%
Pneumococcal Vaccine[1,3]	6	100%	92%	93%
Smoking Cessation Advice[1,3]	1	0%	90%	97%
Surgical Care Improvement Project				
Appropriate VTP Within 24 Hours[5]	0	-	94%	92%
Appropriate Hair Removal[5]	0	-	99%	99%
Appropriate Beta Blocker Usage[5]	0	-	94%	93%
Controlled Postoperative Blood Glucose[5]	0	-	96%	93%
Prophylactic Antibiotic Timing[5]	0	-	97%	97%
Prophylactic Antibiotic Timing (Outpatient)	-	-	93%	92%
Prophylactic Antibiotic Selection[5]	0	-	98%	97%
Prophylactic Antibiotic Select. (Outpatient)	-	-	97%	94%
Prophylactic Antibiotic Stopped[5]	0	-	94%	94%
Recommended VTP Ordered[5]	0	-	95%	94%
Urinary Catheter Removal[5]	0	-	90%	90%
Children's Asthma Care				
Received Systemic Corticosteroids	-	-	-	100%
Received Home Management Plan	-	-	-	71%
Received Reliever Medication	-	-	-	100%
Use of Medical Imaging				
Combination Abdominal CT Scan	-	-	0.152	0.191
Combination Chest CT Scan	-	-	0.033	0.054
Follow-up Mammogram/Ultrasound	-	-	8.1%	8.4%
MRI for Low Back Pain	-	-	33.8%	32.7%
Survey of Patients' Hospital Experiences				
Area Around Room 'Always' Quiet at Night[8]	-	-	-	58%
Doctors 'Always' Communicated Well[8]	-	-	-	80%
Home Recovery Information Given[8]	-	-	-	82%
Hospital Given 9 or 10 on 10 Point Scale[8]	-	-	-	67%
Meds 'Always' Explained Before Given[8]	-	-	-	60%
Nurses 'Always' Communicated Well[8]	-	-	-	76%
Pain 'Always' Well Controlled[8]	-	-	-	69%
Room and Bathroom 'Always' Clean[8]	-	-	-	71%
Timely Help 'Always' Received[8]	-	-	-	64%
Would Definitely Recommend Hospital[8]	-	-	-	69%

Howard County Medical Center

1113 Sherman St
Saint Paul, NE 68873
Type: Critical Access Hospitals
Ownership: Government - Local
Phone: 308-754-4421
Fax: 308-754-4429
Emergency Services: Yes
Beds: 25

Key Personnel:

CEO/President. . . . . Arthur Frable

Measure	Cases	This Hosp.	State Avg.	U.S. Avg.
Heart Attack Care				
ACE Inhibitor or ARB for LVSD[5]	0	-	97%	96%
Aspirin at Arrival[5]	0	-	99%	99%
Aspirin at Discharge[5]	0	-	99%	98%
Beta Blocker at Discharge[5]	0	-	99%	98%
Fibrinolytic Medication Timing[5]	0	-	20%	55%
PCI Within 90 Minutes of Arrival[5]	0	-	91%	90%
Smoking Cessation Advice[5]	0	-	100%	99%
Chest Pain/Possible Heart Attack Care				
Aspirin at Arrival	-	-	96%	95%
Median Time to ECG (minutes)	-	-	7	8
Median Time to Transfer (minutes)	-	-	68	61
Fibrinolytic Medication Timing	-	-	72%	54%
Heart Failure Care				
ACE Inhibitor or ARB for LVSD[5]	0	-	94%	94%
Discharge Instructions[5]	0	-	87%	88%
Evaluation of LVS Function[5]	0	-	96%	98%
Smoking Cessation Advice[5]	0	-	96%	98%
Pneumonia Care				
Appropriate Initial Antibiotic[1]	23	87%	91%	92%
Blood Culture Timing[1]	4	50%	97%	96%
Influenza Vaccine[1]	19	100%	91%	91%
Initial Antibiotic Timing	31	97%	97%	95%
Pneumococcal Vaccine	28	93%	92%	93%
Smoking Cessation Advice[1]	5	80%	90%	97%
Surgical Care Improvement Project				
Appropriate VTP Within 24 Hours[5]	0	-	94%	92%
Appropriate Hair Removal[5]	0	-	99%	99%
Appropriate Beta Blocker Usage[5]	0	-	94%	93%
Controlled Postoperative Blood Glucose[5]	0	-	96%	93%
Prophylactic Antibiotic Timing[5]	0	-	97%	97%
Prophylactic Antibiotic Timing (Outpatient)	-	-	93%	92%
Prophylactic Antibiotic Selection[5]	0	-	98%	97%
Prophylactic Antibiotic Select. (Outpatient)	-	-	97%	94%
Prophylactic Antibiotic Stopped[5]	0	-	94%	94%
Recommended VTP Ordered[5]	0	-	95%	94%
Urinary Catheter Removal[5]	0	-	90%	90%
Children's Asthma Care				
Received Systemic Corticosteroids	-	-	-	100%
Received Home Management Plan	-	-	-	71%
Received Reliever Medication	-	-	-	100%
Use of Medical Imaging				
Combination Abdominal CT Scan	-	-	0.152	0.191
Combination Chest CT Scan	-	-	0.033	0.054
Follow-up Mammogram/Ultrasound	-	-	8.1%	8.4%
MRI for Low Back Pain	-	-	33.8%	32.7%
Survey of Patients' Hospital Experiences				
Area Around Room 'Always' Quiet at Night[8]	-	-	-	58%
Doctors 'Always' Communicated Well[8]	-	-	-	80%
Home Recovery Information Given[8]	-	-	-	82%
Hospital Given 9 or 10 on 10 Point Scale[8]	-	-	-	67%
Meds 'Always' Explained Before Given[8]	-	-	-	60%
Nurses 'Always' Communicated Well[8]	-	-	-	76%
Pain 'Always' Well Controlled[8]	-	-	-	69%
Room and Bathroom 'Always' Clean[8]	-	-	-	71%
Timely Help 'Always' Received[8]	-	-	-	64%
Would Definitely Recommend Hospital[8]	-	-	-	69%

NOTE: Hospital profiles are in alphabetical order by state, then city, then hospital within the city; Rankings exclude hospitals with less than 25 cases except for patient surveys which excludes hospitals with less than 100 cases; (a) 100–299 cases; (1) The number of cases is too small to be sure how well a hospital is performing; (2) The hospital indicated that the data submitted for this measure were based on a sample of cases; (3) Data was collected during a shorter time period (fewer quarters) than the maximum possible time for this measure; (4) Suppressed for one or more quarters by CMS; (5) No data is available from the hospital for this measure; (6) Fewer than 100 patients completed the HCAHPS survey. Use these rates with caution, as the number of surveys may be too low to reliably assess hospital performance; (7) Survey results are based on less than 12 months of data; (8) Survey results are not available for this reporting period; (9) No or very few patients were eligible for the HCAHPS survey. The scores shown, if any, reflect a very small number of surveys; (10) A state average was not calculated because too few hospitals in the state submitted data; (11) There were discrepancies in the data collection process; Please refer to the User's Guide for a full explanation of data.

Alegent Health Memorial Hospital

104 West 17th St Phone: 402-352-2441
Schuyler, NE 68661 Fax: 402-352-2643
URL: www.algent.com
Type: Critical Access Hospitals Emergency Services: Yes
Ownership: Voluntary Non-Profit - Private Beds: 49

Key Personnel:

CEO/President. . . . . Larry Jensen
Chief of Medical Staff . . . . James Martin, MD
Infection Control. . . . . Rose Neuhaus, RN
Quality Assurance . . . . Al Klaasmeyer
Radiology. . . . . Elisa Morgan
Emergency Room . . . . Rita Zelda, RN

Measure	Cases	This Hosp.	State Avg.	U.S. Avg.
Heart Attack Care				
ACE Inhibitor or ARB for LVSD[3]	0	-	97%	96%
Aspirin at Arrival[3]	0	-	99%	99%
Aspirin at Discharge[3]	0	-	99%	98%
Beta Blocker at Discharge[3]	0	-	99%	98%
Fibrinolytic Medication Timing[3]	0	-	20%	55%
PCI Within 90 Minutes of Arrival[3]	0	-	91%	90%
Smoking Cessation Advice[3]	0	-	100%	99%
Chest Pain/Possible Heart Attack Care				
Aspirin at Arrival	-	-	96%	95%
Median Time to ECG (minutes)	-	-	7	8
Median Time to Transfer (minutes)	-	-	68	61
Fibrinolytic Medication Timing	-	-	72%	54%
Heart Failure Care				
ACE Inhibitor or ARB for LVSD[3]	0	-	94%	94%
Discharge Instructions[1,3]	1	100%	87%	88%
Evaluation of LVS Function[1,3]	1	100%	96%	98%
Smoking Cessation Advice[3]	0	-	96%	98%
Pneumonia Care				
Appropriate Initial Antibiotic	0	-	91%	92%
Blood Culture Timing[1]	3	100%	97%	96%
Influenza Vaccine[1]	13	100%	91%	91%
Initial Antibiotic Timing[1]	10	100%	97%	95%
Pneumococcal Vaccine[1]	16	100%	92%	93%
Smoking Cessation Advice[1]	1	100%	90%	97%
Surgical Care Improvement Project				
Appropriate VTP Within 24 Hours[5]	0	-	94%	92%
Appropriate Hair Removal[5]	0	-	99%	99%
Appropriate Beta Blocker Usage[5]	0	-	94%	93%
Controlled Postoperative Blood Glucose[5]	0	-	96%	93%
Prophylactic Antibiotic Timing[5]	0	-	97%	97%
Prophylactic Antibiotic Timing (Outpatient)	-	-	93%	92%
Prophylactic Antibiotic Selection[5]	0	-	98%	97%
Prophylactic Antibiotic Select. (Outpatient)	-	-	97%	94%
Prophylactic Antibiotic Stopped[5]	0	-	94%	94%
Recommended VTP Ordered[5]	0	-	95%	94%
Urinary Catheter Removal[5]	0	-	90%	90%
Children's Asthma Care				
Received Systemic Corticosteroids	-	-	-	100%
Received Home Management Plan	-	-	-	71%
Received Reliever Medication	-	-	-	100%
Use of Medical Imaging				
Combination Abdominal CT Scan	-	-	0.152	0.191
Combination Chest CT Scan	-	-	0.033	0.054
Follow-up Mammogram/Ultrasound	-	-	8.1%	8.4%
MRI for Low Back Pain	-	-	33.8%	32.7%
Survey of Patients' Hospital Experiences				
Area Around Room 'Always' Quiet at Night[6]	<100	75%	-	58%
Doctors 'Always' Communicated Well[6]	<100	84%	-	80%
Home Recovery Information Given[6]	<100	86%	-	82%
Hospital Given 9 or 10 on 10 Point Scale[6]	<100	81%	-	67%
Meds 'Always' Explained Before Given[6]	<100	69%	-	60%
Nurses 'Always' Communicated Well[6]	<100	80%	-	76%
Pain 'Always' Well Controlled[6]	<100	75%	-	69%
Room and Bathroom 'Always' Clean[6]	<100	83%	-	71%
Timely Help 'Always' Received[6]	<100	82%	-	64%
Would Definitely Recommend Hospital	<100	69%	-	69%

Regional West Medical Center

4021 Ave B Phone: 308-635-3711
Scottsbluff, NE 69361 Fax: 308-630-1815
URL: www.rwmc.net
Type: Acute Care Hospitals Emergency Services: Yes
Ownership: Voluntary Non-Profit - Other Beds: 203

Key Personnel:

CEO/President. . . . . Todd S Sorensen, MD
Chief of Medical Staff . . . . James McHugh, MD
Coronary Care . . . . Shirley Barlow
Infection Control. . . . . Marsha Meyer
Operating Room. . . . . Linda Lund
Pediatric In-Patient Care . . . . Robert Flynn
Quality Assurance . . . . Barb Lundgner
Radiology. . . . . Dan Gilbert

Measure	Cases	This Hosp.	State Avg.	U.S. Avg.
Heart Attack Care				
ACE Inhibitor or ARB for LVSD[1]	1	100%	97%	96%
Aspirin at Arrival[1]	19	100%	99%	99%
Aspirin at Discharge[1]	11	100%	99%	98%
Beta Blocker at Discharge[1]	7	100%	99%	98%
Fibrinolytic Medication Timing[1]	1	100%	20%	55%
PCI Within 90 Minutes of Arrival	0	-	91%	90%
Smoking Cessation Advice[1]	3	100%	100%	99%
Chest Pain/Possible Heart Attack Care				
Aspirin at Arrival	50	98%	96%	95%
Median Time to ECG (minutes)	50	5	7	8
Median Time to Transfer (minutes)[1,3]	1	219	68	61
Fibrinolytic Medication Timing[1]	21	76%	72%	54%
Heart Failure Care				
ACE Inhibitor or ARB for LVSD[1]	11	100%	94%	94%
Discharge Instructions	41	61%	87%	88%
Evaluation of LVS Function	58	100%	96%	98%
Smoking Cessation Advice[1]	9	100%	96%	98%
Pneumonia Care				
Appropriate Initial Antibiotic	75	97%	91%	92%
Blood Culture Timing	76	100%	97%	96%
Influenza Vaccine	86	98%	91%	91%
Initial Antibiotic Timing	100	99%	97%	95%
Pneumococcal Vaccine	105	99%	92%	93%
Smoking Cessation Advice	61	100%	90%	97%
Surgical Care Improvement Project				
Appropriate VTP Within 24 Hours[2]	224	94%	94%	92%
Appropriate Hair Removal[2]	520	100%	99%	99%
Appropriate Beta Blocker Usage[2]	122	93%	94%	93%
Controlled Postoperative Blood Glucose[2]	0	-	96%	93%
Prophylactic Antibiotic Timing[2]	391	99%	97%	97%
Prophylactic Antibiotic Timing (Outpatient)	171	98%	93%	92%
Prophylactic Antibiotic Selection[2]	393	98%	98%	97%
Prophylactic Antibiotic Select. (Outpatient)	172	100%	97%	94%
Prophylactic Antibiotic Stopped[2]	378	97%	94%	94%
Recommended VTP Ordered[2]	224	98%	95%	94%
Urinary Catheter Removal[1,2]	20	80%	90%	90%
Children's Asthma Care				
Received Systemic Corticosteroids	-	-	-	100%
Received Home Management Plan	-	-	-	71%
Received Reliever Medication	-	-	-	100%
Use of Medical Imaging				
Combination Abdominal CT Scan	666	0.131	0.152	0.191
Combination Chest CT Scan	444	0.000	0.033	0.054
Follow-up Mammogram/Ultrasound	1,488	9.7%	8.1%	8.4%
MRI for Low Back Pain	300	26.7%	33.8%	32.7%
Survey of Patients' Hospital Experiences				
Area Around Room 'Always' Quiet at Night	300+	56%	-	58%
Doctors 'Always' Communicated Well	300+	80%	-	80%
Home Recovery Information Given	300+	79%	-	82%
Hospital Given 9 or 10 on 10 Point Scale	300+	58%	-	67%
Meds 'Always' Explained Before Given	300+	58%	-	60%
Nurses 'Always' Communicated Well	300+	72%	-	76%
Pain 'Always' Well Controlled	300+	67%	-	69%
Room and Bathroom 'Always' Clean	300+	69%	-	71%
Timely Help 'Always' Received	300+	61%	-	64%
Would Definitely Recommend Hospital	300+	62%	-	69%

Memorial Health Care Systems

300 North Columbia Ave Phone: 402-643-2971
Seward, NE 68434 Fax: 402-646-4639
URL: www.mhcs-seward.org
Type: Critical Access Hospitals Emergency Services: Yes
Ownership: Voluntary Non-Profit - Private Beds: 115

Key Personnel:

CEO/President. . . . . Roger Reamer
Cardiac Laboratory. . . . . Darcy Friedli, RN
Chief of Medical Staff . . . . Barbara E Froehner
Infection Control. . . . . Jan Lucas
Anesthesiology. . . . . Mike George, CRNA

Measure	Cases	This Hosp.	State Avg.	U.S. Avg.
Heart Attack Care				
ACE Inhibitor or ARB for LVSD[3]	0	-	97%	96%
Aspirin at Arrival[3]	0	-	99%	99%
Aspirin at Discharge[3]	0	-	99%	98%
Beta Blocker at Discharge[3]	0	-	99%	98%
Fibrinolytic Medication Timing[3]	0	-	20%	55%
PCI Within 90 Minutes of Arrival[3]	0	-	91%	90%
Smoking Cessation Advice[3]	0	-	100%	99%
Chest Pain/Possible Heart Attack Care				
Aspirin at Arrival	-	-	96%	95%
Median Time to ECG (minutes)	-	-	7	8
Median Time to Transfer (minutes)	-	-	68	61
Fibrinolytic Medication Timing	-	-	72%	54%
Heart Failure Care				
ACE Inhibitor or ARB for LVSD[1]	2	50%	94%	94%
Discharge Instructions[1]	7	14%	87%	88%
Evaluation of LVS Function[1]	11	45%	96%	98%
Smoking Cessation Advice[1]	1	100%	96%	98%
Pneumonia Care				
Appropriate Initial Antibiotic	27	93%	91%	92%
Blood Culture Timing[1]	5	80%	97%	96%
Influenza Vaccine	26	77%	91%	91%
Initial Antibiotic Timing	37	97%	97%	95%
Pneumococcal Vaccine	35	71%	92%	93%
Smoking Cessation Advice[1]	4	25%	90%	97%
Surgical Care Improvement Project				
Appropriate VTP Within 24 Hours[1,3]	1	0%	94%	92%
Appropriate Hair Removal[1,3]	17	76%	99%	99%
Appropriate Beta Blocker Usage[5]	0	-	94%	93%
Controlled Postoperative Blood Glucose[3]	0	-	96%	93%
Prophylactic Antibiotic Timing[1,3]	16	88%	97%	97%
Prophylactic Antibiotic Timing (Outpatient)	-	-	93%	92%
Prophylactic Antibiotic Selection[1,3]	16	25%	98%	97%
Prophylactic Antibiotic Select. (Outpatient)	-	-	97%	94%
Prophylactic Antibiotic Stopped[1,3]	16	100%	94%	94%
Recommended VTP Ordered[1,3]	2	0%	95%	94%
Urinary Catheter Removal	0	-	90%	90%
Children's Asthma Care				
Received Systemic Corticosteroids	-	-	-	100%
Received Home Management Plan	-	-	-	71%
Received Reliever Medication	-	-	-	100%
Use of Medical Imaging				
Combination Abdominal CT Scan	-	-	0.152	0.191
Combination Chest CT Scan	-	-	0.033	0.054
Follow-up Mammogram/Ultrasound	-	-	8.1%	8.4%
MRI for Low Back Pain	-	-	33.8%	32.7%
Survey of Patients' Hospital Experiences				
Area Around Room 'Always' Quiet at Night[8]	-	-	-	58%
Doctors 'Always' Communicated Well[8]	-	-	-	80%
Home Recovery Information Given[8]	-	-	-	82%
Hospital Given 9 or 10 on 10 Point Scale[8]	-	-	-	67%
Meds 'Always' Explained Before Given[8]	-	-	-	60%
Nurses 'Always' Communicated Well[8]	-	-	-	76%
Pain 'Always' Well Controlled[8]	-	-	-	69%
Room and Bathroom 'Always' Clean[8]	-	-	-	71%
Timely Help 'Always' Received[8]	-	-	-	64%
Would Definitely Recommend Hospital[8]	-	-	-	69%

NOTE: Hospital profiles are in alphabetical order by state, then city, then hospital within the city; Rankings exclude hospitals with less than 25 cases except for patient surveys which excludes hospitals with less than 100 cases; (a) 100–299 cases; (1) The number of cases is too small to be sure how well a hospital is performing; (2) The hospital indicated that the data submitted for this measure were based on a sample of cases; (3) Data was collected during a shorter time period (fewer quarters) than the maximum possible time for this measure; (4) Suppressed for one or more quarters by CMS; (5) No data is available from the hospital for this measure; (6) Fewer than 100 patients completed the HCAHPS survey. Use these rates with caution, as the number of surveys may be too low to reliably assess hospital performance; (7) Survey results are based on less than 12 months of data; (8) Survey results are not available for this reporting period; (9) No or very few patients were eligible for the HCAHPS survey. The scores shown, if any, reflect a very small number of surveys; (10) A state average was not calculated because too few hospitals in the state submitted data; (11) There were discrepancies in the data collection process; Please refer to the User's Guide for a full explanation of details.

Memorial Health Center

645 Osage St
Sidney, NE 69162
Phone: 308-254-5825
Fax: 308-254-2300
E-mail: mhchk@wheatbelt.com
URL: www.memorialhealthcenter.org
Type: Critical Access Hospitals
Emergency Services: Yes
Ownership: Voluntary Non-Profit - Private
Beds: 25

Key Personnel:
CEO/President. . . . . Danielle L Gearhart
Chief of Medical Staff . . . . Michael Matthews
Radiology. . . . . Randy Sonnie
Anesthesiology. . . . . Linda Shoemaker

Measure	Cases	This Hosp.	State Avg.	U.S. Avg.
Heart Attack Care				
ACE Inhibitor or ARB for LVSD[1,3]	1	100%	97%	96%
Aspirin at Arrival[1,3]	4	100%	99%	99%
Aspirin at Discharge[1,3]	2	50%	99%	98%
Beta Blocker at Discharge[1,3]	2	50%	99%	98%
Fibrinolytic Medication Timing[3]	0	-	20%	55%
PCI Within 90 Minutes of Arrival[3]	0	-	91%	90%
Smoking Cessation Advice[3]	0	-	100%	99%
Chest Pain/Possible Heart Attack Care				
Aspirin at Arrival	-	-	96%	95%
Median Time to ECG (minutes)	-	-	7	8
Median Time to Transfer (minutes)	-	-	68	61
Fibrinolytic Medication Timing	-	-	72%	54%
Heart Failure Care				
ACE Inhibitor or ARB for LVSD[1]	3	100%	94%	94%
Discharge Instructions[1]	12	0%	87%	88%
Evaluation of LVS Function[1]	14	71%	96%	98%
Smoking Cessation Advice[1]	1	0%	96%	98%
Pneumonia Care				
Appropriate Initial Antibiotic[1]	9	78%	91%	92%
Blood Culture Timing[1]	5	80%	97%	96%
Influenza Vaccine[1]	19	53%	91%	91%
Initial Antibiotic Timing[1]	11	82%	97%	95%
Pneumococcal Vaccine	28	57%	92%	93%
Smoking Cessation Advice[1]	11	0%	90%	97%
Surgical Care Improvement Project				
Appropriate VTP Within 24 Hours[1]	6	50%	94%	92%
Appropriate Hair Removal[1]	8	100%	99%	99%
Appropriate Beta Blocker Usage[5]	0	-	94%	93%
Controlled Postoperative Blood Glucose	0	-	96%	93%
Prophylactic Antibiotic Timing[1]	2	0%	97%	97%
Prophylactic Antibiotic Timing (Outpatient)	-	-	93%	92%
Prophylactic Antibiotic Selection[1]	1	100%	98%	97%
Prophylactic Antibiotic Select. (Outpatient)	-	-	97%	94%
Prophylactic Antibiotic Stopped[1]	1	100%	94%	94%
Recommended VTP Ordered[1]	6	50%	95%	94%
Urinary Catheter Removal[1]	2	0%	90%	90%
Children's Asthma Care				
Received Systemic Corticosteroids	-	-	-	100%
Received Home Management Plan	-	-	-	71%
Received Reliever Medication	-	-	-	100%
Use of Medical Imaging				
Combination Abdominal CT Scan	-	-	0.152	0.191
Combination Chest CT Scan	-	-	0.033	0.054
Follow-up Mammogram/Ultrasound	-	-	8.1%	8.4%
MRI for Low Back Pain	-	-	33.8%	32.7%
Survey of Patients' Hospital Experiences				
Area Around Room 'Always' Quiet at Night	(a)	56%	-	58%
Doctors 'Always' Communicated Well	(a)	85%	-	80%
Home Recovery Information Given	(a)	75%	-	82%
Hospital Given 9 or 10 on 10 Point Scale	(a)	64%	-	67%
Meds 'Always' Explained Before Given	(a)	63%	-	60%
Nurses 'Always' Communicated Well	(a)	75%	-	76%
Pain 'Always' Well Controlled	(a)	75%	-	69%
Room and Bathroom 'Always' Clean	(a)	79%	-	71%
Timely Help 'Always' Received	(a)	72%	-	64%
Would Definitely Recommend Hospital	(a)	58%	-	69%

Brodstone Memorial Hospital

520 East 10th St
Superior, NE 68978
Phone: 402-879-3281
Fax: 402-879-3401
E-mail: jkeelan@brodstonehospital.org
URL: www.brodstonehospital.org
Type: Critical Access Hospitals
Emergency Services: Yes
Ownership: Voluntary Non-Profit - Private
Beds: 25

Key Personnel:
CEO/President. . . . . John Keelan
Chief of Medical Staff . . . . Robert Leibel, MD
Infection Control. . . . . Pam Bower
Operating Room. . . . . Kathe Ely

Measure	Cases	This Hosp.	State Avg.	U.S. Avg.
Heart Attack Care				
ACE Inhibitor or ARB for LVSD[1]	1	100%	97%	96%
Aspirin at Arrival[1]	3	100%	99%	99%
Aspirin at Discharge[1]	3	100%	99%	98%
Beta Blocker at Discharge[1]	2	100%	99%	98%
Fibrinolytic Medication Timing	0	-	20%	55%
PCI Within 90 Minutes of Arrival	0	-	91%	90%
Smoking Cessation Advice	0	-	100%	99%
Chest Pain/Possible Heart Attack Care				
Aspirin at Arrival	-	-	96%	95%
Median Time to ECG (minutes)	-	-	7	8
Median Time to Transfer (minutes)	-	-	68	61
Fibrinolytic Medication Timing	-	-	72%	54%
Heart Failure Care				
ACE Inhibitor or ARB for LVSD[1]	2	100%	94%	94%
Discharge Instructions[1]	13	85%	87%	88%
Evaluation of LVS Function[1]	16	88%	96%	98%
Smoking Cessation Advice[1]	2	100%	96%	98%
Pneumonia Care				
Appropriate Initial Antibiotic[1,3]	5	100%	91%	92%
Blood Culture Timing[1,3]	3	100%	97%	96%
Influenza Vaccine[1]	4	100%	91%	91%
Initial Antibiotic Timing[1,3]	3	100%	97%	95%
Pneumococcal Vaccine[1,3]	8	100%	92%	93%
Smoking Cessation Advice[1,3]	1	100%	90%	97%
Surgical Care Improvement Project				
Appropriate VTP Within 24 Hours[5]	0	-	94%	92%
Appropriate Hair Removal[5]	0	-	99%	99%
Appropriate Beta Blocker Usage[5]	0	-	94%	93%
Controlled Postoperative Blood Glucose[5]	0	-	96%	93%
Prophylactic Antibiotic Timing[5]	0	-	97%	97%
Prophylactic Antibiotic Timing (Outpatient)	-	-	93%	92%
Prophylactic Antibiotic Selection[5]	0	-	98%	97%
Prophylactic Antibiotic Select. (Outpatient)	-	-	97%	94%
Prophylactic Antibiotic Stopped[5]	0	-	94%	94%
Recommended VTP Ordered[5]	0	-	95%	94%
Urinary Catheter Removal[5]	0	-	90%	90%
Children's Asthma Care				
Received Systemic Corticosteroids	-	-	-	100%
Received Home Management Plan	-	-	-	71%
Received Reliever Medication	-	-	-	100%
Use of Medical Imaging				
Combination Abdominal CT Scan	-	-	0.152	0.191
Combination Chest CT Scan	-	-	0.033	0.054
Follow-up Mammogram/Ultrasound	-	-	8.1%	8.4%
MRI for Low Back Pain	-	-	33.8%	32.7%
Survey of Patients' Hospital Experiences				
Area Around Room 'Always' Quiet at Night	(a)	68%	-	58%
Doctors 'Always' Communicated Well	(a)	91%	-	80%
Home Recovery Information Given	(a)	89%	-	82%
Hospital Given 9 or 10 on 10 Point Scale	(a)	81%	-	67%
Meds 'Always' Explained Before Given	(a)	66%	-	60%
Nurses 'Always' Communicated Well	(a)	81%	-	76%
Pain 'Always' Well Controlled	(a)	73%	-	69%
Room and Bathroom 'Always' Clean	(a)	84%	-	71%
Timely Help 'Always' Received	(a)	74%	-	64%
Would Definitely Recommend Hospital	(a)	80%	-	69%

Community Memorial Hospital

1579 Midland St
Syracuse, NE 68446
Phone: 402-269-2011
Fax: 402-269-2795
URL: www.syracusecmh.org
Type: Critical Access Hospitals
Emergency Services: Yes
Ownership: Govt - Hospital Dist/Auth
Beds: 18

Key Personnel:
CEO/President. . . . . Allleen Klaasmeyer
Chief of Medical Staff . . . . Erin Haubschman, MD
Operating Room. . . . . Susan Wilson, RN
Ambulatory Care . . . . Bev Sporhase
Anesthesiology. . . . . Suzanne Wilson
Hemotology Center . . . . Jerel Katen

Measure	Cases	This Hosp.	State Avg.	U.S. Avg.
Heart Attack Care				
ACE Inhibitor or ARB for LVSD[5]	0	-	97%	96%
Aspirin at Arrival[5]	0	-	99%	99%
Aspirin at Discharge[5]	0	-	99%	98%
Beta Blocker at Discharge[5]	0	-	99%	98%
Fibrinolytic Medication Timing[5]	0	-	20%	55%
PCI Within 90 Minutes of Arrival[5]	0	-	91%	90%
Smoking Cessation Advice[5]	0	-	100%	99%
Chest Pain/Possible Heart Attack Care				
Aspirin at Arrival	-	-	96%	95%
Median Time to ECG (minutes)	-	-	7	8
Median Time to Transfer (minutes)	-	-	68	61
Fibrinolytic Medication Timing	-	-	72%	54%
Heart Failure Care				
ACE Inhibitor or ARB for LVSD[1,3]	4	100%	94%	94%
Discharge Instructions[1,3]	3	100%	87%	88%
Evaluation of LVS Function[1,3]	4	100%	96%	98%
Smoking Cessation Advice[3]	0	-	96%	98%
Pneumonia Care				
Appropriate Initial Antibiotic[1,3]	2	100%	91%	92%
Blood Culture Timing[3]	0	-	97%	96%
Influenza Vaccine[1,3]	1	0%	91%	91%
Initial Antibiotic Timing[1,3]	2	100%	97%	95%
Pneumococcal Vaccine[1,3]	2	100%	92%	93%
Smoking Cessation Advice[3]	0	-	90%	97%
Surgical Care Improvement Project				
Appropriate VTP Within 24 Hours[5]	0	-	94%	92%
Appropriate Hair Removal[5]	0	-	99%	99%
Appropriate Beta Blocker Usage[5]	0	-	94%	93%
Controlled Postoperative Blood Glucose[5]	0	-	96%	93%
Prophylactic Antibiotic Timing[5]	0	-	97%	97%
Prophylactic Antibiotic Timing (Outpatient)	-	-	93%	92%
Prophylactic Antibiotic Selection[5]	0	-	98%	97%
Prophylactic Antibiotic Select. (Outpatient)	-	-	97%	94%
Prophylactic Antibiotic Stopped[5]	0	-	94%	94%
Recommended VTP Ordered[5]	0	-	95%	94%
Urinary Catheter Removal[5]	0	-	90%	90%
Children's Asthma Care				
Received Systemic Corticosteroids	-	-	-	100%
Received Home Management Plan	-	-	-	71%
Received Reliever Medication	-	-	-	100%
Use of Medical Imaging				
Combination Abdominal CT Scan	-	-	0.152	0.191
Combination Chest CT Scan	-	-	0.033	0.054
Follow-up Mammogram/Ultrasound	-	-	8.1%	8.4%
MRI for Low Back Pain	-	-	33.8%	32.7%
Survey of Patients' Hospital Experiences				
Area Around Room 'Always' Quiet at Night[8]	-	-	-	58%
Doctors 'Always' Communicated Well[8]	-	-	-	80%
Home Recovery Information Given[8]	-	-	-	82%
Hospital Given 9 or 10 on 10 Point Scale[8]	-	-	-	67%
Meds 'Always' Explained Before Given[8]	-	-	-	60%
Nurses 'Always' Communicated Well[8]	-	-	-	76%
Pain 'Always' Well Controlled[8]	-	-	-	69%
Room and Bathroom 'Always' Clean[8]	-	-	-	71%
Timely Help 'Always' Received[8]	-	-	-	64%
Would Definitely Recommend Hospital[8]	-	-	-	69%

NOTE: Hospital profiles are in alphabetical order by state, then city, then hospital within the city; Rankings exclude hospitals with less than 25 cases except for patient surveys which excludes hospitals with less than 100 cases; (a) 100–299 cases; (1) The number of cases is too small to be sure how well a hospital is performing; (2) The hospital indicated that the data submitted for this measure were based on a sample of cases; (3) Data was collected during a shorter time period (fewer quarters) than the maximum possible time for this measure; (4) Suppressed for one or more quarters by CMS; (5) No data is available from the hospital for this measure; (6) Fewer than 100 patients completed the HCAHPS survey. Use these rates with caution, as the number of surveys may be too low to reliably assess hospital performance; (7) Survey results are based on less than 12 months of data; (8) Survey results are not available for this reporting period; (9) No or very few patients were eligible for the HCAHPS survey. The scores shown, if any, reflect a very small number of surveys; (10) A state average was not calculated because too few hospitals in the state submitted data; (11) There were discrepancies in the data collection process; Please refer to the User's Guide for a full explanation of data.

Johnson County Hospital

202 High St
Tecumseh, NE 68450
Phone: 402-335-3361
Fax: 402-335-6342
Type: Critical Access Hospitals
Emergency Services: Yes
Ownership: Government - Local
Beds: 18

Key Personnel:
CEO/President. . . . . Dianne Newman
Cardiac Laboratory. . . . . J Badertscher
Chief of Medical Staff . . . . Stacey Goodrich
Operating Room. . . . . Jeanne Wolken
Anesthesiology. . . . . James I DeFreece

Measure	Cases	This Hosp.	State Avg.	U.S. Avg.
Heart Attack Care				
ACE Inhibitor or ARB for LVSD[5]	0	-	97%	96%
Aspirin at Arrival[5]	0	-	99%	99%
Aspirin at Discharge[5]	0	-	99%	98%
Beta Blocker at Discharge[5]	0	-	99%	98%
Fibrinolytic Medication Timing[5]	0	-	20%	55%
PCI Within 90 Minutes of Arrival[5]	0	-	91%	90%
Smoking Cessation Advice[5]	0	-	100%	99%
Chest Pain/Possible Heart Attack Care				
Aspirin at Arrival	-	-	96%	95%
Median Time to ECG (minutes)	-	-	7	8
Median Time to Transfer (minutes)	-	-	68	61
Fibrinolytic Medication Timing	-	-	72%	54%
Heart Failure Care				
ACE Inhibitor or ARB for LVSD	0	-	94%	94%
Discharge Instructions[1]	6	83%	87%	88%
Evaluation of LVS Function[1]	11	100%	96%	98%
Smoking Cessation Advice	0	-	96%	98%
Pneumonia Care				
Appropriate Initial Antibiotic[1]	11	91%	91%	92%
Blood Culture Timing[1]	3	100%	97%	96%
Influenza Vaccine[1]	5	100%	91%	91%
Initial Antibiotic Timing[1]	11	91%	97%	95%
Pneumococcal Vaccine[1]	13	85%	92%	93%
Smoking Cessation Advice[1]	2	100%	90%	97%
Surgical Care Improvement Project				
Appropriate VTP Within 24 Hours[1]	2	50%	94%	92%
Appropriate Hair Removal[1]	12	100%	99%	99%
Appropriate Beta Blocker Usage[5]	0	-	94%	93%
Controlled Postoperative Blood Glucose	0	-	96%	93%
Prophylactic Antibiotic Timing[1]	11	100%	97%	97%
Prophylactic Antibiotic Timing (Outpatient)	-	-	93%	92%
Prophylactic Antibiotic Selection[1]	11	100%	98%	97%
Prophylactic Antibiotic Select. (Outpatient)	-	-	97%	94%
Prophylactic Antibiotic Stopped[1]	11	91%	94%	94%
Recommended VTP Ordered[1]	2	50%	95%	94%
Urinary Catheter Removal	0	-	90%	90%
Children's Asthma Care				
Received Systemic Corticosteroids	-	-	-	100%
Received Home Management Plan	-	-	-	71%
Received Reliever Medication	-	-	-	100%
Use of Medical Imaging				
Combination Abdominal CT Scan	-	-	0.152	0.191
Combination Chest CT Scan	-	-	0.033	0.054
Follow-up Mammogram/Ultrasound	-	-	8.1%	8.4%
MRI for Low Back Pain	-	-	33.8%	32.7%
Survey of Patients' Hospital Experiences				
Area Around Room 'Always' Quiet at Night[8]	-	-	-	58%
Doctors 'Always' Communicated Well[8]	-	-	-	80%
Home Recovery Information Given[8]	-	-	-	82%
Hospital Given 9 or 10 on 10 Point Scale[8]	-	-	-	67%
Meds 'Always' Explained Before Given[8]	-	-	-	60%
Nurses 'Always' Communicated Well[8]	-	-	-	76%
Pain 'Always' Well Controlled[8]	-	-	-	69%
Room and Bathroom 'Always' Clean[8]	-	-	-	71%
Timely Help 'Always' Received[8]	-	-	-	64%
Would Definitely Recommend Hospital[8]	-	-	-	69%

Tilden Community Hospital

308 West 2nd
Tilden, NE 68781
Phone: 402-368-5343
Fax: 402-368-7746
E-mail: Info@tildenhospital.org
URL: www.tildenhospital.org
Type: Critical Access Hospitals
Emergency Services: Yes
Ownership: Government - Local
Beds: 20

Key Personnel:
CEO/President. . . . . Lon Knievel
Chief of Medical Staff . . . . Kelly Ellis
Quality Assurance . . . . Anita Morrison
Radiology. . . . . Judy Stout
Ambulatory Care . . . . Anita Morrison
Anesthesiology. . . . . Anita Morrison
Emergency Room . . . . Anita Morrison
Intensive Care Unit. . . . . Anita Morrison

Measure	Cases	This Hosp.	State Avg.	U.S. Avg.
Heart Attack Care				
ACE Inhibitor or ARB for LVSD[5]	0	-	97%	96%
Aspirin at Arrival[5]	0	-	99%	99%
Aspirin at Discharge[5]	0	-	99%	98%
Beta Blocker at Discharge[5]	0	-	99%	98%
Fibrinolytic Medication Timing[5]	0	-	20%	55%
PCI Within 90 Minutes of Arrival[5]	0	-	91%	90%
Smoking Cessation Advice[5]	0	-	100%	99%
Chest Pain/Possible Heart Attack Care				
Aspirin at Arrival[1,3]	1	100%	96%	95%
Median Time to ECG (minutes)[1,3]	1	17	7	8
Median Time to Transfer (minutes)[5]	0	-	68	61
Fibrinolytic Medication Timing[5]	0	-	72%	54%
Heart Failure Care				
ACE Inhibitor or ARB for LVSD[5]	0	-	94%	94%
Discharge Instructions[5]	0	-	87%	88%
Evaluation of LVS Function[5]	0	-	96%	98%
Smoking Cessation Advice[5]	0	-	96%	98%
Pneumonia Care				
Appropriate Initial Antibiotic[1]	4	100%	91%	92%
Blood Culture Timing[1]	1	100%	97%	96%
Influenza Vaccine[1]	3	100%	91%	91%
Initial Antibiotic Timing[1]	2	100%	97%	95%
Pneumococcal Vaccine[1]	4	100%	92%	93%
Smoking Cessation Advice[1]	1	0%	90%	97%
Surgical Care Improvement Project				
Appropriate VTP Within 24 Hours[5]	0	-	94%	92%
Appropriate Hair Removal[5]	0	-	99%	99%
Appropriate Beta Blocker Usage[5]	0	-	94%	93%
Controlled Postoperative Blood Glucose[5]	0	-	96%	93%
Prophylactic Antibiotic Timing[5]	0	-	97%	97%
Prophylactic Antibiotic Timing (Outpatient)[5]	0	-	93%	92%
Prophylactic Antibiotic Selection[5]	0	-	98%	97%
Prophylactic Antibiotic Select. (Outpatient)[5]	0	-	97%	94%
Prophylactic Antibiotic Stopped[5]	0	-	94%	94%
Recommended VTP Ordered[5]	0	-	95%	94%
Urinary Catheter Removal[5]	0	-	90%	90%
Children's Asthma Care				
Received Systemic Corticosteroids	-	-	-	100%
Received Home Management Plan	-	-	-	71%
Received Reliever Medication	-	-	-	100%
Use of Medical Imaging				
Combination Abdominal CT Scan[5]	0	-	0.152	0.191
Combination Chest CT Scan[5]	0	-	0.033	0.054
Follow-up Mammogram/Ultrasound[1]	22	4.5%	8.1%	8.4%
MRI for Low Back Pain[1]	6	0.0%	33.8%	32.7%
Survey of Patients' Hospital Experiences				
Area Around Room 'Always' Quiet at Night[8]	-	-	-	58%
Doctors 'Always' Communicated Well[8]	-	-	-	80%
Home Recovery Information Given[8]	-	-	-	82%
Hospital Given 9 or 10 on 10 Point Scale[8]	-	-	-	67%
Meds 'Always' Explained Before Given[8]	-	-	-	60%
Nurses 'Always' Communicated Well[8]	-	-	-	76%
Pain 'Always' Well Controlled[8]	-	-	-	69%
Room and Bathroom 'Always' Clean[8]	-	-	-	71%
Timely Help 'Always' Received[8]	-	-	-	64%
Would Definitely Recommend Hospital[8]	-	-	-	69%

Cherry County Hospital

510 North Green St
Valentine, NE 69201
Phone: 402-376-2525
Fax: 402-376-1627
URL: www.cchospital.net
Type: Critical Access Hospitals
Emergency Services: Yes
Ownership: Government - Local
Beds: 25

Key Personnel:
Infection Control . . . . Darlene Myer
Operating Room. . . . . Lyreva Nollette

Measure	Cases	This Hosp.	State Avg.	U.S. Avg.
Heart Attack Care				
ACE Inhibitor or ARB for LVSD[3]	0	-	97%	96%
Aspirin at Arrival[1,3]	1	100%	99%	99%
Aspirin at Discharge[1,3]	1	100%	99%	98%
Beta Blocker at Discharge[1,3]	1	100%	99%	98%
Fibrinolytic Medication Timing[3]	0	-	20%	55%
PCI Within 90 Minutes of Arrival[3]	0	-	91%	90%
Smoking Cessation Advice[3]	0	-	100%	99%
Chest Pain/Possible Heart Attack Care				
Aspirin at Arrival	-	-	96%	95%
Median Time to ECG (minutes)	-	-	7	8
Median Time to Transfer (minutes)	-	-	68	61
Fibrinolytic Medication Timing	-	-	72%	54%
Heart Failure Care				
ACE Inhibitor or ARB for LVSD[3]	0	-	94%	94%
Discharge Instructions[1,3]	1	100%	87%	88%
Evaluation of LVS Function[1,3]	1	100%	96%	98%
Smoking Cessation Advice[3]	0	-	96%	98%
Pneumonia Care				
Appropriate Initial Antibiotic[1,2,3]	19	89%	91%	92%
Blood Culture Timing[1,2,3]	5	100%	97%	96%
Influenza Vaccine[1,3]	8	100%	91%	91%
Initial Antibiotic Timing[1,2,3]	22	95%	97%	95%
Pneumococcal Vaccine[1,2,3]	22	95%	92%	93%
Smoking Cessation Advice[1,2,3]	3	100%	90%	97%
Surgical Care Improvement Project				
Appropriate VTP Within 24 Hours[5]	0	-	94%	92%
Appropriate Hair Removal[5]	0	-	99%	99%
Appropriate Beta Blocker Usage[5]	0	-	94%	93%
Controlled Postoperative Blood Glucose[5]	0	-	96%	93%
Prophylactic Antibiotic Timing[5]	0	-	97%	97%
Prophylactic Antibiotic Timing (Outpatient)	-	-	93%	92%
Prophylactic Antibiotic Selection[5]	0	-	98%	97%
Prophylactic Antibiotic Select. (Outpatient)	-	-	97%	94%
Prophylactic Antibiotic Stopped[5]	0	-	94%	94%
Recommended VTP Ordered[5]	0	-	95%	94%
Urinary Catheter Removal[5]	0	-	90%	90%
Children's Asthma Care				
Received Systemic Corticosteroids	-	-	-	100%
Received Home Management Plan	-	-	-	71%
Received Reliever Medication	-	-	-	100%
Use of Medical Imaging				
Combination Abdominal CT Scan	-	-	0.152	0.191
Combination Chest CT Scan	-	-	0.033	0.054
Follow-up Mammogram/Ultrasound	-	-	8.1%	8.4%
MRI for Low Back Pain	-	-	33.8%	32.7%
Survey of Patients' Hospital Experiences				
Area Around Room 'Always' Quiet at Night[8]	-	-	-	58%
Doctors 'Always' Communicated Well[8]	-	-	-	80%
Home Recovery Information Given[8]	-	-	-	82%
Hospital Given 9 or 10 on 10 Point Scale[8]	-	-	-	67%
Meds 'Always' Explained Before Given[8]	-	-	-	60%
Nurses 'Always' Communicated Well[8]	-	-	-	76%
Pain 'Always' Well Controlled[8]	-	-	-	69%
Room and Bathroom 'Always' Clean[8]	-	-	-	71%
Timely Help 'Always' Received[8]	-	-	-	64%
Would Definitely Recommend Hospital[8]	-	-	-	69%

NOTE: Hospital profiles are in alphabetical order by state, then city, then hospital within the city; Rankings exclude hospitals with less than 25 cases except for patient surveys which excludes hospitals with less than 100 cases; (a) 100–299 cases; (1) The number of cases is too small to be sure how well a hospital is performing; (2) The hospital indicated that the data submitted for this measure were based on a sample of cases; (3) Data was collected during a shorter time period (fewer quarters) than the maximum possible time for this measure; (4) Suppressed for one or more quarters by CMS; (5) No data is available from the hospital for this measure; (6) Fewer than 100 patients completed the HCAHPS survey. Use these rates with caution, as the number of surveys may be too low to reliably assess hospital performance; (7) Survey results are based on less than 12 months of data; (8) Survey results are not available for this reporting period; (9) No or very few patients were eligible for the HCAHPS survey. The scores shown, if any, reflect a very small number of surveys; (10) A state average was not calculated because too few hospitals in the state submitted data; (11) There were discrepancies in the data collection process; Please refer to the User's Guide for a full explanation of data.

Saunders Medical Center

1760 County Rd J
Wahoo, NE 68066
E-mail: info@saunders-health.org
URL: www.saunders-health.org
Phone: 402-443-4191
Fax: 402-443-1401
Type: Critical Access Hospitals
Ownership: Government - Local
Emergency Services: Yes
Beds: 25

Key Personnel:

Chief of Medical Staff . . . . Leo Meduna, MD
Infection Control. . . . . Bev Janacek, RN

Measure	Cases	This Hosp.	State Avg.	U.S. Avg.
Heart Attack Care				
ACE Inhibitor or ARB for LVSD[5]	0	-	97%	96%
Aspirin at Arrival[5]	0	-	99%	99%
Aspirin at Discharge[5]	0	-	99%	98%
Beta Blocker at Discharge[5]	0	-	99%	98%
Fibrinolytic Medication Timing[5]	0	-	20%	55%
PCI Within 90 Minutes of Arrival[5]	0	-	91%	90%
Smoking Cessation Advice[5]	0	-	100%	99%
Chest Pain/Possible Heart Attack Care				
Aspirin at Arrival	-	-	96%	95%
Median Time to ECG (minutes)	-	-	7	8
Median Time to Transfer (minutes)	-	-	68	61
Fibrinolytic Medication Timing	-	-	72%	54%
Heart Failure Care				
ACE Inhibitor or ARB for LVSD[3]	0	-	94%	94%
Discharge Instructions[3]	0	-	87%	88%
Evaluation of LVS Function[1,3]	3	100%	96%	98%
Smoking Cessation Advice[3]	0	-	96%	98%
Pneumonia Care				
Appropriate Initial Antibiotic[1,2]	15	100%	91%	92%
Blood Culture Timing[1,2]	10	100%	97%	96%
Influenza Vaccine[1]	19	100%	91%	91%
Initial Antibiotic Timing[1,2]	22	95%	97%	95%
Pneumococcal Vaccine[2]	31	97%	92%	93%
Smoking Cessation Advice[1,2]	2	100%	90%	97%
Surgical Care Improvement Project				
Appropriate VTP Within 24 Hours[5]	0	-	94%	92%
Appropriate Hair Removal[5]	0	-	99%	99%
Appropriate Beta Blocker Usage[5]	0	-	94%	93%
Controlled Postoperative Blood Glucose[5]	0	-	96%	93%
Prophylactic Antibiotic Timing[5]	0	-	97%	97%
Prophylactic Antibiotic Timing (Outpatient)	-	-	93%	92%
Prophylactic Antibiotic Selection[5]	0	-	98%	97%
Prophylactic Antibiotic Select. (Outpatient)	-	-	97%	94%
Prophylactic Antibiotic Stopped[5]	0	-	94%	94%
Recommended VTP Ordered[5]	0	-	95%	94%
Urinary Catheter Removal[5]	0	-	90%	90%
Children's Asthma Care				
Received Systemic Corticosteroids	-	-	-	100%
Received Home Management Plan	-	-	-	71%
Received Reliever Medication	-	-	-	100%
Use of Medical Imaging				
Combination Abdominal CT Scan	-	-	0.152	0.191
Combination Chest CT Scan	-	-	0.033	0.054
Follow-up Mammogram/Ultrasound	-	-	8.1%	8.4%
MRI for Low Back Pain	-	-	33.8%	32.7%
Survey of Patients' Hospital Experiences				
Area Around Room 'Always' Quiet at Night[6]	<100	67%	-	58%
Doctors 'Always' Communicated Well[6]	<100	90%	-	80%
Home Recovery Information Given[6]	<100	80%	-	82%
Hospital Given 9 or 10 on 10 Point Scale[6]	<100	80%	-	67%
Meds 'Always' Explained Before Given[6]	<100	60%	-	60%
Nurses 'Always' Communicated Well[6]	<100	86%	-	76%
Pain 'Always' Well Controlled[6]	<100	79%	-	69%
Room and Bathroom 'Always' Clean[6]	<100	92%	-	71%
Timely Help 'Always' Received[6]	<100	63%	-	64%
Would Definitely Recommend Hospital	<100	87%	-	69%

Providence Medical Center

1200 Providence Rd
Wayne, NE 68787
URL: www.providencemedical.com
Phone: 402-375-3800
Fax: 402-375-7989
Type: Critical Access Hospitals
Ownership: Voluntary Non-Profit - Private
Emergency Services: Yes
Beds: 25

Key Personnel:

Chief of Medical Staff . . . . Matthew Felber
Infection Control. . . . . Kathy Hillier
Operating Room. . . . . Michael Bittles
Quality Assurance . . . . Dennis Spangler
Radiology. . . . . Jeffry Ailes

Measure	Cases	This Hosp.	State Avg.	U.S. Avg.
Heart Attack Care				
ACE Inhibitor or ARB for LVSD[1,3]	1	100%	97%	96%
Aspirin at Arrival[1,3]	5	100%	99%	99%
Aspirin at Discharge[1,3]	4	75%	99%	98%
Beta Blocker at Discharge[1,3]	5	80%	99%	98%
Fibrinolytic Medication Timing[3]	0	-	20%	55%
PCI Within 90 Minutes of Arrival[3]	0	-	91%	90%
Smoking Cessation Advice[3]	0	-	100%	99%
Chest Pain/Possible Heart Attack Care				
Aspirin at Arrival[1]	9	89%	96%	95%
Median Time to ECG (minutes)[1]	9	6	7	8
Median Time to Transfer (minutes)[5]	0	-	68	61
Fibrinolytic Medication Timing[1]	3	0%	72%	54%
Heart Failure Care				
ACE Inhibitor or ARB for LVSD[1]	4	100%	94%	94%
Discharge Instructions[1]	3	100%	87%	88%
Evaluation of LVS Function[1]	13	85%	96%	98%
Smoking Cessation Advice	0	-	96%	98%
Pneumonia Care				
Appropriate Initial Antibiotic[1]	14	86%	91%	92%
Blood Culture Timing[1]	2	50%	97%	96%
Influenza Vaccine[1]	21	86%	91%	91%
Initial Antibiotic Timing[1]	24	96%	97%	95%
Pneumococcal Vaccine	32	91%	92%	93%
Smoking Cessation Advice[1]	4	75%	90%	97%
Surgical Care Improvement Project				
Appropriate VTP Within 24 Hours[1]	4	100%	94%	92%
Appropriate Hair Removal[1]	7	100%	99%	99%
Appropriate Beta Blocker Usage[5]	0	-	94%	93%
Controlled Postoperative Blood Glucose	0	-	96%	93%
Prophylactic Antibiotic Timing[1]	3	100%	97%	97%
Prophylactic Antibiotic Timing (Outpatient)[1]	5	80%	93%	92%
Prophylactic Antibiotic Selection[1]	3	100%	98%	97%
Prophylactic Antibiotic Select. (Outpatient)[1]	16	100%	97%	94%
Prophylactic Antibiotic Stopped[1]	3	100%	94%	94%
Recommended VTP Ordered[1]	4	100%	95%	94%
Urinary Catheter Removal[1]	2	50%	90%	90%
Children's Asthma Care				
Received Systemic Corticosteroids	-	-	-	100%
Received Home Management Plan	-	-	-	71%
Received Reliever Medication	-	-	-	100%
Use of Medical Imaging				
Combination Abdominal CT Scan	92	0.272	0.152	0.191
Combination Chest CT Scan	48	0.000	0.033	0.054
Follow-up Mammogram/Ultrasound	103	7.8%	8.1%	8.4%
MRI for Low Back Pain[1]	22	50.0%	33.8%	32.7%
Survey of Patients' Hospital Experiences				
Area Around Room 'Always' Quiet at Night[8]	-	-	-	58%
Doctors 'Always' Communicated Well[8]	-	-	-	80%
Home Recovery Information Given[8]	-	-	-	82%
Hospital Given 9 or 10 on 10 Point Scale[8]	-	-	-	67%
Meds 'Always' Explained Before Given[8]	-	-	-	60%
Nurses 'Always' Communicated Well[8]	-	-	-	76%
Pain 'Always' Well Controlled[8]	-	-	-	69%
Room and Bathroom 'Always' Clean[8]	-	-	-	71%
Timely Help 'Always' Received[8]	-	-	-	64%
Would Definitely Recommend Hospital[8]	-	-	-	69%

Saint Francis Memorial Hospital

430 North Monitor St
West Point, NE 68788
E-mail: jmeiergerd@fcswp.org
URL: www.fcswp.org/sfmh
Phone: 402-372-2404
Fax: 402-372-2360
Type: Critical Access Hospitals
Ownership: Voluntary Non-Profit - Church
Emergency Services: Yes
Beds: 25

Key Personnel:

CEO/President. . . . . Ronald O Briggs
Chief of Medical Staff . . . . Scott Green
Infection Control. . . . . Karen Spenner, RN
Operating Room. . . . . Gloria Wellman, RN
Patient Relations . . . . Eileen Schlecht, RN

Measure	Cases	This Hosp.	State Avg.	U.S. Avg.
Heart Attack Care				
ACE Inhibitor or ARB for LVSD[1,3]	2	50%	97%	96%
Aspirin at Arrival[1,3]	4	100%	99%	99%
Aspirin at Discharge[1,3]	4	50%	99%	98%
Beta Blocker at Discharge[1,3]	4	100%	99%	98%
Fibrinolytic Medication Timing[3]	0	-	20%	55%
PCI Within 90 Minutes of Arrival[3]	0	-	91%	90%
Smoking Cessation Advice[3]	0	-	100%	99%
Chest Pain/Possible Heart Attack Care				
Aspirin at Arrival	-	-	96%	95%
Median Time to ECG (minutes)	-	-	7	8
Median Time to Transfer (minutes)	-	-	68	61
Fibrinolytic Medication Timing	-	-	72%	54%
Heart Failure Care				
ACE Inhibitor or ARB for LVSD[1]	8	100%	94%	94%
Discharge Instructions[1]	14	93%	87%	88%
Evaluation of LVS Function	26	96%	96%	98%
Smoking Cessation Advice[1]	2	100%	96%	98%
Pneumonia Care				
Appropriate Initial Antibiotic[1]	6	100%	91%	92%
Blood Culture Timing[1]	3	100%	97%	96%
Influenza Vaccine[1]	10	90%	91%	91%
Initial Antibiotic Timing[1]	16	100%	97%	95%
Pneumococcal Vaccine[1]	19	95%	92%	93%
Smoking Cessation Advice[1]	1	100%	90%	97%
Surgical Care Improvement Project				
Appropriate VTP Within 24 Hours[1]	7	100%	94%	92%
Appropriate Hair Removal	33	94%	99%	99%
Appropriate Beta Blocker Usage[5]	0	-	94%	93%
Controlled Postoperative Blood Glucose	0	-	96%	93%
Prophylactic Antibiotic Timing	32	97%	97%	97%
Prophylactic Antibiotic Timing (Outpatient)	-	-	93%	92%
Prophylactic Antibiotic Selection	32	97%	98%	97%
Prophylactic Antibiotic Select. (Outpatient)	-	-	97%	94%
Prophylactic Antibiotic Stopped	32	97%	94%	94%
Recommended VTP Ordered[1]	7	100%	95%	94%
Urinary Catheter Removal[1]	2	100%	90%	90%
Children's Asthma Care				
Received Systemic Corticosteroids	-	-	-	100%
Received Home Management Plan	-	-	-	71%
Received Reliever Medication	-	-	-	100%
Use of Medical Imaging				
Combination Abdominal CT Scan	-	-	0.152	0.191
Combination Chest CT Scan	-	-	0.033	0.054
Follow-up Mammogram/Ultrasound	-	-	8.1%	8.4%
MRI for Low Back Pain	-	-	33.8%	32.7%
Survey of Patients' Hospital Experiences				
Area Around Room 'Always' Quiet at Night	(a)	70%	-	58%
Doctors 'Always' Communicated Well	(a)	84%	-	80%
Home Recovery Information Given	(a)	92%	-	82%
Hospital Given 9 or 10 on 10 Point Scale	(a)	75%	-	67%
Meds 'Always' Explained Before Given	(a)	65%	-	60%
Nurses 'Always' Communicated Well	(a)	79%	-	76%
Pain 'Always' Well Controlled	(a)	74%	-	69%
Room and Bathroom 'Always' Clean	(a)	83%	-	71%
Timely Help 'Always' Received	(a)	75%	-	64%
Would Definitely Recommend Hospital	(a)	74%	-	69%

NOTE: Hospital profiles are in alphabetical order by state, then city, then hospital within the city; Rankings exclude hospitals with less than 25 cases except for patient surveys which excludes hospitals with less than 100 cases; (a) 100–299 cases; (1) The number of cases is too small to be sure how well a hospital is performing; (2) The hospital indicated that the data submitted for this measure were based on a sample of cases; (3) Data was collected during a shorter time period (fewer quarters) than the maximum possible time for this measure; (4) Suppressed for one or more quarters by CMS; (5) No data is available from the hospital for this measure; (6) Fewer than 100 patients completed the HCAHPS survey. Use these rates with caution, as the number of surveys may be too low to reliably assess hospital performance; (7) Survey results are based on less than 12 months of data; (8) Survey results are not available for this reporting period; (9) No or very few patients were eligible for the HCAHPS survey. The scores shown, if any, reflect a very small number of surveys; (10) A state average was not calculated because too few hospitals in the state submitted data; (11) There were discrepancies in the data collection process; Please refer to the User's Guide for a full explanation of data.

Winnebago Ihs Hospital

Hwy 77-75
Winnebago, NE 68071
URL: www.ihs.gov
Type: Acute Care Hospitals
Ownership: Government - Federal
Phone: 402-878-2231
Fax: 402-878-2535
Emergency Services: Yes
Beds: 109

Key Personnel:
CEO/President . . . . Linus Everling
Chief of Medical Staff . . . . Anwar Mohammed
Infection Control . . . . Sharon Wacker
Emergency Room . . . . Deb Saunsoci

Measure	Cases	This Hosp.	State Avg.	U.S. Avg.
Heart Attack Care				
ACE Inhibitor or ARB for LVSD	-	-	97%	96%
Aspirin at Arrival	-	-	99%	99%
Aspirin at Discharge	-	-	99%	98%
Beta Blocker at Discharge	-	-	99%	98%
Fibrinolytic Medication Timing	-	-	20%	55%
PCI Within 90 Minutes of Arrival	-	-	91%	90%
Smoking Cessation Advice	-	-	100%	99%
Chest Pain/Possible Heart Attack Care				
Aspirin at Arrival	-	-	96%	95%
Median Time to ECG (minutes)	-	-	7	8
Median Time to Transfer (minutes)	-	-	68	61
Fibrinolytic Medication Timing	-	-	72%	54%
Heart Failure Care				
ACE Inhibitor or ARB for LVSD	-	-	94%	94%
Discharge Instructions	-	-	87%	88%
Evaluation of LVS Function	-	-	96%	98%
Smoking Cessation Advice	-	-	96%	98%
Pneumonia Care				
Appropriate Initial Antibiotic	-	-	91%	92%
Blood Culture Timing	-	-	97%	96%
Influenza Vaccine	-	-	91%	91%
Initial Antibiotic Timing	-	-	97%	95%
Pneumococcal Vaccine	-	-	92%	93%
Smoking Cessation Advice	-	-	90%	97%
Surgical Care Improvement Project				
Appropriate VTP Within 24 Hours	-	-	94%	92%
Appropriate Hair Removal	-	-	99%	99%
Appropriate Beta Blocker Usage	-	-	94%	93%
Controlled Postoperative Blood Glucose	-	-	96%	93%
Prophylactic Antibiotic Timing	-	-	97%	97%
Prophylactic Antibiotic Timing (Outpatient)	-	-	93%	92%
Prophylactic Antibiotic Selection	-	-	98%	97%
Prophylactic Antibiotic Select. (Outpatient)	-	-	97%	94%
Prophylactic Antibiotic Stopped	-	-	94%	94%
Recommended VTP Ordered	-	-	95%	94%
Urinary Catheter Removal	-	-	90%	90%
Children's Asthma Care				
Received Systemic Corticosteroids	-	-	-	100%
Received Home Management Plan	-	-	-	71%
Received Reliever Medication	-	-	-	100%
Use of Medical Imaging				
Combination Abdominal CT Scan	-	-	0.152	0.191
Combination Chest CT Scan	-	-	0.033	0.054
Follow-up Mammogram/Ultrasound	-	-	8.1%	8.4%
MRI for Low Back Pain	-	-	33.8%	32.7%
Survey of Patients' Hospital Experiences				
Area Around Room 'Always' Quiet at Night	-	-	-	58%
Doctors 'Always' Communicated Well	-	-	-	80%
Home Recovery Information Given	-	-	-	82%
Hospital Given 9 or 10 on 10 Point Scale	-	-	-	67%
Meds 'Always' Explained Before Given	-	-	-	60%
Nurses 'Always' Communicated Well	-	-	-	76%
Pain 'Always' Well Controlled	-	-	-	69%
Room and Bathroom 'Always' Clean	-	-	-	71%
Timely Help 'Always' Received	-	-	-	64%
Would Definitely Recommend Hospital	-	-	-	69%

York General Hospital

2222 Lincoln Ave
York, NE 68467
E-mail: yorkgenhosp@navix.net
URL: www.yorkgeneral.org
Type: Critical Access Hospitals
Ownership: Voluntary Non-Profit - Private
Phone: 402-362-6671
Fax: 402-362-0499
Emergency Services: Yes
Beds: 25

Key Personnel:
CEO/President . . . . Chuck Schulz
Chief of Medical Staff . . . . Ronda K Clark
Quality Assurance . . . . Linda Zieg

Measure	Cases	This Hosp.	State Avg.	U.S. Avg.
Heart Attack Care				
ACE Inhibitor or ARB for LVSD[1,3]	1	100%	97%	96%
Aspirin at Arrival[1,3]	1	100%	99%	99%
Aspirin at Discharge[1,3]	1	100%	99%	98%
Beta Blocker at Discharge[1,3]	1	100%	99%	98%
Fibrinolytic Medication Timing[3]	0	-	20%	55%
PCI Within 90 Minutes of Arrival[3]	0	-	91%	90%
Smoking Cessation Advice[3]	0	-	100%	99%
Chest Pain/Possible Heart Attack Care				
Aspirin at Arrival	-	-	96%	95%
Median Time to ECG (minutes)	-	-	7	8
Median Time to Transfer (minutes)	-	-	68	61
Fibrinolytic Medication Timing	-	-	72%	54%
Heart Failure Care				
ACE Inhibitor or ARB for LVSD[1,3]	2	50%	94%	94%
Discharge Instructions[1,3]	5	40%	87%	88%
Evaluation of LVS Function[1,3]	11	91%	96%	98%
Smoking Cessation Advice[3]	0	-	96%	98%
Pneumonia Care				
Appropriate Initial Antibiotic[1,3]	18	94%	91%	92%
Blood Culture Timing[1,3]	8	100%	97%	96%
Influenza Vaccine[1,3]	10	90%	91%	91%
Initial Antibiotic Timing[3]	27	93%	97%	95%
Pneumococcal Vaccine[3]	27	96%	92%	93%
Smoking Cessation Advice[1,3]	4	75%	90%	97%
Surgical Care Improvement Project				
Appropriate VTP Within 24 Hours[1,3]	18	100%	94%	92%
Appropriate Hair Removal[3]	35	100%	99%	99%
Appropriate Beta Blocker Usage[5]	0	-	94%	93%
Controlled Postoperative Blood Glucose[3]	0	-	96%	93%
Prophylactic Antibiotic Timing[3]	37	100%	97%	97%
Prophylactic Antibiotic Timing (Outpatient)	-	-	93%	92%
Prophylactic Antibiotic Selection[3]	37	100%	98%	97%
Prophylactic Antibiotic Select. (Outpatient)	-	-	97%	94%
Prophylactic Antibiotic Stopped[3]	37	100%	94%	94%
Recommended VTP Ordered[1,3]	18	100%	95%	94%
Urinary Catheter Removal[1]	16	94%	90%	90%
Children's Asthma Care				
Received Systemic Corticosteroids	-	-	-	100%
Received Home Management Plan	-	-	-	71%
Received Reliever Medication	-	-	-	100%
Use of Medical Imaging				
Combination Abdominal CT Scan	-	-	0.152	0.191
Combination Chest CT Scan	-	-	0.033	0.054
Follow-up Mammogram/Ultrasound	-	-	8.1%	8.4%
MRI for Low Back Pain	-	-	33.8%	32.7%
Survey of Patients' Hospital Experiences				
Area Around Room 'Always' Quiet at Night[8]	-	-	-	58%
Doctors 'Always' Communicated Well[8]	-	-	-	80%
Home Recovery Information Given[8]	-	-	-	82%
Hospital Given 9 or 10 on 10 Point Scale[8]	-	-	-	67%
Meds 'Always' Explained Before Given[8]	-	-	-	60%
Nurses 'Always' Communicated Well[8]	-	-	-	76%
Pain 'Always' Well Controlled[8]	-	-	-	69%
Room and Bathroom 'Always' Clean[8]	-	-	-	71%
Timely Help 'Always' Received[8]	-	-	-	64%
Would Definitely Recommend Hospital[8]	-	-	-	69%

NOTE: Hospital profiles are in alphabetical order by state, then city, then hospital within the city; Rankings exclude hospitals with less than 25 cases except for patient surveys which excludes hospitals with less than 100 cases; (a) 100–299 cases; (1) The number of cases is too small to be sure how well a hospital is performing; (2) The hospital indicated that the data submitted for this measure were based on a sample of cases; (3) Data was collected during a shorter time period (fewer quarters) than the maximum possible time for this measure; (4) Suppressed for one or more quarters by CMS; (5) No data is available from the hospital for this measure; (6) Fewer than 100 patients completed the HCAHPS survey. Use these rates with caution, as the number of surveys may be too low to reliably assess hospital performance; (7) Survey results are based on less than 12 months of data; (8) Survey results are not available for this reporting period; (9) No or very few patients were eligible for the HCAHPS survey. The scores shown, if any, reflect a very small number of surveys; (10) A state average was not calculated because too few hospitals in the state submitted data; (11) There were discrepancies in the data collection process; Please refer to the User's Guide for a full explanation of data.

Heart Attack Care

1. ACE Inhibitor or ARB for LVSD

Hospital Name	City	Rate	Cases
Essentia Health-Fargo	Fargo	100%	38
Trinity Hospitals	Minot	100%	25
Altru Hospital	Grand Forks	93%	55
Sanford Medical Center Fargo	Fargo	88%	113

2. Aspirin at Arrival

Hospital Name	City	Rate	Cases
Altru Hospital	Grand Forks	99%	123
Essentia Health-Fargo	Fargo	99%	97
Trinity Hospitals	Minot	99%	133
Medcenter One	Bismarck	98%	92
Saint Alexius Medical Center	Bismarck	98%	105
Sanford Medical Center Fargo	Fargo	97%	196

3. Aspirin at Discharge

Hospital Name	City	Rate	Cases
Altru Hospital	Grand Forks	100%	257
Saint Alexius Medical Center	Bismarck	100%	209
Trinity Hospitals	Minot	100%	240
Sanford Medical Center Fargo	Fargo	99%	568
Essentia Health-Fargo	Fargo	98%	197
Medcenter One	Bismarck	98%	130

4. Beta Blocker at Discharge

Hospital Name	City	Rate	Cases
Saint Alexius Medical Center	Bismarck	100%	202
Trinity Hospitals	Minot	100%	225
Altru Hospital	Grand Forks	99%	245
Medcenter One	Bismarck	98%	129
Sanford Medical Center Fargo	Fargo	98%	565
Essentia Health-Fargo	Fargo	97%	189

6. PCI Within 90 Minutes of Arrival

Hospital Name	City	Rate	Cases
Sanford Medical Center Fargo	Fargo	85%	39
Essentia Health-Fargo	Fargo	83%	30

7. Smoking Cessation Advice

Hospital Name	City	Rate	Cases
Altru Hospital	Grand Forks	100%	84
Medcenter One	Bismarck	100%	41
Saint Alexius Medical Center	Bismarck	100%	72
Sanford Medical Center Fargo	Fargo	100%	201
Trinity Hospitals	Minot	100%	91
Essentia Health-Fargo	Fargo	98%	64

Chest Pain/Possible Heart Attack Care

8. Aspirin at Arrival

Hospital Name	City	Rate	Cases
Jamestown Hospital	Jamestown	98%	64
Mercy Medical Center	Williston	94%	66

9. Median Time to ECG (minutes)

Hospital Name	City	Min.	Cases
Jamestown Hospital	Jamestown	8	67
Mercy Medical Center	Williston	13	68

Heart Failure Care

12. ACE Inhibitor or ARB for LVSD

Hospital Name	City	Rate	Cases
Essentia Health-Fargo	Fargo	98%	44
Trinity Hospitals	Minot	93%	57
Saint Alexius Medical Center	Bismarck	90%	60
Sanford Medical Center Fargo	Fargo	90%	105
Altru Hospital	Grand Forks	89%	70
Medcenter One	Bismarck	82%	39

13. Discharge Instructions

Hospital Name	City	Rate	Cases
Jamestown Hospital	Jamestown	100%	28
Essentia Health-Fargo	Fargo	98%	132
Fargo VA Medical Center	Fargo	96%	73
Medcenter One	Bismarck	96%	130
Sanford Medical Center Fargo	Fargo	93%	289
Altru Hospital	Grand Forks	91%	170
Trinity Hospitals	Minot	90%	178
Mercy Medical Center	Williston	88%	25
Saint Alexius Medical Center	Bismarck	83%	134
Saint Joseph's Hospital & Health Center	Dickinson	74%	50

14. Evaluation of LVS Function

Hospital Name	City	Rate	Cases
Jamestown Hospital	Jamestown	100%	46
Medcenter One	Bismarck	100%	171
Saint Joseph's Hospital & Health Center	Dickinson	100%	75
Sanford Medical Center Fargo	Fargo	100%	385
Trinity Hospitals	Minot	100%	237
Saint Alexius Medical Center	Bismarck	99%	163
Essentia Health-Fargo	Fargo	98%	175
Fargo VA Medical Center	Fargo	98%	82
West River Regional Medical Center	Hettinger	93%	41
Altru Hospital	Grand Forks	90%	215
Heart of America Medical Center	Rugby	74%	35
Mercy Medical Center	Williston	71%	28
Saint Aloisius Medical Center	Harvey	54%	26

15. Smoking Cessation Advice

Hospital Name	City	Rate	Cases
Essentia Health-Fargo	Fargo	100%	31
Medcenter One	Bismarck	100%	27
Saint Alexius Medical Center	Bismarck	100%	27
Trinity Hospitals	Minot	100%	32
Altru Hospital	Grand Forks	98%	45
Sanford Medical Center Fargo	Fargo	96%	57

Pneumonia Care

16. Appropriate Initial Antibiotic

Hospital Name	City	Rate	Cases
Jamestown Hospital	Jamestown	100%	47
Saint Alexius Medical Center[2]	Bismarck	97%	62
Trinity Hospitals	Minot	97%	108
Medcenter One	Bismarck	94%	98
Saint Joseph's Hospital & Health Center	Dickinson	94%	34
Fargo VA Medical Center	Fargo	91%	35
Essentia Health-Fargo	Fargo	90%	79
West River Regional Medical Center	Hettinger	90%	42
Sanford Medical Center Fargo	Fargo	89%	145
Altru Hospital	Grand Forks	70%	141

17. Blood Culture Timing

Hospital Name	City	Rate	Cases
Fargo VA Medical Center	Fargo	100%	30
Saint Alexius Medical Center[2]	Bismarck	99%	115
Sanford Medical Center Fargo	Fargo	99%	218
Jamestown Hospital	Jamestown	98%	57
Saint Joseph's Hospital & Health Center	Dickinson	98%	49
Trinity Hospitals	Minot	98%	220
Essentia Health-Fargo	Fargo	95%	111
Mercy Medical Center	Williston	95%	42
Altru Hospital	Grand Forks	94%	226
Medcenter One	Bismarck	94%	119

18. Influenza Vaccine

Hospital Name	City	Rate	Cases
Jamestown Hospital	Jamestown	100%	32
Mercy Medical Center	Williston	97%	29
Fargo VA Medical Center	Fargo	96%	47
Essentia Health-Fargo	Fargo	93%	75
Trinity Hospitals	Minot	93%	148
Saint Joseph's Hospital & Health Center	Dickinson	90%	41
Sanford Medical Center Fargo	Fargo	90%	236
Saint Alexius Medical Center[2]	Bismarck	88%	85
Medcenter One	Bismarck	84%	69
Altru Hospital	Grand Forks	83%	174
West River Regional Medical Center	Hettinger	78%	41

19. Initial Antibiotic Timing

Hospital Name	City	Rate	Cases
McKenzie County Healthcare Systems	Watford City	100%	26
Saint Joseph's Hospital & Health Center	Dickinson	100%	57
West River Regional Medical Center	Hettinger	100%	74
Mercy Medical Center	Williston	98%	48
Saint Alexius Medical Center[2]	Bismarck	98%	129
Fargo VA Medical Center	Fargo	96%	46
Jamestown Hospital	Jamestown	95%	61
Sanford Medical Center Fargo	Fargo	95%	274
Trinity Hospitals	Minot	95%	214
Essentia Health-Fargo	Fargo	94%	98
Medcenter One	Bismarck	93%	118
Presentation Medical Center	Rolla	93%	30
Altru Hospital	Grand Forks	91%	188

20. Pneumococcal Vaccine

Hospital Name	City	Rate	Cases
Jamestown Hospital	Jamestown	100%	58
Trinity Hospitals	Minot	99%	230
Fargo VA Medical Center	Fargo	97%	58
Saint Joseph's Hospital & Health Center	Dickinson	96%	71
Sanford Medical Center Fargo	Fargo	96%	340
Mercy Medical Center	Williston	95%	44
Saint Alexius Medical Center[2]	Bismarck	94%	144
Essentia Health-Fargo	Fargo	92%	123
West River Regional Medical Center	Hettinger	91%	66
Medcenter One	Bismarck	89%	123
McKenzie County Healthcare Systems	Watford City	88%	25
Altru Hospital	Grand Forks	86%	244
Saint Aloisius Medical Center	Harvey	80%	45
Linton Hospital	Linton	73%	26

21. Smoking Cessation Advice

Hospital Name	City	Rate	Cases
Essentia Health-Fargo	Fargo	100%	35
Trinity Hospitals	Minot	100%	69
Saint Alexius Medical Center[2]	Bismarck	98%	57
Medcenter One	Bismarck	94%	62
Altru Hospital	Grand Forks	92%	116
Sanford Medical Center Fargo	Fargo	91%	164
Fargo VA Medical Center	Fargo	89%	36

Surgical Care Improvement Project

22. Appropriate VTP Within 24 Hours

Hospital Name	City	Rate	Cases
Fargo VA Medical Center[2]	Fargo	100%	81
Sanford Medical Center Fargo[2]	Fargo	98%	267
Essentia Health-Fargo[2]	Fargo	96%	146
Saint Alexius Medical Center[2]	Bismarck	96%	138
Altru Hospital[2]	Grand Forks	94%	233
Mercy Medical Center	Williston	94%	50
Saint Joseph's Hospital & Health Center	Dickinson	92%	38
Medcenter One[2]	Bismarck	87%	253
Trinity Hospitals	Minot	87%	252
Jamestown Hospital	Jamestown	71%	28

23. Appropriate Hair Removal

Hospital Name	City	Rate	Cases
Altru Hospital[2]	Grand Forks	100%	634
Essentia Health-Fargo[2]	Fargo	100%	521
Fargo VA Medical Center[2]	Fargo	100%	151
Jamestown Hospital	Jamestown	100%	68
Medcenter One[2]	Bismarck	100%	841
Mercy Medical Center	Williston	100%	140
Saint Alexius Medical Center[2]	Bismarck	100%	581
Saint Joseph's Hospital & Health Center	Dickinson	100%	131
Trinity Hospitals	Minot	100%	852
Sanford Medical Center Fargo[2]	Fargo	99%	933

24. Appropriate Beta Blocker Usage

Hospital Name	City	Rate	Cases
Saint Alexius Medical Center[2]	Bismarck	96%	204
Saint Joseph's Hospital & Health Center	Dickinson	95%	44
Sanford Medical Center Fargo[2]	Fargo	93%	314
Trinity Hospitals	Minot	93%	298
Essentia Health-Fargo[2]	Fargo	92%	179
Altru Hospital[2]	Grand Forks	89%	227
Medcenter One[2]	Bismarck	87%	273
Fargo VA Medical Center[2]	Fargo	85%	47

25. Controlled Postoperative Blood Glucose

Hospital Name	City	Rate	Cases
Saint Alexius Medical Center[2]	Bismarck	98%	131
Medcenter One[2]	Bismarck	96%	149
Trinity Hospitals	Minot	96%	67
Sanford Medical Center Fargo[2]	Fargo	92%	194
Altru Hospital[2]	Grand Forks	90%	122
Essentia Health-Fargo[2]	Fargo	86%	103

26. Prophylactic Antibiotic Timing

Hospital Name	City	Rate	Cases
Medcenter One[2]	Bismarck	97%	693
Trinity Hospitals	Minot	97%	615
Jamestown Hospital	Jamestown	96%	48
Saint Alexius Medical Center[2]	Bismarck	96%	442
Sanford Medical Center Fargo[2]	Fargo	96%	615
Essentia Health-Fargo[2]	Fargo	95%	370
Fargo VA Medical Center	Fargo	94%	109
Saint Joseph's Hospital & Health Center	Dickinson	94%	106
Altru Hospital[2]	Grand Forks	93%	486

NOTE: Hospital profiles are in alphabetical order by state, then city, then hospital within the city; Rankings exclude hospitals with less than 25 cases except for patient surveys which excludes hospitals with less than 100 cases; (a) 100–299 cases; (1) The number of cases is too small to be sure how well a hospital is performing; (2) The hospital indicated that the data submitted for this measure were based on a sample of cases; (3) Data was collected during a shorter time period (fewer quarters) than the maximum possible time for this measure; (4) Suppressed for one or more quarters by CMS; (5) No data is available from the hospital for this measure; (6) Fewer than 100 patients completed the HCAHPS survey. Use these rates with caution, as the number of surveys may be too low to reliably assess hospital performance; (7) Survey results are based on less than 12 months of data; (8) Survey results are not available for this reporting period; (9) No or very few patients were eligible for the HCAHPS survey. The scores shown, if any, reflect a very small number of surveys; (10) A state average was not calculated because too few hospitals in the state submitted data; (11) There were discrepancies in the data collection process; Please refer to the User's Guide for a full explanation of data.

Hospital Name	City	Rate	Cases
Mercy Medical Center	Williston	93%	97

27. Prophylactic Antibiotic Timing (Outpatient)

Hospital Name	City	Rate	Cases
Sanford Medical Center Fargo	Fargo	98%	586
Mercy Medical Center	Williston	97%	33
Trinity Hospitals	Minot	93%	306
Saint Alexius Medical Center	Bismarck	92%	284
Altru Hospital	Grand Forks	90%	276
Medcenter One	Bismarck	89%	284
Essentia Health-Fargo	Fargo	74%	160

28. Prophylactic Antibiotic Selection

Hospital Name	City	Rate	Cases
Altru Hospital[2]	Grand Forks	98%	489
Fargo VA Medical Center	Fargo	98%	110
Medcenter One[2]	Bismarck	98%	700
Saint Alexius Medical Center[2]	Bismarck	98%	443
Sanford Medical Center Fargo[2]	Fargo	98%	623
Essentia Health-Fargo[2]	Fargo	97%	373
Saint Joseph's Hospital & Health Center	Dickinson	97%	106
Trinity Hospitals	Minot	96%	626
Jamestown Hospital	Jamestown	94%	48
Mercy Medical Center	Williston	94%	98

29. Prophylactic Antibiotic Selection (Outpatient)

Hospital Name	City	Rate	Cases
Altru Hospital	Grand Forks	99%	284
Sanford Medical Center Fargo	Fargo	98%	584
Medcenter One	Bismarck	97%	287
Mercy Medical Center	Williston	97%	32
Trinity Hospitals	Minot	97%	359
Essentia Health-Fargo	Fargo	96%	187
Saint Alexius Medical Center	Bismarck	96%	359

30. Prophylactic Antibiotic Stopped

Hospital Name	City	Rate	Cases
Fargo VA Medical Center	Fargo	100%	108
Saint Alexius Medical Center[2]	Bismarck	99%	425
Medcenter One[2]	Bismarck	97%	677
Saint Joseph's Hospital & Health Center	Dickinson	97%	102
Jamestown Hospital	Jamestown	96%	46
Trinity Hospitals	Minot	96%	589
Altru Hospital[2]	Grand Forks	95%	472
Essentia Health-Fargo[2]	Fargo	95%	331
Mercy Medical Center	Williston	95%	94
Sanford Medical Center Fargo[2]	Fargo	95%	587

31. Recommended VTP Ordered

Hospital Name	City	Rate	Cases
Fargo VA Medical Center[2]	Fargo	100%	81
Sanford Medical Center Fargo[2]	Fargo	98%	267
Saint Joseph's Hospital & Health Center	Dickinson	97%	38
Essentia Health-Fargo[2]	Fargo	96%	147
Mercy Medical Center	Williston	96%	50
Saint Alexius Medical Center[2]	Bismarck	96%	140
Altru Hospital[2]	Grand Forks	94%	233
Trinity Hospitals	Minot	89%	257
Medcenter One[2]	Bismarck	87%	255
Jamestown Hospital	Jamestown	71%	28

32. Urinary Catheter Removal

Hospital Name	City	Rate	Cases
Fargo VA Medical Center[2]	Fargo	97%	86
Saint Alexius Medical Center[2]	Bismarck	97%	117
Trinity Hospitals	Minot	97%	261
Essentia Health-Fargo[2]	Fargo	93%	112
Saint Joseph's Hospital & Health Center	Dickinson	93%	30
Sanford Medical Center Fargo[2]	Fargo	93%	175
Medcenter One[2]	Bismarck	87%	127
Altru Hospital[2]	Grand Forks	83%	126

Use of Medical Imaging

36. Combination Abdominal CT Scan

Hospital Name	City	Ratio	Cases
Medcenter One	Bismarck	0.048	763
Trinity Hospitals	Minot	0.057	863
Unity Medical Center[1]	Grafton	0.077	26
Altru Hospital	Grand Forks	0.087	871
Presentation Medical Center[1]	Rolla	0.220	50
Essentia Health-Fargo	Fargo	0.234	505
Sanford Medical Center Fargo	Fargo	0.250	1662
Saint Alexius Medical Center	Bismarck	0.313	480
Mercy Medical Center	Williston	0.392	97

37. Combination Chest CT Scan

Hospital Name	City	Ratio	Cases
Trinity Hospitals	Minot	0.002	862
Medcenter One	Bismarck	0.003	690
Altru Hospital	Grand Forks	0.004	1391
Essentia Health-Fargo	Fargo	0.005	374
Saint Alexius Medical Center	Bismarck	0.011	525
Sanford Medical Center Fargo	Fargo	0.028	1396
Unity Medical Center[1]	Grafton	0.080	25
Presentation Medical Center[1]	Rolla	0.129	31
Mercy Medical Center[1]	Williston	0.275	40

38. Follow-up Mammogram/Ultrasound

Hospital Name	City	Rate	Cases
Saint Alexius Medical Center	Bismarck	4.3%	351
Trinity Hospitals	Minot	5.3%	2465
Medcenter One	Bismarck	6.6%	1511
Unity Medical Center	Grafton	9.9%	141
Presentation Medical Center[1]	Rolla	10.9%	64
Mercy Medical Center[1]	Williston	13.8%	29
Altru Hospital	Grand Forks	14.2%	2010

39. MRI for Low Back Pain

Hospital Name	City	Rate	Cases
Medcenter One	Bismarck	23.1%	238
Saint Alexius Medical Center	Bismarck	29.1%	327
Altru Hospital	Grand Forks	30.1%	173
Sanford Medical Center Fargo	Fargo	30.9%	375
Essentia Health-Fargo	Fargo	32.2%	171
Trinity Hospitals	Minot	35.7%	244

Survey of Patients' Hospital Experiences

40. Area Around Room 'Always' Quiet at Night

Hospital Name	City	Rate	Cases
P H S Indian Hospital at Belcourt	Belcourt	76%	(a)
Heart of America Medical Center	Rugby	66%	(a)
Jamestown Hospital	Jamestown	63%	300+
Saint Alexius Medical Center	Bismarck	62%	300+
Saint Joseph's Hospital & Health Center	Dickinson	61%	300+
Essentia Health-Fargo	Fargo	57%	300+
Mercy Medical Center	Williston	57%	300+
Sanford Medical Center Fargo	Fargo	52%	300+
Medcenter One	Bismarck	49%	300+
Trinity Hospitals	Minot	46%	300+
Altru Hospital	Grand Forks	44%	300+

41. Doctors 'Always' Communicated Well

Hospital Name	City	Rate	Cases
Mercy Medical Center	Williston	88%	300+
P H S Indian Hospital at Belcourt	Belcourt	87%	(a)
Heart of America Medical Center	Rugby	79%	(a)
Jamestown Hospital	Jamestown	78%	300+
Saint Alexius Medical Center	Bismarck	78%	300+
Saint Joseph's Hospital & Health Center	Dickinson	78%	300+
Essentia Health-Fargo	Fargo	76%	300+
Medcenter One	Bismarck	76%	300+
Altru Hospital	Grand Forks	72%	300+
Sanford Medical Center Fargo	Fargo	72%	300+
Trinity Hospitals	Minot	72%	300+

42. Home Recovery Information Given

Hospital Name	City	Rate	Cases
Heart of America Medical Center	Rugby	89%	(a)
Mercy Medical Center	Williston	89%	300+
Jamestown Hospital	Jamestown	87%	300+
Sanford Medical Center Fargo	Fargo	86%	300+
Altru Hospital	Grand Forks	83%	300+
Saint Alexius Medical Center	Bismarck	83%	300+
Saint Joseph's Hospital & Health Center	Dickinson	83%	300+
Essentia Health-Fargo	Fargo	82%	300+
Medcenter One	Bismarck	82%	300+
Trinity Hospitals	Minot	81%	300+
P H S Indian Hospital at Belcourt	Belcourt	79%	(a)

43. Hospital Given 9 or 10 on 10 Point Scale

Hospital Name	City	Rate	Cases
Heart of America Medical Center	Rugby	75%	(a)
Saint Alexius Medical Center	Bismarck	74%	300+
Medcenter One	Bismarck	70%	300+
Sanford Medical Center Fargo	Fargo	69%	300+
Essentia Health-Fargo	Fargo	68%	300+
Mercy Medical Center	Williston	67%	300+
Jamestown Hospital	Jamestown	63%	300+
Saint Joseph's Hospital & Health Center	Dickinson	63%	300+
Altru Hospital	Grand Forks	57%	300+
Trinity Hospitals	Minot	50%	300+
P H S Indian Hospital at Belcourt	Belcourt	46%	(a)

44. Meds 'Always' Explained Before Given

Hospital Name	City	Rate	Cases
P H S Indian Hospital at Belcourt	Belcourt	71%	(a)
Heart of America Medical Center	Rugby	68%	(a)
Mercy Medical Center	Williston	64%	300+
Saint Joseph's Hospital & Health Center	Dickinson	63%	300+
Jamestown Hospital	Jamestown	60%	300+
Medcenter One	Bismarck	60%	300+
Saint Alexius Medical Center	Bismarck	59%	300+
Essentia Health-Fargo	Fargo	57%	300+
Sanford Medical Center Fargo	Fargo	57%	300+
Altru Hospital	Grand Forks	56%	300+
Trinity Hospitals	Minot	54%	300+

45. Nurses 'Always' Communicated Well

Hospital Name	City	Rate	Cases
Heart of America Medical Center	Rugby	84%	(a)
Jamestown Hospital	Jamestown	80%	300+
Mercy Medical Center	Williston	79%	300+
Saint Joseph's Hospital & Health Center	Dickinson	79%	300+
Saint Alexius Medical Center	Bismarck	77%	300+
Medcenter One	Bismarck	75%	300+
P H S Indian Hospital at Belcourt	Belcourt	74%	(a)
Essentia Health-Fargo	Fargo	73%	300+
Sanford Medical Center Fargo	Fargo	72%	300+
Trinity Hospitals	Minot	71%	300+
Altru Hospital	Grand Forks	69%	300+

46. Pain 'Always' Well Controlled

Hospital Name	City	Rate	Cases
Mercy Medical Center	Williston	75%	300+
P H S Indian Hospital at Belcourt	Belcourt	75%	(a)
Heart of America Medical Center	Rugby	73%	(a)
Jamestown Hospital	Jamestown	73%	300+
Saint Alexius Medical Center	Bismarck	69%	300+
Essentia Health-Fargo	Fargo	68%	300+
Saint Joseph's Hospital & Health Center	Dickinson	67%	300+
Trinity Hospitals	Minot	67%	300+
Medcenter One	Bismarck	64%	300+
Altru Hospital	Grand Forks	61%	300+
Sanford Medical Center Fargo	Fargo	61%	300+

47. Room and Bathroom 'Always' Clean

Hospital Name	City	Rate	Cases
Heart of America Medical Center	Rugby	83%	(a)
Jamestown Hospital	Jamestown	76%	300+
Saint Alexius Medical Center	Bismarck	74%	300+
Saint Joseph's Hospital & Health Center	Dickinson	74%	300+
Mercy Medical Center	Williston	73%	300+
Altru Hospital	Grand Forks	71%	300+
Essentia Health-Fargo	Fargo	70%	300+
Medcenter One	Bismarck	70%	300+
Sanford Medical Center Fargo	Fargo	70%	300+
P H S Indian Hospital at Belcourt	Belcourt	67%	(a)
Trinity Hospitals	Minot	63%	300+

48. Timely Help 'Always' Received

Hospital Name	City	Rate	Cases
Heart of America Medical Center	Rugby	78%	(a)
Jamestown Hospital	Jamestown	75%	300+
Saint Joseph's Hospital & Health Center	Dickinson	72%	300+
Mercy Medical Center	Williston	71%	300+
Saint Alexius Medical Center	Bismarck	68%	300+
Medcenter One	Bismarck	65%	300+
Trinity Hospitals	Minot	64%	300+
Essentia Health-Fargo	Fargo	61%	300+
P H S Indian Hospital at Belcourt	Belcourt	58%	(a)
Sanford Medical Center Fargo	Fargo	57%	300+
Altru Hospital	Grand Forks	55%	300+

49. Would Definitely Recommend Hospital

Hospital Name	City	Rate	Cases
Heart of America Medical Center	Rugby	86%	(a)
Saint Alexius Medical Center	Bismarck	82%	300+
Essentia Health-Fargo	Fargo	78%	300+
Medcenter One	Bismarck	75%	300+
Sanford Medical Center Fargo	Fargo	71%	300+
Mercy Medical Center	Williston	68%	300+
Jamestown Hospital	Jamestown	65%	300+
Saint Joseph's Hospital & Health Center	Dickinson	61%	300+
Altru Hospital	Grand Forks	59%	300+
P H S Indian Hospital at Belcourt	Belcourt	54%	(a)
Trinity Hospitals	Minot	48%	300+

NOTE: Hospital profiles are in alphabetical order by state, then city, then hospital within the city; Rankings exclude hospitals with less than 25 cases except for patient surveys which excludes hospitals with less than 100 cases; (a) 100–299 cases; (1) The number of cases is too small to be sure how well a hospital is performing; (2) The hospital indicated that the data submitted for this measure were based on a sample of cases; (3) Data was collected during a shorter time period (fewer quarters) than the maximum possible time for this measure; (4) Suppressed for one or more quarters by CMS; (5) No data is available from the hospital for this measure; (6) Fewer than 100 patients completed the HCAHPS survey. Use these rates with caution, as the number of surveys may be too low to reliably assess hospital performance; (7) Survey results are based on less than 12 months of data; (8) Survey results are not available for this reporting period; (9) No or very few patients were eligible for the HCAHPS survey. The scores shown, if any, reflect a very small number of surveys; (10) A state average was not calculated because too few hospitals in the state submitted data; (11) There were discrepancies in the data collection process; Please refer to the User's Guide for a full explanation of data.

P H S Indian Hospital at Belcourt - Quentin N Burdick

PO Box 160
Belcourt, ND 58316
Type: Acute Care Hospitals
Ownership: Government - Federal
Phone: 701-477-6111
Fax: 701-477-8410
Emergency Services: Yes
Beds: 29

Key Personnel:

CEO/President. . . . . Levern Parker
Chief of Medical Staff . . . . Penny Wilkie, MD
Infection Control. . . . . Virginia Thomas
Operating Room. . . . . Yvonne Graber
Quality Assurance . . . . Dale Buckles
Emergency Room . . . . Cheryl LaVallie
Intensive Care Unit. . . . . Cheryl LaVallie

Measure	Cases	This Hosp.	State Avg.	U.S. Avg.
Heart Attack Care				
ACE Inhibitor or ARB for LVSD[2,3]	0	-	93%	96%
Aspirin at Arrival[2,3]	0	-	98%	99%
Aspirin at Discharge[1,2,3]	1	100%	99%	98%
Beta Blocker at Discharge[1,2,3]	1	0%	98%	98%
Fibrinolytic Medication Timing[2,3]	0	-	67%	55%
PCI Within 90 Minutes of Arrival[2,3]	0	-	84%	90%
Smoking Cessation Advice[1,2,3]	1	0%	99%	99%
Chest Pain/Possible Heart Attack Care				
Aspirin at Arrival	-	-	96%	95%
Median Time to ECG (minutes)	-	-	11	8
Median Time to Transfer (minutes)	-	-	180	61
Fibrinolytic Medication Timing	-	-	69%	54%
Heart Failure Care				
ACE Inhibitor or ARB for LVSD[2,3]	0	-	90%	94%
Discharge Instructions[1,2,3]	3	0%	89%	88%
Evaluation of LVS Function[1,2,3]	4	0%	94%	98%
Smoking Cessation Advice[2,3]	0	-	97%	98%
Pneumonia Care				
Appropriate Initial Antibiotic[1,2,3]	12	92%	89%	92%
Blood Culture Timing[1,2,3]	6	33%	97%	96%
Influenza Vaccine[1,2]	11	45%	88%	91%
Initial Antibiotic Timing[1,2,3]	15	100%	95%	95%
Pneumococcal Vaccine[1,2,3]	7	86%	93%	93%
Smoking Cessation Advice[1,2,3]	4	25%	91%	97%
Surgical Care Improvement Project				
Appropriate VTP Within 24 Hours[1,2,3]	1	100%	92%	92%
Appropriate Hair Removal[1,2,3]	11	36%	100%	99%
Appropriate Beta Blocker Usage[1,2,3]	1	100%	91%	93%
Controlled Postoperative Blood Glucose[2,3]	0	-	93%	93%
Prophylactic Antibiotic Timing[1,2,3]	8	62%	96%	97%
Prophylactic Antibiotic Timing (Outpatient)	-	-	92%	92%
Prophylactic Antibiotic Selection[1,2,3]	8	50%	97%	97%
Prophylactic Antibiotic Select. (Outpatient)	-	-	97%	94%
Prophylactic Antibiotic Stopped[1,2,3]	8	88%	96%	94%
Recommended VTP Ordered[1,2,3]	1	100%	92%	94%
Urinary Catheter Removal[1,2,3]	1	100%	92%	90%
Children's Asthma Care				
Received Systemic Corticosteroids	-	-	-	100%
Received Home Management Plan	-	-	-	71%
Received Reliever Medication	-	-	-	100%
Use of Medical Imaging				
Combination Abdominal CT Scan	-	-	0.177	0.191
Combination Chest CT Scan	-	-	0.025	0.054
Follow-up Mammogram/Ultrasound	-	-	8%	8.4%
MRI for Low Back Pain	-	-	31.9%	32.7%
Survey of Patients' Hospital Experiences				
Area Around Room 'Always' Quiet at Night	(a)	76%	-	58%
Doctors 'Always' Communicated Well	(a)	87%	-	80%
Home Recovery Information Given	(a)	79%	-	82%
Hospital Given 9 or 10 on 10 Point Scale	(a)	46%	-	67%
Meds 'Always' Explained Before Given	(a)	71%	-	60%
Nurses 'Always' Communicated Well	(a)	74%	-	76%
Pain 'Always' Well Controlled	(a)	75%	-	69%
Room and Bathroom 'Always' Clean	(a)	67%	-	71%
Timely Help 'Always' Received	(a)	58%	-	64%
Would Definitely Recommend Hospital	(a)	54%	-	69%

Medcenter One

300 N 7th St
Bismarck, ND 58506
URL: www.medcenterone.com
Type: Acute Care Hospitals
Ownership: Voluntary Non-Profit - Private
Phone: 701-323-6000
Fax: 701-323-5221
Emergency Services: Yes
Beds: 196

Key Personnel:

CEO/President. . . . . James C Cooper
Chief of Medical Staff . . . . Dr. Les Rainwater
Infection Control. . . . . Jodi Barnum
Operating Room. . . . . Douglas Berglund
Pediatric Ambulatory Care . . . . . . Rafael Ocejo, MD
Pediatric In-Patient Care . . . . Randi Schaeffer
Quality Assurance . . . . Evy Olson
Radiology. . . . . William Cain

Measure	Cases	This Hosp.	State Avg.	U.S. Avg.
Heart Attack Care				
ACE Inhibitor or ARB for LVSD[1]	19	95%	93%	96%
Aspirin at Arrival	92	98%	98%	99%
Aspirin at Discharge	130	98%	99%	98%
Beta Blocker at Discharge	129	98%	98%	98%
Fibrinolytic Medication Timing	0	-	67%	55%
PCI Within 90 Minutes of Arrival[1]	21	90%	84%	90%
Smoking Cessation Advice	41	100%	99%	99%
Chest Pain/Possible Heart Attack Care				
Aspirin at Arrival[5]	0	-	96%	95%
Median Time to ECG (minutes)[5]	0	-	11	8
Median Time to Transfer (minutes)[5]	0	-	180	61
Fibrinolytic Medication Timing[5]	0	-	69%	54%
Heart Failure Care				
ACE Inhibitor or ARB for LVSD	39	82%	90%	94%
Discharge Instructions	130	96%	89%	88%
Evaluation of LVS Function	171	100%	94%	98%
Smoking Cessation Advice	27	100%	97%	98%
Pneumonia Care				
Appropriate Initial Antibiotic	98	94%	89%	92%
Blood Culture Timing	119	94%	97%	96%
Influenza Vaccine	69	84%	88%	91%
Initial Antibiotic Timing	118	93%	95%	95%
Pneumococcal Vaccine	123	89%	93%	93%
Smoking Cessation Advice	62	94%	91%	97%
Surgical Care Improvement Project				
Appropriate VTP Within 24 Hours[2]	253	87%	92%	92%
Appropriate Hair Removal[2]	841	100%	100%	99%
Appropriate Beta Blocker Usage[2]	273	87%	91%	93%
Controlled Postoperative Blood Glucose[2]	149	96%	93%	93%
Prophylactic Antibiotic Timing[2]	693	97%	96%	97%
Prophylactic Antibiotic Timing (Outpatient)	284	89%	92%	92%
Prophylactic Antibiotic Selection[2]	700	98%	97%	97%
Prophylactic Antibiotic Select. (Outpatient)	287	97%	97%	94%
Prophylactic Antibiotic Stopped[2]	677	97%	96%	94%
Recommended VTP Ordered[2]	255	87%	92%	94%
Urinary Catheter Removal[2]	127	87%	92%	90%
Children's Asthma Care				
Received Systemic Corticosteroids	-	-	-	100%
Received Home Management Plan	-	-	-	71%
Received Reliever Medication	-	-	-	100%
Use of Medical Imaging				
Combination Abdominal CT Scan	763	0.048	0.177	0.191
Combination Chest CT Scan	690	0.003	0.025	0.054
Follow-up Mammogram/Ultrasound	1,511	6.6%	8%	8.4%
MRI for Low Back Pain	238	23.1%	31.9%	32.7%
Survey of Patients' Hospital Experiences				
Area Around Room 'Always' Quiet at Night	300+	49%	-	58%
Doctors 'Always' Communicated Well	300+	76%	-	80%
Home Recovery Information Given	300+	82%	-	82%
Hospital Given 9 or 10 on 10 Point Scale	300+	70%	-	67%
Meds 'Always' Explained Before Given	300+	60%	-	60%
Nurses 'Always' Communicated Well	300+	75%	-	76%
Pain 'Always' Well Controlled	300+	64%	-	69%
Room and Bathroom 'Always' Clean	300+	70%	-	71%
Timely Help 'Always' Received	300+	65%	-	64%
Would Definitely Recommend Hospital	300+	75%	-	69%

Saint Alexius Medical Center

900 E Broadway
Bismarck, ND 58501
Type: Acute Care Hospitals
Ownership: Voluntary Non-Profit - Church
Phone: 701-530-7000
Fax: 701-530-7161
Emergency Services: Yes
Beds: 307

Key Personnel:

CEO/President. . . . . Andrew Wilson
Operating Room. . . . . Sue Ebertowski, RN
Pediatric Ambulatory Care . . . . . . Atef Gayed
Pediatric In-Patient Care . . . . Atef Gayed
Quality Assurance . . . . Pam Heinrich
Radiology. . . . . Doug Peterson
Emergency Room . . . . Kathy Seidel

Measure	Cases	This Hosp.	State Avg.	U.S. Avg.
Heart Attack Care				
ACE Inhibitor or ARB for LVSD[1]	23	96%	93%	96%
Aspirin at Arrival	105	98%	98%	99%
Aspirin at Discharge	209	100%	99%	98%
Beta Blocker at Discharge	202	100%	98%	98%
Fibrinolytic Medication Timing	0	-	67%	55%
PCI Within 90 Minutes of Arrival[1]	20	80%	84%	90%
Smoking Cessation Advice	72	100%	99%	99%
Chest Pain/Possible Heart Attack Care				
Aspirin at Arrival[5]	0	-	96%	95%
Median Time to ECG (minutes)[5]	0	-	11	8
Median Time to Transfer (minutes)[5]	0	-	180	61
Fibrinolytic Medication Timing[5]	0	-	69%	54%
Heart Failure Care				
ACE Inhibitor or ARB for LVSD	60	90%	90%	94%
Discharge Instructions	134	83%	89%	88%
Evaluation of LVS Function	163	99%	94%	98%
Smoking Cessation Advice	27	100%	97%	98%
Pneumonia Care				
Appropriate Initial Antibiotic[2]	62	97%	89%	92%
Blood Culture Timing[2]	115	99%	97%	96%
Influenza Vaccine[2]	85	88%	88%	91%
Initial Antibiotic Timing[2]	129	98%	95%	95%
Pneumococcal Vaccine[2]	144	94%	93%	93%
Smoking Cessation Advice[2]	57	98%	91%	97%
Surgical Care Improvement Project				
Appropriate VTP Within 24 Hours[2]	138	96%	92%	92%
Appropriate Hair Removal[2]	581	100%	100%	99%
Appropriate Beta Blocker Usage[2]	204	96%	91%	93%
Controlled Postoperative Blood Glucose[2]	131	98%	93%	93%
Prophylactic Antibiotic Timing[2]	442	96%	96%	97%
Prophylactic Antibiotic Timing (Outpatient)	284	92%	92%	92%
Prophylactic Antibiotic Selection[2]	443	98%	97%	97%
Prophylactic Antibiotic Select. (Outpatient)	359	96%	97%	94%
Prophylactic Antibiotic Stopped[2]	425	99%	96%	94%
Recommended VTP Ordered[2]	140	96%	92%	94%
Urinary Catheter Removal[2]	117	97%	92%	90%
Children's Asthma Care				
Received Systemic Corticosteroids	-	-	-	100%
Received Home Management Plan	-	-	-	71%
Received Reliever Medication	-	-	-	100%
Use of Medical Imaging				
Combination Abdominal CT Scan	480	0.313	0.177	0.191
Combination Chest CT Scan	525	0.011	0.025	0.054
Follow-up Mammogram/Ultrasound	351	4.3%	8%	8.4%
MRI for Low Back Pain	327	29.1%	31.9%	32.7%
Survey of Patients' Hospital Experiences				
Area Around Room 'Always' Quiet at Night	300+	62%	-	58%
Doctors 'Always' Communicated Well	300+	78%	-	80%
Home Recovery Information Given	300+	83%	-	82%
Hospital Given 9 or 10 on 10 Point Scale	300+	74%	-	67%
Meds 'Always' Explained Before Given	300+	59%	-	60%
Nurses 'Always' Communicated Well	300+	77%	-	76%
Pain 'Always' Well Controlled	300+	69%	-	69%
Room and Bathroom 'Always' Clean	300+	74%	-	71%
Timely Help 'Always' Received	300+	68%	-	64%
Would Definitely Recommend Hospital	300+	82%	-	69%

NOTE: Hospital profiles are in alphabetical order by state, then city, then hospital within the city; Rankings exclude hospitals with less than 25 cases except for patient surveys which excludes hospitals with less than 100 cases; (a) 100–299 cases; (1) The number of cases is too small to be sure how well a hospital is performing; (2) The hospital indicated that the data submitted for this measure were based on a sample of cases; (3) Data was collected during a shorter time period (fewer quarters) than the maximum possible time for this measure; (4) Suppressed for one or more quarters by CMS; (5) No data is available from the hospital for this measure; (6) Fewer than 100 patients completed the HCAHPS survey. Use these rates with caution, as the number of surveys may be too low to reliably assess hospital performance; (7) Survey results are based on less than 12 months of data; (8) Survey results are not available for this reporting period; (9) No or very few patients were eligible for the HCAHPS survey. The scores shown, if any, reflect a very small number of surveys; (10) A state average was not calculated because too few hospitals in the state submitted data; (11) There were discrepancies in the data collection process; Please refer to the User's Guide for a full explanation of data.

Saint Andrews Health Center

316 Ohmer Street Phone: 701-228-9300
Bottineau, ND 58318 Fax: 701-228-9384
E-mail: sahc@utma.com
URL: www.standrewshealth.us
Type: Critical Access Hospitals Emergency Services: Yes
Ownership: Voluntary Non-Profit - Church Beds: 25

Key Personnel:

CEO/President . . . . Jodi Atkinson
Chief of Medical Staff . . . . Dinesh Agnihotri, MD
Infection Control . . . . Debra Kleven
Quality Assurance . . . . Jeanne McGuire
Emergency Room . . . . Gwen Wall

Measure	Cases	This Hosp.	State Avg.	U.S. Avg.
Heart Attack Care				
ACE Inhibitor or ARB for LVSD[3]	0	-	93%	96%
Aspirin at Arrival[1,3]	1	100%	98%	99%
Aspirin at Discharge[3]	0	-	99%	98%
Beta Blocker at Discharge[3]	0	-	98%	98%
Fibrinolytic Medication Timing[3]	0	-	67%	55%
PCI Within 90 Minutes of Arrival[3]	0	-	84%	90%
Smoking Cessation Advice[3]	0	-	99%	99%
Chest Pain/Possible Heart Attack Care				
Aspirin at Arrival	-	-	96%	95%
Median Time to ECG (minutes)	-	-	11	8
Median Time to Transfer (minutes)	-	-	180	61
Fibrinolytic Medication Timing	-	-	69%	54%
Heart Failure Care				
ACE Inhibitor or ARB for LVSD[1]	1	100%	90%	94%
Discharge Instructions[1]	6	33%	89%	88%
Evaluation of LVS Function[1]	6	17%	94%	98%
Smoking Cessation Advice	0	-	97%	98%
Pneumonia Care				
Appropriate Initial Antibiotic[1]	6	100%	89%	92%
Blood Culture Timing[1]	3	100%	97%	96%
Influenza Vaccine[1]	6	100%	88%	91%
Initial Antibiotic Timing[1]	8	88%	95%	95%
Pneumococcal Vaccine[1]	11	100%	93%	93%
Smoking Cessation Advice[1]	3	67%	91%	97%
Surgical Care Improvement Project				
Appropriate VTP Within 24 Hours[5]	0	-	92%	92%
Appropriate Hair Removal[5]	0	-	100%	99%
Appropriate Beta Blocker Usage[5]	0	-	91%	93%
Controlled Postoperative Blood Glucose[5]	0	-	93%	93%
Prophylactic Antibiotic Timing[5]	0	-	96%	97%
Prophylactic Antibiotic Timing (Outpatient)	-	-	92%	92%
Prophylactic Antibiotic Selection[5]	0	-	97%	97%
Prophylactic Antibiotic Select. (Outpatient)	-	-	97%	94%
Prophylactic Antibiotic Stopped[5]	0	-	96%	94%
Recommended VTP Ordered[5]	0	-	92%	94%
Urinary Catheter Removal[5]	0	-	92%	90%
Children's Asthma Care				
Received Systemic Corticosteroids	-	-	-	100%
Received Home Management Plan	-	-	-	71%
Received Reliever Medication	-	-	-	100%
Use of Medical Imaging				
Combination Abdominal CT Scan	-	-	0.177	0.191
Combination Chest CT Scan	-	-	0.025	0.054
Follow-up Mammogram/Ultrasound	-	-	8%	8.4%
MRI for Low Back Pain	-	-	31.9%	32.7%
Survey of Patients' Hospital Experiences				
Area Around Room 'Always' Quiet at Night[8]	-	-	-	58%
Doctors 'Always' Communicated Well[8]	-	-	-	80%
Home Recovery Information Given[8]	-	-	-	82%
Hospital Given 9 or 10 on 10 Point Scale[8]	-	-	-	67%
Meds 'Always' Explained Before Given[8]	-	-	-	60%
Nurses 'Always' Communicated Well[8]	-	-	-	76%
Pain 'Always' Well Controlled[8]	-	-	-	69%
Room and Bathroom 'Always' Clean[8]	-	-	-	71%
Timely Help 'Always' Received[8]	-	-	-	64%
Would Definitely Recommend Hospital[8]	-	-	-	69%

Carrington Health Center

PO Box 461 Phone: 701-652-3141
Carrington, ND 58421 Fax: 701-652-2884
URL: www.carringtonhealthcenter.net
Type: Critical Access Hospitals Emergency Services: Yes
Ownership: Voluntary Non-Profit - Church Beds: 25

Key Personnel:

CEO/President . . . . Johnson Smith
Infection Control . . . . Bernardine Anderson
Operating Room . . . . Bernadin Anderson
Quality Assurance . . . . Mariann Doeling

Measure	Cases	This Hosp.	State Avg.	U.S. Avg.
Heart Attack Care				
ACE Inhibitor or ARB for LVSD	0	-	93%	96%
Aspirin at Arrival[1]	4	75%	98%	99%
Aspirin at Discharge[1]	2	50%	99%	98%
Beta Blocker at Discharge[1]	3	67%	98%	98%
Fibrinolytic Medication Timing	0	-	67%	55%
PCI Within 90 Minutes of Arrival	0	-	84%	90%
Smoking Cessation Advice	0	-	99%	99%
Chest Pain/Possible Heart Attack Care				
Aspirin at Arrival	-	-	96%	95%
Median Time to ECG (minutes)	-	-	11	8
Median Time to Transfer (minutes)	-	-	180	61
Fibrinolytic Medication Timing	-	-	69%	54%
Heart Failure Care				
ACE Inhibitor or ARB for LVSD	0	-	90%	94%
Discharge Instructions[1]	11	100%	89%	88%
Evaluation of LVS Function[1]	12	100%	94%	98%
Smoking Cessation Advice	0	-	97%	98%
Pneumonia Care				
Appropriate Initial Antibiotic[1]	5	100%	89%	92%
Blood Culture Timing[1]	3	100%	97%	96%
Influenza Vaccine[1]	5	100%	88%	91%
Initial Antibiotic Timing[1]	15	100%	95%	95%
Pneumococcal Vaccine[1]	20	100%	93%	93%
Smoking Cessation Advice[1]	4	100%	91%	97%
Surgical Care Improvement Project				
Appropriate VTP Within 24 Hours[5]	0	-	92%	92%
Appropriate Hair Removal[5]	0	-	100%	99%
Appropriate Beta Blocker Usage[5]	0	-	91%	93%
Controlled Postoperative Blood Glucose[5]	0	-	93%	93%
Prophylactic Antibiotic Timing[5]	0	-	96%	97%
Prophylactic Antibiotic Timing (Outpatient)	-	-	92%	92%
Prophylactic Antibiotic Selection[5]	0	-	97%	97%
Prophylactic Antibiotic Select. (Outpatient)	-	-	97%	94%
Prophylactic Antibiotic Stopped[5]	0	-	96%	94%
Recommended VTP Ordered[5]	0	-	92%	94%
Urinary Catheter Removal[5]	0	-	92%	90%
Children's Asthma Care				
Received Systemic Corticosteroids	-	-	-	100%
Received Home Management Plan	-	-	-	71%
Received Reliever Medication	-	-	-	100%
Use of Medical Imaging				
Combination Abdominal CT Scan	-	-	0.177	0.191
Combination Chest CT Scan	-	-	0.025	0.054
Follow-up Mammogram/Ultrasound	-	-	8%	8.4%
MRI for Low Back Pain	-	-	31.9%	32.7%
Survey of Patients' Hospital Experiences				
Area Around Room 'Always' Quiet at Night[8]	-	-	-	58%
Doctors 'Always' Communicated Well[8]	-	-	-	80%
Home Recovery Information Given[8]	-	-	-	82%
Hospital Given 9 or 10 on 10 Point Scale[8]	-	-	-	67%
Meds 'Always' Explained Before Given[8]	-	-	-	60%
Nurses 'Always' Communicated Well[8]	-	-	-	76%
Pain 'Always' Well Controlled[8]	-	-	-	69%
Room and Bathroom 'Always' Clean[8]	-	-	-	71%
Timely Help 'Always' Received[8]	-	-	-	64%
Would Definitely Recommend Hospital[8]	-	-	-	69%

Pembina County Memorial Hospital

301 Mountain St East Phone: 701-265-8461
Cavalier, ND 58220 Fax: 701-265-8752
URL: www.cavalierhospital.com
Type: Critical Access Hospitals Emergency Services: Yes
Ownership: Voluntary Non-Profit - Private Beds: 29

Key Personnel:

CEO/President . . . . Everett Butler
Chief of Medical Staff . . . . Hassan Abul-Khoudoud
Quality Assurance . . . . Jodi Thoreson
Emergency Room . . . . Kathelen Duff
Patient Relations . . . . Kathy Duff

Measure	Cases	This Hosp.	State Avg.	U.S. Avg.
Heart Attack Care				
ACE Inhibitor or ARB for LVSD[3]	0	-	93%	96%
Aspirin at Arrival[1,3]	2	100%	98%	99%
Aspirin at Discharge[3]	0	-	99%	98%
Beta Blocker at Discharge[3]	0	-	98%	98%
Fibrinolytic Medication Timing[1,3]	1	100%	67%	55%
PCI Within 90 Minutes of Arrival[3]	0	-	84%	90%
Smoking Cessation Advice[3]	0	-	99%	99%
Chest Pain/Possible Heart Attack Care				
Aspirin at Arrival	-	-	96%	95%
Median Time to ECG (minutes)	-	-	11	8
Median Time to Transfer (minutes)	-	-	180	61
Fibrinolytic Medication Timing	-	-	69%	54%
Heart Failure Care				
ACE Inhibitor or ARB for LVSD[1]	4	25%	90%	94%
Discharge Instructions[1]	5	100%	89%	88%
Evaluation of LVS Function[1]	11	82%	94%	98%
Smoking Cessation Advice[1]	1	100%	97%	98%
Pneumonia Care				
Appropriate Initial Antibiotic[1]	12	100%	89%	92%
Blood Culture Timing	0	-	97%	96%
Influenza Vaccine[1]	6	100%	88%	91%
Initial Antibiotic Timing[1]	3	100%	95%	95%
Pneumococcal Vaccine[1]	7	71%	93%	93%
Smoking Cessation Advice[1]	4	100%	91%	97%
Surgical Care Improvement Project				
Appropriate VTP Within 24 Hours[5]	0	-	92%	92%
Appropriate Hair Removal[5]	0	-	100%	99%
Appropriate Beta Blocker Usage[5]	0	-	91%	93%
Controlled Postoperative Blood Glucose[5]	0	-	93%	93%
Prophylactic Antibiotic Timing[5]	0	-	96%	97%
Prophylactic Antibiotic Timing (Outpatient)	-	-	92%	92%
Prophylactic Antibiotic Selection[5]	0	-	97%	97%
Prophylactic Antibiotic Select. (Outpatient)	-	-	97%	94%
Prophylactic Antibiotic Stopped[5]	0	-	96%	94%
Recommended VTP Ordered[5]	0	-	92%	94%
Urinary Catheter Removal[5]	0	-	92%	90%
Children's Asthma Care				
Received Systemic Corticosteroids	-	-	-	100%
Received Home Management Plan	-	-	-	71%
Received Reliever Medication	-	-	-	100%
Use of Medical Imaging				
Combination Abdominal CT Scan	-	-	0.177	0.191
Combination Chest CT Scan	-	-	0.025	0.054
Follow-up Mammogram/Ultrasound	-	-	8%	8.4%
MRI for Low Back Pain	-	-	31.9%	32.7%
Survey of Patients' Hospital Experiences				
Area Around Room 'Always' Quiet at Night[8]	-	-	-	58%
Doctors 'Always' Communicated Well[8]	-	-	-	80%
Home Recovery Information Given[8]	-	-	-	82%
Hospital Given 9 or 10 on 10 Point Scale[8]	-	-	-	67%
Meds 'Always' Explained Before Given[8]	-	-	-	60%
Nurses 'Always' Communicated Well[8]	-	-	-	76%
Pain 'Always' Well Controlled[8]	-	-	-	69%
Room and Bathroom 'Always' Clean[8]	-	-	-	71%
Timely Help 'Always' Received[8]	-	-	-	64%
Would Definitely Recommend Hospital[8]	-	-	-	69%

NOTE: Hospital profiles are in alphabetical order by state, then city, then hospital within the city; Rankings exclude hospitals with less than 25 cases except for patient surveys which excludes hospitals with less than 100 cases; (a) 100–299 cases; (1) The number of cases is too small to be sure how well a hospital is performing; (2) The hospital indicated that the data submitted for this measure were based on a sample of cases; (3) Data was collected during a shorter time period (fewer quarters) than the maximum possible time for this measure; (4) Suppressed for one or more quarters by CMS; (5) No data is available from the hospital for this measure; (6) Fewer than 100 patients completed the HCAHPS survey. Use these rates with caution, as the number of surveys may be too low to reliably assess hospital performance; (7) Survey results are based on less than 12 months of data; (8) Survey results are not available for this reporting period; (9) No or very few patients were eligible for the HCAHPS survey. The scores shown, if any, reflect a very small number of surveys; (10) A state average was not calculated because too few hospitals in the state submitted data; (11) There were discrepancies in the data collection process; Please refer to the User's Guide for a full explanation of data.

Saint Joseph's Hospital & Health Center

30 West 7th St
Dickinson, ND 58601
Phone: 701-456-4000
Fax: 701-456-4829
E-mail: stjoesinfo@catholichealth.net
URL: www.stjoeshospital.org
Type: Critical Access Hospitals
Emergency Services: Yes
Ownership: Voluntary Non-Profit - Church
Beds: 106

Key Personnel:
CEO/President. . . . . Allan Sonduck
Chief of Medical Staff . . . . Amy Okasa, MD
Infection Control. . . . . Tavia Voll
Operating Room. . . . . Janis Gartner
Quality Assurance . . . . Tavia Voll
Radiology. . . . . Garry Dunn
Hemotology Center . . . . Curtis Prevost
Intensive Care Unit. . . . . Denette Lothspeich

Measure	Cases	This Hosp.	State Avg.	U.S. Avg.
Heart Attack Care				
ACE Inhibitor or ARB for LVSD[1]	4	100%	93%	96%
Aspirin at Arrival[1]	23	100%	98%	99%
Aspirin at Discharge[1]	19	95%	99%	98%
Beta Blocker at Discharge[1]	19	95%	98%	98%
Fibrinolytic Medication Timing[1]	1	0%	67%	55%
PCI Within 90 Minutes of Arrival	0	-	84%	90%
Smoking Cessation Advice[1]	2	100%	99%	99%
Chest Pain/Possible Heart Attack Care				
Aspirin at Arrival	-	-	96%	95%
Median Time to ECG (minutes)	-	-	11	8
Median Time to Transfer (minutes)	-	-	180	61
Fibrinolytic Medication Timing	-	-	69%	54%
Heart Failure Care				
ACE Inhibitor or ARB for LVSD[1]	14	86%	90%	94%
Discharge Instructions	50	74%	89%	88%
Evaluation of LVS Function	75	100%	94%	98%
Smoking Cessation Advice[1]	9	89%	97%	98%
Pneumonia Care				
Appropriate Initial Antibiotic	34	94%	89%	92%
Blood Culture Timing	49	98%	97%	96%
Influenza Vaccine	41	90%	88%	91%
Initial Antibiotic Timing	57	100%	95%	95%
Pneumococcal Vaccine	71	96%	93%	93%
Smoking Cessation Advice[1]	10	90%	91%	97%
Surgical Care Improvement Project				
Appropriate VTP Within 24 Hours	38	92%	92%	92%
Appropriate Hair Removal	131	100%	100%	99%
Appropriate Beta Blocker Usage	44	95%	91%	93%
Controlled Postoperative Blood Glucose	0	-	93%	93%
Prophylactic Antibiotic Timing	106	94%	96%	97%
Prophylactic Antibiotic Timing (Outpatient)	-	-	92%	92%
Prophylactic Antibiotic Selection	106	97%	97%	97%
Prophylactic Antibiotic Select. (Outpatient)	-	-	97%	94%
Prophylactic Antibiotic Stopped	102	97%	96%	94%
Recommended VTP Ordered	38	97%	92%	94%
Urinary Catheter Removal	30	93%	92%	90%
Children's Asthma Care				
Received Systemic Corticosteroids	-	-	-	100%
Received Home Management Plan	-	-	-	71%
Received Reliever Medication	-	-	-	100%
Use of Medical Imaging				
Combination Abdominal CT Scan	-	-	0.177	0.191
Combination Chest CT Scan	-	-	0.025	0.054
Follow-up Mammogram/Ultrasound	-	-	8%	8.4%
MRI for Low Back Pain	-	-	31.9%	32.7%
Survey of Patients' Hospital Experiences				
Area Around Room 'Always' Quiet at Night	300+	61%	-	58%
Doctors 'Always' Communicated Well	300+	78%	-	80%
Home Recovery Information Given	300+	83%	-	82%
Hospital Given 9 or 10 on 10 Point Scale	300+	63%	-	67%
Meds 'Always' Explained Before Given	300+	63%	-	60%
Nurses 'Always' Communicated Well	300+	79%	-	76%
Pain 'Always' Well Controlled	300+	67%	-	69%
Room and Bathroom 'Always' Clean	300+	74%	-	71%
Timely Help 'Always' Received	300+	72%	-	64%
Would Definitely Recommend Hospital	300+	61%	-	69%

Jacobson Memorial Hospital & Care Center

601 East St N
Elgin, ND 58533
Phone: 701-584-2792
Fax: 701-584-3348
Type: Critical Access Hospitals
Emergency Services: Yes
Ownership: Voluntary Non-Profit - Private
Beds: 50

Key Personnel:
CEO/President. . . . . Douglas W Wamack
Chief of Medical Staff . . . . Dakshina Walgampaya, MD
Infection Control. . . . . Nadia Tymkowych
Operating Room. . . . . Thomas Matheson, MD
Quality Assurance . . . . Marian Will
Emergency Room . . . . Marcy Dawson, RN

Measure	Cases	This Hosp.	State Avg.	U.S. Avg.
Heart Attack Care				
ACE Inhibitor or ARB for LVSD[3]	0	-	93%	96%
Aspirin at Arrival[1,3]	1	100%	98%	99%
Aspirin at Discharge[3]	0	-	99%	98%
Beta Blocker at Discharge[3]	0	-	98%	98%
Fibrinolytic Medication Timing[3]	0	-	67%	55%
PCI Within 90 Minutes of Arrival[3]	0	-	84%	90%
Smoking Cessation Advice[3]	0	-	99%	99%
Chest Pain/Possible Heart Attack Care				
Aspirin at Arrival	-	-	96%	95%
Median Time to ECG (minutes)	-	-	11	8
Median Time to Transfer (minutes)	-	-	180	61
Fibrinolytic Medication Timing	-	-	69%	54%
Heart Failure Care				
ACE Inhibitor or ARB for LVSD[5]	0	-	90%	94%
Discharge Instructions[5]	0	-	89%	88%
Evaluation of LVS Function[5]	0	-	94%	98%
Smoking Cessation Advice[5]	0	-	97%	98%
Pneumonia Care				
Appropriate Initial Antibiotic[3]	0	-	89%	92%
Blood Culture Timing[3]	0	-	97%	96%
Influenza Vaccine[5]	0	-	88%	91%
Initial Antibiotic Timing[1,3]	1	100%	95%	95%
Pneumococcal Vaccine[1,3]	2	100%	93%	93%
Smoking Cessation Advice[3]	0	-	91%	97%
Surgical Care Improvement Project				
Appropriate VTP Within 24 Hours[5]	0	-	92%	92%
Appropriate Hair Removal[5]	0	-	100%	99%
Appropriate Beta Blocker Usage[5]	0	-	91%	93%
Controlled Postoperative Blood Glucose[5]	0	-	93%	93%
Prophylactic Antibiotic Timing[5]	0	-	96%	97%
Prophylactic Antibiotic Timing (Outpatient)	-	-	92%	92%
Prophylactic Antibiotic Selection[5]	0	-	97%	97%
Prophylactic Antibiotic Select. (Outpatient)	-	-	97%	94%
Prophylactic Antibiotic Stopped[5]	0	-	96%	94%
Recommended VTP Ordered[5]	0	-	92%	94%
Urinary Catheter Removal[5]	0	-	92%	90%
Children's Asthma Care				
Received Systemic Corticosteroids	-	-	-	100%
Received Home Management Plan	-	-	-	71%
Received Reliever Medication	-	-	-	100%
Use of Medical Imaging				
Combination Abdominal CT Scan	-	-	0.177	0.191
Combination Chest CT Scan	-	-	0.025	0.054
Follow-up Mammogram/Ultrasound	-	-	8%	8.4%
MRI for Low Back Pain	-	-	31.9%	32.7%
Survey of Patients' Hospital Experiences				
Area Around Room 'Always' Quiet at Night[8]	-	-	-	58%
Doctors 'Always' Communicated Well[8]	-	-	-	80%
Home Recovery Information Given[8]	-	-	-	82%
Hospital Given 9 or 10 on 10 Point Scale[8]	-	-	-	67%
Meds 'Always' Explained Before Given[8]	-	-	-	60%
Nurses 'Always' Communicated Well[8]	-	-	-	76%
Pain 'Always' Well Controlled[8]	-	-	-	69%
Room and Bathroom 'Always' Clean[8]	-	-	-	71%
Timely Help 'Always' Received[8]	-	-	-	64%
Would Definitely Recommend Hospital[8]	-	-	-	69%

Essentia Health-Fargo

3000 32nd Ave South
Fargo, ND 58104
Phone: 701-364-8000
Fax: 701-364-8078
URL: www.dakotaclinic.com
Type: Acute Care Hospitals
Emergency Services: Yes
Ownership: Voluntary Non-Profit - Private
Beds: 74

Key Personnel:
CEO/President. . . . . Paul Wilson
Chief of Medical Staff . . . . Michael Priggs
Emergency Room . . . . John R Baugh

Measure	Cases	This Hosp.	State Avg.	U.S. Avg.
Heart Attack Care				
ACE Inhibitor or ARB for LVSD	38	100%	93%	96%
Aspirin at Arrival	97	99%	98%	99%
Aspirin at Discharge	197	98%	99%	98%
Beta Blocker at Discharge	189	97%	98%	98%
Fibrinolytic Medication Timing	0	-	67%	55%
PCI Within 90 Minutes of Arrival	30	83%	84%	90%
Smoking Cessation Advice	64	98%	99%	99%
Chest Pain/Possible Heart Attack Care				
Aspirin at Arrival[5]	0	-	96%	95%
Median Time to ECG (minutes)[5]	0	-	11	8
Median Time to Transfer (minutes)[5]	0	-	180	61
Fibrinolytic Medication Timing[5]	0	-	69%	54%
Heart Failure Care				
ACE Inhibitor or ARB for LVSD	44	98%	90%	94%
Discharge Instructions	132	98%	89%	88%
Evaluation of LVS Function	175	98%	94%	98%
Smoking Cessation Advice	31	100%	97%	98%
Pneumonia Care				
Appropriate Initial Antibiotic	79	90%	89%	92%
Blood Culture Timing	111	95%	97%	96%
Influenza Vaccine	75	93%	88%	91%
Initial Antibiotic Timing	98	94%	95%	95%
Pneumococcal Vaccine	123	92%	93%	93%
Smoking Cessation Advice	35	100%	91%	97%
Surgical Care Improvement Project				
Appropriate VTP Within 24 Hours[2]	146	96%	92%	92%
Appropriate Hair Removal[2]	521	100%	100%	99%
Appropriate Beta Blocker Usage[2]	179	92%	91%	93%
Controlled Postoperative Blood Glucose[2]	103	86%	93%	93%
Prophylactic Antibiotic Timing[2]	370	95%	96%	97%
Prophylactic Antibiotic Timing (Outpatient)	160	74%	92%	92%
Prophylactic Antibiotic Selection[2]	373	97%	97%	97%
Prophylactic Antibiotic Select. (Outpatient)	187	96%	97%	94%
Prophylactic Antibiotic Stopped[2]	331	95%	96%	94%
Recommended VTP Ordered[2]	147	96%	92%	94%
Urinary Catheter Removal[2]	112	93%	92%	90%
Children's Asthma Care				
Received Systemic Corticosteroids	-	-	-	100%
Received Home Management Plan	-	-	-	71%
Received Reliever Medication	-	-	-	100%
Use of Medical Imaging				
Combination Abdominal CT Scan	505	0.234	0.177	0.191
Combination Chest CT Scan	374	0.005	0.025	0.054
Follow-up Mammogram/Ultrasound[5]	0	-	8%	8.4%
MRI for Low Back Pain	171	32.2%	31.9%	32.7%
Survey of Patients' Hospital Experiences				
Area Around Room 'Always' Quiet at Night	300+	57%	-	58%
Doctors 'Always' Communicated Well	300+	76%	-	80%
Home Recovery Information Given	300+	82%	-	82%
Hospital Given 9 or 10 on 10 Point Scale	300+	68%	-	67%
Meds 'Always' Explained Before Given	300+	57%	-	60%
Nurses 'Always' Communicated Well	300+	73%	-	76%
Pain 'Always' Well Controlled	300+	68%	-	69%
Room and Bathroom 'Always' Clean	300+	70%	-	71%
Timely Help 'Always' Received	300+	61%	-	64%
Would Definitely Recommend Hospital	300+	78%	-	69%

NOTE: Hospital profiles are in alphabetical order by state, then city, then hospital within the city; Rankings exclude hospitals with less than 25 cases except for patient surveys which excludes hospitals with less than 100 cases; (a) 100–299 cases; (1) The number of cases is too small to be sure how well a hospital is performing; (2) The hospital indicated that the data submitted for this measure were based on a sample of cases; (3) Data was collected during a shorter time period (fewer quarters) than the maximum possible time for this measure; (4) Suppressed for one or more quarters by CMS; (5) No data is available from the hospital for this measure; (6) Fewer than 100 patients completed the HCAHPS survey. Use these rates with caution, as the number of surveys may be too low to reliably assess hospital performance; (7) Survey results are based on less than 12 months of data; (8) Survey results are not available for this reporting period; (9) No or very few patients were eligible for the HCAHPS survey. The scores shown, if any, reflect a very small number of surveys; (10) A state average was not calculated because too few hospitals in the state submitted data; (11) There were discrepancies in the data collection process; Please refer to the User's Guide for a full explanation of data.

Fargo VA Medical Center

2101 Elm Street
Fargo, ND 58102
Phone: 701-232-3241
Fax: 701-239-3705
Type: Acute Care-Veterans Administration
Emergency Services: No
Ownership: Government - Federal
Beds: 109

Key Personnel:
CEO/President. . . . . Douglas M Kenyon
Chief of Medical Staff. . . . . Steven Julius, MD
Infection Control. . . . . Jan Holmes, RN
Operating Room. . . . . Barbara Franke, RN
Quality Assurance . . . . Julie Bruhn, RN
Emergency Room . . . . Ronald Johnson, MD
Intensive Care Unit. . . . . Kye Grundyson, RN
Patient Relations . . . . Victor Martinez

Measure	Cases	This Hosp.	State Avg.	U.S. Avg.
Heart Attack Care				
ACE Inhibitor or ARB for LVSD[5]	0	-	93%	96%
Aspirin at Arrival[5]	0	-	98%	99%
Aspirin at Discharge[5]	0	-	99%	98%
Beta Blocker at Discharge[5]	0	-	98%	98%
Fibrinolytic Medication Timing[5]	0	-	67%	55%
PCI Within 90 Minutes of Arrival[5]	0	-	84%	90%
Smoking Cessation Advice[5]	0	-	99%	99%
Chest Pain/Possible Heart Attack Care				
Aspirin at Arrival	-	-	96%	95%
Median Time to ECG (minutes)	-	-	11	8
Median Time to Transfer (minutes)	-	-	180	61
Fibrinolytic Medication Timing	-	-	69%	54%
Heart Failure Care				
ACE Inhibitor or ARB for LVSD[1]	24	83%	90%	94%
Discharge Instructions	73	96%	89%	88%
Evaluation of LVS Function	82	98%	94%	98%
Smoking Cessation Advice[1]	22	95%	97%	98%
Pneumonia Care				
Appropriate Initial Antibiotic	35	91%	89%	92%
Blood Culture Timing	30	100%	97%	96%
Influenza Vaccine	47	96%	88%	91%
Initial Antibiotic Timing	46	96%	95%	95%
Pneumococcal Vaccine	58	97%	93%	93%
Smoking Cessation Advice	36	89%	91%	97%
Surgical Care Improvement Project				
Appropriate VTP Within 24 Hours[2]	81	100%	92%	92%
Appropriate Hair Removal[2]	151	100%	100%	99%
Appropriate Beta Blocker Usage[2]	47	85%	91%	93%
Controlled Postoperative Blood Glucose[2,5]	0	-	93%	93%
Prophylactic Antibiotic Timing	109	94%	96%	97%
Prophylactic Antibiotic Timing (Outpatient)	-	-	92%	92%
Prophylactic Antibiotic Selection	110	98%	97%	97%
Prophylactic Antibiotic Select. (Outpatient)	-	-	97%	94%
Prophylactic Antibiotic Stopped	108	100%	96%	94%
Recommended VTP Ordered[2]	81	100%	92%	94%
Urinary Catheter Removal[2]	86	97%	92%	90%
Children's Asthma Care				
Received Systemic Corticosteroids	-	-	-	100%
Received Home Management Plan	-	-	-	71%
Received Reliever Medication	-	-	-	100%
Use of Medical Imaging				
Combination Abdominal CT Scan	-	-	0.177	0.191
Combination Chest CT Scan	-	-	0.025	0.054
Follow-up Mammogram/Ultrasound	-	-	8%	8.4%
MRI for Low Back Pain	-	-	31.9%	32.7%
Survey of Patients' Hospital Experiences				
Area Around Room 'Always' Quiet at Night	-	-	-	58%
Doctors 'Always' Communicated Well	-	-	-	80%
Home Recovery Information Given	-	-	-	82%
Hospital Given 9 or 10 on 10 Point Scale	-	-	-	67%
Meds 'Always' Explained Before Given	-	-	-	60%
Nurses 'Always' Communicated Well	-	-	-	76%
Pain 'Always' Well Controlled	-	-	-	69%
Room and Bathroom 'Always' Clean	-	-	-	71%
Timely Help 'Always' Received	-	-	-	64%
Would Definitely Recommend Hospital	-	-	-	69%

Sanford Medical Center Fargo

801 Broadway North
Fargo, ND 58122
Phone: 701-234-2000
Fax: 701-234-6979
E-mail: feedback@meritcare.com
URL: www.meritcare.com
Type: Acute Care Hospitals
Emergency Services: Yes
Ownership: Voluntary Non-Profit - Private
Beds: 583

Key Personnel:
CEO/President. . . . . Roger Gilbertson, MD
Chief of Medical Staff . . . . Gregory Post, MD
Infection Control. . . . . Joan Cook
Operating Room. . . . . Vicki Beaton
Pediatric Ambulatory Care . . . . . . Ron Miller, MD
Pediatric In-Patient Care . . . . Ron Miller, MD
Quality Assurance . . . . Rhonda Ketterling, MD
Radiology. . . . . Daniel Mickelso, MD

Measure	Cases	This Hosp.	State Avg.	U.S. Avg.
Heart Attack Care				
ACE Inhibitor or ARB for LVSD	113	88%	93%	96%
Aspirin at Arrival	196	97%	98%	99%
Aspirin at Discharge	568	99%	99%	98%
Beta Blocker at Discharge	565	98%	98%	98%
Fibrinolytic Medication Timing	0	-	67%	55%
PCI Within 90 Minutes of Arrival	39	85%	84%	90%
Smoking Cessation Advice	201	100%	99%	99%
Chest Pain/Possible Heart Attack Care				
Aspirin at Arrival[5]	0	-	96%	95%
Median Time to ECG (minutes)[5]	0	-	11	8
Median Time to Transfer (minutes)[5]	0	-	180	61
Fibrinolytic Medication Timing[5]	0	-	69%	54%
Heart Failure Care				
ACE Inhibitor or ARB for LVSD	105	90%	90%	94%
Discharge Instructions	289	93%	89%	88%
Evaluation of LVS Function	385	100%	94%	98%
Smoking Cessation Advice	57	96%	97%	98%
Pneumonia Care				
Appropriate Initial Antibiotic	145	89%	89%	92%
Blood Culture Timing	218	99%	97%	96%
Influenza Vaccine	236	90%	88%	91%
Initial Antibiotic Timing	274	95%	95%	95%
Pneumococcal Vaccine	340	96%	93%	93%
Smoking Cessation Advice	164	91%	91%	97%
Surgical Care Improvement Project				
Appropriate VTP Within 24 Hours[2]	267	98%	92%	92%
Appropriate Hair Removal[2]	933	99%	100%	99%
Appropriate Beta Blocker Usage[2]	314	93%	91%	93%
Controlled Postoperative Blood Glucose[2]	194	92%	93%	93%
Prophylactic Antibiotic Timing[2]	615	96%	96%	97%
Prophylactic Antibiotic Timing (Outpatient)	586	98%	92%	92%
Prophylactic Antibiotic Selection[2]	623	98%	97%	97%
Prophylactic Antibiotic Select. (Outpatient)	584	98%	97%	94%
Prophylactic Antibiotic Stopped[2]	587	95%	96%	94%
Recommended VTP Ordered[2]	267	98%	92%	94%
Urinary Catheter Removal[2]	175	93%	92%	90%
Children's Asthma Care				
Received Systemic Corticosteroids	-	-	-	100%
Received Home Management Plan	-	-	-	71%
Received Reliever Medication	-	-	-	100%
Use of Medical Imaging				
Combination Abdominal CT Scan	1,662	0.250	0.177	0.191
Combination Chest CT Scan	1,396	0.028	0.025	0.054
Follow-up Mammogram/Ultrasound[5]	0	-	8%	8.4%
MRI for Low Back Pain	375	30.9%	31.9%	32.7%
Survey of Patients' Hospital Experiences				
Area Around Room 'Always' Quiet at Night	300+	52%	-	58%
Doctors 'Always' Communicated Well	300+	72%	-	80%
Home Recovery Information Given	300+	86%	-	82%
Hospital Given 9 or 10 on 10 Point Scale	300+	69%	-	67%
Meds 'Always' Explained Before Given	300+	57%	-	60%
Nurses 'Always' Communicated Well	300+	72%	-	76%
Pain 'Always' Well Controlled	300+	61%	-	69%
Room and Bathroom 'Always' Clean	300+	70%	-	71%
Timely Help 'Always' Received	300+	57%	-	64%
Would Definitely Recommend Hospital	300+	71%	-	69%

P H S Indian Hospital at Fort Yates - Standing Rock

10 North River Road
Fort Yates, ND 58538
Phone: 701-854-3831
Fax: 701-854-7399
Type: Acute Care Hospitals
Emergency Services: No
Ownership: Government - Federal
Beds: 12

Key Personnel:
CEO/President. . . . . Lisa Guardipee

Measure	Cases	This Hosp.	State Avg.	U.S. Avg.
Heart Attack Care				
ACE Inhibitor or ARB for LVSD[5]	0	-	93%	96%
Aspirin at Arrival[5]	0	-	98%	99%
Aspirin at Discharge[5]	0	-	99%	98%
Beta Blocker at Discharge[5]	0	-	98%	98%
Fibrinolytic Medication Timing[5]	0	-	67%	55%
PCI Within 90 Minutes of Arrival[5]	0	-	84%	90%
Smoking Cessation Advice[5]	0	-	99%	99%
Chest Pain/Possible Heart Attack Care				
Aspirin at Arrival	-	-	96%	95%
Median Time to ECG (minutes)	-	-	11	8
Median Time to Transfer (minutes)	-	-	180	61
Fibrinolytic Medication Timing	-	-	69%	54%
Heart Failure Care				
ACE Inhibitor or ARB for LVSD[3]	0	-	90%	94%
Discharge Instructions[3]	0	-	89%	88%
Evaluation of LVS Function[3]	0	-	94%	98%
Smoking Cessation Advice[3]	0	-	97%	98%
Pneumonia Care				
Appropriate Initial Antibiotic[1]	12	92%	89%	92%
Blood Culture Timing[1]	4	100%	97%	96%
Influenza Vaccine[1]	9	78%	88%	91%
Initial Antibiotic Timing[1]	18	72%	95%	95%
Pneumococcal Vaccine[1]	6	100%	93%	93%
Smoking Cessation Advice[1]	11	91%	91%	97%
Surgical Care Improvement Project				
Appropriate VTP Within 24 Hours[5]	0	-	92%	92%
Appropriate Hair Removal[5]	0	-	100%	99%
Appropriate Beta Blocker Usage[5]	0	-	91%	93%
Controlled Postoperative Blood Glucose[5]	0	-	93%	93%
Prophylactic Antibiotic Timing[5]	0	-	96%	97%
Prophylactic Antibiotic Timing (Outpatient)	-	-	92%	92%
Prophylactic Antibiotic Selection[5]	0	-	97%	97%
Prophylactic Antibiotic Select. (Outpatient)	-	-	97%	94%
Prophylactic Antibiotic Stopped[5]	0	-	96%	94%
Recommended VTP Ordered[5]	0	-	92%	94%
Urinary Catheter Removal[5]	0	-	92%	90%
Children's Asthma Care				
Received Systemic Corticosteroids	-	-	-	100%
Received Home Management Plan	-	-	-	71%
Received Reliever Medication	-	-	-	100%
Use of Medical Imaging				
Combination Abdominal CT Scan	-	-	0.177	0.191
Combination Chest CT Scan	-	-	0.025	0.054
Follow-up Mammogram/Ultrasound	-	-	8%	8.4%
MRI for Low Back Pain	-	-	31.9%	32.7%
Survey of Patients' Hospital Experiences				
Area Around Room 'Always' Quiet at Night[6]	<100	78%	-	58%
Doctors 'Always' Communicated Well[6]	<100	79%	-	80%
Home Recovery Information Given[6]	<100	81%	-	82%
Hospital Given 9 or 10 on 10 Point Scale[6]	<100	57%	-	67%
Meds 'Always' Explained Before Given[6]	<100	65%	-	60%
Nurses 'Always' Communicated Well[6]	<100	75%	-	76%
Pain 'Always' Well Controlled[6]	<100	71%	-	69%
Room and Bathroom 'Always' Clean[6]	<100	71%	-	71%
Timely Help 'Always' Received[6]	<100	71%	-	64%
Would Definitely Recommend Hospital	<100	66%	-	69%

NOTE: Hospital profiles are in alphabetical order by state, then city, then hospital within the city; Rankings exclude hospitals with less than 25 cases except for patient surveys which excludes hospitals with less than 100 cases; (a) 100–299 cases; (1) The number of cases is too small to be sure how well a hospital is performing; (2) The hospital indicated that the data submitted for this measure were based on a sample of cases; (3) Data was collected during a shorter time period (fewer quarters) than the maximum possible time for this measure; (4) Suppressed for one or more quarters by CMS; (5) No data is available from the hospital for this measure; (6) Fewer than 100 patients completed the HCAHPS survey. Use these rates with caution, as the number of surveys may be too low to reliably assess hospital performance; (7) Survey results are based on less than 12 months of data; (8) Survey results are not available for this reporting period; (9) No or very few patients were eligible for the HCAHPS survey. The scores shown, if any, reflect a very small number of surveys; (10) A state average was not calculated because too few hospitals in the state submitted data; (11) There were discrepancies in the data collection process; Please refer to the User's Guide for a full explanation of data.

Unity Medical Center

164 W 13th Street
Grafton, ND 58237
URL: www.unitymedcenter.com
Type: Critical Access Hospitals
Ownership: Voluntary Non-Profit - Other
Phone: 701-352-1620
Fax: 701-352-1671
Emergency Services: Yes
Beds: 50

Key Personnel:
CEO/President. . . . . Evett A Butler
Infection Control. . . . . Marlene Quanrud
Operating Room. . . . . Delaine Russum

Measure	Cases	This Hosp.	State Avg.	U.S. Avg.
Heart Attack Care				
ACE Inhibitor or ARB for LVSD	-	-	93%	96%
Aspirin at Arrival	-	-	98%	99%
Aspirin at Discharge	-	-	99%	98%
Beta Blocker at Discharge	-	-	98%	98%
Fibrinolytic Medication Timing	-	-	67%	55%
PCI Within 90 Minutes of Arrival	-	-	84%	90%
Smoking Cessation Advice	-	-	99%	99%
Chest Pain/Possible Heart Attack Care				
Aspirin at Arrival[5]	0	-	96%	95%
Median Time to ECG (minutes)[5]	0	-	11	8
Median Time to Transfer (minutes)[5]	0	-	180	61
Fibrinolytic Medication Timing[5]	0	-	69%	54%
Heart Failure Care				
ACE Inhibitor or ARB for LVSD	-	-	90%	94%
Discharge Instructions	-	-	89%	88%
Evaluation of LVS Function	-	-	94%	98%
Smoking Cessation Advice	-	-	97%	98%
Pneumonia Care				
Appropriate Initial Antibiotic	-	-	89%	92%
Blood Culture Timing	-	-	97%	96%
Influenza Vaccine	-	-	88%	91%
Initial Antibiotic Timing	-	-	95%	95%
Pneumococcal Vaccine	-	-	93%	93%
Smoking Cessation Advice	-	-	91%	97%
Surgical Care Improvement Project				
Appropriate VTP Within 24 Hours	-	-	92%	92%
Appropriate Hair Removal	-	-	100%	99%
Appropriate Beta Blocker Usage	-	-	91%	93%
Controlled Postoperative Blood Glucose	-	-	93%	93%
Prophylactic Antibiotic Timing	-	-	96%	97%
Prophylactic Antibiotic Timing (Outpatient)[5]	0	-	92%	92%
Prophylactic Antibiotic Selection	-	-	97%	97%
Prophylactic Antibiotic Select. (Outpatient)[5]	0	-	97%	94%
Prophylactic Antibiotic Stopped	-	-	96%	94%
Recommended VTP Ordered	-	-	92%	94%
Urinary Catheter Removal	-	-	92%	90%
Children's Asthma Care				
Received Systemic Corticosteroids	-	-	-	100%
Received Home Management Plan	-	-	-	71%
Received Reliever Medication	-	-	-	100%
Use of Medical Imaging				
Combination Abdominal CT Scan[1]	26	0.077	0.177	0.191
Combination Chest CT Scan[1]	25	0.080	0.025	0.054
Follow-up Mammogram/Ultrasound	141	9.9%	8%	8.4%
MRI for Low Back Pain[1]	3	100%	31.9%	32.7%
Survey of Patients' Hospital Experiences				
Area Around Room 'Always' Quiet at Night	-	-	-	58%
Doctors 'Always' Communicated Well	-	-	-	80%
Home Recovery Information Given	-	-	-	82%
Hospital Given 9 or 10 on 10 Point Scale	-	-	-	67%
Meds 'Always' Explained Before Given	-	-	-	60%
Nurses 'Always' Communicated Well	-	-	-	76%
Pain 'Always' Well Controlled	-	-	-	69%
Room and Bathroom 'Always' Clean	-	-	-	71%
Timely Help 'Always' Received	-	-	-	64%
Would Definitely Recommend Hospital	-	-	-	69%

Altru Hospital

1200 S Columbia Rd
Grand Forks, ND 58201
E-mail: contactus@altru.org
URL: www.altru.org
Type: Acute Care Hospitals
Ownership: Government - Local
Phone: 701-780-5000
Fax: 701-780-1093
Emergency Services: Yes
Beds: 352

Key Personnel:
CEO/President. . . . . Casey Ryan, MD
Chief of Medical Staff . . . . Norman Byers, MD
Operating Room. . . . . Mary Herbeck
Quality Assurance . . . . Ben Ronstrom
Radiology. . . . . Steve Metcaff
Emergency Room . . . . Tom Alinder
Intensive Care Unit. . . . . Wanda Rosenquist
Patient Relations . . . . Marilyn Troftgrubeen

Measure	Cases	This Hosp.	State Avg.	U.S. Avg.
Heart Attack Care				
ACE Inhibitor or ARB for LVSD	55	93%	93%	96%
Aspirin at Arrival	123	99%	98%	99%
Aspirin at Discharge	257	100%	99%	98%
Beta Blocker at Discharge	245	99%	98%	98%
Fibrinolytic Medication Timing	0	-	67%	55%
PCI Within 90 Minutes of Arrival[1]	20	60%	84%	90%
Smoking Cessation Advice	84	100%	99%	99%
Chest Pain/Possible Heart Attack Care				
Aspirin at Arrival[3]	0	-	96%	95%
Median Time to ECG (minutes)[3]	0	-	11	8
Median Time to Transfer (minutes)[5]	0	-	180	61
Fibrinolytic Medication Timing[5]	0	-	69%	54%
Heart Failure Care				
ACE Inhibitor or ARB for LVSD	70	89%	90%	94%
Discharge Instructions	170	91%	89%	88%
Evaluation of LVS Function	215	90%	94%	98%
Smoking Cessation Advice	45	98%	97%	98%
Pneumonia Care				
Appropriate Initial Antibiotic	141	70%	89%	92%
Blood Culture Timing	226	94%	97%	96%
Influenza Vaccine	174	83%	88%	91%
Initial Antibiotic Timing	188	91%	95%	95%
Pneumococcal Vaccine	244	86%	93%	93%
Smoking Cessation Advice	116	92%	91%	97%
Surgical Care Improvement Project				
Appropriate VTP Within 24 Hours[2]	233	94%	92%	92%
Appropriate Hair Removal[2]	634	100%	100%	99%
Appropriate Beta Blocker Usage[2]	227	89%	91%	93%
Controlled Postoperative Blood Glucose[2]	122	90%	93%	93%
Prophylactic Antibiotic Timing[2]	486	93%	96%	97%
Prophylactic Antibiotic Timing (Outpatient)	276	90%	92%	92%
Prophylactic Antibiotic Selection[2]	489	98%	97%	97%
Prophylactic Antibiotic Select. (Outpatient)	284	99%	97%	94%
Prophylactic Antibiotic Stopped[2]	472	95%	96%	94%
Recommended VTP Ordered[2]	233	94%	92%	94%
Urinary Catheter Removal[2]	126	83%	92%	90%
Children's Asthma Care				
Received Systemic Corticosteroids	-	-	-	100%
Received Home Management Plan	-	-	-	71%
Received Reliever Medication	-	-	-	100%
Use of Medical Imaging				
Combination Abdominal CT Scan	871	0.087	0.177	0.191
Combination Chest CT Scan	1,391	0.004	0.025	0.054
Follow-up Mammogram/Ultrasound	2,010	14.2%	8%	8.4%
MRI for Low Back Pain	173	30.1%	31.9%	32.7%
Survey of Patients' Hospital Experiences				
Area Around Room 'Always' Quiet at Night	300+	44%	-	58%
Doctors 'Always' Communicated Well	300+	72%	-	80%
Home Recovery Information Given	300+	83%	-	82%
Hospital Given 9 or 10 on 10 Point Scale	300+	57%	-	67%
Meds 'Always' Explained Before Given	300+	56%	-	60%
Nurses 'Always' Communicated Well	300+	69%	-	76%
Pain 'Always' Well Controlled	300+	61%	-	69%
Room and Bathroom 'Always' Clean	300+	71%	-	71%
Timely Help 'Always' Received	300+	55%	-	64%
Would Definitely Recommend Hospital	300+	59%	-	69%

Saint Aloisius Medical Center

325 E Brewster St
Harvey, ND 58341
URL: www.staloisius.com
Type: Critical Access Hospitals
Ownership: Voluntary Non-Profit - Church
Phone: 701-324-4651
Fax: 701-324-4651
Emergency Services: Yes
Beds: 131

Key Personnel:
Cardiac Laboratory. . . . . Wayne Zahy
Chief of Medical Staff . . . . Charles Nyhus, MD
Operating Room. . . . . Susanne Levene, RN
Hemotology Center . . . . Candice Thompson

Measure	Cases	This Hosp.	State Avg.	U.S. Avg.
Heart Attack Care				
ACE Inhibitor or ARB for LVSD[1,3]	1	100%	93%	96%
Aspirin at Arrival[1,3]	3	33%	98%	99%
Aspirin at Discharge[1,3]	1	100%	99%	98%
Beta Blocker at Discharge[1,3]	1	100%	98%	98%
Fibrinolytic Medication Timing[3]	0	-	67%	55%
PCI Within 90 Minutes of Arrival[3]	0	-	84%	90%
Smoking Cessation Advice[3]	0	-	99%	99%
Chest Pain/Possible Heart Attack Care				
Aspirin at Arrival	-	-	96%	95%
Median Time to ECG (minutes)	-	-	11	8
Median Time to Transfer (minutes)	-	-	180	61
Fibrinolytic Medication Timing	-	-	69%	54%
Heart Failure Care				
ACE Inhibitor or ARB for LVSD[1]	3	100%	90%	94%
Discharge Instructions[1]	18	83%	89%	88%
Evaluation of LVS Function	26	54%	94%	98%
Smoking Cessation Advice	0	-	97%	98%
Pneumonia Care				
Appropriate Initial Antibiotic[1]	10	70%	89%	92%
Blood Culture Timing[1]	2	50%	97%	96%
Influenza Vaccine[1]	17	71%	88%	91%
Initial Antibiotic Timing[1]	12	83%	95%	95%
Pneumococcal Vaccine	45	80%	93%	93%
Smoking Cessation Advice[1]	6	50%	91%	97%
Surgical Care Improvement Project				
Appropriate VTP Within 24 Hours[5]	0	-	92%	92%
Appropriate Hair Removal[5]	0	-	100%	99%
Appropriate Beta Blocker Usage[5]	0	-	91%	93%
Controlled Postoperative Blood Glucose[5]	0	-	93%	93%
Prophylactic Antibiotic Timing[5]	0	-	96%	97%
Prophylactic Antibiotic Timing (Outpatient)	-	-	92%	92%
Prophylactic Antibiotic Selection[5]	0	-	97%	97%
Prophylactic Antibiotic Select. (Outpatient)	-	-	97%	94%
Prophylactic Antibiotic Stopped[5]	0	-	96%	94%
Recommended VTP Ordered[5]	0	-	92%	94%
Urinary Catheter Removal[5]	0	-	92%	90%
Children's Asthma Care				
Received Systemic Corticosteroids	-	-	-	100%
Received Home Management Plan	-	-	-	71%
Received Reliever Medication	-	-	-	100%
Use of Medical Imaging				
Combination Abdominal CT Scan	-	-	0.177	0.191
Combination Chest CT Scan	-	-	0.025	0.054
Follow-up Mammogram/Ultrasound	-	-	8%	8.4%
MRI for Low Back Pain	-	-	31.9%	32.7%
Survey of Patients' Hospital Experiences				
Area Around Room 'Always' Quiet at Night[8]	-	-	-	58%
Doctors 'Always' Communicated Well[8]	-	-	-	80%
Home Recovery Information Given[8]	-	-	-	82%
Hospital Given 9 or 10 on 10 Point Scale[8]	-	-	-	67%
Meds 'Always' Explained Before Given[8]	-	-	-	60%
Nurses 'Always' Communicated Well[8]	-	-	-	76%
Pain 'Always' Well Controlled[8]	-	-	-	69%
Room and Bathroom 'Always' Clean[8]	-	-	-	71%
Timely Help 'Always' Received[8]	-	-	-	64%
Would Definitely Recommend Hospital[8]	-	-	-	69%

NOTE: Hospital profiles are in alphabetical order by state, then city, then hospital within the city; Rankings exclude hospitals with less than 25 cases except for patient surveys which excludes hospitals with less than 100 cases; (a) 100–299 cases; (1) The number of cases is too small to be sure how well a hospital is performing; (2) The hospital indicated that the data submitted for this measure were based on a sample of cases; (3) Data was collected during a shorter time period (fewer quarters) than the maximum possible time for this measure; (4) Suppressed for one or more quarters by CMS; (5) No data is available from the hospital for this measure; (6) Fewer than 100 patients completed the HCAHPS survey. Use these rates with caution, as the number of surveys may be too low to reliably assess hospital performance; (7) Survey results are based on less than 12 months of data; (8) Survey results are not available for this reporting period; (9) No or very few patients were eligible for the HCAHPS survey. The scores shown, if any, reflect a very small number of surveys; (10) A state average was not calculated because too few hospitals in the state submitted data; (11) There were discrepancies in the data collection process; Please refer to the User's Guide for a full explanation of data.

West River Regional Medical Center

1000 Highway 12
Hettinger, ND 58639
E-mail: jiml@wrhs.com
URL: www.wrhs.com
Phone: 701-567-4561
Fax: 701-567-6364

Type: Critical Access Hospitals
Ownership: Voluntary Non-Profit - Private
Emergency Services: Yes
Beds: 25

Key Personnel:
CEO/President. . . . . James K Long
Operating Room. . . . . Leah Gunther
Quality Assurance . . . . Dana And

Measure	Cases	This Hosp.	State Avg.	U.S. Avg.
Heart Attack Care				
ACE Inhibitor or ARB for LVSD[1,3]	1	100%	93%	96%
Aspirin at Arrival[1,3]	3	100%	98%	99%
Aspirin at Discharge[1,3]	2	100%	99%	98%
Beta Blocker at Discharge[1,3]	2	100%	98%	98%
Fibrinolytic Medication Timing[1,3]	4	75%	67%	55%
PCI Within 90 Minutes of Arrival[3]	0	-	84%	90%
Smoking Cessation Advice[3]	0	-	99%	99%
Chest Pain/Possible Heart Attack Care				
Aspirin at Arrival	-	-	96%	95%
Median Time to ECG (minutes)	-	-	11	8
Median Time to Transfer (minutes)	-	-	180	61
Fibrinolytic Medication Timing	-	-	69%	54%
Heart Failure Care				
ACE Inhibitor or ARB for LVSD[1]	5	100%	90%	94%
Discharge Instructions[1]	21	100%	89%	88%
Evaluation of LVS Function	41	93%	94%	98%
Smoking Cessation Advice[1]	2	100%	97%	98%
Pneumonia Care				
Appropriate Initial Antibiotic	42	90%	89%	92%
Blood Culture Timing[1]	20	100%	97%	96%
Influenza Vaccine	41	78%	88%	91%
Initial Antibiotic Timing	74	100%	95%	95%
Pneumococcal Vaccine	66	91%	93%	93%
Smoking Cessation Advice[1]	14	100%	91%	97%
Surgical Care Improvement Project				
Appropriate VTP Within 24 Hours[1]	15	73%	92%	92%
Appropriate Hair Removal[1]	19	100%	100%	99%
Appropriate Beta Blocker Usage[5]	0	-	91%	93%
Controlled Postoperative Blood Glucose	0	-	93%	93%
Prophylactic Antibiotic Timing[1]	14	79%	96%	97%
Prophylactic Antibiotic Timing (Outpatient)	-	-	92%	92%
Prophylactic Antibiotic Selection[1]	13	92%	97%	97%
Prophylactic Antibiotic Select. (Outpatient)	-	-	97%	94%
Prophylactic Antibiotic Stopped[1]	13	85%	96%	94%
Recommended VTP Ordered[1]	15	73%	92%	94%
Urinary Catheter Removal[1]	2	100%	92%	90%
Children's Asthma Care				
Received Systemic Corticosteroids	-	-	-	100%
Received Home Management Plan	-	-	-	71%
Received Reliever Medication	-	-	-	100%
Use of Medical Imaging				
Combination Abdominal CT Scan	-	-	0.177	0.191
Combination Chest CT Scan	-	-	0.025	0.054
Follow-up Mammogram/Ultrasound	-	-	8%	8.4%
MRI for Low Back Pain	-	-	31.9%	32.7%
Survey of Patients' Hospital Experiences				
Area Around Room 'Always' Quiet at Night[8]	-	-	-	58%
Doctors 'Always' Communicated Well[8]	-	-	-	80%
Home Recovery Information Given[8]	-	-	-	82%
Hospital Given 9 or 10 on 10 Point Scale[8]	-	-	-	67%
Meds 'Always' Explained Before Given[8]	-	-	-	60%
Nurses 'Always' Communicated Well[8]	-	-	-	76%
Pain 'Always' Well Controlled[8]	-	-	-	69%
Room and Bathroom 'Always' Clean[8]	-	-	-	71%
Timely Help 'Always' Received[8]	-	-	-	64%
Would Definitely Recommend Hospital[8]	-	-	-	69%

Hillsboro Medical Center

12 Third Street South East
Hillsboro, ND 58045
E-mail: darleneswanson@meritcare.com
Phone: 701-636-3200
Fax: 701-636-3206

Type: Critical Access Hospitals
Ownership: Voluntary Non-Profit - Private
Emergency Services: Yes
Beds: 20

Key Personnel:
Chief of Medical Staff. . . . . Charles Breen
Infection Control. . . . . Julieeen Rosenberg
Quality Assurance . . . . Jennifer Jacobson

Measure	Cases	This Hosp.	State Avg.	U.S. Avg.
Heart Attack Care				
ACE Inhibitor or ARB for LVSD[3]	0	-	93%	96%
Aspirin at Arrival[3]	0	-	98%	99%
Aspirin at Discharge[3]	0	-	99%	98%
Beta Blocker at Discharge[3]	0	-	98%	98%
Fibrinolytic Medication Timing[3]	0	-	67%	55%
PCI Within 90 Minutes of Arrival[3]	0	-	84%	90%
Smoking Cessation Advice[3]	0	-	99%	99%
Chest Pain/Possible Heart Attack Care				
Aspirin at Arrival[5]	0	-	96%	95%
Median Time to ECG (minutes)[5]	0	-	11	8
Median Time to Transfer (minutes)[5]	0	-	180	61
Fibrinolytic Medication Timing[5]	0	-	69%	54%
Heart Failure Care				
ACE Inhibitor or ARB for LVSD[3]	0	-	90%	94%
Discharge Instructions[1,3]	3	33%	89%	88%
Evaluation of LVS Function[1,3]	6	0%	94%	98%
Smoking Cessation Advice[3]	0	-	97%	98%
Pneumonia Care				
Appropriate Initial Antibiotic[1,3]	9	89%	89%	92%
Blood Culture Timing[3]	0	-	97%	96%
Influenza Vaccine[1]	8	62%	88%	91%
Initial Antibiotic Timing[1,3]	2	100%	95%	95%
Pneumococcal Vaccine[1,3]	5	60%	93%	93%
Smoking Cessation Advice[1,3]	3	67%	91%	97%
Surgical Care Improvement Project				
Appropriate VTP Within 24 Hours[5]	0	-	92%	92%
Appropriate Hair Removal[5]	0	-	100%	99%
Appropriate Beta Blocker Usage[5]	0	-	91%	93%
Controlled Postoperative Blood Glucose[5]	0	-	93%	93%
Prophylactic Antibiotic Timing[5]	0	-	96%	97%
Prophylactic Antibiotic Timing (Outpatient)[5]	0	-	92%	92%
Prophylactic Antibiotic Selection[5]	0	-	97%	97%
Prophylactic Antibiotic Select. (Outpatient)[5]	0	-	97%	94%
Prophylactic Antibiotic Stopped[5]	0	-	96%	94%
Recommended VTP Ordered[5]	0	-	92%	94%
Urinary Catheter Removal[5]	0	-	92%	90%
Children's Asthma Care				
Received Systemic Corticosteroids	-	-	-	100%
Received Home Management Plan	-	-	-	71%
Received Reliever Medication	-	-	-	100%
Use of Medical Imaging				
Combination Abdominal CT Scan[1]	12	0.000	0.177	0.191
Combination Chest CT Scan[1]	21	0.143	0.025	0.054
Follow-up Mammogram/Ultrasound[5]	0	-	8%	8.4%
MRI for Low Back Pain[1]	12	25.0%	31.9%	32.7%
Survey of Patients' Hospital Experiences				
Area Around Room 'Always' Quiet at Night[8]	-	-	-	58%
Doctors 'Always' Communicated Well[8]	-	-	-	80%
Home Recovery Information Given[8]	-	-	-	82%
Hospital Given 9 or 10 on 10 Point Scale[8]	-	-	-	67%
Meds 'Always' Explained Before Given[8]	-	-	-	60%
Nurses 'Always' Communicated Well[8]	-	-	-	76%
Pain 'Always' Well Controlled[8]	-	-	-	69%
Room and Bathroom 'Always' Clean[8]	-	-	-	71%
Timely Help 'Always' Received[8]	-	-	-	64%
Would Definitely Recommend Hospital[8]	-	-	-	69%

Jamestown Hospital

419 5th Street N E
Jamestown, ND 58401
URL: www.jamestownhospital.com
Phone: 701-252-1050
Fax: 701-952-3270

Type: Critical Access Hospitals
Ownership: Voluntary Non-Profit - Other
Emergency Services: Yes
Beds: 85

Key Personnel:
CEO/President. . . . . Martin I Richman
Chief of Medical Staff . . . . Robert Wells, MD
Infection Control. . . . . Jenna Broden
Operating Room. . . . . Linda Todd, RN
Quality Assurance . . . . Martin Richman
Radiology. . . . . Alfonso C Findley
Ambulatory Care . . . . Sheila Krapp
Emergency Room . . . . Sheila Krapp

Measure	Cases	This Hosp.	State Avg.	U.S. Avg.
Heart Attack Care				
ACE Inhibitor or ARB for LVSD[3]	0	-	93%	96%
Aspirin at Arrival[1,3]	4	100%	98%	99%
Aspirin at Discharge[1,3]	3	100%	99%	98%
Beta Blocker at Discharge[1,3]	5	80%	98%	98%
Fibrinolytic Medication Timing[3]	0	-	67%	55%
PCI Within 90 Minutes of Arrival[3]	0	-	84%	90%
Smoking Cessation Advice[1,3]	1	100%	99%	99%
Chest Pain/Possible Heart Attack Care				
Aspirin at Arrival	64	98%	96%	95%
Median Time to ECG (minutes)	67	8	11	8
Median Time to Transfer (minutes)[5]	0	-	180	61
Fibrinolytic Medication Timing[1]	10	70%	69%	54%
Heart Failure Care				
ACE Inhibitor or ARB for LVSD[1]	9	100%	90%	94%
Discharge Instructions	28	100%	89%	88%
Evaluation of LVS Function	46	100%	94%	98%
Smoking Cessation Advice[1]	8	100%	97%	98%
Pneumonia Care				
Appropriate Initial Antibiotic	47	100%	89%	92%
Blood Culture Timing	57	98%	97%	96%
Influenza Vaccine	32	100%	88%	91%
Initial Antibiotic Timing	61	95%	95%	95%
Pneumococcal Vaccine	58	100%	93%	93%
Smoking Cessation Advice[1]	12	100%	91%	97%
Surgical Care Improvement Project				
Appropriate VTP Within 24 Hours	28	71%	92%	92%
Appropriate Hair Removal	68	100%	100%	99%
Appropriate Beta Blocker Usage[1]	16	100%	91%	93%
Controlled Postoperative Blood Glucose	0	-	93%	93%
Prophylactic Antibiotic Timing	48	96%	96%	97%
Prophylactic Antibiotic Timing (Outpatient)[1]	11	73%	92%	92%
Prophylactic Antibiotic Selection	48	94%	97%	97%
Prophylactic Antibiotic Select. (Outpatient)[1]	11	100%	97%	94%
Prophylactic Antibiotic Stopped	46	96%	96%	94%
Recommended VTP Ordered	28	71%	92%	94%
Urinary Catheter Removal[1]	9	78%	92%	90%
Children's Asthma Care				
Received Systemic Corticosteroids	-	-	-	100%
Received Home Management Plan	-	-	-	71%
Received Reliever Medication	-	-	-	100%
Use of Medical Imaging				
Combination Abdominal CT Scan[5]	0	-	0.177	0.191
Combination Chest CT Scan[5]	0	-	0.025	0.054
Follow-up Mammogram/Ultrasound[5]	0	-	8%	8.4%
MRI for Low Back Pain[5]	0	-	31.9%	32.7%
Survey of Patients' Hospital Experiences				
Area Around Room 'Always' Quiet at Night	300+	63%	-	58%
Doctors 'Always' Communicated Well	300+	78%	-	80%
Home Recovery Information Given	300+	87%	-	82%
Hospital Given 9 or 10 on 10 Point Scale	300+	63%	-	67%
Meds 'Always' Explained Before Given	300+	60%	-	60%
Nurses 'Always' Communicated Well	300+	80%	-	76%
Pain 'Always' Well Controlled	300+	73%	-	69%
Room and Bathroom 'Always' Clean	300+	76%	-	71%
Timely Help 'Always' Received	300+	75%	-	64%
Would Definitely Recommend Hospital	300+	65%	-	69%

NOTE: Hospital profiles are in alphabetical order by state, then city, then hospital within the city; Rankings exclude hospitals with less than 25 cases except for patient surveys which excludes hospitals with less than 100 cases; (a) 100–299 cases; (1) The number of cases is too small to be sure how well a hospital is performing; (2) The hospital indicated that the data submitted for this measure were based on a sample of cases; (3) Data was collected during a shorter time period (fewer quarters) than the maximum possible time for this measure; (4) Suppressed for one or more quarters by CMS; (5) No data is available from the hospital for this measure; (6) Fewer than 100 patients completed the HCAHPS survey. Use these rates with caution, as the number of surveys may be too low to reliably assess hospital performance; (7) Survey results are based on less than 12 months of data; (8) Survey results are not available for this reporting period; (9) No or very few patients were eligible for the HCAHPS survey. The scores shown, if any, reflect a very small number of surveys; (10) A state average was not calculated because too few hospitals in the state submitted data; (11) There were discrepancies in the data collection process; Please refer to the User's Guide for a full explanation of data.

Linton Hospital

518 North Broadway Phone: 701-254-4511
Linton, ND 58552 Fax: 701-254-4578
E-mail: info@lintonhospital.com
URL: www.lintonhospital.com
Type: Critical Access Hospitals Emergency Services: Yes
Ownership: Voluntary Non-Profit - Private Beds: 25

Key Personnel:
CEO/President. . . . . Roger Unger
Chief of Medical Staff. . . . . Donald Grinz
Infection Control. . . . . Melanie Jangula, RN
Operating Room. . . . . Joan Wittmeier, RN
Quality Assurance . . . . Nadine Held, LPN
Radiology. . . . . Dennis Kress
Emergency Room . . . . Roger Martin

Measure	Cases	This Hosp.	State Avg.	U.S. Avg.
Heart Attack Care				
ACE Inhibitor or ARB for LVSD[3]	0	-	93%	96%
Aspirin at Arrival[1,3]	8	75%	98%	99%
Aspirin at Discharge[1,3]	6	50%	99%	98%
Beta Blocker at Discharge[1,3]	5	80%	98%	98%
Fibrinolytic Medication Timing[3]	0	-	67%	55%
PCI Within 90 Minutes of Arrival[3]	0	-	84%	90%
Smoking Cessation Advice[1,3]	1	0%	99%	99%
Chest Pain/Possible Heart Attack Care				
Aspirin at Arrival	-	-	96%	95%
Median Time to ECG (minutes)	-	-	11	8
Median Time to Transfer (minutes)	-	-	180	61
Fibrinolytic Medication Timing	-	-	69%	54%
Heart Failure Care				
ACE Inhibitor or ARB for LVSD[1]	1	100%	90%	94%
Discharge Instructions[1]	13	77%	89%	88%
Evaluation of LVS Function[1]	17	35%	94%	98%
Smoking Cessation Advice[1]	2	50%	97%	98%
Pneumonia Care				
Appropriate Initial Antibiotic[1]	12	100%	89%	92%
Blood Culture Timing[1]	6	100%	97%	96%
Influenza Vaccine[1]	21	81%	88%	91%
Initial Antibiotic Timing[1]	24	100%	95%	95%
Pneumococcal Vaccine	26	73%	93%	93%
Smoking Cessation Advice[1]	10	40%	91%	97%
Surgical Care Improvement Project				
Appropriate VTP Within 24 Hours[5]	0	-	92%	92%
Appropriate Hair Removal[5]	0	-	100%	99%
Appropriate Beta Blocker Usage[5]	0	-	91%	93%
Controlled Postoperative Blood Glucose[5]	0	-	93%	93%
Prophylactic Antibiotic Timing[5]	0	-	96%	97%
Prophylactic Antibiotic Timing (Outpatient)	-	-	92%	92%
Prophylactic Antibiotic Selection[5]	0	-	97%	97%
Prophylactic Antibiotic Select. (Outpatient)	-	-	97%	94%
Prophylactic Antibiotic Stopped[5]	0	-	96%	94%
Recommended VTP Ordered[5]	0	-	92%	94%
Urinary Catheter Removal[5]	0	-	92%	90%
Children's Asthma Care				
Received Systemic Corticosteroids	-	-	-	100%
Received Home Management Plan	-	-	-	71%
Received Reliever Medication	-	-	-	100%
Use of Medical Imaging				
Combination Abdominal CT Scan	-	-	0.177	0.191
Combination Chest CT Scan	-	-	0.025	0.054
Follow-up Mammogram/Ultrasound	-	-	8%	8.4%
MRI for Low Back Pain	-	-	31.9%	32.7%
Survey of Patients' Hospital Experiences				
Area Around Room 'Always' Quiet at Night[8]	-	-	-	58%
Doctors 'Always' Communicated Well[8]	-	-	-	80%
Home Recovery Information Given[8]	-	-	-	82%
Hospital Given 9 or 10 on 10 Point Scale[8]	-	-	-	67%
Meds 'Always' Explained Before Given[8]	-	-	-	60%
Nurses 'Always' Communicated Well[8]	-	-	-	76%
Pain 'Always' Well Controlled[8]	-	-	-	69%
Room and Bathroom 'Always' Clean[8]	-	-	-	71%
Timely Help 'Always' Received[8]	-	-	-	64%
Would Definitely Recommend Hospital[8]	-	-	-	69%

Sanford Mayville

42 6th Avenue SE Phone: 701-786-3800
Mayville, ND 58257 Fax: 701-788-2145
Type: Critical Access Hospitals Emergency Services: Yes
Ownership: Voluntary Non-Profit - Other Beds: 25

Key Personnel:
CEO/President. . . . . Roger Baier
Chief of Medical Staff. . . . . Janus McHus
Operating Room. . . . . Cindy Petersen
Quality Assurance . . . . Cynthia Thompson
Radiology. . . . . Lorell Carlson
Emergency Room . . . . Doris Vigen, RN

Measure	Cases	This Hosp.	State Avg.	U.S. Avg.
Heart Attack Care				
ACE Inhibitor or ARB for LVSD[3]	0	-	93%	96%
Aspirin at Arrival[1,3]	4	75%	98%	99%
Aspirin at Discharge[1,3]	3	100%	99%	98%
Beta Blocker at Discharge[1,3]	3	100%	98%	98%
Fibrinolytic Medication Timing[3]	0	-	67%	55%
PCI Within 90 Minutes of Arrival[3]	0	-	84%	90%
Smoking Cessation Advice[3]	0	-	99%	99%
Chest Pain/Possible Heart Attack Care				
Aspirin at Arrival	-	-	96%	95%
Median Time to ECG (minutes)	-	-	11	8
Median Time to Transfer (minutes)	-	-	180	61
Fibrinolytic Medication Timing	-	-	69%	54%
Heart Failure Care				
ACE Inhibitor or ARB for LVSD[1,3]	2	50%	90%	94%
Discharge Instructions[1,3]	4	25%	89%	88%
Evaluation of LVS Function[1,3]	14	71%	94%	98%
Smoking Cessation Advice[1,3]	2	50%	97%	98%
Pneumonia Care				
Appropriate Initial Antibiotic[1,3]	6	67%	89%	92%
Blood Culture Timing[3]	0	-	97%	96%
Influenza Vaccine[1,3]	4	100%	88%	91%
Initial Antibiotic Timing[1,3]	10	100%	95%	95%
Pneumococcal Vaccine[1,3]	9	100%	93%	93%
Smoking Cessation Advice[1,3]	2	100%	91%	97%
Surgical Care Improvement Project				
Appropriate VTP Within 24 Hours[5]	0	-	92%	92%
Appropriate Hair Removal[5]	0	-	100%	99%
Appropriate Beta Blocker Usage[5]	0	-	91%	93%
Controlled Postoperative Blood Glucose[5]	0	-	93%	93%
Prophylactic Antibiotic Timing[5]	0	-	96%	97%
Prophylactic Antibiotic Timing (Outpatient)	-	-	92%	92%
Prophylactic Antibiotic Selection[5]	0	-	97%	97%
Prophylactic Antibiotic Select. (Outpatient)	-	-	97%	94%
Prophylactic Antibiotic Stopped[5]	0	-	96%	94%
Recommended VTP Ordered[5]	0	-	92%	94%
Urinary Catheter Removal[5]	0	-	92%	90%
Children's Asthma Care				
Received Systemic Corticosteroids	-	-	-	100%
Received Home Management Plan	-	-	-	71%
Received Reliever Medication	-	-	-	100%
Use of Medical Imaging				
Combination Abdominal CT Scan	-	-	0.177	0.191
Combination Chest CT Scan	-	-	0.025	0.054
Follow-up Mammogram/Ultrasound	-	-	8%	8.4%
MRI for Low Back Pain	-	-	31.9%	32.7%
Survey of Patients' Hospital Experiences				
Area Around Room 'Always' Quiet at Night[8]	-	-	-	58%
Doctors 'Always' Communicated Well[8]	-	-	-	80%
Home Recovery Information Given[8]	-	-	-	82%
Hospital Given 9 or 10 on 10 Point Scale[8]	-	-	-	67%
Meds 'Always' Explained Before Given[8]	-	-	-	60%
Nurses 'Always' Communicated Well[8]	-	-	-	76%
Pain 'Always' Well Controlled[8]	-	-	-	69%
Room and Bathroom 'Always' Clean[8]	-	-	-	71%
Timely Help 'Always' Received[8]	-	-	-	64%
Would Definitely Recommend Hospital[8]	-	-	-	69%

Trinity Hospitals

407 3rd St SE Phone: 701-857-5000
Minot, ND 58701 Fax: 701-857-5408
E-mail: info@trinityhealth.org
URL: www.trinityhealth.org
Type: Acute Care Hospitals Emergency Services: Yes
Ownership: Voluntary Non-Profit - Other Beds: 441

Key Personnel:
CEO/President. . . . . Terry G Hoff, FACHE
Chief of Medical Staff. . . . . Kevin Collins
Infection Control. . . . . Brenda Lokken
Operating Room. . . . . Nancy Holmes
Quality Assurance . . . . Julie Waldera, RN
Radiology. . . . . James Call
Intensive Care Unit. . . . . Donna Hegle

Measure	Cases	This Hosp.	State Avg.	U.S. Avg.
Heart Attack Care				
ACE Inhibitor or ARB for LVSD	25	100%	93%	96%
Aspirin at Arrival	133	99%	98%	99%
Aspirin at Discharge	240	100%	99%	98%
Beta Blocker at Discharge	225	100%	98%	98%
Fibrinolytic Medication Timing	0	-	67%	55%
PCI Within 90 Minutes of Arrival[1]	23	100%	84%	90%
Smoking Cessation Advice	91	100%	99%	99%
Chest Pain/Possible Heart Attack Care				
Aspirin at Arrival[5]	0	-	96%	95%
Median Time to ECG (minutes)[5]	0	-	11	8
Median Time to Transfer (minutes)[5]	0	-	180	61
Fibrinolytic Medication Timing[5]	0	-	69%	54%
Heart Failure Care				
ACE Inhibitor or ARB for LVSD	57	93%	90%	94%
Discharge Instructions	178	90%	89%	88%
Evaluation of LVS Function	237	100%	94%	98%
Smoking Cessation Advice	32	100%	97%	98%
Pneumonia Care				
Appropriate Initial Antibiotic	108	97%	89%	92%
Blood Culture Timing	220	98%	97%	96%
Influenza Vaccine	148	93%	88%	91%
Initial Antibiotic Timing	214	95%	95%	95%
Pneumococcal Vaccine	230	99%	93%	93%
Smoking Cessation Advice	69	100%	91%	97%
Surgical Care Improvement Project				
Appropriate VTP Within 24 Hours	252	87%	92%	92%
Appropriate Hair Removal	852	100%	100%	99%
Appropriate Beta Blocker Usage	298	93%	91%	93%
Controlled Postoperative Blood Glucose	67	96%	93%	93%
Prophylactic Antibiotic Timing	615	97%	96%	97%
Prophylactic Antibiotic Timing (Outpatient)	306	93%	92%	92%
Prophylactic Antibiotic Selection	626	96%	97%	97%
Prophylactic Antibiotic Select. (Outpatient)	359	97%	97%	94%
Prophylactic Antibiotic Stopped	589	96%	96%	94%
Recommended VTP Ordered	257	89%	92%	94%
Urinary Catheter Removal	261	97%	92%	90%
Children's Asthma Care				
Received Systemic Corticosteroids	-	-	-	100%
Received Home Management Plan	-	-	-	71%
Received Reliever Medication	-	-	-	100%
Use of Medical Imaging				
Combination Abdominal CT Scan	863	0.057	0.177	0.191
Combination Chest CT Scan	862	0.002	0.025	0.054
Follow-up Mammogram/Ultrasound	2,465	5.3%	8%	8.4%
MRI for Low Back Pain	244	35.7%	31.9%	32.7%
Survey of Patients' Hospital Experiences				
Area Around Room 'Always' Quiet at Night	300+	46%	-	58%
Doctors 'Always' Communicated Well	300+	72%	-	80%
Home Recovery Information Given	300+	81%	-	82%
Hospital Given 9 or 10 on 10 Point Scale	300+	50%	-	67%
Meds 'Always' Explained Before Given	300+	54%	-	60%
Nurses 'Always' Communicated Well	300+	71%	-	76%
Pain 'Always' Well Controlled	300+	67%	-	69%
Room and Bathroom 'Always' Clean	300+	63%	-	71%
Timely Help 'Always' Received	300+	64%	-	64%
Would Definitely Recommend Hospital	300+	48%	-	69%

NOTE: Hospital profiles are in alphabetical order by state, then city, then hospital within the city; Rankings exclude hospitals with less than 25 cases except for patient surveys which excludes hospitals with less than 100 cases; (a) 100–299 cases; (1) The number of cases is too small to be sure how well a hospital is performing; (2) The hospital indicated that the data submitted for this measure were based on a sample of cases; (3) Data was collected during a shorter time period (fewer quarters) than the maximum possible time for this measure; (4) Suppressed for one or more quarters by CMS; (5) No data is available from the hospital for this measure; (6) Fewer than 100 patients completed the HCAHPS survey. Use these rates with caution, as the number of surveys may be too low to reliably assess hospital performance; (7) Survey results are based on less than 12 months of data; (8) Survey results are not available for this reporting period; (9) No or very few patients were eligible for the HCAHPS survey. The scores shown, if any, reflect a very small number of surveys; (10) A state average was not calculated because too few hospitals in the state submitted data; (11) There were discrepancies in the data collection process; Please refer to the User's Guide for a full explanation of data.

Northwood Deaconess Health Center

4 N Park St
Northwood, ND 58267
URL: www.ndhc.net
Phone: 701-587-6060
Fax: 701-587-6479
Type: Critical Access Hospitals
Emergency Services: Yes
Ownership: Voluntary Non-Profit - Church
Beds: 89

Key Personnel:

CEO/President. . . . . Pete Antonson
Chief of Medical Staff . . . . Dr Jon Berg
Quality Assurance . . . . Colleen Bomber

Measure	Cases	This Hosp.	State Avg.	U.S. Avg.
Heart Attack Care				
ACE Inhibitor or ARB for LVSD[5]	0	-	93%	96%
Aspirin at Arrival[5]	0	-	98%	99%
Aspirin at Discharge[5]	0	-	99%	98%
Beta Blocker at Discharge[5]	0	-	98%	98%
Fibrinolytic Medication Timing[5]	0	-	67%	55%
PCI Within 90 Minutes of Arrival[5]	0	-	84%	90%
Smoking Cessation Advice[5]	0	-	99%	99%
Chest Pain/Possible Heart Attack Care				
Aspirin at Arrival	-	-	96%	95%
Median Time to ECG (minutes)	-	-	11	8
Median Time to Transfer (minutes)	-	-	180	61
Fibrinolytic Medication Timing	-	-	69%	54%
Heart Failure Care				
ACE Inhibitor or ARB for LVSD[1,3]	1	100%	90%	94%
Discharge Instructions[1,3]	1	0%	89%	88%
Evaluation of LVS Function[1,3]	1	100%	94%	98%
Smoking Cessation Advice[3]	0	-	97%	98%
Pneumonia Care				
Appropriate Initial Antibiotic[1]	4	100%	89%	92%
Blood Culture Timing	0	-	97%	96%
Influenza Vaccine[1]	8	100%	88%	91%
Initial Antibiotic Timing[1]	14	93%	95%	95%
Pneumococcal Vaccine[1]	17	94%	93%	93%
Smoking Cessation Advice	0	-	91%	97%
Surgical Care Improvement Project				
Appropriate VTP Within 24 Hours[5]	0	-	92%	92%
Appropriate Hair Removal[5]	0	-	100%	99%
Appropriate Beta Blocker Usage[5]	0	-	91%	93%
Controlled Postoperative Blood Glucose[5]	0	-	93%	93%
Prophylactic Antibiotic Timing[5]	0	-	96%	97%
Prophylactic Antibiotic Timing (Outpatient)	-	-	92%	92%
Prophylactic Antibiotic Selection[5]	0	-	97%	97%
Prophylactic Antibiotic Select. (Outpatient)	-	-	97%	94%
Prophylactic Antibiotic Stopped[5]	0	-	96%	94%
Recommended VTP Ordered[5]	0	-	92%	94%
Urinary Catheter Removal[5]	0	-	92%	90%
Children's Asthma Care				
Received Systemic Corticosteroids	-	-	-	100%
Received Home Management Plan	-	-	-	71%
Received Reliever Medication	-	-	-	100%
Use of Medical Imaging				
Combination Abdominal CT Scan	-	-	0.177	0.191
Combination Chest CT Scan	-	-	0.025	0.054
Follow-up Mammogram/Ultrasound	-	-	8%	8.4%
MRI for Low Back Pain	-	-	31.9%	32.7%
Survey of Patients' Hospital Experiences				
Area Around Room 'Always' Quiet at Night[8]	-	-	-	58%
Doctors 'Always' Communicated Well[8]	-	-	-	80%
Home Recovery Information Given[8]	-	-	-	82%
Hospital Given 9 or 10 on 10 Point Scale[8]	-	-	-	67%
Meds 'Always' Explained Before Given[8]	-	-	-	60%
Nurses 'Always' Communicated Well[8]	-	-	-	76%
Pain 'Always' Well Controlled[8]	-	-	-	69%
Room and Bathroom 'Always' Clean[8]	-	-	-	71%
Timely Help 'Always' Received[8]	-	-	-	64%
Would Definitely Recommend Hospital[8]	-	-	-	69%

Presentation Medical Center

213 Second Ave NE
Rolla, ND 58367
URL: www.pmc-rolla.com
Phone: 701-477-3161
Fax: 701-477-5564
Type: Critical Access Hospitals
Emergency Services: Yes
Ownership: Voluntary Non-Profit - Church
Beds: 54

Key Personnel:

CEO/President. . . . . Kimber L Wraalstad, CHE
Infection Control. . . . . Bonnie McDougall, RN
Operating Room. . . . . Peggy Hendrickson, RN
Emergency Room . . . . Bonnie McDougall
Intensive Care Unit. . . . . Peggy McPougall

Measure	Cases	This Hosp.	State Avg.	U.S. Avg.
Heart Attack Care				
ACE Inhibitor or ARB for LVSD[5]	0	-	93%	96%
Aspirin at Arrival[5]	0	-	98%	99%
Aspirin at Discharge[5]	0	-	99%	98%
Beta Blocker at Discharge[5]	0	-	98%	98%
Fibrinolytic Medication Timing[5]	0	-	67%	55%
PCI Within 90 Minutes of Arrival[5]	0	-	84%	90%
Smoking Cessation Advice[5]	0	-	99%	99%
Chest Pain/Possible Heart Attack Care				
Aspirin at Arrival[5]	0	-	96%	95%
Median Time to ECG (minutes)[5]	0	-	11	8
Median Time to Transfer (minutes)[5]	0	-	180	61
Fibrinolytic Medication Timing[5]	0	-	69%	54%
Heart Failure Care				
ACE Inhibitor or ARB for LVSD[1]	1	0%	90%	94%
Discharge Instructions[1]	5	100%	89%	88%
Evaluation of LVS Function[1]	13	100%	94%	98%
Smoking Cessation Advice[1]	3	100%	97%	98%
Pneumonia Care				
Appropriate Initial Antibiotic[1]	15	100%	89%	92%
Blood Culture Timing[1]	3	100%	97%	96%
Influenza Vaccine[1]	15	100%	88%	91%
Initial Antibiotic Timing	30	93%	95%	95%
Pneumococcal Vaccine[1]	23	100%	93%	93%
Smoking Cessation Advice[1]	10	80%	91%	97%
Surgical Care Improvement Project				
Appropriate VTP Within 24 Hours[5]	0	-	92%	92%
Appropriate Hair Removal[5]	0	-	100%	99%
Appropriate Beta Blocker Usage[5]	0	-	91%	93%
Controlled Postoperative Blood Glucose[5]	0	-	93%	93%
Prophylactic Antibiotic Timing[5]	0	-	96%	97%
Prophylactic Antibiotic Timing (Outpatient)[5]	0	-	92%	92%
Prophylactic Antibiotic Selection[5]	0	-	97%	97%
Prophylactic Antibiotic Select. (Outpatient)[5]	0	-	97%	94%
Prophylactic Antibiotic Stopped[5]	0	-	96%	94%
Recommended VTP Ordered[5]	0	-	92%	94%
Urinary Catheter Removal[5]	0	-	92%	90%
Children's Asthma Care				
Received Systemic Corticosteroids	-	-	-	100%
Received Home Management Plan	-	-	-	71%
Received Reliever Medication	-	-	-	100%
Use of Medical Imaging				
Combination Abdominal CT Scan[1]	50	0.220	0.177	0.191
Combination Chest CT Scan[1]	31	0.129	0.025	0.054
Follow-up Mammogram/Ultrasound[1]	64	10.9%	8%	8.4%
MRI for Low Back Pain[1]	10	40.0%	31.9%	32.7%
Survey of Patients' Hospital Experiences				
Area Around Room 'Always' Quiet at Night[8]	-	-	-	58%
Doctors 'Always' Communicated Well[8]	-	-	-	80%
Home Recovery Information Given[8]	-	-	-	82%
Hospital Given 9 or 10 on 10 Point Scale[8]	-	-	-	67%
Meds 'Always' Explained Before Given[8]	-	-	-	60%
Nurses 'Always' Communicated Well[8]	-	-	-	76%
Pain 'Always' Well Controlled[8]	-	-	-	69%
Room and Bathroom 'Always' Clean[8]	-	-	-	71%
Timely Help 'Always' Received[8]	-	-	-	64%
Would Definitely Recommend Hospital[8]	-	-	-	69%

Heart of America Medical Center

800 S Main Ave
Rugby, ND 58368
E-mail: admin@hamc.com
URL: www.hamc.com
Phone: 701-776-5261
Fax: 701-776-5448
Type: Critical Access Hospitals
Emergency Services: Yes
Ownership: Voluntary Non-Profit - Other
Beds: 118

Key Personnel:

CEO/President. . . . . Jerry E Jurena
Cardiac Laboratory. . . . . Keri Weick
Chief of Medical Staff . . . . Ron Skipper
Infection Control. . . . . Mary Haugen

Measure	Cases	This Hosp.	State Avg.	U.S. Avg.
Heart Attack Care				
ACE Inhibitor or ARB for LVSD[3]	0	-	93%	96%
Aspirin at Arrival[1,3]	2	100%	98%	99%
Aspirin at Discharge[1,3]	2	100%	99%	98%
Beta Blocker at Discharge[1,3]	2	100%	98%	98%
Fibrinolytic Medication Timing[3]	0	-	67%	55%
PCI Within 90 Minutes of Arrival[3]	0	-	84%	90%
Smoking Cessation Advice[3]	0	-	99%	99%
Chest Pain/Possible Heart Attack Care				
Aspirin at Arrival	-	-	96%	95%
Median Time to ECG (minutes)	-	-	11	8
Median Time to Transfer (minutes)	-	-	180	61
Fibrinolytic Medication Timing	-	-	69%	54%
Heart Failure Care				
ACE Inhibitor or ARB for LVSD[1]	3	100%	90%	94%
Discharge Instructions[1]	20	80%	89%	88%
Evaluation of LVS Function	35	74%	94%	98%
Smoking Cessation Advice[1]	2	50%	97%	98%
Pneumonia Care				
Appropriate Initial Antibiotic[1]	10	80%	89%	92%
Blood Culture Timing[1]	18	100%	97%	96%
Influenza Vaccine[1]	13	100%	88%	91%
Initial Antibiotic Timing[1]	21	90%	95%	95%
Pneumococcal Vaccine[1]	24	92%	93%	93%
Smoking Cessation Advice	0	-	91%	97%
Surgical Care Improvement Project				
Appropriate VTP Within 24 Hours[1]	7	86%	92%	92%
Appropriate Hair Removal[1]	10	100%	100%	99%
Appropriate Beta Blocker Usage[5]	0	-	91%	93%
Controlled Postoperative Blood Glucose	0	-	93%	93%
Prophylactic Antibiotic Timing[1]	3	67%	96%	97%
Prophylactic Antibiotic Timing (Outpatient)	-	-	92%	92%
Prophylactic Antibiotic Selection[1]	3	67%	97%	97%
Prophylactic Antibiotic Select. (Outpatient)	-	-	97%	94%
Prophylactic Antibiotic Stopped[1]	3	100%	96%	94%
Recommended VTP Ordered[1]	8	75%	92%	94%
Urinary Catheter Removal[1]	1	0%	92%	90%
Children's Asthma Care				
Received Systemic Corticosteroids	-	-	-	100%
Received Home Management Plan	-	-	-	71%
Received Reliever Medication	-	-	-	100%
Use of Medical Imaging				
Combination Abdominal CT Scan	-	-	0.177	0.191
Combination Chest CT Scan	-	-	0.025	0.054
Follow-up Mammogram/Ultrasound	-	-	8%	8.4%
MRI for Low Back Pain	-	-	31.9%	32.7%
Survey of Patients' Hospital Experiences				
Area Around Room 'Always' Quiet at Night	(a)	66%	-	58%
Doctors 'Always' Communicated Well	(a)	79%	-	80%
Home Recovery Information Given	(a)	89%	-	82%
Hospital Given 9 or 10 on 10 Point Scale	(a)	75%	-	67%
Meds 'Always' Explained Before Given	(a)	68%	-	60%
Nurses 'Always' Communicated Well	(a)	84%	-	76%
Pain 'Always' Well Controlled	(a)	73%	-	69%
Room and Bathroom 'Always' Clean	(a)	83%	-	71%
Timely Help 'Always' Received	(a)	78%	-	64%
Would Definitely Recommend Hospital	(a)	86%	-	69%

NOTE: Hospital profiles are in alphabetical order by state, then city, then hospital within the city; Rankings exclude hospitals with less than 25 cases except for patient surveys which excludes hospitals with less than 100 cases; (a) 100–299 cases; (1) The number of cases is too small to be sure how well a hospital is performing; (2) The hospital indicated that the data submitted for this measure were based on a sample of cases; (3) Data was collected during a shorter time period (fewer quarters) than the maximum possible time for this measure; (4) Suppressed for one or more quarters by CMS; (5) No data is available from the hospital for this measure; (6) Fewer than 100 patients completed the HCAHPS survey. Use these rates with caution, as the number of surveys may be too low to reliably assess hospital performance; (7) Survey results are based on less than 12 months of data; (8) Survey results are not available for this reporting period; (9) No or very few patients were eligible for the HCAHPS survey. The scores shown, if any, reflect a very small number of surveys; (10) A state average was not calculated because too few hospitals in the state submitted data; (11) There were discrepancies in the data collection process; Please refer to the User's Guide for a full explanation of data.

Mountrail County Medical Center

615 6th St SE Phone: 701-628-2424
Stanley, ND 58784 Fax: 701-628-3274
URL: www.stanleyhealth.org
Type: Critical Access Hospitals Emergency Services: Yes
Ownership: Voluntary Non-Profit - Private Beds: 25
Key Personnel:
Cardiac Laboratory. . . . . Judy Hove
Chief of Medical Staff . . . . Tyrone Langer, MD
Quality Assurance . . . . Ann Nelson

Measure	Cases	This Hosp.	State Avg.	U.S. Avg.
Heart Attack Care				
ACE Inhibitor or ARB for LVSD[5]	0	-	93%	96%
Aspirin at Arrival[5]	0	-	98%	99%
Aspirin at Discharge[5]	0	-	99%	98%
Beta Blocker at Discharge[5]	0	-	98%	98%
Fibrinolytic Medication Timing[5]	0	-	67%	55%
PCI Within 90 Minutes of Arrival[5]	0	-	84%	90%
Smoking Cessation Advice[5]	0	-	99%	99%
Chest Pain/Possible Heart Attack Care				
Aspirin at Arrival	-	-	96%	95%
Median Time to ECG (minutes)	-	-	11	8
Median Time to Transfer (minutes)	-	-	180	61
Fibrinolytic Medication Timing	-	-	69%	54%
Heart Failure Care				
ACE Inhibitor or ARB for LVSD[1,3]	3	100%	90%	94%
Discharge Instructions[1,3]	2	50%	89%	88%
Evaluation of LVS Function[1,3]	7	86%	94%	98%
Smoking Cessation Advice[3]	0	-	97%	98%
Pneumonia Care				
Appropriate Initial Antibiotic[3]	0	-	89%	92%
Blood Culture Timing[3]	0	-	97%	96%
Influenza Vaccine[1]	7	86%	88%	91%
Initial Antibiotic Timing[1,3]	3	100%	95%	95%
Pneumococcal Vaccine[1,3]	6	83%	93%	93%
Smoking Cessation Advice[3]	0	-	91%	97%
Surgical Care Improvement Project				
Appropriate VTP Within 24 Hours[5]	0	-	92%	92%
Appropriate Hair Removal[5]	0	-	100%	99%
Appropriate Beta Blocker Usage[5]	0	-	91%	93%
Controlled Postoperative Blood Glucose[5]	0	-	93%	93%
Prophylactic Antibiotic Timing[5]	0	-	96%	97%
Prophylactic Antibiotic Timing (Outpatient)	-	-	92%	92%
Prophylactic Antibiotic Selection[5]	0	-	97%	97%
Prophylactic Antibiotic Select. (Outpatient)	-	-	97%	94%
Prophylactic Antibiotic Stopped[5]	0	-	96%	94%
Recommended VTP Ordered[5]	0	-	92%	94%
Urinary Catheter Removal[5]	0	-	92%	90%
Children's Asthma Care				
Received Systemic Corticosteroids	-	-	-	100%
Received Home Management Plan	-	-	-	71%
Received Reliever Medication	-	-	-	100%
Use of Medical Imaging				
Combination Abdominal CT Scan	-	-	0.177	0.191
Combination Chest CT Scan	-	-	0.025	0.054
Follow-up Mammogram/Ultrasound	-	-	8%	8.4%
MRI for Low Back Pain	-	-	31.9%	32.7%
Survey of Patients' Hospital Experiences				
Area Around Room 'Always' Quiet at Night[8]	-	-	-	58%
Doctors 'Always' Communicated Well[8]	-	-	-	80%
Home Recovery Information Given[8]	-	-	-	82%
Hospital Given 9 or 10 on 10 Point Scale[8]	-	-	-	67%
Meds 'Always' Explained Before Given[8]	-	-	-	60%
Nurses 'Always' Communicated Well[8]	-	-	-	76%
Pain 'Always' Well Controlled[8]	-	-	-	69%
Room and Bathroom 'Always' Clean[8]	-	-	-	71%
Timely Help 'Always' Received[8]	-	-	-	64%
Would Definitely Recommend Hospital[8]	-	-	-	69%

Tioga Medical Center

810 N Welo St Phone: 701-664-3305
Tioga, ND 58852 Fax: 701-664-3644
URL: www.tiogahealth.org
Type: Critical Access Hospitals Emergency Services: Yes
Ownership: Government - Local Beds: 29
Key Personnel:
CEO/President. . . . . Randy Paderson
Chief of Medical Staff . . . . MV Patel, MD
Infection Control. . . . . Shelley Eide, RN
Operating Room. . . . . Ardith Bingeman, RN
Quality Assurance . . . . Roger Endres

Measure	Cases	This Hosp.	State Avg.	U.S. Avg.
Heart Attack Care				
ACE Inhibitor or ARB for LVSD[5]	0	-	93%	96%
Aspirin at Arrival[5]	0	-	98%	99%
Aspirin at Discharge[5]	0	-	99%	98%
Beta Blocker at Discharge[5]	0	-	98%	98%
Fibrinolytic Medication Timing[5]	0	-	67%	55%
PCI Within 90 Minutes of Arrival[5]	0	-	84%	90%
Smoking Cessation Advice[5]	0	-	99%	99%
Chest Pain/Possible Heart Attack Care				
Aspirin at Arrival	-	-	96%	95%
Median Time to ECG (minutes)	-	-	11	8
Median Time to Transfer (minutes)	-	-	180	61
Fibrinolytic Medication Timing	-	-	69%	54%
Heart Failure Care				
ACE Inhibitor or ARB for LVSD[1]	1	100%	90%	94%
Discharge Instructions[1]	5	60%	89%	88%
Evaluation of LVS Function[1]	12	83%	94%	98%
Smoking Cessation Advice[1]	3	100%	97%	98%
Pneumonia Care				
Appropriate Initial Antibiotic[1]	1	0%	89%	92%
Blood Culture Timing[1]	1	0%	97%	96%
Influenza Vaccine[1]	7	86%	88%	91%
Initial Antibiotic Timing[1]	13	77%	95%	95%
Pneumococcal Vaccine[1]	11	82%	93%	93%
Smoking Cessation Advice[1]	1	100%	91%	97%
Surgical Care Improvement Project				
Appropriate VTP Within 24 Hours[5]	0	-	92%	92%
Appropriate Hair Removal[5]	0	-	100%	99%
Appropriate Beta Blocker Usage[5]	0	-	91%	93%
Controlled Postoperative Blood Glucose[5]	0	-	93%	93%
Prophylactic Antibiotic Timing[5]	0	-	96%	97%
Prophylactic Antibiotic Timing (Outpatient)	-	-	92%	92%
Prophylactic Antibiotic Selection[5]	0	-	97%	97%
Prophylactic Antibiotic Select. (Outpatient)	-	-	97%	94%
Prophylactic Antibiotic Stopped[5]	0	-	96%	94%
Recommended VTP Ordered[5]	0	-	92%	94%
Urinary Catheter Removal[5]	0	-	92%	90%
Children's Asthma Care				
Received Systemic Corticosteroids	-	-	-	100%
Received Home Management Plan	-	-	-	71%
Received Reliever Medication	-	-	-	100%
Use of Medical Imaging				
Combination Abdominal CT Scan	-	-	0.177	0.191
Combination Chest CT Scan	-	-	0.025	0.054
Follow-up Mammogram/Ultrasound	-	-	8%	8.4%
MRI for Low Back Pain	-	-	31.9%	32.7%
Survey of Patients' Hospital Experiences				
Area Around Room 'Always' Quiet at Night[8]	-	-	-	58%
Doctors 'Always' Communicated Well[8]	-	-	-	80%
Home Recovery Information Given[8]	-	-	-	82%
Hospital Given 9 or 10 on 10 Point Scale[8]	-	-	-	67%
Meds 'Always' Explained Before Given[8]	-	-	-	60%
Nurses 'Always' Communicated Well[8]	-	-	-	76%
Pain 'Always' Well Controlled[8]	-	-	-	69%
Room and Bathroom 'Always' Clean[8]	-	-	-	71%
Timely Help 'Always' Received[8]	-	-	-	64%
Would Definitely Recommend Hospital[8]	-	-	-	69%

McKenzie County Healthcare Systems

516 North Main St Phone: 701-842-3000
Watford City, ND 58854 Fax: 701-842-6248
Type: Critical Access Hospitals Emergency Services: Yes
Ownership: Voluntary Non-Profit - Private Beds: 24
Key Personnel:
CEO/President. . . . . Kris Pacheo

Measure	Cases	This Hosp.	State Avg.	U.S. Avg.
Heart Attack Care				
ACE Inhibitor or ARB for LVSD[3]	0	-	93%	96%
Aspirin at Arrival[1,3]	2	100%	98%	99%
Aspirin at Discharge[1,3]	2	100%	99%	98%
Beta Blocker at Discharge[1,3]	2	100%	98%	98%
Fibrinolytic Medication Timing[3]	0	-	67%	55%
PCI Within 90 Minutes of Arrival[3]	0	-	84%	90%
Smoking Cessation Advice[3]	0	-	99%	99%
Chest Pain/Possible Heart Attack Care				
Aspirin at Arrival	-	-	96%	95%
Median Time to ECG (minutes)	-	-	11	8
Median Time to Transfer (minutes)	-	-	180	61
Fibrinolytic Medication Timing	-	-	69%	54%
Heart Failure Care				
ACE Inhibitor or ARB for LVSD	0	-	90%	94%
Discharge Instructions[1]	5	20%	89%	88%
Evaluation of LVS Function[1]	9	44%	94%	98%
Smoking Cessation Advice[1]	1	100%	97%	98%
Pneumonia Care				
Appropriate Initial Antibiotic[1]	15	87%	89%	92%
Blood Culture Timing[1]	12	100%	97%	96%
Influenza Vaccine[1]	18	67%	88%	91%
Initial Antibiotic Timing	26	100%	95%	95%
Pneumococcal Vaccine	25	88%	93%	93%
Smoking Cessation Advice[1]	2	0%	91%	97%
Surgical Care Improvement Project				
Appropriate VTP Within 24 Hours[5]	0	-	92%	92%
Appropriate Hair Removal[5]	0	-	100%	99%
Appropriate Beta Blocker Usage[5]	0	-	91%	93%
Controlled Postoperative Blood Glucose[5]	0	-	93%	93%
Prophylactic Antibiotic Timing[5]	0	-	96%	97%
Prophylactic Antibiotic Timing (Outpatient)	-	-	92%	92%
Prophylactic Antibiotic Selection[5]	0	-	97%	97%
Prophylactic Antibiotic Select. (Outpatient)	-	-	97%	94%
Prophylactic Antibiotic Stopped[5]	0	-	96%	94%
Recommended VTP Ordered[5]	0	-	92%	94%
Urinary Catheter Removal[5]	0	-	92%	90%
Children's Asthma Care				
Received Systemic Corticosteroids	-	-	-	100%
Received Home Management Plan	-	-	-	71%
Received Reliever Medication	-	-	-	100%
Use of Medical Imaging				
Combination Abdominal CT Scan	-	-	0.177	0.191
Combination Chest CT Scan	-	-	0.025	0.054
Follow-up Mammogram/Ultrasound	-	-	8%	8.4%
MRI for Low Back Pain	-	-	31.9%	32.7%
Survey of Patients' Hospital Experiences				
Area Around Room 'Always' Quiet at Night[8]	-	-	-	58%
Doctors 'Always' Communicated Well[8]	-	-	-	80%
Home Recovery Information Given[8]	-	-	-	82%
Hospital Given 9 or 10 on 10 Point Scale[8]	-	-	-	67%
Meds 'Always' Explained Before Given[8]	-	-	-	60%
Nurses 'Always' Communicated Well[8]	-	-	-	76%
Pain 'Always' Well Controlled[8]	-	-	-	69%
Room and Bathroom 'Always' Clean[8]	-	-	-	71%
Timely Help 'Always' Received[8]	-	-	-	64%
Would Definitely Recommend Hospital[8]	-	-	-	69%

NOTE: Hospital profiles are in alphabetical order by state, then city, then hospital within the city; Rankings exclude hospitals with less than 25 cases except for patient surveys which excludes hospitals with less than 100 cases; (a) 100–299 cases; (1) The number of cases is too small to be sure how well a hospital is performing; (2) The hospital indicated that the data submitted for this measure were based on a sample of cases; (3) Data was collected during a shorter time period (fewer quarters) than the maximum possible time for this measure; (4) Suppressed for one or more quarters by CMS; (5) No data is available from the hospital for this measure; (6) Fewer than 100 patients completed the HCAHPS survey. Use these rates with caution, as the number of surveys may be too low to reliably assess hospital performance; (7) Survey results are based on less than 12 months of data; (8) Survey results are not available for this reporting period; (9) No or very few patients were eligible for the HCAHPS survey. The scores shown, if any, reflect a very small number of surveys; (10) A state average was not calculated because too few hospitals in the state submitted data; (11) There were discrepancies in the data collection process; Please refer to the User's Guide for a full explanation of data.

Mercy Medical Center

1301 15th Ave W
Williston, ND 58801
URL: www.mercy-williston.org
Type: Critical Access Hospitals
Ownership: Voluntary Non-Profit - Church
Phone: 701-774-7400
Fax: 701-774-7479
Emergency Services: Yes
Beds: 25

Key Personnel:
Cardiac Laboratory. . . . . Gloria Fenster
Chief of Medical Staff. . . . . B.K Vibeto, MD
Infection Control. . . . . James Moe
Operating Room. . . . . Rod Kerzmann
Quality Assurance . . . . Lori Hahn
Radiology. . . . . Barb Cook
Intensive Care Unit. . . . . Lorrie Antos
Patient Relations . . . . Tami Solberg

Measure	Cases	This Hosp.	State Avg.	U.S. Avg.
Heart Attack Care				
ACE Inhibitor or ARB for LVSD[1]	2	50%	93%	96%
Aspirin at Arrival[1]	5	100%	98%	99%
Aspirin at Discharge[1]	4	100%	99%	98%
Beta Blocker at Discharge[1]	4	75%	98%	98%
Fibrinolytic Medication Timing	0	-	67%	55%
PCI Within 90 Minutes of Arrival	0	-	84%	90%
Smoking Cessation Advice[1]	2	50%	99%	99%
Chest Pain/Possible Heart Attack Care				
Aspirin at Arrival	66	94%	96%	95%
Median Time to ECG (minutes)	68	13	11	8
Median Time to Transfer (minutes)[1]	4	180	180	61
Fibrinolytic Medication Timing[1]	6	67%	69%	54%
Heart Failure Care				
ACE Inhibitor or ARB for LVSD[1]	4	100%	90%	94%
Discharge Instructions	25	88%	89%	88%
Evaluation of LVS Function	28	71%	94%	98%
Smoking Cessation Advice[1]	6	100%	97%	98%
Pneumonia Care				
Appropriate Initial Antibiotic[1]	23	87%	89%	92%
Blood Culture Timing	42	95%	97%	96%
Influenza Vaccine	29	97%	88%	91%
Initial Antibiotic Timing	48	98%	95%	95%
Pneumococcal Vaccine	44	95%	93%	93%
Smoking Cessation Advice[1]	19	74%	91%	97%
Surgical Care Improvement Project				
Appropriate VTP Within 24 Hours	50	94%	92%	92%
Appropriate Hair Removal	140	100%	100%	99%
Appropriate Beta Blocker Usage[1,3]	20	65%	91%	93%
Controlled Postoperative Blood Glucose	0	-	93%	93%
Prophylactic Antibiotic Timing	97	93%	96%	97%
Prophylactic Antibiotic Timing (Outpatient)	33	97%	92%	92%
Prophylactic Antibiotic Selection	98	94%	97%	97%
Prophylactic Antibiotic Select. (Outpatient)	32	97%	97%	94%
Prophylactic Antibiotic Stopped	94	95%	96%	94%
Recommended VTP Ordered	50	96%	92%	94%
Urinary Catheter Removal[1]	8	88%	92%	90%
Children's Asthma Care				
Received Systemic Corticosteroids	-	-	-	100%
Received Home Management Plan	-	-	-	71%
Received Reliever Medication	-	-	-	100%
Use of Medical Imaging				
Combination Abdominal CT Scan	97	0.392	0.177	0.191
Combination Chest CT Scan[1]	40	0.275	0.025	0.054
Follow-up Mammogram/Ultrasound[1]	29	13.8%	8%	8.4%
MRI for Low Back Pain[1]	18	38.9%	31.9%	32.7%
Survey of Patients' Hospital Experiences				
Area Around Room 'Always' Quiet at Night	300+	57%	-	58%
Doctors 'Always' Communicated Well	300+	88%	-	80%
Home Recovery Information Given	300+	89%	-	82%
Hospital Given 9 or 10 on 10 Point Scale	300+	67%	-	67%
Meds 'Always' Explained Before Given	300+	64%	-	60%
Nurses 'Always' Communicated Well	300+	79%	-	76%
Pain 'Always' Well Controlled	300+	75%	-	69%
Room and Bathroom 'Always' Clean	300+	73%	-	71%
Timely Help 'Always' Received	300+	71%	-	64%
Would Definitely Recommend Hospital	300+	68%	-	69%

Wishek Community Hospital

1007 4th Ave S
Wishek, ND 58495
E-mail: wchcbek@bektel.com
URL: www.wishekhospital.com
Type: Critical Access Hospitals
Ownership: Voluntary Non-Profit - Private
Phone: 701-452-2326
Fax: 701-452-2392
Emergency Services: Yes
Beds: 24

Key Personnel:
CEO/President. . . . . Trina Schilling, RN
Chief of Medical Staff. . . . . Amy Smittle, D.O.
Infection Control. . . . . Stacy Wiest
Operating Room. . . . . Calli Klusmann
Quality Assurance . . . . Shelly Glaseman
Radiology. . . . . Jo Vilhauer
Emergency Room . . . . Calli Klusmann
Patient Relations . . . . Katie Lu Bvee

Measure	Cases	This Hosp.	State Avg.	U.S. Avg.
Heart Attack Care				
ACE Inhibitor or ARB for LVSD[3]	0	-	93%	96%
Aspirin at Arrival[1,3]	2	50%	98%	99%
Aspirin at Discharge[1,3]	1	0%	99%	98%
Beta Blocker at Discharge[1,3]	1	0%	98%	98%
Fibrinolytic Medication Timing[3]	0	-	67%	55%
PCI Within 90 Minutes of Arrival[3]	0	-	84%	90%
Smoking Cessation Advice[3]	0	-	99%	99%
Chest Pain/Possible Heart Attack Care				
Aspirin at Arrival	-	-	96%	95%
Median Time to ECG (minutes)	-	-	11	8
Median Time to Transfer (minutes)	-	-	180	61
Fibrinolytic Medication Timing	-	-	69%	54%
Heart Failure Care				
ACE Inhibitor or ARB for LVSD[1,2]	2	100%	90%	94%
Discharge Instructions[1,2]	8	62%	89%	88%
Evaluation of LVS Function[1,2]	14	36%	94%	98%
Smoking Cessation Advice[1,2]	1	0%	97%	98%
Pneumonia Care				
Appropriate Initial Antibiotic[1,2]	4	100%	89%	92%
Blood Culture Timing[1,2]	1	100%	97%	96%
Influenza Vaccine[1,2]	9	78%	88%	91%
Initial Antibiotic Timing[1,2]	7	71%	95%	95%
Pneumococcal Vaccine[1,2]	16	88%	93%	93%
Smoking Cessation Advice[1,2]	3	33%	91%	97%
Surgical Care Improvement Project				
Appropriate VTP Within 24 Hours[5]	0	-	92%	92%
Appropriate Hair Removal[5]	0	-	100%	99%
Appropriate Beta Blocker Usage[5]	0	-	91%	93%
Controlled Postoperative Blood Glucose[5]	0	-	93%	93%
Prophylactic Antibiotic Timing[5]	0	-	96%	97%
Prophylactic Antibiotic Timing (Outpatient)	-	-	92%	92%
Prophylactic Antibiotic Selection[5]	0	-	97%	97%
Prophylactic Antibiotic Select. (Outpatient)	-	-	97%	94%
Prophylactic Antibiotic Stopped[5]	0	-	96%	94%
Recommended VTP Ordered[5]	0	-	92%	94%
Urinary Catheter Removal[5]	0	-	92%	90%
Children's Asthma Care				
Received Systemic Corticosteroids	-	-	-	100%
Received Home Management Plan	-	-	-	71%
Received Reliever Medication	-	-	-	100%
Use of Medical Imaging				
Combination Abdominal CT Scan	-	-	0.177	0.191
Combination Chest CT Scan	-	-	0.025	0.054
Follow-up Mammogram/Ultrasound	-	-	8%	8.4%
MRI for Low Back Pain	-	-	31.9%	32.7%
Survey of Patients' Hospital Experiences				
Area Around Room 'Always' Quiet at Night[8]	-	-	-	58%
Doctors 'Always' Communicated Well[8]	-	-	-	80%
Home Recovery Information Given[8]	-	-	-	82%
Hospital Given 9 or 10 on 10 Point Scale[8]	-	-	-	67%
Meds 'Always' Explained Before Given[8]	-	-	-	60%
Nurses 'Always' Communicated Well[8]	-	-	-	76%
Pain 'Always' Well Controlled[8]	-	-	-	69%
Room and Bathroom 'Always' Clean[8]	-	-	-	71%
Timely Help 'Always' Received[8]	-	-	-	64%
Would Definitely Recommend Hospital[8]	-	-	-	69%

NOTE: Hospital profiles are in alphabetical order by state, then city, then hospital within the city; Rankings exclude hospitals with less than 25 cases except for patient surveys which excludes hospitals with less than 100 cases; (a) 100–299 cases; (1) The number of cases is too small to be sure how well a hospital is performing; (2) The hospital indicated that the data submitted for this measure were based on a sample of cases; (3) Data was collected during a shorter time period (fewer quarters) than the maximum possible time for this measure; (4) Suppressed for one or more quarters by CMS; (5) No data is available from the hospital for this measure; (6) Fewer than 100 patients completed the HCAHPS survey. Use these rates with caution, as the number of surveys may be too low to reliably assess hospital performance; (7) Survey results are based on less than 12 months of data; (8) Survey results are not available for this reporting period; (9) No or very few patients were eligible for the HCAHPS survey. The scores shown, if any, reflect a very small number of surveys; (10) A state average was not calculated because too few hospitals in the state submitted data; (11) There were discrepancies in the data collection process; Please refer to the User's Guide for a full explanation of data.

Heart Attack Care

1. ACE Inhibitor or ARB for LVSD

Hospital Name	City	Rate	Cases
Integris Baptist Medical Center	Oklahoma City	100%	147
O U Medical Center	Oklahoma City	100%	33
Oklahoma Heart Hospital[2]	Oklahoma City	100%	47
Saint Anthony Hospital	Oklahoma City	100%	33
Southcrest Hospital	Tulsa	100%	36
Midwest Regional Medical Center	Midwest City	98%	53
Norman Regional Health System	Norman	97%	36
Saint John Medical Center	Tulsa	97%	119
Comanche County Memorial Hospital	Lawton	92%	40
Saint Francis Hospital	Tulsa	90%	113
Integris Southwest Medical Center	Oklahoma City	88%	52
Hillcrest Medical Center	Tulsa	85%	80
Mercy Memorial Health Center	Ardmore	85%	27

2. Aspirin at Arrival

Hospital Name	City	Rate	Cases
Hillcrest Medical Center	Tulsa	100%	248
Integris Baptist Medical Center	Oklahoma City	100%	293
Integris Grove Hospital[2]	Grove	100%	44
Jane Phillips Medical Center	Bartlesville	100%	120
Medical Center of Southeastern Oklahoma	Durant	100%	39
Midwest Regional Medical Center	Midwest City	100%	263
Norman Regional Health System	Norman	100%	137
O U Medical Center	Oklahoma City	100%	101
Oklahoma Heart Hospital South[2,3]	Oklahoma City	100%	26
Oklahoma State University Medical Center	Tulsa	100%	98
Saint Anthony Hospital	Oklahoma City	100%	144
Southcrest Hospital	Tulsa	100%	131
Stillwater Medical Center	Stillwater	100%	74
Deaconess Hospital	Oklahoma City	99%	82
Integris Bass Baptist Health Center	Enid	99%	78
Oklahoma Heart Hospital[2]	Oklahoma City	99%	98
Saint John Medical Center	Tulsa	99%	499
Integris Southwest Medical Center	Oklahoma City	98%	243
Mercy Memorial Health Center	Ardmore	98%	161
Oklahoma City VA Medical Center	Oklahoma City	98%	133
Saint Francis Hospital	Tulsa	98%	496
Comanche County Memorial Hospital	Lawton	97%	135
Tahlequah City Hospital	Tahlequah	97%	29
Muskogee Regional Medical Center	Muskogee	96%	97
Unity Health Center	Shawnee	96%	74
Saint Mary's Regional Medical Center	Enid	94%	53

3. Aspirin at Discharge

Hospital Name	City	Rate	Cases
Deaconess Hospital	Oklahoma City	100%	106
Integris Baptist Medical Center	Oklahoma City	100%	574
Mercy Memorial Health Center	Ardmore	100%	141
Midwest Regional Medical Center	Midwest City	100%	263
O U Medical Center	Oklahoma City	100%	120
Oklahoma Heart Hospital South[2,3]	Oklahoma City	100%	67
Oklahoma State University Medical Center	Tulsa	100%	143
Saint Francis Hospital	Tulsa	100%	813
Saint John Medical Center	Tulsa	100%	714
Stillwater Medical Center	Stillwater	100%	65
Tahlequah City Hospital	Tahlequah	100%	34
Hillcrest Medical Center	Tulsa	99%	494
Jane Phillips Medical Center	Bartlesville	99%	150
Oklahoma Heart Hospital[2]	Oklahoma City	99%	303
Saint Anthony Hospital	Oklahoma City	99%	222
Comanche County Memorial Hospital	Lawton	98%	283
Norman Regional Health System	Norman	98%	224
Oklahoma City VA Medical Center	Oklahoma City	98%	123
Southcrest Hospital	Tulsa	98%	188
Integris Bass Baptist Health Center	Enid	97%	86
Saint Mary's Regional Medical Center	Enid	97%	58
Integris Grove Hospital[2]	Grove	95%	41
Integris Southwest Medical Center	Oklahoma City	94%	253
Muskogee Regional Medical Center	Muskogee	93%	74
Unity Health Center	Shawnee	93%	42

4. Beta Blocker at Discharge

Hospital Name	City	Rate	Cases
Comanche County Memorial Hospital	Lawton	100%	271
Hillcrest Medical Center	Tulsa	100%	477
Integris Baptist Medical Center	Oklahoma City	100%	515
Jane Phillips Medical Center	Bartlesville	100%	148
Medical Center of Southeastern Oklahoma	Durant	100%	29
O U Medical Center	Oklahoma City	100%	118
Oklahoma Heart Hospital South[2,3]	Oklahoma City	100%	60
Oklahoma State University Medical Center	Tulsa	100%	123
Saint John Medical Center	Tulsa	100%	702
Tahlequah City Hospital	Tahlequah	100%	31
Unity Health Center	Shawnee	100%	31
Deaconess Hospital	Oklahoma City	99%	100
Mercy Memorial Health Center	Ardmore	99%	137
Midwest Regional Medical Center	Midwest City	99%	242
Oklahoma Heart Hospital[2]	Oklahoma City	99%	279
Saint Anthony Hospital	Oklahoma City	99%	210
Saint Francis Hospital	Tulsa	99%	796
Southcrest Hospital	Tulsa	99%	178
Norman Regional Health System	Norman	98%	213
Integris Grove Hospital[2]	Grove	97%	39
Integris Southwest Medical Center	Oklahoma City	97%	237
Muskogee Regional Medical Center	Muskogee	97%	74
Stillwater Medical Center	Stillwater	97%	68
Integris Bass Baptist Health Center	Enid	95%	79
Oklahoma City VA Medical Center	Oklahoma City	95%	121
Saint Mary's Regional Medical Center	Enid	89%	54

6. PCI Within 90 Minutes of Arrival

Hospital Name	City	Rate	Cases
Integris Baptist Medical Center	Oklahoma City	98%	55
Integris Southwest Medical Center	Oklahoma City	98%	48
Jane Phillips Medical Center	Bartlesville	97%	29
Southcrest Hospital	Tulsa	96%	27
Midwest Regional Medical Center	Midwest City	92%	38
Hillcrest Medical Center	Tulsa	91%	34
Norman Regional Health System	Norman	91%	33
Saint John Medical Center	Tulsa	87%	122
Saint Francis Hospital	Tulsa	75%	88
Comanche County Memorial Hospital	Lawton	71%	35

7. Smoking Cessation Advice

Hospital Name	City	Rate	Cases
Comanche County Memorial Hospital	Lawton	100%	129
Deaconess Hospital	Oklahoma City	100%	46
Hillcrest Medical Center	Tulsa	100%	224
Integris Baptist Medical Center	Oklahoma City	100%	239
Integris Bass Baptist Health Center	Enid	100%	36
Integris Southwest Medical Center	Oklahoma City	100%	124
Jane Phillips Medical Center	Bartlesville	100%	69
Mercy Memorial Health Center	Ardmore	100%	59
Midwest Regional Medical Center	Midwest City	100%	99
Muskogee Regional Medical Center	Muskogee	100%	29
Norman Regional Health System	Norman	100%	92
O U Medical Center	Oklahoma City	100%	59
Oklahoma City VA Medical Center	Oklahoma City	100%	50
Oklahoma State University Medical Center	Tulsa	100%	83
Saint Francis Hospital	Tulsa	100%	313
Saint Mary's Regional Medical Center	Enid	100%	29
Southcrest Hospital	Tulsa	100%	73
Stillwater Medical Center	Stillwater	100%	30
Oklahoma Heart Hospital[2]	Oklahoma City	99%	127
Saint Anthony Hospital	Oklahoma City	99%	88
Saint John Medical Center	Tulsa	99%	268
Oklahoma Heart Hospital South[2,3]	Oklahoma City	94%	33

Chest Pain/Possible Heart Attack Care

8. Aspirin at Arrival

Hospital Name	City	Rate	Cases
Cushing Regional Hospital	Cushing	100%	140
Henryetta Medical Center	Henryetta	100%	104
Integris Canadian Valley Hospital	Yukon	100%	79
Medical Center of Southeastern Oklahoma	Durant	100%	44
Ponca City Medical Center	Ponca City	100%	88
Stillwater Medical Center	Stillwater	100%	64
Woodward Regional Hospital	Woodward	100%	29
Claremore Regional Hospital	Claremore	99%	108
Duncan Regional Hospital	Duncan	99%	134
Pauls Valley General Hospital	Pauls Valley	99%	68
Great Plains Regional Medical Center	Elk City	98%	41
Integris Baptist Regional Health Center	Miami	98%	121
Jackson County Memorial Hospital	Altus	98%	96
Valley View Regional Hospital	Ada	98%	63
Integris Mayes County Medical Center	Pryor	97%	116
Oklahoma Heart Hospital	Oklahoma City	97%	31
Unity Health Center	Shawnee	97%	129
Integris Blackwell Regional Hospital	Blackwell	96%	28
Mercy Health Center	Oklahoma City	96%	152
Saint Francis Hospital South	Tulsa	96%	94
Saint John Owasso	Owasso	96%	233
Sequoyah Memorial Hospital	Sallisaw	96%	100
Integris Clinton Regional Hospital	Clinton	95%	58
McCurtain Memorial Hospital	Idabel	95%	80
Integris Marshall County Medical Center	Madill	94%	31
Bailey Medical Center	Owasso	93%	134
Grady Memorial Hospital	Chickasha	93%	105
Integris Grove Hospital	Grove	93%	72
Tahlequah City Hospital	Tahlequah	93%	44
Eastern Oklahoma Medical Center	Poteau	92%	26
Integris Seminole Medical Center	Seminole	92%	106
Pushmataha Cnty-TN of Antlers Hosp Auth	Antlers	92%	36
Purcell Municipal Hospital[3]	Purcell	91%	57
Craig General Hospital	Vinita	90%	73
Mercy Hospital El Reno	El Reno	88%	59
Okmulgee Memorial Hospital	Okmulgee	87%	166
Claremore Indian Hospital	Claremore	86%	145
Share Memorial Hospital	Alva	83%	30
Epic Medical Center	Eufaula	81%	48
Wagoner Community Hospital	Wagoner	81%	37
Choctaw Memorial Hospital[3]	Hugo	71%	31

9. Median Time to ECG (minutes)

Hospital Name	City	Min.	Cases
Oklahoma Heart Hospital	Oklahoma City	1	35
Jackson County Memorial Hospital	Altus	3	99
Integris Baptist Regional Health Center	Miami	4	129
Saint Francis Hospital South	Tulsa	4	97
Medical Center of Southeastern Oklahoma	Durant	5	44
Ponca City Medical Center	Ponca City	5	90
Saint John Owasso	Owasso	5	239
Craig General Hospital	Vinita	6	68
Eastern Oklahoma Medical Center	Poteau	6	29
Integris Clinton Regional Hospital	Clinton	7	61
Integris Mayes County Medical Center	Pryor	7	120
Integris Grove Hospital	Grove	8	74
Claremore Regional Hospital	Claremore	9	115
Cushing Regional Hospital	Cushing	9	145
Duncan Regional Hospital	Duncan	9	137
Great Plains Regional Medical Center	Elk City	9	43
Integris Blackwell Regional Hospital	Blackwell	9	30
Integris Canadian Valley Hospital	Yukon	9	79
Integris Marshall County Medical Center	Madill	9	33
Purcell Municipal Hospital[3]	Purcell	9	61
Sequoyah Memorial Hospital	Sallisaw	9	102
Stillwater Medical Center	Stillwater	9	67
Unity Health Center	Shawnee	9	142
Woodward Regional Hospital	Woodward	9	31
Henryetta Medical Center	Henryetta	10	105
Mercy Health Center	Oklahoma City	10	161
Okmulgee Memorial Hospital	Okmulgee	10	174
Pauls Valley General Hospital	Pauls Valley	10	75
Share Memorial Hospital	Alva	11	32
Bailey Medical Center	Owasso	12	136
McCurtain Memorial Hospital	Idabel	12	83
Valley View Regional Hospital	Ada	12	62
Integris Seminole Medical Center	Seminole	14	113
Mercy Hospital El Reno	El Reno	14	66
Claremore Indian Hospital	Claremore	16	156
Grady Memorial Hospital	Chickasha	16	112
Tahlequah City Hospital	Tahlequah	16	48
Pushmataha Cnty-TN of Antlers Hosp Auth	Antlers	18	38
Wagoner Community Hospital	Wagoner	22	40
Epic Medical Center	Eufaula	24	51
Choctaw Memorial Hospital[3]	Hugo	68	27

Heart Failure Care

12. ACE Inhibitor or ARB for LVSD

Hospital Name	City	Rate	Cases
Integris Bass Baptist Health Center	Enid	100%	28
Medical Center of Southeastern Oklahoma	Durant	100%	85
Midwest Regional Medical Center	Midwest City	100%	123
Oklahoma Heart Hospital South[2,3]	Oklahoma City	100%	30
Saint Francis Hospital	Tulsa	100%	309
Southcrest Hospital	Tulsa	100%	71
Muskogee Regional Medical Center	Muskogee	99%	82
O U Medical Center	Oklahoma City	99%	122
Saint John Medical Center	Tulsa	99%	202
Duncan Regional Hospital	Duncan	98%	43
Integris Baptist Medical Center	Oklahoma City	98%	297
Muskogee VA Medical Center	Muskogee	98%	111
Claremore Regional Hospital	Claremore	97%	31
Deaconess Hospital	Oklahoma City	97%	39
Integris Clinton Regional Hospital	Clinton	97%	30
Jane Phillips Medical Center	Bartlesville	97%	37
Norman Regional Health System	Norman	97%	128
Saint Francis Hospital South	Tulsa	97%	31
Saint Mary's Regional Medical Center	Enid	97%	36
Stillwater Medical Center	Stillwater	97%	35
Unity Health Center	Shawnee	97%	65
Oklahoma City VA Medical Center	Oklahoma City	96%	100
Oklahoma State University Medical Center	Tulsa	96%	77
Tahlequah City Hospital	Tahlequah	96%	47
Oklahoma Heart Hospital[2]	Oklahoma City	95%	132
Saint Anthony Hospital	Oklahoma City	94%	138
Comanche County Memorial Hospital[2]	Lawton	92%	123
Hillcrest Medical Center	Tulsa	90%	220
Mercy Memorial Health Center	Ardmore	90%	51
Integris Southwest Medical Center	Oklahoma City	89%	170
McAlester Regional Health Center	Mcalester	86%	49

NOTE: Hospital profiles are in alphabetical order by state, then city, then hospital within the city; Rankings exclude hospitals with less than 25 cases except for patient surveys which excludes hospitals with less than 100 cases; (a) 100–299 cases; (1) The number of cases is too small to be sure how well a hospital is performing; (2) The hospital indicated that the data submitted for this measure were based on a sample of cases; (3) Data was collected during a shorter time period (fewer quarters) than the maximum possible time for this measure; (4) Suppressed for one or more quarters by CMS; (5) No data is available from the hospital for this measure; (6) Fewer than 100 patients completed the HCAHPS survey. Use these rates with caution, as the number of surveys may be too low to reliably assess hospital performance; (7) Survey results are based on less than 12 months of data; (8) Survey results are not available for this reporting period; (9) No or very few patients were eligible for the HCAHPS survey. The scores shown, if any, reflect a very small number of surveys; (10) A state average was not calculated because too few hospitals in the state submitted data; (11) There were discrepancies in the data collection process; Please refer to the User's Guide for a full explanation of data.

Hospital Name	City	Rate	Cases
Eastern Oklahoma Medical Center	Poteau	84%	37
Jackson County Memorial Hospital	Altus	78%	58
Okmulgee Memorial Hospital	Okmulgee	72%	25

13. Discharge Instructions

Hospital Name	City	Rate	Cases
Cushing Regional Hospital	Cushing	100%	34
Elkview General Hospital	Hobart	100%	32
Integris Bass Baptist Health Center	Enid	100%	76
Integris Canadian Valley Hospital	Yukon	100%	34
Integris Grove Hospital	Grove	100%	57
Integris Mayes County Medical Center	Pryor	100%	27
Medical Center of Southeastern Oklahoma	Durant	100%	250
Oklahoma City VA Medical Center	Oklahoma City	100%	182
Midwest Regional Medical Center	Midwest City	99%	304
Muskogee VA Medical Center	Muskogee	99%	156
Jackson County Memorial Hospital	Altus	97%	118
Ponca City Medical Center	Ponca City	97%	77
Great Plains Regional Medical Center	Elk City	96%	51
Hillcrest Medical Center	Tulsa	96%	520
Integris Marshall County Medical Center	Madill	96%	25
Oklahoma Heart Hospital[2]	Oklahoma City	96%	283
Saint Anthony Hospital	Oklahoma City	96%	312
Saint Francis Hospital	Tulsa	95%	713
Duncan Regional Hospital	Duncan	94%	106
Integris Baptist Regional Health Center	Miami	94%	70
Jane Phillips Medical Center	Bartlesville	94%	110
Saint Francis Hospital South	Tulsa	93%	68
Integris Blackwell Regional Hospital	Blackwell	92%	25
Chickasaw Nation Medical Center	Ada	91%	45
Norman Regional Health System	Norman	91%	276
Southcrest Hospital	Tulsa	91%	163
Oklahoma Heart Hospital South[2,3]	Oklahoma City	89%	56
Pushmataha Cnty-TN of Antlers Hosp Auth	Antlers	89%	28
Woodward Regional Hospital	Woodward	89%	44
O U Medical Center	Oklahoma City	88%	213
Oklahoma State University Medical Center	Tulsa	88%	163
Unity Health Center	Shawnee	87%	110
Integris Baptist Medical Center	Oklahoma City	86%	498
Memorial Hospital of Stilwell	Stilwell	86%	28
Claremore Regional Hospital	Claremore	85%	39
Stillwater Medical Center	Stillwater	85%	62
Integris Seminole Medical Center	Seminole	83%	42
Integris Clinton Regional Hospital	Clinton	82%	50
Integris Southwest Medical Center	Oklahoma City	81%	347
Saint John Medical Center	Tulsa	80%	497
McAlester Regional Health Center	Mcalester	78%	82
Pauls Valley General Hospital	Pauls Valley	78%	58
Tahlequah City Hospital	Tahlequah	78%	98
Saint John Owasso	Owasso	76%	34
Mercy Memorial Health Center	Ardmore	75%	133
Craig General Hospital	Vinita	73%	44
Sayre Memorial Hospital	Sayre	73%	33
Holdenville General Hospital	Holdenville	72%	36
Muskogee Regional Medical Center	Muskogee	72%	203
Southwestern Medical Center	Lawton	72%	32
Deaconess Hospital	Oklahoma City	71%	103
Valley View Regional Hospital	Ada	71%	51
Harmon Memorial Hospital	Hollis	70%	30
Mary Hurley Hospital	Coalgate	69%	36
Mercy Health Center	Oklahoma City	69%	54
Comanche County Memorial Hospital[2]	Lawton	68%	313
Grady Memorial Hospital	Chickasha	67%	58
Okmulgee Memorial Hospital	Okmulgee	67%	49
Saint Mary's Regional Medical Center	Enid	62%	106
Eastern Oklahoma Medical Center	Poteau	61%	99
W W Hastings Indian Hospital	Tahlequah	59%	29
McCurtain Memorial Hospital[2]	Idabel	58%	52
Purcell Municipal Hospital	Purcell	35%	31
Saint John Sapulpa	Sapulpa	15%	33
Choctaw Memorial Hospital	Hugo	4%	81

14. Evaluation of LVS Function

Hospital Name	City	Rate	Cases
Deaconess Hospital	Oklahoma City	100%	135
Duncan Regional Hospital	Duncan	100%	127
Elkview General Hospital	Hobart	100%	41
Integris Baptist Medical Center	Oklahoma City	100%	576
Integris Baptist Regional Health Center	Miami	100%	86
Integris Blackwell Regional Hospital	Blackwell	100%	41
Integris Marshall County Medical Center	Madill	100%	34
Integris Mayes County Medical Center	Pryor	100%	35
Medical Center of Southeastern Oklahoma	Durant	100%	326
Memorial Hospital of Stilwell	Stilwell	100%	36
Midwest Regional Medical Center	Midwest City	100%	375
Muskogee VA Medical Center	Muskogee	100%	178
O U Medical Center	Oklahoma City	100%	227
Oklahoma City VA Medical Center	Oklahoma City	100%	204
Oklahoma Heart Hospital[2]	Oklahoma City	100%	309
Ponca City Medical Center	Ponca City	100%	86
Saint Anthony Hospital	Oklahoma City	100%	355
Saint Francis Hospital	Tulsa	100%	862
Southcrest Hospital	Tulsa	100%	191
Southwestern Medical Center	Lawton	100%	42
Unity Health Center	Shawnee	100%	147
Integris Bass Baptist Health Center	Enid	99%	116
Integris Clinton Regional Hospital	Clinton	99%	74
Jane Phillips Medical Center	Bartlesville	99%	153
Norman Regional Health System	Norman	99%	344
Oklahoma State University Medical Center	Tulsa	99%	182
Saint Francis Hospital South	Tulsa	99%	89
Tahlequah City Hospital	Tahlequah	99%	111
Claremore Regional Hospital	Claremore	98%	48
Hillcrest Medical Center	Tulsa	98%	570
Oklahoma Heart Hospital South[2,3]	Oklahoma City	98%	59
Saint John Medical Center	Tulsa	98%	597
Stillwater Medical Center	Stillwater	98%	82
Woodward Regional Hospital	Woodward	98%	55
Integris Southwest Medical Center	Oklahoma City	97%	418
Mercy Memorial Health Center	Ardmore	97%	153
Sequoyah Memorial Hospital	Sallisaw	97%	32
Comanche County Memorial Hospital[2]	Lawton	96%	356
Eastern Oklahoma Medical Center	Poteau	96%	119
Muskogee Regional Medical Center	Muskogee	96%	256
Integris Canadian Valley Hospital	Yukon	95%	44
Mercy Health Center	Oklahoma City	95%	83
Saint Mary's Regional Medical Center	Enid	95%	168
Integris Seminole Medical Center	Seminole	94%	48
Jackson County Memorial Hospital	Altus	94%	160
Great Plains Regional Medical Center	Elk City	93%	69
McAlester Regional Health Center	Mcalester	93%	101
Valley View Regional Hospital	Ada	93%	70
Cushing Regional Hospital	Cushing	92%	49
W W Hastings Indian Hospital	Tahlequah	92%	36
Saint John Owasso	Owasso	91%	44
Henryetta Medical Center	Henryetta	89%	28
Integris Grove Hospital	Grove	89%	76
Grady Memorial Hospital	Chickasha	88%	77
Weatherford Regional Hospital	Weatherford	88%	33
Okmulgee Memorial Hospital	Okmulgee	85%	65
Purcell Municipal Hospital	Purcell	85%	46
Chickasaw Nation Medical Center	Ada	84%	45
McCurtain Memorial Hospital[2]	Idabel	84%	64
Memorial Hospital & Physician Group	Frederick	83%	36
Pauls Valley General Hospital	Pauls Valley	82%	85
Craig General Hospital	Vinita	79%	56
Logan Medical Center	Guthrie	79%	33
Saint John Sapulpa	Sapulpa	67%	39
Sayre Memorial Hospital	Sayre	61%	46
Mary Hurley Hospital	Coalgate	60%	58
Pushmataha Cnty-TN of Antlers Hosp Auth	Antlers	55%	40
Choctaw Memorial Hospital	Hugo	53%	120
Holdenville General Hospital	Holdenville	48%	60
Harmon Memorial Hospital	Hollis	31%	32

15. Smoking Cessation Advice

Hospital Name	City	Rate	Cases
Deaconess Hospital	Oklahoma City	100%	26
Duncan Regional Hospital	Duncan	100%	35
Integris Baptist Medical Center	Oklahoma City	100%	82
Jackson County Memorial Hospital	Altus	100%	55
Jane Phillips Medical Center	Bartlesville	100%	34
Medical Center of Southeastern Oklahoma	Durant	100%	86
Mercy Memorial Health Center	Ardmore	100%	38
Midwest Regional Medical Center	Midwest City	100%	62
Muskogee Regional Medical Center	Muskogee	100%	62
Muskogee VA Medical Center	Muskogee	100%	59
Norman Regional Health System	Norman	100%	74
O U Medical Center	Oklahoma City	100%	100
Oklahoma City VA Medical Center	Oklahoma City	100%	72
Oklahoma Heart Hospital[2]	Oklahoma City	100%	53
Oklahoma State University Medical Center	Tulsa	100%	50
Saint Francis Hospital	Tulsa	100%	144
Saint Mary's Regional Medical Center	Enid	100%	28
Integris Southwest Medical Center	Oklahoma City	99%	129
Saint John Medical Center	Tulsa	99%	120
Hillcrest Medical Center	Tulsa	98%	154
Saint Anthony Hospital	Oklahoma City	98%	93
Comanche County Memorial Hospital[2]	Lawton	96%	79
McAlester Regional Health Center	Mcalester	96%	25
Eastern Oklahoma Medical Center	Poteau	87%	30
Tahlequah City Hospital	Tahlequah	86%	29
Choctaw Memorial Hospital	Hugo	23%	26

Pneumonia Care

16. Appropriate Initial Antibiotic

Hospital Name	City	Rate	Cases
Bristow Medical Center	Bristow	100%	35
Integris Marshall County Medical Center	Madill	100%	59
Integris Mayes County Medical Center	Pryor	100%	38
Pauls Valley General Hospital	Pauls Valley	100%	56
Saint John Sapulpa	Sapulpa	100%	57
Unity Health Center	Shawnee	100%	116
Ponca City Medical Center	Ponca City	99%	87
Claremore Regional Hospital	Claremore	98%	90
Deaconess Hospital	Oklahoma City	98%	112
Integris Blackwell Regional Hospital	Blackwell	98%	55
Integris Baptist Regional Health Center	Miami	97%	119
Integris Bass Baptist Health Center	Enid	97%	70
Norman Regional Health System[2]	Norman	97%	94
Sayre Memorial Hospital	Sayre	97%	31
Sequoyah Memorial Hospital	Sallisaw	97%	61
Southcrest Hospital	Tulsa	97%	108
Medical Center of Southeastern Oklahoma	Durant	96%	134
Memorial Hospital & Physician Group	Frederick	96%	26
Okmulgee Memorial Hospital	Okmulgee	96%	56
Wagoner Community Hospital	Wagoner	96%	25
Hillcrest Medical Center	Tulsa	95%	147
Integris Seminole Medical Center	Seminole	95%	58
Mercy Health Center	Oklahoma City	95%	147
Oklahoma City VA Medical Center	Oklahoma City	95%	123
Saint John Owasso	Owasso	95%	76
Stillwater Medical Center	Stillwater	95%	98
Tahlequah City Hospital	Tahlequah	95%	78
Claremore Indian Hospital	Claremore	94%	35
Duncan Regional Hospital[2]	Duncan	94%	133
Elkview General Hospital	Hobart	94%	54
Henryetta Medical Center	Henryetta	94%	34
Jane Phillips Medical Center	Bartlesville	94%	126
O U Medical Center	Oklahoma City	94%	87
Saint Anthony Hospital	Oklahoma City	94%	171
W W Hastings Indian Hospital	Tahlequah	94%	47
Comanche County Memorial Hospital[2]	Lawton	93%	137
Integris Grove Hospital	Grove	93%	75
Saint Francis Hospital South	Tulsa	93%	95
Cushing Regional Hospital	Cushing	92%	120
Great Plains Regional Medical Center	Elk City	92%	51
Integris Clinton Regional Hospital	Clinton	92%	63
McCurtain Memorial Hospital	Idabel	92%	64
Midwest Regional Medical Center	Midwest City	92%	210
Pushmataha Cnty-TN of Antlers Hosp Auth	Antlers	92%	36
Saint Mary's Regional Medical Center	Enid	92%	83
Craig General Hospital	Vinita	91%	66
Creek Nation Community Hospital	Okemah	91%	34
Integris Baptist Medical Center[2]	Oklahoma City	91%	121
Jackson County Memorial Hospital	Altus	91%	64
Bailey Medical Center	Owasso	90%	30
McAlester Regional Health Center[2]	Mcalester	89%	28
Saint Francis Hospital	Tulsa	89%	492
Southwestern Medical Center	Lawton	89%	74
Drumright Regional Hospital	Drumright	88%	32
Newman Memorial Hospital	Shattuck	88%	26
Weatherford Regional Hospital	Weatherford	88%	43
Woodward Regional Hospital	Woodward	88%	42
Muskogee VA Medical Center	Muskogee	87%	93
Valley View Regional Hospital	Ada	87%	82
Integris Canadian Valley Hospital[2]	Yukon	86%	90
Kingfisher Regional Hospital	Kingfisher	86%	35
Logan Medical Center	Guthrie	86%	59
Oklahoma State University Medical Center	Tulsa	86%	74
Chickasaw Nation Medical Center	Ada	85%	54
Holdenville General Hospital	Holdenville	85%	27
Muskogee Regional Medical Center	Muskogee	85%	150
Saint John Medical Center[2]	Tulsa	85%	301
Mercy Memorial Health Center	Ardmore	84%	93
Choctaw Memorial Hospital[2]	Hugo	80%	54
Grady Memorial Hospital	Chickasha	80%	50
Mercy Hospital El Reno	El Reno	80%	54
Purcell Municipal Hospital	Purcell	80%	51
Eastern Oklahoma Medical Center	Poteau	79%	94
Integris Southwest Medical Center[2]	Oklahoma City	79%	185
Stroud Regional Medical Center	Stroud	77%	26
Muskogee Community Hospital[2,3]	Muskogee	76%	41
Memorial Hospital of Stilwell	Stilwell	73%	26
Harmon Memorial Hospital	Hollis	57%	46

17. Blood Culture Timing

Hospital Name	City	Rate	Cases
Deaconess Hospital	Oklahoma City	100%	182
Henryetta Medical Center	Henryetta	100%	44
Integris Baptist Medical Center[2]	Oklahoma City	100%	154
Integris Blackwell Regional Hospital	Blackwell	100%	72
Integris Mayes County Medical Center	Pryor	100%	74
Norman Regional Health System[2]	Norman	100%	181
Ponca City Medical Center	Ponca City	100%	97
Saint Francis Hospital South	Tulsa	100%	85
Stillwater Medical Center	Stillwater	100%	140
Unity Health Center	Shawnee	100%	171
Claremore Regional Hospital	Claremore	99%	126

NOTE: Hospital profiles are in alphabetical order by state, then city, then hospital within the city; Rankings exclude hospitals with less than 25 cases except for patient surveys which excludes hospitals with less than 100 cases; (a) 100–299 cases; (1) The number of cases is too small to be sure how well a hospital is performing; (2) The hospital indicated that the data submitted for this measure were based on a sample of cases; (3) Data was collected during a shorter time period (fewer quarters) than the maximum possible time for this measure; (4) Suppressed for one or more quarters by CMS; (5) No data is available from the hospital for this measure; (6) Fewer than 100 patients completed the HCAHPS survey. Use these rates with caution, as the number of surveys may be too low to reliably assess hospital performance; (7) Survey results are based on less than 12 months of data; (8) Survey results are not available for this reporting period; (9) No or very few patients were eligible for the HCAHPS survey. The scores shown, if any, reflect a very small number of surveys; (10) A state average was not calculated because too few hospitals in the state submitted data; (11) There were discrepancies in the data collection process; Please refer to the User's Guide for a full explanation of data.

Hospital Name	City	Rate	Cases
Integris Bass Baptist Health Center	Enid	99%	129
Integris Canadian Valley Hospital[2]	Yukon	99%	110
Medical Center of Southeastern Oklahoma	Durant	99%	159
Muskogee VA Medical Center	Muskogee	99%	177
O U Medical Center	Oklahoma City	99%	203
Saint Mary's Regional Medical Center	Enid	99%	109
Chickasaw Nation Medical Center	Ada	98%	48
Cushing Regional Hospital	Cushing	98%	162
Hillcrest Medical Center	Tulsa	98%	168
Integris Clinton Regional Hospital	Clinton	98%	42
Integris Southwest Medical Center[2]	Oklahoma City	98%	223
Jackson County Memorial Hospital	Altus	98%	52
Oklahoma State University Medical Center	Tulsa	98%	87
Valley View Regional Hospital	Ada	98%	101
Claremore Indian Hospital	Claremore	97%	34
Elkview General Hospital	Hobart	97%	31
Integris Baptist Regional Health Center	Miami	97%	149
McCurtain Memorial Hospital	Idabel	97%	73
Mercy Health Center	Oklahoma City	97%	316
Saint Anthony Hospital	Oklahoma City	97%	250
Saint John Sapulpa	Sapulpa	97%	75
Sequoyah Memorial Hospital	Sallisaw	97%	63
Southcrest Hospital	Tulsa	97%	159
Woodward Regional Hospital	Woodward	97%	39
Bailey Medical Center	Owasso	96%	27
Duncan Regional Hospital[2]	Duncan	96%	210
Grady Memorial Hospital	Chickasha	96%	82
Midwest Regional Medical Center	Midwest City	96%	263
Muskogee Regional Medical Center	Muskogee	96%	281
Oklahoma City VA Medical Center	Oklahoma City	96%	232
Saint John Medical Center[2]	Tulsa	96%	353
Comanche County Memorial Hospital[2]	Lawton	95%	189
Jane Phillips Medical Center	Bartlesville	95%	201
Saint Francis Hospital	Tulsa	95%	840
Integris Grove Hospital	Grove	94%	116
Integris Marshall County Medical Center	Madill	94%	54
Integris Seminole Medical Center	Seminole	94%	69
McAlester Regional Health Center[2]	Mcalester	94%	144
Saint John Owasso	Owasso	94%	79
Craig General Hospital	Vinita	92%	38
Mercy Memorial Health Center	Ardmore	92%	153
Pushmataha Cnty-TN of Antlers Hosp Auth	Antlers	92%	39
Eastern Oklahoma Medical Center	Poteau	90%	84
Holdenville General Hospital	Holdenville	90%	30
Okmulgee Memorial Hospital	Okmulgee	90%	48
Tahlequah City Hospital	Tahlequah	90%	117
Logan Medical Center	Guthrie	89%	62
Southwestern Medical Center	Lawton	88%	68
Mercy Hospital El Reno	El Reno	87%	30
W W Hastings Indian Hospital	Tahlequah	87%	61
Great Plains Regional Medical Center	Elk City	86%	58
Pauls Valley General Hospital	Pauls Valley	86%	56
Purcell Municipal Hospital	Purcell	82%	28
Harmon Memorial Hospital	Hollis	32%	28

18. Influenza Vaccine

Hospital Name	City	Rate	Cases
Integris Mayes County Medical Center	Pryor	100%	47
Medical Center of Southeastern Oklahoma	Durant	100%	156
Mercy Health Center	Oklahoma City	100%	228
Unity Health Center	Shawnee	100%	116
Saint Anthony Hospital	Oklahoma City	99%	201
Great Plains Regional Medical Center	Elk City	98%	58
Southcrest Hospital	Tulsa	98%	125
Deaconess Hospital	Oklahoma City	97%	140
Integris Baptist Medical Center[2]	Oklahoma City	97%	160
O U Medical Center	Oklahoma City	97%	127
Oklahoma State University Medical Center	Tulsa	97%	91
Pauls Valley General Hospital	Pauls Valley	97%	62
Ponca City Medical Center	Ponca City	97%	62
Arbuckle Memorial Hospital	Sulphur	96%	28
Integris Baptist Regional Health Center	Miami	96%	103
Integris Blackwell Regional Hospital	Blackwell	96%	51
Integris Marshall County Medical Center	Madill	96%	51
Norman Regional Health System[2]	Norman	96%	97
Saint Francis Hospital South	Tulsa	96%	71
Elkview General Hospital	Hobart	95%	43
Mercy Memorial Health Center	Ardmore	95%	128
Midwest Regional Medical Center	Midwest City	95%	167
Oklahoma City VA Medical Center	Oklahoma City	95%	169
Sequoyah Memorial Hospital	Sallisaw	95%	43
Cushing Regional Hospital	Cushing	94%	106
Memorial Hospital & Physician Group	Frederick	94%	36
Muskogee VA Medical Center	Muskogee	94%	131
Saint Francis Hospital	Tulsa	94%	587
Duncan Regional Hospital[2]	Duncan	93%	129
Integris Bass Baptist Health Center	Enid	93%	90
Jackson County Memorial Hospital	Altus	93%	54
McAlester Regional Health Center[2]	Mcalester	93%	96
Claremore Regional Hospital	Claremore	92%	87
Integris Seminole Medical Center	Seminole	92%	39
Jane Phillips Medical Center	Bartlesville	92%	145
Memorial Hospital of Stilwell	Stilwell	92%	25
Integris Clinton Regional Hospital	Clinton	91%	44
Weatherford Regional Hospital	Weatherford	91%	45
Integris Southwest Medical Center[2]	Oklahoma City	90%	182
Mercy Hospital El Reno	El Reno	90%	29
Muskogee Regional Medical Center	Muskogee	90%	234
Oklahoma Heart Hospital	Oklahoma City	90%	39
Pushmataha Cnty-TN of Antlers Hosp Auth	Antlers	89%	53
Saint John Owasso	Owasso	89%	46
Integris Grove Hospital	Grove	88%	67
Tahlequah City Hospital	Tahlequah	88%	80
McCurtain Memorial Hospital	Idabel	87%	70
Okmulgee Memorial Hospital	Okmulgee	87%	38
Woodward Regional Hospital	Woodward	87%	38
Saint Mary's Regional Medical Center	Enid	86%	123
Hillcrest Medical Center	Tulsa	85%	157
Integris Canadian Valley Hospital[2]	Yukon	85%	55
Craig General Hospital	Vinita	84%	55
Grady Memorial Hospital	Chickasha	84%	57
Sayre Memorial Hospital	Sayre	84%	37
Holdenville General Hospital	Holdenville	83%	29
Eastern Oklahoma Medical Center	Poteau	82%	67
Henryetta Medical Center	Henryetta	82%	28
Kingfisher Regional Hospital	Kingfisher	80%	30
Harmon Memorial Hospital	Hollis	79%	38
Southwestern Medical Center	Lawton	78%	73
Stillwater Medical Center	Stillwater	77%	96
Saint John Medical Center[2]	Tulsa	75%	310
W W Hastings Indian Hospital	Tahlequah	75%	32
Saint John Sapulpa	Sapulpa	71%	41
Valley View Regional Hospital	Ada	70%	90
Comanche County Memorial Hospital[2]	Lawton	59%	116
Purcell Municipal Hospital	Purcell	55%	44
Logan Medical Center	Guthrie	53%	38
Choctaw Memorial Hospital[2]	Hugo	42%	50
Muskogee Community Hospital[2]	Muskogee	38%	34

19. Initial Antibiotic Timing

Hospital Name	City	Rate	Cases
Bristow Medical Center	Bristow	100%	34
Creek Nation Community Hospital	Okemah	100%	33
Great Plains Regional Medical Center	Elk City	100%	73
Henryetta Medical Center	Henryetta	100%	50
Integris Mayes County Medical Center	Pryor	100%	59
Integris Southwest Medical Center[2]	Oklahoma City	100%	313
Latimer County General Hospital	Wilburton	100%	30
Medical Center of Southeastern Oklahoma	Durant	100%	224
Share Memorial Hospital	Alva	100%	28
Stroud Regional Medical Center	Stroud	100%	26
Tahlequah City Hospital	Tahlequah	100%	141
Cushing Regional Hospital	Cushing	99%	151
Grady Memorial Hospital	Chickasha	99%	94
Integris Baptist Regional Health Center	Miami	99%	181
Integris Blackwell Regional Hospital	Blackwell	99%	90
Integris Grove Hospital	Grove	99%	111
Integris Marshall County Medical Center	Madill	99%	79
Integris Seminole Medical Center	Seminole	99%	82
Oklahoma State University Medical Center	Tulsa	99%	136
Stillwater Medical Center	Stillwater	99%	144
Unity Health Center	Shawnee	99%	184
Valley View Regional Hospital	Ada	99%	109
Deaconess Hospital	Oklahoma City	98%	168
Integris Bass Baptist Health Center	Enid	98%	116
Integris Canadian Valley Hospital[2]	Yukon	98%	120
Integris Clinton Regional Hospital	Clinton	98%	97
Jackson County Memorial Hospital	Altus	98%	87
McAlester Regional Health Center[2]	Mcalester	98%	150
Memorial Hospital of Stilwell	Stilwell	98%	41
Ponca City Medical Center	Ponca City	98%	119
Saint John Owasso	Owasso	98%	92
Southcrest Hospital	Tulsa	98%	151
Woodward Regional Hospital	Woodward	98%	62
Duncan Regional Hospital[2]	Duncan	97%	212
Elkview General Hospital	Hobart	97%	62
Jane Phillips Medical Center	Bartlesville	97%	202
Mercy Health Center	Oklahoma City	97%	258
Midwest Regional Medical Center	Midwest City	97%	332
Newman Memorial Hospital	Shattuck	97%	32
Pushmataha Cnty-TN of Antlers Hosp Auth	Antlers	97%	79
Saint Anthony Hospital	Oklahoma City	97%	238
Saint Mary's Regional Medical Center	Enid	97%	148
Chickasaw Nation Medical Center	Ada	96%	54
Norman Regional Health System[2]	Norman	96%	188
O U Medical Center	Oklahoma City	96%	167
Arbuckle Memorial Hospital	Sulphur	95%	40
Claremore Regional Hospital	Claremore	95%	128
Comanche County Memorial Hospital[2]	Lawton	95%	199
Integris Baptist Medical Center[2]	Oklahoma City	95%	208
Memorial Hospital & Physician Group	Frederick	95%	41
Mercy Memorial Health Center	Ardmore	95%	172
Pauls Valley General Hospital	Pauls Valley	95%	84
Purcell Municipal Hospital	Purcell	95%	83
Weatherford Regional Hospital	Weatherford	95%	73
Saint Francis Hospital South	Tulsa	94%	107
Bailey Medical Center	Owasso	93%	41
Craig General Hospital	Vinita	93%	59
Hillcrest Medical Center	Tulsa	93%	216
Holdenville General Hospital	Holdenville	93%	41
Muskogee VA Medical Center	Muskogee	93%	152
Okmulgee Memorial Hospital	Okmulgee	93%	84
Saint John Sapulpa	Sapulpa	93%	72
Sayre Memorial Hospital	Sayre	93%	67
Sequoyah Memorial Hospital	Sallisaw	93%	100
Claremore Indian Hospital	Claremore	92%	37
McCurtain Memorial Hospital	Idabel	92%	108
Mercy Hospital El Reno	El Reno	92%	66
Drumright Regional Hospital	Drumright	91%	46
Kingfisher Regional Hospital	Kingfisher	91%	53
Oklahoma City VA Medical Center	Oklahoma City	91%	185
Perry Memorial Hospital	Perry	91%	32
Saint Francis Hospital	Tulsa	91%	848
Muskogee Regional Medical Center	Muskogee	90%	330
Saint John Medical Center[2]	Tulsa	90%	431
W W Hastings Indian Hospital	Tahlequah	90%	58
Memorial Hospital of Texas County	Guymon	89%	35
Eastern Oklahoma Medical Center	Poteau	86%	118
Wagoner Community Hospital	Wagoner	86%	29
Choctaw Memorial Hospital[2]	Hugo	82%	84
Southwestern Medical Center	Lawton	81%	108
Logan Medical Center	Guthrie	76%	45
Muskogee Community Hospital[2,3]	Muskogee	76%	33
Harmon Memorial Hospital	Hollis	72%	74

20. Pneumococcal Vaccine

Hospital Name	City	Rate	Cases
Bailey Medical Center	Owasso	100%	25
Great Plains Regional Medical Center	Elk City	100%	78
Integris Seminole Medical Center	Seminole	100%	52
Medical Center of Southeastern Oklahoma	Durant	100%	209
Memorial Hospital of Stilwell	Stilwell	100%	35
Mercy Health Center	Oklahoma City	100%	297
Ponca City Medical Center	Ponca City	100%	95
Saint Francis Hospital South	Tulsa	100%	97
Unity Health Center	Shawnee	100%	158
Integris Baptist Regional Health Center	Miami	99%	137
Integris Blackwell Regional Hospital	Blackwell	99%	67
Claremore Regional Hospital	Claremore	98%	100
Deaconess Hospital	Oklahoma City	98%	170
Duncan Regional Hospital[2]	Duncan	98%	202
Elkview General Hospital	Hobart	98%	43
Integris Clinton Regional Hospital	Clinton	98%	58
Integris Mayes County Medical Center	Pryor	98%	59
Midwest Regional Medical Center	Midwest City	98%	239
Muskogee VA Medical Center	Muskogee	98%	142
Norman Regional Health System[2]	Norman	98%	178
O U Medical Center	Oklahoma City	98%	95
Oklahoma City VA Medical Center	Oklahoma City	98%	162
Saint Anthony Hospital	Oklahoma City	98%	208
Saint Francis Hospital	Tulsa	98%	783
Southcrest Hospital	Tulsa	98%	133
Integris Bass Baptist Health Center	Enid	97%	100
Share Memorial Hospital	Alva	97%	37
Integris Southwest Medical Center[2]	Oklahoma City	96%	221
Mercy Memorial Health Center	Ardmore	96%	166
Oklahoma Heart Hospital	Oklahoma City	96%	57
Sequoyah Memorial Hospital	Sallisaw	96%	55
Integris Baptist Medical Center[2]	Oklahoma City	95%	209
Integris Grove Hospital	Grove	95%	105
Oklahoma State University Medical Center	Tulsa	95%	92
Hillcrest Medical Center	Tulsa	94%	170
Integris Marshall County Medical Center	Madill	94%	70
Memorial Hospital of Texas County	Guymon	94%	31
Southwestern Medical Center	Lawton	94%	88
Cushing Regional Hospital	Cushing	93%	112
Henryetta Medical Center	Henryetta	93%	29
Jackson County Memorial Hospital	Altus	93%	95
Jane Phillips Medical Center	Bartlesville	93%	206
Pauls Valley General Hospital	Pauls Valley	93%	82
Saint John Owasso	Owasso	93%	70
Saint Mary's Regional Medical Center	Enid	93%	156
Tahlequah City Hospital	Tahlequah	93%	127
Grady Memorial Hospital	Chickasha	92%	91
Muskogee Regional Medical Center	Muskogee	92%	293
Okmulgee Memorial Hospital	Okmulgee	92%	52
Pushmataha Cnty-TN of Antlers Hosp Auth	Antlers	92%	66
Woodward Regional Hospital	Woodward	92%	48
McAlester Regional Health Center[2]	Mcalester	91%	135
Sayre Memorial Hospital	Sayre	90%	40

NOTE: Hospital profiles are in alphabetical order by state, then city, then hospital within the city; Rankings exclude hospitals with less than 25 cases except for patient surveys which excludes hospitals with less than 100 cases; (a) 100–299 cases; (1) The number of cases is too small to be sure how well a hospital is performing; (2) The hospital indicated that the data submitted for this measure were based on a sample of cases; (3) Data was collected during a shorter time period (fewer quarters) than the maximum possible time for this measure; (4) Suppressed for one or more quarters by CMS; (5) No data is available from the hospital for this measure; (6) Fewer than 100 patients completed the HCAHPS survey. Use these rates with caution, as the number of surveys may be too low to reliably assess hospital performance; (7) Survey results are based on less than 12 months of data; (8) Survey results are not available for this reporting period; (9) No or very few patients were eligible for the HCAHPS survey. The scores shown, if any, reflect a very small number of surveys; (10) A state average was not calculated because too few hospitals in the state submitted data; (11) There were discrepancies in the data collection process; Please refer to the User's Guide for a full explanation of data.

Hospital Name	City	Rate	Cases
Memorial Hospital & Physician Group	Frederick	87%	39
Mercy Hospital El Reno	El Reno	87%	39
Integris Canadian Valley Hospital[2]	Yukon	86%	77
W W Hastings Indian Hospital	Tahlequah	86%	29
McCurtain Memorial Hospital	Idabel	85%	82
Weatherford Regional Hospital	Weatherford	85%	67
Newman Memorial Hospital	Shattuck	84%	32
Perry Memorial Hospital	Perry	84%	32
Arbuckle Memorial Hospital	Sulphur	83%	36
Harmon Memorial Hospital	Hollis	83%	46
Bristow Medical Center	Bristow	82%	34
Comanche County Memorial Hospital[2]	Lawton	82%	170
Mercy Health Love County[2]	Marietta	81%	26
Eastern Oklahoma Medical Center	Poteau	79%	77
Stillwater Medical Center	Stillwater	79%	155
Craig General Hospital	Vinita	78%	68
Holdenville General Hospital	Holdenville	77%	35
Kingfisher Regional Hospital	Kingfisher	77%	35
Saint John Medical Center[2]	Tulsa	71%	412
Saint John Sapulpa	Sapulpa	71%	49
Chickasaw Nation Medical Center	Ada	69%	29
Valley View Regional Hospital	Ada	69%	109
Stroud Regional Medical Center	Stroud	68%	28
Drumright Regional Hospital	Drumright	56%	27
Logan Medical Center	Guthrie	53%	62
Purcell Municipal Hospital	Purcell	44%	63
Choctaw Memorial Hospital[2]	Hugo	43%	77
Muskogee Community Hospital[2,3]	Muskogee	43%	35

21. Smoking Cessation Advice

Hospital Name	City	Rate	Cases
Claremore Regional Hospital	Claremore	100%	54
Cushing Regional Hospital	Cushing	100%	73
Deaconess Hospital	Oklahoma City	100%	71
Duncan Regional Hospital[2]	Duncan	100%	87
Integris Bass Baptist Health Center	Enid	100%	46
Integris Blackwell Regional Hospital	Blackwell	100%	29
Integris Canadian Valley Hospital[2]	Yukon	100%	38
Integris Clinton Regional Hospital	Clinton	100%	36
Integris Grove Hospital	Grove	100%	35
Integris Marshall County Medical Center	Madill	100%	25
Integris Mayes County Medical Center	Pryor	100%	27
Jackson County Memorial Hospital	Altus	100%	54
Jane Phillips Medical Center	Bartlesville	100%	89
Medical Center of Southeastern Oklahoma	Durant	100%	122
Mercy Health Center	Oklahoma City	100%	94
Mercy Memorial Health Center	Ardmore	100%	85
Midwest Regional Medical Center	Midwest City	100%	143
Muskogee VA Medical Center	Muskogee	100%	67
O U Medical Center	Oklahoma City	100%	147
Oklahoma City VA Medical Center	Oklahoma City	100%	95
Okmulgee Memorial Hospital	Okmulgee	100%	27
Ponca City Medical Center	Ponca City	100%	59
Saint Francis Hospital	Tulsa	100%	313
Saint Francis Hospital South	Tulsa	100%	31
Saint Mary's Regional Medical Center	Enid	100%	55
Sequoyah Memorial Hospital	Sallisaw	100%	43
Unity Health Center	Shawnee	100%	82
Integris Baptist Medical Center[2]	Oklahoma City	99%	78
Muskogee Regional Medical Center	Muskogee	99%	167
Norman Regional Health System[2]	Norman	99%	89
Oklahoma State University Medical Center	Tulsa	99%	104
Saint Anthony Hospital	Oklahoma City	99%	171
Hillcrest Medical Center	Tulsa	98%	177
Integris Baptist Regional Health Center	Miami	98%	66
Integris Seminole Medical Center	Seminole	98%	40
Southcrest Hospital	Tulsa	98%	94
Valley View Regional Hospital	Ada	98%	44
Craig General Hospital	Vinita	97%	34
Integris Southwest Medical Center[2]	Oklahoma City	97%	185
Saint John Medical Center[2]	Tulsa	95%	202
Comanche County Memorial Hospital[2]	Lawton	93%	105
McAlester Regional Health Center[2]	Mcalester	93%	59
Mercy Hospital El Reno	El Reno	93%	27
Saint John Owasso	Owasso	93%	28
Stillwater Medical Center	Stillwater	93%	41
Tahlequah City Hospital	Tahlequah	93%	75
McCurtain Memorial Hospital	Idabel	92%	36
Southwestern Medical Center	Lawton	92%	51
Purcell Municipal Hospital	Purcell	89%	27
Eastern Oklahoma Medical Center	Poteau	88%	43
Grady Memorial Hospital	Chickasha	88%	32
Drumright Regional Hospital	Drumright	86%	29
Pauls Valley General Hospital	Pauls Valley	84%	25
Sayre Memorial Hospital	Sayre	78%	27
Saint John Sapulpa	Sapulpa	69%	26
Logan Medical Center	Guthrie	67%	27
Chickasaw Nation Medical Center	Ada	63%	35
Choctaw Memorial Hospital[2]	Hugo	48%	25

Surgical Care Improvement Project

22. Appropriate VTP Within 24 Hours

Hospital Name	City	Rate	Cases
Chickasaw Nation Medical Center	Ada	100%	26
Claremore Regional Hospital	Claremore	100%	73
Cushing Regional Hospital	Cushing	100%	54
Henryetta Medical Center	Henryetta	100%	29
Integris Baptist Regional Health Center	Miami	99%	77
Oklahoma City VA Medical Center[2]	Oklahoma City	99%	239
Oklahoma State University Medical Center[2]	Tulsa	99%	116
Grady Memorial Hospital	Chickasha	98%	49
Oklahoma Surgical Hospital[2]	Tulsa	98%	80
Unity Health Center	Shawnee	98%	237
Integris Southwest Medical Center[2]	Oklahoma City	97%	199
Mercy Memorial Health Center[2]	Ardmore	97%	233
Muskogee VA Medical Center[2]	Muskogee	97%	76
Medical Center of Southeastern Oklahoma	Durant	96%	81
Midwest Regional Medical Center	Midwest City	96%	245
Ponca City Medical Center	Ponca City	96%	154
Tulsa Spine & Specialty Hospital	Tulsa	96%	28
Comanche County Memorial Hospital[2]	Lawton	95%	291
Integris Bass Baptist Health Center[2]	Enid	95%	112
McBride Clinic Orthopedic Hospital[2]	Oklahoma City	95%	64
Norman Regional Health System[2]	Norman	95%	240
Saint Anthony Hospital[2]	Oklahoma City	95%	331
Southwestern Medical Center	Lawton	95%	106
Bailey Medical Center	Owasso	94%	48
Logan Medical Center	Guthrie	94%	35
Mercy Health Center[2]	Oklahoma City	94%	152
Woodward Regional Hospital	Woodward	94%	64
O U Medical Center[2]	Oklahoma City	93%	299
Oklahoma Heart Hospital	Oklahoma City	93%	43
Southcrest Hospital	Tulsa	93%	175
Jackson County Memorial Hospital[2]	Altus	92%	248
Saint Francis Hospital South	Tulsa	92%	72
Saint John Owasso	Owasso	92%	26
Saint Francis Hospital[2]	Tulsa	91%	732
Integris Grove Hospital	Grove	90%	82
Tahlequah City Hospital	Tahlequah	90%	93
Duncan Regional Hospital[2]	Duncan	89%	142
Great Plains Regional Medical Center	Elk City	89%	74
Hillcrest Medical Center[2]	Tulsa	89%	123
McAlester Regional Health Center[2]	Mcalester	89%	131
W W Hastings Indian Hospital	Tahlequah	89%	45
Deaconess Hospital	Oklahoma City	88%	225
Saint Mary's Regional Medical Center[2]	Enid	88%	174
Stillwater Medical Center	Stillwater	88%	147
Muskogee Regional Medical Center	Muskogee	87%	161
Saint John Medical Center[2]	Tulsa	86%	467
Valley View Regional Hospital	Ada	86%	145
Integris Baptist Medical Center[2]	Oklahoma City	85%	149
Jane Phillips Medical Center[2]	Bartlesville	82%	249
Claremore Indian Hospital[2]	Claremore	81%	32
Integris Canadian Valley Hospital[2]	Yukon	81%	70
Southwestern Regional Medical Center	Tulsa	78%	112
Muskogee Community Hospital[2,3]	Muskogee	51%	57

23. Appropriate Hair Removal

Hospital Name	City	Rate	Cases
Bailey Medical Center	Owasso	100%	136
Chickasaw Nation Medical Center	Ada	100%	130
Claremore Indian Hospital[2]	Claremore	100%	107
Claremore Regional Hospital	Claremore	100%	187
Community Hospital[2]	Oklahoma City	100%	226
Cushing Regional Hospital	Cushing	100%	105
Deaconess Hospital	Oklahoma City	100%	757
Elkview General Hospital	Hobart	100%	38
Henryetta Medical Center	Henryetta	100%	36
Hillcrest Medical Center[2]	Tulsa	100%	614
Integris Baptist Medical Center[2]	Oklahoma City	100%	717
Integris Canadian Valley Hospital[2]	Yukon	100%	230
Integris Grove Hospital	Grove	100%	186
Integris Mayes County Medical Center	Pryor	100%	54
Jackson County Memorial Hospital[2]	Altus	100%	396
Jane Phillips Medical Center[2]	Bartlesville	100%	521
Logan Medical Center	Guthrie	100%	66
McBride Clinic Orthopedic Hospital[2]	Oklahoma City	100%	344
Medical Center of Southeastern Oklahoma	Durant	100%	229
Mercy Memorial Health Center[2]	Ardmore	100%	665
Midwest Regional Medical Center	Midwest City	100%	712
Muskogee VA Medical Center[2]	Muskogee	100%	87
Norman Regional Health System[2]	Norman	100%	776
Northwest Surgical Hospital[2]	Oklahoma City	100%	240
O U Medical Center[2]	Oklahoma City	100%	635
Oklahoma Center for Orthopaedic & Multi-Sp[2]	Oklahoma City	100%	233
Oklahoma City VA Medical Center[2]	Oklahoma City	100%	525
Oklahoma Heart Hospital	Oklahoma City	100%	1284
Oklahoma Heart Hospital South[3]	Oklahoma City	100%	81
Oklahoma State University Medical Center[2]	Tulsa	100%	319
Oklahoma Surgical Hospital[2]	Tulsa	100%	433
Ponca City Medical Center	Ponca City	100%	313
Saint Anthony Hospital[2]	Oklahoma City	100%	1529
Saint Francis Hospital[2]	Tulsa	100%	2287
Saint Francis Hospital South	Tulsa	100%	272
Saint John Medical Center[2]	Tulsa	100%	2490
Saint Mary's Regional Medical Center[2]	Enid	100%	675
Southcrest Hospital	Tulsa	100%	583
Stillwater Medical Center	Stillwater	100%	406
Summit Medical Center	Edmond	100%	31
Tahlequah City Hospital	Tahlequah	100%	345
Tulsa Spine & Specialty Hospital	Tulsa	100%	99
Unity Health Center	Shawnee	100%	392
Valley View Regional Hospital	Ada	100%	316
W W Hastings Indian Hospital	Tahlequah	100%	144
Comanche County Memorial Hospital[2]	Lawton	99%	658
Grady Memorial Hospital	Chickasha	99%	80
Integris Bass Baptist Health Center[2]	Enid	99%	334
Integris Southwest Medical Center[2]	Oklahoma City	99%	578
McAlester Regional Health Center[2]	Mcalester	99%	397
Mercy Health Center[2]	Oklahoma City	99%	357
Muskogee Regional Medical Center	Muskogee	99%	397
Southwestern Medical Center	Lawton	99%	240
Surgical Hospital of Oklahoma[2]	Oklahoma City	99%	179
Duncan Regional Hospital[2]	Duncan	98%	308
Great Plains Regional Medical Center	Elk City	98%	200
Saint John Owasso	Owasso	98%	163
Southwestern Regional Medical Center	Tulsa	98%	125
Integris Baptist Regional Health Center	Miami	97%	149
Muskogee Community Hospital[2,3]	Muskogee	96%	111
Woodward Regional Hospital	Woodward	96%	137
Eastern Oklahoma Medical Center	Poteau	95%	56
Lakeside Women's Hospital	Oklahoma City	94%	78
Memorial Hospital of Stilwell	Stilwell	87%	31

24. Appropriate Beta Blocker Usage

Hospital Name	City	Rate	Cases
Community Hospital[2]	Oklahoma City	100%	49
Midwest Regional Medical Center	Midwest City	100%	185
Northwest Surgical Hospital[2]	Oklahoma City	100%	50
Oklahoma City VA Medical Center[2]	Oklahoma City	100%	257
Oklahoma Surgical Hospital[2]	Tulsa	100%	101
Southcrest Hospital	Tulsa	100%	147
Valley View Regional Hospital	Ada	99%	85
Medical Center of Southeastern Oklahoma	Durant	98%	42
Deaconess Hospital	Oklahoma City	97%	163
Integris Canadian Valley Hospital[2]	Yukon	97%	34
Jane Phillips Medical Center[2]	Bartlesville	96%	77
Oklahoma Heart Hospital	Oklahoma City	96%	594
Unity Health Center	Shawnee	96%	89
Oklahoma Heart Hospital South[3]	Oklahoma City	95%	38
Great Plains Regional Medical Center	Elk City	94%	32
Norman Regional Health System[2]	Norman	94%	190
Saint Anthony Hospital[2]	Oklahoma City	94%	398
Saint John Medical Center[2]	Tulsa	94%	759
Integris Southwest Medical Center[2]	Oklahoma City	93%	186
Mercy Memorial Health Center[2]	Ardmore	93%	176
Ponca City Medical Center	Ponca City	93%	59
Southwestern Medical Center	Lawton	93%	44
Cushing Regional Hospital	Cushing	92%	25
Duncan Regional Hospital[2]	Duncan	92%	91
Muskogee VA Medical Center[2]	Muskogee	92%	39
Saint Francis Hospital South	Tulsa	92%	79
Tahlequah City Hospital	Tahlequah	92%	139
Integris Baptist Regional Health Center	Miami	91%	53
Jackson County Memorial Hospital[2]	Altus	91%	125
Muskogee Regional Medical Center	Muskogee	91%	117
O U Medical Center[2]	Oklahoma City	91%	158
Saint Francis Hospital[2]	Tulsa	91%	651
Integris Bass Baptist Health Center[2]	Enid	90%	82
Integris Grove Hospital	Grove	90%	41
McBride Clinic Orthopedic Hospital[2]	Oklahoma City	90%	93
Hillcrest Medical Center[2]	Tulsa	89%	221
Saint Mary's Regional Medical Center[2]	Enid	89%	163
Stillwater Medical Center	Stillwater	89%	114
Mercy Health Center[2]	Oklahoma City	88%	76
Oklahoma Center for Orthopaedic & Multi-Sp[2]	Oklahoma City	88%	51
Oklahoma State University Medical Center[2]	Tulsa	88%	95
Integris Baptist Medical Center[2]	Oklahoma City	87%	231
McAlester Regional Health Center[2]	Mcalester	86%	56
Claremore Regional Hospital	Claremore	83%	42
Comanche County Memorial Hospital[2]	Lawton	79%	253
Bailey Medical Center	Owasso	69%	32
Muskogee Community Hospital[2,3]	Muskogee	63%	30

25. Controlled Postoperative Blood Glucose

Hospital Name	City	Rate	Cases
Deaconess Hospital	Oklahoma City	100%	57
Oklahoma State University Medical Center[2]	Tulsa	100%	73
Oklahoma City VA Medical Center[2]	Oklahoma City	99%	105

NOTE: Hospital profiles are in alphabetical order by state, then city, then hospital within the city; Rankings exclude hospitals with less than 25 cases except for patient surveys which excludes hospitals with less than 100 cases; (a) 100–299 cases; (1) The number of cases is too small to be sure how well a hospital is performing; (2) The hospital indicated that the data submitted for this measure were based on a sample of cases; (3) Data was collected during a shorter time period (fewer quarters) than the maximum possible time for this measure; (4) Suppressed for one or more quarters by CMS; (5) No data is available from the hospital for this measure; (6) Fewer than 100 patients completed the HCAHPS survey. Use these rates with caution, as the number of surveys may be too low to reliably assess hospital performance; (7) Survey results are based on less than 12 months of data; (8) Survey results are not available for this reporting period; (9) No or very few patients were eligible for the HCAHPS survey. The scores shown, if any, reflect a very small number of surveys; (10) A state average was not calculated because too few hospitals in the state submitted data; (11) There were discrepancies in the data collection process; Please refer to the User's Guide for a full explanation of data.

Hospital Name	City	Rate	Cases
Oklahoma Heart Hospital	Oklahoma City	99%	904
Saint John Medical Center[2]	Tulsa	99%	319
Hillcrest Medical Center[2]	Tulsa	96%	145
Integris Baptist Medical Center[2]	Oklahoma City	96%	170
Saint Anthony Hospital[2]	Oklahoma City	96%	155
Saint Francis Hospital[2]	Tulsa	95%	325
Southcrest Hospital	Tulsa	95%	147
Norman Regional Health System[2]	Norman	93%	58
Integris Bass Baptist Health Center[2]	Enid	91%	69
Oklahoma Heart Hospital South[3]	Oklahoma City	91%	66
Saint Mary's Regional Medical Center[2]	Enid	91%	35
Tahlequah City Hospital	Tahlequah	91%	66
Integris Southwest Medical Center[2]	Oklahoma City	88%	108
Midwest Regional Medical Center	Midwest City	88%	64
O U Medical Center[2]	Oklahoma City	88%	97
Comanche County Memorial Hospital[2]	Lawton	86%	170

26. Prophylactic Antibiotic Timing

Hospital Name	City	Rate	Cases
Lakeside Women's Hospital	Oklahoma City	100%	67
McBride Clinic Orthopedic Hospital[2]	Oklahoma City	100%	255
Oklahoma Heart Hospital	Oklahoma City	100%	1000
Ponca City Medical Center	Ponca City	100%	231
Saint Mary's Regional Medical Center[2]	Enid	100%	520
Southcrest Hospital	Tulsa	100%	405
Tahlequah City Hospital	Tahlequah	100%	248
Claremore Indian Hospital[2]	Claremore	99%	71
Community Hospital[2]	Oklahoma City	99%	189
Integris Baptist Medical Center[2]	Oklahoma City	99%	519
Integris Canadian Valley Hospital[2]	Yukon	99%	168
Integris Southwest Medical Center[2]	Oklahoma City	99%	396
Medical Center of Southeastern Oklahoma	Durant	99%	142
Oklahoma Center for Orthopaedic & Multi-Sp[2]	Oklahoma City	99%	208
Oklahoma Heart Hospital South[3]	Oklahoma City	99%	71
Oklahoma Surgical Hospital[2]	Tulsa	99%	309
Saint Anthony Hospital[2]	Oklahoma City	99%	1258
Unity Health Center	Shawnee	99%	271
Bailey Medical Center	Owasso	98%	108
Deaconess Hospital	Oklahoma City	98%	457
Hillcrest Medical Center[2]	Tulsa	98%	446
Integris Bass Baptist Health Center[2]	Enid	98%	189
Mercy Health Center[2]	Oklahoma City	98%	225
Midwest Regional Medical Center	Midwest City	98%	435
Northwest Surgical Hospital[2]	Oklahoma City	98%	213
O U Medical Center[2]	Oklahoma City	98%	400
Oklahoma State University Medical Center[2]	Tulsa	98%	202
Saint Francis Hospital South	Tulsa	98%	209
Saint John Medical Center[2]	Tulsa	98%	2125
Southwestern Medical Center	Lawton	98%	172
Duncan Regional Hospital[2]	Duncan	97%	229
Integris Baptist Regional Health Center	Miami	97%	117
Integris Grove Hospital	Grove	97%	130
Integris Mayes County Medical Center	Pryor	97%	39
Jackson County Memorial Hospital[2]	Altus	97%	243
Mercy Memorial Health Center[2]	Ardmore	97%	423
Muskogee Regional Medical Center	Muskogee	97%	240
Muskogee VA Medical Center	Muskogee	97%	35
Norman Regional Health System[2]	Norman	97%	491
Oklahoma City VA Medical Center	Oklahoma City	97%	413
Saint John Owasso	Owasso	97%	136
Elkview General Hospital	Hobart	96%	27
McAlester Regional Health Center[2]	Mcalester	96%	284
Jane Phillips Medical Center[2]	Bartlesville	95%	416
Saint Francis Hospital[2]	Tulsa	95%	1875
Southwestern Regional Medical Center	Tulsa	95%	39
Stillwater Medical Center	Stillwater	95%	301
Tulsa Spine & Specialty Hospital	Tulsa	95%	64
Claremore Regional Hospital	Claremore	94%	144
Logan Medical Center	Guthrie	94%	49
Muskogee Community Hospital[2,3]	Muskogee	94%	64
Great Plains Regional Medical Center	Elk City	93%	140
Valley View Regional Hospital	Ada	93%	192
Chickasaw Nation Medical Center	Ada	91%	99
Comanche County Memorial Hospital[2]	Lawton	91%	420
Surgical Hospital of Oklahoma[2]	Oklahoma City	91%	151
Woodward Regional Hospital	Woodward	87%	87
Grady Memorial Hospital	Chickasha	86%	43
Cushing Regional Hospital	Cushing	85%	74
W W Hastings Indian Hospital	Tahlequah	85%	86
Eastern Oklahoma Medical Center	Poteau	81%	36

27. Prophylactic Antibiotic Timing (Outpatient)

Hospital Name	City	Rate	Cases
Grady Memorial Hospital	Chickasha	100%	27
Medical Center of Southeastern Oklahoma	Durant	100%	148
Northwest Surgical Hospital	Oklahoma City	100%	68
Integris Bass Baptist Health Center	Enid	99%	67
Mercy Health Center	Oklahoma City	99%	387
Oklahoma Heart Hospital	Oklahoma City	99%	488
Saint Mary's Regional Medical Center	Enid	99%	265
Community Hospital	Oklahoma City	98%	92
Integris Canadian Valley Hospital	Yukon	97%	38
Integris Grove Hospital	Grove	97%	97
Jackson County Memorial Hospital	Altus	97%	34
Lakeside Women's Hospital[3]	Oklahoma City	97%	233
O U Medical Center	Oklahoma City	97%	575
Oklahoma Surgical Hospital	Tulsa	97%	381
Southcrest Hospital	Tulsa	97%	203
Surgical Hospital of Oklahoma	Oklahoma City	97%	207
Tahlequah City Hospital	Tahlequah	97%	66
Deaconess Hospital	Oklahoma City	96%	429
McAlester Regional Health Center	Mcalester	96%	70
Mercy Memorial Health Center	Ardmore	96%	313
Ponca City Medical Center	Ponca City	96%	78
Saint Francis Hospital	Tulsa	96%	467
Hillcrest Medical Center	Tulsa	94%	620
Integris Mayes County Medical Center	Pryor	94%	53
Midwest Regional Medical Center	Midwest City	94%	156
Norman Regional Health System	Norman	94%	467
Saint Francis Hospital South	Tulsa	94%	108
Claremore Regional Hospital	Claremore	92%	61
Duncan Regional Hospital	Duncan	92%	48
Tulsa Spine & Specialty Hospital	Tulsa	92%	159
Integris Baptist Medical Center	Oklahoma City	91%	367
Saint John Medical Center	Tulsa	91%	454
Stillwater Medical Center	Stillwater	90%	176
Comanche County Memorial Hospital	Lawton	89%	389
Integris Baptist Regional Health Center	Miami	89%	70
Saint John Owasso	Owasso	89%	37
Southwestern Medical Center	Lawton	89%	87
Integris Southwest Medical Center	Oklahoma City	85%	177
Oklahoma Center for Orthopaedic & Multi-Sp	Oklahoma City	85%	268
Southwestern Regional Medical Center	Tulsa	84%	45
Valley View Regional Hospital	Ada	83%	196
Woodward Regional Hospital	Woodward	83%	29
Unity Health Center	Shawnee	82%	50
Muskogee Regional Medical Center	Muskogee	80%	113
Saint Anthony Hospital	Oklahoma City	79%	380
Great Plains Regional Medical Center	Elk City	77%	52
Oklahoma State University Medical Center	Tulsa	77%	84
Jane Phillips Medical Center	Bartlesville	61%	56

28. Prophylactic Antibiotic Selection

Hospital Name	City	Rate	Cases
Elkview General Hospital	Hobart	100%	27
McBride Clinic Orthopedic Hospital[2]	Oklahoma City	100%	255
Mercy Memorial Health Center[2]	Ardmore	100%	429
Muskogee VA Medical Center	Muskogee	100%	36
Northwest Surgical Hospital[2]	Oklahoma City	100%	214
Oklahoma Heart Hospital	Oklahoma City	100%	1027
Oklahoma Heart Hospital South[3]	Oklahoma City	100%	72
Tahlequah City Hospital	Tahlequah	100%	252
Woodward Regional Hospital	Woodward	100%	96
Chickasaw Nation Medical Center	Ada	99%	99
Claremore Regional Hospital	Claremore	99%	147
Comanche County Memorial Hospital[2]	Lawton	99%	427
Hillcrest Medical Center[2]	Tulsa	99%	456
Integris Southwest Medical Center[2]	Oklahoma City	99%	400
Lakeside Women's Hospital	Oklahoma City	99%	71
Medical Center of Southeastern Oklahoma	Durant	99%	142
Norman Regional Health System[2]	Norman	99%	498
Oklahoma City VA Medical Center	Oklahoma City	99%	414
Oklahoma Surgical Hospital[2]	Tulsa	99%	310
Saint Anthony Hospital[2]	Oklahoma City	99%	1263
Saint John Medical Center[2]	Tulsa	99%	2160
Southcrest Hospital	Tulsa	99%	409
Unity Health Center	Shawnee	99%	272
Valley View Regional Hospital	Ada	99%	191
Community Hospital[2]	Oklahoma City	98%	188
Duncan Regional Hospital[2]	Duncan	98%	230
Integris Baptist Medical Center[2]	Oklahoma City	98%	532
Integris Bass Baptist Health Center[2]	Enid	98%	190
Integris Grove Hospital	Grove	98%	131
Jackson County Memorial Hospital[2]	Altus	98%	243
Jane Phillips Medical Center[2]	Bartlesville	98%	418
Logan Medical Center	Guthrie	98%	49
McAlester Regional Health Center[2]	Mcalester	98%	284
Mercy Health Center[2]	Oklahoma City	98%	230
Saint John Owasso	Owasso	98%	137
Saint Mary's Regional Medical Center[2]	Enid	98%	522
Tulsa Spine & Specialty Hospital	Tulsa	98%	64
Bailey Medical Center	Owasso	97%	108
Deaconess Hospital	Oklahoma City	97%	456
Muskogee Regional Medical Center	Muskogee	97%	240
O U Medical Center[2]	Oklahoma City	97%	405
Oklahoma Center for Orthopaedic & Multi-Sp[2]	Oklahoma City	97%	208
Ponca City Medical Center	Ponca City	97%	231
Saint Francis Hospital[2]	Tulsa	97%	1904
Saint Francis Hospital South	Tulsa	97%	210
Southwestern Medical Center	Lawton	97%	173
Southwestern Regional Medical Center	Tulsa	97%	39
Stillwater Medical Center	Stillwater	97%	302
Surgical Hospital of Oklahoma[2]	Oklahoma City	97%	151
Integris Canadian Valley Hospital[2]	Yukon	96%	168
Midwest Regional Medical Center	Midwest City	96%	438
Oklahoma State University Medical Center[2]	Tulsa	96%	208
Integris Baptist Regional Health Center	Miami	95%	117
Great Plains Regional Medical Center	Elk City	94%	141
Cushing Regional Hospital	Cushing	91%	74
W W Hastings Indian Hospital	Tahlequah	91%	87
Claremore Indian Hospital[2]	Claremore	90%	72
Integris Mayes County Medical Center	Pryor	90%	40
Grady Memorial Hospital	Chickasha	88%	43
Eastern Oklahoma Medical Center	Poteau	72%	36
Muskogee Community Hospital[2,3]	Muskogee	70%	67

29. Prophylactic Antibiotic Selection (Outpatient)

Hospital Name	City	Rate	Cases
Community Hospital	Oklahoma City	100%	92
Jackson County Memorial Hospital	Altus	100%	33
Northwest Surgical Hospital	Oklahoma City	100%	68
Oklahoma Heart Hospital	Oklahoma City	100%	488
Saint John Owasso	Owasso	100%	35
Integris Baptist Regional Health Center	Miami	99%	68
Lakeside Women's Hospital[3]	Oklahoma City	99%	228
Medical Center of Southeastern Oklahoma	Durant	99%	148
Saint John Medical Center	Tulsa	99%	433
Southcrest Hospital	Tulsa	99%	200
Claremore Regional Hospital	Claremore	98%	58
Comanche County Memorial Hospital	Lawton	98%	385
O U Medical Center	Oklahoma City	98%	606
Saint Francis Hospital South	Tulsa	98%	106
Deaconess Hospital	Oklahoma City	97%	536
Hillcrest Medical Center	Tulsa	97%	613
Integris Canadian Valley Hospital	Yukon	97%	38
Muskogee Regional Medical Center	Muskogee	97%	98
Norman Regional Health System	Norman	97%	459
Oklahoma Surgical Hospital	Tulsa	97%	377
Ponca City Medical Center	Ponca City	97%	76
Stillwater Medical Center	Stillwater	97%	176
Surgical Hospital of Oklahoma	Oklahoma City	97%	208
Tahlequah City Hospital	Tahlequah	97%	64
Tulsa Spine & Specialty Hospital	Tulsa	97%	156
Duncan Regional Hospital	Duncan	96%	45
Grady Memorial Hospital	Chickasha	96%	27
Integris Mayes County Medical Center	Pryor	96%	50
Mercy Health Center	Oklahoma City	96%	437
Oklahoma Center for Orthopaedic & Multi-Sp	Oklahoma City	96%	232
Unity Health Center	Shawnee	95%	41
Integris Baptist Medical Center	Oklahoma City	94%	373
Integris Bass Baptist Health Center	Enid	94%	67
McAlester Regional Health Center	Mcalester	94%	69
Valley View Regional Hospital	Ada	94%	195
Great Plains Regional Medical Center	Elk City	93%	45
Midwest Regional Medical Center	Midwest City	93%	151
Saint Mary's Regional Medical Center	Enid	93%	273
Woodward Regional Hospital	Woodward	92%	26
Integris Southwest Medical Center	Oklahoma City	91%	171
Oklahoma State University Medical Center	Tulsa	91%	79
Integris Grove Hospital	Grove	90%	97
Southwestern Medical Center	Lawton	89%	81
Southwestern Regional Medical Center	Tulsa	88%	42
Saint Francis Hospital	Tulsa	85%	456
Mercy Memorial Health Center	Ardmore	84%	307
Jane Phillips Medical Center	Bartlesville	74%	34
Saint Anthony Hospital	Oklahoma City	72%	373

30. Prophylactic Antibiotic Stopped

Hospital Name	City	Rate	Cases
Eastern Oklahoma Medical Center	Poteau	100%	36
Integris Mayes County Medical Center	Pryor	100%	39
Medical Center of Southeastern Oklahoma	Durant	100%	138
Muskogee Community Hospital[2,3]	Muskogee	100%	64
Oklahoma Heart Hospital	Oklahoma City	100%	910
McBride Clinic Orthopedic Hospital[2]	Oklahoma City	99%	255
Saint Mary's Regional Medical Center[2]	Enid	99%	501
Deaconess Hospital	Oklahoma City	98%	441
Integris Grove Hospital	Grove	98%	127
Oklahoma Center for Orthopaedic & Multi-Sp[2]	Oklahoma City	98%	208
Oklahoma City VA Medical Center	Oklahoma City	98%	403
Saint Anthony Hospital[2]	Oklahoma City	98%	1201
Unity Health Center	Shawnee	98%	260
Integris Baptist Medical Center[2]	Oklahoma City	97%	484
Integris Bass Baptist Health Center[2]	Enid	97%	185
Muskogee VA Medical Center	Muskogee	97%	33
Oklahoma State University Medical Center[2]	Tulsa	97%	185
Ponca City Medical Center	Ponca City	97%	226
Southcrest Hospital	Tulsa	97%	373
Southwestern Medical Center	Lawton	97%	169
Stillwater Medical Center	Stillwater	97%	292

NOTE: Hospital profiles are in alphabetical order by state, then city, then hospital within the city; Rankings exclude hospitals with less than 25 cases except for patient surveys which excludes hospitals with less than 100 cases; (a) 100–299 cases; (1) The number of cases is too small to be sure how well a hospital is performing; (2) The hospital indicated that the data submitted for this measure were based on a sample of cases; (3) Data was collected during a shorter time period (fewer quarters) than the maximum possible time for this measure; (4) Suppressed for one or more quarters by CMS; (5) No data is available from the hospital for this measure; (6) Fewer than 100 patients completed the HCAHPS survey. Use these rates with caution, as the number of surveys may be too low to reliably assess hospital performance; (7) Survey results are based on less than 12 months of data; (8) Survey results are not available for this reporting period; (9) No or very few patients were eligible for the HCAHPS survey. The scores shown, if any, reflect a very small number of surveys; (10) A state average was not calculated because too few hospitals in the state submitted data; (11) There were discrepancies in the data collection process; Please refer to the User's Guide for a full explanation of data.

Duncan Regional Hospital[2]	Duncan	96%	222
Hillcrest Medical Center[2]	Tulsa	96%	429
Oklahoma Surgical Hospital[2]	Tulsa	96%	308
Saint Francis Hospital South	Tulsa	96%	203
Bailey Medical Center	Owasso	95%	105
Community Hospital[2]	Oklahoma City	95%	187
Grady Memorial Hospital	Chickasha	95%	43
Mercy Health Center[2]	Oklahoma City	95%	216
Mercy Memorial Health Center[2]	Ardmore	95%	382
O U Medical Center[2]	Oklahoma City	95%	365
Oklahoma Heart Hospital South[3]	Oklahoma City	95%	66
Claremore Indian Hospital[2]	Claremore	94%	70
Claremore Regional Hospital	Claremore	94%	141
Comanche County Memorial Hospital[2]	Lawton	94%	402
Jane Phillips Medical Center[2]	Bartlesville	94%	407
Norman Regional Health System[2]	Norman	94%	457
Saint Francis Hospital[2]	Tulsa	94%	1839
Tulsa Spine & Specialty Hospital	Tulsa	94%	63
Woodward Regional Hospital	Woodward	94%	77
Elkview General Hospital	Hobart	93%	27
Integris Canadian Valley Hospital[2]	Yukon	93%	168
Integris Southwest Medical Center[2]	Oklahoma City	93%	370
McAlester Regional Health Center[2]	Mcalester	93%	271
Northwest Surgical Hospital[2]	Oklahoma City	93%	205
Saint John Medical Center[2]	Tulsa	93%	2080
Tahlequah City Hospital	Tahlequah	93%	229
Cushing Regional Hospital	Cushing	92%	73
Muskogee Regional Medical Center	Muskogee	92%	233
Great Plains Regional Medical Center	Elk City	91%	130
Lakeside Women's Hospital	Oklahoma City	91%	67
Integris Baptist Regional Health Center	Miami	90%	114
Chickasaw Nation Medical Center	Ada	89%	98
Saint John Owasso	Owasso	88%	133
Jackson County Memorial Hospital[2]	Altus	86%	237
Midwest Regional Medical Center	Midwest City	83%	418
W W Hastings Indian Hospital	Tahlequah	82%	80
Valley View Regional Hospital	Ada	81%	186
Surgical Hospital of Oklahoma[2]	Oklahoma City	77%	151
Logan Medical Center	Guthrie	72%	43
Southwestern Regional Medical Center	Tulsa	72%	39

31. Recommended VTP Ordered

Hospital Name	City	Rate	Cases
Claremore Regional Hospital	Claremore	100%	73
Cushing Regional Hospital	Cushing	100%	54
Henryetta Medical Center	Henryetta	100%	29
Integris Baptist Regional Health Center	Miami	100%	77
McBride Clinic Orthopedic Hospital[2]	Oklahoma City	100%	64
Saint Francis Hospital South	Tulsa	100%	72
Hillcrest Medical Center[2]	Tulsa	99%	123
Integris Canadian Valley Hospital[2]	Yukon	99%	71
Norman Regional Health System[2]	Norman	99%	241
Oklahoma City VA Medical Center[2]	Oklahoma City	99%	239
Oklahoma State University Medical Center[2]	Tulsa	99%	116
Comanche County Memorial Hospital[2]	Lawton	98%	292
Duncan Regional Hospital[2]	Duncan	98%	142
Grady Memorial Hospital	Chickasha	98%	49
Integris Southwest Medical Center[2]	Oklahoma City	98%	201
Mercy Memorial Health Center[2]	Ardmore	98%	233
Oklahoma Surgical Hospital[2]	Tulsa	98%	80
Ponca City Medical Center	Ponca City	98%	154
Unity Health Center	Shawnee	98%	237
Integris Bass Baptist Health Center[2]	Enid	97%	112
Muskogee VA Medical Center[2]	Muskogee	97%	76
O U Medical Center[2]	Oklahoma City	97%	299
Saint Anthony Hospital[2]	Oklahoma City	97%	331
Saint Francis Hospital[2]	Tulsa	97%	733
Southcrest Hospital	Tulsa	97%	176
Bailey Medical Center	Owasso	96%	48
Medical Center of Southeastern Oklahoma	Durant	96%	81
Midwest Regional Medical Center	Midwest City	96%	247
Saint John Owasso	Owasso	96%	26
Jackson County Memorial Hospital[2]	Altus	95%	248
Woodward Regional Hospital	Woodward	95%	64
Logan Medical Center	Guthrie	94%	35
Mercy Health Center[2]	Oklahoma City	94%	153
Southwestern Medical Center	Lawton	94%	107
Chickasaw Nation Medical Center	Ada	93%	28
Oklahoma Heart Hospital	Oklahoma City	93%	44
Tulsa Spine & Specialty Hospital	Tulsa	93%	29
Deaconess Hospital	Oklahoma City	91%	228
Muskogee Regional Medical Center	Muskogee	91%	161
Integris Grove Hospital	Grove	90%	82
Saint Mary's Regional Medical Center[2]	Enid	90%	175
McAlester Regional Health Center[2]	Mcalester	89%	131
Claremore Indian Hospital[2]	Claremore	88%	32
Great Plains Regional Medical Center	Elk City	88%	76
Jane Phillips Medical Center[2]	Bartlesville	88%	249
Saint John Medical Center[2]	Tulsa	88%	473
Tahlequah City Hospital	Tahlequah	88%	95
Valley View Regional Hospital	Ada	88%	145
Integris Baptist Medical Center[2]	Oklahoma City	87%	155
Southwestern Regional Medical Center	Tulsa	87%	112
Stillwater Medical Center	Stillwater	87%	158
W W Hastings Indian Hospital	Tahlequah	85%	47
Muskogee Community Hospital[2,3]	Muskogee	51%	57

32. Urinary Catheter Removal

Hospital Name	City	Rate	Cases
Community Hospital[2]	Oklahoma City	100%	72
Oklahoma Center for Orthopaedic & Multi-Sp[2]	Oklahoma City	100%	99
Ponca City Medical Center	Ponca City	100%	66
Southcrest Hospital	Tulsa	100%	131
Surgical Hospital of Oklahoma[2]	Oklahoma City	100%	26
Midwest Regional Medical Center	Midwest City	99%	97
Unity Health Center	Shawnee	99%	96
Oklahoma City VA Medical Center[2]	Oklahoma City	98%	53
Integris Baptist Regional Health Center	Miami	97%	39
McAlester Regional Health Center[2]	Mcalester	97%	61
Saint Francis Hospital South	Tulsa	97%	38
Duncan Regional Hospital[2]	Duncan	95%	76
Integris Grove Hospital	Grove	95%	39
Bailey Medical Center	Owasso	93%	27
Hillcrest Medical Center[2]	Tulsa	93%	166
Integris Baptist Medical Center[2]	Oklahoma City	93%	124
Oklahoma Heart Hospital	Oklahoma City	93%	377
Deaconess Hospital	Oklahoma City	92%	48
Integris Southwest Medical Center[2]	Oklahoma City	92%	118
Mercy Health Center[2]	Oklahoma City	92%	25
Saint Anthony Hospital[2]	Oklahoma City	92%	119
Norman Regional Health System[2]	Norman	90%	88
Saint Francis Hospital[2]	Tulsa	88%	339
Comanche County Memorial Hospital[2]	Lawton	87%	137
Integris Bass Baptist Health Center	Enid	87%	55
Muskogee VA Medical Center[2]	Muskogee	87%	39
Saint John Medical Center[2]	Tulsa	87%	198
Stillwater Medical Center	Stillwater	86%	109
Tahlequah City Hospital	Tahlequah	86%	77
O U Medical Center[2]	Oklahoma City	85%	66
Jane Phillips Medical Center[2]	Bartlesville	84%	77
Oklahoma State University Medical Center[2]	Tulsa	84%	45
Oklahoma Heart Hospital South[3]	Oklahoma City	83%	30
Jackson County Memorial Hospital[2]	Altus	75%	99
Muskogee Regional Medical Center	Muskogee	67%	92
Woodward Regional Hospital	Woodward	67%	49
Integris Canadian Valley Hospital[2]	Yukon	62%	61
Mercy Memorial Health Center[2]	Ardmore	57%	35
Saint Mary's Regional Medical Center[2]	Enid	47%	30
Valley View Regional Hospital	Ada	42%	31
Great Plains Regional Medical Center	Elk City	29%	38

Children's Asthma Care

33. Received Systemic Corticosteroids

Hospital Name	City	Rate	Cases
Midwest Regional Medical Center	Midwest City	100%	26
O U Medical Center	Oklahoma City	100%	238

34. Received Home Management Plan of Care

Hospital Name	City	Rate	Cases
Midwest Regional Medical Center	Midwest City	100%	25
O U Medical Center	Oklahoma City	76%	236

35. Received Reliever Medication

Hospital Name	City	Rate	Cases
Midwest Regional Medical Center	Midwest City	100%	26
O U Medical Center	Oklahoma City	100%	238

Use of Medical Imaging

36. Combination Abdominal CT Scan

Hospital Name	City	Ratio	Cases
Jane Phillips Medical Center	Bartlesville	0.013	769
Comanche County Memorial Hospital	Lawton	0.021	1177
Sequoyah Memorial Hospital	Sallisaw	0.030	236
Memorial Hospital & Physician Group[1]	Frederick	0.033	30
Craig General Hospital	Vinita	0.041	317
Perry Memorial Hospital[1]	Perry	0.048	42
Integris Mayes County Medical Center	Pryor	0.060	334
Integris Canadian Valley Hospital	Yukon	0.063	221
Integris Bass Baptist Health Center	Enid	0.076	553
Sayre Memorial Hospital[1]	Sayre	0.089	45
Pauls Valley General Hospital	Pauls Valley	0.093	150
Mercy Hospital El Reno	El Reno	0.094	85
Grady Memorial Hospital	Chickasha	0.102	315
Integris Baptist Regional Health Center	Miami	0.109	192
Norman Regional Health System	Norman	0.109	1216
Stillwater Medical Center	Stillwater	0.109	496
Medical Center of Southeastern Oklahoma	Durant	0.110	317
Latimer County General Hospital[1]	Wilburton	0.111	27
Integris Southwest Medical Center	Oklahoma City	0.134	1146
Memorial Hospital of Stilwell	Stilwell	0.145	76
Duncan Regional Hospital	Duncan	0.150	479
Hillcrest Medical Center	Tulsa	0.154	518
Eastern Oklahoma Medical Center	Poteau	0.166	235
Saint Mary's Regional Medical Center	Enid	0.176	664
Mercy Memorial Health Center	Ardmore	0.182	813
Mercy Health Center	Oklahoma City	0.197	1672
Purcell Municipal Hospital	Purcell	0.257	109
Southcrest Hospital	Tulsa	0.266	376
Integris Baptist Medical Center	Oklahoma City	0.293	774
Bailey Medical Center	Owasso	0.310	155
Kingfisher Regional Hospital	Kingfisher	0.312	154
Deaconess Hospital	Oklahoma City	0.315	568
Southwestern Regional Medical Center	Tulsa	0.317	812
Muskogee Regional Medical Center	Muskogee	0.348	821
Midwest Regional Medical Center	Midwest City	0.390	629
Okmulgee Memorial Hospital	Okmulgee	0.401	147
Oklahoma State University Medical Center	Tulsa	0.412	342
Saint John Owasso	Owasso	0.435	310
Share Memorial Hospital	Alva	0.444	81
Community Hospital	Oklahoma City	0.448	67
Tahlequah City Hospital	Tahlequah	0.480	356
Wagoner Community Hospital	Wagoner	0.500	46
Pushmataha Cnty-TN of Antlers Hosp Auth	Antlers	0.506	83
Southwestern Medical Center	Lawton	0.518	299
Unity Health Center	Shawnee	0.559	472
Cushing Regional Hospital	Cushing	0.565	170
McAlester Regional Health Center	Mcalester	0.571	431
Choctaw Memorial Hospital	Hugo	0.573	96
Bristow Medical Center	Bristow	0.576	66
Integris Clinton Regional Hospital	Clinton	0.581	236
Henryetta Medical Center	Henryetta	0.585	82
Integris Marshall County Medical Center	Madill	0.613	80
Valley View Regional Hospital	Ada	0.614	743
Integris Blackwell Regional Hospital	Blackwell	0.638	130
Saint Anthony Hospital	Oklahoma City	0.638	519
Memorial Hospital of Texas County	Guymon	0.641	117
Woodward Regional Hospital	Woodward	0.664	220
McCurtain Memorial Hospital	Idabel	0.675	114
Saint Francis Hospital	Tulsa	0.678	2007
Ponca City Medical Center	Ponca City	0.703	407
Great Plains Regional Medical Center	Elk City	0.724	290
Saint Francis Hospital South	Tulsa	0.735	359
Integris Seminole Medical Center	Seminole	0.739	115
Saint John Medical Center	Tulsa	0.770	1137
Integris Grove Hospital	Grove	0.773	322
Oklahoma Heart Hospital	Oklahoma City	0.773	309
Northwest Surgical Hospital	Oklahoma City	0.804	107
Elkview General Hospital	Hobart	0.811	111
Claremore Regional Hospital	Claremore	0.839	298
O U Medical Center	Oklahoma City	0.864	1043
Newman Memorial Hospital[1]	Shattuck	0.900	60

37. Combination Chest CT Scan

Hospital Name	City	Ratio	Cases
Bristow Medical Center[1]	Bristow	0.000	38
Henryetta Medical Center	Henryetta	0.000	58
Kingfisher Regional Hospital	Kingfisher	0.000	70
Ponca City Medical Center	Ponca City	0.000	277
Saint Mary's Regional Medical Center	Enid	0.000	558
Unity Health Center	Shawnee	0.000	191
Valley View Regional Hospital	Ada	0.000	256
Comanche County Memorial Hospital	Lawton	0.002	852
Saint Anthony Hospital	Oklahoma City	0.002	457
Jane Phillips Medical Center	Bartlesville	0.004	554
Craig General Hospital	Vinita	0.006	164
Southwestern Regional Medical Center	Tulsa	0.008	921
Integris Bass Baptist Health Center	Enid	0.009	427
Mercy Memorial Health Center	Ardmore	0.009	670
Oklahoma Heart Hospital	Oklahoma City	0.009	224
Integris Baptist Regional Health Center	Miami	0.012	162
Northwest Surgical Hospital	Oklahoma City	0.012	86
Sequoyah Memorial Hospital	Sallisaw	0.012	83
Integris Marshall County Medical Center	Madill	0.016	61
Medical Center of Southeastern Oklahoma	Durant	0.016	183
Pauls Valley General Hospital	Pauls Valley	0.017	59
O U Medical Center	Oklahoma City	0.019	837
Integris Clinton Regional Hospital	Clinton	0.020	150
Hillcrest Medical Center	Tulsa	0.021	438
McAlester Regional Health Center	Mcalester	0.023	307
Stillwater Medical Center	Stillwater	0.024	290
Share Memorial Hospital[1]	Alva	0.025	40
Integris Blackwell Regional Hospital	Blackwell	0.030	67
Mercy Hospital El Reno	El Reno	0.033	60
Integris Southwest Medical Center	Oklahoma City	0.035	922
Purcell Municipal Hospital	Purcell	0.035	86
Community Hospital	Oklahoma City	0.038	52

NOTE: Hospital profiles are in alphabetical order by state, then city, then hospital within the city; Rankings exclude hospitals with less than 25 cases except for patient surveys which excludes hospitals with less than 100 cases; (a) 100–299 cases; (1) The number of cases is too small to be sure how well a hospital is performing; (2) The hospital indicated that the data submitted for this measure were based on a sample of cases; (3) Data was collected during a shorter time period (fewer quarters) than the maximum possible time for this measure; (4) Suppressed for one or more quarters by CMS; (5) No data is available from the hospital for this measure; (6) Fewer than 100 patients completed the HCAHPS survey. Use these rates with caution, as the number of surveys may be too low to reliably assess hospital performance; (7) Survey results are based on less than 12 months of data; (8) Survey results are not available for this reporting period; (9) No or very few patients were eligible for the HCAHPS survey. The scores shown, if any, reflect a very small number of surveys; (10) A state average was not calculated because too few hospitals in the state submitted data; (11) There were discrepancies in the data collection process; Please refer to the User's Guide for a full explanation of data.

Hospital Name	City	Rate	Cases
Integris Mayes County Medical Center	Pryor	0.038	210
Woodward Regional Hospital	Woodward	0.046	130
Integris Grove Hospital	Grove	0.048	230
Norman Regional Health System	Norman	0.048	1205
Saint Francis Hospital	Tulsa	0.051	2053
Southcrest Hospital	Tulsa	0.054	203
Saint Francis Hospital South	Tulsa	0.055	256
Tahlequah City Hospital	Tahlequah	0.059	220
Integris Baptist Medical Center	Oklahoma City	0.060	517
Grady Memorial Hospital	Chickasha	0.067	163
Sayre Memorial Hospital[1]	Sayre	0.071	28
Integris Canadian Valley Hospital	Yukon	0.083	121
Okmulgee Memorial Hospital	Okmulgee	0.085	71
Memorial Hospital of Stilwell[1]	Stilwell	0.096	52
Mercy Health Center	Oklahoma City	0.128	1223
Oklahoma State University Medical Center	Tulsa	0.133	248
Cushing Regional Hospital	Cushing	0.188	96
Duncan Regional Hospital	Duncan	0.197	390
Midwest Regional Medical Center	Midwest City	0.237	439
Latimer County General Hospital[1]	Wilburton	0.240	25
Muskogee Regional Medical Center	Muskogee	0.256	441
Pushmataha Cnty-TN of Antlers Hosp Auth	Antlers	0.277	65
Bailey Medical Center	Owasso	0.311	106
Wagoner Community Hospital[1]	Wagoner	0.370	27
Memorial Hospital of Texas County	Guymon	0.373	75
Eastern Oklahoma Medical Center	Poteau	0.400	110
Deaconess Hospital	Oklahoma City	0.476	332
Saint John Owasso	Owasso	0.478	232
Great Plains Regional Medical Center	Elk City	0.494	164
Southwestern Medical Center	Lawton	0.560	252
Elkview General Hospital	Hobart	0.621	58
Choctaw Memorial Hospital	Hugo	0.625	80
McCurtain Memorial Hospital	Idabel	0.648	91
Saint John Medical Center	Tulsa	0.797	1004
Newman Memorial Hospital[1]	Shattuck	0.808	26
Integris Seminole Medical Center	Seminole	0.819	72
Claremore Regional Hospital	Claremore	0.860	186

38. Follow-up Mammogram/Ultrasound

Hospital Name	City	Rate	Cases
Perry Memorial Hospital	Perry	2.0%	199
Newman Memorial Hospital	Shattuck	2.5%	160
Okmulgee Memorial Hospital	Okmulgee	2.5%	314
Saint Anthony Hospital	Oklahoma City	2.6%	878
Comanche County Memorial Hospital	Lawton	2.9%	1147
Cushing Regional Hospital	Cushing	4.0%	274
Elkview General Hospital	Hobart	4.0%	150
Mercy Memorial Health Center	Ardmore	4.2%	1145
Stillwater Medical Center	Stillwater	4.4%	712
Midwest Regional Medical Center	Midwest City	4.5%	1861
Jane Phillips Medical Center	Bartlesville	4.6%	1524
Muskogee Regional Medical Center	Muskogee	4.6%	1656
Pauls Valley General Hospital	Pauls Valley	4.6%	283
Saint Francis Hospital South	Tulsa	5.2%	518
Saint Francis Hospital	Tulsa	5.8%	2795
Lakeside Women's Hospital	Oklahoma City	6.0%	773
Integris Baptist Regional Health Center	Miami	6.2%	518
Integris Seminole Medical Center	Seminole	6.2%	162
Integris Grove Hospital	Grove	6.5%	688
Integris Blackwell Regional Hospital	Blackwell	6.7%	134
Norman Regional Health System	Norman	6.7%	2695
Southcrest Hospital	Tulsa	6.7%	509
Deaconess Hospital	Oklahoma City	7.0%	834
Valley View Regional Hospital	Ada	7.0%	781
Share Memorial Hospital	Alva	7.1%	85
Integris Baptist Medical Center	Oklahoma City	7.2%	1872
Craig General Hospital	Vinita	7.3%	301
Integris Mayes County Medical Center	Pryor	8.2%	389
Integris Clinton Regional Hospital	Clinton	8.3%	192
Hillcrest Medical Center	Tulsa	8.6%	1447
Integris Southwest Medical Center	Oklahoma City	8.6%	2047
McCurtain Memorial Hospital	Idabel	8.6%	257
Tahlequah City Hospital	Tahlequah	8.7%	564
Unity Health Center	Shawnee	8.8%	399
Bailey Medical Center	Owasso	9.3%	140
Saint Mary's Regional Medical Center	Enid	9.7%	1416
Jackson County Memorial Hospital	Altus	9.8%	569
Claremore Regional Hospital	Claremore	10.4%	472
Grady Memorial Hospital	Chickasha	10.4%	608
Memorial Hospital of Texas County	Guymon	10.5%	133
Mercy Health Center	Oklahoma City	10.7%	2343
Saint John Owasso	Owasso	11.1%	287
Integris Bass Baptist Health Center	Enid	11.3%	808
Medical Center of Southeastern Oklahoma	Durant	11.6%	661
Wagoner Community Hospital	Wagoner	11.6%	86
Integris Canadian Valley Hospital	Yukon	11.7%	291
Eastern Oklahoma Medical Center	Poteau	11.9%	143
Sequoyah Memorial Hospital	Sallisaw	12.1%	199
Choctaw Memorial Hospital	Hugo	12.2%	221
Ponca City Medical Center	Ponca City	12.2%	656
Woodward Regional Hospital	Woodward	12.5%	359
Oklahoma State University Medical Center	Tulsa	12.6%	198
Saint John Medical Center	Tulsa	12.9%	2215
Great Plains Regional Medical Center	Elk City	14.4%	432
Duncan Regional Hospital	Duncan	14.9%	691
Henryetta Medical Center	Henryetta	16.8%	149
Southwestern Regional Medical Center[1]	Tulsa	19.4%	31
Kingfisher Regional Hospital	Kingfisher	20.3%	187
McAlester Regional Health Center	Mcalester	20.3%	512

39. MRI for Low Back Pain

Hospital Name	City	Rate	Cases
Kingfisher Regional Hospital[1]	Kingfisher	21.4%	28
Woodward Regional Hospital[1]	Woodward	25.7%	35
Deaconess Hospital	Oklahoma City	27.2%	151
Great Plains Regional Medical Center	Elk City	27.9%	122
Muskogee Regional Medical Center	Muskogee	29.2%	291
Hillcrest Medical Center	Tulsa	29.4%	109
Integris Grove Hospital	Grove	29.6%	125
Integris Southwest Medical Center	Oklahoma City	29.9%	231
Unity Health Center	Shawnee	29.9%	67
Medical Center of Southeastern Oklahoma	Durant	30.3%	76
Northwest Surgical Hospital	Oklahoma City	30.5%	315
Jackson County Memorial Hospital	Altus	31.6%	76
Saint Francis Hospital	Tulsa	31.6%	392
Stillwater Medical Center	Stillwater	31.6%	136
Mercy Health Center	Oklahoma City	31.9%	373
Oklahoma Spine Hospital	Oklahoma City	31.9%	135
Integris Baptist Regional Health Center	Miami	32.0%	50
O U Medical Center	Oklahoma City	32.1%	112
Oklahoma Surgical Hospital	Tulsa	32.1%	277
Memorial Hospital of Texas County	Guymon	32.7%	49
Community Hospital	Oklahoma City	32.8%	61
Saint Francis Hospital South	Tulsa	32.9%	85
Tahlequah City Hospital	Tahlequah	33.1%	121
Integris Clinton Regional Hospital[1]	Clinton	33.3%	42
McAlester Regional Health Center	Mcalester	33.3%	126
Norman Regional Health System	Norman	33.6%	333
Saint Mary's Regional Medical Center	Enid	33.8%	204
Integris Mayes County Medical Center	Pryor	34.1%	91
Jane Phillips Medical Center	Bartlesville	34.5%	168
Cushing Regional Hospital	Cushing	35.3%	68
Bailey Medical Center	Owasso	35.6%	73
Choctaw Memorial Hospital[1]	Hugo	35.7%	42
Saint John Medical Center	Tulsa	35.8%	201
Valley View Regional Hospital	Ada	36.0%	136
Tulsa Spine & Specialty Hospital	Tulsa	36.1%	252
Comanche County Memorial Hospital	Lawton	36.4%	143
Midwest Regional Medical Center	Midwest City	36.7%	259
Saint Anthony Hospital	Oklahoma City	36.8%	125
Southwestern Medical Center	Lawton	38.7%	111
Claremore Regional Hospital	Claremore	38.9%	90
Sequoyah Memorial Hospital	Sallisaw	39.2%	51
Southcrest Hospital	Tulsa	39.2%	97
Integris Bass Baptist Health Center	Enid	39.5%	114
Duncan Regional Hospital	Duncan	39.8%	128
Oklahoma State University Medical Center	Tulsa	40.9%	44
Mercy Memorial Health Center	Ardmore	41.8%	208
Ponca City Medical Center	Ponca City	42.0%	100
Saint John Owasso	Owasso	42.1%	57
Grady Memorial Hospital	Chickasha	42.4%	66
Integris Marshall County Medical Center	Madill	44.2%	52
Craig General Hospital	Vinita	46.4%	84
Eastern Oklahoma Medical Center	Poteau	52.8%	36
Integris Canadian Valley Hospital	Yukon	53.7%	41
Integris Blackwell Regional Hospital[1]	Blackwell	54.5%	33

Survey of Patients' Hospital Experiences

40. Area Around Room 'Always' Quiet at Night

Hospital Name	City	Rate	Cases
Oklahoma Surgical Hospital	Tulsa	85%	300+
Surgical Hospital of Oklahoma	Oklahoma City	83%	(a)
Tulsa Spine & Specialty Hospital	Tulsa	83%	300+
Oklahoma Center for Orthopaedic & Multi-Sp	Oklahoma City	82%	(a)
Oklahoma Spine Hospital	Oklahoma City	82%	300+
Northwest Surgical Hospital	Oklahoma City	81%	(a)
Orthopedic Hospital	Oklahoma City	79%	(a)
Oklahoma Heart Hospital	Oklahoma City	78%	300+
Bailey Medical Center	Owasso	77%	(a)
Kingfisher Regional Hospital	Kingfisher	76%	(a)
Latimer County General Hospital	Wilburton	75%	(a)
McBride Clinic Orthopedic Hospital	Oklahoma City	75%	300+
Sequoyah Memorial Hospital	Sallisaw	75%	300+
Community Hospital	Oklahoma City	71%	300+
Mercy Hospital El Reno	El Reno	71%	(a)
Sayre Memorial Hospital	Sayre	71%	(a)
McCurtain Memorial Hospital	Idabel	70%	300+
Southwestern Regional Medical Center	Tulsa	69%	(a)
Wagoner Community Hospital	Wagoner	69%	(a)
Deaconess Hospital	Oklahoma City	68%	300+
Integris Seminole Medical Center	Seminole	68%	(a)
Integris Canadian Valley Hospital	Yukon	67%	300+
Newman Memorial Hospital	Shattuck	67%	(a)
Share Memorial Hospital	Alva	67%	(a)
Integris Mayes County Medical Center	Pryor	66%	(a)
Memorial Hospital of Stilwell	Stilwell	66%	300+
Perry Memorial Hospital	Perry	66%	(a)
Saint John Owasso	Owasso	66%	300+
Unity Health Center	Shawnee	66%	300+
Great Plains Regional Medical Center	Elk City	65%	300+
Integris Marshall County Medical Center	Madill	65%	(a)
Logan Medical Center	Guthrie	65%	(a)
Norman Regional Health System	Norman	65%	300+
Claremore Indian Hospital	Claremore	64%	(a)
Henryetta Medical Center	Henryetta	64%	(a)
Integris Baptist Medical Center	Oklahoma City	64%	300+
Purcell Municipal Hospital	Purcell	64%	(a)
W W Hastings Indian Hospital	Tahlequah	64%	300+
Cushing Regional Hospital	Cushing	63%	(a)
Eastern Oklahoma Medical Center	Poteau	63%	(a)
Southwestern Medical Center	Lawton	63%	300+
Integris Grove Hospital	Grove	62%	300+
Ponca City Medical Center	Ponca City	62%	300+
Saint Anthony Hospital	Oklahoma City	62%	300+
Saint Mary's Regional Medical Center	Enid	62%	300+
Epic Medical Center	Eufaula	61%	(a)
Integris Clinton Regional Hospital	Clinton	61%	300+
Memorial Hospital of Texas County	Guymon	61%	(a)
Chickasaw Nation Medical Center	Ada	60%	300+
Choctaw Nation Healthcare	Talihina	60%	(a)
Duncan Regional Hospital	Duncan	60%	300+
Grady Memorial Hospital	Chickasha	60%	300+
Jane Phillips Medical Center	Bartlesville	60%	300+
Lakeside Women's Hospital	Oklahoma City	60%	300+
Mercy Health Center	Oklahoma City	60%	300+
Oklahoma State University Medical Center	Tulsa	60%	300+
Saint Francis Hospital South	Tulsa	60%	300+
Valley View Regional Hospital	Ada	60%	300+
Elkview General Hospital	Hobart	59%	(a)
Hillcrest Medical Center	Tulsa	59%	300+
Integris Bass Baptist Health Center	Enid	59%	300+
Pauls Valley General Hospital	Pauls Valley	59%	300+
Stillwater Medical Center	Stillwater	59%	300+
Woodward Regional Hospital	Woodward	59%	300+
Integris Baptist Regional Health Center	Miami	58%	300+
Saint Francis Hospital	Tulsa	58%	300+
Southcrest Hospital	Tulsa	58%	300+
Integris Blackwell Regional Hospital	Blackwell	57%	(a)
McAlester Regional Health Center	Mcalester	57%	300+
O U Medical Center	Oklahoma City	57%	300+
Saint John Medical Center	Tulsa	57%	300+
Claremore Regional Hospital	Claremore	56%	300+
Integris Southwest Medical Center	Oklahoma City	55%	300+
Medical Center of Southeastern Oklahoma	Durant	55%	300+
Okmulgee Memorial Hospital	Okmulgee	55%	(a)
Mercy Memorial Health Center	Ardmore	54%	300+
Comanche County Memorial Hospital	Lawton	53%	300+
Craig General Hospital	Vinita	53%	300+
Memorial Hospital & Physician Group	Frederick	53%	(a)
Jackson County Memorial Hospital	Altus	51%	300+
Tahlequah City Hospital	Tahlequah	51%	300+
Midwest Regional Medical Center	Midwest City	48%	300+
Muskogee Regional Medical Center	Muskogee	48%	300+
Pushmataha Cnty-TN of Antlers Hosp Auth	Antlers	48%	(a)
Choctaw Memorial Hospital	Hugo	43%	(a)

41. Doctors 'Always' Communicated Well

Hospital Name	City	Rate	Cases
Oklahoma Spine Hospital	Oklahoma City	95%	300+
Integris Marshall County Medical Center	Madill	92%	(a)
Newman Memorial Hospital	Shattuck	91%	(a)
Oklahoma Heart Hospital	Oklahoma City	90%	300+
Purcell Municipal Hospital	Purcell	90%	(a)
Sayre Memorial Hospital	Sayre	90%	(a)
Elkview General Hospital	Hobart	89%	(a)
Surgical Hospital of Oklahoma	Oklahoma City	89%	(a)
Craig General Hospital	Vinita	88%	300+
Lakeside Women's Hospital	Oklahoma City	88%	300+
Oklahoma Center for Orthopaedic & Multi-Sp	Oklahoma City	88%	(a)
Tulsa Spine & Specialty Hospital	Tulsa	88%	300+
Eastern Oklahoma Medical Center	Poteau	87%	(a)
Kingfisher Regional Hospital	Kingfisher	87%	(a)
Logan Medical Center	Guthrie	87%	(a)
McBride Clinic Orthopedic Hospital	Oklahoma City	87%	300+
Northwest Surgical Hospital	Oklahoma City	87%	(a)
Pauls Valley General Hospital	Pauls Valley	87%	300+
Bailey Medical Center	Owasso	86%	(a)
Cushing Regional Hospital	Cushing	86%	(a)
Integris Baptist Regional Health Center	Miami	86%	300+

NOTE: Hospital profiles are in alphabetical order by state, then city, then hospital within the city; Rankings exclude hospitals with less than 25 cases except for patient surveys which excludes hospitals with less than 100 cases; (a) 100–299 cases; (1) The number of cases is too small to be sure how well a hospital is performing; (2) The hospital indicated that the data submitted for this measure were based on a sample of cases; (3) Data was collected during a shorter time period (fewer quarters) than the maximum possible time for this measure; (4) Suppressed for one or more quarters by CMS; (5) No data is available from the hospital for this measure; (6) Fewer than 100 patients completed the HCAHPS survey. Use these rates with caution, as the number of surveys may be too low to reliably assess hospital performance; (7) Survey results are based on less than 12 months of data; (8) Survey results are not available for this reporting period; (9) No or very few patients were eligible for the HCAHPS survey. The scores shown, if any, reflect a very small number of surveys; (10) A state average was not calculated because too few hospitals in the state submitted data; (11) There were discrepancies in the data collection process; Please refer to the User's Guide for a full explanation of data.

Memorial Hospital of Stilwell	Stilwell	86%	300+
Chickasaw Nation Medical Center	Ada	85%	300+
Integris Bass Baptist Health Center	Enid	85%	300+
Integris Mayes County Medical Center	Pryor	85%	(a)
Integris Seminole Medical Center	Seminole	85%	(a)
Latimer County General Hospital	Wilburton	85%	(a)
Oklahoma Surgical Hospital	Tulsa	85%	300+
Southwestern Regional Medical Center	Tulsa	85%	(a)
Unity Health Center	Shawnee	85%	300+
Henryetta Medical Center	Henryetta	84%	(a)
Integris Blackwell Regional Hospital	Blackwell	84%	(a)
Integris Canadian Valley Hospital	Yukon	84%	300+
Integris Clinton Regional Hospital	Clinton	84%	300+
Jackson County Memorial Hospital	Altus	84%	300+
McCurtain Memorial Hospital	Idabel	84%	300+
Mercy Health Center	Oklahoma City	84%	300+
Sequoyah Memorial Hospital	Sallisaw	84%	300+
Duncan Regional Hospital	Duncan	83%	300+
Integris Baptist Medical Center	Oklahoma City	83%	300+
Integris Grove Hospital	Grove	83%	300+
McAlester Regional Health Center	Mcalester	83%	300+
Saint Anthony Hospital	Oklahoma City	83%	300+
Saint John Owasso	Owasso	83%	300+
Saint Mary's Regional Medical Center	Enid	83%	300+
Share Memorial Hospital	Alva	83%	(a)
W W Hastings Indian Hospital	Tahlequah	83%	300+
Choctaw Nation Healthcare	Talihina	82%	(a)
Perry Memorial Hospital	Perry	82%	(a)
Saint Francis Hospital South	Tulsa	82%	300+
Southwestern Medical Center	Lawton	82%	300+
Stillwater Medical Center	Stillwater	82%	300+
Claremore Regional Hospital	Claremore	81%	300+
Jane Phillips Medical Center	Bartlesville	81%	300+
Medical Center of Southeastern Oklahoma	Durant	81%	300+
Norman Regional Health System	Norman	81%	300+
Ponca City Medical Center	Ponca City	81%	300+
Woodward Regional Hospital	Woodward	81%	300+
Deaconess Hospital	Oklahoma City	80%	300+
Grady Memorial Hospital	Chickasha	80%	300+
Mercy Memorial Health Center	Ardmore	80%	300+
Oklahoma State University Medical Center	Tulsa	80%	300+
Okmulgee Memorial Hospital	Okmulgee	80%	(a)
Saint John Medical Center	Tulsa	80%	300+
Comanche County Memorial Hospital	Lawton	79%	300+
Community Hospital	Oklahoma City	79%	300+
Great Plains Regional Medical Center	Elk City	79%	300+
Hillcrest Medical Center	Tulsa	79%	300+
Memorial Hospital & Physician Group	Frederick	79%	(a)
Memorial Hospital of Texas County	Guymon	79%	(a)
Wagoner Community Hospital	Wagoner	79%	(a)
Muskogee Regional Medical Center	Muskogee	78%	300+
O U Medical Center	Oklahoma City	78%	300+
Orthopedic Hospital	Oklahoma City	78%	(a)
Valley View Regional Hospital	Ada	78%	300+
Choctaw Memorial Hospital	Hugo	77%	(a)
Claremore Indian Hospital	Claremore	77%	(a)
Integris Southwest Medical Center	Oklahoma City	77%	300+
Midwest Regional Medical Center	Midwest City	77%	300+
Saint Francis Hospital	Tulsa	77%	300+
Southcrest Hospital	Tulsa	77%	300+
Tahlequah City Hospital	Tahlequah	77%	300+
Pushmataha Cnty-TN of Antlers Hosp Auth	Antlers	76%	(a)
Mercy Hospital El Reno	El Reno	75%	(a)
Epic Medical Center	Eufaula	54%	(a)

42. Home Recovery Information Given

Hospital Name	City	Rate	Cases
McBride Clinic Orthopedic Hospital	Oklahoma City	91%	300+
Oklahoma Heart Hospital	Oklahoma City	89%	300+
Oklahoma Spine Hospital	Oklahoma City	89%	300+
Lakeside Women's Hospital	Oklahoma City	88%	300+
Memorial Hospital of Texas County	Guymon	88%	(a)
Saint Mary's Regional Medical Center	Enid	88%	300+
Integris Marshall County Medical Center	Madill	87%	(a)
Northwest Surgical Hospital	Oklahoma City	87%	(a)
Oklahoma Center for Orthopaedic & Multi-Sp	Oklahoma City	87%	(a)
Bailey Medical Center	Owasso	86%	(a)
Choctaw Nation Healthcare	Talihina	86%	(a)
Community Hospital	Oklahoma City	86%	300+
Perry Memorial Hospital	Perry	86%	(a)
Stillwater Medical Center	Stillwater	86%	300+
Tulsa Spine & Specialty Hospital	Tulsa	86%	300+
Unity Health Center	Shawnee	86%	300+
Chickasaw Nation Medical Center	Ada	85%	300+
Claremore Regional Hospital	Claremore	85%	300+
Logan Medical Center	Guthrie	85%	(a)
Newman Memorial Hospital	Shattuck	85%	(a)
Ponca City Medical Center	Ponca City	85%	300+
Southwestern Regional Medical Center	Tulsa	85%	(a)
Grady Memorial Hospital	Chickasha	84%	300+
Integris Clinton Regional Hospital	Clinton	84%	300+
O U Medical Center	Oklahoma City	84%	300+
Oklahoma Surgical Hospital	Tulsa	84%	300+
Deaconess Hospital	Oklahoma City	83%	300+
Integris Mayes County Medical Center	Pryor	83%	(a)
Jane Phillips Medical Center	Bartlesville	83%	300+
Kingfisher Regional Hospital	Kingfisher	83%	(a)
Saint Francis Hospital South	Tulsa	83%	300+
Surgical Hospital of Oklahoma	Oklahoma City	83%	(a)
Cushing Regional Hospital	Cushing	82%	(a)
Eastern Oklahoma Medical Center	Poteau	82%	(a)
Henryetta Medical Center	Henryetta	82%	(a)
Integris Baptist Regional Health Center	Miami	82%	300+
Jackson County Memorial Hospital	Altus	82%	300+
Norman Regional Health System	Norman	82%	300+
Oklahoma State University Medical Center	Tulsa	82%	300+
Saint Anthony Hospital	Oklahoma City	82%	300+
Craig General Hospital	Vinita	81%	300+
Duncan Regional Hospital	Duncan	81%	300+
Integris Seminole Medical Center	Seminole	81%	(a)
McAlester Regional Health Center	Mcalester	81%	300+
Muskogee Regional Medical Center	Muskogee	81%	300+
Pauls Valley General Hospital	Pauls Valley	81%	300+
Southwestern Medical Center	Lawton	81%	300+
Valley View Regional Hospital	Ada	81%	300+
W W Hastings Indian Hospital	Tahlequah	81%	300+
Great Plains Regional Medical Center	Elk City	80%	300+
Integris Baptist Medical Center	Oklahoma City	80%	300+
Integris Bass Baptist Health Center	Enid	80%	300+
Integris Canadian Valley Hospital	Yukon	80%	300+
Mercy Health Center	Oklahoma City	80%	300+
Mercy Memorial Health Center	Ardmore	80%	300+
Sequoyah Memorial Hospital	Sallisaw	80%	300+
Southcrest Hospital	Tulsa	80%	300+
Woodward Regional Hospital	Woodward	80%	300+
Hillcrest Medical Center	Tulsa	79%	300+
Integris Blackwell Regional Hospital	Blackwell	79%	(a)
Integris Grove Hospital	Grove	79%	300+
Orthopedic Hospital	Oklahoma City	79%	(a)
Saint Francis Hospital	Tulsa	79%	300+
Saint John Owasso	Owasso	79%	300+
Comanche County Memorial Hospital	Lawton	78%	300+
Medical Center of Southeastern Oklahoma	Durant	78%	300+
Midwest Regional Medical Center	Midwest City	78%	300+
Wagoner Community Hospital	Wagoner	78%	(a)
Saint John Medical Center	Tulsa	77%	300+
Tahlequah City Hospital	Tahlequah	77%	300+
Integris Southwest Medical Center	Oklahoma City	76%	300+
Memorial Hospital of Stilwell	Stilwell	76%	300+
Okmulgee Memorial Hospital	Okmulgee	76%	(a)
Elkview General Hospital	Hobart	75%	(a)
Latimer County General Hospital	Wilburton	75%	(a)
Memorial Hospital & Physician Group	Frederick	75%	(a)
Purcell Municipal Hospital	Purcell	75%	(a)
Share Memorial Hospital	Alva	75%	(a)
Sayre Memorial Hospital	Sayre	74%	(a)
Claremore Indian Hospital	Claremore	73%	(a)
McCurtain Memorial Hospital	Idabel	72%	300+
Mercy Hospital El Reno	El Reno	72%	(a)
Pushmataha Cnty-TN of Antlers Hosp Auth	Antlers	67%	(a)
Choctaw Memorial Hospital	Hugo	62%	(a)
Epic Medical Center	Eufaula	60%	(a)

43. Hospital Given 9 or 10 on 10 Point Scale

Hospital Name	City	Rate	Cases
Oklahoma Heart Hospital	Oklahoma City	97%	300+
Oklahoma Spine Hospital	Oklahoma City	91%	300+
Southwestern Regional Medical Center	Tulsa	90%	(a)
Tulsa Spine & Specialty Hospital	Tulsa	88%	300+
Northwest Surgical Hospital	Oklahoma City	87%	(a)
Oklahoma Surgical Hospital	Tulsa	86%	300+
Bailey Medical Center	Owasso	84%	(a)
Lakeside Women's Hospital	Oklahoma City	84%	300+
McBride Clinic Orthopedic Hospital	Oklahoma City	83%	300+
Oklahoma Center for Orthopaedic & Multi-Sp	Oklahoma City	82%	(a)
Surgical Hospital of Oklahoma	Oklahoma City	80%	(a)
Community Hospital	Oklahoma City	77%	300+
Saint Francis Hospital South	Tulsa	77%	300+
Saint John Owasso	Owasso	77%	300+
Sayre Memorial Hospital	Sayre	76%	(a)
Unity Health Center	Shawnee	76%	300+
Perry Memorial Hospital	Perry	75%	(a)
Choctaw Nation Healthcare	Talihina	74%	(a)
Henryetta Medical Center	Henryetta	74%	(a)
Logan Medical Center	Guthrie	74%	(a)
Saint Mary's Regional Medical Center	Enid	74%	300+
Integris Baptist Medical Center	Oklahoma City	73%	300+
Integris Marshall County Medical Center	Madill	73%	(a)
Kingfisher Regional Hospital	Kingfisher	73%	(a)
Mercy Health Center	Oklahoma City	73%	300+
Purcell Municipal Hospital	Purcell	73%	(a)
Newman Memorial Hospital	Shattuck	72%	(a)
Integris Seminole Medical Center	Seminole	71%	(a)
Norman Regional Health System	Norman	71%	300+
Jane Phillips Medical Center	Bartlesville	70%	300+
Sequoyah Memorial Hospital	Sallisaw	70%	300+
Craig General Hospital	Vinita	69%	300+
Share Memorial Hospital	Alva	69%	(a)
W W Hastings Indian Hospital	Tahlequah	69%	300+
Cushing Regional Hospital	Cushing	68%	(a)
Deaconess Hospital	Oklahoma City	68%	300+
Integris Bass Baptist Health Center	Enid	68%	300+
Latimer County General Hospital	Wilburton	68%	(a)
O U Medical Center	Oklahoma City	68%	300+
Saint Anthony Hospital	Oklahoma City	68%	300+
Saint Francis Hospital	Tulsa	68%	300+
Integris Mayes County Medical Center	Pryor	67%	(a)
Memorial Hospital of Stilwell	Stilwell	67%	(a)
Ponca City Medical Center	Ponca City	67%	300+
Stillwater Medical Center	Stillwater	67%	300+
Duncan Regional Hospital	Duncan	66%	300+
Integris Baptist Regional Health Center	Miami	66%	300+
Memorial Hospital of Texas County	Guymon	66%	(a)
Oklahoma State University Medical Center	Tulsa	66%	300+
Pauls Valley General Hospital	Pauls Valley	66%	300+
Saint John Medical Center	Tulsa	66%	300+
Chickasaw Nation Medical Center	Ada	65%	300+
Elkview General Hospital	Hobart	65%	(a)
Integris Blackwell Regional Hospital	Blackwell	65%	(a)
Integris Canadian Valley Hospital	Yukon	65%	300+
Great Plains Regional Medical Center	Elk City	64%	300+
Jackson County Memorial Hospital	Altus	64%	300+
Comanche County Memorial Hospital	Lawton	63%	300+
Hillcrest Medical Center	Tulsa	63%	300+
Integris Clinton Regional Hospital	Clinton	63%	300+
Integris Grove Hospital	Grove	63%	300+
Integris Southwest Medical Center	Oklahoma City	63%	300+
Mercy Hospital El Reno	El Reno	63%	(a)
Southcrest Hospital	Tulsa	63%	300+
Tahlequah City Hospital	Tahlequah	63%	300+
Claremore Indian Hospital	Claremore	62%	(a)
Claremore Regional Hospital	Claremore	62%	300+
Grady Memorial Hospital	Chickasha	62%	300+
Orthopedic Hospital	Oklahoma City	62%	(a)
Southwestern Medical Center	Lawton	62%	300+
Wagoner Community Hospital	Wagoner	61%	(a)
McAlester Regional Health Center	Mcalester	60%	300+
Medical Center of Southeastern Oklahoma	Durant	60%	300+
Eastern Oklahoma Medical Center	Poteau	58%	(a)
Okmulgee Memorial Hospital	Okmulgee	57%	(a)
Valley View Regional Hospital	Ada	57%	300+
Woodward Regional Hospital	Woodward	57%	300+
Memorial Hospital & Physician Group	Frederick	56%	(a)
Mercy Memorial Health Center	Ardmore	56%	300+
McCurtain Memorial Hospital	Idabel	53%	300+
Pushmataha Cnty-TN of Antlers Hosp Auth	Antlers	52%	(a)
Midwest Regional Medical Center	Midwest City	50%	300+
Muskogee Regional Medical Center	Muskogee	47%	300+
Choctaw Memorial Hospital	Hugo	45%	(a)
Epic Medical Center	Eufaula	39%	(a)

44. Meds 'Always' Explained Before Given

Hospital Name	City	Rate	Cases
Oklahoma Heart Hospital	Oklahoma City	78%	300+
Oklahoma Spine Hospital	Oklahoma City	78%	300+
Epic Medical Center	Eufaula	75%	(a)
Tulsa Spine & Specialty Hospital	Tulsa	72%	300+
Choctaw Nation Healthcare	Talihina	71%	(a)
Newman Memorial Hospital	Shattuck	71%	(a)
Northwest Surgical Hospital	Oklahoma City	71%	(a)
Chickasaw Nation Medical Center	Ada	70%	300+
Oklahoma Center for Orthopaedic & Multi-Sp	Oklahoma City	70%	(a)
Oklahoma Surgical Hospital	Tulsa	70%	300+
Purcell Municipal Hospital	Purcell	70%	(a)
W W Hastings Indian Hospital	Tahlequah	70%	300+
Bailey Medical Center	Owasso	69%	(a)
Latimer County General Hospital	Wilburton	69%	(a)
Sequoyah Memorial Hospital	Sallisaw	68%	300+
Southwestern Regional Medical Center	Tulsa	68%	(a)
Surgical Hospital of Oklahoma	Oklahoma City	68%	(a)
Henryetta Medical Center	Henryetta	67%	(a)
Kingfisher Regional Hospital	Kingfisher	67%	(a)
McBride Clinic Orthopedic Hospital	Oklahoma City	67%	300+
Elkview General Hospital	Hobart	66%	(a)
Community Hospital	Oklahoma City	65%	300+
Integris Marshall County Medical Center	Madill	65%	(a)
Jackson County Memorial Hospital	Altus	65%	300+
Memorial Hospital of Stilwell	Stilwell	65%	300+
Claremore Indian Hospital	Claremore	64%	(a)
McCurtain Memorial Hospital	Idabel	64%	300+

NOTE: Hospital profiles are in alphabetical order by state, then city, then hospital within the city; Rankings exclude hospitals with less than 25 cases except for patient surveys which excludes hospitals with less than 100 cases; (a) 100–299 cases; (1) The number of cases is too small to be sure how well a hospital is performing; (2) The hospital indicated that the data submitted for this measure were based on a sample of cases; (3) Data was collected during a shorter time period (fewer quarters) than the maximum possible time for this measure; (4) Suppressed for one or more quarters by CMS; (5) No data is available from the hospital for this measure; (6) Fewer than 100 patients completed the HCAHPS survey. Use these rates with caution, as the number of surveys may be too low to reliably assess hospital performance; (7) Survey results are based on less than 12 months of data; (8) Survey results are not available for this reporting period; (9) No or very few patients were eligible for the HCAHPS survey. The scores shown, if any, reflect a very small number of surveys; (10) A state average was not calculated because too few hospitals in the state submitted data; (11) There were discrepancies in the data collection process; Please refer to the User's Guide for a full explanation of data.

Hospital Name	City	Rate	Cases
Orthopedic Hospital	Oklahoma City	64%	(a)
Perry Memorial Hospital	Perry	64%	(a)
Saint John Owasso	Owasso	64%	300+
McAlester Regional Health Center	Mcalester	63%	300+
Craig General Hospital	Vinita	62%	300+
Integris Baptist Regional Health Center	Miami	62%	300+
Integris Clinton Regional Hospital	Clinton	62%	300+
Lakeside Women's Hospital	Oklahoma City	62%	300+
Sayre Memorial Hospital	Sayre	62%	(a)
Duncan Regional Hospital	Duncan	61%	300+
Pauls Valley General Hospital	Pauls Valley	61%	300+
Unity Health Center	Shawnee	61%	300+
Claremore Regional Hospital	Claremore	60%	300+
Cushing Regional Hospital	Cushing	60%	(a)
Integris Canadian Valley Hospital	Yukon	60%	300+
Integris Grove Hospital	Grove	60%	300+
Integris Mayes County Medical Center	Pryor	60%	(a)
Integris Seminole Medical Center	Seminole	60%	(a)
Mercy Hospital El Reno	El Reno	60%	(a)
Saint Mary's Regional Medical Center	Enid	60%	300+
Tahlequah City Hospital	Tahlequah	60%	300+
Comanche County Memorial Hospital	Lawton	59%	300+
Deaconess Hospital	Oklahoma City	59%	300+
Integris Baptist Medical Center	Oklahoma City	59%	300+
Jane Phillips Medical Center	Bartlesville	59%	300+
Memorial Hospital of Texas County	Guymon	59%	(a)
Ponca City Medical Center	Ponca City	59%	300+
Saint Francis Hospital South	Tulsa	59%	300+
Saint John Medical Center	Tulsa	59%	300+
Valley View Regional Hospital	Ada	59%	300+
Grady Memorial Hospital	Chickasha	58%	300+
Integris Bass Baptist Health Center	Enid	58%	300+
Logan Medical Center	Guthrie	58%	(a)
Medical Center of Southeastern Oklahoma	Durant	58%	300+
Mercy Health Center	Oklahoma City	58%	300+
Norman Regional Health System	Norman	58%	300+
Stillwater Medical Center	Stillwater	58%	300+
Mercy Memorial Health Center	Ardmore	57%	300+
O U Medical Center	Oklahoma City	57%	300+
Oklahoma State University Medical Center	Tulsa	57%	300+
Saint Anthony Hospital	Oklahoma City	57%	300+
Integris Blackwell Regional Hospital	Blackwell	56%	(a)
Share Memorial Hospital	Alva	56%	(a)
Southwestern Medical Center	Lawton	56%	300+
Wagoner Community Hospital	Wagoner	56%	(a)
Woodward Regional Hospital	Woodward	56%	300+
Eastern Oklahoma Medical Center	Poteau	55%	(a)
Great Plains Regional Medical Center	Elk City	55%	300+
Integris Southwest Medical Center	Oklahoma City	55%	300+
Saint Francis Hospital	Tulsa	55%	300+
Hillcrest Medical Center	Tulsa	52%	300+
Midwest Regional Medical Center	Midwest City	52%	300+
Memorial Hospital & Physician Group	Frederick	51%	(a)
Southcrest Hospital	Tulsa	49%	300+
Okmulgee Memorial Hospital	Okmulgee	48%	(a)
Pushmataha Cnty-TN of Antlers Hosp Auth	Antlers	48%	(a)
Muskogee Regional Medical Center	Muskogee	47%	300+
Choctaw Memorial Hospital	Hugo	46%	(a)

45. Nurses 'Always' Communicated Well

Hospital Name	City	Rate	Cases
Oklahoma Heart Hospital	Oklahoma City	93%	300+
Oklahoma Center for Orthopaedic & Multi-Sp	Oklahoma City	89%	(a)
Oklahoma Spine Hospital	Oklahoma City	88%	300+
Northwest Surgical Hospital	Oklahoma City	86%	(a)
Purcell Municipal Hospital	Purcell	86%	(a)
Integris Seminole Medical Center	Seminole	85%	(a)
Tulsa Spine & Specialty Hospital	Tulsa	85%	300+
Oklahoma Surgical Hospital	Tulsa	84%	300+
Lakeside Women's Hospital	Oklahoma City	83%	300+
Latimer County General Hospital	Wilburton	83%	(a)
Surgical Hospital of Oklahoma	Oklahoma City	83%	(a)
Bailey Medical Center	Owasso	82%	(a)
Henryetta Medical Center	Henryetta	82%	(a)
Perry Memorial Hospital	Perry	82%	(a)
W W Hastings Indian Hospital	Tahlequah	82%	300+
Craig General Hospital	Vinita	81%	300+
Elkview General Hospital	Hobart	81%	(a)
Integris Marshall County Medical Center	Madill	81%	(a)
Kingfisher Regional Hospital	Kingfisher	81%	(a)
McBride Clinic Orthopedic Hospital	Oklahoma City	81%	300+
Sequoyah Memorial Hospital	Sallisaw	81%	300+
Share Memorial Hospital	Alva	81%	(a)
Chickasaw Nation Medical Center	Ada	80%	300+
Community Hospital	Oklahoma City	80%	300+
Choctaw Nation Healthcare	Talihina	79%	(a)
Saint John Owasso	Owasso	79%	300+
Southwestern Regional Medical Center	Tulsa	79%	(a)
Integris Baptist Regional Health Center	Miami	78%	300+
Integris Bass Baptist Health Center	Enid	78%	300+
Jackson County Memorial Hospital	Altus	78%	300+
Pauls Valley General Hospital	Pauls Valley	78%	300+
Saint Mary's Regional Medical Center	Enid	78%	300+
Unity Health Center	Shawnee	78%	300+
Integris Mayes County Medical Center	Pryor	77%	(a)
McAlester Regional Health Center	Mcalester	77%	300+
Memorial Hospital of Texas County	Guymon	77%	(a)
Newman Memorial Hospital	Shattuck	77%	(a)
Ponca City Medical Center	Ponca City	77%	300+
Saint Francis Hospital South	Tulsa	77%	300+
Sayre Memorial Hospital	Sayre	77%	(a)
Comanche County Memorial Hospital	Lawton	76%	300+
Cushing Regional Hospital	Cushing	76%	(a)
Grady Memorial Hospital	Chickasha	76%	300+
Integris Canadian Valley Hospital	Yukon	76%	300+
Jane Phillips Medical Center	Bartlesville	76%	300+
Mercy Health Center	Oklahoma City	76%	300+
Saint Anthony Hospital	Oklahoma City	76%	300+
Wagoner Community Hospital	Wagoner	76%	(a)
Duncan Regional Hospital	Duncan	75%	300+
Integris Baptist Medical Center	Oklahoma City	75%	300+
Logan Medical Center	Guthrie	75%	(a)
McCurtain Memorial Hospital	Idabel	75%	300+
Mercy Hospital El Reno	El Reno	75%	(a)
Mercy Memorial Health Center	Ardmore	75%	300+
Norman Regional Health System	Norman	75%	300+
Saint Francis Hospital	Tulsa	75%	300+
Tahlequah City Hospital	Tahlequah	75%	300+
Valley View Regional Hospital	Ada	75%	300+
Integris Blackwell Regional Hospital	Blackwell	74%	(a)
Memorial Hospital of Stilwell	Stilwell	74%	300+
O U Medical Center	Oklahoma City	74%	300+
Saint John Medical Center	Tulsa	74%	300+
Stillwater Medical Center	Stillwater	74%	300+
Eastern Oklahoma Medical Center	Poteau	73%	(a)
Integris Clinton Regional Hospital	Clinton	73%	300+
Integris Grove Hospital	Grove	73%	300+
Claremore Indian Hospital	Claremore	72%	(a)
Deaconess Hospital	Oklahoma City	72%	300+
Medical Center of Southeastern Oklahoma	Durant	72%	300+
Okmulgee Memorial Hospital	Okmulgee	72%	(a)
Orthopedic Hospital	Oklahoma City	72%	(a)
Claremore Regional Hospital	Claremore	71%	300+
Great Plains Regional Medical Center	Elk City	71%	300+
Integris Southwest Medical Center	Oklahoma City	71%	300+
Memorial Hospital & Physician Group	Frederick	71%	(a)
Pushmataha Cnty-TN of Antlers Hosp Auth	Antlers	71%	(a)
Woodward Regional Hospital	Woodward	71%	300+
Hillcrest Medical Center	Tulsa	70%	300+
Oklahoma State University Medical Center	Tulsa	69%	300+
Southwestern Medical Center	Lawton	69%	300+
Southcrest Hospital	Tulsa	68%	300+
Epic Medical Center	Eufaula	67%	(a)
Midwest Regional Medical Center	Midwest City	65%	300+
Muskogee Regional Medical Center	Muskogee	64%	300+
Choctaw Memorial Hospital	Hugo	62%	(a)

46. Pain 'Always' Well Controlled

Hospital Name	City	Rate	Cases
Oklahoma Heart Hospital	Oklahoma City	86%	300+
Epic Medical Center	Eufaula	83%	(a)
Oklahoma Spine Hospital	Oklahoma City	83%	300+
Latimer County General Hospital	Wilburton	81%	(a)
Henryetta Medical Center	Henryetta	78%	(a)
Lakeside Women's Hospital	Oklahoma City	78%	300+
Kingfisher Regional Hospital	Kingfisher	77%	(a)
Newman Memorial Hospital	Shattuck	77%	(a)
Northwest Surgical Hospital	Oklahoma City	77%	(a)
Oklahoma Center for Orthopaedic & Multi-Sp	Oklahoma City	77%	(a)
Tulsa Spine & Specialty Hospital	Tulsa	77%	300+
McBride Clinic Orthopedic Hospital	Oklahoma City	76%	300+
Oklahoma Surgical Hospital	Tulsa	76%	300+
Sayre Memorial Hospital	Sayre	76%	(a)
Share Memorial Hospital	Alva	75%	(a)
Surgical Hospital of Oklahoma	Oklahoma City	75%	(a)
Unity Health Center	Shawnee	75%	300+
W W Hastings Indian Hospital	Tahlequah	75%	300+
Chickasaw Nation Medical Center	Ada	74%	300+
Saint John Owasso	Owasso	74%	300+
Bailey Medical Center	Owasso	73%	(a)
Elkview General Hospital	Hobart	73%	(a)
Integris Baptist Regional Health Center	Miami	73%	300+
Integris Canadian Valley Hospital	Yukon	73%	300+
Mercy Health Center	Oklahoma City	73%	300+
Purcell Municipal Hospital	Purcell	73%	(a)
Craig General Hospital	Vinita	72%	300+
Cushing Regional Hospital	Cushing	72%	(a)
McAlester Regional Health Center	Mcalester	72%	300+
Memorial Hospital of Stilwell	Stilwell	72%	300+
Pauls Valley General Hospital	Pauls Valley	72%	300+
Southwestern Regional Medical Center	Tulsa	72%	(a)
Comanche County Memorial Hospital	Lawton	71%	300+
Jackson County Memorial Hospital	Altus	71%	300+
Logan Medical Center	Guthrie	71%	(a)
Memorial Hospital of Texas County	Guymon	71%	(a)
Norman Regional Health System	Norman	71%	300+
Perry Memorial Hospital	Perry	71%	(a)
Saint Anthony Hospital	Oklahoma City	71%	300+
Saint Mary's Regional Medical Center	Enid	71%	300+
Sequoyah Memorial Hospital	Sallisaw	71%	300+
Valley View Regional Hospital	Ada	71%	300+
Choctaw Nation Healthcare	Talihina	70%	(a)
Deaconess Hospital	Oklahoma City	70%	300+
Integris Baptist Medical Center	Oklahoma City	70%	300+
Integris Mayes County Medical Center	Pryor	70%	(a)
Ponca City Medical Center	Ponca City	70%	300+
Saint Francis Hospital South	Tulsa	70%	300+
Saint John Medical Center	Tulsa	70%	300+
Community Hospital	Oklahoma City	69%	300+
Duncan Regional Hospital	Duncan	69%	300+
Eastern Oklahoma Medical Center	Poteau	69%	(a)
Integris Bass Baptist Health Center	Enid	69%	300+
Integris Grove Hospital	Grove	69%	300+
Integris Southwest Medical Center	Oklahoma City	69%	300+
Jane Phillips Medical Center	Bartlesville	69%	300+
Mercy Hospital El Reno	El Reno	69%	(a)
O U Medical Center	Oklahoma City	69%	300+
Tahlequah City Hospital	Tahlequah	69%	300+
Claremore Regional Hospital	Claremore	68%	300+
Integris Marshall County Medical Center	Madill	68%	(a)
Integris Clinton Regional Hospital	Clinton	67%	300+
Mercy Memorial Health Center	Ardmore	67%	300+
Saint Francis Hospital	Tulsa	67%	300+
Stillwater Medical Center	Stillwater	67%	300+
Wagoner Community Hospital	Wagoner	67%	(a)
Claremore Indian Hospital	Claremore	66%	(a)
Hillcrest Medical Center	Tulsa	66%	300+
Integris Blackwell Regional Hospital	Blackwell	66%	(a)
McCurtain Memorial Hospital	Idabel	66%	300+
Okmulgee Memorial Hospital	Okmulgee	66%	(a)
Southcrest Hospital	Tulsa	66%	300+
Southwestern Medical Center	Lawton	66%	300+
Woodward Regional Hospital	Woodward	66%	300+
Great Plains Regional Medical Center	Elk City	65%	300+
Integris Seminole Medical Center	Seminole	65%	(a)
Medical Center of Southeastern Oklahoma	Durant	65%	300+
Oklahoma State University Medical Center	Tulsa	65%	300+
Pushmataha Cnty-TN of Antlers Hosp Auth	Antlers	65%	(a)
Grady Memorial Hospital	Chickasha	64%	300+
Midwest Regional Medical Center	Midwest City	62%	300+
Memorial Hospital & Physician Group	Frederick	60%	(a)
Orthopedic Hospital	Oklahoma City	60%	(a)
Muskogee Regional Medical Center	Muskogee	59%	300+
Choctaw Memorial Hospital	Hugo	57%	(a)

47. Room and Bathroom 'Always' Clean

Hospital Name	City	Rate	Cases
Oklahoma Spine Hospital	Oklahoma City	91%	300+
Oklahoma Heart Hospital	Oklahoma City	87%	300+
Tulsa Spine & Specialty Hospital	Tulsa	87%	300+
Oklahoma Center for Orthopaedic & Multi-Sp	Oklahoma City	86%	(a)
Northwest Surgical Hospital	Oklahoma City	85%	(a)
Oklahoma Surgical Hospital	Tulsa	84%	300+
Sequoyah Memorial Hospital	Sallisaw	84%	300+
Orthopedic Hospital	Oklahoma City	83%	(a)
Purcell Municipal Hospital	Purcell	83%	(a)
Community Hospital	Oklahoma City	82%	300+
Integris Seminole Medical Center	Seminole	82%	(a)
Latimer County General Hospital	Wilburton	82%	(a)
Perry Memorial Hospital	Perry	82%	(a)
Choctaw Nation Healthcare	Talihina	79%	(a)
Kingfisher Regional Hospital	Kingfisher	79%	(a)
Southwestern Regional Medical Center	Tulsa	79%	(a)
Surgical Hospital of Oklahoma	Oklahoma City	79%	(a)
Integris Clinton Regional Hospital	Clinton	78%	300+
Jane Phillips Medical Center	Bartlesville	78%	300+
Sayre Memorial Hospital	Sayre	78%	(a)
Bailey Medical Center	Owasso	77%	(a)
Elkview General Hospital	Hobart	77%	(a)
Lakeside Women's Hospital	Oklahoma City	77%	300+
Share Memorial Hospital	Alva	77%	(a)
McAlester Regional Health Center	Mcalester	76%	300+
McBride Clinic Orthopedic Hospital	Oklahoma City	76%	300+
Pauls Valley General Hospital	Pauls Valley	76%	300+
Henryetta Medical Center	Henryetta	75%	(a)
Saint John Owasso	Owasso	75%	300+
Integris Marshall County Medical Center	Madill	74%	(a)
Mercy Hospital El Reno	El Reno	74%	(a)
Unity Health Center	Shawnee	74%	300+
Craig General Hospital	Vinita	73%	300+

NOTE: Hospital profiles are in alphabetical order by state, then city, then hospital within the city; Rankings exclude hospitals with less than 25 cases except for patient surveys which excludes hospitals with less than 100 cases; (a) 100–299 cases; (1) The number of cases is too small to be sure how well a hospital is performing; (2) The hospital indicated that the data submitted for this measure were based on a sample of cases; (3) Data was collected during a shorter time period (fewer quarters) than the maximum possible time for this measure; (4) Suppressed for one or more quarters by CMS; (5) No data is available from the hospital for this measure; (6) Fewer than 100 patients completed the HCAHPS survey. Use these rates with caution, as the number of surveys may be too low to reliably assess hospital performance; (7) Survey results are based on less than 12 months of data; (8) Survey results are not available for this reporting period; (9) No or very few patients were eligible for the HCAHPS survey. The scores shown, if any, reflect a very small number of surveys; (10) A state average was not calculated because too few hospitals in the state submitted data; (11) There were discrepancies in the data collection process; Please refer to the User's Guide for a full explanation of data.

Memorial Hospital of Texas County	Guymon	73%	(a)
Jackson County Memorial Hospital	Altus	72%	300+
Saint Francis Hospital South	Tulsa	72%	300+
Integris Bass Baptist Health Center	Enid	71%	300+
Integris Blackwell Regional Hospital	Blackwell	71%	(a)
McCurtain Memorial Hospital	Idabel	71%	300+
Memorial Hospital of Stilwell	Stilwell	71%	300+
Pushmataha Cnty-TN of Antlers Hosp Auth	Antlers	71%	(a)
Integris Baptist Medical Center	Oklahoma City	70%	300+
Newman Memorial Hospital	Shattuck	70%	(a)
Saint Francis Hospital	Tulsa	70%	300+
Wagoner Community Hospital	Wagoner	70%	(a)
Chickasaw Nation Medical Center	Ada	69%	300+
Claremore Regional Hospital	Claremore	69%	300+
Cushing Regional Hospital	Cushing	69%	(a)
Mercy Memorial Health Center	Ardmore	69%	300+
Norman Regional Health System	Norman	69%	300+
Saint Anthony Hospital	Oklahoma City	69%	300+
Saint Mary's Regional Medical Center	Enid	69%	300+
Duncan Regional Hospital	Duncan	68%	300+
Eastern Oklahoma Medical Center	Poteau	68%	(a)
Integris Grove Hospital	Grove	68%	300+
Integris Southwest Medical Center	Oklahoma City	68%	300+
Medical Center of Southeastern Oklahoma	Durant	68%	300+
Mercy Health Center	Oklahoma City	68%	300+
Valley View Regional Hospital	Ada	68%	300+
Woodward Regional Hospital	Woodward	68%	300+
Grady Memorial Hospital	Chickasha	67%	300+
Great Plains Regional Medical Center	Elk City	67%	300+
Integris Baptist Regional Health Center	Miami	67%	300+
Logan Medical Center	Guthrie	67%	(a)
Tahlequah City Hospital	Tahlequah	67%	300+
Ponca City Medical Center	Ponca City	66%	300+
Choctaw Memorial Hospital	Hugo	65%	(a)
Deaconess Hospital	Oklahoma City	65%	300+
Stillwater Medical Center	Stillwater	65%	300+
Claremore Indian Hospital	Claremore	64%	(a)
Integris Canadian Valley Hospital	Yukon	64%	300+
Saint John Medical Center	Tulsa	64%	300+
Comanche County Memorial Hospital	Lawton	63%	300+
Epic Medical Center	Eufaula	63%	(a)
Integris Mayes County Medical Center	Pryor	63%	(a)
Oklahoma State University Medical Center	Tulsa	63%	300+
Memorial Hospital & Physician Group	Frederick	62%	(a)
Hillcrest Medical Center	Tulsa	61%	300+
Southwestern Medical Center	Lawton	61%	300+
O U Medical Center	Oklahoma City	59%	300+
W W Hastings Indian Hospital	Tahlequah	59%	300+
Okmulgee Memorial Hospital	Okmulgee	58%	(a)
Muskogee Regional Medical Center	Muskogee	57%	300+
Southcrest Hospital	Tulsa	57%	300+
Midwest Regional Medical Center	Midwest City	51%	300+

48. Timely Help 'Always' Received

Hospital Name	City	Rate	Cases
Oklahoma Heart Hospital	Oklahoma City	90%	300+
Oklahoma Center for Orthopaedic & Multi-Sp	Oklahoma City	84%	(a)
Oklahoma Spine Hospital	Oklahoma City	83%	300+
Latimer County General Hospital	Wilburton	81%	(a)
Surgical Hospital of Oklahoma	Oklahoma City	80%	(a)
Tulsa Spine & Specialty Hospital	Tulsa	79%	300+
Northwest Surgical Hospital	Oklahoma City	77%	(a)
Choctaw Nation Healthcare	Talihina	75%	(a)
McBride Clinic Orthopedic Hospital	Oklahoma City	75%	300+
Share Memorial Hospital	Alva	75%	(a)
W W Hastings Indian Hospital	Tahlequah	75%	300+
Integris Marshall County Medical Center	Madill	74%	(a)
McCurtain Memorial Hospital	Idabel	74%	300+
Oklahoma Surgical Hospital	Tulsa	74%	300+
Sequoyah Memorial Hospital	Sallisaw	74%	300+
Wagoner Community Hospital	Wagoner	74%	(a)
Elkview General Hospital	Hobart	73%	(a)
Henryetta Medical Center	Henryetta	73%	(a)
Integris Seminole Medical Center	Seminole	73%	(a)
Newman Memorial Hospital	Shattuck	73%	(a)
Community Hospital	Oklahoma City	72%	300+
Orthopedic Hospital	Oklahoma City	72%	(a)
Perry Memorial Hospital	Perry	72%	(a)
Chickasaw Nation Medical Center	Ada	71%	300+
Southwestern Regional Medical Center	Tulsa	71%	(a)
Integris Mayes County Medical Center	Pryor	70%	(a)
Sayre Memorial Hospital	Sayre	70%	(a)
Bailey Medical Center	Owasso	69%	(a)
Claremore Indian Hospital	Claremore	69%	(a)
Jackson County Memorial Hospital	Altus	69%	300+
Kingfisher Regional Hospital	Kingfisher	69%	(a)
Pauls Valley General Hospital	Pauls Valley	69%	300+
Integris Baptist Regional Health Center	Miami	68%	300+
Integris Bass Baptist Health Center	Enid	68%	300+
McAlester Regional Health Center	Mcalester	68%	300+
Saint Francis Hospital South	Tulsa	68%	300+
Unity Health Center	Shawnee	68%	300+
Valley View Regional Hospital	Ada	68%	300+
Craig General Hospital	Vinita	67%	300+
Cushing Regional Hospital	Cushing	67%	(a)
Memorial Hospital of Texas County	Guymon	67%	(a)
Ponca City Medical Center	Ponca City	67%	300+
Epic Medical Center	Eufaula	66%	(a)
Integris Clinton Regional Hospital	Clinton	66%	300+
Memorial Hospital & Physician Group	Frederick	66%	(a)
Memorial Hospital of Stilwell	Stilwell	66%	300+
Mercy Hospital El Reno	El Reno	66%	(a)
Mercy Memorial Health Center	Ardmore	66%	300+
Okmulgee Memorial Hospital	Okmulgee	66%	(a)
Purcell Municipal Hospital	Purcell	66%	(a)
Saint John Owasso	Owasso	66%	300+
Comanche County Memorial Hospital	Lawton	65%	300+
Duncan Regional Hospital	Duncan	65%	300+
Logan Medical Center	Guthrie	65%	(a)
Saint Anthony Hospital	Oklahoma City	65%	300+
Saint Mary's Regional Medical Center	Enid	65%	300+
Integris Baptist Medical Center	Oklahoma City	64%	300+
Integris Blackwell Regional Hospital	Blackwell	64%	(a)
Jane Phillips Medical Center	Bartlesville	64%	300+
Eastern Oklahoma Medical Center	Poteau	63%	(a)
Norman Regional Health System	Norman	63%	300+
Pushmataha Cnty-TN of Antlers Hosp Auth	Antlers	63%	(a)
Stillwater Medical Center	Stillwater	63%	300+
Tahlequah City Hospital	Tahlequah	63%	300+
Woodward Regional Hospital	Woodward	63%	300+
Grady Memorial Hospital	Chickasha	62%	300+
Lakeside Women's Hospital	Oklahoma City	62%	300+
Great Plains Regional Medical Center	Elk City	61%	300+
Mercy Health Center	Oklahoma City	61%	300+
Claremore Regional Hospital	Claremore	60%	300+
Integris Grove Hospital	Grove	59%	300+
Saint Francis Hospital	Tulsa	59%	300+
Deaconess Hospital	Oklahoma City	58%	300+
Integris Canadian Valley Hospital	Yukon	57%	300+
O U Medical Center	Oklahoma City	57%	300+
Saint John Medical Center	Tulsa	57%	300+
Medical Center of Southeastern Oklahoma	Durant	56%	300+
Southwestern Medical Center	Lawton	56%	300+
Hillcrest Medical Center	Tulsa	55%	300+
Integris Southwest Medical Center	Oklahoma City	55%	300+
Choctaw Memorial Hospital	Hugo	53%	(a)
Southcrest Hospital	Tulsa	52%	300+
Midwest Regional Medical Center	Midwest City	49%	300+
Oklahoma State University Medical Center	Tulsa	49%	300+
Muskogee Regional Medical Center	Muskogee	48%	300+

49. Would Definitely Recommend Hospital

Hospital Name	City	Rate	Cases
Oklahoma Heart Hospital	Oklahoma City	99%	300+
Oklahoma Spine Hospital	Oklahoma City	93%	300+
Tulsa Spine & Specialty Hospital	Tulsa	93%	300+
Southwestern Regional Medical Center	Tulsa	92%	(a)
Oklahoma Surgical Hospital	Tulsa	88%	300+
McBride Clinic Orthopedic Hospital	Oklahoma City	87%	300+
Lakeside Women's Hospital	Oklahoma City	86%	300+
Oklahoma Center for Orthopaedic & Multi-Sp	Oklahoma City	86%	(a)
Bailey Medical Center	Owasso	85%	(a)
Saint John Owasso	Owasso	84%	300+
Community Hospital	Oklahoma City	83%	300+
Northwest Surgical Hospital	Oklahoma City	83%	(a)
Mercy Health Center	Oklahoma City	81%	300+
Newman Memorial Hospital	Shattuck	80%	(a)
Saint Francis Hospital South	Tulsa	80%	300+
Surgical Hospital of Oklahoma	Oklahoma City	80%	(a)
Choctaw Nation Healthcare	Talihina	79%	(a)
Integris Baptist Medical Center	Oklahoma City	77%	300+
Integris Bass Baptist Health Center	Enid	75%	300+
Kingfisher Regional Hospital	Kingfisher	74%	(a)
Saint Anthony Hospital	Oklahoma City	74%	300+
Saint Francis Hospital	Tulsa	74%	300+
Saint Mary's Regional Medical Center	Enid	74%	300+
Sayre Memorial Hospital	Sayre	74%	(a)
Henryetta Medical Center	Henryetta	73%	(a)
Saint John Medical Center	Tulsa	73%	300+
Norman Regional Health System	Norman	72%	300+
Purcell Municipal Hospital	Purcell	72%	(a)
Deaconess Hospital	Oklahoma City	71%	300+
Integris Canadian Valley Hospital	Yukon	71%	300+
Logan Medical Center	Guthrie	71%	(a)
Stillwater Medical Center	Stillwater	71%	300+
Chickasaw Nation Medical Center	Ada	70%	300+
Integris Marshall County Medical Center	Madill	70%	(a)
Integris Seminole Medical Center	Seminole	70%	(a)
O U Medical Center	Oklahoma City	70%	300+
W W Hastings Indian Hospital	Tahlequah	70%	300+
Comanche County Memorial Hospital	Lawton	69%	300+
Craig General Hospital	Vinita	69%	300+
Orthopedic Hospital	Oklahoma City	69%	(a)
Unity Health Center	Shawnee	69%	300+
Elkview General Hospital	Hobart	68%	(a)
Memorial Hospital of Stilwell	Stilwell	68%	300+
Oklahoma State University Medical Center	Tulsa	68%	300+
Southcrest Hospital	Tulsa	68%	300+
Tahlequah City Hospital	Tahlequah	68%	300+
Cushing Regional Hospital	Cushing	67%	(a)
Latimer County General Hospital	Wilburton	67%	(a)
Perry Memorial Hospital	Perry	67%	(a)
Wagoner Community Hospital	Wagoner	67%	(a)
Sequoyah Memorial Hospital	Sallisaw	66%	300+
Share Memorial Hospital	Alva	66%	(a)
Southwestern Medical Center	Lawton	66%	300+
Claremore Regional Hospital	Claremore	64%	300+
Duncan Regional Hospital	Duncan	64%	300+
Integris Blackwell Regional Hospital	Blackwell	64%	(a)
Jane Phillips Medical Center	Bartlesville	64%	300+
Integris Clinton Regional Hospital	Clinton	63%	300+
Integris Grove Hospital	Grove	63%	300+
Integris Southwest Medical Center	Oklahoma City	63%	300+
Mercy Hospital El Reno	El Reno	63%	(a)
Hillcrest Medical Center	Tulsa	62%	300+
Jackson County Memorial Hospital	Altus	62%	300+
Medical Center of Southeastern Oklahoma	Durant	62%	300+
Pauls Valley General Hospital	Pauls Valley	62%	300+
Eastern Oklahoma Medical Center	Poteau	61%	(a)
Great Plains Regional Medical Center	Elk City	61%	300+
Integris Baptist Regional Health Center	Miami	61%	300+
McAlester Regional Health Center	Mcalester	60%	300+
Memorial Hospital of Texas County	Guymon	60%	(a)
Ponca City Medical Center	Ponca City	60%	300+
Integris Mayes County Medical Center	Pryor	58%	(a)
Mercy Memorial Health Center	Ardmore	58%	300+
Valley View Regional Hospital	Ada	58%	300+
Claremore Indian Hospital	Claremore	57%	(a)
Grady Memorial Hospital	Chickasha	57%	300+
Memorial Hospital & Physician Group	Frederick	57%	(a)
Pushmataha Cnty-TN of Antlers Hosp Auth	Antlers	56%	(a)
Woodward Regional Hospital	Woodward	54%	300+
McCurtain Memorial Hospital	Idabel	53%	300+
Okmulgee Memorial Hospital	Okmulgee	51%	(a)
Choctaw Memorial Hospital	Hugo	50%	(a)
Midwest Regional Medical Center	Midwest City	50%	300+
Muskogee Regional Medical Center	Muskogee	48%	300+
Epic Medical Center	Eufaula	47%	(a)

NOTE: Hospital profiles are in alphabetical order by state, then city, then hospital within the city; Rankings exclude hospitals with less than 25 cases except for patient surveys which excludes hospitals with less than 100 cases; (a) 100–299 cases; (1) The number of cases is too small to be sure how well a hospital is performing; (2) The hospital indicated that the data submitted for this measure were based on a sample of cases; (3) Data was collected during a shorter time period (fewer quarters) than the maximum possible time for this measure; (4) Suppressed for one or more quarters by CMS; (5) No data is available from the hospital for this measure; (6) Fewer than 100 patients completed the HCAHPS survey. Use these rates with caution, as the number of surveys may be too low to reliably assess hospital performance; (7) Survey results are based on less than 12 months of data; (8) Survey results are not available for this reporting period; (9) No or very few patients were eligible for the HCAHPS survey. The scores shown, if any, reflect a very small number of surveys; (10) A state average was not calculated because too few hospitals in the state submitted data; (11) There were discrepancies in the data collection process; Please refer to the User's Guide for a full explanation of data.

Chickasaw Nation Medical Center

1921 Stonecipher Blvd Phone: 580-436-3980
Ada, OK 74820
URL: www.chickasaw.net
Type: Acute Care Hospitals Emergency Services: Yes
Ownership: Government - Local

Measure	Cases	This Hosp.	State Avg.	U.S. Avg.
Heart Attack Care				
ACE Inhibitor or ARB for LVSD[3]	0	-	95%	96%
Aspirin at Arrival[3]	0	-	98%	99%
Aspirin at Discharge[1,3]	1	100%	98%	98%
Beta Blocker at Discharge[1,3]	1	100%	98%	98%
Fibrinolytic Medication Timing[1,3]	1	0%	42%	55%
PCI Within 90 Minutes of Arrival[3]	0	-	88%	90%
Smoking Cessation Advice[3]	0	-	100%	99%
Chest Pain/Possible Heart Attack Care				
Aspirin at Arrival	-	-	94%	95%
Median Time to ECG (minutes)	-	-	9	8
Median Time to Transfer (minutes)	-	-	75	61
Fibrinolytic Medication Timing	-	-	50%	54%
Heart Failure Care				
ACE Inhibitor or ARB for LVSD[1]	7	57%	94%	94%
Discharge Instructions	45	91%	85%	88%
Evaluation of LVS Function	45	84%	94%	98%
Smoking Cessation Advice[1]	7	86%	97%	98%
Pneumonia Care				
Appropriate Initial Antibiotic	54	85%	91%	92%
Blood Culture Timing	48	98%	96%	96%
Influenza Vaccine[1]	24	92%	89%	91%
Initial Antibiotic Timing	54	96%	95%	95%
Pneumococcal Vaccine	29	69%	91%	93%
Smoking Cessation Advice	35	63%	95%	97%
Surgical Care Improvement Project				
Appropriate VTP Within 24 Hours	26	100%	91%	92%
Appropriate Hair Removal	130	100%	100%	99%
Appropriate Beta Blocker Usage[1]	23	35%	91%	93%
Controlled Postoperative Blood Glucose	0	-	95%	93%
Prophylactic Antibiotic Timing	99	91%	97%	97%
Prophylactic Antibiotic Timing (Outpatient)	-	-	93%	92%
Prophylactic Antibiotic Selection	99	99%	98%	97%
Prophylactic Antibiotic Select. (Outpatient)	-	-	95%	94%
Prophylactic Antibiotic Stopped	98	89%	94%	94%
Recommended VTP Ordered	28	93%	94%	94%
Urinary Catheter Removal[1]	6	83%	87%	90%
Children's Asthma Care				
Received Systemic Corticosteroids	-	-	-	100%
Received Home Management Plan	-	-	-	71%
Received Reliever Medication	-	-	-	100%
Use of Medical Imaging				
Combination Abdominal CT Scan	-	-	0.372	0.191
Combination Chest CT Scan	-	-	0.134	0.054
Follow-up Mammogram/Ultrasound	-	-	8%	8.4%
MRI for Low Back Pain	-	-	34.3%	32.7%
Survey of Patients' Hospital Experiences				
Area Around Room 'Always' Quiet at Night	300+	60%	-	58%
Doctors 'Always' Communicated Well	300+	85%	-	80%
Home Recovery Information Given	300+	85%	-	82%
Hospital Given 9 or 10 on 10 Point Scale	300+	65%	-	67%
Meds 'Always' Explained Before Given	300+	70%	-	60%
Nurses 'Always' Communicated Well	300+	80%	-	76%
Pain 'Always' Well Controlled	300+	74%	-	69%
Room and Bathroom 'Always' Clean	300+	69%	-	71%
Timely Help 'Always' Received	300+	71%	-	64%
Would Definitely Recommend Hospital	300+	70%	-	69%

Valley View Regional Hospital

430 North Monta Vista Phone: 580-421-6074
Ada, OK 74820 Fax: 580-421-1386
URL: www.valleyviewregional.org
Type: Acute Care Hospitals Emergency Services: Yes
Ownership: Voluntary Non-Profit - Private Beds: 180
Key Personnel:
CEO/President. . . . . Ronald Webb
Chief of Medical Staff . . . . James R Powers, MD
Radiology. . . . . John Alcini
Patient Relations . . . . Jackye Ward, MS/RN

Measure	Cases	This Hosp.	State Avg.	U.S. Avg.
Heart Attack Care				
ACE Inhibitor or ARB for LVSD	0	-	95%	96%
Aspirin at Arrival[1]	23	96%	98%	99%
Aspirin at Discharge[1]	13	92%	98%	98%
Beta Blocker at Discharge[1]	13	100%	98%	98%
Fibrinolytic Medication Timing	0	-	42%	55%
PCI Within 90 Minutes of Arrival	0	-	88%	90%
Smoking Cessation Advice[1]	3	100%	100%	99%
Chest Pain/Possible Heart Attack Care				
Aspirin at Arrival	63	98%	94%	95%
Median Time to ECG (minutes)	62	12	9	8
Median Time to Transfer (minutes)[3]	0	-	75	61
Fibrinolytic Medication Timing[1]	12	42%	50%	54%
Heart Failure Care				
ACE Inhibitor or ARB for LVSD[1]	16	100%	94%	94%
Discharge Instructions	51	71%	85%	88%
Evaluation of LVS Function	70	93%	94%	98%
Smoking Cessation Advice[1]	18	89%	97%	98%
Pneumonia Care				
Appropriate Initial Antibiotic	82	87%	91%	92%
Blood Culture Timing	101	98%	96%	96%
Influenza Vaccine	90	70%	89%	91%
Initial Antibiotic Timing	109	99%	95%	95%
Pneumococcal Vaccine	109	69%	91%	93%
Smoking Cessation Advice	44	98%	95%	97%
Surgical Care Improvement Project				
Appropriate VTP Within 24 Hours	145	86%	91%	92%
Appropriate Hair Removal	316	100%	100%	99%
Appropriate Beta Blocker Usage	85	99%	91%	93%
Controlled Postoperative Blood Glucose	0	-	95%	93%
Prophylactic Antibiotic Timing	192	93%	97%	97%
Prophylactic Antibiotic Timing (Outpatient)	196	83%	93%	92%
Prophylactic Antibiotic Selection	191	99%	98%	97%
Prophylactic Antibiotic Select. (Outpatient)	195	94%	95%	94%
Prophylactic Antibiotic Stopped	186	81%	94%	94%
Recommended VTP Ordered	145	88%	94%	94%
Urinary Catheter Removal	31	42%	87%	90%
Children's Asthma Care				
Received Systemic Corticosteroids	-	-	-	100%
Received Home Management Plan	-	-	-	71%
Received Reliever Medication	-	-	-	100%
Use of Medical Imaging				
Combination Abdominal CT Scan	743	0.614	0.372	0.191
Combination Chest CT Scan	256	0.000	0.134	0.054
Follow-up Mammogram/Ultrasound	781	7.0%	8%	8.4%
MRI for Low Back Pain	136	36.0%	34.3%	32.7%
Survey of Patients' Hospital Experiences				
Area Around Room 'Always' Quiet at Night	300+	60%	-	58%
Doctors 'Always' Communicated Well	300+	78%	-	80%
Home Recovery Information Given	300+	81%	-	82%
Hospital Given 9 or 10 on 10 Point Scale	300+	57%	-	67%
Meds 'Always' Explained Before Given	300+	59%	-	60%
Nurses 'Always' Communicated Well	300+	75%	-	76%
Pain 'Always' Well Controlled	300+	71%	-	69%
Room and Bathroom 'Always' Clean	300+	68%	-	71%
Timely Help 'Always' Received	300+	68%	-	64%
Would Definitely Recommend Hospital	300+	58%	-	69%

Jackson County Memorial Hospital

1200 East Pecan Phone: 580-482-4781
Altus, OK 73523 Fax: 580-379-5509
URL: www.jcmh.com
Type: Acute Care Hospitals Emergency Services: Yes
Ownership: Govt - Hospital Dist/Auth Beds: 156
Key Personnel:
CEO/President. . . . . William G Wilson
Chief of Medical Staff . . . . Richard Katseros, MD
Infection Control. . . . . Dorothy Butler
Operating Room. . . . . Mary Stuard
Quality Assurance . . . . Jim King
Emergency Room . . . . Cheryl Simco
Intensive Care Unit. . . . . Becky Braddock
Patient Relations . . . . Bonnie McAskill

Measure	Cases	This Hosp.	State Avg.	U.S. Avg.
Heart Attack Care				
ACE Inhibitor or ARB for LVSD[1]	4	100%	95%	96%
Aspirin at Arrival[1]	22	86%	98%	99%
Aspirin at Discharge[1]	12	92%	98%	98%
Beta Blocker at Discharge[1]	12	92%	98%	98%
Fibrinolytic Medication Timing	0	-	42%	55%
PCI Within 90 Minutes of Arrival	0	-	88%	90%
Smoking Cessation Advice[1]	3	100%	100%	99%
Chest Pain/Possible Heart Attack Care				
Aspirin at Arrival	96	98%	94%	95%
Median Time to ECG (minutes)	99	3	9	8
Median Time to Transfer (minutes)[5]	0	-	75	61
Fibrinolytic Medication Timing[1]	10	80%	50%	54%
Heart Failure Care				
ACE Inhibitor or ARB for LVSD	58	78%	94%	94%
Discharge Instructions	118	97%	85%	88%
Evaluation of LVS Function	160	94%	94%	98%
Smoking Cessation Advice	55	100%	97%	98%
Pneumonia Care				
Appropriate Initial Antibiotic	64	91%	91%	92%
Blood Culture Timing	52	98%	96%	96%
Influenza Vaccine	54	93%	89%	91%
Initial Antibiotic Timing	87	98%	95%	95%
Pneumococcal Vaccine	95	93%	91%	93%
Smoking Cessation Advice	54	100%	95%	97%
Surgical Care Improvement Project				
Appropriate VTP Within 24 Hours[2]	248	92%	91%	92%
Appropriate Hair Removal[2]	396	100%	100%	99%
Appropriate Beta Blocker Usage[2]	125	91%	91%	93%
Controlled Postoperative Blood Glucose[2]	0	-	95%	93%
Prophylactic Antibiotic Timing[2]	243	97%	97%	97%
Prophylactic Antibiotic Timing (Outpatient)	34	97%	93%	92%
Prophylactic Antibiotic Selection[2]	243	98%	98%	97%
Prophylactic Antibiotic Select. (Outpatient)	33	100%	95%	94%
Prophylactic Antibiotic Stopped[2]	237	86%	94%	94%
Recommended VTP Ordered[2]	248	95%	94%	94%
Urinary Catheter Removal[2]	99	75%	87%	90%
Children's Asthma Care				
Received Systemic Corticosteroids	-	-	-	100%
Received Home Management Plan	-	-	-	71%
Received Reliever Medication	-	-	-	100%
Use of Medical Imaging				
Combination Abdominal CT Scan[1]	16	0.063	0.372	0.191
Combination Chest CT Scan[1]	9	0.111	0.134	0.054
Follow-up Mammogram/Ultrasound	569	9.8%	8%	8.4%
MRI for Low Back Pain	76	31.6%	34.3%	32.7%
Survey of Patients' Hospital Experiences				
Area Around Room 'Always' Quiet at Night	300+	51%	-	58%
Doctors 'Always' Communicated Well	300+	84%	-	80%
Home Recovery Information Given	300+	82%	-	82%
Hospital Given 9 or 10 on 10 Point Scale	300+	64%	-	67%
Meds 'Always' Explained Before Given	300+	65%	-	60%
Nurses 'Always' Communicated Well	300+	78%	-	76%
Pain 'Always' Well Controlled	300+	71%	-	69%
Room and Bathroom 'Always' Clean	300+	72%	-	71%
Timely Help 'Always' Received	300+	69%	-	64%
Would Definitely Recommend Hospital	300+	62%	-	69%

NOTE: Hospital profiles are in alphabetical order by state, then city, then hospital within the city; Rankings exclude hospitals with less than 25 cases except for patient surveys which excludes hospitals with less than 100 cases; (a) 100–299 cases; (1) The number of cases is too small to be sure how well a hospital is performing; (2) The hospital indicated that the data submitted for this measure were based on a sample of cases; (3) Data was collected during a shorter time period (fewer quarters) than the maximum possible time for this measure; (4) Suppressed for one or more quarters by CMS; (5) No data is available from the hospital for this measure; (6) Fewer than 100 patients completed the HCAHPS survey. Use these rates with caution, as the number of surveys may be too low to reliably assess hospital performance; (7) Survey results are based on less than 12 months of data; (8) Survey results are not available for this reporting period; (9) No or very few patients were eligible for the HCAHPS survey. The scores shown, if any, reflect a very small number of surveys; (10) A state average was not calculated because too few hospitals in the state submitted data; (11) There were discrepancies in the data collection process; Please refer to the User's Guide for a full explanation of data.

Share Memorial Hospital

800 Share Drive
Alva, OK 73717
Phone: 580-327-2800
Fax: 580-430-3332
Type: Acute Care Hospitals
Emergency Services: Yes
Ownership: Government - Local
Beds: 37

Key Personnel:
CEO/President. . . . . Barbara Oestmann
Chief of Medical Staff . . . . Kirtt Bierig, DO
Infection Control. . . . . Cheryl Ellis, RN
Operating Room. . . . . Kelly Hellar, RN, BSN
Quality Assurance . . . . Dottie Gatz
Emergency Room . . . . Barbara Louthan, RN

Measure	Cases	This Hosp.	State Avg.	U.S. Avg.
Heart Attack Care				
ACE Inhibitor or ARB for LVSD[3]	0	-	95%	96%
Aspirin at Arrival[1,3]	2	0%	98%	99%
Aspirin at Discharge[1,3]	1	0%	98%	98%
Beta Blocker at Discharge[1,3]	1	0%	98%	98%
Fibrinolytic Medication Timing[3]	0	-	42%	55%
PCI Within 90 Minutes of Arrival[3]	0	-	88%	90%
Smoking Cessation Advice[3]	0	-	100%	99%
Chest Pain/Possible Heart Attack Care				
Aspirin at Arrival	30	83%	94%	95%
Median Time to ECG (minutes)	32	11	9	8
Median Time to Transfer (minutes)[5]	0	-	75	61
Fibrinolytic Medication Timing[1,3]	1	0%	50%	54%
Heart Failure Care				
ACE Inhibitor or ARB for LVSD[1]	4	50%	94%	94%
Discharge Instructions[1]	11	91%	85%	88%
Evaluation of LVS Function[1]	20	80%	94%	98%
Smoking Cessation Advice[1]	1	100%	97%	98%
Pneumonia Care				
Appropriate Initial Antibiotic[1]	22	91%	91%	92%
Blood Culture Timing[1]	18	100%	96%	96%
Influenza Vaccine[1]	23	96%	89%	91%
Initial Antibiotic Timing	28	100%	95%	95%
Pneumococcal Vaccine	37	97%	91%	93%
Smoking Cessation Advice[1]	6	67%	95%	97%
Surgical Care Improvement Project				
Appropriate VTP Within 24 Hours[1,2,3]	3	33%	91%	92%
Appropriate Hair Removal[1,2,3]	4	75%	100%	99%
Appropriate Beta Blocker Usage[2,3]	0	-	91%	93%
Controlled Postoperative Blood Glucose[2,3]	0	-	95%	93%
Prophylactic Antibiotic Timing[1,2,3]	3	100%	97%	97%
Prophylactic Antibiotic Timing (Outpatient)[5]	0	-	93%	92%
Prophylactic Antibiotic Selection[1,2,3]	3	100%	98%	97%
Prophylactic Antibiotic Select. (Outpatient)[5]	0	-	95%	94%
Prophylactic Antibiotic Stopped[1,2,3]	3	100%	94%	94%
Recommended VTP Ordered[1,2,3]	3	33%	94%	94%
Urinary Catheter Removal[2,3]	0	-	87%	90%
Children's Asthma Care				
Received Systemic Corticosteroids	-	-	-	100%
Received Home Management Plan	-	-	-	71%
Received Reliever Medication	-	-	-	100%
Use of Medical Imaging				
Combination Abdominal CT Scan	81	0.444	0.372	0.191
Combination Chest CT Scan[1]	40	0.025	0.134	0.054
Follow-up Mammogram/Ultrasound	85	7.1%	8%	8.4%
MRI for Low Back Pain[1]	20	40.0%	34.3%	32.7%
Survey of Patients' Hospital Experiences				
Area Around Room 'Always' Quiet at Night	(a)	67%	-	58%
Doctors 'Always' Communicated Well	(a)	83%	-	80%
Home Recovery Information Given	(a)	75%	-	82%
Hospital Given 9 or 10 on 10 Point Scale	(a)	69%	-	67%
Meds 'Always' Explained Before Given	(a)	56%	-	60%
Nurses 'Always' Communicated Well	(a)	81%	-	76%
Pain 'Always' Well Controlled	(a)	75%	-	69%
Room and Bathroom 'Always' Clean	(a)	77%	-	71%
Timely Help 'Always' Received	(a)	75%	-	64%
Would Definitely Recommend Hospital	(a)	66%	-	69%

Physicians' Hospital in Anadarko

1002 East Central Boulevard
Anadarko, OK 73005
Phone: 405-247-2551
Fax: 405-247-9407
Type: Critical Access Hospitals
Emergency Services: Yes
Ownership: Government - Local
Beds: 25

Key Personnel:
CEO/President. . . . . Alan Riffel
Chief of Medical Staff . . . . Roberta Martin
Radiology. . . . . Craig L Lastine

Measure	Cases	This Hosp.	State Avg.	U.S. Avg.
Heart Attack Care				
ACE Inhibitor or ARB for LVSD[3]	0	-	95%	96%
Aspirin at Arrival[1,3]	1	100%	98%	99%
Aspirin at Discharge[1,3]	1	100%	98%	98%
Beta Blocker at Discharge[1,3]	1	100%	98%	98%
Fibrinolytic Medication Timing[3]	0	-	42%	55%
PCI Within 90 Minutes of Arrival[3]	0	-	88%	90%
Smoking Cessation Advice[3]	0	-	100%	99%
Chest Pain/Possible Heart Attack Care				
Aspirin at Arrival	-	-	94%	95%
Median Time to ECG (minutes)	-	-	9	8
Median Time to Transfer (minutes)	-	-	75	61
Fibrinolytic Medication Timing	-	-	50%	54%
Heart Failure Care				
ACE Inhibitor or ARB for LVSD[3]	0	-	94%	94%
Discharge Instructions[1,3]	4	0%	85%	88%
Evaluation of LVS Function[1,3]	9	11%	94%	98%
Smoking Cessation Advice[3]	0	-	97%	98%
Pneumonia Care				
Appropriate Initial Antibiotic[1,3]	7	100%	91%	92%
Blood Culture Timing[1,3]	5	100%	96%	96%
Influenza Vaccine[1,3]	3	0%	89%	91%
Initial Antibiotic Timing[1,3]	7	100%	95%	95%
Pneumococcal Vaccine[1,3]	12	0%	91%	93%
Smoking Cessation Advice[1,3]	3	33%	95%	97%
Surgical Care Improvement Project				
Appropriate VTP Within 24 Hours[5]	0	-	91%	92%
Appropriate Hair Removal[5]	0	-	100%	99%
Appropriate Beta Blocker Usage[5]	0	-	91%	93%
Controlled Postoperative Blood Glucose[5]	0	-	95%	93%
Prophylactic Antibiotic Timing[5]	0	-	97%	97%
Prophylactic Antibiotic Timing (Outpatient)	-	-	93%	92%
Prophylactic Antibiotic Selection[5]	0	-	98%	97%
Prophylactic Antibiotic Select. (Outpatient)	-	-	95%	94%
Prophylactic Antibiotic Stopped[5]	0	-	94%	94%
Recommended VTP Ordered[5]	0	-	94%	94%
Urinary Catheter Removal[5]	0	-	87%	90%
Children's Asthma Care				
Received Systemic Corticosteroids	-	-	-	100%
Received Home Management Plan	-	-	-	71%
Received Reliever Medication	-	-	-	100%
Use of Medical Imaging				
Combination Abdominal CT Scan	-	-	0.372	0.191
Combination Chest CT Scan	-	-	0.134	0.054
Follow-up Mammogram/Ultrasound	-	-	8%	8.4%
MRI for Low Back Pain	-	-	34.3%	32.7%
Survey of Patients' Hospital Experiences				
Area Around Room 'Always' Quiet at Night[8]	-	-	-	58%
Doctors 'Always' Communicated Well[8]	-	-	-	80%
Home Recovery Information Given[8]	-	-	-	82%
Hospital Given 9 or 10 on 10 Point Scale[8]	-	-	-	67%
Meds 'Always' Explained Before Given[8]	-	-	-	60%
Nurses 'Always' Communicated Well[8]	-	-	-	76%
Pain 'Always' Well Controlled[8]	-	-	-	69%
Room and Bathroom 'Always' Clean[8]	-	-	-	71%
Timely Help 'Always' Received[8]	-	-	-	64%
Would Definitely Recommend Hospital[8]	-	-	-	69%

Pushmataha County-TN of Antlers Hospital Authority

510 East Main Street
Antlers, OK 74523
Phone: 580-298-3341
Fax: 580-298-4713
E-mail: comments@pushhospital.com
URL: www.pushhospital.com
Type: Acute Care Hospitals
Emergency Services: Yes
Ownership: Govt - Hospital Dist/Auth
Beds: 48

Key Personnel:
CEO/President. . . . . Denis Frank
Chief of Medical Staff . . . . Herbert Rowland
Infection Control. . . . . Jane Bates
Emergency Room . . . . Nadine David

Measure	Cases	This Hosp.	State Avg.	U.S. Avg.
Heart Attack Care				
ACE Inhibitor or ARB for LVSD[3]	0	-	95%	96%
Aspirin at Arrival[3]	0	-	98%	99%
Aspirin at Discharge[3]	0	-	98%	98%
Beta Blocker at Discharge[3]	0	-	98%	98%
Fibrinolytic Medication Timing[3]	0	-	42%	55%
PCI Within 90 Minutes of Arrival[3]	0	-	88%	90%
Smoking Cessation Advice[3]	0	-	100%	99%
Chest Pain/Possible Heart Attack Care				
Aspirin at Arrival	36	92%	94%	95%
Median Time to ECG (minutes)	38	18	9	8
Median Time to Transfer (minutes)[5]	0	-	75	61
Fibrinolytic Medication Timing[1]	3	0%	50%	54%
Heart Failure Care				
ACE Inhibitor or ARB for LVSD[1]	9	89%	94%	94%
Discharge Instructions	28	89%	85%	88%
Evaluation of LVS Function	40	55%	94%	98%
Smoking Cessation Advice[1]	5	80%	97%	98%
Pneumonia Care				
Appropriate Initial Antibiotic	36	92%	91%	92%
Blood Culture Timing	39	92%	96%	96%
Influenza Vaccine	53	89%	89%	91%
Initial Antibiotic Timing	79	97%	95%	95%
Pneumococcal Vaccine	66	92%	91%	93%
Smoking Cessation Advice[1]	14	93%	95%	97%
Surgical Care Improvement Project				
Appropriate VTP Within 24 Hours[1,3]	2	100%	91%	92%
Appropriate Hair Removal[1,3]	4	100%	100%	99%
Appropriate Beta Blocker Usage[3]	0	-	91%	93%
Controlled Postoperative Blood Glucose[3]	0	-	95%	93%
Prophylactic Antibiotic Timing[1,3]	4	75%	97%	97%
Prophylactic Antibiotic Timing (Outpatient)[5]	0	-	93%	92%
Prophylactic Antibiotic Selection[1,3]	4	0%	98%	97%
Prophylactic Antibiotic Select. (Outpatient)[5]	0	-	95%	94%
Prophylactic Antibiotic Stopped[1,3]	4	100%	94%	94%
Recommended VTP Ordered[1,3]	2	100%	94%	94%
Urinary Catheter Removal[1,3]	1	100%	87%	90%
Children's Asthma Care				
Received Systemic Corticosteroids	-	-	-	100%
Received Home Management Plan	-	-	-	71%
Received Reliever Medication	-	-	-	100%
Use of Medical Imaging				
Combination Abdominal CT Scan	83	0.506	0.372	0.191
Combination Chest CT Scan	65	0.277	0.134	0.054
Follow-up Mammogram/Ultrasound[5]	0	-	8%	8.4%
MRI for Low Back Pain[5]	0	-	34.3%	32.7%
Survey of Patients' Hospital Experiences				
Area Around Room 'Always' Quiet at Night	(a)	48%	-	58%
Doctors 'Always' Communicated Well	(a)	76%	-	80%
Home Recovery Information Given	(a)	67%	-	82%
Hospital Given 9 or 10 on 10 Point Scale	(a)	52%	-	67%
Meds 'Always' Explained Before Given	(a)	48%	-	60%
Nurses 'Always' Communicated Well	(a)	71%	-	76%
Pain 'Always' Well Controlled	(a)	65%	-	69%
Room and Bathroom 'Always' Clean	(a)	71%	-	71%
Timely Help 'Always' Received	(a)	63%	-	64%
Would Definitely Recommend Hospital	(a)	56%	-	69%

NOTE: Hospital profiles are in alphabetical order by state, then city, then hospital within the city; Rankings exclude hospitals with less than 25 cases except for patient surveys which excludes hospitals with less than 100 cases; (a) 100–299 cases; (1) The number of cases is too small to be sure how well a hospital is performing; (2) The hospital indicated that the data submitted for this measure were based on a sample of cases; (3) Data was collected during a shorter time period (fewer quarters) than the maximum possible time for this measure; (4) Suppressed for one or more quarters by CMS; (5) No data is available from the hospital for this measure; (6) Fewer than 100 patients completed the HCAHPS survey. Use these rates with caution, as the number of surveys may be too low to reliably assess hospital performance; (7) Survey results are based on less than 12 months of data; (8) Survey results are not available for this reporting period; (9) No or very few patients were eligible for the HCAHPS survey. The scores shown, if any, reflect a very small number of surveys; (10) A state average was not calculated because too few hospitals in the state submitted data; (11) There were discrepancies in the data collection process; Please refer to the User's Guide for a full explanation of data.

Mercy Memorial Health Center

1011 Fourteenth Avenue, Northwest
Ardmore, OK 73401
Phone: 405-223-5400
Fax: 580-220-6580
URL: www.mercyok.com/mmhc
Type: Acute Care Hospitals
Emergency Services: Yes
Ownership: Voluntary Non-Profit - Other
Beds: 176
Key Personnel:
CEO/President. . . . . Bobby G Thompson

Measure	Cases	This Hosp.	State Avg.	U.S. Avg.
Heart Attack Care				
ACE Inhibitor or ARB for LVSD	27	85%	95%	96%
Aspirin at Arrival	161	98%	98%	99%
Aspirin at Discharge	141	100%	98%	98%
Beta Blocker at Discharge	137	99%	98%	98%
Fibrinolytic Medication Timing[1]	2	100%	42%	55%
PCI Within 90 Minutes of Arrival[1]	23	65%	88%	90%
Smoking Cessation Advice	59	100%	100%	99%
Chest Pain/Possible Heart Attack Care				
Aspirin at Arrival[1]	15	100%	94%	95%
Median Time to ECG (minutes)[1]	17	8	9	8
Median Time to Transfer (minutes)[5]	0	-	75	61
Fibrinolytic Medication Timing[1,3]	1	100%	50%	54%
Heart Failure Care				
ACE Inhibitor or ARB for LVSD	51	90%	94%	94%
Discharge Instructions	133	75%	85%	88%
Evaluation of LVS Function	153	97%	94%	98%
Smoking Cessation Advice	38	100%	97%	98%
Pneumonia Care				
Appropriate Initial Antibiotic	93	84%	91%	92%
Blood Culture Timing	153	92%	96%	96%
Influenza Vaccine	128	95%	89%	91%
Initial Antibiotic Timing	172	95%	95%	95%
Pneumococcal Vaccine	166	96%	91%	93%
Smoking Cessation Advice	85	100%	95%	97%
Surgical Care Improvement Project				
Appropriate VTP Within 24 Hours[2]	233	97%	91%	92%
Appropriate Hair Removal[2]	665	100%	100%	99%
Appropriate Beta Blocker Usage[2]	176	93%	91%	93%
Controlled Postoperative Blood Glucose[2]	0	-	95%	93%
Prophylactic Antibiotic Timing[2]	423	97%	97%	97%
Prophylactic Antibiotic Timing (Outpatient)	313	96%	93%	92%
Prophylactic Antibiotic Selection[2]	429	100%	98%	97%
Prophylactic Antibiotic Select. (Outpatient)	307	84%	95%	94%
Prophylactic Antibiotic Stopped[2]	382	95%	94%	94%
Recommended VTP Ordered[2]	233	98%	94%	94%
Urinary Catheter Removal[2]	35	57%	87%	90%
Children's Asthma Care				
Received Systemic Corticosteroids	-	-	-	100%
Received Home Management Plan	-	-	-	71%
Received Reliever Medication	-	-	-	100%
Use of Medical Imaging				
Combination Abdominal CT Scan	813	0.182	0.372	0.191
Combination Chest CT Scan	670	0.009	0.134	0.054
Follow-up Mammogram/Ultrasound	1,145	4.2%	8%	8.4%
MRI for Low Back Pain	208	41.8%	34.3%	32.7%
Survey of Patients' Hospital Experiences				
Area Around Room 'Always' Quiet at Night	300+	54%	-	58%
Doctors 'Always' Communicated Well	300+	80%	-	80%
Home Recovery Information Given	300+	80%	-	82%
Hospital Given 9 or 10 on 10 Point Scale	300+	56%	-	67%
Meds 'Always' Explained Before Given	300+	57%	-	60%
Nurses 'Always' Communicated Well	300+	75%	-	76%
Pain 'Always' Well Controlled	300+	67%	-	69%
Room and Bathroom 'Always' Clean	300+	69%	-	71%
Timely Help 'Always' Received	300+	66%	-	64%
Would Definitely Recommend Hospital	300+	58%	-	69%

Atoka Memorial Hospital

1200 West Liberty Road
Atoka, OK 74525
Phone: 580-889-3333
Fax: 580-889-1948
URL: www.atoka-hosp.otnnet.net
Type: Critical Access Hospitals
Emergency Services: Yes
Ownership: Govt - Hospital Dist/Auth
Beds: 25
Key Personnel:
CEO/President. . . . . Charles Young

Measure	Cases	This Hosp.	State Avg.	U.S. Avg.
Heart Attack Care				
ACE Inhibitor or ARB for LVSD[3]	0	-	95%	96%
Aspirin at Arrival[1,3]	1	0%	98%	99%
Aspirin at Discharge[3]	0	-	98%	98%
Beta Blocker at Discharge[3]	0	-	98%	98%
Fibrinolytic Medication Timing[3]	0	-	42%	55%
PCI Within 90 Minutes of Arrival[3]	0	-	88%	90%
Smoking Cessation Advice[3]	0	-	100%	99%
Chest Pain/Possible Heart Attack Care				
Aspirin at Arrival	-	-	94%	95%
Median Time to ECG (minutes)	-	-	9	8
Median Time to Transfer (minutes)	-	-	75	61
Fibrinolytic Medication Timing	-	-	50%	54%
Heart Failure Care				
ACE Inhibitor or ARB for LVSD[1]	1	100%	94%	94%
Discharge Instructions[1]	5	40%	85%	88%
Evaluation of LVS Function[1]	8	12%	94%	98%
Smoking Cessation Advice[1]	1	100%	97%	98%
Pneumonia Care				
Appropriate Initial Antibiotic[1]	15	73%	91%	92%
Blood Culture Timing[1]	1	100%	96%	96%
Influenza Vaccine[1]	11	73%	89%	91%
Initial Antibiotic Timing[1]	20	90%	95%	95%
Pneumococcal Vaccine[1]	20	75%	91%	93%
Smoking Cessation Advice[1]	7	86%	95%	97%
Surgical Care Improvement Project				
Appropriate VTP Within 24 Hours[5]	0	-	91%	92%
Appropriate Hair Removal[5]	0	-	100%	99%
Appropriate Beta Blocker Usage[5]	0	-	91%	93%
Controlled Postoperative Blood Glucose[5]	0	-	95%	93%
Prophylactic Antibiotic Timing[5]	0	-	97%	97%
Prophylactic Antibiotic Timing (Outpatient)	-	-	93%	92%
Prophylactic Antibiotic Selection[5]	0	-	98%	97%
Prophylactic Antibiotic Select. (Outpatient)	-	-	95%	94%
Prophylactic Antibiotic Stopped[5]	0	-	94%	94%
Recommended VTP Ordered[5]	0	-	94%	94%
Urinary Catheter Removal[5]	0	-	87%	90%
Children's Asthma Care				
Received Systemic Corticosteroids	-	-	-	100%
Received Home Management Plan	-	-	-	71%
Received Reliever Medication	-	-	-	100%
Use of Medical Imaging				
Combination Abdominal CT Scan	-	-	0.372	0.191
Combination Chest CT Scan	-	-	0.134	0.054
Follow-up Mammogram/Ultrasound	-	-	8%	8.4%
MRI for Low Back Pain	-	-	34.3%	32.7%
Survey of Patients' Hospital Experiences				
Area Around Room 'Always' Quiet at Night[6]	<100	76%	-	58%
Doctors 'Always' Communicated Well[6]	<100	92%	-	80%
Home Recovery Information Given[6]	<100	83%	-	82%
Hospital Given 9 or 10 on 10 Point Scale[6]	<100	78%	-	67%
Meds 'Always' Explained Before Given[6]	<100	75%	-	60%
Nurses 'Always' Communicated Well[6]	<100	82%	-	76%
Pain 'Always' Well Controlled[6]	<100	83%	-	69%
Room and Bathroom 'Always' Clean[6]	<100	86%	-	71%
Timely Help 'Always' Received[6]	<100	80%	-	64%
Would Definitely Recommend Hospital	<100	79%	-	69%

Jane Phillips Medical Center

3500 East Frank Phillips Boulevard
Bartlesville, OK 74006
Phone: 918-333-7200
Fax: 918-331-1612
URL: www.jpmc.org
Type: Acute Care Hospitals
Emergency Services: Yes
Ownership: Voluntary Non-Profit - Church
Beds: 144
Key Personnel:
CEO/President. . . . . David R Stire
Chief of Medical Staff. . . . . Mark A Robertson MD

Measure	Cases	This Hosp.	State Avg.	U.S. Avg.
Heart Attack Care				
ACE Inhibitor or ARB for LVSD[1]	15	100%	95%	96%
Aspirin at Arrival	120	100%	98%	99%
Aspirin at Discharge	150	99%	98%	98%
Beta Blocker at Discharge	148	100%	98%	98%
Fibrinolytic Medication Timing	0	-	42%	55%
PCI Within 90 Minutes of Arrival	29	97%	88%	90%
Smoking Cessation Advice	69	100%	100%	99%
Chest Pain/Possible Heart Attack Care				
Aspirin at Arrival[5]	0	-	94%	95%
Median Time to ECG (minutes)[5]	0	-	9	8
Median Time to Transfer (minutes)[5]	0	-	75	61
Fibrinolytic Medication Timing[5]	0	-	50%	54%
Heart Failure Care				
ACE Inhibitor or ARB for LVSD	37	97%	94%	94%
Discharge Instructions	110	94%	85%	88%
Evaluation of LVS Function	153	99%	94%	98%
Smoking Cessation Advice	34	100%	97%	98%
Pneumonia Care				
Appropriate Initial Antibiotic	126	94%	91%	92%
Blood Culture Timing	201	95%	96%	96%
Influenza Vaccine	145	92%	89%	91%
Initial Antibiotic Timing	202	97%	95%	95%
Pneumococcal Vaccine	206	93%	91%	93%
Smoking Cessation Advice	89	100%	95%	97%
Surgical Care Improvement Project				
Appropriate VTP Within 24 Hours[2]	249	82%	91%	92%
Appropriate Hair Removal[2]	521	100%	100%	99%
Appropriate Beta Blocker Usage[2]	85	96%	91%	93%
Controlled Postoperative Blood Glucose[2]	0	-	95%	93%
Prophylactic Antibiotic Timing[2]	416	95%	97%	97%
Prophylactic Antibiotic Timing (Outpatient)	56	61%	93%	92%
Prophylactic Antibiotic Selection[2]	418	98%	98%	97%
Prophylactic Antibiotic Select. (Outpatient)	34	74%	95%	94%
Prophylactic Antibiotic Stopped[2]	407	94%	94%	94%
Recommended VTP Ordered[2]	249	88%	94%	94%
Urinary Catheter Removal[2]	77	84%	87%	90%
Children's Asthma Care				
Received Systemic Corticosteroids	-	-	-	100%
Received Home Management Plan	-	-	-	71%
Received Reliever Medication	-	-	-	100%
Use of Medical Imaging				
Combination Abdominal CT Scan	769	0.013	0.372	0.191
Combination Chest CT Scan	554	0.004	0.134	0.054
Follow-up Mammogram/Ultrasound	1,524	4.6%	8%	8.4%
MRI for Low Back Pain	168	34.5%	34.3%	32.7%
Survey of Patients' Hospital Experiences				
Area Around Room 'Always' Quiet at Night	300+	60%	-	58%
Doctors 'Always' Communicated Well	300+	81%	-	80%
Home Recovery Information Given	300+	83%	-	82%
Hospital Given 9 or 10 on 10 Point Scale	300+	70%	-	67%
Meds 'Always' Explained Before Given	300+	59%	-	60%
Nurses 'Always' Communicated Well	300+	76%	-	76%
Pain 'Always' Well Controlled	300+	69%	-	69%
Room and Bathroom 'Always' Clean	300+	78%	-	71%
Timely Help 'Always' Received	300+	64%	-	64%
Would Definitely Recommend Hospital	300+	64%	-	69%

NOTE: Hospital profiles are in alphabetical order by state, then city, then hospital within the city; Rankings exclude hospitals with less than 25 cases except for patient surveys which excludes hospitals with less than 100 cases; (a) 100–299 cases; (1) The number of cases is too small to be sure how well a hospital is performing; (2) The hospital indicated that the data submitted for this measure were based on a sample of cases; (3) Data was collected during a shorter time period (fewer quarters) than the maximum possible time for this measure; (4) Suppressed for one or more quarters by CMS; (5) No data is available from the hospital for this measure; (6) Fewer than 100 patients completed the HCAHPS survey. Use these rates with caution, as the number of surveys may be too low to reliably assess hospital performance; (7) Survey results are based on less than 12 months of data; (8) Survey results are not available for this reporting period; (9) No or very few patients were eligible for the HCAHPS survey. The scores shown, if any, reflect a very small number of surveys; (10) A state average was not calculated because too few hospitals in the state submitted data; (11) There were discrepancies in the data collection process; Please refer to the User's Guide for a full explanation of data.

Beaver County Memorial Hospital

212 East 8th Street
Beaver, OK 73932
Type: Critical Access Hospitals
Ownership: Govt - Hospital Dist/Auth
Phone: 580-625-4551
Fax: 580-625-4212
Emergency Services: Yes
Beds: 24

Key Personnel:
Emergency Room . . . . Deanna Brown

Measure	Cases	This Hosp.	State Avg.	U.S. Avg.
Heart Attack Care				
ACE Inhibitor or ARB for LVSD[5]	0	-	95%	96%
Aspirin at Arrival[5]	0	-	98%	99%
Aspirin at Discharge[5]	0	-	98%	98%
Beta Blocker at Discharge[5]	0	-	98%	98%
Fibrinolytic Medication Timing[5]	0	-	42%	55%
PCI Within 90 Minutes of Arrival[5]	0	-	88%	90%
Smoking Cessation Advice[5]	0	-	100%	99%
Chest Pain/Possible Heart Attack Care				
Aspirin at Arrival	-	-	94%	95%
Median Time to ECG (minutes)	-	-	9	8
Median Time to Transfer (minutes)	-	-	75	61
Fibrinolytic Medication Timing	-	-	50%	54%
Heart Failure Care				
ACE Inhibitor or ARB for LVSD[1]	1	0%	94%	94%
Discharge Instructions[1]	1	0%	85%	88%
Evaluation of LVS Function[1]	3	33%	94%	98%
Smoking Cessation Advice	0	-	97%	98%
Pneumonia Care				
Appropriate Initial Antibiotic[1]	8	75%	91%	92%
Blood Culture Timing	0	-	96%	96%
Influenza Vaccine[1]	11	64%	89%	91%
Initial Antibiotic Timing[1]	11	91%	95%	95%
Pneumococcal Vaccine[1]	10	70%	91%	93%
Smoking Cessation Advice[1]	3	33%	95%	97%
Surgical Care Improvement Project				
Appropriate VTP Within 24 Hours[5]	0	-	91%	92%
Appropriate Hair Removal[5]	0	-	100%	99%
Appropriate Beta Blocker Usage[5]	0	-	91%	93%
Controlled Postoperative Blood Glucose[5]	0	-	95%	93%
Prophylactic Antibiotic Timing[5]	0	-	97%	97%
Prophylactic Antibiotic Timing (Outpatient)	-	-	93%	92%
Prophylactic Antibiotic Selection[5]	0	-	98%	97%
Prophylactic Antibiotic Select. (Outpatient)	-	-	95%	94%
Prophylactic Antibiotic Stopped[5]	0	-	94%	94%
Recommended VTP Ordered[5]	0	-	94%	94%
Urinary Catheter Removal[5]	0	-	87%	90%
Children's Asthma Care				
Received Systemic Corticosteroids	-	-	-	100%
Received Home Management Plan	-	-	-	71%
Received Reliever Medication	-	-	-	100%
Use of Medical Imaging				
Combination Abdominal CT Scan	-	-	0.372	0.191
Combination Chest CT Scan	-	-	0.134	0.054
Follow-up Mammogram/Ultrasound	-	-	8%	8.4%
MRI for Low Back Pain	-	-	34.3%	32.7%
Survey of Patients' Hospital Experiences				
Area Around Room 'Always' Quiet at Night[8]	-	-	-	58%
Doctors 'Always' Communicated Well[8]	-	-	-	80%
Home Recovery Information Given[8]	-	-	-	82%
Hospital Given 9 or 10 on 10 Point Scale[8]	-	-	-	67%
Meds 'Always' Explained Before Given[8]	-	-	-	60%
Nurses 'Always' Communicated Well[8]	-	-	-	76%
Pain 'Always' Well Controlled[8]	-	-	-	69%
Room and Bathroom 'Always' Clean[8]	-	-	-	71%
Timely Help 'Always' Received[8]	-	-	-	64%
Would Definitely Recommend Hospital[8]	-	-	-	69%

Integris Blackwell Regional Hospital

710 South 13th Street
Blackwell, OK 74631
Type: Acute Care Hospitals
Ownership: Voluntary Non-Profit - Private
Phone: 580-363-2311
Fax: 580-363-2339
Emergency Services: No
Beds: 53

Key Personnel:
CEO/President. . . . . James Moore
Chief of Medical Staff. . . . . Dr. Paul Briggs
Infection Control. . . . . Pam Lewellyn
Quality Assurance . . . . Janet Reser, RN
Patient Relations . . . . Cassie Leatherman

Measure	Cases	This Hosp.	State Avg.	U.S. Avg.
Heart Attack Care				
ACE Inhibitor or ARB for LVSD	0	-	95%	96%
Aspirin at Arrival[1]	1	100%	98%	99%
Aspirin at Discharge	0	-	98%	98%
Beta Blocker at Discharge[1]	1	100%	98%	98%
Fibrinolytic Medication Timing	0	-	42%	55%
PCI Within 90 Minutes of Arrival	0	-	88%	90%
Smoking Cessation Advice	0	-	100%	99%
Chest Pain/Possible Heart Attack Care				
Aspirin at Arrival	28	96%	94%	95%
Median Time to ECG (minutes)	30	9	9	8
Median Time to Transfer (minutes)[5]	0	-	75	61
Fibrinolytic Medication Timing[1]	6	83%	50%	54%
Heart Failure Care				
ACE Inhibitor or ARB for LVSD[1]	9	100%	94%	94%
Discharge Instructions	25	92%	85%	88%
Evaluation of LVS Function	41	100%	94%	98%
Smoking Cessation Advice[1]	8	100%	97%	98%
Pneumonia Care				
Appropriate Initial Antibiotic	55	98%	91%	92%
Blood Culture Timing	72	100%	96%	96%
Influenza Vaccine	51	96%	89%	91%
Initial Antibiotic Timing	90	99%	95%	95%
Pneumococcal Vaccine	67	99%	91%	93%
Smoking Cessation Advice	29	100%	95%	97%
Surgical Care Improvement Project				
Appropriate VTP Within 24 Hours[1]	6	83%	91%	92%
Appropriate Hair Removal[1]	17	100%	100%	99%
Appropriate Beta Blocker Usage[1]	2	50%	91%	93%
Controlled Postoperative Blood Glucose	0	-	95%	93%
Prophylactic Antibiotic Timing[1]	9	100%	97%	97%
Prophylactic Antibiotic Timing (Outpatient)[1]	4	75%	93%	92%
Prophylactic Antibiotic Selection[1]	9	100%	98%	97%
Prophylactic Antibiotic Select. (Outpatient)[1]	3	100%	95%	94%
Prophylactic Antibiotic Stopped[1]	8	88%	94%	94%
Recommended VTP Ordered[1]	6	83%	94%	94%
Urinary Catheter Removal[1]	1	0%	87%	90%
Children's Asthma Care				
Received Systemic Corticosteroids	-	-	-	100%
Received Home Management Plan	-	-	-	71%
Received Reliever Medication	-	-	-	100%
Use of Medical Imaging				
Combination Abdominal CT Scan	130	0.638	0.372	0.191
Combination Chest CT Scan	67	0.030	0.134	0.054
Follow-up Mammogram/Ultrasound	134	6.7%	8%	8.4%
MRI for Low Back Pain[1]	33	54.5%	34.3%	32.7%
Survey of Patients' Hospital Experiences				
Area Around Room 'Always' Quiet at Night	(a)	57%	-	58%
Doctors 'Always' Communicated Well	(a)	84%	-	80%
Home Recovery Information Given	(a)	79%	-	82%
Hospital Given 9 or 10 on 10 Point Scale	(a)	65%	-	67%
Meds 'Always' Explained Before Given	(a)	56%	-	60%
Nurses 'Always' Communicated Well	(a)	74%	-	76%
Pain 'Always' Well Controlled	(a)	66%	-	69%
Room and Bathroom 'Always' Clean	(a)	71%	-	71%
Timely Help 'Always' Received	(a)	64%	-	64%
Would Definitely Recommend Hospital	(a)	64%	-	69%

Cimarron Memorial Hospital

100 South Ellis
Boise City, OK 73933
Type: Critical Access Hospitals
Ownership: Government - Local
Phone: 580-544-2501
Fax: 580-544-2517
Emergency Services: Yes
Beds: 64

Key Personnel:
Chief of Medical Staff . . . . JL Wheeler, MD
Operating Room. . . . . Lois Burkhalter
Quality Assurance . . . . Mary Van Leer

Measure	Cases	This Hosp.	State Avg.	U.S. Avg.
Heart Attack Care				
ACE Inhibitor or ARB for LVSD[5]	0	-	95%	96%
Aspirin at Arrival[5]	0	-	98%	99%
Aspirin at Discharge[5]	0	-	98%	98%
Beta Blocker at Discharge[5]	0	-	98%	98%
Fibrinolytic Medication Timing[5]	0	-	42%	55%
PCI Within 90 Minutes of Arrival[5]	0	-	88%	90%
Smoking Cessation Advice[5]	0	-	100%	99%
Chest Pain/Possible Heart Attack Care				
Aspirin at Arrival	-	-	94%	95%
Median Time to ECG (minutes)	-	-	9	8
Median Time to Transfer (minutes)	-	-	75	61
Fibrinolytic Medication Timing	-	-	50%	54%
Heart Failure Care				
ACE Inhibitor or ARB for LVSD[5]	0	-	94%	94%
Discharge Instructions[5]	0	-	85%	88%
Evaluation of LVS Function[5]	0	-	94%	98%
Smoking Cessation Advice[5]	0	-	97%	98%
Pneumonia Care				
Appropriate Initial Antibiotic[5]	0	-	91%	92%
Blood Culture Timing[5]	0	-	96%	96%
Influenza Vaccine[5]	0	-	89%	91%
Initial Antibiotic Timing[5]	0	-	95%	95%
Pneumococcal Vaccine[5]	0	-	91%	93%
Smoking Cessation Advice[5]	0	-	95%	97%
Surgical Care Improvement Project				
Appropriate VTP Within 24 Hours[5]	0	-	91%	92%
Appropriate Hair Removal[5]	0	-	100%	99%
Appropriate Beta Blocker Usage[5]	0	-	91%	93%
Controlled Postoperative Blood Glucose[5]	0	-	95%	93%
Prophylactic Antibiotic Timing[5]	0	-	97%	97%
Prophylactic Antibiotic Timing (Outpatient)	-	-	93%	92%
Prophylactic Antibiotic Selection[5]	0	-	98%	97%
Prophylactic Antibiotic Select. (Outpatient)	-	-	95%	94%
Prophylactic Antibiotic Stopped[5]	0	-	94%	94%
Recommended VTP Ordered[5]	0	-	94%	94%
Urinary Catheter Removal[5]	0	-	87%	90%
Children's Asthma Care				
Received Systemic Corticosteroids	-	-	-	100%
Received Home Management Plan	-	-	-	71%
Received Reliever Medication	-	-	-	100%
Use of Medical Imaging				
Combination Abdominal CT Scan	-	-	0.372	0.191
Combination Chest CT Scan	-	-	0.134	0.054
Follow-up Mammogram/Ultrasound	-	-	8%	8.4%
MRI for Low Back Pain	-	-	34.3%	32.7%
Survey of Patients' Hospital Experiences				
Area Around Room 'Always' Quiet at Night[8]	-	-	-	58%
Doctors 'Always' Communicated Well[8]	-	-	-	80%
Home Recovery Information Given[8]	-	-	-	82%
Hospital Given 9 or 10 on 10 Point Scale[8]	-	-	-	67%
Meds 'Always' Explained Before Given[8]	-	-	-	60%
Nurses 'Always' Communicated Well[8]	-	-	-	76%
Pain 'Always' Well Controlled[8]	-	-	-	69%
Room and Bathroom 'Always' Clean[8]	-	-	-	71%
Timely Help 'Always' Received[8]	-	-	-	64%
Would Definitely Recommend Hospital[8]	-	-	-	69%

NOTE: Hospital profiles are in alphabetical order by state, then city, then hospital within the city; Rankings exclude hospitals with less than 25 cases except for patient surveys which excludes hospitals with less than 100 cases; (a) 100–299 cases; (1) The number of cases is too small to be sure how well a hospital is performing; (2) The hospital indicated that the data submitted for this measure were based on a sample of cases; (3) Data was collected during a shorter time period (fewer quarters) than the maximum possible time for this measure; (4) Suppressed for one or more quarters by CMS; (5) No data is available from the hospital for this measure; (6) Fewer than 100 patients completed the HCAHPS survey. Use these rates with caution, as the number of surveys may be too low to reliably assess hospital performance; (7) Survey results are based on less than 12 months of data; (8) Survey results are not available for this reporting period; (9) No or very few patients were eligible for the HCAHPS survey. The scores shown, if any, reflect a very small number of surveys; (10) A state average was not calculated because too few hospitals in the state submitted data; (11) There were discrepancies in the data collection process; Please refer to the User's Guide for a full explanation of data.

Bristow Medical Center

700 W. 7th
Bristow, OK 74010
Phone: 918-367-2215
Fax: 918-367-9190
Type: Acute Care Hospitals
Emergency Services: No
Ownership: Proprietary
Beds: 30

Key Personnel:
CEO/President.............. Ryan Gehrig
Chief of Medical Staff.......... Dennise Blackstad
Infection Control............. Tina Ordway, RN
Quality Assurance .... Della Allison
Radiology.................. Vivian J Mcdaniel

Measure	Cases	This Hosp.	State Avg.	U.S. Avg.
Heart Attack Care				
ACE Inhibitor or ARB for LVSD[3]	0	-	95%	96%
Aspirin at Arrival[3]	0	-	98%	99%
Aspirin at Discharge[3]	0	-	98%	98%
Beta Blocker at Discharge[3]	0	-	98%	98%
Fibrinolytic Medication Timing[3]	0	-	42%	55%
PCI Within 90 Minutes of Arrival[3]	0	-	88%	90%
Smoking Cessation Advice[3]	0	-	100%	99%
Chest Pain/Possible Heart Attack Care				
Aspirin at Arrival[1,3]	16	100%	94%	95%
Median Time to ECG (minutes)[1,3]	16	14	9	8
Median Time to Transfer (minutes)[5]	0	-	75	61
Fibrinolytic Medication Timing[3]	0	-	50%	54%
Heart Failure Care				
ACE Inhibitor or ARB for LVSD[1]	5	40%	94%	94%
Discharge Instructions[1]	7	100%	85%	88%
Evaluation of LVS Function[1]	8	100%	94%	98%
Smoking Cessation Advice[1]	1	100%	97%	98%
Pneumonia Care				
Appropriate Initial Antibiotic	35	100%	91%	92%
Blood Culture Timing[1]	19	95%	96%	96%
Influenza Vaccine[1]	24	100%	89%	91%
Initial Antibiotic Timing	34	100%	95%	95%
Pneumococcal Vaccine	34	82%	91%	93%
Smoking Cessation Advice[1]	11	91%	95%	97%
Surgical Care Improvement Project				
Appropriate VTP Within 24 Hours[5]	0	-	91%	92%
Appropriate Hair Removal[5]	0	-	100%	99%
Appropriate Beta Blocker Usage[5]	0	-	91%	93%
Controlled Postoperative Blood Glucose[5]	0	-	95%	93%
Prophylactic Antibiotic Timing[5]	0	-	97%	97%
Prophylactic Antibiotic Timing (Outpatient)[5]	0	-	93%	92%
Prophylactic Antibiotic Selection[5]	0	-	98%	97%
Prophylactic Antibiotic Select. (Outpatient)[5]	0	-	95%	94%
Prophylactic Antibiotic Stopped[5]	0	-	94%	94%
Recommended VTP Ordered[5]	0	-	94%	94%
Urinary Catheter Removal[5]	0	-	87%	90%
Children's Asthma Care				
Received Systemic Corticosteroids	-	-	-	100%
Received Home Management Plan	-	-	-	71%
Received Reliever Medication	-	-	-	100%
Use of Medical Imaging				
Combination Abdominal CT Scan	66	0.576	0.372	0.191
Combination Chest CT Scan[1]	38	0.000	0.134	0.054
Follow-up Mammogram/Ultrasound[5]	0	-	8%	8.4%
MRI for Low Back Pain[1]	6	16.7%	34.3%	32.7%
Survey of Patients' Hospital Experiences				
Area Around Room 'Always' Quiet at Night[6]	<100	67%	-	58%
Doctors 'Always' Communicated Well[6]	<100	96%	-	80%
Home Recovery Information Given[6]	<100	81%	-	82%
Hospital Given 9 or 10 on 10 Point Scale[6]	<100	77%	-	67%
Meds 'Always' Explained Before Given[6]	<100	72%	-	60%
Nurses 'Always' Communicated Well[6]	<100	94%	-	76%
Pain 'Always' Well Controlled[6]	<100	91%	-	69%
Room and Bathroom 'Always' Clean[6]	<100	78%	-	71%
Timely Help 'Always' Received[6]	<100	79%	-	64%
Would Definitely Recommend Hospital	<100	83%	-	69%

Harper County Community Hospital

1003 US Highway 64 North
Buffalo, OK 73834
Phone: 580-735-2555
Fax: 580-735-2342
URL: www.hcchospital.com
Type: Critical Access Hospitals
Emergency Services: Yes
Ownership: Voluntary Non-Profit - Other
Beds: 25

Key Personnel:
Chief of Medical Staff.......... N Suthers
Operating Room.............. Paula Lauer, RN
Quality Assurance .... Kim Hudson
Radiology.................. Carl Fieser
Emergency Room .... Paula Lauer, RN
Patient Relations .... Ronna McCubbin

Measure	Cases	This Hosp.	State Avg.	U.S. Avg.
Heart Attack Care				
ACE Inhibitor or ARB for LVSD[5]	0	-	95%	96%
Aspirin at Arrival[5]	0	-	98%	99%
Aspirin at Discharge[5]	0	-	98%	98%
Beta Blocker at Discharge[5]	0	-	98%	98%
Fibrinolytic Medication Timing[5]	0	-	42%	55%
PCI Within 90 Minutes of Arrival[5]	0	-	88%	90%
Smoking Cessation Advice[5]	0	-	100%	99%
Chest Pain/Possible Heart Attack Care				
Aspirin at Arrival	-	-	94%	95%
Median Time to ECG (minutes)	-	-	9	8
Median Time to Transfer (minutes)	-	-	75	61
Fibrinolytic Medication Timing	-	-	50%	54%
Heart Failure Care				
ACE Inhibitor or ARB for LVSD[1]	4	75%	94%	94%
Discharge Instructions[1]	3	67%	85%	88%
Evaluation of LVS Function[1]	6	100%	94%	98%
Smoking Cessation Advice	0	-	97%	98%
Pneumonia Care				
Appropriate Initial Antibiotic[1]	18	89%	91%	92%
Blood Culture Timing[1]	3	100%	96%	96%
Influenza Vaccine[1]	10	100%	89%	91%
Initial Antibiotic Timing[1]	19	100%	95%	95%
Pneumococcal Vaccine[1]	12	100%	91%	93%
Smoking Cessation Advice[1]	8	100%	95%	97%
Surgical Care Improvement Project				
Appropriate VTP Within 24 Hours[5]	0	-	91%	92%
Appropriate Hair Removal[5]	0	-	100%	99%
Appropriate Beta Blocker Usage[5]	0	-	91%	93%
Controlled Postoperative Blood Glucose[5]	0	-	95%	93%
Prophylactic Antibiotic Timing[5]	0	-	97%	97%
Prophylactic Antibiotic Timing (Outpatient)	-	-	93%	92%
Prophylactic Antibiotic Selection[5]	0	-	98%	97%
Prophylactic Antibiotic Select. (Outpatient)	-	-	95%	94%
Prophylactic Antibiotic Stopped[5]	0	-	94%	94%
Recommended VTP Ordered[5]	0	-	94%	94%
Urinary Catheter Removal[5]	0	-	87%	90%
Children's Asthma Care				
Received Systemic Corticosteroids	-	-	-	100%
Received Home Management Plan	-	-	-	71%
Received Reliever Medication	-	-	-	100%
Use of Medical Imaging				
Combination Abdominal CT Scan	-	-	0.372	0.191
Combination Chest CT Scan	-	-	0.134	0.054
Follow-up Mammogram/Ultrasound	-	-	8%	8.4%
MRI for Low Back Pain	-	-	34.3%	32.7%
Survey of Patients' Hospital Experiences				
Area Around Room 'Always' Quiet at Night[6]	<100	81%	-	58%
Doctors 'Always' Communicated Well[6]	<100	94%	-	80%
Home Recovery Information Given[6]	<100	84%	-	82%
Hospital Given 9 or 10 on 10 Point Scale[6]	<100	74%	-	67%
Meds 'Always' Explained Before Given[6]	<100	77%	-	60%
Nurses 'Always' Communicated Well[6]	<100	87%	-	76%
Pain 'Always' Well Controlled[6]	<100	88%	-	69%
Room and Bathroom 'Always' Clean[6]	<100	79%	-	71%
Timely Help 'Always' Received[6]	<100	84%	-	64%
Would Definitely Recommend Hospital	<100	78%	-	69%

Carnegie Tri-County Municipal Hospital

102 North Broadway
Carnegie, OK 73015
Phone: 580-654-1050
Fax: 580-654-2111
Type: Critical Access Hospitals
Emergency Services: Yes
Ownership: Proprietary
Beds: 28

Key Personnel:
CEO/President.............. Barbara Orrell
Chief of Medical Staff.......... Ronald Hill, MD

Measure	Cases	This Hosp.	State Avg.	U.S. Avg.
Heart Attack Care				
ACE Inhibitor or ARB for LVSD[5]	0	-	95%	96%
Aspirin at Arrival[5]	0	-	98%	99%
Aspirin at Discharge[5]	0	-	98%	98%
Beta Blocker at Discharge[5]	0	-	98%	98%
Fibrinolytic Medication Timing[5]	0	-	42%	55%
PCI Within 90 Minutes of Arrival[5]	0	-	88%	90%
Smoking Cessation Advice[5]	0	-	100%	99%
Chest Pain/Possible Heart Attack Care				
Aspirin at Arrival	-	-	94%	95%
Median Time to ECG (minutes)	-	-	9	8
Median Time to Transfer (minutes)	-	-	75	61
Fibrinolytic Medication Timing	-	-	50%	54%
Heart Failure Care				
ACE Inhibitor or ARB for LVSD[5]	0	-	94%	94%
Discharge Instructions[5]	0	-	85%	88%
Evaluation of LVS Function[5]	0	-	94%	98%
Smoking Cessation Advice[5]	0	-	97%	98%
Pneumonia Care				
Appropriate Initial Antibiotic[5]	0	-	91%	92%
Blood Culture Timing[5]	0	-	96%	96%
Influenza Vaccine[5]	0	-	89%	91%
Initial Antibiotic Timing[5]	0	-	95%	95%
Pneumococcal Vaccine[5]	0	-	91%	93%
Smoking Cessation Advice[5]	0	-	95%	97%
Surgical Care Improvement Project				
Appropriate VTP Within 24 Hours[5]	0	-	91%	92%
Appropriate Hair Removal[5]	0	-	100%	99%
Appropriate Beta Blocker Usage[5]	0	-	91%	93%
Controlled Postoperative Blood Glucose[5]	0	-	95%	93%
Prophylactic Antibiotic Timing[5]	0	-	97%	97%
Prophylactic Antibiotic Timing (Outpatient)	-	-	93%	92%
Prophylactic Antibiotic Selection[5]	0	-	98%	97%
Prophylactic Antibiotic Select. (Outpatient)	-	-	95%	94%
Prophylactic Antibiotic Stopped[5]	0	-	94%	94%
Recommended VTP Ordered[5]	0	-	94%	94%
Urinary Catheter Removal[5]	0	-	87%	90%
Children's Asthma Care				
Received Systemic Corticosteroids	-	-	-	100%
Received Home Management Plan	-	-	-	71%
Received Reliever Medication	-	-	-	100%
Use of Medical Imaging				
Combination Abdominal CT Scan	-	-	0.372	0.191
Combination Chest CT Scan	-	-	0.134	0.054
Follow-up Mammogram/Ultrasound	-	-	8%	8.4%
MRI for Low Back Pain	-	-	34.3%	32.7%
Survey of Patients' Hospital Experiences				
Area Around Room 'Always' Quiet at Night[8]	-	-	-	58%
Doctors 'Always' Communicated Well[8]	-	-	-	80%
Home Recovery Information Given[8]	-	-	-	82%
Hospital Given 9 or 10 on 10 Point Scale[8]	-	-	-	67%
Meds 'Always' Explained Before Given[8]	-	-	-	60%
Nurses 'Always' Communicated Well[8]	-	-	-	76%
Pain 'Always' Well Controlled[8]	-	-	-	69%
Room and Bathroom 'Always' Clean[8]	-	-	-	71%
Timely Help 'Always' Received[8]	-	-	-	64%
Would Definitely Recommend Hospital[8]	-	-	-	69%

NOTE: Hospital profiles are in alphabetical order by state, then city, then hospital within the city; Rankings exclude hospitals with less than 25 cases except for patient surveys which excludes hospitals with less than 100 cases; (a) 100–299 cases; (1) The number of cases is too small to be sure how well a hospital is performing; (2) The hospital indicated that the data submitted for this measure were based on a sample of cases; (3) Data was collected during a shorter time period (fewer quarters) than the maximum possible time for this measure; (4) Suppressed for one or more quarters by CMS; (5) No data is available from the hospital for this measure; (6) Fewer than 100 patients completed the HCAHPS survey. Use these rates with caution, as the number of surveys may be too low to reliably assess hospital performance; (7) Survey results are based on less than 12 months of data; (8) Survey results are not available for this reporting period; (9) No or very few patients were eligible for the HCAHPS survey. The scores shown, if any, reflect a very small number of surveys; (10) A state average was not calculated because too few hospitals in the state submitted data; (11) There were discrepancies in the data collection process; Please refer to the User's Guide for a full explanation of data.

Grady Memorial Hospital

2220 Iowa Street
Chickasha, OK 73018
E-mail: jcrump@gradymem.org
URL: www.gradymem.org
Type: Acute Care Hospitals
Ownership: Voluntary Non-Profit - Other
Phone: 405-224-2300
Fax: 405-779-2413
Emergency Services: No
Beds: 99

Key Personnel:
CEO/President. . . . . E Michael Nunamaker
Chief of Medical Staff. . . . . Don R Hess, MD
Infection Control. . . . . Cathy Hamit, RN
Operating Room. . . . . Rick Warden, RN
Quality Assurance . . . . Tawina Wouldridge
Radiology. . . . . James E Milton

Measure	Cases	This Hosp.	State Avg.	U.S. Avg.
Heart Attack Care				
ACE Inhibitor or ARB for LVSD	0	-	95%	96%
Aspirin at Arrival[1]	7	100%	98%	99%
Aspirin at Discharge[1]	3	100%	98%	98%
Beta Blocker at Discharge[1]	1	100%	98%	98%
Fibrinolytic Medication Timing	0	-	42%	55%
PCI Within 90 Minutes of Arrival	0	-	88%	90%
Smoking Cessation Advice	0	-	100%	99%
Chest Pain/Possible Heart Attack Care				
Aspirin at Arrival	105	93%	94%	95%
Median Time to ECG (minutes)	112	16	9	8
Median Time to Transfer (minutes)[1]	3	105	75	61
Fibrinolytic Medication Timing[1]	15	67%	50%	54%
Heart Failure Care				
ACE Inhibitor or ARB for LVSD[1]	18	67%	94%	94%
Discharge Instructions	58	67%	85%	88%
Evaluation of LVS Function	77	88%	94%	98%
Smoking Cessation Advice[1]	13	100%	97%	98%
Pneumonia Care				
Appropriate Initial Antibiotic	50	80%	91%	92%
Blood Culture Timing	82	96%	96%	96%
Influenza Vaccine	57	84%	89%	91%
Initial Antibiotic Timing	94	99%	95%	95%
Pneumococcal Vaccine	91	92%	91%	93%
Smoking Cessation Advice	32	88%	95%	97%
Surgical Care Improvement Project				
Appropriate VTP Within 24 Hours	49	98%	91%	92%
Appropriate Hair Removal	80	99%	100%	99%
Appropriate Beta Blocker Usage[1]	4	100%	91%	93%
Controlled Postoperative Blood Glucose	0	-	95%	93%
Prophylactic Antibiotic Timing	43	86%	97%	97%
Prophylactic Antibiotic Timing (Outpatient)	27	100%	93%	92%
Prophylactic Antibiotic Selection	43	88%	98%	97%
Prophylactic Antibiotic Select. (Outpatient)	27	96%	95%	94%
Prophylactic Antibiotic Stopped	43	95%	94%	94%
Recommended VTP Ordered	49	98%	94%	94%
Urinary Catheter Removal[1]	6	83%	87%	90%
Children's Asthma Care				
Received Systemic Corticosteroids	-	-	-	100%
Received Home Management Plan	-	-	-	71%
Received Reliever Medication	-	-	-	100%
Use of Medical Imaging				
Combination Abdominal CT Scan	315	0.102	0.372	0.191
Combination Chest CT Scan	163	0.067	0.134	0.054
Follow-up Mammogram/Ultrasound	608	10.4%	8%	8.4%
MRI for Low Back Pain	66	42.4%	34.3%	32.7%
Survey of Patients' Hospital Experiences				
Area Around Room 'Always' Quiet at Night	300+	60%	-	58%
Doctors 'Always' Communicated Well	300+	80%	-	80%
Home Recovery Information Given	300+	84%	-	82%
Hospital Given 9 or 10 on 10 Point Scale	300+	62%	-	67%
Meds 'Always' Explained Before Given	300+	58%	-	60%
Nurses 'Always' Communicated Well	300+	76%	-	76%
Pain 'Always' Well Controlled	300+	64%	-	69%
Room and Bathroom 'Always' Clean	300+	67%	-	71%
Timely Help 'Always' Received	300+	62%	-	64%
Would Definitely Recommend Hospital	300+	57%	-	69%

Claremore Indian Hospital

101 South Moore Ave
Claremore, OK 74017
Type: Acute Care Hospitals
Ownership: Government - Federal
Phone: 918-341-8430
Fax: 918-342-6436
Emergency Services: Yes
Beds: 50

Key Personnel:
CEO/President. . . . . James Cussen
Chief of Medical Staff. . . . . Paul Mobley, DO
Infection Control. . . . . Patti V White
Quality Assurance . . . . Donna Francisco
Anesthesiology. . . . . Jeff Belinski, MD
Emergency Room . . . . Donald Bobek

Measure	Cases	This Hosp.	State Avg.	U.S. Avg.
Heart Attack Care				
ACE Inhibitor or ARB for LVSD[2]	0	-	95%	96%
Aspirin at Arrival[1,2]	1	0%	98%	99%
Aspirin at Discharge[1,2]	1	100%	98%	98%
Beta Blocker at Discharge[1,2]	1	100%	98%	98%
Fibrinolytic Medication Timing[2]	0	-	42%	55%
PCI Within 90 Minutes of Arrival[2]	0	-	88%	90%
Smoking Cessation Advice[2]	0	-	100%	99%
Chest Pain/Possible Heart Attack Care				
Aspirin at Arrival	145	86%	94%	95%
Median Time to ECG (minutes)	156	16	9	8
Median Time to Transfer (minutes)[1,3]	2	166	75	61
Fibrinolytic Medication Timing[1]	1	100%	50%	54%
Heart Failure Care				
ACE Inhibitor or ARB for LVSD[1]	3	100%	94%	94%
Discharge Instructions[1]	12	92%	85%	88%
Evaluation of LVS Function[1]	12	92%	94%	98%
Smoking Cessation Advice[1]	1	0%	97%	98%
Pneumonia Care				
Appropriate Initial Antibiotic	35	94%	91%	92%
Blood Culture Timing	34	97%	96%	96%
Influenza Vaccine[1]	14	93%	89%	91%
Initial Antibiotic Timing	37	92%	95%	95%
Pneumococcal Vaccine[1]	8	100%	91%	93%
Smoking Cessation Advice[1]	16	81%	95%	97%
Surgical Care Improvement Project				
Appropriate VTP Within 24 Hours[2]	32	81%	91%	92%
Appropriate Hair Removal[2]	107	100%	100%	99%
Appropriate Beta Blocker Usage[1,2]	11	82%	91%	93%
Controlled Postoperative Blood Glucose[2]	0	-	95%	93%
Prophylactic Antibiotic Timing[2]	71	99%	97%	97%
Prophylactic Antibiotic Timing (Outpatient)[1,3]	17	65%	93%	92%
Prophylactic Antibiotic Selection[2]	72	90%	98%	97%
Prophylactic Antibiotic Select. (Outpatient)[1,3]	12	100%	95%	94%
Prophylactic Antibiotic Stopped[2]	70	94%	94%	94%
Recommended VTP Ordered[2]	32	88%	94%	94%
Urinary Catheter Removal[1]	1	100%	87%	90%
Children's Asthma Care				
Received Systemic Corticosteroids	-	-	-	100%
Received Home Management Plan	-	-	-	71%
Received Reliever Medication	-	-	-	100%
Use of Medical Imaging				
Combination Abdominal CT Scan[5]	0	-	0.372	0.191
Combination Chest CT Scan[5]	0	-	0.134	0.054
Follow-up Mammogram/Ultrasound[5]	0	-	8%	8.4%
MRI for Low Back Pain[5]	0	-	34.3%	32.7%
Survey of Patients' Hospital Experiences				
Area Around Room 'Always' Quiet at Night	(a)	64%	-	58%
Doctors 'Always' Communicated Well	(a)	77%	-	80%
Home Recovery Information Given	(a)	73%	-	82%
Hospital Given 9 or 10 on 10 Point Scale	(a)	62%	-	67%
Meds 'Always' Explained Before Given	(a)	64%	-	60%
Nurses 'Always' Communicated Well	(a)	72%	-	76%
Pain 'Always' Well Controlled	(a)	66%	-	69%
Room and Bathroom 'Always' Clean	(a)	64%	-	71%
Timely Help 'Always' Received	(a)	69%	-	64%
Would Definitely Recommend Hospital	(a)	57%	-	69%

Claremore Regional Hospital

1202 N Muskogee Place
Claremore, OK 74017
URL: www.claremorereghospital.com
Type: Acute Care Hospitals
Ownership: Proprietary
Phone: 918-342-6777
Fax: 918-342-3330
Emergency Services: Yes
Beds: 73

Key Personnel:
CEO/President. . . . . David Chausard
Cardiac Laboratory. . . . . Lilia Turner
Chief of Medical Staff. . . . . Karen Harris
Emergency Room . . . . Jimmy Bible

Measure	Cases	This Hosp.	State Avg.	U.S. Avg.
Heart Attack Care				
ACE Inhibitor or ARB for LVSD[1]	2	100%	95%	96%
Aspirin at Arrival[1]	12	92%	98%	99%
Aspirin at Discharge[1]	4	75%	98%	98%
Beta Blocker at Discharge[1]	5	100%	98%	98%
Fibrinolytic Medication Timing	0	-	42%	55%
PCI Within 90 Minutes of Arrival	0	-	88%	90%
Smoking Cessation Advice[1]	2	100%	100%	99%
Chest Pain/Possible Heart Attack Care				
Aspirin at Arrival	108	99%	94%	95%
Median Time to ECG (minutes)	115	9	9	8
Median Time to Transfer (minutes)[1,3]	8	54	75	61
Fibrinolytic Medication Timing	0	-	50%	54%
Heart Failure Care				
ACE Inhibitor or ARB for LVSD	31	97%	94%	94%
Discharge Instructions	39	85%	85%	88%
Evaluation of LVS Function	48	98%	94%	98%
Smoking Cessation Advice[1]	12	100%	97%	98%
Pneumonia Care				
Appropriate Initial Antibiotic	90	98%	91%	92%
Blood Culture Timing	126	99%	96%	96%
Influenza Vaccine	87	92%	89%	91%
Initial Antibiotic Timing	128	95%	95%	95%
Pneumococcal Vaccine	100	98%	91%	93%
Smoking Cessation Advice	54	100%	95%	97%
Surgical Care Improvement Project				
Appropriate VTP Within 24 Hours	73	100%	91%	92%
Appropriate Hair Removal	187	100%	100%	99%
Appropriate Beta Blocker Usage	42	83%	91%	93%
Controlled Postoperative Blood Glucose	0	-	95%	93%
Prophylactic Antibiotic Timing	144	94%	97%	97%
Prophylactic Antibiotic Timing (Outpatient)	61	92%	93%	92%
Prophylactic Antibiotic Selection	147	99%	98%	97%
Prophylactic Antibiotic Select. (Outpatient)	58	98%	95%	94%
Prophylactic Antibiotic Stopped	141	94%	94%	94%
Recommended VTP Ordered	73	100%	94%	94%
Urinary Catheter Removal[1]	20	90%	87%	90%
Children's Asthma Care				
Received Systemic Corticosteroids	-	-	-	100%
Received Home Management Plan	-	-	-	71%
Received Reliever Medication	-	-	-	100%
Use of Medical Imaging				
Combination Abdominal CT Scan	298	0.839	0.372	0.191
Combination Chest CT Scan	186	0.860	0.134	0.054
Follow-up Mammogram/Ultrasound	472	10.4%	8%	8.4%
MRI for Low Back Pain	90	38.9%	34.3%	32.7%
Survey of Patients' Hospital Experiences				
Area Around Room 'Always' Quiet at Night	300+	56%	-	58%
Doctors 'Always' Communicated Well	300+	81%	-	80%
Home Recovery Information Given	300+	85%	-	82%
Hospital Given 9 or 10 on 10 Point Scale	300+	62%	-	67%
Meds 'Always' Explained Before Given	300+	60%	-	60%
Nurses 'Always' Communicated Well	300+	71%	-	76%
Pain 'Always' Well Controlled	300+	68%	-	69%
Room and Bathroom 'Always' Clean	300+	69%	-	71%
Timely Help 'Always' Received	300+	60%	-	64%
Would Definitely Recommend Hospital	300+	64%	-	69%

NOTE: Hospital profiles are in alphabetical order by state, then city, then hospital within the city; Rankings exclude hospitals with less than 25 cases except for patient surveys which excludes hospitals with less than 100 cases; (a) 100–299 cases; (1) The number of cases is too small to be sure how well a hospital is performing; (2) The hospital indicated that the data submitted for this measure were based on a sample of cases; (3) Data was collected during a shorter time period (fewer quarters) than the maximum possible time for this measure; (4) Suppressed for one or more quarters by CMS; (5) No data is available from the hospital for this measure; (6) Fewer than 100 patients completed the HCAHPS survey. Use these rates with caution, as the number of surveys may be too low to reliably assess hospital performance; (7) Survey results are based on less than 12 months of data; (8) Survey results are not available for this reporting period; (9) No or very few patients were eligible for the HCAHPS survey. The scores shown, if any, reflect a very small number of surveys; (10) A state average was not calculated because too few hospitals in the state submitted data; (11) There were discrepancies in the data collection process; Please refer to the User's Guide for a full explanation of data.

Cleveland Area Hospital

1401 West Pawnee
Cleveland, OK 74020
Phone: 918-358-2501
Type: Critical Access Hospitals
Emergency Services: Yes
Ownership: Govt - Hospital Dist/Auth

Measure	Cases	This Hosp.	State Avg.	U.S. Avg.
Heart Attack Care				
ACE Inhibitor or ARB for LVSD[5]	0	-	95%	96%
Aspirin at Arrival[5]	0	-	98%	99%
Aspirin at Discharge[5]	0	-	98%	98%
Beta Blocker at Discharge[5]	0	-	98%	98%
Fibrinolytic Medication Timing[5]	0	-	42%	55%
PCI Within 90 Minutes of Arrival[5]	0	-	88%	90%
Smoking Cessation Advice[5]	0	-	100%	99%
Chest Pain/Possible Heart Attack Care				
Aspirin at Arrival	-	-	94%	95%
Median Time to ECG (minutes)	-	-	9	8
Median Time to Transfer (minutes)	-	-	75	61
Fibrinolytic Medication Timing	-	-	50%	54%
Heart Failure Care				
ACE Inhibitor or ARB for LVSD[1,3]	1	0%	94%	94%
Discharge Instructions[1,3]	2	0%	85%	88%
Evaluation of LVS Function[1,3]	2	100%	94%	98%
Smoking Cessation Advice[3]	0	-	97%	98%
Pneumonia Care				
Appropriate Initial Antibiotic[1,3]	10	80%	91%	92%
Blood Culture Timing[1,3]	8	75%	96%	96%
Influenza Vaccine[1]	13	62%	89%	91%
Initial Antibiotic Timing[1,3]	15	87%	95%	95%
Pneumococcal Vaccine[1,3]	12	50%	91%	93%
Smoking Cessation Advice[1,3]	2	50%	95%	97%
Surgical Care Improvement Project				
Appropriate VTP Within 24 Hours[5]	0	-	91%	92%
Appropriate Hair Removal[5]	0	-	100%	99%
Appropriate Beta Blocker Usage[5]	0	-	91%	93%
Controlled Postoperative Blood Glucose[5]	0	-	95%	93%
Prophylactic Antibiotic Timing[5]	0	-	97%	97%
Prophylactic Antibiotic Timing (Outpatient)	-	-	93%	92%
Prophylactic Antibiotic Selection[5]	0	-	98%	97%
Prophylactic Antibiotic Select. (Outpatient)	-	-	95%	94%
Prophylactic Antibiotic Stopped[5]	0	-	94%	94%
Recommended VTP Ordered[5]	0	-	94%	94%
Urinary Catheter Removal[5]	0	-	87%	90%
Children's Asthma Care				
Received Systemic Corticosteroids	-	-	-	100%
Received Home Management Plan	-	-	-	71%
Received Reliever Medication	-	-	-	100%
Use of Medical Imaging				
Combination Abdominal CT Scan	-	-	0.372	0.191
Combination Chest CT Scan	-	-	0.134	0.054
Follow-up Mammogram/Ultrasound	-	-	8%	8.4%
MRI for Low Back Pain	-	-	34.3%	32.7%
Survey of Patients' Hospital Experiences				
Area Around Room 'Always' Quiet at Night[8]	-	-	-	58%
Doctors 'Always' Communicated Well[8]	-	-	-	80%
Home Recovery Information Given[8]	-	-	-	82%
Hospital Given 9 or 10 on 10 Point Scale[8]	-	-	-	67%
Meds 'Always' Explained Before Given[8]	-	-	-	60%
Nurses 'Always' Communicated Well[8]	-	-	-	76%
Pain 'Always' Well Controlled[8]	-	-	-	69%
Room and Bathroom 'Always' Clean[8]	-	-	-	71%
Timely Help 'Always' Received[8]	-	-	-	64%
Would Definitely Recommend Hospital[8]	-	-	-	69%

Integris Clinton Regional Hospital

100 North 30th Street
Clinton, OK 73601
Phone: 580-323-2363
Fax: 580-331-1463
URL: www.integris-health.com
Type: Acute Care Hospitals
Emergency Services: Yes
Ownership: Government - Local
Beds: 64

Key Personnel:
CEO/President. . . . . Stanley F Hupfeld
Chief of Medical Staff . . . . Stacy Clothier
Infection Control. . . . . Karol Dillard, RN
Operating Room. . . . . Tom Cashero, RN
Quality Assurance . . . . Bill Kelton
Emergency Room . . . . Tammy Martin, RN
Intensive Care Unit. . . . . Carol Kish, RN

Measure	Cases	This Hosp.	State Avg.	U.S. Avg.
Heart Attack Care				
ACE Inhibitor or ARB for LVSD	0	-	95%	96%
Aspirin at Arrival[1]	5	100%	98%	99%
Aspirin at Discharge[1]	3	100%	98%	98%
Beta Blocker at Discharge[1]	2	100%	98%	98%
Fibrinolytic Medication Timing	0	-	42%	55%
PCI Within 90 Minutes of Arrival	0	-	88%	90%
Smoking Cessation Advice	0	-	100%	99%
Chest Pain/Possible Heart Attack Care				
Aspirin at Arrival	58	95%	94%	95%
Median Time to ECG (minutes)	61	7	9	8
Median Time to Transfer (minutes)[1,3]	1	140	75	61
Fibrinolytic Medication Timing[1]	6	50%	50%	54%
Heart Failure Care				
ACE Inhibitor or ARB for LVSD	30	97%	94%	94%
Discharge Instructions	50	82%	85%	88%
Evaluation of LVS Function	74	99%	94%	98%
Smoking Cessation Advice[1]	10	100%	97%	98%
Pneumonia Care				
Appropriate Initial Antibiotic	63	92%	91%	92%
Blood Culture Timing	42	98%	96%	96%
Influenza Vaccine	44	91%	89%	91%
Initial Antibiotic Timing	97	98%	95%	95%
Pneumococcal Vaccine	58	98%	91%	93%
Smoking Cessation Advice	36	100%	95%	97%
Surgical Care Improvement Project				
Appropriate VTP Within 24 Hours[1]	8	88%	91%	92%
Appropriate Hair Removal[1]	19	100%	100%	99%
Appropriate Beta Blocker Usage[1]	1	100%	91%	93%
Controlled Postoperative Blood Glucose	0	-	95%	93%
Prophylactic Antibiotic Timing[1]	6	83%	97%	97%
Prophylactic Antibiotic Timing (Outpatient)[1]	15	87%	93%	92%
Prophylactic Antibiotic Selection[1]	6	67%	98%	97%
Prophylactic Antibiotic Select. (Outpatient)[1]	13	100%	95%	94%
Prophylactic Antibiotic Stopped[1]	5	100%	94%	94%
Recommended VTP Ordered[1]	8	100%	94%	94%
Urinary Catheter Removal[1]	1	0%	87%	90%
Children's Asthma Care				
Received Systemic Corticosteroids	-	-	-	100%
Received Home Management Plan	-	-	-	71%
Received Reliever Medication	-	-	-	100%
Use of Medical Imaging				
Combination Abdominal CT Scan	236	0.581	0.372	0.191
Combination Chest CT Scan	150	0.020	0.134	0.054
Follow-up Mammogram/Ultrasound	192	8.3%	8%	8.4%
MRI for Low Back Pain[1]	42	33.3%	34.3%	32.7%
Survey of Patients' Hospital Experiences				
Area Around Room 'Always' Quiet at Night	300+	61%	-	58%
Doctors 'Always' Communicated Well	300+	84%	-	80%
Home Recovery Information Given	300+	84%	-	82%
Hospital Given 9 or 10 on 10 Point Scale	300+	63%	-	67%
Meds 'Always' Explained Before Given	300+	62%	-	60%
Nurses 'Always' Communicated Well	300+	73%	-	76%
Pain 'Always' Well Controlled	300+	67%	-	69%
Room and Bathroom 'Always' Clean	300+	78%	-	71%
Timely Help 'Always' Received	300+	66%	-	64%
Would Definitely Recommend Hospital	300+	63%	-	69%

Mary Hurley Hospital

6 North Covington
Coalgate, OK 74538
Phone: 580-927-2327
Fax: 580-927-2432
Type: Critical Access Hospitals
Emergency Services: Yes
Ownership: Proprietary
Beds: 20

Key Personnel:
CEO/President. . . . . Dean Clements
Chief of Medical Staff . . . . R J Alton
Emergency Room . . . . Tommie Stanberry

Measure	Cases	This Hosp.	State Avg.	U.S. Avg.
Heart Attack Care				
ACE Inhibitor or ARB for LVSD[5]	0	-	95%	96%
Aspirin at Arrival[5]	0	-	98%	99%
Aspirin at Discharge[5]	0	-	98%	98%
Beta Blocker at Discharge[5]	0	-	98%	98%
Fibrinolytic Medication Timing[5]	0	-	42%	55%
PCI Within 90 Minutes of Arrival[5]	0	-	88%	90%
Smoking Cessation Advice[5]	0	-	100%	99%
Chest Pain/Possible Heart Attack Care				
Aspirin at Arrival	-	-	94%	95%
Median Time to ECG (minutes)	-	-	9	8
Median Time to Transfer (minutes)	-	-	75	61
Fibrinolytic Medication Timing	-	-	50%	54%
Heart Failure Care				
ACE Inhibitor or ARB for LVSD[1]	9	44%	94%	94%
Discharge Instructions	36	69%	85%	88%
Evaluation of LVS Function	58	60%	94%	98%
Smoking Cessation Advice[1]	9	100%	97%	98%
Pneumonia Care				
Appropriate Initial Antibiotic[1]	10	60%	91%	92%
Blood Culture Timing[1]	1	0%	96%	96%
Influenza Vaccine[1]	11	73%	89%	91%
Initial Antibiotic Timing[1]	14	86%	95%	95%
Pneumococcal Vaccine[1]	15	87%	91%	93%
Smoking Cessation Advice[1]	10	100%	95%	97%
Surgical Care Improvement Project				
Appropriate VTP Within 24 Hours[5]	0	-	91%	92%
Appropriate Hair Removal[5]	0	-	100%	99%
Appropriate Beta Blocker Usage[5]	0	-	91%	93%
Controlled Postoperative Blood Glucose[5]	0	-	95%	93%
Prophylactic Antibiotic Timing[5]	0	-	97%	97%
Prophylactic Antibiotic Timing (Outpatient)	-	-	93%	92%
Prophylactic Antibiotic Selection[5]	0	-	98%	97%
Prophylactic Antibiotic Select. (Outpatient)	-	-	95%	94%
Prophylactic Antibiotic Stopped[5]	0	-	94%	94%
Recommended VTP Ordered[5]	0	-	94%	94%
Urinary Catheter Removal[5]	0	-	87%	90%
Children's Asthma Care				
Received Systemic Corticosteroids	-	-	-	100%
Received Home Management Plan	-	-	-	71%
Received Reliever Medication	-	-	-	100%
Use of Medical Imaging				
Combination Abdominal CT Scan	-	-	0.372	0.191
Combination Chest CT Scan	-	-	0.134	0.054
Follow-up Mammogram/Ultrasound	-	-	8%	8.4%
MRI for Low Back Pain	-	-	34.3%	32.7%
Survey of Patients' Hospital Experiences				
Area Around Room 'Always' Quiet at Night[8]	-	-	-	58%
Doctors 'Always' Communicated Well[8]	-	-	-	80%
Home Recovery Information Given[8]	-	-	-	82%
Hospital Given 9 or 10 on 10 Point Scale[8]	-	-	-	67%
Meds 'Always' Explained Before Given[8]	-	-	-	60%
Nurses 'Always' Communicated Well[8]	-	-	-	76%
Pain 'Always' Well Controlled[8]	-	-	-	69%
Room and Bathroom 'Always' Clean[8]	-	-	-	71%
Timely Help 'Always' Received[8]	-	-	-	64%
Would Definitely Recommend Hospital[8]	-	-	-	69%

NOTE: Hospital profiles are in alphabetical order by state, then city, then hospital within the city; Rankings exclude hospitals with less than 25 cases except for patient surveys which excludes hospitals with less than 100 cases; (a) 100–299 cases; (1) The number of cases is too small to be sure how well a hospital is performing; (2) The hospital indicated that the data submitted for this measure were based on a sample of cases; (3) Data was collected during a shorter time period (fewer quarters) than the maximum possible time for this measure; (4) Suppressed for one or more quarters by CMS; (5) No data is available from the hospital for this measure; (6) Fewer than 100 patients completed the HCAHPS survey. Use these rates with caution, as the number of surveys may be too low to reliably assess hospital performance; (7) Survey results are based on less than 12 months of data; (8) Survey results are not available for this reporting period; (9) No or very few patients were eligible for the HCAHPS survey. The scores shown, if any, reflect a very small number of surveys; (10) A state average was not calculated because too few hospitals in the state submitted data; (11) There were discrepancies in the data collection process; Please refer to the User's Guide for a full explanation of data.

Cordell Memorial Hospital

1220 North Glenn English Street
Cordell, OK 73632
Type: Critical Access Hospitals
Ownership: Govt - Hospital Dist/Auth

Phone: 580-832-3339
Fax: 580-832-5076
Emergency Services: Yes
Beds: 25

Measure	Cases	This Hosp.	State Avg.	U.S. Avg.
Heart Attack Care				
ACE Inhibitor or ARB for LVSD[2,3]	0	-	95%	96%
Aspirin at Arrival[1,2,3]	1	100%	98%	99%
Aspirin at Discharge[1,2,3]	1	100%	98%	98%
Beta Blocker at Discharge[2,3]	0	-	98%	98%
Fibrinolytic Medication Timing[2,3]	0	-	42%	55%
PCI Within 90 Minutes of Arrival[2,3]	0	-	88%	90%
Smoking Cessation Advice[2,3]	0	-	100%	99%
Chest Pain/Possible Heart Attack Care				
Aspirin at Arrival	-	-	94%	95%
Median Time to ECG (minutes)	-	-	9	8
Median Time to Transfer (minutes)	-	-	75	61
Fibrinolytic Medication Timing	-	-	50%	54%
Heart Failure Care				
ACE Inhibitor or ARB for LVSD[2]	0	-	94%	94%
Discharge Instructions[1,2]	1	100%	85%	88%
Evaluation of LVS Function[1,2]	5	20%	94%	98%
Smoking Cessation Advice[2]	0	-	97%	98%
Pneumonia Care				
Appropriate Initial Antibiotic[1,2]	7	71%	91%	92%
Blood Culture Timing[1,2]	4	100%	96%	96%
Influenza Vaccine[1,2]	6	67%	89%	91%
Initial Antibiotic Timing[1,2]	12	100%	95%	95%
Pneumococcal Vaccine[1,2]	16	88%	91%	93%
Smoking Cessation Advice[1,2]	2	100%	95%	97%
Surgical Care Improvement Project				
Appropriate VTP Within 24 Hours[5]	0	-	91%	92%
Appropriate Hair Removal[5]	0	-	100%	99%
Appropriate Beta Blocker Usage[5]	0	-	91%	93%
Controlled Postoperative Blood Glucose[5]	0	-	95%	93%
Prophylactic Antibiotic Timing[5]	0	-	97%	97%
Prophylactic Antibiotic Timing (Outpatient)	-	-	93%	92%
Prophylactic Antibiotic Selection[5]	0	-	98%	97%
Prophylactic Antibiotic Select. (Outpatient)	-	-	95%	94%
Prophylactic Antibiotic Stopped[5]	0	-	94%	94%
Recommended VTP Ordered[5]	0	-	94%	94%
Urinary Catheter Removal[5]	0	-	87%	90%
Children's Asthma Care				
Received Systemic Corticosteroids	-	-	-	100%
Received Home Management Plan	-	-	-	71%
Received Reliever Medication	-	-	-	100%
Use of Medical Imaging				
Combination Abdominal CT Scan	-	-	0.372	0.191
Combination Chest CT Scan	-	-	0.134	0.054
Follow-up Mammogram/Ultrasound	-	-	8%	8.4%
MRI for Low Back Pain	-	-	34.3%	32.7%
Survey of Patients' Hospital Experiences				
Area Around Room 'Always' Quiet at Night[6]	<100	67%	-	58%
Doctors 'Always' Communicated Well[6]	<100	96%	-	80%
Home Recovery Information Given[6]	<100	84%	-	82%
Hospital Given 9 or 10 on 10 Point Scale[6]	<100	90%	-	67%
Meds 'Always' Explained Before Given[6]	<100	71%	-	60%
Nurses 'Always' Communicated Well[6]	<100	91%	-	76%
Pain 'Always' Well Controlled[6]	<100	86%	-	69%
Room and Bathroom 'Always' Clean[6]	<100	93%	-	71%
Timely Help 'Always' Received[6]	<100	85%	-	64%
Would Definitely Recommend Hospital	<100	91%	-	69%

Cushing Regional Hospital

1027 East Cherry Street
Cushing, OK 74023
URL: www.hillcrest.com/cushing
Type: Acute Care Hospitals
Ownership: Proprietary

Phone: 918-225-2915
Fax: 918-225-8202
Emergency Services: Yes
Beds: 99

Key Personnel:
CEO/President. . . . . Ron Cackler
Chief of Medical Staff. . . . . Marylin Peck
Infection Control. . . . . Bernadine Allen, RN
Operating Room. . . . . Fred J Crapse
Quality Assurance . . . . Bernadine Allen, RN
Anesthesiology. . . . . Ray Shofner
Emergency Room . . . . Tom Dotson, MD
Intensive Care Unit. . . . . Jane Stephens

Measure	Cases	This Hosp.	State Avg.	U.S. Avg.
Heart Attack Care				
ACE Inhibitor or ARB for LVSD	0	-	95%	96%
Aspirin at Arrival[1]	8	88%	98%	99%
Aspirin at Discharge[1]	6	83%	98%	98%
Beta Blocker at Discharge[1]	7	100%	98%	98%
Fibrinolytic Medication Timing	0	-	42%	55%
PCI Within 90 Minutes of Arrival	0	-	88%	90%
Smoking Cessation Advice[1]	1	100%	100%	99%
Chest Pain/Possible Heart Attack Care				
Aspirin at Arrival	140	100%	94%	95%
Median Time to ECG (minutes)	145	9	9	8
Median Time to Transfer (minutes)[1]	8	54	75	61
Fibrinolytic Medication Timing	0	-	50%	54%
Heart Failure Care				
ACE Inhibitor or ARB for LVSD[1]	14	64%	94%	94%
Discharge Instructions	34	100%	85%	88%
Evaluation of LVS Function	49	92%	94%	98%
Smoking Cessation Advice[1]	11	100%	97%	98%
Pneumonia Care				
Appropriate Initial Antibiotic	120	92%	91%	92%
Blood Culture Timing	162	98%	96%	96%
Influenza Vaccine	106	94%	89%	91%
Initial Antibiotic Timing	151	99%	95%	95%
Pneumococcal Vaccine	112	93%	91%	93%
Smoking Cessation Advice	73	100%	95%	97%
Surgical Care Improvement Project				
Appropriate VTP Within 24 Hours	54	100%	91%	92%
Appropriate Hair Removal	105	100%	100%	99%
Appropriate Beta Blocker Usage	25	92%	91%	93%
Controlled Postoperative Blood Glucose	0	-	95%	93%
Prophylactic Antibiotic Timing	74	85%	97%	97%
Prophylactic Antibiotic Timing (Outpatient)[1,3]	10	60%	93%	92%
Prophylactic Antibiotic Selection	74	91%	98%	97%
Prophylactic Antibiotic Select. (Outpatient)[1,3]	8	0%	95%	94%
Prophylactic Antibiotic Stopped	73	92%	94%	94%
Recommended VTP Ordered	54	100%	94%	94%
Urinary Catheter Removal[1]	18	78%	87%	90%
Children's Asthma Care				
Received Systemic Corticosteroids	-	-	-	100%
Received Home Management Plan	-	-	-	71%
Received Reliever Medication	-	-	-	100%
Use of Medical Imaging				
Combination Abdominal CT Scan	170	0.565	0.372	0.191
Combination Chest CT Scan	96	0.188	0.134	0.054
Follow-up Mammogram/Ultrasound	274	4.0%	8%	8.4%
MRI for Low Back Pain	68	35.3%	34.3%	32.7%
Survey of Patients' Hospital Experiences				
Area Around Room 'Always' Quiet at Night	(a)	63%	-	58%
Doctors 'Always' Communicated Well	(a)	86%	-	80%
Home Recovery Information Given	(a)	82%	-	82%
Hospital Given 9 or 10 on 10 Point Scale	(a)	68%	-	67%
Meds 'Always' Explained Before Given	(a)	60%	-	60%
Nurses 'Always' Communicated Well	(a)	76%	-	76%
Pain 'Always' Well Controlled	(a)	72%	-	69%
Room and Bathroom 'Always' Clean	(a)	69%	-	71%
Timely Help 'Always' Received	(a)	67%	-	64%
Would Definitely Recommend Hospital	(a)	67%	-	69%

Drumright Regional Hospital

610 West Bypass
Drumright, OK 74030
Type: Critical Access Hospitals
Ownership: Proprietary

Phone: 918-382-2300
Emergency Services: Yes

Measure	Cases	This Hosp.	State Avg.	U.S. Avg.
Heart Attack Care				
ACE Inhibitor or ARB for LVSD[3]	0	-	95%	96%
Aspirin at Arrival[3]	0	-	98%	99%
Aspirin at Discharge[3]	0	-	98%	98%
Beta Blocker at Discharge[3]	0	-	98%	98%
Fibrinolytic Medication Timing[3]	0	-	42%	55%
PCI Within 90 Minutes of Arrival[3]	0	-	88%	90%
Smoking Cessation Advice[3]	0	-	100%	99%
Chest Pain/Possible Heart Attack Care				
Aspirin at Arrival	-	-	94%	95%
Median Time to ECG (minutes)	-	-	9	8
Median Time to Transfer (minutes)	-	-	75	61
Fibrinolytic Medication Timing	-	-	50%	54%
Heart Failure Care				
ACE Inhibitor or ARB for LVSD[1]	2	100%	94%	94%
Discharge Instructions[1]	7	29%	85%	88%
Evaluation of LVS Function[1]	9	89%	94%	98%
Smoking Cessation Advice[1]	2	100%	97%	98%
Pneumonia Care				
Appropriate Initial Antibiotic	32	88%	91%	92%
Blood Culture Timing[1]	4	100%	96%	96%
Influenza Vaccine[1]	24	71%	89%	91%
Initial Antibiotic Timing	46	91%	95%	95%
Pneumococcal Vaccine	27	56%	91%	93%
Smoking Cessation Advice	29	86%	95%	97%
Surgical Care Improvement Project				
Appropriate VTP Within 24 Hours[1]	14	86%	91%	92%
Appropriate Hair Removal[1]	13	92%	100%	99%
Appropriate Beta Blocker Usage[1]	1	0%	91%	93%
Controlled Postoperative Blood Glucose	0	-	95%	93%
Prophylactic Antibiotic Timing[1]	23	83%	97%	97%
Prophylactic Antibiotic Timing (Outpatient)	-	-	93%	92%
Prophylactic Antibiotic Selection[1]	23	43%	98%	97%
Prophylactic Antibiotic Select. (Outpatient)	-	-	95%	94%
Prophylactic Antibiotic Stopped[1]	23	35%	94%	94%
Recommended VTP Ordered[1]	14	86%	94%	94%
Urinary Catheter Removal[1]	1	0%	87%	90%
Children's Asthma Care				
Received Systemic Corticosteroids	-	-	-	100%
Received Home Management Plan	-	-	-	71%
Received Reliever Medication	-	-	-	100%
Use of Medical Imaging				
Combination Abdominal CT Scan	-	-	0.372	0.191
Combination Chest CT Scan	-	-	0.134	0.054
Follow-up Mammogram/Ultrasound	-	-	8%	8.4%
MRI for Low Back Pain	-	-	34.3%	32.7%
Survey of Patients' Hospital Experiences				
Area Around Room 'Always' Quiet at Night[8]	-	-	-	58%
Doctors 'Always' Communicated Well[8]	-	-	-	80%
Home Recovery Information Given[8]	-	-	-	82%
Hospital Given 9 or 10 on 10 Point Scale[8]	-	-	-	67%
Meds 'Always' Explained Before Given[8]	-	-	-	60%
Nurses 'Always' Communicated Well[8]	-	-	-	76%
Pain 'Always' Well Controlled[8]	-	-	-	69%
Room and Bathroom 'Always' Clean[8]	-	-	-	71%
Timely Help 'Always' Received[8]	-	-	-	64%
Would Definitely Recommend Hospital[8]	-	-	-	69%

NOTE: Hospital profiles are in alphabetical order by state, then city, then hospital within the city; Rankings exclude hospitals with less than 25 cases except for patient surveys which excludes hospitals with less than 100 cases; (a) 100–299 cases; (1) The number of cases is too small to be sure how well a hospital is performing; (2) The hospital indicated that the data submitted for this measure were based on a sample of cases; (3) Data was collected during a shorter time period (fewer quarters) than the maximum possible time for this measure; (4) Suppressed for one or more quarters by CMS; (5) No data is available from the hospital for this measure; (6) Fewer than 100 patients completed the HCAHPS survey. Use these rates with caution, as the number of surveys may be too low to reliably assess hospital performance; (7) Survey results are based on less than 12 months of data; (8) Survey results are not available for this reporting period; (9) No or very few patients were eligible for the HCAHPS survey. The scores shown, if any, reflect a very small number of surveys; (10) A state average was not calculated because too few hospitals in the state submitted data; (11) There were discrepancies in the data collection process; Please refer to the User's Guide for a full explanation of data.

Duncan Regional Hospital

1407 Whisenant Drive | Phone: 580-252-5300
Duncan, OK 73533 | Fax: 580-251-8559
URL: www.duncanregional.com
Type: Acute Care Hospitals | Emergency Services: No
Ownership: Proprietary | Beds: 152

Key Personnel:
CEO/President. . . . . Scott Street
Chief of Medical Staff . . . . Jim McGooran, MD
Radiology. . . . . Nelson Uzquiano

Measure	Cases	This Hosp.	State Avg.	U.S. Avg.
Heart Attack Care				
ACE Inhibitor or ARB for LVSD[1]	2	100%	95%	96%
Aspirin at Arrival[1]	14	100%	98%	99%
Aspirin at Discharge[1]	9	100%	98%	98%
Beta Blocker at Discharge[1]	13	100%	98%	98%
Fibrinolytic Medication Timing	0	-	42%	55%
PCI Within 90 Minutes of Arrival	0	-	88%	90%
Smoking Cessation Advice[1]	2	100%	100%	99%
Chest Pain/Possible Heart Attack Care				
Aspirin at Arrival	134	99%	94%	95%
Median Time to ECG (minutes)	137	9	9	8
Median Time to Transfer (minutes)[1,3]	10	141	75	61
Fibrinolytic Medication Timing[1]	13	23%	50%	54%
Heart Failure Care				
ACE Inhibitor or ARB for LVSD	43	98%	94%	94%
Discharge Instructions	106	94%	85%	88%
Evaluation of LVS Function	127	100%	94%	98%
Smoking Cessation Advice	35	100%	97%	98%
Pneumonia Care				
Appropriate Initial Antibiotic[2]	133	94%	91%	92%
Blood Culture Timing[2]	210	96%	96%	96%
Influenza Vaccine[2]	129	93%	89%	91%
Initial Antibiotic Timing[2]	212	97%	95%	95%
Pneumococcal Vaccine[2]	202	98%	91%	93%
Smoking Cessation Advice[2]	87	100%	95%	97%
Surgical Care Improvement Project				
Appropriate VTP Within 24 Hours[2]	142	89%	91%	92%
Appropriate Hair Removal[2]	308	98%	100%	99%
Appropriate Beta Blocker Usage[2]	91	92%	91%	93%
Controlled Postoperative Blood Glucose[2]	0	-	95%	93%
Prophylactic Antibiotic Timing[2]	229	97%	97%	97%
Prophylactic Antibiotic Timing (Outpatient)	48	92%	93%	92%
Prophylactic Antibiotic Selection[2]	230	98%	98%	97%
Prophylactic Antibiotic Select. (Outpatient)	45	96%	95%	94%
Prophylactic Antibiotic Stopped[2]	222	96%	94%	94%
Recommended VTP Ordered[2]	142	98%	94%	94%
Urinary Catheter Removal[2]	76	95%	87%	90%
Children's Asthma Care				
Received Systemic Corticosteroids	-	-	-	100%
Received Home Management Plan	-	-	-	71%
Received Reliever Medication	-	-	-	100%
Use of Medical Imaging				
Combination Abdominal CT Scan	479	0.150	0.372	0.191
Combination Chest CT Scan	390	0.197	0.134	0.054
Follow-up Mammogram/Ultrasound	691	14.9%	8%	8.4%
MRI for Low Back Pain	128	39.8%	34.3%	32.7%
Survey of Patients' Hospital Experiences				
Area Around Room 'Always' Quiet at Night	300+	60%	-	58%
Doctors 'Always' Communicated Well	300+	83%	-	80%
Home Recovery Information Given	300+	81%	-	82%
Hospital Given 9 or 10 on 10 Point Scale	300+	66%	-	67%
Meds 'Always' Explained Before Given	300+	61%	-	60%
Nurses 'Always' Communicated Well	300+	75%	-	76%
Pain 'Always' Well Controlled	300+	69%	-	69%
Room and Bathroom 'Always' Clean	300+	68%	-	71%
Timely Help 'Always' Received	300+	65%	-	64%
Would Definitely Recommend Hospital	300+	64%	-	69%

Medical Center of Southeastern Oklahoma

1800 University Boulevard | Phone: 405-924-3080
Durant, OK 74702 | Fax: 580-924-0422
E-mail: info@mcsohealth.com
URL: www.mcsohealth.com
Type: Acute Care Hospitals | Emergency Services: Yes
Ownership: Proprietary | Beds: 103

Key Personnel:
CEO/President. . . . . Jackie Harms
Chief of Medical Staff . . . . Peter Hedberg, MD
Infection Control. . . . . Vicki Fridle, MT ASCP
Operating Room. . . . . Pat Ferreri, RN
Quality Assurance . . . . Belinda Butlan, RN

Measure	Cases	This Hosp.	State Avg.	U.S. Avg.
Heart Attack Care				
ACE Inhibitor or ARB for LVSD[1]	13	100%	95%	96%
Aspirin at Arrival	39	100%	98%	99%
Aspirin at Discharge[1]	22	100%	98%	98%
Beta Blocker at Discharge	29	100%	98%	98%
Fibrinolytic Medication Timing	0	-	42%	55%
PCI Within 90 Minutes of Arrival	0	-	88%	90%
Smoking Cessation Advice[1]	11	100%	100%	99%
Chest Pain/Possible Heart Attack Care				
Aspirin at Arrival	44	100%	94%	95%
Median Time to ECG (minutes)	44	5	9	8
Median Time to Transfer (minutes)[3]	0	-	75	61
Fibrinolytic Medication Timing[1]	3	100%	50%	54%
Heart Failure Care				
ACE Inhibitor or ARB for LVSD	85	100%	94%	94%
Discharge Instructions	250	100%	85%	88%
Evaluation of LVS Function	326	100%	94%	98%
Smoking Cessation Advice	86	100%	97%	98%
Pneumonia Care				
Appropriate Initial Antibiotic	134	96%	91%	92%
Blood Culture Timing	159	99%	96%	96%
Influenza Vaccine	156	100%	89%	91%
Initial Antibiotic Timing	224	100%	95%	95%
Pneumococcal Vaccine	209	100%	91%	93%
Smoking Cessation Advice	122	100%	95%	97%
Surgical Care Improvement Project				
Appropriate VTP Within 24 Hours	81	96%	91%	92%
Appropriate Hair Removal	229	100%	100%	99%
Appropriate Beta Blocker Usage	42	98%	91%	93%
Controlled Postoperative Blood Glucose	0	-	95%	93%
Prophylactic Antibiotic Timing	142	99%	97%	97%
Prophylactic Antibiotic Timing (Outpatient)	148	100%	93%	92%
Prophylactic Antibiotic Selection	142	99%	98%	97%
Prophylactic Antibiotic Select. (Outpatient)	148	99%	95%	94%
Prophylactic Antibiotic Stopped	138	100%	94%	94%
Recommended VTP Ordered	81	96%	94%	94%
Urinary Catheter Removal[1]	15	87%	87%	90%
Children's Asthma Care				
Received Systemic Corticosteroids[1]	9	100%	-	100%
Received Home Management Plan[1]	9	100%	-	71%
Received Reliever Medication[1]	9	100%	-	100%
Use of Medical Imaging				
Combination Abdominal CT Scan	317	0.110	0.372	0.191
Combination Chest CT Scan	183	0.016	0.134	0.054
Follow-up Mammogram/Ultrasound	661	11.6%	8%	8.4%
MRI for Low Back Pain	76	30.3%	34.3%	32.7%
Survey of Patients' Hospital Experiences				
Area Around Room 'Always' Quiet at Night	300+	55%	-	58%
Doctors 'Always' Communicated Well	300+	81%	-	80%
Home Recovery Information Given	300+	78%	-	82%
Hospital Given 9 or 10 on 10 Point Scale	300+	60%	-	67%
Meds 'Always' Explained Before Given	300+	58%	-	60%
Nurses 'Always' Communicated Well	300+	72%	-	76%
Pain 'Always' Well Controlled	300+	65%	-	69%
Room and Bathroom 'Always' Clean	300+	68%	-	71%
Timely Help 'Always' Received	300+	56%	-	64%
Would Definitely Recommend Hospital	300+	62%	-	69%

Edmond Medical Center

One South Bryant | Phone: 405-341-6100
Edmond, OK 73034 | Fax: 405-359-5500
URL: www.edmondhospital.com
Type: Acute Care Hospitals | Emergency Services: No
Ownership: Proprietary | Beds: 92

Key Personnel:
CEO/President. . . . . Tayo Ficktl
Chief of Medical Staff . . . . Gary Hill, MD
Infection Control. . . . . Barbara McConnell
Operating Room. . . . . Cheryl McConnell
Quality Assurance . . . . Teresa Giffin
Radiology. . . . . Douglas Beall
Emergency Room . . . . Teresa Griffin
Patient Relations . . . . Mike Rhoades

Measure	Cases	This Hosp.	State Avg.	U.S. Avg.
Heart Attack Care				
ACE Inhibitor or ARB for LVSD	-	-	95%	96%
Aspirin at Arrival	-	-	98%	99%
Aspirin at Discharge	-	-	98%	98%
Beta Blocker at Discharge	-	-	98%	98%
Fibrinolytic Medication Timing	-	-	42%	55%
PCI Within 90 Minutes of Arrival	-	-	88%	90%
Smoking Cessation Advice	-	-	100%	99%
Chest Pain/Possible Heart Attack Care				
Aspirin at Arrival	-	-	94%	95%
Median Time to ECG (minutes)	-	-	9	8
Median Time to Transfer (minutes)	-	-	75	61
Fibrinolytic Medication Timing	-	-	50%	54%
Heart Failure Care				
ACE Inhibitor or ARB for LVSD	-	-	94%	94%
Discharge Instructions	-	-	85%	88%
Evaluation of LVS Function	-	-	94%	98%
Smoking Cessation Advice	-	-	97%	98%
Pneumonia Care				
Appropriate Initial Antibiotic	-	-	91%	92%
Blood Culture Timing	-	-	96%	96%
Influenza Vaccine	-	-	89%	91%
Initial Antibiotic Timing	-	-	95%	95%
Pneumococcal Vaccine	-	-	91%	93%
Smoking Cessation Advice	-	-	95%	97%
Surgical Care Improvement Project				
Appropriate VTP Within 24 Hours	-	-	91%	92%
Appropriate Hair Removal	-	-	100%	99%
Appropriate Beta Blocker Usage	-	-	91%	93%
Controlled Postoperative Blood Glucose	-	-	95%	93%
Prophylactic Antibiotic Timing	-	-	97%	97%
Prophylactic Antibiotic Timing (Outpatient)	-	-	93%	92%
Prophylactic Antibiotic Selection	-	-	98%	97%
Prophylactic Antibiotic Select. (Outpatient)	-	-	95%	94%
Prophylactic Antibiotic Stopped	-	-	94%	94%
Recommended VTP Ordered	-	-	94%	94%
Urinary Catheter Removal	-	-	87%	90%
Children's Asthma Care				
Received Systemic Corticosteroids	-	-	-	100%
Received Home Management Plan	-	-	-	71%
Received Reliever Medication	-	-	-	100%
Use of Medical Imaging				
Combination Abdominal CT Scan	-	-	0.372	0.191
Combination Chest CT Scan	-	-	0.134	0.054
Follow-up Mammogram/Ultrasound	-	-	8%	8.4%
MRI for Low Back Pain	-	-	34.3%	32.7%
Survey of Patients' Hospital Experiences				
Area Around Room 'Always' Quiet at Night	-	-	-	58%
Doctors 'Always' Communicated Well	-	-	-	80%
Home Recovery Information Given	-	-	-	82%
Hospital Given 9 or 10 on 10 Point Scale	-	-	-	67%
Meds 'Always' Explained Before Given	-	-	-	60%
Nurses 'Always' Communicated Well	-	-	-	76%
Pain 'Always' Well Controlled	-	-	-	69%
Room and Bathroom 'Always' Clean	-	-	-	71%
Timely Help 'Always' Received	-	-	-	64%
Would Definitely Recommend Hospital	-	-	-	69%

NOTE: Hospital profiles are in alphabetical order by state, then city, then hospital within the city; Rankings exclude hospitals with less than 25 cases except for patient surveys which excludes hospitals with less than 100 cases; (a) 100–299 cases; (1) The number of cases is too small to be sure how well a hospital is performing; (2) The hospital indicated that the data submitted for this measure were based on a sample of cases; (3) Data was collected during a shorter time period (fewer quarters) than the maximum possible time for this measure; (4) Suppressed for one or more quarters by CMS; (5) No data is available from the hospital for this measure; (6) Fewer than 100 patients completed the HCAHPS survey. Use these rates with caution, as the number of surveys may be too low to reliably assess hospital performance; (7) Survey results are based on less than 12 months of data; (8) Survey results are not available for this reporting period; (9) No or very few patients were eligible for the HCAHPS survey. The scores shown, if any, reflect a very small number of surveys; (10) A state average was not calculated because too few hospitals in the state submitted data; (11) There were discrepancies in the data collection process; Please refer to the User's Guide for a full explanation of data.

Summit Medical Center

1800 South Renaissance Boulevard
Edmond, OK 73034
URL: www.weightwise.com
Type: Acute Care Hospitals
Ownership: Proprietary
Phone: 405-359-2400
Emergency Services: No

Measure	Cases	This Hosp.	State Avg.	U.S. Avg.
Heart Attack Care				
ACE Inhibitor or ARB for LVSD[5]	0	-	95%	96%
Aspirin at Arrival[5]	0	-	98%	99%
Aspirin at Discharge[5]	0	-	98%	98%
Beta Blocker at Discharge[5]	0	-	98%	98%
Fibrinolytic Medication Timing[5]	0	-	42%	55%
PCI Within 90 Minutes of Arrival[5]	0	-	88%	90%
Smoking Cessation Advice[5]	0	-	100%	99%
Chest Pain/Possible Heart Attack Care				
Aspirin at Arrival	-	-	94%	95%
Median Time to ECG (minutes)	-	-	9	8
Median Time to Transfer (minutes)	-	-	75	61
Fibrinolytic Medication Timing	-	-	50%	54%
Heart Failure Care				
ACE Inhibitor or ARB for LVSD[5]	0	-	94%	94%
Discharge Instructions[5]	0	-	85%	88%
Evaluation of LVS Function[5]	0	-	94%	98%
Smoking Cessation Advice[5]	0	-	97%	98%
Pneumonia Care				
Appropriate Initial Antibiotic[5]	0	-	91%	92%
Blood Culture Timing[5]	0	-	96%	96%
Influenza Vaccine[5]	0	-	89%	91%
Initial Antibiotic Timing[5]	0	-	95%	95%
Pneumococcal Vaccine[5]	0	-	91%	93%
Smoking Cessation Advice[5]	0	-	95%	97%
Surgical Care Improvement Project				
Appropriate VTP Within 24 Hours[1]	4	50%	91%	92%
Appropriate Hair Removal	31	100%	100%	99%
Appropriate Beta Blocker Usage[1]	2	100%	91%	93%
Controlled Postoperative Blood Glucose	0	-	95%	93%
Prophylactic Antibiotic Timing[1]	15	93%	97%	97%
Prophylactic Antibiotic Timing (Outpatient)	-	-	93%	92%
Prophylactic Antibiotic Selection[1]	16	100%	98%	97%
Prophylactic Antibiotic Select. (Outpatient)	-	-	95%	94%
Prophylactic Antibiotic Stopped[1]	15	100%	94%	94%
Recommended VTP Ordered[1]	4	50%	94%	94%
Urinary Catheter Removal[1]	9	100%	87%	90%
Children's Asthma Care				
Received Systemic Corticosteroids	-	-	-	100%
Received Home Management Plan	-	-	-	71%
Received Reliever Medication	-	-	-	100%
Use of Medical Imaging				
Combination Abdominal CT Scan	-	-	0.372	0.191
Combination Chest CT Scan	-	-	0.134	0.054
Follow-up Mammogram/Ultrasound	-	-	8%	8.4%
MRI for Low Back Pain	-	-	34.3%	32.7%
Survey of Patients' Hospital Experiences				
Area Around Room 'Always' Quiet at Night[6]	<100	89%	-	58%
Doctors 'Always' Communicated Well[6]	<100	88%	-	80%
Home Recovery Information Given[6]	<100	91%	-	82%
Hospital Given 9 or 10 on 10 Point Scale[6]	<100	86%	-	67%
Meds 'Always' Explained Before Given[6]	<100	75%	-	60%
Nurses 'Always' Communicated Well[6]	<100	88%	-	76%
Pain 'Always' Well Controlled[6]	<100	84%	-	69%
Room and Bathroom 'Always' Clean[6]	<100	88%	-	71%
Timely Help 'Always' Received[6]	<100	92%	-	64%
Would Definitely Recommend Hospital	<100	89%	-	69%

Mercy Hospital El Reno

2115 Park View Drive
El Reno, OK 73036
URL: www.parkview-hospital.com
Type: Acute Care Hospitals
Ownership: Government - Local
Phone: 405-262-2640
Fax: 405-422-2521
Emergency Services: Yes
Beds: 54

Key Personnel:
CEO/President. . . . . Lex Smith
Chief of Medical Staff. . . . . Dr Michael Sullivan
Infection Control. . . . . Claudi Eaton, RN
Quality Assurance . . . . Claudia Eaton
Radiology. . . . . Jane Bates, RT(R)

Measure	Cases	This Hosp.	State Avg.	U.S. Avg.
Heart Attack Care				
ACE Inhibitor or ARB for LVSD[3]	0	-	95%	96%
Aspirin at Arrival[3]	0	-	98%	99%
Aspirin at Discharge[3]	0	-	98%	98%
Beta Blocker at Discharge[1,3]	2	0%	98%	98%
Fibrinolytic Medication Timing[3]	0	-	42%	55%
PCI Within 90 Minutes of Arrival[3]	0	-	88%	90%
Smoking Cessation Advice[3]	0	-	100%	99%
Chest Pain/Possible Heart Attack Care				
Aspirin at Arrival	59	88%	94%	95%
Median Time to ECG (minutes)	66	14	9	8
Median Time to Transfer (minutes)[1]	10	76	75	61
Fibrinolytic Medication Timing[1]	1	0%	50%	54%
Heart Failure Care				
ACE Inhibitor or ARB for LVSD[1]	4	50%	94%	94%
Discharge Instructions[1]	15	87%	85%	88%
Evaluation of LVS Function[1]	24	79%	94%	98%
Smoking Cessation Advice[1]	5	80%	97%	98%
Pneumonia Care				
Appropriate Initial Antibiotic	54	80%	91%	92%
Blood Culture Timing	30	87%	96%	96%
Influenza Vaccine	29	90%	89%	91%
Initial Antibiotic Timing	66	92%	95%	95%
Pneumococcal Vaccine	39	87%	91%	93%
Smoking Cessation Advice	27	93%	95%	97%
Surgical Care Improvement Project				
Appropriate VTP Within 24 Hours[1,2]	6	67%	91%	92%
Appropriate Hair Removal[1,2]	16	100%	100%	99%
Appropriate Beta Blocker Usage[1,2]	1	100%	91%	93%
Controlled Postoperative Blood Glucose[2]	0	-	95%	93%
Prophylactic Antibiotic Timing[1,2]	14	100%	97%	97%
Prophylactic Antibiotic Timing (Outpatient)[5]	0	-	93%	92%
Prophylactic Antibiotic Selection[1,2]	14	79%	98%	97%
Prophylactic Antibiotic Select. (Outpatient)[5]	0	-	95%	94%
Prophylactic Antibiotic Stopped[1,2]	14	93%	94%	94%
Recommended VTP Ordered[1,2]	6	67%	94%	94%
Urinary Catheter Removal[1,2]	2	50%	87%	90%
Children's Asthma Care				
Received Systemic Corticosteroids	-	-	-	100%
Received Home Management Plan	-	-	-	71%
Received Reliever Medication	-	-	-	100%
Use of Medical Imaging				
Combination Abdominal CT Scan	85	0.094	0.372	0.191
Combination Chest CT Scan	60	0.033	0.134	0.054
Follow-up Mammogram/Ultrasound[5]	0	-	8%	8.4%
MRI for Low Back Pain[1]	7	57.1%	34.3%	32.7%
Survey of Patients' Hospital Experiences				
Area Around Room 'Always' Quiet at Night	(a)	71%	-	58%
Doctors 'Always' Communicated Well	(a)	75%	-	80%
Home Recovery Information Given	(a)	72%	-	82%
Hospital Given 9 or 10 on 10 Point Scale	(a)	63%	-	67%
Meds 'Always' Explained Before Given	(a)	60%	-	60%
Nurses 'Always' Communicated Well	(a)	75%	-	76%
Pain 'Always' Well Controlled	(a)	69%	-	69%
Room and Bathroom 'Always' Clean	(a)	74%	-	71%
Timely Help 'Always' Received	(a)	66%	-	64%
Would Definitely Recommend Hospital	(a)	63%	-	69%

Great Plains Regional Medical Center

1801 West 3rd Street
Elk City, OK 73644
URL: www.gprmc-ok.com
Type: Acute Care Hospitals
Ownership: Voluntary Non-Profit - Private
Phone: 580-225-2511
Fax: 580-225-9143
Emergency Services: Yes
Beds: 62

Key Personnel:
CEO/President. . . . . Don Ikner
Chief of Medical Staff. . . . . Francis Abraham
Operating Room. . . . . Gwen Fuchs
Quality Assurance . . . . Kimmy Davis
Radiology. . . . . Duane Mills
Emergency Room . . . . Debra Morris
Intensive Care Unit. . . . . Debra Morris

Measure	Cases	This Hosp.	State Avg.	U.S. Avg.
Heart Attack Care				
ACE Inhibitor or ARB for LVSD[1]	1	100%	95%	96%
Aspirin at Arrival[1]	9	89%	98%	99%
Aspirin at Discharge[1]	7	86%	98%	98%
Beta Blocker at Discharge[1]	7	71%	98%	98%
Fibrinolytic Medication Timing	0	-	42%	55%
PCI Within 90 Minutes of Arrival	0	-	88%	90%
Smoking Cessation Advice[1]	1	100%	100%	99%
Chest Pain/Possible Heart Attack Care				
Aspirin at Arrival	41	98%	94%	95%
Median Time to ECG (minutes)	43	9	9	8
Median Time to Transfer (minutes)[5]	0	-	75	61
Fibrinolytic Medication Timing[1]	5	80%	50%	54%
Heart Failure Care				
ACE Inhibitor or ARB for LVSD[1]	9	100%	94%	94%
Discharge Instructions	51	96%	85%	88%
Evaluation of LVS Function	69	93%	94%	98%
Smoking Cessation Advice[1]	10	100%	97%	98%
Pneumonia Care				
Appropriate Initial Antibiotic	51	92%	91%	92%
Blood Culture Timing	58	86%	96%	96%
Influenza Vaccine	58	98%	89%	91%
Initial Antibiotic Timing	73	100%	95%	95%
Pneumococcal Vaccine	78	100%	91%	93%
Smoking Cessation Advice[1]	24	100%	95%	97%
Surgical Care Improvement Project				
Appropriate VTP Within 24 Hours	74	89%	91%	92%
Appropriate Hair Removal	200	98%	100%	99%
Appropriate Beta Blocker Usage	32	94%	91%	93%
Controlled Postoperative Blood Glucose	0	-	95%	93%
Prophylactic Antibiotic Timing	140	93%	97%	97%
Prophylactic Antibiotic Timing (Outpatient)	52	77%	93%	92%
Prophylactic Antibiotic Selection	141	94%	98%	97%
Prophylactic Antibiotic Select. (Outpatient)	45	93%	95%	94%
Prophylactic Antibiotic Stopped	130	91%	94%	94%
Recommended VTP Ordered	76	88%	94%	94%
Urinary Catheter Removal	38	29%	87%	90%
Children's Asthma Care				
Received Systemic Corticosteroids	-	-	-	100%
Received Home Management Plan	-	-	-	71%
Received Reliever Medication	-	-	-	100%
Use of Medical Imaging				
Combination Abdominal CT Scan	290	0.724	0.372	0.191
Combination Chest CT Scan	164	0.494	0.134	0.054
Follow-up Mammogram/Ultrasound	432	14.4%	8%	8.4%
MRI for Low Back Pain	122	27.9%	34.3%	32.7%
Survey of Patients' Hospital Experiences				
Area Around Room 'Always' Quiet at Night	300+	65%	-	58%
Doctors 'Always' Communicated Well	300+	79%	-	80%
Home Recovery Information Given	300+	80%	-	82%
Hospital Given 9 or 10 on 10 Point Scale	300+	64%	-	67%
Meds 'Always' Explained Before Given	300+	55%	-	60%
Nurses 'Always' Communicated Well	300+	71%	-	76%
Pain 'Always' Well Controlled	300+	65%	-	69%
Room and Bathroom 'Always' Clean	300+	67%	-	71%
Timely Help 'Always' Received	300+	61%	-	64%
Would Definitely Recommend Hospital	300+	61%	-	69%

NOTE: Hospital profiles are in alphabetical order by state, then city, then hospital within the city; Rankings exclude hospitals with less than 25 cases except for patient surveys which excludes hospitals with less than 100 cases; (a) 100–299 cases; (1) The number of cases is too small to be sure how well a hospital is performing; (2) The hospital indicated that the data submitted for this measure were based on a sample of cases; (3) Data was collected during a shorter time period (fewer quarters) than the maximum possible time for this measure; (4) Suppressed for one or more quarters by CMS; (5) No data is available from the hospital for this measure; (6) Fewer than 100 patients completed the HCAHPS survey. Use these rates with caution, as the number of surveys may be too low to reliably assess hospital performance; (7) Survey results are based on less than 12 months of data; (8) Survey results are not available for this reporting period; (9) No or very few patients were eligible for the HCAHPS survey. The scores shown, if any, reflect a very small number of surveys; (10) A state average was not calculated because too few hospitals in the state submitted data; (11) There were discrepancies in the data collection process; Please refer to the User's Guide for a full explanation of data.

Integris Bass Baptist Health Center

600 South Monroe
Enid, OK 73701
Phone: 405-233-2300
Fax: 580-233-8922
URL: www.integris-health.com/facilities
Type: Acute Care Hospitals
Emergency Services: Yes
Ownership: Voluntary Non-Profit - Private
Beds: 253

Measure	Cases	This Hosp.	State Avg.	U.S. Avg.
Heart Attack Care				
ACE Inhibitor or ARB for LVSD[1]	8	100%	95%	96%
Aspirin at Arrival	78	99%	98%	99%
Aspirin at Discharge	86	97%	98%	98%
Beta Blocker at Discharge	79	95%	98%	98%
Fibrinolytic Medication Timing	0	-	42%	55%
PCI Within 90 Minutes of Arrival[1]	20	100%	88%	90%
Smoking Cessation Advice	36	100%	100%	99%
Chest Pain/Possible Heart Attack Care				
Aspirin at Arrival[1]	5	80%	94%	95%
Median Time to ECG (minutes)[1]	5	2	9	8
Median Time to Transfer (minutes)[5]	0	-	75	61
Fibrinolytic Medication Timing[3]	0	-	50%	54%
Heart Failure Care				
ACE Inhibitor or ARB for LVSD	28	100%	94%	94%
Discharge Instructions	76	100%	85%	88%
Evaluation of LVS Function	116	99%	94%	98%
Smoking Cessation Advice[1]	19	100%	97%	98%
Pneumonia Care				
Appropriate Initial Antibiotic	70	97%	91%	92%
Blood Culture Timing	129	99%	96%	96%
Influenza Vaccine	90	93%	89%	91%
Initial Antibiotic Timing	116	98%	95%	95%
Pneumococcal Vaccine	100	97%	91%	93%
Smoking Cessation Advice	46	100%	95%	97%
Surgical Care Improvement Project				
Appropriate VTP Within 24 Hours[2]	112	95%	91%	92%
Appropriate Hair Removal[2]	334	99%	100%	99%
Appropriate Beta Blocker Usage[2]	82	90%	91%	93%
Controlled Postoperative Blood Glucose[2]	69	91%	95%	93%
Prophylactic Antibiotic Timing[2]	189	98%	97%	97%
Prophylactic Antibiotic Timing (Outpatient)	67	99%	93%	92%
Prophylactic Antibiotic Selection[2]	190	98%	98%	97%
Prophylactic Antibiotic Select. (Outpatient)	67	94%	95%	94%
Prophylactic Antibiotic Stopped[2]	185	97%	94%	94%
Recommended VTP Ordered[2]	112	97%	94%	94%
Urinary Catheter Removal	55	87%	87%	90%
Children's Asthma Care				
Received Systemic Corticosteroids	-	-	-	100%
Received Home Management Plan	-	-	-	71%
Received Reliever Medication	-	-	-	100%
Use of Medical Imaging				
Combination Abdominal CT Scan	553	0.076	0.372	0.191
Combination Chest CT Scan	427	0.009	0.134	0.054
Follow-up Mammogram/Ultrasound	808	11.3%	8%	8.4%
MRI for Low Back Pain	114	39.5%	34.3%	32.7%
Survey of Patients' Hospital Experiences				
Area Around Room 'Always' Quiet at Night	300+	59%	-	58%
Doctors 'Always' Communicated Well	300+	85%	-	80%
Home Recovery Information Given	300+	80%	-	82%
Hospital Given 9 or 10 on 10 Point Scale	300+	68%	-	67%
Meds 'Always' Explained Before Given	300+	58%	-	60%
Nurses 'Always' Communicated Well	300+	78%	-	76%
Pain 'Always' Well Controlled	300+	69%	-	69%
Room and Bathroom 'Always' Clean	300+	71%	-	71%
Timely Help 'Always' Received	300+	68%	-	64%
Would Definitely Recommend Hospital	300+	75%	-	69%

Saint Mary's Regional Medical Center

305 South 5th Street
Enid, OK 73701
Phone: 580-233-6100
Fax: 580-249-3982
URL: www.stmarysregional.com
Type: Acute Care Hospitals
Emergency Services: Yes
Ownership: Proprietary
Beds: 245

Key Personnel:
CEO/President. . . . . Rick Wallace
Coronary Care . . . . Virginia McCall
Infection Control. . . . . Janie Word
Operating Room. . . . . Robert Ritter
Pediatric In-Patient Care . . . . Kathy Niswander
Quality Assurance . . . . Ann Thain
Intensive Care Unit. . . . . Virginia McCall
Patient Relations . . . . Verla Holguin

Measure	Cases	This Hosp.	State Avg.	U.S. Avg.
Heart Attack Care				
ACE Inhibitor or ARB for LVSD[1]	7	100%	95%	96%
Aspirin at Arrival	53	94%	98%	99%
Aspirin at Discharge	58	97%	98%	98%
Beta Blocker at Discharge	54	89%	98%	98%
Fibrinolytic Medication Timing	0	-	42%	55%
PCI Within 90 Minutes of Arrival[1]	10	60%	88%	90%
Smoking Cessation Advice	29	100%	100%	99%
Chest Pain/Possible Heart Attack Care				
Aspirin at Arrival[1,3]	5	100%	94%	95%
Median Time to ECG (minutes)[1,3]	6	6	9	8
Median Time to Transfer (minutes)[1,3]	1	122	75	61
Fibrinolytic Medication Timing[3]	0	-	50%	54%
Heart Failure Care				
ACE Inhibitor or ARB for LVSD	36	97%	94%	94%
Discharge Instructions	106	62%	85%	88%
Evaluation of LVS Function	168	95%	94%	98%
Smoking Cessation Advice	28	100%	97%	98%
Pneumonia Care				
Appropriate Initial Antibiotic	83	92%	91%	92%
Blood Culture Timing	109	99%	96%	96%
Influenza Vaccine	123	86%	89%	91%
Initial Antibiotic Timing	148	97%	95%	95%
Pneumococcal Vaccine	156	93%	91%	93%
Smoking Cessation Advice	55	100%	95%	97%
Surgical Care Improvement Project				
Appropriate VTP Within 24 Hours[2]	174	88%	91%	92%
Appropriate Hair Removal[2]	675	100%	100%	99%
Appropriate Beta Blocker Usage[2]	163	89%	91%	93%
Controlled Postoperative Blood Glucose[2]	35	91%	95%	93%
Prophylactic Antibiotic Timing[2]	520	100%	97%	97%
Prophylactic Antibiotic Timing (Outpatient)	265	99%	93%	92%
Prophylactic Antibiotic Selection[2]	522	98%	98%	97%
Prophylactic Antibiotic Select. (Outpatient)	273	93%	95%	94%
Prophylactic Antibiotic Stopped[2]	501	99%	94%	94%
Recommended VTP Ordered[2]	175	90%	94%	94%
Urinary Catheter Removal[2]	30	47%	87%	90%
Children's Asthma Care				
Received Systemic Corticosteroids	-	-	-	100%
Received Home Management Plan	-	-	-	71%
Received Reliever Medication	-	-	-	100%
Use of Medical Imaging				
Combination Abdominal CT Scan	664	0.176	0.372	0.191
Combination Chest CT Scan	558	0.000	0.134	0.054
Follow-up Mammogram/Ultrasound	1,416	9.7%	8%	8.4%
MRI for Low Back Pain	204	33.8%	34.3%	32.7%
Survey of Patients' Hospital Experiences				
Area Around Room 'Always' Quiet at Night	300+	62%	-	58%
Doctors 'Always' Communicated Well	300+	83%	-	80%
Home Recovery Information Given	300+	88%	-	82%
Hospital Given 9 or 10 on 10 Point Scale	300+	74%	-	67%
Meds 'Always' Explained Before Given	300+	60%	-	60%
Nurses 'Always' Communicated Well	300+	78%	-	76%
Pain 'Always' Well Controlled	300+	71%	-	69%
Room and Bathroom 'Always' Clean	300+	69%	-	71%
Timely Help 'Always' Received	300+	65%	-	64%
Would Definitely Recommend Hospital	300+	74%	-	69%

Epic Medical Center

1 Hospital Drive
Eufaula, OK 74432
Phone: 918-689-2535
Fax: 918-689-7285
Type: Acute Care Hospitals
Emergency Services: Yes
Ownership: Government - Federal
Beds: 33

Key Personnel:
CEO/President. . . . . Daniel Schaecvle
Infection Control. . . . . Dorothy Merrick
Operating Room. . . . . Vanessa Williams, RN
Quality Assurance . . . . Jerry Manning
Emergency Room . . . . Dorothy Merrick

Measure	Cases	This Hosp.	State Avg.	U.S. Avg.
Heart Attack Care				
ACE Inhibitor or ARB for LVSD[3]	0	-	95%	96%
Aspirin at Arrival[1,3]	1	100%	98%	99%
Aspirin at Discharge[1,3]	1	100%	98%	98%
Beta Blocker at Discharge[1,3]	1	100%	98%	98%
Fibrinolytic Medication Timing[3]	0	-	42%	55%
PCI Within 90 Minutes of Arrival[3]	0	-	88%	90%
Smoking Cessation Advice[3]	0	-	100%	99%
Chest Pain/Possible Heart Attack Care				
Aspirin at Arrival	48	81%	94%	95%
Median Time to ECG (minutes)	51	24	9	8
Median Time to Transfer (minutes)[5]	0	-	75	61
Fibrinolytic Medication Timing[1]	2	0%	50%	54%
Heart Failure Care				
ACE Inhibitor or ARB for LVSD[3]	0	-	94%	94%
Discharge Instructions[1,3]	3	33%	85%	88%
Evaluation of LVS Function[1,3]	5	20%	94%	98%
Smoking Cessation Advice[1,3]	2	50%	97%	98%
Pneumonia Care				
Appropriate Initial Antibiotic[1]	15	87%	91%	92%
Blood Culture Timing[1]	3	67%	96%	96%
Influenza Vaccine[1]	8	88%	89%	91%
Initial Antibiotic Timing[1]	12	83%	95%	95%
Pneumococcal Vaccine[1]	8	25%	91%	93%
Smoking Cessation Advice[1]	8	38%	95%	97%
Surgical Care Improvement Project				
Appropriate VTP Within 24 Hours[5]	0	-	91%	92%
Appropriate Hair Removal[5]	0	-	100%	99%
Appropriate Beta Blocker Usage[5]	0	-	91%	93%
Controlled Postoperative Blood Glucose[5]	0	-	95%	93%
Prophylactic Antibiotic Timing[5]	0	-	97%	97%
Prophylactic Antibiotic Timing (Outpatient)[5]	0	-	93%	92%
Prophylactic Antibiotic Selection[5]	0	-	98%	97%
Prophylactic Antibiotic Select. (Outpatient)[5]	0	-	95%	94%
Prophylactic Antibiotic Stopped[5]	0	-	94%	94%
Recommended VTP Ordered[5]	0	-	94%	94%
Urinary Catheter Removal[5]	0	-	87%	90%
Children's Asthma Care				
Received Systemic Corticosteroids	-	-	-	100%
Received Home Management Plan	-	-	-	71%
Received Reliever Medication	-	-	-	100%
Use of Medical Imaging				
Combination Abdominal CT Scan[5]	0	-	0.372	0.191
Combination Chest CT Scan[5]	0	-	0.134	0.054
Follow-up Mammogram/Ultrasound[5]	0	-	8%	8.4%
MRI for Low Back Pain[5]	0	-	34.3%	32.7%
Survey of Patients' Hospital Experiences				
Area Around Room 'Always' Quiet at Night	(a)	61%	-	58%
Doctors 'Always' Communicated Well	(a)	54%	-	80%
Home Recovery Information Given	(a)	60%	-	82%
Hospital Given 9 or 10 on 10 Point Scale	(a)	39%	-	67%
Meds 'Always' Explained Before Given	(a)	75%	-	60%
Nurses 'Always' Communicated Well	(a)	67%	-	76%
Pain 'Always' Well Controlled	(a)	83%	-	69%
Room and Bathroom 'Always' Clean	(a)	63%	-	71%
Timely Help 'Always' Received	(a)	66%	-	64%
Would Definitely Recommend Hospital	(a)	47%	-	69%

NOTE: Hospital profiles are in alphabetical order by state, then city, then hospital within the city; Rankings exclude hospitals with less than 25 cases except for patient surveys which excludes hospitals with less than 100 cases; (a) 100–299 cases; (1) The number of cases is too small to be sure how well a hospital is performing; (2) The hospital indicated that the data submitted for this measure were based on a sample of cases; (3) Data was collected during a shorter time period (fewer quarters) than the maximum possible time for this measure; (4) Suppressed for one or more quarters by CMS; (5) No data is available from the hospital for this measure; (6) Fewer than 100 patients completed the HCAHPS survey. Use these rates with caution, as the number of surveys may be too low to reliably assess hospital performance; (7) Survey results are based on less than 12 months of data; (8) Survey results are not available for this reporting period; (9) No or very few patients were eligible for the HCAHPS survey. The scores shown, if any, reflect a very small number of surveys; (10) A state average was not calculated because too few hospitals in the state submitted data; (11) There were discrepancies in the data collection process; Please refer to the User's Guide for a full explanation of data.

Fairfax Community Hospital

40 Hospital Road
Fairfax, OK 74637
Phone: 918-642-3291
Fax: 918-642-5161
Type: Critical Access Hospitals
Emergency Services: Yes
Ownership: Proprietary
Beds: 21
Key Personnel:
CEO/President. . . . . Emory Brutigan
Chief of Medical Staff . . . . James Graham
Quality Assurance . . . . Tammy Gibson

Measure	Cases	This Hosp.	State Avg.	U.S. Avg.
Heart Attack Care				
ACE Inhibitor or ARB for LVSD[5]	0	-	95%	96%
Aspirin at Arrival[5]	0	-	98%	99%
Aspirin at Discharge[5]	0	-	98%	98%
Beta Blocker at Discharge[5]	0	-	98%	98%
Fibrinolytic Medication Timing[5]	0	-	42%	55%
PCI Within 90 Minutes of Arrival[5]	0	-	88%	90%
Smoking Cessation Advice[5]	0	-	100%	99%
Chest Pain/Possible Heart Attack Care				
Aspirin at Arrival	-	-	94%	95%
Median Time to ECG (minutes)	-	-	9	8
Median Time to Transfer (minutes)	-	-	75	61
Fibrinolytic Medication Timing	-	-	50%	54%
Heart Failure Care				
ACE Inhibitor or ARB for LVSD[1,3]	4	100%	94%	94%
Discharge Instructions[1,3]	8	75%	85%	88%
Evaluation of LVS Function[1,3]	8	100%	94%	98%
Smoking Cessation Advice[1,3]	1	100%	97%	98%
Pneumonia Care				
Appropriate Initial Antibiotic[1,3]	3	67%	91%	92%
Blood Culture Timing[1,3]	4	100%	96%	96%
Influenza Vaccine[1,3]	3	100%	89%	91%
Initial Antibiotic Timing[1,3]	4	100%	95%	95%
Pneumococcal Vaccine[1,3]	3	100%	91%	93%
Smoking Cessation Advice[1,3]	3	100%	95%	97%
Surgical Care Improvement Project				
Appropriate VTP Within 24 Hours[5]	0	-	91%	92%
Appropriate Hair Removal[5]	0	-	100%	99%
Appropriate Beta Blocker Usage[5]	0	-	91%	93%
Controlled Postoperative Blood Glucose[5]	0	-	95%	93%
Prophylactic Antibiotic Timing[5]	0	-	97%	97%
Prophylactic Antibiotic Timing (Outpatient)	-	-	93%	92%
Prophylactic Antibiotic Selection[5]	0	-	98%	97%
Prophylactic Antibiotic Select. (Outpatient)	-	-	95%	94%
Prophylactic Antibiotic Stopped[5]	0	-	94%	94%
Recommended VTP Ordered[5]	0	-	94%	94%
Urinary Catheter Removal[5]	0	-	87%	90%
Children's Asthma Care				
Received Systemic Corticosteroids	-	-	-	100%
Received Home Management Plan	-	-	-	71%
Received Reliever Medication	-	-	-	100%
Use of Medical Imaging				
Combination Abdominal CT Scan	-	-	0.372	0.191
Combination Chest CT Scan	-	-	0.134	0.054
Follow-up Mammogram/Ultrasound	-	-	8%	8.4%
MRI for Low Back Pain	-	-	34.3%	32.7%
Survey of Patients' Hospital Experiences				
Area Around Room 'Always' Quiet at Night[8]	-	-	-	58%
Doctors 'Always' Communicated Well[8]	-	-	-	80%
Home Recovery Information Given[8]	-	-	-	82%
Hospital Given 9 or 10 on 10 Point Scale[8]	-	-	-	67%
Meds 'Always' Explained Before Given[8]	-	-	-	60%
Nurses 'Always' Communicated Well[8]	-	-	-	76%
Pain 'Always' Well Controlled[8]	-	-	-	69%
Room and Bathroom 'Always' Clean[8]	-	-	-	71%
Timely Help 'Always' Received[8]	-	-	-	64%
Would Definitely Recommend Hospital[8]	-	-	-	69%

Fairview Regional Medical Center

523 East State Road
Fairview, OK 73737
Phone: 580-227-3721
Fax: 580-227-2882
URL: www.fairviewhospital.net
Type: Critical Access Hospitals
Emergency Services: Yes
Ownership: Govt - Hospital Dist/Auth
Beds: 25
Key Personnel:
CEO/President. . . . . Roger Knak
Chief of Medical Staff . . . . Kathy Cain

Measure	Cases	This Hosp.	State Avg.	U.S. Avg.
Heart Attack Care				
ACE Inhibitor or ARB for LVSD[3]	0	-	95%	96%
Aspirin at Arrival[1,3]	1	100%	98%	99%
Aspirin at Discharge[3]	0	-	98%	98%
Beta Blocker at Discharge[3]	0	-	98%	98%
Fibrinolytic Medication Timing[3]	0	-	42%	55%
PCI Within 90 Minutes of Arrival[3]	0	-	88%	90%
Smoking Cessation Advice[3]	0	-	100%	99%
Chest Pain/Possible Heart Attack Care				
Aspirin at Arrival	-	-	94%	95%
Median Time to ECG (minutes)	-	-	9	8
Median Time to Transfer (minutes)	-	-	75	61
Fibrinolytic Medication Timing	-	-	50%	54%
Heart Failure Care				
ACE Inhibitor or ARB for LVSD[3]	0	-	94%	94%
Discharge Instructions[1,3]	5	60%	85%	88%
Evaluation of LVS Function[1,3]	8	12%	94%	98%
Smoking Cessation Advice[3]	0	-	97%	98%
Pneumonia Care				
Appropriate Initial Antibiotic[1]	23	96%	91%	92%
Blood Culture Timing[1]	9	100%	96%	96%
Influenza Vaccine[1]	14	71%	89%	91%
Initial Antibiotic Timing[1]	20	90%	95%	95%
Pneumococcal Vaccine[1]	22	55%	91%	93%
Smoking Cessation Advice[1]	2	100%	95%	97%
Surgical Care Improvement Project				
Appropriate VTP Within 24 Hours[5]	0	-	91%	92%
Appropriate Hair Removal[5]	0	-	100%	99%
Appropriate Beta Blocker Usage[5]	0	-	91%	93%
Controlled Postoperative Blood Glucose[5]	0	-	95%	93%
Prophylactic Antibiotic Timing[5]	0	-	97%	97%
Prophylactic Antibiotic Timing (Outpatient)	-	-	93%	92%
Prophylactic Antibiotic Selection[5]	0	-	98%	97%
Prophylactic Antibiotic Select. (Outpatient)	-	-	95%	94%
Prophylactic Antibiotic Stopped[5]	0	-	94%	94%
Recommended VTP Ordered[5]	0	-	94%	94%
Urinary Catheter Removal[5]	0	-	87%	90%
Children's Asthma Care				
Received Systemic Corticosteroids	-	-	-	100%
Received Home Management Plan	-	-	-	71%
Received Reliever Medication	-	-	-	100%
Use of Medical Imaging				
Combination Abdominal CT Scan	-	-	0.372	0.191
Combination Chest CT Scan	-	-	0.134	0.054
Follow-up Mammogram/Ultrasound	-	-	8%	8.4%
MRI for Low Back Pain	-	-	34.3%	32.7%
Survey of Patients' Hospital Experiences				
Area Around Room 'Always' Quiet at Night[8]	-	-	-	58%
Doctors 'Always' Communicated Well[8]	-	-	-	80%
Home Recovery Information Given[8]	-	-	-	82%
Hospital Given 9 or 10 on 10 Point Scale[8]	-	-	-	67%
Meds 'Always' Explained Before Given[8]	-	-	-	60%
Nurses 'Always' Communicated Well[8]	-	-	-	76%
Pain 'Always' Well Controlled[8]	-	-	-	69%
Room and Bathroom 'Always' Clean[8]	-	-	-	71%
Timely Help 'Always' Received[8]	-	-	-	64%
Would Definitely Recommend Hospital[8]	-	-	-	69%

Memorial Hospital & Physician Group

319 East Josephine
Frederick, OK 73542
Phone: 580-335-7565
Fax: 580-335-7329
Type: Acute Care Hospitals
Emergency Services: Yes
Ownership: Voluntary Non-Profit - Other
Beds: 48
Key Personnel:
CEO/President. . . . . Al Allee
Chief of Medical Staff . . . . Maha Sultan, MD

Measure	Cases	This Hosp.	State Avg.	U.S. Avg.
Heart Attack Care				
ACE Inhibitor or ARB for LVSD[3]	0	-	95%	96%
Aspirin at Arrival[1,3]	1	0%	98%	99%
Aspirin at Discharge[1,3]	1	0%	98%	98%
Beta Blocker at Discharge[1,3]	1	0%	98%	98%
Fibrinolytic Medication Timing[3]	0	-	42%	55%
PCI Within 90 Minutes of Arrival[3]	0	-	88%	90%
Smoking Cessation Advice[3]	0	-	100%	99%
Chest Pain/Possible Heart Attack Care				
Aspirin at Arrival[1]	20	90%	94%	95%
Median Time to ECG (minutes)[1]	19	20	9	8
Median Time to Transfer (minutes)[3]	0	-	75	61
Fibrinolytic Medication Timing	0	-	50%	54%
Heart Failure Care				
ACE Inhibitor or ARB for LVSD[1]	8	100%	94%	94%
Discharge Instructions[1]	24	79%	85%	88%
Evaluation of LVS Function	36	83%	94%	98%
Smoking Cessation Advice[1]	4	100%	97%	98%
Pneumonia Care				
Appropriate Initial Antibiotic	26	96%	91%	92%
Blood Culture Timing[1]	5	100%	96%	96%
Influenza Vaccine	36	94%	89%	91%
Initial Antibiotic Timing	41	95%	95%	95%
Pneumococcal Vaccine	39	87%	91%	93%
Smoking Cessation Advice[1]	23	100%	95%	97%
Surgical Care Improvement Project				
Appropriate VTP Within 24 Hours[5]	0	-	91%	92%
Appropriate Hair Removal[5]	0	-	100%	99%
Appropriate Beta Blocker Usage[5]	0	-	91%	93%
Controlled Postoperative Blood Glucose[5]	0	-	95%	93%
Prophylactic Antibiotic Timing[5]	0	-	97%	97%
Prophylactic Antibiotic Timing (Outpatient)[5]	0	-	93%	92%
Prophylactic Antibiotic Selection[5]	0	-	98%	97%
Prophylactic Antibiotic Select. (Outpatient)[5]	0	-	95%	94%
Prophylactic Antibiotic Stopped[5]	0	-	94%	94%
Recommended VTP Ordered[5]	0	-	94%	94%
Urinary Catheter Removal[5]	0	-	87%	90%
Children's Asthma Care				
Received Systemic Corticosteroids	-	-	-	100%
Received Home Management Plan	-	-	-	71%
Received Reliever Medication	-	-	-	100%
Use of Medical Imaging				
Combination Abdominal CT Scan[1]	30	0.033	0.372	0.191
Combination Chest CT Scan[1]	8	0.000	0.134	0.054
Follow-up Mammogram/Ultrasound[5]	0	-	8%	8.4%
MRI for Low Back Pain[5]	0	-	34.3%	32.7%
Survey of Patients' Hospital Experiences				
Area Around Room 'Always' Quiet at Night	(a)	53%	-	58%
Doctors 'Always' Communicated Well	(a)	79%	-	80%
Home Recovery Information Given	(a)	75%	-	82%
Hospital Given 9 or 10 on 10 Point Scale	(a)	56%	-	67%
Meds 'Always' Explained Before Given	(a)	51%	-	60%
Nurses 'Always' Communicated Well	(a)	71%	-	76%
Pain 'Always' Well Controlled	(a)	60%	-	69%
Room and Bathroom 'Always' Clean	(a)	62%	-	71%
Timely Help 'Always' Received	(a)	66%	-	64%
Would Definitely Recommend Hospital	(a)	57%	-	69%

NOTE: Hospital profiles are in alphabetical order by state, then city, then hospital within the city; Rankings exclude hospitals with less than 25 cases except for patient surveys which excludes hospitals with less than 100 cases; (a) 100–299 cases; (1) The number of cases is too small to be sure how well a hospital is performing; (2) The hospital indicated that the data submitted for this measure were based on a sample of cases; (3) Data was collected during a shorter time period (fewer quarters) than the maximum possible time for this measure; (4) Suppressed for one or more quarters by CMS; (5) No data is available from the hospital for this measure; (6) Fewer than 100 patients completed the HCAHPS survey. Use these rates with caution, as the number of surveys may be too low to reliably assess hospital performance; (7) Survey results are based on less than 12 months of data; (8) Survey results are not available for this reporting period; (9) No or very few patients were eligible for the HCAHPS survey. The scores shown, if any, reflect a very small number of surveys; (10) A state average was not calculated because too few hospitals in the state submitted data; (11) There were discrepancies in the data collection process; Please refer to the User's Guide for a full explanation of data.

Integris Grove Hospital

1001 East 18th Street
Grove, OK 74344
E-mail: cathy.trewyn@integrisok.com
URL: www.integris-health.com
Type: Acute Care Hospitals
Ownership: Voluntary Non-Profit - Other

Phone: 918-786-2243
Fax: 918-787-3403

Emergency Services: Yes
Beds: 58

Key Personnel:
CEO/President. . . . . Greg Martin
Chief of Medical Staff . . . . Richard Tidewell, MD
Infection Control. . . . . Debbie Lawson
Operating Room. . . . . Debbie Berry, RN
Quality Assurance . . . . Dana Chouteau
Radiology. . . . . Michael Foster
Emergency Room . . . . Diane Wilkie

Measure	Cases	This Hosp.	State Avg.	U.S. Avg.
Heart Attack Care				
ACE Inhibitor or ARB for LVSD[1,2]	7	100%	95%	96%
Aspirin at Arrival[2]	44	100%	98%	99%
Aspirin at Discharge[2]	41	95%	98%	98%
Beta Blocker at Discharge[2]	39	97%	98%	98%
Fibrinolytic Medication Timing[2]	0	-	42%	55%
PCI Within 90 Minutes of Arrival[1,2]	4	75%	88%	90%
Smoking Cessation Advice[1,2]	12	100%	100%	99%
Chest Pain/Possible Heart Attack Care				
Aspirin at Arrival	72	93%	94%	95%
Median Time to ECG (minutes)	74	8	9	8
Median Time to Transfer (minutes)[1,3]	4	53	75	61
Fibrinolytic Medication Timing[1]	9	44%	50%	54%
Heart Failure Care				
ACE Inhibitor or ARB for LVSD[1]	15	93%	94%	94%
Discharge Instructions	57	100%	85%	88%
Evaluation of LVS Function	76	89%	94%	98%
Smoking Cessation Advice[1]	17	100%	97%	98%
Pneumonia Care				
Appropriate Initial Antibiotic	75	93%	91%	92%
Blood Culture Timing	116	94%	96%	96%
Influenza Vaccine	67	88%	89%	91%
Initial Antibiotic Timing	111	99%	95%	95%
Pneumococcal Vaccine	105	95%	91%	93%
Smoking Cessation Advice	35	100%	95%	97%
Surgical Care Improvement Project				
Appropriate VTP Within 24 Hours	82	90%	91%	92%
Appropriate Hair Removal	186	100%	100%	99%
Appropriate Beta Blocker Usage	41	90%	91%	93%
Controlled Postoperative Blood Glucose	0	-	95%	93%
Prophylactic Antibiotic Timing	130	97%	97%	97%
Prophylactic Antibiotic Timing (Outpatient)	97	97%	93%	92%
Prophylactic Antibiotic Selection	131	98%	98%	97%
Prophylactic Antibiotic Select. (Outpatient)	97	90%	95%	94%
Prophylactic Antibiotic Stopped	127	98%	94%	94%
Recommended VTP Ordered	82	90%	94%	94%
Urinary Catheter Removal	39	95%	87%	90%
Children's Asthma Care				
Received Systemic Corticosteroids	-	-	-	100%
Received Home Management Plan	-	-	-	71%
Received Reliever Medication	-	-	-	100%
Use of Medical Imaging				
Combination Abdominal CT Scan	322	0.773	0.372	0.191
Combination Chest CT Scan	230	0.048	0.134	0.054
Follow-up Mammogram/Ultrasound	688	6.5%	8%	8.4%
MRI for Low Back Pain	125	29.6%	34.3%	32.7%
Survey of Patients' Hospital Experiences				
Area Around Room 'Always' Quiet at Night	300+	62%	-	58%
Doctors 'Always' Communicated Well	300+	83%	-	80%
Home Recovery Information Given	300+	79%	-	82%
Hospital Given 9 or 10 on 10 Point Scale	300+	63%	-	67%
Meds 'Always' Explained Before Given	300+	60%	-	60%
Nurses 'Always' Communicated Well	300+	73%	-	76%
Pain 'Always' Well Controlled	300+	69%	-	69%
Room and Bathroom 'Always' Clean	300+	68%	-	71%
Timely Help 'Always' Received	300+	59%	-	64%
Would Definitely Recommend Hospital	300+	63%	-	69%

Logan Medical Center

200 South Academy Road
Guthrie, OK 73044
URL: www.loganhosp.com
Type: Critical Access Hospitals
Ownership: Govt - Hospital Dist/Auth

Phone: 405-282-6700
Fax: 405-282-6790

Emergency Services: Yes
Beds: 25

Key Personnel:
CEO/President. . . . . Steve Rowley
Chief of Medical Staff . . . . Todd Krehbiel, MD
Infection Control. . . . . Kaye Freudenberger
Quality Assurance . . . . Anita Valentine, RN
Radiology. . . . . Abe Sims
Emergency Room . . . . Ann Campbell, MD

Measure	Cases	This Hosp.	State Avg.	U.S. Avg.
Heart Attack Care				
ACE Inhibitor or ARB for LVSD[1]	2	100%	95%	96%
Aspirin at Arrival[1]	7	86%	98%	99%
Aspirin at Discharge[1]	4	100%	98%	98%
Beta Blocker at Discharge[1]	3	100%	98%	98%
Fibrinolytic Medication Timing	0	-	42%	55%
PCI Within 90 Minutes of Arrival	0	-	88%	90%
Smoking Cessation Advice	0	-	100%	99%
Chest Pain/Possible Heart Attack Care				
Aspirin at Arrival	-	-	94%	95%
Median Time to ECG (minutes)	-	-	9	8
Median Time to Transfer (minutes)	-	-	75	61
Fibrinolytic Medication Timing	-	-	50%	54%
Heart Failure Care				
ACE Inhibitor or ARB for LVSD[1]	8	50%	94%	94%
Discharge Instructions[1]	11	36%	85%	88%
Evaluation of LVS Function	33	79%	94%	98%
Smoking Cessation Advice[1]	4	75%	97%	98%
Pneumonia Care				
Appropriate Initial Antibiotic	59	86%	91%	92%
Blood Culture Timing	62	89%	96%	96%
Influenza Vaccine	38	53%	89%	91%
Initial Antibiotic Timing	45	76%	95%	95%
Pneumococcal Vaccine	62	53%	91%	93%
Smoking Cessation Advice	27	67%	95%	97%
Surgical Care Improvement Project				
Appropriate VTP Within 24 Hours	35	94%	91%	92%
Appropriate Hair Removal	66	100%	100%	99%
Appropriate Beta Blocker Usage[1]	16	75%	91%	93%
Controlled Postoperative Blood Glucose	0	-	95%	93%
Prophylactic Antibiotic Timing	49	94%	97%	97%
Prophylactic Antibiotic Timing (Outpatient)	-	-	93%	92%
Prophylactic Antibiotic Selection	49	98%	98%	97%
Prophylactic Antibiotic Select. (Outpatient)	-	-	95%	94%
Prophylactic Antibiotic Stopped	43	72%	94%	94%
Recommended VTP Ordered	35	94%	94%	94%
Urinary Catheter Removal[1]	13	46%	87%	90%
Children's Asthma Care				
Received Systemic Corticosteroids	-	-	-	100%
Received Home Management Plan	-	-	-	71%
Received Reliever Medication	-	-	-	100%
Use of Medical Imaging				
Combination Abdominal CT Scan	-	-	0.372	0.191
Combination Chest CT Scan	-	-	0.134	0.054
Follow-up Mammogram/Ultrasound	-	-	8%	8.4%
MRI for Low Back Pain	-	-	34.3%	32.7%
Survey of Patients' Hospital Experiences				
Area Around Room 'Always' Quiet at Night	(a)	65%	-	58%
Doctors 'Always' Communicated Well	(a)	87%	-	80%
Home Recovery Information Given	(a)	85%	-	82%
Hospital Given 9 or 10 on 10 Point Scale	(a)	74%	-	67%
Meds 'Always' Explained Before Given	(a)	58%	-	60%
Nurses 'Always' Communicated Well	(a)	75%	-	76%
Pain 'Always' Well Controlled	(a)	71%	-	69%
Room and Bathroom 'Always' Clean	(a)	67%	-	71%
Timely Help 'Always' Received	(a)	65%	-	64%
Would Definitely Recommend Hospital	(a)	71%	-	69%

Memorial Hospital of Texas County

520 Medical Drive
Guymon, OK 73942
E-mail: mhtchr@iptsi.net
URL: www.mhtcguymon.org
Type: Acute Care Hospitals
Ownership: Government - Local

Phone: 580-338-6515
Fax: 580-338-5722

Emergency Services: Yes
Beds: 42

Key Personnel:
CEO/President. . . . . Tim Starkey
Chief of Medical Staff . . . . Kelly McNurry
Infection Control. . . . . Julie West
Operating Room. . . . . Wayne Caniwell
Quality Assurance . . . . Julie West
Intensive Care Unit. . . . . Jane Brown

Measure	Cases	This Hosp.	State Avg.	U.S. Avg.
Heart Attack Care				
ACE Inhibitor or ARB for LVSD[5]	0	-	95%	96%
Aspirin at Arrival[5]	0	-	98%	99%
Aspirin at Discharge[5]	0	-	98%	98%
Beta Blocker at Discharge[5]	0	-	98%	98%
Fibrinolytic Medication Timing[5]	0	-	42%	55%
PCI Within 90 Minutes of Arrival[5]	0	-	88%	90%
Smoking Cessation Advice[5]	0	-	100%	99%
Chest Pain/Possible Heart Attack Care				
Aspirin at Arrival[1,3]	4	100%	94%	95%
Median Time to ECG (minutes)[1,3]	4	12	9	8
Median Time to Transfer (minutes)[5]	0	-	75	61
Fibrinolytic Medication Timing[1,3]	1	0%	50%	54%
Heart Failure Care				
ACE Inhibitor or ARB for LVSD[5]	0	-	94%	94%
Discharge Instructions[5]	0	-	85%	88%
Evaluation of LVS Function[5]	0	-	94%	98%
Smoking Cessation Advice[5]	0	-	97%	98%
Pneumonia Care				
Appropriate Initial Antibiotic[1]	23	87%	91%	92%
Blood Culture Timing[1]	4	100%	96%	96%
Influenza Vaccine[1]	20	100%	89%	91%
Initial Antibiotic Timing	35	89%	95%	95%
Pneumococcal Vaccine	31	94%	91%	93%
Smoking Cessation Advice[1]	16	88%	95%	97%
Surgical Care Improvement Project				
Appropriate VTP Within 24 Hours[1,3]	3	67%	91%	92%
Appropriate Hair Removal[1,3]	23	100%	100%	99%
Appropriate Beta Blocker Usage[1,3]	4	100%	91%	93%
Controlled Postoperative Blood Glucose[3]	0	-	95%	93%
Prophylactic Antibiotic Timing[1,3]	18	94%	97%	97%
Prophylactic Antibiotic Timing (Outpatient)[5]	0	-	93%	92%
Prophylactic Antibiotic Selection[1,3]	18	100%	98%	97%
Prophylactic Antibiotic Select. (Outpatient)[5]	0	-	95%	94%
Prophylactic Antibiotic Stopped[1,3]	18	100%	94%	94%
Recommended VTP Ordered[1,3]	3	100%	94%	94%
Urinary Catheter Removal[1,3]	1	100%	87%	90%
Children's Asthma Care				
Received Systemic Corticosteroids	-	-	-	100%
Received Home Management Plan	-	-	-	71%
Received Reliever Medication	-	-	-	100%
Use of Medical Imaging				
Combination Abdominal CT Scan	117	0.641	0.372	0.191
Combination Chest CT Scan	75	0.373	0.134	0.054
Follow-up Mammogram/Ultrasound	133	10.5%	8%	8.4%
MRI for Low Back Pain	49	32.7%	34.3%	32.7%
Survey of Patients' Hospital Experiences				
Area Around Room 'Always' Quiet at Night	(a)	61%	-	58%
Doctors 'Always' Communicated Well	(a)	79%	-	80%
Home Recovery Information Given	(a)	88%	-	82%
Hospital Given 9 or 10 on 10 Point Scale	(a)	66%	-	67%
Meds 'Always' Explained Before Given	(a)	59%	-	60%
Nurses 'Always' Communicated Well	(a)	77%	-	76%
Pain 'Always' Well Controlled	(a)	71%	-	69%
Room and Bathroom 'Always' Clean	(a)	73%	-	71%
Timely Help 'Always' Received	(a)	67%	-	64%
Would Definitely Recommend Hospital	(a)	60%	-	69%

NOTE: Hospital profiles are in alphabetical order by state, then city, then hospital within the city; Rankings exclude hospitals with less than 25 cases except for patient surveys which excludes hospitals with less than 100 cases; (a) 100–299 cases; (1) The number of cases is too small to be sure how well a hospital is performing; (2) The hospital indicated that the data submitted for this measure were based on a sample of cases; (3) Data was collected during a shorter time period (fewer quarters) than the maximum possible time for this measure; (4) Suppressed for one or more quarters by CMS; (5) No data is available from the hospital for this measure; (6) Fewer than 100 patients completed the HCAHPS survey. Use these rates with caution, as the number of surveys may be too low to reliably assess hospital performance; (7) Survey results are based on less than 12 months of data; (8) Survey results are not available for this reporting period; (9) No or very few patients were eligible for the HCAHPS survey. The scores shown, if any, reflect a very small number of surveys; (10) A state average was not calculated because too few hospitals in the state submitted data; (11) There were discrepancies in the data collection process; Please refer to the User's Guide for a full explanation of data.

Healdton Mercy Hospital Corporation

918 Southwest 8th Street
Healdton, OK 73438
Type: Critical Access Hospitals
Ownership: Voluntary Non-Profit - Private
Phone: 580-229-0701
Fax: 580-229-0691
Emergency Services: Yes
Beds: 25

Key Personnel:
CEO/President. . . . . Bob Thompson
Infection Control. . . . . Larry Lovelace
Radiology. . . . . Johnny Walker

Measure	Cases	This Hosp.	State Avg.	U.S. Avg.
Heart Attack Care				
ACE Inhibitor or ARB for LVSD[5]	0	-	95%	96%
Aspirin at Arrival[5]	0	-	98%	99%
Aspirin at Discharge[5]	0	-	98%	98%
Beta Blocker at Discharge[5]	0	-	98%	98%
Fibrinolytic Medication Timing[5]	0	-	42%	55%
PCI Within 90 Minutes of Arrival[5]	0	-	88%	90%
Smoking Cessation Advice[5]	0	-	100%	99%
Chest Pain/Possible Heart Attack Care				
Aspirin at Arrival	-	-	94%	95%
Median Time to ECG (minutes)	-	-	9	8
Median Time to Transfer (minutes)	-	-	75	61
Fibrinolytic Medication Timing	-	-	50%	54%
Heart Failure Care				
ACE Inhibitor or ARB for LVSD[3]	0	-	94%	94%
Discharge Instructions[3]	0	-	85%	88%
Evaluation of LVS Function[3]	0	-	94%	98%
Smoking Cessation Advice[3]	0	-	97%	98%
Pneumonia Care				
Appropriate Initial Antibiotic[1,3]	6	100%	91%	92%
Blood Culture Timing[3]	0	-	96%	96%
Influenza Vaccine[1,3]	5	100%	89%	91%
Initial Antibiotic Timing[1,3]	7	100%	95%	95%
Pneumococcal Vaccine[1,3]	7	86%	91%	93%
Smoking Cessation Advice[1,3]	1	100%	95%	97%
Surgical Care Improvement Project				
Appropriate VTP Within 24 Hours[5]	0	-	91%	92%
Appropriate Hair Removal[5]	0	-	100%	99%
Appropriate Beta Blocker Usage[5]	0	-	91%	93%
Controlled Postoperative Blood Glucose[5]	0	-	95%	93%
Prophylactic Antibiotic Timing[5]	0	-	97%	97%
Prophylactic Antibiotic Timing (Outpatient)	-	-	93%	92%
Prophylactic Antibiotic Selection[5]	0	-	98%	97%
Prophylactic Antibiotic Select. (Outpatient)	-	-	95%	94%
Prophylactic Antibiotic Stopped[5]	0	-	94%	94%
Recommended VTP Ordered[5]	0	-	94%	94%
Urinary Catheter Removal[5]	0	-	87%	90%
Children's Asthma Care				
Received Systemic Corticosteroids	-	-	-	100%
Received Home Management Plan	-	-	-	71%
Received Reliever Medication	-	-	-	100%
Use of Medical Imaging				
Combination Abdominal CT Scan	-	-	0.372	0.191
Combination Chest CT Scan	-	-	0.134	0.054
Follow-up Mammogram/Ultrasound	-	-	8%	8.4%
MRI for Low Back Pain	-	-	34.3%	32.7%
Survey of Patients' Hospital Experiences				
Area Around Room 'Always' Quiet at Night[8]	-	-	-	58%
Doctors 'Always' Communicated Well[8]	-	-	-	80%
Home Recovery Information Given[8]	-	-	-	82%
Hospital Given 9 or 10 on 10 Point Scale[8]	-	-	-	67%
Meds 'Always' Explained Before Given[8]	-	-	-	60%
Nurses 'Always' Communicated Well[8]	-	-	-	76%
Pain 'Always' Well Controlled[8]	-	-	-	69%
Room and Bathroom 'Always' Clean[8]	-	-	-	71%
Timely Help 'Always' Received[8]	-	-	-	64%
Would Definitely Recommend Hospital[8]	-	-	-	69%

Henryetta Medical Center

Dewey Bartlett St and Main St
Henryetta, OK 74437
URL: www.hillcrest.com/henryetta
Type: Acute Care Hospitals
Ownership: Government - State
Phone: 918-652-4463
Fax: 918-652-3675
Emergency Services: Yes
Beds: 41

Key Personnel:
CEO/President. . . . . Dee Renshaw
Chief of Medical Staff. . . . . Brent Davis, DO
Infection Control. . . . . Mike Patterson
Operating Room. . . . . James McGee, RN
Quality Assurance . . . . Benita Casselman
Anesthesiology. . . . . Tom Thompson, CRNA
Emergency Room . . . . Brent Davis, DO
Hemotology Center . . . . George Pikler, MD

Measure	Cases	This Hosp.	State Avg.	U.S. Avg.
Heart Attack Care				
ACE Inhibitor or ARB for LVSD[3]	0	-	95%	96%
Aspirin at Arrival[1,3]	2	50%	98%	99%
Aspirin at Discharge[1,3]	1	100%	98%	98%
Beta Blocker at Discharge[1,3]	1	100%	98%	98%
Fibrinolytic Medication Timing[3]	0	-	42%	55%
PCI Within 90 Minutes of Arrival[3]	0	-	88%	90%
Smoking Cessation Advice[3]	0	-	100%	99%
Chest Pain/Possible Heart Attack Care				
Aspirin at Arrival	104	100%	94%	95%
Median Time to ECG (minutes)	105	10	9	8
Median Time to Transfer (minutes)[1,3]	1	45	75	61
Fibrinolytic Medication Timing	0	-	50%	54%
Heart Failure Care				
ACE Inhibitor or ARB for LVSD[1]	12	92%	94%	94%
Discharge Instructions[1]	22	100%	85%	88%
Evaluation of LVS Function	28	89%	94%	98%
Smoking Cessation Advice[1]	4	100%	97%	98%
Pneumonia Care				
Appropriate Initial Antibiotic	34	94%	91%	92%
Blood Culture Timing	44	100%	96%	96%
Influenza Vaccine	28	82%	89%	91%
Initial Antibiotic Timing	50	100%	95%	95%
Pneumococcal Vaccine	29	93%	91%	93%
Smoking Cessation Advice[1]	17	100%	95%	97%
Surgical Care Improvement Project				
Appropriate VTP Within 24 Hours	29	100%	91%	92%
Appropriate Hair Removal	36	100%	100%	99%
Appropriate Beta Blocker Usage[1]	4	100%	91%	93%
Controlled Postoperative Blood Glucose	0	-	95%	93%
Prophylactic Antibiotic Timing[1]	24	100%	97%	97%
Prophylactic Antibiotic Timing (Outpatient)[1,3]	1	100%	93%	92%
Prophylactic Antibiotic Selection[1]	24	100%	98%	97%
Prophylactic Antibiotic Select. (Outpatient)[1,3]	1	100%	95%	94%
Prophylactic Antibiotic Stopped[1]	23	96%	94%	94%
Recommended VTP Ordered	29	100%	94%	94%
Urinary Catheter Removal[1]	5	100%	87%	90%
Children's Asthma Care				
Received Systemic Corticosteroids	-	-	-	100%
Received Home Management Plan	-	-	-	71%
Received Reliever Medication	-	-	-	100%
Use of Medical Imaging				
Combination Abdominal CT Scan	82	0.585	0.372	0.191
Combination Chest CT Scan	58	0.000	0.134	0.054
Follow-up Mammogram/Ultrasound	149	16.8%	8%	8.4%
MRI for Low Back Pain[5]	0	-	34.3%	32.7%
Survey of Patients' Hospital Experiences				
Area Around Room 'Always' Quiet at Night	(a)	64%	-	58%
Doctors 'Always' Communicated Well	(a)	84%	-	80%
Home Recovery Information Given	(a)	82%	-	82%
Hospital Given 9 or 10 on 10 Point Scale	(a)	74%	-	67%
Meds 'Always' Explained Before Given	(a)	67%	-	60%
Nurses 'Always' Communicated Well	(a)	82%	-	76%
Pain 'Always' Well Controlled	(a)	78%	-	69%
Room and Bathroom 'Always' Clean	(a)	75%	-	71%
Timely Help 'Always' Received	(a)	73%	-	64%
Would Definitely Recommend Hospital	(a)	73%	-	69%

Elkview General Hospital

429 West Elm Street
Hobart, OK 73651
URL: www.hobartok.com
Type: Acute Care Hospitals
Ownership: Govt - Hospital Dist/Auth
Phone: 580-726-3324
Fax: 580-726-6041
Emergency Services: Yes
Beds: 50

Measure	Cases	This Hosp.	State Avg.	U.S. Avg.
Heart Attack Care				
ACE Inhibitor or ARB for LVSD[3]	0	-	95%	96%
Aspirin at Arrival[1,3]	1	100%	98%	99%
Aspirin at Discharge[1,3]	1	100%	98%	98%
Beta Blocker at Discharge[3]	0	-	98%	98%
Fibrinolytic Medication Timing[1,3]	1	100%	42%	55%
PCI Within 90 Minutes of Arrival[3]	0	-	88%	90%
Smoking Cessation Advice[1,3]	1	100%	100%	99%
Chest Pain/Possible Heart Attack Care				
Aspirin at Arrival[1]	20	100%	94%	95%
Median Time to ECG (minutes)[1]	20	8	9	8
Median Time to Transfer (minutes)[5]	0	-	75	61
Fibrinolytic Medication Timing[1]	3	67%	50%	54%
Heart Failure Care				
ACE Inhibitor or ARB for LVSD[1]	16	94%	94%	94%
Discharge Instructions	32	100%	85%	88%
Evaluation of LVS Function	41	100%	94%	98%
Smoking Cessation Advice[1]	6	100%	97%	98%
Pneumonia Care				
Appropriate Initial Antibiotic	54	94%	91%	92%
Blood Culture Timing	31	97%	96%	96%
Influenza Vaccine	43	95%	89%	91%
Initial Antibiotic Timing	62	97%	95%	95%
Pneumococcal Vaccine	43	98%	91%	93%
Smoking Cessation Advice[1]	20	100%	95%	97%
Surgical Care Improvement Project				
Appropriate VTP Within 24 Hours[1]	23	70%	91%	92%
Appropriate Hair Removal	38	100%	100%	99%
Appropriate Beta Blocker Usage[1]	4	50%	91%	93%
Controlled Postoperative Blood Glucose	0	-	95%	93%
Prophylactic Antibiotic Timing	27	96%	97%	97%
Prophylactic Antibiotic Timing (Outpatient)[1,3]	2	100%	93%	92%
Prophylactic Antibiotic Selection	27	100%	98%	97%
Prophylactic Antibiotic Select. (Outpatient)[1,3]	2	100%	95%	94%
Prophylactic Antibiotic Stopped	27	93%	94%	94%
Recommended VTP Ordered[1]	23	70%	94%	94%
Urinary Catheter Removal[1]	21	81%	87%	90%
Children's Asthma Care				
Received Systemic Corticosteroids	-	-	-	100%
Received Home Management Plan	-	-	-	71%
Received Reliever Medication	-	-	-	100%
Use of Medical Imaging				
Combination Abdominal CT Scan	111	0.811	0.372	0.191
Combination Chest CT Scan	58	0.621	0.134	0.054
Follow-up Mammogram/Ultrasound	150	4.0%	8%	8.4%
MRI for Low Back Pain[5]	0	-	34.3%	32.7%
Survey of Patients' Hospital Experiences				
Area Around Room 'Always' Quiet at Night	(a)	59%	-	58%
Doctors 'Always' Communicated Well	(a)	89%	-	80%
Home Recovery Information Given	(a)	75%	-	82%
Hospital Given 9 or 10 on 10 Point Scale	(a)	65%	-	67%
Meds 'Always' Explained Before Given	(a)	66%	-	60%
Nurses 'Always' Communicated Well	(a)	81%	-	76%
Pain 'Always' Well Controlled	(a)	73%	-	69%
Room and Bathroom 'Always' Clean	(a)	77%	-	71%
Timely Help 'Always' Received	(a)	73%	-	64%
Would Definitely Recommend Hospital	(a)	68%	-	69%

NOTE: Hospital profiles are in alphabetical order by state, then city, then hospital within the city; Rankings exclude hospitals with less than 25 cases except for patient surveys which excludes hospitals with less than 100 cases; (a) 100–299 cases; (1) The number of cases is too small to be sure how well a hospital is performing; (2) The hospital indicated that the data submitted for this measure were based on a sample of cases; (3) Data was collected during a shorter time period (fewer quarters) than the maximum possible time for this measure; (4) Suppressed for one or more quarters by CMS; (5) No data is available from the hospital for this measure; (6) Fewer than 100 patients completed the HCAHPS survey. Use these rates with caution, as the number of surveys may be too low to reliably assess hospital performance; (7) Survey results are based on less than 12 months of data; (8) Survey results are not available for this reporting period; (9) No or very few patients were eligible for the HCAHPS survey. The scores shown, if any, reflect a very small number of surveys; (10) A state average was not calculated because too few hospitals in the state submitted data; (11) There were discrepancies in the data collection process; Please refer to the User's Guide for a full explanation of data.

Holdenville General Hospital

100 Mcdougal Drive
Holdenville, OK 74848
Phone: 405-379-4200
Type: Critical Access Hospitals
Emergency Services: Yes
Ownership: Govt - Hospital Dist/Auth
Beds: 25

Key Personnel:
CEO/President. . . . . Bridget Cosby, CEO
Chief of Medical Staff. . . . . Tom Osborn, DO
Operating Room. . . . . Jackie Smith
Anesthesiology. . . . . Bill Brasher
Emergency Room . . . . Evin Marshall

Measure	Cases	This Hosp.	State Avg.	U.S. Avg.
Heart Attack Care				
ACE Inhibitor or ARB for LVSD[5]	0	-	95%	96%
Aspirin at Arrival[5]	0	-	98%	99%
Aspirin at Discharge[5]	0	-	98%	98%
Beta Blocker at Discharge[5]	0	-	98%	98%
Fibrinolytic Medication Timing[5]	0	-	42%	55%
PCI Within 90 Minutes of Arrival[5]	0	-	88%	90%
Smoking Cessation Advice[5]	0	-	100%	99%
Chest Pain/Possible Heart Attack Care				
Aspirin at Arrival	-	-	94%	95%
Median Time to ECG (minutes)	-	-	9	8
Median Time to Transfer (minutes)	-	-	75	61
Fibrinolytic Medication Timing	-	-	50%	54%
Heart Failure Care				
ACE Inhibitor or ARB for LVSD[1]	7	71%	94%	94%
Discharge Instructions	36	72%	85%	88%
Evaluation of LVS Function	60	48%	94%	98%
Smoking Cessation Advice[1]	11	82%	97%	98%
Pneumonia Care				
Appropriate Initial Antibiotic	27	85%	91%	92%
Blood Culture Timing	30	90%	96%	96%
Influenza Vaccine	29	83%	89%	91%
Initial Antibiotic Timing	41	93%	95%	95%
Pneumococcal Vaccine	35	77%	91%	93%
Smoking Cessation Advice[1]	17	94%	95%	97%
Surgical Care Improvement Project				
Appropriate VTP Within 24 Hours[5]	0	-	91%	92%
Appropriate Hair Removal[5]	0	-	100%	99%
Appropriate Beta Blocker Usage[5]	0	-	91%	93%
Controlled Postoperative Blood Glucose[5]	0	-	95%	93%
Prophylactic Antibiotic Timing[5]	0	-	97%	97%
Prophylactic Antibiotic Timing (Outpatient)	-	-	93%	92%
Prophylactic Antibiotic Selection[5]	0	-	98%	97%
Prophylactic Antibiotic Select. (Outpatient)	-	-	95%	94%
Prophylactic Antibiotic Stopped[5]	0	-	94%	94%
Recommended VTP Ordered[5]	0	-	94%	94%
Urinary Catheter Removal[5]	0	-	87%	90%
Children's Asthma Care				
Received Systemic Corticosteroids	-	-	-	100%
Received Home Management Plan	-	-	-	71%
Received Reliever Medication	-	-	-	100%
Use of Medical Imaging				
Combination Abdominal CT Scan	-	-	0.372	0.191
Combination Chest CT Scan	-	-	0.134	0.054
Follow-up Mammogram/Ultrasound	-	-	8%	8.4%
MRI for Low Back Pain	-	-	34.3%	32.7%
Survey of Patients' Hospital Experiences				
Area Around Room 'Always' Quiet at Night[8]	-	-	-	58%
Doctors 'Always' Communicated Well[8]	-	-	-	80%
Home Recovery Information Given[8]	-	-	-	82%
Hospital Given 9 or 10 on 10 Point Scale[8]	-	-	-	67%
Meds 'Always' Explained Before Given[8]	-	-	-	60%
Nurses 'Always' Communicated Well[8]	-	-	-	76%
Pain 'Always' Well Controlled[8]	-	-	-	69%
Room and Bathroom 'Always' Clean[8]	-	-	-	71%
Timely Help 'Always' Received[8]	-	-	-	64%
Would Definitely Recommend Hospital[8]	-	-	-	69%

Harmon Memorial Hospital

400 East Chestnut Street
Hollis, OK 73550
Phone: 580-688-3363
Fax: 580-688-2246
Type: Acute Care Hospitals
Emergency Services: No
Ownership: Voluntary Non-Profit - Other
Beds: 22

Measure	Cases	This Hosp.	State Avg.	U.S. Avg.
Heart Attack Care				
ACE Inhibitor or ARB for LVSD	0	-	95%	96%
Aspirin at Arrival[1]	2	50%	98%	99%
Aspirin at Discharge[1]	3	33%	98%	98%
Beta Blocker at Discharge[1]	3	67%	98%	98%
Fibrinolytic Medication Timing	0	-	42%	55%
PCI Within 90 Minutes of Arrival	0	-	88%	90%
Smoking Cessation Advice	0	-	100%	99%
Chest Pain/Possible Heart Attack Care				
Aspirin at Arrival[1]	8	62%	94%	95%
Median Time to ECG (minutes)[1]	8	10	9	8
Median Time to Transfer (minutes)[5]	0	-	75	61
Fibrinolytic Medication Timing[1,3]	3	33%	50%	54%
Heart Failure Care				
ACE Inhibitor or ARB for LVSD[1]	5	80%	94%	94%
Discharge Instructions	30	70%	85%	88%
Evaluation of LVS Function	32	31%	94%	98%
Smoking Cessation Advice[1]	3	67%	97%	98%
Pneumonia Care				
Appropriate Initial Antibiotic	46	57%	91%	92%
Blood Culture Timing	28	32%	96%	96%
Influenza Vaccine	38	79%	89%	91%
Initial Antibiotic Timing	74	72%	95%	95%
Pneumococcal Vaccine	46	83%	91%	93%
Smoking Cessation Advice[1]	22	95%	95%	97%
Surgical Care Improvement Project				
Appropriate VTP Within 24 Hours[5]	0	-	91%	92%
Appropriate Hair Removal[5]	0	-	100%	99%
Appropriate Beta Blocker Usage[5]	0	-	91%	93%
Controlled Postoperative Blood Glucose[5]	0	-	95%	93%
Prophylactic Antibiotic Timing[5]	0	-	97%	97%
Prophylactic Antibiotic Timing (Outpatient)[5]	0	-	93%	92%
Prophylactic Antibiotic Selection[5]	0	-	98%	97%
Prophylactic Antibiotic Select. (Outpatient)[5]	0	-	95%	94%
Prophylactic Antibiotic Stopped[5]	0	-	94%	94%
Recommended VTP Ordered[5]	0	-	94%	94%
Urinary Catheter Removal[5]	0	-	87%	90%
Children's Asthma Care				
Received Systemic Corticosteroids	-	-	-	100%
Received Home Management Plan	-	-	-	71%
Received Reliever Medication	-	-	-	100%
Use of Medical Imaging				
Combination Abdominal CT Scan[1]	3	0.000	0.372	0.191
Combination Chest CT Scan[5]	0	-	0.134	0.054
Follow-up Mammogram/Ultrasound[5]	0	-	8%	8.4%
MRI for Low Back Pain[5]	0	-	34.3%	32.7%
Survey of Patients' Hospital Experiences				
Area Around Room 'Always' Quiet at Night[6]	<100	37%	-	58%
Doctors 'Always' Communicated Well[6]	<100	87%	-	80%
Home Recovery Information Given[6]	<100	73%	-	82%
Hospital Given 9 or 10 on 10 Point Scale[6]	<100	46%	-	67%
Meds 'Always' Explained Before Given[6]	<100	63%	-	60%
Nurses 'Always' Communicated Well[6]	<100	66%	-	76%
Pain 'Always' Well Controlled[6]	<100	51%	-	69%
Room and Bathroom 'Always' Clean[6]	<100	77%	-	71%
Timely Help 'Always' Received[6]	<100	74%	-	64%
Would Definitely Recommend Hospital	<100	64%	-	69%

Choctaw Memorial Hospital

1405 East Kirk Road
Hugo, OK 74743
Phone: 580-317-9500
Fax: 580-326-3541
Type: Acute Care Hospitals
Emergency Services: No
Ownership: Voluntary Non-Profit - Other
Beds: 34

Key Personnel:
CEO/President. . . . . Emmett Sthuster
Chief of Medical Staff . . . . Ted Rowland, MD

Measure	Cases	This Hosp.	State Avg.	U.S. Avg.
Heart Attack Care				
ACE Inhibitor or ARB for LVSD	0	-	95%	96%
Aspirin at Arrival[1]	3	33%	98%	99%
Aspirin at Discharge[1]	2	0%	98%	98%
Beta Blocker at Discharge[1]	3	67%	98%	98%
Fibrinolytic Medication Timing	0	-	42%	55%
PCI Within 90 Minutes of Arrival	0	-	88%	90%
Smoking Cessation Advice	0	-	100%	99%
Chest Pain/Possible Heart Attack Care				
Aspirin at Arrival[3]	31	71%	94%	95%
Median Time to ECG (minutes)[3]	27	68	9	8
Median Time to Transfer (minutes)[1,3]	2	134	75	61
Fibrinolytic Medication Timing[1,3]	2	0%	50%	54%
Heart Failure Care				
ACE Inhibitor or ARB for LVSD[1]	9	100%	94%	94%
Discharge Instructions	81	4%	85%	88%
Evaluation of LVS Function	120	53%	94%	98%
Smoking Cessation Advice	26	23%	97%	98%
Pneumonia Care				
Appropriate Initial Antibiotic[2]	54	80%	91%	92%
Blood Culture Timing[1,2]	21	76%	96%	96%
Influenza Vaccine[2]	50	42%	89%	91%
Initial Antibiotic Timing[2]	84	82%	95%	95%
Pneumococcal Vaccine[2]	77	43%	91%	93%
Smoking Cessation Advice[2]	25	48%	95%	97%
Surgical Care Improvement Project				
Appropriate VTP Within 24 Hours[1]	4	0%	91%	92%
Appropriate Hair Removal[1]	9	22%	100%	99%
Appropriate Beta Blocker Usage[1]	1	0%	91%	93%
Controlled Postoperative Blood Glucose	0	-	95%	93%
Prophylactic Antibiotic Timing[1]	9	56%	97%	97%
Prophylactic Antibiotic Timing (Outpatient)[5]	0	-	93%	92%
Prophylactic Antibiotic Selection[1]	9	33%	98%	97%
Prophylactic Antibiotic Select. (Outpatient)[5]	0	-	95%	94%
Prophylactic Antibiotic Stopped[1]	9	100%	94%	94%
Recommended VTP Ordered[1]	4	0%	94%	94%
Urinary Catheter Removal	0	-	87%	90%
Children's Asthma Care				
Received Systemic Corticosteroids	-	-	-	100%
Received Home Management Plan	-	-	-	71%
Received Reliever Medication	-	-	-	100%
Use of Medical Imaging				
Combination Abdominal CT Scan	96	0.573	0.372	0.191
Combination Chest CT Scan	80	0.625	0.134	0.054
Follow-up Mammogram/Ultrasound	221	12.2%	8%	8.4%
MRI for Low Back Pain[1]	42	35.7%	34.3%	32.7%
Survey of Patients' Hospital Experiences				
Area Around Room 'Always' Quiet at Night	(a)	43%	-	58%
Doctors 'Always' Communicated Well	(a)	77%	-	80%
Home Recovery Information Given	(a)	62%	-	82%
Hospital Given 9 or 10 on 10 Point Scale	(a)	45%	-	67%
Meds 'Always' Explained Before Given	(a)	46%	-	60%
Nurses 'Always' Communicated Well	(a)	62%	-	76%
Pain 'Always' Well Controlled	(a)	57%	-	69%
Room and Bathroom 'Always' Clean	(a)	65%	-	71%
Timely Help 'Always' Received	(a)	53%	-	64%
Would Definitely Recommend Hospital	(a)	50%	-	69%

NOTE: Hospital profiles are in alphabetical order by state, then city, then hospital within the city; Rankings exclude hospitals with less than 25 cases except for patient surveys which excludes hospitals with less than 100 cases; (a) 100–299 cases; (1) The number of cases is too small to be sure how well a hospital is performing; (2) The hospital indicated that the data submitted for this measure were based on a sample of cases; (3) Data was collected during a shorter time period (fewer quarters) than the maximum possible time for this measure; (4) Suppressed for one or more quarters by CMS; (5) No data is available from the hospital for this measure; (6) Fewer than 100 patients completed the HCAHPS survey. Use these rates with caution, as the number of surveys may be too low to reliably assess hospital performance; (7) Survey results are based on less than 12 months of data; (8) Survey results are not available for this reporting period; (9) No or very few patients were eligible for the HCAHPS survey. The scores shown, if any, reflect a very small number of surveys; (10) A state average was not calculated because too few hospitals in the state submitted data; (11) There were discrepancies in the data collection process; Please refer to the User's Guide for a full explanation of data.

McCurtain Memorial Hospital

1301 Lincoln Road
Idabel, OK 74745
Phone: 580-286-7623
Fax: 580-208-3199
Type: Acute Care Hospitals
Emergency Services: No
Ownership: Voluntary Non-Profit - Private
Beds: 111

Key Personnel:

CEO/President. . . . . Brit Messer
Chief of Medical Staff . . . . Jon Maxwell, DO
Infection Control. . . . . Ella Ward, RN
Operating Room. . . . . Anne May
Quality Assurance . . . . Carla Mitchell, RN
Radiology. . . . . R Pritchard, MD
Emergency Room . . . . Faye Gurley
Intensive Care Unit. . . . . Debbie Adams, RN

Measure	Cases	This Hosp.	State Avg.	U.S. Avg.
Heart Attack Care				
ACE Inhibitor or ARB for LVSD	0	-	95%	96%
Aspirin at Arrival[1]	7	100%	98%	99%
Aspirin at Discharge[1]	5	100%	98%	98%
Beta Blocker at Discharge[1]	5	100%	98%	98%
Fibrinolytic Medication Timing	0	-	42%	55%
PCI Within 90 Minutes of Arrival	0	-	88%	90%
Smoking Cessation Advice	0	-	100%	99%
Chest Pain/Possible Heart Attack Care				
Aspirin at Arrival	80	95%	94%	95%
Median Time to ECG (minutes)	83	12	9	8
Median Time to Transfer (minutes)[1,3]	3	95	75	61
Fibrinolytic Medication Timing[1]	2	0%	50%	54%
Heart Failure Care				
ACE Inhibitor or ARB for LVSD[1,2]	11	91%	94%	94%
Discharge Instructions[2]	52	58%	85%	88%
Evaluation of LVS Function[2]	64	84%	94%	98%
Smoking Cessation Advice[1,2]	12	100%	97%	98%
Pneumonia Care				
Appropriate Initial Antibiotic	64	92%	91%	92%
Blood Culture Timing	73	97%	96%	96%
Influenza Vaccine	70	87%	89%	91%
Initial Antibiotic Timing	108	92%	95%	95%
Pneumococcal Vaccine	82	85%	91%	93%
Smoking Cessation Advice	36	92%	95%	97%
Surgical Care Improvement Project				
Appropriate VTP Within 24 Hours[1]	9	89%	91%	92%
Appropriate Hair Removal[1]	24	100%	100%	99%
Appropriate Beta Blocker Usage[1]	3	100%	91%	93%
Controlled Postoperative Blood Glucose	0	-	95%	93%
Prophylactic Antibiotic Timing[1]	23	96%	97%	97%
Prophylactic Antibiotic Timing (Outpatient)[1,3]	4	100%	93%	92%
Prophylactic Antibiotic Selection[1]	23	100%	98%	97%
Prophylactic Antibiotic Select. (Outpatient)[1,3]	4	100%	95%	94%
Prophylactic Antibiotic Stopped[1]	23	91%	94%	94%
Recommended VTP Ordered[1]	9	89%	94%	94%
Urinary Catheter Removal	0	-	87%	90%
Children's Asthma Care				
Received Systemic Corticosteroids	-	-	-	100%
Received Home Management Plan	-	-	-	71%
Received Reliever Medication	-	-	-	100%
Use of Medical Imaging				
Combination Abdominal CT Scan	114	0.675	0.372	0.191
Combination Chest CT Scan	91	0.648	0.134	0.054
Follow-up Mammogram/Ultrasound	257	8.6%	8%	8.4%
MRI for Low Back Pain[1]	22	40.9%	34.3%	32.7%
Survey of Patients' Hospital Experiences				
Area Around Room 'Always' Quiet at Night	300+	70%	-	58%
Doctors 'Always' Communicated Well	300+	84%	-	80%
Home Recovery Information Given	300+	72%	-	82%
Hospital Given 9 or 10 on 10 Point Scale	300+	53%	-	67%
Meds 'Always' Explained Before Given	300+	64%	-	60%
Nurses 'Always' Communicated Well	300+	75%	-	76%
Pain 'Always' Well Controlled	300+	66%	-	69%
Room and Bathroom 'Always' Clean	300+	71%	-	71%
Timely Help 'Always' Received	300+	74%	-	64%
Would Definitely Recommend Hospital	300+	53%	-	69%

Kingfisher Regional Hospital

500 South 9th Street
Kingfisher, OK 73750
Phone: 405-375-3141
Fax: 405-375-6983
E-mail: dbenson@krhhospital.com
URL: www.kingfisherhospital.com
Type: Critical Access Hospitals
Emergency Services: Yes
Ownership: Proprietary
Beds: 25

Key Personnel:

CEO/President. . . . . Steve Jacobson
Chief of Medical Staff . . . . Jb Krablin
Infection Control. . . . . Amanda Mathews
Radiology. . . . . Ted Payne
Emergency Room . . . . Steve Arthurs

Measure	Cases	This Hosp.	State Avg.	U.S. Avg.
Heart Attack Care				
ACE Inhibitor or ARB for LVSD[3]	0	-	95%	96%
Aspirin at Arrival[1,3]	1	100%	98%	99%
Aspirin at Discharge[3]	0	-	98%	98%
Beta Blocker at Discharge[3]	0	-	98%	98%
Fibrinolytic Medication Timing[1,3]	1	0%	42%	55%
PCI Within 90 Minutes of Arrival[3]	0	-	88%	90%
Smoking Cessation Advice[3]	0	-	100%	99%
Chest Pain/Possible Heart Attack Care				
Aspirin at Arrival[1,3]	5	100%	94%	95%
Median Time to ECG (minutes)[1,3]	5	8	9	8
Median Time to Transfer (minutes)[1,3]	1	401	75	61
Fibrinolytic Medication Timing[3]	0	-	50%	54%
Heart Failure Care				
ACE Inhibitor or ARB for LVSD[1,3]	4	100%	94%	94%
Discharge Instructions[1,3]	7	100%	85%	88%
Evaluation of LVS Function[1,3]	9	89%	94%	98%
Smoking Cessation Advice[3]	0	-	97%	98%
Pneumonia Care				
Appropriate Initial Antibiotic	35	86%	91%	92%
Blood Culture Timing[1]	20	80%	96%	96%
Influenza Vaccine	30	80%	89%	91%
Initial Antibiotic Timing	53	91%	95%	95%
Pneumococcal Vaccine	35	77%	91%	93%
Smoking Cessation Advice[1]	7	71%	95%	97%
Surgical Care Improvement Project				
Appropriate VTP Within 24 Hours[5]	0	-	91%	92%
Appropriate Hair Removal[5]	0	-	100%	99%
Appropriate Beta Blocker Usage[5]	0	-	91%	93%
Controlled Postoperative Blood Glucose[5]	0	-	95%	93%
Prophylactic Antibiotic Timing[5]	0	-	97%	97%
Prophylactic Antibiotic Timing (Outpatient)[1,3]	1	0%	93%	92%
Prophylactic Antibiotic Selection[5]	0	-	98%	97%
Prophylactic Antibiotic Select. (Outpatient)[1,3]	1	100%	95%	94%
Prophylactic Antibiotic Stopped[5]	0	-	94%	94%
Recommended VTP Ordered[5]	0	-	94%	94%
Urinary Catheter Removal[5]	0	-	87%	90%
Children's Asthma Care				
Received Systemic Corticosteroids	-	-	-	100%
Received Home Management Plan	-	-	-	71%
Received Reliever Medication	-	-	-	100%
Use of Medical Imaging				
Combination Abdominal CT Scan	154	0.312	0.372	0.191
Combination Chest CT Scan	70	0.000	0.134	0.054
Follow-up Mammogram/Ultrasound	187	20.3%	8%	8.4%
MRI for Low Back Pain[1]	28	21.4%	34.3%	32.7%
Survey of Patients' Hospital Experiences				
Area Around Room 'Always' Quiet at Night	(a)	76%	-	58%
Doctors 'Always' Communicated Well	(a)	87%	-	80%
Home Recovery Information Given	(a)	83%	-	82%
Hospital Given 9 or 10 on 10 Point Scale	(a)	73%	-	67%
Meds 'Always' Explained Before Given	(a)	67%	-	60%
Nurses 'Always' Communicated Well	(a)	81%	-	76%
Pain 'Always' Well Controlled	(a)	77%	-	69%
Room and Bathroom 'Always' Clean	(a)	79%	-	71%
Timely Help 'Always' Received	(a)	69%	-	64%
Would Definitely Recommend Hospital	(a)	74%	-	69%

Comanche County Memorial Hospital

3401 West Gore Boulvard
Lawton, OK 73505
Phone: 580-355-8620
Fax: 580-250-5868
URL: www.memorialhealthsource.org
Type: Acute Care Hospitals
Emergency Services: Yes
Ownership: Govt - Hospital Dist/Auth
Beds: 250

Key Personnel:

CEO/President. . . . . Randall Segler
Chief of Medical Staff . . . . Rick Brittingham
Operating Room. . . . . Marilyn Magid, RN
Pediatric Ambulatory Care . . . . . . Joseph Rarick, MD
Pediatric In-Patient Care . . . . Joseph Rarick, MD
Quality Assurance . . . . Joanne Knecht
Radiology. . . . . Mittie Dragodjvich, MD
Emergency Room . . . . Barbara Clyde, RN

Measure	Cases	This Hosp.	State Avg.	U.S. Avg.
Heart Attack Care				
ACE Inhibitor or ARB for LVSD	40	92%	95%	96%
Aspirin at Arrival	135	97%	98%	99%
Aspirin at Discharge	283	98%	98%	98%
Beta Blocker at Discharge	271	100%	98%	98%
Fibrinolytic Medication Timing[1]	1	0%	42%	55%
PCI Within 90 Minutes of Arrival	35	71%	88%	90%
Smoking Cessation Advice	129	100%	100%	99%
Chest Pain/Possible Heart Attack Care				
Aspirin at Arrival[1]	8	62%	94%	95%
Median Time to ECG (minutes)[1]	7	10	9	8
Median Time to Transfer (minutes)[5]	0	-	75	61
Fibrinolytic Medication Timing[5]	0	-	50%	54%
Heart Failure Care				
ACE Inhibitor or ARB for LVSD[2]	123	92%	94%	94%
Discharge Instructions[2]	313	68%	85%	88%
Evaluation of LVS Function[2]	356	96%	94%	98%
Smoking Cessation Advice[2]	79	96%	97%	98%
Pneumonia Care				
Appropriate Initial Antibiotic[2]	137	93%	91%	92%
Blood Culture Timing[2]	189	95%	96%	96%
Influenza Vaccine[2]	116	59%	89%	91%
Initial Antibiotic Timing[2]	199	95%	95%	95%
Pneumococcal Vaccine[2]	170	82%	91%	93%
Smoking Cessation Advice[2]	105	93%	95%	97%
Surgical Care Improvement Project				
Appropriate VTP Within 24 Hours[2]	291	95%	91%	92%
Appropriate Hair Removal[2]	658	99%	100%	99%
Appropriate Beta Blocker Usage[2]	253	79%	91%	93%
Controlled Postoperative Blood Glucose[2]	170	86%	95%	93%
Prophylactic Antibiotic Timing[2]	420	91%	97%	97%
Prophylactic Antibiotic Timing (Outpatient)	389	89%	93%	92%
Prophylactic Antibiotic Selection[2]	427	99%	98%	97%
Prophylactic Antibiotic Select. (Outpatient)	385	98%	95%	94%
Prophylactic Antibiotic Stopped[2]	402	94%	94%	94%
Recommended VTP Ordered[2]	292	98%	94%	94%
Urinary Catheter Removal[2]	137	87%	87%	90%
Children's Asthma Care				
Received Systemic Corticosteroids	-	-	-	100%
Received Home Management Plan	-	-	-	71%
Received Reliever Medication	-	-	-	100%
Use of Medical Imaging				
Combination Abdominal CT Scan	1,177	0.021	0.372	0.191
Combination Chest CT Scan	852	0.002	0.134	0.054
Follow-up Mammogram/Ultrasound	1,147	2.9%	8%	8.4%
MRI for Low Back Pain	143	36.4%	34.3%	32.7%
Survey of Patients' Hospital Experiences				
Area Around Room 'Always' Quiet at Night	300+	53%	-	58%
Doctors 'Always' Communicated Well	300+	79%	-	80%
Home Recovery Information Given	300+	78%	-	82%
Hospital Given 9 or 10 on 10 Point Scale	300+	63%	-	67%
Meds 'Always' Explained Before Given	300+	59%	-	60%
Nurses 'Always' Communicated Well	300+	76%	-	76%
Pain 'Always' Well Controlled	300+	71%	-	69%
Room and Bathroom 'Always' Clean	300+	63%	-	71%
Timely Help 'Always' Received	300+	65%	-	64%
Would Definitely Recommend Hospital	300+	69%	-	69%

NOTE: Hospital profiles are in alphabetical order by state, then city, then hospital within the city; Rankings exclude hospitals with less than 25 cases except for patient surveys which excludes hospitals with less than 100 cases; (a) 100–299 cases; (1) The number of cases is too small to be sure how well a hospital is performing; (2) The hospital indicated that the data submitted for this measure were based on a sample of cases; (3) Data was collected during a shorter time period (fewer quarters) than the maximum possible time for this measure; (4) Suppressed for one or more quarters by CMS; (5) No data is available from the hospital for this measure; (6) Fewer than 100 patients completed the HCAHPS survey. Use these rates with caution, as the number of surveys may be too low to reliably assess hospital performance; (7) Survey results are based on less than 12 months of data; (8) Survey results are not available for this reporting period; (9) No or very few patients were eligible for the HCAHPS survey. The scores shown, if any, reflect a very small number of surveys; (10) A state average was not calculated because too few hospitals in the state submitted data; (11) There were discrepancies in the data collection process; Please refer to the User's Guide for a full explanation of data.

Southwestern Medical Center

5602 Southwest Lee Boulevard Phone: 580-531-4700
Lawton, OK 73505 Fax: 580-531-4702
URL: www.swmconline.com
Type: Acute Care Hospitals Emergency Services: Yes
Ownership: Proprietary Beds: 162

Key Personnel:
CEO/President. . . . . Thomas L Rine
Chief of Medical Staff . . . . Shane Ross
Radiology. . . . . Randall D Behrmann
Emergency Room . . . . David W Behm

Measure	Cases	This Hosp.	State Avg.	U.S. Avg.
Heart Attack Care				
ACE Inhibitor or ARB for LVSD	0	-	95%	96%
Aspirin at Arrival[1]	3	100%	98%	99%
Aspirin at Discharge	0	-	98%	98%
Beta Blocker at Discharge	0	-	98%	98%
Fibrinolytic Medication Timing	0	-	42%	55%
PCI Within 90 Minutes of Arrival	0	-	88%	90%
Smoking Cessation Advice	0	-	100%	99%
Chest Pain/Possible Heart Attack Care				
Aspirin at Arrival[1,3]	7	100%	94%	95%
Median Time to ECG (minutes)[1,3]	7	43	9	8
Median Time to Transfer (minutes)[3]	0	-	75	61
Fibrinolytic Medication Timing[3]	0	-	50%	54%
Heart Failure Care				
ACE Inhibitor or ARB for LVSD[1]	11	91%	94%	94%
Discharge Instructions	32	72%	85%	88%
Evaluation of LVS Function	42	100%	94%	98%
Smoking Cessation Advice[1]	12	100%	97%	98%
Pneumonia Care				
Appropriate Initial Antibiotic	74	89%	91%	92%
Blood Culture Timing	68	88%	96%	96%
Influenza Vaccine	73	78%	89%	91%
Initial Antibiotic Timing	108	81%	95%	95%
Pneumococcal Vaccine	88	94%	91%	93%
Smoking Cessation Advice	51	92%	95%	97%
Surgical Care Improvement Project				
Appropriate VTP Within 24 Hours	106	95%	91%	92%
Appropriate Hair Removal	240	99%	100%	99%
Appropriate Beta Blocker Usage	44	93%	91%	93%
Controlled Postoperative Blood Glucose	0	-	95%	93%
Prophylactic Antibiotic Timing	172	98%	97%	97%
Prophylactic Antibiotic Timing (Outpatient)	87	89%	93%	92%
Prophylactic Antibiotic Selection	173	97%	98%	97%
Prophylactic Antibiotic Select. (Outpatient)	81	89%	95%	94%
Prophylactic Antibiotic Stopped	169	97%	94%	94%
Recommended VTP Ordered	107	94%	94%	94%
Urinary Catheter Removal[1]	21	48%	87%	90%
Children's Asthma Care				
Received Systemic Corticosteroids	-	-	-	100%
Received Home Management Plan	-	-	-	71%
Received Reliever Medication	-	-	-	100%
Use of Medical Imaging				
Combination Abdominal CT Scan	299	0.518	0.372	0.191
Combination Chest CT Scan	252	0.560	0.134	0.054
Follow-up Mammogram/Ultrasound[5]	0	-	8%	8.4%
MRI for Low Back Pain	111	38.7%	34.3%	32.7%
Survey of Patients' Hospital Experiences				
Area Around Room 'Always' Quiet at Night	300+	63%	-	58%
Doctors 'Always' Communicated Well	300+	82%	-	80%
Home Recovery Information Given	300+	81%	-	82%
Hospital Given 9 or 10 on 10 Point Scale	300+	62%	-	67%
Meds 'Always' Explained Before Given	300+	56%	-	60%
Nurses 'Always' Communicated Well	300+	69%	-	76%
Pain 'Always' Well Controlled	300+	66%	-	69%
Room and Bathroom 'Always' Clean	300+	61%	-	71%
Timely Help 'Always' Received	300+	56%	-	64%
Would Definitely Recommend Hospital	300+	66%	-	69%

USPHS Lawton Indian Hospital

1515 Lawrie Tatum Road Phone: 580-354-5000
Lawton, OK 73507 Fax: 580-353-2914
Type: Acute Care Hospitals Emergency Services: Yes
Ownership: Government - Federal Beds: 48

Key Personnel:
CEO/President. . . . . Hickory Starr Jr
Chief of Medical Staff . . . . Dr Boyce Poolaw, MD
Infection Control. . . . . Sue Burgess
Operating Room. . . . . Dr Pilar
Pediatric Ambulatory Care . . . . . . Bryce Poolaw, MD
Pediatric In-Patient Care . . . . Bryce Poolaw, MD
Quality Assurance . . . . Kevin Whitehead

Measure	Cases	This Hosp.	State Avg.	U.S. Avg.
Heart Attack Care				
ACE Inhibitor or ARB for LVSD[5]	0	-	95%	96%
Aspirin at Arrival[5]	0	-	98%	99%
Aspirin at Discharge[5]	0	-	98%	98%
Beta Blocker at Discharge[5]	0	-	98%	98%
Fibrinolytic Medication Timing[5]	0	-	42%	55%
PCI Within 90 Minutes of Arrival[5]	0	-	88%	90%
Smoking Cessation Advice[5]	0	-	100%	99%
Chest Pain/Possible Heart Attack Care				
Aspirin at Arrival	-	-	94%	95%
Median Time to ECG (minutes)	-	-	9	8
Median Time to Transfer (minutes)	-	-	75	61
Fibrinolytic Medication Timing	-	-	50%	54%
Heart Failure Care				
ACE Inhibitor or ARB for LVSD[1,3]	2	100%	94%	94%
Discharge Instructions[1,3]	5	40%	85%	88%
Evaluation of LVS Function[1,3]	5	80%	94%	98%
Smoking Cessation Advice[1,3]	1	100%	97%	98%
Pneumonia Care				
Appropriate Initial Antibiotic[1]	6	100%	91%	92%
Blood Culture Timing[1]	9	89%	96%	96%
Influenza Vaccine[1]	14	64%	89%	91%
Initial Antibiotic Timing[1]	7	57%	95%	95%
Pneumococcal Vaccine[1]	7	100%	91%	93%
Smoking Cessation Advice[1]	8	25%	95%	97%
Surgical Care Improvement Project				
Appropriate VTP Within 24 Hours[1]	2	50%	91%	92%
Appropriate Hair Removal[1]	10	100%	100%	99%
Appropriate Beta Blocker Usage	0	-	91%	93%
Controlled Postoperative Blood Glucose	0	-	95%	93%
Prophylactic Antibiotic Timing[1]	1	0%	97%	97%
Prophylactic Antibiotic Timing (Outpatient)	-	-	93%	92%
Prophylactic Antibiotic Selection[1]	1	0%	98%	97%
Prophylactic Antibiotic Select. (Outpatient)	-	-	95%	94%
Prophylactic Antibiotic Stopped[1]	1	100%	94%	94%
Recommended VTP Ordered[1]	3	33%	94%	94%
Urinary Catheter Removal[1]	1	100%	87%	90%
Children's Asthma Care				
Received Systemic Corticosteroids	-	-	-	100%
Received Home Management Plan	-	-	-	71%
Received Reliever Medication	-	-	-	100%
Use of Medical Imaging				
Combination Abdominal CT Scan	-	-	0.372	0.191
Combination Chest CT Scan	-	-	0.134	0.054
Follow-up Mammogram/Ultrasound	-	-	8%	8.4%
MRI for Low Back Pain	-	-	34.3%	32.7%
Survey of Patients' Hospital Experiences				
Area Around Room 'Always' Quiet at Night[6]	<100	71%	-	58%
Doctors 'Always' Communicated Well[6]	<100	72%	-	80%
Home Recovery Information Given[6]	<100	79%	-	82%
Hospital Given 9 or 10 on 10 Point Scale[6]	<100	64%	-	67%
Meds 'Always' Explained Before Given[6]	<100	76%	-	60%
Nurses 'Always' Communicated Well[6]	<100	73%	-	76%
Pain 'Always' Well Controlled[6]	<100	78%	-	69%
Room and Bathroom 'Always' Clean[6]	<100	85%	-	71%
Timely Help 'Always' Received[6]	<100	66%	-	64%
Would Definitely Recommend Hospital	<100	64%	-	69%

Lindsay Municipal Hospital

Highway 19 West Phone: 405-756-1404
Lindsay, OK 73052 Fax: 405-756-1476
Type: Acute Care Hospitals Emergency Services: Yes
Ownership: Govt - Hospital Dist/Auth Beds: 25

Key Personnel:
CEO/President. . . . . Norma Howard
Cardiac Laboratory. . . . . Lisa Davis

Measure	Cases	This Hosp.	State Avg.	U.S. Avg.
Heart Attack Care				
ACE Inhibitor or ARB for LVSD[5]	0	-	95%	96%
Aspirin at Arrival[5]	0	-	98%	99%
Aspirin at Discharge[5]	0	-	98%	98%
Beta Blocker at Discharge[5]	0	-	98%	98%
Fibrinolytic Medication Timing[5]	0	-	42%	55%
PCI Within 90 Minutes of Arrival[5]	0	-	88%	90%
Smoking Cessation Advice[5]	0	-	100%	99%
Chest Pain/Possible Heart Attack Care				
Aspirin at Arrival	-	-	94%	95%
Median Time to ECG (minutes)	-	-	9	8
Median Time to Transfer (minutes)	-	-	75	61
Fibrinolytic Medication Timing	-	-	50%	54%
Heart Failure Care				
ACE Inhibitor or ARB for LVSD[5]	0	-	94%	94%
Discharge Instructions[5]	0	-	85%	88%
Evaluation of LVS Function[5]	0	-	94%	98%
Smoking Cessation Advice[5]	0	-	97%	98%
Pneumonia Care				
Appropriate Initial Antibiotic[1,3]	2	100%	91%	92%
Blood Culture Timing[3]	0	-	96%	96%
Influenza Vaccine[5]	0	-	89%	91%
Initial Antibiotic Timing[1,3]	1	100%	95%	95%
Pneumococcal Vaccine[1,3]	1	100%	91%	93%
Smoking Cessation Advice[1,3]	1	100%	95%	97%
Surgical Care Improvement Project				
Appropriate VTP Within 24 Hours[5]	0	-	91%	92%
Appropriate Hair Removal[5]	0	-	100%	99%
Appropriate Beta Blocker Usage[5]	0	-	91%	93%
Controlled Postoperative Blood Glucose[5]	0	-	95%	93%
Prophylactic Antibiotic Timing[5]	0	-	97%	97%
Prophylactic Antibiotic Timing (Outpatient)	-	-	93%	92%
Prophylactic Antibiotic Selection[5]	0	-	98%	97%
Prophylactic Antibiotic Select. (Outpatient)	-	-	95%	94%
Prophylactic Antibiotic Stopped[5]	0	-	94%	94%
Recommended VTP Ordered[5]	0	-	94%	94%
Urinary Catheter Removal[5]	0	-	87%	90%
Children's Asthma Care				
Received Systemic Corticosteroids	-	-	-	100%
Received Home Management Plan	-	-	-	71%
Received Reliever Medication	-	-	-	100%
Use of Medical Imaging				
Combination Abdominal CT Scan	-	-	0.372	0.191
Combination Chest CT Scan	-	-	0.134	0.054
Follow-up Mammogram/Ultrasound	-	-	8%	8.4%
MRI for Low Back Pain	-	-	34.3%	32.7%
Survey of Patients' Hospital Experiences				
Area Around Room 'Always' Quiet at Night[8]	-	-	-	58%
Doctors 'Always' Communicated Well[8]	-	-	-	80%
Home Recovery Information Given[8]	-	-	-	82%
Hospital Given 9 or 10 on 10 Point Scale[8]	-	-	-	67%
Meds 'Always' Explained Before Given[8]	-	-	-	60%
Nurses 'Always' Communicated Well[8]	-	-	-	76%
Pain 'Always' Well Controlled[8]	-	-	-	69%
Room and Bathroom 'Always' Clean[8]	-	-	-	71%
Timely Help 'Always' Received[8]	-	-	-	64%
Would Definitely Recommend Hospital[8]	-	-	-	69%

NOTE: Hospital profiles are in alphabetical order by state, then city, then hospital within the city; Rankings exclude hospitals with less than 25 cases except for patient surveys which excludes hospitals with less than 100 cases; (a) 100–299 cases; (1) The number of cases is too small to be sure how well a hospital is performing; (2) The hospital indicated that the data submitted for this measure were based on a sample of cases; (3) Data was collected during a shorter time period (fewer quarters) than the maximum possible time for this measure; (4) Suppressed for one or more quarters by CMS; (5) No data is available from the hospital for this measure; (6) Fewer than 100 patients completed the HCAHPS survey. Use these rates with caution, as the number of surveys may be too low to reliably assess hospital performance; (7) Survey results are based on less than 12 months of data; (8) Survey results are not available for this reporting period; (9) No or very few patients were eligible for the HCAHPS survey. The scores shown, if any, reflect a very small number of surveys; (10) A state average was not calculated because too few hospitals in the state submitted data; (11) There were discrepancies in the data collection process; Please refer to the User's Guide for a full explanation of data.

Integris Marshall County Medical Center

One Hospital Drive Phone: 580-795-3384
Madill, OK 73446 Fax: 580-795-7080
URL: www.integris-health.com/INTEGRIS
Type: Critical Access Hospitals Emergency Services: Yes
Ownership: Government - Federal Beds: 25
Key Personnel:
CEO/President. . . . . Karen Reynolds
Chief of Medical Staff . . . . Bruck Zimmerman
Infection Control. . . . . Lois Erwin
Operating Room. . . . . Joy Henry, RN
Emergency Room . . . . Carol Gay

Measure	Cases	This Hosp.	State Avg.	U.S. Avg.
Heart Attack Care				
ACE Inhibitor or ARB for LVSD	0	-	95%	96%
Aspirin at Arrival[1]	3	100%	98%	99%
Aspirin at Discharge[1]	1	100%	98%	98%
Beta Blocker at Discharge[1]	1	100%	98%	98%
Fibrinolytic Medication Timing	0	-	42%	55%
PCI Within 90 Minutes of Arrival	0	-	88%	90%
Smoking Cessation Advice	0	-	100%	99%
Chest Pain/Possible Heart Attack Care				
Aspirin at Arrival	31	94%	94%	95%
Median Time to ECG (minutes)	33	9	9	8
Median Time to Transfer (minutes)[5]	0	-	75	61
Fibrinolytic Medication Timing[1]	5	0%	50%	54%
Heart Failure Care				
ACE Inhibitor or ARB for LVSD[1]	11	100%	94%	94%
Discharge Instructions	25	96%	85%	88%
Evaluation of LVS Function	34	100%	94%	98%
Smoking Cessation Advice[1]	12	100%	97%	98%
Pneumonia Care				
Appropriate Initial Antibiotic	59	100%	91%	92%
Blood Culture Timing	54	94%	96%	96%
Influenza Vaccine	51	96%	89%	91%
Initial Antibiotic Timing	79	99%	95%	95%
Pneumococcal Vaccine	70	94%	91%	93%
Smoking Cessation Advice	25	100%	95%	97%
Surgical Care Improvement Project				
Appropriate VTP Within 24 Hours[5]	0	-	91%	92%
Appropriate Hair Removal[5]	0	-	100%	99%
Appropriate Beta Blocker Usage[5]	0	-	91%	93%
Controlled Postoperative Blood Glucose[5]	0	-	95%	93%
Prophylactic Antibiotic Timing[5]	0	-	97%	97%
Prophylactic Antibiotic Timing (Outpatient)[1]	19	100%	93%	92%
Prophylactic Antibiotic Selection[5]	0	-	98%	97%
Prophylactic Antibiotic Select. (Outpatient)[1]	19	89%	95%	94%
Prophylactic Antibiotic Stopped[5]	0	-	94%	94%
Recommended VTP Ordered[5]	0	-	94%	94%
Urinary Catheter Removal[5]	0	-	87%	90%
Children's Asthma Care				
Received Systemic Corticosteroids	-	-	-	100%
Received Home Management Plan	-	-	-	71%
Received Reliever Medication	-	-	-	100%
Use of Medical Imaging				
Combination Abdominal CT Scan	80	0.613	0.372	0.191
Combination Chest CT Scan	61	0.016	0.134	0.054
Follow-up Mammogram/Ultrasound[5]	0	-	8%	8.4%
MRI for Low Back Pain	52	44.2%	34.3%	32.7%
Survey of Patients' Hospital Experiences				
Area Around Room 'Always' Quiet at Night	(a)	65%	-	58%
Doctors 'Always' Communicated Well	(a)	92%	-	80%
Home Recovery Information Given	(a)	87%	-	82%
Hospital Given 9 or 10 on 10 Point Scale	(a)	73%	-	67%
Meds 'Always' Explained Before Given	(a)	65%	-	60%
Nurses 'Always' Communicated Well	(a)	81%	-	76%
Pain 'Always' Well Controlled	(a)	68%	-	69%
Room and Bathroom 'Always' Clean	(a)	74%	-	71%
Timely Help 'Always' Received	(a)	74%	-	64%
Would Definitely Recommend Hospital	(a)	70%	-	69%

Quartz Mountain Medical Center

One Wickersham Drive Phone: 580-782-3353
Mangum, OK 73554 Fax: 580-782-5944
URL: www.mangumhealth.com
Type: Critical Access Hospitals Emergency Services: Yes
Ownership: Proprietary Beds: 25
Key Personnel:
CEO/President. . . . . Jim Ivey

Measure	Cases	This Hosp.	State Avg.	U.S. Avg.
Heart Attack Care				
ACE Inhibitor or ARB for LVSD[3]	0	-	95%	96%
Aspirin at Arrival[3]	0	-	98%	99%
Aspirin at Discharge[3]	0	-	98%	98%
Beta Blocker at Discharge[3]	0	-	98%	98%
Fibrinolytic Medication Timing[3]	0	-	42%	55%
PCI Within 90 Minutes of Arrival[3]	0	-	88%	90%
Smoking Cessation Advice[3]	0	-	100%	99%
Chest Pain/Possible Heart Attack Care				
Aspirin at Arrival	-	-	94%	95%
Median Time to ECG (minutes)	-	-	9	8
Median Time to Transfer (minutes)	-	-	75	61
Fibrinolytic Medication Timing	-	-	50%	54%
Heart Failure Care				
ACE Inhibitor or ARB for LVSD[1,3]	1	100%	94%	94%
Discharge Instructions[1,3]	4	50%	85%	88%
Evaluation of LVS Function[1,3]	4	50%	94%	98%
Smoking Cessation Advice[1,3]	2	50%	97%	98%
Pneumonia Care				
Appropriate Initial Antibiotic[3,1]	7	100%	91%	92%
Blood Culture Timing[1,3]	5	80%	96%	96%
Influenza Vaccine[1,3]	6	83%	89%	91%
Initial Antibiotic Timing[1,3]	8	75%	95%	95%
Pneumococcal Vaccine[1,3]	14	100%	91%	93%
Smoking Cessation Advice[1,3]	3	33%	95%	97%
Surgical Care Improvement Project				
Appropriate VTP Within 24 Hours[5]	0	-	91%	92%
Appropriate Hair Removal[5]	0	-	100%	99%
Appropriate Beta Blocker Usage[5]	0	-	91%	93%
Controlled Postoperative Blood Glucose[5]	0	-	95%	93%
Prophylactic Antibiotic Timing[5]	0	-	97%	97%
Prophylactic Antibiotic Timing (Outpatient)	-	-	93%	92%
Prophylactic Antibiotic Selection[5]	0	-	98%	97%
Prophylactic Antibiotic Select. (Outpatient)	-	-	95%	94%
Prophylactic Antibiotic Stopped[5]	0	-	94%	94%
Recommended VTP Ordered[5]	0	-	94%	94%
Urinary Catheter Removal[5]	0	-	87%	90%
Children's Asthma Care				
Received Systemic Corticosteroids	-	-	-	100%
Received Home Management Plan	-	-	-	71%
Received Reliever Medication	-	-	-	100%
Use of Medical Imaging				
Combination Abdominal CT Scan	-	-	0.372	0.191
Combination Chest CT Scan	-	-	0.134	0.054
Follow-up Mammogram/Ultrasound	-	-	8%	8.4%
MRI for Low Back Pain	-	-	34.3%	32.7%
Survey of Patients' Hospital Experiences				
Area Around Room 'Always' Quiet at Night[8]	-	-	-	58%
Doctors 'Always' Communicated Well[8]	-	-	-	80%
Home Recovery Information Given[8]	-	-	-	82%
Hospital Given 9 or 10 on 10 Point Scale[8]	-	-	-	67%
Meds 'Always' Explained Before Given[8]	-	-	-	60%
Nurses 'Always' Communicated Well[8]	-	-	-	76%
Pain 'Always' Well Controlled[8]	-	-	-	69%
Room and Bathroom 'Always' Clean[8]	-	-	-	71%
Timely Help 'Always' Received[8]	-	-	-	64%
Would Definitely Recommend Hospital[8]	-	-	-	69%

Mercy Health Love County

300 Wanda Street Phone: 580-276-3347
Marietta, OK 73448 Fax: 580-276-2182
URL: www.mercyok.net
Type: Critical Access Hospitals Emergency Services: Yes
Ownership: Proprietary Beds: 30
Key Personnel:
CEO/President. . . . . Diana Smalley

Measure	Cases	This Hosp.	State Avg.	U.S. Avg.
Heart Attack Care				
ACE Inhibitor or ARB for LVSD[3]	0	-	95%	96%
Aspirin at Arrival[1,3]	1	100%	98%	99%
Aspirin at Discharge[1,3]	1	0%	98%	98%
Beta Blocker at Discharge[1,3]	1	100%	98%	98%
Fibrinolytic Medication Timing[3]	0	-	42%	55%
PCI Within 90 Minutes of Arrival[3]	0	-	88%	90%
Smoking Cessation Advice[1,3]	1	100%	100%	99%
Chest Pain/Possible Heart Attack Care				
Aspirin at Arrival	-	-	94%	95%
Median Time to ECG (minutes)	-	-	9	8
Median Time to Transfer (minutes)	-	-	75	61
Fibrinolytic Medication Timing	-	-	50%	54%
Heart Failure Care				
ACE Inhibitor or ARB for LVSD	0	-	94%	94%
Discharge Instructions[1]	13	8%	85%	88%
Evaluation of LVS Function[1]	19	42%	94%	98%
Smoking Cessation Advice[1]	4	100%	97%	98%
Pneumonia Care				
Appropriate Initial Antibiotic[1,2]	3	67%	91%	92%
Blood Culture Timing[1,2]	1	100%	96%	96%
Influenza Vaccine[1]	19	84%	89%	91%
Initial Antibiotic Timing[1,2]	19	63%	95%	95%
Pneumococcal Vaccine[2]	26	81%	91%	93%
Smoking Cessation Advice[1,2]	6	67%	95%	97%
Surgical Care Improvement Project				
Appropriate VTP Within 24 Hours[5]	0	-	91%	92%
Appropriate Hair Removal[5]	0	-	100%	99%
Appropriate Beta Blocker Usage[5]	0	-	91%	93%
Controlled Postoperative Blood Glucose[5]	0	-	95%	93%
Prophylactic Antibiotic Timing[5]	0	-	97%	97%
Prophylactic Antibiotic Timing (Outpatient)	-	-	93%	92%
Prophylactic Antibiotic Selection[5]	0	-	98%	97%
Prophylactic Antibiotic Select. (Outpatient)	-	-	95%	94%
Prophylactic Antibiotic Stopped[5]	0	-	94%	94%
Recommended VTP Ordered[5]	0	-	94%	94%
Urinary Catheter Removal[5]	0	-	87%	90%
Children's Asthma Care				
Received Systemic Corticosteroids	-	-	-	100%
Received Home Management Plan	-	-	-	71%
Received Reliever Medication	-	-	-	100%
Use of Medical Imaging				
Combination Abdominal CT Scan	-	-	0.372	0.191
Combination Chest CT Scan	-	-	0.134	0.054
Follow-up Mammogram/Ultrasound	-	-	8%	8.4%
MRI for Low Back Pain	-	-	34.3%	32.7%
Survey of Patients' Hospital Experiences				
Area Around Room 'Always' Quiet at Night[8]	-	-	-	58%
Doctors 'Always' Communicated Well[8]	-	-	-	80%
Home Recovery Information Given[8]	-	-	-	82%
Hospital Given 9 or 10 on 10 Point Scale[8]	-	-	-	67%
Meds 'Always' Explained Before Given[8]	-	-	-	60%
Nurses 'Always' Communicated Well[8]	-	-	-	76%
Pain 'Always' Well Controlled[8]	-	-	-	69%
Room and Bathroom 'Always' Clean[8]	-	-	-	71%
Timely Help 'Always' Received[8]	-	-	-	64%
Would Definitely Recommend Hospital[8]	-	-	-	69%

NOTE: Hospital profiles are in alphabetical order by state, then city, then hospital within the city; Rankings exclude hospitals with less than 25 cases except for patient surveys which excludes hospitals with less than 100 cases; (a) 100–299 cases; (1) The number of cases is too small to be sure how well a hospital is performing; (2) The hospital indicated that the data submitted for this measure were based on a sample of cases; (3) Data was collected during a shorter time period (fewer quarters) than the maximum possible time for this measure; (4) Suppressed for one or more quarters by CMS; (5) No data is available from the hospital for this measure; (6) Fewer than 100 patients completed the HCAHPS survey. Use these rates with caution, as the number of surveys may be too low to reliably assess hospital performance; (7) Survey results are based on less than 12 months of data; (8) Survey results are not available for this reporting period; (9) No or very few patients were eligible for the HCAHPS survey. The scores shown, if any, reflect a very small number of surveys; (10) A state average was not calculated because too few hospitals in the state submitted data; (11) There were discrepancies in the data collection process; Please refer to the User's Guide for a full explanation of data.

McAlester Regional Health Center

One Clark Bass Boulevard Phone: 918-426-1800
Mcalester, OK 74501 Fax: 918-421-8633
E-mail: nbrinlee@mrhcok.com
URL: www.mrhcok.com
Type: Acute Care Hospitals Emergency Services: Yes
Ownership: Voluntary Non-Profit - Other Beds: 197
Key Personnel:
CEO/President. . . . . Sean Beggs
Chief of Medical Staff . . . . Milton James
Operating Room. . . . . Lem Hodges, RN
Quality Assurance . . . . Kathy Rollins
Radiology. . . . . Bruce O'Brien, MD
Emergency Room . . . . Dennis Staggs

Measure	Cases	This Hosp.	State Avg.	U.S. Avg.
Heart Attack Care				
ACE Inhibitor or ARB for LVSD[1]	3	100%	95%	96%
Aspirin at Arrival[1]	22	82%	98%	99%
Aspirin at Discharge[1]	11	91%	98%	98%
Beta Blocker at Discharge[1]	13	92%	98%	98%
Fibrinolytic Medication Timing	0	-	42%	55%
PCI Within 90 Minutes of Arrival	0	-	88%	90%
Smoking Cessation Advice[1]	4	100%	100%	99%
Chest Pain/Possible Heart Attack Care				
Aspirin at Arrival[5]	0	-	94%	95%
Median Time to ECG (minutes)[5]	0	-	9	8
Median Time to Transfer (minutes)[5]	0	-	75	61
Fibrinolytic Medication Timing[5]	0	-	50%	54%
Heart Failure Care				
ACE Inhibitor or ARB for LVSD	49	86%	94%	94%
Discharge Instructions	82	78%	85%	88%
Evaluation of LVS Function	101	93%	94%	98%
Smoking Cessation Advice	25	96%	97%	98%
Pneumonia Care				
Appropriate Initial Antibiotic[2]	28	89%	91%	92%
Blood Culture Timing[2]	144	94%	96%	96%
Influenza Vaccine[2]	96	93%	89%	91%
Initial Antibiotic Timing[2]	150	98%	95%	95%
Pneumococcal Vaccine[2]	135	91%	91%	93%
Smoking Cessation Advice[2]	59	93%	95%	97%
Surgical Care Improvement Project				
Appropriate VTP Within 24 Hours[2]	131	89%	91%	92%
Appropriate Hair Removal[2]	397	99%	100%	99%
Appropriate Beta Blocker Usage[2]	56	86%	91%	93%
Controlled Postoperative Blood Glucose[2]	0	-	95%	93%
Prophylactic Antibiotic Timing[2]	284	96%	97%	97%
Prophylactic Antibiotic Timing (Outpatient)	70	96%	93%	92%
Prophylactic Antibiotic Selection[2]	284	98%	98%	97%
Prophylactic Antibiotic Select. (Outpatient)	69	94%	95%	94%
Prophylactic Antibiotic Stopped[2]	271	93%	94%	94%
Recommended VTP Ordered[2]	131	89%	94%	94%
Urinary Catheter Removal[2]	61	97%	87%	90%
Children's Asthma Care				
Received Systemic Corticosteroids	-	-	-	100%
Received Home Management Plan	-	-	-	71%
Received Reliever Medication	-	-	-	100%
Use of Medical Imaging				
Combination Abdominal CT Scan	431	0.571	0.372	0.191
Combination Chest CT Scan	307	0.023	0.134	0.054
Follow-up Mammogram/Ultrasound	512	20.3%	8%	8.4%
MRI for Low Back Pain	126	33.3%	34.3%	32.7%
Survey of Patients' Hospital Experiences				
Area Around Room 'Always' Quiet at Night	300+	57%	-	58%
Doctors 'Always' Communicated Well	300+	83%	-	80%
Home Recovery Information Given	300+	81%	-	82%
Hospital Given 9 or 10 on 10 Point Scale	300+	60%	-	67%
Meds 'Always' Explained Before Given	300+	63%	-	60%
Nurses 'Always' Communicated Well	300+	77%	-	76%
Pain 'Always' Well Controlled	300+	72%	-	69%
Room and Bathroom 'Always' Clean	300+	76%	-	71%
Timely Help 'Always' Received	300+	68%	-	64%
Would Definitely Recommend Hospital	300+	60%	-	69%

Integris Baptist Regional Health Center

200 Second Avenue Southwest Phone: 918-542-6611
Miami, OK 74355 Fax: 918-540-7605
URL: www.integris-health.com
Type: Acute Care Hospitals Emergency Services: Yes
Ownership: Voluntary Non-Profit - Other Beds: 124
Key Personnel:
CEO/President. . . . . Joel A Hart

Measure	Cases	This Hosp.	State Avg.	U.S. Avg.
Heart Attack Care				
ACE Inhibitor or ARB for LVSD[1]	1	100%	95%	96%
Aspirin at Arrival[1]	9	89%	98%	99%
Aspirin at Discharge[1]	5	100%	98%	98%
Beta Blocker at Discharge[1]	5	100%	98%	98%
Fibrinolytic Medication Timing	0	-	42%	55%
PCI Within 90 Minutes of Arrival	0	-	88%	90%
Smoking Cessation Advice[1]	1	100%	100%	99%
Chest Pain/Possible Heart Attack Care				
Aspirin at Arrival	121	98%	94%	95%
Median Time to ECG (minutes)	129	4	9	8
Median Time to Transfer (minutes)[3]	0	-	75	61
Fibrinolytic Medication Timing[1]	6	83%	50%	54%
Heart Failure Care				
ACE Inhibitor or ARB for LVSD[1]	18	94%	94%	94%
Discharge Instructions	70	94%	85%	88%
Evaluation of LVS Function	86	100%	94%	98%
Smoking Cessation Advice[1]	17	100%	97%	98%
Pneumonia Care				
Appropriate Initial Antibiotic	119	97%	91%	92%
Blood Culture Timing	149	97%	96%	96%
Influenza Vaccine	103	96%	89%	91%
Initial Antibiotic Timing	181	99%	95%	95%
Pneumococcal Vaccine	137	99%	91%	93%
Smoking Cessation Advice	66	98%	95%	97%
Surgical Care Improvement Project				
Appropriate VTP Within 24 Hours	77	99%	91%	92%
Appropriate Hair Removal	149	97%	100%	99%
Appropriate Beta Blocker Usage	53	91%	91%	93%
Controlled Postoperative Blood Glucose	0	-	95%	93%
Prophylactic Antibiotic Timing	117	97%	97%	97%
Prophylactic Antibiotic Timing (Outpatient)	70	89%	93%	92%
Prophylactic Antibiotic Selection	117	95%	98%	97%
Prophylactic Antibiotic Select. (Outpatient)	68	99%	95%	94%
Prophylactic Antibiotic Stopped	114	90%	94%	94%
Recommended VTP Ordered	77	100%	94%	94%
Urinary Catheter Removal	39	97%	87%	90%
Children's Asthma Care				
Received Systemic Corticosteroids	-	-	-	100%
Received Home Management Plan	-	-	-	71%
Received Reliever Medication	-	-	-	100%
Use of Medical Imaging				
Combination Abdominal CT Scan	192	0.109	0.372	0.191
Combination Chest CT Scan	162	0.012	0.134	0.054
Follow-up Mammogram/Ultrasound	518	6.2%	8%	8.4%
MRI for Low Back Pain	50	32.0%	34.3%	32.7%
Survey of Patients' Hospital Experiences				
Area Around Room 'Always' Quiet at Night	300+	58%	-	58%
Doctors 'Always' Communicated Well	300+	86%	-	80%
Home Recovery Information Given	300+	82%	-	82%
Hospital Given 9 or 10 on 10 Point Scale	300+	66%	-	67%
Meds 'Always' Explained Before Given	300+	62%	-	60%
Nurses 'Always' Communicated Well	300+	78%	-	76%
Pain 'Always' Well Controlled	300+	73%	-	69%
Room and Bathroom 'Always' Clean	300+	67%	-	71%
Timely Help 'Always' Received	300+	68%	-	64%
Would Definitely Recommend Hospital	300+	61%	-	69%

Midwest Regional Medical Center

2825 Parklawn Drive Phone: 405-610-4411
Midwest City, OK 73110 Fax: 405-610-1483
URL: www.midwestregional.com
Type: Acute Care Hospitals Emergency Services: Yes
Ownership: Proprietary Beds: 255
Key Personnel:
CEO/President. . . . . Page Vaughan
Chief of Medical Staff . . . . M Terry Anderson
Radiology. . . . . Chris Degner
Emergency Room . . . . Joel III, MD

Measure	Cases	This Hosp.	State Avg.	U.S. Avg.
Heart Attack Care				
ACE Inhibitor or ARB for LVSD	53	98%	95%	96%
Aspirin at Arrival	263	100%	98%	99%
Aspirin at Discharge	263	100%	98%	98%
Beta Blocker at Discharge	242	99%	98%	98%
Fibrinolytic Medication Timing	0	-	42%	55%
PCI Within 90 Minutes of Arrival	38	92%	88%	90%
Smoking Cessation Advice	99	100%	100%	99%
Chest Pain/Possible Heart Attack Care				
Aspirin at Arrival[1,3]	6	100%	94%	95%
Median Time to ECG (minutes)[1,3]	6	24	9	8
Median Time to Transfer (minutes)[5]	0	-	75	61
Fibrinolytic Medication Timing[5]	0	-	50%	54%
Heart Failure Care				
ACE Inhibitor or ARB for LVSD	123	100%	94%	94%
Discharge Instructions	304	99%	85%	88%
Evaluation of LVS Function	375	100%	94%	98%
Smoking Cessation Advice	62	100%	97%	98%
Pneumonia Care				
Appropriate Initial Antibiotic	210	92%	91%	92%
Blood Culture Timing	263	96%	96%	96%
Influenza Vaccine	167	95%	89%	91%
Initial Antibiotic Timing	332	97%	95%	95%
Pneumococcal Vaccine	239	98%	91%	93%
Smoking Cessation Advice	143	100%	95%	97%
Surgical Care Improvement Project				
Appropriate VTP Within 24 Hours	245	96%	91%	92%
Appropriate Hair Removal	712	100%	100%	99%
Appropriate Beta Blocker Usage	185	100%	91%	93%
Controlled Postoperative Blood Glucose	64	88%	95%	93%
Prophylactic Antibiotic Timing	435	98%	97%	97%
Prophylactic Antibiotic Timing (Outpatient)	156	94%	93%	92%
Prophylactic Antibiotic Selection	438	96%	98%	97%
Prophylactic Antibiotic Select. (Outpatient)	151	93%	95%	94%
Prophylactic Antibiotic Stopped	418	83%	94%	94%
Recommended VTP Ordered	247	96%	94%	94%
Urinary Catheter Removal	97	99%	87%	90%
Children's Asthma Care				
Received Systemic Corticosteroids	26	100%	-	100%
Received Home Management Plan	25	100%	-	71%
Received Reliever Medication	26	100%	-	100%
Use of Medical Imaging				
Combination Abdominal CT Scan	629	0.390	0.372	0.191
Combination Chest CT Scan	439	0.237	0.134	0.054
Follow-up Mammogram/Ultrasound	1,861	4.5%	8%	8.4%
MRI for Low Back Pain	259	36.7%	34.3%	32.7%
Survey of Patients' Hospital Experiences				
Area Around Room 'Always' Quiet at Night	300+	48%	-	58%
Doctors 'Always' Communicated Well	300+	77%	-	80%
Home Recovery Information Given	300+	78%	-	82%
Hospital Given 9 or 10 on 10 Point Scale	300+	50%	-	67%
Meds 'Always' Explained Before Given	300+	52%	-	60%
Nurses 'Always' Communicated Well	300+	65%	-	76%
Pain 'Always' Well Controlled	300+	62%	-	69%
Room and Bathroom 'Always' Clean	300+	51%	-	71%
Timely Help 'Always' Received	300+	49%	-	64%
Would Definitely Recommend Hospital	300+	50%	-	69%

NOTE: Hospital profiles are in alphabetical order by state, then city, then hospital within the city; Rankings exclude hospitals with less than 25 cases except for patient surveys which excludes hospitals with less than 100 cases; (a) 100–299 cases; (1) The number of cases is too small to be sure how well a hospital is performing; (2) The hospital indicated that the data submitted for this measure were based on a sample of cases; (3) Data was collected during a shorter time period (fewer quarters) than the maximum possible time for this measure; (4) Suppressed for one or more quarters by CMS; (5) No data is available from the hospital for this measure; (6) Fewer than 100 patients completed the HCAHPS survey. Use these rates with caution, as the number of surveys may be too low to reliably assess hospital performance; (7) Survey results are based on less than 12 months of data; (8) Survey results are not available for this reporting period; (9) No or very few patients were eligible for the HCAHPS survey. The scores shown, if any, reflect a very small number of surveys; (10) A state average was not calculated because too few hospitals in the state submitted data; (11) There were discrepancies in the data collection process; Please refer to the User's Guide for a full explanation of data.

Muskogee Community Hospital

2900 North Main Street
Muskogee, OK 74402
URL: www.mch-ok.com
Type: Acute Care Hospitals
Ownership: Proprietary
Phone: 918-687-7777
Emergency Services: Yes

Key Personnel:
President . . . . Mark Roberts

Measure	Cases	This Hosp.	State Avg.	U.S. Avg.
Heart Attack Care				
ACE Inhibitor or ARB for LVSD[1,2,3]	1	100%	95%	96%
Aspirin at Arrival[1,2,3]	3	100%	98%	99%
Aspirin at Discharge[1,2,3]	2	100%	98%	98%
Beta Blocker at Discharge[1,2,3]	2	100%	98%	98%
Fibrinolytic Medication Timing[2,3]	0	-	42%	55%
PCI Within 90 Minutes of Arrival[2,3]	0	-	88%	90%
Smoking Cessation Advice[2,3]	0	-	100%	99%
Chest Pain/Possible Heart Attack Care				
Aspirin at Arrival	-	-	94%	95%
Median Time to ECG (minutes)	-	-	9	8
Median Time to Transfer (minutes)	-	-	75	61
Fibrinolytic Medication Timing	-	-	50%	54%
Heart Failure Care				
ACE Inhibitor or ARB for LVSD[1,2,3]	7	86%	94%	94%
Discharge Instructions[1,2,3]	10	30%	85%	88%
Evaluation of LVS Function[1,2,3]	13	62%	94%	98%
Smoking Cessation Advice[1,2,3]	2	50%	97%	98%
Pneumonia Care				
Appropriate Initial Antibiotic[2,3]	41	76%	91%	92%
Blood Culture Timing[1,2,3]	16	94%	96%	96%
Influenza Vaccine[2]	34	38%	89%	91%
Initial Antibiotic Timing[2,3]	33	76%	95%	95%
Pneumococcal Vaccine[2,3]	35	43%	91%	93%
Smoking Cessation Advice[1,2,3]	19	47%	95%	97%
Surgical Care Improvement Project				
Appropriate VTP Within 24 Hours[2,3]	57	51%	91%	92%
Appropriate Hair Removal[2,3]	111	96%	100%	99%
Appropriate Beta Blocker Usage[2,3]	30	63%	91%	93%
Controlled Postoperative Blood Glucose[2,3]	0	-	95%	93%
Prophylactic Antibiotic Timing[2,3]	64	94%	97%	97%
Prophylactic Antibiotic Timing (Outpatient)	-	-	93%	92%
Prophylactic Antibiotic Selection[2,3]	67	70%	98%	97%
Prophylactic Antibiotic Select. (Outpatient)	-	-	95%	94%
Prophylactic Antibiotic Stopped[2,3]	64	100%	94%	94%
Recommended VTP Ordered[2,3]	57	51%	94%	94%
Urinary Catheter Removal[1,2]	10	80%	87%	90%
Children's Asthma Care				
Received Systemic Corticosteroids	-	-	-	100%
Received Home Management Plan	-	-	-	71%
Received Reliever Medication	-	-	-	100%
Use of Medical Imaging				
Combination Abdominal CT Scan	-	-	0.372	0.191
Combination Chest CT Scan	-	-	0.134	0.054
Follow-up Mammogram/Ultrasound	-	-	8%	8.4%
MRI for Low Back Pain	-	-	34.3%	32.7%
Survey of Patients' Hospital Experiences				
Area Around Room 'Always' Quiet at Night[8]	-	-	-	58%
Doctors 'Always' Communicated Well[8]	-	-	-	80%
Home Recovery Information Given[8]	-	-	-	82%
Hospital Given 9 or 10 on 10 Point Scale[8]	-	-	-	67%
Meds 'Always' Explained Before Given[8]	-	-	-	60%
Nurses 'Always' Communicated Well[8]	-	-	-	76%
Pain 'Always' Well Controlled[8]	-	-	-	69%
Room and Bathroom 'Always' Clean[8]	-	-	-	71%
Timely Help 'Always' Received[8]	-	-	-	64%
Would Definitely Recommend Hospital[8]	-	-	-	69%

Muskogee Regional Medical Center

300 Rockefeller Drive
Muskogee, OK 74401
URL: www.muskogeehealth.com
Type: Acute Care Hospitals
Ownership: Govt - Hospital Dist/Auth
Phone: 918-682-5501
Fax: 918-684-2552
Emergency Services: Yes
Beds: 366

Key Personnel:
CEO/President . . . . Kevin Fowler
Cardiac Laboratory . . . . Joy Abbey
Chief of Medical Staff . . . . Gary Lambert, DO
Infection Control . . . . Becky Elliott
Operating Room . . . . Susan Julian
Quality Assurance . . . . Ched Wetz
Radiology . . . . Linda Stubbs

Measure	Cases	This Hosp.	State Avg.	U.S. Avg.
Heart Attack Care				
ACE Inhibitor or ARB for LVSD[1]	17	94%	95%	96%
Aspirin at Arrival	97	96%	98%	99%
Aspirin at Discharge	74	93%	98%	98%
Beta Blocker at Discharge	74	97%	98%	98%
Fibrinolytic Medication Timing[1]	1	0%	42%	55%
PCI Within 90 Minutes of Arrival	0	-	88%	90%
Smoking Cessation Advice	29	100%	100%	99%
Chest Pain/Possible Heart Attack Care				
Aspirin at Arrival[1]	16	94%	94%	95%
Median Time to ECG (minutes)[1]	17	8	9	8
Median Time to Transfer (minutes)[1,3]	1	35	75	61
Fibrinolytic Medication Timing[1]	3	67%	50%	54%
Heart Failure Care				
ACE Inhibitor or ARB for LVSD	82	99%	94%	94%
Discharge Instructions	203	72%	85%	88%
Evaluation of LVS Function	256	96%	94%	98%
Smoking Cessation Advice	62	100%	97%	98%
Pneumonia Care				
Appropriate Initial Antibiotic	150	85%	91%	92%
Blood Culture Timing	281	96%	96%	96%
Influenza Vaccine	234	90%	89%	91%
Initial Antibiotic Timing	330	90%	95%	95%
Pneumococcal Vaccine	293	92%	91%	93%
Smoking Cessation Advice	167	99%	95%	97%
Surgical Care Improvement Project				
Appropriate VTP Within 24 Hours	161	87%	91%	92%
Appropriate Hair Removal	397	99%	100%	99%
Appropriate Beta Blocker Usage	117	91%	91%	93%
Controlled Postoperative Blood Glucose[1]	1	0%	95%	93%
Prophylactic Antibiotic Timing	240	97%	97%	97%
Prophylactic Antibiotic Timing (Outpatient)	113	80%	93%	92%
Prophylactic Antibiotic Selection	240	97%	98%	97%
Prophylactic Antibiotic Select. (Outpatient)	98	97%	95%	94%
Prophylactic Antibiotic Stopped	233	92%	94%	94%
Recommended VTP Ordered	161	91%	94%	94%
Urinary Catheter Removal	92	67%	87%	90%
Children's Asthma Care				
Received Systemic Corticosteroids	-	-	-	100%
Received Home Management Plan	-	-	-	71%
Received Reliever Medication	-	-	-	100%
Use of Medical Imaging				
Combination Abdominal CT Scan	821	0.348	0.372	0.191
Combination Chest CT Scan	441	0.256	0.134	0.054
Follow-up Mammogram/Ultrasound	1,656	4.6%	8%	8.4%
MRI for Low Back Pain	291	29.2%	34.3%	32.7%
Survey of Patients' Hospital Experiences				
Area Around Room 'Always' Quiet at Night	300+	48%	-	58%
Doctors 'Always' Communicated Well	300+	78%	-	80%
Home Recovery Information Given	300+	81%	-	82%
Hospital Given 9 or 10 on 10 Point Scale	300+	47%	-	67%
Meds 'Always' Explained Before Given	300+	47%	-	60%
Nurses 'Always' Communicated Well	300+	64%	-	76%
Pain 'Always' Well Controlled	300+	59%	-	69%
Room and Bathroom 'Always' Clean	300+	57%	-	71%
Timely Help 'Always' Received	300+	48%	-	64%
Would Definitely Recommend Hospital	300+	48%	-	69%

Muskogee VA Medical Center

1011 Honor Heights Drive
Muskogee, OK 74401
URL: www.visn16.med.va.gov/muskogee.asp
Type: Acute Care-Veterans Administration
Ownership: Government - Federal
Phone: 918-577-3000
Fax: 918-577-3648
Emergency Services: No
Beds: 187

Key Personnel:
Chief of Medical Staff . . . . Karen H Gribbin MD, MD
Operating Room . . . . Susan McKinney
Quality Assurance . . . . Linda Fredrick, RN
Patient Relations . . . . Margie Carlton

Measure	Cases	This Hosp.	State Avg.	U.S. Avg.
Heart Attack Care				
ACE Inhibitor or ARB for LVSD[5]	0	-	95%	96%
Aspirin at Arrival[5]	0	-	98%	99%
Aspirin at Discharge[5]	0	-	98%	98%
Beta Blocker at Discharge[5]	0	-	98%	98%
Fibrinolytic Medication Timing[5]	0	-	42%	55%
PCI Within 90 Minutes of Arrival[5]	0	-	88%	90%
Smoking Cessation Advice[5]	0	-	100%	99%
Chest Pain/Possible Heart Attack Care				
Aspirin at Arrival	-	-	94%	95%
Median Time to ECG (minutes)	-	-	9	8
Median Time to Transfer (minutes)	-	-	75	61
Fibrinolytic Medication Timing	-	-	50%	54%
Heart Failure Care				
ACE Inhibitor or ARB for LVSD	111	98%	94%	94%
Discharge Instructions	156	99%	85%	88%
Evaluation of LVS Function	178	100%	94%	98%
Smoking Cessation Advice	59	100%	97%	98%
Pneumonia Care				
Appropriate Initial Antibiotic	93	87%	91%	92%
Blood Culture Timing	177	99%	96%	96%
Influenza Vaccine	131	94%	89%	91%
Initial Antibiotic Timing	152	93%	95%	95%
Pneumococcal Vaccine	142	98%	91%	93%
Smoking Cessation Advice	67	100%	95%	97%
Surgical Care Improvement Project				
Appropriate VTP Within 24 Hours[2]	76	97%	91%	92%
Appropriate Hair Removal[2]	87	100%	100%	99%
Appropriate Beta Blocker Usage[2]	39	92%	91%	93%
Controlled Postoperative Blood Glucose[2,5]	0	-	95%	93%
Prophylactic Antibiotic Timing	35	97%	97%	97%
Prophylactic Antibiotic Timing (Outpatient)	-	-	93%	92%
Prophylactic Antibiotic Selection	36	100%	98%	97%
Prophylactic Antibiotic Select. (Outpatient)	-	-	95%	94%
Prophylactic Antibiotic Stopped	33	97%	94%	94%
Recommended VTP Ordered[2]	76	97%	94%	94%
Urinary Catheter Removal[2]	39	87%	87%	90%
Children's Asthma Care				
Received Systemic Corticosteroids	-	-	-	100%
Received Home Management Plan	-	-	-	71%
Received Reliever Medication	-	-	-	100%
Use of Medical Imaging				
Combination Abdominal CT Scan	-	-	0.372	0.191
Combination Chest CT Scan	-	-	0.134	0.054
Follow-up Mammogram/Ultrasound	-	-	8%	8.4%
MRI for Low Back Pain	-	-	34.3%	32.7%
Survey of Patients' Hospital Experiences				
Area Around Room 'Always' Quiet at Night	-	-	-	58%
Doctors 'Always' Communicated Well	-	-	-	80%
Home Recovery Information Given	-	-	-	82%
Hospital Given 9 or 10 on 10 Point Scale	-	-	-	67%
Meds 'Always' Explained Before Given	-	-	-	60%
Nurses 'Always' Communicated Well	-	-	-	76%
Pain 'Always' Well Controlled	-	-	-	69%
Room and Bathroom 'Always' Clean	-	-	-	71%
Timely Help 'Always' Received	-	-	-	64%
Would Definitely Recommend Hospital	-	-	-	69%

NOTE: Hospital profiles are in alphabetical order by state, then city, then hospital within the city; Rankings exclude hospitals with less than 25 cases except for patient surveys which excludes hospitals with less than 100 cases; (a) 100–299 cases; (1) The number of cases is too small to be sure how well a hospital is performing; (2) The hospital indicated that the data submitted for this measure were based on a sample of cases; (3) Data was collected during a shorter time period (fewer quarters) than the maximum possible time for this measure; (4) Suppressed for one or more quarters by CMS; (5) No data is available from the hospital for this measure; (6) Fewer than 100 patients completed the HCAHPS survey. Use these rates with caution, as the number of surveys may be too low to reliably assess hospital performance; (7) Survey results are based on less than 12 months of data; (8) Survey results are not available for this reporting period; (9) No or very few patients were eligible for the HCAHPS survey. The scores shown, if any, reflect a very small number of surveys; (10) A state average was not calculated because too few hospitals in the state submitted data; (11) There were discrepancies in the data collection process; Please refer to the User's Guide for a full explanation of data.

Norman Regional Health System

901 North Porter | Phone: 405-321-1700
Norman, OK 73070 | Fax: 405-307-1548
URL: www.normanregional.com
Type: Acute Care Hospitals | Emergency Services: Yes
Ownership: Government - Local | Beds: 382

Key Personnel:
CEO/President. . . . . David D Whitaker, FACHE

Measure	Cases	This Hosp.	State Avg.	U.S. Avg.
Heart Attack Care				
ACE Inhibitor or ARB for LVSD	36	97%	95%	96%
Aspirin at Arrival	137	100%	98%	99%
Aspirin at Discharge	224	98%	98%	98%
Beta Blocker at Discharge	213	98%	98%	98%
Fibrinolytic Medication Timing[1]	1	100%	42%	55%
PCI Within 90 Minutes of Arrival	33	91%	88%	90%
Smoking Cessation Advice	92	100%	100%	99%
Chest Pain/Possible Heart Attack Care				
Aspirin at Arrival[1,3]	7	86%	94%	95%
Median Time to ECG (minutes)[1,3]	7	9	9	8
Median Time to Transfer (minutes)[5]	0	-	75	61
Fibrinolytic Medication Timing[3]	0	-	50%	54%
Heart Failure Care				
ACE Inhibitor or ARB for LVSD	128	97%	94%	94%
Discharge Instructions	276	91%	85%	88%
Evaluation of LVS Function	344	99%	94%	98%
Smoking Cessation Advice	74	100%	97%	98%
Pneumonia Care				
Appropriate Initial Antibiotic[2]	94	97%	91%	92%
Blood Culture Timing[2]	181	100%	96%	96%
Influenza Vaccine[2]	97	96%	89%	91%
Initial Antibiotic Timing[2]	188	96%	95%	95%
Pneumococcal Vaccine[2]	178	98%	91%	93%
Smoking Cessation Advice[2]	89	99%	95%	97%
Surgical Care Improvement Project				
Appropriate VTP Within 24 Hours[2]	240	95%	91%	92%
Appropriate Hair Removal[2]	776	100%	100%	99%
Appropriate Beta Blocker Usage[2]	190	94%	91%	93%
Controlled Postoperative Blood Glucose[2]	58	93%	95%	93%
Prophylactic Antibiotic Timing[2]	491	97%	97%	97%
Prophylactic Antibiotic Timing (Outpatient)	467	94%	93%	92%
Prophylactic Antibiotic Selection[2]	498	99%	98%	97%
Prophylactic Antibiotic Select. (Outpatient)	459	97%	95%	94%
Prophylactic Antibiotic Stopped[2]	457	94%	94%	94%
Recommended VTP Ordered[2]	241	99%	94%	94%
Urinary Catheter Removal[2]	88	90%	87%	90%
Children's Asthma Care				
Received Systemic Corticosteroids	-	-	-	100%
Received Home Management Plan	-	-	-	71%
Received Reliever Medication	-	-	-	100%
Use of Medical Imaging				
Combination Abdominal CT Scan	1,216	0.109	0.372	0.191
Combination Chest CT Scan	1,205	0.048	0.134	0.054
Follow-up Mammogram/Ultrasound	2,695	6.7%	8%	8.4%
MRI for Low Back Pain	333	33.6%	34.3%	32.7%
Survey of Patients' Hospital Experiences				
Area Around Room 'Always' Quiet at Night	300+	65%	-	58%
Doctors 'Always' Communicated Well	300+	81%	-	80%
Home Recovery Information Given	300+	82%	-	82%
Hospital Given 9 or 10 on 10 Point Scale	300+	71%	-	67%
Meds 'Always' Explained Before Given	300+	58%	-	60%
Nurses 'Always' Communicated Well	300+	75%	-	76%
Pain 'Always' Well Controlled	300+	71%	-	69%
Room and Bathroom 'Always' Clean	300+	69%	-	71%
Timely Help 'Always' Received	300+	63%	-	64%
Would Definitely Recommend Hospital	300+	72%	-	69%

Okeene Municipal Hospital

207 East F Street | Phone: 580-822-4417
Okeene, OK 73763 | Fax: 580-822-3018
E-mail: sdunham@okeenehospital.com
URL: www.okeenehospital.com
Type: Critical Access Hospitals | Emergency Services: Yes
Ownership: Govt - Hospital Dist/Auth | Beds: 17

Key Personnel:
CEO/President. . . . . Sandra Lamie
Cardiac Laboratory. . . . . Tammy Fisher
Chief of Medical Staff . . . . Ken Parrott, MD
Infection Control. . . . . Pat Lorenz, RN
Operating Room. . . . . Pat Lorenz
Quality Assurance . . . . Pat Lorenz
Anesthesiology. . . . . Ken Parrott, MD
Emergency Room . . . . A Atendido, MD

Measure	Cases	This Hosp.	State Avg.	U.S. Avg.
Heart Attack Care				
ACE Inhibitor or ARB for LVSD[3]	0	-	95%	96%
Aspirin at Arrival[1,3]	1	100%	98%	99%
Aspirin at Discharge[1,3]	1	0%	98%	98%
Beta Blocker at Discharge[1,3]	1	100%	98%	98%
Fibrinolytic Medication Timing[3]	0	-	42%	55%
PCI Within 90 Minutes of Arrival[3]	0	-	88%	90%
Smoking Cessation Advice[3]	0	-	100%	99%
Chest Pain/Possible Heart Attack Care				
Aspirin at Arrival	-	-	94%	95%
Median Time to ECG (minutes)	-	-	9	8
Median Time to Transfer (minutes)	-	-	75	61
Fibrinolytic Medication Timing	-	-	50%	54%
Heart Failure Care				
ACE Inhibitor or ARB for LVSD[1,3]	2	100%	94%	94%
Discharge Instructions[1,3]	5	100%	85%	88%
Evaluation of LVS Function[1,3]	6	67%	94%	98%
Smoking Cessation Advice[3]	0	-	97%	98%
Pneumonia Care				
Appropriate Initial Antibiotic[1]	13	54%	91%	92%
Blood Culture Timing[1]	10	60%	96%	96%
Influenza Vaccine[1]	13	92%	89%	91%
Initial Antibiotic Timing[1]	22	77%	95%	95%
Pneumococcal Vaccine[1]	16	94%	91%	93%
Smoking Cessation Advice[1]	6	17%	95%	97%
Surgical Care Improvement Project				
Appropriate VTP Within 24 Hours[3]	0	-	91%	92%
Appropriate Hair Removal[1,3]	1	100%	100%	99%
Appropriate Beta Blocker Usage[5]	0	-	91%	93%
Controlled Postoperative Blood Glucose[3]	0	-	95%	93%
Prophylactic Antibiotic Timing[1,3]	1	100%	97%	97%
Prophylactic Antibiotic Timing (Outpatient)	-	-	93%	92%
Prophylactic Antibiotic Selection[1,3]	1	0%	98%	97%
Prophylactic Antibiotic Select. (Outpatient)	-	-	95%	94%
Prophylactic Antibiotic Stopped[1,3]	1	0%	94%	94%
Recommended VTP Ordered[3]	0	-	94%	94%
Urinary Catheter Removal[5]	0	-	87%	90%
Children's Asthma Care				
Received Systemic Corticosteroids	-	-	-	100%
Received Home Management Plan	-	-	-	71%
Received Reliever Medication	-	-	-	100%
Use of Medical Imaging				
Combination Abdominal CT Scan	-	-	0.372	0.191
Combination Chest CT Scan	-	-	0.134	0.054
Follow-up Mammogram/Ultrasound	-	-	8%	8.4%
MRI for Low Back Pain	-	-	34.3%	32.7%
Survey of Patients' Hospital Experiences				
Area Around Room 'Always' Quiet at Night[6]	<100	77%	-	58%
Doctors 'Always' Communicated Well[6]	<100	87%	-	80%
Home Recovery Information Given[6]	<100	93%	-	82%
Hospital Given 9 or 10 on 10 Point Scale[6]	<100	87%	-	67%
Meds 'Always' Explained Before Given[6]	<100	73%	-	60%
Nurses 'Always' Communicated Well[6]	<100	89%	-	76%
Pain 'Always' Well Controlled[6]	<100	79%	-	69%
Room and Bathroom 'Always' Clean[6]	<100	87%	-	71%
Timely Help 'Always' Received[6]	<100	89%	-	64%
Would Definitely Recommend Hospital	<100	85%	-	69%

Creek Nation Community Hospital

309 North 14th | Phone: 918-623-1424
Okemah, OK 74859 | Fax: 918-623-9016
URL: www.muscogeenation-nsn.gov
Type: Critical Access Hospitals | Emergency Services: Yes
Ownership: Voluntary Non-Profit - Other | Beds: 39

Key Personnel:
CEO/President. . . . . Judy Aaron
Chief of Medical Staff . . . . Lawrence Vark, DO
Infection Control. . . . . Betty Brown
Operating Room. . . . . Cindy Franks
Quality Assurance . . . . Rick Mathews
Emergency Room . . . . Mark Sullivan, MD

Measure	Cases	This Hosp.	State Avg.	U.S. Avg.
Heart Attack Care				
ACE Inhibitor or ARB for LVSD[3]	0	-	95%	96%
Aspirin at Arrival[3]	0	-	98%	99%
Aspirin at Discharge[3]	0	-	98%	98%
Beta Blocker at Discharge[3]	0	-	98%	98%
Fibrinolytic Medication Timing[3]	0	-	42%	55%
PCI Within 90 Minutes of Arrival[3]	0	-	88%	90%
Smoking Cessation Advice[3]	0	-	100%	99%
Chest Pain/Possible Heart Attack Care				
Aspirin at Arrival	-	-	94%	95%
Median Time to ECG (minutes)	-	-	9	8
Median Time to Transfer (minutes)	-	-	75	61
Fibrinolytic Medication Timing	-	-	50%	54%
Heart Failure Care				
ACE Inhibitor or ARB for LVSD[1]	3	33%	94%	94%
Discharge Instructions[1]	15	53%	85%	88%
Evaluation of LVS Function[1]	16	88%	94%	98%
Smoking Cessation Advice[1]	4	50%	97%	98%
Pneumonia Care				
Appropriate Initial Antibiotic	34	91%	91%	92%
Blood Culture Timing[1]	21	81%	96%	96%
Influenza Vaccine[1]	19	68%	89%	91%
Initial Antibiotic Timing	33	100%	95%	95%
Pneumococcal Vaccine[1]	20	100%	91%	93%
Smoking Cessation Advice[1]	13	85%	95%	97%
Surgical Care Improvement Project				
Appropriate VTP Within 24 Hours[5]	0	-	91%	92%
Appropriate Hair Removal[5]	0	-	100%	99%
Appropriate Beta Blocker Usage[5]	0	-	91%	93%
Controlled Postoperative Blood Glucose[5]	0	-	95%	93%
Prophylactic Antibiotic Timing[5]	0	-	97%	97%
Prophylactic Antibiotic Timing (Outpatient)	-	-	93%	92%
Prophylactic Antibiotic Selection[5]	0	-	98%	97%
Prophylactic Antibiotic Select. (Outpatient)	-	-	95%	94%
Prophylactic Antibiotic Stopped[5]	0	-	94%	94%
Recommended VTP Ordered[5]	0	-	94%	94%
Urinary Catheter Removal[5]	0	-	87%	90%
Children's Asthma Care				
Received Systemic Corticosteroids	-	-	-	100%
Received Home Management Plan	-	-	-	71%
Received Reliever Medication	-	-	-	100%
Use of Medical Imaging				
Combination Abdominal CT Scan	-	-	0.372	0.191
Combination Chest CT Scan	-	-	0.134	0.054
Follow-up Mammogram/Ultrasound	-	-	8%	8.4%
MRI for Low Back Pain	-	-	34.3%	32.7%
Survey of Patients' Hospital Experiences				
Area Around Room 'Always' Quiet at Night[8]	-	-	-	58%
Doctors 'Always' Communicated Well[8]	-	-	-	80%
Home Recovery Information Given[8]	-	-	-	82%
Hospital Given 9 or 10 on 10 Point Scale[8]	-	-	-	67%
Meds 'Always' Explained Before Given[8]	-	-	-	60%
Nurses 'Always' Communicated Well[8]	-	-	-	76%
Pain 'Always' Well Controlled[8]	-	-	-	69%
Room and Bathroom 'Always' Clean[8]	-	-	-	71%
Timely Help 'Always' Received[8]	-	-	-	64%
Would Definitely Recommend Hospital[8]	-	-	-	69%

NOTE: Hospital profiles are in alphabetical order by state, then city, then hospital within the city; Rankings exclude hospitals with less than 25 cases except for patient surveys which excludes hospitals with less than 100 cases; (a) 100–299 cases; (1) The number of cases is too small to be sure how well a hospital is performing; (2) The hospital indicated that the data submitted for this measure were based on a sample of cases; (3) Data was collected during a shorter time period (fewer quarters) than the maximum possible time for this measure; (4) Suppressed for one or more quarters by CMS; (5) No data is available from the hospital for this measure; (6) Fewer than 100 patients completed the HCAHPS survey. Use these rates with caution, as the number of surveys may be too low to reliably assess hospital performance; (7) Survey results are based on less than 12 months of data; (8) Survey results are not available for this reporting period; (9) No or very few patients were eligible for the HCAHPS survey. The scores shown, if any, reflect a very small number of surveys; (10) A state average was not calculated because too few hospitals in the state submitted data; (11) There were discrepancies in the data collection process; Please refer to the User's Guide for a full explanation of data.

Community Hospital

3100 Southwest 89th Street
Oklahoma City, OK 73159
Type: Acute Care Hospitals
Ownership: Proprietary
Phone: 405-602-8100
Emergency Services: Yes

Measure	Cases	This Hosp.	State Avg.	U.S. Avg.
Heart Attack Care				
ACE Inhibitor or ARB for LVSD[5]	0	-	95%	96%
Aspirin at Arrival[5]	0	-	98%	99%
Aspirin at Discharge[5]	0	-	98%	98%
Beta Blocker at Discharge[5]	0	-	98%	98%
Fibrinolytic Medication Timing[5]	0	-	42%	55%
PCI Within 90 Minutes of Arrival[5]	0	-	88%	90%
Smoking Cessation Advice[5]	0	-	100%	99%
Chest Pain/Possible Heart Attack Care				
Aspirin at Arrival[1,3]	9	100%	94%	95%
Median Time to ECG (minutes)[1,3]	11	11	9	8
Median Time to Transfer (minutes)[1,3]	1	54	75	61
Fibrinolytic Medication Timing[3]	0	-	50%	54%
Heart Failure Care				
ACE Inhibitor or ARB for LVSD[5]	0	-	94%	94%
Discharge Instructions[5]	0	-	85%	88%
Evaluation of LVS Function[5]	0	-	94%	98%
Smoking Cessation Advice[5]	0	-	97%	98%
Pneumonia Care				
Appropriate Initial Antibiotic[1,3]	2	100%	91%	92%
Blood Culture Timing[1,3]	3	100%	96%	96%
Influenza Vaccine[3]	0	-	89%	91%
Initial Antibiotic Timing[1,3]	2	100%	95%	95%
Pneumococcal Vaccine[1,3]	1	100%	91%	93%
Smoking Cessation Advice[3]	0	-	95%	97%
Surgical Care Improvement Project				
Appropriate VTP Within 24 Hours[1,2]	21	100%	91%	92%
Appropriate Hair Removal[2]	226	100%	100%	99%
Appropriate Beta Blocker Usage[2]	49	100%	91%	93%
Controlled Postoperative Blood Glucose[2]	0	-	95%	93%
Prophylactic Antibiotic Timing[2]	189	99%	97%	97%
Prophylactic Antibiotic Timing (Outpatient)	92	98%	93%	92%
Prophylactic Antibiotic Selection[2]	188	98%	98%	97%
Prophylactic Antibiotic Select. (Outpatient)	92	100%	95%	94%
Prophylactic Antibiotic Stopped[2]	187	95%	94%	94%
Recommended VTP Ordered[1,2]	21	100%	94%	94%
Urinary Catheter Removal[2]	72	100%	87%	90%
Children's Asthma Care				
Received Systemic Corticosteroids	-	-	-	100%
Received Home Management Plan	-	-	-	71%
Received Reliever Medication	-	-	-	100%
Use of Medical Imaging				
Combination Abdominal CT Scan	67	0.448	0.372	0.191
Combination Chest CT Scan	52	0.038	0.134	0.054
Follow-up Mammogram/Ultrasound[5]	0	-	8%	8.4%
MRI for Low Back Pain	61	32.8%	34.3%	32.7%
Survey of Patients' Hospital Experiences				
Area Around Room 'Always' Quiet at Night	300+	71%	-	58%
Doctors 'Always' Communicated Well	300+	79%	-	80%
Home Recovery Information Given	300+	86%	-	82%
Hospital Given 9 or 10 on 10 Point Scale	300+	77%	-	67%
Meds 'Always' Explained Before Given	300+	65%	-	60%
Nurses 'Always' Communicated Well	300+	80%	-	76%
Pain 'Always' Well Controlled	300+	69%	-	69%
Room and Bathroom 'Always' Clean	300+	82%	-	71%
Timely Help 'Always' Received	300+	72%	-	64%
Would Definitely Recommend Hospital	300+	83%	-	69%

Deaconess Hospital

5501 North Portland Avenue
Oklahoma City, OK 73112
URL: www.deaconessokc.com
Type: Acute Care Hospitals
Ownership: Proprietary
Phone: 405-604-6109
Fax: 405-604-4297
Emergency Services: No
Beds: 313

Key Personnel:
CEO/President. . . . . Paul Dougherty
Chief of Medical Staff. . . . . Ken Whittington, MD
Infection Control. . . . . Carol Shenold, ICP
Quality Assurance . . . . Mary Quisenberg
Radiology. . . . . Kerri Kirchoff, MD
Anesthesiology. . . . . Robin Bayless, MD
Emergency Room . . . . Judi Merning, RN
Intensive Care Unit. . . . . Michelle Engress, RN

Measure	Cases	This Hosp.	State Avg.	U.S. Avg.
Heart Attack Care				
ACE Inhibitor or ARB for LVSD[1]	15	100%	95%	96%
Aspirin at Arrival	82	99%	98%	99%
Aspirin at Discharge	106	100%	98%	98%
Beta Blocker at Discharge	100	99%	98%	98%
Fibrinolytic Medication Timing	0	-	42%	55%
PCI Within 90 Minutes of Arrival[1]	15	87%	88%	90%
Smoking Cessation Advice	46	100%	100%	99%
Chest Pain/Possible Heart Attack Care				
Aspirin at Arrival[1]	7	71%	94%	95%
Median Time to ECG (minutes)[1]	7	9	9	8
Median Time to Transfer (minutes)[5]	0	-	75	61
Fibrinolytic Medication Timing[5]	0	-	50%	54%
Heart Failure Care				
ACE Inhibitor or ARB for LVSD	39	97%	94%	94%
Discharge Instructions	103	71%	85%	88%
Evaluation of LVS Function	135	100%	94%	98%
Smoking Cessation Advice	26	100%	97%	98%
Pneumonia Care				
Appropriate Initial Antibiotic	112	98%	91%	92%
Blood Culture Timing	182	100%	96%	96%
Influenza Vaccine	140	97%	89%	91%
Initial Antibiotic Timing	168	98%	95%	95%
Pneumococcal Vaccine	170	98%	91%	93%
Smoking Cessation Advice	71	100%	95%	97%
Surgical Care Improvement Project				
Appropriate VTP Within 24 Hours	225	88%	91%	92%
Appropriate Hair Removal	757	100%	100%	99%
Appropriate Beta Blocker Usage	163	97%	91%	93%
Controlled Postoperative Blood Glucose	57	100%	95%	93%
Prophylactic Antibiotic Timing	457	98%	97%	97%
Prophylactic Antibiotic Timing (Outpatient)	429	96%	93%	92%
Prophylactic Antibiotic Selection	456	97%	98%	97%
Prophylactic Antibiotic Select. (Outpatient)	536	97%	95%	94%
Prophylactic Antibiotic Stopped	441	98%	94%	94%
Recommended VTP Ordered	228	91%	94%	94%
Urinary Catheter Removal	48	92%	87%	90%
Children's Asthma Care				
Received Systemic Corticosteroids	-	-	-	100%
Received Home Management Plan	-	-	-	71%
Received Reliever Medication	-	-	-	100%
Use of Medical Imaging				
Combination Abdominal CT Scan	568	0.315	0.372	0.191
Combination Chest CT Scan	332	0.476	0.134	0.054
Follow-up Mammogram/Ultrasound	834	7.0%	8%	8.4%
MRI for Low Back Pain	151	27.2%	34.3%	32.7%
Survey of Patients' Hospital Experiences				
Area Around Room 'Always' Quiet at Night	300+	68%	-	58%
Doctors 'Always' Communicated Well	300+	80%	-	80%
Home Recovery Information Given	300+	83%	-	82%
Hospital Given 9 or 10 on 10 Point Scale	300+	68%	-	67%
Meds 'Always' Explained Before Given	300+	59%	-	60%
Nurses 'Always' Communicated Well	300+	72%	-	76%
Pain 'Always' Well Controlled	300+	70%	-	69%
Room and Bathroom 'Always' Clean	300+	65%	-	71%
Timely Help 'Always' Received	300+	58%	-	64%
Would Definitely Recommend Hospital	300+	71%	-	69%

Integris Baptist Medical Center

3300 Northwest Expressway
Oklahoma City, OK 73112
URL: www.integris-health.com
Type: Acute Care Hospitals
Ownership: Voluntary Non-Profit - Private
Phone: 405-949-3011
Fax: 405-945-4997
Emergency Services: Yes
Beds: 577

Key Personnel:
CEO/President. . . . . C Bruce Lawrence
Chief of Medical Staff . . . . Brian Geister, MD
Infection Control. . . . . V Ramgopal, MD
Operating Room. . . . . Connie Harper
Pediatric Ambulatory Care . . . . . . Kevin Moore, MD
Pediatric In-Patient Care . . . . Kevin Moore, MD
Quality Assurance . . . . Bill Wandel
Radiology. . . . . Georgianne Snowden, MD

Measure	Cases	This Hosp.	State Avg.	U.S. Avg.
Heart Attack Care				
ACE Inhibitor or ARB for LVSD	147	100%	95%	96%
Aspirin at Arrival	293	100%	98%	99%
Aspirin at Discharge	574	100%	98%	98%
Beta Blocker at Discharge	515	100%	98%	98%
Fibrinolytic Medication Timing	0	-	42%	55%
PCI Within 90 Minutes of Arrival	55	98%	88%	90%
Smoking Cessation Advice	239	100%	100%	99%
Chest Pain/Possible Heart Attack Care				
Aspirin at Arrival[1]	2	100%	94%	95%
Median Time to ECG (minutes)[1]	2	2	9	8
Median Time to Transfer (minutes)[5]	0	-	75	61
Fibrinolytic Medication Timing[5]	0	-	50%	54%
Heart Failure Care				
ACE Inhibitor or ARB for LVSD	297	98%	94%	94%
Discharge Instructions	498	86%	85%	88%
Evaluation of LVS Function	576	100%	94%	98%
Smoking Cessation Advice	82	100%	97%	98%
Pneumonia Care				
Appropriate Initial Antibiotic[2]	121	91%	91%	92%
Blood Culture Timing[2]	154	100%	96%	96%
Influenza Vaccine[2]	160	97%	89%	91%
Initial Antibiotic Timing[2]	208	95%	95%	95%
Pneumococcal Vaccine[2]	209	95%	91%	93%
Smoking Cessation Advice[2]	78	99%	95%	97%
Surgical Care Improvement Project				
Appropriate VTP Within 24 Hours[2]	149	85%	91%	92%
Appropriate Hair Removal[2]	717	100%	100%	99%
Appropriate Beta Blocker Usage[2]	231	87%	91%	93%
Controlled Postoperative Blood Glucose[2]	170	96%	95%	93%
Prophylactic Antibiotic Timing[2]	519	99%	97%	97%
Prophylactic Antibiotic Timing (Outpatient)	367	91%	93%	92%
Prophylactic Antibiotic Selection[2]	532	98%	98%	97%
Prophylactic Antibiotic Select. (Outpatient)	373	94%	95%	94%
Prophylactic Antibiotic Stopped[2]	484	97%	94%	94%
Recommended VTP Ordered[2]	155	87%	94%	94%
Urinary Catheter Removal[2]	124	93%	87%	90%
Children's Asthma Care				
Received Systemic Corticosteroids	-	-	-	100%
Received Home Management Plan	-	-	-	71%
Received Reliever Medication	-	-	-	100%
Use of Medical Imaging				
Combination Abdominal CT Scan	774	0.293	0.372	0.191
Combination Chest CT Scan	517	0.060	0.134	0.054
Follow-up Mammogram/Ultrasound	1,872	7.2%	8%	8.4%
MRI for Low Back Pain[1]	6	33.3%	34.3%	32.7%
Survey of Patients' Hospital Experiences				
Area Around Room 'Always' Quiet at Night	300+	64%	-	58%
Doctors 'Always' Communicated Well	300+	83%	-	80%
Home Recovery Information Given	300+	80%	-	82%
Hospital Given 9 or 10 on 10 Point Scale	300+	73%	-	67%
Meds 'Always' Explained Before Given	300+	59%	-	60%
Nurses 'Always' Communicated Well	300+	75%	-	76%
Pain 'Always' Well Controlled	300+	70%	-	69%
Room and Bathroom 'Always' Clean	300+	70%	-	71%
Timely Help 'Always' Received	300+	64%	-	64%
Would Definitely Recommend Hospital	300+	77%	-	69%

NOTE: Hospital profiles are in alphabetical order by state, then city, then hospital within the city; Rankings exclude hospitals with less than 25 cases except for patient surveys which excludes hospitals with less than 100 cases; (a) 100–299 cases; (1) The number of cases is too small to be sure how well a hospital is performing; (2) The hospital indicated that the data submitted for this measure were based on a sample of cases; (3) Data was collected during a shorter time period (fewer quarters) than the maximum possible time for this measure; (4) Suppressed for one or more quarters by CMS; (5) No data is available from the hospital for this measure; (6) Fewer than 100 patients completed the HCAHPS survey. Use these rates with caution, as the number of surveys may be too low to reliably assess hospital performance; (7) Survey results are based on less than 12 months of data; (8) Survey results are not available for this reporting period; (9) No or very few patients were eligible for the HCAHPS survey. The scores shown, if any, reflect a very small number of surveys; (10) A state average was not calculated because too few hospitals in the state submitted data; (11) There were discrepancies in the data collection process; Please refer to the User's Guide for a full explanation of data.

Integris Southwest Medical Center

4401 South Western Avenue Phone: 405-636-7777
Oklahoma City, OK 73109 Fax: 405-636-7064
URL: www.integris-health.com
Type: Acute Care Hospitals Emergency Services: Yes
Ownership: Voluntary Non-Profit - Private Beds: 369

Key Personnel:
CEO/President. . . . . Bruce Lawrence
Chief of Medical Staff . . . . Ralph Shadid, MD
Infection Control. . . . . Jennifer Perry
Operating Room. . . . . Jim Lynch
Quality Assurance . . . . Joan Pierce, RN
Radiology. . . . . Dee Tucker
Hemotology Center . . . . Hallie Ennis
Intensive Care Unit. . . . . Darlene Burton

Measure	Cases	This Hosp.	State Avg.	U.S. Avg.
Heart Attack Care				
ACE Inhibitor or ARB for LVSD	52	88%	95%	96%
Aspirin at Arrival	243	98%	98%	99%
Aspirin at Discharge	253	94%	98%	98%
Beta Blocker at Discharge	237	97%	98%	98%
Fibrinolytic Medication Timing[1]	1	100%	42%	55%
PCI Within 90 Minutes of Arrival	48	98%	88%	90%
Smoking Cessation Advice	124	100%	100%	99%
Chest Pain/Possible Heart Attack Care				
Aspirin at Arrival[1]	13	100%	94%	95%
Median Time to ECG (minutes)[1]	14	16	9	8
Median Time to Transfer (minutes)[5]	0	-	75	61
Fibrinolytic Medication Timing[5]	0	-	50%	54%
Heart Failure Care				
ACE Inhibitor or ARB for LVSD	170	89%	94%	94%
Discharge Instructions	347	81%	85%	88%
Evaluation of LVS Function	418	97%	94%	98%
Smoking Cessation Advice	129	99%	97%	98%
Pneumonia Care				
Appropriate Initial Antibiotic[2]	185	79%	91%	92%
Blood Culture Timing[2]	223	98%	96%	96%
Influenza Vaccine[2]	182	90%	89%	91%
Initial Antibiotic Timing[2]	313	100%	95%	95%
Pneumococcal Vaccine[2]	221	96%	91%	93%
Smoking Cessation Advice[2]	185	97%	95%	97%
Surgical Care Improvement Project				
Appropriate VTP Within 24 Hours[2]	199	97%	91%	92%
Appropriate Hair Removal[2]	578	99%	100%	99%
Appropriate Beta Blocker Usage[2]	186	93%	91%	93%
Controlled Postoperative Blood Glucose[2]	108	88%	95%	93%
Prophylactic Antibiotic Timing[2]	396	99%	97%	97%
Prophylactic Antibiotic Timing (Outpatient)	177	85%	93%	92%
Prophylactic Antibiotic Selection[2]	400	99%	98%	97%
Prophylactic Antibiotic Select. (Outpatient)	171	91%	95%	94%
Prophylactic Antibiotic Stopped[2]	370	93%	94%	94%
Recommended VTP Ordered[2]	201	98%	94%	94%
Urinary Catheter Removal[2]	118	92%	87%	90%
Children's Asthma Care				
Received Systemic Corticosteroids	-	-	-	100%
Received Home Management Plan	-	-	-	71%
Received Reliever Medication	-	-	-	100%
Use of Medical Imaging				
Combination Abdominal CT Scan	1,146	0.134	0.372	0.191
Combination Chest CT Scan	922	0.035	0.134	0.054
Follow-up Mammogram/Ultrasound	2,047	8.6%	8%	8.4%
MRI for Low Back Pain	231	29.9%	34.3%	32.7%
Survey of Patients' Hospital Experiences				
Area Around Room 'Always' Quiet at Night	300+	55%	-	58%
Doctors 'Always' Communicated Well	300+	77%	-	80%
Home Recovery Information Given	300+	76%	-	82%
Hospital Given 9 or 10 on 10 Point Scale	300+	63%	-	67%
Meds 'Always' Explained Before Given	300+	55%	-	60%
Nurses 'Always' Communicated Well	300+	71%	-	76%
Pain 'Always' Well Controlled	300+	69%	-	69%
Room and Bathroom 'Always' Clean	300+	68%	-	71%
Timely Help 'Always' Received	300+	55%	-	64%
Would Definitely Recommend Hospital	300+	63%	-	69%

Lakeside Women's Hospital

11200 North Portland Avenue Phone: 405-936-1500
Oklahoma City, OK 73120
Type: Acute Care Hospitals Emergency Services: Yes
Ownership: Proprietary

Key Personnel:
CEO/President. . . . . Kelley Brewer
Emergency Room . . . . Melinda Oldham

Measure	Cases	This Hosp.	State Avg.	U.S. Avg.
Heart Attack Care				
ACE Inhibitor or ARB for LVSD[5]	0	-	95%	96%
Aspirin at Arrival[5]	0	-	98%	99%
Aspirin at Discharge[5]	0	-	98%	98%
Beta Blocker at Discharge[5]	0	-	98%	98%
Fibrinolytic Medication Timing[5]	0	-	42%	55%
PCI Within 90 Minutes of Arrival[5]	0	-	88%	90%
Smoking Cessation Advice[5]	0	-	100%	99%
Chest Pain/Possible Heart Attack Care				
Aspirin at Arrival[5]	0	-	94%	95%
Median Time to ECG (minutes)[5]	0	-	9	8
Median Time to Transfer (minutes)[5]	0	-	75	61
Fibrinolytic Medication Timing[5]	0	-	50%	54%
Heart Failure Care				
ACE Inhibitor or ARB for LVSD[5]	0	-	94%	94%
Discharge Instructions[5]	0	-	85%	88%
Evaluation of LVS Function[5]	0	-	94%	98%
Smoking Cessation Advice[5]	0	-	97%	98%
Pneumonia Care				
Appropriate Initial Antibiotic[5]	0	-	91%	92%
Blood Culture Timing[5]	0	-	96%	96%
Influenza Vaccine[5]	0	-	89%	91%
Initial Antibiotic Timing[5]	0	-	95%	95%
Pneumococcal Vaccine[5]	0	-	91%	93%
Smoking Cessation Advice[5]	0	-	95%	97%
Surgical Care Improvement Project				
Appropriate VTP Within 24 Hours[1]	1	100%	91%	92%
Appropriate Hair Removal	78	94%	100%	99%
Appropriate Beta Blocker Usage[1]	3	100%	91%	93%
Controlled Postoperative Blood Glucose	0	-	95%	93%
Prophylactic Antibiotic Timing	67	100%	97%	97%
Prophylactic Antibiotic Timing (Outpatient)[3]	233	97%	93%	92%
Prophylactic Antibiotic Selection	71	99%	98%	97%
Prophylactic Antibiotic Select. (Outpatient)[3]	228	99%	95%	94%
Prophylactic Antibiotic Stopped	67	91%	94%	94%
Recommended VTP Ordered[1]	1	100%	94%	94%
Urinary Catheter Removal	0	-	87%	90%
Children's Asthma Care				
Received Systemic Corticosteroids	-	-	-	100%
Received Home Management Plan	-	-	-	71%
Received Reliever Medication	-	-	-	100%
Use of Medical Imaging				
Combination Abdominal CT Scan[5]	0	-	0.372	0.191
Combination Chest CT Scan[5]	0	-	0.134	0.054
Follow-up Mammogram/Ultrasound	773	6.0%	8%	8.4%
MRI for Low Back Pain[5]	0	-	34.3%	32.7%
Survey of Patients' Hospital Experiences				
Area Around Room 'Always' Quiet at Night	300+	60%	-	58%
Doctors 'Always' Communicated Well	300+	88%	-	80%
Home Recovery Information Given	300+	88%	-	82%
Hospital Given 9 or 10 on 10 Point Scale	300+	84%	-	67%
Meds 'Always' Explained Before Given	300+	62%	-	60%
Nurses 'Always' Communicated Well	300+	83%	-	76%
Pain 'Always' Well Controlled	300+	78%	-	69%
Room and Bathroom 'Always' Clean	300+	77%	-	71%
Timely Help 'Always' Received	300+	62%	-	64%
Would Definitely Recommend Hospital	300+	86%	-	69%

McBride Clinic Orthopedic Hospital

9600 North Broadway Extension Phone: 405-478-1717
Oklahoma City, OK 73114 Fax: 405-486-2144
URL: www.mcbrideclinic.com
Type: Acute Care Hospitals Emergency Services: No
Ownership: Proprietary

Measure	Cases	This Hosp.	State Avg.	U.S. Avg.
Heart Attack Care				
ACE Inhibitor or ARB for LVSD[3]	0	-	95%	96%
Aspirin at Arrival[1,3]	1	0%	98%	99%
Aspirin at Discharge[3]	0	-	98%	98%
Beta Blocker at Discharge[3]	0	-	98%	98%
Fibrinolytic Medication Timing[3]	0	-	42%	55%
PCI Within 90 Minutes of Arrival[3]	0	-	88%	90%
Smoking Cessation Advice[3]	0	-	100%	99%
Chest Pain/Possible Heart Attack Care				
Aspirin at Arrival[1,3]	1	100%	94%	95%
Median Time to ECG (minutes)[1,3]	1	18	9	8
Median Time to Transfer (minutes)[5]	0	-	75	61
Fibrinolytic Medication Timing[5]	0	-	50%	54%
Heart Failure Care				
ACE Inhibitor or ARB for LVSD[5]	0	-	94%	94%
Discharge Instructions[5]	0	-	85%	88%
Evaluation of LVS Function[5]	0	-	94%	98%
Smoking Cessation Advice[5]	0	-	97%	98%
Pneumonia Care				
Appropriate Initial Antibiotic[5]	0	-	91%	92%
Blood Culture Timing[5]	0	-	96%	96%
Influenza Vaccine[5]	0	-	89%	91%
Initial Antibiotic Timing[5]	0	-	95%	95%
Pneumococcal Vaccine[5]	0	-	91%	93%
Smoking Cessation Advice[5]	0	-	95%	97%
Surgical Care Improvement Project				
Appropriate VTP Within 24 Hours[2]	64	95%	91%	92%
Appropriate Hair Removal[2]	344	100%	100%	99%
Appropriate Beta Blocker Usage[2]	93	90%	91%	93%
Controlled Postoperative Blood Glucose[2]	0	-	95%	93%
Prophylactic Antibiotic Timing[2]	255	100%	97%	97%
Prophylactic Antibiotic Timing (Outpatient)[1]	15	100%	93%	92%
Prophylactic Antibiotic Selection[2]	255	100%	98%	97%
Prophylactic Antibiotic Select. (Outpatient)[1]	15	100%	95%	94%
Prophylactic Antibiotic Stopped[2]	255	99%	94%	94%
Recommended VTP Ordered[2]	64	100%	94%	94%
Urinary Catheter Removal[1,2]	6	67%	87%	90%
Children's Asthma Care				
Received Systemic Corticosteroids	-	-	-	100%
Received Home Management Plan	-	-	-	71%
Received Reliever Medication	-	-	-	100%
Use of Medical Imaging				
Combination Abdominal CT Scan[1]	8	0.875	0.372	0.191
Combination Chest CT Scan[1]	20	0.000	0.134	0.054
Follow-up Mammogram/Ultrasound[5]	0	-	8%	8.4%
MRI for Low Back Pain[5]	0	-	34.3%	32.7%
Survey of Patients' Hospital Experiences				
Area Around Room 'Always' Quiet at Night	300+	75%	-	58%
Doctors 'Always' Communicated Well	300+	87%	-	80%
Home Recovery Information Given	300+	91%	-	82%
Hospital Given 9 or 10 on 10 Point Scale	300+	83%	-	67%
Meds 'Always' Explained Before Given	300+	67%	-	60%
Nurses 'Always' Communicated Well	300+	81%	-	76%
Pain 'Always' Well Controlled	300+	76%	-	69%
Room and Bathroom 'Always' Clean	300+	76%	-	71%
Timely Help 'Always' Received	300+	75%	-	64%
Would Definitely Recommend Hospital	300+	87%	-	69%

NOTE: Hospital profiles are in alphabetical order by state, then city, then hospital within the city; Rankings exclude hospitals with less than 25 cases except for patient surveys which excludes hospitals with less than 100 cases; (a) 100–299 cases; (1) The number of cases is too small to be sure how well a hospital is performing; (2) The hospital indicated that the data submitted for this measure were based on a sample of cases; (3) Data was collected during a shorter time period (fewer quarters) than the maximum possible time for this measure; (4) Suppressed for one or more quarters by CMS; (5) No data is available from the hospital for this measure; (6) Fewer than 100 patients completed the HCAHPS survey. Use these rates with caution, as the number of surveys may be too low to reliably assess hospital performance; (7) Survey results are based on less than 12 months of data; (8) Survey results are not available for this reporting period; (9) No or very few patients were eligible for the HCAHPS survey. The scores shown, if any, reflect a very small number of surveys; (10) A state average was not calculated because too few hospitals in the state submitted data; (11) There were discrepancies in the data collection process; Please refer to the User's Guide for a full explanation of data.

Mercy Health Center

4300 West Memorial Road · Phone: 405-755-1515
Oklahoma City, OK 73120 · Fax: 405-752-3811
URL: www.mercyok.net/mhc
Type: Acute Care Hospitals · Emergency Services: Yes
Ownership: Voluntary Non-Profit - Church · Beds: 351

Key Personnel:
CEO/President. . . . . Bruce F Buchanan
Chief of Medical Staff . . . . William Hughes, MD
Pediatric In-Patient Care . . . . Merl Simmons, MD
Quality Assurance . . . . Cozy Armstrong
Radiology. . . . . Richard Cooke, MD
Anesthesiology. . . . . Bennett Fuller
Emergency Room . . . . Paul Orchutt, MD

Measure	Cases	This Hosp.	State Avg.	U.S. Avg.
Heart Attack Care				
ACE Inhibitor or ARB for LVSD[1]	6	83%	95%	96%
Aspirin at Arrival[1]	21	95%	98%	99%
Aspirin at Discharge[1]	24	96%	98%	98%
Beta Blocker at Discharge[1]	23	87%	98%	98%
Fibrinolytic Medication Timing	0	-	42%	55%
PCI Within 90 Minutes of Arrival	0	-	88%	90%
Smoking Cessation Advice[1]	3	100%	100%	99%
Chest Pain/Possible Heart Attack Care				
Aspirin at Arrival	152	96%	94%	95%
Median Time to ECG (minutes)	161	10	9	8
Median Time to Transfer (minutes)[1]	10	56	75	61
Fibrinolytic Medication Timing	0	-	50%	54%
Heart Failure Care				
ACE Inhibitor or ARB for LVSD[1]	16	81%	94%	94%
Discharge Instructions	54	69%	85%	88%
Evaluation of LVS Function	83	95%	94%	98%
Smoking Cessation Advice[1]	10	100%	97%	98%
Pneumonia Care				
Appropriate Initial Antibiotic	147	95%	91%	92%
Blood Culture Timing	316	97%	96%	96%
Influenza Vaccine	228	100%	89%	91%
Initial Antibiotic Timing	258	97%	95%	95%
Pneumococcal Vaccine	297	100%	91%	93%
Smoking Cessation Advice	94	100%	95%	97%
Surgical Care Improvement Project				
Appropriate VTP Within 24 Hours[2]	152	94%	91%	92%
Appropriate Hair Removal[2]	357	99%	100%	99%
Appropriate Beta Blocker Usage[2]	76	88%	91%	93%
Controlled Postoperative Blood Glucose[2]	0	-	95%	93%
Prophylactic Antibiotic Timing[2]	225	98%	97%	97%
Prophylactic Antibiotic Timing (Outpatient)	387	99%	93%	92%
Prophylactic Antibiotic Selection[2]	230	98%	98%	97%
Prophylactic Antibiotic Select. (Outpatient)	437	96%	95%	94%
Prophylactic Antibiotic Stopped[2]	216	95%	94%	94%
Recommended VTP Ordered[2]	153	94%	94%	94%
Urinary Catheter Removal[2]	25	92%	87%	90%
Children's Asthma Care				
Received Systemic Corticosteroids	-	-	-	100%
Received Home Management Plan	-	-	-	71%
Received Reliever Medication	-	-	-	100%
Use of Medical Imaging				
Combination Abdominal CT Scan	1,672	0.197	0.372	0.191
Combination Chest CT Scan	1,223	0.128	0.134	0.054
Follow-up Mammogram/Ultrasound	2,343	10.7%	8%	8.4%
MRI for Low Back Pain	373	31.9%	34.3%	32.7%
Survey of Patients' Hospital Experiences				
Area Around Room 'Always' Quiet at Night	300+	60%	-	58%
Doctors 'Always' Communicated Well	300+	84%	-	80%
Home Recovery Information Given	300+	80%	-	82%
Hospital Given 9 or 10 on 10 Point Scale	300+	73%	-	67%
Meds 'Always' Explained Before Given	300+	58%	-	60%
Nurses 'Always' Communicated Well	300+	76%	-	76%
Pain 'Always' Well Controlled	300+	73%	-	69%
Room and Bathroom 'Always' Clean	300+	68%	-	71%
Timely Help 'Always' Received	300+	61%	-	64%
Would Definitely Recommend Hospital	300+	81%	-	69%

Northwest Surgical Hospital

9204 North May Avenue · Phone: 404-848-1918
Oklahoma City, OK 73120
Type: Acute Care Hospitals · Emergency Services: No
Ownership: Proprietary · Beds: 9

Key Personnel:
CEO/President. . . . . Debbie Foster

Measure	Cases	This Hosp.	State Avg.	U.S. Avg.
Heart Attack Care				
ACE Inhibitor or ARB for LVSD[5]	0	-	95%	96%
Aspirin at Arrival[5]	0	-	98%	99%
Aspirin at Discharge[5]	0	-	98%	98%
Beta Blocker at Discharge[5]	0	-	98%	98%
Fibrinolytic Medication Timing[5]	0	-	42%	55%
PCI Within 90 Minutes of Arrival[5]	0	-	88%	90%
Smoking Cessation Advice[5]	0	-	100%	99%
Chest Pain/Possible Heart Attack Care				
Aspirin at Arrival[5]	0	-	94%	95%
Median Time to ECG (minutes)[5]	0	-	9	8
Median Time to Transfer (minutes)[5]	0	-	75	61
Fibrinolytic Medication Timing[5]	0	-	50%	54%
Heart Failure Care				
ACE Inhibitor or ARB for LVSD[5]	0	-	94%	94%
Discharge Instructions[5]	0	-	85%	88%
Evaluation of LVS Function[5]	0	-	94%	98%
Smoking Cessation Advice[5]	0	-	97%	98%
Pneumonia Care				
Appropriate Initial Antibiotic[5]	0	-	91%	92%
Blood Culture Timing[5]	0	-	96%	96%
Influenza Vaccine[5]	0	-	89%	91%
Initial Antibiotic Timing[5]	0	-	95%	95%
Pneumococcal Vaccine[5]	0	-	91%	93%
Smoking Cessation Advice[5]	0	-	95%	97%
Surgical Care Improvement Project				
Appropriate VTP Within 24 Hours[1,2]	7	100%	91%	92%
Appropriate Hair Removal[2]	240	100%	100%	99%
Appropriate Beta Blocker Usage[2]	50	100%	91%	93%
Controlled Postoperative Blood Glucose[2]	0	-	95%	93%
Prophylactic Antibiotic Timing[2]	213	98%	97%	97%
Prophylactic Antibiotic Timing (Outpatient)	68	100%	93%	92%
Prophylactic Antibiotic Selection[2]	214	100%	98%	97%
Prophylactic Antibiotic Select. (Outpatient)	68	100%	95%	94%
Prophylactic Antibiotic Stopped[2]	205	93%	94%	94%
Recommended VTP Ordered[1,2]	7	100%	94%	94%
Urinary Catheter Removal[1]	1	100%	87%	90%
Children's Asthma Care				
Received Systemic Corticosteroids	-	-	-	100%
Received Home Management Plan	-	-	-	71%
Received Reliever Medication	-	-	-	100%
Use of Medical Imaging				
Combination Abdominal CT Scan	107	0.804	0.372	0.191
Combination Chest CT Scan	86	0.012	0.134	0.054
Follow-up Mammogram/Ultrasound[5]	0	-	8%	8.4%
MRI for Low Back Pain	315	30.5%	34.3%	32.7%
Survey of Patients' Hospital Experiences				
Area Around Room 'Always' Quiet at Night	(a)	81%	-	58%
Doctors 'Always' Communicated Well	(a)	87%	-	80%
Home Recovery Information Given	(a)	87%	-	82%
Hospital Given 9 or 10 on 10 Point Scale	(a)	87%	-	67%
Meds 'Always' Explained Before Given	(a)	71%	-	60%
Nurses 'Always' Communicated Well	(a)	86%	-	76%
Pain 'Always' Well Controlled	(a)	77%	-	69%
Room and Bathroom 'Always' Clean	(a)	85%	-	71%
Timely Help 'Always' Received	(a)	77%	-	64%
Would Definitely Recommend Hospital	(a)	83%	-	69%

O U Medical Center

1200 Everett Drive · Phone: 405-271-5151
Oklahoma City, OK 73117 · Fax: 405-271-7344
URL: www.oumedcenter.com
Type: Acute Care Hospitals · Emergency Services: Yes
Ownership: Proprietary · Beds: 394

Key Personnel:
CEO/President. . . . . Cole C Eslyn
Chief of Medical Staff . . . . Timothy Coussons, MD
Infection Control. . . . . Margaret Tannehill, RN
Operating Room. . . . . Susan Hollingsworth, RN
Pediatric Ambulatory Care . . . . . . Paul Toubas, MD
Pediatric In-Patient Care . . . . Paul Toubas, MD
Quality Assurance . . . . John Douvillier
Radiology. . . . . Bob Eaton, MD

Measure	Cases	This Hosp.	State Avg.	U.S. Avg.
Heart Attack Care				
ACE Inhibitor or ARB for LVSD	33	100%	95%	96%
Aspirin at Arrival	101	100%	98%	99%
Aspirin at Discharge	120	100%	98%	98%
Beta Blocker at Discharge	118	100%	98%	98%
Fibrinolytic Medication Timing	0	-	42%	55%
PCI Within 90 Minutes of Arrival[1]	20	100%	88%	90%
Smoking Cessation Advice	59	100%	100%	99%
Chest Pain/Possible Heart Attack Care				
Aspirin at Arrival[1,3]	3	100%	94%	95%
Median Time to ECG (minutes)[1,3]	3	5	9	8
Median Time to Transfer (minutes)[5]	0	-	75	61
Fibrinolytic Medication Timing[3]	0	-	50%	54%
Heart Failure Care				
ACE Inhibitor or ARB for LVSD	122	99%	94%	94%
Discharge Instructions	213	88%	85%	88%
Evaluation of LVS Function	227	100%	94%	98%
Smoking Cessation Advice	100	100%	97%	98%
Pneumonia Care				
Appropriate Initial Antibiotic	87	94%	91%	92%
Blood Culture Timing	203	99%	96%	96%
Influenza Vaccine	127	97%	89%	91%
Initial Antibiotic Timing	167	96%	95%	95%
Pneumococcal Vaccine	95	98%	91%	93%
Smoking Cessation Advice	147	100%	95%	97%
Surgical Care Improvement Project				
Appropriate VTP Within 24 Hours[2]	299	93%	91%	92%
Appropriate Hair Removal[2]	635	100%	100%	99%
Appropriate Beta Blocker Usage[2]	158	91%	91%	93%
Controlled Postoperative Blood Glucose[2]	97	88%	95%	93%
Prophylactic Antibiotic Timing[2]	400	98%	97%	97%
Prophylactic Antibiotic Timing (Outpatient)	575	97%	93%	92%
Prophylactic Antibiotic Selection[2]	405	97%	98%	97%
Prophylactic Antibiotic Select. (Outpatient)	606	98%	95%	94%
Prophylactic Antibiotic Stopped[2]	365	95%	94%	94%
Recommended VTP Ordered[2]	299	97%	94%	94%
Urinary Catheter Removal[2]	66	85%	87%	90%
Children's Asthma Care				
Received Systemic Corticosteroids	238	100%	-	100%
Received Home Management Plan	236	76%	-	71%
Received Reliever Medication	238	100%	-	100%
Use of Medical Imaging				
Combination Abdominal CT Scan	1,043	0.864	0.372	0.191
Combination Chest CT Scan	837	0.019	0.134	0.054
Follow-up Mammogram/Ultrasound[5]	0	-	8%	8.4%
MRI for Low Back Pain	112	32.1%	34.3%	32.7%
Survey of Patients' Hospital Experiences				
Area Around Room 'Always' Quiet at Night	300+	57%	-	58%
Doctors 'Always' Communicated Well	300+	78%	-	80%
Home Recovery Information Given	300+	84%	-	82%
Hospital Given 9 or 10 on 10 Point Scale	300+	68%	-	67%
Meds 'Always' Explained Before Given	300+	57%	-	60%
Nurses 'Always' Communicated Well	300+	74%	-	76%
Pain 'Always' Well Controlled	300+	69%	-	69%
Room and Bathroom 'Always' Clean	300+	59%	-	71%
Timely Help 'Always' Received	300+	57%	-	64%
Would Definitely Recommend Hospital	300+	70%	-	69%

NOTE: Hospital profiles are in alphabetical order by state, then city, then hospital within the city; Rankings exclude hospitals with less than 25 cases except for patient surveys which excludes hospitals with less than 100 cases; (a) 100–299 cases; (1) The number of cases is too small to be sure how well a hospital is performing; (2) The hospital indicated that the data submitted for this measure were based on a sample of cases; (3) Data was collected during a shorter time period (fewer quarters) than the maximum possible time for this measure; (4) Suppressed for one or more quarters by CMS; (5) No data is available from the hospital for this measure; (6) Fewer than 100 patients completed the HCAHPS survey. Use these rates with caution, as the number of surveys may be too low to reliably assess hospital performance; (7) Survey results are based on less than 12 months of data; (8) Survey results are not available for this reporting period; (9) No or very few patients were eligible for the HCAHPS survey. The scores shown, if any, reflect a very small number of surveys; (10) A state average was not calculated because too few hospitals in the state submitted data; (11) There were discrepancies in the data collection process; Please refer to the User's Guide for a full explanation of data.

Oklahoma Center for Orthopaedic & Multi-Sp

330 Southwest 80th Street Phone: 405-602-6500
Oklahoma City, OK 73139
Type: Acute Care Hospitals Emergency Services: No
Ownership: Proprietary

Measure	Cases	This Hosp.	State Avg.	U.S. Avg.
Heart Attack Care				
ACE Inhibitor or ARB for LVSD[5]	0	-	95%	96%
Aspirin at Arrival[5]	0	-	98%	99%
Aspirin at Discharge[5]	0	-	98%	98%
Beta Blocker at Discharge[5]	0	-	98%	98%
Fibrinolytic Medication Timing[5]	0	-	42%	55%
PCI Within 90 Minutes of Arrival[5]	0	-	88%	90%
Smoking Cessation Advice[5]	0	-	100%	99%
Chest Pain/Possible Heart Attack Care				
Aspirin at Arrival[5]	0	-	94%	95%
Median Time to ECG (minutes)[5]	0	-	9	8
Median Time to Transfer (minutes)[5]	0	-	75	61
Fibrinolytic Medication Timing[5]	0	-	50%	54%
Heart Failure Care				
ACE Inhibitor or ARB for LVSD[5]	0	-	94%	94%
Discharge Instructions[5]	0	-	85%	88%
Evaluation of LVS Function[5]	0	-	94%	98%
Smoking Cessation Advice[5]	0	-	97%	98%
Pneumonia Care				
Appropriate Initial Antibiotic[5]	0	-	91%	92%
Blood Culture Timing[5]	0	-	96%	96%
Influenza Vaccine[5]	0	-	89%	91%
Initial Antibiotic Timing[5]	0	-	95%	95%
Pneumococcal Vaccine[5]	0	-	91%	93%
Smoking Cessation Advice[5]	0	-	95%	97%
Surgical Care Improvement Project				
Appropriate VTP Within 24 Hours[1,2]	6	100%	91%	92%
Appropriate Hair Removal[2]	233	100%	100%	99%
Appropriate Beta Blocker Usage[2]	51	88%	91%	93%
Controlled Postoperative Blood Glucose[2]	0	-	95%	93%
Prophylactic Antibiotic Timing[2]	208	99%	97%	97%
Prophylactic Antibiotic Timing (Outpatient)	268	85%	93%	92%
Prophylactic Antibiotic Selection[2]	208	97%	98%	97%
Prophylactic Antibiotic Select. (Outpatient)	232	96%	95%	94%
Prophylactic Antibiotic Stopped[2]	208	98%	94%	94%
Recommended VTP Ordered[1,2]	6	100%	94%	94%
Urinary Catheter Removal[2]	99	100%	87%	90%
Children's Asthma Care				
Received Systemic Corticosteroids	-	-	-	100%
Received Home Management Plan	-	-	-	71%
Received Reliever Medication	-	-	-	100%
Use of Medical Imaging				
Combination Abdominal CT Scan[5]	0	-	0.372	0.191
Combination Chest CT Scan[5]	0	-	0.134	0.054
Follow-up Mammogram/Ultrasound[5]	0	-	8%	8.4%
MRI for Low Back Pain[5]	0	-	34.3%	32.7%
Survey of Patients' Hospital Experiences				
Area Around Room 'Always' Quiet at Night	(a)	82%	-	58%
Doctors 'Always' Communicated Well	(a)	88%	-	80%
Home Recovery Information Given	(a)	87%	-	82%
Hospital Given 9 or 10 on 10 Point Scale	(a)	82%	-	67%
Meds 'Always' Explained Before Given	(a)	70%	-	60%
Nurses 'Always' Communicated Well	(a)	89%	-	76%
Pain 'Always' Well Controlled	(a)	77%	-	69%
Room and Bathroom 'Always' Clean	(a)	86%	-	71%
Timely Help 'Always' Received	(a)	84%	-	64%
Would Definitely Recommend Hospital	(a)	86%	-	69%

Oklahoma City VA Medical Center

921 NE 13th Street Phone: 405-270-0501
Oklahoma City, OK 73104 Fax: 405-270-1560
URL: www.va.gov
Type: Acute Care-Veterans Administration Emergency Services: No
Ownership: Government - Federal Beds: 245

Key Personnel:
Chief of Medical Staff.......... D Robert McCaffree, MD
Infection Control.............. Linda Adkins, RN
Operating Room.............. Deborah Hovarter
Quality Assurance .... Jennifer Kubiak
Radiology.................. Max Walters, MD
Ambulatory Care .... M Boyd Shook, MD
Anesthesiology.............. Raghuvender Gauta, MD
Emergency Room .... M Boyd Shook, MD

Measure	Cases	This Hosp.	State Avg.	U.S. Avg.
Heart Attack Care				
ACE Inhibitor or ARB for LVSD[1]	24	92%	95%	96%
Aspirin at Arrival	133	98%	98%	99%
Aspirin at Discharge	123	98%	98%	98%
Beta Blocker at Discharge	121	95%	98%	98%
Fibrinolytic Medication Timing[5]	0	-	42%	55%
PCI Within 90 Minutes of Arrival[1]	15	67%	88%	90%
Smoking Cessation Advice	50	100%	100%	99%
Chest Pain/Possible Heart Attack Care				
Aspirin at Arrival	-	-	94%	95%
Median Time to ECG (minutes)	-	-	9	8
Median Time to Transfer (minutes)	-	-	75	61
Fibrinolytic Medication Timing	-	-	50%	54%
Heart Failure Care				
ACE Inhibitor or ARB for LVSD	100	96%	94%	94%
Discharge Instructions	182	100%	85%	88%
Evaluation of LVS Function	204	100%	94%	98%
Smoking Cessation Advice	72	100%	97%	98%
Pneumonia Care				
Appropriate Initial Antibiotic	123	95%	91%	92%
Blood Culture Timing	232	96%	96%	96%
Influenza Vaccine	169	95%	89%	91%
Initial Antibiotic Timing	185	91%	95%	95%
Pneumococcal Vaccine	162	98%	91%	93%
Smoking Cessation Advice	95	100%	95%	97%
Surgical Care Improvement Project				
Appropriate VTP Within 24 Hours[2]	239	99%	91%	92%
Appropriate Hair Removal[2]	525	100%	100%	99%
Appropriate Beta Blocker Usage[2]	257	100%	91%	93%
Controlled Postoperative Blood Glucose[2]	105	99%	95%	93%
Prophylactic Antibiotic Timing	413	97%	97%	97%
Prophylactic Antibiotic Timing (Outpatient)	-	-	93%	92%
Prophylactic Antibiotic Selection	414	99%	98%	97%
Prophylactic Antibiotic Select. (Outpatient)	-	-	95%	94%
Prophylactic Antibiotic Stopped	403	98%	94%	94%
Recommended VTP Ordered[2]	239	99%	94%	94%
Urinary Catheter Removal[2]	53	98%	87%	90%
Children's Asthma Care				
Received Systemic Corticosteroids	-	-	-	100%
Received Home Management Plan	-	-	-	71%
Received Reliever Medication	-	-	-	100%
Use of Medical Imaging				
Combination Abdominal CT Scan	-	-	0.372	0.191
Combination Chest CT Scan	-	-	0.134	0.054
Follow-up Mammogram/Ultrasound	-	-	8%	8.4%
MRI for Low Back Pain	-	-	34.3%	32.7%
Survey of Patients' Hospital Experiences				
Area Around Room 'Always' Quiet at Night	-	-	-	58%
Doctors 'Always' Communicated Well	-	-	-	80%
Home Recovery Information Given	-	-	-	82%
Hospital Given 9 or 10 on 10 Point Scale	-	-	-	67%
Meds 'Always' Explained Before Given	-	-	-	60%
Nurses 'Always' Communicated Well	-	-	-	76%
Pain 'Always' Well Controlled	-	-	-	69%
Room and Bathroom 'Always' Clean	-	-	-	71%
Timely Help 'Always' Received	-	-	-	64%
Would Definitely Recommend Hospital	-	-	-	69%

Oklahoma Heart Hospital

4050 West Memorial Road Phone: 405-608-3200
Oklahoma City, OK 73120 Fax: 405-608-3396
URL: www.okheart.com
Type: Acute Care Hospitals Emergency Services: Yes
Ownership: Proprietary Beds: 78

Key Personnel:
CEO/President............... John Harvey
Chief of Medical Staff.......... John Harvey, MD
Radiology................... Vance E McCollom

Measure	Cases	This Hosp.	State Avg.	U.S. Avg.
Heart Attack Care				
ACE Inhibitor or ARB for LVSD[2]	47	100%	95%	96%
Aspirin at Arrival[2]	98	99%	98%	99%
Aspirin at Discharge[2]	303	99%	98%	98%
Beta Blocker at Discharge[2]	279	99%	98%	98%
Fibrinolytic Medication Timing[2]	0	-	42%	55%
PCI Within 90 Minutes of Arrival[1,2]	21	76%	88%	90%
Smoking Cessation Advice[2]	127	99%	100%	99%
Chest Pain/Possible Heart Attack Care				
Aspirin at Arrival	31	97%	94%	95%
Median Time to ECG (minutes)	35	1	9	8
Median Time to Transfer (minutes)[5]	0	-	75	61
Fibrinolytic Medication Timing[3]	0	-	50%	54%
Heart Failure Care				
ACE Inhibitor or ARB for LVSD[2]	132	95%	94%	94%
Discharge Instructions[2]	283	96%	85%	88%
Evaluation of LVS Function[2]	309	100%	94%	98%
Smoking Cessation Advice[2]	53	100%	97%	98%
Pneumonia Care				
Appropriate Initial Antibiotic[1]	14	93%	91%	92%
Blood Culture Timing[1]	14	100%	96%	96%
Influenza Vaccine	39	90%	89%	91%
Initial Antibiotic Timing[1]	16	94%	95%	95%
Pneumococcal Vaccine	57	96%	91%	93%
Smoking Cessation Advice[1]	19	100%	95%	97%
Surgical Care Improvement Project				
Appropriate VTP Within 24 Hours	43	93%	91%	92%
Appropriate Hair Removal	1,284	100%	100%	99%
Appropriate Beta Blocker Usage	594	96%	91%	93%
Controlled Postoperative Blood Glucose	904	99%	95%	93%
Prophylactic Antibiotic Timing	1,000	100%	97%	97%
Prophylactic Antibiotic Timing (Outpatient)	488	99%	93%	92%
Prophylactic Antibiotic Selection	1,027	100%	98%	97%
Prophylactic Antibiotic Select. (Outpatient)	488	100%	95%	94%
Prophylactic Antibiotic Stopped	910	100%	94%	94%
Recommended VTP Ordered	44	93%	94%	94%
Urinary Catheter Removal	377	93%	87%	90%
Children's Asthma Care				
Received Systemic Corticosteroids	-	-	-	100%
Received Home Management Plan	-	-	-	71%
Received Reliever Medication	-	-	-	100%
Use of Medical Imaging				
Combination Abdominal CT Scan	309	0.773	0.372	0.191
Combination Chest CT Scan	224	0.009	0.134	0.054
Follow-up Mammogram/Ultrasound[5]	0	-	8%	8.4%
MRI for Low Back Pain[5]	0	-	34.3%	32.7%
Survey of Patients' Hospital Experiences				
Area Around Room 'Always' Quiet at Night	300+	78%	-	58%
Doctors 'Always' Communicated Well	300+	90%	-	80%
Home Recovery Information Given	300+	89%	-	82%
Hospital Given 9 or 10 on 10 Point Scale	300+	97%	-	67%
Meds 'Always' Explained Before Given	300+	78%	-	60%
Nurses 'Always' Communicated Well	300+	93%	-	76%
Pain 'Always' Well Controlled	300+	86%	-	69%
Room and Bathroom 'Always' Clean	300+	87%	-	71%
Timely Help 'Always' Received	300+	90%	-	64%
Would Definitely Recommend Hospital	300+	99%	-	69%

NOTE: Hospital profiles are in alphabetical order by state, then city, then hospital within the city; Rankings exclude hospitals with less than 25 cases except for patient surveys which excludes hospitals with less than 100 cases; (a) 100–299 cases; (1) The number of cases is too small to be sure how well a hospital is performing; (2) The hospital indicated that the data submitted for this measure were based on a sample of cases; (3) Data was collected during a shorter time period (fewer quarters) than the maximum possible time for this measure; (4) Suppressed for one or more quarters by CMS; (5) No data is available from the hospital for this measure; (6) Fewer than 100 patients completed the HCAHPS survey. Use these rates with caution, as the number of surveys may be too low to reliably assess hospital performance; (7) Survey results are based on less than 12 months of data; (8) Survey results are not available for this reporting period; (9) No or very few patients were eligible for the HCAHPS survey. The scores shown, if any, reflect a very small number of surveys; (10) A state average was not calculated because too few hospitals in the state submitted data; (11) There were discrepancies in the data collection process; Please refer to the User's Guide for a full explanation of data.

Oklahoma Heart Hospital South

5200 East I-240 Service Road
Oklahoma City, OK 73135
Phone: 405-628-6000
URL: www.okheart.com/south-campus
Type: Acute Care Hospitals
Emergency Services: Yes
Ownership: Proprietary
Key Personnel:
CEO . . . . John Harvey

Measure	Cases	This Hosp.	State Avg.	U.S. Avg.
Heart Attack Care				
ACE Inhibitor or ARB for LVSD[1,2,3]	13	100%	95%	96%
Aspirin at Arrival[2,3]	26	100%	98%	99%
Aspirin at Discharge[2,3]	67	100%	98%	98%
Beta Blocker at Discharge[2,3]	60	100%	98%	98%
Fibrinolytic Medication Timing[2,3]	0	-	42%	55%
PCI Within 90 Minutes of Arrival[1,2,3]	8	88%	88%	90%
Smoking Cessation Advice[2,3]	33	94%	100%	99%
Chest Pain/Possible Heart Attack Care				
Aspirin at Arrival[1,3]	5	100%	94%	95%
Median Time to ECG (minutes)[1,3]	8	2	9	8
Median Time to Transfer (minutes)[5]	0	-	75	61
Fibrinolytic Medication Timing[5]	0	-	50%	54%
Heart Failure Care				
ACE Inhibitor or ARB for LVSD[2,3]	30	100%	94%	94%
Discharge Instructions[2,3]	56	89%	85%	88%
Evaluation of LVS Function[2,3]	59	98%	94%	98%
Smoking Cessation Advice[1,2,3]	10	100%	97%	98%
Pneumonia Care				
Appropriate Initial Antibiotic[3]	0	-	91%	92%
Blood Culture Timing[1,3]	1	100%	96%	96%
Influenza Vaccine[5]	0	-	89%	91%
Initial Antibiotic Timing[1,3]	2	100%	95%	95%
Pneumococcal Vaccine[1,3]	8	100%	91%	93%
Smoking Cessation Advice[1,3]	1	100%	95%	97%
Surgical Care Improvement Project				
Appropriate VTP Within 24 Hours[3]	0	-	91%	92%
Appropriate Hair Removal[3]	81	100%	100%	99%
Appropriate Beta Blocker Usage[3]	38	95%	91%	93%
Controlled Postoperative Blood Glucose[3]	66	91%	95%	93%
Prophylactic Antibiotic Timing[3]	71	99%	97%	97%
Prophylactic Antibiotic Timing (Outpatient)[1,3]	17	100%	93%	92%
Prophylactic Antibiotic Selection[3]	72	100%	98%	97%
Prophylactic Antibiotic Select. (Outpatient)[1,3]	17	100%	95%	94%
Prophylactic Antibiotic Stopped[3]	66	95%	94%	94%
Recommended VTP Ordered[3]	0	-	94%	94%
Urinary Catheter Removal[3]	30	83%	87%	90%
Children's Asthma Care				
Received Systemic Corticosteroids	-	-	-	100%
Received Home Management Plan	-	-	-	71%
Received Reliever Medication	-	-	-	100%
Use of Medical Imaging				
Combination Abdominal CT Scan	-	-	0.372	0.191
Combination Chest CT Scan	-	-	0.134	0.054
Follow-up Mammogram/Ultrasound	-	-	8%	8.4%
MRI for Low Back Pain	-	-	34.3%	32.7%
Survey of Patients' Hospital Experiences				
Area Around Room 'Always' Quiet at Night[8]	-	-	-	58%
Doctors 'Always' Communicated Well[8]	-	-	-	80%
Home Recovery Information Given[8]	-	-	-	82%
Hospital Given 9 or 10 on 10 Point Scale[8]	-	-	-	67%
Meds 'Always' Explained Before Given[8]	-	-	-	60%
Nurses 'Always' Communicated Well[8]	-	-	-	76%
Pain 'Always' Well Controlled[8]	-	-	-	69%
Room and Bathroom 'Always' Clean[8]	-	-	-	71%
Timely Help 'Always' Received[8]	-	-	-	64%
Would Definitely Recommend Hospital[8]	-	-	-	69%

Oklahoma Spine Hospital

14101 Parkway Commons Drive
Oklahoma City, OK 73134
Phone: 405-749-2700
Fax: 405-749-2783
URL: www.oklahomaspine.com
Type: Acute Care Hospitals
Emergency Services: Yes
Ownership: Proprietary
Beds: 18

Measure	Cases	This Hosp.	State Avg.	U.S. Avg.
Heart Attack Care				
ACE Inhibitor or ARB for LVSD[5]	0	-	95%	96%
Aspirin at Arrival[5]	0	-	98%	99%
Aspirin at Discharge[5]	0	-	98%	98%
Beta Blocker at Discharge[5]	0	-	98%	98%
Fibrinolytic Medication Timing[5]	0	-	42%	55%
PCI Within 90 Minutes of Arrival[5]	0	-	88%	90%
Smoking Cessation Advice[5]	0	-	100%	99%
Chest Pain/Possible Heart Attack Care				
Aspirin at Arrival[5]	0	-	94%	95%
Median Time to ECG (minutes)[5]	0	-	9	8
Median Time to Transfer (minutes)[5]	0	-	75	61
Fibrinolytic Medication Timing[5]	0	-	50%	54%
Heart Failure Care				
ACE Inhibitor or ARB for LVSD[5]	0	-	94%	94%
Discharge Instructions[5]	0	-	85%	88%
Evaluation of LVS Function[5]	0	-	94%	98%
Smoking Cessation Advice[5]	0	-	97%	98%
Pneumonia Care				
Appropriate Initial Antibiotic[2,3]	0	-	91%	92%
Blood Culture Timing[2,3]	0	-	96%	96%
Influenza Vaccine[5]	0	-	89%	91%
Initial Antibiotic Timing[2,3]	0	-	95%	95%
Pneumococcal Vaccine[2,3]	0	-	91%	93%
Smoking Cessation Advice[2,3]	0	-	95%	97%
Surgical Care Improvement Project				
Appropriate VTP Within 24 Hours[1,2]	1	100%	91%	92%
Appropriate Hair Removal[1,2]	18	100%	100%	99%
Appropriate Beta Blocker Usage[1,2]	4	100%	91%	93%
Controlled Postoperative Blood Glucose[2]	0	-	95%	93%
Prophylactic Antibiotic Timing[1,2]	3	67%	97%	97%
Prophylactic Antibiotic Timing (Outpatient)[5]	0	-	93%	92%
Prophylactic Antibiotic Selection[1,2]	2	100%	98%	97%
Prophylactic Antibiotic Select. (Outpatient)[5]	0	-	95%	94%
Prophylactic Antibiotic Stopped[1,2]	2	50%	94%	94%
Recommended VTP Ordered[1,2]	1	100%	94%	94%
Urinary Catheter Removal[2]	0	-	87%	90%
Children's Asthma Care				
Received Systemic Corticosteroids	-	-	-	100%
Received Home Management Plan	-	-	-	71%
Received Reliever Medication	-	-	-	100%
Use of Medical Imaging				
Combination Abdominal CT Scan[1]	3	0.333	0.372	0.191
Combination Chest CT Scan[1]	2	0.000	0.134	0.054
Follow-up Mammogram/Ultrasound[5]	0	-	8%	8.4%
MRI for Low Back Pain	135	31.9%	34.3%	32.7%
Survey of Patients' Hospital Experiences				
Area Around Room 'Always' Quiet at Night	300+	82%	-	58%
Doctors 'Always' Communicated Well	300+	95%	-	80%
Home Recovery Information Given	300+	89%	-	82%
Hospital Given 9 or 10 on 10 Point Scale	300+	91%	-	67%
Meds 'Always' Explained Before Given	300+	78%	-	60%
Nurses 'Always' Communicated Well	300+	88%	-	76%
Pain 'Always' Well Controlled	300+	83%	-	69%
Room and Bathroom 'Always' Clean	300+	91%	-	71%
Timely Help 'Always' Received	300+	83%	-	64%
Would Definitely Recommend Hospital	300+	93%	-	69%

Orthopedic Hospital

1044 SW 44th St, Suite 950
Oklahoma City, OK 73109
Phone: 405-631-3085
Fax: 405-616-2670
URL: www.ortho-ok.com/orthopedichospital
Type: Acute Care Hospitals
Emergency Services: Yes
Ownership: Government - Federal
Key Personnel:
CEO/President. . . . . Joel Frazier, M.D.
Patient Relations . . . . Pam Cannon

Measure	Cases	This Hosp.	State Avg.	U.S. Avg.
Heart Attack Care				
ACE Inhibitor or ARB for LVSD[5]	0	-	95%	96%
Aspirin at Arrival[5]	0	-	98%	99%
Aspirin at Discharge[5]	0	-	98%	98%
Beta Blocker at Discharge[5]	0	-	98%	98%
Fibrinolytic Medication Timing[5]	0	-	42%	55%
PCI Within 90 Minutes of Arrival[5]	0	-	88%	90%
Smoking Cessation Advice[5]	0	-	100%	99%
Chest Pain/Possible Heart Attack Care				
Aspirin at Arrival[5]	0	-	94%	95%
Median Time to ECG (minutes)[5]	0	-	9	8
Median Time to Transfer (minutes)[5]	0	-	75	61
Fibrinolytic Medication Timing[5]	0	-	50%	54%
Heart Failure Care				
ACE Inhibitor or ARB for LVSD[5]	0	-	94%	94%
Discharge Instructions[5]	0	-	85%	88%
Evaluation of LVS Function[5]	0	-	94%	98%
Smoking Cessation Advice[5]	0	-	97%	98%
Pneumonia Care				
Appropriate Initial Antibiotic[5]	0	-	91%	92%
Blood Culture Timing[5]	0	-	96%	96%
Influenza Vaccine[5]	0	-	89%	91%
Initial Antibiotic Timing[5]	0	-	95%	95%
Pneumococcal Vaccine[5]	0	-	91%	93%
Smoking Cessation Advice[5]	0	-	95%	97%
Surgical Care Improvement Project				
Appropriate VTP Within 24 Hours[1,2,3]	4	75%	91%	92%
Appropriate Hair Removal[1,2,3]	11	100%	100%	99%
Appropriate Beta Blocker Usage[1,2,3]	1	100%	91%	93%
Controlled Postoperative Blood Glucose[2,3]	0	-	95%	93%
Prophylactic Antibiotic Timing[1,2,3]	11	55%	97%	97%
Prophylactic Antibiotic Timing (Outpatient)[1,3]	12	100%	93%	92%
Prophylactic Antibiotic Selection[1,2,3]	11	82%	98%	97%
Prophylactic Antibiotic Select. (Outpatient)[1,3]	13	92%	95%	94%
Prophylactic Antibiotic Stopped[1,2,3]	11	100%	94%	94%
Recommended VTP Ordered[1,2,3]	4	75%	94%	94%
Urinary Catheter Removal[1]	7	100%	87%	90%
Children's Asthma Care				
Received Systemic Corticosteroids	-	-	-	100%
Received Home Management Plan	-	-	-	71%
Received Reliever Medication	-	-	-	100%
Use of Medical Imaging				
Combination Abdominal CT Scan[5]	0	-	0.372	0.191
Combination Chest CT Scan[5]	0	-	0.134	0.054
Follow-up Mammogram/Ultrasound[5]	0	-	8%	8.4%
MRI for Low Back Pain[5]	0	-	34.3%	32.7%
Survey of Patients' Hospital Experiences				
Area Around Room 'Always' Quiet at Night	(a)	79%	-	58%
Doctors 'Always' Communicated Well	(a)	78%	-	80%
Home Recovery Information Given	(a)	79%	-	82%
Hospital Given 9 or 10 on 10 Point Scale	(a)	62%	-	67%
Meds 'Always' Explained Before Given	(a)	64%	-	60%
Nurses 'Always' Communicated Well	(a)	72%	-	76%
Pain 'Always' Well Controlled	(a)	60%	-	69%
Room and Bathroom 'Always' Clean	(a)	83%	-	71%
Timely Help 'Always' Received	(a)	72%	-	64%
Would Definitely Recommend Hospital	(a)	69%	-	69%

NOTE: Hospital profiles are in alphabetical order by state, then city, then hospital within the city; Rankings exclude hospitals with less than 25 cases except for patient surveys which excludes hospitals with less than 100 cases; (a) 100–299 cases; (1) The number of cases is too small to be sure how well a hospital is performing; (2) The hospital indicated that the data submitted for this measure were based on a sample of cases; (3) Data was collected during a shorter time period (fewer quarters) than the maximum possible time for this measure; (4) Suppressed for one or more quarters by CMS; (5) No data is available from the hospital for this measure; (6) Fewer than 100 patients completed the HCAHPS survey. Use these rates with caution, as the number of surveys may be too low to reliably assess hospital performance; (7) Survey results are based on less than 12 months of data; (8) Survey results are not available for this reporting period; (9) No or very few patients were eligible for the HCAHPS survey. The scores shown, if any, reflect a very small number of surveys; (10) A state average was not calculated because too few hospitals in the state submitted data; (11) There were discrepancies in the data collection process; Please refer to the User's Guide for a full explanation of data.

Saint Anthony Hospital

1000 North Lee Avenue　Phone: 405-272-7000
Oklahoma City, OK 73101　Fax: 405-272-6592
URL: www.saintsok.com
Type: Acute Care Hospitals　Emergency Services: Yes
Ownership: Voluntary Non-Profit - Church　Beds: 659

Key Personnel:
CEO/President. . . . . Valinda Rutledge
Chief of Medical Staff . . . . Susan Edwards, MD
Infection Control. . . . . Barbara Baker
Quality Assurance . . . . Wanda Fairless
Anesthesiology. . . . . Tin Chen
Emergency Room . . . . Jack Bair, MD

Measure	Cases	This Hosp.	State Avg.	U.S. Avg.
Heart Attack Care				
ACE Inhibitor or ARB for LVSD	33	100%	95%	96%
Aspirin at Arrival	144	100%	98%	99%
Aspirin at Discharge	222	99%	98%	98%
Beta Blocker at Discharge	210	99%	98%	98%
Fibrinolytic Medication Timing	0	-	42%	55%
PCI Within 90 Minutes of Arrival[1]	20	95%	88%	90%
Smoking Cessation Advice	88	99%	100%	99%
Chest Pain/Possible Heart Attack Care				
Aspirin at Arrival[1,3]	1	100%	94%	95%
Median Time to ECG (minutes)[1,3]	1	1	9	8
Median Time to Transfer (minutes)[5]	0	-	75	61
Fibrinolytic Medication Timing[5]	0	-	50%	54%
Heart Failure Care				
ACE Inhibitor or ARB for LVSD	138	94%	94%	94%
Discharge Instructions	312	96%	85%	88%
Evaluation of LVS Function	355	100%	94%	98%
Smoking Cessation Advice	93	98%	97%	98%
Pneumonia Care				
Appropriate Initial Antibiotic	171	94%	91%	92%
Blood Culture Timing	250	97%	96%	96%
Influenza Vaccine	201	99%	89%	91%
Initial Antibiotic Timing	238	97%	95%	95%
Pneumococcal Vaccine	208	98%	91%	93%
Smoking Cessation Advice	171	99%	95%	97%
Surgical Care Improvement Project				
Appropriate VTP Within 24 Hours[2]	331	95%	91%	92%
Appropriate Hair Removal[2]	1,529	100%	100%	99%
Appropriate Beta Blocker Usage[2]	398	94%	91%	93%
Controlled Postoperative Blood Glucose[2]	155	96%	95%	93%
Prophylactic Antibiotic Timing[2]	1,258	99%	97%	97%
Prophylactic Antibiotic Timing (Outpatient)	380	79%	93%	92%
Prophylactic Antibiotic Selection[2]	1,263	99%	98%	97%
Prophylactic Antibiotic Select. (Outpatient)	373	72%	95%	94%
Prophylactic Antibiotic Stopped[2]	1,201	98%	94%	94%
Recommended VTP Ordered[2]	331	97%	94%	94%
Urinary Catheter Removal[2]	119	92%	87%	90%
Children's Asthma Care				
Received Systemic Corticosteroids	-	-	-	100%
Received Home Management Plan	-	-	-	71%
Received Reliever Medication	-	-	-	100%
Use of Medical Imaging				
Combination Abdominal CT Scan	519	0.638	0.372	0.191
Combination Chest CT Scan	457	0.002	0.134	0.054
Follow-up Mammogram/Ultrasound	878	2.6%	8%	8.4%
MRI for Low Back Pain	125	36.8%	34.3%	32.7%
Survey of Patients' Hospital Experiences				
Area Around Room 'Always' Quiet at Night	300+	62%	-	58%
Doctors 'Always' Communicated Well	300+	83%	-	80%
Home Recovery Information Given	300+	82%	-	82%
Hospital Given 9 or 10 on 10 Point Scale	300+	68%	-	67%
Meds 'Always' Explained Before Given	300+	57%	-	60%
Nurses 'Always' Communicated Well	300+	76%	-	76%
Pain 'Always' Well Controlled	300+	71%	-	69%
Room and Bathroom 'Always' Clean	300+	69%	-	71%
Timely Help 'Always' Received	300+	65%	-	64%
Would Definitely Recommend Hospital	300+	74%	-	69%

Surgical Hospital of Oklahoma

100 Southeast 59th Street　Phone: 405-634-9300
Oklahoma City, OK 73129
Type: Acute Care Hospitals　Emergency Services: Yes
Ownership: Proprietary　Beds: 12

Key Personnel:
CEO/President. . . . . Phil Ross

Measure	Cases	This Hosp.	State Avg.	U.S. Avg.
Heart Attack Care				
ACE Inhibitor or ARB for LVSD[5]	0	-	95%	96%
Aspirin at Arrival[5]	0	-	98%	99%
Aspirin at Discharge[5]	0	-	98%	98%
Beta Blocker at Discharge[5]	0	-	98%	98%
Fibrinolytic Medication Timing[5]	0	-	42%	55%
PCI Within 90 Minutes of Arrival[5]	0	-	88%	90%
Smoking Cessation Advice[5]	0	-	100%	99%
Chest Pain/Possible Heart Attack Care				
Aspirin at Arrival[5]	0	-	94%	95%
Median Time to ECG (minutes)[5]	0	-	9	8
Median Time to Transfer (minutes)[5]	0	-	75	61
Fibrinolytic Medication Timing[5]	0	-	50%	54%
Heart Failure Care				
ACE Inhibitor or ARB for LVSD[5]	0	-	94%	94%
Discharge Instructions[5]	0	-	85%	88%
Evaluation of LVS Function[5]	0	-	94%	98%
Smoking Cessation Advice[5]	0	-	97%	98%
Pneumonia Care				
Appropriate Initial Antibiotic[5]	0	-	91%	92%
Blood Culture Timing[5]	0	-	96%	96%
Influenza Vaccine[5]	0	-	89%	91%
Initial Antibiotic Timing[5]	0	-	95%	95%
Pneumococcal Vaccine[5]	0	-	91%	93%
Smoking Cessation Advice[5]	0	-	95%	97%
Surgical Care Improvement Project				
Appropriate VTP Within 24 Hours[1,2]	15	87%	91%	92%
Appropriate Hair Removal[2]	179	99%	100%	99%
Appropriate Beta Blocker Usage[1,2]	21	67%	91%	93%
Controlled Postoperative Blood Glucose[2]	0	-	95%	93%
Prophylactic Antibiotic Timing[2]	151	91%	97%	97%
Prophylactic Antibiotic Timing (Outpatient)	207	97%	93%	92%
Prophylactic Antibiotic Selection[2]	151	97%	98%	97%
Prophylactic Antibiotic Select. (Outpatient)	208	97%	95%	94%
Prophylactic Antibiotic Stopped[2]	151	77%	94%	94%
Recommended VTP Ordered[1,2]	15	87%	94%	94%
Urinary Catheter Removal[2]	26	100%	87%	90%
Children's Asthma Care				
Received Systemic Corticosteroids	-	-	-	100%
Received Home Management Plan	-	-	-	71%
Received Reliever Medication	-	-	-	100%
Use of Medical Imaging				
Combination Abdominal CT Scan[5]	0	-	0.372	0.191
Combination Chest CT Scan[5]	0	-	0.134	0.054
Follow-up Mammogram/Ultrasound[5]	0	-	8%	8.4%
MRI for Low Back Pain[5]	0	-	34.3%	32.7%
Survey of Patients' Hospital Experiences				
Area Around Room 'Always' Quiet at Night	(a)	83%	-	58%
Doctors 'Always' Communicated Well	(a)	89%	-	80%
Home Recovery Information Given	(a)	83%	-	82%
Hospital Given 9 or 10 on 10 Point Scale	(a)	80%	-	67%
Meds 'Always' Explained Before Given	(a)	68%	-	60%
Nurses 'Always' Communicated Well	(a)	83%	-	76%
Pain 'Always' Well Controlled	(a)	75%	-	69%
Room and Bathroom 'Always' Clean	(a)	79%	-	71%
Timely Help 'Always' Received	(a)	80%	-	64%
Would Definitely Recommend Hospital	(a)	80%	-	69%

Okmulgee Memorial Hospital

1401 Morris Drive　Phone: 918-756-4233
Okmulgee, OK 74447　Fax: 918-756-5968
URL: www.okmulgeehospital.com
Type: Acute Care Hospitals　Emergency Services: Yes
Ownership: Voluntary Non-Profit - Private　Beds: 66

Key Personnel:
CEO/President. . . . . Rex Jones
Chief of Medical Staff . . . . Tim Sanford, DO
Infection Control. . . . . Kahty Machetta, RN
Operating Room. . . . . Sara Davis, RN
Quality Assurance . . . . Anita Raley
Radiology. . . . . Dean Fullingim, DO
Emergency Room . . . . Kim Gage, MD

Measure	Cases	This Hosp.	State Avg.	U.S. Avg.
Heart Attack Care				
ACE Inhibitor or ARB for LVSD	0	-	95%	96%
Aspirin at Arrival[1]	2	100%	98%	99%
Aspirin at Discharge[1]	1	0%	98%	98%
Beta Blocker at Discharge[1]	1	100%	98%	98%
Fibrinolytic Medication Timing	0	-	42%	55%
PCI Within 90 Minutes of Arrival	0	-	88%	90%
Smoking Cessation Advice	0	-	100%	99%
Chest Pain/Possible Heart Attack Care				
Aspirin at Arrival	166	87%	94%	95%
Median Time to ECG (minutes)	174	10	9	8
Median Time to Transfer (minutes)[1,3]	3	83	75	61
Fibrinolytic Medication Timing[1]	9	44%	50%	54%
Heart Failure Care				
ACE Inhibitor or ARB for LVSD	25	72%	94%	94%
Discharge Instructions	49	67%	85%	88%
Evaluation of LVS Function	65	85%	94%	98%
Smoking Cessation Advice[1]	19	84%	97%	98%
Pneumonia Care				
Appropriate Initial Antibiotic	56	96%	91%	92%
Blood Culture Timing	48	90%	96%	96%
Influenza Vaccine	38	87%	89%	91%
Initial Antibiotic Timing	84	93%	95%	95%
Pneumococcal Vaccine	52	92%	91%	93%
Smoking Cessation Advice	27	100%	95%	97%
Surgical Care Improvement Project				
Appropriate VTP Within 24 Hours[1]	3	100%	91%	92%
Appropriate Hair Removal[1]	9	100%	100%	99%
Appropriate Beta Blocker Usage[1]	3	67%	91%	93%
Controlled Postoperative Blood Glucose	0	-	95%	93%
Prophylactic Antibiotic Timing[1]	5	100%	97%	97%
Prophylactic Antibiotic Timing (Outpatient)[1,3]	14	86%	93%	92%
Prophylactic Antibiotic Selection[1]	5	100%	98%	97%
Prophylactic Antibiotic Select. (Outpatient)[1,3]	12	100%	95%	94%
Prophylactic Antibiotic Stopped[1]	5	80%	94%	94%
Recommended VTP Ordered[1]	3	100%	94%	94%
Urinary Catheter Removal	0	-	87%	90%
Children's Asthma Care				
Received Systemic Corticosteroids	-	-	-	100%
Received Home Management Plan	-	-	-	71%
Received Reliever Medication	-	-	-	100%
Use of Medical Imaging				
Combination Abdominal CT Scan	147	0.401	0.372	0.191
Combination Chest CT Scan	71	0.085	0.134	0.054
Follow-up Mammogram/Ultrasound	314	2.5%	8%	8.4%
MRI for Low Back Pain[5]	0	-	34.3%	32.7%
Survey of Patients' Hospital Experiences				
Area Around Room 'Always' Quiet at Night	(a)	55%	-	58%
Doctors 'Always' Communicated Well	(a)	80%	-	80%
Home Recovery Information Given	(a)	76%	-	82%
Hospital Given 9 or 10 on 10 Point Scale	(a)	57%	-	67%
Meds 'Always' Explained Before Given	(a)	48%	-	60%
Nurses 'Always' Communicated Well	(a)	72%	-	76%
Pain 'Always' Well Controlled	(a)	66%	-	69%
Room and Bathroom 'Always' Clean	(a)	58%	-	71%
Timely Help 'Always' Received	(a)	66%	-	64%
Would Definitely Recommend Hospital	(a)	51%	-	69%

NOTE: Hospital profiles are in alphabetical order by state, then city, then hospital within the city; Rankings exclude hospitals with less than 25 cases except for patient surveys which excludes hospitals with less than 100 cases; (a) 100–299 cases; (1) The number of cases is too small to be sure how well a hospital is performing; (2) The hospital indicated that the data submitted for this measure were based on a sample of cases; (3) Data was collected during a shorter time period (fewer quarters) than the maximum possible time for this measure; (4) Suppressed for one or more quarters by CMS; (5) No data is available from the hospital for this measure; (6) Fewer than 100 patients completed the HCAHPS survey. Use these rates with caution, as the number of surveys may be too low to reliably assess hospital performance; (7) Survey results are based on less than 12 months of data; (8) Survey results are not available for this reporting period; (9) No or very few patients were eligible for the HCAHPS survey. The scores shown, if any, reflect a very small number of surveys; (10) A state average was not calculated because too few hospitals in the state submitted data; (11) There were discrepancies in the data collection process; Please refer to the User's Guide for a full explanation of data.

Bailey Medical Center

10502 North 110th East Ave
Owasso, OK 74055
Phone: 918-376-8000
URL: www.baileymedicalcenter.com
Type: Acute Care Hospitals
Emergency Services: Yes
Ownership: Government - Local
Beds: 73

Key Personnel:
Cardiology . . . . Eric G Auerbach, MD
Pediatrics. . . . . Lauri S Blesch, MD
Pulmonary Disease . . . . Mark P Britt, MD

Measure	Cases	This Hosp.	State Avg.	U.S. Avg.
Heart Attack Care				
ACE Inhibitor or ARB for LVSD[1]	1	100%	95%	96%
Aspirin at Arrival[1]	4	100%	98%	99%
Aspirin at Discharge[1]	4	100%	98%	98%
Beta Blocker at Discharge[1]	5	100%	98%	98%
Fibrinolytic Medication Timing	0	-	42%	55%
PCI Within 90 Minutes of Arrival	0	-	88%	90%
Smoking Cessation Advice	0	-	100%	99%
Chest Pain/Possible Heart Attack Care				
Aspirin at Arrival	134	93%	94%	95%
Median Time to ECG (minutes)	136	12	9	8
Median Time to Transfer (minutes)[1,3]	2	90	75	61
Fibrinolytic Medication Timing[1]	1	100%	50%	54%
Heart Failure Care				
ACE Inhibitor or ARB for LVSD[1]	5	40%	94%	94%
Discharge Instructions[1]	10	80%	85%	88%
Evaluation of LVS Function[1]	15	100%	94%	98%
Smoking Cessation Advice[1]	1	100%	97%	98%
Pneumonia Care				
Appropriate Initial Antibiotic	30	90%	91%	92%
Blood Culture Timing	27	96%	96%	96%
Influenza Vaccine[1]	21	100%	89%	91%
Initial Antibiotic Timing	41	93%	95%	95%
Pneumococcal Vaccine	25	100%	91%	93%
Smoking Cessation Advice[1]	11	100%	95%	97%
Surgical Care Improvement Project				
Appropriate VTP Within 24 Hours	48	94%	91%	92%
Appropriate Hair Removal	136	100%	100%	99%
Appropriate Beta Blocker Usage	32	69%	91%	93%
Controlled Postoperative Blood Glucose	0	-	95%	93%
Prophylactic Antibiotic Timing	108	98%	97%	97%
Prophylactic Antibiotic Timing (Outpatient)[1]	20	100%	93%	92%
Prophylactic Antibiotic Selection	108	97%	98%	97%
Prophylactic Antibiotic Select. (Outpatient)[1]	20	95%	95%	94%
Prophylactic Antibiotic Stopped	105	95%	94%	94%
Recommended VTP Ordered	48	96%	94%	94%
Urinary Catheter Removal	27	93%	87%	90%
Children's Asthma Care				
Received Systemic Corticosteroids	-	-	-	100%
Received Home Management Plan	-	-	-	71%
Received Reliever Medication	-	-	-	100%
Use of Medical Imaging				
Combination Abdominal CT Scan	155	0.310	0.372	0.191
Combination Chest CT Scan	106	0.311	0.134	0.054
Follow-up Mammogram/Ultrasound	140	9.3%	8%	8.4%
MRI for Low Back Pain	73	35.6%	34.3%	32.7%
Survey of Patients' Hospital Experiences				
Area Around Room 'Always' Quiet at Night	(a)	77%	-	58%
Doctors 'Always' Communicated Well	(a)	86%	-	80%
Home Recovery Information Given	(a)	86%	-	82%
Hospital Given 9 or 10 on 10 Point Scale	(a)	84%	-	67%
Meds 'Always' Explained Before Given	(a)	69%	-	60%
Nurses 'Always' Communicated Well	(a)	82%	-	76%
Pain 'Always' Well Controlled	(a)	73%	-	69%
Room and Bathroom 'Always' Clean	(a)	77%	-	71%
Timely Help 'Always' Received	(a)	69%	-	64%
Would Definitely Recommend Hospital	(a)	85%	-	69%

Saint John Owasso

12451 East 100th Street North
Owasso, OK 74055
Phone: 918-274-5000
URL: www.stjohnowasso.com
Type: Acute Care Hospitals
Emergency Services: Yes
Ownership: Voluntary Non-Profit - Private

Key Personnel:
President/CEO. . . . . M Therese Gottschalk

Measure	Cases	This Hosp.	State Avg.	U.S. Avg.
Heart Attack Care				
ACE Inhibitor or ARB for LVSD	0	-	95%	96%
Aspirin at Arrival[1]	9	100%	98%	99%
Aspirin at Discharge[1]	4	100%	98%	98%
Beta Blocker at Discharge[1]	4	100%	98%	98%
Fibrinolytic Medication Timing	0	-	42%	55%
PCI Within 90 Minutes of Arrival	0	-	88%	90%
Smoking Cessation Advice[1]	1	100%	100%	99%
Chest Pain/Possible Heart Attack Care				
Aspirin at Arrival	233	96%	94%	95%
Median Time to ECG (minutes)	239	5	9	8
Median Time to Transfer (minutes)[1]	16	53	75	61
Fibrinolytic Medication Timing	0	-	50%	54%
Heart Failure Care				
ACE Inhibitor or ARB for LVSD[1]	9	78%	94%	94%
Discharge Instructions	34	76%	85%	88%
Evaluation of LVS Function	44	91%	94%	98%
Smoking Cessation Advice[1]	13	100%	97%	98%
Pneumonia Care				
Appropriate Initial Antibiotic	76	95%	91%	92%
Blood Culture Timing	79	94%	96%	96%
Influenza Vaccine	46	89%	89%	91%
Initial Antibiotic Timing	92	98%	95%	95%
Pneumococcal Vaccine	70	93%	91%	93%
Smoking Cessation Advice	28	93%	95%	97%
Surgical Care Improvement Project				
Appropriate VTP Within 24 Hours	26	92%	91%	92%
Appropriate Hair Removal	163	98%	100%	99%
Appropriate Beta Blocker Usage[1]	23	43%	91%	93%
Controlled Postoperative Blood Glucose	0	-	95%	93%
Prophylactic Antibiotic Timing	136	97%	97%	97%
Prophylactic Antibiotic Timing (Outpatient)	37	89%	93%	92%
Prophylactic Antibiotic Selection	137	98%	98%	97%
Prophylactic Antibiotic Select. (Outpatient)	35	100%	95%	94%
Prophylactic Antibiotic Stopped	133	88%	94%	94%
Recommended VTP Ordered	26	96%	94%	94%
Urinary Catheter Removal[1]	2	50%	87%	90%
Children's Asthma Care				
Received Systemic Corticosteroids	-	-	-	100%
Received Home Management Plan	-	-	-	71%
Received Reliever Medication	-	-	-	100%
Use of Medical Imaging				
Combination Abdominal CT Scan	310	0.435	0.372	0.191
Combination Chest CT Scan	232	0.478	0.134	0.054
Follow-up Mammogram/Ultrasound	287	11.1%	8%	8.4%
MRI for Low Back Pain	57	42.1%	34.3%	32.7%
Survey of Patients' Hospital Experiences				
Area Around Room 'Always' Quiet at Night	300+	66%	-	58%
Doctors 'Always' Communicated Well	300+	83%	-	80%
Home Recovery Information Given	300+	79%	-	82%
Hospital Given 9 or 10 on 10 Point Scale	300+	77%	-	67%
Meds 'Always' Explained Before Given	300+	64%	-	60%
Nurses 'Always' Communicated Well	300+	79%	-	76%
Pain 'Always' Well Controlled	300+	74%	-	69%
Room and Bathroom 'Always' Clean	300+	75%	-	71%
Timely Help 'Always' Received	300+	66%	-	64%
Would Definitely Recommend Hospital	300+	84%	-	69%

Pauls Valley General Hospital

100 Valley Drive
Pauls Valley, OK 73075
Phone: 405-238-5501
Fax: 405-238-5926
URL: www.pvgh.net
Type: Acute Care Hospitals
Emergency Services: Yes
Ownership: Govt - Hospital Dist/Auth
Beds: 72

Key Personnel:
CEO/President. . . . . Charles W Johnston
Chief of Medical Staff. . . . . Charles H Mitchell, MD
Operating Room. . . . . Marty Bashaw, CRNA
Radiology. . . . . Mike Welborn

Measure	Cases	This Hosp.	State Avg.	U.S. Avg.
Heart Attack Care				
ACE Inhibitor or ARB for LVSD	0	-	95%	96%
Aspirin at Arrival[1]	3	67%	98%	99%
Aspirin at Discharge[1]	3	67%	98%	98%
Beta Blocker at Discharge[1]	3	67%	98%	98%
Fibrinolytic Medication Timing	0	-	42%	55%
PCI Within 90 Minutes of Arrival	0	-	88%	90%
Smoking Cessation Advice	0	-	100%	99%
Chest Pain/Possible Heart Attack Care				
Aspirin at Arrival	68	99%	94%	95%
Median Time to ECG (minutes)	75	10	9	8
Median Time to Transfer (minutes)[1,3]	5	117	75	61
Fibrinolytic Medication Timing[1]	5	20%	50%	54%
Heart Failure Care				
ACE Inhibitor or ARB for LVSD[1]	22	95%	94%	94%
Discharge Instructions	58	78%	85%	88%
Evaluation of LVS Function	85	82%	94%	98%
Smoking Cessation Advice[1]	12	100%	97%	98%
Pneumonia Care				
Appropriate Initial Antibiotic	56	100%	91%	92%
Blood Culture Timing	56	86%	96%	96%
Influenza Vaccine	62	97%	89%	91%
Initial Antibiotic Timing	84	95%	95%	95%
Pneumococcal Vaccine	82	93%	91%	93%
Smoking Cessation Advice	25	84%	95%	97%
Surgical Care Improvement Project				
Appropriate VTP Within 24 Hours[1]	14	64%	91%	92%
Appropriate Hair Removal[1]	21	100%	100%	99%
Appropriate Beta Blocker Usage[1]	8	75%	91%	93%
Controlled Postoperative Blood Glucose	0	-	95%	93%
Prophylactic Antibiotic Timing[1]	7	86%	97%	97%
Prophylactic Antibiotic Timing (Outpatient)[5]	0	-	93%	92%
Prophylactic Antibiotic Selection[1]	9	100%	98%	97%
Prophylactic Antibiotic Select. (Outpatient)[5]	0	-	95%	94%
Prophylactic Antibiotic Stopped[1]	7	57%	94%	94%
Recommended VTP Ordered[1]	15	60%	94%	94%
Urinary Catheter Removal[1]	4	100%	87%	90%
Children's Asthma Care				
Received Systemic Corticosteroids	-	-	-	100%
Received Home Management Plan	-	-	-	71%
Received Reliever Medication	-	-	-	100%
Use of Medical Imaging				
Combination Abdominal CT Scan	150	0.093	0.372	0.191
Combination Chest CT Scan	59	0.017	0.134	0.054
Follow-up Mammogram/Ultrasound	283	4.6%	8%	8.4%
MRI for Low Back Pain[5]	0	-	34.3%	32.7%
Survey of Patients' Hospital Experiences				
Area Around Room 'Always' Quiet at Night	300+	59%	-	58%
Doctors 'Always' Communicated Well	300+	87%	-	80%
Home Recovery Information Given	300+	81%	-	82%
Hospital Given 9 or 10 on 10 Point Scale	300+	66%	-	67%
Meds 'Always' Explained Before Given	300+	61%	-	60%
Nurses 'Always' Communicated Well	300+	78%	-	76%
Pain 'Always' Well Controlled	300+	72%	-	69%
Room and Bathroom 'Always' Clean	300+	76%	-	71%
Timely Help 'Always' Received	300+	69%	-	64%
Would Definitely Recommend Hospital	300+	62%	-	69%

NOTE: Hospital profiles are in alphabetical order by state, then city, then hospital within the city; Rankings exclude hospitals with less than 25 cases except for patient surveys which excludes hospitals with less than 100 cases; (a) 100–299 cases; (1) The number of cases is too small to be sure how well a hospital is performing; (2) The hospital indicated that the data submitted for this measure were based on a sample of cases; (3) Data was collected during a shorter time period (fewer quarters) than the maximum possible time for this measure; (4) Suppressed for one or more quarters by CMS; (5) No data is available from the hospital for this measure; (6) Fewer than 100 patients completed the HCAHPS survey. Use these rates with caution, as the number of surveys may be too low to reliably assess hospital performance; (7) Survey results are based on less than 12 months of data; (8) Survey results are not available for this reporting period; (9) No or very few patients were eligible for the HCAHPS survey. The scores shown, if any, reflect a very small number of surveys; (10) A state average was not calculated because too few hospitals in the state submitted data; (11) There were discrepancies in the data collection process; Please refer to the User's Guide for a full explanation of data.

Pawhuska Hospital

1101 East 15th Street
Pawhuska, OK 74056
Phone: 918-287-3232
Fax: 918-287-5145
Type: Critical Access Hospitals
Emergency Services: Yes
Ownership: Proprietary
Beds: 15

Key Personnel:
Chief of Medical Staff.......... Mike Priest, DO
Infection Control.............. Gertrude Greghoff
Quality Assurance .... Karin Arrow Smith
Emergency Room .... Kelly Eaton, RN

Measure	Cases	This Hosp.	State Avg.	U.S. Avg.
Heart Attack Care				
ACE Inhibitor or ARB for LVSD[3]	0	-	95%	96%
Aspirin at Arrival[1,3]	1	0%	98%	99%
Aspirin at Discharge[3]	0	-	98%	98%
Beta Blocker at Discharge[3]	0	-	98%	98%
Fibrinolytic Medication Timing[3]	0	-	42%	55%
PCI Within 90 Minutes of Arrival[3]	0	-	88%	90%
Smoking Cessation Advice[3]	0	-	100%	99%
Chest Pain/Possible Heart Attack Care				
Aspirin at Arrival	-	-	94%	95%
Median Time to ECG (minutes)	-	-	9	8
Median Time to Transfer (minutes)	-	-	75	61
Fibrinolytic Medication Timing	-	-	50%	54%
Heart Failure Care				
ACE Inhibitor or ARB for LVSD[3]	0	-	94%	94%
Discharge Instructions[3]	0	-	85%	88%
Evaluation of LVS Function[1,3]	2	0%	94%	98%
Smoking Cessation Advice[3]	0	-	97%	98%
Pneumonia Care				
Appropriate Initial Antibiotic[1]	4	50%	91%	92%
Blood Culture Timing	0	-	96%	96%
Influenza Vaccine[1]	3	0%	89%	91%
Initial Antibiotic Timing[1]	1	100%	95%	95%
Pneumococcal Vaccine[1]	6	0%	91%	93%
Smoking Cessation Advice[1]	1	100%	95%	97%
Surgical Care Improvement Project				
Appropriate VTP Within 24 Hours[5]	0	-	91%	92%
Appropriate Hair Removal[5]	0	-	100%	99%
Appropriate Beta Blocker Usage[5]	0	-	91%	93%
Controlled Postoperative Blood Glucose[5]	0	-	95%	93%
Prophylactic Antibiotic Timing[5]	0	-	97%	97%
Prophylactic Antibiotic Timing (Outpatient)	-	-	93%	92%
Prophylactic Antibiotic Selection[5]	0	-	98%	97%
Prophylactic Antibiotic Select. (Outpatient)	-	-	95%	94%
Prophylactic Antibiotic Stopped[5]	0	-	94%	94%
Recommended VTP Ordered[5]	0	-	94%	94%
Urinary Catheter Removal[5]	0	-	87%	90%
Children's Asthma Care				
Received Systemic Corticosteroids	-	-	-	100%
Received Home Management Plan	-	-	-	71%
Received Reliever Medication	-	-	-	100%
Use of Medical Imaging				
Combination Abdominal CT Scan	-	-	0.372	0.191
Combination Chest CT Scan	-	-	0.134	0.054
Follow-up Mammogram/Ultrasound	-	-	8%	8.4%
MRI for Low Back Pain	-	-	34.3%	32.7%
Survey of Patients' Hospital Experiences				
Area Around Room 'Always' Quiet at Night[8]	-	-	-	58%
Doctors 'Always' Communicated Well[8]	-	-	-	80%
Home Recovery Information Given[8]	-	-	-	82%
Hospital Given 9 or 10 on 10 Point Scale[8]	-	-	-	67%
Meds 'Always' Explained Before Given[8]	-	-	-	60%
Nurses 'Always' Communicated Well[8]	-	-	-	76%
Pain 'Always' Well Controlled[8]	-	-	-	69%
Room and Bathroom 'Always' Clean[8]	-	-	-	71%
Timely Help 'Always' Received[8]	-	-	-	64%
Would Definitely Recommend Hospital[8]	-	-	-	69%

Perry Memorial Hospital

501 Fourteenth Street
Perry, OK 73077
Phone: 580-336-3541
Fax: 580-336-7209
URL: www.pmh-ok.org
Type: Acute Care Hospitals
Emergency Services: Yes
Ownership: Govt - Hospital Dist/Auth
Beds: 28

Key Personnel:
Radiology.................... James Bullen

Measure	Cases	This Hosp.	State Avg.	U.S. Avg.
Heart Attack Care				
ACE Inhibitor or ARB for LVSD[1,3]	1	100%	95%	96%
Aspirin at Arrival[1,3]	3	100%	98%	99%
Aspirin at Discharge[1,3]	3	67%	98%	98%
Beta Blocker at Discharge[1,3]	3	100%	98%	98%
Fibrinolytic Medication Timing[3]	0	-	42%	55%
PCI Within 90 Minutes of Arrival[3]	0	-	88%	90%
Smoking Cessation Advice[1,3]	1	0%	100%	99%
Chest Pain/Possible Heart Attack Care				
Aspirin at Arrival[1,3]	16	50%	94%	95%
Median Time to ECG (minutes)[1,3]	13	14	9	8
Median Time to Transfer (minutes)[1,3]	1	97	75	61
Fibrinolytic Medication Timing[1,3]	3	0%	50%	54%
Heart Failure Care				
ACE Inhibitor or ARB for LVSD[1]	1	100%	94%	94%
Discharge Instructions[1]	13	69%	85%	88%
Evaluation of LVS Function[1]	21	38%	94%	98%
Smoking Cessation Advice[1]	4	100%	97%	98%
Pneumonia Care				
Appropriate Initial Antibiotic[1]	24	88%	91%	92%
Blood Culture Timing[1]	8	50%	96%	96%
Influenza Vaccine[1]	16	88%	89%	91%
Initial Antibiotic Timing	32	91%	95%	95%
Pneumococcal Vaccine	32	84%	91%	93%
Smoking Cessation Advice[1]	11	73%	95%	97%
Surgical Care Improvement Project				
Appropriate VTP Within 24 Hours[1,3]	1	100%	91%	92%
Appropriate Hair Removal[1,3]	2	100%	100%	99%
Appropriate Beta Blocker Usage[1,3]	1	100%	91%	93%
Controlled Postoperative Blood Glucose[3]	0	-	95%	93%
Prophylactic Antibiotic Timing[3]	0	-	97%	97%
Prophylactic Antibiotic Timing (Outpatient)[5]	0	-	93%	92%
Prophylactic Antibiotic Selection[3]	0	-	98%	97%
Prophylactic Antibiotic Select. (Outpatient)[5]	0	-	95%	94%
Prophylactic Antibiotic Stopped[3]	0	-	94%	94%
Recommended VTP Ordered[1,3]	2	50%	94%	94%
Urinary Catheter Removal[5]	0	-	87%	90%
Children's Asthma Care				
Received Systemic Corticosteroids	-	-	-	100%
Received Home Management Plan	-	-	-	71%
Received Reliever Medication	-	-	-	100%
Use of Medical Imaging				
Combination Abdominal CT Scan[1]	42	0.048	0.372	0.191
Combination Chest CT Scan[1]	11	0.000	0.134	0.054
Follow-up Mammogram/Ultrasound	199	2.0%	8%	8.4%
MRI for Low Back Pain[1]	8	37.5%	34.3%	32.7%
Survey of Patients' Hospital Experiences				
Area Around Room 'Always' Quiet at Night	(a)	66%	-	58%
Doctors 'Always' Communicated Well	(a)	82%	-	80%
Home Recovery Information Given	(a)	86%	-	82%
Hospital Given 9 or 10 on 10 Point Scale	(a)	75%	-	67%
Meds 'Always' Explained Before Given	(a)	64%	-	60%
Nurses 'Always' Communicated Well	(a)	82%	-	76%
Pain 'Always' Well Controlled	(a)	71%	-	69%
Room and Bathroom 'Always' Clean	(a)	82%	-	71%
Timely Help 'Always' Received	(a)	72%	-	64%
Would Definitely Recommend Hospital	(a)	67%	-	69%

Ponca City Medical Center

1900 North 14th Street
Ponca City, OK 74601
Phone: 580-765-3321
Fax: 580-765-0341
URL: www.poncamedcenter.com
Type: Acute Care Hospitals
Emergency Services: Yes
Ownership: Proprietary
Beds: 140

Key Personnel:
CEO/President.................. Dennis Barts
Chief of Medical Staff.......... Krishna Vaidya
Coronary Care.................. Jeanne Stara
Infection Control.............. Cheryle Hiebert
Quality Assurance .... Nancy Nebe
Radiology.................... John Hoy
Emergency Room .... Danny Cassidy, MD
Intensive Care Unit............ Jeanne Stara

Measure	Cases	This Hosp.	State Avg.	U.S. Avg.
Heart Attack Care				
ACE Inhibitor or ARB for LVSD[1]	2	100%	95%	96%
Aspirin at Arrival[1]	15	100%	98%	99%
Aspirin at Discharge[1]	10	100%	98%	98%
Beta Blocker at Discharge[1]	9	100%	98%	98%
Fibrinolytic Medication Timing[1]	2	50%	42%	55%
PCI Within 90 Minutes of Arrival	0	-	88%	90%
Smoking Cessation Advice[1]	3	100%	100%	99%
Chest Pain/Possible Heart Attack Care				
Aspirin at Arrival	88	100%	94%	95%
Median Time to ECG (minutes)	90	5	9	8
Median Time to Transfer (minutes)[1,3]	6	108	75	61
Fibrinolytic Medication Timing[1]	5	60%	50%	54%
Heart Failure Care				
ACE Inhibitor or ARB for LVSD[1]	22	95%	94%	94%
Discharge Instructions	77	97%	85%	88%
Evaluation of LVS Function	86	100%	94%	98%
Smoking Cessation Advice[1]	13	100%	97%	98%
Pneumonia Care				
Appropriate Initial Antibiotic	87	99%	91%	92%
Blood Culture Timing	97	100%	96%	96%
Influenza Vaccine	62	97%	89%	91%
Initial Antibiotic Timing	119	98%	95%	95%
Pneumococcal Vaccine	95	100%	91%	93%
Smoking Cessation Advice	59	100%	95%	97%
Surgical Care Improvement Project				
Appropriate VTP Within 24 Hours	154	96%	91%	92%
Appropriate Hair Removal	313	100%	100%	99%
Appropriate Beta Blocker Usage	59	93%	91%	93%
Controlled Postoperative Blood Glucose	0	-	95%	93%
Prophylactic Antibiotic Timing	231	100%	97%	97%
Prophylactic Antibiotic Timing (Outpatient)	78	96%	93%	92%
Prophylactic Antibiotic Selection	231	97%	98%	97%
Prophylactic Antibiotic Select. (Outpatient)	76	97%	95%	94%
Prophylactic Antibiotic Stopped	226	97%	94%	94%
Recommended VTP Ordered	154	98%	94%	94%
Urinary Catheter Removal	66	100%	87%	90%
Children's Asthma Care				
Received Systemic Corticosteroids	-	-	-	100%
Received Home Management Plan	-	-	-	71%
Received Reliever Medication	-	-	-	100%
Use of Medical Imaging				
Combination Abdominal CT Scan	407	0.703	0.372	0.191
Combination Chest CT Scan	277	0.000	0.134	0.054
Follow-up Mammogram/Ultrasound	656	12.2%	8%	8.4%
MRI for Low Back Pain	100	42.0%	34.3%	32.7%
Survey of Patients' Hospital Experiences				
Area Around Room 'Always' Quiet at Night	300+	62%	-	58%
Doctors 'Always' Communicated Well	300+	81%	-	80%
Home Recovery Information Given	300+	85%	-	82%
Hospital Given 9 or 10 on 10 Point Scale	300+	67%	-	67%
Meds 'Always' Explained Before Given	300+	59%	-	60%
Nurses 'Always' Communicated Well	300+	77%	-	76%
Pain 'Always' Well Controlled	300+	70%	-	69%
Room and Bathroom 'Always' Clean	300+	66%	-	71%
Timely Help 'Always' Received	300+	67%	-	64%
Would Definitely Recommend Hospital	300+	60%	-	69%

NOTE: Hospital profiles are in alphabetical order by state, then city, then hospital within the city; Rankings exclude hospitals with less than 25 cases except for patient surveys which excludes hospitals with less than 100 cases; (a) 100–299 cases; (1) The number of cases is too small to be sure how well a hospital is performing; (2) The hospital indicated that the data submitted for this measure were based on a sample of cases; (3) Data was collected during a shorter time period (fewer quarters) than the maximum possible time for this measure; (4) Suppressed for one or more quarters by CMS; (5) No data is available from the hospital for this measure; (6) Fewer than 100 patients completed the HCAHPS survey. Use these rates with caution, as the number of surveys may be too low to reliably assess hospital performance; (7) Survey results are based on less than 12 months of data; (8) Survey results are not available for this reporting period; (9) No or very few patients were eligible for the HCAHPS survey. The scores shown, if any, reflect a very small number of surveys; (10) A state average was not calculated because too few hospitals in the state submitted data; (11) There were discrepancies in the data collection process; Please refer to the User's Guide for a full explanation of data.

Eastern Oklahoma Medical Center

105 Wall Street
Poteau, OK 74953
URL: www.eomchospital.com
Type: Acute Care Hospitals
Ownership: Voluntary Non-Profit - Other

Phone: 918-647-8161
Fax: 918-635-3358
Emergency Services: Yes
Beds: 84

Key Personnel:

CEO/President. . . . . Terry Buckner
Infection Control. . . . . Connie Moody
Operating Room. . . . . Ron Huddleston, RN
Quality Assurance . . . . Connie Moody
Anesthesiology. . . . . Vickie Smalley
Emergency Room . . . . Jonathan Clark, MD
Intensive Care Unit. . . . . Sue Hall

Measure	Cases	This Hosp.	State Avg.	U.S. Avg.
Heart Attack Care				
ACE Inhibitor or ARB for LVSD[1]	1	100%	95%	96%
Aspirin at Arrival[1]	14	79%	98%	99%
Aspirin at Discharge[1]	7	71%	98%	98%
Beta Blocker at Discharge[1]	9	56%	98%	98%
Fibrinolytic Medication Timing	0	-	42%	55%
PCI Within 90 Minutes of Arrival	0	-	88%	90%
Smoking Cessation Advice[1]	1	100%	100%	99%
Chest Pain/Possible Heart Attack Care				
Aspirin at Arrival	26	92%	94%	95%
Median Time to ECG (minutes)	29	6	9	8
Median Time to Transfer (minutes)[1,3]	1	146	75	61
Fibrinolytic Medication Timing[1]	8	88%	50%	54%
Heart Failure Care				
ACE Inhibitor or ARB for LVSD	37	84%	94%	94%
Discharge Instructions	99	61%	85%	88%
Evaluation of LVS Function	119	96%	94%	98%
Smoking Cessation Advice	30	87%	97%	98%
Pneumonia Care				
Appropriate Initial Antibiotic	94	79%	91%	92%
Blood Culture Timing	84	90%	96%	96%
Influenza Vaccine	67	82%	89%	91%
Initial Antibiotic Timing	118	86%	95%	95%
Pneumococcal Vaccine	77	79%	91%	93%
Smoking Cessation Advice	43	88%	95%	97%
Surgical Care Improvement Project				
Appropriate VTP Within 24 Hours[1]	17	65%	91%	92%
Appropriate Hair Removal	56	95%	100%	99%
Appropriate Beta Blocker Usage[1]	10	70%	91%	93%
Controlled Postoperative Blood Glucose	0	-	95%	93%
Prophylactic Antibiotic Timing	36	81%	97%	97%
Prophylactic Antibiotic Timing (Outpatient)[1]	5	40%	93%	92%
Prophylactic Antibiotic Selection	36	72%	98%	97%
Prophylactic Antibiotic Select. (Outpatient)[1]	2	100%	95%	94%
Prophylactic Antibiotic Stopped	36	100%	94%	94%
Recommended VTP Ordered[1]	18	61%	94%	94%
Urinary Catheter Removal[1]	8	88%	87%	90%
Children's Asthma Care				
Received Systemic Corticosteroids	-	-	-	100%
Received Home Management Plan	-	-	-	71%
Received Reliever Medication	-	-	-	100%
Use of Medical Imaging				
Combination Abdominal CT Scan	235	0.166	0.372	0.191
Combination Chest CT Scan	110	0.400	0.134	0.054
Follow-up Mammogram/Ultrasound	143	11.9%	8%	8.4%
MRI for Low Back Pain	36	52.8%	34.3%	32.7%
Survey of Patients' Hospital Experiences				
Area Around Room 'Always' Quiet at Night	(a)	63%	-	58%
Doctors 'Always' Communicated Well	(a)	87%	-	80%
Home Recovery Information Given	(a)	82%	-	82%
Hospital Given 9 or 10 on 10 Point Scale	(a)	58%	-	67%
Meds 'Always' Explained Before Given	(a)	55%	-	60%
Nurses 'Always' Communicated Well	(a)	73%	-	76%
Pain 'Always' Well Controlled	(a)	69%	-	69%
Room and Bathroom 'Always' Clean	(a)	68%	-	71%
Timely Help 'Always' Received	(a)	63%	-	64%
Would Definitely Recommend Hospital	(a)	61%	-	69%

Prague Community Hospital

1322 Klabsuba Avenue
Prague, OK 74864
URL: www.praguehospital.com
Type: Critical Access Hospitals
Ownership: Voluntary Non-Profit - Private

Phone: 405-567-4922
Fax: 405-567-4290
Emergency Services: Yes
Beds: 25

Key Personnel:

CEO/President. . . . . Joan Walters
Chief of Medical Staff . . . . Bonnie Bennett
Quality Assurance . . . . Joan Walters
Radiology. . . . . Bates
Emergency Room . . . . Alexander Frank MD

Measure	Cases	This Hosp.	State Avg.	U.S. Avg.
Heart Attack Care				
ACE Inhibitor or ARB for LVSD[5]	0	-	95%	96%
Aspirin at Arrival[5]	0	-	98%	99%
Aspirin at Discharge[5]	0	-	98%	98%
Beta Blocker at Discharge[5]	0	-	98%	98%
Fibrinolytic Medication Timing[5]	0	-	42%	55%
PCI Within 90 Minutes of Arrival[5]	0	-	88%	90%
Smoking Cessation Advice[5]	0	-	100%	99%
Chest Pain/Possible Heart Attack Care				
Aspirin at Arrival	-	-	94%	95%
Median Time to ECG (minutes)	-	-	9	8
Median Time to Transfer (minutes)	-	-	75	61
Fibrinolytic Medication Timing	-	-	50%	54%
Heart Failure Care				
ACE Inhibitor or ARB for LVSD[3]	0	-	94%	94%
Discharge Instructions[1,3]	5	60%	85%	88%
Evaluation of LVS Function[1,3]	4	25%	94%	98%
Smoking Cessation Advice[3]	0	-	97%	98%
Pneumonia Care				
Appropriate Initial Antibiotic[1,3]	18	100%	91%	92%
Blood Culture Timing[1,3]	10	90%	96%	96%
Influenza Vaccine[1]	9	78%	89%	91%
Initial Antibiotic Timing[1,3]	17	94%	95%	95%
Pneumococcal Vaccine[1,3]	13	92%	91%	93%
Smoking Cessation Advice[1,3]	3	100%	95%	97%
Surgical Care Improvement Project				
Appropriate VTP Within 24 Hours[5]	0	-	91%	92%
Appropriate Hair Removal[5]	0	-	100%	99%
Appropriate Beta Blocker Usage[5]	0	-	91%	93%
Controlled Postoperative Blood Glucose[5]	0	-	95%	93%
Prophylactic Antibiotic Timing[5]	0	-	97%	97%
Prophylactic Antibiotic Timing (Outpatient)	-	-	93%	92%
Prophylactic Antibiotic Selection[5]	0	-	98%	97%
Prophylactic Antibiotic Select. (Outpatient)	-	-	95%	94%
Prophylactic Antibiotic Stopped[5]	0	-	94%	94%
Recommended VTP Ordered[5]	0	-	94%	94%
Urinary Catheter Removal[5]	0	-	87%	90%
Children's Asthma Care				
Received Systemic Corticosteroids	-	-	-	100%
Received Home Management Plan	-	-	-	71%
Received Reliever Medication	-	-	-	100%
Use of Medical Imaging				
Combination Abdominal CT Scan	-	-	0.372	0.191
Combination Chest CT Scan	-	-	0.134	0.054
Follow-up Mammogram/Ultrasound	-	-	8%	8.4%
MRI for Low Back Pain	-	-	34.3%	32.7%
Survey of Patients' Hospital Experiences				
Area Around Room 'Always' Quiet at Night[8]	-	-	-	58%
Doctors 'Always' Communicated Well[8]	-	-	-	80%
Home Recovery Information Given[8]	-	-	-	82%
Hospital Given 9 or 10 on 10 Point Scale[8]	-	-	-	67%
Meds 'Always' Explained Before Given[8]	-	-	-	60%
Nurses 'Always' Communicated Well[8]	-	-	-	76%
Pain 'Always' Well Controlled[8]	-	-	-	69%
Room and Bathroom 'Always' Clean[8]	-	-	-	71%
Timely Help 'Always' Received[8]	-	-	-	64%
Would Definitely Recommend Hospital[8]	-	-	-	69%

Integris Mayes County Medical Center

111 North Bailey Street
Pryor, OK 74361
E-mail: white@integris-health.com
URL: www.integris-health.com
Type: Acute Care Hospitals
Ownership: Voluntary Non-Profit - Other

Phone: 918-825-1600
Fax: 918-825-7668
Emergency Services: Yes
Beds: 73

Key Personnel:

Chief of Medical Staff . . . . Paul Battles, DO
Quality Assurance . . . . Jean Poppino
Radiology. . . . . Steve Davenport
Emergency Room . . . . Chris DeLong, DO

Measure	Cases	This Hosp.	State Avg.	U.S. Avg.
Heart Attack Care				
ACE Inhibitor or ARB for LVSD	0	-	95%	96%
Aspirin at Arrival[1]	3	100%	98%	99%
Aspirin at Discharge[1]	1	100%	98%	98%
Beta Blocker at Discharge[1]	1	100%	98%	98%
Fibrinolytic Medication Timing	0	-	42%	55%
PCI Within 90 Minutes of Arrival	0	-	88%	90%
Smoking Cessation Advice	0	-	100%	99%
Chest Pain/Possible Heart Attack Care				
Aspirin at Arrival	116	97%	94%	95%
Median Time to ECG (minutes)	120	7	9	8
Median Time to Transfer (minutes)[1,3]	2	94	75	61
Fibrinolytic Medication Timing[1]	5	60%	50%	54%
Heart Failure Care				
ACE Inhibitor or ARB for LVSD[1]	12	83%	94%	94%
Discharge Instructions	27	100%	85%	88%
Evaluation of LVS Function	35	100%	94%	98%
Smoking Cessation Advice[1]	5	100%	97%	98%
Pneumonia Care				
Appropriate Initial Antibiotic	38	100%	91%	92%
Blood Culture Timing	74	100%	96%	96%
Influenza Vaccine	47	100%	89%	91%
Initial Antibiotic Timing	59	100%	95%	95%
Pneumococcal Vaccine	59	98%	91%	93%
Smoking Cessation Advice	27	100%	95%	97%
Surgical Care Improvement Project				
Appropriate VTP Within 24 Hours[1]	12	92%	91%	92%
Appropriate Hair Removal	54	100%	100%	99%
Appropriate Beta Blocker Usage[1]	13	100%	91%	93%
Controlled Postoperative Blood Glucose	0	-	95%	93%
Prophylactic Antibiotic Timing	39	97%	97%	97%
Prophylactic Antibiotic Timing (Outpatient)	53	94%	93%	92%
Prophylactic Antibiotic Selection	40	90%	98%	97%
Prophylactic Antibiotic Select. (Outpatient)	50	96%	95%	94%
Prophylactic Antibiotic Stopped	39	100%	94%	94%
Recommended VTP Ordered[1]	12	92%	94%	94%
Urinary Catheter Removal[1]	11	100%	87%	90%
Children's Asthma Care				
Received Systemic Corticosteroids	-	-	-	100%
Received Home Management Plan	-	-	-	71%
Received Reliever Medication	-	-	-	100%
Use of Medical Imaging				
Combination Abdominal CT Scan	334	0.060	0.372	0.191
Combination Chest CT Scan	210	0.038	0.134	0.054
Follow-up Mammogram/Ultrasound	389	8.2%	8%	8.4%
MRI for Low Back Pain	91	34.1%	34.3%	32.7%
Survey of Patients' Hospital Experiences				
Area Around Room 'Always' Quiet at Night	(a)	66%	-	58%
Doctors 'Always' Communicated Well	(a)	85%	-	80%
Home Recovery Information Given	(a)	83%	-	82%
Hospital Given 9 or 10 on 10 Point Scale	(a)	67%	-	67%
Meds 'Always' Explained Before Given	(a)	60%	-	60%
Nurses 'Always' Communicated Well	(a)	77%	-	76%
Pain 'Always' Well Controlled	(a)	70%	-	69%
Room and Bathroom 'Always' Clean	(a)	63%	-	71%
Timely Help 'Always' Received	(a)	70%	-	64%
Would Definitely Recommend Hospital	(a)	58%	-	69%

NOTE: Hospital profiles are in alphabetical order by state, then city, then hospital within the city; Rankings exclude hospitals with less than 25 cases except for patient surveys which excludes hospitals with less than 100 cases; (a) 100–299 cases; (1) The number of cases is too small to be sure how well a hospital is performing; (2) The hospital indicated that the data submitted for this measure were based on a sample of cases; (3) Data was collected during a shorter time period (fewer quarters) than the maximum possible time for this measure; (4) Suppressed for one or more quarters by CMS; (5) No data is available from the hospital for this measure; (6) Fewer than 100 patients completed the HCAHPS survey. Use these rates with caution, as the number of surveys may be too low to reliably assess hospital performance; (7) Survey results are based on less than 12 months of data; (8) Survey results are not available for this reporting period; (9) No or very few patients were eligible for the HCAHPS survey. The scores shown, if any, reflect a very small number of surveys; (10) A state average was not calculated because too few hospitals in the state submitted data; (11) There were discrepancies in the data collection process; Please refer to the User's Guide for a full explanation of data.

Purcell Municipal Hospital

1500 North Green Avenue
Purcell, OK 73080
Phone: 405-527-6524
Fax: 405-527-6963
Type: Acute Care Hospitals
Emergency Services: Yes
Ownership: Govt - Hospital Dist/Auth
Beds: 39

Key Personnel:
CEO/President. . . . . Curtis Pryor
Chief of Medical Staff . . . . Jill Watson, MD
Infection Control. . . . . Pam Kaiser, RN
Operating Room. . . . . Angela Garrett, RN
Quality Assurance . . . . Pam Kaiser, RN
Emergency Room . . . . Donn A Avila, RN

Measure	Cases	This Hosp.	State Avg.	U.S. Avg.
Heart Attack Care				
ACE Inhibitor or ARB for LVSD[3]	0	-	95%	96%
Aspirin at Arrival[1,3]	1	100%	98%	99%
Aspirin at Discharge[3]	0	-	98%	98%
Beta Blocker at Discharge[3]	0	-	98%	98%
Fibrinolytic Medication Timing[3]	0	-	42%	55%
PCI Within 90 Minutes of Arrival[3]	0	-	88%	90%
Smoking Cessation Advice[3]	0	-	100%	99%
Chest Pain/Possible Heart Attack Care				
Aspirin at Arrival[3]	57	91%	94%	95%
Median Time to ECG (minutes)[3]	61	9	9	8
Median Time to Transfer (minutes)[1,3]	1	135	75	61
Fibrinolytic Medication Timing[1,3]	3	100%	50%	54%
Heart Failure Care				
ACE Inhibitor or ARB for LVSD[1]	9	67%	94%	94%
Discharge Instructions	31	35%	85%	88%
Evaluation of LVS Function	46	85%	94%	98%
Smoking Cessation Advice[1]	9	56%	97%	98%
Pneumonia Care				
Appropriate Initial Antibiotic	51	80%	91%	92%
Blood Culture Timing	28	82%	96%	96%
Influenza Vaccine	44	55%	89%	91%
Initial Antibiotic Timing	83	95%	95%	95%
Pneumococcal Vaccine	63	44%	91%	93%
Smoking Cessation Advice	27	89%	95%	97%
Surgical Care Improvement Project				
Appropriate VTP Within 24 Hours[3]	0	-	91%	92%
Appropriate Hair Removal[1,3]	2	100%	100%	99%
Appropriate Beta Blocker Usage[3]	0	-	91%	93%
Controlled Postoperative Blood Glucose[3]	0	-	95%	93%
Prophylactic Antibiotic Timing[1,3]	2	100%	97%	97%
Prophylactic Antibiotic Timing (Outpatient)[5]	0	-	93%	92%
Prophylactic Antibiotic Selection[1,3]	2	50%	98%	97%
Prophylactic Antibiotic Select. (Outpatient)[5]	0	-	95%	94%
Prophylactic Antibiotic Stopped[1,3]	2	100%	94%	94%
Recommended VTP Ordered[3]	0	-	94%	94%
Urinary Catheter Removal[3]	0	-	87%	90%
Children's Asthma Care				
Received Systemic Corticosteroids	-	-	-	100%
Received Home Management Plan	-	-	-	71%
Received Reliever Medication	-	-	-	100%
Use of Medical Imaging				
Combination Abdominal CT Scan	109	0.257	0.372	0.191
Combination Chest CT Scan	86	0.035	0.134	0.054
Follow-up Mammogram/Ultrasound[5]	0	-	8%	8.4%
MRI for Low Back Pain[5]	0	-	34.3%	32.7%
Survey of Patients' Hospital Experiences				
Area Around Room 'Always' Quiet at Night	(a)	64%	-	58%
Doctors 'Always' Communicated Well	(a)	90%	-	80%
Home Recovery Information Given	(a)	75%	-	82%
Hospital Given 9 or 10 on 10 Point Scale	(a)	73%	-	67%
Meds 'Always' Explained Before Given	(a)	70%	-	60%
Nurses 'Always' Communicated Well	(a)	86%	-	76%
Pain 'Always' Well Controlled	(a)	73%	-	69%
Room and Bathroom 'Always' Clean	(a)	83%	-	71%
Timely Help 'Always' Received	(a)	66%	-	64%
Would Definitely Recommend Hospital	(a)	72%	-	69%

Sequoyah Memorial Hospital

213 East Redwood
Sallisaw, OK 74955
Phone: 918-774-1100
Fax: 918-774-1142
URL: www.smhok.com
Type: Acute Care Hospitals
Emergency Services: Yes
Ownership: Voluntary Non-Profit - Other
Beds: 41

Key Personnel:
CEO/President. . . . . Chuck Wade
Chief of Medical Staff . . . . William E Wood

Measure	Cases	This Hosp.	State Avg.	U.S. Avg.
Heart Attack Care				
ACE Inhibitor or ARB for LVSD[3]	0	-	95%	96%
Aspirin at Arrival[1,3]	1	100%	98%	99%
Aspirin at Discharge[3]	0	-	98%	98%
Beta Blocker at Discharge[3]	0	-	98%	98%
Fibrinolytic Medication Timing[3]	0	-	42%	55%
PCI Within 90 Minutes of Arrival[3]	0	-	88%	90%
Smoking Cessation Advice[3]	0	-	100%	99%
Chest Pain/Possible Heart Attack Care				
Aspirin at Arrival	100	96%	94%	95%
Median Time to ECG (minutes)	102	9	9	8
Median Time to Transfer (minutes)[5]	0	-	75	61
Fibrinolytic Medication Timing[1]	4	50%	50%	54%
Heart Failure Care				
ACE Inhibitor or ARB for LVSD[1]	9	67%	94%	94%
Discharge Instructions[1]	19	100%	85%	88%
Evaluation of LVS Function	32	97%	94%	98%
Smoking Cessation Advice[1]	10	100%	97%	98%
Pneumonia Care				
Appropriate Initial Antibiotic	61	97%	91%	92%
Blood Culture Timing	63	97%	96%	96%
Influenza Vaccine	43	95%	89%	91%
Initial Antibiotic Timing	100	93%	95%	95%
Pneumococcal Vaccine	55	96%	91%	93%
Smoking Cessation Advice	43	100%	95%	97%
Surgical Care Improvement Project				
Appropriate VTP Within 24 Hours[5]	0	-	91%	92%
Appropriate Hair Removal[5]	0	-	100%	99%
Appropriate Beta Blocker Usage[5]	0	-	91%	93%
Controlled Postoperative Blood Glucose[5]	0	-	95%	93%
Prophylactic Antibiotic Timing[5]	0	-	97%	97%
Prophylactic Antibiotic Timing (Outpatient)[1,3]	2	50%	93%	92%
Prophylactic Antibiotic Selection[5]	0	-	98%	97%
Prophylactic Antibiotic Select. (Outpatient)[1,3]	1	100%	95%	94%
Prophylactic Antibiotic Stopped[5]	0	-	94%	94%
Recommended VTP Ordered[5]	0	-	94%	94%
Urinary Catheter Removal[5]	0	-	87%	90%
Children's Asthma Care				
Received Systemic Corticosteroids	-	-	-	100%
Received Home Management Plan	-	-	-	71%
Received Reliever Medication	-	-	-	100%
Use of Medical Imaging				
Combination Abdominal CT Scan	236	0.030	0.372	0.191
Combination Chest CT Scan	83	0.012	0.134	0.054
Follow-up Mammogram/Ultrasound	199	12.1%	8%	8.4%
MRI for Low Back Pain	51	39.2%	34.3%	32.7%
Survey of Patients' Hospital Experiences				
Area Around Room 'Always' Quiet at Night	300+	75%	-	58%
Doctors 'Always' Communicated Well	300+	84%	-	80%
Home Recovery Information Given	300+	80%	-	82%
Hospital Given 9 or 10 on 10 Point Scale	300+	70%	-	67%
Meds 'Always' Explained Before Given	300+	68%	-	60%
Nurses 'Always' Communicated Well	300+	81%	-	76%
Pain 'Always' Well Controlled	300+	71%	-	69%
Room and Bathroom 'Always' Clean	300+	84%	-	71%
Timely Help 'Always' Received	300+	74%	-	64%
Would Definitely Recommend Hospital	300+	66%	-	69%

Saint John Sapulpa

1004 East Bryan
Sapulpa, OK 74066
Phone: 918-224-4280
Fax: 918-224-4395
Type: Critical Access Hospitals
Emergency Services: Yes
Ownership: Voluntary Non-Profit - Private
Beds: 113

Key Personnel:
CEO/President. . . . . Raymond Replogle
Chief of Medical Staff . . . . Roger Wilson
Infection Control. . . . . Peggy Ault
Operating Room. . . . . Kurt Lane
Quality Assurance . . . . Faye Massey
Emergency Room . . . . Beatrice Lewis, RN

Measure	Cases	This Hosp.	State Avg.	U.S. Avg.
Heart Attack Care				
ACE Inhibitor or ARB for LVSD[5]	0	-	95%	96%
Aspirin at Arrival[5]	0	-	98%	99%
Aspirin at Discharge[5]	0	-	98%	98%
Beta Blocker at Discharge[5]	0	-	98%	98%
Fibrinolytic Medication Timing[5]	0	-	42%	55%
PCI Within 90 Minutes of Arrival[5]	0	-	88%	90%
Smoking Cessation Advice[5]	0	-	100%	99%
Chest Pain/Possible Heart Attack Care				
Aspirin at Arrival	-	-	94%	95%
Median Time to ECG (minutes)	-	-	9	8
Median Time to Transfer (minutes)	-	-	75	61
Fibrinolytic Medication Timing	-	-	50%	54%
Heart Failure Care				
ACE Inhibitor or ARB for LVSD[1]	10	70%	94%	94%
Discharge Instructions	33	15%	85%	88%
Evaluation of LVS Function	39	67%	94%	98%
Smoking Cessation Advice[1]	13	62%	97%	98%
Pneumonia Care				
Appropriate Initial Antibiotic	57	100%	91%	92%
Blood Culture Timing	75	97%	96%	96%
Influenza Vaccine	41	71%	89%	91%
Initial Antibiotic Timing	72	93%	95%	95%
Pneumococcal Vaccine	49	71%	91%	93%
Smoking Cessation Advice	26	69%	95%	97%
Surgical Care Improvement Project				
Appropriate VTP Within 24 Hours[5]	0	-	91%	92%
Appropriate Hair Removal[5]	0	-	100%	99%
Appropriate Beta Blocker Usage[5]	0	-	91%	93%
Controlled Postoperative Blood Glucose[5]	0	-	95%	93%
Prophylactic Antibiotic Timing[5]	0	-	97%	97%
Prophylactic Antibiotic Timing (Outpatient)	-	-	93%	92%
Prophylactic Antibiotic Selection[5]	0	-	98%	97%
Prophylactic Antibiotic Select. (Outpatient)	-	-	95%	94%
Prophylactic Antibiotic Stopped[5]	0	-	94%	94%
Recommended VTP Ordered[5]	0	-	94%	94%
Urinary Catheter Removal[5]	0	-	87%	90%
Children's Asthma Care				
Received Systemic Corticosteroids	-	-	-	100%
Received Home Management Plan	-	-	-	71%
Received Reliever Medication	-	-	-	100%
Use of Medical Imaging				
Combination Abdominal CT Scan	-	-	0.372	0.191
Combination Chest CT Scan	-	-	0.134	0.054
Follow-up Mammogram/Ultrasound	-	-	8%	8.4%
MRI for Low Back Pain	-	-	34.3%	32.7%
Survey of Patients' Hospital Experiences				
Area Around Room 'Always' Quiet at Night[8]	-	-	-	58%
Doctors 'Always' Communicated Well[8]	-	-	-	80%
Home Recovery Information Given[8]	-	-	-	82%
Hospital Given 9 or 10 on 10 Point Scale[8]	-	-	-	67%
Meds 'Always' Explained Before Given[8]	-	-	-	60%
Nurses 'Always' Communicated Well[8]	-	-	-	76%
Pain 'Always' Well Controlled[8]	-	-	-	69%
Room and Bathroom 'Always' Clean[8]	-	-	-	71%
Timely Help 'Always' Received[8]	-	-	-	64%
Would Definitely Recommend Hospital[8]	-	-	-	69%

NOTE: Hospital profiles are in alphabetical order by state, then city, then hospital within the city; Rankings exclude hospitals with less than 25 cases except for patient surveys which excludes hospitals with less than 100 cases; (a) 100–299 cases; (1) The number of cases is too small to be sure how well a hospital is performing; (2) The hospital indicated that the data submitted for this measure were based on a sample of cases; (3) Data was collected during a shorter time period (fewer quarters) than the maximum possible time for this measure; (4) Suppressed for one or more quarters by CMS; (5) No data is available from the hospital for this measure; (6) Fewer than 100 patients completed the HCAHPS survey. Use these rates with caution, as the number of surveys may be too low to reliably assess hospital performance; (7) Survey results are based on less than 12 months of data; (8) Survey results are not available for this reporting period; (9) No or very few patients were eligible for the HCAHPS survey. The scores shown, if any, reflect a very small number of surveys; (10) A state average was not calculated because too few hospitals in the state submitted data; (11) There were discrepancies in the data collection process; Please refer to the User's Guide for a full explanation of data.

Sayre Memorial Hospital

911 Hospital Drive
Sayre, OK 73662
Phone: 580-928-5541
Fax: 580-928-3523
Type: Acute Care Hospitals
Emergency Services: No
Ownership: Govt - Hospital Dist/Auth
Beds: 46

Key Personnel:
Chief of Medical Staff . . . . Mel Robison
Emergency Room . . . . Kenneth Whinery, MD

Measure	Cases	This Hosp.	State Avg.	U.S. Avg.
Heart Attack Care				
ACE Inhibitor or ARB for LVSD[1,3]	1	100%	95%	96%
Aspirin at Arrival[1,3]	4	75%	98%	99%
Aspirin at Discharge[1,3]	4	50%	98%	98%
Beta Blocker at Discharge[1,3]	3	33%	98%	98%
Fibrinolytic Medication Timing[3]	0	-	42%	55%
PCI Within 90 Minutes of Arrival[3]	0	-	88%	90%
Smoking Cessation Advice[1,3]	1	0%	100%	99%
Chest Pain/Possible Heart Attack Care				
Aspirin at Arrival[1]	22	91%	94%	95%
Median Time to ECG (minutes)[1]	24	20	9	8
Median Time to Transfer (minutes)[5]	0	-	75	61
Fibrinolytic Medication Timing[1,3]	1	0%	50%	54%
Heart Failure Care				
ACE Inhibitor or ARB for LVSD[1]	10	60%	94%	94%
Discharge Instructions	33	73%	85%	88%
Evaluation of LVS Function	46	61%	94%	98%
Smoking Cessation Advice[1]	6	67%	97%	98%
Pneumonia Care				
Appropriate Initial Antibiotic	31	97%	91%	92%
Blood Culture Timing[1]	15	93%	96%	96%
Influenza Vaccine	37	84%	89%	91%
Initial Antibiotic Timing	67	93%	95%	95%
Pneumococcal Vaccine	40	90%	91%	93%
Smoking Cessation Advice	27	78%	95%	97%
Surgical Care Improvement Project				
Appropriate VTP Within 24 Hours[5]	0	-	91%	92%
Appropriate Hair Removal[5]	0	-	100%	99%
Appropriate Beta Blocker Usage[5]	0	-	91%	93%
Controlled Postoperative Blood Glucose[5]	0	-	95%	93%
Prophylactic Antibiotic Timing[5]	0	-	97%	97%
Prophylactic Antibiotic Timing (Outpatient)[5]	0	-	93%	92%
Prophylactic Antibiotic Selection[5]	0	-	98%	97%
Prophylactic Antibiotic Select. (Outpatient)[5]	0	-	95%	94%
Prophylactic Antibiotic Stopped[5]	0	-	94%	94%
Recommended VTP Ordered[5]	0	-	94%	94%
Urinary Catheter Removal[5]	0	-	87%	90%
Children's Asthma Care				
Received Systemic Corticosteroids	-	-	-	100%
Received Home Management Plan	-	-	-	71%
Received Reliever Medication	-	-	-	100%
Use of Medical Imaging				
Combination Abdominal CT Scan[1]	45	0.089	0.372	0.191
Combination Chest CT Scan[1]	28	0.071	0.134	0.054
Follow-up Mammogram/Ultrasound[5]	0	-	8%	8.4%
MRI for Low Back Pain[5]	0	-	34.3%	32.7%
Survey of Patients' Hospital Experiences				
Area Around Room 'Always' Quiet at Night	(a)	71%	-	58%
Doctors 'Always' Communicated Well	(a)	90%	-	80%
Home Recovery Information Given	(a)	74%	-	82%
Hospital Given 9 or 10 on 10 Point Scale	(a)	76%	-	67%
Meds 'Always' Explained Before Given	(a)	62%	-	60%
Nurses 'Always' Communicated Well	(a)	77%	-	76%
Pain 'Always' Well Controlled	(a)	76%	-	69%
Room and Bathroom 'Always' Clean	(a)	78%	-	71%
Timely Help 'Always' Received	(a)	70%	-	64%
Would Definitely Recommend Hospital	(a)	74%	-	69%

Seiling Community Hospital

Us Highway 60 Northeast
Seiling, OK 73663
Phone: 580-922-7361
Fax: 580-922-7718
Type: Critical Access Hospitals
Emergency Services: Yes
Ownership: Government - Local
Beds: 18

Key Personnel:
CEO/President . . . . Deryl Gulliford, PhD

Measure	Cases	This Hosp.	State Avg.	U.S. Avg.
Heart Attack Care				
ACE Inhibitor or ARB for LVSD[1,3]	1	100%	95%	96%
Aspirin at Arrival[1,3]	1	100%	98%	99%
Aspirin at Discharge[1,3]	1	100%	98%	98%
Beta Blocker at Discharge[1,3]	1	0%	98%	98%
Fibrinolytic Medication Timing[3]	0	-	42%	55%
PCI Within 90 Minutes of Arrival[3]	0	-	88%	90%
Smoking Cessation Advice[3]	0	-	100%	99%
Chest Pain/Possible Heart Attack Care				
Aspirin at Arrival	-	-	94%	95%
Median Time to ECG (minutes)	-	-	9	8
Median Time to Transfer (minutes)	-	-	75	61
Fibrinolytic Medication Timing	-	-	50%	54%
Heart Failure Care				
ACE Inhibitor or ARB for LVSD[1,3]	2	100%	94%	94%
Discharge Instructions[3]	0	-	85%	88%
Evaluation of LVS Function[1,3]	2	100%	94%	98%
Smoking Cessation Advice[3]	0	-	97%	98%
Pneumonia Care				
Appropriate Initial Antibiotic[1,3]	13	62%	91%	92%
Blood Culture Timing[1,3]	1	100%	96%	96%
Influenza Vaccine[1]	17	71%	89%	91%
Initial Antibiotic Timing[1,3]	9	67%	95%	95%
Pneumococcal Vaccine[1,3]	18	78%	91%	93%
Smoking Cessation Advice[1,3]	2	0%	95%	97%
Surgical Care Improvement Project				
Appropriate VTP Within 24 Hours[5]	0	-	91%	92%
Appropriate Hair Removal[5]	0	-	100%	99%
Appropriate Beta Blocker Usage[5]	0	-	91%	93%
Controlled Postoperative Blood Glucose[5]	0	-	95%	93%
Prophylactic Antibiotic Timing[5]	0	-	97%	97%
Prophylactic Antibiotic Timing (Outpatient)	-	-	93%	92%
Prophylactic Antibiotic Selection[5]	0	-	98%	97%
Prophylactic Antibiotic Select. (Outpatient)	-	-	95%	94%
Prophylactic Antibiotic Stopped[5]	0	-	94%	94%
Recommended VTP Ordered[5]	0	-	94%	94%
Urinary Catheter Removal[5]	0	-	87%	90%
Children's Asthma Care				
Received Systemic Corticosteroids	-	-	-	100%
Received Home Management Plan	-	-	-	71%
Received Reliever Medication	-	-	-	100%
Use of Medical Imaging				
Combination Abdominal CT Scan	-	-	0.372	0.191
Combination Chest CT Scan	-	-	0.134	0.054
Follow-up Mammogram/Ultrasound	-	-	8%	8.4%
MRI for Low Back Pain	-	-	34.3%	32.7%
Survey of Patients' Hospital Experiences				
Area Around Room 'Always' Quiet at Night[8]	-	-	-	58%
Doctors 'Always' Communicated Well[8]	-	-	-	80%
Home Recovery Information Given[8]	-	-	-	82%
Hospital Given 9 or 10 on 10 Point Scale[8]	-	-	-	67%
Meds 'Always' Explained Before Given[8]	-	-	-	60%
Nurses 'Always' Communicated Well[8]	-	-	-	76%
Pain 'Always' Well Controlled[8]	-	-	-	69%
Room and Bathroom 'Always' Clean[8]	-	-	-	71%
Timely Help 'Always' Received[8]	-	-	-	64%
Would Definitely Recommend Hospital[8]	-	-	-	69%

Integris Seminole Medical Center

2401 Wrangler Boulevard
Seminole, OK 74868
Phone: 405-303-4000
Fax: 405-303-4150
URL: www.seminolemedicalcenter.com
Type: Acute Care Hospitals
Emergency Services: Yes
Ownership: Government - Federal
Beds: 32

Key Personnel:
CEO/President . . . . Mike Schuster
Chief of Medical Staff . . . . Rodney McCrory
Infection Control . . . . Troy Sainder, RN
Operating Room . . . . Dana Taylor, RNFA
Quality Assurance . . . . Brenda Swanson
Emergency Room . . . . Mark Macklin, RN
Patient Relations . . . . Darlene Cornelious

Measure	Cases	This Hosp.	State Avg.	U.S. Avg.
Heart Attack Care				
ACE Inhibitor or ARB for LVSD[3]	0	-	95%	96%
Aspirin at Arrival[1,3]	4	100%	98%	99%
Aspirin at Discharge[1,3]	4	100%	98%	98%
Beta Blocker at Discharge[1,3]	3	100%	98%	98%
Fibrinolytic Medication Timing[3]	0	-	42%	55%
PCI Within 90 Minutes of Arrival[3]	0	-	88%	90%
Smoking Cessation Advice[1,3]	1	100%	100%	99%
Chest Pain/Possible Heart Attack Care				
Aspirin at Arrival	106	92%	94%	95%
Median Time to ECG (minutes)	113	14	9	8
Median Time to Transfer (minutes)[5]	0	-	75	61
Fibrinolytic Medication Timing[1]	5	20%	50%	54%
Heart Failure Care				
ACE Inhibitor or ARB for LVSD[1]	10	100%	94%	94%
Discharge Instructions	42	83%	85%	88%
Evaluation of LVS Function	48	94%	94%	98%
Smoking Cessation Advice[1]	9	100%	97%	98%
Pneumonia Care				
Appropriate Initial Antibiotic	58	95%	91%	92%
Blood Culture Timing	69	94%	96%	96%
Influenza Vaccine	39	92%	89%	91%
Initial Antibiotic Timing	82	99%	95%	95%
Pneumococcal Vaccine	52	100%	91%	93%
Smoking Cessation Advice	40	98%	95%	97%
Surgical Care Improvement Project				
Appropriate VTP Within 24 Hours[1]	10	90%	91%	92%
Appropriate Hair Removal[1]	12	100%	100%	99%
Appropriate Beta Blocker Usage[1]	3	33%	91%	93%
Controlled Postoperative Blood Glucose	0	-	95%	93%
Prophylactic Antibiotic Timing[1]	4	50%	97%	97%
Prophylactic Antibiotic Timing (Outpatient)[1]	19	95%	93%	92%
Prophylactic Antibiotic Selection[1]	4	100%	98%	97%
Prophylactic Antibiotic Select. (Outpatient)[1]	18	100%	95%	94%
Prophylactic Antibiotic Stopped[1]	4	50%	94%	94%
Recommended VTP Ordered[1]	10	90%	94%	94%
Urinary Catheter Removal[1]	3	67%	87%	90%
Children's Asthma Care				
Received Systemic Corticosteroids	-	-	-	100%
Received Home Management Plan	-	-	-	71%
Received Reliever Medication	-	-	-	100%
Use of Medical Imaging				
Combination Abdominal CT Scan	115	0.739	0.372	0.191
Combination Chest CT Scan	72	0.819	0.134	0.054
Follow-up Mammogram/Ultrasound	162	6.2%	8%	8.4%
MRI for Low Back Pain[1]	2	0.0%	34.3%	32.7%
Survey of Patients' Hospital Experiences				
Area Around Room 'Always' Quiet at Night	(a)	68%	-	58%
Doctors 'Always' Communicated Well	(a)	85%	-	80%
Home Recovery Information Given	(a)	81%	-	82%
Hospital Given 9 or 10 on 10 Point Scale	(a)	71%	-	67%
Meds 'Always' Explained Before Given	(a)	60%	-	60%
Nurses 'Always' Communicated Well	(a)	85%	-	76%
Pain 'Always' Well Controlled	(a)	65%	-	69%
Room and Bathroom 'Always' Clean	(a)	82%	-	71%
Timely Help 'Always' Received	(a)	73%	-	64%
Would Definitely Recommend Hospital	(a)	70%	-	69%

NOTE: Hospital profiles are in alphabetical order by state, then city, then hospital within the city; Rankings exclude hospitals with less than 25 cases except for patient surveys which excludes hospitals with less than 100 cases; (a) 100–299 cases; (1) The number of cases is too small to be sure how well a hospital is performing; (2) The hospital indicated that the data submitted for this measure were based on a sample of cases; (3) Data was collected during a shorter time period (fewer quarters) than the maximum possible time for this measure; (4) Suppressed for one or more quarters by CMS; (5) No data is available from the hospital for this measure; (6) Fewer than 100 patients completed the HCAHPS survey. Use these rates with caution, as the number of surveys may be too low to reliably assess hospital performance; (7) Survey results are based on less than 12 months of data; (8) Survey results are not available for this reporting period; (9) No or very few patients were eligible for the HCAHPS survey. The scores shown, if any, reflect a very small number of surveys; (10) A state average was not calculated because too few hospitals in the state submitted data; (11) There were discrepancies in the data collection process; Please refer to the User's Guide for a full explanation of data.

Newman Memorial Hospital

905 South Main Street
Shattuck, OK 73858
Phone: 580-938-2551
Fax: 580-938-2309
Type: Acute Care Hospitals
Emergency Services: Yes
Ownership: Govt - Hospital Dist/Auth
Beds: 27

Key Personnel:
CEO/President. . . . . Gary W Mitchell, CHE
Infection Control. . . . . Gwen Stafford, RN
Operating Room. . . . . Brenda Huenergardt
Anesthesiology. . . . . Greg Farrar, CRNA

Measure	Cases	This Hosp.	State Avg.	U.S. Avg.
Heart Attack Care				
ACE Inhibitor or ARB for LVSD[1,3]	2	100%	95%	96%
Aspirin at Arrival[1,3]	7	100%	98%	99%
Aspirin at Discharge[1,3]	6	83%	98%	98%
Beta Blocker at Discharge[1,3]	6	100%	98%	98%
Fibrinolytic Medication Timing[3]	0	-	42%	55%
PCI Within 90 Minutes of Arrival[3]	0	-	88%	90%
Smoking Cessation Advice[1,3]	1	100%	100%	99%
Chest Pain/Possible Heart Attack Care				
Aspirin at Arrival[1]	15	80%	94%	95%
Median Time to ECG (minutes)[1]	15	61	9	8
Median Time to Transfer (minutes)[1,3]	2	204	75	61
Fibrinolytic Medication Timing[1]	1	0%	50%	54%
Heart Failure Care				
ACE Inhibitor or ARB for LVSD[1]	2	100%	94%	94%
Discharge Instructions[1]	17	53%	85%	88%
Evaluation of LVS Function[1]	22	45%	94%	98%
Smoking Cessation Advice[1]	1	100%	97%	98%
Pneumonia Care				
Appropriate Initial Antibiotic	26	88%	91%	92%
Blood Culture Timing[1]	5	100%	96%	96%
Influenza Vaccine[1]	17	76%	89%	91%
Initial Antibiotic Timing	32	97%	95%	95%
Pneumococcal Vaccine	32	84%	91%	93%
Smoking Cessation Advice[1]	7	100%	95%	97%
Surgical Care Improvement Project				
Appropriate VTP Within 24 Hours[1,2]	4	100%	91%	92%
Appropriate Hair Removal[1,2]	7	100%	100%	99%
Appropriate Beta Blocker Usage[1,2]	2	50%	91%	93%
Controlled Postoperative Blood Glucose[2]	0	-	95%	93%
Prophylactic Antibiotic Timing[1,2]	3	100%	97%	97%
Prophylactic Antibiotic Timing (Outpatient)[5]	0	-	93%	92%
Prophylactic Antibiotic Selection[1,2]	3	100%	98%	97%
Prophylactic Antibiotic Select. (Outpatient)[5]	0	-	95%	94%
Prophylactic Antibiotic Stopped[1,2]	3	100%	94%	94%
Recommended VTP Ordered[1,2]	4	100%	94%	94%
Urinary Catheter Removal[1]	1	100%	87%	90%
Children's Asthma Care				
Received Systemic Corticosteroids	-	-	-	100%
Received Home Management Plan	-	-	-	71%
Received Reliever Medication	-	-	-	100%
Use of Medical Imaging				
Combination Abdominal CT Scan[1]	60	0.900	0.372	0.191
Combination Chest CT Scan[1]	26	0.808	0.134	0.054
Follow-up Mammogram/Ultrasound	160	2.5%	8%	8.4%
MRI for Low Back Pain[1]	20	45.0%	34.3%	32.7%
Survey of Patients' Hospital Experiences				
Area Around Room 'Always' Quiet at Night	(a)	67%	-	58%
Doctors 'Always' Communicated Well	(a)	91%	-	80%
Home Recovery Information Given	(a)	85%	-	82%
Hospital Given 9 or 10 on 10 Point Scale	(a)	72%	-	67%
Meds 'Always' Explained Before Given	(a)	71%	-	60%
Nurses 'Always' Communicated Well	(a)	77%	-	76%
Pain 'Always' Well Controlled	(a)	77%	-	69%
Room and Bathroom 'Always' Clean	(a)	70%	-	71%
Timely Help 'Always' Received	(a)	73%	-	64%
Would Definitely Recommend Hospital	(a)	80%	-	69%

Unity Health Center

1102 W Macarthur
Shawnee, OK 74804
Phone: 405-273-2270
E-mail: info@uhcenter.com
URL: www.unityhealthcenter.com
Type: Acute Care Hospitals
Emergency Services: Yes
Ownership: Voluntary Non-Profit - Other

Key Personnel:
CEO/President. . . . . Charles E. Skillings
Chief of Medical Staff . . . . Linda E. Brown

Measure	Cases	This Hosp.	State Avg.	U.S. Avg.
Heart Attack Care				
ACE Inhibitor or ARB for LVSD[1]	7	100%	95%	96%
Aspirin at Arrival	74	96%	98%	99%
Aspirin at Discharge	42	93%	98%	98%
Beta Blocker at Discharge	31	100%	98%	98%
Fibrinolytic Medication Timing[1]	2	0%	42%	55%
PCI Within 90 Minutes of Arrival	0	-	88%	90%
Smoking Cessation Advice[1]	15	100%	100%	99%
Chest Pain/Possible Heart Attack Care				
Aspirin at Arrival	129	97%	94%	95%
Median Time to ECG (minutes)	142	9	9	8
Median Time to Transfer (minutes)[1]	9	62	75	61
Fibrinolytic Medication Timing[1]	17	65%	50%	54%
Heart Failure Care				
ACE Inhibitor or ARB for LVSD	65	97%	94%	94%
Discharge Instructions	110	87%	85%	88%
Evaluation of LVS Function	147	100%	94%	98%
Smoking Cessation Advice[1]	24	100%	97%	98%
Pneumonia Care				
Appropriate Initial Antibiotic	116	100%	91%	92%
Blood Culture Timing	171	100%	96%	96%
Influenza Vaccine	116	100%	89%	91%
Initial Antibiotic Timing	184	99%	95%	95%
Pneumococcal Vaccine	158	100%	91%	93%
Smoking Cessation Advice	82	100%	95%	97%
Surgical Care Improvement Project				
Appropriate VTP Within 24 Hours	237	98%	91%	92%
Appropriate Hair Removal	392	100%	100%	99%
Appropriate Beta Blocker Usage	89	96%	91%	93%
Controlled Postoperative Blood Glucose	0	-	95%	93%
Prophylactic Antibiotic Timing	271	99%	97%	97%
Prophylactic Antibiotic Timing (Outpatient)	50	82%	93%	92%
Prophylactic Antibiotic Selection	272	99%	98%	97%
Prophylactic Antibiotic Select. (Outpatient)	41	95%	95%	94%
Prophylactic Antibiotic Stopped	260	98%	94%	94%
Recommended VTP Ordered	237	98%	94%	94%
Urinary Catheter Removal	96	99%	87%	90%
Children's Asthma Care				
Received Systemic Corticosteroids	-	-	-	100%
Received Home Management Plan	-	-	-	71%
Received Reliever Medication	-	-	-	100%
Use of Medical Imaging				
Combination Abdominal CT Scan	472	0.559	0.372	0.191
Combination Chest CT Scan	191	0.000	0.134	0.054
Follow-up Mammogram/Ultrasound	399	8.8%	8%	8.4%
MRI for Low Back Pain	67	29.9%	34.3%	32.7%
Survey of Patients' Hospital Experiences				
Area Around Room 'Always' Quiet at Night	300+	66%	-	58%
Doctors 'Always' Communicated Well	300+	85%	-	80%
Home Recovery Information Given	300+	86%	-	82%
Hospital Given 9 or 10 on 10 Point Scale	300+	76%	-	67%
Meds 'Always' Explained Before Given	300+	61%	-	60%
Nurses 'Always' Communicated Well	300+	78%	-	76%
Pain 'Always' Well Controlled	300+	75%	-	69%
Room and Bathroom 'Always' Clean	300+	74%	-	71%
Timely Help 'Always' Received	300+	68%	-	64%
Would Definitely Recommend Hospital	300+	69%	-	69%

Haskell County Healthcare System

401 Northwest H Street
Stigler, OK 74462
Phone: 918-967-4682
Fax: 918-967-8694
E-mail: info@hchs.otnnet.net
URL: www.hchs.otnnet.net
Type: Acute Care Hospitals
Emergency Services: Yes
Ownership: Voluntary Non-Profit - Other
Beds: 40

Key Personnel:
CEO/President. . . . . Leon Balila
Chief of Medical Staff . . . . Stephen Woodson, DO
Infection Control. . . . . Joyce Johnson
Quality Assurance . . . . Stacy Holland
Emergency Room . . . . George Bullard, RN

Measure	Cases	This Hosp.	State Avg.	U.S. Avg.
Heart Attack Care				
ACE Inhibitor or ARB for LVSD	-	-	95%	96%
Aspirin at Arrival	-	-	98%	99%
Aspirin at Discharge	-	-	98%	98%
Beta Blocker at Discharge	-	-	98%	98%
Fibrinolytic Medication Timing	-	-	42%	55%
PCI Within 90 Minutes of Arrival	-	-	88%	90%
Smoking Cessation Advice	-	-	100%	99%
Chest Pain/Possible Heart Attack Care				
Aspirin at Arrival	-	-	94%	95%
Median Time to ECG (minutes)	-	-	9	8
Median Time to Transfer (minutes)	-	-	75	61
Fibrinolytic Medication Timing	-	-	50%	54%
Heart Failure Care				
ACE Inhibitor or ARB for LVSD	-	-	94%	94%
Discharge Instructions	-	-	85%	88%
Evaluation of LVS Function	-	-	94%	98%
Smoking Cessation Advice	-	-	97%	98%
Pneumonia Care				
Appropriate Initial Antibiotic	-	-	91%	92%
Blood Culture Timing	-	-	96%	96%
Influenza Vaccine	-	-	89%	91%
Initial Antibiotic Timing	-	-	95%	95%
Pneumococcal Vaccine	-	-	91%	93%
Smoking Cessation Advice	-	-	95%	97%
Surgical Care Improvement Project				
Appropriate VTP Within 24 Hours	-	-	91%	92%
Appropriate Hair Removal	-	-	100%	99%
Appropriate Beta Blocker Usage	-	-	91%	93%
Controlled Postoperative Blood Glucose	-	-	95%	93%
Prophylactic Antibiotic Timing	-	-	97%	97%
Prophylactic Antibiotic Timing (Outpatient)	-	-	93%	92%
Prophylactic Antibiotic Selection	-	-	98%	97%
Prophylactic Antibiotic Select. (Outpatient)	-	-	95%	94%
Prophylactic Antibiotic Stopped	-	-	94%	94%
Recommended VTP Ordered	-	-	94%	94%
Urinary Catheter Removal	-	-	87%	90%
Children's Asthma Care				
Received Systemic Corticosteroids	-	-	-	100%
Received Home Management Plan	-	-	-	71%
Received Reliever Medication	-	-	-	100%
Use of Medical Imaging				
Combination Abdominal CT Scan	-	-	0.372	0.191
Combination Chest CT Scan	-	-	0.134	0.054
Follow-up Mammogram/Ultrasound	-	-	8%	8.4%
MRI for Low Back Pain	-	-	34.3%	32.7%
Survey of Patients' Hospital Experiences				
Area Around Room 'Always' Quiet at Night	-	-	-	58%
Doctors 'Always' Communicated Well	-	-	-	80%
Home Recovery Information Given	-	-	-	82%
Hospital Given 9 or 10 on 10 Point Scale	-	-	-	67%
Meds 'Always' Explained Before Given	-	-	-	60%
Nurses 'Always' Communicated Well	-	-	-	76%
Pain 'Always' Well Controlled	-	-	-	69%
Room and Bathroom 'Always' Clean	-	-	-	71%
Timely Help 'Always' Received	-	-	-	64%
Would Definitely Recommend Hospital	-	-	-	69%

NOTE: Hospital profiles are in alphabetical order by state, then city, then hospital within the city; Rankings exclude hospitals with less than 25 cases except for patient surveys which excludes hospitals with less than 100 cases; (a) 100–299 cases; (1) The number of cases is too small to be sure how well a hospital is performing; (2) The hospital indicated that the data submitted for this measure were based on a sample of cases; (3) Data was collected during a shorter time period (fewer quarters) than the maximum possible time for this measure; (4) Suppressed for one or more quarters by CMS; (5) No data is available from the hospital for this measure; (6) Fewer than 100 patients completed the HCAHPS survey. Use these rates with caution, as the number of surveys may be too low to reliably assess hospital performance; (7) Survey results are based on less than 12 months of data; (8) Survey results are not available for this reporting period; (9) No or very few patients were eligible for the HCAHPS survey. The scores shown, if any, reflect a very small number of surveys; (10) A state average was not calculated because too few hospitals in the state submitted data; (11) There were discrepancies in the data collection process; Please refer to the User's Guide for a full explanation of data.

Stillwater Medical Center

1323 West 6th Street
Stillwater, OK 74076
Phone: 405-372-1480
Fax: 405-372-9552
E-mail: info@stillwater-medical.org
URL: www.stillwater-medical.org
Type: Acute Care Hospitals
Emergency Services: Yes
Ownership: Govt - Hospital Dist/Auth
Beds: 128

Key Personnel:
CEO/President. . . . . Jerry Moeller
Chief of Medical Staff. . . . . Karen Hendren
Quality Assurance . . . . Cheryl Wilkinson
Radiology. . . . . J Bullen
Patient Relations . . . . Bonnie Peterson

Measure	Cases	This Hosp.	State Avg.	U.S. Avg.
Heart Attack Care				
ACE Inhibitor or ARB for LVSD[1]	7	71%	95%	96%
Aspirin at Arrival	74	100%	98%	99%
Aspirin at Discharge	65	100%	98%	98%
Beta Blocker at Discharge	68	97%	98%	98%
Fibrinolytic Medication Timing[1]	4	25%	42%	55%
PCI Within 90 Minutes of Arrival[1]	6	100%	88%	90%
Smoking Cessation Advice	30	100%	100%	99%
Chest Pain/Possible Heart Attack Care				
Aspirin at Arrival	64	100%	94%	95%
Median Time to ECG (minutes)	67	9	9	8
Median Time to Transfer (minutes)[1]	8	98	75	61
Fibrinolytic Medication Timing[1]	5	20%	50%	54%
Heart Failure Care				
ACE Inhibitor or ARB for LVSD	35	97%	94%	94%
Discharge Instructions	62	85%	85%	88%
Evaluation of LVS Function	82	98%	94%	98%
Smoking Cessation Advice[1]	18	100%	97%	98%
Pneumonia Care				
Appropriate Initial Antibiotic	98	95%	91%	92%
Blood Culture Timing	140	100%	96%	96%
Influenza Vaccine	96	77%	89%	91%
Initial Antibiotic Timing	144	99%	95%	95%
Pneumococcal Vaccine	155	79%	91%	93%
Smoking Cessation Advice	41	93%	95%	97%
Surgical Care Improvement Project				
Appropriate VTP Within 24 Hours	147	88%	91%	92%
Appropriate Hair Removal	406	100%	100%	99%
Appropriate Beta Blocker Usage	114	89%	91%	93%
Controlled Postoperative Blood Glucose	0	-	95%	93%
Prophylactic Antibiotic Timing	301	95%	97%	97%
Prophylactic Antibiotic Timing (Outpatient)	176	90%	93%	92%
Prophylactic Antibiotic Selection	302	97%	98%	97%
Prophylactic Antibiotic Select. (Outpatient)	176	97%	95%	94%
Prophylactic Antibiotic Stopped	292	97%	94%	94%
Recommended VTP Ordered	158	87%	94%	94%
Urinary Catheter Removal	109	86%	87%	90%
Children's Asthma Care				
Received Systemic Corticosteroids	-	-	-	100%
Received Home Management Plan	-	-	-	71%
Received Reliever Medication	-	-	-	100%
Use of Medical Imaging				
Combination Abdominal CT Scan	496	0.109	0.372	0.191
Combination Chest CT Scan	290	0.024	0.134	0.054
Follow-up Mammogram/Ultrasound	712	4.4%	8%	8.4%
MRI for Low Back Pain	136	31.6%	34.3%	32.7%
Survey of Patients' Hospital Experiences				
Area Around Room 'Always' Quiet at Night	300+	59%	-	58%
Doctors 'Always' Communicated Well	300+	82%	-	80%
Home Recovery Information Given	300+	86%	-	82%
Hospital Given 9 or 10 on 10 Point Scale	300+	67%	-	67%
Meds 'Always' Explained Before Given	300+	58%	-	60%
Nurses 'Always' Communicated Well	300+	74%	-	76%
Pain 'Always' Well Controlled	300+	67%	-	69%
Room and Bathroom 'Always' Clean	300+	65%	-	71%
Timely Help 'Always' Received	300+	63%	-	64%
Would Definitely Recommend Hospital	300+	71%	-	69%

Memorial Hospital of Stilwell

1401 West Locust
Stilwell, OK 74960
Phone: 918-696-3101
Fax: 918-696-3388
Type: Acute Care Hospitals
Emergency Services: Yes
Ownership: Government - Federal
Beds: 50

Key Personnel:
CEO/President. . . . . Alan L Adams

Measure	Cases	This Hosp.	State Avg.	U.S. Avg.
Heart Attack Care				
ACE Inhibitor or ARB for LVSD	0	-	95%	96%
Aspirin at Arrival[1]	4	100%	98%	99%
Aspirin at Discharge[1]	3	67%	98%	98%
Beta Blocker at Discharge[1]	4	25%	98%	98%
Fibrinolytic Medication Timing	0	-	42%	55%
PCI Within 90 Minutes of Arrival	0	-	88%	90%
Smoking Cessation Advice	0	-	100%	99%
Chest Pain/Possible Heart Attack Care				
Aspirin at Arrival[1]	16	88%	94%	95%
Median Time to ECG (minutes)[1]	16	19	9	8
Median Time to Transfer (minutes)[5]	0	-	75	61
Fibrinolytic Medication Timing[1,3]	2	50%	50%	54%
Heart Failure Care				
ACE Inhibitor or ARB for LVSD[1]	15	93%	94%	94%
Discharge Instructions	28	86%	85%	88%
Evaluation of LVS Function	36	100%	94%	98%
Smoking Cessation Advice[1]	7	100%	97%	98%
Pneumonia Care				
Appropriate Initial Antibiotic	26	73%	91%	92%
Blood Culture Timing[1]	13	100%	96%	96%
Influenza Vaccine	25	92%	89%	91%
Initial Antibiotic Timing	41	98%	95%	95%
Pneumococcal Vaccine	35	100%	91%	93%
Smoking Cessation Advice[1]	12	83%	95%	97%
Surgical Care Improvement Project				
Appropriate VTP Within 24 Hours[1]	8	88%	91%	92%
Appropriate Hair Removal	31	87%	100%	99%
Appropriate Beta Blocker Usage[1]	3	67%	91%	93%
Controlled Postoperative Blood Glucose	0	-	95%	93%
Prophylactic Antibiotic Timing[1]	24	88%	97%	97%
Prophylactic Antibiotic Timing (Outpatient)[1,3]	5	80%	93%	92%
Prophylactic Antibiotic Selection[1]	24	92%	98%	97%
Prophylactic Antibiotic Select. (Outpatient)[1,3]	5	100%	95%	94%
Prophylactic Antibiotic Stopped[1]	24	100%	94%	94%
Recommended VTP Ordered[1]	8	88%	94%	94%
Urinary Catheter Removal[1]	7	100%	87%	90%
Children's Asthma Care				
Received Systemic Corticosteroids	-	-	-	100%
Received Home Management Plan	-	-	-	71%
Received Reliever Medication	-	-	-	100%
Use of Medical Imaging				
Combination Abdominal CT Scan	76	0.145	0.372	0.191
Combination Chest CT Scan[1]	52	0.096	0.134	0.054
Follow-up Mammogram/Ultrasound[5]	0	-	8%	8.4%
MRI for Low Back Pain[1]	21	42.9%	34.3%	32.7%
Survey of Patients' Hospital Experiences				
Area Around Room 'Always' Quiet at Night	300+	66%	-	58%
Doctors 'Always' Communicated Well	300+	86%	-	80%
Home Recovery Information Given	300+	76%	-	82%
Hospital Given 9 or 10 on 10 Point Scale	300+	67%	-	67%
Meds 'Always' Explained Before Given	300+	65%	-	60%
Nurses 'Always' Communicated Well	300+	74%	-	76%
Pain 'Always' Well Controlled	300+	72%	-	69%
Room and Bathroom 'Always' Clean	300+	71%	-	71%
Timely Help 'Always' Received	300+	66%	-	64%
Would Definitely Recommend Hospital	300+	68%	-	69%

Stroud Regional Medical Center

2308 Highway 66 West
Stroud, OK 74079
Phone: 918-968-3571
Fax: 918-968-4814
Type: Critical Access Hospitals
Emergency Services: Yes
Ownership: Government - Federal
Beds: 25

Key Personnel:
CEO/President. . . . . Regina Peters
Chief of Medical Staff. . . . . Dr. Ken Darvin
Infection Control. . . . . Linda Wolff
Quality Assurance . . . . Donna Buchanan
Radiology. . . . . Brenda McGinnis
Anesthesiology. . . . . Monica McKinney
Emergency Room . . . . Tammy McElroy
Intensive Care Unit. . . . . Donna Buchanan

Measure	Cases	This Hosp.	State Avg.	U.S. Avg.
Heart Attack Care				
ACE Inhibitor or ARB for LVSD[5]	0	-	95%	96%
Aspirin at Arrival[5]	0	-	98%	99%
Aspirin at Discharge[5]	0	-	98%	98%
Beta Blocker at Discharge[5]	0	-	98%	98%
Fibrinolytic Medication Timing[5]	0	-	42%	55%
PCI Within 90 Minutes of Arrival[5]	0	-	88%	90%
Smoking Cessation Advice[5]	0	-	100%	99%
Chest Pain/Possible Heart Attack Care				
Aspirin at Arrival	-	-	94%	95%
Median Time to ECG (minutes)	-	-	9	8
Median Time to Transfer (minutes)	-	-	75	61
Fibrinolytic Medication Timing	-	-	50%	54%
Heart Failure Care				
ACE Inhibitor or ARB for LVSD[1]	2	50%	94%	94%
Discharge Instructions[1]	7	86%	85%	88%
Evaluation of LVS Function[1]	14	50%	94%	98%
Smoking Cessation Advice	0	-	97%	98%
Pneumonia Care				
Appropriate Initial Antibiotic	26	77%	91%	92%
Blood Culture Timing[1]	20	90%	96%	96%
Influenza Vaccine[1]	23	70%	89%	91%
Initial Antibiotic Timing	26	100%	95%	95%
Pneumococcal Vaccine	28	68%	91%	93%
Smoking Cessation Advice[1]	7	29%	95%	97%
Surgical Care Improvement Project				
Appropriate VTP Within 24 Hours[1,3]	3	33%	91%	92%
Appropriate Hair Removal[1,3]	4	100%	100%	99%
Appropriate Beta Blocker Usage[1,3]	1	100%	91%	93%
Controlled Postoperative Blood Glucose[3]	0	-	95%	93%
Prophylactic Antibiotic Timing[1,3]	3	33%	97%	97%
Prophylactic Antibiotic Timing (Outpatient)	-	-	93%	92%
Prophylactic Antibiotic Selection[1,3]	3	100%	98%	97%
Prophylactic Antibiotic Select. (Outpatient)	-	-	95%	94%
Prophylactic Antibiotic Stopped[1,3]	3	100%	94%	94%
Recommended VTP Ordered[1,3]	3	33%	94%	94%
Urinary Catheter Removal	0	-	87%	90%
Children's Asthma Care				
Received Systemic Corticosteroids	-	-	-	100%
Received Home Management Plan	-	-	-	71%
Received Reliever Medication	-	-	-	100%
Use of Medical Imaging				
Combination Abdominal CT Scan	-	-	0.372	0.191
Combination Chest CT Scan	-	-	0.134	0.054
Follow-up Mammogram/Ultrasound	-	-	8%	8.4%
MRI for Low Back Pain	-	-	34.3%	32.7%
Survey of Patients' Hospital Experiences				
Area Around Room 'Always' Quiet at Night[8]	-	-	-	58%
Doctors 'Always' Communicated Well[8]	-	-	-	80%
Home Recovery Information Given[8]	-	-	-	82%
Hospital Given 9 or 10 on 10 Point Scale[8]	-	-	-	67%
Meds 'Always' Explained Before Given[8]	-	-	-	60%
Nurses 'Always' Communicated Well[8]	-	-	-	76%
Pain 'Always' Well Controlled[8]	-	-	-	69%
Room and Bathroom 'Always' Clean[8]	-	-	-	71%
Timely Help 'Always' Received[8]	-	-	-	64%
Would Definitely Recommend Hospital[8]	-	-	-	69%

NOTE: Hospital profiles are in alphabetical order by state, then city, then hospital within the city; Rankings exclude hospitals with less than 25 cases except for patient surveys which excludes hospitals with less than 100 cases; (a) 100–299 cases; (1) The number of cases is too small to be sure how well a hospital is performing; (2) The hospital indicated that the data submitted for this measure were based on a sample of cases; (3) Data was collected during a shorter time period (fewer quarters) than the maximum possible time for this measure; (4) Suppressed for one or more quarters by CMS; (5) No data is available from the hospital for this measure; (6) Fewer than 100 patients completed the HCAHPS survey. Use these rates with caution, as the number of surveys may be too low to reliably assess hospital performance; (7) Survey results are based on less than 12 months of data; (8) Survey results are not available for this reporting period; (9) No or very few patients were eligible for the HCAHPS survey. The scores shown, if any, reflect a very small number of surveys; (10) A state average was not calculated because too few hospitals in the state submitted data; (11) There were discrepancies in the data collection process; Please refer to the User's Guide for a full explanation of data.

Arbuckle Memorial Hospital

2011 West Broadway Phone: 580-622-2161
Sulphur, OK 73086 Fax: 580-622-2763
E-mail: webmaster@arbucklehospital.com
URL: www.arbucklehospital.com
Type: Critical Access Hospitals Emergency Services: Yes
Ownership: Voluntary Non-Profit - Other Beds: 25
Key Personnel:
Chief of Medical Staff.......... Atonio Lee, MD

Measure	Cases	This Hosp.	State Avg.	U.S. Avg.
Heart Attack Care				
ACE Inhibitor or ARB for LVSD[3]	0	-	95%	96%
Aspirin at Arrival[3]	0	-	98%	99%
Aspirin at Discharge[3]	0	-	98%	98%
Beta Blocker at Discharge[3]	0	-	98%	98%
Fibrinolytic Medication Timing[3]	0	-	42%	55%
PCI Within 90 Minutes of Arrival[3]	0	-	88%	90%
Smoking Cessation Advice[3]	0	-	100%	99%
Chest Pain/Possible Heart Attack Care				
Aspirin at Arrival	-	-	94%	95%
Median Time to ECG (minutes)	-	-	9	8
Median Time to Transfer (minutes)	-	-	75	61
Fibrinolytic Medication Timing	-	-	50%	54%
Heart Failure Care				
ACE Inhibitor or ARB for LVSD[1]	3	100%	94%	94%
Discharge Instructions[1]	7	43%	85%	88%
Evaluation of LVS Function[1]	18	78%	94%	98%
Smoking Cessation Advice[1]	2	50%	97%	98%
Pneumonia Care				
Appropriate Initial Antibiotic[1]	24	79%	91%	92%
Blood Culture Timing[1]	22	91%	96%	96%
Influenza Vaccine	28	96%	89%	91%
Initial Antibiotic Timing	40	95%	95%	95%
Pneumococcal Vaccine	36	83%	91%	93%
Smoking Cessation Advice[1]	18	67%	95%	97%
Surgical Care Improvement Project				
Appropriate VTP Within 24 Hours[5]	0	-	91%	92%
Appropriate Hair Removal[5]	0	-	100%	99%
Appropriate Beta Blocker Usage[5]	0	-	91%	93%
Controlled Postoperative Blood Glucose[5]	0	-	95%	93%
Prophylactic Antibiotic Timing[5]	0	-	97%	97%
Prophylactic Antibiotic Timing (Outpatient)	-	-	93%	92%
Prophylactic Antibiotic Selection[5]	0	-	98%	97%
Prophylactic Antibiotic Select. (Outpatient)	-	-	95%	94%
Prophylactic Antibiotic Stopped[5]	0	-	94%	94%
Recommended VTP Ordered[5]	0	-	94%	94%
Urinary Catheter Removal[5]	0	-	87%	90%
Children's Asthma Care				
Received Systemic Corticosteroids	-	-	-	100%
Received Home Management Plan	-	-	-	71%
Received Reliever Medication	-	-	-	100%
Use of Medical Imaging				
Combination Abdominal CT Scan	-	-	0.372	0.191
Combination Chest CT Scan	-	-	0.134	0.054
Follow-up Mammogram/Ultrasound	-	-	8%	8.4%
MRI for Low Back Pain	-	-	34.3%	32.7%
Survey of Patients' Hospital Experiences				
Area Around Room 'Always' Quiet at Night[8]	-	-	-	58%
Doctors 'Always' Communicated Well[8]	-	-	-	80%
Home Recovery Information Given[8]	-	-	-	82%
Hospital Given 9 or 10 on 10 Point Scale[8]	-	-	-	67%
Meds 'Always' Explained Before Given[8]	-	-	-	60%
Nurses 'Always' Communicated Well[8]	-	-	-	76%
Pain 'Always' Well Controlled[8]	-	-	-	69%
Room and Bathroom 'Always' Clean[8]	-	-	-	71%
Timely Help 'Always' Received[8]	-	-	-	64%
Would Definitely Recommend Hospital[8]	-	-	-	69%

Tahlequah City Hospital

1400 East Downing Street Phone: 918-456-0641
Tahlequah, OK 74465 Fax: 918-456-8886
Type: Acute Care Hospitals Emergency Services: Yes
Ownership: Voluntary Non-Profit - Other Beds: 82
Key Personnel:
CEO/President.................. Gary L Jepson
Chief of Medical Staff.......... Herbert Littleton, DO
Infection Control............... Cheri Olgesbee, RN
Quality Assurance............. Gloria Hoover
Radiology..................... Mark Whitley, MD
Anesthesiology................ M Adele King, DO
Emergency Room.............. John Galdamez, DO

Measure	Cases	This Hosp.	State Avg.	U.S. Avg.
Heart Attack Care				
ACE Inhibitor or ARB for LVSD[1]	2	100%	95%	96%
Aspirin at Arrival	29	97%	98%	99%
Aspirin at Discharge	34	100%	98%	98%
Beta Blocker at Discharge	31	100%	98%	98%
Fibrinolytic Medication Timing	0	-	42%	55%
PCI Within 90 Minutes of Arrival[1]	1	0%	88%	90%
Smoking Cessation Advice[1]	15	100%	100%	99%
Chest Pain/Possible Heart Attack Care				
Aspirin at Arrival	44	93%	94%	95%
Median Time to ECG (minutes)	48	16	9	8
Median Time to Transfer (minutes)[3]	0	-	75	61
Fibrinolytic Medication Timing[1]	5	80%	50%	54%
Heart Failure Care				
ACE Inhibitor or ARB for LVSD	47	96%	94%	94%
Discharge Instructions	98	78%	85%	88%
Evaluation of LVS Function	111	99%	94%	98%
Smoking Cessation Advice	29	86%	97%	98%
Pneumonia Care				
Appropriate Initial Antibiotic	78	95%	91%	92%
Blood Culture Timing	117	90%	96%	96%
Influenza Vaccine	80	88%	89%	91%
Initial Antibiotic Timing	141	100%	95%	95%
Pneumococcal Vaccine	127	93%	91%	93%
Smoking Cessation Advice	75	93%	95%	97%
Surgical Care Improvement Project				
Appropriate VTP Within 24 Hours	93	90%	91%	92%
Appropriate Hair Removal	345	100%	100%	99%
Appropriate Beta Blocker Usage	139	92%	91%	93%
Controlled Postoperative Blood Glucose	66	91%	95%	93%
Prophylactic Antibiotic Timing	248	100%	97%	97%
Prophylactic Antibiotic Timing (Outpatient)	66	97%	93%	92%
Prophylactic Antibiotic Selection	252	100%	98%	97%
Prophylactic Antibiotic Select. (Outpatient)	64	97%	95%	94%
Prophylactic Antibiotic Stopped	229	93%	94%	94%
Recommended VTP Ordered	95	88%	94%	94%
Urinary Catheter Removal	77	86%	87%	90%
Children's Asthma Care				
Received Systemic Corticosteroids	-	-	-	100%
Received Home Management Plan	-	-	-	71%
Received Reliever Medication	-	-	-	100%
Use of Medical Imaging				
Combination Abdominal CT Scan	356	0.480	0.372	0.191
Combination Chest CT Scan	220	0.059	0.134	0.054
Follow-up Mammogram/Ultrasound	564	8.7%	8%	8.4%
MRI for Low Back Pain	121	33.1%	34.3%	32.7%
Survey of Patients' Hospital Experiences				
Area Around Room 'Always' Quiet at Night	300+	51%	-	58%
Doctors 'Always' Communicated Well	300+	77%	-	80%
Home Recovery Information Given	300+	77%	-	82%
Hospital Given 9 or 10 on 10 Point Scale	300+	63%	-	67%
Meds 'Always' Explained Before Given	300+	60%	-	60%
Nurses 'Always' Communicated Well	300+	75%	-	76%
Pain 'Always' Well Controlled	300+	69%	-	69%
Room and Bathroom 'Always' Clean	300+	67%	-	71%
Timely Help 'Always' Received	300+	63%	-	64%
Would Definitely Recommend Hospital	300+	68%	-	69%

W W Hastings Indian Hospital

100 S Bliss Avenue Phone: 918-458-3100
Tahlequah, OK 74464 Fax: 918-458-3262
URL: www.ihs.gov
Type: Acute Care Hospitals Emergency Services: Yes
Ownership: Government - Federal Beds: 58
Key Personnel:
CEO/President.............. Edwin McLemore
Quality Assurance .... James Clevenger

Measure	Cases	This Hosp.	State Avg.	U.S. Avg.
Heart Attack Care				
ACE Inhibitor or ARB for LVSD[5]	0	-	95%	96%
Aspirin at Arrival[5]	0	-	98%	99%
Aspirin at Discharge[5]	0	-	98%	98%
Beta Blocker at Discharge[5]	0	-	98%	98%
Fibrinolytic Medication Timing[5]	0	-	42%	55%
PCI Within 90 Minutes of Arrival[5]	0	-	88%	90%
Smoking Cessation Advice[5]	0	-	100%	99%
Chest Pain/Possible Heart Attack Care				
Aspirin at Arrival	-	-	94%	95%
Median Time to ECG (minutes)	-	-	9	8
Median Time to Transfer (minutes)	-	-	75	61
Fibrinolytic Medication Timing	-	-	50%	54%
Heart Failure Care				
ACE Inhibitor or ARB for LVSD[1]	9	100%	94%	94%
Discharge Instructions	29	59%	85%	88%
Evaluation of LVS Function	36	92%	94%	98%
Smoking Cessation Advice[1]	5	80%	97%	98%
Pneumonia Care				
Appropriate Initial Antibiotic	47	94%	91%	92%
Blood Culture Timing	61	87%	96%	96%
Influenza Vaccine	32	75%	89%	91%
Initial Antibiotic Timing	58	90%	95%	95%
Pneumococcal Vaccine	29	86%	91%	93%
Smoking Cessation Advice[1]	20	50%	95%	97%
Surgical Care Improvement Project				
Appropriate VTP Within 24 Hours	45	89%	91%	92%
Appropriate Hair Removal	144	100%	100%	99%
Appropriate Beta Blocker Usage[1]	20	95%	91%	93%
Controlled Postoperative Blood Glucose	0	-	95%	93%
Prophylactic Antibiotic Timing	86	85%	97%	97%
Prophylactic Antibiotic Timing (Outpatient)	-	-	93%	92%
Prophylactic Antibiotic Selection	87	91%	98%	97%
Prophylactic Antibiotic Select. (Outpatient)	-	-	95%	94%
Prophylactic Antibiotic Stopped	80	82%	94%	94%
Recommended VTP Ordered	47	85%	94%	94%
Urinary Catheter Removal[1]	13	85%	87%	90%
Children's Asthma Care				
Received Systemic Corticosteroids	-	-	-	100%
Received Home Management Plan	-	-	-	71%
Received Reliever Medication	-	-	-	100%
Use of Medical Imaging				
Combination Abdominal CT Scan	-	-	0.372	0.191
Combination Chest CT Scan	-	-	0.134	0.054
Follow-up Mammogram/Ultrasound	-	-	8%	8.4%
MRI for Low Back Pain	-	-	34.3%	32.7%
Survey of Patients' Hospital Experiences				
Area Around Room 'Always' Quiet at Night	300+	64%	-	58%
Doctors 'Always' Communicated Well	300+	83%	-	80%
Home Recovery Information Given	300+	81%	-	82%
Hospital Given 9 or 10 on 10 Point Scale	300+	69%	-	67%
Meds 'Always' Explained Before Given	300+	70%	-	60%
Nurses 'Always' Communicated Well	300+	82%	-	76%
Pain 'Always' Well Controlled	300+	75%	-	69%
Room and Bathroom 'Always' Clean	300+	59%	-	71%
Timely Help 'Always' Received	300+	75%	-	64%
Would Definitely Recommend Hospital	300+	70%	-	69%

NOTE: Hospital profiles are in alphabetical order by state, then city, then hospital within the city; Rankings exclude hospitals with less than 25 cases except for patient surveys which excludes hospitals with less than 100 cases; (a) 100–299 cases; (1) The number of cases is too small to be sure how well a hospital is performing; (2) The hospital indicated that the data submitted for this measure were based on a sample of cases; (3) Data was collected during a shorter time period (fewer quarters) than the maximum possible time for this measure; (4) Suppressed for one or more quarters by CMS; (5) No data is available from the hospital for this measure; (6) Fewer than 100 patients completed the HCAHPS survey. Use these rates with caution, as the number of surveys may be too low to reliably assess hospital performance; (7) Survey results are based on less than 12 months of data; (8) Survey results are not available for this reporting period; (9) No or very few patients were eligible for the HCAHPS survey. The scores shown, if any, reflect a very small number of surveys; (10) A state average was not calculated because too few hospitals in the state submitted data; (11) There were discrepancies in the data collection process; Please refer to the User's Guide for a full explanation of data.

Choctaw Nation Healthcare

1 Choctaw Way
Talihina, OK 74571
URL: www.choctawnationhealth.com
Type: Acute Care Hospitals
Ownership: Government - Federal
Phone: 918-567-7000
Fax: 918-567-7026
Emergency Services: Yes
Beds: 37

Key Personnel:
Chief of Medical Staff . . . . Dr Thomas Bonien
Operating Room. . . . . Jumelle, Antoine, RN
Pediatric Ambulatory Care . . . . . . Valerie Taylor, LPN
Quality Assurance . . . . David Wharton
Radiology. . . . . hakel Creel
Patient Relations . . . . Maggie Hayes

Measure	Cases	This Hosp.	State Avg.	U.S. Avg.
Heart Attack Care				
ACE Inhibitor or ARB for LVSD[3]	0	-	95%	96%
Aspirin at Arrival[1,3]	1	100%	98%	99%
Aspirin at Discharge[1,3]	1	100%	98%	98%
Beta Blocker at Discharge[1,3]	1	100%	98%	98%
Fibrinolytic Medication Timing[3]	0	-	42%	55%
PCI Within 90 Minutes of Arrival[3]	0	-	88%	90%
Smoking Cessation Advice[3]	0	-	100%	99%
Chest Pain/Possible Heart Attack Care				
Aspirin at Arrival	-	-	94%	95%
Median Time to ECG (minutes)	-	-	9	8
Median Time to Transfer (minutes)	-	-	75	61
Fibrinolytic Medication Timing	-	-	50%	54%
Heart Failure Care				
ACE Inhibitor or ARB for LVSD[1,3]	3	67%	94%	94%
Discharge Instructions[1,3]	7	86%	85%	88%
Evaluation of LVS Function[1,3]	7	100%	94%	98%
Smoking Cessation Advice[1,3]	2	100%	97%	98%
Pneumonia Care				
Appropriate Initial Antibiotic[1,3]	19	95%	91%	92%
Blood Culture Timing[1,3]	17	82%	96%	96%
Influenza Vaccine[1]	9	56%	89%	91%
Initial Antibiotic Timing[1,3]	14	100%	95%	95%
Pneumococcal Vaccine[1,3]	8	75%	91%	93%
Smoking Cessation Advice[1,3]	5	100%	95%	97%
Surgical Care Improvement Project				
Appropriate VTP Within 24 Hours[1,3]	2	0%	91%	92%
Appropriate Hair Removal[1,3]	11	100%	100%	99%
Appropriate Beta Blocker Usage[1,3]	1	0%	91%	93%
Controlled Postoperative Blood Glucose[3]	0	-	95%	93%
Prophylactic Antibiotic Timing[1,3]	9	89%	97%	97%
Prophylactic Antibiotic Timing (Outpatient)	-	-	93%	92%
Prophylactic Antibiotic Selection[1,3]	8	88%	98%	97%
Prophylactic Antibiotic Select. (Outpatient)	-	-	95%	94%
Prophylactic Antibiotic Stopped[1,3]	8	100%	94%	94%
Recommended VTP Ordered[1,3]	2	0%	94%	94%
Urinary Catheter Removal[1]	2	100%	87%	90%
Children's Asthma Care				
Received Systemic Corticosteroids	-	-	-	100%
Received Home Management Plan	-	-	-	71%
Received Reliever Medication	-	-	-	100%
Use of Medical Imaging				
Combination Abdominal CT Scan	-	-	0.372	0.191
Combination Chest CT Scan	-	-	0.134	0.054
Follow-up Mammogram/Ultrasound	-	-	8%	8.4%
MRI for Low Back Pain	-	-	34.3%	32.7%
Survey of Patients' Hospital Experiences				
Area Around Room 'Always' Quiet at Night	(a)	60%	-	58%
Doctors 'Always' Communicated Well	(a)	82%	-	80%
Home Recovery Information Given	(a)	86%	-	82%
Hospital Given 9 or 10 on 10 Point Scale	(a)	74%	-	67%
Meds 'Always' Explained Before Given	(a)	71%	-	60%
Nurses 'Always' Communicated Well	(a)	79%	-	76%
Pain 'Always' Well Controlled	(a)	70%	-	69%
Room and Bathroom 'Always' Clean	(a)	79%	-	71%
Timely Help 'Always' Received	(a)	75%	-	64%
Would Definitely Recommend Hospital	(a)	79%	-	69%

Johnston Memorial Hospital

1000 South Byrd
Tishomingo, OK 73460
Type: Critical Access Hospitals
Ownership: Voluntary Non-Profit - Private
Phone: 580-371-2327
Fax: 580-371-2127
Emergency Services: Yes
Beds: 25

Key Personnel:
Chief of Medical Staff . . . . Richard H Tidwell, MD
Infection Control. . . . . Carolyn Pearson, RN
Operating Room. . . . . Carol Hewitt, RN

Measure	Cases	This Hosp.	State Avg.	U.S. Avg.
Heart Attack Care				
ACE Inhibitor or ARB for LVSD[5]	0	-	95%	96%
Aspirin at Arrival[5]	0	-	98%	99%
Aspirin at Discharge[5]	0	-	98%	98%
Beta Blocker at Discharge[5]	0	-	98%	98%
Fibrinolytic Medication Timing[5]	0	-	42%	55%
PCI Within 90 Minutes of Arrival[5]	0	-	88%	90%
Smoking Cessation Advice[5]	0	-	100%	99%
Chest Pain/Possible Heart Attack Care				
Aspirin at Arrival	-	-	94%	95%
Median Time to ECG (minutes)	-	-	9	8
Median Time to Transfer (minutes)	-	-	75	61
Fibrinolytic Medication Timing	-	-	50%	54%
Heart Failure Care				
ACE Inhibitor or ARB for LVSD[3]	0	-	94%	94%
Discharge Instructions[1,3]	3	67%	85%	88%
Evaluation of LVS Function[1,3]	6	0%	94%	98%
Smoking Cessation Advice[3]	0	-	97%	98%
Pneumonia Care				
Appropriate Initial Antibiotic[3]	0	-	91%	92%
Blood Culture Timing[3]	0	-	96%	96%
Influenza Vaccine[5]	0	-	89%	91%
Initial Antibiotic Timing[1,3]	3	67%	95%	95%
Pneumococcal Vaccine[1,3]	1	0%	91%	93%
Smoking Cessation Advice[1,3]	1	100%	95%	97%
Surgical Care Improvement Project				
Appropriate VTP Within 24 Hours[5]	0	-	91%	92%
Appropriate Hair Removal[5]	0	-	100%	99%
Appropriate Beta Blocker Usage[5]	0	-	91%	93%
Controlled Postoperative Blood Glucose[5]	0	-	95%	93%
Prophylactic Antibiotic Timing[5]	0	-	97%	97%
Prophylactic Antibiotic Timing (Outpatient)	-	-	93%	92%
Prophylactic Antibiotic Selection[5]	0	-	98%	97%
Prophylactic Antibiotic Select. (Outpatient)	-	-	95%	94%
Prophylactic Antibiotic Stopped[5]	0	-	94%	94%
Recommended VTP Ordered[5]	0	-	94%	94%
Urinary Catheter Removal[5]	0	-	87%	90%
Children's Asthma Care				
Received Systemic Corticosteroids	-	-	-	100%
Received Home Management Plan	-	-	-	71%
Received Reliever Medication	-	-	-	100%
Use of Medical Imaging				
Combination Abdominal CT Scan	-	-	0.372	0.191
Combination Chest CT Scan	-	-	0.134	0.054
Follow-up Mammogram/Ultrasound	-	-	8%	8.4%
MRI for Low Back Pain	-	-	34.3%	32.7%
Survey of Patients' Hospital Experiences				
Area Around Room 'Always' Quiet at Night[8]	-	-	-	58%
Doctors 'Always' Communicated Well[8]	-	-	-	80%
Home Recovery Information Given[8]	-	-	-	82%
Hospital Given 9 or 10 on 10 Point Scale[8]	-	-	-	67%
Meds 'Always' Explained Before Given[8]	-	-	-	60%
Nurses 'Always' Communicated Well[8]	-	-	-	76%
Pain 'Always' Well Controlled[8]	-	-	-	69%
Room and Bathroom 'Always' Clean[8]	-	-	-	71%
Timely Help 'Always' Received[8]	-	-	-	64%
Would Definitely Recommend Hospital[8]	-	-	-	69%

Hillcrest Medical Center

1120 South Utica Avenue
Tulsa, OK 74104
URL: www.hillcrest.com
Type: Acute Care Hospitals
Ownership: Voluntary Non-Profit - Other
Phone: 918-579-1000
Fax: 918-584-6636
Emergency Services: Yes
Beds: 607

Key Personnel:
CEO/President. . . . . Steve Dobbs
Chief of Medical Staff . . . . D Decker, MD
Operating Room. . . . . Robert L Archer
Quality Assurance . . . . Liz Ross
Emergency Room . . . . Susan Messon

Measure	Cases	This Hosp.	State Avg.	U.S. Avg.
Heart Attack Care				
ACE Inhibitor or ARB for LVSD	80	85%	95%	96%
Aspirin at Arrival	248	100%	98%	99%
Aspirin at Discharge	494	99%	98%	98%
Beta Blocker at Discharge	477	100%	98%	98%
Fibrinolytic Medication Timing[1]	1	100%	42%	55%
PCI Within 90 Minutes of Arrival	34	91%	88%	90%
Smoking Cessation Advice	224	100%	100%	99%
Chest Pain/Possible Heart Attack Care				
Aspirin at Arrival[3]	0	-	94%	95%
Median Time to ECG (minutes)[3]	0	-	9	8
Median Time to Transfer (minutes)[5]	0	-	75	61
Fibrinolytic Medication Timing[5]	0	-	50%	54%
Heart Failure Care				
ACE Inhibitor or ARB for LVSD	220	90%	94%	94%
Discharge Instructions	520	96%	85%	88%
Evaluation of LVS Function	570	98%	94%	98%
Smoking Cessation Advice	154	98%	97%	98%
Pneumonia Care				
Appropriate Initial Antibiotic	147	95%	91%	92%
Blood Culture Timing	168	98%	96%	96%
Influenza Vaccine	157	85%	89%	91%
Initial Antibiotic Timing	216	93%	95%	95%
Pneumococcal Vaccine	170	94%	91%	93%
Smoking Cessation Advice	177	98%	95%	97%
Surgical Care Improvement Project				
Appropriate VTP Within 24 Hours[2]	123	89%	91%	92%
Appropriate Hair Removal[2]	614	100%	100%	99%
Appropriate Beta Blocker Usage[2]	221	89%	91%	93%
Controlled Postoperative Blood Glucose[2]	145	96%	95%	93%
Prophylactic Antibiotic Timing[2]	446	98%	97%	97%
Prophylactic Antibiotic Timing (Outpatient)	620	94%	93%	92%
Prophylactic Antibiotic Selection[2]	456	99%	98%	97%
Prophylactic Antibiotic Select. (Outpatient)	613	97%	95%	94%
Prophylactic Antibiotic Stopped[2]	429	96%	94%	94%
Recommended VTP Ordered[2]	123	99%	94%	94%
Urinary Catheter Removal[2]	166	93%	87%	90%
Children's Asthma Care				
Received Systemic Corticosteroids	-	-	-	100%
Received Home Management Plan	-	-	-	71%
Received Reliever Medication	-	-	-	100%
Use of Medical Imaging				
Combination Abdominal CT Scan	518	0.154	0.372	0.191
Combination Chest CT Scan	438	0.021	0.134	0.054
Follow-up Mammogram/Ultrasound	1,447	8.6%	8%	8.4%
MRI for Low Back Pain	109	29.4%	34.3%	32.7%
Survey of Patients' Hospital Experiences				
Area Around Room 'Always' Quiet at Night	300+	59%	-	58%
Doctors 'Always' Communicated Well	300+	79%	-	80%
Home Recovery Information Given	300+	79%	-	82%
Hospital Given 9 or 10 on 10 Point Scale	300+	63%	-	67%
Meds 'Always' Explained Before Given	300+	52%	-	60%
Nurses 'Always' Communicated Well	300+	70%	-	76%
Pain 'Always' Well Controlled	300+	66%	-	69%
Room and Bathroom 'Always' Clean	300+	61%	-	71%
Timely Help 'Always' Received	300+	55%	-	64%
Would Definitely Recommend Hospital	300+	62%	-	69%

NOTE: Hospital profiles are in alphabetical order by state, then city, then hospital within the city; Rankings exclude hospitals with less than 25 cases except for patient surveys which excludes hospitals with less than 100 cases; (a) 100–299 cases; (1) The number of cases is too small to be sure how well a hospital is performing; (2) The hospital indicated that the data submitted for this measure were based on a sample of cases; (3) Data was collected during a shorter time period (fewer quarters) than the maximum possible time for this measure; (4) Suppressed for one or more quarters by CMS; (5) No data is available from the hospital for this measure; (6) Fewer than 100 patients completed the HCAHPS survey. Use these rates with caution, as the number of surveys may be too low to reliably assess hospital performance; (7) Survey results are based on less than 12 months of data; (8) Survey results are not available for this reporting period; (9) No or very few patients were eligible for the HCAHPS survey. The scores shown, if any, reflect a very small number of surveys; (10) A state average was not calculated because too few hospitals in the state submitted data; (11) There were discrepancies in the data collection process; Please refer to the User's Guide for a full explanation of data.

Oklahoma State University Medical Center

744 West 9th Street Phone: 918-587-2561
Tulsa, OK 74127 Fax: 918-599-1750
URL: www.tulsaregional.com
Type: Acute Care Hospitals Emergency Services: Yes
Ownership: Proprietary Beds: 415

Key Personnel:
CEO/President. . . . . Jan Slater
Chief of Medical Staff . . . . Jenny Alexopulos, DO
Infection Control. . . . . Janet Bacon
Operating Room. . . . . Nellie Rhea
Radiology. . . . . Maureen Miller
Anesthesiology. . . . . Kimberly Dullge
Emergency Room . . . . Jan Emmons
Intensive Care Unit. . . . . Eric Burch

Measure	Cases	This Hosp.	State Avg.	U.S. Avg.
Heart Attack Care				
ACE Inhibitor or ARB for LVSD[1]	23	100%	95%	96%
Aspirin at Arrival	98	100%	98%	99%
Aspirin at Discharge	143	100%	98%	98%
Beta Blocker at Discharge	123	100%	98%	98%
Fibrinolytic Medication Timing	0	-	42%	55%
PCI Within 90 Minutes of Arrival[1]	20	100%	88%	90%
Smoking Cessation Advice	83	100%	100%	99%
Chest Pain/Possible Heart Attack Care				
Aspirin at Arrival[1,3]	2	100%	94%	95%
Median Time to ECG (minutes)[1,3]	2	6	9	8
Median Time to Transfer (minutes)[5]	0	-	75	61
Fibrinolytic Medication Timing[5]	0	-	50%	54%
Heart Failure Care				
ACE Inhibitor or ARB for LVSD	77	96%	94%	94%
Discharge Instructions	163	88%	85%	88%
Evaluation of LVS Function	182	99%	94%	98%
Smoking Cessation Advice	50	100%	97%	98%
Pneumonia Care				
Appropriate Initial Antibiotic	74	86%	91%	92%
Blood Culture Timing	87	98%	96%	96%
Influenza Vaccine	91	97%	89%	91%
Initial Antibiotic Timing	136	99%	95%	95%
Pneumococcal Vaccine	92	95%	91%	93%
Smoking Cessation Advice	104	99%	95%	97%
Surgical Care Improvement Project				
Appropriate VTP Within 24 Hours[2]	116	99%	91%	92%
Appropriate Hair Removal[2]	319	100%	100%	99%
Appropriate Beta Blocker Usage[2]	95	88%	91%	93%
Controlled Postoperative Blood Glucose[2]	73	100%	95%	93%
Prophylactic Antibiotic Timing[2]	202	98%	97%	97%
Prophylactic Antibiotic Timing (Outpatient)	84	77%	93%	92%
Prophylactic Antibiotic Selection[2]	208	96%	98%	97%
Prophylactic Antibiotic Select. (Outpatient)	79	91%	95%	94%
Prophylactic Antibiotic Stopped[2]	185	97%	94%	94%
Recommended VTP Ordered[2]	116	99%	94%	94%
Urinary Catheter Removal[2]	45	84%	87%	90%
Children's Asthma Care				
Received Systemic Corticosteroids	-	-	-	100%
Received Home Management Plan	-	-	-	71%
Received Reliever Medication	-	-	-	100%
Use of Medical Imaging				
Combination Abdominal CT Scan	342	0.412	0.372	0.191
Combination Chest CT Scan	248	0.133	0.134	0.054
Follow-up Mammogram/Ultrasound	198	12.6%	8%	8.4%
MRI for Low Back Pain	44	40.9%	34.3%	32.7%
Survey of Patients' Hospital Experiences				
Area Around Room 'Always' Quiet at Night	300+	60%	-	58%
Doctors 'Always' Communicated Well	300+	80%	-	80%
Home Recovery Information Given	300+	82%	-	82%
Hospital Given 9 or 10 on 10 Point Scale	300+	66%	-	67%
Meds 'Always' Explained Before Given	300+	57%	-	60%
Nurses 'Always' Communicated Well	300+	69%	-	76%
Pain 'Always' Well Controlled	300+	65%	-	69%
Room and Bathroom 'Always' Clean	300+	63%	-	71%
Timely Help 'Always' Received	300+	49%	-	64%
Would Definitely Recommend Hospital	300+	68%	-	69%

Oklahoma Surgical Hospital

2408 East 81st Street, Suite 300 Phone: 918-477-5000
Tulsa, OK 74137
URL: www.oklahomasurgicalhospital.com
Type: Acute Care Hospitals Emergency Services: Yes
Ownership: Proprietary

Key Personnel:
President/CEO. . . . . Rick Ferguson

Measure	Cases	This Hosp.	State Avg.	U.S. Avg.
Heart Attack Care				
ACE Inhibitor or ARB for LVSD[5]	0	-	95%	96%
Aspirin at Arrival[5]	0	-	98%	99%
Aspirin at Discharge[5]	0	-	98%	98%
Beta Blocker at Discharge[5]	0	-	98%	98%
Fibrinolytic Medication Timing[5]	0	-	42%	55%
PCI Within 90 Minutes of Arrival[5]	0	-	88%	90%
Smoking Cessation Advice[5]	0	-	100%	99%
Chest Pain/Possible Heart Attack Care				
Aspirin at Arrival[5]	0	-	94%	95%
Median Time to ECG (minutes)[5]	0	-	9	8
Median Time to Transfer (minutes)[5]	0	-	75	61
Fibrinolytic Medication Timing[5]	0	-	50%	54%
Heart Failure Care				
ACE Inhibitor or ARB for LVSD[5]	0	-	94%	94%
Discharge Instructions[5]	0	-	85%	88%
Evaluation of LVS Function[5]	0	-	94%	98%
Smoking Cessation Advice[5]	0	-	97%	98%
Pneumonia Care				
Appropriate Initial Antibiotic[5]	0	-	91%	92%
Blood Culture Timing[5]	0	-	96%	96%
Influenza Vaccine[5]	0	-	89%	91%
Initial Antibiotic Timing[5]	0	-	95%	95%
Pneumococcal Vaccine[5]	0	-	91%	93%
Smoking Cessation Advice[5]	0	-	95%	97%
Surgical Care Improvement Project				
Appropriate VTP Within 24 Hours[2]	80	98%	91%	92%
Appropriate Hair Removal[2]	433	100%	100%	99%
Appropriate Beta Blocker Usage[2]	101	100%	91%	93%
Controlled Postoperative Blood Glucose[2]	0	-	95%	93%
Prophylactic Antibiotic Timing[2]	309	99%	97%	97%
Prophylactic Antibiotic Timing (Outpatient)	381	97%	93%	92%
Prophylactic Antibiotic Selection[2]	310	99%	98%	97%
Prophylactic Antibiotic Select. (Outpatient)	377	97%	95%	94%
Prophylactic Antibiotic Stopped[2]	308	96%	94%	94%
Recommended VTP Ordered[2]	80	98%	94%	94%
Urinary Catheter Removal[1,2]	16	88%	87%	90%
Children's Asthma Care				
Received Systemic Corticosteroids	-	-	-	100%
Received Home Management Plan	-	-	-	71%
Received Reliever Medication	-	-	-	100%
Use of Medical Imaging				
Combination Abdominal CT Scan[1]	7	0.857	0.372	0.191
Combination Chest CT Scan[1]	4	0.750	0.134	0.054
Follow-up Mammogram/Ultrasound[5]	0	-	8%	8.4%
MRI for Low Back Pain	277	32.1%	34.3%	32.7%
Survey of Patients' Hospital Experiences				
Area Around Room 'Always' Quiet at Night	300+	85%	-	58%
Doctors 'Always' Communicated Well	300+	85%	-	80%
Home Recovery Information Given	300+	84%	-	82%
Hospital Given 9 or 10 on 10 Point Scale	300+	86%	-	67%
Meds 'Always' Explained Before Given	300+	70%	-	60%
Nurses 'Always' Communicated Well	300+	84%	-	76%
Pain 'Always' Well Controlled	300+	76%	-	69%
Room and Bathroom 'Always' Clean	300+	84%	-	71%
Timely Help 'Always' Received	300+	74%	-	64%
Would Definitely Recommend Hospital	300+	88%	-	69%

Pinnacle Specialty Hospital

2408 East 81st Street, Suite 600 Phone: 918-392-2780
Tulsa, OK 74137
URL: www.pinnaclespecialtyhospital.com
Type: Acute Care Hospitals Emergency Services: Yes
Ownership: Proprietary

Measure	Cases	This Hosp.	State Avg.	U.S. Avg.
Heart Attack Care				
ACE Inhibitor or ARB for LVSD[5]	0	-	95%	96%
Aspirin at Arrival[5]	0	-	98%	99%
Aspirin at Discharge[5]	0	-	98%	98%
Beta Blocker at Discharge[5]	0	-	98%	98%
Fibrinolytic Medication Timing[5]	0	-	42%	55%
PCI Within 90 Minutes of Arrival[5]	0	-	88%	90%
Smoking Cessation Advice[5]	0	-	100%	99%
Chest Pain/Possible Heart Attack Care				
Aspirin at Arrival	-	-	94%	95%
Median Time to ECG (minutes)	-	-	9	8
Median Time to Transfer (minutes)	-	-	75	61
Fibrinolytic Medication Timing	-	-	50%	54%
Heart Failure Care				
ACE Inhibitor or ARB for LVSD[5]	0	-	94%	94%
Discharge Instructions[5]	0	-	85%	88%
Evaluation of LVS Function[5]	0	-	94%	98%
Smoking Cessation Advice[5]	0	-	97%	98%
Pneumonia Care				
Appropriate Initial Antibiotic[5]	0	-	91%	92%
Blood Culture Timing[5]	0	-	96%	96%
Influenza Vaccine[5]	0	-	89%	91%
Initial Antibiotic Timing[5]	0	-	95%	95%
Pneumococcal Vaccine[5]	0	-	91%	93%
Smoking Cessation Advice[5]	0	-	95%	97%
Surgical Care Improvement Project				
Appropriate VTP Within 24 Hours[5]	0	-	91%	92%
Appropriate Hair Removal[5]	0	-	100%	99%
Appropriate Beta Blocker Usage[5]	0	-	91%	93%
Controlled Postoperative Blood Glucose[5]	0	-	95%	93%
Prophylactic Antibiotic Timing[5]	0	-	97%	97%
Prophylactic Antibiotic Timing (Outpatient)	-	-	93%	92%
Prophylactic Antibiotic Selection[5]	0	-	98%	97%
Prophylactic Antibiotic Select. (Outpatient)	-	-	95%	94%
Prophylactic Antibiotic Stopped[5]	0	-	94%	94%
Recommended VTP Ordered[5]	0	-	94%	94%
Urinary Catheter Removal[5]	0	-	87%	90%
Children's Asthma Care				
Received Systemic Corticosteroids	-	-	-	100%
Received Home Management Plan	-	-	-	71%
Received Reliever Medication	-	-	-	100%
Use of Medical Imaging				
Combination Abdominal CT Scan	-	-	0.372	0.191
Combination Chest CT Scan	-	-	0.134	0.054
Follow-up Mammogram/Ultrasound	-	-	8%	8.4%
MRI for Low Back Pain	-	-	34.3%	32.7%
Survey of Patients' Hospital Experiences				
Area Around Room 'Always' Quiet at Night[8]	-	-	-	58%
Doctors 'Always' Communicated Well[8]	-	-	-	80%
Home Recovery Information Given[8]	-	-	-	82%
Hospital Given 9 or 10 on 10 Point Scale[8]	-	-	-	67%
Meds 'Always' Explained Before Given[8]	-	-	-	60%
Nurses 'Always' Communicated Well[8]	-	-	-	76%
Pain 'Always' Well Controlled[8]	-	-	-	69%
Room and Bathroom 'Always' Clean[8]	-	-	-	71%
Timely Help 'Always' Received[8]	-	-	-	64%
Would Definitely Recommend Hospital[8]	-	-	-	69%

NOTE: Hospital profiles are in alphabetical order by state, then city, then hospital within the city; Rankings exclude hospitals with less than 25 cases except for patient surveys which excludes hospitals with less than 100 cases; (a) 100–299 cases; (1) The number of cases is too small to be sure how well a hospital is performing; (2) The hospital indicated that the data submitted for this measure were based on a sample of cases; (3) Data was collected during a shorter time period (fewer quarters) than the maximum possible time for this measure; (4) Suppressed for one or more quarters by CMS; (5) No data is available from the hospital for this measure; (6) Fewer than 100 patients completed the HCAHPS survey. Use these rates with caution, as the number of surveys may be too low to reliably assess hospital performance; (7) Survey results are based on less than 12 months of data; (8) Survey results are not available for this reporting period; (9) No or very few patients were eligible for the HCAHPS survey. The scores shown, if any, reflect a very small number of surveys; (10) A state average was not calculated because too few hospitals in the state submitted data; (11) There were discrepancies in the data collection process; Please refer to the User's Guide for a full explanation of data.

Saint Francis Hospital

6161 South Yale
Tulsa, OK 74136
Phone: 918-494-2200
Fax: 918-494-4501
E-mail: webadministrator@saintfrancis.com
URL: www.saintfrancis.com
Type: Acute Care Hospitals
Emergency Services: Yes
Ownership: Voluntary Non-Profit - Other
Beds: 897

Key Personnel:

CEO/President. . . . . Jake Henry, Jr
Cardiac Laboratory. . . . . James Whiteneck, MD
Infection Control. . . . . Dee Copeland, RN
Quality Assurance . . . . Jane Sharpe, RN
Radiology. . . . . R Krieger, MD
Anesthesiology. . . . . Mel Mercer Jr, MD
Emergency Room . . . . Frank Mitchell, MD

Measure	Cases	This Hosp.	State Avg.	U.S. Avg.
Heart Attack Care				
ACE Inhibitor or ARB for LVSD	113	90%	95%	96%
Aspirin at Arrival	496	98%	98%	99%
Aspirin at Discharge	813	100%	98%	98%
Beta Blocker at Discharge	796	99%	98%	98%
Fibrinolytic Medication Timing[1]	1	0%	42%	55%
PCI Within 90 Minutes of Arrival	88	75%	88%	90%
Smoking Cessation Advice	313	100%	100%	99%
Chest Pain/Possible Heart Attack Care				
Aspirin at Arrival[5]	0	-	94%	95%
Median Time to ECG (minutes)[5]	0	-	9	8
Median Time to Transfer (minutes)[5]	0	-	75	61
Fibrinolytic Medication Timing[5]	0	-	50%	54%
Heart Failure Care				
ACE Inhibitor or ARB for LVSD	309	100%	94%	94%
Discharge Instructions	713	95%	85%	88%
Evaluation of LVS Function	862	100%	94%	98%
Smoking Cessation Advice	144	100%	97%	98%
Pneumonia Care				
Appropriate Initial Antibiotic	492	89%	91%	92%
Blood Culture Timing	840	95%	96%	96%
Influenza Vaccine	587	94%	89%	91%
Initial Antibiotic Timing	848	91%	95%	95%
Pneumococcal Vaccine	783	98%	91%	93%
Smoking Cessation Advice	313	100%	95%	97%
Surgical Care Improvement Project				
Appropriate VTP Within 24 Hours[2]	732	91%	91%	92%
Appropriate Hair Removal[2]	2,287	100%	100%	99%
Appropriate Beta Blocker Usage[2]	651	91%	91%	93%
Controlled Postoperative Blood Glucose[2]	325	95%	95%	93%
Prophylactic Antibiotic Timing[2]	1,875	95%	97%	97%
Prophylactic Antibiotic Timing (Outpatient)	467	96%	93%	92%
Prophylactic Antibiotic Selection[2]	1,904	97%	98%	97%
Prophylactic Antibiotic Select. (Outpatient)	456	85%	95%	94%
Prophylactic Antibiotic Stopped[2]	1,839	94%	94%	94%
Recommended VTP Ordered[2]	733	97%	94%	94%
Urinary Catheter Removal[2]	339	88%	87%	90%
Children's Asthma Care				
Received Systemic Corticosteroids	-	-	-	100%
Received Home Management Plan	-	-	-	71%
Received Reliever Medication	-	-	-	100%
Use of Medical Imaging				
Combination Abdominal CT Scan	2,007	0.678	0.372	0.191
Combination Chest CT Scan	2,053	0.051	0.134	0.054
Follow-up Mammogram/Ultrasound	2,795	5.8%	8%	8.4%
MRI for Low Back Pain	392	31.6%	34.3%	32.7%
Survey of Patients' Hospital Experiences				
Area Around Room 'Always' Quiet at Night	300+	58%	-	58%
Doctors 'Always' Communicated Well	300+	77%	-	80%
Home Recovery Information Given	300+	79%	-	82%
Hospital Given 9 or 10 on 10 Point Scale	300+	68%	-	67%
Meds 'Always' Explained Before Given	300+	55%	-	60%
Nurses 'Always' Communicated Well	300+	75%	-	76%
Pain 'Always' Well Controlled	300+	67%	-	69%
Room and Bathroom 'Always' Clean	300+	70%	-	71%
Timely Help 'Always' Received	300+	59%	-	64%
Would Definitely Recommend Hospital	300+	74%	-	69%

Saint Francis Hospital South

10501 East 91st Street South
Tulsa, OK 74133
Phone: 918-307-6000
E-mail: webadministrator@saintfrancis.com
URL: www.saintfrancis.com
Type: Acute Care Hospitals
Emergency Services: Yes
Ownership: Proprietary
Beds: 76

Key Personnel:

CEO/President. . . . . Jake Henry, Jr.
Chief of Medical Staff. . . . . David Thomas

Measure	Cases	This Hosp.	State Avg.	U.S. Avg.
Heart Attack Care				
ACE Inhibitor or ARB for LVSD[1,3]	2	100%	95%	96%
Aspirin at Arrival[1,3]	7	100%	98%	99%
Aspirin at Discharge[1,3]	4	100%	98%	98%
Beta Blocker at Discharge[1,3]	4	100%	98%	98%
Fibrinolytic Medication Timing[3]	0	-	42%	55%
PCI Within 90 Minutes of Arrival[3]	0	-	88%	90%
Smoking Cessation Advice[3]	0	-	100%	99%
Chest Pain/Possible Heart Attack Care				
Aspirin at Arrival	94	96%	94%	95%
Median Time to ECG (minutes)	97	4	9	8
Median Time to Transfer (minutes)[1]	10	48	75	61
Fibrinolytic Medication Timing	0	-	50%	54%
Heart Failure Care				
ACE Inhibitor or ARB for LVSD	31	97%	94%	94%
Discharge Instructions	68	93%	85%	88%
Evaluation of LVS Function	89	99%	94%	98%
Smoking Cessation Advice[1]	7	100%	97%	98%
Pneumonia Care				
Appropriate Initial Antibiotic	95	93%	91%	92%
Blood Culture Timing	85	100%	96%	96%
Influenza Vaccine	71	96%	89%	91%
Initial Antibiotic Timing	107	94%	95%	95%
Pneumococcal Vaccine	97	100%	91%	93%
Smoking Cessation Advice	31	100%	95%	97%
Surgical Care Improvement Project				
Appropriate VTP Within 24 Hours	72	92%	91%	92%
Appropriate Hair Removal	272	100%	100%	99%
Appropriate Beta Blocker Usage	79	92%	91%	93%
Controlled Postoperative Blood Glucose	0	-	95%	93%
Prophylactic Antibiotic Timing	209	98%	97%	97%
Prophylactic Antibiotic Timing (Outpatient)	108	94%	93%	92%
Prophylactic Antibiotic Selection	210	97%	98%	97%
Prophylactic Antibiotic Select. (Outpatient)	106	98%	95%	94%
Prophylactic Antibiotic Stopped	203	96%	94%	94%
Recommended VTP Ordered	72	100%	94%	94%
Urinary Catheter Removal	38	97%	87%	90%
Children's Asthma Care				
Received Systemic Corticosteroids	-	-	-	100%
Received Home Management Plan	-	-	-	71%
Received Reliever Medication	-	-	-	100%
Use of Medical Imaging				
Combination Abdominal CT Scan	359	0.735	0.372	0.191
Combination Chest CT Scan	256	0.055	0.134	0.054
Follow-up Mammogram/Ultrasound	518	5.2%	8%	8.4%
MRI for Low Back Pain	85	32.9%	34.3%	32.7%
Survey of Patients' Hospital Experiences				
Area Around Room 'Always' Quiet at Night	300+	60%	-	58%
Doctors 'Always' Communicated Well	300+	82%	-	80%
Home Recovery Information Given	300+	83%	-	82%
Hospital Given 9 or 10 on 10 Point Scale	300+	77%	-	67%
Meds 'Always' Explained Before Given	300+	59%	-	60%
Nurses 'Always' Communicated Well	300+	77%	-	76%
Pain 'Always' Well Controlled	300+	70%	-	69%
Room and Bathroom 'Always' Clean	300+	72%	-	71%
Timely Help 'Always' Received	300+	68%	-	64%
Would Definitely Recommend Hospital	300+	80%	-	69%

Saint John Medical Center

1923 South Utica Avenue
Tulsa, OK 74104
Phone: 918-744-2345
URL: www.sjmc.org
Type: Acute Care Hospitals
Emergency Services: Yes
Ownership: Voluntary Non-Profit - Church

Key Personnel:

CEO . . . . Charles Anderson

Measure	Cases	This Hosp.	State Avg.	U.S. Avg.
Heart Attack Care				
ACE Inhibitor or ARB for LVSD	119	97%	95%	96%
Aspirin at Arrival	499	99%	98%	99%
Aspirin at Discharge	714	100%	98%	98%
Beta Blocker at Discharge	702	100%	98%	98%
Fibrinolytic Medication Timing	0	-	42%	55%
PCI Within 90 Minutes of Arrival	122	87%	88%	90%
Smoking Cessation Advice	268	99%	100%	99%
Chest Pain/Possible Heart Attack Care				
Aspirin at Arrival[3]	0	-	94%	95%
Median Time to ECG (minutes)[3]	0	-	9	8
Median Time to Transfer (minutes)[5]	0	-	75	61
Fibrinolytic Medication Timing[5]	0	-	50%	54%
Heart Failure Care				
ACE Inhibitor or ARB for LVSD	202	99%	94%	94%
Discharge Instructions	497	80%	85%	88%
Evaluation of LVS Function	597	98%	94%	98%
Smoking Cessation Advice	120	99%	97%	98%
Pneumonia Care				
Appropriate Initial Antibiotic[2]	301	85%	91%	92%
Blood Culture Timing[2]	353	96%	96%	96%
Influenza Vaccine[2]	310	75%	89%	91%
Initial Antibiotic Timing[2]	431	90%	95%	95%
Pneumococcal Vaccine[2]	412	71%	91%	93%
Smoking Cessation Advice[2]	202	95%	95%	97%
Surgical Care Improvement Project				
Appropriate VTP Within 24 Hours[2]	467	86%	91%	92%
Appropriate Hair Removal[2]	2,490	100%	100%	99%
Appropriate Beta Blocker Usage[2]	759	94%	91%	93%
Controlled Postoperative Blood Glucose[2]	319	99%	95%	93%
Prophylactic Antibiotic Timing[2]	2,125	98%	97%	97%
Prophylactic Antibiotic Timing (Outpatient)	454	91%	93%	92%
Prophylactic Antibiotic Selection[2]	2,160	99%	98%	97%
Prophylactic Antibiotic Select. (Outpatient)	433	99%	95%	94%
Prophylactic Antibiotic Stopped[2]	2,080	93%	94%	94%
Recommended VTP Ordered[2]	473	88%	94%	94%
Urinary Catheter Removal[2]	198	87%	87%	90%
Children's Asthma Care				
Received Systemic Corticosteroids	-	-	-	100%
Received Home Management Plan	-	-	-	71%
Received Reliever Medication	-	-	-	100%
Use of Medical Imaging				
Combination Abdominal CT Scan	1,137	0.770	0.372	0.191
Combination Chest CT Scan	1,004	0.797	0.134	0.054
Follow-up Mammogram/Ultrasound	2,215	12.9%	8%	8.4%
MRI for Low Back Pain	201	35.8%	34.3%	32.7%
Survey of Patients' Hospital Experiences				
Area Around Room 'Always' Quiet at Night	300+	57%	-	58%
Doctors 'Always' Communicated Well	300+	80%	-	80%
Home Recovery Information Given	300+	77%	-	82%
Hospital Given 9 or 10 on 10 Point Scale	300+	66%	-	67%
Meds 'Always' Explained Before Given	300+	59%	-	60%
Nurses 'Always' Communicated Well	300+	74%	-	76%
Pain 'Always' Well Controlled	300+	70%	-	69%
Room and Bathroom 'Always' Clean	300+	64%	-	71%
Timely Help 'Always' Received	300+	57%	-	64%
Would Definitely Recommend Hospital	300+	73%	-	69%

NOTE: Hospital profiles are in alphabetical order by state, then city, then hospital within the city; Rankings exclude hospitals with less than 25 cases except for patient surveys which excludes hospitals with less than 100 cases; (a) 100–299 cases; (1) The number of cases is too small to be sure how well a hospital is performing; (2) The hospital indicated that the data submitted for this measure were based on a sample of cases; (3) Data was collected during a shorter time period (fewer quarters) than the maximum possible time for this measure; (4) Suppressed for one or more quarters by CMS; (5) No data is available from the hospital for this measure; (6) Fewer than 100 patients completed the HCAHPS survey. Use these rates with caution, as the number of surveys may be too low to reliably assess hospital performance; (7) Survey results are based on less than 12 months of data; (8) Survey results are not available for this reporting period; (9) No or very few patients were eligible for the HCAHPS survey. The scores shown, if any, reflect a very small number of surveys; (10) A state average was not calculated because too few hospitals in the state submitted data; (11) There were discrepancies in the data collection process; Please refer to the User's Guide for a full explanation of data.

Southcrest Hospital

8801 South 101st East Avenue
Tulsa, OK 74133
Phone: 918-294-4000
Fax: 918-294-4809
URL: www.southcresthospital.com
Type: Acute Care Hospitals
Emergency Services: Yes
Ownership: Proprietary
Beds: 180

Key Personnel:
CEO/President. . . . . Anthonry R Young
Cardiac Laboratory. . . . . Ernest Pickpring
Quality Assurance . . . . Judy Dodson
Radiology. . . . . M Nguyen

Measure	Cases	This Hosp.	State Avg.	U.S. Avg.
Heart Attack Care				
ACE Inhibitor or ARB for LVSD	36	100%	95%	96%
Aspirin at Arrival	131	100%	98%	99%
Aspirin at Discharge	188	98%	98%	98%
Beta Blocker at Discharge	178	99%	98%	98%
Fibrinolytic Medication Timing	0	-	42%	55%
PCI Within 90 Minutes of Arrival	27	96%	88%	90%
Smoking Cessation Advice	73	100%	100%	99%
Chest Pain/Possible Heart Attack Care				
Aspirin at Arrival[1]	12	100%	94%	95%
Median Time to ECG (minutes)[1]	13	21	9	8
Median Time to Transfer (minutes)[5]	0	-	75	61
Fibrinolytic Medication Timing[3]	0	-	50%	54%
Heart Failure Care				
ACE Inhibitor or ARB for LVSD	71	100%	94%	94%
Discharge Instructions	163	91%	85%	88%
Evaluation of LVS Function	191	100%	94%	98%
Smoking Cessation Advice[1]	22	100%	97%	98%
Pneumonia Care				
Appropriate Initial Antibiotic	108	97%	91%	92%
Blood Culture Timing	159	97%	96%	96%
Influenza Vaccine	125	98%	89%	91%
Initial Antibiotic Timing	151	98%	95%	95%
Pneumococcal Vaccine	133	98%	91%	93%
Smoking Cessation Advice	94	98%	95%	97%
Surgical Care Improvement Project				
Appropriate VTP Within 24 Hours	175	93%	91%	92%
Appropriate Hair Removal	583	100%	100%	99%
Appropriate Beta Blocker Usage	147	100%	91%	93%
Controlled Postoperative Blood Glucose	147	95%	95%	93%
Prophylactic Antibiotic Timing	405	100%	97%	97%
Prophylactic Antibiotic Timing (Outpatient)	203	97%	93%	92%
Prophylactic Antibiotic Selection	409	99%	98%	97%
Prophylactic Antibiotic Select. (Outpatient)	200	99%	95%	94%
Prophylactic Antibiotic Stopped	373	97%	94%	94%
Recommended VTP Ordered	176	97%	94%	94%
Urinary Catheter Removal	131	100%	87%	90%
Children's Asthma Care				
Received Systemic Corticosteroids	-	-	-	100%
Received Home Management Plan	-	-	-	71%
Received Reliever Medication	-	-	-	100%
Use of Medical Imaging				
Combination Abdominal CT Scan	376	0.266	0.372	0.191
Combination Chest CT Scan	203	0.054	0.134	0.054
Follow-up Mammogram/Ultrasound	509	6.7%	8%	8.4%
MRI for Low Back Pain	97	39.2%	34.3%	32.7%
Survey of Patients' Hospital Experiences				
Area Around Room 'Always' Quiet at Night	300+	58%	-	58%
Doctors 'Always' Communicated Well	300+	77%	-	80%
Home Recovery Information Given	300+	80%	-	82%
Hospital Given 9 or 10 on 10 Point Scale	300+	63%	-	67%
Meds 'Always' Explained Before Given	300+	49%	-	60%
Nurses 'Always' Communicated Well	300+	68%	-	76%
Pain 'Always' Well Controlled	300+	66%	-	69%
Room and Bathroom 'Always' Clean	300+	57%	-	71%
Timely Help 'Always' Received	300+	52%	-	64%
Would Definitely Recommend Hospital	300+	68%	-	69%

Southwestern Regional Medical Center

10109 East 79th Street South
Tulsa, OK 74133
Phone: 918-496-5000
Type: Acute Care Hospitals
Emergency Services: No
Ownership: Proprietary
Beds: 42

Key Personnel:
CEO/President. . . . . Jim Brewer
Radiology. . . . . Ed McKay

Measure	Cases	This Hosp.	State Avg.	U.S. Avg.
Heart Attack Care				
ACE Inhibitor or ARB for LVSD[5]	0	-	95%	96%
Aspirin at Arrival[5]	0	-	98%	99%
Aspirin at Discharge[5]	0	-	98%	98%
Beta Blocker at Discharge[5]	0	-	98%	98%
Fibrinolytic Medication Timing[5]	0	-	42%	55%
PCI Within 90 Minutes of Arrival[5]	0	-	88%	90%
Smoking Cessation Advice[5]	0	-	100%	99%
Chest Pain/Possible Heart Attack Care				
Aspirin at Arrival[5]	0	-	94%	95%
Median Time to ECG (minutes)[5]	0	-	9	8
Median Time to Transfer (minutes)[5]	0	-	75	61
Fibrinolytic Medication Timing[5]	0	-	50%	54%
Heart Failure Care				
ACE Inhibitor or ARB for LVSD[3]	0	-	94%	94%
Discharge Instructions[1,3]	1	100%	85%	88%
Evaluation of LVS Function[1,3]	1	100%	94%	98%
Smoking Cessation Advice[3]	0	-	97%	98%
Pneumonia Care				
Appropriate Initial Antibiotic	0	-	91%	92%
Blood Culture Timing	0	-	96%	96%
Influenza Vaccine[1]	4	25%	89%	91%
Initial Antibiotic Timing[1]	2	100%	95%	95%
Pneumococcal Vaccine[1]	2	100%	91%	93%
Smoking Cessation Advice[1]	9	67%	95%	97%
Surgical Care Improvement Project				
Appropriate VTP Within 24 Hours	112	78%	91%	92%
Appropriate Hair Removal	125	98%	100%	99%
Appropriate Beta Blocker Usage[1]	14	71%	91%	93%
Controlled Postoperative Blood Glucose	0	-	95%	93%
Prophylactic Antibiotic Timing	39	95%	97%	97%
Prophylactic Antibiotic Timing (Outpatient)	45	84%	93%	92%
Prophylactic Antibiotic Selection	39	97%	98%	97%
Prophylactic Antibiotic Select. (Outpatient)	42	88%	95%	94%
Prophylactic Antibiotic Stopped	39	72%	94%	94%
Recommended VTP Ordered	112	87%	94%	94%
Urinary Catheter Removal[1]	18	61%	87%	90%
Children's Asthma Care				
Received Systemic Corticosteroids	-	-	-	100%
Received Home Management Plan	-	-	-	71%
Received Reliever Medication	-	-	-	100%
Use of Medical Imaging				
Combination Abdominal CT Scan	812	0.317	0.372	0.191
Combination Chest CT Scan	921	0.008	0.134	0.054
Follow-up Mammogram/Ultrasound[1]	31	19.4%	8%	8.4%
MRI for Low Back Pain[1]	2	50.0%	34.3%	32.7%
Survey of Patients' Hospital Experiences				
Area Around Room 'Always' Quiet at Night	(a)	69%	-	58%
Doctors 'Always' Communicated Well	(a)	85%	-	80%
Home Recovery Information Given	(a)	85%	-	82%
Hospital Given 9 or 10 on 10 Point Scale	(a)	90%	-	67%
Meds 'Always' Explained Before Given	(a)	68%	-	60%
Nurses 'Always' Communicated Well	(a)	79%	-	76%
Pain 'Always' Well Controlled	(a)	72%	-	69%
Room and Bathroom 'Always' Clean	(a)	79%	-	71%
Timely Help 'Always' Received	(a)	71%	-	64%
Would Definitely Recommend Hospital	(a)	92%	-	69%

Tulsa Spine & Specialty Hospital

6901 South Olympia Avenue
Tulsa, OK 74132
Phone: 918-388-5701
URL: www.tulsaspinehospital.com
Type: Acute Care Hospitals
Emergency Services: Yes
Ownership: Voluntary Non-Profit - Private

Measure	Cases	This Hosp.	State Avg.	U.S. Avg.
Heart Attack Care				
ACE Inhibitor or ARB for LVSD[5]	0	-	95%	96%
Aspirin at Arrival[5]	0	-	98%	99%
Aspirin at Discharge[5]	0	-	98%	98%
Beta Blocker at Discharge[5]	0	-	98%	98%
Fibrinolytic Medication Timing[5]	0	-	42%	55%
PCI Within 90 Minutes of Arrival[5]	0	-	88%	90%
Smoking Cessation Advice[5]	0	-	100%	99%
Chest Pain/Possible Heart Attack Care				
Aspirin at Arrival[5]	0	-	94%	95%
Median Time to ECG (minutes)[5]	0	-	9	8
Median Time to Transfer (minutes)[5]	0	-	75	61
Fibrinolytic Medication Timing[5]	0	-	50%	54%
Heart Failure Care				
ACE Inhibitor or ARB for LVSD[5]	0	-	94%	94%
Discharge Instructions[5]	0	-	85%	88%
Evaluation of LVS Function[5]	0	-	94%	98%
Smoking Cessation Advice[5]	0	-	97%	98%
Pneumonia Care				
Appropriate Initial Antibiotic[5]	0	-	91%	92%
Blood Culture Timing[5]	0	-	96%	96%
Influenza Vaccine[5]	0	-	89%	91%
Initial Antibiotic Timing[5]	0	-	95%	95%
Pneumococcal Vaccine[5]	0	-	91%	93%
Smoking Cessation Advice[5]	0	-	95%	97%
Surgical Care Improvement Project				
Appropriate VTP Within 24 Hours	28	96%	91%	92%
Appropriate Hair Removal	99	100%	100%	99%
Appropriate Beta Blocker Usage[1]	21	76%	91%	93%
Controlled Postoperative Blood Glucose	0	-	95%	93%
Prophylactic Antibiotic Timing	64	95%	97%	97%
Prophylactic Antibiotic Timing (Outpatient)	159	92%	93%	92%
Prophylactic Antibiotic Selection	64	98%	98%	97%
Prophylactic Antibiotic Select. (Outpatient)	156	97%	95%	94%
Prophylactic Antibiotic Stopped	63	94%	94%	94%
Recommended VTP Ordered	29	93%	94%	94%
Urinary Catheter Removal[1]	7	86%	87%	90%
Children's Asthma Care				
Received Systemic Corticosteroids	-	-	-	100%
Received Home Management Plan	-	-	-	71%
Received Reliever Medication	-	-	-	100%
Use of Medical Imaging				
Combination Abdominal CT Scan[1]	6	0.167	0.372	0.191
Combination Chest CT Scan[1]	5	0.400	0.134	0.054
Follow-up Mammogram/Ultrasound[5]	0	-	8%	8.4%
MRI for Low Back Pain	252	36.1%	34.3%	32.7%
Survey of Patients' Hospital Experiences				
Area Around Room 'Always' Quiet at Night	300+	83%	-	58%
Doctors 'Always' Communicated Well	300+	88%	-	80%
Home Recovery Information Given	300+	86%	-	82%
Hospital Given 9 or 10 on 10 Point Scale	300+	88%	-	67%
Meds 'Always' Explained Before Given	300+	72%	-	60%
Nurses 'Always' Communicated Well	300+	85%	-	76%
Pain 'Always' Well Controlled	300+	77%	-	69%
Room and Bathroom 'Always' Clean	300+	87%	-	71%
Timely Help 'Always' Received	300+	79%	-	64%
Would Definitely Recommend Hospital	300+	93%	-	69%

NOTE: Hospital profiles are in alphabetical order by state, then city, then hospital within the city; Rankings exclude hospitals with less than 25 cases except for patient surveys which excludes hospitals with less than 100 cases; (a) 100–299 cases; (1) The number of cases is too small to be sure how well a hospital is performing; (2) The hospital indicated that the data submitted for this measure were based on a sample of cases; (3) Data was collected during a shorter time period (fewer quarters) than the maximum possible time for this measure; (4) Suppressed for one or more quarters by CMS; (5) No data is available from the hospital for this measure; (6) Fewer than 100 patients completed the HCAHPS survey. Use these rates with caution, as the number of surveys may be too low to reliably assess hospital performance; (7) Survey results are based on less than 12 months of data; (8) Survey results are not available for this reporting period; (9) No or very few patients were eligible for the HCAHPS survey. The scores shown, if any, reflect a very small number of surveys; (10) A state average was not calculated because too few hospitals in the state submitted data; (11) There were discrepancies in the data collection process; Please refer to the User's Guide for a full explanation of data.

Craig General Hospital

735 North Foreman
Vinita, OK 74301
Phone: 918-256-7551
Fax: 918-256-3703
URL: www.craiggeneralhospital.com
Type: Acute Care Hospitals
Emergency Services: Yes
Ownership: Voluntary Non-Profit - Other
Beds: 62

Key Personnel:
CEO/President. . . . . B Joe Gunn, EdD
Chief of Medical Staff . . . . Robert F Villareal, MD
Infection Control. . . . . Gwen Barbaree
Quality Assurance . . . . Bill Dennis
Radiology. . . . . Laura Arrowsmith
Emergency Room . . . . Barbara Hodges

Measure	Cases	This Hosp.	State Avg.	U.S. Avg.
Heart Attack Care				
ACE Inhibitor or ARB for LVSD[1]	2	50%	95%	96%
Aspirin at Arrival[1]	9	67%	98%	99%
Aspirin at Discharge[1]	7	43%	98%	98%
Beta Blocker at Discharge[1]	7	43%	98%	98%
Fibrinolytic Medication Timing	0	-	42%	55%
PCI Within 90 Minutes of Arrival	0	-	88%	90%
Smoking Cessation Advice[1]	1	100%	100%	99%
Chest Pain/Possible Heart Attack Care				
Aspirin at Arrival	73	90%	94%	95%
Median Time to ECG (minutes)	68	6	9	8
Median Time to Transfer (minutes)[1,3]	5	90	75	61
Fibrinolytic Medication Timing[1]	3	0%	50%	54%
Heart Failure Care				
ACE Inhibitor or ARB for LVSD[1]	13	69%	94%	94%
Discharge Instructions	44	73%	85%	88%
Evaluation of LVS Function	56	79%	94%	98%
Smoking Cessation Advice[1]	9	100%	97%	98%
Pneumonia Care				
Appropriate Initial Antibiotic	66	91%	91%	92%
Blood Culture Timing	38	92%	96%	96%
Influenza Vaccine	55	84%	89%	91%
Initial Antibiotic Timing	59	93%	95%	95%
Pneumococcal Vaccine	68	78%	91%	93%
Smoking Cessation Advice	34	97%	95%	97%
Surgical Care Improvement Project				
Appropriate VTP Within 24 Hours[1,3]	4	75%	91%	92%
Appropriate Hair Removal[1,3]	14	100%	100%	99%
Appropriate Beta Blocker Usage[1,3]	1	0%	91%	93%
Controlled Postoperative Blood Glucose[3]	0	-	95%	93%
Prophylactic Antibiotic Timing[1,3]	13	100%	97%	97%
Prophylactic Antibiotic Timing (Outpatient)[1,3]	9	89%	93%	92%
Prophylactic Antibiotic Selection[1,3]	13	92%	98%	97%
Prophylactic Antibiotic Select. (Outpatient)[1,3]	8	100%	95%	94%
Prophylactic Antibiotic Stopped[1,3]	11	100%	94%	94%
Recommended VTP Ordered[1,3]	4	100%	94%	94%
Urinary Catheter Removal	0	-	87%	90%
Children's Asthma Care				
Received Systemic Corticosteroids	-	-	-	100%
Received Home Management Plan	-	-	-	71%
Received Reliever Medication	-	-	-	100%
Use of Medical Imaging				
Combination Abdominal CT Scan	317	0.041	0.372	0.191
Combination Chest CT Scan	164	0.006	0.134	0.054
Follow-up Mammogram/Ultrasound	301	7.3%	8%	8.4%
MRI for Low Back Pain	84	46.4%	34.3%	32.7%
Survey of Patients' Hospital Experiences				
Area Around Room 'Always' Quiet at Night	300+	53%	-	58%
Doctors 'Always' Communicated Well	300+	88%	-	80%
Home Recovery Information Given	300+	81%	-	82%
Hospital Given 9 or 10 on 10 Point Scale	300+	69%	-	67%
Meds 'Always' Explained Before Given	300+	62%	-	60%
Nurses 'Always' Communicated Well	300+	81%	-	76%
Pain 'Always' Well Controlled	300+	72%	-	69%
Room and Bathroom 'Always' Clean	300+	73%	-	71%
Timely Help 'Always' Received	300+	67%	-	64%
Would Definitely Recommend Hospital	300+	69%	-	69%

Wagoner Community Hospital

1200 West Cherokee Street
Wagoner, OK 74467
Phone: 918-485-5514
Fax: 918-485-9701
Type: Acute Care Hospitals
Emergency Services: Yes
Ownership: Govt - Hospital Dist/Auth
Beds: 100

Key Personnel:
CEO/President. . . . . John Crawford
Chief of Medical Staff . . . . Chris Roberts
Intensive Care Unit. . . . . Louie Easter

Measure	Cases	This Hosp.	State Avg.	U.S. Avg.
Heart Attack Care				
ACE Inhibitor or ARB for LVSD[3]	0	-	95%	96%
Aspirin at Arrival[1,3]	3	100%	98%	99%
Aspirin at Discharge[1,3]	2	100%	98%	98%
Beta Blocker at Discharge[1,3]	2	100%	98%	98%
Fibrinolytic Medication Timing[3]	0	-	42%	55%
PCI Within 90 Minutes of Arrival[3]	0	-	88%	90%
Smoking Cessation Advice[3]	0	-	100%	99%
Chest Pain/Possible Heart Attack Care				
Aspirin at Arrival	37	81%	94%	95%
Median Time to ECG (minutes)	40	22	9	8
Median Time to Transfer (minutes)[1,3]	1	135	75	61
Fibrinolytic Medication Timing[1]	1	0%	50%	54%
Heart Failure Care				
ACE Inhibitor or ARB for LVSD[1]	9	89%	94%	94%
Discharge Instructions[1]	23	78%	85%	88%
Evaluation of LVS Function[1]	22	82%	94%	98%
Smoking Cessation Advice[1]	5	100%	97%	98%
Pneumonia Care				
Appropriate Initial Antibiotic	25	96%	91%	92%
Blood Culture Timing[1]	14	100%	96%	96%
Influenza Vaccine[1]	16	81%	89%	91%
Initial Antibiotic Timing	29	86%	95%	95%
Pneumococcal Vaccine[1]	16	88%	91%	93%
Smoking Cessation Advice[1]	12	100%	95%	97%
Surgical Care Improvement Project				
Appropriate VTP Within 24 Hours[5]	0	-	91%	92%
Appropriate Hair Removal[5]	0	-	100%	99%
Appropriate Beta Blocker Usage[5]	0	-	91%	93%
Controlled Postoperative Blood Glucose[5]	0	-	95%	93%
Prophylactic Antibiotic Timing[5]	0	-	97%	97%
Prophylactic Antibiotic Timing (Outpatient)[5]	0	-	93%	92%
Prophylactic Antibiotic Selection[5]	0	-	98%	97%
Prophylactic Antibiotic Select. (Outpatient)[5]	0	-	95%	94%
Prophylactic Antibiotic Stopped[5]	0	-	94%	94%
Recommended VTP Ordered[5]	0	-	94%	94%
Urinary Catheter Removal[5]	0	-	87%	90%
Children's Asthma Care				
Received Systemic Corticosteroids	-	-	-	100%
Received Home Management Plan	-	-	-	71%
Received Reliever Medication	-	-	-	100%
Use of Medical Imaging				
Combination Abdominal CT Scan	46	0.500	0.372	0.191
Combination Chest CT Scan[1]	27	0.370	0.134	0.054
Follow-up Mammogram/Ultrasound	86	11.6%	8%	8.4%
MRI for Low Back Pain[1]	14	21.4%	34.3%	32.7%
Survey of Patients' Hospital Experiences				
Area Around Room 'Always' Quiet at Night	(a)	69%	-	58%
Doctors 'Always' Communicated Well	(a)	79%	-	80%
Home Recovery Information Given	(a)	78%	-	82%
Hospital Given 9 or 10 on 10 Point Scale	(a)	61%	-	67%
Meds 'Always' Explained Before Given	(a)	56%	-	60%
Nurses 'Always' Communicated Well	(a)	76%	-	76%
Pain 'Always' Well Controlled	(a)	67%	-	69%
Room and Bathroom 'Always' Clean	(a)	70%	-	71%
Timely Help 'Always' Received	(a)	74%	-	64%
Would Definitely Recommend Hospital	(a)	67%	-	69%

Watonga Municipal Hospital

500 North Clarence Nash Boulevard
Watonga, OK 73772
Phone: 580-623-7211
Fax: 580-623-7206
E-mail: wmhosp@pldi.net
URL: www.watongahospital.com
Type: Critical Access Hospitals
Emergency Services: Yes
Ownership: Govt - Hospital Dist/Auth
Beds: 25

Key Personnel:
CEO/President. . . . . Brenda Doyel
Quality Assurance . . . . Kathy Vermillion

Measure	Cases	This Hosp.	State Avg.	U.S. Avg.
Heart Attack Care				
ACE Inhibitor or ARB for LVSD[3]	0	-	95%	96%
Aspirin at Arrival[1,3]	1	100%	98%	99%
Aspirin at Discharge[3]	0	-	98%	98%
Beta Blocker at Discharge[3]	0	-	98%	98%
Fibrinolytic Medication Timing[3]	0	-	42%	55%
PCI Within 90 Minutes of Arrival[3]	0	-	88%	90%
Smoking Cessation Advice[3]	0	-	100%	99%
Chest Pain/Possible Heart Attack Care				
Aspirin at Arrival	-	-	94%	95%
Median Time to ECG (minutes)	-	-	9	8
Median Time to Transfer (minutes)	-	-	75	61
Fibrinolytic Medication Timing	-	-	50%	54%
Heart Failure Care				
ACE Inhibitor or ARB for LVSD[1,3]	3	100%	94%	94%
Discharge Instructions[1,3]	8	62%	85%	88%
Evaluation of LVS Function[1,3]	13	46%	94%	98%
Smoking Cessation Advice[1,3]	3	67%	97%	98%
Pneumonia Care				
Appropriate Initial Antibiotic[1,3]	19	100%	91%	92%
Blood Culture Timing[1,3]	11	100%	96%	96%
Influenza Vaccine[1]	11	73%	89%	91%
Initial Antibiotic Timing[1,3]	2	50%	95%	95%
Pneumococcal Vaccine[1,3]	11	73%	91%	93%
Smoking Cessation Advice[1,3]	5	40%	95%	97%
Surgical Care Improvement Project				
Appropriate VTP Within 24 Hours[5]	0	-	91%	92%
Appropriate Hair Removal[5]	0	-	100%	99%
Appropriate Beta Blocker Usage[5]	0	-	91%	93%
Controlled Postoperative Blood Glucose[5]	0	-	95%	93%
Prophylactic Antibiotic Timing[5]	0	-	97%	97%
Prophylactic Antibiotic Timing (Outpatient)	-	-	93%	92%
Prophylactic Antibiotic Selection[5]	0	-	98%	97%
Prophylactic Antibiotic Select. (Outpatient)	-	-	95%	94%
Prophylactic Antibiotic Stopped[5]	0	-	94%	94%
Recommended VTP Ordered[5]	0	-	94%	94%
Urinary Catheter Removal[5]	0	-	87%	90%
Children's Asthma Care				
Received Systemic Corticosteroids	-	-	-	100%
Received Home Management Plan	-	-	-	71%
Received Reliever Medication	-	-	-	100%
Use of Medical Imaging				
Combination Abdominal CT Scan	-	-	0.372	0.191
Combination Chest CT Scan	-	-	0.134	0.054
Follow-up Mammogram/Ultrasound	-	-	8%	8.4%
MRI for Low Back Pain	-	-	34.3%	32.7%
Survey of Patients' Hospital Experiences				
Area Around Room 'Always' Quiet at Night[6]	<100	64%	-	58%
Doctors 'Always' Communicated Well[6]	<100	85%	-	80%
Home Recovery Information Given[6]	<100	72%	-	82%
Hospital Given 9 or 10 on 10 Point Scale[6]	<100	53%	-	67%
Meds 'Always' Explained Before Given[6]	<100	56%	-	60%
Nurses 'Always' Communicated Well[6]	<100	68%	-	76%
Pain 'Always' Well Controlled[6]	<100	69%	-	69%
Room and Bathroom 'Always' Clean[6]	<100	68%	-	71%
Timely Help 'Always' Received[6]	<100	74%	-	64%
Would Definitely Recommend Hospital	<100	58%	-	69%

NOTE: Hospital profiles are in alphabetical order by state, then city, then hospital within the city; Rankings exclude hospitals with less than 25 cases except for patient surveys which excludes hospitals with less than 100 cases; (a) 100–299 cases; (1) The number of cases is too small to be sure how well a hospital is performing; (2) The hospital indicated that the data submitted for this measure were based on a sample of cases; (3) Data was collected during a shorter time period (fewer quarters) than the maximum possible time for this measure; (4) Suppressed for one or more quarters by CMS; (5) No data is available from the hospital for this measure; (6) Fewer than 100 patients completed the HCAHPS survey. Use these rates with caution, as the number of surveys may be too low to reliably assess hospital performance; (7) Survey results are based on less than 12 months of data; (8) Survey results are not available for this reporting period; (9) No or very few patients were eligible for the HCAHPS survey. The scores shown, if any, reflect a very small number of surveys; (10) A state average was not calculated because too few hospitals in the state submitted data; (11) There were discrepancies in the data collection process; Please refer to the User's Guide for a full explanation of data.

Jefferson County Hospital

Intersection Hyws 81 & 70
Waurika, OK 73573
Type: Critical Access Hospitals
Ownership: Govt - Hospital Dist/Auth
Phone: 580-228-2244
Fax: 580-228-3410
Emergency Services: Yes
Beds: 25

Key Personnel:
CEO/President. . . . . Buck McKinney Jr
Chief of Medical Staff. . . . . Harold Start, MD
Infection Control. . . . . Pam Jackson, RN
Quality Assurance . . . . Buck McKinley, Jr
Emergency Room . . . . Steven Hwshay, DO

Measure	Cases	This Hosp.	State Avg.	U.S. Avg.
Heart Attack Care				
ACE Inhibitor or ARB for LVSD[5]	0	-	95%	96%
Aspirin at Arrival[5]	0	-	98%	99%
Aspirin at Discharge[5]	0	-	98%	98%
Beta Blocker at Discharge[5]	0	-	98%	98%
Fibrinolytic Medication Timing[5]	0	-	42%	55%
PCI Within 90 Minutes of Arrival[5]	0	-	88%	90%
Smoking Cessation Advice[5]	0	-	100%	99%
Chest Pain/Possible Heart Attack Care				
Aspirin at Arrival	-	-	94%	95%
Median Time to ECG (minutes)	-	-	9	8
Median Time to Transfer (minutes)	-	-	75	61
Fibrinolytic Medication Timing	-	-	50%	54%
Heart Failure Care				
ACE Inhibitor or ARB for LVSD[5]	0	-	94%	94%
Discharge Instructions[5]	0	-	85%	88%
Evaluation of LVS Function[5]	0	-	94%	98%
Smoking Cessation Advice[5]	0	-	97%	98%
Pneumonia Care				
Appropriate Initial Antibiotic[1,3]	4	100%	91%	92%
Blood Culture Timing[1,3]	1	100%	96%	96%
Influenza Vaccine[1]	9	22%	89%	91%
Initial Antibiotic Timing[1,3]	10	100%	95%	95%
Pneumococcal Vaccine[1,3]	7	14%	91%	93%
Smoking Cessation Advice[1,3]	3	67%	95%	97%
Surgical Care Improvement Project				
Appropriate VTP Within 24 Hours[5]	0	-	91%	92%
Appropriate Hair Removal[5]	0	-	100%	99%
Appropriate Beta Blocker Usage[5]	0	-	91%	93%
Controlled Postoperative Blood Glucose[5]	0	-	95%	93%
Prophylactic Antibiotic Timing[5]	0	-	97%	97%
Prophylactic Antibiotic Timing (Outpatient)	-	-	93%	92%
Prophylactic Antibiotic Selection[5]	0	-	98%	97%
Prophylactic Antibiotic Select. (Outpatient)	-	-	95%	94%
Prophylactic Antibiotic Stopped[5]	0	-	94%	94%
Recommended VTP Ordered[5]	0	-	94%	94%
Urinary Catheter Removal[5]	0	-	87%	90%
Children's Asthma Care				
Received Systemic Corticosteroids	-	-	-	100%
Received Home Management Plan	-	-	-	71%
Received Reliever Medication	-	-	-	100%
Use of Medical Imaging				
Combination Abdominal CT Scan	-	-	0.372	0.191
Combination Chest CT Scan	-	-	0.134	0.054
Follow-up Mammogram/Ultrasound	-	-	8%	8.4%
MRI for Low Back Pain	-	-	34.3%	32.7%
Survey of Patients' Hospital Experiences				
Area Around Room 'Always' Quiet at Night[8]	-	-	-	58%
Doctors 'Always' Communicated Well[8]	-	-	-	80%
Home Recovery Information Given[8]	-	-	-	82%
Hospital Given 9 or 10 on 10 Point Scale[8]	-	-	-	67%
Meds 'Always' Explained Before Given[8]	-	-	-	60%
Nurses 'Always' Communicated Well[8]	-	-	-	76%
Pain 'Always' Well Controlled[8]	-	-	-	69%
Room and Bathroom 'Always' Clean[8]	-	-	-	71%
Timely Help 'Always' Received[8]	-	-	-	64%
Would Definitely Recommend Hospital[8]	-	-	-	69%

Weatherford Regional Hospital

3701 E Main
Weatherford, OK 73096
URL: www.weatherfordhospital.com
Type: Critical Access Hospitals
Ownership: Govt - Hospital Dist/Auth
Phone: 580-772-5551
Fax: 580-774-4764
Emergency Services: Yes
Beds: 49

Key Personnel:
CEO/President. . . . . Debbie Howe
Operating Room. . . . . Ollie Brooks
Radiology. . . . . John Hamlin
Emergency Room . . . . Sergio DeMier

Measure	Cases	This Hosp.	State Avg.	U.S. Avg.
Heart Attack Care				
ACE Inhibitor or ARB for LVSD	0	-	95%	96%
Aspirin at Arrival[1]	2	50%	98%	99%
Aspirin at Discharge[1]	1	0%	98%	98%
Beta Blocker at Discharge[1]	2	50%	98%	98%
Fibrinolytic Medication Timing	0	-	42%	55%
PCI Within 90 Minutes of Arrival	0	-	88%	90%
Smoking Cessation Advice	0	-	100%	99%
Chest Pain/Possible Heart Attack Care				
Aspirin at Arrival	-	-	94%	95%
Median Time to ECG (minutes)	-	-	9	8
Median Time to Transfer (minutes)	-	-	75	61
Fibrinolytic Medication Timing	-	-	50%	54%
Heart Failure Care				
ACE Inhibitor or ARB for LVSD[1]	9	78%	94%	94%
Discharge Instructions[1]	19	89%	85%	88%
Evaluation of LVS Function	33	88%	94%	98%
Smoking Cessation Advice[1]	4	75%	97%	98%
Pneumonia Care				
Appropriate Initial Antibiotic	43	88%	91%	92%
Blood Culture Timing[1]	19	89%	96%	96%
Influenza Vaccine	45	91%	89%	91%
Initial Antibiotic Timing	73	95%	95%	95%
Pneumococcal Vaccine	67	85%	91%	93%
Smoking Cessation Advice[1]	18	56%	95%	97%
Surgical Care Improvement Project				
Appropriate VTP Within 24 Hours[5]	0	-	91%	92%
Appropriate Hair Removal[5]	0	-	100%	99%
Appropriate Beta Blocker Usage[5]	0	-	91%	93%
Controlled Postoperative Blood Glucose[5]	0	-	95%	93%
Prophylactic Antibiotic Timing[5]	0	-	97%	97%
Prophylactic Antibiotic Timing (Outpatient)	-	-	93%	92%
Prophylactic Antibiotic Selection[5]	0	-	98%	97%
Prophylactic Antibiotic Select. (Outpatient)	-	-	95%	94%
Prophylactic Antibiotic Stopped[5]	0	-	94%	94%
Recommended VTP Ordered[5]	0	-	94%	94%
Urinary Catheter Removal[5]	0	-	87%	90%
Children's Asthma Care				
Received Systemic Corticosteroids	-	-	-	100%
Received Home Management Plan	-	-	-	71%
Received Reliever Medication	-	-	-	100%
Use of Medical Imaging				
Combination Abdominal CT Scan	-	-	0.372	0.191
Combination Chest CT Scan	-	-	0.134	0.054
Follow-up Mammogram/Ultrasound	-	-	8%	8.4%
MRI for Low Back Pain	-	-	34.3%	32.7%
Survey of Patients' Hospital Experiences				
Area Around Room 'Always' Quiet at Night[8]	-	-	-	58%
Doctors 'Always' Communicated Well[8]	-	-	-	80%
Home Recovery Information Given[8]	-	-	-	82%
Hospital Given 9 or 10 on 10 Point Scale[8]	-	-	-	67%
Meds 'Always' Explained Before Given[8]	-	-	-	60%
Nurses 'Always' Communicated Well[8]	-	-	-	76%
Pain 'Always' Well Controlled[8]	-	-	-	69%
Room and Bathroom 'Always' Clean[8]	-	-	-	71%
Timely Help 'Always' Received[8]	-	-	-	64%
Would Definitely Recommend Hospital[8]	-	-	-	69%

Latimer County General Hospital

806 State Highway 2 North
Wilburton, OK 74578
Type: Acute Care Hospitals
Ownership: Voluntary Non-Profit - Other
Phone: 918-465-2391
Fax: 918-465-5169
Emergency Services: No
Beds: 33

Key Personnel:
CEO/President. . . . . Sue Mings
Chief of Medical Staff. . . . . Ricardo Valbuena
Emergency Room . . . . Lynda Willmoen

Measure	Cases	This Hosp.	State Avg.	U.S. Avg.
Heart Attack Care				
ACE Inhibitor or ARB for LVSD[3]	0	-	95%	96%
Aspirin at Arrival[1,3]	2	0%	98%	99%
Aspirin at Discharge[1,3]	1	0%	98%	98%
Beta Blocker at Discharge[1,3]	1	100%	98%	98%
Fibrinolytic Medication Timing[3]	0	-	42%	55%
PCI Within 90 Minutes of Arrival[3]	0	-	88%	90%
Smoking Cessation Advice[1,3]	1	0%	100%	99%
Chest Pain/Possible Heart Attack Care				
Aspirin at Arrival[1,3]	15	73%	94%	95%
Median Time to ECG (minutes)[1,3]	16	26	9	8
Median Time to Transfer (minutes)[5]	0	-	75	61
Fibrinolytic Medication Timing[1,3]	2	50%	50%	54%
Heart Failure Care				
ACE Inhibitor or ARB for LVSD[1]	2	50%	94%	94%
Discharge Instructions[1]	13	100%	85%	88%
Evaluation of LVS Function[1]	13	46%	94%	98%
Smoking Cessation Advice[1]	2	100%	97%	98%
Pneumonia Care				
Appropriate Initial Antibiotic[1]	17	82%	91%	92%
Blood Culture Timing[1]	12	100%	96%	96%
Influenza Vaccine[1]	18	89%	89%	91%
Initial Antibiotic Timing	30	100%	95%	95%
Pneumococcal Vaccine[1]	21	81%	91%	93%
Smoking Cessation Advice[1]	13	85%	95%	97%
Surgical Care Improvement Project				
Appropriate VTP Within 24 Hours[5]	0	-	91%	92%
Appropriate Hair Removal[5]	0	-	100%	99%
Appropriate Beta Blocker Usage[5]	0	-	91%	93%
Controlled Postoperative Blood Glucose[5]	0	-	95%	93%
Prophylactic Antibiotic Timing[5]	0	-	97%	97%
Prophylactic Antibiotic Timing (Outpatient)[5]	0	-	93%	92%
Prophylactic Antibiotic Selection[5]	0	-	98%	97%
Prophylactic Antibiotic Select. (Outpatient)[5]	0	-	95%	94%
Prophylactic Antibiotic Stopped[5]	0	-	94%	94%
Recommended VTP Ordered[5]	0	-	94%	94%
Urinary Catheter Removal[5]	0	-	87%	90%
Children's Asthma Care				
Received Systemic Corticosteroids	-	-	-	100%
Received Home Management Plan	-	-	-	71%
Received Reliever Medication	-	-	-	100%
Use of Medical Imaging				
Combination Abdominal CT Scan[1]	27	0.111	0.372	0.191
Combination Chest CT Scan[1]	25	0.240	0.134	0.054
Follow-up Mammogram/Ultrasound[5]	0	-	8%	8.4%
MRI for Low Back Pain[5]	0	-	34.3%	32.7%
Survey of Patients' Hospital Experiences				
Area Around Room 'Always' Quiet at Night	(a)	75%	-	58%
Doctors 'Always' Communicated Well	(a)	85%	-	80%
Home Recovery Information Given	(a)	75%	-	82%
Hospital Given 9 or 10 on 10 Point Scale	(a)	68%	-	67%
Meds 'Always' Explained Before Given	(a)	69%	-	60%
Nurses 'Always' Communicated Well	(a)	83%	-	76%
Pain 'Always' Well Controlled	(a)	81%	-	69%
Room and Bathroom 'Always' Clean	(a)	82%	-	71%
Timely Help 'Always' Received	(a)	81%	-	64%
Would Definitely Recommend Hospital	(a)	67%	-	69%

NOTE: Hospital profiles are in alphabetical order by state, then city, then hospital within the city; Rankings exclude hospitals with less than 25 cases except for patient surveys which excludes hospitals with less than 100 cases; (a) 100–299 cases; (1) The number of cases is too small to be sure how well a hospital is performing; (2) The hospital indicated that the data submitted for this measure were based on a sample of cases; (3) Data was collected during a shorter time period (fewer quarters) than the maximum possible time for this measure; (4) Suppressed for one or more quarters by CMS; (5) No data is available from the hospital for this measure; (6) Fewer than 100 patients completed the HCAHPS survey. Use these rates with caution, as the number of surveys may be too low to reliably assess hospital performance; (7) Survey results are based on less than 12 months of data; (8) Survey results are not available for this reporting period; (9) No or very few patients were eligible for the HCAHPS survey. The scores shown, if any, reflect a very small number of surveys; (10) A state average was not calculated because too few hospitals in the state submitted data; (11) There were discrepancies in the data collection process; Please refer to the User's Guide for a full explanation of data.

Woodward Regional Hospital

900 17th Street
Woodward, OK 73801
Phone: 580-256-5511
Fax: 580-254-8431
E-mail: bhubbard@woodwardhospital.com
URL: www.woodwardhospital.com
Type: Acute Care Hospitals
Emergency Services: Yes
Ownership: Proprietary
Beds: 87

Key Personnel:
CEO/President. . . . . Troy Taubenheim, CPA
Quality Assurance . . . . Martha Syms, RN, BSN
Emergency Room . . . . Liz Sizelove, RN

Measure	Cases	This Hosp.	State Avg.	U.S. Avg.
Heart Attack Care				
ACE Inhibitor or ARB for LVSD[1]	1	100%	95%	96%
Aspirin at Arrival[1]	8	100%	98%	99%
Aspirin at Discharge[1]	5	100%	98%	98%
Beta Blocker at Discharge[1]	5	100%	98%	98%
Fibrinolytic Medication Timing	0	-	42%	55%
PCI Within 90 Minutes of Arrival	0	-	88%	90%
Smoking Cessation Advice[1]	1	100%	100%	99%
Chest Pain/Possible Heart Attack Care				
Aspirin at Arrival	29	100%	94%	95%
Median Time to ECG (minutes)	31	9	9	8
Median Time to Transfer (minutes)[1,3]	3	148	75	61
Fibrinolytic Medication Timing[1]	8	50%	50%	54%
Heart Failure Care				
ACE Inhibitor or ARB for LVSD[1]	10	100%	94%	94%
Discharge Instructions	44	89%	85%	88%
Evaluation of LVS Function	55	98%	94%	98%
Smoking Cessation Advice[1]	5	100%	97%	98%
Pneumonia Care				
Appropriate Initial Antibiotic	42	88%	91%	92%
Blood Culture Timing	39	97%	96%	96%
Influenza Vaccine	38	87%	89%	91%
Initial Antibiotic Timing	62	98%	95%	95%
Pneumococcal Vaccine	48	92%	91%	93%
Smoking Cessation Advice[1]	21	100%	95%	97%
Surgical Care Improvement Project				
Appropriate VTP Within 24 Hours	64	94%	91%	92%
Appropriate Hair Removal	137	96%	100%	99%
Appropriate Beta Blocker Usage[1]	21	62%	91%	93%
Controlled Postoperative Blood Glucose	0	-	95%	93%
Prophylactic Antibiotic Timing	87	87%	97%	97%
Prophylactic Antibiotic Timing (Outpatient)	29	83%	93%	92%
Prophylactic Antibiotic Selection	96	100%	98%	97%
Prophylactic Antibiotic Select. (Outpatient)	26	92%	95%	94%
Prophylactic Antibiotic Stopped	77	94%	94%	94%
Recommended VTP Ordered	64	95%	94%	94%
Urinary Catheter Removal	49	67%	87%	90%
Children's Asthma Care				
Received Systemic Corticosteroids	-	-	-	100%
Received Home Management Plan	-	-	-	71%
Received Reliever Medication	-	-	-	100%
Use of Medical Imaging				
Combination Abdominal CT Scan	220	0.664	0.372	0.191
Combination Chest CT Scan	130	0.046	0.134	0.054
Follow-up Mammogram/Ultrasound	359	12.5%	8%	8.4%
MRI for Low Back Pain[1]	35	25.7%	34.3%	32.7%
Survey of Patients' Hospital Experiences				
Area Around Room 'Always' Quiet at Night	300+	59%	-	58%
Doctors 'Always' Communicated Well	300+	81%	-	80%
Home Recovery Information Given	300+	80%	-	82%
Hospital Given 9 or 10 on 10 Point Scale	300+	57%	-	67%
Meds 'Always' Explained Before Given	300+	56%	-	60%
Nurses 'Always' Communicated Well	300+	71%	-	76%
Pain 'Always' Well Controlled	300+	66%	-	69%
Room and Bathroom 'Always' Clean	300+	68%	-	71%
Timely Help 'Always' Received	300+	63%	-	64%
Would Definitely Recommend Hospital	300+	54%	-	69%

Integris Canadian Valley Hospital

1201 Health Center Parkway
Yukon, OK 73099
Phone: 405-717-7999
Type: Acute Care Hospitals
Emergency Services: Yes
Ownership: Voluntary Non-Profit - Other

Measure	Cases	This Hosp.	State Avg.	U.S. Avg.
Heart Attack Care				
ACE Inhibitor or ARB for LVSD[1]	1	100%	95%	96%
Aspirin at Arrival[1]	14	100%	98%	99%
Aspirin at Discharge[1]	12	100%	98%	98%
Beta Blocker at Discharge[1]	11	91%	98%	98%
Fibrinolytic Medication Timing	0	-	42%	55%
PCI Within 90 Minutes of Arrival	0	-	88%	90%
Smoking Cessation Advice[1]	1	100%	100%	99%
Chest Pain/Possible Heart Attack Care				
Aspirin at Arrival	79	100%	94%	95%
Median Time to ECG (minutes)	79	9	9	8
Median Time to Transfer (minutes)[1]	7	40	75	61
Fibrinolytic Medication Timing[1]	1	0%	50%	54%
Heart Failure Care				
ACE Inhibitor or ARB for LVSD[1]	13	92%	94%	94%
Discharge Instructions	34	100%	85%	88%
Evaluation of LVS Function	44	95%	94%	98%
Smoking Cessation Advice[1]	3	100%	97%	98%
Pneumonia Care				
Appropriate Initial Antibiotic[2]	90	86%	91%	92%
Blood Culture Timing[2]	110	99%	96%	96%
Influenza Vaccine[2]	55	85%	89%	91%
Initial Antibiotic Timing[2]	120	98%	95%	95%
Pneumococcal Vaccine[2]	77	86%	91%	93%
Smoking Cessation Advice[2]	38	100%	95%	97%
Surgical Care Improvement Project				
Appropriate VTP Within 24 Hours[2]	70	81%	91%	92%
Appropriate Hair Removal[2]	230	100%	100%	99%
Appropriate Beta Blocker Usage[2]	34	97%	91%	93%
Controlled Postoperative Blood Glucose[2]	0	-	95%	93%
Prophylactic Antibiotic Timing[2]	168	99%	97%	97%
Prophylactic Antibiotic Timing (Outpatient)	38	97%	93%	92%
Prophylactic Antibiotic Selection[2]	168	96%	98%	97%
Prophylactic Antibiotic Select. (Outpatient)	38	97%	95%	94%
Prophylactic Antibiotic Stopped[2]	168	93%	94%	94%
Recommended VTP Ordered[2]	71	99%	94%	94%
Urinary Catheter Removal[2]	61	62%	87%	90%
Children's Asthma Care				
Received Systemic Corticosteroids	-	-	-	100%
Received Home Management Plan	-	-	-	71%
Received Reliever Medication	-	-	-	100%
Use of Medical Imaging				
Combination Abdominal CT Scan	221	0.063	0.372	0.191
Combination Chest CT Scan	121	0.083	0.134	0.054
Follow-up Mammogram/Ultrasound	291	11.7%	8%	8.4%
MRI for Low Back Pain	41	53.7%	34.3%	32.7%
Survey of Patients' Hospital Experiences				
Area Around Room 'Always' Quiet at Night	300+	67%	-	58%
Doctors 'Always' Communicated Well	300+	84%	-	80%
Home Recovery Information Given	300+	80%	-	82%
Hospital Given 9 or 10 on 10 Point Scale	300+	65%	-	67%
Meds 'Always' Explained Before Given	300+	60%	-	60%
Nurses 'Always' Communicated Well	300+	76%	-	76%
Pain 'Always' Well Controlled	300+	73%	-	69%
Room and Bathroom 'Always' Clean	300+	64%	-	71%
Timely Help 'Always' Received	300+	57%	-	64%
Would Definitely Recommend Hospital	300+	71%	-	69%

NOTE: Hospital profiles are in alphabetical order by state, then city, then hospital within the city; Rankings exclude hospitals with less than 25 cases except for patient surveys which excludes hospitals with less than 100 cases; (a) 100–299 cases; (1) The number of cases is too small to be sure how well a hospital is performing; (2) The hospital indicated that the data submitted for this measure were based on a sample of cases; (3) Data was collected during a shorter time period (fewer quarters) than the maximum possible time for this measure; (4) Suppressed for one or more quarters by CMS; (5) No data is available from the hospital for this measure; (6) Fewer than 100 patients completed the HCAHPS survey. Use these rates with caution, as the number of surveys may be too low to reliably assess hospital performance; (7) Survey results are based on less than 12 months of data; (8) Survey results are not available for this reporting period; (9) No or very few patients were eligible for the HCAHPS survey. The scores shown, if any, reflect a very small number of surveys; (10) A state average was not calculated because too few hospitals in the state submitted data; (11) There were discrepancies in the data collection process; Please refer to the User's Guide for a full explanation of data.

Heart Attack Care

1. ACE Inhibitor or ARB for LVSD

Hospital Name	City	Rate	Cases
Rapid City Regional Hospital	Rapid City	100%	61
Avera Heart Hospital of South Dakota	Sioux Falls	98%	88
Sanford Usd Medical Center	Sioux Falls	92%	59

2. Aspirin at Arrival

Hospital Name	City	Rate	Cases
Avera St Lukes	Aberdeen	100%	56
Prairie Lakes Hospital	Watertown	100%	57
Avera Heart Hospital of South Dakota	Sioux Falls	99%	87
Rapid City Regional Hospital	Rapid City	99%	195
Sanford Usd Medical Center	Sioux Falls	98%	178
Avera Mckennan Hosp & Univ Health Ctr	Sioux Falls	97%	60

3. Aspirin at Discharge

Hospital Name	City	Rate	Cases
Avera Mckennan Hosp & Univ Health Ctr	Sioux Falls	100%	64
Avera St Lukes	Aberdeen	100%	59
Sanford Usd Medical Center	Sioux Falls	100%	345
Avera Heart Hospital of South Dakota	Sioux Falls	99%	599
Rapid City Regional Hospital	Rapid City	98%	402
Prairie Lakes Hospital	Watertown	97%	61

4. Beta Blocker at Discharge

Hospital Name	City	Rate	Cases
Avera Heart Hospital of South Dakota	Sioux Falls	100%	593
Avera Mckennan Hosp & Univ Health Ctr	Sioux Falls	100%	69
Avera St Lukes	Aberdeen	100%	54
Prairie Lakes Hospital	Watertown	98%	56
Rapid City Regional Hospital	Rapid City	98%	380
Sanford Usd Medical Center	Sioux Falls	98%	336

6. PCI Within 90 Minutes of Arrival

Hospital Name	City	Rate	Cases
Sanford Usd Medical Center	Sioux Falls	91%	32
Rapid City Regional Hospital	Rapid City	76%	46

7. Smoking Cessation Advice

Hospital Name	City	Rate	Cases
Rapid City Regional Hospital	Rapid City	100%	145
Sanford Usd Medical Center	Sioux Falls	100%	125
Avera Heart Hospital of South Dakota	Sioux Falls	99%	165

Chest Pain/Possible Heart Attack Care

8. Aspirin at Arrival

Hospital Name	City	Rate	Cases
Avera Queen of Peace	Mitchell	100%	56
Avera Sacred Heart Hospital	Yankton	98%	41
Brookings Hospital	Brookings	93%	54
Spearfish Regional Hospital	Spearfish	92%	40

9. Median Time to ECG (minutes)

Hospital Name	City	Min.	Cases
Spearfish Regional Hospital	Spearfish	2	40
Brookings Hospital	Brookings	6	58
Avera Sacred Heart Hospital	Yankton	8	43
Avera Queen of Peace	Mitchell	12	57

Heart Failure Care

12. ACE Inhibitor or ARB for LVSD

Hospital Name	City	Rate	Cases
Avera Heart Hospital of South Dakota	Sioux Falls	97%	61
Sioux Falls VA Medical Center	Sioux Falls	96%	26
Rapid City Regional Hospital	Rapid City	95%	83
Avera Mckennan Hosp & Univ Health Ctr	Sioux Falls	94%	62
Sanford Usd Medical Center	Sioux Falls	90%	84
Prairie Lakes Hospital	Watertown	85%	27

13. Discharge Instructions

Hospital Name	City	Rate	Cases
Avera Queen of Peace	Mitchell	100%	46
Avera Sacred Heart Hospital	Yankton	100%	57
Avera Heart Hospital of South Dakota	Sioux Falls	99%	124
Sioux Falls VA Medical Center	Sioux Falls	98%	52
Avera St Lukes	Aberdeen	95%	80
VA Black Hills Healthcare Sys-Fort Meade	Fort Meade	92%	53
Avera Mckennan Hosp & Univ Health Ctr	Sioux Falls	91%	175
Rapid City Regional Hospital	Rapid City	87%	241
Sanford Usd Medical Center	Sioux Falls	84%	210
Prairie Lakes Hospital	Watertown	79%	63

14. Evaluation of LVS Function

Hospital Name	City	Rate	Cases
Avera Sacred Heart Hospital	Yankton	100%	100
Saint Marys Hospital	Pierre	100%	26
Sioux Falls VA Medical Center	Sioux Falls	100%	56
VA Black Hills Healthcare Sys-Fort Meade	Fort Meade	100%	58
Avera Heart Hospital of South Dakota	Sioux Falls	99%	142
Avera Mckennan Hosp & Univ Health Ctr	Sioux Falls	99%	228
Avera Queen of Peace	Mitchell	99%	76
Avera St Lukes	Aberdeen	99%	131
Rapid City Regional Hospital	Rapid City	99%	296
Sanford Usd Medical Center	Sioux Falls	96%	280
Prairie Lakes Hospital	Watertown	93%	87
Avera Gregory Healthcare Center	Gregory	85%	26
Huron Regional Medical Center	Huron	85%	34

15. Smoking Cessation Advice

Hospital Name	City	Rate	Cases
Rapid City Regional Hospital	Rapid City	98%	53
Sanford Usd Medical Center	Sioux Falls	98%	40

Pneumonia Care

16. Appropriate Initial Antibiotic

Hospital Name	City	Rate	Cases
Avera Sacred Heart Hospital	Yankton	100%	63
Spearfish Regional Hospital	Spearfish	100%	37
Avera Queen of Peace	Mitchell	99%	76
Avera Mckennan Hosp & Univ Health Ctr	Sioux Falls	97%	94
Brookings Hospital	Brookings	97%	32
Prairie Lakes Hospital	Watertown	96%	141
Avera St Lukes	Aberdeen	95%	87
Sioux Falls VA Medical Center	Sioux Falls	93%	28
Rapid City Regional Hospital	Rapid City	91%	136
VA Black Hills Healthcare Sys-Fort Meade	Fort Meade	90%	48
Saint Marys Hospital	Pierre	89%	28
Avera Gregory Healthcare Center	Gregory	88%	41
Sanford Usd Medical Center	Sioux Falls	87%	144
Huron Regional Medical Center[2]	Huron	71%	59

17. Blood Culture Timing

Hospital Name	City	Rate	Cases
Avera Queen of Peace	Mitchell	100%	61
Saint Marys Hospital	Pierre	100%	30
Sioux Falls VA Medical Center	Sioux Falls	100%	33
VA Black Hills Healthcare Sys-Fort Meade	Fort Meade	100%	44
Avera St Lukes	Aberdeen	98%	97
Avera Sacred Heart Hospital	Yankton	97%	110
Sanford Usd Medical Center	Sioux Falls	97%	143
Brookings Hospital	Brookings	96%	26
Rapid City Regional Hospital	Rapid City	96%	178
Avera Mckennan Hosp & Univ Health Ctr	Sioux Falls	95%	94
Prairie Lakes Hospital	Watertown	94%	127
Huron Regional Medical Center[2]	Huron	93%	41

18. Influenza Vaccine

Hospital Name	City	Rate	Cases
Avera Queen of Peace	Mitchell	100%	71
Avera St Lukes	Aberdeen	100%	75
Avera Gregory Healthcare Center	Gregory	98%	49
Avera Sacred Heart Hospital	Yankton	98%	114
Avera Mckennan Hosp & Univ Health Ctr	Sioux Falls	97%	157
Rapid City Regional Hospital	Rapid City	96%	220
Sanford Usd Medical Center	Sioux Falls	94%	175
Spearfish Regional Hospital	Spearfish	93%	29
Huron Regional Medical Center[2]	Huron	92%	50
Prairie Lakes Hospital	Watertown	92%	107
VA Black Hills Healthcare Sys-Fort Meade	Fort Meade	90%	29
Saint Marys Hospital	Pierre	87%	38
Brookings Hospital	Brookings	83%	35

19. Initial Antibiotic Timing

Hospital Name	City	Rate	Cases
Avera Queen of Peace	Mitchell	100%	110
Brookings Hospital	Brookings	100%	49
Avera Sacred Heart Hospital	Yankton	99%	171
Prairie Lakes Hospital	Watertown	98%	176
Avera Mckennan Hosp & Univ Health Ctr	Sioux Falls	97%	167
Avera St Lukes	Aberdeen	97%	132
Sioux Falls VA Medical Center	Sioux Falls	97%	38
Saint Marys Hospital	Pierre	96%	47
Rapid City Regional Hospital	Rapid City	95%	276
Spearfish Regional Hospital	Spearfish	95%	39
VA Black Hills Healthcare Sys-Fort Meade	Fort Meade	95%	62
Sanford Usd Medical Center	Sioux Falls	93%	194
Sturgis Regional Hospital	Sturgis	92%	26
Huron Regional Medical Center[2]	Huron	84%	57
Avera Gregory Healthcare Center	Gregory	64%	28
PHS Indian Hospital at Rosebud[2,3]	Rosebud	58%	40

20. Pneumococcal Vaccine

Hospital Name	City	Rate	Cases
Avera Queen of Peace	Mitchell	100%	120
Sioux Falls VA Medical Center	Sioux Falls	100%	32
VA Black Hills Healthcare Sys-Fort Meade	Fort Meade	100%	47
Avera St Lukes	Aberdeen	99%	122
Avera Sacred Heart Hospital	Yankton	98%	148
Avera Gregory Healthcare Center	Gregory	97%	71
Saint Marys Hospital	Pierre	96%	55
Rapid City Regional Hospital	Rapid City	95%	273
Sanford Usd Medical Center	Sioux Falls	95%	284
Avera Mckennan Hosp & Univ Health Ctr	Sioux Falls	94%	179
Prairie Lakes Hospital	Watertown	93%	193
Huron Regional Medical Center[2]	Huron	86%	65
Brookings Hospital	Brookings	85%	55
Sturgis Regional Hospital	Sturgis	82%	28
Spearfish Regional Hospital	Spearfish	80%	49

21. Smoking Cessation Advice

Hospital Name	City	Rate	Cases
Avera Mckennan Hosp & Univ Health Ctr	Sioux Falls	100%	86
Avera Queen of Peace	Mitchell	100%	26
Avera Sacred Heart Hospital	Yankton	100%	40
Avera St Lukes	Aberdeen	100%	46
Rapid City Regional Hospital	Rapid City	100%	147
Sanford Usd Medical Center	Sioux Falls	97%	122
Prairie Lakes Hospital	Watertown	77%	35

Surgical Care Improvement Project

22. Appropriate VTP Within 24 Hours

Hospital Name	City	Rate	Cases
Avera Queen of Peace	Mitchell	100%	80
Sioux Falls Surgical Hospital	Sioux Falls	100%	33
Sioux Falls VA Medical Center[2]	Sioux Falls	99%	104
Avera Sacred Heart Hospital	Yankton	97%	157
Lewis and Clark Specialty Hospital[2]	Yankton	97%	35
Saint Marys Hospital[2]	Pierre	97%	78
Spearfish Regional Hospital	Spearfish	96%	50
Siouxland Surgery Center Lp[2]	Dakota Dunes	94%	31
Sanford Usd Medical Center[2]	Sioux Falls	93%	261
Rapid City Regional Hospital[2]	Rapid City	92%	193
Avera Mckennan Hosp & Univ Health Ctr[2]	Sioux Falls	89%	148
Avera St Lukes	Aberdeen	82%	185
Prairie Lakes Hospital[2]	Watertown	81%	130
Huron Regional Medical Center	Huron	79%	57

23. Appropriate Hair Removal

Hospital Name	City	Rate	Cases
Avera Heart Hospital of South Dakota	Sioux Falls	100%	440
Avera Queen of Peace	Mitchell	100%	195
Avera St Lukes	Aberdeen	100%	517
Black Hills Surgical Hospital[2]	Rapid City	100%	257
Brookings Hospital	Brookings	100%	49
Dakota Plains Surgical Center[2]	Aberdeen	100%	277
Huron Regional Medical Center	Huron	100%	81
Lewis and Clark Specialty Hospital[2]	Yankton	100%	118
Prairie Lakes Hospital[2]	Watertown	100%	383
Saint Marys Hospital[2]	Pierre	100%	204
Same Day Surgery Center[2,3]	Rapid City	100%	29
Sanford Usd Medical Center[2]	Sioux Falls	100%	1500
Sioux Falls Surgical Hospital	Sioux Falls	100%	679
Sioux Falls VA Medical Center[2]	Sioux Falls	100%	184
Siouxland Surgery Center Lp[2]	Dakota Dunes	100%	353
Spearfish Regional Hospital	Spearfish	100%	226
Avera Mckennan Hosp & Univ Health Ctr[2]	Sioux Falls	99%	377
Rapid City Regional Hospital[2]	Rapid City	98%	471
Spearfish Regional Surgery Center	Spearfish	98%	51
Avera Sacred Heart Hospital	Yankton	97%	344

24. Appropriate Beta Blocker Usage

Hospital Name	City	Rate	Cases
Avera Heart Hospital of South Dakota	Sioux Falls	100%	218
Avera Sacred Heart Hospital	Yankton	100%	86
Black Hills Surgical Hospital[2]	Rapid City	100%	44
Saint Marys Hospital[2]	Pierre	98%	56
Spearfish Regional Hospital	Spearfish	98%	53
Dakota Plains Surgical Center[2]	Aberdeen	97%	60
Lewis and Clark Specialty Hospital[2]	Yankton	96%	26
Avera Queen of Peace	Mitchell	95%	61
Sanford Usd Medical Center[2]	Sioux Falls	95%	400
Sioux Falls Surgical Hospital	Sioux Falls	93%	139
Sioux Falls VA Medical Center[2]	Sioux Falls	93%	84

NOTE: Hospital profiles are in alphabetical order by state, then city, then hospital within the city; Rankings exclude hospitals with less than 25 cases except for patient surveys which excludes hospitals with less than 100 cases; (a) 100–299 cases; (1) The number of cases is too small to be sure how well a hospital is performing; (2) The hospital indicated that the data submitted for this measure were based on a sample of cases; (3) Data was collected during a shorter time period (fewer quarters) than the maximum possible time for this measure; (4) Suppressed for one or more quarters by CMS; (5) No data is available from the hospital for this measure; (6) Fewer than 100 patients completed the HCAHPS survey. Use these rates with caution, as the number of surveys may be too low to reliably assess hospital performance; (7) Survey results are based on less than 12 months of data; (8) Survey results are not available for this reporting period; (9) No or very few patients were eligible for the HCAHPS survey. The scores shown, if any, reflect a very small number of surveys; (10) A state average was not calculated because too few hospitals in the state submitted data; (11) There were discrepancies in the data collection process; Please refer to the User's Guide for a full explanation of data.

Hospital Name	City	Rate	Cases
Avera St Lukes	Aberdeen	91%	152
Avera Mckennan Hosp & Univ Health Ctr[2]	Sioux Falls	89%	121
Rapid City Regional Hospital[2]	Rapid City	89%	178
Siouxland Surgery Center Lp[2]	Dakota Dunes	86%	95
Prairie Lakes Hospital[2]	Watertown	85%	122

25. Controlled Postoperative Blood Glucose

Hospital Name	City	Rate	Cases
Avera Heart Hospital of South Dakota	Sioux Falls	98%	360
Rapid City Regional Hospital[2]	Rapid City	95%	118
Sanford Usd Medical Center[2]	Sioux Falls	95%	202

26. Prophylactic Antibiotic Timing

Hospital Name	City	Rate	Cases
Dakota Plains Surgical Center[2]	Aberdeen	100%	267
Lewis and Clark Specialty Hospital[2]	Yankton	100%	110
Avera Heart Hospital of South Dakota	Sioux Falls	99%	382
Avera Mckennan Hosp & Univ Health Ctr[2]	Sioux Falls	99%	222
Avera Queen of Peace	Mitchell	99%	126
Sioux Falls Surgical Hospital	Sioux Falls	99%	658
Siouxland Surgery Center Lp[2]	Dakota Dunes	98%	303
Black Hills Surgical Hospital[2]	Rapid City	97%	237
Prairie Lakes Hospital[2]	Watertown	97%	284
Sanford Usd Medical Center[2]	Sioux Falls	97%	1181
Spearfish Regional Hospital	Spearfish	97%	199
Spearfish Regional Surgery Center	Spearfish	97%	38
Avera Sacred Heart Hospital	Yankton	96%	200
Rapid City Regional Hospital[2]	Rapid City	96%	323
Sioux Falls VA Medical Center	Sioux Falls	96%	132
Avera St Lukes	Aberdeen	95%	368
Saint Marys Hospital[2]	Pierre	95%	161
Same Day Surgery Center[2,3]	Rapid City	94%	36
Huron Regional Medical Center	Huron	90%	49
Brookings Hospital	Brookings	83%	41

27. Prophylactic Antibiotic Timing (Outpatient)

Hospital Name	City	Rate	Cases
Dakota Plains Surgical Center	Aberdeen	100%	55
Lewis and Clark Specialty Hospital	Yankton	100%	34
Avera Queen of Peace	Mitchell	99%	75
Sioux Falls Surgical Hospital	Sioux Falls	99%	298
Black Hills Surgical Hospital	Rapid City	98%	504
Siouxland Surgery Center Lp	Dakota Dunes	98%	314
Avera Mckennan Hosp & Univ Health Ctr	Sioux Falls	97%	316
Avera Heart Hospital of South Dakota	Sioux Falls	96%	295
Saint Marys Hospital	Pierre	96%	26
Sanford Usd Medical Center	Sioux Falls	96%	646
Prairie Lakes Hospital	Watertown	95%	107
Avera Sacred Heart Hospital	Yankton	94%	105
Rapid City Regional Hospital	Rapid City	94%	288
Avera St Lukes	Aberdeen	70%	101

28. Prophylactic Antibiotic Selection

Hospital Name	City	Rate	Cases
Avera Heart Hospital of South Dakota	Sioux Falls	100%	383
Dakota Plains Surgical Center[2]	Aberdeen	100%	268
Rapid City Regional Hospital[2]	Rapid City	100%	325
Sioux Falls Surgical Hospital	Sioux Falls	100%	658
Siouxland Surgery Center Lp[2]	Dakota Dunes	100%	303
Avera Sacred Heart Hospital	Yankton	99%	202
Sioux Falls VA Medical Center	Sioux Falls	99%	135
Avera Queen of Peace	Mitchell	98%	126
Lewis and Clark Specialty Hospital[2]	Yankton	98%	110
Saint Marys Hospital[2]	Pierre	98%	161
Brookings Hospital	Brookings	97%	38
Avera Mckennan Hosp & Univ Health Ctr[2]	Sioux Falls	96%	222
Avera St Lukes	Aberdeen	96%	370
Black Hills Surgical Hospital[2]	Rapid City	96%	238
Huron Regional Medical Center	Huron	96%	49
Sanford Usd Medical Center[2]	Sioux Falls	96%	1186
Prairie Lakes Hospital[2]	Watertown	95%	291
Spearfish Regional Hospital	Spearfish	95%	199
Spearfish Regional Surgery Center	Spearfish	95%	38
Same Day Surgery Center[2,3]	Rapid City	94%	36

29. Prophylactic Antibiotic Selection (Outpatient)

Hospital Name	City	Rate	Cases
Avera Heart Hospital of South Dakota	Sioux Falls	100%	295
Dakota Plains Surgical Center	Aberdeen	100%	55
Black Hills Surgical Hospital	Rapid City	99%	502
Sioux Falls Surgical Hospital	Sioux Falls	98%	295
Siouxland Surgery Center Lp	Dakota Dunes	98%	311
Avera Queen of Peace	Mitchell	97%	75
Prairie Lakes Hospital	Watertown	97%	104
Avera Mckennan Hosp & Univ Health Ctr	Sioux Falls	96%	314
Avera Sacred Heart Hospital	Yankton	96%	103
Saint Marys Hospital	Pierre	96%	26
Sanford Usd Medical Center	Sioux Falls	96%	646
Rapid City Regional Hospital	Rapid City	95%	277
Avera St Lukes	Aberdeen	85%	81
Lewis and Clark Specialty Hospital	Yankton	41%	34

30. Prophylactic Antibiotic Stopped

Hospital Name	City	Rate	Cases
Avera Heart Hospital of South Dakota	Sioux Falls	100%	380
Sioux Falls Surgical Hospital	Sioux Falls	99%	658
Sioux Falls VA Medical Center	Sioux Falls	98%	131
Siouxland Surgery Center Lp[2]	Dakota Dunes	98%	301
Avera Queen of Peace	Mitchell	97%	119
Black Hills Surgical Hospital[2]	Rapid City	97%	237
Saint Marys Hospital[2]	Pierre	97%	156
Avera Mckennan Hosp & Univ Health Ctr[2]	Sioux Falls	96%	211
Avera Sacred Heart Hospital	Yankton	96%	192
Prairie Lakes Hospital[2]	Watertown	96%	275
Sanford Usd Medical Center[2]	Sioux Falls	96%	1127
Avera St Lukes	Aberdeen	95%	361
Brookings Hospital	Brookings	95%	37
Spearfish Regional Hospital	Spearfish	94%	198
Dakota Plains Surgical Center[2]	Aberdeen	91%	267
Rapid City Regional Hospital[2]	Rapid City	91%	294
Same Day Surgery Center[2,3]	Rapid City	91%	35
Lewis and Clark Specialty Hospital[2]	Yankton	90%	109
Spearfish Regional Surgery Center	Spearfish	89%	37
Huron Regional Medical Center	Huron	82%	49

31. Recommended VTP Ordered

Hospital Name	City	Rate	Cases
Sioux Falls Surgical Hospital	Sioux Falls	100%	33
Avera Queen of Peace	Mitchell	99%	81
Sioux Falls VA Medical Center[2]	Sioux Falls	99%	104
Avera Sacred Heart Hospital	Yankton	98%	157
Lewis and Clark Specialty Hospital[2]	Yankton	97%	35
Saint Marys Hospital[2]	Pierre	97%	78
Sanford Usd Medical Center[2]	Sioux Falls	96%	263
Spearfish Regional Hospital	Spearfish	96%	50
Rapid City Regional Hospital[2]	Rapid City	94%	193
Siouxland Surgery Center Lp[2]	Dakota Dunes	94%	31
Avera Mckennan Hosp & Univ Health Ctr[2]	Sioux Falls	92%	149
Prairie Lakes Hospital[2]	Watertown	84%	131
Avera St Lukes	Aberdeen	81%	190
Huron Regional Medical Center	Huron	81%	57

32. Urinary Catheter Removal

Hospital Name	City	Rate	Cases
Black Hills Surgical Hospital[2]	Rapid City	100%	89
Dakota Plains Surgical Center[2]	Aberdeen	100%	138
Sioux Falls Surgical Hospital	Sioux Falls	100%	206
Spearfish Regional Hospital	Spearfish	99%	81
Avera Heart Hospital of South Dakota	Sioux Falls	96%	114
Sioux Falls VA Medical Center[2]	Sioux Falls	95%	96
Sanford Usd Medical Center[2]	Sioux Falls	92%	219
Prairie Lakes Hospital[2]	Watertown	91%	101
Avera St Lukes	Aberdeen	86%	112
Rapid City Regional Hospital[2]	Rapid City	63%	93
Avera Mckennan Hosp & Univ Health Ctr[2]	Sioux Falls	61%	77
Avera Sacred Heart Hospital	Yankton	38%	29

Children's Asthma Care

33. Received Systemic Corticosteroids

Hospital Name	City	Rate	Cases
Sanford Usd Medical Center	Sioux Falls	100%	64

34. Received Home Management Plan of Care

Hospital Name	City	Rate	Cases
Sanford Usd Medical Center	Sioux Falls	95%	63

35. Received Reliever Medication

Hospital Name	City	Rate	Cases
Sanford Usd Medical Center	Sioux Falls	100%	65

Use of Medical Imaging

36. Combination Abdominal CT Scan

Hospital Name	City	Ratio	Cases
Fall River Hospital[1]	Hot Springs	0.000	42
Sturgis Regional Hospital	Sturgis	0.038	52
Rapid City Regional Hospital	Rapid City	0.061	958
Custer Regional Hospital	Custer	0.068	74
Spearfish Regional Hospital	Spearfish	0.080	250
Avera Mckennan Hosp & Univ Health Ctr	Sioux Falls	0.083	824
Brookings Hospital	Brookings	0.092	152
Avera Heart Hospital of South Dakota[1]	Sioux Falls	0.123	57
Black Hills Surgical Hospital[1]	Rapid City	0.237	38
Sanford Usd Medical Center	Sioux Falls	0.245	1299
Avera Sacred Heart Hospital	Yankton	0.365	115
Wagner Community Memorial Hospital[1]	Wagner	0.500	30
Avera St Lukes	Aberdeen	0.647	896
Prairie Lakes Hospital	Watertown	0.747	245
Saint Marys Hospital	Pierre	0.782	280
Platte Health Center[1]	Platte	0.800	35
Avera Queen of Peace	Mitchell	0.841	340
Avera St Benedict Health Center	Parkston	0.901	71

37. Combination Chest CT Scan

Hospital Name	City	Ratio	Cases
Fall River Hospital[1]	Hot Springs	0.000	30
Rapid City Regional Hospital	Rapid City	0.000	810
Sanford Usd Medical Center	Sioux Falls	0.000	906
Spearfish Regional Hospital	Spearfish	0.000	141
Sturgis Regional Hospital[1]	Sturgis	0.000	33
Avera Mckennan Hosp & Univ Health Ctr	Sioux Falls	0.008	721
Saint Marys Hospital	Pierre	0.023	174
Brookings Hospital	Brookings	0.032	93
Custer Regional Hospital[1]	Custer	0.059	51
Black Hills Surgical Hospital[1]	Rapid City	0.114	44
Avera Heart Hospital of South Dakota[1]	Sioux Falls	0.122	41
Platte Health Center[1]	Platte	0.250	32
Avera St Lukes	Aberdeen	0.266	770
Avera St Benedict Health Center[1]	Parkston	0.278	36
Avera Queen of Peace	Mitchell	0.339	180
Avera Sacred Heart Hospital	Yankton	0.459	37
Prairie Lakes Hospital	Watertown	0.683	218

38. Follow-up Mammogram/Ultrasound

Hospital Name	City	Rate	Cases
Saint Marys Hospital	Pierre	2.0%	651
Bowdle Hospital[1]	Bowdle	4.8%	42
Wagner Community Memorial Hospital	Wagner	4.9%	81
Spearfish Regional Hospital	Spearfish	5.4%	259
Avera Queen of Peace	Mitchell	6.6%	997
Avera Sacred Heart Hospital	Yankton	6.7%	285
Rapid City Regional Hospital	Rapid City	7.8%	307
Avera Mckennan Hosp & Univ Health Ctr	Sioux Falls	8.3%	762
Avera St Benedict Health Center	Parkston	8.9%	235
Platte Health Center	Platte	9.6%	114
Prairie Lakes Hospital[1]	Watertown	11.3%	62
Avera St Lukes	Aberdeen	11.6%	1709
Sturgis Regional Hospital	Sturgis	19.5%	128

39. MRI for Low Back Pain

Hospital Name	City	Rate	Cases
Dakota Plains Surgical Center	Aberdeen	24.1%	116
Sioux Falls Surgical Hospital[1]	Sioux Falls	24.3%	37
Avera St Lukes	Aberdeen	25.0%	216
Avera Mckennan Hosp & Univ Health Ctr	Sioux Falls	25.6%	227
Prairie Lakes Hospital	Watertown	27.0%	63
Avera Sacred Heart Hospital	Yankton	28.7%	122
Brookings Hospital	Brookings	29.6%	54
Avera Queen of Peace	Mitchell	31.4%	156
Sanford Usd Medical Center	Sioux Falls	31.8%	412
Rapid City Regional Hospital	Rapid City	35.4%	274
Black Hills Surgical Hospital	Rapid City	36.1%	485
Spearfish Regional Hospital	Spearfish	38.5%	91
Saint Marys Hospital	Pierre	39.8%	83

Survey of Patients' Hospital Experiences

40. Area Around Room 'Always' Quiet at Night

Hospital Name	City	Rate	Cases
Black Hills Surgical Hospital	Rapid City	87%	300+
Sioux Falls Surgical Hospital	Sioux Falls	87%	300+
Dakota Plains Surgical Center	Aberdeen	84%	(a)
Siouxland Surgery Center Lp	Dakota Dunes	84%	300+
Lewis and Clark Specialty Hospital	Yankton	83%	(a)
Avera Dells Area Health Center	Dell Rapids	78%	(a)
Avera St Benedict Health Center	Parkston	74%	(a)
Lead-Deadwood Regional Hospital	Deadwood	73%	(a)
Avera Gregory Healthcare Center	Gregory	68%	(a)
Avera Heart Hospital of South Dakota	Sioux Falls	68%	300+
Avera Sacred Heart Hospital	Yankton	64%	300+
Brookings Hospital	Brookings	64%	300+
Milbank Area Hospital/Avera Health	Milbank	63%	(a)
Avera Hand County Memorial Hospital	Miller	61%	(a)
Avera St Lukes	Aberdeen	61%	300+
Avera Queen of Peace	Mitchell	60%	300+
Spearfish Regional Hospital	Spearfish	60%	300+
Wagner Community Memorial Hospital	Wagner	60%	(a)
Mobridge Regional Hospital[11]	Mobridge	59%	(a)
Sanford Usd Medical Center	Sioux Falls	58%	300+
Sanford Vermillion Hospital	Vermillion	58%	(a)
Saint Marys Hospital	Pierre	57%	(a)

NOTE: Hospital profiles are in alphabetical order by state, then city, then hospital within the city; Rankings exclude hospitals with less than 25 cases except for patient surveys which excludes hospitals with less than 100 cases; (a) 100–299 cases; (1) The number of cases is too small to be sure how well a hospital is performing; (2) The hospital indicated that the data submitted for this measure were based on a sample of cases; (3) Data was collected during a shorter time period (fewer quarters) than the maximum possible time for this measure; (4) Suppressed for one or more quarters by CMS; (5) No data is available from the hospital for this measure; (6) Fewer than 100 patients completed the HCAHPS survey. Use these rates with caution, as the number of surveys may be too low to reliably assess hospital performance; (7) Survey results are based on less than 12 months of data; (8) Survey results are not available for this reporting period; (9) No or very few patients were eligible for the HCAHPS survey. The scores shown, if any, reflect a very small number of surveys; (10) A state average was not calculated because too few hospitals in the state submitted data; (11) There were discrepancies in the data collection process; Please refer to the User's Guide for a full explanation of data.

Hospital Name	City	Rate	Cases
Prairie Lakes Hospital	Watertown	56%	300+
Avera Mckennan Hosp & Univ Health Ctr	Sioux Falls	55%	300+
Sturgis Regional Hospital	Sturgis	52%	(a)
Rapid City Regional Hospital	Rapid City	44%	300+

41. Doctors 'Always' Communicated Well

Hospital Name	City	Rate	Cases
Dakota Plains Surgical Center	Aberdeen	92%	(a)
Lead-Deadwood Regional Hospital	Deadwood	92%	(a)
Sturgis Regional Hospital	Sturgis	91%	(a)
Avera Dells Area Health Center	Dell Rapids	89%	(a)
Black Hills Surgical Hospital	Rapid City	89%	300+
Lewis and Clark Specialty Hospital	Yankton	89%	(a)
Wagner Community Memorial Hospital	Wagner	87%	(a)
Sanford Vermillion Hospital	Vermillion	86%	(a)
Siouxland Surgery Center Lp	Dakota Dunes	86%	300+
Prairie Lakes Hospital	Watertown	85%	300+
Sioux Falls Surgical Hospital	Sioux Falls	85%	300+
Avera Queen of Peace	Mitchell	84%	300+
Avera St Benedict Health Center	Parkston	84%	(a)
Mobridge Regional Hospital[11]	Mobridge	84%	(a)
Spearfish Regional Hospital	Spearfish	84%	300+
Avera Sacred Heart Hospital	Yankton	83%	300+
Brookings Hospital	Brookings	83%	300+
Saint Marys Hospital	Pierre	82%	(a)
Avera Hand County Memorial Hospital	Miller	81%	(a)
Avera Heart Hospital of South Dakota	Sioux Falls	81%	300+
Avera St Lukes	Aberdeen	80%	300+
Milbank Area Hospital/Avera Health	Milbank	80%	(a)
Avera Gregory Healthcare Center	Gregory	79%	(a)
Sanford Usd Medical Center	Sioux Falls	79%	300+
Rapid City Regional Hospital	Rapid City	78%	300+
Avera Mckennan Hosp & Univ Health Ctr	Sioux Falls	77%	300+

42. Home Recovery Information Given

Hospital Name	City	Rate	Cases
Black Hills Surgical Hospital	Rapid City	94%	300+
Dakota Plains Surgical Center	Aberdeen	94%	(a)
Sioux Falls Surgical Hospital	Sioux Falls	90%	300+
Siouxland Surgery Center Lp	Dakota Dunes	88%	300+
Lewis and Clark Specialty Hospital	Yankton	87%	(a)
Avera St Lukes	Aberdeen	86%	300+
Brookings Hospital	Brookings	86%	300+
Avera Dells Area Health Center	Dell Rapids	85%	(a)
Milbank Area Hospital/Avera Health	Milbank	85%	(a)
Avera Mckennan Hosp & Univ Health Ctr	Sioux Falls	84%	300+
Lead-Deadwood Regional Hospital	Deadwood	84%	(a)
Sanford Usd Medical Center	Sioux Falls	84%	300+
Sturgis Regional Hospital	Sturgis	84%	(a)
Avera Heart Hospital of South Dakota	Sioux Falls	83%	300+
Avera Queen of Peace	Mitchell	83%	300+
Saint Marys Hospital	Pierre	83%	(a)
Avera St Benedict Health Center	Parkston	82%	(a)
Prairie Lakes Hospital	Watertown	82%	300+
Rapid City Regional Hospital	Rapid City	82%	300+
Sanford Vermillion Hospital	Vermillion	82%	(a)
Avera Sacred Heart Hospital	Yankton	81%	300+
Spearfish Regional Hospital	Spearfish	81%	300+
Mobridge Regional Hospital[11]	Mobridge	76%	(a)
Avera Hand County Memorial Hospital	Miller	74%	(a)
Wagner Community Memorial Hospital	Wagner	73%	(a)
Avera Gregory Healthcare Center	Gregory	71%	(a)

43. Hospital Given 9 or 10 on 10 Point Scale

Hospital Name	City	Rate	Cases
Black Hills Surgical Hospital	Rapid City	92%	300+
Dakota Plains Surgical Center	Aberdeen	92%	(a)
Avera Dells Area Health Center	Dell Rapids	89%	(a)
Sioux Falls Surgical Hospital	Sioux Falls	88%	300+
Siouxland Surgery Center Lp	Dakota Dunes	87%	300+
Avera Heart Hospital of South Dakota	Sioux Falls	86%	300+
Lewis and Clark Specialty Hospital	Yankton	85%	(a)
Lead-Deadwood Regional Hospital	Deadwood	84%	(a)
Sturgis Regional Hospital	Sturgis	80%	(a)
Avera Hand County Memorial Hospital	Miller	78%	(a)
Avera St Benedict Health Center	Parkston	78%	(a)
Sanford Usd Medical Center	Sioux Falls	75%	300+
Avera Sacred Heart Hospital	Yankton	73%	300+
Avera Gregory Healthcare Center	Gregory	71%	(a)
Wagner Community Memorial Hospital	Wagner	71%	(a)
Spearfish Regional Hospital	Spearfish	70%	300+
Avera Mckennan Hosp & Univ Health Ctr	Sioux Falls	68%	300+
Mobridge Regional Hospital[11]	Mobridge	68%	(a)
Prairie Lakes Hospital	Watertown	68%	300+
Avera Queen of Peace	Mitchell	67%	300+
Milbank Area Hospital/Avera Health	Milbank	67%	(a)
Saint Marys Hospital	Pierre	66%	(a)
Avera St Lukes	Aberdeen	64%	300+
Brookings Hospital	Brookings	62%	300+
Rapid City Regional Hospital	Rapid City	61%	300+
Sanford Vermillion Hospital	Vermillion	59%	(a)

44. Meds 'Always' Explained Before Given

Hospital Name	City	Rate	Cases
Dakota Plains Surgical Center	Aberdeen	77%	(a)
Black Hills Surgical Hospital	Rapid City	76%	300+
Lead-Deadwood Regional Hospital	Deadwood	74%	(a)
Sioux Falls Surgical Hospital	Sioux Falls	74%	300+
Siouxland Surgery Center Lp	Dakota Dunes	72%	300+
Avera Dells Area Health Center	Dell Rapids	71%	(a)
Lewis and Clark Specialty Hospital	Yankton	69%	(a)
Avera Heart Hospital of South Dakota	Sioux Falls	68%	300+
Avera Sacred Heart Hospital	Yankton	67%	300+
Avera St Benedict Health Center	Parkston	66%	(a)
Milbank Area Hospital/Avera Health	Milbank	66%	(a)
Sturgis Regional Hospital	Sturgis	66%	(a)
Avera Gregory Healthcare Center	Gregory	65%	(a)
Avera Queen of Peace	Mitchell	65%	300+
Mobridge Regional Hospital[11]	Mobridge	65%	(a)
Wagner Community Memorial Hospital	Wagner	65%	(a)
Brookings Hospital	Brookings	64%	300+
Prairie Lakes Hospital	Watertown	64%	300+
Avera St Lukes	Aberdeen	63%	300+
Spearfish Regional Hospital	Spearfish	62%	300+
Avera Hand County Memorial Hospital	Miller	61%	(a)
Sanford Usd Medical Center	Sioux Falls	60%	300+
Avera Mckennan Hosp & Univ Health Ctr	Sioux Falls	59%	300+
Saint Marys Hospital	Pierre	59%	(a)
Rapid City Regional Hospital	Rapid City	57%	300+
Sanford Vermillion Hospital	Vermillion	57%	(a)

45. Nurses 'Always' Communicated Well

Hospital Name	City	Rate	Cases
Avera Dells Area Health Center	Dell Rapids	89%	(a)
Dakota Plains Surgical Center	Aberdeen	88%	(a)
Lead-Deadwood Regional Hospital	Deadwood	88%	(a)
Lewis and Clark Specialty Hospital	Yankton	88%	(a)
Sioux Falls Surgical Hospital	Sioux Falls	88%	300+
Siouxland Surgery Center Lp	Dakota Dunes	88%	300+
Black Hills Surgical Hospital	Rapid City	85%	300+
Avera Heart Hospital of South Dakota	Sioux Falls	84%	300+
Sturgis Regional Hospital	Sturgis	84%	(a)
Avera Hand County Memorial Hospital	Miller	83%	(a)
Avera St Benedict Health Center	Parkston	83%	(a)
Milbank Area Hospital/Avera Health	Milbank	82%	(a)
Brookings Hospital	Brookings	81%	300+
Avera Sacred Heart Hospital	Yankton	80%	300+
Avera St Lukes	Aberdeen	79%	300+
Wagner Community Memorial Hospital	Wagner	79%	(a)
Avera Gregory Healthcare Center	Gregory	78%	(a)
Mobridge Regional Hospital[11]	Mobridge	78%	(a)
Spearfish Regional Hospital	Spearfish	78%	300+
Avera Queen of Peace	Mitchell	76%	300+
Prairie Lakes Hospital	Watertown	76%	300+
Saint Marys Hospital	Pierre	76%	(a)
Sanford Usd Medical Center	Sioux Falls	76%	300+
Avera Mckennan Hosp & Univ Health Ctr	Sioux Falls	74%	300+
Rapid City Regional Hospital	Rapid City	73%	300+
Sanford Vermillion Hospital	Vermillion	70%	(a)

46. Pain 'Always' Well Controlled

Hospital Name	City	Rate	Cases
Avera Dells Area Health Center	Dell Rapids	78%	(a)
Dakota Plains Surgical Center	Aberdeen	78%	(a)
Black Hills Surgical Hospital	Rapid City	77%	300+
Siouxland Surgery Center Lp	Dakota Dunes	76%	300+
Avera Gregory Healthcare Center	Gregory	75%	(a)
Avera Heart Hospital of South Dakota	Sioux Falls	75%	300+
Lewis and Clark Specialty Hospital	Yankton	75%	(a)
Sioux Falls Surgical Hospital	Sioux Falls	75%	300+
Avera Sacred Heart Hospital	Yankton	73%	300+
Prairie Lakes Hospital	Watertown	72%	300+
Sturgis Regional Hospital	Sturgis	72%	(a)
Avera St Benedict Health Center	Parkston	71%	(a)
Milbank Area Hospital/Avera Health	Milbank	71%	(a)
Spearfish Regional Hospital	Spearfish	71%	300+
Lead-Deadwood Regional Hospital	Deadwood	70%	(a)
Sanford Usd Medical Center	Sioux Falls	70%	300+
Avera Queen of Peace	Mitchell	69%	300+
Brookings Hospital	Brookings	69%	300+
Rapid City Regional Hospital	Rapid City	69%	300+
Wagner Community Memorial Hospital	Wagner	68%	(a)
Avera St Lukes	Aberdeen	67%	300+
Saint Marys Hospital	Pierre	66%	(a)
Avera Hand County Memorial Hospital	Miller	65%	(a)
Sanford Vermillion Hospital	Vermillion	65%	(a)
Avera Mckennan Hosp & Univ Health Ctr	Sioux Falls	64%	300+
Mobridge Regional Hospital[11]	Mobridge	60%	(a)

47. Room and Bathroom 'Always' Clean

Hospital Name	City	Rate	Cases
Lead-Deadwood Regional Hospital	Deadwood	93%	(a)
Avera Dells Area Health Center	Dell Rapids	91%	(a)
Dakota Plains Surgical Center	Aberdeen	89%	(a)
Avera St Benedict Health Center	Parkston	88%	(a)
Black Hills Surgical Hospital	Rapid City	87%	300+
Lewis and Clark Specialty Hospital	Yankton	87%	(a)
Sioux Falls Surgical Hospital	Sioux Falls	87%	300+
Avera Heart Hospital of South Dakota	Sioux Falls	84%	300+
Sturgis Regional Hospital	Sturgis	84%	(a)
Avera Gregory Healthcare Center	Gregory	83%	(a)
Wagner Community Memorial Hospital	Wagner	83%	(a)
Milbank Area Hospital/Avera Health	Milbank	81%	(a)
Mobridge Regional Hospital[11]	Mobridge	81%	(a)
Siouxland Surgery Center Lp	Dakota Dunes	81%	300+
Avera Hand County Memorial Hospital	Miller	80%	(a)
Avera Sacred Heart Hospital	Yankton	79%	300+
Avera St Lukes	Aberdeen	77%	300+
Avera Queen of Peace	Mitchell	76%	300+
Prairie Lakes Hospital	Watertown	76%	300+
Rapid City Regional Hospital	Rapid City	76%	300+
Spearfish Regional Hospital	Spearfish	76%	300+
Brookings Hospital	Brookings	74%	300+
Avera Mckennan Hosp & Univ Health Ctr	Sioux Falls	70%	300+
Saint Marys Hospital	Pierre	67%	(a)
Sanford Usd Medical Center	Sioux Falls	67%	300+
Sanford Vermillion Hospital	Vermillion	63%	(a)

48. Timely Help 'Always' Received

Hospital Name	City	Rate	Cases
Lead-Deadwood Regional Hospital	Deadwood	91%	(a)
Siouxland Surgery Center Lp	Dakota Dunes	91%	300+
Dakota Plains Surgical Center	Aberdeen	89%	(a)
Lewis and Clark Specialty Hospital	Yankton	87%	(a)
Sioux Falls Surgical Hospital	Sioux Falls	87%	300+
Black Hills Surgical Hospital	Rapid City	86%	300+
Sturgis Regional Hospital	Sturgis	83%	(a)
Avera Hand County Memorial Hospital	Miller	80%	(a)
Spearfish Regional Hospital	Spearfish	79%	300+
Avera Heart Hospital of South Dakota	Sioux Falls	78%	300+
Avera Dells Area Health Center	Dell Rapids	74%	(a)
Avera St Benedict Health Center	Parkston	73%	(a)
Brookings Hospital	Brookings	73%	300+
Wagner Community Memorial Hospital	Wagner	72%	(a)
Avera St Lukes	Aberdeen	70%	300+
Prairie Lakes Hospital	Watertown	70%	300+
Avera Sacred Heart Hospital	Yankton	69%	300+
Mobridge Regional Hospital[11]	Mobridge	69%	(a)
Rapid City Regional Hospital	Rapid City	68%	300+
Milbank Area Hospital/Avera Health	Milbank	67%	(a)
Sanford Usd Medical Center	Sioux Falls	67%	300+
Saint Marys Hospital	Pierre	65%	(a)
Avera Queen of Peace	Mitchell	64%	300+
Sanford Vermillion Hospital	Vermillion	63%	(a)
Avera Gregory Healthcare Center	Gregory	60%	(a)
Avera Mckennan Hosp & Univ Health Ctr	Sioux Falls	58%	300+

49. Would Definitely Recommend Hospital

Hospital Name	City	Rate	Cases
Dakota Plains Surgical Center	Aberdeen	96%	(a)
Black Hills Surgical Hospital	Rapid City	93%	300+
Avera Heart Hospital of South Dakota	Sioux Falls	90%	300+
Lewis and Clark Specialty Hospital	Yankton	90%	(a)
Sioux Falls Surgical Hospital	Sioux Falls	90%	300+
Siouxland Surgery Center Lp	Dakota Dunes	89%	300+
Lead-Deadwood Regional Hospital	Deadwood	88%	(a)
Avera Dells Area Health Center	Dell Rapids	85%	(a)
Avera St Benedict Health Center	Parkston	80%	(a)
Sanford Usd Medical Center	Sioux Falls	78%	300+
Avera Mckennan Hosp & Univ Health Ctr	Sioux Falls	75%	300+
Sturgis Regional Hospital	Sturgis	75%	(a)
Avera Hand County Memorial Hospital	Miller	74%	(a)
Milbank Area Hospital/Avera Health	Milbank	73%	(a)
Avera Gregory Healthcare Center	Gregory	72%	(a)
Spearfish Regional Hospital	Spearfish	72%	300+
Avera Sacred Heart Hospital	Yankton	70%	300+
Wagner Community Memorial Hospital	Wagner	70%	(a)
Avera Queen of Peace	Mitchell	69%	300+
Prairie Lakes Hospital	Watertown	67%	300+
Brookings Hospital	Brookings	65%	300+
Saint Marys Hospital	Pierre	65%	(a)
Sanford Vermillion Hospital	Vermillion	65%	(a)
Mobridge Regional Hospital[11]	Mobridge	63%	(a)
Avera St Lukes	Aberdeen	62%	300+
Rapid City Regional Hospital	Rapid City	62%	300+

NOTE: Hospital profiles are in alphabetical order by state, then city, then hospital within the city; Rankings exclude hospitals with less than 25 cases except for patient surveys which excludes hospitals with less than 100 cases; (a) 100–299 cases; (1) The number of cases is too small to be sure how well a hospital is performing; (2) The hospital indicated that the data submitted for this measure were based on a sample of cases; (3) Data was collected during a shorter time period (fewer quarters) than the maximum possible time for this measure; (4) Suppressed for one or more quarters by CMS; (5) No data is available from the hospital for this measure; (6) Fewer than 100 patients completed the HCAHPS survey. Use these rates with caution, as the number of surveys may be too low to reliably assess hospital performance; (7) Survey results are based on less than 12 months of data; (8) Survey results are not available for this reporting period; (9) No or very few patients were eligible for the HCAHPS survey. The scores shown, if any, reflect a very small number of surveys; (10) A state average was not calculated because too few hospitals in the state submitted data; (11) There were discrepancies in the data collection process; Please refer to the User's Guide for a full explanation of data.

Avera St Lukes

305 S State St
Aberdeen, SD 57401
URL: www.averastlukes.org
Type: Acute Care Hospitals
Ownership: Voluntary Non-Profit - Other
Phone: 605-622-5000
Fax: 605-622-5041
Emergency Services: No
Beds: 137

Key Personnel:
CEO/President. . . . . Ron L Jacobson
Chief of Medical Staff . . . . John Fritz
Infection Control. . . . . Jolynn Zeller
Operating Room. . . . . Kathy Nipp
Quality Assurance . . . . Pat Cavanaugh
Radiology. . . . . Melchor Aguilar, MD

Measure	Cases	This Hosp.	State Avg.	U.S. Avg.
Heart Attack Care				
ACE Inhibitor or ARB for LVSD[1]	5	100%	96%	96%
Aspirin at Arrival	56	100%	98%	99%
Aspirin at Discharge	59	100%	99%	98%
Beta Blocker at Discharge	54	100%	98%	98%
Fibrinolytic Medication Timing	0	-	45%	55%
PCI Within 90 Minutes of Arrival[1]	11	100%	87%	90%
Smoking Cessation Advice[1]	10	100%	99%	99%
Chest Pain/Possible Heart Attack Care				
Aspirin at Arrival[1]	13	92%	96%	95%
Median Time to ECG (minutes)[1]	14	4	7	8
Median Time to Transfer (minutes)[1,3]	1	82	84	61
Fibrinolytic Medication Timing[3]	0	-	54%	54%
Heart Failure Care				
ACE Inhibitor or ARB for LVSD[1]	19	100%	90%	94%
Discharge Instructions	80	95%	85%	88%
Evaluation of LVS Function	131	99%	93%	98%
Smoking Cessation Advice[1]	19	100%	93%	98%
Pneumonia Care				
Appropriate Initial Antibiotic	87	95%	91%	92%
Blood Culture Timing	97	98%	95%	96%
Influenza Vaccine	75	100%	94%	91%
Initial Antibiotic Timing	132	97%	94%	95%
Pneumococcal Vaccine	122	99%	93%	93%
Smoking Cessation Advice	46	100%	92%	97%
Surgical Care Improvement Project				
Appropriate VTP Within 24 Hours	185	82%	90%	92%
Appropriate Hair Removal	517	100%	100%	99%
Appropriate Beta Blocker Usage	152	91%	93%	93%
Controlled Postoperative Blood Glucose	0	-	96%	93%
Prophylactic Antibiotic Timing	368	95%	97%	97%
Prophylactic Antibiotic Timing (Outpatient)	101	70%	96%	92%
Prophylactic Antibiotic Selection	370	96%	98%	97%
Prophylactic Antibiotic Select. (Outpatient)	81	85%	97%	94%
Prophylactic Antibiotic Stopped	361	95%	96%	94%
Recommended VTP Ordered	190	81%	91%	94%
Urinary Catheter Removal	112	86%	89%	90%
Children's Asthma Care				
Received Systemic Corticosteroids	-	-	-	100%
Received Home Management Plan	-	-	-	71%
Received Reliever Medication	-	-	-	100%
Use of Medical Imaging				
Combination Abdominal CT Scan	896	0.647	0.325	0.191
Combination Chest CT Scan	770	0.266	0.116	0.054
Follow-up Mammogram/Ultrasound	1,709	11.6%	7.6%	8.4%
MRI for Low Back Pain	216	25.0%	31.3%	32.7%
Survey of Patients' Hospital Experiences				
Area Around Room 'Always' Quiet at Night	300+	61%	-	58%
Doctors 'Always' Communicated Well	300+	80%	-	80%
Home Recovery Information Given	300+	86%	-	82%
Hospital Given 9 or 10 on 10 Point Scale	300+	64%	-	67%
Meds 'Always' Explained Before Given	300+	63%	-	60%
Nurses 'Always' Communicated Well	300+	79%	-	76%
Pain 'Always' Well Controlled	300+	67%	-	69%
Room and Bathroom 'Always' Clean	300+	77%	-	71%
Timely Help 'Always' Received	300+	70%	-	64%
Would Definitely Recommend Hospital	300+	62%	-	69%

Dakota Plains Surgical Center

701 8th Avenue NW, Suite C
Aberdeen, SD 57401
Type: Acute Care Hospitals
Ownership: Proprietary
Phone: 605-225-3300
Emergency Services: No

Measure	Cases	This Hosp.	State Avg.	U.S. Avg.
Heart Attack Care				
ACE Inhibitor or ARB for LVSD[5]	0	-	96%	96%
Aspirin at Arrival[5]	0	-	98%	99%
Aspirin at Discharge[5]	0	-	99%	98%
Beta Blocker at Discharge[5]	0	-	98%	98%
Fibrinolytic Medication Timing[5]	0	-	45%	55%
PCI Within 90 Minutes of Arrival[5]	0	-	87%	90%
Smoking Cessation Advice[5]	0	-	99%	99%
Chest Pain/Possible Heart Attack Care				
Aspirin at Arrival[5]	0	-	96%	95%
Median Time to ECG (minutes)[5]	0	-	7	8
Median Time to Transfer (minutes)[5]	0	-	84	61
Fibrinolytic Medication Timing[5]	0	-	54%	54%
Heart Failure Care				
ACE Inhibitor or ARB for LVSD[5]	0	-	90%	94%
Discharge Instructions[5]	0	-	85%	88%
Evaluation of LVS Function[5]	0	-	93%	98%
Smoking Cessation Advice[5]	0	-	93%	98%
Pneumonia Care				
Appropriate Initial Antibiotic[5]	0	-	91%	92%
Blood Culture Timing[5]	0	-	95%	96%
Influenza Vaccine[5]	0	-	94%	91%
Initial Antibiotic Timing[5]	0	-	94%	95%
Pneumococcal Vaccine[5]	0	-	93%	93%
Smoking Cessation Advice[5]	0	-	92%	97%
Surgical Care Improvement Project				
Appropriate VTP Within 24 Hours[1,2]	11	100%	90%	92%
Appropriate Hair Removal[2]	277	100%	100%	99%
Appropriate Beta Blocker Usage[2]	60	97%	93%	93%
Controlled Postoperative Blood Glucose[2]	0	-	96%	93%
Prophylactic Antibiotic Timing[2]	267	100%	97%	97%
Prophylactic Antibiotic Timing (Outpatient)	55	100%	96%	92%
Prophylactic Antibiotic Selection[2]	268	100%	98%	97%
Prophylactic Antibiotic Select. (Outpatient)	55	100%	97%	94%
Prophylactic Antibiotic Stopped[2]	267	91%	96%	94%
Recommended VTP Ordered[1,2]	11	100%	91%	94%
Urinary Catheter Removal[2]	138	100%	89%	90%
Children's Asthma Care				
Received Systemic Corticosteroids	-	-	-	100%
Received Home Management Plan	-	-	-	71%
Received Reliever Medication	-	-	-	100%
Use of Medical Imaging				
Combination Abdominal CT Scan[5]	0	-	0.325	0.191
Combination Chest CT Scan[5]	0	-	0.116	0.054
Follow-up Mammogram/Ultrasound[5]	0	-	7.6%	8.4%
MRI for Low Back Pain	116	24.1%	31.3%	32.7%
Survey of Patients' Hospital Experiences				
Area Around Room 'Always' Quiet at Night	(a)	84%	-	58%
Doctors 'Always' Communicated Well	(a)	92%	-	80%
Home Recovery Information Given	(a)	94%	-	82%
Hospital Given 9 or 10 on 10 Point Scale	(a)	92%	-	67%
Meds 'Always' Explained Before Given	(a)	77%	-	60%
Nurses 'Always' Communicated Well	(a)	88%	-	76%
Pain 'Always' Well Controlled	(a)	78%	-	69%
Room and Bathroom 'Always' Clean	(a)	89%	-	71%
Timely Help 'Always' Received	(a)	89%	-	64%
Would Definitely Recommend Hospital	(a)	96%	-	69%

Bowdle Hospital

8001 W 5th
Bowdle, SD 57428
E-mail: kkarst@midca.net
URL: www.bowdlehealthcarecenter.com
Type: Critical Access Hospitals
Ownership: Government - Local
Phone: 605-285-6146
Fax: 605-285-6410
Emergency Services: Yes
Beds: 50

Key Personnel:
CEO/President. . . . . Mike Piper
Quality Assurance . . . . Karen Karst

Measure	Cases	This Hosp.	State Avg.	U.S. Avg.
Heart Attack Care				
ACE Inhibitor or ARB for LVSD	-	-	96%	96%
Aspirin at Arrival	-	-	98%	99%
Aspirin at Discharge	-	-	99%	98%
Beta Blocker at Discharge	-	-	98%	98%
Fibrinolytic Medication Timing	-	-	45%	55%
PCI Within 90 Minutes of Arrival	-	-	87%	90%
Smoking Cessation Advice	-	-	99%	99%
Chest Pain/Possible Heart Attack Care				
Aspirin at Arrival[1]	6	100%	96%	95%
Median Time to ECG (minutes)[1]	6	32	7	8
Median Time to Transfer (minutes)[5]	0	-	84	61
Fibrinolytic Medication Timing[3]	0	-	54%	54%
Heart Failure Care				
ACE Inhibitor or ARB for LVSD	-	-	90%	94%
Discharge Instructions	-	-	85%	88%
Evaluation of LVS Function	-	-	93%	98%
Smoking Cessation Advice	-	-	93%	98%
Pneumonia Care				
Appropriate Initial Antibiotic	-	-	91%	92%
Blood Culture Timing	-	-	95%	96%
Influenza Vaccine	-	-	94%	91%
Initial Antibiotic Timing	-	-	94%	95%
Pneumococcal Vaccine	-	-	93%	93%
Smoking Cessation Advice	-	-	92%	97%
Surgical Care Improvement Project				
Appropriate VTP Within 24 Hours	-	-	90%	92%
Appropriate Hair Removal	-	-	100%	99%
Appropriate Beta Blocker Usage	-	-	93%	93%
Controlled Postoperative Blood Glucose	-	-	96%	93%
Prophylactic Antibiotic Timing	-	-	97%	97%
Prophylactic Antibiotic Timing (Outpatient)[5]	0	-	96%	92%
Prophylactic Antibiotic Selection	-	-	98%	97%
Prophylactic Antibiotic Select. (Outpatient)[5]	0	-	97%	94%
Prophylactic Antibiotic Stopped	-	-	96%	94%
Recommended VTP Ordered	-	-	91%	94%
Urinary Catheter Removal	-	-	89%	90%
Children's Asthma Care				
Received Systemic Corticosteroids	-	-	-	100%
Received Home Management Plan	-	-	-	71%
Received Reliever Medication	-	-	-	100%
Use of Medical Imaging				
Combination Abdominal CT Scan[1]	12	0.167	0.325	0.191
Combination Chest CT Scan[1]	15	0.133	0.116	0.054
Follow-up Mammogram/Ultrasound[1]	42	4.8%	7.6%	8.4%
MRI for Low Back Pain[5]	0	-	31.3%	32.7%
Survey of Patients' Hospital Experiences				
Area Around Room 'Always' Quiet at Night	-	-	-	58%
Doctors 'Always' Communicated Well	-	-	-	80%
Home Recovery Information Given	-	-	-	82%
Hospital Given 9 or 10 on 10 Point Scale	-	-	-	67%
Meds 'Always' Explained Before Given	-	-	-	60%
Nurses 'Always' Communicated Well	-	-	-	76%
Pain 'Always' Well Controlled	-	-	-	69%
Room and Bathroom 'Always' Clean	-	-	-	71%
Timely Help 'Always' Received	-	-	-	64%
Would Definitely Recommend Hospital	-	-	-	69%

NOTE: Hospital profiles are in alphabetical order by state, then city, then hospital within the city; Rankings exclude hospitals with less than 25 cases except for patient surveys which excludes hospitals with less than 100 cases; (a) 100–299 cases; (1) The number of cases is too small to be sure how well a hospital is performing; (2) The hospital indicated that the data submitted for this measure were based on a sample of cases; (3) Data was collected during a shorter time period (fewer quarters) than the maximum possible time for this measure; (4) Suppressed for one or more quarters by CMS; (5) No data is available from the hospital for this measure; (6) Fewer than 100 patients completed the HCAHPS survey. Use these rates with caution, as the number of surveys may be too low to reliably assess hospital performance; (7) Survey results are based on less than 12 months of data; (8) Survey results are not available for this reporting period; (9) No or very few patients were eligible for the HCAHPS survey. The scores shown, if any, reflect a very small number of surveys; (10) A state average was not calculated because too few hospitals in the state submitted data; (11) There were discrepancies in the data collection process; Please refer to the User's Guide for a full explanation of data.

Brookings Hospital

300 22nd Ave
Brookings, SD 57006
URL: www.brookingshospital.org
Type: Acute Care Hospitals
Ownership: Government - Local
Phone: 605-696-7701
Fax: 605-696-7770
Emergency Services: No
Beds: 128

Key Personnel:

CEO/President. . . . . Kevin Coffey
Chief of Medical Staff. . . . . Richard S Hieb
Quality Assurance . . . . Dianna Eberf
Radiology. . . . . Randi Hart

Measure	Cases	This Hosp.	State Avg.	U.S. Avg.
Heart Attack Care				
ACE Inhibitor or ARB for LVSD[1]	1	0%	96%	96%
Aspirin at Arrival[1]	17	88%	98%	99%
Aspirin at Discharge[1]	12	100%	99%	98%
Beta Blocker at Discharge[1]	12	83%	98%	98%
Fibrinolytic Medication Timing	0	-	45%	55%
PCI Within 90 Minutes of Arrival	0	-	87%	90%
Smoking Cessation Advice[1]	1	0%	99%	99%
Chest Pain/Possible Heart Attack Care				
Aspirin at Arrival	54	93%	96%	95%
Median Time to ECG (minutes)	58	6	7	8
Median Time to Transfer (minutes)[1]	2	207	84	61
Fibrinolytic Medication Timing[1]	3	67%	54%	54%
Heart Failure Care				
ACE Inhibitor or ARB for LVSD[1]	10	50%	90%	94%
Discharge Instructions[1]	13	54%	85%	88%
Evaluation of LVS Function[1]	22	64%	93%	98%
Smoking Cessation Advice[1]	2	0%	93%	98%
Pneumonia Care				
Appropriate Initial Antibiotic	32	97%	91%	92%
Blood Culture Timing	26	96%	95%	96%
Influenza Vaccine	35	83%	94%	91%
Initial Antibiotic Timing	49	100%	94%	95%
Pneumococcal Vaccine	55	85%	93%	93%
Smoking Cessation Advice[1]	13	69%	92%	97%
Surgical Care Improvement Project				
Appropriate VTP Within 24 Hours[1]	18	50%	90%	92%
Appropriate Hair Removal	49	100%	100%	99%
Appropriate Beta Blocker Usage[1]	12	92%	93%	93%
Controlled Postoperative Blood Glucose	0	-	96%	93%
Prophylactic Antibiotic Timing	41	83%	97%	97%
Prophylactic Antibiotic Timing (Outpatient)[1,3]	7	100%	96%	92%
Prophylactic Antibiotic Selection	38	97%	98%	97%
Prophylactic Antibiotic Select. (Outpatient)[1,3]	7	100%	97%	94%
Prophylactic Antibiotic Stopped	37	95%	96%	94%
Recommended VTP Ordered[1]	18	83%	91%	94%
Urinary Catheter Removal[1]	7	71%	89%	90%
Children's Asthma Care				
Received Systemic Corticosteroids	-	-	-	100%
Received Home Management Plan	-	-	-	71%
Received Reliever Medication	-	-	-	100%
Use of Medical Imaging				
Combination Abdominal CT Scan	152	0.092	0.325	0.191
Combination Chest CT Scan	93	0.032	0.116	0.054
Follow-up Mammogram/Ultrasound[5]	0	-	7.6%	8.4%
MRI for Low Back Pain	54	29.6%	31.3%	32.7%
Survey of Patients' Hospital Experiences				
Area Around Room 'Always' Quiet at Night	300+	64%	-	58%
Doctors 'Always' Communicated Well	300+	83%	-	80%
Home Recovery Information Given	300+	86%	-	82%
Hospital Given 9 or 10 on 10 Point Scale	300+	62%	-	67%
Meds 'Always' Explained Before Given	300+	64%	-	60%
Nurses 'Always' Communicated Well	300+	81%	-	76%
Pain 'Always' Well Controlled	300+	69%	-	69%
Room and Bathroom 'Always' Clean	300+	74%	-	71%
Timely Help 'Always' Received	300+	73%	-	64%
Would Definitely Recommend Hospital	300+	65%	-	69%

Sanford Mid-Dakota Hospital

300 S Byron
Chamberlain, SD 57325
URL: sanfordmiddakota.org
Type: Critical Access Hospitals
Ownership: Voluntary Non-Profit - Private
Phone: 605-734-5511
Fax: 605-234-7118
Emergency Services: Yes
Beds: 25

Key Personnel:

CEO/President. . . . . Maureen Cadwell, FHFMA
Chief of Medical Staff. . . . . John Jones, MD
Infection Control. . . . . Diane Blasius
Operating Room. . . . . Donna Greensfeild, RN
Quality Assurance . . . . Nancy McDonald, RN
Radiology. . . . . Tom Davis
Emergency Room . . . . Stephanie Feltman, RN
Intensive Care Unit. . . . . Jayson Pullman, RN

Measure	Cases	This Hosp.	State Avg.	U.S. Avg.
Heart Attack Care				
ACE Inhibitor or ARB for LVSD[3]	0	-	96%	96%
Aspirin at Arrival[1,3]	1	100%	98%	99%
Aspirin at Discharge[1,3]	1	100%	99%	98%
Beta Blocker at Discharge[1,3]	1	100%	98%	98%
Fibrinolytic Medication Timing[3]	0	-	45%	55%
PCI Within 90 Minutes of Arrival[3]	0	-	87%	90%
Smoking Cessation Advice[3]	0	-	99%	99%
Chest Pain/Possible Heart Attack Care				
Aspirin at Arrival	-	-	96%	95%
Median Time to ECG (minutes)	-	-	7	8
Median Time to Transfer (minutes)	-	-	84	61
Fibrinolytic Medication Timing	-	-	54%	54%
Heart Failure Care				
ACE Inhibitor or ARB for LVSD[1,3]	2	100%	90%	94%
Discharge Instructions[1,3]	10	0%	85%	88%
Evaluation of LVS Function[1,3]	14	50%	93%	98%
Smoking Cessation Advice[1,3]	1	100%	93%	98%
Pneumonia Care				
Appropriate Initial Antibiotic[1,3]	6	50%	91%	92%
Blood Culture Timing[1,3]	5	80%	95%	96%
Influenza Vaccine[1]	8	75%	94%	91%
Initial Antibiotic Timing[1,3]	12	83%	94%	95%
Pneumococcal Vaccine[1,3]	5	60%	93%	93%
Smoking Cessation Advice[1,3]	6	100%	92%	97%
Surgical Care Improvement Project				
Appropriate VTP Within 24 Hours[1,3]	1	100%	90%	92%
Appropriate Hair Removal[3,1]	1	100%	100%	99%
Appropriate Beta Blocker Usage[5]	0	-	93%	93%
Controlled Postoperative Blood Glucose[3]	0	-	96%	93%
Prophylactic Antibiotic Timing[1,3]	1	100%	97%	97%
Prophylactic Antibiotic Timing (Outpatient)	-	-	96%	92%
Prophylactic Antibiotic Selection[1,3]	1	100%	98%	97%
Prophylactic Antibiotic Select. (Outpatient)	-	-	97%	94%
Prophylactic Antibiotic Stopped[1,3]	1	100%	96%	94%
Recommended VTP Ordered[1,3]	1	100%	91%	94%
Urinary Catheter Removal[5]	0	-	89%	90%
Children's Asthma Care				
Received Systemic Corticosteroids	-	-	-	100%
Received Home Management Plan	-	-	-	71%
Received Reliever Medication	-	-	-	100%
Use of Medical Imaging				
Combination Abdominal CT Scan	-	-	0.325	0.191
Combination Chest CT Scan	-	-	0.116	0.054
Follow-up Mammogram/Ultrasound	-	-	7.6%	8.4%
MRI for Low Back Pain	-	-	31.3%	32.7%
Survey of Patients' Hospital Experiences				
Area Around Room 'Always' Quiet at Night[6]	<100	62%	-	58%
Doctors 'Always' Communicated Well[6]	<100	77%	-	80%
Home Recovery Information Given[6]	<100	79%	-	82%
Hospital Given 9 or 10 on 10 Point Scale[6]	<100	66%	-	67%
Meds 'Always' Explained Before Given[6]	<100	55%	-	60%
Nurses 'Always' Communicated Well[6]	<100	77%	-	76%
Pain 'Always' Well Controlled[6]	<100	71%	-	69%
Room and Bathroom 'Always' Clean[6]	<100	71%	-	71%
Timely Help 'Always' Received[6]	<100	66%	-	64%
Would Definitely Recommend Hospital	<100	61%	-	69%

Custer Regional Hospital

1039 Montgomery Street
Custer, SD 57730
URL: www.rcrh.org/Facilities
Type: Critical Access Hospitals
Ownership: Voluntary Non-Profit - Private
Phone: 605-673-2229
Fax: 605-673-3586
Emergency Services: Yes
Beds: 16

Key Personnel:

Chief of Medical Staff. . . . . Sarah Schryvers
Infection Control. . . . . Wendy Honomichl
Quality Assurance . . . . Nancy Hargens
Radiology. . . . . Brian R Baxter

Measure	Cases	This Hosp.	State Avg.	U.S. Avg.
Heart Attack Care				
ACE Inhibitor or ARB for LVSD[5]	0	-	96%	96%
Aspirin at Arrival[5]	0	-	98%	99%
Aspirin at Discharge[5]	0	-	99%	98%
Beta Blocker at Discharge[5]	0	-	98%	98%
Fibrinolytic Medication Timing[5]	0	-	45%	55%
PCI Within 90 Minutes of Arrival[5]	0	-	87%	90%
Smoking Cessation Advice[5]	0	-	99%	99%
Chest Pain/Possible Heart Attack Care				
Aspirin at Arrival[1]	23	100%	96%	95%
Median Time to ECG (minutes)[1]	23	4	7	8
Median Time to Transfer (minutes)[5]	0	-	84	61
Fibrinolytic Medication Timing[1,3]	2	50%	54%	54%
Heart Failure Care				
ACE Inhibitor or ARB for LVSD[1]	3	67%	90%	94%
Discharge Instructions[1]	14	86%	85%	88%
Evaluation of LVS Function[1]	16	94%	93%	98%
Smoking Cessation Advice[1]	4	100%	93%	98%
Pneumonia Care				
Appropriate Initial Antibiotic[1]	8	100%	91%	92%
Blood Culture Timing[1]	9	100%	95%	96%
Influenza Vaccine[1]	4	100%	94%	91%
Initial Antibiotic Timing[1]	19	100%	94%	95%
Pneumococcal Vaccine[1]	16	94%	93%	93%
Smoking Cessation Advice[1]	4	100%	92%	97%
Surgical Care Improvement Project				
Appropriate VTP Within 24 Hours[5]	0	-	90%	92%
Appropriate Hair Removal[5]	0	-	100%	99%
Appropriate Beta Blocker Usage[5]	0	-	93%	93%
Controlled Postoperative Blood Glucose[5]	0	-	96%	93%
Prophylactic Antibiotic Timing[5]	0	-	97%	97%
Prophylactic Antibiotic Timing (Outpatient)[5]	0	-	96%	92%
Prophylactic Antibiotic Selection[5]	0	-	98%	97%
Prophylactic Antibiotic Select. (Outpatient)[5]	0	-	97%	94%
Prophylactic Antibiotic Stopped[5]	0	-	96%	94%
Recommended VTP Ordered[5]	0	-	91%	94%
Urinary Catheter Removal[5]	0	-	89%	90%
Children's Asthma Care				
Received Systemic Corticosteroids	-	-	-	100%
Received Home Management Plan	-	-	-	71%
Received Reliever Medication	-	-	-	100%
Use of Medical Imaging				
Combination Abdominal CT Scan	74	0.068	0.325	0.191
Combination Chest CT Scan[1]	51	0.059	0.116	0.054
Follow-up Mammogram/Ultrasound[5]	0	-	7.6%	8.4%
MRI for Low Back Pain[1]	10	60.0%	31.3%	32.7%
Survey of Patients' Hospital Experiences				
Area Around Room 'Always' Quiet at Night[6]	<100	70%	-	58%
Doctors 'Always' Communicated Well[6]	<100	84%	-	80%
Home Recovery Information Given[6]	<100	89%	-	82%
Hospital Given 9 or 10 on 10 Point Scale[6]	<100	73%	-	67%
Meds 'Always' Explained Before Given[6]	<100	73%	-	60%
Nurses 'Always' Communicated Well[6]	<100	77%	-	76%
Pain 'Always' Well Controlled[6]	<100	64%	-	69%
Room and Bathroom 'Always' Clean[6]	<100	83%	-	71%
Timely Help 'Always' Received[6]	<100	81%	-	64%
Would Definitely Recommend Hospital	<100	75%	-	69%

NOTE: Hospital profiles are in alphabetical order by state, then city, then hospital within the city; Rankings exclude hospitals with less than 25 cases except for patient surveys which excludes hospitals with less than 100 cases; (a) 100–299 cases; (1) The number of cases is too small to be sure how well a hospital is performing; (2) The hospital indicated that the data submitted for this measure were based on a sample of cases; (3) Data was collected during a shorter time period (fewer quarters) than the maximum possible time for this measure; (4) Suppressed for one or more quarters by CMS; (5) No data is available from the hospital for this measure; (6) Fewer than 100 patients completed the HCAHPS survey. Use these rates with caution, as the number of surveys may be too low to reliably assess hospital performance; (7) Survey results are based on less than 12 months of data; (8) Survey results are not available for this reporting period; (9) No or very few patients were eligible for the HCAHPS survey. The scores shown, if any, reflect a very small number of surveys; (10) A state average was not calculated because too few hospitals in the state submitted data; (11) There were discrepancies in the data collection process; Please refer to the User's Guide for a full explanation of data.

Siouxland Surgery Center Lp

600 Sioux Point Road Phone: 605-232-3332
Dakota Dunes, SD 57049
Type: Acute Care Hospitals Emergency Services: No
Ownership: Proprietary Beds: 10
Key Personnel:
CEO/President. . . . . Greg Miner

Measure	Cases	This Hosp.	State Avg.	U.S. Avg.
Heart Attack Care				
ACE Inhibitor or ARB for LVSD[5]	0	-	96%	96%
Aspirin at Arrival[5]	0	-	98%	99%
Aspirin at Discharge[5]	0	-	99%	98%
Beta Blocker at Discharge[5]	0	-	98%	98%
Fibrinolytic Medication Timing[5]	0	-	45%	55%
PCI Within 90 Minutes of Arrival[5]	0	-	87%	90%
Smoking Cessation Advice[5]	0	-	99%	99%
Chest Pain/Possible Heart Attack Care				
Aspirin at Arrival[5]	0	-	96%	95%
Median Time to ECG (minutes)[5]	0	-	7	8
Median Time to Transfer (minutes)[5]	0	-	84	61
Fibrinolytic Medication Timing[5]	0	-	54%	54%
Heart Failure Care				
ACE Inhibitor or ARB for LVSD[5]	0	-	90%	94%
Discharge Instructions[5]	0	-	85%	88%
Evaluation of LVS Function[5]	0	-	93%	98%
Smoking Cessation Advice[5]	0	-	93%	98%
Pneumonia Care				
Appropriate Initial Antibiotic[5]	0	-	91%	92%
Blood Culture Timing[5]	0	-	95%	96%
Influenza Vaccine[5]	0	-	94%	91%
Initial Antibiotic Timing[5]	0	-	94%	95%
Pneumococcal Vaccine[5]	0	-	93%	93%
Smoking Cessation Advice[5]	0	-	92%	97%
Surgical Care Improvement Project				
Appropriate VTP Within 24 Hours[2]	31	94%	90%	92%
Appropriate Hair Removal[2]	353	100%	100%	99%
Appropriate Beta Blocker Usage[2]	95	86%	93%	93%
Controlled Postoperative Blood Glucose[2]	0	-	96%	93%
Prophylactic Antibiotic Timing[2]	303	98%	97%	97%
Prophylactic Antibiotic Timing (Outpatient)	314	98%	96%	92%
Prophylactic Antibiotic Selection[2]	303	100%	98%	97%
Prophylactic Antibiotic Select. (Outpatient)	311	98%	97%	94%
Prophylactic Antibiotic Stopped[2]	301	98%	96%	94%
Recommended VTP Ordered[2]	31	94%	91%	94%
Urinary Catheter Removal[1,2]	9	100%	89%	90%
Children's Asthma Care				
Received Systemic Corticosteroids	-	-	-	100%
Received Home Management Plan	-	-	-	71%
Received Reliever Medication	-	-	-	100%
Use of Medical Imaging				
Combination Abdominal CT Scan[1]	7	0.714	0.325	0.191
Combination Chest CT Scan[1]	14	0.214	0.116	0.054
Follow-up Mammogram/Ultrasound[5]	0	-	7.6%	8.4%
MRI for Low Back Pain[1]	15	13.3%	31.3%	32.7%
Survey of Patients' Hospital Experiences				
Area Around Room 'Always' Quiet at Night	300+	84%	-	58%
Doctors 'Always' Communicated Well	300+	86%	-	80%
Home Recovery Information Given	300+	88%	-	82%
Hospital Given 9 or 10 on 10 Point Scale	300+	87%	-	67%
Meds 'Always' Explained Before Given	300+	72%	-	60%
Nurses 'Always' Communicated Well	300+	88%	-	76%
Pain 'Always' Well Controlled	300+	76%	-	69%
Room and Bathroom 'Always' Clean	300+	81%	-	71%
Timely Help 'Always' Received	300+	91%	-	64%
Would Definitely Recommend Hospital	300+	89%	-	69%

Avera Desmet Memorial Hospital

306 Prairie Avenue SW Phone: 605-854-3329
De Smet, SD 57231 Fax: 605-854-3161
E-mail: info@desmetmemorial.org
URL: www.desmetmemorial.org
Type: Critical Access Hospitals Emergency Services: Yes
Ownership: Voluntary Non-Profit - Other Beds: 17
Key Personnel:
Chief of Medical Staff. . . . . John A Berg

Measure	Cases	This Hosp.	State Avg.	U.S. Avg.
Heart Attack Care				
ACE Inhibitor or ARB for LVSD[5]	0	-	96%	96%
Aspirin at Arrival[5]	0	-	98%	99%
Aspirin at Discharge[5]	0	-	99%	98%
Beta Blocker at Discharge[5]	0	-	98%	98%
Fibrinolytic Medication Timing[5]	0	-	45%	55%
PCI Within 90 Minutes of Arrival[5]	0	-	87%	90%
Smoking Cessation Advice[5]	0	-	99%	99%
Chest Pain/Possible Heart Attack Care				
Aspirin at Arrival	-	-	96%	95%
Median Time to ECG (minutes)	-	-	7	8
Median Time to Transfer (minutes)	-	-	84	61
Fibrinolytic Medication Timing	-	-	54%	54%
Heart Failure Care				
ACE Inhibitor or ARB for LVSD[3]	0	-	90%	94%
Discharge Instructions[3]	0	-	85%	88%
Evaluation of LVS Function[1,3]	1	0%	93%	98%
Smoking Cessation Advice[3]	0	-	93%	98%
Pneumonia Care				
Appropriate Initial Antibiotic[1,3]	7	86%	91%	92%
Blood Culture Timing[1,3]	2	100%	95%	96%
Influenza Vaccine[1,3]	6	100%	94%	91%
Initial Antibiotic Timing[1,3]	6	100%	94%	95%
Pneumococcal Vaccine[1,3]	7	71%	93%	93%
Smoking Cessation Advice[1,3]	2	0%	92%	97%
Surgical Care Improvement Project				
Appropriate VTP Within 24 Hours[5]	0	-	90%	92%
Appropriate Hair Removal[5]	0	-	100%	99%
Appropriate Beta Blocker Usage[5]	0	-	93%	93%
Controlled Postoperative Blood Glucose[5]	0	-	96%	93%
Prophylactic Antibiotic Timing[5]	0	-	97%	97%
Prophylactic Antibiotic Timing (Outpatient)	-	-	96%	92%
Prophylactic Antibiotic Selection[5]	0	-	98%	97%
Prophylactic Antibiotic Select. (Outpatient)	-	-	97%	94%
Prophylactic Antibiotic Stopped[5]	0	-	96%	94%
Recommended VTP Ordered[5]	0	-	91%	94%
Urinary Catheter Removal[5]	0	-	89%	90%
Children's Asthma Care				
Received Systemic Corticosteroids	-	-	-	100%
Received Home Management Plan	-	-	-	71%
Received Reliever Medication	-	-	-	100%
Use of Medical Imaging				
Combination Abdominal CT Scan	-	-	0.325	0.191
Combination Chest CT Scan	-	-	0.116	0.054
Follow-up Mammogram/Ultrasound	-	-	7.6%	8.4%
MRI for Low Back Pain	-	-	31.3%	32.7%
Survey of Patients' Hospital Experiences				
Area Around Room 'Always' Quiet at Night[6]	<100	68%	-	58%
Doctors 'Always' Communicated Well[6]	<100	80%	-	80%
Home Recovery Information Given[6]	<100	77%	-	82%
Hospital Given 9 or 10 on 10 Point Scale[6]	<100	85%	-	67%
Meds 'Always' Explained Before Given[6]	<100	67%	-	60%
Nurses 'Always' Communicated Well[6]	<100	85%	-	76%
Pain 'Always' Well Controlled[6]	<100	80%	-	69%
Room and Bathroom 'Always' Clean[6]	<100	93%	-	71%
Timely Help 'Always' Received[6]	<100	83%	-	64%
Would Definitely Recommend Hospital	<100	72%	-	69%

Lead-Deadwood Regional Hospital

61 Charles Street Phone: 605-722-6101
Deadwood, SD 57732 Fax: 605-719-6163
Type: Critical Access Hospitals Emergency Services: Yes
Ownership: Voluntary Non-Profit - Private Beds: 18
Key Personnel:
CEO/President. . . . . Sherry Bea Smith, BSN, MPA
Chief of Medical Staff. . . . . James J Holloway, MD
Infection Control. . . . . Joanne Baer, RN
Operating Room. . . . . Karen Schleenaut, MD
Quality Assurance . . . . Joanne Baer, RN

Measure	Cases	This Hosp.	State Avg.	U.S. Avg.
Heart Attack Care				
ACE Inhibitor or ARB for LVSD[5]	0	-	96%	96%
Aspirin at Arrival[5]	0	-	98%	99%
Aspirin at Discharge[5]	0	-	99%	98%
Beta Blocker at Discharge[5]	0	-	98%	98%
Fibrinolytic Medication Timing[5]	0	-	45%	55%
PCI Within 90 Minutes of Arrival[5]	0	-	87%	90%
Smoking Cessation Advice[5]	0	-	99%	99%
Chest Pain/Possible Heart Attack Care				
Aspirin at Arrival	-	-	96%	95%
Median Time to ECG (minutes)	-	-	7	8
Median Time to Transfer (minutes)	-	-	84	61
Fibrinolytic Medication Timing	-	-	54%	54%
Heart Failure Care				
ACE Inhibitor or ARB for LVSD[3]	0	-	90%	94%
Discharge Instructions[1,3]	2	100%	85%	88%
Evaluation of LVS Function[1,3]	3	100%	93%	98%
Smoking Cessation Advice[3]	0	-	93%	98%
Pneumonia Care				
Appropriate Initial Antibiotic[3]	0	-	91%	92%
Blood Culture Timing[3]	0	-	95%	96%
Influenza Vaccine[3]	0	-	94%	91%
Initial Antibiotic Timing[3]	0	-	94%	95%
Pneumococcal Vaccine[3]	0	-	93%	93%
Smoking Cessation Advice[3]	0	-	92%	97%
Surgical Care Improvement Project				
Appropriate VTP Within 24 Hours[5]	0	-	90%	92%
Appropriate Hair Removal[5]	0	-	100%	99%
Appropriate Beta Blocker Usage[5]	0	-	93%	93%
Controlled Postoperative Blood Glucose[5]	0	-	96%	93%
Prophylactic Antibiotic Timing[5]	0	-	97%	97%
Prophylactic Antibiotic Timing (Outpatient)	-	-	96%	92%
Prophylactic Antibiotic Selection[5]	0	-	98%	97%
Prophylactic Antibiotic Select. (Outpatient)	-	-	97%	94%
Prophylactic Antibiotic Stopped[5]	0	-	96%	94%
Recommended VTP Ordered[5]	0	-	91%	94%
Urinary Catheter Removal[5]	0	-	89%	90%
Children's Asthma Care				
Received Systemic Corticosteroids	-	-	-	100%
Received Home Management Plan	-	-	-	71%
Received Reliever Medication	-	-	-	100%
Use of Medical Imaging				
Combination Abdominal CT Scan	-	-	0.325	0.191
Combination Chest CT Scan	-	-	0.116	0.054
Follow-up Mammogram/Ultrasound	-	-	7.6%	8.4%
MRI for Low Back Pain	-	-	31.3%	32.7%
Survey of Patients' Hospital Experiences				
Area Around Room 'Always' Quiet at Night	(a)	73%	-	58%
Doctors 'Always' Communicated Well	(a)	92%	-	80%
Home Recovery Information Given	(a)	84%	-	82%
Hospital Given 9 or 10 on 10 Point Scale	(a)	84%	-	67%
Meds 'Always' Explained Before Given	(a)	74%	-	60%
Nurses 'Always' Communicated Well	(a)	88%	-	76%
Pain 'Always' Well Controlled	(a)	70%	-	69%
Room and Bathroom 'Always' Clean	(a)	93%	-	71%
Timely Help 'Always' Received	(a)	91%	-	64%
Would Definitely Recommend Hospital	(a)	88%	-	69%

NOTE: Hospital profiles are in alphabetical order by state, then city, then hospital within the city; Rankings exclude hospitals with less than 25 cases except for patient surveys which excludes hospitals with less than 100 cases; (a) 100–299 cases; (1) The number of cases is too small to be sure how well a hospital is performing; (2) The hospital indicated that the data submitted for this measure were based on a sample of cases; (3) Data was collected during a shorter time period (fewer quarters) than the maximum possible time for this measure; (4) Suppressed for one or more quarters by CMS; (5) No data is available from the hospital for this measure; (6) Fewer than 100 patients completed the HCAHPS survey. Use these rates with caution, as the number of surveys may be too low to reliably assess hospital performance; (7) Survey results are based on less than 12 months of data; (8) Survey results are not available for this reporting period; (9) No or very few patients were eligible for the HCAHPS survey. The scores shown, if any, reflect a very small number of surveys; (10) A state average was not calculated because too few hospitals in the state submitted data; (11) There were discrepancies in the data collection process; Please refer to the User's Guide for a full explanation of data.

Avera Dells Area Health Center

909 N Iowa Ave
Dell Rapids, SD 57022
URL: www.avera.org/avera/facilities
Type: Critical Access Hospitals
Ownership: Voluntary Non-Profit - Church
Phone: 605-428-5431
Fax: 605-428-3906
Emergency Services: Yes
Beds: 21

Key Personnel:
CEO/President. . . . . James A Faulwell
Chief of Medical Staff . . . . Dr. Shawn Culey
Radiology. . . . . Daryl C Rife

Measure	Cases	This Hosp.	State Avg.	U.S. Avg.
Heart Attack Care				
ACE Inhibitor or ARB for LVSD[2,3]	0	-	96%	96%
Aspirin at Arrival[1,2,3]	3	100%	98%	99%
Aspirin at Discharge[1,2,3]	2	100%	99%	98%
Beta Blocker at Discharge[1,2,3]	2	100%	98%	98%
Fibrinolytic Medication Timing[1,2,3]	1	0%	45%	55%
PCI Within 90 Minutes of Arrival[2,3]	0	-	87%	90%
Smoking Cessation Advice[2,3]	0	-	99%	99%
Chest Pain/Possible Heart Attack Care				
Aspirin at Arrival	-	-	96%	95%
Median Time to ECG (minutes)	-	-	7	8
Median Time to Transfer (minutes)	-	-	84	61
Fibrinolytic Medication Timing	-	-	54%	54%
Heart Failure Care				
ACE Inhibitor or ARB for LVSD[1,2]	3	100%	90%	94%
Discharge Instructions[1,2]	12	83%	85%	88%
Evaluation of LVS Function[1,2]	12	58%	93%	98%
Smoking Cessation Advice[1,2]	1	100%	93%	98%
Pneumonia Care				
Appropriate Initial Antibiotic[1,2]	11	100%	91%	92%
Blood Culture Timing[1,2]	1	100%	95%	96%
Influenza Vaccine[1,2]	13	92%	94%	91%
Initial Antibiotic Timing[1,2]	11	100%	94%	95%
Pneumococcal Vaccine[1,2]	18	89%	93%	93%
Smoking Cessation Advice[1,2]	1	100%	92%	97%
Surgical Care Improvement Project				
Appropriate VTP Within 24 Hours[5]	0	-	90%	92%
Appropriate Hair Removal[5]	0	-	100%	99%
Appropriate Beta Blocker Usage[5]	0	-	93%	93%
Controlled Postoperative Blood Glucose[5]	0	-	96%	93%
Prophylactic Antibiotic Timing[5]	0	-	97%	97%
Prophylactic Antibiotic Timing (Outpatient)	-	-	96%	92%
Prophylactic Antibiotic Selection[5]	0	-	98%	97%
Prophylactic Antibiotic Select. (Outpatient)	-	-	97%	94%
Prophylactic Antibiotic Stopped[5]	0	-	96%	94%
Recommended VTP Ordered[5]	0	-	91%	94%
Urinary Catheter Removal[5]	0	-	89%	90%
Children's Asthma Care				
Received Systemic Corticosteroids	-	-	-	100%
Received Home Management Plan	-	-	-	71%
Received Reliever Medication	-	-	-	100%
Use of Medical Imaging				
Combination Abdominal CT Scan	-	-	0.325	0.191
Combination Chest CT Scan	-	-	0.116	0.054
Follow-up Mammogram/Ultrasound	-	-	7.6%	8.4%
MRI for Low Back Pain	-	-	31.3%	32.7%
Survey of Patients' Hospital Experiences				
Area Around Room 'Always' Quiet at Night	(a)	78%	-	58%
Doctors 'Always' Communicated Well	(a)	89%	-	80%
Home Recovery Information Given	(a)	85%	-	82%
Hospital Given 9 or 10 on 10 Point Scale	(a)	89%	-	67%
Meds 'Always' Explained Before Given	(a)	71%	-	60%
Nurses 'Always' Communicated Well	(a)	89%	-	76%
Pain 'Always' Well Controlled	(a)	78%	-	69%
Room and Bathroom 'Always' Clean	(a)	91%	-	71%
Timely Help 'Always' Received	(a)	74%	-	64%
Would Definitely Recommend Hospital	(a)	85%	-	69%

PHS Indian Hospital at Eagle Butte

317 Main Street
Eagle Butte, SD 57625
URL: www.ihs.gov
Type: Acute Care Hospitals
Ownership: Government - Federal
Phone: 605-964-3005
Fax: 605-964-1169
Emergency Services: No
Beds: 27

Key Personnel:
Chief of Medical Staff . . . . Margaret Upell
Infection Control. . . . . Margaret Zephier, RN
Quality Assurance . . . . Cyndi Halfred

Measure	Cases	This Hosp.	State Avg.	U.S. Avg.
Heart Attack Care				
ACE Inhibitor or ARB for LVSD[5]	0	-	96%	96%
Aspirin at Arrival[5]	0	-	98%	99%
Aspirin at Discharge[5]	0	-	99%	98%
Beta Blocker at Discharge[5]	0	-	98%	98%
Fibrinolytic Medication Timing[5]	0	-	45%	55%
PCI Within 90 Minutes of Arrival[5]	0	-	87%	90%
Smoking Cessation Advice[5]	0	-	99%	99%
Chest Pain/Possible Heart Attack Care				
Aspirin at Arrival	-	-	96%	95%
Median Time to ECG (minutes)	-	-	7	8
Median Time to Transfer (minutes)	-	-	84	61
Fibrinolytic Medication Timing	-	-	54%	54%
Heart Failure Care				
ACE Inhibitor or ARB for LVSD[3]	0	-	90%	94%
Discharge Instructions[1,3]	1	0%	85%	88%
Evaluation of LVS Function[1,3]	1	0%	93%	98%
Smoking Cessation Advice[1,3]	1	0%	93%	98%
Pneumonia Care				
Appropriate Initial Antibiotic[1,2,3]	2	50%	91%	92%
Blood Culture Timing[2,3]	0	-	95%	96%
Influenza Vaccine[1,3]	1	0%	94%	91%
Initial Antibiotic Timing[1,2,3]	1	100%	94%	95%
Pneumococcal Vaccine[1,2,3]	2	100%	93%	93%
Smoking Cessation Advice[2,3]	0	-	92%	97%
Surgical Care Improvement Project				
Appropriate VTP Within 24 Hours[5]	0	-	90%	92%
Appropriate Hair Removal[5]	0	-	100%	99%
Appropriate Beta Blocker Usage[5]	0	-	93%	93%
Controlled Postoperative Blood Glucose[5]	0	-	96%	93%
Prophylactic Antibiotic Timing[5]	0	-	97%	97%
Prophylactic Antibiotic Timing (Outpatient)	-	-	96%	92%
Prophylactic Antibiotic Selection[5]	0	-	98%	97%
Prophylactic Antibiotic Select. (Outpatient)	-	-	97%	94%
Prophylactic Antibiotic Stopped[5]	0	-	96%	94%
Recommended VTP Ordered[5]	0	-	91%	94%
Urinary Catheter Removal[5]	0	-	89%	90%
Children's Asthma Care				
Received Systemic Corticosteroids	-	-	-	100%
Received Home Management Plan	-	-	-	71%
Received Reliever Medication	-	-	-	100%
Use of Medical Imaging				
Combination Abdominal CT Scan	-	-	0.325	0.191
Combination Chest CT Scan	-	-	0.116	0.054
Follow-up Mammogram/Ultrasound	-	-	7.6%	8.4%
MRI for Low Back Pain	-	-	31.3%	32.7%
Survey of Patients' Hospital Experiences				
Area Around Room 'Always' Quiet at Night[9,11,6]	<100	93%	-	58%
Doctors 'Always' Communicated Well[9,11,6]	<100	84%	-	80%
Home Recovery Information Given[9,11,6]	<100	48%	-	82%
Hospital Given 9 or 10 on 10 Point Scale[9,11,6]	<100	51%	-	67%
Meds 'Always' Explained Before Given[9,11,6]	<100	93%	-	60%
Nurses 'Always' Communicated Well[9,11,6]	<100	90%	-	76%
Pain 'Always' Well Controlled[9,11,6]	<100	95%	-	69%
Room and Bathroom 'Always' Clean[9,11,6]	<100	58%	-	71%
Timely Help 'Always' Received[9,11,6]	<100	98%	-	64%
Would Definitely Recommend Hospital[9,11]	<100	52%	-	69%

Avera Flandreau Medical Center Hospital

214 North Prairie Avenue
Flandreau, SD 57028
URL: www.flandreaumedical.org
Type: Critical Access Hospitals
Ownership: Government - Local
Phone: 605-997-2433
Fax: 605-997-3611
Emergency Services: Yes
Beds: 18

Key Personnel:
Chief of Medical Staff . . . . Gary Bruning, DO
Patient Relations . . . . Marie Myers, RN

Measure	Cases	This Hosp.	State Avg.	U.S. Avg.
Heart Attack Care				
ACE Inhibitor or ARB for LVSD[3]	0	-	96%	96%
Aspirin at Arrival[3]	0	-	98%	99%
Aspirin at Discharge[3]	0	-	99%	98%
Beta Blocker at Discharge[3]	0	-	98%	98%
Fibrinolytic Medication Timing[3]	0	-	45%	55%
PCI Within 90 Minutes of Arrival[3]	0	-	87%	90%
Smoking Cessation Advice[3]	0	-	99%	99%
Chest Pain/Possible Heart Attack Care				
Aspirin at Arrival	-	-	96%	95%
Median Time to ECG (minutes)	-	-	7	8
Median Time to Transfer (minutes)	-	-	84	61
Fibrinolytic Medication Timing	-	-	54%	54%
Heart Failure Care				
ACE Inhibitor or ARB for LVSD[1]	1	100%	90%	94%
Discharge Instructions[1]	4	100%	85%	88%
Evaluation of LVS Function[1]	6	50%	93%	98%
Smoking Cessation Advice	0	-	93%	98%
Pneumonia Care				
Appropriate Initial Antibiotic[1]	10	90%	91%	92%
Blood Culture Timing	0	-	95%	96%
Influenza Vaccine[1]	12	58%	94%	91%
Initial Antibiotic Timing[1]	12	100%	94%	95%
Pneumococcal Vaccine[1]	14	93%	93%	93%
Smoking Cessation Advice[1]	1	100%	92%	97%
Surgical Care Improvement Project				
Appropriate VTP Within 24 Hours[5]	0	-	90%	92%
Appropriate Hair Removal[5]	0	-	100%	99%
Appropriate Beta Blocker Usage[5]	0	-	93%	93%
Controlled Postoperative Blood Glucose[5]	0	-	96%	93%
Prophylactic Antibiotic Timing[5]	0	-	97%	97%
Prophylactic Antibiotic Timing (Outpatient)	-	-	96%	92%
Prophylactic Antibiotic Selection[5]	0	-	98%	97%
Prophylactic Antibiotic Select. (Outpatient)	-	-	97%	94%
Prophylactic Antibiotic Stopped[5]	0	-	96%	94%
Recommended VTP Ordered[5]	0	-	91%	94%
Urinary Catheter Removal[5]	0	-	89%	90%
Children's Asthma Care				
Received Systemic Corticosteroids	-	-	-	100%
Received Home Management Plan	-	-	-	71%
Received Reliever Medication	-	-	-	100%
Use of Medical Imaging				
Combination Abdominal CT Scan	-	-	0.325	0.191
Combination Chest CT Scan	-	-	0.116	0.054
Follow-up Mammogram/Ultrasound	-	-	7.6%	8.4%
MRI for Low Back Pain	-	-	31.3%	32.7%
Survey of Patients' Hospital Experiences				
Area Around Room 'Always' Quiet at Night[6]	<100	68%	-	58%
Doctors 'Always' Communicated Well[6]	<100	86%	-	80%
Home Recovery Information Given[6]	<100	69%	-	82%
Hospital Given 9 or 10 on 10 Point Scale[6]	<100	67%	-	67%
Meds 'Always' Explained Before Given[6]	<100	58%	-	60%
Nurses 'Always' Communicated Well[6]	<100	78%	-	76%
Pain 'Always' Well Controlled[6]	<100	67%	-	69%
Room and Bathroom 'Always' Clean[6]	<100	77%	-	71%
Timely Help 'Always' Received[6]	<100	85%	-	64%
Would Definitely Recommend Hospital	<100	71%	-	69%

NOTE: Hospital profiles are in alphabetical order by state, then city, then hospital within the city; Rankings exclude hospitals with less than 25 cases except for patient surveys which excludes hospitals with less than 100 cases; (a) 100–299 cases; (1) The number of cases is too small to be sure how well a hospital is performing; (2) The hospital indicated that the data submitted for this measure were based on a sample of cases; (3) Data was collected during a shorter time period (fewer quarters) than the maximum possible time for this measure; (4) Suppressed for one or more quarters by CMS; (5) No data is available from the hospital for this measure; (6) Fewer than 100 patients completed the HCAHPS survey. Use these rates with caution, as the number of surveys may be too low to reliably assess hospital performance; (7) Survey results are based on less than 12 months of data; (8) Survey results are not available for this reporting period; (9) No or very few patients were eligible for the HCAHPS survey. The scores shown, if any, reflect a very small number of surveys; (10) A state average was not calculated because too few hospitals in the state submitted data; (11) There were discrepancies in the data collection process; Please refer to the User's Guide for a full explanation of data.

VA Black Hills Healthcare System - Fort Meade

113 Comanche Road Phone: 605-347-2511
Fort Meade, SD 57741 Fax: 605-720-7171
URL: www.va.gov
Type: Acute Care-Veterans Administration Emergency Services: No
Ownership: Government - Federal Beds: 318

Key Personnel:
Chief of Medical Staff.......... Craig J. Fisher, MD
Quality Assurance .... Sandra Simensen, RN
Radiology.................. Nathan Pulcher
Anesthesiology............... Rodney Hines
Emergency Room .... Moriah Walker
Intensive Care Unit........... Robert Vosler
Patient Relations .... Clyde Walton

Measure	Cases	This Hosp.	State Avg.	U.S. Avg.
Heart Attack Care				
ACE Inhibitor or ARB for LVSD[5]	0	-	96%	96%
Aspirin at Arrival[5]	0	-	98%	99%
Aspirin at Discharge[5]	0	-	99%	98%
Beta Blocker at Discharge[5]	0	-	98%	98%
Fibrinolytic Medication Timing[5]	0	-	45%	55%
PCI Within 90 Minutes of Arrival[5]	0	-	87%	90%
Smoking Cessation Advice[5]	0	-	99%	99%
Chest Pain/Possible Heart Attack Care				
Aspirin at Arrival	-	-	96%	95%
Median Time to ECG (minutes)	-	-	7	8
Median Time to Transfer (minutes)	-	-	84	61
Fibrinolytic Medication Timing	-	-	54%	54%
Heart Failure Care				
ACE Inhibitor or ARB for LVSD[1]	20	95%	90%	94%
Discharge Instructions	53	92%	85%	88%
Evaluation of LVS Function	58	100%	93%	98%
Smoking Cessation Advice[1]	14	100%	93%	98%
Pneumonia Care				
Appropriate Initial Antibiotic	48	90%	91%	92%
Blood Culture Timing	44	100%	95%	96%
Influenza Vaccine	29	90%	94%	91%
Initial Antibiotic Timing	62	95%	94%	95%
Pneumococcal Vaccine	47	100%	93%	93%
Smoking Cessation Advice[1]	19	79%	92%	97%
Surgical Care Improvement Project				
Appropriate VTP Within 24 Hours[2,5]	0	-	90%	92%
Appropriate Hair Removal[2,5]	0	-	100%	99%
Appropriate Beta Blocker Usage[2,5]	0	-	93%	93%
Controlled Postoperative Blood Glucose[2,5]	0	-	96%	93%
Prophylactic Antibiotic Timing[5]	0	-	97%	97%
Prophylactic Antibiotic Timing (Outpatient)	-	-	96%	92%
Prophylactic Antibiotic Selection[5]	0	-	98%	97%
Prophylactic Antibiotic Select. (Outpatient)	-	-	97%	94%
Prophylactic Antibiotic Stopped[5]	0	-	96%	94%
Recommended VTP Ordered[2,5]	0	-	91%	94%
Urinary Catheter Removal[2,5]	0	-	89%	90%
Children's Asthma Care				
Received Systemic Corticosteroids	-	-	-	100%
Received Home Management Plan	-	-	-	71%
Received Reliever Medication	-	-	-	100%
Use of Medical Imaging				
Combination Abdominal CT Scan	-	-	0.325	0.191
Combination Chest CT Scan	-	-	0.116	0.054
Follow-up Mammogram/Ultrasound	-	-	7.6%	8.4%
MRI for Low Back Pain	-	-	31.3%	32.7%
Survey of Patients' Hospital Experiences				
Area Around Room 'Always' Quiet at Night	-	-	-	58%
Doctors 'Always' Communicated Well	-	-	-	80%
Home Recovery Information Given	-	-	-	82%
Hospital Given 9 or 10 on 10 Point Scale	-	-	-	67%
Meds 'Always' Explained Before Given	-	-	-	60%
Nurses 'Always' Communicated Well	-	-	-	76%
Pain 'Always' Well Controlled	-	-	-	69%
Room and Bathroom 'Always' Clean	-	-	-	71%
Timely Help 'Always' Received	-	-	-	64%
Would Definitely Recommend Hospital	-	-	-	69%

Avera Gregory Healthcare Center

400 Park Street Phone: 605-835-8394
Gregory, SD 57533 Fax: 605-835-9422
URL: www.gregoryhealthcare.org
Type: Critical Access Hospitals Emergency Services: Yes
Ownership: Voluntary Non-Profit - Church Beds: 81

Key Personnel:
CEO/President............... Carol Varland
Chief of Medical Staff.......... R Nemer, MD

Measure	Cases	This Hosp.	State Avg.	U.S. Avg.
Heart Attack Care				
ACE Inhibitor or ARB for LVSD[1,3]	2	100%	96%	96%
Aspirin at Arrival[1,3]	4	50%	98%	99%
Aspirin at Discharge[1,3]	4	75%	99%	98%
Beta Blocker at Discharge[1,3]	4	75%	98%	98%
Fibrinolytic Medication Timing[3]	0	-	45%	55%
PCI Within 90 Minutes of Arrival[3]	0	-	87%	90%
Smoking Cessation Advice[3]	0	-	99%	99%
Chest Pain/Possible Heart Attack Care				
Aspirin at Arrival	-	-	96%	95%
Median Time to ECG (minutes)	-	-	7	8
Median Time to Transfer (minutes)	-	-	84	61
Fibrinolytic Medication Timing	-	-	54%	54%
Heart Failure Care				
ACE Inhibitor or ARB for LVSD[1]	10	80%	90%	94%
Discharge Instructions[1]	11	82%	85%	88%
Evaluation of LVS Function	26	85%	93%	98%
Smoking Cessation Advice[1]	1	0%	93%	98%
Pneumonia Care				
Appropriate Initial Antibiotic	41	88%	91%	92%
Blood Culture Timing[1]	1	100%	95%	96%
Influenza Vaccine	49	98%	94%	91%
Initial Antibiotic Timing	28	64%	94%	95%
Pneumococcal Vaccine	71	97%	93%	93%
Smoking Cessation Advice[1]	6	100%	92%	97%
Surgical Care Improvement Project				
Appropriate VTP Within 24 Hours[5]	0	-	90%	92%
Appropriate Hair Removal[5]	0	-	100%	99%
Appropriate Beta Blocker Usage[5]	0	-	93%	93%
Controlled Postoperative Blood Glucose[5]	0	-	96%	93%
Prophylactic Antibiotic Timing[5]	0	-	97%	97%
Prophylactic Antibiotic Timing (Outpatient)	-	-	96%	92%
Prophylactic Antibiotic Selection[5]	0	-	98%	97%
Prophylactic Antibiotic Select. (Outpatient)	-	-	97%	94%
Prophylactic Antibiotic Stopped[5]	0	-	96%	94%
Recommended VTP Ordered[5]	0	-	91%	94%
Urinary Catheter Removal[5]	0	-	89%	90%
Children's Asthma Care				
Received Systemic Corticosteroids	-	-	-	100%
Received Home Management Plan	-	-	-	71%
Received Reliever Medication	-	-	-	100%
Use of Medical Imaging				
Combination Abdominal CT Scan	-	-	0.325	0.191
Combination Chest CT Scan	-	-	0.116	0.054
Follow-up Mammogram/Ultrasound	-	-	7.6%	8.4%
MRI for Low Back Pain	-	-	31.3%	32.7%
Survey of Patients' Hospital Experiences				
Area Around Room 'Always' Quiet at Night	(a)	68%	-	58%
Doctors 'Always' Communicated Well	(a)	79%	-	80%
Home Recovery Information Given	(a)	71%	-	82%
Hospital Given 9 or 10 on 10 Point Scale	(a)	71%	-	67%
Meds 'Always' Explained Before Given	(a)	65%	-	60%
Nurses 'Always' Communicated Well	(a)	78%	-	76%
Pain 'Always' Well Controlled	(a)	75%	-	69%
Room and Bathroom 'Always' Clean	(a)	83%	-	71%
Timely Help 'Always' Received	(a)	60%	-	64%
Would Definitely Recommend Hospital	(a)	72%	-	69%

Fall River Hospital

1201 Highway 71 South Phone: 605-745-8910
Hot Springs, SD 57747
URL: fallriverhealthservices.com/hospital.php
Type: Critical Access Hospitals Emergency Services: Yes
Ownership: Government - Local Beds: 11

Measure	Cases	This Hosp.	State Avg.	U.S. Avg.
Heart Attack Care				
ACE Inhibitor or ARB for LVSD[5]	0	-	96%	96%
Aspirin at Arrival[5]	0	-	98%	99%
Aspirin at Discharge[5]	0	-	99%	98%
Beta Blocker at Discharge[5]	0	-	98%	98%
Fibrinolytic Medication Timing[5]	0	-	45%	55%
PCI Within 90 Minutes of Arrival[5]	0	-	87%	90%
Smoking Cessation Advice[5]	0	-	99%	99%
Chest Pain/Possible Heart Attack Care				
Aspirin at Arrival[5]	0	-	96%	95%
Median Time to ECG (minutes)[5]	0	-	7	8
Median Time to Transfer (minutes)[5]	0	-	84	61
Fibrinolytic Medication Timing[5]	0	-	54%	54%
Heart Failure Care				
ACE Inhibitor or ARB for LVSD[5]	0	-	90%	94%
Discharge Instructions[5]	0	-	85%	88%
Evaluation of LVS Function[5]	0	-	93%	98%
Smoking Cessation Advice[5]	0	-	93%	98%
Pneumonia Care				
Appropriate Initial Antibiotic[5]	0	-	91%	92%
Blood Culture Timing[5]	0	-	95%	96%
Influenza Vaccine[5]	0	-	94%	91%
Initial Antibiotic Timing[5]	0	-	94%	95%
Pneumococcal Vaccine[5]	0	-	93%	93%
Smoking Cessation Advice[5]	0	-	92%	97%
Surgical Care Improvement Project				
Appropriate VTP Within 24 Hours[5]	0	-	90%	92%
Appropriate Hair Removal[5]	0	-	100%	99%
Appropriate Beta Blocker Usage[5]	0	-	93%	93%
Controlled Postoperative Blood Glucose[5]	0	-	96%	93%
Prophylactic Antibiotic Timing[5]	0	-	97%	97%
Prophylactic Antibiotic Timing (Outpatient)[5]	0	-	96%	92%
Prophylactic Antibiotic Selection[5]	0	-	98%	97%
Prophylactic Antibiotic Select. (Outpatient)[5]	0	-	97%	94%
Prophylactic Antibiotic Stopped[5]	0	-	96%	94%
Recommended VTP Ordered[5]	0	-	91%	94%
Urinary Catheter Removal[5]	0	-	89%	90%
Children's Asthma Care				
Received Systemic Corticosteroids	-	-	-	100%
Received Home Management Plan	-	-	-	71%
Received Reliever Medication	-	-	-	100%
Use of Medical Imaging				
Combination Abdominal CT Scan[1]	42	0.000	0.325	0.191
Combination Chest CT Scan[1]	30	0.000	0.116	0.054
Follow-up Mammogram/Ultrasound[5]	0	-	7.6%	8.4%
MRI for Low Back Pain[1]	10	30.0%	31.3%	32.7%
Survey of Patients' Hospital Experiences				
Area Around Room 'Always' Quiet at Night[8]	-	-	-	58%
Doctors 'Always' Communicated Well[8]	-	-	-	80%
Home Recovery Information Given[8]	-	-	-	82%
Hospital Given 9 or 10 on 10 Point Scale[8]	-	-	-	67%
Meds 'Always' Explained Before Given[8]	-	-	-	60%
Nurses 'Always' Communicated Well[8]	-	-	-	76%
Pain 'Always' Well Controlled[8]	-	-	-	69%
Room and Bathroom 'Always' Clean[8]	-	-	-	71%
Timely Help 'Always' Received[8]	-	-	-	64%
Would Definitely Recommend Hospital[8]	-	-	-	69%

NOTE: Hospital profiles are in alphabetical order by state, then city, then hospital within the city; Rankings exclude hospitals with less than 25 cases except for patient surveys which excludes hospitals with less than 100 cases; (a) 100–299 cases; (1) The number of cases is too small to be sure how well a hospital is performing; (2) The hospital indicated that the data submitted for this measure were based on a sample of cases; (3) Data was collected during a shorter time period (fewer quarters) than the maximum possible time for this measure; (4) Suppressed for one or more quarters by CMS; (5) No data is available from the hospital for this measure; (6) Fewer than 100 patients completed the HCAHPS survey. Use these rates with caution, as the number of surveys may be too low to reliably assess hospital performance; (7) Survey results are based on less than 12 months of data; (8) Survey results are not available for this reporting period; (9) No or very few patients were eligible for the HCAHPS survey. The scores shown, if any, reflect a very small number of surveys; (10) A state average was not calculated because too few hospitals in the state submitted data; (11) There were discrepancies in the data collection process; Please refer to the User's Guide for a full explanation of data.

Holy Infant Hospital

512 Main Street, Box 158
Hoven, SD 57450
Phone: 605-948-2262
Fax: 605-948-2379
Type: Acute Care Hospitals
Emergency Services: No
Ownership: Voluntary Non-Profit - Other
Beds: 26

Key Personnel:
Chief of Medical Staff . . . . Dion Rameriz, MD
Quality Assurance . . . . Angie Hageman

Measure	Cases	This Hosp.	State Avg.	U.S. Avg.
Heart Attack Care				
ACE Inhibitor or ARB for LVSD[5]	0	-	96%	96%
Aspirin at Arrival[5]	0	-	98%	99%
Aspirin at Discharge[5]	0	-	99%	98%
Beta Blocker at Discharge[5]	0	-	98%	98%
Fibrinolytic Medication Timing[5]	0	-	45%	55%
PCI Within 90 Minutes of Arrival[5]	0	-	87%	90%
Smoking Cessation Advice[5]	0	-	99%	99%
Chest Pain/Possible Heart Attack Care				
Aspirin at Arrival[1,3]	1	100%	96%	95%
Median Time to ECG (minutes)[1,3]	1	80	7	8
Median Time to Transfer (minutes)[5]	0	-	84	61
Fibrinolytic Medication Timing[5]	0	-	54%	54%
Heart Failure Care				
ACE Inhibitor or ARB for LVSD[5]	0	-	90%	94%
Discharge Instructions[5]	0	-	85%	88%
Evaluation of LVS Function[5]	0	-	93%	98%
Smoking Cessation Advice[5]	0	-	93%	98%
Pneumonia Care				
Appropriate Initial Antibiotic[5]	0	-	91%	92%
Blood Culture Timing[5]	0	-	95%	96%
Influenza Vaccine[5]	0	-	94%	91%
Initial Antibiotic Timing[5]	0	-	94%	95%
Pneumococcal Vaccine[5]	0	-	93%	93%
Smoking Cessation Advice[5]	0	-	92%	97%
Surgical Care Improvement Project				
Appropriate VTP Within 24 Hours[5]	0	-	90%	92%
Appropriate Hair Removal[5]	0	-	100%	99%
Appropriate Beta Blocker Usage[5]	0	-	93%	93%
Controlled Postoperative Blood Glucose[5]	0	-	96%	93%
Prophylactic Antibiotic Timing[5]	0	-	97%	97%
Prophylactic Antibiotic Timing (Outpatient)[5]	0	-	96%	92%
Prophylactic Antibiotic Selection[5]	0	-	98%	97%
Prophylactic Antibiotic Select. (Outpatient)[5]	0	-	97%	94%
Prophylactic Antibiotic Stopped[5]	0	-	96%	94%
Recommended VTP Ordered[5]	0	-	91%	94%
Urinary Catheter Removal[5]	0	-	89%	90%
Children's Asthma Care				
Received Systemic Corticosteroids	-	-	-	100%
Received Home Management Plan	-	-	-	71%
Received Reliever Medication	-	-	-	100%
Use of Medical Imaging				
Combination Abdominal CT Scan[5]	0	-	0.325	0.191
Combination Chest CT Scan[5]	0	-	0.116	0.054
Follow-up Mammogram/Ultrasound[1]	7	0.0%	7.6%	8.4%
MRI for Low Back Pain[5]	0	-	31.3%	32.7%
Survey of Patients' Hospital Experiences				
Area Around Room 'Always' Quiet at Night[9]	-	-	-	58%
Doctors 'Always' Communicated Well[9]	-	-	-	80%
Home Recovery Information Given[9]	-	-	-	82%
Hospital Given 9 or 10 on 10 Point Scale[9]	-	-	-	67%
Meds 'Always' Explained Before Given[9]	-	-	-	60%
Nurses 'Always' Communicated Well[9]	-	-	-	76%
Pain 'Always' Well Controlled[9]	-	-	-	69%
Room and Bathroom 'Always' Clean[9]	-	-	-	71%
Timely Help 'Always' Received[9]	-	-	-	64%
Would Definitely Recommend Hospital[9]	-	-	-	69%

Huron Regional Medical Center

172 Fourth Street SE
Huron, SD 57350
Phone: 605-353-6200
Fax: 605-353-6300
URL: www.huronregional.org
Type: Critical Access Hospitals
Emergency Services: Yes
Ownership: Voluntary Non-Profit - Private
Beds: 25

Key Personnel:
CEO/President. . . . . John Single
Chief of Medical Staff . . . . Cy Hartvedt
Infection Control . . . . Janice Farrar, RN
Operating Room. . . . . Kris Brandt
Quality Assurance . . . . Janice Farrar
Radiology. . . . . Rick Janes
Emergency Room . . . . Pat Woulridge

Measure	Cases	This Hosp.	State Avg.	U.S. Avg.
Heart Attack Care				
ACE Inhibitor or ARB for LVSD[1,2]	5	100%	96%	96%
Aspirin at Arrival[1,2]	18	100%	98%	99%
Aspirin at Discharge[1,2]	7	100%	99%	98%
Beta Blocker at Discharge[1,2]	7	71%	98%	98%
Fibrinolytic Medication Timing[1,2]	1	100%	45%	55%
PCI Within 90 Minutes of Arrival[5]	0	-	87%	90%
Smoking Cessation Advice[1,2]	1	0%	99%	99%
Chest Pain/Possible Heart Attack Care				
Aspirin at Arrival	-	-	96%	95%
Median Time to ECG (minutes)	-	-	7	8
Median Time to Transfer (minutes)	-	-	84	61
Fibrinolytic Medication Timing	-	-	54%	54%
Heart Failure Care				
ACE Inhibitor or ARB for LVSD[1]	7	71%	90%	94%
Discharge Instructions[1]	21	90%	85%	88%
Evaluation of LVS Function	34	85%	93%	98%
Smoking Cessation Advice[1]	2	50%	93%	98%
Pneumonia Care				
Appropriate Initial Antibiotic[2]	59	71%	91%	92%
Blood Culture Timing[2]	41	93%	95%	96%
Influenza Vaccine[2]	50	92%	94%	91%
Initial Antibiotic Timing[2]	57	84%	94%	95%
Pneumococcal Vaccine[2]	65	86%	93%	93%
Smoking Cessation Advice[1,2]	17	76%	92%	97%
Surgical Care Improvement Project				
Appropriate VTP Within 24 Hours	57	79%	90%	92%
Appropriate Hair Removal	81	100%	100%	99%
Appropriate Beta Blocker Usage[5]	0	-	93%	93%
Controlled Postoperative Blood Glucose[5]	0	-	96%	93%
Prophylactic Antibiotic Timing	49	90%	97%	97%
Prophylactic Antibiotic Timing (Outpatient)	-	-	96%	92%
Prophylactic Antibiotic Selection	49	96%	98%	97%
Prophylactic Antibiotic Select. (Outpatient)	-	-	97%	94%
Prophylactic Antibiotic Stopped	49	82%	96%	94%
Recommended VTP Ordered	57	81%	91%	94%
Urinary Catheter Removal[1]	11	27%	89%	90%
Children's Asthma Care				
Received Systemic Corticosteroids	-	-	-	100%
Received Home Management Plan	-	-	-	71%
Received Reliever Medication	-	-	-	100%
Use of Medical Imaging				
Combination Abdominal CT Scan	-	-	0.325	0.191
Combination Chest CT Scan	-	-	0.116	0.054
Follow-up Mammogram/Ultrasound	-	-	7.6%	8.4%
MRI for Low Back Pain	-	-	31.3%	32.7%
Survey of Patients' Hospital Experiences				
Area Around Room 'Always' Quiet at Night[8]	-	-	-	58%
Doctors 'Always' Communicated Well[8]	-	-	-	80%
Home Recovery Information Given[8]	-	-	-	82%
Hospital Given 9 or 10 on 10 Point Scale[8]	-	-	-	67%
Meds 'Always' Explained Before Given[8]	-	-	-	60%
Nurses 'Always' Communicated Well[8]	-	-	-	76%
Pain 'Always' Well Controlled[8]	-	-	-	69%
Room and Bathroom 'Always' Clean[8]	-	-	-	71%
Timely Help 'Always' Received[8]	-	-	-	64%
Would Definitely Recommend Hospital[8]	-	-	-	69%

Madison Community Hospital

917 N Washington Ave
Madison, SD 57042
Phone: 605-256-6551
Fax: 605-256-6469
E-mail: info@madisonhospital.com
URL: www.madisonhospital.com
Type: Critical Access Hospitals
Emergency Services: Yes
Ownership: Voluntary Non-Profit - Private
Beds: 25

Key Personnel:
Chief of Medical Staff . . . . RG Sample, MD
Infection Control . . . . Kathy Hansen
Quality Assurance . . . . Jennifer Eimers
Emergency Room . . . . Donna Quade

Measure	Cases	This Hosp.	State Avg.	U.S. Avg.
Heart Attack Care				
ACE Inhibitor or ARB for LVSD[3]	0	-	96%	96%
Aspirin at Arrival[3]	0	-	98%	99%
Aspirin at Discharge[3]	0	-	99%	98%
Beta Blocker at Discharge[3]	0	-	98%	98%
Fibrinolytic Medication Timing[3]	0	-	45%	55%
PCI Within 90 Minutes of Arrival[3]	0	-	87%	90%
Smoking Cessation Advice[3]	0	-	99%	99%
Chest Pain/Possible Heart Attack Care				
Aspirin at Arrival	-	-	96%	95%
Median Time to ECG (minutes)	-	-	7	8
Median Time to Transfer (minutes)	-	-	84	61
Fibrinolytic Medication Timing	-	-	54%	54%
Heart Failure Care				
ACE Inhibitor or ARB for LVSD	0	-	90%	94%
Discharge Instructions[1]	1	0%	85%	88%
Evaluation of LVS Function[1]	9	44%	93%	98%
Smoking Cessation Advice	0	-	93%	98%
Pneumonia Care				
Appropriate Initial Antibiotic[1]	19	89%	91%	92%
Blood Culture Timing[1]	2	100%	95%	96%
Influenza Vaccine[1]	12	92%	94%	91%
Initial Antibiotic Timing[1]	12	92%	94%	95%
Pneumococcal Vaccine[1]	17	94%	93%	93%
Smoking Cessation Advice[1]	7	43%	92%	97%
Surgical Care Improvement Project				
Appropriate VTP Within 24 Hours[1]	9	67%	90%	92%
Appropriate Hair Removal[1]	11	100%	100%	99%
Appropriate Beta Blocker Usage[5]	0	-	93%	93%
Controlled Postoperative Blood Glucose	0	-	96%	93%
Prophylactic Antibiotic Timing[1]	2	100%	97%	97%
Prophylactic Antibiotic Timing (Outpatient)	-	-	96%	92%
Prophylactic Antibiotic Selection[1]	2	100%	98%	97%
Prophylactic Antibiotic Select. (Outpatient)	-	-	97%	94%
Prophylactic Antibiotic Stopped[1]	2	100%	96%	94%
Recommended VTP Ordered[1]	9	67%	91%	94%
Urinary Catheter Removal[1]	3	67%	89%	90%
Children's Asthma Care				
Received Systemic Corticosteroids	-	-	-	100%
Received Home Management Plan	-	-	-	71%
Received Reliever Medication	-	-	-	100%
Use of Medical Imaging				
Combination Abdominal CT Scan	-	-	0.325	0.191
Combination Chest CT Scan	-	-	0.116	0.054
Follow-up Mammogram/Ultrasound	-	-	7.6%	8.4%
MRI for Low Back Pain	-	-	31.3%	32.7%
Survey of Patients' Hospital Experiences				
Area Around Room 'Always' Quiet at Night[8]	-	-	-	58%
Doctors 'Always' Communicated Well[8]	-	-	-	80%
Home Recovery Information Given[8]	-	-	-	82%
Hospital Given 9 or 10 on 10 Point Scale[8]	-	-	-	67%
Meds 'Always' Explained Before Given[8]	-	-	-	60%
Nurses 'Always' Communicated Well[8]	-	-	-	76%
Pain 'Always' Well Controlled[8]	-	-	-	69%
Room and Bathroom 'Always' Clean[8]	-	-	-	71%
Timely Help 'Always' Received[8]	-	-	-	64%
Would Definitely Recommend Hospital[8]	-	-	-	69%

NOTE: Hospital profiles are in alphabetical order by state, then city, then hospital within the city; Rankings exclude hospitals with less than 25 cases except for patient surveys which excludes hospitals with less than 100 cases; (a) 100–299 cases; (1) The number of cases is too small to be sure how well a hospital is performing; (2) The hospital indicated that the data submitted for this measure were based on a sample of cases; (3) Data was collected during a shorter time period (fewer quarters) than the maximum possible time for this measure; (4) Suppressed for one or more quarters by CMS; (5) No data is available from the hospital for this measure; (6) Fewer than 100 patients completed the HCAHPS survey. Use these rates with caution, as the number of surveys may be too low to reliably assess hospital performance; (7) Survey results are based on less than 12 months of data; (8) Survey results are not available for this reporting period; (9) No or very few patients were eligible for the HCAHPS survey. The scores shown, if any, reflect a very small number of surveys; (10) A state average was not calculated because too few hospitals in the state submitted data; (11) There were discrepancies in the data collection process; Please refer to the User's Guide for a full explanation of data.

Milbank Area Hospital/Avera Health

901 E Virgil Ave Phone: 605-432-4538
Milbank, SD 57252
URL: www1.averahealth.org
Type: Critical Access Hospitals Emergency Services: Yes
Ownership: Voluntary Non-Profit - Private

Key Personnel:
Administrator . . . . Natalie Gauer
Radiology. . . . . Amanda Sommers

Measure	Cases	This Hosp.	State Avg.	U.S. Avg.
Heart Attack Care				
ACE Inhibitor or ARB for LVSD[3]	0	-	96%	96%
Aspirin at Arrival[1,3]	1	100%	98%	99%
Aspirin at Discharge[1,3]	1	0%	99%	98%
Beta Blocker at Discharge[1,3]	1	100%	98%	98%
Fibrinolytic Medication Timing[3]	0	-	45%	55%
PCI Within 90 Minutes of Arrival[3]	0	-	87%	90%
Smoking Cessation Advice[3]	0	-	99%	99%
Chest Pain/Possible Heart Attack Care				
Aspirin at Arrival	-	-	96%	95%
Median Time to ECG (minutes)	-	-	7	8
Median Time to Transfer (minutes)	-	-	84	61
Fibrinolytic Medication Timing	-	-	54%	54%
Heart Failure Care				
ACE Inhibitor or ARB for LVSD[1,3]	2	100%	90%	94%
Discharge Instructions[1,3]	7	100%	85%	88%
Evaluation of LVS Function[1,3]	11	91%	93%	98%
Smoking Cessation Advice[3]	0	-	93%	98%
Pneumonia Care				
Appropriate Initial Antibiotic[1,3]	8	100%	91%	92%
Blood Culture Timing[3]	0	-	95%	96%
Influenza Vaccine[1]	6	83%	94%	91%
Initial Antibiotic Timing[1,3]	5	100%	94%	95%
Pneumococcal Vaccine[1,3]	11	91%	93%	93%
Smoking Cessation Advice[3]	0	-	92%	97%
Surgical Care Improvement Project				
Appropriate VTP Within 24 Hours[5]	0	-	90%	92%
Appropriate Hair Removal[5]	0	-	100%	99%
Appropriate Beta Blocker Usage[5]	0	-	93%	93%
Controlled Postoperative Blood Glucose[5]	0	-	96%	93%
Prophylactic Antibiotic Timing[5]	0	-	97%	97%
Prophylactic Antibiotic Timing (Outpatient)	-	-	96%	92%
Prophylactic Antibiotic Selection[5]	0	-	98%	97%
Prophylactic Antibiotic Select. (Outpatient)	-	-	97%	94%
Prophylactic Antibiotic Stopped[5]	0	-	96%	94%
Recommended VTP Ordered[5]	0	-	91%	94%
Urinary Catheter Removal[5]	0	-	89%	90%
Children's Asthma Care				
Received Systemic Corticosteroids	-	-	-	100%
Received Home Management Plan	-	-	-	71%
Received Reliever Medication	-	-	-	100%
Use of Medical Imaging				
Combination Abdominal CT Scan	-	-	0.325	0.191
Combination Chest CT Scan	-	-	0.116	0.054
Follow-up Mammogram/Ultrasound	-	-	7.6%	8.4%
MRI for Low Back Pain	-	-	31.3%	32.7%
Survey of Patients' Hospital Experiences				
Area Around Room 'Always' Quiet at Night	(a)	63%	-	58%
Doctors 'Always' Communicated Well	(a)	80%	-	80%
Home Recovery Information Given	(a)	85%	-	82%
Hospital Given 9 or 10 on 10 Point Scale	(a)	67%	-	67%
Meds 'Always' Explained Before Given	(a)	66%	-	60%
Nurses 'Always' Communicated Well	(a)	82%	-	76%
Pain 'Always' Well Controlled	(a)	71%	-	69%
Room and Bathroom 'Always' Clean	(a)	81%	-	71%
Timely Help 'Always' Received	(a)	67%	-	64%
Would Definitely Recommend Hospital	(a)	73%	-	69%

Avera Hand County Memorial Hospital and Clinic

300 W 5th St Phone: 605-853-2421
Miller, SD 57362 Fax: 605-853-0333
URL: www.avera.org
Type: Critical Access Hospitals Emergency Services: Yes
Ownership: Government - Local Beds: 25

Key Personnel:
Chief of Medical Staff . . . . Joel Huber
Radiology. . . . . Daryl C Rife

Measure	Cases	This Hosp.	State Avg.	U.S. Avg.
Heart Attack Care				
ACE Inhibitor or ARB for LVSD[3]	0	-	96%	96%
Aspirin at Arrival[1,3]	1	100%	98%	99%
Aspirin at Discharge[3]	0	-	99%	98%
Beta Blocker at Discharge[3]	0	-	98%	98%
Fibrinolytic Medication Timing[3]	0	-	45%	55%
PCI Within 90 Minutes of Arrival[3]	0	-	87%	90%
Smoking Cessation Advice[3]	0	-	99%	99%
Chest Pain/Possible Heart Attack Care				
Aspirin at Arrival	-	-	96%	95%
Median Time to ECG (minutes)	-	-	7	8
Median Time to Transfer (minutes)	-	-	84	61
Fibrinolytic Medication Timing	-	-	54%	54%
Heart Failure Care				
ACE Inhibitor or ARB for LVSD[1,3]	5	60%	90%	94%
Discharge Instructions[1,3]	4	75%	85%	88%
Evaluation of LVS Function[1,3]	14	93%	93%	98%
Smoking Cessation Advice[3]	0	-	93%	98%
Pneumonia Care				
Appropriate Initial Antibiotic[1]	7	71%	91%	92%
Blood Culture Timing	0	-	95%	96%
Influenza Vaccine[1]	9	100%	94%	91%
Initial Antibiotic Timing[1]	9	100%	94%	95%
Pneumococcal Vaccine[1]	13	77%	93%	93%
Smoking Cessation Advice	0	-	92%	97%
Surgical Care Improvement Project				
Appropriate VTP Within 24 Hours[5]	0	-	90%	92%
Appropriate Hair Removal[5]	0	-	100%	99%
Appropriate Beta Blocker Usage[5]	0	-	93%	93%
Controlled Postoperative Blood Glucose[5]	0	-	96%	93%
Prophylactic Antibiotic Timing[5]	0	-	97%	97%
Prophylactic Antibiotic Timing (Outpatient)	-	-	96%	92%
Prophylactic Antibiotic Selection[5]	0	-	98%	97%
Prophylactic Antibiotic Select. (Outpatient)	-	-	97%	94%
Prophylactic Antibiotic Stopped[5]	0	-	96%	94%
Recommended VTP Ordered[5]	0	-	91%	94%
Urinary Catheter Removal[5]	0	-	89%	90%
Children's Asthma Care				
Received Systemic Corticosteroids	-	-	-	100%
Received Home Management Plan	-	-	-	71%
Received Reliever Medication	-	-	-	100%
Use of Medical Imaging				
Combination Abdominal CT Scan	-	-	0.325	0.191
Combination Chest CT Scan	-	-	0.116	0.054
Follow-up Mammogram/Ultrasound	-	-	7.6%	8.4%
MRI for Low Back Pain	-	-	31.3%	32.7%
Survey of Patients' Hospital Experiences				
Area Around Room 'Always' Quiet at Night	(a)	61%	-	58%
Doctors 'Always' Communicated Well	(a)	81%	-	80%
Home Recovery Information Given	(a)	74%	-	82%
Hospital Given 9 or 10 on 10 Point Scale	(a)	78%	-	67%
Meds 'Always' Explained Before Given	(a)	61%	-	60%
Nurses 'Always' Communicated Well	(a)	83%	-	76%
Pain 'Always' Well Controlled	(a)	65%	-	69%
Room and Bathroom 'Always' Clean	(a)	80%	-	71%
Timely Help 'Always' Received	(a)	80%	-	64%
Would Definitely Recommend Hospital	(a)	74%	-	69%

Avera Queen of Peace

525 N Foster Phone: 605-995-2000
Mitchell, SD 57301 Fax: 605-995-2441
URL: www.averaqueenofpeace.org
Type: Acute Care Hospitals Emergency Services: Yes
Ownership: Voluntary Non-Profit - Church Beds: 120

Key Personnel:
CEO/President. . . . . Thomas P Rasmusson
Chief of Medical Staff . . . . Jerome Howe
Quality Assurance . . . . Brenda Olson
Radiology. . . . . Calvin F Andersen
Emergency Room . . . . Kathy Herttinger, RN

Measure	Cases	This Hosp.	State Avg.	U.S. Avg.
Heart Attack Care				
ACE Inhibitor or ARB for LVSD[1]	1	100%	96%	96%
Aspirin at Arrival[1]	14	100%	98%	99%
Aspirin at Discharge[1]	8	100%	99%	98%
Beta Blocker at Discharge[1]	6	100%	98%	98%
Fibrinolytic Medication Timing	0	-	45%	55%
PCI Within 90 Minutes of Arrival	0	-	87%	90%
Smoking Cessation Advice[1]	1	100%	99%	99%
Chest Pain/Possible Heart Attack Care				
Aspirin at Arrival	56	100%	96%	95%
Median Time to ECG (minutes)	57	12	7	8
Median Time to Transfer (minutes)[1,3]	2	106	84	61
Fibrinolytic Medication Timing[1]	10	50%	54%	54%
Heart Failure Care				
ACE Inhibitor or ARB for LVSD[1]	12	92%	90%	94%
Discharge Instructions	46	100%	85%	88%
Evaluation of LVS Function	76	99%	93%	98%
Smoking Cessation Advice[1]	6	100%	93%	98%
Pneumonia Care				
Appropriate Initial Antibiotic	76	99%	91%	92%
Blood Culture Timing	61	100%	95%	96%
Influenza Vaccine	71	100%	94%	91%
Initial Antibiotic Timing	110	100%	94%	95%
Pneumococcal Vaccine	120	100%	93%	93%
Smoking Cessation Advice	26	100%	92%	97%
Surgical Care Improvement Project				
Appropriate VTP Within 24 Hours	80	100%	90%	92%
Appropriate Hair Removal	195	100%	100%	99%
Appropriate Beta Blocker Usage	61	95%	93%	93%
Controlled Postoperative Blood Glucose	0	-	96%	93%
Prophylactic Antibiotic Timing	126	99%	97%	97%
Prophylactic Antibiotic Timing (Outpatient)	75	99%	96%	92%
Prophylactic Antibiotic Selection	126	98%	98%	97%
Prophylactic Antibiotic Select. (Outpatient)	75	97%	97%	94%
Prophylactic Antibiotic Stopped	119	97%	96%	94%
Recommended VTP Ordered	81	99%	91%	94%
Urinary Catheter Removal[1]	11	91%	89%	90%
Children's Asthma Care				
Received Systemic Corticosteroids	-	-	-	100%
Received Home Management Plan	-	-	-	71%
Received Reliever Medication	-	-	-	100%
Use of Medical Imaging				
Combination Abdominal CT Scan	340	0.841	0.325	0.191
Combination Chest CT Scan	180	0.339	0.116	0.054
Follow-up Mammogram/Ultrasound	997	6.6%	7.6%	8.4%
MRI for Low Back Pain	156	31.4%	31.3%	32.7%
Survey of Patients' Hospital Experiences				
Area Around Room 'Always' Quiet at Night	300+	60%	-	58%
Doctors 'Always' Communicated Well	300+	84%	-	80%
Home Recovery Information Given	300+	83%	-	82%
Hospital Given 9 or 10 on 10 Point Scale	300+	67%	-	67%
Meds 'Always' Explained Before Given	300+	65%	-	60%
Nurses 'Always' Communicated Well	300+	76%	-	76%
Pain 'Always' Well Controlled	300+	69%	-	69%
Room and Bathroom 'Always' Clean	300+	76%	-	71%
Timely Help 'Always' Received	300+	64%	-	64%
Would Definitely Recommend Hospital	300+	69%	-	69%

NOTE: Hospital profiles are in alphabetical order by state, then city, then hospital within the city; Rankings exclude hospitals with less than 25 cases except for patient surveys which excludes hospitals with less than 100 cases; (a) 100–299 cases; (1) The number of cases is too small to be sure how well a hospital is performing; (2) The hospital indicated that the data submitted for this measure were based on a sample of cases; (3) Data was collected during a shorter time period (fewer quarters) than the maximum possible time for this measure; (4) Suppressed for one or more quarters by CMS; (5) No data is available from the hospital for this measure; (6) Fewer than 100 patients completed the HCAHPS survey. Use these rates with caution, as the number of surveys may be too low to reliably assess hospital performance; (7) Survey results are based on less than 12 months of data; (8) Survey results are not available for this reporting period; (9) No or very few patients were eligible for the HCAHPS survey. The scores shown, if any, reflect a very small number of surveys; (10) A state average was not calculated because too few hospitals in the state submitted data; (11) There were discrepancies in the data collection process; Please refer to the User's Guide for a full explanation of data.

Mobridge Regional Hospital

1401 10th Ave West
Mobridge, SD 57601
Phone: 605-845-3692
Fax: 605-845-8252
URL: www.mobridgehospital.org
Type: Critical Access Hospitals
Emergency Services: Yes
Ownership: Government - Local
Beds: 25

Key Personnel:

CEO/President. . . . . Angie Svihovec
Cardiac Laboratory. . . . . Deb Brekke
Infection Control. . . . . June Volk
Quality Assurance . . . . Diane Blom

Measure	Cases	This Hosp.	State Avg.	U.S. Avg.
Heart Attack Care				
ACE Inhibitor or ARB for LVSD[3]	0	-	96%	96%
Aspirin at Arrival[1,3]	1	100%	98%	99%
Aspirin at Discharge[1,3]	1	100%	99%	98%
Beta Blocker at Discharge[1,3]	1	100%	98%	98%
Fibrinolytic Medication Timing[3]	0	-	45%	55%
PCI Within 90 Minutes of Arrival[3]	0	-	87%	90%
Smoking Cessation Advice[3]	0	-	99%	99%
Chest Pain/Possible Heart Attack Care				
Aspirin at Arrival	-	-	96%	95%
Median Time to ECG (minutes)	-	-	7	8
Median Time to Transfer (minutes)	-	-	84	61
Fibrinolytic Medication Timing	-	-	54%	54%
Heart Failure Care				
ACE Inhibitor or ARB for LVSD[1,3]	3	100%	90%	94%
Discharge Instructions[1,3]	3	33%	85%	88%
Evaluation of LVS Function[1,3]	7	86%	93%	98%
Smoking Cessation Advice[3]	0	-	93%	98%
Pneumonia Care				
Appropriate Initial Antibiotic[1,3]	7	100%	91%	92%
Blood Culture Timing[1,3]	2	100%	95%	96%
Influenza Vaccine[1]	13	100%	94%	91%
Initial Antibiotic Timing[1,3]	3	100%	94%	95%
Pneumococcal Vaccine[1,3]	15	93%	93%	93%
Smoking Cessation Advice[1,3]	3	100%	92%	97%
Surgical Care Improvement Project				
Appropriate VTP Within 24 Hours[3]	0	-	90%	92%
Appropriate Hair Removal[1,3]	2	0%	100%	99%
Appropriate Beta Blocker Usage[1,3]	2	50%	93%	93%
Controlled Postoperative Blood Glucose[3]	0	-	96%	93%
Prophylactic Antibiotic Timing[3]	0	-	97%	97%
Prophylactic Antibiotic Timing (Outpatient)	-	-	96%	92%
Prophylactic Antibiotic Selection[3]	0	-	98%	97%
Prophylactic Antibiotic Select. (Outpatient)	-	-	97%	94%
Prophylactic Antibiotic Stopped[3]	0	-	96%	94%
Recommended VTP Ordered[3]	0	-	91%	94%
Urinary Catheter Removal[5]	0	-	89%	90%
Children's Asthma Care				
Received Systemic Corticosteroids	-	-	-	100%
Received Home Management Plan	-	-	-	71%
Received Reliever Medication	-	-	-	100%
Use of Medical Imaging				
Combination Abdominal CT Scan	-	-	0.325	0.191
Combination Chest CT Scan	-	-	0.116	0.054
Follow-up Mammogram/Ultrasound	-	-	7.6%	8.4%
MRI for Low Back Pain	-	-	31.3%	32.7%
Survey of Patients' Hospital Experiences				
Area Around Room 'Always' Quiet at Night[11]	(a)	59%	-	58%
Doctors 'Always' Communicated Well[11]	(a)	84%	-	80%
Home Recovery Information Given[11]	(a)	76%	-	82%
Hospital Given 9 or 10 on 10 Point Scale[11]	(a)	68%	-	67%
Meds 'Always' Explained Before Given[11]	(a)	65%	-	60%
Nurses 'Always' Communicated Well[11]	(a)	78%	-	76%
Pain 'Always' Well Controlled[11]	(a)	60%	-	69%
Room and Bathroom 'Always' Clean[11]	(a)	81%	-	71%
Timely Help 'Always' Received[11]	(a)	69%	-	64%
Would Definitely Recommend Hospital[11]	(a)	63%	-	69%

Avera St Benedict Health Center

401 West Glynn Drive
Parkston, SD 57366
Phone: 605-928-3311
Fax: 605-928-7368
URL: www.averastbenedict.org
Type: Critical Access Hospitals
Emergency Services: Yes
Ownership: Voluntary Non-Profit - Private
Beds: 25

Key Personnel:

Chief of Medical Staff . . . . Toni Vanderpol
Infection Control. . . . . Brenda Stoebner
Operating Room. . . . . Kynan Trail, RN
Quality Assurance . . . . Brenda Stoebner
Radiology. . . . . Carey Buhler
Anesthesiology. . . . . Ken Travnick
Emergency Room . . . . Phillip D Barker, DO
Intensive Care Unit. . . . . Denise Muntefering

Measure	Cases	This Hosp.	State Avg.	U.S. Avg.
Heart Attack Care				
ACE Inhibitor or ARB for LVSD[1,3]	1	0%	96%	96%
Aspirin at Arrival[1,3]	2	100%	98%	99%
Aspirin at Discharge[1,3]	1	100%	99%	98%
Beta Blocker at Discharge[1,3]	1	0%	98%	98%
Fibrinolytic Medication Timing[3]	0	-	45%	55%
PCI Within 90 Minutes of Arrival[3]	0	-	87%	90%
Smoking Cessation Advice[3]	0	-	99%	99%
Chest Pain/Possible Heart Attack Care				
Aspirin at Arrival[5]	0	-	96%	95%
Median Time to ECG (minutes)[5]	0	-	7	8
Median Time to Transfer (minutes)[5]	0	-	84	61
Fibrinolytic Medication Timing[5]	0	-	54%	54%
Heart Failure Care				
ACE Inhibitor or ARB for LVSD[1,3]	1	0%	90%	94%
Discharge Instructions[1,3]	3	33%	85%	88%
Evaluation of LVS Function[1,3]	8	100%	93%	98%
Smoking Cessation Advice[1,3]	1	100%	93%	98%
Pneumonia Care				
Appropriate Initial Antibiotic[1,3]	4	100%	91%	92%
Blood Culture Timing[1,3]	3	100%	95%	96%
Influenza Vaccine[1,3]	6	100%	94%	91%
Initial Antibiotic Timing[1,3]	13	100%	94%	95%
Pneumococcal Vaccine[1,3]	22	95%	93%	93%
Smoking Cessation Advice[1,3]	2	50%	92%	97%
Surgical Care Improvement Project				
Appropriate VTP Within 24 Hours[5]	0	-	90%	92%
Appropriate Hair Removal[5]	0	-	100%	99%
Appropriate Beta Blocker Usage[5]	0	-	93%	93%
Controlled Postoperative Blood Glucose[5]	0	-	96%	93%
Prophylactic Antibiotic Timing[5]	0	-	97%	97%
Prophylactic Antibiotic Timing (Outpatient)[5]	0	-	96%	92%
Prophylactic Antibiotic Selection[5]	0	-	98%	97%
Prophylactic Antibiotic Select. (Outpatient)[5]	0	-	97%	94%
Prophylactic Antibiotic Stopped[5]	0	-	96%	94%
Recommended VTP Ordered[5]	0	-	91%	94%
Urinary Catheter Removal[5]	0	-	89%	90%
Children's Asthma Care				
Received Systemic Corticosteroids	-	-	-	100%
Received Home Management Plan	-	-	-	71%
Received Reliever Medication	-	-	-	100%
Use of Medical Imaging				
Combination Abdominal CT Scan	71	0.901	0.325	0.191
Combination Chest CT Scan[1]	36	0.278	0.116	0.054
Follow-up Mammogram/Ultrasound	235	8.9%	7.6%	8.4%
MRI for Low Back Pain[1]	10	40.0%	31.3%	32.7%
Survey of Patients' Hospital Experiences				
Area Around Room 'Always' Quiet at Night	(a)	74%	-	58%
Doctors 'Always' Communicated Well	(a)	84%	-	80%
Home Recovery Information Given	(a)	82%	-	82%
Hospital Given 9 or 10 on 10 Point Scale	(a)	78%	-	67%
Meds 'Always' Explained Before Given	(a)	66%	-	60%
Nurses 'Always' Communicated Well	(a)	83%	-	76%
Pain 'Always' Well Controlled	(a)	71%	-	69%
Room and Bathroom 'Always' Clean	(a)	88%	-	71%
Timely Help 'Always' Received	(a)	73%	-	64%
Would Definitely Recommend Hospital	(a)	80%	-	69%

Saint Marys Hospital

801 E Sioux
Pierre, SD 57501
Phone: 605-224-3100
Fax: 605-224-3429
URL: www.st-marys.com
Type: Acute Care Hospitals
Emergency Services: Yes
Ownership: Voluntary Non-Profit - Church
Beds: 83

Key Personnel:

CEO/President. . . . . Chad Cooper
Infection Control. . . . . Jeanne Vogel
Operating Room. . . . . Jackie Neilan
Quality Assurance . . . . Anita Baker
Radiology. . . . . Ben Shoup
Emergency Room . . . . Robin Gadd
Patient Relations . . . . Nick Brandner

Measure	Cases	This Hosp.	State Avg.	U.S. Avg.
Heart Attack Care				
ACE Inhibitor or ARB for LVSD	0	-	96%	96%
Aspirin at Arrival[1]	6	100%	98%	99%
Aspirin at Discharge[1]	5	80%	99%	98%
Beta Blocker at Discharge[1]	5	60%	98%	98%
Fibrinolytic Medication Timing[1]	6	17%	45%	55%
PCI Within 90 Minutes of Arrival	0	-	87%	90%
Smoking Cessation Advice[1]	2	100%	99%	99%
Chest Pain/Possible Heart Attack Care				
Aspirin at Arrival[1]	17	100%	96%	95%
Median Time to ECG (minutes)[1]	18	10	7	8
Median Time to Transfer (minutes)[5]	0	-	84	61
Fibrinolytic Medication Timing[1,3]	4	75%	54%	54%
Heart Failure Care				
ACE Inhibitor or ARB for LVSD[1]	9	67%	90%	94%
Discharge Instructions[1]	19	100%	85%	88%
Evaluation of LVS Function	26	100%	93%	98%
Smoking Cessation Advice[1]	4	100%	93%	98%
Pneumonia Care				
Appropriate Initial Antibiotic	28	89%	91%	92%
Blood Culture Timing	30	100%	95%	96%
Influenza Vaccine	38	87%	94%	91%
Initial Antibiotic Timing	47	96%	94%	95%
Pneumococcal Vaccine	55	96%	93%	93%
Smoking Cessation Advice[1]	16	100%	92%	97%
Surgical Care Improvement Project				
Appropriate VTP Within 24 Hours[2]	78	97%	90%	92%
Appropriate Hair Removal[2]	204	100%	100%	99%
Appropriate Beta Blocker Usage[2]	56	98%	93%	93%
Controlled Postoperative Blood Glucose[2]	0	-	96%	93%
Prophylactic Antibiotic Timing[2]	161	95%	97%	97%
Prophylactic Antibiotic Timing (Outpatient)	26	96%	96%	92%
Prophylactic Antibiotic Selection[2]	161	98%	98%	97%
Prophylactic Antibiotic Select. (Outpatient)	26	96%	97%	94%
Prophylactic Antibiotic Stopped[2]	156	97%	96%	94%
Recommended VTP Ordered[2]	78	97%	91%	94%
Urinary Catheter Removal[1,2]	10	90%	89%	90%
Children's Asthma Care				
Received Systemic Corticosteroids	-	-	-	100%
Received Home Management Plan	-	-	-	71%
Received Reliever Medication	-	-	-	100%
Use of Medical Imaging				
Combination Abdominal CT Scan	280	0.782	0.325	0.191
Combination Chest CT Scan	174	0.023	0.116	0.054
Follow-up Mammogram/Ultrasound	651	2.0%	7.6%	8.4%
MRI for Low Back Pain	83	39.8%	31.3%	32.7%
Survey of Patients' Hospital Experiences				
Area Around Room 'Always' Quiet at Night	(a)	57%	-	58%
Doctors 'Always' Communicated Well	(a)	82%	-	80%
Home Recovery Information Given	(a)	83%	-	82%
Hospital Given 9 or 10 on 10 Point Scale	(a)	66%	-	67%
Meds 'Always' Explained Before Given	(a)	59%	-	60%
Nurses 'Always' Communicated Well	(a)	76%	-	76%
Pain 'Always' Well Controlled	(a)	66%	-	69%
Room and Bathroom 'Always' Clean	(a)	67%	-	71%
Timely Help 'Always' Received	(a)	65%	-	64%
Would Definitely Recommend Hospital	(a)	65%	-	69%

NOTE: Hospital profiles are in alphabetical order by state, then city, then hospital within the city; Rankings exclude hospitals with less than 25 cases except for patient surveys which excludes hospitals with less than 100 cases; (a) 100–299 cases; (1) The number of cases is too small to be sure how well a hospital is performing; (2) The hospital indicated that the data submitted for this measure were based on a sample of cases; (3) Data was collected during a shorter time period (fewer quarters) than the maximum possible time for this measure; (4) Suppressed for one or more quarters by CMS; (5) No data is available from the hospital for this measure; (6) Fewer than 100 patients completed the HCAHPS survey. Use these rates with caution, as the number of surveys may be too low to reliably assess hospital performance; (7) Survey results are based on less than 12 months of data; (8) Survey results are not available for this reporting period; (9) No or very few patients were eligible for the HCAHPS survey. The scores shown, if any, reflect a very small number of surveys; (10) A state average was not calculated because too few hospitals in the state submitted data; (11) There were discrepancies in the data collection process; Please refer to the User's Guide for a full explanation of data.

PHS Indian Hospital at Pine Ridge

East Highway 18 Phone: 605-867-5131
Pine Ridge, SD 57770 Fax: 605-867-3271
URL: www.ihs.gov
Type: Acute Care Hospitals Emergency Services: No
Ownership: Government - Federal Beds: 45

Key Personnel:
Chief of Medical Staff.......... Andy Hurst, MD
Infection Control.............. Alice Sierra
Quality Assurance .... Kathey Wilson Ecoffey

Measure	Cases	This Hosp.	State Avg.	U.S. Avg.
Heart Attack Care				
ACE Inhibitor or ARB for LVSD[3]	0	-	96%	96%
Aspirin at Arrival[3]	0	-	98%	99%
Aspirin at Discharge[3]	0	-	99%	98%
Beta Blocker at Discharge[3]	0	-	98%	98%
Fibrinolytic Medication Timing[3]	0	-	45%	55%
PCI Within 90 Minutes of Arrival[3]	0	-	87%	90%
Smoking Cessation Advice[3]	0	-	99%	99%
Chest Pain/Possible Heart Attack Care				
Aspirin at Arrival	-	-	96%	95%
Median Time to ECG (minutes)	-	-	7	8
Median Time to Transfer (minutes)	-	-	84	61
Fibrinolytic Medication Timing	-	-	54%	54%
Heart Failure Care				
ACE Inhibitor or ARB for LVSD[1]	1	0%	90%	94%
Discharge Instructions[1]	15	0%	85%	88%
Evaluation of LVS Function[1]	16	19%	93%	98%
Smoking Cessation Advice[1]	2	50%	93%	98%
Pneumonia Care				
Appropriate Initial Antibiotic[1]	18	67%	91%	92%
Blood Culture Timing[1]	20	70%	95%	96%
Influenza Vaccine[1]	8	62%	94%	91%
Initial Antibiotic Timing[1]	23	83%	94%	95%
Pneumococcal Vaccine[1]	14	93%	93%	93%
Smoking Cessation Advice[1]	9	0%	92%	97%
Surgical Care Improvement Project				
Appropriate VTP Within 24 Hours[3]	0	-	90%	92%
Appropriate Hair Removal[1,3]	8	100%	100%	99%
Appropriate Beta Blocker Usage[1,3]	1	100%	93%	93%
Controlled Postoperative Blood Glucose[3]	0	-	96%	93%
Prophylactic Antibiotic Timing[1,3]	5	40%	97%	97%
Prophylactic Antibiotic Timing (Outpatient)	-	-	96%	92%
Prophylactic Antibiotic Selection[1,3]	4	100%	98%	97%
Prophylactic Antibiotic Select. (Outpatient)	-	-	97%	94%
Prophylactic Antibiotic Stopped[1,3]	4	75%	96%	94%
Recommended VTP Ordered[3]	0	-	91%	94%
Urinary Catheter Removal[1]	1	100%	89%	90%
Children's Asthma Care				
Received Systemic Corticosteroids	-	-	-	100%
Received Home Management Plan	-	-	-	71%
Received Reliever Medication	-	-	-	100%
Use of Medical Imaging				
Combination Abdominal CT Scan	-	-	0.325	0.191
Combination Chest CT Scan	-	-	0.116	0.054
Follow-up Mammogram/Ultrasound	-	-	7.6%	8.4%
MRI for Low Back Pain	-	-	31.3%	32.7%
Survey of Patients' Hospital Experiences				
Area Around Room 'Always' Quiet at Night[11,6]	<100	42%	-	58%
Doctors 'Always' Communicated Well[11,6]	<100	57%	-	80%
Home Recovery Information Given[11,6]	<100	64%	-	82%
Hospital Given 9 or 10 on 10 Point Scale[11,6]	<100	46%	-	67%
Meds 'Always' Explained Before Given[11,6]	<100	42%	-	60%
Nurses 'Always' Communicated Well[11,6]	<100	53%	-	76%
Pain 'Always' Well Controlled[11,6]	<100	44%	-	69%
Room and Bathroom 'Always' Clean[11,6]	<100	58%	-	71%
Timely Help 'Always' Received[11,6]	<100	45%	-	64%
Would Definitely Recommend Hospital[11]	<100	34%	-	69%

Platte Health Center

601 E 7th St Phone: 605-337-3364
Platte, SD 57369 Fax: 605-337-2670
Type: Critical Access Hospitals Emergency Services: Yes
Ownership: Voluntary Non-Profit - Private Beds: 15

Key Personnel:
CEO/President............... Mark Burkett
Chief of Medical Staff.......... John Bentv
Infection Control.............. Jan Stahnke
Operating Room.............. Linda Fito
Quality Assurance .... Nancy Nachtigal
Emergency Room .... Jerome Bentz, MD

Measure	Cases	This Hosp.	State Avg.	U.S. Avg.
Heart Attack Care				
ACE Inhibitor or ARB for LVSD[5]	0	-	96%	96%
Aspirin at Arrival[5]	0	-	98%	99%
Aspirin at Discharge[5]	0	-	99%	98%
Beta Blocker at Discharge[5]	0	-	98%	98%
Fibrinolytic Medication Timing[5]	0	-	45%	55%
PCI Within 90 Minutes of Arrival[5]	0	-	87%	90%
Smoking Cessation Advice[5]	0	-	99%	99%
Chest Pain/Possible Heart Attack Care				
Aspirin at Arrival[5]	0	-	96%	95%
Median Time to ECG (minutes)[5]	0	-	7	8
Median Time to Transfer (minutes)[5]	0	-	84	61
Fibrinolytic Medication Timing[5]	0	-	54%	54%
Heart Failure Care				
ACE Inhibitor or ARB for LVSD[1,3]	4	100%	90%	94%
Discharge Instructions[1,3]	3	33%	85%	88%
Evaluation of LVS Function[1,3]	5	80%	93%	98%
Smoking Cessation Advice[3]	0	-	93%	98%
Pneumonia Care				
Appropriate Initial Antibiotic[1]	12	92%	91%	92%
Blood Culture Timing[1]	6	83%	95%	96%
Influenza Vaccine[1]	5	100%	94%	91%
Initial Antibiotic Timing[1]	23	87%	94%	95%
Pneumococcal Vaccine[1]	19	100%	93%	93%
Smoking Cessation Advice[1]	2	100%	92%	97%
Surgical Care Improvement Project				
Appropriate VTP Within 24 Hours[5]	0	-	90%	92%
Appropriate Hair Removal[5]	0	-	100%	99%
Appropriate Beta Blocker Usage[5]	0	-	93%	93%
Controlled Postoperative Blood Glucose[5]	0	-	96%	93%
Prophylactic Antibiotic Timing[5]	0	-	97%	97%
Prophylactic Antibiotic Timing (Outpatient)[5]	0	-	96%	92%
Prophylactic Antibiotic Selection[5]	0	-	98%	97%
Prophylactic Antibiotic Select. (Outpatient)[5]	0	-	97%	94%
Prophylactic Antibiotic Stopped[5]	0	-	96%	94%
Recommended VTP Ordered[5]	0	-	91%	94%
Urinary Catheter Removal[5]	0	-	89%	90%
Children's Asthma Care				
Received Systemic Corticosteroids	-	-	-	100%
Received Home Management Plan	-	-	-	71%
Received Reliever Medication	-	-	-	100%
Use of Medical Imaging				
Combination Abdominal CT Scan[1]	35	0.800	0.325	0.191
Combination Chest CT Scan[1]	32	0.250	0.116	0.054
Follow-up Mammogram/Ultrasound	114	9.6%	7.6%	8.4%
MRI for Low Back Pain[1]	15	26.7%	31.3%	32.7%
Survey of Patients' Hospital Experiences				
Area Around Room 'Always' Quiet at Night[6]	<100	68%	-	58%
Doctors 'Always' Communicated Well[6]	<100	84%	-	80%
Home Recovery Information Given[6]	<100	70%	-	82%
Hospital Given 9 or 10 on 10 Point Scale[6]	<100	77%	-	67%
Meds 'Always' Explained Before Given[6]	<100	76%	-	60%
Nurses 'Always' Communicated Well[6]	<100	80%	-	76%
Pain 'Always' Well Controlled[6]	<100	79%	-	69%
Room and Bathroom 'Always' Clean[6]	<100	83%	-	71%
Timely Help 'Always' Received[6]	<100	80%	-	64%
Would Definitely Recommend Hospital	<100	79%	-	69%

Black Hills Surgical Hospital

1868 Lombardy Dr Phone: 605-721-4900
Rapid City, SD 57703
Type: Acute Care Hospitals Emergency Services: Yes
Ownership: Proprietary

Key Personnel:
CEO/President............... William May
Chief of Medical Staff.......... Dave Johnson MD
Radiology.................. Nicholas Wilson
Patient Relations .... Debbie Mertes

Measure	Cases	This Hosp.	State Avg.	U.S. Avg.
Heart Attack Care				
ACE Inhibitor or ARB for LVSD[5]	0	-	96%	96%
Aspirin at Arrival[5]	0	-	98%	99%
Aspirin at Discharge[5]	0	-	99%	98%
Beta Blocker at Discharge[5]	0	-	98%	98%
Fibrinolytic Medication Timing[5]	0	-	45%	55%
PCI Within 90 Minutes of Arrival[5]	0	-	87%	90%
Smoking Cessation Advice[5]	0	-	99%	99%
Chest Pain/Possible Heart Attack Care				
Aspirin at Arrival[5]	0	-	96%	95%
Median Time to ECG (minutes)[5]	0	-	7	8
Median Time to Transfer (minutes)[5]	0	-	84	61
Fibrinolytic Medication Timing[5]	0	-	54%	54%
Heart Failure Care				
ACE Inhibitor or ARB for LVSD[5]	0	-	90%	94%
Discharge Instructions[5]	0	-	85%	88%
Evaluation of LVS Function[5]	0	-	93%	98%
Smoking Cessation Advice[5]	0	-	93%	98%
Pneumonia Care				
Appropriate Initial Antibiotic[5]	0	-	91%	92%
Blood Culture Timing[5]	0	-	95%	96%
Influenza Vaccine[5]	0	-	94%	91%
Initial Antibiotic Timing[5]	0	-	94%	95%
Pneumococcal Vaccine[5]	0	-	93%	93%
Smoking Cessation Advice[5]	0	-	92%	97%
Surgical Care Improvement Project				
Appropriate VTP Within 24 Hours[1,2]	21	86%	90%	92%
Appropriate Hair Removal[2]	257	100%	100%	99%
Appropriate Beta Blocker Usage[2]	44	100%	93%	93%
Controlled Postoperative Blood Glucose[2]	0	-	96%	93%
Prophylactic Antibiotic Timing[2]	237	97%	97%	97%
Prophylactic Antibiotic Timing (Outpatient)	504	98%	96%	92%
Prophylactic Antibiotic Selection[2]	238	96%	98%	97%
Prophylactic Antibiotic Select. (Outpatient)	502	99%	97%	94%
Prophylactic Antibiotic Stopped[2]	237	97%	96%	94%
Recommended VTP Ordered[1,2]	21	86%	91%	94%
Urinary Catheter Removal[2]	89	100%	89%	90%
Children's Asthma Care				
Received Systemic Corticosteroids	-	-	-	100%
Received Home Management Plan	-	-	-	71%
Received Reliever Medication	-	-	-	100%
Use of Medical Imaging				
Combination Abdominal CT Scan[1]	38	0.237	0.325	0.191
Combination Chest CT Scan[1]	44	0.114	0.116	0.054
Follow-up Mammogram/Ultrasound[5]	0	-	7.6%	8.4%
MRI for Low Back Pain	485	36.1%	31.3%	32.7%
Survey of Patients' Hospital Experiences				
Area Around Room 'Always' Quiet at Night	300+	87%	-	58%
Doctors 'Always' Communicated Well	300+	89%	-	80%
Home Recovery Information Given	300+	94%	-	82%
Hospital Given 9 or 10 on 10 Point Scale	300+	92%	-	67%
Meds 'Always' Explained Before Given	300+	76%	-	60%
Nurses 'Always' Communicated Well	300+	85%	-	76%
Pain 'Always' Well Controlled	300+	77%	-	69%
Room and Bathroom 'Always' Clean	300+	87%	-	71%
Timely Help 'Always' Received	300+	86%	-	64%
Would Definitely Recommend Hospital	300+	93%	-	69%

NOTE: Hospital profiles are in alphabetical order by state, then city, then hospital within the city; Rankings exclude hospitals with less than 25 cases except for patient surveys which excludes hospitals with less than 100 cases; (a) 100–299 cases; (1) The number of cases is too small to be sure how well a hospital is performing; (2) The hospital indicated that the data submitted for this measure were based on a sample of cases; (3) Data was collected during a shorter time period (fewer quarters) than the maximum possible time for this measure; (4) Suppressed for one or more quarters by CMS; (5) No data is available from the hospital for this measure; (6) Fewer than 100 patients completed the HCAHPS survey. Use these rates with caution, as the number of surveys may be too low to reliably assess hospital performance; (7) Survey results are based on less than 12 months of data; (8) Survey results are not available for this reporting period; (9) No or very few patients were eligible for the HCAHPS survey. The scores shown, if any, reflect a very small number of surveys; (10) A state average was not calculated because too few hospitals in the state submitted data; (11) There were discrepancies in the data collection process; Please refer to the User's Guide for a full explanation of data.

PHS Indian Hospital at Rapid City - Sioux San

3200 Canyon Lake Dr
Rapid City, SD 57702
URL: www.ihs.gov
Type: Acute Care Hospitals
Ownership: Government - Federal
Phone: 605-355-2500
Fax: 605-355-2504
Emergency Services: Yes
Beds: 32

Measure	Cases	This Hosp.	State Avg.	U.S. Avg.
Heart Attack Care				
ACE Inhibitor or ARB for LVSD[5]	0	-	96%	96%
Aspirin at Arrival[5]	0	-	98%	99%
Aspirin at Discharge[5]	0	-	99%	98%
Beta Blocker at Discharge[5]	0	-	98%	98%
Fibrinolytic Medication Timing[5]	0	-	45%	55%
PCI Within 90 Minutes of Arrival[5]	0	-	87%	90%
Smoking Cessation Advice[5]	0	-	99%	99%
Chest Pain/Possible Heart Attack Care				
Aspirin at Arrival	-	-	96%	95%
Median Time to ECG (minutes)	-	-	7	8
Median Time to Transfer (minutes)	-	-	84	61
Fibrinolytic Medication Timing	-	-	54%	54%
Heart Failure Care				
ACE Inhibitor or ARB for LVSD[5]	0	-	90%	94%
Discharge Instructions[5]	0	-	85%	88%
Evaluation of LVS Function[5]	0	-	93%	98%
Smoking Cessation Advice[5]	0	-	93%	98%
Pneumonia Care				
Appropriate Initial Antibiotic[1,3]	8	88%	91%	92%
Blood Culture Timing[1,3]	6	83%	95%	96%
Influenza Vaccine[1,3]	3	33%	94%	91%
Initial Antibiotic Timing[1,3]	6	100%	94%	95%
Pneumococcal Vaccine[1,3]	3	100%	93%	93%
Smoking Cessation Advice[1,3]	6	50%	92%	97%
Surgical Care Improvement Project				
Appropriate VTP Within 24 Hours[5]	0	-	90%	92%
Appropriate Hair Removal[5]	0	-	100%	99%
Appropriate Beta Blocker Usage[5]	0	-	93%	93%
Controlled Postoperative Blood Glucose[5]	0	-	96%	93%
Prophylactic Antibiotic Timing[5]	0	-	97%	97%
Prophylactic Antibiotic Timing (Outpatient)	-	-	96%	92%
Prophylactic Antibiotic Selection[5]	0	-	98%	97%
Prophylactic Antibiotic Select. (Outpatient)	-	-	97%	94%
Prophylactic Antibiotic Stopped[5]	0	-	96%	94%
Recommended VTP Ordered[5]	0	-	91%	94%
Urinary Catheter Removal[5]	0	-	89%	90%
Children's Asthma Care				
Received Systemic Corticosteroids	-	-	-	100%
Received Home Management Plan	-	-	-	71%
Received Reliever Medication	-	-	-	100%
Use of Medical Imaging				
Combination Abdominal CT Scan	-	-	0.325	0.191
Combination Chest CT Scan	-	-	0.116	0.054
Follow-up Mammogram/Ultrasound	-	-	7.6%	8.4%
MRI for Low Back Pain	-	-	31.3%	32.7%
Survey of Patients' Hospital Experiences				
Area Around Room 'Always' Quiet at Night[9,11,6]	<100	69%	-	58%
Doctors 'Always' Communicated Well[9,11,6]	<100	88%	-	80%
Home Recovery Information Given[9,11,6]	<100	48%	-	82%
Hospital Given 9 or 10 on 10 Point Scale[9,11,6]	<100	49%	-	67%
Meds 'Always' Explained Before Given[9,11,6]	<100	97%	-	60%
Nurses 'Always' Communicated Well[9,11,6]	<100	84%	-	76%
Pain 'Always' Well Controlled[9,11,6]	<100	61%	-	69%
Room and Bathroom 'Always' Clean[9,11,6]	<100	78%	-	71%
Timely Help 'Always' Received[9,11,6]	<100	91%	-	64%
Would Definitely Recommend Hospital[9,11]	<100	36%	-	69%

Rapid City Regional Hospital

353 Fairmont Blvd
Rapid City, SD 57701
E-mail: humanresources@rcrh.org
URL: www.rcrh.org
Type: Acute Care Hospitals
Ownership: Voluntary Non-Profit - Private
Phone: 605-719-1000
Fax: 605-719-8053
Emergency Services: Yes
Beds: 310

Key Personnel:
CEO/President. . . . . Timothy Sughrue
Cardiac Laboratory. . . . . Alex Schabauer
Chief of Medical Staff. . . . . Charles Hart
Operating Room. . . . . Marcia Taylor
Quality Assurance . . . . Mary Masten
Intensive Care Unit. . . . . Sherry Smith

Measure	Cases	This Hosp.	State Avg.	U.S. Avg.
Heart Attack Care				
ACE Inhibitor or ARB for LVSD	61	100%	96%	96%
Aspirin at Arrival	195	99%	98%	99%
Aspirin at Discharge	402	98%	99%	98%
Beta Blocker at Discharge	380	98%	98%	98%
Fibrinolytic Medication Timing	0	-	45%	55%
PCI Within 90 Minutes of Arrival	46	76%	87%	90%
Smoking Cessation Advice	145	100%	99%	99%
Chest Pain/Possible Heart Attack Care				
Aspirin at Arrival[3]	0	-	96%	95%
Median Time to ECG (minutes)[3]	0	-	7	8
Median Time to Transfer (minutes)[5]	0	-	84	61
Fibrinolytic Medication Timing[5]	0	-	54%	54%
Heart Failure Care				
ACE Inhibitor or ARB for LVSD	83	95%	90%	94%
Discharge Instructions	241	87%	85%	88%
Evaluation of LVS Function	296	99%	93%	98%
Smoking Cessation Advice	53	98%	93%	98%
Pneumonia Care				
Appropriate Initial Antibiotic	136	91%	91%	92%
Blood Culture Timing	178	96%	95%	96%
Influenza Vaccine	220	96%	94%	91%
Initial Antibiotic Timing	276	95%	94%	95%
Pneumococcal Vaccine	273	95%	93%	93%
Smoking Cessation Advice	147	100%	92%	97%
Surgical Care Improvement Project				
Appropriate VTP Within 24 Hours[2]	193	92%	90%	92%
Appropriate Hair Removal[2]	471	98%	100%	99%
Appropriate Beta Blocker Usage[2]	178	89%	93%	93%
Controlled Postoperative Blood Glucose[2]	118	95%	96%	93%
Prophylactic Antibiotic Timing[2]	323	96%	97%	97%
Prophylactic Antibiotic Timing (Outpatient)	288	94%	96%	92%
Prophylactic Antibiotic Selection[2]	325	100%	98%	97%
Prophylactic Antibiotic Select. (Outpatient)	277	95%	97%	94%
Prophylactic Antibiotic Stopped[2]	294	91%	96%	94%
Recommended VTP Ordered[2]	193	94%	91%	94%
Urinary Catheter Removal[2]	93	63%	89%	90%
Children's Asthma Care				
Received Systemic Corticosteroids	-	-	-	100%
Received Home Management Plan	-	-	-	71%
Received Reliever Medication	-	-	-	100%
Use of Medical Imaging				
Combination Abdominal CT Scan	958	0.061	0.325	0.191
Combination Chest CT Scan	810	0.000	0.116	0.054
Follow-up Mammogram/Ultrasound	307	7.8%	7.6%	8.4%
MRI for Low Back Pain	274	35.4%	31.3%	32.7%
Survey of Patients' Hospital Experiences				
Area Around Room 'Always' Quiet at Night	300+	44%	-	58%
Doctors 'Always' Communicated Well	300+	78%	-	80%
Home Recovery Information Given	300+	82%	-	82%
Hospital Given 9 or 10 on 10 Point Scale	300+	61%	-	67%
Meds 'Always' Explained Before Given	300+	57%	-	60%
Nurses 'Always' Communicated Well	300+	73%	-	76%
Pain 'Always' Well Controlled	300+	69%	-	69%
Room and Bathroom 'Always' Clean	300+	76%	-	71%
Timely Help 'Always' Received	300+	68%	-	64%
Would Definitely Recommend Hospital	300+	62%	-	69%

Same Day Surgery Center

651 Cathedral Drive
Rapid City, SD 57701
URL: www.samedaysurgerycenter.org
Type: Acute Care Hospitals
Ownership: Voluntary Non-Profit - Other
Phone: 605-719-5000
Fax: 605-719-5055
Emergency Services: Yes
Beds: 8

Key Personnel:
CEO/President. . . . . Doris Fritts

Measure	Cases	This Hosp.	State Avg.	U.S. Avg.
Heart Attack Care				
ACE Inhibitor or ARB for LVSD[5]	0	-	96%	96%
Aspirin at Arrival[5]	0	-	98%	99%
Aspirin at Discharge[5]	0	-	99%	98%
Beta Blocker at Discharge[5]	0	-	98%	98%
Fibrinolytic Medication Timing[5]	0	-	45%	55%
PCI Within 90 Minutes of Arrival[5]	0	-	87%	90%
Smoking Cessation Advice[5]	0	-	99%	99%
Chest Pain/Possible Heart Attack Care				
Aspirin at Arrival[5]	0	-	96%	95%
Median Time to ECG (minutes)[5]	0	-	7	8
Median Time to Transfer (minutes)[5]	0	-	84	61
Fibrinolytic Medication Timing[5]	0	-	54%	54%
Heart Failure Care				
ACE Inhibitor or ARB for LVSD[5]	0	-	90%	94%
Discharge Instructions[5]	0	-	85%	88%
Evaluation of LVS Function[5]	0	-	93%	98%
Smoking Cessation Advice[5]	0	-	93%	98%
Pneumonia Care				
Appropriate Initial Antibiotic[5]	0	-	91%	92%
Blood Culture Timing[5]	0	-	95%	96%
Influenza Vaccine[5]	0	-	94%	91%
Initial Antibiotic Timing[5]	0	-	94%	95%
Pneumococcal Vaccine[5]	0	-	93%	93%
Smoking Cessation Advice[5]	0	-	92%	97%
Surgical Care Improvement Project				
Appropriate VTP Within 24 Hours[1,2,3]	1	100%	90%	92%
Appropriate Hair Removal[2,3]	29	100%	100%	99%
Appropriate Beta Blocker Usage[2,3]	0	-	93%	93%
Controlled Postoperative Blood Glucose[2,3]	0	-	96%	93%
Prophylactic Antibiotic Timing[2,3]	36	94%	97%	97%
Prophylactic Antibiotic Timing (Outpatient)[5]	0	-	96%	92%
Prophylactic Antibiotic Selection[2,3]	36	94%	98%	97%
Prophylactic Antibiotic Select. (Outpatient)[5]	0	-	97%	94%
Prophylactic Antibiotic Stopped[2,3]	35	91%	96%	94%
Recommended VTP Ordered[1,2,3]	1	100%	91%	94%
Urinary Catheter Removal[2]	0	-	89%	90%
Children's Asthma Care				
Received Systemic Corticosteroids	-	-	-	100%
Received Home Management Plan	-	-	-	71%
Received Reliever Medication	-	-	-	100%
Use of Medical Imaging				
Combination Abdominal CT Scan[5]	0	-	0.325	0.191
Combination Chest CT Scan[5]	0	-	0.116	0.054
Follow-up Mammogram/Ultrasound[5]	0	-	7.6%	8.4%
MRI for Low Back Pain[5]	0	-	31.3%	32.7%
Survey of Patients' Hospital Experiences				
Area Around Room 'Always' Quiet at Night[8]	-	-	-	58%
Doctors 'Always' Communicated Well[8]	-	-	-	80%
Home Recovery Information Given[8]	-	-	-	82%
Hospital Given 9 or 10 on 10 Point Scale[8]	-	-	-	67%
Meds 'Always' Explained Before Given[8]	-	-	-	60%
Nurses 'Always' Communicated Well[8]	-	-	-	76%
Pain 'Always' Well Controlled[8]	-	-	-	69%
Room and Bathroom 'Always' Clean[8]	-	-	-	71%
Timely Help 'Always' Received[8]	-	-	-	64%
Would Definitely Recommend Hospital[8]	-	-	-	69%

NOTE: Hospital profiles are in alphabetical order by state, then city, then hospital within the city; Rankings exclude hospitals with less than 25 cases except for patient surveys which excludes hospitals with less than 100 cases; (a) 100–299 cases; (1) The number of cases is too small to be sure how well a hospital is performing; (2) The hospital indicated that the data submitted for this measure were based on a sample of cases; (3) Data was collected during a shorter time period (fewer quarters) than the maximum possible time for this measure; (4) Suppressed for one or more quarters by CMS; (5) No data is available from the hospital for this measure; (6) Fewer than 100 patients completed the HCAHPS survey. Use these rates with caution, as the number of surveys may be too low to reliably assess hospital performance; (7) Survey results are based on less than 12 months of data; (8) Survey results are not available for this reporting period; (9) No or very few patients were eligible for the HCAHPS survey. The scores shown, if any, reflect a very small number of surveys; (10) A state average was not calculated because too few hospitals in the state submitted data; (11) There were discrepancies in the data collection process; Please refer to the User's Guide for a full explanation of data.

Community Memorial Hospital

111 W 10th Ave Phone: 605-472-1110
Redfield, SD 57469 Fax: 605-472-0331
URL: www.redfield-sd.com/hospital
Type: Critical Access Hospitals Emergency Services: Yes
Ownership: Government - Local Beds: 25
Key Personnel:
CEO/President. . . . . William E Bestor

Measure	Cases	This Hosp.	State Avg.	U.S. Avg.
Heart Attack Care				
ACE Inhibitor or ARB for LVSD[5]	0	-	96%	96%
Aspirin at Arrival[5]	0	-	98%	99%
Aspirin at Discharge[5]	0	-	99%	98%
Beta Blocker at Discharge[5]	0	-	98%	98%
Fibrinolytic Medication Timing[5]	0	-	45%	55%
PCI Within 90 Minutes of Arrival[5]	0	-	87%	90%
Smoking Cessation Advice[5]	0	-	99%	99%
Chest Pain/Possible Heart Attack Care				
Aspirin at Arrival	-	-	96%	95%
Median Time to ECG (minutes)	-	-	7	8
Median Time to Transfer (minutes)	-	-	84	61
Fibrinolytic Medication Timing	-	-	54%	54%
Heart Failure Care				
ACE Inhibitor or ARB for LVSD[1,3]	3	67%	90%	94%
Discharge Instructions[1,3]	4	25%	85%	88%
Evaluation of LVS Function[1,3]	6	83%	93%	98%
Smoking Cessation Advice[1,3]	1	100%	93%	98%
Pneumonia Care				
Appropriate Initial Antibiotic[1,3]	4	100%	91%	92%
Blood Culture Timing[1,3]	1	100%	95%	96%
Influenza Vaccine[1,3]	7	100%	94%	91%
Initial Antibiotic Timing[1,3]	12	100%	94%	95%
Pneumococcal Vaccine[1,3]	9	89%	93%	93%
Smoking Cessation Advice[1,3]	1	100%	92%	97%
Surgical Care Improvement Project				
Appropriate VTP Within 24 Hours[5]	0	-	90%	92%
Appropriate Hair Removal[5]	0	-	100%	99%
Appropriate Beta Blocker Usage[5]	0	-	93%	93%
Controlled Postoperative Blood Glucose[5]	0	-	96%	93%
Prophylactic Antibiotic Timing[5]	0	-	97%	97%
Prophylactic Antibiotic Timing (Outpatient)	-	-	96%	92%
Prophylactic Antibiotic Selection[5]	0	-	98%	97%
Prophylactic Antibiotic Select. (Outpatient)	-	-	97%	94%
Prophylactic Antibiotic Stopped[5]	0	-	96%	94%
Recommended VTP Ordered[5]	0	-	91%	94%
Urinary Catheter Removal[5]	0	-	89%	90%
Children's Asthma Care				
Received Systemic Corticosteroids	-	-	-	100%
Received Home Management Plan	-	-	-	71%
Received Reliever Medication	-	-	-	100%
Use of Medical Imaging				
Combination Abdominal CT Scan	-	-	0.325	0.191
Combination Chest CT Scan	-	-	0.116	0.054
Follow-up Mammogram/Ultrasound	-	-	7.6%	8.4%
MRI for Low Back Pain	-	-	31.3%	32.7%
Survey of Patients' Hospital Experiences				
Area Around Room 'Always' Quiet at Night[8]	-	-	-	58%
Doctors 'Always' Communicated Well[8]	-	-	-	80%
Home Recovery Information Given[8]	-	-	-	82%
Hospital Given 9 or 10 on 10 Point Scale[8]	-	-	-	67%
Meds 'Always' Explained Before Given[8]	-	-	-	60%
Nurses 'Always' Communicated Well[8]	-	-	-	76%
Pain 'Always' Well Controlled[8]	-	-	-	69%
Room and Bathroom 'Always' Clean[8]	-	-	-	71%
Timely Help 'Always' Received[8]	-	-	-	64%
Would Definitely Recommend Hospital[8]	-	-	-	69%

PHS Indian Hospital at Rosebud

400 Soldier Creek Road Phone: 605-747-2231
Rosebud, SD 57570 Fax: 605-747-2216
URL: www.ihs.gov
Type: Acute Care Hospitals Emergency Services: No
Ownership: Government - Federal Beds: 35
Key Personnel:
Chief of Medical Staff . . . . Dr. Timothy Ryscon
Emergency Room . . . . Pam Pourier

Measure	Cases	This Hosp.	State Avg.	U.S. Avg.
Heart Attack Care				
ACE Inhibitor or ARB for LVSD[3]	0	-	96%	96%
Aspirin at Arrival[1,3]	7	86%	98%	99%
Aspirin at Discharge[1,3]	5	80%	99%	98%
Beta Blocker at Discharge[1,3]	5	60%	98%	98%
Fibrinolytic Medication Timing[3]	0	-	45%	55%
PCI Within 90 Minutes of Arrival[3]	0	-	87%	90%
Smoking Cessation Advice[1,3]	3	0%	99%	99%
Chest Pain/Possible Heart Attack Care				
Aspirin at Arrival[5]	0	-	96%	95%
Median Time to ECG (minutes)[5]	0	-	7	8
Median Time to Transfer (minutes)[5]	0	-	84	61
Fibrinolytic Medication Timing[5]	0	-	54%	54%
Heart Failure Care				
ACE Inhibitor or ARB for LVSD[2,3]	0	-	90%	94%
Discharge Instructions[1,2,3]	18	22%	85%	88%
Evaluation of LVS Function[1,2,3]	18	17%	93%	98%
Smoking Cessation Advice[1,2,3]	2	50%	93%	98%
Pneumonia Care				
Appropriate Initial Antibiotic[1,2,3]	11	82%	91%	92%
Blood Culture Timing[1,2,3]	17	71%	95%	96%
Influenza Vaccine[1]	20	75%	94%	91%
Initial Antibiotic Timing[2,3]	40	58%	94%	95%
Pneumococcal Vaccine[1,2,3]	16	75%	93%	93%
Smoking Cessation Advice[1,2,3]	14	29%	92%	97%
Surgical Care Improvement Project				
Appropriate VTP Within 24 Hours[3]	0	-	90%	92%
Appropriate Hair Removal[1,3]	1	0%	100%	99%
Appropriate Beta Blocker Usage[3]	0	-	93%	93%
Controlled Postoperative Blood Glucose[3]	0	-	96%	93%
Prophylactic Antibiotic Timing[3]	0	-	97%	97%
Prophylactic Antibiotic Timing (Outpatient)[5]	0	-	96%	92%
Prophylactic Antibiotic Selection[3]	0	-	98%	97%
Prophylactic Antibiotic Select. (Outpatient)[5]	0	-	97%	94%
Prophylactic Antibiotic Stopped[3]	0	-	96%	94%
Recommended VTP Ordered[3]	0	-	91%	94%
Urinary Catheter Removal[3]	0	-	89%	90%
Children's Asthma Care				
Received Systemic Corticosteroids	-	-	-	100%
Received Home Management Plan	-	-	-	71%
Received Reliever Medication	-	-	-	100%
Use of Medical Imaging				
Combination Abdominal CT Scan[5]	0	-	0.325	0.191
Combination Chest CT Scan[5]	0	-	0.116	0.054
Follow-up Mammogram/Ultrasound[5]	0	-	7.6%	8.4%
MRI for Low Back Pain[5]	0	-	31.3%	32.7%
Survey of Patients' Hospital Experiences				
Area Around Room 'Always' Quiet at Night[8]	-	-	-	58%
Doctors 'Always' Communicated Well[8]	-	-	-	80%
Home Recovery Information Given[8]	-	-	-	82%
Hospital Given 9 or 10 on 10 Point Scale[8]	-	-	-	67%
Meds 'Always' Explained Before Given[8]	-	-	-	60%
Nurses 'Always' Communicated Well[8]	-	-	-	76%
Pain 'Always' Well Controlled[8]	-	-	-	69%
Room and Bathroom 'Always' Clean[8]	-	-	-	71%
Timely Help 'Always' Received[8]	-	-	-	64%
Would Definitely Recommend Hospital[8]	-	-	-	69%

Landmann-Jungman Memorial Hospital

600 Billars St Phone: 605-583-2226
Scotland, SD 57059 Fax: 605-583-4557
E-mail: jay.plucker@mckennan.org
URL: www.ljmh.org
Type: Critical Access Hospitals Emergency Services: Yes
Ownership: Government - Local Beds: 25
Key Personnel:
Chief of Medical Staff . . . . Manuel Ramos, MD
Operating Room. . . . . Sherry Fisher, RN

Measure	Cases	This Hosp.	State Avg.	U.S. Avg.
Heart Attack Care				
ACE Inhibitor or ARB for LVSD[5]	0	-	96%	96%
Aspirin at Arrival[5]	0	-	98%	99%
Aspirin at Discharge[5]	0	-	99%	98%
Beta Blocker at Discharge[5]	0	-	98%	98%
Fibrinolytic Medication Timing[5]	0	-	45%	55%
PCI Within 90 Minutes of Arrival[5]	0	-	87%	90%
Smoking Cessation Advice[5]	0	-	99%	99%
Chest Pain/Possible Heart Attack Care				
Aspirin at Arrival	-	-	96%	95%
Median Time to ECG (minutes)	-	-	7	8
Median Time to Transfer (minutes)	-	-	84	61
Fibrinolytic Medication Timing	-	-	54%	54%
Heart Failure Care				
ACE Inhibitor or ARB for LVSD[1,3]	2	50%	90%	94%
Discharge Instructions[1,3]	2	50%	85%	88%
Evaluation of LVS Function[1,3]	6	100%	93%	98%
Smoking Cessation Advice[3]	0	-	93%	98%
Pneumonia Care				
Appropriate Initial Antibiotic[1,3]	3	100%	91%	92%
Blood Culture Timing[5]	0	-	95%	96%
Influenza Vaccine[1]	9	100%	94%	91%
Initial Antibiotic Timing[1,3]	1	100%	94%	95%
Pneumococcal Vaccine[1,3]	11	82%	93%	93%
Smoking Cessation Advice[1,3]	1	100%	92%	97%
Surgical Care Improvement Project				
Appropriate VTP Within 24 Hours[5]	0	-	90%	92%
Appropriate Hair Removal[5]	0	-	100%	99%
Appropriate Beta Blocker Usage[5]	0	-	93%	93%
Controlled Postoperative Blood Glucose[5]	0	-	96%	93%
Prophylactic Antibiotic Timing[5]	0	-	97%	97%
Prophylactic Antibiotic Timing (Outpatient)	-	-	96%	92%
Prophylactic Antibiotic Selection[5]	0	-	98%	97%
Prophylactic Antibiotic Select. (Outpatient)	-	-	97%	94%
Prophylactic Antibiotic Stopped[5]	0	-	96%	94%
Recommended VTP Ordered[5]	0	-	91%	94%
Urinary Catheter Removal[5]	0	-	89%	90%
Children's Asthma Care				
Received Systemic Corticosteroids	-	-	-	100%
Received Home Management Plan	-	-	-	71%
Received Reliever Medication	-	-	-	100%
Use of Medical Imaging				
Combination Abdominal CT Scan	-	-	0.325	0.191
Combination Chest CT Scan	-	-	0.116	0.054
Follow-up Mammogram/Ultrasound	-	-	7.6%	8.4%
MRI for Low Back Pain	-	-	31.3%	32.7%
Survey of Patients' Hospital Experiences				
Area Around Room 'Always' Quiet at Night[8]	-	-	-	58%
Doctors 'Always' Communicated Well[8]	-	-	-	80%
Home Recovery Information Given[8]	-	-	-	82%
Hospital Given 9 or 10 on 10 Point Scale[8]	-	-	-	67%
Meds 'Always' Explained Before Given[8]	-	-	-	60%
Nurses 'Always' Communicated Well[8]	-	-	-	76%
Pain 'Always' Well Controlled[8]	-	-	-	69%
Room and Bathroom 'Always' Clean[8]	-	-	-	71%
Timely Help 'Always' Received[8]	-	-	-	64%
Would Definitely Recommend Hospital[8]	-	-	-	69%

NOTE: Hospital profiles are in alphabetical order by state, then city, then hospital within the city; Rankings exclude hospitals with less than 25 cases except for patient surveys which excludes hospitals with less than 100 cases; (a) 100–299 cases; (1) The number of cases is too small to be sure how well a hospital is performing; (2) The hospital indicated that the data submitted for this measure were based on a sample of cases; (3) Data was collected during a shorter time period (fewer quarters) than the maximum possible time for this measure; (4) Suppressed for one or more quarters by CMS; (5) No data is available from the hospital for this measure; (6) Fewer than 100 patients completed the HCAHPS survey. Use these rates with caution, as the number of surveys may be too low to reliably assess hospital performance; (7) Survey results are based on less than 12 months of data; (8) Survey results are not available for this reporting period; (9) No or very few patients were eligible for the HCAHPS survey. The scores shown, if any, reflect a very small number of surveys; (10) A state average was not calculated because too few hospitals in the state submitted data; (11) There were discrepancies in the data collection process; Please refer to the User's Guide for a full explanation of data.

Avera Heart Hospital of South Dakota

4500 W 69th St Phone: 605-977-7000
Sioux Falls, SD 57108
Type: Acute Care Hospitals Emergency Services: No
Ownership: Proprietary
Key Personnel:
CEO/President. . . . . John Soderholm
Anesthesiology. . . . . Ty White

Measure	Cases	This Hosp.	State Avg.	U.S. Avg.
Heart Attack Care				
ACE Inhibitor or ARB for LVSD	88	98%	96%	96%
Aspirin at Arrival	87	99%	98%	99%
Aspirin at Discharge	599	99%	99%	98%
Beta Blocker at Discharge	593	100%	98%	98%
Fibrinolytic Medication Timing	0	-	45%	55%
PCI Within 90 Minutes of Arrival[1]	13	100%	87%	90%
Smoking Cessation Advice	165	99%	99%	99%
Chest Pain/Possible Heart Attack Care				
Aspirin at Arrival[1]	5	100%	96%	95%
Median Time to ECG (minutes)[1]	5	7	7	8
Median Time to Transfer (minutes)[5]	0	-	84	61
Fibrinolytic Medication Timing[5]	0	-	54%	54%
Heart Failure Care				
ACE Inhibitor or ARB for LVSD	61	97%	90%	94%
Discharge Instructions	124	99%	85%	88%
Evaluation of LVS Function	142	99%	93%	98%
Smoking Cessation Advice[1]	19	100%	93%	98%
Pneumonia Care				
Appropriate Initial Antibiotic[1]	2	50%	91%	92%
Blood Culture Timing[1]	5	100%	95%	96%
Influenza Vaccine[1]	7	100%	94%	91%
Initial Antibiotic Timing[1]	1	0%	94%	95%
Pneumococcal Vaccine[1]	12	100%	93%	93%
Smoking Cessation Advice[1]	3	100%	92%	97%
Surgical Care Improvement Project				
Appropriate VTP Within 24 Hours[1]	12	75%	90%	92%
Appropriate Hair Removal	440	100%	100%	99%
Appropriate Beta Blocker Usage	218	100%	93%	93%
Controlled Postoperative Blood Glucose	360	98%	96%	93%
Prophylactic Antibiotic Timing	382	99%	97%	97%
Prophylactic Antibiotic Timing (Outpatient)	295	96%	96%	92%
Prophylactic Antibiotic Selection	383	100%	98%	97%
Prophylactic Antibiotic Select. (Outpatient)	295	100%	97%	94%
Prophylactic Antibiotic Stopped	380	100%	96%	94%
Recommended VTP Ordered[1]	12	75%	91%	94%
Urinary Catheter Removal	114	96%	89%	90%
Children's Asthma Care				
Received Systemic Corticosteroids	-	-	-	100%
Received Home Management Plan	-	-	-	71%
Received Reliever Medication	-	-	-	100%
Use of Medical Imaging				
Combination Abdominal CT Scan[1]	57	0.123	0.325	0.191
Combination Chest CT Scan[1]	41	0.122	0.116	0.054
Follow-up Mammogram/Ultrasound[5]	0	-	7.6%	8.4%
MRI for Low Back Pain[5]	0	-	31.3%	32.7%
Survey of Patients' Hospital Experiences				
Area Around Room 'Always' Quiet at Night	300+	68%	-	58%
Doctors 'Always' Communicated Well	300+	81%	-	80%
Home Recovery Information Given	300+	83%	-	82%
Hospital Given 9 or 10 on 10 Point Scale	300+	86%	-	67%
Meds 'Always' Explained Before Given	300+	68%	-	60%
Nurses 'Always' Communicated Well	300+	84%	-	76%
Pain 'Always' Well Controlled	300+	75%	-	69%
Room and Bathroom 'Always' Clean	300+	84%	-	71%
Timely Help 'Always' Received	300+	78%	-	64%
Would Definitely Recommend Hospital	300+	90%	-	69%

Avera Mckennan Hospital & University Health Center

800 E 21st St Phone: 605-322-8000
Sioux Falls, SD 57117 Fax: 605-322-7822
E-mail: info@mckennan.org
URL: www.mckennan.org
Type: Acute Care Hospitals Emergency Services: Yes
Ownership: Voluntary Non-Profit - Private Beds: 490
Key Personnel:
CEO/President. . . . . Frederick W Slunecka
Infection Control. . . . . Don Tomac
Emergency Room . . . . Howard Burns

Measure	Cases	This Hosp.	State Avg.	U.S. Avg.
Heart Attack Care				
ACE Inhibitor or ARB for LVSD[1]	14	100%	96%	96%
Aspirin at Arrival	60	97%	98%	99%
Aspirin at Discharge	64	100%	99%	98%
Beta Blocker at Discharge	69	100%	98%	98%
Fibrinolytic Medication Timing[1]	1	100%	45%	55%
PCI Within 90 Minutes of Arrival[1]	19	79%	87%	90%
Smoking Cessation Advice[1]	24	100%	99%	99%
Chest Pain/Possible Heart Attack Care				
Aspirin at Arrival[5]	0	-	96%	95%
Median Time to ECG (minutes)[5]	0	-	7	8
Median Time to Transfer (minutes)[5]	0	-	84	61
Fibrinolytic Medication Timing[5]	0	-	54%	54%
Heart Failure Care				
ACE Inhibitor or ARB for LVSD	62	94%	90%	94%
Discharge Instructions	175	91%	85%	88%
Evaluation of LVS Function	228	99%	93%	98%
Smoking Cessation Advice[1]	22	100%	93%	98%
Pneumonia Care				
Appropriate Initial Antibiotic	94	97%	91%	92%
Blood Culture Timing	94	95%	95%	96%
Influenza Vaccine	157	97%	94%	91%
Initial Antibiotic Timing	167	97%	94%	95%
Pneumococcal Vaccine	179	94%	93%	93%
Smoking Cessation Advice	86	100%	92%	97%
Surgical Care Improvement Project				
Appropriate VTP Within 24 Hours[2]	148	89%	90%	92%
Appropriate Hair Removal[2]	377	99%	100%	99%
Appropriate Beta Blocker Usage[2]	121	89%	93%	93%
Controlled Postoperative Blood Glucose[1,2]	1	0%	96%	93%
Prophylactic Antibiotic Timing[2]	222	99%	97%	97%
Prophylactic Antibiotic Timing (Outpatient)	316	97%	96%	92%
Prophylactic Antibiotic Selection[2]	222	96%	98%	97%
Prophylactic Antibiotic Select. (Outpatient)	314	96%	97%	94%
Prophylactic Antibiotic Stopped[2]	211	96%	96%	94%
Recommended VTP Ordered[2]	149	92%	91%	94%
Urinary Catheter Removal[2]	77	61%	89%	90%
Children's Asthma Care				
Received Systemic Corticosteroids	-	-	-	100%
Received Home Management Plan	-	-	-	71%
Received Reliever Medication	-	-	-	100%
Use of Medical Imaging				
Combination Abdominal CT Scan	824	0.083	0.325	0.191
Combination Chest CT Scan	721	0.008	0.116	0.054
Follow-up Mammogram/Ultrasound	762	8.3%	7.6%	8.4%
MRI for Low Back Pain	227	25.6%	31.3%	32.7%
Survey of Patients' Hospital Experiences				
Area Around Room 'Always' Quiet at Night	300+	55%	-	58%
Doctors 'Always' Communicated Well	300+	77%	-	80%
Home Recovery Information Given	300+	84%	-	82%
Hospital Given 9 or 10 on 10 Point Scale	300+	68%	-	67%
Meds 'Always' Explained Before Given	300+	59%	-	60%
Nurses 'Always' Communicated Well	300+	74%	-	76%
Pain 'Always' Well Controlled	300+	64%	-	69%
Room and Bathroom 'Always' Clean	300+	70%	-	71%
Timely Help 'Always' Received	300+	58%	-	64%
Would Definitely Recommend Hospital	300+	75%	-	69%

Sanford Usd Medical Center

1305 W 18th St Phone: 605-333-1000
Sioux Falls, SD 57117 Fax: 605-328-1577
E-mail: info@sanfordhealth.org
URL: www.sanfordhealth.org
Type: Acute Care Hospitals Emergency Services: Yes
Ownership: Voluntary Non-Profit - Other Beds: 477
Key Personnel:
CEO/President. . . . . Kelby K Krabbenhoft
Chief of Medical Staff. . . . . Barbara Hall, MD
Infection Control. . . . . Lisa Docken, RN
Pediatric Ambulatory Care . . . . . . Dave Munson, MD
Pediatric In-Patient Care . . . . Dave Munson, MD
Quality Assurance . . . . Jeannine Schwarting
Radiology. . . . . Daryl Wierda, MD
Emergency Room . . . . Becky Nelson, MD

Measure	Cases	This Hosp.	State Avg.	U.S. Avg.
Heart Attack Care				
ACE Inhibitor or ARB for LVSD	59	92%	96%	96%
Aspirin at Arrival	178	98%	98%	99%
Aspirin at Discharge	345	100%	99%	98%
Beta Blocker at Discharge	336	98%	98%	98%
Fibrinolytic Medication Timing	0	-	45%	55%
PCI Within 90 Minutes of Arrival	32	91%	87%	90%
Smoking Cessation Advice	125	100%	99%	99%
Chest Pain/Possible Heart Attack Care				
Aspirin at Arrival[3]	0	-	96%	95%
Median Time to ECG (minutes)[3]	0	-	7	8
Median Time to Transfer (minutes)[5]	0	-	84	61
Fibrinolytic Medication Timing[5]	0	-	54%	54%
Heart Failure Care				
ACE Inhibitor or ARB for LVSD	84	90%	90%	94%
Discharge Instructions	210	84%	85%	88%
Evaluation of LVS Function	280	96%	93%	98%
Smoking Cessation Advice	40	98%	93%	98%
Pneumonia Care				
Appropriate Initial Antibiotic	144	87%	91%	92%
Blood Culture Timing	143	97%	95%	96%
Influenza Vaccine	175	94%	94%	91%
Initial Antibiotic Timing	194	93%	94%	95%
Pneumococcal Vaccine	284	95%	93%	93%
Smoking Cessation Advice	122	97%	92%	97%
Surgical Care Improvement Project				
Appropriate VTP Within 24 Hours[2]	261	93%	90%	92%
Appropriate Hair Removal[2]	1,500	100%	100%	99%
Appropriate Beta Blocker Usage[2]	400	95%	93%	93%
Controlled Postoperative Blood Glucose[2]	202	95%	96%	93%
Prophylactic Antibiotic Timing[2]	1,181	97%	97%	97%
Prophylactic Antibiotic Timing (Outpatient)	646	96%	96%	92%
Prophylactic Antibiotic Selection[2]	1,186	96%	98%	97%
Prophylactic Antibiotic Select. (Outpatient)	646	96%	97%	94%
Prophylactic Antibiotic Stopped[2]	1,127	96%	96%	94%
Recommended VTP Ordered[2]	263	96%	91%	94%
Urinary Catheter Removal[2]	219	92%	89%	90%
Children's Asthma Care				
Received Systemic Corticosteroids	64	100%	-	100%
Received Home Management Plan	63	95%	-	71%
Received Reliever Medication	65	100%	-	100%
Use of Medical Imaging				
Combination Abdominal CT Scan	1,299	0.245	0.325	0.191
Combination Chest CT Scan	906	0.000	0.116	0.054
Follow-up Mammogram/Ultrasound[5]	0	-	7.6%	8.4%
MRI for Low Back Pain	412	31.8%	31.3%	32.7%
Survey of Patients' Hospital Experiences				
Area Around Room 'Always' Quiet at Night	300+	58%	-	58%
Doctors 'Always' Communicated Well	300+	79%	-	80%
Home Recovery Information Given	300+	84%	-	82%
Hospital Given 9 or 10 on 10 Point Scale	300+	75%	-	67%
Meds 'Always' Explained Before Given	300+	60%	-	60%
Nurses 'Always' Communicated Well	300+	76%	-	76%
Pain 'Always' Well Controlled	300+	70%	-	69%
Room and Bathroom 'Always' Clean	300+	67%	-	71%
Timely Help 'Always' Received	300+	67%	-	64%
Would Definitely Recommend Hospital	300+	78%	-	69%

NOTE: Hospital profiles are in alphabetical order by state, then city, then hospital within the city; Rankings exclude hospitals with less than 25 cases except for patient surveys which excludes hospitals with less than 100 cases; (a) 100–299 cases; (1) The number of cases is too small to be sure how well a hospital is performing; (2) The hospital indicated that the data submitted for this measure were based on a sample of cases; (3) Data was collected during a shorter time period (fewer quarters) than the maximum possible time for this measure; (4) Suppressed for one or more quarters by CMS; (5) No data is available from the hospital for this measure; (6) Fewer than 100 patients completed the HCAHPS survey. Use these rates with caution, as the number of surveys may be too low to reliably assess hospital performance; (7) Survey results are based on less than 12 months of data; (8) Survey results are not available for this reporting period; (9) No or very few patients were eligible for the HCAHPS survey. The scores shown, if any, reflect a very small number of surveys; (10) A state average was not calculated because too few hospitals in the state submitted data; (11) There were discrepancies in the data collection process; Please refer to the User's Guide for a full explanation of data.

Sioux Falls Surgical Hospital

910 East 20th Street
Sioux Falls, SD 57105
URL: www.sfsurgical.com
Type: Acute Care Hospitals
Ownership: Proprietary
Phone: 605-334-6730
Fax: 605-334-8096
Emergency Services: Yes
Beds: 13

Key Personnel:
CEO/President. . . . . Douglas V. Johnson

Measure	Cases	This Hosp.	State Avg.	U.S. Avg.
Heart Attack Care				
ACE Inhibitor or ARB for LVSD[5]	0	-	96%	96%
Aspirin at Arrival[5]	0	-	98%	99%
Aspirin at Discharge[5]	0	-	99%	98%
Beta Blocker at Discharge[5]	0	-	98%	98%
Fibrinolytic Medication Timing[5]	0	-	45%	55%
PCI Within 90 Minutes of Arrival[5]	0	-	87%	90%
Smoking Cessation Advice[5]	0	-	99%	99%
Chest Pain/Possible Heart Attack Care				
Aspirin at Arrival[5]	0	-	96%	95%
Median Time to ECG (minutes)[5]	0	-	7	8
Median Time to Transfer (minutes)[5]	0	-	84	61
Fibrinolytic Medication Timing[5]	0	-	54%	54%
Heart Failure Care				
ACE Inhibitor or ARB for LVSD[5]	0	-	90%	94%
Discharge Instructions[5]	0	-	85%	88%
Evaluation of LVS Function[5]	0	-	93%	98%
Smoking Cessation Advice[5]	0	-	93%	98%
Pneumonia Care				
Appropriate Initial Antibiotic[5]	0	-	91%	92%
Blood Culture Timing[5]	0	-	95%	96%
Influenza Vaccine[5]	0	-	94%	91%
Initial Antibiotic Timing[5]	0	-	94%	95%
Pneumococcal Vaccine[5]	0	-	93%	93%
Smoking Cessation Advice[5]	0	-	92%	97%
Surgical Care Improvement Project				
Appropriate VTP Within 24 Hours	33	100%	90%	92%
Appropriate Hair Removal	679	100%	100%	99%
Appropriate Beta Blocker Usage	139	93%	93%	93%
Controlled Postoperative Blood Glucose	0	-	96%	93%
Prophylactic Antibiotic Timing	658	99%	97%	97%
Prophylactic Antibiotic Timing (Outpatient)	298	99%	96%	92%
Prophylactic Antibiotic Selection	658	100%	98%	97%
Prophylactic Antibiotic Select. (Outpatient)	295	98%	97%	94%
Prophylactic Antibiotic Stopped	658	99%	96%	94%
Recommended VTP Ordered	33	100%	91%	94%
Urinary Catheter Removal	206	100%	89%	90%
Children's Asthma Care				
Received Systemic Corticosteroids	-	-	-	100%
Received Home Management Plan	-	-	-	71%
Received Reliever Medication	-	-	-	100%
Use of Medical Imaging				
Combination Abdominal CT Scan[5]	0	-	0.325	0.191
Combination Chest CT Scan[5]	0	-	0.116	0.054
Follow-up Mammogram/Ultrasound[5]	0	-	7.6%	8.4%
MRI for Low Back Pain[1]	37	24.3%	31.3%	32.7%
Survey of Patients' Hospital Experiences				
Area Around Room 'Always' Quiet at Night	300+	87%	-	58%
Doctors 'Always' Communicated Well	300+	85%	-	80%
Home Recovery Information Given	300+	90%	-	82%
Hospital Given 9 or 10 on 10 Point Scale	300+	88%	-	67%
Meds 'Always' Explained Before Given	300+	74%	-	60%
Nurses 'Always' Communicated Well	300+	88%	-	76%
Pain 'Always' Well Controlled	300+	75%	-	69%
Room and Bathroom 'Always' Clean	300+	87%	-	71%
Timely Help 'Always' Received	300+	87%	-	64%
Would Definitely Recommend Hospital	300+	90%	-	69%

Sioux Falls VA Medical Center

2501 West 22nd Street
Sioux Falls, SD 57117
URL: www.va.gov
Type: Acute Care-Veterans Administration
Ownership: Government - Federal
Phone: 605-336-3230
Fax: 605-333-6878
Emergency Services: No
Beds: 259

Key Personnel:
CEO/President. . . . . Vincent Crawford
Chief of Medical Staff . . . . William Becker, MD
Infection Control. . . . . Jeanld Tjaden, RN
Operating Room. . . . . Sandra Vander Woude
Quality Assurance . . . . Sandra Frazer
Hemotology Center . . . . Michael Robinson, MD
Intensive Care Unit. . . . . Elizabeth Flinn, RN
Patient Relations . . . . Rita Loving, RN

Measure	Cases	This Hosp.	State Avg.	U.S. Avg.
Heart Attack Care				
ACE Inhibitor or ARB for LVSD[5]	0	-	96%	96%
Aspirin at Arrival[5]	0	-	98%	99%
Aspirin at Discharge[5]	0	-	99%	98%
Beta Blocker at Discharge[5]	0	-	98%	98%
Fibrinolytic Medication Timing[5]	0	-	45%	55%
PCI Within 90 Minutes of Arrival[5]	0	-	87%	90%
Smoking Cessation Advice[5]	0	-	99%	99%
Chest Pain/Possible Heart Attack Care				
Aspirin at Arrival	-	-	96%	95%
Median Time to ECG (minutes)	-	-	7	8
Median Time to Transfer (minutes)	-	-	84	61
Fibrinolytic Medication Timing	-	-	54%	54%
Heart Failure Care				
ACE Inhibitor or ARB for LVSD	26	96%	90%	94%
Discharge Instructions	52	98%	85%	88%
Evaluation of LVS Function	56	100%	93%	98%
Smoking Cessation Advice[1]	12	100%	93%	98%
Pneumonia Care				
Appropriate Initial Antibiotic	28	93%	91%	92%
Blood Culture Timing	33	100%	95%	96%
Influenza Vaccine[1]	16	100%	94%	91%
Initial Antibiotic Timing	38	97%	94%	95%
Pneumococcal Vaccine	32	100%	93%	93%
Smoking Cessation Advice[1]	10	90%	92%	97%
Surgical Care Improvement Project				
Appropriate VTP Within 24 Hours[2]	104	99%	90%	92%
Appropriate Hair Removal[2]	184	100%	100%	99%
Appropriate Beta Blocker Usage[2]	84	93%	93%	93%
Controlled Postoperative Blood Glucose[2,5]	0	-	96%	93%
Prophylactic Antibiotic Timing	132	96%	97%	97%
Prophylactic Antibiotic Timing (Outpatient)	-	-	96%	92%
Prophylactic Antibiotic Selection	135	99%	98%	97%
Prophylactic Antibiotic Select. (Outpatient)	-	-	97%	94%
Prophylactic Antibiotic Stopped	131	98%	96%	94%
Recommended VTP Ordered[2]	104	99%	91%	94%
Urinary Catheter Removal[2]	96	95%	89%	90%
Children's Asthma Care				
Received Systemic Corticosteroids	-	-	-	100%
Received Home Management Plan	-	-	-	71%
Received Reliever Medication	-	-	-	100%
Use of Medical Imaging				
Combination Abdominal CT Scan	-	-	0.325	0.191
Combination Chest CT Scan	-	-	0.116	0.054
Follow-up Mammogram/Ultrasound	-	-	7.6%	8.4%
MRI for Low Back Pain	-	-	31.3%	32.7%
Survey of Patients' Hospital Experiences				
Area Around Room 'Always' Quiet at Night	-	-	-	58%
Doctors 'Always' Communicated Well	-	-	-	80%
Home Recovery Information Given	-	-	-	82%
Hospital Given 9 or 10 on 10 Point Scale	-	-	-	67%
Meds 'Always' Explained Before Given	-	-	-	60%
Nurses 'Always' Communicated Well	-	-	-	76%
Pain 'Always' Well Controlled	-	-	-	69%
Room and Bathroom 'Always' Clean	-	-	-	71%
Timely Help 'Always' Received	-	-	-	64%
Would Definitely Recommend Hospital	-	-	-	69%

Spearfish Regional Hospital

1440 N Main St
Spearfish, SD 57783
URL: www.rcrh.org
Type: Acute Care Hospitals
Ownership: Voluntary Non-Profit - Private
Phone: 605-644-4000
Fax: 605-644-4011
Emergency Services: No
Beds: 40

Key Personnel:
Cardiac Laboratory. . . . . Dawn Koehler
Infection Control. . . . . Jennifer Jones
Radiology. . . . . Kristin Ulmer
Anesthesiology. . . . . Chuck Austin
Emergency Room . . . . Kathy Culver

Measure	Cases	This Hosp.	State Avg.	U.S. Avg.
Heart Attack Care				
ACE Inhibitor or ARB for LVSD	0	-	96%	96%
Aspirin at Arrival[1]	5	80%	98%	99%
Aspirin at Discharge[1]	3	100%	99%	98%
Beta Blocker at Discharge[1]	2	100%	98%	98%
Fibrinolytic Medication Timing[1]	1	100%	45%	55%
PCI Within 90 Minutes of Arrival	0	-	87%	90%
Smoking Cessation Advice	0	-	99%	99%
Chest Pain/Possible Heart Attack Care				
Aspirin at Arrival	40	92%	96%	95%
Median Time to ECG (minutes)	40	2	7	8
Median Time to Transfer (minutes)[5]	0	-	84	61
Fibrinolytic Medication Timing[1,3]	6	50%	54%	54%
Heart Failure Care				
ACE Inhibitor or ARB for LVSD[1]	6	100%	90%	94%
Discharge Instructions[1]	13	62%	85%	88%
Evaluation of LVS Function[1]	20	85%	93%	98%
Smoking Cessation Advice	0	-	93%	98%
Pneumonia Care				
Appropriate Initial Antibiotic	37	100%	91%	92%
Blood Culture Timing[1]	15	100%	95%	96%
Influenza Vaccine	29	93%	94%	91%
Initial Antibiotic Timing	39	95%	94%	95%
Pneumococcal Vaccine	49	80%	93%	93%
Smoking Cessation Advice[1]	11	100%	92%	97%
Surgical Care Improvement Project				
Appropriate VTP Within 24 Hours	50	96%	90%	92%
Appropriate Hair Removal	226	100%	100%	99%
Appropriate Beta Blocker Usage	53	98%	93%	93%
Controlled Postoperative Blood Glucose	0	-	96%	93%
Prophylactic Antibiotic Timing	199	97%	97%	97%
Prophylactic Antibiotic Timing (Outpatient)[1]	16	100%	96%	92%
Prophylactic Antibiotic Selection	199	95%	98%	97%
Prophylactic Antibiotic Select. (Outpatient)[1]	16	100%	97%	94%
Prophylactic Antibiotic Stopped	198	94%	96%	94%
Recommended VTP Ordered	50	96%	91%	94%
Urinary Catheter Removal	81	99%	89%	90%
Children's Asthma Care				
Received Systemic Corticosteroids	-	-	-	100%
Received Home Management Plan	-	-	-	71%
Received Reliever Medication	-	-	-	100%
Use of Medical Imaging				
Combination Abdominal CT Scan	250	0.080	0.325	0.191
Combination Chest CT Scan	141	0.000	0.116	0.054
Follow-up Mammogram/Ultrasound	259	5.4%	7.6%	8.4%
MRI for Low Back Pain	91	38.5%	31.3%	32.7%
Survey of Patients' Hospital Experiences				
Area Around Room 'Always' Quiet at Night	300+	60%	-	58%
Doctors 'Always' Communicated Well	300+	84%	-	80%
Home Recovery Information Given	300+	81%	-	82%
Hospital Given 9 or 10 on 10 Point Scale	300+	70%	-	67%
Meds 'Always' Explained Before Given	300+	62%	-	60%
Nurses 'Always' Communicated Well	300+	78%	-	76%
Pain 'Always' Well Controlled	300+	71%	-	69%
Room and Bathroom 'Always' Clean	300+	76%	-	71%
Timely Help 'Always' Received	300+	79%	-	64%
Would Definitely Recommend Hospital	300+	72%	-	69%

NOTE: Hospital profiles are in alphabetical order by state, then city, then hospital within the city; Rankings exclude hospitals with less than 25 cases except for patient surveys which excludes hospitals with less than 100 cases; (a) 100–299 cases; (1) The number of cases is too small to be sure how well a hospital is performing; (2) The hospital indicated that the data submitted for this measure were based on a sample of cases; (3) Data was collected during a shorter time period (fewer quarters) than the maximum possible time for this measure; (4) Suppressed for one or more quarters by CMS; (5) No data is available from the hospital for this measure; (6) Fewer than 100 patients completed the HCAHPS survey. Use these rates with caution, as the number of surveys may be too low to reliably assess hospital performance; (7) Survey results are based on less than 12 months of data; (8) Survey results are not available for this reporting period; (9) No or very few patients were eligible for the HCAHPS survey. The scores shown, if any, reflect a very small number of surveys; (10) A state average was not calculated because too few hospitals in the state submitted data; (11) There were discrepancies in the data collection process; Please refer to the User's Guide for a full explanation of data.

Spearfish Regional Surgery Center

1316 10th St Phone: 605-642-3113
Spearfish, SD 57783
Type: Acute Care Hospitals Emergency Services: Yes
Ownership: Voluntary Non-Profit - Other Beds: 6
Key Personnel:
CEO/President. . . . . Mike Delano

Measure	Cases	This Hosp.	State Avg.	U.S. Avg.
Heart Attack Care				
ACE Inhibitor or ARB for LVSD[5]	0	-	96%	96%
Aspirin at Arrival[5]	0	-	98%	99%
Aspirin at Discharge[5]	0	-	99%	98%
Beta Blocker at Discharge[5]	0	-	98%	98%
Fibrinolytic Medication Timing[5]	0	-	45%	55%
PCI Within 90 Minutes of Arrival[5]	0	-	87%	90%
Smoking Cessation Advice[5]	0	-	99%	99%
Chest Pain/Possible Heart Attack Care				
Aspirin at Arrival[5]	0	-	96%	95%
Median Time to ECG (minutes)[5]	0	-	7	8
Median Time to Transfer (minutes)[5]	0	-	84	61
Fibrinolytic Medication Timing[5]	0	-	54%	54%
Heart Failure Care				
ACE Inhibitor or ARB for LVSD[5]	0	-	90%	94%
Discharge Instructions[5]	0	-	85%	88%
Evaluation of LVS Function[5]	0	-	93%	98%
Smoking Cessation Advice[5]	0	-	93%	98%
Pneumonia Care				
Appropriate Initial Antibiotic[5]	0	-	91%	92%
Blood Culture Timing[5]	0	-	95%	96%
Influenza Vaccine[5]	0	-	94%	91%
Initial Antibiotic Timing[5]	0	-	94%	95%
Pneumococcal Vaccine[5]	0	-	93%	93%
Smoking Cessation Advice[5]	0	-	92%	97%
Surgical Care Improvement Project				
Appropriate VTP Within 24 Hours[1]	10	90%	90%	92%
Appropriate Hair Removal	51	98%	100%	99%
Appropriate Beta Blocker Usage[1]	5	80%	93%	93%
Controlled Postoperative Blood Glucose	0	-	96%	93%
Prophylactic Antibiotic Timing	38	97%	97%	97%
Prophylactic Antibiotic Timing (Outpatient)[1,3]	10	90%	96%	92%
Prophylactic Antibiotic Selection	38	95%	98%	97%
Prophylactic Antibiotic Select. (Outpatient)[1,3]	9	100%	97%	94%
Prophylactic Antibiotic Stopped	37	89%	96%	94%
Recommended VTP Ordered[1]	10	90%	91%	94%
Urinary Catheter Removal[1]	15	100%	89%	90%
Children's Asthma Care				
Received Systemic Corticosteroids	-	-	-	100%
Received Home Management Plan	-	-	-	71%
Received Reliever Medication	-	-	-	100%
Use of Medical Imaging				
Combination Abdominal CT Scan[5]	0	-	0.325	0.191
Combination Chest CT Scan[5]	0	-	0.116	0.054
Follow-up Mammogram/Ultrasound[5]	0	-	7.6%	8.4%
MRI for Low Back Pain[5]	0	-	31.3%	32.7%
Survey of Patients' Hospital Experiences				
Area Around Room 'Always' Quiet at Night[6]	<100	70%	-	58%
Doctors 'Always' Communicated Well[6]	<100	92%	-	80%
Home Recovery Information Given[6]	<100	94%	-	82%
Hospital Given 9 or 10 on 10 Point Scale[6]	<100	89%	-	67%
Meds 'Always' Explained Before Given[6]	<100	66%	-	60%
Nurses 'Always' Communicated Well[6]	<100	86%	-	76%
Pain 'Always' Well Controlled[6]	<100	76%	-	69%
Room and Bathroom 'Always' Clean[6]	<100	80%	-	71%
Timely Help 'Always' Received[6]	<100	91%	-	64%
Would Definitely Recommend Hospital	<100	86%	-	69%

Sturgis Regional Hospital

949 Harmon Street Phone: 605-720-2400
Sturgis, SD 57785 Fax: 605-720-0338
URL: www.rcrh.org
Type: Critical Access Hospitals Emergency Services: Yes
Ownership: Voluntary Non-Profit - Private Beds: 25
Key Personnel:
CEO/President. . . . . Van D Hyde
Chief of Medical Staff . . . . George Tenter
Infection Control. . . . . Glea Beck
Operating Room. . . . . Ron Owen
Quality Assurance . . . . Marilyn Johnson
Emergency Room . . . . Lynn Simons

Measure	Cases	This Hosp.	State Avg.	U.S. Avg.
Heart Attack Care				
ACE Inhibitor or ARB for LVSD[3]	0	-	96%	96%
Aspirin at Arrival[1,3]	1	100%	98%	99%
Aspirin at Discharge[1,3]	1	100%	99%	98%
Beta Blocker at Discharge[1,3]	1	100%	98%	98%
Fibrinolytic Medication Timing[3]	0	-	45%	55%
PCI Within 90 Minutes of Arrival[3]	0	-	87%	90%
Smoking Cessation Advice[3]	0	-	99%	99%
Chest Pain/Possible Heart Attack Care				
Aspirin at Arrival[1]	21	100%	96%	95%
Median Time to ECG (minutes)[1]	23	7	7	8
Median Time to Transfer (minutes)[3]	0	-	84	61
Fibrinolytic Medication Timing[3]	0	-	54%	54%
Heart Failure Care				
ACE Inhibitor or ARB for LVSD[1]	4	75%	90%	94%
Discharge Instructions[1]	8	100%	85%	88%
Evaluation of LVS Function[1]	11	73%	93%	98%
Smoking Cessation Advice	0	-	93%	98%
Pneumonia Care				
Appropriate Initial Antibiotic[1]	22	95%	91%	92%
Blood Culture Timing[1]	3	100%	95%	96%
Influenza Vaccine[1]	23	83%	94%	91%
Initial Antibiotic Timing	26	92%	94%	95%
Pneumococcal Vaccine	28	82%	93%	93%
Smoking Cessation Advice[1]	11	91%	92%	97%
Surgical Care Improvement Project				
Appropriate VTP Within 24 Hours[5]	0	-	90%	92%
Appropriate Hair Removal[5]	0	-	100%	99%
Appropriate Beta Blocker Usage[5]	0	-	93%	93%
Controlled Postoperative Blood Glucose[5]	0	-	96%	93%
Prophylactic Antibiotic Timing[5]	0	-	97%	97%
Prophylactic Antibiotic Timing (Outpatient)[5]	0	-	96%	92%
Prophylactic Antibiotic Selection[5]	0	-	98%	97%
Prophylactic Antibiotic Select. (Outpatient)[5]	0	-	97%	94%
Prophylactic Antibiotic Stopped[5]	0	-	96%	94%
Recommended VTP Ordered[5]	0	-	91%	94%
Urinary Catheter Removal[5]	0	-	89%	90%
Children's Asthma Care				
Received Systemic Corticosteroids	-	-	-	100%
Received Home Management Plan	-	-	-	71%
Received Reliever Medication	-	-	-	100%
Use of Medical Imaging				
Combination Abdominal CT Scan	52	0.038	0.325	0.191
Combination Chest CT Scan[1]	33	0.000	0.116	0.054
Follow-up Mammogram/Ultrasound	128	19.5%	7.6%	8.4%
MRI for Low Back Pain[1]	18	27.8%	31.3%	32.7%
Survey of Patients' Hospital Experiences				
Area Around Room 'Always' Quiet at Night	(a)	52%	-	58%
Doctors 'Always' Communicated Well	(a)	91%	-	80%
Home Recovery Information Given	(a)	84%	-	82%
Hospital Given 9 or 10 on 10 Point Scale	(a)	80%	-	67%
Meds 'Always' Explained Before Given	(a)	66%	-	60%
Nurses 'Always' Communicated Well	(a)	84%	-	76%
Pain 'Always' Well Controlled	(a)	72%	-	69%
Room and Bathroom 'Always' Clean	(a)	84%	-	71%
Timely Help 'Always' Received	(a)	83%	-	64%
Would Definitely Recommend Hospital	(a)	75%	-	69%

Sanford Vermillion Hospital

20 South Plum Street Phone: 605-624-2611
Vermillion, SD 57069 Fax: 605-624-4001
E-mail: info@sanfordvermillion.org
URL: www.sanfordvermillion.org
Type: Critical Access Hospitals Emergency Services: Yes
Ownership: Voluntary Non-Profit - Private Beds: 25
Key Personnel:
CEO/President. . . . . John Paulsa
Chief of Medical Staff . . . . W Dendinger, MD
Infection Control. . . . . Tammy Spiers
Operating Room. . . . . John Jorgensen
Anesthesiology. . . . . Jim Sundit

Measure	Cases	This Hosp.	State Avg.	U.S. Avg.
Heart Attack Care				
ACE Inhibitor or ARB for LVSD[1,3]	1	100%	96%	96%
Aspirin at Arrival[3]	0	-	98%	99%
Aspirin at Discharge[1,3]	1	100%	99%	98%
Beta Blocker at Discharge[1,3]	1	100%	98%	98%
Fibrinolytic Medication Timing[3]	0	-	45%	55%
PCI Within 90 Minutes of Arrival[3]	0	-	87%	90%
Smoking Cessation Advice[3]	0	-	99%	99%
Chest Pain/Possible Heart Attack Care				
Aspirin at Arrival	-	-	96%	95%
Median Time to ECG (minutes)	-	-	7	8
Median Time to Transfer (minutes)	-	-	84	61
Fibrinolytic Medication Timing	-	-	54%	54%
Heart Failure Care				
ACE Inhibitor or ARB for LVSD[1]	4	100%	90%	94%
Discharge Instructions[1]	13	38%	85%	88%
Evaluation of LVS Function[1]	17	100%	93%	98%
Smoking Cessation Advice	0	-	93%	98%
Pneumonia Care				
Appropriate Initial Antibiotic[1]	16	100%	91%	92%
Blood Culture Timing[1]	8	100%	95%	96%
Influenza Vaccine[1]	9	89%	94%	91%
Initial Antibiotic Timing[1]	19	89%	94%	95%
Pneumococcal Vaccine[1]	16	81%	93%	93%
Smoking Cessation Advice[1]	4	100%	92%	97%
Surgical Care Improvement Project				
Appropriate VTP Within 24 Hours[1,3]	1	0%	90%	92%
Appropriate Hair Removal[1,3]	5	100%	100%	99%
Appropriate Beta Blocker Usage[5]	0	-	93%	93%
Controlled Postoperative Blood Glucose[3]	0	-	96%	93%
Prophylactic Antibiotic Timing[1,3]	4	75%	97%	97%
Prophylactic Antibiotic Timing (Outpatient)	-	-	96%	92%
Prophylactic Antibiotic Selection[1,3]	5	100%	98%	97%
Prophylactic Antibiotic Select. (Outpatient)	-	-	97%	94%
Prophylactic Antibiotic Stopped[1,3]	4	100%	96%	94%
Recommended VTP Ordered[1,3]	3	0%	91%	94%
Urinary Catheter Removal[1]	1	100%	89%	90%
Children's Asthma Care				
Received Systemic Corticosteroids	-	-	-	100%
Received Home Management Plan	-	-	-	71%
Received Reliever Medication	-	-	-	100%
Use of Medical Imaging				
Combination Abdominal CT Scan	-	-	0.325	0.191
Combination Chest CT Scan	-	-	0.116	0.054
Follow-up Mammogram/Ultrasound	-	-	7.6%	8.4%
MRI for Low Back Pain	-	-	31.3%	32.7%
Survey of Patients' Hospital Experiences				
Area Around Room 'Always' Quiet at Night	(a)	58%	-	58%
Doctors 'Always' Communicated Well	(a)	86%	-	80%
Home Recovery Information Given	(a)	82%	-	82%
Hospital Given 9 or 10 on 10 Point Scale	(a)	59%	-	67%
Meds 'Always' Explained Before Given	(a)	57%	-	60%
Nurses 'Always' Communicated Well	(a)	70%	-	76%
Pain 'Always' Well Controlled	(a)	65%	-	69%
Room and Bathroom 'Always' Clean	(a)	63%	-	71%
Timely Help 'Always' Received	(a)	63%	-	64%
Would Definitely Recommend Hospital	(a)	65%	-	69%

NOTE: Hospital profiles are in alphabetical order by state, then city, then hospital within the city; Rankings exclude hospitals with less than 25 cases except for patient surveys which excludes hospitals with less than 100 cases; (a) 100–299 cases; (1) The number of cases is too small to be sure how well a hospital is performing; (2) The hospital indicated that the data submitted for this measure were based on a sample of cases; (3) Data was collected during a shorter time period (fewer quarters) than the maximum possible time for this measure; (4) Suppressed for one or more quarters by CMS; (5) No data is available from the hospital for this measure; (6) Fewer than 100 patients completed the HCAHPS survey. Use these rates with caution, as the number of surveys may be too low to reliably assess hospital performance; (7) Survey results are based on less than 12 months of data; (8) Survey results are not available for this reporting period; (9) No or very few patients were eligible for the HCAHPS survey. The scores shown, if any, reflect a very small number of surveys; (10) A state average was not calculated because too few hospitals in the state submitted data; (11) There were discrepancies in the data collection process; Please refer to the User's Guide for a full explanation of data.

Wagner Community Memorial Hospital

513 3rd St SW Phone: 605-384-3611
Wagner, SD 57380 Fax: 605-384-3232
URL: www.avera.org
Type: Critical Access Hospitals Emergency Services: Yes
Ownership: Government - Local Beds: 20
Key Personnel:
Chief of Medical Staff.......... GA Bubak, MD
Infection Control............. Marcia Podzimek
Emergency Room .... Judith Neilsen

Measure	Cases	This Hosp.	State Avg.	U.S. Avg.
Heart Attack Care				
ACE Inhibitor or ARB for LVSD[5]	0	-	96%	96%
Aspirin at Arrival[5]	0	-	98%	99%
Aspirin at Discharge[5]	0	-	99%	98%
Beta Blocker at Discharge[5]	0	-	98%	98%
Fibrinolytic Medication Timing[5]	0	-	45%	55%
PCI Within 90 Minutes of Arrival[5]	0	-	87%	90%
Smoking Cessation Advice[5]	0	-	99%	99%
Chest Pain/Possible Heart Attack Care				
Aspirin at Arrival[5]	0	-	96%	95%
Median Time to ECG (minutes)[5]	0	-	7	8
Median Time to Transfer (minutes)[5]	0	-	84	61
Fibrinolytic Medication Timing[5]	0	-	54%	54%
Heart Failure Care				
ACE Inhibitor or ARB for LVSD[1,3]	3	67%	90%	94%
Discharge Instructions[1,3]	5	60%	85%	88%
Evaluation of LVS Function[1,3]	12	83%	93%	98%
Smoking Cessation Advice[3]	0	-	93%	98%
Pneumonia Care				
Appropriate Initial Antibiotic[1,3]	13	69%	91%	92%
Blood Culture Timing[1,3]	4	100%	95%	96%
Influenza Vaccine[5]	0	-	94%	91%
Initial Antibiotic Timing[1,3]	19	95%	94%	95%
Pneumococcal Vaccine[1,3]	14	29%	93%	93%
Smoking Cessation Advice[1,3]	1	0%	92%	97%
Surgical Care Improvement Project				
Appropriate VTP Within 24 Hours[5]	0	-	90%	92%
Appropriate Hair Removal[5]	0	-	100%	99%
Appropriate Beta Blocker Usage[5]	0	-	93%	93%
Controlled Postoperative Blood Glucose[5]	0	-	96%	93%
Prophylactic Antibiotic Timing[5]	0	-	97%	97%
Prophylactic Antibiotic Timing (Outpatient)[5]	0	-	96%	92%
Prophylactic Antibiotic Selection[5]	0	-	98%	97%
Prophylactic Antibiotic Select. (Outpatient)[5]	0	-	97%	94%
Prophylactic Antibiotic Stopped[5]	0	-	96%	94%
Recommended VTP Ordered[5]	0	-	91%	94%
Urinary Catheter Removal[5]	0	-	89%	90%
Children's Asthma Care				
Received Systemic Corticosteroids	-	-	-	100%
Received Home Management Plan	-	-	-	71%
Received Reliever Medication	-	-	-	100%
Use of Medical Imaging				
Combination Abdominal CT Scan[1]	30	0.500	0.325	0.191
Combination Chest CT Scan[1]	10	0.800	0.116	0.054
Follow-up Mammogram/Ultrasound	81	4.9%	7.6%	8.4%
MRI for Low Back Pain[1]	7	0.0%	31.3%	32.7%
Survey of Patients' Hospital Experiences				
Area Around Room 'Always' Quiet at Night	(a)	60%	-	58%
Doctors 'Always' Communicated Well	(a)	87%	-	80%
Home Recovery Information Given	(a)	73%	-	82%
Hospital Given 9 or 10 on 10 Point Scale	(a)	71%	-	67%
Meds 'Always' Explained Before Given	(a)	65%	-	60%
Nurses 'Always' Communicated Well	(a)	79%	-	76%
Pain 'Always' Well Controlled	(a)	68%	-	69%
Room and Bathroom 'Always' Clean	(a)	83%	-	71%
Timely Help 'Always' Received	(a)	72%	-	64%
Would Definitely Recommend Hospital	(a)	70%	-	69%

Prairie Lakes Hospital

401 9th Avenue NW Phone: 605-882-7000
Watertown, SD 57201 Fax: 605-882-7726
E-mail: info@prairielakes.com
URL: www.prairielakes.com
Type: Acute Care Hospitals Emergency Services: Yes
Ownership: Voluntary Non-Profit - Private Beds: 81
Key Personnel:
CEO/President............... Paul Hanson
Chief of Medical Staff.......... Dan Reiffenberger, MD
Infection Control............. Shannon Britt
Operating Room.............. Alan Christensen
Radiology................... William Bishop
Emergency Room .... Elliott Filler
Intensive Care Unit............ Debra Pederson
Patient Relations .... Jill Fuller

Measure	Cases	This Hosp.	State Avg.	U.S. Avg.
Heart Attack Care				
ACE Inhibitor or ARB for LVSD[1]	9	89%	96%	96%
Aspirin at Arrival	57	100%	98%	99%
Aspirin at Discharge	61	97%	99%	98%
Beta Blocker at Discharge	56	98%	98%	98%
Fibrinolytic Medication Timing	0	-	45%	55%
PCI Within 90 Minutes of Arrival[1]	20	95%	87%	90%
Smoking Cessation Advice[1]	13	100%	99%	99%
Chest Pain/Possible Heart Attack Care				
Aspirin at Arrival[1]	6	67%	96%	95%
Median Time to ECG (minutes)[1]	5	7	7	8
Median Time to Transfer (minutes)[5]	0	-	84	61
Fibrinolytic Medication Timing[5]	0	-	54%	54%
Heart Failure Care				
ACE Inhibitor or ARB for LVSD	27	85%	90%	94%
Discharge Instructions	63	79%	85%	88%
Evaluation of LVS Function	87	93%	93%	98%
Smoking Cessation Advice[1]	9	67%	93%	98%
Pneumonia Care				
Appropriate Initial Antibiotic	141	96%	91%	92%
Blood Culture Timing	127	94%	95%	96%
Influenza Vaccine	107	92%	94%	91%
Initial Antibiotic Timing	176	98%	94%	95%
Pneumococcal Vaccine	193	93%	93%	93%
Smoking Cessation Advice	35	77%	92%	97%
Surgical Care Improvement Project				
Appropriate VTP Within 24 Hours[2]	130	81%	90%	92%
Appropriate Hair Removal[2]	383	100%	100%	99%
Appropriate Beta Blocker Usage[2]	122	85%	93%	93%
Controlled Postoperative Blood Glucose[2]	0	-	96%	93%
Prophylactic Antibiotic Timing[2]	284	97%	97%	97%
Prophylactic Antibiotic Timing (Outpatient)	107	95%	96%	92%
Prophylactic Antibiotic Selection[2]	291	95%	98%	97%
Prophylactic Antibiotic Select. (Outpatient)	104	97%	97%	94%
Prophylactic Antibiotic Stopped[2]	275	96%	96%	94%
Recommended VTP Ordered[2]	131	84%	91%	94%
Urinary Catheter Removal[2]	101	91%	89%	90%
Children's Asthma Care				
Received Systemic Corticosteroids	-	-	-	100%
Received Home Management Plan	-	-	-	71%
Received Reliever Medication	-	-	-	100%
Use of Medical Imaging				
Combination Abdominal CT Scan	245	0.747	0.325	0.191
Combination Chest CT Scan	218	0.683	0.116	0.054
Follow-up Mammogram/Ultrasound[1]	62	11.3%	7.6%	8.4%
MRI for Low Back Pain	63	27.0%	31.3%	32.7%
Survey of Patients' Hospital Experiences				
Area Around Room 'Always' Quiet at Night	300+	56%	-	58%
Doctors 'Always' Communicated Well	300+	85%	-	80%
Home Recovery Information Given	300+	82%	-	82%
Hospital Given 9 or 10 on 10 Point Scale	300+	68%	-	67%
Meds 'Always' Explained Before Given	300+	64%	-	60%
Nurses 'Always' Communicated Well	300+	76%	-	76%
Pain 'Always' Well Controlled	300+	72%	-	69%
Room and Bathroom 'Always' Clean	300+	76%	-	71%
Timely Help 'Always' Received	300+	70%	-	64%
Would Definitely Recommend Hospital	300+	67%	-	69%

Avera Weskota Memorial Medical Center

604 1st St NE Phone: 605-539-1201
Wessington Springs, SD 57382 Fax: 605-995-2441
URL: www.averaweskota.org
Type: Critical Access Hospitals Emergency Services: Yes
Ownership: Voluntary Non-Profit - Church Beds: 28
Key Personnel:
Chief of Medical Staff.......... Tom Dehan
Emergency Room .... Grace Edwyetr

Measure	Cases	This Hosp.	State Avg.	U.S. Avg.
Heart Attack Care				
ACE Inhibitor or ARB for LVSD[5]	0	-	96%	96%
Aspirin at Arrival[5]	0	-	98%	99%
Aspirin at Discharge[5]	0	-	99%	98%
Beta Blocker at Discharge[5]	0	-	98%	98%
Fibrinolytic Medication Timing[5]	0	-	45%	55%
PCI Within 90 Minutes of Arrival[5]	0	-	87%	90%
Smoking Cessation Advice[5]	0	-	99%	99%
Chest Pain/Possible Heart Attack Care				
Aspirin at Arrival	-	-	96%	95%
Median Time to ECG (minutes)	-	-	7	8
Median Time to Transfer (minutes)	-	-	84	61
Fibrinolytic Medication Timing	-	-	54%	54%
Heart Failure Care				
ACE Inhibitor or ARB for LVSD[1,3]	1	100%	90%	94%
Discharge Instructions[1,3]	3	100%	85%	88%
Evaluation of LVS Function[1,3]	6	17%	93%	98%
Smoking Cessation Advice[3]	0	-	93%	98%
Pneumonia Care				
Appropriate Initial Antibiotic[1]	8	88%	91%	92%
Blood Culture Timing[1]	1	100%	95%	96%
Influenza Vaccine[1]	6	100%	94%	91%
Initial Antibiotic Timing[1]	11	100%	94%	95%
Pneumococcal Vaccine[1]	16	100%	93%	93%
Smoking Cessation Advice[1]	2	50%	92%	97%
Surgical Care Improvement Project				
Appropriate VTP Within 24 Hours[5]	0	-	90%	92%
Appropriate Hair Removal[5]	0	-	100%	99%
Appropriate Beta Blocker Usage[5]	0	-	93%	93%
Controlled Postoperative Blood Glucose[5]	0	-	96%	93%
Prophylactic Antibiotic Timing[5]	0	-	97%	97%
Prophylactic Antibiotic Timing (Outpatient)		-	96%	92%
Prophylactic Antibiotic Selection[5]	0	-	98%	97%
Prophylactic Antibiotic Select. (Outpatient)		-	97%	94%
Prophylactic Antibiotic Stopped[5]	0	-	96%	94%
Recommended VTP Ordered[5]	0	-	91%	94%
Urinary Catheter Removal[5]	0	-	89%	90%
Children's Asthma Care				
Received Systemic Corticosteroids	-	-	-	100%
Received Home Management Plan	-	-	-	71%
Received Reliever Medication	-	-	-	100%
Use of Medical Imaging				
Combination Abdominal CT Scan	-	-	0.325	0.191
Combination Chest CT Scan	-	-	0.116	0.054
Follow-up Mammogram/Ultrasound	-	-	7.6%	8.4%
MRI for Low Back Pain	-	-	31.3%	32.7%
Survey of Patients' Hospital Experiences				
Area Around Room 'Always' Quiet at Night[6]	<100	74%	-	58%
Doctors 'Always' Communicated Well[6]	<100	81%	-	80%
Home Recovery Information Given[6]	<100	77%	-	82%
Hospital Given 9 or 10 on 10 Point Scale[6]	<100	73%	-	67%
Meds 'Always' Explained Before Given[6]	<100	73%	-	60%
Nurses 'Always' Communicated Well[6]	<100	80%	-	76%
Pain 'Always' Well Controlled[6]	<100	68%	-	69%
Room and Bathroom 'Always' Clean[6]	<100	87%	-	71%
Timely Help 'Always' Received[6]	<100	71%	-	64%
Would Definitely Recommend Hospital	<100	76%	-	69%

NOTE: Hospital profiles are in alphabetical order by state, then city, then hospital within the city; Rankings exclude hospitals with less than 25 cases except for patient surveys which excludes hospitals with less than 100 cases; (a) 100–299 cases; (1) The number of cases is too small to be sure how well a hospital is performing; (2) The hospital indicated that the data submitted for this measure were based on a sample of cases; (3) Data was collected during a shorter time period (fewer quarters) than the maximum possible time for this measure; (4) Suppressed for one or more quarters by CMS; (5) No data is available from the hospital for this measure; (6) Fewer than 100 patients completed the HCAHPS survey. Use these rates with caution, as the number of surveys may be too low to reliably assess hospital performance; (7) Survey results are based on less than 12 months of data; (8) Survey results are not available for this reporting period; (9) No or very few patients were eligible for the HCAHPS survey. The scores shown, if any, reflect a very small number of surveys; (10) A state average was not calculated because too few hospitals in the state submitted data; (11) There were discrepancies in the data collection process; Please refer to the User's Guide for a full explanation of data.

Winner Regional Healthcare Center

745 East 8th Street
Winner, SD 57580
Phone: 605-842-7100
Fax: 605-842-7198
E-mail: info@winnerregional.org
URL: www.winnerregional.org
Type: Critical Access Hospitals
Emergency Services: Yes
Ownership: Voluntary Non-Profit - Private
Beds: 97

Key Personnel:
CEO/President. . . . . Michael Hall
Chief of Medical Staff . . . . Tony Berg
Infection Control. . . . . Ellen Storms
Operating Room. . . . . Thomas Kosina
Quality Assurance . . . . Wendy Heath, PRO
Anesthesiology. . . . . Nancy Rehr
Emergency Room . . . . Gregg Tobin, MD

Measure	Cases	This Hosp.	State Avg.	U.S. Avg.
Heart Attack Care				
ACE Inhibitor or ARB for LVSD	0	-	96%	96%
Aspirin at Arrival[1]	2	50%	98%	99%
Aspirin at Discharge	0	-	99%	98%
Beta Blocker at Discharge	0	-	98%	98%
Fibrinolytic Medication Timing	0	-	45%	55%
PCI Within 90 Minutes of Arrival	0	-	87%	90%
Smoking Cessation Advice	0	-	99%	99%
Chest Pain/Possible Heart Attack Care				
Aspirin at Arrival	-	-	96%	95%
Median Time to ECG (minutes)	-	-	7	8
Median Time to Transfer (minutes)	-	-	84	61
Fibrinolytic Medication Timing	-	-	54%	54%
Heart Failure Care				
ACE Inhibitor or ARB for LVSD[1]	5	20%	90%	94%
Discharge Instructions[1]	15	67%	85%	88%
Evaluation of LVS Function[1]	18	44%	93%	98%
Smoking Cessation Advice[1]	2	0%	93%	98%
Pneumonia Care				
Appropriate Initial Antibiotic[1]	6	33%	91%	92%
Blood Culture Timing[1]	4	25%	95%	96%
Influenza Vaccine[1]	7	86%	94%	91%
Initial Antibiotic Timing[1]	11	82%	94%	95%
Pneumococcal Vaccine[1]	13	77%	93%	93%
Smoking Cessation Advice[1]	4	50%	92%	97%
Surgical Care Improvement Project				
Appropriate VTP Within 24 Hours[1]	3	0%	90%	92%
Appropriate Hair Removal[1]	10	100%	100%	99%
Appropriate Beta Blocker Usage[5]	0	-	93%	93%
Controlled Postoperative Blood Glucose	0	-	96%	93%
Prophylactic Antibiotic Timing[1]	6	100%	97%	97%
Prophylactic Antibiotic Timing (Outpatient)	-	-	96%	92%
Prophylactic Antibiotic Selection[1]	7	29%	98%	97%
Prophylactic Antibiotic Select. (Outpatient)	-	-	97%	94%
Prophylactic Antibiotic Stopped[1]	6	100%	96%	94%
Recommended VTP Ordered[1]	3	0%	91%	94%
Urinary Catheter Removal[1]	2	50%	89%	90%
Children's Asthma Care				
Received Systemic Corticosteroids	-	-	-	100%
Received Home Management Plan	-	-	-	71%
Received Reliever Medication	-	-	-	100%
Use of Medical Imaging				
Combination Abdominal CT Scan	-	-	0.325	0.191
Combination Chest CT Scan	-	-	0.116	0.054
Follow-up Mammogram/Ultrasound	-	-	7.6%	8.4%
MRI for Low Back Pain	-	-	31.3%	32.7%
Survey of Patients' Hospital Experiences				
Area Around Room 'Always' Quiet at Night[8]	-	-	-	58%
Doctors 'Always' Communicated Well[8]	-	-	-	80%
Home Recovery Information Given[8]	-	-	-	82%
Hospital Given 9 or 10 on 10 Point Scale[8]	-	-	-	67%
Meds 'Always' Explained Before Given[8]	-	-	-	60%
Nurses 'Always' Communicated Well[8]	-	-	-	76%
Pain 'Always' Well Controlled[8]	-	-	-	69%
Room and Bathroom 'Always' Clean[8]	-	-	-	71%
Timely Help 'Always' Received[8]	-	-	-	64%
Would Definitely Recommend Hospital[8]	-	-	-	69%

Avera Sacred Heart Hospital

501 Summit
Yankton, SD 57078
Phone: 605-668-8000
Fax: 605-665-0170
Type: Acute Care Hospitals
Emergency Services: Yes
Ownership: Voluntary Non-Profit - Church
Beds: 144

Key Personnel:
CEO/President. . . . . Pamela Rezac, PhD
Chief of Medical Staff . . . . David Barnes
Infection Control. . . . . Jan Johnson
Operating Room. . . . . Cindy Miller
Pediatric Ambulatory Care . . . . . . David Withrow, MD
Pediatric In-Patient Care . . . . . . Mark Brown, MD
Quality Assurance . . . . Jean Hunhoff
Radiology. . . . . Thomas Posch

Measure	Cases	This Hosp.	State Avg.	U.S. Avg.
Heart Attack Care				
ACE Inhibitor or ARB for LVSD[1]	4	100%	96%	96%
Aspirin at Arrival[1]	22	100%	98%	99%
Aspirin at Discharge[1]	19	100%	99%	98%
Beta Blocker at Discharge[1]	18	100%	98%	98%
Fibrinolytic Medication Timing[1]	1	100%	45%	55%
PCI Within 90 Minutes of Arrival	0	-	87%	90%
Smoking Cessation Advice[1]	2	100%	99%	99%
Chest Pain/Possible Heart Attack Care				
Aspirin at Arrival	41	98%	96%	95%
Median Time to ECG (minutes)	43	8	7	8
Median Time to Transfer (minutes)[1]	2	71	84	61
Fibrinolytic Medication Timing[1]	10	50%	54%	54%
Heart Failure Care				
ACE Inhibitor or ARB for LVSD[1]	22	100%	90%	94%
Discharge Instructions	57	100%	85%	88%
Evaluation of LVS Function	100	100%	93%	98%
Smoking Cessation Advice[1]	12	100%	93%	98%
Pneumonia Care				
Appropriate Initial Antibiotic	63	100%	91%	92%
Blood Culture Timing	110	97%	95%	96%
Influenza Vaccine	114	98%	94%	91%
Initial Antibiotic Timing	171	99%	94%	95%
Pneumococcal Vaccine	148	98%	93%	93%
Smoking Cessation Advice	40	100%	92%	97%
Surgical Care Improvement Project				
Appropriate VTP Within 24 Hours	157	97%	90%	92%
Appropriate Hair Removal	344	97%	100%	99%
Appropriate Beta Blocker Usage	86	100%	93%	93%
Controlled Postoperative Blood Glucose	0	-	96%	93%
Prophylactic Antibiotic Timing	200	96%	97%	97%
Prophylactic Antibiotic Timing (Outpatient)	105	94%	96%	92%
Prophylactic Antibiotic Selection	202	99%	98%	97%
Prophylactic Antibiotic Select. (Outpatient)	103	96%	97%	94%
Prophylactic Antibiotic Stopped	192	96%	96%	94%
Recommended VTP Ordered	157	98%	91%	94%
Urinary Catheter Removal	29	38%	89%	90%
Children's Asthma Care				
Received Systemic Corticosteroids	-	-	-	100%
Received Home Management Plan	-	-	-	71%
Received Reliever Medication	-	-	-	100%
Use of Medical Imaging				
Combination Abdominal CT Scan	115	0.365	0.325	0.191
Combination Chest CT Scan	37	0.459	0.116	0.054
Follow-up Mammogram/Ultrasound	285	6.7%	7.6%	8.4%
MRI for Low Back Pain	122	28.7%	31.3%	32.7%
Survey of Patients' Hospital Experiences				
Area Around Room 'Always' Quiet at Night	300+	64%	-	58%
Doctors 'Always' Communicated Well	300+	83%	-	80%
Home Recovery Information Given	300+	81%	-	82%
Hospital Given 9 or 10 on 10 Point Scale	300+	73%	-	67%
Meds 'Always' Explained Before Given	300+	67%	-	60%
Nurses 'Always' Communicated Well	300+	80%	-	76%
Pain 'Always' Well Controlled	300+	73%	-	69%
Room and Bathroom 'Always' Clean	300+	79%	-	71%
Timely Help 'Always' Received	300+	69%	-	64%
Would Definitely Recommend Hospital	300+	70%	-	69%

Lewis and Clark Specialty Hospital

2601 Fox Run Parkway
Yankton, SD 57078
Phone: 605-665-5100
Type: Acute Care Hospitals
Emergency Services: No
Ownership: Proprietary

Key Personnel:
CEO/President. . . . . Michelle Weidner-Jordan

Measure	Cases	This Hosp.	State Avg.	U.S. Avg.
Heart Attack Care				
ACE Inhibitor or ARB for LVSD[5]	0	-	96%	96%
Aspirin at Arrival[5]	0	-	98%	99%
Aspirin at Discharge[5]	0	-	99%	98%
Beta Blocker at Discharge[5]	0	-	98%	98%
Fibrinolytic Medication Timing[5]	0	-	45%	55%
PCI Within 90 Minutes of Arrival[5]	0	-	87%	90%
Smoking Cessation Advice[5]	0	-	99%	99%
Chest Pain/Possible Heart Attack Care				
Aspirin at Arrival[5]	0	-	96%	95%
Median Time to ECG (minutes)[5]	0	-	7	8
Median Time to Transfer (minutes)[5]	0	-	84	61
Fibrinolytic Medication Timing[5]	0	-	54%	54%
Heart Failure Care				
ACE Inhibitor or ARB for LVSD[5]	0	-	90%	94%
Discharge Instructions[5]	0	-	85%	88%
Evaluation of LVS Function[5]	0	-	93%	98%
Smoking Cessation Advice[5]	0	-	93%	98%
Pneumonia Care				
Appropriate Initial Antibiotic[5]	0	-	91%	92%
Blood Culture Timing[5]	0	-	95%	96%
Influenza Vaccine[5]	0	-	94%	91%
Initial Antibiotic Timing[5]	0	-	94%	95%
Pneumococcal Vaccine[5]	0	-	93%	93%
Smoking Cessation Advice[5]	0	-	92%	97%
Surgical Care Improvement Project				
Appropriate VTP Within 24 Hours[2]	35	97%	90%	92%
Appropriate Hair Removal[2]	118	100%	100%	99%
Appropriate Beta Blocker Usage[2]	26	96%	93%	93%
Controlled Postoperative Blood Glucose[2]	0	-	96%	93%
Prophylactic Antibiotic Timing[2]	110	100%	97%	97%
Prophylactic Antibiotic Timing (Outpatient)	34	100%	96%	92%
Prophylactic Antibiotic Selection[2]	110	98%	98%	97%
Prophylactic Antibiotic Select. (Outpatient)	34	41%	97%	94%
Prophylactic Antibiotic Stopped[2]	109	90%	96%	94%
Recommended VTP Ordered[2]	35	97%	91%	94%
Urinary Catheter Removal[1,2]	3	67%	89%	90%
Children's Asthma Care				
Received Systemic Corticosteroids	-	-	-	100%
Received Home Management Plan	-	-	-	71%
Received Reliever Medication	-	-	-	100%
Use of Medical Imaging				
Combination Abdominal CT Scan[5]	0	-	0.325	0.191
Combination Chest CT Scan[5]	0	-	0.116	0.054
Follow-up Mammogram/Ultrasound[5]	0	-	7.6%	8.4%
MRI for Low Back Pain[1]	8	25.0%	31.3%	32.7%
Survey of Patients' Hospital Experiences				
Area Around Room 'Always' Quiet at Night	(a)	83%	-	58%
Doctors 'Always' Communicated Well	(a)	89%	-	80%
Home Recovery Information Given	(a)	87%	-	82%
Hospital Given 9 or 10 on 10 Point Scale	(a)	85%	-	67%
Meds 'Always' Explained Before Given	(a)	69%	-	60%
Nurses 'Always' Communicated Well	(a)	88%	-	76%
Pain 'Always' Well Controlled	(a)	75%	-	69%
Room and Bathroom 'Always' Clean	(a)	87%	-	71%
Timely Help 'Always' Received	(a)	87%	-	64%
Would Definitely Recommend Hospital	(a)	90%	-	69%

NOTE: Hospital profiles are in alphabetical order by state, then city, then hospital within the city; Rankings exclude hospitals with less than 25 cases except for patient surveys which excludes hospitals with less than 100 cases; (a) 100–299 cases; (1) The number of cases is too small to be sure how well a hospital is performing; (2) The hospital indicated that the data submitted for this measure were based on a sample of cases; (3) Data was collected during a shorter time period (fewer quarters) than the maximum possible time for this measure; (4) Suppressed for one or more quarters by CMS; (5) No data is available from the hospital for this measure; (6) Fewer than 100 patients completed the HCAHPS survey. Use these rates with caution, as the number of surveys may be too low to reliably assess hospital performance; (7) Survey results are based on less than 12 months of data; (8) Survey results are not available for this reporting period; (9) No or very few patients were eligible for the HCAHPS survey. The scores shown, if any, reflect a very small number of surveys; (10) A state average was not calculated because too few hospitals in the state submitted data; (11) There were discrepancies in the data collection process; Please refer to the User's Guide for a full explanation of data.

Heart Attack Care

1. ACE Inhibitor or ARB for LVSD

Hospital Name	City	Rate	Cases
Aurora St Lukes Medical Center	Milwaukee	100%	157
Bellin Memorial Hospital	Green Bay	100%	34
Froedtert Memorial Lutheran Hospital	Milwaukee	100%	31
Luther Hospital Mayo Health System	Eau Claire	100%	33
Saint Clare's Hospital of Weston	Weston	100%	43
Saint Elizabeth Hospital	Appleton	100%	26
Saint Josephs Hospital	Marshfield	100%	55
Waukesha Memorial Hospital[2]	Waukesha	100%	47
Appleton Medical Center	Appleton	98%	59
Gundersen Luth Medical Center	La Crosse	98%	52
Aspirus Wausau Hospital[2]	Wausau	97%	29
Columbia St Mary's Hospital Ozaukee	Mequon	97%	33
Saint Agnes Hospital	Fond Du Lac	96%	26
Saint Mary's Hospital	Madison	96%	83
Meriter Hospital[2]	Madison	95%	40
Univ of Wisconsin Hosps & Clinics Auth[2]	Madison	95%	42
Columbia St Marys Hosp Milwaukee	Milwaukee	94%	31
Sacred Heart Hospital	Eau Claire	94%	33
Wheaton Franciscan Healthcare - All Saints	Racine	88%	26

2. Aspirin at Arrival

Hospital Name	City	Rate	Cases
Appleton Medical Center	Appleton	100%	134
Aspirus Wausau Hospital[2]	Wausau	100%	118
Aurora Baycare Medical Center	Green Bay	100%	52
Aurora Medical Center Manitowoc County	Two Rivers	100%	27
Aurora Medical Center Oshkosh	Oshkosh	100%	43
Aurora St Lukes Medical Center	Milwaukee	100%	615
Aurora West Allis Medical Center	West Allis	100%	53
Columbia St Marys Hosp Milwaukee	Milwaukee	100%	115
Community Memorial Hospital	Menomonee Fls	100%	125
Gundersen Luth Medical Center	La Crosse	100%	165
Madison VA Medical Center	Madison	100%	49
Memorial Medical Center	Ashland	100%	27
Mercy Medical Center of Oshkosh	Oshkosh	100%	53
Meriter Hospital[2]	Madison	100%	190
Milwaukee VA Medical Center	Milwaukee	100%	37
Sacred Heart Hospital	Eau Claire	100%	92
Saint Clare's Hospital of Weston	Weston	100%	69
Saint Elizabeth Hospital	Appleton	100%	110
Saint Mary's Hospital	Madison	100%	206
Saint Marys Hospital Medical Center	Green Bay	100%	98
Theda Clark Medical Center	Neenah	100%	70
Wheaton Franciscan Healthcare - All Saints	Racine	100%	193
Bellin Memorial Hospital	Green Bay	99%	189
Columbia St Mary's Hospital Ozaukee	Mequon	99%	190
Franciscan Skemp La Crosse Hospital	La Crosse	99%	81
Froedtert Memorial Lutheran Hospital	Milwaukee	99%	159
Mercy Health Sys Corp	Janesville	99%	124
Saint Agnes Hospital	Fond Du Lac	99%	136
Saint Josephs Hospital	Marshfield	99%	170
Saint Vincent Hospital	Green Bay	99%	136
United Hospital System	Kenosha	99%	153
Waukesha Memorial Hospital[2]	Waukesha	99%	216
Wheaton Franciscan - St Joseph	Milwaukee	99%	177
Wheaton Franciscan Healthcare - St Francis	Milwaukee	99%	77
Aurora Sheboygan Memorial Medical Center	Sheboygan	98%	40
Bay Area Medical Center	Marinette	98%	112
Luther Hospital Mayo Health System	Eau Claire	98%	107
Oconomowoc Memorial Hospital	Oconomowoc	98%	57
Univ of Wisconsin Hosps & Clinics Auth[2]	Madison	98%	112
Holy Family Memorial	Manitowoc	97%	62
Saint Nicholas Hospital	Sheboygan	96%	26
Beloit Memorial Hospital	Beloit	95%	84
Aurora Medical Center - Washington County	Hartford	87%	39

3. Aspirin at Discharge

Hospital Name	City	Rate	Cases
Appleton Medical Center	Appleton	100%	261
Aspirus Wausau Hospital[2]	Wausau	100%	251
Aurora Medical Center Oshkosh	Oshkosh	100%	41
Aurora St Lukes Medical Center	Milwaukee	100%	1006
Aurora West Allis Medical Center	West Allis	100%	26
Columbia St Marys Hosp Milwaukee	Milwaukee	100%	146
Luther Hospital Mayo Health System	Eau Claire	100%	245
Madison VA Medical Center	Madison	100%	56
Mercy Health Sys Corp	Janesville	100%	158
Meriter Hospital[2]	Madison	100%	266
Milwaukee VA Medical Center	Milwaukee	100%	39
Oconomowoc Memorial Hospital	Oconomowoc	100%	52
Sacred Heart Hospital	Eau Claire	100%	189
Saint Clare's Hospital of Weston	Weston	100%	243
Saint Elizabeth Hospital	Appleton	100%	156
Saint Josephs Hospital	Marshfield	100%	302
Saint Mary's Hospital	Madison	100%	445
Wheaton Franciscan - St Joseph	Milwaukee	100%	213
Wheaton Franciscan Healthcare - All Saints	Racine	100%	188
Bellin Memorial Hospital	Green Bay	99%	359
Community Memorial Hospital	Menomonee Fls	99%	132
Froedtert Memorial Lutheran Hospital	Milwaukee	99%	195
Gundersen Luth Medical Center	La Crosse	99%	324
Saint Vincent Hospital	Green Bay	99%	164
Theda Clark Medical Center	Neenah	99%	70
United Hospital System	Kenosha	99%	146
Univ of Wisconsin Hosps & Clinics Auth[2]	Madison	99%	275
Aurora Baycare Medical Center	Green Bay	98%	137
Columbia St Mary's Hospital Ozaukee	Mequon	98%	212
Holy Family Memorial	Manitowoc	98%	53
Mercy Medical Center of Oshkosh	Oshkosh	98%	60
Waukesha Memorial Hospital[2]	Waukesha	98%	202
Saint Agnes Hospital	Fond Du Lac	97%	153
Saint Marys Hospital Medical Center	Green Bay	97%	94
Wheaton Franciscan Healthcare - St Francis	Milwaukee	97%	73
Bay Area Medical Center	Marinette	96%	78
Franciscan Skemp La Crosse Hospital	La Crosse	95%	111
Aurora Sheboygan Memorial Medical Center	Sheboygan	94%	32
Beloit Memorial Hospital	Beloit	94%	69
Memorial Medical Center	Ashland	93%	28
Aurora Medical Center - Washington County	Hartford	88%	26

4. Beta Blocker at Discharge

Hospital Name	City	Rate	Cases
Aspirus Wausau Hospital[2]	Wausau	100%	250
Aurora Medical Center Oshkosh	Oshkosh	100%	37
Aurora St Lukes Medical Center	Milwaukee	100%	952
Aurora West Allis Medical Center	West Allis	100%	29
Bellin Memorial Hospital	Green Bay	100%	353
Franciscan Skemp La Crosse Hospital	La Crosse	100%	111
Gundersen Luth Medical Center	La Crosse	100%	325
Luther Hospital Mayo Health System	Eau Claire	100%	246
Madison VA Medical Center	Madison	100%	52
Mercy Health Sys Corp	Janesville	100%	154
Milwaukee VA Medical Center	Milwaukee	100%	36
Saint Clare's Hospital of Weston	Weston	100%	231
Saint Elizabeth Hospital	Appleton	100%	150
Saint Mary's Hospital	Madison	100%	433
Univ of Wisconsin Hosps & Clinics Auth[2]	Madison	100%	262
Wheaton Franciscan Healthcare - All Saints	Racine	100%	184
Appleton Medical Center	Appleton	99%	264
Sacred Heart Hospital	Eau Claire	99%	184
Saint Josephs Hospital	Marshfield	99%	338
Wheaton Franciscan - St Joseph	Milwaukee	99%	202
Wheaton Franciscan Healthcare - St Francis	Milwaukee	99%	78
Aurora Baycare Medical Center	Green Bay	98%	132
Columbia St Marys Hosp Milwaukee	Milwaukee	98%	145
Community Memorial Hospital	Menomonee Fls	98%	124
Froedtert Memorial Lutheran Hospital	Milwaukee	98%	192
Mercy Medical Center of Oshkosh	Oshkosh	98%	49
Meriter Hospital[2]	Madison	98%	251
Oconomowoc Memorial Hospital	Oconomowoc	98%	52
Saint Marys Hospital Medical Center	Green Bay	98%	95
Theda Clark Medical Center	Neenah	98%	62
Waukesha Memorial Hospital[2]	Waukesha	98%	199
Bay Area Medical Center	Marinette	97%	79
Beloit Memorial Hospital	Beloit	97%	71
Saint Vincent Hospital	Green Bay	97%	156
Columbia St Mary's Hospital Ozaukee	Mequon	96%	213
United Hospital System	Kenosha	96%	135
Saint Agnes Hospital	Fond Du Lac	94%	131
Aurora Medical Center - Washington County	Hartford	93%	30
Aurora Sheboygan Memorial Medical Center	Sheboygan	93%	29
Holy Family Memorial	Manitowoc	92%	51
Memorial Medical Center	Ashland	89%	27

6. PCI Within 90 Minutes of Arrival

Hospital Name	City	Rate	Cases
Aspirus Wausau Hospital[2]	Wausau	100%	33
Bellin Memorial Hospital	Green Bay	100%	36
Community Memorial Hospital	Menomonee Fls	100%	27
Appleton Medical Center	Appleton	97%	32
Meriter Hospital[2]	Madison	96%	47
Aurora St Lukes Medical Center	Milwaukee	95%	93
Gundersen Luth Medical Center	La Crosse	94%	33
Saint Mary's Hospital	Madison	92%	40
Mercy Health Sys Corp	Janesville	91%	32
Waukesha Memorial Hospital[2]	Waukesha	91%	35
Wheaton Franciscan Healthcare - All Saints	Racine	91%	46
Saint Marys Hospital Medical Center	Green Bay	90%	30
Saint Vincent Hospital	Green Bay	90%	29
Saint Agnes Hospital	Fond Du Lac	88%	34
United Hospital System	Kenosha	83%	35
Wheaton Franciscan - St Joseph	Milwaukee	83%	48
Columbia St Mary's Hospital Ozaukee	Mequon	76%	49

7. Smoking Cessation Advice

Hospital Name	City	Rate	Cases
Aspirus Wausau Hospital[2]	Wausau	100%	80
Aurora St Lukes Medical Center	Milwaukee	100%	328
Bellin Memorial Hospital	Green Bay	100%	115
Community Memorial Hospital	Menomonee Fls	100%	26
Franciscan Skemp La Crosse Hospital	La Crosse	100%	40
Gundersen Luth Medical Center	La Crosse	100%	110
Luther Hospital Mayo Health System	Eau Claire	100%	83
Madison VA Medical Center	Madison	100%	27
Meriter Hospital[2]	Madison	100%	68
Sacred Heart Hospital	Eau Claire	100%	66
Saint Agnes Hospital	Fond Du Lac	100%	51
Saint Clare's Hospital of Weston	Weston	100%	84
Saint Elizabeth Hospital	Appleton	100%	51
Saint Josephs Hospital	Marshfield	100%	93
Saint Mary's Hospital	Madison	100%	127
Saint Marys Hospital Medical Center	Green Bay	100%	31
Theda Clark Medical Center	Neenah	100%	26
United Hospital System	Kenosha	100%	66
Univ of Wisconsin Hosps & Clinics Auth[2]	Madison	100%	96
Waukesha Memorial Hospital[2]	Waukesha	100%	46
Wheaton Franciscan Healthcare - All Saints	Racine	100%	68
Aurora Baycare Medical Center	Green Bay	98%	46
Columbia St Mary's Hospital Ozaukee	Mequon	98%	55
Columbia St Marys Hosp Milwaukee	Milwaukee	98%	43
Saint Vincent Hospital	Green Bay	98%	57
Appleton Medical Center	Appleton	97%	108
Wheaton Franciscan - St Joseph	Milwaukee	97%	78
Wheaton Franciscan Healthcare - St Francis	Milwaukee	96%	27
Mercy Health Sys Corp	Janesville	94%	69
Froedtert Memorial Lutheran Hospital	Milwaukee	92%	73

Chest Pain/Possible Heart Attack Care

8. Aspirin at Arrival

Hospital Name	City	Rate	Cases
Aurora Medical Center Kenosha	Kenosha	100%	71
Aurora Medical Center Manitowoc County	Two Rivers	100%	75
Bay Area Medical Center	Marinette	100%	72
Calumet Medical Center	Chilton	100%	45
Ministry St Michaels Hosp-Stevens Point	Stevens Point	100%	205
Monroe Clinic	Monroe	100%	69
Our Lady of Victory Hospital	Stanley	100%	42
Saint Nicholas Hospital	Sheboygan	100%	71
Spooner Health System	Spooner	100%	25
Watertown Regional Medical Center	Watertown	100%	66
Aurora Lakeland Medical Center	Elkhorn	99%	91
Beaver Dam Com Hospital	Beaver Dam	99%	134
Howard Young Medical Center	Woodruff	99%	135
Lakeview Medical Center	Rice Lake	99%	116
Mercy Walworth Hospital & Medical Center	Lake Geneva	99%	146
Aurora Sheboygan Memorial Medical Center	Sheboygan	98%	99
Berlin Memorial Hospital	Berlin	98%	81
Memorial Health Center	Medford	98%	86
Ministry St Marys Hospital	Rhinelander	98%	117
Prairie Du Chien Memorial Hospital[3]	Prairie Du Chien	98%	40
Saint Clare Hospital Health Svcs	Baraboo	98%	63
Shawano Medical Center	Shawano	98%	83
Aurora West Allis Medical Center	West Allis	97%	144
Saint Josephs Hospital	Chippewa Falls	97%	133
Beloit Memorial Hospital	Beloit	96%	49
Fort Healthcare	Fort Atkinson	96%	124
Reedsburg Area Medical Center	Reedsburg	96%	46
Riverview Hospital Assoc	Wisc. Rapids	96%	206
Southwest Health Center	Platteville	96%	46
Divine Savior Healthcare	Portage	95%	99
Mile Bluff Medical Center	Mauston	95%	79
Aurora Medical Center - Washington County	Hartford	94%	98
Grant Regional Health Center	Lancaster	94%	32
Wheaton Franciscan Healthcare-Elmbrook	Brookfield	94%	49
Moundview Memorial Hospital and Clinics[3]	Friendship	93%	29
River Falls Area Hospital	River Falls	93%	27
Wheaton Franciscan Healthcare - Franklin	Franklin	93%	54
Sauk Prairie Memorial Hospital	Prairie Du Sac	92%	63
Aurora Memorial Hospital Burlington	Burlington	90%	40
Black River Memorial Hospital	Black River Falls	90%	77
St Josephs Community Hosp West Bend	West Bend	88%	132

9. Median Time to ECG (minutes)

Hospital Name	City	Min.	Cases
Aurora Memorial Hospital Burlington	Burlington	0	41
Berlin Memorial Hospital	Berlin	0	81
Mile Bluff Medical Center	Mauston	0	80
Bay Area Medical Center	Marinette	1	75
Saint Clare Hospital Health Svcs	Baraboo	3	63
Shawano Medical Center	Shawano	3	89
Black River Memorial Hospital	Black River Falls	4	86
Lakeview Medical Center	Rice Lake	4	118

NOTE: Hospital profiles are in alphabetical order by state, then city, then hospital within the city; Rankings exclude hospitals with less than 25 cases except for patient surveys which excludes hospitals with less than 100 cases; (a) 100–299 cases; (1) The number of cases is too small to be sure how well a hospital is performing; (2) The hospital indicated that the data submitted for this measure were based on a sample of cases; (3) Data was collected during a shorter time period (fewer quarters) than the maximum possible time for this measure; (4) Suppressed for one or more quarters by CMS; (5) No data is available from the hospital for this measure; (6) Fewer than 100 patients completed the HCAHPS survey. Use these rates with caution, as the number of surveys may be too low to reliably assess hospital performance; (7) Survey results are based on less than 12 months of data; (8) Survey results are not available for this reporting period; (9) No or very few patients were eligible for the HCAHPS survey. The scores shown, if any, reflect a very small number of surveys; (10) A state average was not calculated because too few hospitals in the state submitted data; (11) There were discrepancies in the data collection process; Please refer to the User's Guide for a full explanation of data.

Memorial Health Center	Medford	4	88
Reedsburg Area Medical Center	Reedsburg	4	48
Calumet Medical Center	Chilton	5	47
Ministry St Marys Hospital	Rhinelander	5	126
Monroe Clinic	Monroe	5	70
Our Lady of Victory Hospital	Stanley	5	43
Prairie Du Chien Memorial Hospital[3]	Prairie Du Chien	5	39
Aurora Lakeland Medical Center	Elkhorn	6	93
Aurora Medical Center Kenosha	Kenosha	6	73
Aurora Sheboygan Memorial Medical Center	Sheboygan	6	99
Mercy Walworth Hospital & Medical Center	Lake Geneva	6	151
Wheaton Franciscan Healthcare-Elmbrook	Brookfield	6	50
Wheaton Franciscan Healthcare - Franklin	Franklin	6	59
Fort Healthcare	Fort Atkinson	7	127
Howard Young Medical Center	Woodruff	7	135
Saint Nicholas Hospital	Sheboygan	7	73
Beaver Dam Com Hospital	Beaver Dam	8	138
Grant Regional Health Center	Lancaster	8	32
Saint Josephs Hospital	Chippewa Falls	8	138
River Falls Area Hospital	River Falls	9	29
St Josephs Community Hosp West Bend	West Bend	9	133
Watertown Regional Medical Center	Watertown	9	67
Aurora Medical Center - Washington County	Hartford	10	103
Aurora Medical Center Manitowoc County	Two Rivers	10	77
Divine Savior Healthcare	Portage	10	103
Ministry St Michaels Hosp-Stevens Point	Stevens Point	10	214
Sauk Prairie Memorial Hospital	Prairie Du Sac	10	67
Wheaton Franciscan - St Joseph	Milwaukee	10	25
Aurora West Allis Medical Center	West Allis	12	148
Beloit Memorial Hospital	Beloit	12	51
Moundview Memorial Hospital and Clinics[3]	Friendship	12	31
Riverview Hospital Assoc	Wisc. Rapids	12	214
Southwest Health Center	Platteville	12	46
Spooner Health System	Spooner	24	27

10. Median Time to Transfer (minutes)

Hospital Name	City	Min.	Cases
Ministry St Michaels Hosp-Stevens Point	Stevens Point	27	27
Aurora Sheboygan Memorial Medical Center	Sheboygan	44	29

Heart Failure Care

12. ACE Inhibitor or ARB for LVSD

Hospital Name	City	Rate	Cases
Aurora West Allis Medical Center	West Allis	100%	34
Community Memorial Hospital	Menomonee Fls	100%	71
Holy Family Memorial	Manitowoc	100%	25
Ministry St Michaels Hosp-Stevens Point	Stevens Point	100%	31
Saint Clare's Hospital of Weston	Weston	100%	31
Saint Elizabeth Hospital	Appleton	100%	32
Saint Josephs Hospital	Marshfield	100%	104
Wheaton Franciscan Healthcare - All Saints	Racine	99%	155
Aurora St Lukes Medical Center	Milwaukee	98%	545
Luther Hospital Mayo Health System	Eau Claire	98%	49
Saint Agnes Hospital	Fond Du Lac	98%	54
Univ of Wisconsin Hosps & Clinics Auth[2]	Madison	98%	90
Aurora Sheboygan Memorial Medical Center	Sheboygan	97%	30
Franciscan Skemp La Crosse Hospital	La Crosse	97%	36
Froedtert Memorial Lutheran Hospital[2]	Milwaukee	97%	119
Madison VA Medical Center	Madison	97%	39
Saint Marys Hospital Medical Center	Green Bay	97%	29
Saint Nicholas Hospital	Sheboygan	97%	33
Waukesha Memorial Hospital[2]	Waukesha	97%	75
Columbia St Marys Hosp Milwaukee	Milwaukee	96%	139
Gundersen Luth Medical Center	La Crosse	96%	47
Mercy Health Sys Corp[2]	Janesville	96%	56
Milwaukee VA Medical Center	Milwaukee	96%	84
Wheaton Franciscan - St Joseph	Milwaukee	96%	233
Aurora Medical Center Kenosha	Kenosha	95%	39
Sacred Heart Hospital	Eau Claire	95%	42
Wheaton Franciscan Healthcare - St Francis	Milwaukee	95%	73
Columbia St Mary's Hospital Ozaukee	Mequon	94%	82
United Hospital System	Kenosha	94%	141
Appleton Medical Center	Appleton	93%	58
Saint Mary's Hospital	Madison	93%	122
Aspirus Wausau Hospital[2]	Wausau	92%	51
Aurora Baycare Medical Center	Green Bay	92%	36
Meriter Hospital	Madison	92%	99
Mercy Medical Center of Oshkosh	Oshkosh	90%	40
Bellin Memorial Hospital	Green Bay	89%	57
Beloit Memorial Hospital	Beloit	88%	52
Saint Vincent Hospital	Green Bay	88%	43
Wheaton Franciscan Healthcare-Elmbrook	Brookfield	87%	31
Bay Area Medical Center	Marinette	85%	41
St Josephs Community Hosp West Bend	West Bend	81%	27
Memorial Medical Center	Ashland	60%	25

13. Discharge Instructions

Hospital Name	City	Rate	Cases
Gundersen Luth Medical Center	La Crosse	100%	119
Ministry St Marys Hospital	Rhinelander	100%	63
Monroe Clinic	Monroe	100%	59
Aurora Memorial Hospital Burlington	Burlington	99%	72
Saint Clare's Hospital of Weston	Weston	99%	111
Aurora Sheboygan Memorial Medical Center	Sheboygan	97%	78
Community Memorial Hospital	Oconto Falls	97%	37
Holy Family Memorial	Manitowoc	97%	59
Lakeview Medical Center	Rice Lake	97%	59
Milwaukee VA Medical Center	Milwaukee	97%	215
Madison VA Medical Center	Madison	96%	136
Luther Hospital Mayo Health System	Eau Claire	95%	192
Mercy Health Sys Corp[2]	Janesville	95%	169
Saint Clare Hospital Health Svcs	Baraboo	95%	40
Aurora Medical Center - Washington County	Hartford	94%	49
Meriter Hospital	Madison	94%	239
Sacred Heart Hospital	Eau Claire	93%	105
Saint Elizabeth Hospital	Appleton	93%	134
Saint Marys Hospital Medical Center	Green Bay	93%	97
Appleton Medical Center	Appleton	92%	168
Aurora Medical Center Manitowoc County	Two Rivers	92%	26
Bellin Memorial Hospital	Green Bay	92%	165
Langlade Hospital	Antigo	92%	25
Theda Clark Medical Center	Neenah	92%	72
St Josephs Community Hosp West Bend	West Bend	91%	57
Saint Mary's Hospital	Madison	91%	341
Aurora St Lukes Medical Center	Milwaukee	90%	1201
Saint Josephs Hospital	Marshfield	90%	298
Aurora West Allis Medical Center	West Allis	89%	114
Bay Area Medical Center	Marinette	89%	116
Mercy Medical Center of Oshkosh	Oshkosh	88%	77
Saint Vincent Hospital	Green Bay	87%	132
Wheaton Franciscan Healthcare - All Saints	Racine	87%	382
Waukesha Memorial Hospital[2]	Waukesha	86%	221
Ministry St Michaels Hosp-Stevens Point	Stevens Point	85%	67
Riverview Hospital Assoc	Wisc. Rapids	85%	71
Beloit Memorial Hospital	Beloit	84%	148
Burnett Medical Center	Grantsburg	84%	25
Memorial Medical Center	Ashland	84%	49
Saint Josephs Hospital	Chippewa Falls	84%	37
United Hospital System	Kenosha	84%	254
Wheaton Franciscan Healthcare - St Francis	Milwaukee	84%	144
Aurora Medical Center Oshkosh	Oshkosh	83%	52
Wheaton Franciscan - St Joseph	Milwaukee	83%	450
Aurora Medical Center Kenosha	Kenosha	82%	73
Saint Agnes Hospital	Fond Du Lac	82%	99
Saint Croix Regional Medical Center	Saint Croix Falls	82%	50
Saint Nicholas Hospital	Sheboygan	81%	43
Aspirus Wausau Hospital[2]	Wausau	80%	205
Community Memorial Hospital	Menomonee Fls	80%	152
Columbia St Marys Hosp Milwaukee	Milwaukee	78%	264
Door County Memorial Hospital	Sturgeon Bay	78%	65
Aurora Baycare Medical Center	Green Bay	77%	82
Univ of Wisconsin Hosps & Clinics Auth[2]	Madison	77%	231
Red Cedar Med Ctr-Mayo Health System	Menomonie	76%	51
Columbia St Mary's Hospital Ozaukee	Mequon	75%	163
Froedtert Memorial Lutheran Hospital[2]	Milwaukee	75%	255
Wheaton Franciscan Healthcare-Elmbrook	Brookfield	74%	76
Reedsburg Area Medical Center	Reedsburg	73%	45
Richland Hospital	Richland Center	73%	30
Aurora Lakeland Medical Center	Elkhorn	72%	50
Oconomowoc Memorial Hospital	Oconomowoc	72%	58
Howard Young Medical Center	Woodruff	67%	57
Franciscan Skemp La Crosse Hospital	La Crosse	64%	83
Fort Healthcare	Fort Atkinson	63%	54
Shawano Medical Center	Shawano	62%	39
Mile Bluff Medical Center	Mauston	61%	33
Beaver Dam Com Hospital	Beaver Dam	60%	48
Watertown Regional Medical Center	Watertown	60%	43
Westfields Hospital	New Richmond	59%	29
Divine Savior Healthcare	Portage	42%	48

14. Evaluation of LVS Function

Hospital Name	City	Rate	Cases
Aspirus Wausau Hospital[2]	Wausau	100%	238
Aurora Baycare Medical Center	Green Bay	100%	107
Aurora Lakeland Medical Center	Elkhorn	100%	55
Aurora Medical Center Oshkosh	Oshkosh	100%	66
Aurora Memorial Hospital Burlington	Burlington	100%	87
Aurora Sheboygan Memorial Medical Center	Sheboygan	100%	101
Aurora St Lukes Medical Center	Milwaukee	100%	1435
Aurora West Allis Medical Center	West Allis	100%	187
Bellin Memorial Hospital	Green Bay	100%	202
Beloit Memorial Hospital	Beloit	100%	194
Door County Memorial Hospital	Sturgeon Bay	100%	74
Good Samaritan Health Center	Merrill	100%	25
Holy Family Memorial	Manitowoc	100%	101
Langlade Hospital	Antigo	100%	28
Luther Hospital Mayo Health System	Eau Claire	100%	264
Luther Midelfort-Northland Mayo Hlth Sys	Barron	100%	27
Madison VA Medical Center	Madison	100%	147
Mercy Medical Center of Oshkosh	Oshkosh	100%	110
Meriter Hospital	Madison	100%	302
Milwaukee VA Medical Center	Milwaukee	100%	218
Ministry Eagle River Memorial Hospital	Eagle River	100%	28
Ministry St Marys Hospital	Rhinelander	100%	90
Ministry St Michaels Hosp-Stevens Point	Stevens Point	100%	117
Monroe Clinic	Monroe	100%	77
Oconomowoc Memorial Hospital	Oconomowoc	100%	82
Our Lady of Victory Hospital	Stanley	100%	25
Riverview Hospital Assoc	Wisc. Rapids	100%	102
Sacred Heart Hospital	Eau Claire	100%	139
Saint Agnes Hospital	Fond Du Lac	100%	143
Saint Clare Hospital Health Svcs	Baraboo	100%	52
Saint Elizabeth Hospital	Appleton	100%	174
Saint Josephs Hospital	Marshfield	100%	392
Tomah Memorial Hospital	Tomah	100%	25
Watertown Regional Medical Center	Watertown	100%	54
Wheaton Franciscan Healthcare - All Saints	Racine	100%	491
Community Memorial Hospital	Menomonee Fls	99%	204
Franciscan Skemp La Crosse Hospital	La Crosse	99%	126
Froedtert Memorial Lutheran Hospital[2]	Milwaukee	99%	300
Gundersen Luth Medical Center	La Crosse	99%	153
Lakeview Medical Center	Rice Lake	99%	72
Saint Clare's Hospital of Weston	Weston	99%	144
St Josephs Community Hosp West Bend	West Bend	99%	80
Saint Nicholas Hospital	Sheboygan	99%	68
United Hospital System	Kenosha	99%	320
Univ of Wisconsin Hosps & Clinics Auth[2]	Madison	99%	264
Wheaton Franciscan - St Joseph	Milwaukee	99%	524
Wheaton Franciscan Healthcare-Elmbrook	Brookfield	99%	116
Wheaton Franciscan Healthcare - St Francis	Milwaukee	99%	189
Appleton Medical Center	Appleton	98%	211
Aurora Medical Center Kenosha	Kenosha	98%	90
Howard Young Medical Center	Woodruff	98%	62
Saint Josephs Hospital	Chippewa Falls	98%	55
Saint Mary's Hospital	Madison	98%	465
Waukesha Memorial Hospital[2]	Waukesha	98%	286
Aurora Medical Center - Washington County	Hartford	97%	71
Aurora Medical Center Manitowoc County	Two Rivers	97%	38
Columbia St Marys Hosp Milwaukee	Milwaukee	97%	332
Red Cedar Med Ctr-Mayo Health System	Menomonie	97%	79
Saint Marys Hospital Medical Center	Green Bay	97%	130
Saint Vincent Hospital	Green Bay	97%	161
Sauk Prairie Memorial Hospital	Prairie Du Sac	97%	30
Bay Area Medical Center	Marinette	96%	164
Mercy Health Sys Corp[2]	Janesville	96%	205
Mile Bluff Medical Center	Mauston	96%	46
Columbia St Mary's Hospital Ozaukee	Mequon	95%	247
Fort Healthcare	Fort Atkinson	95%	79
Ripon Medical Center	Ripon	94%	33
Stoughton Hospital	Stoughton	93%	30
Theda Clark Medical Center	Neenah	93%	107
Vernon Memorial Hospital	Viroqua	93%	27
Wild Rose Com Memorial Hospital	Wild Rose	93%	28
Reedsburg Area Medical Center	Reedsburg	91%	57
Shawano Medical Center	Shawano	90%	58
Southwest Health Center	Platteville	90%	31
Upland Hills Health	Dodgeville	89%	28
Prairie Du Chien Memorial Hospital	Prairie Du Chien	88%	33
Waupun Memorial Hospital	Waupun	88%	26
Beaver Dam Com Hospital	Beaver Dam	87%	69
Columbus Community Hospital	Columbus	87%	31
Berlin Memorial Hospital	Berlin	84%	44
Burnett Medical Center	Grantsburg	84%	31
Memorial Medical Center	Ashland	84%	63
Community Memorial Hospital	Oconto Falls	79%	47
Divine Savior Healthcare	Portage	78%	60
Westfields Hospital	New Richmond	78%	37
Richland Hospital	Richland Center	68%	37
Saint Croix Regional Medical Center	Saint Croix Falls	67%	61
Amery Regional Medical Center	Amery	48%	31

15. Smoking Cessation Advice

Hospital Name	City	Rate	Cases
Aspirus Wausau Hospital[2]	Wausau	100%	27
Aurora Medical Center Kenosha	Kenosha	100%	27
Aurora St Lukes Medical Center	Milwaukee	100%	288
Beloit Memorial Hospital	Beloit	100%	32
Madison VA Medical Center	Madison	100%	44
Mercy Health Sys Corp[2]	Janesville	100%	35
Milwaukee VA Medical Center	Milwaukee	100%	47
Saint Mary's Hospital	Madison	100%	55
United Hospital System	Kenosha	100%	51
Univ of Wisconsin Hosps & Clinics Auth[2]	Madison	100%	47
Waukesha Memorial Hospital[2]	Waukesha	100%	25
Wheaton Franciscan - St Joseph	Milwaukee	100%	203
Wheaton Franciscan Healthcare - All Saints	Racine	100%	120

NOTE: Hospital profiles are in alphabetical order by state, then city, then hospital within the city; Rankings exclude hospitals with less than 25 cases except for patient surveys which excludes hospitals with less than 100 cases; (a) 100–299 cases; (1) The number of cases is too small to be sure how well a hospital is performing; (2) The hospital indicated that the data submitted for this measure were based on a sample of cases; (3) Data was collected during a shorter time period (fewer quarters) than the maximum possible time for this measure; (4) Suppressed for one or more quarters by CMS; (5) No data is available from the hospital for this measure; (6) Fewer than 100 patients completed the HCAHPS survey. Use these rates with caution, as the number of surveys may be too low to reliably assess hospital performance; (7) Survey results are based on less than 12 months of data; (8) Survey results are not available for this reporting period; (9) No or very few patients were eligible for the HCAHPS survey. The scores shown, if any, reflect a very small number of surveys; (10) A state average was not calculated because too few hospitals in the state submitted data; (11) There were discrepancies in the data collection process; Please refer to the User's Guide for a full explanation of data.

Wheaton Franciscan Healthcare - St Francis	Milwaukee	100%	28
Community Memorial Hospital	Menomonee Fls	97%	29
Saint Josephs Hospital	Marshfield	97%	32
Saint Clare's Hospital of Weston	Weston	96%	27
Meriter Hospital	Madison	95%	38
Columbia St Marys Hosp Milwaukee	Milwaukee	91%	65
Froedtert Memorial Lutheran Hospital[2]	Milwaukee	88%	76

Pneumonia Care

16. Appropriate Initial Antibiotic

Hospital Name	City	Rate	Cases
Langlade Hospital	Antigo	100%	37
Madison VA Medical Center	Madison	100%	43
Ministry St Marys Hospital	Rhinelander	100%	73
Monroe Clinic	Monroe	100%	73
Red Cedar Med Ctr-Mayo Health System	Menomonie	100%	42
Wheaton Franciscan - St Joseph	Milwaukee	100%	138
Aurora Lakeland Medical Center	Elkhorn	99%	79
Froedtert Memorial Lutheran Hospital[2]	Milwaukee	99%	80
Aurora Medical Center Oshkosh	Oshkosh	98%	54
Beaver Dam Com Hospital	Beaver Dam	98%	59
Lakeview Medical Center	Rice Lake	98%	44
Saint Agnes Hospital[2]	Fond Du Lac	98%	90
Saint Mary's Hospital	Madison	98%	165
Watertown Regional Medical Center	Watertown	98%	56
Waukesha Memorial Hospital[2]	Waukesha	98%	83
Wheaton Franciscan Healthcare - All Saints	Racine	98%	129
Aurora Medical Center Kenosha	Kenosha	97%	103
Memorial Hospital Lafayette County	Darlington	97%	29
Milwaukee VA Medical Center	Milwaukee	97%	69
Ministry St Michaels Hosp-Stevens Point	Stevens Point	97%	109
Oconomowoc Memorial Hospital	Oconomowoc	97%	59
Saint Clare Hospital Health Svcs	Baraboo	97%	69
Saint Clare's Hospital of Weston	Weston	97%	36
Saint Elizabeth Hospital	Appleton	97%	95
Waupun Memorial Hospital	Waupun	97%	32
Wheaton Franciscan Healthcare-Elmbrook	Brookfield	97%	65
Wheaton Franciscan Healthcare - St Francis	Milwaukee	97%	99
Aurora West Allis Medical Center	West Allis	96%	137
Holy Family Memorial	Manitowoc	96%	54
Mercy Medical Center of Oshkosh	Oshkosh	96%	49
Stoughton Hospital	Stoughton	96%	26
Wheaton Franciscan Healthcare - Franklin	Franklin	96%	27
Appleton Medical Center	Appleton	95%	123
Aspirus Wausau Hospital[2]	Wausau	95%	66
Aurora Memorial Hospital Burlington	Burlington	95%	78
Aurora St Lukes Medical Center	Milwaukee	95%	488
Bellin Memorial Hospital	Green Bay	95%	81
Community Memorial Hospital	Menomonee Fls	95%	127
Divine Savior Healthcare	Portage	95%	55
Luther Hospital Mayo Health System	Eau Claire	95%	108
Reedsburg Area Medical Center	Reedsburg	95%	65
Saint Nicholas Hospital	Sheboygan	95%	76
Aurora Medical Center Manitowoc County	Two Rivers	94%	36
Bay Area Medical Center	Marinette	94%	80
Black River Memorial Hospital	Black River Falls	94%	31
Door County Memorial Hospital	Sturgeon Bay	94%	49
Saint Croix Regional Medical Center	Saint Croix Falls	94%	48
Saint Marys Hospital Medical Center	Green Bay	94%	66
Aurora Baycare Medical Center	Green Bay	93%	46
Aurora Sheboygan Memorial Medical Center	Sheboygan	93%	41
Fort Healthcare	Fort Atkinson	93%	45
Memorial Medical Center	Ashland	93%	73
Saint Josephs Hospital	Marshfield	93%	103
Sauk Prairie Memorial Hospital	Prairie Du Sac	93%	27
United Hospital System[2]	Kenosha	93%	102
Baldwin Area Medical Center	Baldwin	92%	38
Franciscan Skemp La Crosse Hospital[2]	La Crosse	92%	80
Howard Young Medical Center	Woodruff	92%	62
Mercy Health Sys Corp[2]	Janesville	92%	119
New London Family Medical Center	New London	92%	25
Riverview Hospital Assoc	Wisc. Rapids	91%	54
Saint Josephs Hospital	Chippewa Falls	91%	45
Shawano Medical Center	Shawano	91%	65
Beloit Memorial Hospital	Beloit	90%	59
Columbia St Marys Hosp Milwaukee	Milwaukee	90%	154
Gundersen Luth Medical Center	La Crosse	90%	89
Memorial Health Center	Medford	90%	30
Meriter Hospital	Madison	90%	115
Prairie Du Chien Memorial Hospital	Prairie Du Chien	90%	40
Saint Vincent Hospital	Green Bay	90%	69
Sacred Heart Hospital	Eau Claire	89%	74
St Josephs Community Hosp West Bend	West Bend	89%	81
Theda Clark Medical Center	Neenah	89%	56
Univ of Wisconsin Hosps & Clinics Auth[2]	Madison	89%	37
Westfields Hospital	New Richmond	89%	28
Aurora Medical Center - Washington County	Hartford	87%	38
Columbia St Mary's Hospital Ozaukee	Mequon	85%	121
Riverside Medical Center	Waupaca	85%	33
Southwest Health Center	Platteville	84%	45
Vernon Memorial Hospital	Viroqua	79%	63
Columbus Community Hospital	Columbus	78%	45
Cumberland Memorial Hospital	Cumberland	76%	33

17. Blood Culture Timing

Hospital Name	City	Rate	Cases
Aurora Medical Center Oshkosh	Oshkosh	100%	73
Aurora Sheboygan Memorial Medical Center	Sheboygan	100%	55
Aurora West Allis Medical Center	West Allis	100%	220
Bellin Memorial Hospital	Green Bay	100%	104
Calumet Medical Center[2]	Chilton	100%	33
Good Samaritan Health Center	Merrill	100%	41
Lakeview Medical Center	Rice Lake	100%	60
Mercy Medical Center of Oshkosh	Oshkosh	100%	71
Milwaukee VA Medical Center	Milwaukee	100%	77
Monroe Clinic	Monroe	100%	133
Oconomowoc Memorial Hospital	Oconomowoc	100%	94
Red Cedar Med Ctr-Mayo Health System	Menomonie	100%	37
Ripon Medical Center	Ripon	100%	31
Saint Clare's Hospital of Weston	Weston	100%	63
Stoughton Hospital	Stoughton	100%	49
Tomah Memorial Hospital	Tomah	100%	35
Wheaton Franciscan Healthcare-Elmbrook	Brookfield	100%	91
Aurora Lakeland Medical Center	Elkhorn	99%	73
Aurora St Lukes Medical Center	Milwaukee	99%	752
Luther Hospital Mayo Health System	Eau Claire	99%	159
Ministry St Marys Hospital	Rhinelander	99%	88
Saint Elizabeth Hospital	Appleton	99%	158
Saint Nicholas Hospital	Sheboygan	99%	92
Shawano Medical Center	Shawano	99%	77
Watertown Regional Medical Center	Watertown	99%	95
Waukesha Memorial Hospital[2]	Waukesha	99%	158
Wheaton Franciscan Healthcare - All Saints	Racine	99%	343
Aurora Baycare Medical Center	Green Bay	98%	59
Aurora Medical Center Kenosha	Kenosha	98%	129
Aurora Medical Center Manitowoc County	Two Rivers	98%	44
Aurora Memorial Hospital Burlington	Burlington	98%	121
Columbia St Mary's Hospital Ozaukee	Mequon	98%	180
Community Memorial Hospital	Menomonee Fls	98%	197
Door County Memorial Hospital	Sturgeon Bay	98%	58
Fort Healthcare	Fort Atkinson	98%	65
Madison VA Medical Center	Madison	98%	81
Memorial Health Center	Medford	98%	42
Mercy Health Sys Corp[2]	Janesville	98%	185
Ministry St Michaels Hosp-Stevens Point	Stevens Point	98%	166
Reedsburg Area Medical Center	Reedsburg	98%	40
Saint Agnes Hospital[2]	Fond Du Lac	98%	129
Saint Josephs Hospital	Chippewa Falls	98%	51
Saint Vincent Hospital	Green Bay	98%	115
Theda Clark Medical Center	Neenah	98%	64
Wheaton Franciscan - St Joseph	Milwaukee	98%	291
Flambeau Hospital[2]	Park Falls	97%	32
Franciscan Skemp La Crosse Hospital[2]	La Crosse	97%	110
Hayward Area Memorial Hospital[3]	Hayward	97%	29
Langlade Hospital	Antigo	97%	33
Memorial Medical Center	Ashland	97%	79
Mile Bluff Medical Center	Mauston	97%	37
Sacred Heart Hospital	Eau Claire	97%	120
Saint Mary's Hospital	Madison	97%	254
Tri County Memorial Hospital	Whitehall	97%	30
Waupun Memorial Hospital	Waupun	97%	33
Wheaton Franciscan Healthcare - Franklin	Franklin	97%	35
Wheaton Franciscan Healthcare - St Francis	Milwaukee	97%	170
Appleton Medical Center	Appleton	96%	178
Bay Area Medical Center	Marinette	96%	114
Columbia St Marys Hosp Milwaukee	Milwaukee	96%	225
Franciscan Skemp Sparta Hospital	Sparta	96%	26
Holy Family Memorial	Manitowoc	96%	78
Howard Young Medical Center	Woodruff	96%	72
St Josephs Community Hosp West Bend	West Bend	96%	126
Saint Marys Hospital Medical Center	Green Bay	96%	114
Univ of Wisconsin Hosps & Clinics Auth[2]	Madison	96%	83
Aspirus Wausau Hospital[2]	Wausau	95%	102
Beaver Dam Com Hospital	Beaver Dam	95%	66
Southwest Health Center	Platteville	95%	38
Beloit Memorial Hospital	Beloit	94%	50
Froedtert Memorial Lutheran Hospital[2]	Milwaukee	94%	151
Meriter Hospital	Madison	94%	166
Prairie Du Chien Memorial Hospital	Prairie Du Chien	94%	49
Gundersen Luth Medical Center	La Crosse	92%	121
Saint Croix Regional Medical Center	Saint Croix Falls	92%	60
Aurora Medical Center - Washington County	Hartford	91%	55
Riverview Hospital Assoc	Wisc. Rapids	91%	78
Upland Hills Health	Dodgeville	91%	46
Divine Savior Healthcare	Portage	90%	52
United Hospital System[2]	Kenosha	90%	165
Berlin Memorial Hospital	Berlin	89%	44
Riverside Medical Center	Waupaca	89%	71
Saint Clare Hospital Health Svcs	Baraboo	89%	96
Luther Midelfort-Northland Mayo Hlth Sys	Barron	88%	25
Columbus Community Hospital	Columbus	86%	43
Saint Josephs Hospital	Marshfield	86%	72
Richland Hospital	Richland Center	85%	26

18. Influenza Vaccine

Hospital Name	City	Rate	Cases
Aurora Memorial Hospital Burlington	Burlington	100%	85
Holy Family Memorial	Manitowoc	100%	53
Langlade Hospital	Antigo	100%	26
Madison VA Medical Center	Madison	100%	57
Milwaukee VA Medical Center	Milwaukee	100%	67
Reedsburg Area Medical Center	Reedsburg	100%	43
Stoughton Hospital	Stoughton	100%	32
Tomah Memorial Hospital	Tomah	100%	27
Vernon Memorial Hospital	Viroqua	100%	45
Waupun Memorial Hospital	Waupun	100%	29
Wheaton Franciscan Healthcare - All Saints	Racine	100%	203
Aurora West Allis Medical Center	West Allis	99%	175
Saint Agnes Hospital[2]	Fond Du Lac	99%	92
Bellin Memorial Hospital	Green Bay	98%	58
Luther Hospital Mayo Health System	Eau Claire	98%	138
Saint Josephs Hospital	Chippewa Falls	98%	40
United Hospital System[2]	Kenosha	98%	103
Aurora Medical Center Kenosha	Kenosha	97%	86
Aurora Medical Center Manitowoc County	Two Rivers	97%	33
Ministry St Michaels Hosp-Stevens Point	Stevens Point	97%	121
Monroe Clinic	Monroe	97%	92
Oconomowoc Memorial Hospital	Oconomowoc	97%	63
Sacred Heart Hospital	Eau Claire	97%	88
Saint Mary's Hospital	Madison	97%	274
Univ of Wisconsin Hosps & Clinics Auth[2]	Madison	97%	74
Waukesha Memorial Hospital[2]	Waukesha	97%	97
Fort Healthcare	Fort Atkinson	96%	51
Franciscan Skemp La Crosse Hospital[2]	La Crosse	96%	120
Mercy Medical Center of Oshkosh	Oshkosh	96%	75
Saint Elizabeth Hospital	Appleton	96%	123
Watertown Regional Medical Center	Watertown	96%	48
Aurora Lakeland Medical Center	Elkhorn	95%	57
Aurora St Lukes Medical Center	Milwaukee	95%	520
Aurora Medical Center - Washington County	Hartford	94%	33
Columbia St Marys Hosp Milwaukee	Milwaukee	94%	144
Froedtert Memorial Lutheran Hospital[2]	Milwaukee	94%	105
Mercy Health Sys Corp	Janesville	94%	139
Riverside Medical Center	Waupaca	94%	35
Saint Josephs Hospital	Marshfield	94%	143
Saint Marys Hospital Medical Center	Green Bay	94%	54
Saint Nicholas Hospital	Sheboygan	94%	80
Aspirus Wausau Hospital[2]	Wausau	93%	85
Aurora Medical Center Oshkosh	Oshkosh	93%	54
Aurora Sheboygan Memorial Medical Center	Sheboygan	93%	59
Lakeview Medical Center	Rice Lake	93%	46
Ministry St Marys Hospital	Rhinelander	93%	61
Riverview Hospital Assoc	Wisc. Rapids	93%	42
Wheaton Franciscan Healthcare-Elmbrook	Brookfield	93%	68
Wheaton Franciscan Healthcare - St Francis	Milwaukee	93%	123
Columbia St Mary's Hospital Ozaukee	Mequon	92%	113
Saint Vincent Hospital	Green Bay	92%	88
Wheaton Franciscan - St Joseph	Milwaukee	92%	130
Upland Hills Health	Dodgeville	91%	32
Beloit Memorial Hospital	Beloit	90%	63
Door County Memorial Hospital	Sturgeon Bay	90%	42
Meriter Hospital	Madison	90%	143
Theda Clark Medical Center	Neenah	90%	51
Community Memorial Hospital	Menomonee Fls	89%	135
Divine Savior Healthcare	Portage	88%	40
St Josephs Community Hosp West Bend	West Bend	87%	93
Baldwin Area Medical Center	Baldwin	86%	37
Howard Young Medical Center	Woodruff	86%	36
Saint Clare's Hospital of Weston	Weston	86%	44
Southwest Health Center	Platteville	85%	33
Appleton Medical Center	Appleton	84%	146
Saint Clare Hospital Health Svcs	Baraboo	84%	61
Beaver Dam Com Hospital	Beaver Dam	83%	41
Shawano Medical Center	Shawano	82%	50
Gundersen Luth Medical Center	La Crosse	81%	129
Richland Hospital	Richland Center	81%	31
Aurora Baycare Medical Center	Green Bay	79%	56
Bay Area Medical Center	Marinette	79%	89
Memorial Medical Center	Ashland	79%	48
Cumberland Memorial Hospital	Cumberland	77%	31
Prairie Du Chien Memorial Hospital	Prairie Du Chien	75%	36
Mile Bluff Medical Center	Mauston	73%	49
Saint Croix Regional Medical Center	Saint Croix Falls	70%	40
Memorial Health Center	Medford	69%	26
Amery Regional Medical Center	Amery	56%	34
Columbus Community Hospital	Columbus	43%	28

NOTE: Hospital profiles are in alphabetical order by state, then city, then hospital within the city; Rankings exclude hospitals with less than 25 cases except for patient surveys which excludes hospitals with less than 100 cases; (a) 100–299 cases; (1) The number of cases is too small to be sure how well a hospital is performing; (2) The hospital indicated that the data submitted for this measure were based on a sample of cases; (3) Data was collected during a shorter time period (fewer quarters) than the maximum possible time for this measure; (4) Suppressed for one or more quarters by CMS; (5) No data is available from the hospital for this measure; (6) Fewer than 100 patients completed the HCAHPS survey. Use these rates with caution, as the number of surveys may be too low to reliably assess hospital performance; (7) Survey results are based on less than 12 months of data; (8) Survey results are not available for this reporting period; (9) No or very few patients were eligible for the HCAHPS survey. The scores shown, if any, reflect a very small number of surveys; (10) A state average was not calculated because too few hospitals in the state submitted data; (11) There were discrepancies in the data collection process; Please refer to the User's Guide for a full explanation of data.

19. Initial Antibiotic Timing

Hospital Name	City	Rate	Cases
Aurora Medical Center Oshkosh	Oshkosh	100%	78
Aurora Memorial Hospital Burlington	Burlington	100%	124
Black River Memorial Hospital	Black River Falls	100%	37
Calumet Medical Center[2]	Chilton	100%	28
Flambeau Hospital[2]	Park Falls	100%	33
Franciscan Skemp Sparta Hospital	Sparta	100%	26
Good Samaritan Health Center	Merrill	100%	49
Gundersen Luth Medical Center	La Crosse	100%	131
Hayward Area Memorial Hospital[3]	Hayward	100%	34
Lakeview Medical Center	Rice Lake	100%	71
Langlade Hospital	Antigo	100%	42
Madison VA Medical Center	Madison	100%	67
Memorial Health Center	Medford	100%	46
Mercy Medical Center of Oshkosh	Oshkosh	100%	95
New London Family Medical Center	New London	100%	33
Our Lady of Victory Hospital[2]	Stanley	100%	30
Red Cedar Med Ctr-Mayo Health System	Menomonie	100%	51
Ripon Medical Center	Ripon	100%	32
Saint Agnes Hospital[2]	Fond Du Lac	100%	119
Saint Clare's Hospital of Weston	Weston	100%	76
Shawano Medical Center	Shawano	100%	83
Theda Clark Medical Center	Neenah	100%	74
Vernon Memorial Hospital	Viroqua	100%	66
Waupun Memorial Hospital	Waupun	100%	44
Wheaton Franciscan Healthcare - Franklin	Franklin	100%	29
Aurora Lakeland Medical Center	Elkhorn	99%	91
Aurora St Lukes Medical Center	Milwaukee	99%	894
Bay Area Medical Center	Marinette	99%	132
Beaver Dam Com Hospital	Beaver Dam	99%	76
Bellin Memorial Hospital	Green Bay	99%	103
Memorial Medical Center	Ashland	99%	78
Monroe Clinic	Monroe	99%	121
Saint Clare Hospital Health Svcs	Baraboo	99%	102
St Josephs Community Hosp West Bend	West Bend	99%	119
Saint Mary's Hospital	Madison	99%	287
Saint Marys Hospital Medical Center	Green Bay	99%	110
Waukesha Memorial Hospital[2]	Waukesha	99%	148
Wheaton Franciscan - St Joseph	Milwaukee	99%	276
Wheaton Franciscan Healthcare - All Saints	Racine	99%	285
Aurora Medical Center Kenosha	Kenosha	98%	118
Aurora West Allis Medical Center	West Allis	98%	250
Columbia St Mary's Hospital Ozaukee	Mequon	98%	196
Door County Memorial Hospital	Sturgeon Bay	98%	64
Fort Healthcare	Fort Atkinson	98%	82
Howard Young Medical Center	Woodruff	98%	82
Ministry St Michaels Hosp-Stevens Point	Stevens Point	98%	172
Saint Elizabeth Hospital	Appleton	98%	153
Saint Josephs Hospital	Marshfield	98%	144
Stoughton Hospital	Stoughton	98%	45
Watertown Regional Medical Center	Watertown	98%	101
Wheaton Franciscan Healthcare - St Francis	Milwaukee	98%	160
Aspirus Wausau Hospital[2]	Wausau	97%	113
Aurora Sheboygan Memorial Medical Center	Sheboygan	97%	77
Columbia St Marys Hosp Milwaukee	Milwaukee	97%	252
Community Memorial Hospital	Menomonee Fls	97%	213
Cumberland Memorial Hospital	Cumberland	97%	39
Holy Family Memorial	Manitowoc	97%	73
Hudson Hospital[3]	Hudson	97%	29
Memorial Hospital Lafayette County	Darlington	97%	39
Mercy Health Sys Corp[2]	Janesville	97%	185
Ministry St Marys Hospital	Rhinelander	97%	100
Oconomowoc Memorial Hospital	Oconomowoc	97%	90
Prairie Du Chien Memorial Hospital	Prairie Du Chien	97%	60
Reedsburg Area Medical Center	Reedsburg	97%	67
Sacred Heart Hospital	Eau Claire	97%	132
Saint Josephs Hospital	Chippewa Falls	97%	61
Tri County Memorial Hospital	Whitehall	97%	31
Univ of Wisconsin Hosps & Clinics Auth[2]	Madison	97%	78
Wheaton Franciscan Healthcare-Elmbrook	Brookfield	97%	92
Aurora Baycare Medical Center	Green Bay	96%	73
Froedtert Memorial Lutheran Hospital[2]	Milwaukee	96%	197
Grant Regional Health Center	Lancaster	96%	28
Meriter Hospital	Madison	96%	192
Richland Hospital	Richland Center	96%	28
Saint Croix Regional Medical Center	Saint Croix Falls	96%	68
Saint Vincent Hospital	Green Bay	96%	121
Appleton Medical Center	Appleton	95%	198
Beloit Memorial Hospital	Beloit	95%	73
Divine Savior Healthcare	Portage	95%	74
Franciscan Skemp La Crosse Hospital[2]	La Crosse	95%	110
Riverview Hospital Assoc	Wisc. Rapids	95%	78
Saint Nicholas Hospital	Sheboygan	95%	94
Southwest Health Center	Platteville	95%	58
Amery Regional Medical Center	Amery	94%	62
Aurora Medical Center Manitowoc County	Two Rivers	94%	52
Baldwin Area Medical Center	Baldwin	94%	54
Columbus Community Hospital	Columbus	94%	32
Luther Hospital Mayo Health System	Eau Claire	94%	163
Mile Bluff Medical Center	Mauston	94%	95
Tomah Memorial Hospital	Tomah	93%	29
United Hospital System[2]	Kenosha	93%	175
Upland Hills Health	Dodgeville	93%	43
Aurora Medical Center - Washington County	Hartford	90%	59
Milwaukee VA Medical Center	Milwaukee	87%	103
Berlin Memorial Hospital	Berlin	84%	50
Riverside Medical Center	Waupaca	84%	70

20. Pneumococcal Vaccine

Hospital Name	City	Rate	Cases
Aurora Memorial Hospital Burlington	Burlington	100%	112
Calumet Medical Center[2]	Chilton	100%	30
Fort Healthcare	Fort Atkinson	100%	74
Good Samaritan Health Center	Merrill	100%	29
Holy Family Memorial	Manitowoc	100%	68
Madison VA Medical Center	Madison	100%	77
Milwaukee VA Medical Center	Milwaukee	100%	67
River Falls Area Hospital	River Falls	100%	29
Vernon Memorial Hospital	Viroqua	100%	78
Waupun Memorial Hospital	Waupun	100%	47
Aurora Lakeland Medical Center	Elkhorn	99%	90
Aurora Medical Center Oshkosh	Oshkosh	99%	70
Aurora West Allis Medical Center	West Allis	99%	221
Franciscan Skemp La Crosse Hospital[2]	La Crosse	99%	160
Reedsburg Area Medical Center	Reedsburg	99%	68
Riverside Medical Center	Waupaca	99%	73
Saint Clare's Hospital of Weston	Weston	99%	82
Saint Mary's Hospital	Madison	99%	381
Watertown Regional Medical Center	Watertown	99%	88
Waukesha Memorial Hospital[2]	Waukesha	99%	146
Wheaton Franciscan Healthcare - All Saints	Racine	99%	302
Aurora St Lukes Medical Center	Milwaukee	98%	684
Langlade Hospital	Antigo	98%	41
Luther Hospital Mayo Health System	Eau Claire	98%	197
Monroe Clinic	Monroe	98%	128
Tomah Memorial Hospital	Tomah	98%	44
Flambeau Hospital[2]	Park Falls	97%	37
Hayward Area Memorial Hospital[3]	Hayward	97%	29
Lakeview Medical Center	Rice Lake	97%	78
Meriter Hospital	Madison	97%	219
Our Lady of Victory Hospital[2]	Stanley	97%	32
Sacred Heart Hospital	Eau Claire	97%	117
Saint Agnes Hospital[2]	Fond Du Lac	97%	131
Saint Elizabeth Hospital	Appleton	97%	173
Saint Josephs Hospital	Marshfield	97%	206
Stoughton Hospital	Stoughton	97%	60
United Hospital System[2]	Kenosha	97%	125
Aspirus Wausau Hospital[2]	Wausau	96%	124
Bellin Memorial Hospital	Green Bay	96%	85
Black River Memorial Hospital	Black River Falls	96%	26
Franciscan Skemp Sparta Hospital	Sparta	96%	27
Gundersen Luth Medical Center	La Crosse	96%	194
Howard Young Medical Center	Woodruff	96%	71
Ministry St Michaels Hosp-Stevens Point	Stevens Point	96%	169
Oconomowoc Memorial Hospital	Oconomowoc	96%	93
Sauk Prairie Memorial Hospital	Prairie Du Sac	96%	27
Univ of Wisconsin Hosps & Clinics Auth[2]	Madison	96%	80
Aurora Medical Center Kenosha	Kenosha	95%	103
Door County Memorial Hospital	Sturgeon Bay	95%	61
Mercy Health Sys Corp[2]	Janesville	95%	168
Wheaton Franciscan Healthcare-Elmbrook	Brookfield	95%	93
Wheaton Franciscan Healthcare - St Francis	Milwaukee	95%	174
Appleton Medical Center	Appleton	94%	183
Aurora Medical Center - Washington County	Hartford	94%	51
Aurora Medical Center Manitowoc County	Two Rivers	94%	47
Aurora Sheboygan Memorial Medical Center	Sheboygan	94%	96
Bay Area Medical Center	Marinette	94%	129
Riverview Hospital Assoc	Wisc. Rapids	94%	67
Saint Vincent Hospital	Green Bay	94%	111
Southwest Health Center	Platteville	94%	50
Theda Clark Medical Center	Neenah	94%	71
Wheaton Franciscan - St Joseph	Milwaukee	94%	176
Saint Clare Hospital Health Svcs	Baraboo	93%	86
St Josephs Community Hosp West Bend	West Bend	93%	125
Saint Josephs Hospital	Chippewa Falls	93%	61
Saint Marys Hospital Medical Center	Green Bay	93%	88
Wheaton Franciscan Healthcare - Franklin	Franklin	93%	29
Aurora Baycare Medical Center	Green Bay	92%	61
Froedtert Memorial Lutheran Hospital[2]	Milwaukee	92%	130
Saint Nicholas Hospital	Sheboygan	92%	97
Mercy Medical Center of Oshkosh	Oshkosh	91%	111
Prairie Du Chien Memorial Hospital	Prairie Du Chien	91%	66
Columbia St Marys Hosp Milwaukee	Milwaukee	90%	188
Red Cedar Med Ctr-Mayo Health System	Menomonie	90%	42
Rusk County Memorial Hospital	Ladysmith	90%	30
Community Memorial Hospital	Menomonee Fls	89%	217
Hudson Hospital[3]	Hudson	89%	27
Cumberland Memorial Hospital	Cumberland	88%	48
Ministry St Marys Hospital	Rhinelander	87%	86
Ripon Medical Center	Ripon	87%	31
New London Family Medical Center	New London	86%	36
Upland Hills Health	Dodgeville	86%	43
Beloit Memorial Hospital	Beloit	85%	86
Columbia St Mary's Hospital Ozaukee	Mequon	84%	195
Memorial Hospital Lafayette County	Darlington	84%	44
Beaver Dam Com Hospital	Beaver Dam	83%	66
Shawano Medical Center	Shawano	83%	75
Memorial Medical Center	Ashland	82%	77
Berlin Memorial Hospital	Berlin	81%	42
Baldwin Area Medical Center	Baldwin	80%	41
Divine Savior Healthcare	Portage	72%	68
Saint Croix Regional Medical Center	Saint Croix Falls	70%	69
Richland Hospital	Richland Center	68%	47
Westfields Hospital	New Richmond	67%	36
Columbus Community Hospital	Columbus	62%	50
Memorial Health Center	Medford	62%	45
Tri County Memorial Hospital	Whitehall	61%	36
Mile Bluff Medical Center	Mauston	57%	70
Grant Regional Health Center	Lancaster	56%	27
Amery Regional Medical Center	Amery	52%	58

21. Smoking Cessation Advice

Hospital Name	City	Rate	Cases
Aurora Lakeland Medical Center	Elkhorn	100%	46
Aurora Medical Center Kenosha	Kenosha	100%	51
Aurora Medical Center Oshkosh	Oshkosh	100%	25
Aurora Memorial Hospital Burlington	Burlington	100%	45
Aurora Sheboygan Memorial Medical Center	Sheboygan	100%	31
Aurora West Allis Medical Center	West Allis	100%	76
Beloit Memorial Hospital	Beloit	100%	33
Gundersen Luth Medical Center	La Crosse	100%	69
Luther Hospital Mayo Health System	Eau Claire	100%	68
Mercy Medical Center of Oshkosh	Oshkosh	100%	34
Ministry St Marys Hospital	Rhinelander	100%	30
Monroe Clinic	Monroe	100%	32
Oconomowoc Memorial Hospital	Oconomowoc	100%	25
Saint Elizabeth Hospital	Appleton	100%	49
St Josephs Community Hosp West Bend	West Bend	100%	29
Saint Mary's Hospital	Madison	100%	111
Saint Marys Hospital Medical Center	Green Bay	100%	38
Shawano Medical Center	Shawano	100%	30
Theda Clark Medical Center	Neenah	100%	30
Univ of Wisconsin Hosps & Clinics Auth[2]	Madison	100%	37
Waukesha Memorial Hospital[2]	Waukesha	100%	36
Aurora St Lukes Medical Center	Milwaukee	99%	364
Meriter Hospital	Madison	99%	72
Saint Josephs Hospital	Marshfield	99%	69
United Hospital System[2]	Kenosha	99%	82
Appleton Medical Center	Appleton	98%	52
Aspirus Wausau Hospital[2]	Wausau	98%	47
Milwaukee VA Medical Center	Milwaukee	98%	46
Bellin Memorial Hospital	Green Bay	97%	35
Ministry St Michaels Hosp-Stevens Point	Stevens Point	97%	32
Saint Agnes Hospital[2]	Fond Du Lac	97%	29
Saint Clare Hospital Health Svcs	Baraboo	97%	34
Sacred Heart Hospital	Eau Claire	96%	48
Bay Area Medical Center	Marinette	95%	41
Saint Vincent Hospital	Green Bay	95%	40
Wheaton Franciscan - St Joseph	Milwaukee	95%	162
Mercy Health Sys Corp[2]	Janesville	94%	84
Wheaton Franciscan Healthcare - All Saints	Racine	94%	105
Community Memorial Hospital	Menomonee Fls	93%	44
Franciscan Skemp La Crosse Hospital[2]	La Crosse	92%	48
Wheaton Franciscan Healthcare - St Francis	Milwaukee	92%	62
Columbia St Marys Hosp Milwaukee	Milwaukee	88%	72
Saint Nicholas Hospital	Sheboygan	87%	38
Columbia St Mary's Hospital Ozaukee	Mequon	84%	43
Froedtert Memorial Lutheran Hospital[2]	Milwaukee	75%	63

Surgical Care Improvement Project

22. Appropriate VTP Within 24 Hours

Hospital Name	City	Rate	Cases
Lakeview Medical Center[2]	Rice Lake	100%	54
Vernon Memorial Hospital	Viroqua	100%	64
Fort Healthcare[2]	Fort Atkinson	99%	118
Luther Hospital Mayo Health System	Eau Claire	99%	392
Wheaton Franciscan Healthcare - All Saints[2]	Racine	99%	208
Appleton Medical Center[2]	Appleton	98%	285
Aurora Memorial Hospital Burlington[2]	Burlington	98%	122
Milwaukee VA Medical Center[2]	Milwaukee	98%	172
Monroe Clinic[2]	Monroe	98%	91
Saint Josephs Hospital	Chippewa Falls	98%	58
Univ of Wisconsin Hosps & Clinics Auth[2]	Madison	98%	220
Aurora Medical Center Kenosha[2]	Kenosha	97%	115
Berlin Memorial Hospital[2]	Berlin	97%	39
Madison VA Medical Center[2]	Madison	97%	98
Mercy Walworth Hospital & Medical Center	Lake Geneva	97%	37
Saint Josephs Hospital	Marshfield	97%	646

NOTE: Hospital profiles are in alphabetical order by state, then city, then hospital within the city; Rankings exclude hospitals with less than 25 cases except for patient surveys which excludes hospitals with less than 100 cases; (a) 100–299 cases; (1) The number of cases is too small to be sure how well a hospital is performing; (2) The hospital indicated that the data submitted for this measure were based on a sample of cases; (3) Data was collected during a shorter time period (fewer quarters) than the maximum possible time for this measure; (4) Suppressed for one or more quarters by CMS; (5) No data is available from the hospital for this measure; (6) Fewer than 100 patients completed the HCAHPS survey. Use these rates with caution, as the number of surveys may be too low to reliably assess hospital performance; (7) Survey results are based on less than 12 months of data; (8) Survey results are not available for this reporting period; (9) No or very few patients were eligible for the HCAHPS survey. The scores shown, if any, reflect a very small number of surveys; (10) A state average was not calculated because too few hospitals in the state submitted data; (11) There were discrepancies in the data collection process; Please refer to the User's Guide for a full explanation of data.

Shawano Medical Center	Shawano	97%	31
Amery Regional Medical Center[3]	Amery	97%	27
Franciscan Skemp La Crosse Hospital	La Crosse	96%	327
Langlade Hospital	Antigo	96%	47
Meriter Hospital[2]	Madison	96%	123
Saint Agnes Hospital[2]	Fond Du Lac	96%	180
Saint Nicholas Hospital	Sheboygan	96%	126
Aurora Medical Center Oshkosh[2]	Oshkosh	95%	81
Aurora Sheboygan Memorial Medical Center[2]	Sheboygan	95%	132
Aurora St Lukes Medical Center[2]	Milwaukee	95%	597
Mercy Health Sys Corp[2]	Janesville	95%	499
Saint Mary's Hospital[2]	Madison	95%	405
United Hospital System[2]	Kenosha	95%	213
Wheaton Franciscan - St Joseph[2]	Milwaukee	95%	303
Divine Savior Healthcare	Portage	94%	54
Oak Leaf Surgcl Hospital	Eau Claire	94%	48
River Falls Area Hospital	River Falls	94%	50
Aspirus Wausau Hospital[2]	Wausau	93%	88
Aurora West Allis Medical Center[2]	West Allis	93%	258
Froedtert Memorial Lutheran Hospital[2]	Milwaukee	93%	267
Ministry St Michaels Hosp-Stevens Point	Stevens Point	93%	137
Riverview Hospital Assoc	Wisc. Rapids	93%	72
Waukesha Memorial Hospital[2]	Waukesha	93%	173
Bellin Memorial Hospital[2]	Green Bay	92%	129
Door County Memorial Hospital	Sturgeon Bay	92%	48
Holy Family Memorial	Manitowoc	92%	93
Saint Clare's Hospital of Weston	Weston	92%	73
Stoughton Hospital	Stoughton	92%	25
Theda Clark Medical Center[2]	Neenah	92%	123
Saint Vincent Hospital[2]	Green Bay	91%	160
Saint Clare Hospital Health Svcs	Baraboo	90%	42
Saint Marys Hospital Medical Center	Green Bay	90%	167
Aurora Baycare Medical Center[2]	Green Bay	89%	104
Aurora Medical Center - Washington County[2]	Hartford	89%	47
Columbia St Mary's Hospital Ozaukee[2]	Mequon	89%	184
Wheaton Franciscan Healthcare-Elmbrook[2]	Brookfield	89%	154
Beaver Dam Com Hospital	Beaver Dam	88%	112
Community Memorial Hospital[2]	Menomonee Fls	88%	193
Ministry St Marys Hospital	Rhinelander	88%	95
Sacred Heart Hospital[2]	Eau Claire	88%	192
Sauk Prairie Memorial Hospital	Prairie Du Sac	88%	77
Beloit Memorial Hospital	Beloit	87%	125
Saint Elizabeth Hospital[2]	Appleton	87%	143
Watertown Regional Medical Center	Watertown	87%	76
Columbia St Marys Hosp Milwaukee[2]	Milwaukee	85%	323
Oconomowoc Memorial Hospital[2]	Oconomowoc	85%	96
St Josephs Community Hosp West Bend	West Bend	85%	109
Mercy Medical Center of Oshkosh[2]	Oshkosh	84%	150
Wheaton Franciscan Healthcare - St Francis[2]	Milwaukee	84%	147
Aurora Lakeland Medical Center[2]	Elkhorn	83%	81
Aurora Medical Center Manitowoc County[2]	Two Rivers	83%	46
Gundersen Luth Medical Center[2]	La Crosse	81%	241
Howard Young Medical Center	Woodruff	80%	113
Memorial Medical Center	Ashland	77%	75
Mile Bluff Medical Center	Mauston	77%	35
Bay Area Medical Center	Marinette	74%	101

23. Appropriate Hair Removal

Hospital Name	City	Rate	Cases
Appleton Medical Center[2]	Appleton	100%	1291
Aspirus Wausau Hospital[2]	Wausau	100%	547
Aurora Baycare Medical Center[2]	Green Bay	100%	632
Aurora Lakeland Medical Center[2]	Elkhorn	100%	179
Aurora Medical Center - Washington County[2]	Hartford	100%	266
Aurora Medical Center Kenosha[2]	Kenosha	100%	374
Aurora Medical Center Manitowoc County[2]	Two Rivers	100%	263
Aurora Medical Center Oshkosh[2]	Oshkosh	100%	330
Aurora Memorial Hospital Burlington[2]	Burlington	100%	381
Aurora Sheboygan Memorial Medical Center[2]	Sheboygan	100%	589
Aurora St Lukes Medical Center[2]	Milwaukee	100%	2572
Aurora West Allis Medical Center[2]	West Allis	100%	811
Bellin Memorial Hospital[2]	Green Bay	100%	771
Berlin Memorial Hospital[2]	Berlin	100%	173
Calumet Medical Center[2]	Chilton	100%	50
Columbia St Mary's Hospital Ozaukee[2]	Mequon	100%	553
Columbia St Marys Hosp Milwaukee[2]	Milwaukee	100%	800
Columbus Community Hospital	Columbus	100%	76
Community Memorial Hospital[2]	Menomonee Fls	100%	618
Divine Savior Healthcare	Portage	100%	112
Door County Memorial Hospital	Sturgeon Bay	100%	110
Fort Healthcare[2]	Fort Atkinson	100%	322
Franciscan Skemp La Crosse Hospital	La Crosse	100%	803
Froedtert Memorial Lutheran Hospital[2]	Milwaukee	100%	753
Good Samaritan Health Center[2]	Merrill	100%	72
Grant Regional Health Center	Lancaster	100%	41
Gundersen Luth Medical Center[2]	La Crosse	100%	1040
Holy Family Memorial	Manitowoc	100%	426
Howard Young Medical Center	Woodruff	100%	392
Lakeview Medical Center[2]	Rice Lake	100%	367
Langlade Hospital	Antigo	100%	94
Luther Hospital Mayo Health System	Eau Claire	100%	1405
Luther Midelfort-Northland Mayo Hlth Sys	Barron	100%	40
Madison VA Medical Center[2]	Madison	100%	274
Memorial Health Center	Medford	100%	46
Memorial Hospital Lafayette County	Darlington	100%	34
Memorial Medical Center	Ashland	100%	151
Mercy Health Sys Corp[2]	Janesville	100%	1048
Mercy Walworth Hospital & Medical Center	Lake Geneva	100%	113
Midwest Orthopedic Specialty Hospital[2,3]	Franklin	100%	131
Ministry St Marys Hospital	Rhinelander	100%	460
Ministry St Michaels Hosp-Stevens Point	Stevens Point	100%	559
Oak Leaf Surgcl Hospital	Eau Claire	100%	347
Oconomowoc Memorial Hospital[2]	Oconomowoc	100%	373
Orthopaedic Hospital of Wisconsin[2]	Glendale	100%	134
Prairie Du Chien Memorial Hospital	Prairie Du Chien	100%	35
Red Cedar Med Ctr-Mayo Health System	Menomonie	100%	125
Reedsburg Area Medical Center[2]	Reedsburg	100%	86
Richland Hospital	Richland Center	100%	64
River Falls Area Hospital	River Falls	100%	182
Riverview Hospital Assoc	Wisc. Rapids	100%	527
Sacred Heart Hospital[2]	Eau Claire	100%	513
Saint Agnes Hospital[2]	Fond Du Lac	100%	535
Saint Clare Hospital Health Svcs	Baraboo	100%	149
Saint Clare's Hospital of Weston	Weston	100%	804
Saint Elizabeth Hospital[2]	Appleton	100%	557
Saint Josephs Hospital	Chippewa Falls	100%	233
Saint Josephs Hospital	Marshfield	100%	1932
Saint Nicholas Hospital	Sheboygan	100%	409
Saint Vincent Hospital[2]	Green Bay	100%	692
Sauk Prairie Memorial Hospital	Prairie Du Sac	100%	749
Shawano Medical Center	Shawano	100%	70
Southwest Health Center[3]	Platteville	100%	53
Stoughton Hospital	Stoughton	100%	67
Theda Clark Medical Center[2]	Neenah	100%	494
Vernon Memorial Hospital	Viroqua	100%	556
Waupun Memorial Hospital	Waupun	100%	84
Wheaton Franciscan - St Joseph[2]	Milwaukee	100%	787
Wheaton Franciscan Healthcare - All Saints[2]	Racine	100%	628
Wheaton Franciscan Healthcare - St Francis[2]	Milwaukee	100%	503
Bay Area Medical Center	Marinette	99%	278
Mercy Medical Center of Oshkosh[2]	Oshkosh	99%	364
Meriter Hospital[2]	Madison	99%	544
Mile Bluff Medical Center	Mauston	99%	165
Milwaukee VA Medical Center[2]	Milwaukee	99%	295
Monroe Clinic[2]	Monroe	99%	321
Saint Mary's Hospital[2]	Madison	99%	1819
Saint Marys Hospital Medical Center	Green Bay	99%	543
United Hospital System[2]	Kenosha	99%	598
Univ of Wisconsin Hosps & Clinics Auth[2]	Madison	99%	647
Watertown Regional Medical Center	Watertown	99%	221
Waukesha Memorial Hospital[2]	Waukesha	99%	616
Wheaton Franciscan Healthcare-Elmbrook[2]	Brookfield	99%	393
Beloit Memorial Hospital	Beloit	98%	440
Beaver Dam Com Hospital	Beaver Dam	97%	290
Upland Hills Health	Dodgeville	97%	37
St Josephs Community Hosp West Bend	West Bend	96%	340
Black River Memorial Hospital	Black River Falls	91%	56

24. Appropriate Beta Blocker Usage

Hospital Name	City	Rate	Cases
Aurora Memorial Hospital Burlington[2]	Burlington	100%	109
Madison VA Medical Center[2]	Madison	100%	125
Saint Clare Hospital Health Svcs	Baraboo	100%	38
Sauk Prairie Memorial Hospital	Prairie Du Sac	100%	183
Univ of Wisconsin Hosps & Clinics Auth[2]	Madison	100%	231
Aurora Medical Center - Washington County[2]	Hartford	99%	83
Aurora Medical Center Manitowoc County[2]	Two Rivers	99%	83
Aurora Sheboygan Memorial Medical Center[2]	Sheboygan	98%	177
Bellin Memorial Hospital[2]	Green Bay	98%	283
Oak Leaf Surgcl Hospital	Eau Claire	98%	80
Aurora St Lukes Medical Center[2]	Milwaukee	97%	936
Aurora West Allis Medical Center[2]	West Allis	97%	190
Luther Hospital Mayo Health System	Eau Claire	97%	561
Mercy Medical Center of Oshkosh[2]	Oshkosh	97%	108
Mile Bluff Medical Center	Mauston	97%	29
Ministry St Michaels Hosp-Stevens Point	Stevens Point	97%	191
Saint Agnes Hospital[2]	Fond Du Lac	97%	146
Wheaton Franciscan - St Joseph[2]	Milwaukee	97%	220
Aurora Baycare Medical Center[2]	Green Bay	96%	246
Aurora Medical Center Oshkosh[2]	Oshkosh	96%	103
Saint Elizabeth Hospital[2]	Appleton	96%	199
Saint Marys Hospital Medical Center	Green Bay	96%	157
Wheaton Franciscan Healthcare - All Saints[2]	Racine	96%	185
Aspirus Wausau Hospital[2]	Wausau	95%	248
Lakeview Medical Center[2]	Rice Lake	95%	116
Riverview Hospital Assoc	Wisc. Rapids	95%	152
Saint Clare's Hospital of Weston	Weston	95%	300
Saint Josephs Hospital	Marshfield	95%	634
Aurora Medical Center Kenosha[2]	Kenosha	94%	90
Bay Area Medical Center	Marinette	94%	95
Mercy Health Sys Corp[2]	Janesville	94%	270
Oconomowoc Memorial Hospital[2]	Oconomowoc	94%	72
Saint Mary's Hospital[2]	Madison	94%	578
Theda Clark Medical Center[2]	Neenah	94%	139
Froedtert Memorial Lutheran Hospital[2]	Milwaukee	93%	240
Wheaton Franciscan Healthcare - St Francis[2]	Milwaukee	93%	129
Aurora Lakeland Medical Center[2]	Elkhorn	92%	61
Saint Josephs Hospital	Chippewa Falls	92%	65
Howard Young Medical Center	Woodruff	91%	103
River Falls Area Hospital	River Falls	90%	30
Appleton Medical Center[2]	Appleton	89%	447
Ministry St Marys Hospital	Rhinelander	89%	134
Vernon Memorial Hospital	Viroqua	89%	208
Milwaukee VA Medical Center[2]	Milwaukee	88%	113
Beaver Dam Com Hospital	Beaver Dam	87%	90
Franciscan Skemp La Crosse Hospital	La Crosse	87%	255
Memorial Medical Center	Ashland	87%	52
Sacred Heart Hospital[2]	Eau Claire	87%	171
Holy Family Memorial	Manitowoc	86%	138
St Josephs Community Hosp West Bend	West Bend	86%	63
Saint Vincent Hospital[2]	Green Bay	86%	300
Beloit Memorial Hospital	Beloit	85%	124
Gundersen Luth Medical Center[2]	La Crosse	85%	427
Saint Nicholas Hospital	Sheboygan	85%	100
Waukesha Memorial Hospital[2]	Waukesha	85%	226
Wheaton Franciscan Healthcare-Elmbrook[2]	Brookfield	85%	95
Midwest Orthopedic Specialty Hospital[2,3]	Franklin	84%	32
Monroe Clinic[2]	Monroe	84%	100
Fort Healthcare[2]	Fort Atkinson	83%	77
Door County Memorial Hospital	Sturgeon Bay	82%	28
United Hospital System[2]	Kenosha	82%	151
Watertown Regional Medical Center	Watertown	82%	76
Columbia St Marys Hosp Milwaukee[2]	Milwaukee	81%	234
Meriter Hospital[2]	Madison	81%	136
Community Memorial Hospital[2]	Menomonee Fls	80%	176
Columbia St Mary's Hospital Ozaukee[2]	Mequon	79%	159
Divine Savior Healthcare	Portage	79%	33
Reedsburg Area Medical Center[2]	Reedsburg	73%	33
Orthopaedic Hospital of Wisconsin[2]	Glendale	68%	25

25. Controlled Postoperative Blood Glucose

Hospital Name	City	Rate	Cases
Madison VA Medical Center[2]	Madison	100%	41
Aurora Baycare Medical Center[2]	Green Bay	99%	144
Wheaton Franciscan - St Joseph[2]	Milwaukee	99%	159
Luther Hospital Mayo Health System	Eau Claire	98%	230
Milwaukee VA Medical Center[2]	Milwaukee	98%	46
Aurora St Lukes Medical Center[2]	Milwaukee	97%	606
Saint Agnes Hospital[2]	Fond Du Lac	97%	65
Saint Clare's Hospital of Weston	Weston	97%	144
Saint Vincent Hospital[2]	Green Bay	97%	156
Bellin Memorial Hospital[2]	Green Bay	96%	245
Gundersen Luth Medical Center[2]	La Crosse	96%	242
Aspirus Wausau Hospital[2]	Wausau	95%	145
Mercy Health Sys Corp[2]	Janesville	95%	66
Meriter Hospital[2]	Madison	95%	115
Columbia St Marys Hosp Milwaukee[2]	Milwaukee	93%	112
Sacred Heart Hospital[2]	Eau Claire	93%	43
Waukesha Memorial Hospital[2]	Waukesha	93%	153
Beloit Memorial Hospital	Beloit	92%	38
Columbia St Mary's Hospital Ozaukee[2]	Mequon	92%	131
Community Memorial Hospital[2]	Menomonee Fls	92%	105
Saint Mary's Hospital[2]	Madison	92%	316
Saint Elizabeth Hospital[2]	Appleton	91%	151
Saint Josephs Hospital	Marshfield	90%	323
Appleton Medical Center[2]	Appleton	88%	255
Wheaton Franciscan Healthcare - All Saints[2]	Racine	86%	71
Wheaton Franciscan Healthcare - St Francis[2]	Milwaukee	85%	59
Froedtert Memorial Lutheran Hospital[2]	Milwaukee	84%	159
Univ of Wisconsin Hosps & Clinics Auth[2]	Madison	84%	133
United Hospital System[2]	Kenosha	82%	94

26. Prophylactic Antibiotic Timing

Hospital Name	City	Rate	Cases
Black River Memorial Hospital	Black River Falls	100%	51
Calumet Medical Center[2]	Chilton	100%	35
Good Samaritan Health Center[2]	Merrill	100%	45
Memorial Hospital Lafayette County	Darlington	100%	29
Mercy Walworth Hospital & Medical Center	Lake Geneva	100%	99
Ministry St Michaels Hosp-Stevens Point	Stevens Point	100%	418
Oak Leaf Surgcl Hospital	Eau Claire	100%	276
Riverview Hospital Assoc	Wisc. Rapids	100%	447
Saint Clare's Hospital of Weston	Weston	100%	624
Saint Josephs Hospital	Chippewa Falls	100%	192
Stoughton Hospital	Stoughton	100%	47
Aspirus Wausau Hospital[2]	Wausau	99%	389
Aurora Baycare Medical Center[2]	Green Bay	99%	487
Aurora Medical Center - Washington County[2]	Hartford	99%	204
Aurora Medical Center Manitowoc County[2]	Two Rivers	99%	145
Aurora Medical Center Oshkosh[2]	Oshkosh	99%	250

NOTE: Hospital profiles are in alphabetical order by state, then city, then hospital within the city; Rankings exclude hospitals with less than 25 cases except for patient surveys which excludes hospitals with less than 100 cases; (a) 100–299 cases; (1) The number of cases is too small to be sure how well a hospital is performing; (2) The hospital indicated that the data submitted for this measure were based on a sample of cases; (3) Data was collected during a shorter time period (fewer quarters) than the maximum possible time for this measure; (4) Suppressed for one or more quarters by CMS; (5) No data is available from the hospital for this measure; (6) Fewer than 100 patients completed the HCAHPS survey. Use these rates with caution, as the number of surveys may be too low to reliably assess hospital performance; (7) Survey results are based on less than 12 months of data; (8) Survey results are not available for this reporting period; (9) No or very few patients were eligible for the HCAHPS survey. The scores shown, if any, reflect a very small number of surveys; (10) A state average was not calculated because too few hospitals in the state submitted data; (11) There were discrepancies in the data collection process; Please refer to the User's Guide for a full explanation of data.

Hospital Name	City	Rate	Cases
Aurora Memorial Hospital Burlington[2]	Burlington	99%	241
Aurora St Lukes Medical Center[2]	Milwaukee	99%	1970
Aurora West Allis Medical Center[2]	West Allis	99%	651
Bellin Memorial Hospital[2]	Green Bay	99%	575
Franciscan Skemp La Crosse Hospital	La Crosse	99%	589
Lakeview Medical Center[2]	Rice Lake	99%	311
Madison VA Medical Center	Madison	99%	167
Oconomowoc Memorial Hospital[2]	Oconomowoc	99%	260
Orthopaedic Hospital of Wisconsin[2]	Glendale	99%	105
Saint Agnes Hospital[2]	Fond Du Lac	99%	372
Saint Elizabeth Hospital[2]	Appleton	99%	409
Sauk Prairie Memorial Hospital	Prairie Du Sac	99%	678
Watertown Regional Medical Center	Watertown	99%	158
Aurora Lakeland Medical Center[2]	Elkhorn	98%	108
Aurora Medical Center Kenosha[2]	Kenosha	98%	252
Aurora Sheboygan Memorial Medical Center[2]	Sheboygan	98%	468
Holy Family Memorial	Manitowoc	98%	304
Howard Young Medical Center	Woodruff	98%	281
Langlade Hospital	Antigo	98%	51
Luther Hospital Mayo Health System	Eau Claire	98%	943
Mercy Health Sys Corp[2]	Janesville	98%	717
Ministry St Marys Hospital	Rhinelander	98%	364
River Falls Area Hospital	River Falls	98%	133
Saint Clare Hospital Health Svcs	Baraboo	98%	123
Saint Mary's Hospital[2]	Madison	98%	1460
Saint Vincent Hospital[2]	Green Bay	98%	487
Shawano Medical Center	Shawano	98%	41
Theda Clark Medical Center[2]	Neenah	98%	331
Waukesha Memorial Hospital[2]	Waukesha	98%	447
Wheaton Franciscan - St Joseph[2]	Milwaukee	98%	452
Mercy Medical Center of Oshkosh[2]	Oshkosh	97%	226
Saint Josephs Hospital	Marshfield	97%	1163
Saint Marys Hospital Medical Center	Green Bay	97%	416
Wheaton Franciscan Healthcare - All Saints[2]	Racine	97%	376
Appleton Medical Center[2]	Appleton	96%	1032
Meriter Hospital[2]	Madison	96%	423
Midwest Orthopedic Specialty Hospital[2,3]	Franklin	96%	90
Mile Bluff Medical Center	Mauston	96%	136
Sacred Heart Hospital[2]	Eau Claire	96%	366
St Josephs Community Hosp West Bend	West Bend	96%	237
Wheaton Franciscan Healthcare-Elmbrook[2]	Brookfield	96%	256
Bay Area Medical Center	Marinette	95%	171
Columbia St Mary's Hospital Ozaukee[2]	Mequon	95%	407
Columbia St Marys Hosp Milwaukee[2]	Milwaukee	95%	552
Divine Savior Healthcare	Portage	95%	83
Memorial Health Center	Medford	95%	40
Red Cedar Med Ctr-Mayo Health System	Menomonie	95%	94
Waupun Memorial Hospital	Waupun	95%	66
Wheaton Franciscan Healthcare - St Francis[2]	Milwaukee	95%	327
Beloit Memorial Hospital	Beloit	94%	321
Gundersen Luth Medical Center[2]	La Crosse	94%	721
Memorial Medical Center	Ashland	94%	127
Univ of Wisconsin Hosps & Clinics Auth[2]	Madison	94%	408
Froedtert Memorial Lutheran Hospital[2]	Milwaukee	93%	453
Milwaukee VA Medical Center	Milwaukee	93%	208
Reedsburg Area Medical Center[2]	Reedsburg	93%	76
Saint Nicholas Hospital	Sheboygan	93%	281
Baldwin Area Medical Center	Baldwin	92%	49
Community Memorial Hospital[2]	Menomonee Fls	91%	447
Fort Healthcare[2]	Fort Atkinson	91%	213
Ladd Memorial Hospital	Osceola	91%	76
Berlin Memorial Hospital[2]	Berlin	90%	145
Door County Memorial Hospital	Sturgeon Bay	90%	82
Grant Regional Health Center	Lancaster	90%	31
United Hospital System[2]	Kenosha	90%	408
Community Memorial Hospital	Oconto Falls	89%	38
Saint Croix Regional Medical Center	Saint Croix Falls	89%	80
Vernon Memorial Hospital	Viroqua	89%	492
Luther Midelfort-Northland Mayo Hlth Sys	Barron	87%	30
Richland Hospital	Richland Center	87%	61
Monroe Clinic[2]	Monroe	86%	222
Southwest Health Center[3]	Platteville	86%	50
Beaver Dam Com Hospital	Beaver Dam	82%	217
Prairie Du Chien Memorial Hospital	Prairie Du Chien	76%	25

27. Prophylactic Antibiotic Timing (Outpatient)

Hospital Name	City	Rate	Cases
Holy Family Memorial	Manitowoc	100%	122
Sauk Prairie Memorial Hospital	Prairie Du Sac	100%	67
Aurora Sheboygan Memorial Medical Center	Sheboygan	99%	342
Oak Leaf Surgcl Hospital	Eau Claire	99%	143
Saint Clare's Hospital of Weston	Weston	98%	119
Saint Josephs Hospital	Chippewa Falls	98%	43
Mercy Walworth Hospital & Medical Center	Lake Geneva	97%	29
Aspirus Wausau Hospital	Wausau	96%	408
Fort Healthcare	Fort Atkinson	96%	166
Luther Hospital Mayo Health System	Eau Claire	96%	315
Saint Elizabeth Hospital	Appleton	96%	482
Saint Vincent Hospital	Green Bay	96%	338
Theda Clark Medical Center	Neenah	96%	655
Wheaton Franciscan Healthcare - Franklin	Franklin	96%	26
Orthopaedic Hospital of Wisconsin[3]	Glendale	95%	130
Sacred Heart Hospital	Eau Claire	95%	334
Saint Mary's Hospital	Madison	95%	639
Appleton Medical Center	Appleton	94%	499
Aurora Medical Center - Washington County	Hartford	94%	117
Divine Savior Healthcare	Portage	94%	51
Gundersen Luth Medical Center	La Crosse	94%	742
Mercy Medical Center of Oshkosh	Oshkosh	94%	286
Wheaton Franciscan - St Joseph	Milwaukee	94%	561
Aurora Medical Center Kenosha	Kenosha	93%	294
Bellin Memorial Hospital	Green Bay	93%	755
Community Memorial Hospital	Menomonee Fls	93%	406
Howard Young Medical Center	Woodruff	93%	44
Lakeview Medical Center	Rice Lake	93%	43
Riverview Hospital Assoc	Wisc. Rapids	93%	54
Saint Agnes Hospital	Fond Du Lac	93%	360
Saint Clare Hospital Health Svcs	Baraboo	93%	69
Saint Josephs Hospital	Marshfield	93%	439
Wheaton Franciscan Healthcare - All Saints	Racine	93%	400
Wheaton Franciscan Healthcare - St Francis	Milwaukee	93%	288
Aurora Baycare Medical Center	Green Bay	92%	503
Bay Area Medical Center	Marinette	92%	115
Aurora St Lukes Medical Center	Milwaukee	91%	1058
Froedtert Memorial Lutheran Hospital	Milwaukee	91%	472
Midwest Orthopedic Specialty Hospital[3]	Franklin	91%	91
Aurora Medical Center Oshkosh	Oshkosh	90%	218
Saint Marys Hospital Medical Center	Green Bay	90%	253
Aurora West Allis Medical Center	West Allis	89%	214
Columbia St Marys Hosp Milwaukee	Milwaukee	89%	391
Meriter Hospital	Madison	89%	256
Monroe Clinic	Monroe	89%	82
Berlin Memorial Hospital	Berlin	88%	50
Columbia St Mary's Hospital Ozaukee	Mequon	87%	124
Watertown Regional Medical Center	Watertown	87%	191
Beloit Memorial Hospital	Beloit	86%	137
Oconomowoc Memorial Hospital	Oconomowoc	86%	114
Waukesha Memorial Hospital	Waukesha	86%	523
Wheaton Franciscan Healthcare-Elmbrook	Brookfield	86%	263
Mercy Health Sys Corp	Janesville	85%	175
St Josephs Community Hosp West Bend	West Bend	85%	89
Aurora Lakeland Medical Center	Elkhorn	84%	58
Ministry St Marys Hospital	Rhinelander	84%	76
Ministry St Michaels Hosp-Stevens Point	Stevens Point	84%	50
Southwest Health Center	Platteville	84%	50
Aurora Memorial Hospital Burlington	Burlington	82%	195
Univ of Wisconsin Hosps & Clinics Auth	Madison	82%	266
Reedsburg Area Medical Center	Reedsburg	81%	53
Mile Bluff Medical Center	Mauston	80%	50
Saint Nicholas Hospital	Sheboygan	80%	87
Aurora Medical Center Manitowoc County	Two Rivers	75%	81
Franciscan Skemp La Crosse Hospital	La Crosse	75%	176
United Hospital System	Kenosha	73%	188
Beaver Dam Com Hospital	Beaver Dam	47%	78

28. Prophylactic Antibiotic Selection

Hospital Name	City	Rate	Cases
Appleton Medical Center[2]	Appleton	100%	1048
Aurora Medical Center Oshkosh[2]	Oshkosh	100%	251
Baldwin Area Medical Center	Baldwin	100%	49
Beaver Dam Com Hospital	Beaver Dam	100%	219
Calumet Medical Center[2]	Chilton	100%	36
Good Samaritan Health Center[2]	Merrill	100%	45
Grant Regional Health Center	Lancaster	100%	31
Memorial Hospital Lafayette County	Darlington	100%	30
Midwest Orthopedic Specialty Hospital[2,3]	Franklin	100%	90
Milwaukee VA Medical Center	Milwaukee	100%	209
Ministry St Marys Hospital	Rhinelander	100%	365
Orthopaedic Hospital of Wisconsin[2]	Glendale	100%	106
Reedsburg Area Medical Center[2]	Reedsburg	100%	76
Saint Clare Hospital Health Svcs	Baraboo	100%	123
Saint Elizabeth Hospital[2]	Appleton	100%	412
Saint Marys Hospital Medical Center	Green Bay	100%	416
Shawano Medical Center	Shawano	100%	41
Southwest Health Center[3]	Platteville	100%	49
Stoughton Hospital	Stoughton	100%	48
Vernon Memorial Hospital	Viroqua	100%	492
Waupun Memorial Hospital	Waupun	100%	67
Wheaton Franciscan - St Joseph[2]	Milwaukee	100%	455
Aspirus Wausau Hospital[2]	Wausau	99%	401
Aurora Baycare Medical Center[2]	Green Bay	99%	493
Aurora Medical Center Kenosha[2]	Kenosha	99%	252
Aurora Medical Center Manitowoc County[2]	Two Rivers	99%	146
Aurora Sheboygan Memorial Medical Center[2]	Sheboygan	99%	468
Aurora West Allis Medical Center[2]	West Allis	99%	654
Door County Memorial Hospital	Sturgeon Bay	99%	82
Holy Family Memorial	Manitowoc	99%	308
Ladd Memorial Hospital	Osceola	99%	76
Lakeview Medical Center[2]	Rice Lake	99%	314
Luther Hospital Mayo Health System	Eau Claire	99%	967
Madison VA Medical Center	Madison	99%	167
Mercy Walworth Hospital & Medical Center	Lake Geneva	99%	99
Meriter Hospital[2]	Madison	99%	424
Ministry St Michaels Hosp-Stevens Point	Stevens Point	99%	425
River Falls Area Hospital	River Falls	99%	133
Saint Clare's Hospital of Weston	Weston	99%	630
Saint Mary's Hospital[2]	Madison	99%	1469
Saint Nicholas Hospital	Sheboygan	99%	280
Sauk Prairie Memorial Hospital	Prairie Du Sac	99%	689
Aurora Medical Center - Washington County[2]	Hartford	98%	204
Aurora Memorial Hospital Burlington[2]	Burlington	98%	244
Aurora St Lukes Medical Center[2]	Milwaukee	98%	1997
Bellin Memorial Hospital[2]	Green Bay	98%	593
Columbia St Mary's Hospital Ozaukee[2]	Mequon	98%	408
Columbia St Marys Hosp Milwaukee[2]	Milwaukee	98%	560
Fort Healthcare[2]	Fort Atkinson	98%	214
Franciscan Skemp La Crosse Hospital	La Crosse	98%	596
Howard Young Medical Center	Woodruff	98%	285
Langlade Hospital	Antigo	98%	51
Mercy Medical Center of Oshkosh[2]	Oshkosh	98%	226
Oak Leaf Surgcl Hospital	Eau Claire	98%	277
Oconomowoc Memorial Hospital[2]	Oconomowoc	98%	260
Saint Agnes Hospital[2]	Fond Du Lac	98%	375
Theda Clark Medical Center[2]	Neenah	98%	332
Watertown Regional Medical Center	Watertown	98%	160
Wheaton Franciscan Healthcare - All Saints[2]	Racine	98%	386
Wheaton Franciscan Healthcare-Elmbrook[2]	Brookfield	98%	261
Wheaton Franciscan Healthcare - St Francis[2]	Milwaukee	98%	329
Bay Area Medical Center	Marinette	97%	172
Beloit Memorial Hospital	Beloit	97%	319
Berlin Memorial Hospital[2]	Berlin	97%	147
Froedtert Memorial Lutheran Hospital[2]	Milwaukee	97%	470
Mercy Health Sys Corp[2]	Janesville	97%	719
Riverview Hospital Assoc	Wisc. Rapids	97%	447
Saint Josephs Hospital	Chippewa Falls	97%	192
Saint Josephs Hospital	Marshfield	97%	1190
Saint Vincent Hospital[2]	Green Bay	97%	501
Aurora Lakeland Medical Center[2]	Elkhorn	96%	108
Community Memorial Hospital[2]	Menomonee Fls	96%	455
Gundersen Luth Medical Center[2]	La Crosse	96%	734
Mile Bluff Medical Center	Mauston	96%	136
Red Cedar Med Ctr-Mayo Health System	Menomonie	96%	94
Saint Croix Regional Medical Center	Saint Croix Falls	96%	80
Univ of Wisconsin Hosps & Clinics Auth[2]	Madison	96%	420
Divine Savior Healthcare	Portage	95%	83
Memorial Health Center	Medford	95%	40
United Hospital System[2]	Kenosha	95%	419
Waukesha Memorial Hospital[2]	Waukesha	95%	455
Memorial Medical Center	Ashland	94%	126
Monroe Clinic[2]	Monroe	93%	214
Richland Hospital	Richland Center	93%	61
Sacred Heart Hospital[2]	Eau Claire	93%	368
Black River Memorial Hospital	Black River Falls	92%	51
St Josephs Community Hosp West Bend	West Bend	92%	236
Community Memorial Hospital	Oconto Falls	89%	38
Luther Midelfort-Northland Mayo Hlth Sys	Barron	86%	28

29. Prophylactic Antibiotic Selection (Outpatient)

Hospital Name	City	Rate	Cases
Midwest Orthopedic Specialty Hospital[3]	Franklin	100%	90
Orthopaedic Hospital of Wisconsin[3]	Glendale	100%	130
Saint Josephs Hospital	Chippewa Falls	100%	43
Wheaton Franciscan Healthcare - Franklin	Franklin	100%	25
Saint Mary's Hospital	Madison	99%	636
Wheaton Franciscan - St Joseph	Milwaukee	99%	551
Aurora Baycare Medical Center	Green Bay	98%	494
Aurora Sheboygan Memorial Medical Center	Sheboygan	98%	340
Beaver Dam Com Hospital	Beaver Dam	98%	40
Bellin Memorial Hospital	Green Bay	98%	722
Divine Savior Healthcare	Portage	98%	50
Fort Healthcare	Fort Atkinson	98%	163
Holy Family Memorial	Manitowoc	98%	122
Lakeview Medical Center	Rice Lake	98%	42
Luther Hospital Mayo Health System	Eau Claire	98%	312
Mercy Medical Center of Oshkosh	Oshkosh	98%	290
Mile Bluff Medical Center	Mauston	98%	40
Ministry St Michaels Hosp-Stevens Point	Stevens Point	98%	45
Saint Clare's Hospital of Weston	Weston	98%	117
Southwest Health Center	Platteville	98%	47
Theda Clark Medical Center	Neenah	98%	656
Aurora Medical Center Kenosha	Kenosha	97%	286
Aurora Medical Center Manitowoc County	Two Rivers	97%	66
Franciscan Skemp La Crosse Hospital	La Crosse	97%	153
Mercy Walworth Hospital & Medical Center	Lake Geneva	97%	29
Meriter Hospital	Madison	97%	251
Monroe Clinic	Monroe	97%	115
Saint Clare Hospital Health Svcs	Baraboo	97%	64
Saint Elizabeth Hospital	Appleton	97%	476
Saint Josephs Hospital	Marshfield	97%	437
Saint Vincent Hospital	Green Bay	97%	332

NOTE: Hospital profiles are in alphabetical order by state, then city, then hospital within the city; Rankings exclude hospitals with less than 25 cases except for patient surveys which excludes hospitals with less than 100 cases; (a) 100–299 cases; (1) The number of cases is too small to be sure how well a hospital is performing; (2) The hospital indicated that the data submitted for this measure were based on a sample of cases; (3) Data was collected during a shorter time period (fewer quarters) than the maximum possible time for this measure; (4) Suppressed for one or more quarters by CMS; (5) No data is available from the hospital for this measure; (6) Fewer than 100 patients completed the HCAHPS survey. Use these rates with caution, as the number of surveys may be too low to reliably assess hospital performance; (7) Survey results are based on less than 12 months of data; (8) Survey results are not available for this reporting period; (9) No or very few patients were eligible for the HCAHPS survey. The scores shown, if any, reflect a very small number of surveys; (10) A state average was not calculated because too few hospitals in the state submitted data; (11) There were discrepancies in the data collection process; Please refer to the User's Guide for a full explanation of data.

Univ of Wisconsin Hosps & Clinics Auth	Madison	97%	488
Wheaton Franciscan Healthcare - All Saints	Racine	97%	494
Wheaton Franciscan Healthcare - St Francis	Milwaukee	97%	281
Aurora Medical Center - Washington County	Hartford	96%	111
Aurora St Lukes Medical Center	Milwaukee	96%	1031
Aurora West Allis Medical Center	West Allis	96%	203
Bay Area Medical Center	Marinette	96%	110
Columbia St Mary's Hospital Ozaukee	Mequon	96%	114
Gundersen Luth Medical Center	La Crosse	96%	742
Riverview Hospital Assoc	Wisc. Rapids	96%	51
Sacred Heart Hospital	Eau Claire	96%	331
Saint Agnes Hospital	Fond Du Lac	96%	343
Saint Marys Hospital Medical Center	Green Bay	96%	244
Aspirus Wausau Hospital	Wausau	95%	400
Aurora Medical Center Oshkosh	Oshkosh	94%	212
Beloit Memorial Hospital	Beloit	94%	125
Berlin Memorial Hospital	Berlin	94%	47
Froedtert Memorial Lutheran Hospital	Milwaukee	94%	572
Wheaton Franciscan Healthcare-Elmbrook	Brookfield	94%	300
Howard Young Medical Center	Woodruff	93%	41
Watertown Regional Medical Center	Watertown	93%	216
Aurora Lakeland Medical Center	Elkhorn	92%	53
Appleton Medical Center	Appleton	91%	500
Columbia St Marys Hosp Milwaukee	Milwaukee	91%	394
Mercy Health Sys Corp	Janesville	91%	150
Oak Leaf Surgcl Hospital	Eau Claire	91%	142
Saint Nicholas Hospital	Sheboygan	91%	85
Sauk Prairie Memorial Hospital	Prairie Du Sac	91%	67
United Hospital System	Kenosha	91%	265
Community Memorial Hospital	Menomonee Fls	90%	398
Reedsburg Area Medical Center	Reedsburg	90%	50
St Josephs Community Hosp West Bend	West Bend	90%	78
Waukesha Memorial Hospital	Waukesha	89%	538
Aurora Memorial Hospital Burlington	Burlington	88%	224
Oconomowoc Memorial Hospital	Oconomowoc	87%	109
Ministry St Marys Hospital	Rhinelander	85%	73

30. Prophylactic Antibiotic Stopped

Hospital Name	City	Rate	Cases
Aurora Memorial Hospital Burlington[2]	Burlington	100%	229
Good Samaritan Health Center[2]	Merrill	100%	45
Grant Regional Health Center	Lancaster	100%	31
Ladd Memorial Hospital	Osceola	100%	76
Madison VA Medical Center	Madison	100%	162
Midwest Orthopedic Specialty Hospital[2,3]	Franklin	100%	85
Aurora Baycare Medical Center[2]	Green Bay	99%	457
Aurora Sheboygan Memorial Medical Center[2]	Sheboygan	99%	453
Lakeview Medical Center[2]	Rice Lake	99%	305
Red Cedar Med Ctr-Mayo Health System	Menomonie	99%	94
Reedsburg Area Medical Center[2]	Reedsburg	99%	74
Aurora Medical Center - Washington County[2]	Hartford	98%	201
Aurora Medical Center Manitowoc County[2]	Two Rivers	98%	144
Bellin Memorial Hospital[2]	Green Bay	98%	569
Franciscan Skemp La Crosse Hospital	La Crosse	98%	565
Howard Young Medical Center	Woodruff	98%	275
Langlade Hospital	Antigo	98%	49
Luther Hospital Mayo Health System	Eau Claire	98%	877
Meriter Hospital[2]	Madison	98%	415
Ministry St Marys Hospital	Rhinelander	98%	358
Ministry St Michaels Hosp-Stevens Point	Stevens Point	98%	413
Monroe Clinic[2]	Monroe	98%	203
Oconomowoc Memorial Hospital[2]	Oconomowoc	98%	255
River Falls Area Hospital	River Falls	98%	128
Riverview Hospital Assoc	Wisc. Rapids	98%	446
Saint Clare's Hospital of Weston	Weston	98%	617
Saint Josephs Hospital	Chippewa Falls	98%	191
Saint Marys Hospital Medical Center	Green Bay	98%	412
Aspirus Wausau Hospital[2]	Wausau	97%	372
Aurora St Lukes Medical Center[2]	Milwaukee	97%	1894
Aurora West Allis Medical Center[2]	West Allis	97%	628
Gundersen Luth Medical Center[2]	La Crosse	97%	708
Memorial Health Center	Medford	97%	39
Mercy Walworth Hospital & Medical Center	Lake Geneva	97%	99
Saint Croix Regional Medical Center	Saint Croix Falls	97%	79
Sauk Prairie Memorial Hospital	Prairie Du Sac	97%	674
Univ of Wisconsin Hosps & Clinics Auth[2]	Madison	97%	383
Waukesha Memorial Hospital[2]	Waukesha	97%	439
Waupun Memorial Hospital	Waupun	97%	66
Wheaton Franciscan - St Joseph[2]	Milwaukee	97%	413
Aurora Lakeland Medical Center[2]	Elkhorn	96%	91
Aurora Medical Center Oshkosh[2]	Oshkosh	96%	245
Baldwin Area Medical Center	Baldwin	96%	49
Black River Memorial Hospital	Black River Falls	96%	50
Saint Nicholas Hospital	Sheboygan	96%	261
Southwest Health Center[3]	Platteville	96%	48
Theda Clark Medical Center[2]	Neenah	96%	319
Wheaton Franciscan Healthcare - All Saints[2]	Racine	96%	350
Wheaton Franciscan Healthcare-Elmbrook[2]	Brookfield	96%	248
Appleton Medical Center[2]	Appleton	95%	999
Aurora Medical Center Kenosha[2]	Kenosha	95%	244
Community Memorial Hospital[2]	Menomonee Fls	95%	441
Door County Memorial Hospital	Sturgeon Bay	95%	78
Orthopaedic Hospital of Wisconsin[2]	Glendale	95%	105
Saint Mary's Hospital[2]	Madison	95%	1409
Shawano Medical Center	Shawano	95%	39
Froedtert Memorial Lutheran Hospital[2]	Milwaukee	94%	427
Oak Leaf Surgcl Hospital	Eau Claire	94%	274
Saint Elizabeth Hospital[2]	Appleton	94%	391
St Josephs Community Hosp West Bend	West Bend	94%	228
United Hospital System[2]	Kenosha	94%	394
Vernon Memorial Hospital	Viroqua	94%	481
Wheaton Franciscan Healthcare - St Francis[2]	Milwaukee	94%	301
Beloit Memorial Hospital	Beloit	93%	310
Fort Healthcare[2]	Fort Atkinson	93%	205
Holy Family Memorial	Manitowoc	93%	294
Luther Midelfort-Northland Mayo Hlth Sys	Barron	93%	28
Milwaukee VA Medical Center	Milwaukee	93%	207
Richland Hospital	Richland Center	93%	61
Saint Agnes Hospital[2]	Fond Du Lac	93%	353
Saint Vincent Hospital[2]	Green Bay	93%	446
Berlin Memorial Hospital[2]	Berlin	92%	145
Columbia St Mary's Hospital Ozaukee[2]	Mequon	92%	393
Columbia St Marys Hosp Milwaukee[2]	Milwaukee	92%	540
Mercy Medical Center of Oshkosh[2]	Oshkosh	92%	224
Calumet Medical Center[2]	Chilton	91%	35
Mile Bluff Medical Center	Mauston	91%	133
Stoughton Hospital	Stoughton	91%	47
Watertown Regional Medical Center	Watertown	91%	151
Memorial Hospital Lafayette County	Darlington	90%	29
Saint Clare Hospital Health Svcs	Baraboo	90%	121
Beaver Dam Com Hospital	Beaver Dam	89%	208
Divine Savior Healthcare	Portage	89%	79
Mercy Health Sys Corp[2]	Janesville	89%	691
Sacred Heart Hospital[2]	Eau Claire	89%	348
Saint Josephs Hospital	Marshfield	89%	1152
Community Memorial Hospital	Oconto Falls	86%	36
Bay Area Medical Center	Marinette	83%	161
Memorial Medical Center	Ashland	79%	125

31. Recommended VTP Ordered

Hospital Name	City	Rate	Cases
Lakeview Medical Center[2]	Rice Lake	100%	54
Mercy Walworth Hospital & Medical Center	Lake Geneva	100%	37
River Falls Area Hospital	River Falls	100%	50
Vernon Memorial Hospital	Viroqua	100%	64
Wheaton Franciscan Healthcare - All Saints[2]	Racine	100%	208
Aurora Memorial Hospital Burlington[2]	Burlington	99%	122
Aurora Sheboygan Memorial Medical Center[2]	Sheboygan	99%	132
Fort Healthcare[2]	Fort Atkinson	99%	118
Luther Hospital Mayo Health System	Eau Claire	99%	393
Milwaukee VA Medical Center[2]	Milwaukee	99%	172
Monroe Clinic[2]	Monroe	99%	91
Appleton Medical Center[2]	Appleton	98%	285
Aspirus Wausau Hospital[2]	Wausau	98%	88
Aurora Medical Center Kenosha[2]	Kenosha	98%	115
Meriter Hospital[2]	Madison	98%	123
Saint Josephs Hospital	Chippewa Falls	98%	58
Saint Josephs Hospital	Marshfield	98%	647
Saint Nicholas Hospital	Sheboygan	98%	126
Univ of Wisconsin Hosps & Clinics Auth[2]	Madison	98%	220
Wheaton Franciscan - St Joseph[2]	Milwaukee	98%	303
Aurora St Lukes Medical Center[2]	Milwaukee	97%	603
Aurora West Allis Medical Center[2]	West Allis	97%	258
Madison VA Medical Center[2]	Madison	97%	98
Shawano Medical Center	Shawano	97%	31
Amery Regional Medical Center[3]	Amery	96%	27
Aurora Medical Center Oshkosh[2]	Oshkosh	96%	81
Franciscan Skemp La Crosse Hospital	La Crosse	96%	327
Mercy Health Sys Corp[2]	Janesville	96%	499
Saint Agnes Hospital[2]	Fond Du Lac	96%	182
Saint Mary's Hospital[2]	Madison	96%	405
Stoughton Hospital	Stoughton	96%	25
Berlin Memorial Hospital[2]	Berlin	95%	40
Froedtert Memorial Lutheran Hospital[2]	Milwaukee	95%	271
Holy Family Memorial	Manitowoc	95%	93
Saint Vincent Hospital[2]	Green Bay	95%	160
United Hospital System[2]	Kenosha	95%	213
Bellin Memorial Hospital[2]	Green Bay	94%	129
Divine Savior Healthcare	Portage	94%	54
Door County Memorial Hospital	Sturgeon Bay	94%	48
Langlade Hospital	Antigo	94%	48
Ministry St Michaels Hosp-Stevens Point	Stevens Point	94%	137
Oak Leaf Surgcl Hospital	Eau Claire	94%	48
Riverview Hospital Assoc	Wisc. Rapids	94%	72
Theda Clark Medical Center[2]	Neenah	94%	125
Waukesha Memorial Hospital[2]	Waukesha	94%	173
Columbia St Mary's Hospital Ozaukee[2]	Mequon	93%	184
Columbia St Marys Hosp Milwaukee[2]	Milwaukee	93%	323
Ministry St Marys Hospital	Rhinelander	93%	96
Beloit Memorial Hospital	Beloit	92%	125
Saint Clare's Hospital of Weston	Weston	92%	73
Wheaton Franciscan Healthcare - St Francis[2]	Milwaukee	92%	147
Sacred Heart Hospital[2]	Eau Claire	91%	193
Aurora Baycare Medical Center[2]	Green Bay	90%	105
Community Memorial Hospital[2]	Menomonee Fls	90%	193
Saint Clare Hospital Health Svcs	Baraboo	90%	42
Saint Elizabeth Hospital[2]	Appleton	90%	143
Saint Marys Hospital Medical Center	Green Bay	90%	167
Sauk Prairie Memorial Hospital	Prairie Du Sac	90%	77
Aurora Medical Center - Washington County[2]	Hartford	89%	47
Wheaton Franciscan Healthcare-Elmbrook[2]	Brookfield	89%	155
Beaver Dam Com Hospital	Beaver Dam	88%	112
Aurora Medical Center Manitowoc County[2]	Two Rivers	87%	46
Watertown Regional Medical Center	Watertown	87%	77
Oconomowoc Memorial Hospital[2]	Oconomowoc	86%	96
Aurora Lakeland Medical Center[2]	Elkhorn	85%	81
Howard Young Medical Center	Woodruff	85%	113
Mercy Medical Center of Oshkosh[2]	Oshkosh	85%	150
St Josephs Community Hosp West Bend	West Bend	85%	110
Gundersen Luth Medical Center[2]	La Crosse	83%	241
Mile Bluff Medical Center	Mauston	83%	35
Bay Area Medical Center	Marinette	76%	102
Memorial Medical Center	Ashland	75%	77

32. Urinary Catheter Removal

Hospital Name	City	Rate	Cases
Midwest Orthopedic Specialty Hospital[2]	Franklin	100%	63
Red Cedar Med Ctr-Mayo Health System	Menomonie	100%	34
Wheaton Franciscan Healthcare - All Saints[2]	Racine	100%	66
Aurora Medical Center - Washington County[2]	Hartford	99%	98
Aurora Memorial Hospital Burlington[2]	Burlington	99%	117
Aurora Sheboygan Memorial Medical Center[2]	Sheboygan	99%	245
Oak Leaf Surgcl Hospital	Eau Claire	99%	79
Sauk Prairie Memorial Hospital	Prairie Du Sac	99%	240
Lakeview Medical Center[2]	Rice Lake	98%	122
Theda Clark Medical Center[2]	Neenah	98%	135
Howard Young Medical Center	Woodruff	97%	114
Luther Hospital Mayo Health System	Eau Claire	97%	319
Ministry St Michaels Hosp-Stevens Point	Stevens Point	97%	155
Waukesha Memorial Hospital[2]	Waukesha	97%	185
Aurora Medical Center Oshkosh[2]	Oshkosh	96%	45
Columbia St Mary's Hospital Ozaukee[2]	Mequon	96%	134
Mercy Medical Center of Oshkosh[2]	Oshkosh	96%	113
Mercy Walworth Hospital & Medical Center	Lake Geneva	96%	50
Aurora Medical Center Kenosha[2]	Kenosha	95%	110
Aurora St Lukes Medical Center[2]	Milwaukee	95%	781
Saint Agnes Hospital[2]	Fond Du Lac	95%	132
Saint Josephs Hospital	Chippewa Falls	95%	42
Saint Marys Hospital Medical Center	Green Bay	95%	223
Aurora Lakeland Medical Center[2]	Elkhorn	94%	54
Bellin Memorial Hospital[2]	Green Bay	94%	127
Holy Family Memorial	Manitowoc	94%	103
Saint Mary's Hospital[2]	Madison	94%	556
Watertown Regional Medical Center	Watertown	94%	67
Milwaukee VA Medical Center[2]	Milwaukee	93%	138
Saint Clare's Hospital of Weston	Weston	93%	155
Aurora Baycare Medical Center[2]	Green Bay	92%	83
Madison VA Medical Center[2]	Madison	92%	73
Saint Clare Hospital Health Svcs	Baraboo	92%	48
Saint Elizabeth Hospital[2]	Appleton	92%	146
Aspirus Wausau Hospital[2]	Wausau	91%	89
Berlin Memorial Hospital[2]	Berlin	91%	54
Ministry St Marys Hospital	Rhinelander	91%	35
Oconomowoc Memorial Hospital[2]	Oconomowoc	91%	92
Orthopaedic Hospital of Wisconsin[2]	Glendale	91%	103
United Hospital System[2]	Kenosha	91%	163
Mercy Health Sys Corp	Janesville	90%	267
Univ of Wisconsin Hosps & Clinics Auth[2]	Madison	90%	168
Aurora West Allis Medical Center[2]	West Allis	89%	117
Franciscan Skemp La Crosse Hospital	La Crosse	89%	198
Gundersen Luth Medical Center[2]	La Crosse	89%	291
Saint Nicholas Hospital	Sheboygan	89%	102
Beaver Dam Com Hospital	Beaver Dam	88%	103
Beloit Memorial Hospital	Beloit	88%	59
Meriter Hospital[2]	Madison	88%	89
Vernon Memorial Hospital	Viroqua	87%	79
Columbia St Marys Hosp Milwaukee[2]	Milwaukee	86%	191
Door County Memorial Hospital	Sturgeon Bay	86%	36
Wheaton Franciscan Healthcare-Elmbrook[2]	Brookfield	86%	100
Froedtert Memorial Lutheran Hospital[2]	Milwaukee	84%	166
Sacred Heart Hospital[2]	Eau Claire	83%	127
Appleton Medical Center[2]	Appleton	81%	170
St Josephs Community Hosp West Bend	West Bend	81%	63
Wheaton Franciscan - St Joseph[2]	Milwaukee	80%	103
Wheaton Franciscan Healthcare - St Francis[2]	Milwaukee	80%	49
Monroe Clinic[2]	Monroe	78%	41
Community Memorial Hospital[2]	Menomonee Fls	76%	156
Saint Josephs Hospital	Marshfield	75%	387
Saint Vincent Hospital[2]	Green Bay	73%	73

NOTE: Hospital profiles are in alphabetical order by state, then city, then hospital within the city; Rankings exclude hospitals with less than 25 cases except for patient surveys which excludes hospitals with less than 100 cases; (a) 100–299 cases; (1) The number of cases is too small to be sure how well a hospital is performing; (2) The hospital indicated that the data submitted for this measure were based on a sample of cases; (3) Data was collected during a shorter time period (fewer quarters) than the maximum possible time for this measure; (4) Suppressed for one or more quarters by CMS; (5) No data is available from the hospital for this measure; (6) Fewer than 100 patients completed the HCAHPS survey. Use these rates with caution, as the number of surveys may be too low to reliably assess hospital performance; (7) Survey results are based on less than 12 months of data; (8) Survey results are not available for this reporting period; (9) No or very few patients were eligible for the HCAHPS survey. The scores shown, if any, reflect a very small number of surveys; (10) A state average was not calculated because too few hospitals in the state submitted data; (11) There were discrepancies in the data collection process; Please refer to the User's Guide for a full explanation of data.

Use of Medical Imaging

36. Combination Abdominal CT Scan

Hospital Name	City	Ratio	Cases
Saint Clare's Hospital of Weston[1]	Weston	0.000	42
Riverview Hospital Assoc	Wisc. Rapids	0.006	489
Gundersen Luth Medical Center	La Crosse	0.011	190
Aurora Medical Center - Washington County	Hartford	0.017	118
Moundview Memorial Hospital and Clinics	Friendship	0.018	109
Our Lady of Victory Hospital	Stanley	0.018	55
St Josephs Community Hosp West Bend	West Bend	0.018	284
Bellin Memorial Hospital	Green Bay	0.019	154
River Falls Area Hospital	River Falls	0.020	147
Saint Mary's Hospital	Madison	0.020	351
Saint Josephs Community Health Services[1]	Hillsboro	0.024	42
Saint Josephs Hospital	Chippewa Falls	0.024	255
Saint Marys Hospital Superior	Superior	0.029	206
Mercy Health Sys Corp	Janesville	0.032	894
Divine Savior Healthcare	Portage	0.034	203
Reedsburg Area Medical Center	Reedsburg	0.038	185
Memorial Health Center	Medford	0.039	206
Community Memorial Hospital	Menomonee Fls	0.040	274
Saint Vincent Hospital	Green Bay	0.040	547
Prairie Du Chien Memorial Hospital	Prairie Du Chien	0.042	167
Aurora West Allis Medical Center	West Allis	0.044	960
Franciscan Skemp La Crosse Hospital	La Crosse	0.047	704
Aurora Baycare Medical Center	Green Bay	0.048	480
Monroe Clinic	Monroe	0.048	415
Black River Memorial Hospital	Black River Falls	0.049	103
Saint Josephs Hospital[1]	Marshfield	0.049	41
Howard Young Medical Center	Woodruff	0.053	114
Saint Nicholas Hospital	Sheboygan	0.053	472
Aurora Lakeland Medical Center	Elkhorn	0.055	597
Appleton Medical Center	Appleton	0.057	783
Boscobel Area Health Care[1]	Boscobel	0.057	35
Spooner Health System	Spooner	0.057	88
Saint Clare Hospital Health Svcs	Baraboo	0.058	310
Lakeview Medical Center	Rice Lake	0.062	275
Meriter Hospital	Madison	0.062	531
Aurora Medical Center Manitowoc County	Two Rivers	0.063	304
Southwest Health Center	Platteville	0.063	175
Saint Marys Hospital Medical Center	Green Bay	0.065	354
Mercy Medical Center of Oshkosh	Oshkosh	0.068	340
Good Samaritan Health Center	Merrill	0.070	157
Aspirus Wausau Hospital	Wausau	0.072	430
Ministry St Michaels Hosp-Stevens Point	Stevens Point	0.072	585
Univ of Wisconsin Hosps & Clinics Auth	Madison	0.073	2268
Vernon Memorial Hospital	Viroqua	0.073	96
Aurora Memorial Hospital Burlington	Burlington	0.074	448
Sacred Heart Hospital	Tomahawk	0.078	103
Watertown Regional Medical Center	Watertown	0.078	437
Columbia St Mary's Hospital Ozaukee	Mequon	0.080	754
Ministry St Marys Hospital	Rhinelander	0.080	487
Theda Clark Medical Center	Neenah	0.081	447
Aurora Medical Center Kenosha	Kenosha	0.082	535
Ministry Eagle River Memorial Hospital	Eagle River	0.082	196
Shawano Medical Center	Shawano	0.082	182
Columbia St Marys Hosp Milwaukee	Milwaukee	0.083	1088
Grant Regional Health Center	Lancaster	0.086	70
Oconomowoc Memorial Hospital	Oconomowoc	0.088	385
Aurora St Lukes Medical Center	Milwaukee	0.090	2729
Luther Hospital Mayo Health System	Eau Claire	0.093	785
Saint Elizabeth Hospital	Appleton	0.097	486
Calumet Medical Center	Chilton	0.102	88
Bay Area Medical Center	Marinette	0.103	583
Berlin Memorial Hospital	Berlin	0.104	241
Mile Bluff Medical Center	Mauston	0.107	178
United Hospital System	Kenosha	0.108	1101
Mercy Walworth Hospital & Medical Center	Lake Geneva	0.111	198
Holy Family Memorial	Manitowoc	0.113	310
Memorial Hospital Lafayette County	Darlington	0.114	70
Sauk Prairie Memorial Hospital	Prairie Du Sac	0.115	165
Sacred Heart Hospital	Eau Claire	0.120	493
Saint Agnes Hospital	Fond Du Lac	0.128	553
Aurora Sheboygan Memorial Medical Center	Sheboygan	0.132	448
Froedtert Memorial Lutheran Hospital	Milwaukee	0.134	2119
Wheaton Franciscan Healthcare - All Saints	Racine	0.134	1108
Aurora Medical Center Oshkosh	Oshkosh	0.136	484
Waukesha Memorial Hospital	Waukesha	0.136	1410
Wheaton Franciscan Healthcare-Elmbrook	Brookfield	0.140	598
Wheaton Franciscan - St Joseph	Milwaukee	0.178	533
Fort Healthcare	Fort Atkinson	0.374	617
Beloit Memorial Hospital	Beloit	0.376	218
Wheaton Franciscan Healthcare - St Francis	Milwaukee	0.568	410
Beaver Dam Com Hospital	Beaver Dam	0.612	379
Wheaton Franciscan Healthcare - Franklin	Franklin	0.641	64

37. Combination Chest CT Scan

Hospital Name	City	Ratio	Cases
Aurora Lakeland Medical Center	Elkhorn	0.000	535
Aurora Medical Center - Washington County	Hartford	0.000	124
Aurora Medical Center Oshkosh	Oshkosh	0.000	396
Bellin Memorial Hospital	Green Bay	0.000	110
Beloit Memorial Hospital	Beloit	0.000	125
Memorial Health Center	Medford	0.000	126
Moundview Memorial Hospital and Clinics	Friendship	0.000	99
Reedsburg Area Medical Center	Reedsburg	0.000	79
River Falls Area Hospital	River Falls	0.000	90
Riverview Hospital Assoc	Wisc. Rapids	0.000	359
Sacred Heart Hospital	Tomahawk	0.000	54
Saint Clare's Hospital of Weston[1]	Weston	0.000	31
Saint Marys Hospital Superior	Superior	0.000	111
Spooner Health System[1]	Spooner	0.000	44
Froedtert Memorial Lutheran Hospital	Milwaukee	0.002	2078
Theda Clark Medical Center	Neenah	0.002	424
Appleton Medical Center	Appleton	0.003	869
Aurora Baycare Medical Center	Green Bay	0.003	307
Fort Healthcare	Fort Atkinson	0.003	353
Ministry St Marys Hospital	Rhinelander	0.003	339
Aspirus Wausau Hospital	Wausau	0.005	436
Aurora West Allis Medical Center	West Allis	0.005	586
Berlin Memorial Hospital	Berlin	0.005	216
Franciscan Skemp La Crosse Hospital	La Crosse	0.005	581
Luther Hospital Mayo Health System	Eau Claire	0.005	928
Mile Bluff Medical Center	Mauston	0.005	186
Saint Nicholas Hospital	Sheboygan	0.006	353
Columbia St Mary's Hospital Ozaukee	Mequon	0.007	874
Aurora Medical Center Manitowoc County	Two Rivers	0.008	260
Columbia St Marys Hosp Milwaukee	Milwaukee	0.008	944
Mercy Medical Center of Oshkosh	Oshkosh	0.008	255
United Hospital System	Kenosha	0.008	765
Univ of Wisconsin Hosps & Clinics Auth	Madison	0.008	2607
Divine Savior Healthcare	Portage	0.010	206
Aurora St Lukes Medical Center	Milwaukee	0.011	2789
Sacred Heart Hospital	Eau Claire	0.012	486
Shawano Medical Center	Shawano	0.012	169
Gundersen Luth Medical Center	La Crosse	0.013	78
Saint Elizabeth Hospital	Appleton	0.013	377
Howard Young Medical Center	Woodruff	0.014	71
Vernon Memorial Hospital	Viroqua	0.015	68
Saint Marys Hospital Medical Center	Green Bay	0.016	189
Wheaton Franciscan Healthcare - All Saints	Racine	0.016	1131
Aurora Sheboygan Memorial Medical Center	Sheboygan	0.019	310
Ministry St Michaels Hosp-Stevens Point	Stevens Point	0.019	323
Monroe Clinic	Monroe	0.019	215
Black River Memorial Hospital	Black River Falls	0.021	48
Southwest Health Center	Platteville	0.021	95
Aurora Memorial Hospital Burlington	Burlington	0.022	364
Saint Vincent Hospital	Green Bay	0.023	394
Mercy Health Sys Corp	Janesville	0.024	697
Oconomowoc Memorial Hospital	Oconomowoc	0.024	334
Community Memorial Hospital	Menomonee Fls	0.026	228
Ministry Eagle River Memorial Hospital	Eagle River	0.027	112
St Josephs Community Hosp West Bend	West Bend	0.027	301
Lakeview Medical Center	Rice Lake	0.028	283
Wheaton Franciscan Healthcare - Franklin[1]	Franklin	0.029	35
Bay Area Medical Center	Marinette	0.030	271
Good Samaritan Health Center	Merrill	0.030	66
Saint Agnes Hospital	Fond Du Lac	0.030	534
Saint Josephs Hospital	Chippewa Falls	0.031	194
Meriter Hospital	Madison	0.035	398
Grant Regional Health Center	Lancaster	0.036	56
Wheaton Franciscan Healthcare - St Francis	Milwaukee	0.038	289
Saint Clare Hospital Health Svcs	Baraboo	0.039	178
Prairie Du Chien Memorial Hospital	Prairie Du Chien	0.053	75
Saint Mary's Hospital[1]	Madison	0.056	54
Waukesha Memorial Hospital	Waukesha	0.060	1549
Aurora Medical Center Kenosha	Kenosha	0.061	441
Watertown Regional Medical Center	Watertown	0.063	301
Wheaton Franciscan - St Joseph	Milwaukee	0.069	346
Wheaton Franciscan Healthcare-Elmbrook	Brookfield	0.080	339
Mercy Walworth Hospital & Medical Center	Lake Geneva	0.085	129
Holy Family Memorial	Manitowoc	0.101	288
Sauk Prairie Memorial Hospital	Prairie Du Sac	0.152	105
Memorial Hospital Lafayette County[1]	Darlington	0.321	28
Beaver Dam Com Hospital	Beaver Dam	0.596	250

38. Follow-up Mammogram/Ultrasound

Hospital Name	City	Rate	Cases
Fort Healthcare	Fort Atkinson	1.1%	846
Bay Area Medical Center	Marinette	1.3%	540
Memorial Health Center	Medford	1.8%	275
United Hospital System	Kenosha	2.6%	2143
Boscobel Area Health Care	Boscobel	2.8%	142
Community Memorial Hospital	Menomonee Fls	3.1%	98
Mercy Walworth Hospital & Medical Center	Lake Geneva	3.2%	283
Bellin Memorial Hospital	Green Bay	3.4%	955
Moundview Memorial Hospital and Clinics	Friendship	3.7%	190
Good Samaritan Health Center	Merrill	3.8%	369
Mercy Health Sys Corp	Janesville	3.9%	535
Beloit Memorial Hospital	Beloit	4.2%	429
Saint Marys Hospital Superior	Superior	4.4%	543
Saint Nicholas Hospital	Sheboygan	4.8%	377
Beaver Dam Com Hospital	Beaver Dam	5.3%	717
Berlin Memorial Hospital	Berlin	5.6%	444
Univ of Wisconsin Hosps & Clinics Auth	Madison	5.9%	1660
Aurora West Allis Medical Center	West Allis	6.3%	1870
Ministry St Marys Hospital	Rhinelander	6.4%	792
Prairie Du Chien Memorial Hospital	Prairie Du Chien	6.6%	286
Froedtert Memorial Lutheran Hospital	Milwaukee	6.9%	1374
Sacred Heart Hospital	Tomahawk	7.0%	199
Saint Vincent Hospital	Green Bay	7.0%	370
Aurora St Lukes Medical Center	Milwaukee	7.4%	2244
Riverview Hospital Assoc	Wisc. Rapids	7.6%	1077
Shawano Medical Center	Shawano	7.7%	261
Wheaton Franciscan Healthcare - All Saints	Racine	7.8%	2565
Appleton Medical Center	Appleton	7.9%	632
Aurora Medical Center Kenosha	Kenosha	7.9%	682
River Falls Area Hospital	River Falls	7.9%	328
Aspirus Wausau Hospital	Wausau	8.0%	928
Saint Marys Hospital Medical Center	Green Bay	8.0%	199
Mile Bluff Medical Center	Mauston	8.1%	520
Aurora Medical Center Oshkosh	Oshkosh	8.3%	903
Aurora Memorial Hospital Burlington	Burlington	8.3%	965
Aurora Lakeland Medical Center	Elkhorn	8.4%	463
Southwest Health Center	Platteville	8.4%	227
Watertown Regional Medical Center	Watertown	8.6%	699
Saint Josephs Hospital	Chippewa Falls	8.7%	173
Calumet Medical Center	Chilton	8.9%	146
Aurora Baycare Medical Center	Green Bay	9.0%	621
Holy Family Memorial	Manitowoc	9.0%	881
Columbia St Mary's Hospital Ozaukee	Mequon	9.2%	1153
Oconomowoc Memorial Hospital	Oconomowoc	9.5%	749
Vernon Memorial Hospital	Viroqua	9.5%	241
Wheaton Franciscan - St Joseph	Milwaukee	9.6%	1726
Lakeview Medical Center	Rice Lake	9.8%	256
Columbia St Marys Hosp Milwaukee	Milwaukee	9.9%	3028
Grant Regional Health Center	Lancaster	10.0%	190
Saint Josephs Community Health Services	Hillsboro	10.2%	88
Our Lady of Victory Hospital	Stanley	10.3%	117
Saint Clare Hospital Health Svcs	Baraboo	10.4%	335
Memorial Hospital Lafayette County	Darlington	10.6%	104
Mercy Medical Center of Oshkosh	Oshkosh	10.7%	797
Wheaton Franciscan Healthcare-Elmbrook	Brookfield	10.8%	729
Sauk Prairie Memorial Hospital	Prairie Du Sac	11.0%	536
Ministry St Michaels Hosp-Stevens Point	Stevens Point	11.1%	1057
Spooner Health System	Spooner	11.1%	243
Saint Elizabeth Hospital	Appleton	11.3%	915
Theda Clark Medical Center	Neenah	11.5%	590
Waukesha Memorial Hospital	Waukesha	11.5%	2047
Monroe Clinic	Monroe	11.6%	1065
Sacred Heart Hospital	Eau Claire	11.6%	311
Saint Agnes Hospital	Fond Du Lac	12.6%	1196
Reedsburg Area Medical Center	Reedsburg	13.8%	254
Divine Savior Healthcare	Portage	14.4%	464
Wheaton Franciscan Healthcare - St Francis	Milwaukee	15.7%	1044
Wheaton Franciscan Healthcare - Franklin[1]	Franklin	17.9%	28
Howard Young Medical Center[1]	Woodruff	22.4%	58
Ministry Eagle River Memorial Hospital	Eagle River	22.9%	345

39. MRI for Low Back Pain

Hospital Name	City	Rate	Cases
Prairie Du Chien Memorial Hospital[1]	Prairie Du Chien	4.5%	44
Aurora Sheboygan Memorial Medical Center[1]	Sheboygan	15.8%	38
Beaver Dam Com Hospital[1]	Beaver Dam	18.0%	50
Community Memorial Hospital[1]	Menomonee Fls	18.4%	38
Divine Savior Healthcare[1]	Portage	19.2%	52
Mercy Walworth Hospital & Medical Center	Lake Geneva	23.5%	68
Columbia St Mary's Hospital Ozaukee	Mequon	24.2%	132
Aspirus Wausau Hospital[1]	Wausau	24.5%	53
Saint Elizabeth Hospital	Appleton	24.6%	65
Berlin Memorial Hospital[1]	Berlin	25.0%	40
Sacred Heart Hospital	Eau Claire	25.1%	167
Aurora Medical Center Oshkosh	Oshkosh	25.2%	151
Luther Hospital Mayo Health System	Eau Claire	25.8%	240
Ministry St Marys Hospital	Rhinelander	26.7%	131
Monroe Clinic	Monroe	26.8%	123
Froedtert Memorial Lutheran Hospital	Milwaukee	27.1%	203
Wheaton Franciscan - St Joseph	Milwaukee	27.3%	132
Aurora St Lukes Medical Center	Milwaukee	27.8%	345
Orthopaedic Hospital of Wisconsin	Glendale	28.1%	89
Univ of Wisconsin Hosps & Clinics Auth	Madison	28.1%	342
Lakeview Medical Center	Rice Lake	28.6%	84
Saint Nicholas Hospital	Sheboygan	28.6%	70
River Falls Area Hospital[1]	River Falls	29.0%	31
Saint Agnes Hospital	Fond Du Lac	29.8%	141
Aurora Lakeland Medical Center	Elkhorn	30.2%	63
Memorial Health Center[1]	Medford	30.3%	33
Columbia St Marys Hosp Milwaukee	Milwaukee	30.7%	264
St Josephs Community Hosp West Bend	West Bend	31.1%	103

NOTE: Hospital profiles are in alphabetical order by state, then city, then hospital within the city; Rankings exclude hospitals with less than 25 cases except for patient surveys which excludes hospitals with less than 100 cases; (a) 100–299 cases; (1) The number of cases is too small to be sure how well a hospital is performing; (2) The hospital indicated that the data submitted for this measure were based on a sample of cases; (3) Data was collected during a shorter time period (fewer quarters) than the maximum possible time for this measure; (4) Suppressed for one or more quarters by CMS; (5) No data is available from the hospital for this measure; (6) Fewer than 100 patients completed the HCAHPS survey. Use these rates with caution, as the number of surveys may be too low to reliably assess hospital performance; (7) Survey results are based on less than 12 months of data; (8) Survey results are not available for this reporting period; (9) No or very few patients were eligible for the HCAHPS survey. The scores shown, if any, reflect a very small number of surveys; (10) A state average was not calculated because too few hospitals in the state submitted data; (11) There were discrepancies in the data collection process; Please refer to the User's Guide for a full explanation of data.

Mercy Medical Center of Oshkosh	Oshkosh	31.2%	77
Fort Healthcare	Fort Atkinson	31.4%	70
Watertown Regional Medical Center	Watertown	31.5%	92
Aurora Memorial Hospital Burlington	Burlington	31.7%	145
Aurora Medical Center Kenosha	Kenosha	31.8%	110
Wheaton Franciscan Healthcare - St Francis	Milwaukee	31.8%	88
Holy Family Memorial	Manitowoc	31.9%	119
Black River Memorial Hospital[1]	Black River Falls	32.1%	28
Ministry Eagle River Memorial Hospital	Eagle River	32.1%	56
Oconomowoc Memorial Hospital	Oconomowoc	32.4%	145
United Hospital System	Kenosha	32.4%	207
Riverview Hospital Assoc	Wisc. Rapids	32.8%	67
Wheaton Franciscan Healthcare - All Saints	Racine	33.1%	284
Mercy Health Sys Corp	Janesville	33.3%	177
Sauk Prairie Memorial Hospital	Prairie Du Sac	33.3%	75
Vernon Memorial Hospital[1]	Viroqua	33.3%	30
Appleton Medical Center	Appleton	33.9%	124
Aurora Medical Center - Washington County	Hartford	33.9%	62
Mile Bluff Medical Center	Mauston	34.4%	61
Howard Young Medical Center[1]	Woodruff	34.5%	29
Waukesha Memorial Hospital	Waukesha	35.2%	349
Wheaton Franciscan Healthcare-Elmbrook	Brookfield	35.3%	204
Franciscan Skemp La Crosse Hospital	La Crosse	35.8%	173
Aurora Baycare Medical Center	Green Bay	35.9%	217
Ministry St Michaels Hosp-Stevens Point	Stevens Point	36.9%	84
Aurora Medical Center Manitowoc County	Two Rivers	38.8%	85
Reedsburg Area Medical Center	Reedsburg	39.2%	79
Good Samaritan Health Center[1]	Merrill	39.4%	33
Bay Area Medical Center	Marinette	40.2%	107
Saint Josephs Hospital	Chippewa Falls	41.0%	61
Theda Clark Medical Center	Neenah	41.2%	102
Spooner Health System[1]	Spooner	41.4%	29
Beloit Memorial Hospital	Beloit	42.0%	131
Aurora West Allis Medical Center	West Allis	42.1%	126
Saint Vincent Hospital	Green Bay	43.2%	44
Shawano Medical Center	Shawano	46.2%	39
Southwest Health Center[1]	Platteville	52.0%	25

Survey of Patients' Hospital Experiences

40. Area Around Room 'Always' Quiet at Night

Hospital Name	City	Rate	Cases
Oak Leaf Surgcl Hospital	Eau Claire	80%	300+
Orthopaedic Hospital of Wisconsin	Glendale	78%	300+
Wheaton Franciscan Healthcare - Franklin	Franklin	78%	(a)
Grant Regional Health Center	Lancaster	74%	(a)
Columbia Center	Mequon	73%	300+
Black River Memorial Hospital	Black River Falls	72%	(a)
Hayward Area Memorial Hospital	Hayward	72%	300+
St Josephs Community Hosp West Bend	West Bend	72%	300+
Ladd Memorial Hosptial[11]	Osceola	71%	(a)
Tomah Memorial Hospital	Tomah	71%	300+
Aurora Baycare Medical Center	Green Bay	70%	300+
Ministry Eagle River Memorial Hospital	Eagle River	70%	(a)
Red Cedar Med Ctr-Mayo Health System	Menomonie	70%	300+
Sacred Heart Hospital	Tomahawk	70%	(a)
Stoughton Hospital	Stoughton	70%	(a)
Wheaton Franciscan - St Joseph	Milwaukee	69%	300+
Columbus Community Hospital	Columbus	68%	300+
Memorial Health Center	Medford	68%	(a)
Waupun Memorial Hospital	Waupun	68%	300+
Southwest Health Center	Platteville	67%	300+
Ripon Medical Center	Ripon	66%	300+
Riverview Hospital Assoc	Wisc. Rapids	66%	300+
Shawano Medical Center	Shawano	66%	300+
Calumet Medical Center	Chilton	65%	(a)
Fort Healthcare	Fort Atkinson	65%	300+
Ministry St Michaels Hosp-Stevens Point	Stevens Point	65%	300+
Reedsburg Area Medical Center	Reedsburg	65%	300+
Riverside Medical Center	Waupaca	65%	300+
Saint Vincent Hospital	Green Bay	65%	300+
Aurora Medical Center Oshkosh	Oshkosh	64%	300+
Hudson Hospital	Hudson	64%	300+
Saint Clare Hospital Health Svcs	Baraboo	64%	300+
Upland Hills Health	Dodgeville	64%	300+
Waukesha Memorial Hospital	Waukesha	64%	300+
Aspirus Wausau Hospital	Wausau	63%	300+
Aurora Medical Center Manitowoc County	Two Rivers	63%	300+
Memorial Hospital Lafayette County[11]	Darlington	63%	(a)
Oconomowoc Memorial Hospital	Oconomowoc	63%	300+
Saint Josephs Hospital	Chippewa Falls	63%	300+
Saint Mary's Hospital	Madison	63%	300+
Bellin Memorial Hospital	Green Bay	62%	300+
Good Samaritan Health Center	Merrill	62%	(a)
River Falls Area Hospital	River Falls	62%	300+
Watertown Regional Medical Center	Watertown	62%	300+
Door County Memorial Hospital	Sturgeon Bay	61%	300+
Flambeau Hospital	Park Falls	61%	(a)
Luther Midelfort-Northland Mayo Hlth Sys	Barron	61%	(a)
Monroe Clinic	Monroe	61%	300+
Westfields Hospital	New Richmond	61%	300+
Aurora Medical Center - Washington County	Hartford	60%	300+
Aurora Medical Center Kenosha	Kenosha	60%	300+
Bay Area Medical Center	Marinette	60%	300+
Vernon Memorial Hospital	Viroqua	60%	300+
Wild Rose Com Memorial Hospital	Wild Rose	60%	(a)
Aurora Sheboygan Memorial Medical Center	Sheboygan	59%	300+
Aurora West Allis Medical Center	West Allis	59%	300+
Beaver Dam Com Hospital	Beaver Dam	59%	300+
Lakeview Medical Center	Rice Lake	59%	300+
Our Lady of Victory Hospital	Stanley	59%	(a)
Beloit Memorial Hospital	Beloit	58%	300+
Berlin Memorial Hospital	Berlin	58%	300+
Community Memorial Hospital	Oconto Falls	58%	300+
Divine Savior Healthcare	Portage	58%	300+
Luther Midelfort-Chippewa Vly Mayo Hlth	Bloomer	58%	(a)
Luther Midelfort-Oakridge Mayo Hlth Sys	Osseo	58%	(a)
Meriter Hospital	Madison	58%	300+
New London Family Medical Center	New London	58%	(a)
Saint Agnes Hospital	Fond Du Lac	58%	300+
Saint Marys Hospital Medical Center	Green Bay	58%	300+
Sauk Prairie Memorial Hospital	Prairie Du Sac	58%	300+
Tri County Memorial Hospital	Whitehall	58%	(a)
Columbia St Marys Hosp Milwaukee	Milwaukee	57%	300+
Cumberland Memorial Hospital	Cumberland	57%	(a)
Prairie Du Chien Memorial Hospital	Prairie Du Chien	57%	300+
Sacred Heart Hospital	Eau Claire	57%	300+
Wheaton Franciscan Healthcare-Elmbrook	Brookfield	57%	300+
Boscobel Area Health Care	Boscobel	56%	(a)
Community Memorial Hospital	Menomonee Fls	56%	300+
Memorial Medical Center	Ashland	56%	300+
Memorial Medical Center	Neillsville	56%	(a)
Mercy Medical Center of Oshkosh	Oshkosh	56%	300+
Richland Hospital	Richland Center	56%	300+
Aurora Memorial Hospital Burlington	Burlington	55%	300+
Langlade Hospital	Antigo	55%	300+
Theda Clark Medical Center	Neenah	55%	300+
Univ of Wisconsin Hosps & Clinics Auth	Madison	55%	300+
Saint Croix Regional Medical Center	Saint Croix Falls	54%	300+
Saint Elizabeth Hospital	Appleton	54%	300+
Saint Nicholas Hospital	Sheboygan	54%	300+
Burnett Medical Center	Grantsburg	53%	(a)
Gundersen Luth Medical Center	La Crosse	53%	300+
Luther Hospital Mayo Health System	Eau Claire	53%	300+
Wheaton Franciscan Healthcare - All Saints	Racine	53%	300+
Mile Bluff Medical Center	Mauston	52%	300+
Franciscan Skemp La Crosse Hospital	La Crosse	51%	300+
Holy Family Memorial	Manitowoc	51%	300+
Saint Clare's Hospital of Weston	Weston	51%	300+
Spooner Health System	Spooner	51%	(a)
Howard Young Medical Center	Woodruff	50%	300+
Saint Josephs Hospital	Marshfield	50%	300+
Wheaton Franciscan Healthcare - St Francis	Milwaukee	50%	300+
Columbia St Mary's Hospital Ozaukee	Mequon	49%	300+
Froedtert Memorial Lutheran Hospital	Milwaukee	49%	300+
Mercy Health Sys Corp	Janesville	49%	300+
Ministry St Marys Hospital	Rhinelander	49%	300+
Appleton Medical Center	Appleton	48%	300+
United Hospital System	Kenosha	48%	300+
Aurora St Lukes Medical Center	Milwaukee	47%	300+
Aurora Lakeland Medical Center	Elkhorn	46%	300+

41. Doctors 'Always' Communicated Well

Hospital Name	City	Rate	Cases
Oak Leaf Surgcl Hospital	Eau Claire	94%	300+
Grant Regional Health Center	Lancaster	91%	(a)
Hayward Area Memorial Hospital	Hayward	91%	300+
Columbia Center	Mequon	90%	300+
Orthopaedic Hospital of Wisconsin	Glendale	90%	300+
Black River Memorial Hospital	Black River Falls	89%	(a)
Upland Hills Health	Dodgeville	88%	300+
Ladd Memorial Hosptial[11]	Osceola	87%	(a)
Prairie Du Chien Memorial Hospital	Prairie Du Chien	87%	300+
Red Cedar Med Ctr-Mayo Health System	Menomonie	87%	300+
Tomah Memorial Hospital	Tomah	87%	300+
Tri County Memorial Hospital	Whitehall	87%	(a)
Vernon Memorial Hospital	Viroqua	87%	300+
Luther Midelfort-Oakridge Mayo Hlth Sys	Osseo	86%	(a)
Sacred Heart Hospital	Tomahawk	86%	(a)
Spooner Health System	Spooner	86%	(a)
Berlin Memorial Hospital	Berlin	85%	300+
Calumet Medical Center	Chilton	85%	(a)
Luther Hospital Mayo Health System	Eau Claire	85%	300+
Sauk Prairie Memorial Hospital	Prairie Du Sac	85%	300+
Columbus Community Hospital	Columbus	84%	300+
Door County Memorial Hospital	Sturgeon Bay	84%	300+
Hudson Hospital	Hudson	84%	300+
Memorial Medical Center	Ashland	84%	300+
Mile Bluff Medical Center	Mauston	84%	300+
Reedsburg Area Medical Center	Reedsburg	84%	300+
Richland Hospital	Richland Center	84%	300+
River Falls Area Hospital	River Falls	84%	300+
Stoughton Hospital	Stoughton	84%	(a)
Waupun Memorial Hospital	Waupun	84%	300+
Wheaton Franciscan Healthcare - Franklin	Franklin	84%	(a)
Beaver Dam Com Hospital	Beaver Dam	83%	300+
Cumberland Memorial Hospital	Cumberland	83%	(a)
Good Samaritan Health Center	Merrill	83%	(a)
Langlade Hospital	Antigo	83%	300+
Memorial Hospital Lafayette County[11]	Darlington	83%	(a)
Riverview Hospital Assoc	Wisc. Rapids	83%	300+
Saint Clare Hospital Health Svcs	Baraboo	83%	300+
Saint Elizabeth Hospital	Appleton	83%	300+
St Josephs Community Hosp West Bend	West Bend	83%	300+
Saint Josephs Hospital	Chippewa Falls	83%	300+
Southwest Health Center	Platteville	83%	300+
Wild Rose Com Memorial Hospital	Wild Rose	83%	(a)
Aurora Medical Center Manitowoc County	Two Rivers	82%	300+
Columbia St Mary's Hospital Ozaukee	Mequon	82%	300+
Community Memorial Hospital	Oconto Falls	82%	300+
Lakeview Medical Center	Rice Lake	82%	300+
Memorial Health Center	Medford	82%	(a)
Our Lady of Victory Hospital	Stanley	82%	(a)
Ripon Medical Center	Ripon	82%	300+
Riverside Medical Center	Waupaca	82%	300+
Sacred Heart Hospital	Eau Claire	82%	300+
Saint Croix Regional Medical Center	Saint Croix Falls	82%	300+
Saint Marys Hospital Medical Center	Green Bay	82%	300+
Westfields Hospital	New Richmond	82%	300+
Wheaton Franciscan Healthcare-Elmbrook	Brookfield	82%	300+
Aspirus Wausau Hospital	Wausau	81%	300+
Aurora Baycare Medical Center	Green Bay	81%	300+
Aurora Medical Center - Washington County	Hartford	81%	300+
Aurora Sheboygan Memorial Medical Center	Sheboygan	81%	300+
Beloit Memorial Hospital	Beloit	81%	300+
Boscobel Area Health Care	Boscobel	81%	(a)
Community Memorial Hospital	Menomonee Fls	81%	300+
Gundersen Luth Medical Center	La Crosse	81%	300+
Luther Midelfort-Chippewa Vly Mayo Hlth	Bloomer	81%	(a)
Luther Midelfort-Northland Mayo Hlth Sys	Barron	81%	(a)
Mercy Medical Center of Oshkosh	Oshkosh	81%	300+
Ministry St Marys Hospital	Rhinelander	81%	300+
Saint Nicholas Hospital	Sheboygan	81%	300+
Saint Vincent Hospital	Green Bay	81%	300+
Shawano Medical Center	Shawano	81%	300+
Aurora Lakeland Medical Center	Elkhorn	80%	300+
Aurora Medical Center Oshkosh	Oshkosh	80%	300+
Bellin Memorial Hospital	Green Bay	80%	300+
Divine Savior Healthcare	Portage	80%	300+
Meriter Hospital	Madison	80%	300+
Ministry Eagle River Memorial Hospital	Eagle River	80%	(a)
Monroe Clinic	Monroe	80%	300+
Oconomowoc Memorial Hospital	Oconomowoc	80%	300+
Saint Agnes Hospital	Fond Du Lac	80%	300+
Waukesha Memorial Hospital	Waukesha	80%	300+
Columbia St Marys Hosp Milwaukee	Milwaukee	79%	300+
Flambeau Hospital	Park Falls	79%	(a)
Fort Healthcare	Fort Atkinson	79%	300+
Franciscan Skemp La Crosse Hospital	La Crosse	79%	300+
Froedtert Memorial Lutheran Hospital	Milwaukee	79%	300+
Ministry St Michaels Hosp-Stevens Point	Stevens Point	79%	300+
Wheaton Franciscan - St Joseph	Milwaukee	79%	300+
Appleton Medical Center	Appleton	78%	300+
Aurora Medical Center Kenosha	Kenosha	78%	300+
Aurora Memorial Hospital Burlington	Burlington	78%	300+
Bay Area Medical Center	Marinette	78%	300+
Burnett Medical Center	Grantsburg	78%	(a)
Holy Family Memorial	Manitowoc	78%	300+
Howard Young Medical Center	Woodruff	78%	300+
Mercy Health Sys Corp	Janesville	78%	300+
Theda Clark Medical Center	Neenah	78%	300+
Memorial Medical Center	Neillsville	77%	(a)
New London Family Medical Center	New London	77%	(a)
Saint Mary's Hospital	Madison	77%	300+
Wheaton Franciscan Healthcare - All Saints	Racine	77%	300+
Wheaton Franciscan Healthcare - St Francis	Milwaukee	77%	300+
Aurora West Allis Medical Center	West Allis	76%	300+
Saint Clare's Hospital of Weston	Weston	76%	300+
Univ of Wisconsin Hosps & Clinics Auth	Madison	76%	300+
United Hospital System	Kenosha	75%	300+
Watertown Regional Medical Center	Watertown	75%	300+
Aurora St Lukes Medical Center	Milwaukee	74%	300+
Saint Josephs Hospital	Marshfield	73%	300+

42. Home Recovery Information Given

Hospital Name	City	Rate	Cases
Langlade Hospital	Antigo	93%	300+
Oak Leaf Surgcl Hospital	Eau Claire	93%	300+
Black River Memorial Hospital	Black River Falls	92%	(a)
Sacred Heart Hospital	Tomahawk	91%	(a)

NOTE: Hospital profiles are in alphabetical order by state, then city, then hospital within the city; Rankings exclude hospitals with less than 25 cases except for patient surveys which excludes hospitals with less than 100 cases; (a) 100–299 cases; (1) The number of cases is too small to be sure how well a hospital is performing; (2) The hospital indicated that the data submitted for this measure were based on a sample of cases; (3) Data was collected during a shorter time period (fewer quarters) than the maximum possible time for this measure; (4) Suppressed for one or more quarters by CMS; (5) No data is available from the hospital for this measure; (6) Fewer than 100 patients completed the HCAHPS survey. Use these rates with caution, as the number of surveys may be too low to reliably assess hospital performance; (7) Survey results are based on less than 12 months of data; (8) Survey results are not available for this reporting period; (9) No or very few patients were eligible for the HCAHPS survey. The scores shown, if any, reflect a very small number of surveys; (10) A state average was not calculated because too few hospitals in the state submitted data; (11) There were discrepancies in the data collection process; Please refer to the User's Guide for a full explanation of data.

Saint Clare's Hospital of Weston	Weston	91%	300+
Tomah Memorial Hospital	Tomah	91%	300+
Upland Hills Health	Dodgeville	91%	300+
Bellin Memorial Hospital	Green Bay	90%	300+
Monroe Clinic	Monroe	90%	300+
Southwest Health Center	Platteville	90%	300+
Stoughton Hospital	Stoughton	90%	(a)
Vernon Memorial Hospital	Viroqua	90%	300+
Aurora Medical Center Oshkosh	Oshkosh	89%	300+
Aurora Sheboygan Memorial Medical Center	Sheboygan	89%	300+
Columbia Center	Mequon	89%	300+
Ladd Memorial Hosptial[11]	Osceola	89%	(a)
Ministry St Marys Hospital	Rhinelander	89%	300+
Orthopaedic Hospital of Wisconsin	Glendale	89%	300+
Prairie Du Chien Memorial Hospital	Prairie Du Chien	89%	300+
Saint Mary's Hospital	Madison	89%	300+
Aurora Medical Center - Washington County	Hartford	88%	300+
Aurora Medical Center Manitowoc County	Two Rivers	88%	300+
Good Samaritan Health Center	Merrill	88%	(a)
Gundersen Luth Medical Center	La Crosse	88%	300+
Luther Hospital Mayo Health System	Eau Claire	88%	300+
Luther Midelfort-Chippewa Vly Mayo Hlth	Bloomer	88%	(a)
Memorial Hospital Lafayette County[11]	Darlington	88%	(a)
Mercy Medical Center of Oshkosh	Oshkosh	88%	300+
Meriter Hospital	Madison	88%	300+
Reedsburg Area Medical Center	Reedsburg	88%	300+
River Falls Area Hospital	River Falls	88%	300+
Saint Elizabeth Hospital	Appleton	88%	300+
Saint Josephs Hospital	Chippewa Falls	88%	300+
Sauk Prairie Memorial Hospital	Prairie Du Sac	88%	300+
Univ of Wisconsin Hosps & Clinics Auth	Madison	88%	300+
Appleton Medical Center	Appleton	87%	300+
Aspirus Wausau Hospital	Wausau	87%	300+
Aurora Baycare Medical Center	Green Bay	87%	300+
Aurora Memorial Hospital Burlington	Burlington	87%	300+
Beaver Dam Com Hospital	Beaver Dam	87%	300+
Calumet Medical Center	Chilton	87%	(a)
Holy Family Memorial	Manitowoc	87%	300+
Oconomowoc Memorial Hospital	Oconomowoc	87%	300+
Red Cedar Med Ctr-Mayo Health System	Menomonie	87%	300+
Riverside Medical Center	Waupaca	87%	300+
Sacred Heart Hospital	Eau Claire	87%	300+
Saint Croix Regional Medical Center	Saint Croix Falls	87%	300+
St Josephs Community Hosp West Bend	West Bend	87%	300+
Saint Josephs Hospital	Marshfield	87%	300+
Saint Vincent Hospital	Green Bay	87%	300+
Waukesha Memorial Hospital	Waukesha	87%	300+
Waupun Memorial Hospital	Waupun	87%	300+
Wheaton Franciscan Healthcare - All Saints	Racine	87%	300+
Aurora Lakeland Medical Center	Elkhorn	86%	300+
Burnett Medical Center	Grantsburg	86%	(a)
Community Memorial Hospital	Menomonee Fls	86%	300+
Fort Healthcare	Fort Atkinson	86%	300+
Hudson Hospital	Hudson	86%	300+
Lakeview Medical Center	Rice Lake	86%	300+
Ministry St Michaels Hosp-Stevens Point	Stevens Point	86%	300+
Saint Agnes Hospital	Fond Du Lac	86%	300+
Saint Marys Hospital Medical Center	Green Bay	86%	300+
Theda Clark Medical Center	Neenah	86%	300+
Westfields Hospital	New Richmond	86%	300+
Aurora Medical Center Kenosha	Kenosha	85%	300+
Aurora St Lukes Medical Center	Milwaukee	85%	300+
Berlin Memorial Hospital	Berlin	85%	300+
Boscobel Area Health Care	Boscobel	85%	(a)
Columbus Community Hospital	Columbus	85%	300+
Community Memorial Hospital	Oconto Falls	85%	300+
Cumberland Memorial Hospital	Cumberland	85%	(a)
Divine Savior Healthcare	Portage	85%	300+
Door County Memorial Hospital	Sturgeon Bay	85%	300+
Froedtert Memorial Lutheran Hospital	Milwaukee	85%	300+
Hayward Area Memorial Hospital	Hayward	85%	300+
Memorial Health Center	Medford	85%	(a)
Memorial Medical Center	Ashland	85%	300+
Mercy Health Sys Corp	Janesville	85%	300+
Ripon Medical Center	Ripon	85%	300+
Riverview Hospital Assoc	Wisc. Rapids	85%	300+
Saint Clare Hospital Health Svcs	Baraboo	85%	300+
Bay Area Medical Center	Marinette	84%	300+
Franciscan Skemp La Crosse Hospital	La Crosse	84%	300+
Luther Midelfort-Oakridge Mayo Hlth Sys	Osseo	84%	(a)
Ministry Eagle River Memorial Hospital	Eagle River	84%	(a)
Our Lady of Victory Hospital	Stanley	84%	(a)
Richland Hospital	Richland Center	84%	300+
Saint Nicholas Hospital	Sheboygan	84%	300+
Spooner Health System	Spooner	84%	(a)
Watertown Regional Medical Center	Watertown	84%	300+
Wheaton Franciscan - St Joseph	Milwaukee	84%	300+
Wild Rose Com Memorial Hospital	Wild Rose	84%	(a)
Aurora West Allis Medical Center	West Allis	83%	300+
Beloit Memorial Hospital	Beloit	83%	300+
Memorial Medical Center	Neillsville	83%	(a)
Mile Bluff Medical Center	Mauston	83%	300+
Wheaton Franciscan Healthcare-Elmbrook	Brookfield	83%	300+
Columbia St Marys Hosp Milwaukee	Milwaukee	82%	300+
Grant Regional Health Center	Lancaster	82%	(a)
Luther Midelfort-Northland Mayo Hlth Sys	Barron	82%	(a)
New London Family Medical Center	New London	82%	(a)
United Hospital System	Kenosha	82%	300+
Wheaton Franciscan Healthcare - St Francis	Milwaukee	82%	300+
Flambeau Hospital	Park Falls	81%	(a)
Howard Young Medical Center	Woodruff	81%	300+
Shawano Medical Center	Shawano	81%	300+
Wheaton Franciscan Healthcare - Franklin	Franklin	80%	(a)
Columbia St Mary's Hospital Ozaukee	Mequon	79%	300+
Tri County Memorial Hospital	Whitehall	79%	(a)

43. Hospital Given 9 or 10 on 10 Point Scale

Hospital Name	City	Rate	Cases
Oak Leaf Surgcl Hospital	Eau Claire	97%	300+
Columbia Center	Mequon	89%	300+
Orthopaedic Hospital of Wisconsin	Glendale	87%	300+
Ladd Memorial Hosptial[11]	Osceola	83%	(a)
Luther Midelfort-Oakridge Mayo Hlth Sys	Osseo	83%	(a)
Stoughton Hospital	Stoughton	83%	(a)
Wheaton Franciscan Healthcare - Franklin	Franklin	83%	(a)
Black River Memorial Hospital	Black River Falls	82%	(a)
Our Lady of Victory Hospital	Stanley	82%	(a)
Sauk Prairie Memorial Hospital	Prairie Du Sac	82%	300+
Meriter Hospital	Madison	80%	300+
Grant Regional Health Center	Lancaster	79%	(a)
Hudson Hospital	Hudson	79%	300+
Saint Mary's Hospital	Madison	79%	300+
Waupun Memorial Hospital	Waupun	79%	300+
Gundersen Luth Medical Center	La Crosse	78%	300+
Luther Hospital Mayo Health System	Eau Claire	78%	300+
Sacred Heart Hospital	Tomahawk	78%	(a)
Waukesha Memorial Hospital	Waukesha	78%	300+
Bellin Memorial Hospital	Green Bay	77%	300+
Calumet Medical Center	Chilton	77%	(a)
Mercy Medical Center of Oshkosh	Oshkosh	77%	300+
Southwest Health Center	Platteville	77%	300+
Univ of Wisconsin Hosps & Clinics Auth	Madison	77%	300+
Upland Hills Health	Dodgeville	77%	300+
Aurora Baycare Medical Center	Green Bay	76%	300+
Luther Midelfort-Chippewa Vly Mayo Hlth	Bloomer	76%	(a)
Prairie Du Chien Memorial Hospital	Prairie Du Chien	76%	300+
Aurora Medical Center Manitowoc County	Two Rivers	75%	300+
Cumberland Memorial Hospital	Cumberland	75%	(a)
Door County Memorial Hospital	Sturgeon Bay	75%	300+
Froedtert Memorial Lutheran Hospital	Milwaukee	75%	300+
Hayward Area Memorial Hospital	Hayward	75%	300+
Memorial Health Center	Medford	75%	(a)
Red Cedar Med Ctr-Mayo Health System	Menomonie	75%	300+
Tri County Memorial Hospital	Whitehall	75%	(a)
Columbus Community Hospital	Columbus	74%	300+
Franciscan Skemp La Crosse Hospital	La Crosse	74%	300+
River Falls Area Hospital	River Falls	74%	300+
Saint Croix Regional Medical Center	Saint Croix Falls	74%	300+
Saint Josephs Hospital	Chippewa Falls	74%	300+
Vernon Memorial Hospital	Viroqua	74%	300+
Aurora Medical Center Oshkosh	Oshkosh	73%	300+
Aurora Sheboygan Memorial Medical Center	Sheboygan	73%	300+
Berlin Memorial Hospital	Berlin	73%	300+
Community Memorial Hospital	Menomonee Fls	73%	300+
Memorial Hospital Lafayette County[11]	Darlington	73%	(a)
Oconomowoc Memorial Hospital	Oconomowoc	73%	300+
Ripon Medical Center	Ripon	73%	300+
Sacred Heart Hospital	Eau Claire	73%	300+
Saint Clare's Hospital of Weston	Weston	73%	300+
Saint Elizabeth Hospital	Appleton	73%	300+
Westfields Hospital	New Richmond	73%	300+
Aspirus Wausau Hospital	Wausau	72%	300+
Monroe Clinic	Monroe	72%	300+
Riverview Hospital Assoc	Wisc. Rapids	72%	300+
Saint Marys Hospital Medical Center	Green Bay	72%	300+
Theda Clark Medical Center	Neenah	72%	300+
Wild Rose Com Memorial Hospital	Wild Rose	72%	(a)
Langlade Hospital	Antigo	71%	300+
Reedsburg Area Medical Center	Reedsburg	71%	300+
St Josephs Community Hosp West Bend	West Bend	71%	300+
Saint Josephs Hospital	Marshfield	71%	300+
Saint Vincent Hospital	Green Bay	71%	300+
Burnett Medical Center	Grantsburg	70%	(a)
Richland Hospital	Richland Center	70%	300+
Saint Clare Hospital Health Svcs	Baraboo	70%	300+
Tomah Memorial Hospital	Tomah	70%	300+
Aurora West Allis Medical Center	West Allis	69%	300+
Beaver Dam Com Hospital	Beaver Dam	69%	300+
Columbia St Mary's Hospital Ozaukee	Mequon	69%	300+
Flambeau Hospital	Park Falls	69%	(a)
Aurora Medical Center Kenosha	Kenosha	68%	300+
Lakeview Medical Center	Rice Lake	68%	300+
Memorial Medical Center	Ashland	68%	300+
Memorial Medical Center	Neillsville	68%	(a)
Saint Agnes Hospital	Fond Du Lac	68%	300+
Aurora Medical Center - Washington County	Hartford	67%	300+
Beloit Memorial Hospital	Beloit	67%	300+
Good Samaritan Health Center	Merrill	67%	(a)
Wheaton Franciscan - St Joseph	Milwaukee	67%	300+
Appleton Medical Center	Appleton	66%	300+
Luther Midelfort-Northland Mayo Hlth Sys	Barron	66%	(a)
Riverside Medical Center	Waupaca	66%	300+
Spooner Health System	Spooner	66%	(a)
Aurora St Lukes Medical Center	Milwaukee	65%	300+
Boscobel Area Health Care	Boscobel	65%	(a)
Howard Young Medical Center	Woodruff	65%	300+
Shawano Medical Center	Shawano	65%	300+
Ministry Eagle River Memorial Hospital	Eagle River	64%	(a)
United Hospital System	Kenosha	64%	300+
Wheaton Franciscan Healthcare-Elmbrook	Brookfield	64%	300+
Fort Healthcare	Fort Atkinson	63%	300+
Holy Family Memorial	Manitowoc	63%	300+
Mile Bluff Medical Center	Mauston	63%	300+
Ministry St Michaels Hosp-Stevens Point	Stevens Point	63%	300+
Watertown Regional Medical Center	Watertown	63%	300+
Saint Nicholas Hospital	Sheboygan	62%	300+
Aurora Memorial Hospital Burlington	Burlington	61%	300+
Community Memorial Hospital	Oconto Falls	61%	300+
Columbia St Marys Hosp Milwaukee	Milwaukee	60%	300+
Ministry St Marys Hospital	Rhinelander	60%	300+
New London Family Medical Center	New London	60%	(a)
Divine Savior Healthcare	Portage	59%	300+
Wheaton Franciscan Healthcare - All Saints	Racine	58%	300+
Mercy Health Sys Corp	Janesville	57%	300+
Bay Area Medical Center	Marinette	56%	300+
Aurora Lakeland Medical Center	Elkhorn	55%	300+
Wheaton Franciscan Healthcare - St Francis	Milwaukee	55%	300+

44. Meds 'Always' Explained Before Given

Hospital Name	City	Rate	Cases
Oak Leaf Surgcl Hospital	Eau Claire	80%	300+
Sacred Heart Hospital	Tomahawk	80%	(a)
Grant Regional Health Center	Lancaster	76%	(a)
Langlade Hospital	Antigo	75%	300+
Memorial Hospital Lafayette County[11]	Darlington	75%	(a)
Red Cedar Med Ctr-Mayo Health System	Menomonie	74%	300+
Ladd Memorial Hosptial[11]	Osceola	73%	(a)
Orthopaedic Hospital of Wisconsin	Glendale	73%	300+
Waupun Memorial Hospital	Waupun	73%	300+
Black River Memorial Hospital	Black River Falls	72%	(a)
Columbia Center	Mequon	72%	300+
Wild Rose Com Memorial Hospital	Wild Rose	71%	(a)
Hudson Hospital	Hudson	70%	300+
Prairie Du Chien Memorial Hospital	Prairie Du Chien	70%	300+
Sauk Prairie Memorial Hospital	Prairie Du Sac	70%	300+
Aurora Medical Center Oshkosh	Oshkosh	69%	300+
Tomah Memorial Hospital	Tomah	69%	300+
Tri County Memorial Hospital	Whitehall	69%	(a)
Wheaton Franciscan Healthcare - Franklin	Franklin	69%	(a)
Berlin Memorial Hospital	Berlin	68%	300+
Door County Memorial Hospital	Sturgeon Bay	68%	300+
Hayward Area Memorial Hospital	Hayward	68%	300+
Ripon Medical Center	Ripon	68%	300+
Riverview Hospital Assoc	Wisc. Rapids	68%	300+
St Josephs Community Hosp West Bend	West Bend	68%	300+
Upland Hills Health	Dodgeville	68%	300+
Aurora Baycare Medical Center	Green Bay	67%	300+
Aurora Sheboygan Memorial Medical Center	Sheboygan	67%	300+
Bellin Memorial Hospital	Green Bay	67%	300+
Columbus Community Hospital	Columbus	67%	300+
Lakeview Medical Center	Rice Lake	67%	300+
Memorial Medical Center	Ashland	67%	300+
Mercy Medical Center of Oshkosh	Oshkosh	67%	300+
Saint Clare Hospital Health Svcs	Baraboo	67%	300+
Saint Josephs Hospital	Chippewa Falls	67%	300+
Saint Mary's Hospital	Madison	67%	300+
Westfields Hospital	New Richmond	67%	300+
Gundersen Luth Medical Center	La Crosse	66%	300+
Luther Midelfort-Northland Mayo Hlth Sys	Barron	66%	(a)
Ministry St Michaels Hosp-Stevens Point	Stevens Point	66%	300+
Monroe Clinic	Monroe	66%	300+
Oconomowoc Memorial Hospital	Oconomowoc	66%	300+
Saint Croix Regional Medical Center	Saint Croix Falls	66%	300+
Saint Marys Hospital Medical Center	Green Bay	66%	300+
Saint Vincent Hospital	Green Bay	66%	300+
Southwest Health Center	Platteville	66%	300+
Spooner Health System	Spooner	66%	(a)
Stoughton Hospital	Stoughton	66%	(a)
Aurora Medical Center - Washington County	Hartford	65%	300+
Beaver Dam Com Hospital	Beaver Dam	65%	300+
Calumet Medical Center	Chilton	65%	(a)

NOTE: Hospital profiles are in alphabetical order by state, then city, then hospital within the city; Rankings exclude hospitals with less than 25 cases except for patient surveys which excludes hospitals with less than 100 cases; (a) 100–299 cases; (1) The number of cases is too small to be sure how well a hospital is performing; (2) The hospital indicated that the data submitted for this measure were based on a sample of cases; (3) Data was collected during a shorter time period (fewer quarters) than the maximum possible time for this measure; (4) Suppressed for one or more quarters by CMS; (5) No data is available from the hospital for this measure; (6) Fewer than 100 patients completed the HCAHPS survey. Use these rates with caution, as the number of surveys may be too low to reliably assess hospital performance; (7) Survey results are based on less than 12 months of data; (8) Survey results are not available for this reporting period; (9) No or very few patients were eligible for the HCAHPS survey. The scores shown, if any, reflect a very small number of surveys; (10) A state average was not calculated because too few hospitals in the state submitted data; (11) There were discrepancies in the data collection process; Please refer to the User's Guide for a full explanation of data.

Hospital Name	City	Rate	Cases
Good Samaritan Health Center	Merrill	65%	(a)
Luther Hospital Mayo Health System	Eau Claire	65%	300+
Luther Midelfort-Oakridge Mayo Hlth Sys	Osseo	65%	(a)
Mile Bluff Medical Center	Mauston	65%	300+
Sacred Heart Hospital	Eau Claire	65%	300+
Univ of Wisconsin Hosps & Clinics Auth	Madison	65%	300+
Aurora Medical Center Manitowoc County	Two Rivers	64%	300+
Beloit Memorial Hospital	Beloit	64%	300+
Divine Savior Healthcare	Portage	64%	300+
Flambeau Hospital	Park Falls	64%	(a)
Franciscan Skemp La Crosse Hospital	La Crosse	64%	300+
River Falls Area Hospital	River Falls	64%	300+
Riverside Medical Center	Waupaca	64%	300+
Saint Elizabeth Hospital	Appleton	64%	300+
Vernon Memorial Hospital	Viroqua	64%	300+
Wheaton Franciscan - St Joseph	Milwaukee	64%	300+
Aspirus Wausau Hospital	Wausau	63%	300+
Howard Young Medical Center	Woodruff	63%	300+
Mercy Health Sys Corp	Janesville	63%	300+
Our Lady of Victory Hospital	Stanley	63%	(a)
Theda Clark Medical Center	Neenah	63%	300+
Waukesha Memorial Hospital	Waukesha	63%	300+
Boscobel Area Health Care	Boscobel	62%	(a)
Columbia St Marys Hosp Milwaukee	Milwaukee	62%	300+
Community Memorial Hospital	Oconto Falls	62%	300+
Holy Family Memorial	Manitowoc	62%	300+
Memorial Health Center	Medford	62%	(a)
Meriter Hospital	Madison	62%	300+
Reedsburg Area Medical Center	Reedsburg	62%	300+
Richland Hospital	Richland Center	62%	300+
Saint Clare's Hospital of Weston	Weston	62%	300+
Shawano Medical Center	Shawano	62%	300+
Watertown Regional Medical Center	Watertown	62%	300+
Community Memorial Hospital	Menomonee Fls	61%	300+
Cumberland Memorial Hospital	Cumberland	61%	(a)
Ministry Eagle River Memorial Hospital	Eagle River	61%	(a)
Saint Josephs Hospital	Marshfield	61%	300+
Bay Area Medical Center	Marinette	60%	300+
Burnett Medical Center	Grantsburg	60%	(a)
Froedtert Memorial Lutheran Hospital	Milwaukee	60%	300+
Ministry St Marys Hospital	Rhinelander	60%	300+
Saint Agnes Hospital	Fond Du Lac	60%	300+
Appleton Medical Center	Appleton	59%	300+
Aurora Memorial Hospital Burlington	Burlington	59%	300+
Aurora St Lukes Medical Center	Milwaukee	59%	300+
Columbia St Mary's Hospital Ozaukee	Mequon	59%	300+
Saint Nicholas Hospital	Sheboygan	59%	300+
Wheaton Franciscan Healthcare-Elmbrook	Brookfield	59%	300+
Aurora Medical Center Kenosha	Kenosha	58%	300+
Aurora West Allis Medical Center	West Allis	58%	300+
New London Family Medical Center	New London	58%	(a)
Aurora Lakeland Medical Center	Elkhorn	57%	300+
Fort Healthcare	Fort Atkinson	57%	300+
Luther Midelfort-Chippewa Vly Mayo Hlth	Bloomer	57%	(a)
Memorial Medical Center	Neillsville	57%	(a)
United Hospital System	Kenosha	57%	300+
Wheaton Franciscan Healthcare - All Saints	Racine	57%	300+
Wheaton Franciscan Healthcare - St Francis	Milwaukee	57%	300+

45. Nurses 'Always' Communicated Well

Hospital Name	City	Rate	Cases
Oak Leaf Surgcl Hospital	Eau Claire	92%	300+
Orthopaedic Hospital of Wisconsin	Glendale	90%	300+
Grant Regional Health Center	Lancaster	87%	(a)
Calumet Medical Center	Chilton	86%	(a)
Stoughton Hospital	Stoughton	86%	(a)
Luther Midelfort-Oakridge Mayo Hlth Sys	Osseo	85%	(a)
Sacred Heart Hospital	Tomahawk	85%	(a)
Waupun Memorial Hospital	Waupun	85%	300+
Wheaton Franciscan Healthcare - Franklin	Franklin	85%	(a)
Columbia Center	Mequon	84%	300+
Door County Memorial Hospital	Sturgeon Bay	84%	300+
Hudson Hospital	Hudson	84%	300+
Our Lady of Victory Hospital	Stanley	84%	(a)
Ripon Medical Center	Ripon	84%	300+
Tri County Memorial Hospital	Whitehall	84%	(a)
Black River Memorial Hospital	Black River Falls	83%	(a)
Ladd Memorial Hospital[11]	Osceola	83%	(a)
Aurora Medical Center Manitowoc County	Two Rivers	82%	300+
Berlin Memorial Hospital	Berlin	82%	300+
Flambeau Hospital	Park Falls	82%	(a)
Hayward Area Memorial Hospital	Hayward	82%	300+
Langlade Hospital	Antigo	82%	300+
Memorial Health Center	Medford	82%	(a)
Monroe Clinic	Monroe	82%	300+
Prairie Du Chien Memorial Hospital	Prairie Du Chien	82%	300+
Riverview Hospital Assoc	Wisc. Rapids	82%	300+
Saint Mary's Hospital	Madison	82%	300+
Sauk Prairie Memorial Hospital	Prairie Du Sac	82%	300+
Spooner Health System	Spooner	82%	(a)
Vernon Memorial Hospital	Viroqua	82%	300+
Aurora Sheboygan Memorial Medical Center	Sheboygan	81%	300+
Beaver Dam Com Hospital	Beaver Dam	81%	300+
Bellin Memorial Hospital	Green Bay	81%	300+
Memorial Hospital Lafayette County[11]	Darlington	81%	(a)
Red Cedar Med Ctr-Mayo Health System	Menomonie	81%	300+
Reedsburg Area Medical Center	Reedsburg	81%	300+
Saint Elizabeth Hospital	Appleton	81%	300+
Tomah Memorial Hospital	Tomah	81%	300+
Upland Hills Health	Dodgeville	81%	300+
Boscobel Area Health Care	Boscobel	80%	(a)
Froedtert Memorial Lutheran Hospital	Milwaukee	80%	300+
Gundersen Luth Medical Center	La Crosse	80%	300+
Mercy Medical Center of Oshkosh	Oshkosh	80%	300+
Oconomowoc Memorial Hospital	Oconomowoc	80%	300+
River Falls Area Hospital	River Falls	80%	300+
Sacred Heart Hospital	Eau Claire	80%	300+
Saint Clare Hospital Health Svcs	Baraboo	80%	300+
Saint Josephs Hospital	Chippewa Falls	80%	300+
Westfields Hospital	New Richmond	80%	300+
Aspirus Wausau Hospital	Wausau	79%	300+
Aurora Baycare Medical Center	Green Bay	79%	300+
Aurora Medical Center Oshkosh	Oshkosh	79%	300+
Beloit Memorial Hospital	Beloit	79%	300+
Community Memorial Hospital	Menomonee Fls	79%	300+
Lakeview Medical Center	Rice Lake	79%	300+
Luther Hospital Mayo Health System	Eau Claire	79%	300+
Richland Hospital	Richland Center	79%	300+
St Josephs Community Hosp West Bend	West Bend	79%	300+
Univ of Wisconsin Hosps & Clinics Auth	Madison	79%	300+
Wild Rose Com Memorial Hospital	Wild Rose	79%	(a)
Aurora Medical Center - Washington County	Hartford	78%	300+
Community Memorial Hospital	Oconto Falls	78%	300+
Cumberland Memorial Hospital	Cumberland	78%	(a)
Good Samaritan Health Center	Merrill	78%	(a)
Meriter Hospital	Madison	78%	300+
Southwest Health Center	Platteville	78%	300+
Waukesha Memorial Hospital	Waukesha	78%	300+
Columbia St Mary's Hospital Ozaukee	Mequon	77%	300+
Memorial Medical Center	Ashland	77%	300+
Mercy Health Sys Corp	Janesville	77%	300+
Ministry Eagle River Memorial Hospital	Eagle River	77%	(a)
Saint Agnes Hospital	Fond Du Lac	77%	300+
Saint Marys Hospital Medical Center	Green Bay	77%	300+
Saint Vincent Hospital	Green Bay	77%	300+
Shawano Medical Center	Shawano	77%	300+
Theda Clark Medical Center	Neenah	77%	300+
Wheaton Franciscan - St Joseph	Milwaukee	77%	300+
Aurora Memorial Hospital Burlington	Burlington	76%	300+
Bay Area Medical Center	Marinette	76%	300+
Holy Family Memorial	Manitowoc	76%	300+
Howard Young Medical Center	Woodruff	76%	300+
Ministry St Michaels Hosp-Stevens Point	Stevens Point	76%	300+
Saint Croix Regional Medical Center	Saint Croix Falls	76%	300+
Wheaton Franciscan Healthcare-Elmbrook	Brookfield	76%	300+
Aurora Lakeland Medical Center	Elkhorn	75%	300+
Fort Healthcare	Fort Atkinson	75%	300+
Luther Midelfort-Chippewa Vly Mayo Hlth	Bloomer	75%	(a)
Mile Bluff Medical Center	Mauston	75%	300+
Ministry St Marys Hospital	Rhinelander	75%	300+
Saint Clare's Hospital of Weston	Weston	75%	300+
Saint Josephs Hospital	Marshfield	75%	300+
Appleton Medical Center	Appleton	74%	300+
Aurora West Allis Medical Center	West Allis	74%	300+
Columbus Community Hospital	Columbus	74%	300+
Divine Savior Healthcare	Portage	74%	300+
Franciscan Skemp La Crosse Hospital	La Crosse	74%	300+
Luther Midelfort-Northland Mayo Hlth Sys	Barron	74%	(a)
Memorial Medical Center	Neillsville	74%	(a)
Riverside Medical Center	Waupaca	74%	300+
Watertown Regional Medical Center	Watertown	74%	300+
Wheaton Franciscan Healthcare - All Saints	Racine	74%	300+
Aurora Medical Center Kenosha	Kenosha	73%	300+
Aurora St Lukes Medical Center	Milwaukee	73%	300+
Columbia St Marys Hosp Milwaukee	Milwaukee	73%	300+
United Hospital System	Kenosha	73%	300+
Burnett Medical Center	Grantsburg	71%	(a)
Wheaton Franciscan Healthcare - St Francis	Milwaukee	71%	300+
Saint Nicholas Hospital	Sheboygan	70%	300+
New London Family Medical Center	New London	69%	(a)

46. Pain 'Always' Well Controlled

Hospital Name	City	Rate	Cases
Calumet Medical Center	Chilton	82%	(a)
Grant Regional Health Center	Lancaster	81%	(a)
Orthopaedic Hospital of Wisconsin	Glendale	81%	300+
Columbia Center	Mequon	80%	300+
Oak Leaf Surgcl Hospital	Eau Claire	79%	300+
Burnett Medical Center	Grantsburg	78%	(a)
Waupun Memorial Hospital	Waupun	78%	300+
Wheaton Franciscan Healthcare - Franklin	Franklin	78%	(a)
Our Lady of Victory Hospital	Stanley	77%	(a)
Hudson Hospital	Hudson	76%	300+
Prairie Du Chien Memorial Hospital	Prairie Du Chien	76%	300+
Stoughton Hospital	Stoughton	76%	(a)
Boscobel Area Health Care	Boscobel	75%	(a)
Memorial Health Center	Medford	75%	(a)
Ripon Medical Center	Ripon	75%	300+
River Falls Area Hospital	River Falls	75%	300+
Upland Hills Health	Dodgeville	75%	300+
Aurora Medical Center Manitowoc County	Two Rivers	74%	300+
Black River Memorial Hospital	Black River Falls	74%	(a)
Langlade Hospital	Antigo	74%	300+
Ministry Eagle River Memorial Hospital	Eagle River	74%	(a)
Aurora Medical Center Oshkosh	Oshkosh	73%	300+
Aurora Sheboygan Memorial Medical Center	Sheboygan	73%	300+
Door County Memorial Hospital	Sturgeon Bay	73%	300+
Hayward Area Memorial Hospital	Hayward	73%	300+
Memorial Hospital Lafayette County[11]	Darlington	73%	(a)
Red Cedar Med Ctr-Mayo Health System	Menomonie	73%	300+
Riverview Hospital Assoc	Wisc. Rapids	73%	300+
Spooner Health System	Spooner	73%	(a)
Aurora Baycare Medical Center	Green Bay	72%	300+
Aurora Memorial Hospital Burlington	Burlington	72%	300+
Bellin Memorial Hospital	Green Bay	72%	300+
Beloit Memorial Hospital	Beloit	72%	300+
Cumberland Memorial Hospital	Cumberland	72%	(a)
Flambeau Hospital	Park Falls	72%	(a)
Froedtert Memorial Lutheran Hospital	Milwaukee	72%	300+
Sacred Heart Hospital	Eau Claire	72%	300+
Saint Agnes Hospital	Fond Du Lac	72%	300+
Saint Elizabeth Hospital	Appleton	72%	300+
St Josephs Community Hosp West Bend	West Bend	72%	300+
Saint Josephs Hospital	Chippewa Falls	72%	300+
Saint Mary's Hospital	Madison	72%	300+
Saint Marys Hospital Medical Center	Green Bay	72%	300+
Vernon Memorial Hospital	Viroqua	72%	300+
Gundersen Luth Medical Center	La Crosse	71%	300+
Lakeview Medical Center	Rice Lake	71%	300+
Luther Hospital Mayo Health System	Eau Claire	71%	300+
Mercy Medical Center of Oshkosh	Oshkosh	71%	300+
Monroe Clinic	Monroe	71%	300+
Sacred Heart Hospital	Tomahawk	71%	(a)
Wild Rose Com Memorial Hospital	Wild Rose	71%	(a)
Aurora Medical Center - Washington County	Hartford	70%	300+
Bay Area Medical Center	Marinette	70%	300+
Berlin Memorial Hospital	Berlin	70%	300+
Community Memorial Hospital	Menomonee Fls	70%	300+
Ladd Memorial Hosptial[11]	Osceola	70%	(a)
Memorial Medical Center	Ashland	70%	300+
Saint Vincent Hospital	Green Bay	70%	300+
Sauk Prairie Memorial Hospital	Prairie Du Sac	70%	300+
Southwest Health Center	Platteville	70%	300+
Tomah Memorial Hospital	Tomah	70%	300+
Westfields Hospital	New Richmond	70%	300+
Wheaton Franciscan - St Joseph	Milwaukee	70%	300+
Aspirus Wausau Hospital	Wausau	69%	300+
Columbus Community Hospital	Columbus	69%	300+
Community Memorial Hospital	Oconto Falls	69%	300+
Holy Family Memorial	Manitowoc	69%	300+
Luther Hospital Midelfort-Chippewa Vly Mayo Hlth	Bloomer	69%	(a)
Luther Midelfort-Oakridge Mayo Hlth Sys	Osseo	69%	(a)
Saint Clare's Hospital of Weston	Weston	69%	300+
Saint Croix Regional Medical Center	Saint Croix Falls	69%	300+
Waukesha Memorial Hospital	Waukesha	69%	300+
Aurora Lakeland Medical Center	Elkhorn	68%	300+
Beaver Dam Com Hospital	Beaver Dam	68%	300+
Columbia St Mary's Hospital Ozaukee	Mequon	68%	300+
Divine Savior Healthcare	Portage	68%	300+
Luther Midelfort-Northland Mayo Hlth Sys	Barron	68%	(a)
Mercy Health Sys Corp	Janesville	68%	300+
Ministry St Michaels Hosp-Stevens Point	Stevens Point	68%	300+
Reedsburg Area Medical Center	Reedsburg	68%	300+
Saint Nicholas Hospital	Sheboygan	68%	300+
Theda Clark Medical Center	Neenah	68%	300+
Univ of Wisconsin Hosps & Clinics Auth	Madison	68%	300+
Wheaton Franciscan Healthcare-Elmbrook	Brookfield	68%	300+
Franciscan Skemp La Crosse Hospital	La Crosse	67%	300+
Howard Young Medical Center	Woodruff	67%	300+
New London Family Medical Center	New London	67%	(a)
Oconomowoc Memorial Hospital	Oconomowoc	67%	300+
Shawano Medical Center	Shawano	67%	300+
United Hospital System	Kenosha	67%	300+
Watertown Regional Medical Center	Watertown	67%	300+
Columbia St Marys Hosp Milwaukee	Milwaukee	66%	300+
Mile Bluff Medical Center	Mauston	66%	300+
Ministry St Marys Hospital	Rhinelander	66%	300+
Richland Hospital	Richland Center	66%	300+
Saint Clare Hospital Health Svcs	Baraboo	66%	300+
Wheaton Franciscan Healthcare - All Saints	Racine	66%	300+
Aurora St Lukes Medical Center	Milwaukee	65%	300+

NOTE: Hospital profiles are in alphabetical order by state, then city, then hospital within the city; Rankings exclude hospitals with less than 25 cases except for patient surveys which excludes hospitals with less than 100 cases; (a) 100–299 cases; (1) The number of cases is too small to be sure how well a hospital is performing; (2) The hospital indicated that the data submitted for this measure were based on a sample of cases; (3) Data was collected during a shorter time period (fewer quarters) than the maximum possible time for this measure; (4) Suppressed for one or more quarters by CMS; (5) No data is available from the hospital for this measure; (6) Fewer than 100 patients completed the HCAHPS survey. Use these rates with caution, as the number of surveys may be too low to reliably assess hospital performance; (7) Survey results are based on less than 12 months of data; (8) Survey results are not available for this reporting period; (9) No or very few patients were eligible for the HCAHPS survey. The scores shown, if any, reflect a very small number of surveys; (10) A state average was not calculated because too few hospitals in the state submitted data; (11) There were discrepancies in the data collection process; Please refer to the User's Guide for a full explanation of data.

Aurora West Allis Medical Center	West Allis	65%	300+
Fort Healthcare	Fort Atkinson	65%	300+
Meriter Hospital	Madison	65%	300+
Saint Josephs Hospital	Marshfield	65%	300+
Tri County Memorial Hospital	Whitehall	65%	(a)
Appleton Medical Center	Appleton	64%	300+
Riverside Medical Center	Waupaca	64%	300+
Aurora Medical Center Kenosha	Kenosha	63%	300+
Good Samaritan Health Center	Merrill	63%	(a)
Memorial Medical Center	Neillsville	61%	(a)
Wheaton Franciscan Healthcare - St Francis	Milwaukee	61%	300+

47. Room and Bathroom 'Always' Clean

Hospital Name	City	Rate	Cases
Our Lady of Victory Hospital	Stanley	94%	(a)
Aurora Medical Center Manitowoc County	Two Rivers	89%	300+
Calumet Medical Center	Chilton	89%	(a)
Tri County Memorial Hospital	Whitehall	89%	(a)
Memorial Hospital Lafayette County[11]	Darlington	88%	(a)
Vernon Memorial Hospital	Viroqua	88%	300+
Flambeau Hospital	Park Falls	87%	(a)
Riverview Hospital Assoc	Wisc. Rapids	87%	300+
Boscobel Area Health Care	Boscobel	86%	(a)
Southwest Health Center	Platteville	86%	300+
Stoughton Hospital	Stoughton	86%	(a)
Burnett Medical Center	Grantsburg	85%	(a)
Columbus Community Hospital	Columbus	85%	300+
Ministry Eagle River Memorial Hospital	Eagle River	85%	(a)
Richland Hospital	Richland Center	85%	300+
Upland Hills Health	Dodgeville	85%	300+
Langlade Hospital	Antigo	84%	300+
Luther Midelfort-Oakridge Mayo Hlth Sys	Osseo	84%	(a)
Prairie Du Chien Memorial Hospital	Prairie Du Chien	84%	300+
Sacred Heart Hospital	Tomahawk	84%	(a)
Westfields Hospital	New Richmond	84%	300+
Memorial Medical Center	Ashland	83%	300+
Oak Leaf Surgcl Hospital	Eau Claire	83%	300+
Hayward Area Memorial Hospital	Hayward	82%	300+
Ladd Memorial Hosptial[11]	Osceola	82%	(a)
Red Cedar Med Ctr-Mayo Health System	Menomonie	82%	300+
Door County Memorial Hospital	Sturgeon Bay	81%	300+
Memorial Medical Center	Neillsville	81%	(a)
Ripon Medical Center	Ripon	81%	300+
Sauk Prairie Memorial Hospital	Prairie Du Sac	81%	300+
Waupun Memorial Hospital	Waupun	81%	300+
Aurora Baycare Medical Center	Green Bay	80%	300+
Beaver Dam Com Hospital	Beaver Dam	80%	300+
Black River Memorial Hospital	Black River Falls	80%	(a)
Cumberland Memorial Hospital	Cumberland	80%	(a)
Memorial Health Center	Medford	80%	(a)
Orthopaedic Hospital of Wisconsin	Glendale	80%	300+
Reedsburg Area Medical Center	Reedsburg	80%	300+
Saint Croix Regional Medical Center	Saint Croix Falls	80%	300+
Berlin Memorial Hospital	Berlin	79%	300+
Columbia Center	Mequon	79%	300+
Luther Midelfort-Chippewa Vly Mayo Hlth	Bloomer	79%	(a)
Meriter Hospital	Madison	79%	300+
Saint Marys Hospital Medical Center	Green Bay	79%	300+
Shawano Medical Center	Shawano	79%	300+
Tomah Memorial Hospital	Tomah	79%	300+
Waukesha Memorial Hospital	Waukesha	79%	300+
Aurora Medical Center - Washington County	Hartford	78%	300+
Bellin Memorial Hospital	Green Bay	78%	300+
Luther Hospital Mayo Health System	Eau Claire	78%	300+
New London Family Medical Center	New London	78%	(a)
Oconomowoc Memorial Hospital	Oconomowoc	78%	300+
Riverside Medical Center	Waupaca	78%	300+
Saint Vincent Hospital	Green Bay	78%	300+
United Hospital System	Kenosha	78%	300+
Wheaton Franciscan Healthcare - Franklin	Franklin	78%	(a)
Wild Rose Com Memorial Hospital	Wild Rose	78%	(a)
Bay Area Medical Center	Marinette	77%	300+
Grant Regional Health Center	Lancaster	77%	(a)
Holy Family Memorial	Manitowoc	77%	300+
Lakeview Medical Center	Rice Lake	77%	300+
Mercy Medical Center of Oshkosh	Oshkosh	77%	300+
Mile Bluff Medical Center	Mauston	77%	300+
River Falls Area Hospital	River Falls	77%	300+
Sacred Heart Hospital	Eau Claire	77%	300+
Saint Agnes Hospital	Fond Du Lac	77%	300+
Saint Josephs Hospital	Chippewa Falls	77%	300+
Aurora Sheboygan Memorial Medical Center	Sheboygan	76%	300+
Good Samaritan Health Center	Merrill	76%	(a)
St Josephs Community Hosp West Bend	West Bend	76%	300+
Aurora Medical Center Oshkosh	Oshkosh	75%	300+
Beloit Memorial Hospital	Beloit	75%	300+
Divine Savior Healthcare	Portage	75%	300+
Gundersen Luth Medical Center	La Crosse	75%	300+
Monroe Clinic	Monroe	75%	300+
Aurora Medical Center Kenosha	Kenosha	74%	300+
Aurora Memorial Hospital Burlington	Burlington	74%	300+
Mercy Health Sys Corp	Janesville	74%	300+
Ministry St Michaels Hosp-Stevens Point	Stevens Point	74%	300+
Saint Clare Hospital Health Svcs	Baraboo	74%	300+
Saint Clare's Hospital of Weston	Weston	74%	300+
Saint Josephs Hospital	Marshfield	74%	300+
Saint Mary's Hospital	Madison	74%	300+
Theda Clark Medical Center	Neenah	74%	300+
Watertown Regional Medical Center	Watertown	74%	300+
Aspirus Wausau Hospital	Wausau	73%	300+
Community Memorial Hospital	Menomonee Fls	73%	300+
Howard Young Medical Center	Woodruff	73%	300+
Saint Elizabeth Hospital	Appleton	73%	300+
Univ of Wisconsin Hosps & Clinics Auth	Madison	73%	300+
Franciscan Skemp La Crosse Hospital	La Crosse	72%	300+
Spooner Health System	Spooner	72%	(a)
Appleton Medical Center	Appleton	71%	300+
Luther Midelfort-Northland Mayo Hlth Sys	Barron	71%	(a)
Aurora West Allis Medical Center	West Allis	70%	300+
Hudson Hospital	Hudson	70%	300+
Ministry St Marys Hospital	Rhinelander	70%	300+
Fort Healthcare	Fort Atkinson	69%	300+
Aurora St Lukes Medical Center	Milwaukee	68%	300+
Columbia St Mary's Hospital Ozaukee	Mequon	68%	300+
Community Memorial Hospital	Oconto Falls	68%	300+
Wheaton Franciscan Healthcare - All Saints	Racine	68%	300+
Aurora Lakeland Medical Center	Elkhorn	67%	300+
Wheaton Franciscan - St Joseph	Milwaukee	67%	300+
Wheaton Franciscan Healthcare-Elmbrook	Brookfield	67%	300+
Wheaton Franciscan Healthcare - St Francis	Milwaukee	65%	300+
Froedtert Memorial Lutheran Hospital	Milwaukee	64%	300+
Saint Nicholas Hospital	Sheboygan	62%	300+
Columbia St Marys Hosp Milwaukee	Milwaukee	60%	300+

48. Timely Help 'Always' Received

Hospital Name	City	Rate	Cases
Oak Leaf Surgcl Hospital	Eau Claire	89%	300+
Grant Regional Health Center	Lancaster	86%	(a)
Orthopaedic Hospital of Wisconsin	Glendale	84%	300+
Black River Memorial Hospital	Black River Falls	82%	(a)
Flambeau Hospital	Park Falls	81%	(a)
Our Lady of Victory Hospital	Stanley	81%	(a)
Tri County Memorial Hospital	Whitehall	80%	(a)
Red Cedar Med Ctr-Mayo Health System	Menomonie	79%	300+
River Falls Area Hospital	River Falls	79%	300+
Columbia Center	Mequon	78%	300+
Vernon Memorial Hospital	Viroqua	78%	300+
Waupun Memorial Hospital	Waupun	78%	300+
Berlin Memorial Hospital	Berlin	77%	300+
Burnett Medical Center	Grantsburg	77%	(a)
Prairie Du Chien Memorial Hospital	Prairie Du Chien	77%	300+
Ripon Medical Center	Ripon	77%	300+
Sacred Heart Hospital	Tomahawk	77%	(a)
Ministry Eagle River Memorial Hospital	Eagle River	76%	(a)
Wheaton Franciscan Healthcare - Franklin	Franklin	76%	(a)
Bellin Memorial Hospital	Green Bay	75%	300+
Cumberland Memorial Hospital	Cumberland	75%	(a)
Luther Midelfort-Oakridge Mayo Hlth Sys	Osseo	75%	(a)
Boscobel Area Health Care	Boscobel	74%	(a)
Calumet Medical Center	Chilton	74%	(a)
Hudson Hospital	Hudson	74%	300+
Ladd Memorial Hosptial[11]	Osceola	74%	(a)
Lakeview Medical Center	Rice Lake	74%	300+
Memorial Medical Center	Ashland	74%	300+
Saint Josephs Hospital	Chippewa Falls	74%	300+
Sauk Prairie Memorial Hospital	Prairie Du Sac	74%	300+
Upland Hills Health	Dodgeville	74%	300+
Community Memorial Hospital	Oconto Falls	73%	300+
Door County Memorial Hospital	Sturgeon Bay	73%	300+
Luther Hospital Mayo Health System	Eau Claire	73%	300+
Memorial Hospital Lafayette County[11]	Darlington	73%	(a)
Stoughton Hospital	Stoughton	73%	(a)
Hayward Area Memorial Hospital	Hayward	72%	300+
Memorial Health Center	Medford	72%	(a)
Memorial Medical Center	Neillsville	72%	(a)
Mercy Medical Center of Oshkosh	Oshkosh	72%	300+
Saint Croix Regional Medical Center	Saint Croix Falls	72%	300+
Spooner Health System	Spooner	72%	(a)
Westfields Hospital	New Richmond	72%	300+
Wild Rose Com Memorial Hospital	Wild Rose	72%	(a)
Aurora Medical Center Manitowoc County	Two Rivers	70%	300+
Columbus Community Hospital	Columbus	70%	300+
Riverview Hospital Assoc	Wisc. Rapids	70%	300+
Saint Clare Hospital Health Svcs	Baraboo	70%	300+
Shawano Medical Center	Shawano	70%	300+
Southwest Health Center	Platteville	70%	300+
Tomah Memorial Hospital	Tomah	70%	300+
Watertown Regional Medical Center	Watertown	70%	300+
Beloit Memorial Hospital	Beloit	69%	300+
Good Samaritan Health Center	Merrill	69%	(a)
Howard Young Medical Center	Woodruff	69%	300+
Luther Midelfort-Northland Mayo Hlth Sys	Barron	69%	(a)
United Hospital System	Kenosha	69%	300+
Aurora Baycare Medical Center	Green Bay	68%	300+
Aurora Medical Center Oshkosh	Oshkosh	68%	300+
Monroe Clinic	Monroe	68%	300+
Richland Hospital	Richland Center	68%	300+
Sacred Heart Hospital	Eau Claire	68%	300+
Saint Clare's Hospital of Weston	Weston	68%	300+
Saint Elizabeth Hospital	Appleton	68%	300+
Aurora Medical Center - Washington County	Hartford	67%	300+
Gundersen Luth Medical Center	La Crosse	67%	300+
Langlade Hospital	Antigo	67%	300+
Reedsburg Area Medical Center	Reedsburg	67%	300+
Beaver Dam Com Hospital	Beaver Dam	66%	300+
Community Memorial Hospital	Menomonee Fls	66%	300+
Oconomowoc Memorial Hospital	Oconomowoc	66%	300+
Riverside Medical Center	Waupaca	66%	300+
Wheaton Franciscan - St Joseph	Milwaukee	66%	300+
Aspirus Wausau Hospital	Wausau	65%	300+
Divine Savior Healthcare	Portage	65%	300+
Saint Mary's Hospital	Madison	65%	300+
Waukesha Memorial Hospital	Waukesha	65%	300+
Appleton Medical Center	Appleton	64%	300+
Aurora Lakeland Medical Center	Elkhorn	64%	300+
Aurora Sheboygan Memorial Medical Center	Sheboygan	64%	300+
Meriter Hospital	Madison	64%	300+
Ministry St Michaels Hosp-Stevens Point	Stevens Point	64%	300+
Bay Area Medical Center	Marinette	63%	300+
Froedtert Memorial Lutheran Hospital	Milwaukee	63%	300+
Luther Midelfort-Chippewa Vly Mayo Hlth	Bloomer	63%	(a)
Mercy Health Sys Corp	Janesville	63%	300+
Mile Bluff Medical Center	Mauston	63%	300+
St Josephs Community Hosp West Bend	West Bend	63%	300+
Saint Marys Hospital Medical Center	Green Bay	63%	300+
Aurora Memorial Hospital Burlington	Burlington	62%	300+
Fort Healthcare	Fort Atkinson	62%	300+
Holy Family Memorial	Manitowoc	62%	300+
New London Family Medical Center	New London	62%	(a)
Saint Josephs Hospital	Marshfield	62%	300+
Saint Vincent Hospital	Green Bay	62%	300+
Theda Clark Medical Center	Neenah	62%	300+
Univ of Wisconsin Hosps & Clinics Auth	Madison	62%	300+
Ministry St Marys Hospital	Rhinelander	61%	300+
Franciscan Skemp La Crosse Hospital	La Crosse	60%	300+
Saint Agnes Hospital	Fond Du Lac	60%	300+
Wheaton Franciscan Healthcare-Elmbrook	Brookfield	60%	300+
Aurora Medical Center Kenosha	Kenosha	59%	300+
Columbia St Marys Hosp Milwaukee	Milwaukee	58%	300+
Columbia St Mary's Hospital Ozaukee	Mequon	57%	300+
Saint Nicholas Hospital	Sheboygan	57%	300+
Wheaton Franciscan Healthcare - All Saints	Racine	55%	300+
Wheaton Franciscan Healthcare - St Francis	Milwaukee	55%	300+
Aurora West Allis Medical Center	West Allis	54%	300+
Aurora St Lukes Medical Center	Milwaukee	53%	300+

49. Would Definitely Recommend Hospital

Hospital Name	City	Rate	Cases
Oak Leaf Surgcl Hospital	Eau Claire	96%	300+
Columbia Center	Mequon	91%	300+
Orthopaedic Hospital of Wisconsin	Glendale	89%	300+
Stoughton Hospital	Stoughton	89%	(a)
Sauk Prairie Memorial Hospital	Prairie Du Sac	88%	300+
Luther Hospital Mayo Health System	Eau Claire	85%	300+
Meriter Hospital	Madison	85%	300+
Wheaton Franciscan Healthcare - Franklin	Franklin	85%	(a)
Hudson Hospital	Hudson	84%	300+
Ladd Memorial Hosptial[11]	Osceola	84%	(a)
Gundersen Luth Medical Center	La Crosse	83%	300+
Saint Mary's Hospital	Madison	83%	300+
Univ of Wisconsin Hosps & Clinics Auth	Madison	83%	300+
Black River Memorial Hospital	Black River Falls	82%	(a)
Waukesha Memorial Hospital	Waukesha	82%	300+
Bellin Memorial Hospital	Green Bay	81%	300+
Froedtert Memorial Lutheran Hospital	Milwaukee	81%	300+
Aurora Baycare Medical Center	Green Bay	80%	300+
Luther Midelfort-Oakridge Mayo Hlth Sys	Osseo	79%	(a)
Memorial Hospital Lafayette County[11]	Darlington	79%	(a)
Sacred Heart Hospital	Eau Claire	79%	300+
Upland Hills Health	Dodgeville	79%	300+
Aspirus Wausau Hospital	Wausau	78%	300+
Calumet Medical Center	Chilton	78%	(a)
Hayward Area Memorial Hospital	Hayward	78%	300+
Luther Midelfort-Chippewa Vly Mayo Hlth	Bloomer	78%	(a)
Mercy Medical Center of Oshkosh	Oshkosh	78%	300+
Theda Clark Medical Center	Neenah	78%	300+
Aurora Medical Center Manitowoc County	Two Rivers	77%	300+
Vernon Memorial Hospital	Viroqua	77%	300+
Aurora Medical Center Oshkosh	Oshkosh	76%	300+
Franciscan Skemp La Crosse Hospital	La Crosse	76%	300+

NOTE: Hospital profiles are in alphabetical order by state, then city, then hospital within the city; Rankings exclude hospitals with less than 25 cases except for patient surveys which excludes hospitals with less than 100 cases; (a) 100–299 cases; (1) The number of cases is too small to be sure how well a hospital is performing; (2) The hospital indicated that the data submitted for this measure were based on a sample of cases; (3) Data was collected during a shorter time period (fewer quarters) than the maximum possible time for this measure; (4) Suppressed for one or more quarters by CMS; (5) No data is available from the hospital for this measure; (6) Fewer than 100 patients completed the HCAHPS survey. Use these rates with caution, as the number of surveys may be too low to reliably assess hospital performance; (7) Survey results are based on less than 12 months of data; (8) Survey results are not available for this reporting period; (9) No or very few patients were eligible for the HCAHPS survey. The scores shown, if any, reflect a very small number of surveys; (10) A state average was not calculated because too few hospitals in the state submitted data; (11) There were discrepancies in the data collection process; Please refer to the User's Guide for a full explanation of data.

Our Lady of Victory Hospital	Stanley	76%	(a)
Reedsburg Area Medical Center	Reedsburg	76%	300+
Saint Clare's Hospital of Weston	Weston	76%	300+
Saint Elizabeth Hospital	Appleton	76%	300+
Appleton Medical Center	Appleton	75%	300+
Community Memorial Hospital	Menomonee Fls	75%	300+
Monroe Clinic	Monroe	75%	300+
Oconomowoc Memorial Hospital	Oconomowoc	75%	300+
Saint Croix Regional Medical Center	Saint Croix Falls	75%	300+
Saint Josephs Hospital	Chippewa Falls	75%	300+
Tomah Memorial Hospital	Tomah	75%	300+
Aurora Sheboygan Memorial Medical Center	Sheboygan	74%	300+
Columbia St Mary's Hospital Ozaukee	Mequon	74%	300+
Grant Regional Health Center	Lancaster	74%	(a)
River Falls Area Hospital	River Falls	74%	300+
Saint Marys Hospital Medical Center	Green Bay	74%	300+
Saint Vincent Hospital	Green Bay	74%	300+
Tri County Memorial Hospital	Whitehall	74%	(a)
Waupun Memorial Hospital	Waupun	74%	300+
Columbus Community Hospital	Columbus	73%	300+
Door County Memorial Hospital	Sturgeon Bay	73%	300+
Red Cedar Med Ctr-Mayo Health System	Menomonie	73%	300+
Saint Josephs Hospital	Marshfield	73%	300+
Southwest Health Center	Platteville	73%	300+
Westfields Hospital	New Richmond	73%	300+
Aurora West Allis Medical Center	West Allis	72%	300+
Berlin Memorial Hospital	Berlin	72%	300+
Riverview Hospital Assoc	Wisc. Rapids	72%	300+
Saint Clare Hospital Health Svcs	Baraboo	72%	300+
St Josephs Community Hosp West Bend	West Bend	72%	300+
Wheaton Franciscan - St Joseph	Milwaukee	71%	300+
Aurora Medical Center Kenosha	Kenosha	70%	300+
Aurora St Lukes Medical Center	Milwaukee	70%	300+
Beaver Dam Com Hospital	Beaver Dam	70%	300+
Cumberland Memorial Hospital	Cumberland	70%	(a)
Lakeview Medical Center	Rice Lake	70%	300+
Memorial Health Center	Medford	70%	(a)
Richland Hospital	Richland Center	70%	300+
Ripon Medical Center	Ripon	70%	300+
Sacred Heart Hospital	Tomahawk	70%	(a)
Saint Nicholas Hospital	Sheboygan	70%	300+
Beloit Memorial Hospital	Beloit	69%	300+
Wild Rose Com Memorial Hospital	Wild Rose	69%	(a)
Aurora Medical Center - Washington County	Hartford	68%	300+
Holy Family Memorial	Manitowoc	68%	300+
Langlade Hospital	Antigo	68%	300+
Flambeau Hospital	Park Falls	67%	(a)
Howard Young Medical Center	Woodruff	67%	300+
Prairie Du Chien Memorial Hospital	Prairie Du Chien	67%	300+
Wheaton Franciscan Healthcare-Elmbrook	Brookfield	67%	300+
Fort Healthcare	Fort Atkinson	66%	300+
Luther Midelfort-Northland Mayo Hlth Sys	Barron	66%	(a)
Ministry St Michaels Hosp-Stevens Point	Stevens Point	66%	300+
Saint Agnes Hospital	Fond Du Lac	66%	300+
United Hospital System	Kenosha	66%	300+
Burnett Medical Center	Grantsburg	65%	(a)
Spooner Health System	Spooner	65%	(a)
Memorial Medical Center	Ashland	64%	300+
Riverside Medical Center	Waupaca	64%	300+
Aurora Memorial Hospital Burlington	Burlington	63%	300+
Columbia St Marys Hosp Milwaukee	Milwaukee	63%	300+
Good Samaritan Health Center	Merrill	63%	(a)
Boscobel Area Health Care	Boscobel	62%	(a)
Mile Bluff Medical Center	Mauston	62%	300+
Shawano Medical Center	Shawano	62%	300+
Memorial Medical Center	Neillsville	61%	(a)
Watertown Regional Medical Center	Watertown	61%	300+
Ministry St Marys Hospital	Rhinelander	60%	300+
Wheaton Franciscan Healthcare - St Francis	Milwaukee	60%	300+
Bay Area Medical Center	Marinette	59%	300+
Community Memorial Hospital	Oconto Falls	59%	300+
New London Family Medical Center	New London	59%	(a)
Aurora Lakeland Medical Center	Elkhorn	58%	300+
Ministry Eagle River Memorial Hospital	Eagle River	58%	(a)
Divine Savior Healthcare	Portage	57%	300+
Mercy Health Sys Corp	Janesville	54%	300+
Wheaton Franciscan Healthcare - All Saints	Racine	54%	300+

NOTE: Hospital profiles are in alphabetical order by state, then city, then hospital within the city; Rankings exclude hospitals with less than 25 cases except for patient surveys which excludes hospitals with less than 100 cases; (a) 100–299 cases; (1) The number of cases is too small to be sure how well a hospital is performing; (2) The hospital indicated that the data submitted for this measure were based on a sample of cases; (3) Data was collected during a shorter time period (fewer quarters) than the maximum possible time for this measure; (4) Suppressed for one or more quarters by CMS; (5) No data is available from the hospital for this measure; (6) Fewer than 100 patients completed the HCAHPS survey. Use these rates with caution, as the number of surveys may be too low to reliably assess hospital performance; (7) Survey results are based on less than 12 months of data; (8) Survey results are not available for this reporting period; (9) No or very few patients were eligible for the HCAHPS survey. The scores shown, if any, reflect a very small number of surveys; (10) A state average was not calculated because too few hospitals in the state submitted data; (11) There were discrepancies in the data collection process; Please refer to the User's Guide for a full explanation of data.

Amery Regional Medical Center

265 Griffin Street East Phone: 715-268-0300
Amery, WI 54001 Fax: 715-268-1376
Type: Critical Access Hospitals Emergency Services: Yes
Ownership: Voluntary Non-Profit - Private Beds: 29

Key Personnel:
CEO/President. . . . . Michael Karuschak Jr
Chief of Medical Staff . . . . Craig Johnson, MD CMO
Infection Control. . . . . Nancy Magnine
Operating Room. . . . . James P Quenan
Radiology. . . . . Thomas M Pelant
Hemotology Center . . . . Pat Derrington

Measure	Cases	This Hosp.	State Avg.	U.S. Avg.
Heart Attack Care				
ACE Inhibitor or ARB for LVSD[5]	0	-	97%	96%
Aspirin at Arrival[5]	0	-	99%	99%
Aspirin at Discharge[5]	0	-	99%	98%
Beta Blocker at Discharge[5]	0	-	99%	98%
Fibrinolytic Medication Timing[5]	0	-	0%	55%
PCI Within 90 Minutes of Arrival[5]	0	-	89%	90%
Smoking Cessation Advice[5]	0	-	99%	99%
Chest Pain/Possible Heart Attack Care				
Aspirin at Arrival	-	-	96%	95%
Median Time to ECG (minutes)	-	-	7	8
Median Time to Transfer (minutes)	-	-	49	61
Fibrinolytic Medication Timing	-	-	63%	54%
Heart Failure Care				
ACE Inhibitor or ARB for LVSD[1]	4	50%	95%	94%
Discharge Instructions[1]	21	100%	86%	88%
Evaluation of LVS Function	31	48%	97%	98%
Smoking Cessation Advice	0	-	97%	98%
Pneumonia Care				
Appropriate Initial Antibiotic[1]	9	56%	94%	92%
Blood Culture Timing[1]	23	91%	97%	96%
Influenza Vaccine	34	56%	92%	91%
Initial Antibiotic Timing	62	94%	97%	95%
Pneumococcal Vaccine	58	52%	93%	93%
Smoking Cessation Advice[1]	9	89%	95%	97%
Surgical Care Improvement Project				
Appropriate VTP Within 24 Hours[3]	27	96%	93%	92%
Appropriate Hair Removal[5]	0	-	100%	99%
Appropriate Beta Blocker Usage[1,3]	19	100%	92%	93%
Controlled Postoperative Blood Glucose[3]	0	-	93%	93%
Prophylactic Antibiotic Timing[1,3]	13	69%	97%	97%
Prophylactic Antibiotic Timing (Outpatient)	-	-	91%	92%
Prophylactic Antibiotic Selection[1,3]	13	54%	98%	97%
Prophylactic Antibiotic Select. (Outpatient)	-	-	96%	94%
Prophylactic Antibiotic Stopped[1,3]	13	100%	95%	94%
Recommended VTP Ordered[3]	27	96%	94%	94%
Urinary Catheter Removal[5]	0	-	91%	90%
Children's Asthma Care				
Received Systemic Corticosteroids	-	-	-	100%
Received Home Management Plan	-	-	-	71%
Received Reliever Medication	-	-	-	100%
Use of Medical Imaging				
Combination Abdominal CT Scan	-	-	0.106	0.191
Combination Chest CT Scan	-	-	0.027	0.054
Follow-up Mammogram/Ultrasound	-	-	8.4%	8.4%
MRI for Low Back Pain	-	-	31.8%	32.7%
Survey of Patients' Hospital Experiences				
Area Around Room 'Always' Quiet at Night[8]	-	-	-	58%
Doctors 'Always' Communicated Well[8]	-	-	-	80%
Home Recovery Information Given[8]	-	-	-	82%
Hospital Given 9 or 10 on 10 Point Scale[8]	-	-	-	67%
Meds 'Always' Explained Before Given[8]	-	-	-	60%
Nurses 'Always' Communicated Well[8]	-	-	-	76%
Pain 'Always' Well Controlled[8]	-	-	-	69%
Room and Bathroom 'Always' Clean[8]	-	-	-	71%
Timely Help 'Always' Received[8]	-	-	-	64%
Would Definitely Recommend Hospital[8]	-	-	-	69%

Langlade Hospital

112 E Fifth St Phone: 715-623-2331
Antigo, WI 54409 Fax: 715-623-9440
URL: www.langladememorial.org
Type: Critical Access Hospitals Emergency Services: Yes
Ownership: Voluntary Non-Profit - Church Beds: 25

Key Personnel:
CEO/President. . . . . Dave Schneider
Chief of Medical Staff . . . . Jay Turnbull
Infection Control. . . . . Sandy Leider
Operating Room. . . . . Frank Burkett, RN
Radiology. . . . . Joseph McCausli
Anesthesiology. . . . . Jim Leek, MD
Emergency Room . . . . Randy Waskin

Measure	Cases	This Hosp.	State Avg.	U.S. Avg.
Heart Attack Care				
ACE Inhibitor or ARB for LVSD[5]	0	-	97%	96%
Aspirin at Arrival[5]	0	-	99%	99%
Aspirin at Discharge[5]	0	-	99%	98%
Beta Blocker at Discharge[5]	0	-	99%	98%
Fibrinolytic Medication Timing[5]	0	-	0%	55%
PCI Within 90 Minutes of Arrival[5]	0	-	89%	90%
Smoking Cessation Advice[5]	0	-	99%	99%
Chest Pain/Possible Heart Attack Care				
Aspirin at Arrival	-	-	96%	95%
Median Time to ECG (minutes)	-	-	7	8
Median Time to Transfer (minutes)	-	-	49	61
Fibrinolytic Medication Timing	-	-	63%	54%
Heart Failure Care				
ACE Inhibitor or ARB for LVSD[1]	4	100%	95%	94%
Discharge Instructions	25	92%	86%	88%
Evaluation of LVS Function	28	100%	97%	98%
Smoking Cessation Advice[1]	2	100%	97%	98%
Pneumonia Care				
Appropriate Initial Antibiotic	37	100%	94%	92%
Blood Culture Timing	33	97%	97%	96%
Influenza Vaccine	26	100%	92%	91%
Initial Antibiotic Timing	42	100%	97%	95%
Pneumococcal Vaccine	41	98%	93%	93%
Smoking Cessation Advice[1]	11	100%	95%	97%
Surgical Care Improvement Project				
Appropriate VTP Within 24 Hours	47	96%	93%	92%
Appropriate Hair Removal	94	100%	100%	99%
Appropriate Beta Blocker Usage[5]	0	-	92%	93%
Controlled Postoperative Blood Glucose	0	-	93%	93%
Prophylactic Antibiotic Timing	51	98%	97%	97%
Prophylactic Antibiotic Timing (Outpatient)	-	-	91%	92%
Prophylactic Antibiotic Selection	51	98%	98%	97%
Prophylactic Antibiotic Select. (Outpatient)	-	-	96%	94%
Prophylactic Antibiotic Stopped	49	98%	95%	94%
Recommended VTP Ordered	48	94%	94%	94%
Urinary Catheter Removal[1]	6	100%	91%	90%
Children's Asthma Care				
Received Systemic Corticosteroids	-	-	-	100%
Received Home Management Plan	-	-	-	71%
Received Reliever Medication	-	-	-	100%
Use of Medical Imaging				
Combination Abdominal CT Scan	-	-	0.106	0.191
Combination Chest CT Scan	-	-	0.027	0.054
Follow-up Mammogram/Ultrasound	-	-	8.4%	8.4%
MRI for Low Back Pain	-	-	31.8%	32.7%
Survey of Patients' Hospital Experiences				
Area Around Room 'Always' Quiet at Night	300+	55%	-	58%
Doctors 'Always' Communicated Well	300+	83%	-	80%
Home Recovery Information Given	300+	93%	-	82%
Hospital Given 9 or 10 on 10 Point Scale	300+	71%	-	67%
Meds 'Always' Explained Before Given	300+	75%	-	60%
Nurses 'Always' Communicated Well	300+	82%	-	76%
Pain 'Always' Well Controlled	300+	74%	-	69%
Room and Bathroom 'Always' Clean	300+	84%	-	71%
Timely Help 'Always' Received	300+	67%	-	64%
Would Definitely Recommend Hospital	300+	68%	-	69%

Appleton Medical Center

1818 N Meade St Phone: 920-731-4101
Appleton, WI 54911 Fax: 920-738-6319
URL: www.thedacare.org
Type: Acute Care Hospitals Emergency Services: Yes
Ownership: Voluntary Non-Profit - Private Beds: 160

Key Personnel:
CEO/President. . . . . Dean Gruner, MD
Chief of Medical Staff . . . . Greg Long, MD
Infection Control. . . . . Steve DuBois
Operating Room. . . . . Sherry Cheadle
Pediatric Ambulatory Care . . . . . . Eileen C Jekot, MD
Pediatric In-Patient Care . . . . . . Eileen C Jekot, MD
Quality Assurance . . . . Sally Podoski
Radiology. . . . . Timothy A Bernauer, MD

Measure	Cases	This Hosp.	State Avg.	U.S. Avg.
Heart Attack Care				
ACE Inhibitor or ARB for LVSD	59	98%	97%	96%
Aspirin at Arrival	134	100%	99%	99%
Aspirin at Discharge	261	100%	99%	98%
Beta Blocker at Discharge	264	99%	99%	98%
Fibrinolytic Medication Timing	0	-	0%	55%
PCI Within 90 Minutes of Arrival	32	97%	89%	90%
Smoking Cessation Advice	108	97%	99%	99%
Chest Pain/Possible Heart Attack Care				
Aspirin at Arrival[1,3]	3	100%	96%	95%
Median Time to ECG (minutes)[1,3]	3	5	7	8
Median Time to Transfer (minutes)[5]	0	-	49	61
Fibrinolytic Medication Timing[5]	0	-	63%	54%
Heart Failure Care				
ACE Inhibitor or ARB for LVSD	58	93%	95%	94%
Discharge Instructions	168	92%	86%	88%
Evaluation of LVS Function	211	98%	97%	98%
Smoking Cessation Advice[1]	16	88%	97%	98%
Pneumonia Care				
Appropriate Initial Antibiotic	123	95%	94%	92%
Blood Culture Timing	178	96%	97%	96%
Influenza Vaccine	146	84%	92%	91%
Initial Antibiotic Timing	198	95%	97%	95%
Pneumococcal Vaccine	183	94%	93%	93%
Smoking Cessation Advice	52	98%	95%	97%
Surgical Care Improvement Project				
Appropriate VTP Within 24 Hours[2]	285	98%	93%	92%
Appropriate Hair Removal[2]	1,291	100%	100%	99%
Appropriate Beta Blocker Usage[2]	447	89%	92%	93%
Controlled Postoperative Blood Glucose[2]	255	88%	93%	93%
Prophylactic Antibiotic Timing[2]	1,032	96%	97%	97%
Prophylactic Antibiotic Timing (Outpatient)	499	94%	91%	92%
Prophylactic Antibiotic Selection[2]	1,048	100%	98%	97%
Prophylactic Antibiotic Select. (Outpatient)	500	91%	96%	94%
Prophylactic Antibiotic Stopped[2]	999	95%	95%	94%
Recommended VTP Ordered[2]	285	98%	94%	94%
Urinary Catheter Removal[2]	170	81%	91%	90%
Children's Asthma Care				
Received Systemic Corticosteroids	-	-	-	100%
Received Home Management Plan	-	-	-	71%
Received Reliever Medication	-	-	-	100%
Use of Medical Imaging				
Combination Abdominal CT Scan	783	0.057	0.106	0.191
Combination Chest CT Scan	869	0.003	0.027	0.054
Follow-up Mammogram/Ultrasound	632	7.9%	8.4%	8.4%
MRI for Low Back Pain	124	33.9%	31.8%	32.7%
Survey of Patients' Hospital Experiences				
Area Around Room 'Always' Quiet at Night	300+	48%	-	58%
Doctors 'Always' Communicated Well	300+	78%	-	80%
Home Recovery Information Given	300+	87%	-	82%
Hospital Given 9 or 10 on 10 Point Scale	300+	66%	-	67%
Meds 'Always' Explained Before Given	300+	59%	-	60%
Nurses 'Always' Communicated Well	300+	74%	-	76%
Pain 'Always' Well Controlled	300+	64%	-	69%
Room and Bathroom 'Always' Clean	300+	71%	-	71%
Timely Help 'Always' Received	300+	64%	-	64%
Would Definitely Recommend Hospital	300+	75%	-	69%

NOTE: Hospital profiles are in alphabetical order by state, then city, then hospital within the city; Rankings exclude hospitals with less than 25 cases except for patient surveys which excludes hospitals with less than 100 cases; (a) 100–299 cases; (1) The number of cases is too small to be sure how well a hospital is performing; (2) The hospital indicated that the data submitted for this measure were based on a sample of cases; (3) Data was collected during a shorter time period (fewer quarters) than the maximum possible time for this measure; (4) Suppressed for one or more quarters by CMS; (5) No data is available from the hospital for this measure; (6) Fewer than 100 patients completed the HCAHPS survey. Use these rates with caution, as the number of surveys may be too low to reliably assess hospital performance; (7) Survey results are based on less than 12 months of data; (8) Survey results are not available for this reporting period; (9) No or very few patients were eligible for the HCAHPS survey. The scores shown, if any, reflect a very small number of surveys; (10) A state average was not calculated because too few hospitals in the state submitted data; (11) There were discrepancies in the data collection process; Please refer to the User's Guide for a full explanation of data.

Saint Elizabeth Hospital

1506 S Oneida St
Appleton, WI 54915
URL: www.affinityhealth.org
Type: Acute Care Hospitals
Ownership: Voluntary Non-Profit - Private
Phone: 920-738-2000
Fax: 920-831-1324
Emergency Services: Yes
Beds: 352

Key Personnel:
CEO/President . . . . Daniel E Neufelder
Operating Room. . . . . Eileen Leinweber
Pediatric In-Patient Care . . . . C Green, MD
Quality Assurance . . . . Cheryl Schmidt
Radiology. . . . . Robert Kinde, MD
Emergency Room . . . . Rosemary Dvorachek, RN

Measure	Cases	This Hosp.	State Avg.	U.S. Avg.
Heart Attack Care				
ACE Inhibitor or ARB for LVSD	26	100%	97%	96%
Aspirin at Arrival	110	100%	99%	99%
Aspirin at Discharge	156	100%	99%	98%
Beta Blocker at Discharge	150	100%	99%	98%
Fibrinolytic Medication Timing	0	-	0%	55%
PCI Within 90 Minutes of Arrival[1]	24	100%	89%	90%
Smoking Cessation Advice	51	100%	99%	99%
Chest Pain/Possible Heart Attack Care				
Aspirin at Arrival[1,3]	2	100%	96%	95%
Median Time to ECG (minutes)[1,3]	2	4	7	8
Median Time to Transfer (minutes)[5]	0	-	49	61
Fibrinolytic Medication Timing[5]	0	-	63%	54%
Heart Failure Care				
ACE Inhibitor or ARB for LVSD	32	100%	95%	94%
Discharge Instructions	134	93%	86%	88%
Evaluation of LVS Function	174	100%	97%	98%
Smoking Cessation Advice[1]	19	100%	97%	98%
Pneumonia Care				
Appropriate Initial Antibiotic	95	97%	94%	92%
Blood Culture Timing	158	99%	97%	96%
Influenza Vaccine	123	96%	92%	91%
Initial Antibiotic Timing	153	98%	97%	95%
Pneumococcal Vaccine	173	97%	93%	93%
Smoking Cessation Advice	49	100%	95%	97%
Surgical Care Improvement Project				
Appropriate VTP Within 24 Hours[2]	143	87%	93%	92%
Appropriate Hair Removal[2]	557	100%	100%	99%
Appropriate Beta Blocker Usage[2]	199	96%	92%	93%
Controlled Postoperative Blood Glucose[2]	151	91%	93%	93%
Prophylactic Antibiotic Timing[2]	409	99%	97%	97%
Prophylactic Antibiotic Timing (Outpatient)	482	96%	91%	92%
Prophylactic Antibiotic Selection[2]	412	100%	98%	97%
Prophylactic Antibiotic Select. (Outpatient)	476	97%	96%	94%
Prophylactic Antibiotic Stopped[2]	391	94%	95%	94%
Recommended VTP Ordered[2]	143	90%	94%	94%
Urinary Catheter Removal[2]	146	92%	91%	90%
Children's Asthma Care				
Received Systemic Corticosteroids	-	-	-	100%
Received Home Management Plan	-	-	-	71%
Received Reliever Medication	-	-	-	100%
Use of Medical Imaging				
Combination Abdominal CT Scan	486	0.097	0.106	0.191
Combination Chest CT Scan	377	0.013	0.027	0.054
Follow-up Mammogram/Ultrasound	915	11.3%	8.4%	8.4%
MRI for Low Back Pain	65	24.6%	31.8%	32.7%
Survey of Patients' Hospital Experiences				
Area Around Room 'Always' Quiet at Night	300+	54%	-	58%
Doctors 'Always' Communicated Well	300+	83%	-	80%
Home Recovery Information Given	300+	88%	-	82%
Hospital Given 9 or 10 on 10 Point Scale	300+	73%	-	67%
Meds 'Always' Explained Before Given	300+	64%	-	60%
Nurses 'Always' Communicated Well	300+	81%	-	76%
Pain 'Always' Well Controlled	300+	72%	-	69%
Room and Bathroom 'Always' Clean	300+	73%	-	71%
Timely Help 'Always' Received	300+	68%	-	64%
Would Definitely Recommend Hospital	300+	76%	-	69%

Franciscan Skemp Arcadia

464 S St Joseph Ave
Arcadia, WI 54612
URL: www.mayohealthsystem.org
Type: Critical Access Hospitals
Ownership: Voluntary Non-Profit - Church
Phone: 608-323-3341
Fax: 608-323-3694
Emergency Services: Yes
Beds: 25

Key Personnel:
Chief of Medical Staff. . . . . Dr Burggraf
Infection Control. . . . . Mary Klonecki, RN
Quality Assurance . . . . Darlene Feltes
Radiology. . . . . Lawrence D Furlong Jr
Anesthesiology. . . . . Fred Kaminsky, CRNA
Patient Relations . . . . Diane Holmay

Measure	Cases	This Hosp.	State Avg.	U.S. Avg.
Heart Attack Care				
ACE Inhibitor or ARB for LVSD[5]	0	-	97%	96%
Aspirin at Arrival[5]	0	-	99%	99%
Aspirin at Discharge[5]	0	-	99%	98%
Beta Blocker at Discharge[5]	0	-	99%	98%
Fibrinolytic Medication Timing[5]	0	-	0%	55%
PCI Within 90 Minutes of Arrival[5]	0	-	89%	90%
Smoking Cessation Advice[5]	0	-	99%	99%
Chest Pain/Possible Heart Attack Care				
Aspirin at Arrival	-	-	96%	95%
Median Time to ECG (minutes)	-	-	7	8
Median Time to Transfer (minutes)	-	-	49	61
Fibrinolytic Medication Timing	-	-	63%	54%
Heart Failure Care				
ACE Inhibitor or ARB for LVSD[1]	1	100%	95%	94%
Discharge Instructions[1]	6	50%	86%	88%
Evaluation of LVS Function[1]	12	92%	97%	98%
Smoking Cessation Advice[1]	2	100%	97%	98%
Pneumonia Care				
Appropriate Initial Antibiotic[1]	3	100%	94%	92%
Blood Culture Timing[1]	1	100%	97%	96%
Influenza Vaccine[1]	1	0%	92%	91%
Initial Antibiotic Timing[1]	3	100%	97%	95%
Pneumococcal Vaccine[1]	2	50%	93%	93%
Smoking Cessation Advice	0	-	95%	97%
Surgical Care Improvement Project				
Appropriate VTP Within 24 Hours[5]	0	-	93%	92%
Appropriate Hair Removal[5]	0	-	100%	99%
Appropriate Beta Blocker Usage[5]	0	-	92%	93%
Controlled Postoperative Blood Glucose[5]	0	-	93%	93%
Prophylactic Antibiotic Timing[1]	18	94%	97%	97%
Prophylactic Antibiotic Timing (Outpatient)	-	-	91%	92%
Prophylactic Antibiotic Selection[1]	18	83%	98%	97%
Prophylactic Antibiotic Select. (Outpatient)	-	-	96%	94%
Prophylactic Antibiotic Stopped[1]	18	94%	95%	94%
Recommended VTP Ordered[5]	0	-	94%	94%
Urinary Catheter Removal	0	-	91%	90%
Children's Asthma Care				
Received Systemic Corticosteroids	-	-	-	100%
Received Home Management Plan	-	-	-	71%
Received Reliever Medication	-	-	-	100%
Use of Medical Imaging				
Combination Abdominal CT Scan	-	-	0.106	0.191
Combination Chest CT Scan	-	-	0.027	0.054
Follow-up Mammogram/Ultrasound	-	-	8.4%	8.4%
MRI for Low Back Pain	-	-	31.8%	32.7%
Survey of Patients' Hospital Experiences				
Area Around Room 'Always' Quiet at Night[6]	<100	60%	-	58%
Doctors 'Always' Communicated Well[6]	<100	81%	-	80%
Home Recovery Information Given[6]	<100	79%	-	82%
Hospital Given 9 or 10 on 10 Point Scale[6]	<100	61%	-	67%
Meds 'Always' Explained Before Given[6]	<100	61%	-	60%
Nurses 'Always' Communicated Well[6]	<100	84%	-	76%
Pain 'Always' Well Controlled[6]	<100	73%	-	69%
Room and Bathroom 'Always' Clean[6]	<100	63%	-	71%
Timely Help 'Always' Received[6]	<100	83%	-	64%
Would Definitely Recommend Hospital	<100	72%	-	69%

Memorial Medical Center

1615 Maple Ln
Ashland, WI 54806
URL: www.ashlandmmc.com
Type: Critical Access Hospitals
Ownership: Voluntary Non-Profit - Private
Phone: 715-685-5500
Fax: 715-682-4022
Emergency Services: Yes
Beds: 100

Key Personnel:
CEO/President. . . . . Daniel J Hymans
Chief of Medical Staff. . . . . Andrew Matheus
Infection Control. . . . . Keith Henry, MD
Radiology. . . . . Fredrick E Ekberg
Emergency Room . . . . Donald Patton
Patient Relations . . . . Dan Adams

Measure	Cases	This Hosp.	State Avg.	U.S. Avg.
Heart Attack Care				
ACE Inhibitor or ARB for LVSD[1]	6	100%	97%	96%
Aspirin at Arrival	27	100%	99%	99%
Aspirin at Discharge	28	93%	99%	98%
Beta Blocker at Discharge	27	89%	99%	98%
Fibrinolytic Medication Timing	0	-	0%	55%
PCI Within 90 Minutes of Arrival	0	-	89%	90%
Smoking Cessation Advice[1]	3	100%	99%	99%
Chest Pain/Possible Heart Attack Care				
Aspirin at Arrival	-	-	96%	95%
Median Time to ECG (minutes)	-	-	7	8
Median Time to Transfer (minutes)	-	-	49	61
Fibrinolytic Medication Timing	-	-	63%	54%
Heart Failure Care				
ACE Inhibitor or ARB for LVSD	25	60%	95%	94%
Discharge Instructions	49	84%	86%	88%
Evaluation of LVS Function	63	84%	97%	98%
Smoking Cessation Advice[1]	7	71%	97%	98%
Pneumonia Care				
Appropriate Initial Antibiotic	73	93%	94%	92%
Blood Culture Timing	79	97%	97%	96%
Influenza Vaccine	48	79%	92%	91%
Initial Antibiotic Timing	78	99%	97%	95%
Pneumococcal Vaccine	77	82%	93%	93%
Smoking Cessation Advice[1]	22	86%	95%	97%
Surgical Care Improvement Project				
Appropriate VTP Within 24 Hours	75	77%	93%	92%
Appropriate Hair Removal	151	100%	100%	99%
Appropriate Beta Blocker Usage	52	87%	92%	93%
Controlled Postoperative Blood Glucose[5]	0	-	93%	93%
Prophylactic Antibiotic Timing	127	94%	97%	97%
Prophylactic Antibiotic Timing (Outpatient)	-	-	91%	92%
Prophylactic Antibiotic Selection	126	94%	98%	97%
Prophylactic Antibiotic Select. (Outpatient)	-	-	96%	94%
Prophylactic Antibiotic Stopped	125	79%	95%	94%
Recommended VTP Ordered	77	75%	94%	94%
Urinary Catheter Removal[1]	7	100%	91%	90%
Children's Asthma Care				
Received Systemic Corticosteroids	-	-	-	100%
Received Home Management Plan	-	-	-	71%
Received Reliever Medication	-	-	-	100%
Use of Medical Imaging				
Combination Abdominal CT Scan	-	-	0.106	0.191
Combination Chest CT Scan	-	-	0.027	0.054
Follow-up Mammogram/Ultrasound	-	-	8.4%	8.4%
MRI for Low Back Pain	-	-	31.8%	32.7%
Survey of Patients' Hospital Experiences				
Area Around Room 'Always' Quiet at Night	300+	56%	-	58%
Doctors 'Always' Communicated Well	300+	84%	-	80%
Home Recovery Information Given	300+	85%	-	82%
Hospital Given 9 or 10 on 10 Point Scale	300+	68%	-	67%
Meds 'Always' Explained Before Given	300+	67%	-	60%
Nurses 'Always' Communicated Well	300+	77%	-	76%
Pain 'Always' Well Controlled	300+	70%	-	69%
Room and Bathroom 'Always' Clean	300+	83%	-	71%
Timely Help 'Always' Received	300+	74%	-	64%
Would Definitely Recommend Hospital	300+	64%	-	69%

NOTE: Hospital profiles are in alphabetical order by state, then city, then hospital within the city; Rankings exclude hospitals with less than 25 cases except for patient surveys which excludes hospitals with less than 100 cases; (a) 100–299 cases; (1) The number of cases is too small to be sure how well a hospital is performing; (2) The hospital indicated that the data submitted for this measure were based on a sample of cases; (3) Data was collected during a shorter time period (fewer quarters) than the maximum possible time for this measure; (4) Suppressed for one or more quarters by CMS; (5) No data is available from the hospital for this measure; (6) Fewer than 100 patients completed the HCAHPS survey. Use these rates with caution, as the number of surveys may be too low to reliably assess hospital performance; (7) Survey results are based on less than 12 months of data; (8) Survey results are not available for this reporting period; (9) No or very few patients were eligible for the HCAHPS survey. The scores shown, if any, reflect a very small number of surveys; (10) A state average was not calculated because too few hospitals in the state submitted data; (11) There were discrepancies in the data collection process; Please refer to the User's Guide for a full explanation of data.

Baldwin Area Medical Center

730 10th Ave
Baldwin, WI 54002
Phone: 715-684-3311
Fax: 715-684-4757
E-mail: baldhosp@baldwin-telecom.net
URL: www.baldwin-hospital.com
Type: Critical Access Hospitals
Emergency Services: Yes
Ownership: Voluntary Non-Profit - Private
Beds: 33

Key Personnel:

CEO/President. . . . . Alison Page
Quality Assurance . . . . Peggy Swedine
Radiology. . . . . Mark Doyscher
Emergency Room . . . . Joel Stoeckeler, MD
Patient Relations . . . . Jean Peavey

Measure	Cases	This Hosp.	State Avg.	U.S. Avg.
Heart Attack Care				
ACE Inhibitor or ARB for LVSD[5]	0	-	97%	96%
Aspirin at Arrival[5]	0	-	99%	99%
Aspirin at Discharge[5]	0	-	99%	98%
Beta Blocker at Discharge[5]	0	-	99%	98%
Fibrinolytic Medication Timing[5]	0	-	0%	55%
PCI Within 90 Minutes of Arrival[5]	0	-	89%	90%
Smoking Cessation Advice[5]	0	-	99%	99%
Chest Pain/Possible Heart Attack Care				
Aspirin at Arrival	-	-	96%	95%
Median Time to ECG (minutes)	-	-	7	8
Median Time to Transfer (minutes)	-	-	49	61
Fibrinolytic Medication Timing	-	-	63%	54%
Heart Failure Care				
ACE Inhibitor or ARB for LVSD[1]	2	100%	95%	94%
Discharge Instructions[1]	8	88%	86%	88%
Evaluation of LVS Function[1]	11	91%	97%	98%
Smoking Cessation Advice[1]	2	100%	97%	98%
Pneumonia Care				
Appropriate Initial Antibiotic	38	92%	94%	92%
Blood Culture Timing[1]	23	100%	97%	96%
Influenza Vaccine	37	86%	92%	91%
Initial Antibiotic Timing	54	94%	97%	95%
Pneumococcal Vaccine	41	80%	93%	93%
Smoking Cessation Advice[1]	12	92%	95%	97%
Surgical Care Improvement Project				
Appropriate VTP Within 24 Hours[5]	0	-	93%	92%
Appropriate Hair Removal[5]	0	-	100%	99%
Appropriate Beta Blocker Usage[5]	0	-	92%	93%
Controlled Postoperative Blood Glucose[5]	0	-	93%	93%
Prophylactic Antibiotic Timing	49	92%	97%	97%
Prophylactic Antibiotic Timing (Outpatient)	-	-	91%	92%
Prophylactic Antibiotic Selection	49	100%	98%	97%
Prophylactic Antibiotic Select. (Outpatient)	-	-	96%	94%
Prophylactic Antibiotic Stopped	49	96%	95%	94%
Recommended VTP Ordered[5]	0	-	94%	94%
Urinary Catheter Removal[5]	0	-	91%	90%
Children's Asthma Care				
Received Systemic Corticosteroids	-	-	-	100%
Received Home Management Plan	-	-	-	71%
Received Reliever Medication	-	-	-	100%
Use of Medical Imaging				
Combination Abdominal CT Scan	-	-	0.106	0.191
Combination Chest CT Scan	-	-	0.027	0.054
Follow-up Mammogram/Ultrasound	-	-	8.4%	8.4%
MRI for Low Back Pain	-	-	31.8%	32.7%
Survey of Patients' Hospital Experiences				
Area Around Room 'Always' Quiet at Night[8]	-	-	-	58%
Doctors 'Always' Communicated Well[8]	-	-	-	80%
Home Recovery Information Given[8]	-	-	-	82%
Hospital Given 9 or 10 on 10 Point Scale[8]	-	-	-	67%
Meds 'Always' Explained Before Given[8]	-	-	-	60%
Nurses 'Always' Communicated Well[8]	-	-	-	76%
Pain 'Always' Well Controlled[8]	-	-	-	69%
Room and Bathroom 'Always' Clean[8]	-	-	-	71%
Timely Help 'Always' Received[8]	-	-	-	64%
Would Definitely Recommend Hospital[8]	-	-	-	69%

Saint Clare Hospital Health Svcs

707 14th St
Baraboo, WI 53913
Phone: 608-356-1400
Fax: 608-356-1367
URL: www.stclare.com
Type: Acute Care Hospitals
Emergency Services: Yes
Ownership: Voluntary Non-Profit - Private
Beds: 62

Key Personnel:

CEO/President. . . . . Sandra Anderson
Chief of Medical Staff . . . . Erich Herbest
Emergency Room . . . . Theresa Weiland

Measure	Cases	This Hosp.	State Avg.	U.S. Avg.
Heart Attack Care				
ACE Inhibitor or ARB for LVSD[1]	1	100%	97%	96%
Aspirin at Arrival[1]	3	100%	99%	99%
Aspirin at Discharge[1]	2	100%	99%	98%
Beta Blocker at Discharge	0	-	99%	98%
Fibrinolytic Medication Timing	0	-	0%	55%
PCI Within 90 Minutes of Arrival	0	-	89%	90%
Smoking Cessation Advice	0	-	99%	99%
Chest Pain/Possible Heart Attack Care				
Aspirin at Arrival	63	98%	96%	95%
Median Time to ECG (minutes)	63	3	7	8
Median Time to Transfer (minutes)[1,3]	7	26	49	61
Fibrinolytic Medication Timing[1]	1	100%	63%	54%
Heart Failure Care				
ACE Inhibitor or ARB for LVSD[1]	16	100%	95%	94%
Discharge Instructions	40	95%	86%	88%
Evaluation of LVS Function	52	100%	97%	98%
Smoking Cessation Advice[1]	3	100%	97%	98%
Pneumonia Care				
Appropriate Initial Antibiotic	69	97%	94%	92%
Blood Culture Timing	96	89%	97%	96%
Influenza Vaccine	61	84%	92%	91%
Initial Antibiotic Timing	102	99%	97%	95%
Pneumococcal Vaccine	86	93%	93%	93%
Smoking Cessation Advice	34	97%	95%	97%
Surgical Care Improvement Project				
Appropriate VTP Within 24 Hours	42	90%	93%	92%
Appropriate Hair Removal	149	100%	100%	99%
Appropriate Beta Blocker Usage	38	100%	92%	93%
Controlled Postoperative Blood Glucose	0	-	93%	93%
Prophylactic Antibiotic Timing	123	98%	97%	97%
Prophylactic Antibiotic Timing (Outpatient)	69	93%	91%	92%
Prophylactic Antibiotic Selection	123	100%	98%	97%
Prophylactic Antibiotic Select. (Outpatient)	64	97%	96%	94%
Prophylactic Antibiotic Stopped	121	90%	95%	94%
Recommended VTP Ordered	42	90%	94%	94%
Urinary Catheter Removal	48	92%	91%	90%
Children's Asthma Care				
Received Systemic Corticosteroids	-	-	-	100%
Received Home Management Plan	-	-	-	71%
Received Reliever Medication	-	-	-	100%
Use of Medical Imaging				
Combination Abdominal CT Scan	310	0.058	0.106	0.191
Combination Chest CT Scan	178	0.039	0.027	0.054
Follow-up Mammogram/Ultrasound	335	10.4%	8.4%	8.4%
MRI for Low Back Pain[1]	2	0.0%	31.8%	32.7%
Survey of Patients' Hospital Experiences				
Area Around Room 'Always' Quiet at Night	300+	64%	-	58%
Doctors 'Always' Communicated Well	300+	83%	-	80%
Home Recovery Information Given	300+	85%	-	82%
Hospital Given 9 or 10 on 10 Point Scale	300+	70%	-	67%
Meds 'Always' Explained Before Given	300+	67%	-	60%
Nurses 'Always' Communicated Well	300+	80%	-	76%
Pain 'Always' Well Controlled	300+	66%	-	69%
Room and Bathroom 'Always' Clean	300+	74%	-	71%
Timely Help 'Always' Received	300+	70%	-	64%
Would Definitely Recommend Hospital	300+	72%	-	69%

Luther Midelfort - Northland Mayo Health System

1222 E Woodland Ave
Barron, WI 54812
Phone: 715-537-3186
Fax: 715-537-9023
URL: www.luthermidelfortnorthland.org
Type: Critical Access Hospitals
Emergency Services: Yes
Ownership: Voluntary Non-Profit - Other
Beds: 29

Key Personnel:

Chief of Medical Staff . . . . Michael Damroth
Infection Control. . . . . Kim Droege
Operating Room. . . . . Lorna Larson, RN
Quality Assurance . . . . Lori Springer
Anesthesiology. . . . . Tom Thomsen
Emergency Room . . . . Lorna Larson, RN

Measure	Cases	This Hosp.	State Avg.	U.S. Avg.
Heart Attack Care				
ACE Inhibitor or ARB for LVSD	0	-	97%	96%
Aspirin at Arrival[1]	8	100%	99%	99%
Aspirin at Discharge[1]	5	100%	99%	98%
Beta Blocker at Discharge[1]	5	100%	99%	98%
Fibrinolytic Medication Timing	0	-	0%	55%
PCI Within 90 Minutes of Arrival[5]	0	-	89%	90%
Smoking Cessation Advice	0	-	99%	99%
Chest Pain/Possible Heart Attack Care				
Aspirin at Arrival	-	-	96%	95%
Median Time to ECG (minutes)	-	-	7	8
Median Time to Transfer (minutes)	-	-	49	61
Fibrinolytic Medication Timing	-	-	63%	54%
Heart Failure Care				
ACE Inhibitor or ARB for LVSD[1]	7	100%	95%	94%
Discharge Instructions[1]	21	100%	86%	88%
Evaluation of LVS Function	27	100%	97%	98%
Smoking Cessation Advice[1]	2	100%	97%	98%
Pneumonia Care				
Appropriate Initial Antibiotic[1]	13	92%	94%	92%
Blood Culture Timing	25	88%	97%	96%
Influenza Vaccine[1]	14	86%	92%	91%
Initial Antibiotic Timing[1]	21	100%	97%	95%
Pneumococcal Vaccine[1]	23	100%	93%	93%
Smoking Cessation Advice[1]	4	75%	95%	97%
Surgical Care Improvement Project				
Appropriate VTP Within 24 Hours[1]	18	94%	93%	92%
Appropriate Hair Removal	40	100%	100%	99%
Appropriate Beta Blocker Usage[1]	12	100%	92%	93%
Controlled Postoperative Blood Glucose[5]	0	-	93%	93%
Prophylactic Antibiotic Timing	30	87%	97%	97%
Prophylactic Antibiotic Timing (Outpatient)	-	-	91%	92%
Prophylactic Antibiotic Selection	28	86%	98%	97%
Prophylactic Antibiotic Select. (Outpatient)	-	-	96%	94%
Prophylactic Antibiotic Stopped	28	93%	95%	94%
Recommended VTP Ordered[1]	18	94%	94%	94%
Urinary Catheter Removal[1]	4	75%	91%	90%
Children's Asthma Care				
Received Systemic Corticosteroids	-	-	-	100%
Received Home Management Plan	-	-	-	71%
Received Reliever Medication	-	-	-	100%
Use of Medical Imaging				
Combination Abdominal CT Scan	-	-	0.106	0.191
Combination Chest CT Scan	-	-	0.027	0.054
Follow-up Mammogram/Ultrasound	-	-	8.4%	8.4%
MRI for Low Back Pain	-	-	31.8%	32.7%
Survey of Patients' Hospital Experiences				
Area Around Room 'Always' Quiet at Night	(a)	61%	-	58%
Doctors 'Always' Communicated Well	(a)	81%	-	80%
Home Recovery Information Given	(a)	82%	-	82%
Hospital Given 9 or 10 on 10 Point Scale	(a)	66%	-	67%
Meds 'Always' Explained Before Given	(a)	66%	-	60%
Nurses 'Always' Communicated Well	(a)	74%	-	76%
Pain 'Always' Well Controlled	(a)	68%	-	69%
Room and Bathroom 'Always' Clean	(a)	71%	-	71%
Timely Help 'Always' Received	(a)	69%	-	64%
Would Definitely Recommend Hospital	(a)	66%	-	69%

NOTE: Hospital profiles are in alphabetical order by state, then city, then hospital within the city; Rankings exclude hospitals with less than 25 cases except for patient surveys which excludes hospitals with less than 100 cases; (a) 100–299 cases; (1) The number of cases is too small to be sure how well a hospital is performing; (2) The hospital indicated that the data submitted for this measure were based on a sample of cases; (3) Data was collected during a shorter time period (fewer quarters) than the maximum possible time for this measure; (4) Suppressed for one or more quarters by CMS; (5) No data is available from the hospital for this measure; (6) Fewer than 100 patients completed the HCAHPS survey. Use these rates with caution, as the number of surveys may be too low to reliably assess hospital performance; (7) Survey results are based on less than 12 months of data; (8) Survey results are not available for this reporting period; (9) No or very few patients were eligible for the HCAHPS survey. The scores shown, if any, reflect a very small number of surveys; (10) A state average was not calculated because too few hospitals in the state submitted data; (11) There were discrepancies in the data collection process; Please refer to the User's Guide for a full explanation of data.

Beaver Dam Com Hospital

707 S University Ave
Beaver Dam, WI 53916
Type: Acute Care Hospitals
Ownership: Voluntary Non-Profit - Private
Phone: 920-887-7181
Fax: 920-887-3422
Emergency Services: Yes
Beds: 125

Key Personnel:
CEO/President. . . . . John R Landdeck
Operating Room. . . . . Julie Nampel
Quality Assurance . . . . Sue Williams
Radiology. . . . . John Sweeney
Ambulatory Care . . . . Sandra Tiedt
Emergency Room . . . . Judy MacDonald

Measure	Cases	This Hosp.	State Avg.	U.S. Avg.
Heart Attack Care				
ACE Inhibitor or ARB for LVSD[1]	2	100%	97%	96%
Aspirin at Arrival[1]	15	100%	99%	99%
Aspirin at Discharge[1]	10	100%	99%	98%
Beta Blocker at Discharge[1]	9	100%	99%	98%
Fibrinolytic Medication Timing	0	-	0%	55%
PCI Within 90 Minutes of Arrival	0	-	89%	90%
Smoking Cessation Advice[1]	1	100%	99%	99%
Chest Pain/Possible Heart Attack Care				
Aspirin at Arrival	134	99%	96%	95%
Median Time to ECG (minutes)	138	8	7	8
Median Time to Transfer (minutes)[1]	14	80	49	61
Fibrinolytic Medication Timing[1]	1	0%	63%	54%
Heart Failure Care				
ACE Inhibitor or ARB for LVSD[1]	17	88%	95%	94%
Discharge Instructions	48	60%	86%	88%
Evaluation of LVS Function	69	87%	97%	98%
Smoking Cessation Advice[1]	9	89%	97%	98%
Pneumonia Care				
Appropriate Initial Antibiotic	59	98%	94%	92%
Blood Culture Timing	66	95%	97%	96%
Influenza Vaccine	41	83%	92%	91%
Initial Antibiotic Timing	76	99%	97%	95%
Pneumococcal Vaccine	66	83%	93%	93%
Smoking Cessation Advice[1]	12	92%	95%	97%
Surgical Care Improvement Project				
Appropriate VTP Within 24 Hours	112	88%	93%	92%
Appropriate Hair Removal	290	97%	100%	99%
Appropriate Beta Blocker Usage	90	87%	92%	93%
Controlled Postoperative Blood Glucose	0	-	93%	93%
Prophylactic Antibiotic Timing	217	82%	97%	97%
Prophylactic Antibiotic Timing (Outpatient)	78	47%	91%	92%
Prophylactic Antibiotic Selection	219	100%	98%	97%
Prophylactic Antibiotic Select. (Outpatient)	40	98%	96%	94%
Prophylactic Antibiotic Stopped	208	89%	95%	94%
Recommended VTP Ordered	112	88%	94%	94%
Urinary Catheter Removal	103	88%	91%	90%
Children's Asthma Care				
Received Systemic Corticosteroids	-	-	-	100%
Received Home Management Plan	-	-	-	71%
Received Reliever Medication	-	-	-	100%
Use of Medical Imaging				
Combination Abdominal CT Scan	379	0.612	0.106	0.191
Combination Chest CT Scan	250	0.596	0.027	0.054
Follow-up Mammogram/Ultrasound	717	5.3%	8.4%	8.4%
MRI for Low Back Pain[1]	50	18.0%	31.8%	32.7%
Survey of Patients' Hospital Experiences				
Area Around Room 'Always' Quiet at Night	300+	59%	-	58%
Doctors 'Always' Communicated Well	300+	83%	-	80%
Home Recovery Information Given	300+	87%	-	82%
Hospital Given 9 or 10 on 10 Point Scale	300+	69%	-	67%
Meds 'Always' Explained Before Given	300+	65%	-	60%
Nurses 'Always' Communicated Well	300+	81%	-	76%
Pain 'Always' Well Controlled	300+	68%	-	69%
Room and Bathroom 'Always' Clean	300+	80%	-	71%
Timely Help 'Always' Received	300+	66%	-	64%
Would Definitely Recommend Hospital	300+	70%	-	69%

Beloit Memorial Hospital

1969 W Hart Rd
Beloit, WI 53511
Type: Acute Care Hospitals
Ownership: Voluntary Non-Profit - Private
Phone: 608-364-5011
Fax: 608-364-5356
Emergency Services: Yes
Beds: 174

Key Personnel:
CEO/President. . . . . Gregory K Britton
Cardiac Laboratory. . . . . Larry Bergen
Chief of Medical Staff. . . . . Shamshad A Anjum
Infection Control. . . . . Karen Draves
Operating Room. . . . . Shirley Fischer
Radiology. . . . . Bilal A Ahmed

Measure	Cases	This Hosp.	State Avg.	U.S. Avg.
Heart Attack Care				
ACE Inhibitor or ARB for LVSD[1]	16	94%	97%	96%
Aspirin at Arrival	84	95%	99%	99%
Aspirin at Discharge	69	94%	99%	98%
Beta Blocker at Discharge	71	97%	99%	98%
Fibrinolytic Medication Timing[1]	2	0%	0%	55%
PCI Within 90 Minutes of Arrival	0	-	89%	90%
Smoking Cessation Advice[1]	17	94%	99%	99%
Chest Pain/Possible Heart Attack Care				
Aspirin at Arrival	49	96%	96%	95%
Median Time to ECG (minutes)	51	12	7	8
Median Time to Transfer (minutes)[1]	7	64	49	61
Fibrinolytic Medication Timing[1]	3	0%	63%	54%
Heart Failure Care				
ACE Inhibitor or ARB for LVSD	52	88%	95%	94%
Discharge Instructions	148	84%	86%	88%
Evaluation of LVS Function	194	100%	97%	98%
Smoking Cessation Advice	32	100%	97%	98%
Pneumonia Care				
Appropriate Initial Antibiotic	59	90%	94%	92%
Blood Culture Timing	50	94%	97%	96%
Influenza Vaccine	63	90%	92%	91%
Initial Antibiotic Timing	73	95%	97%	95%
Pneumococcal Vaccine	86	85%	93%	93%
Smoking Cessation Advice	33	100%	95%	97%
Surgical Care Improvement Project				
Appropriate VTP Within 24 Hours	125	87%	93%	92%
Appropriate Hair Removal	440	98%	100%	99%
Appropriate Beta Blocker Usage	124	85%	92%	93%
Controlled Postoperative Blood Glucose	38	92%	93%	93%
Prophylactic Antibiotic Timing	321	94%	97%	97%
Prophylactic Antibiotic Timing (Outpatient)	137	86%	91%	92%
Prophylactic Antibiotic Selection	319	97%	98%	97%
Prophylactic Antibiotic Select. (Outpatient)	125	94%	96%	94%
Prophylactic Antibiotic Stopped	310	93%	95%	94%
Recommended VTP Ordered	125	92%	94%	94%
Urinary Catheter Removal	59	88%	91%	90%
Children's Asthma Care				
Received Systemic Corticosteroids	-	-	-	100%
Received Home Management Plan	-	-	-	71%
Received Reliever Medication	-	-	-	100%
Use of Medical Imaging				
Combination Abdominal CT Scan	218	0.376	0.106	0.191
Combination Chest CT Scan	125	0.000	0.027	0.054
Follow-up Mammogram/Ultrasound	429	4.2%	8.4%	8.4%
MRI for Low Back Pain	131	42.0%	31.8%	32.7%
Survey of Patients' Hospital Experiences				
Area Around Room 'Always' Quiet at Night	300+	58%	-	58%
Doctors 'Always' Communicated Well	300+	81%	-	80%
Home Recovery Information Given	300+	83%	-	82%
Hospital Given 9 or 10 on 10 Point Scale	300+	67%	-	67%
Meds 'Always' Explained Before Given	300+	64%	-	60%
Nurses 'Always' Communicated Well	300+	79%	-	76%
Pain 'Always' Well Controlled	300+	72%	-	69%
Room and Bathroom 'Always' Clean	300+	75%	-	71%
Timely Help 'Always' Received	300+	69%	-	64%
Would Definitely Recommend Hospital	300+	69%	-	69%

Berlin Memorial Hospital

225 Memorial Drive
Berlin, WI 54923
Type: Critical Access Hospitals
Ownership: Voluntary Non-Profit - Private
Phone: 920-361-1313
Fax: 920-361-5318
Emergency Services: Yes
Beds: 61

Key Personnel:
CEO/President. . . . . Craig WC Schmidt
Chief of Medical Staff. . . . . Jeff Carroll, MD
Infection Control. . . . . Kathy Beier
Quality Assurance . . . . Kathy Beier
Anesthesiology. . . . . Daniel Resop, MD
Emergency Room . . . . Dan Perrault, MD
Intensive Care Unit. . . . . Kelly Schmude

Measure	Cases	This Hosp.	State Avg.	U.S. Avg.
Heart Attack Care				
ACE Inhibitor or ARB for LVSD[5]	0	-	97%	96%
Aspirin at Arrival[5]	0	-	99%	99%
Aspirin at Discharge[5]	0	-	99%	98%
Beta Blocker at Discharge[5]	0	-	99%	98%
Fibrinolytic Medication Timing[5]	0	-	0%	55%
PCI Within 90 Minutes of Arrival[5]	0	-	89%	90%
Smoking Cessation Advice[5]	0	-	99%	99%
Chest Pain/Possible Heart Attack Care				
Aspirin at Arrival	81	98%	96%	95%
Median Time to ECG (minutes)	81	0	7	8
Median Time to Transfer (minutes)	0	-	49	61
Fibrinolytic Medication Timing	0	-	63%	54%
Heart Failure Care				
ACE Inhibitor or ARB for LVSD[1]	9	78%	95%	94%
Discharge Instructions[1]	20	90%	86%	88%
Evaluation of LVS Function	44	84%	97%	98%
Smoking Cessation Advice[1]	6	83%	97%	98%
Pneumonia Care				
Appropriate Initial Antibiotic[1]	23	57%	94%	92%
Blood Culture Timing	44	89%	97%	96%
Influenza Vaccine[1]	24	83%	92%	91%
Initial Antibiotic Timing	50	84%	97%	95%
Pneumococcal Vaccine	42	81%	93%	93%
Smoking Cessation Advice[1]	10	60%	95%	97%
Surgical Care Improvement Project				
Appropriate VTP Within 24 Hours[2]	39	97%	93%	92%
Appropriate Hair Removal[2]	173	100%	100%	99%
Appropriate Beta Blocker Usage[5]	0	-	92%	93%
Controlled Postoperative Blood Glucose[5]	0	-	93%	93%
Prophylactic Antibiotic Timing[2]	145	90%	97%	97%
Prophylactic Antibiotic Timing (Outpatient)	50	88%	91%	92%
Prophylactic Antibiotic Selection[2]	147	97%	98%	97%
Prophylactic Antibiotic Select. (Outpatient)	47	94%	96%	94%
Prophylactic Antibiotic Stopped[2]	145	92%	95%	94%
Recommended VTP Ordered[2]	40	95%	94%	94%
Urinary Catheter Removal[2]	54	91%	91%	90%
Children's Asthma Care				
Received Systemic Corticosteroids	-	-	-	100%
Received Home Management Plan	-	-	-	71%
Received Reliever Medication	-	-	-	100%
Use of Medical Imaging				
Combination Abdominal CT Scan	241	0.104	0.106	0.191
Combination Chest CT Scan	216	0.005	0.027	0.054
Follow-up Mammogram/Ultrasound	444	5.6%	8.4%	8.4%
MRI for Low Back Pain[1]	40	25.0%	31.8%	32.7%
Survey of Patients' Hospital Experiences				
Area Around Room 'Always' Quiet at Night	300+	58%	-	58%
Doctors 'Always' Communicated Well	300+	85%	-	80%
Home Recovery Information Given	300+	85%	-	82%
Hospital Given 9 or 10 on 10 Point Scale	300+	73%	-	67%
Meds 'Always' Explained Before Given	300+	68%	-	60%
Nurses 'Always' Communicated Well	300+	82%	-	76%
Pain 'Always' Well Controlled	300+	70%	-	69%
Room and Bathroom 'Always' Clean	300+	79%	-	71%
Timely Help 'Always' Received	300+	77%	-	64%
Would Definitely Recommend Hospital	300+	72%	-	69%

NOTE: Hospital profiles are in alphabetical order by state, then city, then hospital within the city; Rankings exclude hospitals with less than 25 cases except for patient surveys which excludes hospitals with less than 100 cases; (a) 100–299 cases; (1) The number of cases is too small to be sure how well a hospital is performing; (2) The hospital indicated that the data submitted for this measure were based on a sample of cases; (3) Data was collected during a shorter time period (fewer quarters) than the maximum possible time for this measure; (4) Suppressed for one or more quarters by CMS; (5) No data is available from the hospital for this measure; (6) Fewer than 100 patients completed the HCAHPS survey. Use these rates with caution, as the number of surveys may be too low to reliably assess hospital performance; (7) Survey results are based on less than 12 months of data; (8) Survey results are not available for this reporting period; (9) No or very few patients were eligible for the HCAHPS survey. The scores shown, if any, reflect a very small number of surveys; (10) A state average was not calculated because too few hospitals in the state submitted data; (11) There were discrepancies in the data collection process; Please refer to the User's Guide for a full explanation of data.

Black River Memorial Hospital

711 W Adams St | Phone: 715-284-5361
Black River Falls, WI 54615 | Fax: 715-284-7166
URL: www.brmh.net
Type: Critical Access Hospitals | Emergency Services: Yes
Ownership: Voluntary Non-Profit - Private | Beds: 51

Key Personnel:
CEO/President. . . . . Stanley J Gaynor
Quality Assurance . . . . Mary Bestwait
Radiology. . . . . Mary Ewing
Emergency Room . . . . Barb Holderman, RN

Measure	Cases	This Hosp.	State Avg.	U.S. Avg.
Heart Attack Care				
ACE Inhibitor or ARB for LVSD[1,3]	1	100%	97%	96%
Aspirin at Arrival[1,3]	2	100%	99%	99%
Aspirin at Discharge[1,3]	2	100%	99%	98%
Beta Blocker at Discharge[1,3]	2	100%	99%	98%
Fibrinolytic Medication Timing[3]	0	-	0%	55%
PCI Within 90 Minutes of Arrival[3]	0	-	89%	90%
Smoking Cessation Advice[3]	0	-	99%	99%
Chest Pain/Possible Heart Attack Care				
Aspirin at Arrival	77	90%	96%	95%
Median Time to ECG (minutes)	86	4	7	8
Median Time to Transfer (minutes)[1]	8	82	49	61
Fibrinolytic Medication Timing[1]	4	0%	63%	54%
Heart Failure Care				
ACE Inhibitor or ARB for LVSD[1]	5	100%	95%	94%
Discharge Instructions[1]	17	94%	86%	88%
Evaluation of LVS Function[1]	22	59%	97%	98%
Smoking Cessation Advice[1]	1	100%	97%	98%
Pneumonia Care				
Appropriate Initial Antibiotic	31	94%	94%	92%
Blood Culture Timing[1]	19	100%	97%	96%
Influenza Vaccine[1]	20	95%	92%	91%
Initial Antibiotic Timing	37	100%	97%	95%
Pneumococcal Vaccine	26	96%	93%	93%
Smoking Cessation Advice[1]	11	64%	95%	97%
Surgical Care Improvement Project				
Appropriate VTP Within 24 Hours[5]	0	-	93%	92%
Appropriate Hair Removal	56	91%	100%	99%
Appropriate Beta Blocker Usage[5]	0	-	92%	93%
Controlled Postoperative Blood Glucose	0	-	93%	93%
Prophylactic Antibiotic Timing	51	100%	97%	97%
Prophylactic Antibiotic Timing (Outpatient)[1]	23	87%	91%	92%
Prophylactic Antibiotic Selection	51	92%	98%	97%
Prophylactic Antibiotic Select. (Outpatient)[1]	23	96%	96%	94%
Prophylactic Antibiotic Stopped	50	96%	95%	94%
Recommended VTP Ordered[5]	0	-	94%	94%
Urinary Catheter Removal[1]	18	56%	91%	90%
Children's Asthma Care				
Received Systemic Corticosteroids	-	-	-	100%
Received Home Management Plan	-	-	-	71%
Received Reliever Medication	-	-	-	100%
Use of Medical Imaging				
Combination Abdominal CT Scan	103	0.049	0.106	0.191
Combination Chest CT Scan	48	0.021	0.027	0.054
Follow-up Mammogram/Ultrasound[5]	0	-	8.4%	8.4%
MRI for Low Back Pain[1]	28	32.1%	31.8%	32.7%
Survey of Patients' Hospital Experiences				
Area Around Room 'Always' Quiet at Night	(a)	72%	-	58%
Doctors 'Always' Communicated Well	(a)	89%	-	80%
Home Recovery Information Given	(a)	92%	-	82%
Hospital Given 9 or 10 on 10 Point Scale	(a)	82%	-	67%
Meds 'Always' Explained Before Given	(a)	72%	-	60%
Nurses 'Always' Communicated Well	(a)	83%	-	76%
Pain 'Always' Well Controlled	(a)	74%	-	69%
Room and Bathroom 'Always' Clean	(a)	80%	-	71%
Timely Help 'Always' Received	(a)	82%	-	64%
Would Definitely Recommend Hospital	(a)	82%	-	69%

Luther Midelfort - Chippewa Valley Mayo Health System

1501 Thompson St | Phone: 715-568-2000
Bloomer, WI 54724 | Fax: 715-568-2000
E-mail: kerg.mary@mayo.edu
Type: Critical Access Hospitals | Emergency Services: Yes
Ownership: Voluntary Non-Profit - Other | Beds: 37

Key Personnel:
CEO/President. . . . . John Larson, MD
Chief of Medical Staff . . . . Richard Gladitsch, MD
Infection Control. . . . . Mel Crisp
Operating Room. . . . . Gail Anderson
Quality Assurance . . . . Kay Dahlka

Measure	Cases	This Hosp.	State Avg.	U.S. Avg.
Heart Attack Care				
ACE Inhibitor or ARB for LVSD[5]	0	-	97%	96%
Aspirin at Arrival[5]	0	-	99%	99%
Aspirin at Discharge[5]	0	-	99%	98%
Beta Blocker at Discharge[5]	0	-	99%	98%
Fibrinolytic Medication Timing[5]	0	-	0%	55%
PCI Within 90 Minutes of Arrival[5]	0	-	89%	90%
Smoking Cessation Advice[5]	0	-	99%	99%
Chest Pain/Possible Heart Attack Care				
Aspirin at Arrival	-	-	96%	95%
Median Time to ECG (minutes)	-	-	7	8
Median Time to Transfer (minutes)	-	-	49	61
Fibrinolytic Medication Timing	-	-	63%	54%
Heart Failure Care				
ACE Inhibitor or ARB for LVSD	0	-	95%	94%
Discharge Instructions[1]	4	75%	86%	88%
Evaluation of LVS Function[1]	8	100%	97%	98%
Smoking Cessation Advice	0	-	97%	98%
Pneumonia Care				
Appropriate Initial Antibiotic[1]	11	100%	94%	92%
Blood Culture Timing[1]	12	83%	97%	96%
Influenza Vaccine[1]	10	80%	92%	91%
Initial Antibiotic Timing[1]	12	100%	97%	95%
Pneumococcal Vaccine[1]	10	100%	93%	93%
Smoking Cessation Advice[1]	7	100%	95%	97%
Surgical Care Improvement Project				
Appropriate VTP Within 24 Hours[3]	0	-	93%	92%
Appropriate Hair Removal[1,3]	1	100%	100%	99%
Appropriate Beta Blocker Usage[5]	0	-	92%	93%
Controlled Postoperative Blood Glucose[3]	0	-	93%	93%
Prophylactic Antibiotic Timing[3]	0	-	97%	97%
Prophylactic Antibiotic Timing (Outpatient)	-	-	91%	92%
Prophylactic Antibiotic Selection[3]	0	-	98%	97%
Prophylactic Antibiotic Select. (Outpatient)	-	-	96%	94%
Prophylactic Antibiotic Stopped[3]	0	-	95%	94%
Recommended VTP Ordered[3]	0	-	94%	94%
Urinary Catheter Removal[5]	0	-	91%	90%
Children's Asthma Care				
Received Systemic Corticosteroids	-	-	-	100%
Received Home Management Plan	-	-	-	71%
Received Reliever Medication	-	-	-	100%
Use of Medical Imaging				
Combination Abdominal CT Scan	-	-	0.106	0.191
Combination Chest CT Scan	-	-	0.027	0.054
Follow-up Mammogram/Ultrasound	-	-	8.4%	8.4%
MRI for Low Back Pain	-	-	31.8%	32.7%
Survey of Patients' Hospital Experiences				
Area Around Room 'Always' Quiet at Night	(a)	58%	-	58%
Doctors 'Always' Communicated Well	(a)	81%	-	80%
Home Recovery Information Given	(a)	88%	-	82%
Hospital Given 9 or 10 on 10 Point Scale	(a)	76%	-	67%
Meds 'Always' Explained Before Given	(a)	57%	-	60%
Nurses 'Always' Communicated Well	(a)	75%	-	76%
Pain 'Always' Well Controlled	(a)	69%	-	69%
Room and Bathroom 'Always' Clean	(a)	79%	-	71%
Timely Help 'Always' Received	(a)	63%	-	64%
Would Definitely Recommend Hospital	(a)	78%	-	69%

Boscobel Area Health Care

205 Parker St | Phone: 608-375-4112
Boscobel, WI 53805 | Fax: 608-375-5463
URL: www.boscobelhealth.com
Type: Critical Access Hospitals | Emergency Services: Yes
Ownership: Voluntary Non-Profit - Private | Beds: 123

Key Personnel:
Chief of Medical Staff. . . . . Thomas Pelz
Infection Control. . . . . Sally N Rosemeyer, RN
Quality Assurance . . . . Sally N Rosemeyer, RN
Intensive Care Unit. . . . . Nancy Nelson

Measure	Cases	This Hosp.	State Avg.	U.S. Avg.
Heart Attack Care				
ACE Inhibitor or ARB for LVSD[3]	0	-	97%	96%
Aspirin at Arrival[1,3]	1	100%	99%	99%
Aspirin at Discharge[3]	0	-	99%	98%
Beta Blocker at Discharge[3]	0	-	99%	98%
Fibrinolytic Medication Timing[3]	0	-	0%	55%
PCI Within 90 Minutes of Arrival[3]	0	-	89%	90%
Smoking Cessation Advice[3]	0	-	99%	99%
Chest Pain/Possible Heart Attack Care				
Aspirin at Arrival[1,3]	16	100%	96%	95%
Median Time to ECG (minutes)[1,3]	15	10	7	8
Median Time to Transfer (minutes)[1,3]	2	127	49	61
Fibrinolytic Medication Timing[1,3]	2	50%	63%	54%
Heart Failure Care				
ACE Inhibitor or ARB for LVSD[1]	3	67%	95%	94%
Discharge Instructions[1]	8	100%	86%	88%
Evaluation of LVS Function[1]	17	53%	97%	98%
Smoking Cessation Advice	0	-	97%	98%
Pneumonia Care				
Appropriate Initial Antibiotic[1]	7	71%	94%	92%
Blood Culture Timing[1]	4	100%	97%	96%
Influenza Vaccine[1]	5	60%	92%	91%
Initial Antibiotic Timing[1]	9	89%	97%	95%
Pneumococcal Vaccine[1]	11	9%	93%	93%
Smoking Cessation Advice[1]	1	0%	95%	97%
Surgical Care Improvement Project				
Appropriate VTP Within 24 Hours[1]	8	62%	93%	92%
Appropriate Hair Removal[1]	14	93%	100%	99%
Appropriate Beta Blocker Usage[5]	0	-	92%	93%
Controlled Postoperative Blood Glucose	0	-	93%	93%
Prophylactic Antibiotic Timing[1]	9	89%	97%	97%
Prophylactic Antibiotic Timing (Outpatient)[1]	9	78%	91%	92%
Prophylactic Antibiotic Selection[1]	9	100%	98%	97%
Prophylactic Antibiotic Select. (Outpatient)[1]	7	100%	96%	94%
Prophylactic Antibiotic Stopped[1]	9	56%	95%	94%
Recommended VTP Ordered[1]	8	62%	94%	94%
Urinary Catheter Removal[1]	4	75%	91%	90%
Children's Asthma Care				
Received Systemic Corticosteroids	-	-	-	100%
Received Home Management Plan	-	-	-	71%
Received Reliever Medication	-	-	-	100%
Use of Medical Imaging				
Combination Abdominal CT Scan[1]	35	0.057	0.106	0.191
Combination Chest CT Scan[1]	18	0.000	0.027	0.054
Follow-up Mammogram/Ultrasound	142	2.8%	8.4%	8.4%
MRI for Low Back Pain[1]	6	16.7%	31.8%	32.7%
Survey of Patients' Hospital Experiences				
Area Around Room 'Always' Quiet at Night	(a)	56%	-	58%
Doctors 'Always' Communicated Well	(a)	81%	-	80%
Home Recovery Information Given	(a)	85%	-	82%
Hospital Given 9 or 10 on 10 Point Scale	(a)	65%	-	67%
Meds 'Always' Explained Before Given	(a)	62%	-	60%
Nurses 'Always' Communicated Well	(a)	80%	-	76%
Pain 'Always' Well Controlled	(a)	75%	-	69%
Room and Bathroom 'Always' Clean	(a)	86%	-	71%
Timely Help 'Always' Received	(a)	74%	-	64%
Would Definitely Recommend Hospital	(a)	62%	-	69%

NOTE: Hospital profiles are in alphabetical order by state, then city, then hospital within the city; Rankings exclude hospitals with less than 25 cases except for patient surveys which excludes hospitals with less than 100 cases; (a) 100–299 cases; (1) The number of cases is too small to be sure how well a hospital is performing; (2) The hospital indicated that the data submitted for this measure were based on a sample of cases; (3) Data was collected during a shorter time period (fewer quarters) than the maximum possible time for this measure; (4) Suppressed for one or more quarters by CMS; (5) No data is available from the hospital for this measure; (6) Fewer than 100 patients completed the HCAHPS survey. Use these rates with caution, as the number of surveys may be too low to reliably assess hospital performance; (7) Survey results are based on less than 12 months of data; (8) Survey results are not available for this reporting period; (9) No or very few patients were eligible for the HCAHPS survey. The scores shown, if any, reflect a very small number of surveys; (10) A state average was not calculated because too few hospitals in the state submitted data; (11) There were discrepancies in the data collection process; Please refer to the User's Guide for a full explanation of data.

Wheaton Franciscan Healthcare - Elmbrook Memorial

19333 W North Ave — Phone: 262-785-2000
Brookfield, WI 53045 — Fax: 262-785-2444
URL: www.mywheaton.org
Type: Acute Care Hospitals — Emergency Services: Yes
Ownership: Voluntary Non-Profit - Church — Beds: 166

Key Personnel:
CEO/President. . . . . Kimry A Johnsrud
Ambulatory Care . . . . Monica Marton

Measure	Cases	This Hosp.	State Avg.	U.S. Avg.
Heart Attack Care				
ACE Inhibitor or ARB for LVSD[1]	1	100%	97%	96%
Aspirin at Arrival[1]	9	89%	99%	99%
Aspirin at Discharge[1]	4	100%	99%	98%
Beta Blocker at Discharge[1]	3	100%	99%	98%
Fibrinolytic Medication Timing	0	-	0%	55%
PCI Within 90 Minutes of Arrival	0	-	89%	90%
Smoking Cessation Advice	0	-	99%	99%
Chest Pain/Possible Heart Attack Care				
Aspirin at Arrival	49	94%	96%	95%
Median Time to ECG (minutes)	50	6	7	8
Median Time to Transfer (minutes)[1]	4	50	49	61
Fibrinolytic Medication Timing	0	-	63%	54%
Heart Failure Care				
ACE Inhibitor or ARB for LVSD	31	87%	95%	94%
Discharge Instructions	76	74%	86%	88%
Evaluation of LVS Function	116	99%	97%	98%
Smoking Cessation Advice[1]	15	100%	97%	98%
Pneumonia Care				
Appropriate Initial Antibiotic	65	97%	94%	92%
Blood Culture Timing	91	100%	97%	96%
Influenza Vaccine	68	93%	92%	91%
Initial Antibiotic Timing	92	97%	97%	95%
Pneumococcal Vaccine	93	95%	93%	93%
Smoking Cessation Advice[1]	18	94%	95%	97%
Surgical Care Improvement Project				
Appropriate VTP Within 24 Hours[2]	154	89%	93%	92%
Appropriate Hair Removal[2]	393	99%	100%	99%
Appropriate Beta Blocker Usage[2]	95	85%	92%	93%
Controlled Postoperative Blood Glucose[2]	0	-	93%	93%
Prophylactic Antibiotic Timing[2]	256	96%	97%	97%
Prophylactic Antibiotic Timing (Outpatient)	263	86%	91%	92%
Prophylactic Antibiotic Selection[2]	261	98%	98%	97%
Prophylactic Antibiotic Select. (Outpatient)	300	94%	96%	94%
Prophylactic Antibiotic Stopped[2]	248	96%	95%	94%
Recommended VTP Ordered[2]	155	89%	94%	94%
Urinary Catheter Removal[2]	100	86%	91%	90%
Children's Asthma Care				
Received Systemic Corticosteroids	-	-	-	100%
Received Home Management Plan	-	-	-	71%
Received Reliever Medication	-	-	-	100%
Use of Medical Imaging				
Combination Abdominal CT Scan	598	0.140	0.106	0.191
Combination Chest CT Scan	339	0.080	0.027	0.054
Follow-up Mammogram/Ultrasound	729	10.8%	8.4%	8.4%
MRI for Low Back Pain	204	35.3%	31.8%	32.7%
Survey of Patients' Hospital Experiences				
Area Around Room 'Always' Quiet at Night	300+	57%	-	58%
Doctors 'Always' Communicated Well	300+	82%	-	80%
Home Recovery Information Given	300+	83%	-	82%
Hospital Given 9 or 10 on 10 Point Scale	300+	64%	-	67%
Meds 'Always' Explained Before Given	300+	59%	-	60%
Nurses 'Always' Communicated Well	300+	76%	-	76%
Pain 'Always' Well Controlled	300+	68%	-	69%
Room and Bathroom 'Always' Clean	300+	67%	-	71%
Timely Help 'Always' Received	300+	60%	-	64%
Would Definitely Recommend Hospital	300+	67%	-	69%

Aurora Memorial Hospital Burlington

252 Mchenry St — Phone: 262-767-6000
Burlington, WI 53105 — Fax: 262-767-6380
URL: www.aurorahealthcare.org
Type: Acute Care Hospitals — Emergency Services: Yes
Ownership: Voluntary Non-Profit - Private — Beds: 123

Key Personnel:
Chief of Medical Staff . . . . Laurence Tempelis, MD
Infection Control. . . . . Gwria McPeek
Operating Room. . . . . Joseph Majewski
Quality Assurance . . . . Barb Bigler
Anesthesiology. . . . . S Joshi, MD
Emergency Room . . . . John Linstroth, MD
Intensive Care Unit. . . . . Diane Huck

Measure	Cases	This Hosp.	State Avg.	U.S. Avg.
Heart Attack Care				
ACE Inhibitor or ARB for LVSD[1]	4	100%	97%	96%
Aspirin at Arrival[1]	24	100%	99%	99%
Aspirin at Discharge[1]	15	100%	99%	98%
Beta Blocker at Discharge[1]	14	100%	99%	98%
Fibrinolytic Medication Timing	0	-	0%	55%
PCI Within 90 Minutes of Arrival	0	-	89%	90%
Smoking Cessation Advice[1]	1	100%	99%	99%
Chest Pain/Possible Heart Attack Care				
Aspirin at Arrival	40	90%	96%	95%
Median Time to ECG (minutes)	41	0	7	8
Median Time to Transfer (minutes)[1]	9	49	49	61
Fibrinolytic Medication Timing[1]	1	100%	63%	54%
Heart Failure Care				
ACE Inhibitor or ARB for LVSD[1]	23	100%	95%	94%
Discharge Instructions	72	99%	86%	88%
Evaluation of LVS Function	87	100%	97%	98%
Smoking Cessation Advice[1]	21	100%	97%	98%
Pneumonia Care				
Appropriate Initial Antibiotic	78	95%	94%	92%
Blood Culture Timing	121	98%	97%	96%
Influenza Vaccine	85	100%	92%	91%
Initial Antibiotic Timing	124	100%	97%	95%
Pneumococcal Vaccine	112	100%	93%	93%
Smoking Cessation Advice	45	100%	95%	97%
Surgical Care Improvement Project				
Appropriate VTP Within 24 Hours[2]	122	98%	93%	92%
Appropriate Hair Removal[2]	381	100%	100%	99%
Appropriate Beta Blocker Usage[2]	109	100%	92%	93%
Controlled Postoperative Blood Glucose[2]	0	-	93%	93%
Prophylactic Antibiotic Timing[2]	241	99%	97%	97%
Prophylactic Antibiotic Timing (Outpatient)	195	82%	91%	92%
Prophylactic Antibiotic Selection[2]	244	98%	98%	97%
Prophylactic Antibiotic Select. (Outpatient)	224	88%	96%	94%
Prophylactic Antibiotic Stopped[2]	229	100%	95%	94%
Recommended VTP Ordered[2]	122	99%	94%	94%
Urinary Catheter Removal[2]	117	99%	91%	90%
Children's Asthma Care				
Received Systemic Corticosteroids	-	-	-	100%
Received Home Management Plan	-	-	-	71%
Received Reliever Medication	-	-	-	100%
Use of Medical Imaging				
Combination Abdominal CT Scan	448	0.074	0.106	0.191
Combination Chest CT Scan	364	0.022	0.027	0.054
Follow-up Mammogram/Ultrasound	965	8.3%	8.4%	8.4%
MRI for Low Back Pain	145	31.7%	31.8%	32.7%
Survey of Patients' Hospital Experiences				
Area Around Room 'Always' Quiet at Night	300+	55%	-	58%
Doctors 'Always' Communicated Well	300+	78%	-	80%
Home Recovery Information Given	300+	87%	-	82%
Hospital Given 9 or 10 on 10 Point Scale	300+	61%	-	67%
Meds 'Always' Explained Before Given	300+	59%	-	60%
Nurses 'Always' Communicated Well	300+	76%	-	76%
Pain 'Always' Well Controlled	300+	72%	-	69%
Room and Bathroom 'Always' Clean	300+	74%	-	71%
Timely Help 'Always' Received	300+	62%	-	64%
Would Definitely Recommend Hospital	300+	63%	-	69%

Calumet Medical Center

614 Memorial Dr — Phone: 920-849-2386
Chilton, WI 53014 — Fax: 920-849-7510
URL: www.ministryhealth.org
Type: Critical Access Hospitals — Emergency Services: Yes
Ownership: Voluntary Non-Profit - Private — Beds: 29

Key Personnel:
CEO/President. . . . . Travis Anderson
Radiology. . . . . Corbin Asbury

Measure	Cases	This Hosp.	State Avg.	U.S. Avg.
Heart Attack Care				
ACE Inhibitor or ARB for LVSD[5]	0	-	97%	96%
Aspirin at Arrival[5]	0	-	99%	99%
Aspirin at Discharge[5]	0	-	99%	98%
Beta Blocker at Discharge[5]	0	-	99%	98%
Fibrinolytic Medication Timing[5]	0	-	0%	55%
PCI Within 90 Minutes of Arrival[5]	0	-	89%	90%
Smoking Cessation Advice[5]	0	-	99%	99%
Chest Pain/Possible Heart Attack Care				
Aspirin at Arrival	45	100%	96%	95%
Median Time to ECG (minutes)	47	5	7	8
Median Time to Transfer (minutes)[1]	12	44	49	61
Fibrinolytic Medication Timing	0	-	63%	54%
Heart Failure Care				
ACE Inhibitor or ARB for LVSD[1,2]	3	100%	95%	94%
Discharge Instructions[1,2]	11	100%	86%	88%
Evaluation of LVS Function[1,2]	19	100%	97%	98%
Smoking Cessation Advice[1,2]	2	100%	97%	98%
Pneumonia Care				
Appropriate Initial Antibiotic[1,2]	23	100%	94%	92%
Blood Culture Timing[2]	33	100%	97%	96%
Influenza Vaccine[1]	15	100%	92%	91%
Initial Antibiotic Timing[2]	28	100%	97%	95%
Pneumococcal Vaccine[2]	30	100%	93%	93%
Smoking Cessation Advice[1,2]	3	100%	95%	97%
Surgical Care Improvement Project				
Appropriate VTP Within 24 Hours[1,2]	12	100%	93%	92%
Appropriate Hair Removal[2]	50	100%	100%	99%
Appropriate Beta Blocker Usage[1,2]	22	100%	92%	93%
Controlled Postoperative Blood Glucose[2]	0	-	93%	93%
Prophylactic Antibiotic Timing[2]	35	100%	97%	97%
Prophylactic Antibiotic Timing (Outpatient)[5]	0	-	91%	92%
Prophylactic Antibiotic Selection[2]	36	100%	98%	97%
Prophylactic Antibiotic Select. (Outpatient)[5]	0	-	96%	94%
Prophylactic Antibiotic Stopped[2]	35	91%	95%	94%
Recommended VTP Ordered[1,2]	12	100%	94%	94%
Urinary Catheter Removal[1]	8	75%	91%	90%
Children's Asthma Care				
Received Systemic Corticosteroids	-	-	-	100%
Received Home Management Plan	-	-	-	71%
Received Reliever Medication	-	-	-	100%
Use of Medical Imaging				
Combination Abdominal CT Scan	88	0.102	0.106	0.191
Combination Chest CT Scan[1]	19	0.000	0.027	0.054
Follow-up Mammogram/Ultrasound	146	8.9%	8.4%	8.4%
MRI for Low Back Pain[1]	7	28.6%	31.8%	32.7%
Survey of Patients' Hospital Experiences				
Area Around Room 'Always' Quiet at Night	(a)	65%	-	58%
Doctors 'Always' Communicated Well	(a)	85%	-	80%
Home Recovery Information Given	(a)	87%	-	82%
Hospital Given 9 or 10 on 10 Point Scale	(a)	77%	-	67%
Meds 'Always' Explained Before Given	(a)	65%	-	60%
Nurses 'Always' Communicated Well	(a)	86%	-	76%
Pain 'Always' Well Controlled	(a)	82%	-	69%
Room and Bathroom 'Always' Clean	(a)	89%	-	71%
Timely Help 'Always' Received	(a)	74%	-	64%
Would Definitely Recommend Hospital	(a)	78%	-	69%

NOTE: Hospital profiles are in alphabetical order by state, then city, then hospital within the city; Rankings exclude hospitals with less than 25 cases except for patient surveys which excludes hospitals with less than 100 cases; (a) 100–299 cases; (1) The number of cases is too small to be sure how well a hospital is performing; (2) The hospital indicated that the data submitted for this measure were based on a sample of cases; (3) Data was collected during a shorter time period (fewer quarters) than the maximum possible time for this measure; (4) Suppressed for one or more quarters by CMS; (5) No data is available from the hospital for this measure; (6) Fewer than 100 patients completed the HCAHPS survey. Use these rates with caution, as the number of surveys may be too low to reliably assess hospital performance; (7) Survey results are based on less than 12 months of data; (8) Survey results are not available for this reporting period; (9) No or very few patients were eligible for the HCAHPS survey. The scores shown, if any, reflect a very small number of surveys; (10) A state average was not calculated because too few hospitals in the state submitted data; (11) There were discrepancies in the data collection process; Please refer to the User's Guide for a full explanation of data.

Saint Josephs Hospital

2661 County Hwy I
Chippewa Falls, WI 54729
URL: www.stjoeschipfalls.com
Type: Acute Care Hospitals
Ownership: Voluntary Non-Profit - Church
Phone: 715-717-7200
Fax: 715-726-3204
Emergency Services: Yes
Beds: 193

Key Personnel:
CEO/President. . . . . David Fish
Chief of Medical Staff . . . . Jeffrey Brown, MD
Infection Control. . . . . Debra Neitge
Operating Room. . . . . Gary Wulff, RN
Quality Assurance . . . . Raymond Myers
Radiology. . . . . Mark A Augustyn
Ambulatory Care . . . . Gary Wolff, RN
Emergency Room . . . . Patrick Ayer

Measure	Cases	This Hosp.	State Avg.	U.S. Avg.
Heart Attack Care				
ACE Inhibitor or ARB for LVSD[1]	1	100%	97%	96%
Aspirin at Arrival[1]	8	88%	99%	99%
Aspirin at Discharge[1]	7	100%	99%	98%
Beta Blocker at Discharge[1]	5	80%	99%	98%
Fibrinolytic Medication Timing	0	-	0%	55%
PCI Within 90 Minutes of Arrival	0	-	89%	90%
Smoking Cessation Advice	0	-	99%	99%
Chest Pain/Possible Heart Attack Care				
Aspirin at Arrival	133	97%	96%	95%
Median Time to ECG (minutes)	138	8	7	8
Median Time to Transfer (minutes)[1]	14	63	49	61
Fibrinolytic Medication Timing	0	-	63%	54%
Heart Failure Care				
ACE Inhibitor or ARB for LVSD[1]	16	88%	95%	94%
Discharge Instructions	37	84%	86%	88%
Evaluation of LVS Function	55	98%	97%	98%
Smoking Cessation Advice[1]	3	100%	97%	98%
Pneumonia Care				
Appropriate Initial Antibiotic	45	91%	94%	92%
Blood Culture Timing	51	98%	97%	96%
Influenza Vaccine	40	98%	92%	91%
Initial Antibiotic Timing	61	97%	97%	95%
Pneumococcal Vaccine	61	93%	93%	93%
Smoking Cessation Advice[1]	17	100%	95%	97%
Surgical Care Improvement Project				
Appropriate VTP Within 24 Hours	58	98%	93%	92%
Appropriate Hair Removal	233	100%	100%	99%
Appropriate Beta Blocker Usage	65	92%	92%	93%
Controlled Postoperative Blood Glucose	0	-	93%	93%
Prophylactic Antibiotic Timing	192	100%	97%	97%
Prophylactic Antibiotic Timing (Outpatient)	43	98%	91%	92%
Prophylactic Antibiotic Selection	192	97%	98%	97%
Prophylactic Antibiotic Select. (Outpatient)	43	100%	96%	94%
Prophylactic Antibiotic Stopped	191	98%	95%	94%
Recommended VTP Ordered	58	98%	94%	94%
Urinary Catheter Removal	42	95%	91%	90%
Children's Asthma Care				
Received Systemic Corticosteroids	-	-	-	100%
Received Home Management Plan	-	-	-	71%
Received Reliever Medication	-	-	-	100%
Use of Medical Imaging				
Combination Abdominal CT Scan	255	0.024	0.106	0.191
Combination Chest CT Scan	194	0.031	0.027	0.054
Follow-up Mammogram/Ultrasound	173	8.7%	8.4%	8.4%
MRI for Low Back Pain	61	41.0%	31.8%	32.7%
Survey of Patients' Hospital Experiences				
Area Around Room 'Always' Quiet at Night	300+	63%	-	58%
Doctors 'Always' Communicated Well	300+	83%	-	80%
Home Recovery Information Given	300+	88%	-	82%
Hospital Given 9 or 10 on 10 Point Scale	300+	74%	-	67%
Meds 'Always' Explained Before Given	300+	67%	-	60%
Nurses 'Always' Communicated Well	300+	80%	-	76%
Pain 'Always' Well Controlled	300+	72%	-	69%
Room and Bathroom 'Always' Clean	300+	77%	-	71%
Timely Help 'Always' Received	300+	74%	-	64%
Would Definitely Recommend Hospital	300+	75%	-	69%

Columbus Community Hospital

1515 Park Ave
Columbus, WI 53925
Type: Critical Access Hospitals
Ownership: Voluntary Non-Profit - Private
Phone: 920-623-2200
Emergency Services: Yes

Key Personnel:
CEO/President. . . . . Ed Harding

Measure	Cases	This Hosp.	State Avg.	U.S. Avg.
Heart Attack Care				
ACE Inhibitor or ARB for LVSD[5]	0	-	97%	96%
Aspirin at Arrival[5]	0	-	99%	99%
Aspirin at Discharge[5]	0	-	99%	98%
Beta Blocker at Discharge[5]	0	-	99%	98%
Fibrinolytic Medication Timing[5]	0	-	0%	55%
PCI Within 90 Minutes of Arrival[5]	0	-	89%	90%
Smoking Cessation Advice[5]	0	-	99%	99%
Chest Pain/Possible Heart Attack Care				
Aspirin at Arrival	-	-	96%	95%
Median Time to ECG (minutes)	-	-	7	8
Median Time to Transfer (minutes)	-	-	49	61
Fibrinolytic Medication Timing	-	-	63%	54%
Heart Failure Care				
ACE Inhibitor or ARB for LVSD[1]	9	100%	95%	94%
Discharge Instructions[1]	20	45%	86%	88%
Evaluation of LVS Function	31	87%	97%	98%
Smoking Cessation Advice[1]	2	0%	97%	98%
Pneumonia Care				
Appropriate Initial Antibiotic	45	78%	94%	92%
Blood Culture Timing	43	86%	97%	96%
Influenza Vaccine	28	43%	92%	91%
Initial Antibiotic Timing	32	94%	97%	95%
Pneumococcal Vaccine	50	62%	93%	93%
Smoking Cessation Advice[1]	4	25%	95%	97%
Surgical Care Improvement Project				
Appropriate VTP Within 24 Hours[5]	0	-	93%	92%
Appropriate Hair Removal	76	100%	100%	99%
Appropriate Beta Blocker Usage[5]	0	-	92%	93%
Controlled Postoperative Blood Glucose	0	-	93%	93%
Prophylactic Antibiotic Timing[5]	0	-	97%	97%
Prophylactic Antibiotic Timing (Outpatient)	-	-	91%	92%
Prophylactic Antibiotic Selection[5]	0	-	98%	97%
Prophylactic Antibiotic Select. (Outpatient)	-	-	96%	94%
Prophylactic Antibiotic Stopped[5]	0	-	95%	94%
Recommended VTP Ordered[5]	0	-	94%	94%
Urinary Catheter Removal[1]	12	92%	91%	90%
Children's Asthma Care				
Received Systemic Corticosteroids	-	-	-	100%
Received Home Management Plan	-	-	-	71%
Received Reliever Medication	-	-	-	100%
Use of Medical Imaging				
Combination Abdominal CT Scan	-	-	0.106	0.191
Combination Chest CT Scan	-	-	0.027	0.054
Follow-up Mammogram/Ultrasound	-	-	8.4%	8.4%
MRI for Low Back Pain	-	-	31.8%	32.7%
Survey of Patients' Hospital Experiences				
Area Around Room 'Always' Quiet at Night	300+	68%	-	58%
Doctors 'Always' Communicated Well	300+	84%	-	80%
Home Recovery Information Given	300+	85%	-	82%
Hospital Given 9 or 10 on 10 Point Scale	300+	74%	-	67%
Meds 'Always' Explained Before Given	300+	67%	-	60%
Nurses 'Always' Communicated Well	300+	74%	-	76%
Pain 'Always' Well Controlled	300+	69%	-	69%
Room and Bathroom 'Always' Clean	300+	85%	-	71%
Timely Help 'Always' Received	300+	70%	-	64%
Would Definitely Recommend Hospital	300+	73%	-	69%

Cumberland Memorial Hospital

1110 7th Avenue
Cumberland, WI 54829
URL: www.cumberlandhelathcare.com
Type: Critical Access Hospitals
Ownership: Voluntary Non-Profit - Other
Phone: 715-822-2741
Fax: 715-822-2740
Emergency Services: Yes
Beds: 40

Key Personnel:
CEO/President. . . . . Robert J Hansen
Chief of Medical Staff . . . . B Ankarlo, MD
Infection Control. . . . . Toniann Knutson, RN
Operating Room. . . . . Sarah Lunquist, RN
Quality Assurance . . . . Nancy Ruppel
Radiology. . . . . Laurie Lien
Anesthesiology. . . . . Jeff Kuehn, CRNA
Emergency Room . . . . Janet Peterson, RN

Measure	Cases	This Hosp.	State Avg.	U.S. Avg.
Heart Attack Care				
ACE Inhibitor or ARB for LVSD[5]	0	-	97%	96%
Aspirin at Arrival[5]	0	-	99%	99%
Aspirin at Discharge[5]	0	-	99%	98%
Beta Blocker at Discharge[5]	0	-	99%	98%
Fibrinolytic Medication Timing[5]	0	-	0%	55%
PCI Within 90 Minutes of Arrival[5]	0	-	89%	90%
Smoking Cessation Advice[5]	0	-	99%	99%
Chest Pain/Possible Heart Attack Care				
Aspirin at Arrival	-	-	96%	95%
Median Time to ECG (minutes)	-	-	7	8
Median Time to Transfer (minutes)	-	-	49	61
Fibrinolytic Medication Timing	-	-	63%	54%
Heart Failure Care				
ACE Inhibitor or ARB for LVSD[1,3]	2	50%	95%	94%
Discharge Instructions[1,3]	9	78%	86%	88%
Evaluation of LVS Function[1,3]	16	31%	97%	98%
Smoking Cessation Advice[1,3]	2	100%	97%	98%
Pneumonia Care				
Appropriate Initial Antibiotic	33	76%	94%	92%
Blood Culture Timing[1]	4	100%	97%	96%
Influenza Vaccine	31	77%	92%	91%
Initial Antibiotic Timing	39	97%	97%	95%
Pneumococcal Vaccine	48	88%	93%	93%
Smoking Cessation Advice[1]	6	67%	95%	97%
Surgical Care Improvement Project				
Appropriate VTP Within 24 Hours[5]	0	-	93%	92%
Appropriate Hair Removal[5]	0	-	100%	99%
Appropriate Beta Blocker Usage[5]	0	-	92%	93%
Controlled Postoperative Blood Glucose[5]	0	-	93%	93%
Prophylactic Antibiotic Timing[5]	0	-	97%	97%
Prophylactic Antibiotic Timing (Outpatient)	-	-	91%	92%
Prophylactic Antibiotic Selection[5]	0	-	98%	97%
Prophylactic Antibiotic Select. (Outpatient)	-	-	96%	94%
Prophylactic Antibiotic Stopped[5]	0	-	95%	94%
Recommended VTP Ordered[5]	0	-	94%	94%
Urinary Catheter Removal[5]	0	-	91%	90%
Children's Asthma Care				
Received Systemic Corticosteroids	-	-	-	100%
Received Home Management Plan	-	-	-	71%
Received Reliever Medication	-	-	-	100%
Use of Medical Imaging				
Combination Abdominal CT Scan	-	-	0.106	0.191
Combination Chest CT Scan	-	-	0.027	0.054
Follow-up Mammogram/Ultrasound	-	-	8.4%	8.4%
MRI for Low Back Pain	-	-	31.8%	32.7%
Survey of Patients' Hospital Experiences				
Area Around Room 'Always' Quiet at Night	(a)	57%	-	58%
Doctors 'Always' Communicated Well	(a)	83%	-	80%
Home Recovery Information Given	(a)	85%	-	82%
Hospital Given 9 or 10 on 10 Point Scale	(a)	75%	-	67%
Meds 'Always' Explained Before Given	(a)	61%	-	60%
Nurses 'Always' Communicated Well	(a)	78%	-	76%
Pain 'Always' Well Controlled	(a)	72%	-	69%
Room and Bathroom 'Always' Clean	(a)	80%	-	71%
Timely Help 'Always' Received	(a)	75%	-	64%
Would Definitely Recommend Hospital	(a)	70%	-	69%

NOTE: Hospital profiles are in alphabetical order by state, then city, then hospital within the city; Rankings exclude hospitals with less than 25 cases except for patient surveys which excludes hospitals with less than 100 cases; (a) 100–299 cases; (1) The number of cases is too small to be sure how well a hospital is performing; (2) The hospital indicated that the data submitted for this measure were based on a sample of cases; (3) Data was collected during a shorter time period (fewer quarters) than the maximum possible time for this measure; (4) Suppressed for one or more quarters by CMS; (5) No data is available from the hospital for this measure; (6) Fewer than 100 patients completed the HCAHPS survey. Use these rates with caution, as the number of surveys may be too low to reliably assess hospital performance; (7) Survey results are based on less than 12 months of data; (8) Survey results are not available for this reporting period; (9) No or very few patients were eligible for the HCAHPS survey. The scores shown, if any, reflect a very small number of surveys; (10) A state average was not calculated because too few hospitals in the state submitted data; (11) There were discrepancies in the data collection process; Please refer to the User's Guide for a full explanation of data.

Memorial Hospital Lafayette County

800 Clay St | Phone: 608-776-4466
Darlington, WI 53530 | Fax: 608-776-5701
URL: www.mhlc-mhf.org
Type: Critical Access Hospitals | Emergency Services: Yes
Ownership: Government - Local | Beds: 25

Key Personnel:
Chief of Medical Staff.......... Michael Robiolio, MD
Infection Control.............. Pamela Gould
Operating Room.............. Dr Scott Gibson, RN
Quality Assurance .... Karla Blackbourn
Radiology.................... Dr Mark F Rich

Measure	Cases	This Hosp.	State Avg.	U.S. Avg.
Heart Attack Care				
ACE Inhibitor or ARB for LVSD[1,3]	1	100%	97%	96%
Aspirin at Arrival[1,3]	3	100%	99%	99%
Aspirin at Discharge[1,3]	2	100%	99%	98%
Beta Blocker at Discharge[1,3]	2	100%	99%	98%
Fibrinolytic Medication Timing[3]	0	-	0%	55%
PCI Within 90 Minutes of Arrival[5]	0	-	89%	90%
Smoking Cessation Advice[3]	0	-	99%	99%
Chest Pain/Possible Heart Attack Care				
Aspirin at Arrival[1]	15	100%	96%	95%
Median Time to ECG (minutes)[1]	18	12	7	8
Median Time to Transfer (minutes)[1,3]	1	70	49	61
Fibrinolytic Medication Timing	0	-	63%	54%
Heart Failure Care				
ACE Inhibitor or ARB for LVSD[1]	4	75%	95%	94%
Discharge Instructions[1]	18	72%	86%	88%
Evaluation of LVS Function[1]	22	95%	97%	98%
Smoking Cessation Advice	0	-	97%	98%
Pneumonia Care				
Appropriate Initial Antibiotic	29	97%	94%	92%
Blood Culture Timing[1]	6	100%	97%	96%
Influenza Vaccine[1]	20	95%	92%	91%
Initial Antibiotic Timing	39	97%	97%	95%
Pneumococcal Vaccine	44	84%	93%	93%
Smoking Cessation Advice[1]	6	83%	95%	97%
Surgical Care Improvement Project				
Appropriate VTP Within 24 Hours[1]	3	100%	93%	92%
Appropriate Hair Removal	34	100%	100%	99%
Appropriate Beta Blocker Usage[1]	9	100%	92%	93%
Controlled Postoperative Blood Glucose	0	-	93%	93%
Prophylactic Antibiotic Timing	29	100%	97%	97%
Prophylactic Antibiotic Timing (Outpatient)[1,3]	7	71%	91%	92%
Prophylactic Antibiotic Selection	30	100%	98%	97%
Prophylactic Antibiotic Select. (Outpatient)[1,3]	5	100%	96%	94%
Prophylactic Antibiotic Stopped	29	90%	95%	94%
Recommended VTP Ordered[1]	3	100%	94%	94%
Urinary Catheter Removal	0	-	91%	90%
Children's Asthma Care				
Received Systemic Corticosteroids	-	-	-	100%
Received Home Management Plan	-	-	-	71%
Received Reliever Medication	-	-	-	100%
Use of Medical Imaging				
Combination Abdominal CT Scan	70	0.114	0.106	0.191
Combination Chest CT Scan[1]	28	0.321	0.027	0.054
Follow-up Mammogram/Ultrasound	104	10.6%	8.4%	8.4%
MRI for Low Back Pain[1]	13	23.1%	31.8%	32.7%
Survey of Patients' Hospital Experiences				
Area Around Room 'Always' Quiet at Night[11]	(a)	63%	-	58%
Doctors 'Always' Communicated Well[11]	(a)	83%	-	80%
Home Recovery Information Given[11]	(a)	88%	-	82%
Hospital Given 9 or 10 on 10 Point Scale[11]	(a)	73%	-	67%
Meds 'Always' Explained Before Given[11]	(a)	75%	-	60%
Nurses 'Always' Communicated Well[11]	(a)	81%	-	76%
Pain 'Always' Well Controlled[11]	(a)	73%	-	69%
Room and Bathroom 'Always' Clean[11]	(a)	88%	-	71%
Timely Help 'Always' Received[11]	(a)	73%	-	64%
Would Definitely Recommend Hospital[11]	(a)	79%	-	69%

Upland Hills Health

800 Compassion Way | Phone: 608-930-8000
Dodgeville, WI 53533 | Fax: 608-930-7250
URL: www.uplandhillshealth.org
Type: Critical Access Hospitals | Emergency Services: Yes
Ownership: Voluntary Non-Profit - Private | Beds: 69

Key Personnel:
CEO/President................ Steve Deal
Chief of Medical Staff.......... Phyllis Fritsch
Infection Control.............. Maria Leary
Operating Room.............. Dr Young Kim
Pediatric Ambulatory Care ...... Samy Desouky
Quality Assurance .... Christine Harrsion
Radiology.................... Lynette Collins, MD
Emergency Room .... Gary Grunow

Measure	Cases	This Hosp.	State Avg.	U.S. Avg.
Heart Attack Care				
ACE Inhibitor or ARB for LVSD[5]	0	-	97%	96%
Aspirin at Arrival[5]	0	-	99%	99%
Aspirin at Discharge[5]	0	-	99%	98%
Beta Blocker at Discharge[5]	0	-	99%	98%
Fibrinolytic Medication Timing[5]	0	-	0%	55%
PCI Within 90 Minutes of Arrival[5]	0	-	89%	90%
Smoking Cessation Advice[5]	0	-	99%	99%
Chest Pain/Possible Heart Attack Care				
Aspirin at Arrival	-	-	96%	95%
Median Time to ECG (minutes)	-	-	7	8
Median Time to Transfer (minutes)	-	-	49	61
Fibrinolytic Medication Timing	-	-	63%	54%
Heart Failure Care				
ACE Inhibitor or ARB for LVSD[1]	5	100%	95%	94%
Discharge Instructions[1]	21	100%	86%	88%
Evaluation of LVS Function	28	89%	97%	98%
Smoking Cessation Advice[1]	2	50%	97%	98%
Pneumonia Care				
Appropriate Initial Antibiotic[1]	8	62%	94%	92%
Blood Culture Timing	46	91%	97%	96%
Influenza Vaccine	32	91%	92%	91%
Initial Antibiotic Timing	43	93%	97%	95%
Pneumococcal Vaccine	43	86%	93%	93%
Smoking Cessation Advice[1]	5	80%	95%	97%
Surgical Care Improvement Project				
Appropriate VTP Within 24 Hours[5]	0	-	93%	92%
Appropriate Hair Removal	37	97%	100%	99%
Appropriate Beta Blocker Usage[5]	0	-	92%	93%
Controlled Postoperative Blood Glucose	0	-	93%	93%
Prophylactic Antibiotic Timing[1]	15	80%	97%	97%
Prophylactic Antibiotic Timing (Outpatient)	-	-	91%	92%
Prophylactic Antibiotic Selection[1]	15	80%	98%	97%
Prophylactic Antibiotic Select. (Outpatient)	-	-	96%	94%
Prophylactic Antibiotic Stopped[1]	15	93%	95%	94%
Recommended VTP Ordered[5]	0	-	94%	94%
Urinary Catheter Removal[1]	3	67%	91%	90%
Children's Asthma Care				
Received Systemic Corticosteroids	-	-	-	100%
Received Home Management Plan	-	-	-	71%
Received Reliever Medication	-	-	-	100%
Use of Medical Imaging				
Combination Abdominal CT Scan	-	-	0.106	0.191
Combination Chest CT Scan	-	-	0.027	0.054
Follow-up Mammogram/Ultrasound	-	-	8.4%	8.4%
MRI for Low Back Pain	-	-	31.8%	32.7%
Survey of Patients' Hospital Experiences				
Area Around Room 'Always' Quiet at Night	300+	64%	-	58%
Doctors 'Always' Communicated Well	300+	88%	-	80%
Home Recovery Information Given	300+	91%	-	82%
Hospital Given 9 or 10 on 10 Point Scale	300+	77%	-	67%
Meds 'Always' Explained Before Given	300+	68%	-	60%
Nurses 'Always' Communicated Well	300+	81%	-	76%
Pain 'Always' Well Controlled	300+	75%	-	69%
Room and Bathroom 'Always' Clean	300+	85%	-	71%
Timely Help 'Always' Received	300+	74%	-	64%
Would Definitely Recommend Hospital	300+	79%	-	69%

Ministry Eagle River Memorial Hospital

201 Hospital Rd | Phone: 715-356-8000
Eagle River, WI 54521 | Fax: 715-479-0395
Type: Critical Access Hospitals | Emergency Services: Yes
Ownership: Voluntary Non-Profit - Church | Beds: 29

Key Personnel:
Chief of Medical Staff.......... Dr. Terrance Moe
Operating Room.............. Rich Foster, RN
Emergency Room .... Karen Sturdevent

Measure	Cases	This Hosp.	State Avg.	U.S. Avg.
Heart Attack Care				
ACE Inhibitor or ARB for LVSD[3]	0	-	97%	96%
Aspirin at Arrival[1,3]	2	100%	99%	99%
Aspirin at Discharge[1,3]	1	100%	99%	98%
Beta Blocker at Discharge[3]	0	-	99%	98%
Fibrinolytic Medication Timing[3]	0	-	0%	55%
PCI Within 90 Minutes of Arrival[3]	0	-	89%	90%
Smoking Cessation Advice[3]	0	-	99%	99%
Chest Pain/Possible Heart Attack Care				
Aspirin at Arrival[1,3]	15	100%	96%	95%
Median Time to ECG (minutes)[1,3]	15	8	7	8
Median Time to Transfer (minutes)[5]	0	-	49	61
Fibrinolytic Medication Timing[1,3]	1	100%	63%	54%
Heart Failure Care				
ACE Inhibitor or ARB for LVSD[1]	1	100%	95%	94%
Discharge Instructions[1]	20	75%	86%	88%
Evaluation of LVS Function	28	100%	97%	98%
Smoking Cessation Advice[1]	6	100%	97%	98%
Pneumonia Care				
Appropriate Initial Antibiotic[1]	5	40%	94%	92%
Blood Culture Timing[1]	7	86%	97%	96%
Influenza Vaccine[1]	11	82%	92%	91%
Initial Antibiotic Timing[1]	15	100%	97%	95%
Pneumococcal Vaccine[1]	15	93%	93%	93%
Smoking Cessation Advice[1]	5	100%	95%	97%
Surgical Care Improvement Project				
Appropriate VTP Within 24 Hours[5]	0	-	93%	92%
Appropriate Hair Removal[5]	0	-	100%	99%
Appropriate Beta Blocker Usage[5]	0	-	92%	93%
Controlled Postoperative Blood Glucose[5]	0	-	93%	93%
Prophylactic Antibiotic Timing[5]	0	-	97%	97%
Prophylactic Antibiotic Timing (Outpatient)[5]	0	-	91%	92%
Prophylactic Antibiotic Selection[5]	0	-	98%	97%
Prophylactic Antibiotic Select. (Outpatient)[5]	0	-	96%	94%
Prophylactic Antibiotic Stopped[5]	0	-	95%	94%
Recommended VTP Ordered[5]	0	-	94%	94%
Urinary Catheter Removal[5]	0	-	91%	90%
Children's Asthma Care				
Received Systemic Corticosteroids	-	-	-	100%
Received Home Management Plan	-	-	-	71%
Received Reliever Medication	-	-	-	100%
Use of Medical Imaging				
Combination Abdominal CT Scan	196	0.082	0.106	0.191
Combination Chest CT Scan	112	0.027	0.027	0.054
Follow-up Mammogram/Ultrasound	345	22.9%	8.4%	8.4%
MRI for Low Back Pain	56	32.1%	31.8%	32.7%
Survey of Patients' Hospital Experiences				
Area Around Room 'Always' Quiet at Night	(a)	70%	-	58%
Doctors 'Always' Communicated Well	(a)	80%	-	80%
Home Recovery Information Given	(a)	84%	-	82%
Hospital Given 9 or 10 on 10 Point Scale	(a)	64%	-	67%
Meds 'Always' Explained Before Given	(a)	61%	-	60%
Nurses 'Always' Communicated Well	(a)	77%	-	76%
Pain 'Always' Well Controlled	(a)	74%	-	69%
Room and Bathroom 'Always' Clean	(a)	85%	-	71%
Timely Help 'Always' Received	(a)	76%	-	64%
Would Definitely Recommend Hospital	(a)	58%	-	69%

NOTE: Hospital profiles are in alphabetical order by state, then city, then hospital within the city; Rankings exclude hospitals with less than 25 cases except for patient surveys which excludes hospitals with less than 100 cases; (a) 100–299 cases; (1) The number of cases is too small to be sure how well a hospital is performing; (2) The hospital indicated that the data submitted for this measure were based on a sample of cases; (3) Data was collected during a shorter time period (fewer quarters) than the maximum possible time for this measure; (4) Suppressed for one or more quarters by CMS; (5) No data is available from the hospital for this measure; (6) Fewer than 100 patients completed the HCAHPS survey. Use these rates with caution, as the number of surveys may be too low to reliably assess hospital performance; (7) Survey results are based on less than 12 months of data; (8) Survey results are not available for this reporting period; (9) No or very few patients were eligible for the HCAHPS survey. The scores shown, if any, reflect a very small number of surveys; (10) A state average was not calculated because too few hospitals in the state submitted data; (11) There were discrepancies in the data collection process; Please refer to the User's Guide for a full explanation of data.

Luther Hospital Mayo Health System

1221 Whipple St Phone: 715-838-3311
Eau Claire, WI 54703
URL: www.luthermidelfort.org
Type: Acute Care Hospitals Emergency Services: Yes
Ownership: Voluntary Non-Profit - Private Beds: 304

Key Personnel:
CEO/President. . . . . Randall Linton, MD
Chief of Medical Staff . . . . David Henly, MD
Infection Control. . . . . Susan Shea
Operating Room. . . . . Gary Welch
Pediatric Ambulatory Care . . . . . . Melody Dodge
Pediatric In-Patient Care . . . . Kelly Buchheltz
Quality Assurance . . . . Ed Wittrock
Radiology. . . . . Zan Degen

Measure	Cases	This Hosp.	State Avg.	U.S. Avg.
Heart Attack Care				
ACE Inhibitor or ARB for LVSD	33	100%	97%	96%
Aspirin at Arrival	107	98%	99%	99%
Aspirin at Discharge	245	100%	99%	98%
Beta Blocker at Discharge	246	100%	99%	98%
Fibrinolytic Medication Timing	0	-	0%	55%
PCI Within 90 Minutes of Arrival[1]	12	92%	89%	90%
Smoking Cessation Advice	83	100%	99%	99%
Chest Pain/Possible Heart Attack Care				
Aspirin at Arrival[1,3]	3	100%	96%	95%
Median Time to ECG (minutes)[1,3]	3	13	7	8
Median Time to Transfer (minutes)[5]	0	-	49	61
Fibrinolytic Medication Timing[5]	0	-	63%	54%
Heart Failure Care				
ACE Inhibitor or ARB for LVSD	49	98%	95%	94%
Discharge Instructions	192	95%	86%	88%
Evaluation of LVS Function	264	100%	97%	98%
Smoking Cessation Advice[1]	18	100%	97%	98%
Pneumonia Care				
Appropriate Initial Antibiotic	108	95%	94%	92%
Blood Culture Timing	159	99%	97%	96%
Influenza Vaccine	138	98%	92%	91%
Initial Antibiotic Timing	163	94%	97%	95%
Pneumococcal Vaccine	197	98%	93%	93%
Smoking Cessation Advice	68	100%	95%	97%
Surgical Care Improvement Project				
Appropriate VTP Within 24 Hours	392	99%	93%	92%
Appropriate Hair Removal	1,405	100%	100%	99%
Appropriate Beta Blocker Usage	561	97%	92%	93%
Controlled Postoperative Blood Glucose	230	98%	93%	93%
Prophylactic Antibiotic Timing	943	98%	97%	97%
Prophylactic Antibiotic Timing (Outpatient)	315	96%	91%	92%
Prophylactic Antibiotic Selection	967	99%	98%	97%
Prophylactic Antibiotic Select. (Outpatient)	312	98%	96%	94%
Prophylactic Antibiotic Stopped	877	98%	95%	94%
Recommended VTP Ordered	393	99%	94%	94%
Urinary Catheter Removal	319	97%	91%	90%
Children's Asthma Care				
Received Systemic Corticosteroids	-	-	-	100%
Received Home Management Plan	-	-	-	71%
Received Reliever Medication	-	-	-	100%
Use of Medical Imaging				
Combination Abdominal CT Scan	785	0.093	0.106	0.191
Combination Chest CT Scan	928	0.005	0.027	0.054
Follow-up Mammogram/Ultrasound[5]	0	-	8.4%	8.4%
MRI for Low Back Pain	240	25.8%	31.8%	32.7%
Survey of Patients' Hospital Experiences				
Area Around Room 'Always' Quiet at Night	300+	53%	-	58%
Doctors 'Always' Communicated Well	300+	85%	-	80%
Home Recovery Information Given	300+	88%	-	82%
Hospital Given 9 or 10 on 10 Point Scale	300+	78%	-	67%
Meds 'Always' Explained Before Given	300+	65%	-	60%
Nurses 'Always' Communicated Well	300+	79%	-	76%
Pain 'Always' Well Controlled	300+	71%	-	69%
Room and Bathroom 'Always' Clean	300+	78%	-	71%
Timely Help 'Always' Received	300+	73%	-	64%
Would Definitely Recommend Hospital	300+	85%	-	69%

Oak Leaf Surgcl Hospital

3802 Oakwood Mall Dr Phone: 715-831-8130
Eau Claire, WI 54701
E-mail: info@oakleafsurgical.com
URL: www.oakleafsurgical.com
Type: Acute Care Hospitals Emergency Services: Yes
Ownership: Proprietary Beds: 13

Measure	Cases	This Hosp.	State Avg.	U.S. Avg.
Heart Attack Care				
ACE Inhibitor or ARB for LVSD[5]	0	-	97%	96%
Aspirin at Arrival[5]	0	-	99%	99%
Aspirin at Discharge[5]	0	-	99%	98%
Beta Blocker at Discharge[5]	0	-	99%	98%
Fibrinolytic Medication Timing[5]	0	-	0%	55%
PCI Within 90 Minutes of Arrival[5]	0	-	89%	90%
Smoking Cessation Advice[5]	0	-	99%	99%
Chest Pain/Possible Heart Attack Care				
Aspirin at Arrival[5]	0	-	96%	95%
Median Time to ECG (minutes)[5]	0	-	7	8
Median Time to Transfer (minutes)[5]	0	-	49	61
Fibrinolytic Medication Timing[5]	0	-	63%	54%
Heart Failure Care				
ACE Inhibitor or ARB for LVSD[5]	0	-	95%	94%
Discharge Instructions[5]	0	-	86%	88%
Evaluation of LVS Function[5]	0	-	97%	98%
Smoking Cessation Advice[5]	0	-	97%	98%
Pneumonia Care				
Appropriate Initial Antibiotic[5]	0	-	94%	92%
Blood Culture Timing[5]	0	-	97%	96%
Influenza Vaccine[5]	0	-	92%	91%
Initial Antibiotic Timing[5]	0	-	97%	95%
Pneumococcal Vaccine[5]	0	-	93%	93%
Smoking Cessation Advice[5]	0	-	95%	97%
Surgical Care Improvement Project				
Appropriate VTP Within 24 Hours	48	94%	93%	92%
Appropriate Hair Removal	347	100%	100%	99%
Appropriate Beta Blocker Usage	80	98%	92%	93%
Controlled Postoperative Blood Glucose	0	-	93%	93%
Prophylactic Antibiotic Timing	276	100%	97%	97%
Prophylactic Antibiotic Timing (Outpatient)	143	99%	91%	92%
Prophylactic Antibiotic Selection	277	98%	98%	97%
Prophylactic Antibiotic Select. (Outpatient)	142	91%	96%	94%
Prophylactic Antibiotic Stopped	274	94%	95%	94%
Recommended VTP Ordered	48	94%	94%	94%
Urinary Catheter Removal	79	99%	91%	90%
Children's Asthma Care				
Received Systemic Corticosteroids	-	-	-	100%
Received Home Management Plan	-	-	-	71%
Received Reliever Medication	-	-	-	100%
Use of Medical Imaging				
Combination Abdominal CT Scan[5]	0	-	0.106	0.191
Combination Chest CT Scan[5]	0	-	0.027	0.054
Follow-up Mammogram/Ultrasound[5]	0	-	8.4%	8.4%
MRI for Low Back Pain[5]	0	-	31.8%	32.7%
Survey of Patients' Hospital Experiences				
Area Around Room 'Always' Quiet at Night	300+	80%	-	58%
Doctors 'Always' Communicated Well	300+	94%	-	80%
Home Recovery Information Given	300+	93%	-	82%
Hospital Given 9 or 10 on 10 Point Scale	300+	97%	-	67%
Meds 'Always' Explained Before Given	300+	80%	-	60%
Nurses 'Always' Communicated Well	300+	92%	-	76%
Pain 'Always' Well Controlled	300+	79%	-	69%
Room and Bathroom 'Always' Clean	300+	83%	-	71%
Timely Help 'Always' Received	300+	89%	-	64%
Would Definitely Recommend Hospital	300+	96%	-	69%

Sacred Heart Hospital

900 W Clairemont Ave Phone: 715-717-4131
Eau Claire, WI 54701
URL: www.sacredhearteauclaire.org
Type: Acute Care Hospitals Emergency Services: Yes
Ownership: Voluntary Non-Profit - Church Beds: 344

Key Personnel:
CEO/President. . . . . Steve Ronstrom
Cardiac Laboratory. . . . . Nancy DeMars
Chief of Medical Staff . . . . Richard Daniels, MD
Infection Control. . . . . Donna Moraska
Operating Room. . . . . Loren Lortscher
Pediatric In-Patient Care . . . . Brook Steele
Quality Assurance . . . . Dawn Garcia
Radiology. . . . . Michael Dillon

Measure	Cases	This Hosp.	State Avg.	U.S. Avg.
Heart Attack Care				
ACE Inhibitor or ARB for LVSD	33	94%	97%	96%
Aspirin at Arrival	92	100%	99%	99%
Aspirin at Discharge	189	100%	99%	98%
Beta Blocker at Discharge	184	99%	99%	98%
Fibrinolytic Medication Timing	0	-	0%	55%
PCI Within 90 Minutes of Arrival[1]	20	85%	89%	90%
Smoking Cessation Advice	66	100%	99%	99%
Chest Pain/Possible Heart Attack Care				
Aspirin at Arrival[1,3]	3	67%	96%	95%
Median Time to ECG (minutes)[1,3]	4	14	7	8
Median Time to Transfer (minutes)[5]	0	-	49	61
Fibrinolytic Medication Timing[5]	0	-	63%	54%
Heart Failure Care				
ACE Inhibitor or ARB for LVSD	42	95%	95%	94%
Discharge Instructions	105	93%	86%	88%
Evaluation of LVS Function	139	100%	97%	98%
Smoking Cessation Advice[1]	18	100%	97%	98%
Pneumonia Care				
Appropriate Initial Antibiotic	74	89%	94%	92%
Blood Culture Timing	120	97%	97%	96%
Influenza Vaccine	88	97%	92%	91%
Initial Antibiotic Timing	132	97%	97%	95%
Pneumococcal Vaccine	117	97%	93%	93%
Smoking Cessation Advice	48	96%	95%	97%
Surgical Care Improvement Project				
Appropriate VTP Within 24 Hours[2]	192	88%	93%	92%
Appropriate Hair Removal[2]	513	100%	100%	99%
Appropriate Beta Blocker Usage[2]	171	87%	92%	93%
Controlled Postoperative Blood Glucose[2]	43	93%	93%	93%
Prophylactic Antibiotic Timing[2]	366	96%	97%	97%
Prophylactic Antibiotic Timing (Outpatient)	334	95%	91%	92%
Prophylactic Antibiotic Selection[2]	368	93%	98%	97%
Prophylactic Antibiotic Select. (Outpatient)	331	96%	96%	94%
Prophylactic Antibiotic Stopped[2]	348	89%	95%	94%
Recommended VTP Ordered[2]	193	91%	94%	94%
Urinary Catheter Removal[2]	127	83%	91%	90%
Children's Asthma Care				
Received Systemic Corticosteroids	-	-	-	100%
Received Home Management Plan	-	-	-	71%
Received Reliever Medication	-	-	-	100%
Use of Medical Imaging				
Combination Abdominal CT Scan	493	0.120	0.106	0.191
Combination Chest CT Scan	486	0.012	0.027	0.054
Follow-up Mammogram/Ultrasound	311	11.6%	8.4%	8.4%
MRI for Low Back Pain	167	25.1%	31.8%	32.7%
Survey of Patients' Hospital Experiences				
Area Around Room 'Always' Quiet at Night	300+	57%	-	58%
Doctors 'Always' Communicated Well	300+	82%	-	80%
Home Recovery Information Given	300+	87%	-	82%
Hospital Given 9 or 10 on 10 Point Scale	300+	73%	-	67%
Meds 'Always' Explained Before Given	300+	65%	-	60%
Nurses 'Always' Communicated Well	300+	80%	-	76%
Pain 'Always' Well Controlled	300+	72%	-	69%
Room and Bathroom 'Always' Clean	300+	77%	-	71%
Timely Help 'Always' Received	300+	68%	-	64%
Would Definitely Recommend Hospital	300+	79%	-	69%

NOTE: Hospital profiles are in alphabetical order by state, then city, then hospital within the city; Rankings exclude hospitals with less than 25 cases except for patient surveys which excludes hospitals with less than 100 cases; (a) 100–299 cases; (1) The number of cases is too small to be sure how well a hospital is performing; (2) The hospital indicated that the data submitted for this measure were based on a sample of cases; (3) Data was collected during a shorter time period (fewer quarters) than the maximum possible time for this measure; (4) Suppressed for one or more quarters by CMS; (5) No data is available from the hospital for this measure; (6) Fewer than 100 patients completed the HCAHPS survey. Use these rates with caution, as the number of surveys may be too low to reliably assess hospital performance; (7) Survey results are based on less than 12 months of data; (8) Survey results are not available for this reporting period; (9) No or very few patients were eligible for the HCAHPS survey. The scores shown, if any, reflect a very small number of surveys; (10) A state average was not calculated because too few hospitals in the state submitted data; (11) There were discrepancies in the data collection process; Please refer to the User's Guide for a full explanation of data.

Edgerton Hospital and Health Services

313 Stoughton Rd Phone: 608-884-3441
Edgerton, WI 53534 Fax: 608-884-1659
E-mail: mchinfo@edgertonhospital.com
URL: www.edgertonhospital.com
Type: Critical Access Hospitals Emergency Services: Yes
Ownership: Voluntary Non-Profit - Private Beds: 86

Key Personnel:
CEO/President. . . . . Jim Pernau
Chief of Medical Staff . . . . Dennis Litsheim, MD
Operating Room. . . . . Shelley Mcguire
Quality Assurance . . . . Sue Alusin, POPP
Radiology. . . . . Roberta Nelson
Emergency Room . . . . Christine Langemo, MD

Measure	Cases	This Hosp.	State Avg.	U.S. Avg.
Heart Attack Care				
ACE Inhibitor or ARB for LVSD[5]	0	-	97%	96%
Aspirin at Arrival[5]	0	-	99%	99%
Aspirin at Discharge[5]	0	-	99%	98%
Beta Blocker at Discharge[5]	0	-	99%	98%
Fibrinolytic Medication Timing[5]	0	-	0%	55%
PCI Within 90 Minutes of Arrival[5]	0	-	89%	90%
Smoking Cessation Advice[5]	0	-	99%	99%
Chest Pain/Possible Heart Attack Care				
Aspirin at Arrival	-	-	96%	95%
Median Time to ECG (minutes)	-	-	7	8
Median Time to Transfer (minutes)	-	-	49	61
Fibrinolytic Medication Timing	-	-	63%	54%
Heart Failure Care				
ACE Inhibitor or ARB for LVSD[5]	0	-	95%	94%
Discharge Instructions[5]	0	-	86%	88%
Evaluation of LVS Function[5]	0	-	97%	98%
Smoking Cessation Advice[5]	0	-	97%	98%
Pneumonia Care				
Appropriate Initial Antibiotic[5]	0	-	94%	92%
Blood Culture Timing[5]	0	-	97%	96%
Influenza Vaccine[5]	0	-	92%	91%
Initial Antibiotic Timing[5]	0	-	97%	95%
Pneumococcal Vaccine[5]	0	-	93%	93%
Smoking Cessation Advice[5]	0	-	95%	97%
Surgical Care Improvement Project				
Appropriate VTP Within 24 Hours[5]	0	-	93%	92%
Appropriate Hair Removal[5]	0	-	100%	99%
Appropriate Beta Blocker Usage[5]	0	-	92%	93%
Controlled Postoperative Blood Glucose[5]	0	-	93%	93%
Prophylactic Antibiotic Timing[5]	0	-	97%	97%
Prophylactic Antibiotic Timing (Outpatient)	-	-	91%	92%
Prophylactic Antibiotic Selection[5]	0	-	98%	97%
Prophylactic Antibiotic Select. (Outpatient)	-	-	96%	94%
Prophylactic Antibiotic Stopped[5]	0	-	95%	94%
Recommended VTP Ordered[5]	0	-	94%	94%
Urinary Catheter Removal[5]	0	-	91%	90%
Children's Asthma Care				
Received Systemic Corticosteroids	-	-	-	100%
Received Home Management Plan	-	-	-	71%
Received Reliever Medication	-	-	-	100%
Use of Medical Imaging				
Combination Abdominal CT Scan	-	-	0.106	0.191
Combination Chest CT Scan	-	-	0.027	0.054
Follow-up Mammogram/Ultrasound	-	-	8.4%	8.4%
MRI for Low Back Pain	-	-	31.8%	32.7%
Survey of Patients' Hospital Experiences				
Area Around Room 'Always' Quiet at Night[6]	<100	59%	-	58%
Doctors 'Always' Communicated Well[6]	<100	82%	-	80%
Home Recovery Information Given[6]	<100	96%	-	82%
Hospital Given 9 or 10 on 10 Point Scale[6]	<100	70%	-	67%
Meds 'Always' Explained Before Given[6]	<100	73%	-	60%
Nurses 'Always' Communicated Well[6]	<100	81%	-	76%
Pain 'Always' Well Controlled[6]	<100	71%	-	69%
Room and Bathroom 'Always' Clean[6]	<100	84%	-	71%
Timely Help 'Always' Received[6]	<100	74%	-	64%
Would Definitely Recommend Hospital	<100	75%	-	69%

Aurora Lakeland Medical Center

W3985 County Rd Nn Phone: 262-741-2000
Elkhorn, WI 53121
URL: www.aurorahealthcare.org/facilities
Type: Acute Care Hospitals Emergency Services: Yes
Ownership: Voluntary Non-Profit - Private Beds: 99

Measure	Cases	This Hosp.	State Avg.	U.S. Avg.
Heart Attack Care				
ACE Inhibitor or ARB for LVSD[1]	5	100%	97%	96%
Aspirin at Arrival[1]	15	100%	99%	99%
Aspirin at Discharge[1]	7	100%	99%	98%
Beta Blocker at Discharge[1]	8	100%	99%	98%
Fibrinolytic Medication Timing	0	-	0%	55%
PCI Within 90 Minutes of Arrival	0	-	89%	90%
Smoking Cessation Advice[1]	2	100%	99%	99%
Chest Pain/Possible Heart Attack Care				
Aspirin at Arrival	91	99%	96%	95%
Median Time to ECG (minutes)	93	6	7	8
Median Time to Transfer (minutes)[1]	12	43	49	61
Fibrinolytic Medication Timing	0	-	63%	54%
Heart Failure Care				
ACE Inhibitor or ARB for LVSD[1]	20	95%	95%	94%
Discharge Instructions	50	72%	86%	88%
Evaluation of LVS Function	55	100%	97%	98%
Smoking Cessation Advice[1]	8	100%	97%	98%
Pneumonia Care				
Appropriate Initial Antibiotic	79	99%	94%	92%
Blood Culture Timing	73	99%	97%	96%
Influenza Vaccine	57	95%	92%	91%
Initial Antibiotic Timing	91	99%	97%	95%
Pneumococcal Vaccine	90	99%	93%	93%
Smoking Cessation Advice	46	100%	95%	97%
Surgical Care Improvement Project				
Appropriate VTP Within 24 Hours[2]	81	83%	93%	92%
Appropriate Hair Removal[2]	179	100%	100%	99%
Appropriate Beta Blocker Usage[2]	61	92%	92%	93%
Controlled Postoperative Blood Glucose[2]	0	-	93%	93%
Prophylactic Antibiotic Timing[2]	108	98%	97%	97%
Prophylactic Antibiotic Timing (Outpatient)	58	84%	91%	92%
Prophylactic Antibiotic Selection[2]	108	96%	98%	97%
Prophylactic Antibiotic Select. (Outpatient)	53	92%	96%	94%
Prophylactic Antibiotic Stopped[2]	91	96%	95%	94%
Recommended VTP Ordered[2]	81	85%	94%	94%
Urinary Catheter Removal[2]	54	94%	91%	90%
Children's Asthma Care				
Received Systemic Corticosteroids	-	-	-	100%
Received Home Management Plan	-	-	-	71%
Received Reliever Medication	-	-	-	100%
Use of Medical Imaging				
Combination Abdominal CT Scan	597	0.055	0.106	0.191
Combination Chest CT Scan	535	0.000	0.027	0.054
Follow-up Mammogram/Ultrasound	463	8.4%	8.4%	8.4%
MRI for Low Back Pain	63	30.2%	31.8%	32.7%
Survey of Patients' Hospital Experiences				
Area Around Room 'Always' Quiet at Night	300+	46%	-	58%
Doctors 'Always' Communicated Well	300+	80%	-	80%
Home Recovery Information Given	300+	86%	-	82%
Hospital Given 9 or 10 on 10 Point Scale	300+	55%	-	67%
Meds 'Always' Explained Before Given	300+	57%	-	60%
Nurses 'Always' Communicated Well	300+	75%	-	76%
Pain 'Always' Well Controlled	300+	68%	-	69%
Room and Bathroom 'Always' Clean	300+	67%	-	71%
Timely Help 'Always' Received	300+	64%	-	64%
Would Definitely Recommend Hospital	300+	58%	-	69%

Saint Agnes Hospital

430 E Divison St Phone: 920-926-5408
Fond Du Lac, WI 54935 Fax: 920-926-4306
URL: www.agnesian.com
Type: Acute Care Hospitals Emergency Services: Yes
Ownership: Voluntary Non-Profit - Private Beds: 330

Key Personnel:
CEO/President. . . . . Robert A Fale
Cardiac Laboratory. . . . . Jim Mugan
Chief of Medical Staff . . . . Theodore Miller, MD
Infection Control. . . . . Kayla Ericksen
Operating Room. . . . . James Avery
Pediatric In-Patient Care . . . . . . Maria Zahn
Quality Assurance . . . . Cathic Aschenbrenner
Radiology. . . . . Missy Tate

Measure	Cases	This Hosp.	State Avg.	U.S. Avg.
Heart Attack Care				
ACE Inhibitor or ARB for LVSD	26	96%	97%	96%
Aspirin at Arrival	136	99%	99%	99%
Aspirin at Discharge	153	97%	99%	98%
Beta Blocker at Discharge	131	94%	99%	98%
Fibrinolytic Medication Timing	0	-	0%	55%
PCI Within 90 Minutes of Arrival	34	88%	89%	90%
Smoking Cessation Advice	51	100%	99%	99%
Chest Pain/Possible Heart Attack Care				
Aspirin at Arrival[1,3]	4	50%	96%	95%
Median Time to ECG (minutes)[1,3]	4	8	7	8
Median Time to Transfer (minutes)[5]	0	-	49	61
Fibrinolytic Medication Timing[5]	0	-	63%	54%
Heart Failure Care				
ACE Inhibitor or ARB for LVSD	54	98%	95%	94%
Discharge Instructions	99	82%	86%	88%
Evaluation of LVS Function	143	100%	97%	98%
Smoking Cessation Advice[1]	21	100%	97%	98%
Pneumonia Care				
Appropriate Initial Antibiotic[2]	90	98%	94%	92%
Blood Culture Timing[2]	129	98%	97%	96%
Influenza Vaccine[2]	92	99%	92%	91%
Initial Antibiotic Timing[2]	119	100%	97%	95%
Pneumococcal Vaccine[2]	131	97%	93%	93%
Smoking Cessation Advice[2]	29	97%	95%	97%
Surgical Care Improvement Project				
Appropriate VTP Within 24 Hours[2]	180	96%	93%	92%
Appropriate Hair Removal[2]	535	100%	100%	99%
Appropriate Beta Blocker Usage[2]	146	97%	92%	93%
Controlled Postoperative Blood Glucose[2]	65	97%	93%	93%
Prophylactic Antibiotic Timing[2]	372	99%	97%	97%
Prophylactic Antibiotic Timing (Outpatient)	360	93%	91%	92%
Prophylactic Antibiotic Selection[2]	375	98%	98%	97%
Prophylactic Antibiotic Select. (Outpatient)	343	96%	96%	94%
Prophylactic Antibiotic Stopped[2]	353	93%	95%	94%
Recommended VTP Ordered[2]	182	96%	94%	94%
Urinary Catheter Removal[2]	132	95%	91%	90%
Children's Asthma Care				
Received Systemic Corticosteroids	-	-	-	100%
Received Home Management Plan	-	-	-	71%
Received Reliever Medication	-	-	-	100%
Use of Medical Imaging				
Combination Abdominal CT Scan	553	0.128	0.106	0.191
Combination Chest CT Scan	534	0.030	0.027	0.054
Follow-up Mammogram/Ultrasound	1,196	12.6%	8.4%	8.4%
MRI for Low Back Pain	141	29.8%	31.8%	32.7%
Survey of Patients' Hospital Experiences				
Area Around Room 'Always' Quiet at Night	300+	58%	-	58%
Doctors 'Always' Communicated Well	300+	80%	-	80%
Home Recovery Information Given	300+	86%	-	82%
Hospital Given 9 or 10 on 10 Point Scale	300+	68%	-	67%
Meds 'Always' Explained Before Given	300+	60%	-	60%
Nurses 'Always' Communicated Well	300+	77%	-	76%
Pain 'Always' Well Controlled	300+	72%	-	69%
Room and Bathroom 'Always' Clean	300+	77%	-	71%
Timely Help 'Always' Received	300+	60%	-	64%
Would Definitely Recommend Hospital	300+	66%	-	69%

NOTE: Hospital profiles are in alphabetical order by state, then city, then hospital within the city; Rankings exclude hospitals with less than 25 cases except for patient surveys which excludes hospitals with less than 100 cases; (a) 100–299 cases; (1) The number of cases is too small to be sure how well a hospital is performing; (2) The hospital indicated that the data submitted for this measure were based on a sample of cases; (3) Data was collected during a shorter time period (fewer quarters) than the maximum possible time for this measure; (4) Suppressed for one or more quarters by CMS; (5) No data is available from the hospital for this measure; (6) Fewer than 100 patients completed the HCAHPS survey. Use these rates with caution, as the number of surveys may be too low to reliably assess hospital performance; (7) Survey results are based on less than 12 months of data; (8) Survey results are not available for this reporting period; (9) No or very few patients were eligible for the HCAHPS survey. The scores shown, if any, reflect a very small number of surveys; (10) A state average was not calculated because too few hospitals in the state submitted data; (11) There were discrepancies in the data collection process; Please refer to the User's Guide for a full explanation of data.

Fort Healthcare

611 Sherman Ave E Phone: 920-568-5000
Fort Atkinson, WI 53538 Fax: 920-568-5412
E-mail: sally.hink@famhs.org
URL: www.forthealthcare.com
Type: Acute Care Hospitals Emergency Services: Yes
Ownership: Voluntary Non-Profit - Private Beds: 110
Key Personnel:
CEO/President. . . . . Michael Wallace
Chief of Medical Staff . . . . Pam Kuehl, MD
Coronary Care . . . . Linda Smith, RN
Quality Assurance . . . . Marie Wiesmann, RN
Radiology. . . . . Edgardo Jiongco, MD
Emergency Room . . . . Harold Wilson, RN

Measure	Cases	This Hosp.	State Avg.	U.S. Avg.
Heart Attack Care				
ACE Inhibitor or ARB for LVSD[1,3]	1	100%	97%	96%
Aspirin at Arrival[1,3]	7	100%	99%	99%
Aspirin at Discharge[1,3]	5	100%	99%	98%
Beta Blocker at Discharge[1,3]	5	80%	99%	98%
Fibrinolytic Medication Timing[3]	0	-	0%	55%
PCI Within 90 Minutes of Arrival[3]	0	-	89%	90%
Smoking Cessation Advice[3]	0	-	99%	99%
Chest Pain/Possible Heart Attack Care				
Aspirin at Arrival	124	96%	96%	95%
Median Time to ECG (minutes)	127	7	7	8
Median Time to Transfer (minutes)[1]	12	66	49	61
Fibrinolytic Medication Timing	0	-	63%	54%
Heart Failure Care				
ACE Inhibitor or ARB for LVSD[1]	13	92%	95%	94%
Discharge Instructions	54	63%	86%	88%
Evaluation of LVS Function	79	95%	97%	98%
Smoking Cessation Advice[1]	12	100%	97%	98%
Pneumonia Care				
Appropriate Initial Antibiotic	45	93%	94%	92%
Blood Culture Timing	65	98%	97%	96%
Influenza Vaccine	51	96%	92%	91%
Initial Antibiotic Timing	82	98%	97%	95%
Pneumococcal Vaccine	74	100%	93%	93%
Smoking Cessation Advice[1]	20	90%	95%	97%
Surgical Care Improvement Project				
Appropriate VTP Within 24 Hours[2]	118	99%	93%	92%
Appropriate Hair Removal[2]	322	100%	100%	99%
Appropriate Beta Blocker Usage[2]	77	83%	92%	93%
Controlled Postoperative Blood Glucose[2]	0	-	93%	93%
Prophylactic Antibiotic Timing[2]	213	91%	97%	97%
Prophylactic Antibiotic Timing (Outpatient)	166	96%	91%	92%
Prophylactic Antibiotic Selection[2]	214	98%	98%	97%
Prophylactic Antibiotic Select. (Outpatient)	163	98%	96%	94%
Prophylactic Antibiotic Stopped[2]	205	93%	95%	94%
Recommended VTP Ordered[2]	118	99%	94%	94%
Urinary Catheter Removal[1,2]	19	95%	91%	90%
Children's Asthma Care				
Received Systemic Corticosteroids	-	-	-	100%
Received Home Management Plan	-	-	-	71%
Received Reliever Medication	-	-	-	100%
Use of Medical Imaging				
Combination Abdominal CT Scan	617	0.374	0.106	0.191
Combination Chest CT Scan	353	0.003	0.027	0.054
Follow-up Mammogram/Ultrasound	846	1.1%	8.4%	8.4%
MRI for Low Back Pain	70	31.4%	31.8%	32.7%
Survey of Patients' Hospital Experiences				
Area Around Room 'Always' Quiet at Night	300+	65%	-	58%
Doctors 'Always' Communicated Well	300+	79%	-	80%
Home Recovery Information Given	300+	86%	-	82%
Hospital Given 9 or 10 on 10 Point Scale	300+	63%	-	67%
Meds 'Always' Explained Before Given	300+	57%	-	60%
Nurses 'Always' Communicated Well	300+	75%	-	76%
Pain 'Always' Well Controlled	300+	65%	-	69%
Room and Bathroom 'Always' Clean	300+	69%	-	71%
Timely Help 'Always' Received	300+	62%	-	64%
Would Definitely Recommend Hospital	300+	66%	-	69%

Midwest Orthopedic Specialty Hospital

10101 South 27th Street, 2nd Floor Phone: 414-325-4518
Franklin, WI 53132
URL: www.mymosh.com
Type: Acute Care Hospitals Emergency Services: No
Ownership: Voluntary Non-Profit - Private Beds: 31

Measure	Cases	This Hosp.	State Avg.	U.S. Avg.
Heart Attack Care				
ACE Inhibitor or ARB for LVSD[5]	0	-	97%	96%
Aspirin at Arrival[5]	0	-	99%	99%
Aspirin at Discharge[5]	0	-	99%	98%
Beta Blocker at Discharge[5]	0	-	99%	98%
Fibrinolytic Medication Timing[5]	0	-	0%	55%
PCI Within 90 Minutes of Arrival[5]	0	-	89%	90%
Smoking Cessation Advice[5]	0	-	99%	99%
Chest Pain/Possible Heart Attack Care				
Aspirin at Arrival[5]	0	-	96%	95%
Median Time to ECG (minutes)[5]	0	-	7	8
Median Time to Transfer (minutes)[5]	0	-	49	61
Fibrinolytic Medication Timing[5]	0	-	63%	54%
Heart Failure Care				
ACE Inhibitor or ARB for LVSD[5]	0	-	95%	94%
Discharge Instructions[5]	0	-	86%	88%
Evaluation of LVS Function[5]	0	-	97%	98%
Smoking Cessation Advice[5]	0	-	97%	98%
Pneumonia Care				
Appropriate Initial Antibiotic[5]	0	-	94%	92%
Blood Culture Timing[5]	0	-	97%	96%
Influenza Vaccine[5]	0	-	92%	91%
Initial Antibiotic Timing[5]	0	-	97%	95%
Pneumococcal Vaccine[5]	0	-	93%	93%
Smoking Cessation Advice[5]	0	-	95%	97%
Surgical Care Improvement Project				
Appropriate VTP Within 24 Hours[1,2,3]	5	100%	93%	92%
Appropriate Hair Removal[2,3]	131	100%	100%	99%
Appropriate Beta Blocker Usage[2,3]	32	84%	92%	93%
Controlled Postoperative Blood Glucose[2,3]	0	-	93%	93%
Prophylactic Antibiotic Timing[2,3]	90	96%	97%	97%
Prophylactic Antibiotic Timing (Outpatient)[3]	91	91%	91%	92%
Prophylactic Antibiotic Selection[2,3]	90	100%	98%	97%
Prophylactic Antibiotic Select. (Outpatient)[3]	90	100%	96%	94%
Prophylactic Antibiotic Stopped[2,3]	85	100%	95%	94%
Recommended VTP Ordered[1,2,3]	5	100%	94%	94%
Urinary Catheter Removal[2]	63	100%	91%	90%
Children's Asthma Care				
Received Systemic Corticosteroids	-	-	-	100%
Received Home Management Plan	-	-	-	71%
Received Reliever Medication	-	-	-	100%
Use of Medical Imaging				
Combination Abdominal CT Scan[5]	0	-	0.106	0.191
Combination Chest CT Scan[5]	0	-	0.027	0.054
Follow-up Mammogram/Ultrasound[5]	0	-	8.4%	8.4%
MRI for Low Back Pain[5]	0	-	31.8%	32.7%
Survey of Patients' Hospital Experiences				
Area Around Room 'Always' Quiet at Night[8]	-	-	-	58%
Doctors 'Always' Communicated Well[8]	-	-	-	80%
Home Recovery Information Given[8]	-	-	-	82%
Hospital Given 9 or 10 on 10 Point Scale[8]	-	-	-	67%
Meds 'Always' Explained Before Given[8]	-	-	-	60%
Nurses 'Always' Communicated Well[8]	-	-	-	76%
Pain 'Always' Well Controlled[8]	-	-	-	69%
Room and Bathroom 'Always' Clean[8]	-	-	-	71%
Timely Help 'Always' Received[8]	-	-	-	64%
Would Definitely Recommend Hospital[8]	-	-	-	69%

Wheaton Franciscan Healthcare - Franklin

10101 South 27th Street Phone: 414-325-4700
Franklin, WI 53132
URL: www.mywheaton.org
Type: Acute Care Hospitals Emergency Services: Yes
Ownership: Voluntary Non-Profit - Private
Key Personnel:
President. . . . . Daniel Mattes

Measure	Cases	This Hosp.	State Avg.	U.S. Avg.
Heart Attack Care				
ACE Inhibitor or ARB for LVSD[5]	0	-	97%	96%
Aspirin at Arrival[5]	0	-	99%	99%
Aspirin at Discharge[5]	0	-	99%	98%
Beta Blocker at Discharge[5]	0	-	99%	98%
Fibrinolytic Medication Timing[5]	0	-	0%	55%
PCI Within 90 Minutes of Arrival[5]	0	-	89%	90%
Smoking Cessation Advice[5]	0	-	99%	99%
Chest Pain/Possible Heart Attack Care				
Aspirin at Arrival	54	93%	96%	95%
Median Time to ECG (minutes)	59	6	7	8
Median Time to Transfer (minutes)[1,3]	4	44	49	61
Fibrinolytic Medication Timing	0	-	63%	54%
Heart Failure Care				
ACE Inhibitor or ARB for LVSD[1]	9	78%	95%	94%
Discharge Instructions[1]	18	72%	86%	88%
Evaluation of LVS Function[1]	21	100%	97%	98%
Smoking Cessation Advice[1]	2	100%	97%	98%
Pneumonia Care				
Appropriate Initial Antibiotic	27	96%	94%	92%
Blood Culture Timing	35	97%	97%	96%
Influenza Vaccine[1]	24	92%	92%	91%
Initial Antibiotic Timing	29	100%	97%	95%
Pneumococcal Vaccine	29	93%	93%	93%
Smoking Cessation Advice[1]	9	100%	95%	97%
Surgical Care Improvement Project				
Appropriate VTP Within 24 Hours[1]	5	20%	93%	92%
Appropriate Hair Removal[1]	16	100%	100%	99%
Appropriate Beta Blocker Usage[1]	2	100%	92%	93%
Controlled Postoperative Blood Glucose	0	-	93%	93%
Prophylactic Antibiotic Timing[1]	9	78%	97%	97%
Prophylactic Antibiotic Timing (Outpatient)	26	96%	91%	92%
Prophylactic Antibiotic Selection[1]	10	100%	98%	97%
Prophylactic Antibiotic Select. (Outpatient)	25	100%	96%	94%
Prophylactic Antibiotic Stopped[1]	9	100%	95%	94%
Recommended VTP Ordered[1]	5	40%	94%	94%
Urinary Catheter Removal[1]	2	50%	91%	90%
Children's Asthma Care				
Received Systemic Corticosteroids	-	-	-	100%
Received Home Management Plan	-	-	-	71%
Received Reliever Medication	-	-	-	100%
Use of Medical Imaging				
Combination Abdominal CT Scan	64	0.641	0.106	0.191
Combination Chest CT Scan[1]	35	0.029	0.027	0.054
Follow-up Mammogram/Ultrasound[1]	28	17.9%	8.4%	8.4%
MRI for Low Back Pain[1]	17	11.8%	31.8%	32.7%
Survey of Patients' Hospital Experiences				
Area Around Room 'Always' Quiet at Night	(a)	78%	-	58%
Doctors 'Always' Communicated Well	(a)	84%	-	80%
Home Recovery Information Given	(a)	80%	-	82%
Hospital Given 9 or 10 on 10 Point Scale	(a)	83%	-	67%
Meds 'Always' Explained Before Given	(a)	69%	-	60%
Nurses 'Always' Communicated Well	(a)	85%	-	76%
Pain 'Always' Well Controlled	(a)	78%	-	69%
Room and Bathroom 'Always' Clean	(a)	78%	-	71%
Timely Help 'Always' Received	(a)	76%	-	64%
Would Definitely Recommend Hospital	(a)	85%	-	69%

NOTE: Hospital profiles are in alphabetical order by state, then city, then hospital within the city; Rankings exclude hospitals with less than 25 cases except for patient surveys which excludes hospitals with less than 100 cases; (a) 100–299 cases; (1) The number of cases is too small to be sure how well a hospital is performing; (2) The hospital indicated that the data submitted for this measure were based on a sample of cases; (3) Data was collected during a shorter time period (fewer quarters) than the maximum possible time for this measure; (4) Suppressed for one or more quarters by CMS; (5) No data is available from the hospital for this measure; (6) Fewer than 100 patients completed the HCAHPS survey. Use these rates with caution, as the number of surveys may be too low to reliably assess hospital performance; (7) Survey results are based on less than 12 months of data; (8) Survey results are not available for this reporting period; (9) No or very few patients were eligible for the HCAHPS survey. The scores shown, if any, reflect a very small number of surveys; (10) A state average was not calculated because too few hospitals in the state submitted data; (11) There were discrepancies in the data collection process; Please refer to the User's Guide for a full explanation of data.

Moundview Memorial Hospital and Clinics

402 W Lake St
Friendship, WI 53934
Phone: 608-339-3331
Fax: 608-339-9385
E-mail: medwards@acmh.com
URL: www.acmh.com
Type: Critical Access Hospitals
Emergency Services: Yes
Ownership: Government - Local
Beds: 29

Key Personnel:

Chief of Medical Staff.......... Martin Janssen, MD
Emergency Room .... M Esmaili, MD

Measure	Cases	This Hosp.	State Avg.	U.S. Avg.
Heart Attack Care				
ACE Inhibitor or ARB for LVSD[5]	0	-	97%	96%
Aspirin at Arrival[5]	0	-	99%	99%
Aspirin at Discharge[5]	0	-	99%	98%
Beta Blocker at Discharge[5]	0	-	99%	98%
Fibrinolytic Medication Timing[5]	0	-	0%	55%
PCI Within 90 Minutes of Arrival[5]	0	-	89%	90%
Smoking Cessation Advice[5]	0	-	99%	99%
Chest Pain/Possible Heart Attack Care				
Aspirin at Arrival[3]	29	93%	96%	95%
Median Time to ECG (minutes)[3]	31	12	7	8
Median Time to Transfer (minutes)[5]	0	-	49	61
Fibrinolytic Medication Timing[3]	0	-	63%	54%
Heart Failure Care				
ACE Inhibitor or ARB for LVSD[1,3]	1	100%	95%	94%
Discharge Instructions[1,3]	7	57%	86%	88%
Evaluation of LVS Function[1,3]	9	89%	97%	98%
Smoking Cessation Advice[1,3]	2	100%	97%	98%
Pneumonia Care				
Appropriate Initial Antibiotic[1,3]	6	100%	94%	92%
Blood Culture Timing[1,3]	2	100%	97%	96%
Influenza Vaccine[1]	10	90%	92%	91%
Initial Antibiotic Timing[1,3]	11	82%	97%	95%
Pneumococcal Vaccine[1,3]	10	90%	93%	93%
Smoking Cessation Advice[1,3]	4	100%	95%	97%
Surgical Care Improvement Project				
Appropriate VTP Within 24 Hours[5]	0	-	93%	92%
Appropriate Hair Removal[5]	0	-	100%	99%
Appropriate Beta Blocker Usage[5]	0	-	92%	93%
Controlled Postoperative Blood Glucose[5]	0	-	93%	93%
Prophylactic Antibiotic Timing[5]	0	-	97%	97%
Prophylactic Antibiotic Timing (Outpatient)[1,3]	7	86%	91%	92%
Prophylactic Antibiotic Selection[5]	0	-	98%	97%
Prophylactic Antibiotic Select. (Outpatient)[1,3]	6	0%	96%	94%
Prophylactic Antibiotic Stopped[5]	0	-	95%	94%
Recommended VTP Ordered[5]	0	-	94%	94%
Urinary Catheter Removal[5]	0	-	91%	90%
Children's Asthma Care				
Received Systemic Corticosteroids	-	-	-	100%
Received Home Management Plan	-	-	-	71%
Received Reliever Medication	-	-	-	100%
Use of Medical Imaging				
Combination Abdominal CT Scan	109	0.018	0.106	0.191
Combination Chest CT Scan	99	0.000	0.027	0.054
Follow-up Mammogram/Ultrasound	190	3.7%	8.4%	8.4%
MRI for Low Back Pain[1]	11	54.5%	31.8%	32.7%
Survey of Patients' Hospital Experiences				
Area Around Room 'Always' Quiet at Night[6]	<100	58%	-	58%
Doctors 'Always' Communicated Well[6]	<100	69%	-	80%
Home Recovery Information Given[6]	<100	80%	-	82%
Hospital Given 9 or 10 on 10 Point Scale[6]	<100	60%	-	67%
Meds 'Always' Explained Before Given[6]	<100	64%	-	60%
Nurses 'Always' Communicated Well[6]	<100	82%	-	76%
Pain 'Always' Well Controlled[6]	<100	66%	-	69%
Room and Bathroom 'Always' Clean[6]	<100	86%	-	71%
Timely Help 'Always' Received[6]	<100	77%	-	64%
Would Definitely Recommend Hospital	<100	60%	-	69%

Orthopaedic Hospital of Wisconsin

475 W River Woods Pkwy
Glendale, WI 53212
Phone: 414-961-6800
Fax: 414-961-6738
URL: www.ohow.org
Type: Acute Care Hospitals
Emergency Services: No
Ownership: Voluntary Non-Profit - Other

Key Personnel:

CEO/President............... Susan Henckel

Measure	Cases	This Hosp.	State Avg.	U.S. Avg.
Heart Attack Care				
ACE Inhibitor or ARB for LVSD[5]	0	-	97%	96%
Aspirin at Arrival[5]	0	-	99%	99%
Aspirin at Discharge[5]	0	-	99%	98%
Beta Blocker at Discharge[5]	0	-	99%	98%
Fibrinolytic Medication Timing[5]	0	-	0%	55%
PCI Within 90 Minutes of Arrival[5]	0	-	89%	90%
Smoking Cessation Advice[5]	0	-	99%	99%
Chest Pain/Possible Heart Attack Care				
Aspirin at Arrival[5]	0	-	96%	95%
Median Time to ECG (minutes)[5]	0	-	7	8
Median Time to Transfer (minutes)[5]	0	-	49	61
Fibrinolytic Medication Timing[5]	0	-	63%	54%
Heart Failure Care				
ACE Inhibitor or ARB for LVSD[5]	0	-	95%	94%
Discharge Instructions[5]	0	-	86%	88%
Evaluation of LVS Function[5]	0	-	97%	98%
Smoking Cessation Advice[5]	0	-	97%	98%
Pneumonia Care				
Appropriate Initial Antibiotic[5]	0	-	94%	92%
Blood Culture Timing[5]	0	-	97%	96%
Influenza Vaccine[5]	0	-	92%	91%
Initial Antibiotic Timing[5]	0	-	97%	95%
Pneumococcal Vaccine[5]	0	-	93%	93%
Smoking Cessation Advice[5]	0	-	95%	97%
Surgical Care Improvement Project				
Appropriate VTP Within 24 Hours[1,2]	19	95%	93%	92%
Appropriate Hair Removal[2]	134	100%	100%	99%
Appropriate Beta Blocker Usage[2]	25	68%	92%	93%
Controlled Postoperative Blood Glucose[2]	0	-	93%	93%
Prophylactic Antibiotic Timing[2]	105	99%	97%	97%
Prophylactic Antibiotic Timing (Outpatient)[3]	130	95%	91%	92%
Prophylactic Antibiotic Selection[2]	106	100%	98%	97%
Prophylactic Antibiotic Select. (Outpatient)[3]	130	100%	96%	94%
Prophylactic Antibiotic Stopped[2]	105	95%	95%	94%
Recommended VTP Ordered[1,2]	19	95%	94%	94%
Urinary Catheter Removal[2]	103	91%	91%	90%
Children's Asthma Care				
Received Systemic Corticosteroids	-	-	-	100%
Received Home Management Plan	-	-	-	71%
Received Reliever Medication	-	-	-	100%
Use of Medical Imaging				
Combination Abdominal CT Scan[5]	0	-	0.106	0.191
Combination Chest CT Scan[5]	0	-	0.027	0.054
Follow-up Mammogram/Ultrasound[5]	0	-	8.4%	8.4%
MRI for Low Back Pain	89	28.1%	31.8%	32.7%
Survey of Patients' Hospital Experiences				
Area Around Room 'Always' Quiet at Night	300+	78%	-	58%
Doctors 'Always' Communicated Well	300+	90%	-	80%
Home Recovery Information Given	300+	89%	-	82%
Hospital Given 9 or 10 on 10 Point Scale	300+	87%	-	67%
Meds 'Always' Explained Before Given	300+	73%	-	60%
Nurses 'Always' Communicated Well	300+	90%	-	76%
Pain 'Always' Well Controlled	300+	81%	-	69%
Room and Bathroom 'Always' Clean	300+	80%	-	71%
Timely Help 'Always' Received	300+	84%	-	64%
Would Definitely Recommend Hospital	300+	89%	-	69%

Burnett Medical Center

257 W St George Ave
Grantsburg, WI 54840
Phone: 715-463-5353
Fax: 715-463-2423
E-mail: info@burnettmedicalcenter.com
URL: www.burnettmedicalcenter.com
Type: Critical Access Hospitals
Emergency Services: Yes
Ownership: Voluntary Non-Profit - Private
Beds: 78

Key Personnel:

CEO/President.............. Gordy Lewis
Cardiac Laboratory............ Terry Giles
Chief of Medical Staff.......... Blasé Vitale
Infection Control............. Debra Stigar
Quality Assurance .... Susan Smith
Anesthesiology.............. Gregory Pekkala

Measure	Cases	This Hosp.	State Avg.	U.S. Avg.
Heart Attack Care				
ACE Inhibitor or ARB for LVSD[3]	0	-	97%	96%
Aspirin at Arrival[1,3]	2	50%	99%	99%
Aspirin at Discharge[1,3]	1	100%	99%	98%
Beta Blocker at Discharge[1,3]	1	0%	99%	98%
Fibrinolytic Medication Timing[3]	0	-	0%	55%
PCI Within 90 Minutes of Arrival[3]	0	-	89%	90%
Smoking Cessation Advice[1,3]	1	100%	99%	99%
Chest Pain/Possible Heart Attack Care				
Aspirin at Arrival	-	-	96%	95%
Median Time to ECG (minutes)	-	-	7	8
Median Time to Transfer (minutes)	-	-	49	61
Fibrinolytic Medication Timing	-	-	63%	54%
Heart Failure Care				
ACE Inhibitor or ARB for LVSD[1]	2	100%	95%	94%
Discharge Instructions	25	84%	86%	88%
Evaluation of LVS Function	31	84%	97%	98%
Smoking Cessation Advice[1]	5	100%	97%	98%
Pneumonia Care				
Appropriate Initial Antibiotic[1]	21	100%	94%	92%
Blood Culture Timing[1]	14	93%	97%	96%
Influenza Vaccine[1]	11	100%	92%	91%
Initial Antibiotic Timing[1]	16	94%	97%	95%
Pneumococcal Vaccine[1]	20	85%	93%	93%
Smoking Cessation Advice[1]	4	100%	95%	97%
Surgical Care Improvement Project				
Appropriate VTP Within 24 Hours[5]	0	-	93%	92%
Appropriate Hair Removal[5]	0	-	100%	99%
Appropriate Beta Blocker Usage[5]	0	-	92%	93%
Controlled Postoperative Blood Glucose[5]	0	-	93%	93%
Prophylactic Antibiotic Timing[1,3]	12	67%	97%	97%
Prophylactic Antibiotic Timing (Outpatient)	-	-	91%	92%
Prophylactic Antibiotic Selection[1,3]	12	58%	98%	97%
Prophylactic Antibiotic Select. (Outpatient)	-	-	96%	94%
Prophylactic Antibiotic Stopped[1,3]	12	100%	95%	94%
Recommended VTP Ordered[5]	0	-	94%	94%
Urinary Catheter Removal[3]	0	-	91%	90%
Children's Asthma Care				
Received Systemic Corticosteroids	-	-	-	100%
Received Home Management Plan	-	-	-	71%
Received Reliever Medication	-	-	-	100%
Use of Medical Imaging				
Combination Abdominal CT Scan	-	-	0.106	0.191
Combination Chest CT Scan	-	-	0.027	0.054
Follow-up Mammogram/Ultrasound	-	-	8.4%	8.4%
MRI for Low Back Pain	-	-	31.8%	32.7%
Survey of Patients' Hospital Experiences				
Area Around Room 'Always' Quiet at Night	(a)	53%	-	58%
Doctors 'Always' Communicated Well	(a)	78%	-	80%
Home Recovery Information Given	(a)	86%	-	82%
Hospital Given 9 or 10 on 10 Point Scale	(a)	70%	-	67%
Meds 'Always' Explained Before Given	(a)	60%	-	60%
Nurses 'Always' Communicated Well	(a)	71%	-	76%
Pain 'Always' Well Controlled	(a)	78%	-	69%
Room and Bathroom 'Always' Clean	(a)	85%	-	71%
Timely Help 'Always' Received	(a)	77%	-	64%
Would Definitely Recommend Hospital	(a)	65%	-	69%

NOTE: Hospital profiles are in alphabetical order by state, then city, then hospital within the city; Rankings exclude hospitals with less than 25 cases except for patient surveys which excludes hospitals with less than 100 cases; (a) 100–299 cases; (1) The number of cases is too small to be sure how well a hospital is performing; (2) The hospital indicated that the data submitted for this measure were based on a sample of cases; (3) Data was collected during a shorter time period (fewer quarters) than the maximum possible time for this measure; (4) Suppressed for one or more quarters by CMS; (5) No data is available from the hospital for this measure; (6) Fewer than 100 patients completed the HCAHPS survey. Use these rates with caution, as the number of surveys may be too low to reliably assess hospital performance; (7) Survey results are based on less than 12 months of data; (8) Survey results are not available for this reporting period; (9) No or very few patients were eligible for the HCAHPS survey. The scores shown, if any, reflect a very small number of surveys; (10) A state average was not calculated because too few hospitals in the state submitted data; (11) There were discrepancies in the data collection process; Please refer to the User's Guide for a full explanation of data.

Aurora Baycare Medical Center

2845 Greenbrier Rd
Green Bay, WI 54311
Phone: 920-288-8000
URL: www.aurorabaycare.com
Type: Acute Care Hospitals
Emergency Services: Yes
Ownership: Proprietary
Beds: 167
Key Personnel:
CEO/President............... Daniel Meyer

Measure	Cases	This Hosp.	State Avg.	U.S. Avg.
Heart Attack Care				
ACE Inhibitor or ARB for LVSD[1]	22	100%	97%	96%
Aspirin at Arrival	52	100%	99%	99%
Aspirin at Discharge	137	98%	99%	98%
Beta Blocker at Discharge	132	98%	99%	98%
Fibrinolytic Medication Timing	0	-	0%	55%
PCI Within 90 Minutes of Arrival[1]	2	50%	89%	90%
Smoking Cessation Advice	46	98%	99%	99%
Chest Pain/Possible Heart Attack Care				
Aspirin at Arrival[3]	0	-	96%	95%
Median Time to ECG (minutes)[3]	0	-	7	8
Median Time to Transfer (minutes)[5]	0	-	49	61
Fibrinolytic Medication Timing[5]	0	-	63%	54%
Heart Failure Care				
ACE Inhibitor or ARB for LVSD	36	92%	95%	94%
Discharge Instructions	82	77%	86%	88%
Evaluation of LVS Function	107	100%	97%	98%
Smoking Cessation Advice[1]	6	100%	97%	98%
Pneumonia Care				
Appropriate Initial Antibiotic	46	93%	94%	92%
Blood Culture Timing	59	98%	97%	96%
Influenza Vaccine	56	79%	92%	91%
Initial Antibiotic Timing	73	96%	97%	95%
Pneumococcal Vaccine	61	92%	93%	93%
Smoking Cessation Advice[1]	24	96%	95%	97%
Surgical Care Improvement Project				
Appropriate VTP Within 24 Hours[2]	104	89%	93%	92%
Appropriate Hair Removal[2]	632	100%	100%	99%
Appropriate Beta Blocker Usage[2]	246	96%	92%	93%
Controlled Postoperative Blood Glucose[2]	144	99%	93%	93%
Prophylactic Antibiotic Timing[2]	487	99%	97%	97%
Prophylactic Antibiotic Timing (Outpatient)	503	92%	91%	92%
Prophylactic Antibiotic Selection[2]	493	99%	98%	97%
Prophylactic Antibiotic Select. (Outpatient)	494	98%	96%	94%
Prophylactic Antibiotic Stopped[2]	457	99%	95%	94%
Recommended VTP Ordered[2]	105	90%	94%	94%
Urinary Catheter Removal[2]	83	92%	91%	90%
Children's Asthma Care				
Received Systemic Corticosteroids	-	-	-	100%
Received Home Management Plan	-	-	-	71%
Received Reliever Medication	-	-	-	100%
Use of Medical Imaging				
Combination Abdominal CT Scan	480	0.048	0.106	0.191
Combination Chest CT Scan	307	0.003	0.027	0.054
Follow-up Mammogram/Ultrasound	621	9.0%	8.4%	8.4%
MRI for Low Back Pain	217	35.9%	31.8%	32.7%
Survey of Patients' Hospital Experiences				
Area Around Room 'Always' Quiet at Night	300+	70%	-	58%
Doctors 'Always' Communicated Well	300+	81%	-	80%
Home Recovery Information Given	300+	87%	-	82%
Hospital Given 9 or 10 on 10 Point Scale	300+	76%	-	67%
Meds 'Always' Explained Before Given	300+	67%	-	60%
Nurses 'Always' Communicated Well	300+	79%	-	76%
Pain 'Always' Well Controlled	300+	72%	-	69%
Room and Bathroom 'Always' Clean	300+	80%	-	71%
Timely Help 'Always' Received	300+	68%	-	64%
Would Definitely Recommend Hospital	300+	80%	-	69%

Bellin Memorial Hospital

744 S Webster Ave
Green Bay, WI 54305
Phone: 920-433-3500
Fax: 920-433-7971
URL: www.bellin.org
Type: Acute Care Hospitals
Emergency Services: Yes
Ownership: Voluntary Non-Profit - Private
Beds: 167
Key Personnel:
CEO/President.............. George F Kerwin

Measure	Cases	This Hosp.	State Avg.	U.S. Avg.
Heart Attack Care				
ACE Inhibitor or ARB for LVSD	34	100%	97%	96%
Aspirin at Arrival	189	99%	99%	99%
Aspirin at Discharge	359	99%	99%	98%
Beta Blocker at Discharge	353	100%	99%	98%
Fibrinolytic Medication Timing	0	-	0%	55%
PCI Within 90 Minutes of Arrival	36	100%	89%	90%
Smoking Cessation Advice	115	100%	99%	99%
Chest Pain/Possible Heart Attack Care				
Aspirin at Arrival[5]	0	-	96%	95%
Median Time to ECG (minutes)[5]	0	-	7	8
Median Time to Transfer (minutes)[5]	0	-	49	61
Fibrinolytic Medication Timing[5]	0	-	63%	54%
Heart Failure Care				
ACE Inhibitor or ARB for LVSD	57	89%	95%	94%
Discharge Instructions	165	92%	86%	88%
Evaluation of LVS Function	202	100%	97%	98%
Smoking Cessation Advice[1]	22	91%	97%	98%
Pneumonia Care				
Appropriate Initial Antibiotic	81	95%	94%	92%
Blood Culture Timing	104	100%	97%	96%
Influenza Vaccine	58	98%	92%	91%
Initial Antibiotic Timing	103	99%	97%	95%
Pneumococcal Vaccine	85	96%	93%	93%
Smoking Cessation Advice	35	97%	95%	97%
Surgical Care Improvement Project				
Appropriate VTP Within 24 Hours[2]	129	92%	93%	92%
Appropriate Hair Removal[2]	771	100%	100%	99%
Appropriate Beta Blocker Usage[2]	283	98%	92%	93%
Controlled Postoperative Blood Glucose[2]	245	96%	93%	93%
Prophylactic Antibiotic Timing[2]	575	99%	97%	97%
Prophylactic Antibiotic Timing (Outpatient)	755	93%	91%	92%
Prophylactic Antibiotic Selection[2]	593	98%	98%	97%
Prophylactic Antibiotic Select. (Outpatient)	722	98%	96%	94%
Prophylactic Antibiotic Stopped[2]	569	98%	95%	94%
Recommended VTP Ordered[2]	129	94%	94%	94%
Urinary Catheter Removal[2]	127	94%	91%	90%
Children's Asthma Care				
Received Systemic Corticosteroids	-	-	-	100%
Received Home Management Plan	-	-	-	71%
Received Reliever Medication	-	-	-	100%
Use of Medical Imaging				
Combination Abdominal CT Scan	154	0.019	0.106	0.191
Combination Chest CT Scan	110	0.000	0.027	0.054
Follow-up Mammogram/Ultrasound	955	3.4%	8.4%	8.4%
MRI for Low Back Pain[1]	3	66.7%	31.8%	32.7%
Survey of Patients' Hospital Experiences				
Area Around Room 'Always' Quiet at Night	300+	62%	-	58%
Doctors 'Always' Communicated Well	300+	80%	-	80%
Home Recovery Information Given	300+	90%	-	82%
Hospital Given 9 or 10 on 10 Point Scale	300+	77%	-	67%
Meds 'Always' Explained Before Given	300+	67%	-	60%
Nurses 'Always' Communicated Well	300+	81%	-	76%
Pain 'Always' Well Controlled	300+	72%	-	69%
Room and Bathroom 'Always' Clean	300+	78%	-	71%
Timely Help 'Always' Received	300+	75%	-	64%
Would Definitely Recommend Hospital	300+	81%	-	69%

Saint Marys Hospital Medical Center

1726 Shawano Ave
Green Bay, WI 54303
Phone: 920-498-4200
Fax: 920-498-1861
E-mail: info@stmgb.org
URL: www.stmgb.org
Type: Acute Care Hospitals
Emergency Services: Yes
Ownership: Voluntary Non-Profit - Other
Beds: 94
Key Personnel:
CEO/President............... James G Coller
Cardiac Laboratory.......... Daniel Doran
Operating Room.............. Jane Beyer
Radiology................... Henry Kenneth Feider
Ambulatory Care .... Lawrence Connors
Emergency Room .... Karen Ann Stanlaw

Measure	Cases	This Hosp.	State Avg.	U.S. Avg.
Heart Attack Care				
ACE Inhibitor or ARB for LVSD[1]	22	100%	97%	96%
Aspirin at Arrival	98	100%	99%	99%
Aspirin at Discharge	94	97%	99%	98%
Beta Blocker at Discharge	95	98%	99%	98%
Fibrinolytic Medication Timing	0	-	0%	55%
PCI Within 90 Minutes of Arrival	30	90%	89%	90%
Smoking Cessation Advice	31	100%	99%	99%
Chest Pain/Possible Heart Attack Care				
Aspirin at Arrival[1]	4	100%	96%	95%
Median Time to ECG (minutes)[1]	5	9	7	8
Median Time to Transfer (minutes)[5]	0	-	49	61
Fibrinolytic Medication Timing[3]	0	-	63%	54%
Heart Failure Care				
ACE Inhibitor or ARB for LVSD	29	97%	95%	94%
Discharge Instructions	97	93%	86%	88%
Evaluation of LVS Function	130	97%	97%	98%
Smoking Cessation Advice[1]	16	100%	97%	98%
Pneumonia Care				
Appropriate Initial Antibiotic	66	94%	94%	92%
Blood Culture Timing	114	96%	97%	96%
Influenza Vaccine	54	94%	92%	91%
Initial Antibiotic Timing	110	99%	97%	95%
Pneumococcal Vaccine	88	93%	93%	93%
Smoking Cessation Advice	38	100%	95%	97%
Surgical Care Improvement Project				
Appropriate VTP Within 24 Hours	167	90%	93%	92%
Appropriate Hair Removal	543	99%	100%	99%
Appropriate Beta Blocker Usage	157	96%	92%	93%
Controlled Postoperative Blood Glucose	0	-	93%	93%
Prophylactic Antibiotic Timing	416	97%	97%	97%
Prophylactic Antibiotic Timing (Outpatient)	253	90%	91%	92%
Prophylactic Antibiotic Selection	416	100%	98%	97%
Prophylactic Antibiotic Select. (Outpatient)	244	96%	96%	94%
Prophylactic Antibiotic Stopped	412	98%	95%	94%
Recommended VTP Ordered	167	90%	94%	94%
Urinary Catheter Removal	223	95%	91%	90%
Children's Asthma Care				
Received Systemic Corticosteroids	-	-	-	100%
Received Home Management Plan	-	-	-	71%
Received Reliever Medication	-	-	-	100%
Use of Medical Imaging				
Combination Abdominal CT Scan	354	0.065	0.106	0.191
Combination Chest CT Scan	189	0.016	0.027	0.054
Follow-up Mammogram/Ultrasound	199	8.0%	8.4%	8.4%
MRI for Low Back Pain[5]	0	-	31.8%	32.7%
Survey of Patients' Hospital Experiences				
Area Around Room 'Always' Quiet at Night	300+	58%	-	58%
Doctors 'Always' Communicated Well	300+	82%	-	80%
Home Recovery Information Given	300+	86%	-	82%
Hospital Given 9 or 10 on 10 Point Scale	300+	72%	-	67%
Meds 'Always' Explained Before Given	300+	66%	-	60%
Nurses 'Always' Communicated Well	300+	77%	-	76%
Pain 'Always' Well Controlled	300+	72%	-	69%
Room and Bathroom 'Always' Clean	300+	79%	-	71%
Timely Help 'Always' Received	300+	63%	-	64%
Would Definitely Recommend Hospital	300+	74%	-	69%

NOTE: Hospital profiles are in alphabetical order by state, then city, then hospital within the city; Rankings exclude hospitals with less than 25 cases except for patient surveys which excludes hospitals with less than 100 cases; (a) 100–299 cases; (1) The number of cases is too small to be sure how well a hospital is performing; (2) The hospital indicated that the data submitted for this measure were based on a sample of cases; (3) Data was collected during a shorter time period (fewer quarters) than the maximum possible time for this measure; (4) Suppressed for one or more quarters by CMS; (5) No data is available from the hospital for this measure; (6) Fewer than 100 patients completed the HCAHPS survey. Use these rates with caution, as the number of surveys may be too low to reliably assess hospital performance; (7) Survey results are based on less than 12 months of data; (8) Survey results are not available for this reporting period; (9) No or very few patients were eligible for the HCAHPS survey. The scores shown, if any, reflect a very small number of surveys; (10) A state average was not calculated because too few hospitals in the state submitted data; (11) There were discrepancies in the data collection process; Please refer to the User's Guide for a full explanation of data.

Saint Vincent Hospital

835 S Van Buren St Phone: 920-433-0111
Green Bay, WI 54301 Fax: 920-431-3151
URL: www.stvincenthospital.org
Type: Acute Care Hospitals Emergency Services: Yes
Ownership: Voluntary Non-Profit - Church Beds: 547

Key Personnel:
CEO/President. . . . . James Coller
Chief of Medical Staff . . . . David Rentmeester, MD
Infection Control. . . . . Nancy Lorenzoni
Operating Room. . . . . Mary Ann Sallenbach
Pediatric In-Patient Care . . . . Joel Anent, MD
Radiology. . . . . Henry Feider, MD
Anesthesiology. . . . . Brian Johnson, MD
Emergency Room . . . . Kenneth Johnson

Measure	Cases	This Hosp.	State Avg.	U.S. Avg.
Heart Attack Care				
ACE Inhibitor or ARB for LVSD[1]	17	88%	97%	96%
Aspirin at Arrival	136	99%	99%	99%
Aspirin at Discharge	164	99%	99%	98%
Beta Blocker at Discharge	156	97%	99%	98%
Fibrinolytic Medication Timing	0	-	0%	55%
PCI Within 90 Minutes of Arrival	29	90%	89%	90%
Smoking Cessation Advice	57	98%	99%	99%
Chest Pain/Possible Heart Attack Care				
Aspirin at Arrival[1,3]	1	100%	96%	95%
Median Time to ECG (minutes)[1,3]	1	3	7	8
Median Time to Transfer (minutes)[5]	0	-	49	61
Fibrinolytic Medication Timing[5]	0	-	63%	54%
Heart Failure Care				
ACE Inhibitor or ARB for LVSD	43	88%	95%	94%
Discharge Instructions	132	87%	86%	88%
Evaluation of LVS Function	161	97%	97%	98%
Smoking Cessation Advice[1]	23	100%	97%	98%
Pneumonia Care				
Appropriate Initial Antibiotic	69	90%	94%	92%
Blood Culture Timing	115	98%	97%	96%
Influenza Vaccine	88	92%	92%	91%
Initial Antibiotic Timing	121	96%	97%	95%
Pneumococcal Vaccine	111	94%	93%	93%
Smoking Cessation Advice	40	95%	95%	97%
Surgical Care Improvement Project				
Appropriate VTP Within 24 Hours[2]	160	91%	93%	92%
Appropriate Hair Removal[2]	692	100%	100%	99%
Appropriate Beta Blocker Usage[2]	300	86%	92%	93%
Controlled Postoperative Blood Glucose[2]	156	97%	93%	93%
Prophylactic Antibiotic Timing[2]	487	98%	97%	97%
Prophylactic Antibiotic Timing (Outpatient)	338	96%	91%	92%
Prophylactic Antibiotic Selection[2]	501	97%	98%	97%
Prophylactic Antibiotic Select. (Outpatient)	332	97%	96%	94%
Prophylactic Antibiotic Stopped[2]	446	93%	95%	94%
Recommended VTP Ordered[2]	160	95%	94%	94%
Urinary Catheter Removal[2]	73	73%	91%	90%
Children's Asthma Care				
Received Systemic Corticosteroids	-	-	-	100%
Received Home Management Plan	-	-	-	71%
Received Reliever Medication	-	-	-	100%
Use of Medical Imaging				
Combination Abdominal CT Scan	547	0.040	0.106	0.191
Combination Chest CT Scan	394	0.023	0.027	0.054
Follow-up Mammogram/Ultrasound	370	7.0%	8.4%	8.4%
MRI for Low Back Pain	44	43.2%	31.8%	32.7%
Survey of Patients' Hospital Experiences				
Area Around Room 'Always' Quiet at Night	300+	65%	-	58%
Doctors 'Always' Communicated Well	300+	81%	-	80%
Home Recovery Information Given	300+	87%	-	82%
Hospital Given 9 or 10 on 10 Point Scale	300+	71%	-	67%
Meds 'Always' Explained Before Given	300+	66%	-	60%
Nurses 'Always' Communicated Well	300+	77%	-	76%
Pain 'Always' Well Controlled	300+	70%	-	69%
Room and Bathroom 'Always' Clean	300+	78%	-	71%
Timely Help 'Always' Received	300+	62%	-	64%
Would Definitely Recommend Hospital	300+	74%	-	69%

Aurora Medical Center - Washington County

1032 E Sumner St Phone: 262-673-2300
Hartford, WI 53027
URL: www.aurorahealthcare.org
Type: Acute Care Hospitals Emergency Services: Yes
Ownership: Voluntary Non-Profit - Private

Key Personnel:
Administrator . . . . Mark Schwartz

Measure	Cases	This Hosp.	State Avg.	U.S. Avg.
Heart Attack Care				
ACE Inhibitor or ARB for LVSD[1]	4	100%	97%	96%
Aspirin at Arrival	39	87%	99%	99%
Aspirin at Discharge	26	88%	99%	98%
Beta Blocker at Discharge	30	93%	99%	98%
Fibrinolytic Medication Timing	0	-	0%	55%
PCI Within 90 Minutes of Arrival	0	-	89%	90%
Smoking Cessation Advice	0	-	99%	99%
Chest Pain/Possible Heart Attack Care				
Aspirin at Arrival	98	94%	96%	95%
Median Time to ECG (minutes)	103	10	7	8
Median Time to Transfer (minutes)[1,3]	3	35	49	61
Fibrinolytic Medication Timing	0	-	63%	54%
Heart Failure Care				
ACE Inhibitor or ARB for LVSD[1]	17	94%	95%	94%
Discharge Instructions	49	94%	86%	88%
Evaluation of LVS Function	71	97%	97%	98%
Smoking Cessation Advice[1]	5	100%	97%	98%
Pneumonia Care				
Appropriate Initial Antibiotic	38	87%	94%	92%
Blood Culture Timing	55	91%	97%	96%
Influenza Vaccine	33	94%	92%	91%
Initial Antibiotic Timing	59	90%	97%	95%
Pneumococcal Vaccine	51	94%	93%	93%
Smoking Cessation Advice[1]	12	100%	95%	97%
Surgical Care Improvement Project				
Appropriate VTP Within 24 Hours[2]	47	89%	93%	92%
Appropriate Hair Removal[2]	266	100%	100%	99%
Appropriate Beta Blocker Usage[2]	83	99%	92%	93%
Controlled Postoperative Blood Glucose[2]	0	-	93%	93%
Prophylactic Antibiotic Timing[2]	204	99%	97%	97%
Prophylactic Antibiotic Timing (Outpatient)	117	94%	91%	92%
Prophylactic Antibiotic Selection[2]	204	98%	98%	97%
Prophylactic Antibiotic Select. (Outpatient)	111	96%	96%	94%
Prophylactic Antibiotic Stopped[2]	201	98%	95%	94%
Recommended VTP Ordered[2]	47	89%	94%	94%
Urinary Catheter Removal[2]	98	99%	91%	90%
Children's Asthma Care				
Received Systemic Corticosteroids	-	-	-	100%
Received Home Management Plan	-	-	-	71%
Received Reliever Medication	-	-	-	100%
Use of Medical Imaging				
Combination Abdominal CT Scan	118	0.017	0.106	0.191
Combination Chest CT Scan	124	0.000	0.027	0.054
Follow-up Mammogram/Ultrasound[5]	0	-	8.4%	8.4%
MRI for Low Back Pain	62	33.9%	31.8%	32.7%
Survey of Patients' Hospital Experiences				
Area Around Room 'Always' Quiet at Night	300+	60%	-	58%
Doctors 'Always' Communicated Well	300+	81%	-	80%
Home Recovery Information Given	300+	88%	-	82%
Hospital Given 9 or 10 on 10 Point Scale	300+	67%	-	67%
Meds 'Always' Explained Before Given	300+	65%	-	60%
Nurses 'Always' Communicated Well	300+	78%	-	76%
Pain 'Always' Well Controlled	300+	70%	-	69%
Room and Bathroom 'Always' Clean	300+	78%	-	71%
Timely Help 'Always' Received	300+	67%	-	64%
Would Definitely Recommend Hospital	300+	68%	-	69%

Hayward Area Memorial Hospital

11040 N State Rd 77 Phone: 715-934-4321
Hayward, WI 54843 Fax: 715-934-4272
URL: www.hamhnh.com
Type: Critical Access Hospitals Emergency Services: Yes
Ownership: Voluntary Non-Profit - Private Beds: 25

Key Personnel:
CEO/President. . . . . Barbara Peickert
Chief of Medical Staff . . . . Ravinder Vir, MD
Operating Room. . . . . Jane McPeak

Measure	Cases	This Hosp.	State Avg.	U.S. Avg.
Heart Attack Care				
ACE Inhibitor or ARB for LVSD[3]	0	-	97%	96%
Aspirin at Arrival[1,3]	4	75%	99%	99%
Aspirin at Discharge[1,3]	4	75%	99%	98%
Beta Blocker at Discharge[1,3]	5	80%	99%	98%
Fibrinolytic Medication Timing[5]	0	-	0%	55%
PCI Within 90 Minutes of Arrival[5]	0	-	89%	90%
Smoking Cessation Advice[3]	0	-	99%	99%
Chest Pain/Possible Heart Attack Care				
Aspirin at Arrival	-	-	96%	95%
Median Time to ECG (minutes)	-	-	7	8
Median Time to Transfer (minutes)	-	-	49	61
Fibrinolytic Medication Timing	-	-	63%	54%
Heart Failure Care				
ACE Inhibitor or ARB for LVSD[1,3]	2	100%	95%	94%
Discharge Instructions[1,3]	9	100%	86%	88%
Evaluation of LVS Function[1,3]	14	64%	97%	98%
Smoking Cessation Advice[3]	0	-	97%	98%
Pneumonia Care				
Appropriate Initial Antibiotic[1,3]	23	91%	94%	92%
Blood Culture Timing[3]	29	97%	97%	96%
Influenza Vaccine[1]	20	75%	92%	91%
Initial Antibiotic Timing[3]	34	100%	97%	95%
Pneumococcal Vaccine[3]	29	97%	93%	93%
Smoking Cessation Advice[1,3]	15	87%	95%	97%
Surgical Care Improvement Project				
Appropriate VTP Within 24 Hours[1,3]	4	75%	93%	92%
Appropriate Hair Removal[1,3]	8	100%	100%	99%
Appropriate Beta Blocker Usage[1,3]	2	100%	92%	93%
Controlled Postoperative Blood Glucose[3]	0	-	93%	93%
Prophylactic Antibiotic Timing[1,3]	1	0%	97%	97%
Prophylactic Antibiotic Timing (Outpatient)	-	-	91%	92%
Prophylactic Antibiotic Selection[1,3]	1	0%	98%	97%
Prophylactic Antibiotic Select. (Outpatient)	-	-	96%	94%
Prophylactic Antibiotic Stopped[1,3]	1	100%	95%	94%
Recommended VTP Ordered[1,3]	5	60%	94%	94%
Urinary Catheter Removal[1]	2	100%	91%	90%
Children's Asthma Care				
Received Systemic Corticosteroids	-	-	-	100%
Received Home Management Plan	-	-	-	71%
Received Reliever Medication	-	-	-	100%
Use of Medical Imaging				
Combination Abdominal CT Scan	-	-	0.106	0.191
Combination Chest CT Scan	-	-	0.027	0.054
Follow-up Mammogram/Ultrasound	-	-	8.4%	8.4%
MRI for Low Back Pain	-	-	31.8%	32.7%
Survey of Patients' Hospital Experiences				
Area Around Room 'Always' Quiet at Night	300+	72%	-	58%
Doctors 'Always' Communicated Well	300+	91%	-	80%
Home Recovery Information Given	300+	85%	-	82%
Hospital Given 9 or 10 on 10 Point Scale	300+	75%	-	67%
Meds 'Always' Explained Before Given	300+	68%	-	60%
Nurses 'Always' Communicated Well	300+	82%	-	76%
Pain 'Always' Well Controlled	300+	73%	-	69%
Room and Bathroom 'Always' Clean	300+	82%	-	71%
Timely Help 'Always' Received	300+	72%	-	64%
Would Definitely Recommend Hospital	300+	78%	-	69%

NOTE: Hospital profiles are in alphabetical order by state, then city, then hospital within the city; Rankings exclude hospitals with less than 25 cases except for patient surveys which excludes hospitals with less than 100 cases; (a) 100–299 cases; (1) The number of cases is too small to be sure how well a hospital is performing; (2) The hospital indicated that the data submitted for this measure were based on a sample of cases; (3) Data was collected during a shorter time period (fewer quarters) than the maximum possible time for this measure; (4) Suppressed for one or more quarters by CMS; (5) No data is available from the hospital for this measure; (6) Fewer than 100 patients completed the HCAHPS survey. Use these rates with caution, as the number of surveys may be too low to reliably assess hospital performance; (7) Survey results are based on less than 12 months of data; (8) Survey results are not available for this reporting period; (9) No or very few patients were eligible for the HCAHPS survey. The scores shown, if any, reflect a very small number of surveys; (10) A state average was not calculated because too few hospitals in the state submitted data; (11) There were discrepancies in the data collection process; Please refer to the User's Guide for a full explanation of data.

Saint Josephs Community Health Services

400 Water Ave Phone: 608-489-8000
Hillsboro, WI 54634 Fax: 608-489-8181
E-mail: kcoblentz@stjhealthcare.org
URL: www.stjhealthcare.org
Type: Critical Access Hospitals Emergency Services: Yes
Ownership: Voluntary Non-Profit - Private Beds: 125
Key Personnel:
CEO/President. . . . . Bill Bruce
Chief of Medical Staff . . . . Tim Brieske
Emergency Room . . . . Mary Charles, RN

Measure	Cases	This Hosp.	State Avg.	U.S. Avg.
Heart Attack Care				
ACE Inhibitor or ARB for LVSD[5]	0	-	97%	96%
Aspirin at Arrival[5]	0	-	99%	99%
Aspirin at Discharge[5]	0	-	99%	98%
Beta Blocker at Discharge[5]	0	-	99%	98%
Fibrinolytic Medication Timing[5]	0	-	0%	55%
PCI Within 90 Minutes of Arrival[5]	0	-	89%	90%
Smoking Cessation Advice[5]	0	-	99%	99%
Chest Pain/Possible Heart Attack Care				
Aspirin at Arrival[1]	10	70%	96%	95%
Median Time to ECG (minutes)[1]	9	14	7	8
Median Time to Transfer (minutes)[1,3]	1	95	49	61
Fibrinolytic Medication Timing[3]	0	-	63%	54%
Heart Failure Care				
ACE Inhibitor or ARB for LVSD[1]	2	100%	95%	94%
Discharge Instructions[1]	11	64%	86%	88%
Evaluation of LVS Function[1]	13	77%	97%	98%
Smoking Cessation Advice[1]	2	50%	97%	98%
Pneumonia Care				
Appropriate Initial Antibiotic[1]	14	79%	94%	92%
Blood Culture Timing[1]	4	75%	97%	96%
Influenza Vaccine[1]	10	100%	92%	91%
Initial Antibiotic Timing[1]	15	87%	97%	95%
Pneumococcal Vaccine[1]	12	75%	93%	93%
Smoking Cessation Advice[1]	4	75%	95%	97%
Surgical Care Improvement Project				
Appropriate VTP Within 24 Hours[1,3]	3	100%	93%	92%
Appropriate Hair Removal[1,3]	5	100%	100%	99%
Appropriate Beta Blocker Usage[1,3]	3	100%	92%	93%
Controlled Postoperative Blood Glucose[3]	0	-	93%	93%
Prophylactic Antibiotic Timing[1,3]	4	75%	97%	97%
Prophylactic Antibiotic Timing (Outpatient)[1,3]	3	100%	91%	92%
Prophylactic Antibiotic Selection[1,3]	4	100%	98%	97%
Prophylactic Antibiotic Select. (Outpatient)[1,3]	3	100%	96%	94%
Prophylactic Antibiotic Stopped[1,3]	4	100%	95%	94%
Recommended VTP Ordered[1,3]	3	100%	94%	94%
Urinary Catheter Removal[1]	4	100%	91%	90%
Children's Asthma Care				
Received Systemic Corticosteroids	-	-	-	100%
Received Home Management Plan	-	-	-	71%
Received Reliever Medication	-	-	-	100%
Use of Medical Imaging				
Combination Abdominal CT Scan[1]	42	0.024	0.106	0.191
Combination Chest CT Scan[1]	17	0.059	0.027	0.054
Follow-up Mammogram/Ultrasound	88	10.2%	8.4%	8.4%
MRI for Low Back Pain[1]	11	36.4%	31.8%	32.7%
Survey of Patients' Hospital Experiences				
Area Around Room 'Always' Quiet at Night[6]	<100	55%	-	58%
Doctors 'Always' Communicated Well[6]	<100	91%	-	80%
Home Recovery Information Given[6]	<100	91%	-	82%
Hospital Given 9 or 10 on 10 Point Scale[6]	<100	68%	-	67%
Meds 'Always' Explained Before Given[6]	<100	66%	-	60%
Nurses 'Always' Communicated Well[6]	<100	84%	-	76%
Pain 'Always' Well Controlled[6]	<100	76%	-	69%
Room and Bathroom 'Always' Clean[6]	<100	89%	-	71%
Timely Help 'Always' Received[6]	<100	73%	-	64%
Would Definitely Recommend Hospital	<100	69%	-	69%

Hudson Hospital

405 Stageline Road Phone: 715-531-6000
Hudson, WI 54016 Fax: 715-531-6011
E-mail: codonovan@hudsonhospital.org
URL: www.hudsonhospital.org
Type: Critical Access Hospitals Emergency Services: Yes
Ownership: Voluntary Non-Profit - Other Beds: 29
Key Personnel:
CEO/President. . . . . Marian Furlong
Chief of Medical Staff . . . . Gregory Young
Quality Assurance . . . . Linda Ehlers
Emergency Room . . . . Luke Albretch

Measure	Cases	This Hosp.	State Avg.	U.S. Avg.
Heart Attack Care				
ACE Inhibitor or ARB for LVSD[1,3]	1	100%	97%	96%
Aspirin at Arrival[1,3]	3	100%	99%	99%
Aspirin at Discharge[1,3]	4	100%	99%	98%
Beta Blocker at Discharge[1,3]	4	75%	99%	98%
Fibrinolytic Medication Timing[5]	0	-	0%	55%
PCI Within 90 Minutes of Arrival[5]	0	-	89%	90%
Smoking Cessation Advice[3]	0	-	99%	99%
Chest Pain/Possible Heart Attack Care				
Aspirin at Arrival	-	-	96%	95%
Median Time to ECG (minutes)	-	-	7	8
Median Time to Transfer (minutes)	-	-	49	61
Fibrinolytic Medication Timing	-	-	63%	54%
Heart Failure Care				
ACE Inhibitor or ARB for LVSD[1,3]	8	88%	95%	94%
Discharge Instructions[1,3]	15	93%	86%	88%
Evaluation of LVS Function[1,3]	18	83%	97%	98%
Smoking Cessation Advice[1,3]	2	100%	97%	98%
Pneumonia Care				
Appropriate Initial Antibiotic[1,3]	17	88%	94%	92%
Blood Culture Timing[1,3]	5	80%	97%	96%
Influenza Vaccine[1,3]	15	93%	92%	91%
Initial Antibiotic Timing[3]	29	97%	97%	95%
Pneumococcal Vaccine[3]	27	89%	93%	93%
Smoking Cessation Advice[1,3]	4	100%	95%	97%
Surgical Care Improvement Project				
Appropriate VTP Within 24 Hours[5]	0	-	93%	92%
Appropriate Hair Removal[5]	0	-	100%	99%
Appropriate Beta Blocker Usage[5]	0	-	92%	93%
Controlled Postoperative Blood Glucose[5]	0	-	93%	93%
Prophylactic Antibiotic Timing[5]	0	-	97%	97%
Prophylactic Antibiotic Timing (Outpatient)	-	-	91%	92%
Prophylactic Antibiotic Selection[5]	0	-	98%	97%
Prophylactic Antibiotic Select. (Outpatient)	-	-	96%	94%
Prophylactic Antibiotic Stopped[5]	0	-	95%	94%
Recommended VTP Ordered[5]	0	-	94%	94%
Urinary Catheter Removal[5]	0	-	91%	90%
Children's Asthma Care				
Received Systemic Corticosteroids	-	-	-	100%
Received Home Management Plan	-	-	-	71%
Received Reliever Medication	-	-	-	100%
Use of Medical Imaging				
Combination Abdominal CT Scan	-	-	0.106	0.191
Combination Chest CT Scan	-	-	0.027	0.054
Follow-up Mammogram/Ultrasound	-	-	8.4%	8.4%
MRI for Low Back Pain	-	-	31.8%	32.7%
Survey of Patients' Hospital Experiences				
Area Around Room 'Always' Quiet at Night	300+	64%	-	58%
Doctors 'Always' Communicated Well	300+	84%	-	80%
Home Recovery Information Given	300+	86%	-	82%
Hospital Given 9 or 10 on 10 Point Scale	300+	79%	-	67%
Meds 'Always' Explained Before Given	300+	70%	-	60%
Nurses 'Always' Communicated Well	300+	84%	-	76%
Pain 'Always' Well Controlled	300+	76%	-	69%
Room and Bathroom 'Always' Clean	300+	70%	-	71%
Timely Help 'Always' Received	300+	74%	-	64%
Would Definitely Recommend Hospital	300+	84%	-	69%

Mercy Health Sys Corp

1000 Mineral Point Ave Phone: 608-756-6161
Janesville, WI 53548 Fax: 608-756-6168
URL: www.mercyhealthsystem.org
Type: Acute Care Hospitals Emergency Services: Yes
Ownership: Voluntary Non-Profit - Private Beds: 275
Key Personnel:
CEO/President. . . . . Javon R Bea
Cardiac Laboratory. . . . . Lubin Kan
Chief of Medical Staff . . . . Blaine Nowak
Operating Room. . . . . Linda Nevenschwander
Emergency Room . . . . France Keilhauer

Measure	Cases	This Hosp.	State Avg.	U.S. Avg.
Heart Attack Care				
ACE Inhibitor or ARB for LVSD[1]	19	100%	97%	96%
Aspirin at Arrival	124	99%	99%	99%
Aspirin at Discharge	158	100%	99%	98%
Beta Blocker at Discharge	154	100%	99%	98%
Fibrinolytic Medication Timing	0	-	0%	55%
PCI Within 90 Minutes of Arrival	32	91%	89%	90%
Smoking Cessation Advice	69	94%	99%	99%
Chest Pain/Possible Heart Attack Care				
Aspirin at Arrival[1]	21	100%	96%	95%
Median Time to ECG (minutes)[1]	23	6	7	8
Median Time to Transfer (minutes)[5]	0	-	49	61
Fibrinolytic Medication Timing[3]	0	-	63%	54%
Heart Failure Care				
ACE Inhibitor or ARB for LVSD[2]	56	96%	95%	94%
Discharge Instructions[2]	169	95%	86%	88%
Evaluation of LVS Function[2]	205	96%	97%	98%
Smoking Cessation Advice[2]	35	100%	97%	98%
Pneumonia Care				
Appropriate Initial Antibiotic[2]	119	92%	94%	92%
Blood Culture Timing[2]	185	98%	97%	96%
Influenza Vaccine	139	94%	92%	91%
Initial Antibiotic Timing[2]	185	97%	97%	95%
Pneumococcal Vaccine[2]	168	95%	93%	93%
Smoking Cessation Advice[2]	84	94%	95%	97%
Surgical Care Improvement Project				
Appropriate VTP Within 24 Hours[2]	499	95%	93%	92%
Appropriate Hair Removal[2]	1,048	100%	100%	99%
Appropriate Beta Blocker Usage[2]	270	94%	92%	93%
Controlled Postoperative Blood Glucose[2]	66	95%	93%	93%
Prophylactic Antibiotic Timing[2]	717	98%	97%	97%
Prophylactic Antibiotic Timing (Outpatient)	175	85%	91%	92%
Prophylactic Antibiotic Selection[2]	719	97%	98%	97%
Prophylactic Antibiotic Select. (Outpatient)	150	91%	96%	94%
Prophylactic Antibiotic Stopped[2]	691	89%	95%	94%
Recommended VTP Ordered[2]	499	96%	94%	94%
Urinary Catheter Removal	267	90%	91%	90%
Children's Asthma Care				
Received Systemic Corticosteroids	-	-	-	100%
Received Home Management Plan	-	-	-	71%
Received Reliever Medication	-	-	-	100%
Use of Medical Imaging				
Combination Abdominal CT Scan	894	0.032	0.106	0.191
Combination Chest CT Scan	697	0.024	0.027	0.054
Follow-up Mammogram/Ultrasound	535	3.9%	8.4%	8.4%
MRI for Low Back Pain	177	33.3%	31.8%	32.7%
Survey of Patients' Hospital Experiences				
Area Around Room 'Always' Quiet at Night	300+	49%	-	58%
Doctors 'Always' Communicated Well	300+	78%	-	80%
Home Recovery Information Given	300+	85%	-	82%
Hospital Given 9 or 10 on 10 Point Scale	300+	57%	-	67%
Meds 'Always' Explained Before Given	300+	63%	-	60%
Nurses 'Always' Communicated Well	300+	77%	-	76%
Pain 'Always' Well Controlled	300+	68%	-	69%
Room and Bathroom 'Always' Clean	300+	74%	-	71%
Timely Help 'Always' Received	300+	63%	-	64%
Would Definitely Recommend Hospital	300+	54%	-	69%

NOTE: Hospital profiles are in alphabetical order by state, then city, then hospital within the city; Rankings exclude hospitals with less than 25 cases except for patient surveys which excludes hospitals with less than 100 cases; (a) 100–299 cases; (1) The number of cases is too small to be sure how well a hospital is performing; (2) The hospital indicated that the data submitted for this measure were based on a sample of cases; (3) Data was collected during a shorter time period (fewer quarters) than the maximum possible time for this measure; (4) Suppressed for one or more quarters by CMS; (5) No data is available from the hospital for this measure; (6) Fewer than 100 patients completed the HCAHPS survey. Use these rates with caution, as the number of surveys may be too low to reliably assess hospital performance; (7) Survey results are based on less than 12 months of data; (8) Survey results are not available for this reporting period; (9) No or very few patients were eligible for the HCAHPS survey. The scores shown, if any, reflect a very small number of surveys; (10) A state average was not calculated because too few hospitals in the state submitted data; (11) There were discrepancies in the data collection process; Please refer to the User's Guide for a full explanation of data.

Aurora Medical Center Kenosha

10400 75th St Phone: 262-948-5600
Kenosha, WI 53142 Fax: 262-942-5828
URL: www.aurorahealthcare.org
Type: Acute Care Hospitals Emergency Services: Yes
Ownership: Voluntary Non-Profit - Private Beds: 72

Key Personnel:
CEO/President. . . . . Chris Olson
Chief of Medical Staff. . . . . John M Agaiby
Radiology. Martin R Crain

Measure	Cases	This Hosp.	State Avg.	U.S. Avg.
Heart Attack Care				
ACE Inhibitor or ARB for LVSD[1]	4	100%	97%	96%
Aspirin at Arrival[1]	21	95%	99%	99%
Aspirin at Discharge[1]	16	100%	99%	98%
Beta Blocker at Discharge[1]	16	100%	99%	98%
Fibrinolytic Medication Timing	0	-	0%	55%
PCI Within 90 Minutes of Arrival	0	-	89%	90%
Smoking Cessation Advice[1]	1	100%	99%	99%
Chest Pain/Possible Heart Attack Care				
Aspirin at Arrival	71	100%	96%	95%
Median Time to ECG (minutes)	73	6	7	8
Median Time to Transfer (minutes)[1]	15	41	49	61
Fibrinolytic Medication Timing	0	-	63%	54%
Heart Failure Care				
ACE Inhibitor or ARB for LVSD	39	95%	95%	94%
Discharge Instructions	73	82%	86%	88%
Evaluation of LVS Function	90	98%	97%	98%
Smoking Cessation Advice	27	100%	97%	98%
Pneumonia Care				
Appropriate Initial Antibiotic	103	97%	94%	92%
Blood Culture Timing	129	98%	97%	96%
Influenza Vaccine	86	97%	92%	91%
Initial Antibiotic Timing	118	98%	97%	95%
Pneumococcal Vaccine	103	95%	93%	93%
Smoking Cessation Advice	51	100%	95%	97%
Surgical Care Improvement Project				
Appropriate VTP Within 24 Hours[2]	115	97%	93%	92%
Appropriate Hair Removal[2]	374	100%	100%	99%
Appropriate Beta Blocker Usage[2]	90	94%	92%	93%
Controlled Postoperative Blood Glucose[2]	0	-	93%	93%
Prophylactic Antibiotic Timing[2]	252	98%	97%	97%
Prophylactic Antibiotic Timing (Outpatient)	294	93%	91%	92%
Prophylactic Antibiotic Selection[2]	252	99%	98%	97%
Prophylactic Antibiotic Select. (Outpatient)	286	97%	96%	94%
Prophylactic Antibiotic Stopped[2]	244	95%	95%	94%
Recommended VTP Ordered[2]	115	98%	94%	94%
Urinary Catheter Removal[2]	110	95%	91%	90%
Children's Asthma Care				
Received Systemic Corticosteroids	-	-	-	100%
Received Home Management Plan	-	-	-	71%
Received Reliever Medication	-	-	-	100%
Use of Medical Imaging				
Combination Abdominal CT Scan	535	0.082	0.106	0.191
Combination Chest CT Scan	441	0.061	0.027	0.054
Follow-up Mammogram/Ultrasound	682	7.9%	8.4%	8.4%
MRI for Low Back Pain	110	31.8%	31.8%	32.7%
Survey of Patients' Hospital Experiences				
Area Around Room 'Always' Quiet at Night	300+	60%	-	58%
Doctors 'Always' Communicated Well	300+	78%	-	80%
Home Recovery Information Given	300+	85%	-	82%
Hospital Given 9 or 10 on 10 Point Scale	300+	68%	-	67%
Meds 'Always' Explained Before Given	300+	58%	-	60%
Nurses 'Always' Communicated Well	300+	73%	-	76%
Pain 'Always' Well Controlled	300+	63%	-	69%
Room and Bathroom 'Always' Clean	300+	74%	-	71%
Timely Help 'Always' Received	300+	59%	-	64%
Would Definitely Recommend Hospital	300+	70%	-	69%

United Hospital System

6308 Eighth Ave Phone: 262-656-2368
Kenosha, WI 53143 Fax: 262-656-2124
E-mail: webmaster@uhsi.org
Type: Acute Care Hospitals Emergency Services: Yes
Ownership: Government - Local Beds: 315

Key Personnel:
CEO/President. . . . . Robert Cook
Infection Control. . . . . Jim Johnson
Operating Room. . . . . Dorothy Barca, RN
Quality Assurance . . . . Mary Becker

Measure	Cases	This Hosp.	State Avg.	U.S. Avg.
Heart Attack Care				
ACE Inhibitor or ARB for LVSD[1]	21	100%	97%	96%
Aspirin at Arrival	153	99%	99%	99%
Aspirin at Discharge	146	99%	99%	98%
Beta Blocker at Discharge	135	96%	99%	98%
Fibrinolytic Medication Timing	0	-	0%	55%
PCI Within 90 Minutes of Arrival	35	83%	89%	90%
Smoking Cessation Advice	66	100%	99%	99%
Chest Pain/Possible Heart Attack Care				
Aspirin at Arrival[1]	6	83%	96%	95%
Median Time to ECG (minutes)[1]	7	9	7	8
Median Time to Transfer (minutes)[5]	0	-	49	61
Fibrinolytic Medication Timing[3]	0	-	63%	54%
Heart Failure Care				
ACE Inhibitor or ARB for LVSD	141	94%	95%	94%
Discharge Instructions	254	84%	86%	88%
Evaluation of LVS Function	320	99%	97%	98%
Smoking Cessation Advice	51	100%	97%	98%
Pneumonia Care				
Appropriate Initial Antibiotic[2]	102	93%	94%	92%
Blood Culture Timing[2]	165	90%	97%	96%
Influenza Vaccine[2]	103	98%	92%	91%
Initial Antibiotic Timing[2]	175	93%	97%	95%
Pneumococcal Vaccine[2]	125	97%	93%	93%
Smoking Cessation Advice[2]	82	99%	95%	97%
Surgical Care Improvement Project				
Appropriate VTP Within 24 Hours[2]	213	95%	93%	92%
Appropriate Hair Removal[2]	598	99%	100%	99%
Appropriate Beta Blocker Usage[2]	151	82%	92%	93%
Controlled Postoperative Blood Glucose[2]	94	82%	93%	93%
Prophylactic Antibiotic Timing[2]	408	90%	97%	97%
Prophylactic Antibiotic Timing (Outpatient)	188	73%	91%	92%
Prophylactic Antibiotic Selection[2]	419	95%	98%	97%
Prophylactic Antibiotic Select. (Outpatient)	265	91%	96%	94%
Prophylactic Antibiotic Stopped[2]	394	94%	95%	94%
Recommended VTP Ordered[2]	213	95%	94%	94%
Urinary Catheter Removal[2]	163	91%	91%	90%
Children's Asthma Care				
Received Systemic Corticosteroids	-	-	-	100%
Received Home Management Plan	-	-	-	71%
Received Reliever Medication	-	-	-	100%
Use of Medical Imaging				
Combination Abdominal CT Scan	1,101	0.108	0.106	0.191
Combination Chest CT Scan	765	0.008	0.027	0.054
Follow-up Mammogram/Ultrasound	2,143	2.6%	8.4%	8.4%
MRI for Low Back Pain	207	32.4%	31.8%	32.7%
Survey of Patients' Hospital Experiences				
Area Around Room 'Always' Quiet at Night	300+	48%	-	58%
Doctors 'Always' Communicated Well	300+	75%	-	80%
Home Recovery Information Given	300+	82%	-	82%
Hospital Given 9 or 10 on 10 Point Scale	300+	64%	-	67%
Meds 'Always' Explained Before Given	300+	57%	-	60%
Nurses 'Always' Communicated Well	300+	73%	-	76%
Pain 'Always' Well Controlled	300+	67%	-	69%
Room and Bathroom 'Always' Clean	300+	78%	-	71%
Timely Help 'Always' Received	300+	69%	-	64%
Would Definitely Recommend Hospital	300+	66%	-	69%

Franciscan Skemp La Crosse Hospital

700 West Ave S Phone: 608-785-0940
La Crosse, WI 54601 Fax: 608-791-9504
URL: www.mayohealthsytem.org
Type: Acute Care Hospitals Emergency Services: Yes
Ownership: Voluntary Non-Profit - Private Beds: 350

Key Personnel:
CEO/President. . . . . Robert E Nesse, MD
Infection Control. . . . . Madeline McDonald
Operating Room. . . . . Charlotte Baier, RN
Pediatric In-Patient Care . . . . David Smith, MD
Radiology. . . . . Gary Wood, MD
Emergency Room . . . . Sue McBride
Intensive Care Unit. . . . . Jacalyn Lee
Patient Relations . . . . Diane Holmay

Measure	Cases	This Hosp.	State Avg.	U.S. Avg.
Heart Attack Care				
ACE Inhibitor or ARB for LVSD[1]	22	95%	97%	96%
Aspirin at Arrival	81	99%	99%	99%
Aspirin at Discharge	111	95%	99%	98%
Beta Blocker at Discharge	111	100%	99%	98%
Fibrinolytic Medication Timing	0	-	0%	55%
PCI Within 90 Minutes of Arrival[1]	24	83%	89%	90%
Smoking Cessation Advice	40	100%	99%	99%
Chest Pain/Possible Heart Attack Care				
Aspirin at Arrival[1]	7	100%	96%	95%
Median Time to ECG (minutes)[1]	7	22	7	8
Median Time to Transfer (minutes)[1,3]	1	75	49	61
Fibrinolytic Medication Timing[3]	0	-	63%	54%
Heart Failure Care				
ACE Inhibitor or ARB for LVSD	36	97%	95%	94%
Discharge Instructions	83	64%	86%	88%
Evaluation of LVS Function	126	99%	97%	98%
Smoking Cessation Advice[1]	20	100%	97%	98%
Pneumonia Care				
Appropriate Initial Antibiotic[2]	80	92%	94%	92%
Blood Culture Timing[2]	110	97%	97%	96%
Influenza Vaccine[2]	120	96%	92%	91%
Initial Antibiotic Timing[2]	110	95%	97%	95%
Pneumococcal Vaccine[2]	160	99%	93%	93%
Smoking Cessation Advice[2]	48	92%	95%	97%
Surgical Care Improvement Project				
Appropriate VTP Within 24 Hours	327	96%	93%	92%
Appropriate Hair Removal	803	100%	100%	99%
Appropriate Beta Blocker Usage	255	87%	92%	93%
Controlled Postoperative Blood Glucose	0	-	93%	93%
Prophylactic Antibiotic Timing	589	99%	97%	97%
Prophylactic Antibiotic Timing (Outpatient)	176	75%	91%	92%
Prophylactic Antibiotic Selection	596	98%	98%	97%
Prophylactic Antibiotic Select. (Outpatient)	153	97%	96%	94%
Prophylactic Antibiotic Stopped	565	98%	95%	94%
Recommended VTP Ordered	327	96%	94%	94%
Urinary Catheter Removal	198	89%	91%	90%
Children's Asthma Care				
Received Systemic Corticosteroids	-	-	-	100%
Received Home Management Plan	-	-	-	71%
Received Reliever Medication	-	-	-	100%
Use of Medical Imaging				
Combination Abdominal CT Scan	704	0.047	0.106	0.191
Combination Chest CT Scan	581	0.005	0.027	0.054
Follow-up Mammogram/Ultrasound[5]	0	-	8.4%	8.4%
MRI for Low Back Pain	173	35.8%	31.8%	32.7%
Survey of Patients' Hospital Experiences				
Area Around Room 'Always' Quiet at Night	300+	51%	-	58%
Doctors 'Always' Communicated Well	300+	79%	-	80%
Home Recovery Information Given	300+	84%	-	82%
Hospital Given 9 or 10 on 10 Point Scale	300+	74%	-	67%
Meds 'Always' Explained Before Given	300+	64%	-	60%
Nurses 'Always' Communicated Well	300+	74%	-	76%
Pain 'Always' Well Controlled	300+	67%	-	69%
Room and Bathroom 'Always' Clean	300+	72%	-	71%
Timely Help 'Always' Received	300+	60%	-	64%
Would Definitely Recommend Hospital	300+	76%	-	69%

NOTE: Hospital profiles are in alphabetical order by state, then city, then hospital within the city; Rankings exclude hospitals with less than 25 cases except for patient surveys which excludes hospitals with less than 100 cases; (a) 100–299 cases; (1) The number of cases is too small to be sure how well a hospital is performing; (2) The hospital indicated that the data submitted for this measure were based on a sample of cases; (3) Data was collected during a shorter time period (fewer quarters) than the maximum possible time for this measure; (4) Suppressed for one or more quarters by CMS; (5) No data is available from the hospital for this measure; (6) Fewer than 100 patients completed the HCAHPS survey. Use these rates with caution, as the number of surveys may be too low to reliably assess hospital performance; (7) Survey results are based on less than 12 months of data; (8) Survey results are not available for this reporting period; (9) No or very few patients were eligible for the HCAHPS survey. The scores shown, if any, reflect a very small number of surveys; (10) A state average was not calculated because too few hospitals in the state submitted data; (11) There were discrepancies in the data collection process; Please refer to the User's Guide for a full explanation of data.

Gundersen Luth Medical Center

1910 South Ave
La Crosse, WI 54601
Phone: 608-782-7300
Fax: 608-775-5594
E-mail: careers@gundluth.org
URL: www.gundluth.org
Type: Acute Care Hospitals
Emergency Services: Yes
Ownership: Voluntary Non-Profit - Private
Beds: 325

Key Personnel:
CEO/President. . . . . Jeffrey E Thompson, MD
Chief of Medical Staff . . . . Julio Bird, MD
Infection Control. . . . . William Agger, MD
Quality Assurance . . . . Jean Krause
Radiology. . . . . Eugene Valentini, MD
Emergency Room . . . . Stephanie Schwartz
Hemotology Center . . . . Wayne Bottner, MD
Intensive Care Unit. . . . . Mary Lu Gerke, RN

Measure	Cases	This Hosp.	State Avg.	U.S. Avg.
Heart Attack Care				
ACE Inhibitor or ARB for LVSD	52	98%	97%	96%
Aspirin at Arrival	165	100%	99%	99%
Aspirin at Discharge	324	99%	99%	98%
Beta Blocker at Discharge	325	100%	99%	98%
Fibrinolytic Medication Timing	0	-	0%	55%
PCI Within 90 Minutes of Arrival	33	94%	89%	90%
Smoking Cessation Advice	110	100%	99%	99%
Chest Pain/Possible Heart Attack Care				
Aspirin at Arrival[3]	0	-	96%	95%
Median Time to ECG (minutes)[3]	0	-	7	8
Median Time to Transfer (minutes)[5]	0	-	49	61
Fibrinolytic Medication Timing[5]	0	-	63%	54%
Heart Failure Care				
ACE Inhibitor or ARB for LVSD	47	96%	95%	94%
Discharge Instructions	119	100%	86%	88%
Evaluation of LVS Function	153	99%	97%	98%
Smoking Cessation Advice[1]	22	100%	97%	98%
Pneumonia Care				
Appropriate Initial Antibiotic	89	90%	94%	92%
Blood Culture Timing	121	92%	97%	96%
Influenza Vaccine	129	81%	92%	91%
Initial Antibiotic Timing	131	100%	97%	95%
Pneumococcal Vaccine	194	96%	93%	93%
Smoking Cessation Advice	69	100%	95%	97%
Surgical Care Improvement Project				
Appropriate VTP Within 24 Hours[2]	241	81%	93%	92%
Appropriate Hair Removal[2]	1,040	100%	100%	99%
Appropriate Beta Blocker Usage[2]	427	85%	92%	93%
Controlled Postoperative Blood Glucose[2]	242	96%	93%	93%
Prophylactic Antibiotic Timing[2]	721	94%	97%	97%
Prophylactic Antibiotic Timing (Outpatient)	742	94%	91%	92%
Prophylactic Antibiotic Selection[2]	734	96%	98%	97%
Prophylactic Antibiotic Select. (Outpatient)	742	96%	96%	94%
Prophylactic Antibiotic Stopped[2]	708	97%	95%	94%
Recommended VTP Ordered[2]	241	83%	94%	94%
Urinary Catheter Removal[2]	291	89%	91%	90%
Children's Asthma Care				
Received Systemic Corticosteroids	-	-	-	100%
Received Home Management Plan	-	-	-	71%
Received Reliever Medication	-	-	-	100%
Use of Medical Imaging				
Combination Abdominal CT Scan	190	0.011	0.106	0.191
Combination Chest CT Scan	78	0.013	0.027	0.054
Follow-up Mammogram/Ultrasound[5]	0	-	8.4%	8.4%
MRI for Low Back Pain[1]	17	35.3%	31.8%	32.7%
Survey of Patients' Hospital Experiences				
Area Around Room 'Always' Quiet at Night	300+	53%	-	58%
Doctors 'Always' Communicated Well	300+	81%	-	80%
Home Recovery Information Given	300+	88%	-	82%
Hospital Given 9 or 10 on 10 Point Scale	300+	78%	-	67%
Meds 'Always' Explained Before Given	300+	66%	-	60%
Nurses 'Always' Communicated Well	300+	80%	-	76%
Pain 'Always' Well Controlled	300+	71%	-	69%
Room and Bathroom 'Always' Clean	300+	75%	-	71%
Timely Help 'Always' Received	300+	67%	-	64%
Would Definitely Recommend Hospital	300+	83%	-	69%

Rusk County Memorial Hospital

900 College Ave West
Ladysmith, WI 54848
Phone: 715-532-5561
Fax: 715-532-9809
E-mail: info@ruskhospital.org
URL: www.ruskhospital.org
Type: Critical Access Hospitals
Emergency Services: Yes
Ownership: Voluntary Non-Profit - Other
Beds: 25

Key Personnel:
CEO/President. . . . . J Michael Shaw
Chief of Medical Staff . . . . Dr John Ziemer
Quality Assurance . . . . Lorene Reisner
Radiology. . . . . Mark A Augustyn
Emergency Room . . . . Mary Schneider

Measure	Cases	This Hosp.	State Avg.	U.S. Avg.
Heart Attack Care				
ACE Inhibitor or ARB for LVSD[3]	0	-	97%	96%
Aspirin at Arrival[1,3]	2	100%	99%	99%
Aspirin at Discharge[3]	0	-	99%	98%
Beta Blocker at Discharge[3]	0	-	99%	98%
Fibrinolytic Medication Timing[3]	0	-	0%	55%
PCI Within 90 Minutes of Arrival[3]	0	-	89%	90%
Smoking Cessation Advice[3]	0	-	99%	99%
Chest Pain/Possible Heart Attack Care				
Aspirin at Arrival	-	-	96%	95%
Median Time to ECG (minutes)	-	-	7	8
Median Time to Transfer (minutes)	-	-	49	61
Fibrinolytic Medication Timing	-	-	63%	54%
Heart Failure Care				
ACE Inhibitor or ARB for LVSD[1]	7	43%	95%	94%
Discharge Instructions[1]	16	69%	86%	88%
Evaluation of LVS Function[1]	22	91%	97%	98%
Smoking Cessation Advice	0	-	97%	98%
Pneumonia Care				
Appropriate Initial Antibiotic[1]	23	83%	94%	92%
Blood Culture Timing[1]	18	78%	97%	96%
Influenza Vaccine[1]	21	81%	92%	91%
Initial Antibiotic Timing[1]	23	87%	97%	95%
Pneumococcal Vaccine	30	90%	93%	93%
Smoking Cessation Advice[1]	8	50%	95%	97%
Surgical Care Improvement Project				
Appropriate VTP Within 24 Hours[5]	0	-	93%	92%
Appropriate Hair Removal[5]	0	-	100%	99%
Appropriate Beta Blocker Usage[5]	0	-	92%	93%
Controlled Postoperative Blood Glucose[5]	0	-	93%	93%
Prophylactic Antibiotic Timing[5]	0	-	97%	97%
Prophylactic Antibiotic Timing (Outpatient)	-	-	91%	92%
Prophylactic Antibiotic Selection[5]	0	-	98%	97%
Prophylactic Antibiotic Select. (Outpatient)	-	-	96%	94%
Prophylactic Antibiotic Stopped[5]	0	-	95%	94%
Recommended VTP Ordered[5]	0	-	94%	94%
Urinary Catheter Removal[5]	0	-	91%	90%
Children's Asthma Care				
Received Systemic Corticosteroids	-	-	-	100%
Received Home Management Plan	-	-	-	71%
Received Reliever Medication	-	-	-	100%
Use of Medical Imaging				
Combination Abdominal CT Scan	-	-	0.106	0.191
Combination Chest CT Scan	-	-	0.027	0.054
Follow-up Mammogram/Ultrasound	-	-	8.4%	8.4%
MRI for Low Back Pain	-	-	31.8%	32.7%
Survey of Patients' Hospital Experiences				
Area Around Room 'Always' Quiet at Night[8]	-	-	-	58%
Doctors 'Always' Communicated Well[8]	-	-	-	80%
Home Recovery Information Given[8]	-	-	-	82%
Hospital Given 9 or 10 on 10 Point Scale[8]	-	-	-	67%
Meds 'Always' Explained Before Given[8]	-	-	-	60%
Nurses 'Always' Communicated Well[8]	-	-	-	76%
Pain 'Always' Well Controlled[8]	-	-	-	69%
Room and Bathroom 'Always' Clean[8]	-	-	-	71%
Timely Help 'Always' Received[8]	-	-	-	64%
Would Definitely Recommend Hospital[8]	-	-	-	69%

Mercy Walworth Hospital & Medical Center

N2950 State Road 67
Lake Geneva, WI 53147
Phone: 262-245-0535
Type: Critical Access Hospitals
Emergency Services: Yes
Ownership: Voluntary Non-Profit - Private

Key Personnel:
CEO/President. . . . . Sheridan Yerk

Measure	Cases	This Hosp.	State Avg.	U.S. Avg.
Heart Attack Care				
ACE Inhibitor or ARB for LVSD[5]	0	-	97%	96%
Aspirin at Arrival[5]	0	-	99%	99%
Aspirin at Discharge[5]	0	-	99%	98%
Beta Blocker at Discharge[5]	0	-	99%	98%
Fibrinolytic Medication Timing[5]	0	-	0%	55%
PCI Within 90 Minutes of Arrival[5]	0	-	89%	90%
Smoking Cessation Advice[5]	0	-	99%	99%
Chest Pain/Possible Heart Attack Care				
Aspirin at Arrival	146	99%	96%	95%
Median Time to ECG (minutes)	151	6	7	8
Median Time to Transfer (minutes)[1,3]	13	45	49	61
Fibrinolytic Medication Timing	0	-	63%	54%
Heart Failure Care				
ACE Inhibitor or ARB for LVSD[5]	0	-	95%	94%
Discharge Instructions[5]	0	-	86%	88%
Evaluation of LVS Function[5]	0	-	97%	98%
Smoking Cessation Advice[5]	0	-	97%	98%
Pneumonia Care				
Appropriate Initial Antibiotic[1,3]	11	100%	94%	92%
Blood Culture Timing[1,3]	10	80%	97%	96%
Influenza Vaccine[1]	11	91%	92%	91%
Initial Antibiotic Timing[1,3]	10	90%	97%	95%
Pneumococcal Vaccine[1,3]	5	100%	93%	93%
Smoking Cessation Advice[1,3]	5	100%	95%	97%
Surgical Care Improvement Project				
Appropriate VTP Within 24 Hours	37	97%	93%	92%
Appropriate Hair Removal	113	100%	100%	99%
Appropriate Beta Blocker Usage[1]	22	86%	92%	93%
Controlled Postoperative Blood Glucose	0	-	93%	93%
Prophylactic Antibiotic Timing	99	100%	97%	97%
Prophylactic Antibiotic Timing (Outpatient)	29	97%	91%	92%
Prophylactic Antibiotic Selection	99	99%	98%	97%
Prophylactic Antibiotic Select. (Outpatient)	29	97%	96%	94%
Prophylactic Antibiotic Stopped	99	97%	95%	94%
Recommended VTP Ordered	37	100%	94%	94%
Urinary Catheter Removal	50	96%	91%	90%
Children's Asthma Care				
Received Systemic Corticosteroids	-	-	-	100%
Received Home Management Plan	-	-	-	71%
Received Reliever Medication	-	-	-	100%
Use of Medical Imaging				
Combination Abdominal CT Scan	198	0.111	0.106	0.191
Combination Chest CT Scan	129	0.085	0.027	0.054
Follow-up Mammogram/Ultrasound	283	3.2%	8.4%	8.4%
MRI for Low Back Pain	68	23.5%	31.8%	32.7%
Survey of Patients' Hospital Experiences				
Area Around Room 'Always' Quiet at Night[8]	-	-	-	58%
Doctors 'Always' Communicated Well[8]	-	-	-	80%
Home Recovery Information Given[8]	-	-	-	82%
Hospital Given 9 or 10 on 10 Point Scale[8]	-	-	-	67%
Meds 'Always' Explained Before Given[8]	-	-	-	60%
Nurses 'Always' Communicated Well[8]	-	-	-	76%
Pain 'Always' Well Controlled[8]	-	-	-	69%
Room and Bathroom 'Always' Clean[8]	-	-	-	71%
Timely Help 'Always' Received[8]	-	-	-	64%
Would Definitely Recommend Hospital[8]	-	-	-	69%

NOTE: Hospital profiles are in alphabetical order by state, then city, then hospital within the city; Rankings exclude hospitals with less than 25 cases except for patient surveys which excludes hospitals with less than 100 cases; (a) 100–299 cases; (1) The number of cases is too small to be sure how well a hospital is performing; (2) The hospital indicated that the data submitted for this measure were based on a sample of cases; (3) Data was collected during a shorter time period (fewer quarters) than the maximum possible time for this measure; (4) Suppressed for one or more quarters by CMS; (5) No data is available from the hospital for this measure; (6) Fewer than 100 patients completed the HCAHPS survey. Use these rates with caution, as the number of surveys may be too low to reliably assess hospital performance; (7) Survey results are based on less than 12 months of data; (8) Survey results are not available for this reporting period; (9) No or very few patients were eligible for the HCAHPS survey. The scores shown, if any, reflect a very small number of surveys; (10) A state average was not calculated because too few hospitals in the state submitted data; (11) There were discrepancies in the data collection process; Please refer to the User's Guide for a full explanation of data.

Grant Regional Health Center

507 S Monroe St
Lancaster, WI 53813
Phone: 608-723-2143
Fax: 608-723-4464
URL: www.grantregional.com
Type: Critical Access Hospitals
Emergency Services: Yes
Ownership: Voluntary Non-Profit - Private
Beds: 29

Key Personnel:

CEO/President. . . . . Nicole Clapp
Chief of Medical Staff. . . . . Sunil Sharma, MD
Infection Control. . . . . Kandi Auel
Operating Room. . . . . James Yurcek
Quality Assurance . . . . Nicole Clapp, RN
Anesthesiology. . . . . David Bainbridge
Emergency Room . . . . Robert Smith, MD
Patient Relations . . . . Nicole Clapp

Measure	Cases	This Hosp.	State Avg.	U.S. Avg.
Heart Attack Care				
ACE Inhibitor or ARB for LVSD[5]	0	-	97%	96%
Aspirin at Arrival[5]	0	-	99%	99%
Aspirin at Discharge[5]	0	-	99%	98%
Beta Blocker at Discharge[5]	0	-	99%	98%
Fibrinolytic Medication Timing[5]	0	-	0%	55%
PCI Within 90 Minutes of Arrival[5]	0	-	89%	90%
Smoking Cessation Advice[5]	0	-	99%	99%
Chest Pain/Possible Heart Attack Care				
Aspirin at Arrival	32	94%	96%	95%
Median Time to ECG (minutes)	32	8	7	8
Median Time to Transfer (minutes)[1,3]	2	138	49	61
Fibrinolytic Medication Timing[1]	2	50%	63%	54%
Heart Failure Care				
ACE Inhibitor or ARB for LVSD[1]	4	50%	95%	94%
Discharge Instructions[1]	8	75%	86%	88%
Evaluation of LVS Function[1]	17	47%	97%	98%
Smoking Cessation Advice	0	-	97%	98%
Pneumonia Care				
Appropriate Initial Antibiotic[1]	18	94%	94%	92%
Blood Culture Timing[1]	16	88%	97%	96%
Influenza Vaccine[1]	15	87%	92%	91%
Initial Antibiotic Timing	28	96%	97%	95%
Pneumococcal Vaccine	27	56%	93%	93%
Smoking Cessation Advice[1]	5	100%	95%	97%
Surgical Care Improvement Project				
Appropriate VTP Within 24 Hours[1]	13	100%	93%	92%
Appropriate Hair Removal	41	100%	100%	99%
Appropriate Beta Blocker Usage[1]	7	100%	92%	93%
Controlled Postoperative Blood Glucose	0	-	93%	93%
Prophylactic Antibiotic Timing	31	90%	97%	97%
Prophylactic Antibiotic Timing (Outpatient)[1,3]	7	57%	91%	92%
Prophylactic Antibiotic Selection	31	100%	98%	97%
Prophylactic Antibiotic Select. (Outpatient)[1,3]	4	100%	96%	94%
Prophylactic Antibiotic Stopped	31	100%	95%	94%
Recommended VTP Ordered[1]	15	87%	94%	94%
Urinary Catheter Removal[1]	14	100%	91%	90%
Children's Asthma Care				
Received Systemic Corticosteroids	-	-	-	100%
Received Home Management Plan	-	-	-	71%
Received Reliever Medication	-	-	-	100%
Use of Medical Imaging				
Combination Abdominal CT Scan	70	0.086	0.106	0.191
Combination Chest CT Scan	56	0.036	0.027	0.054
Follow-up Mammogram/Ultrasound	190	10.0%	8.4%	8.4%
MRI for Low Back Pain[1]	14	50.0%	31.8%	32.7%
Survey of Patients' Hospital Experiences				
Area Around Room 'Always' Quiet at Night	(a)	74%	-	58%
Doctors 'Always' Communicated Well	(a)	91%	-	80%
Home Recovery Information Given	(a)	82%	-	82%
Hospital Given 9 or 10 on 10 Point Scale	(a)	79%	-	67%
Meds 'Always' Explained Before Given	(a)	76%	-	60%
Nurses 'Always' Communicated Well	(a)	87%	-	76%
Pain 'Always' Well Controlled	(a)	81%	-	69%
Room and Bathroom 'Always' Clean	(a)	77%	-	71%
Timely Help 'Always' Received	(a)	86%	-	64%
Would Definitely Recommend Hospital	(a)	74%	-	69%

Madison VA Medical Center

2500 Overlook Terrace
Madison, WI 53705
Phone: 608-256-1901
Fax: 608-280-7096
URL: www.madison.va.gov
Type: Acute Care-Veterans Administration
Emergency Services: No
Ownership: Government - Federal
Beds: 87

Key Personnel:

Cardiac Laboratory. . . . . Judith Werner, RN
Chief of Medical Staff. . . . . Alan J Bridges, MD
Coronary Care . . . . Karen Anderson, RN
Infection Control. . . . . Linda McKinley, RN
Operating Room. . . . . Tami Essman, RN
Radiology. . . . . James J Vesely, MD

Measure	Cases	This Hosp.	State Avg.	U.S. Avg.
Heart Attack Care				
ACE Inhibitor or ARB for LVSD[1]	9	100%	97%	96%
Aspirin at Arrival	49	100%	99%	99%
Aspirin at Discharge	56	100%	99%	98%
Beta Blocker at Discharge	52	100%	99%	98%
Fibrinolytic Medication Timing[5]	0	-	0%	55%
PCI Within 90 Minutes of Arrival[1]	8	25%	89%	90%
Smoking Cessation Advice	27	100%	99%	99%
Chest Pain/Possible Heart Attack Care				
Aspirin at Arrival	-	-	96%	95%
Median Time to ECG (minutes)	-	-	7	8
Median Time to Transfer (minutes)	-	-	49	61
Fibrinolytic Medication Timing	-	-	63%	54%
Heart Failure Care				
ACE Inhibitor or ARB for LVSD	39	97%	95%	94%
Discharge Instructions	136	96%	86%	88%
Evaluation of LVS Function	147	100%	97%	98%
Smoking Cessation Advice	44	100%	97%	98%
Pneumonia Care				
Appropriate Initial Antibiotic	43	100%	94%	92%
Blood Culture Timing	81	98%	97%	96%
Influenza Vaccine	57	100%	92%	91%
Initial Antibiotic Timing	67	100%	97%	95%
Pneumococcal Vaccine	77	100%	93%	93%
Smoking Cessation Advice[1]	21	100%	95%	97%
Surgical Care Improvement Project				
Appropriate VTP Within 24 Hours[2]	98	97%	93%	92%
Appropriate Hair Removal[2]	274	100%	100%	99%
Appropriate Beta Blocker Usage[2]	125	100%	92%	93%
Controlled Postoperative Blood Glucose[2]	41	100%	93%	93%
Prophylactic Antibiotic Timing	167	99%	97%	97%
Prophylactic Antibiotic Timing (Outpatient)	-	-	91%	92%
Prophylactic Antibiotic Selection	167	99%	98%	97%
Prophylactic Antibiotic Select. (Outpatient)	-	-	96%	94%
Prophylactic Antibiotic Stopped	162	100%	95%	94%
Recommended VTP Ordered[2]	98	97%	94%	94%
Urinary Catheter Removal[2]	73	92%	91%	90%
Children's Asthma Care				
Received Systemic Corticosteroids	-	-	-	100%
Received Home Management Plan	-	-	-	71%
Received Reliever Medication	-	-	-	100%
Use of Medical Imaging				
Combination Abdominal CT Scan	-	-	0.106	0.191
Combination Chest CT Scan	-	-	0.027	0.054
Follow-up Mammogram/Ultrasound	-	-	8.4%	8.4%
MRI for Low Back Pain	-	-	31.8%	32.7%
Survey of Patients' Hospital Experiences				
Area Around Room 'Always' Quiet at Night	-	-	-	58%
Doctors 'Always' Communicated Well	-	-	-	80%
Home Recovery Information Given	-	-	-	82%
Hospital Given 9 or 10 on 10 Point Scale	-	-	-	67%
Meds 'Always' Explained Before Given	-	-	-	60%
Nurses 'Always' Communicated Well	-	-	-	76%
Pain 'Always' Well Controlled	-	-	-	69%
Room and Bathroom 'Always' Clean	-	-	-	71%
Timely Help 'Always' Received	-	-	-	64%
Would Definitely Recommend Hospital	-	-	-	69%

Meriter Hospital

202 S Park St
Madison, WI 53715
Phone: 608-417-6210
Fax: 608-417-6568
URL: www.meriter.com
Type: Acute Care Hospitals
Emergency Services: Yes
Ownership: Voluntary Non-Profit - Private
Beds: 448

Key Personnel:

CEO/President. . . . . James L Woodward
Chief of Medical Staff. . . . . Geoffrey Priest MD

Measure	Cases	This Hosp.	State Avg.	U.S. Avg.
Heart Attack Care				
ACE Inhibitor or ARB for LVSD[2]	40	95%	97%	96%
Aspirin at Arrival[2]	190	100%	99%	99%
Aspirin at Discharge[2]	266	100%	99%	98%
Beta Blocker at Discharge[2]	251	98%	99%	98%
Fibrinolytic Medication Timing[2]	0	-	0%	55%
PCI Within 90 Minutes of Arrival[2]	47	96%	89%	90%
Smoking Cessation Advice[2]	68	100%	99%	99%
Chest Pain/Possible Heart Attack Care				
Aspirin at Arrival[5]	0	-	96%	95%
Median Time to ECG (minutes)[5]	0	-	7	8
Median Time to Transfer (minutes)[5]	0	-	49	61
Fibrinolytic Medication Timing[5]	0	-	63%	54%
Heart Failure Care				
ACE Inhibitor or ARB for LVSD	99	92%	95%	94%
Discharge Instructions	239	94%	86%	88%
Evaluation of LVS Function	302	100%	97%	98%
Smoking Cessation Advice	38	95%	97%	98%
Pneumonia Care				
Appropriate Initial Antibiotic	115	90%	94%	92%
Blood Culture Timing	166	94%	97%	96%
Influenza Vaccine	143	90%	92%	91%
Initial Antibiotic Timing	192	96%	97%	95%
Pneumococcal Vaccine	219	97%	93%	93%
Smoking Cessation Advice	72	99%	95%	97%
Surgical Care Improvement Project				
Appropriate VTP Within 24 Hours[2]	123	96%	93%	92%
Appropriate Hair Removal[2]	544	99%	100%	99%
Appropriate Beta Blocker Usage[2]	136	81%	92%	93%
Controlled Postoperative Blood Glucose[2]	115	95%	93%	93%
Prophylactic Antibiotic Timing[2]	423	96%	97%	97%
Prophylactic Antibiotic Timing (Outpatient)	256	89%	91%	92%
Prophylactic Antibiotic Selection[2]	424	99%	98%	97%
Prophylactic Antibiotic Select. (Outpatient)	251	97%	96%	94%
Prophylactic Antibiotic Stopped[2]	415	98%	95%	94%
Recommended VTP Ordered[2]	123	98%	94%	94%
Urinary Catheter Removal[2]	89	88%	91%	90%
Children's Asthma Care				
Received Systemic Corticosteroids	-	-	-	100%
Received Home Management Plan	-	-	-	71%
Received Reliever Medication	-	-	-	100%
Use of Medical Imaging				
Combination Abdominal CT Scan	531	0.062	0.106	0.191
Combination Chest CT Scan	398	0.035	0.027	0.054
Follow-up Mammogram/Ultrasound[5]	0	-	8.4%	8.4%
MRI for Low Back Pain[5]	0	-	31.8%	32.7%
Survey of Patients' Hospital Experiences				
Area Around Room 'Always' Quiet at Night	300+	58%	-	58%
Doctors 'Always' Communicated Well	300+	80%	-	80%
Home Recovery Information Given	300+	88%	-	82%
Hospital Given 9 or 10 on 10 Point Scale	300+	80%	-	67%
Meds 'Always' Explained Before Given	300+	62%	-	60%
Nurses 'Always' Communicated Well	300+	78%	-	76%
Pain 'Always' Well Controlled	300+	65%	-	69%
Room and Bathroom 'Always' Clean	300+	79%	-	71%
Timely Help 'Always' Received	300+	64%	-	64%
Would Definitely Recommend Hospital	300+	85%	-	69%

NOTE: Hospital profiles are in alphabetical order by state, then city, then hospital within the city; Rankings exclude hospitals with less than 25 cases except for patient surveys which excludes hospitals with less than 100 cases; (a) 100–299 cases; (1) The number of cases is too small to be sure how well a hospital is performing; (2) The hospital indicated that the data submitted for this measure were based on a sample of cases; (3) Data was collected during a shorter time period (fewer quarters) than the maximum possible time for this measure; (4) Suppressed for one or more quarters by CMS; (5) No data is available from the hospital for this measure; (6) Fewer than 100 patients completed the HCAHPS survey. Use these rates with caution, as the number of surveys may be too low to reliably assess hospital performance; (7) Survey results are based on less than 12 months of data; (8) Survey results are not available for this reporting period; (9) No or very few patients were eligible for the HCAHPS survey. The scores shown, if any, reflect a very small number of surveys; (10) A state average was not calculated because too few hospitals in the state submitted data; (11) There were discrepancies in the data collection process; Please refer to the User's Guide for a full explanation of data.

Saint Mary's Hospital

700 South Park St Phone: 608-251-6100
Madison, WI 53715 Fax: 608-258-5711
URL: www.stmarysmadison.com
Type: Acute Care Hospitals Emergency Services: Yes
Ownership: Voluntary Non-Profit - Other Beds: 440

Key Personnel:
CEO/President. . . . . Frank Byrne
Chief of Medical Staff . . . . Joan V Brown, MD
Coronary Care . . . . Jody De Rosa
Infection Control. . . . . Chuck Zeisser
Operating Room. . . . . Beverly Beine
Pediatric In-Patient Care . . . . Diane Buss
Quality Assurance . . . . Vicki Scheel
Emergency Room . . . . Audra Thompson

Measure	Cases	This Hosp.	State Avg.	U.S. Avg.
Heart Attack Care				
ACE Inhibitor or ARB for LVSD	83	96%	97%	96%
Aspirin at Arrival	206	100%	99%	99%
Aspirin at Discharge	445	100%	99%	98%
Beta Blocker at Discharge	433	100%	99%	98%
Fibrinolytic Medication Timing	0	-	0%	55%
PCI Within 90 Minutes of Arrival	40	92%	89%	90%
Smoking Cessation Advice	127	100%	99%	99%
Chest Pain/Possible Heart Attack Care				
Aspirin at Arrival[1]	15	100%	96%	95%
Median Time to ECG (minutes)[1]	15	5	7	8
Median Time to Transfer (minutes)[5]	0	-	49	61
Fibrinolytic Medication Timing[5]	0	-	63%	54%
Heart Failure Care				
ACE Inhibitor or ARB for LVSD	122	93%	95%	94%
Discharge Instructions	341	91%	86%	88%
Evaluation of LVS Function	465	98%	97%	98%
Smoking Cessation Advice	55	100%	97%	98%
Pneumonia Care				
Appropriate Initial Antibiotic	165	98%	94%	92%
Blood Culture Timing	254	97%	97%	96%
Influenza Vaccine	274	97%	92%	91%
Initial Antibiotic Timing	287	99%	97%	95%
Pneumococcal Vaccine	381	99%	93%	93%
Smoking Cessation Advice	111	100%	95%	97%
Surgical Care Improvement Project				
Appropriate VTP Within 24 Hours[2]	405	95%	93%	92%
Appropriate Hair Removal[2]	1,819	99%	100%	99%
Appropriate Beta Blocker Usage[2]	578	94%	92%	93%
Controlled Postoperative Blood Glucose[2]	316	92%	93%	93%
Prophylactic Antibiotic Timing[2]	1,460	98%	97%	97%
Prophylactic Antibiotic Timing (Outpatient)	639	95%	91%	92%
Prophylactic Antibiotic Selection[2]	1,469	99%	98%	97%
Prophylactic Antibiotic Select. (Outpatient)	636	99%	96%	94%
Prophylactic Antibiotic Stopped[2]	1,409	95%	95%	94%
Recommended VTP Ordered[2]	405	96%	94%	94%
Urinary Catheter Removal[2]	556	94%	91%	90%
Children's Asthma Care				
Received Systemic Corticosteroids	-	-	-	100%
Received Home Management Plan	-	-	-	71%
Received Reliever Medication	-	-	-	100%
Use of Medical Imaging				
Combination Abdominal CT Scan	351	0.020	0.106	0.191
Combination Chest CT Scan[1]	54	0.056	0.027	0.054
Follow-up Mammogram/Ultrasound[5]	0	-	8.4%	8.4%
MRI for Low Back Pain[1]	1	0.0%	31.8%	32.7%
Survey of Patients' Hospital Experiences				
Area Around Room 'Always' Quiet at Night	300+	63%	-	58%
Doctors 'Always' Communicated Well	300+	77%	-	80%
Home Recovery Information Given	300+	89%	-	82%
Hospital Given 9 or 10 on 10 Point Scale	300+	79%	-	67%
Meds 'Always' Explained Before Given	300+	67%	-	60%
Nurses 'Always' Communicated Well	300+	82%	-	76%
Pain 'Always' Well Controlled	300+	72%	-	69%
Room and Bathroom 'Always' Clean	300+	74%	-	71%
Timely Help 'Always' Received	300+	65%	-	64%
Would Definitely Recommend Hospital	300+	83%	-	69%

University of Wisconsin Hospitals & Clinics Authority

600 Highland Avenue Phone: 608-263-8991
Madison, WI 53792 Fax: 608-263-9830
URL: uwhealth.org
Type: Acute Care Hospitals Emergency Services: Yes
Ownership: Govt - Hospital Dist/Auth Beds: 512

Key Personnel:
CEO/President. . . . . Donna Katen-Bahansky
Chief of Medical Staff . . . . Carl Getto
Infection Control. . . . . Dennis Maki MD
Pediatric Ambulatory Care . . . . . . Ellen Wald
Quality Assurance . . . . Mark S Kirschbaum
Radiology. . . . . Thomas Grist
Anesthesiology. . . . . Robert Pearce MD
Emergency Room . . . . Joseph Cline MD

Measure	Cases	This Hosp.	State Avg.	U.S. Avg.
Heart Attack Care				
ACE Inhibitor or ARB for LVSD[2]	42	95%	97%	96%
Aspirin at Arrival[2]	112	98%	99%	99%
Aspirin at Discharge[2]	275	99%	99%	98%
Beta Blocker at Discharge[2]	262	100%	99%	98%
Fibrinolytic Medication Timing[2]	0	-	0%	55%
PCI Within 90 Minutes of Arrival[1,2]	14	93%	89%	90%
Smoking Cessation Advice[2]	96	100%	99%	99%
Chest Pain/Possible Heart Attack Care				
Aspirin at Arrival[5]	0	-	96%	95%
Median Time to ECG (minutes)[5]	0	-	7	8
Median Time to Transfer (minutes)[5]	0	-	49	61
Fibrinolytic Medication Timing[5]	0	-	63%	54%
Heart Failure Care				
ACE Inhibitor or ARB for LVSD[2]	90	98%	95%	94%
Discharge Instructions[2]	231	77%	86%	88%
Evaluation of LVS Function[2]	264	99%	97%	98%
Smoking Cessation Advice[2]	47	100%	97%	98%
Pneumonia Care				
Appropriate Initial Antibiotic[2]	37	89%	94%	92%
Blood Culture Timing[2]	83	96%	97%	96%
Influenza Vaccine[2]	74	97%	92%	91%
Initial Antibiotic Timing[2]	78	97%	97%	95%
Pneumococcal Vaccine[2]	80	96%	93%	93%
Smoking Cessation Advice[2]	37	100%	95%	97%
Surgical Care Improvement Project				
Appropriate VTP Within 24 Hours[2]	220	98%	93%	92%
Appropriate Hair Removal[2]	647	99%	100%	99%
Appropriate Beta Blocker Usage[2]	231	100%	92%	93%
Controlled Postoperative Blood Glucose[2]	133	84%	93%	93%
Prophylactic Antibiotic Timing[2]	408	94%	97%	97%
Prophylactic Antibiotic Timing (Outpatient)	266	82%	91%	92%
Prophylactic Antibiotic Selection[2]	420	96%	98%	97%
Prophylactic Antibiotic Select. (Outpatient)	488	97%	96%	94%
Prophylactic Antibiotic Stopped[2]	383	97%	95%	94%
Recommended VTP Ordered[2]	220	98%	94%	94%
Urinary Catheter Removal[2]	168	90%	91%	90%
Children's Asthma Care				
Received Systemic Corticosteroids	-	-	-	100%
Received Home Management Plan	-	-	-	71%
Received Reliever Medication	-	-	-	100%
Use of Medical Imaging				
Combination Abdominal CT Scan	2,268	0.073	0.106	0.191
Combination Chest CT Scan	2,607	0.008	0.027	0.054
Follow-up Mammogram/Ultrasound	1,660	5.9%	8.4%	8.4%
MRI for Low Back Pain	342	28.1%	31.8%	32.7%
Survey of Patients' Hospital Experiences				
Area Around Room 'Always' Quiet at Night	300+	55%	-	58%
Doctors 'Always' Communicated Well	300+	76%	-	80%
Home Recovery Information Given	300+	88%	-	82%
Hospital Given 9 or 10 on 10 Point Scale	300+	77%	-	67%
Meds 'Always' Explained Before Given	300+	65%	-	60%
Nurses 'Always' Communicated Well	300+	79%	-	76%
Pain 'Always' Well Controlled	300+	68%	-	69%
Room and Bathroom 'Always' Clean	300+	73%	-	71%
Timely Help 'Always' Received	300+	62%	-	64%
Would Definitely Recommend Hospital	300+	83%	-	69%

Holy Family Memorial

2300 Western Ave Phone: 920-684-2011
Manitowoc, WI 54221 Fax: 920-320-8576
URL: www.hfmhealth.org
Type: Acute Care Hospitals Emergency Services: Yes
Ownership: Voluntary Non-Profit - Other Beds: 303

Key Personnel:
CEO/President. . . . . Mark Herzog
Chief of Medical Staff . . . . Steven Driggers, MD
Infection Control. . . . . Mike Helgesen
Operating Room. . . . . Lisa Sherman
Quality Assurance . . . . Betty Hove
Radiology. . . . . Carrie Wasmuth
Emergency Room . . . . Mary Coenen
Intensive Care Unit. . . . . Mary Coenen

Measure	Cases	This Hosp.	State Avg.	U.S. Avg.
Heart Attack Care				
ACE Inhibitor or ARB for LVSD[1]	10	90%	97%	96%
Aspirin at Arrival	62	97%	99%	99%
Aspirin at Discharge	53	98%	99%	98%
Beta Blocker at Discharge	51	92%	99%	98%
Fibrinolytic Medication Timing	0	-	0%	55%
PCI Within 90 Minutes of Arrival[1]	9	67%	89%	90%
Smoking Cessation Advice[1]	10	100%	99%	99%
Chest Pain/Possible Heart Attack Care				
Aspirin at Arrival[1]	15	80%	96%	95%
Median Time to ECG (minutes)[1]	16	5	7	8
Median Time to Transfer (minutes)[1,3]	4	49	49	61
Fibrinolytic Medication Timing[3]	0	-	63%	54%
Heart Failure Care				
ACE Inhibitor or ARB for LVSD	25	100%	95%	94%
Discharge Instructions	59	97%	86%	88%
Evaluation of LVS Function	101	100%	97%	98%
Smoking Cessation Advice[1]	12	100%	97%	98%
Pneumonia Care				
Appropriate Initial Antibiotic	54	96%	94%	92%
Blood Culture Timing	78	96%	97%	96%
Influenza Vaccine	53	100%	92%	91%
Initial Antibiotic Timing	73	97%	97%	95%
Pneumococcal Vaccine	68	100%	93%	93%
Smoking Cessation Advice[1]	19	100%	95%	97%
Surgical Care Improvement Project				
Appropriate VTP Within 24 Hours	93	92%	93%	92%
Appropriate Hair Removal	426	100%	100%	99%
Appropriate Beta Blocker Usage	138	86%	92%	93%
Controlled Postoperative Blood Glucose	0	-	93%	93%
Prophylactic Antibiotic Timing	304	98%	97%	97%
Prophylactic Antibiotic Timing (Outpatient)	122	100%	91%	92%
Prophylactic Antibiotic Selection	308	99%	98%	97%
Prophylactic Antibiotic Select. (Outpatient)	122	98%	96%	94%
Prophylactic Antibiotic Stopped	294	93%	95%	94%
Recommended VTP Ordered	93	95%	94%	94%
Urinary Catheter Removal	103	94%	91%	90%
Children's Asthma Care				
Received Systemic Corticosteroids	-	-	-	100%
Received Home Management Plan	-	-	-	71%
Received Reliever Medication	-	-	-	100%
Use of Medical Imaging				
Combination Abdominal CT Scan	310	0.113	0.106	0.191
Combination Chest CT Scan	288	0.101	0.027	0.054
Follow-up Mammogram/Ultrasound	881	9.0%	8.4%	8.4%
MRI for Low Back Pain	119	31.9%	31.8%	32.7%
Survey of Patients' Hospital Experiences				
Area Around Room 'Always' Quiet at Night	300+	51%	-	58%
Doctors 'Always' Communicated Well	300+	78%	-	80%
Home Recovery Information Given	300+	87%	-	82%
Hospital Given 9 or 10 on 10 Point Scale	300+	63%	-	67%
Meds 'Always' Explained Before Given	300+	62%	-	60%
Nurses 'Always' Communicated Well	300+	76%	-	76%
Pain 'Always' Well Controlled	300+	69%	-	69%
Room and Bathroom 'Always' Clean	300+	77%	-	71%
Timely Help 'Always' Received	300+	62%	-	64%
Would Definitely Recommend Hospital	300+	68%	-	69%

NOTE: Hospital profiles are in alphabetical order by state, then city, then hospital within the city; Rankings exclude hospitals with less than 25 cases except for patient surveys which excludes hospitals with less than 100 cases; (a) 100–299 cases; (1) The number of cases is too small to be sure how well a hospital is performing; (2) The hospital indicated that the data submitted for this measure were based on a sample of cases; (3) Data was collected during a shorter time period (fewer quarters) than the maximum possible time for this measure; (4) Suppressed for one or more quarters by CMS; (5) No data is available from the hospital for this measure; (6) Fewer than 100 patients completed the HCAHPS survey. Use these rates with caution, as the number of surveys may be too low to reliably assess hospital performance; (7) Survey results are based on less than 12 months of data; (8) Survey results are not available for this reporting period; (9) No or very few patients were eligible for the HCAHPS survey. The scores shown, if any, reflect a very small number of surveys; (10) A state average was not calculated because too few hospitals in the state submitted data; (11) There were discrepancies in the data collection process; Please refer to the User's Guide for a full explanation of data.

Bay Area Medical Center

3100 Shore Dr
Marinette, WI 54143
URL: www.bamc.org
Type: Acute Care Hospitals
Ownership: Voluntary Non-Profit - Private
Phone: 715-735-6621
Fax: 715-735-6241
Emergency Services: Yes
Beds: 99

Key Personnel:
CEO/President. . . . . David Olson
Chief of Medical Staff . . . . Adam Ankrum
Radiology. . . . . David J Balison

Measure	Cases	This Hosp.	State Avg.	U.S. Avg.
Heart Attack Care				
ACE Inhibitor or ARB for LVSD[1]	15	73%	97%	96%
Aspirin at Arrival	112	98%	99%	99%
Aspirin at Discharge	78	96%	99%	98%
Beta Blocker at Discharge	79	97%	99%	98%
Fibrinolytic Medication Timing	0	-	0%	55%
PCI Within 90 Minutes of Arrival[1]	4	75%	89%	90%
Smoking Cessation Advice[1]	15	93%	99%	99%
Chest Pain/Possible Heart Attack Care				
Aspirin at Arrival	72	100%	96%	95%
Median Time to ECG (minutes)	75	1	7	8
Median Time to Transfer (minutes)[1,3]	4	78	49	61
Fibrinolytic Medication Timing[1]	9	89%	63%	54%
Heart Failure Care				
ACE Inhibitor or ARB for LVSD	41	85%	95%	94%
Discharge Instructions	116	89%	86%	88%
Evaluation of LVS Function	164	96%	97%	98%
Smoking Cessation Advice[1]	22	95%	97%	98%
Pneumonia Care				
Appropriate Initial Antibiotic	80	94%	94%	92%
Blood Culture Timing	114	96%	97%	96%
Influenza Vaccine	89	79%	92%	91%
Initial Antibiotic Timing	132	99%	97%	95%
Pneumococcal Vaccine	129	94%	93%	93%
Smoking Cessation Advice	41	95%	95%	97%
Surgical Care Improvement Project				
Appropriate VTP Within 24 Hours	101	74%	93%	92%
Appropriate Hair Removal	278	99%	100%	99%
Appropriate Beta Blocker Usage	95	94%	92%	93%
Controlled Postoperative Blood Glucose	0	-	93%	93%
Prophylactic Antibiotic Timing	171	95%	97%	97%
Prophylactic Antibiotic Timing (Outpatient)	115	92%	91%	92%
Prophylactic Antibiotic Selection	172	97%	98%	97%
Prophylactic Antibiotic Select. (Outpatient)	110	96%	96%	94%
Prophylactic Antibiotic Stopped	161	83%	95%	94%
Recommended VTP Ordered	102	76%	94%	94%
Urinary Catheter Removal[1]	21	81%	91%	90%
Children's Asthma Care				
Received Systemic Corticosteroids	-	-	-	100%
Received Home Management Plan	-	-	-	71%
Received Reliever Medication	-	-	-	100%
Use of Medical Imaging				
Combination Abdominal CT Scan	583	0.103	0.106	0.191
Combination Chest CT Scan	271	0.030	0.027	0.054
Follow-up Mammogram/Ultrasound	540	1.3%	8.4%	8.4%
MRI for Low Back Pain	107	40.2%	31.8%	32.7%
Survey of Patients' Hospital Experiences				
Area Around Room 'Always' Quiet at Night	300+	60%	-	58%
Doctors 'Always' Communicated Well	300+	78%	-	80%
Home Recovery Information Given	300+	84%	-	82%
Hospital Given 9 or 10 on 10 Point Scale	300+	56%	-	67%
Meds 'Always' Explained Before Given	300+	60%	-	60%
Nurses 'Always' Communicated Well	300+	76%	-	76%
Pain 'Always' Well Controlled	300+	70%	-	69%
Room and Bathroom 'Always' Clean	300+	77%	-	71%
Timely Help 'Always' Received	300+	63%	-	64%
Would Definitely Recommend Hospital	300+	59%	-	69%

Saint Josephs Hospital

611 St Joseph Ave
Marshfield, WI 54449
E-mail: sjhweb@stjosephs-marshfield.org
URL: www.stjosephs-marshfield.org
Type: Acute Care Hospitals
Ownership: Voluntary Non-Profit - Church
Phone: 715-387-7850
Fax: 715-387-5240
Emergency Services: Yes
Beds: 500

Key Personnel:
CEO/President. . . . . Michael A Schmidt
Chief of Medical Staff . . . . Fredrick Wesbrook, MD
Infection Control. . . . . Thomas L Sell, MD
Pediatric Ambulatory Care . . . . . . George J Hoehn, III, DP
Pediatric In-Patient Care . . . . George J Hoehn, III, DP
Quality Assurance . . . . Paul Nedd
Radiology. . . . . Tim Swan, MD

Measure	Cases	This Hosp.	State Avg.	U.S. Avg.
Heart Attack Care				
ACE Inhibitor or ARB for LVSD	55	100%	97%	96%
Aspirin at Arrival	170	99%	99%	99%
Aspirin at Discharge	302	100%	99%	98%
Beta Blocker at Discharge	338	99%	99%	98%
Fibrinolytic Medication Timing	0	-	0%	55%
PCI Within 90 Minutes of Arrival[1]	24	100%	89%	90%
Smoking Cessation Advice	93	100%	99%	99%
Chest Pain/Possible Heart Attack Care				
Aspirin at Arrival[5]	0	-	96%	95%
Median Time to ECG (minutes)[5]	0	-	7	8
Median Time to Transfer (minutes)[5]	0	-	49	61
Fibrinolytic Medication Timing[5]	0	-	63%	54%
Heart Failure Care				
ACE Inhibitor or ARB for LVSD	104	100%	95%	94%
Discharge Instructions	298	90%	86%	88%
Evaluation of LVS Function	392	100%	97%	98%
Smoking Cessation Advice	32	97%	97%	98%
Pneumonia Care				
Appropriate Initial Antibiotic	103	93%	94%	92%
Blood Culture Timing	72	86%	97%	96%
Influenza Vaccine	143	94%	92%	91%
Initial Antibiotic Timing	144	98%	97%	95%
Pneumococcal Vaccine	206	97%	93%	93%
Smoking Cessation Advice	69	99%	95%	97%
Surgical Care Improvement Project				
Appropriate VTP Within 24 Hours	646	97%	93%	92%
Appropriate Hair Removal	1,932	100%	100%	99%
Appropriate Beta Blocker Usage	634	95%	92%	93%
Controlled Postoperative Blood Glucose	323	90%	93%	93%
Prophylactic Antibiotic Timing	1,163	97%	97%	97%
Prophylactic Antibiotic Timing (Outpatient)	439	93%	91%	92%
Prophylactic Antibiotic Selection	1,190	97%	98%	97%
Prophylactic Antibiotic Select. (Outpatient)	437	97%	96%	94%
Prophylactic Antibiotic Stopped	1,152	89%	95%	94%
Recommended VTP Ordered	647	98%	94%	94%
Urinary Catheter Removal	387	75%	91%	90%
Children's Asthma Care				
Received Systemic Corticosteroids	-	-	-	100%
Received Home Management Plan	-	-	-	71%
Received Reliever Medication	-	-	-	100%
Use of Medical Imaging				
Combination Abdominal CT Scan[1]	41	0.049	0.106	0.191
Combination Chest CT Scan[1]	16	0.000	0.027	0.054
Follow-up Mammogram/Ultrasound[5]	0	-	8.4%	8.4%
MRI for Low Back Pain[5]	0	-	31.8%	32.7%
Survey of Patients' Hospital Experiences				
Area Around Room 'Always' Quiet at Night	300+	50%	-	58%
Doctors 'Always' Communicated Well	300+	73%	-	80%
Home Recovery Information Given	300+	87%	-	82%
Hospital Given 9 or 10 on 10 Point Scale	300+	71%	-	67%
Meds 'Always' Explained Before Given	300+	61%	-	60%
Nurses 'Always' Communicated Well	300+	75%	-	76%
Pain 'Always' Well Controlled	300+	65%	-	69%
Room and Bathroom 'Always' Clean	300+	74%	-	71%
Timely Help 'Always' Received	300+	62%	-	64%
Would Definitely Recommend Hospital	300+	73%	-	69%

Mile Bluff Medical Center

1050 Division St
Mauston, WI 53948
Type: Acute Care Hospitals
Ownership: Proprietary
Phone: 608-847-6161
Fax: 608-847-6017
Emergency Services: Yes
Beds: 100

Key Personnel:
CEO/President. . . . . James M O'Keefe

Measure	Cases	This Hosp.	State Avg.	U.S. Avg.
Heart Attack Care				
ACE Inhibitor or ARB for LVSD	0	-	97%	96%
Aspirin at Arrival[1]	10	90%	99%	99%
Aspirin at Discharge[1]	6	100%	99%	98%
Beta Blocker at Discharge[1]	6	67%	99%	98%
Fibrinolytic Medication Timing[1]	1	0%	0%	55%
PCI Within 90 Minutes of Arrival	0	-	89%	90%
Smoking Cessation Advice	0	-	99%	99%
Chest Pain/Possible Heart Attack Care				
Aspirin at Arrival	79	95%	96%	95%
Median Time to ECG (minutes)	80	0	7	8
Median Time to Transfer (minutes)[1]	6	161	49	61
Fibrinolytic Medication Timing[1]	3	33%	63%	54%
Heart Failure Care				
ACE Inhibitor or ARB for LVSD[1]	5	100%	95%	94%
Discharge Instructions	33	61%	86%	88%
Evaluation of LVS Function	46	96%	97%	98%
Smoking Cessation Advice[1]	3	0%	97%	98%
Pneumonia Care				
Appropriate Initial Antibiotic[1]	3	100%	94%	92%
Blood Culture Timing	37	97%	97%	96%
Influenza Vaccine	49	73%	92%	91%
Initial Antibiotic Timing	95	94%	97%	95%
Pneumococcal Vaccine	70	57%	93%	93%
Smoking Cessation Advice[1]	22	45%	95%	97%
Surgical Care Improvement Project				
Appropriate VTP Within 24 Hours	35	77%	93%	92%
Appropriate Hair Removal	165	99%	100%	99%
Appropriate Beta Blocker Usage	29	97%	92%	93%
Controlled Postoperative Blood Glucose	0	-	93%	93%
Prophylactic Antibiotic Timing	136	96%	97%	97%
Prophylactic Antibiotic Timing (Outpatient)	50	80%	91%	92%
Prophylactic Antibiotic Selection	136	96%	98%	97%
Prophylactic Antibiotic Select. (Outpatient)	40	98%	96%	94%
Prophylactic Antibiotic Stopped	133	91%	95%	94%
Recommended VTP Ordered	35	83%	94%	94%
Urinary Catheter Removal[1]	14	100%	91%	90%
Children's Asthma Care				
Received Systemic Corticosteroids	-	-	-	100%
Received Home Management Plan	-	-	-	71%
Received Reliever Medication	-	-	-	100%
Use of Medical Imaging				
Combination Abdominal CT Scan	178	0.107	0.106	0.191
Combination Chest CT Scan	186	0.005	0.027	0.054
Follow-up Mammogram/Ultrasound	520	8.1%	8.4%	8.4%
MRI for Low Back Pain	61	34.4%	31.8%	32.7%
Survey of Patients' Hospital Experiences				
Area Around Room 'Always' Quiet at Night	300+	52%	-	58%
Doctors 'Always' Communicated Well	300+	84%	-	80%
Home Recovery Information Given	300+	83%	-	82%
Hospital Given 9 or 10 on 10 Point Scale	300+	63%	-	67%
Meds 'Always' Explained Before Given	300+	65%	-	60%
Nurses 'Always' Communicated Well	300+	75%	-	76%
Pain 'Always' Well Controlled	300+	66%	-	69%
Room and Bathroom 'Always' Clean	300+	77%	-	71%
Timely Help 'Always' Received	300+	63%	-	64%
Would Definitely Recommend Hospital	300+	62%	-	69%

NOTE: Hospital profiles are in alphabetical order by state, then city, then hospital within the city; Rankings exclude hospitals with less than 25 cases except for patient surveys which excludes hospitals with less than 100 cases; (a) 100–299 cases; (1) The number of cases is too small to be sure how well a hospital is performing; (2) The hospital indicated that the data submitted for this measure were based on a sample of cases; (3) Data was collected during a shorter time period (fewer quarters) than the maximum possible time for this measure; (4) Suppressed for one or more quarters by CMS; (5) No data is available from the hospital for this measure; (6) Fewer than 100 patients completed the HCAHPS survey. Use these rates with caution, as the number of surveys may be too low to reliably assess hospital performance; (7) Survey results are based on less than 12 months of data; (8) Survey results are not available for this reporting period; (9) No or very few patients were eligible for the HCAHPS survey. The scores shown, if any, reflect a very small number of surveys; (10) A state average was not calculated because too few hospitals in the state submitted data; (11) There were discrepancies in the data collection process; Please refer to the User's Guide for a full explanation of data.

Memorial Health Center

135 S Gibson St
Medford, WI 54451
Phone: 715-748-8100
Fax: 715-748-8199
URL: www.memhc.com
Type: Critical Access Hospitals
Emergency Services: Yes
Ownership: Voluntary Non-Profit - Other
Beds: 164

Key Personnel:

Chief of Medical Staff.......... Mark Reuter
Infection Control............. Jane Schiszik
Operating Room............. Erik Branstetter
Quality Assurance .... Carol Ahles
Radiology.................. Steve Liegel, MD

Measure	Cases	This Hosp.	State Avg.	U.S. Avg.
Heart Attack Care				
ACE Inhibitor or ARB for LVSD[5]	0	-	97%	96%
Aspirin at Arrival[5]	0	-	99%	99%
Aspirin at Discharge[5]	0	-	99%	98%
Beta Blocker at Discharge[5]	0	-	99%	98%
Fibrinolytic Medication Timing[5]	0	-	0%	55%
PCI Within 90 Minutes of Arrival[5]	0	-	89%	90%
Smoking Cessation Advice[5]	0	-	99%	99%
Chest Pain/Possible Heart Attack Care				
Aspirin at Arrival	86	98%	96%	95%
Median Time to ECG (minutes)	88	4	7	8
Median Time to Transfer (minutes)[1,3]	10	30	49	61
Fibrinolytic Medication Timing[1]	3	33%	63%	54%
Heart Failure Care				
ACE Inhibitor or ARB for LVSD[1]	7	100%	95%	94%
Discharge Instructions[1]	8	100%	86%	88%
Evaluation of LVS Function[1]	18	100%	97%	98%
Smoking Cessation Advice[1]	1	0%	97%	98%
Pneumonia Care				
Appropriate Initial Antibiotic	30	90%	94%	92%
Blood Culture Timing	42	98%	97%	96%
Influenza Vaccine	26	69%	92%	91%
Initial Antibiotic Timing	46	100%	97%	95%
Pneumococcal Vaccine	45	62%	93%	93%
Smoking Cessation Advice[1]	1	100%	95%	97%
Surgical Care Improvement Project				
Appropriate VTP Within 24 Hours[1]	9	89%	93%	92%
Appropriate Hair Removal	46	100%	100%	99%
Appropriate Beta Blocker Usage[5]	0	-	92%	93%
Controlled Postoperative Blood Glucose	0	-	93%	93%
Prophylactic Antibiotic Timing	40	95%	97%	97%
Prophylactic Antibiotic Timing (Outpatient)[1,3]	7	100%	91%	92%
Prophylactic Antibiotic Selection	40	95%	98%	97%
Prophylactic Antibiotic Select. (Outpatient)[1,3]	7	100%	96%	94%
Prophylactic Antibiotic Stopped	39	97%	95%	94%
Recommended VTP Ordered[1]	9	89%	94%	94%
Urinary Catheter Removal[1]	1	100%	91%	90%
Children's Asthma Care				
Received Systemic Corticosteroids	-	-	-	100%
Received Home Management Plan	-	-	-	71%
Received Reliever Medication	-	-	-	100%
Use of Medical Imaging				
Combination Abdominal CT Scan	206	0.039	0.106	0.191
Combination Chest CT Scan	126	0.000	0.027	0.054
Follow-up Mammogram/Ultrasound	275	1.8%	8.4%	8.4%
MRI for Low Back Pain[1]	33	30.3%	31.8%	32.7%
Survey of Patients' Hospital Experiences				
Area Around Room 'Always' Quiet at Night	(a)	68%	-	58%
Doctors 'Always' Communicated Well	(a)	82%	-	80%
Home Recovery Information Given	(a)	85%	-	82%
Hospital Given 9 or 10 on 10 Point Scale	(a)	75%	-	67%
Meds 'Always' Explained Before Given	(a)	62%	-	60%
Nurses 'Always' Communicated Well	(a)	82%	-	76%
Pain 'Always' Well Controlled	(a)	75%	-	69%
Room and Bathroom 'Always' Clean	(a)	80%	-	71%
Timely Help 'Always' Received	(a)	72%	-	64%
Would Definitely Recommend Hospital	(a)	70%	-	69%

Community Memorial Hospital

W180 N8085 Town Hall Rd
Menomonee Falls, WI 53051
Phone: 262-251-1000
Fax: 262-253-7169
E-mail: jkohlbeck@communitymemorial.com
URL: www.communitymemorial.com
Type: Acute Care Hospitals
Emergency Services: Yes
Ownership: Voluntary Non-Profit - Private
Beds: 237

Key Personnel:

CEO/President............... William E Bestor
Cardiac Laboratory............ Karl Raaum
Chief of Medical Staff.......... Charles Holmburg, MD
Infection Control............. Margaret Bell
Operating Room............. Saleem Bakhtiar
Quality Assurance .... Georgeann Ellison
Radiology.................. Robert Nichols

Measure	Cases	This Hosp.	State Avg.	U.S. Avg.
Heart Attack Care				
ACE Inhibitor or ARB for LVSD[1]	21	90%	97%	96%
Aspirin at Arrival	125	100%	99%	99%
Aspirin at Discharge	132	99%	99%	98%
Beta Blocker at Discharge	124	98%	99%	98%
Fibrinolytic Medication Timing	0	-	0%	55%
PCI Within 90 Minutes of Arrival	27	100%	89%	90%
Smoking Cessation Advice	26	100%	99%	99%
Chest Pain/Possible Heart Attack Care				
Aspirin at Arrival[1]	8	100%	96%	95%
Median Time to ECG (minutes)[1]	10	12	7	8
Median Time to Transfer (minutes)[5]	0	-	49	61
Fibrinolytic Medication Timing[5]	0	-	63%	54%
Heart Failure Care				
ACE Inhibitor or ARB for LVSD	71	100%	95%	94%
Discharge Instructions	152	80%	86%	88%
Evaluation of LVS Function	204	99%	97%	98%
Smoking Cessation Advice	29	97%	97%	98%
Pneumonia Care				
Appropriate Initial Antibiotic	127	95%	94%	92%
Blood Culture Timing	197	98%	97%	96%
Influenza Vaccine	135	89%	92%	91%
Initial Antibiotic Timing	213	97%	97%	95%
Pneumococcal Vaccine	217	89%	93%	93%
Smoking Cessation Advice	44	93%	95%	97%
Surgical Care Improvement Project				
Appropriate VTP Within 24 Hours[2]	193	88%	93%	92%
Appropriate Hair Removal[2]	618	100%	100%	99%
Appropriate Beta Blocker Usage[2]	176	80%	92%	93%
Controlled Postoperative Blood Glucose[2]	105	92%	93%	93%
Prophylactic Antibiotic Timing[2]	447	91%	97%	97%
Prophylactic Antibiotic Timing (Outpatient)	406	93%	91%	92%
Prophylactic Antibiotic Selection[2]	455	96%	98%	97%
Prophylactic Antibiotic Select. (Outpatient)	398	90%	96%	94%
Prophylactic Antibiotic Stopped[2]	441	95%	95%	94%
Recommended VTP Ordered[2]	193	90%	94%	94%
Urinary Catheter Removal[2]	156	76%	91%	90%
Children's Asthma Care				
Received Systemic Corticosteroids	-	-	-	100%
Received Home Management Plan	-	-	-	71%
Received Reliever Medication	-	-	-	100%
Use of Medical Imaging				
Combination Abdominal CT Scan	274	0.040	0.106	0.191
Combination Chest CT Scan	228	0.026	0.027	0.054
Follow-up Mammogram/Ultrasound	98	3.1%	8.4%	8.4%
MRI for Low Back Pain[1]	38	18.4%	31.8%	32.7%
Survey of Patients' Hospital Experiences				
Area Around Room 'Always' Quiet at Night	300+	56%	-	58%
Doctors 'Always' Communicated Well	300+	81%	-	80%
Home Recovery Information Given	300+	86%	-	82%
Hospital Given 9 or 10 on 10 Point Scale	300+	73%	-	67%
Meds 'Always' Explained Before Given	300+	61%	-	60%
Nurses 'Always' Communicated Well	300+	79%	-	76%
Pain 'Always' Well Controlled	300+	70%	-	69%
Room and Bathroom 'Always' Clean	300+	73%	-	71%
Timely Help 'Always' Received	300+	66%	-	64%
Would Definitely Recommend Hospital	300+	75%	-	69%

Red Cedar Medical Center-Mayo Health System

2321 Stout Rd
Menomonie, WI 54751
Phone: 715-235-5531
Fax: 715-233-7645
URL: www.mayohealthsystem.org
Type: Critical Access Hospitals
Emergency Services: Yes
Ownership: Voluntary Non-Profit - Private
Beds: 25

Key Personnel:

CEO/President............... Tom Miller
Chief of Medical Staff.......... D Spendsen, MD

Measure	Cases	This Hosp.	State Avg.	U.S. Avg.
Heart Attack Care				
ACE Inhibitor or ARB for LVSD[1]	1	100%	97%	96%
Aspirin at Arrival[1]	6	100%	99%	99%
Aspirin at Discharge[1]	4	100%	99%	98%
Beta Blocker at Discharge[1]	4	100%	99%	98%
Fibrinolytic Medication Timing	0	-	0%	55%
PCI Within 90 Minutes of Arrival[5]	0	-	89%	90%
Smoking Cessation Advice[1]	1	100%	99%	99%
Chest Pain/Possible Heart Attack Care				
Aspirin at Arrival	-	-	96%	95%
Median Time to ECG (minutes)	-	-	7	8
Median Time to Transfer (minutes)	-	-	49	61
Fibrinolytic Medication Timing	-	-	63%	54%
Heart Failure Care				
ACE Inhibitor or ARB for LVSD[1]	9	78%	95%	94%
Discharge Instructions	51	76%	86%	88%
Evaluation of LVS Function	79	97%	97%	98%
Smoking Cessation Advice[1]	9	100%	97%	98%
Pneumonia Care				
Appropriate Initial Antibiotic	42	100%	94%	92%
Blood Culture Timing	37	100%	97%	96%
Influenza Vaccine[1]	22	77%	92%	91%
Initial Antibiotic Timing	51	100%	97%	95%
Pneumococcal Vaccine	42	90%	93%	93%
Smoking Cessation Advice[1]	7	86%	95%	97%
Surgical Care Improvement Project				
Appropriate VTP Within 24 Hours[5]	0	-	93%	92%
Appropriate Hair Removal	125	100%	100%	99%
Appropriate Beta Blocker Usage[5]	0	-	92%	93%
Controlled Postoperative Blood Glucose	0	-	93%	93%
Prophylactic Antibiotic Timing	94	95%	97%	97%
Prophylactic Antibiotic Timing (Outpatient)	-	-	91%	92%
Prophylactic Antibiotic Selection	94	96%	98%	97%
Prophylactic Antibiotic Select. (Outpatient)	-	-	96%	94%
Prophylactic Antibiotic Stopped	94	99%	95%	94%
Recommended VTP Ordered[5]	0	-	94%	94%
Urinary Catheter Removal	34	100%	91%	90%
Children's Asthma Care				
Received Systemic Corticosteroids	-	-	-	100%
Received Home Management Plan	-	-	-	71%
Received Reliever Medication	-	-	-	100%
Use of Medical Imaging				
Combination Abdominal CT Scan	-	-	0.106	0.191
Combination Chest CT Scan	-	-	0.027	0.054
Follow-up Mammogram/Ultrasound	-	-	8.4%	8.4%
MRI for Low Back Pain	-	-	31.8%	32.7%
Survey of Patients' Hospital Experiences				
Area Around Room 'Always' Quiet at Night	300+	70%	-	58%
Doctors 'Always' Communicated Well	300+	87%	-	80%
Home Recovery Information Given	300+	87%	-	82%
Hospital Given 9 or 10 on 10 Point Scale	300+	75%	-	67%
Meds 'Always' Explained Before Given	300+	74%	-	60%
Nurses 'Always' Communicated Well	300+	81%	-	76%
Pain 'Always' Well Controlled	300+	73%	-	69%
Room and Bathroom 'Always' Clean	300+	82%	-	71%
Timely Help 'Always' Received	300+	79%	-	64%
Would Definitely Recommend Hospital	300+	73%	-	69%

NOTE: Hospital profiles are in alphabetical order by state, then city, then hospital within the city; Rankings exclude hospitals with less than 25 cases except for patient surveys which excludes hospitals with less than 100 cases; (a) 100–299 cases; (1) The number of cases is too small to be sure how well a hospital is performing; (2) The hospital indicated that the data submitted for this measure were based on a sample of cases; (3) Data was collected during a shorter time period (fewer quarters) than the maximum possible time for this measure; (4) Suppressed for one or more quarters by CMS; (5) No data is available from the hospital for this measure; (6) Fewer than 100 patients completed the HCAHPS survey. Use these rates with caution, as the number of surveys may be too low to reliably assess hospital performance; (7) Survey results are based on less than 12 months of data; (8) Survey results are not available for this reporting period; (9) No or very few patients were eligible for the HCAHPS survey. The scores shown, if any, reflect a very small number of surveys; (10) A state average was not calculated because too few hospitals in the state submitted data; (11) There were discrepancies in the data collection process; Please refer to the User's Guide for a full explanation of data.

Columbia Center

13125 N Port Washington Rd Phone: 262-243-7408
Mequon, WI 53097
URL: www.columbiacenter.org
Type: Acute Care Hospitals Emergency Services: No
Ownership: Voluntary Non-Profit - Private

Measure	Cases	This Hosp.	State Avg.	U.S. Avg.
Heart Attack Care				
ACE Inhibitor or ARB for LVSD[5]	0	-	97%	96%
Aspirin at Arrival[5]	0	-	99%	99%
Aspirin at Discharge[5]	0	-	99%	98%
Beta Blocker at Discharge[5]	0	-	99%	98%
Fibrinolytic Medication Timing[5]	0	-	0%	55%
PCI Within 90 Minutes of Arrival[5]	0	-	89%	90%
Smoking Cessation Advice[5]	0	-	99%	99%
Chest Pain/Possible Heart Attack Care				
Aspirin at Arrival[5]	0	-	96%	95%
Median Time to ECG (minutes)[5]	0	-	7	8
Median Time to Transfer (minutes)[5]	0	-	49	61
Fibrinolytic Medication Timing[5]	0	-	63%	54%
Heart Failure Care				
ACE Inhibitor or ARB for LVSD[5]	0	-	95%	94%
Discharge Instructions[5]	0	-	86%	88%
Evaluation of LVS Function[5]	0	-	97%	98%
Smoking Cessation Advice[5]	0	-	97%	98%
Pneumonia Care				
Appropriate Initial Antibiotic[5]	0	-	94%	92%
Blood Culture Timing[5]	0	-	97%	96%
Influenza Vaccine[5]	0	-	92%	91%
Initial Antibiotic Timing[5]	0	-	97%	95%
Pneumococcal Vaccine[5]	0	-	93%	93%
Smoking Cessation Advice[5]	0	-	95%	97%
Surgical Care Improvement Project				
Appropriate VTP Within 24 Hours[5]	0	-	93%	92%
Appropriate Hair Removal[5]	0	-	100%	99%
Appropriate Beta Blocker Usage[5]	0	-	92%	93%
Controlled Postoperative Blood Glucose[5]	0	-	93%	93%
Prophylactic Antibiotic Timing[5]	0	-	97%	97%
Prophylactic Antibiotic Timing (Outpatient)[5]	0	-	91%	92%
Prophylactic Antibiotic Selection[5]	0	-	98%	97%
Prophylactic Antibiotic Select. (Outpatient)[5]	0	-	96%	94%
Prophylactic Antibiotic Stopped[5]	0	-	95%	94%
Recommended VTP Ordered[5]	0	-	94%	94%
Urinary Catheter Removal[5]	0	-	91%	90%
Children's Asthma Care				
Received Systemic Corticosteroids	-	-	-	100%
Received Home Management Plan	-	-	-	71%
Received Reliever Medication	-	-	-	100%
Use of Medical Imaging				
Combination Abdominal CT Scan[5]	0	-	0.106	0.191
Combination Chest CT Scan[5]	0	-	0.027	0.054
Follow-up Mammogram/Ultrasound[5]	0	-	8.4%	8.4%
MRI for Low Back Pain[5]	0	-	31.8%	32.7%
Survey of Patients' Hospital Experiences				
Area Around Room 'Always' Quiet at Night	300+	73%	-	58%
Doctors 'Always' Communicated Well	300+	90%	-	80%
Home Recovery Information Given	300+	89%	-	82%
Hospital Given 9 or 10 on 10 Point Scale	300+	89%	-	67%
Meds 'Always' Explained Before Given	300+	72%	-	60%
Nurses 'Always' Communicated Well	300+	84%	-	76%
Pain 'Always' Well Controlled	300+	80%	-	69%
Room and Bathroom 'Always' Clean	300+	79%	-	71%
Timely Help 'Always' Received	300+	78%	-	64%
Would Definitely Recommend Hospital	300+	91%	-	69%

Columbia St Mary's Hospital Ozaukee

13111 N Port Washington Rd Phone: 262-243-7300
Mequon, WI 53097
Type: Acute Care Hospitals Emergency Services: Yes
Ownership: Voluntary Non-Profit - Church
Key Personnel:
CEO/President. . . . . Leo Brideau

Measure	Cases	This Hosp.	State Avg.	U.S. Avg.
Heart Attack Care				
ACE Inhibitor or ARB for LVSD	33	97%	97%	96%
Aspirin at Arrival	190	99%	99%	99%
Aspirin at Discharge	212	98%	99%	98%
Beta Blocker at Discharge	213	96%	99%	98%
Fibrinolytic Medication Timing	0	-	0%	55%
PCI Within 90 Minutes of Arrival	49	76%	89%	90%
Smoking Cessation Advice	55	98%	99%	99%
Chest Pain/Possible Heart Attack Care				
Aspirin at Arrival[1,3]	4	75%	96%	95%
Median Time to ECG (minutes)[1,3]	4	6	7	8
Median Time to Transfer (minutes)[1,3]	1	430	49	61
Fibrinolytic Medication Timing[3]	0	-	63%	54%
Heart Failure Care				
ACE Inhibitor or ARB for LVSD	82	94%	95%	94%
Discharge Instructions	163	75%	86%	88%
Evaluation of LVS Function	247	95%	97%	98%
Smoking Cessation Advice[1]	23	74%	97%	98%
Pneumonia Care				
Appropriate Initial Antibiotic	121	85%	94%	92%
Blood Culture Timing	180	98%	97%	96%
Influenza Vaccine	113	92%	92%	91%
Initial Antibiotic Timing	196	98%	97%	95%
Pneumococcal Vaccine	195	84%	93%	93%
Smoking Cessation Advice	43	84%	95%	97%
Surgical Care Improvement Project				
Appropriate VTP Within 24 Hours[2]	184	89%	93%	92%
Appropriate Hair Removal[2]	553	100%	100%	99%
Appropriate Beta Blocker Usage[2]	159	79%	92%	93%
Controlled Postoperative Blood Glucose[2]	131	92%	93%	93%
Prophylactic Antibiotic Timing[2]	407	95%	97%	97%
Prophylactic Antibiotic Timing (Outpatient)	124	87%	91%	92%
Prophylactic Antibiotic Selection[2]	408	98%	98%	97%
Prophylactic Antibiotic Select. (Outpatient)	114	96%	96%	94%
Prophylactic Antibiotic Stopped[2]	393	92%	95%	94%
Recommended VTP Ordered[2]	184	93%	94%	94%
Urinary Catheter Removal[2]	134	96%	91%	90%
Children's Asthma Care				
Received Systemic Corticosteroids	-	-	-	100%
Received Home Management Plan	-	-	-	71%
Received Reliever Medication	-	-	-	100%
Use of Medical Imaging				
Combination Abdominal CT Scan	754	0.080	0.106	0.191
Combination Chest CT Scan	874	0.007	0.027	0.054
Follow-up Mammogram/Ultrasound	1,153	9.2%	8.4%	8.4%
MRI for Low Back Pain	132	24.2%	31.8%	32.7%
Survey of Patients' Hospital Experiences				
Area Around Room 'Always' Quiet at Night	300+	49%	-	58%
Doctors 'Always' Communicated Well	300+	82%	-	80%
Home Recovery Information Given	300+	79%	-	82%
Hospital Given 9 or 10 on 10 Point Scale	300+	69%	-	67%
Meds 'Always' Explained Before Given	300+	59%	-	60%
Nurses 'Always' Communicated Well	300+	77%	-	76%
Pain 'Always' Well Controlled	300+	68%	-	69%
Room and Bathroom 'Always' Clean	300+	68%	-	71%
Timely Help 'Always' Received	300+	57%	-	64%
Would Definitely Recommend Hospital	300+	74%	-	69%

Good Samaritan Health Center

601 S Center Ave Phone: 715-536-5511
Merrill, WI 54452 Fax: 715-539-2170
Type: Critical Access Hospitals Emergency Services: Yes
Ownership: Voluntary Non-Profit - Church Beds: 73
Key Personnel:
CEO/President. . . . . Michael Hammer
Chief of Medical Staff . . . . Ronald Krajnik
Infection Control. . . . . Cheryl Jahns, RN
Operating Room. . . . . Cheryl Johns
Anesthesiology. . . . . James J Schuh, MD
Emergency Room . . . . Jeffrey Moore, MD

Measure	Cases	This Hosp.	State Avg.	U.S. Avg.
Heart Attack Care				
ACE Inhibitor or ARB for LVSD[1]	1	100%	97%	96%
Aspirin at Arrival[1]	2	100%	99%	99%
Aspirin at Discharge[1]	3	100%	99%	98%
Beta Blocker at Discharge[1]	3	100%	99%	98%
Fibrinolytic Medication Timing	0	-	0%	55%
PCI Within 90 Minutes of Arrival	0	-	89%	90%
Smoking Cessation Advice[1]	1	100%	99%	99%
Chest Pain/Possible Heart Attack Care				
Aspirin at Arrival[5]	0	-	96%	95%
Median Time to ECG (minutes)[5]	0	-	7	8
Median Time to Transfer (minutes)[5]	0	-	49	61
Fibrinolytic Medication Timing[5]	0	-	63%	54%
Heart Failure Care				
ACE Inhibitor or ARB for LVSD[1]	5	100%	95%	94%
Discharge Instructions[1]	16	100%	86%	88%
Evaluation of LVS Function	25	100%	97%	98%
Smoking Cessation Advice[1]	1	100%	97%	98%
Pneumonia Care				
Appropriate Initial Antibiotic[1]	24	100%	94%	92%
Blood Culture Timing	41	100%	97%	96%
Influenza Vaccine[1]	15	100%	92%	91%
Initial Antibiotic Timing	49	100%	97%	95%
Pneumococcal Vaccine	29	100%	93%	93%
Smoking Cessation Advice[1]	16	100%	95%	97%
Surgical Care Improvement Project				
Appropriate VTP Within 24 Hours[1,2]	21	100%	93%	92%
Appropriate Hair Removal[2]	72	100%	100%	99%
Appropriate Beta Blocker Usage[1,2]	18	100%	92%	93%
Controlled Postoperative Blood Glucose[2]	0	-	93%	93%
Prophylactic Antibiotic Timing[2]	45	100%	97%	97%
Prophylactic Antibiotic Timing (Outpatient)[5]	0	-	91%	92%
Prophylactic Antibiotic Selection[2]	45	100%	98%	97%
Prophylactic Antibiotic Select. (Outpatient)[5]	0	-	96%	94%
Prophylactic Antibiotic Stopped[2]	45	100%	95%	94%
Recommended VTP Ordered[1,2]	21	100%	94%	94%
Urinary Catheter Removal[1,2]	4	100%	91%	90%
Children's Asthma Care				
Received Systemic Corticosteroids	-	-	-	100%
Received Home Management Plan	-	-	-	71%
Received Reliever Medication	-	-	-	100%
Use of Medical Imaging				
Combination Abdominal CT Scan	157	0.070	0.106	0.191
Combination Chest CT Scan	66	0.030	0.027	0.054
Follow-up Mammogram/Ultrasound	369	3.8%	8.4%	8.4%
MRI for Low Back Pain[1]	33	39.4%	31.8%	32.7%
Survey of Patients' Hospital Experiences				
Area Around Room 'Always' Quiet at Night	(a)	62%	-	58%
Doctors 'Always' Communicated Well	(a)	83%	-	80%
Home Recovery Information Given	(a)	88%	-	82%
Hospital Given 9 or 10 on 10 Point Scale	(a)	67%	-	67%
Meds 'Always' Explained Before Given	(a)	65%	-	60%
Nurses 'Always' Communicated Well	(a)	78%	-	76%
Pain 'Always' Well Controlled	(a)	63%	-	69%
Room and Bathroom 'Always' Clean	(a)	76%	-	71%
Timely Help 'Always' Received	(a)	69%	-	64%
Would Definitely Recommend Hospital	(a)	63%	-	69%

NOTE: Hospital profiles are in alphabetical order by state, then city, then hospital within the city; Rankings exclude hospitals with less than 25 cases except for patient surveys which excludes hospitals with less than 100 cases; (a) 100–299 cases; (1) The number of cases is too small to be sure how well a hospital is performing; (2) The hospital indicated that the data submitted for this measure were based on a sample of cases; (3) Data was collected during a shorter time period (fewer quarters) than the maximum possible time for this measure; (4) Suppressed for one or more quarters by CMS; (5) No data is available from the hospital for this measure; (6) Fewer than 100 patients completed the HCAHPS survey. Use these rates with caution, as the number of surveys may be too low to reliably assess hospital performance; (7) Survey results are based on less than 12 months of data; (8) Survey results are not available for this reporting period; (9) No or very few patients were eligible for the HCAHPS survey. The scores shown, if any, reflect a very small number of surveys; (10) A state average was not calculated because too few hospitals in the state submitted data; (11) There were discrepancies in the data collection process; Please refer to the User's Guide for a full explanation of data.

Aurora St Lukes Medical Center

2900 W Oklahoma Ave Phone: 414-649-6000
Milwaukee, WI 53215 Fax: 414-649-7982
URL: www.aurorahealthcare.org
Type: Acute Care Hospitals Emergency Services: Yes
Ownership: Voluntary Non-Profit - Private Beds: 600

Key Personnel:
CEO/President. . . . . Mark Ambrosius
Chief of Medical Staff . . . . Ann Tylenda
Infection Control. . . . . Lousie Cunningham
Operating Room. . . . . Lisa Hillyer, RN
Pediatric Ambulatory Care . . . . . . Ruth Rademacher
Pediatric In-Patient Care . . . . . . Ruth Rademacher
Quality Assurance . . . . Kathy Ptak
Emergency Room . . . . Heidi J Harkins

Measure	Cases	This Hosp.	State Avg.	U.S. Avg.
Heart Attack Care				
ACE Inhibitor or ARB for LVSD	157	100%	97%	96%
Aspirin at Arrival	615	100%	99%	99%
Aspirin at Discharge	1,006	100%	99%	98%
Beta Blocker at Discharge	952	100%	99%	98%
Fibrinolytic Medication Timing	0	-	0%	55%
PCI Within 90 Minutes of Arrival	93	95%	89%	90%
Smoking Cessation Advice	328	100%	99%	99%
Chest Pain/Possible Heart Attack Care				
Aspirin at Arrival[1,3]	7	100%	96%	95%
Median Time to ECG (minutes)[1,3]	7	6	7	8
Median Time to Transfer (minutes)[5]	0	-	49	61
Fibrinolytic Medication Timing[5]	0	-	63%	54%
Heart Failure Care				
ACE Inhibitor or ARB for LVSD	545	98%	95%	94%
Discharge Instructions	1,201	90%	86%	88%
Evaluation of LVS Function	1,435	100%	97%	98%
Smoking Cessation Advice	288	100%	97%	98%
Pneumonia Care				
Appropriate Initial Antibiotic	488	95%	94%	92%
Blood Culture Timing	752	99%	97%	96%
Influenza Vaccine	520	95%	92%	91%
Initial Antibiotic Timing	894	99%	97%	95%
Pneumococcal Vaccine	684	98%	93%	93%
Smoking Cessation Advice	364	99%	95%	97%
Surgical Care Improvement Project				
Appropriate VTP Within 24 Hours[2]	597	95%	93%	92%
Appropriate Hair Removal[2]	2,572	100%	100%	99%
Appropriate Beta Blocker Usage[2]	936	97%	92%	93%
Controlled Postoperative Blood Glucose[2]	606	97%	93%	93%
Prophylactic Antibiotic Timing[2]	1,970	99%	97%	97%
Prophylactic Antibiotic Timing (Outpatient)	1,058	91%	91%	92%
Prophylactic Antibiotic Selection[2]	1,997	98%	98%	97%
Prophylactic Antibiotic Select. (Outpatient)	1,031	96%	96%	94%
Prophylactic Antibiotic Stopped[2]	1,894	97%	95%	94%
Recommended VTP Ordered[2]	603	97%	94%	94%
Urinary Catheter Removal[2]	781	95%	91%	90%
Children's Asthma Care				
Received Systemic Corticosteroids	-	-	-	100%
Received Home Management Plan	-	-	-	71%
Received Reliever Medication	-	-	-	100%
Use of Medical Imaging				
Combination Abdominal CT Scan	2,729	0.090	0.106	0.191
Combination Chest CT Scan	2,789	0.011	0.027	0.054
Follow-up Mammogram/Ultrasound	2,244	7.4%	8.4%	8.4%
MRI for Low Back Pain	345	27.8%	31.8%	32.7%
Survey of Patients' Hospital Experiences				
Area Around Room 'Always' Quiet at Night	300+	47%	-	58%
Doctors 'Always' Communicated Well	300+	74%	-	80%
Home Recovery Information Given	300+	85%	-	82%
Hospital Given 9 or 10 on 10 Point Scale	300+	65%	-	67%
Meds 'Always' Explained Before Given	300+	59%	-	60%
Nurses 'Always' Communicated Well	300+	73%	-	76%
Pain 'Always' Well Controlled	300+	65%	-	69%
Room and Bathroom 'Always' Clean	300+	68%	-	71%
Timely Help 'Always' Received	300+	53%	-	64%
Would Definitely Recommend Hospital	300+	70%	-	69%

Columbia St Marys Hospital Milwaukee (Col & Milw Campus)

2323 N Lake Dr Phone: 414-291-1210
Milwaukee, WI 53211 Fax: 414-291-1048
URL: columbia-stmarys.com
Type: Acute Care Hospitals Emergency Services: Yes
Ownership: Voluntary Non-Profit - Church Beds: 314

Key Personnel:
CEO/President. . . . . Sr Bernice Coreil, DC
Coronary Care . . . . Andrew W Allen
Operating Room. . . . . Jane Ryan
Quality Assurance . . . . James K Beckmann, Jr

Measure	Cases	This Hosp.	State Avg.	U.S. Avg.
Heart Attack Care				
ACE Inhibitor or ARB for LVSD	31	94%	97%	96%
Aspirin at Arrival	115	100%	99%	99%
Aspirin at Discharge	146	100%	99%	98%
Beta Blocker at Discharge	145	98%	99%	98%
Fibrinolytic Medication Timing	0	-	0%	55%
PCI Within 90 Minutes of Arrival[1]	17	53%	89%	90%
Smoking Cessation Advice	43	98%	99%	99%
Chest Pain/Possible Heart Attack Care				
Aspirin at Arrival[1,3]	4	75%	96%	95%
Median Time to ECG (minutes)[1,3]	4	10	7	8
Median Time to Transfer (minutes)[5]	0	-	49	61
Fibrinolytic Medication Timing[5]	0	-	63%	54%
Heart Failure Care				
ACE Inhibitor or ARB for LVSD	139	96%	95%	94%
Discharge Instructions	264	78%	86%	88%
Evaluation of LVS Function	332	97%	97%	98%
Smoking Cessation Advice	65	91%	97%	98%
Pneumonia Care				
Appropriate Initial Antibiotic	154	90%	94%	92%
Blood Culture Timing	225	96%	97%	96%
Influenza Vaccine	144	94%	92%	91%
Initial Antibiotic Timing	252	97%	97%	95%
Pneumococcal Vaccine	188	90%	93%	93%
Smoking Cessation Advice	72	88%	95%	97%
Surgical Care Improvement Project				
Appropriate VTP Within 24 Hours[2]	323	85%	93%	92%
Appropriate Hair Removal[2]	800	100%	100%	99%
Appropriate Beta Blocker Usage[2]	234	81%	92%	93%
Controlled Postoperative Blood Glucose[2]	112	93%	93%	93%
Prophylactic Antibiotic Timing[2]	552	95%	97%	97%
Prophylactic Antibiotic Timing (Outpatient)	391	89%	91%	92%
Prophylactic Antibiotic Selection[2]	560	98%	98%	97%
Prophylactic Antibiotic Select. (Outpatient)	394	91%	96%	94%
Prophylactic Antibiotic Stopped[2]	540	92%	95%	94%
Recommended VTP Ordered[2]	323	93%	94%	94%
Urinary Catheter Removal[2]	191	86%	91%	90%
Children's Asthma Care				
Received Systemic Corticosteroids	-	-	-	100%
Received Home Management Plan	-	-	-	71%
Received Reliever Medication	-	-	-	100%
Use of Medical Imaging				
Combination Abdominal CT Scan	1,088	0.083	0.106	0.191
Combination Chest CT Scan	944	0.008	0.027	0.054
Follow-up Mammogram/Ultrasound	3,028	9.9%	8.4%	8.4%
MRI for Low Back Pain	264	30.7%	31.8%	32.7%
Survey of Patients' Hospital Experiences				
Area Around Room 'Always' Quiet at Night	300+	57%	-	58%
Doctors 'Always' Communicated Well	300+	79%	-	80%
Home Recovery Information Given	300+	82%	-	82%
Hospital Given 9 or 10 on 10 Point Scale	300+	60%	-	67%
Meds 'Always' Explained Before Given	300+	62%	-	60%
Nurses 'Always' Communicated Well	300+	73%	-	76%
Pain 'Always' Well Controlled	300+	66%	-	69%
Room and Bathroom 'Always' Clean	300+	60%	-	71%
Timely Help 'Always' Received	300+	58%	-	64%
Would Definitely Recommend Hospital	300+	63%	-	69%

Froedtert Memorial Lutheran Hospital

9200 W Wisconsin Ave Phone: 414-805-3000
Milwaukee, WI 53226 Fax: 414-805-7790
URL: www.froedtert.com
Type: Acute Care Hospitals Emergency Services: Yes
Ownership: Voluntary Non-Profit - Private Beds: 413

Key Personnel:
CEO/President. . . . . William D Petasnick
Chief of Medical Staff . . . . Marcelle Neuberg, MD
Coronary Care . . . . Safwan Jaradeh, MD
Infection Control. . . . . Michael Frank, MD
Pediatric Ambulatory Care . . . . . . Robert M Kliegman, MD
Pediatric In-Patient Care . . . . . . Robert M Kliegman, MD
Quality Assurance . . . . Mary Wolbert
Radiology. . . . . James Youker, MD

Measure	Cases	This Hosp.	State Avg.	U.S. Avg.
Heart Attack Care				
ACE Inhibitor or ARB for LVSD	31	100%	97%	96%
Aspirin at Arrival	159	99%	99%	99%
Aspirin at Discharge	195	99%	99%	98%
Beta Blocker at Discharge	192	98%	99%	98%
Fibrinolytic Medication Timing	0	-	0%	55%
PCI Within 90 Minutes of Arrival[1]	23	70%	89%	90%
Smoking Cessation Advice	73	92%	99%	99%
Chest Pain/Possible Heart Attack Care				
Aspirin at Arrival[1]	3	67%	96%	95%
Median Time to ECG (minutes)[1]	3	82	7	8
Median Time to Transfer (minutes)[5]	0	-	49	61
Fibrinolytic Medication Timing[5]	0	-	63%	54%
Heart Failure Care				
ACE Inhibitor or ARB for LVSD[2]	119	97%	95%	94%
Discharge Instructions[2]	255	75%	86%	88%
Evaluation of LVS Function[2]	300	99%	97%	98%
Smoking Cessation Advice[2]	76	88%	97%	98%
Pneumonia Care				
Appropriate Initial Antibiotic[2]	80	99%	94%	92%
Blood Culture Timing[2]	151	94%	97%	96%
Influenza Vaccine[2]	105	94%	92%	91%
Initial Antibiotic Timing[2]	197	96%	97%	95%
Pneumococcal Vaccine[2]	130	92%	93%	93%
Smoking Cessation Advice[2]	63	75%	95%	97%
Surgical Care Improvement Project				
Appropriate VTP Within 24 Hours[2]	267	93%	93%	92%
Appropriate Hair Removal[2]	753	100%	100%	99%
Appropriate Beta Blocker Usage[2]	240	93%	92%	93%
Controlled Postoperative Blood Glucose[2]	159	84%	93%	93%
Prophylactic Antibiotic Timing[2]	453	93%	97%	97%
Prophylactic Antibiotic Timing (Outpatient)	472	91%	91%	92%
Prophylactic Antibiotic Selection[2]	470	97%	98%	97%
Prophylactic Antibiotic Select. (Outpatient)	572	94%	96%	94%
Prophylactic Antibiotic Stopped[2]	427	94%	95%	94%
Recommended VTP Ordered[2]	271	95%	94%	94%
Urinary Catheter Removal[2]	166	84%	91%	90%
Children's Asthma Care				
Received Systemic Corticosteroids	-	-	-	100%
Received Home Management Plan	-	-	-	71%
Received Reliever Medication	-	-	-	100%
Use of Medical Imaging				
Combination Abdominal CT Scan	2,119	0.134	0.106	0.191
Combination Chest CT Scan	2,078	0.002	0.027	0.054
Follow-up Mammogram/Ultrasound	1,374	6.9%	8.4%	8.4%
MRI for Low Back Pain	203	27.1%	31.8%	32.7%
Survey of Patients' Hospital Experiences				
Area Around Room 'Always' Quiet at Night	300+	49%	-	58%
Doctors 'Always' Communicated Well	300+	79%	-	80%
Home Recovery Information Given	300+	85%	-	82%
Hospital Given 9 or 10 on 10 Point Scale	300+	75%	-	67%
Meds 'Always' Explained Before Given	300+	60%	-	60%
Nurses 'Always' Communicated Well	300+	80%	-	76%
Pain 'Always' Well Controlled	300+	72%	-	69%
Room and Bathroom 'Always' Clean	300+	64%	-	71%
Timely Help 'Always' Received	300+	63%	-	64%
Would Definitely Recommend Hospital	300+	81%	-	69%

NOTE: Hospital profiles are in alphabetical order by state, then city, then hospital within the city; Rankings exclude hospitals with less than 25 cases except for patient surveys which excludes hospitals with less than 100 cases; (a) 100–299 cases; (1) The number of cases is too small to be sure how well a hospital is performing; (2) The hospital indicated that the data submitted for this measure were based on a sample of cases; (3) Data was collected during a shorter time period (fewer quarters) than the maximum possible time for this measure; (4) Suppressed for one or more quarters by CMS; (5) No data is available from the hospital for this measure; (6) Fewer than 100 patients completed the HCAHPS survey. Use these rates with caution, as the number of surveys may be too low to reliably assess hospital performance; (7) Survey results are based on less than 12 months of data; (8) Survey results are not available for this reporting period; (9) No or very few patients were eligible for the HCAHPS survey. The scores shown, if any, reflect a very small number of surveys; (10) A state average was not calculated because too few hospitals in the state submitted data; (11) There were discrepancies in the data collection process; Please refer to the User's Guide for a full explanation of data.

Milwaukee VA Medical Center

5000 W. National Avenue
Milwaukee, WI 53295
Phone: 414-384-2000
URL: www.milwaukee.va.gov
Type: Acute Care-Veterans Administration
Emergency Services: No
Ownership: Government - Federal
Beds: 168

Measure	Cases	This Hosp.	State Avg.	U.S. Avg.
Heart Attack Care				
ACE Inhibitor or ARB for LVSD[1]	9	100%	97%	96%
Aspirin at Arrival	37	100%	99%	99%
Aspirin at Discharge	39	100%	99%	98%
Beta Blocker at Discharge	36	100%	99%	98%
Fibrinolytic Medication Timing[5]	0	-	0%	55%
PCI Within 90 Minutes of Arrival[1]	5	0%	89%	90%
Smoking Cessation Advice[1]	13	100%	99%	99%
Chest Pain/Possible Heart Attack Care				
Aspirin at Arrival	-	-	96%	95%
Median Time to ECG (minutes)	-	-	7	8
Median Time to Transfer (minutes)	-	-	49	61
Fibrinolytic Medication Timing	-	-	63%	54%
Heart Failure Care				
ACE Inhibitor or ARB for LVSD	84	96%	95%	94%
Discharge Instructions	215	97%	86%	88%
Evaluation of LVS Function	218	100%	97%	98%
Smoking Cessation Advice	47	100%	97%	98%
Pneumonia Care				
Appropriate Initial Antibiotic	69	97%	94%	92%
Blood Culture Timing	77	100%	97%	96%
Influenza Vaccine	67	100%	92%	91%
Initial Antibiotic Timing	103	87%	97%	95%
Pneumococcal Vaccine	67	100%	93%	93%
Smoking Cessation Advice	46	98%	95%	97%
Surgical Care Improvement Project				
Appropriate VTP Within 24 Hours[2]	172	98%	93%	92%
Appropriate Hair Removal[2]	295	99%	100%	99%
Appropriate Beta Blocker Usage[2]	113	88%	92%	93%
Controlled Postoperative Blood Glucose[2]	46	98%	93%	93%
Prophylactic Antibiotic Timing	208	93%	97%	97%
Prophylactic Antibiotic Timing (Outpatient)	-	-	91%	92%
Prophylactic Antibiotic Selection	209	100%	98%	97%
Prophylactic Antibiotic Select. (Outpatient)	-	-	96%	94%
Prophylactic Antibiotic Stopped	207	93%	95%	94%
Recommended VTP Ordered[2]	172	99%	94%	94%
Urinary Catheter Removal[2]	138	93%	91%	90%
Children's Asthma Care				
Received Systemic Corticosteroids	-	-	-	100%
Received Home Management Plan	-	-	-	71%
Received Reliever Medication	-	-	-	100%
Use of Medical Imaging				
Combination Abdominal CT Scan	-	-	0.106	0.191
Combination Chest CT Scan	-	-	0.027	0.054
Follow-up Mammogram/Ultrasound	-	-	8.4%	8.4%
MRI for Low Back Pain	-	-	31.8%	32.7%
Survey of Patients' Hospital Experiences				
Area Around Room 'Always' Quiet at Night	-	-	-	58%
Doctors 'Always' Communicated Well	-	-	-	80%
Home Recovery Information Given	-	-	-	82%
Hospital Given 9 or 10 on 10 Point Scale	-	-	-	67%
Meds 'Always' Explained Before Given	-	-	-	60%
Nurses 'Always' Communicated Well	-	-	-	76%
Pain 'Always' Well Controlled	-	-	-	69%
Room and Bathroom 'Always' Clean	-	-	-	71%
Timely Help 'Always' Received	-	-	-	64%
Would Definitely Recommend Hospital	-	-	-	69%

Wheaton Franciscan - St Joseph

5000 W Chambers St
Milwaukee, WI 53210
Phone: 414-447-2000
Fax: 414-874-4394
URL: www.wfhealthcare.org
Type: Acute Care Hospitals
Emergency Services: Yes
Ownership: Voluntary Non-Profit - Church
Beds: 595

Key Personnel:
CEO/President. . . . . Debra Standridge
Cardiac Laboratory. . . . . David Kasun
Chief of Medical Staff . . . . Tod Poremski, MD
Infection Control. . . . . Mary Luzinski
Operating Room. . . . . Kathy Madsen
Quality Assurance . . . . Patty Vail
Radiology. . . . . Rob Weisbecker

Measure	Cases	This Hosp.	State Avg.	U.S. Avg.
Heart Attack Care				
ACE Inhibitor or ARB for LVSD[1]	23	96%	97%	96%
Aspirin at Arrival	177	99%	99%	99%
Aspirin at Discharge	213	100%	99%	98%
Beta Blocker at Discharge	202	99%	99%	98%
Fibrinolytic Medication Timing	0	-	0%	55%
PCI Within 90 Minutes of Arrival	48	83%	89%	90%
Smoking Cessation Advice	78	97%	99%	99%
Chest Pain/Possible Heart Attack Care				
Aspirin at Arrival[1]	22	64%	96%	95%
Median Time to ECG (minutes)	25	10	7	8
Median Time to Transfer (minutes)[5]	0	-	49	61
Fibrinolytic Medication Timing[5]	0	-	63%	54%
Heart Failure Care				
ACE Inhibitor or ARB for LVSD	233	96%	95%	94%
Discharge Instructions	450	83%	86%	88%
Evaluation of LVS Function	524	99%	97%	98%
Smoking Cessation Advice	203	100%	97%	98%
Pneumonia Care				
Appropriate Initial Antibiotic	138	100%	94%	92%
Blood Culture Timing	291	98%	97%	96%
Influenza Vaccine	130	92%	92%	91%
Initial Antibiotic Timing	276	99%	97%	95%
Pneumococcal Vaccine	176	94%	93%	93%
Smoking Cessation Advice	162	95%	95%	97%
Surgical Care Improvement Project				
Appropriate VTP Within 24 Hours[2]	303	95%	93%	92%
Appropriate Hair Removal[2]	787	100%	100%	99%
Appropriate Beta Blocker Usage[2]	220	97%	92%	93%
Controlled Postoperative Blood Glucose[2]	159	99%	93%	93%
Prophylactic Antibiotic Timing[2]	452	98%	97%	97%
Prophylactic Antibiotic Timing (Outpatient)	561	94%	91%	92%
Prophylactic Antibiotic Selection[2]	455	100%	98%	97%
Prophylactic Antibiotic Select. (Outpatient)	551	99%	96%	94%
Prophylactic Antibiotic Stopped[2]	413	97%	95%	94%
Recommended VTP Ordered[2]	303	98%	94%	94%
Urinary Catheter Removal[2]	103	80%	91%	90%
Children's Asthma Care				
Received Systemic Corticosteroids	-	-	-	100%
Received Home Management Plan	-	-	-	71%
Received Reliever Medication	-	-	-	100%
Use of Medical Imaging				
Combination Abdominal CT Scan	533	0.178	0.106	0.191
Combination Chest CT Scan	346	0.069	0.027	0.054
Follow-up Mammogram/Ultrasound	1,726	9.6%	8.4%	8.4%
MRI for Low Back Pain	132	27.3%	31.8%	32.7%
Survey of Patients' Hospital Experiences				
Area Around Room 'Always' Quiet at Night	300+	69%	-	58%
Doctors 'Always' Communicated Well	300+	79%	-	80%
Home Recovery Information Given	300+	84%	-	82%
Hospital Given 9 or 10 on 10 Point Scale	300+	67%	-	67%
Meds 'Always' Explained Before Given	300+	64%	-	60%
Nurses 'Always' Communicated Well	300+	77%	-	76%
Pain 'Always' Well Controlled	300+	70%	-	69%
Room and Bathroom 'Always' Clean	300+	67%	-	71%
Timely Help 'Always' Received	300+	66%	-	64%
Would Definitely Recommend Hospital	300+	71%	-	69%

Wheaton Franciscan Healthcare - St Francis

3237 S 16th St
Milwaukee, WI 53215
Phone: 414-647-5000
Fax: 414-647-5565
URL: www.mywheaton.org
Type: Acute Care Hospitals
Emergency Services: Yes
Ownership: Voluntary Non-Profit - Church
Beds: 260

Key Personnel:
Chief of Medical Staff . . . . Parmod Kumar, MD
Infection Control. . . . . Pat Skonieczny, RN
Operating Room. . . . . Jean Tetlaff, RN
Pediatric Ambulatory Care . . . . . . Chandra Shivpuri, MD
Quality Assurance . . . . Joanne Mercer
Radiology. . . . . Bruce Cardone, MD

Measure	Cases	This Hosp.	State Avg.	U.S. Avg.
Heart Attack Care				
ACE Inhibitor or ARB for LVSD[1]	17	94%	97%	96%
Aspirin at Arrival	77	99%	99%	99%
Aspirin at Discharge	73	97%	99%	98%
Beta Blocker at Discharge	78	99%	99%	98%
Fibrinolytic Medication Timing	0	-	0%	55%
PCI Within 90 Minutes of Arrival[1]	19	74%	89%	90%
Smoking Cessation Advice	27	96%	99%	99%
Chest Pain/Possible Heart Attack Care				
Aspirin at Arrival[1]	9	100%	96%	95%
Median Time to ECG (minutes)[1]	10	4	7	8
Median Time to Transfer (minutes)[5]	0	-	49	61
Fibrinolytic Medication Timing[5]	0	-	63%	54%
Heart Failure Care				
ACE Inhibitor or ARB for LVSD	73	95%	95%	94%
Discharge Instructions	144	84%	86%	88%
Evaluation of LVS Function	189	99%	97%	98%
Smoking Cessation Advice	28	100%	97%	98%
Pneumonia Care				
Appropriate Initial Antibiotic	99	97%	94%	92%
Blood Culture Timing	170	97%	97%	96%
Influenza Vaccine	123	93%	92%	91%
Initial Antibiotic Timing	160	98%	97%	95%
Pneumococcal Vaccine	174	95%	93%	93%
Smoking Cessation Advice	62	92%	95%	97%
Surgical Care Improvement Project				
Appropriate VTP Within 24 Hours[2]	147	84%	93%	92%
Appropriate Hair Removal[2]	503	100%	100%	99%
Appropriate Beta Blocker Usage[2]	129	93%	92%	93%
Controlled Postoperative Blood Glucose[2]	59	85%	93%	93%
Prophylactic Antibiotic Timing[2]	327	95%	97%	97%
Prophylactic Antibiotic Timing (Outpatient)	288	93%	91%	92%
Prophylactic Antibiotic Selection[2]	329	98%	98%	97%
Prophylactic Antibiotic Select. (Outpatient)	281	97%	96%	94%
Prophylactic Antibiotic Stopped[2]	301	94%	95%	94%
Recommended VTP Ordered[2]	147	92%	94%	94%
Urinary Catheter Removal[2]	49	80%	91%	90%
Children's Asthma Care				
Received Systemic Corticosteroids	-	-	-	100%
Received Home Management Plan	-	-	-	71%
Received Reliever Medication	-	-	-	100%
Use of Medical Imaging				
Combination Abdominal CT Scan	410	0.568	0.106	0.191
Combination Chest CT Scan	289	0.038	0.027	0.054
Follow-up Mammogram/Ultrasound	1,044	15.7%	8.4%	8.4%
MRI for Low Back Pain	88	31.8%	31.8%	32.7%
Survey of Patients' Hospital Experiences				
Area Around Room 'Always' Quiet at Night	300+	50%	-	58%
Doctors 'Always' Communicated Well	300+	77%	-	80%
Home Recovery Information Given	300+	82%	-	82%
Hospital Given 9 or 10 on 10 Point Scale	300+	55%	-	67%
Meds 'Always' Explained Before Given	300+	57%	-	60%
Nurses 'Always' Communicated Well	300+	71%	-	76%
Pain 'Always' Well Controlled	300+	61%	-	69%
Room and Bathroom 'Always' Clean	300+	65%	-	71%
Timely Help 'Always' Received	300+	55%	-	64%
Would Definitely Recommend Hospital	300+	60%	-	69%

NOTE: Hospital profiles are in alphabetical order by state, then city, then hospital within the city; Rankings exclude hospitals with less than 25 cases except for patient surveys which excludes hospitals with less than 100 cases; (a) 100–299 cases; (1) The number of cases is too small to be sure how well a hospital is performing; (2) The hospital indicated that the data submitted for this measure were based on a sample of cases; (3) Data was collected during a shorter time period (fewer quarters) than the maximum possible time for this measure; (4) Suppressed for one or more quarters by CMS; (5) No data is available from the hospital for this measure; (6) Fewer than 100 patients completed the HCAHPS survey. Use these rates with caution, as the number of surveys may be too low to reliably assess hospital performance; (7) Survey results are based on less than 12 months of data; (8) Survey results are not available for this reporting period; (9) No or very few patients were eligible for the HCAHPS survey. The scores shown, if any, reflect a very small number of surveys; (10) A state average was not calculated because too few hospitals in the state submitted data; (11) There were discrepancies in the data collection process; Please refer to the User's Guide for a full explanation of data.

Monroe Clinic

515 22nd Ave
Monroe, WI 53566
Phone: 608-324-1000
Fax: 608-324-1114
E-mail: questions@monroeclinic.org
URL: www.themonroeclinic.org
Type: Acute Care Hospitals
Emergency Services: Yes
Ownership: Voluntary Non-Profit - Church
Beds: 221

Key Personnel:
CEO/President. . . . . Julie Wilke
Chief of Medical Staff . . . . John Frey, MD
Operating Room. . . . . Nicholas Maxwell
Quality Assurance . . . . Dorothy White
Emergency Room . . . . Amy Fargo-Young

Measure	Cases	This Hosp.	State Avg.	U.S. Avg.
Heart Attack Care				
ACE Inhibitor or ARB for LVSD[1]	1	100%	97%	96%
Aspirin at Arrival[1]	14	100%	99%	99%
Aspirin at Discharge[1]	9	100%	99%	98%
Beta Blocker at Discharge[1]	10	100%	99%	98%
Fibrinolytic Medication Timing	0	-	0%	55%
PCI Within 90 Minutes of Arrival	0	-	89%	90%
Smoking Cessation Advice	0	-	99%	99%
Chest Pain/Possible Heart Attack Care				
Aspirin at Arrival	69	100%	96%	95%
Median Time to ECG (minutes)	70	5	7	8
Median Time to Transfer (minutes)[1]	3	47	49	61
Fibrinolytic Medication Timing[1]	6	100%	63%	54%
Heart Failure Care				
ACE Inhibitor or ARB for LVSD[1]	17	100%	95%	94%
Discharge Instructions	59	100%	86%	88%
Evaluation of LVS Function	77	100%	97%	98%
Smoking Cessation Advice[1]	9	100%	97%	98%
Pneumonia Care				
Appropriate Initial Antibiotic	73	100%	94%	92%
Blood Culture Timing	133	100%	97%	96%
Influenza Vaccine	92	97%	92%	91%
Initial Antibiotic Timing	121	99%	97%	95%
Pneumococcal Vaccine	128	98%	93%	93%
Smoking Cessation Advice	32	100%	95%	97%
Surgical Care Improvement Project				
Appropriate VTP Within 24 Hours[2]	91	98%	93%	92%
Appropriate Hair Removal[2]	321	99%	100%	99%
Appropriate Beta Blocker Usage[2]	100	84%	92%	93%
Controlled Postoperative Blood Glucose[2]	0	-	93%	93%
Prophylactic Antibiotic Timing[2]	222	86%	97%	97%
Prophylactic Antibiotic Timing (Outpatient)	82	89%	91%	92%
Prophylactic Antibiotic Selection[2]	214	93%	98%	97%
Prophylactic Antibiotic Select. (Outpatient)	115	97%	96%	94%
Prophylactic Antibiotic Stopped[2]	203	98%	95%	94%
Recommended VTP Ordered[2]	91	99%	94%	94%
Urinary Catheter Removal[2]	41	78%	91%	90%
Children's Asthma Care				
Received Systemic Corticosteroids	-	-	-	100%
Received Home Management Plan	-	-	-	71%
Received Reliever Medication	-	-	-	100%
Use of Medical Imaging				
Combination Abdominal CT Scan	415	0.048	0.106	0.191
Combination Chest CT Scan	215	0.019	0.027	0.054
Follow-up Mammogram/Ultrasound	1,065	11.6%	8.4%	8.4%
MRI for Low Back Pain	123	26.8%	31.8%	32.7%
Survey of Patients' Hospital Experiences				
Area Around Room 'Always' Quiet at Night	300+	61%	-	58%
Doctors 'Always' Communicated Well	300+	80%	-	80%
Home Recovery Information Given	300+	90%	-	82%
Hospital Given 9 or 10 on 10 Point Scale	300+	72%	-	67%
Meds 'Always' Explained Before Given	300+	66%	-	60%
Nurses 'Always' Communicated Well	300+	82%	-	76%
Pain 'Always' Well Controlled	300+	71%	-	69%
Room and Bathroom 'Always' Clean	300+	75%	-	71%
Timely Help 'Always' Received	300+	68%	-	64%
Would Definitely Recommend Hospital	300+	75%	-	69%

Theda Clark Medical Center

130 2nd St
Neenah, WI 54956
Phone: 920-729-3100
Fax: 920-729-3167
URL: www.thedacare.org
Type: Acute Care Hospitals
Emergency Services: Yes
Ownership: Voluntary Non-Profit - Private
Beds: 250

Key Personnel:
CEO/President. . . . . John Toussaint, MD
Chief of Medical Staff . . . . Steven Knaus, MD
Operating Room. . . . . Sherry Cheadle
Pediatric Ambulatory Care . . . . . Eileen Jekot, MD
Pediatric In-Patient Care . . . . . . Eileen Jekot, MD
Quality Assurance . . . . Sally Podoski
Radiology. . . . . Thomas Tolly, MD

Measure	Cases	This Hosp.	State Avg.	U.S. Avg.
Heart Attack Care				
ACE Inhibitor or ARB for LVSD[1]	12	92%	97%	96%
Aspirin at Arrival	70	100%	99%	99%
Aspirin at Discharge	70	99%	99%	98%
Beta Blocker at Discharge	62	98%	99%	98%
Fibrinolytic Medication Timing[1]	1	0%	0%	55%
PCI Within 90 Minutes of Arrival[1]	20	90%	89%	90%
Smoking Cessation Advice	26	100%	99%	99%
Chest Pain/Possible Heart Attack Care				
Aspirin at Arrival[1]	12	100%	96%	95%
Median Time to ECG (minutes)[1]	12	2	7	8
Median Time to Transfer (minutes)[1,3]	1	32	49	61
Fibrinolytic Medication Timing[3]	0	-	63%	54%
Heart Failure Care				
ACE Inhibitor or ARB for LVSD[1]	10	100%	95%	94%
Discharge Instructions	72	92%	86%	88%
Evaluation of LVS Function	107	93%	97%	98%
Smoking Cessation Advice[1]	10	100%	97%	98%
Pneumonia Care				
Appropriate Initial Antibiotic	56	89%	94%	92%
Blood Culture Timing	64	98%	97%	96%
Influenza Vaccine	51	90%	92%	91%
Initial Antibiotic Timing	74	100%	97%	95%
Pneumococcal Vaccine	71	94%	93%	93%
Smoking Cessation Advice	30	100%	95%	97%
Surgical Care Improvement Project				
Appropriate VTP Within 24 Hours[2]	123	92%	93%	92%
Appropriate Hair Removal[2]	494	100%	100%	99%
Appropriate Beta Blocker Usage[2]	139	94%	92%	93%
Controlled Postoperative Blood Glucose[2]	0	-	93%	93%
Prophylactic Antibiotic Timing[2]	331	98%	97%	97%
Prophylactic Antibiotic Timing (Outpatient)	655	96%	91%	92%
Prophylactic Antibiotic Selection[2]	332	98%	98%	97%
Prophylactic Antibiotic Select. (Outpatient)	656	98%	96%	94%
Prophylactic Antibiotic Stopped[2]	319	96%	95%	94%
Recommended VTP Ordered[2]	125	94%	94%	94%
Urinary Catheter Removal[2]	135	98%	91%	90%
Children's Asthma Care				
Received Systemic Corticosteroids[1]	11	100%	-	100%
Received Home Management Plan[1]	11	9%	-	71%
Received Reliever Medication[1]	11	100%	-	100%
Use of Medical Imaging				
Combination Abdominal CT Scan	447	0.081	0.106	0.191
Combination Chest CT Scan	424	0.002	0.027	0.054
Follow-up Mammogram/Ultrasound	590	11.5%	8.4%	8.4%
MRI for Low Back Pain	102	41.2%	31.8%	32.7%
Survey of Patients' Hospital Experiences				
Area Around Room 'Always' Quiet at Night	300+	55%	-	58%
Doctors 'Always' Communicated Well	300+	78%	-	80%
Home Recovery Information Given	300+	86%	-	82%
Hospital Given 9 or 10 on 10 Point Scale	300+	72%	-	67%
Meds 'Always' Explained Before Given	300+	63%	-	60%
Nurses 'Always' Communicated Well	300+	77%	-	76%
Pain 'Always' Well Controlled	300+	68%	-	69%
Room and Bathroom 'Always' Clean	300+	74%	-	71%
Timely Help 'Always' Received	300+	62%	-	64%
Would Definitely Recommend Hospital	300+	78%	-	69%

Memorial Medical Center

216 Sunset Place
Neillsville, WI 54456
Phone: 715-743-3101
Fax: 715-743-6245
Type: Critical Access Hospitals
Emergency Services: Yes
Ownership: Voluntary Non-Profit - Other
Beds: 28

Key Personnel:
CEO/President. . . . . Scott Polenz
Chief of Medical Staff . . . . Timothy Meyer, MD
Infection Control . . . . Ann Rust
Operating Room. . . . . Karen King
Emergency Room . . . . Karen King, RN

Measure	Cases	This Hosp.	State Avg.	U.S. Avg.
Heart Attack Care				
ACE Inhibitor or ARB for LVSD[3]	0	-	97%	96%
Aspirin at Arrival[1,3]	4	100%	99%	99%
Aspirin at Discharge[1,3]	4	100%	99%	98%
Beta Blocker at Discharge[1,3]	3	67%	99%	98%
Fibrinolytic Medication Timing[3]	0	-	0%	55%
PCI Within 90 Minutes of Arrival[3]	0	-	89%	90%
Smoking Cessation Advice[3]	0	-	99%	99%
Chest Pain/Possible Heart Attack Care				
Aspirin at Arrival	-	-	96%	95%
Median Time to ECG (minutes)	-	-	7	8
Median Time to Transfer (minutes)	-	-	49	61
Fibrinolytic Medication Timing	-	-	63%	54%
Heart Failure Care				
ACE Inhibitor or ARB for LVSD[1]	2	100%	95%	94%
Discharge Instructions[1]	11	73%	86%	88%
Evaluation of LVS Function[1]	19	58%	97%	98%
Smoking Cessation Advice	0	-	97%	98%
Pneumonia Care				
Appropriate Initial Antibiotic[1]	19	89%	94%	92%
Blood Culture Timing[1]	9	100%	97%	96%
Influenza Vaccine[1]	21	90%	92%	91%
Initial Antibiotic Timing[1]	21	95%	97%	95%
Pneumococcal Vaccine[1]	23	87%	93%	93%
Smoking Cessation Advice[1]	4	100%	95%	97%
Surgical Care Improvement Project				
Appropriate VTP Within 24 Hours[5]	0	-	93%	92%
Appropriate Hair Removal[5]	0	-	100%	99%
Appropriate Beta Blocker Usage[5]	0	-	92%	93%
Controlled Postoperative Blood Glucose[5]	0	-	93%	93%
Prophylactic Antibiotic Timing[5]	0	-	97%	97%
Prophylactic Antibiotic Timing (Outpatient)	-	-	91%	92%
Prophylactic Antibiotic Selection[5]	0	-	98%	97%
Prophylactic Antibiotic Select. (Outpatient)	-	-	96%	94%
Prophylactic Antibiotic Stopped[5]	0	-	95%	94%
Recommended VTP Ordered[5]	0	-	94%	94%
Urinary Catheter Removal[5]	0	-	91%	90%
Children's Asthma Care				
Received Systemic Corticosteroids	-	-	-	100%
Received Home Management Plan	-	-	-	71%
Received Reliever Medication	-	-	-	100%
Use of Medical Imaging				
Combination Abdominal CT Scan	-	-	0.106	0.191
Combination Chest CT Scan	-	-	0.027	0.054
Follow-up Mammogram/Ultrasound	-	-	8.4%	8.4%
MRI for Low Back Pain	-	-	31.8%	32.7%
Survey of Patients' Hospital Experiences				
Area Around Room 'Always' Quiet at Night	(a)	56%	-	58%
Doctors 'Always' Communicated Well	(a)	77%	-	80%
Home Recovery Information Given	(a)	83%	-	82%
Hospital Given 9 or 10 on 10 Point Scale	(a)	68%	-	67%
Meds 'Always' Explained Before Given	(a)	57%	-	60%
Nurses 'Always' Communicated Well	(a)	74%	-	76%
Pain 'Always' Well Controlled	(a)	61%	-	69%
Room and Bathroom 'Always' Clean	(a)	81%	-	71%
Timely Help 'Always' Received	(a)	72%	-	64%
Would Definitely Recommend Hospital	(a)	61%	-	69%

NOTE: Hospital profiles are in alphabetical order by state, then city, then hospital within the city; Rankings exclude hospitals with less than 25 cases except for patient surveys which excludes hospitals with less than 100 cases; (a) 100–299 cases; (1) The number of cases is too small to be sure how well a hospital is performing; (2) The hospital indicated that the data submitted for this measure were based on a sample of cases; (3) Data was collected during a shorter time period (fewer quarters) than the maximum possible time for this measure; (4) Suppressed for one or more quarters by CMS; (5) No data is available from the hospital for this measure; (6) Fewer than 100 patients completed the HCAHPS survey. Use these rates with caution, as the number of surveys may be too low to reliably assess hospital performance; (7) Survey results are based on less than 12 months of data; (8) Survey results are not available for this reporting period; (9) No or very few patients were eligible for the HCAHPS survey. The scores shown, if any, reflect a very small number of surveys; (10) A state average was not calculated because too few hospitals in the state submitted data; (11) There were discrepancies in the data collection process; Please refer to the User's Guide for a full explanation of data.

New London Family Medical Center

1405 Mill St
New London, WI 54961
E-mail: dmente@ahs.fv.org
Phone: 920-531-2000
Fax: 920-531-2098
Type: Critical Access Hospitals
Emergency Services: Yes
Ownership: Voluntary Non-Profit - Private
Beds: 75

Key Personnel:
CEO/President. . . . . Paul Gurgel
Quality Assurance . . . . Barb Neely
Emergency Room . . . . Randy Schoenrock
Intensive Care Unit. . . . . Randy Shoenrock

Measure	Cases	This Hosp.	State Avg.	U.S. Avg.
Heart Attack Care				
ACE Inhibitor or ARB for LVSD[5]	0	-	97%	96%
Aspirin at Arrival[5]	0	-	99%	99%
Aspirin at Discharge[5]	0	-	99%	98%
Beta Blocker at Discharge[5]	0	-	99%	98%
Fibrinolytic Medication Timing[5]	0	-	0%	55%
PCI Within 90 Minutes of Arrival[5]	0	-	89%	90%
Smoking Cessation Advice[5]	0	-	99%	99%
Chest Pain/Possible Heart Attack Care				
Aspirin at Arrival	-	-	96%	95%
Median Time to ECG (minutes)	-	-	7	8
Median Time to Transfer (minutes)	-	-	49	61
Fibrinolytic Medication Timing	-	-	63%	54%
Heart Failure Care				
ACE Inhibitor or ARB for LVSD[5]	0	-	95%	94%
Discharge Instructions[5]	0	-	86%	88%
Evaluation of LVS Function[5]	0	-	97%	98%
Smoking Cessation Advice[5]	0	-	97%	98%
Pneumonia Care				
Appropriate Initial Antibiotic	25	92%	94%	92%
Blood Culture Timing[1]	18	94%	97%	96%
Influenza Vaccine[1]	19	68%	92%	91%
Initial Antibiotic Timing	33	100%	97%	95%
Pneumococcal Vaccine	36	86%	93%	93%
Smoking Cessation Advice[1]	6	100%	95%	97%
Surgical Care Improvement Project				
Appropriate VTP Within 24 Hours[5]	0	-	93%	92%
Appropriate Hair Removal[5]	0	-	100%	99%
Appropriate Beta Blocker Usage[5]	0	-	92%	93%
Controlled Postoperative Blood Glucose[5]	0	-	93%	93%
Prophylactic Antibiotic Timing[5]	0	-	97%	97%
Prophylactic Antibiotic Timing (Outpatient)	-	-	91%	92%
Prophylactic Antibiotic Selection[5]	0	-	98%	97%
Prophylactic Antibiotic Select. (Outpatient)	-	-	96%	94%
Prophylactic Antibiotic Stopped[5]	0	-	95%	94%
Recommended VTP Ordered[5]	0	-	94%	94%
Urinary Catheter Removal[5]	0	-	91%	90%
Children's Asthma Care				
Received Systemic Corticosteroids	-	-	-	100%
Received Home Management Plan	-	-	-	71%
Received Reliever Medication	-	-	-	100%
Use of Medical Imaging				
Combination Abdominal CT Scan	-	-	0.106	0.191
Combination Chest CT Scan	-	-	0.027	0.054
Follow-up Mammogram/Ultrasound	-	-	8.4%	8.4%
MRI for Low Back Pain	-	-	31.8%	32.7%
Survey of Patients' Hospital Experiences				
Area Around Room 'Always' Quiet at Night	(a)	58%	-	58%
Doctors 'Always' Communicated Well	(a)	77%	-	80%
Home Recovery Information Given	(a)	82%	-	82%
Hospital Given 9 or 10 on 10 Point Scale	(a)	60%	-	67%
Meds 'Always' Explained Before Given	(a)	58%	-	60%
Nurses 'Always' Communicated Well	(a)	69%	-	76%
Pain 'Always' Well Controlled	(a)	67%	-	69%
Room and Bathroom 'Always' Clean	(a)	78%	-	71%
Timely Help 'Always' Received	(a)	62%	-	64%
Would Definitely Recommend Hospital	(a)	59%	-	69%

Westfields Hospital

535 Hospital Rd
New Richmond, WI 54017
Phone: 715-246-2101
Fax: 715-243-7203
Type: Critical Access Hospitals
Emergency Services: Yes
Ownership: Voluntary Non-Profit - Private
Beds: 227

Key Personnel:
Chief of Medical Staff . . . . David O DeGear, MD
Infection Control. . . . . Charlene Mayry, RN
Operating Room. . . . . Michael Melby
Quality Assurance . . . . Charlene Mayry, RN
Radiology. . . . . Todd M Arsenault
Emergency Room . . . . David De Gear, MD

Measure	Cases	This Hosp.	State Avg.	U.S. Avg.
Heart Attack Care				
ACE Inhibitor or ARB for LVSD[3]	0	-	97%	96%
Aspirin at Arrival[1,3]	2	50%	99%	99%
Aspirin at Discharge[1,3]	1	100%	99%	98%
Beta Blocker at Discharge[1,3]	2	100%	99%	98%
Fibrinolytic Medication Timing[5]	0	-	0%	55%
PCI Within 90 Minutes of Arrival[5]	0	-	89%	90%
Smoking Cessation Advice[3]	0	-	99%	99%
Chest Pain/Possible Heart Attack Care				
Aspirin at Arrival	-	-	96%	95%
Median Time to ECG (minutes)	-	-	7	8
Median Time to Transfer (minutes)	-	-	49	61
Fibrinolytic Medication Timing	-	-	63%	54%
Heart Failure Care				
ACE Inhibitor or ARB for LVSD[1]	3	33%	95%	94%
Discharge Instructions	29	59%	86%	88%
Evaluation of LVS Function	37	78%	97%	98%
Smoking Cessation Advice[1]	1	100%	97%	98%
Pneumonia Care				
Appropriate Initial Antibiotic	28	89%	94%	92%
Blood Culture Timing[1]	6	100%	97%	96%
Influenza Vaccine[1]	23	61%	92%	91%
Initial Antibiotic Timing[1]	20	95%	97%	95%
Pneumococcal Vaccine	36	67%	93%	93%
Smoking Cessation Advice[1]	5	100%	95%	97%
Surgical Care Improvement Project				
Appropriate VTP Within 24 Hours[5]	0	-	93%	92%
Appropriate Hair Removal[5]	0	-	100%	99%
Appropriate Beta Blocker Usage[5]	0	-	92%	93%
Controlled Postoperative Blood Glucose[5]	0	-	93%	93%
Prophylactic Antibiotic Timing[5]	0	-	97%	97%
Prophylactic Antibiotic Timing (Outpatient)	-	-	91%	92%
Prophylactic Antibiotic Selection[5]	0	-	98%	97%
Prophylactic Antibiotic Select. (Outpatient)	-	-	96%	94%
Prophylactic Antibiotic Stopped[5]	0	-	95%	94%
Recommended VTP Ordered[5]	0	-	94%	94%
Urinary Catheter Removal[5]	0	-	91%	90%
Children's Asthma Care				
Received Systemic Corticosteroids	-	-	-	100%
Received Home Management Plan	-	-	-	71%
Received Reliever Medication	-	-	-	100%
Use of Medical Imaging				
Combination Abdominal CT Scan	-	-	0.106	0.191
Combination Chest CT Scan	-	-	0.027	0.054
Follow-up Mammogram/Ultrasound	-	-	8.4%	8.4%
MRI for Low Back Pain	-	-	31.8%	32.7%
Survey of Patients' Hospital Experiences				
Area Around Room 'Always' Quiet at Night	300+	61%	-	58%
Doctors 'Always' Communicated Well	300+	82%	-	80%
Home Recovery Information Given	300+	86%	-	82%
Hospital Given 9 or 10 on 10 Point Scale	300+	73%	-	67%
Meds 'Always' Explained Before Given	300+	67%	-	60%
Nurses 'Always' Communicated Well	300+	80%	-	76%
Pain 'Always' Well Controlled	300+	70%	-	69%
Room and Bathroom 'Always' Clean	300+	84%	-	71%
Timely Help 'Always' Received	300+	72%	-	64%
Would Definitely Recommend Hospital	300+	73%	-	69%

Oconomowoc Memorial Hospital

791 E Summit Ave
Oconomowoc, WI 53066
Phone: 262-569-9400
Fax: 262-560-4527
Type: Acute Care Hospitals
Emergency Services: Yes
Ownership: Voluntary Non-Profit - Other
Beds: 77

Key Personnel:
CEO/President. . . . . Douglas Guy
Chief of Medical Staff . . . . Brian Lipman, MD
Patient Relations . . . . Martha Klug

Measure	Cases	This Hosp.	State Avg.	U.S. Avg.
Heart Attack Care				
ACE Inhibitor or ARB for LVSD[1]	9	100%	97%	96%
Aspirin at Arrival	57	98%	99%	99%
Aspirin at Discharge	52	100%	99%	98%
Beta Blocker at Discharge	52	98%	99%	98%
Fibrinolytic Medication Timing	0	-	0%	55%
PCI Within 90 Minutes of Arrival[1]	13	92%	89%	90%
Smoking Cessation Advice[1]	15	100%	99%	99%
Chest Pain/Possible Heart Attack Care				
Aspirin at Arrival[1,3]	3	100%	96%	95%
Median Time to ECG (minutes)[1,3]	4	6	7	8
Median Time to Transfer (minutes)[5]	0	-	49	61
Fibrinolytic Medication Timing[5]	0	-	63%	54%
Heart Failure Care				
ACE Inhibitor or ARB for LVSD[1]	20	100%	95%	94%
Discharge Instructions	58	72%	86%	88%
Evaluation of LVS Function	82	100%	97%	98%
Smoking Cessation Advice[1]	6	100%	97%	98%
Pneumonia Care				
Appropriate Initial Antibiotic	59	97%	94%	92%
Blood Culture Timing	94	100%	97%	96%
Influenza Vaccine	63	97%	92%	91%
Initial Antibiotic Timing	90	97%	97%	95%
Pneumococcal Vaccine	93	96%	93%	93%
Smoking Cessation Advice	25	100%	95%	97%
Surgical Care Improvement Project				
Appropriate VTP Within 24 Hours[2]	96	85%	93%	92%
Appropriate Hair Removal[2]	373	100%	100%	99%
Appropriate Beta Blocker Usage[2]	72	94%	92%	93%
Controlled Postoperative Blood Glucose[2]	0	-	93%	93%
Prophylactic Antibiotic Timing[2]	260	99%	97%	97%
Prophylactic Antibiotic Timing (Outpatient)	114	86%	91%	92%
Prophylactic Antibiotic Selection[2]	260	98%	98%	97%
Prophylactic Antibiotic Select. (Outpatient)	109	87%	96%	94%
Prophylactic Antibiotic Stopped[2]	255	98%	95%	94%
Recommended VTP Ordered[2]	96	86%	94%	94%
Urinary Catheter Removal[2]	92	91%	91%	90%
Children's Asthma Care				
Received Systemic Corticosteroids	-	-	-	100%
Received Home Management Plan	-	-	-	71%
Received Reliever Medication	-	-	-	100%
Use of Medical Imaging				
Combination Abdominal CT Scan	385	0.088	0.106	0.191
Combination Chest CT Scan	334	0.024	0.027	0.054
Follow-up Mammogram/Ultrasound	749	9.5%	8.4%	8.4%
MRI for Low Back Pain	145	32.4%	31.8%	32.7%
Survey of Patients' Hospital Experiences				
Area Around Room 'Always' Quiet at Night	300+	63%	-	58%
Doctors 'Always' Communicated Well	300+	80%	-	80%
Home Recovery Information Given	300+	87%	-	82%
Hospital Given 9 or 10 on 10 Point Scale	300+	73%	-	67%
Meds 'Always' Explained Before Given	300+	66%	-	60%
Nurses 'Always' Communicated Well	300+	80%	-	76%
Pain 'Always' Well Controlled	300+	67%	-	69%
Room and Bathroom 'Always' Clean	300+	78%	-	71%
Timely Help 'Always' Received	300+	66%	-	64%
Would Definitely Recommend Hospital	300+	75%	-	69%

NOTE: Hospital profiles are in alphabetical order by state, then city, then hospital within the city; Rankings exclude hospitals with less than 25 cases except for patient surveys which excludes hospitals with less than 100 cases; (a) 100–299 cases; (1) The number of cases is too small to be sure how well a hospital is performing; (2) The hospital indicated that the data submitted for this measure were based on a sample of cases; (3) Data was collected during a shorter time period (fewer quarters) than the maximum possible time for this measure; (4) Suppressed for one or more quarters by CMS; (5) No data is available from the hospital for this measure; (6) Fewer than 100 patients completed the HCAHPS survey. Use these rates with caution, as the number of surveys may be too low to reliably assess hospital performance; (7) Survey results are based on less than 12 months of data; (8) Survey results are not available for this reporting period; (9) No or very few patients were eligible for the HCAHPS survey. The scores shown, if any, reflect a very small number of surveys; (10) A state average was not calculated because too few hospitals in the state submitted data; (11) There were discrepancies in the data collection process; Please refer to the User's Guide for a full explanation of data.

Oconto Hospital & Medical Center

820 Arbutus Ave
Oconto, WI 54153
Phone: 920-835-1100
URL: www.ocontohospital.com
Type: Critical Access Hospitals
Emergency Services: Yes
Ownership: Voluntary Non-Profit - Private

Measure	Cases	This Hosp.	State Avg.	U.S. Avg.
Heart Attack Care				
ACE Inhibitor or ARB for LVSD[5]	0	-	97%	96%
Aspirin at Arrival[5]	0	-	99%	99%
Aspirin at Discharge[5]	0	-	99%	98%
Beta Blocker at Discharge[5]	0	-	99%	98%
Fibrinolytic Medication Timing[5]	0	-	0%	55%
PCI Within 90 Minutes of Arrival[5]	0	-	89%	90%
Smoking Cessation Advice[5]	0	-	99%	99%
Chest Pain/Possible Heart Attack Care				
Aspirin at Arrival	-	-	96%	95%
Median Time to ECG (minutes)	-	-	7	8
Median Time to Transfer (minutes)	-	-	49	61
Fibrinolytic Medication Timing	-	-	63%	54%
Heart Failure Care				
ACE Inhibitor or ARB for LVSD[5]	0	-	95%	94%
Discharge Instructions[5]	0	-	86%	88%
Evaluation of LVS Function[5]	0	-	97%	98%
Smoking Cessation Advice[5]	0	-	97%	98%
Pneumonia Care				
Appropriate Initial Antibiotic[5]	0	-	94%	92%
Blood Culture Timing[5]	0	-	97%	96%
Influenza Vaccine[5]	0	-	92%	91%
Initial Antibiotic Timing[5]	0	-	97%	95%
Pneumococcal Vaccine[5]	0	-	93%	93%
Smoking Cessation Advice[5]	0	-	95%	97%
Surgical Care Improvement Project				
Appropriate VTP Within 24 Hours[5]	0	-	93%	92%
Appropriate Hair Removal[5]	0	-	100%	99%
Appropriate Beta Blocker Usage[5]	0	-	92%	93%
Controlled Postoperative Blood Glucose[5]	0	-	93%	93%
Prophylactic Antibiotic Timing[5]	0	-	97%	97%
Prophylactic Antibiotic Timing (Outpatient)	-	-	91%	92%
Prophylactic Antibiotic Selection[5]	0	-	98%	97%
Prophylactic Antibiotic Select. (Outpatient)	-	-	96%	94%
Prophylactic Antibiotic Stopped[5]	0	-	95%	94%
Recommended VTP Ordered[5]	0	-	94%	94%
Urinary Catheter Removal[5]	0	-	91%	90%
Children's Asthma Care				
Received Systemic Corticosteroids	-	-	-	100%
Received Home Management Plan	-	-	-	71%
Received Reliever Medication	-	-	-	100%
Use of Medical Imaging				
Combination Abdominal CT Scan	-	-	0.106	0.191
Combination Chest CT Scan	-	-	0.027	0.054
Follow-up Mammogram/Ultrasound	-	-	8.4%	8.4%
MRI for Low Back Pain	-	-	31.8%	32.7%
Survey of Patients' Hospital Experiences				
Area Around Room 'Always' Quiet at Night[8]	-	-	-	58%
Doctors 'Always' Communicated Well[8]	-	-	-	80%
Home Recovery Information Given[8]	-	-	-	82%
Hospital Given 9 or 10 on 10 Point Scale[8]	-	-	-	67%
Meds 'Always' Explained Before Given[8]	-	-	-	60%
Nurses 'Always' Communicated Well[8]	-	-	-	76%
Pain 'Always' Well Controlled[8]	-	-	-	69%
Room and Bathroom 'Always' Clean[8]	-	-	-	71%
Timely Help 'Always' Received[8]	-	-	-	64%
Would Definitely Recommend Hospital[8]	-	-	-	69%

Community Memorial Hospital

855 S Main St
Oconto Falls, WI 54154
Phone: 920-846-3444
Fax: 920-846-4244
URL: www.cmhospital.org
Type: Critical Access Hospitals
Emergency Services: Yes
Ownership: Voluntary Non-Profit - Private
Beds: 25

Key Personnel:
CEO/President. . . . . Jim VanDornick
Chief of Medical Staff . . . . Genadi Maltinski, MD
Infection Control. . . . . Debbie Wesolowski
Operating Room. . . . . Kathy Micoley
Quality Assurance . . . . Debbie Wesolowski
Radiology. . . . . Arthur Stiennon
Emergency Room . . . . Vallie Kaprelian
Hemotology Center . . . . Judy Sylema

Measure	Cases	This Hosp.	State Avg.	U.S. Avg.
Heart Attack Care				
ACE Inhibitor or ARB for LVSD[1,3]	1	100%	97%	96%
Aspirin at Arrival[1,3]	5	100%	99%	99%
Aspirin at Discharge[1,3]	5	100%	99%	98%
Beta Blocker at Discharge[1,3]	5	80%	99%	98%
Fibrinolytic Medication Timing[3]	0	-	0%	55%
PCI Within 90 Minutes of Arrival[5]	0	-	89%	90%
Smoking Cessation Advice[1,3]	1	100%	99%	99%
Chest Pain/Possible Heart Attack Care				
Aspirin at Arrival	-	-	96%	95%
Median Time to ECG (minutes)	-	-	7	8
Median Time to Transfer (minutes)	-	-	49	61
Fibrinolytic Medication Timing	-	-	63%	54%
Heart Failure Care				
ACE Inhibitor or ARB for LVSD[1]	9	67%	95%	94%
Discharge Instructions	37	97%	86%	88%
Evaluation of LVS Function	47	79%	97%	98%
Smoking Cessation Advice[1]	5	100%	97%	98%
Pneumonia Care				
Appropriate Initial Antibiotic[1]	22	82%	94%	92%
Blood Culture Timing[1]	17	94%	97%	96%
Influenza Vaccine[1]	18	83%	92%	91%
Initial Antibiotic Timing[1]	20	90%	97%	95%
Pneumococcal Vaccine[1]	22	95%	93%	93%
Smoking Cessation Advice[1]	8	100%	95%	97%
Surgical Care Improvement Project				
Appropriate VTP Within 24 Hours[5]	0	-	93%	92%
Appropriate Hair Removal[5]	0	-	100%	99%
Appropriate Beta Blocker Usage[5]	0	-	92%	93%
Controlled Postoperative Blood Glucose[5]	0	-	93%	93%
Prophylactic Antibiotic Timing	38	89%	97%	97%
Prophylactic Antibiotic Timing (Outpatient)	-	-	91%	92%
Prophylactic Antibiotic Selection	38	89%	98%	97%
Prophylactic Antibiotic Select. (Outpatient)	-	-	96%	94%
Prophylactic Antibiotic Stopped	36	86%	95%	94%
Recommended VTP Ordered[5]	0	-	94%	94%
Urinary Catheter Removal[5]	0	-	91%	90%
Children's Asthma Care				
Received Systemic Corticosteroids	-	-	-	100%
Received Home Management Plan	-	-	-	71%
Received Reliever Medication	-	-	-	100%
Use of Medical Imaging				
Combination Abdominal CT Scan	-	-	0.106	0.191
Combination Chest CT Scan	-	-	0.027	0.054
Follow-up Mammogram/Ultrasound	-	-	8.4%	8.4%
MRI for Low Back Pain	-	-	31.8%	32.7%
Survey of Patients' Hospital Experiences				
Area Around Room 'Always' Quiet at Night	300+	58%	-	58%
Doctors 'Always' Communicated Well	300+	82%	-	80%
Home Recovery Information Given	300+	85%	-	82%
Hospital Given 9 or 10 on 10 Point Scale	300+	61%	-	67%
Meds 'Always' Explained Before Given	300+	62%	-	60%
Nurses 'Always' Communicated Well	300+	78%	-	76%
Pain 'Always' Well Controlled	300+	69%	-	69%
Room and Bathroom 'Always' Clean	300+	68%	-	71%
Timely Help 'Always' Received	300+	73%	-	64%
Would Definitely Recommend Hospital	300+	59%	-	69%

Ladd Memorial Hosptial

2600 65th Avenue
Osceola, WI 54020
Phone: 715-294-2111
URL: www.osceolamedicalcenter.com
Type: Critical Access Hospitals
Emergency Services: Yes
Ownership: Voluntary Non-Profit - Private
Beds: 42

Key Personnel:
CEO/President. . . . . Jeff Meyer
Chief of Medical Staff . . . . Robert Dybvig, MD
Infection Control. . . . . Pam Carlson, RN
Operating Room. . . . . Warren Abell, DO
Quality Assurance . . . . Dawn Olson
Radiology. . . . . Brad Feltz, RT, RRT
Emergency Room . . . . Kelly Johnson, RN
Hemotology Center . . . . Dody Lunde, RN

Measure	Cases	This Hosp.	State Avg.	U.S. Avg.
Heart Attack Care				
ACE Inhibitor or ARB for LVSD[5]	0	-	97%	96%
Aspirin at Arrival[5]	0	-	99%	99%
Aspirin at Discharge[5]	0	-	99%	98%
Beta Blocker at Discharge[5]	0	-	99%	98%
Fibrinolytic Medication Timing[5]	0	-	0%	55%
PCI Within 90 Minutes of Arrival[5]	0	-	89%	90%
Smoking Cessation Advice[5]	0	-	99%	99%
Chest Pain/Possible Heart Attack Care				
Aspirin at Arrival	-	-	96%	95%
Median Time to ECG (minutes)	-	-	7	8
Median Time to Transfer (minutes)	-	-	49	61
Fibrinolytic Medication Timing	-	-	63%	54%
Heart Failure Care				
ACE Inhibitor or ARB for LVSD[1]	2	0%	95%	94%
Discharge Instructions[1]	14	100%	86%	88%
Evaluation of LVS Function[1]	18	56%	97%	98%
Smoking Cessation Advice[1]	3	67%	97%	98%
Pneumonia Care				
Appropriate Initial Antibiotic[1,3]	4	75%	94%	92%
Blood Culture Timing[1,3]	5	80%	97%	96%
Influenza Vaccine[1]	10	50%	92%	91%
Initial Antibiotic Timing[1,3]	8	88%	97%	95%
Pneumococcal Vaccine[1,3]	10	80%	93%	93%
Smoking Cessation Advice[3]	0	-	95%	97%
Surgical Care Improvement Project				
Appropriate VTP Within 24 Hours[5]	0	-	93%	92%
Appropriate Hair Removal[5]	0	-	100%	99%
Appropriate Beta Blocker Usage[5]	0	-	92%	93%
Controlled Postoperative Blood Glucose[5]	0	-	93%	93%
Prophylactic Antibiotic Timing	76	91%	97%	97%
Prophylactic Antibiotic Timing (Outpatient)	-	-	91%	92%
Prophylactic Antibiotic Selection	76	99%	98%	97%
Prophylactic Antibiotic Select. (Outpatient)	-	-	96%	94%
Prophylactic Antibiotic Stopped	76	100%	95%	94%
Recommended VTP Ordered[5]	0	-	94%	94%
Urinary Catheter Removal[1]	1	100%	91%	90%
Children's Asthma Care				
Received Systemic Corticosteroids	-	-	-	100%
Received Home Management Plan	-	-	-	71%
Received Reliever Medication	-	-	-	100%
Use of Medical Imaging				
Combination Abdominal CT Scan	-	-	0.106	0.191
Combination Chest CT Scan	-	-	0.027	0.054
Follow-up Mammogram/Ultrasound	-	-	8.4%	8.4%
MRI for Low Back Pain	-	-	31.8%	32.7%
Survey of Patients' Hospital Experiences				
Area Around Room 'Always' Quiet at Night[11]	(a)	71%	-	58%
Doctors 'Always' Communicated Well[11]	(a)	87%	-	80%
Home Recovery Information Given[11]	(a)	89%	-	82%
Hospital Given 9 or 10 on 10 Point Scale[11]	(a)	83%	-	67%
Meds 'Always' Explained Before Given[11]	(a)	73%	-	60%
Nurses 'Always' Communicated Well[11]	(a)	83%	-	76%
Pain 'Always' Well Controlled[11]	(a)	70%	-	69%
Room and Bathroom 'Always' Clean[11]	(a)	82%	-	71%
Timely Help 'Always' Received[11]	(a)	74%	-	64%
Would Definitely Recommend Hospital[11]	(a)	84%	-	69%

NOTE: Hospital profiles are in alphabetical order by state, then city, then hospital within the city; Rankings exclude hospitals with less than 25 cases except for patient surveys which excludes hospitals with less than 100 cases; (a) 100–299 cases; (1) The number of cases is too small to be sure how well a hospital is performing; (2) The hospital indicated that the data submitted for this measure were based on a sample of cases; (3) Data was collected during a shorter time period (fewer quarters) than the maximum possible time for this measure; (4) Suppressed for one or more quarters by CMS; (5) No data is available from the hospital for this measure; (6) Fewer than 100 patients completed the HCAHPS survey. Use these rates with caution, as the number of surveys may be too low to reliably assess hospital performance; (7) Survey results are based on less than 12 months of data; (8) Survey results are not available for this reporting period; (9) No or very few patients were eligible for the HCAHPS survey. The scores shown, if any, reflect a very small number of surveys; (10) A state average was not calculated because too few hospitals in the state submitted data; (11) There were discrepancies in the data collection process; Please refer to the User's Guide for a full explanation of data.

Aurora Medical Center Oshkosh

855 N Westhaven Drive Phone: 920-456-6000
Oshkosh, WI 54904
URL: www.aurorahealthcare.org
Type: Acute Care Hospitals Emergency Services: Yes
Ownership: Voluntary Non-Profit - Private Beds: 49

Key Personnel:
CEO/President. . . . . Mark A Schwartz
Chief of Medical Staff. . . . . D Erbes, MD
Emergency Room . . . . David Madenburg, DO

Measure	Cases	This Hosp.	State Avg.	U.S. Avg.
Heart Attack Care				
ACE Inhibitor or ARB for LVSD[1]	2	100%	97%	96%
Aspirin at Arrival	43	100%	99%	99%
Aspirin at Discharge	41	100%	99%	98%
Beta Blocker at Discharge	37	100%	99%	98%
Fibrinolytic Medication Timing	0	-	0%	55%
PCI Within 90 Minutes of Arrival[1]	18	83%	89%	90%
Smoking Cessation Advice[1]	14	100%	99%	99%
Chest Pain/Possible Heart Attack Care				
Aspirin at Arrival[1]	8	100%	96%	95%
Median Time to ECG (minutes)[1]	8	6	7	8
Median Time to Transfer (minutes)[1,3]	1	118	49	61
Fibrinolytic Medication Timing[3]	0	-	63%	54%
Heart Failure Care				
ACE Inhibitor or ARB for LVSD[1]	15	100%	95%	94%
Discharge Instructions	52	83%	86%	88%
Evaluation of LVS Function	66	100%	97%	98%
Smoking Cessation Advice[1]	3	100%	97%	98%
Pneumonia Care				
Appropriate Initial Antibiotic	54	98%	94%	92%
Blood Culture Timing	73	100%	97%	96%
Influenza Vaccine	54	93%	92%	91%
Initial Antibiotic Timing	78	100%	97%	95%
Pneumococcal Vaccine	70	99%	93%	93%
Smoking Cessation Advice	25	100%	95%	97%
Surgical Care Improvement Project				
Appropriate VTP Within 24 Hours[2]	81	95%	93%	92%
Appropriate Hair Removal[2]	330	100%	100%	99%
Appropriate Beta Blocker Usage[2]	103	96%	92%	93%
Controlled Postoperative Blood Glucose[2]	0	-	93%	93%
Prophylactic Antibiotic Timing[2]	250	99%	97%	97%
Prophylactic Antibiotic Timing (Outpatient)	218	90%	91%	92%
Prophylactic Antibiotic Selection[2]	251	100%	98%	97%
Prophylactic Antibiotic Select. (Outpatient)	212	94%	96%	94%
Prophylactic Antibiotic Stopped[2]	245	96%	95%	94%
Recommended VTP Ordered[2]	81	96%	94%	94%
Urinary Catheter Removal[2]	45	96%	91%	90%
Children's Asthma Care				
Received Systemic Corticosteroids	-	-	-	100%
Received Home Management Plan	-	-	-	71%
Received Reliever Medication	-	-	-	100%
Use of Medical Imaging				
Combination Abdominal CT Scan	484	0.136	0.106	0.191
Combination Chest CT Scan	396	0.000	0.027	0.054
Follow-up Mammogram/Ultrasound	903	8.3%	8.4%	8.4%
MRI for Low Back Pain	151	25.2%	31.8%	32.7%
Survey of Patients' Hospital Experiences				
Area Around Room 'Always' Quiet at Night	300+	64%	-	58%
Doctors 'Always' Communicated Well	300+	80%	-	80%
Home Recovery Information Given	300+	89%	-	82%
Hospital Given 9 or 10 on 10 Point Scale	300+	73%	-	67%
Meds 'Always' Explained Before Given	300+	69%	-	60%
Nurses 'Always' Communicated Well	300+	79%	-	76%
Pain 'Always' Well Controlled	300+	73%	-	69%
Room and Bathroom 'Always' Clean	300+	75%	-	71%
Timely Help 'Always' Received	300+	68%	-	64%
Would Definitely Recommend Hospital	300+	76%	-	69%

Mercy Medical Center of Oshkosh

500 S Oakwood Rd Phone: 920-223-2000
Oshkosh, WI 54904 Fax: 920-223-0599
URL: www.ministryhealth.org
Type: Acute Care Hospitals Emergency Services: Yes
Ownership: Voluntary Non-Profit - Church Beds: 234

Key Personnel:
CEO/President. . . . . Kevin Nolan
Chief of Medical Staff. . . . . JJ Hanusa, MD
Operating Room. . . . . Florette Raffi
Pediatric Ambulatory Care . . . . . . Mark Kehrberg
Pediatric In-Patient Care . . . . Mark Kehrberg

Measure	Cases	This Hosp.	State Avg.	U.S. Avg.
Heart Attack Care				
ACE Inhibitor or ARB for LVSD[1]	13	92%	97%	96%
Aspirin at Arrival	53	100%	99%	99%
Aspirin at Discharge	60	98%	99%	98%
Beta Blocker at Discharge	49	98%	99%	98%
Fibrinolytic Medication Timing	0	-	0%	55%
PCI Within 90 Minutes of Arrival[1]	13	85%	89%	90%
Smoking Cessation Advice[1]	22	100%	99%	99%
Chest Pain/Possible Heart Attack Care				
Aspirin at Arrival[1,3]	6	100%	96%	95%
Median Time to ECG (minutes)[1,3]	7	5	7	8
Median Time to Transfer (minutes)[1,3]	1	33	49	61
Fibrinolytic Medication Timing[3]	0	-	63%	54%
Heart Failure Care				
ACE Inhibitor or ARB for LVSD	40	90%	95%	94%
Discharge Instructions	77	88%	86%	88%
Evaluation of LVS Function	110	100%	97%	98%
Smoking Cessation Advice[1]	19	100%	97%	98%
Pneumonia Care				
Appropriate Initial Antibiotic	49	96%	94%	92%
Blood Culture Timing	71	100%	97%	96%
Influenza Vaccine	75	96%	92%	91%
Initial Antibiotic Timing	95	100%	97%	95%
Pneumococcal Vaccine	111	91%	93%	93%
Smoking Cessation Advice	34	100%	95%	97%
Surgical Care Improvement Project				
Appropriate VTP Within 24 Hours[2]	150	84%	93%	92%
Appropriate Hair Removal[2]	364	99%	100%	99%
Appropriate Beta Blocker Usage[2]	108	97%	92%	93%
Controlled Postoperative Blood Glucose[2]	0	-	93%	93%
Prophylactic Antibiotic Timing[2]	226	97%	97%	97%
Prophylactic Antibiotic Timing (Outpatient)	286	94%	91%	92%
Prophylactic Antibiotic Selection[2]	226	98%	98%	97%
Prophylactic Antibiotic Select. (Outpatient)	290	98%	96%	94%
Prophylactic Antibiotic Stopped[2]	224	92%	95%	94%
Recommended VTP Ordered[2]	150	85%	94%	94%
Urinary Catheter Removal[2]	113	96%	91%	90%
Children's Asthma Care				
Received Systemic Corticosteroids	-	-	-	100%
Received Home Management Plan	-	-	-	71%
Received Reliever Medication	-	-	-	100%
Use of Medical Imaging				
Combination Abdominal CT Scan	340	0.068	0.106	0.191
Combination Chest CT Scan	255	0.008	0.027	0.054
Follow-up Mammogram/Ultrasound	797	10.7%	8.4%	8.4%
MRI for Low Back Pain	77	31.2%	31.8%	32.7%
Survey of Patients' Hospital Experiences				
Area Around Room 'Always' Quiet at Night	300+	56%	-	58%
Doctors 'Always' Communicated Well	300+	81%	-	80%
Home Recovery Information Given	300+	88%	-	82%
Hospital Given 9 or 10 on 10 Point Scale	300+	77%	-	67%
Meds 'Always' Explained Before Given	300+	67%	-	60%
Nurses 'Always' Communicated Well	300+	80%	-	76%
Pain 'Always' Well Controlled	300+	71%	-	69%
Room and Bathroom 'Always' Clean	300+	77%	-	71%
Timely Help 'Always' Received	300+	72%	-	64%
Would Definitely Recommend Hospital	300+	78%	-	69%

Luther Midelfort - Oakridge Mayo Health System

13025 8th St Phone: 715-597-3121
Osseo, WI 54758 Fax: 715-597-6250
URL: www.mhs.mayo.edu
Type: Critical Access Hospitals Emergency Services: Yes
Ownership: Voluntary Non-Profit - Other Beds: 68

Key Personnel:
CEO/President. . . . . Mike Ryan
Chief of Medical Staff. . . . . Thomas Screneck
Infection Control. . . . . Sarah Berquist
Emergency Room . . . . Margaret Lunde, RN
Patient Relations . . . . Cori Mc Reynolds

Measure	Cases	This Hosp.	State Avg.	U.S. Avg.
Heart Attack Care				
ACE Inhibitor or ARB for LVSD[5]	0	-	97%	96%
Aspirin at Arrival[5]	0	-	99%	99%
Aspirin at Discharge[5]	0	-	99%	98%
Beta Blocker at Discharge[5]	0	-	99%	98%
Fibrinolytic Medication Timing[5]	0	-	0%	55%
PCI Within 90 Minutes of Arrival[5]	0	-	89%	90%
Smoking Cessation Advice[5]	0	-	99%	99%
Chest Pain/Possible Heart Attack Care				
Aspirin at Arrival	-	-	96%	95%
Median Time to ECG (minutes)	-	-	7	8
Median Time to Transfer (minutes)	-	-	49	61
Fibrinolytic Medication Timing	-	-	63%	54%
Heart Failure Care				
ACE Inhibitor or ARB for LVSD	0	-	95%	94%
Discharge Instructions[1]	2	100%	86%	88%
Evaluation of LVS Function[1]	5	80%	97%	98%
Smoking Cessation Advice	0	-	97%	98%
Pneumonia Care				
Appropriate Initial Antibiotic[1]	13	100%	94%	92%
Blood Culture Timing[1]	16	100%	97%	96%
Influenza Vaccine[1]	8	100%	92%	91%
Initial Antibiotic Timing[1]	16	100%	97%	95%
Pneumococcal Vaccine[1]	18	94%	93%	93%
Smoking Cessation Advice[1]	8	100%	95%	97%
Surgical Care Improvement Project				
Appropriate VTP Within 24 Hours[5]	0	-	93%	92%
Appropriate Hair Removal[5]	0	-	100%	99%
Appropriate Beta Blocker Usage[5]	0	-	92%	93%
Controlled Postoperative Blood Glucose[5]	0	-	93%	93%
Prophylactic Antibiotic Timing[5]	0	-	97%	97%
Prophylactic Antibiotic Timing (Outpatient)	-	-	91%	92%
Prophylactic Antibiotic Selection[5]	0	-	98%	97%
Prophylactic Antibiotic Select. (Outpatient)	-	-	96%	94%
Prophylactic Antibiotic Stopped[5]	0	-	95%	94%
Recommended VTP Ordered[5]	0	-	94%	94%
Urinary Catheter Removal[5]	0	-	91%	90%
Children's Asthma Care				
Received Systemic Corticosteroids	-	-	-	100%
Received Home Management Plan	-	-	-	71%
Received Reliever Medication	-	-	-	100%
Use of Medical Imaging				
Combination Abdominal CT Scan	-	-	0.106	0.191
Combination Chest CT Scan	-	-	0.027	0.054
Follow-up Mammogram/Ultrasound	-	-	8.4%	8.4%
MRI for Low Back Pain	-	-	31.8%	32.7%
Survey of Patients' Hospital Experiences				
Area Around Room 'Always' Quiet at Night	(a)	58%	-	58%
Doctors 'Always' Communicated Well	(a)	86%	-	80%
Home Recovery Information Given	(a)	84%	-	82%
Hospital Given 9 or 10 on 10 Point Scale	(a)	83%	-	67%
Meds 'Always' Explained Before Given	(a)	65%	-	60%
Nurses 'Always' Communicated Well	(a)	85%	-	76%
Pain 'Always' Well Controlled	(a)	69%	-	69%
Room and Bathroom 'Always' Clean	(a)	84%	-	71%
Timely Help 'Always' Received	(a)	75%	-	64%
Would Definitely Recommend Hospital	(a)	79%	-	69%

NOTE: Hospital profiles are in alphabetical order by state, then city, then hospital within the city; Rankings exclude hospitals with less than 25 cases except for patient surveys which excludes hospitals with less than 100 cases; (a) 100–299 cases; (1) The number of cases is too small to be sure how well a hospital is performing; (2) The hospital indicated that the data submitted for this measure were based on a sample of cases; (3) Data was collected during a shorter time period (fewer quarters) than the maximum possible time for this measure; (4) Suppressed for one or more quarters by CMS; (5) No data is available from the hospital for this measure; (6) Fewer than 100 patients completed the HCAHPS survey. Use these rates with caution, as the number of surveys may be too low to reliably assess hospital performance; (7) Survey results are based on less than 12 months of data; (8) Survey results are not available for this reporting period; (9) No or very few patients were eligible for the HCAHPS survey. The scores shown, if any, reflect a very small number of surveys; (10) A state average was not calculated because too few hospitals in the state submitted data; (11) There were discrepancies in the data collection process; Please refer to the User's Guide for a full explanation of data.

Flambeau Hospital

98 Sherry Ave, P0 Box 310
Park Falls, WI 54552
Phone: 715-762-7500
Fax: 715-762-7545
URL: www.ministryhealth.org
Type: Critical Access Hospitals
Emergency Services: Yes
Ownership: Voluntary Non-Profit - Private
Beds: 42

Key Personnel:

Chief of Medical Staff.......... Sue Seidl
Infection Control............. Timothy J Lindgren, MD
Operating Room............. Liz Schreiber
Quality Assurance .... Robert Pflanz
Emergency Room .... Robert C Becker, MD

Measure	Cases	This Hosp.	State Avg.	U.S. Avg.
Heart Attack Care				
ACE Inhibitor or ARB for LVSD[1,3]	1	100%	97%	96%
Aspirin at Arrival[1,3]	7	100%	99%	99%
Aspirin at Discharge[1,3]	3	100%	99%	98%
Beta Blocker at Discharge[1,3]	5	100%	99%	98%
Fibrinolytic Medication Timing[3]	0	-	0%	55%
PCI Within 90 Minutes of Arrival[3]	0	-	89%	90%
Smoking Cessation Advice[3]	0	-	99%	99%
Chest Pain/Possible Heart Attack Care				
Aspirin at Arrival	-	-	96%	95%
Median Time to ECG (minutes)	-	-	7	8
Median Time to Transfer (minutes)	-	-	49	61
Fibrinolytic Medication Timing	-	-	63%	54%
Heart Failure Care				
ACE Inhibitor or ARB for LVSD[1]	6	100%	95%	94%
Discharge Instructions[1]	11	82%	86%	88%
Evaluation of LVS Function[1]	18	100%	97%	98%
Smoking Cessation Advice[1]	3	100%	97%	98%
Pneumonia Care				
Appropriate Initial Antibiotic[1,2]	22	82%	94%	92%
Blood Culture Timing[2]	32	97%	97%	96%
Influenza Vaccine[1,2]	16	94%	92%	91%
Initial Antibiotic Timing[2]	33	100%	97%	95%
Pneumococcal Vaccine[2]	37	97%	93%	93%
Smoking Cessation Advice[1,2]	9	100%	95%	97%
Surgical Care Improvement Project				
Appropriate VTP Within 24 Hours[5]	0	-	93%	92%
Appropriate Hair Removal[5]	0	-	100%	99%
Appropriate Beta Blocker Usage[5]	0	-	92%	93%
Controlled Postoperative Blood Glucose[5]	0	-	93%	93%
Prophylactic Antibiotic Timing[5]	0	-	97%	97%
Prophylactic Antibiotic Timing (Outpatient)	-	-	91%	92%
Prophylactic Antibiotic Selection[5]	0	-	98%	97%
Prophylactic Antibiotic Select. (Outpatient)	-	-	96%	94%
Prophylactic Antibiotic Stopped[5]	0	-	95%	94%
Recommended VTP Ordered[5]	0	-	94%	94%
Urinary Catheter Removal[5]	0	-	91%	90%
Children's Asthma Care				
Received Systemic Corticosteroids	-	-	-	100%
Received Home Management Plan	-	-	-	71%
Received Reliever Medication	-	-	-	100%
Use of Medical Imaging				
Combination Abdominal CT Scan	-	-	0.106	0.191
Combination Chest CT Scan	-	-	0.027	0.054
Follow-up Mammogram/Ultrasound	-	-	8.4%	8.4%
MRI for Low Back Pain	-	-	31.8%	32.7%
Survey of Patients' Hospital Experiences				
Area Around Room 'Always' Quiet at Night	(a)	61%	-	58%
Doctors 'Always' Communicated Well	(a)	79%	-	80%
Home Recovery Information Given	(a)	81%	-	82%
Hospital Given 9 or 10 on 10 Point Scale	(a)	69%	-	67%
Meds 'Always' Explained Before Given	(a)	64%	-	60%
Nurses 'Always' Communicated Well	(a)	82%	-	76%
Pain 'Always' Well Controlled	(a)	72%	-	69%
Room and Bathroom 'Always' Clean	(a)	87%	-	71%
Timely Help 'Always' Received	(a)	81%	-	64%
Would Definitely Recommend Hospital	(a)	67%	-	69%

Southwest Health Center

1400 East Side Rd
Platteville, WI 53818
Phone: 608-342-4701
Fax: 608-342-5035
E-mail: hr@southwesthealth.org
URL: www.southwesthealth.org
Type: Critical Access Hospitals
Emergency Services: Yes
Ownership: Voluntary Non-Profit - Other
Beds: 119

Key Personnel:

CEO/President.............. Anne Klawiter
Chief of Medical Staff.......... Kevin Carr
Operating Room............. Allen Rebchook
Quality Assurance .... Pat Moxness
Emergency Room .... Paul Mariskanish

Measure	Cases	This Hosp.	State Avg.	U.S. Avg.
Heart Attack Care				
ACE Inhibitor or ARB for LVSD[3]	0	-	97%	96%
Aspirin at Arrival[1,3]	1	100%	99%	99%
Aspirin at Discharge[3]	0	-	99%	98%
Beta Blocker at Discharge[3]	0	-	99%	98%
Fibrinolytic Medication Timing[3]	0	-	0%	55%
PCI Within 90 Minutes of Arrival[3]	0	-	89%	90%
Smoking Cessation Advice[3]	0	-	99%	99%
Chest Pain/Possible Heart Attack Care				
Aspirin at Arrival	46	96%	96%	95%
Median Time to ECG (minutes)	46	12	7	8
Median Time to Transfer (minutes)[1,3]	2	55	49	61
Fibrinolytic Medication Timing[1]	1	0%	63%	54%
Heart Failure Care				
ACE Inhibitor or ARB for LVSD[1]	5	100%	95%	94%
Discharge Instructions[1]	16	88%	86%	88%
Evaluation of LVS Function	31	90%	97%	98%
Smoking Cessation Advice[1]	1	100%	97%	98%
Pneumonia Care				
Appropriate Initial Antibiotic	45	84%	94%	92%
Blood Culture Timing	38	95%	97%	96%
Influenza Vaccine	33	85%	92%	91%
Initial Antibiotic Timing	58	95%	97%	95%
Pneumococcal Vaccine	50	94%	93%	93%
Smoking Cessation Advice[1]	7	100%	95%	97%
Surgical Care Improvement Project				
Appropriate VTP Within 24 Hours[5]	0	-	93%	92%
Appropriate Hair Removal[3]	53	100%	100%	99%
Appropriate Beta Blocker Usage[5]	0	-	92%	93%
Controlled Postoperative Blood Glucose[3]	0	-	93%	93%
Prophylactic Antibiotic Timing[3]	50	86%	97%	97%
Prophylactic Antibiotic Timing (Outpatient)	50	84%	91%	92%
Prophylactic Antibiotic Selection[3]	49	100%	98%	97%
Prophylactic Antibiotic Select. (Outpatient)	47	98%	96%	94%
Prophylactic Antibiotic Stopped[3]	48	96%	95%	94%
Recommended VTP Ordered[5]	0	-	94%	94%
Urinary Catheter Removal[5]	0	-	91%	90%
Children's Asthma Care				
Received Systemic Corticosteroids	-	-	-	100%
Received Home Management Plan	-	-	-	71%
Received Reliever Medication	-	-	-	100%
Use of Medical Imaging				
Combination Abdominal CT Scan	175	0.063	0.106	0.191
Combination Chest CT Scan	95	0.021	0.027	0.054
Follow-up Mammogram/Ultrasound	227	8.4%	8.4%	8.4%
MRI for Low Back Pain[1]	25	52.0%	31.8%	32.7%
Survey of Patients' Hospital Experiences				
Area Around Room 'Always' Quiet at Night	300+	67%	-	58%
Doctors 'Always' Communicated Well	300+	83%	-	80%
Home Recovery Information Given	300+	90%	-	82%
Hospital Given 9 or 10 on 10 Point Scale	300+	77%	-	67%
Meds 'Always' Explained Before Given	300+	66%	-	60%
Nurses 'Always' Communicated Well	300+	78%	-	76%
Pain 'Always' Well Controlled	300+	70%	-	69%
Room and Bathroom 'Always' Clean	300+	86%	-	71%
Timely Help 'Always' Received	300+	70%	-	64%
Would Definitely Recommend Hospital	300+	73%	-	69%

Divine Savior Healthcare

2817 New Pinery Rd
Portage, WI 53901
Phone: 608-742-4131
Fax: 608-742-6098
URL: www.dshealthcare.com
Type: Acute Care Hospitals
Emergency Services: Yes
Ownership: Voluntary Non-Profit - Church
Beds: 162

Key Personnel:

CEO/President.............. Michael T Decker
Chief of Medical Staff.......... Susan Kreckman
Infection Control............. Wanda Lowry
Operating Room............. Allison Mitchell, RN
Quality Assurance .... Laura Lindquist, RN
Emergency Room .... Jeffry Snyder, MD
Intensive Care Unit............ Melissa Bradbury, RN

Measure	Cases	This Hosp.	State Avg.	U.S. Avg.
Heart Attack Care				
ACE Inhibitor or ARB for LVSD[1,3]	2	100%	97%	96%
Aspirin at Arrival[1,3]	3	100%	99%	99%
Aspirin at Discharge[1,3]	3	100%	99%	98%
Beta Blocker at Discharge[1,3]	3	100%	99%	98%
Fibrinolytic Medication Timing[3]	0	-	0%	55%
PCI Within 90 Minutes of Arrival[3]	0	-	89%	90%
Smoking Cessation Advice[3]	0	-	99%	99%
Chest Pain/Possible Heart Attack Care				
Aspirin at Arrival	99	95%	96%	95%
Median Time to ECG (minutes)	103	10	7	8
Median Time to Transfer (minutes)[1,3]	14	42	49	61
Fibrinolytic Medication Timing[1]	2	50%	63%	54%
Heart Failure Care				
ACE Inhibitor or ARB for LVSD[1]	13	92%	95%	94%
Discharge Instructions	48	42%	86%	88%
Evaluation of LVS Function	60	78%	97%	98%
Smoking Cessation Advice[1]	5	80%	97%	98%
Pneumonia Care				
Appropriate Initial Antibiotic	55	95%	94%	92%
Blood Culture Timing	52	90%	97%	96%
Influenza Vaccine	40	88%	92%	91%
Initial Antibiotic Timing	74	95%	97%	95%
Pneumococcal Vaccine	68	72%	93%	93%
Smoking Cessation Advice[1]	22	68%	95%	97%
Surgical Care Improvement Project				
Appropriate VTP Within 24 Hours	54	94%	93%	92%
Appropriate Hair Removal	112	100%	100%	99%
Appropriate Beta Blocker Usage	33	79%	92%	93%
Controlled Postoperative Blood Glucose	0	-	93%	93%
Prophylactic Antibiotic Timing	83	95%	97%	97%
Prophylactic Antibiotic Timing (Outpatient)	51	94%	91%	92%
Prophylactic Antibiotic Selection	83	95%	98%	97%
Prophylactic Antibiotic Select. (Outpatient)	50	98%	96%	94%
Prophylactic Antibiotic Stopped	79	89%	95%	94%
Recommended VTP Ordered	54	94%	94%	94%
Urinary Catheter Removal[1]	20	90%	91%	90%
Children's Asthma Care				
Received Systemic Corticosteroids	-	-	-	100%
Received Home Management Plan	-	-	-	71%
Received Reliever Medication	-	-	-	100%
Use of Medical Imaging				
Combination Abdominal CT Scan	203	0.034	0.106	0.191
Combination Chest CT Scan	206	0.010	0.027	0.054
Follow-up Mammogram/Ultrasound	464	14.4%	8.4%	8.4%
MRI for Low Back Pain[1]	52	19.2%	31.8%	32.7%
Survey of Patients' Hospital Experiences				
Area Around Room 'Always' Quiet at Night	300+	58%	-	58%
Doctors 'Always' Communicated Well	300+	80%	-	80%
Home Recovery Information Given	300+	85%	-	82%
Hospital Given 9 or 10 on 10 Point Scale	300+	59%	-	67%
Meds 'Always' Explained Before Given	300+	64%	-	60%
Nurses 'Always' Communicated Well	300+	74%	-	76%
Pain 'Always' Well Controlled	300+	68%	-	69%
Room and Bathroom 'Always' Clean	300+	75%	-	71%
Timely Help 'Always' Received	300+	65%	-	64%
Would Definitely Recommend Hospital	300+	57%	-	69%

NOTE: Hospital profiles are in alphabetical order by state, then city, then hospital within the city; Rankings exclude hospitals with less than 25 cases except for patient surveys which excludes hospitals with less than 100 cases; (a) 100–299 cases; (1) The number of cases is too small to be sure how well a hospital is performing; (2) The hospital indicated that the data submitted for this measure were based on a sample of cases; (3) Data was collected during a shorter time period (fewer quarters) than the maximum possible time for this measure; (4) Suppressed for one or more quarters by CMS; (5) No data is available from the hospital for this measure; (6) Fewer than 100 patients completed the HCAHPS survey. Use these rates with caution, as the number of surveys may be too low to reliably assess hospital performance; (7) Survey results are based on less than 12 months of data; (8) Survey results are not available for this reporting period; (9) No or very few patients were eligible for the HCAHPS survey. The scores shown, if any, reflect a very small number of surveys; (10) A state average was not calculated because too few hospitals in the state submitted data; (11) There were discrepancies in the data collection process; Please refer to the User's Guide for a full explanation of data.

Prairie Du Chien Memorial Hospital

705 E Taylor St — Phone: 608-357-2000
Prairie Du Chien, WI 53821 — Fax: 608-357-2100
Type: Critical Access Hospitals — Emergency Services: Yes
Ownership: Voluntary Non-Profit - Private — Beds: 43

Key Personnel:
CEO/President. . . . . Harold W Brown
Chief of Medical Staff . . . . Walter Boisrert, MD
Infection Control. . . . . Ruth Mundt, RN
Operating Room. . . . . Kathy Kurt, RN
Quality Assurance . . . . Jacqueline Johnsrud, RN
Emergency Room . . . . Kurt Jorgensen, MD
Intensive Care Unit. . . . . Jean Bacon, RN

Measure	Cases	This Hosp.	State Avg.	U.S. Avg.
Heart Attack Care				
ACE Inhibitor or ARB for LVSD[1]	2	100%	97%	96%
Aspirin at Arrival[1]	7	100%	99%	99%
Aspirin at Discharge[1]	4	100%	99%	98%
Beta Blocker at Discharge[1]	5	100%	99%	98%
Fibrinolytic Medication Timing	0	-	0%	55%
PCI Within 90 Minutes of Arrival[5]	0	-	89%	90%
Smoking Cessation Advice[1]	1	100%	99%	99%
Chest Pain/Possible Heart Attack Care				
Aspirin at Arrival[3]	40	98%	96%	95%
Median Time to ECG (minutes)[3]	39	5	7	8
Median Time to Transfer (minutes)[3]	0	-	49	61
Fibrinolytic Medication Timing[1,3]	8	75%	63%	54%
Heart Failure Care				
ACE Inhibitor or ARB for LVSD[1]	3	100%	95%	94%
Discharge Instructions[1]	21	90%	86%	88%
Evaluation of LVS Function	33	88%	97%	98%
Smoking Cessation Advice[1]	2	100%	97%	98%
Pneumonia Care				
Appropriate Initial Antibiotic	40	90%	94%	92%
Blood Culture Timing	49	94%	97%	96%
Influenza Vaccine	36	75%	92%	91%
Initial Antibiotic Timing	60	97%	97%	95%
Pneumococcal Vaccine	66	91%	93%	93%
Smoking Cessation Advice[1]	8	100%	95%	97%
Surgical Care Improvement Project				
Appropriate VTP Within 24 Hours[1]	22	100%	93%	92%
Appropriate Hair Removal	35	100%	100%	99%
Appropriate Beta Blocker Usage[5]	0	-	92%	93%
Controlled Postoperative Blood Glucose	0	-	93%	93%
Prophylactic Antibiotic Timing	25	76%	97%	97%
Prophylactic Antibiotic Timing (Outpatient)[5]	0	-	91%	92%
Prophylactic Antibiotic Selection[1]	24	96%	98%	97%
Prophylactic Antibiotic Select. (Outpatient)[5]	0	-	96%	94%
Prophylactic Antibiotic Stopped[1]	24	100%	95%	94%
Recommended VTP Ordered[1]	22	100%	94%	94%
Urinary Catheter Removal[1]	21	90%	91%	90%
Children's Asthma Care				
Received Systemic Corticosteroids	-	-	-	100%
Received Home Management Plan	-	-	-	71%
Received Reliever Medication	-	-	-	100%
Use of Medical Imaging				
Combination Abdominal CT Scan	167	0.042	0.106	0.191
Combination Chest CT Scan	75	0.053	0.027	0.054
Follow-up Mammogram/Ultrasound	286	6.6%	8.4%	8.4%
MRI for Low Back Pain[1]	44	4.5%	31.8%	32.7%
Survey of Patients' Hospital Experiences				
Area Around Room 'Always' Quiet at Night	300+	57%	-	58%
Doctors 'Always' Communicated Well	300+	87%	-	80%
Home Recovery Information Given	300+	89%	-	82%
Hospital Given 9 or 10 on 10 Point Scale	300+	76%	-	67%
Meds 'Always' Explained Before Given	300+	70%	-	60%
Nurses 'Always' Communicated Well	300+	82%	-	76%
Pain 'Always' Well Controlled	300+	76%	-	69%
Room and Bathroom 'Always' Clean	300+	84%	-	71%
Timely Help 'Always' Received	300+	77%	-	64%
Would Definitely Recommend Hospital	300+	67%	-	69%

Sauk Prairie Memorial Hospital

80 First St — Phone: 608-643-3311
Prairie Du Sac, WI 53578 — Fax: 608-643-7151
URL: www.spmh.org
Type: Acute Care Hospitals — Emergency Services: Yes
Ownership: Voluntary Non-Profit - Private — Beds: 36

Key Personnel:
CEO/President. . . . . Larry Schroeder
Chief of Medical Staff . . . . Norbert R Straub
Infection Control. . . . . Sandra Schlender, RN
Operating Room. . . . . John A DeGiovanni, RN
Quality Assurance . . . . Jackie Smith
Anesthesiology. . . . . Mark Sparr
Emergency Room . . . . Connie Henery

Measure	Cases	This Hosp.	State Avg.	U.S. Avg.
Heart Attack Care				
ACE Inhibitor or ARB for LVSD[1]	2	50%	97%	96%
Aspirin at Arrival[1]	3	67%	99%	99%
Aspirin at Discharge[1]	2	50%	99%	98%
Beta Blocker at Discharge[1]	3	67%	99%	98%
Fibrinolytic Medication Timing	0	-	0%	55%
PCI Within 90 Minutes of Arrival	0	-	89%	90%
Smoking Cessation Advice	0	-	99%	99%
Chest Pain/Possible Heart Attack Care				
Aspirin at Arrival	63	92%	96%	95%
Median Time to ECG (minutes)	67	10	7	8
Median Time to Transfer (minutes)[1]	9	95	49	61
Fibrinolytic Medication Timing	0	-	63%	54%
Heart Failure Care				
ACE Inhibitor or ARB for LVSD[1]	4	50%	95%	94%
Discharge Instructions[1]	24	100%	86%	88%
Evaluation of LVS Function	30	97%	97%	98%
Smoking Cessation Advice[1]	1	100%	97%	98%
Pneumonia Care				
Appropriate Initial Antibiotic	27	93%	94%	92%
Blood Culture Timing[1]	12	92%	97%	96%
Influenza Vaccine[1]	18	100%	92%	91%
Initial Antibiotic Timing[1]	21	86%	97%	95%
Pneumococcal Vaccine	27	96%	93%	93%
Smoking Cessation Advice[1]	13	100%	95%	97%
Surgical Care Improvement Project				
Appropriate VTP Within 24 Hours	77	88%	93%	92%
Appropriate Hair Removal	749	100%	100%	99%
Appropriate Beta Blocker Usage	183	100%	92%	93%
Controlled Postoperative Blood Glucose	0	-	93%	93%
Prophylactic Antibiotic Timing	678	99%	97%	97%
Prophylactic Antibiotic Timing (Outpatient)	67	100%	91%	92%
Prophylactic Antibiotic Selection	689	99%	98%	97%
Prophylactic Antibiotic Select. (Outpatient)	67	91%	96%	94%
Prophylactic Antibiotic Stopped	674	97%	95%	94%
Recommended VTP Ordered	77	90%	94%	94%
Urinary Catheter Removal	240	99%	91%	90%
Children's Asthma Care				
Received Systemic Corticosteroids	-	-	-	100%
Received Home Management Plan	-	-	-	71%
Received Reliever Medication	-	-	-	100%
Use of Medical Imaging				
Combination Abdominal CT Scan	165	0.115	0.106	0.191
Combination Chest CT Scan	105	0.152	0.027	0.054
Follow-up Mammogram/Ultrasound	536	11.0%	8.4%	8.4%
MRI for Low Back Pain	75	33.3%	31.8%	32.7%
Survey of Patients' Hospital Experiences				
Area Around Room 'Always' Quiet at Night	300+	58%	-	58%
Doctors 'Always' Communicated Well	300+	85%	-	80%
Home Recovery Information Given	300+	88%	-	82%
Hospital Given 9 or 10 on 10 Point Scale	300+	82%	-	67%
Meds 'Always' Explained Before Given	300+	70%	-	60%
Nurses 'Always' Communicated Well	300+	82%	-	76%
Pain 'Always' Well Controlled	300+	70%	-	69%
Room and Bathroom 'Always' Clean	300+	81%	-	71%
Timely Help 'Always' Received	300+	74%	-	64%
Would Definitely Recommend Hospital	300+	88%	-	69%

Wheaton Franciscan Healthcare - All Saints

3801 Spring St — Phone: 262-687-4011
Racine, WI 53405 — Fax: 262-687-2674
URL: www.mywheaton.org
Type: Acute Care Hospitals — Emergency Services: Yes
Ownership: Voluntary Non-Profit - Church — Beds: 226

Key Personnel:
CEO/President. . . . . John D Oliverio
Chief of Medical Staff . . . . Sharee ChanceLawson, MD
Coronary Care . . . . Carol Meils
Operating Room. . . . . James Waltenberger, RN
Pediatric In-Patient Care . . . . Scott Meyer, MD
Quality Assurance . . . . Donna Brossard
Emergency Room . . . . Margrett Malnory
Patient Relations . . . . Rose Fowler

Measure	Cases	This Hosp.	State Avg.	U.S. Avg.
Heart Attack Care				
ACE Inhibitor or ARB for LVSD	26	88%	97%	96%
Aspirin at Arrival	193	100%	99%	99%
Aspirin at Discharge	188	100%	99%	98%
Beta Blocker at Discharge	184	100%	99%	98%
Fibrinolytic Medication Timing[1]	1	0%	0%	55%
PCI Within 90 Minutes of Arrival	46	91%	89%	90%
Smoking Cessation Advice	68	100%	99%	99%
Chest Pain/Possible Heart Attack Care				
Aspirin at Arrival[1]	9	78%	96%	95%
Median Time to ECG (minutes)[1]	8	8	7	8
Median Time to Transfer (minutes)[5]	0	-	49	61
Fibrinolytic Medication Timing[3]	0	-	63%	54%
Heart Failure Care				
ACE Inhibitor or ARB for LVSD	155	99%	95%	94%
Discharge Instructions	382	87%	86%	88%
Evaluation of LVS Function	491	100%	97%	98%
Smoking Cessation Advice	120	100%	97%	98%
Pneumonia Care				
Appropriate Initial Antibiotic	129	98%	94%	92%
Blood Culture Timing	343	99%	97%	96%
Influenza Vaccine	203	100%	92%	91%
Initial Antibiotic Timing	285	99%	97%	95%
Pneumococcal Vaccine	302	99%	93%	93%
Smoking Cessation Advice	105	94%	95%	97%
Surgical Care Improvement Project				
Appropriate VTP Within 24 Hours[2]	208	99%	93%	92%
Appropriate Hair Removal[2]	628	100%	100%	99%
Appropriate Beta Blocker Usage[2]	185	96%	92%	93%
Controlled Postoperative Blood Glucose[2]	71	86%	93%	93%
Prophylactic Antibiotic Timing[2]	376	97%	97%	97%
Prophylactic Antibiotic Timing (Outpatient)	400	93%	91%	92%
Prophylactic Antibiotic Selection[2]	386	98%	98%	97%
Prophylactic Antibiotic Select. (Outpatient)	494	97%	96%	94%
Prophylactic Antibiotic Stopped[2]	350	96%	95%	94%
Recommended VTP Ordered[2]	208	100%	94%	94%
Urinary Catheter Removal[2]	66	100%	91%	90%
Children's Asthma Care				
Received Systemic Corticosteroids	-	-	-	100%
Received Home Management Plan	-	-	-	71%
Received Reliever Medication	-	-	-	100%
Use of Medical Imaging				
Combination Abdominal CT Scan	1,108	0.134	0.106	0.191
Combination Chest CT Scan	1,131	0.016	0.027	0.054
Follow-up Mammogram/Ultrasound	2,565	7.8%	8.4%	8.4%
MRI for Low Back Pain	284	33.1%	31.8%	32.7%
Survey of Patients' Hospital Experiences				
Area Around Room 'Always' Quiet at Night	300+	53%	-	58%
Doctors 'Always' Communicated Well	300+	77%	-	80%
Home Recovery Information Given	300+	87%	-	82%
Hospital Given 9 or 10 on 10 Point Scale	300+	58%	-	67%
Meds 'Always' Explained Before Given	300+	57%	-	60%
Nurses 'Always' Communicated Well	300+	74%	-	76%
Pain 'Always' Well Controlled	300+	66%	-	69%
Room and Bathroom 'Always' Clean	300+	68%	-	71%
Timely Help 'Always' Received	300+	55%	-	64%
Would Definitely Recommend Hospital	300+	54%	-	69%

NOTE: Hospital profiles are in alphabetical order by state, then city, then hospital within the city; Rankings exclude hospitals with less than 25 cases except for patient surveys which excludes hospitals with less than 100 cases; (a) 100–299 cases; (1) The number of cases is too small to be sure how well a hospital is performing; (2) The hospital indicated that the data submitted for this measure were based on a sample of cases; (3) Data was collected during a shorter time period (fewer quarters) than the maximum possible time for this measure; (4) Suppressed for one or more quarters by CMS; (5) No data is available from the hospital for this measure; (6) Fewer than 100 patients completed the HCAHPS survey. Use these rates with caution, as the number of surveys may be too low to reliably assess hospital performance; (7) Survey results are based on less than 12 months of data; (8) Survey results are not available for this reporting period; (9) No or very few patients were eligible for the HCAHPS survey. The scores shown, if any, reflect a very small number of surveys; (10) A state average was not calculated because too few hospitals in the state submitted data; (11) There were discrepancies in the data collection process; Please refer to the User's Guide for a full explanation of data.

Reedsburg Area Medical Center

2000 N Dewey Ave
Reedsburg, WI 53959
Phone: 608-524-6487
Fax: 608-524-6566
URL: www.ramchealth.com
Type: Critical Access Hospitals
Emergency Services: Yes
Ownership: Voluntary Non-Profit - Private

Key Personnel:

CEO/President. . . . . Bob Van Meeteren
Chief of Medical Staff . . . . K M Hoffmann, MD
Infection Control. . . . . Peg Dobrovelny
Operating Room. . . . . Pat Peterson
Radiology. . . . . Douglas R Andrews
Anesthesiology. . . . . Ken Olson, CRNA MS
Emergency Room . . . . Janet Bolk
Intensive Care Unit. . . . . Janet Volk

Measure	Cases	This Hosp.	State Avg.	U.S. Avg.
Heart Attack Care				
ACE Inhibitor or ARB for LVSD[3]	0	-	97%	96%
Aspirin at Arrival[1,3]	2	100%	99%	99%
Aspirin at Discharge[1,3]	2	100%	99%	98%
Beta Blocker at Discharge[1,3]	2	100%	99%	98%
Fibrinolytic Medication Timing[3]	0	-	0%	55%
PCI Within 90 Minutes of Arrival[5]	0	-	89%	90%
Smoking Cessation Advice[3]	0	-	99%	99%
Chest Pain/Possible Heart Attack Care				
Aspirin at Arrival	46	96%	96%	95%
Median Time to ECG (minutes)	48	4	7	8
Median Time to Transfer (minutes)[1]	14	64	49	61
Fibrinolytic Medication Timing[1]	2	50%	63%	54%
Heart Failure Care				
ACE Inhibitor or ARB for LVSD[1]	13	85%	95%	94%
Discharge Instructions	45	73%	86%	88%
Evaluation of LVS Function	57	91%	97%	98%
Smoking Cessation Advice[1]	4	100%	97%	98%
Pneumonia Care				
Appropriate Initial Antibiotic	65	95%	94%	92%
Blood Culture Timing	40	98%	97%	96%
Influenza Vaccine	43	100%	92%	91%
Initial Antibiotic Timing	67	97%	97%	95%
Pneumococcal Vaccine	68	99%	93%	93%
Smoking Cessation Advice[1]	21	100%	95%	97%
Surgical Care Improvement Project				
Appropriate VTP Within 24 Hours[1,2]	23	87%	93%	92%
Appropriate Hair Removal[2]	86	100%	100%	99%
Appropriate Beta Blocker Usage[2]	33	73%	92%	93%
Controlled Postoperative Blood Glucose[5]	0	-	93%	93%
Prophylactic Antibiotic Timing[2]	76	93%	97%	97%
Prophylactic Antibiotic Timing (Outpatient)	53	81%	91%	92%
Prophylactic Antibiotic Selection[2]	76	100%	98%	97%
Prophylactic Antibiotic Select. (Outpatient)	50	90%	96%	94%
Prophylactic Antibiotic Stopped[2]	74	99%	95%	94%
Recommended VTP Ordered[1,2]	23	87%	94%	94%
Urinary Catheter Removal[1]	8	100%	91%	90%
Children's Asthma Care				
Received Systemic Corticosteroids	-	-	-	100%
Received Home Management Plan	-	-	-	71%
Received Reliever Medication	-	-	-	100%
Use of Medical Imaging				
Combination Abdominal CT Scan	185	0.038	0.106	0.191
Combination Chest CT Scan	79	0.000	0.027	0.054
Follow-up Mammogram/Ultrasound	254	13.8%	8.4%	8.4%
MRI for Low Back Pain	79	39.2%	31.8%	32.7%
Survey of Patients' Hospital Experiences				
Area Around Room 'Always' Quiet at Night	300+	65%	-	58%
Doctors 'Always' Communicated Well	300+	84%	-	80%
Home Recovery Information Given	300+	88%	-	82%
Hospital Given 9 or 10 on 10 Point Scale	300+	71%	-	67%
Meds 'Always' Explained Before Given	300+	62%	-	60%
Nurses 'Always' Communicated Well	300+	81%	-	76%
Pain 'Always' Well Controlled	300+	68%	-	69%
Room and Bathroom 'Always' Clean	300+	80%	-	71%
Timely Help 'Always' Received	300+	67%	-	64%
Would Definitely Recommend Hospital	300+	76%	-	69%

Ministry St Marys Hospital

2251 North Shore Dr
Rhinelander, WI 54501
Phone: 715-361-2000
Fax: 715-361-2011
URL: www.ministryhealth.org
Type: Acute Care Hospitals
Emergency Services: Yes
Ownership: Voluntary Non-Profit - Private
Beds: 73

Key Personnel:

CEO/President. . . . . Kevin O'Donnell
Cardiac Laboratory. . . . . Kathy Grill, RN
Chief of Medical Staff . . . . Judith Pagano, MD
Infection Control. . . . . Karen Wiedeman, RN
Operating Room. . . . . Gary Tiesling
Pediatric In-Patient Care . . . . Rene Iannarelli
Quality Assurance . . . . Ann Zenk
Radiology. . . . . Kathi Senoraske

Measure	Cases	This Hosp.	State Avg.	U.S. Avg.
Heart Attack Care				
ACE Inhibitor or ARB for LVSD[1]	2	100%	97%	96%
Aspirin at Arrival[1]	18	100%	99%	99%
Aspirin at Discharge[1]	12	92%	99%	98%
Beta Blocker at Discharge[1]	13	85%	99%	98%
Fibrinolytic Medication Timing	0	-	0%	55%
PCI Within 90 Minutes of Arrival	0	-	89%	90%
Smoking Cessation Advice	0	-	99%	99%
Chest Pain/Possible Heart Attack Care				
Aspirin at Arrival	117	98%	96%	95%
Median Time to ECG (minutes)	126	5	7	8
Median Time to Transfer (minutes)[3]	0	-	49	61
Fibrinolytic Medication Timing[1]	11	64%	63%	54%
Heart Failure Care				
ACE Inhibitor or ARB for LVSD[1]	13	100%	95%	94%
Discharge Instructions	63	100%	86%	88%
Evaluation of LVS Function	90	100%	97%	98%
Smoking Cessation Advice[1]	8	100%	97%	98%
Pneumonia Care				
Appropriate Initial Antibiotic	73	100%	94%	92%
Blood Culture Timing	88	99%	97%	96%
Influenza Vaccine	61	93%	92%	91%
Initial Antibiotic Timing	100	97%	97%	95%
Pneumococcal Vaccine	86	87%	93%	93%
Smoking Cessation Advice	30	100%	95%	97%
Surgical Care Improvement Project				
Appropriate VTP Within 24 Hours	95	88%	93%	92%
Appropriate Hair Removal	460	100%	100%	99%
Appropriate Beta Blocker Usage	134	89%	92%	93%
Controlled Postoperative Blood Glucose	0	-	93%	93%
Prophylactic Antibiotic Timing	364	98%	97%	97%
Prophylactic Antibiotic Timing (Outpatient)	76	84%	91%	92%
Prophylactic Antibiotic Selection	365	100%	98%	97%
Prophylactic Antibiotic Select. (Outpatient)	73	85%	96%	94%
Prophylactic Antibiotic Stopped	358	98%	95%	94%
Recommended VTP Ordered	96	93%	94%	94%
Urinary Catheter Removal	35	91%	91%	90%
Children's Asthma Care				
Received Systemic Corticosteroids	-	-	-	100%
Received Home Management Plan	-	-	-	71%
Received Reliever Medication	-	-	-	100%
Use of Medical Imaging				
Combination Abdominal CT Scan	487	0.080	0.106	0.191
Combination Chest CT Scan	339	0.003	0.027	0.054
Follow-up Mammogram/Ultrasound	792	6.4%	8.4%	8.4%
MRI for Low Back Pain	131	26.7%	31.8%	32.7%
Survey of Patients' Hospital Experiences				
Area Around Room 'Always' Quiet at Night	300+	49%	-	58%
Doctors 'Always' Communicated Well	300+	81%	-	80%
Home Recovery Information Given	300+	89%	-	82%
Hospital Given 9 or 10 on 10 Point Scale	300+	60%	-	67%
Meds 'Always' Explained Before Given	300+	60%	-	60%
Nurses 'Always' Communicated Well	300+	75%	-	76%
Pain 'Always' Well Controlled	300+	66%	-	69%
Room and Bathroom 'Always' Clean	300+	70%	-	71%
Timely Help 'Always' Received	300+	61%	-	64%
Would Definitely Recommend Hospital	300+	60%	-	69%

Lakeview Medical Center

1700 West Stout Street
Rice Lake, WI 54868
Phone: 715-234-1515
Fax: 715-234-4465
URL: www.lakeviewmedical.com
Type: Acute Care Hospitals
Emergency Services: Yes
Ownership: Voluntary Non-Profit - Private
Beds: 75

Measure	Cases	This Hosp.	State Avg.	U.S. Avg.
Heart Attack Care				
ACE Inhibitor or ARB for LVSD	0	-	97%	96%
Aspirin at Arrival[1]	16	94%	99%	99%
Aspirin at Discharge[1]	8	100%	99%	98%
Beta Blocker at Discharge[1]	7	100%	99%	98%
Fibrinolytic Medication Timing	0	-	0%	55%
PCI Within 90 Minutes of Arrival	0	-	89%	90%
Smoking Cessation Advice[1]	1	100%	99%	99%
Chest Pain/Possible Heart Attack Care				
Aspirin at Arrival	116	99%	96%	95%
Median Time to ECG (minutes)	118	4	7	8
Median Time to Transfer (minutes)[1]	10	51	49	61
Fibrinolytic Medication Timing[1]	1	0%	63%	54%
Heart Failure Care				
ACE Inhibitor or ARB for LVSD[1]	12	92%	95%	94%
Discharge Instructions	59	97%	86%	88%
Evaluation of LVS Function	72	99%	97%	98%
Smoking Cessation Advice[1]	12	75%	97%	98%
Pneumonia Care				
Appropriate Initial Antibiotic	44	98%	94%	92%
Blood Culture Timing	60	100%	97%	96%
Influenza Vaccine	46	93%	92%	91%
Initial Antibiotic Timing	71	100%	97%	95%
Pneumococcal Vaccine	78	97%	93%	93%
Smoking Cessation Advice[1]	19	100%	95%	97%
Surgical Care Improvement Project				
Appropriate VTP Within 24 Hours[2]	54	100%	93%	92%
Appropriate Hair Removal[2]	367	100%	100%	99%
Appropriate Beta Blocker Usage[2]	116	95%	92%	93%
Controlled Postoperative Blood Glucose[2]	0	-	93%	93%
Prophylactic Antibiotic Timing[2]	311	99%	97%	97%
Prophylactic Antibiotic Timing (Outpatient)	43	93%	91%	92%
Prophylactic Antibiotic Selection[2]	314	99%	98%	97%
Prophylactic Antibiotic Select. (Outpatient)	42	98%	96%	94%
Prophylactic Antibiotic Stopped[2]	305	99%	95%	94%
Recommended VTP Ordered[2]	54	100%	94%	94%
Urinary Catheter Removal[2]	122	98%	91%	90%
Children's Asthma Care				
Received Systemic Corticosteroids	-	-	-	100%
Received Home Management Plan	-	-	-	71%
Received Reliever Medication	-	-	-	100%
Use of Medical Imaging				
Combination Abdominal CT Scan	275	0.062	0.106	0.191
Combination Chest CT Scan	283	0.028	0.027	0.054
Follow-up Mammogram/Ultrasound	256	9.8%	8.4%	8.4%
MRI for Low Back Pain	84	28.6%	31.8%	32.7%
Survey of Patients' Hospital Experiences				
Area Around Room 'Always' Quiet at Night	300+	59%	-	58%
Doctors 'Always' Communicated Well	300+	82%	-	80%
Home Recovery Information Given	300+	86%	-	82%
Hospital Given 9 or 10 on 10 Point Scale	300+	68%	-	67%
Meds 'Always' Explained Before Given	300+	67%	-	60%
Nurses 'Always' Communicated Well	300+	79%	-	76%
Pain 'Always' Well Controlled	300+	71%	-	69%
Room and Bathroom 'Always' Clean	300+	77%	-	71%
Timely Help 'Always' Received	300+	74%	-	64%
Would Definitely Recommend Hospital	300+	70%	-	69%

NOTE: Hospital profiles are in alphabetical order by state, then city, then hospital within the city; Rankings exclude hospitals with less than 25 cases except for patient surveys which excludes hospitals with less than 100 cases; (a) 100–299 cases; (1) The number of cases is too small to be sure how well a hospital is performing; (2) The hospital indicated that the data submitted for this measure were based on a sample of cases; (3) Data was collected during a shorter time period (fewer quarters) than the maximum possible time for this measure; (4) Suppressed for one or more quarters by CMS; (5) No data is available from the hospital for this measure; (6) Fewer than 100 patients completed the HCAHPS survey. Use these rates with caution, as the number of surveys may be too low to reliably assess hospital performance; (7) Survey results are based on less than 12 months of data; (8) Survey results are not available for this reporting period; (9) No or very few patients were eligible for the HCAHPS survey. The scores shown, if any, reflect a very small number of surveys; (10) A state average was not calculated because too few hospitals in the state submitted data; (11) There were discrepancies in the data collection process; Please refer to the User's Guide for a full explanation of data.

Richland Hospital

333 E Second St
Richland Center, WI 53581
E-mail: hr@richlandhospial.com
URL: www.richlandhospital.com
Type: Critical Access Hospitals
Ownership: Voluntary Non-Profit - Private

Phone: 608-647-6321
Fax: 608-647-6235
Emergency Services: Yes
Beds: 25

Key Personnel:
CEO/President. . . . . Steve Nockerts
Patient Relations . . . . Richard Lee

Measure	Cases	This Hosp.	State Avg.	U.S. Avg.
Heart Attack Care				
ACE Inhibitor or ARB for LVSD[1]	3	100%	97%	96%
Aspirin at Arrival[1]	9	100%	99%	99%
Aspirin at Discharge[1]	8	100%	99%	98%
Beta Blocker at Discharge[1]	10	80%	99%	98%
Fibrinolytic Medication Timing	0	-	0%	55%
PCI Within 90 Minutes of Arrival[5]	0	-	89%	90%
Smoking Cessation Advice	0	-	99%	99%
Chest Pain/Possible Heart Attack Care				
Aspirin at Arrival	-	-	96%	95%
Median Time to ECG (minutes)	-	-	7	8
Median Time to Transfer (minutes)	-	-	49	61
Fibrinolytic Medication Timing	-	-	63%	54%
Heart Failure Care				
ACE Inhibitor or ARB for LVSD[1]	6	83%	95%	94%
Discharge Instructions	30	73%	86%	88%
Evaluation of LVS Function	37	68%	97%	98%
Smoking Cessation Advice[1]	4	25%	97%	98%
Pneumonia Care				
Appropriate Initial Antibiotic[1]	18	94%	94%	92%
Blood Culture Timing	26	85%	97%	96%
Influenza Vaccine	31	81%	92%	91%
Initial Antibiotic Timing	28	96%	97%	95%
Pneumococcal Vaccine	47	68%	93%	93%
Smoking Cessation Advice[1]	6	67%	95%	97%
Surgical Care Improvement Project				
Appropriate VTP Within 24 Hours[1]	20	75%	93%	92%
Appropriate Hair Removal	64	100%	100%	99%
Appropriate Beta Blocker Usage[5]	0	-	92%	93%
Controlled Postoperative Blood Glucose	0	-	93%	93%
Prophylactic Antibiotic Timing	61	87%	97%	97%
Prophylactic Antibiotic Timing (Outpatient)	-	-	91%	92%
Prophylactic Antibiotic Selection	61	93%	98%	97%
Prophylactic Antibiotic Select. (Outpatient)	-	-	96%	94%
Prophylactic Antibiotic Stopped	61	93%	95%	94%
Recommended VTP Ordered[1]	20	75%	94%	94%
Urinary Catheter Removal[1]	20	100%	91%	90%
Children's Asthma Care				
Received Systemic Corticosteroids	-	-	-	100%
Received Home Management Plan	-	-	-	71%
Received Reliever Medication	-	-	-	100%
Use of Medical Imaging				
Combination Abdominal CT Scan	-	-	0.106	0.191
Combination Chest CT Scan	-	-	0.027	0.054
Follow-up Mammogram/Ultrasound	-	-	8.4%	8.4%
MRI for Low Back Pain	-	-	31.8%	32.7%
Survey of Patients' Hospital Experiences				
Area Around Room 'Always' Quiet at Night	300+	56%	-	58%
Doctors 'Always' Communicated Well	300+	84%	-	80%
Home Recovery Information Given	300+	84%	-	82%
Hospital Given 9 or 10 on 10 Point Scale	300+	70%	-	67%
Meds 'Always' Explained Before Given	300+	62%	-	60%
Nurses 'Always' Communicated Well	300+	79%	-	76%
Pain 'Always' Well Controlled	300+	66%	-	69%
Room and Bathroom 'Always' Clean	300+	85%	-	71%
Timely Help 'Always' Received	300+	68%	-	64%
Would Definitely Recommend Hospital	300+	70%	-	69%

Ripon Medical Center

933 Newbury St, Box 390
Ripon, WI 54971
E-mail: info@riponmedicalcenter.com
URL: www.riponmedicalcenter.com
Type: Critical Access Hospitals
Ownership: Voluntary Non-Profit - Private

Phone: 920-748-3101
Fax: 920-748-9104
Emergency Services: Yes
Beds: 25

Key Personnel:
CEO/President. . . . . Jim Tavary
Cardiac Laboratory. . . . . Sandy Schaffer
Chief of Medical Staff . . . . Michael Combs, MD
Operating Room. . . . . Cheryl O'Grady-Ritch
Quality Assurance . . . . Pam Schmitz
Emergency Room . . . . Tami Moffat-Keenlanc
Patient Relations . . . . Jean Surguy

Measure	Cases	This Hosp.	State Avg.	U.S. Avg.
Heart Attack Care				
ACE Inhibitor or ARB for LVSD[5]	0	-	97%	96%
Aspirin at Arrival[5]	0	-	99%	99%
Aspirin at Discharge[5]	0	-	99%	98%
Beta Blocker at Discharge[5]	0	-	99%	98%
Fibrinolytic Medication Timing[5]	0	-	0%	55%
PCI Within 90 Minutes of Arrival[5]	0	-	89%	90%
Smoking Cessation Advice[5]	0	-	99%	99%
Chest Pain/Possible Heart Attack Care				
Aspirin at Arrival	-	-	96%	95%
Median Time to ECG (minutes)	-	-	7	8
Median Time to Transfer (minutes)	-	-	49	61
Fibrinolytic Medication Timing	-	-	63%	54%
Heart Failure Care				
ACE Inhibitor or ARB for LVSD[1]	5	40%	95%	94%
Discharge Instructions[1]	22	82%	86%	88%
Evaluation of LVS Function	33	94%	97%	98%
Smoking Cessation Advice[1]	2	100%	97%	98%
Pneumonia Care				
Appropriate Initial Antibiotic[1]	22	95%	94%	92%
Blood Culture Timing	31	100%	97%	96%
Influenza Vaccine[1]	19	74%	92%	91%
Initial Antibiotic Timing	32	100%	97%	95%
Pneumococcal Vaccine	31	87%	93%	93%
Smoking Cessation Advice[1]	3	100%	95%	97%
Surgical Care Improvement Project				
Appropriate VTP Within 24 Hours[5]	0	-	93%	92%
Appropriate Hair Removal[5]	0	-	100%	99%
Appropriate Beta Blocker Usage[5]	0	-	92%	93%
Controlled Postoperative Blood Glucose[5]	0	-	93%	93%
Prophylactic Antibiotic Timing[5]	0	-	97%	97%
Prophylactic Antibiotic Timing (Outpatient)	-	-	91%	92%
Prophylactic Antibiotic Selection[5]	0	-	98%	97%
Prophylactic Antibiotic Select. (Outpatient)	-	-	96%	94%
Prophylactic Antibiotic Stopped[5]	0	-	95%	94%
Recommended VTP Ordered[5]	0	-	94%	94%
Urinary Catheter Removal[5]	0	-	91%	90%
Children's Asthma Care				
Received Systemic Corticosteroids	-	-	-	100%
Received Home Management Plan	-	-	-	71%
Received Reliever Medication	-	-	-	100%
Use of Medical Imaging				
Combination Abdominal CT Scan	-	-	0.106	0.191
Combination Chest CT Scan	-	-	0.027	0.054
Follow-up Mammogram/Ultrasound	-	-	8.4%	8.4%
MRI for Low Back Pain	-	-	31.8%	32.7%
Survey of Patients' Hospital Experiences				
Area Around Room 'Always' Quiet at Night	300+	66%	-	58%
Doctors 'Always' Communicated Well	300+	82%	-	80%
Home Recovery Information Given	300+	85%	-	82%
Hospital Given 9 or 10 on 10 Point Scale	300+	73%	-	67%
Meds 'Always' Explained Before Given	300+	68%	-	60%
Nurses 'Always' Communicated Well	300+	84%	-	76%
Pain 'Always' Well Controlled	300+	75%	-	69%
Room and Bathroom 'Always' Clean	300+	81%	-	71%
Timely Help 'Always' Received	300+	77%	-	64%
Would Definitely Recommend Hospital	300+	70%	-	69%

River Falls Area Hospital

1629 E Division St
River Falls, WI 54022
URL: www.allina.com
Type: Critical Access Hospitals
Ownership: Voluntary Non-Profit - Private

Phone: 715-426-6155
Fax: 715-426-4555
Emergency Services: Yes
Beds: 25

Key Personnel:
CEO/President. . . . . David Miller
Chief of Medical Staff . . . . Dan Zimmerman
Infection Control. . . . . Lori Carlick
Operating Room. . . . . Matthew C Clayton, RN
Emergency Room . . . . Karen Swenson, RN

Measure	Cases	This Hosp.	State Avg.	U.S. Avg.
Heart Attack Care				
ACE Inhibitor or ARB for LVSD[3]	0	-	97%	96%
Aspirin at Arrival[1,3]	3	67%	99%	99%
Aspirin at Discharge[1,3]	1	100%	99%	98%
Beta Blocker at Discharge[1,3]	1	100%	99%	98%
Fibrinolytic Medication Timing[3]	0	-	0%	55%
PCI Within 90 Minutes of Arrival[3]	0	-	89%	90%
Smoking Cessation Advice[3]	0	-	99%	99%
Chest Pain/Possible Heart Attack Care				
Aspirin at Arrival	27	93%	96%	95%
Median Time to ECG (minutes)	29	9	7	8
Median Time to Transfer (minutes)[1]	7	35	49	61
Fibrinolytic Medication Timing	0	-	63%	54%
Heart Failure Care				
ACE Inhibitor or ARB for LVSD[1]	7	100%	95%	94%
Discharge Instructions[1]	18	94%	86%	88%
Evaluation of LVS Function[1]	21	100%	97%	98%
Smoking Cessation Advice[1]	2	100%	97%	98%
Pneumonia Care				
Appropriate Initial Antibiotic[1]	17	100%	94%	92%
Blood Culture Timing[1]	10	100%	97%	96%
Influenza Vaccine[1]	17	100%	92%	91%
Initial Antibiotic Timing[1]	22	100%	97%	95%
Pneumococcal Vaccine	29	100%	93%	93%
Smoking Cessation Advice[1]	5	100%	95%	97%
Surgical Care Improvement Project				
Appropriate VTP Within 24 Hours	50	94%	93%	92%
Appropriate Hair Removal	182	100%	100%	99%
Appropriate Beta Blocker Usage	30	90%	92%	93%
Controlled Postoperative Blood Glucose[5]	0	-	93%	93%
Prophylactic Antibiotic Timing	133	98%	97%	97%
Prophylactic Antibiotic Timing (Outpatient)[1,3]	13	85%	91%	92%
Prophylactic Antibiotic Selection	133	99%	98%	97%
Prophylactic Antibiotic Select. (Outpatient)[3,1]	12	100%	96%	94%
Prophylactic Antibiotic Stopped	128	98%	95%	94%
Recommended VTP Ordered	50	100%	94%	94%
Urinary Catheter Removal[1]	11	91%	91%	90%
Children's Asthma Care				
Received Systemic Corticosteroids	-	-	-	100%
Received Home Management Plan	-	-	-	71%
Received Reliever Medication	-	-	-	100%
Use of Medical Imaging				
Combination Abdominal CT Scan	147	0.020	0.106	0.191
Combination Chest CT Scan	90	0.000	0.027	0.054
Follow-up Mammogram/Ultrasound	328	7.9%	8.4%	8.4%
MRI for Low Back Pain[1]	31	29.0%	31.8%	32.7%
Survey of Patients' Hospital Experiences				
Area Around Room 'Always' Quiet at Night	300+	62%	-	58%
Doctors 'Always' Communicated Well	300+	84%	-	80%
Home Recovery Information Given	300+	88%	-	82%
Hospital Given 9 or 10 on 10 Point Scale	300+	74%	-	67%
Meds 'Always' Explained Before Given	300+	64%	-	60%
Nurses 'Always' Communicated Well	300+	80%	-	76%
Pain 'Always' Well Controlled	300+	75%	-	69%
Room and Bathroom 'Always' Clean	300+	77%	-	71%
Timely Help 'Always' Received	300+	79%	-	64%
Would Definitely Recommend Hospital	300+	74%	-	69%

NOTE: Hospital profiles are in alphabetical order by state, then city, then hospital within the city; Rankings exclude hospitals with less than 25 cases except for patient surveys which excludes hospitals with less than 100 cases; (a) 100–299 cases; (1) The number of cases is too small to be sure how well a hospital is performing; (2) The hospital indicated that the data submitted for this measure were based on a sample of cases; (3) Data was collected during a shorter time period (fewer quarters) than the maximum possible time for this measure; (4) Suppressed for one or more quarters by CMS; (5) No data is available from the hospital for this measure; (6) Fewer than 100 patients completed the HCAHPS survey. Use these rates with caution, as the number of surveys may be too low to reliably assess hospital performance; (7) Survey results are based on less than 12 months of data; (8) Survey results are not available for this reporting period; (9) No or very few patients were eligible for the HCAHPS survey. The scores shown, if any, reflect a very small number of surveys; (10) A state average was not calculated because too few hospitals in the state submitted data; (11) There were discrepancies in the data collection process; Please refer to the User's Guide for a full explanation of data.

Saint Croix Regional Medical Center

235 State Street Phone: 715-483-3261
Saint Croix Falls, WI 54024 Fax: 340-772-7398
URL: www.scrmc.org
Type: Critical Access Hospitals Emergency Services: Yes
Ownership: Voluntary Non-Profit - Private Beds: 25

Key Personnel:
CEO/President. . . . . Lenny Libis
Cardiac Laboratory. . . . . Deb Leal
Infection Control. . . . . Wanda Brown
Quality Assurance . . . . Carol Thornton
Radiology. . . . . Kathy Coffman
Emergency Room . . . . Mary Erickson
Intensive Care Unit. . . . . Kari Peer

Measure	Cases	This Hosp.	State Avg.	U.S. Avg.
Heart Attack Care				
ACE Inhibitor or ARB for LVSD[5]	0	-	97%	96%
Aspirin at Arrival[5]	0	-	99%	99%
Aspirin at Discharge[5]	0	-	99%	98%
Beta Blocker at Discharge[5]	0	-	99%	98%
Fibrinolytic Medication Timing[5]	0	-	0%	55%
PCI Within 90 Minutes of Arrival[5]	0	-	89%	90%
Smoking Cessation Advice[5]	0	-	99%	99%
Chest Pain/Possible Heart Attack Care				
Aspirin at Arrival	-	-	96%	95%
Median Time to ECG (minutes)	-	-	7	8
Median Time to Transfer (minutes)	-	-	49	61
Fibrinolytic Medication Timing	-	-	63%	54%
Heart Failure Care				
ACE Inhibitor or ARB for LVSD[1]	12	100%	95%	94%
Discharge Instructions	50	82%	86%	88%
Evaluation of LVS Function	61	67%	97%	98%
Smoking Cessation Advice[1]	8	62%	97%	98%
Pneumonia Care				
Appropriate Initial Antibiotic	48	94%	94%	92%
Blood Culture Timing	60	92%	97%	96%
Influenza Vaccine	40	70%	92%	91%
Initial Antibiotic Timing	68	96%	97%	95%
Pneumococcal Vaccine	69	70%	93%	93%
Smoking Cessation Advice[1]	14	57%	95%	97%
Surgical Care Improvement Project				
Appropriate VTP Within 24 Hours[5]	0	-	93%	92%
Appropriate Hair Removal[5]	0	-	100%	99%
Appropriate Beta Blocker Usage[5]	0	-	92%	93%
Controlled Postoperative Blood Glucose[5]	0	-	93%	93%
Prophylactic Antibiotic Timing	80	89%	97%	97%
Prophylactic Antibiotic Timing (Outpatient)	-	-	91%	92%
Prophylactic Antibiotic Selection	80	96%	98%	97%
Prophylactic Antibiotic Select. (Outpatient)	-	-	96%	94%
Prophylactic Antibiotic Stopped	79	97%	95%	94%
Recommended VTP Ordered[5]	0	-	94%	94%
Urinary Catheter Removal[5]	0	-	91%	90%
Children's Asthma Care				
Received Systemic Corticosteroids	-	-	-	100%
Received Home Management Plan	-	-	-	71%
Received Reliever Medication	-	-	-	100%
Use of Medical Imaging				
Combination Abdominal CT Scan	-	-	0.106	0.191
Combination Chest CT Scan	-	-	0.027	0.054
Follow-up Mammogram/Ultrasound	-	-	8.4%	8.4%
MRI for Low Back Pain	-	-	31.8%	32.7%
Survey of Patients' Hospital Experiences				
Area Around Room 'Always' Quiet at Night	300+	54%	-	58%
Doctors 'Always' Communicated Well	300+	82%	-	80%
Home Recovery Information Given	300+	87%	-	82%
Hospital Given 9 or 10 on 10 Point Scale	300+	74%	-	67%
Meds 'Always' Explained Before Given	300+	66%	-	60%
Nurses 'Always' Communicated Well	300+	76%	-	76%
Pain 'Always' Well Controlled	300+	69%	-	69%
Room and Bathroom 'Always' Clean	300+	80%	-	71%
Timely Help 'Always' Received	300+	72%	-	64%
Would Definitely Recommend Hospital	300+	75%	-	69%

Shawano Medical Center

309 N Bartlette St Phone: 715-526-2111
Shawano, WI 54166 Fax: 715-526-7205
E-mail: smc@shawanomed.org
URL: www.shawanomed.org
Type: Critical Access Hospitals Emergency Services: Yes
Ownership: Voluntary Non-Profit - Other Beds: 25

Key Personnel:
CEO/President. . . . . Dorothy Erdmann
Chief of Medical Staff. . . . . Amy Slagle, MD
Infection Control. . . . . Kim Marquardt, RN
Operating Room. . . . . Steve Schenk, RN
Quality Assurance . . . . Dennis Jalter, RN
Radiology. . . . . Paul Ho
Intensive Care Unit. . . . . Arlene Calkins, RN
Patient Relations . . . . Penny Block

Measure	Cases	This Hosp.	State Avg.	U.S. Avg.
Heart Attack Care				
ACE Inhibitor or ARB for LVSD[5]	0	-	97%	96%
Aspirin at Arrival[5]	0	-	99%	99%
Aspirin at Discharge[5]	0	-	99%	98%
Beta Blocker at Discharge[5]	0	-	99%	98%
Fibrinolytic Medication Timing[5]	0	-	0%	55%
PCI Within 90 Minutes of Arrival[5]	0	-	89%	90%
Smoking Cessation Advice[5]	0	-	99%	99%
Chest Pain/Possible Heart Attack Care				
Aspirin at Arrival	83	98%	96%	95%
Median Time to ECG (minutes)	89	3	7	8
Median Time to Transfer (minutes)[1]	11	40	49	61
Fibrinolytic Medication Timing	0	-	63%	54%
Heart Failure Care				
ACE Inhibitor or ARB for LVSD[1]	18	100%	95%	94%
Discharge Instructions	39	62%	86%	88%
Evaluation of LVS Function	58	90%	97%	98%
Smoking Cessation Advice[1]	7	100%	97%	98%
Pneumonia Care				
Appropriate Initial Antibiotic	65	91%	94%	92%
Blood Culture Timing	77	99%	97%	96%
Influenza Vaccine	50	82%	92%	91%
Initial Antibiotic Timing	83	100%	97%	95%
Pneumococcal Vaccine	75	83%	93%	93%
Smoking Cessation Advice	30	100%	95%	97%
Surgical Care Improvement Project				
Appropriate VTP Within 24 Hours	31	97%	93%	92%
Appropriate Hair Removal	70	100%	100%	99%
Appropriate Beta Blocker Usage[1]	19	84%	92%	93%
Controlled Postoperative Blood Glucose	0	-	93%	93%
Prophylactic Antibiotic Timing	41	98%	97%	97%
Prophylactic Antibiotic Timing (Outpatient)[1]	11	100%	91%	92%
Prophylactic Antibiotic Selection	41	100%	98%	97%
Prophylactic Antibiotic Select. (Outpatient)[1]	11	100%	96%	94%
Prophylactic Antibiotic Stopped	39	95%	95%	94%
Recommended VTP Ordered	31	97%	94%	94%
Urinary Catheter Removal[1]	3	100%	91%	90%
Children's Asthma Care				
Received Systemic Corticosteroids	-	-	-	100%
Received Home Management Plan	-	-	-	71%
Received Reliever Medication	-	-	-	100%
Use of Medical Imaging				
Combination Abdominal CT Scan	182	0.082	0.106	0.191
Combination Chest CT Scan	169	0.012	0.027	0.054
Follow-up Mammogram/Ultrasound	261	7.7%	8.4%	8.4%
MRI for Low Back Pain	39	46.2%	31.8%	32.7%
Survey of Patients' Hospital Experiences				
Area Around Room 'Always' Quiet at Night	300+	66%	-	58%
Doctors 'Always' Communicated Well	300+	81%	-	80%
Home Recovery Information Given	300+	81%	-	82%
Hospital Given 9 or 10 on 10 Point Scale	300+	65%	-	67%
Meds 'Always' Explained Before Given	300+	62%	-	60%
Nurses 'Always' Communicated Well	300+	77%	-	76%
Pain 'Always' Well Controlled	300+	67%	-	69%
Room and Bathroom 'Always' Clean	300+	79%	-	71%
Timely Help 'Always' Received	300+	70%	-	64%
Would Definitely Recommend Hospital	300+	62%	-	69%

Aurora Sheboygan Memorial Medical Center

2629 N 7th St Phone: 920-451-5000
Sheboygan, WI 53083 Fax: 920-451-5333
URL: www.aurorahealthcare.org/facilities
Type: Acute Care Hospitals Emergency Services: Yes
Ownership: Voluntary Non-Profit - Private

Key Personnel:
CEO/President. . . . . Bobbe Tiegen

Measure	Cases	This Hosp.	State Avg.	U.S. Avg.
Heart Attack Care				
ACE Inhibitor or ARB for LVSD[1]	6	83%	97%	96%
Aspirin at Arrival	40	98%	99%	99%
Aspirin at Discharge	32	94%	99%	98%
Beta Blocker at Discharge	29	93%	99%	98%
Fibrinolytic Medication Timing	0	-	0%	55%
PCI Within 90 Minutes of Arrival	0	-	89%	90%
Smoking Cessation Advice[1]	4	100%	99%	99%
Chest Pain/Possible Heart Attack Care				
Aspirin at Arrival	99	98%	96%	95%
Median Time to ECG (minutes)	99	6	7	8
Median Time to Transfer (minutes)	29	44	49	61
Fibrinolytic Medication Timing	0	-	63%	54%
Heart Failure Care				
ACE Inhibitor or ARB for LVSD	30	97%	95%	94%
Discharge Instructions	78	97%	86%	88%
Evaluation of LVS Function	101	100%	97%	98%
Smoking Cessation Advice[1]	13	100%	97%	98%
Pneumonia Care				
Appropriate Initial Antibiotic	41	93%	94%	92%
Blood Culture Timing	55	100%	97%	96%
Influenza Vaccine	59	93%	92%	91%
Initial Antibiotic Timing	77	97%	97%	95%
Pneumococcal Vaccine	96	94%	93%	93%
Smoking Cessation Advice	31	100%	95%	97%
Surgical Care Improvement Project				
Appropriate VTP Within 24 Hours[2]	132	95%	93%	92%
Appropriate Hair Removal[2]	589	100%	100%	99%
Appropriate Beta Blocker Usage[2]	177	98%	92%	93%
Controlled Postoperative Blood Glucose[2]	0	-	93%	93%
Prophylactic Antibiotic Timing[2]	468	98%	97%	97%
Prophylactic Antibiotic Timing (Outpatient)	342	99%	91%	92%
Prophylactic Antibiotic Selection[2]	468	99%	98%	97%
Prophylactic Antibiotic Select. (Outpatient)	340	98%	96%	94%
Prophylactic Antibiotic Stopped[2]	453	99%	95%	94%
Recommended VTP Ordered[2]	132	99%	94%	94%
Urinary Catheter Removal[2]	245	99%	91%	90%
Children's Asthma Care				
Received Systemic Corticosteroids	-	-	-	100%
Received Home Management Plan	-	-	-	71%
Received Reliever Medication	-	-	-	100%
Use of Medical Imaging				
Combination Abdominal CT Scan	448	0.132	0.106	0.191
Combination Chest CT Scan	310	0.019	0.027	0.054
Follow-up Mammogram/Ultrasound[5]	0	-	8.4%	8.4%
MRI for Low Back Pain[1]	38	15.8%	31.8%	32.7%
Survey of Patients' Hospital Experiences				
Area Around Room 'Always' Quiet at Night	300+	59%	-	58%
Doctors 'Always' Communicated Well	300+	81%	-	80%
Home Recovery Information Given	300+	89%	-	82%
Hospital Given 9 or 10 on 10 Point Scale	300+	73%	-	67%
Meds 'Always' Explained Before Given	300+	67%	-	60%
Nurses 'Always' Communicated Well	300+	81%	-	76%
Pain 'Always' Well Controlled	300+	73%	-	69%
Room and Bathroom 'Always' Clean	300+	76%	-	71%
Timely Help 'Always' Received	300+	64%	-	64%
Would Definitely Recommend Hospital	300+	74%	-	69%

NOTE: Hospital profiles are in alphabetical order by state, then city, then hospital within the city; Rankings exclude hospitals with less than 25 cases except for patient surveys which excludes hospitals with less than 100 cases; (a) 100–299 cases; (1) The number of cases is too small to be sure how well a hospital is performing; (2) The hospital indicated that the data submitted for this measure were based on a sample of cases; (3) Data was collected during a shorter time period (fewer quarters) than the maximum possible time for this measure; (4) Suppressed for one or more quarters by CMS; (5) No data is available from the hospital for this measure; (6) Fewer than 100 patients completed the HCAHPS survey. Use these rates with caution, as the number of surveys may be too low to reliably assess hospital performance; (7) Survey results are based on less than 12 months of data; (8) Survey results are not available for this reporting period; (9) No or very few patients were eligible for the HCAHPS survey. The scores shown, if any, reflect a very small number of surveys; (10) A state average was not calculated because too few hospitals in the state submitted data; (11) There were discrepancies in the data collection process; Please refer to the User's Guide for a full explanation of data.

Saint Nicholas Hospital

3100 Superior Ave
Sheboygan, WI 53081
Phone: 920-459-8300
Fax: 920-451-7280
URL: www.stnicholashospital.org
Type: Acute Care Hospitals
Emergency Services: Yes
Ownership: Voluntary Non-Profit - Church
Beds: 185

Key Personnel:
Chief of Medical Staff.......... Philip Walker, MD
Infection Control.............. Sally Korff
Operating Room.............. Christine McCann, RN
Pediatric Ambulatory Care ...... William L Trager, MD
Pediatric In-Patient Care .... William L Trager, MD
Quality Assurance .... Kathie Lensen
Radiology.................. William Pao, MD

Measure	Cases	This Hosp.	State Avg.	U.S. Avg.
Heart Attack Care				
ACE Inhibitor or ARB for LVSD[1]	9	89%	97%	96%
Aspirin at Arrival	26	96%	99%	99%
Aspirin at Discharge[1]	23	83%	99%	98%
Beta Blocker at Discharge[1]	23	91%	99%	98%
Fibrinolytic Medication Timing	0	-	0%	55%
PCI Within 90 Minutes of Arrival	0	-	89%	90%
Smoking Cessation Advice[1]	2	100%	99%	99%
Chest Pain/Possible Heart Attack Care				
Aspirin at Arrival	71	100%	96%	95%
Median Time to ECG (minutes)	73	7	7	8
Median Time to Transfer (minutes)[1]	21	37	49	61
Fibrinolytic Medication Timing[1]	1	100%	63%	54%
Heart Failure Care				
ACE Inhibitor or ARB for LVSD	33	97%	95%	94%
Discharge Instructions	43	81%	86%	88%
Evaluation of LVS Function	68	99%	97%	98%
Smoking Cessation Advice[1]	2	0%	97%	98%
Pneumonia Care				
Appropriate Initial Antibiotic	76	95%	94%	92%
Blood Culture Timing	92	99%	97%	96%
Influenza Vaccine	80	94%	92%	91%
Initial Antibiotic Timing	94	95%	97%	95%
Pneumococcal Vaccine	97	92%	93%	93%
Smoking Cessation Advice	38	87%	95%	97%
Surgical Care Improvement Project				
Appropriate VTP Within 24 Hours	126	96%	93%	92%
Appropriate Hair Removal	409	100%	100%	99%
Appropriate Beta Blocker Usage	100	85%	92%	93%
Controlled Postoperative Blood Glucose	0	-	93%	93%
Prophylactic Antibiotic Timing	281	93%	97%	97%
Prophylactic Antibiotic Timing (Outpatient)	87	80%	91%	92%
Prophylactic Antibiotic Selection	280	99%	98%	97%
Prophylactic Antibiotic Select. (Outpatient)	85	91%	96%	94%
Prophylactic Antibiotic Stopped	261	96%	95%	94%
Recommended VTP Ordered	126	98%	94%	94%
Urinary Catheter Removal	102	89%	91%	90%
Children's Asthma Care				
Received Systemic Corticosteroids	-	-	-	100%
Received Home Management Plan	-	-	-	71%
Received Reliever Medication	-	-	-	100%
Use of Medical Imaging				
Combination Abdominal CT Scan	472	0.053	0.106	0.191
Combination Chest CT Scan	353	0.006	0.027	0.054
Follow-up Mammogram/Ultrasound	377	4.8%	8.4%	8.4%
MRI for Low Back Pain	70	28.6%	31.8%	32.7%
Survey of Patients' Hospital Experiences				
Area Around Room 'Always' Quiet at Night	300+	54%	-	58%
Doctors 'Always' Communicated Well	300+	81%	-	80%
Home Recovery Information Given	300+	84%	-	82%
Hospital Given 9 or 10 on 10 Point Scale	300+	62%	-	67%
Meds 'Always' Explained Before Given	300+	59%	-	60%
Nurses 'Always' Communicated Well	300+	70%	-	76%
Pain 'Always' Well Controlled	300+	68%	-	69%
Room and Bathroom 'Always' Clean	300+	62%	-	71%
Timely Help 'Always' Received	300+	57%	-	64%
Would Definitely Recommend Hospital	300+	70%	-	69%

Indianhead Medical Center

113 4th Ave
Shell Lake, WI 54871
Phone: 715-468-7833
Type: Critical Access Hospitals
Emergency Services: Yes
Ownership: Voluntary Non-Profit - Private

Measure	Cases	This Hosp.	State Avg.	U.S. Avg.
Heart Attack Care				
ACE Inhibitor or ARB for LVSD[3]	0	-	97%	96%
Aspirin at Arrival[3]	0	-	99%	99%
Aspirin at Discharge[3]	0	-	99%	98%
Beta Blocker at Discharge[3]	0	-	99%	98%
Fibrinolytic Medication Timing[3]	0	-	0%	55%
PCI Within 90 Minutes of Arrival[3]	0	-	89%	90%
Smoking Cessation Advice[3]	0	-	99%	99%
Chest Pain/Possible Heart Attack Care				
Aspirin at Arrival	-	-	96%	95%
Median Time to ECG (minutes)	-	-	7	8
Median Time to Transfer (minutes)	-	-	49	61
Fibrinolytic Medication Timing	-	-	63%	54%
Heart Failure Care				
ACE Inhibitor or ARB for LVSD[1]	6	50%	95%	94%
Discharge Instructions[1]	13	69%	86%	88%
Evaluation of LVS Function[1]	15	87%	97%	98%
Smoking Cessation Advice[1]	3	100%	97%	98%
Pneumonia Care				
Appropriate Initial Antibiotic[1]	7	100%	94%	92%
Blood Culture Timing	0	-	97%	96%
Influenza Vaccine[1]	7	57%	92%	91%
Initial Antibiotic Timing[1]	10	100%	97%	95%
Pneumococcal Vaccine[1]	9	56%	93%	93%
Smoking Cessation Advice[1]	2	100%	95%	97%
Surgical Care Improvement Project				
Appropriate VTP Within 24 Hours[5]	0	-	93%	92%
Appropriate Hair Removal[5]	0	-	100%	99%
Appropriate Beta Blocker Usage[5]	0	-	92%	93%
Controlled Postoperative Blood Glucose[5]	0	-	93%	93%
Prophylactic Antibiotic Timing[5]	0	-	97%	97%
Prophylactic Antibiotic Timing (Outpatient)	-	-	91%	92%
Prophylactic Antibiotic Selection[5]	0	-	98%	97%
Prophylactic Antibiotic Select. (Outpatient)	-	-	96%	94%
Prophylactic Antibiotic Stopped[5]	0	-	95%	94%
Recommended VTP Ordered[5]	0	-	94%	94%
Urinary Catheter Removal[5]	0	-	91%	90%
Children's Asthma Care				
Received Systemic Corticosteroids	-	-	-	100%
Received Home Management Plan	-	-	-	71%
Received Reliever Medication	-	-	-	100%
Use of Medical Imaging				
Combination Abdominal CT Scan	-	-	0.106	0.191
Combination Chest CT Scan	-	-	0.027	0.054
Follow-up Mammogram/Ultrasound	-	-	8.4%	8.4%
MRI for Low Back Pain	-	-	31.8%	32.7%
Survey of Patients' Hospital Experiences				
Area Around Room 'Always' Quiet at Night[8]	-	-	-	58%
Doctors 'Always' Communicated Well[8]	-	-	-	80%
Home Recovery Information Given[8]	-	-	-	82%
Hospital Given 9 or 10 on 10 Point Scale[8]	-	-	-	67%
Meds 'Always' Explained Before Given[8]	-	-	-	60%
Nurses 'Always' Communicated Well[8]	-	-	-	76%
Pain 'Always' Well Controlled[8]	-	-	-	69%
Room and Bathroom 'Always' Clean[8]	-	-	-	71%
Timely Help 'Always' Received[8]	-	-	-	64%
Would Definitely Recommend Hospital[8]	-	-	-	69%

Franciscan Skemp Sparta Hospital

310 W Main St
Sparta, WI 54656
Phone: 608-269-2132
Fax: 608-269-4562
URL: www.mayohealthsystem.org/mhs/live/page.cfm
Type: Critical Access Hospitals
Emergency Services: Yes
Ownership: Voluntary Non-Profit - Church
Beds: 25

Key Personnel:
CEO/President............... Darlene Feltes, MD
Chief of Medical Staff.......... J Alan Fleischmann
Operating Room.............. Toni Eddy-Ballman
Quality Assurance .... Vicki Williams
Patient Relations .... John T Brennan

Measure	Cases	This Hosp.	State Avg.	U.S. Avg.
Heart Attack Care				
ACE Inhibitor or ARB for LVSD[5]	0	-	97%	96%
Aspirin at Arrival[5]	0	-	99%	99%
Aspirin at Discharge[5]	0	-	99%	98%
Beta Blocker at Discharge[5]	0	-	99%	98%
Fibrinolytic Medication Timing[5]	0	-	0%	55%
PCI Within 90 Minutes of Arrival[5]	0	-	89%	90%
Smoking Cessation Advice[5]	0	-	99%	99%
Chest Pain/Possible Heart Attack Care				
Aspirin at Arrival	-	-	96%	95%
Median Time to ECG (minutes)	-	-	7	8
Median Time to Transfer (minutes)	-	-	49	61
Fibrinolytic Medication Timing	-	-	63%	54%
Heart Failure Care				
ACE Inhibitor or ARB for LVSD[1]	1	100%	95%	94%
Discharge Instructions[1]	3	33%	86%	88%
Evaluation of LVS Function[1]	15	80%	97%	98%
Smoking Cessation Advice[1]	2	100%	97%	98%
Pneumonia Care				
Appropriate Initial Antibiotic[1]	23	96%	94%	92%
Blood Culture Timing	26	96%	97%	96%
Influenza Vaccine[1]	19	89%	92%	91%
Initial Antibiotic Timing	26	100%	97%	95%
Pneumococcal Vaccine	27	96%	93%	93%
Smoking Cessation Advice[1]	4	100%	95%	97%
Surgical Care Improvement Project				
Appropriate VTP Within 24 Hours[5]	0	-	93%	92%
Appropriate Hair Removal[5]	0	-	100%	99%
Appropriate Beta Blocker Usage[5]	0	-	92%	93%
Controlled Postoperative Blood Glucose[5]	0	-	93%	93%
Prophylactic Antibiotic Timing[5]	0	-	97%	97%
Prophylactic Antibiotic Timing (Outpatient)	-	-	91%	92%
Prophylactic Antibiotic Selection[5]	0	-	98%	97%
Prophylactic Antibiotic Select. (Outpatient)	-	-	96%	94%
Prophylactic Antibiotic Stopped[5]	0	-	95%	94%
Recommended VTP Ordered[5]	0	-	94%	94%
Urinary Catheter Removal[5]	0	-	91%	90%
Children's Asthma Care				
Received Systemic Corticosteroids	-	-	-	100%
Received Home Management Plan	-	-	-	71%
Received Reliever Medication	-	-	-	100%
Use of Medical Imaging				
Combination Abdominal CT Scan	-	-	0.106	0.191
Combination Chest CT Scan	-	-	0.027	0.054
Follow-up Mammogram/Ultrasound	-	-	8.4%	8.4%
MRI for Low Back Pain	-	-	31.8%	32.7%
Survey of Patients' Hospital Experiences				
Area Around Room 'Always' Quiet at Night[6]	<100	61%	-	58%
Doctors 'Always' Communicated Well[6]	<100	88%	-	80%
Home Recovery Information Given[6]	<100	70%	-	82%
Hospital Given 9 or 10 on 10 Point Scale[6]	<100	66%	-	67%
Meds 'Always' Explained Before Given[6]	<100	51%	-	60%
Nurses 'Always' Communicated Well[6]	<100	82%	-	76%
Pain 'Always' Well Controlled[6]	<100	57%	-	69%
Room and Bathroom 'Always' Clean[6]	<100	67%	-	71%
Timely Help 'Always' Received[6]	<100	84%	-	64%
Would Definitely Recommend Hospital	<100	54%	-	69%

NOTE: Hospital profiles are in alphabetical order by state, then city, then hospital within the city; Rankings exclude hospitals with less than 25 cases except for patient surveys which excludes hospitals with less than 100 cases; (a) 100–299 cases; (1) The number of cases is too small to be sure how well a hospital is performing; (2) The hospital indicated that the data submitted for this measure were based on a sample of cases; (3) Data was collected during a shorter time period (fewer quarters) than the maximum possible time for this measure; (4) Suppressed for one or more quarters by CMS; (5) No data is available from the hospital for this measure; (6) Fewer than 100 patients completed the HCAHPS survey. Use these rates with caution, as the number of surveys may be too low to reliably assess hospital performance; (7) Survey results are based on less than 12 months of data; (8) Survey results are not available for this reporting period; (9) No or very few patients were eligible for the HCAHPS survey. The scores shown, if any, reflect a very small number of surveys; (10) A state average was not calculated because too few hospitals in the state submitted data; (11) There were discrepancies in the data collection process; Please refer to the User's Guide for a full explanation of data.

Spooner Health System

819 Ash St Phone: 715-635-2111
Spooner, WI 54801 Fax: 715-635-6846
E-mail: shs@spoonerhealthsystem.com
URL: www.spoonerhealthsystem.com
Type: Critical Access Hospitals Emergency Services: Yes
Ownership: Voluntary Non-Profit - Private Beds: 130

Key Personnel:
Chief of Medical Staff . . . . Laura Boelke, MD
Emergency Room . . . . Linda Trent

Measure	Cases	This Hosp.	State Avg.	U.S. Avg.
Heart Attack Care				
ACE Inhibitor or ARB for LVSD[3]	0	-	97%	96%
Aspirin at Arrival[1,3]	1	100%	99%	99%
Aspirin at Discharge[1,3]	1	100%	99%	98%
Beta Blocker at Discharge[1,3]	1	100%	99%	98%
Fibrinolytic Medication Timing[3]	0	-	0%	55%
PCI Within 90 Minutes of Arrival[5]	0	-	89%	90%
Smoking Cessation Advice[3]	0	-	99%	99%
Chest Pain/Possible Heart Attack Care				
Aspirin at Arrival	25	100%	96%	95%
Median Time to ECG (minutes)	27	24	7	8
Median Time to Transfer (minutes)[1,3]	5	180	49	61
Fibrinolytic Medication Timing[1]	3	67%	63%	54%
Heart Failure Care				
ACE Inhibitor or ARB for LVSD[1]	4	100%	95%	94%
Discharge Instructions[1]	8	100%	86%	88%
Evaluation of LVS Function[1]	14	100%	97%	98%
Smoking Cessation Advice	0	-	97%	98%
Pneumonia Care				
Appropriate Initial Antibiotic[1]	20	80%	94%	92%
Blood Culture Timing[1]	17	82%	97%	96%
Influenza Vaccine[1]	10	100%	92%	91%
Initial Antibiotic Timing[1]	15	100%	97%	95%
Pneumococcal Vaccine[1]	22	100%	93%	93%
Smoking Cessation Advice[1]	6	100%	95%	97%
Surgical Care Improvement Project				
Appropriate VTP Within 24 Hours[5]	0	-	93%	92%
Appropriate Hair Removal[5]	0	-	100%	99%
Appropriate Beta Blocker Usage[5]	0	-	92%	93%
Controlled Postoperative Blood Glucose[5]	0	-	93%	93%
Prophylactic Antibiotic Timing[5]	0	-	97%	97%
Prophylactic Antibiotic Timing (Outpatient)[5]	0	-	91%	92%
Prophylactic Antibiotic Selection[5]	0	-	98%	97%
Prophylactic Antibiotic Select. (Outpatient)[5]	0	-	96%	94%
Prophylactic Antibiotic Stopped[5]	0	-	95%	94%
Recommended VTP Ordered[5]	0	-	94%	94%
Urinary Catheter Removal[5]	0	-	91%	90%
Children's Asthma Care				
Received Systemic Corticosteroids	-	-	-	100%
Received Home Management Plan	-	-	-	71%
Received Reliever Medication	-	-	-	100%
Use of Medical Imaging				
Combination Abdominal CT Scan	88	0.057	0.106	0.191
Combination Chest CT Scan[1]	44	0.000	0.027	0.054
Follow-up Mammogram/Ultrasound	243	11.1%	8.4%	8.4%
MRI for Low Back Pain[1]	29	41.4%	31.8%	32.7%
Survey of Patients' Hospital Experiences				
Area Around Room 'Always' Quiet at Night	(a)	51%	-	58%
Doctors 'Always' Communicated Well	(a)	86%	-	80%
Home Recovery Information Given	(a)	84%	-	82%
Hospital Given 9 or 10 on 10 Point Scale	(a)	66%	-	67%
Meds 'Always' Explained Before Given	(a)	66%	-	60%
Nurses 'Always' Communicated Well	(a)	82%	-	76%
Pain 'Always' Well Controlled	(a)	73%	-	69%
Room and Bathroom 'Always' Clean	(a)	72%	-	71%
Timely Help 'Always' Received	(a)	72%	-	64%
Would Definitely Recommend Hospital	(a)	65%	-	69%

Our Lady of Victory Hospital

1120 Pine St Phone: 715-644-5571
Stanley, WI 54768 Fax: 715-644-6221
E-mail: papiernk@OLVH.ORG
URL: www.ministryhealth.org
Type: Critical Access Hospitals Emergency Services: Yes
Ownership: Voluntary Non-Profit - Private Beds: 25

Key Personnel:
CEO/President. . . . . Cynthia Eichman
Chief of Medical Staff. . . . . Sharon Hayward, MD
Infection Control. . . . . Toni Smith, RN
Operating Room. . . . . Debra Savina, RN
Quality Assurance . . . . Carol Meyer
Anesthesiology. . . . . Dwight Perkins
Emergency Room . . . . Badal Raval, MD

Measure	Cases	This Hosp.	State Avg.	U.S. Avg.
Heart Attack Care				
ACE Inhibitor or ARB for LVSD[1,3]	1	100%	97%	96%
Aspirin at Arrival[1,3]	2	50%	99%	99%
Aspirin at Discharge[1,3]	2	100%	99%	98%
Beta Blocker at Discharge[1,3]	2	100%	99%	98%
Fibrinolytic Medication Timing[3]	0	-	0%	55%
PCI Within 90 Minutes of Arrival[5]	0	-	89%	90%
Smoking Cessation Advice[1,3]	1	100%	99%	99%
Chest Pain/Possible Heart Attack Care				
Aspirin at Arrival	42	100%	96%	95%
Median Time to ECG (minutes)	43	5	7	8
Median Time to Transfer (minutes)[1,3]	3	75	49	61
Fibrinolytic Medication Timing[1]	3	33%	63%	54%
Heart Failure Care				
ACE Inhibitor or ARB for LVSD[1]	10	100%	95%	94%
Discharge Instructions[1]	14	100%	86%	88%
Evaluation of LVS Function	25	100%	97%	98%
Smoking Cessation Advice	0	-	97%	98%
Pneumonia Care				
Appropriate Initial Antibiotic[1,2]	22	91%	94%	92%
Blood Culture Timing[1,2]	23	100%	97%	96%
Influenza Vaccine[1]	18	100%	92%	91%
Initial Antibiotic Timing[2]	30	100%	97%	95%
Pneumococcal Vaccine[2]	32	97%	93%	93%
Smoking Cessation Advice[1,2]	2	100%	95%	97%
Surgical Care Improvement Project				
Appropriate VTP Within 24 Hours[1,3]	1	100%	93%	92%
Appropriate Hair Removal[1,3]	1	100%	100%	99%
Appropriate Beta Blocker Usage[3]	0	-	92%	93%
Controlled Postoperative Blood Glucose[5]	0	-	93%	93%
Prophylactic Antibiotic Timing[3]	0	-	97%	97%
Prophylactic Antibiotic Timing (Outpatient)[1,3]	4	50%	91%	92%
Prophylactic Antibiotic Selection[3]	0	-	98%	97%
Prophylactic Antibiotic Select. (Outpatient)[1,3]	2	100%	96%	94%
Prophylactic Antibiotic Stopped[3]	0	-	95%	94%
Recommended VTP Ordered[1,3]	1	100%	94%	94%
Urinary Catheter Removal[5]	0	-	91%	90%
Children's Asthma Care				
Received Systemic Corticosteroids	-	-	-	100%
Received Home Management Plan	-	-	-	71%
Received Reliever Medication	-	-	-	100%
Use of Medical Imaging				
Combination Abdominal CT Scan	55	0.018	0.106	0.191
Combination Chest CT Scan[1]	17	0.059	0.027	0.054
Follow-up Mammogram/Ultrasound	117	10.3%	8.4%	8.4%
MRI for Low Back Pain[1]	13	38.5%	31.8%	32.7%
Survey of Patients' Hospital Experiences				
Area Around Room 'Always' Quiet at Night	(a)	59%	-	58%
Doctors 'Always' Communicated Well	(a)	82%	-	80%
Home Recovery Information Given	(a)	84%	-	82%
Hospital Given 9 or 10 on 10 Point Scale	(a)	82%	-	67%
Meds 'Always' Explained Before Given	(a)	63%	-	60%
Nurses 'Always' Communicated Well	(a)	84%	-	76%
Pain 'Always' Well Controlled	(a)	77%	-	69%
Room and Bathroom 'Always' Clean	(a)	94%	-	71%
Timely Help 'Always' Received	(a)	81%	-	64%
Would Definitely Recommend Hospital	(a)	76%	-	69%

Ministry St Michaels Hospital of Stevens Point

900 Illinois Ave Phone: 715-346-5000
Stevens Point, WI 54481 Fax: 715-343-3133
URL: www.saintmichaelshospital.org
Type: Acute Care Hospitals Emergency Services: Yes
Ownership: Voluntary Non-Profit - Church Beds: 129

Key Personnel:
CEO/President. . . . . Jeffrey L Martin
Chief of Medical Staff . . . . Mark Fenlon, MD
Infection Control. . . . . Artie Sadlemyer
Operating Room. . . . . Steve King, RN
Pediatric In-Patient Care . . . . Thomas McIntee, MD
Quality Assurance . . . . Gloria Field
Emergency Room . . . . Paulette Bessen
Hemotology Center . . . . Russ Shifton

Measure	Cases	This Hosp.	State Avg.	U.S. Avg.
Heart Attack Care				
ACE Inhibitor or ARB for LVSD[1]	4	75%	97%	96%
Aspirin at Arrival[1]	15	100%	99%	99%
Aspirin at Discharge[1]	9	100%	99%	98%
Beta Blocker at Discharge[1]	12	100%	99%	98%
Fibrinolytic Medication Timing	0	-	0%	55%
PCI Within 90 Minutes of Arrival	0	-	89%	90%
Smoking Cessation Advice	0	-	99%	99%
Chest Pain/Possible Heart Attack Care				
Aspirin at Arrival	205	100%	96%	95%
Median Time to ECG (minutes)	214	10	7	8
Median Time to Transfer (minutes)	27	27	49	61
Fibrinolytic Medication Timing	0	-	63%	54%
Heart Failure Care				
ACE Inhibitor or ARB for LVSD	31	100%	95%	94%
Discharge Instructions	67	85%	86%	88%
Evaluation of LVS Function	117	100%	97%	98%
Smoking Cessation Advice[1]	10	100%	97%	98%
Pneumonia Care				
Appropriate Initial Antibiotic	109	97%	94%	92%
Blood Culture Timing	166	98%	97%	96%
Influenza Vaccine	121	97%	92%	91%
Initial Antibiotic Timing	172	98%	97%	95%
Pneumococcal Vaccine	169	96%	93%	93%
Smoking Cessation Advice	32	97%	95%	97%
Surgical Care Improvement Project				
Appropriate VTP Within 24 Hours	137	93%	93%	92%
Appropriate Hair Removal	559	100%	100%	99%
Appropriate Beta Blocker Usage	191	97%	92%	93%
Controlled Postoperative Blood Glucose	0	-	93%	93%
Prophylactic Antibiotic Timing	418	100%	97%	97%
Prophylactic Antibiotic Timing (Outpatient)	50	84%	91%	92%
Prophylactic Antibiotic Selection	425	99%	98%	97%
Prophylactic Antibiotic Select. (Outpatient)	45	98%	96%	94%
Prophylactic Antibiotic Stopped	413	98%	95%	94%
Recommended VTP Ordered	137	94%	94%	94%
Urinary Catheter Removal	155	97%	91%	90%
Children's Asthma Care				
Received Systemic Corticosteroids	-	-	-	100%
Received Home Management Plan	-	-	-	71%
Received Reliever Medication	-	-	-	100%
Use of Medical Imaging				
Combination Abdominal CT Scan	585	0.072	0.106	0.191
Combination Chest CT Scan	323	0.019	0.027	0.054
Follow-up Mammogram/Ultrasound	1,057	11.1%	8.4%	8.4%
MRI for Low Back Pain	84	36.9%	31.8%	32.7%
Survey of Patients' Hospital Experiences				
Area Around Room 'Always' Quiet at Night	300+	65%	-	58%
Doctors 'Always' Communicated Well	300+	79%	-	80%
Home Recovery Information Given	300+	86%	-	82%
Hospital Given 9 or 10 on 10 Point Scale	300+	63%	-	67%
Meds 'Always' Explained Before Given	300+	66%	-	60%
Nurses 'Always' Communicated Well	300+	76%	-	76%
Pain 'Always' Well Controlled	300+	68%	-	69%
Room and Bathroom 'Always' Clean	300+	74%	-	71%
Timely Help 'Always' Received	300+	64%	-	64%
Would Definitely Recommend Hospital	300+	66%	-	69%

NOTE: Hospital profiles are in alphabetical order by state, then city, then hospital within the city; Rankings exclude hospitals with less than 25 cases except for patient surveys which excludes hospitals with less than 100 cases; (a) 100–299 cases; (1) The number of cases is too small to be sure how well a hospital is performing; (2) The hospital indicated that the data submitted for this measure were based on a sample of cases; (3) Data was collected during a shorter time period (fewer quarters) than the maximum possible time for this measure; (4) Suppressed for one or more quarters by CMS; (5) No data is available from the hospital for this measure; (6) Fewer than 100 patients completed the HCAHPS survey. Use these rates with caution, as the number of surveys may be too low to reliably assess hospital performance; (7) Survey results are based on less than 12 months of data; (8) Survey results are not available for this reporting period; (9) No or very few patients were eligible for the HCAHPS survey. The scores shown, if any, reflect a very small number of surveys; (10) A state average was not calculated because too few hospitals in the state submitted data; (11) There were discrepancies in the data collection process; Please refer to the User's Guide for a full explanation of data.

Stoughton Hospital

900 Ridge St
Stoughton, WI 53589
Phone: 608-873-6611
Fax: 608-873-2234
E-mail: info@stoughtonhospital.com
URL: www.stoughtonhospital.com
Type: Critical Access Hospitals
Emergency Services: Yes
Ownership: Voluntary Non-Profit - Private
Beds: 32

Key Personnel:

CEO/President. . . . . Terence J Brenny
Chief of Medical Staff . . . . Joyce Brehm
Infection Control. . . . . Joyce Williams
Operating Room. . . . . Ronald E Beresky
Quality Assurance . . . . Joyce Williams
Ambulatory Care . . . . Teresa De Nucci

Measure	Cases	This Hosp.	State Avg.	U.S. Avg.
Heart Attack Care				
ACE Inhibitor or ARB for LVSD[5]	0	-	97%	96%
Aspirin at Arrival[5]	0	-	99%	99%
Aspirin at Discharge[5]	0	-	99%	98%
Beta Blocker at Discharge[5]	0	-	99%	98%
Fibrinolytic Medication Timing[5]	0	-	0%	55%
PCI Within 90 Minutes of Arrival[5]	0	-	89%	90%
Smoking Cessation Advice[5]	0	-	99%	99%
Chest Pain/Possible Heart Attack Care				
Aspirin at Arrival	-	-	96%	95%
Median Time to ECG (minutes)	-	-	7	8
Median Time to Transfer (minutes)	-	-	49	61
Fibrinolytic Medication Timing	-	-	63%	54%
Heart Failure Care				
ACE Inhibitor or ARB for LVSD[1]	6	83%	95%	94%
Discharge Instructions[1]	21	95%	86%	88%
Evaluation of LVS Function	30	93%	97%	98%
Smoking Cessation Advice	0	-	97%	98%
Pneumonia Care				
Appropriate Initial Antibiotic	26	96%	94%	92%
Blood Culture Timing	49	100%	97%	96%
Influenza Vaccine	32	100%	92%	91%
Initial Antibiotic Timing	45	98%	97%	95%
Pneumococcal Vaccine	60	97%	93%	93%
Smoking Cessation Advice[1]	8	88%	95%	97%
Surgical Care Improvement Project				
Appropriate VTP Within 24 Hours	25	92%	93%	92%
Appropriate Hair Removal	67	100%	100%	99%
Appropriate Beta Blocker Usage[5]	0	-	92%	93%
Controlled Postoperative Blood Glucose	0	-	93%	93%
Prophylactic Antibiotic Timing	47	100%	97%	97%
Prophylactic Antibiotic Timing (Outpatient)	-	-	91%	92%
Prophylactic Antibiotic Selection	48	100%	98%	97%
Prophylactic Antibiotic Select. (Outpatient)	-	-	96%	94%
Prophylactic Antibiotic Stopped	47	91%	95%	94%
Recommended VTP Ordered	25	96%	94%	94%
Urinary Catheter Removal[1]	6	100%	91%	90%
Children's Asthma Care				
Received Systemic Corticosteroids	-	-	-	100%
Received Home Management Plan	-	-	-	71%
Received Reliever Medication	-	-	-	100%
Use of Medical Imaging				
Combination Abdominal CT Scan	-	-	0.106	0.191
Combination Chest CT Scan	-	-	0.027	0.054
Follow-up Mammogram/Ultrasound	-	-	8.4%	8.4%
MRI for Low Back Pain	-	-	31.8%	32.7%
Survey of Patients' Hospital Experiences				
Area Around Room 'Always' Quiet at Night	(a)	70%	-	58%
Doctors 'Always' Communicated Well	(a)	84%	-	80%
Home Recovery Information Given	(a)	90%	-	82%
Hospital Given 9 or 10 on 10 Point Scale	(a)	83%	-	67%
Meds 'Always' Explained Before Given	(a)	66%	-	60%
Nurses 'Always' Communicated Well	(a)	86%	-	76%
Pain 'Always' Well Controlled	(a)	76%	-	69%
Room and Bathroom 'Always' Clean	(a)	86%	-	71%
Timely Help 'Always' Received	(a)	73%	-	64%
Would Definitely Recommend Hospital	(a)	89%	-	69%

Door County Memorial Hospital

323 South 18th Avenue
Sturgeon Bay, WI 54235
Phone: 920-743-5566
Fax: 920-743-8165
E-mail: dcmhinfo@dcmh.org
URL: www.doorcountymemorial.org
Type: Critical Access Hospitals
Emergency Services: Yes
Ownership: Voluntary Non-Profit - Church
Beds: 89

Key Personnel:

CEO/President. . . . . Gerald M Worrick
Chief of Medical Staff . . . . James M Lewis, MD
Coronary Care . . . . Sherri Christenson, RN
Infection Control. . . . . Julie Pinney, RN
Operating Room. . . . . Jody Boes, RN
Quality Assurance . . . . Christa Kraus

Measure	Cases	This Hosp.	State Avg.	U.S. Avg.
Heart Attack Care				
ACE Inhibitor or ARB for LVSD[1]	1	100%	97%	96%
Aspirin at Arrival[1]	7	100%	99%	99%
Aspirin at Discharge[1]	7	100%	99%	98%
Beta Blocker at Discharge[1]	7	100%	99%	98%
Fibrinolytic Medication Timing	0	-	0%	55%
PCI Within 90 Minutes of Arrival	0	-	89%	90%
Smoking Cessation Advice	0	-	99%	99%
Chest Pain/Possible Heart Attack Care				
Aspirin at Arrival	-	-	96%	95%
Median Time to ECG (minutes)	-	-	7	8
Median Time to Transfer (minutes)	-	-	49	61
Fibrinolytic Medication Timing	-	-	63%	54%
Heart Failure Care				
ACE Inhibitor or ARB for LVSD[1]	19	89%	95%	94%
Discharge Instructions	65	78%	86%	88%
Evaluation of LVS Function	74	100%	97%	98%
Smoking Cessation Advice[1]	5	100%	97%	98%
Pneumonia Care				
Appropriate Initial Antibiotic	49	94%	94%	92%
Blood Culture Timing	58	98%	97%	96%
Influenza Vaccine	42	90%	92%	91%
Initial Antibiotic Timing	64	98%	97%	95%
Pneumococcal Vaccine	61	95%	93%	93%
Smoking Cessation Advice[1]	12	100%	95%	97%
Surgical Care Improvement Project				
Appropriate VTP Within 24 Hours	48	92%	93%	92%
Appropriate Hair Removal	110	100%	100%	99%
Appropriate Beta Blocker Usage	28	82%	92%	93%
Controlled Postoperative Blood Glucose[5]	0	-	93%	93%
Prophylactic Antibiotic Timing	82	90%	97%	97%
Prophylactic Antibiotic Timing (Outpatient)	-	-	91%	92%
Prophylactic Antibiotic Selection	82	99%	98%	97%
Prophylactic Antibiotic Select. (Outpatient)	-	-	96%	94%
Prophylactic Antibiotic Stopped	78	95%	95%	94%
Recommended VTP Ordered	48	94%	94%	94%
Urinary Catheter Removal	36	86%	91%	90%
Children's Asthma Care				
Received Systemic Corticosteroids	-	-	-	100%
Received Home Management Plan	-	-	-	71%
Received Reliever Medication	-	-	-	100%
Use of Medical Imaging				
Combination Abdominal CT Scan	-	-	0.106	0.191
Combination Chest CT Scan	-	-	0.027	0.054
Follow-up Mammogram/Ultrasound	-	-	8.4%	8.4%
MRI for Low Back Pain	-	-	31.8%	32.7%
Survey of Patients' Hospital Experiences				
Area Around Room 'Always' Quiet at Night	300+	61%	-	58%
Doctors 'Always' Communicated Well	300+	84%	-	80%
Home Recovery Information Given	300+	85%	-	82%
Hospital Given 9 or 10 on 10 Point Scale	300+	75%	-	67%
Meds 'Always' Explained Before Given	300+	68%	-	60%
Nurses 'Always' Communicated Well	300+	84%	-	76%
Pain 'Always' Well Controlled	300+	73%	-	69%
Room and Bathroom 'Always' Clean	300+	81%	-	71%
Timely Help 'Always' Received	300+	73%	-	64%
Would Definitely Recommend Hospital	300+	73%	-	69%

Aurora Medical Center

36500 Aurora Drive
Summit, WI 53066
Phone: 262-434-1000
URL: www.aurorahealthcare.org
Type: Acute Care Hospitals
Emergency Services: Yes
Ownership: Voluntary Non-Profit - Private

Key Personnel:

Radiology. . . . . Ellen L Ziaja, MD
Emergency . . . . Mike Kefer, MD

Measure	Cases	This Hosp.	State Avg.	U.S. Avg.
Heart Attack Care				
ACE Inhibitor or ARB for LVSD[5]	0	-	97%	96%
Aspirin at Arrival[5]	0	-	99%	99%
Aspirin at Discharge[5]	0	-	99%	98%
Beta Blocker at Discharge[5]	0	-	99%	98%
Fibrinolytic Medication Timing[5]	0	-	0%	55%
PCI Within 90 Minutes of Arrival[5]	0	-	89%	90%
Smoking Cessation Advice[5]	0	-	99%	99%
Chest Pain/Possible Heart Attack Care				
Aspirin at Arrival	-	-	96%	95%
Median Time to ECG (minutes)	-	-	7	8
Median Time to Transfer (minutes)	-	-	49	61
Fibrinolytic Medication Timing	-	-	63%	54%
Heart Failure Care				
ACE Inhibitor or ARB for LVSD[5]	0	-	95%	94%
Discharge Instructions[5]	0	-	86%	88%
Evaluation of LVS Function[5]	0	-	97%	98%
Smoking Cessation Advice[5]	0	-	97%	98%
Pneumonia Care				
Appropriate Initial Antibiotic[5]	0	-	94%	92%
Blood Culture Timing[5]	0	-	97%	96%
Influenza Vaccine[5]	0	-	92%	91%
Initial Antibiotic Timing[5]	0	-	97%	95%
Pneumococcal Vaccine[5]	0	-	93%	93%
Smoking Cessation Advice[5]	0	-	95%	97%
Surgical Care Improvement Project				
Appropriate VTP Within 24 Hours[5]	0	-	93%	92%
Appropriate Hair Removal[5]	0	-	100%	99%
Appropriate Beta Blocker Usage[5]	0	-	92%	93%
Controlled Postoperative Blood Glucose[5]	0	-	93%	93%
Prophylactic Antibiotic Timing[5]	0	-	97%	97%
Prophylactic Antibiotic Timing (Outpatient)	-	-	91%	92%
Prophylactic Antibiotic Selection[5]	0	-	98%	97%
Prophylactic Antibiotic Select. (Outpatient)	-	-	96%	94%
Prophylactic Antibiotic Stopped[5]	0	-	95%	94%
Recommended VTP Ordered[5]	0	-	94%	94%
Urinary Catheter Removal[5]	0	-	91%	90%
Children's Asthma Care				
Received Systemic Corticosteroids	-	-	-	100%
Received Home Management Plan	-	-	-	71%
Received Reliever Medication	-	-	-	100%
Use of Medical Imaging				
Combination Abdominal CT Scan	-	-	0.106	0.191
Combination Chest CT Scan	-	-	0.027	0.054
Follow-up Mammogram/Ultrasound	-	-	8.4%	8.4%
MRI for Low Back Pain	-	-	31.8%	32.7%
Survey of Patients' Hospital Experiences				
Area Around Room 'Always' Quiet at Night[8]	-	-	-	58%
Doctors 'Always' Communicated Well[8]	-	-	-	80%
Home Recovery Information Given[8]	-	-	-	82%
Hospital Given 9 or 10 on 10 Point Scale[8]	-	-	-	67%
Meds 'Always' Explained Before Given[8]	-	-	-	60%
Nurses 'Always' Communicated Well[8]	-	-	-	76%
Pain 'Always' Well Controlled[8]	-	-	-	69%
Room and Bathroom 'Always' Clean[8]	-	-	-	71%
Timely Help 'Always' Received[8]	-	-	-	64%
Would Definitely Recommend Hospital[8]	-	-	-	69%

NOTE: Hospital profiles are in alphabetical order by state, then city, then hospital within the city; Rankings exclude hospitals with less than 25 cases except for patient surveys which excludes hospitals with less than 100 cases; (a) 100–299 cases; (1) The number of cases is too small to be sure how well a hospital is performing; (2) The hospital indicated that the data submitted for this measure were based on a sample of cases; (3) Data was collected during a shorter time period (fewer quarters) than the maximum possible time for this measure; (4) Suppressed for one or more quarters by CMS; (5) No data is available from the hospital for this measure; (6) Fewer than 100 patients completed the HCAHPS survey. Use these rates with caution, as the number of surveys may be too low to reliably assess hospital performance; (7) Survey results are based on less than 12 months of data; (8) Survey results are not available for this reporting period; (9) No or very few patients were eligible for the HCAHPS survey. The scores shown, if any, reflect a very small number of surveys; (10) A state average was not calculated because too few hospitals in the state submitted data; (11) There were discrepancies in the data collection process; Please refer to the User's Guide for a full explanation of data.

Saint Marys Hospital Superior

3500 Tower Ave
Superior, WI 54880
URL: www.smdc.org
Type: Critical Access Hospitals
Ownership: Voluntary Non-Profit - Private
Phone: 715-395-5400
Fax: 715-392-8395
Emergency Services: Yes
Beds: 25

Key Personnel:
CEO/President.............. Peter E Person, MD
Chief of Medical Staff.......... Timothy Burke, MD
Infection Control.............. Tim Sandor
Quality Assurance .... Don Diklich

Measure	Cases	This Hosp.	State Avg.	U.S. Avg.
Heart Attack Care				
ACE Inhibitor or ARB for LVSD[5]	0	-	97%	96%
Aspirin at Arrival[5]	0	-	99%	99%
Aspirin at Discharge[5]	0	-	99%	98%
Beta Blocker at Discharge[5]	0	-	99%	98%
Fibrinolytic Medication Timing[5]	0	-	0%	55%
PCI Within 90 Minutes of Arrival[5]	0	-	89%	90%
Smoking Cessation Advice[5]	0	-	99%	99%
Chest Pain/Possible Heart Attack Care				
Aspirin at Arrival[1,3]	16	81%	96%	95%
Median Time to ECG (minutes)[1,3]	15	26	7	8
Median Time to Transfer (minutes)[1,3]	2	40	49	61
Fibrinolytic Medication Timing[3]	0	-	63%	54%
Heart Failure Care				
ACE Inhibitor or ARB for LVSD[1]	3	100%	95%	94%
Discharge Instructions[1]	12	42%	86%	88%
Evaluation of LVS Function[1]	15	73%	97%	98%
Smoking Cessation Advice[1]	2	50%	97%	98%
Pneumonia Care				
Appropriate Initial Antibiotic[1]	9	78%	94%	92%
Blood Culture Timing[1]	3	100%	97%	96%
Influenza Vaccine[1]	7	71%	92%	91%
Initial Antibiotic Timing[1]	13	85%	97%	95%
Pneumococcal Vaccine[1]	13	100%	93%	93%
Smoking Cessation Advice[1]	2	100%	95%	97%
Surgical Care Improvement Project				
Appropriate VTP Within 24 Hours[5]	0	-	93%	92%
Appropriate Hair Removal[5]	0	-	100%	99%
Appropriate Beta Blocker Usage[5]	0	-	92%	93%
Controlled Postoperative Blood Glucose[5]	0	-	93%	93%
Prophylactic Antibiotic Timing[5]	0	-	97%	97%
Prophylactic Antibiotic Timing (Outpatient)[1,3]	3	67%	91%	92%
Prophylactic Antibiotic Selection[5]	0	-	98%	97%
Prophylactic Antibiotic Select. (Outpatient)[1,3]	2	100%	96%	94%
Prophylactic Antibiotic Stopped[5]	0	-	95%	94%
Recommended VTP Ordered[5]	0	-	94%	94%
Urinary Catheter Removal[5]	0	-	91%	90%
Children's Asthma Care				
Received Systemic Corticosteroids	-	-	-	100%
Received Home Management Plan	-	-	-	71%
Received Reliever Medication	-	-	-	100%
Use of Medical Imaging				
Combination Abdominal CT Scan	206	0.029	0.106	0.191
Combination Chest CT Scan	111	0.000	0.027	0.054
Follow-up Mammogram/Ultrasound	543	4.4%	8.4%	8.4%
MRI for Low Back Pain[5]	0	-	31.8%	32.7%
Survey of Patients' Hospital Experiences				
Area Around Room 'Always' Quiet at Night[8]	-	-	-	58%
Doctors 'Always' Communicated Well[8]	-	-	-	80%
Home Recovery Information Given[8]	-	-	-	82%
Hospital Given 9 or 10 on 10 Point Scale[8]	-	-	-	67%
Meds 'Always' Explained Before Given[8]	-	-	-	60%
Nurses 'Always' Communicated Well[8]	-	-	-	76%
Pain 'Always' Well Controlled[8]	-	-	-	69%
Room and Bathroom 'Always' Clean[8]	-	-	-	71%
Timely Help 'Always' Received[8]	-	-	-	64%
Would Definitely Recommend Hospital[8]	-	-	-	69%

Tomah Memorial Hospital

321 Butts Ave
Tomah, WI 54660
URL: www.tomahhospital.org
Type: Critical Access Hospitals
Ownership: Voluntary Non-Profit - Private
Phone: 608-372-2181
Fax: 608-374-0289
Emergency Services: Yes
Beds: 25

Key Personnel:
CEO/President.............. Philip J Stuart
Chief of Medical Staff.......... Robb Kline, MD
Infection Control.............. Jan Path
Quality Assurance .... Shelly Egstad
Anesthesiology............... David Demask
Emergency Room .... Robb Kline, MD

Measure	Cases	This Hosp.	State Avg.	U.S. Avg.
Heart Attack Care				
ACE Inhibitor or ARB for LVSD[1]	2	100%	97%	96%
Aspirin at Arrival[1]	16	100%	99%	99%
Aspirin at Discharge[1]	15	87%	99%	98%
Beta Blocker at Discharge[1]	15	100%	99%	98%
Fibrinolytic Medication Timing	0	-	0%	55%
PCI Within 90 Minutes of Arrival[5]	0	-	89%	90%
Smoking Cessation Advice[1]	1	100%	99%	99%
Chest Pain/Possible Heart Attack Care				
Aspirin at Arrival	-	-	96%	95%
Median Time to ECG (minutes)	-	-	7	8
Median Time to Transfer (minutes)	-	-	49	61
Fibrinolytic Medication Timing	-	-	63%	54%
Heart Failure Care				
ACE Inhibitor or ARB for LVSD[1]	4	75%	95%	94%
Discharge Instructions[1]	15	100%	86%	88%
Evaluation of LVS Function	25	100%	97%	98%
Smoking Cessation Advice[1]	1	100%	97%	98%
Pneumonia Care				
Appropriate Initial Antibiotic[1]	24	88%	94%	92%
Blood Culture Timing	35	100%	97%	96%
Influenza Vaccine	27	100%	92%	91%
Initial Antibiotic Timing	29	93%	97%	95%
Pneumococcal Vaccine	44	98%	93%	93%
Smoking Cessation Advice[1]	12	100%	95%	97%
Surgical Care Improvement Project				
Appropriate VTP Within 24 Hours[5]	0	-	93%	92%
Appropriate Hair Removal[1,3]	3	100%	100%	99%
Appropriate Beta Blocker Usage[5]	0	-	92%	93%
Controlled Postoperative Blood Glucose[3]	0	-	93%	93%
Prophylactic Antibiotic Timing[5]	0	-	97%	97%
Prophylactic Antibiotic Timing (Outpatient)	-	-	91%	92%
Prophylactic Antibiotic Selection[5]	0	-	98%	97%
Prophylactic Antibiotic Select. (Outpatient)	-	-	96%	94%
Prophylactic Antibiotic Stopped[5]	0	-	95%	94%
Recommended VTP Ordered[5]	0	-	94%	94%
Urinary Catheter Removal[3]	0	-	91%	90%
Children's Asthma Care				
Received Systemic Corticosteroids	-	-	-	100%
Received Home Management Plan	-	-	-	71%
Received Reliever Medication	-	-	-	100%
Use of Medical Imaging				
Combination Abdominal CT Scan	-	-	0.106	0.191
Combination Chest CT Scan	-	-	0.027	0.054
Follow-up Mammogram/Ultrasound	-	-	8.4%	8.4%
MRI for Low Back Pain	-	-	31.8%	32.7%
Survey of Patients' Hospital Experiences				
Area Around Room 'Always' Quiet at Night	300+	71%	-	58%
Doctors 'Always' Communicated Well	300+	87%	-	80%
Home Recovery Information Given	300+	91%	-	82%
Hospital Given 9 or 10 on 10 Point Scale	300+	70%	-	67%
Meds 'Always' Explained Before Given	300+	69%	-	60%
Nurses 'Always' Communicated Well	300+	81%	-	76%
Pain 'Always' Well Controlled	300+	70%	-	69%
Room and Bathroom 'Always' Clean	300+	79%	-	71%
Timely Help 'Always' Received	300+	70%	-	64%
Would Definitely Recommend Hospital	300+	75%	-	69%

Tomah VA Medical Center

500 East Veterans Street
Tomah, WI 54660
URL: www.tomah.va.gov
Type: Acute Care-Veterans Administration
Ownership: Government - Federal
Phone: 608-372-3971
Emergency Services: No

Measure	Cases	This Hosp.	State Avg.	U.S. Avg.
Heart Attack Care				
ACE Inhibitor or ARB for LVSD[5]	0	-	97%	96%
Aspirin at Arrival[5]	0	-	99%	99%
Aspirin at Discharge[5]	0	-	99%	98%
Beta Blocker at Discharge[5]	0	-	99%	98%
Fibrinolytic Medication Timing[5]	0	-	0%	55%
PCI Within 90 Minutes of Arrival[5]	0	-	89%	90%
Smoking Cessation Advice[5]	0	-	99%	99%
Chest Pain/Possible Heart Attack Care				
Aspirin at Arrival	-	-	96%	95%
Median Time to ECG (minutes)	-	-	7	8
Median Time to Transfer (minutes)	-	-	49	61
Fibrinolytic Medication Timing	-	-	63%	54%
Heart Failure Care				
ACE Inhibitor or ARB for LVSD[5]	0	-	95%	94%
Discharge Instructions[5]	0	-	86%	88%
Evaluation of LVS Function[5]	0	-	97%	98%
Smoking Cessation Advice[5]	0	-	97%	98%
Pneumonia Care				
Appropriate Initial Antibiotic[5]	0	-	94%	92%
Blood Culture Timing[5]	0	-	97%	96%
Influenza Vaccine[5]	0	-	92%	91%
Initial Antibiotic Timing[5]	0	-	97%	95%
Pneumococcal Vaccine[5]	0	-	93%	93%
Smoking Cessation Advice[5]	0	-	95%	97%
Surgical Care Improvement Project				
Appropriate VTP Within 24 Hours[2,5]	0	-	93%	92%
Appropriate Hair Removal[2,5]	0	-	100%	99%
Appropriate Beta Blocker Usage[2,5]	0	-	92%	93%
Controlled Postoperative Blood Glucose[2,5]	0	-	93%	93%
Prophylactic Antibiotic Timing[5]	0	-	97%	97%
Prophylactic Antibiotic Timing (Outpatient)	-	-	91%	92%
Prophylactic Antibiotic Selection[5]	0	-	98%	97%
Prophylactic Antibiotic Select. (Outpatient)	-	-	96%	94%
Prophylactic Antibiotic Stopped[5]	0	-	95%	94%
Recommended VTP Ordered[2,5]	0	-	94%	94%
Urinary Catheter Removal[2,5]	0	-	91%	90%
Children's Asthma Care				
Received Systemic Corticosteroids	-	-	-	100%
Received Home Management Plan	-	-	-	71%
Received Reliever Medication	-	-	-	100%
Use of Medical Imaging				
Combination Abdominal CT Scan	-	-	0.106	0.191
Combination Chest CT Scan	-	-	0.027	0.054
Follow-up Mammogram/Ultrasound	-	-	8.4%	8.4%
MRI for Low Back Pain	-	-	31.8%	32.7%
Survey of Patients' Hospital Experiences				
Area Around Room 'Always' Quiet at Night	-	-	-	58%
Doctors 'Always' Communicated Well	-	-	-	80%
Home Recovery Information Given	-	-	-	82%
Hospital Given 9 or 10 on 10 Point Scale	-	-	-	67%
Meds 'Always' Explained Before Given	-	-	-	60%
Nurses 'Always' Communicated Well	-	-	-	76%
Pain 'Always' Well Controlled	-	-	-	69%
Room and Bathroom 'Always' Clean	-	-	-	71%
Timely Help 'Always' Received	-	-	-	64%
Would Definitely Recommend Hospital	-	-	-	69%

NOTE: Hospital profiles are in alphabetical order by state, then city, then hospital within the city; Rankings exclude hospitals with less than 25 cases except for patient surveys which excludes hospitals with less than 100 cases; (a) 100–299 cases; (1) The number of cases is too small to be sure how well a hospital is performing; (2) The hospital indicated that the data submitted for this measure were based on a sample of cases; (3) Data was collected during a shorter time period (fewer quarters) than the maximum possible time for this measure; (4) Suppressed for one or more quarters by CMS; (5) No data is available from the hospital for this measure; (6) Fewer than 100 patients completed the HCAHPS survey. Use these rates with caution, as the number of surveys may be too low to reliably assess hospital performance; (7) Survey results are based on less than 12 months of data; (8) Survey results are not available for this reporting period; (9) No or very few patients were eligible for the HCAHPS survey. The scores shown, if any, reflect a very small number of surveys; (10) A state average was not calculated because too few hospitals in the state submitted data; (11) There were discrepancies in the data collection process; Please refer to the User's Guide for a full explanation of data.

Sacred Heart Hospital

401 W Mohawk Dr Ste 100
Tomahawk, WI 54487
Phone: 715-453-7700
Fax: 715-361-2006
URL: www.ministryhealth.org
Type: Critical Access Hospitals
Emergency Services: Yes
Ownership: Voluntary Non-Profit - Church
Beds: 18

Key Personnel:
CEO/President. . . . . Monica Hilt
Chief of Medical Staff. . . . . Ron Cortte, MD
Infection Control. . . . . Karen Wiedema, RN
Quality Assurance . . . . Karen Wiedeman
Emergency Room . . . . Paula Gebauer, RN

Measure	Cases	This Hosp.	State Avg.	U.S. Avg.
Heart Attack Care				
ACE Inhibitor or ARB for LVSD[3]	0	-	97%	96%
Aspirin at Arrival[3]	0	-	99%	99%
Aspirin at Discharge[3]	0	-	99%	98%
Beta Blocker at Discharge[3]	0	-	99%	98%
Fibrinolytic Medication Timing[3]	0	-	0%	55%
PCI Within 90 Minutes of Arrival[3]	0	-	89%	90%
Smoking Cessation Advice[3]	0	-	99%	99%
Chest Pain/Possible Heart Attack Care				
Aspirin at Arrival[5]	0	-	96%	95%
Median Time to ECG (minutes)[5]	0	-	7	8
Median Time to Transfer (minutes)[5]	0	-	49	61
Fibrinolytic Medication Timing[5]	0	-	63%	54%
Heart Failure Care				
ACE Inhibitor or ARB for LVSD[1,3]	3	100%	95%	94%
Discharge Instructions[1,3]	8	100%	86%	88%
Evaluation of LVS Function[1,3]	9	100%	97%	98%
Smoking Cessation Advice[1,3]	2	100%	97%	98%
Pneumonia Care				
Appropriate Initial Antibiotic[1,3]	15	100%	94%	92%
Blood Culture Timing[1,3]	11	91%	97%	96%
Influenza Vaccine[1,3]	1	100%	92%	91%
Initial Antibiotic Timing[1,3]	19	100%	97%	95%
Pneumococcal Vaccine[1,3]	22	100%	93%	93%
Smoking Cessation Advice[1,3]	2	100%	95%	97%
Surgical Care Improvement Project				
Appropriate VTP Within 24 Hours[5]	0	-	93%	92%
Appropriate Hair Removal[5]	0	-	100%	99%
Appropriate Beta Blocker Usage[5]	0	-	92%	93%
Controlled Postoperative Blood Glucose[5]	0	-	93%	93%
Prophylactic Antibiotic Timing[5]	0	-	97%	97%
Prophylactic Antibiotic Timing (Outpatient)[5]	0	-	91%	92%
Prophylactic Antibiotic Selection[5]	0	-	98%	97%
Prophylactic Antibiotic Select. (Outpatient)[5]	0	-	96%	94%
Prophylactic Antibiotic Stopped[5]	0	-	95%	94%
Recommended VTP Ordered[5]	0	-	94%	94%
Urinary Catheter Removal[5]	0	-	91%	90%
Children's Asthma Care				
Received Systemic Corticosteroids	-	-	-	100%
Received Home Management Plan	-	-	-	71%
Received Reliever Medication	-	-	-	100%
Use of Medical Imaging				
Combination Abdominal CT Scan	103	0.078	0.106	0.191
Combination Chest CT Scan	54	0.000	0.027	0.054
Follow-up Mammogram/Ultrasound	199	7.0%	8.4%	8.4%
MRI for Low Back Pain[5]	0	-	31.8%	32.7%
Survey of Patients' Hospital Experiences				
Area Around Room 'Always' Quiet at Night	(a)	70%	-	58%
Doctors 'Always' Communicated Well	(a)	86%	-	80%
Home Recovery Information Given	(a)	91%	-	82%
Hospital Given 9 or 10 on 10 Point Scale	(a)	78%	-	67%
Meds 'Always' Explained Before Given	(a)	80%	-	60%
Nurses 'Always' Communicated Well	(a)	85%	-	76%
Pain 'Always' Well Controlled	(a)	71%	-	69%
Room and Bathroom 'Always' Clean	(a)	84%	-	71%
Timely Help 'Always' Received	(a)	77%	-	64%
Would Definitely Recommend Hospital	(a)	70%	-	69%

Aurora Medical Center Manitowoc County

5000 Memorial Dr
Two Rivers, WI 54241
Phone: 920-794-5000
Fax: 920-794-5487
URL: www.aurorahealthcare.org
Type: Acute Care Hospitals
Emergency Services: Yes
Ownership: Voluntary Non-Profit - Private
Beds: 73

Key Personnel:
Chief of Medical Staff. . . . . Glenn Smith, MD
Infection Control. . . . . Vicki Grimstad
Operating Room. . . . . Per Anderas, RN
Pediatric Ambulatory Care . . . . . . Ali A Mir, MD
Pediatric In-Patient Care . . . . Ali A Mir, MD
Quality Assurance . . . . Vicki Grimstad
Emergency Room . . . . James Hermann, MD
Intensive Care Unit. . . . . M Swoboda, RN

Measure	Cases	This Hosp.	State Avg.	U.S. Avg.
Heart Attack Care				
ACE Inhibitor or ARB for LVSD[1]	6	100%	97%	96%
Aspirin at Arrival	27	100%	99%	99%
Aspirin at Discharge[1]	19	100%	99%	98%
Beta Blocker at Discharge[1]	21	100%	99%	98%
Fibrinolytic Medication Timing	0	-	0%	55%
PCI Within 90 Minutes of Arrival	0	-	89%	90%
Smoking Cessation Advice	0	-	99%	99%
Chest Pain/Possible Heart Attack Care				
Aspirin at Arrival	75	100%	96%	95%
Median Time to ECG (minutes)	77	10	7	8
Median Time to Transfer (minutes)[1]	11	59	49	61
Fibrinolytic Medication Timing	0	-	63%	54%
Heart Failure Care				
ACE Inhibitor or ARB for LVSD[1]	15	100%	95%	94%
Discharge Instructions	26	92%	86%	88%
Evaluation of LVS Function	38	97%	97%	98%
Smoking Cessation Advice	0	-	97%	98%
Pneumonia Care				
Appropriate Initial Antibiotic	36	94%	94%	92%
Blood Culture Timing	44	98%	97%	96%
Influenza Vaccine	33	97%	92%	91%
Initial Antibiotic Timing	52	94%	97%	95%
Pneumococcal Vaccine	47	94%	93%	93%
Smoking Cessation Advice[1]	12	100%	95%	97%
Surgical Care Improvement Project				
Appropriate VTP Within 24 Hours[2]	46	83%	93%	92%
Appropriate Hair Removal[2]	263	100%	100%	99%
Appropriate Beta Blocker Usage[2]	83	99%	92%	93%
Controlled Postoperative Blood Glucose[2]	0	-	93%	93%
Prophylactic Antibiotic Timing[2]	145	99%	97%	97%
Prophylactic Antibiotic Timing (Outpatient)	81	75%	91%	92%
Prophylactic Antibiotic Selection[2]	146	99%	98%	97%
Prophylactic Antibiotic Select. (Outpatient)	66	97%	96%	94%
Prophylactic Antibiotic Stopped[2]	144	98%	95%	94%
Recommended VTP Ordered[2]	46	87%	94%	94%
Urinary Catheter Removal[1,2]	8	75%	91%	90%
Children's Asthma Care				
Received Systemic Corticosteroids	-	-	-	100%
Received Home Management Plan	-	-	-	71%
Received Reliever Medication	-	-	-	100%
Use of Medical Imaging				
Combination Abdominal CT Scan	304	0.063	0.106	0.191
Combination Chest CT Scan	260	0.008	0.027	0.054
Follow-up Mammogram/Ultrasound[5]	0	-	8.4%	8.4%
MRI for Low Back Pain	85	38.8%	31.8%	32.7%
Survey of Patients' Hospital Experiences				
Area Around Room 'Always' Quiet at Night	300+	63%	-	58%
Doctors 'Always' Communicated Well	300+	82%	-	80%
Home Recovery Information Given	300+	88%	-	82%
Hospital Given 9 or 10 on 10 Point Scale	300+	75%	-	67%
Meds 'Always' Explained Before Given	300+	64%	-	60%
Nurses 'Always' Communicated Well	300+	82%	-	76%
Pain 'Always' Well Controlled	300+	74%	-	69%
Room and Bathroom 'Always' Clean	300+	89%	-	71%
Timely Help 'Always' Received	300+	70%	-	64%
Would Definitely Recommend Hospital	300+	77%	-	69%

Vernon Memorial Hospital

507 Main St
Viroqua, WI 54665
Phone: 608-637-2101
Fax: 608-637-2141
E-mail: jsteiner@vmh.org
URL: www.vmh.org
Type: Critical Access Hospitals
Emergency Services: Yes
Ownership: Voluntary Non-Profit - Private
Beds: 25

Key Personnel:
CEO/President. . . . . Garith Steiner
Chief of Medical Staff. . . . . Jeff Lawrence
Infection Control. . . . . Romelle Heisel
Operating Room. . . . . Sue Heitman
Quality Assurance . . . . Sue Sullivan
Ambulatory Care . . . . Sue Heitman
Anesthesiology. . . . . Arnold Nomann
Emergency Room . . . . Anthony Macasaet

Measure	Cases	This Hosp.	State Avg.	U.S. Avg.
Heart Attack Care				
ACE Inhibitor or ARB for LVSD[1]	1	100%	97%	96%
Aspirin at Arrival[1]	4	100%	99%	99%
Aspirin at Discharge[1]	1	100%	99%	98%
Beta Blocker at Discharge[1]	1	100%	99%	98%
Fibrinolytic Medication Timing	0	-	0%	55%
PCI Within 90 Minutes of Arrival	0	-	89%	90%
Smoking Cessation Advice	0	-	99%	99%
Chest Pain/Possible Heart Attack Care				
Aspirin at Arrival[1,3]	4	100%	96%	95%
Median Time to ECG (minutes)[1,3]	6	8	7	8
Median Time to Transfer (minutes)[1,3]	1	34	49	61
Fibrinolytic Medication Timing[3]	0	-	63%	54%
Heart Failure Care				
ACE Inhibitor or ARB for LVSD[1]	6	100%	95%	94%
Discharge Instructions[1]	18	61%	86%	88%
Evaluation of LVS Function	27	93%	97%	98%
Smoking Cessation Advice[1]	3	100%	97%	98%
Pneumonia Care				
Appropriate Initial Antibiotic	63	79%	94%	92%
Blood Culture Timing[1]	16	94%	97%	96%
Influenza Vaccine	45	100%	92%	91%
Initial Antibiotic Timing	66	100%	97%	95%
Pneumococcal Vaccine	78	100%	93%	93%
Smoking Cessation Advice[1]	13	92%	95%	97%
Surgical Care Improvement Project				
Appropriate VTP Within 24 Hours	64	100%	93%	92%
Appropriate Hair Removal	556	100%	100%	99%
Appropriate Beta Blocker Usage	208	89%	92%	93%
Controlled Postoperative Blood Glucose[5]	0	-	93%	93%
Prophylactic Antibiotic Timing	492	89%	97%	97%
Prophylactic Antibiotic Timing (Outpatient)[1,3]	5	100%	91%	92%
Prophylactic Antibiotic Selection	492	100%	98%	97%
Prophylactic Antibiotic Select. (Outpatient)[1,3]	5	100%	96%	94%
Prophylactic Antibiotic Stopped	481	94%	95%	94%
Recommended VTP Ordered	64	100%	94%	94%
Urinary Catheter Removal	79	87%	91%	90%
Children's Asthma Care				
Received Systemic Corticosteroids	-	-	-	100%
Received Home Management Plan	-	-	-	71%
Received Reliever Medication	-	-	-	100%
Use of Medical Imaging				
Combination Abdominal CT Scan	96	0.073	0.106	0.191
Combination Chest CT Scan	68	0.015	0.027	0.054
Follow-up Mammogram/Ultrasound	241	9.5%	8.4%	8.4%
MRI for Low Back Pain[1]	30	33.3%	31.8%	32.7%
Survey of Patients' Hospital Experiences				
Area Around Room 'Always' Quiet at Night	300+	60%	-	58%
Doctors 'Always' Communicated Well	300+	87%	-	80%
Home Recovery Information Given	300+	90%	-	82%
Hospital Given 9 or 10 on 10 Point Scale	300+	74%	-	67%
Meds 'Always' Explained Before Given	300+	64%	-	60%
Nurses 'Always' Communicated Well	300+	82%	-	76%
Pain 'Always' Well Controlled	300+	72%	-	69%
Room and Bathroom 'Always' Clean	300+	88%	-	71%
Timely Help 'Always' Received	300+	78%	-	64%
Would Definitely Recommend Hospital	300+	77%	-	69%

NOTE: Hospital profiles are in alphabetical order by state, then city, then hospital within the city; Rankings exclude hospitals with less than 25 cases except for patient surveys which excludes hospitals with less than 100 cases; (a) 100–299 cases; (1) The number of cases is too small to be sure how well a hospital is performing; (2) The hospital indicated that the data submitted for this measure were based on a sample of cases; (3) Data was collected during a shorter time period (fewer quarters) than the maximum possible time for this measure; (4) Suppressed for one or more quarters by CMS; (5) No data is available from the hospital for this measure; (6) Fewer than 100 patients completed the HCAHPS survey. Use these rates with caution, as the number of surveys may be too low to reliably assess hospital performance; (7) Survey results are based on less than 12 months of data; (8) Survey results are not available for this reporting period; (9) No or very few patients were eligible for the HCAHPS survey. The scores shown, if any, reflect a very small number of surveys; (10) A state average was not calculated because too few hospitals in the state submitted data; (11) There were discrepancies in the data collection process; Please refer to the User's Guide for a full explanation of data.

Watertown Regional Medical Center

125 Hospital Dr
Watertown, WI 53098
Phone: 920-261-4210
Fax: 920-261-3940
URL: www.watertownmemorialhospital.com
Type: Acute Care Hospitals — Emergency Services: Yes
Ownership: Voluntary Non-Profit - Private — Beds: 95

Key Personnel:
CEO/President. . . . . John Kosanovich
Chief of Medical Staff . . . . James Milford, MD
Infection Control. . . . . Linda Gehring
Pediatric In-Patient Care . . . . Barb Quest, RN
Quality Assurance . . . . Tricia Price
Radiology. . . . . Jeffrey Van Beek
Intensive Care Unit. . . . . Barb Quest, RN
Patient Relations . . . . Tom Peterson

Measure	Cases	This Hosp.	State Avg.	U.S. Avg.
Heart Attack Care				
ACE Inhibitor or ARB for LVSD[1]	1	0%	97%	96%
Aspirin at Arrival[1]	8	100%	99%	99%
Aspirin at Discharge[1]	3	100%	99%	98%
Beta Blocker at Discharge[1]	5	80%	99%	98%
Fibrinolytic Medication Timing	0	-	0%	55%
PCI Within 90 Minutes of Arrival	0	-	89%	90%
Smoking Cessation Advice	0	-	99%	99%
Chest Pain/Possible Heart Attack Care				
Aspirin at Arrival	66	100%	96%	95%
Median Time to ECG (minutes)	67	9	7	8
Median Time to Transfer (minutes)[1]	5	67	49	61
Fibrinolytic Medication Timing[1]	5	80%	63%	54%
Heart Failure Care				
ACE Inhibitor or ARB for LVSD[1]	13	100%	95%	94%
Discharge Instructions	43	60%	86%	88%
Evaluation of LVS Function	54	100%	97%	98%
Smoking Cessation Advice[1]	6	100%	97%	98%
Pneumonia Care				
Appropriate Initial Antibiotic	56	98%	94%	92%
Blood Culture Timing	95	99%	97%	96%
Influenza Vaccine	48	96%	92%	91%
Initial Antibiotic Timing	101	98%	97%	95%
Pneumococcal Vaccine	88	99%	93%	93%
Smoking Cessation Advice[1]	18	94%	95%	97%
Surgical Care Improvement Project				
Appropriate VTP Within 24 Hours	76	87%	93%	92%
Appropriate Hair Removal	221	99%	100%	99%
Appropriate Beta Blocker Usage	76	82%	92%	93%
Controlled Postoperative Blood Glucose	0	-	93%	93%
Prophylactic Antibiotic Timing	158	99%	97%	97%
Prophylactic Antibiotic Timing (Outpatient)	191	87%	91%	92%
Prophylactic Antibiotic Selection	160	98%	98%	97%
Prophylactic Antibiotic Select. (Outpatient)	216	93%	96%	94%
Prophylactic Antibiotic Stopped	151	91%	95%	94%
Recommended VTP Ordered	77	87%	94%	94%
Urinary Catheter Removal	67	94%	91%	90%
Children's Asthma Care				
Received Systemic Corticosteroids	-	-	-	100%
Received Home Management Plan	-	-	-	71%
Received Reliever Medication	-	-	-	100%
Use of Medical Imaging				
Combination Abdominal CT Scan	437	0.078	0.106	0.191
Combination Chest CT Scan	301	0.063	0.027	0.054
Follow-up Mammogram/Ultrasound	699	8.6%	8.4%	8.4%
MRI for Low Back Pain	92	31.5%	31.8%	32.7%
Survey of Patients' Hospital Experiences				
Area Around Room 'Always' Quiet at Night	300+	62%	-	58%
Doctors 'Always' Communicated Well	300+	75%	-	80%
Home Recovery Information Given	300+	84%	-	82%
Hospital Given 9 or 10 on 10 Point Scale	300+	63%	-	67%
Meds 'Always' Explained Before Given	300+	62%	-	60%
Nurses 'Always' Communicated Well	300+	74%	-	76%
Pain 'Always' Well Controlled	300+	67%	-	69%
Room and Bathroom 'Always' Clean	300+	74%	-	71%
Timely Help 'Always' Received	300+	70%	-	64%
Would Definitely Recommend Hospital	300+	61%	-	69%

Waukesha Memorial Hospital

725 American Ave
Waukesha, WI 53188
Phone: 262-928-1000
Fax: 262-928-7810
URL: www.waukeshamemorial.org
Type: Acute Care Hospitals — Emergency Services: Yes
Ownership: Voluntary Non-Profit - Private — Beds: 301

Key Personnel:
CEO/President. . . . . Ed Olson

Measure	Cases	This Hosp.	State Avg.	U.S. Avg.
Heart Attack Care				
ACE Inhibitor or ARB for LVSD[2]	47	100%	97%	96%
Aspirin at Arrival[2]	216	99%	99%	99%
Aspirin at Discharge[2]	202	98%	99%	98%
Beta Blocker at Discharge[2]	199	98%	99%	98%
Fibrinolytic Medication Timing[2]	0	-	0%	55%
PCI Within 90 Minutes of Arrival[2]	35	91%	89%	90%
Smoking Cessation Advice[2]	46	100%	99%	99%
Chest Pain/Possible Heart Attack Care				
Aspirin at Arrival[1]	5	100%	96%	95%
Median Time to ECG (minutes)[1]	5	5	7	8
Median Time to Transfer (minutes)[5]	0	-	49	61
Fibrinolytic Medication Timing[3]	0	-	63%	54%
Heart Failure Care				
ACE Inhibitor or ARB for LVSD[2]	75	97%	95%	94%
Discharge Instructions[2]	221	86%	86%	88%
Evaluation of LVS Function[2]	286	98%	97%	98%
Smoking Cessation Advice[2]	25	100%	97%	98%
Pneumonia Care				
Appropriate Initial Antibiotic[2]	83	98%	94%	92%
Blood Culture Timing[2]	158	99%	97%	96%
Influenza Vaccine[2]	97	97%	92%	91%
Initial Antibiotic Timing[2]	148	99%	97%	95%
Pneumococcal Vaccine[2]	146	99%	93%	93%
Smoking Cessation Advice[2]	36	100%	95%	97%
Surgical Care Improvement Project				
Appropriate VTP Within 24 Hours[2]	173	93%	93%	92%
Appropriate Hair Removal[2]	616	99%	100%	99%
Appropriate Beta Blocker Usage[2]	226	85%	92%	93%
Controlled Postoperative Blood Glucose[2]	153	93%	93%	93%
Prophylactic Antibiotic Timing[2]	447	98%	97%	97%
Prophylactic Antibiotic Timing (Outpatient)	523	86%	91%	92%
Prophylactic Antibiotic Selection[2]	455	95%	98%	97%
Prophylactic Antibiotic Select. (Outpatient)	538	89%	96%	94%
Prophylactic Antibiotic Stopped[2]	439	97%	95%	94%
Recommended VTP Ordered[2]	173	94%	94%	94%
Urinary Catheter Removal[2]	185	97%	91%	90%
Children's Asthma Care				
Received Systemic Corticosteroids	-	-	-	100%
Received Home Management Plan	-	-	-	71%
Received Reliever Medication	-	-	-	100%
Use of Medical Imaging				
Combination Abdominal CT Scan	1,410	0.136	0.106	0.191
Combination Chest CT Scan	1,549	0.060	0.027	0.054
Follow-up Mammogram/Ultrasound	2,047	11.5%	8.4%	8.4%
MRI for Low Back Pain	349	35.2%	31.8%	32.7%
Survey of Patients' Hospital Experiences				
Area Around Room 'Always' Quiet at Night	300+	64%	-	58%
Doctors 'Always' Communicated Well	300+	80%	-	80%
Home Recovery Information Given	300+	87%	-	82%
Hospital Given 9 or 10 on 10 Point Scale	300+	78%	-	67%
Meds 'Always' Explained Before Given	300+	63%	-	60%
Nurses 'Always' Communicated Well	300+	78%	-	76%
Pain 'Always' Well Controlled	300+	69%	-	69%
Room and Bathroom 'Always' Clean	300+	79%	-	71%
Timely Help 'Always' Received	300+	65%	-	64%
Would Definitely Recommend Hospital	300+	82%	-	69%

Riverside Medical Center

800 Riverside Dr
Waupaca, WI 54981
Phone: 715-258-1000
Fax: 715-256-2083
URL: www.riversidemedical.org
Type: Critical Access Hospitals — Emergency Services: Yes
Ownership: Voluntary Non-Profit - Private — Beds: 77

Key Personnel:
CEO/President. . . . . Phil Kambic
Radiology. . . . . Corbin Asbury

Measure	Cases	This Hosp.	State Avg.	U.S. Avg.
Heart Attack Care				
ACE Inhibitor or ARB for LVSD[5]	0	-	97%	96%
Aspirin at Arrival[5]	0	-	99%	99%
Aspirin at Discharge[5]	0	-	99%	98%
Beta Blocker at Discharge[5]	0	-	99%	98%
Fibrinolytic Medication Timing[5]	0	-	0%	55%
PCI Within 90 Minutes of Arrival[5]	0	-	89%	90%
Smoking Cessation Advice[5]	0	-	99%	99%
Chest Pain/Possible Heart Attack Care				
Aspirin at Arrival	-	-	96%	95%
Median Time to ECG (minutes)	-	-	7	8
Median Time to Transfer (minutes)	-	-	49	61
Fibrinolytic Medication Timing	-	-	63%	54%
Heart Failure Care				
ACE Inhibitor or ARB for LVSD[5]	0	-	95%	94%
Discharge Instructions[5]	0	-	86%	88%
Evaluation of LVS Function[5]	0	-	97%	98%
Smoking Cessation Advice[5]	0	-	97%	98%
Pneumonia Care				
Appropriate Initial Antibiotic	33	85%	94%	92%
Blood Culture Timing	71	89%	97%	96%
Influenza Vaccine	35	94%	92%	91%
Initial Antibiotic Timing	70	84%	97%	95%
Pneumococcal Vaccine	73	99%	93%	93%
Smoking Cessation Advice[1]	13	77%	95%	97%
Surgical Care Improvement Project				
Appropriate VTP Within 24 Hours[5]	0	-	93%	92%
Appropriate Hair Removal[5]	0	-	100%	99%
Appropriate Beta Blocker Usage[5]	0	-	92%	93%
Controlled Postoperative Blood Glucose[5]	0	-	93%	93%
Prophylactic Antibiotic Timing[5]	0	-	97%	97%
Prophylactic Antibiotic Timing (Outpatient)	-	-	91%	92%
Prophylactic Antibiotic Selection[5]	0	-	98%	97%
Prophylactic Antibiotic Select. (Outpatient)	-	-	96%	94%
Prophylactic Antibiotic Stopped[5]	0	-	95%	94%
Recommended VTP Ordered[5]	0	-	94%	94%
Urinary Catheter Removal[5]	0	-	91%	90%
Children's Asthma Care				
Received Systemic Corticosteroids	-	-	-	100%
Received Home Management Plan	-	-	-	71%
Received Reliever Medication	-	-	-	100%
Use of Medical Imaging				
Combination Abdominal CT Scan	-	-	0.106	0.191
Combination Chest CT Scan	-	-	0.027	0.054
Follow-up Mammogram/Ultrasound	-	-	8.4%	8.4%
MRI for Low Back Pain	-	-	31.8%	32.7%
Survey of Patients' Hospital Experiences				
Area Around Room 'Always' Quiet at Night	300+	65%	-	58%
Doctors 'Always' Communicated Well	300+	82%	-	80%
Home Recovery Information Given	300+	87%	-	82%
Hospital Given 9 or 10 on 10 Point Scale	300+	66%	-	67%
Meds 'Always' Explained Before Given	300+	64%	-	60%
Nurses 'Always' Communicated Well	300+	74%	-	76%
Pain 'Always' Well Controlled	300+	64%	-	69%
Room and Bathroom 'Always' Clean	300+	78%	-	71%
Timely Help 'Always' Received	300+	66%	-	64%
Would Definitely Recommend Hospital	300+	64%	-	69%

NOTE: Hospital profiles are in alphabetical order by state, then city, then hospital within the city; Rankings exclude hospitals with less than 25 cases except for patient surveys which excludes hospitals with less than 100 cases; (a) 100–299 cases; (1) The number of cases is too small to be sure how well a hospital is performing; (2) The hospital indicated that the data submitted for this measure were based on a sample of cases; (3) Data was collected during a shorter time period (fewer quarters) than the maximum possible time for this measure; (4) Suppressed for one or more quarters by CMS; (5) No data is available from the hospital for this measure; (6) Fewer than 100 patients completed the HCAHPS survey. Use these rates with caution, as the number of surveys may be too low to reliably assess hospital performance; (7) Survey results are based on less than 12 months of data; (8) Survey results are not available for this reporting period; (9) No or very few patients were eligible for the HCAHPS survey. The scores shown, if any, reflect a very small number of surveys; (10) A state average was not calculated because too few hospitals in the state submitted data; (11) There were discrepancies in the data collection process; Please refer to the User's Guide for a full explanation of data.

Waupun Memorial Hospital

620 W Brown St Phone: 920-324-6530
Waupun, WI 53963 Fax: 920-324-2085
URL: www.agnesian.com
Type: Critical Access Hospitals Emergency Services: Yes
Ownership: Voluntary Non-Profit - Church Beds: 25

Key Personnel:
Infection Control. . . . . Kayla Ericksen, RN
Emergency Room . . . . Patricia M Demery, RN

Measure	Cases	This Hosp.	State Avg.	U.S. Avg.
Heart Attack Care				
ACE Inhibitor or ARB for LVSD[5]	0	-	97%	96%
Aspirin at Arrival[5]	0	-	99%	99%
Aspirin at Discharge[5]	0	-	99%	98%
Beta Blocker at Discharge[5]	0	-	99%	98%
Fibrinolytic Medication Timing[5]	0	-	0%	55%
PCI Within 90 Minutes of Arrival[5]	0	-	89%	90%
Smoking Cessation Advice[5]	0	-	99%	99%
Chest Pain/Possible Heart Attack Care				
Aspirin at Arrival	-	-	96%	95%
Median Time to ECG (minutes)	-	-	7	8
Median Time to Transfer (minutes)	-	-	49	61
Fibrinolytic Medication Timing	-	-	63%	54%
Heart Failure Care				
ACE Inhibitor or ARB for LVSD[1]	6	83%	95%	94%
Discharge Instructions[1]	21	95%	86%	88%
Evaluation of LVS Function	26	88%	97%	98%
Smoking Cessation Advice[1]	3	100%	97%	98%
Pneumonia Care				
Appropriate Initial Antibiotic	32	97%	94%	92%
Blood Culture Timing	33	97%	97%	96%
Influenza Vaccine	29	100%	92%	91%
Initial Antibiotic Timing	44	100%	97%	95%
Pneumococcal Vaccine	47	100%	93%	93%
Smoking Cessation Advice[1]	8	100%	95%	97%
Surgical Care Improvement Project				
Appropriate VTP Within 24 Hours[1]	23	96%	93%	92%
Appropriate Hair Removal	84	100%	100%	99%
Appropriate Beta Blocker Usage[1]	23	100%	92%	93%
Controlled Postoperative Blood Glucose[5]	0	-	93%	93%
Prophylactic Antibiotic Timing	66	95%	97%	97%
Prophylactic Antibiotic Timing (Outpatient)		-	91%	92%
Prophylactic Antibiotic Selection	67	100%	98%	97%
Prophylactic Antibiotic Select. (Outpatient)	-	-	96%	94%
Prophylactic Antibiotic Stopped	66	97%	95%	94%
Recommended VTP Ordered[1]	23	100%	94%	94%
Urinary Catheter Removal[1]	21	100%	91%	90%
Children's Asthma Care				
Received Systemic Corticosteroids	-	-	-	100%
Received Home Management Plan	-	-	-	71%
Received Reliever Medication	-	-	-	100%
Use of Medical Imaging				
Combination Abdominal CT Scan	-	-	0.106	0.191
Combination Chest CT Scan	-	-	0.027	0.054
Follow-up Mammogram/Ultrasound	-	-	8.4%	8.4%
MRI for Low Back Pain	-	-	31.8%	32.7%
Survey of Patients' Hospital Experiences				
Area Around Room 'Always' Quiet at Night	300+	68%	-	58%
Doctors 'Always' Communicated Well	300+	84%	-	80%
Home Recovery Information Given	300+	87%	-	82%
Hospital Given 9 or 10 on 10 Point Scale	300+	79%	-	67%
Meds 'Always' Explained Before Given	300+	73%	-	60%
Nurses 'Always' Communicated Well	300+	85%	-	76%
Pain 'Always' Well Controlled	300+	78%	-	69%
Room and Bathroom 'Always' Clean	300+	81%	-	71%
Timely Help 'Always' Received	300+	78%	-	64%
Would Definitely Recommend Hospital	300+	74%	-	69%

Aspirus Wausau Hospital

333 Pine Ridge Blvd Phone: 715-847-2121
Wausau, WI 54401 Fax: 715-847-2017
URL: www.aspirus.org
Type: Acute Care Hospitals Emergency Services: Yes
Ownership: Proprietary Beds: 321

Key Personnel:
CEO/President. . . . . Paul A Spaude
Cardiac Laboratory. . . . . Scott Gavavet
Chief of Medical Staff . . . . Chuck Shabirro
Infection Control. . . . . Jeanine Bresnahan
Operating Room. . . . . Anne Hanzel
Quality Assurance . . . . Michelle Boylaneuser
Radiology. . . . . Kevin Drorocl

Measure	Cases	This Hosp.	State Avg.	U.S. Avg.
Heart Attack Care				
ACE Inhibitor or ARB for LVSD[2]	29	97%	97%	96%
Aspirin at Arrival[2]	118	100%	99%	99%
Aspirin at Discharge[2]	251	100%	99%	98%
Beta Blocker at Discharge[2]	250	100%	99%	98%
Fibrinolytic Medication Timing[2]	0	-	0%	55%
PCI Within 90 Minutes of Arrival[2]	33	100%	89%	90%
Smoking Cessation Advice[2]	80	100%	99%	99%
Chest Pain/Possible Heart Attack Care				
Aspirin at Arrival[5]	0	-	96%	95%
Median Time to ECG (minutes)[5]	0	-	7	8
Median Time to Transfer (minutes)[5]	0	-	49	61
Fibrinolytic Medication Timing[5]	0	-	63%	54%
Heart Failure Care				
ACE Inhibitor or ARB for LVSD[2]	51	92%	95%	94%
Discharge Instructions[2]	205	80%	86%	88%
Evaluation of LVS Function[2]	238	100%	97%	98%
Smoking Cessation Advice[2]	27	100%	97%	98%
Pneumonia Care				
Appropriate Initial Antibiotic[2]	66	95%	94%	92%
Blood Culture Timing[2]	102	95%	97%	96%
Influenza Vaccine[2]	85	93%	92%	91%
Initial Antibiotic Timing[2]	113	97%	97%	95%
Pneumococcal Vaccine[2]	124	96%	93%	93%
Smoking Cessation Advice[2]	47	98%	95%	97%
Surgical Care Improvement Project				
Appropriate VTP Within 24 Hours[2]	88	93%	93%	92%
Appropriate Hair Removal[2]	547	100%	100%	99%
Appropriate Beta Blocker Usage[2]	248	95%	92%	93%
Controlled Postoperative Blood Glucose[2]	145	95%	93%	93%
Prophylactic Antibiotic Timing[2]	389	99%	97%	97%
Prophylactic Antibiotic Timing (Outpatient)	408	96%	91%	92%
Prophylactic Antibiotic Selection[2]	401	99%	98%	97%
Prophylactic Antibiotic Select. (Outpatient)	400	95%	96%	94%
Prophylactic Antibiotic Stopped[2]	372	97%	95%	94%
Recommended VTP Ordered[2]	88	98%	94%	94%
Urinary Catheter Removal[2]	89	91%	91%	90%
Children's Asthma Care				
Received Systemic Corticosteroids	-	-	-	100%
Received Home Management Plan	-	-	-	71%
Received Reliever Medication	-	-	-	100%
Use of Medical Imaging				
Combination Abdominal CT Scan	430	0.072	0.106	0.191
Combination Chest CT Scan	436	0.005	0.027	0.054
Follow-up Mammogram/Ultrasound	928	8.0%	8.4%	8.4%
MRI for Low Back Pain[1]	53	24.5%	31.8%	32.7%
Survey of Patients' Hospital Experiences				
Area Around Room 'Always' Quiet at Night	300+	63%	-	58%
Doctors 'Always' Communicated Well	300+	81%	-	80%
Home Recovery Information Given	300+	87%	-	82%
Hospital Given 9 or 10 on 10 Point Scale	300+	72%	-	67%
Meds 'Always' Explained Before Given	300+	63%	-	60%
Nurses 'Always' Communicated Well	300+	79%	-	76%
Pain 'Always' Well Controlled	300+	69%	-	69%
Room and Bathroom 'Always' Clean	300+	73%	-	71%
Timely Help 'Always' Received	300+	65%	-	64%
Would Definitely Recommend Hospital	300+	78%	-	69%

Aurora West Allis Medical Center

8901 W Lincoln Ave Phone: 414-328-6000
West Allis, WI 53227 Fax: 414-328-8536
URL: www.aurorahealthcare.org
Type: Acute Care Hospitals Emergency Services: Yes
Ownership: Voluntary Non-Profit - Private Beds: 250

Key Personnel:
CEO/President. . . . . Richard Kellar
Chief of Medical Staff . . . . Jeffery Showers
Pediatric Ambulatory Care . . . . . . Michael Gutzeit, MD
Pediatric In-Patient Care . . . . . . Michael Gutzeit, MD
Quality Assurance . . . . Vicki Volp
Radiology. . . . . Perry M Gould, MD
Emergency Room . . . . Wendy Roberts, RN
Intensive Care Unit. . . . . Larry Conrad

Measure	Cases	This Hosp.	State Avg.	U.S. Avg.
Heart Attack Care				
ACE Inhibitor or ARB for LVSD[1]	8	100%	97%	96%
Aspirin at Arrival	53	100%	99%	99%
Aspirin at Discharge	26	100%	99%	98%
Beta Blocker at Discharge	29	100%	99%	98%
Fibrinolytic Medication Timing	0	-	0%	55%
PCI Within 90 Minutes of Arrival	0	-	89%	90%
Smoking Cessation Advice[1]	1	100%	99%	99%
Chest Pain/Possible Heart Attack Care				
Aspirin at Arrival	144	97%	96%	95%
Median Time to ECG (minutes)	148	12	7	8
Median Time to Transfer (minutes)[1]	15	38	49	61
Fibrinolytic Medication Timing	0	-	63%	54%
Heart Failure Care				
ACE Inhibitor or ARB for LVSD	34	100%	95%	94%
Discharge Instructions	114	89%	86%	88%
Evaluation of LVS Function	187	100%	97%	98%
Smoking Cessation Advice[1]	15	100%	97%	98%
Pneumonia Care				
Appropriate Initial Antibiotic	137	96%	94%	92%
Blood Culture Timing	220	100%	97%	96%
Influenza Vaccine	175	99%	92%	91%
Initial Antibiotic Timing	250	98%	97%	95%
Pneumococcal Vaccine	221	99%	93%	93%
Smoking Cessation Advice	76	100%	95%	97%
Surgical Care Improvement Project				
Appropriate VTP Within 24 Hours[2]	258	93%	93%	92%
Appropriate Hair Removal[2]	811	100%	100%	99%
Appropriate Beta Blocker Usage[2]	190	97%	92%	93%
Controlled Postoperative Blood Glucose[2]	0	-	93%	93%
Prophylactic Antibiotic Timing[2]	651	99%	97%	97%
Prophylactic Antibiotic Timing (Outpatient)	214	89%	91%	92%
Prophylactic Antibiotic Selection[2]	654	99%	98%	97%
Prophylactic Antibiotic Select. (Outpatient)	203	96%	96%	94%
Prophylactic Antibiotic Stopped[2]	628	97%	95%	94%
Recommended VTP Ordered[2]	258	97%	94%	94%
Urinary Catheter Removal[2]	117	89%	91%	90%
Children's Asthma Care				
Received Systemic Corticosteroids	-	-	-	100%
Received Home Management Plan	-	-	-	71%
Received Reliever Medication	-	-	-	100%
Use of Medical Imaging				
Combination Abdominal CT Scan	960	0.044	0.106	0.191
Combination Chest CT Scan	586	0.005	0.027	0.054
Follow-up Mammogram/Ultrasound	1,870	6.3%	8.4%	8.4%
MRI for Low Back Pain	126	42.1%	31.8%	32.7%
Survey of Patients' Hospital Experiences				
Area Around Room 'Always' Quiet at Night	300+	59%	-	58%
Doctors 'Always' Communicated Well	300+	76%	-	80%
Home Recovery Information Given	300+	83%	-	82%
Hospital Given 9 or 10 on 10 Point Scale	300+	69%	-	67%
Meds 'Always' Explained Before Given	300+	58%	-	60%
Nurses 'Always' Communicated Well	300+	74%	-	76%
Pain 'Always' Well Controlled	300+	65%	-	69%
Room and Bathroom 'Always' Clean	300+	70%	-	71%
Timely Help 'Always' Received	300+	54%	-	64%
Would Definitely Recommend Hospital	300+	72%	-	69%

NOTE: Hospital profiles are in alphabetical order by state, then city, then hospital within the city; Rankings exclude hospitals with less than 25 cases except for patient surveys which excludes hospitals with less than 100 cases; (a) 100–299 cases; (1) The number of cases is too small to be sure how well a hospital is performing; (2) The hospital indicated that the data submitted for this measure were based on a sample of cases; (3) Data was collected during a shorter time period (fewer quarters) than the maximum possible time for this measure; (4) Suppressed for one or more quarters by CMS; (5) No data is available from the hospital for this measure; (6) Fewer than 100 patients completed the HCAHPS survey. Use these rates with caution, as the number of surveys may be too low to reliably assess hospital performance; (7) Survey results are based on less than 12 months of data; (8) Survey results are not available for this reporting period; (9) No or very few patients were eligible for the HCAHPS survey. The scores shown, if any, reflect a very small number of surveys; (10) A state average was not calculated because too few hospitals in the state submitted data; (11) There were discrepancies in the data collection process; Please refer to the User's Guide for a full explanation of data.

Saint Josephs Community Hospital West Bend

3200 Pleasant Valley Road Phone: 262-334-5533
West Bend, WI 53095 Fax: 262-334-8484
URL: www.stjosephswb.com
Type: Acute Care Hospitals Emergency Services: Yes
Ownership: Voluntary Non-Profit - Private Beds: 80

Key Personnel:
CEO/President. . . . . Michael Laird
Chief of Medical Staff . . . . G Michael Mosley, MD
Infection Control. . . . . Pat Pearson
Quality Assurance . . . . Karen Ernisse
Radiology. . . . . Donna Lawien
Anesthesiology. . . . . Eric Breckenridge, DO
Emergency Room . . . . Mary Lewis, MD

Measure	Cases	This Hosp.	State Avg.	U.S. Avg.
Heart Attack Care				
ACE Inhibitor or ARB for LVSD[1]	2	100%	97%	96%
Aspirin at Arrival[1]	11	73%	99%	99%
Aspirin at Discharge[1]	7	57%	99%	98%
Beta Blocker at Discharge[1]	8	100%	99%	98%
Fibrinolytic Medication Timing	0	-	0%	55%
PCI Within 90 Minutes of Arrival	0	-	89%	90%
Smoking Cessation Advice[1]	1	100%	99%	99%
Chest Pain/Possible Heart Attack Care				
Aspirin at Arrival	132	88%	96%	95%
Median Time to ECG (minutes)	133	9	7	8
Median Time to Transfer (minutes)[1]	24	54	49	61
Fibrinolytic Medication Timing	0	-	63%	54%
Heart Failure Care				
ACE Inhibitor or ARB for LVSD	27	81%	95%	94%
Discharge Instructions	57	91%	86%	88%
Evaluation of LVS Function	80	99%	97%	98%
Smoking Cessation Advice[1]	7	100%	97%	98%
Pneumonia Care				
Appropriate Initial Antibiotic	81	89%	94%	92%
Blood Culture Timing	126	96%	97%	96%
Influenza Vaccine	93	87%	92%	91%
Initial Antibiotic Timing	119	99%	97%	95%
Pneumococcal Vaccine	125	93%	93%	93%
Smoking Cessation Advice	29	100%	95%	97%
Surgical Care Improvement Project				
Appropriate VTP Within 24 Hours	109	85%	93%	92%
Appropriate Hair Removal	340	96%	100%	99%
Appropriate Beta Blocker Usage	63	86%	92%	93%
Controlled Postoperative Blood Glucose	0	-	93%	93%
Prophylactic Antibiotic Timing	237	96%	97%	97%
Prophylactic Antibiotic Timing (Outpatient)	89	85%	91%	92%
Prophylactic Antibiotic Selection	236	92%	98%	97%
Prophylactic Antibiotic Select. (Outpatient)	78	90%	96%	94%
Prophylactic Antibiotic Stopped	228	94%	95%	94%
Recommended VTP Ordered	110	85%	94%	94%
Urinary Catheter Removal	63	81%	91%	90%
Children's Asthma Care				
Received Systemic Corticosteroids	-	-	-	100%
Received Home Management Plan	-	-	-	71%
Received Reliever Medication	-	-	-	100%
Use of Medical Imaging				
Combination Abdominal CT Scan	284	0.018	0.106	0.191
Combination Chest CT Scan	301	0.027	0.027	0.054
Follow-up Mammogram/Ultrasound[1]	17	23.5%	8.4%	8.4%
MRI for Low Back Pain	103	31.1%	31.8%	32.7%
Survey of Patients' Hospital Experiences				
Area Around Room 'Always' Quiet at Night	300+	72%	-	58%
Doctors 'Always' Communicated Well	300+	83%	-	80%
Home Recovery Information Given	300+	87%	-	82%
Hospital Given 9 or 10 on 10 Point Scale	300+	71%	-	67%
Meds 'Always' Explained Before Given	300+	68%	-	60%
Nurses 'Always' Communicated Well	300+	79%	-	76%
Pain 'Always' Well Controlled	300+	72%	-	69%
Room and Bathroom 'Always' Clean	300+	76%	-	71%
Timely Help 'Always' Received	300+	63%	-	64%
Would Definitely Recommend Hospital	300+	72%	-	69%

Saint Clare's Hospital of Weston

3400 Ministry Parkway Phone: 715-393-3000
Weston, WI 54476
E-mail: saintclare@ministryhealth.org
URL: ministryhealth.org
Type: Acute Care Hospitals Emergency Services: Yes
Ownership: Voluntary Non-Profit - Private

Key Personnel:
Chief of Medical Staff . . . . Larry Hegland
Patient Relations . . . . Colleen Hoerneman

Measure	Cases	This Hosp.	State Avg.	U.S. Avg.
Heart Attack Care				
ACE Inhibitor or ARB for LVSD	43	100%	97%	96%
Aspirin at Arrival	69	100%	99%	99%
Aspirin at Discharge	243	100%	99%	98%
Beta Blocker at Discharge	231	100%	99%	98%
Fibrinolytic Medication Timing	0	-	0%	55%
PCI Within 90 Minutes of Arrival[1]	19	95%	89%	90%
Smoking Cessation Advice	84	100%	99%	99%
Chest Pain/Possible Heart Attack Care				
Aspirin at Arrival[3]	0	-	96%	95%
Median Time to ECG (minutes)[3]	0	-	7	8
Median Time to Transfer (minutes)[5]	0	-	49	61
Fibrinolytic Medication Timing[5]	0	-	63%	54%
Heart Failure Care				
ACE Inhibitor or ARB for LVSD	31	100%	95%	94%
Discharge Instructions	111	99%	86%	88%
Evaluation of LVS Function	144	99%	97%	98%
Smoking Cessation Advice	27	96%	97%	98%
Pneumonia Care				
Appropriate Initial Antibiotic	36	97%	94%	92%
Blood Culture Timing	63	100%	97%	96%
Influenza Vaccine	44	86%	92%	91%
Initial Antibiotic Timing	76	100%	97%	95%
Pneumococcal Vaccine	82	99%	93%	93%
Smoking Cessation Advice[1]	23	100%	95%	97%
Surgical Care Improvement Project				
Appropriate VTP Within 24 Hours	73	92%	93%	92%
Appropriate Hair Removal	804	100%	100%	99%
Appropriate Beta Blocker Usage	300	95%	92%	93%
Controlled Postoperative Blood Glucose	144	97%	93%	93%
Prophylactic Antibiotic Timing	624	100%	97%	97%
Prophylactic Antibiotic Timing (Outpatient)	119	98%	91%	92%
Prophylactic Antibiotic Selection	630	99%	98%	97%
Prophylactic Antibiotic Select. (Outpatient)	117	98%	96%	94%
Prophylactic Antibiotic Stopped	617	98%	95%	94%
Recommended VTP Ordered	73	92%	94%	94%
Urinary Catheter Removal	155	93%	91%	90%
Children's Asthma Care				
Received Systemic Corticosteroids	-	-	-	100%
Received Home Management Plan	-	-	-	71%
Received Reliever Medication	-	-	-	100%
Use of Medical Imaging				
Combination Abdominal CT Scan[1]	42	0.000	0.106	0.191
Combination Chest CT Scan[1]	31	0.000	0.027	0.054
Follow-up Mammogram/Ultrasound[5]	0	-	8.4%	8.4%
MRI for Low Back Pain[1]	5	20.0%	31.8%	32.7%
Survey of Patients' Hospital Experiences				
Area Around Room 'Always' Quiet at Night	300+	51%	-	58%
Doctors 'Always' Communicated Well	300+	76%	-	80%
Home Recovery Information Given	300+	91%	-	82%
Hospital Given 9 or 10 on 10 Point Scale	300+	73%	-	67%
Meds 'Always' Explained Before Given	300+	62%	-	60%
Nurses 'Always' Communicated Well	300+	75%	-	76%
Pain 'Always' Well Controlled	300+	69%	-	69%
Room and Bathroom 'Always' Clean	300+	74%	-	71%
Timely Help 'Always' Received	300+	68%	-	64%
Would Definitely Recommend Hospital	300+	76%	-	69%

Tri County Memorial Hospital

18601 Lincoln St Phone: 715-538-4361
Whitehall, WI 54773 Fax: 715-538-4343
Type: Critical Access Hospitals Emergency Services: Yes
Ownership: Voluntary Non-Profit - Private Beds: 93

Key Personnel:
CEO/President. . . . . Ronald B Fields
Chief of Medical Staff . . . . Joanne Selkurt

Measure	Cases	This Hosp.	State Avg.	U.S. Avg.
Heart Attack Care				
ACE Inhibitor or ARB for LVSD[5]	0	-	97%	96%
Aspirin at Arrival[5]	0	-	99%	99%
Aspirin at Discharge[5]	0	-	99%	98%
Beta Blocker at Discharge[5]	0	-	99%	98%
Fibrinolytic Medication Timing[5]	0	-	0%	55%
PCI Within 90 Minutes of Arrival[5]	0	-	89%	90%
Smoking Cessation Advice[5]	0	-	99%	99%
Chest Pain/Possible Heart Attack Care				
Aspirin at Arrival	-	-	96%	95%
Median Time to ECG (minutes)	-	-	7	8
Median Time to Transfer (minutes)	-	-	49	61
Fibrinolytic Medication Timing	-	-	63%	54%
Heart Failure Care				
ACE Inhibitor or ARB for LVSD[1,3]	7	57%	95%	94%
Discharge Instructions[1,3]	15	100%	86%	88%
Evaluation of LVS Function[1,3]	23	65%	97%	98%
Smoking Cessation Advice[1,3]	1	100%	97%	98%
Pneumonia Care				
Appropriate Initial Antibiotic[1]	22	73%	94%	92%
Blood Culture Timing	30	97%	97%	96%
Influenza Vaccine[1]	24	38%	92%	91%
Initial Antibiotic Timing	31	97%	97%	95%
Pneumococcal Vaccine	36	61%	93%	93%
Smoking Cessation Advice[1]	6	83%	95%	97%
Surgical Care Improvement Project				
Appropriate VTP Within 24 Hours[5]	0	-	93%	92%
Appropriate Hair Removal[5]	0	-	100%	99%
Appropriate Beta Blocker Usage[5]	0	-	92%	93%
Controlled Postoperative Blood Glucose[5]	0	-	93%	93%
Prophylactic Antibiotic Timing[5]	0	-	97%	97%
Prophylactic Antibiotic Timing (Outpatient)	-	-	91%	92%
Prophylactic Antibiotic Selection[5]	0	-	98%	97%
Prophylactic Antibiotic Select. (Outpatient)	-	-	96%	94%
Prophylactic Antibiotic Stopped[5]	0	-	95%	94%
Recommended VTP Ordered[5]	0	-	94%	94%
Urinary Catheter Removal[5]	0	-	91%	90%
Children's Asthma Care				
Received Systemic Corticosteroids	-	-	-	100%
Received Home Management Plan	-	-	-	71%
Received Reliever Medication	-	-	-	100%
Use of Medical Imaging				
Combination Abdominal CT Scan	-	-	0.106	0.191
Combination Chest CT Scan	-	-	0.027	0.054
Follow-up Mammogram/Ultrasound	-	-	8.4%	8.4%
MRI for Low Back Pain	-	-	31.8%	32.7%
Survey of Patients' Hospital Experiences				
Area Around Room 'Always' Quiet at Night	(a)	58%	-	58%
Doctors 'Always' Communicated Well	(a)	87%	-	80%
Home Recovery Information Given	(a)	79%	-	82%
Hospital Given 9 or 10 on 10 Point Scale	(a)	75%	-	67%
Meds 'Always' Explained Before Given	(a)	69%	-	60%
Nurses 'Always' Communicated Well	(a)	84%	-	76%
Pain 'Always' Well Controlled	(a)	65%	-	69%
Room and Bathroom 'Always' Clean	(a)	89%	-	71%
Timely Help 'Always' Received	(a)	80%	-	64%
Would Definitely Recommend Hospital	(a)	74%	-	69%

NOTE: Hospital profiles are in alphabetical order by state, then city, then hospital within the city; Rankings exclude hospitals with less than 25 cases except for patient surveys which excludes hospitals with less than 100 cases; (a) 100–299 cases; (1) The number of cases is too small to be sure how well a hospital is performing; (2) The hospital indicated that the data submitted for this measure were based on a sample of cases; (3) Data was collected during a shorter time period (fewer quarters) than the maximum possible time for this measure; (4) Suppressed for one or more quarters by CMS; (5) No data is available from the hospital for this measure; (6) Fewer than 100 patients completed the HCAHPS survey. Use these rates with caution, as the number of surveys may be too low to reliably assess hospital performance; (7) Survey results are based on less than 12 months of data; (8) Survey results are not available for this reporting period; (9) No or very few patients were eligible for the HCAHPS survey. The scores shown, if any, reflect a very small number of surveys; (10) A state average was not calculated because too few hospitals in the state submitted data; (11) There were discrepancies in the data collection process; Please refer to the User's Guide for a full explanation of data.

Wild Rose Com Memorial Hospital

601 Grove Ave
Wild Rose, WI 54984
Phone: 920-622-3257
Fax: 920-622-5593
URL: www.wildrosehospital.org
Type: Critical Access Hospitals
Emergency Services: Yes
Ownership: Voluntary Non-Profit - Private
Beds: 25

Key Personnel:
CEO/President............... Donald Caves
Chief of Medical Staff.......... Chad Voskuil, MD
Infection Control.............. Becky Brooks
Operating Room............... Cathy Truebl
Anesthesiology............... Dan Resop, MD

Measure	Cases	This Hosp.	State Avg.	U.S. Avg.
Heart Attack Care				
ACE Inhibitor or ARB for LVSD[3]	0	-	97%	96%
Aspirin at Arrival[1,3]	1	100%	99%	99%
Aspirin at Discharge[1,3]	2	100%	99%	98%
Beta Blocker at Discharge[3]	0	-	99%	98%
Fibrinolytic Medication Timing[5]	0	-	0%	55%
PCI Within 90 Minutes of Arrival[5]	0	-	89%	90%
Smoking Cessation Advice[1,3]	1	0%	99%	99%
Chest Pain/Possible Heart Attack Care				
Aspirin at Arrival	-	-	96%	95%
Median Time to ECG (minutes)	-	-	7	8
Median Time to Transfer (minutes)	-	-	49	61
Fibrinolytic Medication Timing	-	-	63%	54%
Heart Failure Care				
ACE Inhibitor or ARB for LVSD[1]	7	57%	95%	94%
Discharge Instructions[1]	16	88%	86%	88%
Evaluation of LVS Function	28	93%	97%	98%
Smoking Cessation Advice[1]	3	100%	97%	98%
Pneumonia Care				
Appropriate Initial Antibiotic[1]	19	89%	94%	92%
Blood Culture Timing[1]	24	88%	97%	96%
Influenza Vaccine[1]	11	91%	92%	91%
Initial Antibiotic Timing[1]	24	92%	97%	95%
Pneumococcal Vaccine[1]	19	89%	93%	93%
Smoking Cessation Advice[1]	8	100%	95%	97%
Surgical Care Improvement Project				
Appropriate VTP Within 24 Hours[5]	0	-	93%	92%
Appropriate Hair Removal[5]	0	-	100%	99%
Appropriate Beta Blocker Usage[5]	0	-	92%	93%
Controlled Postoperative Blood Glucose[5]	0	-	93%	93%
Prophylactic Antibiotic Timing[5]	0	-	97%	97%
Prophylactic Antibiotic Timing (Outpatient)	-	-	91%	92%
Prophylactic Antibiotic Selection[5]	0	-	98%	97%
Prophylactic Antibiotic Select. (Outpatient)	-	-	96%	94%
Prophylactic Antibiotic Stopped[5]	0	-	95%	94%
Recommended VTP Ordered[5]	0	-	94%	94%
Urinary Catheter Removal[5]	0	-	91%	90%
Children's Asthma Care				
Received Systemic Corticosteroids	-	-	-	100%
Received Home Management Plan	-	-	-	71%
Received Reliever Medication	-	-	-	100%
Use of Medical Imaging				
Combination Abdominal CT Scan	-	-	0.106	0.191
Combination Chest CT Scan	-	-	0.027	0.054
Follow-up Mammogram/Ultrasound	-	-	8.4%	8.4%
MRI for Low Back Pain	-	-	31.8%	32.7%
Survey of Patients' Hospital Experiences				
Area Around Room 'Always' Quiet at Night	(a)	60%	-	58%
Doctors 'Always' Communicated Well	(a)	83%	-	80%
Home Recovery Information Given	(a)	84%	-	82%
Hospital Given 9 or 10 on 10 Point Scale	(a)	72%	-	67%
Meds 'Always' Explained Before Given	(a)	71%	-	60%
Nurses 'Always' Communicated Well	(a)	79%	-	76%
Pain 'Always' Well Controlled	(a)	71%	-	69%
Room and Bathroom 'Always' Clean	(a)	78%	-	71%
Timely Help 'Always' Received	(a)	72%	-	64%
Would Definitely Recommend Hospital	(a)	69%	-	69%

Riverview Hospital Assoc

410 Dewey St
Wisconsin Rapids, WI 54495
Phone: 715-423-6060
Fax: 715-421-7551
Type: Acute Care Hospitals
Emergency Services: Yes
Ownership: Voluntary Non-Profit - Private
Beds: 99

Key Personnel:
CEO/President............... Celse A Berard
Chief of Medical Staff.......... Daniel Lucas
Operating Room............... Kathleen Schultz, RN
Quality Assurance............ Jim Mohr
Radiology.................... James V Kiernan
Emergency Room............ Ron R Greenburg, DO

Measure	Cases	This Hosp.	State Avg.	U.S. Avg.
Heart Attack Care				
ACE Inhibitor or ARB for LVSD[1]	2	100%	97%	96%
Aspirin at Arrival[1]	12	100%	99%	99%
Aspirin at Discharge[1]	9	100%	99%	98%
Beta Blocker at Discharge[1]	7	100%	99%	98%
Fibrinolytic Medication Timing	0	-	0%	55%
PCI Within 90 Minutes of Arrival	0	-	89%	90%
Smoking Cessation Advice	0	-	99%	99%
Chest Pain/Possible Heart Attack Care				
Aspirin at Arrival	206	96%	96%	95%
Median Time to ECG (minutes)	214	12	7	8
Median Time to Transfer (minutes)[1,3]	14	30	49	61
Fibrinolytic Medication Timing	0	-	63%	54%
Heart Failure Care				
ACE Inhibitor or ARB for LVSD[1]	20	90%	95%	94%
Discharge Instructions	71	85%	86%	88%
Evaluation of LVS Function	102	100%	97%	98%
Smoking Cessation Advice[1]	5	100%	97%	98%
Pneumonia Care				
Appropriate Initial Antibiotic	54	91%	94%	92%
Blood Culture Timing	78	91%	97%	96%
Influenza Vaccine	42	93%	92%	91%
Initial Antibiotic Timing	78	95%	97%	95%
Pneumococcal Vaccine	67	94%	93%	93%
Smoking Cessation Advice[1]	18	94%	95%	97%
Surgical Care Improvement Project				
Appropriate VTP Within 24 Hours	72	93%	93%	92%
Appropriate Hair Removal	527	100%	100%	99%
Appropriate Beta Blocker Usage	152	95%	92%	93%
Controlled Postoperative Blood Glucose	0	-	93%	93%
Prophylactic Antibiotic Timing	447	100%	97%	97%
Prophylactic Antibiotic Timing (Outpatient)	54	93%	91%	92%
Prophylactic Antibiotic Selection	447	97%	98%	97%
Prophylactic Antibiotic Select. (Outpatient)	51	96%	96%	94%
Prophylactic Antibiotic Stopped	446	98%	95%	94%
Recommended VTP Ordered	72	94%	94%	94%
Urinary Catheter Removal[1]	17	59%	91%	90%
Children's Asthma Care				
Received Systemic Corticosteroids	-	-	-	100%
Received Home Management Plan	-	-	-	71%
Received Reliever Medication	-	-	-	100%
Use of Medical Imaging				
Combination Abdominal CT Scan	489	0.006	0.106	0.191
Combination Chest CT Scan	359	0.000	0.027	0.054
Follow-up Mammogram/Ultrasound	1,077	7.6%	8.4%	8.4%
MRI for Low Back Pain	67	32.8%	31.8%	32.7%
Survey of Patients' Hospital Experiences				
Area Around Room 'Always' Quiet at Night	300+	66%	-	58%
Doctors 'Always' Communicated Well	300+	83%	-	80%
Home Recovery Information Given	300+	85%	-	82%
Hospital Given 9 or 10 on 10 Point Scale	300+	72%	-	67%
Meds 'Always' Explained Before Given	300+	68%	-	60%
Nurses 'Always' Communicated Well	300+	82%	-	76%
Pain 'Always' Well Controlled	300+	73%	-	69%
Room and Bathroom 'Always' Clean	300+	87%	-	71%
Timely Help 'Always' Received	300+	70%	-	64%
Would Definitely Recommend Hospital	300+	72%	-	69%

Howard Young Medical Center

240 Maple St
Woodruff, WI 54568
Phone: 715-356-8000
Fax: 715-356-8691
URL: www.ministryhealth.org
Type: Acute Care Hospitals
Emergency Services: Yes
Ownership: Voluntary Non-Profit - Church
Beds: 99

Key Personnel:
CEO/President............... Sheila Clough
Chief of Medical Staff.......... Michael Schaars, MD
Infection Control.............. Chris Brost, RN
Operating Room............... Kim Mears
Quality Assurance............ Judy Nelson
Emergency Room............ Rick Brodhead, MD

Measure	Cases	This Hosp.	State Avg.	U.S. Avg.
Heart Attack Care				
ACE Inhibitor or ARB for LVSD[1]	1	100%	97%	96%
Aspirin at Arrival[1]	5	80%	99%	99%
Aspirin at Discharge[1]	5	100%	99%	98%
Beta Blocker at Discharge[1]	5	100%	99%	98%
Fibrinolytic Medication Timing	0	-	0%	55%
PCI Within 90 Minutes of Arrival	0	-	89%	90%
Smoking Cessation Advice[1]	3	67%	99%	99%
Chest Pain/Possible Heart Attack Care				
Aspirin at Arrival	135	99%	96%	95%
Median Time to ECG (minutes)	135	7	7	8
Median Time to Transfer (minutes)[1,3]	1	50	49	61
Fibrinolytic Medication Timing[1]	16	75%	63%	54%
Heart Failure Care				
ACE Inhibitor or ARB for LVSD[1]	16	94%	95%	94%
Discharge Instructions	57	67%	86%	88%
Evaluation of LVS Function	62	98%	97%	98%
Smoking Cessation Advice[1]	11	100%	97%	98%
Pneumonia Care				
Appropriate Initial Antibiotic	62	92%	94%	92%
Blood Culture Timing	72	96%	97%	96%
Influenza Vaccine	36	86%	92%	91%
Initial Antibiotic Timing	82	98%	97%	95%
Pneumococcal Vaccine	71	96%	93%	93%
Smoking Cessation Advice[1]	21	100%	95%	97%
Surgical Care Improvement Project				
Appropriate VTP Within 24 Hours	113	80%	93%	92%
Appropriate Hair Removal	392	100%	100%	99%
Appropriate Beta Blocker Usage	103	91%	92%	93%
Controlled Postoperative Blood Glucose	0	-	93%	93%
Prophylactic Antibiotic Timing	281	98%	97%	97%
Prophylactic Antibiotic Timing (Outpatient)	44	93%	91%	92%
Prophylactic Antibiotic Selection	285	98%	98%	97%
Prophylactic Antibiotic Select. (Outpatient)	41	93%	96%	94%
Prophylactic Antibiotic Stopped	275	98%	95%	94%
Recommended VTP Ordered	113	85%	94%	94%
Urinary Catheter Removal	114	97%	91%	90%
Children's Asthma Care				
Received Systemic Corticosteroids	-	-	-	100%
Received Home Management Plan	-	-	-	71%
Received Reliever Medication	-	-	-	100%
Use of Medical Imaging				
Combination Abdominal CT Scan	114	0.053	0.106	0.191
Combination Chest CT Scan	71	0.014	0.027	0.054
Follow-up Mammogram/Ultrasound[1]	58	22.4%	8.4%	8.4%
MRI for Low Back Pain[1]	29	34.5%	31.8%	32.7%
Survey of Patients' Hospital Experiences				
Area Around Room 'Always' Quiet at Night	300+	50%	-	58%
Doctors 'Always' Communicated Well	300+	78%	-	80%
Home Recovery Information Given	300+	81%	-	82%
Hospital Given 9 or 10 on 10 Point Scale	300+	65%	-	67%
Meds 'Always' Explained Before Given	300+	63%	-	60%
Nurses 'Always' Communicated Well	300+	76%	-	76%
Pain 'Always' Well Controlled	300+	67%	-	69%
Room and Bathroom 'Always' Clean	300+	73%	-	71%
Timely Help 'Always' Received	300+	69%	-	64%
Would Definitely Recommend Hospital	300+	67%	-	69%

NOTE: Hospital profiles are in alphabetical order by state, then city, then hospital within the city; Rankings exclude hospitals with less than 25 cases except for patient surveys which excludes hospitals with less than 100 cases; (a) 100–299 cases; (1) The number of cases is too small to be sure how well a hospital is performing; (2) The hospital indicated that the data submitted for this measure were based on a sample of cases; (3) Data was collected during a shorter time period (fewer quarters) than the maximum possible time for this measure; (4) Suppressed for one or more quarters by CMS; (5) No data is available from the hospital for this measure; (6) Fewer than 100 patients completed the HCAHPS survey. Use these rates with caution, as the number of surveys may be too low to reliably assess hospital performance; (7) Survey results are based on less than 12 months of data; (8) Survey results are not available for this reporting period; (9) No or very few patients were eligible for the HCAHPS survey. The scores shown, if any, reflect a very small number of surveys; (10) A state average was not calculated because too few hospitals in the state submitted data; (11) There were discrepancies in the data collection process; Please refer to the User's Guide for a full explanation of data.

Hospital	Heart Attack Care 1	2	3	4	5	6	7	Chest Pain/Possible Heart Attack Care 8	9	10	11	Heart Failure Care 12	13	14	15
ILLINOIS															
Abraham Lincoln Memorial Hospital, Lincoln, IL	**-** 0	**100** 1	**100** 1	**100** 1	**-** 0	**-** 0	**-** 0	**97** 191	**4** 197	**-** 0	**-** 0	**100** 3	**100** 10	**100** 20	**100** 1
Adventist Bolingbrook Hospital, Bolingbrook, IL	**80** 10	**100** 84	**100** 68	**99** 70	**-** 0	**95** 20	**100** 30	**73** 11	**9** 10	**-** 0	**-** 0	**98** 61	**56** 142	**99** 175	**92** 26
Adventist Glenoaks, Glendale Heights, IL	**100** 4	**97** 37	**100** 26	**100** 24	**-** 0	**100** 5	**100** 10	**100** 3	**0** 3	**-** 0	**-** 0	**91** 34	**61** 54	**96** 78	**100** 16
Adventist La Grange Memorial Hospital, La Grange, IL	**100** 14	**100** 134	**100** 117	**100** 114	**-** 0	**90** 31	**100** 44	**100** 2	**4** 2	**-** 0	**-** 0	**99** 81	**81** 243	**100** 327	**100** 32
Advocate Christ Hospital & Medical Center, Oak Lawn, IL	**100** 55	**99** 256	**100** 305	**100** 295	**-** 0	**100** 45	**100** 109	**94** 16	**4** 17	**-** 0	**-** 0	**100** 115	**99** 255	**100** 344	**100** 52
Advocate Condell Medical Center, Libertyville, IL	**100** 32	**100** 221	**100** 215	**100** 201	**-** 0	**100** 62	**100** 76	**100** 6	**16** 6	**-** 0	**-** 0	**100** 107	**92** 325	**100** 428	**100** 48
Advocate Eureka Hospital, Eureka, IL	**-** 0	**-** 0	**-** 0	**-** 0	**-** 0	**-** 0	**-** 0	**100** 21	**4** 21	**118** 2	**-** 0	**90** 10	**78** 9	**100** 23	**100** 1
Advocate Good Samaritan Hospital, Downers Grove, IL	**100** 52	**100** 240	**100** 226	**100** 224	**-** 0	**98** 61	**100** 55	**100** 2	**21** 2	**-** 0	**-** 0	**100** 161	**99** 337	**100** 456	**100** 43
Advocate Good Shepherd Hospital, Barrington, IL	**100** 31	**100** 210	**100** 217	**100** 214	**-** 0	**93** 41	**100** 73	**100** 1	**9** 1	**-** 0	**-** 0	**94** 72	**90** 218	**100** 314	**100** 41
Advocate Illinois Masonic Medical Center, Chicago, IL	**100** 20	**100** 127	**100** 173	**100** 169	**100** 1	**85** 13	**100** 64	**0** 1	**0** 1	**-** 0	**-** 0	**98** 124	**97** 233	**100** 307	**100** 76
Advocate Lutheran General Hospital, Park Ridge, IL	**100** 43	**100** 255	**99** 241	**100** 236	**-** 0	**98** 50	**100** 61	**75** 4	**7** 5	**-** 0	**-** 0	**99** 187	**99** 374	**100** 518	**100** 49
Advocate South Suburban Hospital, Hazel Crest, IL	**100** 27	**100** 148	**100** 126	**100** 133	**-** 0	**100** 19	**100** 53	**71** 7	**4** 7	**-** 0	**-** 0	**99** 133	**93** 260	**100** 314	**100** 85
Advocate Trinity Hospital, Chicago, IL	**100** 18	**99** 167	**100** 112	**100** 112	**-** 0	**100** 12	**98** 46	**88** 16	**9** 17	**136** 1	**-** 0	**99** 171	**87** 386	**99** 439	**100** 119
Alexian Brothers Medical Center, Elk Grove Village, IL	**94** 49	**99** 213	**100** 249	**99** 245	**-** 0	**98** 58	**100** 85	**100** 4	**5** 4	**-** 0	**-** 0	**94** 137	**96** 398	**100** 497	**100** 44
Alton Memorial Hospital, Alton, IL	**91** 11	**100** 95	**100** 80	**100** 84	**100** 1	**100** 3	**100** 31	**97** 68	**6** 65	**51** 5	**-** 0	**94** 72	**82** 171	**100** 226	**100** 42
Anderson Hospital, Maryville, IL	**100** 11	**96** 113	**99** 97	**100** 97	**-** 0	**86** 14	**100** 30	**98** 86	**1** 87	**45** 31	**-** 0	**96** 79	**82** 167	**100** 249	**98** 45
Blessing Hospital, Quincy, IL	**97** 30	**100** 212	**100** 247	**96** 236	**-** 0	**97** 32	**100** 82	**100** 5	**8** 6	**-** 0	**-** 0	**84** 89	**93** 223	**99** 351	**100** 49
Bromenn Healthcare, Normal, IL	**100** 16	**99** 159	**99** 165	**98** 161	**-** 0	**94** 31	**100** 66	**100** 1	**1** 1	**-** 0	**-** 0	**97** 92	**83** 185	**100** 245	**100** 8
Carle Foundation Hospital, Urbana, IL	**92** 60	**99** 161	**100** 278	**99** 270	**-** 0	**89** 19	**100** 101	**100** 2	**60** 2	**-** 0	**-** 0	**98** 119	**88** 244	**100** 300	**100** 44
Carlinville Area Hospital, Carlinville, IL	**100** 1	**75** 4	**50** 2	**67** 3	**-** 0	**-** 0	**-** 0	**-** -	**-** -	**-** -	**-** -	**100** 3	**88** 8	**89** 19	**-** 0
Centegra Health System - McHenry Hospital, Mchenry, IL	**91** 34	**99** 226	**98** 290	**97** 299	**-** 0	**80** 50	**99** 102	**86** 7	**13** 7	**-** 0	**-** 0	**92** 90	**95** 260	**99** 331	**98** 49
Centegra Health System - Woodstock Hospital, Woodstock, IL	**100** 5	**95** 59	**100** 25	**93** 28	**-** 0	**-** 0	**80** 5	**94** 51	**5** 53	**50** 9	**-** 0	**89** 18	**91** 79	**96** 121	**94** 18
Central Dupage Hospital, Winfield, IL	**97** 34	**99** 190	**100** 198	**99** 192	**-** 0	**89** 53	**100** 54	**-** 0	**-** 0	**-** 0	**-** 0	**100** 106	**96** 338	**100** 415	**100** 61
CGH Medical Center, Sterling, IL	**100** 13	**100** 80	**99** 69	**99** 67	**-** 0	**81** 21	**100** 24	**98** 89	**9** 90	**407** 3	**0** 1	**97** 36	**84** 179	**100** 219	**100** 20
Clay County Hospital, Flora, IL	**-** 0	**91** 11	**100** 4	**100** 3	**-** 0	**-** 0	**100** 1	**98** 58	**15** 54	**-** 0	**-** 0	**91** 11	**90** 29	**98** 44	**100** 5
Community Memorial Hospital, Staunton, IL	**0** 1	**75** 8	**83** 6	**86** 7	**-** 0	**-** 0	**-** 0	**-** -	**-** -	**-** -	**-** -	**50** 4	**50** 6	**75** 8	**-** 0
Copley Memorial Hospital, Aurora, IL	**97** 29	**99** 182	**99** 183	**100** 179	**-** 0	**97** 35	**100** 77	**92** 12	**7** 11	**-** 0	**-** 0	**98** 63	**97** 203	**99** 275	**100** 46
Crawford Memorial Hospital, Robinson, IL	**100** 2	**100** 8	**100** 4	**100** 3	**-** 0	**-** 0	**-** 0	**-** -	**-** -	**-** -	**-** -	**92** 13	**80** 30	**91** 46	**67** 3
Crossroads Community Hospital, Mount Vernon, IL	**100** 1	**100** 3	**100** 3	**100** 2	**-** 0	**-** 0	**-** 0	**100** 47	**2** 49	**48** 4	**-** 0	**100** 14	**89** 28	**100** 38	**100** 4
Decatur Memorial Hospital, Decatur, IL	**98** 57	**100** 172	**100** 220	**100** 224	**-** 0	**97** 31	**100** 86	**-** 0	**-** 0	**-** 0	**-** 0	**90** 147	**98** 312	**99** 407	**100** 54
Delnor Community Hospital, Geneva, IL	**100** 10	**99** 100	**100** 86	**100** 89	**-** 0	**94** 33	**100** 23	**100** 12	**6** 12	**-** 0	**-** 0	**100** 44	**90** 149	**100** 203	**100** 33
Dr John Warner Hospital, Clinton, IL	**-** 0	**-** 0	**-** 0	**-** 0	**-** 0	**-** 0	**-** 0	**-** -	**-** -	**-** -	**-** -	**-** 0	**-** 0	**-** 0	**-** 0
Edward Hospital, Naperville, IL	**98** 44	**100** 214	**99** 231	**99** 222	**-** 0	**85** 33	**100** 61	**100** 12	**8** 11	**-** 0	**-** 0	**95** 143	**86** 336	**100** 434	**100** 48
Elmhurst Memorial Hospital, Elmhurst, IL	**100** 38	**100** 213	**100** 201	**100** 196	**-** 0	**97** 33	**100** 48	**-** 0	**-** 0	**-** 0	**-** 0	**98** 90	**100** 229	**100** 308	**100** 37
Evanston Hospital, Evanston, IL	**96** 50	**99** 412	**99** 392	**99** 384	**-** 0	**96** 82	**100** 70	**-** 0	**-** 0	**-** 0	**-** 0	**95** 231	**96** 695	**100** 993	**96** 85
Fairfield Memorial Hospital, Fairfield, IL	**100** 1	**80** 10	**50** 6	**50** 6	**-** 0	**-** 0	**-** 0	**95** 76	**10** 82	**-** 0	**-** 0	**55** 11	**75** 16	**100** 29	**50** 2
Fayette County Hospital, Vandalia, IL	**-** 0	**50** 2	**67** 3	**67** 3	**-** 0	**-** 0	**-** 0	**-** -	**-** -	**-** -	**-** -	**57** 7	**87** 15	**85** 26	**60** 5
Ferrell Hospital Community Foundations, Eldorado, IL	**-** 0	**100** 1	**-** 0	**-** 0	**-** 0	**-** 0	**-** 0	**-** -	**-** -	**-** -	**-** -	**50** 2	**27** 15	**58** 19	**75** 4
Fhn Memorial Hospital, Freeport, IL	**100** 12	**100** 65	**98** 58	**98** 58	**-** 0	**100** 5	**100** 13	**100** 35	**6** 35	**61** 8	**33** 3	**97** 59	**87** 100	**100** 164	**75** 16
Galesburg Cottage Hospital, Galesburg, IL	**100** 3	**100** 35	**96** 28	**100** 28	**-** 0	**-** 0	**100** 7	**100** 70	**8** 74	**62** 4	**33** 3	**95** 22	**89** 56	**99** 102	**100** 19
Gateway Regional Medical Center, Granite City, IL	**100** 11	**100** 91	**100** 73	**100** 60	**-** 0	**100** 1	**100** 30	**100** 42	**11** 46	**58** 2	**100** 1	**100** 44	**88** 137	**100** 160	**100** 48
Genesis Medical Center Illini Campus, Silvis, IL	**100** 77	**98** 115	**99** 113	**100** 105	**-** 0	**86** 21	**100** 37	**100** 35	**6** 39	**127** 1	**-** 0	**94** 70	**95** 140	**100** 214	**100** 25
Gibson Community Hospital, Gibson City, IL	**-** 0	**-** 0	**-** 0	**-** 0	**-** 0	**-** 0	**-** 0	**-** -	**-** -	**-** -	**-** -	**83** 6	**100** 8	**100** 16	**100** 2
Good Samaritan Regional Health Center, Mount Vernon, IL	**93** 54	**98** 141	**100** 274	**100** 269	**0** 1	**80** 20	**100** 121	**91** 23	**7** 26	**-** 0	**-** 0	**94** 67	**94** 163	**100** 193	**100** 34
Graham Hospital Association, Canton, IL	**100** 2	**88** 8	**100** 3	**100** 3	**-** 0	**-** 0	**-** 0	**95** 76	**9** 76	**58** 19	**-** 0	**77** 35	**88** 60	**86** 108	**88** 8
Greenville Regional Hospital, Greenville, IL	**-** 0	**100** 1	**100** 1	**50** 2	**-** 0	**-** 0	**-** 0	**97** 32	**11** 33	**47** 2	**0** 1	**57** 7	**100** 12	**90** 20	**100** 2
Hamilton Memorial Hospital District, Mcleansboro, IL	**-** 0	**-** 0	**-** 0	**-** 0	**-** 0	**-** 0	**-** 0	**-** -	**-** -	**-** -	**-** -	**92** 13	**91** 32	**100** 52	**71** 7
Hammond Henry Hospital, Geneseo, IL	**-** 0	**-** 0	**-** 0	**-** 0	**-** 0	**-** 0	**-** 0	**-** -	**-** -	**-** -	**-** -	**-** 0	**-** 0	**-** 0	**-** 0
Hardin County General Hospital, Rosiclare, IL	**-** 0	**-** 0	**-** 0	**-** 0	**-** 0	**-** 0	**-** 0	**98** 50	**7** 55	**-** 0	**33** 3	**100** 5	**100** 19	**100** 29	**100** 7
Harrisburg Medical Center, Harrisburg, IL	**100** 2	**100** 16	**100** 9	**100** 7	**-** 0	**-** 0	**100** 1	**97** 129	**5** 134	**26** 4	**-** 0	**100** 19	**100** 67	**94** 100	**100** 12
Heartland Regional Medical Center, Marion, IL	**84** 19	**98** 56	**97** 78	**97** 78	**-** 0	**83** 12	**100** 33	**67** 6	**5** 7	**-** 0	**-** 0	**98** 62	**59** 116	**99** 136	**100** 25
Herrin Hospital, Herrin, IL	**57** 7	**97** 29	**94** 18	**100** 18	**-** 0	**-** 0	**100** 6	**96** 157	**2** 164	**26** 24	**-** 0	**82** 50	**70** 141	**99** 177	**100** 31
Hillsboro Area Hospital, Hillsboro, IL	**-** 0	**80** 5	**100** 4	**100** 3	**-** 0	**-** 0	**100** 1	**-** -	**-** -	**-** -	**-** -	**100** 6	**100** 21	**100** 33	**100** 6
Hines VA Medical Center, Hines, IL	**100** 10	**97** 36	**100** 33	**100** 27	**-** 0	**20** 5	**100** 14	**-** -	**-** -	**-** -	**-** -	**100** 121	**98** 248	**100** 271	**100** 61
Hinsdale Hospital, Hinsdale, IL	**88** 16	**100** 89	**100** 94	**99** 101	**-** 0	**100** 17	**100** 23	**-** 0	**-** 0	**-** 0	**-** 0	**88** 75	**79** 163	**100** 249	**100** 24
Holy Cross Hospital, Chicago, IL	**69** 32	**90** 105	**83** 89	**84** 86	**0** 1	**14** 14	**90** 40	**85** 20	**7** 21	**-** 0	**-** 0	**83** 164	**65** 291	**95** 302	**97** 106
Hoopeston Community Memorial Hospital, Hoopeston, IL	**-** 0	**-** 0	**-** 0	**-** 0	**-** 0	**-** 0	**-** 0	**-** -	**-** -	**-** -	**-** -	**88** 8	**97** 32	**82** 39	**100** 5
Hopedale Medical Complex, Hopedale, IL	**-** 0	**-** 0	**-** 0	**-** 0	**-** 0	**-** 0	**-** 0	**-** -	**-** -	**-** -	**-** -	**-** 0	**-** 0	**-** 0	**-** 0
Illini Community Hospital, Pittsfield, IL	**-** 0	**-** 0	**-** 0	**-** 0	**-** 0	**-** 0	**-** 0	**-** 0	**-** 0	**-** 0	**-** 0	**83** 6	**70** 10	**88** 24	**100** 3
Illinois Valley Community Hospital, Peru, IL	**100** 2	**100** 7	**100** 5	**100** 6	**0** 1	**-** 0	**-** 0	**100** 52	**4** 55	**60** 7	**50** 2	**100** 22	**79** 61	**94** 82	**100** 11
Ingalls Memorial Hospital, Harvey, IL	**92** 40	**99** 201	**98** 196	**98** 198	**-** 0	**100** 20	**100** 65	**93** 46	**10** 46	**32** 6	**-** 0	**95** 95	**92** 257	**99** 307	**100** 48
Iroquois Memorial Hospital, Watseka, IL	**100** 3	**91** 22	**75** 12	**100** 11	**100** 2	**-** 0	**67** 3	**100** 13	**9** 15	**50** 1	**100** 1	**88** 24	**60** 52	**92** 79	**92** 12
Jackson Park Hospital, Chicago, IL	**100** 2	**100** 23	**100** 10	**100** 10	**-** 0	**-** 0	**-** 0	**-** 0	**-** 0	**-** 0	**-** 0	**100** 159	**100** 270	**100** 302	**100** 134
Jersey Community Hospital, Jerseyville, IL	**67** 3	**95** 20	**94** 16	**75** 16	**-** 0	**-** 0	**100** 1	**94** 65	**6** 68	**65** 1	**33** 3	**84** 25	**96** 54	**85** 86	**100** 9
Jesse Brown VA Medical Ctr-VA Chicago Healthcare, Chicago, IL	**83** 6	**100** 43	**100** 42	**98** 40	**-** 0	**86** 7	**100** 20	**-** -	**-** -	**-** -	**-** -	**97** 154	**100** 259	**100** 288	**100** 102
John & Mary Kirby Hospital, Monticello, IL	**-** 0	**-** 0	**-** 0	**-** 0	**-** 0	**-** 0	**-** 0	**-** -	**-** -	**-** -	**-** -	**100** 5	**100** 5[a]	**92** 12	**100** 2

NOTE: The first number in each column (boldface) is the score, the second number is the number of patients; Please refer to the main entry for footnotes; (a) 100-299
MEASURES: ***Heart Attack Care:*** *1. ACE Inhibitor or ARB for LVSD; 2. Aspirin at Arrival; 3. Aspirin at Discharge; 4. Beta Blocker at Discharge; 5. Fibrinolytic Medication Timing; 6. PCI Within 90 Minutes of Arrival; 7. Smoking Cessation Advice;* ***Chest Pain/Possible Heart Attack Care:*** *8. Aspirin at Arrival; 9. Median Time to ECG (minutes); 10. Median Time to Transfer (minutes); 11. Fibrinolytic Medication Timing;* ***Heart Failure Care:*** *12. ACE Inhibitor or ARB for LVSD; 13. Discharge Instructions; 14. Evaluation of LVS Function; 15. Smoking Cessation Advice*

Hospital	Heart Attack Care							Chest Pain/Possible Heart Attack Care				Heart Failure Care			
	1	2	3	4	5	6	7	8	9	10	11	12	13	14	15
John H Stroger Jr Hospital, Chicago, IL	100 34	99 178	98 189	99 184	- 0	71 7	100 82	- 0	- 0	- 0	- 0	98 134	69 300	97 308	99 94
Katherine Shaw Bethea Hospital, Dixon, IL	100 8	98 54	100 50	100 45	100 2	75 4	100 19	100 15	10 15	- 0	50 2	100 27	93 91	100 131	100 25
Kewanee Hospital, Kewanee, IL	- 0	- 0	100 1	50 2	- 0	- 0	- 0	- -	- -	- -	- -	89 9	85 27	89 45	100 7
Kishwaukee Community Hospital, Dekalb, IL	80 5	98 65	95 58	100 55	0 1	76 25	100 26	95 19	20 20	- 0	- 0	96 52	78 117	99 154	100 25
Lake Forest Hospital, Lake Forest, IL	100 7	100 53	98 43	100 41	- 0	80 10	100 10	100 33	6 40	28 3	- 0	100 46	98 146	100 179	100 8
Lawrence County Memorial Hospital, Lawrenceville, IL	100 2	100 3	100 3	100 2	- 0	- 0	- 0	- -	- -	- -	- -	100 19	100 24	91 46	100 8
Little Company of Mary Hospital, Evergreen Park, IL	100 22	100 109	100 81	100 79	- 0	94 18	100 20	71 7	4 8	- 0	- 0	100 93	84 263	100 327	100 66
Loretto Hospital, Chicago, IL	- 0	92 12	100 2	100 3	- 0	- 0	- 0	92 12	15 13	- 0	0 1	100 46	100 101	100 141	100 41
Louis A Weiss Memorial Hospital, Chicago, IL	100 25	100 109	99 95	99 104	- 0	83 12	100 37	- 0	- 0	- 0	- 0	98 103	98 203	100 275	100 70
Loyola Gottlieb Memorial Hospital, Melrose Park, IL	100 44	99 174	100 157	100 171	- 0	65 23	100 51	- 0	- 0	- 0	- 0	100 79	87 275	100 335	100 40
Loyola University Medical Center, Maywood, IL	100 33	100 157	100 178	99 167	- 0	100 30	100 55	- 0	- 0	- 0	- 0	98 261	94 601	100 690	98 132
Macneal Hospital, Berwyn, IL	98 45	100 209	98 185	98 186	- 0	96 45	100 61	100 2	6 2	- 0	- 0	99 137	95 306	100 379	100 52
Marion Illinois VA Medical Center, Marion, IL	- 0	- 0	- 0	- 0	- 0	- 0	- 0	- -	- -	- -	- -	93 57	99 135	100 143	100 22
Marshall Browning Hospital, Du Quoin, IL	- 0	100 1	100 1	100 1	- 0	- 0	- 0	- -	- -	- -	- -	67 9	55 20	64 28	33 3
Mason District Hospital, Havana, IL	- 0	- 0	- 0	- 0	- 0	- 0	- 0	- -	- -	- -	- -	100 7	92 12	100 26	100 3
McDonough District Hospital, Macomb, IL	100 1	100 6	75 4	100 4	- 0	- 0	- 0	94 81	7 85	57 3	100 1	84 31	63 49	99 91	89 9
Memorial Hospital, Belleville, IL	99 68	98 301	99 285	99 279	- 0	94 34	100 78	100 20	2 21	- 0	- 0	98 182	85 492	99 603	100 114
Memorial Hospital, Chester, IL	- 0	100 1	100 1	100 1	- 0	- 0	- 0	100 41	6 44	68 1	- 0	100 10	76 29	100 41	100 7
Memorial Hospital of Carbondale, Carbondale, IL	99 74	98 119	99 394	99 383	- 0	97 29	99 169	- 0	- 0	- 0	- 0	88 76	67 178	99 213	98 44
Memorial Medical Center, Springfield, IL	94 77	99 344	99 520	99 495	- 0	99 71	99 183	100 6	20 6	- 0	- 0	98 183	94 444	100 557	100 95
Mendota Community Hospital, Mendota, IL	- 0	100 3	100 2	100 2	0 1	- 0	- 0	- 0	- 0	- 0	- 0	100 9	82 22	100 35	100 2
Mercer County Hospital, Aledo, IL	- 0	- 0	- 0	- 0	- 0	- 0	- 0	- -	- -	- -	- -	- 0	- 0	- 0	- 0
Mercy Harvard Hospital, Harvard, IL	- 0	- 0	- 0	- 0	- 0	- 0	- 0	100 16	6 17	42 2	- 0	100 6	100 15	100 24	50 2
Mercy Hospital and Medical Center, Chicago, IL	96 48	97 194	94 180	96 167	- 0	56 16	100 55	- 0	- 0	- 0	- 0	92 168	89 275	96 307	100 62
Methodist Hospital of Chicago, Chicago, IL	100 2	100 11	100 7	67 6	- 0	- 0	100 1	- 0	- 0	- 0	- 0	92 13	50 6	98 48	100 17
Methodist Medical Center of Illinois, Peoria, IL	98 41	99 116	100 211	100 212	- 0	93 27	100 97	- 0	- 0	- 0	- 0	100 106	93 238	100 310	100 69
Metrosouth Medical Center, Blue Island, IL	92 36	100 110	96 107	91 103	- 0	81 27	100 37	100 14	8 15	- 0	- 0	85 253	94 521	100 588	99 97
Midwest Medical Center, Galena, IL	- 0	- 0	- 0	- 0	- 0	- 0	- 0	- -	- -	- -	- -	- 0	- 0	- 0	- 0
Midwestern Region Medical Center, Zion, IL	- 0	- 0	- 0	- 0	- 0	- 0	- 0	100 1	17 1	- 0	- 0	100 3	67 3	100 3	100 2
Morris Hospital & Healthcare Centers, Morris, IL	100 10	100 81	100 67	100 66	- 0	100 18	100 28	100 8	8 8	76 4	- 0	90 48	89 143	100 183	100 26
Mount Sinai Hospital Medical Center, Chicago, IL	98 44	99 115	100 153	100 130	- 0	50 16	100 67	- 0	- 0	- 0	- 0	95 157	98 275	99 302	100 124
North Chicago VA Medical Center, North Chicago, IL	100 1	100 11	100 4	100 4	- 0	- 0	100 1	- -	- -	- -	- -	100 34	93 68	100 73	100 32
Northwest Community Hospital, Arlington Heights, IL	91 33	99 390	97 349	99 339	- 0	93 59	98 66	57 7	4 7	- 0	- 0	100 52	95 189	100 306	100 18
Northwestern Memorial Hospital, Chicago, IL	96 46	99 294	98 299	98 281	- 0	91 45	100 72	- 0	- 0	- 0	- 0	98 318	97 768	100 852	100 149
Norwegian-American Hospital, Chicago, IL	100 3	100 37	96 24	83 24	- 0	14 7	100 9	100 3	2 3	300 1	- 0	85 87	67 159	99 210	100 54
Oak Forest Hospital, Oak Forest, IL	- 0	67 3	100 1	100 1	- 0	- 0	- 0	95 37	16 37	162 6	- 0	98 110	91 202	98 202	98 62
OSF Holy Family Medical Center, Monmouth, IL	- 0	100 1	- 0	- 0	- 0	- 0	- 0	100 33	6 35	60 5	0 3	67 6	90 20	53 30	100 7
Ottawa Regional Hospital & Healthcare Center, Ottawa, IL	- 0	- 0	- 0	- 0	- 0	- 0	- 0	100 70	5 75	102 1	75 8	83 24	84 56	95 79	89 9
Our Lady of the Resurrection Medical Center, Chicago, IL	100 29	100 224	100 182	100 165	- 0	86 36	100 50	100 32	3 31	- 0	- 0	100 71	94 249	100 414	100 67
Palos Community Hospital, Palos Heights, IL	94 33	99 276	99 254	100 241	- 0	92 48	100 75	76 29	0 29	- 0	- 0	98 48	90 207	100 266	100 30
Pana Community Hospital, Pana, IL	- 0	- 0	- 0	- 0	- 0	- 0	- 0	- -	- -	- -	- -	82 11	81 21	88 33	100 1
Paris Community Hospital, Paris, IL	- 0	100 3	50 2	- 0	- 0	- 0	- 0	- -	- -	- -	- -	100 8	100 17	95 39	100 3
Passavant Area Hospital, Jacksonville, IL	- 0	100 6	100 3	100 3	- 0	- 0	100 1	94 298	14 301	53 29	0 1	88 26	82 82	95 123	100 23
Pekin Memorial Hospital, Pekin, IL	100 5	98 41	100 29	100 30	- 0	- 0	100 6	94 54	5 55	56 4	- 0	100 33	95 92	100 111	100 22
Perry Memorial Hospital, Princeton, IL	100 2	67 3	75 4	80 5	- 0	- 0	- 0	- -	- -	- -	- -	78 9	98 44	81 59	40 5
Pinckneyville Community Hospital, Pinckneyville, IL	- 0	- 0	- 0	- 0	- 0	- 0	- 0	- -	- -	- -	- -	86 7	100 8	93 15	100 1
Proctor Hospital, Peoria, IL	100 11	100 66	100 67	100 68	- 0	95 19	100 20	- 0	- 0	- 0	- 0	100 40	92 95	100 145	100 9
Provena Covenant Medical Center - Urbana, Urbana, IL	88 41	93 90	97 190	97 192	40 5	90 10	99 87	88 8	5 8	- 0	- 0	89 104	96 228	100 284	100 52
Provena Mercy Medical Center, Aurora, IL	95 21	98 110	100 118	98 121	- 0	73 22	100 34	80 5	9 5	- 0	- 0	80 76	95 147	96 197	100 26
Provena St Joseph Medical Center, Joliet, IL	100 49	99 309	100 296	99 299	- 0	88 56	100 78	100 8	12 8	- 0	- 0	99 93	83 239	99 307	100 24
Provena St Marys Hospital, Kankakee, IL	100 13	100 57	100 50	100 48	- 0	100 17	100 21	100 4	11 5	- 0	- 0	96 56	79 102	100 125	100 37
Provena United Samaritans Medical Center - Logan, Danville, IL	92 12	97 69	88 32	98 48	- 0	- 0	100 7	89 128	11 129	64 21	18 11	92 96	87 197	97 275	98 46
Provena-Saint Joseph Hospital, Elgin, IL	83 18	96 125	95 124	98 121	- 0	93 27	100 40	100 2	2 2	- 0	- 0	74 68	75 151	90 210	97 37
Provident Hospital of Chicago, Chicago, IL	100 1	100 11	100 4	100 4	- 0	- 0	100 1	100 35	103 37	771 3	0 1	97 152	96 266	100 276	99 122
Red Bud Regional Hospital, Red Bud, IL	- 0	100 1	- 0	100 1	- 0	- 0	- 0	98 93	6 98	56 6	- 0	89 9	82 17	100 41	100 7
Resurrection Medical Center, Chicago, IL	100 41	99 342	99 314	98 293	- 0	84 63	100 75	94 16	9 17	- 0	- 0	87 142	78 393	100 609	100 49
RHC St Francis Hospital, Evanston, IL	69 13	98 106	100 101	88 96	- 0	88 24	100 24	100 4	8 4	- 0	- 0	87 84	94 224	98 304	100 44
Richland Memorial Hospital, Olney, IL	100 1	86 7	83 6	83 6	- 0	- 0	67 3	83 36	20 37	85 5	33 3	71 24	70 57	89 87	75 8
Riverside Medical Center, Kankakee, IL	95 21	97 113	99 104	96 106	- 0	94 36	97 39	0 2	4 2	- 0	- 0	92 86	94 173	98 222	92 40
Rochelle Community Hospital, Rochelle, IL	- 0	100 4	100 3	100 3	- 0	- 0	- 0	- -	- -	- -	- -	18 11	91 23	97 30	25 4
Rockford Memorial Hospital, Rockford, IL	97 30	99 161	99 220	100 219	- 0	87 31	100 80	- 0	- 0	- 0	- 0	100 73	89 193	100 270	100 60
Roseland Community Hospital, Chicago, IL	56 9	87 23	85 20	80 20	- 0	- 0	86 7	88 24	36 24	- 0	- 0	70 101	98 239	86 259	98 93
Rush Oak Park Hospital, Oak Park, IL	100 4	96 25	95 19	100 19	- 0	100 1	100 9	100 17	6 16	35 7	- 0	92 61	83 152	94 196	100 32
Rush University Medical Center, Chicago, IL	94 35	100 90	99 128	98 122	- 0	100 13	98 40	- 0	- 0	- 0	- 0	99 155	81 283	100 298	94 53
Sacred Heart Hospital, Chicago, IL	- 0	50 2	0 1	50 2	- 0	- 0	- 0	- 0	- 0	- 0	- 0	68 34	34 132	89 144	87 23
Saint Alexius Medical Center, Hoffman Estates, IL	96 24	100 173	100 144	99 146	- 0	93 41	100 54	91 11	7 13	130 1	- 0	92 64	96 277	100 397	100 44
Saint Anthony Hospital, Chicago, IL	100 2	95 19	100 8	100 7	- 0	- 0	100 1	100 23	13 23	49 1	50 2	87 69	79 123	97 140	100 24

NOTE: The first number in each column (boldface) is the score, the second number is the number of patients; Please refer to the main entry for footnotes; (a) 100-299
*MEASURES: **Heart Attack Care:** 1. ACE Inhibitor or ARB for LVSD; 2. Aspirin at Arrival; 3. Aspirin at Discharge; 4. Beta Blocker at Discharge; 5. Fibrinolytic Medication Timing; 6. PCI Within 90 Minutes of Arrival; 7. Smoking Cessation Advice; **Chest Pain/Possible Heart Attack Care:** 8. Aspirin at Arrival; 9. Median Time to ECG (minutes); 10. Median Time to Transfer (minutes); 11. Fibrinolytic Medication Timing; **Heart Failure Care:** 12. ACE Inhibitor or ARB for LVSD; 13. Discharge Instructions; 14. Evaluation of LVS Function; 15. Smoking Cessation Advice*

Hospital	Heart Attack Care							Chest Pain/Possible Heart Attack Care				Heart Failure Care			
	1	2	3	4	5	6	7	8	9	10	11	12	13	14	15
Saint Anthony Medical Center, Rockford, IL	**96** 45	**99** 222	**99** 258	**95** 254	- 0	**80** 50	**100** 84	**100** 7	**16** 8	- 0	- 0	**89** 94	**94** 215	**99** 301	**100** 26
Saint Anthony's Health Center, Alton, IL	**83** 6	**96** 45	**95** 42	**95** 43	- 0	**86** 7	**100** 12	**95** 21	**12** 22	**62** 9	- 0	**93** 46	**78** 117	**98** 165	**100** 28
Saint Anthonys Memorial Hospital, Effingham, IL	**75** 8	**84** 19	**85** 20	**95** 20	- 0	- 0	**100** 2	**95** 187	**12** 193	- 0	**0** 1	**95** 41	**83** 139	**98** 178	**97** 31
Saint Bernard Hospital, Chicago, IL	**100** 3	**96** 23	**75** 12	**75** 12	- 0	- 0	**100** 4	**95** 100	**0** 104	**104** 22	- 0	**80** 122	**98** 314	**97** 345	**100** 162
Saint Elizabeth Hospital, Belleville, IL	**100** 38	**98** 170	**100** 229	**99** 224	- 0	**100** 29	**100** 88	**89** 9	**0** 10	- 0	- 0	**91** 134	**83** 379	**98** 456	**98** 66
Saint Francis Hospital, Litchfield, IL	- 0	- 0	- 0	- 0	- 0	- 0	- 0	- -	- -	- -	- -	**100** 6	**100** 25	**82** 40	**80** 5
Saint Francis Medical Center, Peoria, IL	**99** 77	**99** 217	**100** 547	**99** 541	- 0	**98** 50	**100** 209	**0** 1	**17** 1	- 0	- 0	**97** 183	**85** 385	**100** 492	**100** 108
Saint James Hospital, Pontiac, IL	- 0	**100** 3	**100** 2	**100** 1	- 0	- 0	- 0	**95** 99	**8** 105	**54** 8	**0** 2	**100** 14	**100** 25	**100** 35	**100** 4
Saint James Hospital-Olympia Fields, Olympia Fields, IL	**95** 56	**99** 306	**99** 288	**99** 304	- 0	**95** 20	**100** 84	**90** 31	**6** 34	- 0	- 0	**92** 276	**87** 655	**99** 806	**100** 153
Saint Johns Hospital, Springfield, IL	**99** 116	**100** 158	**100** 559	**100** 546	- 0	**100** 43	**100** 228	- 0	- 0	- 0	- 0	**100** 112	**92** 244	**100** 295	**100** 91
Saint Joseph Hospital, Chicago, IL	**100** 9	**99** 68	**100** 74	**100** 64	- 0	**69** 13	**100** 14	- 0	- 0	- 0	- 0	**94** 63	**99** 195	**100** 280	**100** 26
Saint Joseph Medical Center, Bloomington, IL	**91** 22	**100** 111	**100** 145	**99** 140	- 0	**73** 33	**100** 65	**50** 2	**12** 2	- 0	- 0	**94** 66	**98** 124	**99** 163	**100** 30
Saint Joseph Memorial Hospital, Murphysboro, IL	**100** 1	**100** 2	- 0	**100** 1	- 0	- 0	**100** 1	- 0	- 0	- 0	- 0	**100** 3	**96** 26	**100** 35	**100** 5
Saint Joseph's Hospital, Highland, IL	- 0	- 0	- 0	- 0	- 0	- 0	- 0	- -	- -	- -	- -	**83** 6	**100** 14	**90** 30	**100** 3
Saint Josephs Hospital, Breese, IL	- 0	**100** 1	- 0	- 0	- 0	- 0	- 0	**100** 86	**7** 88	**40** 9	- 0	**87** 15	**90** 30	**98** 47	**100** 6
Saint Margarets Hospital, Spring Valley, IL	**100** 2	**100** 4	**100** 3	**100** 3	- 0	- 0	**100** 1	**98** 45	**6** 48	**68** 6	**50** 2	**95** 19	**78** 55	**100** 91	**73** 11
Saint Mary & Elizabeth Med Ctr-Division Campus, Chicago, IL	**100** 25	**100** 159	**100** 157	**100** 160	- 0	**96** 27	**98** 54	**100** 78	**6** 81	**27** 1	- 0	**100** 134	**100** 330	**100** 391	**100** 85
Saint Mary Medical Center, Galesburg, IL	**100** 7	**98** 40	**96** 26	**100** 26	- 0	- 0	**100** 5	**98** 105	**9** 107	**59** 24	**33** 3	**96** 45	**89** 72	**100** 109	**85** 26
Saint Marys Hospital, Streator, IL	**100** 1	**89** 28	**95** 20	**100** 22	- 0	- 0	**100** 2	**100** 46	**7** 46	**73** 3	**25** 4	**100** 18	**90** 51	**96** 84	**100** 7
Saint Marys Hospital, Centralia, IL	**100** 3	**100** 48	**100** 31	**100** 34	- 0	- 0	**100** 8	**94** 131	**8** 138	**48** 10	- 0	**100** 47	**100** 147	**100** 204	**100** 30
Saint Marys Hospital, Decatur, IL	**100** 9	**98** 47	**97** 34	**95** 38	- 0	- 0	**100** 9	**100** 40	**12** 42	**91** 5	- 0	**100** 55	**88** 165	**100** 227	**100** 44
Salem Township Hospital, Salem, IL	- 0	- 0	- 0	- 0	- 0	- 0	- 0	- -	- -	- -	- -	**86** 7	**86** 28	**62** 45	**100** 7
Sarah Bush Lincoln Health Center, Mattoon, IL	**100** 4	**97** 37	**100** 20	**100** 25	- 0	- 0	**100** 4	**95** 176	**11** 182	**71** 15	**25** 4	**100** 52	**96** 173	**100** 234	**100** 50
Sarah D Culbertson Memorial Hospital, Rushville, IL	- 0	- 0	- 0	- 0	- 0	- 0	- 0	- -	- -	- -	- -	**100** 2	**67** 3	**50** 8	- 0
Shelby Memorial Hospital, Shelbyville, IL	- 0	**100** 4	**100** 2	**100** 2	- 0	- 0	- 0	**92** 62	**6** 66	**129** 4	**25** 4	**67** 6	**68** 31	**89** 91	**100** 5
Sherman Hospital, Elgin, IL	**100** 20	**100** 161	**99** 162	**100** 164	- 0	**96** 49	**100** 50	**100** 2	**10** 3	- 0	- 0	**96** 71	**96** 268	**98** 342	**98** 49
Silver Cross Hospital, Joliet, IL	**100** 47	**99** 192	**100** 176	**99** 171	- 0	**94** 50	**100** 53	**94** 17	**3** 17	**92** 1	- 0	**98** 128	**89** 312	**100** 420	**100** 67
Skokie Hospital, Skokie, IL	**88** 17	**100** 120	**99** 106	**94** 103	- 0	**91** 23	**100** 17	- 0	- 0	- 0	- 0	**92** 79	**71** 196	**97** 318	**89** 9
South Shore Hospital, Chicago, IL	**100** 2	**84** 38	**94** 16	**89** 19	- 0	- 0	**88** 8	**100** 5	**13** 5	- 0	- 0	**92** 64	**66** 183	**89** 235	**98** 44
Sparta Community Hospital, Sparta, IL	- 0	**100** 2	- 0	- 0	- 0	- 0	- 0	- -	- -	- -	- -	- 0	- 0	- 0	**100** 4
Swedish American Hospital, Rockford, IL	**98** 42	**100** 218	**100** 233	**100** 229	- 0	**93** 43	**100** 86	**96** 50	**6** 50	**43** 1	- 0	**97** 132	**89** 311	**100** 426	**100** 96
Swedish Covenant Hospital, Chicago, IL	**98** 61	**96** 275	**98** 248	**94** 249	- 0	**86** 22	**100** 49	**82** 49	**8** 54	**62** 1	- 0	**92** 171	**87** 341	**99** 467	**98** 56
Taylorville Memorial Hospital, Taylorville, IL	**100** 1	**80** 5	**100** 2	**100** 2	- 0	- 0	- 0	**82** 22	**3** 22	- 0	- 0	**96** 24	**100** 43	**98** 63	**89** 9
Thomas H Boyd Memorial Hospital, Carrollton, IL	- 0	- 0	- 0	- 0	- 0	- 0	- 0	- -	- -	- -	- -	- 0	**14** 7	**0** 15	**100** 1
Thorek Memorial Hospital, Chicago, IL	**50** 2	**95** 21	**78** 9	**67** 9	- 0	- 0	**100** 1	**100** 1	**12** 1	- 0	- 0	**71** 34	**90** 89	**100** 129	**91** 23
Touchette Regional Hospital, Centreville, IL	**100** 1	**92** 26	**100** 10	**67** 9	**0** 2	- 0	**100** 4	**100** 17	**9** 18	- 0	**0** 2	**94** 69	**70** 159	**96** 171	**97** 75
Trinity Rock Island, Rock Island, IL	**98** 62	**100** 252	**99** 391	**98** 364	- 0	**91** 45	**100** 135	**82** 11	**9** 11	- 0	- 0	**98** 82	**97** 207	**99** 288	**100** 36
Union County Hospital, Anna, IL	- 0	**100** 1	**100** 1	**100** 1	- 0	- 0	- 0	**96** 82	**9** 83	**42** 14	- 0	**88** 17	**83** 29	**95** 37	**100** 11
The University of Chicago Medical Center, Chicago, IL	**97** 38	**100** 96	**99** 137	**98** 131	- 0	**94** 18	**100** 44	**71** 34	**15** 35	- 0	- 0	**100** 123	**87** 254	**100** 280	**98** 48
University of Illinois Hospital, Chicago, IL	**94** 18	**98** 59	**98** 80	**96** 79	- 0	**80** 15	**100** 33	**100** 1	**349** 1	- 0	- 0	**95** 132	**55** 252	**100** 271	**100** 72
VA Illiana Healthcare System - Danville, Danville, IL	- 0	- 0	- 0	- 0	- 0	- 0	- 0	- -	- -	- -	- -	**95** 39	**86** 73	**100** 73	**100** 23
Valley West Community Hospital, Sandwich, IL	- 0	**100** 6	**25** 4	**75** 4	- 0	- 0	- 0	- -	- -	- -	- -	**100** 7	**82** 22	**96** 26	**50** 2
Vista Medical Center East, Waukegan, IL	**96** 25	**98** 132	**94** 122	**95** 125	**100** 2	**83** 23	**100** 49	**75** 4	**0** 4	- 0	- 0	**96** 103	**90** 282	**99** 342	**100** 71
Vista Medical Center West, Waukegan, IL	- 0	- 0	- 0	- 0	- 0	- 0	- 0	**100** 105	**13** 111	**101** 1	- 0	- 0	- 0	- 0	- 0
Wabash General Hospital, Mount Carmel, IL	**100** 2	**100** 5	**100** 4	**100** 5	- 0	- 0	- 0	**94** 71	**8** 72	**72** 5	- 0	**100** 15	**91** 34	**93** 54	**67** 9
West Suburban Medical Center, Oak Park, IL	**93** 14	**100** 74	**89** 57	**96** 69	- 0	**50** 10	**100** 32	**100** 5	**9** 5	- 0	- 0	**93** 126	**94** 288	**99** 316	**99** 106
Westlake Community Hospital, Melrose Park, IL	**100** 7	**98** 41	**100** 37	**97** 39	- 0	**75** 4	**100** 17	- 0	- 0	- 0	- 0	**94** 82	**84** 170	**100** 213	**100** 36
INDIANA															
Adams Memorial Hospital, Decatur, IN	**100** 5	**100** 19	**100** 13	**100** 12	**0** 1	- 0	**33** 3	- -	- -	- -	- -	**100** 20	**83** 66	**99** 87	**100** 8
Ball Memorial Hospital, Muncie, IN	**97** 74	**99** 241	**99** 335	**99** 323	- 0	**92** 60	**99** 142	**100** 10	**3** 15	- 0	- 0	**96** 104	**99** 214	**99** 301	**100** 52
Bedford Regional Medical Center, Bedford, IN	**100** 5	**92** 37	**97** 34	**100** 33	- 0	- 0	**89** 9	**100** 23	**6** 25	**66** 2	- 0	**79** 24	**84** 43	**95** 55	**100** 10
Blackford Community Hospital, Hartford City, IN	- -	- -	- -	- -	- -	- -	- -	- 0	- 0	- 0	- 0	- -	- -	- -	- -
Bloomington Hospital, Bloomington, IN	**98** 47	**99** 277	**100** 358	**100** 357	- 0	**95** 56	**100** 143	**100** 2	**8** 2	- 0	- 0	**95** 91	**94** 189	**99** 262	**94** 53
Bluffton Regional Medical Center, Bluffton, IN	- 0	**100** 15	**100** 13	**100** 14	**0** 1	- 0	**100** 2	**98** 63	**4** 65	**42** 15	- 0	**100** 23	**100** 36	**100** 53	**100** 1
Cameron Memorial Community Hospital, Angola, IN	- 0	- 0	- 0	- 0	- 0	- 0	- 0	**97** 153	**6** 158	**53** 24	**0** 2	**100** 10	**97** 32	**83** 47	**100** 6
Clark Memorial Hospital, Jeffersonville, IN	**89** 38	**97** 167	**97** 181	**98** 186	**100** 1	**97** 36	**100** 78	**91** 11	**5** 11	**139** 1	- 0	**88** 102	**88** 264	**99** 337	**100** 65
Columbus Regional Hospital, Columbus, IN	**89** 36	**99** 195	**99** 242	**98** 235	- 0	**98** 46	**100** 61	**100** 16	**2** 19	- 0	- 0	**96** 98	**68** 190	**99** 247	**100** 45
Community Hospital, Munster, IN	**100** 18	**96** 164	**98** 153	**96** 132	- 0	**93** 28	**100** 51	**56** 9	**15** 9	- 0	- 0	**94** 67	**73** 232	**96** 295	**100** 38
Community Hospital East, Indianapolis, IN	**100** 30	**99** 113	**99** 109	**100** 108	- 0	**93** 29	**100** 50	**95** 21	**4** 22	**159** 1	- 0	**92** 91	**74** 231	**99** 285	**100** 75
Community Hospital North, Indianapolis, IN	**100** 2	**67** 6	**100** 3	**67** 3	- 0	- 0	**100** 1	**91** 131	**12** 139	**62** 14	- 0	**75** 20	**82** 67	**95** 110	**100** 13
Community Hospital of Anderson & Madison Co, Anderson, IN	**100** 16	**98** 54	**89** 37	**100** 49	- 0	**33** 3	**100** 13	**99** 84	**10** 89	**41** 19	- 0	**100** 66	**97** 178	**100** 232	**100** 49
Community Hospital of Bremen, Bremen, IN	- 0	- 0	- 0	- 0	- 0	- 0	- 0	- 0	- 0	- 0	- 0	- 0	**100** 2	**50** 2	**100** 2
Community Hospital South, Indianapolis, IN	**93** 28	**100** 93	**100** 132	**100** 126	- 0	**83** 29	**100** 61	**92** 12	**6** 14	**263** 2	- 0	**93** 76	**71** 159	**99** 211	**100** 44
Daviess Community Hospital, Washington, IN	- 0	**100** 8	**100** 7	**88** 8	- 0	- 0	**100** 1	**99** 77	**5** 83	**65** 8	**0** 1	**88** 8	**46** 35	**94** 49	**80** 5
Deaconess Hospital, Evansville, IN	**87** 71	**96** 261	**98** 391	**95** 373	**0** 1	**98** 55	**97** 154	**97** 823	**5** 854	**38** 28	- 0	**81** 234	**63** 548	**93** 729	**90** 183
Dearborn County Hospital, Lawrenceburg, IN	**75** 4	**100** 47	**100** 26	**96** 26	**67** 6	- 0	**100** 7	**99** 134	**8** 140	**194** 2	**73** 15	**79** 33	**64** 86	**98** 104	**100** 25
Decatur County Memorial Hospital, Greensburg, IN	**100** 1	**100** 2	**100** 2	**100** 2	- 0	- 0	**50** 2	**98** 138	**11** 149	**88** 7	**75** 4	**88** 8	**95** 39	**100** 67	**100** 5

NOTE: The first number in each column (boldface) is the score, the second number is the number of patients; Please refer to the main entry for footnotes; (a) 100-299
*MEASURES: **Heart Attack Care:** 1. ACE Inhibitor or ARB for LVSD; 2. Aspirin at Arrival; 3. Aspirin at Discharge; 4. Beta Blocker at Discharge; 5. Fibrinolytic Medication Timing; 6. PCI Within 90 Minutes of Arrival; 7. Smoking Cessation Advice; **Chest Pain/Possible Heart Attack Care:** 8. Aspirin at Arrival; 9. Median Time to ECG (minutes); 10. Median Time to Transfer (minutes); 11. Fibrinolytic Medication Timing; **Heart Failure Care:** 12. ACE Inhibitor or ARB for LVSD; 13. Discharge Instructions; 14. Evaluation of LVS Function; 15. Smoking Cessation Advice*

Hospital	Heart Attack Care							Chest Pain/Possible Heart Attack Care				Heart Failure Care			
	1	2	3	4	5	6	7	8	9	10	11	12	13	14	15
Dekalb Memorial Hospital, Auburn, IN	**100** 1	**93** 14	**92** 13	**100** 14	- 0	- 0	**100** 1	**96** 112	**10** 115	**48** 3	**67** 3	**82** 11	**79** 38	**98** 59	**100** 7
Dukes Memorial Hospital, Peru, IN	- 0	**80** 5	**100** 3	**67** 3	- 0	- 0	- 0	**98** 172	**7** 181	**50** 18	- 0	**100** 9	**95** 20	**94** 31	**100** 3
Dupont Hospital, Fort Wayne, IN	- 0	**100** 6	**100** 4	**100** 2	- 0	- 0	- 0	**100** 65	**4** 68	**46** 8	- 0	**100** 14	**100** 35	**100** 39	**100** 5
Elkhart General Hospital, Elkhart, IN	**97** 62	**99** 296	**97** 329	**95** 296	- 0	**98** 49	**100** 135	**91** 11	**11** 13	- 0	- 0	**87** 237	**70** 417	**99** 549	**100** 95
Fayette Regional Health System, Connersville, IN	**100** 3	**100** 15	**100** 10	**100** 11	- 0	- 0	**100** 2	**94** 97	**7** 102	**44** 8	- 0	**100** 28	**93** 57	**100** 88	**100** 12
Floyd Memorial Hospital and Health Services, New Albany, IN	**96** 83	**100** 257	**98** 298	**98** 273	- 0	**94** 51	**100** 113	**100** 1	**39** 1	- 0	- 0	**89** 95	**90** 286	**97** 388	**100** 63
Franciscan Physicians Hospital, Munster, IN	**100** 1	**100** 12	**100** 8	**100** 10	- 0	**100** 1	**100** 2	- 0	- 0	- 0	- 0	**88** 17	**72** 43	**98** 44	**80** 5
Franciscan St Anthony Health - Crown Point, Crown Point, IN	**95** 19	**99** 162	**99** 142	**97** 149	- 0	**94** 36	**100** 67	- 0	- 0	- 0	- 0	**87** 83	**83** 196	**99** 270	**98** 46
Franciscan St Anthony Health - Michigan City, Michigan City, IN	**100** 26	**99** 135	**99** 119	**99** 113	- 0	**100** 20	**94** 52	**100** 1	**4** 2	- 0	- 0	**100** 84	**100** 204	**100** 231	**100** 52
Franciscan St Margaret Health - Dyer, Dyer, IN	**100** 16	**99** 100	**100** 93	**98** 98	- 0	**100** 20	**100** 33	- 0	- 0	- 0	- 0	**94** 77	**94** 200	**98** 244	**100** 29
Franciscan St Margaret Health - Hammond, Hammond, IN	**93** 42	**98** 215	**99** 208	**96** 198	- 0	**87** 38	**99** 80	**94** 17	**6** 20	- 0	- 0	**97** 115	**82** 293	**97** 333	**100** 100
Gibson General Hospital, Princeton, IN	- 0	- 0	- 0	- 0	- 0	- 0	- 0	- -	- -	- -	- -	**100** 6	**83** 6	**95** 19	**100** 1
Good Samaritan Hospital, Vincennes, IN	**97** 31	**99** 101	**98** 131	**96** 135	- 0	**90** 31	**96** 51	**83** 6	**7** 7	- 0	- 0	**86** 98	**87** 200	**93** 266	**97** 35
Greene County General Hospital, Linton, IN	- 0	**100** 1	- 0	- 0	- 0	- 0	- 0	- -	- -	- -	- -	**86** 7	**94** 33	**63** 52	**100** 5
Hancock Regional Hospital, Greenfield, IN	**75** 4	**100** 24	**100** 20	**100** 17	- 0	**0** 1	**100** 3	**93** 81	**4** 84	**70** 9	- 0	**95** 22	**66** 53	**96** 84	**100** 14
Harrison County Hospital, Corydon, IN	**0** 2	**100** 5	**100** 4	**75** 4	- 0	- 0	**0** 1	**94** 87	**6** 97	**57** 20	**0** 1	**100** 7	**87** 23	**97** 39	**100** 9
The Heart Hospital at Deaconess Gateway, Newburgh, IN	**89** 27	**100** 2	**99** 136	**96** 139	- 0	- 0	**91** 54	- 0	- 0	- 0	- 0	**67** 24	**69** 54	**94** 70	**90** 21
Hendricks Regional Health, Danville, IN	**95** 22	**99** 72	**100** 59	**98** 53	- 0	**100** 2	**100** 9	**94** 174	**10** 176	**58** 25	- 0	**92** 48	**85** 106	**97** 146	**100** 22
Henry County Memorial Hospital, New Castle, IN	**100** 1	**100** 10	**100** 5	**100** 5	- 0	- 0	**100** 1	**97** 240	**4** 268	**22** 4	**100** 1	**100** 38	**95** 80	**100** 111	**100** 24
Howard Regional Health System, Kokomo, IN	**100** 35	**100** 112	**100** 110	**100** 107	- 0	**100** 39	**100** 55	**97** 30	**6** 33	**51** 7	- 0	**98** 41	**100** 104	**99** 156	**100** 24
The Indiana Heart Hospital, Indianapolis, IN	**96** 73	**99** 145	**99** 352	**99** 330	- 0	**94** 51	**100** 130	**100** 14	**4** 15	- 0	- 0	**98** 147	**98** 326	**99** 377	**100** 60
Indiana Orthopaedic Hospital, Indianapolis, IN	- 0	- 0	- 0	- 0	- 0	- 0	- 0	- 0	- 0	- 0	- 0	- 0	- 0	- 0	- 0
Indiana University Health, Indianapolis, IN	**100** 100	**99** 357	**99** 537	**100** 515	- 0	**97** 96	**100** 221	- 0	- 0	- 0	- 0	**99** 346	**92** 731	**100** 879	**100** 213
Indiana University Health Arnett Hospital, Lafayette, IN	**87** 30	**100** 147	**99** 152	**98** 145	- 0	**93** 14	**98** 50	- 0	- 0	- 0	- 0	**82** 49	**55** 132	**99** 193	**96** 24
Indiana University Health North Hospital, Carmel, IN	**91** 11	**100** 29	**97** 31	**90** 30	- 0	**25** 4	**100** 5	- 0	- 0	- 0	- 0	**91** 23	**84** 56	**100** 76	**100** 5
Indiana University Health West Hospital, Avon, IN	**88** 8	**96** 89	**99** 70	**95** 63	- 0	- 0	**100** 15	**93** 56	**8** 58	**43** 15	- 0	**90** 39	**88** 108	**100** 153	**100** 15
Indianapolis VA Medical Center, Indianapolis, IN	**92** 13	**100** 111	**99** 112	**100** 111	- 0	**47** 15	**98** 47	- -	- -	- -	- -	**97** 117	**100** 287	**100** 314	**98** 102
IU Health Goshen Hospital, Goshen, IN	**100** 11	**100** 54	**100** 46	**100** 45	- 0	**100** 7	**100** 16	**100** 71	**5** 72	**43** 19	**100** 3	**100** 73	**91** 129	**100** 185	**100** 31
Jasper County Hospital, Rensselaer, IN	- 0	**100** 4	**100** 3	**100** 3	- 0	- 0	- 0	- -	- -	- -	- -	**67** 9	**91** 22	**98** 41	**80** 5
Jay County Hospital, Portland, IN	- 0	**0** 1	**100** 1	**100** 2	- 0	- 0	**100** 1	**87** 106	**6** 112	- 0	- 0	**100** 7	**56** 9	**67** 15	**100** 1
Johnson Memorial Hospital, Franklin, IN	- 0	**92** 12	**100** 1	**100** 3	- 0	- 0	**100** 1	**98** 46	**2** 69	**31** 15	- 0	**88** 17	**63** 54	**97** 75	**100** 14
Kentuckiana Medical Center, Clarksville, IN	**100** 7	**100** 1	**100** 8	**100** 7	- 0	- 0	**100** 3	- 0	- 0	- 0	- 0	**100** 10	**100** 15	**82** 17	**100** 3
The King's Daughters' Hospital and Health Services, Madison, IN	**100** 1	**96** 25	**100** 14	**89** 9	- 0	- 0	**100** 2	**99** 122	**8** 124	**154** 2	**92** 12	**96** 23	**99** 108	**99** 143	**100** 24
Kosciusko Community Hospital, Warsaw, IN	**83** 6	**98** 42	**100** 24	**100** 20	- 0	- 0	**100** 3	**98** 228	**4** 234	**41** 19	- 0	**94** 36	**96** 100	**99** 150	**100** 25
Laporte Hospital and Health Services, La Porte, IN	**86** 22	**100** 107	**100** 112	**100** 99	**0** 1	**95** 20	**100** 46	**100** 1	**15** 1	- 0	- 0	**100** 92	**89** 160	**100** 212	**100** 25
Lutheran Hospital of Indiana, Fort Wayne, IN	**97** 99	**98** 225	**100** 553	**99** 516	- 0	**96** 45	**100** 201	- 0	- 0	- 0	- 0	**95** 158	**86** 397	**98** 507	**100** 77
Major Hospital, Shelbyville, IN	- 0	**100** 6	**100** 4	**100** 4	- 0	- 0	**100** 1	**96** 100	**4** 105	**44** 18	- 0	**93** 28	**76** 51	**100** 72	**100** 10
Margaret Mary Community Hospital, Batesville, IN	- 0	- 0	- 0	- 0	- 0	- 0	- 0	**96** 114	**6** 118	**76** 6	**33** 9	**86** 14	**96** 50	**99** 74	**100** 13
Marion General Hospital, Marion, IN	**80** 5	**97** 39	**90** 29	**94** 31	- 0	**100** 1	**100** 4	**94** 207	**6** 215	**56** 40	**0** 2	**90** 63	**87** 118	**99** 189	**100** 32
Memorial Hospital, Logansport, IN	**100** 1	**100** 3	**100** 3	**100** 3	- 0	- 0	- 0	**96** 96	**6** 125	**74** 12	**33** 3	**89** 19	**100** 38	**100** 55	**100** 7
Memorial Hospital and Health Care Center, Jasper, IN	**77** 22	**98** 123	**99** 159	**99** 143	- 0	**83** 18	**98** 63	- 0	- 0	- 0	- 0	**84** 67	**70** 149	**94** 212	**91** 22
Memorial Hospital of South Bend, South Bend, IN	**100** 27	**98** 252	**99** 266	**100** 252	- 0	**100** 55	**98** 96	- 0	- 0	- 0	- 0	**99** 113	**94** 318	**100** 403	**100** 103
Methodist Hospitals, Gary, IN	**90** 49	**94** 215	**92** 190	**92** 196	- 0	**28** 18	**100** 81	- 0	- 0	- 0	- 0	**98** 142	**52** 269	**99** 317	**100** 81
Monroe Hospital, Bloomington, IN	- 0	**75** 4	**100** 2	**50** 2	**33** 3	- 0	- 0	**100** 9	**8** 11	**80** 3	**0** 2	**100** 8	**59** 22	**76** 37	**100** 2
Morgan Hospital and Medical Center, Martinsville, IN	**100** 2	**100** 14	**100** 7	**100** 9	- 0	- 0	- 0	**94** 50	**2** 52	**32** 1	- 0	**94** 17	**100** 70	**99** 88	**100** 12
Orthopaedic Hospital at Parkview North, Fort Wayne, IN	- 0	- 0	- 0	- 0	- 0	- 0	- 0	- 0	- 0	- 0	- 0	- 0	- 0	- 0	- 0
The Orthopaedic Hosp of Lutheran Health Network, Fort Wayne, IN	- 0	- 0	- 0	- 0	- 0	- 0	- 0	- 0	- 0	- 0	- 0	- 0	- 0	- 0	- 0
Parkview Hospital, Fort Wayne, IN	**94** 86	**99** 267	**100** 555	**100** 547	**0** 1	**93** 60	**100** 216	**100** 7	**5** 7	- 0	- 0	**96** 92	**78** 223	**99** 294	**100** 58
Parkview Huntington Hospital, Huntington, IN	- 0	**100** 1	**100** 1	**0** 1	- 0	- 0	- 0	**96** 107	**8** 109	**42** 5	**100** 1	**100** 14	**84** 37	**96** 52	**100** 8
Parkview Lagrange Hospital, Lagrange, IN	- 0	**100** 1	**100** 1	**100** 1	- 0	- 0	- 0	**99** 75	**5** 75	**58** 7	**0** 1	**60** 5	**77** 13	**100** 19	**100** 2
Parkview Noble Hospital, Kendallville, IN	- 0	**100** 4	**100** 4	**100** 4	- 0	- 0	**100** 2	**97** 96	**4** 100	**46** 2	**67** 3	**67** 12	**85** 41	**93** 61	**100** 10
Parkview Whitley Hospital, Columbia City, IN	- 0	- 0	- 0	- 0	- 0	- 0	- 0	**97** 158	**6** 159	**31** 8	**100** 1	**80** 5	**81** 26	**90** 41	**100** 8
Perry County Memorial Hospital, Tell City, IN	**67** 3	**83** 6	**100** 4	**100** 3	- 0	- 0	- 0	- -	- -	- -	- -	**69** 13	**74** 23	**79** 33	**80** 5
Physicians' Medical Center, New Albany, IN	- 0	- 0	- 0	- 0	- 0	- 0	- 0	- 0	- 0	- 0	- 0	- 0	- 0	- 0	- 0
Pinnacle Hospital, Crown Point, IN	- 0	- 0	- 0	- 0	- 0	- 0	- 0	- 0	- 0	- 0	- 0	**60** 10	**60** 20	**78** 27	**67** 3
Porter Valparaiso Hospital Campus, Valparaiso, IN	**96** 24	**100** 155	**100** 179	**100** 176	- 0	**90** 39	**100** 70	**89** 19	**7** 22	- 0	- 0	**100** 112	**100** 252	**100** 323	**100** 36
Putnam County Hospital, Greencastle, IN	**100** 1	**100** 4	**100** 4	**100** 4	- 0	- 0	- 0	- -	- -	- -	- -	**100** 15	**100** 21	**100** 30	**100** 3
Reid Hospital & Health Care Services, Richmond, IN	**100** 57	**100** 286	**100** 350	**100** 338	- 0	**97** 62	**100** 114	**80** 5	**1** 5	- 0	- 0	**99** 97	**94** 277	**99** 383	**100** 67
Riverview Hospital, Noblesville, IN	**100** 21	**100** 101	**100** 97	**100** 97	- 0	**93** 28	**100** 35	**100** 2	**2** 2	- 0	- 0	**97** 34	**92** 66	**99** 110	**100** 15
Rush Memorial Hospital, Rushville, IN	- -	- -	- -	- -	- -	- -	- -	- 0	- 0	- 0	- 0	- -	- -	- -	- -
Saint Catherine Hospital, East Chicago, IN	**100** 7	**100** 63	**100** 53	**100** 59	- 0	**89** 9	**100** 22	**100** 2	**0** 1	- 0	- 0	**100** 75	**97** 276	**100** 338	**100** 66
Saint Catherine Regional Hospital, Charlestown, IN	- 0	**67** 6	**100** 3	**67** 3	**0** 2	- 0	**100** 2	**100** 24	**9** 23	- 0	**0** 1	**60** 15	**78** 27	**94** 32	**100** 7
Saint Clare Medical Center, Crawfordsville, IN	**0** 1	**100** 5	**100** 3	**100** 2	- 0	- 0	- 0	**92** 165	**9** 167	**44** 6	- 0	**83** 24	**94** 70	**85** 106	**100** 4
Saint Elizabeth Central, Lafayette, IN	**97** 33	**100** 98	**99** 167	**100** 163	- 0	**96** 27	**100** 59	**95** 76	**5** 80	- 0	- 0	**92** 80	**79** 135	**98** 195	**100** 25
Saint Elizabeth East, Lafayette, IN	**100** 10	**100** 47	**100** 79	**100** 75	**100** 1	**85** 13	**100** 26	**91** 67	**8** 69	**46** 6	- 0	**91** 23	**67** 55	**99** 81	**100** 12
Saint Francis Hospital and Health Centers, Beech Grove, IN	**100** 2	**95** 20	**100** 15	**100** 14	- 0	- 0	**100** 1	**97** 105	**7** 109	**36** 5	- 0	**79** 39	**72** 85	**99** 164	**100** 17
Saint Francis Hosp & Health Ctrs-Indianapolis, Indianapolis, IN	**98** 91	**99** 303	**100** 492	**100** 473	- 0	**97** 92	**99** 192	**67** 70	**9** 75	- 0	- 0	**94** 145	**88** 394	**99** 453	**100** 73

NOTE: The first number in each column (boldface) is the score, the second number is the number of patients; Please refer to the main entry for footnotes; (a) 100-299
*MEASURES: **Heart Attack Care:** 1. ACE Inhibitor or ARB for LVSD; 2. Aspirin at Arrival; 3. Aspirin at Discharge; 4. Beta Blocker at Discharge; 5. Fibrinolytic Medication Timing; 6. PCI Within 90 Minutes of Arrival; 7. Smoking Cessation Advice; **Chest Pain/Possible Heart Attack Care:** 8. Aspirin at Arrival; 9. Median Time to ECG (minutes); 10. Median Time to Transfer (minutes); 11. Fibrinolytic Medication Timing; **Heart Failure Care:** 12. ACE Inhibitor or ARB for LVSD; 13. Discharge Instructions; 14. Evaluation of LVS Function; 15. Smoking Cessation Advice*

Hospital	Heart Attack Care							Chest Pain/Possible Heart Attack Care				Heart Failure Care			
	1	2	3	4	5	6	7	8	9	10	11	12	13	14	15
Saint Francis Hospital Mooresville, Mooresville, IN	100 1	100 7	100 5	100 5	- 0	- 0	- 0	94 171	8 177	33 7	- 0	78 9	76 21	97 32	100 2
Saint John's Health System, Anderson, IN	100 3	98 46	100 25	100 29	- 0	- 0	100 2	98 113	8 117	400 22	- 0	92 51	95 110	95 160	100 34
Saint Joseph Hospital, Fort Wayne, IN	100 18	98 51	99 150	100 145	- 0	86 14	100 70	100 2	6 3	- 0	- 0	100 60	100 153	100 188	100 48
Saint Joseph Hospital & Health Center, Kokomo, IN	100 2	100 8	100 6	100 6	- 0	- 0	100 1	96 106	8 106	41 35	- 0	78 46	70 82	95 122	100 18
Saint Joseph Regional Medical Center, Mishawaka, IN	100 20	100 223	100 257	99 249	- 0	95 44	100 90	100 7	11 7	- 0	- 0	96 112	96 363	100 478	100 101
Saint Joseph's Regional Medical Center - Plymouth, Plymouth, IN	100 6	100 34	95 22	96 24	- 0	- 0	100 6	100 44	7 45	- 0	67 15	96 23	92 60	100 90	100 22
Saint Mary Medical Center, Hobart, IN	100 18	99 100	95 93	97 96	- 0	71 17	97 38	100 2	34 2	- 0	- 0	96 113	99 234	100 270	100 26
Saint Mary's Medical Center of Evansville, Evansville, IN	94 68	98 203	99 293	99 287	- 0	100 44	100 117	- 0	- 0	- 0	- 0	89 153	83 327	97 420	100 65
Saint Mary's Warrick Hospital, Boonville, IN	- 0	100 1	- 0	- 0	- 0	- 0	- 0	- -	- -	- -	- -	100 13	31 16	81 27	100 2
Saint Vincent Carmel Hospital, Carmel, IN	100 1	100 4	100 1	100 3	- 0	- 0	- 0	93 137	7 140	70 14	100 2	100 8	80 20	89 38	100 2
Saint Vincent Clay Hospital, Brazil, IN	- 0	100 1	- 0	100 1	- 0	- 0	100 1	- -	- -	- -	- -	89 9	100 21	87 31	100 4
Saint Vincent Dunn Hospital, Bedford, IN	100 14	99 81	100 92	100 88	- 0	100 21	100 32	97 75	3 80	37 17	- 0	95 22	98 55	97 88	94 18
Saint Vincent Frankfort Hospital, Frankfort, IN	100 1	100 1	100 1	100 1	- 0	- 0	- 0	- -	- -	- -	- -	100 3	82 11	82 17	100 2
Saint Vincent Heart Center of Indiana, Indianapolis, IN	98 245	100 129	99 1064	99 1039	- 0	100 20	100 386	78 9	5 12	- 0	- 0	68 203	88 383	100 447	100 63
Saint Vincent Hospital & Health Services, Indianapolis, IN	98 80	98 265	100 365	99 350	- 0	71 38	100 100	87 60	6 60	52 3	- 0	95 254	68 629	96 832	100 125
Saint Vincent Jennings Hospital, North Vernon, IN	- 0	- 0	- 0	- 0	- 0	- 0	- 0	- -	- -	- -	- -	100 8	43 7	100 8	100 4
Saint Vincent Mercy Hospital, Elwood, IN	- 0	100 1	100 1	100 1	- 0	- 0	- 0	97 60	2 72	- 0	75 4	89 9	57 21	84 25	100 3
Saint Vincent Randolph Hospital, Winchester, IN	- 0	100 3	100 2	100 2	- 0	- 0	- 0	- 0	- 0	- 0	- 0	82 17	74 43	86 44	92 12
Saint Vincent Salem Hospital, Salem, IN	- -	- -	- -	- -	- -	- -	- -	- 0	- 0	- 0	- 0	- -	- -	- -	- -
Saint Vincent Williamsport Hospital, Williamsport, IN	- 0	100 2	100 2	100 2	- 0	- 0	- 0	- -	- -	- -	- -	83 12	100 26	98 46	100 4
Schneck Medical Center, Seymour, IN	- 0	100 12	100 8	90 10	- 0	- 0	100 2	95 170	8 183	53 11	- 0	84 19	88 56	97 73	94 16
Scott Memorial Hospital, Scottsburg, IN	- 0	57 7	- 0	100 1	- 0	- 0	- 0	- -	- -	- -	- -	100 14	90 31	83 29	100 9
Starke Memorial Hospital, Knox, IN	- 0	100 3	100 1	100 1	- 0	- 0	- 0	83 66	6 71	67 11	- 0	75 8	77 26	81 27	88 8
Sullivan County Community Hospital, Sullivan, IN	- 0	100 8	100 5	100 5	- 0	- 0	100 1	97 132	4 142	32 15	100 1	38 13	78 23	74 42	67 6
Surgical Hospital of Munster, Munster, IN	- 0	- 0	- 0	- 0	- 0	- 0	- 0	- 0	- 0	- 0	- 0	- 0	- 0	- 0	- 0
Terre Haute Regional Hospital, Terre Haute, IN	100 30	99 76	99 125	99 129	- 0	100 13	100 65	100 2	5 3	- 0	- 0	100 56	91 173	100 212	100 59
Tipton Hospital, Tipton, IN	100 1	100 1	100 1	100 1	- 0	- 0	- 0	- -	- -	- -	- -	100 14	100 26	100 48	100 5
Union Hospital, Terre Haute, IN	96 81	98 245	100 321	99 314	- 0	87 46	100 115	86 14	8 14	- 0	- 0	96 185	84 470	100 570	100 67
Union Hospital Clinton, Clinton, IN	- 0	100 1	- 0	- 0	- 0	- 0	- 0	99 148	5 155	46 10	- 0	100 12	62 34	100 41	100 6
Unity Medical and Surgical Hospital, Mishawaka, IN	- 0	- 0	- 0	- 0	- 0	- 0	- 0	- -	- -	- -	- -	- 0	- 0	- 0	- 0
VA Northern Indiana Healthcare System - Marion, Marion, IN	- 0	- 0	- 0	- 0	- 0	- 0	- 0	- -	- -	- -	- -	85 26	98 100	99 106	92 24
Wabash County Hospital, Wabash, IN	- 0	100 3	100 2	100 1	- 0	- 0	- 0	- -	- -	- -	- -	73 11	90 21	90 39	100 4
Westview Hospital, Indianapolis, IN	100 1	67 3	50 2	100 2	0 1	- 0	- 0	87 15	6 15	- 0	- 0	67 15	59 51	99 68	93 15
White County Memorial Hospital, Monticello, IN	- 0	75 4	100 4	100 4	- 0	- 0	100 1	- -	- -	- -	- -	67 12	95 20	81 31	100 3
William N Wishard Memorial Hospital, Indianapolis, IN	98 42	98 249	98 228	94 221	- 0	90 10	100 132	- 0	- 0	- 0	- 0	90 189	97 371	98 409	99 169
Witham Health Services, Lebanon, IN	100 3	88 17	100 16	88 16	- 0	- 0	100 2	92 87	8 90	- 0	- 0	91 11	45 55	89 75	100 5
The Women's Hospital, Newburgh, IN	- 0	- 0	- 0	- 0	- 0	- 0	- 0	- 0	- 0	- 0	- 0	- 0	- 0	- 0	- 0
IOWA															
Adair County Memorial Hospital, Greenfield, IA	- 0	- 0	- 0	- 0	- 0	- 0	- 0	- -	- -	- -	- -	- 0	- 0	- 0	- 0
Alegent Health Community Memorial Hospital, Missouri Valley, IA	- 0	100 1	100 1	100 1	- 0	- 0	- 0	- -	- -	- -	- -	100 6	100 17	100 41	100 2
Alegent Health Mercy Hospital, Council Bluffs, IA	100 11	99 115	100 103	100 106	- 0	97 39	100 44	100 3	48 3	- 0	- 0	100 23	92 103	99 132	100 35
Alegent Health Mercy Hospital, Corning, IA	- 0	100 1	100 1	100 1	- 0	- 0	- 0	- -	- -	- -	- -	100 4	100 14	100 16	100 1
Allen Memorial Hospital, Waterloo, IA	94 48	99 168	100 237	100 233	- 0	97 31	100 79	90 29	8 29	- 0	- 0	95 104	92 233	100 300	98 47
Audubon County Memorial Hospital, Audubon, IA	- 0	- 0	- 0	- 0	- 0	- 0	- 0	100 5	1 5	- 0	0 2	100 2	88 8	55 11	0 2
Avera Holy Family Health, Estherville, IA	- 0	- 0	0 1	100 1	- 0	- 0	- 0	- -	- -	- -	- -	75 8	100 16	97 33	100 1
Baum Harmon Mercy Hospital, Primghar, IA	- 0	- 0	- 0	- 0	- 0	- 0	- 0	- -	- -	- -	- -	- 0	0 2	0 6	0 1
Belmond Medical Center, Belmond, IA	- 0	100 1	- 0	- 0	- 0	- 0	- 0	96 25	4 28	- 0	0 2	- 0	0 1	100 1	- 0
Boone County Hospital, Boone, IA	- 0	89 9	75 8	100 7	- 0	- 0	- 0	- 0	- 0	- 0	- 0	100 4	86 14	93 29	100 2
Broadlawns Medical Center, Des Moines, IA	100 1	100 3	100 4	100 4	- 0	- 0	100 3	98 52	12 54	46 5	- 0	100 16	69 36	98 44	95 20
Buchanan County Health Center, Independence, IA	- 0	- 0	- 0	- 0	- 0	- 0	- 0	- -	- -	- -	- -	100 1	100 5	57 7	- 0
Buena Vista Regional Medical Center, Storm Lake, IA	100 1	100 8	100 6	100 5	- 0	- 0	- 0	- -	- -	- -	- -	100 6	60 10	100 18	- 0
Burgess Health Center, Onawa, IA	- 0	100 1	- 0	- 0	- 0	- 0	- 0	- -	- -	- -	- -	100 4	93 15	100 20	100 6
Cass County Memorial Hospital, Atlantic, IA	100 1	100 3	100 4	100 4	- 0	- 0	- 0	100 50	6 48	72 11	- 0	100 14	89 9	100 30	100 1
Central Community Hospital, Elkader, IA	- 0	100 1	100 1	100 1	- 0	- 0	100 1	- -	- -	- -	- -	- 0	50 2	67 9	- 0
Cherokee Regional Medical Center, Cherokee, IA	- 0	- 0	- 0	- 0	- 0	- 0	- 0	- -	- -	- -	- -	42 12	71 14	86 37	100 6
Clarinda Regional Health Center, Clarinda, IA	- 0	- 0	- 0	- 0	- 0	- 0	- 0	- -	- -	- -	- -	100 3	75 4	71 7	100 1
Clarke County Hospital, Osceola, IA	- 0	- 0	- 0	- 0	- 0	- 0	- 0	96 28	11 29	62 4	- 0	0 1	75 4	86 7	100 1
Covenant Medical Center, Waterloo, IA	86 7	100 56	100 81	97 73	- 0	89 27	100 32	100 5	4 5	102 1	- 0	86 28	91 89	99 130	100 14
Crawford County Memorial Hospital, Denison, IA	50 2	100 1	100 1	100 3	- 0	- 0	- 0	- -	- -	- -	- -	75 4	64 11	68 22	- 0
Dallas County Hospital, Perry, IA	- 0	- 0	- 0	- 0	- 0	- 0	- 0	100 29	2 28	25 1	- 0	100 1	80 5	100 8	100 1
Davis County Hospital, Bloomfield, IA	- 0	0 1	0 1	0 1	- 0	- 0	- 0	62 8	9 10	- 0	- 0	100 1	42 24	33 30	- 0
Decatur County Hospital, Leon, IA	- 0	- 0	- 0	- 0	- 0	- 0	- 0	- -	- -	- -	- -	100 2	22 9	29 14	100 1
Ellsworth Municipal Hospital, Iowa Falls, IA	- 0	100 1	100 2	50 2	- 0	- 0	- 0	- -	- -	- -	- -	100 3	100 21	45 40	67 3
The Finley Hospital, Dubuque, IA	100 10	95 40	92 38	97 35	- 0	- 0	100 5	100 44	9 44	28 5	- 0	100 24	84 57	99 82	92 12
Floyd Valley Hospital, Le Mars, IA	- 0	- 0	- 0	- 0	- 0	- 0	- 0	- -	- -	- -	- -	71 7	88 32	98 44	100 2
Fort Madison Community Hospital, Fort Madison, IA	100 2	100 17	100 13	92 13	- 0	- 0	100 4	96 52	3 53	102 8	75 4	100 18	100 37	100 58	100 11
Franklin General Hospital, Hampton, IA	- 0	100 1	- 0	- 0	- 0	- 0	- 0	- -	- -	- -	- -	0 2	56 9	75 12	33 3

NOTE: The first number in each column (boldface) is the score, the second number is the number of patients; Please refer to the main entry for footnotes; (a) 100-299
*MEASURES: **Heart Attack Care:** 1. ACE Inhibitor or ARB for LVSD; 2. Aspirin at Arrival; 3. Aspirin at Discharge; 4. Beta Blocker at Discharge; 5. Fibrinolytic Medication Timing; 6. PCI Within 90 Minutes of Arrival; 7. Smoking Cessation Advice; **Chest Pain/Possible Heart Attack Care:** 8. Aspirin at Arrival; 9. Median Time to ECG (minutes); 10. Median Time to Transfer (minutes); 11. Fibrinolytic Medication Timing; **Heart Failure Care:** 12. ACE Inhibitor or ARB for LVSD; 13. Discharge Instructions; 14. Evaluation of LVS Function; 15. Smoking Cessation Advice*

Hospital	Heart Attack Care							Chest Pain/Possible Heart Attack Care				Heart Failure Care			
	1	2	3	4	5	6	7	8	9	10	11	12	13	14	15
Genesis Medical Center - Davenport, Davenport, IA	**97** 63	**99** 147	**100** 297	**99** 282	- 0	**96** 26	**100** 102	**85** 20	**4** 20	- 0	- 0	**98** 103	**90** 239	**100** 305	**100** 55
Genesis Medical Center-Dewitt, Dewitt, IA	- 0	- 0	- 0	- 0	- 0	- 0	- 0	**96** 49	**1** 51	**30** 7	**100** 1	**100** 2	**100** 8	**100** 10	**100** 1
Great River Medical Center, West Burlington, IA	**89** 18	**98** 139	**97** 125	**94** 125	- 0	**81** 16	**84** 38	**93** 103	**12** 106	**66** 4	**40** 5	**84** 56	**92** 122	**90** 168	**95** 19
Greater Regional Medical Center, Creston, IA	- 0	**100** 6	**100** 4	**100** 4	- 0	- 0	- 0	- -	- -	- -	- -	**100** 5	**87** 15	**69** 16	**100** 1
Greene County Medical Center, Jefferson, IA	- 0	**100** 1	**100** 1	**100** 1	- 0	- 0	- 0	- -	- -	- -	- -	- 0	**88** 8	**53** 17	**50** 2
Grinnell Regional Medical Center, Grinnell, IA	**50** 4	**100** 14	**88** 8	**100** 8	- 0	- 0	**100** 1	**95** 61	**5** 67	**68** 4	**100** 1	**75** 8	**86** 28	**100** 48	**100** 5
Grundy County Memorial Hospital, Grundy Center, IA	- 0	- 0	- 0	- 0	- 0	- 0	- 0	**100** 30	**4** 32	**39** 1	- 0	**100** 1	**100** 13	**100** 17	- 0
Guthrie County Hospital, Guthrie Center, IA	- -	- -	- -	- -	- -	- -	- -	- 0	- 0	- 0	- 0	- -	- -	- -	- -
Guttenberg Municipal Hospital, Guttenberg, IA	- 0	**100** 2	- 0	- 0	- 0	- 0	- 0	- -	- -	- -	- -	- 0	**50** 6	**87** 15	**50** 2
Hancock County Memorial Hospital, Britt, IA	- 0	- 0	- 0	- 0	- 0	- 0	- 0	- -	- -	- -	- -	**100** 5	**90** 10	**89** 19	- 0
Hawarden Community Hospital, Hawarden, IA	- 0	- 0	- 0	- 0	- 0	- 0	- 0	- -	- -	- -	- -	- 0	- 0	- 0	- 0
Hegg Memorial Health Center, Rock Valley, IA	- 0	- 0	- 0	- 0	- 0	- 0	- 0	- 0	- 0	- 0	- 0	**100** 2	**50** 2	**83** 6	- 0
Henry County Health Center, Mount Pleasant, IA	- 0	**100** 4	**50** 2	**50** 2	- 0	- 0	- 0	- -	- -	- -	- -	**100** 2	**44** 9	**72** 18	**100** 2
Horn Memorial Hospital, Ida Grove, IA	- 0	- 0	- 0	- 0	- 0	- 0	- 0	- -	- -	- -	- -	**0** 1	**15** 13	**24** 21	**40** 5
Iowa City VA Medical Center, Iowa City, IA	**100** 6	**100** 35	**96** 26	**93** 27	- 0	**50** 2	**86** 7	- -	- -	- -	- -	**100** 34	**100** 101	**100** 106	**100** 30
Iowa Lutheran Hospital, Des Moines, IA	**94** 16	**98** 121	**100** 116	**98** 112	- 0	**85** 27	**97** 33	**100** 3	**24** 3	- 0	- 0	**98** 60	**55** 159	**99** 191	**100** 26
Iowa Methodist Medical Center, Des Moines, IA	**97** 38	**98** 147	**99** 268	**99** 258	- 0	**85** 33	**100** 65	**86** 7	**11** 7	- 0	- 0	**89** 63	**69** 198	**98** 244	**100** 34
Jackson County Regional Health Center, Maquoketa, IA	- 0	- 0	- 0	- 0	- 0	- 0	- 0	- -	- -	- -	- -	**0** 1	**25** 4	**60** 5	- 0
Jefferson County Health Center, Fairfield, IA	- 0	**100** 1	**100** 2	**100** 2	- 0	- 0	**100** 1	- -	- -	- -	- -	**100** 1	**100** 4	**100** 9	**100** 1
Jennie Edmundson Hospital, Council Bluffs, IA	**100** 20	**98** 107	**97** 93	**98** 91	- 0	**86** 21	**97** 29	- 0	- 0	- 0	- 0	**100** 39	**100** 113	**94** 138	**87** 23
Jones Regional Medical Center, Anamosa, IA	- 0	- 0	- 0	- 0	- 0	- 0	- 0	- -	- -	- -	- -	- 0	**91** 11	**87** 15	- 0
Keokuk Area Hospital, Keokuk, IA	**100** 2	**100** 20	**92** 12	**92** 12	- 0	- 0	**100** 1	**91** 66	**11** 69	**44** 1	**71** 7	**68** 19	**88** 82	**97** 101	**100** 20
Knoxville Hospital & Clinics, Knoxville, IA	- 0	- 0	- 0	- 0	- 0	- 0	- 0	- -	- -	- -	- -	**75** 4	**94** 18	**82** 22	**83** 6
Kossuth Regional Health Center, Algona, IA	- 0	- 0	- 0	- 0	- 0	- 0	- 0	- -	- -	- -	- -	**89** 9	**91** 11	**83** 24	- 0
Lakes Regional Healthcare, Spirit Lake, IA	- 0	**100** 5	**100** 4	**100** 4	- 0	- 0	- 0	**100** 69	**5** 68	- 0	**62** 8	**100** 1	**91** 23	**91** 32	**100** 3
Lucas County Health Center, Chariton, IA	- 0	**100** 2	**100** 1	**0** 1	- 0	- 0	- 0	- -	- -	- -	- -	**100** 2	**27** 11	**58** 19	**0** 1
Madison County Memorial Hospital, Winterset, IA	- 0	**100** 3	**100** 3	**75** 4	- 0	- 0	**100** 1	- -	- -	- -	- -	**50** 2	**100** 10	**72** 18	**100** 1
Mahaska Health Partnership, Oskaloosa, IA	- 0	- 0	- 0	- 0	- 0	- 0	- 0	**100** 52	**6** 56	**86** 5	**0** 1	**77** 13	**75** 32	**98** 55	**86** 7
Manning Regional Healthcare Center, Manning, IA	- 0	- 0	- 0	- 0	- 0	- 0	- 0	- -	- -	- -	- -	**0** 1	**33** 3	**60** 5	**0** 1
Marengo Memorial Hospital, Marengo, IA	- 0	- 0	- 0	- 0	- 0	- 0	- 0	**100** 3	**2** 3	- 0	- 0	- 0	- 0	- 0	- 0
Marshalltown Medical & Surgical Center, Marshalltown, IA	**88** 8	**98** 56	**98** 52	**98** 52	- 0	**100** 19	**100** 16	**100** 19	**7** 18	- 0	- 0	**100** 22	**77** 48	**99** 73	**100** 12
Mary Greeley Medical Center, Ames, IA	**100** 27	**100** 114	**100** 129	**100** 132	- 0	**100** 15	**100** 34	**100** 3	**2** 3	- 0	- 0	**100** 50	**85** 123	**100** 173	**100** 15
Mercy Hospital, Iowa City, IA	**96** 28	**100** 113	**100** 221	**98** 214	- 0	**91** 23	**100** 61	**100** 2	**14** 2	- 0	- 0	**97** 70	**97** 177	**100** 212	**100** 17
Mercy Hospital of Franciscan Sisters-Oelwein, Oelwein, IA	- 0	- 0	- 0	- 0	- 0	- 0	- 0	- -	- -	- -	- -	**100** 1	**82** 11	**91** 22	**100** 3
Mercy Medical Center-Cedar Rapids, Cedar Rapids, IA	**100** 25	**100** 205	**100** 198	**100** 186	- 0	**100** 49	**100** 67	**100** 6	**2** 6	- 0	- 0	**93** 29	**82** 128	**100** 194	**88** 25
Mercy Medical Center-Centerville, Centerville, IA	**100** 1	**100** 1	**67** 3	**100** 3	- 0	- 0	**100** 1	- -	- -	- -	- -	**100** 3	**80** 15	**100** 27	**100** 2
Mercy Medical Center-Clinton, Clinton, IA	**86** 7	**99** 124	**97** 102	**97** 100	**50** 2	**81** 16	**100** 39	**96** 23	**5** 23	**97** 1	- 0	**93** 46	**78** 134	**99** 184	**100** 22
Mercy Medical Center-Des Moines, Des Moines, IA	**99** 82	**99** 343	**100** 639	**100** 625	- 0	**99** 99	**100** 248	**100** 3	**7** 3	- 0	- 0	**100** 126	**98** 403	**100** 509	**100** 70
Mercy Medical Center-Dubuque, Dubuque, IA	**100** 25	**100** 133	**99** 224	**100** 214	- 0	**94** 33	**100** 65	**100** 5	**9** 5	- 0	- 0	**98** 47	**95** 146	**100** 181	**100** 25
Mercy Medical Center-Dyersville, Dyersville, IA	- 0	- 0	- 0	- 0	- 0	- 0	- 0	- 0	- 0	- 0	- 0	**100** 1	**50** 4	**50** 6	- 0
Mercy Medical Center-New Hampton, New Hampton, IA	**75** 4	**100** 6	**100** 6	**83** 6	- 0	- 0	**100** 1	- -	- -	- -	- -	**100** 6	**83** 6	**69** 13	**50** 2
Mercy Medical Center-North Iowa, Mason City, IA	**99** 69	**100** 156	**100** 252	**100** 245	- 0	**94** 17	**100** 76	**83** 6	**25** 6	- 0	- 0	**99** 120	**97** 207	**99** 319	**100** 33
Mercy Medical Center-Sioux City, Sioux City, IA	**100** 49	**100** 223	**98** 364	**99** 367	- 0	**95** 38	**100** 116	- 0	- 0	- 0	- 0	**99** 89	**99** 202	**99** 251	**100** 62
Monroe County Hospital, Albia, IA	- 0	- 0	- 0	- 0	- 0	- 0	- 0	- -	- -	- -	- -	**40** 5	**89** 9	**56** 18	**100** 2
Montgomery County Memorial Hospital, Red Oak, IA	- 0	**100** 8	**100** 9	**75** 8	- 0	- 0	**100** 1	- -	- -	- -	- -	**80** 5	**88** 16	**95** 37	**100** 2
Myrtue Medical Center, Harlan, IA	- 0	- 0	- 0	- 0	- 0	- 0	- 0	- 0	- 0	- 0	- 0	**100** 12	**87** 15	**100** 37	**75** 4
Orange City Area Health System, Orange City, IA	**100** 2	**100** 9	**100** 7	**100** 6	- 0	- 0	- 0	- -	- -	- -	- -	**100** 4	**92** 12	**85** 13	**100** 1
Osceola Community Hospital, Sibley, IA	- 0	- 0	- 0	- 0	- 0	- 0	- 0	- -	- -	- -	- -	**25** 4	**100** 3	**100** 7	- 0
Ottumwa Regional Health Center, Ottumwa, IA	**100** 3	**95** 22	**100** 18	**95** 21	- 0	- 0	**75** 4	**90** 103	**9** 105	**94** 22	**0** 7	**96** 24	**83** 96	**89** 128	**100** 18
Palmer Lutheran Health Center, West Union, IA	- 0	- 0	- 0	- 0	- 0	- 0	- 0	- 0	- 0	- 0	- 0	**100** 4	**100** 6	**73** 15	**100** 1
Palo Alto County Hospital, Emmetsburg, IA	- 0	- 0	- 0	- 0	- 0	- 0	- 0	- -	- -	- -	- -	- 0	- 0	- 0	- 0
Pella Regional Health Center, Pella, IA	**100** 1	**100** 2	**100** 2	**50** 2	- 0	- 0	- 0	- -	- -	- -	- -	**93** 15	**100** 28	**98** 43	**100** 3
Regional Health Services of Howard County, Cresco, IA	- 0	- 0	- 0	- 0	- 0	- 0	- 0	- -	- -	- -	- -	**100** 2	**20** 5	**45** 11	**100** 1
Regional Medical Center, Manchester, IA	- 0	- 0	- 0	- 0	- 0	- 0	- 0	- -	- -	- -	- -	**100** 5	**100** 10	**100** 17	**100** 3
Ringgold County Hospital, Mount Ayr, IA	- 0	- 0	- 0	- 0	- 0	- 0	- 0	- -	- -	- -	- -	**100** 2	**0** 9	**82** 11	- 0
Saint Anthony Regional Hospital, Carroll, IA	**100** 1	**100** 5	**100** 3	**100** 3	- 0	- 0	- 0	**100** 42	**11** 44	**148** 1	**57** 7	**100** 11	**94** 36	**96** 51	**100** 4
Saint Lukes Hospital, Cedar Rapids, IA	**96** 27	**100** 214	**100** 258	**100** 252	**100** 1	**96** 49	**99** 86	**95** 21	**12** 22	- 0	- 0	**97** 29	**96** 159	**99** 185	**100** 19
Saint Lukes Regional Medical Center, Sioux City, IA	**100** 5	**100** 30	**100** 29	**100** 30	- 0	**100** 5	**100** 8	**100** 17	**4** 17	**37** 13	- 0	**100** 26	**97** 72	**99** 94	**100** 10
Sanford Hospital Rock Rapids, Rock Rapids, IA	- 0	- 0	- 0	- 0	- 0	- 0	- 0	- -	- -	- -	- -	- 0	**67** 3	**40** 5	- 0
Sanford Sheldon Medical Center, Sheldon, IA	- 0	- 0	- 0	- 0	- 0	- 0	- 0	- -	- -	- -	- -	**50** 2	**78** 9	**71** 14	- 0
Sartori Memorial Hospital, Cedar Falls, IA	**100** 2	**88** 8	**80** 5	**100** 5	- 0	- 0	- 0	**100** 8	**5** 8	**50** 2	- 0	**50** 2	**75** 12	**100** 25	**100** 2
Shenandoah Medical Center, Shenandoah, IA	- 0	- 0	- 0	- 0	- 0	- 0	- 0	- -	- -	- -	- -	- 0	**100** 5	**44** 9	**100** 2
Sioux Center Community Hospital, Sioux Center, IA	- 0	- 0	- 0	- 0	- 0	- 0	- 0	- 0	- 0	- 0	- 0	**100** 1	**100** 2	**100** 6	- 0
Skiff Medical Center, Newton, IA	**100** 1	**80** 10	**75** 8	**75** 8	- 0	- 0	**100** 1	**96** 52	**5** 52	**54** 8	- 0	**79** 14	**86** 44	**78** 64	**90** 10
Spencer Municipal Hospital, Spencer, IA	- 0	- 0	- 0	- 0	- 0	- 0	- 0	**100** 37	**13** 38	**115** 1	**0** 2	**87** 15	**93** 27	**98** 45	**100** 8
Stewart Memorial Community Hospital, Lake City, IA	- 0	**100** 2	**100** 1	**100** 1	- 0	- 0	- 0	- -	- -	- -	- -	**100** 5	**71** 17	**83** 23	**0** 1
Story County Hospital, Nevada, IA	- 0	- 0	- 0	- 0	- 0	- 0	- 0	- -	- -	- -	- -	**100** 1	**0** 1	**50** 2	- 0

NOTE: The first number in each column (boldface) is the score, the second number is the number of patients; Please refer to the main entry for footnotes; (a) 100-299
*MEASURES: **Heart Attack Care:** 1. ACE Inhibitor or ARB for LVSD; 2. Aspirin at Arrival; 3. Aspirin at Discharge; 4. Beta Blocker at Discharge; 5. Fibrinolytic Medication Timing; 6. PCI Within 90 Minutes of Arrival; 7. Smoking Cessation Advice; **Chest Pain/Possible Heart Attack Care:** 8. Aspirin at Arrival; 9. Median Time to ECG (minutes); 10. Median Time to Transfer (minutes); 11. Fibrinolytic Medication Timing; **Heart Failure Care:** 12. ACE Inhibitor or ARB for LVSD; 13. Discharge Instructions; 14. Evaluation of LVS Function; 15. Smoking Cessation Advice*

Hospital	Heart Attack Care							Chest Pain/Possible Heart Attack Care				Heart Failure Care			
	1	2	3	4	5	6	7	8	9	10	11	12	13	14	15
Trinity Bettendorf, Bettendorf, IA	75 8	100 49	100 49	100 44	- 0	70 10	100 16	100 16	8 17	50 1	- 0	100 23	100 49	98 65	100 10
Trinity Muscatine, Muscatine, IA	100 2	100 5	100 5	100 5	- 0	- 0	- 0	100 114	9 114	65 5	50 2	100 16	100 25	100 45	100 5
Trinity Regional Medical Center, Fort Dodge, IA	98 41	97 104	100 189	99 187	- 0	97 30	100 61	100 11	6 11	- 0	- 0	97 64	84 133	98 179	100 22
University of Iowa Hospital & Clinics, Iowa City, IA	83 42	100 79	100 245	99 240	- 0	81 16	97 102	75 4	9 4	- 0	- 0	91 121	55 255	98 284	97 67
VA Central Iowa Healthcare System, Des Moines, IA	- 0	- 0	- 0	- 0	- 0	- 0	- 0	- -	- -	- -	- -	94 17	96 46	100 47	100 9
Van Buren County Hospital, Keosauqua, IA	100 1	67 3	67 3	33 3	- 0	- 0	- 0	- -	- -	- -	- -	71 7	83 6	91 23	- 0
Van Diest Medical Center, Webster City, IA	- 0	100 6	83 6	57 7	- 0	- 0	100 1	- -	- -	- -	- -	62 8	72 43	87 63	100 3
Veterans Memorial Hospital, Waukon, IA	- 0	- 0	- 0	- 0	- 0	- 0	- 0	- -	- -	- -	- -	50 8	100 12	76 21	100 1
Washington County Hospital, Washington, IA	- 0	- 0	- 0	- 0	- 0	- 0	- 0	- -	- -	- -	- -	100 6	50 6	67 15	100 1
Waverly Health Center, Waverly, IA	100 1	100 1	100 1	100 1	- 0	- 0	- 0	97 92	5 95	96 2	- 0	100 4	62 16	68 22	- 0
Wayne County Hospital, Corydon, IA	- 0	100 4	100 3	67 3	- 0	- 0	- 0	- -	- -	- -	- -	0 1	92 12	77 13	- 0
Winneshiek Medical Center, Decorah, IA	100 1	100 5	100 1	100 2	- 0	- 0	- 0	- -	- -	- -	- -	100 12	100 26	100 45	100 2
Wright Medical Center, Clarion, IA	- 0	- 0	- 0	- 0	- 0	- 0	- 0	- -	- -	- -	- -	- 0	- 0	- 0	- 0
KANSAS															
Allen County Hospital, Iola, KS	- 0	100 1	100 1	50 4	- 0	- 0	100 1	97 87	18 94	- 0	100 3	60 5	92 13	89 28	100 4
Anderson County Hospital, Garnett, KS	- 0	- 0	100 1	- 0	- 0	- 0	- 0	100 33	11 34	88 2	- 0	100 3	33 6	100 9	- 0
Ashland Health Center, Ashland, KS	- 0	- 0	- 0	- 0	- 0	- 0	- 0	- -	- -	- -	- -	100 1	100 1	75 4	- 0
Atchison Hospital, Atchison, KS	- 0	- 0	- 0	- 0	- 0	- 0	- 0	- -	- -	- -	- -	- 0	- 0	- 0	- 0
Bob Wilson Memorial Grant County Hospital, Ulysses, KS	- 0	0 1	0 1	0 1	- 0	- 0	- 0	87 23	8 22	- 0	- 0	100 3	23 13	82 17	0 2
Central Kansas Medical Center, Great Bend, KS	- 0	100 2	- 0	- 0	- 0	- 0	- 0	93 70	18 72	131 1	0 2	100 1	50 16	92 24	100 6
Cheyenne County Hospital, Saint Francis, KS	- 0	- 0	- 0	- 0	- 0	- 0	- 0	- -	- -	- -	- -	20 5	0 2	100 8	- 0
Clara Barton Hospital, Hoisington, KS	- 0	- 0	- 0	- 0	- 0	- 0	- 0	- 0	- 0	- 0	- 0	0 1	0 4	33 9	- 0
Clay County Medical Center, Clay Center, KS	- 0	- 0	- 0	- 0	- 0	- 0	- 0	- -	- -	- -	- -	- 0	57 7	21 14	0 1
Cloud County Health Center, Concordia, KS	0 1	100 2	100 2	100 2	- 0	- 0	100 1	- -	- -	- -	- -	83 6	79 33	48 50	56 9
Coffey County Hospital, Burlington, KS	- 0	100 2	- 0	- 0	- 0	- 0	- 0	84 31	9 32	- 0	0 1	62 8	27 37	38 61	100 1
Coffeyville Regional Medical Center, Coffeyville, KS	75 4	88 17	73 11	64 11	- 0	- 0	50 2	75 8	3 9	90 1	- 0	62 42	69 91	93 131	82 17
Comanche County Hospital, Coldwater, KS	- 0	- 0	- 0	- 0	- 0	- 0	- 0	- -	- -	- -	- -	- 0	- 0	- 0	- 0
Community Hospital - Onaga and St Marys Campus, Onaga, KS	- 0	- 0	- 0	- 0	- 0	- 0	- 0	- -	- -	- -	- -	50 6	45 11	73 30	- 0
Cushing Memorial Hospital, Leavenworth, KS	- 0	67 3	100 2	- 0	- 0	- 0	- 0	97 29	14 30	1067 2	- 0	100 13	54 24	88 33	100 5
Doctors Hospital, Leawood, KS	- 0	- 0	- 0	- 0	- 0	- 0	- 0	- 0	- 0	- 0	- 0	- 0	- 0	- 0	- 0
Edwards County Hospital, Kinsley, KS	- 0	- 0	- 0	- 0	- 0	- 0	- 0	- -	- -	- -	- -	- 0	100 1	50 2	- 0
Ellsworth County Medical Center, Ellsworth, KS	100 1	70 10	88 8	90 10	- 0	- 0	- 0	- 0	- 0	- 0	- 0	60 10	58 19	82 34	33 3
Fredonia Regional Hospital, Fredonia, KS	- 0	- 0	- 0	- 0	- 0	- 0	- 0	- -	- -	- -	- -	- 0	33 3	33 6	- 0
Galichia Heart Hospital, Wichita, KS	94 18	98 66	99 110	100 97	0 3	88 8	100 42	100 2	5051 2	- 0	- 0	95 58	100 213	99 251	100 39
Geary Community Hospital, Junction City, KS	100 2	83 6	75 4	100 4	- 0	- 0	- 0	93 29	13 25	109 3	100 2	91 11	57 30	77 39	80 5
Girard Medical Center, Girard, KS	- 0	- 0	- 0	- 0	- 0	- 0	- 0	- -	- -	- -	- -	67 6	83 18	86 29	100 6
Goodland Regional Medical Center, Goodland, KS	- 0	- 0	- 0	- 0	- 0	- 0	- 0	- -	- -	- -	- -	- 0	- 0	- 0	- 0
Gove County Medical Center, Quinter, KS	- 0	- 0	- 0	- 0	- 0	- 0	- 0	- -	- -	- -	- -	- 0	- 0	- 0	- 0
Graham County Hospital, Hill City, KS	- 0	- 0	- 0	- 0	- 0	- 0	- 0	100 16	10 17	- 0	0 1	100 5	25 12	47 38	0 11
Great Bend Regional Hospital, Great Bend, KS	- 0	100 1	100 1	100 1	- 0	- 0	0 1	80 35	17 35	- 0	- 0	0 1	8 12	15 13	- 0
Greeley County Health Services, Tribune, KS	- 0	- 0	- 0	- 0	- 0	- 0	- 0	- -	- -	- -	- -	- 0	0 2	0 3	- 0
Greenwood County Hospital, Eureka, KS	- 0	- 0	- 0	- 0	0 1	- 0	- 0	- -	- -	- -	- -	100 1	22 9	12 17	100 1
Grisell Memorial Hospital District #1, Ransom, KS	- 0	- 0	- 0	- 0	- 0	- 0	- 0	- -	- -	- -	- -	- 0	- 0	- 0	- 0
Hamilton County Hospital, Syracuse, KS	- 0	- 0	- 0	- 0	- 0	- 0	- 0	- -	- -	- -	- -	- 0	0 1	0 3	- 0
Harper Hospital District #5, Harper, KS	- 0	- 0	- 0	- 0	- 0	- 0	- 0	- -	- -	- -	- -	- 0	0 3	0 5	- 0
Hays Medical Center, Hays, KS	100 27	99 81	100 220	99 208	- 0	50 8	100 68	100 1	7 2	- 0	- 0	98 57	84 133	99 170	95 19
Heartland Surgical Spec Hospital, Overland Park, KS	- 0	- 0	- 0	- 0	- 0	- 0	- 0	- 0	- 0	- 0	- 0	- 0	- 0	- 0	- 0
Herington Municipal Hospital, Herington, KS	- 0	- 0	- 0	- 0	- 0	- 0	- 0	- -	- -	- -	- -	- 0	- 0	- 0	- 0
Hiawatha Community Hospital, Hiawatha, KS	0 1	100 2	100 2	100 1	- 0	- 0	- 0	- -	- -	- -	- -	67 3	89 9	56 18	100 2
Hillsboro Community Hospital, Hillsboro, KS	- 0	100 1	100 1	100 1	- 0	- 0	- 0	62 8	10 8	- 0	- 0	100 1	40 5	75 8	0 2
Hodgeman County Health Center, Jetmore, KS	- 0	- 0	- 0	- 0	- 0	- 0	- 0	- -	- -	- -	- -	- 0	- 0	- 0	- 0
Holton Community Hospital, Holton, KS	- 0	- 0	- 0	- 0	- 0	- 0	- 0	- 0	- 0	- 0	- 0	0 2	50 4	62 8	- 0
Jefferson County Memorial Hospital, Winchester, KS	- 0	- 0	- 0	- 0	- 0	- 0	- 0	- -	- -	- -	- -	- 0	- 0	- 0	- 0
Jewell County Hospital, Mankato, KS	- 0	- 0	- 0	- 0	- 0	- 0	- 0	- -	- -	- -	- -	- 0	- 0	- 0	- 0
Kansas City Orthopaedic Institute, Leawood, KS	- 0	- 0	- 0	- 0	- 0	- 0	- 0	- 0	- 0	- 0	- 0	- 0	- 0	- 0	- 0
Kansas Heart Hospital, Wichita, KS	93 27	89 35	100 221	98 208	- 0	100 1	94 66	- 0	- 0	- 0	- 0	97 39	91 104	100 118	100 22
Kansas Medical Center, Andover, KS	93 15	96 24	95 88	92 77	- 0	100 5	100 27	67 3	17 3	- 0	- 0	96 25	81 54	97 63	90 10
Kansas Spine Hospital, Wichita, KS	- 0	- 0	- 0	- 0	- 0	- 0	- 0	- 0	- 0	- 0	- 0	- 0	- 0	- 0	- 0
Kansas Surgery & Recovery Center, Wichita, KS	- 0	- 0	- 0	- 0	- 0	- 0	- 0	- 0	- 0	- 0	- 0	- 0	- 0	- 0	- 0
Kearny County Hospital, Lakin, KS	- 0	- 0	- 0	- 0	- 0	- 0	- 0	- -	- -	- -	- -	50 4	92 13	73 15	100 3
Kingman Community Hospital, Kingman, KS	- 0	- 0	- 0	- 0	- 0	- 0	- 0	- -	- -	- -	- -	100 2	50 2	90 10	100 1
Kiowa District Hospital, Kiowa, KS	- 0	- 0	- 0	- 0	- 0	- 0	- 0	92 12	10 12	100 1	50 2	- 0	- 0	- 0	- 0
Labette Health, Parsons, KS	- 0	88 8	100 4	50 4	- 0	- 0	100 1	96 68	6 68	50 6	100 3	80 10	60 25	97 32	100 4
Lawrence Memorial Hospital, Lawrence, KS	100 17	100 89	100 80	100 72	- 0	100 25	100 28	100 27	4 27	17 5	- 0	100 32	100 91	100 125	100 20
Lindsborg Community Hospital, Lindsborg, KS	100 1	100 1	100 1	100 1	- 0	- 0	- 0	- -	- -	- -	- -	- 0	33 3	89 9	100 1
Manhattan Surgical Hospital, Manhattan, KS	- 0	- 0	- 0	- 0	- 0	- 0	- 0	- 0	- 0	- 0	- 0	- 0	- 0	- 0	- 0
Meade District Hospital, Meade, KS	- 0	100 2	100 2	100 2	- 0	- 0	- 0	- -	- -	- -	- -	50 4	27 15	82 17	- 0

NOTE: The first number in each column (boldface) is the score, the second number is the number of patients; Please refer to the main entry for footnotes; (a) 100-299
MEASURES: ***Heart Attack Care:*** *1. ACE Inhibitor or ARB for LVSD; 2. Aspirin at Arrival; 3. Aspirin at Discharge; 4. Beta Blocker at Discharge; 5. Fibrinolytic Medication Timing; 6. PCI Within 90 Minutes of Arrival; 7. Smoking Cessation Advice;* ***Chest Pain/Possible Heart Attack Care:*** *8. Aspirin at Arrival; 9. Median Time to ECG (minutes); 10. Median Time to Transfer (minutes); 11. Fibrinolytic Medication Timing;* ***Heart Failure Care:*** *12. ACE Inhibitor or ARB for LVSD; 13. Discharge Instructions; 14. Evaluation of LVS Function; 15. Smoking Cessation Advice*

Hospital	Heart Attack Care 1	2	3	4	5	6	7	Chest Pain/Possible Heart Attack Care 8	9	10	11	Heart Failure Care 12	13	14	15
Memorial Hospital, Mcpherson, KS	- 0	25 4	25 4	100 4	- 0	- 0	- 0	96 110	14 112	- 0	- 0	86 7	57 21	87 30	100 1
Memorial Hospital, Abilene, KS	- 0	100 4	100 2	100 3	- 0	- 0	- 0	- -	- -	- -	- -	50 2	9 11	79 33	0 1
Menorah Medical Center, Overland Park, KS	100 8	97 35	100 39	100 36	- 0	92 12	100 9	- 0	- 0	- 0	- 0	100 25	98 95	100 138	100 7
Mercy Health Center, Fort Scott, KS	100 1	86 7	100 3	80 5	- 0	- 0	- 0	92 63	12 64	131 3	0 7	95 22	91 44	100 77	100 6
Mercy Hospital, Moundridge, KS	0 2	100 3	0 3	0 3	- 0	- 0	- 0	- 0	- 0	- 0	- 0	80 10	67 9	88 16	- 0
Mercy Hospital of Kansas Independence, Independence, KS	100 1	100 4	100 4	67 3	- 0	- 0	100 1	89 56	6 56	79 2	0 1	88 8	86 29	100 41	100 6
Mercy Regional Health Center, Manhattan, KS	100 8	100 71	97 76	92 73	0 1	83 18	100 26	74 27	13 27	- 0	50 2	83 24	69 59	92 76	100 15
Miami County Medical Center, Paola, KS	100 1	100 2	100 1	100 1	- 0	- 0	- 0	86 69	16 70	28 9	- 0	100 3	100 3	100 8	- 0
Mitchell County Hospital Health Systems, Beloit, KS	100 2	100 7	100 5	100 6	- 0	- 0	0 1	- -	- -	- -	- -	88 8	59 17	97 33	100 1
Morris County Hospital, Council Grove, KS	- 0	100 2	100 2	100 2	- 0	- 0	- 0	- -	- -	- -	- -	83 6	25 28	33 57	43 7
Morton County Hospital, Elkhart, KS	- 0	100 1	- 0	- 0	- 0	- 0	- 0	- 0	- 0	- 0	- 0	100 4	0 16	57 42	60 5
Nemaha Valley Community Hospital, Seneca, KS	- 0	- 0	- 0	- 0	- 0	- 0	- 0	- -	- -	- -	- -	- 0	50 6	6 16	- 0
Neosho Memorial Regional Medical Center, Chanute, KS	100 1	100 7	100 5	75 4	- 0	- 0	100 2	100 43	8 45	162 2	- 0	100 15	100 43	100 69	86 7
Ness County Hospital District #2, Ness City, KS	- 0	- 0	- 0	- 0	- 0	- 0	- 0	- -	- -	- -	- -	- 0	- 0	- 0	- 0
Newman Regional Health, Emporia, KS	- 0	100 10	100 8	86 7	- 0	- 0	100 1	93 128	3 135	40 6	36 11	79 29	72 53	86 93	92 12
Newton Medical Center, Newton, KS	100 2	92 25	95 20	100 20	- 0	- 0	100 3	85 82	15 88	76 3	50 2	77 22	37 57	86 125	85 20
Norton County Hospital, Norton, KS	- 0	- 0	- 0	- 0	- 0	- 0	- 0	- -	- -	- -	- -	- 0	- 0	- 0	- 0
Olathe Medical Center, Olathe, KS	100 39	99 189	99 221	97 211	- 0	93 41	100 78	- 0	- 0	- 0	- 0	91 67	82 182	98 260	100 32
Osborne County Memorial Hospital, Osborne, KS	- 0	- 0	- 0	- 0	- 0	- 0	- 0	- -	- -	- -	- -	- 0	- 0	- 0	- 0
Oswego Community Hospital, Oswego, KS	- 0	- 0	- 0	- 0	- 0	- 0	- 0	- -	- -	- -	- -	- 0	- 0	- 0	- 0
Ottawa County Health Center, Minneapolis, KS	- 0	- 0	- 0	- 0	- 0	- 0	- 0	77 13	15 13	- 0	- 0	- 0	- 0	- 0	- 0
Overland Park Regional Medical Center, Overland Park, KS	100 16	100 106	100 106	100 96	- 0	96 27	100 28	- 0	- 0	- 0	- 0	100 47	94 123	100 162	100 12
Phillips County Hospital, Phillipsburg, KS	- 0	- 0	- 0	- 0	- 0	- 0	- 0	- -	- -	- -	- -	- 0	- 0	0 1	- 0
Pratt Regional Medical Center, Pratt, KS	- 0	100 1	100 1	100 1	- 0	- 0	- 0	91 70	12 70	- 0	- 0	100 2	54 26	33 30	33 3
Promise Regional Medical Center Hutchinson, Hutchinson, KS	92 25	100 135	98 170	92 145	- 0	77 31	100 55	100 12	10 12	- 0	- 0	93 46	91 94	96 140	100 17
Providence Medical Center, Kansas City, KS	94 33	99 148	99 154	98 151	- 0	92 36	100 67	- 0	- 0	- 0	- 0	89 130	78 263	99 319	100 72
Ransom Memorial Hospital, Ottawa, KS	100 1	50 4	33 3	100 2	- 0	- 0	100 2	94 49	5 48	36 4	- 0	100 2	87 15	100 23	100 4
Republic County Hospital, Belleville, KS	- 0	100 6	80 5	100 5	- 0	- 0	- 0	- -	- -	- -	- -	- 0	- 0	- 0	- 0
Russell Regional Hospital, Russell, KS	- 0	- 0	- 0	- 0	- 0	- 0	- 0	- -	- -	- -	- -	- 0	- 0	- 0	- 0
Sabetha Community Hospital, Sabetha, KS	- 0	- 0	- 0	- 0	- 0	- 0	- 0	- -	- -	- -	- -	100 3	25 4	100 8	0 1
Saint Catherine Hospital, Garden City, KS	100 5	100 29	100 36	100 35	- 0	100 4	100 15	90 20	11 19	104 1	0 2	100 10	94 34	95 40	100 6
Saint Francis Health Center, Topeka, KS	100 28	98 112	99 168	98 159	- 0	100 32	100 64	- 0	- 0	- 0	- 0	94 80	90 174	99 229	98 50
Saint John Hospital, Leavenworth, KS	- 0	100 10	80 5	100 5	- 0	- 0	- 0	100 16	12 16	175 1	- 0	95 21	98 45	99 72	91 11
Saint Luke Hospital & Living Center, Marion, KS	- 0	- 0	- 0	- 0	- 0	- 0	- 0	- -	- -	- -	- -	- 0	33 6	62 8	100 1
Saint Luke's South Hospital, Overland Park, KS	100 8	100 80	97 79	100 77	- 0	85 13	100 18	100 9	9 9	- 0	- 0	98 44	76 118	99 137	100 10
Salina Regional Health Center, Salina, KS	93 28	99 96	99 142	99 134	53 17	0 4	100 47	100 6	6 6	- 0	- 0	100 26	98 63	88 86	100 11
Salina Surgical Hospital, Salina, KS	- 0	- 0	- 0	- 0	- 0	- 0	- 0	- 0	- 0	- 0	- 0	- 0	- 0	- 0	- 0
Scott County Hospital, Scott City, KS	- 0	- 0	- 0	- 0	- 0	- 0	- 0	- -	- -	- -	- -	67 3	11 9	24 21	0 1
Sedan City Hospital, Sedan, KS	- 0	- 0	- 0	- 0	- 0	- 0	- 0	- -	- -	- -	- -	- 0	- 0	- 0	- 0
Shawnee Mission Medical Center, Shawnee Mission, KS	92 38	99 185	100 208	100 201	- 0	97 38	100 61	88 8	8 9	- 0	- 0	97 112	84 292	99 375	100 47
Sheridan County Hospital, Hoxie, KS	- 0	- 0	- 0	- 0	- 0	- 0	- 0	- -	- -	- -	- -	- 0	- 0	- 0	- 0
Smith County Memorial Hospital, Smith Center, KS	- 0	100 1	100 1	100 1	- 0	- 0	- 0	100 1	22 1	- 0	- 0	- 0	14 7	50 12	0 1
South Central Ks Regional Medical Center, Arkansas City, KS	100 1	100 3	100 3	50 4	0 1	- 0	100 1	89 47	12 47	156 2	25 4	100 4	33 21	75 28	100 2
Southwest Medical Center, Liberal, KS	- 0	100 2	100 2	50 2	- 0	- 0	- 0	96 45	12 46	140 1	60 5	69 13	79 24	89 27	100 2
Stormont-Vail Healthcare, Topeka, KS	100 45	99 190	99 283	100 285	- 0	100 49	100 101	- 0	- 0	- 0	- 0	94 88	90 234	100 334	100 56
Summit Surgical, Hutchinson, KS	- 0	- 0	- 0	- 0	- 0	- 0	- 0	- 0	- 0	- 0	- 0	- 0	- 0	- 0	- 0
Sumner Regional Medical Center, Wellington, KS	- 0	- 0	- 0	- 0	- 0	- 0	- 0	92 87	10 88	- 0	0 1	0 2	78 9	41 17	100 1
Susan B Allen Memorial Hospital, El Dorado, KS	100 1	100 1	100 1	100 1	- 0	- 0	- 0	95 150	8 153	64 2	50 2	75 8	96 26	100 50	100 7
Trego County Lemke Memorial Hospital, Wa Keeney, KS	- 0	- 0	- 0	- 0	- 0	- 0	- 0	- -	- -	- -	- -	100 5	8 12	63 38	0 1
University of Kansas Hospital, Kansas City, KS	94 36	100 109	100 187	100 176	- 0	96 23	100 85	- 0	- 0	- 0	- 0	99 136	97 376	100 420	100 98
VA Eastern Kansas Healthcare System, Leavenworth, KS	100 1	100 13	100 4	100 5	- 0	- 0	100 2	- -	- -	- -	- -	100 41	93 102	100 113	96 23
Via Christi Hospital Pittsburg, Pittsburg, KS	78 9	98 58	85 54	92 50	100 2	86 7	100 11	100 21	7 21	98 1	100 5	80 44	79 67	98 102	100 18
Via Christi Hospital Wichita - Saint Teresa, Wichita, KS	- 0	- 0	- 0	- 0	- 0	- 0	- 0	- -	- -	- -	- -	- 0	- 0	- 0	- 0
Via Christi Hospitals Wichita, Wichita, KS	96 50	99 272	99 298	98 280	- 0	81 53	100 124	100 6	14 6	- 0	- 0	90 99	95 265	99 329	100 79
Wamego City Hospital, Wamego, KS	- 0	100 3	100 2	100 2	- 0	- 0	- 0	- 0	- 0	- 0	- 0	100 2	100 9	78 18	100 4
Washington County Hospital, Washington, KS	- 0	100 2	100 2	100 1	- 0	- 0	0 1	- -	- -	- -	- -	100 1	0 2	67 3	- 0
Wesley Medical Center, Wichita, KS	100 43	99 252	100 355	100 337	- 0	94 63	100 134	- 0	- 0	- 0	- 0	100 94	96 216	100 302	100 43
Western Plains Medical Complex, Dodge City, KS	100 4	100 24	100 31	96 24	- 0	100 3	100 13	100 17	9 17	- 0	- 0	95 20	89 37	98 50	100 3
Wichita County Health Center, Leoti, KS	- 0	- 0	- 0	- 0	- 0	- 0	- 0	- -	- -	- -	- -	- 0	- 0	- 0	- 0
Wichita VA Medical Center, Wichita, KS	- 0	- 0	- 0	- 0	- 0	- 0	- 0	- -	- -	- -	- -	100 32	100 74	100 81	100 24
William Newton Hospital, Winfield, KS	50 2	100 6	100 5	100 6	- 0	- 0	0 1	95 82	4 84	132 1	17 6	100 2	60 5	80 15	100 1
Wilson Medical Center, Neodesha, KS	- 0	- 0	- 0	- 0	- 0	- 0	- 0	- -	- -	- -	- -	- 0	0 3	0 3	- 0
MICHIGAN															
Allegan General Hospital, Allegan, MI	100 1	100 6	80 5	75 4	- 0	- 0	100 3	- -	- -	- -	- -	68 22	98 59	100 75	100 18
Allegiance Health, Jackson, MI	94 53	99 354	99 333	99 329	- 0	99 77	99 108	100 8	6 11	- 0	- 0	94 124	87 341	100 430	100 84
Alpena Regional Medical Center, Alpena, MI	100 5	98 47	97 29	96 27	100 1	- 0	100 7	98 108	9 113	233 1	67 15	90 61	84 152	97 197	100 26
Aspirus Grand View Hospital, Ironwood, MI	100 1	100 9	100 5	100 6	- 0	- 0	- 0	- -	- -	- -	- -	100 15	100 24	100 40	100 4

NOTE: The first number in each column (boldface) is the score, the second number is the number of patients; Please refer to the main entry for footnotes; (a) 100-299
*MEASURES: **Heart Attack Care:** 1. ACE Inhibitor or ARB for LVSD; 2. Aspirin at Arrival; 3. Aspirin at Discharge; 4. Beta Blocker at Discharge; 5. Fibrinolytic Medication Timing; 6. PCI Within 90 Minutes of Arrival; 7. Smoking Cessation Advice; **Chest Pain/Possible Heart Attack Care:** 8. Aspirin at Arrival; 9. Median Time to ECG (minutes); 10. Median Time to Transfer (minutes); 11. Fibrinolytic Medication Timing; **Heart Failure Care:** 12. ACE Inhibitor or ARB for LVSD; 13. Discharge Instructions; 14. Evaluation of LVS Function; 15. Smoking Cessation Advice*

Hospital	Heart Attack Care							Chest Pain/Possible Heart Attack Care				Heart Failure Care			
	1	2	3	4	5	6	7	8	9	10	11	12	13	14	15
Baraga County Memorial Hospital, L'Anse, MI	- 0	- 0	- 0	- 0	- 0	- 0	- 0	- -	- -	- -	- -	- 0	- 0	- 0	- 0
Battle Creek Health System, Battle Creek, MI	92 25	100 134	99 90	99 94	- 0	- 0	100 25	97 115	16 118	56 12	- 0	99 117	84 381	100 449	100 118
Battle Creek VA Medical Center, Battle Creek, MI	- 0	- 0	- 0	- 0	- 0	- 0	- 0	- -	- -	- -	- -	60 5	100 14	100 15	100 5
Bay Regional Medical Center, Bay City, MI	96 74	97 204	99 318	96 310	- 0	91 53	100 132	100 1	23 1	- 0	- 0	88 174	99 502	96 601	99 81
Beaumont Hospital - Grosse Pointe, Grosse Pointe, MI	100 7	100 63	100 39	100 38	- 0	- 0	100 4	89 27	10 26	56 9	- 0	97 135	97 326	100 375	100 70
Bell Memorial Hospital, Ishpeming, MI	- 0	100 4	67 3	100 3	- 0	- 0	- 0	- -	- -	- -	- -	- 0	0 3	100 3	- 0
Borgess Medical Center, Kalamazoo, MI	92 53	100 98	99 276	99 267	- 0	88 17	100 119	100 1	10 1	- 0	- 0	90 71	83 228	99 279	98 46
Borgess-Lee Memorial Hospital, Dowagiac, MI	67 3	100 16	100 9	100 8	0 2	- 0	100 1	- -	- -	- -	- -	90 10	83 47	98 52	100 7
Botsford Hospital, Farmington Hills, MI	95 40	100 241	90 157	93 153	- 0	86 29	100 34	95 39	6 40	73 7	- 0	92 170	99 462	97 612	98 112
Brighton Hospital, Brighton, MI	- 0	- 0	- 0	- 0	- 0	- 0	- 0	- 0	- 0	- 0	- 0	- 0	- 0	- 0	- 0
Bronson Lakeview Hospital, Paw Paw, MI	- 0	100 2	100 2	100 2	- 0	- 0	- 0	- -	- -	- -	- -	94 16	100 37	100 38	100 6
Bronson Methodist Hospital, Kalamazoo, MI	94 69	99 278	99 413	99 413	0 1	85 72	100 151	75 4	36 4	- 0	- 0	98 149	94 497	99 579	100 103
Bronson Vicksburg Hospital, Vicksburg, MI	- 0	- 0	- 0	- 0	- 0	- 0	- 0	100 34	3 37	58 4	- 0	- 0	- 0	- 0	- 0
Caro Community Hospital, Caro, MI	- 0	- 0	- 0	- 0	- 0	- 0	- 0	- -	- -	- -	- -	67 3	83 6	100 10	50 2
Carson City Hospital, Carson City, MI	100 2	100 7	100 5	100 5	- 0	- 0	- 0	100 130	13 131	108 4	100 3	82 11	92 26	95 37	100 4
Central Michigan Community Hospital, Mount Pleasant, MI	100 2	100 27	100 18	94 17	- 0	- 0	100 6	99 92	7 95	61 1	82 11	97 31	98 84	100 112	100 7
Charlevoix Area Hospital, Charlevoix, MI	- 0	- 0	100 1	100 1	- 0	- 0	- 0	- -	- -	- -	- -	- 0	100 1	100 1	100 1
Cheboygan Memorial Hospital, Cheboygan, MI	- -	- -	- -	- -	- -	- -	- -	- -	- -	- -	- -	- -	- -	- -	- -
Chelsea Community Hospital, Chelsea, MI	100 3	100 8	100 7	100 7	- 0	- 0	- 0	98 89	9 95	52 12	- 0	92 13	96 49	100 63	100 8
Children's Hospital of Michigan, Detroit, MI	- -	- -	- -	- -	- -	- -	- -	- -	- -	- -	- -	- -	- -	- -	- -
Chippewa County War Memorial Hospital, Sault Sainte Marie, MI	80 5	97 37	100 21	100 20	- 0	- 0	100 1	99 105	13 107	307 1	67 3	94 33	94 82	100 96	92 13
Clinton Memorial Hospital, Saint Johns, MI	- 0	100 1	- 0	100 1	- 0	- 0	- 0	- 0	- 0	- 0	- 0	100 13	94 36	100 46	100 2
Community Health Center of Branch County, Coldwater, MI	- 0	100 9	100 6	100 7	- 0	- 0	100 1	95 234	10 243	65 13	0 2	100 16	100 82	100 98	100 17
Community Hospital, Watervliet, MI	100 1	100 3	100 2	0 1	- 0	- 0	- 0	93 112	11 117	- 0	- 0	83 6	82 38	68 41	100 7
Covenant Medical Center, Saginaw, MI	96 83	98 369	98 452	99 436	- 0	88 33	100 151	100 3	8 4	- 0	- 0	98 228	83 573	99 701	100 124
Crittenton Hospital Medical Center, Rochester, MI	100 25	98 141	98 128	99 122	- 0	91 22	100 38	100 6	13 6	- 0	- 0	98 130	91 287	99 368	100 43
Deckerville Community Hospital, Deckerville, MI	- 0	- 0	- 0	- 0	- 0	- 0	- 0	- 0	- 0	- 0	- 0	- 0	- 0	- 0	- 0
Detroit (John D. Dingell) VA Medical Center, Detroit, MI	100 3	94 18	100 12	100 12	- 0	- 0	100 4	- -	- -	- -	- -	96 82	75 148	100 155	100 31
Detroit Receiving Hospital & Univ Health Center, Detroit, MI	100 21	100 68	98 58	98 61	- 0	- 0	94 17	100 626	15 663	28 78	100 1	95 277	100 521	100 578	100 237
Dickinson County Memorial Hospital, Iron Mountain, MI	100 2	100 33	100 18	100 19	- 0	- 0	100 3	96 94	10 97	225 1	67 9	100 13	96 67	99 100	100 14
Doctor's Hospital of Michigan, Pontiac, MI	50 2	100 11	75 8	86 7	- 0	- 0	- 0	95 38	12 38	130 2	- 0	90 20	78 89	83 103	90 21
Eaton Rapids Medical Center, Eaton Rapids, MI	- 0	100 3	100 1	100 1	- 0	- 0	- 0	88 68	16 78	105 3	25 4	100 6	94 31	97 29	100 3
Edward W Sparrow Hospital, Lansing, MI	99 70	99 266	100 410	100 403	- 0	81 36	100 146	67 3	18 3	- 0	- 0	95 191	80 467	98 559	100 120
Emma L Bixby Medical Center, Adrian, MI	100 14	98 54	97 38	98 42	- 0	- 0	75 4	85 197	11 202	- 0	0 2	98 48	89 90	99 117	100 13
Garden City Hospital, Garden City, MI	96 24	97 204	90 140	96 135	- 0	96 54	100 46	97 86	5 87	118 4	- 0	92 85	90 321	96 401	100 71
Genesys Regional Medical Center - Health Park, Grand Blanc, MI	91 68	100 424	100 424	99 394	- 0	82 62	100 154	- 0	- 0	- 0	- 0	99 137	98 394	100 464	100 88
Gratiot Medical Center, Alma, MI	50 4	94 34	87 23	100 23	0 1	- 0	100 5	98 95	5 100	160 7	38 13	82 38	71 155	100 224	100 25
Harbor Beach Community Hospital, Harbor Beach, MI	- 0	- 0	- 0	- 0	- 0	- 0	- 0	- -	- -	- -	- -	- 0	- 0	- 0	- 0
Harper University Hospital, Detroit, MI	100 76	99 149	99 355	99 351	- 0	94 16	100 144	94 35	14 34	- 0	- 0	96 257	88 676	100 786	100 193
Hayes Green Beach Memorial Hospital, Charlotte, MI	- 0	100 3	100 2	100 2	- 0	- 0	- 0	- -	- -	- -	- -	100 8	100 24	100 27	100 4
Healthsource Saginaw, Saginaw, MI	- 0	- 0	- 0	- 0	- 0	- 0	- 0	- 0	- 0	- 0	- 0	- 0	- 0	- 0	- 0
Henry Ford Hospital, Detroit, MI	97 158	99 581	99 898	98 884	- 0	100 36	100 310	100 69	11 71	- 0	- 0	91 172	85 354	99 396	99 102
Henry Ford Macomb Hospital, Clinton Township, MI	100 85	100 476	100 451	100 450	- 0	100 77	100 137	98 51	16 57	- 0	- 0	100 78	94 271	100 338	100 37
Henry Ford West Bloomfield Hospital, West Bloomfield, MI	94 16	98 90	94 65	97 60	- 0	- 0	100 9	- 0	- 0	- 0	- 0	81 97	62 225	98 281	100 19
Henry Ford Wyandotte Hospital, Wyandotte, MI	88 33	98 235	97 170	97 163	- 0	73 44	100 69	91 225	8 236	54 3	- 0	93 199	82 560	99 672	100 115
Herrick Memorial Hospital, Tecumseh, MI	67 3	100 9	86 7	88 8	- 0	- 0	- 0	- -	- -	- -	- -	93 14	92 36	98 42	100 4
Hills & Dales General Hospital, Cass City, MI	- 0	- 0	- 0	- 0	- 0	- 0	- 0	92 36	15 38	83 1	67 3	0 3	50 12	60 15	- 0
Hillsdale Community Health Center, Hillsdale, MI	33 6	95 21	79 14	82 17	- 0	- 0	100 4	96 50	10 54	60 7	- 0	82 38	64 66	90 88	83 12
Holland Community Hospital, Holland, MI	100 9	100 105	100 73	100 77	- 0	96 26	100 19	97 36	9 38	- 0	- 0	100 36	92 88	100 120	100 8
Hurley Medical Center, Flint, MI	90 31	99 175	98 117	96 117	0 1	72 29	100 65	83 12	8 12	130 1	- 0	99 133	88 336	96 362	99 132
Huron Medical Center, Bad Axe, MI	100 2	100 6	100 3	83 6	- 0	- 0	- 0	98 105	10 113	- 0	33 3	100 5	100 29	98 46	100 5
Huron Valley-Sinai Hospital, Commerce Twp, MI	86 29	99 157	95 111	94 113	- 0	98 45	100 34	94 36	6 37	- 0	- 0	93 100	86 276	98 350	100 57
Ingham Regional Medical Center, Lansing, MI	87 86	97 226	98 321	99 313	- 0	89 37	98 121	100 2	23 2	- 0	- 0	83 190	92 463	97 516	100 79
Ionia County Memorial Hospital, Ionia, MI	- 0	- 0	- 0	- 0	- 0	- 0	- 0	- 0	- 0	- 0	- 0	100 4	77 22	96 24	100 5
Iron Mountain VA Medical Center, Iron Mountain, MI	100 1	100 3	100 2	100 2	0 1	- 0	- 0	- -	- -	- -	- -	100 19	97 39	98 53	86 7
Karmanos Cancer Center, Detroit, MI	- 0	- 0	- 0	- 0	- 0	- 0	- 0	- 0	- 0	- 0	- 0	50 2	29 7	86 7	0 1
Lakeland Hospital - St Joseph, Saint Joseph, MI	87 71	99 332	100 340	98 322	75 4	82 40	100 119	100 12	16 16	- 0	- 0	97 179	93 403	99 498	100 110
Lapeer Regional Medical Center, Lapeer, MI	56 9	88 59	84 32	94 33	- 0	- 0	100 4	97 77	3 78	35 32	- 0	93 45	81 155	98 193	100 18
Marlette Regional Hospital, Marlette, MI	100 1	88 8	83 6	100 6	- 0	- 0	100 1	96 79	11 82	139 8	40 5	62 13	65 31	85 33	25 4
Marquette General Hospital, Marquette, MI	90 59	100 86	100 351	97 337	- 0	63 19	98 122	100 1	7 1	- 0	- 0	98 41	85 140	94 171	100 31
McKenzie Memorial Hospital, Sandusky, MI	- 0	- 0	- 0	- 0	- 0	- 0	- 0	92 75	7 77	247 3	0 2	- 0	- 0	- 0	- 0
Mclaren Regional Medical Center, Flint, MI	100 72	99 344	99 407	99 408	0 1	92 76	100 144	100 5	4 6	- 0	- 0	93 262	83 655	96 770	99 118
Mecosta County Medical Center, Big Rapids, MI	- 0	92 12	100 9	89 9	- 0	- 0	100 1	97 138	10 146	- 0	75 8	90 20	89 55	92 63	100 11
Memorial Healthcare, Owosso, MI	86 7	95 19	89 18	100 18	- 0	- 0	100 2	96 150	12 154	245 2	55 11	91 22	85 53	99 82	100 13
Memorial Medical Center of West Michigan, Ludington, MI	100 2	100 12	100 5	100 5	- 0	- 0	- 0	99 78	8 80	54 4	56 9	88 16	90 48	93 57	100 4
Mercy Health Partners - Hackley Campus, Muskegon, MI	100 4	100 19	100 11	100 13	- 0	- 0	100 1	89 45	6 47	41 19	- 0	100 42	96 79	100 101	100 30
Mercy Health Partners - Mercy Campus, Muskegon, MI	98 59	100 243	100 365	100 359	100 1	80 54	100 147	83 6	6 5	- 0	- 0	98 94	97 212	99 246	100 51

NOTE: The first number in each column (boldface) is the score, the second number is the number of patients; Please refer to the main entry for footnotes; (a) 100-299
*MEASURES: **Heart Attack Care:** 1. ACE Inhibitor or ARB for LVSD; 2. Aspirin at Arrival; 3. Aspirin at Discharge; 4. Beta Blocker at Discharge; 5. Fibrinolytic Medication Timing; 6. PCI Within 90 Minutes of Arrival; 7. Smoking Cessation Advice; **Chest Pain/Possible Heart Attack Care:** 8. Aspirin at Arrival; 9. Median Time to ECG (minutes); 10. Median Time to Transfer (minutes); 11. Fibrinolytic Medication Timing; **Heart Failure Care:** 12. ACE Inhibitor or ARB for LVSD; 13. Discharge Instructions; 14. Evaluation of LVS Function; 15. Smoking Cessation Advice*

Hospital	Heart Attack Care							Chest Pain/Possible Heart Attack Care				Heart Failure Care			
	1	2	3	4	5	6	7	8	9	10	11	12	13	14	15
Mercy Hospital - Cadillac, Cadillac, MI	100 10	100 51	95 39	95 39	- 0	- 0	100 8	100 75	10 74	153 6	80 5	94 33	94 102	100 120	100 22
Mercy Hospital - Grayling, Grayling, MI	80 5	97 34	90 20	91 23	- 0	- 0	100 4	98 190	5 194	35 3	81 21	87 38	96 81	100 98	100 23
Mercy Memorial Hospital System, Monroe, MI	100 17	98 144	98 60	100 61	67 9	- 0	100 3	97 73	6 78	68 4	62 8	100 81	94 191	100 280	100 54
Metro Health Hospital, Wyoming, MI	100 20	100 140	97 116	99 110	- 0	88 43	100 43	100 7	6 7	- 0	- 0	95 61	72 159	100 195	100 36
Midmichigan Medical Center-Clare, Clare, MI	100 1	100 15	77 13	93 14	- 0	- 0	100 2	95 100	15 104	120 2	54 13	80 41	76 131	96 151	97 36
Midmichigan Medical Center-Gladwin, Gladwin, MI	- 0	100 2	100 1	- 0	- 0	- 0	- 0	99 75	9 76	86 2	25 8	91 11	98 47	100 66	100 11
Midmichigan Medical Center-Midland, Midland, MI	95 57	100 128	99 267	100 268	- 0	88 26	98 98	100 11	9 11	- 0	- 0	96 69	82 218	99 262	94 49
Mount Clemens Regional Medical Center, Mount Clemens, MI	93 30	99 253	99 240	100 227	- 0	97 67	96 102	94 16	4 16	- 0	- 0	81 167	50 406	98 494	96 77
Munson Medical Center, Traverse City, MI	97 154	100 430	100 892	99 816	- 0	83 71	100 304	- 0	- 0	- 0	- 0	94 145	93 482	100 536	99 73
North Ottawa Community Hospital, Grand Haven, MI	100 1	100 6	100 5	100 6	- 0	- 0	100 1	100 43	6 45	56 14	- 0	92 12	88 34	100 49	100 4
Northern Michigan Regional Hospital, Petoskey, MI	98 57	100 129	99 356	99 335	- 0	83 29	100 126	- 0	- 0	- 0	- 0	97 119	87 244	99 274	100 40
Northstar Health System, Iron River, MI	- 0	- 0	- 0	- 0	- 0	- 0	- 0	- -	- -	- -	- -	70 10	50 32	80 45	83 6
Oakland Regional Hospital, Southfield, MI	- 0	- 0	- 0	- 0	- 0	- 0	- 0	- 0	- 0	- 0	- 0	- 0	0 1	0 1	- 0
Oaklawn Hospital, Marshall, MI	100 1	100 9	100 6	100 7	- 0	- 0	100 1	98 320	9 333	40 9	- 0	86 14	94 69	100 85	93 15
Oakwood Annapolis Hospital, Wayne, MI	100 24	100 116	100 85	100 83	- 0	89 28	100 37	91 56	0 58	- 0	- 0	92 109	92 270	99 337	100 83
Oakwood Heritage Hospital, Taylor, MI	100 8	100 32	100 22	100 24	- 0	- 0	100 4	89 101	9 108	55 5	- 0	100 51	97 99	100 167	100 33
Oakwood Hospital and Medical Center, Dearborn, MI	99 240	100 581	100 939	99 965	- 0	89 84	100 338	84 90	4 94	56 2	- 0	98 475	92 1053	100 1263	100 292
Oakwood Southshore Medical Center, Trenton, MI	100 17	99 112	97 70	100 71	- 0	86 29	100 27	92 63	6 66	40 1	- 0	94 95	95 230	99 287	100 38
Otsego Memorial Hospital, Gaylord, MI	100 2	100 5	100 4	100 6	- 0	- 0	- 0	96 157	8 162	48 10	40 10	100 15	95 56	95 66	100 9
Paul Oliver Memorial Hospital, Frankfort, MI	- -	- -	- -	- -	- -	- -	- -	- 0	- 0	- 0	- 0	- -	- -	- -	- -
Pennock Hospital, Hastings, MI	100 2	100 14	100 6	100 8	- 0	- 0	100 1	97 60	10 61	28 5	- 0	100 28	98 97	100 107	100 8
Poh Medical Center, Pontiac, MI	89 9	95 38	97 33	100 35	- 0	- 0	100 9	91 91	5 95	49 10	- 0	95 80	39 192	100 221	77 77
Port Huron Hospital, Port Huron, MI	92 76	100 239	98 313	97 312	- 0	76 50	100 106	50 2	16 2	- 0	- 0	97 103	88 265	98 325	91 55
Portage Health Hospital, Hancock, MI	100 3	100 12	100 8	100 9	- 0	- 0	- 0	100 46	6 46	- 0	25 4	100 15	96 47	98 62	86 7
Providence Hospital and Medical Centers, Southfield, MI	100 83	99 254	99 421	99 404	- 0	95 37	100 120	100 36	8 37	- 0	- 0	99 422	88 1022	100 1248	99 159
Saginaw VA Medical Center, Saginaw, MI	- 0	100 5	100 2	100 2	- 0	- 0	- 0	- -	- -	- -	- -	100 17	100 33	100 41	100 5
Saint Francis Hospital, Escanaba, MI	75 4	100 20	100 15	100 16	- 0	- 0	100 2	97 132	14 144	165 1	67 15	96 28	92 86	95 106	100 6
Saint John Hospital and Medical Center, Detroit, MI	93 101	99 347	98 426	98 430	- 0	90 72	99 158	95 101	7 107	50 2	- 0	98 288	93 662	99 763	99 162
Saint John Macomb-Oakland Hospital, Warren, MI	97 66	99 318	98 301	99 291	- 0	85 54	100 108	96 77	14 79	54 18	- 0	97 320	95 850	99 1048	99 177
Saint John River District Hospital, East China, MI	- 0	100 5	100 1	100 2	- 0	- 0	- 0	100 46	2 48	142 2	- 0	100 23	100 61	99 93	100 13
Saint Joseph Mercy Hospital, Ann Arbor, MI	98 104	99 508	98 732	99 690	- 0	91 103	100 200	48 50	12 43	- 0	- 0	94 276	95 654	99 791	100 90
Saint Joseph Mercy Livingston Hospital, Howell, MI	100 1	100 13	90 10	90 10	- 0	- 0	- 0	75 367	9 369	66 12	0 1	97 31	95 96	100 131	100 8
Saint Joseph Mercy Oakland, Pontiac, MI	100 69	100 253	99 305	99 290	- 0	90 48	100 96	100 12	12 13	- 0	- 0	96 109	94 255	99 298	100 53
Saint Joseph Mercy Port Huron, Port Huron, MI	100 7	100 31	100 24	100 25	- 0	- 0	100 6	100 33	13 32	52 9	- 0	97 31	91 108	100 146	100 30
Saint Joseph Mercy Saline Hospital, Saline, MI	- 0	100 4	100 2	100 1	- 0	- 0	- 0	75 272	10 275	69 9	- 0	100 4	96 24	100 34	100 2
Saint Mary Mercy Hospital, Livonia, MI	95 43	99 253	95 170	99 188	- 0	89 64	100 33	89 124	10 129	- 0	- 0	92 146	96 353	100 517	100 44
Saint Mary's Health Care, Grand Rapids, MI	100 14	98 111	100 75	100 75	- 0	85 26	100 33	100 14	6 13	40 1	- 0	99 83	93 258	100 310	100 67
Saint Mary's of Michigan Medical Center, Saginaw, MI	92 51	98 120	95 282	98 270	- 0	64 14	99 103	82 17	11 18	- 0	- 0	92 102	77 249	100 301	97 63
Saint Mary's Standish Community Hospital, Standish, MI	- 0	100 1	0 1	100 1	- 0	- 0	- 0	100 49	16 52	32 2	67 3	100 2	89 19	81 32	67 3
Schoolcraft Memorial Hospital, Manistique, MI	- 0	- 0	- 0	- 0	100 1	- 0	- 0	- -	- -	- -	- -	- 0	- 0	- 0	- 0
Sheridan Community Hospital, Sheridan, MI	- 0	0 1	0 1	100 1	- 0	- 0	- 0	- -	- -	- -	- -	- 0	- 0	- 0	- 0
Sinai-Grace Hospital, Detroit, MI	100 68	99 323	99 285	98 278	- 0	76 33	96 113	85 27	10 29	- 0	- 0	91 440	88 887	99 1042	98 396
South Haven Community Hospital, South Haven, MI	100 1	100 3	100 3	100 3	- 0	- 0	- 0	99 121	9 128	110 4	57 7	94 16	91 44	94 50	64 11
Southeast Michigan Surgical Hospital, Warren, MI	- 0	- 0	- 0	- 0	- 0	- 0	- 0	- 0	- 0	- 0	- 0	- 0	- 0	- 0	- 0
Spectrum Health - Butterworth Campus, Grand Rapids, MI	100 130	99 424	100 855	100 830	- 0	94 108	99 310	- 0	- 0	- 0	- 0	98 350	89 904	100 1066	100 160
Spectrum Health - Reed City Campus, Reed City, MI	0 1	100 3	100 3	100 3	- 0	- 0	- 0	100 83	5 83	34 10	50 2	91 11	92 26	100 35	80 5
Spectrum Health Gerber Memorial, Fremont, MI	100 1	100 5	100 4	100 4	- 0	- 0	- 0	99 126	10 130	55 15	60 5	100 19	96 51	100 61	100 13
Spectrum Health United Memorial - Kelsey Campus, Lakeview, MI	- 0	100 1	- 0	100 1	- 0	- 0	- 0	100 68	9 73	28 4	0 1	60 5	92 12	100 17	100 4
Spectrum Health United Memorial - United Campus, Greenville, MI	- 0	92 12	100 7	100 5	- 0	- 0	100 1	99 110	6 113	57 10	- 0	100 15	99 68	100 96	100 12
Straith Hospital for Special Surgery, Southfield, MI	- 0	- 0	- 0	- 0	- 0	- 0	- 0	- 0	- 0	- 0	- 0	- 0	- 0	- 0	- 0
Sturgis Hospital, Sturgis, MI	- 0	100 4	75 4	67 3	- 0	- 0	- 0	78 18	7 19	120 1	- 0	80 15	92 50	97 60	100 7
Tawas Saint Joseph Hospital, Tawas City, MI	100 1	100 4	100 2	100 2	- 0	- 0	- 0	97 289	9 298	104 6	36 14	95 22	99 73	99 88	100 14
Three Rivers Health, Three Rivers, MI	- 0	- 0	- 0	- 0	- 0	- 0	- 0	94 152	18 164	76 23	100 2	76 17	93 58	95 80	100 12
University of Michigan Health System, Ann Arbor, MI	100 68	100 246	100 351	100 322	- 0	94 64	100 121	- 0	- 0	- 0	- 0	99 289	99 710	100 800	100 104
VA Ann Arbor Healthcare System, Ann Arbor, MI	86 7	100 45	100 50	100 48	- 0	100 1	100 15	- -	- -	- -	- -	95 57	98 140	100 151	96 26
West Branch Regional Medical Center, West Branch, MI	100 1	100 18	100 10	100 12	- 0	- 0	100 1	94 153	9 166	- 0	95 21	97 35	94 128	97 152	100 26
West Shore Medical Center, Manistee, MI	100 1	88 8	60 5	80 5	- 0	- 0	- 0	95 63	10 66	26 3	100 1	100 14	42 38	100 49	100 2
William Beaumont Hospital, Royal Oak, MI	100 107	100 601	100 619	100 590	- 0	97 69	100 143	100 6	0 8	- 0	- 0	98 369	93 1063	100 1306	100 177
William Beaumont Hospital-Troy, Troy, MI	100 84	100 438	100 414	100 417	- 0	99 71	100 120	54 26	8 28	73 1	- 0	100 156	99 506	100 616	100 70
Zeeland Community Hospital, Zeeland, MI	100 1	100 8	100 5	100 4	- 0	- 0	- 0	100 51	11 53	38 9	- 0	92 13	97 60	100 70	100 10
MINNESOTA															
Abbott Northwestern Hospital, Minneapolis, MN	100 113	100 223	100 837	100 806	- 0	96 51	100 249	100 1	0 1	- 0	- 0	99 268	92 551	100 679	100 117
Albany Area Hospital, Albany, MN	- 0	- 0	- 0	- 0	- 0	- 0	- 0	- 0	- 0	- 0	- 0	100 1	100 6	10 10	100 1
Appleton Municipal Hospital, Appleton, MN	- 0	100 1	100 1	100 1	- 0	- 0	- 0	- -	- -	- -	- -	- 0	0 1	100 3	- 0
Austin Medical Center, Austin, MN	100 1	100 5	100 4	100 3	- 0	- 0	- 0	99 90	8 95	126 2	80 5	100 30	97 77	100 112	100 6
Avera Marshall Regional Medical Center, Marshall, MN	- 0	100 4	100 2	100 2	- 0	- 0	- 0	94 35	0 35	60 2	100 1	83 6	82 11	100 18	- 0
Bigfork Valley Hospital, Bigfork, MN	- 0	- 0	- 0	- 0	- 0	- 0	- 0	- 0	- 0	- 0	- 0	100 1	42 12	85 13	100 1

NOTE: The first number in each column (boldface) is the score, the second number is the number of patients; Please refer to the main entry for footnotes; (a) 100-299
*MEASURES: **Heart Attack Care:** 1. ACE Inhibitor or ARB for LVSD; 2. Aspirin at Arrival; 3. Aspirin at Discharge; 4. Beta Blocker at Discharge; 5. Fibrinolytic Medication Timing; 6. PCI Within 90 Minutes of Arrival; 7. Smoking Cessation Advice; **Chest Pain/Possible Heart Attack Care:** 8. Aspirin at Arrival; 9. Median Time to ECG (minutes); 10. Median Time to Transfer (minutes); 11. Fibrinolytic Medication Timing; **Heart Failure Care:** 12. ACE Inhibitor or ARB for LVSD; 13. Discharge Instructions; 14. Evaluation of LVS Function; 15. Smoking Cessation Advice*

Hospital	Heart Attack Care							Chest Pain/Possible Heart Attack Care				Heart Failure Care			
	1	2	3	4	5	6	7	8	9	10	11	12	13	14	15
Bridges Medical Services, Ada, MN	- 0	- 0	- 0	- 0	- 0	- 0	- 0	- 0	- 0	- 0	- 0	- 0	**75** 4	**0** 2	**0** 1
Buffalo Hospital, Buffalo, MN	**100** 2	**100** 5	**100** 4	**100** 4	- 0	- 0	- 0	**100** 94	**9** 100	**48** 11	- 0	**100** 7	**95** 38	**100** 61	**100** 4
Cambridge Medical Center, Cambridge, MN	**100** 3	**90** 10	**100** 6	**100** 8	- 0	- 0	**100** 1	**100** 75	**2** 76	**44** 5	- 0	**100** 12	**95** 38	**100** 50	**100** 8
Cannon Falls Medical Center Mayo, Cannon Falls, MN	- 0	- 0	- 0	- 0	- 0	- 0	- 0	- 0	- 0	- 0	- 0	**100** 3	**86** 7	**94** 16	- 0
Cass Lake Indian Health Services Hospital, Cass Lake, MN	- -	- -	- -	- -	- -	- -	- -	- 0	- 0	- 0	- 0	- -	- -	- -	- -
Centracare Health System - Long Prairie, Long Prairie, MN	- 0	**100** 2	**100** 2	**50** 2	- 0	- 0	- 0	**93** 29	**0** 28	**38** 5	- 0	**100** 4	**0** 8	**62** 13	**100** 2
Centracare Health System - Melrose Hospital, Melrose, MN	- 0	**50** 2	**50** 2	**100** 2	- 0	- 0	- 0	- 0	- 0	- 0	- 0	**100** 1	**0** 1	**100** 1	- 0
Children's Hospitals & Clinics, Minneapolis, MN	- -	- -	- -	- -	- -	- -	- -	- -	- -	- -	- -	- -	- -	- -	- -
Chippewa County Hospital, Montevideo, MN	- 0	**100** 3	**100** 2	**100** 2	- 0	- 0	- 0	- 0	- 0	- 0	- 0	**83** 6	**31** 13	**70** 23	**0** 2
Clearwater Health Services, Bagley, MN	- 0	- 0	- 0	- 0	- 0	- 0	- 0	- -	- -	- -	- -	- 0	**0** 2	**0** 2	**0** 1
Community Memorial Hospital, Cloquet, MN	**100** 1	**100** 4	**100** 3	**100** 4	- 0	- 0	**100** 1	**98** 55	**5** 54	**42** 7	- 0	**100** 9	**85** 13	**100** 19	**100** 3
Cook County Northshore Hospital, Grand Marais, MN	- 0	- 0	- 0	- 0	- 0	- 0	- 0	- -	- -	- -	- -	- 0	**0** 3	**67** 3	- 0
Cook Hospital, Cook, MN	- 0	**100** 1	**100** 1	**100** 1	- 0	- 0	- 0	- -	- -	- -	- -	**100** 1	**8** 13	**19** 16	**100** 1
Cuyuna Regional Medical Center, Crosby, MN	- 0	**80** 5	**100** 3	**100** 4	- 0	- 0	- 0	- -	- -	- -	- -	**75** 4	**70** 20	**69** 35	**100** 1
Deer River Healthcare Center, Deer River, MN	- 0	**100** 5	**100** 3	**100** 4	- 0	- 0	- 0	**90** 20	**11** 20	**122** 1	- 0	**100** 3	**32** 19	**67** 21	**33** 6
District One Hospital, Faribault, MN	- 0	**100** 2	**100** 2	**50** 2	- 0	- 0	- 0	**99** 117	**5** 123	**50** 15	**0** 1	**100** 9	**86** 29	**95** 38	**100** 2
Douglas County Hospital, Alexandria, MN	**100** 1	**100** 8	**100** 5	**75** 4	- 0	- 0	- 0	**98** 127	**4** 126	**56** 12	- 0	**97** 29	**84** 45	**95** 87	**100** 10
Ely Bloomenson Community Hospital, Ely, MN	- 0	**100** 1	**100** 1	**100** 1	- 0	- 0	- 0	- -	- -	- -	- -	**100** 3	**33** 6	**75** 8	**100** 1
Essentia Health Duluth, Duluth, MN	- 0	- 0	**100** 1	**100** 1	- 0	- 0	- 0	- 0	- 0	- 0	- 0	**100** 1	**9** 11	**79** 19	**67** 3
Essentia Health Fosston, Fosston, MN	- 0	**100** 2	**100** 2	**100** 1	- 0	- 0	- 0	**100** 1	**12** 1	**90** 1	- 0	**100** 9	**100** 16	**97** 36	**100** 6
Essentia Health Sandstone, Sandstone, MN	- 0	**100** 3	**100** 3	**100** 3	- 0	- 0	- 0	**92** 25	**10** 26	**114** 3	**0** 3	**100** 2	**36** 14	**55** 22	**100** 3
Essentia Health St Joseph's Medical Center, Brainerd, MN	**75** 4	**94** 33	**96** 24	**100** 22	- 0	- 0	**100** 3	**99** 159	**9** 164	**28** 21	- 0	**78** 54	**73** 126	**96** 191	**100** 23
Essentia Health St Mary's Medical Center, Duluth, MN	**93** 58	**98** 99	**99** 350	**99** 338	- 0	**77** 13	**99** 128	**80** 5	**27** 6	- 0	- 0	**91** 100	**82** 215	**100** 255	**98** 58
Fairmont Medical Center, Fairmont, MN	**80** 5	**100** 25	**100** 16	**93** 14	- 0	- 0	**100** 2	**98** 42	**5** 42	**66** 4	**20** 5	**96** 23	**93** 44	**98** 103	**100** 5
Fairview Lakes Health Services, Wyoming, MN	**100** 4	**100** 15	**100** 7	**100** 13	- 0	- 0	- 0	**98** 186	**8** 189	**51** 15	- 0	**92** 26	**96** 67	**100** 76	**100** 15
Fairview Northland Regional Hospital, Princeton, MN	**100** 5	**100** 26	**100** 19	**100** 20	- 0	- 0	**100** 1	**97** 72	**7** 77	**56** 10	- 0	**100** 16	**100** 44	**100** 63	**100** 6
Fairview Red Wing Hospital, Red Wing, MN	**100** 3	**100** 12	**100** 8	**100** 9	- 0	- 0	- 0	**100** 91	**5** 92	**85** 5	**33** 3	**100** 2	**97** 34	**100** 47	**100** 4
Fairview Ridges Hospital, Burnsville, MN	**100** 7	**100** 69	**98** 60	**100** 59	**100** 1	- 0	**100** 21	**100** 101	**14** 109	**54** 29	- 0	**95** 40	**99** 122	**99** 151	**100** 29
Fairview Southdale Hospital, Edina, MN	**99** 92	**100** 334	**100** 439	**100** 428	- 0	**98** 63	**100** 115	**100** 5	**5** 5	- 0	- 0	**97** 120	**97** 255	**99** 359	**100** 45
Glacial Ridge Hospital, Glenwood, MN	- 0	**89** 9	**100** 6	**86** 7	**0** 1	- 0	- 0	- 0	- 0	- 0	- 0	**60** 5	**0** 14	**80** 25	- 0
Glencoe Regional Health Services, Glencoe, MN	- 0	- 0	- 0	- 0	- 0	- 0	- 0	**95** 37	**8** 38	**79** 1	- 0	**100** 6	**42** 12	**97** 33	**75** 4
Grand Itasca Clinic and Hospital, Grand Rapids, MN	**100** 3	**100** 16	**100** 14	**100** 12	- 0	- 0	- 0	**100** 71	**4** 68	**70** 3	**67** 6	**100** 16	**77** 43	**96** 52	**57** 7
Healtheast St John's Hospital, Maplewood, MN	**100** 8	**100** 55	**100** 25	**100** 27	- 0	- 0	**100** 2	**97** 111	**13** 110	**62** 31	- 0	**100** 44	**84** 166	**99** 212	**100** 25
Healtheast Woodwinds Hospital, Woodbury, MN	**100** 2	**100** 20	**100** 8	**100** 6	- 0	- 0	**100** 1	**96** 81	**6** 81	**55** 19	**100** 1	**88** 26	**81** 78	**98** 100	**100** 15
Hendricks Community Hospital, Hendricks, MN	- 0	**100** 1	**100** 2	**100** 2	- 0	- 0	**0** 1	- 0	- 0	- 0	- 0	**100** 2	**0** 3	**78** 9	**0** 1
Hennepin County Medical Center, Minneapolis, MN	**100** 43	**100** 200	**100** 198	**98** 188	**100** 2	**90** 49	**100** 83	- 0	- 0	- 0	- 0	**99** 142	**90** 262	**100** 331	**100** 132
Holy Trinity Hospital, Graceville, MN	- 0	**100** 2	**50** 2	**100** 1	- 0	- 0	- 0	- 0	- 0	- 0	- 0	- 0	**0** 1	**50** 2	- 0
Hutchinson Area Health Care, Hutchinson, MN	- 0	**100** 5	**100** 5	**80** 5	- 0	- 0	- 0	**99** 87	**6** 87	- 0	**62** 8	**94** 17	**94** 47	**97** 70	**100** 4
Immanuel-St Josephs-Mayo Health System, Mankato, MN	**100** 39	**100** 165	**100** 226	**100** 210	- 0	**93** 29	**100** 57	**100** 1	**34** 1	- 0	- 0	**98** 45	**89** 144	**100** 198	**100** 16
Johnson Memorial Hospital, Dawson, MN	- 0	**100** 2	**100** 2	**100** 1	- 0	- 0	- 0	- 0	- 0	- 0	- 0	**100** 1	**50** 4	**100** 6	- 0
Kanabec Hospital, Mora, MN	- 0	**100** 2	**50** 2	**100** 1	- 0	- 0	- 0	**92** 40	**7** 41	- 0	- 0	**74** 19	**97** 30	**85** 48	**100** 6
Kittson Memorial Hospital, Hallock, MN	- 0	**100** 1	**100** 1	**100** 1	- 0	- 0	- 0	- 0	- 0	- 0	- 0	- 0	**80** 5	**0** 8	- 0
Lake City Medical Center Mayo Health System, Lake City, MN	**100** 2	**100** 4	**100** 4	**100** 4	- 0	- 0	- 0	- 0	- 0	- 0	- 0	- 0	**12** 8	**67** 9	- 0
Lake Region Healthcare Corporation, Fergus Falls, MN	**100** 3	**97** 30	**95** 19	**95** 19	- 0	- 0	**100** 2	**95** 57	**6** 59	**141** 1	**83** 12	**100** 26	**85** 54	**100** 79	**100** 3
Lake View Memorial Hospital, Two Harbors, MN	- 0	- 0	- 0	- 0	- 0	- 0	- 0	- -	- -	- -	- -	**33** 3	**57** 7	**56** 9	**0** 3
Lakeside Medical Center, Pine City, MN	- 0	- 0	- 0	- 0	- 0	- 0	- 0	- 0	- 0	- 0	- 0	- 0	- 0	- 0	- 0
Lakeview Memorial Hospital, Stillwater, MN	**100** 1	**100** 6	**100** 3	**100** 4	- 0	- 0	- 0	**92** 60	**3** 60	**30** 14	- 0	**100** 15	**97** 35	**98** 50	**83** 6
Lakewood Health Center, Baudette, MN	- 0	**100** 3	**100** 2	**100** 2	- 0	- 0	- 0	- 0	- 0	- 0	- 0	**100** 4	**83** 6	**100** 13	**100** 1
Lakewood Health System, Staples, MN	- 0	**100** 2	**100** 1	**100** 1	- 0	- 0	- 0	- -	- -	- -	- -	**67** 3	**0** 16	**54** 24	**100** 3
Lifecare Medical Center, Roseau, MN	- 0	**100** 2	**100** 2	**100** 2	**0** 1	- 0	- 0	**99** 82	**6** 85	- 0	**33** 6	**82** 11	**100** 16	**97** 30	**100** 2
Madelia Community Hospital, Madelia, MN	- 0	**100** 1	- 0	- 0	- 0	- 0	- 0	- -	- -	- -	- -	**82** 11	**85** 13	**100** 23	- 0
Madison Hospital, Madison, MN	- 0	- 0	- 0	- 0	- 0	- 0	- 0	- 0	- 0	- 0	- 0	**0** 1	**40** 5	**22** 9	- 0
Mahnomen Health Center, Mahnomen, MN	- 0	- 0	- 0	- 0	- 0	- 0	- 0	- 0	- 0	- 0	- 0	**0** 1	**33** 3	**33** 3	**100** 1
Maple Grove Hospital, Maple Grove, MN	- 0	- 0	- 0	- 0	- 0	- 0	- 0	- -	- -	- -	- -	- 0	- 0	- 0	- 0
Mayo Clinic - Methodist Hospital, Rochester, MN	- 0	- 0	- 0	- 0	- 0	- 0	- 0	- 0	- 0	- 0	- 0	**100** 1	**50** 12	**100** 12	**100** 1
Mayo Clinic - Saint Marys Hospital, Rochester, MN	**100** 45	**100** 128	**100** 302	**100** 294	- 0	**95** 22	**100** 75	**100** 2	**8** 2	- 0	- 0	**99** 80	**94** 207	**100** 277	**100** 24
Meeker Memorial Hospital, Litchfield, MN	**100** 1	- 0	**100** 1	**100** 1	- 0	- 0	- 0	**75** 8	**14** 8	- 0	- 0	**91** 11	**36** 22	**63** 41	**44** 9
Mercy Hospital, Coon Rapids, MN	**100** 61	**99** 326	**100** 439	**99** 437	**100** 1	**91** 91	**100** 174	**83** 6	**4** 7	- 0	- 0	**99** 89	**95** 254	**100** 306	**100** 58
Mercy Hospital & Health Care Center, Moose Lake, MN	- 0	**100** 4	**100** 1	**100** 1	- 0	- 0	- 0	- 0	- 0	- 0	- 0	- 0	**73** 11	**93** 15	- 0
Mille Lacs Health System, Onamia, MN	- 0	**100** 1	**100** 1	**100** 1	- 0	- 0	- 0	- -	- -	- -	- -	**89** 9	**96** 25	**90** 30	**67** 3
Minneapolis VA Medical Center, Minneapolis, MN	**100** 17	**98** 132	**100** 143	**100** 139	- 0	**50** 10	**100** 33	- -	- -	- -	- -	**100** 56	**95** 175	**100** 201	**100** 20
Minnesota Valley Health Center, Le Sueur, MN	- 0	**100** 1	**100** 1	**100** 1	- 0	- 0	- 0	- 0	- 0	- 0	- 0	**100** 1	**0** 1	**100** 2	- 0
Municipal Hospital and Granite Manor, Granite Falls, MN	- 0	**67** 3	**50** 2	**100** 3	- 0	- 0	- 0	**100** 19	**19** 18	**143** 1	**100** 1	- 0	**100** 4	**91** 11	- 0
Murray County Memorial Hospital, Slayton, MN	- 0	- 0	- 0	- 0	- 0	- 0	- 0	- 0	- 0	- 0	- 0	- 0	**0** 2	**50** 4	- 0
Naeve Hospital, Albert Lea, MN	**78** 9	**98** 43	**94** 36	**94** 36	- 0	- 0	**100** 2	**94** 129	**7** 130	**80** 4	**50** 4	**100** 18	**57** 49	**92** 73	**100** 10
New River Medical Center, Monticello, MN	- 0	**100** 3	**100** 1	**100** 1	- 0	- 0	- 0	- 0	- 0	- 0	- 0	**100** 9	**95** 38	**98** 48	**100** 4
New Ulm Medical Center, New Ulm, MN	**100** 1	**80** 10	**100** 5	**100** 4	- 0	- 0	- 0	**100** 48	**4** 46	**260** 1	**75** 4	**91** 11	**97** 39	**100** 62	**100** 8

NOTE: The first number in each column (boldface) is the score, the second number is the number of patients; Please refer to the main entry for footnotes; (a) 100-299
*MEASURES: **Heart Attack Care:** 1. ACE Inhibitor or ARB for LVSD; 2. Aspirin at Arrival; 3. Aspirin at Discharge; 4. Beta Blocker at Discharge; 5. Fibrinolytic Medication Timing; 6. PCI Within 90 Minutes of Arrival; 7. Smoking Cessation Advice; **Chest Pain/Possible Heart Attack Care:** 8. Aspirin at Arrival; 9. Median Time to ECG (minutes); 10. Median Time to Transfer (minutes); 11. Fibrinolytic Medication Timing; **Heart Failure Care:** 12. ACE Inhibitor or ARB for LVSD; 13. Discharge Instructions; 14. Evaluation of LVS Function; 15. Smoking Cessation Advice*

Hospital	Heart Attack Care							Chest Pain/Possible Heart Attack Care				Heart Failure Care			
	1	2	3	4	5	6	7	8	9	10	11	12	13	14	15
North Country Regional Hospital, Bemidji, MN	**100** 3	**100** 13	**100** 9	**100** 9	- 0	- 0	**100** 1	**94** 125	**8** 127	**545** 2	**89** 9	**89** 28	**76** 70	**99** 84	**100** 23
North Memorial Medical Center, Robbinsdale, MN	**100** 49	**100** 263	**100** 271	**99** 277	- 0	**100** 62	**95** 79	- 0	- 0	- 0	- 0	**99** 77	**79** 229	**99** 296	**93** 43
North Valley Health Center, Warren, MN	- 0	- 0	- 0	- 0	- 0	- 0	- 0	- -	- -	- -	- -	**100** 2	**50** 2	**50** 4	- 0
Northern Pines Medical Center, Aurora, MN	- 0	- 0	- 0	- 0	- 0	- 0	- 0	- 0	- 0	- 0	- 0	**100** 1	**17** 6	**33** 9	**0** 1
Northfield Hospital, Northfield, MN	**100** 1	**92** 12	**80** 10	**89** 9	- 0	- 0	**100** 1	**99** 73	**2** 75	**57** 9	**50** 2	**73** 11	**67** 30	**98** 47	**75** 8
Olmsted Medical Center, Rochester, MN	- 0	- 0	- 0	- 0	- 0	- 0	- 0	**92** 59	**7** 60	- 0	- 0	**100** 6	**71** 14	**95** 20	**67** 3
Ortonville Area Health Services, Ortonville, MN	**100** 1	**100** 4	**100** 3	**75** 4	- 0	- 0	- 0	**100** 3	**4** 4	- 0	**100** 1	**83** 6	**88** 8	**71** 14	**50** 2
Owatonna Hospital, Owatonna, MN	- 0	**100** 10	**100** 8	**100** 8	- 0	- 0	**100** 1	**94** 110	**8** 111	**62** 4	**80** 5	**100** 8	**89** 35	**100** 55	**100** 4
Park Nicollet Methodist Hospital, Saint Louis Park, MN	**98** 50	**100** 301	**100** 337	**99** 337	- 0	**94** 53	**100** 82	**100** 5	**16** 5	- 0	- 0	**98** 133	**91** 280	**99** 386	**100** 47
Paynesville Area Hospital, Paynesville, MN	- 0	**100** 2	**100** 2	**100** 2	- 0	- 0	- 0	**100** 18	**5** 20	**32** 4	- 0	**100** 6	**62** 13	**100** 17	- 0
Perham Memorial Hospital, Perham, MN	- 0	**100** 11	**100** 9	**100** 10	- 0	- 0	- 0	**98** 48	**7** 48	- 0	**75** 4	**100** 2	**89** 9	**62** 21	**50** 2
Phillips Eye Institute, Minneapolis, MN	- 0	- 0	- 0	- 0	- 0	- 0	- 0	- 0	- 0	- 0	- 0	- 0	- 0	- 0	- 0
Pipestone County Medical Center, Pipestone, MN	**100** 1	**100** 4	**75** 4	**100** 4	**100** 1	- 0	- 0	- 0	- 0	- 0	- 0	**75** 8	**55** 11	**89** 19	- 0
Prairie Ridge Hospital and Health Services, Elbow Lake, MN	- 0	- 0	- 0	- 0	- 0	- 0	- 0	- -	- -	- -	- -	**86** 7	**14** 7	**70** 10	**0** 1
Queen of Peace Hospital, New Prague, MN	- 0	**100** 5	**100** 1	**100** 2	- 0	- 0	- 0	**100** 27	**8** 29	**65** 4	- -	**88** 8	**95** 20	**94** 35	**100** 2
Rainy Lake Medical Center, Int'l Falls, MN	- 0	**0** 1	- 0	- 0	- 0	- 0	- 0	- -	- -	- -	- -	- 0	**67** 6	**14** 7	- 0
Red Lake Hospital, Redlake, MN	- 0	- 0	- 0	- 0	- 0	- 0	- 0	- -	- -	- -	- -	**100** 3	**100** 7	**100** 6	- 0
Redwood Area Hospital, Redwood Falls, MN	**0** 1	**100** 5	**100** 3	**67** 3	- 0	- 0	- 0	- 0	- 0	- 0	- 0	**80** 5	**90** 10	**80** 20	**100** 1
Regina Medical Center, Hastings, MN	- 0	**100** 12	**100** 11	**100** 12	- 0	- 0	- 0	**93** 185	**7** 191	**26** 15	- 0	**100** 14	**95** 37	**100** 52	**100** 5
Regions Hospital, Saint Paul, MN	**100** 65	**100** 307	**99** 417	**99** 419	- 0	**98** 61	**100** 151	**80** 5	**9** 5	- 0	- 0	**99** 115	**93** 309	**100** 381	**100** 95
Renville County Hospital and Clinics, Olivia, MN	**100** 1	**100** 2	**50** 2	**50** 2	**100** 1	- 0	- 0	- 0	- 0	- 0	- 0	**100** 2	**30** 10	**58** 19	**50** 2
Rice Memorial Hospital, Willmar, MN	**100** 1	**100** 19	**92** 12	**93** 14	- 0	- 0	- 0	**97** 75	**8** 77	**56** 9	- 0	**82** 17	**83** 36	**97** 58	**75** 4
Ridgeview Medical Center, Waconia, MN	**100** 7	**100** 33	**96** 24	**100** 24	- 0	- 0	**100** 3	**92** 63	**10** 59	**42** 34	- 0	**91** 34	**96** 68	**100** 113	**93** 15
River's Edge Hospital & Clinic, Saint Peter, MN	- 0	**100** 5	**100** 3	**100** 3	- 0	- 0	- 0	**97** 76	**5** 77	**36** 3	- 0	**100** 3	**33** 6	**83** 12	**100** 1
Riverview Hospital, Crookston, MN	- 0	**100** 4	**75** 4	**100** 2	- 0	- 0	- 0	**80** 20	**15** 21	**49** 3	- 0	**75** 12	**45** 20	**87** 38	**50** 2
Riverwood Healthcare Center, Aitkin, MN	**100** 2	**100** 3	**100** 2	**100** 2	- 0	- 0	- 0	- -	- -	- -	- -	**100** 5	**70** 23	**92** 24	**100** 1
Saint Cloud Hospital, Saint Cloud, MN	**93** 92	**100** 213	**100** 664	**99** 640	- 0	**87** 62	**100** 218	**92** 12	**11** 13	- 0	- 0	**97** 229	**89** 499	**100** 679	**100** 72
Saint Cloud VA Medical Center, Saint Cloud, MN	- 0	- 0	- 0	- 0	- 0	- 0	- 0	- -	- -	- -	- -	- 0	- 0	- 0	- 0
Saint Elizabeth Medical Center, Wabasha, MN	**100** 1	**100** 2	**100** 2	**100** 2	- 0	- 0	- 0	- -	- -	- -	- -	**100** 5	**85** 13	**92** 13	**100** 1
Saint Francis Healthcare Campus, Breckenridge, MN	- 0	**100** 9	**88** 8	**67** 6	- 0	- 0	- 0	- 0	- 0	- 0	- 0	**100** 3	**86** 36	**95** 42	**67** 3
Saint Francis Regional Medical Center, Shakopee, MN	- 0	**100** 15	**100** 6	**100** 6	- 0	- 0	**100** 2	**100** 98	**6** 100	**80** 2	- 0	**100** 25	**96** 73	**99** 93	**100** 11
Saint Gabriels Hospital, Little Falls, MN	**100** 1	**100** 2	**100** 2	**100** 3	- 0	- 0	- 0	**100** 32	**6** 33	**38** 10	- 0	**100** 6	**100** 16	**90** 30	**100** 2
Saint James Medical Center-Mayo Health Sys, Saint James, MN	- 0	- 0	- 0	- 0	- 0	- 0	- 0	- 0	- 0	- 0	- 0	**100** 1	**60** 5	**75** 8	**50** 2
Saint Joseph's Hospital, Saint Paul, MN	**100** 60	**100** 152	**99** 327	**99** 315	- 0	**100** 24	**100** 94	**50** 2	**7** 3	- 0	- 0	**100** 96	**83** 175	**100** 234	**100** 34
Saint Josephs Area Health Services, Park Rapids, MN	- 0	**75** 4	**50** 2	**0** 1	**0** 1	- 0	- 0	**95** 42	**13** 43	**33** 1	**0** 2	**100** 8	**91** 23	**93** 30	**100** 4
Saint Lukes Hospital, Duluth, MN	**100** 18	**100** 122	**99** 165	**99** 164	- 0	**96** 24	**96** 55	- 0	- 0	- 0	- 0	**96** 75	**78** 147	**99** 199	**97** 35
Saint Marys Regional Health Center, Detroit Lakes, MN	**100** 1	**100** 12	**100** 9	**100** 9	- 0	- 0	- 0	**99** 77	**7** 81	**44** 5	**17** 6	**50** 2	**89** 9	**100** 19	**100** 4
Saint Michaels Hospital & Nursing Home, Sauk Centre, MN	- 0	- 0	- 0	- 0	- 0	- 0	- 0	- 0	- 0	- 0	- 0	**0** 1	**43** 7	**67** 9	- 0
Sanford Canby Medical Center, Canby, MN	- 0	**50** 2	**50** 2	**100** 2	- 0	- 0	- 0	**80** 5	**4** 6	- 0	- 0	**100** 1	**33** 3	**80** 5	- 0
Sanford Jackson Medical Center, Jackson, MN	- 0	**100** 1	**100** 1	**100** 1	- 0	- 0	- 0	**100** 14	**8** 15	- 0	**20** 5	- 0	**100** 1	**50** 4	- 0
Sanford Luverne Medical Center, Luverne, MN	**67** 3	**86** 7	**67** 6	**83** 6	- 0	- 0	- 0	- 0	- 0	- 0	- 0	**0** 2	**100** 6	**73** 15	- 0
Sanford Medical Center Thief River Falls, Thief River Falls, MN	**100** 1	**80** 5	**67** 3	**75** 4	- 0	- 0	- 0	- -	- -	- -	- -	**88** 8	**56** 18	**90** 40	**100** 2
Sanford Tracy, Tracy, MN	- 0	- 0	- 0	- 0	- 0	- 0	- 0	- -	- -	- -	- -	**50** 2	**50** 2	**50** 4	**100** 1
Sanford Westbrook Medical Center, Westbrook, MN	- 0	- 0	- 0	- 0	- 0	- 0	- 0	- 0	- 0	- 0	- 0	- 0	**0** 1	**100** 4	**0** 1
Sanford Worthington Medical Center, Worthington, MN	- 0	**100** 3	**100** 1	**50** 2	- 0	- 0	- 0	**97** 61	**7** 62	**100** 3	**100** 3	**100** 5	**79** 19	**73** 26	**0** 1
Sibley Medical Center, Arlington, MN	- 0	- 0	- 0	- 0	- 0	- 0	- 0	- 0	- 0	- 0	- 0	- 0	- 0	- 0	- 0
Sleepy Eye Municipal Hospital, Sleepy Eye, MN	- 0	- 0	- 0	- 0	- 0	- 0	- 0	- 0	- 0	- 0	- 0	**100** 1	**64** 11	**41** 17	**100** 1
Springfield Medical Center Mayo Health System, Springfield, MN	**50** 2	**67** 3	**67** 3	**100** 3	- 0	- 0	- 0	**100** 1	**5** 1	- 0	- 0	**100** 3	**40** 15	**86** 22	**50** 2
Stevens Community Medical Center, Morris, MN	**50** 2	**89** 9	**86** 7	**83** 6	- 0	- 0	- 0	- 0	- 0	- 0	- 0	**67** 6	**24** 21	**44** 36	- 0
Swift County Benson Hospital, Benson, MN	- 0	**50** 2	**100** 1	**100** 1	- 0	- 0	- 0	- 0	- 0	- 0	- 0	**100** 1	**100** 2	**50** 14	**0** 1
Tri County Hospital, Wadena, MN	**100** 1	**100** 5	**100** 4	**100** 5	- 0	- 0	- 0	**71** 24	**9** 25	- 0	- 0	**60** 5	**85** 34	**78** 50	**83** 6
Tyler Healthcare Center, Tyler, MN	- 0	**100** 1	**100** 1	**100** 1	**0** 1	- 0	- 0	**100** 4	**27** 4	- 0	- 0	**0** 1	**0** 1	**60** 5	- 0
United Hospital, Saint Paul, MN	**95** 61	**99** 296	**100** 427	**99** 399	- 0	**94** 80	**99** 134	**100** 2	**22** 3	- 0	- 0	**99** 168	**93** 372	**100** 478	**99** 73
United Hospital District, Blue Earth, MN	**50** 2	**100** 4	**100** 4	**100** 3	- 0	- 0	- 0	**93** 15	**4** 15	**118** 2	**50** 2	**100** 2	**38** 13	**78** 18	**0** 1
Unity Hospital, Fridley, MN	- 0	**100** 40	**100** 20	**100** 23	- 0	- 0	**100** 3	**99** 88	**4** 88	**32** 15	- 0	**100** 37	**99** 141	**100** 160	**95** 21
University Medical Center - Mesabi/Mesaba Clinics, Hibbing, MN	**83** 6	**93** 27	**95** 20	**89** 18	- 0	- 0	**67** 3	**100** 87	**7** 90	**66** 7	**100** 1	**97** 30	**84** 69	**96** 90	**100** 15
University of Minnesota Medical Ctr-Fairview, Minneapolis, MN	**100** 34	**100** 110	**99** 198	**99** 188	- 0	**91** 11	**100** 71	**100** 1	**10** 1	- 0	- 0	**98** 117	**97** 264	**100** 322	**100** 53
Virginia Regional Medical Center, Virginia, MN	**100** 2	**100** 7	**100** 6	**83** 6	- 0	- 0	- 0	**96** 93	**10** 95	**49** 9	**0** 1	**82** 11	**76** 21	**96** 49	**67** 3
Waseca Medical Center - Mayo Health System, Waseca, MN	- 0	- 0	- 0	- 0	- 0	- 0	- 0	- 0	- 0	- 0	- 0	**100** 1	**73** 11	**100** 12	**100** 1
Wheaton Community Hospital, Wheaton, MN	- 0	**100** 1	**100** 1	**100** 1	- 0	- 0	- 0	- 0	- 0	- 0	- 0	- 0	- 0	- 0	- 0
Windom Area Hospital, Windom, MN	- 0	**100** 2	**100** 2	**100** 2	**0** 1	- 0	- 0	**100** 36	**19** 37	- 0	**0** 1	**88** 8	**73** 15	**52** 21	**67** 3
Winona Health Services, Winona, MN	**100** 3	**95** 20	**93** 14	**100** 14	- 0	- 0	- 0	**99** 90	**6** 95	**40** 1	**100** 3	**100** 25	**90** 49	**100** 82	**100** 12
MISSOURI															
Advanced Healthcare Medical Center, Ellington, MO	- 0	- 0	- 0	- 0	- 0	- 0	- 0	- -	- -	- -	- -	**100** 1	**67** 9	**27** 15	**100** 1
Audrain Medical Center, Mexico, MO	**100** 5	**100** 43	**100** 41	**95** 42	- 0	**93** 14	**100** 22	**100** 12	**8** 12	**105** 1	- 0	**98** 55	**90** 122	**99** 165	**100** 25
Barnes Jewish Hospital, Saint Louis, MO	**97** 135	**99** 408	**99** 629	**99** 583	- 0	**98** 57	**100** 217	**67** 3	**8** 3	- 0	- 0	**97** 382	**92** 731	**100** 817	**100** 228
Barnes-Jewish St Peters Hospital, Saint Peters, MO	**100** 24	**98** 179	**98** 183	**98** 186	- 0	**86** 29	**100** 61	**95** 19	**1** 19	**1646** 1	- 0	**100** 28	**92** 122	**98** 154	**100** 15

NOTE: The first number in each column (boldface) is the score, the second number is the number of patients; Please refer to the main entry for footnotes; (a) 100-299

*MEASURES: **Heart Attack Care:** 1. ACE Inhibitor or ARB for LVSD; 2. Aspirin at Arrival; 3. Aspirin at Discharge; 4. Beta Blocker at Discharge; 5. Fibrinolytic Medication Timing; 6. PCI Within 90 Minutes of Arrival; 7. Smoking Cessation Advice; **Chest Pain/Possible Heart Attack Care:** 8. Aspirin at Arrival; 9. Median Time to ECG (minutes); 10. Median Time to Transfer (minutes); 11. Fibrinolytic Medication Timing; **Heart Failure Care:** 12. ACE Inhibitor or ARB for LVSD; 13. Discharge Instructions; 14. Evaluation of LVS Function; 15. Smoking Cessation Advice*

Hospital	Heart Attack Care							Chest Pain/Possible Heart Attack Care				Heart Failure Care			
	1	2	3	4	5	6	7	8	9	10	11	12	13	14	15
Barnes-Jewish West County Hospital, Creve Coeur, MO	**100** 1	**100** 9	**100** 7	**100** 6	- 0	- 0	**100** 1	**97** 64	**8** 64	**86** 8	- 0	**100** 25	**90** 96	**99** 109	**100** 7
Barton County Memorial Hospital, Lamar, MO	**100** 1	**100** 8	**83** 6	**100** 6	- 0	- 0	- 0	- -	- -	- -	- -	- 0	**55** 20	**39** 33	- 0
Bates County Memorial Hospital, Butler, MO	- 0	**100** 3	**100** 3	**0** 3	- 0	- 0	- 0	**91** 53	**18** 56	**55** 1	**0** 1	**33** 3	**92** 49	**45** 91	**92** 12
Boone Hospital Center, Columbia, MO	**97** 117	**100** 219	**100** 469	**99** 453	- 0	**93** 54	**100** 152	**100** 1	**28** 2	- 0	- 0	**95** 222	**91** 429	**99** 513	**100** 68
Bothwell Regional Health Center, Sedalia, MO	**93** 14	**97** 58	**100** 34	**94** 36	**0** 4	- 0	**100** 10	**95** 85	**19** 86	**81** 10	- 0	**87** 52	**83** 133	**99** 164	**100** 22
Callaway Community Hospital, Fulton, MO	- 0	**100** 1	- 0	- 0	- 0	- 0	- 0	**92** 75	**8** 77	**80** 5	- 0	**100** 4	**86** 21	**94** 32	**100** 4
Cameron Regional Medical Center, Cameron, MO	**0** 1	**89** 9	**100** 7	**100** 8	- 0	- 0	**100** 2	**98** 99	**9** 105	**65** 7	- 0	**67** 3	**84** 25	**79** 52	**83** 6
Capital Region Medical Center, Jefferson City, MO	**100** 27	**100** 143	**99** 137	**98** 132	- 0	**100** 25	**100** 41	**73** 11	**1** 11	- 0	- 0	**100** 70	**94** 176	**100** 225	**100** 33
Carroll County Memorial Hospital, Carrollton, MO	- 0	- 0	- 0	- 0	- 0	- 0	- 0	- -	- -	- -	- -	- 0	- 0	- 0	- 0
Cass Medical Center, Harrisonville, MO	**100** 1	**75** 4	**100** 3	**67** 3	- 0	- 0	- 0	- -	- -	- -	- -	**69** 16	**75** 40	**92** 50	**83** 6
Centerpoint Medical Center of Independence, Independence, MO	**100** 54	**100** 313	**100** 323	**99** 292	- 0	**93** 68	**100** 117	**100** 4	**8** 4	- 0	- 0	**100** 122	**96** 325	**100** 424	**100** 93
Childrens Mercy Hospital, Kansas City, MO	- -	- -	- -	- -	- -	- -	- -	- -	- -	- -	- -	- -	- -	- -	- -
Christian Hospital Northeast, Saint Louis, MO	**99** 91	**99** 302	**100** 409	**100** 393	- 0	**94** 33	**100** 154	**79** 28	**4** 30	- 0	- 0	**97** 214	**81** 556	**99** 655	**99** 144
Christian Hospital Northwest, Florissant, MO	- 0	- 0	- 0	- 0	- 0	- 0	- 0	**96** 322	**9** 333	**69** 5	- 0	- 0	- 0	- 0	- 0
Citizens Memorial Hospital, Bolivar, MO	**100** 2	**86** 35	**86** 35	**100** 34	- 0	**67** 3	**100** 9	**98** 86	**24** 96	**94** 4	**0** 2	**95** 20	**91** 44	**85** 73	**100** 16
Columbia Missouri VA Medical Center, Columbia, MO	**100** 5	**100** 49	**100** 48	**96** 51	- 0	**57** 7	**100** 15	- -	- -	- -	- -	**100** 48	**100** 137	**99** 153	**100** 23
Community Hospital Association, Fairfax, MO	- 0	- 0	- 0	- 0	- 0	- 0	- 0	- -	- -	- -	- -	**25** 4	**71** 7	**83** 12	- 0
Cooper County Memorial Hospital, Boonville, MO	- 0	**100** 5	**75** 4	**100** 3	- 0	- 0	**0** 1	**96** 56	**8** 58	**34** 8	- 0	**100** 10	**100** 13	**87** 31	**80** 5
Cox Medical Center, Springfield, MO	**93** 94	**99** 422	**98** 519	**99** 502	**0** 2	**89** 74	**100** 226	**80** 5	**2** 5	- 0	- 0	**95** 171	**97** 415	**100** 496	**100** 172
Cox Monett Hospital, Monett, MO	**100** 1	**100** 4	**100** 2	**100** 3	- 0	- 0	- 0	- -	- -	- -	- -	**88** 8	**100** 16	**100** 18	**100** 1
Des Peres Hospital, Saint Louis, MO	**100** 21	**99** 73	**99** 178	**99** 176	- 0	**89** 19	**100** 64	**100** 1	**4** 1	- 0	- 0	**98** 83	**93** 205	**100** 256	**100** 46
Fitzgibbon Memorial Hospital, Marshall, MO	**100** 1	**100** 2	**100** 1	**67** 3	- 0	- 0	- 0	**87** 126	**12** 132	**45** 8	**50** 4	**75** 4	**58** 38	**66** 50	**83** 6
Forest Park Hospital, Saint Louis, MO	**100** 1	**83** 6	**100** 1	**100** 1	- 0	- 0	- 0	**96** 24	**20** 25	- 0	- 0	**72** 29	**67** 63	**88** 85	**100** 26
Freeman Health System - Freeman West, Joplin, MO	**100** 51	**100** 205	**99** 371	**98** 312	- 0	**85** 52	**99** 192	**100** 2	**6** 2	- 0	- 0	**95** 81	**73** 223	**99** 267	**93** 54
Freeman Neosho Hospital, Neosho, MO	**100** 2	**100** 3	**100** 2	**100** 2	- 0	- 0	- 0	- -	- -	- -	- -	**94** 18	**87** 30	**100** 49	**100** 9
Golden Valley Memorial Hospital, Clinton, MO	**100** 1	**100** 9	**67** 6	**80** 5	- 0	- 0	**100** 2	**96** 135	**4** 141	**42** 3	**0** 3	**94** 31	**76** 55	**99** 107	**100** 16
Hannibal Regional Hospital, Hannibal, MO	**89** 18	**99** 102	**100** 97	**99** 96	- 0	**86** 35	**100** 33	**93** 14	**8** 15	- 0	- 0	**91** 58	**98** 129	**98** 172	**100** 40
Harrison County Community Hospital, Bethany, MO	- 0	- 0	- 0	- 0	- 0	- 0	- 0	- -	- -	- -	- -	**0** 2	**57** 7	**75** 8	**100** 1
Heartland Regional Medical Center, Saint Joseph, MO	**100** 36	**100** 299	**100** 391	**100** 384	- 0	**96** 52	**100** 160	**100** 8	**6** 8	- 0	- 0	**100** 128	**100** 297	**100** 388	**100** 66
Hedrick Medical Center, Chillicothe, MO	- 0	**100** 4	**100** 3	**100** 2	- 0	- 0	- 0	**96** 179	**9** 186	**70** 11	**50** 2	**100** 2	**88** 16	**92** 26	**100** 2
Hermann Area District Hospital, Hermann, MO	- 0	- 0	- 0	- 0	- 0	- 0	- 0	- -	- -	- -	- -	- 0	**29** 7	**65** 20	- 0
Jefferson Regional Medical Center, Crystal City, MO	**97** 38	**99** 200	**100** 260	**100** 252	- 0	**95** 43	**100** 110	**100** 30	**6** 32	- 0	- 0	**100** 108	**96** 297	**99** 419	**100** 91
Kansas City VA Medical Center, Kansas City, MO	**100** 4	**89** 28	**100** 22	**100** 18	- 0	**0** 1	**100** 8	- -	- -	- -	- -	**95** 74	**93** 177	**100** 202	**100** 55
Lafayette Regional Health Center, Lexington, MO	**100** 1	**100** 2	**100** 2	**100** 2	- 0	- 0	- 0	**100** 43	**6** 42	**46** 2	- 0	**100** 2	**100** 6	**100** 14	**50** 2
Lake Regional Health System, Osage Beach, MO	**96** 28	**98** 220	**99** 207	**98** 208	- 0	**74** 43	**100** 94	**100** 14	**8** 14	- 0	- 0	**92** 80	**85** 208	**100** 248	**97** 58
Lee's Summit Medical Center, Lee's Summit, MO	**100** 13	**100** 104	**100** 95	**100** 90	- 0	**97** 32	**100** 32	**100** 3	**7** 4	- 0	- 0	**100** 27	**79** 58	**99** 86	**100** 15
Liberty Hospital, Liberty, MO	**89** 27	**96** 111	**98** 119	**96** 112	- 0	**80** 15	**100** 39	**93** 58	**10** 59	**40** 16	- 0	**90** 98	**75** 208	**97** 272	**100** 52
Lincoln County Medical Center, Troy, MO	- 0	- 0	- 0	- 0	- 0	- 0	- 0	- -	- -	- -	- -	**100** 4	**72** 18	**96** 28	**100** 2
McCune-Brooks Hospital, Carthage, MO	**100** 1	**43** 7	**100** 4	**100** 3	- 0	- 0	- 0	- -	- -	- -	- -	**78** 9	**84** 25	**81** 36	**100** 4
Mineral Area Regional Medical Center, Farmington, MO	- 0	**100** 4	**100** 3	**100** 3	- 0	- 0	**100** 1	**99** 90	**7** 94	**49** 6	**12** 8	**76** 25	**71** 82	**95** 119	**96** 23
Missouri Baptist Hospital Sullivan, Sullivan, MO	**100** 5	**100** 15	**92** 13	**100** 13	- 0	- 0	**100** 2	**94** 163	**3** 163	**49** 10	- 0	**100** 17	**96** 55	**100** 78	**100** 12
Missouri Baptist Medical Center, Town and Country, MO	**98** 96	**99** 229	**100** 466	**100** 453	- 0	**94** 32	**100** 128	**0** 2	**0** 2	- 0	- 0	**92** 198	**87** 539	**100** 716	**100** 69
Missouri Delta Medical Center, Sikeston, MO	**89** 9	**87** 31	**88** 25	**88** 26	- 0	- 0	**100** 10	**95** 100	**12** 104	**64** 6	**50** 6	**92** 75	**84** 172	**98** 223	**100** 49
Missouri Southern Healthcare, Dexter, MO	- 0	**93** 15	**64** 11	**91** 11	- 0	- 0	- 0	**90** 90	**13** 94	**119** 6	**50** 4	**90** 10	**36** 72	**46** 93	**93** 15
Moberly Regional Medical Center, Moberly, MO	- 0	**100** 25	**100** 17	**100** 17	- 0	- 0	**100** 1	**97** 114	**9** 121	**64** 13	**40** 5	**100** 16	**93** 41	**99** 70	**100** 14
Nevada Regional Medical Center, Nevada, MO	**100** 1	**75** 4	**67** 3	**100** 3	- 0	- 0	- 0	**96** 97	**10** 99	**195** 3	**10** 10	**73** 15	**83** 35	**87** 46	**100** 5
North Kansas City Hospital, North Kansas City, MO	**98** 120	**100** 293	**99** 369	**99** 367	- 0	**98** 80	**100** 155	- 0	- 0	- 0	- 0	**94** 132	**96** 367	**97** 411	**100** 66
Northeast Regional Medical Center, Kirksville, MO	- 0	**100** 12	**100** 9	**89** 9	- 0	- 0	**100** 3	**100** 42	**3** 43	**192** 5	**75** 4	**100** 10	**100** 31	**98** 46	**100** 8
Northwest Medical Center, Albany, MO	- 0	- 0	- 0	- 0	- 0	- 0	- 0	- -	- -	- -	- -	- 0	- 0	- 0	- 0
Ozarks Community Hospital, Springfield, MO	- 0	**60** 5	**33** 3	**67** 3	- 0	- 0	- 0	**92** 24	**22** 26	**108** 2	**0** 1	**60** 5	**22** 9	**88** 26	**100** 3
Ozarks Medical Center, West Plains, MO	**70** 10	**99** 100	**96** 95	**94** 96	**100** 1	**84** 19	**100** 35	**93** 74	**11** 80	**121** 2	**33** 6	**83** 30	**90** 79	**96** 99	**100** 17
Parkland Health Center, Farmington, MO	**100** 3	**96** 24	**100** 13	**83** 12	- 0	- 0	**100** 1	**97** 256	**8** 266	**54** 25	- 0	**97** 32	**80** 81	**100** 111	**100** 23
Pemiscot Memorial Hospital, Hayti, MO	**0** 1	**70** 10	**14** 7	**29** 7	- 0	- 0	**0** 2	**100** 17	**30** 17	- 0	**33** 6	**48** 21	**16** 115	**62** 137	**61** 36
Perry County Memorial Hospital, Perryville, MO	- 0	**100** 3	**100** 2	**100** 2	- 0	- 0	- 0	- -	- -	- -	- -	**100** 3	**57** 14	**83** 23	**100** 3
Pershing Memorial Hospital, Brookfield, MO	- 0	- 0	- 0	- 0	- 0	- 0	- 0	- -	- -	- -	- -	- 0	**64** 11	**26** 19	- 0
Phelps County Regional Medical Center, Rolla, MO	**100** 10	**94** 68	**95** 42	**95** 43	- 0	- 0	**100** 9	**96** 151	**12** 156	**135** 11	**0** 5	**96** 81	**90** 141	**97** 193	**100** 37
Pike County Memorial Hospital, Louisiana, MO	- 0	- 0	**100** 1	**0** 1	- 0	- 0	- 0	- -	- -	- -	- -	**100** 6	**100** 21	**100** 31	**100** 10
Poplar Bluff Regional Medical Center, Poplar Bluff, MO	**100** 33	**99** 107	**100** 130	**100** 122	- 0	**100** 29	**100** 70	**89** 9	**6** 9	- 0	- 0	**99** 91	**100** 269	**99** 330	**100** 60
Poplar Bluff VA Medical Center, Poplar Bluff, MO	- 0	**100** 3	**100** 2	**100** 3	**100** 3	- 0	- 0	- -	- -	- -	- -	**90** 21	**100** 96	**97** 107	**100** 20
Progress West Healthcare Center, O'Fallon, MO	**100** 1	**100** 13	**100** 6	**100** 6	- 0	- 0	- 0	**94** 33	**4** 33	**33** 3	- 0	**100** 21	**91** 46	**97** 58	**100** 9
Putnam County Memorial Hospital, Unionville, MO	- 0	**0** 1	**0** 1	**0** 1	- 0	- 0	- 0	- -	- -	- -	- -	**89** 9	**90** 10	**80** 25	**50** 2
Ray County Memorial Hospital, Richmond, MO	- 0	**0** 1	**0** 1	**0** 1	- 0	- 0	- 0	- -	- -	- -	- -	**50** 8	**79** 19	**88** 33	**67** 6
Research Belton Hospital, Belton, MO	- 0	**100** 8	**100** 8	**100** 7	- 0	- 0	**100** 1	**100** 78	**5** 81	**35** 5	- 0	**100** 6	**96** 25	**100** 33	**100** 5
Research Medical Center, Kansas City, MO	**100** 44	**100** 143	**100** 242	**100** 225	- 0	**100** 29	**99** 97	**100** 3	**5** 3	- 0	- 0	**99** 121	**98** 258	**100** 310	**100** 93
Ripley County Memorial Hospital, Doniphan, MO	**0** 1	**100** 1	**100** 1	**100** 1	- 0	- 0	- 0	**91** 44	**17** 46	**79** 2	- 0	**50** 4	**74** 27	**57** 30	**100** 3
SAC-Osage Hospital, Osceola, MO	- 0	- 0	- 0	- 0	- 0	- 0	- 0	**47** 19	**7** 17	**90** 3	**33** 3	**100** 1	**50** 16	**4** 24	**67** 6
Saint Alexius Hospital, Saint Louis, MO	**100** 3	**90** 21	**100** 9	**89** 9	- 0	- 0	**100** 5	**75** 4	**23** 4	**37** 1	- 0	**88** 40	**73** 112	**100** 146	**100** 41

NOTE: The first number in each column (boldface) is the score, the second number is the number of patients; Please refer to the main entry for footnotes; (a) 100-299
*MEASURES: **Heart Attack Care:** 1. ACE Inhibitor or ARB for LVSD; 2. Aspirin at Arrival; 3. Aspirin at Discharge; 4. Beta Blocker at Discharge; 5. Fibrinolytic Medication Timing; 6. PCI Within 90 Minutes of Arrival; 7. Smoking Cessation Advice; **Chest Pain/Possible Heart Attack Care:** 8. Aspirin at Arrival; 9. Median Time to ECG (minutes); 10. Median Time to Transfer (minutes); 11. Fibrinolytic Medication Timing; **Heart Failure Care:** 12. ACE Inhibitor or ARB for LVSD; 13. Discharge Instructions; 14. Evaluation of LVS Function; 15. Smoking Cessation Advice*

Hospital	Heart Attack Care							Chest Pain/Possible Heart Attack Care				Heart Failure Care			
	1	2	3	4	5	6	7	8	9	10	11	12	13	14	15
Saint Anthony's Medical Center, Saint Louis, MO	82 61	98 317	96 312	97 309	- 0	86 66	91 112	100 6	10 6	- 0	- 0	79 126	68 244	98 327	89 45
Saint Francis Hospital, Maryville, MO	- 0	100 4	100 2	100 3	- 0	- 0	- 0	93 71	6 74	60 2	- 0	100 14	100 19	100 42	100 2
Saint Francis Hospital, Mountain View, MO	- 0	- 0	- 0	- 0	- 0	- 0	- 0	- -	- -	- -	- -	- 0	100 4	100 7	100 2
Saint Francis Medical Center, Cape Girardeau, MO	100 37	98 127	100 186	99 182	- 0	96 27	100 81	0 1	5 1	- 0	- 0	97 97	88 264	99 328	100 60
Saint John's Regional Health Center, Springfield, MO	96 79	100 236	98 369	99 338	- 0	95 75	99 136	92 12	11 12	- 0	- 0	93 135	84 298	99 366	93 58
Saint John's Regional Medical Center, Joplin, MO	97 90	99 204	99 311	97 307	100 2	97 33	100 141	100 1	7 1	- 0	- 0	93 151	85 296	99 353	100 69
Saint Johns Hospital - Aurora, Aurora, MO	- 0	- 0	- 0	- 0	- 0	- 0	- 0	- -	- -	- -	- -	100 3	100 12	94 16	100 2
Saint Johns Hospital - Cassville, Cassville, MO	- 0	- 0	- 0	- 0	- 0	- 0	- 0	- -	- -	- -	- -	86 7	94 18	91 22	100 5
Saint Johns Hospital-Lebanon, Lebanon, MO	100 2	100 5	100 3	100 4	- 0	- 0	- 0	97 215	12 230	73 1	27 11	83 24	87 62	84 75	85 20
Saint Johns Mercy Hospital, Washington, MO	100 3	100 25	100 20	95 19	- 0	- 0	100 2	98 217	9 215	76 30	33 3	97 36	96 135	99 197	100 22
Saint Johns Mercy Medical Center, Saint Louis, MO	100 49	99 280	99 395	99 388	- 0	88 34	98 95	85 72	10 71	- 0	- 0	97 174	84 514	100 669	100 75
Saint Joseph Medical Center, Kansas City, MO	98 51	99 184	100 230	100 218	- 0	79 42	100 82	83 6	0 1	- 0	- 0	100 135	99 305	100 395	100 52
Saint Louis University Hospital, Saint Louis, MO	100 35	98 110	100 116	99 108	- 0	96 24	100 59	100 2	13 2	- 0	- 0	99 202	99 296	99 356	100 97
Saint Louis-John Cochran VA Medical Center, Saint Louis, MO	100 14	100 91	100 98	99 91	100 1	90 10	94 48	- -	- -	- -	- -	97 158	98 382	100 389	94 137
Saint Luke's East Lee's Summit Hospital, Lees Summit, MO	100 12	100 121	99 113	99 110	- 0	100 23	100 29	85 26	2 31	- 0	- 0	97 58	74 140	98 162	100 21
Saint Lukes Cancer Institute, Kansas City, MO	- 0	- 0	- 0	- 0	- 0	- 0	- 0	- 0	- 0	- 0	- 0	- 0	0 1	100 1	- 0
Saint Lukes Hospital, Chesterfield, MO	97 33	100 281	100 301	100 298	- 0	100 39	100 66	100 1	7 1	- 0	- 0	97 143	91 354	99 471	100 39
Saint Lukes Hospital of Kansas City, Kansas City, MO	100 64	100 167	100 441	100 434	- 0	94 31	100 157	100 2	9 2	- 0	- 0	100 210	76 385	100 456	100 107
Saint Lukes Northland Hospital, Kansas City, MO	100 5	100 79	99 71	98 63	- 0	79 14	100 28	96 45	6 45	465 7	- 0	89 35	86 77	100 93	100 15
Saint Mary's Medical Center, Blue Springs, MO	94 16	98 106	100 92	98 89	- 0	87 15	98 47	100 6	- 0	- 0	- 0	87 30	88 52	100 79	95 19
Saint Marys Health Center, Jefferson City, MO	100 20	100 119	100 114	100 115	- 0	100 27	100 38	100 15	4 15	- 0	- 0	100 62	100 155	100 184	100 23
Salem Memorial District Hospital, Salem, MO	100 1	50 2	100 1	100 1	- 0	- 0	- 0	- -	- -	- -	- -	100 4	75 24	41 32	100 2
Scotland County Hospital, Memphis, MO	- 0	- 0	- 0	- 0	- 0	- 0	- 0	- -	- -	- -	- -	100 4	12 16	39 23	50 4
Skaggs Community Health Center, Branson, MO	88 34	99 188	100 190	99 178	- 0	100 35	97 76	100 2	12 2	- 0	- 0	86 94	84 194	99 224	96 54
Southeast Missouri Hospital, Cape Girardeau, MO	90 52	99 155	96 254	96 251	0 2	89 35	98 134	100 3	7 3	- 0	- 0	86 98	67 232	98 294	94 54
SSM Depaul Health Center, Bridgeton, MO	88 100	98 313	98 327	99 318	- 0	78 37	100 131	67 21	6 21	- 0	- 0	90 114	88 252	98 316	100 49
SSM St Clare Health Center, Fenton, MO	94 47	100 219	98 263	98 245	- 0	98 45	100 94	- 0	- 0	- 0	- 0	94 95	88 224	100 290	100 51
SSM St Joseph Health Center, Saint Charles, MO	94 53	98 241	98 356	99 356	- 0	75 51	100 135	88 8	9 9	- 0	- 0	90 84	94 213	100 267	100 52
SSM St Joseph Hospital West, Lake Saint Louis, MO	100 6	96 52	100 24	100 23	- 0	- 0	100 3	96 96	8 97	41 9	- 0	100 45	92 170	99 227	100 48
SSM St Marys Health Center, Richmond Heights, MO	100 30	100 167	100 158	100 148	- 0	100 31	100 48	- 0	- 0	- 0	- 0	99 86	95 268	100 317	100 57
Ste Genevieve County Memorial Hospital, Sainte Genevieve, MO	- 0	100 1	100 1	100 1	- 0	- 0	- 0	- -	- -	- -	- -	75 4	100 16	94 35	100 3
Sullivan County Memorial Hospital, Milan, MO	- 0	- 0	- 0	- 0	- 0	- 0	- 0	- 0	- 0	- 0	- 0	0 1	40 5	27 11	100 1
Texas County Memorial Hospital, Houston, MO	100 2	90 10	88 8	100 9	- 0	- 0	- 0	96 106	14 114	- 0	43 7	90 10	75 24	73 30	67 3
Truman Medical Center - Hospital Hill, Kansas City, MO	100 12	98 50	100 61	100 62	- 0	78 9	100 44	100 1	- 0	- 0	- 0	99 176	77 272	100 306	99 152
Truman Medical Center Lakewood, Kansas City, MO	- 0	100 1	- 0	- 0	- 0	- 0	- 0	100 2	14 2	- 0	- 0	97 34	87 67	97 71	100 29
Twin Rivers Regional Medical Center, Kennett, MO	100 5	100 14	100 8	100 8	- 0	- 0	100 1	100 63	5 67	- 0	67 3	100 26	100 72	100 92	100 16
University of Missouri Health Care, Columbia, MO	95 56	99 127	100 249	99 241	- 0	97 38	99 121	100 2	3 3	- 0	- 0	95 105	89 177	100 224	98 63
Washington County Memorial Hospital, Potosi, MO	- 0	- 0	- 0	- 0	- 0	- 0	- 0	- -	- -	- -	- -	67 3	60 15	60 15	50 2
Western Missouri Medical Center, Warrensburg, MO	100 1	87 15	100 6	86 7	- 0	- 0	- 0	95 261	12 278	- 0	- 0	64 11	59 22	88 42	80 5
Women's and Children's Hospital, Columbia, MO	- 0	100 5	100 4	100 4	- 0	0 1	100 1	100 9	20 10	45 1	- 0	75 4	29 7	100 9	- 0
Wright Memorial Hospital, Trenton, MO	- 0	100 4	100 3	100 2	- 0	- 0	- 0	98 59	19 65	80 2	- 0	100 10	91 43	92 61	100 11
NEBRASKA															
Alegent Health Bergan Mercy Medical Center, Omaha, NE	100 30	99 160	100 208	100 204	- 0	93 28	100 73	100 4	6 4	- 0	- 0	95 81	92 215	100 275	100 41
Alegent Health Immanuel Medical Center, Omaha, NE	100 17	100 101	100 128	100 125	- 0	89 28	100 52	100 5	5 5	- 0	- 0	100 50	100 108	100 153	100 29
Alegent Health Lakeside Hospital, Omaha, NE	91 11	99 113	100 99	100 98	- 0	94 33	100 27	90 10	3 10	53 2	- 0	100 32	94 93	100 153	100 13
Alegent Health Memorial Hospital, Schuyler, NE	- 0	- 0	- 0	- 0	- 0	- 0	- 0	- -	- -	- -	- -	- 0	100 1	100 1	- 0
Alegent Health Midlands Hospital, Papillion, NE	100 15	100 79	100 72	100 72	- 0	100 37	100 28	90 20	8 23	- 0	- 0	100 33	95 74	100 105	100 13
Annie Jeffrey Memorial County Health Center, Osceola, NE	- 0	- 0	- 0	- 0	- 0	- 0	- 0	- -	- -	- -	- -	- 0	- 0	- 0	- 0
Antelope Memorial Hospital, Neligh, NE	- 0	100 1	100 1	100 2	- 0	- 0	- 0	- -	- -	- -	- -	- 0	100 1	0 1	- 0
Avera Creighton Hospital, Creighton, NE	100 1	0 1	0 1	100 1	- 0	- 0	- 0	- -	- -	- -	- -	- 0	- 0	- 0	- 0
Avera St Anthony's Hospital, O'Neill, NE	- 0	- 0	- 0	- 0	- 0	- 0	- 0	- -	- -	- -	- -	100 5	67 9	55 22	- 0
Beatrice Community Hospital & Health Center, Beatrice, NE	- 0	- 0	- 0	- 0	- 0	- 0	- 0	- 0	- 0	- 0	- 0	100 5	100 19	97 34	100 2
Bellevue Medical Center, Bellevue, NE	- 0	- 0	- 0	- 0	- 0	- 0	- 0	- -	- -	- -	- -	- 0	- 0	- 0	- 0
Boone County Health Center, Albion, NE	- 0	100 5	100 3	100 3	0 1	- 0	- 0	- -	- -	- -	- -	83 6	77 13	68 22	- 0
Box Butte General Hospital, Alliance, NE	- 0	100 1	100 1	100 1	- 0	- 0	- 0	- -	- -	- -	- -	- 0	62 13	23 22	100 3
Brodstone Memorial Hospital, Superior, NE	100 1	100 3	100 3	100 2	- 0	- 0	- 0	- -	- -	- -	- -	100 2	85 13	88 16	100 2
Brown County Hospital, Ainsworth, NE	- 0	75 4	50 4	75 4	0 1	- 0	- 0	- -	- -	- -	- -	0 2	50 2	40 5	100 1
Bryanlgh Medical Center, Lincoln, NE	97 75	100 208	100 430	100 422	- 0	97 36	100 152	100 3	4 3	- 0	- 0	99 129	94 304	100 377	100 57
Butler County Health Care Center, David City, NE	- 0	100 1	0 1	- 0	- 0	- 0	- 0	- -	- -	- -	- -	100 2	67 9	54 13	0 1
Callaway District Hospital, Callaway, NE	- 0	- 0	- 0	- 0	- 0	- 0	- 0	- -	- -	- -	- -	- 0	- 0	- 0	- 0
Chadron Community Hospital and Health Services, Chadron, NE	- 0	100 3	- 0	- 0	- 0	- 0	- 0	- -	- -	- -	- -	- 0	57 7	67 15	50 2
Chase County Community Hospital, Imperial, NE	- 0	- 0	- 0	- 0	- 0	- 0	- 0	- -	- -	- -	- -	- 0	0 1	0 3	- 0
Cherry County Hospital, Valentine, NE	- 0	100 1	100 1	100 1	- 0	- 0	- 0	- -	- -	- -	- -	- 0	100 1	100 1	- 0
Children's Hospital & Medical Center, Omaha, NE	- -	- -	- -	- -	- -	- -	- -	- -	- -	- -	- -	- -	- -	- -	- -
Columbus Community Hospital, Columbus, NE	100 3	78 9	100 7	100 7	- 0	- 0	- 0	98 123	7 134	50 3	100 7	75 12	81 21	100 31	100 2
Community Hospital, Mccook, NE	- 0	100 4	100 2	100 1	0 1	- 0	- 0	95 21	11 20	110 1	100 1	71 7	77 22	81 31	100 2
Community Medical Center, Falls City, NE	- 0	- 0	- 0	- 0	- 0	- 0	- 0	94 17	17 16	- 0	- 0	83 6	73 11	88 17	100 2

NOTE: The first number in each column (boldface) is the score, the second number is the number of patients; Please refer to the main entry for footnotes; (a) 100-299
MEASURES: ***Heart Attack Care:*** *1. ACE Inhibitor or ARB for LVSD; 2. Aspirin at Arrival; 3. Aspirin at Discharge; 4. Beta Blocker at Discharge; 5. Fibrinolytic Medication Timing; 6. PCI Within 90 Minutes of Arrival; 7. Smoking Cessation Advice;* ***Chest Pain/Possible Heart Attack Care:*** *8. Aspirin at Arrival; 9. Median Time to ECG (minutes); 10. Median Time to Transfer (minutes); 11. Fibrinolytic Medication Timing;* ***Heart Failure Care:*** *12. ACE Inhibitor or ARB for LVSD; 13. Discharge Instructions; 14. Evaluation of LVS Function; 15. Smoking Cessation Advice*

Hospital	Heart Attack Care 1	2	3	4	5	6	7	Chest Pain/Possible Heart Attack Care 8	9	10	11	Heart Failure Care 12	13	14	15
Community Memorial Hospital, Syracuse, NE	- 0	- 0	- 0	- 0	- 0	- 0	- 0	- -	- -	- -	- -	100 4	100 3	100 4	- 0
Cozad Community Hospital, Cozad, NE	- 0	- 0	- 0	- 0	- 0	- 0	- 0	- -	- -	- -	- -	- 0	0 3	50 10	0 1
Creighton University Medical Center - Saint Joseph, Omaha, NE	100 68	99 123	100 275	100 264	- 0	100 20	100 105	100 3	0 3	- 0	- 0	98 116	96 249	99 291	100 101
Crete Area Medical Center, Crete, NE	- 0	100 1	100 1	100 1	- 0	- 0	- 0	- -	- -	- -	- -	50 2	44 9	86 14	- 0
Dundy County Hospital, Benkelman, NE	100 1	100 1	100 1	100 1	- 0	- 0	0 1	- -	- -	- -	- -	- 0	- 0	- 0	- 0
Faith Regional Health Services, Norfolk, NE	95 19	97 74	100 108	100 106	0 1	83 6	100 31	100 2	3 2	- 0	- 0	96 28	74 43	99 79	100 6
Fillmore County Hospital, Geneva, NE	- 0	100 1	100 1	100 1	- 0	- 0	- 0	- -	- -	- -	- -	- 0	0 7	45 11	- 0
Franklin County Memorial Hospital, Franklin, NE	- 0	- 0	- 0	- 0	- 0	- 0	- 0	- -	- -	- -	- -	- 0	0 4	50 6	- 0
Fremont Area Medical Center, Fremont, NE	100 3	100 28	100 27	100 24	- 0	100 3	100 6	100 38	6 38	56 2	100 1	100 16	100 35	100 79	100 5
Garden County Health Services, Oshkosh, NE	- 0	- 0	- 0	- 0	- 0	- 0	- 0	- -	- -	- -	- -	- 0	0 1	0 1	- 0
Good Samaritan Hospital, Kearney, NE	94 32	99 75	99 177	97 169	- 0	71 21	99 67	- 0	- 0	- 0	- 0	89 45	82 111	99 150	100 25
Gordon Memorial Hospital District, Gordon, NE	- 0	- 0	- 0	- 0	- 0	- 0	- 0	- -	- -	- -	- -	- 0	- 0	- 0	- 0
Gothenburg Memorial Hospital, Gothenburg, NE	- 0	- 0	- 0	- 0	- 0	- 0	- 0	- -	- -	- -	- -	100 1	50 2	33 6	- 0
Great Plains Regional Medical Center, North Platte, NE	100 2	100 16	100 17	100 14	- 0	- 0	100 3	100 55	7 56	- 0	87 15	95 20	86 70	98 102	100 14
Harlan County Health System, Alma, NE	100 1	0 1	100 1	100 1	- 0	- 0	- 0	- -	- -	- -	- -	100 1	100 3	100 3	- 0
Henderson Health Care Services, Henderson, NE	- 0	- 0	- 0	- 0	- 0	- 0	- 0	- -	- -	- -	- -	- 0	- 0	- 0	- 0
Howard County Medical Center, Saint Paul, NE	- 0	- 0	- 0	- 0	- 0	- 0	- 0	- -	- -	- -	- -	- 0	- 0	- 0	- 0
Jefferson Community Health Center, Fairbury, NE	100 1	100 1	100 1	100 1	- 0	- 0	- 0	100 27	23 32	- 0	- 0	100 1	100 2	100 5	- 0
Jennie M Melham Memorial Medical Center, Broken Bow, NE	100 1	100 3	100 4	100 4	- 0	- 0	- 0	- -	- -	- -	- -	33 9	92 26	91 35	20 5
Johnson County Hospital, Tecumseh, NE	- 0	- 0	- 0	- 0	- 0	- 0	- 0	- -	- -	- -	- -	- 0	83 6	100 11	- 0
Kearney County Health Services Hospital, Minden, NE	- 0	- 0	- 0	- 0	- 0	- 0	- 0	- -	- -	- -	- -	- 0	- 0	- 0	- 0
Kimball Health Services, Kimball, NE	- 0	- 0	- 0	- 0	- 0	- 0	- 0	- -	- -	- -	- -	100 1	33 3	100 4	0 2
Lincoln Surgical Hospital, Lincoln, NE	- 0	- 0	- 0	- 0	- 0	- 0	- 0	- 0	- 0	- 0	- 0	- 0	- 0	- 0	- 0
Litzenberg Memorial County Hospital, Central City, NE	- 0	- 0	- 0	- 0	- 0	- 0	- 0	- -	- -	- -	- -	- 0	100 4	100 10	- 0
Mary Lanning Memorial Hospital, Hastings, NE	100 2	100 32	93 27	79 24	- 0	- 0	100 6	97 30	10 32	84 2	50 6	88 40	87 78	96 109	67 6
Memorial Community Hospital, Blair, NE	- 0	100 3	100 2	100 2	- 0	- 0	100 1	- -	- -	- -	- -	100 3	100 6	100 16	100 3
Memorial Health Care Systems, Seward, NE	- 0	- 0	- 0	- 0	- 0	- 0	- 0	- -	- -	- -	- -	50 2	14 7	45 11	100 1
Memorial Health Center, Sidney, NE	100 1	100 4	50 2	50 2	- 0	- 0	- 0	- -	- -	- -	- -	100 3	0 12	71 14	0 1
Memorial Hospital, Aurora, NE	- 0	50 2	50 2	100 1	- 0	- 0	- 0	- -	- -	- -	- -	100 1	50 2	100 6	- 0
Midwest Surgical Hospital, Omaha, NE	- 0	- 0	- 0	- 0	- 0	- 0	- 0	- 0	- 0	- 0	- 0	- 0	- 0	- 0	- 0
Morrill County Community Hospital, Bridgeport, NE	- 0	- 0	- 0	- 0	- 0	- 0	- 0	- -	- -	- -	- -	- 0	- 0	- 0	- 0
Nebraska Heart Hospital, Lincoln, NE	100 45	100 29	100 371	100 343	- 0	- 0	100 113	- 0	- 0	- 0	- 0	96 137	86 227	100 263	100 42
The Nebraska Medical Center, Omaha, NE	90 41	98 210	98 273	97 267	- 0	85 34	99 111	91 33	12 32	- 0	- 0	90 114	79 240	100 287	98 55
The Nebraska Methodist Hospital, Omaha, NE	100 42	99 136	100 181	97 180	- 0	83 35	98 49	- 0	- 0	- 0	- 0	99 114	98 244	100 323	100 37
Nebraska Orthopaedic Hospital, Omaha, NE	- 0	- 0	- 0	- 0	- 0	- 0	- 0	- 0	- 0	- 0	- 0	- 0	- 0	- 0	- 0
Nemaha County Hospital, Auburn, NE	- 0	- 0	- 0	- 0	- 0	- 0	- 0	- -	- -	- -	- -	- 0	100 2	100 4	- 0
Niobrara Valley Hospital, Lynch, NE	- 0	- 0	- 0	- 0	- 0	- 0	- 0	- -	- -	- -	- -	- 0	- 0	- 0	- 0
Oakland Mercy Hospital, Oakland, NE	- 0	- 0	- 0	- 0	- 0	- 0	- 0	- -	- -	- -	- -	33 3	20 5	62 8	50 4
Ogallala Community Hospital, Ogallala, NE	- 0	100 1	- 0	100 1	- 0	- 0	- 0	83 18	6 16	230 1	20 5	100 8	100 21	100 24	100 1
Omaha VA Medical Center, Omaha, NE	- 0	- 0	- 0	- 0	- 0	- 0	- 0	- -	- -	- -	- -	100 48	99 125	100 154	96 26
Osmond General Hospital, Osmond, NE	- 0	- 0	- 0	- 0	- 0	- 0	- 0	- -	- -	- -	- -	- 0	- 0	- 0	- 0
Pawnee County Memorial Hospital, Pawnee City, NE	- 0	- 0	- 0	- 0	- 0	- 0	- 0	- -	- -	- -	- -	- 0	- 0	- 0	- 0
Pender Community Hospital, Pender, NE	- 0	- 0	- 0	- 0	- 0	- 0	- 0	- -	- -	- -	- -	100 2	50 8	45 11	0 2
Perkins County Health Services, Grant, NE	- 0	- 0	- 0	- 0	- 0	- 0	- 0	- -	- -	- -	- -	- 0	100 1	0 3	0 1
Phelps Memorial Health Center, Holdrege, NE	0 1	80 5	100 1	100 2	- 0	- 0	- 0	- -	- -	- -	- -	40 5	100 9	97 29	0 1
Plainview Public Hospital, Plainview, NE	- 0	100 1	100 1	100 1	- 0	- 0	- 0	- -	- -	- -	- -	- 0	- 0	0 1	- 0
Providence Medical Center, Wayne, NE	100 1	100 5	75 4	80 5	- 0	- 0	- 0	89 9	6 9	- 0	0 3	100 4	100 3	85 13	- 0
Regional West Medical Center, Scottsbluff, NE	100 1	100 19	100 11	100 7	100 1	- 0	100 3	98 50	5 50	219 1	76 21	100 11	61 41	100 58	100 9
Rock County Hospital, Bassett, NE	- 0	- 0	- 0	- 0	- 0	- 0	- 0	- -	- -	- -	- -	- 0	- 0	- 0	- 0
Saint Elizabeth Regional Medical Center, Lincoln, NE	90 20	100 98	100 112	99 107	- 0	96 23	100 30	100 7	8 7	- 0	- 0	86 59	77 167	96 209	100 29
Saint Francis Medical Center, Grand Island, NE	100 12	99 83	99 81	100 81	- 0	94 16	100 28	93 58	2 59	68 2	100 1	97 33	96 89	94 130	100 15
Saint Francis Memorial Hospital, West Point, NE	50 2	100 4	50 4	100 4	- 0	- 0	- 0	- -	- -	- -	- -	100 8	93 14	96 26	100 2
Saint Mary's Community Hospital, Nebraska City, NE	100 2	67 3	67 3	100 4	- 0	- 0	- 0	- -	- -	- -	- -	100 4	50 6	100 11	50 2
Saunders Medical Center, Wahoo, NE	- 0	- 0	- 0	- 0	- 0	- 0	- 0	- -	- -	- -	- -	- 0	- 0	100 3	- 0
Thayer County Health Services, Hebron, NE	100 1	67 3	100 1	67 3	- 0	- 0	- 0	- -	- -	- -	- -	75 4	87 15	89 18	0 1
Tilden Community Hospital, Tilden, NE	- 0	- 0	- 0	- 0	- 0	- 0	- 0	100 1	17 1	- 0	- 0	- 0	- 0	- 0	- 0
Tri Valley Health System, Cambridge, NE	- 0	100 1	100 1	100 1	- 0	- 0	- 0	- -	- -	- -	- -	100 2	67 9	74 19	100 2
Tri-County Area Hospital District, Lexington, NE	100 3	100 5	100 5	100 5	- 0	- 0	- 0	- 0	- 0	- 0	- 0	100 8	100 11	93 15	100 1
Valley County Health System, Ord, NE	- 0	- 0	- 0	- 0	- 0	- 0	- 0	- -	- -	- -	- -	100 2	29 7	89 9	0 1
Warren Memorial Hospital, Friend, NE	- 0	- 0	- 0	- 0	- 0	- 0	- 0	- -	- -	- -	- -	- 0	- 0	- 0	- 0
Webster County Community Hospital, Red Cloud, NE	- 0	- 0	- 0	- 0	- 0	- 0	- 0	- -	- -	- -	- -	100 6	75 4	90 10	0 1
West Holt Memorial Hospital, Atkinson, NE	- 0	- 0	- 0	- 0	- 0	- 0	- 0	- -	- -	- -	- -	- 0	- 0	- 0	- 0
Winnebago Ihs Hospital, Winnebago, NE	- -	- -	- -	- -	- -	- -	- -	- -	- -	- -	- -	- -	- -	- -	- -
York General Hospital, York, NE	100 1	100 1	100 1	100 1	- 0	- 0	- 0	- -	- -	- -	- -	50 2	40 5	91 11	- 0
NORTH DAKOTA															
Altru Hospital, Grand Forks, ND	93 55	99 123	100 257	99 245	- 0	60 20	100 84	- 0	- 0	- 0	- 0	89 70	91 170	90 215	98 45
Carrington Health Center, Carrington, ND	- 0	75 4	50 2	67 3	- 0	- 0	- 0	- 0	- 0	- 0	- 0	- 0	100 11	100 12	- 0

NOTE: The first number in each column (boldface) is the score, the second number is the number of patients; Please refer to the main entry for footnotes; (a) 100-299
*MEASURES: **Heart Attack Care:** 1. ACE Inhibitor or ARB for LVSD; 2. Aspirin at Arrival; 3. Aspirin at Discharge; 4. Beta Blocker at Discharge; 5. Fibrinolytic Medication Timing; 6. PCI Within 90 Minutes of Arrival; 7. Smoking Cessation Advice; **Chest Pain/Possible Heart Attack Care:** 8. Aspirin at Arrival; 9. Median Time to ECG (minutes); 10. Median Time to Transfer (minutes); 11. Fibrinolytic Medication Timing; **Heart Failure Care:** 12. ACE Inhibitor or ARB for LVSD; 13. Discharge Instructions; 14. Evaluation of LVS Function; 15. Smoking Cessation Advice*

Hospital	Heart Attack Care							Chest Pain/Possible Heart Attack Care				Heart Failure Care			
	1	2	3	4	5	6	7	8	9	10	11	12	13	14	15
Essentia Health-Fargo, Fargo, ND	100 38	99 97	98 197	97 189	- 0	83 30	98 64	- 0	- 0	- 0	- 0	98 44	98 132	98 175	100 31
Fargo VA Medical Center, Fargo, ND	- 0	- 0	- 0	- 0	- 0	- 0	- 0	- -	- -	- -	- -	83 24	96 73	98 82	95 22
Heart of America Medical Center, Rugby, ND	- 0	100 2	100 2	100 2	- 0	- 0	- 0	- -	- -	- -	- -	100 3	80 20	74 35	50 2
Hillsboro Medical Center, Hillsboro, ND	- 0	- 0	- 0	- 0	- 0	- 0	- 0	- 0	- 0	- 0	- 0	- 0	33 3	0 6	- 0
Jacobson Memorial Hospital & Care Center, Elgin, ND	- 0	100 1	- 0	- 0	- 0	- 0	- 0	- -	- -	- -	- -	- 0	- 0	- 0	- 0
Jamestown Hospital, Jamestown, ND	- 0	100 4	100 3	80 5	- 0	- 0	100 1	98 64	8 67	- 0	70 10	100 9	100 28	100 46	100 8
Linton Hospital, Linton, ND	- 0	75 8	50 6	80 5	- 0	- 0	0 1	- -	- -	- -	- -	100 1	77 13	35 17	50 2
McKenzie County Healthcare Systems, Watford City, ND	- 0	100 2	100 2	100 2	- 0	- 0	- 0	- -	- -	- -	- -	- 0	20 5	44 9	100 1
Medcenter One, Bismarck, ND	95 19	98 92	98 130	98 129	- 0	90 21	100 41	- 0	- 0	- 0	- 0	82 39	96 130	100 171	100 27
Mercy Medical Center, Williston, ND	50 2	100 5	100 4	75 4	- 0	- 0	50 2	94 66	13 68	180 4	67 6	100 4	88 25	71 28	100 6
Mountrail County Medical Center, Stanley, ND	- 0	- 0	- 0	- 0	- 0	- 0	- 0	- -	- -	- -	- -	100 3	50 2	86 7	- 0
Northwood Deaconess Health Center, Northwood, ND	- 0	- 0	- 0	- 0	- 0	- 0	- 0	- -	- -	- -	- -	100 1	0 1	100 1	- 0
P H S Indian Hospital at Belcourt - Quentin N Burdick, Belcourt, ND	- 0	- 0	100 1	0 1	- 0	- 0	0 1	- -	- -	- -	- -	- 0	0 3	0 4	- 0
P H S Indian Hospital at Fort Yates-Standing Rock, Fort Yates, ND	- 0	- 0	- 0	- 0	- 0	- 0	- 0	- -	- -	- -	- -	- 0	- 0	- 0	- 0
Pembina County Memorial Hospital, Cavalier, ND	- 0	100 2	- 0	- 0	100 1	- 0	- 0	- -	- -	- -	- -	25 4	100 5	82 11	100 1
Presentation Medical Center, Rolla, ND	- 0	- 0	- 0	- 0	- 0	- 0	- 0	- 0	- 0	- 0	- 0	0 1	100 5	100 13	100 3
Saint Alexius Medical Center, Bismarck, ND	96 23	98 105	100 209	100 202	- 0	80 20	100 72	- 0	- 0	- 0	- 0	90 60	83 134	99 163	100 27
Saint Aloisius Medical Center, Harvey, ND	100 1	33 3	100 1	100 1	- 0	- 0	- 0	- -	- -	- -	- -	100 3	83 18	54 26	- 0
Saint Andrews Health Center, Bottineau, ND	- 0	100 1	- 0	- 0	- 0	- 0	- 0	- -	- -	- -	- -	100 1	33 6	17 6	- 0
Saint Joseph's Hospital & Health Center, Dickinson, ND	100 4	100 23	95 19	95 19	0 1	- 0	100 2	- -	- -	- -	- -	86 14	74 50	100 75	89 9
Sanford Mayville, Mayville, ND	- 0	75 4	100 3	100 3	- 0	- 0	- 0	- -	- -	- -	- -	50 2	25 4	71 14	50 2
Sanford Medical Center Fargo, Fargo, ND	88 113	97 196	99 568	98 565	- 0	85 39	100 201	- 0	- 0	- 0	- 0	90 105	93 289	100 385	96 57
Tioga Medical Center, Tioga, ND	- 0	- 0	- 0	- 0	- 0	- 0	- 0	- -	- -	- -	- -	100 1	60 5	83 12	100 3
Trinity Hospitals, Minot, ND	100 25	99 133	100 240	100 225	- 0	100 23	100 91	- 0	- 0	- 0	- 0	93 57	90 178	100 237	100 32
Unity Medical Center, Grafton, ND	- -	- -	- -	- -	- -	- -	- -	- 0	- 0	- 0	- 0	- -	- -	- -	- -
West River Regional Medical Center, Hettinger, ND	100 1	100 3	100 2	100 2	75 4	- 0	- 0	- -	- -	- -	- -	100 5	100 21	93 41	100 2
Wishek Community Hospital, Wishek, ND	- 0	50 2	0 1	0 1	- 0	- 0	- 0	- -	- -	- -	- -	100 2	62 8	36 14	0 1
OKLAHOMA															
Arbuckle Memorial Hospital, Sulphur, OK	- 0	- 0	- 0	- 0	- 0	- 0	- 0	- -	- -	- -	- -	100 3	43 7	78 18	50 2
Atoka Memorial Hospital, Atoka, OK	- 0	0 1	- 0	- 0	- 0	- 0	- 0	- -	- -	- -	- -	100 1	40 5	12 8	100 1
Bailey Medical Center, Owasso, OK	100 1	100 4	100 4	100 5	- 0	- 0	- 0	93 134	12 136	90 2	100 1	40 5	80 10	100 15	100 1
Beaver County Memorial Hospital, Beaver, OK	- 0	- 0	- 0	- 0	- 0	- 0	- 0	- -	- -	- -	- -	0 1	0 1	33 3	- 0
Bristow Medical Center, Bristow, OK	- 0	- 0	- 0	- 0	- 0	- 0	- 0	100 16	14 16	- 0	- 0	40 5	100 7	100 8	100 1
Carnegie Tri-County Municipal Hospital, Carnegie, OK	- 0	- 0	- 0	- 0	- 0	- 0	- 0	- -	- -	- -	- -	- 0	- 0	- 0	- 0
Chickasaw Nation Medical Center, Ada, OK	- 0	- 0	100 1	100 1	0 1	- 0	- 0	- -	- -	- -	- -	57 7	91 45	84 45	86 7
Choctaw Memorial Hospital, Hugo, OK	- 0	33 3	0 2	67 3	- 0	- 0	- 0	71 31	68 27	134 2	0 2	100 9	4 81	53 120	23 26
Choctaw Nation Healthcare, Talihina, OK	- 0	100 1	100 1	100 1	- 0	- 0	- 0	- -	- -	- -	- -	67 3	86 7	100 7	100 2
Cimarron Memorial Hospital, Boise City, OK	- 0	- 0	- 0	- 0	- 0	- 0	- 0	- -	- -	- -	- -	- 0	- 0	- 0	- 0
Claremore Indian Hospital, Claremore, OK	- 0	0 1	100 1	100 1	- 0	- 0	- 0	86 145	16 156	166 2	100 1	100 3	92 12	92 12	0 1
Claremore Regional Hospital, Claremore, OK	100 2	92 12	75 4	100 5	- 0	- 0	100 2	99 108	9 115	54 8	- 0	97 31	85 39	98 48	100 12
Cleveland Area Hospital, Cleveland, OK	- 0	- 0	- 0	- 0	- 0	- 0	- 0	- -	- -	- -	- -	0 1	0 2	100 2	- 0
Comanche County Memorial Hospital, Lawton, OK	92 40	97 135	98 283	100 271	0 1	71 35	100 129	62 8	10 7	- 0	- 0	92 123	68 313	96 356	96 79
Community Hospital, Oklahoma City, OK	- 0	- 0	- 0	- 0	- 0	- 0	- 0	100 9	11 11	54 1	- 0	- 0	- 0	- 0	- 0
Cordell Memorial Hospital, Cordell, OK	- 0	100 1	100 1	- 0	- 0	- 0	- 0	- -	- -	- -	- -	- 0	100 1	20 5	- 0
Craig General Hospital, Vinita, OK	50 2	67 9	43 7	43 7	- 0	- 0	100 1	90 73	6 68	90 5	0 3	69 13	73 44	79 56	100 9
Creek Nation Community Hospital, Okemah, OK	- 0	- 0	- 0	- 0	- 0	- 0	- 0	- -	- -	- -	- -	33 3	53 15	88 16	50 4
Cushing Regional Hospital, Cushing, OK	- 0	88 8	83 6	100 7	- 0	- 0	100 1	100 140	9 145	54 8	- 0	64 14	100 34	92 49	100 11
Deaconess Hospital, Oklahoma City, OK	100 15	99 82	100 106	99 100	- 0	87 15	100 46	71 7	9 7	- 0	- 0	97 39	71 103	100 135	100 26
Drumright Regional Hospital, Drumright, OK	- 0	- 0	- 0	- 0	- 0	- 0	- 0	- -	- -	- -	- -	100 2	29 7	89 9	100 2
Duncan Regional Hospital, Duncan, OK	100 2	100 14	100 9	100 13	- 0	- 0	100 2	99 134	9 137	141 10	23 13	98 43	94 106	100 127	100 35
Eastern Oklahoma Medical Center, Poteau, OK	100 1	79 14	71 7	56 9	- 0	- 0	100 1	92 26	6 29	146 1	88 8	84 37	61 99	96 119	87 30
Edmond Medical Center, Edmond, OK	- -	- -	- -	- -	- -	- -	- -	- -	- -	- -	- -	- -	- -	- -	- -
Elkview General Hospital, Hobart, OK	- 0	100 1	100 1	- 0	100 1	- 0	100 1	100 20	8 20	- 0	67 3	94 16	100 32	100 41	100 6
Epic Medical Center, Eufaula, OK	- 0	100 1	100 1	100 1	- 0	- 0	- 0	81 48	24 51	- 0	0 2	- 0	33 3	20 5	50 2
Fairfax Community Hospital, Fairfax, OK	- 0	- 0	- 0	- 0	- 0	- 0	- 0	- -	- -	- -	- -	100 4	75 8	100 8	100 1
Fairview Regional Medical Center, Fairview, OK	- 0	100 1	- 0	- 0	- 0	- 0	- 0	- -	- -	- -	- -	- 0	60 5	12 8	- 0
Grady Memorial Hospital, Chickasha, OK	- 0	100 7	100 3	100 1	- 0	- 0	- 0	93 105	16 112	105 3	67 15	67 18	67 58	88 77	100 13
Great Plains Regional Medical Center, Elk City, OK	100 1	89 9	86 7	71 7	- 0	- 0	100 1	98 41	9 43	- 0	80 5	100 9	96 51	93 69	100 10
Harmon Memorial Hospital, Hollis, OK	- 0	50 2	33 3	67 3	- 0	- 0	- 0	62 8	10 8	- 0	33 3	80 5	70 30	31 32	67 3
Harper County Community Hospital, Buffalo, OK	- 0	- 0	- 0	- 0	- 0	- 0	- 0	- -	- -	- -	- -	75 4	67 3	100 6	- 0
Haskell County Healthcare System, Stigler, OK	- -	- -	- -	- -	- -	- -	- -	- -	- -	- -	- -	- -	- -	- -	- -
Healdton Mercy Hospital Corporation, Healdton, OK	- 0	- 0	- 0	- 0	- 0	- 0	- 0	- -	- -	- -	- -	- 0	- 0	- 0	- 0
Henryetta Medical Center, Henryetta, OK	- 0	50 2	100 1	100 1	- 0	- 0	- 0	100 104	10 105	45 1	- 0	92 12	100 22	89 28	100 4
Hillcrest Medical Center, Tulsa, OK	85 80	100 248	99 494	100 477	100 1	91 34	100 224	- 0	- 0	- 0	- 0	90 220	96 520	98 570	98 154
Holdenville General Hospital, Holdenville, OK	- 0	- 0	- 0	- 0	- 0	- 0	- 0	- -	- -	- -	- -	71 7	72 36	48 60	82 11
Integris Baptist Medical Center, Oklahoma City, OK	100 147	100 293	100 574	100 515	- 0	98 55	100 239	100 2	2 2	- 0	- 0	98 297	86 498	100 576	100 82
Integris Baptist Regional Health Center, Miami, OK	100 1	89 9	100 5	100 5	- 0	- 0	100 1	98 121	4 129	- 0	83 6	94 18	94 70	100 86	100 17

NOTE: The first number in each column (boldface) is the score, the second number is the number of patients; Please refer to the main entry for footnotes; (a) 100-299
*MEASURES: **Heart Attack Care:** 1. ACE Inhibitor or ARB for LVSD; 2. Aspirin at Arrival; 3. Aspirin at Discharge; 4. Beta Blocker at Discharge; 5. Fibrinolytic Medication Timing; 6. PCI Within 90 Minutes of Arrival; 7. Smoking Cessation Advice; **Chest Pain/Possible Heart Attack Care:** 8. Aspirin at Arrival; 9. Median Time to ECG (minutes); 10. Median Time to Transfer (minutes); 11. Fibrinolytic Medication Timing; **Heart Failure Care:** 12. ACE Inhibitor or ARB for LVSD; 13. Discharge Instructions; 14. Evaluation of LVS Function; 15. Smoking Cessation Advice*

Hospital	Heart Attack Care							Chest Pain/Possible Heart Attack Care				Heart Failure Care			
	1	2	3	4	5	6	7	8	9	10	11	12	13	14	15
Integris Bass Baptist Health Center, Enid, OK	100 8	99 78	97 86	95 79	- 0	100 20	100 36	80 5	2 5	- 0	- 0	100 28	100 76	99 116	100 19
Integris Blackwell Regional Hospital, Blackwell, OK	- 0	100 1	- 0	100 1	- 0	- 0	- 0	96 28	9 30	- 0	83 6	100 9	92 25	100 41	100 8
Integris Canadian Valley Hospital, Yukon, OK	100 1	100 14	100 12	91 11	- 0	- 0	100 1	100 79	9 79	40 7	0 1	92 13	100 34	95 44	100 3
Integris Clinton Regional Hospital, Clinton, OK	- 0	100 5	100 3	100 2	- 0	- 0	- 0	95 58	7 61	140 1	50 6	97 30	82 50	99 74	100 10
Integris Grove Hospital, Grove, OK	100 7	100 44	95 41	97 39	- 0	75 4	100 12	93 72	8 74	53 4	44 9	93 15	100 57	89 76	100 17
Integris Marshall County Medical Center, Madill, OK	- 0	100 3	100 1	100 1	- 0	- 0	- 0	94 31	9 33	- 0	0 5	100 11	96 25	100 34	100 12
Integris Mayes County Medical Center, Pryor, OK	- 0	100 3	100 1	100 1	- 0	- 0	- 0	97 116	7 120	94 2	60 5	83 12	100 27	100 35	100 5
Integris Seminole Medical Center, Seminole, OK	- 0	100 4	100 4	100 3	- 0	- 0	100 1	92 106	14 113	- 0	20 5	100 10	83 42	94 48	100 9
Integris Southwest Medical Center, Oklahoma City, OK	88 52	98 243	94 253	97 237	100 1	98 48	100 124	100 13	16 14	- 0	- 0	89 170	81 347	97 418	99 129
Jackson County Memorial Hospital, Altus, OK	100 4	86 22	92 12	92 12	- 0	- 0	100 3	98 96	3 99	- 0	80 10	78 58	97 118	94 160	100 55
Jane Phillips Medical Center, Bartlesville, OK	100 15	100 120	99 150	100 148	- 0	97 29	100 69	- 0	- 0	- 0	- 0	97 37	94 110	99 153	100 34
Jefferson County Hospital, Waurika, OK	- 0	- 0	- 0	- 0	- 0	- 0	- 0	- -	- -	- -	- -	- 0	- 0	- 0	- 0
Johnston Memorial Hospital, Tishomingo, OK	- 0	- 0	- 0	- 0	- 0	- 0	- 0	- -	- -	- -	- -	- 0	67 3	0 6	- 0
Kingfisher Regional Hospital, Kingfisher, OK	- 0	100 1	- 0	- 0	0 1	- 0	- 0	100 5	8 5	401 1	- 0	100 4	100 7	89 9	- 0
Lakeside Women's Hospital, Oklahoma City, OK	- 0	- 0	- 0	- 0	- 0	- 0	- 0	- 0	- 0	- 0	- 0	- 0	- 0	- 0	- 0
Latimer County General Hospital, Wilburton, OK	- 0	0 2	0 1	100 1	- 0	- 0	0 1	73 15	26 16	- 0	50 2	50 2	100 13	46 13	100 2
Lindsay Municipal Hospital, Lindsay, OK	- 0	- 0	- 0	- 0	- 0	- 0	- 0	- -	- -	- -	- -	- 0	- 0	- 0	- 0
Logan Medical Center, Guthrie, OK	100 2	86 7	100 4	100 3	- 0	- 0	- 0	- -	- -	- -	- -	50 8	36 11	79 33	75 4
Mary Hurley Hospital, Coalgate, OK	- 0	- 0	- 0	- 0	- 0	- 0	- 0	- -	- -	- -	- -	44 9	69 36	60 58	100 9
McAlester Regional Health Center, Mcalester, OK	100 3	82 22	91 11	92 13	- 0	- 0	100 4	- 0	- 0	- 0	- 0	86 49	78 82	93 101	96 25
McBride Clinic Orthopedic Hospital, Oklahoma City, OK	- 0	0 1	- 0	- 0	- 0	- 0	- 0	100 1	18 1	- 0	- 0	- 0	- 0	- 0	- 0
McCurtain Memorial Hospital, Idabel, OK	- 0	100 7	100 5	100 5	- 0	- 0	- 0	95 80	12 83	95 3	0 2	91 11	58 52	84 64	100 12
Medical Center of Southeastern Oklahoma, Durant, OK	100 13	100 39	100 22	100 29	- 0	- 0	100 11	100 44	5 44	- 0	100 3	100 85	100 250	100 326	100 86
Memorial Hospital & Physician Group, Frederick, OK	- 0	0 1	0 1	0 1	- 0	- 0	- 0	90 20	20 19	- 0	- 0	100 8	79 24	83 36	100 4
Memorial Hospital of Stilwell, Stilwell, OK	- 0	100 4	67 3	25 4	- 0	- 0	- 0	88 16	19 16	- 0	50 2	93 15	86 28	100 36	100 7
Memorial Hospital of Texas County, Guymon, OK	- 0	- 0	- 0	- 0	- 0	- 0	- 0	100 4	12 4	- 0	0 1	- 0	- 0	- 0	- 0
Mercy Health Center, Oklahoma City, OK	83 6	95 21	96 24	87 23	- 0	- 0	100 3	96 152	10 161	56 10	- 0	81 16	69 54	95 83	100 10
Mercy Health Love County, Marietta, OK	- 0	100 1	0 1	100 1	- 0	- 0	100 1	- -	- -	- -	- -	- 0	8 13	42 19	100 4
Mercy Hospital El Reno, El Reno, OK	- 0	- 0	- 0	0 2	- 0	- 0	- 0	88 59	14 66	76 10	0 1	50 4	87 15	79 24	80 5
Mercy Memorial Health Center, Ardmore, OK	85 27	98 161	100 141	99 137	100 2	65 23	100 59	100 15	8 17	- 0	100 1	90 51	75 133	97 153	100 38
Midwest Regional Medical Center, Midwest City, OK	98 53	100 263	100 263	99 242	- 0	92 38	100 99	100 6	24 6	- 0	- 0	100 123	99 304	100 375	100 62
Muskogee Community Hospital, Muskogee, OK	100 1	100 3	100 2	100 2	- 0	- 0	- 0	- -	- -	- -	- -	86 7	30 10	62 13	50 2
Muskogee Regional Medical Center, Muskogee, OK	94 17	96 97	93 74	97 74	0 1	- 0	100 29	94 16	8 17	35 1	67 3	99 82	72 203	96 256	100 62
Muskogee VA Medical Center, Muskogee, OK	- 0	- 0	- 0	- 0	- 0	- 0	- 0	- -	- -	- -	- -	98 111	99 156	100 178	100 59
Newman Memorial Hospital, Shattuck, OK	100 2	100 7	83 6	100 6	- 0	- 0	100 1	80 15	61 15	204 2	0 1	100 2	53 17	45 22	100 1
Norman Regional Health System, Norman, OK	97 36	100 137	98 224	98 213	100 1	91 33	100 92	86 7	9 7	- 0	- 0	97 128	91 276	99 344	100 74
Northwest Surgical Hospital, Oklahoma City, OK	- 0	- 0	- 0	- 0	- 0	- 0	- 0	- 0	- 0	- 0	- 0	- 0	- 0	- 0	- 0
O U Medical Center, Oklahoma City, OK	100 33	100 101	100 120	100 118	- 0	100 20	100 59	100 3	5 3	- 0	- 0	99 122	88 213	100 227	100 100
Okeene Municipal Hospital, Okeene, OK	- 0	100 1	0 1	100 1	- 0	- 0	- 0	- -	- -	- -	- -	100 2	100 5	67 6	- 0
Oklahoma Center for Orthopaedic & Multi-Sp, Oklahoma City, OK	- 0	- 0	- 0	- 0	- 0	- 0	- 0	- 0	- 0	- 0	- 0	- 0	- 0	- 0	- 0
Oklahoma City VA Medical Center, Oklahoma City, OK	92 24	98 133	98 123	95 121	- 0	67 15	100 50	- -	- -	- -	- -	96 100	100 182	100 204	100 72
Oklahoma Heart Hospital, Oklahoma City, OK	100 47	99 98	99 303	99 279	- 0	76 21	99 127	97 31	1 35	- 0	- 0	95 132	96 283	100 309	100 53
Oklahoma Heart Hospital South, Oklahoma City, OK	100 13	100 26	100 67	100 60	- 0	88 8	94 33	100 5	2 8	- 0	- 0	100 30	89 56	98 59	100 10
Oklahoma Spine Hospital, Oklahoma City, OK	- 0	- 0	- 0	- 0	- 0	- 0	- 0	- 0	- 0	- 0	- 0	- 0	- 0	- 0	- 0
Oklahoma State University Medical Center, Tulsa, OK	100 23	100 98	100 143	100 123	- 0	100 20	100 83	100 2	6 2	- 0	- 0	96 77	88 163	99 182	100 50
Oklahoma Surgical Hospital, Tulsa, OK	- 0	- 0	- 0	- 0	- 0	- 0	- 0	- 0	- 0	- 0	- 0	- 0	- 0	- 0	- 0
Okmulgee Memorial Hospital, Okmulgee, OK	- 0	100 2	0 1	100 1	- 0	- 0	- 0	87 166	10 174	83 3	44 9	72 25	67 49	85 65	84 19
Orthopedic Hospital, Oklahoma City, OK	- 0	- 0	- 0	- 0	- 0	- 0	- 0	- 0	- 0	- 0	- 0	- 0	- 0	- 0	- 0
Pauls Valley General Hospital, Pauls Valley, OK	- 0	67 3	67 3	67 3	- 0	- 0	- 0	99 68	10 75	117 5	20 5	95 22	78 58	82 85	100 12
Pawhuska Hospital, Pawhuska, OK	- 0	0 1	- 0	- 0	- 0	- 0	- 0	- -	- -	- -	- -	- 0	- 0	0 2	- 0
Perry Memorial Hospital, Perry, OK	100 1	100 3	67 3	100 3	- 0	- 0	0 1	50 16	14 13	97 1	0 3	100 1	69 13	38 21	100 4
Physicians' Hospital in Anadarko, Anadarko, OK	- 0	100 1	100 1	100 1	- 0	- 0	- 0	- -	- -	- -	- -	- 0	0 4	11 9	- 0
Pinnacle Specialty Hospital, Tulsa, OK	- 0	- 0	- 0	- 0	- 0	- 0	- 0	- -	- -	- -	- -	- 0	- 0	- 0	- 0
Ponca City Medical Center, Ponca City, OK	100 2	100 15	100 10	100 9	50 2	- 0	100 3	100 88	5 90	108 6	60 5	95 22	97 77	100 86	100 13
Prague Community Hospital, Prague, OK	- 0	- 0	- 0	- 0	- 0	- 0	- 0	- -	- -	- -	- -	- 0	60 5	25 4	- 0
Purcell Municipal Hospital, Purcell, OK	- 0	100 1	- 0	- 0	- 0	- 0	- 0	91 57	9 61	135 1	100 3	67 9	35 31	85 46	56 9
Pushmataha County-TN of Antlers Hospital Authority, Antlers, OK	- 0	- 0	- 0	- 0	- 0	- 0	- 0	92 36	18 38	- 0	0 3	89 9	89 28	55 40	80 5
Quartz Mountain Medical Center, Mangum, OK	- 0	- 0	- 0	- 0	- 0	- 0	- 0	- -	- -	- -	- -	100 1	50 4	50 4	50 2
Saint Anthony Hospital, Oklahoma City, OK	100 33	100 144	99 222	99 210	- 0	95 20	99 88	100 1	1 1	- 0	- 0	94 138	96 312	100 355	98 93
Saint Francis Hospital, Tulsa, OK	90 113	98 496	100 813	99 796	0 1	75 88	100 313	- 0	- 0	- 0	- 0	100 309	95 713	100 862	100 144
Saint Francis Hospital South, Tulsa, OK	100 2	100 7	100 4	100 4	- 0	- 0	- 0	96 94	4 97	48 10	- 0	97 31	93 68	99 89	100 7
Saint John Medical Center, Tulsa, OK	97 119	99 499	100 714	100 702	- 0	87 122	99 268	- 0	- 0	- 0	- 0	99 202	80 497	98 597	99 120
Saint John Owasso, Owasso, OK	- 0	100 9	100 4	100 4	- 0	- 0	100 1	96 233	5 239	53 16	- 0	78 9	76 34	91 44	100 13
Saint John Sapulpa, Sapulpa, OK	- 0	- 0	- 0	- 0	- 0	- 0	- 0	- -	- -	- -	- -	70 10	15 33	67 39	62 13
Saint Mary's Regional Medical Center, Enid, OK	100 7	94 53	97 58	89 54	- 0	60 10	100 29	100 5	6 6	122 1	- 0	97 36	62 106	95 168	100 28
Sayre Memorial Hospital, Sayre, OK	100 1	75 4	50 4	33 3	- 0	- 0	0 1	91 22	20 24	- 0	0 1	60 10	73 33	61 46	67 6
Seiling Community Hospital, Seiling, OK	100 1	100 1	100 1	0 1	- 0	- 0	- 0	- -	- -	- -	- -	100 2	- 0	100 2	- 0

NOTE: The first number in each column (boldface) is the score, the second number is the number of patients; Please refer to the main entry for footnotes; (a) 100-299
*MEASURES: **Heart Attack Care:** 1. ACE Inhibitor or ARB for LVSD; 2. Aspirin at Arrival; 3. Aspirin at Discharge; 4. Beta Blocker at Discharge; 5. Fibrinolytic Medication Timing; 6. PCI Within 90 Minutes of Arrival; 7. Smoking Cessation Advice; **Chest Pain/Possible Heart Attack Care:** 8. Aspirin at Arrival; 9. Median Time to ECG (minutes); 10. Median Time to Transfer (minutes); 11. Fibrinolytic Medication Timing; **Heart Failure Care:** 12. ACE Inhibitor or ARB for LVSD; 13. Discharge Instructions; 14. Evaluation of LVS Function; 15. Smoking Cessation Advice*

Hospital	Heart Attack Care							Chest Pain/Possible Heart Attack Care				Heart Failure Care			
	1	2	3	4	5	6	7	8	9	10	11	12	13	14	15
Sequoyah Memorial Hospital, Sallisaw, OK	- 0	100 1	- 0	- 0	- 0	- 0	- 0	96 100	9 102	- 0	50 4	67 9	100 19	97 32	100 10
Share Memorial Hospital, Alva, OK	- 0	0 2	0 1	0 1	- 0	- 0	- 0	83 30	11 32	- 0	0 1	50 4	91 11	80 20	100 1
Southcrest Hospital, Tulsa, OK	100 36	100 131	98 188	99 178	- 0	96 27	100 73	100 12	21 13	- 0	- 0	100 71	91 163	100 191	100 22
Southwestern Medical Center, Lawton, OK	- 0	100 3	- 0	- 0	- 0	- 0	- 0	100 7	43 7	- 0	- 0	91 11	72 32	100 42	100 12
Southwestern Regional Medical Center, Tulsa, OK	- 0	- 0	- 0	- 0	- 0	- 0	- 0	- 0	- 0	- 0	- 0	- 0	100 1	100 1	- 0
Stillwater Medical Center, Stillwater, OK	71 7	100 74	100 65	97 68	25 4	100 6	100 30	100 64	9 67	98 8	20 5	97 35	85 62	98 82	100 18
Stroud Regional Medical Center, Stroud, OK	- 0	- 0	- 0	- 0	- 0	- 0	- 0	- -	- -	- -	- -	50 2	86 7	50 14	- 0
Summit Medical Center, Edmond, OK	- 0	- 0	- 0	- 0	- 0	- 0	- 0	- -	- -	- -	- -	- 0	- 0	- 0	- 0
Surgical Hospital of Oklahoma, Oklahoma City, OK	- 0	- 0	- 0	- 0	- 0	- 0	- 0	- 0	- 0	- 0	- 0	- 0	- 0	- 0	- 0
Tahlequah City Hospital, Tahlequah, OK	100 2	97 29	100 34	100 31	- 0	0 1	100 15	93 44	16 48	- 0	80 5	96 47	78 98	99 111	86 29
Tulsa Spine & Specialty Hospital, Tulsa, OK	- 0	- 0	- 0	- 0	- 0	- 0	- 0	- 0	- 0	- 0	- 0	- 0	- 0	- 0	- 0
Unity Health Center, Shawnee, OK	100 7	96 74	93 42	100 31	0 2	- 0	100 15	97 129	9 142	62 9	65 17	97 65	87 110	100 147	100 24
USPHS Lawton Indian Hospital, Lawton, OK	- 0	- 0	- 0	- 0	- 0	- 0	- 0	- -	- -	- -	- -	100 2	40 5	80 5	100 1
Valley View Regional Hospital, Ada, OK	- 0	96 23	92 13	100 13	- 0	- 0	100 3	98 63	12 62	- 0	42 12	100 16	71 51	93 70	89 18
W W Hastings Indian Hospital, Tahlequah, OK	- 0	- 0	- 0	- 0	- 0	- 0	- 0	- -	- -	- -	- -	100 9	59 29	92 36	80 5
Wagoner Community Hospital, Wagoner, OK	- 0	100 3	100 2	100 2	- 0	- 0	- 0	81 37	22 40	135 1	0 1	89 9	78 23	82 22	100 5
Watonga Municipal Hospital, Watonga, OK	- 0	100 1	- 0	- 0	- 0	- 0	- 0	- -	- -	- -	- -	100 3	62 8	46 13	67 3
Weatherford Regional Hospital, Weatherford, OK	- 0	50 2	0 1	50 2	- 0	- 0	- 0	- -	- -	- -	- -	78 9	89 19	88 33	75 4
Woodward Regional Hospital, Woodward, OK	100 1	100 8	100 5	100 5	- 0	- 0	100 1	100 29	9 31	148 3	50 8	100 10	89 44	98 55	100 5
SOUTH DAKOTA															
Avera Dells Area Health Center, Dell Rapids, SD	- 0	100 3	100 2	100 2	0 1	- 0	- 0	- -	- -	- -	- -	100 3	83 12	58 12	100 1
Avera Desmet Memorial Hospital, De Smet, SD	- 0	- 0	- 0	- 0	- 0	- 0	- 0	- -	- -	- -	- -	- 0	- 0	0 1	- 0
Avera Flandreau Medical Center Hospital, Flandreau, SD	- 0	- 0	- 0	- 0	- 0	- 0	- 0	- -	- -	- -	- -	100 1	100 4	50 6	- 0
Avera Gregory Healthcare Center, Gregory, SD	100 2	50 4	75 4	75 4	- 0	- 0	- 0	- -	- -	- -	- -	80 10	82 11	85 26	0 1
Avera Hand County Memorial Hospital and Clinic, Miller, SD	- 0	100 1	- 0	- 0	- 0	- 0	- 0	- -	- -	- -	- -	60 5	75 4	93 14	- 0
Avera Heart Hospital of South Dakota, Sioux Falls, SD	98 88	99 87	99 599	100 593	- 0	100 13	99 165	100 5	7 5	- 0	- 0	97 61	99 124	99 142	100 19
Avera Mckennan Hospital & University Health Ctr, Sioux Falls, SD	100 14	97 60	100 64	100 69	100 1	79 19	100 24	- 0	- 0	- 0	- 0	94 62	91 175	99 228	100 22
Avera Queen of Peace, Mitchell, SD	100 1	100 14	100 8	100 6	- 0	- 0	100 1	100 56	12 57	106 2	50 10	92 12	100 46	99 76	100 6
Avera Sacred Heart Hospital, Yankton, SD	100 4	100 22	100 19	100 18	100 1	- 0	100 2	98 41	8 43	71 2	50 10	100 22	100 57	100 100	100 12
Avera St Benedict Health Center, Parkston, SD	0 1	100 2	100 1	0 1	- 0	- 0	- 0	- 0	- 0	- 0	- 0	0 1	33 3	100 8	100 1
Avera St Lukes, Aberdeen, SD	100 5	100 56	100 59	100 54	- 0	100 11	100 10	92 13	4 14	82 1	- 0	100 19	95 80	99 131	100 19
Avera Weskota Memorial Medical Center, Wessington Springs, SD	- 0	- 0	- 0	- 0	- 0	- 0	- 0	- -	- -	- -	- -	100 1	100 3	17 6	- 0
Black Hills Surgical Hospital, Rapid City, SD	- 0	- 0	- 0	- 0	- 0	- 0	- 0	- 0	- 0	- 0	- 0	- 0	- 0	- 0	- 0
Bowdle Hospital, Bowdle, SD	- -	- -	- -	- -	- -	- -	- -	100 6	32 6	- 0	- 0	- 0	- 0	- 0	- 0
Brookings Hospital, Brookings, SD	0 1	88 17	100 12	83 12	- 0	- 0	0 1	93 54	6 58	207 2	67 3	50 10	54 13	64 22	0 2
Community Memorial Hospital, Redfield, SD	- 0	- 0	- 0	- 0	- 0	- 0	- 0	- -	- -	- -	- -	67 3	25 4	83 6	100 1
Custer Regional Hospital, Custer, SD	- 0	- 0	- 0	- 0	- 0	- 0	- 0	100 23	4 23	- 0	50 2	67 3	86 14	94 16	100 4
Dakota Plains Surgical Center, Aberdeen, SD	- 0	- 0	- 0	- 0	- 0	- 0	- 0	- 0	- 0	- 0	- 0	- 0	- 0	- 0	- 0
Fall River Hospital, Hot Springs, SD	- 0	- 0	- 0	- 0	- 0	- 0	- 0	- 0	- 0	- 0	- 0	- 0	- 0	- 0	- 0
Holy Infant Hospital, Hoven, SD	- 0	- 0	- 0	- 0	- 0	- 0	- 0	100 1	80 1	- 0	- 0	- 0	- 0	- 0	- 0
Huron Regional Medical Center, Huron, SD	100 5	100 18	100 7	71 7	100 1	- 0	0 1	- -	- -	- -	- -	71 7	90 21	85 34	50 2
Landmann-Jungman Memorial Hospital, Scotland, SD	- 0	- 0	- 0	- 0	- 0	- 0	- 0	- -	- -	- -	- -	50 2	50 2	100 6	- 0
Lead-Deadwood Regional Hospital, Deadwood, SD	- 0	- 0	- 0	- 0	- 0	- 0	- 0	- -	- -	- -	- -	- 0	100 2	100 3	- 0
Lewis and Clark Specialty Hospital, Yankton, SD	- 0	- 0	- 0	- 0	- 0	- 0	- 0	- 0	- 0	- 0	- 0	- 0	- 0	- 0	- 0
Madison Community Hospital, Madison, SD	- 0	- 0	- 0	- 0	- 0	- 0	- 0	- -	- -	- -	- -	- 0	0 1	44 9	- 0
Milbank Area Hospital/Avera Health, Milbank, SD	- 0	100 1	0 1	100 1	- 0	- 0	- 0	- -	- -	- -	- -	100 2	100 7	91 11	- 0
Mobridge Regional Hospital, Mobridge, SD	- 0	100 1	100 1	100 1	- 0	- 0	- 0	- -	- -	- -	- -	100 3	33 3	86 7	- 0
PHS Indian Hospital at Eagle Butte, Eagle Butte, SD	- 0	- 0	- 0	- 0	- 0	- 0	- 0	- -	- -	- -	- -	- 0	0 1	0 1	0 1
PHS Indian Hospital at Pine Ridge, Pine Ridge, SD	- 0	- 0	- 0	- 0	- 0	- 0	- 0	- -	- -	- -	- -	0 1	0 15	19 16	50 2
PHS Indian Hospital at Rapid City - Sioux San, Rapid City, SD	- 0	- 0	- 0	- 0	- 0	- 0	- 0	- -	- -	- -	- -	- 0	- 0	- 0	- 0
PHS Indian Hospital at Rosebud, Rosebud, SD	- 0	86 7	80 5	60 5	- 0	- 0	0 3	- 0	- 0	- 0	- 0	- 0	22 18	17 18	50 2
Platte Health Center, Platte, SD	- 0	- 0	- 0	- 0	- 0	- 0	- 0	- 0	- 0	- 0	- 0	100 4	33 3	80 5	- 0
Prairie Lakes Hospital, Watertown, SD	89 9	100 57	97 61	98 56	- 0	95 20	100 13	67 6	7 5	- 0	- 0	85 27	79 63	93 87	67 9
Rapid City Regional Hospital, Rapid City, SD	100 61	99 195	98 402	98 380	- 0	76 46	100 145	- 0	- 0	- 0	- 0	95 83	87 241	99 296	98 53
Saint Marys Hospital, Pierre, SD	- 0	100 6	80 5	60 5	17 6	- 0	100 2	100 17	10 18	- 0	75 4	67 9	100 19	100 26	100 4
Same Day Surgery Center, Rapid City, SD	- 0	- 0	- 0	- 0	- 0	- 0	- 0	- 0	- 0	- 0	- 0	- 0	- 0	- 0	- 0
Sanford Mid-Dakota Hospital, Chamberlain, SD	- 0	100 1	100 1	100 1	- 0	- 0	- 0	- -	- -	- -	- -	100 2	0 10	50 14	100 1
Sanford Usd Medical Center, Sioux Falls, SD	92 59	98 178	100 345	98 336	- 0	91 32	100 125	- 0	- 0	- 0	- 0	90 84	84 210	96 280	98 40
Sanford Vermillion Hospital, Vermillion, SD	100 1	- 0	100 1	100 1	- 0	- 0	- 0	- -	- -	- -	- -	100 4	38 13	100 17	- 0
Sioux Falls Surgical Hospital, Sioux Falls, SD	- 0	- 0	- 0	- 0	- 0	- 0	- 0	- 0	- 0	- 0	- 0	- 0	- 0	- 0	- 0
Sioux Falls VA Medical Center, Sioux Falls, SD	- 0	- 0	- 0	- 0	- 0	- 0	- 0	- -	- -	- -	- -	96 26	98 52	100 56	100 12
Siouxland Surgery Center Lp, Dakota Dunes, SD	- 0	- 0	- 0	- 0	- 0	- 0	- 0	- 0	- 0	- 0	- 0	- 0	- 0	- 0	- 0
Spearfish Regional Hospital, Spearfish, SD	- 0	80 5	100 3	100 2	100 1	- 0	- 0	92 40	2 40	- 0	50 6	100 6	62 13	85 20	- 0
Spearfish Regional Surgery Center, Spearfish, SD	- 0	- 0	- 0	- 0	- 0	- 0	- 0	- 0	- 0	- 0	- 0	- 0	- 0	- 0	- 0
Sturgis Regional Hospital, Sturgis, SD	- 0	100 1	100 1	100 1	- 0	- 0	- 0	100 21	7 23	- 0	- 0	75 4	100 8	73 11	- 0
VA Black Hills Healthcare System - Fort Meade, Fort Meade, SD	- 0	- 0	- 0	- 0	- 0	- 0	- 0	- -	- -	- -	- -	95 20	92 53	100 58	100 14
Wagner Community Memorial Hospital, Wagner, SD	- 0	- 0	- 0	- 0	- 0	- 0	- 0	- 0	- 0	- 0	- 0	67 3	60 5	83 12	- 0

NOTE: The first number in each column (boldface) is the score, the second number is the number of patients; Please refer to the main entry for footnotes; (a) 100-299
*MEASURES: **Heart Attack Care:** 1. ACE Inhibitor or ARB for LVSD; 2. Aspirin at Arrival; 3. Aspirin at Discharge; 4. Beta Blocker at Discharge; 5. Fibrinolytic Medication Timing; 6. PCI Within 90 Minutes of Arrival; 7. Smoking Cessation Advice; **Chest Pain/Possible Heart Attack Care:** 8. Aspirin at Arrival; 9. Median Time to ECG (minutes); 10. Median Time to Transfer (minutes); 11. Fibrinolytic Medication Timing; **Heart Failure Care:** 12. ACE Inhibitor or ARB for LVSD; 13. Discharge Instructions; 14. Evaluation of LVS Function; 15. Smoking Cessation Advice*

Hospital	Heart Attack Care							Chest Pain/Possible Heart Attack Care				Heart Failure Care			
	1	2	3	4	5	6	7	8	9	10	11	12	13	14	15
Winner Regional Healthcare Center, Winner, SD	- 0	**50** 2	- 0	- 0	- 0	- 0	- 0	- -	- -	- -	- -	**20** 5	**67** 15	**44** 18	**0** 2
WISCONSIN															
Amery Regional Medical Center, Amery, WI	- 0	- 0	- 0	- 0	- 0	- 0	- 0	- -	- -	- -	- -	**50** 4	**100** 21	**48** 31	- 0
Appleton Medical Center, Appleton, WI	**98** 59	**100** 134	**100** 261	**99** 264	- 0	**97** 32	**97** 108	**100** 3	**5** 3	- 0	- 0	**93** 58	**92** 168	**98** 211	**88** 16
Aspirus Wausau Hospital, Wausau, WI	**97** 29	**100** 118	**100** 251	**100** 250	- 0	**100** 33	**100** 80	- 0	- 0	- 0	- 0	**92** 51	**80** 205	**100** 238	**100** 27
Aurora Baycare Medical Center, Green Bay, WI	**100** 22	**100** 52	**98** 137	**98** 132	- 0	**50** 2	**98** 46	- 0	- 0	- 0	- 0	**92** 36	**77** 82	**100** 107	**100** 6
Aurora Lakeland Medical Center, Elkhorn, WI	**100** 5	**100** 15	**100** 7	**100** 8	- 0	- 0	**100** 2	**99** 91	**6** 93	**43** 12	- 0	**95** 20	**72** 50	**100** 55	**100** 8
Aurora Medical Center, Summit, WI	- 0	- 0	- 0	- 0	- 0	- 0	- 0	- -	- -	- -	- -	- 0	- 0	- 0	- 0
Aurora Medical Center - Washington County, Hartford, WI	**100** 4	**87** 39	**88** 26	**93** 30	- 0	- 0	- 0	**94** 98	**10** 103	**35** 3	- 0	**94** 17	**94** 49	**97** 71	**100** 5
Aurora Medical Center Kenosha, Kenosha, WI	**100** 4	**95** 21	**100** 16	**100** 16	- 0	- 0	**100** 1	**100** 71	**6** 73	**41** 15	- 0	**95** 39	**82** 73	**98** 90	**100** 27
Aurora Medical Center Manitowoc County, Two Rivers, WI	**100** 6	**100** 27	**100** 19	**100** 21	- 0	- 0	- 0	**100** 75	**10** 77	**59** 11	- 0	**100** 15	**92** 26	**97** 38	- 0
Aurora Medical Center Oshkosh, Oshkosh, WI	**100** 2	**100** 43	**100** 41	**100** 37	- 0	**83** 18	**100** 14	**100** 8	**6** 8	**118** 1	- 0	**100** 15	**83** 52	**100** 66	**100** 3
Aurora Memorial Hospital Burlington, Burlington, WI	**100** 4	**100** 24	**100** 15	**100** 14	- 0	- 0	**100** 1	**90** 40	**0** 41	**49** 9	**100** 1	**100** 23	**99** 72	**100** 87	**100** 21
Aurora Sheboygan Memorial Medical Center, Sheboygan, WI	**83** 6	**98** 40	**94** 32	**93** 29	- 0	- 0	**100** 4	**98** 99	**6** 99	**44** 29	- 0	**97** 30	**97** 78	**100** 101	**100** 13
Aurora St Lukes Medical Center, Milwaukee, WI	**100** 157	**100** 615	**100** 1006	**100** 952	- 0	**95** 93	**100** 328	**100** 7	**6** 7	- 0	- 0	**98** 545	**90** 1201	**100** 1435	**100** 288
Aurora West Allis Medical Center, West Allis, WI	**100** 8	**100** 53	**100** 26	**100** 29	- 0	- 0	**100** 1	**97** 144	**12** 148	**38** 15	- 0	**100** 34	**89** 114	**100** 187	**100** 15
Baldwin Area Medical Center, Baldwin, WI	- 0	- 0	- 0	- 0	- 0	- 0	- 0	- -	- -	- -	- -	**100** 2	**88** 8	**91** 11	**100** 2
Bay Area Medical Center, Marinette, WI	**73** 15	**98** 112	**96** 78	**97** 79	- 0	**75** 4	**93** 15	**100** 72	**1** 75	**78** 4	**89** 9	**85** 41	**89** 116	**96** 164	**95** 22
Beaver Dam Com Hospital, Beaver Dam, WI	**100** 2	**100** 15	**100** 10	**100** 9	- 0	- 0	**100** 1	**99** 134	**8** 138	**80** 14	**0** 1	**88** 17	**60** 48	**87** 69	**89** 9
Bellin Memorial Hospital, Green Bay, WI	**100** 34	**99** 189	**99** 359	**100** 353	- 0	**100** 36	**100** 115	- 0	- 0	- 0	- 0	**89** 57	**92** 165	**100** 202	**91** 22
Beloit Memorial Hospital, Beloit, WI	**94** 16	**95** 84	**94** 69	**97** 71	**0** 2	- 0	**94** 17	**96** 49	**12** 51	**64** 7	**0** 3	**88** 52	**84** 148	**100** 194	**100** 32
Berlin Memorial Hospital, Berlin, WI	- 0	- 0	- 0	- 0	- 0	- 0	- 0	**98** 81	**0** 81	- 0	- 0	**78** 9	**90** 20	**84** 44	**83** 6
Black River Memorial Hospital, Black River Falls, WI	**100** 1	**100** 2	**100** 2	**100** 2	- 0	- 0	- 0	**90** 77	**4** 86	**82** 8	**0** 4	**100** 5	**94** 17	**59** 22	**100** 1
Boscobel Area Health Care, Boscobel, WI	- 0	**100** 1	- 0	- 0	- 0	- 0	- 0	**100** 16	**10** 15	**127** 2	**50** 2	**67** 3	**100** 8	**53** 17	- 0
Burnett Medical Center, Grantsburg, WI	- 0	**50** 2	**100** 1	**0** 1	- 0	- 0	**100** 1	- -	- -	- -	- -	**100** 2	**84** 25	**84** 31	**100** 5
Calumet Medical Center, Chilton, WI	- 0	- 0	- 0	- 0	- 0	- 0	- 0	**100** 45	**5** 47	**44** 12	- 0	**100** 3	**100** 11	**100** 19	**100** 2
Columbia Center, Mequon, WI	- 0	- 0	- 0	- 0	- 0	- 0	- 0	- 0	- 0	- 0	- 0	- 0	- 0	- 0	- 0
Columbia St Mary's Hospital Ozaukee, Mequon, WI	**97** 33	**99** 190	**98** 212	**96** 213	- 0	**76** 49	**98** 55	**75** 4	**6** 4	**430** 1	- 0	**94** 82	**75** 163	**95** 247	**74** 23
Columbia St Marys Hospital Milwaukee, Milwaukee, WI	**94** 31	**100** 115	**100** 146	**98** 145	- 0	**53** 17	**98** 43	**75** 4	**10** 4	- 0	- 0	**96** 139	**78** 264	**97** 332	**91** 65
Columbus Community Hospital, Columbus, WI	- 0	- 0	- 0	- 0	- 0	- 0	- 0	- -	- -	- -	- -	**100** 9	**45** 20	**87** 31	**0** 2
Community Memorial Hospital, Menomonee Falls, WI	**90** 21	**100** 125	**99** 132	**98** 124	- 0	**100** 27	**100** 26	**100** 8	**12** 10	- 0	- 0	**100** 71	**80** 152	**99** 204	**97** 29
Community Memorial Hospital, Oconto Falls, WI	**100** 1	**100** 5	**100** 5	**80** 5	- 0	- 0	**100** 1	- -	- -	- -	- -	**67** 9	**97** 37	**79** 47	**100** 5
Cumberland Memorial Hospital, Cumberland, WI	- 0	- 0	- 0	- 0	- 0	- 0	- 0	- -	- -	- -	- -	**50** 2	**78** 9	**31** 16	**100** 2
Divine Savior Healthcare, Portage, WI	**100** 2	**100** 3	**100** 3	**100** 3	- 0	- 0	- 0	**95** 99	**10** 103	**42** 14	**50** 2	**92** 13	**42** 48	**78** 60	**80** 5
Door County Memorial Hospital, Sturgeon Bay, WI	**100** 1	**100** 7	**100** 7	**100** 7	- 0	- 0	- 0	- -	- -	- -	- -	**89** 19	**78** 65	**100** 74	**100** 5
Edgerton Hospital and Health Services, Edgerton, WI	- 0	- 0	- 0	- 0	- 0	- 0	- 0	- -	- -	- -	- -	- 0	- 0	- 0	- 0
Flambeau Hospital, Park Falls, WI	**100** 1	**100** 7	**100** 3	**100** 5	- 0	- 0	- 0	- -	- -	- -	- -	**100** 6	**82** 11	**100** 18	**100** 3
Fort Healthcare, Fort Atkinson, WI	**100** 1	**100** 7	**100** 5	**80** 5	- 0	- 0	- 0	**96** 124	**7** 127	**66** 12	- 0	**92** 13	**63** 54	**95** 79	**100** 12
Franciscan Skemp Arcadia, Arcadia, WI	- 0	- 0	- 0	- 0	- 0	- 0	- 0	- -	- -	- -	- -	**100** 1	**50** 6	**92** 12	**100** 2
Franciscan Skemp La Crosse Hospital, La Crosse, WI	**95** 22	**99** 81	**95** 111	**100** 111	- 0	**83** 24	**100** 40	**100** 7	**22** 7	**75** 1	- 0	**97** 36	**64** 83	**99** 126	**100** 20
Franciscan Skemp Sparta Hospital, Sparta, WI	- 0	- 0	- 0	- 0	- 0	- 0	- 0	- -	- -	- -	- -	**100** 1	**33** 3	**80** 15	**100** 2
Froedtert Memorial Lutheran Hospital, Milwaukee, WI	**100** 31	**99** 159	**99** 195	**98** 192	- 0	**70** 23	**92** 73	**67** 3	**82** 3	- 0	- 0	**97** 119	**75** 255	**99** 300	**88** 76
Good Samaritan Health Center, Merrill, WI	**100** 1	**100** 2	**100** 3	**100** 3	- 0	- 0	**100** 1	- 0	- 0	- 0	- 0	**100** 5	**100** 16	**100** 25	**100** 1
Grant Regional Health Center, Lancaster, WI	- 0	- 0	- 0	- 0	- 0	- 0	- 0	**94** 32	**8** 32	**138** 2	**50** 2	**50** 4	**75** 8	**47** 17	- 0
Gundersen Luth Medical Center, La Crosse, WI	**98** 52	**100** 165	**99** 324	**100** 325	- 0	**94** 33	**100** 110	- 0	- 0	- 0	- 0	**96** 47	**100** 119	**99** 153	**100** 22
Hayward Area Memorial Hospital, Hayward, WI	- 0	**75** 4	**75** 4	**80** 5	- 0	- 0	- 0	- -	- -	- -	- -	**100** 2	**100** 9	**64** 14	- 0
Holy Family Memorial, Manitowoc, WI	**90** 10	**97** 62	**98** 53	**92** 51	- 0	**67** 9	**100** 10	**80** 15	**5** 16	**49** 4	- 0	**100** 25	**97** 59	**100** 101	**100** 12
Howard Young Medical Center, Woodruff, WI	**100** 1	**80** 5	**100** 5	**100** 5	- 0	- 0	**67** 3	**99** 135	**7** 135	**50** 1	**75** 16	**94** 16	**67** 57	**98** 62	**100** 11
Hudson Hospital, Hudson, WI	**100** 1	**100** 3	**100** 4	**75** 4	- 0	- 0	- 0	- -	- -	- -	- -	**88** 8	**93** 15	**83** 18	**100** 2
Indianhead Medical Center, Shell Lake, WI	- 0	- 0	- 0	- 0	- 0	- 0	- 0	- -	- -	- -	- -	**50** 6	**69** 13	**87** 15	**100** 3
Ladd Memorial Hosptial, Osceola, WI	- 0	- 0	- 0	- 0	- 0	- 0	- 0	- -	- -	- -	- -	**0** 2	**100** 14	**56** 18	**67** 3
Lakeview Medical Center, Rice Lake, WI	- 0	**94** 16	**100** 8	**100** 7	- 0	- 0	**100** 1	**99** 116	**4** 118	**51** 10	**0** 1	**92** 12	**97** 59	**99** 72	**75** 12
Langlade Hospital, Antigo, WI	- 0	- 0	- 0	- 0	- 0	- 0	- 0	- -	- -	- -	- -	**100** 4	**92** 25	**100** 28	**100** 2
Luther Hospital Mayo Health System, Eau Claire, WI	**100** 33	**98** 107	**100** 245	**100** 246	- 0	**92** 12	**100** 83	**100** 3	**13** 3	- 0	- 0	**98** 49	**95** 192	**100** 264	**100** 18
Luther Midelfort - Chippewa Valley Mayo Health Sys, Bloomer, WI	- 0	- 0	- 0	- 0	- 0	- 0	- 0	- -	- -	- -	- -	- 0	**75** 4	**100** 8	- 0
Luther Midelfort - Northland Mayo Health System, Barron, WI	- 0	**100** 8	**100** 5	**100** 5	- 0	- 0	- 0	- -	- -	- -	- -	**100** 7	**100** 21	**100** 27	**100** 2
Luther Midelfort - Oakridge Mayo Health System, Osseo, WI	- 0	- 0	- 0	- 0	- 0	- 0	- 0	- -	- -	- -	- -	- 0	**100** 2	**80** 5	- 0
Madison VA Medical Center, Madison, WI	**100** 9	**100** 49	**100** 56	**100** 52	- 0	**25** 8	**100** 27	- -	- -	- -	- -	**97** 39	**96** 136	**100** 147	**100** 44
Memorial Health Center, Medford, WI	- 0	- 0	- 0	- 0	- 0	- 0	- 0	**98** 86	**4** 88	**30** 10	**33** 3	**100** 7	**100** 8	**100** 18	**0** 1
Memorial Hospital Lafayette County, Darlington, WI	**100** 1	**100** 3	**100** 2	**100** 2	- 0	- 0	- 0	**100** 15	**12** 18	**70** 1	- 0	**75** 4	**72** 18	**95** 22	- 0
Memorial Medical Center, Neillsville, WI	- 0	**100** 4	**100** 4	**67** 3	- 0	- 0	- 0	- -	- -	- -	- -	**100** 2	**73** 11	**58** 19	- 0
Memorial Medical Center, Ashland, WI	**100** 6	**100** 27	**93** 28	**89** 27	- 0	- 0	**100** 3	- -	- -	- -	- -	**60** 25	**84** 49	**84** 63	**71** 7
Mercy Health Sys Corp, Janesville, WI	**100** 19	**99** 124	**100** 158	**100** 154	- 0	**91** 32	**94** 69	**100** 21	**6** 23	- 0	- 0	**96** 56	**95** 169	**96** 205	**100** 35
Mercy Medical Center of Oshkosh, Oshkosh, WI	**92** 13	**100** 53	**98** 60	**98** 49	- 0	**85** 13	**100** 22	**100** 6	**5** 7	**33** 1	- 0	**90** 40	**88** 77	**100** 110	**100** 19
Mercy Walworth Hospital & Medical Center, Lake Geneva, WI	- 0	- 0	- 0	- 0	- 0	- 0	- 0	**99** 146	**6** 151	**45** 13	- 0	- 0	- 0	- 0	- 0
Meriter Hospital, Madison, WI	**95** 40	**100** 190	**100** 266	**98** 251	- 0	**96** 47	**100** 68	- 0	- 0	- 0	- 0	**92** 99	**94** 239	**100** 302	**95** 38
Midwest Orthopedic Specialty Hospital, Franklin, WI	- 0	- 0	- 0	- 0	- 0	- 0	- 0	- 0	- 0	- 0	- 0	- 0	- 0	- 0	- 0

NOTE: The first number in each column (boldface) is the score, the second number is the number of patients; Please refer to the main entry for footnotes; (a) 100-299
MEASURES: ***Heart Attack Care:*** *1. ACE Inhibitor or ARB for LVSD; 2. Aspirin at Arrival; 3. Aspirin at Discharge; 4. Beta Blocker at Discharge; 5. Fibrinolytic Medication Timing; 6. PCI Within 90 Minutes of Arrival; 7. Smoking Cessation Advice;* ***Chest Pain/Possible Heart Attack Care:*** *8. Aspirin at Arrival; 9. Median Time to ECG (minutes); 10. Median Time to Transfer (minutes); 11. Fibrinolytic Medication Timing;* ***Heart Failure Care:*** *12. ACE Inhibitor or ARB for LVSD; 13. Discharge Instructions; 14. Evaluation of LVS Function; 15. Smoking Cessation Advice*

Hospital	Heart Attack Care							Chest Pain/Possible Heart Attack Care				Heart Failure Care			
	1	2	3	4	5	6	7	8	9	10	11	12	13	14	15
Mile Bluff Medical Center, Mauston, WI	- 0	90 10	100 6	67 6	0 1	- 0	- 0	95 79	0 80	161 6	33 3	100 5	61 33	96 46	0 3
Milwaukee VA Medical Center, Milwaukee, WI	100 9	100 37	100 39	100 36	- 0	0 5	100 13	- -	- -	- -	- -	96 84	97 215	100 218	100 47
Ministry Eagle River Memorial Hospital, Eagle River, WI	- 0	100 2	100 1	- 0	- 0	- 0	- 0	100 15	8 15	- 0	100 1	100 1	75 20	100 28	100 6
Ministry St Marys Hospital, Rhinelander, WI	100 2	100 18	92 12	85 13	- 0	- 0	- 0	98 117	5 126	- 0	64 11	100 13	100 63	100 90	100 8
Ministry St Michaels Hospital of Stevens Point, Stevens Point, WI	75 4	100 15	100 9	100 12	- 0	- 0	- 0	100 205	10 214	27 27	- 0	100 31	85 67	100 117	100 10
Monroe Clinic, Monroe, WI	100 1	100 14	100 9	100 10	- 0	- 0	- 0	100 69	5 70	47 3	100 6	100 17	100 59	100 77	100 9
Moundview Memorial Hospital and Clinics, Friendship, WI	- 0	- 0	- 0	- 0	- 0	- 0	- 0	93 29	12 31	- 0	- 0	100 1	57 7	89 9	100 2
New London Family Medical Center, New London, WI	- 0	- 0	- 0	- 0	- 0	- 0	- 0	- -	- -	- -	- -	- 0	- 0	- 0	- 0
Oak Leaf Surgcl Hospital, Eau Claire, WI	- 0	- 0	- 0	- 0	- 0	- 0	- 0	- 0	- 0	- 0	- 0	- 0	- 0	- 0	- 0
Oconomowoc Memorial Hospital, Oconomowoc, WI	100 9	98 57	100 52	98 52	- 0	92 13	100 15	100 3	6 4	- 0	- 0	100 20	72 58	100 82	100 6
Oconto Hospital & Medical Center, Oconto, WI	- 0	- 0	- 0	- 0	- 0	- 0	- 0	- -	- -	- -	- -	- 0	- 0	- 0	- 0
Orthopaedic Hospital of Wisconsin, Glendale, WI	- 0	- 0	- 0	- 0	- 0	- 0	- 0	- 0	- 0	- 0	- 0	- 0	- 0	- 0	- 0
Our Lady of Victory Hospital, Stanley, WI	100 1	50 2	100 2	100 2	- 0	- 0	100 1	100 42	5 43	75 3	33 3	100 10	100 14	100 25	- 0
Prairie Du Chien Memorial Hospital, Prairie Du Chien, WI	100 2	100 7	100 4	100 5	- 0	- 0	100 1	98 40	5 39	- 0	75 8	100 3	90 21	88 33	100 2
Red Cedar Medical Center-Mayo Health System, Menomonie, WI	100 1	100 6	100 4	100 4	- 0	- 0	100 1	- -	- -	- -	- -	78 9	76 51	97 79	100 9
Reedsburg Area Medical Center, Reedsburg, WI	- 0	100 2	100 2	100 2	- 0	- 0	- 0	96 46	4 48	64 14	50 2	85 13	73 45	91 57	100 4
Richland Hospital, Richland Center, WI	100 3	100 9	100 8	80 10	- 0	- 0	- 0	- -	- -	- -	- -	83 6	73 30	68 37	25 4
Ripon Medical Center, Ripon, WI	- 0	- 0	- 0	- 0	- 0	- 0	- 0	- -	- -	- -	- -	40 5	82 22	94 33	100 2
River Falls Area Hospital, River Falls, WI	- 0	67 3	100 1	100 1	- 0	- 0	- 0	93 27	9 29	35 7	- 0	100 7	94 18	100 21	100 2
Riverside Medical Center, Waupaca, WI	- 0	- 0	- 0	- 0	- 0	- 0	- 0	- -	- -	- -	- -	- 0	- 0	- 0	- 0
Riverview Hospital Assoc, Wisconsin Rapids, WI	100 2	100 12	100 9	100 7	- 0	- 0	- 0	96 206	12 214	30 14	- 0	90 20	85 71	100 102	100 5
Rusk County Memorial Hospital, Ladysmith, WI	- 0	100 2	- 0	- 0	- 0	- 0	- 0	- -	- -	- -	- -	43 7	69 16	91 22	- 0
Sacred Heart Hospital, Eau Claire, WI	94 33	100 92	100 189	99 184	- 0	85 20	100 66	67 3	14 4	- 0	- 0	95 42	93 105	100 139	100 18
Sacred Heart Hospital, Tomahawk, WI	- 0	- 0	- 0	- 0	- 0	- 0	- 0	- 0	- 0	- 0	- 0	100 3	100 8	100 9	100 2
Saint Agnes Hospital, Fond Du Lac, WI	96 26	99 136	97 153	94 131	- 0	88 34	100 51	50 4	8 4	- 0	- 0	98 54	82 99	100 143	100 21
Saint Clare Hospital Health Svcs, Baraboo, WI	100 1	100 3	100 2	- 0	- 0	- 0	- 0	98 63	3 63	26 7	100 1	100 16	95 40	100 52	100 3
Saint Clare's Hospital of Weston, Weston, WI	100 43	100 69	100 243	100 231	- 0	95 19	100 84	- 0	- 0	- 0	- 0	100 31	99 111	99 144	96 27
Saint Croix Regional Medical Center, Saint Croix Falls, WI	- 0	- 0	- 0	- 0	- 0	- 0	- 0	- -	- -	- -	- -	100 12	82 50	67 61	62 8
Saint Elizabeth Hospital, Appleton, WI	100 26	100 110	100 156	100 150	- 0	100 24	100 51	100 2	4 2	- 0	- 0	100 32	93 134	100 174	100 19
Saint Josephs Community Health Services, Hillsboro, WI	- 0	- 0	- 0	- 0	- 0	- 0	- 0	70 10	14 9	95 1	- 0	100 2	64 11	77 13	50 2
Saint Josephs Community Hospital West Bend, West Bend, WI	100 2	73 11	57 7	100 8	- 0	- 0	100 1	88 132	9 133	54 24	- 0	81 27	91 57	99 80	100 7
Saint Josephs Hospital, Chippewa Falls, WI	100 1	88 8	100 7	80 5	- 0	- 0	- 0	97 133	8 138	63 14	- 0	88 16	84 37	98 55	100 3
Saint Josephs Hospital, Marshfield, WI	100 55	99 170	100 302	99 338	- 0	100 24	100 93	- 0	- 0	- 0	- 0	100 104	90 298	100 392	97 32
Saint Mary's Hospital, Madison, WI	96 83	100 206	100 445	100 433	- 0	92 40	100 127	100 15	5 15	- 0	- 0	93 122	91 341	98 465	100 55
Saint Marys Hospital Medical Center, Green Bay, WI	100 22	100 98	97 94	98 95	- 0	90 30	100 31	100 4	9 5	- 0	- 0	97 29	93 97	97 130	100 16
Saint Marys Hospital Superior, Superior, WI	- 0	- 0	- 0	- 0	- 0	- 0	- 0	81 16	26 15	40 2	- 0	100 3	42 12	73 15	50 2
Saint Nicholas Hospital, Sheboygan, WI	89 9	96 26	83 23	91 23	- 0	- 0	100 2	100 71	7 73	37 21	100 1	97 33	81 43	99 68	0 2
Saint Vincent Hospital, Green Bay, WI	88 17	99 136	99 164	97 156	- 0	90 29	98 57	100 1	3 1	- 0	- 0	88 43	87 132	97 161	100 23
Sauk Prairie Memorial Hospital, Prairie Du Sac, WI	50 2	67 3	50 2	67 3	- 0	- 0	- 0	92 63	10 67	95 9	- 0	50 4	100 24	97 30	100 1
Shawano Medical Center, Shawano, WI	- 0	- 0	- 0	- 0	- 0	- 0	- 0	98 83	3 89	40 11	- 0	100 18	62 39	90 58	100 7
Southwest Health Center, Platteville, WI	- 0	100 1	- 0	- 0	- 0	- 0	- 0	96 46	12 46	55 2	0 1	100 5	88 16	90 31	100 1
Spooner Health System, Spooner, WI	- 0	100 1	100 1	100 1	- 0	- 0	- 0	100 25	24 27	180 5	67 3	100 4	100 8	100 14	- 0
Stoughton Hospital, Stoughton, WI	- 0	- 0	- 0	- 0	- 0	- 0	- 0	- -	- -	- -	- -	83 6	95 21	93 30	- 0
Theda Clark Medical Center, Neenah, WI	92 12	100 70	99 70	98 62	0 1	90 20	100 26	100 12	2 12	32 1	- 0	100 10	92 72	93 107	100 10
Tomah Memorial Hospital, Tomah, WI	100 2	100 16	87 15	100 15	- 0	- 0	100 1	- -	- -	- -	- -	75 4	100 15	100 25	100 1
Tomah VA Medical Center, Tomah, WI	- 0	- 0	- 0	- 0	- 0	- 0	- 0	- -	- -	- -	- -	- 0	- 0	- 0	- 0
Tri County Memorial Hospital, Whitehall, WI	- 0	- 0	- 0	- 0	- 0	- 0	- 0	- -	- -	- -	- -	57 7	100 15	65 23	100 1
United Hospital System, Kenosha, WI	100 21	99 153	99 146	96 135	- 0	83 35	100 66	83 6	9 7	- 0	- 0	94 141	84 254	99 320	100 51
University of Wisconsin Hospitals & Clinics Authority, Madison, WI	95 42	98 112	99 275	100 262	- 0	93 14	100 96	- 0	- 0	- 0	- 0	98 90	77 231	99 264	100 47
Upland Hills Health, Dodgeville, WI	- 0	- 0	- 0	- 0	- 0	- 0	- 0	- -	- -	- -	- -	100 5	100 21	89 28	50 2
Vernon Memorial Hospital, Viroqua, WI	100 1	100 4	100 1	100 1	- 0	- 0	- 0	100 4	8 6	34 1	- 0	100 6	61 18	93 27	100 3
Watertown Regional Medical Center, Watertown, WI	0 1	100 8	100 3	80 5	- 0	- 0	- 0	100 66	9 67	67 5	80 5	100 13	60 43	100 54	100 6
Waukesha Memorial Hospital, Waukesha, WI	100 47	99 216	98 202	98 199	- 0	91 35	100 46	100 5	5 5	- 0	- 0	97 75	86 221	98 286	100 25
Waupun Memorial Hospital, Waupun, WI	- 0	- 0	- 0	- 0	- 0	- 0	- 0	- -	- -	- -	- -	83 6	95 21	88 26	100 3
Westfields Hospital, New Richmond, WI	- 0	50 2	100 1	100 2	- 0	- 0	- 0	- -	- -	- -	- -	33 3	59 29	78 37	100 1
Wheaton Franciscan - St Joseph, Milwaukee, WI	96 23	99 177	100 213	99 202	- 0	83 48	97 78	64 22	10 25	- 0	- 0	96 233	83 450	99 524	100 203
Wheaton Franciscan Healthcare - All Saints, Racine, WI	88 26	100 193	100 188	100 184	0 1	91 46	100 68	78 9	8 8	- 0	- 0	99 155	87 382	100 491	100 120
Wheaton Franciscan Healthcare-Elmbrook Mem, Brookfield, WI	100 1	89 9	100 4	100 3	- 0	- 0	- 0	94 49	6 50	50 4	- 0	87 31	74 76	99 116	100 15
Wheaton Franciscan Healthcare - Franklin, Franklin, WI	- 0	- 0	- 0	- 0	- 0	- 0	- 0	93 54	6 59	44 4	- 0	78 9	72 18	100 21	100 2
Wheaton Franciscan Healthcare - St Francis, Milwaukee, WI	94 17	99 77	97 73	99 78	- 0	74 19	96 27	100 9	4 10	- 0	- 0	95 73	84 144	99 189	100 28
Wild Rose Com Memorial Hospital, Wild Rose, WI	- 0	100 1	100 2	- 0	- 0	- 0	0 1	- -	- -	- -	- -	57 7	88 16	93 28	100 3

NOTE: The first number in each column (boldface) is the score, the second number is the number of patients; Please refer to the main entry for footnotes; (a) 100-299

*MEASURES: **Heart Attack Care:** 1. ACE Inhibitor or ARB for LVSD; 2. Aspirin at Arrival; 3. Aspirin at Discharge; 4. Beta Blocker at Discharge; 5. Fibrinolytic Medication Timing; 6. PCI Within 90 Minutes of Arrival; 7. Smoking Cessation Advice; **Chest Pain/Possible Heart Attack Care:** 8. Aspirin at Arrival; 9. Median Time to ECG (minutes); 10. Median Time to Transfer (minutes); 11. Fibrinolytic Medication Timing; **Heart Failure Care:** 12. ACE Inhibitor or ARB for LVSD; 13. Discharge Instructions; 14. Evaluation of LVS Function; 15. Smoking Cessation Advice*

Hospital	Pneumonia Care						Surgical Care Improvement Project										
	16	17	18	19	20	21	22	23	24	25	26	27	28	29	30	31	32
ILLINOIS																	
Abraham Lincoln Memorial Hospital, Lincoln, IL	90 31	96 53	100 39	98 54	98 63	100 9	100 19	100 64	100 12	- 0	98 41	- 0	100 42	- 0	100 40	100 19	100 16
Adventist Bolingbrook Hospital, Bolingbrook, IL	96 110	98 162	97 87	96 164	96 109	100 45	88 83	99 149	97 33	- 0	89 79	85 111	91 77	88 108	64 75	92 83	92 26
Adventist Glenoaks, Glendale Heights, IL	89 27	99 89	91 35	97 65	100 41	100 17	93 43	100 90	55 20	- 0	100 35	77 31	100 35	89 27	97 34	91 44	60 10
Adventist La Grange Memorial Hospital, La Grange, IL	97 148	100 266	90 160	99 310	93 274	100 47	96 178	100 411	97 138	100 55	97 283	93 155	98 283	98 149	94 270	97 178	83 99
Advocate Christ Hospital & Medical Center, Oak Lawn, IL	95 65	98 54	99 110	98 140	99 167	96 50	98 212	100 741	93 303	95 145	99 488	97 728	97 499	95 723	98 461	99 212	86 111
Advocate Condell Medical Center, Libertyville, IL	96 85	99 135	100 89	98 156	99 132	100 40	94 189	100 609	99 201	99 120	98 425	94 446	98 429	98 442	96 398	94 189	93 125
Advocate Eureka Hospital, Eureka, IL	100 16	100 21	95 19	100 24	97 32	100 4	- 0	- 0	- 0	- 0	- 0	- 0	- 0	- 0	- 0	- 0	- 0
Advocate Good Samaritan Hospital, Downers Grove, IL	96 142	99 227	97 167	99 236	96 258	100 72	97 203	100 612	97 198	98 132	100 439	96 323	98 442	98 317	98 425	98 203	91 82
Advocate Good Shepherd Hospital, Barrington, IL	95 101	100 234	100 132	100 201	99 211	100 58	98 153	100 594	98 243	100 134	98 425	97 396	99 436	98 391	96 416	98 153	97 137
Advocate Illinois Masonic Medical Center, Chicago, IL	98 60	100 145	99 79	100 113	97 92	96 57	97 217	100 607	96 182	90 86	99 432	99 401	97 435	98 476	98 406	97 217	96 106
Advocate Lutheran General Hospital, Park Ridge, IL	93 150	100 267	99 201	99 280	99 305	100 63	96 211	100 641	99 233	92 108	100 460	99 730	97 464	98 727	96 434	99 211	97 116
Advocate South Suburban Hospital, Hazel Crest, IL	97 75	97 58	99 86	100 141	99 133	100 54	98 159	100 415	98 126	- 0	99 295	97 220	100 298	99 219	97 271	99 159	99 69
Advocate Trinity Hospital, Chicago, IL	93 143	97 202	99 143	94 203	98 168	99 82	100 147	100 402	95 129	- 0	100 256	94 115	98 256	96 113	93 245	100 147	87 46
Alexian Brothers Medical Center, Elk Grove Village, IL	89 202	99 306	85 256	96 320	94 378	99 93	97 269	100 728	99 278	94 141	98 481	97 518	96 487	95 515	95 414	98 269	91 158
Alton Memorial Hospital, Alton, IL	87 187	99 271	89 167	97 279	89 228	100 105	95 134	100 333	100 92	- 0	98 239	94 142	99 242	94 144	96 226	96 134	83 109
Anderson Hospital, Maryville, IL	93 103	97 189	100 98	95 161	93 140	100 76	97 228	100 512	91 119	- 0	96 362	96 288	97 368	97 283	93 347	97 228	92 72
Blessing Hospital, Quincy, IL	94 234	99 438	95 291	99 436	96 405	100 160	95 245	100 663	88 208	95 85	97 405	88 271	97 412	96 248	94 383	95 246	70 79
Bromenn Healthcare, Normal, IL	97 94	94 216	93 145	90 194	93 191	100 38	86 204	100 771	90 196	99 67	97 543	89 229	97 545	96 213	95 521	89 204	85 81
Carle Foundation Hospital, Urbana, IL	95 78	98 99	97 75	98 126	95 110	100 51	95 130	100 604	98 261	91 137	95 422	93 435	99 446	93 434	97 413	95 130	95 106
Carlinville Area Hospital, Carlinville, IL	93 29	88 24	95 20	97 31	91 33	100 5	- 0	- 0	- 0	- 0	- 0	- -	- 0	- -	- 0	- 0	- 0
Centegra Health System - McHenry Hospital, Mchenry, IL	87 141	99 230	75 152	96 246	73 211	96 85	78 235	100 758	97 275	96 136	94 557	81 163	97 559	96 150	88 536	85 236	74 214
Centegra Health System - Woodstock Hospital, Woodstock, IL	93 99	96 154	73 104	99 158	62 135	95 56	87 162	100 622	93 167	- 0	93 491	77 84	97 492	94 71	94 481	88 162	93 146
Central Dupage Hospital, Winfield, IL	96 189	98 215	90 174	98 249	92 212	100 80	99 95	100 553	98 182	100 105	99 391	97 490	99 394	98 483	97 375	100 95	96 100
CGH Medical Center, Sterling, IL	93 89	98 126	93 107	95 168	96 139	97 38	96 242	99 444	81 149	- 0	97 307	93 57	96 307	85 55	96 303	96 242	85 117
Clay County Hospital, Flora, IL	94 49	100 68	94 35	97 74	93 54	100 19	100 7	100 7	- 0	- 0	100 3	33 6	67 3	100 4	67 3	100 7	100 2
Community Memorial Hospital, Staunton, IL	92 13	62 8	89 9	100 13	73 11	67 6	0 1	100 7	- 0	- 0	20 5	- -	100 4	- -	100 4	0 1	- 0
Copley Memorial Hospital, Aurora, IL	92 119	97 154	93 81	99 173	92 119	100 55	94 199	100 840	94 274	98 97	99 669	99 303	97 675	97 301	93 656	96 199	94 249
Crawford Memorial Hospital, Robinson, IL	88 26	96 47	97 31	- 0	97 33	88 17	81 21	100 54	- 0	- 0	87 46	- -	91 47	- -	74 46	86 21	50 4
Crossroads Community Hospital, Mount Vernon, IL	89 56	100 70	89 46	99 75	100 70	100 27	90 51	99 188	100 49	- 0	99 146	90 48	99 146	96 85	91 140	98 51	91 35
Decatur Memorial Hospital, Decatur, IL	91 187	98 301	92 216	99 289	90 292	100 92	93 294	100 809	100 284	95 97	100 583	96 406	99 588	98 394	97 572	93 294	94 238
Delnor Community Hospital, Geneva, IL	97 127	99 105	99 132	99 213	100 226	100 40	98 172	100 466	97 145	- 0	98 317	98 109	96 316	90 109	96 304	99 172	84 50
Dr John Warner Hospital, Clinton, IL	- 0	- 0	- 0	- 0	- 0	- 0	- 0	- 0	- 0	- 0	- 0	- -	- 0	- -	- 0	- 0	- 0
Edward Hospital, Naperville, IL	95 248	100 438	97 277	97 439	97 408	99 113	96 635	100 1858	99 570	96 211	97 1228	98 474	100 1240	98 470	96 1167	97 635	91 555
Elmhurst Memorial Hospital, Elmhurst, IL	93 82	99 151	95 100	96 136	94 143	100 35	92 213	100 543	99 171	99 112	99 368	96 167	99 375	91 163	98 354	94 213	84 99
Evanston Hospital, Evanston, IL	97 106	98 180	98 129	99 165	97 194	100 34	99 537	100 1658	100 461	99 225	99 1123	99 623	98 1132	94 619	99 1080	99 537	98 260
Fairfield Memorial Hospital, Fairfield, IL	73 22	100 28	100 30	92 36	100 35	100 10	100 30	100 43	- 0	- 0	100 21	97 36	100 22	86 36	100 21	100 30	75 4
Fayette County Hospital, Vandalia, IL	73 15	93 15	84 31	95 42	88 33	80 10	- 0	100 1	- 0	- 0	0 1	- -	- 0	- -	- 0	- 0	100 1
Ferrell Hospital Community Foundations, Eldorado, IL	82 28	90 10	78 27	91 34	91 35	90 21	100 1	0 1	- 0	- 0	0 1	- -	0 1	- -	100 1	100 1	- 0
Fhn Memorial Hospital, Freeport, IL	92 91	97 145	96 92	99 141	95 126	86 37	91 115	100 429	94 133	- 0	99 291	92 92	94 292	99 142	99 276	97 115	95 21
Galesburg Cottage Hospital, Galesburg, IL	95 60	99 116	99 104	99 108	98 111	100 36	99 115	100 244	94 82	- 0	98 171	97 108	97 172	92 106	97 161	98 117	99 81
Gateway Regional Medical Center, Granite City, IL	100 50	100 113	96 51	99 99	98 62	100 54	99 100	100 255	100 46	- 0	99 202	97 73	100 203	96 72	99 202	99 100	99 69
Genesis Medical Center Illini Campus, Silvis, IL	97 102	100 161	96 111	98 161	98 133	96 51	97 134	100 422	100 98	- 0	100 313	99 108	98 312	97 107	96 305	99 135	94 18
Gibson Community Hospital, Gibson City, IL	90 42	97 38	96 25	100 50	95 40	92 13	73 37	92 106	84 31	- 0	94 82	- -	99 83	- -	93 82	73 37	94 47
Good Samaritan Regional Health Center, Mount Vernon, IL	93 107	100 135	98 125	98 171	100 164	100 59	97 237	100 647	96 231	98 52	96 502	93 193	99 510	90 191	94 476	97 238	81 31
Graham Hospital Association, Canton, IL	92 36	97 66	96 46	98 65	90 60	95 19	96 69	100 215	88 51	- 0	95 131	92 80	95 134	89 75	93 128	93 71	94 54
Greenville Regional Hospital, Greenville, IL	83 30	92 52	70 23	96 51	74 47	91 11	50 10	92 13	67 3	- 0	67 6	83 6	43 7	50 6	100 6	50 10	100 1
Hamilton Memorial Hospital District, Mcleansboro, IL	73 22	92 13	100 22	100 27	96 27	87 15	100 1	100 1	- 0	- 0	0 1	- -	100 1	- -	100 1	100 1	100 1
Hammond Henry Hospital, Geneseo, IL	- 0	- 0	- 0	- 0	- 0	- 0	92 38	100 111	- 0	- 0	98 88	- -	93 88	- -	93 87	95 38	33 9
Hardin County General Hospital, Rosiclare, IL	97 37	98 57	97 36	98 57	98 51	100 18	- 0	- 0	- 0	- 0	- 0	- 0	- 0	- 0	- 0	- 0	- 0
Harrisburg Medical Center, Harrisburg, IL	78 93	78 93	93 91	97 154	91 127	97 31	56 18	100 34	71 7	- 0	90 21	- 0	80 20	- 0	100 20	56 18	100 2
Heartland Regional Medical Center, Marion, IL	85 68	99 115	83 107	95 117	88 152	100 59	93 186	100 483	88 155	90 21	96 316	94 207	99 318	93 213	82 292	96 186	81 42
Herrin Hospital, Herrin, IL	88 95	100 119	88 144	92 177	90 177	96 92	90 173	100 277	93 102	- 0	92 198	81 37	95 198	91 33	88 183	94 173	96 89
Hillsboro Area Hospital, Hillsboro, IL	98 42	97 30	100 36	100 51	100 52	100 14	- 0	100 1	100 1	- 0	- 0	- -	- 0	- -	- 0	- 0	- 0
Hines VA Medical Center, Hines, IL	95 66	100 129	98 112	95 132	99 149	100 78	97 78	100 252	100 143	92 108	98 158	- -	99 158	- -	100 155	97 78	100 138
Hinsdale Hospital, Hinsdale, IL	86 120	97 243	88 142	97 217	89 240	97 38	95 144	100 440	96 120	88 77	95 309	96 278	100 313	99 272	94 292	99 144	98 80
Holy Cross Hospital, Chicago, IL	76 72	94 103	68 56	81 119	84 86	81 48	89 142	98 215	77 61	- 0	91 123	74 58	91 124	73 49	79 121	96 142	39 36
Hoopeston Community Memorial Hospital, Hoopeston, IL	97 30	70 57	100 23	93 27	78 49	73 11	67 3	100 13	- 0	- 0	100 7	- -	100 6	- -	100 6	67 3	100 9
Hopedale Medical Complex, Hopedale, IL	- 0	- 0	- 0	- 0	- 0	- 0	- 0	- 0	- 0	- 0	- 0	- -	- 0	- -	- 0	- 0	- 0
Illini Community Hospital, Pittsfield, IL	95 19	95 19	100 14	97 33	96 28	100 8	0 3	86 7	- 0	- 0	- 0	- 0	- 0	- 0	- 0	0 3	- 0
Illinois Valley Community Hospital, Peru, IL	79 67	93 82	93 67	95 95	93 108	100 19	97 71	100 248	100 81	- 0	96 200	89 136	100 200	93 132	92 200	96 72	100 96
Ingalls Memorial Hospital, Harvey, IL	90 94	98 123	86 84	95 146	96 90	100 51	91 138	100 452	95 130	89 37	97 332	94 107	99 335	98 104	97 321	96 138	95 78
Iroquois Memorial Hospital, Watseka, IL	85 84	90 122	95 64	93 118	97 117	90 29	92 25	100 87	96 24	- 0	96 69	100 31	97 69	84 31	94 65	92 25	100 2
Jackson Park Hospital, Chicago, IL	11 152	100 82	58 53	87 172	63 52	100 61	- 0	91 47	50 2	- 0	6 17	- 0	73 15	- 0	80 15	0 30	- 0
Jersey Community Hospital, Jerseyville, IL	83 83	97 116	94 64	99 108	87 94	96 26	75 16	100 49	83 12	- 0	88 32	93 14	91 32	95 39	90 31	71 17	100 1
Jesse Brown VA Medical Ctr-VA Chicago Healthcare, Chicago, IL	92 51	100 71	100 72	87 93	99 80	98 62	99 136	99 177	100 59	- 0	95 83	- -	98 86	- -	97 79	99 136	100 79
John & Mary Kirby Hospital, Monticello, IL	97 35	96 45	79 28	93 45	90 41	100 10	- 0	- 0	- 0	- 0	- 0	- -	- 0	- -	- 0	- 0	- 0
John H Stroger Jr Hospital, Chicago, IL	70 121	87 166	59 68	65 190	42 36	97 102	89 204	98 453	83 132	83 92	93 268	96 141	92 266	87 140	93 257	89 204	66 47

NOTE: The first number in each column (boldface) is the score, the second number is the number of patients; Please refer to the main entry for footnotes; (a) 100-299

*MEASURES: **Pneumonia Care:** 16. Appropriate Initial Antibiotic; 17. Blood Culture Timing; 18. Influenza Vaccine; 19. Initial Antibiotic Timing; 20. Pneumococcal Vaccine; 21. Smoking Cessation Advice; **Surgical Care Improvement Project:** 22. Appropriate VTP Within 24 Hours; 23. Appropriate Hair Removal; 24. Appropriate Beta Blocker Usage; 25. Controlled Postoperative Blood Glucose; 26. Prophylactic Antibiotic Timing; 27. Prophylactic Antibiotic Timing (Outpatient); 28. Prophylactic Antibiotic Selection; 29. Prophylactic Antibiotic Selection (Outpatient); 30. Prophylactic Antibiotic Stopped; 31. Recommended VTP Ordered; 32. Urinary Catheter Removal*

Hospital	Pneumonia Care						Surgical Care Improvement Project										
	16	17	18	19	20	21	22	23	24	25	26	27	28	29	30	31	32
Katherine Shaw Bethea Hospital, Dixon, IL	95 44	100 70	98 56	100 85	96 79	100 30	100 95	100 290	100 86	- 0	100 197	96 84	99 198	99 81	97 153	100 95	100 31
Kewanee Hospital, Kewanee, IL	92 36	94 49	88 41	98 47	88 48	93 15	100 20	100 50	100 13	- 0	100 29	- -	97 29	- -	82 28	100 20	100 4
Kishwaukee Community Hospital, Dekalb, IL	90 93	97 101	75 105	93 137	92 147	94 32	86 138	99 382	89 115	- 0	91 269	86 123	91 266	96 117	94 257	91 138	93 90
Lake Forest Hospital, Lake Forest, IL	95 114	97 207	93 99	98 158	96 137	100 34	91 268	100 822	94 181	- 0	98 640	96 327	98 642	97 327	96 638	93 268	94 248
Lawrence County Memorial Hospital, Lawrenceville, IL	50 12	97 30	94 17	100 36	76 25	100 5	- 0	- 0	- 0	- 0	- 0	- -	- 0	- -	- 0	- 0	- 0
Little Company of Mary Hospital, Evergreen Park, IL	94 82	100 116	100 79	98 143	96 143	100 49	99 240	100 478	98 118	- 0	99 283	96 242	98 285	99 239	99 247	100 240	100 66
Loretto Hospital, Chicago, IL	78 55	95 101	100 51	88 113	100 59	100 36	67 18	100 32	86 7	- 0	40 5	75 24	83 6	95 19	100 4	63 19	100 1
Louis A Weiss Memorial Hospital, Chicago, IL	88 52	98 201	98 112	98 176	96 171	96 56	96 171	100 412	92 133	83 23	97 245	76 147	98 245	84 257	96 231	98 171	97 117
Loyola Gottlieb Memorial Hospital, Melrose Park, IL	88 69	97 78	96 99	95 141	96 112	100 31	81 192	100 428	90 118	97 64	97 306	97 62	91 305	95 60	92 295	86 194	92 96
Loyola University Medical Center, Maywood, IL	93 92	96 255	89 158	91 219	95 217	100 68	97 175	100 576	89 245	89 138	98 381	93 268	96 387	93 486	94 370	98 175	95 142
Macneal Hospital, Berwyn, IL	91 150	95 235	91 150	96 223	96 208	100 83	98 258	96 738	96 248	88 80	98 539	74 388	98 559	79 317	97 513	99 258	96 190
Marion Illinois VA Medical Center, Marion, IL	88 80	96 112	85 79	94 17	95 85	100 50	- 0	- 0	- 0	- 0	- 0	- -	- 0	- -	- 0	- 0	- 0
Marshall Browning Hospital, Du Quoin, IL	79 14	95 22	61 18	80 15	23 22	50 6	- 0	- 0	- 0	- 0	- 0	- -	- 0	- -	- 0	- 0	- 0
Mason District Hospital, Havana, IL	100 19	88 8	100 16	100 26	100 30	83 6	100 3	100 4	- 0	- 0	100 2	- -	100 2	- -	100 2	100 3	- 0
McDonough District Hospital, Macomb, IL	98 41	96 51	93 60	93 70	93 84	92 12	89 45	100 107	72 29	- 0	94 70	80 45	99 70	97 36	86 66	89 46	77 22
Memorial Hospital, Belleville, IL	95 235	95 375	98 222	95 345	100 299	99 143	95 208	100 647	98 251	98 125	98 421	92 494	98 426	95 499	96 409	97 209	85 146
Memorial Hospital, Chester, IL	95 43	100 33	90 39	96 54	93 44	100 13	100 10	100 22	78 9	- 0	89 18	52 21	100 18	88 17	100 17	100 10	100 4
Memorial Hospital of Carbondale, Carbondale, IL	93 61	96 106	87 106	95 127	90 119	95 84	95 378	100 1084	90 414	96 201	97 714	95 452	94 718	98 438	93 679	95 384	88 246
Memorial Medical Center, Springfield, IL	91 291	97 390	88 311	95 532	91 507	97 231	93 194	100 1051	97 440	94 248	98 842	94 655	98 847	93 648	97 813	97 194	93 219
Mendota Community Hospital, Mendota, IL	83 6	100 31	100 14	100 18	97 31	100 3	100 19	100 24	89 9	- 0	67 3	- 0	67 3	- 0	100 3	100 19	100 5
Mercer County Hospital, Aledo, IL	- 0	- 0	- 0	- 0	- 0	- 0	- 0	- 0	- 0	- 0	- 0	- -	- 0	- -	- 0	- 0	- 0
Mercy Harvard Hospital, Harvard, IL	100 12	100 15	100 17	94 17	92 13	100 4	89 19	100 47	86 7	- 0	96 26	96 26	96 26	96 26	96 26	89 19	100 20
Mercy Hospital and Medical Center, Chicago, IL	95 77	93 130	51 91	91 148	37 128	100 69	88 248	100 618	59 180	92 84	91 382	80 148	94 382	83 134	90 366	98 248	84 138
Methodist Hospital of Chicago, Chicago, IL	56 9	88 113	79 89	87 148	74 90	91 101	83 23	100 32	91 11	- 0	50 6	92 36	88 8	97 33	83 6	83 23	- 0
Methodist Medical Center of Illinois, Peoria, IL	97 149	99 194	98 182	100 224	98 257	100 106	92 184	100 906	95 289	96 135	99 715	95 337	99 728	93 329	97 679	95 184	96 233
Metrosouth Medical Center, Blue Island, IL	85 120	92 173	83 120	91 201	85 159	100 67	88 185	91 532	70 159	47 79	97 383	90 278	98 389	96 261	94 355	89 185	84 128
Midwest Medical Center, Galena, IL	100 1	67 3	- 0	100 6	80 5	0 1	- 0	- 0	- 0	- 0	- 0	- -	- 0	- -	- 0	- 0	- 0
Midwestern Region Medical Center, Zion, IL	50 4	100 8	75 12	88 17	100 5	90 10	92 187	100 210	83 35	- 0	94 71	96 28	96 71	96 28	90 63	99 187	45 22
Morris Hospital & Healthcare Centers, Morris, IL	80 103	94 156	94 111	97 151	96 160	98 61	91 92	100 321	93 85	- 0	98 244	97 292	98 245	86 319	88 242	92 92	98 100
Mount Sinai Hospital Medical Center, Chicago, IL	96 95	99 203	78 54	96 135	91 101	100 107	96 110	100 306	88 74	97 34	99 172	84 74	96 175	99 208	94 155	99 110	98 43
North Chicago VA Medical Center, North Chicago, IL	97 62	100 72	100 23	97 70	100 24	100 33	- 0	- 0	- 0	- 0	- 0	- -	- 0	- -	- 0	- 0	- 0
Northwest Community Hospital, Arlington Heights, IL	94 83	93 149	94 94	98 156	89 141	82 22	91 182	84 670	94 225	91 160	87 487	90 350	95 488	88 366	93 457	94 182	82 147
Northwestern Memorial Hospital, Chicago, IL	97 135	99 401	93 274	96 359	95 301	99 149	94 200	100 711	86 222	96 144	97 437	97 561	99 451	97 554	94 416	98 200	84 192
Norwegian-American Hospital, Chicago, IL	83 71	89 98	74 50	81 118	60 48	100 34	42 43	100 92	56 9	- 0	95 40	81 43	85 39	97 36	64 36	51 47	67 6
Oak Forest Hospital, Oak Forest, IL	94 49	98 56	88 17	87 45	57 7	95 20	100 7	100 8	- 0	- 0	100 2	100 12	100 2	92 12	100 2	100 7	100 1
OSF Holy Family Medical Center, Monmouth, IL	100 2	100 10	86 14	100 16	89 19	50 2	56 9	100 9	- 0	- 0	100 4	100 8	100 4	100 8	75 4	56 9	50 2
Ottawa Regional Hospital & Healthcare Center, Ottawa, IL	96 103	95 155	90 120	99 171	96 149	93 55	92 92	100 214	100 44	- 0	99 143	88 57	99 145	96 53	92 136	96 92	92 39
Our Lady of the Resurrection Medical Center, Chicago, IL	96 130	100 159	100 164	99 246	100 223	100 101	98 202	100 353	100 59	- 0	97 149	88 98	94 150	92 90	98 135	99 202	94 47
Palos Community Hospital, Palos Heights, IL	93 82	93 144	95 93	97 129	94 152	94 35	91 233	100 632	85 207	97 133	98 415	96 224	98 423	97 222	93 401	94 234	79 84
Pana Community Hospital, Pana, IL	85 20	96 25	75 12	- 0	81 21	100 9	- 0	- 0	- 0	- 0	- 0	- -	- 0	- -	- 0	- 0	- 0
Paris Community Hospital, Paris, IL	88 24	100 17	94 18	100 39	94 35	93 15	67 6	100 7	50 2	- 0	100 4	- -	75 4	- -	100 4	67 6	100 3
Passavant Area Hospital, Jacksonville, IL	93 135	94 227	96 141	100 210	98 172	100 62	74 105	100 353	70 110	- 0	99 276	96 70	96 278	80 69	96 263	76 106	78 18
Pekin Memorial Hospital, Pekin, IL	91 119	98 250	99 123	99 231	98 188	99 68	97 153	100 357	93 84	- 0	97 227	63 19	96 229	94 18	95 219	97 153	98 98
Perry Memorial Hospital, Princeton, IL	85 40	94 52	72 47	96 74	67 66	83 18	73 33	78 49	62 8	- 0	90 20	- -	95 20	- -	89 19	73 33	100 4
Pinckneyville Community Hospital, Pinckneyville, IL	100 12	92 13	100 6	100 9	91 11	100 4	100 1	100 1	- 0	- 0	- 0	- -	- 0	- -	- 0	100 1	- 0
Proctor Hospital, Peoria, IL	100 106	99 200	98 125	99 184	97 195	95 40	92 140	100 793	91 270	94 66	99 630	91 123	99 634	88 117	94 623	96 140	96 291
Provena Covenant Medical Center - Urbana, Urbana, IL	87 92	97 148	89 125	94 157	85 168	100 73	77 180	100 617	82 215	90 106	95 438	95 286	96 442	95 276	92 418	82 180	83 163
Provena Mercy Medical Center, Aurora, IL	86 94	89 170	87 86	93 157	83 115	100 47	85 158	100 636	87 207	91 159	93 470	86 174	97 478	87 171	91 429	85 158	70 184
Provena St Joseph Medical Center, Joliet, IL	88 77	91 111	97 73	92 139	89 124	100 45	99 190	100 615	100 220	88 133	97 477	90 378	94 479	95 361	86 441	99 190	95 124
Provena St Marys Hospital, Kankakee, IL	80 84	92 145	92 77	97 151	91 101	100 70	92 134	100 411	90 84	- 0	98 285	92 199	97 284	93 191	94 271	92 134	97 119
Provena United Samaritans Medical Center - Logan, Danville, IL	92 147	92 174	86 175	94 218	93 240	100 85	73 139	100 253	82 85	- 0	96 155	79 48	95 155	92 38	84 148	88 139	65 26
Provena-Saint Joseph Hospital, Elgin, IL	88 77	94 129	78 85	96 125	98 121	92 36	87 191	98 416	91 134	98 43	97 264	78 109	98 265	97 118	87 247	91 191	88 50
Provident Hospital of Chicago, Chicago, IL	95 131	83 151	97 67	79 156	84 44	98 108	100 39	100 85	100 6	100 1	93 67	93 72	95 66	87 77	98 64	100 39	100 2
Red Bud Regional Hospital, Red Bud, IL	93 42	99 69	95 38	100 67	99 70	100 4	100 6	100 42	100 7	- 0	100 35	94 18	94 35	100 17	94 35	100 6	50 2
Resurrection Medical Center, Chicago, IL	96 180	100 452	90 268	97 406	91 412	99 73	85 213	100 620	86 230	96 127	99 434	95 199	98 445	89 196	93 416	95 213	81 118
RHC St Francis Hospital, Evanston, IL	75 173	98 422	92 255	97 385	92 333	100 64	92 335	99 572	73 136	83 64	97 364	82 73	96 367	88 67	89 332	95 335	63 78
Richland Memorial Hospital, Olney, IL	89 62	100 69	71 89	98 92	88 114	89 36	69 29	100 105	68 22	- 0	90 84	85 26	95 80	96 24	88 76	77 30	25 4
Riverside Medical Center, Kankakee, IL	83 108	98 235	97 142	98 220	99 190	88 77	83 127	99 517	91 196	89 121	97 352	93 381	97 359	92 378	87 328	83 127	92 111
Rochelle Community Hospital, Rochelle, IL	78 27	100 32	86 22	97 38	68 34	75 8	93 15	86 22	- 0	- 0	80 10	- -	82 11	- -	89 9	93 15	100 3
Rockford Memorial Hospital, Rockford, IL	98 178	99 324	91 221	95 348	92 289	100 120	86 254	100 1032	96 349	89 149	99 575	98 361	98 593	97 357	93 547	92 259	70 127
Roseland Community Hospital, Chicago, IL	66 118	75 77	16 77	76 143	19 85	100 54	21 39	69 96	80 10	- 0	89 19	0 2	83 18	- 0	94 18	15 55	45 20
Rush Oak Park Hospital, Oak Park, IL	83 58	96 56	98 58	92 91	94 84	100 28	88 181	99 378	89 110	- 0	96 211	82 40	98 212	92 37	91 202	93 182	94 124
Rush University Medical Center, Chicago, IL	82 40	94 109	78 50	94 96	80 74	95 38	97 193	100 624	83 175	89 90	96 397	93 414	96 398	88 406	95 379	98 193	89 110
Sacred Heart Hospital, Chicago, IL	83 6	100 5	80 5	55 11	89 9	100 2	68 37	100 89	88 16	- 0	56 43	73 44	90 42	88 42	57 42	78 40	50 10
Saint Alexius Medical Center, Hoffman Estates, IL	95 165	99 329	98 250	94 290	99 355	100 112	97 209	100 466	91 101	- 0	99 309	94 321	97 311	98 316	98 284	98 209	91 94
Saint Anthony Hospital, Chicago, IL	84 75	99 128	68 66	94 124	66 76	100 40	74 53	99 107	83 12	- 0	85 46	88 120	85 46	91 106	66 44	72 54	80 5
Saint Anthony Medical Center, Rockford, IL	83 115	98 212	94 143	98 190	94 222	100 71	84 256	100 1204	95 450	91 182	98 964	93 369	99 974	95 363	96 943	95 256	85 97
Saint Anthony's Health Center, Alton, IL	85 92	96 142	85 117	97 148	92 154	99 73	86 80	100 307	97 91	- 0	96 239	88 49	96 242	98 112	92 225	98 80	95 93

NOTE: The first number in each column (boldface) is the score, the second number is the number of patients; Please refer to the main entry for footnotes; (a) 100-299
*MEASURES: **Pneumonia Care:** 16. Appropriate Initial Antibiotic; 17. Blood Culture Timing; 18. Influenza Vaccine; 19. Initial Antibiotic Timing; 20. Pneumococcal Vaccine; 21. Smoking Cessation Advice; **Surgical Care Improvement Project:** 22. Appropriate VTP Within 24 Hours; 23. Appropriate Hair Removal; 24. Appropriate Beta Blocker Usage; 25. Controlled Postoperative Blood Glucose; 26. Prophylactic Antibiotic Timing; 27. Prophylactic Antibiotic Timing (Outpatient); 28. Prophylactic Antibiotic Selection; 29. Prophylactic Antibiotic Selection (Outpatient); 30. Prophylactic Antibiotic Stopped; 31. Recommended VTP Ordered; 32. Urinary Catheter Removal*

Hospital	Pneumonia Care						Surgical Care Improvement Project										
	16	17	18	19	20	21	22	23	24	25	26	27	28	29	30	31	32
Saint Anthonys Memorial Hospital, Effingham, IL	**89** 117	**94** 161	**92** 107	**93** 170	**89** 179	**94** 67	**94** 364	**99** 921	**94** 268	**-** 0	**91** 690	**68** 76	**97** 695	**99** 71	**96** 666	**94** 367	**96** 274
Saint Bernard Hospital, Chicago, IL	**88** 120	**97** 245	**97** 86	**92** 298	**90** 126	**97** 102	**89** 65	**100** 115	**100** 10	**-** 0	**89** 38	**10** 10	**82** 38	**100** 1	**78** 36	**83** 70	**60** 5
Saint Elizabeth Hospital, Belleville, IL	**86** 199	**98** 277	**94** 200	**96** 343	**94** 263	**95** 128	**84** 180	**99** 485	**94** 189	**87** 113	**94** 313	**91** 179	**95** 317	**94** 207	**89** 299	**91** 180	**70** 89
Saint Francis Hospital, Litchfield, IL	**84** 38	**90** 49	**70** 23	**90** 52	**70** 47	**82** 22	**33** 39	**85** 48	**79** 19	**-** 0	**88** 50	**-** -	**86** 50	**-** -	**60** 50	**33** 39	**56** 18
Saint Francis Medical Center, Peoria, IL	**96** 217	**92** 310	**92** 288	**96** 386	**91** 380	**100** 203	**93** 436	**100** 1769	**78** 622	**84** 351	**97** 1417	**92** 320	**98** 1430	**90** 315	**92** 1372	**96** 436	**86** 439
Saint James Hospital, Pontiac, IL	**92** 48	**95** 61	**98** 47	**95** 61	**100** 54	**100** 30	**87** 55	**100** 154	**86** 51	**-** 0	**98** 105	**100** 24	**99** 108	**100** 24	**97** 95	**89** 55	**100** 47
Saint James Hospital-Olympia Fields, Olympia Fields, IL	**90** 121	**96** 274	**90** 147	**95** 289	**93** 197	**100** 100	**93** 269	**99** 702	**84** 225	**88** 99	**94** 424	**81** 265	**99** 429	**86** 246	**93** 391	**97** 270	**87** 70
Saint Johns Hospital, Springfield, IL	**87** 61	**96** 53	**79** 84	**89** 88	**80** 123	**100** 73	**78** 161	**100** 711	**93** 301	**94** 180	**97** 510	**93** 428	**99** 518	**96** 423	**97** 482	**86** 161	**93** 199
Saint Joseph Hospital, Chicago, IL	**89** 75	**98** 149	**99** 111	**97** 146	**98** 145	**100** 34	**89** 152	**100** 515	**84** 143	**93** 58	**97** 389	**93** 161	**94** 392	**95** 154	**89** 381	**92** 152	**92** 38
Saint Joseph Medical Center, Bloomington, IL	**88** 101	**100** 88	**90** 104	**96** 128	**97** 129	**100** 62	**91** 172	**100** 750	**90** 237	**80** 87	**98** 541	**99** 189	**98** 546	**99** 189	**91** 514	**92** 172	**91** 163
Saint Joseph Memorial Hospital, Murphysboro, IL	**96** 28	**100** 43	**100** 31	**100** 18	**97** 38	**100** 15	**100** 3	**100** 3	**-** 0	**-** 0	**100** 1	**-** 0	**100** 1	**-** 0	**100** 1	**100** 3	**100** 1
Saint Joseph's Hospital, Highland, IL	**86** 29	**100** 23	**96** 25	**90** 31	**85** 33	**100** 12	**78** 27	**100** 37	**50** 10	**-** 0	**93** 27	**-** -	**96** 27	**-** -	**81** 27	**81** 27	**73** 15
Saint Josephs Hospital, Breese, IL	**89** 72	**100** 89	**97** 70	**98** 99	**100** 92	**100** 32	**89** 53	**100** 123	**100** 21	**-** 0	**97** 79	**85** 39	**97** 79	**94** 34	**90** 78	**89** 53	**72** 25
Saint Margarets Hospital, Spring Valley, IL	**88** 40	**98** 49	**91** 54	**98** 102	**94** 82	**87** 15	**98** 81	**99** 335	**89** 100	**-** 0	**92** 242	**93** 44	**98** 241	**89** 44	**96** 227	**99** 81	**100** 102
Saint Mary & Elizabeth Med Ctr-Division Campus, Chicago, IL	**95** 208	**100** 352	**95** 149	**98** 329	**96** 181	**100** 138	**93** 202	**100** 458	**95** 133	**91** 54	**99** 297	**91** 198	**96** 297	**96** 184	**94** 287	**95** 202	**89** 54
Saint Mary Medical Center, Galesburg, IL	**92** 142	**99** 176	**91** 137	**98** 217	**95** 181	**92** 77	**96** 181	**100** 347	**96** 103	**-** 0	**98** 231	**98** 47	**99** 234	**93** 46	**93** 218	**97** 182	**95** 106
Saint Marys Hospital, Streator, IL	**95** 65	**100** 93	**98** 90	**98** 120	**98** 115	**88** 43	**98** 89	**100** 173	**100** 60	**-** 0	**99** 113	**88** 67	**96** 113	**97** 63	**93** 110	**99** 89	**93** 45
Saint Marys Hospital, Centralia, IL	**93** 84	**100** 142	**100** 142	**98** 206	**100** 180	**100** 86	**99** 121	**100** 288	**99** 81	**-** 0	**100** 168	**79** 52	**99** 168	**88** 42	**99** 152	**98** 122	**100** 45
Saint Marys Hospital, Decatur, IL	**88** 104	**94** 144	**99** 106	**95** 153	**100** 127	**100** 54	**92** 144	**100** 336	**100** 91	**-** 0	**98** 235	**97** 111	**97** 236	**99** 145	**92** 221	**93** 145	**94** 48
Salem Township Hospital, Salem, IL	**72** 25	**88** 32	**81** 26	**92** 24	**62** 34	**93** 14	**100** 19	**100** 21	**-** 0	**-** 0	**64** 14	**-** -	**93** 14	**-** -	**100** 12	**100** 19	**100** 1
Sarah Bush Lincoln Health Center, Mattoon, IL	**93** 105	**95** 99	**81** 135	**97** 184	**100** 174	**100** 74	**95** 171	**100** 520	**94** 147	**-** 0	**98** 382	**98** 122	**97** 387	**88** 122	**93** 349	**95** 173	**72** 75
Sarah D Culbertson Memorial Hospital, Rushville, IL	**100** 15	**100** 12	**58** 12	**94** 17	**88** 16	**50** 8	**-** 0	**100** 3	**-** 0	**-** 0	**25** 4	**-** -	**100** 4	**-** -	**50** 4	**-** 0	**-** 0
Shelby Memorial Hospital, Shelbyville, IL	**90** 20	**79** 38	**54** 35	**88** 43	**51** 53	**75** 8	**-** 0	**-** 0	**-** 0	**-** 0	**-** 0	**-** 0	**-** 0	**-** 0	**-** 0	**-** 0	**-** 0
Sherman Hospital, Elgin, IL	**98** 133	**100** 235	**98** 129	**95** 219	**95** 187	**96** 74	**100** 320	**100** 884	**98** 293	**98** 101	**99** 552	**65** 220	**97** 555	**82** 220	**100** 503	**100** 320	**100** 24
Silver Cross Hospital, Joliet, IL	**94** 193	**97** 241	**99** 232	**100** 346	**99** 293	**100** 125	**96** 178	**100** 679	**95** 153	**-** 0	**100** 509	**97** 378	**99** 509	**96** 371	**98** 480	**97** 179	**99** 167
Skokie Hospital, Skokie, IL	**90** 93	**95** 88	**92** 119	**98** 172	**86** 199	**94** 16	**100** 153	**100** 518	**100** 161	**92** 53	**98** 347	**97** 192	**99** 350	**96** 191	**96** 343	**100** 153	**99** 150
South Shore Hospital, Chicago, IL	**67** 45	**85** 100	**23** 62	**83** 109	**19** 84	**100** 19	**59** 34	**97** 78	**92** 12	**-** 0	**38** 39	**85** 13	**80** 40	**100** 14	**87** 39	**41** 49	**20** 10
Sparta Community Hospital, Sparta, IL	**93** 44	**95** 21	**-** 0	**98** 53	**-** 0	**95** 20	**-** 0	**-** 0	**-** 0	**-** 0	**-** 0	**-** -	**-** 0	**-** -	**-** 0	**-** 0	**-** 0
Swedish American Hospital, Rockford, IL	**94** 170	**94** 261	**92** 176	**95** 263	**93** 227	**100** 133	**88** 286	**100** 1210	**96** 380	**93** 163	**99** 942	**96** 312	**98** 956	**97** 307	**98** 883	**93** 287	**89** 164
Swedish Covenant Hospital, Chicago, IL	**89** 189	**95** 356	**78** 267	**95** 296	**89** 369	**100** 64	**81** 160	**98** 421	**96** 127	**93** 72	**93** 271	**76** 142	**90** 274	**85** 117	**89** 259	**84** 160	**66** 82
Taylorville Memorial Hospital, Taylorville, IL	**77** 48	**89** 90	**98** 81	**95** 119	**100** 146	**100** 30	**100** 3	**98** 50	**-** 0	**-** 0	**98** 45	**-** 0	**100** 45	**-** 0	**89** 44	**100** 3	**-** 0
Thomas H Boyd Memorial Hospital, Carrollton, IL	**44** 9	**83** 6	**100** 2	**92** 13	**56** 16	**80** 5	**-** 0	**-** 0	**-** 0	**-** 0	**-** 0	**-** -	**-** 0	**-** -	**-** 0	**-** 0	**-** 0
Thorek Memorial Hospital, Chicago, IL	**97** 36	**94** 71	**99** 74	**93** 69	**98** 81	**96** 25	**98** 41	**100** 79	**86** 14	**-** 0	**100** 43	**93** 27	**98** 43	**100** 25	**97** 36	**98** 41	**100** 4
Touchette Regional Hospital, Centreville, IL	**89** 44	**96** 51	**89** 27	**93** 58	**83** 18	**96** 25	**68** 28	**100** 70	**75** 8	**-** 0	**98** 44	**6** 36	**98** 45	**78** 9	**91** 44	**66** 29	**75** 8
Trinity Rock Island, Rock Island, IL	**97** 71	**99** 125	**91** 94	**97** 128	**99** 142	**96** 50	**85** 136	**100** 512	**97** 184	**94** 114	**98** 357	**97** 478	**99** 366	**92** 475	**97** 352	**94** 136	**97** 62
Union County Hospital, Anna, IL	**97** 36	**96** 57	**93** 42	**96** 55	**98** 57	**100** 20	**-** 0	**100** 1	**-** 0	**-** 0	**100** 1	**100** 4	**100** 1	**100** 4	**100** 1	**-** 0	**-** 0
The University of Chicago Medical Center, Chicago, IL	**94** 18	**98** 53	**100** 55	**98** 44	**97** 58	**100** 35	**99** 195	**100** 571	**94** 159	**94** 121	**99** 377	**88** 286	**99** 386	**94** 486	**98** 352	**99** 195	**82** 130
University of Illinois Hospital, Chicago, IL	**82** 51	**98** 130	**72** 68	**91** 139	**84** 76	**100** 54	**97** 222	**100** 420	**93** 135	**85** 52	**99** 275	**88** 200	**97** 282	**94** 223	**97** 259	**99** 222	**91** 85
VA Illiana Healthcare System - Danville, Danville, IL	**96** 25	**100** 29	**93** 29	**96** 45	**97** 32	**100** 23	**100** 12	**100** 20	**100** 11	**-** 0	**86** 14	**-** -	**100** 14	**-** -	**92** 13	**100** 12	**67** 3
Valley West Community Hospital, Sandwich, IL	**100** 23	**94** 31	**81** 16	**97** 35	**92** 26	**78** 9	**61** 33	**100** 69	**-** 0	**-** 0	**100** 35	**-** -	**91** 35	**-** -	**94** 35	**73** 33	**91** 11
Vista Medical Center East, Waukegan, IL	**82** 93	**97** 113	**98** 119	**94** 168	**100** 144	**98** 62	**92** 123	**100** 510	**96** 123	**98** 45	**99** 361	**98** 162	**97** 363	**98** 166	**98** 348	**95** 123	**93** 101
Vista Medical Center West, Waukegan, IL	**-** 0	**-** 0	**-** 0	**-** 0	**-** 0	**-** 0	**-** 0	**-** 0	**-** 0	**-** 0	**-** 0	**-** 0	**-** 0	**-** 0	**-** 0	**-** 0	**-** 0
Wabash General Hospital, Mount Carmel, IL	**86** 50	**90** 51	**85** 48	**100** 64	**79** 78	**95** 19	**98** 51	**100** 74	**87** 31	**-** 0	**93** 67	**80** 10	**93** 67	**100** 8	**97** 65	**100** 51	**97** 29
West Suburban Medical Center, Oak Park, IL	**88** 86	**97** 176	**83** 78	**95** 161	**86** 91	**100** 71	**99** 146	**100** 461	**94** 115	**78** 41	**99** 322	**95** 142	**94** 326	**92** 138	**97** 318	**99** 146	**92** 49
Westlake Community Hospital, Melrose Park, IL	**97** 35	**100** 73	**85** 54	**97** 69	**91** 58	**100** 21	**96** 75	**100** 175	**100** 36	**78** 18	**96** 109	**85** 93	**94** 110	**88** 84	**94** 90	**96** 75	**100** 10
INDIANA																	
Adams Memorial Hospital, Decatur, IN	**82** 84	**92** 87	**92** 64	**95** 95	**90** 97	**100** 17	**85** 13	**87** 52	**50** 12	**-** 0	**55** 20	**-** -	**86** 21	**-** -	**80** 20	**71** 17	**89** 9
Ball Memorial Hospital, Muncie, IN	**99** 203	**98** 328	**94** 279	**97** 299	**96** 363	**98** 177	**94** 288	**100** 822	**100** 261	**99** 132	**97** 606	**95** 504	**100** 613	**98** 525	**98** 564	**95** 288	**94** 228
Bedford Regional Medical Center, Bedford, IN	**82** 56	**97** 102	**95** 37	**99** 92	**99** 75	**89** 37	**100** 53	**100** 131	**90** 31	**-** 0	**98** 99	**100** 15	**98** 99	**93** 15	**98** 95	**100** 53	**73** 30
Blackford Community Hospital, Hartford City, IN	**-** -	**-** -	**-** -	**-** -	**-** -	**-** -	**-** -	**-** -	**-** -	**-** -	**-** 0	**-** 0	**-** 0	**-** 0	**-** -	**-** -	**-** -
Bloomington Hospital, Bloomington, IN	**94** 199	**97** 296	**94** 227	**98** 287	**97** 299	**97** 130	**89** 349	**100** 1204	**95** 379	**95** 144	**96** 775	**95** 851	**99** 780	**95** 837	**97** 748	**90** 351	**95** 360
Bluffton Regional Medical Center, Bluffton, IN	**100** 81	**100** 92	**99** 75	**100** 119	**100** 115	**100** 23	**100** 50	**100** 140	**100** 39	**-** 0	**99** 101	**98** 42	**100** 101	**95** 42	**99** 96	**100** 50	**94** 17
Cameron Memorial Community Hospital, Angola, IN	**92** 53	**100** 42	**96** 56	**98** 90	**99** 68	**89** 18	**86** 14	**100** 29	**-** 0	**-** 0	**75** 12	**79** 39	**100** 12	**95** 38	**100** 11	**86** 14	**75** 4
Clark Memorial Hospital, Jeffersonville, IN	**95** 227	**97** 328	**96** 258	**94** 315	**96** 278	**100** 180	**90** 285	**100** 642	**99** 176	**-** 0	**100** 449	**92** 395	**98** 453	**94** 377	**96** 431	**94** 285	**94** 156
Columbus Regional Hospital, Columbus, IN	**95** 144	**98** 218	**99** 163	**99** 215	**98** 210	**100** 120	**90** 192	**100** 734	**95** 242	**93** 56	**99** 471	**96** 386	**99** 469	**97** 381	**96** 426	**93** 192	**98** 208
Community Hospital, Munster, IN	**91** 81	**93** 147	**94** 90	**96** 156	**93** 138	**100** 40	**78** 226	**100** 703	**90** 230	**98** 151	**93** 495	**94** 589	**97** 502	**96** 615	**92** 465	**84** 226	**86** 138
Community Hospital East, Indianapolis, IN	**92** 91	**94** 131	**84** 73	**99** 146	**89** 102	**100** 54	**93** 151	**100** 396	**96** 103	**-** 0	**96** 248	**76** 364	**96** 251	**85** 353	**97** 243	**94** 151	**87** 46
Community Hospital North, Indianapolis, IN	**89** 74	**95** 132	**92** 72	**97** 125	**91** 114	**100** 40	**96** 165	**100** 442	**97** 92	**100** 1	**97** 306	**89** 480	**97** 308	**93** 460	**97** 283	**96** 168	**97** 35
Community Hospital of Anderson & Madison Co, Anderson, IN	**93** 100	**83** 75	**97** 101	**96** 155	**97** 148	**100** 67	**87** 133	**100** 486	**100** 138	**-** 0	**97** 360	**97** 183	**99** 360	**99** 184	**96** 351	**87** 134	**94** 124
Community Hospital of Bremen, Bremen, IN	**100** 2	**100** 5	**-** 0	**100** 6	**100** 3	**100** 2	**-** 0	**-** 0	**-** 0	**-** 0	**-** 0	**-** 0	**-** 0	**-** 0	**-** 0	**-** 0	**-** 0
Community Hospital South, Indianapolis, IN	**94** 83	**94** 125	**85** 75	**95** 143	**91** 142	**100** 38	**91** 130	**100** 457	**97** 116	**-** 0	**95** 307	**86** 324	**95** 308	**91** 315	**96** 298	**92** 130	**100** 79
Daviess Community Hospital, Washington, IN	**91** 92	**94** 144	**79** 97	**99** 122	**75** 141	**82** 56	**56** 32	**100** 54	**86** 7	**-** 0	**96** 24	**94** 18	**96** 24	**100** 17	**71** 21	**56** 32	**86** 14
Deaconess Hospital, Evansville, IN	**96** 180	**95** 252	**87** 297	**97** 320	**91** 362	**93** 183	**84** 192	**99** 818	**91** 278	**92** 108	**91** 552	**85** 1277	**98** 556	**93** 1277	**85** 518	**90** 197	**81** 85
Dearborn County Hospital, Lawrenceburg, IN	**92** 102	**92** 145	**97** 108	**94** 162	**98** 139	**100** 76	**89** 118	**100** 261	**90** 71	**-** 0	**92** 181	**70** 88	**98** 183	**93** 134	**94** 179	**93** 118	**87** 54
Decatur County Memorial Hospital, Greensburg, IN	**83** 29	**89** 37	**100** 28	**98** 47	**97** 34	**100** 22	**55** 22	**100** 109	**100** 23	**-** 0	**98** 65	**86** 35	**100** 66	**97** 31	**95** 62	**59** 22	**97** 34
Dekalb Memorial Hospital, Auburn, IN	**100** 72	**100** 70	**97** 59	**100** 97	**98** 86	**100** 42	**93** 30	**100** 70	**92** 13	**-** 0	**100** 36	**97** 113	**94** 36	**100** 113	**97** 35	**100** 30	**100** 4
Dukes Memorial Hospital, Peru, IN	**97** 36	**97** 36	**86** 37	**100** 54	**94** 51	**100** 19	**64** 11	**100** 22	**100** 4	**-** 0	**92** 12	**100** 46	**91** 11	**98** 46	**91** 11	**82** 11	**100** 2
Dupont Hospital, Fort Wayne, IN	**100** 47	**100** 55	**100** 32	**100** 50	**100** 34	**100** 17	**100** 89	**100** 598	**100** 142	**-** 0	**100** 476	**100** 465	**100** 477	**99** 466	**100** 461	**100** 89	**98** 60

NOTE: The first number in each column (boldface) is the score, the second number is the number of patients; Please refer to the main entry for footnotes; (a) 100-299
*MEASURES: **Pneumonia Care:** 16. Appropriate Initial Antibiotic; 17. Blood Culture Timing; 18. Influenza Vaccine; 19. Initial Antibiotic Timing; 20. Pneumococcal Vaccine; 21. Smoking Cessation Advice; **Surgical Care Improvement Project:** 22. Appropriate VTP Within 24 Hours; 23. Appropriate Hair Removal; 24. Appropriate Beta Blocker Usage; 25. Controlled Postoperative Blood Glucose; 26. Prophylactic Antibiotic Timing; 27. Prophylactic Antibiotic Timing (Outpatient); 28. Prophylactic Antibiotic Selection; 29. Prophylactic Antibiotic Selection (Outpatient); 30. Prophylactic Antibiotic Stopped; 31. Recommended VTP Ordered; 32. Urinary Catheter Removal*

Hospital	Pneumonia Care							Surgical Care Improvement Project									
	16	17	18	19	20	21	22	23	24	25	26	27	28	29	30	31	32
Elkhart General Hospital, Elkhart, IN	88 163	96 53	87 167	96 285	87 199	98 122	93 164	100 933	94 247	97 228	97 691	92 290	95 708	95 286	94 655	95 164	99 230
Fayette Regional Health System, Connersville, IN	93 97	99 121	99 82	99 143	100 130	100 79	97 30	99 99	97 29	- 0	99 83	81 43	95 83	92 39	97 78	97 30	100 22
Floyd Memorial Hospital and Health Services, New Albany, IN	93 216	97 424	85 325	97 376	95 386	99 186	79 234	100 741	100 242	94 144	96 441	97 327	98 444	89 317	90 407	81 235	96 178
Franciscan Physicians Hospital, Munster, IN	89 18	- 0	85 20	100 22	88 16	100 5	88 40	99 84	100 30	85 26	98 52	95 76	98 53	99 75	92 48	92 40	69 16
Franciscan St Anthony Health - Crown Point, Crown Point, IN	88 78	98 126	95 79	97 145	98 124	98 47	81 194	100 455	87 113	77 66	99 322	96 275	94 326	92 267	85 314	85 194	73 99
Franciscan St Anthony Health - Michigan City, Michigan City, IN	99 72	99 98	94 62	97 113	97 97	100 53	99 162	100 401	95 132	93 29	96 269	63 229	98 272	96 169	98 249	99 162	96 102
Franciscan St Margaret Health - Dyer, Dyer, IN	95 92	96 155	90 98	95 155	85 117	97 32	94 208	99 384	99 107	90 40	98 240	77 197	98 241	89 225	95 223	97 208	86 37
Franciscan St Margaret Health - Hammond, Hammond, IN	94 82	97 197	94 89	97 208	93 117	100 86	91 144	99 416	97 118	83 92	99 249	84 122	97 260	92 129	97 236	97 146	76 51
Gibson General Hospital, Princeton, IN	93 29	91 47	95 21	96 45	97 30	96 24	- 0	- 0	- 0	- 0	- 0	- -	- 0	- -	- 0	- 0	- 0
Good Samaritan Hospital, Vincennes, IN	88 120	99 156	99 184	97 195	98 194	95 76	92 168	100 604	96 165	92 51	99 405	97 168	99 413	95 166	97 384	94 168	91 45
Greene County General Hospital, Linton, IN	81 27	93 29	74 27	95 44	80 45	94 16	- 0	- 0	- 0	- 0	- 0	- -	- 0	- -	- 0	- 0	- 0
Hancock Regional Hospital, Greenfield, IN	94 87	97 106	91 85	95 132	89 119	100 44	90 116	100 333	69 99	- 0	95 241	81 133	98 239	93 122	97 232	91 116	95 62
Harrison County Hospital, Corydon, IN	80 75	89 64	85 71	95 94	92 104	80 40	100 28	98 42	100 8	- 0	94 17	95 22	95 19	100 21	81 16	100 28	92 13
The Heart Hospital at Deaconess Gateway, Newburgh, IN	- 0	- 0	100 3	- 0	50 2	100 2	100 4	99 171	87 95	95 163	90 102	70 128	100 106	98 128	87 100	100 4	98 99
Hendricks Regional Health, Danville, IN	79 125	90 134	93 118	98 174	89 159	100 51	95 112	99 358	79 97	- 0	97 258	91 215	97 258	87 207	95 254	96 112	89 116
Henry County Memorial Hospital, New Castle, IN	93 106	96 112	100 78	99 157	100 121	100 57	95 111	100 359	97 177	- 0	99 276	95 157	100 279	95 151	98 266	95 111	98 45
Howard Regional Health System, Kokomo, IN	91 126	98 145	95 144	94 174	96 167	100 80	73 84	100 251	85 91	95 38	99 165	91 57	96 166	96 56	85 155	90 84	81 53
The Indiana Heart Hospital, Indianapolis, IN	80 5	100 6	92 12	100 4	88 17	100 6	100 12	100 604	81 333	95 349	99 466	96 330	99 474	100 325	93 440	100 12	96 226
Indiana Orthopaedic Hospital, Indianapolis, IN	- 0	- 0	- 0	- 0	- 0	- 0	100 6	100 236	97 113	- 0	100 168	100 486	100 168	100 486	96 168	100 6	100 21
Indiana University Health, Indianapolis, IN	87 45	94 103	89 84	97 107	92 96	97 67	96 263	100 752	92 218	95 115	97 510	95 783	97 515	92 906	95 467	97 264	90 146
Indiana University Health Arnett Hospital, Lafayette, IN	91 82	97 143	90 89	96 135	94 126	93 41	88 154	100 432	94 142	95 92	98 294	85 369	99 296	96 351	88 269	92 154	78 104
Indiana University Health North Hospital, Carmel, IN	86 49	94 51	85 48	95 57	80 59	100 12	96 72	100 286	99 67	- 0	99 215	98 423	99 219	95 419	99 207	96 72	89 85
Indiana University Health West Hospital, Avon, IN	99 73	88 153	95 77	99 122	99 123	100 55	89 104	100 271	80 44	- 0	99 172	96 190	99 172	98 186	92 164	95 104	79 70
Indianapolis VA Medical Center, Indianapolis, IN	98 115	99 185	99 131	94 195	100 155	96 110	97 191	100 469	94 272	93 102	99 346	- -	99 358	- -	95 331	99 191	96 203
IU Health Goshen Hospital, Goshen, IN	95 104	95 121	99 87	100 131	99 113	100 57	88 216	100 585	94 140	- 0	98 378	85 117	97 383	96 118	93 367	89 219	86 108
Jasper County Hospital, Rensselaer, IN	82 39	77 44	73 37	93 54	87 53	92 13	- 0	100 20	- 0	- 0	95 20	- -	80 20	- -	89 19	- 0	- 0
Jay County Hospital, Portland, IN	91 34	89 47	95 38	90 62	89 47	69 16	38 16	100 31	0 1	- 0	64 11	- 0	100 16	- 0	100 11	38 16	100 3
Johnson Memorial Hospital, Franklin, IN	93 83	94 98	84 56	99 88	97 79	100 31	93 73	100 163	97 35	- 0	96 102	96 96	95 101	95 94	97 98	95 74	88 33
Kentuckiana Medical Center, Clarksville, IN	- 0	- 0	44 9	58 19	48 25	71 7	100 3	97 68	97 39	92 49	57 56	- 0	100 58	- 0	93 56	100 3	- 0
The King's Daughters' Hospital and Health Services, Madison, IN	96 116	99 134	100 117	99 188	100 148	100 87	94 89	100 203	95 43	- 0	98 110	90 60	100 110	95 55	96 107	96 89	97 32
Kosciusko Community Hospital, Warsaw, IN	95 97	98 147	98 86	97 144	98 112	100 41	97 71	100 321	100 75	- 0	100 244	97 99	97 245	99 97	97 237	97 71	100 21
Laporte Hospital and Health Services, La Porte, IN	86 93	91 179	91 113	96 169	93 146	100 81	87 153	98 472	93 135	94 51	97 345	80 192	98 343	92 173	96 326	90 154	94 101
Lutheran Hospital of Indiana, Fort Wayne, IN	86 132	98 198	97 189	95 207	99 198	99 98	94 486	100 1498	92 626	89 350	98 687	98 1463	99 709	99 1457	93 636	96 487	82 222
Major Hospital, Shelbyville, IN	97 89	99 150	100 89	100 135	100 142	100 59	96 57	100 148	91 46	- 0	93 95	96 45	100 95	100 45	93 90	96 57	91 44
Margaret Mary Community Hospital, Batesville, IN	99 67	97 92	87 77	100 95	80 105	100 38	76 50	99 160	85 33	- 0	98 120	75 68	98 120	85 60	90 117	76 50	95 20
Marion General Hospital, Marion, IN	95 127	98 130	93 123	96 166	95 139	90 70	94 277	100 498	91 156	- 0	96 359	86 142	94 361	94 133	93 345	93 286	95 42
Memorial Hospital, Logansport, IN	85 81	97 74	94 64	97 114	98 94	100 43	74 27	100 137	100 7	- 0	94 101	93 126	91 102	97 121	98 101	74 27	40 5
Memorial Hospital and Health Care Center, Jasper, IN	90 97	93 97	92 93	99 135	96 129	91 45	82 119	100 631	97 183	- 0	95 507	83 127	97 508	95 110	95 491	82 121	93 92
Memorial Hospital of South Bend, South Bend, IN	85 167	99 172	93 157	94 236	98 216	98 94	79 217	99 815	79 227	87 164	92 591	87 677	94 598	75 654	95 573	81 218	80 115
Methodist Hospitals, Gary, IN	76 50	93 108	84 83	93 138	78 119	100 48	91 186	100 493	90 144	87 77	98 332	96 326	93 337	86 323	90 317	94 188	83 84
Monroe Hospital, Bloomington, IN	100 9	100 39	94 16	94 18	69 32	100 21	89 27	100 183	93 14	- 0	96 146	92 13	97 144	92 13	100 144	86 28	100 72
Morgan Hospital and Medical Center, Martinsville, IN	69 58	98 88	87 53	95 94	93 70	100 30	100 33	100 70	47 15	- 0	85 27	38 72	93 28	89 38	80 25	100 33	100 12
Orthopaedic Hospital at Parkview North, Fort Wayne, IN	- 0	- 0	- 0	- 0	- 0	- 0	100 23	100 269	90 83	- 0	96 201	96 347	100 201	99 344	97 199	100 23	98 110
The Orthopaedic Hosp of Lutheran Health Network, Fort Wayne, IN	- 0	- 0	- 0	- 0	- 0	- 0	97 138	100 1101	97 370	- 0	100 947	99 819	100 950	100 818	99 932	98 138	98 132
Parkview Hospital, Fort Wayne, IN	96 91	85 95	99 91	95 129	99 135	100 55	92 180	100 729	93 280	96 175	95 524	96 721	98 541	97 716	94 509	92 182	94 123
Parkview Huntington Hospital, Huntington, IN	92 59	95 56	96 55	100 87	92 74	100 31	100 47	100 114	95 40	- 0	97 96	92 99	99 96	89 92	96 95	100 47	89 19
Parkview Lagrange Hospital, Lagrange, IN	98 44	100 22	93 28	100 49	94 36	100 13	100 30	100 59	75 4	- 0	92 52	95 20	100 52	100 20	94 50	100 30	90 10
Parkview Noble Hospital, Kendallville, IN	98 59	99 72	96 52	97 79	97 75	100 37	90 20	99 85	93 14	- 0	97 66	92 26	99 67	92 25	95 64	86 21	92 12
Parkview Whitley Hospital, Columbia City, IN	96 50	96 45	97 32	98 58	96 51	100 20	92 26	100 69	95 19	- 0	98 54	90 42	100 54	95 41	94 50	92 26	100 15
Perry County Memorial Hospital, Tell City, IN	72 36	98 45	98 46	91 58	95 60	83 23	- 0	- 0	- 0	- 0	- 0	- -	- 0	- -	- 0	- 0	- 0
Physicians' Medical Center, New Albany, IN	- 0	- 0	- 0	- 0	- 0	- 0	100 8	99 152	79 28	- 0	97 143	91 187	87 143	79 194	99 143	100 8	90 41
Pinnacle Hospital, Crown Point, IN	58 12	- 0	76 17	73 15	67 24	100 3	50 2	100 18	100 2	- 0	78 9	81 21	89 9	84 19	100 9	50 2	33 3
Porter Valparaiso Hospital Campus, Valparaiso, IN	90 146	94 259	95 228	93 247	96 272	100 100	81 236	100 1056	97 331	85 118	98 764	91 527	98 769	95 510	96 745	85 236	85 156
Putnam County Hospital, Greencastle, IN	86 37	91 66	98 44	95 63	98 62	93 14	87 23	98 40	100 3	- 0	84 19	- -	79 19	- -	76 17	87 23	100 8
Reid Hospital & Health Care Services, Richmond, IN	98 291	100 483	99 396	99 452	100 527	100 210	98 230	100 819	93 296	95 165	99 571	93 382	99 584	97 385	99 526	98 230	95 146
Riverview Hospital, Noblesville, IN	84 86	96 114	98 99	95 125	96 123	97 35	97 140	100 569	98 178	89 46	99 403	99 177	98 402	94 176	93 390	97 140	98 167
Rush Memorial Hospital, Rushville, IN	- -	- -	- -	- -	- -	- -	- -	- -	- -	- -	- 0	- 0	- 0	- 0	- -	- -	- -
Saint Catherine Hospital, East Chicago, IN	92 92	94 101	89 71	96 120	93 67	100 73	97 119	100 307	95 78	98 56	100 201	83 87	99 204	94 82	94 180	98 119	96 71
Saint Catherine Regional Hospital, Charlestown, IN	78 36	77 22	91 23	94 35	89 27	100 19	67 6	78 9	100 1	- 0	25 4	0 5	40 5	- 0	75 4	67 6	100 1
Saint Clare Medical Center, Crawfordsville, IN	88 67	95 60	87 47	99 87	78 69	100 17	83 48	100 158	97 33	- 0	99 140	90 51	99 142	100 47	92 140	86 49	100 55
Saint Elizabeth Central, Lafayette, IN	86 71	99 83	95 85	97 102	91 131	100 39	94 17	100 273	96 91	96 46	97 225	99 198	98 226	99 198	97 212	94 17	95 19
Saint Elizabeth East, Lafayette, IN	85 46	95 44	96 54	93 71	87 70	100 27	82 185	100 756	94 205	100 27	99 531	98 625	99 533	96 620	98 513	91 185	91 102
Saint Francis Hospital and Health Centers, Beech Grove, IN	70 110	86 175	90 194	89 193	91 256	99 115	98 276	100 744	91 268	- 0	97 442	91 267	98 442	97 258	96 412	99 276	88 82
Saint Francis Hosp & Health Ctrs-Indianapolis, Indianapolis, IN	76 144	84 133	92 112	86 153	90 154	98 58	93 151	100 863	92 379	95 401	98 575	91 653	97 587	95 641	97 551	96 151	96 169
Saint Francis Hospital Mooresville, Mooresville, IN	68 73	95 60	93 44	100 80	86 65	100 22	99 203	100 811	83 225	- 0	98 597	85 95	98 597	94 89	95 593	99 203	99 400
Saint John's Health System, Anderson, IN	80 91	98 147	95 78	98 138	96 171	96 73	86 104	100 360	98 89	- 0	98 234	94 178	96 235	98 180	92 231	86 104	97 91
Saint Joseph Hospital, Fort Wayne, IN	89 38	97 39	97 33	98 53	100 26	100 37	90 39	100 140	98 44	98 42	96 90	95 73	98 91	97 72	97 87	95 39	100 11
Saint Joseph Hospital & Health Center, Kokomo, IN	85 110	99 167	94 135	95 165	96 159	100 76	83 83	100 295	94 108	- 0	97 228	91 175	94 228	90 169	85 224	83 84	87 90

NOTE: The first number in each column (boldface) is the score, the second number is the number of patients; Please refer to the main entry for footnotes; (a) 100-299
*MEASURES: **Pneumonia Care:** 16. Appropriate Initial Antibiotic; 17. Blood Culture Timing; 18. Influenza Vaccine; 19. Initial Antibiotic Timing; 20. Pneumococcal Vaccine; 21. Smoking Cessation Advice; **Surgical Care Improvement Project:** 22. Appropriate VTP Within 24 Hours; 23. Appropriate Hair Removal; 24. Appropriate Beta Blocker Usage; 25. Controlled Postoperative Blood Glucose; 26. Prophylactic Antibiotic Timing; 27. Prophylactic Antibiotic Timing (Outpatient); 28. Prophylactic Antibiotic Selection; 29. Prophylactic Antibiotic Selection (Outpatient); 30. Prophylactic Antibiotic Stopped; 31. Recommended VTP Ordered; 32. Urinary Catheter Removal*

Hospital	Pneumonia Care						Surgical Care Improvement Project										
	16	17	18	19	20	21	22	23	24	25	26	27	28	29	30	31	32
Saint Joseph Regional Medical Center, Mishawaka, IN	**97** 230	**98** 222	**99** 205	**98** 373	**99** 303	**100** 131	**91** 143	**100** 695	**93** 186	**94** 140	**98** 510	**96** 350	**98** 517	**99** 340	**96** 495	**92** 143	**94** 87
Saint Joseph's Regional Medical Center - Plymouth, Plymouth, IN	**90** 67	**99** 72	**98** 65	**100** 103	**99** 88	**100** 36	**95** 38	**100** 196	**95** 42	- 0	**100** 164	**98** 40	**99** 165	**100** 40	**97** 159	**100** 38	**100** 5
Saint Mary Medical Center, Hobart, IN	**82** 74	**100** 96	**98** 64	**95** 128	**93** 98	**98** 52	**79** 150	**99** 532	**94** 151	**77** 65	**99** 367	**94** 394	**98** 365	**97** 390	**92** 355	**81** 151	**79** 91
Saint Mary's Medical Center of Evansville, Evansville, IN	**96** 166	**98** 240	**89** 205	**96** 288	**94** 271	**99** 171	**91** 229	**99** 1429	**91** 467	**89** 186	**96** 1122	**92** 1292	**99** 1136	**95** 1273	**96** 1107	**94** 230	**94** 335
Saint Mary's Warrick Hospital, Boonville, IN	**94** 34	**73** 30	**92** 25	- 0	**79** 33	**71** 21	- 0	- 0	- 0	- 0	- 0	- -	- 0	- -	- 0	- 0	- 0
Saint Vincent Carmel Hospital, Carmel, IN	**57** 51	**86** 80	**76** 34	**91** 74	**85** 48	**100** 14	**90** 89	**100** 303	**89** 72	- 0	**97** 227	**90** 98	**99** 228	**93** 92	**97** 226	**88** 92	**93** 15
Saint Vincent Clay Hospital, Brazil, IN	**100** 11	**85** 20	**77** 13	**100** 22	**65** 17	**57** 7	**92** 13	**100** 21	**100** 3	- 0	**62** 8	- -	**75** 12	- -	**57** 7	**100** 13	**50** 4
Saint Vincent Dunn Hospital, Bedford, IN	**90** 48	**94** 66	**98** 55	**100** 72	**97** 73	**100** 26	**96** 27	**100** 50	**54** 13	- 0	**100** 24	**91** 23	**93** 29	**81** 21	**80** 20	**96** 27	**40** 5
Saint Vincent Frankfort Hospital, Frankfort, IN	**82** 44	**94** 50	**91** 35	**95** 61	**94** 48	**100** 11	**100** 22	**94** 31	**91** 11	- 0	**97** 29	- -	**97** 29	- -	**97** 29	**100** 22	**0** 2
Saint Vincent Heart Center of Indiana, Indianapolis, IN	**100** 4	**100** 5	**17** 6	**100** 5	**46** 13	**100** 1	- 0	**100** 358	**95** 184	**97** 294	**98** 200	**74** 349	**100** 204	**93** 349	**98** 193	- 0	**86** 101
Saint Vincent Hospital & Health Services, Indianapolis, IN	**75** 151	**95** 256	**88** 249	**93** 260	**89** 316	**100** 148	**86** 193	**99** 793	**89** 323	**92** 203	**98** 532	**89** 913	**97** 538	**94** 872	**95** 526	**87** 194	**83** 190
Saint Vincent Jennings Hospital, North Vernon, IN	**83** 30	**69** 13	**100** 8	**83** 23	**91** 23	**100** 9	- 0	- 0	- 0	- 0	- 0	- -	- 0	- -	- 0	- 0	- 0
Saint Vincent Mercy Hospital, Elwood, IN	**95** 37	**90** 49	**92** 24	**96** 54	**84** 44	**100** 22	**100** 7	**100** 11	**100** 1	- 0	**67** 3	- 0	**100** 3	- 0	**100** 3	**88** 8	**100** 1
Saint Vincent Randolph Hospital, Winchester, IN	**92** 25	**93** 45	**89** 28	**96** 56	**93** 43	**92** 12	- 0	**100** 2	- 0	- 0	**100** 2	- 0	**100** 2	- 0	**100** 2	- 0	- 0
Saint Vincent Salem Hospital, Salem, IN	- -	- -	- -	- -	- -	- -	- -	- -	- -	- -	- 0	- 0	- 0	- 0	- -	- -	- -
Saint Vincent Williamsport Hospital, Williamsport, IN	**90** 29	**93** 46	**97** 30	**95** 44	**100** 39	**100** 12	- 0	**100** 12	**100** 1	- 0	**100** 12	- -	**100** 12	- -	**75** 12	- 0	- 0
Schneck Medical Center, Seymour, IN	**97** 64	**99** 99	**100** 78	**98** 118	**100** 125	**94** 53	**91** 76	**100** 247	**97** 65	- 0	**99** 170	**97** 114	**99** 171	**96** 113	**96** 163	**93** 76	**75** 4
Scott Memorial Hospital, Scottsburg, IN	**91** 54	**85** 55	**100** 30	**94** 63	**96** 45	**96** 25	**0** 2	**93** 14	**100** 1	- 0	**60** 5	- -	**0** 4	- -	**100** 4	**0** 3	- 0
Starke Memorial Hospital, Knox, IN	**82** 39	**92** 49	**62** 26	**93** 54	**76** 25	**89** 27	**100** 7	**100** 12	**100** 6	- 0	**86** 7	**80** 15	**100** 8	**86** 14	**67** 6	**100** 7	**100** 1
Sullivan County Community Hospital, Sullivan, IN	**93** 44	**88** 50	**69** 29	**98** 62	**86** 44	**81** 27	**89** 18	**100** 30	**78** 9	- 0	**89** 19	**33** 3	**84** 19	**0** 1	**71** 17	**95** 19	**75** 4
Surgical Hospital of Munster, Munster, IN	- 0	- 0	- 0	- 0	- 0	- 0	**100** 5	**100** 80	**100** 9	- 0	**83** 69	**80** 30	**72** 69	**96** 27	**100** 69	**100** 5	**94** 17
Terre Haute Regional Hospital, Terre Haute, IN	**94** 78	**100** 111	**100** 103	**99** 112	**100** 95	**100** 82	**100** 119	**100** 381	**99** 146	**94** 72	**100** 274	**100** 223	**98** 276	**98** 223	**98** 232	**100** 119	**100** 50
Tipton Hospital, Tipton, IN	**86** 35	**97** 39	**92** 37	**92** 49	**98** 50	**100** 11	**98** 47	**100** 130	**97** 36	- 0	**100** 91	- -	**98** 90	- -	**96** 90	**98** 47	**100** 44
Union Hospital, Terre Haute, IN	**90** 238	**94** 139	**94** 288	**93** 368	**98** 351	**100** 188	**92** 413	**99** 1188	**89** 453	**95** 194	**97** 732	**95** 850	**96** 731	**95** 840	**92** 674	**95** 415	**88** 267
Union Hospital Clinton, Clinton, IN	**97** 36	**90** 21	**100** 18	**96** 48	**98** 40	**93** 29	**92** 13	**100** 23	**62** 8	- 0	**91** 11	- 0	**100** 11	- 0	**100** 11	**100** 13	**75** 4
Unity Medical and Surgical Hospital, Mishawaka, IN	- 0	- 0	- 0	- 0	- 0	- 0	- 0	- 0	- 0	- 0	- 0	- -	- 0	- -	- 0	- 0	- 0
VA Northern Indiana Healthcare System - Marion, Marion, IN	**100** 44	**100** 46	**95** 44	**98** 52	**100** 54	**85** 26	- 0	- 0	- 0	- 0	- 0	- -	- 0	- -	- 0	- 0	- 0
Wabash County Hospital, Wabash, IN	**82** 33	**100** 33	**93** 29	**100** 30	**82** 39	**100** 9	**67** 15	**100** 35	**40** 5	- 0	**64** 14	- -	**100** 14	- -	**93** 14	**67** 15	**75** 4
Westview Hospital, Indianapolis, IN	**85** 34	**98** 53	**91** 46	**92** 53	**100** 50	**97** 30	**82** 45	**100** 132	**87** 31	- 0	**94** 84	**88** 51	**94** 82	**97** 63	**96** 79	**84** 45	**100** 9
White County Memorial Hospital, Monticello, IN	**86** 59	**90** 71	**57** 47	**97** 76	**85** 59	**94** 33	- 0	**100** 9	- 0	- 0	**60** 5	- -	**100** 4	- -	**100** 4	- 0	**100** 1
William N Wishard Memorial Hospital, Indianapolis, IN	**95** 92	**98** 130	**77** 47	**93** 134	**87** 67	**100** 83	**94** 180	**99** 345	**100** 61	- 0	**98** 238	**88** 80	**98** 241	**96** 96	**94** 234	**95** 181	**96** 85
Witham Health Services, Lebanon, IN	**87** 54	**87** 82	**79** 48	**100** 82	**96** 52	**88** 32	**80** 54	**100** 118	**81** 31	- 0	**71** 92	**61** 18	**99** 91	**93** 14	**91** 88	**83** 54	**82** 28
The Women's Hospital, Newburgh, IN	- 0	- 0	- 0	- 0	- 0	- 0	**95** 19	**100** 189	**100** 20	- 0	**94** 141	**98** 474	**99** 141	**97** 473	**97** 133	**95** 19	**100** 2
IOWA																	
Adair County Memorial Hospital, Greenfield, IA	- 0	- 0	- 0	- 0	- 0	- 0	- 0	- 0	- 0	- 0	- 0	- -	- 0	- -	- 0	- 0	- 0
Alegent Health Community Memorial Hospital, Missouri Valley, IA	**100** 29	**100** 27	**100** 25	**100** 27	**100** 39	**100** 5	**100** 2	**100** 3	- 0	- 0	**100** 1	- -	**100** 1	- -	**100** 1	**100** 2	- 0
Alegent Health Mercy Hospital, Council Bluffs, IA	**99** 95	**100** 137	**97** 74	**100** 142	**100** 93	**100** 62	**97** 167	**100** 712	**99** 231	- 0	**99** 494	**99** 80	**99** 497	**100** 80	**99** 480	**98** 167	**100** 8
Alegent Health Mercy Hospital, Corning, IA	**100** 8	**100** 3	**100** 2	**100** 9	**100** 8	**100** 4	**100** 2	**100** 7	- 0	- 0	**100** 6	- -	**100** 6	- -	**100** 6	**100** 2	**100** 1
Allen Memorial Hospital, Waterloo, IA	**92** 92	**97** 147	**96** 145	**94** 142	**96** 206	**98** 61	**96** 138	**100** 469	**96** 180	**97** 94	**100** 310	**92** 370	**99** 314	**98** 348	**98** 300	**97** 138	**97** 62
Audubon County Memorial Hospital, Audubon, IA	**100** 8	**100** 14	**100** 9	**93** 14	**100** 14	**100** 3	**75** 4	**100** 5	- 0	- 0	**100** 4	**100** 13	**100** 4	**93** 15	**75** 4	**75** 4	**100** 2
Avera Holy Family Health, Estherville, IA	**97** 30	**92** 12	**74** 23	**100** 39	**94** 34	**100** 12	- 0	- 0	- 0	- 0	- 0	- -	- 0	- -	- 0	- 0	- 0
Baum Harmon Mercy Hospital, Primghar, IA	- 0	- 0	- 0	- 0	**100** 1	- 0	- 0	- 0	- 0	- 0	- 0	- -	- 0	- -	- 0	- 0	- 0
Belmond Medical Center, Belmond, IA	**67** 18	**60** 5	**85** 13	**95** 21	**68** 19	**86** 7	- 0	**100** 4	- 0	- 0	**67** 3	**100** 1	**100** 3	**100** 1	**100** 3	- 0	- 0
Boone County Hospital, Boone, IA	**78** 50	**88** 41	**97** 37	**95** 64	**91** 54	**87** 15	**87** 15	**98** 60	**83** 12	- 0	**84** 50	- 0	**96** 48	- 0	**89** 47	**87** 15	- 0
Broadlawns Medical Center, Des Moines, IA	**92** 62	**98** 57	**81** 27	**94** 72	**75** 16	**100** 60	**92** 50	**100** 74	**58** 12	- 0	**93** 41	**90** 59	**93** 41	**100** 58	**95** 39	**94** 50	**95** 22
Buchanan County Health Center, Independence, IA	**94** 16	**96** 23	**100** 8	**95** 20	**89** 28	**67** 3	- 0	- 0	- 0	- 0	- 0	- -	- 0	- -	- 0	- 0	- 0
Buena Vista Regional Medical Center, Storm Lake, IA	**81** 32	**74** 23	**94** 32	**81** 43	**98** 44	**50** 16	**71** 45	**96** 99	- 0	- 0	**89** 76	- -	**99** 75	- -	**92** 74	**71** 45	**86** 28
Burgess Health Center, Onawa, IA	**87** 30	**95** 44	**100** 46	**100** 49	**100** 56	**100** 18	**100** 1	**100** 1	- 0	- 0	- 0	- -	- 0	- -	- 0	**100** 1	- 0
Cass County Memorial Hospital, Atlantic, IA	**87** 30	**96** 25	**100** 30	**100** 40	**100** 56	**83** 12	**54** 13	**100** 21	- 0	- 0	**83** 6	- 0	**100** 7	- 0	**40** 5	**54** 13	**71** 7
Central Community Hospital, Elkader, IA	**75** 4	**100** 6	**100** 6	**88** 8	**100** 8	- 0	- 0	**100** 2	- 0	- 0	**0** 1	- -	**100** 1	- -	**100** 1	**0** 1	- 0
Cherokee Regional Medical Center, Cherokee, IA	**93** 30	**92** 12	**94** 31	**93** 41	**98** 52	**56** 9	- 0	- 0	- 0	- 0	- 0	- -	- 0	- -	- 0	- 0	- 0
Clarinda Regional Health Center, Clarinda, IA	**100** 20	**94** 18	**89** 28	**94** 35	**93** 45	**100** 9	- 0	- 0	- 0	- 0	- 0	- -	- 0	- -	- 0	- 0	- 0
Clarke County Hospital, Osceola, IA	**100** 14	**93** 15	**92** 12	**93** 15	**100** 16	- 0	- 0	- 0	- 0	- 0	- 0	- 0	- 0	- 0	- 0	- 0	- 0
Covenant Medical Center, Waterloo, IA	**93** 73	**94** 95	**99** 74	**93** 107	**99** 101	**100** 40	**91** 332	**100** 564	**93** 160	- 0	**97** 377	**87** 454	**98** 374	**96** 417	**89** 357	**91** 334	**86** 138
Crawford County Memorial Hospital, Denison, IA	**96** 25	**100** 21	**85** 20	**97** 37	**93** 27	**100** 8	- 0	- 0	- 0	- 0	- 0	- -	- 0	- -	- 0	- 0	- 0
Dallas County Hospital, Perry, IA	**91** 11	**92** 13	**89** 9	**94** 18	**90** 20	- 0	- 0	- 0	- 0	- 0	- 0	- 0	- 0	- 0	- 0	- 0	- 0
Davis County Hospital, Bloomfield, IA	**71** 7	**40** 5	**100** 1	**100** 6	**90** 10	**25** 4	- 0	**100** 1	- 0	- 0	**100** 1	- 0	**100** 1	- 0	**100** 1	- 0	- 0
Decatur County Hospital, Leon, IA	**100** 3	**100** 3	**67** 3	**100** 1	**71** 7	**100** 3	- 0	- 0	- 0	- 0	- 0	- -	- 0	- -	- 0	- 0	- 0
Ellsworth Municipal Hospital, Iowa Falls, IA	**89** 18	**100** 10	**86** 21	**89** 27	**76** 41	**83** 6	- 0	- 0	- 0	- 0	- 0	- -	- 0	- -	- 0	- 0	- 0
The Finley Hospital, Dubuque, IA	**98** 65	**97** 128	**93** 82	**99** 98	**97** 150	**100** 32	**93** 139	**100** 310	**97** 66	- 0	**100** 208	**95** 197	**99** 208	**95** 190	**97** 201	**94** 139	**90** 81
Floyd Valley Hospital, Le Mars, IA	**100** 32	**100** 51	**100** 30	**98** 53	**98** 50	**100** 4	**100** 23	**100** 76	- 0	- 0	**98** 60	- -	**100** 60	- -	**98** 59	**100** 23	**100** 4
Fort Madison Community Hospital, Fort Madison, IA	**96** 48	**100** 63	**92** 51	**98** 66	**100** 69	**100** 27	**100** 38	**100** 110	**97** 39	- 0	**99** 86	**93** 42	**94** 86	**98** 46	**98** 86	**100** 38	**100** 34
Franklin General Hospital, Hampton, IA	**88** 8	**75** 4	**86** 7	**89** 9	**82** 11	**75** 4	- 0	- 0	- 0	- 0	- 0	- -	- 0	- -	- 0	- 0	- 0
Genesis Medical Center - Davenport, Davenport, IA	**100** 79	**99** 143	**95** 102	**96** 160	**94** 143	**99** 72	**91** 177	**100** 666	**95** 237	**94** 159	**99** 493	**96** 654	**98** 503	**97** 650	**94** 470	**92** 177	**91** 109
Genesis Medical Center-Dewitt, Dewitt, IA	**100** 5	**100** 6	**100** 11	**92** 13	**100** 15	**100** 2	- 0	- 0	- 0	- 0	- 0	**100** 5	- 0	**100** 5	- 0	- 0	- 0
Great River Medical Center, West Burlington, IA	**90** 115	**96** 121	**93** 115	**99** 147	**97** 153	**90** 52	**94** 248	**99** 620	**88** 190	- 0	**98** 421	**90** 217	**97** 423	**96** 200	**94** 399	**96** 251	**96** 201
Greater Regional Medical Center, Creston, IA	**85** 20	**100** 9	**62** 16	**93** 29	**70** 23	**100** 6	**93** 15	**88** 32	- 0	- 0	**94** 17	- -	**83** 18	- -	**100** 17	**88** 16	**100** 1
Greene County Medical Center, Jefferson, IA	**68** 19	**91** 11	**71** 17	**87** 15	**65** 23	**0** 3	**40** 10	**100** 16	- 0	- 0	**89** 9	- -	**89** 9	- -	**89** 9	**40** 10	**67** 3

NOTE: The first number in each column (boldface) is the score, the second number is the number of patients; Please refer to the main entry for footnotes; (a) 100-299

*MEASURES: **Pneumonia Care:** 16. Appropriate Initial Antibiotic; 17. Blood Culture Timing; 18. Influenza Vaccine; 19. Initial Antibiotic Timing; 20. Pneumococcal Vaccine; 21. Smoking Cessation Advice; **Surgical Care Improvement Project:** 22. Appropriate VTP Within 24 Hours; 23. Appropriate Hair Removal; 24. Appropriate Beta Blocker Usage; 25. Controlled Postoperative Blood Glucose; 26. Prophylactic Antibiotic Timing; 27. Prophylactic Antibiotic Timing (Outpatient); 28. Prophylactic Antibiotic Selection; 29. Prophylactic Antibiotic Selection (Outpatient); 30. Prophylactic Antibiotic Stopped; 31. Recommended VTP Ordered; 32. Urinary Catheter Removal*

Hospital	Pneumonia Care						Surgical Care Improvement Project										
	16	17	18	19	20	21	22	23	24	25	26	27	28	29	30	31	32
Grinnell Regional Medical Center, Grinnell, IA	91 43	98 41	100 30	100 57	100 49	100 20	100 44	100 98	90 31	- 0	95 37	100 35	95 38	94 35	91 35	100 44	92 12
Grundy County Memorial Hospital, Grundy Center, IA	100 11	100 9	100 6	100 12	100 13	100 1	89 19	100 41	- 0	- 0	98 40	- 0	100 40	- 0	92 40	89 19	0 1
Guthrie County Hospital, Guthrie Center, IA	- -	- -	- -	- -	- -	- -	- -	- -	- -	- -	- 0	- 0	- 0	- 0	- -	- -	- -
Guttenberg Municipal Hospital, Guttenberg, IA	86 22	100 12	69 16	95 21	89 19	71 7	- 0	- 0	- 0	- 0	- 0	- -	- 0	- -	- 0	- 0	- 0
Hancock County Memorial Hospital, Britt, IA	92 12	100 23	77 22	94 32	88 24	100 11	- 0	- 0	- 0	- 0	- 0	- -	- 0	- -	- 0	- 0	- 0
Hawarden Community Hospital, Hawarden, IA	100 4	100 5	100 5	100 7	100 9	0 2	- 0	- 0	- 0	- 0	- 0	- -	- 0	- -	- 0	- 0	- 0
Hegg Memorial Health Center, Rock Valley, IA	100 4	100 2	100 7	100 9	100 13	- 0	- 0	- 0	- 0	- 0	- 0	- 0	- 0	- 0	- 0	- 0	- 0
Henry County Health Center, Mount Pleasant, IA	88 25	92 24	95 20	100 30	87 30	100 7	- 0	100 7	- 0	- 0	60 5	- -	50 6	- -	60 5	- 0	100 1
Horn Memorial Hospital, Ida Grove, IA	- 0	- 0	- 0	- 0	- 0	- 0	- 0	- 0	- 0	- 0	- 0	- -	- 0	- -	- 0	- 0	- 0
Iowa City VA Medical Center, Iowa City, IA	91 23	100 34	89 36	90 29	100 38	100 28	98 130	100 252	98 94	- 0	96 175	- -	99 174	- -	92 171	98 130	99 142
Iowa Lutheran Hospital, Des Moines, IA	94 86	92 92	97 74	100 115	93 120	89 47	82 125	100 431	99 121	79 86	98 299	89 226	98 304	97 217	95 271	82 129	96 82
Iowa Methodist Medical Center, Des Moines, IA	79 67	98 82	93 75	95 106	95 109	97 32	96 168	100 632	99 180	80 123	95 456	95 710	97 462	97 705	96 437	97 168	95 169
Jackson County Regional Health Center, Maquoketa, IA	89 18	100 19	88 17	96 27	83 29	50 4	50 2	100 4	- 0	- 0	- 0	- -	- 0	- -	- 0	50 2	- 0
Jefferson County Health Center, Fairfield, IA	85 27	89 18	75 20	80 5	88 25	100 4	82 17	96 26	- 0	- 0	81 16	- -	94 16	- -	73 15	94 17	33 3
Jennie Edmundson Hospital, Council Bluffs, IA	90 88	97 159	80 111	95 197	93 164	88 57	76 146	98 468	100 143	- 0	96 369	92 214	95 368	94 203	92 368	80 146	94 128
Jones Regional Medical Center, Anamosa, IA	96 24	96 23	100 27	96 28	85 40	100 5	- 0	- 0	- 0	- 0	- 0	- -	- 0	- -	- 0	- 0	- 0
Keokuk Area Hospital, Keokuk, IA	89 57	93 43	100 55	96 77	96 82	96 28	87 23	100 44	92 12	- 0	92 24	88 24	92 24	100 22	91 22	100 23	80 5
Knoxville Hospital & Clinics, Knoxville, IA	87 31	81 27	100 16	88 41	97 33	67 9	- 0	100 8	- 0	- 0	100 1	- -	50 2	- -	100 1	75 4	- 0
Kossuth Regional Health Center, Algona, IA	- 0	86 7	73 15	- 0	80 20	82 11	40 5	100 5	- 0	- 0	100 2	- -	100 2	- -	100 2	40 5	0 2
Lakes Regional Healthcare, Spirit Lake, IA	86 43	100 54	92 39	97 70	94 70	100 13	100 55	99 102	100 21	- 0	98 85	83 23	96 85	95 22	96 83	100 55	100 30
Lucas County Health Center, Chariton, IA	93 15	100 17	78 23	96 23	86 28	0 2	10 10	89 19	50 4	- 0	80 10	- -	100 10	- -	67 9	10 10	86 7
Madison County Memorial Hospital, Winterset, IA	91 22	67 6	86 21	100 43	88 40	100 7	- 0	0 1	- 0	- 0	- 0	- -	- 0	- -	- 0	- 0	100 1
Mahaska Health Partnership, Oskaloosa, IA	82 33	100 42	100 32	98 44	100 47	50 12	100 27	100 96	100 24	- 0	99 80	100 5	99 80	100 5	88 73	100 27	96 27
Manning Regional Healthcare Center, Manning, IA	78 9	90 10	85 13	88 8	83 23	100 1	100 3	100 4	- 0	- 0	0 1	- -	100 1	- -	100 1	100 3	0 1
Marengo Memorial Hospital, Marengo, IA	40 10	73 11	67 3	62 8	60 10	100 1	- 0	- 0	- 0	- 0	- 0	- 0	- 0	- 0	- 0	- 0	- 0
Marshalltown Medical & Surgical Center, Marshalltown, IA	97 64	98 105	100 63	100 95	100 111	100 28	98 62	100 219	99 69	- 0	98 180	98 97	97 179	99 96	98 175	98 62	92 13
Mary Greeley Medical Center, Ames, IA	90 107	99 141	95 116	99 166	96 181	100 52	98 353	100 732	99 192	- 0	100 526	96 334	99 527	100 347	99 505	99 353	100 71
Mercy Hospital, Iowa City, IA	89 82	99 112	86 76	94 109	94 125	100 31	78 411	99 1241	99 385	90 113	97 918	94 198	99 920	98 195	89 893	82 411	91 375
Mercy Hospital of Franciscan Sisters-Oelwein, Oelwein, IA	100 18	95 21	93 15	97 33	100 32	86 7	86 14	100 17	100 4	- 0	60 5	- -	100 4	- -	100 3	86 14	100 1
Mercy Medical Center-Cedar Rapids, Cedar Rapids, IA	91 57	98 100	95 74	96 101	95 118	90 41	95 115	100 349	94 125	- 0	99 231	98 814	98 234	99 813	95 186	98 115	92 78
Mercy Medical Center-Centerville, Centerville, IA	93 28	96 25	70 30	100 38	87 46	100 18	75 12	100 43	60 10	- 0	100 39	- -	85 39	- -	87 38	92 12	100 2
Mercy Medical Center-Clinton, Clinton, IA	96 157	98 222	93 172	96 239	96 261	97 95	93 112	100 218	89 66	- 0	97 132	95 87	94 132	97 86	95 125	93 112	91 55
Mercy Medical Center-Des Moines, Des Moines, IA	99 276	99 545	95 364	98 501	97 452	97 237	97 190	100 794	95 315	79 175	97 537	93 654	99 548	96 646	98 500	98 190	85 120
Mercy Medical Center-Dubuque, Dubuque, IA	97 79	99 127	100 99	98 113	99 150	100 35	89 134	100 519	99 174	96 83	98 394	96 278	98 403	99 273	97 380	93 134	97 160
Mercy Medical Center-Dyersville, Dyersville, IA	80 5	100 3	100 3	100 4	100 4	- 0	- 0	- 0	- 0	- 0	- 0	- 0	- 0	- 0	- 0	- 0	- 0
Mercy Medical Center-New Hampton, New Hampton, IA	100 8	100 15	100 11	100 17	80 20	50 4	- 0	- 0	- 0	- 0	- 0	- -	- 0	- -	- 0	- 0	- 0
Mercy Medical Center-North Iowa, Mason City, IA	91 143	100 186	92 142	97 190	96 225	99 75	95 288	100 1158	92 437	94 185	99 798	99 809	99 805	98 806	97 757	95 288	88 107
Mercy Medical Center-Sioux City, Sioux City, IA	96 120	99 146	98 216	97 210	97 271	100 111	97 383	100 879	94 304	94 78	99 406	92 111	98 419	97 106	92 375	97 385	84 83
Monroe County Hospital, Albia, IA	75 4	80 5	50 8	75 4	67 15	0 2	0 1	100 1	- 0	- 0	100 1	- -	0 1	- -	100 1	0 1	- 0
Montgomery County Memorial Hospital, Red Oak, IA	81 27	94 18	100 38	97 34	100 52	100 9	100 18	100 29	- 0	- 0	100 11	- -	91 11	- -	100 11	100 18	60 5
Myrtue Medical Center, Harlan, IA	91 32	100 47	92 26	100 53	100 53	85 13	- 0	- 0	- 0	- 0	- 0	- 0	- 0	- 0	- 0	- 0	- 0
Orange City Area Health System, Orange City, IA	89 37	96 28	91 23	98 42	88 42	50 2	100 4	98 43	- 0	- 0	83 41	- -	100 39	- -	95 39	67 15	- 0
Osceola Community Hospital, Sibley, IA	50 2	100 1	- 0	75 4	100 3	- 0	100 1	100 5	- 0	- 0	100 5	- -	100 5	- -	100 5	100 1	- 0
Ottumwa Regional Health Center, Ottumwa, IA	93 91	97 129	91 89	95 129	94 117	100 28	81 98	100 211	87 60	- 0	97 169	66 97	97 171	97 68	88 162	80 99	25 4
Palmer Lutheran Health Center, West Union, IA	100 6	90 10	75 8	89 9	92 12	- 0	- 0	- 0	- 0	- 0	- 0	- 0	- 0	- 0	- 0	- 0	- 0
Palo Alto County Hospital, Emmetsburg, IA	97 30	100 9	84 19	96 45	86 37	67 3	- 0	- 0	- 0	- 0	- 0	- -	- 0	- -	- 0	- 0	- 0
Pella Regional Health Center, Pella, IA	80 51	96 45	85 48	95 55	85 66	75 12	80 44	100 129	73 33	- 0	90 94	- -	99 92	- -	98 90	82 44	86 7
Regional Health Services of Howard County, Cresco, IA	100 2	100 1	100 2	100 5	50 6	- 0	- 0	- 0	- 0	- 0	- 0	- -	- 0	- -	- 0	- 0	- 0
Regional Medical Center, Manchester, IA	100 18	100 26	100 11	100 25	100 26	80 5	- 0	- 0	- 0	- 0	- 0	- -	- 0	- -	- 0	- 0	- 0
Ringgold County Hospital, Mount Ayr, IA	71 7	- 0	86 7	78 9	93 14	0 1	- 0	- 0	- 0	- 0	- 0	- -	- 0	- -	- 0	- 0	- 0
Saint Anthony Regional Hospital, Carroll, IA	91 44	100 29	93 42	98 63	89 73	95 20	100 213	100 274	97 101	- 0	99 210	95 59	99 213	98 56	96 206	100 213	96 85
Saint Lukes Hospital, Cedar Rapids, IA	96 55	95 81	92 74	99 86	97 115	100 41	92 109	99 494	95 229	89 134	99 361	97 582	99 366	99 581	95 309	95 109	92 144
Saint Lukes Regional Medical Center, Sioux City, IA	91 127	99 141	98 118	99 171	97 185	100 87	95 222	100 687	96 157	- 0	98 500	88 102	96 499	97 97	94 460	94 224	54 26
Sanford Hospital Rock Rapids, Rock Rapids, IA	78 9	100 3	100 9	100 13	94 17	50 2	100 2	100 2	- 0	- 0	- 0	- -	- 0	- -	- 0	100 2	0 1
Sanford Sheldon Medical Center, Sheldon, IA	86 35	86 36	89 35	93 56	81 57	100 5	- 0	- 0	- 0	- 0	- 0	- -	- 0	- -	- 0	- 0	- 0
Sartori Memorial Hospital, Cedar Falls, IA	100 19	100 32	100 19	97 34	100 37	100 5	92 100	100 145	97 38	- 0	98 91	67 21	98 91	88 17	97 88	92 101	93 43
Shenandoah Medical Center, Shenandoah, IA	100 12	100 20	69 16	95 19	77 30	100 6	50 2	93 15	67 3	- 0	71 14	- -	64 14	- -	93 14	100 2	50 2
Sioux Center Community Hospital, Sioux Center, IA	100 14	100 10	100 11	94 16	100 14	75 4	75 4	100 10	100 2	- 0	100 9	- 0	100 9	- 0	100 9	75 4	0 1
Skiff Medical Center, Newton, IA	83 24	100 15	82 28	95 41	67 42	92 12	95 41	100 177	98 53	- 0	98 144	88 32	97 146	96 28	88 143	98 41	100 5
Spencer Municipal Hospital, Spencer, IA	90 50	96 52	96 72	100 75	96 89	100 16	100 92	100 222	94 51	- 0	97 147	88 108	100 144	97 102	96 142	100 92	97 60
Stewart Memorial Community Hospital, Lake City, IA	100 18	100 13	100 29	100 34	97 33	100 5	100 2	100 5	- 0	- 0	83 6	- -	100 6	- -	100 6	100 2	- 0
Story County Hospital, Nevada, IA	73 11	75 4	42 12	100 15	56 16	100 3	- 0	- 0	- 0	- 0	- 0	- -	- 0	- -	- 0	- 0	- 0
Trinity Bettendorf, Bettendorf, IA	98 54	98 89	98 49	99 76	96 70	100 20	100 45	100 253	96 77	- 0	100 169	96 162	100 172	99 160	98 164	100 45	96 24
Trinity Muscatine, Muscatine, IA	98 51	98 54	100 35	98 59	100 52	100 21	100 39	100 89	100 24	- 0	91 33	98 43	97 35	100 43	97 32	100 39	100 9
Trinity Regional Medical Center, Fort Dodge, IA	89 115	98 219	98 124	99 201	99 197	100 79	89 80	100 321	93 116	97 70	98 227	90 182	96 231	98 179	100 217	89 80	93 71
University of Iowa Hospital & Clinics, Iowa City, IA	88 33	93 58	67 69	96 54	85 73	92 60	95 204	99 604	63 167	88 115	99 391	89 532	97 399	95 596	93 370	95 205	85 146
VA Central Iowa Healthcare System, Des Moines, IA	100 21	95 41	70 27	95 37	97 29	94 16	100 80	100 108	100 48	- 0	98 54	- -	96 54	- -	100 53	100 80	97 35
Van Buren County Hospital, Keosauqua, IA	79 19	94 17	59 22	0 1	65 26	100 8	- 0	- 0	- 0	- 0	- 0	- -	- 0	- -	- 0	- 0	- 0

NOTE: The first number in each column (boldface) is the score, the second number is the number of patients; Please refer to the main entry for footnotes; (a) 100-299

*MEASURES: **Pneumonia Care:** 16. Appropriate Initial Antibiotic; 17. Blood Culture Timing; 18. Influenza Vaccine; 19. Initial Antibiotic Timing; 20. Pneumococcal Vaccine; 21. Smoking Cessation Advice; **Surgical Care Improvement Project:** 22. Appropriate VTP Within 24 Hours; 23. Appropriate Hair Removal; 24. Appropriate Beta Blocker Usage; 25. Controlled Postoperative Blood Glucose; 26. Prophylactic Antibiotic Timing; 27. Prophylactic Antibiotic Timing (Outpatient); 28. Prophylactic Antibiotic Selection; 29. Prophylactic Antibiotic Selection (Outpatient); 30. Prophylactic Antibiotic Stopped; 31. Recommended VTP Ordered; 32. Urinary Catheter Removal*

Hospital	Pneumonia Care						Surgical Care Improvement Project										
	16	17	18	19	20	21	22	23	24	25	26	27	28	29	30	31	32
Van Diest Medical Center, Webster City, IA	**85** 46	**100** 27	**90** 40	**98** 60	**90** 51	**100** 10	**100** 5	**96** 27	- 0	- 0	**100** 24	- -	**88** 25	- -	**96** 23	**100** 5	- 0
Veterans Memorial Hospital, Waukon, IA	**91** 23	**91** 23	**81** 26	**86** 29	**88** 48	**50** 8	**100** 4	**100** 25	- 0	- 0	**96** 24	- -	**100** 24	- -	**96** 24	**100** 4	- 0
Washington County Hospital, Washington, IA	**64** 11	**100** 6	**48** 23	**91** 23	**33** 18	**67** 3	- 0	**100** 10	- 0	- 0	**100** 10	- -	**60** 10	- -	**100** 10	- 0	- 0
Waverly Health Center, Waverly, IA	**100** 30	**98** 40	**90** 21	**97** 39	**95** 41	**100** 4	**97** 29	**100** 49	- 0	- 0	**98** 41	**94** 35	**93** 41	**88** 34	**92** 39	**100** 29	**100** 6
Wayne County Hospital, Corydon, IA	**86** 21	**67** 6	**100** 11	**91** 23	**82** 17	**86** 7	**100** 12	**100** 18	**100** 5	- 0	**88** 16	- -	**100** 16	- -	**19** 16	**100** 12	**83** 6
Winneshiek Medical Center, Decorah, IA	**97** 33	**100** 59	**100** 37	**100** 67	**100** 68	**100** 4	**67** 3	**100** 4	- 0	- 0	**67** 3	- -	**67** 3	- -	**67** 3	**67** 3	**100** 1
Wright Medical Center, Clarion, IA	**86** 21	**96** 24	**64** 14	**0** 1	**50** 22	**50** 2	**100** 22	**100** 307	- 0	- 0	**99** 249	- -	**98** 249	- -	**98** 246	**100** 22	**33** 3
KANSAS																	
Allen County Hospital, Iola, KS	**100** 30	**100** 25	**100** 33	**100** 50	**96** 47	**100** 13	**83** 12	**100** 25	**100** 2	- 0	**91** 11	**100** 1	**91** 11	**100** 1	**100** 10	**92** 12	**0** 1
Anderson County Hospital, Garnett, KS	**100** 10	**100** 9	**100** 10	**75** 12	**89** 18	**50** 2	- 0	- 0	- 0	- 0	- 0	- 0	- 0	- 0	- 0	- 0	- 0
Ashland Health Center, Ashland, KS	**83** 6	- 0	**100** 1	**100** 5	**100** 9	**0** 2	- 0	- 0	- 0	- 0	- 0	- -	- 0	- -	- 0	- 0	- 0
Atchison Hospital, Atchison, KS	- 0	- 0	- 0	- 0	- 0	- 0	- 0	- 0	- 0	- 0	- 0	- -	- 0	- -	- 0	- 0	- 0
Bob Wilson Memorial Grant County Hospital, Ulysses, KS	**83** 12	**88** 8	**67** 15	**94** 18	**54** 24	**60** 5	**89** 9	**95** 21	**60** 5	- 0	**92** 13	- 0	**46** 13	- 0	**100** 13	**89** 9	**50** 6
Central Kansas Medical Center, Great Bend, KS	**81** 32	**100** 36	**73** 30	**97** 38	**82** 38	**100** 8	**93** 28	**100** 61	**87** 15	- 0	**93** 44	**92** 74	**95** 44	**96** 72	**95** 44	**93** 28	**91** 11
Cheyenne County Hospital, Saint Francis, KS	**0** 2	**0** 1	- 0	**0** 2	**60** 5	- 0	- 0	- 0	- 0	- 0	- 0	- -	- 0	- -	- 0	- 0	- 0
Clara Barton Hospital, Hoisington, KS	**79** 14	**100** 6	**56** 9	**94** 16	**50** 14	**67** 3	**60** 5	**93** 14	- 0	- 0	**91** 11	- 0	**73** 11	- 0	**91** 11	**60** 5	**100** 3
Clay County Medical Center, Clay Center, KS	**71** 17	**75** 12	**80** 20	**71** 17	**100** 35	**50** 4	- 0	- 0	- 0	- 0	- 0	- -	- 0	- -	- 0	- 0	- 0
Cloud County Health Center, Concordia, KS	**94** 17	**80** 10	**68** 19	**97** 34	**59** 32	**100** 2	**0** 4	**86** 7	**100** 1	- 0	**100** 4	- -	**100** 5	- -	**100** 4	**0** 4	- 0
Coffey County Hospital, Burlington, KS	**97** 39	**100** 7	**68** 47	**98** 56	**65** 57	**50** 20	**67** 3	**77** 30	**40** 5	- 0	**62** 26	**46** 13	**100** 26	**67** 12	**80** 25	**67** 3	**100** 11
Coffeyville Regional Medical Center, Coffeyville, KS	**75** 59	**98** 55	**93** 82	**90** 40	**83** 128	**73** 44	**81** 57	**100** 113	**92** 26	- 0	**89** 38	**88** 50	**100** 40	**94** 69	**97** 32	**79** 58	**88** 16
Comanche County Hospital, Coldwater, KS	- 0	- 0	**75** 4	**100** 2	**83** 6	- 0	- 0	- 0	- 0	- 0	- 0	- -	- 0	- -	- 0	- 0	- 0
Community Hospital - Onaga and St Marys Campus, Onaga, KS	**95** 19	**100** 2	**72** 32	**100** 32	**64** 36	**38** 8	- 0	- 0	- 0	- 0	- 0	- -	- 0	- -	- 0	- 0	- 0
Cushing Memorial Hospital, Leavenworth, KS	**89** 47	**98** 48	**100** 26	**98** 52	**91** 46	**96** 25	**96** 26	**100** 74	**88** 16	- 0	**94** 53	**86** 36	**96** 53	**63** 35	**98** 52	**96** 26	**86** 14
Doctors Hospital, Leawood, KS	- 0	- 0	- 0	- 0	- 0	- 0	- 0	**100** 12	**88** 8	- 0	**73** 11	**77** 39	**91** 11	**92** 36	**100** 11	- 0	**0** 1
Edwards County Hospital, Kinsley, KS	**88** 8	**100** 1	**75** 4	**86** 7	**83** 6	**50** 2	- 0	- 0	- 0	- 0	- 0	- -	- 0	- -	- 0	- 0	- 0
Ellsworth County Medical Center, Ellsworth, KS	**47** 19	**100** 14	**72** 25	**89** 36	**70** 43	**89** 9	- 0	- 0	- 0	- 0	- 0	- 0	- 0	- 0	- 0	- 0	- 0
Fredonia Regional Hospital, Fredonia, KS	**88** 8	- 0	**83** 6	**33** 3	**89** 9	**50** 4	- 0	- 0	- 0	- 0	- 0	- -	- 0	- -	- 0	- 0	- 0
Galichia Heart Hospital, Wichita, KS	**71** 59	**77** 73	**92** 63	**84** 79	**89** 101	**100** 26	**69** 52	**97** 310	**92** 120	**82** 183	**91** 221	**94** 170	**97** 220	**98** 168	**91** 209	**70** 54	**94** 78
Geary Community Hospital, Junction City, KS	**77** 30	**88** 17	**72** 36	**87** 52	**89** 53	**95** 20	**73** 52	**99** 178	**73** 41	- 0	**74** 133	**84** 19	**92** 132	**90** 20	**90** 130	**74** 54	**78** 59
Girard Medical Center, Girard, KS	**87** 15	**98** 41	**78** 23	- 0	**89** 45	**91** 11	**67** 12	**100** 17	**25** 4	- 0	**100** 9	- -	**100** 10	- -	**86** 7	**75** 12	**75** 4
Goodland Regional Medical Center, Goodland, KS	- 0	- 0	- 0	- 0	- 0	- 0	- 0	- 0	- 0	- 0	- 0	- -	- 0	- -	- 0	- 0	- 0
Gove County Medical Center, Quinter, KS	**38** 16	- 0	**74** 23	**100** 24	**49** 35	**0** 1	- 0	- 0	- 0	- 0	- 0	- -	- 0	- -	- 0	- 0	- 0
Graham County Hospital, Hill City, KS	**100** 11	**100** 3	**27** 11	**85** 13	**64** 11	**0** 6	- 0	- 0	- 0	- 0	- 0	- 0	- 0	- 0	- 0	- 0	- 0
Great Bend Regional Hospital, Great Bend, KS	**55** 11	**86** 7	**25** 16	**100** 17	**45** 22	**0** 3	**92** 157	**99** 351	**82** 88	- 0	**87** 311	**71** 28	**96** 311	**100** 20	**81** 306	**90** 161	**59** 137
Greeley County Health Services, Tribune, KS	**100** 1	- 0	**0** 3	**0** 1	**0** 3	- 0	- 0	- 0	- 0	- 0	- 0	- -	- 0	- -	- 0	- 0	- 0
Greenwood County Hospital, Eureka, KS	**41** 22	**60** 5	**67** 24	**93** 42	**61** 38	**100** 10	- 0	- 0	- 0	- 0	- 0	- -	- 0	- -	- 0	- 0	- 0
Grisell Memorial Hospital District #1, Ransom, KS	**100** 7	**100** 1	**86** 7	**100** 7	**100** 9	**100** 1	- 0	- 0	- 0	- 0	- 0	- -	- 0	- -	- 0	- 0	- 0
Hamilton County Hospital, Syracuse, KS	**71** 7	**40** 5	**0** 4	**73** 11	**25** 4	**50** 2	- 0	- 0	- 0	- 0	- 0	- -	- 0	- -	- 0	- 0	- 0
Harper Hospital District #5, Harper, KS	**70** 10	- 0	**58** 12	**100** 10	**64** 11	**25** 4	- 0	- 0	- 0	- 0	- 0	- -	- 0	- -	- 0	- 0	- 0
Hays Medical Center, Hays, KS	**73** 56	**91** 81	**78** 94	**94** 78	**81** 144	**100** 47	**88** 203	**100** 555	**96** 179	**90** 81	**89** 363	**80** 241	**90** 369	**92** 212	**86** 340	**90** 203	**75** 116
Heartland Surgical Spec Hospital, Overland Park, KS	- 0	- 0	- 0	- 0	- 0	- 0	**100** 12	**99** 102	**72** 32	- 0	**99** 84	**97** 352	**100** 84	**99** 349	**95** 80	**100** 12	**93** 44
Herington Municipal Hospital, Herington, KS	- 0	- 0	- 0	- 0	- 0	**0** 1	- 0	- 0	- 0	- 0	- 0	- -	- 0	- -	- 0	- 0	- 0
Hiawatha Community Hospital, Hiawatha, KS	**71** 7	**77** 13	**70** 23	**0** 3	**73** 22	**100** 6	**100** 4	**100** 19	- 0	- 0	**38** 13	- -	**100** 12	- -	**92** 12	**36** 11	**100** 2
Hillsboro Community Hospital, Hillsboro, KS	**25** 4	**100** 1	**75** 4	**100** 2	**75** 4	- 0	- 0	- 0	- 0	- 0	- 0	- 0	- 0	- 0	- 0	- 0	- 0
Hodgeman County Health Center, Jetmore, KS	**33** 21	**0** 3	**91** 11	**88** 25	**95** 21	**67** 3	- 0	- 0	- 0	- 0	- 0	- -	- 0	- -	- 0	- 0	- 0
Holton Community Hospital, Holton, KS	**87** 15	**100** 1	**100** 7	**100** 15	**84** 19	**60** 5	- 0	- 0	- 0	- 0	- 0	- 0	- 0	- 0	- 0	- 0	- 0
Jefferson County Memorial Hospital, Winchester, KS	- 0	- 0	- 0	- 0	- 0	- 0	- 0	- 0	- 0	- 0	- 0	- -	- 0	- -	- 0	- 0	- 0
Jewell County Hospital, Mankato, KS	- 0	- 0	- 0	- 0	- 0	- 0	- 0	- 0	- 0	- 0	- 0	- -	- 0	- -	- 0	- 0	- 0
Kansas City Orthopaedic Institute, Leawood, KS	- 0	- 0	- 0	- 0	- 0	- 0	**100** 11	**100** 184	**100** 15	- 0	**97** 158	**100** 21	**100** 158	**100** 21	**95** 158	**100** 11	- 0
Kansas Heart Hospital, Wichita, KS	- 0	- 0	**100** 5	- 0	**100** 5	**100** 4	**95** 44	**99** 450	**90** 201	**93** 287	**97** 343	**97** 263	**100** 352	**97** 265	**96** 337	**98** 44	**96** 68
Kansas Medical Center, Andover, KS	**82** 11	**94** 16	**85** 13	**92** 13	**74** 27	**100** 5	**94** 49	**98** 389	**84** 158	**87** 164	**93** 274	**99** 181	**100** 277	**99** 181	**89** 270	**94** 50	**89** 134
Kansas Spine Hospital, Wichita, KS	- 0	- 0	- 0	- 0	- 0	- 0	**98** 42	**100** 66	**69** 26	- 0	**96** 49	**99** 315	**100** 49	**100** 315	**0** 49	**98** 42	**93** 29
Kansas Surgery & Recovery Center, Wichita, KS	- 0	- 0	- 0	- 0	- 0	- 0	**100** 22	**100** 361	**85** 66	- 0	**99** 361	**100** 109	**100** 361	**100** 109	**96** 361	**100** 22	**100** 4
Kearny County Hospital, Lakin, KS	**100** 5	**100** 1	**80** 5	**71** 7	**88** 8	**100** 1	- 0	- 0	- 0	- 0	- 0	- -	- 0	- -	- 0	- 0	- 0
Kingman Community Hospital, Kingman, KS	**92** 24	**83** 6	**100** 20	**100** 28	**100** 36	**100** 6	**40** 5	**100** 7	**50** 2	- 0	**29** 7	- -	**57** 7	- -	**57** 7	**40** 5	**100** 3
Kiowa District Hospital, Kiowa, KS	**78** 9	- 0	**22** 9	**90** 10	**18** 11	**33** 3	- 0	- 0	- 0	- 0	- 0	- 0	- 0	- 0	- 0	- 0	- 0
Labette Health, Parsons, KS	**91** 43	**99** 68	**90** 59	**96** 69	**82** 72	**97** 32	**84** 115	**100** 601	**84** 173	- 0	**98** 485	**91** 76	**99** 486	**95** 73	**99** 460	**92** 115	**90** 62
Lawrence Memorial Hospital, Lawrence, KS	**97** 89	**94** 109	**98** 87	**99** 120	**99** 123	**100** 53	**90** 222	**100** 626	**91** 128	- 0	**99** 451	**96** 161	**98** 452	**97** 255	**98** 442	**94** 223	**95** 172
Lindsborg Community Hospital, Lindsborg, KS	**57** 7	- 0	**92** 13	**100** 12	**58** 19	- 0	- 0	- 0	- 0	- 0	- 0	- -	- 0	- -	- 0	- 0	- 0
Manhattan Surgical Hospital, Manhattan, KS	- 0	- 0	- 0	- 0	- 0	- 0	**100** 1	**98** 233	**56** 16	- 0	**98** 229	**98** 148	**95** 228	**96** 149	**92** 228	**100** 1	- 0
Meade District Hospital, Meade, KS	**59** 27	**100** 4	**85** 33	**98** 41	**77** 53	**0** 2	**100** 15	**100** 57	- 0	- 0	**100** 53	- -	**94** 53	- -	**100** 53	**100** 15	- 0
Memorial Hospital, Mcpherson, KS	**97** 35	**100** 31	**84** 43	**98** 65	**82** 61	**88** 8	**90** 20	**100** 31	**100** 6	- 0	**73** 11	**50** 2	**90** 10	**100** 2	**100** 10	**90** 20	**75** 4
Memorial Hospital, Abilene, KS	**64** 22	**83** 18	**76** 29	**96** 25	**58** 36	**50** 4	- 0	- 0	- 0	- 0	- 0	- -	- 0	- -	- 0	- 0	- 0
Menorah Medical Center, Overland Park, KS	**94** 88	**97** 135	**100** 95	**99** 118	**100** 132	**100** 35	**93** 178	**100** 526	**94** 127	**78** 36	**98** 352	**98** 333	**98** 355	**99** 332	**96** 340	**97** 179	**92** 73
Mercy Health Center, Fort Scott, KS	**100** 40	**100** 53	**96** 52	**100** 61	**100** 79	**100** 23	**83** 30	**100** 102	**79** 19	- 0	**100** 68	**77** 13	**91** 69	**92** 13	**99** 67	**83** 30	**75** 12
Mercy Hospital, Moundridge, KS	**100** 7	- 0	**57** 7	**88** 16	**80** 20	- 0	- 0	- 0	- 0	- 0	- 0	- 0	- 0	- 0	- 0	- 0	- 0
Mercy Hospital of Kansas Independence, Independence, KS	**81** 16	**93** 27	**100** 23	**100** 37	**97** 31	**100** 12	**85** 33	**100** 66	**67** 15	- 0	**94** 49	**89** 28	**94** 48	**100** 25	**98** 47	**97** 33	**33** 9
Mercy Regional Health Center, Manhattan, KS	**94** 67	**96** 74	**80** 64	**94** 96	**90** 88	**98** 42	**86** 125	**99** 625	**90** 142	- 0	**95** 444	**83** 120	**98** 442	**99** 107	**97** 436	**87** 127	**96** 135

NOTE: The first number in each column (boldface) is the score, the second number is the number of patients; Please refer to the main entry for footnotes; (a) 100-299

*MEASURES: **Pneumonia Care:** 16. Appropriate Initial Antibiotic; 17. Blood Culture Timing; 18. Influenza Vaccine; 19. Initial Antibiotic Timing; 20. Pneumococcal Vaccine; 21. Smoking Cessation Advice; **Surgical Care Improvement Project:** 22. Appropriate VTP Within 24 Hours; 23. Appropriate Hair Removal; 24. Appropriate Beta Blocker Usage; 25. Controlled Postoperative Blood Glucose; 26. Prophylactic Antibiotic Timing; 27. Prophylactic Antibiotic Timing (Outpatient); 28. Prophylactic Antibiotic Selection; 29. Prophylactic Antibiotic Selection (Outpatient); 30. Prophylactic Antibiotic Stopped; 31. Recommended VTP Ordered; 32. Urinary Catheter Removal*

Hospital	Pneumonia Care						Surgical Care Improvement Project										
	16	17	18	19	20	21	22	23	24	25	26	27	28	29	30	31	32
Miami County Medical Center, Paola, KS	**95** 19	**100** 23	**100** 20	**96** 27	**93** 14	**100** 15	**100** 30	**100** 139	**88** 25	- 0	**98** 90	**90** 20	**100** 90	**95** 19	**91** 88	**100** 30	**89** 44
Mitchell County Hospital Health Systems, Beloit, KS	**59** 29	**88** 26	**77** 31	**92** 53	**82** 50	**100** 5	**80** 10	**100** 18	**100** 6	- 0	**91** 11	- -	**91** 11	- -	**100** 9	**80** 10	**100** 5
Morris County Hospital, Council Grove, KS	**93** 14	**100** 1	**9** 11	**100** 18	**15** 26	**100** 3	- 0	- 0	- 0	- 0	- 0	- -	- 0	- -	- 0	- 0	- 0
Morton County Hospital, Elkhart, KS	**29** 28	**80** 10	**35** 20	**79** 14	**48** 31	**70** 10	- 0	- 0	- 0	- 0	- 0	**0** 3	- 0	- 0	- 0	- 0	- 0
Nemaha Valley Community Hospital, Seneca, KS	**94** 17	**0** 1	**88** 8	**91** 11	**68** 22	**20** 5	**0** 3	**100** 3	- 0	- 0	**0** 1	- -	**100** 1	- -	**100** 1	**0** 3	**100** 1
Neosho Memorial Regional Medical Center, Chanute, KS	**94** 50	**100** 85	**95** 64	**100** 113	**97** 86	**98** 47	**92** 24	**100** 48	**89** 9	- 0	**100** 21	**100** 77	**100** 21	**92** 80	**90** 20	**92** 24	**100** 9
Ness County Hospital District #2, Ness City, KS	**100** 8	**100** 6	**72** 18	**100** 11	**67** 18	**0** 1	- 0	- 0	- 0	- 0	- 0	- -	- 0	- -	- 0	- 0	- 0
Newman Regional Health, Emporia, KS	**91** 57	**96** 50	**78** 45	**96** 71	**88** 68	**97** 31	**55** 102	**98** 219	**78** 54	- 0	**89** 149	**93** 60	**95** 149	**91** 58	**90** 146	**70** 102	**78** 64
Newton Medical Center, Newton, KS	**88** 78	**92** 78	**77** 78	**91** 117	**92** 127	**91** 33	**80** 172	**100** 509	**91** 141	- 0	**90** 370	**73** 90	**86** 363	**96** 117	**92** 347	**87** 175	**82** 139
Norton County Hospital, Norton, KS	**29** 7	- 0	**80** 10	**90** 10	**53** 17	- 0	- 0	- 0	- 0	- 0	- 0	- -	- 0	- -	- 0	- 0	- 0
Olathe Medical Center, Olathe, KS	**83** 122	**98** 172	**87** 173	**98** 197	**96** 200	**100** 94	**93** 307	**100** 1069	**95** 357	**94** 108	**96** 778	**95** 653	**97** 786	**98** 643	**94** 746	**96** 307	**91** 316
Osborne County Memorial Hospital, Osborne, KS	- 0	- 0	- 0	- 0	- 0	- 0	- 0	- 0	- 0	- 0	- 0	- -	- 0	- -	- 0	- 0	- 0
Oswego Community Hospital, Oswego, KS	- 0	- 0	- 0	- 0	- 0	- 0	- 0	- 0	- 0	- 0	- 0	- -	- 0	- -	- 0	- 0	- 0
Ottawa County Health Center, Minneapolis, KS	**86** 7	**100** 1	**57** 7	**100** 9	**70** 10	**0** 1	- 0	- 0	- 0	- 0	- 0	- 0	- 0	- 0	- 0	- 0	- 0
Overland Park Regional Medical Center, Overland Park, KS	**100** 72	**99** 148	**97** 105	**99** 133	**99** 137	**98** 49	**96** 189	**100** 562	**99** 166	**93** 61	**98** 379	**97** 642	**99** 384	**98** 628	**97** 351	**97** 190	**97** 61
Phillips County Hospital, Phillipsburg, KS	**100** 2	- 0	**62** 8	**88** 8	**75** 8	- 0	- 0	- 0	- 0	- 0	- 0	- -	- 0	- -	- 0	- 0	- 0
Pratt Regional Medical Center, Pratt, KS	**79** 38	**100** 16	**74** 31	**98** 46	**63** 54	**50** 10	**98** 107	**99** 198	**63** 52	- 0	**98** 147	**100** 35	**95** 148	**97** 35	**99** 146	**98** 107	**90** 63
Promise Regional Medical Center Hutchinson, Hutchinson, KS	**83** 123	**96** 120	**95** 151	**93** 179	**94** 219	**100** 71	**71** 253	**100** 844	**69** 229	**83** 143	**86** 559	**77** 285	**95** 558	**84** 274	**81** 542	**72** 255	**84** 217
Providence Medical Center, Kansas City, KS	**92** 109	**98** 170	**93** 111	**98** 181	**98** 152	**100** 94	**85** 155	**99** 608	**94** 190	**98** 65	**99** 457	**95** 336	**99** 467	**98** 327	**99** 432	**90** 155	**92** 133
Ransom Memorial Hospital, Ottawa, KS	**95** 42	**100** 57	**95** 41	**97** 67	**96** 69	**96** 28	**97** 35	**100** 111	**88** 17	- 0	**91** 95	**75** 20	**91** 94	**98** 61	**98** 88	**100** 35	**94** 16
Republic County Hospital, Belleville, KS	**73** 15	- 0	**62** 13	**95** 21	**59** 27	**100** 4	**89** 9	**100** 15	- 0	- 0	**80** 15	- -	**100** 15	- -	**93** 15	**89** 9	**40** 5
Russell Regional Hospital, Russell, KS	**56** 9	**60** 5	**75** 8	**87** 15	**31** 16	**25** 8	- 0	- 0	- 0	- 0	- 0	- -	- 0	- -	- 0	- 0	- 0
Sabetha Community Hospital, Sabetha, KS	**100** 14	**100** 2	**75** 8	**100** 13	**73** 11	**0** 3	**50** 2	**100** 2	- 0	- 0	**100** 1	- -	**100** 1	- -	**100** 1	**50** 2	- 0
Saint Catherine Hospital, Garden City, KS	**93** 58	**97** 71	**98** 50	**92** 97	**97** 60	**100** 36	**94** 158	**100** 321	**99** 73	- 0	**99** 241	**100** 71	**96** 241	**96** 71	**69** 240	**94** 158	**83** 76
Saint Francis Health Center, Topeka, KS	**95** 159	**100** 208	**99** 178	**98** 250	**99** 238	**99** 111	**96** 180	**100** 910	**100** 293	**98** 118	**97** 730	**93** 581	**100** 740	**97** 567	**99** 700	**97** 180	**99** 265
Saint John Hospital, Leavenworth, KS	**91** 46	**100** 46	**98** 43	**96** 56	**92** 40	**97** 33	**56** 25	**100** 44	**100** 15	- 0	**90** 21	**96** 27	**81** 21	**93** 28	**86** 21	**60** 25	**57** 7
Saint Luke Hospital & Living Center, Marion, KS	**86** 7	- 0	**33** 3	**100** 6	**100** 3	**50** 2	- 0	- 0	- 0	- 0	- 0	- -	- 0	- -	- 0	- 0	- 0
Saint Luke's South Hospital, Overland Park, KS	**94** 62	**99** 77	**94** 64	**96** 85	**97** 101	**88** 25	**87** 134	**100** 757	**94** 208	- 0	**100** 589	**93** 140	**100** 594	**90** 135	**96** 575	**92** 134	**85** 26
Salina Regional Health Center, Salina, KS	**91** 91	**98** 130	**100** 107	**97** 144	**99** 157	**100** 50	**92** 352	**100** 776	**93** 260	**96** 82	**98** 447	**82** 164	**98** 457	**87** 144	**95** 421	**95** 352	**76** 88
Salina Surgical Hospital, Salina, KS	- 0	- 0	- 0	- 0	- 0	- 0	**94** 77	**100** 623	**99** 145	- 0	**99** 568	**88** 75	**99** 568	**94** 68	**92** 562	**95** 77	**81** 16
Scott County Hospital, Scott City, KS	**57** 7	**33** 3	**71** 7	**0** 1	**40** 10	**50** 2	- 0	- 0	- 0	- 0	- 0	- -	- 0	- -	- 0	- 0	- 0
Sedan City Hospital, Sedan, KS	- 0	- 0	- 0	- 0	- 0	- 0	- 0	- 0	- 0	- 0	- 0	- -	- 0	- -	- 0	- 0	- 0
Shawnee Mission Medical Center, Shawnee Mission, KS	**93** 268	**98** 257	**90** 234	**95** 336	**95** 295	**99** 99	**95** 398	**100** 1366	**86** 417	**99** 169	**97** 1083	**83** 676	**98** 1088	**95** 609	**95** 1041	**96** 400	**79** 173
Sheridan County Hospital, Hoxie, KS	**25** 4	**100** 2	**82** 11	**83** 12	**75** 20	**67** 3	- 0	- 0	- 0	- 0	- 0	- -	- 0	- -	- 0	- 0	- 0
Smith County Memorial Hospital, Smith Center, KS	**83** 6	**80** 5	**22** 9	**100** 15	**92** 13	**0** 3	- 0	**100** 1	- 0	- 0	**0** 1	- 0	- 0	- 0	- 0	- 0	- 0
South Central Ks Regional Medical Center, Arkansas City, KS	**79** 19	**100** 6	**89** 27	**94** 36	**87** 31	**91** 11	**67** 42	**100** 70	**94** 18	- 0	**98** 44	**100** 2	**96** 45	**0** 2	**100** 44	**69** 42	**63** 30
Southwest Medical Center, Liberal, KS	**95** 22	**84** 19	**55** 20	**100** 33	**72** 29	**71** 7	**89** 80	**100** 104	**94** 18	- 0	**91** 55	**95** 213	**98** 53	**97** 210	**94** 48	**89** 80	**74** 31
Stormont-Vail Healthcare, Topeka, KS	**88** 147	**96** 235	**98** 207	**97** 267	**100** 253	**100** 121	**89** 262	**100** 1228	**97** 424	**89** 187	**99** 962	**95** 806	**97** 974	**94** 800	**95** 925	**94** 264	**85** 155
Summit Surgical, Hutchinson, KS	- 0	- 0	- 0	- 0	- 0	- 0	**100** 2	**100** 293	**98** 42	- 0	**99** 279	**100** 11	**99** 279	**100** 11	**100** 278	**100** 2	**100** 79
Sumner Regional Medical Center, Wellington, KS	**73** 22	**100** 3	**83** 24	**92** 26	**90** 31	**73** 11	**100** 6	**100** 12	**25** 4	- 0	**67** 6	**100** 6	**100** 6	**100** 6	**67** 6	**100** 6	- 0
Susan B Allen Memorial Hospital, El Dorado, KS	**94** 53	**100** 42	**88** 51	**97** 60	**81** 69	**100** 35	**96** 25	**100** 116	**93** 14	- 0	**98** 93	**98** 46	**94** 96	**100** 45	**93** 91	**96** 25	**100** 9
Trego County Lemke Memorial Hospital, Wa Keeney, KS	**81** 31	**80** 10	**68** 25	**89** 38	**32** 56	**0** 6	- 0	- 0	- 0	- 0	- 0	- -	- 0	- -	- 0	- 0	- 0
University of Kansas Hospital, Kansas City, KS	**96** 112	**95** 275	**98** 181	**93** 241	**97** 189	**100** 147	**93** 246	**99** 588	**89** 178	**99** 126	**97** 381	**89** 452	**96** 386	**98** 445	**95** 365	**95** 246	**90** 132
VA Eastern Kansas Healthcare System, Leavenworth, KS	**92** 65	**98** 116	**97** 87	**95** 117	**100** 80	**100** 65	**100** 6	**100** 8	**100** 2	- 0	- 0	- -	- 0	- -	- 0	**100** 6	**100** 4
Via Christi Hospital Pittsburg, Pittsburg, KS	**87** 79	**100** 120	**71** 86	**98** 122	**89** 120	**96** 53	**90** 109	**99** 293	**80** 71	- 0	**98** 192	**94** 67	**96** 196	**94** 67	**86** 177	**94** 109	**56** 39
Via Christi Hospital Wichita - Saint Teresa, Wichita, KS	- 0	- 0	- 0	- 0	- 0	- 0	- 0	- 0	- 0	- 0	- 0	- -	- 0	- -	- 0	- 0	- 0
Via Christi Hospitals Wichita, Wichita, KS	**86** 72	**94** 175	**80** 89	**93** 168	**79** 142	**96** 90	**85** 292	**100** 841	**82** 237	**97** 151	**97** 557	**97** 598	**97** 558	**97** 592	**91** 533	**90** 294	**78** 126
Wamego City Hospital, Wamego, KS	**67** 3	- 0	**80** 5	**100** 4	**67** 9	**100** 3	- 0	- 0	- 0	- 0	- 0	- 0	- 0	- 0	- 0	- 0	- 0
Washington County Hospital, Washington, KS	**100** 3	- 0	**83** 12	**73** 15	**93** 15	- 0	- 0	- 0	- 0	- 0	- 0	- -	- 0	- -	- 0	- 0	- 0
Wesley Medical Center, Wichita, KS	**97** 75	**98** 95	**100** 97	**95** 108	**99** 144	**100** 64	**99** 296	**100** 823	**96** 226	**89** 168	**100** 540	**97** 704	**99** 551	**98** 701	**98** 503	**99** 296	**97** 89
Western Plains Medical Complex, Dodge City, KS	**96** 47	**97** 72	**95** 55	**96** 83	**96** 81	**100** 24	**93** 76	**99** 240	**93** 55	- 0	**95** 178	**94** 79	**98** 178	**99** 77	**91** 170	**95** 76	**83** 12
Wichita County Health Center, Leoti, KS	- 0	- 0	- 0	- 0	- 0	- 0	- 0	- 0	- 0	- 0	- 0	- -	- 0	- -	- 0	- 0	- 0
Wichita VA Medical Center, Wichita, KS	**93** 46	**100** 70	**98** 54	**96** 57	**100** 48	**100** 37	**99** 69	**100** 106	**100** 31	- 0	**99** 67	- -	**100** 66	- -	**93** 60	**99** 69	**88** 8
William Newton Hospital, Winfield, KS	**88** 24	**94** 32	**89** 35	**98** 51	**87** 46	**90** 10	**73** 11	**100** 74	- 0	- 0	**88** 50	**86** 21	**94** 51	**95** 20	**98** 49	**71** 14	**67** 3
Wilson Medical Center, Neodesha, KS	**33** 6	**88** 8	**25** 4	**88** 8	**33** 6	**40** 5	- 0	- 0	- 0	- 0	- 0	- -	- 0	- -	- 0	- 0	- 0
MICHIGAN																	
Allegan General Hospital, Allegan, MI	**79** 43	**96** 56	**81** 47	**97** 64	**87** 52	**89** 19	**73** 73	**100** 157	- 0	- 0	**96** 126	- -	**96** 127	- -	**91** 126	**72** 74	**81** 16
Allegiance Health, Jackson, MI	**93** 99	**98** 124	**95** 87	**95** 140	**97** 125	**97** 76	**95** 164	**100** 619	**96** 267	**94** 107	**97** 433	**92** 420	**98** 434	**92** 408	**98** 410	**96** 164	**96** 69
Alpena Regional Medical Center, Alpena, MI	**95** 95	**98** 129	**87** 101	**97** 126	**88** 138	**98** 53	**97** 115	**99** 415	**84** 125	- 0	**96** 299	**88** 166	**92** 300	**93** 155	**95** 284	**97** 115	**95** 95
Aspirus Grand View Hospital, Ironwood, MI	**98** 54	**99** 87	**100** 36	**100** 79	**100** 68	**100** 12	- 0	**100** 81	- 0	- 0	**100** 43	- -	**98** 43	- -	**87** 39	- 0	**100** 10
Baraga County Memorial Hospital, L'Anse, MI	- 0	- 0	- 0	- 0	- 0	- 0	- 0	- 0	- 0	- 0	- 0	- -	- 0	- -	- 0	- 0	- 0
Battle Creek Health System, Battle Creek, MI	**95** 223	**99** 367	**97** 235	**98** 337	**99** 275	**100** 163	**94** 179	**100** 986	**93** 264	**0** 1	**99** 800	**98** 248	**99** 806	**98** 251	**97** 741	**95** 179	**100** 279
Battle Creek VA Medical Center, Battle Creek, MI	**67** 12	- 0	**86** 14	**90** 21	**100** 14	**100** 14	- 0	- 0	- 0	- 0	- 0	- -	- 0	- -	- 0	- 0	- 0
Bay Regional Medical Center, Bay City, MI	**90** 136	**97** 159	**81** 140	**97** 241	**92** 201	**98** 85	**86** 394	**100** 1514	**93** 522	**92** 387	**98** 995	**73** 460	**96** 1013	**94** 450	**96** 975	**89** 394	**81** 267
Beaumont Hospital - Grosse Pointe, Grosse Pointe, MI	**94** 177	**98** 202	**93** 168	**99** 243	**96** 211	**95** 88	**96** 225	**100** 693	**95** 214	- 0	**99** 513	**90** 230	**99** 516	**99** 218	**97** 497	**97** 225	**98** 172
Bell Memorial Hospital, Ishpeming, MI	**92** 13	**88** 16	- 0	**100** 15	**69** 16	**67** 6	- 0	- 0	- 0	- 0	- 0	- -	- 0	- -	- 0	- 0	- 0
Borgess Medical Center, Kalamazoo, MI	**92** 53	**96** 91	**86** 72	**93** 116	**95** 101	**98** 41	**93** 116	**100** 567	**98** 206	**96** 132	**97** 418	**77** 620	**97** 426	**95** 598	**97** 402	**95** 116	**93** 106
Borgess-Lee Memorial Hospital, Dowagiac, MI	**78** 36	**96** 28	**65** 20	**96** 45	**85** 34	**87** 15	**74** 23	**93** 29	- 0	- 0	**82** 11	- -	**73** 11	- -	**64** 11	**74** 23	**100** 8

NOTE: The first number in each column (boldface) is the score, the second number is the number of patients; Please refer to the main entry for footnotes; (a) 100-299
*MEASURES: **Pneumonia Care:** 16. Appropriate Initial Antibiotic; 17. Blood Culture Timing; 18. Influenza Vaccine; 19. Initial Antibiotic Timing; 20. Pneumococcal Vaccine; 21. Smoking Cessation Advice; **Surgical Care Improvement Project:** 22. Appropriate VTP Within 24 Hours; 23. Appropriate Hair Removal; 24. Appropriate Beta Blocker Usage; 25. Controlled Postoperative Blood Glucose; 26. Prophylactic Antibiotic Timing; 27. Prophylactic Antibiotic Timing (Outpatient); 28. Prophylactic Antibiotic Selection; 29. Prophylactic Antibiotic Selection (Outpatient); 30. Prophylactic Antibiotic Stopped; 31. Recommended VTP Ordered; 32. Urinary Catheter Removal*

Hospital	Pneumonia Care						Surgical Care Improvement Project										
	16	17	18	19	20	21	22	23	24	25	26	27	28	29	30	31	32
Botsford Hospital, Farmington Hills, MI	92 115	95 294	89 124	96 250	96 189	99 79	99 267	100 666	98 189	- 0	97 502	91 240	99 504	96 224	97 480	99 267	94 199
Brighton Hospital, Brighton, MI	- 0	- 0	- 0	- 0	- 0	- 0	- 0	- 0	- 0	- 0	- 0	- 0	- 0	- 0	- 0	- 0	- 0
Bronson Lakeview Hospital, Paw Paw, MI	98 60	93 61	100 44	99 79	98 59	100 36	- 0	- 0	- 0	- 0	- 0	- -	- 0	- -	- 0	- 0	- 0
Bronson Methodist Hospital, Kalamazoo, MI	94 260	92 349	95 148	95 384	90 332	98 188	90 384	100 1477	98 455	100 201	97 1198	90 396	98 1201	97 376	98 1169	96 384	93 336
Bronson Vicksburg Hospital, Vicksburg, MI	- 0	- 0	- 0	- 0	- 0	- 0	- 0	- 0	- 0	- 0	- 0	- 0	- 0	- 0	- 0	- 0	- 0
Caro Community Hospital, Caro, MI	100 12	100 13	58 12	89 9	73 11	50 2	- 0	83 6	- 0	- 0	83 6	- -	100 6	- -	100 6	- 0	100 3
Carson City Hospital, Carson City, MI	91 45	92 37	87 31	93 46	89 35	100 14	98 66	95 219	77 31	- 0	90 197	77 39	93 200	88 34	92 193	100 66	78 54
Central Michigan Community Hospital, Mount Pleasant, MI	99 131	97 179	95 116	98 181	99 165	100 62	90 41	100 276	97 76	- 0	98 229	86 65	97 228	92 60	94 219	93 41	98 43
Charlevoix Area Hospital, Charlevoix, MI	100 9	67 9	- 0	100 12	44 9	- 0	- 0	- 0	- 0	- 0	- 0	- -	- 0	- -	- 0	- 0	- 0
Cheboygan Memorial Hospital, Cheboygan, MI	- -	- -	- -	- -	- -	- -	- -	- -	- -	- -	- -	- -	- -	- -	- -	- -	- -
Chelsea Community Hospital, Chelsea, MI	92 72	97 99	100 59	96 83	100 82	97 30	100 281	100 887	100 197	- 0	100 741	99 136	100 743	99 151	99 732	100 281	96 246
Children's Hospital of Michigan, Detroit, MI	- -	- -	- -	- -	- -	- -	- -	- -	- -	- -	- -	- -	- -	- -	- -	- -	- -
Chippewa County War Memorial Hospital, Sault Sainte Marie, MI	99 86	96 114	92 53	98 126	99 105	90 42	98 89	100 248	95 77	- 0	99 197	93 27	99 197	89 57	98 192	97 90	95 97
Clinton Memorial Hospital, Saint Johns, MI	97 33	89 37	96 27	98 40	95 41	100 11	100 27	100 59	- 0	- 0	98 40	- 0	92 39	- 0	92 39	96 28	100 13
Community Health Center of Branch County, Coldwater, MI	93 105	98 121	94 67	96 128	98 93	100 50	85 117	100 275	99 76	- 0	98 165	80 82	95 164	96 71	90 159	86 117	73 77
Community Hospital, Watervliet, MI	94 66	82 61	94 36	91 66	91 53	100 27	91 45	100 137	77 39	- 0	89 122	71 7	98 123	100 5	97 122	89 46	92 61
Covenant Medical Center, Saginaw, MI	90 224	91 400	91 369	97 448	93 488	100 226	88 226	97 824	89 291	86 132	96 535	89 625	96 545	94 591	70 518	89 228	87 100
Crittenton Hospital Medical Center, Rochester, MI	88 121	83 165	91 129	96 191	94 214	96 48	91 148	100 546	97 186	97 77	98 400	85 247	99 405	91 227	95 370	91 148	78 69
Deckerville Community Hospital, Deckerville, MI	100 8	100 6	60 5	91 11	75 8	0 2	- 0	- 0	- 0	- 0	- 0	- 0	- 0	- 0	- 0	- 0	- 0
Detroit (John D. Dingell) VA Medical Center, Detroit, MI	92 52	99 74	96 47	96 67	97 36	100 38	96 161	100 281	96 109	- 0	97 191	- -	97 192	- -	95 188	98 161	91 32
Detroit Receiving Hospital & Univ Health Center, Detroit, MI	98 98	98 333	95 142	98 315	97 115	98 165	91 362	100 608	98 119	0 1	100 277	95 73	100 279	93 71	96 274	92 362	93 204
Dickinson County Memorial Hospital, Iron Mountain, MI	97 73	99 86	98 62	98 90	96 90	100 33	98 149	100 320	98 84	- 0	99 236	64 39	97 236	93 27	97 230	98 149	90 20
Doctor's Hospital of Michigan, Pontiac, MI	79 33	96 46	89 28	86 50	87 30	72 29	89 89	99 132	84 25	- 0	42 57	52 94	80 51	61 75	92 50	91 90	78 41
Eaton Rapids Medical Center, Eaton Rapids, MI	95 22	95 19	80 15	95 21	69 13	100 5	- 0	- 0	- 0	- 0	- 0	89 64	- 0	98 63	- 0	- 0	- 0
Edward W Sparrow Hospital, Lansing, MI	93 305	94 404	85 366	93 500	87 436	100 222	87 442	98 1697	91 416	89 187	92 1370	87 599	97 1383	88 581	96 1333	94 442	81 204
Emma L Bixby Medical Center, Adrian, MI	90 62	92 96	93 75	96 96	95 96	100 42	89 112	100 274	97 60	- 0	98 195	94 87	98 195	58 84	96 189	89 114	97 70
Garden City Hospital, Garden City, MI	91 170	96 260	86 139	96 258	89 178	100 80	91 306	99 634	96 193	- 0	91 391	84 257	95 394	61 244	94 370	97 306	88 153
Genesys Regional Medical Center - Health Park, Grand Blanc, MI	90 96	94 171	93 164	94 211	98 200	100 90	92 410	94 1555	96 562	94 160	98 1320	81 479	96 1333	87 488	94 1251	98 411	96 391
Gratiot Medical Center, Alma, MI	94 109	100 91	88 105	98 160	94 125	100 44	79 154	100 345	89 112	- 0	95 219	71 156	88 219	91 117	82 211	79 156	88 72
Harbor Beach Community Hospital, Harbor Beach, MI	75 8	62 8	100 4	88 8	83 6	0 2	- 0	- 0	- 0	- 0	- 0	- -	- 0	- -	- 0	- 0	- 0
Harper University Hospital, Detroit, MI	99 71	98 177	98 100	92 169	100 109	100 47	91 155	100 615	99 167	78 99	100 414	61 590	95 428	85 476	93 383	88 162	78 87
Hayes Green Beach Memorial Hospital, Charlotte, MI	100 42	99 67	97 32	100 59	98 50	100 23	95 20	100 46	100 2	- 0	94 31	- -	87 30	- -	97 30	95 20	60 5
Healthsource Saginaw, Saginaw, MI	- 0	- 0	- 0	- 0	- 0	- 0	- 0	- 0	- 0	- 0	- 0	- 0	- 0	- 0	- 0	- 0	- 0
Henry Ford Hospital, Detroit, MI	91 64	93 188	79 101	92 135	76 116	100 80	98 300	100 842	70 320	96 181	97 571	79 476	99 583	86 907	93 561	99 300	89 198
Henry Ford Macomb Hospital, Clinton Township, MI	95 315	97 476	91 293	95 497	94 472	100 160	98 379	100 1559	95 534	96 168	98 1264	94 352	99 1271	95 344	97 1216	99 379	97 461
Henry Ford West Bloomfield Hospital, West Bloomfield, MI	83 119	84 219	62 123	94 213	62 196	96 25	97 240	99 661	78 158	- 0	96 445	77 140	98 443	73 273	94 435	98 241	93 214
Henry Ford Wyandotte Hospital, Wyandotte, MI	93 292	97 419	97 307	97 519	96 432	100 237	99 208	100 482	92 158	- 0	94 308	88 334	98 310	88 325	94 285	100 208	69 42
Herrick Memorial Hospital, Tecumseh, MI	96 45	98 62	86 42	92 64	97 58	94 17	- 0	- 0	- 0	- 0	- 0	- -	- 0	- -	- 0	- 0	- 0
Hills & Dales General Hospital, Cass City, MI	83 18	80 15	67 9	100 8	38 16	67 3	50 6	56 9	- 0	- 0	100 2	75 4	100 2	100 3	50 2	50 6	100 1
Hillsdale Community Health Center, Hillsdale, MI	89 114	89 111	52 90	85 134	42 128	91 65	80 59	99 246	79 73	- 0	79 184	66 38	79 176	81 32	83 173	78 60	90 62
Holland Community Hospital, Holland, MI	99 138	99 250	99 163	100 232	100 228	100 66	99 156	100 654	100 160	- 0	100 500	100 301	99 504	98 300	100 490	99 156	97 33
Hurley Medical Center, Flint, MI	81 121	97 109	86 80	90 179	79 102	99 100	95 175	99 443	91 98	- 0	99 286	70 172	97 287	88 153	94 272	97 176	92 75
Huron Medical Center, Bad Axe, MI	91 33	100 60	81 27	100 52	88 52	100 7	91 23	100 178	100 44	- 0	99 148	73 11	97 149	92 26	100 146	91 23	97 33
Huron Valley-Sinai Hospital, Commerce Twp, MI	97 117	96 212	89 124	99 192	97 156	97 69	93 179	100 657	94 161	- 0	98 489	74 196	99 502	94 158	96 486	93 179	91 185
Ingham Regional Medical Center, Lansing, MI	90 233	84 196	87 166	92 274	92 238	99 122	88 190	100 1240	91 380	85 240	97 957	79 574	93 969	90 547	93 944	92 190	80 171
Ionia County Memorial Hospital, Ionia, MI	87 31	91 23	92 12	90 29	78 23	79 14	75 4	86 7	- 0	- 0	100 1	- 0	0 1	- 0	100 1	100 4	100 1
Iron Mountain VA Medical Center, Iron Mountain, MI	95 20	96 27	100 14	100 2	100 30	100 14	- 0	- 0	- 0	- 0	- 0	- -	- 0	- -	- 0	- 0	- 0
Karmanos Cancer Center, Detroit, MI	0 1	0 1	67 24	50 10	94 17	91 11	93 227	100 355	99 96	- 0	98 130	53 95	89 130	78 67	92 129	96 230	50 48
Lakeland Hospital - St Joseph, Saint Joseph, MI	95 234	98 296	94 247	92 373	96 332	99 169	98 294	99 964	92 292	98 126	99 632	93 391	96 643	92 381	99 610	98 294	95 215
Lapeer Regional Medical Center, Lapeer, MI	92 190	100 252	98 127	97 231	98 206	98 65	97 128	100 517	97 158	- 0	99 396	96 81	100 398	97 79	97 386	98 128	100 1
Marlette Regional Hospital, Marlette, MI	90 68	78 59	61 38	89 79	49 53	60 20	68 25	68 37	- 0	- 0	88 25	68 19	87 23	100 15	100 22	68 25	91 11
Marquette General Hospital, Marquette, MI	82 57	99 99	85 94	97 97	83 128	100 52	86 126	91 517	87 170	96 125	97 373	76 640	98 376	86 593	89 366	89 126	79 94
McKenzie Memorial Hospital, Sandusky, MI	100 21	83 12	78 18	95 22	95 21	33 3	90 10	94 16	50 2	- 0	100 8	100 10	100 8	100 10	88 8	90 10	40 5
Mclaren Regional Medical Center, Flint, MI	97 215	96 103	88 225	90 346	91 301	100 115	93 291	100 1345	91 426	84 252	98 1069	93 428	97 1091	96 419	95 1018	97 291	79 152
Mecosta County Medical Center, Big Rapids, MI	88 72	98 93	87 62	99 75	92 74	100 30	86 28	100 227	83 54	- 0	93 199	27 83	95 199	91 23	94 195	83 29	91 56
Memorial Healthcare, Owosso, MI	89 91	86 127	93 76	96 122	99 92	100 47	87 138	100 333	95 79	- 0	96 222	94 126	95 220	92 122	94 216	92 140	95 100
Memorial Medical Center of West Michigan, Ludington, MI	93 57	97 120	92 50	97 97	96 82	89 28	79 126	99 299	95 91	- 0	98 242	73 26	98 244	96 26	94 239	80 126	100 15
Mercy Health Partners - Hackley Campus, Muskegon, MI	97 133	97 214	93 86	100 203	96 124	95 76	97 278	98 992	90 221	- 0	93 646	91 320	98 637	98 328	99 631	96 281	95 64
Mercy Health Partners - Mercy Campus, Muskegon, MI	93 119	97 193	95 113	98 176	95 159	98 88	92 298	100 1450	89 440	95 217	95 1088	93 482	99 1087	97 595	95 1051	93 299	95 382
Mercy Hospital - Cadillac, Cadillac, MI	94 97	94 151	100 82	98 128	98 117	100 42	93 86	100 422	90 102	- 0	96 322	93 153	97 322	82 151	96 318	94 86	97 102
Mercy Hospital - Grayling, Grayling, MI	96 93	100 132	99 72	97 132	96 112	98 48	94 63	100 209	96 53	- 0	99 138	97 99	98 142	98 96	93 133	94 63	100 16
Mercy Memorial Hospital System, Monroe, MI	95 162	99 278	98 160	98 257	99 217	100 120	94 244	100 728	99 193	- 0	98 522	85 117	99 524	98 107	96 493	95 244	100 19
Metro Health Hospital, Wyoming, MI	98 90	96 194	99 77	99 159	99 101	100 47	91 144	100 458	86 99	- 0	97 322	94 258	97 323	97 298	96 308	94 144	90 97
Midmichigan Medical Center-Clare, Clare, MI	89 76	93 59	93 55	94 109	96 77	98 45	83 54	100 109	94 36	- 0	92 60	93 15	87 60	89 18	95 56	85 54	92 26
Midmichigan Medical Center-Gladwin, Gladwin, MI	95 38	96 45	95 22	94 53	100 41	100 15	- 0	- 0	- 0	- 0	- 0	- 0	- 0	- 0	- 0	- 0	- 0
Midmichigan Medical Center-Midland, Midland, MI	93 87	97 145	87 78	94 121	91 125	96 57	94 154	100 710	96 213	95 126	93 486	91 391	98 491	91 378	96 471	94 154	94 170
Mount Clemens Regional Medical Center, Mount Clemens, MI	89 184	94 277	82 202	95 288	76 234	98 135	96 298	99 1177	68 405	85 119	96 847	90 244	97 856	95 235	94 762	98 298	94 294
Munson Medical Center, Traverse City, MI	100 228	98 386	100 219	99 318	100 342	99 160	97 254	100 920	98 269	95 169	96 586	90 339	99 596	97 390	98 568	98 255	94 113

NOTE: The first number in each column (boldface) is the score, the second number is the number of patients; Please refer to the main entry for footnotes; (a) 100-299
MEASURES: ***Pneumonia Care:*** *16. Appropriate Initial Antibiotic; 17. Blood Culture Timing; 18. Influenza Vaccine; 19. Initial Antibiotic Timing; 20. Pneumococcal Vaccine; 21. Smoking Cessation Advice;* ***Surgical Care Improvement Project:*** *22. Appropriate VTP Within 24 Hours; 23. Appropriate Hair Removal; 24. Appropriate Beta Blocker Usage; 25. Controlled Postoperative Blood Glucose; 26. Prophylactic Antibiotic Timing; 27. Prophylactic Antibiotic Timing (Outpatient); 28. Prophylactic Antibiotic Selection; 29. Prophylactic Antibiotic Selection (Outpatient); 30. Prophylactic Antibiotic Stopped; 31. Recommended VTP Ordered; 32. Urinary Catheter Removal*

Hospital	Pneumonia Care						Surgical Care Improvement Project										
	16	17	18	19	20	21	22	23	24	25	26	27	28	29	30	31	32
North Ottawa Community Hospital, Grand Haven, MI	90 50	99 88	94 50	100 80	98 63	100 17	97 65	100 257	90 67	- 0	100 203	99 80	98 205	95 87	99 201	97 65	100 94
Northern Michigan Regional Hospital, Petoskey, MI	93 83	97 129	92 106	90 125	96 137	98 63	93 145	99 615	92 223	93 125	97 447	84 362	99 458	95 334	91 427	90 155	89 105
Northstar Health System, Iron River, MI	93 28	87 77	74 68	96 78	72 93	96 23	- 0	- 0	- 0	- 0	- 0	- -	- 0	- -	- 0	- 0	- 0
Oakland Regional Hospital, Southfield, MI	- 0	- 0	- 0	- 0	- 0	- 0	100 10	97 33	86 7	- 0	84 32	98 49	100 32	98 49	100 31	100 10	80 5
Oaklawn Hospital, Marshall, MI	98 80	98 93	100 59	97 118	98 90	97 33	97 116	100 568	97 148	- 0	99 426	93 67	98 427	96 70	98 422	97 116	95 117
Oakwood Annapolis Hospital, Wayne, MI	94 163	98 268	100 154	95 294	100 186	100 104	91 180	100 448	93 136	- 0	98 312	91 284	98 313	92 318	94 299	94 184	60 20
Oakwood Heritage Hospital, Taylor, MI	97 144	99 297	100 168	97 286	100 207	100 105	99 90	100 314	96 93	- 0	100 234	81 16	99 235	88 16	100 224	99 90	100 37
Oakwood Hospital and Medical Center, Dearborn, MI	96 370	96 285	82 347	94 572	89 475	100 224	98 516	100 1665	93 657	93 387	98 1267	96 320	99 1281	96 344	94 1197	99 518	77 266
Oakwood Southshore Medical Center, Trenton, MI	97 209	97 269	97 188	97 325	97 257	100 101	99 149	100 549	93 181	- 0	99 403	83 133	99 403	93 126	98 392	99 149	74 35
Otsego Memorial Hospital, Gaylord, MI	100 59	95 80	96 46	99 76	92 78	100 18	100 45	100 217	97 63	- 0	90 169	78 27	98 168	100 23	97 167	100 45	100 62
Paul Oliver Memorial Hospital, Frankfort, MI	- -	- -	- -	- -	- -	- -	- -	- -	- -	- -	- 0	- 0	- 0	- 0	- -	- -	- -
Pennock Hospital, Hastings, MI	98 86	97 104	98 56	95 115	100 93	100 28	85 73	100 266	98 59	- 0	100 202	88 68	97 202	83 60	97 201	89 74	84 25
Poh Medical Center, Pontiac, MI	88 88	95 84	92 64	94 113	91 79	73 67	92 105	100 291	78 64	- 0	99 178	79 100	95 184	76 88	86 170	94 106	86 88
Port Huron Hospital, Port Huron, MI	96 189	95 261	93 169	91 279	94 239	97 97	99 280	98 836	81 260	99 150	97 613	90 142	97 616	99 136	98 587	99 280	74 246
Portage Health Hospital, Hancock, MI	89 28	95 37	86 22	100 44	92 37	93 15	95 64	100 200	92 51	- 0	99 171	69 29	99 173	88 52	93 162	98 64	80 40
Providence Hospital and Medical Centers, Southfield, MI	98 409	96 526	95 386	97 656	93 495	99 157	96 785	100 2310	93 709	97 218	98 1577	95 884	99 1597	99 866	96 1431	97 785	94 564
Saginaw VA Medical Center, Saginaw, MI	96 28	100 24	95 21	97 36	100 23	100 18	- 0	- 0	- 0	- 0	- 0	- -	- 0	- -	- 0	- 0	- 0
Saint Francis Hospital, Escanaba, MI	88 81	93 139	97 104	97 119	96 141	100 42	93 57	100 139	95 20	- 0	100 74	71 42	93 74	100 30	99 73	93 57	100 15
Saint John Hospital and Medical Center, Detroit, MI	96 267	95 205	94 271	95 449	97 300	99 187	98 394	100 1512	98 515	95 260	98 1213	94 642	98 1228	97 622	96 1155	99 394	96 198
Saint John Macomb-Oakland Hospital, Warren, MI	96 387	98 454	98 442	96 634	99 600	98 251	99 406	100 1366	97 460	94 192	97 1068	91 446	99 1079	97 422	97 971	99 407	97 310
Saint John River District Hospital, East China, MI	95 78	100 85	98 80	100 96	99 95	96 23	96 45	100 105	100 24	- 0	100 45	96 47	100 45	100 46	100 45	96 45	100 20
Saint Joseph Mercy Hospital, Ann Arbor, MI	88 285	92 137	78 412	94 512	79 496	100 180	95 242	100 827	88 279	97 175	98 577	97 921	97 584	97 936	97 560	98 243	75 202
Saint Joseph Mercy Livingston Hospital, Howell, MI	89 103	95 110	91 81	96 142	89 132	100 28	86 93	100 310	78 67	- 0	97 227	86 96	97 227	95 113	95 223	87 93	78 108
Saint Joseph Mercy Oakland, Pontiac, MI	95 84	100 77	88 83	94 126	93 116	100 58	99 161	100 630	96 201	94 130	99 459	99 421	99 473	98 438	98 426	99 161	92 143
Saint Joseph Mercy Port Huron, Port Huron, MI	87 78	99 125	98 83	99 133	97 95	100 56	99 165	100 415	95 142	- 0	98 316	91 32	99 318	94 32	97 272	100 165	98 177
Saint Joseph Mercy Saline Hospital, Saline, MI	100 51	81 16	89 46	98 66	84 64	100 11	85 13	100 56	91 11	- 0	94 47	98 50	100 47	98 50	98 45	85 13	93 15
Saint Mary Mercy Hospital, Livonia, MI	91 205	98 313	94 266	97 433	95 439	100 75	90 364	100 898	91 264	100 2	96 520	92 253	99 524	95 243	95 504	92 365	88 221
Saint Mary's Health Care, Grand Rapids, MI	97 195	100 330	95 209	99 362	97 257	99 123	98 162	100 596	96 179	- 0	96 397	95 314	98 389	90 307	97 373	99 162	96 135
Saint Mary's of Michigan Medical Center, Saginaw, MI	93 46	93 99	81 81	96 83	81 104	98 51	93 188	100 566	94 230	90 124	99 388	98 430	98 391	97 438	96 376	94 188	79 94
Saint Mary's Standish Community Hospital, Standish, MI	86 22	96 49	100 32	100 46	100 40	95 21	100 9	100 10	100 1	- 0	0 3	100 3	67 3	100 3	100 2	100 9	- 0
Schoolcraft Memorial Hospital, Manistique, MI	100 19	79 19	80 10	89 27	80 20	43 7	- 0	- 0	- 0	- 0	- 0	- -	- 0	- -	- 0	- 0	- 0
Sheridan Community Hospital, Sheridan, MI	74 23	75 16	94 16	100 20	80 15	50 4	0 1	100 1	- 0	- 0	100 1	- -	100 1	- -	100 1	0 1	100 1
Sinai-Grace Hospital, Detroit, MI	97 183	89 446	92 212	97 396	94 256	100 153	98 280	100 862	99 210	96 82	98 555	73 487	99 563	82 379	98 529	98 281	97 223
South Haven Community Hospital, South Haven, MI	98 44	96 50	94 31	96 54	98 45	100 16	100 13	100 101	95 20	- 0	99 82	85 13	95 82	82 11	100 81	100 13	100 29
Southeast Michigan Surgical Hospital, Warren, MI	- 0	- 0	- 0	- 0	- 0	- 0	100 2	100 8	100 2	- 0	38 8	89 108	100 8	99 106	100 8	100 2	100 7
Spectrum Health - Butterworth Campus, Grand Rapids, MI	97 600	97 1062	96 631	97 948	99 822	97 282	99 262	100 1143	95 383	98 187	95 750	96 1225	98 761	96 1197	98 715	100 262	90 323
Spectrum Health - Reed City Campus, Reed City, MI	98 52	93 85	96 27	97 73	98 60	100 15	100 1	100 16	- 0	- 0	100 14	94 18	100 14	76 17	100 14	100 1	- 0
Spectrum Health Gerber Memorial, Fremont, MI	96 92	98 132	100 69	99 118	98 100	100 41	90 73	100 330	94 68	- 0	99 266	85 27	99 267	91 23	96 260	89 74	87 15
Spectrum Health United Memorial - Kelsey Campus, Lakeview, MI	100 26	100 27	100 11	100 24	100 24	100 11	- 0	- 0	- 0	- 0	- 0	- 0	- 0	100 9	- 0	- 0	- 0
Spectrum Health United Memorial - United Campus, Greenville, MI	95 107	98 186	100 114	100 165	100 149	100 50	91 70	100 202	97 34	- 0	99 145	93 55	100 146	98 53	100 137	99 70	95 37
Straith Hospital for Special Surgery, Southfield, MI	- 0	- 0	- 0	- 0	- 0	- 0	- 0	- 0	- 0	- 0	- 0	- 0	- 0	- 0	- 0	- 0	- 0
Sturgis Hospital, Sturgis, MI	88 50	97 59	97 37	95 77	95 65	71 17	96 49	99 127	96 27	- 0	90 89	75 75	99 89	95 58	87 87	98 49	100 24
Tawas Saint Joseph Hospital, Tawas City, MI	95 95	93 144	97 74	98 133	97 113	100 54	100 45	100 223	95 76	- 0	97 151	94 63	99 154	97 62	99 148	100 45	100 41
Three Rivers Health, Three Rivers, MI	91 46	93 58	71 28	96 56	81 47	78 23	71 21	98 94	94 17	- 0	98 57	- 0	93 58	- 0	100 57	71 21	94 18
University of Michigan Health System, Ann Arbor, MI	93 203	98 324	88 268	96 403	93 296	100 155	99 699	98 2332	80 887	98 651	98 1735	74 541	99 1766	88 694	93 1625	99 700	89 683
VA Ann Arbor Healthcare System, Ann Arbor, MI	87 47	95 78	85 54	95 81	93 60	98 45	94 163	100 488	100 291	94 163	96 363	- -	99 363	- -	87 350	97 163	96 199
West Branch Regional Medical Center, West Branch, MI	91 81	94 118	90 58	95 106	92 101	100 33	96 175	98 335	100 112	- 0	89 270	100 63	98 269	92 63	86 259	97 175	96 57
West Shore Medical Center, Manistee, MI	98 43	90 31	82 38	97 63	88 59	89 18	79 76	99 185	95 60	- 0	99 116	83 18	97 117	94 16	97 113	88 76	92 53
William Beaumont Hospital, Royal Oak, MI	94 86	96 121	97 116	95 177	99 154	98 51	97 309	100 977	96 363	94 176	96 645	94 727	99 663	91 732	97 609	99 309	87 236
William Beaumont Hospital-Troy, Troy, MI	95 147	96 165	97 154	93 230	98 219	99 76	89 162	100 688	97 277	92 153	96 456	91 471	99 457	94 464	98 388	93 162	93 148
Zeeland Community Hospital, Zeeland, MI	100 44	100 112	96 57	98 100	100 100	100 27	96 50	100 251	97 64	- 0	99 196	95 57	97 198	100 54	98 188	96 50	100 16
MINNESOTA																	
Abbott Northwestern Hospital, Minneapolis, MN	93 116	97 213	97 175	98 216	97 256	99 143	94 216	100 814	96 303	97 138	98 557	93 524	98 563	95 505	96 528	96 216	93 187
Albany Area Hospital, Albany, MN	67 6	- 0	50 4	89 9	77 13	0 1	- 0	100 1	- 0	- 0	0 1	- 0	100 1	- 0	100 1	- 0	- 0
Appleton Municipal Hospital, Appleton, MN	- 0	- 0	- 0	100 1	100 1	- 0	- 0	- 0	- 0	- 0	- 0	- -	- 0	- -	- 0	- 0	- 0
Austin Medical Center, Austin, MN	93 115	99 172	98 99	100 168	98 182	91 33	96 125	100 241	97 96	- 0	100 208	88 32	98 209	100 35	100 204	98 125	97 78
Avera Marshall Regional Medical Center, Marshall, MN	60 48	92 37	76 21	76 54	93 44	88 8	90 20	100 86	100 13	- 0	79 81	88 16	99 80	81 16	84 80	86 21	95 40
Bigfork Valley Hospital, Bigfork, MN	100 5	86 7	80 10	79 14	71 14	100 3	100 17	100 62	54 28	- 0	96 55	- 0	100 55	- 0	96 55	100 17	100 33
Bridges Medical Services, Ada, MN	89 9	- 0	40 10	85 13	55 11	0 2	- 0	- 0	- 0	- 0	- 0	- 0	- 0	- 0	- 0	- 0	- 0
Buffalo Hospital, Buffalo, MN	95 40	93 42	100 29	98 52	100 45	100 18	100 51	100 219	100 48	- 0	98 161	95 82	99 163	96 79	97 151	100 51	100 58
Cambridge Medical Center, Cambridge, MN	90 52	98 81	100 40	100 63	97 67	100 22	97 35	99 257	98 66	- 0	98 194	89 19	98 196	100 20	98 186	100 35	96 53
Cannon Falls Medical Center Mayo, Cannon Falls, MN	100 8	75 4	100 10	100 8	93 15	100 5	100 11	100 27	86 14	- 0	100 24	- 0	100 24	- 0	96 24	100 11	100 10
Cass Lake Indian Health Services Hospital, Cass Lake, MN	- -	- -	- -	- -	- -	- -	- -	- -	- -	- -	- 0	- 0	- 0	- 0	- -	- -	- -
Centracare Health System - Long Prairie, Long Prairie, MN	83 12	100 10	47 15	95 21	71 24	17 6	100 3	100 8	- 0	- 0	86 7	60 10	86 7	86 7	86 7	100 3	- 0
Centracare Health System - Melrose Hospital, Melrose, MN	50 6	0 1	0 1	- 0	100 8	100 1	- 0	100 2	- 0	- 0	0 2	- 0	100 2	- 0	100 2	- 0	- 0
Children's Hospitals & Clinics, Minneapolis, MN	- -	- -	- -	- -	- -	- -	- -	- -	- -	- -	- -	- -	- -	- -	- -	- -	- -
Chippewa County Hospital, Montevideo, MN	78 9	82 17	67 12	100 16	62 29	60 5	88 25	76 38	89 9	- 0	73 33	- 0	94 31	- 0	77 31	85 26	100 15
Clearwater Health Services, Bagley, MN	100 3	- 0	- 0	100 7	20 5	0 1	- 0	- 0	- 0	- 0	- 0	- -	- 0	- -	- 0	- 0	- 0

NOTE: The first number in each column (boldface) is the score, the second number is the number of patients; Please refer to the main entry for footnotes; (a) 100-299
*MEASURES: **Pneumonia Care:** 16. Appropriate Initial Antibiotic; 17. Blood Culture Timing; 18. Influenza Vaccine; 19. Initial Antibiotic Timing; 20. Pneumococcal Vaccine; 21. Smoking Cessation Advice; **Surgical Care Improvement Project:** 22. Appropriate VTP Within 24 Hours; 23. Appropriate Hair Removal; 24. Appropriate Beta Blocker Usage; 25. Controlled Postoperative Blood Glucose; 26. Prophylactic Antibiotic Timing; 27. Prophylactic Antibiotic Timing (Outpatient); 28. Prophylactic Antibiotic Selection; 29. Prophylactic Antibiotic Selection (Outpatient); 30. Prophylactic Antibiotic Stopped; 31. Recommended VTP Ordered; 32. Urinary Catheter Removal*

Hospital	Pneumonia Care						Surgical Care Improvement Project										
	16	17	18	19	20	21	22	23	24	25	26	27	28	29	30	31	32
Community Memorial Hospital, Cloquet, MN	91 43	94 31	100 26	96 57	100 41	100 13	97 39	100 121	96 28	- 0	99 105	100 12	100 107	100 12	97 104	97 39	90 29
Cook County Northshore Hospital, Grand Marais, MN	100 1	100 2	0 1	67 3	0 3	100 1	- 0	- 0	- 0	- 0	- 0	- -	- 0	- -	- 0	- 0	- 0
Cook Hospital, Cook, MN	43 14	100 3	67 6	79 19	24 17	0 2	- 0	- 0	- 0	- 0	- 0	- -	- 0	- -	- 0	- 0	- 0
Cuyuna Regional Medical Center, Crosby, MN	92 25	95 19	33 27	82 38	67 42	62 8	100 17	76 96	88 33	- 0	33 73	- -	99 70	- -	99 70	100 17	100 13
Deer River Healthcare Center, Deer River, MN	84 19	73 11	100 11	71 17	90 20	100 3	43 7	71 7	100 2	- 0	20 5	75 8	60 5	100 8	100 5	43 7	100 1
District One Hospital, Faribault, MN	89 57	98 54	98 57	99 84	100 80	88 17	86 59	100 173	94 50	- 0	96 154	90 52	97 152	98 50	93 151	86 59	97 33
Douglas County Hospital, Alexandria, MN	85 72	91 88	98 82	98 122	95 151	100 29	92 139	100 422	96 130	- 0	91 306	91 179	96 306	97 172	99 294	94 139	94 115
Ely Bloomenson Community Hospital, Ely, MN	89 9	100 3	80 5	100 10	86 14	100 1	- 0	- 0	- 0	- 0	- 0	- -	- 0	- -	- 0	- 0	- 0
Essentia Health Duluth, Duluth, MN	- 0	- 0	73 15	- 0	89 19	94 16	100 4	100 212	80 25	- 0	96 188	74 293	97 191	95 367	89 187	100 4	100 1
Essentia Health Fosston, Fosston, MN	100 8	100 5	100 10	100 16	100 17	100 2	100 8	100 18	- 0	- 0	100 16	- 0	100 16	- 0	100 16	100 8	100 5
Essentia Health Sandstone, Sandstone, MN	75 16	89 9	57 14	84 19	84 19	100 6	- 0	- 0	- 0	- 0	- 0	0 1	- 0	100 1	- 0	- 0	- 0
Essentia Health St Joseph's Medical Center, Brainerd, MN	85 65	99 108	91 70	99 106	86 132	90 40	98 89	100 348	92 99	- 0	96 257	91 47	96 257	93 45	94 247	98 89	76 21
Essentia Health St Mary's Medical Center, Duluth, MN	91 54	97 66	92 93	95 97	98 121	97 74	97 201	100 765	93 321	95 170	96 534	95 521	98 556	97 523	97 512	99 201	85 220
Fairmont Medical Center, Fairmont, MN	95 79	100 94	97 94	98 114	98 129	93 28	97 71	100 211	100 82	- 0	96 163	77 39	98 163	86 56	99 157	97 71	91 45
Fairview Lakes Health Services, Wyoming, MN	87 67	97 87	96 55	96 98	99 89	100 24	94 103	100 440	93 161	- 0	96 347	90 173	99 350	99 167	99 334	97 103	97 32
Fairview Northland Regional Hospital, Princeton, MN	96 69	100 101	100 60	100 99	100 84	100 39	100 42	100 217	97 61	- 0	99 176	89 53	100 178	94 49	98 173	100 42	100 10
Fairview Red Wing Hospital, Red Wing, MN	100 62	98 63	100 36	100 74	100 61	100 21	100 39	100 214	100 68	- 0	99 165	100 52	98 167	92 65	98 161	100 39	100 56
Fairview Ridges Hospital, Burnsville, MN	94 115	96 238	96 134	97 222	97 168	100 47	79 160	100 767	87 222	- 0	98 620	95 253	100 622	99 249	97 616	91 160	95 326
Fairview Southdale Hospital, Edina, MN	89 206	99 304	93 221	96 311	96 294	100 70	94 357	100 2200	98 799	94 203	99 1882	70 662	99 1900	98 597	96 1811	96 357	96 477
Glacial Ridge Hospital, Glenwood, MN	96 25	- 0	17 30	86 37	36 45	50 6	86 7	100 12	25 4	- 0	80 5	- 0	80 5	- 0	100 5	86 7	100 4
Glencoe Regional Health Services, Glencoe, MN	80 15	75 4	91 11	94 18	94 16	100 1	91 23	100 74	80 25	- 0	94 67	92 12	94 67	100 12	100 67	91 23	100 6
Grand Itasca Clinic and Hospital, Grand Rapids, MN	96 49	90 62	100 52	99 68	93 70	90 21	93 58	92 211	98 57	- 0	94 155	100 14	97 147	97 36	100 147	93 58	82 28
Healtheast St John's Hospital, Maplewood, MN	95 103	98 131	98 92	97 146	96 142	100 37	93 292	100 899	87 208	- 0	96 760	99 204	97 766	95 203	98 740	95 292	82 78
Healtheast Woodwinds Hospital, Woodbury, MN	94 79	99 98	94 69	100 99	93 84	100 27	92 132	100 1153	96 272	- 0	100 1013	94 200	99 1015	98 191	98 998	92 132	95 101
Hendricks Community Hospital, Hendricks, MN	67 3	0 1	0 2	33 3	17 6	- 0	100 3	100 13	- 0	- 0	62 13	- 0	100 13	- 0	62 13	100 3	100 4
Hennepin County Medical Center, Minneapolis, MN	90 119	77 242	95 151	91 246	95 118	100 169	93 165	100 396	94 111	94 65	97 271	95 172	97 276	88 168	98 256	96 165	87 60
Holy Trinity Hospital, Graceville, MN	100 1	100 5	100 6	100 10	100 9	0 1	- 0	- 0	- 0	- 0	- 0	0 1	- 0	0 1	- 0	- 0	- 0
Hutchinson Area Health Care, Hutchinson, MN	96 45	94 50	92 36	98 60	95 62	100 11	99 67	100 195	97 64	- 0	94 144	84 45	92 146	98 40	100 136	100 67	94 16
Immanuel-St Josephs-Mayo Health System, Mankato, MN	90 96	93 94	93 135	97 156	91 173	91 46	95 223	100 533	94 152	- 0	99 307	95 100	97 305	97 99	96 292	96 224	86 85
Johnson Memorial Hospital, Dawson, MN	86 7	100 1	90 10	100 16	93 14	67 3	- 0	- 0	- 0	- 0	- 0	- 0	- 0	- 0	- 0	- 0	- 0
Kanabec Hospital, Mora, MN	95 39	100 31	96 23	96 53	86 50	100 7	96 46	97 78	68 22	- 0	93 75	5 22	100 75	100 2	91 75	100 46	100 22
Kittson Memorial Hospital, Hallock, MN	71 7	- 0	14 7	91 11	14 14	- 0	- 0	- 0	- 0	- 0	- 0	- 0	- 0	- 0	- 0	- 0	- 0
Lake City Medical Center Mayo Health System, Lake City, MN	67 3	67 6	75 4	89 9	38 8	67 3	100 12	100 33	- 0	- 0	90 29	- 0	100 29	- 0	100 29	100 12	50 16
Lake Region Healthcare Corporation, Fergus Falls, MN	94 63	96 96	98 84	95 104	100 109	100 23	90 115	100 260	93 59	- 0	90 193	83 72	96 193	93 73	97 190	93 115	98 45
Lake View Memorial Hospital, Two Harbors, MN	67 9	67 6	100 9	100 12	91 11	0 2	- 0	- 0	- 0	- 0	- 0	- -	- 0	- -	- 0	- 0	- 0
Lakeside Medical Center, Pine City, MN	- 0	- 0	- 0	- 0	- 0	- 0	- 0	- 0	- 0	- 0	- 0	- 0	- 0	- 0	- 0	- 0	- 0
Lakeview Memorial Hospital, Stillwater, MN	100 25	94 31	79 19	96 45	85 27	89 9	84 69	100 463	84 98	- 0	97 302	95 207	99 302	94 207	100 295	87 69	88 16
Lakewood Health Center, Baudette, MN	80 5	100 1	100 8	100 9	82 11	50 2	- 0	- 0	- 0	- 0	- 0	- 0	- 0	- 0	- 0	- 0	- 0
Lakewood Health System, Staples, MN	85 34	94 35	43 28	88 59	61 46	75 12	86 7	100 65	- 0	- 0	40 65	- -	98 56	- -	91 55	86 7	100 2
Lifecare Medical Center, Roseau, MN	94 18	100 11	95 19	100 33	100 37	100 9	50 2	100 9	0 1	- 0	67 6	- 0	100 6	- 0	83 6	100 2	67 3
Madelia Community Hospital, Madelia, MN	86 14	100 4	75 12	95 19	94 16	50 2	100 3	100 4	- 0	- 0	100 1	- -	100 1	- -	100 1	100 3	100 1
Madison Hospital, Madison, MN	20 5	- 0	44 9	89 9	33 12	50 2	- 0	- 0	- 0	- 0	- 0	- 0	- 0	- 0	- 0	- 0	- 0
Mahnomen Health Center, Mahnomen, MN	80 5	- 0	50 2	80 10	56 9	100 1	- 0	- 0	- 0	- 0	- 0	- 0	- 0	- 0	- 0	- 0	- 0
Maple Grove Hospital, Maple Grove, MN	- 0	- 0	- 0	- 0	- 0	- 0	- 0	- 0	- 0	- 0	- 0	- -	- 0	- -	- 0	- 0	- 0
Mayo Clinic - Methodist Hospital, Rochester, MN	- 0	- 0	76 33	71 7	92 36	100 6	99 202	99 666	99 164	- 0	98 412	95 329	99 411	97 566	99 403	100 202	94 78
Mayo Clinic - Saint Marys Hospital, Rochester, MN	88 32	88 78	94 87	92 104	96 135	97 31	98 259	100 786	98 337	87 254	96 408	84 628	98 438	98 581	95 392	99 259	79 158
Meeker Memorial Hospital, Litchfield, MN	90 10	100 8	88 8	71 17	88 17	80 5	86 22	74 27	- 0	- 0	85 26	100 2	92 26	100 2	100 26	83 24	100 9
Mercy Hospital, Coon Rapids, MN	96 170	94 165	94 160	95 245	99 201	99 107	97 165	100 667	97 279	98 141	97 434	97 443	100 447	98 443	99 414	99 165	88 104
Mercy Hospital & Health Care Center, Moose Lake, MN	97 31	96 27	100 21	97 38	97 34	100 7	82 28	100 68	- 0	- 0	89 63	- 0	100 64	- 0	94 62	82 28	50 16
Mille Lacs Health System, Onamia, MN	100 12	95 21	55 11	97 32	88 16	80 15	83 6	93 14	- 0	- 0	100 12	- -	100 12	- -	100 12	83 6	- 0
Minneapolis VA Medical Center, Minneapolis, MN	96 46	98 81	97 70	95 98	100 120	100 24	97 206	100 498	97 230	91 181	99 392	- -	97 396	- -	97 384	98 206	97 157
Minnesota Valley Health Center, Le Sueur, MN	83 6	100 2	100 2	100 6	100 4	- 0	- 0	- 0	- 0	- 0	- 0	- 0	- 0	- 0	- 0	- 0	- 0
Municipal Hospital and Granite Manor, Granite Falls, MN	94 16	90 10	94 16	96 24	90 30	67 3	- 0	- 0	- 0	- 0	- 0	- 0	- 0	- 0	- 0	- 0	- 0
Murray County Memorial Hospital, Slayton, MN	90 10	- 0	50 6	- 0	46 13	33 3	100 3	94 18	- 0	- 0	93 15	- 0	100 15	- 0	100 15	100 3	100 9
Naeve Hospital, Albert Lea, MN	73 55	90 87	98 53	91 98	98 100	70 10	97 144	100 347	96 94	- 0	99 272	76 38	99 277	100 30	98 266	97 145	97 90
New River Medical Center, Monticello, MN	95 43	97 58	100 27	100 60	96 45	100 11	100 10	100 55	100 2	- 0	98 49	- 0	100 49	- 0	93 46	100 10	67 9
New Ulm Medical Center, New Ulm, MN	92 24	98 42	89 36	100 46	100 57	100 12	100 49	100 155	98 60	- 0	99 107	50 42	100 107	91 22	100 106	100 49	100 18
North Country Regional Hospital, Bemidji, MN	90 63	89 102	96 72	92 114	99 107	98 43	85 280	100 613	89 177	- 0	96 509	82 72	96 512	94 66	94 499	84 282	87 128
North Memorial Medical Center, Robbinsdale, MN	82 95	93 147	86 122	98 181	83 150	86 57	72 165	100 650	98 247	71 156	95 498	91 262	97 511	95 253	94 493	72 166	83 191
North Valley Health Center, Warren, MN	90 10	100 1	62 13	100 15	20 15	50 2	- 0	- 0	- 0	- 0	- 0	- -	- 0	- -	- 0	- 0	- 0
Northern Pines Medical Center, Aurora, MN	50 2	100 2	50 2	100 4	75 4	- 0	- 0	- 0	- 0	- 0	- 0	- 0	- 0	- 0	- 0	- 0	- 0
Northfield Hospital, Northfield, MN	96 46	94 34	62 24	98 45	85 39	100 11	91 57	100 193	90 51	- 0	97 162	85 52	98 163	96 45	96 157	96 57	97 36
Olmsted Medical Center, Rochester, MN	83 29	90 31	71 17	82 34	84 32	88 8	83 76	100 287	99 90	- 0	89 251	89 106	96 248	95 101	97 246	83 76	95 82
Ortonville Area Health Services, Ortonville, MN	100 12	100 1	100 3	100 2	80 10	100 1	0 2	100 10	- 0	- 0	50 4	- 0	100 2	- 0	100 2	0 2	- 0
Owatonna Hospital, Owatonna, MN	91 35	95 20	96 26	98 40	96 50	100 11	82 39	100 272	99 88	- 0	97 224	97 91	97 222	99 90	98 215	85 39	99 71
Park Nicollet Methodist Hospital, Saint Louis Park, MN	92 217	96 328	98 325	97 350	97 457	100 115	91 187	100 822	91 328	97 175	99 602	93 570	99 611	97 538	98 556	89 192	79 211
Paynesville Area Hospital, Paynesville, MN	100 7	100 3	80 5	100 5	78 9	80 5	100 12	98 47	85 13	- 0	98 53	56 36	98 53	71 38	87 52	100 12	92 12
Perham Memorial Hospital, Perham, MN	89 27	78 9	78 23	97 34	79 42	75 4	83 12	100 23	100 8	- 0	72 18	- 0	78 18	- 0	94 18	83 12	100 4

NOTE: The first number in each column (boldface) is the score, the second number is the number of patients; Please refer to the main entry for footnotes; (a) 100-299
*MEASURES: **Pneumonia Care:** 16. Appropriate Initial Antibiotic; 17. Blood Culture Timing; 18. Influenza Vaccine; 19. Initial Antibiotic Timing; 20. Pneumococcal Vaccine; 21. Smoking Cessation Advice; **Surgical Care Improvement Project:** 22. Appropriate VTP Within 24 Hours; 23. Appropriate Hair Removal; 24. Appropriate Beta Blocker Usage; 25. Controlled Postoperative Blood Glucose; 26. Prophylactic Antibiotic Timing; 27. Prophylactic Antibiotic Timing (Outpatient); 28. Prophylactic Antibiotic Selection; 29. Prophylactic Antibiotic Selection (Outpatient); 30. Prophylactic Antibiotic Stopped; 31. Recommended VTP Ordered; 32. Urinary Catheter Removal*

Hospital	Pneumonia Care 16	17	18	19	20	21	Surgical Care Improvement Project 22	23	24	25	26	27	28	29	30	31	32
Phillips Eye Institute, Minneapolis, MN	- 0	- 0	- 0	- 0	- 0	- 0	- 0	- 0	- 0	- 0	- 0	- 0	- 0	- 0	- 0	- 0	- 0
Pipestone County Medical Center, Pipestone, MN	**93** 15	**100** 4	**94** 17	**93** 15	**95** 20	**100** 5	**100** 14	**100** 47	**71** 7	- 0	**81** 37	- 0	**97** 37	- 0	**94** 36	**100** 14	**100** 5
Prairie Ridge Hospital and Health Services, Elbow Lake, MN	**67** 6	**0** 2	**0** 4	**71** 7	**41** 17	**33** 6	- 0	- 0	- 0	- 0	- 0	- -	- 0	- -	- 0	- 0	- 0
Queen of Peace Hospital, New Prague, MN	**92** 24	**98** 40	**94** 32	**100** 42	**89** 47	**100** 6	**94** 33	**100** 129	**90** 30	- 0	**95** 115	**60** 5	**94** 111	**95** 19	**96** 107	**97** 34	**84** 32
Rainy Lake Medical Center, Int'l Falls, MN	**67** 3	**50** 2	**0** 3	- 0	**0** 2	**100** 1	- 0	- 0	- 0	- 0	- 0	- -	- 0	- -	- 0	- 0	- 0
Red Lake Hospital, Redlake, MN	**54** 13	**70** 10	**20** 5	**71** 14	**33** 3	**80** 5	- 0	- 0	- 0	- 0	- 0	- -	- 0	- -	- 0	- 0	- 0
Redwood Area Hospital, Redwood Falls, MN	**88** 17	**100** 12	**94** 16	**96** 23	**92** 25	**78** 9	- 0	- 0	- 0	- 0	- 0	- 0	- 0	- 0	- 0	- 0	- 0
Regina Medical Center, Hastings, MN	**97** 33	**96** 52	**100** 36	**100** 58	**100** 50	**92** 12	**98** 64	**100** 245	**100** 34	- 0	**95** 182	**94** 82	**97** 182	**96** 79	**100** 181	**98** 64	**97** 31
Regions Hospital, Saint Paul, MN	**99** 165	**94** 162	**95** 223	**96** 306	**98** 250	**99** 157	**86** 209	**100** 692	**93** 254	**96** 136	**96** 465	**96** 321	**100** 479	**97** 317	**98** 447	**92** 209	**96** 180
Renville County Hospital and Clinics, Olivia, MN	**90** 10	- 0	**78** 9	**100** 5	**100** 8	**100** 2	- 0	- 0	- 0	- 0	- 0	- 0	- 0	- 0	- 0	- 0	- 0
Rice Memorial Hospital, Willmar, MN	**88** 69	**97** 86	**94** 70	**98** 117	**91** 127	**89** 19	**90** 104	**100** 274	**84** 63	- 0	**89** 201	**79** 73	**97** 199	**95** 66	**97** 195	**93** 104	**84** 85
Ridgeview Medical Center, Waconia, MN	**89** 108	**97** 154	**96** 84	**97** 139	**96** 136	**100** 31	**100** 121	**100** 433	**100** 76	- 0	**95** 294	**96** 152	**97** 298	**98** 158	**100** 294	**100** 121	**86** 56
River's Edge Hospital & Clinic, Saint Peter, MN	**95** 19	**94** 18	**94** 17	**100** 22	**100** 17	**91** 11	- 0	- 0	- 0	- 0	- 0	**100** 1	- 0	**100** 1	- 0	- 0	- 0
Riverview Hospital, Crookston, MN	**95** 20	**100** 19	**81** 21	**94** 36	**86** 36	**60** 5	**84** 31	**100** 72	**88** 16	- 0	**85** 55	**100** 8	**95** 55	**100** 8	**89** 54	**90** 31	**70** 10
Riverwood Healthcare Center, Aitkin, MN	**94** 16	**79** 14	**86** 14	**92** 13	**88** 24	**80** 5	**95** 19	**100** 59	- 0	- 0	**90** 49	- -	**90** 48	- -	**90** 48	**95** 19	**100** 5
Saint Cloud Hospital, Saint Cloud, MN	**92** 186	**96** 243	**97** 244	**98** 298	**97** 342	**100** 138	**92** 152	**100** 665	**95** 248	**88** 152	**96** 461	**89** 412	**98** 476	**95** 411	**97** 431	**92** 152	**87** 111
Saint Cloud VA Medical Center, Saint Cloud, MN	- 0	- 0	- 0	- 0	- 0	- 0	- 0	- 0	- 0	- 0	- 0	- -	- 0	- -	- 0	- 0	- 0
Saint Elizabeth Medical Center, Wabasha, MN	**92** 13	**92** 12	**100** 7	**93** 15	**94** 16	**100** 1	**96** 25	**100** 36	- 0	- 0	**90** 31	- 0	**97** 32	- 0	**87** 30	**96** 25	**100** 14
Saint Francis Healthcare Campus, Breckenridge, MN	**77** 43	**100** 6	**97** 33	**93** 43	**98** 60	**100** 20	**60** 30	**93** 44	**56** 9	- 0	**62** 26	- 0	**92** 25	- 0	**84** 25	**60** 30	**50** 4
Saint Francis Regional Medical Center, Shakopee, MN	**98** 100	**100** 87	**99** 89	**100** 131	**100** 116	**100** 47	**90** 115	**100** 478	**94** 136	- 0	**97** 327	**97** 106	**99** 328	**98** 103	**100** 318	**94** 115	**100** 46
Saint Gabriels Hospital, Little Falls, MN	**81** 58	**98** 55	**97** 30	**99** 71	**97** 62	**100** 15	**83** 46	**99** 219	**87** 54	- 0	**91** 186	**100** 10	**99** 184	**100** 10	**96** 178	**85** 46	**100** 40
Saint James Medical Center-Mayo Health Sys, Saint James, MN	**71** 7	**100** 2	**100** 7	**67** 3	**100** 10	**0** 1	- 0	- 0	- 0	- 0	- 0	- 0	- 0	- 0	- 0	- 0	- 0
Saint Joseph's Hospital, Saint Paul, MN	**92** 75	**98** 86	**95** 93	**97** 143	**89** 136	**100** 42	**89** 225	**99** 902	**93** 327	**93** 191	**99** 698	**95** 264	**99** 707	**95** 260	**97** 662	**89** 225	**83** 158
Saint Josephs Area Health Services, Park Rapids, MN	**83** 41	**93** 42	**96** 27	**96** 47	**88** 56	**100** 12	**97** 88	**99** 119	**62** 21	- 0	**90** 20	**75** 4	**90** 20	**100** 3	**84** 19	**97** 88	**87** 23
Saint Lukes Hospital, Duluth, MN	**89** 106	**99** 144	**95** 126	**94** 177	**94** 194	**86** 100	**82** 164	**100** 477	**97** 152	**93** 85	**97** 354	**93** 135	**99** 354	**92** 132	**95** 348	**86** 164	**73** 71
Saint Marys Regional Health Center, Detroit Lakes, MN	**92** 59	**98** 44	**89** 37	**95** 66	**100** 57	**95** 20	**72** 50	**100** 245	**94** 64	- 0	**99** 198	**100** 27	**98** 200	**100** 27	**97** 192	**76** 50	**97** 69
Saint Michaels Hospital & Nursing Home, Sauk Centre, MN	**73** 11	- 0	**83** 6	**94** 16	**82** 17	**100** 1	- 0	- 0	- 0	- 0	**57** 7	- 0	**100** 4	- 0	**100** 4	- 0	- 0
Sanford Canby Medical Center, Canby, MN	**75** 8	**100** 1	**67** 9	**87** 15	**75** 20	- 0	**70** 10	**93** 14	**100** 5	- 0	**91** 11	**0** 2	**82** 11	- 0	**100** 11	**70** 10	**50** 4
Sanford Jackson Medical Center, Jackson, MN	**90** 10	**100** 9	**100** 7	**100** 16	**94** 16	**0** 1	- 0	- 0	- 0	- 0	- 0	- 0	- 0	- 0	- 0	- 0	- 0
Sanford Luverne Medical Center, Luverne, MN	**100** 19	**100** 4	**86** 21	**93** 28	**90** 29	**0** 2	**100** 4	**89** 9	**100** 2	- 0	**100** 7	- 0	**100** 7	- 0	**100** 6	**100** 4	- 0
Sanford Medical Center Thief River Falls, Thief River Falls, MN	**86** 22	**89** 18	**84** 32	**98** 54	**83** 54	**50** 8	**85** 26	**98** 114	**87** 31	- 0	**91** 110	- -	**94** 108	- -	**95** 107	**85** 26	**95** 39
Sanford Tracy, Tracy, MN	**88** 8	**50** 2	**86** 7	**94** 16	**69** 13	**100** 3	- 0	- 0	- 0	- 0	- 0	- -	- 0	- -	- 0	- 0	- 0
Sanford Westbrook Medical Center, Westbrook, MN	**100** 2	- 0	**100** 2	**100** 4	**100** 2	**100** 1	- 0	- 0	- 0	- 0	- 0	- 0	- 0	- 0	- 0	- 0	- 0
Sanford Worthington Medical Center, Worthington, MN	**84** 19	**96** 24	**90** 20	**100** 28	**71** 31	**83** 6	**91** 23	**100** 89	**100** 24	- 0	**91** 76	**87** 30	**100** 76	**100** 31	**100** 75	**92** 24	**65** 20
Sibley Medical Center, Arlington, MN	**84** 19	**71** 7	**87** 15	**100** 3	**83** 23	**80** 5	- 0	- 0	- 0	- 0	- 0	- 0	- 0	- 0	- 0	- 0	- 0
Sleepy Eye Municipal Hospital, Sleepy Eye, MN	**100** 7	**100** 2	**100** 3	**93** 14	**60** 10	**50** 2	**100** 1	**100** 2	- 0	- 0	**33** 3	- 0	**67** 3	- 0	**100** 2	**100** 1	- 0
Springfield Medical Center Mayo Health System, Springfield, MN	**100** 5	**100** 3	**78** 9	**100** 10	**79** 19	**50** 2	**0** 1	**100** 1	**100** 1	- 0	- 0	**33** 3	- 0	**100** 2	- 0	**0** 1	- 0
Stevens Community Medical Center, Morris, MN	**84** 32	**94** 17	**74** 38	**100** 40	**70** 53	**88** 8	**88** 24	**74** 50	**67** 12	- 0	**91** 46	- 0	**100** 46	- 0	**100** 46	**88** 24	**64** 11
Swift County Benson Hospital, Benson, MN	**43** 7	**100** 1	**86** 7	**100** 15	**69** 16	**100** 2	**79** 19	**14** 35	**31** 13	- 0	**94** 31	- 0	**100** 32	- 0	**100** 31	**79** 19	**87** 15
Tri County Hospital, Wadena, MN	**86** 29	**97** 30	**78** 41	**100** 74	**82** 57	**91** 11	**75** 24	**100** 51	**64** 11	- 0	**95** 20	**20** 5	**90** 20	**67** 12	**79** 19	**75** 24	**50** 2
Tyler Healthcare Center, Tyler, MN	**60** 5	**67** 3	**100** 1	**80** 5	**100** 4	**33** 3	- 0	- 0	- 0	- 0	- 0	**100** 1	- 0	**0** 1	- 0	- 0	- 0
United Hospital, Saint Paul, MN	**95** 152	**96** 196	**95** 203	**97** 201	**99** 245	**99** 96	**93** 159	**100** 738	**96** 257	**97** 173	**97** 544	**86** 469	**98** 549	**73** 434	**96** 514	**95** 159	**90** 130
United Hospital District, Blue Earth, MN	- 0	**88** 24	**100** 17	**92** 37	**100** 37	**100** 3	**100** 8	**100** 41	- 0	- 0	**91** 33	- 0	**100** 33	- 0	**97** 33	**100** 8	**84** 19
Unity Hospital, Fridley, MN	**97** 138	**95** 226	**99** 142	**99** 209	**100** 188	**100** 92	**99** 166	**100** 492	**93** 172	- 0	**98** 299	**97** 152	**98** 300	**98** 152	**96** 281	**100** 166	**96** 23
University Medical Center - Mesabi/Mesaba Clinics, Hibbing, MN	**92** 93	**97** 69	**92** 61	**100** 118	**95** 86	**87** 45	**89** 63	**100** 125	**94** 16	- 0	**97** 79	**93** 14	**96** 82	**100** 13	**95** 75	**89** 63	**86** 14
University of Minnesota Medical Ctr-Fairview, Minneapolis, MN	**90** 83	**97** 196	**88** 139	**98** 156	**91** 154	**100** 94	**95** 433	**100** 1026	**97** 298	**94** 127	**99** 758	**95** 377	**98** 766	**94** 470	**97** 725	**96** 434	**92** 402
Virginia Regional Medical Center, Virginia, MN	**86** 36	**86** 22	**76** 29	**89** 54	**86** 50	**95** 20	**80** 65	**100** 171	**81** 58	- 0	**97** 128	**97** 32	**95** 130	**97** 31	**95** 120	**83** 65	**86** 51
Waseca Medical Center - Mayo Health System, Waseca, MN	**94** 17	**100** 20	**83** 12	**82** 11	**79** 19	**50** 2	- 0	- 0	- 0	- 0	- 0	- 0	- 0	- 0	- 0	- 0	- 0
Wheaton Community Hospital, Wheaton, MN	**100** 1	- 0	**100** 1	**100** 3	**80** 5	- 0	- 0	- 0	- 0	- 0	- 0	- 0	- 0	- 0	- 0	- 0	- 0
Windom Area Hospital, Windom, MN	**100** 5	**100** 5	**100** 5	**100** 7	**100** 7	**0** 1	- 0	- 0	- 0	- 0	- 0	- 0	- 0	- 0	- 0	- 0	- 0
Winona Health Services, Winona, MN	**91** 66	**98** 108	**99** 73	**100** 106	**99** 109	**100** 32	**92** 75	**100** 176	**100** 52	- 0	**98** 133	**92** 71	**88** 133	**93** 92	**92** 131	**92** 75	**80** 40
MISSOURI																	
Advanced Healthcare Medical Center, Ellington, MO	**89** 9	**100** 1	**50** 6	**100** 11	**67** 6	**80** 5	- 0	- 0	- 0	- 0	- 0	- -	- 0	- -	- 0	- 0	- 0
Audrain Medical Center, Mexico, MO	**95** 56	**100** 68	**97** 67	**100** 82	**94** 86	**100** 31	**93** 60	**100** 287	**88** 72	- 0	**99** 220	**94** 108	**97** 223	**99** 106	**94** 217	**95** 60	**69** 13
Barnes Jewish Hospital, Saint Louis, MO	**92** 169	**93** 103	**91** 273	**91** 386	**90** 270	**98** 198	**96** 261	**100** 896	**92** 240	**93** 148	**98** 570	**96** 765	**99** 579	**91** 751	**97** 546	**96** 262	**84** 211
Barnes-Jewish St Peters Hospital, Saint Peters, MO	**96** 184	**99** 269	**89** 174	**97** 265	**96** 206	**100** 96	**96** 186	**100** 420	**99** 94	- 0	**93** 254	**93** 255	**96** 254	**96** 248	**96** 244	**96** 187	**81** 99
Barnes-Jewish West County Hospital, Creve Coeur, MO	**95** 38	**90** 39	**81** 27	**98** 55	**93** 43	**100** 7	**97** 178	**100** 882	**99** 148	- 0	**93** 636	**96** 339	**100** 639	**92** 338	**93** 632	**95** 181	**95** 248
Barton County Memorial Hospital, Lamar, MO	**92** 40	**91** 23	**53** 43	**95** 64	**58** 55	**100** 23	- 0	- 0	- 0	- 0	- 0	- -	- 0	- -	- 0	- 0	- 0
Bates County Memorial Hospital, Butler, MO	**76** 46	**86** 44	**66** 44	**99** 80	**87** 60	**100** 13	**80** 30	**86** 37	**75** 4	- 0	**91** 23	**81** 16	**100** 23	**73** 15	**82** 22	**77** 31	**75** 12
Boone Hospital Center, Columbia, MO	**86** 139	**100** 179	**89** 204	**97** 229	**93** 291	**99** 83	**95** 182	**100** 911	**95** 263	**94** 186	**97** 674	**97** 724	**97** 681	**90** 714	**96** 668	**94** 183	**93** 252
Bothwell Regional Health Center, Sedalia, MO	**95** 132	**99** 84	**71** 90	**94** 153	**85** 178	**100** 73	**66** 89	**99** 389	**82** 97	- 0	**97** 280	**90** 154	**96** 279	**95** 169	**94** 274	**71** 89	**97** 92
Callaway Community Hospital, Fulton, MO	**100** 21	**96** 26	**88** 17	**94** 32	**94** 32	**100** 15	**75** 4	**100** 10	**80** 5	- 0	**100** 5	**100** 2	**80** 5	**100** 2	**75** 4	**75** 4	- 0
Cameron Regional Medical Center, Cameron, MO	**94** 52	**92** 61	**91** 57	**97** 112	**93** 92	**90** 51	**92** 48	**99** 95	**89** 28	- 0	**92** 65	**76** 17	**97** 65	**93** 15	**86** 63	**92** 48	**94** 17
Capital Region Medical Center, Jefferson City, MO	**89** 89	**99** 141	**100** 115	**96** 148	**99** 142	**100** 60	**96** 158	**100** 545	**97** 179	**92** 86	**98** 373	**97** 258	**97** 377	**94** 254	**97** 359	**99** 158	**95** 148
Carroll County Memorial Hospital, Carrollton, MO	- 0	- 0	- 0	- 0	- 0	- 0	- 0	- 0	- 0	- 0	- 0	- -	- 0	- -	- 0	- 0	- 0
Cass Medical Center, Harrisonville, MO	**88** 59	**98** 59	**84** 49	**99** 86	**95** 64	**97** 37	**88** 33	**95** 64	**78** 9	- 0	**92** 50	- -	**96** 50	- -	**88** 49	**88** 33	**91** 22
Centerpoint Medical Center of Independence, Independence, MO	**92** 194	**99** 329	**97** 189	**98** 304	**98** 249	**100** 117	**92** 233	**100** 621	**99** 159	**99** 110	**100** 414	**99** 531	**99** 421	**99** 529	**95** 398	**96** 234	**97** 75
Childrens Mercy Hospital, Kansas City, MO	- -	- -	- -	- -	- -	- -	- -	- -	- -	- -	- -	- -	- -	- -	- -	- -	- -

NOTE: The first number in each column (boldface) is the score, the second number is the number of patients; Please refer to the main entry for footnotes; (a) 100-299
*MEASURES: **Pneumonia Care:** 16. Appropriate Initial Antibiotic; 17. Blood Culture Timing; 18. Influenza Vaccine; 19. Initial Antibiotic Timing; 20. Pneumococcal Vaccine; 21. Smoking Cessation Advice; **Surgical Care Improvement Project:** 22. Appropriate VTP Within 24 Hours; 23. Appropriate Hair Removal; 24. Appropriate Beta Blocker Usage; 25. Controlled Postoperative Blood Glucose; 26. Prophylactic Antibiotic Timing; 27. Prophylactic Antibiotic Timing (Outpatient); 28. Prophylactic Antibiotic Selection; 29. Prophylactic Antibiotic Selection (Outpatient); 30. Prophylactic Antibiotic Stopped; 31. Recommended VTP Ordered; 32. Urinary Catheter Removal*

Hospital	Pneumonia Care							Surgical Care Improvement Project									
	16	17	18	19	20	21	22	23	24	25	26	27	28	29	30	31	32
Christian Hospital Northeast, Saint Louis, MO	**95** 155	**97** 278	**81** 213	**91** 289	**88** 243	**100** 149	**96** 320	**100** 828	**99** 283	**97** 182	**98** 459	**94** 346	**86** 474	**97** 338	**97** 410	**98** 320	**85** 132
Christian Hospital Northwest, Florissant, MO	- 0	- 0	- 0	- 0	- 0	- 0	- 0	- 0	- 0	- 0	- 0	- 0	- 0	- 0	- 0	- 0	- 0
Citizens Memorial Hospital, Bolivar, MO	**79** 71	**96** 117	**97** 77	**92** 133	**96** 108	**95** 58	**96** 120	**100** 231	**84** 61	- 0	**97** 156	**98** 173	**97** 155	**94** 175	**91** 152	**96** 120	**96** 57
Columbia Missouri VA Medical Center, Columbia, MO	**90** 39	**97** 65	**90** 61	**96** 51	**99** 86	**100** 31	**100** 93	**100** 275	**100** 131	**99** 100	**94** 173	- -	**100** 172	- -	**100** 172	**100** 93	**99** 137
Community Hospital Association, Fairfax, MO	**81** 16	- 0	**83** 12	**91** 22	**82** 22	**75** 4	- 0	- 0	- 0	- 0	- 0	- -	- 0	- -	- 0	- 0	- 0
Cooper County Memorial Hospital, Boonville, MO	**93** 27	**96** 23	**94** 31	**87** 15	**81** 32	**85** 13	- 0	- 0	- 0	- 0	- 0	- 0	- 0	- 0	- 0	- 0	- 0
Cox Medical Center, Springfield, MO	**94** 190	**99** 283	**98** 212	**97** 235	**98** 230	**97** 137	**95** 234	**100** 685	**95** 231	**97** 147	**97** 494	**97** 778	**97** 502	**97** 776	**89** 479	**95** 234	**56** 156
Cox Monett Hospital, Monett, MO	**95** 58	**93** 59	**88** 50	**96** 69	**91** 57	**92** 26	**92** 13	**95** 21	**100** 7	- 0	**67** 18	- -	**94** 18	- -	**76** 17	**100** 13	**14** 7
Des Peres Hospital, Saint Louis, MO	**93** 134	**99** 263	**100** 162	**98** 260	**100** 241	**100** 78	**96** 142	**100** 464	**97** 179	**94** 125	**97** 321	**97** 537	**97** 328	**99** 532	**91** 304	**98** 142	**91** 105
Fitzgibbon Memorial Hospital, Marshall, MO	**87** 68	**99** 76	**75** 68	**89** 87	**82** 95	**92** 36	**85** 27	**100** 63	**71** 7	- 0	**90** 40	**95** 106	**98** 40	**98** 101	**76** 38	**85** 27	**87** 15
Forest Park Hospital, Saint Louis, MO	**92** 50	**93** 56	**97** 33	**96** 67	**93** 27	**97** 31	**69** 13	**100** 25	**33** 3	- 0	**80** 10	**65** 17	**100** 10	**93** 14	**89** 9	**69** 13	**0** 1
Freeman Health System - Freeman West, Joplin, MO	**89** 64	**96** 138	**91** 108	**97** 133	**96** 139	**98** 111	**97** 255	**100** 820	**84** 259	**93** 179	**96** 598	**93** 554	**99** 610	**95** 534	**88** 565	**97** 258	**82** 122
Freeman Neosho Hospital, Neosho, MO	**98** 47	**100** 43	**90** 48	**97** 66	**96** 55	**97** 37	- 0	- 0	- 0	- 0	- 0	- -	- 0	- -	- 0	- 0	- 0
Golden Valley Memorial Hospital, Clinton, MO	**96** 91	**100** 77	**98** 62	**99** 121	**99** 95	**100** 48	**88** 40	**100** 109	**75** 20	- 0	**99** 74	**88** 34	**97** 74	**79** 34	**89** 71	**98** 40	**84** 19
Hannibal Regional Hospital, Hannibal, MO	**90** 136	**95** 185	**77** 162	**95** 221	**94** 245	**100** 97	**93** 152	**100** 632	**95** 224	- 0	**97** 461	**91** 89	**97** 460	**95** 86	**96** 457	**97** 152	**53** 32
Harrison County Community Hospital, Bethany, MO	**67** 9	**91** 11	**76** 17	**100** 15	**93** 27	**33** 6	- 0	- 0	- 0	- 0	- 0	- -	- 0	- -	- 0	- 0	- 0
Heartland Regional Medical Center, Saint Joseph, MO	**97** 332	**100** 453	**99** 324	**99** 432	**100** 462	**100** 217	**98** 250	**100** 1141	**100** 444	**94** 254	**100** 941	**99** 693	**100** 951	**97** 687	**99** 888	**98** 251	**97** 277
Hedrick Medical Center, Chillicothe, MO	**83** 29	**95** 41	**95** 37	**98** 58	**98** 54	**88** 8	**0** 5	**100** 16	**100** 2	- 0	**90** 10	**75** 4	**73** 11	**67** 3	**100** 10	**0** 5	**50** 2
Hermann Area District Hospital, Hermann, MO	**94** 17	**90** 10	**53** 17	**93** 28	**46** 24	**100** 11	- 0	- 0	- 0	- 0	- 0	- -	- 0	- -	- 0	- 0	- 0
Jefferson Regional Medical Center, Crystal City, MO	**91** 197	**98** 321	**96** 210	**99** 328	**92** 264	**100** 162	**94** 155	**100** 488	**90** 126	**89** 57	**95** 339	**85** 149	**95** 341	**95** 141	**92** 331	**94** 155	**86** 42
Kansas City VA Medical Center, Kansas City, MO	**94** 80	**99** 122	**90** 125	**93** 123	**98** 126	**100** 57	**96** 113	**100** 152	**93** 41	- 0	**100** 79	- -	**100** 79	- -	**93** 76	**97** 113	**98** 59
Lafayette Regional Health Center, Lexington, MO	**95** 55	**100** 55	**100** 48	**99** 67	**100** 60	**100** 25	**94** 18	**100** 22	**83** 6	- 0	**100** 15	**88** 26	**100** 15	**96** 23	**100** 13	**94** 18	**100** 2
Lake Regional Health System, Osage Beach, MO	**92** 149	**97** 185	**97** 107	**96** 181	**97** 168	**97** 79	**80** 201	**100** 385	**93** 108	**96** 52	**90** 258	**82** 213	**92** 259	**92** 192	**87** 250	**80** 205	**91** 94
Lee's Summit Medical Center, Lee's Summit, MO	**100** 59	**98** 99	**100** 58	**100** 105	**100** 98	**100** 28	**98** 119	**100** 350	**98** 85	- 0	**100** 232	**90** 79	**99** 233	**97** 75	**97** 224	**100** 119	**87** 30
Liberty Hospital, Liberty, MO	**92** 159	**96** 206	**96** 180	**98** 264	**97** 243	**98** 130	**87** 318	**99** 827	**94** 243	**98** 58	**94** 490	**93** 407	**99** 494	**95** 398	**93** 469	**94** 320	**78** 100
Lincoln County Medical Center, Troy, MO	**96** 27	**93** 44	**94** 34	**98** 54	**88** 43	**83** 24	**100** 24	**98** 47	**57** 7	- 0	**84** 38	- -	**78** 37	- -	**81** 32	**100** 24	**29** 7
McCune-Brooks Hospital, Carthage, MO	**88** 42	**93** 58	**84** 32	**99** 69	**84** 45	**74** 23	**97** 32	**97** 203	- 0	- 0	**94** 182	- -	**99** 182	- -	**86** 182	**97** 32	**100** 12
Mineral Area Regional Medical Center, Farmington, MO	**93** 112	**99** 125	**93** 94	**99** 139	**93** 103	**96** 71	**95** 21	**100** 72	**75** 28	- 0	**88** 40	**83** 89	**92** 40	**95** 81	**95** 38	**91** 22	**88** 24
Missouri Baptist Hospital Sullivan, Sullivan, MO	**95** 96	**98** 122	**97** 61	**96** 127	**97** 95	**100** 48	**100** 21	**100** 36	**100** 6	- 0	**93** 14	**80** 54	**93** 14	**93** 44	**93** 14	**100** 21	**33** 9
Missouri Baptist Medical Center, Town and Country, MO	**95** 234	**99** 408	**97** 356	**95** 431	**97** 505	**100** 120	**96** 214	**100** 921	**97** 307	**99** 187	**98** 606	**97** 767	**98** 627	**92** 756	**96** 586	**97** 214	**85** 198
Missouri Delta Medical Center, Sikeston, MO	**90** 115	**90** 128	**77** 117	**93** 163	**82** 154	**100** 108	**83** 72	**100** 184	**96** 28	- 0	**96** 106	**96** 71	**88** 105	**97** 68	**90** 93	**89** 72	**100** 7
Missouri Southern Healthcare, Dexter, MO	**83** 65	**95** 41	**78** 77	**96** 94	**85** 105	**89** 38	**68** 22	**100** 25	**83** 6	- 0	**100** 7	**50** 4	**14** 7	**100** 3	**100** 6	**73** 22	**88** 8
Moberly Regional Medical Center, Moberly, MO	**95** 58	**98** 84	**94** 67	**96** 97	**99** 106	**100** 45	**98** 48	**100** 115	**92** 36	- 0	**98** 81	**96** 83	**99** 82	**99** 82	**95** 77	**100** 48	**62** 16
Nevada Regional Medical Center, Nevada, MO	**90** 39	**100** 19	**86** 37	**100** 54	**77** 47	**100** 26	**85** 27	**100** 34	**55** 11	- 0	**86** 21	**97** 39	**100** 21	**95** 39	**89** 18	**96** 27	**83** 12
North Kansas City Hospital, North Kansas City, MO	**94** 170	**96** 189	**96** 159	**96** 281	**95** 249	**98** 123	**80** 353	**99** 938	**90** 316	**98** 181	**95** 659	**90** 761	**96** 669	**96** 722	**94** 633	**87** 353	**89** 195
Northeast Regional Medical Center, Kirksville, MO	**88** 34	**96** 113	**88** 91	**94** 119	**96** 137	**100** 66	**98** 90	**100** 246	**100** 69	- 0	**96** 159	**94** 72	**97** 160	**97** 70	**95** 145	**98** 90	**89** 45
Northwest Medical Center, Albany, MO	- 0	- 0	- 0	- 0	- 0	- 0	- 0	- 0	- 0	- 0	- 0	- 0	- 0	- 0	- 0	- 0	- 0
Ozarks Community Hospital, Springfield, MO	**86** 50	**98** 49	**98** 46	**97** 75	**100** 58	**95** 39	**90** 21	**100** 62	**25** 12	- 0	**95** 64	**90** 70	**95** 63	**90** 70	**92** 61	**95** 21	**92** 13
Ozarks Medical Center, West Plains, MO	**83** 136	**96** 171	**68** 120	**88** 207	**79** 166	**97** 71	**87** 119	**100** 261	**80** 81	**95** 19	**96** 184	**95** 222	**98** 184	**93** 219	**86** 174	**87** 121	**78** 45
Parkland Health Center, Farmington, MO	**95** 102	**98** 139	**97** 101	**94** 148	**94** 122	**100** 77	**100** 29	**100** 113	**76** 29	- 0	**97** 76	**100** 43	**97** 77	**89** 44	**96** 73	**100** 29	**82** 17
Pemiscot Memorial Hospital, Hayti, MO	**76** 37	**94** 17	**48** 29	**72** 43	**43** 23	**55** 22	**61** 18	**16** 19	**75** 4	- 0	**17** 6	**50** 10	**25** 4	**67** 9	**100** 4	**67** 18	**50** 2
Perry County Memorial Hospital, Perryville, MO	**94** 16	**97** 39	**89** 36	**98** 50	**88** 48	**100** 11	**82** 11	**100** 22	**67** 3	- 0	**100** 13	- -	**100** 13	- -	**92** 12	**82** 11	**75** 4
Pershing Memorial Hospital, Brookfield, MO	**56** 16	**90** 10	- 0	**92** 25	**75** 20	**100** 6	- 0	- 0	- 0	- 0	- 0	- -	- 0	- -	- 0	- 0	- 0
Phelps County Regional Medical Center, Rolla, MO	**87** 164	**91** 221	**90** 144	**96** 216	**96** 192	**100** 99	**85** 197	**100** 383	**84** 96	- 0	**99** 260	**97** 208	**98** 261	**95** 202	**94** 255	**87** 197	**67** 100
Pike County Memorial Hospital, Louisiana, MO	**93** 27	**89** 19	**96** 28	**97** 34	**100** 30	**100** 9	- 0	- 0	- 0	- 0	- 0	- -	- 0	- -	- 0	- 0	- 0
Poplar Bluff Regional Medical Center, Poplar Bluff, MO	**91** 137	**97** 233	**100** 161	**94** 216	**100** 219	**100** 116	**96** 200	**100** 763	**99** 218	**92** 115	**98** 531	**99** 223	**96** 539	**95** 222	**96** 473	**98** 200	**100** 130
Poplar Bluff VA Medical Center, Poplar Bluff, MO	**92** 25	**100** 16	**95** 20	**100** 8	**97** 33	**100** 13	- 0	- 0	- 0	- 0	- 0	- -	- 0	- -	- 0	- 0	- 0
Progress West Healthcare Center, O'Fallon, MO	**100** 88	**99** 93	**85** 60	**98** 85	**96** 52	**100** 38	**95** 75	**100** 350	**82** 97	- 0	**98** 286	**89** 46	**99** 286	**88** 43	**98** 279	**95** 75	**98** 133
Putnam County Memorial Hospital, Unionville, MO	**94** 18	**100** 3	**88** 16	**95** 22	**77** 22	**71** 7	- 0	- 0	- 0	- 0	- 0	- -	- 0	- -	- 0	- 0	- 0
Ray County Memorial Hospital, Richmond, MO	**75** 16	**100** 3	**75** 12	**95** 19	**93** 28	**71** 7	- 0	- 0	- 0	- 0	- 0	- -	- 0	- -	- 0	- 0	- 0
Research Belton Hospital, Belton, MO	**90** 41	**98** 64	**97** 35	**100** 59	**98** 44	**95** 21	**98** 45	**100** 223	**100** 59	- 0	**99** 177	**100** 32	**98** 177	**100** 32	**99** 172	**98** 45	**97** 66
Research Medical Center, Kansas City, MO	**87** 87	**97** 154	**95** 186	**96** 163	**99** 187	**98** 133	**96** 252	**100** 723	**88** 239	**93** 147	**98** 476	**96** 312	**98** 480	**95** 324	**96** 420	**96** 252	**74** 108
Ripley County Memorial Hospital, Doniphan, MO	**87** 30	**92** 37	**67** 33	**93** 44	**73** 45	**95** 20	- 0	- 0	- 0	- 0	- 0	- 0	- 0	- 0	- 0	- 0	- 0
SAC-Osage Hospital, Osceola, MO	**75** 12	**33** 6	**18** 11	**71** 14	**33** 15	**100** 7	- 0	- 0	- 0	- 0	- 0	- 0	- 0	- 0	- 0	- 0	- 0
Saint Alexius Hospital, Saint Louis, MO	**84** 91	**96** 108	**98** 89	**92** 125	**94** 94	**100** 88	**91** 45	**100** 82	**82** 17	- 0	**90** 20	**50** 16	**100** 20	**96** 25	**94** 17	**94** 47	**62** 8
Saint Anthony's Medical Center, Saint Louis, MO	**87** 129	**96** 141	**81** 128	**95** 215	**90** 186	**94** 77	**92** 324	**100** 1177	**90** 358	**88** 204	**97** 816	**96** 434	**97** 833	**99** 433	**92** 790	**94** 327	**68** 149
Saint Francis Hospital, Maryville, MO	**97** 35	**97** 31	**100** 28	**96** 54	**100** 42	**100** 15	**98** 43	**100** 110	**100** 27	- 0	**99** 100	**100** 18	**99** 102	**94** 18	**97** 91	**98** 43	**100** 7
Saint Francis Hospital, Mountain View, MO	**82** 76	**94** 65	**97** 65	**95** 95	**99** 91	**100** 23	- 0	- 0	- 0	- 0	- 0	- -	- 0	- -	- 0	- 0	- 0
Saint Francis Medical Center, Cape Girardeau, MO	**91** 213	**99** 355	**79** 274	**97** 315	**89** 354	**99** 164	**93** 368	**100** 1243	**94** 401	**95** 222	**98** 757	**96** 843	**98** 778	**91** 832	**96** 744	**94** 369	**86** 209
Saint John's Regional Health Center, Springfield, MO	**98** 83	**95** 99	**95** 110	**96** 104	**95** 125	**94** 79	**89** 173	**100** 689	**89** 231	**92** 146	**97** 489	**96** 596	**98** 495	**98** 592	**91** 476	**90** 173	**86** 154
Saint John's Regional Medical Center, Joplin, MO	**91** 201	**97** 325	**94** 328	**96** 427	**97** 407	**100** 239	**94** 399	**100** 1080	**98** 346	**95** 155	**99** 659	**97** 235	**99** 666	**100** 230	**95** 626	**95** 404	**85** 152
Saint Johns Hospital - Aurora, Aurora, MO	**98** 53	**100** 46	**95** 38	**97** 71	**98** 51	**100** 30	- 0	- 0	- 0	- 0	- 0	- -	- 0	- -	- 0	- 0	- 0
Saint Johns Hospital - Cassville, Cassville, MO	**100** 34	**93** 27	**100** 21	**100** 38	**100** 25	**100** 17	- 0	- 0	- 0	- 0	- 0	- -	- 0	- -	- 0	- 0	- 0
Saint Johns Hospital-Lebanon, Lebanon, MO	**91** 107	**98** 133	**93** 74	**97** 150	**96** 118	**95** 42	**99** 90	**100** 231	**96** 79	- 0	**96** 190	**80** 46	**97** 189	**97** 38	**95** 185	**97** 92	**93** 75
Saint Johns Mercy Hospital, Washington, MO	**93** 85	**94** 81	**100** 76	**99** 143	**99** 120	**100** 47	**95** 119	**100** 306	**85** 85	- 0	**97** 206	**96** 224	**99** 207	**98** 218	**98** 198	**97** 119	**93** 72
Saint Johns Mercy Medical Center, Saint Louis, MO	**95** 91	**92** 145	**80** 87	**99** 151	**89** 148	**100** 53	**95** 143	**100** 609	**97** 176	**98** 127	**98** 405	**98** 698	**99** 417	**98** 746	**98** 386	**97** 143	**91** 105
Saint Joseph Medical Center, Kansas City, MO	**87** 159	**97** 264	**88** 199	**93** 275	**89** 266	**97** 77	**83** 157	**100** 491	**95** 138	**92** 108	**96** 358	**95** 395	**96** 362	**96** 385	**96** 346	**85** 157	**92** 60
Saint Louis University Hospital, Saint Louis, MO	**98** 82	**93** 131	**99** 133	**92** 157	**98** 111	**99** 137	**96** 230	**100** 442	**95** 138	**92** 64	**98** 199	**95** 171	**99** 205	**90** 163	**97** 177	**98** 230	**92** 99

NOTE: The first number in each column (boldface) is the score, the second number is the number of patients; Please refer to the main entry for footnotes; (a) 100-299

MEASURES: ***Pneumonia Care:*** *16. Appropriate Initial Antibiotic; 17. Blood Culture Timing; 18. Influenza Vaccine; 19. Initial Antibiotic Timing; 20. Pneumococcal Vaccine; 21. Smoking Cessation Advice;* ***Surgical Care Improvement Project:*** *22. Appropriate VTP Within 24 Hours; 23. Appropriate Hair Removal; 24. Appropriate Beta Blocker Usage; 25. Controlled Postoperative Blood Glucose; 26. Prophylactic Antibiotic Timing; 27. Prophylactic Antibiotic Timing (Outpatient); 28. Prophylactic Antibiotic Selection; 29. Prophylactic Antibiotic Selection (Outpatient); 30. Prophylactic Antibiotic Stopped; 31. Recommended VTP Ordered; 32. Urinary Catheter Removal*

Hospital	Pneumonia Care						Surgical Care Improvement Project										
	16	17	18	19	20	21	22	23	24	25	26	27	28	29	30	31	32
Saint Louis-John Cochran VA Medical Center, Saint Louis, MO	100 49	99 86	89 62	95 80	98 45	97 63	96 182	100 260	91 80	- 0	96 162	- -	99 162	- -	92 158	98 182	100 106
Saint Luke's East Lee's Summit Hospital, Lees Summit, MO	92 120	97 155	95 106	96 158	97 151	95 41	87 145	100 533	96 138	- 0	99 308	93 170	98 308	96 169	95 300	98 145	82 22
Saint Lukes Cancer Institute, Kansas City, MO	- 0	100 1	100 2	100 1	100 2	100 1	80 15	100 84	85 13	- 0	98 53	94 51	94 54	98 50	96 52	100 15	100 1
Saint Lukes Hospital, Chesterfield, MO	80 169	98 255	78 308	94 346	85 434	100 109	95 317	95 995	92 320	95 194	94 727	92 1049	98 751	96 1027	93 695	98 318	85 117
Saint Lukes Hospital of Kansas City, Kansas City, MO	79 89	98 146	89 164	93 205	93 215	100 98	88 298	99 1190	97 507	91 391	96 822	97 529	98 834	97 523	97 781	92 298	96 228
Saint Lukes Northland Hospital, Kansas City, MO	92 93	98 108	100 97	95 138	97 101	100 58	88 110	100 269	98 59	- 0	100 180	86 51	98 182	98 50	97 174	92 110	73 33
Saint Mary's Medical Center, Blue Springs, MO	88 119	97 204	90 112	96 203	92 166	93 55	91 133	100 282	92 53	- 0	98 184	97 66	98 185	98 66	95 183	95 133	86 64
Saint Marys Health Center, Jefferson City, MO	98 66	100 174	100 133	100 212	100 152	100 85	100 186	100 589	100 161	100 66	100 384	100 314	100 388	99 314	100 370	100 186	100 73
Salem Memorial District Hospital, Salem, MO	87 15	89 38	95 44	90 59	98 54	86 21	- 0	- 0	- 0	- 0	- 0	- -	- 0	- -	- 0	- 0	- 0
Scotland County Hospital, Memphis, MO	67 12	89 27	79 29	97 38	81 47	57 14	- 0	- 0	- 0	- 0	- 0	- -	- 0	- -	- 0	- 0	- 0
Skaggs Community Health Center, Branson, MO	94 124	97 187	96 104	96 159	95 150	89 79	92 100	100 426	92 125	91 70	96 308	82 150	96 308	86 138	90 251	96 100	89 94
Southeast Missouri Hospital, Cape Girardeau, MO	92 126	97 231	91 150	92 196	95 198	89 104	84 164	100 653	89 241	79 168	99 408	95 565	96 418	90 553	93 397	91 166	83 86
SSM Depaul Health Center, Bridgeton, MO	95 97	97 118	76 74	90 148	91 136	100 90	95 197	99 849	97 238	99 159	98 595	93 395	99 604	96 388	96 566	96 197	79 96
SSM St Clare Health Center, Fenton, MO	96 111	96 122	91 77	92 143	90 131	100 69	95 244	100 802	99 229	96 204	97 575	96 516	98 585	97 512	94 557	97 244	95 189
SSM St Joseph Health Center, Saint Charles, MO	96 70	95 88	91 82	94 108	98 135	100 62	98 249	100 781	96 281	96 156	97 577	97 492	99 581	96 487	98 565	100 249	91 159
SSM St Joseph Hospital West, Lake Saint Louis, MO	95 92	98 124	95 81	94 125	96 134	100 79	99 227	100 537	97 105	- 0	98 376	89 214	99 377	95 212	98 366	100 227	91 92
SSM St Marys Health Center, Richmond Heights, MO	97 74	94 97	83 78	85 136	95 125	96 74	94 289	99 768	97 209	96 103	97 550	96 584	98 555	99 580	93 516	96 292	90 87
Ste Genevieve County Memorial Hospital, Sainte Genevieve, MO	100 20	91 23	85 13	100 27	57 21	100 16	- 0	100 8	- 0	- 0	100 7	- -	100 7	- -	100 7	- 0	- 0
Sullivan County Memorial Hospital, Milan, MO	75 4	100 5	25 4	80 10	29 7	100 4	- 0	- 0	- 0	- 0	- 0	- 0	- 0	- 0	- 0	- 0	- 0
Texas County Memorial Hospital, Houston, MO	76 76	96 85	82 62	95 101	81 88	96 27	100 3	100 9	67 3	- 0	33 3	- 0	100 2	- 0	0 2	100 3	- 0
Truman Medical Center - Hospital Hill, Kansas City, MO	87 89	98 138	97 59	91 152	92 38	99 146	92 138	99 316	92 71	- 0	99 223	79 207	99 226	96 189	95 213	94 139	92 24
Truman Medical Center Lakewood, Kansas City, MO	92 84	98 94	94 52	88 109	92 39	98 48	86 29	100 232	98 42	- 0	100 209	100 66	98 210	98 66	100 208	86 29	75 4
Twin Rivers Regional Medical Center, Kennett, MO	98 48	97 110	100 59	99 106	100 76	100 48	100 24	100 79	100 16	- 0	98 50	100 11	94 53	100 11	98 48	100 24	100 13
University of Missouri Health Care, Columbia, MO	83 64	98 125	93 137	79 118	96 137	98 89	98 501	100 911	92 278	99 93	98 192	90 344	95 201	96 402	90 136	98 502	94 128
Washington County Memorial Hospital, Potosi, MO	90 59	93 82	82 28	96 75	79 56	76 38	- 0	- 0	- 0	- 0	- 0	- -	- 0	- -	- 0	- 0	- 0
Western Missouri Medical Center, Warrensburg, MO	79 71	94 69	75 64	98 118	77 84	84 31	82 73	100 210	90 39	- 0	99 173	96 51	97 176	55 49	96 160	86 73	98 42
Women's and Children's Hospital, Columbia, MO	88 8	100 8	67 6	90 10	50 6	83 6	99 162	100 562	93 126	- 0	93 375	96 372	98 376	96 370	96 373	99 162	97 176
Wright Memorial Hospital, Trenton, MO	96 28	100 47	90 20	94 51	80 41	100 11	100 1	100 3	- 0	- 0	- 0	- 0	- 0	- 0	- 0	100 1	100 1
NEBRASKA																	
Alegent Health Bergan Mercy Medical Center, Omaha, NE	97 116	99 150	100 126	98 182	99 154	100 61	94 244	100 1574	98 589	98 228	96 1292	94 469	97 1294	97 460	98 1247	95 245	91 448
Alegent Health Immanuel Medical Center, Omaha, NE	100 58	99 102	100 72	99 138	100 111	100 56	99 114	100 272	100 85	- 0	100 146	89 362	100 148	97 343	96 134	100 114	98 65
Alegent Health Lakeside Hospital, Omaha, NE	95 85	98 118	99 102	100 149	98 127	100 37	96 151	100 423	99 149	- 0	100 261	90 168	99 262	98 161	99 254	97 151	98 97
Alegent Health Memorial Hospital, Schuyler, NE	- 0	100 3	100 13	100 10	100 16	100 1	- 0	- 0	- 0	- 0	- 0	- -	- 0	- -	- 0	- 0	- 0
Alegent Health Midlands Hospital, Papillion, NE	100 63	100 97	100 49	100 96	100 80	100 21	98 59	100 126	100 31	- 0	97 66	94 90	95 66	99 88	100 64	98 59	100 17
Annie Jeffrey Memorial County Health Center, Osceola, NE	100 7	100 4	100 7	90 10	92 12	- 0	- 0	- 0	- 0	- 0	- 0	- -	- 0	- -	- 0	- 0	- 0
Antelope Memorial Hospital, Neligh, NE	71 7	- 0	71 7	100 8	74 27	100 1	- 0	- 0	- 0	- 0	- 0	- -	- 0	- -	- 0	- 0	- 0
Avera Creighton Hospital, Creighton, NE	92 25	100 1	100 16	100 20	97 34	88 8	- 0	- 0	- 0	- 0	- 0	- -	- 0	- -	- 0	- 0	- 0
Avera St Anthony's Hospital, O'Neill, NE	89 54	83 6	89 44	97 68	91 56	50 14	98 42	100 53	- 0	- 0	76 45	- -	88 43	- -	93 41	100 42	100 23
Beatrice Community Hospital & Health Center, Beatrice, NE	92 36	92 72	95 42	98 65	93 57	80 15	67 18	100 46	- 0	- 0	98 42	- 0	93 42	- 0	97 39	83 18	100 4
Bellevue Medical Center, Bellevue, NE	- 0	- 0	- 0	- 0	- 0	- 0	- 0	- 0	- 0	- 0	- 0	- -	- 0	- -	- 0	- 0	- 0
Boone County Health Center, Albion, NE	94 32	67 6	100 33	96 54	97 59	75 8	100 9	100 18	- 0	- 0	88 17	- -	100 17	- -	94 16	100 9	- 0
Box Butte General Hospital, Alliance, NE	85 48	96 26	23 35	0 1	20 41	79 19	- 0	- 0	- 0	- 0	- 0	- -	- 0	- -	- 0	- 0	- 0
Brodstone Memorial Hospital, Superior, NE	100 5	100 3	100 4	100 3	100 8	100 1	- 0	- 0	- 0	- 0	- 0	- -	- 0	- -	- 0	- 0	- 0
Brown County Hospital, Ainsworth, NE	86 7	100 1	43 7	100 11	62 16	25 4	- 0	- 0	- 0	- 0	- 0	- -	- 0	- -	- 0	- 0	- 0
Bryanlgh Medical Center, Lincoln, NE	95 139	97 186	97 180	99 244	98 265	99 94	92 285	100 1176	94 430	96 291	98 810	99 603	96 830	98 601	90 764	94 288	74 102
Butler County Health Care Center, David City, NE	90 10	- 0	75 12	100 11	79 14	- 0	100 2	100 18	- 0	- 0	86 22	- -	86 22	- -	95 22	100 2	- 0
Callaway District Hospital, Callaway, NE	- 0	- 0	- 0	- 0	- 0	- 0	- 0	- 0	- 0	- 0	- 0	- -	- 0	- -	- 0	- 0	- 0
Chadron Community Hospital and Health Services, Chadron, NE	91 11	- 0	44 9	92 13	80 20	60 5	33 6	100 7	- 0	- 0	33 3	- -	0 3	- -	100 3	29 7	100 1
Chase County Community Hospital, Imperial, NE	67 6	- 0	67 3	100 7	43 7	100 1	100 3	50 4	- 0	- 0	50 4	- -	75 4	- -	75 4	100 3	100 1
Cherry County Hospital, Valentine, NE	89 19	100 5	100 8	95 22	95 22	100 3	- 0	- 0	- 0	- 0	- 0	- -	- 0	- -	- 0	- 0	- 0
Children's Hospital & Medical Center, Omaha, NE	- -	- -	- -	- -	- -	- -	- -	- -	- -	- -	- -	- -	- -	- -	- -	- -	- -
Columbus Community Hospital, Columbus, NE	98 40	100 54	98 50	100 67	99 78	100 12	98 122	100 231	95 77	- 0	98 169	93 68	98 168	94 65	96 163	98 122	91 11
Community Hospital, Mccook, NE	100 19	100 22	87 39	100 51	94 49	91 11	98 54	100 99	- 0	- 0	91 82	- 0	88 82	- 0	96 81	98 54	85 20
Community Medical Center, Falls City, NE	100 10	100 3	100 9	88 16	88 17	100 5	50 2	100 3	- 0	- 0	100 2	- 0	50 2	- 0	50 2	50 2	0 2
Community Memorial Hospital, Syracuse, NE	100 2	- 0	0 1	100 2	100 2	- 0	- 0	- 0	- 0	- 0	- 0	- -	- 0	- -	- 0	- 0	- 0
Cozad Community Hospital, Cozad, NE	100 5	- 0	67 3	100 5	75 4	0 1	- 0	- 0	- 0	- 0	- 0	- -	- 0	- -	- 0	- 0	- 0
Creighton University Medical Center - Saint Joseph, Omaha, NE	98 54	99 118	97 86	97 111	99 96	100 64	93 189	100 607	95 231	95 173	99 407	97 259	99 408	98 258	97 386	95 189	83 95
Crete Area Medical Center, Crete, NE	89 9	100 4	78 9	94 17	69 16	100 3	- 0	- 0	- 0	- 0	- 0	- -	- 0	- -	- 0	- 0	- 0
Dundy County Hospital, Benkelman, NE	82 17	75 4	100 10	92 24	70 20	75 8	- 0	100 1	- 0	- 0	100 1	- -	100 1	- -	100 1	- 0	- 0
Faith Regional Health Services, Norfolk, NE	100 44	100 78	96 54	99 88	100 86	96 25	98 194	100 667	98 248	82 55	99 489	99 136	99 491	99 136	98 473	99 194	93 30
Fillmore County Hospital, Geneva, NE	100 6	100 2	100 8	100 9	92 12	- 0	71 7	100 10	- 0	- 0	67 9	- -	100 10	- -	78 9	71 7	67 3
Franklin County Memorial Hospital, Franklin, NE	100 10	100 1	100 9	100 17	100 8	67 3	- 0	- 0	- 0	- 0	- 0	- -	- 0	- -	- 0	- 0	- 0
Fremont Area Medical Center, Fremont, NE	94 63	99 88	91 66	99 98	99 95	95 20	100 96	100 474	100 126	- 0	98 361	79 53	99 361	87 53	91 355	100 96	94 69
Garden County Health Services, Oshkosh, NE	50 2	100 1	83 6	100 2	29 7	0 2	- 0	- 0	- 0	- 0	- 0	- -	- 0	- -	- 0	- 0	- 0
Good Samaritan Hospital, Kearney, NE	90 97	98 66	90 105	97 134	93 147	90 41	93 404	99 1167	91 406	99 133	97 783	93 517	99 789	98 502	93 748	96 404	69 134
Gordon Memorial Hospital District, Gordon, NE	78 9	100 2	92 12	94 18	93 14	100 6	- 0	- 0	- 0	- 0	- 0	- -	- 0	- -	- 0	- 0	- 0
Gothenburg Memorial Hospital, Gothenburg, NE	100 5	- 0	100 5	100 5	90 10	100 2	- 0	- 0	- 0	- 0	- 0	- -	- 0	- -	- 0	- 0	- 0
Great Plains Regional Medical Center, North Platte, NE	98 90	99 141	94 83	99 136	97 133	98 45	93 115	100 342	97 115	- 0	99 240	100 151	100 240	99 152	97 234	97 115	100 25

NOTE: The first number in each column (boldface) is the score, the second number is the number of patients; Please refer to the main entry for footnotes; (a) 100-299
*MEASURES: **Pneumonia Care:** 16. Appropriate Initial Antibiotic; 17. Blood Culture Timing; 18. Influenza Vaccine; 19. Initial Antibiotic Timing; 20. Pneumococcal Vaccine; 21. Smoking Cessation Advice; **Surgical Care Improvement Project:** 22. Appropriate VTP Within 24 Hours; 23. Appropriate Hair Removal; 24. Appropriate Beta Blocker Usage; 25. Controlled Postoperative Blood Glucose; 26. Prophylactic Antibiotic Timing; 27. Prophylactic Antibiotic Timing (Outpatient); 28. Prophylactic Antibiotic Selection; 29. Prophylactic Antibiotic Selection (Outpatient); 30. Prophylactic Antibiotic Stopped; 31. Recommended VTP Ordered; 32. Urinary Catheter Removal*

Hospital	Pneumonia Care						Surgical Care Improvement Project										
	16	17	18	19	20	21	22	23	24	25	26	27	28	29	30	31	32
Harlan County Health System, Alma, NE	86 7	100 1	86 7	100 3	71 7	100 1	- 0	- 0	- 0	- 0	- 0	- -	- 0	- -	- 0	- 0	- 0
Henderson Health Care Services, Henderson, NE	- 0	- 0	100 3	100 2	100 3	- 0	- 0	- 0	- 0	- 0	- 0	- -	- 0	- -	- 0	- 0	- 0
Howard County Medical Center, Saint Paul, NE	87 23	50 4	100 19	97 31	93 28	80 5	- 0	- 0	- 0	- 0	- 0	- -	- 0	- -	- 0	- 0	- 0
Jefferson Community Health Center, Fairbury, NE	100 14	100 2	91 11	100 17	100 17	100 4	100 6	100 19	- 0	- 0	100 14	- 0	100 14	- 0	93 14	100 6	100 5
Jennie M Melham Memorial Medical Center, Broken Bow, NE	90 42	100 17	91 46	95 61	82 74	12 8	- 0	- 0	- 0	- 0	- 0	- -	- 0	- -	- 0	- 0	- 0
Johnson County Hospital, Tecumseh, NE	91 11	100 3	100 5	91 11	85 13	100 2	50 2	100 12	- 0	- 0	100 11	- -	100 11	- -	91 11	50 2	- 0
Kearney County Health Services Hospital, Minden, NE	100 2	100 1	100 4	50 2	50 6	- 0	- 0	- 0	- 0	- 0	- 0	- -	- 0	- -	- 0	- 0	- 0
Kimball Health Services, Kimball, NE	100 5	- 0	40 5	100 5	33 6	100 1	- 0	- 0	- 0	- 0	- 0	- -	- 0	- -	- 0	- 0	- 0
Lincoln Surgical Hospital, Lincoln, NE	- 0	- 0	- 0	- 0	- 0	- 0	100 29	100 484	100 91	- 0	98 432	98 372	100 433	99 367	100 430	100 29	100 69
Litzenberg Memorial County Hospital, Central City, NE	100 18	100 2	100 16	100 33	98 40	73 11	- 0	- 0	- 0	- 0	- 0	- -	- 0	- -	- 0	- 0	- 0
Mary Lanning Memorial Hospital, Hastings, NE	94 83	98 101	95 81	98 125	97 121	69 29	93 204	99 593	96 128	- 0	96 508	46 116	97 508	94 109	78 495	92 206	76 93
Memorial Community Hospital, Blair, NE	100 19	100 19	100 23	100 18	100 29	100 9	100 4	100 13	- 0	- 0	100 8	- -	100 9	- -	100 8	100 4	- 0
Memorial Health Care Systems, Seward, NE	93 27	80 5	77 26	97 37	71 35	25 4	0 1	76 17	- 0	- 0	88 16	- -	25 16	- -	100 16	0 2	- 0
Memorial Health Center, Sidney, NE	78 9	80 5	53 19	82 11	57 28	0 11	50 6	100 8	- 0	- 0	0 2	- -	100 1	- -	100 1	50 6	0 2
Memorial Hospital, Aurora, NE	100 11	- 0	100 10	100 13	100 18	50 2	100 12	96 28	- 0	- 0	88 24	- -	92 24	- -	100 23	100 12	100 6
Midwest Surgical Hospital, Omaha, NE	- 0	- 0	- 0	- 0	- 0	- 0	100 2	100 129	78 40	- 0	94 123	94 409	99 121	98 403	99 121	100 2	100 59
Morrill County Community Hospital, Bridgeport, NE	100 3	- 0	- 0	- 0	33 3	0 1	- 0	- 0	- 0	- 0	- 0	- -	- 0	- -	- 0	- 0	- 0
Nebraska Heart Hospital, Lincoln, NE	100 2	- 0	88 8	100 3	73 15	100 2	86 21	100 327	95 180	93 169	98 213	98 398	100 218	99 397	96 205	90 21	100 2
The Nebraska Medical Center, Omaha, NE	81 47	96 110	83 76	94 83	84 102	92 65	88 196	100 580	88 256	91 124	96 361	86 382	99 371	95 365	97 349	91 198	85 162
The Nebraska Methodist Hospital, Omaha, NE	72 204	95 251	93 207	92 308	95 356	91 58	96 683	97 2394	99 300	98 287	95 1654	92 450	97 1675	92 438	94 1590	97 684	98 531
Nebraska Orthopaedic Hospital, Omaha, NE	- 0	- 0	- 0	- 0	- 0	- 0	100 20	99 231	90 77	- 0	99 164	99 147	100 164	100 147	95 164	100 20	97 64
Nemaha County Hospital, Auburn, NE	100 5	100 1	100 1	88 8	86 7	100 2	- 0	100 1	- 0	- 0	100 1	- -	100 1	- -	100 1	- 0	- 0
Niobrara Valley Hospital, Lynch, NE	- 0	- 0	- 0	100 1	- 0	- 0	- 0	- 0	- 0	- 0	- 0	- -	- 0	- -	- 0	- 0	- 0
Oakland Mercy Hospital, Oakland, NE	80 5	90 10	67 9	94 16	69 13	75 8	- 0	- 0	- 0	- 0	- 0	- -	- 0	- -	- 0	- 0	- 0
Ogallala Community Hospital, Ogallala, NE	100 25	100 9	83 12	100 21	90 31	100 6	100 18	100 35	- 0	- 0	97 30	100 2	100 30	100 2	93 29	100 18	- 0
Omaha VA Medical Center, Omaha, NE	96 28	100 63	94 67	94 68	98 80	100 36	98 130	100 298	97 117	- 0	97 206	- -	100 207	- -	98 200	98 130	96 144
Osmond General Hospital, Osmond, NE	0 1	- 0	- 0	50 2	60 5	- 0	- 0	- 0	- 0	- 0	- 0	- -	- 0	- -	- 0	- 0	- 0
Pawnee County Memorial Hospital, Pawnee City, NE	100 7	100 3	50 8	80 5	50 8	25 4	- 0	- 0	- 0	- 0	- 0	- -	- 0	- -	- 0	- 0	- 0
Pender Community Hospital, Pender, NE	76 25	100 4	90 20	100 31	83 29	80 5	100 1	43 7	- 0	- 0	83 6	- -	100 6	- -	100 6	100 1	- 0
Perkins County Health Services, Grant, NE	50 4	0 1	80 5	57 7	83 6	25 4	- 0	- 0	- 0	- 0	- 0	- -	- 0	- -	- 0	- 0	- 0
Phelps Memorial Health Center, Holdrege, NE	88 26	83 6	89 53	90 51	94 62	100 5	100 33	100 81	- 0	- 0	93 71	- -	96 71	- -	91 66	97 34	80 5
Plainview Public Hospital, Plainview, NE	100 6	100 1	100 4	86 7	91 11	100 1	- 0	- 0	- 0	- 0	- 0	- -	- 0	- -	- 0	- 0	- 0
Providence Medical Center, Wayne, NE	86 14	50 2	86 21	96 24	91 32	75 4	100 4	100 7	- 0	- 0	100 3	80 5	100 3	100 16	100 3	100 4	50 2
Regional West Medical Center, Scottsbluff, NE	97 75	100 76	98 86	99 100	99 105	100 61	94 224	100 520	93 122	- 0	99 391	98 171	98 393	100 172	97 378	98 224	80 20
Rock County Hospital, Bassett, NE	- 0	- 0	- 0	- 0	- 0	- 0	- 0	- 0	- 0	- 0	- 0	- -	- 0	- -	- 0	- 0	- 0
Saint Elizabeth Regional Medical Center, Lincoln, NE	96 90	96 152	88 82	97 162	92 148	100 34	76 197	100 647	75 183	96 54	95 354	93 495	97 356	94 487	96 336	82 197	78 72
Saint Francis Medical Center, Grand Island, NE	90 118	99 202	87 158	98 207	91 210	100 72	95 198	100 694	89 228	- 0	100 448	88 84	99 451	96 77	94 423	97 198	87 174
Saint Francis Memorial Hospital, West Point, NE	100 6	100 3	90 10	100 16	95 19	100 1	100 7	94 33	- 0	- 0	97 32	- -	97 32	- -	97 32	100 7	100 2
Saint Mary's Community Hospital, Nebraska City, NE	89 19	100 16	94 18	97 36	100 32	71 7	100 1	100 13	- 0	- 0	82 11	- -	100 12	- -	100 10	100 1	- 0
Saunders Medical Center, Wahoo, NE	100 15	100 10	100 19	95 22	97 31	100 2	- 0	- 0	- 0	- 0	- 0	- -	- 0	- -	- 0	- 0	- 0
Thayer County Health Services, Hebron, NE	100 7	100 1	85 13	100 13	89 19	0 2	89 9	100 20	- 0	- 0	89 18	- -	94 18	- -	100 18	100 9	50 8
Tilden Community Hospital, Tilden, NE	100 4	100 1	100 3	100 2	100 4	0 1	- 0	- 0	- 0	- 0	- 0	- 0	- 0	- 0	- 0	- 0	- 0
Tri Valley Health System, Cambridge, NE	96 26	100 3	68 31	92 39	70 40	100 6	100 1	100 2	- 0	- 0	100 2	- -	0 2	- -	100 2	100 1	- 0
Tri-County Area Hospital District, Lexington, NE	100 28	92 13	95 22	100 45	98 40	100 9	100 16	100 45	100 9	- 0	95 39	- 0	100 39	- 0	100 39	100 16	100 10
Valley County Health System, Ord, NE	93 15	92 13	50 10	100 18	77 22	20 5	- 0	- 0	- 0	- 0	- 0	- -	- 0	- -	- 0	- 0	- 0
Warren Memorial Hospital, Friend, NE	- 0	- 0	- 0	- 0	- 0	- 0	- 0	- 0	- 0	- 0	- 0	- -	- 0	- -	- 0	- 0	- 0
Webster County Community Hospital, Red Cloud, NE	100 2	- 0	100 4	- 0	100 6	0 1	- 0	- 0	- 0	- 0	- 0	- -	- 0	- -	- 0	- 0	- 0
West Holt Memorial Hospital, Atkinson, NE	50 4	- 0	80 5	100 6	86 7	67 3	- 0	- 0	- 0	- 0	- 0	- -	- 0	- -	- 0	- 0	- 0
Winnebago Ihs Hospital, Winnebago, NE	- -	- -	- -	- -	- -	- -	- -	- -	- -	- -	- -	- -	- -	- -	- -	- -	- -
York General Hospital, York, NE	94 18	100 8	90 10	93 27	96 27	75 4	100 18	100 35	- 0	- 0	100 37	- -	100 37	- -	100 37	100 18	94 16
NORTH DAKOTA																	
Altru Hospital, Grand Forks, ND	70 141	94 226	83 174	91 188	86 244	92 116	94 233	100 634	89 227	90 122	93 486	90 276	98 489	99 284	95 472	94 233	83 126
Carrington Health Center, Carrington, ND	100 5	100 3	100 5	100 15	100 20	100 4	- 0	- 0	- 0	- 0	- 0	- -	- 0	- -	- 0	- 0	- 0
Essentia Health-Fargo, Fargo, ND	90 79	95 111	93 75	94 98	92 123	100 35	96 146	100 521	92 179	86 103	95 370	74 160	97 373	96 187	95 331	96 147	93 112
Fargo VA Medical Center, Fargo, ND	91 35	100 30	96 47	96 46	97 58	89 36	100 81	100 151	85 47	- 0	94 109	- -	98 110	- -	100 108	100 81	97 86
Heart of America Medical Center, Rugby, ND	80 10	100 18	100 13	90 21	92 24	- 0	86 7	100 10	- 0	- 0	67 3	- -	67 3	- -	100 3	75 8	0 1
Hillsboro Medical Center, Hillsboro, ND	89 9	- 0	62 8	100 2	60 5	67 3	- 0	- 0	- 0	- 0	- 0	- 0	- 0	- 0	- 0	- 0	- 0
Jacobson Memorial Hospital & Care Center, Elgin, ND	- 0	- 0	- 0	100 1	100 2	- 0	- 0	- 0	- 0	- 0	- 0	- -	- 0	- -	- 0	- 0	- 0
Jamestown Hospital, Jamestown, ND	100 47	98 57	100 32	95 61	100 58	100 12	71 28	100 68	100 16	- 0	96 48	73 11	94 48	100 11	96 46	71 28	78 9
Linton Hospital, Linton, ND	100 12	100 6	81 21	100 24	73 26	40 10	- 0	- 0	- 0	- 0	- 0	- -	- 0	- -	- 0	- 0	- 0
McKenzie County Healthcare Systems, Watford City, ND	87 15	100 12	67 18	100 26	88 25	0 2	- 0	- 0	- 0	- 0	- 0	- -	- 0	- -	- 0	- 0	- 0
Medcenter One, Bismarck, ND	94 98	94 119	84 69	93 118	89 123	94 62	87 253	100 841	87 273	96 149	97 693	89 284	98 700	97 287	97 677	87 255	87 127
Mercy Medical Center, Williston, ND	87 23	95 42	97 29	98 48	95 44	74 19	94 50	100 140	65 20	- 0	93 97	97 33	94 98	97 32	95 94	96 50	88 8
Mountrail County Medical Center, Stanley, ND	- 0	- 0	86 7	100 3	83 6	- 0	- 0	- 0	- 0	- 0	- 0	- -	- 0	- -	- 0	- 0	- 0
Northwood Deaconess Health Center, Northwood, ND	100 4	- 0	100 8	93 14	94 17	- 0	- 0	- 0	- 0	- 0	- 0	- -	- 0	- -	- 0	- 0	- 0
P H S Indian Hospital at Belcourt - Quentin N Burdick, Belcourt, ND	92 12	33 6	45 11	100 15	86 7	25 4	100 1	36 11	100 1	- 0	62 8	- -	50 8	- -	88 8	100 1	100 1
P H S Indian Hospital at Fort Yates-Standing Rock, Fort Yates, ND	92 12	100 4	78 9	72 18	100 6	91 11	- 0	- 0	- 0	- 0	- 0	- -	- 0	- -	- 0	- 0	- 0
Pembina County Memorial Hospital, Cavalier, ND	100 12	- 0	100 6	100 3	71 7	100 4	- 0	- 0	- 0	- 0	- 0	- -	- 0	- -	- 0	- 0	- 0

NOTE: The first number in each column (boldface) is the score, the second number is the number of patients; Please refer to the main entry for footnotes; (a) 100-299
MEASURES: ***Pneumonia Care:*** *16. Appropriate Initial Antibiotic; 17. Blood Culture Timing; 18. Influenza Vaccine; 19. Initial Antibiotic Timing; 20. Pneumococcal Vaccine; 21. Smoking Cessation Advice;* ***Surgical Care Improvement Project:*** *22. Appropriate VTP Within 24 Hours; 23. Appropriate Hair Removal; 24. Appropriate Beta Blocker Usage; 25. Controlled Postoperative Blood Glucose; 26. Prophylactic Antibiotic Timing; 27. Prophylactic Antibiotic Timing (Outpatient); 28. Prophylactic Antibiotic Selection; 29. Prophylactic Antibiotic Selection (Outpatient); 30. Prophylactic Antibiotic Stopped; 31. Recommended VTP Ordered; 32. Urinary Catheter Removal*

Hospital	Pneumonia Care						Surgical Care Improvement Project										
	16	17	18	19	20	21	22	23	24	25	26	27	28	29	30	31	32
Presentation Medical Center, Rolla, ND	**100** 15	**100** 3	**100** 15	**93** 30	**100** 23	**80** 10	- 0	- 0	- 0	- 0	- 0	- 0	- 0	- 0	- 0	- 0	- 0
Saint Alexius Medical Center, Bismarck, ND	**97** 62	**99** 115	**88** 85	**98** 129	**94** 144	**98** 57	**96** 138	**100** 581	**96** 204	**98** 131	**96** 442	**92** 284	**98** 443	**96** 359	**99** 425	**96** 140	**97** 117
Saint Aloisius Medical Center, Harvey, ND	**70** 10	**50** 2	**71** 17	**83** 12	**80** 45	**50** 6	- 0	- 0	- 0	- 0	- 0	- -	- 0	- -	- 0	- 0	- 0
Saint Andrews Health Center, Bottineau, ND	**100** 6	**100** 3	**100** 6	**88** 8	**100** 11	**67** 3	- 0	- 0	- 0	- 0	- 0	- -	- 0	- -	- 0	- 0	- 0
Saint Joseph's Hospital & Health Center, Dickinson, ND	**94** 34	**98** 49	**90** 41	**100** 57	**96** 71	**90** 10	**92** 38	**100** 131	**95** 44	- 0	**94** 106	- -	**97** 106	- -	**97** 102	**97** 38	**93** 30
Sanford Mayville, Mayville, ND	**67** 6	- 0	**100** 4	**100** 10	**100** 9	**100** 2	- 0	- 0	- 0	- 0	- 0	- -	- 0	- -	- 0	- 0	- 0
Sanford Medical Center Fargo, Fargo, ND	**89** 145	**99** 218	**90** 236	**95** 274	**96** 340	**91** 164	**98** 267	**99** 933	**93** 314	**92** 194	**96** 615	**98** 586	**98** 623	**98** 584	**95** 587	**98** 267	**93** 175
Tioga Medical Center, Tioga, ND	**0** 1	**0** 1	**86** 7	**77** 13	**82** 11	**100** 1	- 0	- 0	- 0	- 0	- 0	- -	- 0	- -	- 0	- 0	- 0
Trinity Hospitals, Minot, ND	**97** 108	**98** 220	**93** 148	**95** 214	**99** 230	**100** 69	**87** 252	**100** 852	**93** 298	**96** 67	**97** 615	**93** 306	**96** 626	**97** 359	**96** 589	**89** 257	**97** 261
Unity Medical Center, Grafton, ND	- -	- -	- -	- -	- -	- -	- -	- -	- -	- -	- 0	- 0	- 0	- 0	- -	- -	- -
West River Regional Medical Center, Hettinger, ND	**90** 42	**100** 20	**78** 41	**100** 74	**91** 66	**100** 14	**73** 15	**100** 19	- 0	- 0	**79** 14	- -	**92** 13	- -	**85** 13	**73** 15	**100** 2
Wishek Community Hospital, Wishek, ND	**100** 4	**100** 1	**78** 9	**71** 7	**88** 16	**33** 3	- 0	- 0	- 0	- 0	- 0	- -	- 0	- -	- 0	- 0	- 0
OKLAHOMA																	
Arbuckle Memorial Hospital, Sulphur, OK	**79** 24	**91** 22	**96** 28	**95** 40	**83** 36	**67** 18	- 0	- 0	- 0	- 0	- 0	- -	- 0	- -	- 0	- 0	- 0
Atoka Memorial Hospital, Atoka, OK	**73** 15	**100** 1	**73** 11	**90** 20	**75** 20	**86** 7	- 0	- 0	- 0	- 0	- 0	- -	- 0	- -	- 0	- 0	- 0
Bailey Medical Center, Owasso, OK	**90** 30	**96** 27	**100** 21	**93** 41	**100** 25	**100** 11	**94** 48	**100** 136	**69** 32	- 0	**98** 108	**100** 20	**97** 108	**95** 20	**95** 105	**96** 48	**93** 27
Beaver County Memorial Hospital, Beaver, OK	**75** 8	- 0	**64** 11	**91** 11	**70** 10	**33** 3	- 0	- 0	- 0	- 0	- 0	- -	- 0	- -	- 0	- 0	- 0
Bristow Medical Center, Bristow, OK	**100** 35	**95** 19	**100** 24	**100** 34	**82** 34	**91** 11	- 0	- 0	- 0	- 0	- 0	- 0	- 0	- 0	- 0	- 0	- 0
Carnegie Tri-County Municipal Hospital, Carnegie, OK	- 0	- 0	- 0	- 0	- 0	- 0	- 0	- 0	- 0	- 0	- 0	- 0	- 0	- 0	- 0	- 0	- 0
Chickasaw Nation Medical Center, Ada, OK	**85** 54	**98** 48	**92** 24	**96** 54	**69** 29	**63** 35	**100** 26	**100** 130	**35** 23	- 0	**91** 99	- -	**99** 99	- -	**89** 98	**93** 28	**83** 6
Choctaw Memorial Hospital, Hugo, OK	**80** 54	**76** 21	**42** 50	**82** 84	**43** 77	**48** 25	**0** 4	**22** 9	**0** 1	- 0	**56** 9	- 0	**33** 9	- 0	**100** 9	**0** 4	- 0
Choctaw Nation Healthcare, Talihina, OK	**95** 19	**82** 17	**56** 9	**100** 14	**75** 8	**100** 5	**0** 2	**100** 11	**0** 1	- 0	**89** 9	- -	**88** 8	- -	**100** 8	**0** 2	**100** 2
Cimarron Memorial Hospital, Boise City, OK	- 0	- 0	- 0	- 0	- 0	- 0	- 0	- 0	- 0	- 0	- 0	- -	- 0	- -	- 0	- 0	- 0
Claremore Indian Hospital, Claremore, OK	**94** 35	**97** 34	**93** 14	**92** 37	**100** 8	**81** 16	**81** 32	**100** 107	**82** 11	- 0	**99** 71	**65** 17	**90** 72	**100** 12	**94** 70	**88** 32	**100** 1
Claremore Regional Hospital, Claremore, OK	**98** 90	**99** 126	**92** 87	**95** 128	**98** 100	**100** 54	**100** 73	**100** 187	**83** 42	- 0	**94** 144	**92** 61	**99** 147	**98** 58	**94** 141	**100** 73	**90** 20
Cleveland Area Hospital, Cleveland, OK	**80** 10	**75** 8	**62** 13	**87** 15	**50** 12	**50** 2	- 0	- 0	- 0	- 0	- 0	- -	- 0	- -	- 0	- 0	- 0
Comanche County Memorial Hospital, Lawton, OK	**93** 137	**95** 189	**59** 116	**95** 199	**82** 170	**93** 105	**95** 291	**99** 658	**79** 253	**86** 170	**91** 420	**89** 389	**99** 427	**98** 385	**94** 402	**98** 292	**87** 137
Community Hospital, Oklahoma City, OK	**100** 2	**100** 3	- 0	**100** 2	**100** 1	- 0	**100** 21	**100** 226	**100** 49	- 0	**99** 189	**98** 92	**98** 188	**100** 92	**95** 187	**100** 21	**100** 72
Cordell Memorial Hospital, Cordell, OK	**71** 7	**100** 4	**67** 6	**100** 12	**88** 16	**100** 2	- 0	- 0	- 0	- 0	- 0	- -	- 0	- -	- 0	- 0	- 0
Craig General Hospital, Vinita, OK	**91** 66	**92** 38	**84** 55	**93** 59	**78** 68	**97** 34	**75** 4	**100** 14	**0** 1	- 0	**100** 13	**89** 9	**92** 13	**100** 8	**100** 11	**100** 4	- 0
Creek Nation Community Hospital, Okemah, OK	**91** 34	**81** 21	**68** 19	**100** 33	**100** 20	**85** 13	- 0	- 0	- 0	- 0	- 0	- -	- 0	- -	- 0	- 0	- 0
Cushing Regional Hospital, Cushing, OK	**92** 120	**98** 162	**94** 106	**99** 151	**93** 112	**100** 73	**100** 54	**100** 105	**92** 25	- 0	**85** 74	**60** 10	**91** 74	**0** 8	**92** 73	**100** 54	**78** 18
Deaconess Hospital, Oklahoma City, OK	**98** 112	**100** 182	**97** 140	**98** 168	**98** 170	**100** 71	**88** 225	**100** 757	**97** 163	**100** 57	**98** 457	**96** 429	**97** 456	**97** 536	**98** 441	**91** 228	**92** 48
Drumright Regional Hospital, Drumright, OK	**88** 32	**100** 4	**71** 24	**91** 46	**56** 27	**86** 29	**86** 14	**92** 13	**0** 1	- 0	**83** 23	- -	**43** 23	- -	**35** 23	**86** 14	**0** 1
Duncan Regional Hospital, Duncan, OK	**94** 133	**96** 210	**93** 129	**97** 212	**98** 202	**100** 87	**89** 142	**98** 308	**92** 91	- 0	**97** 229	**92** 48	**98** 230	**96** 45	**96** 222	**98** 142	**95** 76
Eastern Oklahoma Medical Center, Poteau, OK	**79** 94	**90** 84	**82** 67	**86** 118	**79** 77	**88** 43	**65** 17	**95** 56	**70** 10	- 0	**81** 36	**40** 5	**72** 36	**100** 2	**100** 36	**61** 18	**88** 8
Edmond Medical Center, Edmond, OK	- -	- -	- -	- -	- -	- -	- -	- -	- -	- -	- -	- -	- -	- -	- -	- -	- -
Elkview General Hospital, Hobart, OK	**94** 54	**97** 31	**95** 43	**97** 62	**98** 43	**100** 20	**70** 23	**100** 38	**50** 4	- 0	**96** 27	**100** 2	**100** 27	**100** 2	**93** 27	**70** 23	**81** 21
Epic Medical Center, Eufaula, OK	**87** 15	**67** 3	**88** 8	**83** 12	**25** 8	**38** 8	- 0	- 0	- 0	- 0	- 0	- 0	- 0	- 0	- 0	- 0	- 0
Fairfax Community Hospital, Fairfax, OK	**67** 3	**100** 4	**100** 3	**100** 4	**100** 3	**100** 3	- 0	- 0	- 0	- 0	- 0	- -	- 0	- -	- 0	- 0	- 0
Fairview Regional Medical Center, Fairview, OK	**96** 23	**100** 9	**71** 14	**90** 20	**55** 22	**100** 2	- 0	- 0	- 0	- 0	- 0	- -	- 0	- -	- 0	- 0	- 0
Grady Memorial Hospital, Chickasha, OK	**80** 50	**96** 82	**84** 57	**99** 94	**92** 91	**88** 32	**98** 49	**99** 80	**100** 4	- 0	**86** 43	**100** 27	**88** 43	**96** 27	**95** 43	**98** 49	**83** 6
Great Plains Regional Medical Center, Elk City, OK	**92** 51	**86** 58	**98** 58	**100** 73	**100** 78	**100** 24	**89** 74	**98** 200	**94** 32	- 0	**93** 140	**77** 52	**94** 141	**93** 45	**91** 130	**88** 76	**29** 38
Harmon Memorial Hospital, Hollis, OK	**57** 46	**32** 28	**79** 38	**72** 74	**83** 46	**95** 22	- 0	- 0	- 0	- 0	- 0	- 0	- 0	- 0	- 0	- 0	- 0
Harper County Community Hospital, Buffalo, OK	**89** 18	**100** 3	**100** 10	**100** 19	**100** 12	**100** 8	- 0	- 0	- 0	- 0	- 0	- -	- 0	- -	- 0	- 0	- 0
Haskell County Healthcare System, Stigler, OK	- -	- -	- -	- -	- -	- -	- -	- -	- -	- -	- -	- -	- -	- -	- -	- -	- -
Healdton Mercy Hospital Corporation, Healdton, OK	**100** 6	- 0	**100** 5	**100** 7	**86** 7	**100** 1	- 0	- 0	- 0	- 0	- 0	- -	- 0	- -	- 0	- 0	- 0
Henryetta Medical Center, Henryetta, OK	**94** 34	**100** 44	**82** 28	**100** 50	**93** 29	**100** 17	**100** 29	**100** 36	**100** 4	- 0	**100** 24	**100** 1	**100** 24	**100** 1	**96** 23	**100** 29	**100** 5
Hillcrest Medical Center, Tulsa, OK	**95** 147	**98** 168	**85** 157	**93** 216	**94** 170	**98** 177	**89** 123	**100** 614	**89** 221	**96** 145	**98** 446	**94** 620	**99** 456	**97** 613	**96** 429	**99** 123	**93** 166
Holdenville General Hospital, Holdenville, OK	**85** 27	**90** 30	**83** 29	**93** 41	**77** 35	**94** 17	- 0	- 0	- 0	- 0	- 0	- -	- 0	- -	- 0	- 0	- 0
Integris Baptist Medical Center, Oklahoma City, OK	**91** 121	**100** 154	**97** 160	**95** 208	**95** 209	**99** 78	**85** 149	**100** 717	**87** 231	**96** 170	**99** 519	**91** 367	**98** 532	**94** 373	**97** 484	**87** 155	**93** 124
Integris Baptist Regional Health Center, Miami, OK	**97** 119	**97** 149	**96** 103	**99** 181	**99** 137	**98** 66	**99** 77	**97** 149	**91** 53	- 0	**97** 117	**89** 70	**95** 117	**99** 68	**90** 114	**100** 77	**97** 39
Integris Bass Baptist Health Center, Enid, OK	**97** 70	**99** 129	**93** 90	**98** 116	**97** 100	**100** 46	**95** 112	**99** 334	**90** 82	**91** 69	**98** 189	**99** 67	**98** 190	**94** 67	**97** 185	**97** 112	**87** 55
Integris Blackwell Regional Hospital, Blackwell, OK	**98** 55	**100** 72	**96** 51	**99** 90	**99** 67	**100** 29	**83** 6	**100** 17	**50** 2	- 0	**100** 9	**75** 4	**100** 9	**100** 3	**88** 8	**83** 6	**0** 1
Integris Canadian Valley Hospital, Yukon, OK	**86** 90	**99** 110	**85** 55	**98** 120	**86** 77	**100** 38	**81** 70	**100** 230	**97** 34	- 0	**99** 168	**97** 38	**96** 168	**97** 38	**93** 168	**99** 71	**62** 61
Integris Clinton Regional Hospital, Clinton, OK	**92** 63	**98** 42	**91** 44	**98** 97	**98** 58	**100** 36	**88** 8	**100** 19	**100** 1	- 0	**83** 6	**87** 15	**67** 6	**100** 13	**100** 5	**100** 8	**0** 1
Integris Grove Hospital, Grove, OK	**93** 75	**94** 116	**88** 67	**99** 111	**95** 105	**100** 35	**90** 82	**100** 186	**90** 41	- 0	**97** 130	**97** 97	**98** 131	**90** 97	**98** 127	**90** 82	**95** 39
Integris Marshall County Medical Center, Madill, OK	**100** 59	**94** 54	**96** 51	**99** 79	**94** 70	**100** 25	- 0	- 0	- 0	- 0	- 0	**100** 19	- 0	**89** 19	- 0	- 0	- 0
Integris Mayes County Medical Center, Pryor, OK	**100** 38	**100** 74	**100** 47	**100** 59	**98** 59	**100** 27	**92** 12	**100** 54	**100** 13	- 0	**97** 39	**94** 53	**90** 40	**96** 50	**100** 39	**92** 12	**100** 11
Integris Seminole Medical Center, Seminole, OK	**95** 58	**94** 69	**92** 39	**99** 82	**100** 52	**98** 40	**90** 10	**100** 12	**33** 3	- 0	**50** 4	**95** 19	**100** 4	**100** 18	**50** 4	**90** 10	**67** 3
Integris Southwest Medical Center, Oklahoma City, OK	**79** 185	**98** 223	**90** 182	**100** 313	**96** 221	**97** 185	**97** 199	**99** 578	**93** 186	**88** 108	**99** 396	**85** 177	**99** 400	**91** 171	**93** 370	**98** 201	**92** 118
Jackson County Memorial Hospital, Altus, OK	**91** 64	**98** 52	**93** 54	**98** 87	**93** 95	**100** 54	**92** 248	**100** 396	**91** 125	- 0	**97** 243	**97** 34	**98** 243	**100** 33	**86** 237	**95** 248	**75** 99
Jane Phillips Medical Center, Bartlesville, OK	**94** 126	**95** 201	**92** 145	**97** 202	**93** 206	**100** 89	**82** 249	**100** 521	**96** 85	- 0	**95** 416	**61** 56	**98** 418	**74** 34	**94** 407	**88** 249	**84** 77
Jefferson County Hospital, Waurika, OK	**100** 4	**100** 1	**22** 9	**100** 10	**14** 7	**67** 3	- 0	- 0	- 0	- 0	- 0	- -	- 0	- -	- 0	- 0	- 0
Johnston Memorial Hospital, Tishomingo, OK	- 0	- 0	- 0	**67** 3	**0** 1	**100** 1	- 0	- 0	- 0	- 0	- 0	- -	- 0	- -	- 0	- 0	- 0
Kingfisher Regional Hospital, Kingfisher, OK	**86** 35	**80** 20	**80** 30	**91** 53	**77** 35	**71** 7	- 0	- 0	- 0	- 0	- 0	**0** 1	- 0	**100** 1	- 0	- 0	- 0
Lakeside Women's Hospital, Oklahoma City, OK	- 0	- 0	- 0	- 0	- 0	- 0	**100** 1	**94** 78	**100** 3	- 0	**100** 67	**97** 233	**99** 71	**99** 228	**91** 67	**100** 1	- 0
Latimer County General Hospital, Wilburton, OK	**82** 17	**100** 12	**89** 18	**100** 30	**81** 21	**85** 13	- 0	- 0	- 0	- 0	- 0	- 0	- 0	- 0	- 0	- 0	- 0

NOTE: The first number in each column (boldface) is the score, the second number is the number of patients; Please refer to the main entry for footnotes; (a) 100-299
*MEASURES: **Pneumonia Care:** 16. Appropriate Initial Antibiotic; 17. Blood Culture Timing; 18. Influenza Vaccine; 19. Initial Antibiotic Timing; 20. Pneumococcal Vaccine; 21. Smoking Cessation Advice; **Surgical Care Improvement Project:** 22. Appropriate VTP Within 24 Hours; 23. Appropriate Hair Removal; 24. Appropriate Beta Blocker Usage; 25. Controlled Postoperative Blood Glucose; 26. Prophylactic Antibiotic Timing; 27. Prophylactic Antibiotic Timing (Outpatient); 28. Prophylactic Antibiotic Selection; 29. Prophylactic Antibiotic Selection (Outpatient); 30. Prophylactic Antibiotic Stopped; 31. Recommended VTP Ordered; 32. Urinary Catheter Removal*

Hospital	Pneumonia Care							Surgical Care Improvement Project									
	16	17	18	19	20	21	22	23	24	25	26	27	28	29	30	31	32
Lindsay Municipal Hospital, Lindsay, OK	100 2	- 0	- 0	100 1	100 1	100 1	- 0	- 0	- 0	- 0	- 0	- -	- 0	- -	- 0	- 0	- 0
Logan Medical Center, Guthrie, OK	86 59	89 62	53 38	76 45	53 62	67 27	94 35	100 66	75 16	- 0	94 49	- -	98 49	- -	72 43	94 35	46 13
Mary Hurley Hospital, Coalgate, OK	60 10	0 1	73 11	86 14	87 15	100 10	- 0	- 0	- 0	- 0	- 0	- -	- 0	- -	- 0	- 0	- 0
McAlester Regional Health Center, Mcalester, OK	89 28	94 144	93 96	98 150	91 135	93 59	89 131	99 397	86 56	- 0	96 284	96 70	98 284	94 69	93 271	89 131	97 61
McBride Clinic Orthopedic Hospital, Oklahoma City, OK	- 0	- 0	- 0	- 0	- 0	- 0	95 64	100 344	90 93	- 0	100 255	100 15	100 255	100 15	99 255	100 64	67 6
McCurtain Memorial Hospital, Idabel, OK	92 64	97 73	87 70	92 108	85 82	92 36	89 9	100 24	100 3	- 0	96 23	100 4	100 23	100 4	91 23	89 9	- 0
Medical Center of Southeastern Oklahoma, Durant, OK	96 134	99 159	100 156	100 224	100 209	100 122	96 81	100 229	98 42	- 0	99 142	100 148	99 142	99 148	100 138	96 81	87 15
Memorial Hospital & Physician Group, Frederick, OK	96 26	100 5	94 36	95 41	87 39	100 23	- 0	- 0	- 0	- 0	- 0	- 0	- 0	- 0	- 0	- 0	- 0
Memorial Hospital of Stilwell, Stilwell, OK	73 26	100 13	92 25	98 41	100 35	83 12	88 8	87 31	67 3	- 0	88 24	80 5	92 24	100 5	100 24	88 8	100 7
Memorial Hospital of Texas County, Guymon, OK	87 23	100 4	100 20	89 35	94 31	88 16	67 3	100 23	100 4	- 0	94 18	- 0	100 18	- 0	100 18	100 3	100 1
Mercy Health Center, Oklahoma City, OK	95 147	97 316	100 228	97 258	100 297	100 94	94 152	99 357	88 76	- 0	98 225	99 387	98 230	96 437	95 216	94 153	92 25
Mercy Health Love County, Marietta, OK	67 3	100 1	84 19	63 19	81 26	67 6	- 0	- 0	- 0	- 0	- 0	- -	- 0	- -	- 0	- 0	- 0
Mercy Hospital El Reno, El Reno, OK	80 54	87 30	90 29	92 66	87 39	93 27	67 6	100 16	100 1	- 0	100 14	- 0	79 14	- 0	93 14	67 6	50 2
Mercy Memorial Health Center, Ardmore, OK	84 93	92 153	95 128	95 172	96 166	100 85	97 233	100 665	93 176	- 0	97 423	96 313	100 429	84 307	95 382	98 233	57 35
Midwest Regional Medical Center, Midwest City, OK	92 210	96 263	95 167	97 332	98 239	100 143	96 245	100 712	100 185	88 64	98 435	94 156	96 438	93 151	83 418	96 247	99 97
Muskogee Community Hospital, Muskogee, OK	76 41	94 16	38 34	76 33	43 35	47 19	51 57	96 111	63 30	- 0	94 64	- -	70 67	- -	100 64	51 57	80 10
Muskogee Regional Medical Center, Muskogee, OK	85 150	96 281	90 234	90 330	92 293	99 167	87 161	99 397	91 117	0 1	97 240	80 113	97 240	97 98	92 233	91 161	67 92
Muskogee VA Medical Center, Muskogee, OK	87 93	99 177	94 131	93 152	98 142	100 67	97 76	100 87	92 39	- 0	97 35	- -	100 36	- -	97 33	97 76	87 39
Newman Memorial Hospital, Shattuck, OK	88 26	100 5	76 17	97 32	84 32	100 7	100 4	100 7	50 2	- 0	100 3	- 0	100 3	- 0	100 3	100 4	100 1
Norman Regional Health System, Norman, OK	97 94	100 181	96 97	96 188	98 178	99 89	95 240	100 776	94 190	93 58	97 491	94 467	99 498	97 459	94 457	99 241	90 88
Northwest Surgical Hospital, Oklahoma City, OK	- 0	- 0	- 0	- 0	- 0	- 0	100 7	100 240	100 50	- 0	98 213	100 68	100 214	100 68	93 205	100 7	100 1
O U Medical Center, Oklahoma City, OK	94 87	99 203	97 127	96 167	98 95	100 147	93 299	100 635	91 158	88 97	98 400	97 575	97 405	98 606	95 365	97 299	85 66
Okeene Municipal Hospital, Okeene, OK	54 13	60 10	92 13	77 22	94 16	17 6	- 0	100 1	- 0	- 0	100 1	- -	0 1	- -	0 1	- 0	- 0
Oklahoma Center for Orthopaedic & Multi-Sp, Oklahoma City, OK	- 0	- 0	- 0	- 0	- 0	- 0	100 6	100 233	88 51	- 0	99 208	85 268	97 208	96 232	98 208	100 6	100 99
Oklahoma City VA Medical Center, Oklahoma City, OK	95 123	96 232	95 169	91 185	98 162	100 95	99 239	100 525	100 257	99 105	97 413	- -	99 414	- -	98 403	99 239	98 53
Oklahoma Heart Hospital, Oklahoma City, OK	93 14	100 14	90 39	94 16	96 57	100 19	93 43	100 1284	96 594	99 904	100 1000	99 488	100 1027	100 488	100 910	93 44	93 377
Oklahoma Heart Hospital South, Oklahoma City, OK	- 0	100 1	- 0	100 2	100 8	100 1	- 0	100 81	95 38	91 66	99 71	100 17	100 72	100 17	95 66	- 0	83 30
Oklahoma Spine Hospital, Oklahoma City, OK	- 0	- 0	- 0	- 0	- 0	- 0	100 1	100 18	100 4	- 0	67 3	- 0	100 2	- 0	50 2	100 1	- 0
Oklahoma State University Medical Center, Tulsa, OK	86 74	98 87	97 91	99 136	95 92	99 104	99 116	100 319	88 95	100 73	98 202	77 84	96 208	91 79	97 185	99 116	84 45
Oklahoma Surgical Hospital, Tulsa, OK	- 0	- 0	- 0	- 0	- 0	- 0	98 80	100 433	100 101	- 0	99 309	97 381	99 310	97 377	96 308	98 80	88 16
Okmulgee Memorial Hospital, Okmulgee, OK	96 56	90 48	87 38	93 84	92 52	100 27	100 3	100 9	67 3	- 0	100 5	86 14	100 5	100 12	80 5	100 3	- 0
Orthopedic Hospital, Oklahoma City, OK	- 0	- 0	- 0	- 0	- 0	- 0	75 4	100 11	100 1	- 0	55 11	100 12	82 11	92 13	100 11	75 4	100 7
Pauls Valley General Hospital, Pauls Valley, OK	100 56	86 56	97 62	95 84	93 82	84 25	64 14	100 21	75 8	- 0	86 7	- 0	100 9	- 0	57 7	60 15	100 4
Pawhuska Hospital, Pawhuska, OK	50 4	- 0	0 3	100 1	0 6	100 1	- 0	- 0	- 0	- 0	- 0	- -	- 0	- -	- 0	- 0	- 0
Perry Memorial Hospital, Perry, OK	88 24	50 8	88 16	91 32	84 32	73 11	100 1	100 2	100 1	- 0	- 0	- 0	- 0	- 0	- 0	50 2	- 0
Physicians' Hospital in Anadarko, Anadarko, OK	100 7	100 5	0 3	100 7	0 12	33 3	- 0	- 0	- 0	- 0	- 0	- -	- 0	- -	- 0	- 0	- 0
Pinnacle Specialty Hospital, Tulsa, OK	- 0	- 0	- 0	- 0	- 0	- 0	- 0	- 0	- 0	- 0	- 0	- -	- 0	- -	- 0	- 0	- 0
Ponca City Medical Center, Ponca City, OK	99 87	100 97	97 62	98 119	100 95	100 59	96 154	100 313	93 59	- 0	100 231	96 78	97 231	97 76	97 226	98 154	100 66
Prague Community Hospital, Prague, OK	100 18	90 10	78 9	94 17	92 13	100 3	- 0	- 0	- 0	- 0	- 0	- -	- 0	- -	- 0	- 0	- 0
Purcell Municipal Hospital, Purcell, OK	80 51	82 28	55 44	95 83	44 63	89 27	- 0	100 2	- 0	- 0	100 2	- 0	50 2	- 0	100 2	- 0	- 0
Pushmataha County-TN of Antlers Hospital Authority, Antlers, OK	92 36	92 39	89 53	97 79	92 66	93 14	100 2	100 4	- 0	- 0	75 4	- 0	0 4	- 0	100 4	100 2	100 1
Quartz Mountain Medical Center, Mangum, OK	100 7	80 5	83 6	75 8	100 14	33 3	- 0	- 0	- 0	- 0	- 0	- -	- 0	- -	- 0	- 0	- 0
Saint Anthony Hospital, Oklahoma City, OK	94 171	97 250	99 201	97 238	98 208	99 171	95 331	100 1529	94 398	96 155	99 1258	79 380	99 1263	72 373	98 1201	97 331	92 119
Saint Francis Hospital, Tulsa, OK	89 492	95 840	94 587	91 848	98 783	100 313	91 732	100 2287	91 651	95 325	95 1875	96 467	97 1904	85 456	94 1839	97 733	88 339
Saint Francis Hospital South, Tulsa, OK	93 95	100 85	96 71	94 107	100 97	100 31	92 72	100 272	92 79	- 0	98 209	94 108	97 210	98 106	96 203	100 72	97 38
Saint John Medical Center, Tulsa, OK	85 301	96 353	75 310	90 431	71 412	95 202	86 467	100 2490	94 759	99 319	98 2125	91 454	99 2160	99 433	93 2080	88 473	87 198
Saint John Owasso, Owasso, OK	95 76	94 79	89 46	98 92	93 70	93 28	92 26	98 163	43 23	- 0	97 136	89 37	98 137	100 35	88 133	96 26	50 2
Saint John Sapulpa, Sapulpa, OK	100 57	97 75	71 41	93 72	71 49	69 26	- 0	- 0	- 0	- 0	- 0	- -	- 0	- -	- 0	- 0	- 0
Saint Mary's Regional Medical Center, Enid, OK	92 83	99 109	86 123	97 148	93 156	100 55	88 174	100 675	89 163	91 35	100 520	99 265	98 522	93 273	99 501	90 175	47 30
Sayre Memorial Hospital, Sayre, OK	97 31	93 15	84 37	93 67	90 40	78 27	- 0	- 0	- 0	- 0	- 0	- 0	- 0	- 0	- 0	- 0	- 0
Seiling Community Hospital, Seiling, OK	62 13	100 1	71 17	67 9	78 18	0 2	- 0	- 0	- 0	- 0	- 0	- -	- 0	- -	- 0	- 0	- 0
Sequoyah Memorial Hospital, Sallisaw, OK	97 61	97 63	95 43	93 100	96 55	100 43	- 0	- 0	- 0	- 0	- 0	50 2	- 0	100 1	- 0	- 0	- 0
Share Memorial Hospital, Alva, OK	91 22	100 18	96 23	100 28	97 37	67 6	33 3	75 4	- 0	- 0	100 3	- 0	100 3	- 0	100 3	33 3	- 0
Southcrest Hospital, Tulsa, OK	97 108	97 159	98 125	98 151	98 133	98 94	93 175	100 583	100 147	95 147	100 405	97 203	99 409	99 200	97 373	97 176	100 131
Southwestern Medical Center, Lawton, OK	89 74	88 68	78 73	81 108	94 88	92 51	95 106	99 240	93 44	- 0	98 172	89 87	97 173	89 81	97 169	94 107	48 21
Southwestern Regional Medical Center, Tulsa, OK	- 0	- 0	25 4	100 2	100 2	67 9	78 112	98 125	71 14	- 0	95 39	84 45	97 39	88 42	72 39	87 112	61 18
Stillwater Medical Center, Stillwater, OK	95 98	100 140	77 96	99 144	79 155	93 41	88 147	100 406	89 114	- 0	95 301	90 176	97 302	97 176	97 292	87 158	86 109
Stroud Regional Medical Center, Stroud, OK	77 26	90 20	70 23	100 26	68 28	29 7	33 3	100 4	100 1	- 0	33 3	- -	100 3	- -	100 3	33 3	- 0
Summit Medical Center, Edmond, OK	- 0	- 0	- 0	- 0	- 0	- 0	50 4	100 31	100 2	- 0	93 15	- -	100 16	- -	100 15	50 4	100 9
Surgical Hospital of Oklahoma, Oklahoma City, OK	- 0	- 0	- 0	- 0	- 0	- 0	87 15	99 179	67 21	- 0	91 151	97 207	97 151	97 208	77 151	87 15	100 26
Tahlequah City Hospital, Tahlequah, OK	95 78	90 117	88 80	100 141	93 127	93 75	90 93	100 345	92 139	91 66	100 248	97 66	100 252	97 64	93 229	88 95	86 77
Tulsa Spine & Specialty Hospital, Tulsa, OK	- 0	- 0	- 0	- 0	- 0	- 0	96 28	100 99	76 21	- 0	95 64	92 159	98 64	97 156	94 63	93 29	86 7
Unity Health Center, Shawnee, OK	100 116	100 171	100 116	99 184	100 158	100 82	98 237	100 392	96 89	- 0	99 271	82 50	99 272	95 41	98 260	98 237	99 96
USPHS Lawton Indian Hospital, Lawton, OK	100 6	89 9	64 14	57 7	100 7	25 8	50 2	100 10	- 0	- 0	0 1	- -	0 1	- -	100 1	33 3	100 1
Valley View Regional Hospital, Ada, OK	87 82	98 101	70 90	99 109	69 109	98 44	86 145	100 316	99 85	- 0	93 192	83 196	99 191	94 195	81 186	88 145	42 31
W W Hastings Indian Hospital, Tahlequah, OK	94 47	87 61	75 32	90 58	86 29	50 20	89 45	100 144	95 20	- 0	85 86	- -	91 87	- -	82 80	85 47	85 13
Wagoner Community Hospital, Wagoner, OK	96 25	100 14	81 16	86 29	88 16	100 12	- 0	- 0	- 0	- 0	- 0	- 0	- 0	- 0	- 0	- 0	- 0
Watonga Municipal Hospital, Watonga, OK	100 19	100 11	73 11	50 2	73 11	40 5	- 0	- 0	- 0	- 0	- 0	- -	- 0	- -	- 0	- 0	- 0

NOTE: The first number in each column (boldface) is the score, the second number is the number of patients; Please refer to the main entry for footnotes; (a) 100-299

*MEASURES: **Pneumonia Care:** 16. Appropriate Initial Antibiotic; 17. Blood Culture Timing; 18. Influenza Vaccine; 19. Initial Antibiotic Timing; 20. Pneumococcal Vaccine; 21. Smoking Cessation Advice; **Surgical Care Improvement Project:** 22. Appropriate VTP Within 24 Hours; 23. Appropriate Hair Removal; 24. Appropriate Beta Blocker Usage; 25. Controlled Postoperative Blood Glucose; 26. Prophylactic Antibiotic Timing; 27. Prophylactic Antibiotic Timing (Outpatient); 28. Prophylactic Antibiotic Selection; 29. Prophylactic Antibiotic Selection (Outpatient); 30. Prophylactic Antibiotic Stopped; 31. Recommended VTP Ordered; 32. Urinary Catheter Removal*

Hospital	Pneumonia Care						Surgical Care Improvement Project										
	16	17	18	19	20	21	22	23	24	25	26	27	28	29	30	31	32
Weatherford Regional Hospital, Weatherford, OK	88 43	89 19	91 45	95 73	85 67	56 18	- 0	- 0	- 0	- 0	- 0	- -	- 0	- -	- 0	- 0	- 0
Woodward Regional Hospital, Woodward, OK	88 42	97 39	87 38	98 62	92 48	100 21	94 64	96 137	62 21	- 0	87 87	83 29	100 96	92 26	94 77	95 64	67 49
SOUTH DAKOTA																	
Avera Dells Area Health Center, Dell Rapids, SD	100 11	100 1	92 13	100 11	89 18	100 1	- 0	- 0	- 0	- 0	- 0	- -	- 0	- -	- 0	- 0	- 0
Avera Desmet Memorial Hospital, De Smet, SD	86 7	100 2	100 6	100 6	71 7	0 2	- 0	- 0	- 0	- 0	- 0	- -	- 0	- -	- 0	- 0	- 0
Avera Flandreau Medical Center Hospital, Flandreau, SD	90 10	- 0	58 12	100 12	93 14	100 1	- 0	- 0	- 0	- 0	- 0	- -	- 0	- -	- 0	- 0	- 0
Avera Gregory Healthcare Center, Gregory, SD	88 41	100 1	98 49	64 28	97 71	100 6	- 0	- 0	- 0	- 0	- 0	- -	- 0	- -	- 0	- 0	- 0
Avera Hand County Memorial Hospital and Clinic, Miller, SD	71 7	- 0	100 9	100 9	77 13	- 0	- 0	- 0	- 0	- 0	- 0	- -	- 0	- -	- 0	- 0	- 0
Avera Heart Hospital of South Dakota, Sioux Falls, SD	50 2	100 5	100 7	0 1	100 12	100 3	75 12	100 440	100 218	98 360	99 382	96 295	100 383	100 295	100 380	75 12	96 114
Avera Mckennan Hospital & University Health Ctr, Sioux Falls, SD	97 94	95 94	97 157	97 167	94 179	100 86	89 148	99 377	89 121	0 1	99 222	97 316	96 222	96 314	96 211	92 149	61 77
Avera Queen of Peace, Mitchell, SD	99 76	100 61	100 71	100 110	100 120	100 26	100 80	100 195	95 61	- 0	99 126	99 75	98 126	97 75	97 119	99 81	91 11
Avera Sacred Heart Hospital, Yankton, SD	100 63	97 110	98 114	99 171	98 148	100 40	97 157	97 344	100 86	- 0	96 200	94 105	99 202	96 103	96 192	98 157	38 29
Avera St Benedict Health Center, Parkston, SD	100 4	100 3	100 6	100 13	95 22	50 2	- 0	- 0	- 0	- 0	- 0	- 0	- 0	- 0	- 0	- 0	- 0
Avera St Lukes, Aberdeen, SD	95 87	98 97	100 75	97 132	99 122	100 46	82 185	100 517	91 152	- 0	95 368	70 101	96 370	85 81	95 361	81 190	86 112
Avera Weskota Memorial Medical Center, Wessington Springs, SD	88 8	100 1	100 6	100 11	100 16	50 2	- 0	- 0	- 0	- 0	- 0	- -	- 0	- -	- 0	- 0	- 0
Black Hills Surgical Hospital, Rapid City, SD	- 0	- 0	- 0	- 0	- 0	- 0	86 21	100 257	100 44	- 0	97 237	98 504	96 238	99 502	97 237	86 21	100 89
Bowdle Hospital, Bowdle, SD	- -	- -	- -	- -	- -	- -	- -	- -	- -	- -	- 0	- 0	- 0	- 0	- -	- -	- -
Brookings Hospital, Brookings, SD	97 32	96 26	83 35	100 49	85 55	69 13	50 18	100 49	92 12	- 0	83 41	100 7	97 38	100 7	95 37	83 18	71 7
Community Memorial Hospital, Redfield, SD	100 4	100 1	100 7	100 12	89 9	100 1	- 0	- 0	- 0	- 0	- 0	- -	- 0	- -	- 0	- 0	- 0
Custer Regional Hospital, Custer, SD	100 8	100 9	100 4	100 19	94 16	100 4	- 0	- 0	- 0	- 0	- 0	- 0	- 0	- 0	- 0	- 0	- 0
Dakota Plains Surgical Center, Aberdeen, SD	- 0	- 0	- 0	- 0	- 0	- 0	100 11	100 277	97 60	- 0	100 267	100 55	100 268	100 55	91 267	100 11	100 138
Fall River Hospital, Hot Springs, SD	- 0	- 0	- 0	- 0	- 0	- 0	- 0	- 0	- 0	- 0	- 0	- 0	- 0	- 0	- 0	- 0	- 0
Holy Infant Hospital, Hoven, SD	- 0	- 0	- 0	- 0	- 0	- 0	- 0	- 0	- 0	- 0	- 0	- 0	- 0	- 0	- 0	- 0	- 0
Huron Regional Medical Center, Huron, SD	71 59	93 41	92 50	84 57	86 65	76 17	79 57	100 81	- 0	- 0	90 49	- -	96 49	- -	82 49	81 57	27 11
Landmann-Jungman Memorial Hospital, Scotland, SD	100 3	- 0	100 9	100 1	82 11	100 1	- 0	- 0	- 0	- 0	- 0	- -	- 0	- -	- 0	- 0	- 0
Lead-Deadwood Regional Hospital, Deadwood, SD	- 0	- 0	- 0	- 0	- 0	- 0	- 0	- 0	- 0	- 0	- 0	- -	- 0	- -	- 0	- 0	- 0
Lewis and Clark Specialty Hospital, Yankton, SD	- 0	- 0	- 0	- 0	- 0	- 0	97 35	100 118	96 26	- 0	100 110	100 34	98 110	41 34	90 109	97 35	67 3
Madison Community Hospital, Madison, SD	89 19	100 2	92 12	92 12	94 17	43 7	67 9	100 11	- 0	- 0	100 2	- -	100 2	- -	100 2	67 9	67 3
Milbank Area Hospital/Avera Health, Milbank, SD	100 8	- 0	83 6	100 5	91 11	- 0	- 0	- 0	- 0	- 0	- 0	- -	- 0	- -	- 0	- 0	- 0
Mobridge Regional Hospital, Mobridge, SD	100 7	100 2	100 13	100 3	93 15	100 3	- 0	0 2	50 2	- 0	- 0	- -	- 0	- -	- 0	- 0	- 0
PHS Indian Hospital at Eagle Butte, Eagle Butte, SD	50 2	- 0	0 1	100 1	100 2	- 0	- 0	- 0	- 0	- 0	- 0	- -	- 0	- -	- 0	- 0	- 0
PHS Indian Hospital at Pine Ridge, Pine Ridge, SD	67 18	70 20	62 8	83 23	93 14	0 9	- 0	100 8	100 1	- 0	40 5	- -	100 4	- -	75 4	- 0	100 1
PHS Indian Hospital at Rapid City - Sioux San, Rapid City, SD	88 8	83 6	33 3	100 6	100 3	50 6	- 0	- 0	- 0	- 0	- 0	- -	- 0	- -	- 0	- 0	- 0
PHS Indian Hospital at Rosebud, Rosebud, SD	82 11	71 17	75 20	58 40	75 16	29 14	- 0	0 1	- 0	- 0	- 0	- 0	- 0	- 0	- 0	- 0	- 0
Platte Health Center, Platte, SD	92 12	83 6	100 5	87 23	100 19	100 2	- 0	- 0	- 0	- 0	- 0	- 0	- 0	- 0	- 0	- 0	- 0
Prairie Lakes Hospital, Watertown, SD	96 141	94 127	92 107	98 176	93 193	77 35	81 130	100 383	85 122	- 0	97 284	95 107	95 291	97 104	96 275	84 131	91 101
Rapid City Regional Hospital, Rapid City, SD	91 136	96 178	96 220	95 276	95 273	100 147	92 193	98 471	89 178	95 118	96 323	94 288	100 325	95 277	91 294	94 193	63 93
Saint Marys Hospital, Pierre, SD	89 28	100 30	87 38	96 47	96 55	100 16	97 78	100 204	98 56	- 0	95 161	96 26	98 161	96 26	97 156	97 78	90 10
Same Day Surgery Center, Rapid City, SD	- 0	- 0	- 0	- 0	- 0	- 0	100 1	100 29	- 0	- 0	94 36	- 0	94 36	- 0	91 35	100 1	- 0
Sanford Mid-Dakota Hospital, Chamberlain, SD	50 6	80 5	75 8	83 12	60 5	100 6	100 1	100 1	- 0	- 0	100 1	- -	100 1	- -	100 1	100 1	- 0
Sanford Usd Medical Center, Sioux Falls, SD	87 144	97 143	94 175	93 194	95 284	97 122	93 261	100 1500	95 400	95 202	97 1181	96 646	96 1186	96 646	96 1127	96 263	92 219
Sanford Vermillion Hospital, Vermillion, SD	100 16	100 8	89 9	89 19	81 16	100 4	0 1	100 5	- 0	- 0	75 4	- -	100 5	- -	100 4	0 3	100 1
Sioux Falls Surgical Hospital, Sioux Falls, SD	- 0	- 0	- 0	- 0	- 0	- 0	100 33	100 679	93 139	- 0	99 658	99 298	100 658	98 295	99 658	100 33	100 206
Sioux Falls VA Medical Center, Sioux Falls, SD	93 28	100 33	100 16	97 38	100 32	90 10	99 104	100 184	93 84	- 0	96 132	- -	99 135	- -	98 131	99 104	95 96
Siouxland Surgery Center Lp, Dakota Dunes, SD	- 0	- 0	- 0	- 0	- 0	- 0	94 31	100 353	86 95	- 0	98 303	98 314	100 303	98 311	98 301	94 31	100 9
Spearfish Regional Hospital, Spearfish, SD	100 37	100 15	93 29	95 39	80 49	100 11	96 50	100 226	98 53	- 0	97 199	100 16	95 199	100 16	94 198	96 50	99 81
Spearfish Regional Surgery Center, Spearfish, SD	- 0	- 0	- 0	- 0	- 0	- 0	90 10	98 51	80 5	- 0	97 38	90 10	95 38	100 9	89 37	90 10	100 15
Sturgis Regional Hospital, Sturgis, SD	95 22	100 3	83 23	92 26	82 28	91 11	- 0	- 0	- 0	- 0	- 0	- 0	- 0	- 0	- 0	- 0	- 0
VA Black Hills Healthcare System - Fort Meade, Fort Meade, SD	90 48	100 44	90 29	95 62	100 47	79 19	- 0	- 0	- 0	- 0	- 0	- -	- 0	- -	- 0	- 0	- 0
Wagner Community Memorial Hospital, Wagner, SD	69 13	100 4	- 0	95 19	29 14	0 1	- 0	- 0	- 0	- 0	- 0	- 0	- 0	- 0	- 0	- 0	- 0
Winner Regional Healthcare Center, Winner, SD	33 6	25 4	86 7	82 11	77 13	50 4	0 3	100 10	- 0	- 0	100 6	- -	29 7	- -	100 6	0 3	50 2
WISCONSIN																	
Amery Regional Medical Center, Amery, WI	56 9	91 23	56 34	94 62	52 58	89 9	96 27	- 0	100 19	- 0	69 13	- -	54 13	- -	100 13	96 27	- 0
Appleton Medical Center, Appleton, WI	95 123	96 178	84 146	95 198	94 183	98 52	98 285	100 1291	89 447	88 255	96 1032	94 499	100 1048	91 500	95 999	98 285	81 170
Aspirus Wausau Hospital, Wausau, WI	95 66	95 102	93 85	97 113	96 124	98 47	93 88	100 547	95 248	95 145	99 389	96 408	99 401	95 400	97 372	98 88	91 89
Aurora Baycare Medical Center, Green Bay, WI	93 46	98 59	79 56	96 73	92 61	96 24	89 104	100 632	96 246	99 144	99 487	92 503	99 493	98 494	99 457	90 105	92 83
Aurora Lakeland Medical Center, Elkhorn, WI	99 79	99 73	95 57	99 91	99 90	100 46	83 81	100 179	92 61	- 0	98 108	84 58	96 108	92 53	96 91	85 81	94 54
Aurora Medical Center, Summit, WI	- 0	- 0	- 0	- 0	- 0	- 0	- 0	- 0	- 0	- 0	- 0	- -	- 0	- -	- 0	- 0	- 0
Aurora Medical Center - Washington County, Hartford, WI	87 38	91 55	94 33	90 59	94 51	100 12	89 47	100 266	99 83	- 0	99 204	94 117	98 204	96 111	98 201	89 47	99 98
Aurora Medical Center Kenosha, Kenosha, WI	97 103	98 129	97 86	98 118	95 103	100 51	97 115	100 374	94 90	- 0	98 252	93 294	99 252	97 286	95 244	98 115	95 110
Aurora Medical Center Manitowoc County, Two Rivers, WI	94 36	98 44	97 33	94 52	94 47	100 12	83 46	100 263	99 83	- 0	99 145	75 81	99 146	97 66	98 144	87 46	75 8
Aurora Medical Center Oshkosh, Oshkosh, WI	98 54	100 73	93 54	100 78	99 70	100 25	95 81	100 330	96 103	- 0	99 250	90 218	100 251	94 212	96 245	96 81	96 45
Aurora Memorial Hospital Burlington, Burlington, WI	95 78	98 121	100 85	100 124	100 112	100 45	98 122	100 381	100 109	- 0	99 241	82 195	98 244	88 224	100 229	99 122	99 117
Aurora Sheboygan Memorial Medical Center, Sheboygan, WI	93 41	100 55	93 59	97 77	94 96	100 31	95 132	100 589	98 177	- 0	98 468	99 342	99 468	98 340	99 453	99 132	99 245
Aurora St Lukes Medical Center, Milwaukee, WI	95 488	99 752	95 520	99 894	98 684	99 364	95 597	100 2572	97 936	97 606	99 1970	91 1058	98 1997	96 1031	97 1894	97 603	95 781
Aurora West Allis Medical Center, West Allis, WI	96 137	100 220	99 175	98 250	99 221	100 76	93 258	100 811	97 190	- 0	99 651	89 214	99 654	96 203	97 628	97 258	89 117
Baldwin Area Medical Center, Baldwin, WI	92 38	100 23	86 37	94 54	80 41	92 12	- 0	- 0	- 0	- 0	92 49	- -	100 49	- -	96 49	- 0	- 0
Bay Area Medical Center, Marinette, WI	94 80	96 114	79 89	99 132	94 129	95 41	74 101	99 278	94 95	- 0	95 171	92 115	97 172	96 110	83 161	76 102	81 21

NOTE: The first number in each column (boldface) is the score, the second number is the number of patients; Please refer to the main entry for footnotes; (a) 100-299
*MEASURES: **Pneumonia Care:** 16. Appropriate Initial Antibiotic; 17. Blood Culture Timing; 18. Influenza Vaccine; 19. Initial Antibiotic Timing; 20. Pneumococcal Vaccine; 21. Smoking Cessation Advice; **Surgical Care Improvement Project:** 22. Appropriate VTP Within 24 Hours; 23. Appropriate Hair Removal; 24. Appropriate Beta Blocker Usage; 25. Controlled Postoperative Blood Glucose; 26. Prophylactic Antibiotic Timing; 27. Prophylactic Antibiotic Timing (Outpatient); 28. Prophylactic Antibiotic Selection; 29. Prophylactic Antibiotic Selection (Outpatient); 30. Prophylactic Antibiotic Stopped; 31. Recommended VTP Ordered; 32. Urinary Catheter Removal*

Hospital	Pneumonia Care							Surgical Care Improvement Project									
	16	17	18	19	20	21	22	23	24	25	26	27	28	29	30	31	32
Beaver Dam Com Hospital, Beaver Dam, WI	**98** 59	**95** 66	**83** 41	**99** 76	**83** 66	**92** 12	**88** 112	**97** 290	**87** 90	- 0	**82** 217	**47** 78	**100** 219	**98** 40	**89** 208	**88** 112	**88** 103
Bellin Memorial Hospital, Green Bay, WI	**95** 81	**100** 104	**98** 58	**99** 103	**96** 85	**97** 35	**92** 129	**100** 771	**98** 283	**96** 245	**99** 575	**93** 755	**98** 593	**98** 722	**98** 569	**94** 129	**94** 127
Beloit Memorial Hospital, Beloit, WI	**90** 59	**94** 50	**90** 63	**95** 73	**85** 86	**100** 33	**87** 125	**98** 440	**85** 124	**92** 38	**94** 321	**86** 137	**97** 319	**94** 125	**93** 310	**92** 125	**88** 59
Berlin Memorial Hospital, Berlin, WI	**57** 23	**89** 44	**83** 24	**84** 50	**81** 42	**60** 10	**97** 39	**100** 173	- 0	- 0	**90** 145	**88** 50	**97** 147	**94** 47	**92** 145	**95** 40	**91** 54
Black River Memorial Hospital, Black River Falls, WI	**94** 31	**100** 19	**95** 20	**100** 37	**96** 26	**64** 11	- 0	**91** 56	- 0	- 0	**100** 51	**87** 23	**92** 51	**96** 23	**96** 50	- 0	**56** 18
Boscobel Area Health Care, Boscobel, WI	**71** 7	**100** 4	**60** 5	**89** 9	**9** 11	**0** 1	**62** 8	**93** 14	- 0	- 0	**89** 9	**78** 9	**100** 9	**100** 7	**56** 9	**62** 8	**75** 4
Burnett Medical Center, Grantsburg, WI	**100** 21	**93** 14	**100** 11	**94** 16	**85** 20	**100** 4	- 0	- 0	- 0	- 0	**67** 12	- -	**58** 12	- -	**100** 12	- 0	- 0
Calumet Medical Center, Chilton, WI	**100** 23	**100** 33	**100** 15	**100** 28	**100** 30	**100** 3	**100** 12	**100** 50	**100** 22	- 0	**100** 35	- 0	**100** 36	- 0	**91** 35	**100** 12	**75** 8
Columbia Center, Mequon, WI	- 0	- 0	- 0	- 0	- 0	- 0	- 0	- 0	- 0	- 0	- 0	- 0	- 0	- 0	- 0	- 0	- 0
Columbia St Mary's Hospital Ozaukee, Mequon, WI	**85** 121	**98** 180	**92** 113	**98** 196	**84** 195	**84** 43	**89** 184	**100** 553	**79** 159	**92** 131	**95** 407	**87** 124	**98** 408	**96** 114	**92** 393	**93** 184	**96** 134
Columbia St Marys Hospital Milwaukee, Milwaukee, WI	**90** 154	**96** 225	**94** 144	**97** 252	**90** 188	**88** 72	**85** 323	**100** 800	**81** 234	**93** 112	**95** 552	**89** 391	**98** 560	**91** 394	**92** 540	**93** 323	**86** 191
Columbus Community Hospital, Columbus, WI	**78** 45	**86** 43	**43** 28	**94** 32	**62** 50	**25** 4	- 0	**100** 76	- 0	- 0	- 0	- -	- 0	- -	- 0	- 0	**92** 12
Community Memorial Hospital, Menomonee Falls, WI	**95** 127	**98** 197	**89** 135	**97** 213	**89** 217	**93** 44	**88** 193	**100** 618	**80** 176	**92** 105	**91** 447	**93** 406	**96** 455	**90** 398	**95** 441	**90** 193	**76** 156
Community Memorial Hospital, Oconto Falls, WI	**82** 22	**94** 17	**83** 18	**90** 20	**95** 22	**100** 8	- 0	- 0	- 0	- 0	**89** 38	- -	**89** 38	- -	**86** 36	- 0	- 0
Cumberland Memorial Hospital, Cumberland, WI	**76** 33	**100** 4	**77** 31	**97** 39	**88** 48	**67** 6	- 0	- 0	- 0	- 0	- 0	- -	- 0	- -	- 0	- 0	- 0
Divine Savior Healthcare, Portage, WI	**95** 55	**90** 52	**88** 40	**95** 74	**72** 68	**68** 22	**94** 54	**100** 112	**79** 33	- 0	**95** 83	**94** 51	**95** 83	**98** 50	**89** 79	**94** 54	**90** 20
Door County Memorial Hospital, Sturgeon Bay, WI	**94** 49	**98** 58	**90** 42	**98** 64	**95** 61	**100** 12	**92** 48	**100** 110	**82** 28	- 0	**90** 82	- -	**99** 82	- -	**95** 78	**94** 48	**86** 36
Edgerton Hospital and Health Services, Edgerton, WI	- 0	- 0	- 0	- 0	- 0	- 0	- 0	- 0	- 0	- 0	- 0	- -	- 0	- -	- 0	- 0	- 0
Flambeau Hospital, Park Falls, WI	**82** 22	**97** 32	**94** 16	**100** 33	**97** 37	**100** 9	- 0	- 0	- 0	- 0	- 0	- -	- 0	- -	- 0	- 0	- 0
Fort Healthcare, Fort Atkinson, WI	**93** 45	**98** 65	**96** 51	**98** 82	**100** 74	**90** 20	**99** 118	**100** 322	**83** 77	- 0	**91** 213	**96** 166	**98** 214	**98** 163	**93** 205	**99** 118	**95** 19
Franciscan Skemp Arcadia, Arcadia, WI	**100** 3	**100** 1	**0** 1	**100** 3	**50** 2	- 0	- 0	- 0	- 0	- 0	**94** 18	- -	**83** 18	- -	**94** 18	- 0	- 0
Franciscan Skemp La Crosse Hospital, La Crosse, WI	**92** 80	**97** 110	**96** 120	**95** 110	**99** 160	**92** 48	**96** 327	**100** 803	**87** 255	- 0	**99** 589	**75** 176	**98** 596	**97** 153	**98** 565	**96** 327	**89** 198
Franciscan Skemp Sparta Hospital, Sparta, WI	**96** 23	**96** 26	**89** 19	**100** 26	**96** 27	**100** 4	- 0	- 0	- 0	- 0	- 0	- -	- 0	- -	- 0	- 0	- 0
Froedtert Memorial Lutheran Hospital, Milwaukee, WI	**99** 80	**94** 151	**94** 105	**96** 197	**92** 130	**75** 63	**93** 267	**100** 753	**93** 240	**84** 159	**93** 453	**91** 472	**97** 470	**94** 572	**94** 427	**95** 271	**84** 166
Good Samaritan Health Center, Merrill, WI	**100** 24	**100** 41	**100** 15	**100** 49	**100** 29	**100** 16	**100** 21	**100** 72	**100** 18	- 0	**100** 45	- 0	**100** 45	- 0	**100** 45	**100** 21	**100** 4
Grant Regional Health Center, Lancaster, WI	**94** 18	**88** 16	**87** 15	**96** 28	**56** 27	**100** 5	**100** 13	**100** 41	**100** 7	- 0	**90** 31	**57** 7	**100** 31	**100** 4	**100** 31	**87** 15	**100** 14
Gundersen Luth Medical Center, La Crosse, WI	**90** 89	**92** 121	**81** 129	**100** 131	**96** 194	**100** 69	**81** 241	**100** 1040	**85** 427	**96** 242	**94** 721	**94** 742	**96** 734	**96** 742	**97** 708	**83** 241	**89** 291
Hayward Area Memorial Hospital, Hayward, WI	**91** 23	**97** 29	**75** 20	**100** 34	**97** 29	**87** 15	**75** 4	**100** 8	**100** 2	- 0	**0** 1	- -	**0** 1	- -	**100** 1	**60** 5	**100** 2
Holy Family Memorial, Manitowoc, WI	**96** 54	**96** 78	**100** 53	**97** 73	**100** 68	**100** 19	**92** 93	**100** 426	**86** 138	- 0	**98** 304	**100** 122	**99** 308	**98** 122	**93** 294	**95** 93	**94** 103
Howard Young Medical Center, Woodruff, WI	**92** 62	**96** 72	**86** 36	**98** 82	**96** 71	**100** 21	**80** 113	**100** 392	**91** 103	- 0	**98** 281	**93** 44	**98** 285	**93** 41	**98** 275	**85** 113	**97** 114
Hudson Hospital, Hudson, WI	**88** 17	**80** 5	**93** 15	**97** 29	**89** 27	**100** 4	- 0	- 0	- 0	- 0	- 0	- -	- 0	- -	- 0	- 0	- 0
Indianhead Medical Center, Shell Lake, WI	**100** 7	- 0	**57** 7	**100** 10	**56** 9	**100** 2	- 0	- 0	- 0	- 0	- 0	- -	- 0	- -	- 0	- 0	- 0
Ladd Memorial Hosptial, Osceola, WI	**75** 4	**80** 5	**50** 10	**88** 8	**80** 10	- 0	- 0	- 0	- 0	- 0	**91** 76	- -	**99** 76	- -	**100** 76	- 0	**100** 1
Lakeview Medical Center, Rice Lake, WI	**98** 44	**100** 60	**93** 46	**100** 71	**97** 78	**100** 19	**100** 54	**100** 367	**95** 116	- 0	**99** 311	**93** 43	**99** 314	**98** 42	**99** 305	**100** 54	**98** 122
Langlade Hospital, Antigo, WI	**100** 37	**97** 33	**100** 26	**100** 42	**98** 41	**100** 11	**96** 47	**100** 94	- 0	- 0	**98** 51	- -	**98** 51	- -	**98** 49	**94** 48	**100** 6
Luther Hospital Mayo Health System, Eau Claire, WI	**95** 108	**99** 159	**98** 138	**94** 163	**98** 197	**100** 68	**99** 392	**100** 1405	**97** 561	**98** 230	**98** 943	**96** 315	**99** 967	**98** 312	**98** 877	**99** 393	**97** 319
Luther Midelfort - Chippewa Valley Mayo Health Sys, Bloomer, WI	**100** 11	**83** 12	**80** 10	**100** 12	**100** 10	**100** 7	- 0	**100** 1	- 0	- 0	- 0	- -	- 0	- -	- 0	- 0	- 0
Luther Midelfort - Northland Mayo Health System, Barron, WI	**92** 13	**88** 25	**86** 14	**100** 21	**100** 23	**75** 4	**94** 18	**100** 40	**100** 12	- 0	**87** 30	- -	**86** 28	- -	**93** 28	**94** 18	**75** 4
Luther Midelfort - Oakridge Mayo Health System, Osseo, WI	**100** 13	**100** 16	**100** 8	**100** 16	**94** 18	**100** 8	- 0	- 0	- 0	- 0	- 0	- -	- 0	- -	- 0	- 0	- 0
Madison VA Medical Center, Madison, WI	**100** 43	**98** 81	**100** 57	**100** 67	**100** 77	**100** 21	**97** 98	**100** 274	**100** 125	**100** 41	**99** 167	- -	**99** 167	- -	**100** 162	**97** 98	**92** 73
Memorial Health Center, Medford, WI	**90** 30	**98** 42	**69** 26	**100** 46	**62** 45	**100** 1	**89** 9	**100** 46	- 0	- 0	**95** 40	**100** 7	**95** 40	**100** 7	**97** 39	**89** 9	**100** 1
Memorial Hospital Lafayette County, Darlington, WI	**97** 29	**100** 6	**95** 20	**97** 39	**84** 44	**83** 6	**100** 3	**100** 34	**100** 9	- 0	**100** 29	**71** 7	**100** 30	**100** 5	**90** 29	**100** 3	- 0
Memorial Medical Center, Neillsville, WI	**89** 19	**100** 9	**90** 21	**95** 21	**87** 23	**100** 4	- 0	- 0	- 0	- 0	- 0	- -	- 0	- -	- 0	- 0	- 0
Memorial Medical Center, Ashland, WI	**93** 73	**97** 79	**79** 48	**99** 78	**82** 77	**86** 22	**77** 75	**100** 151	**87** 52	- 0	**94** 127	- -	**94** 126	- -	**79** 125	**75** 77	**100** 7
Mercy Health Sys Corp, Janesville, WI	**92** 119	**98** 185	**94** 139	**97** 185	**95** 168	**94** 84	**95** 499	**100** 1048	**94** 270	**95** 66	**98** 717	**85** 175	**97** 719	**91** 150	**89** 691	**96** 499	**90** 267
Mercy Medical Center of Oshkosh, Oshkosh, WI	**96** 49	**100** 71	**96** 75	**100** 95	**91** 111	**100** 34	**84** 150	**99** 364	**97** 108	- 0	**97** 226	**94** 286	**98** 226	**98** 290	**92** 224	**85** 150	**96** 113
Mercy Walworth Hospital & Medical Center, Lake Geneva, WI	**100** 11	**80** 10	**91** 11	**90** 10	**100** 5	**100** 5	**97** 37	**100** 113	**86** 22	- 0	**100** 99	**97** 29	**99** 99	**97** 29	**97** 99	**100** 37	**96** 50
Meriter Hospital, Madison, WI	**90** 115	**94** 166	**90** 143	**96** 192	**97** 219	**99** 72	**96** 123	**99** 544	**81** 136	**95** 115	**96** 423	**89** 256	**99** 424	**97** 251	**98** 415	**98** 123	**88** 89
Midwest Orthopedic Specialty Hospital, Franklin, WI	- 0	- 0	- 0	- 0	- 0	- 0	**100** 5	**100** 131	**84** 32	- 0	**96** 90	**91** 91	**100** 90	**100** 90	**100** 85	**100** 5	**100** 63
Mile Bluff Medical Center, Mauston, WI	**100** 3	**97** 37	**73** 49	**94** 95	**57** 70	**45** 22	**77** 35	**99** 165	**97** 29	- 0	**96** 136	**80** 50	**96** 136	**98** 40	**91** 133	**83** 35	**100** 14
Milwaukee VA Medical Center, Milwaukee, WI	**97** 69	**100** 77	**100** 67	**87** 103	**100** 67	**98** 46	**98** 172	**99** 295	**88** 113	**98** 46	**93** 208	- -	**100** 209	- -	**93** 207	**99** 172	**93** 138
Ministry Eagle River Memorial Hospital, Eagle River, WI	**40** 5	**86** 7	**82** 11	**100** 15	**93** 15	**100** 5	- 0	- 0	- 0	- 0	- 0	- 0	- 0	- 0	- 0	- 0	- 0
Ministry St Marys Hospital, Rhinelander, WI	**100** 73	**99** 88	**93** 61	**97** 100	**87** 86	**100** 30	**88** 95	**100** 460	**89** 134	- 0	**98** 364	**84** 76	**100** 365	**85** 73	**98** 358	**93** 96	**91** 35
Ministry St Michaels Hospital of Stevens Point, Stevens Point, WI	**97** 109	**98** 166	**97** 121	**98** 172	**96** 169	**97** 32	**93** 137	**100** 559	**97** 191	- 0	**100** 418	**84** 50	**99** 425	**98** 45	**98** 413	**94** 137	**97** 155
Monroe Clinic, Monroe, WI	**100** 73	**100** 133	**97** 92	**99** 121	**98** 128	**100** 32	**98** 91	**99** 321	**84** 100	- 0	**86** 222	**89** 82	**93** 214	**97** 115	**98** 203	**99** 91	**78** 41
Moundview Memorial Hospital and Clinics, Friendship, WI	**100** 6	**100** 2	**90** 10	**82** 11	**90** 10	**100** 4	- 0	- 0	- 0	- 0	- 0	**86** 7	- 0	**0** 6	- 0	- 0	- 0
New London Family Medical Center, New London, WI	**92** 25	**94** 18	**68** 19	**100** 33	**86** 36	**100** 6	- 0	- 0	- 0	- 0	- 0	- -	- 0	- -	- 0	- 0	- 0
Oak Leaf Surgcl Hospital, Eau Claire, WI	- 0	- 0	- 0	- 0	- 0	- 0	**94** 48	**100** 347	**98** 80	- 0	**100** 276	**99** 143	**98** 277	**91** 142	**94** 274	**94** 48	**99** 79
Oconomowoc Memorial Hospital, Oconomowoc, WI	**97** 59	**100** 94	**97** 63	**97** 90	**96** 93	**100** 25	**85** 96	**100** 373	**94** 72	- 0	**99** 260	**86** 114	**98** 260	**87** 109	**98** 255	**86** 96	**91** 92
Oconto Hospital & Medical Center, Oconto, WI	- 0	- 0	- 0	- 0	- 0	- 0	- 0	- 0	- 0	- 0	- 0	- -	- 0	- -	- 0	- 0	- 0
Orthopaedic Hospital of Wisconsin, Glendale, WI	- 0	- 0	- 0	- 0	- 0	- 0	**95** 19	**100** 134	**68** 25	- 0	**99** 105	**95** 130	**100** 106	**100** 130	**95** 105	**95** 19	**91** 103
Our Lady of Victory Hospital, Stanley, WI	**91** 22	**100** 23	**100** 18	**100** 30	**97** 32	**100** 2	**100** 1	**100** 1	- 0	- 0	- 0	**50** 4	- 0	**100** 2	- 0	**100** 1	- 0
Prairie Du Chien Memorial Hospital, Prairie Du Chien, WI	**90** 40	**94** 49	**75** 36	**97** 60	**91** 66	**100** 8	**100** 22	**100** 35	- 0	- 0	**76** 25	- 0	**96** 24	- 0	**100** 24	**100** 22	**90** 21
Red Cedar Medical Center-Mayo Health System, Menomonie, WI	**100** 42	**100** 37	**77** 22	**100** 51	**90** 42	**86** 7	- 0	**100** 125	- 0	- 0	**95** 94	- -	**96** 94	- -	**99** 94	- 0	**100** 34
Reedsburg Area Medical Center, Reedsburg, WI	**95** 65	**98** 40	**100** 43	**97** 67	**99** 68	**100** 21	**87** 23	**100** 86	**73** 33	- 0	**93** 76	**81** 53	**100** 76	**90** 50	**99** 74	**87** 23	**100** 8
Richland Hospital, Richland Center, WI	**94** 18	**85** 26	**81** 31	**96** 28	**68** 47	**67** 6	**75** 20	**100** 64	- 0	- 0	**87** 61	- -	**93** 61	- -	**93** 61	**75** 20	**100** 20
Ripon Medical Center, Ripon, WI	**95** 22	**100** 31	**74** 19	**100** 32	**87** 31	**100** 3	- 0	- 0	- 0	- 0	- 0	- -	- 0	- -	- 0	- 0	- 0
River Falls Area Hospital, River Falls, WI	**100** 17	**100** 10	**100** 17	**100** 22	**100** 29	**100** 5	**94** 50	**100** 182	**90** 30	- 0	**98** 133	**85** 13	**99** 133	**100** 12	**98** 128	**100** 50	**91** 11

NOTE: The first number in each column (boldface) is the score, the second number is the number of patients; Please refer to the main entry for footnotes; (a) 100-299
*MEASURES: **Pneumonia Care:** 16. Appropriate Initial Antibiotic; 17. Blood Culture Timing; 18. Influenza Vaccine; 19. Initial Antibiotic Timing; 20. Pneumococcal Vaccine; 21. Smoking Cessation Advice; **Surgical Care Improvement Project:** 22. Appropriate VTP Within 24 Hours; 23. Appropriate Hair Removal; 24. Appropriate Beta Blocker Usage; 25. Controlled Postoperative Blood Glucose; 26. Prophylactic Antibiotic Timing; 27. Prophylactic Antibiotic Timing (Outpatient); 28. Prophylactic Antibiotic Selection; 29. Prophylactic Antibiotic Selection (Outpatient); 30. Prophylactic Antibiotic Stopped; 31. Recommended VTP Ordered; 32. Urinary Catheter Removal*

Hospital	Pneumonia Care							Surgical Care Improvement Project									
	16	17	18	19	20	21	22	23	24	25	26	27	28	29	30	31	32
Riverside Medical Center, Waupaca, WI	**85** 33	**89** 71	**94** 35	**84** 70	**99** 73	**77** 13	- 0	- 0	- 0	- 0	- 0	- -	- 0	- -	- 0	- 0	- 0
Riverview Hospital Assoc, Wisconsin Rapids, WI	**91** 54	**91** 78	**93** 42	**95** 78	**94** 67	**94** 18	**93** 72	**100** 527	**95** 152	- 0	**100** 447	**93** 54	**97** 447	**96** 51	**98** 446	**94** 72	**59** 17
Rusk County Memorial Hospital, Ladysmith, WI	**83** 23	**78** 18	**81** 21	**87** 23	**90** 30	**50** 8	- 0	- 0	- 0	- 0	- 0	- -	- 0	- -	- 0	- 0	- 0
Sacred Heart Hospital, Eau Claire, WI	**89** 74	**97** 120	**97** 88	**97** 132	**97** 117	**96** 48	**88** 192	**100** 513	**87** 171	**93** 43	**96** 366	**95** 334	**93** 368	**96** 331	**89** 348	**91** 193	**83** 127
Sacred Heart Hospital, Tomahawk, WI	**100** 15	**91** 11	**100** 1	**100** 19	**100** 22	**100** 2	- 0	- 0	- 0	- 0	- 0	- 0	- 0	- 0	- 0	- 0	- 0
Saint Agnes Hospital, Fond Du Lac, WI	**98** 90	**98** 129	**99** 92	**100** 119	**97** 131	**97** 29	**96** 180	**100** 535	**97** 146	**97** 65	**99** 372	**93** 360	**98** 375	**96** 343	**93** 353	**96** 182	**95** 132
Saint Clare Hospital Health Svcs, Baraboo, WI	**97** 69	**89** 96	**84** 61	**99** 102	**93** 86	**97** 34	**90** 42	**100** 149	**100** 38	- 0	**98** 123	**93** 69	**100** 123	**97** 64	**90** 121	**90** 42	**92** 48
Saint Clare's Hospital of Weston, Weston, WI	**97** 36	**100** 63	**86** 44	**100** 76	**99** 82	**100** 23	**92** 73	**100** 804	**95** 300	**97** 144	**100** 624	**98** 119	**99** 630	**98** 117	**98** 617	**92** 73	**93** 155
Saint Croix Regional Medical Center, Saint Croix Falls, WI	**94** 48	**92** 60	**70** 40	**96** 68	**70** 69	**57** 14	- 0	- 0	- 0	- 0	**89** 80	- -	**96** 80	- -	**97** 79	- 0	- 0
Saint Elizabeth Hospital, Appleton, WI	**97** 95	**99** 158	**96** 123	**98** 153	**97** 173	**100** 49	**87** 143	**100** 557	**96** 199	**91** 151	**99** 409	**96** 482	**100** 412	**97** 476	**94** 391	**90** 143	**92** 146
Saint Josephs Community Health Services, Hillsboro, WI	**79** 14	**75** 4	**100** 10	**87** 15	**75** 12	**75** 4	**100** 3	**100** 5	**100** 3	- 0	**75** 4	**100** 3	**100** 4	**100** 3	**100** 4	**100** 3	**100** 4
Saint Josephs Community Hospital West Bend, West Bend, WI	**89** 81	**96** 126	**87** 93	**99** 119	**93** 125	**100** 29	**85** 109	**96** 340	**86** 63	- 0	**96** 237	**85** 89	**92** 236	**90** 78	**94** 228	**85** 110	**81** 63
Saint Josephs Hospital, Chippewa Falls, WI	**91** 45	**98** 51	**98** 40	**97** 61	**93** 61	**100** 17	**98** 58	**100** 233	**92** 65	- 0	**100** 192	**98** 43	**97** 192	**100** 43	**98** 191	**98** 58	**95** 42
Saint Josephs Hospital, Marshfield, WI	**93** 103	**86** 72	**94** 143	**98** 144	**97** 206	**99** 69	**97** 646	**100** 1932	**95** 634	**90** 323	**97** 1163	**93** 439	**97** 1190	**97** 437	**89** 1152	**98** 647	**75** 387
Saint Mary's Hospital, Madison, WI	**98** 165	**97** 254	**97** 274	**99** 287	**99** 381	**100** 111	**95** 405	**99** 1819	**94** 578	**92** 316	**98** 1460	**95** 639	**99** 1469	**99** 636	**95** 1409	**96** 405	**94** 556
Saint Marys Hospital Medical Center, Green Bay, WI	**94** 66	**96** 114	**94** 54	**99** 110	**93** 88	**100** 38	**90** 167	**99** 543	**96** 157	- 0	**97** 416	**90** 253	**100** 416	**96** 244	**98** 412	**90** 167	**95** 223
Saint Marys Hospital Superior, Superior, WI	**78** 9	**100** 3	**71** 7	**85** 13	**100** 13	**100** 2	- 0	- 0	- 0	- 0	- 0	**67** 3	- 0	**100** 2	- 0	- 0	- 0
Saint Nicholas Hospital, Sheboygan, WI	**95** 76	**99** 92	**94** 80	**95** 94	**92** 97	**87** 38	**96** 126	**100** 409	**85** 100	- 0	**93** 281	**80** 87	**99** 280	**91** 85	**96** 261	**98** 126	**89** 102
Saint Vincent Hospital, Green Bay, WI	**90** 69	**98** 115	**92** 88	**96** 121	**94** 111	**95** 40	**91** 160	**100** 692	**86** 300	**97** 156	**98** 487	**96** 338	**97** 501	**97** 332	**93** 446	**95** 160	**73** 73
Sauk Prairie Memorial Hospital, Prairie Du Sac, WI	**93** 27	**92** 12	**100** 18	**86** 21	**96** 27	**100** 13	**88** 77	**100** 749	**100** 183	- 0	**99** 678	**100** 67	**99** 689	**91** 67	**97** 674	**90** 77	**99** 240
Shawano Medical Center, Shawano, WI	**91** 65	**99** 77	**82** 50	**100** 83	**83** 75	**100** 30	**97** 31	**100** 70	**84** 19	- 0	**98** 41	**100** 11	**100** 41	**100** 11	**95** 39	**97** 31	**100** 3
Southwest Health Center, Platteville, WI	**84** 45	**95** 38	**85** 33	**95** 58	**94** 50	**100** 7	- 0	**100** 53	- 0	- 0	**86** 50	**84** 50	**100** 49	**98** 47	**96** 48	- 0	- 0
Spooner Health System, Spooner, WI	**80** 20	**82** 17	**100** 10	**100** 15	**100** 22	**100** 6	- 0	- 0	- 0	- 0	- 0	- 0	- 0	- 0	- 0	- 0	- 0
Stoughton Hospital, Stoughton, WI	**96** 26	**100** 49	**100** 32	**98** 45	**97** 60	**88** 8	**92** 25	**100** 67	- 0	- 0	**100** 47	- -	**100** 48	- -	**91** 47	**96** 25	**100** 6
Theda Clark Medical Center, Neenah, WI	**89** 56	**98** 64	**90** 51	**100** 74	**94** 71	**100** 30	**92** 123	**100** 494	**94** 139	- 0	**98** 331	**96** 655	**98** 332	**98** 656	**96** 319	**94** 125	**98** 135
Tomah Memorial Hospital, Tomah, WI	**88** 24	**100** 35	**100** 27	**93** 29	**98** 44	**100** 12	- 0	**100** 3	- 0	- 0	- 0	- -	- 0	- -	- 0	- 0	- 0
Tomah VA Medical Center, Tomah, WI	- 0	- 0	- 0	- 0	- 0	- 0	- 0	- 0	- 0	- 0	- 0	- -	- 0	- -	- 0	- 0	- 0
Tri County Memorial Hospital, Whitehall, WI	**73** 22	**97** 30	**38** 24	**97** 31	**61** 36	**83** 6	- 0	- 0	- 0	- 0	- 0	- -	- 0	- -	- 0	- 0	- 0
United Hospital System, Kenosha, WI	**93** 102	**90** 165	**98** 103	**93** 175	**97** 125	**99** 82	**95** 213	**99** 598	**82** 151	**82** 94	**90** 408	**73** 188	**95** 419	**91** 265	**94** 394	**95** 213	**91** 163
University of Wisconsin Hospitals & Clinics Authority, Madison, WI	**89** 37	**96** 83	**97** 74	**97** 78	**96** 80	**100** 37	**98** 220	**99** 647	**100** 231	**84** 133	**94** 408	**82** 266	**96** 420	**97** 488	**97** 383	**98** 220	**90** 168
Upland Hills Health, Dodgeville, WI	**62** 8	**91** 46	**91** 32	**93** 43	**86** 43	**80** 5	- 0	**97** 37	- 0	- 0	**80** 15	- -	**80** 15	- -	**93** 15	- 0	**67** 3
Vernon Memorial Hospital, Viroqua, WI	**79** 63	**94** 16	**100** 45	**100** 66	**100** 78	**92** 13	**100** 64	**100** 556	**89** 208	- 0	**89** 492	**100** 5	**100** 492	**100** 5	**94** 481	**100** 64	**87** 79
Watertown Regional Medical Center, Watertown, WI	**98** 56	**99** 95	**96** 48	**98** 101	**99** 88	**94** 18	**87** 76	**99** 221	**82** 76	- 0	**99** 158	**87** 191	**98** 160	**93** 216	**91** 151	**87** 77	**94** 67
Waukesha Memorial Hospital, Waukesha, WI	**98** 83	**99** 158	**97** 97	**99** 148	**99** 146	**100** 36	**93** 173	**99** 616	**85** 226	**93** 153	**98** 447	**86** 523	**95** 455	**89** 538	**97** 439	**94** 173	**97** 185
Waupun Memorial Hospital, Waupun, WI	**97** 32	**97** 33	**100** 29	**100** 44	**100** 47	**100** 8	**96** 23	**100** 84	**100** 23	- 0	**95** 66	- -	**100** 67	- -	**97** 66	**100** 23	**100** 21
Westfields Hospital, New Richmond, WI	**89** 28	**100** 6	**61** 23	**95** 20	**67** 36	**100** 5	- 0	- 0	- 0	- 0	- 0	- -	- 0	- -	- 0	- 0	- 0
Wheaton Franciscan - St Joseph, Milwaukee, WI	**100** 138	**98** 291	**92** 130	**99** 276	**94** 176	**95** 162	**95** 303	**100** 787	**97** 220	**99** 159	**98** 452	**94** 561	**100** 455	**99** 551	**97** 413	**98** 303	**80** 103
Wheaton Franciscan Healthcare - All Saints, Racine, WI	**98** 129	**99** 343	**100** 203	**99** 285	**99** 302	**94** 105	**99** 208	**100** 628	**96** 185	**86** 71	**97** 376	**93** 400	**98** 386	**97** 494	**96** 350	**100** 208	**100** 66
Wheaton Franciscan Healthcare-Elmbrook Mem, Brookfield, WI	**97** 65	**100** 91	**93** 68	**97** 92	**95** 93	**94** 18	**89** 154	**99** 393	**85** 95	- 0	**96** 256	**86** 263	**98** 261	**94** 300	**96** 248	**89** 155	**86** 100
Wheaton Franciscan Healthcare - Franklin, Franklin, WI	**96** 27	**97** 35	**92** 24	**100** 29	**93** 29	**100** 9	**20** 5	**100** 16	**100** 2	- 0	**78** 9	**96** 26	**100** 10	**100** 25	**100** 9	**40** 5	**50** 2
Wheaton Franciscan Healthcare - St Francis, Milwaukee, WI	**97** 99	**97** 170	**93** 123	**98** 160	**95** 174	**92** 62	**84** 147	**100** 503	**93** 129	**85** 59	**95** 327	**93** 288	**98** 329	**97** 281	**94** 301	**92** 147	**80** 49
Wild Rose Com Memorial Hospital, Wild Rose, WI	**89** 19	**88** 24	**91** 11	**92** 24	**89** 19	**100** 8	- 0	- 0	- 0	- 0	- 0	- -	- 0	- -	- 0	- 0	- 0

NOTE: The first number in each column (boldface) is the score, the second number is the number of patients; Please refer to the main entry for footnotes; (a) 100-299
*MEASURES: **Pneumonia Care:** 16. Appropriate Initial Antibiotic; 17. Blood Culture Timing; 18. Influenza Vaccine; 19. Initial Antibiotic Timing; 20. Pneumococcal Vaccine; 21. Smoking Cessation Advice; **Surgical Care Improvement Project:** 22. Appropriate VTP Within 24 Hours; 23. Appropriate Hair Removal; 24. Appropriate Beta Blocker Usage; 25. Controlled Postoperative Blood Glucose; 26. Prophylactic Antibiotic Timing; 27. Prophylactic Antibiotic Timing (Outpatient); 28. Prophylactic Antibiotic Selection; 29. Prophylactic Antibiotic Selection (Outpatient); 30. Prophylactic Antibiotic Stopped; 31. Recommended VTP Ordered; 32. Urinary Catheter Removal*

Hospital	Children's Asthma Care			Use of Medical Imaging				Survey of Patients' Hospital Experiences									
	33	34	35	36	37	38	39	40	41	42	43	44	45	46	47	48	49
ILLINOIS																	
Abraham Lincoln Memorial Hospital, Lincoln, IL	- -	- -	- -	**0.102** 459	**0.025** 315	**7.7** 427	**47.8** 90	**64** (a)	**91** (a)	**89** (a)	**73** (a)	**66** (a)	**81** (a)	**76** (a)	**79** (a)	**72** (a)	**78** (a)
Adventist Bolingbrook Hospital, Bolingbrook, IL	- -	- -	- -	**0.101** 159	**0.095** 63	**11.8** 187	**35.3** 34	**66** 300+	**75** 300+	**82** 300+	**63** 300+	**53** 300+	**66** 300+	**63** 300+	**70** 300+	**55** 300+	**65** 300+
Adventist Glenoaks, Glendale Heights, IL	- -	- -	- -	**0.081** 124	**0.053** 57	**8.1** 111	**40.0** 20	**51** 300+	**73** 300+	**80** 300+	**51** 300+	**54** 300+	**64** 300+	**61** 300+	**65** 300+	**55** 300+	**56** 300+
Adventist La Grange Memorial Hospital, La Grange, IL	- -	- -	- -	**0.093** 873	**0.007** 703	**12.3** 1600	**32.2** 143	**62** 300+	**78** 300+	**85** 300+	**66** 300+	**54** 300+	**70** 300+	**66** 300+	**70** 300+	**57** 300+	**70** 300+
Advocate Christ Hospital & Medical Center, Oak Lawn, IL	- -	- -	- -	**0.087** 1349	**0.038** 1483	**7.8** 2229	**37.6** 117	**49** 300+	**77** 300+	**84** 300+	**66** 300+	**60** 300+	**79** 300+	**72** 300+	**67** 300+	**64** 300+	**68** 300+
Advocate Condell Medical Center, Libertyville, IL	- -	- -	- -	**0.397** 1271	**0.338** 932	**14.5** 1460	**35.0** 197	**45** 300+	**74** 300+	**76** 300+	**58** 300+	**54** 300+	**70** 300+	**65** 300+	**69** 300+	**55** 300+	**62** 300+
Advocate Eureka Hospital, Eureka, IL	- -	- -	- -	**0.806** 124	**0.684** 95	**4.5** 222	**41.9** 31	- -	- -	- -	- -	- -	- -	- -	- -	- -	- -
Advocate Good Samaritan Hospital, Downers Grove, IL	- -	- -	- -	**0.156** 1183	**0.073** 1155	**11.6** 2270	**32.7** 156	**50** 300+	**80** 300+	**83** 300+	**71** 300+	**62** 300+	**78** 300+	**70** 300+	**71** 300+	**64** 300+	**77** 300+
Advocate Good Shepherd Hospital, Barrington, IL	- -	- -	- -	**0.125** 999	**0.020** 909	**9.0** 1483	**34.6** 104	**44** 300+	**78** 300+	**83** 300+	**66** 300+	**60** 300+	**77** 300+	**69** 300+	**72** 300+	**59** 300+	**72** 300+
Advocate Illinois Masonic Medical Center, Chicago, IL	- -	- -	- -	**0.122** 641	**0.034** 528	**7.8** 982	**39.2** 143	**49** 300+	**77** 300+	**80** 300+	**65** 300+	**61** 300+	**75** 300+	**69** 300+	**70** 300+	**62** 300+	**69** 300+
Advocate Lutheran General Hospital, Park Ridge, IL	- -	- -	- -	**0.058** 2202	**0.036** 1767	**6.2** 3625	**31.2** 247	**54** 300+	**78** 300+	**85** 300+	**72** 300+	**61** 300+	**76** 300+	**70** 300+	**73** 300+	**60** 300+	**76** 300+
Advocate South Suburban Hospital, Hazel Crest, IL	- -	- -	- -	**0.094** 732	**0.052** 497	**9.7** 1087	**34.7** 95	**52** 300+	**78** 300+	**79** 300+	**61** 300+	**59** 300+	**75** 300+	**68** 300+	**66** 300+	**59** 300+	**63** 300+
Advocate Trinity Hospital, Chicago, IL	- -	- -	- -	**0.049** 389	**0.053** 246	**12.7** 880	**36.5** 63	**58** 300+	**74** 300+	**69** 300+	**54** 300+	**56** 300+	**73** 300+	**68** 300+	**67** 300+	**56** 300+	**52** 300+
Alexian Brothers Medical Center, Elk Grove Village, IL	- -	- -	- -	**0.520** 1701	**0.019** 1477	**7.3** 2615	**31.1** 235	**53** 300+	**80** 300+	**83** 300+	**71** 300+	**61** 300+	**79** 300+	**69** 300+	**77** 300+	**63** 300+	**77** 300+
Alton Memorial Hospital, Alton, IL	- -	- -	- -	**0.114** 888	**0.018** 509	**2.0** 1181	**33.3** 3	**60** 300+	**84** 300+	**84** 300+	**71** 300+	**58** 300+	**80** 300+	**72** 300+	**73** 300+	**61** 300+	**78** 300+
Anderson Hospital, Maryville, IL	- -	- -	- -	**0.197** 656	**0.016** 793	**12.2** 755	**30.9** 139	**51** 300+	**80** 300+	**81** 300+	**61** 300+	**55** 300+	**73** 300+	**67** 300+	**72** 300+	**60** 300+	**69** 300+
Blessing Hospital, Quincy, IL	- -	- -	- -	**0.061** 526	**0.002** 426	**7.1** 1554	**28.9** 121	**45** 300+	**78** 300+	**86** 300+	**65** 300+	**60** 300+	**79** 300+	**70** 300+	**73** 300+	**62** 300+	**64** 300+
Bromenn Healthcare, Normal, IL	- -	- -	- -	**0.682** 446	**0.476** 590	**4.8** 1164	**35.0** 120	**58** 300+	**81** 300+	**88** 300+	**74** 300+	**56** 300+	**79** 300+	**74** 300+	**71** 300+	**60** 300+	**78** 300+
Carle Foundation Hospital, Urbana, IL	- -	- -	- -	**0.009** 233	**0.000** 171	- 0	**0.0** 4	**50** 300+	**81** 300+	**83** 300+	**75** 300+	**63** 300+	**80** 300+	**70** 300+	**66** 300+	**64** 300+	**80** 300+
Carlinville Area Hospital, Carlinville, IL	- -	- -	- -	- -	- -	- -	- -	**57** (a)	**85** (a)	**87** (a)	**76** (a)	**68** (a)	**85** (a)	**83** (a)	**89** (a)	**71** (a)	**73** (a)
Centegra Health System - McHenry Hospital, Mchenry, IL	- -	- -	- -	**0.699** 933	**0.046** 659	**5.2** 1336	**31.7** 249	**41** 300+	**77** 300+	**86** 300+	**65** 300+	**60** 300+	**77** 300+	**70** 300+	**76** 300+	**65** 300+	**68** 300+
Centegra Health System - Woodstock Hospital, Woodstock, IL	- -	- -	- -	**0.711** 523	**0.025** 317	**3.4** 860	**28.9** 121	**45** 300+	**78** 300+	**87** 300+	**64** 300+	**59** 300+	**76** 300+	**70** 300+	**79** 300+	**65** 300+	**68** 300+
Central Dupage Hospital, Winfield, IL	- -	- -	- -	**0.324** 1480	**0.017** 1469	**4.4** 2668	**34.5** 220	**51** 300+	**80** 300+	**89** 300+	**79** 300+	**60** 300+	**81** 300+	**73** 300+	**70** 300+	**65** 300+	**81** 300+
CGH Medical Center, Sterling, IL	- -	- -	- -	**0.337** 600	**0.341** 384	**10.1** 503	**32.1** 137	**55** 300+	**80** 300+	**84** 300+	**66** 300+	**63** 300+	**74** 300+	**71** 300+	**78** 300+	**69** 300+	**66** 300+
Clay County Hospital, Flora, IL	- -	- -	- -	**0.567** 263	**0.032** 218	**6.5** 385	**33.3** 12	- -	- -	- -	- -	- -	- -	- -	- -	- -	- -
Community Memorial Hospital, Staunton, IL	- -	- -	- -	- -	- -	- -	- -	- -	- -	- -	- -	- -	- -	- -	- -	- -	- -
Copley Memorial Hospital, Aurora, IL	- -	- -	- -	**0.066** 785	**0.025** 487	**7.3** 725	**34.7** 95	**52** 300+	**79** 300+	**82** 300+	**67** 300+	**60** 300+	**74** 300+	**69** 300+	**65** 300+	**56** 300+	**73** 300+
Crawford Memorial Hospital, Robinson, IL	- -	- -	- -	- -	- -	- -	- -	**56** (a)	**86** (a)	**89** (a)	**64** (a)	**69** (a)	**82** (a)	**74** (a)	**79** (a)	**74** (a)	**60** (a)
Crossroads Community Hospital, Mount Vernon, IL	- -	- -	- -	**0.413** 208	**0.375** 96	**7.9** 453	**38.5** 26	**52** 300+	**82** 300+	**84** 300+	**63** 300+	**57** 300+	**74** 300+	**69** 300+	**71** 300+	**57** 300+	**62** 300+
Decatur Memorial Hospital, Decatur, IL	- -	- -	- -	**0.045** 2382	**0.006** 1876	**9.2** 3058	**38.3** 626	**56** 300+	**78** 300+	**86** 300+	**67** 300+	**56** 300+	**74** 300+	**66** 300+	**65** 300+	**58** 300+	**73** 300+
Delnor Community Hospital, Geneva, IL	- -	- -	- -	**0.561** 974	**0.357** 770	**12.4** 1093	**30.7** 140	**64** 300+	**81** 300+	**86** 300+	**75** 300+	**63** 300+	**80** 300+	**71** 300+	**75** 300+	**64** 300+	**77** 300+
Dr John Warner Hospital, Clinton, IL	- -	- -	- -	- -	- -	- -	- -	- -	- -	- -	- -	- -	- -	- -	- -	- -	- -
Edward Hospital, Naperville, IL	- -	- -	- -	**0.715** 1754	**0.698** 1439	**11.4** 2536	**32.8** 341	**62** 300+	**82** 300+	**84** 300+	**74** 300+	**62** 300+	**78** 300+	**72** 300+	**68** 300+	**60** 300+	**81** 300+
Elmhurst Memorial Hospital, Elmhurst, IL	- -	- -	- -	**0.155** 1591	**0.041** 1321	**13.0** 2231	**32.9** 471	**49** 300+	**81** 300+	**83** 300+	**63** 300+	**60** 300+	**75** 300+	**68** 300+	**62** 300+	**57** 300+	**68** 300+
Evanston Hospital, Evanston, IL	- -	- -	- -	**0.236** 5038	**0.040** 5565	**4.4** 9551	**31.1** 1226	**57** 300+	**77** 300+	**81** 300+	**70** 300+	**56** 300+	**74** 300+	**67** 300+	**69** 300+	**56** 300+	**76** 300+
Fairfield Memorial Hospital, Fairfield, IL	- -	- -	- -	**0.533** 390	**0.042** 238	**0.5** 365	**45.7** 35	- -	- -	- -	- -	- -	- -	- -	- -	- -	- -
Fayette County Hospital, Vandalia, IL	- -	- -	- -	- -	- -	- -	- -	- -	- -	- -	- -	- -	- -	- -	- -	- -	- -
Ferrell Hospital Community Foundations, Eldorado, IL	- -	- -	- -	- -	- -	- -	- -	- -	- -	- -	- -	- -	- -	- -	- -	- -	- -
Fhn Memorial Hospital, Freeport, IL	- -	- -	- -	**0.073** 508	**0.003** 353	**5.8** 1016	**33.6** 143	**54** 300+	**76** 300+	**80** 300+	**61** 300+	**61** 300+	**76** 300+	**65** 300+	**69** 300+	**59** 300+	**55** 300+
Galesburg Cottage Hospital, Galesburg, IL	- -	- -	- -	**0.704** 247	**0.677** 229	**4.8** 705	**38.1** 84	**56** 300+	**84** 300+	**85** 300+	**62** 300+	**59** 300+	**73** 300+	**66** 300+	**66** 300+	**58** 300+	**61** 300+
Gateway Regional Medical Center, Granite City, IL	- -	- -	- -	**0.217** 309	**0.029** 205	**6.5** 525	**24.5** 98	**54** 300+	**79** 300+	**77** 300+	**56** 300+	**57** 300+	**72** 300+	**62** 300+	**62** 300+	**54** 300+	**53** 300+
Genesis Medical Center Illini Campus, Silvis, IL	- -	- -	- -	**0.044** 362	**0.100** 261	**10.3** 847	**25.4** 71	**54** 300+	**80** 300+	**84** 300+	**72** 300+	**59** 300+	**77** 300+	**71** 300+	**70** 300+	**63** 300+	**75** 300+
Gibson Community Hospital, Gibson City, IL	- -	- -	- -	- -	- -	- -	- -	**65** 300+	**86** 300+	**91** 300+	**83** 300+	**68** 300+	**82** 300+	**77** 300+	**78** 300+	**75** 300+	**81** 300+
Good Samaritan Regional Health Center, Mount Vernon, IL	- -	- -	- -	**0.612** 737	**0.187** 422	**6.5** 910	**41.8** 122	**50** 300+	**78** 300+	**86** 300+	**67** 300+	**63** 300+	**80** 300+	**73** 300+	**75** 300+	**68** 300+	**72** 300+
Graham Hospital Association, Canton, IL	- -	- -	- -	**0.719** 366	**0.732** 246	**1.6** 500	**50.5** 95	**49** 300+	**84** 300+	**83** 300+	**67** 300+	**60** 300+	**79** 300+	**68** 300+	**74** 300+	**67** 300+	**61** 300+
Greenville Regional Hospital, Greenville, IL	- -	- -	- -	**0.773** 375	**0.679** 243	- 0	**44.8** 29	**60** (a)	**74** (a)	**83** (a)	**62** (a)	**53** (a)	**77** (a)	**69** (a)	**70** (a)	**62** (a)	**62** (a)
Hamilton Memorial Hospital District, Mcleansboro, IL	- -	- -	- -	- -	- -	- -	- -	- -	- -	- -	- -	- -	- -	- -	- -	- -	- -
Hammond Henry Hospital, Geneseo, IL	- -	- -	- -	- -	- -	- -	- -	**60** 300+	**87** 300+	**83** 300+	**78** 300+	**71** 300+	**84** 300+	**75** 300+	**78** 300+	**77** 300+	**77** 300+
Hardin County General Hospital, Rosiclare, IL	- -	- -	- -	**0.318** 85	**0.743** 35	**6.8** 88	**31.8** 22	- -	- -	- -	- -	- -	- -	- -	- -	- -	- -
Harrisburg Medical Center, Harrisburg, IL	- -	- -	- -	**0.526** 390	**0.654** 301	**5.3** 695	- 0	**55** 300+	**80** 300+	**78** 300+	**65** 300+	**57** 300+	**76** 300+	**68** 300+	**71** 300+	**64** 300+	**61** 300+
Heartland Regional Medical Center, Marion, IL	- -	- -	- -	**0.095** 518	**0.021** 282	**8.0** 425	**26.3** 80	**52** 300+	**75** 300+	**80** 300+	**55** 300+	**52** 300+	**68** 300+	**63** 300+	**66** 300+	**56** 300+	**52** 300+
Herrin Hospital, Herrin, IL	- -	- -	- -	**0.107** 1080	**0.074** 679	**6.4** 1111	**43.7** 167	**48** 300+	**85** 300+	**87** 300+	**72** 300+	**64** 300+	**78** 300+	**70** 300+	**76** 300+	**65** 300+	**78** 300+
Hillsboro Area Hospital, Hillsboro, IL	- -	- -	- -	- -	- -	- -	- -	**53** (a)	**78** (a)	**81** (a)	**70** (a)	**65** (a)	**81** (a)	**72** (a)	**73** (a)	**70** (a)	**64** (a)
Hines VA Medical Center, Hines, IL	- -	- -	- -	- -	- -	- -	- -	- -	- -	- -	- -	- -	- -	- -	- -	- -	- -
Hinsdale Hospital, Hinsdale, IL	- -	- -	- -	**0.241** 909	**0.011** 704	**10.6** 3031	**27.7** 137	**49** 300+	**76** 300+	**83** 300+	**65** 300+	**54** 300+	**70** 300+	**66** 300+	**73** 300+	**58** 300+	**68** 300+
Holy Cross Hospital, Chicago, IL	- -	- -	- -	**0.016** 306	**0.000** 218	**1.9** 526	**31.0** 42	**49** 300+	**68** 300+	**70** 300+	**45** 300+	**47** 300+	**63** 300+	**55** 300+	**61** 300+	**46** 300+	**43** 300+
Hoopeston Community Memorial Hospital, Hoopeston, IL	- -	- -	- -	- -	- -	- -	- -	- -	- -	- -	- -	- -	- -	- -	- -	- -	- -
Hopedale Medical Complex, Hopedale, IL	- -	- -	- -	- -	- -	- -	- -	- -	- -	- -	- -	- -	- -	- -	- -	- -	- -
Illini Community Hospital, Pittsfield, IL	- -	- -	- -	**0.080** 188	**0.013** 153	**6.7** 330	**32.0** 25	**64** (a)	**85** (a)	**87** (a)	**77** (a)	**69** (a)	**85** (a)	**76** (a)	**84** (a)	**79** (a)	**69** (a)
Illinois Valley Community Hospital, Peru, IL	- -	- -	- -	**0.126** 405	**0.011** 285	**5.9** 746	**31.8** 179	**58** 300+	**88** 300+	**88** 300+	**75** 300+	**72** 300+	**86** 300+	**76** 300+	**83** 300+	**79** 300+	**77** 300+
Ingalls Memorial Hospital, Harvey, IL	- -	- -	- -	**0.082** 1471	**0.014** 1451	**8.6** 2589	**33.7** 323	**51** 300+	**75** 300+	**76** 300+	**61** 300+	**53** 300+	**69** 300+	**66** 300+	**62** 300+	**51** 300+	**65** 300+
Iroquois Memorial Hospital, Watseka, IL	- -	- -	- -	**0.495** 218	**0.393** 122	**11.7** 409	**48.5** 33	**54** 300+	**78** 300+	**83** 300+	**65** 300+	**61** 300+	**78** 300+	**72** 300+	**79** 300+	**72** 300+	**60** 300+
Jackson Park Hospital, Chicago, IL	- -	- -	- -	**0.075** 53	**0.000** 44	**7.1** 99	- 0	**48** 300+	**68** 300+	**61** 300+	**31** 300+	**45** 300+	**54** 300+	**49** 300+	**56** 300+	**38** 300+	**30** 300+
Jersey Community Hospital, Jerseyville, IL	- -	- -	- -	**0.527** 256	**0.078** 90	**9.2** 346	**33.3** 51	**63** 300+	**81** 300+	**79** 300+	**68** 300+	**62** 300+	**79** 300+	**72** 300+	**80** 300+	**76** 300+	**62** 300+
Jesse Brown VA Medical Ctr-VA Chicago Healthcare, Chicago, IL	- -	- -	- -	- -	- -	- -	- -	- -	- -	- -	- -	- -	- -	- -	- -	- -	- -
John & Mary Kirby Hospital, Monticello, IL	- -	- -	- -	- -	- -	- -	- -	- -	- -	- -	- -	- -	- -	- -	- -	- -	- -

NOTE: The first number in each column (boldface) is the score, the second number is the number of patients; Please refer to the main entry for footnotes; (a) 100-299
*MEASURES: **Children's Asthma Care:** 33. Received Systemic Corticosteroids; 34. Received Home Management Plan of Care; 35. Received Reliever Medication; **Use of Medical Imaging:** 36. Combination Abdominal CT Scan; 37. Combination Chest CT Scan; 38. Follow-up Mammogram/Ultrasound; 39. MRI for Low Back Pain; **Survey of Patients' Hospital Experiences:** 40. Area Around Room 'Always' Quiet at Night; 41. Doctors 'Always' Communicated Well; 42. Home Recovery Information Given; 43. Hospital Given 9 or 10 on 10 Point Scale; 44. Meds 'Always' Explained Before Given; 45. Nurses 'Always' Communicated Well; 46. Pain 'Always' Well Controlled; 47. Room and Bathroom 'Always' Clean; 48. Timely Help 'Always' Received; 49. Would Definitely Recommend Hospital*

Hospital	Children's Asthma Care			Use of Medical Imaging				Survey of Patients' Hospital Experiences									
	33	34	35	36	37	38	39	40	41	42	43	44	45	46	47	48	49
John H Stroger Jr Hospital, Chicago, IL	- -	- -	- -	0.631 740	0.013 78	- 0	38.2 34	55 300+	79 300+	74 300+	52 300+	52 300+	62 300+	63 300+	52 300+	50 300+	61 300+
Katherine Shaw Bethea Hospital, Dixon, IL	- -	- -	- -	0.592 326	0.538 195	15.1 819	28.2 117	55 300+	83 300+	86 300+	73 300+	62 300+	82 300+	75 300+	75 300+	73 300+	77 300+
Kewanee Hospital, Kewanee, IL	- -	- -	- -	- -	- -	- -	- -	74 (a)	84 (a)	82 (a)	62 (a)	66 (a)	75 (a)	70 (a)	84 (a)	57 (a)	56 (a)
Kishwaukee Community Hospital, Dekalb, IL	- -	- -	- -	0.046 457	0.013 311	7.9 508	37.5 40	55 300+	81 300+	81 300+	67 300+	57 300+	75 300+	69 300+	76 300+	58 300+	69 300+
Lake Forest Hospital, Lake Forest, IL	- -	- -	- -	0.739 983	0.682 737	14.9 2527	29.6 233	52 300+	81 300+	83 300+	73 300+	58 300+	75 300+	69 300+	73 300+	59 300+	76 300+
Lawrence County Memorial Hospital, Lawrenceville, IL	- -	- -	- -	- -	- -	- -	- -	- -	- -	- -	- -	- -	- -	- -	- -	- -	- -
Little Company of Mary Hospital, Evergreen Park, IL	- -	- -	- -	0.125 977	0.023 887	11.9 1729	32.0 103	51 300+	79 300+	79 300+	65 300+	55 300+	75 300+	69 300+	65 300+	60 300+	67 300+
Loretto Hospital, Chicago, IL	- -	- -	- -	0.022 46	0.000 25	8.6 58	- 0	48 (a)	69 (a)	58 (a)	41 (a)	41 (a)	59 (a)	50 (a)	57 (a)	39 (a)	39 (a)
Louis A Weiss Memorial Hospital, Chicago, IL	- -	- -	- -	0.109 549	0.008 475	6.3 571	27.0 126	57 300+	77 300+	75 300+	62 300+	56 300+	72 300+	66 300+	71 300+	59 300+	63 300+
Loyola Gottlieb Memorial Hospital, Melrose Park, IL	- -	- -	- -	0.237 603	0.135 325	7.1 1288	36.5 189	49 300+	79 300+	77 300+	57 300+	57 300+	74 300+	69 300+	69 300+	58 300+	60 300+
Loyola University Medical Center, Maywood, IL	97 38	81 37	100 38	0.214 2704	0.016 2392	7.0 2282	28.9 377	53 300+	77 300+	82 300+	66 300+	58 300+	73 300+	67 300+	65 300+	54 300+	72 300+
Macneal Hospital, Berwyn, IL	- -	- -	- -	0.140 608	0.125 506	9.4 1330	25.0 8	50 300+	80 300+	81 300+	61 300+	58 300+	77 300+	71 300+	72 300+	63 300+	64 300+
Marion Illinois VA Medical Center, Marion, IL	- -	- -	- -	- -	- -	- -	- -	- -	- -	- -	- -	- -	- -	- -	- -	- -	- -
Marshall Browning Hospital, Du Quoin, IL	- -	- -	- -	- -	- -	- -	- -	- -	- -	- -	- -	- -	- -	- -	- -	- -	- -
Mason District Hospital, Havana, IL	- -	- -	- -	- -	- -	- -	- -	58 <100	87 <100	89 <100	88 <100	72 <100	87 <100	76 <100	85 <100	81 <100	83 <100
McDonough District Hospital, Macomb, IL	- -	- -	- -	0.733 330	0.217 373	6.5 642	31.0 58	56 300+	84 300+	90 300+	65 300+	59 300+	78 300+	73 300+	81 300+	72 300+	64 300+
Memorial Hospital, Belleville, IL	- -	- -	- -	0.102 1377	0.053 941	10.4 1803	32.8 268	56 300+	78 300+	80 300+	70 300+	59 300+	78 300+	70 300+	69 300+	61 300+	74 300+
Memorial Hospital, Chester, IL	- -	- -	- -	0.090 211	0.000 115	8.5 235	22.6 31	- -	- -	- -	- -	- -	- -	- -	- -	- -	- -
Memorial Hospital of Carbondale, Carbondale, IL	- -	- -	- -	0.112 721	0.029 385	7.2 1923	41.7 127	60 300+	80 300+	86 300+	74 300+	63 300+	79 300+	72 300+	76 300+	66 300+	82 300+
Memorial Medical Center, Springfield, IL	- -	- -	- -	0.093 1873	0.017 1692	7.2 3066	33.8 391	43 300+	78 300+	80 300+	65 300+	56 300+	75 300+	67 300+	60 300+	57 300+	74 300+
Mendota Community Hospital, Mendota, IL	- -	- -	- -	0.077 235	0.029 140	7.5 334	32.5 40	57 300+	86 300+	87 300+	68 300+	63 300+	83 300+	72 300+	80 300+	77 300+	65 300+
Mercer County Hospital, Aledo, IL	- -	- -	- -	- -	- -	- -	- -	- -	- -	- -	- -	- -	- -	- -	- -	- -	- -
Mercy Harvard Hospital, Harvard, IL	- -	- -	- -	0.033 92	0.051 78	5.6 89	60.0 5	- -	- -	- -	- -	- -	- -	- -	- -	- -	- -
Mercy Hospital and Medical Center, Chicago, IL	- -	- -	- -	0.118 619	0.083 336	4.2 1510	33.6 140	64 300+	80 300+	79 300+	68 300+	57 300+	77 300+	69 300+	71 300+	56 300+	77 300+
Methodist Hospital of Chicago, Chicago, IL	- -	- -	- -	0.494 81	0.329 73	10.3 116	50.0 2	52 (a)	72 (a)	71 (a)	63 (a)	45 (a)	60 (a)	50 (a)	77 (a)	39 (a)	60 (a)
Methodist Medical Center of Illinois, Peoria, IL	- -	- -	- -	0.224 1116	0.036 881	12.0 2032	31.3 310	60 300+	80 300+	86 300+	77 300+	65 300+	83 300+	75 300+	78 300+	68 300+	81 300+
Metrosouth Medical Center, Blue Island, IL	- -	- -	- -	0.074 457	0.000 445	10.7 671	28.8 59	51 300+	78 300+	71 300+	54 300+	57 300+	70 300+	63 300+	65 300+	57 300+	57 300+
Midwest Medical Center, Galena, IL	- -	- -	- -	- -	- -	- -	- -	- -	- -	- -	- -	- -	- -	- -	- -	- -	- -
Midwestern Region Medical Center, Zion, IL	- -	- -	- -	0.974 694	0.000 760	3.9 205	25.0 8	60 300+	85 300+	91 300+	86 300+	69 300+	80 300+	79 300+	74 300+	69 300+	91 300+
Morris Hospital & Healthcare Centers, Morris, IL	- -	- -	- -	0.092 649	0.015 459	7.0 788	32.9 164	57 300+	85 300+	86 300+	78 300+	61 300+	82 300+	74 300+	78 300+	72 300+	82 300+
Mount Sinai Hospital Medical Center, Chicago, IL	- -	- -	- -	0.146 328	0.072 250	5.4 411	60.7 28	49 300+	74 300+	76 300+	51 300+	56 300+	63 300+	61 300+	53 300+	42 300+	52 300+
North Chicago VA Medical Center, North Chicago, IL	- -	- -	- -	- -	- -	- -	- -	- -	- -	- -	- -	- -	- -	- -	- -	- -	- -
Northwest Community Hospital, Arlington Heights, IL	- -	- -	- -	0.090 3470	0.025 2628	7.7 5143	31.0 575	39 300+	71 300+	77 300+	58 300+	51 300+	68 300+	64 300+	61 300+	54 300+	65 300+
Northwestern Memorial Hospital, Chicago, IL	- -	- -	- -	0.201 4159	0.001 4348	8.4 3743	29.5 774	64 300+	77 300+	77 300+	77 300+	59 300+	73 300+	69 300+	68 300+	59 300+	82 300+
Norwegian-American Hospital, Chicago, IL	- -	- -	- -	0.072 181	0.000 57	7.7 287	26.7 15	40 300+	66 300+	70 300+	45 300+	40 300+	52 300+	52 300+	56 300+	44 300+	44 300+
Oak Forest Hospital, Oak Forest, IL	- -	- -	- -	0.000 18	0.083 12	- 0	- 0	62 300+	78 300+	77 300+	59 300+	58 300+	78 300+	69 300+	65 300+	67 300+	66 300+
OSF Holy Family Medical Center, Monmouth, IL	- -	- -	- -	0.699 73	0.839 62	4.0 300	42.6 47	63 (a)	77 (a)	87 (a)	72 (a)	52 (a)	77 (a)	67 (a)	82 (a)	75 (a)	66 (a)
Ottawa Regional Hospital & Healthcare Center, Ottawa, IL	- -	- -	- -	0.118 509	0.022 408	21.0 352	27.6 127	52 300+	78 300+	85 300+	62 300+	61 300+	78 300+	68 300+	77 300+	69 300+	63 300+
Our Lady of the Resurrection Medical Center, Chicago, IL	- -	- -	- -	0.399 501	0.272 334	9.3 924	29.7 74	42 300+	72 300+	79 300+	49 300+	53 300+	66 300+	62 300+	64 300+	56 300+	51 300+
Palos Community Hospital, Palos Heights, IL	- -	- -	- -	0.059 1969	0.010 2265	11.2 2785	- 0	43 300+	80 300+	81 300+	63 300+	59 300+	76 300+	70 300+	66 300+	60 300+	68 300+
Pana Community Hospital, Pana, IL	- -	- -	- -	- -	- -	- -	- -	- -	- -	- -	- -	- -	- -	- -	- -	- -	- -
Paris Community Hospital, Paris, IL	- -	- -	- -	- -	- -	- -	- -	- -	- -	- -	- -	- -	- -	- -	- -	- -	- -
Passavant Area Hospital, Jacksonville, IL	- -	- -	- -	0.026 498	0.007 299	5.3 1016	41.5 135	55 300+	80 300+	84 300+	68 300+	60 300+	76 300+	73 300+	76 300+	61 300+	64 300+
Pekin Memorial Hospital, Pekin, IL	- -	- -	- -	0.094 682	0.008 532	15.7 739	24.6 118	50 300+	81 300+	84 300+	68 300+	59 300+	77 300+	70 300+	72 300+	70 300+	65 300+
Perry Memorial Hospital, Princeton, IL	- -	- -	- -	- -	- -	- -	- -	- -	- -	- -	- -	- -	- -	- -	- -	- -	- -
Pinckneyville Community Hospital, Pinckneyville, IL	- -	- -	- -	- -	- -	- -	- -	65 (a)	88 (a)	95 (a)	66 (a)	66 (a)	82 (a)	81 (a)	78 (a)	78 (a)	61 (a)
Proctor Hospital, Peoria, IL	- -	- -	- -	0.675 425	0.532 278	8.9 440	34.7 95	56 300+	79 300+	87 300+	73 300+	54 300+	73 300+	69 300+	69 300+	59 300+	78 300+
Provena Covenant Medical Center - Urbana, Urbana, IL	- -	- -	- -	0.010 305	0.006 162	9.2 338	25.4 59	60 300+	79 300+	84 300+	65 300+	59 300+	78 300+	70 300+	66 300+	62 300+	73 300+
Provena Mercy Medical Center, Aurora, IL	- -	- -	- -	0.080 388	0.045 222	16.3 443	28.3 106	57 300+	77 300+	84 300+	61 300+	58 300+	74 300+	63 300+	67 300+	55 300+	64 300+
Provena St Joseph Medical Center, Joliet, IL	- -	- -	- -	0.360 1073	0.171 914	5.6 2201	27.9 330	67 300+	77 300+	84 300+	67 300+	54 300+	73 300+	72 300+	65 300+	55 300+	70 300+
Provena St Marys Hospital, Kankakee, IL	- -	- -	- -	0.137 510	0.037 271	9.0 679	30.4 112	61 300+	80 300+	84 300+	74 300+	61 300+	79 300+	72 300+	75 300+	67 300+	77 300+
Provena United Samaritans Medical Center - Logan, Danville, IL	- -	- -	- -	0.411 474	0.171 456	18.2 335	37.0 208	66 300+	85 300+	87 300+	68 300+	63 300+	80 300+	71 300+	66 300+	64 300+	55 300+
Provena-Saint Joseph Hospital, Elgin, IL	- -	- -	- -	0.240 563	0.236 394	10.2 768	34.3 70	65 300+	77 300+	87 300+	68 300+	58 300+	73 300+	70 300+	73 300+	54 300+	72 300+
Provident Hospital of Chicago, Chicago, IL	- -	- -	- -	0.000 70	0.000 42	0.0 4	- 0	68 300+	80 300+	76 300+	51 300+	59 300+	69 300+	66 300+	64 300+	53 300+	53 300+
Red Bud Regional Hospital, Red Bud, IL	- -	- -	- -	0.250 204	0.278 115	16.2 303	30.0 10	57 (a)	84 (a)	84 (a)	72 (a)	59 (a)	79 (a)	78 (a)	75 (a)	56 (a)	67 (a)
Resurrection Medical Center, Chicago, IL	- -	- -	- -	0.144 1585	0.093 1079	15.1 2446	37.2 352	40 300+	75 300+	79 300+	55 300+	54 300+	69 300+	64 300+	54 300+	51 300+	59 300+
RHC St Francis Hospital, Evanston, IL	- -	- -	- -	0.380 626	0.330 454	14.2 1123	42.0 69	42 300+	73 300+	79 300+	58 300+	48 300+	69 300+	63 300+	63 300+	57 300+	62 300+
Richland Memorial Hospital, Olney, IL	- -	- -	- -	0.702 238	0.429 210	2.2 224	29.2 24	64 300+	85 300+	87 300+	71 300+	64 300+	79 300+	75 300+	64 300+	69 300+	74 300+
Riverside Medical Center, Kankakee, IL	- -	- -	- -	0.165 901	0.169 485	8.2 1741	32.9 426	51 300+	78 300+	83 300+	71 300+	61 300+	79 300+	70 300+	69 300+	67 300+	78 300+
Rochelle Community Hospital, Rochelle, IL	- -	- -	- -	- -	- -	- -	- -	73 (a)	82 (a)	87 (a)	82 (a)	72 (a)	84 (a)	79 (a)	87 (a)	85 (a)	79 (a)
Rockford Memorial Hospital, Rockford, IL	- -	- -	- -	0.098 697	0.003 682	- 0	29.8 248	55 300+	74 300+	81 300+	63 300+	56 300+	72 300+	64 300+	69 300+	51 300+	67 300+
Roseland Community Hospital, Chicago, IL	- -	- -	- -	0.350 60	0.211 38	2.9 68	- 0	57 300+	75 300+	66 300+	43 300+	47 300+	60 300+	57 300+	61 300+	38 300+	40 300+
Rush Oak Park Hospital, Oak Park, IL	- -	- -	- -	0.468 325	0.006 177	6.1 890	0.0 1	63 300+	79 300+	75 300+	60 300+	57 300+	72 300+	70 300+	66 300+	59 300+	64 300+
Rush University Medical Center, Chicago, IL	- -	- -	- -	0.140 328	0.050 160	9.0 2038	6.3 16	53 300+	76 300+	83 300+	70 300+	60 300+	77 300+	68 300+	61 300+	59 300+	76 300+
Sacred Heart Hospital, Chicago, IL	- -	- -	- -	0.632 57	0.529 34	7.7 195	15.0 60	57 300+	76 300+	70 300+	47 300+	51 300+	62 300+	64 300+	62 300+	47 300+	55 300+
Saint Alexius Medical Center, Hoffman Estates, IL	- -	- -	- -	0.337 962	0.175 936	8.1 1166	34.6 156	42 300+	79 300+	81 300+	66 300+	59 300+	80 300+	71 300+	70 300+	66 300+	68 300+
Saint Anthony Hospital, Chicago, IL	- -	- -	- -	0.028 106	0.017 60	4.3 209	24.1 29	44 300+	77 300+	73 300+	67 300+	52 300+	65 300+	60 300+	58 300+	52 300+	65 300+

NOTE: The first number in each column (boldface) is the score, the second number is the number of patients; Please refer to the main entry for footnotes; (a) 100-299
*MEASURES: **Children's Asthma Care:** 33. Received Systemic Corticosteroids; 34. Received Home Management Plan of Care; 35. Received Reliever Medication; **Use of Medical Imaging:** 36. Combination Abdominal CT Scan; 37. Combination Chest CT Scan; 38. Follow-up Mammogram/Ultrasound; 39. MRI for Low Back Pain; **Survey of Patients' Hospital Experiences:** 40. Area Around Room 'Always' Quiet at Night; 41. Doctors 'Always' Communicated Well; 42. Home Recovery Information Given; 43. Hospital Given 9 or 10 on 10 Point Scale; 44. Meds 'Always' Explained Before Given; 45. Nurses 'Always' Communicated Well; 46. Pain 'Always' Well Controlled; 47. Room and Bathroom 'Always' Clean; 48. Timely Help 'Always' Received; 49. Would Definitely Recommend Hospital*

Hospital	Children's Asthma Care			Use of Medical Imaging				Survey of Patients' Hospital Experiences									
	33	34	35	36	37	38	39	40	41	42	43	44	45	46	47	48	49
Saint Anthony Medical Center, Rockford, IL	- -	- -	- -	**0.076** 1154	**0.001** 1032	**8.7** 1381	**35.8** 193	**45** 300+	**76** 300+	**82** 300+	**70** 300+	**61** 300+	**76** 300+	**69** 300+	**73** 300+	**63** 300+	**73** 300+
Saint Anthony's Health Center, Alton, IL	- -	- -	- -	**0.310** 491	**0.072** 207	**7.3** 871	**33.0** 88	**54** 300+	**78** 300+	**84** 300+	**66** 300+	**61** 300+	**74** 300+	**67** 300+	**71** 300+	**59** 300+	**68** 300+
Saint Anthonys Memorial Hospital, Effingham, IL	- -	- -	- -	**0.751** 995	**0.006** 642	**9.1** 1567	**35.6** 160	**53** 300+	**80** 300+	**81** 300+	**66** 300+	**61** 300+	**74** 300+	**66** 300+	**71** 300+	**62** 300+	**67** 300+
Saint Bernard Hospital, Chicago, IL	- -	- -	- -	**0.607** 112	**0.000** 79	**3.6** 112	- 0	**58** 300+	**70** 300+	**72** 300+	**43** 300+	**51** 300+	**64** 300+	**59** 300+	**65** 300+	**51** 300+	**39** 300+
Saint Elizabeth Hospital, Belleville, IL	- -	- -	- -	**0.484** 826	**0.200** 715	**16.0** 1446	**33.3** 114	**52** 300+	**77** 300+	**81** 300+	**57** 300+	**52** 300+	**70** 300+	**64** 300+	**58** 300+	**52** 300+	**61** 300+
Saint Francis Hospital, Litchfield, IL	- -	- -	- -	- -	- -	- -	- -	**65** 300+	**83** 300+	**81** 300+	**70** 300+	**63** 300+	**79** 300+	**71** 300+	**83** 300+	**66** 300+	**64** 300+
Saint Francis Medical Center, Peoria, IL	- -	- -	- -	**0.142** 1625	**0.027** 1262	**8.7** 4488	**34.0** 350	**49** 300+	**78** 300+	**83** 300+	**68** 300+	**59** 300+	**77** 300+	**69** 300+	**72** 300+	**57** 300+	**71** 300+
Saint James Hospital, Pontiac, IL	- -	- -	- -	**0.072** 416	**0.039** 279	**10.2** 783	**29.7** 101	**53** 300+	**84** 300+	**90** 300+	**70** 300+	**63** 300+	**80** 300+	**73** 300+	**79** 300+	**76** 300+	**71** 300+
Saint James Hospital-Olympia Fields, Olympia Fields, IL	- -	- -	- -	**0.208** 711	**0.109** 548	**6.7** 1319	**38.2** 123	**49** 300+	**75** 300+	**75** 300+	**57** 300+	**56** 300+	**72** 300+	**67** 300+	**65** 300+	**55** 300+	**58** 300+
Saint Johns Hospital, Springfield, IL	**99** 88	**60** 88	**100** 88	**0.460** 755	**0.169** 813	**12.4** 1812	**40.0** 160	**54** 300+	**79** 300+	**81** 300+	**69** 300+	**59** 300+	**74** 300+	**66** 300+	**68** 300+	**61** 300+	**73** 300+
Saint Joseph Hospital, Chicago, IL	- -	- -	- -	**0.129** 458	**0.006** 316	**7.4** 1035	**34.9** 83	**52** 300+	**78** 300+	**81** 300+	**64** 300+	**59** 300+	**70** 300+	**63** 300+	**65** 300+	**55** 300+	**67** 300+
Saint Joseph Medical Center, Bloomington, IL	- -	- -	- -	**0.722** 324	**0.615** 351	**5.3** 525	**28.2** 103	**63** 300+	**83** 300+	**83** 300+	**75** 300+	**64** 300+	**80** 300+	**71** 300+	**77** 300+	**67** 300+	**78** 300+
Saint Joseph Memorial Hospital, Murphysboro, IL	- -	- -	- -	**0.136** 396	**0.078** 115	- 0	**19.4** 31	**63** (a)	**81** (a)	**86** (a)	**75** (a)	**69** (a)	**84** (a)	**72** (a)	**88** (a)	**79** (a)	**79** (a)
Saint Joseph's Hospital, Highland, IL	- -	- -	- -	- -	- -	- -	- -	**59** (a)	**84** (a)	**85** (a)	**72** (a)	**63** (a)	**84** (a)	**80** (a)	**86** (a)	**66** (a)	**71** (a)
Saint Josephs Hospital, Breese, IL	- -	- -	- -	**0.204** 275	**0.051** 217	**7.5** 612	**37.7** 53	**69** 300+	**86** 300+	**85** 300+	**81** 300+	**73** 300+	**87** 300+	**78** 300+	**85** 300+	**72** 300+	**83** 300+
Saint Margarets Hospital, Spring Valley, IL	- -	- -	- -	**0.134** 276	**0.032** 217	**6.9** 563	**31.6** 76	**53** 300+	**86** 300+	**85** 300+	**62** 300+	**64** 300+	**77** 300+	**66** 300+	**73** 300+	**60** 300+	**67** 300+
Saint Mary & Elizabeth Med Ctr-Division Campus, Chicago, IL	- -	- -	- -	**0.201** 671	**0.007** 151	**5.6** 481	**36.7** 109	**58** 300+	**77** 300+	**78** 300+	**67** 300+	**52** 300+	**67** 300+	**64** 300+	**63** 300+	**55** 300+	**66** 300+
Saint Mary Medical Center, Galesburg, IL	- -	- -	- -	**0.068** 472	**0.012** 343	**6.6** 1323	**28.5** 123	**57** 300+	**83** 300+	**89** 300+	**75** 300+	**67** 300+	**81** 300+	**73** 300+	**75** 300+	**75** 300+	**83** 300+
Saint Marys Hospital, Streator, IL	- -	- -	- -	**0.566** 274	**0.560** 234	**5.5** 860	**33.8** 80	**56** 300+	**81** 300+	**85** 300+	**61** 300+	**60** 300+	**76** 300+	**70** 300+	**77** 300+	**68** 300+	**63** 300+
Saint Marys Hospital, Centralia, IL	- -	- -	- -	**0.728** 691	**0.195** 430	**6.2** 728	**39.6** 106	**62** 300+	**82** 300+	**87** 300+	**77** 300+	**64** 300+	**85** 300+	**80** 300+	**85** 300+	**78** 300+	**76** 300+
Saint Marys Hospital, Decatur, IL	- -	- -	- -	**0.062** 513	**0.011** 369	**6.1** 919	**35.3** 187	**59** 300+	**77** 300+	**81** 300+	**62** 300+	**54** 300+	**70** 300+	**62** 300+	**62** 300+	**53** 300+	**69** 300+
Salem Township Hospital, Salem, IL	- -	- -	- -	- -	- -	- -	- -	**60** (a)	**88** (a)	**83** (a)	**75** (a)	**66** (a)	**84** (a)	**75** (a)	**88** (a)	**73** (a)	**72** (a)
Sarah Bush Lincoln Health Center, Mattoon, IL	- -	- -	- -	**0.076** 828	**0.000** 612	**5.8** 1535	**34.3** 181	**56** 300+	**85** 300+	**89** 300+	**73** 300+	**68** 300+	**82** 300+	**73** 300+	**73** 300+	**70** 300+	**74** 300+
Sarah D Culbertson Memorial Hospital, Rushville, IL	- -	- -	- -	- -	- -	- -	- -	- -	- -	- -	- -	- -	- -	- -	- -	- -	- -
Shelby Memorial Hospital, Shelbyville, IL	- -	- -	- -	**0.037** 161	**0.012** 86	**19.0** 195	**20.0** 25	**50** (a)	**80** (a)	**74** (a)	**56** (a)	**59** (a)	**75** (a)	**65** (a)	**79** (a)	**60** (a)	**44** (a)
Sherman Hospital, Elgin, IL	- -	- -	- -	**0.243** 787	**0.147** 620	**6.8** 1663	**36.0** 100	**62** 300+	**74** 300+	**82** 300+	**67** 300+	**57** 300+	**76** 300+	**68** 300+	**74** 300+	**59** 300+	**73** 300+
Silver Cross Hospital, Joliet, IL	- -	- -	- -	**0.082** 672	**0.048** 681	**8.3** 942	**35.5** 211	**56** 300+	**78** 300+	**78** 300+	**71** 300+	**61** 300+	**78** 300+	**71** 300+	**71** 300+	**62** 300+	**72** 300+
Skokie Hospital, Skokie, IL	- -	- -	- -	**0.464** 317	**0.593** 204	**8.1** 2398	**28.6** 7	**48** 300+	**74** 300+	**73** 300+	**51** 300+	**49** 300+	**68** 300+	**57** 300+	**60** 300+	**49** 300+	**60** 300+
South Shore Hospital, Chicago, IL	- -	- -	- -	**0.013** 78	**0.041** 49	**2.2** 179	- 0	**56** 300+	**70** 300+	**56** 300+	**41** 300+	**48** 300+	**63** 300+	**57** 300+	**61** 300+	**47** 300+	**38** 300+
Sparta Community Hospital, Sparta, IL	- -	- -	- -	- -	- -	- -	- -	- -	- -	- -	- -	- -	- -	- -	- -	- -	- -
Swedish American Hospital, Rockford, IL	- -	- -	- -	**0.059** 1062	**0.002** 1002	**8.7** 2740	**33.7** 252	**55** 300+	**77** 300+	**81** 300+	**66** 300+	**59** 300+	**76** 300+	**70** 300+	**72** 300+	**67** 300+	**72** 300+
Swedish Covenant Hospital, Chicago, IL	- -	- -	- -	**0.132** 1085	**0.018** 786	**7.3** 1556	**35.9** 281	**41** 300+	**74** 300+	**80** 300+	**56** 300+	**51** 300+	**65** 300+	**60** 300+	**57** 300+	**50** 300+	**61** 300+
Taylorville Memorial Hospital, Taylorville, IL	- -	- -	- -	**0.034** 357	**0.003** 310	**7.3** 641	**66.3** 80	**45** 300+	**84** 300+	**76** 300+	**68** 300+	**62** 300+	**78** 300+	**70** 300+	**76** 300+	**64** 300+	**68** 300+
Thomas H Boyd Memorial Hospital, Carrollton, IL	- -	- -	- -	- -	- -	- -	- -	- -	- -	- -	- -	- -	- -	- -	- -	- -	- -
Thorek Memorial Hospital, Chicago, IL	- -	- -	- -	**0.834** 181	**0.319** 94	**17.9** 173	**22.2** 36	**52** 300+	**71** 300+	**75** 300+	**48** 300+	**46** 300+	**60** 300+	**56** 300+	**65** 300+	**44** 300+	**47** 300+
Touchette Regional Hospital, Centreville, IL	- -	- -	- -	**0.000** 71	**0.000** 50	**6.7** 223	**44.4** 9	**64** (a)	**80** (a)	**77** (a)	**48** (a)	**51** (a)	**70** (a)	**60** (a)	**64** (a)	**47** (a)	**53** (a)
Trinity Rock Island, Rock Island, IL	- -	- -	- -	**0.059** 1113	**0.069** 763	**10.9** 2177	- 0	**50** 300+	**78** 300+	**86** 300+	**62** 300+	**61** 300+	**72** 300+	**67** 300+	**69** 300+	**49** 300+	**64** 300+
Union County Hospital, Anna, IL	- -	- -	- -	**0.207** 276	**0.000** 130	**8.7** 358	**34.5** 29	**63** (a)	**85** (a)	**77** (a)	**63** (a)	**61** (a)	**75** (a)	**69** (a)	**72** (a)	**63** (a)	**57** (a)
The University of Chicago Medical Center, Chicago, IL	**100** 239	**7** 239	**100** 239	**0.076** 3622	**0.001** 4244	**6.0** 2377	**35.1** 285	**48** 300+	**79** 300+	**80** 300+	**63** 300+	**56** 300+	**71** 300+	**65** 300+	**60** 300+	**55** 300+	**70** 300+
University of Illinois Hospital, Chicago, IL	- -	- -	- -	**0.232** 788	**0.048** 794	**4.1** 701	**32.5** 154	**55** 300+	**81** 300+	**81** 300+	**59** 300+	**68** 300+	**69** 300+	**71** 300+	**64** 300+	**61** 300+	**63** 300+
VA Illiana Healthcare System - Danville, Danville, IL	- -	- -	- -	- -	- -	- -	- -	- -	- -	- -	- -	- -	- -	- -	- -	- -	- -
Valley West Community Hospital, Sandwich, IL	- -	- -	- -	- -	- -	- -	- -	**73** 300+	**85** 300+	**81** 300+	**71** 300+	**63** 300+	**82** 300+	**76** 300+	**79** 300+	**72** 300+	**72** 300+
Vista Medical Center East, Waukegan, IL	- -	- -	- -	**0.569** 861	**0.551** 615	**4.3** 1916	**26.6** 128	**48** 300+	**75** 300+	**74** 300+	**52** 300+	**52** 300+	**63** 300+	**61** 300+	**57** 300+	**47** 300+	**48** 300+
Vista Medical Center West, Waukegan, IL	- -	- -	- -	**0.217** 23	**0.500** 2	- 0	- 0	- -	- -	- -	- -	- -	- -	- -	- -	- -	- -
Wabash General Hospital, Mount Carmel, IL	- -	- -	- -	**0.420** 212	**0.403** 144	**6.6** 211	**42.4** 33	- -	- -	- -	- -	- -	- -	- -	- -	- -	- -
West Suburban Medical Center, Oak Park, IL	- -	- -	- -	**0.229** 528	**0.233** 352	**6.3** 160	**37.5** 64	**60** 300+	**80** 300+	**83** 300+	**63** 300+	**62** 300+	**70** 300+	**68** 300+	**66** 300+	**49** 300+	**61** 300+
Westlake Community Hospital, Melrose Park, IL	- -	- -	- -	**0.219** 224	**0.000** 124	**8.5** 435	**37.9** 29	**55** 300+	**82** 300+	**79** 300+	**67** 300+	**60** 300+	**77** 300+	**72** 300+	**70** 300+	**61** 300+	**66** 300+
INDIANA																	
Adams Memorial Hospital, Decatur, IN	- -	- -	- -	- -	- -	- -	- -	- -	- -	- -	- -	- -	- -	- -	- -	- -	- -
Ball Memorial Hospital, Muncie, IN	- -	- -	- -	**0.051** 1127	**0.053** 584	**8.3** 2460	**38.2** 186	**54** 300+	**80** 300+	**84** 300+	**68** 300+	**61** 300+	**78** 300+	**74** 300+	**70** 300+	**61** 300+	**65** 300+
Bedford Regional Medical Center, Bedford, IN	- -	- -	- -	**0.354** 452	**0.363** 245	**3.2** 598	**38.6** 83	**44** 300+	**84** 300+	**83** 300+	**72** 300+	**67** 300+	**79** 300+	**71** 300+	**76** 300+	**68** 300+	**72** 300+
Blackford Community Hospital, Hartford City, IN	- -	- -	- -	**0.059** 220	**0.016** 126	**12.0** 241	**36.6** 41	- -	- -	- -	- -	- -	- -	- -	- -	- -	- -
Bloomington Hospital, Bloomington, IN	- -	- -	- -	**0.044** 589	**0.016** 255	- 0	**23.6** 144	**47** 300+	**80** 300+	**85** 300+	**70** 300+	**59** 300+	**75** 300+	**69** 300+	**66** 300+	**64** 300+	**74** 300+
Bluffton Regional Medical Center, Bluffton, IN	- -	- -	- -	**0.022** 231	**0.039** 153	**7.7** 673	**31.9** 94	**60** 300+	**79** 300+	**86** 300+	**73** 300+	**66** 300+	**81** 300+	**73** 300+	**78** 300+	**67** 300+	**70** 300+
Cameron Memorial Community Hospital, Angola, IN	- -	- -	- -	**0.241** 303	**0.010** 205	**8.0** 411	**29.3** 75	**58** 300+	**84** 300+	**81** 300+	**69** 300+	**61** 300+	**83** 300+	**75** 300+	**83** 300+	**81** 300+	**69** 300+
Clark Memorial Hospital, Jeffersonville, IN	- -	- -	- -	**0.726** 1042	**0.007** 1013	**6.2** 1524	**40.6** 207	**53** 300+	**82** 300+	**74** 300+	**72** 300+	**64** 300+	**80** 300+	**73** 300+	**77** 300+	**67** 300+	**74** 300+
Columbus Regional Hospital, Columbus, IN	- -	- -	- -	**0.025** 563	**0.005** 553	**9.7** 1283	**35.7** 84	**44** 300+	**83** 300+	**79** 300+	**71** 300+	**58** 300+	**77** 300+	**71** 300+	**79** 300+	**64** 300+	**72** 300+
Community Hospital, Munster, IN	- -	- -	- -	**0.333** 1973	**0.300** 1384	**4.3** 2396	**35.5** 341	**55** 300+	**82** 300+	**83** 300+	**77** 300+	**65** 300+	**82** 300+	**74** 300+	**78** 300+	**69** 300+	**80** 300+
Community Hospital East, Indianapolis, IN	- -	- -	- -	**0.210** 1135	**0.161** 974	**8.7** 2278	**34.0** 438	**49** 300+	**74** 300+	**79** 300+	**61** 300+	**53** 300+	**69** 300+	**66** 300+	**65** 300+	**60** 300+	**66** 300+
Community Hospital North, Indianapolis, IN	- -	- -	- -	**0.231** 888	**0.198** 774	**9.1** 1178	**35.3** 354	**61** 300+	**77** 300+	**79** 300+	**72** 300+	**55** 300+	**71** 300+	**68** 300+	**69** 300+	**55** 300+	**79** 300+
Community Hospital of Anderson & Madison Co, Anderson, IN	- -	- -	- -	**0.075** 755	**0.005** 600	**12.2** 1357	**37.7** 199	**56** 300+	**83** 300+	**85** 300+	**74** 300+	**62** 300+	**79** 300+	**71** 300+	**73** 300+	**67** 300+	**77** 300+
Community Hospital of Bremen, Bremen, IN	- -	- -	- -	**0.048** 83	**0.019** 52	**5.5** 200	**30.6** 36	- -	- -	- -	- -	- -	- -	- -	- -	- -	- -
Community Hospital South, Indianapolis, IN	- -	- -	- -	**0.058** 533	**0.077** 392	**7.1** 778	**38.0** 121	**47** 300+	**76** 300+	**78** 300+	**68** 300+	**54** 300+	**73** 300+	**68** 300+	**67** 300+	**61** 300+	**71** 300+
Daviess Community Hospital, Washington, IN	- -	- -	- -	**0.830** 229	**0.500** 128	**9.3** 452	**36.2** 69	**57** 300+	**80** 300+	**81** 300+	**63** 300+	**57** 300+	**71** 300+	**67** 300+	**76** 300+	**69** 300+	**58** 300+
Deaconess Hospital, Evansville, IN	- -	- -	- -	**0.047** 1714	**0.007** 1279	- 0	**39.4** 340	**58** 300+	**77** 300+	**78** 300+	**68** 300+	**58** 300+	**75** 300+	**67** 300+	**69** 300+	**59** 300+	**72** 300+
Dearborn County Hospital, Lawrenceburg, IN	- -	- -	- -	**0.466** 620	**0.089** 427	**7.2** 847	**29.5** 129	**55** 300+	**79** 300+	**77** 300+	**63** 300+	**58** 300+	**77** 300+	**67** 300+	**80** 300+	**68** 300+	**64** 300+
Decatur County Memorial Hospital, Greensburg, IN	- -	- -	- -	**0.612** 196	**0.160** 119	**3.8** 445	**22.9** 48	**51** (a)	**87** (a)	**90** (a)	**65** (a)	**59** (a)	**79** (a)	**73** (a)	**69** (a)	**67** (a)	**64** (a)

NOTE: The first number in each column (boldface) is the score, the second number is the number of patients; Please refer to the main entry for footnotes; (a) 100-299
*MEASURES: **Children's Asthma Care:** 33. Received Systemic Corticosteroids; 34. Received Home Management Plan of Care; 35. Received Reliever Medication; **Use of Medical Imaging:** 36. Combination Abdominal CT Scan; 37. Combination Chest CT Scan; 38. Follow-up Mammogram/Ultrasound; 39. MRI for Low Back Pain; **Survey of Patients' Hospital Experiences:** 40. Area Around Room 'Always' Quiet at Night; 41. Doctors 'Always' Communicated Well; 42. Home Recovery Information Given; 43. Hospital Given 9 or 10 on 10 Point Scale; 44. Meds 'Always' Explained Before Given; 45. Nurses 'Always' Communicated Well; 46. Pain 'Always' Well Controlled; 47. Room and Bathroom 'Always' Clean; 48. Timely Help 'Always' Received; 49. Would Definitely Recommend Hospital*

Hospital	Children's Asthma Care			Use of Medical Imaging				Survey of Patients' Hospital Experiences									
	33	34	35	36	37	38	39	40	41	42	43	44	45	46	47	48	49
Dekalb Memorial Hospital, Auburn, IN	- -	- -	- -	0.360 344	0.000 149	11.0 365	30.0 50	55 300+	90 300+	86 300+	79 300+	68 300+	81 300+	75 300+	79 300+	77 300+	76 300+
Dukes Memorial Hospital, Peru, IN	- -	- -	- -	0.032 249	0.019 208	6.4 299	31.5 54	65 (a)	83 (a)	88 (a)	64 (a)	65 (a)	77 (a)	75 (a)	67 (a)	70 (a)	66 (a)
Dupont Hospital, Fort Wayne, IN	- -	- -	- -	0.068 324	0.022 182	7.5 308	36.0 75	58 300+	79 300+	85 300+	77 300+	55 300+	77 300+	72 300+	72 300+	65 300+	79 300+
Elkhart General Hospital, Elkhart, IN	- -	- -	- -	0.067 983	0.010 813	8.2 2280	33.2 196	52 300+	75 300+	78 300+	68 300+	54 300+	73 300+	68 300+	73 300+	61 300+	69 300+
Fayette Regional Health System, Connersville, IN	- -	- -	- -	0.053 245	0.013 156	5.7 370	31.5 73	67 300+	84 300+	88 300+	71 300+	69 300+	82 300+	77 300+	84 300+	76 300+	66 300+
Floyd Memorial Hospital and Health Services, New Albany, IN	- -	- -	- -	0.648 1127	0.043 889	8.5 1540	31.9 188	65 300+	83 300+	82 300+	80 300+	59 300+	79 300+	68 300+	71 300+	69 300+	82 300+
Franciscan Physicians Hospital, Munster, IN	- -	- -	- -	0.808 26	0.250 24	6.7 60	38.5 13	66 300+	81 300+	83 300+	76 300+	63 300+	82 300+	73 300+	82 300+	76 300+	74 300+
Franciscan St Anthony Health - Crown Point, Crown Point, IN	- -	- -	- -	0.333 1035	0.445 760	7.4 1644	28.8 212	49 300+	77 300+	84 300+	68 300+	57 300+	75 300+	68 300+	77 300+	55 300+	73 300+
Franciscan St Anthony Health - Michigan City, Michigan City, IN	- -	- -	- -	0.437 506	0.556 399	2.2 1210	37.1 167	51 300+	82 300+	80 300+	67 300+	61 300+	80 300+	74 300+	71 300+	67 300+	68 300+
Franciscan St Margaret Health - Dyer, Dyer, IN	- -	- -	- -	0.594 424	0.112 268	4.1 440	30.8 133	49 300+	77 300+	74 300+	64 300+	54 300+	73 300+	66 300+	72 300+	57 300+	65 300+
Franciscan St Margaret Health - Hammond, Hammond, IN	- -	- -	- -	0.586 517	0.033 364	4.9 652	31.0 116	58 300+	72 300+	72 300+	56 300+	52 300+	70 300+	62 300+	70 300+	53 300+	57 300+
Gibson General Hospital, Princeton, IN	- -	- -	- -	- -	- -	- -	- -	64 (a)	85 (a)	82 (a)	73 (a)	58 (a)	82 (a)	71 (a)	75 (a)	73 (a)	68 (a)
Good Samaritan Hospital, Vincennes, IN	- -	- -	- -	0.507 1034	0.114 603	4.9 1542	31.6 171	55 300+	83 300+	89 300+	76 300+	65 300+	84 300+	78 300+	87 300+	76 300+	79 300+
Greene County General Hospital, Linton, IN	- -	- -	- -	- -	- -	- -	- -	- -	- -	- -	- -	- -	- -	- -	- -	- -	- -
Hancock Regional Hospital, Greenfield, IN	- -	- -	- -	0.085 600	0.021 521	7.2 1156	35.6 160	57 300+	82 300+	83 300+	73 300+	60 300+	78 300+	72 300+	76 300+	67 300+	72 300+
Harrison County Hospital, Corydon, IN	- -	- -	- -	0.704 379	0.131 222	10.1 505	39.5 81	59 300+	88 300+	89 300+	71 300+	70 300+	81 300+	71 300+	82 300+	71 300+	71 300+
The Heart Hospital at Deaconess Gateway, Newburgh, IN	- -	- -	- -	- 0	- 0	- 0	- 0	- -	- -	- -	- -	- -	- -	- -	- -	- -	- -
Hendricks Regional Health, Danville, IN	- -	- -	- -	0.292 920	0.107 514	9.6 1235	37.7 220	59 300+	83 300+	91 300+	81 300+	60 300+	79 300+	71 300+	77 300+	62 300+	83 300+
Henry County Memorial Hospital, New Castle, IN	- -	- -	- -	0.060 629	0.027 299	4.1 1010	35.3 136	58 300+	83 300+	85 300+	71 300+	64 300+	81 300+	74 300+	75 300+	66 300+	70 300+
Howard Regional Health System, Kokomo, IN	- -	- -	- -	0.018 856	0.010 1025	9.1 997	33.3 12	57 300+	82 300+	81 300+	68 300+	63 300+	79 300+	74 300+	70 300+	63 300+	71 300+
The Indiana Heart Hospital, Indianapolis, IN	- -	- -	- -	0.120 92	0.087 173	- 0	- 0	66 300+	81 300+	83 300+	84 300+	55 300+	81 300+	73 300+	78 300+	74 300+	87 300+
Indiana Orthopaedic Hospital, Indianapolis, IN	- -	- -	- -	0.000 1	0.000 18	- 0	31.9 141	76 300+	88 300+	93 300+	90 300+	72 300+	87 300+	79 300+	89 300+	80 300+	91 300+
Indiana University Health, Indianapolis, IN	- -	- -	- -	0.093 3827	0.011 3506	6.8 3069	42.6 568	51 300+	74 300+	80 300+	65 300+	56 300+	71 300+	68 300+	63 300+	52 300+	68 300+
Indiana University Health Arnett Hospital, Lafayette, IN	- -	- -	- -	0.100 70	0.024 42	- 0	64.7 17	68 300+	72 300+	82 300+	74 300+	57 300+	76 300+	70 300+	75 300+	61 300+	77 300+
Indiana University Health North Hospital, Carmel, IN	100 80	90 80	100 80	0.079 419	0.009 347	7.8 422	44.6 83	67 300+	82 300+	82 300+	83 300+	56 300+	75 300+	70 300+	69 300+	60 300+	84 300+
Indiana University Health West Hospital, Avon, IN	- -	- -	- -	0.064 623	0.013 532	11.8 524	34.5 145	60 300+	78 300+	80 300+	77 300+	54 300+	71 300+	63 300+	74 300+	60 300+	77 300+
Indianapolis VA Medical Center, Indianapolis, IN	- -	- -	- -	- -	- -	- -	- -	- -	- -	- -	- -	- -	- -	- -	- -	- -	- -
IU Health Goshen Hospital, Goshen, IN	- -	- -	- -	0.056 660	0.013 535	8.6 1448	34.6 127	53 300+	78 300+	81 300+	71 300+	59 300+	78 300+	71 300+	77 300+	70 300+	74 300+
Jasper County Hospital, Rensselaer, IN	- -	- -	- -	- -	- -	- -	- -	- -	- -	- -	- -	- -	- -	- -	- -	- -	- -
Jay County Hospital, Portland, IN	- -	- -	- -	0.183 268	0.115 104	14.8 345	43.1 51	71 (a)	85 (a)	88 (a)	75 (a)	68 (a)	80 (a)	75 (a)	71 (a)	74 (a)	74 (a)
Johnson Memorial Hospital, Franklin, IN	- -	- -	- -	0.042 504	0.000 295	5.4 683	34.2 76	56 300+	84 300+	85 300+	72 300+	65 300+	81 300+	69 300+	75 300+	68 300+	71 300+
Kentuckiana Medical Center, Clarksville, IN	- -	- -	- -	- 0	- 0	- 0	- 0	- -	- -	- -	- -	- -	- -	- -	- -	- -	- -
The King's Daughters' Hospital and Health Services, Madison, IN	- -	- -	- -	0.768 603	0.765 349	3.8 945	35.4 82	52 300+	82 300+	86 300+	65 300+	61 300+	78 300+	70 300+	74 300+	72 300+	62 300+
Kosciusko Community Hospital, Warsaw, IN	- -	- -	- -	0.497 493	0.396 283	1.2 660	32.3 198	51 300+	82 300+	83 300+	64 300+	57 300+	75 300+	70 300+	69 300+	58 300+	59 300+
Laporte Hospital and Health Services, La Porte, IN	- -	- -	- -	0.479 735	0.698 504	17.6 1154	31.8 296	51 300+	75 300+	86 300+	64 300+	56 300+	75 300+	67 300+	70 300+	63 300+	66 300+
Lutheran Hospital of Indiana, Fort Wayne, IN	- -	- -	- -	0.046 654	0.004 459	- 0	28.0 25	46 300+	76 300+	86 300+	75 300+	57 300+	77 300+	70 300+	68 300+	65 300+	78 300+
Major Hospital, Shelbyville, IN	- -	- -	- -	0.328 393	0.143 300	4.9 716	27.6 145	57 300+	83 300+	84 300+	72 300+	65 300+	83 300+	73 300+	82 300+	75 300+	72 300+
Margaret Mary Community Hospital, Batesville, IN	- -	- -	- -	0.169 344	0.186 231	14.7 416	32.8 61	56 300+	88 300+	84 300+	82 300+	64 300+	86 300+	79 300+	84 300+	76 300+	85 300+
Marion General Hospital, Marion, IN	- -	- -	- -	0.690 1039	0.787 601	10.6 1784	36.9 244	52 300+	85 300+	83 300+	69 300+	68 300+	83 300+	74 300+	74 300+	73 300+	66 300+
Memorial Hospital, Logansport, IN	- -	- -	- -	0.707 464	0.041 290	9.9 1017	37.5 144	58 300+	82 300+	81 300+	65 300+	64 300+	80 300+	74 300+	78 300+	73 300+	64 300+
Memorial Hospital and Health Care Center, Jasper, IN	- -	- -	- -	0.638 937	0.775 668	10.3 1386	34.0 159	67 300+	87 300+	77 300+	77 300+	63 300+	83 300+	72 300+	84 300+	68 300+	78 300+
Memorial Hospital of South Bend, South Bend, IN	- -	- -	- -	0.103 757	0.026 623	6.5 1224	0.0 1	43 300+	80 300+	84 300+	74 300+	57 300+	76 300+	72 300+	68 300+	66 300+	76 300+
Methodist Hospitals, Gary, IN	- -	- -	- -	0.315 1090	0.337 603	7.7 1459	36.0 136	47 300+	74 300+	79 300+	49 300+	52 300+	68 300+	66 300+	61 300+	52 300+	52 300+
Monroe Hospital, Bloomington, IN	- -	- -	- -	0.029 205	0.030 99	- 0	30.4 56	68 300+	84 300+	78 300+	74 300+	59 300+	80 300+	73 300+	85 300+	67 300+	77 300+
Morgan Hospital and Medical Center, Martinsville, IN	- -	- -	- -	0.129 271	0.040 177	12.9 420	34.6 52	63 300+	79 300+	75 300+	59 300+	60 300+	71 300+	66 300+	66 300+	62 300+	57 300+
Orthopaedic Hospital at Parkview North, Fort Wayne, IN	- -	- -	- -	- 0	- 0	- 0	- 0	68 300+	87 300+	91 300+	80 300+	67 300+	79 300+	66 300+	72 300+	72 300+	82 300+
The Orthopaedic Hosp of Lutheran Health Network, Fort Wayne, IN	- -	- -	- -	- 0	- 0	- 0	32.9 73	66 300+	82 300+	90 300+	76 300+	58 300+	77 300+	69 300+	72 300+	68 300+	80 300+
Parkview Hospital, Fort Wayne, IN	- -	- -	- -	0.277 1080	0.025 730	- 0	43.5 177	61 300+	84 300+	87 300+	76 300+	64 300+	83 300+	77 300+	74 300+	68 300+	78 300+
Parkview Huntington Hospital, Huntington, IN	- -	- -	- -	0.263 213	0.071 127	12.1 338	37.1 62	62 300+	85 300+	89 300+	77 300+	62 300+	84 300+	76 300+	75 300+	74 300+	75 300+
Parkview Lagrange Hospital, Lagrange, IN	- -	- -	- -	0.011 179	0.157 83	7.4 270	45.2 42	61 (a)	85 (a)	84 (a)	80 (a)	59 (a)	79 (a)	73 (a)	79 (a)	71 (a)	75 (a)
Parkview Noble Hospital, Kendallville, IN	- -	- -	- -	0.031 353	0.000 149	9.2 382	35.3 102	62 300+	87 300+	89 300+	78 300+	70 300+	82 300+	76 300+	80 300+	72 300+	77 300+
Parkview Whitley Hospital, Columbia City, IN	- -	- -	- -	0.262 214	0.045 134	6.0 332	35.5 62	64 300+	89 300+	90 300+	79 300+	69 300+	87 300+	81 300+	78 300+	79 300+	78 300+
Perry County Memorial Hospital, Tell City, IN	- -	- -	- -	- -	- -	- -	- -	- -	- -	- -	- -	- -	- -	- -	- -	- -	- -
Physicians' Medical Center, New Albany, IN	- -	- -	- -	- 0	- 0	- 0	- 0	84 (a)	91 (a)	85 (a)	83 (a)	75 (a)	84 (a)	77 (a)	75 (a)	83 (a)	83 (a)
Pinnacle Hospital, Crown Point, IN	- -	- -	- -	0.326 92	0.192 73	- 0	38.0 79	- -	- -	- -	- -	- -	- -	- -	- -	- -	- -
Porter Valparaiso Hospital Campus, Valparaiso, IN	- -	- -	- -	0.629 1328	0.583 911	8.7 1834	35.1 350	49 300+	77 300+	81 300+	58 300+	55 300+	72 300+	67 300+	63 300+	51 300+	60 300+
Putnam County Hospital, Greencastle, IN	- -	- -	- -	- -	- -	- -	- -	- -	- -	- -	- -	- -	- -	- -	- -	- -	- -
Reid Hospital & Health Care Services, Richmond, IN	- -	- -	- -	0.110 1288	0.006 806	5.6 2179	35.9 348	54 300+	79 300+	84 300+	71 300+	57 300+	76 300+	68 300+	84 300+	59 300+	73 300+
Riverview Hospital, Noblesville, IN	- -	- -	- -	0.059 544	0.016 435	9.7 1032	31.0 126	57 300+	82 300+	86 300+	72 300+	64 300+	76 300+	71 300+	76 300+	62 300+	72 300+
Rush Memorial Hospital, Rushville, IN	- -	- -	- -	0.068 191	0.000 92	7.4 188	48.1 27	- -	- -	- -	- -	- -	- -	- -	- -	- -	- -
Saint Catherine Hospital, East Chicago, IN	- -	- -	- -	0.453 406	0.008 244	4.3 559	42.0 112	59 300+	78 300+	80 300+	70 300+	63 300+	79 300+	72 300+	74 300+	67 300+	71 300+
Saint Catherine Regional Hospital, Charlestown, IN	- -	- -	- -	0.146 103	0.143 133	11.9 109	32.1 28	51 (a)	76 (a)	67 (a)	51 (a)	45 (a)	68 (a)	57 (a)	54 (a)	54 (a)	52 (a)
Saint Clare Medical Center, Crawfordsville, IN	- -	- -	- -	0.046 539	0.032 312	6.4 748	30.5 128	51 300+	80 300+	80 300+	59 300+	56 300+	74 300+	64 300+	68 300+	61 300+	59 300+
Saint Elizabeth Central, Lafayette, IN	- -	- -	- -	0.072 594	0.007 611	7.4 2043	39.3 28	47 300+	75 300+	84 300+	65 300+	54 300+	77 300+	71 300+	68 300+	58 300+	70 300+
Saint Elizabeth East, Lafayette, IN	- -	- -	- -	0.425 1401	0.012 1259	0.0 1	36.2 329	59 300+	80 300+	86 300+	66 300+	58 300+	78 300+	74 300+	77 300+	60 300+	72 300+
Saint Francis Hospital and Health Centers, Beech Grove, IN	- -	- -	- -	0.066 455	0.004 257	- 0	45.9 61	52 300+	73 300+	83 300+	69 300+	56 300+	75 300+	72 300+	69 300+	59 300+	72 300+
Saint Francis Hosp & Health Ctrs-Indianapolis, Indianapolis, IN	- -	- -	- -	0.129 1547	0.030 941	8.8 2338	33.0 427	53 300+	80 300+	85 300+	76 300+	58 300+	77 300+	70 300+	72 300+	69 300+	79 300+

NOTE: The first number in each column (boldface) is the score, the second number is the number of patients; Please refer to the main entry for footnotes; (a) 100-299
*MEASURES: **Children's Asthma Care:** 33. Received Systemic Corticosteroids; 34. Received Home Management Plan of Care; 35. Received Reliever Medication; **Use of Medical Imaging:** 36. Combination Abdominal CT Scan; 37. Combination Chest CT Scan; 38. Follow-up Mammogram/Ultrasound; 39. MRI for Low Back Pain; **Survey of Patients' Hospital Experiences:** 40. Area Around Room 'Always' Quiet at Night; 41. Doctors 'Always' Communicated Well; 42. Home Recovery Information Given; 43. Hospital Given 9 or 10 on 10 Point Scale; 44. Meds 'Always' Explained Before Given; 45. Nurses 'Always' Communicated Well; 46. Pain 'Always' Well Controlled; 47. Room and Bathroom 'Always' Clean; 48. Timely Help 'Always' Received; 49. Would Definitely Recommend Hospital*

Hospital	Children's Asthma Care			Use of Medical Imaging				Survey of Patients' Hospital Experiences									
	33	34	35	36	37	38	39	40	41	42	43	44	45	46	47	48	49
Saint Francis Hospital Mooresville, Mooresville, IN	- -	- -	- -	0.118 313	0.120 184	6.7 627	39.2 79	65 300+	83 300+	87 300+	79 300+	65 300+	80 300+	73 300+	79 300+	64 300+	84 300+
Saint John's Health System, Anderson, IN	- -	- -	- -	0.111 915	0.028 928	10.2 1805	37.4 270	53 300+	83 300+	86 300+	71 300+	59 300+	80 300+	70 300+	77 300+	67 300+	76 300+
Saint Joseph Hospital, Fort Wayne, IN	- -	- -	- -	0.110 181	0.010 98	5.4 387	33.3 9	58 300+	80 300+	88 300+	69 300+	60 300+	76 300+	71 300+	74 300+	66 300+	69 300+
Saint Joseph Hospital & Health Center, Kokomo, IN	- -	- -	- -	0.091 656	0.006 505	9.6 688	39.4 132	50 300+	80 300+	80 300+	73 300+	58 300+	74 300+	67 300+	72 300+	62 300+	79 300+
Saint Joseph Regional Medical Center, Mishawaka, IN	- -	- -	- -	0.051 763	0.002 465	14.4 1262	- 0	60 300+	79 300+	85 300+	73 300+	57 300+	77 300+	70 300+	68 300+	62 300+	77 300+
Saint Joseph's Regional Medical Center - Plymouth, Plymouth, IN	- -	- -	- -	0.023 432	0.000 292	13.4 543	- 0	58 300+	83 300+	87 300+	79 300+	64 300+	82 300+	74 300+	72 300+	74 300+	77 300+
Saint Mary Medical Center, Hobart, IN	- -	- -	- -	0.426 940	0.395 851	6.8 878	37.0 184	57 300+	79 300+	84 300+	74 300+	61 300+	80 300+	71 300+	77 300+	66 300+	80 300+
Saint Mary's Medical Center of Evansville, Evansville, IN	- -	- -	- -	0.024 1366	0.002 1285	- 0	35.5 293	60 300+	83 300+	87 300+	77 300+	63 300+	79 300+	70 300+	75 300+	68 300+	82 300+
Saint Mary's Warrick Hospital, Boonville, IN	- -	- -	- -	- -	- -	- -	- -	- -	- -	- -	- -	- -	- -	- -	- -	- -	- -
Saint Vincent Carmel Hospital, Carmel, IN	- -	- -	- -	0.096 437	0.000 210	10.8 427	32.7 220	62 300+	84 300+	83 300+	81 300+	61 300+	83 300+	77 300+	75 300+	70 300+	85 300+
Saint Vincent Clay Hospital, Brazil, IN	- -	- -	- -	- -	- -	- -	- -	46 (a)	85 (a)	78 (a)	62 (a)	55 (a)	78 (a)	70 (a)	79 (a)	60 (a)	56 (a)
Saint Vincent Dunn Hospital, Bedford, IN	- -	- -	- -	0.030 333	0.006 155	11.6 311	18.8 32	65 300+	88 300+	86 300+	77 300+	72 300+	83 300+	73 300+	74 300+	77 300+	74 300+
Saint Vincent Frankfort Hospital, Frankfort, IN	- -	- -	- -	- -	- -	- -	- -	65 (a)	85 (a)	82 (a)	77 (a)	68 (a)	85 (a)	73 (a)	74 (a)	74 (a)	67 (a)
Saint Vincent Heart Center of Indiana, Indianapolis, IN	- -	- -	- -	0.205 39	0.327 52	- 0	17.6 17	57 300+	84 300+	85 300+	87 300+	63 300+	85 300+	77 300+	77 300+	77 300+	92 300+
Saint Vincent Hospital & Health Services, Indianapolis, IN	- -	- -	- -	0.078 2054	0.003 1694	9.1 2738	34.4 392	60 300+	80 300+	82 300+	77 300+	61 300+	77 300+	72 300+	68 300+	63 300+	80 300+
Saint Vincent Jennings Hospital, North Vernon, IN	- -	- -	- -	- -	- -	- -	- -	63 <100	85 <100	77 <100	64 <100	66 <100	86 <100	75 <100	94 <100	80 <100	70 <100
Saint Vincent Mercy Hospital, Elwood, IN	- -	- -	- -	0.218 211	0.000 115	22.2 329	23.9 46	47 (a)	82 (a)	85 (a)	72 (a)	63 (a)	83 (a)	74 (a)	68 (a)	65 (a)	68 (a)
Saint Vincent Randolph Hospital, Winchester, IN	- -	- -	- -	0.112 233	0.022 139	7.4 311	34.4 32	55 (a)	82 (a)	82 (a)	66 (a)	63 (a)	74 (a)	69 (a)	72 (a)	70 (a)	61 (a)
Saint Vincent Salem Hospital, Salem, IN	- -	- -	- -	0.801 166	0.315 108	16.7 198	39.5 43	- -	- -	- -	- -	- -	- -	- -	- -	- -	- -
Saint Vincent Williamsport Hospital, Williamsport, IN	- -	- -	- -	- -	- -	- -	- -	52 (a)	82 (a)	84 (a)	68 (a)	64 (a)	83 (a)	69 (a)	87 (a)	78 (a)	68 (a)
Schneck Medical Center, Seymour, IN	- -	- -	- -	0.041 589	0.005 365	10.1 704	40.4 104	67 300+	85 300+	84 300+	75 300+	64 300+	82 300+	76 300+	78 300+	72 300+	78 300+
Scott Memorial Hospital, Scottsburg, IN	- -	- -	- -	- -	- -	- -	- -	63 (a)	85 (a)	81 (a)	73 (a)	73 (a)	87 (a)	79 (a)	82 (a)	79 (a)	72 (a)
Starke Memorial Hospital, Knox, IN	- -	- -	- -	0.543 210	0.555 110	14.9 175	44.4 54	62 (a)	78 (a)	71 (a)	54 (a)	55 (a)	83 (a)	67 (a)	84 (a)	72 (a)	56 (a)
Sullivan County Community Hospital, Sullivan, IN	- -	- -	- -	0.394 284	0.042 215	2.8 211	51.2 43	64 (a)	78 (a)	80 (a)	67 (a)	59 (a)	77 (a)	69 (a)	83 (a)	75 (a)	72 (a)
Surgical Hospital of Munster, Munster, IN	- -	- -	- -	- 0	- 0	- 0	- 0	90 <100	89 <100	92 <100	90 <100	82 <100	92 <100	86 <100	87 <100	92 <100	91 <100
Terre Haute Regional Hospital, Terre Haute, IN	100 11	82 11	100 11	0.216 361	0.133 256	12.1 578	21.1 19	55 300+	82 300+	88 300+	71 300+	62 300+	78 300+	72 300+	74 300+	67 300+	74 300+
Tipton Hospital, Tipton, IN	- -	- -	- -	- -	- -	- -	- -	66 300+	88 300+	88 300+	81 300+	59 300+	82 300+	71 300+	81 300+	68 300+	81 300+
Union Hospital, Terre Haute, IN	- -	- -	- -	0.050 845	0.005 421	11.4 2073	30.7 215	49 300+	75 300+	84 300+	66 300+	54 300+	73 300+	65 300+	72 300+	63 300+	71 300+
Union Hospital Clinton, Clinton, IN	- -	- -	- -	0.438 313	0.534 178	7.7 234	- 0	53 300+	81 300+	83 300+	70 300+	65 300+	80 300+	74 300+	75 300+	75 300+	68 300+
Unity Medical and Surgical Hospital, Mishawaka, IN	- -	- -	- -	- -	- -	- -	- -	- -	- -	- -	- -	- -	- -	- -	- -	- -	- -
VA Northern Indiana Healthcare System - Marion, Marion, IN	- -	- -	- -	- -	- -	- -	- -	- -	- -	- -	- -	- -	- -	- -	- -	- -	- -
Wabash County Hospital, Wabash, IN	- -	- -	- -	- -	- -	- -	- -	60 (a)	79 (a)	86 (a)	71 (a)	62 (a)	86 (a)	78 (a)	84 (a)	81 (a)	66 (a)
Westview Hospital, Indianapolis, IN	- -	- -	- -	0.012 162	0.000 86	2.7 261	29.8 47	58 300+	82 300+	81 300+	67 300+	53 300+	71 300+	64 300+	68 300+	57 300+	67 300+
White County Memorial Hospital, Monticello, IN	- -	- -	- -	- -	- -	- -	- -	- -	- -	- -	- -	- -	- -	- -	- -	- -	- -
William N Wishard Memorial Hospital, Indianapolis, IN	- -	- -	- -	0.099 750	0.043 557	8.4 1353	28.9 190	57 300+	79 300+	82 300+	70 300+	58 300+	72 300+	68 300+	66 300+	56 300+	71 300+
Witham Health Services, Lebanon, IN	- -	- -	- -	0.094 436	0.015 331	11.8 576	31.9 94	60 300+	83 300+	80 300+	73 300+	62 300+	79 300+	72 300+	75 300+	69 300+	74 300+
The Women's Hospital, Newburgh, IN	- -	- -	- -	- 0	- 0	- 0	- 0	69 300+	84 300+	88 300+	86 300+	57 300+	79 300+	72 300+	82 300+	67 300+	86 300+
IOWA																	
Adair County Memorial Hospital, Greenfield, IA	- -	- -	- -	- -	- -	- -	- -	- -	- -	- -	- -	- -	- -	- -	- -	- -	- -
Alegent Health Community Memorial Hospital, Missouri Valley, IA	- -	- -	- -	- -	- -	- -	- -	65 <100	87 <100	89 <100	74 <100	70 <100	80 <100	73 <100	83 <100	71 <100	61 <100
Alegent Health Mercy Hospital, Council Bluffs, IA	- -	- -	- -	0.149 496	0.025 275	3.3 693	34.6 130	67 300+	79 300+	88 300+	74 300+	61 300+	80 300+	73 300+	72 300+	61 300+	79 300+
Alegent Health Mercy Hospital, Corning, IA	- -	- -	- -	- -	- -	- -	- -	70 <100	86 <100	84 <100	86 <100	64 <100	81 <100	76 <100	80 <100	77 <100	83 <100
Allen Memorial Hospital, Waterloo, IA	- -	- -	- -	0.046 1144	0.006 715	8.0 2129	30.4 207	55 300+	74 300+	83 300+	67 300+	58 300+	74 300+	67 300+	72 300+	55 300+	69 300+
Audubon County Memorial Hospital, Audubon, IA	- -	- -	- -	0.148 115	0.051 59	3.8 133	22.2 18	63 <100	90 <100	78 <100	84 <100	65 <100	77 <100	79 <100	92 <100	78 <100	78 <100
Avera Holy Family Health, Estherville, IA	- -	- -	- -	- -	- -	- -	- -	64 (a)	86 (a)	85 (a)	76 (a)	62 (a)	84 (a)	67 (a)	81 (a)	70 (a)	80 (a)
Baum Harmon Mercy Hospital, Primghar, IA	- -	- -	- -	- -	- -	- -	- -	- -	- -	- -	- -	- -	- -	- -	- -	- -	- -
Belmond Medical Center, Belmond, IA	- -	- -	- -	0.143 42	0.026 39	10.1 109	28.6 7	75 <100	96 <100	84 <100	89 <100	79 <100	91 <100	79 <100	80 <100	89 <100	86 <100
Boone County Hospital, Boone, IA	- -	- -	- -	0.783 138	0.062 97	7.0 499	24.6 57	63 300+	82 300+	85 300+	74 300+	61 300+	76 300+	65 300+	80 300+	66 300+	73 300+
Broadlawns Medical Center, Des Moines, IA	- -	- -	- -	0.042 72	0.175 63	29.6 206	20.0 5	61 300+	80 300+	83 300+	63 300+	61 300+	76 300+	71 300+	66 300+	61 300+	68 300+
Buchanan County Health Center, Independence, IA	- -	- -	- -	- -	- -	- -	- -	67 (a)	83 (a)	79 (a)	66 (a)	60 (a)	77 (a)	73 (a)	79 (a)	77 (a)	68 (a)
Buena Vista Regional Medical Center, Storm Lake, IA	- -	- -	- -	- -	- -	- -	- -	- -	- -	- -	- -	- -	- -	- -	- -	- -	- -
Burgess Health Center, Onawa, IA	- -	- -	- -	- -	- -	- -	- -	60 (a)	86 (a)	85 (a)	80 (a)	67 (a)	83 (a)	77 (a)	81 (a)	68 (a)	80 (a)
Cass County Memorial Hospital, Atlantic, IA	- -	- -	- -	0.029 208	0.135 141	6.5 445	37.5 32	66 (a)	78 (a)	84 (a)	63 (a)	59 (a)	77 (a)	69 (a)	76 (a)	71 (a)	60 (a)
Central Community Hospital, Elkader, IA	- -	- -	- -	- -	- -	- -	- -	- -	- -	- -	- -	- -	- -	- -	- -	- -	- -
Cherokee Regional Medical Center, Cherokee, IA	- -	- -	- -	- -	- -	- -	- -	- -	- -	- -	- -	- -	- -	- -	- -	- -	- -
Clarinda Regional Health Center, Clarinda, IA	- -	- -	- -	- -	- -	- -	- -	60 (a)	87 (a)	76 (a)	68 (a)	67 (a)	81 (a)	77 (a)	82 (a)	79 (a)	67 (a)
Clarke County Hospital, Osceola, IA	- -	- -	- -	0.117 103	0.037 54	2.7 146	43.8 16	76 (a)	87 (a)	88 (a)	78 (a)	69 (a)	87 (a)	71 (a)	91 (a)	76 (a)	76 (a)
Covenant Medical Center, Waterloo, IA	- -	- -	- -	0.046 585	0.004 679	7.3 1275	31.6 171	54 300+	76 300+	80 300+	61 300+	52 300+	71 300+	59 300+	71 300+	58 300+	65 300+
Crawford County Memorial Hospital, Denison, IA	- -	- -	- -	- -	- -	- -	- -	- -	- -	- -	- -	- -	- -	- -	- -	- -	- -
Dallas County Hospital, Perry, IA	- -	- -	- -	0.290 107	0.400 60	6.6 152	33.3 21	74 <100	83 <100	84 <100	81 <100	77 <100	88 <100	81 <100	84 <100	83 <100	86 <100
Davis County Hospital, Bloomfield, IA	- -	- -	- -	0.724 105	0.000 31	3.2 189	33.3 27	54 (a)	87 (a)	84 (a)	67 (a)	60 (a)	81 (a)	68 (a)	83 (a)	73 (a)	70 (a)
Decatur County Hospital, Leon, IA	- -	- -	- -	- -	- -	- -	- -	- -	- -	- -	- -	- -	- -	- -	- -	- -	- -
Ellsworth Municipal Hospital, Iowa Falls, IA	- -	- -	- -	- -	- -	- -	- -	- -	- -	- -	- -	- -	- -	- -	- -	- -	- -
The Finley Hospital, Dubuque, IA	- -	- -	- -	0.074 564	0.029 489	15.7 217	31.4 315	59 300+	80 300+	89 300+	72 300+	61 300+	78 300+	68 300+	77 300+	64 300+	74 300+
Floyd Valley Hospital, Le Mars, IA	- -	- -	- -	- -	- -	- -	- -	74 300+	87 300+	88 300+	79 300+	71 300+	83 300+	79 300+	89 300+	73 300+	77 300+
Fort Madison Community Hospital, Fort Madison, IA	- -	- -	- -	0.775 258	0.031 162	12.6 564	37.5 72	61 300+	80 300+	83 300+	74 300+	61 300+	80 300+	68 300+	72 300+	70 300+	75 300+
Franklin General Hospital, Hampton, IA	- -	- -	- -	- -	- -	- -	- -	- -	- -	- -	- -	- -	- -	- -	- -	- -	- -

NOTE: The first number in each column (boldface) is the score, the second number is the number of patients; Please refer to the main entry for footnotes; (a) 100-299

*MEASURES: **Children's Asthma Care:** 33. Received Systemic Corticosteroids; 34. Received Home Management Plan of Care; 35. Received Reliever Medication; **Use of Medical Imaging:** 36. Combination Abdominal CT Scan; 37. Combination Chest CT Scan; 38. Follow-up Mammogram/Ultrasound; 39. MRI for Low Back Pain; **Survey of Patients' Hospital Experiences:** 40. Area Around Room 'Always' Quiet at Night; 41. Doctors 'Always' Communicated Well; 42. Home Recovery Information Given; 43. Hospital Given 9 or 10 on 10 Point Scale; 44. Meds 'Always' Explained Before Given; 45. Nurses 'Always' Communicated Well; 46. Pain 'Always' Well Controlled; 47. Room and Bathroom 'Always' Clean; 48. Timely Help 'Always' Received; 49. Would Definitely Recommend Hospital*

Hospital	Children's Asthma Care			Use of Medical Imaging				Survey of Patients' Hospital Experiences									
	33	34	35	36	37	38	39	40	41	42	43	44	45	46	47	48	49
Genesis Medical Center - Davenport, Davenport, IA	-	-	-	**0.033** 1171	**0.016** 1200	**10.2** 1620	**28.1** 135	**54** 300+	**79** 300+	**81** 300+	**69** 300+	**60** 300+	**78** 300+	**70** 300+	**71** 300+	**64** 300+	**75** 300+
Genesis Medical Center-Dewitt, Dewitt, IA	-	-	-	**0.000** 38	**0.045** 44	**10.9** 320	**33.3** 9	-	-	-	-	-	-	-	-	-	-
Great River Medical Center, West Burlington, IA	-	-	-	**0.741** 854	**0.078** 774	**8.2** 1411	**28.4** 201	**55** 300+	**79** 300+	**84** 300+	**68** 300+	**62** 300+	**78** 300+	**70** 300+	**71** 300+	**64** 300+	**69** 300+
Greater Regional Medical Center, Creston, IA	-	-	-	-	-	-	-	**62** 300+	**84** 300+	**80** 300+	**70** 300+	**68** 300+	**82** 300+	**69** 300+	**78** 300+	**76** 300+	**67** 300+
Greene County Medical Center, Jefferson, IA	-	-	-	-	-	-	-	-	-	-	-	-	-	-	-	-	-
Grinnell Regional Medical Center, Grinnell, IA	-	-	-	**0.099** 262	**0.063** 144	**18.3** 449	**30.4** 79	**67** 300+	**85** 300+	**87** 300+	**72** 300+	**67** 300+	**81** 300+	**73** 300+	**81** 300+	**74** 300+	**74** 300+
Grundy County Memorial Hospital, Grundy Center, IA	-	-	-	**0.037** 54	**0.000** 31	**5.2** 213	**37.5** 8	**72** <100	**81** <100	**89** <100	**80** <100	**64** <100	**77** <100	**72** <100	**80** <100	**67** <100	**87** <100
Guthrie County Hospital, Guthrie Center, IA	-	-	-	**0.091** 77	**0.080** 50	**12.2** 123	**26.3** 19	-	-	-	-	-	-	-	-	-	-
Guttenberg Municipal Hospital, Guttenberg, IA	-	-	-	-	-	-	-	**70** (a)	**88** (a)	**84** (a)	**77** (a)	**71** (a)	**85** (a)	**72** (a)	**87** (a)	**79** (a)	**82** (a)
Hancock County Memorial Hospital, Britt, IA	-	-	-	-	-	-	-	-	-	-	-	-	-	-	-	-	-
Hawarden Community Hospital, Hawarden, IA	-	-	-	-	-	-	-	**88** <100	**84** <100	**69** <100	**77** <100	**80** <100	**83** <100	**62** <100	**87** <100	**88** <100	**78** <100
Hegg Memorial Health Center, Rock Valley, IA	-	-	-	**0.127** 55	**0.182** 22	**9.5** 105	**18.2** 11	**67** (a)	**84** (a)	**86** (a)	**81** (a)	**80** (a)	**82** (a)	**73** (a)	**82** (a)	**74** (a)	**86** (a)
Henry County Health Center, Mount Pleasant, IA	-	-	-	-	-	-	-	**65** (a)	**89** (a)	**84** (a)	**75** (a)	**61** (a)	**82** (a)	**69** (a)	**64** (a)	**75** (a)	**68** (a)
Horn Memorial Hospital, Ida Grove, IA	-	-	-	-	-	-	-	-	-	-	-	-	-	-	-	-	-
Iowa City VA Medical Center, Iowa City, IA	-	-	-	-	-	-	-	-	-	-	-	-	-	-	-	-	-
Iowa Lutheran Hospital, Des Moines, IA	-	-	-	**0.058** 462	**0.171** 245	**26.8** 1043	**29.4** 102	**56** 300+	**75** 300+	**84** 300+	**70** 300+	**58** 300+	**74** 300+	**67** 300+	**72** 300+	**60** 300+	**75** 300+
Iowa Methodist Medical Center, Des Moines, IA	-	-	-	**0.094** 479	**0.147** 109	- 0	**36.4** 44	**61** 300+	**77** 300+	**82** 300+	**72** 300+	**59** 300+	**75** 300+	**67** 300+	**70** 300+	**59** 300+	**77** 300+
Jackson County Regional Health Center, Maquoketa, IA	-	-	-	-	-	-	-	**71** (a)	**84** (a)	**80** (a)	**63** (a)	**62** (a)	**76** (a)	**74** (a)	**77** (a)	**65** (a)	**59** (a)
Jefferson County Health Center, Fairfield, IA	-	-	-	-	-	-	-	**73** (a)	**85** (a)	**80** (a)	**81** (a)	**58** (a)	**89** (a)	**74** (a)	**89** (a)	**81** (a)	**78** (a)
Jennie Edmundson Hospital, Council Bluffs, IA	-	-	-	**0.110** 573	**0.013** 396	**10.4** 1046	**32.8** 180	**57** 300+	**85** 300+	**87** 300+	**73** 300+	**65** 300+	**82** 300+	**71** 300+	**73** 300+	**68** 300+	**74** 300+
Jones Regional Medical Center, Anamosa, IA	-	-	-	-	-	-	-	-	-	-	-	-	-	-	-	-	-
Keokuk Area Hospital, Keokuk, IA	-	-	-	**0.250** 284	**0.506** 87	**4.1** 583	**24.5** 53	**46** (a)	**77** (a)	**80** (a)	**61** (a)	**55** (a)	**71** (a)	**62** (a)	**74** (a)	**54** (a)	**55** (a)
Knoxville Hospital & Clinics, Knoxville, IA	-	-	-	-	-	-	-	**49** (a)	**91** (a)	**84** (a)	**68** (a)	**64** (a)	**79** (a)	**70** (a)	**81** (a)	**67** (a)	**71** (a)
Kossuth Regional Health Center, Algona, IA	-	-	-	-	-	-	-	-	-	-	-	-	-	-	-	-	-
Lakes Regional Healthcare, Spirit Lake, IA	-	-	-	**0.395** 86	**0.300** 50	**0.9** 327	**32.1** 53	**67** 300+	**83** 300+	**88** 300+	**74** 300+	**65** 300+	**80** 300+	**71** 300+	**77** 300+	**71** 300+	**74** 300+
Lucas County Health Center, Chariton, IA	-	-	-	-	-	-	-	-	-	-	-	-	-	-	-	-	-
Madison County Memorial Hospital, Winterset, IA	-	-	-	-	-	-	-	-	-	-	-	-	-	-	-	-	-
Mahaska Health Partnership, Oskaloosa, IA	-	-	-	**0.711** 173	**0.025** 79	**2.1** 421	**35.7** 42	**55** (a)	**88** (a)	**81** (a)	**70** (a)	**62** (a)	**80** (a)	**70** (a)	**73** (a)	**61** (a)	**67** (a)
Manning Regional Healthcare Center, Manning, IA	-	-	-	-	-	-	-	-	-	-	-	-	-	-	-	-	-
Marengo Memorial Hospital, Marengo, IA	-	-	-	**0.073** 41	**0.053** 19	- 0	**20.0** 10	-	-	-	-	-	-	-	-	-	-
Marshalltown Medical & Surgical Center, Marshalltown, IA	-	-	-	**0.023** 302	**0.000** 188	**13.1** 628	**44.9** 49	**53** 300+	**80** 300+	**85** 300+	**65** 300+	**60** 300+	**75** 300+	**65** 300+	**70** 300+	**56** 300+	**60** 300+
Mary Greeley Medical Center, Ames, IA	-	-	-	**0.010** 203	**0.225** 129	**10.5** 190	**14.8** 27	**47** 300+	**81** 300+	**84** 300+	**67** 300+	**56** 300+	**75** 300+	**65** 300+	**69** 300+	**59** 300+	**74** 300+
Mercy Hospital, Iowa City, IA	-	-	-	**0.067** 625	**0.002** 583	**7.7** 1189	**28.3** 269	**58** 300+	**85** 300+	**92** 300+	**76** 300+	**66** 300+	**81** 300+	**69** 300+	**70** 300+	**72** 300+	**86** 300+
Mercy Hospital of Franciscan Sisters-Oelwein, Oelwein, IA	-	-	-	-	-	-	-	**72** (a)	**85** (a)	**88** (a)	**70** (a)	**63** (a)	**86** (a)	**77** (a)	**87** (a)	**71** (a)	**67** (a)
Mercy Medical Center-Cedar Rapids, Cedar Rapids, IA	-	-	-	**0.075** 783	**0.008** 529	**7.4** 2686	**31.8** 340	**68** 300+	**79** 300+	**83** 300+	**75** 300+	**62** 300+	**76** 300+	**64** 300+	**68** 300+	**58** 300+	**81** 300+
Mercy Medical Center-Centerville, Centerville, IA	-	-	-	-	-	-	-	-	-	-	-	-	-	-	-	-	-
Mercy Medical Center-Clinton, Clinton, IA	-	-	-	**0.625** 168	**0.315** 111	**1.0** 392	**0.0** 2	**58** 300+	**75** 300+	**86** 300+	**66** 300+	**61** 300+	**79** 300+	**73** 300+	**65** 300+	**65** 300+	**61** 300+
Mercy Medical Center-Des Moines, Des Moines, IA	-	-	-	**0.017** 1496	**0.021** 1214	**6.5** 3240	**36.5** 304	**56** 300+	**77** 300+	**85** 300+	**71** 300+	**59** 300+	**76** 300+	**67** 300+	**68** 300+	**57** 300+	**74** 300+
Mercy Medical Center-Dubuque, Dubuque, IA	-	-	-	**0.165** 393	**0.125** 176	**23.3** 30	**29.8** 47	**58** 300+	**81** 300+	**90** 300+	**77** 300+	**61** 300+	**77** 300+	**71** 300+	**71** 300+	**63** 300+	**81** 300+
Mercy Medical Center-Dyersville, Dyersville, IA	-	-	-	- 0	- 0	**10.1** 109	- 0	-	-	-	-	-	-	-	-	-	-
Mercy Medical Center-New Hampton, New Hampton, IA	-	-	-	-	-	-	-	-	-	-	-	-	-	-	-	-	-
Mercy Medical Center-North Iowa, Mason City, IA	-	-	-	**0.081** 1032	**0.015** 1156	**10.7** 2698	**0.0** 2	**54** 300+	**77** 300+	**87** 300+	**68** 300+	**58** 300+	**77** 300+	**69** 300+	**71** 300+	**67** 300+	**71** 300+
Mercy Medical Center-Sioux City, Sioux City, IA	-	-	-	**0.422** 535	**0.010** 298	**4.6** 393	**37.1** 143	**52** 300+	**78** 300+	**86** 300+	**71** 300+	**59** 300+	**77** 300+	**71** 300+	**71** 300+	**64** 300+	**75** 300+
Monroe County Hospital, Albia, IA	-	-	-	-	-	-	-	-	-	-	-	-	-	-	-	-	-
Montgomery County Memorial Hospital, Red Oak, IA	-	-	-	-	-	-	-	**60** (a)	**89** (a)	**90** (a)	**81** (a)	**67** (a)	**84** (a)	**75** (a)	**73** (a)	**74** (a)	**81** (a)
Myrtue Medical Center, Harlan, IA	-	-	-	**0.133** 195	**0.091** 88	**9.0** 423	**39.0** 41	**57** 300+	**87** 300+	**84** 300+	**73** 300+	**61** 300+	**81** 300+	**69** 300+	**84** 300+	**65** 300+	**72** 300+
Orange City Area Health System, Orange City, IA	-	-	-	-	-	-	-	-	-	-	-	-	-	-	-	-	-
Osceola Community Hospital, Sibley, IA	-	-	-	-	-	-	-	**72** (a)	**83** (a)	**78** (a)	**83** (a)	**66** (a)	**82** (a)	**71** (a)	**92** (a)	**80** (a)	**79** (a)
Ottumwa Regional Health Center, Ottumwa, IA	-	-	-	**0.433** 30	**0.160** 25	**3.2** 1120	**37.1** 97	**65** 300+	**82** 300+	**84** 300+	**65** 300+	**62** 300+	**78** 300+	**71** 300+	**80** 300+	**71** 300+	**64** 300+
Palmer Lutheran Health Center, West Union, IA	-	-	-	**0.020** 98	**0.000** 37	- 0	**33.3** 18	-	-	-	-	-	-	-	-	-	-
Palo Alto County Hospital, Emmetsburg, IA	-	-	-	-	-	-	-	-	-	-	-	-	-	-	-	-	-
Pella Regional Health Center, Pella, IA	-	-	-	-	-	-	-	**66** 300+	**88** 300+	**85** 300+	**84** 300+	**68** 300+	**82** 300+	**68** 300+	**80** 300+	**71** 300+	**82** 300+
Regional Health Services of Howard County, Cresco, IA	-	-	-	-	-	-	-	-	-	-	-	-	-	-	-	-	-
Regional Medical Center, Manchester, IA	-	-	-	-	-	-	-	-	-	-	-	-	-	-	-	-	-
Ringgold County Hospital, Mount Ayr, IA	-	-	-	-	-	-	-	-	-	-	-	-	-	-	-	-	-
Saint Anthony Regional Hospital, Carroll, IA	-	-	-	**0.055** 343	**0.014** 212	**8.5** 519	**19.0** 100	**68** 300+	**84** 300+	**86** 300+	**82** 300+	**65** 300+	**81** 300+	**72** 300+	**81** 300+	**71** 300+	**82** 300+
Saint Lukes Hospital, Cedar Rapids, IA	-	-	-	**0.112** 881	**0.048** 580	**8.3** 1591	**29.8** 312	**61** 300+	**78** 300+	**89** 300+	**77** 300+	**62** 300+	**79** 300+	**71** 300+	**75** 300+	**61** 300+	**82** 300+
Saint Lukes Regional Medical Center, Sioux City, IA	-	-	-	**0.601** 258	**0.156** 90	- 0	**33.3** 12	**47** 300+	**74** 300+	**83** 300+	**68** 300+	**58** 300+	**73** 300+	**65** 300+	**70** 300+	**58** 300+	**76** 300+
Sanford Hospital Rock Rapids, Rock Rapids, IA	-	-	-	-	-	-	-	**59** (a)	**85** (a)	**80** (a)	**85** (a)	**60** (a)	**79** (a)	**70** (a)	**87** (a)	**78** (a)	**79** (a)
Sanford Sheldon Medical Center, Sheldon, IA	-	-	-	-	-	-	-	**49** (a)	**82** (a)	**76** (a)	**68** (a)	**60** (a)	**73** (a)	**67** (a)	**73** (a)	**60** (a)	**72** (a)
Sartori Memorial Hospital, Cedar Falls, IA	-	-	-	**0.006** 168	**0.000** 102	**5.4** 516	**25.0** 48	**69** 300+	**82** 300+	**83** 300+	**71** 300+	**61** 300+	**78** 300+	**71** 300+	**79** 300+	**58** 300+	**74** 300+
Shenandoah Medical Center, Shenandoah, IA	-	-	-	-	-	-	-	**47** <100	**89** <100	**83** <100	**68** <100	**70** <100	**76** <100	**67** <100	**65** <100	**69** <100	**69** <100
Sioux Center Community Hospital, Sioux Center, IA	-	-	-	**0.197** 76	**0.119** 42	**9.1** 197	**11.1** 27	**60** (a)	**81** (a)	**82** (a)	**79** (a)	**66** (a)	**83** (a)	**72** (a)	**77** (a)	**75** (a)	**80** (a)
Skiff Medical Center, Newton, IA	-	-	-	**0.030** 236	**0.019** 105	**3.6** 638	**26.9** 52	**55** 300+	**85** 300+	**83** 300+	**68** 300+	**60** 300+	**79** 300+	**68** 300+	**67** 300+	**66** 300+	**69** 300+
Spencer Municipal Hospital, Spencer, IA	-	-	-	**0.223** 282	**0.179** 207	**10.7** 568	**32.1** 112	**67** 300+	**80** 300+	**87** 300+	**76** 300+	**63** 300+	**78** 300+	**71** 300+	**82** 300+	**68** 300+	**76** 300+
Stewart Memorial Community Hospital, Lake City, IA	-	-	-	-	-	-	-	**61** (a)	**79** (a)	**83** (a)	**80** (a)	**66** (a)	**81** (a)	**69** (a)	**91** (a)	**72** (a)	**79** (a)
Story County Hospital, Nevada, IA	-	-	-	-	-	-	-	-	-	-	-	-	-	-	-	-	-

NOTE: The first number in each column (boldface) is the score, the second number is the number of patients; Please refer to the main entry for footnotes; (a) 100-299

*MEASURES: **Children's Asthma Care:** 33. Received Systemic Corticosteroids; 34. Received Home Management Plan of Care; 35. Received Reliever Medication; **Use of Medical Imaging:** 36. Combination Abdominal CT Scan; 37. Combination Chest CT Scan; 38. Follow-up Mammogram/Ultrasound; 39. MRI for Low Back Pain; **Survey of Patients' Hospital Experiences:** 40. Area Around Room 'Always' Quiet at Night; 41. Doctors 'Always' Communicated Well; 42. Home Recovery Information Given; 43. Hospital Given 9 or 10 on 10 Point Scale; 44. Meds 'Always' Explained Before Given; 45. Nurses 'Always' Communicated Well; 46. Pain 'Always' Well Controlled; 47. Room and Bathroom 'Always' Clean; 48. Timely Help 'Always' Received; 49. Would Definitely Recommend Hospital*

Hospital	Children's Asthma Care			Use of Medical Imaging				Survey of Patients' Hospital Experiences									
	33	34	35	36	37	38	39	40	41	42	43	44	45	46	47	48	49
Trinity Bettendorf, Bettendorf, IA	- -	- -	- -	**0.055** 255	**0.083** 132	**14.7** 251	- 0	**65** 300+	**79** 300+	**87** 300+	**74** 300+	**62** 300+	**76** 300+	**69** 300+	**76** 300+	**63** 300+	**78** 300+
Trinity Muscatine, Muscatine, IA	- -	- -	- -	**0.024** 210	**0.000** 125	**4.0** 570	**28.2** 39	**49** 300+	**84** 300+	**82** 300+	**58** 300+	**62** 300+	**75** 300+	**67** 300+	**73** 300+	**67** 300+	**60** 300+
Trinity Regional Medical Center, Fort Dodge, IA	- -	- -	- -	**0.011** 380	**0.002** 445	- 0	**31.4** 159	**53** 300+	**82** 300+	**89** 300+	**69** 300+	**63** 300+	**78** 300+	**72** 300+	**75** 300+	**63** 300+	**67** 300+
University of Iowa Hospital & Clinics, Iowa City, IA	- -	- -	- -	**0.091** 1602	**0.015** 1581	**9.4** 1121	**23.4** 205	**44** 300+	**75** 300+	**84** 300+	**66** 300+	**55** 300+	**72** 300+	**62** 300+	**66** 300+	**55** 300+	**77** 300+
VA Central Iowa Healthcare System, Des Moines, IA	- -	- -	- -	- -	- -	- -	- -	- -	- -	- -	- -	- -	- -	- -	- -	- -	- -
Van Buren County Hospital, Keosauqua, IA	- -	- -	- -	- -	- -	- -	- -	- -	- -	- -	- -	- -	- -	- -	- -	- -	- -
Van Diest Medical Center, Webster City, IA	- -	- -	- -	- -	- -	- -	- -	**56** (a)	**86** (a)	**81** (a)	**68** (a)	**61** (a)	**80** (a)	**78** (a)	**80** (a)	**74** (a)	**64** (a)
Veterans Memorial Hospital, Waukon, IA	- -	- -	- -	- -	- -	- -	- -	- -	- -	- -	- -	- -	- -	- -	- -	- -	- -
Washington County Hospital, Washington, IA	- -	- -	- -	- -	- -	- -	- -	**61** (a)	**86** (a)	**81** (a)	**70** (a)	**61** (a)	**81** (a)	**70** (a)	**80** (a)	**66** (a)	**69** (a)
Waverly Health Center, Waverly, IA	- -	- -	- -	**0.011** 275	**0.000** 124	**4.8** 540	**27.6** 58	**77** 300+	**88** 300+	**88** 300+	**84** 300+	**73** 300+	**84** 300+	**76** 300+	**89** 300+	**74** 300+	**86** 300+
Wayne County Hospital, Corydon, IA	- -	- -	- -	- -	- -	- -	- -	- -	- -	- -	- -	- -	- -	- -	- -	- -	- -
Winneshiek Medical Center, Decorah, IA	- -	- -	- -	- -	- -	- -	- -	- -	- -	- -	- -	- -	- -	- -	- -	- -	- -
Wright Medical Center, Clarion, IA	- -	- -	- -	- -	- -	- -	- -	**69** 300+	**85** 300+	**90** 300+	**83** 300+	**62** 300+	**85** 300+	**77** 300+	**79** 300+	**78** 300+	**85** 300+
KANSAS																	
Allen County Hospital, Iola, KS	- -	- -	- -	**0.758** 182	**0.015** 66	**0.8** 260	**53.7** 41	- -	- -	- -	- -	- -	- -	- -	- -	- -	- -
Anderson County Hospital, Garnett, KS	- -	- -	- -	**0.131** 107	**0.294** 34	**1.9** 162	**26.7** 15	**68** <100	**92** <100	**78** <100	**80** <100	**76** <100	**85** <100	**76** <100	**86** <100	**78** <100	**89** <100
Ashland Health Center, Ashland, KS	- -	- -	- -	- -	- -	- -	- -	- -	- -	- -	- -	- -	- -	- -	- -	- -	- -
Atchison Hospital, Atchison, KS	- -	- -	- -	- -	- -	- -	- -	- -	- -	- -	- -	- -	- -	- -	- -	- -	- -
Bob Wilson Memorial Grant County Hospital, Ulysses, KS	- -	- -	- -	**0.089** 56	**0.071** 28	**7.0** 114	**55.6** 9	**71** (a)	**83** (a)	**76** (a)	**64** (a)	**56** (a)	**76** (a)	**70** (a)	**77** (a)	**68** (a)	**62** (a)
Central Kansas Medical Center, Great Bend, KS	- -	- -	- -	**0.039** 727	**0.015** 710	**5.3** 437	**35.7** 70	**62** (a)	**81** (a)	**89** (a)	**70** (a)	**60** (a)	**77** (a)	**67** (a)	**67** (a)	**73** (a)	**68** (a)
Cheyenne County Hospital, Saint Francis, KS	- -	- -	- -	- -	- -	- -	- -	- -	- -	- -	- -	- -	- -	- -	- -	- -	- -
Clara Barton Hospital, Hoisington, KS	- -	- -	- -	**0.392** 189	**0.079** 139	**2.5** 163	**36.0** 25	- -	- -	- -	- -	- -	- -	- -	- -	- -	- -
Clay County Medical Center, Clay Center, KS	- -	- -	- -	- -	- -	- -	- -	- -	- -	- -	- -	- -	- -	- -	- -	- -	- -
Cloud County Health Center, Concordia, KS	- -	- -	- -	- -	- -	- -	- -	- -	- -	- -	- -	- -	- -	- -	- -	- -	- -
Coffey County Hospital, Burlington, KS	- -	- -	- -	**0.902** 112	**0.288** 59	**2.5** 243	**30.8** 52	**66** 300+	**84** 300+	**83** 300+	**76** 300+	**63** 300+	**78** 300+	**70** 300+	**80** 300+	**68** 300+	**78** 300+
Coffeyville Regional Medical Center, Coffeyville, KS	- -	- -	- -	**0.082** 389	**0.004** 236	**11.1** 497	**31.1** 45	**49** 300+	**80** 300+	**77** 300+	**61** 300+	**58** 300+	**73** 300+	**65** 300+	**66** 300+	**60** 300+	**59** 300+
Comanche County Hospital, Coldwater, KS	- -	- -	- -	- -	- -	- -	- -	- -	- -	- -	- -	- -	- -	- -	- -	- -	- -
Community Hospital - Onaga and St Marys Campus, Onaga, KS	- -	- -	- -	- -	- -	- -	- -	- -	- -	- -	- -	- -	- -	- -	- -	- -	- -
Cushing Memorial Hospital, Leavenworth, KS	- -	- -	- -	**0.302** 106	**0.012** 81	**7.6** 341	- 0	**60** (a)	**78** (a)	**82** (a)	**62** (a)	**64** (a)	**76** (a)	**70** (a)	**75** (a)	**72** (a)	**67** (a)
Doctors Hospital, Leawood, KS	- -	- -	- -	**0.000** 2	- 0	- 0	**33.3** 9	**91** (a)	**84** (a)	**87** (a)	**80** (a)	**62** (a)	**86** (a)	**75** (a)	**85** (a)	**77** (a)	**83** (a)
Edwards County Hospital, Kinsley, KS	- -	- -	- -	- -	- -	- -	- -	- -	- -	- -	- -	- -	- -	- -	- -	- -	- -
Ellsworth County Medical Center, Ellsworth, KS	- -	- -	- -	**0.402** 107	**0.044** 68	**4.7** 128	**47.6** 21	**60** (a)	**83** (a)	**71** (a)	**77** (a)	**66** (a)	**76** (a)	**64** (a)	**82** (a)	**71** (a)	**71** (a)
Fredonia Regional Hospital, Fredonia, KS	- -	- -	- -	- -	- -	- -	- -	- -	- -	- -	- -	- -	- -	- -	- -	- -	- -
Galichia Heart Hospital, Wichita, KS	- -	- -	- -	**0.401** 167	**0.504** 133	- 0	- 0	**61** 300+	**74** 300+	**80** 300+	**73** 300+	**50** 300+	**77** 300+	**70** 300+	**71** 300+	**63** 300+	**78** 300+
Geary Community Hospital, Junction City, KS	- -	- -	- -	**0.036** 247	**0.011** 185	**4.2** 647	**34.6** 52	**65** 300+	**85** 300+	**86** 300+	**68** 300+	**65** 300+	**77** 300+	**68** 300+	**72** 300+	**64** 300+	**70** 300+
Girard Medical Center, Girard, KS	- -	- -	- -	- -	- -	- -	- -	- -	- -	- -	- -	- -	- -	- -	- -	- -	- -
Goodland Regional Medical Center, Goodland, KS	- -	- -	- -	- -	- -	- -	- -	- -	- -	- -	- -	- -	- -	- -	- -	- -	- -
Gove County Medical Center, Quinter, KS	- -	- -	- -	- -	- -	- -	- -	- -	- -	- -	- -	- -	- -	- -	- -	- -	- -
Graham County Hospital, Hill City, KS	- -	- -	- -	**0.648** 88	**0.035** 85	**9.8** 92	**32.0** 25	- -	- -	- -	- -	- -	- -	- -	- -	- -	- -
Great Bend Regional Hospital, Great Bend, KS	- -	- -	- -	- 0	- 0	- 0	- 0	**68** 300+	**86** 300+	**80** 300+	**76** 300+	**63** 300+	**78** 300+	**72** 300+	**75** 300+	**72** 300+	**80** 300+
Greeley County Health Services, Tribune, KS	- -	- -	- -	- -	- -	- -	- -	- -	- -	- -	- -	- -	- -	- -	- -	- -	- -
Greenwood County Hospital, Eureka, KS	- -	- -	- -	- -	- -	- -	- -	- -	- -	- -	- -	- -	- -	- -	- -	- -	- -
Grisell Memorial Hospital District #1, Ransom, KS	- -	- -	- -	- -	- -	- -	- -	- -	- -	- -	- -	- -	- -	- -	- -	- -	- -
Hamilton County Hospital, Syracuse, KS	- -	- -	- -	- -	- -	- -	- -	- -	- -	- -	- -	- -	- -	- -	- -	- -	- -
Harper Hospital District #5, Harper, KS	- -	- -	- -	- -	- -	- -	- -	- -	- -	- -	- -	- -	- -	- -	- -	- -	- -
Hays Medical Center, Hays, KS	- -	- -	- -	**0.586** 630	**0.006** 710	**5.5** 1025	**41.3** 160	**63** 300+	**78** 300+	**86** 300+	**70** 300+	**61** 300+	**76** 300+	**68** 300+	**74** 300+	**60** 300+	**71** 300+
Heartland Surgical Spec Hospital, Overland Park, KS	- -	- -	- -	**0.375** 32	**0.400** 5	- 0	**30.2** 169	**82** 300+	**85** 300+	**87** 300+	**91** 300+	**69** 300+	**85** 300+	**76** 300+	**81** 300+	**85** 300+	**91** 300+
Herington Municipal Hospital, Herington, KS	- -	- -	- -	- -	- -	- -	- -	- -	- -	- -	- -	- -	- -	- -	- -	- -	- -
Hiawatha Community Hospital, Hiawatha, KS	- -	- -	- -	- -	- -	- -	- -	- -	- -	- -	- -	- -	- -	- -	- -	- -	- -
Hillsboro Community Hospital, Hillsboro, KS	- -	- -	- -	**0.296** 27	**0.000** 14	- 0	**30.0** 10	- -	- -	- -	- -	- -	- -	- -	- -	- -	- -
Hodgeman County Health Center, Jetmore, KS	- -	- -	- -	- -	- -	- -	- -	- -	- -	- -	- -	- -	- -	- -	- -	- -	- -
Holton Community Hospital, Holton, KS	- -	- -	- -	**0.247** 93	**0.050** 40	**4.0** 201	**44.7** 38	- -	- -	- -	- -	- -	- -	- -	- -	- -	- -
Jefferson County Memorial Hospital, Winchester, KS	- -	- -	- -	- -	- -	- -	- -	- -	- -	- -	- -	- -	- -	- -	- -	- -	- -
Jewell County Hospital, Mankato, KS	- -	- -	- -	- -	- -	- -	- -	- -	- -	- -	- -	- -	- -	- -	- -	- -	- -
Kansas City Orthopaedic Institute, Leawood, KS	- -	- -	- -	- 0	- 0	- 0	**29.3** 150	**68** 300+	**91** 300+	**93** 300+	**89** 300+	**74** 300+	**85** 300+	**79** 300+	**80** 300+	**89** 300+	**93** 300+
Kansas Heart Hospital, Wichita, KS	- -	- -	- -	**1.000** 1	**1.000** 1	- 0	- 0	**59** 300+	**86** 300+	**79** 300+	**87** 300+	**67** 300+	**86** 300+	**75** 300+	**90** 300+	**83** 300+	**91** 300+
Kansas Medical Center, Andover, KS	- -	- -	- -	**0.355** 110	**0.131** 84	- 0	- 0	**70** 300+	**84** 300+	**86** 300+	**83** 300+	**65** 300+	**82** 300+	**70** 300+	**80** 300+	**74** 300+	**79** 300+
Kansas Spine Hospital, Wichita, KS	- -	- -	- -	**0.833** 6	**1.000** 7	- 0	**26.7** 161	**76** 300+	**84** 300+	**87** 300+	**83** 300+	**66** 300+	**81** 300+	**73** 300+	**77** 300+	**73** 300+	**84** 300+
Kansas Surgery & Recovery Center, Wichita, KS	- -	- -	- -	**0.500** 10	**0.545** 11	- 0	**26.7** 217	**64** 300+	**88** 300+	**87** 300+	**80** 300+	**66** 300+	**80** 300+	**73** 300+	**80** 300+	**69** 300+	**84** 300+
Kearny County Hospital, Lakin, KS	- -	- -	- -	- -	- -	- -	- -	- -	- -	- -	- -	- -	- -	- -	- -	- -	- -
Kingman Community Hospital, Kingman, KS	- -	- -	- -	- -	- -	- -	- -	**54** (a)	**87** (a)	**82** (a)	**78** (a)	**62** (a)	**86** (a)	**74** (a)	**70** (a)	**72** (a)	**76** (a)
Kiowa District Hospital, Kiowa, KS	- -	- -	- -	**0.647** 17	**0.769** 13	- 0	**50.0** 4	- -	- -	- -	- -	- -	- -	- -	- -	- -	- -
Labette Health, Parsons, KS	- -	- -	- -	**0.829** 439	**0.483** 298	**3.2** 409	**40.6** 165	**58** 300+	**81** 300+	**89** 300+	**70** 300+	**54** 300+	**77** 300+	**68** 300+	**74** 300+	**67** 300+	**68** 300+
Lawrence Memorial Hospital, Lawrence, KS	- -	- -	- -	**0.133** 976	**0.000** 660	**7.0** 2133	**37.7** 316	**56** 300+	**83** 300+	**88** 300+	**73** 300+	**65** 300+	**78** 300+	**68** 300+	**72** 300+	**66** 300+	**76** 300+
Lindsborg Community Hospital, Lindsborg, KS	- -	- -	- -	- -	- -	- -	- -	- -	- -	- -	- -	- -	- -	- -	- -	- -	- -
Manhattan Surgical Hospital, Manhattan, KS	- -	- -	- -	- 0	- 0	- 0	- 0	**93** (a)	**95** (a)	**89** (a)	**95** (a)	**72** (a)	**90** (a)	**83** (a)	**90** (a)	**89** (a)	**94** (a)
Meade District Hospital, Meade, KS	- -	- -	- -	- -	- -	- -	- -	- -	- -	- -	- -	- -	- -	- -	- -	- -	- -

NOTE: The first number in each column (boldface) is the score, the second number is the number of patients; Please refer to the main entry for footnotes; (a) 100-299
*MEASURES: **Children's Asthma Care:** 33. Received Systemic Corticosteroids; 34. Received Home Management Plan of Care; 35. Received Reliever Medication; **Use of Medical Imaging:** 36. Combination Abdominal CT Scan; 37. Combination Chest CT Scan; 38. Follow-up Mammogram/Ultrasound; 39. MRI for Low Back Pain; **Survey of Patients' Hospital Experiences:** 40. Area Around Room 'Always' Quiet at Night; 41. Doctors 'Always' Communicated Well; 42. Home Recovery Information Given; 43. Hospital Given 9 or 10 on 10 Point Scale; 44. Meds 'Always' Explained Before Given; 45. Nurses 'Always' Communicated Well; 46. Pain 'Always' Well Controlled; 47. Room and Bathroom 'Always' Clean; 48. Timely Help 'Always' Received; 49. Would Definitely Recommend Hospital*

Hospital	Children's Asthma Care 33	34	35	Use of Medical Imaging 36	37	38	39	Survey of Patients' Hospital Experiences 40	41	42	43	44	45	46	47	48	49
Memorial Hospital, Mcpherson, KS	-	-	-	**0.656** 320	**0.028** 283	**9.9** 514	**30.6** 62	**57** 300+	**82** 300+	**80** 300+	**66** 300+	**59** 300+	**74** 300+	**69** 300+	**71** 300+	**67** 300+	**65** 300+
Memorial Hospital, Abilene, KS	-	-	-	-	-	-	-	-	-	-	-	-	-	-	-	-	-
Menorah Medical Center, Overland Park, KS	-	-	-	**0.102** 392	**0.014** 437	**11.2** 824	**41.9** 86	**60** 300+	**79** 300+	**86** 300+	**67** 300+	**58** 300+	**72** 300+	**68** 300+	**57** 300+	**56** 300+	**72** 300+
Mercy Health Center, Fort Scott, KS	-	-	-	**0.111** 216	**0.069** 131	**9.2** 469	**36.7** 49	**68** 300+	**85** 300+	**83** 300+	**69** 300+	**62** 300+	**82** 300+	**72** 300+	**77** 300+	**75** 300+	**61** 300+
Mercy Hospital, Moundridge, KS	-	-	-	- 0	- 0	- 0	- 0	**73** (a)	**88** (a)	**80** (a)	**85** (a)	**62** (a)	**84** (a)	**75** (a)	**86** (a)	**80** (a)	**87** (a)
Mercy Hospital of Kansas Independence, Independence, KS	-	-	-	**0.730** 148	**0.056** 90	**6.3** 384	**42.9** 42	**60** (a)	**87** (a)	**86** (a)	**69** (a)	**64** (a)	**78** (a)	**75** (a)	**75** (a)	**75** (a)	**66** (a)
Mercy Regional Health Center, Manhattan, KS	-	-	-	**0.088** 273	**0.000** 194	**7.5** 1442	**25.7** 35	**62** 300+	**83** 300+	**86** 300+	**69** 300+	**58** 300+	**78** 300+	**73** 300+	**68** 300+	**65** 300+	**73** 300+
Miami County Medical Center, Paola, KS	-	-	-	**0.015** 202	**0.000** 105	**8.5** 496	**34.5** 58	**76** (a)	**87** (a)	**87** (a)	**84** (a)	**74** (a)	**83** (a)	**77** (a)	**76** (a)	**73** (a)	**79** (a)
Mitchell County Hospital Health Systems, Beloit, KS	-	-	-	-	-	-	-	-	-	-	-	-	-	-	-	-	-
Morris County Hospital, Council Grove, KS	-	-	-	-	-	-	-	-	-	-	-	-	-	-	-	-	-
Morton County Hospital, Elkhart, KS	-	-	-	**0.600** 35	**0.467** 15	**9.5** 42	**37.5** 8	**43** (a)	**85** (a)	**67** (a)	**59** (a)	**46** (a)	**68** (a)	**61** (a)	**67** (a)	**53** (a)	**69** (a)
Nemaha Valley Community Hospital, Seneca, KS	-	-	-	-	-	-	-	-	-	-	-	-	-	-	-	-	-
Neosho Memorial Regional Medical Center, Chanute, KS	-	-	-	**0.062** 306	**0.038** 211	**3.5** 425	**43.4** 53	**71** 300+	**88** 300+	**87** 300+	**81** 300+	**67** 300+	**86** 300+	**77** 300+	**85** 300+	**77** 300+	**79** 300+
Ness County Hospital District #2, Ness City, KS	-	-	-	-	-	-	-	-	-	-	-	-	-	-	-	-	-
Newman Regional Health, Emporia, KS	-	-	-	**0.849** 370	**0.004** 251	- 0	**30.6** 180	**57** 300+	**79** 300+	**77** 300+	**61** 300+	**60** 300+	**73** 300+	**68** 300+	**74** 300+	**62** 300+	**54** 300+
Newton Medical Center, Newton, KS	-	-	-	**0.760** 288	**0.000** 193	**7.2** 947	**25.6** 78	**56** 300+	**83** 300+	**82** 300+	**79** 300+	**59** 300+	**78** 300+	**72** 300+	**76** 300+	**67** 300+	**82** 300+
Norton County Hospital, Norton, KS	-	-	-	-	-	-	-	-	-	-	-	-	-	-	-	-	-
Olathe Medical Center, Olathe, KS	-	-	-	**0.024** 706	**0.003** 684	**9.9** 1292	**37.8** 283	**56** 300+	**80** 300+	**87** 300+	**73** 300+	**61** 300+	**75** 300+	**69** 300+	**63** 300+	**61** 300+	**76** 300+
Osborne County Memorial Hospital, Osborne, KS	-	-	-	-	-	-	-	-	-	-	-	-	-	-	-	-	-
Oswego Community Hospital, Oswego, KS	-	-	-	-	-	-	-	-	-	-	-	-	-	-	-	-	-
Ottawa County Health Center, Minneapolis, KS	-	-	-	**1.000** 4	**0.250** 4	- 0	- 0	-	-	-	-	-	-	-	-	-	-
Overland Park Regional Medical Center, Overland Park, KS	-	-	-	**0.084** 275	**0.055** 217	**8.5** 376	**31.7** 41	**54** 300+	**80** 300+	**86** 300+	**66** 300+	**56** 300+	**73** 300+	**69** 300+	**63** 300+	**56** 300+	**68** 300+
Phillips County Hospital, Phillipsburg, KS	-	-	-	-	-	-	-	-	-	-	-	-	-	-	-	-	-
Pratt Regional Medical Center, Pratt, KS	-	-	-	**0.761** 255	**0.299** 204	**9.2** 609	**33.9** 121	**66** 300+	**85** 300+	**82** 300+	**73** 300+	**65** 300+	**83** 300+	**76** 300+	**77** 300+	**74** 300+	**78** 300+
Promise Regional Medical Center Hutchinson, Hutchinson, KS	-	-	-	**0.019** 320	**0.000** 139	- 0	**29.2** 72	**47** 300+	**75** 300+	**79** 300+	**61** 300+	**52** 300+	**70** 300+	**63** 300+	**66** 300+	**56** 300+	**62** 300+
Providence Medical Center, Kansas City, KS	-	-	-	**0.023** 385	**0.049** 425	**7.4** 488	**23.5** 51	**52** 300+	**72** 300+	**79** 300+	**60** 300+	**57** 300+	**70** 300+	**61** 300+	**61** 300+	**59** 300+	**58** 300+
Ransom Memorial Hospital, Ottawa, KS	-	-	-	**0.057** 244	**0.000** 177	**9.8** 439	**27.5** 80	**55** 300+	**87** 300+	**85** 300+	**70** 300+	**60** 300+	**80** 300+	**71** 300+	**69** 300+	**70** 300+	**72** 300+
Republic County Hospital, Belleville, KS	-	-	-	-	-	-	-	-	-	-	-	-	-	-	-	-	-
Russell Regional Hospital, Russell, KS	-	-	-	-	-	-	-	-	-	-	-	-	-	-	-	-	-
Sabetha Community Hospital, Sabetha, KS	-	-	-	-	-	-	-	**59** <100	**92** <100	**80** <100	**84** <100	**70** <100	**88** <100	**80** <100	**84** <100	**81** <100	**92** <100
Saint Catherine Hospital, Garden City, KS	-	-	-	**0.457** 341	**0.000** 143	**0.9** 423	**37.7** 77	**53** 300+	**80** 300+	**84** 300+	**63** 300+	**56** 300+	**70** 300+	**68** 300+	**68** 300+	**56** 300+	**62** 300+
Saint Francis Health Center, Topeka, KS	-	-	-	**0.111** 1053	**0.018** 554	**5.1** 2599	**35.5** 394	**51** 300+	**76** 300+	**82** 300+	**68** 300+	**62** 300+	**76** 300+	**72** 300+	**63** 300+	**62** 300+	**74** 300+
Saint John Hospital, Leavenworth, KS	-	-	-	**0.046** 151	**0.029** 137	**2.7** 377	- 0	**44** (a)	**74** (a)	**75** (a)	**57** (a)	**53** (a)	**72** (a)	**65** (a)	**66** (a)	**65** (a)	**63** (a)
Saint Luke Hospital & Living Center, Marion, KS	-	-	-	-	-	-	-	-	-	-	-	-	-	-	-	-	-
Saint Luke's South Hospital, Overland Park, KS	-	-	-	**0.224** 361	**0.052** 230	**8.5** 672	**30.5** 131	**61** 300+	**77** 300+	**85** 300+	**79** 300+	**62** 300+	**75** 300+	**72** 300+	**71** 300+	**72** 300+	**79** 300+
Salina Regional Health Center, Salina, KS	-	-	-	**0.275** 516	**0.002** 540	**7.3** 232	**32.1** 187	**54** 300+	**81** 300+	**80** 300+	**69** 300+	**57** 300+	**74** 300+	**63** 300+	**73** 300+	**58** 300+	**73** 300+
Salina Surgical Hospital, Salina, KS	-	-	-	- 0	- 0	- 0	- 0	**80** 300+	**89** 300+	**89** 300+	**95** 300+	**80** 300+	**92** 300+	**79** 300+	**89** 300+	**89** 300+	**94** 300+
Scott County Hospital, Scott City, KS	-	-	-	-	-	-	-	-	-	-	-	-	-	-	-	-	-
Sedan City Hospital, Sedan, KS	-	-	-	-	-	-	-	-	-	-	-	-	-	-	-	-	-
Shawnee Mission Medical Center, Shawnee Mission, KS	-	-	-	**0.138** 821	**0.081** 431	**6.9** 2262	**29.5** 315	**55** 300+	**76** 300+	**86** 300+	**69** 300+	**60** 300+	**73** 300+	**69** 300+	**66** 300+	**57** 300+	**72** 300+
Sheridan County Hospital, Hoxie, KS	-	-	-	-	-	-	-	-	-	-	-	-	-	-	-	-	-
Smith County Memorial Hospital, Smith Center, KS	-	-	-	**0.143** 63	**0.100** 60	**10.1** 169	**58.8** 34	-	-	-	-	-	-	-	-	-	-
South Central Ks Regional Medical Center, Arkansas City, KS	-	-	-	**0.834** 145	**0.023** 130	**8.8** 240	**23.8** 42	**69** (a)	**90** (a)	**85** (a)	**66** (a)	**67** (a)	**79** (a)	**73** (a)	**75** (a)	**71** (a)	**65** (a)
Southwest Medical Center, Liberal, KS	-	-	-	**0.683** 221	**0.719** 139	**5.3** 303	**38.6** 70	**53** 300+	**80** 300+	**83** 300+	**66** 300+	**64** 300+	**73** 300+	**69** 300+	**75** 300+	**62** 300+	**67** 300+
Stormont-Vail Healthcare, Topeka, KS	-	-	-	**0.072** 1314	**0.008** 660	- 0	**37.2** 527	**66** 300+	**82** 300+	**85** 300+	**75** 300+	**60** 300+	**77** 300+	**69** 300+	**69** 300+	**65** 300+	**78** 300+
Summit Surgical, Hutchinson, KS	-	-	-	- 0	- 0	- 0	- 0	**81** (a)	**88** (a)	**90** (a)	**88** (a)	**63** (a)	**88** (a)	**75** (a)	**82** (a)	**84** (a)	**90** (a)
Sumner Regional Medical Center, Wellington, KS	-	-	-	**0.647** 139	**0.067** 75	**7.4** 282	**52.6** 57	**61** <100	**90** <100	**76** <100	**72** <100	**65** <100	**77** <100	**69** <100	**84** <100	**66** <100	**78** <100
Susan B Allen Memorial Hospital, El Dorado, KS	-	-	-	**0.014** 420	**0.003** 342	**22.0** 554	**23.9** 159	**58** 300+	**85** 300+	**81** 300+	**72** 300+	**61** 300+	**75** 300+	**68** 300+	**69** 300+	**66** 300+	**71** 300+
Trego County Lemke Memorial Hospital, Wa Keeney, KS	-	-	-	-	-	-	-	-	-	-	-	-	-	-	-	-	-
University of Kansas Hospital, Kansas City, KS	-	-	-	**0.764** 1617	**0.005** 1980	**10.2** 1327	**27.4** 146	**60** 300+	**80** 300+	**88** 300+	**75** 300+	**66** 300+	**79** 300+	**69** 300+	**68** 300+	**63** 300+	**79** 300+
VA Eastern Kansas Healthcare System, Leavenworth, KS	-	-	-	-	-	-	-	-	-	-	-	-	-	-	-	-	-
Via Christi Hospital Pittsburg, Pittsburg, KS	-	-	-	**0.383** 439	**0.105** 285	**5.7** 757	**28.8** 73	**60** 300+	**86** 300+	**85** 300+	**72** 300+	**69** 300+	**80** 300+	**73** 300+	**74** 300+	**67** 300+	**68** 300+
Via Christi Hospital Wichita - Saint Teresa, Wichita, KS	-	-	-	-	-	-	-	-	-	-	-	-	-	-	-	-	-
Via Christi Hospitals Wichita, Wichita, KS	-	-	-	**0.634** 1437	**0.097** 781	**8.7** 1022	**50.0** 2	**46** 300+	**74** 300+	**78** 300+	**64** 300+	**53** 300+	**69** 300+	**62** 300+	**66** 300+	**50** 300+	**69** 300+
Wamego City Hospital, Wamego, KS	-	-	-	**0.057** 53	**0.121** 33	**6.1** 165	**38.9** 18	**56** <100	**80** <100	**76** <100	**78** <100	**59** <100	**74** <100	**57** <100	**80** <100	**74** <100	**80** <100
Washington County Hospital, Washington, KS	-	-	-	-	-	-	-	-	-	-	-	-	-	-	-	-	-
Wesley Medical Center, Wichita, KS	**99** 112	**85** 111	**100** 112	**0.575** 1064	**0.109** 477	**6.0** 265	**31.5** 130	**54** 300+	**78** 300+	**81** 300+	**62** 300+	**53** 300+	**69** 300+	**65** 300+	**61** 300+	**53** 300+	**63** 300+
Western Plains Medical Complex, Dodge City, KS	-	-	-	**0.406** 133	**0.086** 70	**5.9** 119	**46.7** 15	**50** 300+	**79** 300+	**77** 300+	**62** 300+	**55** 300+	**73** 300+	**68** 300+	**60** 300+	**55** 300+	**55** 300+
Wichita County Health Center, Leoti, KS	-	-	-	-	-	-	-	-	-	-	-	-	-	-	-	-	-
Wichita VA Medical Center, Wichita, KS	-	-	-	-	-	-	-	-	-	-	-	-	-	-	-	-	-
William Newton Hospital, Winfield, KS	-	-	-	**0.838** 247	**0.004** 249	**9.8** 579	**37.7** 69	**63** (a)	**84** (a)	**83** (a)	**68** (a)	**71** (a)	**81** (a)	**74** (a)	**76** (a)	**70** (a)	**72** (a)
Wilson Medical Center, Neodesha, KS	-	-	-	-	-	-	-	-	-	-	-	-	-	-	-	-	-
MICHIGAN																	
Allegan General Hospital, Allegan, MI	-	-	-	-	-	-	-	**66** (a)	**81** (a)	**89** (a)	**78** (a)	**58** (a)	**82** (a)	**75** (a)	**81** (a)	**76** (a)	**77** (a)
Allegiance Health, Jackson, MI	-	-	-	**0.060** 1644	**0.001** 1117	**3.6** 2442	**26.0** 423	**58** 300+	**76** 300+	**84** 300+	**66** 300+	**60** 300+	**77** 300+	**67** 300+	**69** 300+	**67** 300+	**64** 300+
Alpena Regional Medical Center, Alpena, MI	-	-	-	**0.164** 1011	**0.102** 777	**7.5** 1631	**39.3** 257	**37** (a)	**73** (a)	**78** (a)	**60** (a)	**48** (a)	**63** (a)	**57** (a)	**59** (a)	**55** (a)	**52** (a)
Aspirus Grand View Hospital, Ironwood, MI	-	-	-	-	-	-	-	-	-	-	-	-	-	-	-	-	-

NOTE: The first number in each column (boldface) is the score, the second number is the number of patients; Please refer to the main entry for footnotes; (a) 100-299
*MEASURES: **Children's Asthma Care:** 33. Received Systemic Corticosteroids; 34. Received Home Management Plan of Care; 35. Received Reliever Medication; **Use of Medical Imaging:** 36. Combination Abdominal CT Scan; 37. Combination Chest CT Scan; 38. Follow-up Mammogram/Ultrasound; 39. MRI for Low Back Pain; **Survey of Patients' Hospital Experiences:** 40. Area Around Room 'Always' Quiet at Night; 41. Doctors 'Always' Communicated Well; 42. Home Recovery Information Given; 43. Hospital Given 9 or 10 on 10 Point Scale; 44. Meds 'Always' Explained Before Given; 45. Nurses 'Always' Communicated Well; 46. Pain 'Always' Well Controlled; 47. Room and Bathroom 'Always' Clean; 48. Timely Help 'Always' Received; 49. Would Definitely Recommend Hospital*

Hospital	Children's Asthma Care			Use of Medical Imaging				Survey of Patients' Hospital Experiences									
	33	34	35	36	37	38	39	40	41	42	43	44	45	46	47	48	49
Baraga County Memorial Hospital, L'Anse, MI	- -	- -	- -	- -	- -	- -	- -	- -	- -	- -	- -	- -	- -	- -	- -	- -	- -
Battle Creek Health System, Battle Creek, MI	- -	- -	- -	**0.034** 1160	**0.009** 694	**4.3** 1745	**33.2** 220	**54** 300+	**76** 300+	**88** 300+	**64** 300+	**59** 300+	**76** 300+	**69** 300+	**69** 300+	**67** 300+	**59** 300+
Battle Creek VA Medical Center, Battle Creek, MI	- -	- -	- -	- -	- -	- -	- -	- -	- -	- -	- -	- -	- -	- -	- -	- -	- -
Bay Regional Medical Center, Bay City, MI	- -	- -	- -	**0.089** 1135	**0.029** 864	**4.3** 2019	**37.3** 415	**45** 300+	**76** 300+	**83** 300+	**63** 300+	**59** 300+	**76** 300+	**69** 300+	**65** 300+	**67** 300+	**66** 300+
Beaumont Hospital - Grosse Pointe, Grosse Pointe, MI	- -	- -	- -	**0.057** 703	**0.004** 550	**4.5** 819	**26.7** 116	**51** 300+	**78** 300+	**80** 300+	**69** 300+	**60** 300+	**75** 300+	**69** 300+	**67** 300+	**60** 300+	**71** 300+
Bell Memorial Hospital, Ishpeming, MI	- -	- -	- -	- -	- -	- -	- -	- -	- -	- -	- -	- -	- -	- -	- -	- -	- -
Borgess Medical Center, Kalamazoo, MI	- -	- -	- -	**0.157** 1205	**0.095** 1005	**10.8** 1607	**33.0** 469	**52** 300+	**75** 300+	**85** 300+	**67** 300+	**56** 300+	**71** 300+	**67** 300+	**67** 300+	**52** 300+	**71** 300+
Borgess-Lee Memorial Hospital, Dowagiac, MI	- -	- -	- -	- -	- -	- -	- -	**58** (a)	**68** (a)	**73** (a)	**63** (a)	**54** (a)	**72** (a)	**59** (a)	**80** (a)	**66** (a)	**64** (a)
Botsford Hospital, Farmington Hills, MI	- -	- -	- -	**0.090** 1124	**0.032** 816	**8.3** 1044	**30.1** 93	**44** 300+	**76** 300+	**83** 300+	**60** 300+	**48** 300+	**71** 300+	**64** 300+	**62** 300+	**59** 300+	**65** 300+
Brighton Hospital, Brighton, MI	- -	- -	- -	- 0	- 0	- 0	- 0	- -	- -	- -	- -	- -	- -	- -	- -	- -	- -
Bronson Lakeview Hospital, Paw Paw, MI	- -	- -	- -	- -	- -	- -	- -	**60** (a)	**85** (a)	**87** (a)	**69** (a)	**59** (a)	**81** (a)	**74** (a)	**73** (a)	**76** (a)	**69** (a)
Bronson Methodist Hospital, Kalamazoo, MI	**99** 87	**83** 87	**99** 87	**0.073** 1162	**0.003** 657	**6.1** 1020	**29.6** 324	**58** 300+	**80** 300+	**85** 300+	**78** 300+	**61** 300+	**79** 300+	**73** 300+	**74** 300+	**63** 300+	**82** 300+
Bronson Vicksburg Hospital, Vicksburg, MI	- -	- -	- -	- 0	- 0	**4.4** 272	- 0	- -	- -	- -	- -	- -	- -	- -	- -	- -	- -
Caro Community Hospital, Caro, MI	- -	- -	- -	- -	- -	- -	- -	**55** <100	**80** <100	**83** <100	**72** <100	**42** <100	**74** <100	**69** <100	**72** <100	**78** <100	**64** <100
Carson City Hospital, Carson City, MI	- -	- -	- -	**0.094** 235	**0.032** 187	**12.9** 294	**42.9** 133	**59** 300+	**83** 300+	**85** 300+	**73** 300+	**62** 300+	**77** 300+	**68** 300+	**78** 300+	**72** 300+	**70** 300+
Central Michigan Community Hospital, Mount Pleasant, MI	- -	- -	- -	**0.036** 388	**0.036** 338	**6.3** 492	**34.0** 103	**54** 300+	**81** 300+	**90** 300+	**75** 300+	**61** 300+	**81** 300+	**73** 300+	**72** 300+	**74** 300+	**77** 300+
Charlevoix Area Hospital, Charlevoix, MI	- -	- -	- -	- -	- -	- -	- -	- -	- -	- -	- -	- -	- -	- -	- -	- -	- -
Cheboygan Memorial Hospital, Cheboygan, MI	- -	- -	- -	- -	- -	- -	- -	- -	- -	- -	- -	- -	- -	- -	- -	- -	- -
Chelsea Community Hospital, Chelsea, MI	- -	- -	- -	**0.098** 356	**0.040** 200	**10.9** 847	**24.8** 161	**66** 300+	**83** 300+	**88** 300+	**82** 300+	**69** 300+	**83** 300+	**72** 300+	**79** 300+	**74** 300+	**85** 300+
Children's Hospital of Michigan, Detroit, MI	**100** 401	**84** 401	**100** 401	- -	- -	- -	- -	- -	- -	- -	- -	- -	- -	- -	- -	- -	- -
Chippewa County War Memorial Hospital, Sault Sainte Marie, MI	- -	- -	- -	**0.785** 330	**0.168** 262	**10.5** 599	**41.2** 165	**53** 300+	**83** 300+	**83** 300+	**68** 300+	**58** 300+	**82** 300+	**71** 300+	**76** 300+	**77** 300+	**68** 300+
Clinton Memorial Hospital, Saint Johns, MI	- -	- -	- -	**0.064** 311	**0.000** 213	**4.9** 243	**26.8** 82	**57** 300+	**87** 300+	**86** 300+	**82** 300+	**66** 300+	**83** 300+	**77** 300+	**84** 300+	**69** 300+	**79** 300+
Community Health Center of Branch County, Coldwater, MI	- -	- -	- -	**0.251** 351	**0.176** 261	**5.6** 622	**28.2** 85	**51** 300+	**76** 300+	**86** 300+	**67** 300+	**64** 300+	**77** 300+	**66** 300+	**67** 300+	**61** 300+	**61** 300+
Community Hospital, Watervliet, MI	- -	- -	- -	**0.038** 212	**0.016** 128	**7.0** 342	**28.6** 63	**64** (a)	**83** (a)	**88** (a)	**74** (a)	**60** (a)	**79** (a)	**77** (a)	**74** (a)	**79** (a)	**75** (a)
Covenant Medical Center, Saginaw, MI	- -	- -	- -	**0.196** 1615	**0.238** 1086	**4.6** 2883	**37.2** 401	**44** 300+	**77** 300+	**86** 300+	**67** 300+	**59** 300+	**79** 300+	**73** 300+	**66** 300+	**67** 300+	**73** 300+
Crittenton Hospital Medical Center, Rochester, MI	- -	- -	- -	**0.151** 820	**0.014** 698	**7.9** 1401	**50.0** 2	**58** 300+	**79** 300+	**82** 300+	**71** 300+	**54** 300+	**78** 300+	**70** 300+	**67** 300+	**64** 300+	**73** 300+
Deckerville Community Hospital, Deckerville, MI	- -	- -	- -	**0.031** 32	**0.000** 22	**15.4** 117	- 0	**61** <100	**79** <100	**81** <100	**68** <100	**65** <100	**83** <100	**62** <100	**71** <100	**69** <100	**60** <100
Detroit (John D. Dingell) VA Medical Center, Detroit, MI	- -	- -	- -	- -	- -	- -	- -	- -	- -	- -	- -	- -	- -	- -	- -	- -	- -
Detroit Receiving Hospital & Univ Health Center, Detroit, MI	- -	- -	- -	**0.221** 421	**0.201** 309	- 0	- 0	**56** 300+	**75** 300+	**79** 300+	**62** 300+	**56** 300+	**72** 300+	**63** 300+	**60** 300+	**63** 300+	**65** 300+
Dickinson County Memorial Hospital, Iron Mountain, MI	- -	- -	- -	**0.097** 464	**0.013** 399	**6.7** 765	**31.9** 204	**61** 300+	**83** 300+	**83** 300+	**64** 300+	**62** 300+	**78** 300+	**73** 300+	**84** 300+	**69** 300+	**66** 300+
Doctor's Hospital of Michigan, Pontiac, MI	- -	- -	- -	**0.214** 262	**0.027** 188	**3.2** 818	**30.8** 39	**58** 300+	**74** 300+	**79** 300+	**58** 300+	**58** 300+	**75** 300+	**67** 300+	**72** 300+	**62** 300+	**61** 300+
Eaton Rapids Medical Center, Eaton Rapids, MI	- -	- -	- -	**0.286** 161	**0.424** 59	**8.3** 205	**22.2** 18	- -	- -	- -	- -	- -	- -	- -	- -	- -	- -
Edward W Sparrow Hospital, Lansing, MI	- -	- -	- -	**0.079** 1265	**0.002** 979	**4.8** 1194	- 0	**48** 300+	**74** 300+	**86** 300+	**67** 300+	**61** 300+	**77** 300+	**71** 300+	**65** 300+	**60** 300+	**74** 300+
Emma L Bixby Medical Center, Adrian, MI	- -	- -	- -	**0.051** 585	**0.031** 356	**10.8** 945	**30.8** 130	**55** 300+	**82** 300+	**83** 300+	**67** 300+	**64** 300+	**76** 300+	**73** 300+	**75** 300+	**69** 300+	**63** 300+
Garden City Hospital, Garden City, MI	- -	- -	- -	**0.116** 782	**0.006** 668	**8.9** 415	**26.7** 120	**43** 300+	**77** 300+	**79** 300+	**60** 300+	**59** 300+	**71** 300+	**67** 300+	**69** 300+	**62** 300+	**63** 300+
Genesys Regional Medical Center - Health Park, Grand Blanc, MI	- -	- -	- -	**0.047** 916	**0.393** 580	**31.8** 374	- 0	**45** 300+	**75** 300+	**81** 300+	**66** 300+	**57** 300+	**73** 300+	**68** 300+	**61** 300+	**66** 300+	**69** 300+
Gratiot Medical Center, Alma, MI	**100** 11	**0** 11	**100** 11	**0.065** 480	**0.015** 539	**2.1** 811	**35.3** 190	**64** 300+	**82** 300+	**88** 300+	**76** 300+	**65** 300+	**82** 300+	**67** 300+	**78** 300+	**68** 300+	**75** 300+
Harbor Beach Community Hospital, Harbor Beach, MI	- -	- -	- -	- -	- -	- -	- -	**61** <100	**89** <100	**89** <100	**86** <100	**70** <100	**87** <100	**77** <100	**88** <100	**76** <100	**89** <100
Harper University Hospital, Detroit, MI	- -	- -	- -	**0.108** 636	**0.005** 558	- 0	**21.4** 350	**59** 300+	**77** 300+	**77** 300+	**65** 300+	**59** 300+	**76** 300+	**67** 300+	**67** 300+	**64** 300+	**65** 300+
Hayes Green Beach Memorial Hospital, Charlotte, MI	- -	- -	- -	- -	- -	- -	- -	**59** (a)	**77** (a)	**85** (a)	**72** (a)	**54** (a)	**78** (a)	**73** (a)	**80** (a)	**67** (a)	**72** (a)
Healthsource Saginaw, Saginaw, MI	- -	- -	- -	- 0	- 0	- 0	- 0	- -	- -	- -	- -	- -	- -	- -	- -	- -	- -
Henry Ford Hospital, Detroit, MI	- -	- -	- -	**0.061** 3298	**0.023** 3061	**10.7** 5254	**32.7** 447	**54** 300+	**75** 300+	**82** 300+	**67** 300+	**59** 300+	**75** 300+	**67** 300+	**68** 300+	**60** 300+	**68** 300+
Henry Ford Macomb Hospital, Clinton Township, MI	- -	- -	- -	**0.210** 1019	**0.174** 745	**9.9** 1851	**26.1** 161	**48** 300+	**77** 300+	**82** 300+	**62** 300+	**58** 300+	**76** 300+	**68** 300+	**70** 300+	**62** 300+	**66** 300+
Henry Ford West Bloomfield Hospital, West Bloomfield, MI	- -	- -	- -	- 0	- 0	- 0	- 0	**75** 300+	**80** 300+	**82** 300+	**81** 300+	**64** 300+	**78** 300+	**70** 300+	**68** 300+	**68** 300+	**82** 300+
Henry Ford Wyandotte Hospital, Wyandotte, MI	- -	- -	- -	**0.030** 1215	**0.033** 1120	**8.3** 1228	**26.3** 319	**48** 300+	**76** 300+	**77** 300+	**64** 300+	**60** 300+	**75** 300+	**66** 300+	**68** 300+	**62** 300+	**63** 300+
Herrick Memorial Hospital, Tecumseh, MI	- -	- -	- -	- -	- -	- -	- -	**58** 300+	**75** 300+	**82** 300+	**64** 300+	**58** 300+	**73** 300+	**66** 300+	**78** 300+	**62** 300+	**64** 300+
Hills & Dales General Hospital, Cass City, MI	- -	- -	- -	**0.325** 160	**0.536** 84	**10.1** 158	- 0	**69** (a)	**82** (a)	**79** (a)	**74** (a)	**68** (a)	**82** (a)	**66** (a)	**78** (a)	**86** (a)	**69** (a)
Hillsdale Community Health Center, Hillsdale, MI	- -	- -	- -	**0.273** 326	**0.055** 256	**10.0** 653	**35.2** 142	**51** 300+	**77** 300+	**78** 300+	**58** 300+	**57** 300+	**74** 300+	**66** 300+	**73** 300+	**62** 300+	**54** 300+
Holland Community Hospital, Holland, MI	- -	- -	- -	**0.079** 726	**0.044** 454	**4.3** 1383	**40.6** 229	**55** 300+	**83** 300+	**90** 300+	**79** 300+	**64** 300+	**79** 300+	**70** 300+	**80** 300+	**68** 300+	**80** 300+
Hurley Medical Center, Flint, MI	- -	- -	- -	**0.137** 489	**0.127** 307	**9.9** 142	- 0	**48** 300+	**73** 300+	**82** 300+	**61** 300+	**56** 300+	**73** 300+	**67** 300+	**60** 300+	**60** 300+	**64** 300+
Huron Medical Center, Bad Axe, MI	- -	- -	- -	**0.102** 354	**0.083** 133	**3.0** 428	- 0	**59** 300+	**83** 300+	**89** 300+	**77** 300+	**63** 300+	**80** 300+	**75** 300+	**76** 300+	**75** 300+	**75** 300+
Huron Valley-Sinai Hospital, Commerce Twp, MI	- -	- -	- -	**0.099** 547	**0.002** 582	**6.4** 815	**26.4** 174	**53** 300+	**79** 300+	**80** 300+	**68** 300+	**61** 300+	**77** 300+	**67** 300+	**66** 300+	**65** 300+	**71** 300+
Ingham Regional Medical Center, Lansing, MI	- -	- -	- -	**0.157** 904	**0.032** 555	**2.7** 911	**30.0** 170	**49** 300+	**77** 300+	**84** 300+	**63** 300+	**54** 300+	**74** 300+	**64** 300+	**68** 300+	**58** 300+	**70** 300+
Ionia County Memorial Hospital, Ionia, MI	- -	- -	- -	**0.073** 164	**0.204** 98	**10.2** 187	**37.5** 32	- -	- -	- -	- -	- -	- -	- -	- -	- -	- -
Iron Mountain VA Medical Center, Iron Mountain, MI	- -	- -	- -	- -	- -	- -	- -	- -	- -	- -	- -	- -	- -	- -	- -	- -	- -
Karmanos Cancer Center, Detroit, MI	- -	- -	- -	**0.125** 1164	**0.024** 2088	**4.7** 2378	**22.7** 22	**61** 300+	**77** 300+	**88** 300+	**78** 300+	**68** 300+	**83** 300+	**74** 300+	**66** 300+	**68** 300+	**80** 300+
Lakeland Hospital - St Joseph, Saint Joseph, MI	- -	- -	- -	**0.093** 1890	**0.011** 1229	**6.7** 2810	**29.8** 275	**56** 300+	**79** 300+	**80** 300+	**64** 300+	**57** 300+	**74** 300+	**70** 300+	**78** 300+	**62** 300+	**60** 300+
Lapeer Regional Medical Center, Lapeer, MI	- -	- -	- -	**0.097** 454	**0.006** 358	- 0	**34.7** 193	**47** 300+	**73** 300+	**80** 300+	**59** 300+	**60** 300+	**72** 300+	**67** 300+	**73** 300+	**57** 300+	**58** 300+
Marlette Regional Hospital, Marlette, MI	- -	- -	- -	**0.187** 252	**0.125** 200	**5.7** 283	- 0	**59** (a)	**85** (a)	**84** (a)	**71** (a)	**62** (a)	**75** (a)	**73** (a)	**77** (a)	**60** (a)	**79** (a)
Marquette General Hospital, Marquette, MI	- -	- -	- -	**0.724** 638	**0.387** 553	**15.6** 909	**41.5** 207	**48** 300+	**78** 300+	**86** 300+	**64** 300+	**58** 300+	**72** 300+	**62** 300+	**73** 300+	**62** 300+	**69** 300+
McKenzie Memorial Hospital, Sandusky, MI	- -	- -	- -	**0.058** 138	**0.018** 112	**12.0** 167	- 0	**54** <100	**80** <100	**89** <100	**75** <100	**69** <100	**81** <100	**74** <100	**75** <100	**78** <100	**73** <100
Mclaren Regional Medical Center, Flint, MI	- -	- -	- -	**0.429** 1408	**0.001** 1214	**6.4** 1642	**25.0** 4	**44** 300+	**72** 300+	**77** 300+	**59** 300+	**54** 300+	**69** 300+	**65** 300+	**56** 300+	**53** 300+	**62** 300+
Mecosta County Medical Center, Big Rapids, MI	- -	- -	- -	**0.488** 330	**0.032** 310	**8.6** 571	**35.1** 154	**61** 300+	**79** 300+	**85** 300+	**69** 300+	**61** 300+	**73** 300+	**69** 300+	**62** 300+	**66** 300+	**68** 300+
Memorial Healthcare, Owosso, MI	- -	- -	- -	**0.029** 655	**0.005** 576	**7.3** 1438	**32.4** 207	**51** 300+	**71** 300+	**81** 300+	**54** 300+	**54** 300+	**71** 300+	**65** 300+	**74** 300+	**60** 300+	**57** 300+
Memorial Medical Center of West Michigan, Ludington, MI	- -	- -	- -	**0.664** 580	**0.893** 506	**5.7** 1037	**31.2** 154	**56** 300+	**81** 300+	**85** 300+	**67** 300+	**61** 300+	**76** 300+	**71** 300+	**68** 300+	**72** 300+	**64** 300+
Mercy Health Partners - Hackley Campus, Muskegon, MI	- -	- -	- -	**0.091** 789	**0.108** 471	**6.5** 1745	**34.1** 264	**50** 300+	**79** 300+	**84** 300+	**68** 300+	**62** 300+	**75** 300+	**70** 300+	**61** 300+	**64** 300+	**72** 300+
Mercy Health Partners - Mercy Campus, Muskegon, MI	- -	- -	- -	**0.016** 903	**0.061** 821	**4.7** 1547	**32.4** 552	**52** 300+	**78** 300+	**86** 300+	**68** 300+	**57** 300+	**73** 300+	**68** 300+	**66** 300+	**63** 300+	**70** 300+

NOTE: The first number in each column (boldface) is the score, the second number is the number of patients; Please refer to the main entry for footnotes; (a) 100-299
*MEASURES: **Children's Asthma Care:** 33. Received Systemic Corticosteroids; 34. Received Home Management Plan of Care; 35. Received Reliever Medication; **Use of Medical Imaging:** 36. Combination Abdominal CT Scan; 37. Combination Chest CT Scan; 38. Follow-up Mammogram/Ultrasound; 39. MRI for Low Back Pain; **Survey of Patients' Hospital Experiences:** 40. Area Around Room 'Always' Quiet at Night; 41. Doctors 'Always' Communicated Well; 42. Home Recovery Information Given; 43. Hospital Given 9 or 10 on 10 Point Scale; 44. Meds 'Always' Explained Before Given; 45. Nurses 'Always' Communicated Well; 46. Pain 'Always' Well Controlled; 47. Room and Bathroom 'Always' Clean; 48. Timely Help 'Always' Received; 49. Would Definitely Recommend Hospital*

Hospital	Children's Asthma Care 33	34	35	Use of Medical Imaging 36	37	38	39	Survey of Patients' Hospital Experiences 40	41	42	43	44	45	46	47	48	49
Mercy Hospital - Cadillac, Cadillac, MI	-	-	-	**0.024** 638	**0.005** 440	**6.5** 842	**38.5** 262	**61** 300+	**81** 300+	**88** 300+	**76** 300+	**65** 300+	**80** 300+	**73** 300+	**68** 300+	**74** 300+	**73** 300+
Mercy Hospital - Grayling, Grayling, MI	-	-	-	**0.115** 460	**0.039** 409	**11.2** 1083	**54.5** 220	**58** 300+	**80** 300+	**89** 300+	**71** 300+	**64** 300+	**80** 300+	**73** 300+	**71** 300+	**71** 300+	**71** 300+
Mercy Memorial Hospital System, Monroe, MI	-	-	-	**0.057** 840	**0.006** 708	**6.9** 1229	**25.6** 129	**47** 300+	**76** 300+	**75** 300+	**54** 300+	**56** 300+	**73** 300+	**65** 300+	**63** 300+	**60** 300+	**46** 300+
Metro Health Hospital, Wyoming, MI	-	-	-	**0.098** 945	**0.120** 581	**11.9** 1050	**29.4** 282	**64** 300+	**80** 300+	**88** 300+	**79** 300+	**63** 300+	**77** 300+	**72** 300+	**75** 300+	**61** 300+	**80** 300+
Midmichigan Medical Center-Clare, Clare, MI	-	-	-	**0.072** 362	**0.145** 249	**7.7** 794	**37.5** 128	**63** 300+	**82** 300+	**86** 300+	**66** 300+	**59** 300+	**75** 300+	**75** 300+	**72** 300+	**71** 300+	**60** 300+
Midmichigan Medical Center-Gladwin, Gladwin, MI	-	-	-	**0.054** 331	**0.065** 399	**3.8** 636	**35.2** 88	**72** (a)	**87** (a)	**87** (a)	**71** (a)	**59** (a)	**82** (a)	**77** (a)	**69** (a)	**75** (a)	**66** (a)
Midmichigan Medical Center-Midland, Midland, MI	-	-	-	**0.061** 1238	**0.026** 956	**5.9** 2207	**30.1** 489	**52** 300+	**81** 300+	**83** 300+	**73** 300+	**60** 300+	**76** 300+	**75** 300+	**67** 300+	**67** 300+	**75** 300+
Mount Clemens Regional Medical Center, Mount Clemens, MI	-	-	-	**0.328** 1212	**0.124** 964	- 0	**0.0** 1	**44** 300+	**76** 300+	**80** 300+	**58** 300+	**55** 300+	**71** 300+	**65** 300+	**63** 300+	**57** 300+	**59** 300+
Munson Medical Center, Traverse City, MI	-	-	-	**0.034** 1305	**0.003** 901	**8.8** 2443	**32.3** 542	**52** 300+	**81** 300+	**86** 300+	**83** 300+	**65** 300+	**83** 300+	**73** 300+	**71** 300+	**71** 300+	**85** 300+
North Ottawa Community Hospital, Grand Haven, MI	-	-	-	**0.049** 185	**0.170** 159	**6.0** 662	**37.3** 59	**70** 300+	**80** 300+	**88** 300+	**75** 300+	**61** 300+	**78** 300+	**71** 300+	**71** 300+	**72** 300+	**75** 300+
Northern Michigan Regional Hospital, Petoskey, MI	-	-	-	**0.053** 837	**0.000** 827	**4.0** 1214	**36.9** 206	**51** 300+	**82** 300+	**90** 300+	**75** 300+	**70** 300+	**80** 300+	**75** 300+	**66** 300+	**69** 300+	**78** 300+
Northstar Health System, Iron River, MI	-	-	-	-	-	-	-	-	-	-	-	-	-	-	-	-	-
Oakland Regional Hospital, Southfield, MI	-	-	-	- 0	- 0	- 0	**25.9** 27	**67** <100	**83** <100	**84** <100	**67** <100	**66** <100	**83** <100	**81** <100	**81** <100	**65** <100	**74** <100
Oaklawn Hospital, Marshall, MI	-	-	-	**0.017** 526	**0.000** 361	**3.6** 913	**36.4** 44	**67** 300+	**81** 300+	**88** 300+	**79** 300+	**61** 300+	**79** 300+	**74** 300+	**72** 300+	**73** 300+	**83** 300+
Oakwood Annapolis Hospital, Wayne, MI	-	-	-	**0.104** 548	**0.062** 308	**10.9** 742	**20.4** 152	**52** 300+	**78** 300+	**74** 300+	**59** 300+	**63** 300+	**76** 300+	**70** 300+	**68** 300+	**59** 300+	**60** 300+
Oakwood Heritage Hospital, Taylor, MI	-	-	-	**0.035** 254	**0.022** 268	**7.1** 1012	**28.2** 110	**51** 300+	**76** 300+	**79** 300+	**60** 300+	**58** 300+	**75** 300+	**71** 300+	**66** 300+	**59** 300+	**62** 300+
Oakwood Hospital and Medical Center, Dearborn, MI	-	-	-	**0.063** 1724	**0.036** 1438	**5.8** 2597	**24.8** 202	**48** 300+	**79** 300+	**77** 300+	**66** 300+	**61** 300+	**80** 300+	**71** 300+	**67** 300+	**64** 300+	**68** 300+
Oakwood Southshore Medical Center, Trenton, MI	-	-	-	**0.124** 704	**0.013** 533	**11.2** 519	**27.7** 130	**61** 300+	**81** 300+	**81** 300+	**73** 300+	**63** 300+	**78** 300+	**73** 300+	**75** 300+	**65** 300+	**74** 300+
Otsego Memorial Hospital, Gaylord, MI	-	-	-	**0.052** 383	**0.000** 305	**11.4** 431	**41.5** 135	**57** 300+	**86** 300+	**83** 300+	**68** 300+	**66** 300+	**78** 300+	**71** 300+	**71** 300+	**69** 300+	**68** 300+
Paul Oliver Memorial Hospital, Frankfort, MI	-	-	-	**0.035** 141	**0.013** 76	**8.2** 403	- 0	-	-	-	-	-	-	-	-	-	-
Pennock Hospital, Hastings, MI	-	-	-	**0.064** 342	**0.015** 200	**10.2** 695	**34.1** 123	**57** 300+	**83** 300+	**86** 300+	**72** 300+	**55** 300+	**75** 300+	**67** 300+	**61** 300+	**61** 300+	**73** 300+
Poh Medical Center, Pontiac, MI	-	-	-	**0.147** 395	**0.059** 272	**16.4** 341	- 0	**48** 300+	**70** 300+	**75** 300+	**60** 300+	**54** 300+	**71** 300+	**68** 300+	**74** 300+	**60** 300+	**59** 300+
Port Huron Hospital, Port Huron, MI	-	-	-	**0.030** 897	**0.002** 833	**12.4** 1448	- 0	**51** 300+	**77** 300+	**81** 300+	**67** 300+	**58** 300+	**79** 300+	**71** 300+	**71** 300+	**64** 300+	**70** 300+
Portage Health Hospital, Hancock, MI	-	-	-	**0.087** 196	**0.013** 153	**12.2** 353	**30.2** 96	**60** 300+	**81** 300+	**83** 300+	**69** 300+	**66** 300+	**79** 300+	**70** 300+	**79** 300+	**74** 300+	**76** 300+
Providence Hospital and Medical Centers, Southfield, MI	-	-	-	**0.073** 2330	**0.012** 1788	**4.7** 4175	**26.7** 424	**56** 300+	**77** 300+	**77** 300+	**68** 300+	**54** 300+	**74** 300+	**65** 300+	**64** 300+	**60** 300+	**72** 300+
Saginaw VA Medical Center, Saginaw, MI	-	-	-	-	-	-	-	-	-	-	-	-	-	-	-	-	-
Saint Francis Hospital, Escanaba, MI	-	-	-	**0.847** 472	**0.847** 405	**4.9** 667	**43.8** 112	**47** 300+	**83** 300+	**84** 300+	**68** 300+	**61** 300+	**83** 300+	**74** 300+	**76** 300+	**74** 300+	**65** 300+
Saint John Hospital and Medical Center, Detroit, MI	-	-	-	**0.155** 1107	**0.170** 778	**2.5** 2562	**29.6** 294	**54** 300+	**73** 300+	**79** 300+	**62** 300+	**57** 300+	**75** 300+	**67** 300+	**58** 300+	**54** 300+	**67** 300+
Saint John Macomb-Oakland Hospital, Warren, MI	-	-	-	**0.348** 1539	**0.007** 992	**4.4** 2133	**23.9** 205	**41** 300+	**70** 300+	**74** 300+	**57** 300+	**54** 300+	**70** 300+	**65** 300+	**59** 300+	**55** 300+	**55** 300+
Saint John River District Hospital, East China, MI	-	-	-	**0.040** 272	**0.014** 218	**18.7** 504	- 0	**52** 300+	**79** 300+	**82** 300+	**68** 300+	**57** 300+	**76** 300+	**74** 300+	**78** 300+	**69** 300+	**65** 300+
Saint Joseph Mercy Hospital, Ann Arbor, MI	-	-	-	**0.103** 2089	**0.011** 1498	**7.4** 3075	**30.8** 370	**57** 300+	**78** 300+	**86** 300+	**74** 300+	**61** 300+	**76** 300+	**67** 300+	**72** 300+	**64** 300+	**80** 300+
Saint Joseph Mercy Livingston Hospital, Howell, MI	-	-	-	**0.042** 552	**0.021** 233	**7.2** 585	**28.2** 110	**59** 300+	**78** 300+	**89** 300+	**70** 300+	**64** 300+	**80** 300+	**73** 300+	**69** 300+	**75** 300+	**72** 300+
Saint Joseph Mercy Oakland, Pontiac, MI	-	-	-	**0.152** 999	**0.084** 818	**6.4** 1613	**24.5** 282	**51** 300+	**76** 300+	**83** 300+	**66** 300+	**57** 300+	**73** 300+	**66** 300+	**58** 300+	**56** 300+	**70** 300+
Saint Joseph Mercy Port Huron, Port Huron, MI	-	-	-	**0.020** 345	**0.000** 383	**16.7** 701	- 0	**63** 300+	**78** 300+	**85** 300+	**68** 300+	**57** 300+	**75** 300+	**68** 300+	**73** 300+	**63** 300+	**68** 300+
Saint Joseph Mercy Saline Hospital, Saline, MI	-	-	-	**0.092** 380	**0.005** 204	**6.7** 525	**36.8** 223	**71** (a)	**80** (a)	**90** (a)	**74** (a)	**63** (a)	**80** (a)	**73** (a)	**68** (a)	**74** (a)	**77** (a)
Saint Mary Mercy Hospital, Livonia, MI	-	-	-	**0.463** 1108	**0.370** 1222	**12.4** 1401	**24.8** 258	**42** 300+	**76** 300+	**82** 300+	**62** 300+	**53** 300+	**74** 300+	**68** 300+	**57** 300+	**57** 300+	**64** 300+
Saint Mary's Health Care, Grand Rapids, MI	-	-	-	**0.078** 1051	**0.032** 875	**5.7** 1769	**34.8** 244	**62** 300+	**80** 300+	**88** 300+	**73** 300+	**63** 300+	**77** 300+	**70** 300+	**69** 300+	**63** 300+	**75** 300+
Saint Mary's of Michigan Medical Center, Saginaw, MI	-	-	-	**0.143** 1205	**0.202** 889	**7.1** 1558	**37.3** 576	**44** 300+	**74** 300+	**84** 300+	**57** 300+	**52** 300+	**67** 300+	**63** 300+	**62** 300+	**60** 300+	**63** 300+
Saint Mary's Standish Community Hospital, Standish, MI	-	-	-	**0.097** 331	**0.053** 281	**7.3** 262	**45.5** 66	-	-	-	-	-	-	-	-	-	-
Schoolcraft Memorial Hospital, Manistique, MI	-	-	-	-	-	-	-	-	-	-	-	-	-	-	-	-	-
Sheridan Community Hospital, Sheridan, MI	-	-	-	-	-	-	-	-	-	-	-	-	-	-	-	-	-
Sinai-Grace Hospital, Detroit, MI	-	-	-	**0.182** 939	**0.022** 912	**12.8** 1235	**25.2** 222	**60** 300+	**74** 300+	**76** 300+	**56** 300+	**54** 300+	**73** 300+	**67** 300+	**67** 300+	**62** 300+	**51** 300+
South Haven Community Hospital, South Haven, MI	-	-	-	**0.073** 218	**0.058** 103	**1.6** 305	**39.1** 46	**53** (a)	**83** (a)	**86** (a)	**69** (a)	**63** (a)	**78** (a)	**71** (a)	**68** (a)	**69** (a)	**66** (a)
Southeast Michigan Surgical Hospital, Warren, MI	-	-	-	- 0	- 0	- 0	- 0	**83** <100	**82** <100	**88** <100	**86** <100	**77** <100	**91** <100	**74** <100	**90** <100	**90** <100	**84** <100
Spectrum Health - Butterworth Campus, Grand Rapids, MI	**98** 185	**78** 185	**100** 185	**0.045** 2656	**0.045** 1622	**9.0** 4174	**36.0** 702	**50** 300+	**77** 300+	**85** 300+	**72** 300+	**59** 300+	**79** 300+	**70** 300+	**71** 300+	**64** 300+	**78** 300+
Spectrum Health - Reed City Campus, Reed City, MI	-	-	-	**0.042** 479	**0.056** 321	**10.9** 366	**39.1** 64	**59** (a)	**84** (a)	**88** (a)	**76** (a)	**70** (a)	**84** (a)	**78** (a)	**81** (a)	**74** (a)	**75** (a)
Spectrum Health Gerber Memorial, Fremont, MI	-	-	-	**0.010** 415	**0.014** 367	**7.1** 709	**43.9** 82	**57** 300+	**83** 300+	**89** 300+	**73** 300+	**69** 300+	**82** 300+	**74** 300+	**71** 300+	**72** 300+	**69** 300+
Spectrum Health United Memorial - Kelsey Campus, Lakeview, MI	-	-	-	**0.044** 91	**0.034** 58	**3.1** 194	- 0	**60** (a)	**78** (a)	**82** (a)	**80** (a)	**69** (a)	**88** (a)	**78** (a)	**92** (a)	**83** (a)	**80** (a)
Spectrum Health United Memorial - United Campus, Greenville, MI	-	-	-	**0.053** 543	**0.003** 350	**5.2** 601	**26.4** 239	**60** 300+	**84** 300+	**85** 300+	**71** 300+	**66** 300+	**78** 300+	**72** 300+	**79** 300+	**62** 300+	**72** 300+
Straith Hospital for Special Surgery, Southfield, MI	-	-	-	- 0	- 0	- 0	- 0	-	-	-	-	-	-	-	-	-	-
Sturgis Hospital, Sturgis, MI	-	-	-	**0.931** 218	**0.835** 182	**5.1** 534	**34.0** 50	**61** 300+	**82** 300+	**83** 300+	**73** 300+	**58** 300+	**77** 300+	**71** 300+	**69** 300+	**70** 300+	**67** 300+
Tawas Saint Joseph Hospital, Tawas City, MI	-	-	-	**0.125** 654	**0.093** 377	**6.9** 1172	**41.7** 223	**58** 300+	**80** 300+	**85** 300+	**73** 300+	**60** 300+	**80** 300+	**76** 300+	**70** 300+	**71** 300+	**70** 300+
Three Rivers Health, Three Rivers, MI	-	-	-	**0.062** 341	**0.013** 149	**6.4** 344	**41.4** 70	**43** (a)	**70** (a)	**84** (a)	**60** (a)	**59** (a)	**72** (a)	**60** (a)	**69** (a)	**60** (a)	**58** (a)
University of Michigan Health System, Ann Arbor, MI	-	-	-	**0.102** 2805	**0.004** 3659	**8.5** 2433	**22.7** 396	**42** 300+	**78** 300+	**88** 300+	**74** 300+	**60** 300+	**77** 300+	**68** 300+	**61** 300+	**62** 300+	**83** 300+
VA Ann Arbor Healthcare System, Ann Arbor, MI	-	-	-	-	-	-	-	-	-	-	-	-	-	-	-	-	-
West Branch Regional Medical Center, West Branch, MI	-	-	-	**0.157** 762	**0.041** 955	**3.6** 505	**36.3** 237	**54** 300+	**81** 300+	**87** 300+	**72** 300+	**56** 300+	**78** 300+	**73** 300+	**71** 300+	**69** 300+	**75** 300+
West Shore Medical Center, Manistee, MI	-	-	-	- 0	- 0	- 0	- 0	**63** 300+	**86** 300+	**85** 300+	**74** 300+	**68** 300+	**81** 300+	**74** 300+	**76** 300+	**75** 300+	**69** 300+
William Beaumont Hospital, Royal Oak, MI	-	-	-	**0.072** 3843	**0.023** 3829	**7.4** 6797	**26.0** 781	**42** 300+	**78** 300+	**84** 300+	**69** 300+	**56** 300+	**75** 300+	**70** 300+	**64** 300+	**56** 300+	**72** 300+
William Beaumont Hospital-Troy, Troy, MI	-	-	-	**0.137** 2371	**0.018** 2328	**7.2** 3408	**26.4** 606	**44** 300+	**79** 300+	**80** 300+	**69** 300+	**56** 300+	**75** 300+	**69** 300+	**68** 300+	**63** 300+	**77** 300+
Zeeland Community Hospital, Zeeland, MI	-	-	-	**0.065** 186	**0.104** 67	**7.0** 372	**31.0** 29	**64** 300+	**83** 300+	**90** 300+	**83** 300+	**63** 300+	**82** 300+	**73** 300+	**80** 300+	**70** 300+	**87** 300+
MINNESOTA																	
Abbott Northwestern Hospital, Minneapolis, MN	-	-	-	**0.074** 1685	**0.014** 1699	**4.2** 2250	**34.8** 302	**52** 300+	**78** 300+	**86** 300+	**70** 300+	**58** 300+	**75** 300+	**67** 300+	**65** 300+	**64** 300+	**78** 300+
Albany Area Hospital, Albany, MN	-	-	-	**0.070** 43	**0.000** 18	**5.3** 76	**60.0** 15	**69** <100	**87** <100	**88** <100	**82** <100	**66** <100	**83** <100	**73** <100	**77** <100	**85** <100	**81** <100
Appleton Municipal Hospital, Appleton, MN	-	-	-	-	-	-	-	-	-	-	-	-	-	-	-	-	-
Austin Medical Center, Austin, MN	-	-	-	**0.369** 279	**0.240** 167	**5.8** 1115	**35.3** 51	**52** 300+	**79** 300+	**78** 300+	**64** 300+	**63** 300+	**76** 300+	**66** 300+	**80** 300+	**62** 300+	**63** 300+
Avera Marshall Regional Medical Center, Marshall, MN	-	-	-	**0.108** 241	**0.008** 132	**10.7** 112	**26.1** 46	**59** 300+	**77** 300+	**83** 300+	**61** 300+	**55** 300+	**73** 300+	**67** 300+	**71** 300+	**57** 300+	**66** 300+
Bigfork Valley Hospital, Bigfork, MN	-	-	-	**0.000** 33	**0.043** 23	**4.9** 122	**27.3** 11	**71** (a)	**90** (a)	**90** (a)	**88** (a)	**80** (a)	**88** (a)	**83** (a)	**93** (a)	**93** (a)	**93** (a)

NOTE: The first number in each column (boldface) is the score, the second number is the number of patients; Please refer to the main entry for footnotes; (a) 100-299

*MEASURES: **Children's Asthma Care:** 33. Received Systemic Corticosteroids; 34. Received Home Management Plan of Care; 35. Received Reliever Medication; **Use of Medical Imaging:** 36. Combination Abdominal CT Scan; 37. Combination Chest CT Scan; 38. Follow-up Mammogram/Ultrasound; 39. MRI for Low Back Pain; **Survey of Patients' Hospital Experiences:** 40. Area Around Room 'Always' Quiet at Night; 41. Doctors 'Always' Communicated Well; 42. Home Recovery Information Given; 43. Hospital Given 9 or 10 on 10 Point Scale; 44. Meds 'Always' Explained Before Given; 45. Nurses 'Always' Communicated Well; 46. Pain 'Always' Well Controlled; 47. Room and Bathroom 'Always' Clean; 48. Timely Help 'Always' Received; 49. Would Definitely Recommend Hospital*

Hospital	Children's Asthma Care			Use of Medical Imaging				Survey of Patients' Hospital Experiences									
	33	34	35	36	37	38	39	40	41	42	43	44	45	46	47	48	49
Bridges Medical Services, Ada, MN	- -	- -	- -	**0.412** 17	**0.545** 11	**9.1** 44	**20.0** 10	- -	- -	- -	- -	- -	- -	- -	- -	- -	- -
Buffalo Hospital, Buffalo, MN	- -	- -	- -	**0.034** 295	**0.005** 220	**1.6** 248	**33.0** 88	**57** 300+	**79** 300+	**87** 300+	**65** 300+	**61** 300+	**79** 300+	**68** 300+	**75** 300+	**67** 300+	**67** 300+
Cambridge Medical Center, Cambridge, MN	- -	- -	- -	**0.041** 366	**0.019** 269	**4.8** 686	**43.3** 120	**60** 300+	**80** 300+	**87** 300+	**65** 300+	**60** 300+	**77** 300+	**67** 300+	**69** 300+	**73** 300+	**67** 300+
Cannon Falls Medical Center Mayo, Cannon Falls, MN	- -	- -	- -	**0.360** 25	**0.188** 16	**7.2** 97	**11.1** 9	- -	- -	- -	- -	- -	- -	- -	- -	- -	- -
Cass Lake Indian Health Services Hospital, Cass Lake, MN	- -	- -	- -	- 0	- 0	- 0	- 0	- -	- -	- -	- -	- -	- -	- -	- -	- -	- -
Centracare Health System - Long Prairie, Long Prairie, MN	- -	- -	- -	**0.063** 80	**0.020** 49	**4.5** 89	**68.4** 19	- -	- -	- -	- -	- -	- -	- -	- -	- -	- -
Centracare Health System - Melrose Hospital, Melrose, MN	- -	- -	- -	**0.062** 65	**0.000** 43	**7.0** 201	**42.1** 19	- -	- -	- -	- -	- -	- -	- -	- -	- -	- -
Children's Hospitals & Clinics, Minneapolis, MN	**98** 331	**41** 331	**100** 331	- -	- -	- -	- -	- -	- -	- -	- -	- -	- -	- -	- -	- -	- -
Chippewa County Hospital, Montevideo, MN	- -	- -	- -	**0.804** 97	**0.051** 59	**4.9** 267	**38.1** 21	**63** 300+	**84** 300+	**84** 300+	**67** 300+	**53** 300+	**71** 300+	**62** 300+	**74** 300+	**64** 300+	**69** 300+
Clearwater Health Services, Bagley, MN	- -	- -	- -	- -	- -	- -	- -	- -	- -	- -	- -	- -	- -	- -	- -	- -	- -
Community Memorial Hospital, Cloquet, MN	- -	- -	- -	**0.073** 193	**0.000** 105	**3.3** 90	**50.0** 32	**58** 300+	**84** 300+	**80** 300+	**68** 300+	**66** 300+	**78** 300+	**69** 300+	**77** 300+	**75** 300+	**69** 300+
Cook County Northshore Hospital, Grand Marais, MN	- -	- -	- -	- -	- -	- -	- -	- -	- -	- -	- -	- -	- -	- -	- -	- -	- -
Cook Hospital, Cook, MN	- -	- -	- -	- -	- -	- -	- -	- -	- -	- -	- -	- -	- -	- -	- -	- -	- -
Cuyuna Regional Medical Center, Crosby, MN	- -	- -	- -	- -	- -	- -	- -	**63** 300+	**84** 300+	**86** 300+	**78** 300+	**69** 300+	**83** 300+	**70** 300+	**77** 300+	**74** 300+	**87** 300+
Deer River Healthcare Center, Deer River, MN	- -	- -	- -	**0.014** 73	**0.018** 55	**6.6** 136	**36.0** 25	- -	- -	- -	- -	- -	- -	- -	- -	- -	- -
District One Hospital, Faribault, MN	- -	- -	- -	**0.050** 240	**0.048** 209	**13.2** 53	**49.2** 61	**64** 300+	**81** 300+	**83** 300+	**69** 300+	**62** 300+	**76** 300+	**70** 300+	**75** 300+	**72** 300+	**67** 300+
Douglas County Hospital, Alexandria, MN	- -	- -	- -	**0.047** 297	**0.004** 224	**3.3** 61	**35.1** 222	**56** 300+	**80** 300+	**87** 300+	**74** 300+	**63** 300+	**77** 300+	**70** 300+	**82** 300+	**69** 300+	**74** 300+
Ely Bloomenson Community Hospital, Ely, MN	- -	- -	- -	- -	- -	- -	- -	**58** (a)	**80** (a)	**73** (a)	**64** (a)	**57** (a)	**75** (a)	**78** (a)	**78** (a)	**77** (a)	**65** (a)
Essentia Health Duluth, Duluth, MN	- -	- -	- -	- 0	- 0	- 0	- 0	**46** 300+	**83** 300+	**88** 300+	**68** 300+	**64** 300+	**77** 300+	**70** 300+	**70** 300+	**68** 300+	**71** 300+
Essentia Health Fosston, Fosston, MN	- -	- -	- -	**0.000** 50	**0.000** 35	**8.0** 88	**41.2** 17	**61** (a)	**89** (a)	**89** (a)	**78** (a)	**65** (a)	**83** (a)	**77** (a)	**80** (a)	**76** (a)	**82** (a)
Essentia Health Sandstone, Sandstone, MN	- -	- -	- -	**0.074** 54	**0.000** 30	**3.3** 61	**46.2** 13	- -	- -	- -	- -	- -	- -	- -	- -	- -	- -
Essentia Health St Joseph's Medical Center, Brainerd, MN	- -	- -	- -	**0.046** 648	**0.000** 679	**5.4** 1511	**37.6** 210	**61** 300+	**79** 300+	**86** 300+	**69** 300+	**62** 300+	**78** 300+	**70** 300+	**77** 300+	**70** 300+	**68** 300+
Essentia Health St Mary's Medical Center, Duluth, MN	- -	- -	- -	**0.215** 636	**0.031** 351	- 0	- 0	**46** 300+	**80** 300+	**85** 300+	**61** 300+	**57** 300+	**73** 300+	**67** 300+	**59** 300+	**62** 300+	**73** 300+
Fairmont Medical Center, Fairmont, MN	- -	- -	- -	**0.065** 306	**0.000** 214	**6.3** 649	**26.9** 93	**55** 300+	**82** 300+	**84** 300+	**63** 300+	**59** 300+	**74** 300+	**69** 300+	**70** 300+	**60** 300+	**63** 300+
Fairview Lakes Health Services, Wyoming, MN	- -	- -	- -	**0.089** 493	**0.006** 499	**4.9** 815	**33.5** 173	**52** 300+	**80** 300+	**82** 300+	**68** 300+	**63** 300+	**76** 300+	**70** 300+	**73** 300+	**71** 300+	**71** 300+
Fairview Northland Regional Hospital, Princeton, MN	- -	- -	- -	**0.032** 281	**0.005** 209	**8.6** 617	**32.3** 62	**57** 300+	**81** 300+	**85** 300+	**73** 300+	**64** 300+	**78** 300+	**73** 300+	**77** 300+	**71** 300+	**71** 300+
Fairview Red Wing Hospital, Red Wing, MN	- -	- -	- -	**0.076** 185	**0.041** 146	**3.9** 584	**37.1** 89	**63** 300+	**82** 300+	**86** 300+	**70** 300+	**62** 300+	**77** 300+	**72** 300+	**76** 300+	**75** 300+	**72** 300+
Fairview Ridges Hospital, Burnsville, MN	- -	- -	- -	**0.048** 684	**0.005** 651	**10.8** 908	**41.4** 99	**56** 300+	**76** 300+	**87** 300+	**68** 300+	**60** 300+	**72** 300+	**62** 300+	**68** 300+	**62** 300+	**72** 300+
Fairview Southdale Hospital, Edina, MN	- -	- -	- -	**0.086** 954	**0.007** 854	**6.6** 728	**44.4** 108	**49** 300+	**76** 300+	**84** 300+	**61** 300+	**58** 300+	**71** 300+	**64** 300+	**65** 300+	**57** 300+	**68** 300+
Glacial Ridge Hospital, Glenwood, MN	- -	- -	- -	**0.413** 92	**0.029** 70	**7.9** 203	**38.5** 26	- -	- -	- -	- -	- -	- -	- -	- -	- -	- -
Glencoe Regional Health Services, Glencoe, MN	- -	- -	- -	**0.064** 218	**0.000** 96	**6.1** 293	**47.7** 44	**64** 300+	**84** 300+	**82** 300+	**71** 300+	**58** 300+	**75** 300+	**67** 300+	**79** 300+	**66** 300+	**74** 300+
Grand Itasca Clinic and Hospital, Grand Rapids, MN	- -	- -	- -	**0.106** 273	**0.011** 184	**5.1** 740	**36.5** 85	**62** 300+	**83** 300+	**83** 300+	**69** 300+	**61** 300+	**79** 300+	**71** 300+	**72** 300+	**71** 300+	**68** 300+
Healtheast St John's Hospital, Maplewood, MN	- -	- -	- -	**0.079** 903	**0.015** 523	**4.2** 2809	**41.0** 166	**49** 300+	**72** 300+	**87** 300+	**66** 300+	**55** 300+	**72** 300+	**68** 300+	**70** 300+	**57** 300+	**68** 300+
Healtheast Woodwinds Hospital, Woodbury, MN	- -	- -	- -	**0.037** 565	**0.003** 370	**9.1** 1139	**42.1** 133	**70** 300+	**76** 300+	**88** 300+	**78** 300+	**65** 300+	**76** 300+	**69** 300+	**70** 300+	**67** 300+	**80** 300+
Hendricks Community Hospital, Hendricks, MN	- -	- -	- -	**0.161** 56	**0.088** 34	**2.2** 138	**38.5** 13	- -	- -	- -	- -	- -	- -	- -	- -	- -	- -
Hennepin County Medical Center, Minneapolis, MN	**100** 36	**89** 36	**100** 36	**0.074** 435	**0.002** 439	**8.4** 735	**26.3** 38	**48** 300+	**72** 300+	**84** 300+	**60** 300+	**53** 300+	**65** 300+	**60** 300+	**63** 300+	**48** 300+	**63** 300+
Holy Trinity Hospital, Graceville, MN	- -	- -	- -	**0.174** 23	**0.063** 16	**13.1** 61	**75.0** 4	- -	- -	- -	- -	- -	- -	- -	- -	- -	- -
Hutchinson Area Health Care, Hutchinson, MN	- -	- -	- -	**0.060** 281	**0.000** 216	**5.8** 591	**27.0** 74	**63** 300+	**82** 300+	**86** 300+	**70** 300+	**61** 300+	**76** 300+	**69** 300+	**74** 300+	**66** 300+	**72** 300+
Immanuel-St Josephs-Mayo Health System, Mankato, MN	- -	- -	- -	**0.070** 569	**0.002** 401	**5.7** 454	**25.0** 64	**44** 300+	**72** 300+	**79** 300+	**58** 300+	**57** 300+	**69** 300+	**62** 300+	**67** 300+	**57** 300+	**59** 300+
Johnson Memorial Hospital, Dawson, MN	- -	- -	- -	**0.840** 25	**0.200** 10	**5.9** 85	**0.0** 7	**80** <100	**89** <100	**87** <100	**84** <100	**66** <100	**90** <100	**65** <100	**86** <100	**81** <100	**91** <100
Kanabec Hospital, Mora, MN	- -	- -	- -	**0.064** 220	**0.031** 131	**5.5** 237	**32.7** 52	**55** 300+	**76** 300+	**84** 300+	**65** 300+	**65** 300+	**75** 300+	**68** 300+	**75** 300+	**71** 300+	**66** 300+
Kittson Memorial Hospital, Hallock, MN	- -	- -	- -	**0.429** 14	**0.182** 11	**4.7** 85	**66.7** 3	- -	- -	- -	- -	- -	- -	- -	- -	- -	- -
Lake City Medical Center Mayo Health System, Lake City, MN	- -	- -	- -	**0.114** 44	**0.000** 18	**11.3** 247	**27.3** 11	**60** (a)	**83** (a)	**80** (a)	**73** (a)	**59** (a)	**77** (a)	**70** (a)	**83** (a)	**70** (a)	**77** (a)
Lake Region Healthcare Corporation, Fergus Falls, MN	- -	- -	- -	**0.118** 373	**0.032** 252	**5.0** 783	**36.5** 85	**63** (a)	**81** (a)	**90** (a)	**76** (a)	**67** (a)	**81** (a)	**74** (a)	**83** (a)	**72** (a)	**74** (a)
Lake View Memorial Hospital, Two Harbors, MN	- -	- -	- -	- -	- -	- -	- -	- -	- -	- -	- -	- -	- -	- -	- -	- -	- -
Lakeside Medical Center, Pine City, MN	- -	- -	- -	**0.100** 20	**0.059** 17	- 0	**50.0** 6	- -	- -	- -	- -	- -	- -	- -	- -	- -	- -
Lakeview Memorial Hospital, Stillwater, MN	- -	- -	- -	**0.050** 457	**0.007** 289	**4.2** 991	**45.9** 146	**66** 300+	**85** 300+	**89** 300+	**81** 300+	**72** 300+	**84** 300+	**77** 300+	**77** 300+	**79** 300+	**84** 300+
Lakewood Health Center, Baudette, MN	- -	- -	- -	**0.190** 42	**0.087** 23	**11.0** 91	**30.8** 13	**62** <100	**84** <100	**88** <100	**81** <100	**62** <100	**84** <100	**68** <100	**87** <100	**82** <100	**81** <100
Lakewood Health System, Staples, MN	- -	- -	- -	- -	- -	- -	- -	**73** 300+	**87** 300+	**87** 300+	**85** 300+	**66** 300+	**85** 300+	**77** 300+	**82** 300+	**76** 300+	**88** 300+
Lifecare Medical Center, Roseau, MN	- -	- -	- -	**0.011** 95	**0.000** 79	**9.4** 171	**80.0** 20	**65** (a)	**86** (a)	**86** (a)	**69** (a)	**68** (a)	**75** (a)	**70** (a)	**82** (a)	**74** (a)	**67** (a)
Madelia Community Hospital, Madelia, MN	- -	- -	- -	- -	- -	- -	- -	- -	- -	- -	- -	- -	- -	- -	- -	- -	- -
Madison Hospital, Madison, MN	- -	- -	- -	**0.875** 24	**0.167** 24	**9.0** 78	**60.0** 5	- -	- -	- -	- -	- -	- -	- -	- -	- -	- -
Mahnomen Health Center, Mahnomen, MN	- -	- -	- -	**0.000** 25	**0.000** 10	**7.7** 65	**28.6** 7	- -	- -	- -	- -	- -	- -	- -	- -	- -	- -
Maple Grove Hospital, Maple Grove, MN	- -	- -	- -	- -	- -	- -	- -	- -	- -	- -	- -	- -	- -	- -	- -	- -	- -
Mayo Clinic - Methodist Hospital, Rochester, MN	- -	- -	- -	**0.101** 189	**0.006** 155	- 0	**17.6** 17	**58** 300+	**83** 300+	**88** 300+	**80** 300+	**65** 300+	**81** 300+	**69** 300+	**68** 300+	**68** 300+	**83** 300+
Mayo Clinic - Saint Marys Hospital, Rochester, MN	- -	- -	- -	**0.047** 576	**0.008** 260	- 0	**20.0** 20	**62** 300+	**82** 300+	**84** 300+	**81** 300+	**67** 300+	**79** 300+	**73** 300+	**74** 300+	**70** 300+	**85** 300+
Meeker Memorial Hospital, Litchfield, MN	- -	- -	- -	**0.864** 110	**0.081** 62	**2.5** 275	**20.0** 25	**80** (a)	**83** (a)	**83** (a)	**75** (a)	**61** (a)	**80** (a)	**73** (a)	**83** (a)	**73** (a)	**76** (a)
Mercy Hospital, Coon Rapids, MN	- -	- -	- -	**0.046** 842	**0.017** 823	- 0	**48.3** 58	**56** 300+	**75** 300+	**87** 300+	**65** 300+	**60** 300+	**76** 300+	**67** 300+	**68** 300+	**63** 300+	**71** 300+
Mercy Hospital & Health Care Center, Moose Lake, MN	- -	- -	- -	**0.102** 88	**0.000** 70	**4.0** 226	**38.1** 21	- -	- -	- -	- -	- -	- -	- -	- -	- -	- -
Mille Lacs Health System, Onamia, MN	- -	- -	- -	- -	- -	- -	- -	**60** (a)	**88** (a)	**88** (a)	**67** (a)	**66** (a)	**81** (a)	**69** (a)	**76** (a)	**74** (a)	**68** (a)
Minneapolis VA Medical Center, Minneapolis, MN	- -	- -	- -	- -	- -	- -	- -	- -	- -	- -	- -	- -	- -	- -	- -	- -	- -
Minnesota Valley Health Center, Le Sueur, MN	- -	- -	- -	**0.024** 42	**0.000** 14	- 0	**33.3** 3	- -	- -	- -	- -	- -	- -	- -	- -	- -	- -
Municipal Hospital and Granite Manor, Granite Falls, MN	- -	- -	- -	**0.080** 87	**0.000** 64	**4.8** 189	**14.3** 14	- -	- -	- -	- -	- -	- -	- -	- -	- -	- -
Murray County Memorial Hospital, Slayton, MN	- -	- -	- -	**0.067** 60	**0.000** 27	**6.5** 155	**14.3** 14	- -	- -	- -	- -	- -	- -	- -	- -	- -	- -
Naeve Hospital, Albert Lea, MN	- -	- -	- -	**0.053** 399	**0.000** 137	**8.4** 857	**27.8** 72	**58** 300+	**83** 300+	**81** 300+	**70** 300+	**67** 300+	**82** 300+	**70** 300+	**81** 300+	**71** 300+	**73** 300+
New River Medical Center, Monticello, MN	- -	- -	- -	**0.071** 155	**0.000** 86	**9.3** 182	**25.7** 35	**64** 300+	**77** 300+	**83** 300+	**63** 300+	**60** 300+	**77** 300+	**70** 300+	**81** 300+	**66** 300+	**68** 300+
New Ulm Medical Center, New Ulm, MN	- -	- -	- -	**0.084** 263	**0.025** 202	**4.2** 622	**26.6** 64	**58** 300+	**83** 300+	**87** 300+	**65** 300+	**61** 300+	**74** 300+	**64** 300+	**75** 300+	**71** 300+	**68** 300+

NOTE: The first number in each column (boldface) is the score, the second number is the number of patients; Please refer to the main entry for footnotes; (a) 100-299

*MEASURES: **Children's Asthma Care:** 33. Received Systemic Corticosteroids; 34. Received Home Management Plan of Care; 35. Received Reliever Medication; **Use of Medical Imaging:** 36. Combination Abdominal CT Scan; 37. Combination Chest CT Scan; 38. Follow-up Mammogram/Ultrasound; 39. MRI for Low Back Pain; **Survey of Patients' Hospital Experiences:** 40. Area Around Room 'Always' Quiet at Night; 41. Doctors 'Always' Communicated Well; 42. Home Recovery Information Given; 43. Hospital Given 9 or 10 on 10 Point Scale; 44. Meds 'Always' Explained Before Given; 45. Nurses 'Always' Communicated Well; 46. Pain 'Always' Well Controlled; 47. Room and Bathroom 'Always' Clean; 48. Timely Help 'Always' Received; 49. Would Definitely Recommend Hospital*

Hospital	Children's Asthma Care			Use of Medical Imaging				Survey of Patients' Hospital Experiences									
	33	34	35	36	37	38	39	40	41	42	43	44	45	46	47	48	49
North Country Regional Hospital, Bemidji, MN	- -	- -	- -	0.023 222	0.000 74	7.8 51	41.6 101	58 300+	78 300+	82 300+	63 300+	59 300+	72 300+	64 300+	71 300+	57 300+	62 300+
North Memorial Medical Center, Robbinsdale, MN	- -	- -	- -	0.083 1034	0.016 943	6.9 711	54.3 210	52 300+	73 300+	81 300+	56 300+	54 300+	68 300+	66 300+	60 300+	52 300+	64 300+
North Valley Health Center, Warren, MN	- -	- -	- -	- -	- -	- -	- -	- -	- -	- -	- -	- -	- -	- -	- -	- -	- -
Northern Pines Medical Center, Aurora, MN	- -	- -	- -	0.000 32	0.000 25	- 0	- 0	- -	- -	- -	- -	- -	- -	- -	- -	- -	- -
Northfield Hospital, Northfield, MN	- -	- -	- -	0.065 107	0.020 100	11.3 133	23.1 39	58 300+	81 300+	86 300+	70 300+	62 300+	72 300+	67 300+	65 300+	64 300+	74 300+
Olmsted Medical Center, Rochester, MN	- -	- -	- -	0.344 227	0.253 146	5.7 1053	14.6 41	57 300+	80 300+	90 300+	73 300+	67 300+	75 300+	69 300+	70 300+	70 300+	82 300+
Ortonville Area Health Services, Ortonville, MN	- -	- -	- -	0.924 66	0.054 56	5.1 216	42.1 19	59 (a)	82 (a)	75 (a)	67 (a)	55 (a)	77 (a)	64 (a)	77 (a)	69 (a)	70 (a)
Owatonna Hospital, Owatonna, MN	- -	- -	- -	0.373 158	0.152 99	6.7 15	- 0	54 300+	78 300+	85 300+	60 300+	59 300+	73 300+	67 300+	70 300+	67 300+	67 300+
Park Nicollet Methodist Hospital, Saint Louis Park, MN	- -	- -	- -	0.067 1318	0.022 959	- 0	45.0 300	44 300+	75 300+	76 300+	54 300+	58 300+	65 300+	64 300+	57 300+	51 300+	65 300+
Paynesville Area Hospital, Paynesville, MN	- -	- -	- -	0.068 148	0.007 144	5.3 264	38.1 21	76 (a)	82 (a)	85 (a)	77 (a)	66 (a)	84 (a)	71 (a)	84 (a)	79 (a)	76 (a)
Perham Memorial Hospital, Perham, MN	- -	- -	- -	0.039 102	0.000 67	8.0 262	34.8 23	- -	- -	- -	- -	- -	- -	- -	- -	- -	- -
Phillips Eye Institute, Minneapolis, MN	- -	- -	- -	- 0	- 0	- 0	- 0	88 (a)	91 (a)	86 (a)	86 (a)	76 (a)	92 (a)	79 (a)	89 (a)	94 (a)	93 (a)
Pipestone County Medical Center, Pipestone, MN	- -	- -	- -	0.375 120	0.094 32	1.7 293	46.2 26	62 (a)	79 (a)	82 (a)	62 (a)	64 (a)	74 (a)	67 (a)	78 (a)	61 (a)	67 (a)
Prairie Ridge Hospital and Health Services, Elbow Lake, MN	- -	- -	- -	- -	- -	- -	- -	- -	- -	- -	- -	- -	- -	- -	- -	- -	- -
Queen of Peace Hospital, New Prague, MN	- -	- -	- -	0.131 237	0.006 158	4.3 418	27.5 69	65 300+	84 300+	88 300+	78 300+	72 300+	87 300+	76 300+	88 300+	85 300+	79 300+
Rainy Lake Medical Center, Int'l Falls, MN	- -	- -	- -	- -	- -	- -	- -	63 (a)	83 (a)	88 (a)	63 (a)	63 (a)	76 (a)	69 (a)	75 (a)	74 (a)	63 (a)
Red Lake Hospital, Redlake, MN	- -	- -	- -	- -	- -	- -	- -	84 <100	71 <100	70 <100	65 <100	66 <100	82 <100	74 <100	65 <100	23 <100	40 <100
Redwood Area Hospital, Redwood Falls, MN	- -	- -	- -	0.043 140	0.011 89	4.5 67	24.2 33	77 (a)	82 (a)	90 (a)	72 (a)	67 (a)	81 (a)	70 (a)	86 (a)	82 (a)	70 (a)
Regina Medical Center, Hastings, MN	- -	- -	- -	0.049 284	0.005 197	5.0 279	22.5 40	70 300+	82 300+	83 300+	72 300+	64 300+	78 300+	70 300+	72 300+	73 300+	74 300+
Regions Hospital, Saint Paul, MN	- -	- -	- -	0.148 1491	0.002 1324	9.2 1265	56.9 320	57 300+	77 300+	85 300+	66 300+	60 300+	74 300+	65 300+	70 300+	62 300+	71 300+
Renville County Hospital and Clinics, Olivia, MN	- -	- -	- -	0.649 37	0.031 32	7.6 172	31.3 16	- -	- -	- -	- -	- -	- -	- -	- -	- -	- -
Rice Memorial Hospital, Willmar, MN	- -	- -	- -	0.054 148	0.000 77	2.7 222	45.8 24	66 300+	82 300+	86 300+	71 300+	64 300+	77 300+	70 300+	73 300+	71 300+	71 300+
Ridgeview Medical Center, Waconia, MN	- -	- -	- -	0.037 515	0.002 427	3.5 462	51.0 147	66 300+	80 300+	83 300+	79 300+	64 300+	75 300+	66 300+	83 300+	69 300+	85 300+
River's Edge Hospital & Clinic, Saint Peter, MN	- -	- -	- -	0.032 95	0.000 74	6.0 251	46.2 13	75 <100	91 <100	90 <100	86 <100	76 <100	86 <100	77 <100	92 <100	86 <100	91 <100
Riverview Hospital, Crookston, MN	- -	- -	- -	0.033 91	0.043 69	3.9 335	17.9 56	62 (a)	83 (a)	83 (a)	67 (a)	61 (a)	76 (a)	61 (a)	70 (a)	69 (a)	75 (a)
Riverwood Healthcare Center, Aitkin, MN	- -	- -	- -	- -	- -	- -	- -	59 300+	79 300+	85 300+	77 300+	63 300+	77 300+	75 300+	84 300+	76 300+	79 300+
Saint Cloud Hospital, Saint Cloud, MN	- -	- -	- -	0.026 1399	0.003 1472	6.0 1525	43.3 277	62 300+	80 300+	84 300+	73 300+	65 300+	78 300+	69 300+	75 300+	71 300+	75 300+
Saint Cloud VA Medical Center, Saint Cloud, MN	- -	- -	- -	- -	- -	- -	- -	- -	- -	- -	- -	- -	- -	- -	- -	- -	- -
Saint Elizabeth Medical Center, Wabasha, MN	- -	- -	- -	0.049 61	0.034 58	9.4 266	16.7 18	65 (a)	84 (a)	85 (a)	83 (a)	72 (a)	80 (a)	71 (a)	87 (a)	84 (a)	80 (a)
Saint Francis Healthcare Campus, Breckenridge, MN	- -	- -	- -	0.112 170	0.136 88	3.0 133	28.6 56	61 (a)	87 (a)	83 (a)	73 (a)	72 (a)	79 (a)	73 (a)	78 (a)	72 (a)	74 (a)
Saint Francis Regional Medical Center, Shakopee, MN	- -	- -	- -	0.044 525	0.033 366	3.4 533	39.8 103	67 300+	78 300+	86 300+	70 300+	61 300+	77 300+	69 300+	75 300+	68 300+	74 300+
Saint Gabriels Hospital, Little Falls, MN	- -	- -	- -	0.068 207	0.006 162	9.0 466	48.4 64	74 (a)	85 (a)	87 (a)	77 (a)	65 (a)	81 (a)	74 (a)	81 (a)	77 (a)	77 (a)
Saint James Medical Center-Mayo Health Sys, Saint James, MN	- -	- -	- -	0.043 46	0.100 20	4.3 161	54.5 11	73 <100	76 <100	70 <100	61 <100	42 <100	70 <100	73 <100	81 <100	71 <100	64 <100
Saint Joseph's Hospital, Saint Paul, MN	- -	- -	- -	0.068 399	0.011 273	7.6 683	38.7 62	50 300+	70 300+	82 300+	63 300+	52 300+	69 300+	59 300+	63 300+	53 300+	71 300+
Saint Josephs Area Health Services, Park Rapids, MN	- -	- -	- -	0.235 293	0.018 217	9.4 551	36.1 83	68 300+	82 300+	89 300+	76 300+	68 300+	83 300+	74 300+	79 300+	71 300+	78 300+
Saint Lukes Hospital, Duluth, MN	- -	- -	- -	0.222 919	0.009 814	11.0 1350	- 0	57 300+	80 300+	84 300+	70 300+	65 300+	75 300+	66 300+	68 300+	61 300+	77 300+
Saint Marys Regional Health Center, Detroit Lakes, MN	- -	- -	- -	0.122 189	0.112 170	- 0	27.3 44	62 300+	82 300+	81 300+	68 300+	61 300+	78 300+	71 300+	77 300+	73 300+	68 300+
Saint Michaels Hospital & Nursing Home, Sauk Centre, MN	- -	- -	- -	0.013 77	0.016 63	8.6 186	16.0 25	- -	- -	- -	- -	- -	- -	- -	- -	- -	- -
Sanford Canby Medical Center, Canby, MN	- -	- -	- -	0.761 46	0.385 26	2.1 191	35.0 20	56 (a)	77 (a)	85 (a)	73 (a)	63 (a)	81 (a)	59 (a)	79 (a)	70 (a)	64 (a)
Sanford Jackson Medical Center, Jackson, MN	- -	- -	- -	0.304 23	0.133 15	10.5 105	60.0 10	63 <100	69 <100	72 <100	59 <100	57 <100	78 <100	59 <100	67 <100	61 <100	49 <100
Sanford Luverne Medical Center, Luverne, MN	- -	- -	- -	0.180 89	0.175 40	7.1 367	33.3 57	65 (a)	83 (a)	77 (a)	75 (a)	63 (a)	78 (a)	72 (a)	81 (a)	76 (a)	82 (a)
Sanford Medical Center Thief River Falls, Thief River Falls, MN	- -	- -	- -	- -	- -	- -	- -	61 300+	76 300+	77 300+	55 300+	57 300+	73 300+	67 300+	75 300+	64 300+	57 300+
Sanford Tracy, Tracy, MN	- -	- -	- -	- -	- -	- -	- -	58 <100	69 <100	80 <100	72 <100	53 <100	81 <100	50 <100	87 <100	79 <100	75 <100
Sanford Westbrook Medical Center, Westbrook, MN	- -	- -	- -	0.333 18	0.000 13	6.3 95	33.3 3	71 <100	82 <100	84 <100	86 <100	74 <100	95 <100	58 <100	82 <100	87 <100	87 <100
Sanford Worthington Medical Center, Worthington, MN	- -	- -	- -	0.087 138	0.018 56	- 0	38.6 44	63 300+	74 300+	84 300+	65 300+	61 300+	76 300+	65 300+	83 300+	69 300+	64 300+
Sibley Medical Center, Arlington, MN	- -	- -	- -	0.037 82	0.066 91	2.9 104	18.2 11	- -	- -	- -	- -	- -	- -	- -	- -	- -	- -
Sleepy Eye Municipal Hospital, Sleepy Eye, MN	- -	- -	- -	0.065 124	0.000 49	2.9 104	23.5 17	- -	- -	- -	- -	- -	- -	- -	- -	- -	- -
Springfield Medical Center Mayo Health System, Springfield, MN	- -	- -	- -	0.054 56	0.000 23	4.4 206	40.0 20	73 (a)	86 (a)	78 (a)	80 (a)	63 (a)	82 (a)	69 (a)	93 (a)	82 (a)	82 (a)
Stevens Community Medical Center, Morris, MN	- -	- -	- -	0.129 170	0.036 83	14.6 192	27.3 22	- -	- -	- -	- -	- -	- -	- -	- -	- -	- -
Swift County Benson Hospital, Benson, MN	- -	- -	- -	0.068 73	0.031 65	2.8 143	62.5 8	69 (a)	81 (a)	85 (a)	83 (a)	58 (a)	81 (a)	74 (a)	87 (a)	82 (a)	82 (a)
Tri County Hospital, Wadena, MN	- -	- -	- -	0.051 196	0.000 111	4.3 258	40.0 40	60 300+	84 300+	81 300+	71 300+	68 300+	79 300+	71 300+	81 300+	73 300+	71 300+
Tyler Healthcare Center, Tyler, MN	- -	- -	- -	0.431 58	0.368 19	10.5 86	30.8 13	63 <100	79 <100	76 <100	65 <100	44 <100	80 <100	75 <100	75 <100	74 <100	72 <100
United Hospital, Saint Paul, MN	- -	- -	- -	0.064 746	0.005 412	8.6 1247	43.1 109	48 300+	75 300+	83 300+	63 300+	57 300+	73 300+	66 300+	63 300+	61 300+	70 300+
United Hospital District, Blue Earth, MN	- -	- -	- -	0.000 104	0.000 70	9.0 255	39.1 23	74 (a)	88 (a)	88 (a)	81 (a)	67 (a)	88 (a)	77 (a)	86 (a)	79 (a)	84 (a)
Unity Hospital, Fridley, MN	- -	- -	- -	0.024 594	0.002 614	- 0	39.3 28	50 300+	76 300+	86 300+	60 300+	56 300+	72 300+	64 300+	64 300+	57 300+	64 300+
University Medical Center - Mesabi/Mesaba Clinics, Hibbing, MN	- -	- -	- -	0.085 260	0.000 220	5.5 383	51.9 106	60 300+	87 300+	86 300+	68 300+	67 300+	81 300+	71 300+	76 300+	68 300+	65 300+
University of Minnesota Medical Ctr-Fairview, Minneapolis, MN	100 31	19 32	100 32	0.026 1332	0.008 1423	6.1 604	42.3 104	47 300+	73 300+	84 300+	62 300+	59 300+	70 300+	65 300+	62 300+	56 300+	69 300+
Virginia Regional Medical Center, Virginia, MN	- -	- -	- -	0.417 424	0.014 276	12.6 231	37.5 128	54 300+	80 300+	81 300+	65 300+	60 300+	78 300+	71 300+	76 300+	72 300+	62 300+
Waseca Medical Center - Mayo Health System, Waseca, MN	- -	- -	- -	0.127 102	0.021 47	6.8 221	26.7 15	60 <100	78 <100	89 <100	62 <100	69 <100	78 <100	68 <100	77 <100	66 <100	67 <100
Wheaton Community Hospital, Wheaton, MN	- -	- -	- -	0.141 64	0.179 28	4.3 162	33.3 15	- -	- -	- -	- -	- -	- -	- -	- -	- -	- -
Windom Area Hospital, Windom, MN	- -	- -	- -	0.040 100	0.043 47	13.2 129	45.5 22	65 (a)	84 (a)	80 (a)	72 (a)	61 (a)	84 (a)	69 (a)	84 (a)	74 (a)	75 (a)
Winona Health Services, Winona, MN	- -	- -	- -	0.069 245	0.041 122	3.5 677	47.7 44	54 300+	79 300+	82 300+	61 300+	55 300+	73 300+	63 300+	71 300+	64 300+	65 300+
MISSOURI																	
Advanced Healthcare Medical Center, Ellington, MO	- -	- -	- -	- -	- -	- -	- -	- -	- -	- -	- -	- -	- -	- -	- -	- -	- -
Audrain Medical Center, Mexico, MO	- -	- -	- -	0.520 481	0.156 333	6.2 1041	35.7 129	55 300+	79 300+	87 300+	66 300+	58 300+	76 300+	72 300+	77 300+	71 300+	64 300+
Barnes Jewish Hospital, Saint Louis, MO	- -	- -	- -	0.121 4449	0.022 4518	7.1 4757	30.0 533	55 300+	79 300+	87 300+	67 300+	60 300+	73 300+	70 300+	66 300+	53 300+	72 300+
Barnes-Jewish St Peters Hospital, Saint Peters, MO	- -	- -	- -	0.137 761	0.052 749	7.7 979	30.6 72	62 300+	84 300+	86 300+	77 300+	65 300+	82 300+	72 300+	70 300+	63 300+	81 300+

NOTE: The first number in each column (boldface) is the score, the second number is the number of patients; Please refer to the main entry for footnotes; (a) 100-299

*MEASURES: **Children's Asthma Care:** 33. Received Systemic Corticosteroids; 34. Received Home Management Plan of Care; 35. Received Reliever Medication; **Use of Medical Imaging:** 36. Combination Abdominal CT Scan; 37. Combination Chest CT Scan; 38. Follow-up Mammogram/Ultrasound; 39. MRI for Low Back Pain; **Survey of Patients' Hospital Experiences:** 40. Area Around Room 'Always' Quiet at Night; 41. Doctors 'Always' Communicated Well; 42. Home Recovery Information Given; 43. Hospital Given 9 or 10 on 10 Point Scale; 44. Meds 'Always' Explained Before Given; 45. Nurses 'Always' Communicated Well; 46. Pain 'Always' Well Controlled; 47. Room and Bathroom 'Always' Clean; 48. Timely Help 'Always' Received; 49. Would Definitely Recommend Hospital*

Hospital	Children's Asthma Care			Use of Medical Imaging				Survey of Patients' Hospital Experiences									
	33	34	35	36	37	38	39	40	41	42	43	44	45	46	47	48	49
Barnes-Jewish West County Hospital, Creve Coeur, MO	- -	- -	- -	**0.103** 846	**0.014** 814	**6.4** 672	**29.0** 155	**64** 300+	**84** 300+	**87** 300+	**78** 300+	**60** 300+	**82** 300+	**77** 300+	**71** 300+	**72** 300+	**79** 300+
Barton County Memorial Hospital, Lamar, MO	- -	- -	- -	- -	- -	- -	- -	- -	- -	- -	- -	- -	- -	- -	- -	- -	- -
Bates County Memorial Hospital, Butler, MO	- -	- -	- -	**0.056** 215	**0.000** 119	**7.0** 270	**28.6** 63	**56** 300+	**76** 300+	**83** 300+	**69** 300+	**58** 300+	**75** 300+	**68** 300+	**71** 300+	**63** 300+	**71** 300+
Boone Hospital Center, Columbia, MO	- -	- -	- -	**0.170** 1483	**0.011** 1012	**3.1** 2578	**36.8** 465	**60** 300+	**87** 300+	**89** 300+	**78** 300+	**73** 300+	**84** 300+	**71** 300+	**75** 300+	**69** 300+	**83** 300+
Bothwell Regional Health Center, Sedalia, MO	- -	- -	- -	**0.730** 788	**0.000** 649	**1.2** 752	**37.1** 237	**63** 300+	**83** 300+	**85** 300+	**70** 300+	**66** 300+	**81** 300+	**74** 300+	**81** 300+	**76** 300+	**67** 300+
Callaway Community Hospital, Fulton, MO	- -	- -	- -	**0.784** 111	**0.014** 69	**9.5** 264	**42.9** 35	**48** (a)	**81** (a)	**80** (a)	**58** (a)	**63** (a)	**71** (a)	**65** (a)	**66** (a)	**68** (a)	**50** (a)
Cameron Regional Medical Center, Cameron, MO	- -	- -	- -	**0.061** 310	**0.022** 136	**4.4** 295	**45.1** 51	**49** 300+	**67** 300+	**77** 300+	**52** 300+	**46** 300+	**63** 300+	**58** 300+	**69** 300+	**52** 300+	**50** 300+
Capital Region Medical Center, Jefferson City, MO	- -	- -	- -	**0.409** 802	**0.056** 695	**13.9** 1083	**47.5** 297	**62** 300+	**82** 300+	**82** 300+	**77** 300+	**59** 300+	**80** 300+	**72** 300+	**76** 300+	**66** 300+	**81** 300+
Carroll County Memorial Hospital, Carrollton, MO	- -	- -	- -	- -	- -	- -	- -	- -	- -	- -	- -	- -	- -	- -	- -	- -	- -
Cass Medical Center, Harrisonville, MO	- -	- -	- -	- -	- -	- -	- -	- -	- -	- -	- -	- -	- -	- -	- -	- -	- -
Centerpoint Medical Center of Independence, Independence, MO	- -	- -	- -	**0.050** 539	**0.010** 288	**6.2** 1273	**31.7** 104	**66** 300+	**78** 300+	**88** 300+	**68** 300+	**58** 300+	**75** 300+	**70** 300+	**69** 300+	**62** 300+	**68** 300+
Childrens Mercy Hospital, Kansas City, MO	**100** 446	**63** 446	**100** 449	- -	- -	- -	- -	- -	- -	- -	- -	- -	- -	- -	- -	- -	- -
Christian Hospital Northeast, Saint Louis, MO	- -	- -	- -	**0.522** 783	**0.003** 672	**10.9** 522	**39.1** 87	**71** 300+	**84** 300+	**84** 300+	**68** 300+	**67** 300+	**83** 300+	**73** 300+	**69** 300+	**64** 300+	**67** 300+
Christian Hospital Northwest, Florissant, MO	- -	- -	- -	**0.438** 240	**0.110** 191	**12.5** 861	**26.3** 38	- -	- -	- -	- -	- -	- -	- -	- -	- -	- -
Citizens Memorial Hospital, Bolivar, MO	- -	- -	- -	**0.358** 383	**0.310** 255	**3.6** 583	**39.6** 139	**56** 300+	**82** 300+	**83** 300+	**69** 300+	**60** 300+	**79** 300+	**72** 300+	**79** 300+	**68** 300+	**67** 300+
Columbia Missouri VA Medical Center, Columbia, MO	- -	- -	- -	- -	- -	- -	- -	- -	- -	- -	- -	- -	- -	- -	- -	- -	- -
Community Hospital Association, Fairfax, MO	- -	- -	- -	- -	- -	- -	- -	- -	- -	- -	- -	- -	- -	- -	- -	- -	- -
Cooper County Memorial Hospital, Boonville, MO	- -	- -	- -	**0.755** 94	**0.607** 56	- 0	**18.2** 11	**60** <100	**83** <100	**81** <100	**60** <100	**51** <100	**72** <100	**63** <100	**62** <100	**61** <100	**71** <100
Cox Medical Center, Springfield, MO	- -	- -	- -	**0.048** 1960	**0.002** 1322	**9.2** 2956	**34.9** 601	**44** 300+	**79** 300+	**79** 300+	**61** 300+	**53** 300+	**72** 300+	**63** 300+	**65** 300+	**58** 300+	**68** 300+
Cox Monett Hospital, Monett, MO	- -	- -	- -	- -	- -	- -	- -	**70** (a)	**89** (a)	**81** (a)	**74** (a)	**71** (a)	**83** (a)	**79** (a)	**77** (a)	**77** (a)	**71** (a)
Des Peres Hospital, Saint Louis, MO	- -	- -	- -	**0.621** 243	**0.000** 90	**6.0** 150	**39.6** 111	**55** 300+	**82** 300+	**83** 300+	**64** 300+	**58** 300+	**74** 300+	**69** 300+	**67** 300+	**62** 300+	**69** 300+
Fitzgibbon Memorial Hospital, Marshall, MO	- -	- -	- -	**0.017** 288	**0.025** 119	**3.4** 557	**46.8** 94	**54** 300+	**79** 300+	**84** 300+	**67** 300+	**60** 300+	**76** 300+	**71** 300+	**66** 300+	**68** 300+	**58** 300+
Forest Park Hospital, Saint Louis, MO	- -	- -	- -	**0.444** 117	**0.000** 63	**2.9** 380	**52.6** 19	**61** (a)	**77** (a)	**67** (a)	**55** (a)	**61** (a)	**79** (a)	**76** (a)	**55** (a)	**57** (a)	**54** (a)
Freeman Health System - Freeman West, Joplin, MO	- -	- -	- -	**0.523** 1154	**0.612** 842	**3.8** 2505	**31.2** 609	**52** 300+	**76** 300+	**82** 300+	**65** 300+	**57** 300+	**74** 300+	**68** 300+	**66** 300+	**56** 300+	**70** 300+
Freeman Neosho Hospital, Neosho, MO	- -	- -	- -	- -	- -	- -	- -	**52** 300+	**83** 300+	**84** 300+	**73** 300+	**62** 300+	**78** 300+	**69** 300+	**79** 300+	**70** 300+	**71** 300+
Golden Valley Memorial Hospital, Clinton, MO	- -	- -	- -	**0.083** 444	**0.084** 285	**5.1** 830	**31.9** 191	**53** 300+	**83** 300+	**82** 300+	**64** 300+	**57** 300+	**76** 300+	**69** 300+	**81** 300+	**67** 300+	**63** 300+
Hannibal Regional Hospital, Hannibal, MO	- -	- -	- -	**0.653** 245	**0.133** 143	**12.1** 174	**31.5** 108	**53** 300+	**83** 300+	**87** 300+	**74** 300+	**62** 300+	**81** 300+	**70** 300+	**70** 300+	**68** 300+	**71** 300+
Harrison County Community Hospital, Bethany, MO	- -	- -	- -	- -	- -	- -	- -	- -	- -	- -	- -	- -	- -	- -	- -	- -	- -
Heartland Regional Medical Center, Saint Joseph, MO	- -	- -	- -	**0.135** 1438	**0.070** 1277	**7.5** 2395	**36.5** 373	**62** 300+	**81** 300+	**83** 300+	**67** 300+	**62** 300+	**80** 300+	**71** 300+	**70** 300+	**60** 300+	**66** 300+
Hedrick Medical Center, Chillicothe, MO	- -	- -	- -	**0.029** 240	**0.051** 197	**9.1** 274	**32.1** 53	**69** (a)	**78** (a)	**79** (a)	**65** (a)	**55** (a)	**75** (a)	**64** (a)	**80** (a)	**71** (a)	**57** (a)
Hermann Area District Hospital, Hermann, MO	- -	- -	- -	- -	- -	- -	- -	- -	- -	- -	- -	- -	- -	- -	- -	- -	- -
Jefferson Regional Medical Center, Crystal City, MO	- -	- -	- -	**0.336** 836	**0.005** 624	**8.2** 926	**35.8** 109	**46** 300+	**75** 300+	**75** 300+	**62** 300+	**56** 300+	**74** 300+	**67** 300+	**68** 300+	**63** 300+	**61** 300+
Kansas City VA Medical Center, Kansas City, MO	- -	- -	- -	- -	- -	- -	- -	- -	- -	- -	- -	- -	- -	- -	- -	- -	- -
Lafayette Regional Health Center, Lexington, MO	- -	- -	- -	**0.020** 201	**0.051** 137	**11.8** 221	**46.0** 63	**56** (a)	**82** (a)	**85** (a)	**70** (a)	**64** (a)	**79** (a)	**68** (a)	**77** (a)	**66** (a)	**65** (a)
Lake Regional Health System, Osage Beach, MO	- -	- -	- -	**0.719** 556	**0.706** 361	**6.1** 1094	**32.9** 70	**54** 300+	**78** 300+	**85** 300+	**66** 300+	**61** 300+	**76** 300+	**69** 300+	**78** 300+	**70** 300+	**66** 300+
Lee's Summit Medical Center, Lee's Summit, MO	- -	- -	- -	**0.140** 272	**0.094** 160	**15.6** 572	**36.5** 63	**66** 300+	**76** 300+	**85** 300+	**72** 300+	**57** 300+	**75** 300+	**70** 300+	**72** 300+	**61** 300+	**72** 300+
Liberty Hospital, Liberty, MO	- -	- -	- -	**0.092** 1087	**0.002** 593	**3.7** 2377	**37.4** 281	**50** 300+	**77** 300+	**82** 300+	**75** 300+	**62** 300+	**76** 300+	**64** 300+	**71** 300+	**61** 300+	**77** 300+
Lincoln County Medical Center, Troy, MO	- -	- -	- -	- -	- -	- -	- -	**61** (a)	**83** (a)	**84** (a)	**67** (a)	**70** (a)	**81** (a)	**71** (a)	**80** (a)	**74** (a)	**65** (a)
McCune-Brooks Hospital, Carthage, MO	- -	- -	- -	- -	- -	- -	- -	**64** 300+	**88** 300+	**88** 300+	**83** 300+	**64** 300+	**84** 300+	**78** 300+	**80** 300+	**85** 300+	**85** 300+
Mineral Area Regional Medical Center, Farmington, MO	- -	- -	- -	**0.126** 277	**0.064** 110	**4.3** 444	**34.7** 98	**59** 300+	**85** 300+	**83** 300+	**62** 300+	**57** 300+	**75** 300+	**67** 300+	**72** 300+	**62** 300+	**63** 300+
Missouri Baptist Hospital Sullivan, Sullivan, MO	- -	- -	- -	**0.025** 316	**0.002** 423	**7.7** 456	**47.8** 67	**68** 300+	**86** 300+	**85** 300+	**79** 300+	**67** 300+	**83** 300+	**76** 300+	**81** 300+	**73** 300+	**71** 300+
Missouri Baptist Medical Center, Town and Country, MO	- -	- -	- -	**0.044** 1663	**0.000** 2226	**7.6** 2421	**31.6** 383	**51** 300+	**83** 300+	**85** 300+	**73** 300+	**61** 300+	**75** 300+	**69** 300+	**64** 300+	**59** 300+	**76** 300+
Missouri Delta Medical Center, Sikeston, MO	- -	- -	- -	**0.627** 327	**0.021** 194	**7.5** 738	**60.8** 74	**61** 300+	**84** 300+	**77** 300+	**65** 300+	**67** 300+	**78** 300+	**75** 300+	**83** 300+	**67** 300+	**62** 300+
Missouri Southern Healthcare, Dexter, MO	- -	- -	- -	**0.470** 217	**0.017** 117	**8.1** 406	**26.3** 38	**59** 300+	**87** 300+	**76** 300+	**66** 300+	**60** 300+	**81** 300+	**71** 300+	**79** 300+	**73** 300+	**65** 300+
Moberly Regional Medical Center, Moberly, MO	- -	- -	- -	**0.506** 233	**0.057** 230	**11.8** 288	**31.6** 38	**61** 300+	**81** 300+	**89** 300+	**66** 300+	**56** 300+	**74** 300+	**66** 300+	**72** 300+	**63** 300+	**60** 300+
Nevada Regional Medical Center, Nevada, MO	- -	- -	- -	**0.409** 269	**0.008** 118	**4.4** 411	**51.7** 58	**58** (a)	**88** (a)	**86** (a)	**59** (a)	**56** (a)	**75** (a)	**61** (a)	**84** (a)	**71** (a)	**56** (a)
North Kansas City Hospital, North Kansas City, MO	- -	- -	- -	**0.093** 1477	**0.034** 1088	**15.7** 949	**36.2** 442	**56** 300+	**80** 300+	**80** 300+	**72** 300+	**59** 300+	**75** 300+	**68** 300+	**69** 300+	**63** 300+	**78** 300+
Northeast Regional Medical Center, Kirksville, MO	- -	- -	- -	**0.425** 374	**0.104** 337	**7.3** 740	**43.8** 48	**61** 300+	**80** 300+	**85** 300+	**66** 300+	**58** 300+	**75** 300+	**66** 300+	**70** 300+	**59** 300+	**59** 300+
Northwest Medical Center, Albany, MO	- -	- -	- -	- -	- -	- -	- -	- -	- -	- -	- -	- -	- -	- -	- -	- -	- -
Ozarks Community Hospital, Springfield, MO	- -	- -	- -	**0.198** 177	**0.047** 64	- 0	**39.3** 107	**63** 300+	**88** 300+	**80** 300+	**74** 300+	**66** 300+	**80** 300+	**71** 300+	**83** 300+	**73** 300+	**80** 300+
Ozarks Medical Center, West Plains, MO	- -	- -	- -	**0.238** 480	**0.000** 308	**9.6** 793	**41.9** 136	**57** 300+	**83** 300+	**83** 300+	**64** 300+	**58** 300+	**79** 300+	**73** 300+	**72** 300+	**72** 300+	**66** 300+
Parkland Health Center, Farmington, MO	- -	- -	- -	**0.074** 852	**0.126** 541	**5.5** 947	**33.9** 174	**60** 300+	**88** 300+	**85** 300+	**78** 300+	**74** 300+	**86** 300+	**79** 300+	**74** 300+	**78** 300+	**77** 300+
Pemiscot Memorial Hospital, Hayti, MO	- -	- -	- -	**0.100** 290	**0.114** 105	**2.8** 251	**35.0** 40	**46** 300+	**82** 300+	**62** 300+	**40** 300+	**47** 300+	**60** 300+	**56** 300+	**57** 300+	**48** 300+	**40** 300+
Perry County Memorial Hospital, Perryville, MO	- -	- -	- -	- -	- -	- -	- -	- -	- -	- -	- -	- -	- -	- -	- -	- -	- -
Pershing Memorial Hospital, Brookfield, MO	- -	- -	- -	- -	- -	- -	- -	- -	- -	- -	- -	- -	- -	- -	- -	- -	- -
Phelps County Regional Medical Center, Rolla, MO	- -	- -	- -	**0.378** 526	**0.005** 398	**2.9** 1595	**41.5** 205	**52** 300+	**81** 300+	**84** 300+	**62** 300+	**56** 300+	**80** 300+	**71** 300+	**77** 300+	**64** 300+	**63** 300+
Pike County Memorial Hospital, Louisiana, MO	- -	- -	- -	- -	- -	- -	- -	- -	- -	- -	- -	- -	- -	- -	- -	- -	- -
Poplar Bluff Regional Medical Center, Poplar Bluff, MO	**100** 61	**100** 61	**100** 61	**0.115** 356	**0.068** 192	**6.4** 738	**39.4** 71	**44** 300+	**76** 300+	**73** 300+	**44** 300+	**52** 300+	**67** 300+	**65** 300+	**57** 300+	**61** 300+	**45** 300+
Poplar Bluff VA Medical Center, Poplar Bluff, MO	- -	- -	- -	- -	- -	- -	- -	- -	- -	- -	- -	- -	- -	- -	- -	- -	- -
Progress West Healthcare Center, O'Fallon, MO	- -	- -	- -	**0.059** 119	**0.000** 91	**5.4** 93	**23.8** 21	**67** 300+	**83** 300+	**85** 300+	**80** 300+	**65** 300+	**80** 300+	**72** 300+	**75** 300+	**65** 300+	**82** 300+
Putnam County Memorial Hospital, Unionville, MO	- -	- -	- -	- -	- -	- -	- -	- -	- -	- -	- -	- -	- -	- -	- -	- -	- -
Ray County Memorial Hospital, Richmond, MO	- -	- -	- -	- -	- -	- -	- -	- -	- -	- -	- -	- -	- -	- -	- -	- -	- -
Research Belton Hospital, Belton, MO	- -	- -	- -	**0.163** 196	**0.125** 112	**14.1** 467	**38.3** 47	**65** 300+	**78** 300+	**87** 300+	**70** 300+	**58** 300+	**77** 300+	**72** 300+	**67** 300+	**66** 300+	**65** 300+
Research Medical Center, Kansas City, MO	- -	- -	- -	**0.182** 752	**0.140** 479	**7.3** 1030	**35.9** 142	**64** 300+	**81** 300+	**85** 300+	**66** 300+	**59** 300+	**76** 300+	**69** 300+	**63** 300+	**59** 300+	**64** 300+
Ripley County Memorial Hospital, Doniphan, MO	- -	- -	- -	**0.000** 55	**0.000** 52	- 0	**20.0** 15	**42** (a)	**79** (a)	**82** (a)	**57** (a)	**55** (a)	**73** (a)	**51** (a)	**77** (a)	**68** (a)	**55** (a)
SAC-Osage Hospital, Osceola, MO	- -	- -	- -	**0.735** 68	**0.024** 42	**2.5** 161	**43.5** 23	**58** (a)	**82** (a)	**75** (a)	**59** (a)	**69** (a)	**81** (a)	**63** (a)	**81** (a)	**70** (a)	**64** (a)
Saint Alexius Hospital, Saint Louis, MO	- -	- -	- -	**0.087** 138	**0.074** 54	**7.0** 327	**50.0** 2	**59** 300+	**84** 300+	**78** 300+	**65** 300+	**61** 300+	**78** 300+	**71** 300+	**64** 300+	**62** 300+	**65** 300+

NOTE: The first number in each column (boldface) is the score, the second number is the number of patients; Please refer to the main entry for footnotes; (a) 100-299
*MEASURES: **Children's Asthma Care:** 33. Received Systemic Corticosteroids; 34. Received Home Management Plan of Care; 35. Received Reliever Medication; **Use of Medical Imaging:** 36. Combination Abdominal CT Scan; 37. Combination Chest CT Scan; 38. Follow-up Mammogram/Ultrasound; 39. MRI for Low Back Pain; **Survey of Patients' Hospital Experiences:** 40. Area Around Room 'Always' Quiet at Night; 41. Doctors 'Always' Communicated Well; 42. Home Recovery Information Given; 43. Hospital Given 9 or 10 on 10 Point Scale; 44. Meds 'Always' Explained Before Given; 45. Nurses 'Always' Communicated Well; 46. Pain 'Always' Well Controlled; 47. Room and Bathroom 'Always' Clean; 48. Timely Help 'Always' Received; 49. Would Definitely Recommend Hospital*

Hospital	Children's Asthma Care			Use of Medical Imaging				Survey of Patients' Hospital Experiences									
	33	34	35	36	37	38	39	40	41	42	43	44	45	46	47	48	49
Saint Anthony's Medical Center, Saint Louis, MO	-	-	-	**0.666** 1358	**0.008** 828	**6.6** 2726	**31.6** 275	**59** 300+	**77** 300+	**80** 300+	**62** 300+	**55** 300+	**75** 300+	**70** 300+	**69** 300+	**56** 300+	**61** 300+
Saint Francis Hospital, Maryville, MO	-	-	-	**0.049** 285	**0.023** 177	**4.4** 436	**28.9** 76	**68** 300+	**85** 300+	**82** 300+	**74** 300+	**66** 300+	**82** 300+	**72** 300+	**88** 300+	**76** 300+	**71** 300+
Saint Francis Hospital, Mountain View, MO	-	-	-	-	-	-	-	-	-	-	-	-	-	-	-	-	-
Saint Francis Medical Center, Cape Girardeau, MO	-	-	-	**0.401** 1340	**0.002** 872	**8.6** 1799	**28.3** 378	**57** 300+	**82** 300+	**83** 300+	**74** 300+	**67** 300+	**81** 300+	**71** 300+	**75** 300+	**63** 300+	**80** 300+
Saint John's Regional Health Center, Springfield, MO	-	-	-	**0.017** 2112	**0.001** 1712	**8.6** 4865	**40.8** 660	**60** 300+	**82** 300+	**87** 300+	**80** 300+	**65** 300+	**80** 300+	**73** 300+	**79** 300+	**67** 300+	**83** 300+
Saint John's Regional Medical Center, Joplin, MO	-	-	-	**0.025** 1123	**0.001** 876	**7.5** 1878	**36.2** 301	**58** 300+	**80** 300+	**85** 300+	**72** 300+	**56** 300+	**77** 300+	**72** 300+	**72** 300+	**62** 300+	**75** 300+
Saint Johns Hospital - Aurora, Aurora, MO	-	-	-	-	-	-	-	-	-	-	-	-	-	-	-	-	-
Saint Johns Hospital - Cassville, Cassville, MO	-	-	-	-	-	-	-	-	-	-	-	-	-	-	-	-	-
Saint Johns Hospital-Lebanon, Lebanon, MO	-	-	-	**0.040** 346	**0.018** 164	**7.3** 560	**67.5** 77	**53** 300+	**83** 300+	**86** 300+	**66** 300+	**65** 300+	**76** 300+	**66** 300+	**83** 300+	**66** 300+	**67** 300+
Saint Johns Mercy Hospital, Washington, MO	-	-	-	**0.038** 529	**0.000** 412	**4.2** 686	**40.3** 129	**57** 300+	**83** 300+	**82** 300+	**63** 300+	**61** 300+	**75** 300+	**68** 300+	**75** 300+	**59** 300+	**67** 300+
Saint Johns Mercy Medical Center, Saint Louis, MO	**100** 195	**69** 194	**100** 195	**0.057** 2017	**0.009** 1514	**5.2** 3740	**37.0** 411	**59** 300+	**79** 300+	**77** 300+	**75** 300+	**52** 300+	**78** 300+	**69** 300+	**70** 300+	**62** 300+	**79** 300+
Saint Joseph Medical Center, Kansas City, MO	-	-	-	**0.272** 1054	**0.121** 696	**10.8** 1626	**32.1** 355	**53** 300+	**81** 300+	**88** 300+	**67** 300+	**56** 300+	**73** 300+	**68** 300+	**60** 300+	**55** 300+	**73** 300+
Saint Louis University Hospital, Saint Louis, MO	-	-	-	**0.373** 807	**0.076** 621	**5.0** 340	**32.3** 31	**57** 300+	**78** 300+	**86** 300+	**67** 300+	**65** 300+	**72** 300+	**66** 300+	**67** 300+	**60** 300+	**71** 300+
Saint Louis-John Cochran VA Medical Center, Saint Louis, MO	-	-	-	-	-	-	-	-	-	-	-	-	-	-	-	-	-
Saint Luke's East Lee's Summit Hospital, Lees Summit, MO	-	-	-	**0.050** 537	**0.041** 197	**11.8** 408	**38.0** 121	**68** 300+	**80** 300+	**86** 300+	**83** 300+	**63** 300+	**79** 300+	**71** 300+	**79** 300+	**65** 300+	**86** 300+
Saint Lukes Cancer Institute, Kansas City, MO	-	-	-	**0.000** 3	**0.000** 3	**9.5** 1341	- 0	**59** (a)	**86** (a)	**89** (a)	**74** (a)	**73** (a)	**85** (a)	**70** (a)	**71** (a)	**81** (a)	**87** (a)
Saint Lukes Hospital, Chesterfield, MO	-	-	-	**0.076** 1482	**0.007** 1364	**6.5** 5188	**31.0** 474	**58** 300+	**81** 300+	**81** 300+	**80** 300+	**61** 300+	**77** 300+	**72** 300+	**72** 300+	**62** 300+	**84** 300+
Saint Lukes Hospital of Kansas City, Kansas City, MO	-	-	-	**0.018** 342	**0.157** 83	- 0	**30.4** 23	**56** 300+	**80** 300+	**85** 300+	**72** 300+	**63** 300+	**78** 300+	**74** 300+	**68** 300+	**66** 300+	**81** 300+
Saint Lukes Northland Hospital, Kansas City, MO	-	-	-	**0.102** 333	**0.004** 236	**9.7** 639	**48.3** 58	**61** 300+	**78** 300+	**84** 300+	**73** 300+	**64** 300+	**76** 300+	**70** 300+	**73** 300+	**60** 300+	**77** 300+
Saint Mary's Medical Center, Blue Springs, MO	-	-	-	**0.063** 459	**0.048** 270	**10.6** 756	**39.2** 102	**58** 300+	**78** 300+	**88** 300+	**71** 300+	**58** 300+	**78** 300+	**70** 300+	**67** 300+	**64** 300+	**73** 300+
Saint Marys Health Center, Jefferson City, MO	-	-	-	**0.164** 317	**0.005** 184	**12.6** 910	**38.9** 131	**59** 300+	**84** 300+	**84** 300+	**76** 300+	**62** 300+	**84** 300+	**75** 300+	**77** 300+	**67** 300+	**80** 300+
Salem Memorial District Hospital, Salem, MO	-	-	-	-	-	-	-	-	-	-	-	-	-	-	-	-	-
Scotland County Hospital, Memphis, MO	-	-	-	-	-	-	-	-	-	-	-	-	-	-	-	-	-
Skaggs Community Health Center, Branson, MO	-	-	-	**0.054** 829	**0.038** 714	**11.2** 1068	**30.5** 272	**56** 300+	**80** 300+	**78** 300+	**64** 300+	**55** 300+	**74** 300+	**64** 300+	**72** 300+	**63** 300+	**69** 300+
Southeast Missouri Hospital, Cape Girardeau, MO	-	-	-	**0.660** 698	**0.119** 614	- 0	**33.2** 226	**67** 300+	**81** 300+	**88** 300+	**80** 300+	**64** 300+	**85** 300+	**74** 300+	**76** 300+	**72** 300+	**85** 300+
SSM Depaul Health Center, Bridgeton, MO	-	-	-	**0.503** 723	**0.081** 507	**7.5** 876	**32.6** 227	**58** 300+	**78** 300+	**82** 300+	**63** 300+	**59** 300+	**74** 300+	**68** 300+	**62** 300+	**56** 300+	**67** 300+
SSM St Clare Health Center, Fenton, MO	-	-	-	**0.732** 347	**0.113** 231	**7.8** 1108	**33.8** 68	**72** 300+	**80** 300+	**86** 300+	**78** 300+	**60** 300+	**78** 300+	**71** 300+	**78** 300+	**63** 300+	**81** 300+
SSM St Joseph Health Center, Saint Charles, MO	-	-	-	**0.079** 768	**0.029** 589	**6.6** 576	**37.0** 135	**54** 300+	**76** 300+	**85** 300+	**68** 300+	**60** 300+	**76** 300+	**68** 300+	**69** 300+	**65** 300+	**70** 300+
SSM St Joseph Hospital West, Lake Saint Louis, MO	-	-	-	**0.070** 682	**0.006** 482	**6.4** 691	**42.9** 91	**53** 300+	**77** 300+	**84** 300+	**70** 300+	**61** 300+	**78** 300+	**70** 300+	**65** 300+	**62** 300+	**75** 300+
SSM St Marys Health Center, Richmond Heights, MO	**100** 291	**90** 291	**100** 291	**0.677** 899	**0.010** 493	**12.3** 1630	**40.4** 104	**53** 300+	**76** 300+	**81** 300+	**63** 300+	**55** 300+	**74** 300+	**66** 300+	**61** 300+	**58** 300+	**66** 300+
Ste Genevieve County Memorial Hospital, Sainte Genevieve, MO	-	-	-	-	-	-	-	**53** 300+	**84** 300+	**87** 300+	**69** 300+	**61** 300+	**80** 300+	**68** 300+	**77** 300+	**67** 300+	**70** 300+
Sullivan County Memorial Hospital, Milan, MO	-	-	-	**0.536** 28	**0.667** 6	- 0	**43.8** 16	-	-	-	-	-	-	-	-	-	-
Texas County Memorial Hospital, Houston, MO	-	-	-	**0.123** 227	**0.066** 137	**4.3** 396	**45.5** 22	**53** 300+	**79** 300+	**81** 300+	**59** 300+	**59** 300+	**72** 300+	**62** 300+	**82** 300+	**59** 300+	**55** 300+
Truman Medical Center - Hospital Hill, Kansas City, MO	-	-	-	**0.102** 283	**0.012** 242	**12.5** 607	**40.5** 42	**53** 300+	**72** 300+	**81** 300+	**55** 300+	**58** 300+	**68** 300+	**61** 300+	**62** 300+	**52** 300+	**58** 300+
Truman Medical Center Lakewood, Kansas City, MO	-	-	-	**0.085** 82	**0.000** 50	**12.0** 250	**46.2** 13	**58** 300+	**77** 300+	**83** 300+	**68** 300+	**61** 300+	**76** 300+	**65** 300+	**70** 300+	**62** 300+	**69** 300+
Twin Rivers Regional Medical Center, Kennett, MO	**100** 14	**100** 15	**100** 15	**0.204** 265	**0.227** 176	**2.5** 356	**31.3** 128	**47** 300+	**80** 300+	**79** 300+	**52** 300+	**52** 300+	**69** 300+	**58** 300+	**58** 300+	**52** 300+	**55** 300+
University of Missouri Health Care, Columbia, MO	-	-	-	**0.273** 1075	**0.042** 1213	**8.3** 2817	**29.0** 62	**50** 300+	**72** 300+	**85** 300+	**60** 300+	**54** 300+	**72** 300+	**65** 300+	**66** 300+	**58** 300+	**68** 300+
Washington County Memorial Hospital, Potosi, MO	-	-	-	-	-	-	-	-	-	-	-	-	-	-	-	-	-
Western Missouri Medical Center, Warrensburg, MO	-	-	-	**0.033** 239	**0.009** 235	**5.5** 544	**26.0** 100	**54** 300+	**81** 300+	**86** 300+	**59** 300+	**64** 300+	**77** 300+	**69** 300+	**79** 300+	**61** 300+	**60** 300+
Women's and Children's Hospital, Columbia, MO	-	-	-	**0.717** 159	**0.091** 121	**11.4** 405	**31.0** 129	**63** 300+	**76** 300+	**87** 300+	**73** 300+	**55** 300+	**75** 300+	**69** 300+	**77** 300+	**68** 300+	**76** 300+
Wright Memorial Hospital, Trenton, MO	-	-	-	**0.127** 158	**0.146** 151	**9.6** 249	**36.4** 44	**59** (a)	**86** (a)	**75** (a)	**63** (a)	**66** (a)	**78** (a)	**68** (a)	**77** (a)	**68** (a)	**55** (a)
NEBRASKA																	
Alegent Health Bergan Mercy Medical Center, Omaha, NE	-	-	-	**0.061** 1290	**0.000** 1190	**5.7** 751	**38.0** 326	**58** 300+	**80** 300+	**86** 300+	**69** 300+	**59** 300+	**77** 300+	**70** 300+	**63** 300+	**58** 300+	**70** 300+
Alegent Health Immanuel Medical Center, Omaha, NE	-	-	-	**0.085** 658	**0.013** 640	**3.8** 681	**37.7** 204	**64** 300+	**80** 300+	**88** 300+	**73** 300+	**61** 300+	**78** 300+	**70** 300+	**73** 300+	**60** 300+	**72** 300+
Alegent Health Lakeside Hospital, Omaha, NE	-	-	-	**0.074** 353	**0.013** 228	**6.7** 744	**32.7** 101	**59** 300+	**82** 300+	**88** 300+	**72** 300+	**57** 300+	**77** 300+	**70** 300+	**69** 300+	**60** 300+	**75** 300+
Alegent Health Memorial Hospital, Schuyler, NE	-	-	-	-	-	-	-	**75** <100	**84** <100	**86** <100	**81** <100	**69** <100	**80** <100	**75** <100	**83** <100	**82** <100	**69** <100
Alegent Health Midlands Hospital, Papillion, NE	-	-	-	**0.113** 462	**0.030** 329	**5.4** 925	**40.6** 101	**63** 300+	**81** 300+	**87** 300+	**73** 300+	**61** 300+	**77** 300+	**73** 300+	**80** 300+	**70** 300+	**70** 300+
Annie Jeffrey Memorial County Health Center, Osceola, NE	-	-	-	-	-	-	-	-	-	-	-	-	-	-	-	-	-
Antelope Memorial Hospital, Neligh, NE	-	-	-	-	-	-	-	-	-	-	-	-	-	-	-	-	-
Avera Creighton Hospital, Creighton, NE	-	-	-	-	-	-	-	**52** <100	**81** <100	**79** <100	**71** <100	**51** <100	**78** <100	**73** <100	**84** <100	**70** <100	**70** <100
Avera St Anthony's Hospital, O'Neill, NE	-	-	-	-	-	-	-	**47** 300+	**83** 300+	**82** 300+	**70** 300+	**60** 300+	**79** 300+	**71** 300+	**81** 300+	**72** 300+	**73** 300+
Beatrice Community Hospital & Health Center, Beatrice, NE	-	-	-	**0.087** 344	**0.037** 214	**13.3** 660	**36.2** 69	**59** (a)	**78** (a)	**76** (a)	**46** (a)	**38** (a)	**68** (a)	**60** (a)	**64** (a)	**70** (a)	**44** (a)
Bellevue Medical Center, Bellevue, NE	-	-	-	-	-	-	-	-	-	-	-	-	-	-	-	-	-
Boone County Health Center, Albion, NE	-	-	-	-	-	-	-	-	-	-	-	-	-	-	-	-	-
Box Butte General Hospital, Alliance, NE	-	-	-	-	-	-	-	**50** (a)	**86** (a)	**87** (a)	**65** (a)	**55** (a)	**75** (a)	**73** (a)	**84** (a)	**81** (a)	**65** (a)
Brodstone Memorial Hospital, Superior, NE	-	-	-	-	-	-	-	**68** (a)	**91** (a)	**89** (a)	**81** (a)	**66** (a)	**81** (a)	**73** (a)	**84** (a)	**74** (a)	**80** (a)
Brown County Hospital, Ainsworth, NE	-	-	-	-	-	-	-	-	-	-	-	-	-	-	-	-	-
Bryanlgh Medical Center, Lincoln, NE	-	-	-	**0.072** 1336	**0.085** 729	**9.3** 2860	**34.7** 245	**60** 300+	**76** 300+	**89** 300+	**74** 300+	**60** 300+	**74** 300+	**66** 300+	**73** 300+	**63** 300+	**79** 300+
Butler County Health Care Center, David City, NE	-	-	-	-	-	-	-	-	-	-	-	-	-	-	-	-	-
Callaway District Hospital, Callaway, NE	-	-	-	-	-	-	-	-	-	-	-	-	-	-	-	-	-
Chadron Community Hospital and Health Services, Chadron, NE	-	-	-	-	-	-	-	-	-	-	-	-	-	-	-	-	-
Chase County Community Hospital, Imperial, NE	-	-	-	-	-	-	-	-	-	-	-	-	-	-	-	-	-
Cherry County Hospital, Valentine, NE	-	-	-	-	-	-	-	-	-	-	-	-	-	-	-	-	-
Children's Hospital & Medical Center, Omaha, NE	**100** 59	**93** 61	**100** 61	-	-	-	-	-	-	-	-	-	-	-	-	-	-
Columbus Community Hospital, Columbus, NE	-	-	-	**0.771** 389	**0.011** 348	**1.2** 734	**28.2** 85	**51** 300+	**83** 300+	**89** 300+	**74** 300+	**63** 300+	**79** 300+	**71** 300+	**78** 300+	**71** 300+	**74** 300+
Community Hospital, Mccook, NE	-	-	-	**0.009** 221	**0.072** 195	**13.5** 349	**21.5** 65	**49** 300+	**84** 300+	**80** 300+	**65** 300+	**60** 300+	**76** 300+	**68** 300+	**75** 300+	**70** 300+	**68** 300+
Community Medical Center, Falls City, NE	-	-	-	**0.155** 103	**0.041** 73	**4.6** 109	**33.3** 36	-	-	-	-	-	-	-	-	-	-

NOTE: The first number in each column (boldface) is the score, the second number is the number of patients; Please refer to the main entry for footnotes; (a) 100-299
*MEASURES: **Children's Asthma Care:** 33. Received Systemic Corticosteroids; 34. Received Home Management Plan of Care; 35. Received Reliever Medication; **Use of Medical Imaging:** 36. Combination Abdominal CT Scan; 37. Combination Chest CT Scan; 38. Follow-up Mammogram/Ultrasound; 39. MRI for Low Back Pain; **Survey of Patients' Hospital Experiences:** 40. Area Around Room 'Always' Quiet at Night; 41. Doctors 'Always' Communicated Well; 42. Home Recovery Information Given; 43. Hospital Given 9 or 10 on 10 Point Scale; 44. Meds 'Always' Explained Before Given; 45. Nurses 'Always' Communicated Well; 46. Pain 'Always' Well Controlled; 47. Room and Bathroom 'Always' Clean; 48. Timely Help 'Always' Received; 49. Would Definitely Recommend Hospital*

Hospital	Children's Asthma Care			Use of Medical Imaging				Survey of Patients' Hospital Experiences									
	33	34	35	36	37	38	39	40	41	42	43	44	45	46	47	48	49
Community Memorial Hospital, Syracuse, NE	- -	- -	- -	- -	- -	- -	- -	- -	- -	- -	- -	- -	- -	- -	- -	- -	- -
Cozad Community Hospital, Cozad, NE	- -	- -	- -	- -	- -	- -	- -	- -	- -	- -	- -	- -	- -	- -	- -	- -	- -
Creighton University Medical Center - Saint Joseph, Omaha, NE	- -	- -	- -	**0.368** 345	**0.073** 395	**8.8** 512	**41.2** 51	**56** 300+	**79** 300+	**83** 300+	**66** 300+	**62** 300+	**77** 300+	**69** 300+	**67** 300+	**65** 300+	**69** 300+
Crete Area Medical Center, Crete, NE	- -	- -	- -	- -	- -	- -	- -	**68** <100	**86** <100	**83** <100	**80** <100	**62** <100	**77** <100	**65** <100	**82** <100	**56** <100	**72** <100
Dundy County Hospital, Benkelman, NE	- -	- -	- -	- -	- -	- -	- -	- -	- -	- -	- -	- -	- -	- -	- -	- -	- -
Faith Regional Health Services, Norfolk, NE	- -	- -	- -	**0.746** 578	**0.037** 647	**5.4** 607	**22.5** 129	**42** 300+	**79** 300+	**86** 300+	**60** 300+	**58** 300+	**77** 300+	**67** 300+	**77** 300+	**62** 300+	**65** 300+
Fillmore County Hospital, Geneva, NE	- -	- -	- -	- -	- -	- -	- -	- -	- -	- -	- -	- -	- -	- -	- -	- -	- -
Franklin County Memorial Hospital, Franklin, NE	- -	- -	- -	- -	- -	- -	- -	- -	- -	- -	- -	- -	- -	- -	- -	- -	- -
Fremont Area Medical Center, Fremont, NE	- -	- -	- -	**0.772** 526	**0.003** 613	**3.5** 1420	**26.1** 207	**56** 300+	**83** 300+	**86** 300+	**71** 300+	**65** 300+	**81** 300+	**73** 300+	**80** 300+	**69** 300+	**68** 300+
Garden County Health Services, Oshkosh, NE	- -	- -	- -	- -	- -	- -	- -	- -	- -	- -	- -	- -	- -	- -	- -	- -	- -
Good Samaritan Hospital, Kearney, NE	- -	- -	- -	**0.077** 491	**0.019** 429	**7.1** 707	**31.5** 200	**56** 300+	**79** 300+	**84** 300+	**67** 300+	**59** 300+	**75** 300+	**67** 300+	**72** 300+	**58** 300+	**72** 300+
Gordon Memorial Hospital District, Gordon, NE	- -	- -	- -	- -	- -	- -	- -	- -	- -	- -	- -	- -	- -	- -	- -	- -	- -
Gothenburg Memorial Hospital, Gothenburg, NE	- -	- -	- -	- -	- -	- -	- -	- -	- -	- -	- -	- -	- -	- -	- -	- -	- -
Great Plains Regional Medical Center, North Platte, NE	- -	- -	- -	**0.052** 737	**0.032** 564	**9.9** 1184	**29.7** 256	**48** 300+	**79** 300+	**83** 300+	**61** 300+	**58** 300+	**71** 300+	**66** 300+	**70** 300+	**67** 300+	**62** 300+
Harlan County Health System, Alma, NE	- -	- -	- -	- -	- -	- -	- -	- -	- -	- -	- -	- -	- -	- -	- -	- -	- -
Henderson Health Care Services, Henderson, NE	- -	- -	- -	- -	- -	- -	- -	- -	- -	- -	- -	- -	- -	- -	- -	- -	- -
Howard County Medical Center, Saint Paul, NE	- -	- -	- -	- -	- -	- -	- -	- -	- -	- -	- -	- -	- -	- -	- -	- -	- -
Jefferson Community Health Center, Fairbury, NE	- -	- -	- -	**0.071** 85	**0.016** 63	**10.0** 221	**20.0** 15	- -	- -	- -	- -	- -	- -	- -	- -	- -	- -
Jennie M Melham Memorial Medical Center, Broken Bow, NE	- -	- -	- -	- -	- -	- -	- -	- -	- -	- -	- -	- -	- -	- -	- -	- -	- -
Johnson County Hospital, Tecumseh, NE	- -	- -	- -	- -	- -	- -	- -	- -	- -	- -	- -	- -	- -	- -	- -	- -	- -
Kearney County Health Services Hospital, Minden, NE	- -	- -	- -	- -	- -	- -	- -	- -	- -	- -	- -	- -	- -	- -	- -	- -	- -
Kimball Health Services, Kimball, NE	- -	- -	- -	- -	- -	- -	- -	**74** <100	**89** <100	**73** <100	**87** <100	**67** <100	**89** <100	**81** <100	**94** <100	**77** <100	**68** <100
Lincoln Surgical Hospital, Lincoln, NE	- -	- -	- -	- 0	- 0	- 0	- 0	**80** 300+	**87** 300+	**96** 300+	**89** 300+	**72** 300+	**86** 300+	**75** 300+	**89** 300+	**85** 300+	**89** 300+
Litzenberg Memorial County Hospital, Central City, NE	- -	- -	- -	- -	- -	- -	- -	- -	- -	- -	- -	- -	- -	- -	- -	- -	- -
Mary Lanning Memorial Hospital, Hastings, NE	- -	- -	- -	**0.048** 417	**0.080** 515	**9.2** 607	**24.7** 85	**55** 300+	**80** 300+	**86** 300+	**67** 300+	**64** 300+	**77** 300+	**70** 300+	**78** 300+	**60** 300+	**71** 300+
Memorial Community Hospital, Blair, NE	- -	- -	- -	- -	- -	- -	- -	**74** <100	**86** <100	**90** <100	**89** <100	**57** <100	**85** <100	**77** <100	**87** <100	**79** <100	**76** <100
Memorial Health Care Systems, Seward, NE	- -	- -	- -	- -	- -	- -	- -	- -	- -	- -	- -	- -	- -	- -	- -	- -	- -
Memorial Health Center, Sidney, NE	- -	- -	- -	- -	- -	- -	- -	**56** (a)	**85** (a)	**75** (a)	**64** (a)	**63** (a)	**75** (a)	**75** (a)	**79** (a)	**72** (a)	**58** (a)
Memorial Hospital, Aurora, NE	- -	- -	- -	- -	- -	- -	- -	- -	- -	- -	- -	- -	- -	- -	- -	- -	- -
Midwest Surgical Hospital, Omaha, NE	- -	- -	- -	- 0	- 0	- 0	- 0	**91** 300+	**93** 300+	**92** 300+	**95** 300+	**81** 300+	**91** 300+	**82** 300+	**90** 300+	**92** 300+	**94** 300+
Morrill County Community Hospital, Bridgeport, NE	- -	- -	- -	- -	- -	- -	- -	- -	- -	- -	- -	- -	- -	- -	- -	- -	- -
Nebraska Heart Hospital, Lincoln, NE	- -	- -	- -	- 0	**0.000** 1	- 0	- 0	**49** 300+	**76** 300+	**82** 300+	**80** 300+	**58** 300+	**78** 300+	**66** 300+	**82** 300+	**73** 300+	**84** 300+
The Nebraska Medical Center, Omaha, NE	- -	- -	- -	**0.072** 1644	**0.002** 1954	**7.2** 1888	**33.1** 239	**55** 300+	**76** 300+	**84** 300+	**71** 300+	**60** 300+	**77** 300+	**67** 300+	**68** 300+	**62** 300+	**77** 300+
The Nebraska Methodist Hospital, Omaha, NE	- -	- -	- -	**0.052** 1493	**0.013** 1465	**6.3** 1277	**35.9** 340	**46** 300+	**82** 300+	**87** 300+	**71** 300+	**60** 300+	**79** 300+	**72** 300+	**63** 300+	**62** 300+	**74** 300+
Nebraska Orthopaedic Hospital, Omaha, NE	- -	- -	- -	- 0	- 0	- 0	**35.3** 85	**81** 300+	**84** 300+	**93** 300+	**85** 300+	**67** 300+	**86** 300+	**72** 300+	**75** 300+	**78** 300+	**88** 300+
Nemaha County Hospital, Auburn, NE	- -	- -	- -	- -	- -	- -	- -	**64** <100	**84** <100	**88** <100	**88** <100	**71** <100	**85** <100	**79** <100	**90** <100	**84** <100	**79** <100
Niobrara Valley Hospital, Lynch, NE	- -	- -	- -	- -	- -	- -	- -	- -	- -	- -	- -	- -	- -	- -	- -	- -	- -
Oakland Mercy Hospital, Oakland, NE	- -	- -	- -	- -	- -	- -	- -	- -	- -	- -	- -	- -	- -	- -	- -	- -	- -
Ogallala Community Hospital, Ogallala, NE	- -	- -	- -	**0.040** 150	**0.025** 79	**10.3** 204	**40.0** 15	**61** (a)	**87** (a)	**86** (a)	**74** (a)	**65** (a)	**78** (a)	**72** (a)	**86** (a)	**74** (a)	**72** (a)
Omaha VA Medical Center, Omaha, NE	- -	- -	- -	- -	- -	- -	- -	- -	- -	- -	- -	- -	- -	- -	- -	- -	- -
Osmond General Hospital, Osmond, NE	- -	- -	- -	- -	- -	- -	- -	**57** <100	**79** <100	**69** <100	**71** <100	**63** <100	**83** <100	**59** <100	**75** <100	**73** <100	**64** <100
Pawnee County Memorial Hospital, Pawnee City, NE	- -	- -	- -	- -	- -	- -	- -	- -	- -	- -	- -	- -	- -	- -	- -	- -	- -
Pender Community Hospital, Pender, NE	- -	- -	- -	- -	- -	- -	- -	**61** (a)	**91** (a)	**80** (a)	**75** (a)	**70** (a)	**79** (a)	**73** (a)	**83** (a)	**78** (a)	**77** (a)
Perkins County Health Services, Grant, NE	- -	- -	- -	- -	- -	- -	- -	- -	- -	- -	- -	- -	- -	- -	- -	- -	- -
Phelps Memorial Health Center, Holdrege, NE	- -	- -	- -	- -	- -	- -	- -	**54** 300+	**84** 300+	**80** 300+	**72** 300+	**60** 300+	**75** 300+	**69** 300+	**84** 300+	**65** 300+	**75** 300+
Plainview Public Hospital, Plainview, NE	- -	- -	- -	- -	- -	- -	- -	- -	- -	- -	- -	- -	- -	- -	- -	- -	- -
Providence Medical Center, Wayne, NE	- -	- -	- -	**0.272** 92	**0.000** 48	**7.8** 103	**50.0** 22	- -	- -	- -	- -	- -	- -	- -	- -	- -	- -
Regional West Medical Center, Scottsbluff, NE	- -	- -	- -	**0.131** 666	**0.000** 444	**9.7** 1488	**26.7** 300	**56** 300+	**80** 300+	**79** 300+	**58** 300+	**58** 300+	**72** 300+	**67** 300+	**69** 300+	**61** 300+	**62** 300+
Rock County Hospital, Bassett, NE	- -	- -	- -	- -	- -	- -	- -	- -	- -	- -	- -	- -	- -	- -	- -	- -	- -
Saint Elizabeth Regional Medical Center, Lincoln, NE	- -	- -	- -	**0.054** 847	**0.005** 563	**12.2** 1693	**37.4** 147	**57** 300+	**77** 300+	**90** 300+	**72** 300+	**58** 300+	**76** 300+	**68** 300+	**69** 300+	**58** 300+	**78** 300+
Saint Francis Medical Center, Grand Island, NE	- -	- -	- -	**0.012** 241	**0.025** 121	**5.3** 1337	**17.6** 17	**63** 300+	**78** 300+	**88** 300+	**72** 300+	**61** 300+	**74** 300+	**67** 300+	**73** 300+	**64** 300+	**71** 300+
Saint Francis Memorial Hospital, West Point, NE	- -	- -	- -	- -	- -	- -	- -	**70** (a)	**84** (a)	**92** (a)	**75** (a)	**65** (a)	**79** (a)	**74** (a)	**83** (a)	**75** (a)	**74** (a)
Saint Mary's Community Hospital, Nebraska City, NE	- -	- -	- -	- -	- -	- -	- -	- -	- -	- -	- -	- -	- -	- -	- -	- -	- -
Saunders Medical Center, Wahoo, NE	- -	- -	- -	- -	- -	- -	- -	**67** <100	**90** <100	**80** <100	**80** <100	**60** <100	**86** <100	**79** <100	**92** <100	**63** <100	**87** <100
Thayer County Health Services, Hebron, NE	- -	- -	- -	- -	- -	- -	- -	- -	- -	- -	- -	- -	- -	- -	- -	- -	- -
Tilden Community Hospital, Tilden, NE	- -	- -	- -	- 0	- 0	**4.5** 22	**0.0** 6	- -	- -	- -	- -	- -	- -	- -	- -	- -	- -
Tri Valley Health System, Cambridge, NE	- -	- -	- -	- -	- -	- -	- -	**58** (a)	**88** (a)	**83** (a)	**67** (a)	**62** (a)	**77** (a)	**64** (a)	**74** (a)	**70** (a)	**73** (a)
Tri-County Area Hospital District, Lexington, NE	- -	- -	- -	**0.041** 73	**0.130** 54	**2.2** 185	**36.4** 11	**62** (a)	**79** (a)	**82** (a)	**64** (a)	**61** (a)	**76** (a)	**68** (a)	**77** (a)	**62** (a)	**63** (a)
Valley County Health System, Ord, NE	- -	- -	- -	- -	- -	- -	- -	- -	- -	- -	- -	- -	- -	- -	- -	- -	- -
Warren Memorial Hospital, Friend, NE	- -	- -	- -	- -	- -	- -	- -	- -	- -	- -	- -	- -	- -	- -	- -	- -	- -
Webster County Community Hospital, Red Cloud, NE	- -	- -	- -	- -	- -	- -	- -	- -	- -	- -	- -	- -	- -	- -	- -	- -	- -
West Holt Memorial Hospital, Atkinson, NE	- -	- -	- -	- -	- -	- -	- -	- -	- -	- -	- -	- -	- -	- -	- -	- -	- -
Winnebago Ihs Hospital, Winnebago, NE	- -	- -	- -	- -	- -	- -	- -	- -	- -	- -	- -	- -	- -	- -	- -	- -	- -
York General Hospital, York, NE	- -	- -	- -	- -	- -	- -	- -	- -	- -	- -	- -	- -	- -	- -	- -	- -	- -
NORTH DAKOTA																	
Altru Hospital, Grand Forks, ND	- -	- -	- -	**0.087** 871	**0.004** 1391	**14.2** 2010	**30.1** 173	**44** 300+	**72** 300+	**83** 300+	**57** 300+	**56** 300+	**69** 300+	**61** 300+	**71** 300+	**55** 300+	**59** 300+
Carrington Health Center, Carrington, ND	- -	- -	- -	- -	- -	- -	- -	- -	- -	- -	- -	- -	- -	- -	- -	- -	- -

NOTE: The first number in each column (boldface) is the score, the second number is the number of patients; Please refer to the main entry for footnotes; (a) 100-299
*MEASURES: **Children's Asthma Care:** 33. Received Systemic Corticosteroids; 34. Received Home Management Plan of Care; 35. Received Reliever Medication; **Use of Medical Imaging:** 36. Combination Abdominal CT Scan; 37. Combination Chest CT Scan; 38. Follow-up Mammogram/Ultrasound; 39. MRI for Low Back Pain; **Survey of Patients' Hospital Experiences:** 40. Area Around Room 'Always' Quiet at Night; 41. Doctors 'Always' Communicated Well; 42. Home Recovery Information Given; 43. Hospital Given 9 or 10 on 10 Point Scale; 44. Meds 'Always' Explained Before Given; 45. Nurses 'Always' Communicated Well; 46. Pain 'Always' Well Controlled; 47. Room and Bathroom 'Always' Clean; 48. Timely Help 'Always' Received; 49. Would Definitely Recommend Hospital*

Hospital	Children's Asthma Care			Use of Medical Imaging				Survey of Patients' Hospital Experiences									
	33	34	35	36	37	38	39	40	41	42	43	44	45	46	47	48	49
Essentia Health-Fargo, Fargo, ND	- -	- -	- -	0.234 505	0.005 374	- 0	32.2 171	57 300+	76 300+	82 300+	68 300+	57 300+	73 300+	68 300+	70 300+	61 300+	78 300+
Fargo VA Medical Center, Fargo, ND	- -	- -	- -	- -	- -	- -	- -	- -	- -	- -	- -	- -	- -	- -	- -	- -	- -
Heart of America Medical Center, Rugby, ND	- -	- -	- -	- -	- -	- -	- -	66 (a)	79 (a)	89 (a)	75 (a)	68 (a)	84 (a)	73 (a)	83 (a)	78 (a)	86 (a)
Hillsboro Medical Center, Hillsboro, ND	- -	- -	- -	0.000 12	0.143 21	- 0	25.0 12	- -	- -	- -	- -	- -	- -	- -	- -	- -	- -
Jacobson Memorial Hospital & Care Center, Elgin, ND	- -	- -	- -	- -	- -	- -	- -	- -	- -	- -	- -	- -	- -	- -	- -	- -	- -
Jamestown Hospital, Jamestown, ND	- -	- -	- -	- 0	- 0	- 0	- 0	63 300+	78 300+	87 300+	63 300+	60 300+	80 300+	73 300+	76 300+	75 300+	65 300+
Linton Hospital, Linton, ND	- -	- -	- -	- -	- -	- -	- -	- -	- -	- -	- -	- -	- -	- -	- -	- -	- -
McKenzie County Healthcare Systems, Watford City, ND	- -	- -	- -	- -	- -	- -	- -	- -	- -	- -	- -	- -	- -	- -	- -	- -	- -
Medcenter One, Bismarck, ND	- -	- -	- -	0.048 763	0.003 690	6.6 1511	23.1 238	49 300+	76 300+	82 300+	70 300+	60 300+	75 300+	64 300+	70 300+	65 300+	75 300+
Mercy Medical Center, Williston, ND	- -	- -	- -	0.392 97	0.275 40	13.8 29	38.9 18	57 300+	88 300+	89 300+	67 300+	64 300+	79 300+	75 300+	73 300+	71 300+	68 300+
Mountrail County Medical Center, Stanley, ND	- -	- -	- -	- -	- -	- -	- -	- -	- -	- -	- -	- -	- -	- -	- -	- -	- -
Northwood Deaconess Health Center, Northwood, ND	- -	- -	- -	- -	- -	- -	- -	- -	- -	- -	- -	- -	- -	- -	- -	- -	- -
P H S Indian Hospital at Belcourt - Quentin N Burdick, Belcourt, ND	- -	- -	- -	- -	- -	- -	- -	76 (a)	87 (a)	79 (a)	46 (a)	71 (a)	74 (a)	75 (a)	67 (a)	58 (a)	54 (a)
P H S Indian Hospital at Fort Yates-Standing Rock, Fort Yates, ND	- -	- -	- -	- -	- -	- -	- -	78 <100	79 <100	81 <100	57 <100	65 <100	75 <100	71 <100	71 <100	71 <100	66 <100
Pembina County Memorial Hospital, Cavalier, ND	- -	- -	- -	- -	- -	- -	- -	- -	- -	- -	- -	- -	- -	- -	- -	- -	- -
Presentation Medical Center, Rolla, ND	- -	- -	- -	0.220 50	0.129 31	10.9 64	40.0 10	- -	- -	- -	- -	- -	- -	- -	- -	- -	- -
Saint Alexius Medical Center, Bismarck, ND	- -	- -	- -	0.313 480	0.011 525	4.3 351	29.1 327	62 300+	78 300+	83 300+	74 300+	59 300+	77 300+	69 300+	74 300+	68 300+	82 300+
Saint Aloisius Medical Center, Harvey, ND	- -	- -	- -	- -	- -	- -	- -	- -	- -	- -	- -	- -	- -	- -	- -	- -	- -
Saint Andrews Health Center, Bottineau, ND	- -	- -	- -	- -	- -	- -	- -	- -	- -	- -	- -	- -	- -	- -	- -	- -	- -
Saint Joseph's Hospital & Health Center, Dickinson, ND	- -	- -	- -	- -	- -	- -	- -	61 300+	78 300+	83 300+	63 300+	63 300+	79 300+	67 300+	74 300+	72 300+	61 300+
Sanford Mayville, Mayville, ND	- -	- -	- -	- -	- -	- -	- -	- -	- -	- -	- -	- -	- -	- -	- -	- -	- -
Sanford Medical Center Fargo, Fargo, ND	- -	- -	- -	0.250 1662	0.028 1396	- 0	30.9 375	52 300+	72 300+	86 300+	69 300+	57 300+	72 300+	61 300+	70 300+	57 300+	71 300+
Tioga Medical Center, Tioga, ND	- -	- -	- -	- -	- -	- -	- -	- -	- -	- -	- -	- -	- -	- -	- -	- -	- -
Trinity Hospitals, Minot, ND	- -	- -	- -	0.057 863	0.002 862	5.3 2465	35.7 244	46 300+	72 300+	81 300+	50 300+	54 300+	71 300+	67 300+	63 300+	64 300+	48 300+
Unity Medical Center, Grafton, ND	- -	- -	- -	0.077 26	0.080 25	9.9 141	100 3	- -	- -	- -	- -	- -	- -	- -	- -	- -	- -
West River Regional Medical Center, Hettinger, ND	- -	- -	- -	- -	- -	- -	- -	- -	- -	- -	- -	- -	- -	- -	- -	- -	- -
Wishek Community Hospital, Wishek, ND	- -	- -	- -	- -	- -	- -	- -	- -	- -	- -	- -	- -	- -	- -	- -	- -	- -
OKLAHOMA																	
Arbuckle Memorial Hospital, Sulphur, OK	- -	- -	- -	- -	- -	- -	- -	- -	- -	- -	- -	- -	- -	- -	- -	- -	- -
Atoka Memorial Hospital, Atoka, OK	- -	- -	- -	- -	- -	- -	- -	76 <100	92 <100	83 <100	78 <100	75 <100	82 <100	83 <100	86 <100	80 <100	79 <100
Bailey Medical Center, Owasso, OK	- -	- -	- -	0.310 155	0.311 106	9.3 140	35.6 73	77 (a)	86 (a)	86 (a)	84 (a)	69 (a)	82 (a)	73 (a)	77 (a)	69 (a)	85 (a)
Beaver County Memorial Hospital, Beaver, OK	- -	- -	- -	- -	- -	- -	- -	- -	- -	- -	- -	- -	- -	- -	- -	- -	- -
Bristow Medical Center, Bristow, OK	- -	- -	- -	0.576 66	0.000 38	- 0	16.7 6	67 <100	96 <100	81 <100	77 <100	72 <100	94 <100	91 <100	78 <100	79 <100	83 <100
Carnegie Tri-County Municipal Hospital, Carnegie, OK	- -	- -	- -	- -	- -	- -	- -	- -	- -	- -	- -	- -	- -	- -	- -	- -	- -
Chickasaw Nation Medical Center, Ada, OK	- -	- -	- -	- -	- -	- -	- -	60 300+	85 300+	85 300+	65 300+	70 300+	80 300+	74 300+	69 300+	71 300+	70 300+
Choctaw Memorial Hospital, Hugo, OK	- -	- -	- -	0.573 96	0.625 80	12.2 221	35.7 42	43 (a)	77 (a)	62 (a)	45 (a)	46 (a)	62 (a)	57 (a)	65 (a)	53 (a)	50 (a)
Choctaw Nation Healthcare, Talihina, OK	- -	- -	- -	- -	- -	- -	- -	60 (a)	82 (a)	86 (a)	74 (a)	71 (a)	79 (a)	70 (a)	79 (a)	75 (a)	79 (a)
Cimarron Memorial Hospital, Boise City, OK	- -	- -	- -	- -	- -	- -	- -	- -	- -	- -	- -	- -	- -	- -	- -	- -	- -
Claremore Indian Hospital, Claremore, OK	- -	- -	- -	- 0	- 0	- 0	- 0	64 (a)	77 (a)	73 (a)	62 (a)	64 (a)	72 (a)	66 (a)	64 (a)	69 (a)	57 (a)
Claremore Regional Hospital, Claremore, OK	- -	- -	- -	0.839 298	0.860 186	10.4 472	38.9 90	56 300+	81 300+	85 300+	62 300+	60 300+	71 300+	68 300+	69 300+	60 300+	64 300+
Cleveland Area Hospital, Cleveland, OK	- -	- -	- -	- -	- -	- -	- -	- -	- -	- -	- -	- -	- -	- -	- -	- -	- -
Comanche County Memorial Hospital, Lawton, OK	- -	- -	- -	0.021 1177	0.002 852	2.9 1147	36.4 143	53 300+	79 300+	78 300+	63 300+	59 300+	76 300+	71 300+	63 300+	65 300+	69 300+
Community Hospital, Oklahoma City, OK	- -	- -	- -	0.448 67	0.038 52	- 0	32.8 61	71 300+	79 300+	86 300+	77 300+	65 300+	80 300+	69 300+	82 300+	72 300+	83 300+
Cordell Memorial Hospital, Cordell, OK	- -	- -	- -	- -	- -	- -	- -	67 <100	96 <100	84 <100	90 <100	71 <100	91 <100	86 <100	93 <100	85 <100	91 <100
Craig General Hospital, Vinita, OK	- -	- -	- -	0.041 317	0.006 164	7.3 301	46.4 84	53 300+	88 300+	81 300+	69 300+	62 300+	81 300+	72 300+	73 300+	67 300+	69 300+
Creek Nation Community Hospital, Okemah, OK	- -	- -	- -	- -	- -	- -	- -	- -	- -	- -	- -	- -	- -	- -	- -	- -	- -
Cushing Regional Hospital, Cushing, OK	- -	- -	- -	0.565 170	0.188 96	4.0 274	35.3 68	63 (a)	86 (a)	82 (a)	68 (a)	60 (a)	76 (a)	72 (a)	69 (a)	67 (a)	67 (a)
Deaconess Hospital, Oklahoma City, OK	- -	- -	- -	0.315 568	0.476 332	7.0 834	27.2 151	68 300+	80 300+	83 300+	68 300+	59 300+	72 300+	70 300+	65 300+	58 300+	71 300+
Drumright Regional Hospital, Drumright, OK	- -	- -	- -	- -	- -	- -	- -	- -	- -	- -	- -	- -	- -	- -	- -	- -	- -
Duncan Regional Hospital, Duncan, OK	- -	- -	- -	0.150 479	0.197 390	14.9 691	39.8 128	60 300+	83 300+	81 300+	66 300+	61 300+	75 300+	69 300+	68 300+	65 300+	64 300+
Eastern Oklahoma Medical Center, Poteau, OK	- -	- -	- -	0.166 235	0.400 110	11.9 143	52.8 36	63 (a)	87 (a)	82 (a)	58 (a)	55 (a)	73 (a)	69 (a)	68 (a)	63 (a)	61 (a)
Edmond Medical Center, Edmond, OK	- -	- -	- -	- -	- -	- -	- -	- -	- -	- -	- -	- -	- -	- -	- -	- -	- -
Elkview General Hospital, Hobart, OK	- -	- -	- -	0.811 111	0.621 58	4.0 150	- 0	59 (a)	89 (a)	75 (a)	65 (a)	66 (a)	81 (a)	73 (a)	77 (a)	73 (a)	68 (a)
Epic Medical Center, Eufaula, OK	- -	- -	- -	- 0	- 0	- 0	- 0	61 (a)	54 (a)	60 (a)	39 (a)	75 (a)	67 (a)	83 (a)	63 (a)	66 (a)	47 (a)
Fairfax Community Hospital, Fairfax, OK	- -	- -	- -	- -	- -	- -	- -	- -	- -	- -	- -	- -	- -	- -	- -	- -	- -
Fairview Regional Medical Center, Fairview, OK	- -	- -	- -	- -	- -	- -	- -	- -	- -	- -	- -	- -	- -	- -	- -	- -	- -
Grady Memorial Hospital, Chickasha, OK	- -	- -	- -	0.102 315	0.067 163	10.4 608	42.4 66	60 300+	80 300+	84 300+	62 300+	58 300+	76 300+	64 300+	67 300+	62 300+	57 300+
Great Plains Regional Medical Center, Elk City, OK	- -	- -	- -	0.724 290	0.494 164	14.4 432	27.9 122	65 300+	79 300+	80 300+	64 300+	55 300+	71 300+	65 300+	67 300+	61 300+	61 300+
Harmon Memorial Hospital, Hollis, OK	- -	- -	- -	0.000 3	- 0	- 0	- 0	37 <100	87 <100	73 <100	46 <100	63 <100	66 <100	51 <100	77 <100	74 <100	64 <100
Harper County Community Hospital, Buffalo, OK	- -	- -	- -	- -	- -	- -	- -	81 <100	94 <100	84 <100	74 <100	77 <100	87 <100	88 <100	79 <100	84 <100	78 <100
Haskell County Healthcare System, Stigler, OK	- -	- -	- -	- -	- -	- -	- -	- -	- -	- -	- -	- -	- -	- -	- -	- -	- -
Healdton Mercy Hospital Corporation, Healdton, OK	- -	- -	- -	- -	- -	- -	- -	- -	- -	- -	- -	- -	- -	- -	- -	- -	- -
Henryetta Medical Center, Henryetta, OK	- -	- -	- -	0.585 82	0.000 58	16.8 149	- 0	64 (a)	84 (a)	82 (a)	74 (a)	67 (a)	82 (a)	78 (a)	75 (a)	73 (a)	73 (a)
Hillcrest Medical Center, Tulsa, OK	- -	- -	- -	0.154 518	0.021 438	8.6 1447	29.4 109	59 300+	79 300+	79 300+	63 300+	52 300+	70 300+	66 300+	61 300+	55 300+	62 300+
Holdenville General Hospital, Holdenville, OK	- -	- -	- -	- -	- -	- -	- -	- -	- -	- -	- -	- -	- -	- -	- -	- -	- -
Integris Baptist Medical Center, Oklahoma City, OK	- -	- -	- -	0.293 774	0.060 517	7.2 1872	33.3 6	64 300+	83 300+	80 300+	73 300+	59 300+	75 300+	70 300+	70 300+	64 300+	77 300+
Integris Baptist Regional Health Center, Miami, OK	- -	- -	- -	0.109 192	0.012 162	6.2 518	32.0 50	58 300+	86 300+	82 300+	66 300+	62 300+	78 300+	73 300+	67 300+	68 300+	61 300+

NOTE: The first number in each column (boldface) is the score, the second number is the number of patients; Please refer to the main entry for footnotes; (a) 100-299
*MEASURES: **Children's Asthma Care:** 33. Received Systemic Corticosteroids; 34. Received Home Management Plan of Care; 35. Received Reliever Medication; **Use of Medical Imaging:** 36. Combination Abdominal CT Scan; 37. Combination Chest CT Scan; 38. Follow-up Mammogram/Ultrasound; 39. MRI for Low Back Pain; **Survey of Patients' Hospital Experiences:** 40. Area Around Room 'Always' Quiet at Night; 41. Doctors 'Always' Communicated Well; 42. Home Recovery Information Given; 43. Hospital Given 9 or 10 on 10 Point Scale; 44. Meds 'Always' Explained Before Given; 45. Nurses 'Always' Communicated Well; 46. Pain 'Always' Well Controlled; 47. Room and Bathroom 'Always' Clean; 48. Timely Help 'Always' Received; 49. Would Definitely Recommend Hospital*

Hospital	Children's Asthma Care			Use of Medical Imaging				Survey of Patients' Hospital Experiences									
	33	34	35	36	37	38	39	40	41	42	43	44	45	46	47	48	49
Integris Bass Baptist Health Center, Enid, OK	- -	- -	- -	0.076 553	0.009 427	11.3 808	39.5 114	59 300+	85 300+	80 300+	68 300+	58 300+	78 300+	69 300+	71 300+	68 300+	75 300+
Integris Blackwell Regional Hospital, Blackwell, OK	- -	- -	- -	0.638 130	0.030 67	6.7 134	54.5 33	57 (a)	84 (a)	79 (a)	65 (a)	56 (a)	74 (a)	66 (a)	71 (a)	64 (a)	64 (a)
Integris Canadian Valley Hospital, Yukon, OK	- -	- -	- -	0.063 221	0.083 121	11.7 291	53.7 41	67 300+	84 300+	80 300+	65 300+	60 300+	76 300+	73 300+	64 300+	57 300+	71 300+
Integris Clinton Regional Hospital, Clinton, OK	- -	- -	- -	0.581 236	0.020 150	8.3 192	33.3 42	61 300+	84 300+	84 300+	63 300+	62 300+	73 300+	67 300+	78 300+	66 300+	63 300+
Integris Grove Hospital, Grove, OK	- -	- -	- -	0.773 322	0.048 230	6.5 688	29.6 125	62 300+	83 300+	79 300+	63 300+	60 300+	73 300+	69 300+	68 300+	59 300+	63 300+
Integris Marshall County Medical Center, Madill, OK	- -	- -	- -	0.613 80	0.016 61	- 0	44.2 52	65 (a)	92 (a)	87 (a)	73 (a)	65 (a)	81 (a)	68 (a)	74 (a)	74 (a)	70 (a)
Integris Mayes County Medical Center, Pryor, OK	- -	- -	- -	0.060 334	0.038 210	8.2 389	34.1 91	66 (a)	85 (a)	83 (a)	67 (a)	60 (a)	77 (a)	70 (a)	63 (a)	70 (a)	58 (a)
Integris Seminole Medical Center, Seminole, OK	- -	- -	- -	0.739 115	0.819 72	6.2 162	0.0 2	68 (a)	85 (a)	81 (a)	71 (a)	60 (a)	85 (a)	65 (a)	82 (a)	73 (a)	70 (a)
Integris Southwest Medical Center, Oklahoma City, OK	- -	- -	- -	0.134 1146	0.035 922	8.6 2047	29.9 231	55 300+	77 300+	76 300+	63 300+	55 300+	71 300+	69 300+	68 300+	55 300+	63 300+
Jackson County Memorial Hospital, Altus, OK	- -	- -	- -	0.063 16	0.111 9	9.8 569	31.6 76	51 300+	84 300+	82 300+	64 300+	65 300+	78 300+	71 300+	72 300+	69 300+	62 300+
Jane Phillips Medical Center, Bartlesville, OK	- -	- -	- -	0.013 769	0.004 554	4.6 1524	34.5 168	60 300+	81 300+	83 300+	70 300+	59 300+	76 300+	69 300+	78 300+	64 300+	64 300+
Jefferson County Hospital, Waurika, OK	- -	- -	- -	- -	- -	- -	- -	- -	- -	- -	- -	- -	- -	- -	- -	- -	- -
Johnston Memorial Hospital, Tishomingo, OK	- -	- -	- -	- -	- -	- -	- -	- -	- -	- -	- -	- -	- -	- -	- -	- -	- -
Kingfisher Regional Hospital, Kingfisher, OK	- -	- -	- -	0.312 154	0.000 70	20.3 187	21.4 28	76 (a)	87 (a)	83 (a)	73 (a)	67 (a)	81 (a)	77 (a)	79 (a)	69 (a)	74 (a)
Lakeside Women's Hospital, Oklahoma City, OK	- -	- -	- -	- 0	- 0	6.0 773	- 0	60 300+	88 300+	88 300+	84 300+	62 300+	83 300+	78 300+	77 300+	62 300+	86 300+
Latimer County General Hospital, Wilburton, OK	- -	- -	- -	0.111 27	0.240 25	- 0	- 0	75 (a)	85 (a)	75 (a)	68 (a)	69 (a)	83 (a)	81 (a)	82 (a)	81 (a)	67 (a)
Lindsay Municipal Hospital, Lindsay, OK	- -	- -	- -	- -	- -	- -	- -	- -	- -	- -	- -	- -	- -	- -	- -	- -	- -
Logan Medical Center, Guthrie, OK	- -	- -	- -	- -	- -	- -	- -	65 (a)	87 (a)	85 (a)	74 (a)	58 (a)	75 (a)	71 (a)	67 (a)	65 (a)	71 (a)
Mary Hurley Hospital, Coalgate, OK	- -	- -	- -	- -	- -	- -	- -	- -	- -	- -	- -	- -	- -	- -	- -	- -	- -
McAlester Regional Health Center, Mcalester, OK	- -	- -	- -	0.571 431	0.023 307	20.3 512	33.3 126	57 300+	83 300+	81 300+	60 300+	63 300+	77 300+	72 300+	76 300+	68 300+	60 300+
McBride Clinic Orthopedic Hospital, Oklahoma City, OK	- -	- -	- -	0.875 8	0.000 20	- 0	- 0	75 300+	87 300+	91 300+	83 300+	67 300+	81 300+	76 300+	76 300+	75 300+	87 300+
McCurtain Memorial Hospital, Idabel, OK	- -	- -	- -	0.675 114	0.648 91	8.6 257	40.9 22	70 300+	84 300+	72 300+	53 300+	64 300+	75 300+	66 300+	71 300+	74 300+	53 300+
Medical Center of Southeastern Oklahoma, Durant, OK	100 9	100 9	100 9	0.110 317	0.016 183	11.6 661	30.3 76	55 300+	81 300+	78 300+	60 300+	58 300+	72 300+	65 300+	68 300+	56 300+	62 300+
Memorial Hospital & Physician Group, Frederick, OK	- -	- -	- -	0.033 30	0.000 8	- 0	- 0	53 (a)	79 (a)	75 (a)	56 (a)	51 (a)	71 (a)	60 (a)	62 (a)	66 (a)	57 (a)
Memorial Hospital of Stilwell, Stilwell, OK	- -	- -	- -	0.145 76	0.096 52	- 0	42.9 21	66 300+	86 300+	76 300+	67 300+	65 300+	74 300+	72 300+	71 300+	66 300+	68 300+
Memorial Hospital of Texas County, Guymon, OK	- -	- -	- -	0.641 117	0.373 75	10.5 133	32.7 49	61 (a)	79 (a)	88 (a)	66 (a)	59 (a)	77 (a)	71 (a)	73 (a)	67 (a)	60 (a)
Mercy Health Center, Oklahoma City, OK	- -	- -	- -	0.197 1672	0.128 1223	10.7 2343	31.9 373	60 300+	84 300+	80 300+	73 300+	58 300+	76 300+	73 300+	68 300+	61 300+	81 300+
Mercy Health Love County, Marietta, OK	- -	- -	- -	- -	- -	- -	- -	- -	- -	- -	- -	- -	- -	- -	- -	- -	- -
Mercy Hospital El Reno, El Reno, OK	- -	- -	- -	0.094 85	0.033 60	- 0	57.1 7	71 (a)	75 (a)	72 (a)	63 (a)	60 (a)	75 (a)	69 (a)	74 (a)	66 (a)	63 (a)
Mercy Memorial Health Center, Ardmore, OK	- -	- -	- -	0.182 813	0.009 670	4.2 1145	41.8 208	54 300+	80 300+	80 300+	56 300+	57 300+	75 300+	67 300+	69 300+	66 300+	58 300+
Midwest Regional Medical Center, Midwest City, OK	100 26	100 25	100 26	0.390 629	0.237 439	4.5 1861	36.7 259	48 300+	77 300+	78 300+	50 300+	52 300+	65 300+	62 300+	51 300+	49 300+	50 300+
Muskogee Community Hospital, Muskogee, OK	- -	- -	- -	- -	- -	- -	- -	- -	- -	- -	- -	- -	- -	- -	- -	- -	- -
Muskogee Regional Medical Center, Muskogee, OK	- -	- -	- -	0.348 821	0.256 441	4.6 1656	29.2 291	48 300+	78 300+	81 300+	47 300+	47 300+	64 300+	59 300+	57 300+	48 300+	48 300+
Muskogee VA Medical Center, Muskogee, OK	- -	- -	- -	- -	- -	- -	- -	- -	- -	- -	- -	- -	- -	- -	- -	- -	- -
Newman Memorial Hospital, Shattuck, OK	- -	- -	- -	0.900 60	0.808 26	2.5 160	45.0 20	67 (a)	91 (a)	85 (a)	72 (a)	71 (a)	77 (a)	77 (a)	70 (a)	73 (a)	80 (a)
Norman Regional Health System, Norman, OK	- -	- -	- -	0.109 1216	0.048 1205	6.7 2695	33.6 333	65 300+	81 300+	82 300+	71 300+	58 300+	75 300+	71 300+	69 300+	63 300+	72 300+
Northwest Surgical Hospital, Oklahoma City, OK	- -	- -	- -	0.804 107	0.012 86	- 0	30.5 315	81 (a)	87 (a)	87 (a)	87 (a)	71 (a)	86 (a)	77 (a)	85 (a)	77 (a)	83 (a)
O U Medical Center, Oklahoma City, OK	100 238	76 236	100 238	0.864 1043	0.019 837	- 0	32.1 112	57 300+	78 300+	84 300+	68 300+	57 300+	74 300+	69 300+	59 300+	57 300+	70 300+
Okeene Municipal Hospital, Okeene, OK	- -	- -	- -	- -	- -	- -	- -	77 <100	87 <100	93 <100	87 <100	73 <100	89 <100	79 <100	87 <100	89 <100	85 <100
Oklahoma Center for Orthopaedic & Multi-Sp, Oklahoma City, OK	- -	- -	- -	- 0	- 0	- 0	- 0	82 (a)	88 (a)	87 (a)	82 (a)	70 (a)	89 (a)	77 (a)	86 (a)	84 (a)	86 (a)
Oklahoma City VA Medical Center, Oklahoma City, OK	- -	- -	- -	- -	- -	- -	- -	- -	- -	- -	- -	- -	- -	- -	- -	- -	- -
Oklahoma Heart Hospital, Oklahoma City, OK	- -	- -	- -	0.773 309	0.009 224	- 0	- 0	78 300+	90 300+	89 300+	97 300+	78 300+	93 300+	86 300+	87 300+	90 300+	99 300+
Oklahoma Heart Hospital South, Oklahoma City, OK	- -	- -	- -	- -	- -	- -	- -	- -	- -	- -	- -	- -	- -	- -	- -	- -	- -
Oklahoma Spine Hospital, Oklahoma City, OK	- -	- -	- -	0.333 3	0.000 2	- 0	31.9 135	82 300+	95 300+	89 300+	91 300+	78 300+	88 300+	83 300+	91 300+	83 300+	93 300+
Oklahoma State University Medical Center, Tulsa, OK	- -	- -	- -	0.412 342	0.133 248	12.6 198	40.9 44	60 300+	80 300+	82 300+	66 300+	57 300+	69 300+	65 300+	63 300+	49 300+	68 300+
Oklahoma Surgical Hospital, Tulsa, OK	- -	- -	- -	0.857 7	0.750 4	- 0	32.1 277	85 300+	85 300+	84 300+	86 300+	70 300+	84 300+	76 300+	84 300+	74 300+	88 300+
Okmulgee Memorial Hospital, Okmulgee, OK	- -	- -	- -	0.401 147	0.085 71	2.5 314	- 0	55 (a)	80 (a)	76 (a)	57 (a)	48 (a)	72 (a)	66 (a)	58 (a)	66 (a)	51 (a)
Orthopedic Hospital, Oklahoma City, OK	- -	- -	- -	- 0	- 0	- 0	- 0	79 (a)	78 (a)	79 (a)	62 (a)	64 (a)	72 (a)	60 (a)	83 (a)	72 (a)	69 (a)
Pauls Valley General Hospital, Pauls Valley, OK	- -	- -	- -	0.093 150	0.017 59	4.6 283	- 0	59 300+	87 300+	81 300+	66 300+	61 300+	78 300+	72 300+	76 300+	69 300+	62 300+
Pawhuska Hospital, Pawhuska, OK	- -	- -	- -	- -	- -	- -	- -	- -	- -	- -	- -	- -	- -	- -	- -	- -	- -
Perry Memorial Hospital, Perry, OK	- -	- -	- -	0.048 42	0.000 11	2.0 199	37.5 8	66 (a)	82 (a)	86 (a)	75 (a)	64 (a)	82 (a)	71 (a)	82 (a)	72 (a)	67 (a)
Physicians' Hospital in Anadarko, Anadarko, OK	- -	- -	- -	- -	- -	- -	- -	- -	- -	- -	- -	- -	- -	- -	- -	- -	- -
Pinnacle Specialty Hospital, Tulsa, OK	- -	- -	- -	- -	- -	- -	- -	- -	- -	- -	- -	- -	- -	- -	- -	- -	- -
Ponca City Medical Center, Ponca City, OK	- -	- -	- -	0.703 407	0.000 277	12.2 656	42.0 100	62 300+	81 300+	85 300+	67 300+	59 300+	77 300+	70 300+	66 300+	67 300+	60 300+
Prague Community Hospital, Prague, OK	- -	- -	- -	- -	- -	- -	- -	- -	- -	- -	- -	- -	- -	- -	- -	- -	- -
Purcell Municipal Hospital, Purcell, OK	- -	- -	- -	0.257 109	0.035 86	- 0	- 0	64 (a)	90 (a)	75 (a)	73 (a)	70 (a)	86 (a)	73 (a)	83 (a)	66 (a)	72 (a)
Pushmataha County-TN of Antlers Hospital Authority, Antlers, OK	- -	- -	- -	0.506 83	0.277 65	- 0	- 0	48 (a)	76 (a)	67 (a)	52 (a)	48 (a)	71 (a)	65 (a)	71 (a)	63 (a)	56 (a)
Quartz Mountain Medical Center, Mangum, OK	- -	- -	- -	- -	- -	- -	- -	- -	- -	- -	- -	- -	- -	- -	- -	- -	- -
Saint Anthony Hospital, Oklahoma City, OK	- -	- -	- -	0.638 519	0.002 457	2.6 878	36.8 125	62 300+	83 300+	82 300+	68 300+	57 300+	76 300+	71 300+	69 300+	65 300+	74 300+
Saint Francis Hospital, Tulsa, OK	- -	- -	- -	0.678 2007	0.051 2053	5.8 2795	31.6 392	58 300+	77 300+	79 300+	68 300+	55 300+	75 300+	67 300+	70 300+	59 300+	74 300+
Saint Francis Hospital South, Tulsa, OK	- -	- -	- -	0.735 359	0.055 256	5.2 518	32.9 85	60 300+	82 300+	83 300+	77 300+	59 300+	77 300+	70 300+	72 300+	68 300+	80 300+
Saint John Medical Center, Tulsa, OK	- -	- -	- -	0.770 1137	0.797 1004	12.9 2215	35.8 201	57 300+	80 300+	77 300+	66 300+	59 300+	74 300+	70 300+	64 300+	57 300+	73 300+
Saint John Owasso, Owasso, OK	- -	- -	- -	0.435 310	0.478 232	11.1 287	42.1 57	66 300+	83 300+	79 300+	77 300+	64 300+	79 300+	74 300+	75 300+	66 300+	84 300+
Saint John Sapulpa, Sapulpa, OK	- -	- -	- -	- -	- -	- -	- -	- -	- -	- -	- -	- -	- -	- -	- -	- -	- -
Saint Mary's Regional Medical Center, Enid, OK	- -	- -	- -	0.176 664	0.000 558	9.7 1416	33.8 204	62 300+	83 300+	88 300+	74 300+	60 300+	78 300+	71 300+	69 300+	65 300+	74 300+
Sayre Memorial Hospital, Sayre, OK	- -	- -	- -	0.089 45	0.071 28	- 0	- 0	71 (a)	90 (a)	74 (a)	76 (a)	62 (a)	77 (a)	76 (a)	78 (a)	70 (a)	74 (a)
Seiling Community Hospital, Seiling, OK	- -	- -	- -	- -	- -	- -	- -	- -	- -	- -	- -	- -	- -	- -	- -	- -	- -

NOTE: The first number in each column (boldface) is the score, the second number is the number of patients; Please refer to the main entry for footnotes; (a) 100-299
MEASURES: ***Children's Asthma Care:*** *33. Received Systemic Corticosteroids; 34. Received Home Management Plan of Care; 35. Received Reliever Medication;* ***Use of Medical Imaging:*** *36. Combination Abdominal CT Scan; 37. Combination Chest CT Scan; 38. Follow-up Mammogram/Ultrasound; 39. MRI for Low Back Pain;* ***Survey of Patients' Hospital Experiences:*** *40. Area Around Room 'Always' Quiet at Night; 41. Doctors 'Always' Communicated Well; 42. Home Recovery Information Given; 43. Hospital Given 9 or 10 on 10 Point Scale; 44. Meds 'Always' Explained Before Given; 45. Nurses 'Always' Communicated Well; 46. Pain 'Always' Well Controlled; 47. Room and Bathroom 'Always' Clean; 48. Timely Help 'Always' Received; 49. Would Definitely Recommend Hospital*

Hospital	Children's Asthma Care			Use of Medical Imaging				Survey of Patients' Hospital Experiences									
	33	34	35	36	37	38	39	40	41	42	43	44	45	46	47	48	49
Sequoyah Memorial Hospital, Sallisaw, OK	- -	- -	- -	0.030 236	0.012 83	12.1 199	39.2 51	75 300+	84 300+	80 300+	70 300+	68 300+	81 300+	71 300+	84 300+	74 300+	66 300+
Share Memorial Hospital, Alva, OK	- -	- -	- -	0.444 81	0.025 40	7.1 85	40.0 20	67 (a)	83 (a)	75 (a)	69 (a)	56 (a)	81 (a)	75 (a)	77 (a)	75 (a)	66 (a)
Southcrest Hospital, Tulsa, OK	- -	- -	- -	0.266 376	0.054 203	6.7 509	39.2 97	58 300+	77 300+	80 300+	63 300+	49 300+	68 300+	66 300+	57 300+	52 300+	68 300+
Southwestern Medical Center, Lawton, OK	- -	- -	- -	0.518 299	0.560 252	- 0	38.7 111	63 300+	82 300+	81 300+	62 300+	56 300+	69 300+	66 300+	61 300+	56 300+	66 300+
Southwestern Regional Medical Center, Tulsa, OK	- -	- -	- -	0.317 812	0.008 921	19.4 31	50.0 2	69 (a)	85 (a)	85 (a)	90 (a)	68 (a)	79 (a)	72 (a)	79 (a)	71 (a)	92 (a)
Stillwater Medical Center, Stillwater, OK	- -	- -	- -	0.109 496	0.024 290	4.4 712	31.6 136	59 300+	82 300+	86 300+	67 300+	58 300+	74 300+	67 300+	65 300+	63 300+	71 300+
Stroud Regional Medical Center, Stroud, OK	- -	- -	- -	- -	- -	- -	- -	- -	- -	- -	- -	- -	- -	- -	- -	- -	- -
Summit Medical Center, Edmond, OK	- -	- -	- -	- -	- -	- -	- -	89 <100	88 <100	91 <100	86 <100	75 <100	88 <100	84 <100	88 <100	92 <100	89 <100
Surgical Hospital of Oklahoma, Oklahoma City, OK	- -	- -	- -	- 0	- 0	- 0	- 0	83 (a)	89 (a)	83 (a)	80 (a)	68 (a)	83 (a)	75 (a)	79 (a)	80 (a)	80 (a)
Tahlequah City Hospital, Tahlequah, OK	- -	- -	- -	0.480 356	0.059 220	8.7 564	33.1 121	51 300+	77 300+	77 300+	63 300+	60 300+	75 300+	69 300+	67 300+	63 300+	68 300+
Tulsa Spine & Specialty Hospital, Tulsa, OK	- -	- -	- -	0.167 6	0.400 5	- 0	36.1 252	83 300+	88 300+	86 300+	88 300+	72 300+	85 300+	77 300+	87 300+	79 300+	93 300+
Unity Health Center, Shawnee, OK	- -	- -	- -	0.559 472	0.000 191	8.8 399	29.9 67	66 300+	85 300+	86 300+	76 300+	61 300+	78 300+	75 300+	74 300+	68 300+	69 300+
USPHS Lawton Indian Hospital, Lawton, OK	- -	- -	- -	- -	- -	- -	- -	71 <100	72 <100	79 <100	64 <100	76 <100	73 <100	78 <100	85 <100	66 <100	64 <100
Valley View Regional Hospital, Ada, OK	- -	- -	- -	0.614 743	0.000 256	7.0 781	36.0 136	60 300+	78 300+	81 300+	57 300+	59 300+	75 300+	71 300+	68 300+	68 300+	58 300+
W W Hastings Indian Hospital, Tahlequah, OK	- -	- -	- -	- -	- -	- -	- -	64 300+	83 300+	81 300+	69 300+	70 300+	82 300+	75 300+	59 300+	75 300+	70 300+
Wagoner Community Hospital, Wagoner, OK	- -	- -	- -	0.500 46	0.370 27	11.6 86	21.4 14	69 (a)	79 (a)	78 (a)	61 (a)	56 (a)	76 (a)	67 (a)	70 (a)	74 (a)	67 (a)
Watonga Municipal Hospital, Watonga, OK	- -	- -	- -	- -	- -	- -	- -	64 <100	85 <100	72 <100	53 <100	56 <100	68 <100	69 <100	68 <100	74 <100	58 <100
Weatherford Regional Hospital, Weatherford, OK	- -	- -	- -	- -	- -	- -	- -	- -	- -	- -	- -	- -	- -	- -	- -	- -	- -
Woodward Regional Hospital, Woodward, OK	- -	- -	- -	0.664 220	0.046 130	12.5 359	25.7 35	59 300+	81 300+	80 300+	57 300+	56 300+	71 300+	66 300+	68 300+	63 300+	54 300+
SOUTH DAKOTA																	
Avera Dells Area Health Center, Dell Rapids, SD	- -	- -	- -	- -	- -	- -	- -	78 (a)	89 (a)	85 (a)	89 (a)	71 (a)	89 (a)	78 (a)	91 (a)	74 (a)	85 (a)
Avera Desmet Memorial Hospital, De Smet, SD	- -	- -	- -	- -	- -	- -	- -	68 <100	80 <100	77 <100	85 <100	67 <100	85 <100	80 <100	93 <100	83 <100	72 <100
Avera Flandreau Medical Center Hospital, Flandreau, SD	- -	- -	- -	- -	- -	- -	- -	68 <100	86 <100	69 <100	67 <100	58 <100	78 <100	67 <100	77 <100	85 <100	71 <100
Avera Gregory Healthcare Center, Gregory, SD	- -	- -	- -	- -	- -	- -	- -	68 (a)	79 (a)	71 (a)	71 (a)	65 (a)	78 (a)	75 (a)	83 (a)	60 (a)	72 (a)
Avera Hand County Memorial Hospital and Clinic, Miller, SD	- -	- -	- -	- -	- -	- -	- -	61 (a)	81 (a)	74 (a)	78 (a)	61 (a)	83 (a)	65 (a)	80 (a)	80 (a)	74 (a)
Avera Heart Hospital of South Dakota, Sioux Falls, SD	- -	- -	- -	0.123 57	0.122 41	- 0	- 0	68 300+	81 300+	83 300+	86 300+	68 300+	84 300+	75 300+	84 300+	78 300+	90 300+
Avera Mckennan Hospital & University Health Ctr, Sioux Falls, SD	- -	- -	- -	0.083 824	0.008 721	8.3 762	25.6 227	55 300+	77 300+	84 300+	68 300+	59 300+	74 300+	64 300+	70 300+	58 300+	75 300+
Avera Queen of Peace, Mitchell, SD	- -	- -	- -	0.841 340	0.339 180	6.6 997	31.4 156	60 300+	84 300+	83 300+	67 300+	65 300+	76 300+	69 300+	76 300+	64 300+	69 300+
Avera Sacred Heart Hospital, Yankton, SD	- -	- -	- -	0.365 115	0.459 37	6.7 285	28.7 122	64 300+	83 300+	81 300+	73 300+	67 300+	80 300+	73 300+	79 300+	69 300+	70 300+
Avera St Benedict Health Center, Parkston, SD	- -	- -	- -	0.901 71	0.278 36	8.9 235	40.0 10	74 (a)	84 (a)	82 (a)	78 (a)	66 (a)	83 (a)	71 (a)	88 (a)	73 (a)	80 (a)
Avera St Lukes, Aberdeen, SD	- -	- -	- -	0.647 896	0.266 770	11.6 1709	25.0 216	61 300+	80 300+	86 300+	64 300+	63 300+	79 300+	67 300+	77 300+	70 300+	62 300+
Avera Weskota Memorial Medical Center, Wessington Springs, SD	- -	- -	- -	- -	- -	- -	- -	74 <100	81 <100	77 <100	73 <100	73 <100	80 <100	68 <100	87 <100	71 <100	76 <100
Black Hills Surgical Hospital, Rapid City, SD	- -	- -	- -	0.237 38	0.114 44	- 0	36.1 485	87 300+	89 300+	94 300+	92 300+	76 300+	85 300+	77 300+	87 300+	86 300+	93 300+
Bowdle Hospital, Bowdle, SD	- -	- -	- -	0.167 12	0.133 15	4.8 42	- 0	- -	- -	- -	- -	- -	- -	- -	- -	- -	- -
Brookings Hospital, Brookings, SD	- -	- -	- -	0.092 152	0.032 93	- 0	29.6 54	64 300+	83 300+	86 300+	62 300+	64 300+	81 300+	69 300+	74 300+	73 300+	65 300+
Community Memorial Hospital, Redfield, SD	- -	- -	- -	- -	- -	- -	- -	- -	- -	- -	- -	- -	- -	- -	- -	- -	- -
Custer Regional Hospital, Custer, SD	- -	- -	- -	0.068 74	0.059 51	- 0	60.0 10	70 <100	84 <100	89 <100	73 <100	73 <100	77 <100	64 <100	83 <100	81 <100	75 <100
Dakota Plains Surgical Center, Aberdeen, SD	- -	- -	- -	- 0	- 0	- 0	24.1 116	84 (a)	92 (a)	94 (a)	92 (a)	77 (a)	88 (a)	78 (a)	89 (a)	89 (a)	96 (a)
Fall River Hospital, Hot Springs, SD	- -	- -	- -	0.000 42	0.000 30	- 0	30.0 10	- -	- -	- -	- -	- -	- -	- -	- -	- -	- -
Holy Infant Hospital, Hoven, SD	- -	- -	- -	- 0	- 0	0.0 7	- 0	- -	- -	- -	- -	- -	- -	- -	- -	- -	- -
Huron Regional Medical Center, Huron, SD	- -	- -	- -	- -	- -	- -	- -	- -	- -	- -	- -	- -	- -	- -	- -	- -	- -
Landmann-Jungman Memorial Hospital, Scotland, SD	- -	- -	- -	- -	- -	- -	- -	- -	- -	- -	- -	- -	- -	- -	- -	- -	- -
Lead-Deadwood Regional Hospital, Deadwood, SD	- -	- -	- -	- -	- -	- -	- -	73 (a)	92 (a)	84 (a)	84 (a)	74 (a)	88 (a)	70 (a)	93 (a)	91 (a)	88 (a)
Lewis and Clark Specialty Hospital, Yankton, SD	- -	- -	- -	- 0	- 0	- 0	25.0 8	83 (a)	89 (a)	87 (a)	85 (a)	69 (a)	88 (a)	75 (a)	87 (a)	87 (a)	90 (a)
Madison Community Hospital, Madison, SD	- -	- -	- -	- -	- -	- -	- -	- -	- -	- -	- -	- -	- -	- -	- -	- -	- -
Milbank Area Hospital/Avera Health, Milbank, SD	- -	- -	- -	- -	- -	- -	- -	63 (a)	80 (a)	85 (a)	67 (a)	66 (a)	82 (a)	71 (a)	81 (a)	67 (a)	73 (a)
Mobridge Regional Hospital, Mobridge, SD	- -	- -	- -	- -	- -	- -	- -	59 (a)	84 (a)	76 (a)	68 (a)	65 (a)	78 (a)	60 (a)	81 (a)	69 (a)	63 (a)
PHS Indian Hospital at Eagle Butte, Eagle Butte, SD	- -	- -	- -	- -	- -	- -	- -	93 <100	84 <100	48 <100	51 <100	93 <100	90 <100	95 <100	58 <100	98 <100	52 <100
PHS Indian Hospital at Pine Ridge, Pine Ridge, SD	- -	- -	- -	- -	- -	- -	- -	42 <100	57 <100	64 <100	46 <100	42 <100	53 <100	44 <100	58 <100	45 <100	34 <100
PHS Indian Hospital at Rapid City - Sioux San, Rapid City, SD	- -	- -	- -	- -	- -	- -	- -	69 <100	88 <100	48 <100	49 <100	97 <100	84 <100	61 <100	78 <100	91 <100	36 <100
PHS Indian Hospital at Rosebud, Rosebud, SD	- -	- -	- -	- 0	- 0	- 0	- 0	- -	- -	- -	- -	- -	- -	- -	- -	- -	- -
Platte Health Center, Platte, SD	- -	- -	- -	0.800 35	0.250 32	9.6 114	26.7 15	68 <100	84 <100	70 <100	77 <100	76 <100	80 <100	79 <100	83 <100	80 <100	79 <100
Prairie Lakes Hospital, Watertown, SD	- -	- -	- -	0.747 245	0.683 218	11.3 62	27.0 63	56 300+	85 300+	82 300+	68 300+	64 300+	76 300+	72 300+	76 300+	70 300+	67 300+
Rapid City Regional Hospital, Rapid City, SD	- -	- -	- -	0.061 958	0.000 810	7.8 307	35.4 274	44 300+	78 300+	82 300+	61 300+	57 300+	73 300+	69 300+	76 300+	68 300+	62 300+
Saint Marys Hospital, Pierre, SD	- -	- -	- -	0.782 280	0.023 174	2.0 651	39.8 83	57 (a)	82 (a)	83 (a)	66 (a)	59 (a)	76 (a)	66 (a)	67 (a)	65 (a)	65 (a)
Same Day Surgery Center, Rapid City, SD	- -	- -	- -	- 0	- 0	- 0	- 0	- -	- -	- -	- -	- -	- -	- -	- -	- -	- -
Sanford Mid-Dakota Hospital, Chamberlain, SD	- -	- -	- -	- -	- -	- -	- -	62 <100	77 <100	79 <100	66 <100	55 <100	77 <100	71 <100	71 <100	66 <100	61 <100
Sanford Usd Medical Center, Sioux Falls, SD	100 64	95 63	100 65	0.245 1299	0.000 906	- 0	31.8 412	58 300+	79 300+	84 300+	75 300+	60 300+	76 300+	70 300+	67 300+	67 300+	78 300+
Sanford Vermillion Hospital, Vermillion, SD	- -	- -	- -	- -	- -	- -	- -	58 (a)	86 (a)	82 (a)	59 (a)	57 (a)	70 (a)	65 (a)	63 (a)	63 (a)	65 (a)
Sioux Falls Surgical Hospital, Sioux Falls, SD	- -	- -	- -	- 0	- 0	- 0	24.3 37	87 300+	85 300+	90 300+	88 300+	74 300+	88 300+	75 300+	87 300+	87 300+	90 300+
Sioux Falls VA Medical Center, Sioux Falls, SD	- -	- -	- -	- -	- -	- -	- -	- -	- -	- -	- -	- -	- -	- -	- -	- -	- -
Siouxland Surgery Center Lp, Dakota Dunes, SD	- -	- -	- -	0.714 7	0.214 14	- 0	13.3 15	84 300+	86 300+	88 300+	87 300+	72 300+	88 300+	76 300+	81 300+	91 300+	89 300+
Spearfish Regional Hospital, Spearfish, SD	- -	- -	- -	0.080 250	0.000 141	5.4 259	38.5 91	60 300+	84 300+	81 300+	70 300+	62 300+	78 300+	71 300+	76 300+	79 300+	72 300+
Spearfish Regional Surgery Center, Spearfish, SD	- -	- -	- -	- 0	- 0	- 0	- 0	70 <100	92 <100	94 <100	89 <100	66 <100	86 <100	76 <100	80 <100	91 <100	86 <100
Sturgis Regional Hospital, Sturgis, SD	- -	- -	- -	0.038 52	0.000 33	19.5 128	27.8 18	52 (a)	91 (a)	84 (a)	80 (a)	66 (a)	84 (a)	72 (a)	84 (a)	83 (a)	75 (a)
VA Black Hills Healthcare System - Fort Meade, Fort Meade, SD	- -	- -	- -	- -	- -	- -	- -	- -	- -	- -	- -	- -	- -	- -	- -	- -	- -
Wagner Community Memorial Hospital, Wagner, SD	- -	- -	- -	0.500 30	0.800 10	4.9 81	0.0 7	60 (a)	87 (a)	73 (a)	71 (a)	65 (a)	79 (a)	68 (a)	83 (a)	72 (a)	70 (a)

NOTE: The first number in each column (boldface) is the score, the second number is the number of patients; Please refer to the main entry for footnotes; (a) 100-299
*MEASURES: **Children's Asthma Care:** 33. Received Systemic Corticosteroids; 34. Received Home Management Plan of Care; 35. Received Reliever Medication; **Use of Medical Imaging:** 36. Combination Abdominal CT Scan; 37. Combination Chest CT Scan; 38. Follow-up Mammogram/Ultrasound; 39. MRI for Low Back Pain; **Survey of Patients' Hospital Experiences:** 40. Area Around Room 'Always' Quiet at Night; 41. Doctors 'Always' Communicated Well; 42. Home Recovery Information Given; 43. Hospital Given 9 or 10 on 10 Point Scale; 44. Meds 'Always' Explained Before Given; 45. Nurses 'Always' Communicated Well; 46. Pain 'Always' Well Controlled; 47. Room and Bathroom 'Always' Clean; 48. Timely Help 'Always' Received; 49. Would Definitely Recommend Hospital*

Hospital	Children's Asthma Care			Use of Medical Imaging				Survey of Patients' Hospital Experiences									
	33	34	35	36	37	38	39	40	41	42	43	44	45	46	47	48	49
Winner Regional Healthcare Center, Winner, SD	-	-	-	-	-	-	-	-	-	-	-	-	-	-	-	-	-
WISCONSIN																	
Amery Regional Medical Center, Amery, WI	-	-	-	-	-	-	-	-	-	-	-	-	-	-	-	-	-
Appleton Medical Center, Appleton, WI	-	-	-	**0.057** 783	**0.003** 869	**7.9** 632	**33.9** 124	**48** 300+	**78** 300+	**87** 300+	**66** 300+	**59** 300+	**74** 300+	**64** 300+	**71** 300+	**64** 300+	**75** 300+
Aspirus Wausau Hospital, Wausau, WI	-	-	-	**0.072** 430	**0.005** 436	**8.0** 928	**24.5** 53	**63** 300+	**81** 300+	**87** 300+	**72** 300+	**63** 300+	**79** 300+	**69** 300+	**73** 300+	**65** 300+	**78** 300+
Aurora Baycare Medical Center, Green Bay, WI	-	-	-	**0.048** 480	**0.003** 307	**9.0** 621	**35.9** 217	**70** 300+	**81** 300+	**87** 300+	**76** 300+	**67** 300+	**79** 300+	**72** 300+	**80** 300+	**68** 300+	**80** 300+
Aurora Lakeland Medical Center, Elkhorn, WI	-	-	-	**0.055** 597	**0.000** 535	**8.4** 463	**30.2** 63	**46** 300+	**80** 300+	**86** 300+	**55** 300+	**57** 300+	**75** 300+	**68** 300+	**67** 300+	**64** 300+	**58** 300+
Aurora Medical Center, Summit, WI	-	-	-	-	-	-	-	-	-	-	-	-	-	-	-	-	-
Aurora Medical Center - Washington County, Hartford, WI	-	-	-	**0.017** 118	**0.000** 124	- 0	**33.9** 62	**60** 300+	**81** 300+	**88** 300+	**67** 300+	**65** 300+	**78** 300+	**70** 300+	**78** 300+	**67** 300+	**68** 300+
Aurora Medical Center Kenosha, Kenosha, WI	-	-	-	**0.082** 535	**0.061** 441	**7.9** 682	**31.8** 110	**60** 300+	**78** 300+	**85** 300+	**68** 300+	**58** 300+	**73** 300+	**63** 300+	**74** 300+	**59** 300+	**70** 300+
Aurora Medical Center Manitowoc County, Two Rivers, WI	-	-	-	**0.063** 304	**0.008** 260	- 0	**38.8** 85	**63** 300+	**82** 300+	**88** 300+	**75** 300+	**64** 300+	**82** 300+	**74** 300+	**89** 300+	**70** 300+	**77** 300+
Aurora Medical Center Oshkosh, Oshkosh, WI	-	-	-	**0.136** 484	**0.000** 396	**8.3** 903	**25.2** 151	**64** 300+	**80** 300+	**89** 300+	**73** 300+	**69** 300+	**79** 300+	**73** 300+	**75** 300+	**68** 300+	**76** 300+
Aurora Memorial Hospital Burlington, Burlington, WI	-	-	-	**0.074** 448	**0.022** 364	**8.3** 965	**31.7** 145	**55** 300+	**78** 300+	**87** 300+	**61** 300+	**59** 300+	**76** 300+	**72** 300+	**74** 300+	**62** 300+	**63** 300+
Aurora Sheboygan Memorial Medical Center, Sheboygan, WI	-	-	-	**0.132** 448	**0.019** 310	- 0	**15.8** 38	**59** 300+	**81** 300+	**89** 300+	**73** 300+	**67** 300+	**81** 300+	**73** 300+	**76** 300+	**64** 300+	**74** 300+
Aurora St Lukes Medical Center, Milwaukee, WI	-	-	-	**0.090** 2729	**0.011** 2789	**7.4** 2244	**27.8** 345	**47** 300+	**74** 300+	**85** 300+	**65** 300+	**59** 300+	**73** 300+	**65** 300+	**68** 300+	**53** 300+	**70** 300+
Aurora West Allis Medical Center, West Allis, WI	-	-	-	**0.044** 960	**0.005** 586	**6.3** 1870	**42.1** 126	**59** 300+	**76** 300+	**83** 300+	**69** 300+	**58** 300+	**74** 300+	**65** 300+	**70** 300+	**54** 300+	**72** 300+
Baldwin Area Medical Center, Baldwin, WI	-	-	-	-	-	-	-	-	-	-	-	-	-	-	-	-	-
Bay Area Medical Center, Marinette, WI	-	-	-	**0.103** 583	**0.030** 271	**1.3** 540	**40.2** 107	**60** 300+	**78** 300+	**84** 300+	**56** 300+	**60** 300+	**76** 300+	**70** 300+	**77** 300+	**63** 300+	**59** 300+
Beaver Dam Com Hospital, Beaver Dam, WI	-	-	-	**0.612** 379	**0.596** 250	**5.3** 717	**18.0** 50	**59** 300+	**83** 300+	**87** 300+	**69** 300+	**65** 300+	**81** 300+	**68** 300+	**80** 300+	**66** 300+	**70** 300+
Bellin Memorial Hospital, Green Bay, WI	-	-	-	**0.019** 154	**0.000** 110	**3.4** 955	**66.7** 3	**62** 300+	**80** 300+	**90** 300+	**77** 300+	**67** 300+	**81** 300+	**72** 300+	**78** 300+	**75** 300+	**81** 300+
Beloit Memorial Hospital, Beloit, WI	-	-	-	**0.376** 218	**0.000** 125	**4.2** 429	**42.0** 131	**58** 300+	**81** 300+	**83** 300+	**67** 300+	**64** 300+	**79** 300+	**72** 300+	**75** 300+	**69** 300+	**69** 300+
Berlin Memorial Hospital, Berlin, WI	-	-	-	**0.104** 241	**0.005** 216	**5.6** 444	**25.0** 40	**58** 300+	**85** 300+	**85** 300+	**73** 300+	**68** 300+	**82** 300+	**70** 300+	**79** 300+	**77** 300+	**72** 300+
Black River Memorial Hospital, Black River Falls, WI	-	-	-	**0.049** 103	**0.021** 48	- 0	**32.1** 28	**72** (a)	**89** (a)	**92** (a)	**82** (a)	**72** (a)	**83** (a)	**74** (a)	**80** (a)	**82** (a)	**82** (a)
Boscobel Area Health Care, Boscobel, WI	-	-	-	**0.057** 35	**0.000** 18	**2.8** 142	**16.7** 6	**56** (a)	**81** (a)	**85** (a)	**65** (a)	**62** (a)	**80** (a)	**75** (a)	**86** (a)	**74** (a)	**62** (a)
Burnett Medical Center, Grantsburg, WI	-	-	-	-	-	-	-	**53** (a)	**78** (a)	**86** (a)	**70** (a)	**60** (a)	**71** (a)	**78** (a)	**85** (a)	**77** (a)	**65** (a)
Calumet Medical Center, Chilton, WI	-	-	-	**0.102** 88	**0.000** 19	**8.9** 146	**28.6** 7	**65** (a)	**85** (a)	**87** (a)	**77** (a)	**65** (a)	**86** (a)	**82** (a)	**89** (a)	**74** (a)	**78** (a)
Columbia Center, Mequon, WI	-	-	-	- 0	- 0	- 0	- 0	**73** 300+	**90** 300+	**89** 300+	**89** 300+	**72** 300+	**84** 300+	**80** 300+	**79** 300+	**78** 300+	**91** 300+
Columbia St Mary's Hospital Ozaukee, Mequon, WI	-	-	-	**0.080** 754	**0.007** 874	**9.2** 1153	**24.2** 132	**49** 300+	**82** 300+	**79** 300+	**69** 300+	**59** 300+	**77** 300+	**68** 300+	**68** 300+	**57** 300+	**74** 300+
Columbia St Marys Hospital Milwaukee, Milwaukee, WI	-	-	-	**0.083** 1088	**0.008** 944	**9.9** 3028	**30.7** 264	**57** 300+	**79** 300+	**82** 300+	**60** 300+	**62** 300+	**73** 300+	**66** 300+	**60** 300+	**58** 300+	**63** 300+
Columbus Community Hospital, Columbus, WI	-	-	-	-	-	-	-	**68** 300+	**84** 300+	**85** 300+	**74** 300+	**67** 300+	**74** 300+	**69** 300+	**85** 300+	**70** 300+	**73** 300+
Community Memorial Hospital, Menomonee Falls, WI	-	-	-	**0.040** 274	**0.026** 228	**3.1** 98	**18.4** 38	**56** 300+	**81** 300+	**86** 300+	**73** 300+	**61** 300+	**79** 300+	**70** 300+	**73** 300+	**66** 300+	**75** 300+
Community Memorial Hospital, Oconto Falls, WI	-	-	-	-	-	-	-	**58** 300+	**82** 300+	**85** 300+	**61** 300+	**62** 300+	**78** 300+	**69** 300+	**68** 300+	**73** 300+	**59** 300+
Cumberland Memorial Hospital, Cumberland, WI	-	-	-	-	-	-	-	**57** (a)	**83** (a)	**85** (a)	**75** (a)	**61** (a)	**78** (a)	**72** (a)	**80** (a)	**75** (a)	**70** (a)
Divine Savior Healthcare, Portage, WI	-	-	-	**0.034** 203	**0.010** 206	**14.4** 464	**19.2** 52	**58** 300+	**80** 300+	**85** 300+	**59** 300+	**64** 300+	**74** 300+	**68** 300+	**75** 300+	**65** 300+	**57** 300+
Door County Memorial Hospital, Sturgeon Bay, WI	-	-	-	-	-	-	-	**61** 300+	**84** 300+	**85** 300+	**75** 300+	**68** 300+	**84** 300+	**73** 300+	**81** 300+	**73** 300+	**73** 300+
Edgerton Hospital and Health Services, Edgerton, WI	-	-	-	-	-	-	-	**59** <100	**82** <100	**96** <100	**70** <100	**73** <100	**81** <100	**71** <100	**84** <100	**74** <100	**75** <100
Flambeau Hospital, Park Falls, WI	-	-	-	-	-	-	-	**61** (a)	**79** (a)	**81** (a)	**69** (a)	**64** (a)	**82** (a)	**72** (a)	**87** (a)	**81** (a)	**67** (a)
Fort Healthcare, Fort Atkinson, WI	-	-	-	**0.374** 617	**0.003** 353	**1.1** 846	**31.4** 70	**65** 300+	**79** 300+	**86** 300+	**63** 300+	**57** 300+	**75** 300+	**65** 300+	**69** 300+	**62** 300+	**66** 300+
Franciscan Skemp Arcadia, Arcadia, WI	-	-	-	-	-	-	-	**60** <100	**81** <100	**79** <100	**61** <100	**61** <100	**84** <100	**73** <100	**63** <100	**83** <100	**72** <100
Franciscan Skemp La Crosse Hospital, La Crosse, WI	-	-	-	**0.047** 704	**0.005** 581	- 0	**35.8** 173	**51** 300+	**79** 300+	**84** 300+	**74** 300+	**64** 300+	**74** 300+	**67** 300+	**72** 300+	**60** 300+	**76** 300+
Franciscan Skemp Sparta Hospital, Sparta, WI	-	-	-	-	-	-	-	**61** <100	**88** <100	**70** <100	**66** <100	**51** <100	**82** <100	**57** <100	**67** <100	**84** <100	**54** <100
Froedtert Memorial Lutheran Hospital, Milwaukee, WI	-	-	-	**0.134** 2119	**0.002** 2078	**6.9** 1374	**27.1** 203	**49** 300+	**79** 300+	**85** 300+	**75** 300+	**60** 300+	**80** 300+	**72** 300+	**64** 300+	**63** 300+	**81** 300+
Good Samaritan Health Center, Merrill, WI	-	-	-	**0.070** 157	**0.030** 66	**3.8** 369	**39.4** 33	**62** (a)	**83** (a)	**88** (a)	**67** (a)	**65** (a)	**78** (a)	**63** (a)	**76** (a)	**69** (a)	**63** (a)
Grant Regional Health Center, Lancaster, WI	-	-	-	**0.086** 70	**0.036** 56	**10.0** 190	**50.0** 14	**74** (a)	**91** (a)	**82** (a)	**79** (a)	**76** (a)	**87** (a)	**81** (a)	**77** (a)	**86** (a)	**74** (a)
Gundersen Luth Medical Center, La Crosse, WI	-	-	-	**0.011** 190	**0.013** 78	- 0	**35.3** 17	**53** 300+	**81** 300+	**88** 300+	**78** 300+	**66** 300+	**80** 300+	**71** 300+	**75** 300+	**67** 300+	**83** 300+
Hayward Area Memorial Hospital, Hayward, WI	-	-	-	-	-	-	-	**72** 300+	**91** 300+	**85** 300+	**75** 300+	**68** 300+	**82** 300+	**73** 300+	**82** 300+	**72** 300+	**78** 300+
Holy Family Memorial, Manitowoc, WI	-	-	-	**0.113** 310	**0.101** 288	**9.0** 881	**31.9** 119	**51** 300+	**78** 300+	**87** 300+	**63** 300+	**62** 300+	**76** 300+	**69** 300+	**77** 300+	**62** 300+	**68** 300+
Howard Young Medical Center, Woodruff, WI	-	-	-	**0.053** 114	**0.014** 71	**22.4** 58	**34.5** 29	**50** 300+	**78** 300+	**81** 300+	**65** 300+	**63** 300+	**76** 300+	**67** 300+	**73** 300+	**69** 300+	**67** 300+
Hudson Hospital, Hudson, WI	-	-	-	-	-	-	-	**64** 300+	**84** 300+	**86** 300+	**79** 300+	**70** 300+	**84** 300+	**76** 300+	**70** 300+	**74** 300+	**84** 300+
Indianhead Medical Center, Shell Lake, WI	-	-	-	-	-	-	-	-	-	-	-	-	-	-	-	-	-
Ladd Memorial Hosptial, Osceola, WI	-	-	-	-	-	-	-	**71** (a)	**87** (a)	**89** (a)	**83** (a)	**73** (a)	**83** (a)	**70** (a)	**82** (a)	**74** (a)	**84** (a)
Lakeview Medical Center, Rice Lake, WI	-	-	-	**0.062** 275	**0.028** 283	**9.8** 256	**28.6** 84	**59** 300+	**82** 300+	**86** 300+	**68** 300+	**67** 300+	**79** 300+	**71** 300+	**77** 300+	**74** 300+	**70** 300+
Langlade Hospital, Antigo, WI	-	-	-	-	-	-	-	**55** 300+	**83** 300+	**93** 300+	**71** 300+	**75** 300+	**82** 300+	**74** 300+	**84** 300+	**67** 300+	**68** 300+
Luther Hospital Mayo Health System, Eau Claire, WI	-	-	-	**0.093** 785	**0.005** 928	- 0	**25.8** 240	**53** 300+	**85** 300+	**88** 300+	**78** 300+	**65** 300+	**79** 300+	**71** 300+	**78** 300+	**73** 300+	**85** 300+
Luther Midelfort - Chippewa Valley Mayo Health Sys, Bloomer, WI	-	-	-	-	-	-	-	**58** (a)	**81** (a)	**88** (a)	**76** (a)	**57** (a)	**75** (a)	**69** (a)	**79** (a)	**63** (a)	**78** (a)
Luther Midelfort - Northland Mayo Health System, Barron, WI	-	-	-	-	-	-	-	**61** (a)	**81** (a)	**82** (a)	**66** (a)	**66** (a)	**74** (a)	**68** (a)	**71** (a)	**69** (a)	**66** (a)
Luther Midelfort - Oakridge Mayo Health System, Osseo, WI	-	-	-	-	-	-	-	**58** (a)	**86** (a)	**84** (a)	**83** (a)	**65** (a)	**85** (a)	**69** (a)	**84** (a)	**75** (a)	**79** (a)
Madison VA Medical Center, Madison, WI	-	-	-	-	-	-	-	-	-	-	-	-	-	-	-	-	-
Memorial Health Center, Medford, WI	-	-	-	**0.039** 206	**0.000** 126	**1.8** 275	**30.3** 33	**68** (a)	**82** (a)	**85** (a)	**75** (a)	**62** (a)	**82** (a)	**75** (a)	**80** (a)	**72** (a)	**70** (a)
Memorial Hospital Lafayette County, Darlington, WI	-	-	-	**0.114** 70	**0.321** 28	**10.6** 104	**23.1** 13	**63** (a)	**83** (a)	**88** (a)	**73** (a)	**75** (a)	**81** (a)	**73** (a)	**88** (a)	**73** (a)	**79** (a)
Memorial Medical Center, Neillsville, WI	-	-	-	-	-	-	-	**56** (a)	**77** (a)	**83** (a)	**68** (a)	**57** (a)	**74** (a)	**61** (a)	**81** (a)	**72** (a)	**61** (a)
Memorial Medical Center, Ashland, WI	-	-	-	-	-	-	-	**56** 300+	**84** 300+	**85** 300+	**68** 300+	**67** 300+	**77** 300+	**70** 300+	**83** 300+	**74** 300+	**64** 300+
Mercy Health Sys Corp, Janesville, WI	-	-	-	**0.032** 894	**0.024** 697	**3.9** 535	**33.3** 177	**49** 300+	**78** 300+	**85** 300+	**57** 300+	**63** 300+	**77** 300+	**68** 300+	**74** 300+	**63** 300+	**54** 300+
Mercy Medical Center of Oshkosh, Oshkosh, WI	-	-	-	**0.068** 340	**0.008** 255	**10.7** 797	**31.2** 77	**56** 300+	**81** 300+	**88** 300+	**77** 300+	**67** 300+	**80** 300+	**71** 300+	**77** 300+	**72** 300+	**78** 300+
Mercy Walworth Hospital & Medical Center, Lake Geneva, WI	-	-	-	**0.111** 198	**0.085** 129	**3.2** 283	**23.5** 68	-	-	-	-	-	-	-	-	-	-
Meriter Hospital, Madison, WI	-	-	-	**0.062** 531	**0.035** 398	- 0	- 0	**58** 300+	**80** 300+	**88** 300+	**80** 300+	**62** 300+	**78** 300+	**65** 300+	**79** 300+	**64** 300+	**85** 300+
Midwest Orthopedic Specialty Hospital, Franklin, WI	-	-	-	- 0	- 0	- 0	- 0	-	-	-	-	-	-	-	-	-	-

NOTE: The first number in each column (boldface) is the score, the second number is the number of patients; Please refer to the main entry for footnotes; (a) 100-299

*MEASURES: **Children's Asthma Care:** 33. Received Systemic Corticosteroids; 34. Received Home Management Plan of Care; 35. Received Reliever Medication; **Use of Medical Imaging:** 36. Combination Abdominal CT Scan; 37. Combination Chest CT Scan; 38. Follow-up Mammogram/Ultrasound; 39. MRI for Low Back Pain; **Survey of Patients' Hospital Experiences:** 40. Area Around Room 'Always' Quiet at Night; 41. Doctors 'Always' Communicated Well; 42. Home Recovery Information Given; 43. Hospital Given 9 or 10 on 10 Point Scale; 44. Meds 'Always' Explained Before Given; 45. Nurses 'Always' Communicated Well; 46. Pain 'Always' Well Controlled; 47. Room and Bathroom 'Always' Clean; 48. Timely Help 'Always' Received; 49. Would Definitely Recommend Hospital*

Hospital	Children's Asthma Care 33	34	35	Use of Medical Imaging 36	37	38	39	Survey of Patients' Hospital Experiences 40	41	42	43	44	45	46	47	48	49
Mile Bluff Medical Center, Mauston, WI	-	-	-	**0.107** 178	**0.005** 186	**8.1** 520	**34.4** 61	**52** 300+	**84** 300+	**83** 300+	**63** 300+	**65** 300+	**75** 300+	**66** 300+	**77** 300+	**63** 300+	**62** 300+
Milwaukee VA Medical Center, Milwaukee, WI	-	-	-	-	-	-	-	-	-	-	-	-	-	-	-	-	-
Ministry Eagle River Memorial Hospital, Eagle River, WI	-	-	-	**0.082** 196	**0.027** 112	**22.9** 345	**32.1** 56	**70** (a)	**80** (a)	**84** (a)	**64** (a)	**61** (a)	**77** (a)	**74** (a)	**85** (a)	**76** (a)	**58** (a)
Ministry St Marys Hospital, Rhinelander, WI	-	-	-	**0.080** 487	**0.003** 339	**6.4** 792	**26.7** 131	**49** 300+	**81** 300+	**89** 300+	**60** 300+	**60** 300+	**75** 300+	**66** 300+	**70** 300+	**61** 300+	**60** 300+
Ministry St Michaels Hospital of Stevens Point, Stevens Point, WI	-	-	-	**0.072** 585	**0.019** 323	**11.1** 1057	**36.9** 84	**65** 300+	**79** 300+	**86** 300+	**63** 300+	**66** 300+	**76** 300+	**68** 300+	**74** 300+	**64** 300+	**66** 300+
Monroe Clinic, Monroe, WI	-	-	-	**0.048** 415	**0.019** 215	**11.6** 1065	**26.8** 123	**61** 300+	**80** 300+	**90** 300+	**72** 300+	**66** 300+	**82** 300+	**71** 300+	**75** 300+	**68** 300+	**75** 300+
Moundview Memorial Hospital and Clinics, Friendship, WI	-	-	-	**0.018** 109	**0.000** 99	**3.7** 190	**54.5** 11	**58** <100	**69** <100	**80** <100	**60** <100	**64** <100	**82** <100	**66** <100	**86** <100	**77** <100	**60** <100
New London Family Medical Center, New London, WI	-	-	-	-	-	-	-	**58** (a)	**77** (a)	**82** (a)	**60** (a)	**58** (a)	**69** (a)	**67** (a)	**78** (a)	**62** (a)	**59** (a)
Oak Leaf Surgcl Hospital, Eau Claire, WI	-	-	-	- 0	- 0	- 0	- 0	**80** 300+	**94** 300+	**93** 300+	**97** 300+	**80** 300+	**92** 300+	**79** 300+	**83** 300+	**89** 300+	**96** 300+
Oconomowoc Memorial Hospital, Oconomowoc, WI	-	-	-	**0.088** 385	**0.024** 334	**9.5** 749	**32.4** 145	**63** 300+	**80** 300+	**87** 300+	**73** 300+	**66** 300+	**80** 300+	**67** 300+	**78** 300+	**66** 300+	**75** 300+
Oconto Hospital & Medical Center, Oconto, WI	-	-	-	-	-	-	-	-	-	-	-	-	-	-	-	-	-
Orthopaedic Hospital of Wisconsin, Glendale, WI	-	-	-	- 0	- 0	- 0	**28.1** 89	**78** 300+	**90** 300+	**89** 300+	**87** 300+	**73** 300+	**90** 300+	**81** 300+	**80** 300+	**84** 300+	**89** 300+
Our Lady of Victory Hospital, Stanley, WI	-	-	-	**0.018** 55	**0.059** 17	**10.3** 117	**38.5** 13	**59** (a)	**82** (a)	**84** (a)	**82** (a)	**63** (a)	**84** (a)	**77** (a)	**94** (a)	**81** (a)	**76** (a)
Prairie Du Chien Memorial Hospital, Prairie Du Chien, WI	-	-	-	**0.042** 167	**0.053** 75	**6.6** 286	**4.5** 44	**57** 300+	**87** 300+	**89** 300+	**76** 300+	**70** 300+	**82** 300+	**76** 300+	**84** 300+	**77** 300+	**67** 300+
Red Cedar Medical Center-Mayo Health System, Menomonie, WI	-	-	-	-	-	-	-	**70** 300+	**87** 300+	**87** 300+	**75** 300+	**74** 300+	**81** 300+	**73** 300+	**82** 300+	**79** 300+	**73** 300+
Reedsburg Area Medical Center, Reedsburg, WI	-	-	-	**0.038** 185	**0.000** 79	**13.8** 254	**39.2** 79	**65** 300+	**84** 300+	**88** 300+	**71** 300+	**62** 300+	**81** 300+	**68** 300+	**80** 300+	**67** 300+	**76** 300+
Richland Hospital, Richland Center, WI	-	-	-	-	-	-	-	**56** 300+	**84** 300+	**84** 300+	**70** 300+	**62** 300+	**79** 300+	**66** 300+	**85** 300+	**68** 300+	**70** 300+
Ripon Medical Center, Ripon, WI	-	-	-	-	-	-	-	**66** 300+	**82** 300+	**85** 300+	**73** 300+	**68** 300+	**84** 300+	**75** 300+	**81** 300+	**77** 300+	**70** 300+
River Falls Area Hospital, River Falls, WI	-	-	-	**0.020** 147	**0.000** 90	**7.9** 328	**29.0** 31	**62** 300+	**84** 300+	**88** 300+	**74** 300+	**64** 300+	**80** 300+	**75** 300+	**77** 300+	**79** 300+	**74** 300+
Riverside Medical Center, Waupaca, WI	-	-	-	-	-	-	-	**65** 300+	**82** 300+	**87** 300+	**66** 300+	**64** 300+	**74** 300+	**64** 300+	**78** 300+	**66** 300+	**64** 300+
Riverview Hospital Assoc, Wisconsin Rapids, WI	-	-	-	**0.006** 489	**0.000** 359	**7.6** 1077	**32.8** 67	**66** 300+	**83** 300+	**85** 300+	**72** 300+	**68** 300+	**82** 300+	**73** 300+	**87** 300+	**70** 300+	**72** 300+
Rusk County Memorial Hospital, Ladysmith, WI	-	-	-	-	-	-	-	-	-	-	-	-	-	-	-	-	-
Sacred Heart Hospital, Eau Claire, WI	-	-	-	**0.120** 493	**0.012** 486	**11.6** 311	**25.1** 167	**57** 300+	**82** 300+	**87** 300+	**73** 300+	**65** 300+	**80** 300+	**72** 300+	**77** 300+	**68** 300+	**79** 300+
Sacred Heart Hospital, Tomahawk, WI	-	-	-	**0.078** 103	**0.000** 54	**7.0** 199	- 0	**70** (a)	**86** (a)	**91** (a)	**78** (a)	**80** (a)	**85** (a)	**71** (a)	**84** (a)	**77** (a)	**70** (a)
Saint Agnes Hospital, Fond Du Lac, WI	-	-	-	**0.128** 553	**0.030** 534	**12.6** 1196	**29.8** 141	**58** 300+	**80** 300+	**86** 300+	**68** 300+	**60** 300+	**77** 300+	**72** 300+	**77** 300+	**60** 300+	**66** 300+
Saint Clare Hospital Health Svcs, Baraboo, WI	-	-	-	**0.058** 310	**0.039** 178	**10.4** 335	**0.0** 2	**64** 300+	**83** 300+	**85** 300+	**70** 300+	**67** 300+	**80** 300+	**66** 300+	**74** 300+	**70** 300+	**72** 300+
Saint Clare's Hospital of Weston, Weston, WI	-	-	-	**0.000** 42	**0.000** 31	- 0	**20.0** 5	**51** 300+	**76** 300+	**91** 300+	**73** 300+	**62** 300+	**75** 300+	**69** 300+	**74** 300+	**68** 300+	**76** 300+
Saint Croix Regional Medical Center, Saint Croix Falls, WI	-	-	-	-	-	-	-	**54** 300+	**82** 300+	**87** 300+	**74** 300+	**66** 300+	**76** 300+	**69** 300+	**80** 300+	**72** 300+	**75** 300+
Saint Elizabeth Hospital, Appleton, WI	-	-	-	**0.097** 486	**0.013** 377	**11.3** 915	**24.6** 65	**54** 300+	**83** 300+	**88** 300+	**73** 300+	**64** 300+	**81** 300+	**72** 300+	**73** 300+	**68** 300+	**76** 300+
Saint Josephs Community Health Services, Hillsboro, WI	-	-	-	**0.024** 42	**0.059** 17	**10.2** 88	**36.4** 11	**55** <100	**91** <100	**91** <100	**68** <100	**66** <100	**84** <100	**76** <100	**89** <100	**73** <100	**69** <100
Saint Josephs Community Hospital West Bend, West Bend, WI	-	-	-	**0.018** 284	**0.027** 301	**23.5** 17	**31.1** 103	**72** 300+	**83** 300+	**87** 300+	**71** 300+	**68** 300+	**79** 300+	**72** 300+	**76** 300+	**63** 300+	**72** 300+
Saint Josephs Hospital, Chippewa Falls, WI	-	-	-	**0.024** 255	**0.031** 194	**8.7** 173	**41.0** 61	**63** 300+	**83** 300+	**88** 300+	**74** 300+	**67** 300+	**80** 300+	**72** 300+	**77** 300+	**74** 300+	**75** 300+
Saint Josephs Hospital, Marshfield, WI	-	-	-	**0.049** 41	**0.000** 16	- 0	- 0	**50** 300+	**73** 300+	**87** 300+	**71** 300+	**61** 300+	**75** 300+	**65** 300+	**74** 300+	**62** 300+	**73** 300+
Saint Mary's Hospital, Madison, WI	-	-	-	**0.020** 351	**0.056** 54	- 0	**0.0** 1	**63** 300+	**77** 300+	**89** 300+	**79** 300+	**67** 300+	**82** 300+	**72** 300+	**74** 300+	**65** 300+	**83** 300+
Saint Marys Hospital Medical Center, Green Bay, WI	-	-	-	**0.065** 354	**0.016** 189	**8.0** 199	- 0	**58** 300+	**82** 300+	**86** 300+	**72** 300+	**66** 300+	**77** 300+	**72** 300+	**79** 300+	**63** 300+	**74** 300+
Saint Marys Hospital Superior, Superior, WI	-	-	-	**0.029** 206	**0.000** 111	**4.4** 543	- 0	-	-	-	-	-	-	-	-	-	-
Saint Nicholas Hospital, Sheboygan, WI	-	-	-	**0.053** 472	**0.006** 353	**4.8** 377	**28.6** 70	**54** 300+	**81** 300+	**84** 300+	**62** 300+	**59** 300+	**70** 300+	**68** 300+	**62** 300+	**57** 300+	**70** 300+
Saint Vincent Hospital, Green Bay, WI	-	-	-	**0.040** 547	**0.023** 394	**7.0** 370	**43.2** 44	**65** 300+	**81** 300+	**87** 300+	**71** 300+	**66** 300+	**77** 300+	**70** 300+	**78** 300+	**62** 300+	**74** 300+
Sauk Prairie Memorial Hospital, Prairie Du Sac, WI	-	-	-	**0.115** 165	**0.152** 105	**11.0** 536	**33.3** 75	**58** 300+	**85** 300+	**88** 300+	**82** 300+	**70** 300+	**82** 300+	**70** 300+	**81** 300+	**74** 300+	**88** 300+
Shawano Medical Center, Shawano, WI	-	-	-	**0.082** 182	**0.012** 169	**7.7** 261	**46.2** 39	**66** 300+	**81** 300+	**81** 300+	**65** 300+	**62** 300+	**77** 300+	**67** 300+	**79** 300+	**70** 300+	**62** 300+
Southwest Health Center, Platteville, WI	-	-	-	**0.063** 175	**0.021** 95	**8.4** 227	**52.0** 25	**67** 300+	**83** 300+	**90** 300+	**77** 300+	**66** 300+	**78** 300+	**70** 300+	**86** 300+	**70** 300+	**73** 300+
Spooner Health System, Spooner, WI	-	-	-	**0.057** 88	**0.000** 44	**11.1** 243	**41.4** 29	**51** (a)	**86** (a)	**84** (a)	**66** (a)	**66** (a)	**82** (a)	**73** (a)	**72** (a)	**72** (a)	**65** (a)
Stoughton Hospital, Stoughton, WI	-	-	-	-	-	-	-	**70** (a)	**84** (a)	**90** (a)	**83** (a)	**66** (a)	**86** (a)	**76** (a)	**86** (a)	**73** (a)	**89** (a)
Theda Clark Medical Center, Neenah, WI	**100** 11	**9** 11	**100** 11	**0.081** 447	**0.002** 424	**11.5** 590	**41.2** 102	**55** 300+	**78** 300+	**86** 300+	**72** 300+	**63** 300+	**77** 300+	**68** 300+	**74** 300+	**62** 300+	**78** 300+
Tomah Memorial Hospital, Tomah, WI	-	-	-	-	-	-	-	**71** 300+	**87** 300+	**91** 300+	**70** 300+	**69** 300+	**81** 300+	**70** 300+	**79** 300+	**70** 300+	**75** 300+
Tomah VA Medical Center, Tomah, WI	-	-	-	-	-	-	-	-	-	-	-	-	-	-	-	-	-
Tri County Memorial Hospital, Whitehall, WI	-	-	-	-	-	-	-	**58** (a)	**87** (a)	**79** (a)	**75** (a)	**69** (a)	**84** (a)	**65** (a)	**89** (a)	**80** (a)	**74** (a)
United Hospital System, Kenosha, WI	-	-	-	**0.108** 1101	**0.008** 765	**2.6** 2143	**32.4** 207	**48** 300+	**75** 300+	**82** 300+	**64** 300+	**57** 300+	**73** 300+	**67** 300+	**78** 300+	**69** 300+	**66** 300+
University of Wisconsin Hospitals & Clinics Authority, Madison, WI	-	-	-	**0.073** 2268	**0.008** 2607	**5.9** 1660	**28.1** 342	**55** 300+	**76** 300+	**88** 300+	**77** 300+	**65** 300+	**79** 300+	**68** 300+	**73** 300+	**62** 300+	**83** 300+
Upland Hills Health, Dodgeville, WI	-	-	-	-	-	-	-	**64** 300+	**88** 300+	**91** 300+	**77** 300+	**68** 300+	**81** 300+	**75** 300+	**85** 300+	**74** 300+	**79** 300+
Vernon Memorial Hospital, Viroqua, WI	-	-	-	**0.073** 96	**0.015** 68	**9.5** 241	**33.3** 30	**60** 300+	**87** 300+	**90** 300+	**74** 300+	**64** 300+	**82** 300+	**72** 300+	**88** 300+	**78** 300+	**77** 300+
Watertown Regional Medical Center, Watertown, WI	-	-	-	**0.078** 437	**0.063** 301	**8.6** 699	**31.5** 92	**62** 300+	**75** 300+	**84** 300+	**63** 300+	**62** 300+	**74** 300+	**67** 300+	**74** 300+	**70** 300+	**61** 300+
Waukesha Memorial Hospital, Waukesha, WI	-	-	-	**0.136** 1410	**0.060** 1549	**11.5** 2047	**35.2** 349	**64** 300+	**80** 300+	**87** 300+	**78** 300+	**63** 300+	**78** 300+	**69** 300+	**79** 300+	**65** 300+	**82** 300+
Waupun Memorial Hospital, Waupun, WI	-	-	-	-	-	-	-	**68** 300+	**84** 300+	**87** 300+	**79** 300+	**73** 300+	**85** 300+	**78** 300+	**81** 300+	**78** 300+	**74** 300+
Westfields Hospital, New Richmond, WI	-	-	-	-	-	-	-	**61** 300+	**82** 300+	**86** 300+	**73** 300+	**67** 300+	**80** 300+	**70** 300+	**84** 300+	**72** 300+	**73** 300+
Wheaton Franciscan - St Joseph, Milwaukee, WI	-	-	-	**0.178** 533	**0.069** 346	**9.6** 1726	**27.3** 132	**69** 300+	**79** 300+	**84** 300+	**67** 300+	**64** 300+	**77** 300+	**70** 300+	**67** 300+	**66** 300+	**71** 300+
Wheaton Franciscan Healthcare - All Saints, Racine, WI	-	-	-	**0.134** 1108	**0.016** 1131	**7.8** 2565	**33.1** 284	**53** 300+	**77** 300+	**87** 300+	**58** 300+	**57** 300+	**74** 300+	**66** 300+	**68** 300+	**55** 300+	**54** 300+
Wheaton Franciscan Healthcare-Elmbrook Mem, Brookfield, WI	-	-	-	**0.140** 598	**0.080** 339	**10.8** 729	**35.3** 204	**57** 300+	**82** 300+	**83** 300+	**64** 300+	**59** 300+	**76** 300+	**68** 300+	**67** 300+	**60** 300+	**67** 300+
Wheaton Franciscan Healthcare - Franklin, Franklin, WI	-	-	-	**0.641** 64	**0.029** 35	**17.9** 28	**11.8** 17	**78** (a)	**84** (a)	**80** (a)	**83** (a)	**69** (a)	**85** (a)	**78** (a)	**78** (a)	**76** (a)	**85** (a)
Wheaton Franciscan Healthcare - St Francis, Milwaukee, WI	-	-	-	**0.568** 410	**0.038** 289	**15.7** 1044	**31.8** 88	**50** 300+	**77** 300+	**82** 300+	**55** 300+	**57** 300+	**71** 300+	**61** 300+	**65** 300+	**55** 300+	**60** 300+
Wild Rose Com Memorial Hospital, Wild Rose, WI	-	-	-	-	-	-	-	**60** (a)	**83** (a)	**84** (a)	**72** (a)	**71** (a)	**79** (a)	**71** (a)	**78** (a)	**72** (a)	**69** (a)

NOTE: The first number in each column (boldface) is the score, the second number is the number of patients; Please refer to the main entry for footnotes; (a) 100-299
*MEASURES: **Children's Asthma Care:** 33. Received Systemic Corticosteroids; 34. Received Home Management Plan of Care; 35. Received Reliever Medication; **Use of Medical Imaging:** 36. Combination Abdominal CT Scan; 37. Combination Chest CT Scan; 38. Follow-up Mammogram/Ultrasound; 39. MRI for Low Back Pain; **Survey of Patients' Hospital Experiences:** 40. Area Around Room 'Always' Quiet at Night; 41. Doctors 'Always' Communicated Well; 42. Home Recovery Information Given; 43. Hospital Given 9 or 10 on 10 Point Scale; 44. Meds 'Always' Explained Before Given; 45. Nurses 'Always' Communicated Well; 46. Pain 'Always' Well Controlled; 47. Room and Bathroom 'Always' Clean; 48. Timely Help 'Always' Received; 49. Would Definitely Recommend Hospital*

Hospitals whose Heart Attack 30-Day Mortality Rate is Better (Lower) than the U.S. National Rate

Hospital	City	State	Phone	Web Site
Advocate Good Shepherd Hospital	Barrington	Illinois	847-381-9600	www.advocatehealth.com
Alameda Hospital	Alameda	California	510-522-3700	www.alamedahospital.org
Arizona Heart Hospital	Phoenix	Arizona	602-532-1000	www.azhearthospital.com
Arkansas Heart Hospital	Little Rock	Arkansas	501-219-7000	www.arheart.com
Aurora St Lukes Medical Center	Milwaukee	Wisconsin	414-649-6000	www.aurorahealthcare.org
Avera Heart Hospital of South Dakota	Sioux Falls	South Dakota	605-977-7000	
Banner Good Samaritan Medical Center	Phoenix	Arizona	602-239-2000	www.bannerhealth.com
Baptist Hospital East	Louisville	Kentucky	502-897-8100	www.baptisteast.com
Barnes Jewish Hospital	Saint Louis	Missouri	314-747-3000	www.barnesjewish.org
Bayhealth - Kent General Hospital	Dover	Delaware	302-744-7001	www.bayhealth.org/about/kent.asp
Baystate Medical Center	Springfield	Massachusetts	413-794-0000	www.baystatehealth.com
Bellin Memorial Hospital	Green Bay	Wisconsin	920-433-3500	www.bellin.org
Beth Israel Deaconess Medical Center	Boston	Massachusetts	617-667-7000	www.bidmc.harvard.edu
Boone Hospital Center	Columbia	Missouri	573-815-8000	
Cape Cod Hospital	Hyannis	Massachusetts	508-771-1800	www.capecodhealth.org
Carolinas Medical Center-Northeast	Concord	North Carolina	704-783-3000	www.northeastmedical.org
Cedars-Sinai Medical Center	Los Angeles	California	310-423-5000	www.cedars-sinai.edu
Christian Hospital Northeast	Saint Louis	Missouri	314-653-5000	www.christianhospital.org
Clear Lake Regional Medical Center	Webster	Texas	281-332-2511	www.clearlakermc.com
Community Regional Medical Center	Lorain	Ohio	440-960-3295	
Conemaugh Valley Memorial Hospital	Johnstown	Pennsylvania	814-534-9000	www.conemaugh.org
Doylestown Hospital	Doylestown	Pennsylvania	215-345-2200	www.dh.org
Durham Regional Hospital	Durham	North Carolina	919-620-1078	durhamregional.org
Edward Hospital	Naperville	Illinois	630-527-3000	www.edward.org
Emh Regional Medical Center	Elyria	Ohio	440-329-7500	
Englewood Hospital and Medical Center	Englewood	New Jersey	201-894-3000	www.englewoodhospital.com
Ephraim Mcdowell Regional Medical Center	Danville	Kentucky	859-239-2409	www.emrmc.com
Evanston Hospital	Evanston	Illinois	847-432-8000	www.enh.org
Franciscan St Margaret Health - Hammond	Hammond	Indiana	219-932-2300	www.smmhc.com
Hackensack University Medical Center	Hackensack	New Jersey	201-996-2000	www.humed.com
Heart Hospital of Austin	Austin	Texas	512-407-7581	www.hearthospitalofaustin.com
Heart Hospital of New Mexico	Albuquerque	New Mexico	505-724-2000	www.hearthospitalnm.com
Henry Ford Hospital	Detroit	Michigan	313-916-2600	www.henryfordhospital.com
Henry Ford Macomb Hospital	Clinton Township	Michigan	586-263-2300	www.stjoe-macomb.com
Holy Name Medical Center	Teaneck	New Jersey	201-833-3000	www.holyname.org
Inova Fairfax Hospital	Falls Church	Virginia	703-776-3332	www.inova.org
John T Mather Memorial Hospital of Port Jefferson	Port Jefferson	New York	631-473-1320	www.matherhospital.com
Lahey Clinic Hospital	Burlington	Massachusetts	781-744-5100	www.lahey.org
Lehigh Valley Hospital	Allentown	Pennsylvania	610-402-2273	www.lvhhn.org
Lenox Hill Hospital	New York	New York	212-439-2345	www.lenoxhillhospital.org
Los Robles Hospital & Medical Center	Thousand Oaks	California	805-497-2727	www.losrobleshospital.com
Maimonides Medical Center	Brooklyn	New York	718-283-6000	www.maimonidesmed.org
Marlborough Hospital	Marlborough	Massachusetts	508-481-5000	
Mary Hitchcock Memorial Hospital	Lebanon	New Hampshire	603-650-5000	www.dhmc.org
Massachusetts General Hospital	Boston	Massachusetts	617-726-2000	www.massgeneral.org
Mayo Clinic - Saint Marys Hospital	Rochester	Minnesota	507-255-5123	www.mayoclinic.org/saintmaryshospital
Memorial Medical Center	Springfield	Illinois	217-788-3000	www.memorialmedical.com
Memorial Mission Hospital and Asheville Surgery Center	Asheville	North Carolina	828-213-1111	www.missionhospitals.org
Meriter Hospital	Madison	Wisconsin	608-417-6210	www.meriter.com
The Methodist Hospital	Houston	Texas	713-790-2221	www.methodisthealth.com
Methodist Medical Center of Oak Ridge	Oak Ridge	Tennessee	865-835-1000	www.mmcoakridge.com
Methodist Willowbrook Hospital	Houston	Texas	281-477-1000	
Middlesex Hospital	Middletown	Connecticut	860-344-6000	www.midhosp.org
Midwest Regional Medical Center	Midwest City	Oklahoma	405-610-4411	www.midwestregional.com
Montefiore Medical Center	Bronx	New York	718-920-4321	www.montefiore.org
Morton Plant Hospital	Clearwater	Florida	727-462-7000	www.measehospitals.com
Mount Sinai Hospital	New York	New York	212-241-7981	www.mountsinai.org
Mount Sinai Medical Center	Miami Beach	Florida	305-674-2121	www.msmc.com
Munson Medical Center	Traverse City	Michigan	231-935-5000	www.munsonhealthcare.org
Naples Community Hospital	Naples	Florida	239-436-5000	www.nchmd.org
New York-Presbyterian Hospital	New York	New York	212-746-4189	www.nyp.org
Newton-Wellesley Hospital	Newton	Massachusetts	617-243-6000	www.nwh.org
Northeast Georgia Medical Center	Gainesville	Georgia	770-535-3553	www.nghs.com
Norwalk Hospital Association	Norwalk	Connecticut	203-852-2000	www.norwalkhosp.org

Hospital	City	State	Phone	Web Site
NYU Hospitals Center	New York	New York	212-263-7300	www.med.nyu.edu
Ohio State University Hospitals	Columbus	Ohio	614-293-9700	www.jamesline.com
Palm Beach Gardens Medical Center	Palm Beach Gardens	Florida	561-622-1411	www.pbgmc.com
Park Nicollet Methodist Hospital	Saint Louis Park	Minnesota	952-993-5000	www.parknicollet.com/methodist
Providence Hospital and Medical Centers	Southfield	Michigan	248-849-3011	www.stjohn.org/Providence
Rochester General Hospital	Rochester	New York	585-922-4000	www.rochestergeneral.org
Saint John's Health Center	Santa Monica	California	310-829-5511	www.stjohns.org
Saint Marys Hospital	Waterbury	Connecticut	203-574-6000	
Sarasota Memorial Hospital	Sarasota	Florida	941-917-9000	www.smh.com
Seton Medical Center Austin	Austin	Texas	512-324-1000	www.seton.net
Sinai Hospital of Baltimore	Baltimore	Maryland	410-601-5131	www.sinai-balt.com
Southcoast Hospital Group	Fall River	Massachusetts	508-679-3131	www.southcoast.org/charlton
Saint Elizabeth Medical Center North	Covington	Kentucky	859-292-2000	www.stelizabeth.com
Saint Francis Hospital and Health Centers-Indianapolis	Indianapolis	Indiana	317-865-5001	www.stfrancishospitals.org
Saint Francis Hospital - Roslyn	Roslyn	New York	516-562-6000	www.stfrancisheartcenter.com
Saint Johns Hospital	Springfield	Illinois	217-544-6464	www.st-johns.org
Saint Joseph Hospital	Bethpage	New York	516-579-6000	www.newislandhospital.org
Saint Joseph Mercy Hospital	Ann Arbor	Michigan	734-712-3791	
Saint Lukes Episcopal Hospital	Houston	Texas	832-355-1000	www.sleh.com
Saint Mary's Hospital	Madison	Wisconsin	608-251-6100	www.stmarysmadison.com
Saint Vincent Heart Center of Indiana	Indianapolis	Indiana	317-583-5000	www.theheartcenter.com
Saint Vincent's Medical Center	Bridgeport	Connecticut	203-576-5551	www.stvincents.org
Stamford Hospital	Stamford	Connecticut	203-276-1000	www.stamhealth.org
Tallahassee Memorial Healthcare	Tallahassee	Florida	850-431-1155	www.tmh.org
Texsan Heart Hospital	San Antonio	Texas	210-736-8013	www.texsanhearthospital.com
The Nebraska Methodist Hospital	Omaha	Nebraska	402-390-4000	www.bestcare.org
UMass Memorial Medical Center	Worcester	Massachusetts	508-334-1000	www.umassmemorial.org
University of Michigan Health System	Ann Arbor	Michigan	734-764-1505	www.med.umich.edu
UPMC Passavant	Pittsburgh	Pennsylvania	412-367-6700	passavant.upmc.com
Waterbury Hospital	Waterbury	Connecticut	203-573-6000	www.waterburyhospital.org
Yale-New Haven Hospital	New Haven	Connecticut	203-688-4242	www.ynhh.org

Note: Table shows hospitals nationwide whose Acute Myocardial Infarction 30-day risk-adjusted mortality rate is better (lower) than U.S. rate of 16.2%

Hospitals whose Heart Attack 30-Day Mortality Rate is Worse (Higher) than the U.S. National Rate

Hospital	City	State	Phone	Web Site
Albemarle Hospital Authority	Elizabeth City	North Carolina	252-335-0531	www.albemarlehealth.org
Arkansas Methodist Medical Center	Paragould	Arkansas	870-239-7000	www.arkansasmethodist.org
Baptist Memorial Hospital Huntingdon	Huntingdon	Tennessee	731-986-4461	www.bmhcc.org
Baxter Regional Medical Center	Mountain Home	Arkansas	870-508-1000	www.baxterregional.org
Brookdale Hospital Medical Center	Brooklyn	New York	718-240-5966	www.brookdalehospital.org
Brooklyn Hospital Center at Downtown Campus	Brooklyn	New York	718-250-8000	www.tbh.org
Cape Coral Hospital	Cape Coral	Florida	239-574-2323	
Catawba Valley Medical Center	Hickory	North Carolina	828-326-3809	www.catawbavalleymc.org
Clearfield Hospital	Clearfield	Pennsylvania	814-765-5341	www.clearfieldhosp.org
Community Regional Medical Center	Fresno	California	559-459-6000	www.communitymedical.org
Danville Regional Medical Center	Danville	Virginia	434-799-2100	www.danvilleregional.org
Dyersburg Regional Medical Center	Dyersburg	Tennessee	731-285-2410	
Edward W Sparrow Hospital	Lansing	Michigan	517-364-5000	www.sparrow.org
Erie County Medical Center	Buffalo	New York	716-898-3936	www.ecmc.edu
Forrest General Hospital	Hattiesburg	Mississippi	601-288-7000	www.forrestgeneral.com
Good Samaritan Hospital & Rehab Center	Puyallup	Washington	253-848-6661	www.multicare.org/goodsam
Great River Medical Center	Blytheville	Arkansas	870-838-7300	www.greatrivermc.com
Hospital Damas	Ponce	Puerto Rico	787-840-8460	
Howard Regional Health System	Kokomo	Indiana	765-453-8371	www.howardcommunity.org
Hurley Medical Center	Flint	Michigan	810-257-9000	www.hurleymc.com
Jefferson Regional Medical Center	Pine Bluff	Arkansas	870-541-7100	www.jrmc.org
Kennewick General Hospital	Kennewick	Washington	509-586-6111	www.kennewickgeneral.com
Kettering Medical Center - Sycamore	Miamisburg	Ohio	937-384-8776	www.khnetwork.org/sycamore
Lafayette General Medical Center	Lafayette	Louisiana	337-289-7991	www.lafayettegeneral.org
Laredo Medical Center	Laredo	Texas	956-796-5000	www.laredomedical.com
Manatee Memorial Hospital	Bradenton	Florida	941-746-5111	www.manateememorial.com
Massena Memorial Hospital	Massena	New York	315-764-1711	www.massenahospital.org
Mena Regional Health System	Mena	Arkansas	479-394-6100	
Mercy Memorial Health Center	Ardmore	Oklahoma	405-223-5400	www.mercyok.com/mmhc
Nassau University Medical Center	East Meadow	New York	516-572-0123	www.numc.edu
Navarro Regional Hospital	Corsicana	Texas	903-654-6800	www.navarrohospital.com
North Broward Medical Center	Pompano Beach	Florida	954-786-6950	www.browardhealth.org
Piedmont Medical Center	Rock Hill	South Carolina	803-329-1234	www.piedmontmedicalcenter.com
Raleigh General Hospital	Beckley	West Virginia	304-256-4100	
Schuylkill Medical Center - South Jackson Street	Pottsville	Pennsylvania	570-621-5000	www.pottsvillehospital.com
Seton Medical Center	Daly City	California	650-992-4000	www.setonmedicalcenter.org
Southwest Mississippi Regional Medical Center	Mccomb	Mississippi	601-249-5500	www.smrmc.com
Saint Francis Hospital	Columbus	Georgia	706-596-4020	wecareforlife.com
Saint Joseph Medical Center	Tacoma	Washington	253-627-4101	www.fhshealth.org
Saint Joseph's Regional Medical Center	Paterson	New Jersey	973-754-2000	www.sjhmc.org
Saint Lucie Medical Center	Port Saint Lucie	Florida	772-335-4000	www.stluciemed.com
Saint Mary's Regional Medical Center	Enid	Oklahoma	580-233-6100	www.stmarysregional.com
University Medical Center	Lubbock	Texas	806-775-8200	www.teamumc.org
Virginia Commonwealth University Health System	Richmond	Virginia	804-828-0938	www.vcuhealth.org
Wheaton Franciscan Healthcare - St Francis	Milwaukee	Wisconsin	414-647-5000	www.mywheaton.org

Note: Table shows hospitals nationwide whose Acute Myocardial Infarction 30-day risk-adjusted mortality rate is worse (higher) than U.S. rate of 16.2%

Hospitals whose Heart Failure 30-Day Mortality Rate is Better (Lower) than the U.S. National Rate

Hospital	City	State	Phone	Web Site
Adventist La Grange Memorial Hospital	La Grange	Illinois	708-352-1200	www.keepingyouwell.com
Advocate Good Samaritan Hospital	Downers Grove	Illinois	630-275-5900	www.advocatehealth.com/gsam
Advocate Good Shepherd Hospital	Barrington	Illinois	847-381-9600	www.advocatehealth.com
Advocate Illinois Masonic Medical Center	Chicago	Illinois	773-975-1600	www.advocatehealth.com/immc
Advocate South Suburban Hospital	Hazel Crest	Illinois	708-799-8000	www.advocatehealth.com
Advocate Trinity Hospital	Chicago	Illinois	773-967-2000	www.advocatehealth.com/trin
Alexian Brothers Medical Center	Elk Grove Village	Illinois	847-437-5500	www.alexian.org
Alle Kiski Medical Center	Natrona	Pennsylvania	412-224-5100	www.wpahs.org
Anna Jaques Hospital	Newburyport	Massachusetts	978-463-1000	www.ajh.org
Ashtabula County Medical Center	Ashtabula	Ohio	440-997-2262	www.acmchealth.org
Audrain Medical Center	Mexico	Missouri	573-582-5000	www.audrainmedicalcenter.com
Aventura Hospital and Medical Center	Aventura	Florida	305-682-7000	www.aventurahospital.com
Baptist Hospital East	Louisville	Kentucky	502-897-8100	www.baptisteast.com
Baptist Medical Center	San Antonio	Texas	210-297-1020	www.baptisthealthsystem.org
Baptist Memorial Hospital	Memphis	Tennessee	901-226-5000	www.bmhcc.org
Barnes Jewish Hospital	Saint Louis	Missouri	314-747-3000	www.barnesjewish.org
Bay Medical Center	Panama City	Florida	850-769-1511	www.baymedical.org
Bay Regional Medical Center	Bay City	Michigan	989-894-3000	www.baymed.org
Baylor Medical Center at Garland	Garland	Texas	972-487-5000	www.baylorhealth.com
Bayonne Hospital Center	Bayonne	New Jersey	201-858-5000	www.bayonnemedicalcenter.org
Beaumont Hospital - Grosse Pointe	Grosse Pointe	Michigan	313-343-1000	www.beaumonthospitals.com
Beth Israel Deaconess Medical Center	Boston	Massachusetts	617-667-7000	www.bidmc.harvard.edu
Beth Israel Medical Center	New York	New York	212-420-2000	www.wehealny.org
Brandon Regional Hospital	Brandon	Florida	813-681-5551	www.brandonregionalhospital.com
Brigham and Women's Hosptial	Boston	Massachusetts	617-732-5500	www.brighamandwomens.org
Bronx-Lebanon Hospital Center	Bronx	New York	212-588-7000	www.bronx-leb.org
Brookwood Medical Center	Birmingham	Alabama	205-877-1000	www.bwmc.com
Cedars-Sinai Medical Center	Los Angeles	California	310-423-5000	www.cedars-sinai.edu
Centinela Hospital Medical Center	Inglewood	California	310-673-4660	www.centinelafreeman.com
Centrastate Medical Center	Freehold	New Jersey	732-431-2000	www.centrastate.com
Charlotte Regional Medical Center	Punta Gorda	Florida	941-639-3131	www.charlotteregional.com
Christus Spohn Hospital Alice	Alice	Texas	361-661-8000	www.christusspohn.org
Citizens Medical Center	Victoria	Texas	361-573-9181	www.citizensmedicalcenter.org
Cleveland Clinic	Cleveland	Ohio	216-444-2200	www.clevelandclinic.org
Cleveland Clinic Hospital	Weston	Florida	954-689-5000	www.clevelandclinic.org
Community Hospital	Munster	Indiana	219-836-1600	www.comhs.org/community
Community Medical Center	Toms River	New Jersey	732-557-8000	www.sbhcs.com
D C H Regional Medical Center	Tuscaloosa	Alabama	205-759-7111	www.dchsystem.com
Deborah Heart and Lung Center	Browns Mills	New Jersey	609-893-6611	
East Orange General Hospital	East Orange	New Jersey	973-266-4401	www.evh.org
Easton Hospital	Easton	Pennsylvania	610-250-4076	www.easton-hospital.com
Elmhurst Memorial Hospital	Elmhurst	Illinois	630-833-1400	www.emhc.org
Emory University Hospital	Atlanta	Georgia	404-686-8500	www.emoryhealthcare.org
Englewood Hospital and Medical Center	Englewood	New Jersey	201-894-3000	www.englewoodhospital.com
Evanston Hospital	Evanston	Illinois	847-432-8000	www.enh.org
Fairview Hospital	Cleveland	Ohio	216-476-7000	www.fairviewhospital.org
Fairview Southdale Hospital	Edina	Minnesota	952-924-5000	www.fairview.org
Faulkner Hospital	Boston	Massachusetts	617-983-7000	
Firsthealth Moore Regional Hospital	Pinehurst	North Carolina	910-715-1000	www.firsthealth.org
Flagler Hospital	Saint Augustine	Florida	904-819-4426	www.flaglerhospital.com
Florida Hospital	Orlando	Florida	407-303-1976	www.floridahospital.com
Florida Hospital Fish Memorial	Orange City	Florida	386-917-5000	www.fhfishmemorial.org
Franciscan St Margaret Health - Hammond	Hammond	Indiana	219-932-2300	www.smmhc.com
Franklin Square Hospital Center	Baltimore	Maryland	443-777-7850	www.franklinsquare.org
Froedtert Memorial Lutheran Hospital	Milwaukee	Wisconsin	414-805-3000	www.froedtert.com
Garfield Medical Center	Monterey Park	California	626-573-2222	www.garfieldmedicalcenter.com
Genesys Regional Medical Center - Health Park	Grand Blanc	Michigan	810-606-5000	www.genesys.org
Glendale Adventist Medical Center	Glendale	California	818-409-8202	www.glendaleadventist.com
Glendale Memorial Hospital & Health Center	Glendale	California	818-502-1900	www.glendalememorialhospital.org
Good Samaritan Hospital	Baltimore	Maryland	443-444-3902	www.goodsam-md.org
Good Samaritan Hospital	Dayton	Ohio	937-278-2612	
Grand View Hospital	Sellersville	Pennsylvania	215-453-4615	www.gvh.org
Grandview Hospital & Medical Center	Dayton	Ohio	937-723-4988	www.kmcnetwork.org
Griffin Hospital	Derby	Connecticut	203-732-7500	www.griffinhealth.org

Hospital	City	State	Phone	Web Site
Hackensack University Medical Center	Hackensack	New Jersey	201-996-2000	www.humed.com
Hahnemann University Hospital	Philadelphia	Pennsylvania	215-762-7000	www.hahnemannhospital.com
Hamilton General Hospital	Hamilton	Texas	254-386-3151	www.hamiltonhospital.org
Hamot Medical Center	Erie	Pennsylvania	814-877-6000	www.hamot.org
Harper University Hospital	Detroit	Michigan	313-745-6211	www.harperhospital.org
Hazleton General Hospital	Hazleton	Pennsylvania	570-501-4000	www.ghha.org
Henry Ford Hospital	Detroit	Michigan	313-916-2600	www.henryfordhospital.com
Highlands Regional Medical Center	Sebring	Florida	863-385-6101	www.highlandsregional.com
Hillcrest Hospital	Mayfield Heights	Ohio	440-312-4500	www.hillcresthospital.org
Holy Name Medical Center	Teaneck	New Jersey	201-833-3000	www.holyname.org
Holy Redeemer Hospital and Medical Center	Meadowbrook	Pennsylvania	215-947-3000	www.holyredeemer.com
Hospital of St Raphael	New Haven	Connecticut	203-789-3000	www.srhs.org
Houston Medical Center	Warner Robins	Georgia	478-922-4281	www.hhc.org
Huntington Memorial Hospital	Pasadena	California	626-397-5000	www.huntingtonhospital.com
Huron Hospital	Cleveland	Ohio	216-761-3300	
Huron Valley-Sinai Hospital	Commerce Township	Michigan	248-937-3370	www.hvsh.org
Ingalls Memorial Hospital	Harvey	Illinois	708-333-2300	www.ingalls.org
Inova Alexandria Hospital	Alexandria	Virginia	703-504-3000	www.inova.com/inovapublic.srt/iah/index.jsp
Jeanes Hospital	Philadelphia	Pennsylvania	215-728-2000	www.jeanes.com
Jersey Shore University Medical Center	Neptune	New Jersey	732-775-5500	www.meridianhealth.com
Jewish Hospital & St Mary's Healthcare	Louisville	Kentucky	502-587-4011	www.jhhs.org
Johns Hopkins Bayview Medical Center	Baltimore	Maryland	410-550-0123	www.hopkinsbayview.org
Kingsbrook Jewish Medical Center	Brooklyn	New York	718-604-5789	www.kingsbrook.org
Lake Region Healthcare Corporation	Fergus Falls	Minnesota	218-736-8000	www.lrhc.org
Lakewood Hospital	Lakewood	Ohio	216-529-4200	www.lakewoodhospital.org
Lehigh Valley Hospital	Allentown	Pennsylvania	610-402-2273	www.lvhhn.org
Lehigh Valley Hospital - Muhlenberg	Bethlehem	Pennsylvania	610-402-2273	www.lvhn.org
Lenox Hill Hospital	New York	New York	212-439-2345	www.lenoxhillhospital.org
Liberty Hospital	Liberty	Missouri	816-781-7200	www.libertyhospital.org
Little Company of Mary Hospital	Evergreen Park	Illinois	708-422-6200	www.lcmh.org
Loyola University Medical Center	Maywood	Illinois	708-216-9000	www.lumc.edu
Maimonides Medical Center	Brooklyn	New York	718-283-6000	www.maimonidesmed.org
Main Line Hospital Bryn Mawr Campus	Bryn Mawr	Pennsylvania	610-526-3000	www.mainlinehealth.org
Main Line Hospital Lankenau	Wynnewood	Pennsylvania	610-645-2000	www.mainlinehealth.org/lh
Maryland General Hospital	Baltimore	Maryland	410-225-8996	www.marylandgeneral.org
Marymount Hospital	Garfield Heights	Ohio	216-581-0500	www.marymount.org
Massachusetts General Hospital	Boston	Massachusetts	617-726-2000	www.massgeneral.org
Mayo Clinic - Saint Marys Hospital	Rochester	Minnesota	507-255-5123	www.mayoclinic.org/saintmaryshospital
Mclaren Regional Medical Center	Flint	Michigan	810-342-2000	www.mclaren.org
Memorial Health University Medical Center	Savannah	Georgia	912-350-8000	www.memorialhealth.com
Memorial Hermann Hospital System	Houston	Texas	713-448-6796	www.memorialhermann.org
Memorial Hospital	Manchester	Kentucky	606-598-5104	www.manchestermemorial.com
Mercy Hospital	Miami	Florida	305-285-2121	www.mercymiami.com
Meriter Hospital	Madison	Wisconsin	608-417-6210	www.meriter.com
The Methodist Hospital	Houston	Texas	713-790-2221	www.methodisthealth.com
Methodist Hospitals	Gary	Indiana	219-886-4601	www.methodisthospital.org
Metrosouth Medical Center	Blue Island	Illinois	708-597-2000	www.stfrancisblueisland.com
Miami Valley Hospital	Dayton	Ohio	937-208-8000	www.miamivalleyhospital.com
Missouri Baptist Medical Center	Town and Country	Missouri	314-996-5000	www.missouribaptistmedicalcenter.org
Montefiore Medical Center	Bronx	New York	718-920-4321	www.montefiore.org
Mount Auburn Hospital	Cambridge	Massachusetts	617-492-3500	
Mount Sinai Hospital	New York	New York	212-241-7981	www.mountsinai.org
Mount Sinai Medical Center	Miami Beach	Florida	305-674-2121	www.msmc.com
Natchitoches Regional Medical Center	Natchitoches	Louisiana	318-352-1200	www.natchitocheshospital.org
Nebraska Heart Hospital	Lincoln	Nebraska	402-328-3000	www.neheart.com
New York Methodist Hospital	Brooklyn	New York	718-780-3000	www.nym.org
New York-Presbyterian Hospital	New York	New York	212-746-4189	www.nyp.org
Newton-Wellesley Hospital	Newton	Massachusetts	617-243-6000	www.nwh.org
North Kansas City Hospital	North Kansas City	Missouri	816-691-2000	www.nkch.org
North Shore Medical Center	Salem	Massachusetts	978-741-1215	
Northeast Georgia Medical Center	Gainesville	Georgia	770-535-3553	www.nghs.com
Northwestern Memorial Hospital	Chicago	Illinois	312-926-2000	www.nmh.org
Norwood Hospital	Norwood	Massachusetts	508-772-1000	www.caritasnorwood.org
NYU Hospitals Center	New York	New York	212-263-7300	www.med.nyu.edu
Oakwood Annapolis Hospital	Wayne	Michigan	734-467-4175	www.oakwood.org
Oakwood Hospital and Medical Center	Dearborn	Michigan	313-593-7125	www.oakwood.org
Oklahoma Heart Hospital	Oklahoma City	Oklahoma	405-608-3200	www.okheart.com

Hospital	City	State	Phone	Web Site
Olympia Medical Center	Los Angeles	California	310-657-5900	www.olympiamc.com
Orange Regional Medical Center	Goshen	New York	845-343-2424	
Our Lady of Bellefonte Hospital	Ashland	Kentucky	606-833-3600	www.olbh.com
Pacific Alliance Medical Center	Los Angeles	California	213-624-8411	www.pamc.net
Piedmont Hospital	Atlanta	Georgia	404-605-5000	www.piedmonthospital.org
Princeton Community Hospital	Princeton	West Virginia	304-487-7260	www.pchonline.org
Provena St Joseph Medical Center	Joliet	Illinois	815-725-7133	www.provena.org/stjoes
Providence Hospital	Washington	District of Columbia	202-269-7000	www.provhosp.org
Providence Hospital and Medical Centers	Southfield	Michigan	248-849-3011	www.stjohn.org/Providence
RHC St Francis Hospital	Evanston	Illinois	847-316-4000	www.reshealth.org
Rio Grande Regional Hospital	Mcallen	Texas	956-632-6000	www.riohealth.com
Rush University Medical Center	Chicago	Illinois	312-942-5000	www.ruch.edu
Saint Anne's Hospital	Fall River	Massachusetts	508-674-5600	www.saintanneshospital.org
Saint Barnabas Medical Center	Livingston	New Jersey	973-322-5000	www.saintbarnabas.com
Saint Joseph Hospital	Chicago	Illinois	773-665-3000	www.res-health.org
Saint Michael's Medical Center	Newark	New Jersey	973-877-5350	www.cathedralhealth.org
Saint Vincent Health Center	Erie	Pennsylvania	814-452-5000	www.svhs.org
Saint Vincent Medical Center	Los Angeles	California	213-484-7111	
Scripps Mercy Hospital	San Diego	California	619-294-8111	www.scrippshealth.org
Sharp Chula Vista Medical Center	Chula Vista	California	619-502-5800	www.sharp.com
Sherman Oaks Hospital	Sherman Oaks	California	818-981-7111	www.shermanoakshospital.com
Sinai-Grace Hospital	Detroit	Michigan	313-966-3300	www.sinaigrace.org
Southcoast Hospital Group	Fall River	Massachusetts	508-679-3131	www.southcoast.org/charlton
Southeast Alabama Medical Center	Dothan	Alabama	334-793-8701	www.samc.org
Southwest General Health Center	Middleburg Heights	Ohio	440-816-8000	www.swgeneral.com
Saint Alexius Medical Center	Hoffman Estates	Illinois	847-843-2000	www.alexianbrothershealth.org
Saint Catherine Hospital	East Chicago	Indiana	219-392-7004	www.comhs.org/stcatherine
Saint Elizabeth Ft Thomas	Fort Thomas	Kentucky	859-572-3100	www.cardinalhill.org
Saint Elizabeth's Medical Center	Brighton	Massachusetts	617-789-3000	www.semc.org
Saint Francis Hospital & Medical Center	Hartford	Connecticut	860-714-4000	www.saintfranciscare.com
Saint Francis Hospital - Roslyn	Roslyn	New York	516-562-6000	www.stfrancisheartcenter.com
Saint James Hospital & Health Center-Olympia Fields	Olympia Fields	Illinois	708-747-4000	
Saint John Hospital and Medical Center	Detroit	Michigan	313-343-4000	www.stjohnprovidence.org
Saint John Macomb-Oakland Hospital-Macomb Center	Warren	Michigan	586-573-5000	www.stjohn.org
Saint John Medical Center	Westlake	Ohio	440-835-8000	www.sjws.net
Saint John's Riverside Hospital	Yonkers	New York	914-964-4444	www.riversidehealth.org
Saint Joseph Hospital	Bethpage	New York	516-579-6000	www.newislandhospital.org
Saint Josephs Hospital	Marshfield	Wisconsin	715-387-7850	www.stjosephs-marshfield.org
Saint Luke's Cornwall Hospital	Newburgh	New York	845-561-4400	www.stlukeshospital.org
Saint Luke's Roosevelt Hospital	New York	New York	212-523-4000	www.wehealny.org
Saint Lukes Episcopal Hospital	Houston	Texas	832-355-1000	www.sleh.com
Saint Vincent Charity Medical Center	Cleveland	Ohio	216-861-6200	
Saint Vincent Hospital & Health Services	Indianapolis	Indiana	317-338-7000	www.indianapolis.stvincent.org
Suburban Hospital	Bethesda	Maryland	301-896-2576	www.suburbanhospital.org
Swedish Covenant Hospital	Chicago	Illinois	773-878-8200	
Thomas Jefferson University Hospital	Philadelphia	Pennsylvania	215-955-6000	www.jeffersonhospital.org
Tomball Regional Hospital	Tomball	Texas	281-351-1623	www.tomballhospital.org
Trumbull Memorial Hospital	Warren	Ohio	330-841-9820	www.trumhosp.org
Union Hospital	Dover	Ohio	330-343-3311	www.unionhospital.org
University Hospital - Stony Brook	Stony Brook	New York	631-444-4000	www.stonybrookmedicalcenter.org
UPMC Mckeesport	McKeesport	Pennsylvania	412-664-2000	www.selectmedicalcorp.com
UPMC Presbyterian Shadyside	Pittsburgh	Pennsylvania	412-647-8788	www.upmc.edu
Upper Valley Medical Center	Troy	Ohio	937-440-7853	www.uvmc.com
Valley Baptist Medical Center	Harlingen	Texas	956-389-1100	www.vbmc.org
Valley Hospital	Ridgewood	New Jersey	201-447-8000	www.valleyhealth.com
Virtua West Jersey Hospitals Berlin	Berlin	New Jersey	856-322-3200	
Washington Hospital Center	Washington	District of Columbia	202-877-7000	www.whcenter.org
Wellstar Kennestone Hospital	Marietta	Georgia	770-793-5000	www.wellstar.org
West Hills Hospital & Medical Center	West Hills	California	818-676-4100	www.westhillshospital.com
Western Pennsylvania Hospital - Forbes Regional Campus	Monroeville	Pennsylvania	412-858-2000	www.wpahs.org
Wheaton Franciscan - St Joseph	Milwaukee	Wisconsin	414-447-2000	www.wfhealthcare.org
William Beaumont Hospital-Troy	Troy	Michigan	248-964-8800	www.beaumonthospitals.com
Willis Knighton Medical Center	Shreveport	Louisiana	318-632-4000	www.wkhs.com//Locations/MedicalCenter.aspx
Wyckoff Heights Medical Center	Brooklyn	New York	718-963-7272	www.wyckoffhospital.org
Yale-New Haven Hospital	New Haven	Connecticut	203-688-4242	www.ynhh.org

Note: Table shows hospitals nationwide whose Heart Failure 30-day risk-adjusted mortality rate is better (lower) than U.S. rate of 11.2%

Hospitals whose Heart Failure 30-Day Mortality Rate is Worse (Higher) than the U.S. National Rate

Hospital	City	State	Phone	Web Site
Adventist Medical Center	Portland	Oregon	503-257-2500	www.adventisthealth.com
Aiken Regional Medical Center	Aiken	South Carolina	803-641-5900	www.aikenregional.com
Alamance Regional Medical Center	Burlington	North Carolina	336-538-7000	www.armc.com
Albany Memorial Hospital	Albany	New York	518-471-3221	www.nehealth.com
American Legion Hospital	Crowley	Louisiana	337-788-6400	
Athens Regional Medical Center	Athens	Tennessee	423-745-1411	www.athensrmc.com
Auburn Regional Medical Center	Auburn	Washington	253-833-7711	www.armcuhs.com/p1.html
Aurora Sheboygan Memorial Medical Center	Sheboygan	Wisconsin	920-451-5000	www.aurorahealthcare.org/facilities
Bay Area Hospital	Coos Bay	Oregon	541-269-8111	www.bayareahospital.org
Beloit Memorial Hospital	Beloit	Wisconsin	608-364-5011	
Blake Medical Center	Bradenton	Florida	941-792-6611	www.blakemedicalcenter.com
Blanchard Valley Hospital	Findlay	Ohio	419-423-4500	www.bvha.org
Blessing Hospital	Quincy	Illinois	217-223-5811	www.blessinghealthsystem.org
Bromenn Healthcare	Normal	Illinois	309-454-1400	
Camden Clark Memorial Hospital	Parkersburg	West Virginia	304-424-2111	www.ccmh.org
Capital Region Medical Center	Jefferson City	Missouri	573-632-5000	www.crmc.org
Centerpoint Medical Center of Independence	Independence	Missouri	816-698-7000	
Central Washington Hospital	Wenatchee	Washington	509-662-1511	www.cwhs.com
Clarion Hospital	Clarion	Pennsylvania	814-226-9500	www.clarionhospital.org
Columbia St Mary's Hospital Ozaukee	Mequon	Wisconsin	262-243-7300	
Community Health Center of Branch County	Coldwater	Michigan	517-279-5400	www.chcbc.com
Community Hospitals and Wellness Centers	Bryan	Ohio	419-636-1131	www.chwchospital.com
Conway Regional Medical Center	Conway	Arkansas	501-329-3831	www.conwayregional.org
Cox Medical Center	Springfield	Missouri	417-269-6000	www.coxhealth.com
Danville Regional Medical Center	Danville	Virginia	434-799-2100	www.danvilleregional.org
Decatur County General Hospital	Parsons	Tennessee	731-847-3031	www.dcgh.org
Decatur Memorial Hospital	Decatur	Illinois	217-877-8121	www.dmhcares.org
Desert Regional Medical Center	Palm Springs	California	760-323-6511	www.desertmedctr.com
Dixie Regional Medical Center	Saint George	Utah	435-251-1000	intermountainhealthcare.org
El Centro Regional Medical Center	El Centro	California	760-339-7100	www.ecrmc.org
Fayette Regional Health System	Connersville	Indiana	765-825-5131	www.fayettememorial.org
Ferrell Hospital Community Foundations	Eldorado	Illinois	618-273-3361	
Fhn Memorial Hospital	Freeport	Illinois	815-235-4131	www.fhn.org
Fletcher Allen Hospital of Vermont	Burlington	Vermont	802-847-0000	www.fletcherallen.org
Forrest General Hospital	Hattiesburg	Mississippi	601-288-7000	www.forrestgeneral.com
Geisinger Medical Center	Danville	Pennsylvania	570-271-6211	www.geisinger.org
Good Samaritan Hospital	Kearney	Nebraska	308-865-7900	www.gshs.org
Good Samaritan Hospital	Lebanon	Pennsylvania	717-270-7500	www.gshleb.org
Grossmont Hospital	La Mesa	California	619-465-0711	www.sharp.com
Halifax Health Medical Center	Daytona Beach	Florida	386-254-4000	www.halifax.org
Harrison Medical Center	Bremerton	Washington	360-377-3911	www.harrisonmedical.org
Harton Regional Medical Center	Tullahoma	Tennessee	931-393-3000	www.hartonmedicalcenter.com
Hendrick Medical Center	Abilene	Texas	325-670-2000	www.ehendrick.org
Henry County Medical Center	Paris	Tennessee	731-642-1220	www.hcmc-tn.org
Highland Hospital	Rochester	New York	585-473-2200	www.urmc.rochester.edu
Holzer Medical Center	Gallipolis	Ohio	740-446-5000	www.holzer.org
Indian River Medical Center	Vero Beach	Florida	772-567-4311	www.irmh.com
Integris Grove Hospital	Grove	Oklahoma	918-786-2243	www.integris-health.com
Kadlec Regional Medical Center	Richland	Washington	509-946-4611	www.kadlecmed.org
Kenmore Mercy Hospital	Kenmore	New York	716-447-6100	www.chsbuffalo.org
Kennewick General Hospital	Kennewick	Washington	509-586-6111	www.kennewickgeneral.com
Lafayette General Medical Center	Lafayette	Louisiana	337-289-7991	www.lafayettegeneral.org
Lake Charles Memorial Hospital	Lake Charles	Louisiana	337-494-3200	www.lcmh.com
Lake Granbury Medical Center	Granbury	Texas	817-573-2683	www.lakegranburymedicalcenter.com
Laporte Hospital and Health Services	La Porte	Indiana	219-326-1234	www.laportehealth.org
Lodi Memorial Hospital	Lodi	California	209-334-3411	www.lodihealth.org
Manatee Memorial Hospital	Bradenton	Florida	941-746-5111	www.manateememorial.com
Marian Medical Center	Santa Maria	California	805-739-3000	www.marinmedicalcenter.org
Marietta Memorial Hospital	Marietta	Ohio	740-374-1400	www.mmhospital.org
Marion General Hospital	Columbia	Mississippi	601-736-6303	
McNairy Regional Hospital	Selmer	Tennessee	731-645-3221	www.mcnairyregionalhospital.com
Memorial Healthcare	Owosso	Michigan	989-723-5211	www.memorialhealthcare.org
Memorial Hospital of Martinsville & Henry County	Martinsville	Virginia	276-666-7200	www.martinsvillehospital.com
Memorial Medical Center	Las Cruces	New Mexico	575-522-8641	www.mmclc.org

Hospital	City	State	Phone	Web Site
Mercy Medical Center Redding	Redding	California	530-225-6102	www.redding.mercy.org
Mercy Medical Center-North Iowa	Mason City	Iowa	641-422-7000	www.mercynorthiowa.com
Metro Health Hospital	Wyoming	Michigan	616-252-7200	www.metrohealth.net
Mid-Columbia Medical Center	The Dalles	Oregon	541-296-1111	www.mcmc.net
Midland Memorial Hospital	Midland	Texas	432-685-1111	www.midland-memorial.com
Mississippi Baptist Medical Center	Jackson	Mississippi	601-968-1000	www.mbmc.org
Missouri Delta Medical Center	Sikeston	Missouri	573-471-1600	www.missouridelta.com
Mount Nittany Medical Center	State College	Pennsylvania	814-231-7000	www.mountnittany.org
Munroe Regional Medical Center	Ocala	Florida	352-351-7200	www.munroeregional.com
National Park Medical Center	Hot Springs	Arkansas	501-321-1000	www.nationalparkmedical.com
NEA Baptist Memorial Hospital	Jonesboro	Arkansas	870-972-7000	www.baptistonline.com
North Mississippi Medical Center	Tupelo	Mississippi	662-377-7176	www.nmhs.net/nmmc
Northwest Hospital	Seattle	Washington	206-364-0500	www.nwhospital.org
Northwestern Medical Center	Saint Albans	Vermont	802-524-1231	www.northwesternmedicalcenter.org
Ogden Regional Medical Center	Ogden	Utah	801-479-2111	
Oneida Healthcare Center	Oneida	New York	315-363-6000	www.oneidahealthcare.org
Otto Kaiser Memorial Hospital	Kenedy	Texas	830-583-3401	www.okmh.net
Our Lady of the Lake Regional Medical Center	Baton Rouge	Louisiana	225-765-8902	www.ololrmc.com
Peacehealth St Joseph Medical Center	Bellingham	Washington	360-734-5400	www.peacehealth.org
Piedmont Medical Center	Rock Hill	South Carolina	803-329-1234	www.piedmontmedicalcenter.com
Pikeville Medical Center	Pikeville	Kentucky	606-437-3500	www.pikevillehospital.org
Providence St Peter Hospital	Olympia	Washington	360-491-9480	www.providence.org/swsa
Putnam Community Medical Center	Palatka	Florida	386-326-8500	www.pcmcfl.com
Rideout Memorial Hospital	Marysville	California	530-749-4300	www.frhg.org
Riverside Medical Center	Waupaca	Wisconsin	715-258-1000	www.riversidemedical.org
Riverview Hospital	Noblesville	Indiana	317-776-7108	www.riverviewhospital.org
Saint Clare Hospital	Lakewood	Washington	253-588-1711	www.fhshealth.org
Saint Francis Medical Center	Peoria	Illinois	309-655-2000	www.osfsaintfrancis.org
Salem Hospital	Salem	Oregon	503-561-2278	www.salemhospital.org
Salina Regional Health Center	Salina	Kansas	785-452-7000	www.srhc.com
Saline Memorial Hospital	Benton	Arkansas	501-776-6000	www.salinememorial.org
Samaritan Hospital	Troy	New York	518-271-3225	www.nehealth.com
Samaritan North Lincoln Hospital	Lincoln City	Oregon	541-994-3661	www.samhealth.org/shs_facilities
Self Regional Healthcare	Greenwood	South Carolina	864-227-4111	www.selfregional.org
Sentara Leigh Hospital	Norfolk	Virginia	757-261-6601	www.sentara.com
Sheridan Memorial Hospital	Sheridan	Wyoming	307-672-1000	www.sheridanhospital.org
Sierra View District Hospital	Porterville	California	559-784-1110	www.sierra-view.com
Skyridge Medical Center	Cleveland	Tennessee	423-339-4132	www.skyridgemedcenter.com
South County Hospital	Wakefield	Rhode Island	401-782-8000	www.schospital.com
South Georgia Medical Center	Valdosta	Georgia	229-333-1020	www.sgmc.org
Southampton Hospital	Southampton	New York	516-726-8200	www.southamptonhospital.org
Southwestern Medical Center	Lawton	Oklahoma	580-531-4700	www.swmconline.com
Southwestern Vermont Medical Center	Bennington	Vermont	802-442-6361	www.svhealthcare.org
Sparks Regional Medical Center	Fort Smith	Arkansas	501-441-4000	www.sparks.org
Saint Agnes Hospital	Fond Du Lac	Wisconsin	920-926-5408	www.agnesian.com
Saint Anthony's Healthcare Center	Morrilton	Arkansas	501-977-2300	stvincenthealth.com
Saint Bernards Medical Center	Jonesboro	Arkansas	870-972-4100	www.sbrmc.com
Saint Francis Hospital	Litchfield	Illinois	217-324-2191	www.stfrancis-litchfield.org
Saint Francis Hospital	Columbus	Georgia	706-596-4020	wecareforlife.com
Saint Francis Medical Center	Cape Girardeau	Missouri	573-331-3000	www.sfmc.net
Saint Joseph Hospital	Eureka	California	707-443-8051	www.stjosepheureka.org
Saint Joseph Hospital	Nashua	New Hampshire	603-882-3000	www.stjosephhospital.com
Saint Joseph Medical Center	Tacoma	Washington	253-627-4101	www.fhshealth.org
Saint Josephs Medical Center of Stockton	Stockton	California	209-943-2000	www.stjosephscares.org
Saint Josephs Mercy Health Center	Hot Springs	Arkansas	501-622-1000	www.saintjosephs.com
Saint Lucie Medical Center	Port Saint Lucie	Florida	772-335-4000	www.stluciemed.com
Saint Mary Medical Center	Langhorne	Pennsylvania	215-750-2003	www.stmaryhealthcare.org
Saint Mary's Medical Center	Huntington	West Virginia	304-526-1234	www.st-marys.org
Saint Peter's Hospital	Helena	Montana	406-442-2100	www.stpetes.org
Summa Health Systems Hospitals	Akron	Ohio	330-375-3000	www.summahealth.org
Summit Medical Center	Hermitage	Tennessee	615-316-3000	www.summitmedctr.com
Sutter Auburn Faith Hospital	Auburn	California	530-888-4500	www.sutterauburnfaith.org
Sycamore Shoals Hospital	Elizabethton	Tennessee	423-542-1300	www.msha.com
Tacoma General Allenmore Hospital	Tacoma	Washington	253-403-1000	www.multicare.org
Tallahassee Memorial Healthcare	Tallahassee	Florida	850-431-1155	www.tmh.org
Thibodaux Regional Medical Center	Thibodaux	Louisiana	985-447-5500	www.thibodaux.com
Three Rivers Community Hospital	Grants Pass	Oregon	541-472-7000	www.asante.org

Hospital	City	State	Phone	Web Site
Trident Medical Center	Charleston	South Carolina	843-797-8800	www.tridenthealthsystem.com
Trinity Medical Center East & Trinity Medical Center West	Steubenville	Ohio	740-264-7212	www.trinityhealth.com
United Memorial Medical Center	Batavia	New York	585-343-6030	www.ummc.org
United Regional Health Care System	Wichita Falls	Texas	940-764-3055	www.urhcs.org
Upson Regional Medical Center	Thomaston	Georgia	706-647-8111	www.urmc.org
Virtua Memorial Hospital of Burlington County	Mount Holly	New Jersey	609-914-6200	www.virtua.org
White County Medical Center	Searcy	Arkansas	501-278-3100	www.centralarkhospital.com
Wilkes-Barre General Hospital	Wilkes-Barre	Pennsylvania	570-829-8111	www.wvhcs.org

Note: Table shows hospitals nationwide whose Heart Failure 30-day risk-adjusted mortality rate is worse (higher) than U.S. rate of 11.2%

Hospitals whose Pneumonia 30-Day Mortality Rate is Better (Lower) than the U.S. National Rate

Hospital	City	State	Phone	Web Site
Abbott Northwestern Hospital	Minneapolis	Minnesota	612-863-4000	www.abbottnorthwestern.com
Advocate Good Samaritan Hospital	Downers Grove	Illinois	630-275-5900	www.advocatehealth.com/gsam
Advocate South Suburban Hospital	Hazel Crest	Illinois	708-799-8000	www.advocatehealth.com
Akron General Medical Center	Akron	Ohio	330-344-6000	www.akrongeneral.org
Alexian Brothers Medical Center	Elk Grove Village	Illinois	847-437-5500	www.alexian.org
Alhambra Hospital Medical Center	Alhambra	California	626-570-1606	www.alhambrahospital.com
Alle Kiski Medical Center	Natrona	Pennsylvania	412-224-5100	www.wpahs.org
Anmed Health	Anderson	South Carolina	864-261-1109	www.anmed.com
Aultman Hospital	Canton	Ohio	330-452-9911	www.aultman.com
Aurelia Osborn Fox Memorial Hospital	Oneonta	New York	607-423-2000	www.foxcarenetwork.com
Aurora West Allis Medical Center	West Allis	Wisconsin	414-328-6000	www.aurorahealthcare.org
Austin Medical Center	Austin	Minnesota	507-433-7351	www.mayohealthsystem.org
Aventura Hospital and Medical Center	Aventura	Florida	305-682-7000	www.aventurahospital.com
Baptist Medical Center	San Antonio	Texas	210-297-1020	www.baptisthealthsystem.org
Bay Medical Center	Panama City	Florida	850-769-1511	www.baymedical.org
Bayshore Community Hospital	Holmdel	New Jersey	732-739-5900	www.bchs.com
Bayshore Medical Center	Pasadena	Texas	713-359-2000	www.bayshoremedical.com
Berkshire Medical Center	Pittsfield	Massachusetts	413-447-2000	www.berkshirehealthsystems.org
Beth Israel Deaconess Medical Center	Boston	Massachusetts	617-667-7000	www.bidmc.harvard.edu
Beth Israel Medical Center	New York	New York	212-420-2000	www.wehealny.org
Betsy Johnson Regional Hospital	Dunn	North Carolina	910-892-7161	www.bjrh.org
Boca Raton Regional Hospital	Boca Raton	Florida	561-362-5002	
Bon Secours - St Francis Xavier Hospital	Charleston	South Carolina	843-402-1000	www.stfrancishealth.org
Boston Medical Center Corporation	Boston	Massachusetts	617-638-8000	www.bmc.org
Bronx-Lebanon Hospital Center	Bronx	New York	212-588-7000	www.bronx-leb.org
Calvert Memorial Hospital	Prince Frederick	Maryland	410-535-8239	www.calverthospital.com
Candler Hospital	Savannah	Georgia	912-819-6000	
Cape Regional Medical Center	Cape May Court House	New Jersey	609-463-2000	www.caperegional.com
Cedars-Sinai Medical Center	Los Angeles	California	310-423-5000	www.cedars-sinai.edu
Centura Health-Penrose St Francis Health Services	Colorado Springs	Colorado	719-776-5000	www.centurahealth.com
Centura Health-Porter Adventist Hospital	Denver	Colorado	303-778-1955	www.centura.org
Christ Hospital	Cincinnati	Ohio	513-585-2771	www.thechristhospital.com
Christus St Michael Health System	Texarkana	Texas	903-614-1000	www.christusstmichael.org
Clark Regional Medical Center	Winchester	Kentucky	859-745-3500	www.clarkregional.org
Coffeyville Regional Medical Center	Coffeyville	Kansas	620-252-1200	www.crmcinc.com
Community Hospital	Munster	Indiana	219-836-1600	www.comhs.org/community
Community Medical Center	Toms River	New Jersey	732-557-8000	www.sbhcs.com
The Cooley Dickinson Hospital	Northampton	Massachusetts	413-582-2000	www.cooley-dickinson.org
Coral Gables Hospital	Coral Gables	Florida	305-445-8461	www.coralgableshospital.com
Covenant Medical Center	Lubbock	Texas	806-725-6000	www.covenanthealth.org
Crittenden Health System	Marion	Kentucky	270-965-5281	www.crittenden-health.org
Cumberland River Hospital	Celina	Tennessee	931-243-3581	
D C H Regional Medical Center	Tuscaloosa	Alabama	205-759-7111	www.dchsystem.com
Danbury Hospital	Danbury	Connecticut	203-797-7000	www.danburyhospital.com
Delray Medical Center	Delray Beach	Florida	561-498-4440	www.delraymedicalctr.com
Doctors Hospital	Dallas	Texas	214-324-6100	www.doctorshospitaldallas.com
Doctors Hospital	Coral Gables	Florida	305-666-2111	www.baptisthealth.net
East Valley Hospital Medical Center	Glendora	California	626-335-0231	www.eastvalleyhospital.org
Easton Hospital	Easton	Pennsylvania	610-250-4076	www.easton-hospital.com
Elmhurst Memorial Hospital	Elmhurst	Illinois	630-833-1400	www.emhc.org
Emh Regional Medical Center	Elyria	Ohio	440-329-7500	
Encino Hospital Medical Center	Encino	California	818-995-5000	www.encino-tarzana.com
Essentia Health St Joseph's Medical Center	Brainerd	Minnesota	218-829-2861	www.sjmcmn.org
Evanston Hospital	Evanston	Illinois	847-432-8000	www.enh.org
Evergreen Hospital Medical Center	Kirkland	Washington	425-899-1000	www.evergreenhospital.org
Exeter Hospital	Exeter	New Hampshire	603-778-7311	
Fairview Hospital	Cleveland	Ohio	216-476-7000	www.fairviewhospital.org
Falmouth Hospital	Falmouth	Massachusetts	508-548-5300	www.capecodhealth.com
Faxton-St Luke's Healthcare	Utica	New York	315-798-6000	
Flagler Hospital	Saint Augustine	Florida	904-819-4426	www.flaglerhospital.com
Florida Hospital	Orlando	Florida	407-303-1976	www.floridahospital.com
Franciscan St Margaret Health - Hammond	Hammond	Indiana	219-932-2300	www.smmhc.com
Franklin Square Hospital Center	Baltimore	Maryland	443-777-7850	www.franklinsquare.org
Frederick Memorial Hospital	Frederick	Maryland	240-566-3300	www.fmh.org

Hospital	City	State	Phone	Web Site
Genesys Regional Medical Center - Health Park	Grand Blanc	Michigan	810-606-5000	www.genesys.org
Good Samaritan Hospital	Baltimore	Maryland	443-444-3902	www.goodsam-md.org
Good Samaritan Medical Center	West Palm Beach	Florida	561-655-5511	www.goodsamartianmc.com
Greater Baltimore Medical Center	Baltimore	Maryland	443-849-2121	www.gbmc.org
Gulf Coast Medical Center	Panama City	Florida	850-747-7926	www.egulfcoastmedical.com
Hackensack University Medical Center	Hackensack	New Jersey	201-996-2000	www.humed.com
Hackettstown Regional Medical Center	Hackettstown	New Jersey	908-852-5100	www.hrmcnj.org
Hallmark Health System	Melrose	Massachusetts	781-979-3000	www.hallmarkhealth.org
Hamilton General Hospital	Hamilton	Texas	254-386-3151	www.hamiltonhospital.org
Hamot Medical Center	Erie	Pennsylvania	814-877-6000	www.hamot.org
Harmon Memorial Hospital	Hollis	Oklahoma	580-688-3363	
Harper University Hospital	Detroit	Michigan	313-745-6211	www.harperhospital.org
Hazleton General Hospital	Hazleton	Pennsylvania	570-501-4000	www.ghha.org
Henry Ford Macomb Hospital	Clinton Township	Michigan	586-263-2300	www.stjoe-macomb.com
Hillcrest Hospital	Mayfield Heights	Ohio	440-312-4500	www.hillcresthospital.org
Homestead Hospital	Homestead	Florida	786-243-8000	www.baptisthealth.net
The Hospital of Central Connecticut	New Britain	Connecticut	860-224-5011	www.thocc.org
Hospital of St Raphael	New Haven	Connecticut	203-789-3000	www.srhs.org
Houston Medical Center	Warner Robins	Georgia	478-922-4281	www.hhc.org
Howard Regional Health System	Kokomo	Indiana	765-453-8371	www.howardcommunity.org
Huntington Hospital	Huntington	New York	631-351-2000	www.hunthosp.org
Huntington Memorial Hospital	Pasadena	California	626-397-5000	www.huntingtonhospital.com
Ingalls Memorial Hospital	Harvey	Illinois	708-333-2300	www.ingalls.org
Inland Hospital	Waterville	Maine	207-861-3000	www.inlandhospital.org
Integris Clinton Regional Hospital	Clinton	Oklahoma	580-323-2363	www.integris-health.com
Integris Southwest Medical Center	Oklahoma City	Oklahoma	405-636-7777	www.integris-health.com
J C Blair Memorial Hospital	Huntingdon	Pennsylvania	814-643-2290	www.jcblair.org
John Muir Medical Center - Walnut Creek Campus	Walnut Creek	California	925-939-3000	www.jmmdhs.com
Jupiter Medical Center	Jupiter	Florida	561-747-2234	www.jupitermed.com
Kingsbrook Jewish Medical Center	Brooklyn	New York	718-604-5789	www.kingsbrook.org
Lake Forest Hospital	Lake Forest	Illinois	847-234-5600	www.lakeforesthospital.com
Lakewood Hospital	Lakewood	Ohio	216-529-4200	www.lakewoodhospital.org
Laredo Medical Center	Laredo	Texas	956-796-5000	www.laredomedical.com
Larkin Community Hospital	South Miami	Florida	305-284-7500	www.larkinhospital.com
Lawrence General Hospital	Lawrence	Massachusetts	978-683-4000	www.lawrencegeneral.org
Lehigh Valley Hospital	Allentown	Pennsylvania	610-402-2273	www.lvhhn.org
Lehigh Valley Hospital - Muhlenberg	Bethlehem	Pennsylvania	610-402-2273	www.lvhn.org
Liberty Hospital	Liberty	Missouri	816-781-7200	www.libertyhospital.org
Lutheran Medical Center	Brooklyn	New York	718-630-8000	www.lmcmc.com
Maimonides Medical Center	Brooklyn	New York	718-283-6000	www.maimonidesmed.org
Main Line Hospital Lankenau	Wynnewood	Pennsylvania	610-645-2000	www.mainlinehealth.org/lh
Mainland Medical Center	Texas City	Texas	409-938-5000	www.mainlandmedical.com
Marshall Medical Center (1-Rh)	Placerville	California	530-622-1441	www.marshallmedical.org
Mary Greeley Medical Center	Ames	Iowa	515-239-2011	www.mgmc.org
Massachusetts General Hospital	Boston	Massachusetts	617-726-2000	www.massgeneral.org
Mayo Clinic Hospital	Phoenix	Arizona	480-515-6296	www.mayoclinic.org
Mclaren Regional Medical Center	Flint	Michigan	810-342-2000	www.mclaren.org
Memorial Hospital York	York	Pennsylvania	717-843-8623	www.mhyork.org
Mercy Health Partners - Hackley Campus	Muskegon	Michigan	231-726-3511	www.hackley.org
Mercy Hospital	Iowa City	Iowa	319-339-0300	www.mercyiowacity.org
Mercy Hospital - Grayling	Grayling	Michigan	989-348-5461	www.mercygrayling.munsonhealthcare.org
Mercy Hospital	Miami	Florida	305-285-2121	www.mercymiami.com
Methodist Hospital	San Antonio	Texas	210-575-4000	www.mh.sahealth.com
Methodist Hospital of Chicago	Chicago	Illinois	773-271-9040	www.methodistchicago.org
The Methodist Hospital	Houston	Texas	713-790-2221	www.methodisthealth.com
Metrosouth Medical Center	Blue Island	Illinois	708-597-2000	www.stfrancisblueisland.com
Miami Valley Hospital	Dayton	Ohio	937-208-8000	www.miamivalleyhospital.com
Mission Regional Medical Center	Mission	Texas	956-323-9000	www.missionhospital.org
Missouri Baptist Medical Center	Town and Country	Missouri	314-996-5000	www.missouribaptistmedicalcenter.org
Monmouth Medical Center	Long Branch	New Jersey	732-222-5200	www.sbhcs.com
Montgomery General Hospital	Olney	Maryland	301-774-8771	www.montgomerygeneral.com
Mount Auburn Hospital	Cambridge	Massachusetts	617-492-3500	
Mount Sinai Hospital	New York	New York	212-241-7981	www.mountsinai.org
Mount Sinai Medical Center	Miami Beach	Florida	305-674-2121	www.msmc.com
Munson Medical Center	Traverse City	Michigan	231-935-5000	www.munsonhealthcare.org
Natchitoches Regional Medical Center	Natchitoches	Louisiana	318-352-1200	www.natchitocheshospital.org
New York-Presbyterian Hospital	New York	New York	212-746-4189	www.nyp.org

Hospital	City	State	Phone	Web Site
Newton-Wellesley Hospital	Newton	Massachusetts	617-243-6000	www.nwh.org
North Kansas City Hospital	North Kansas City	Missouri	816-691-2000	www.nkch.org
North Shore Medical Center	Salem	Massachusetts	978-741-1215	
Norwood Hospital	Norwood	Massachusetts	508-772-1000	www.caritasnorwood.org
NYU Hospitals Center	New York	New York	212-263-7300	www.med.nyu.edu
O'Bleness Memorial Hospital	Athens	Ohio	740-593-5551	www.obleness.org
Ocean Medical Center	Brick	New Jersey	732-840-2200	www.meridianhealth.com/mcoc.cfm/ind
Ouachita County Medical Center	Camden	Arkansas	870-836-1000	www.ouachitamedcenter.com
Pacific Alliance Medical Center	Los Angeles	California	213-624-8411	www.pamc.net
Palos Community Hospital	Palos Heights	Illinois	708-923-4000	www.paloshospital.org
Park Nicollet Methodist Hospital	Saint Louis Park	Minnesota	952-993-5000	www.parknicollet.com/methodist
Parkview Adventist Medical Center	Brunswick	Maine	207-373-2000	www.parkviewamc.org
Parkview Medical Center	Pueblo	Colorado	719-584-4000	www.parkviewmc.com
Peninsula Regional Medical Center	Salisbury	Maryland	410-543-7116	www.peninsula.org
Perry Hospital	Perry	Georgia	478-987-3600	www.hhc.org
Piedmont Fayette Hospital	Fayetteville	Georgia	770-719-7071	www.fayettehospital.org
Piedmont Hospital	Atlanta	Georgia	404-605-5000	www.piedmonthospital.org
Presbyterian Intercommunity Hospital	Whittier	California	526-698-0811	www.whittierpres.com
Provena-Saint Joseph Hospital	Elgin	Illinois	847-695-3200	www.provenasaintjoeph.com
Provena St Joseph Medical Center	Joliet	Illinois	815-725-7133	www.provena.org/stjoes
Providence Hospital and Medical Centers	Southfield	Michigan	248-849-3011	www.stjohn.org/Providence
Providence Medical Center	Kansas City	Kansas	913-596-3930	www.providence-health.org
Putnam Hospital Center	Carmel	New York	914-279-5711	www.putnamhospital.org
Raritan Bay Medical Center	Perth Amboy	New Jersey	732-442-3700	
Rex Hospital	Raleigh	North Carolina	919-784-3100	www.rexhealth.com
Richland Parish Hospital-Delhi	Delhi	Louisiana	318-878-5171	www.delhihospital.com
Rogue Valley Medical Center	Medford	Oregon	541-789-7000	www.asante.org
Saint John's Health Center	Santa Monica	California	310-829-5511	www.stjohns.org
Saint John's Health System	Anderson	Indiana	765-649-2511	www.stjohnshealthsystem.org
Saint Joseph Hospital	Chicago	Illinois	773-665-3000	www.res-health.org
Saint Joseph Hospital London	London	Kentucky	606-330-6000	www.sjhlex.org
Saint Marys Hospital	Waterbury	Connecticut	203-574-6000	
Saint Vincent Medical Center	Los Angeles	California	213-484-7111	
San Gabriel Valley Medical Center	San Gabriel	California	626-289-5454	www.sangabrielvalleymedctr.org
San Luis Valley Regional Medical Center	Alamosa	Colorado	719-589-2511	www.slvrmc.org
Scripps Mercy Hospital	San Diego	California	619-294-8111	www.scrippshealth.org
Seton Northwest Hospital	Austin	Texas	512-324-6000	www.seton.net
Seton Medical Center Austin	Austin	Texas	512-324-1000	www.seton.net
Shore Memorial Hospital	Somers Point	New Jersey	609-653-3545	www.shorememorial.org
Skaggs Community Health Center	Branson	Missouri	417-335-7000	www.skaggs.net
Skokie Hospital	Skokie	Illinois	847-677-9600	
South Pointe Hospital	Warrensville Heights	Ohio	216-491-6000	www.southpointehospital.org
Southampton Hospital	Southampton	New York	516-726-8200	www.southamptonhospital.org
Southeast Alabama Medical Center	Dothan	Alabama	334-793-8701	www.samc.org
Southern Ohio Medical Center	Portsmouth	Ohio	740-354-5000	www.somc.org
Southwest General Health Center	Middleburg Heights	Ohio	440-816-8000	www.swgeneral.com
SSM St Joseph Hospital West	Lake Saint Louis	Missouri	636-625-5200	
Saint Alexius Medical Center	Hoffman Estates	Illinois	847-843-2000	www.alexianbrothershealth.org
Saint Cloud Hospital	Saint Cloud	Minnesota	320-251-2700	www.centracare.com
Saint Francis Health Center	Topeka	Kansas	785-295-8000	www.stfrancistopeka.org
Saint Francis Hospital and Health Centers-Indianapolis	Indianapolis	Indiana	317-865-5001	www.stfrancishospitals.org
Saint Francis Hospital - Roslyn	Roslyn	New York	516-562-6000	www.stfrancisheartcenter.com
Saint John Medical Center	Westlake	Ohio	440-835-8000	www.sjws.net
Saint John's Episcopal Hospital at South Shore	Far Rockaway	New York	718-869-7000	
Saint John's Riverside Hospital	Yonkers	New York	914-964-4444	www.riversidehealth.org
Saint Joseph Health Center	Warren	Ohio	330-841-4000	
Saint Luke's Hospital Bethlehem	Bethlehem	Pennsylvania	610-954-4000	www.slhn-lehighvalley.org
Saint Lukes Hospital	Cedar Rapids	Iowa	319-369-7211	www.crstlukes.com
Saint Lukes Hospital	Chesterfield	Missouri	314-434-1500	www.goodhealthmatters.com
Saint Mary & Elizabeth Medical Center-Division Campus	Chicago	Illinois	312-633-5896	www.reshealth.org
Saint Mary Medical Center	Long Beach	California	562-491-9000	www.stmarymedicalcenter.org
Saint Mary Medical Center	Hobart	Indiana	219-942-0551	
Saint Marys Hospital	Centralia	Illinois	618-436-8000	www.stmarys-goodsamaritan.com
Saint Vincent Hospital & Health Services	Indianapolis	Indiana	317-338-7000	www.indianapolis.stvincent.org
Suburban Hospital	Bethesda	Maryland	301-896-2576	www.suburbanhospital.org
Swedish Covenant Hospital	Chicago	Illinois	773-878-8200	
Texas Health Harris Methodist Hospital - SW Fort Worth	Fort Worth	Texas	817-433-5000	www.texahealth.org

Hospital	City	State	Phone	Web Site
Tomball Regional Hospital	Tomball	Texas	281-351-1623	www.tomballhospital.org
Tri-City Regional Medical Center	Hawaiian Gardens	California	562-860-0401	www.tri-cityrmc.org
Tuba City Regional Health Care Corporation	Tuba City	Arizona	928-283-2501	www.tcrhcc.org
Unicoi County Memorial Hospital	Erwin	Tennessee	423-743-3141	
United Hospital Center	Bridgeport	West Virginia	681-342-1000	www.uhcwv.org
University of Michigan Health System	Ann Arbor	Michigan	734-764-1505	www.med.umich.edu
UPMC Presbyterian Shadyside	Pittsburgh	Pennsylvania	412-647-8788	www.upmc.edu
Valley Baptist Medical Center	Harlingen	Texas	956-389-1100	www.vbmc.org
Valley Baptist Medical Center - Brownsville	Brownsville	Texas	956-544-1400	www.brownsvillemedical.com
Valley Hospital	Ridgewood	New Jersey	201-447-8000	www.valleyhealth.com
Via Christi Hospitals Wichita	Wichita	Kansas	316-268-5000	www.via-christi.org
Virginia Mason Medical Center	Seattle	Washington	206-223-6600	www.vmmc.org
Wadley Regional Medical Center	Texarkana	Texas	903-798-8000	www.wadleyhealth.com
Western Pennsylvania Hospital - Forbes Regional Campus	Monroeville	Pennsylvania	412-858-2000	www.wpahs.org
Westlake Regional Hospital	Columbia	Kentucky	270-384-4753	www.westlake-healthcare.org
William Beaumont Hospital	Royal Oak	Michigan	248-898-5000	www.beaumonthospitals.com
William Beaumont Hospital-Troy	Troy	Michigan	248-964-8800	www.beaumonthospitals.com
Willis Knighton Bossier Health Center	Bossier City	Louisiana	318-212-7000	www.wkhs.com/Locations/Bossier.aspx
Willis Knighton Medical Center	Shreveport	Louisiana	318-632-4000	www.wkhs.com//Locations/MedicalCenter.aspx
Winchester Hospital	Winchester	Massachusetts	781-729-9000	www.winchesterhospital.org
Yale-New Haven Hospital	New Haven	Connecticut	203-688-4242	www.ynhh.org

Note: Table shows hospitals nationwide whose Pneumonia 30-day risk-adjusted mortality rate is better (lower) than U.S. rate of 11.6%

Hospitals whose Pneumonia 30-Day Mortality Rate is Worse (Higher) than the U.S. National Rate

Hospital	City	State	Phone	Web Site
Abilene Regional Medical Center	Abilene	Texas	325-428-1000	www.abileneregional.com
Adventist Medical Center	Portland	Oregon	503-257-2500	www.adventisthealth.com
Aiken Regional Medical Center	Aiken	South Carolina	803-641-5900	www.aikenregional.com
Athens Regional Medical Center	Athens	Tennessee	423-745-1411	www.athensrmc.com
Aurora Lakeland Medical Center	Elkhorn	Wisconsin	262-741-2000	www.aurorahealthcare.org/facilities
Baptist Memorial Hospital Golden Triangle	Columbus	Mississippi	662-244-1500	www.bmhcc.org/facilities/goldentriangle
Baylor Medical Center at Waxahachie	Waxahachie	Texas	972-923-7000	www.bhcs.com/locations/waxahachie
Beloit Memorial Hospital	Beloit	Wisconsin	608-364-5011	
Blanchard Valley Hospital	Findlay	Ohio	419-423-4500	www.bvha.org
Blessing Hospital	Quincy	Illinois	217-223-5811	www.blessinghealthsystem.org
Boulder City Hospital	Boulder City	Nevada	702-293-4111	www.bouldercityhospital.org
Bromenn Healthcare	Normal	Illinois	309-454-1400	
Cabell-Huntington Hospital	Huntington	West Virginia	304-526-2000	www.cabellhuntington.org
Cameron Regional Medical Center	Cameron	Missouri	816-632-2101	www.cameronregional.org
Cannon Memorial Hospital	Pickens	South Carolina	864-878-4791	www.cannonhospital.org
Canton-Potsdam Hospital	Potsdam	New York	315-265-3300	www.cphospital.org
Capital Region Medical Center	Jefferson City	Missouri	573-632-5000	www.crmc.org
Carilion Medical Center	Roanoke	Virginia	540-981-7000	www.carilion.com/crmh
Carlisle Regional Medical Center	Carlisle	Pennsylvania	717-249-1212	www.carlislermc.com
Carolina East Medical Center	New Bern	North Carolina	252-633-8640	www.cravenhealthcare.org
Carson Tahoe Regional Medical Center	Carson City	Nevada	775-445-8000	www.carsontahoehospital.com
Carteret General Hospital	Morehead City	North Carolina	252-808-6000	www.ccgh.org
Cass Medical Center	Harrisonville	Missouri	816-380-5888	www.cassregional.org
Catawba Valley Medical Center	Hickory	North Carolina	828-326-3809	www.catawbavalleymc.org
Chadron Community Hospital and Health Services	Chadron	Nebraska	308-432-5586	www.chadronhospital.com
Citrus Memorial Hospital	Inverness	Florida	352-726-1551	www.citrusmh.com
Clarinda Regional Health Center	Clarinda	Iowa	712-542-2176	www.clarindahealth.com
Coleman County Medical Center	Coleman	Texas	325-625-2135	
Community-General Hospital of Greater Syracuse	Syracuse	New York	315-492-5011	www.cgh.org
Concord Hospital	Concord	New Hampshire	603-225-2711	www.concordhospital.org
Conway Regional Medical Center	Conway	Arkansas	501-329-3831	www.conwayregional.org
Corona Regional Medical Center	Corona	California	951-737-4343	www.coronaregional.com
Covenant Hospital Plainview	Plainview	Texas	806-296-5531	www.covenantplainview.org
Covington County Hospital	Collins	Mississippi	601-765-6711	
Dameron Hospital	Stockton	California	209-944-5550	www.dameronhospital.org
Danville Regional Medical Center	Danville	Virginia	434-799-2100	www.danvilleregional.org
Decatur County General Hospital	Parsons	Tennessee	731-847-3031	www.dcgh.org
Delano Regional Medical Center	Delano	California	661-725-4800	www.drmc.com
Dyersburg Regional Medical Center	Dyersburg	Tennessee	731-285-2410	
Eastern Niagara Hospital	Lockport	New York	716-514-5700	
Elliot Hospital	Manchester	New Hampshire	603-669-5300	www.elliothospital.org
Elmhurst Hospital Center	Elmhurst	New York	718-334-1141	nyc.gov
Emanuel Medical Center	Turlock	California	209-667-4200	www.emanuelmedicalcenter.org
Fairchild Medical Center	Yreka	California	530-842-4121	www.fairchildmed.org
Fairview Park Hospital	Dublin	Georgia	478-274-3100	www.fairviewparkhospital.com
Firelands Regional Medical Center	Sandusky	Ohio	419-557-7400	www.firelands.com
Fletcher Allen Hospital of Vermont	Burlington	Vermont	802-847-0000	www.fletcherallen.org
Flushing Hospital Medical Center	Flushing	New York	718-670-5000	www.flushinghospital.org
Frye Regional Medical Center	Hickory	North Carolina	828-322-6070	www.fryemedctr.com
Gateway Medical Center	Clarksville	Tennessee	931-502-1000	www.todaysgateway.com
Good Samaritan Hospital	San Jose	California	408-559-2011	www.goodsamsj.org
Good Samaritan Hospital	Lebanon	Pennsylvania	717-270-7500	www.gshleb.org
Greater Regional Medical Center	Creston	Iowa	641-782-7091	
Guadalupe Regional Medical Center	Seguin	Texas	830-379-2411	www.gvh.com
Hammond Henry Hospital	Geneseo	Illinois	309-944-6431	www.hammondhenry.com
Hanford Community Medical Center	Hanford	California	559-582-9000	www.hanfordhealth.com
Hardin Medical Center	Savannah	Tennessee	731-926-8121	
Hardin Memorial Hospital	Kenton	Ohio	419-673-0761	www.hardinmemorial.org
Harrison County Hospital	Corydon	Indiana	812-738-4251	www.hchin.org
Harrison Memorial Hospital	Cynthiana	Kentucky	859-234-2300	www.harrisonmemhosp.com
Hart County Hospital	Hartwell	Georgia	706-856-6113	www.tycobbhealthcaresystem.org
Hawaii Medical Center East	Honolulu	Hawaii	808-547-6011	www.hawaiimedcent.com
Hemet Valley Medical Center	Hemet	California	951-652-2811	www.valleyhealthsystem.com/hemmain
Herrin Hospital	Herrin	Illinois	618-942-2171	www.sih.net

Hospital	City	State	Phone	Web Site
Hi-Desert Medical Center	Joshua Tree	California	760-366-6285	www.hdmc.org
Holdenville General Hospital	Holdenville	Oklahoma	405-379-4200	
Holland Community Hospital	Holland	Michigan	616-392-5141	www.hoho.org
Hospital De La Concepcion	San German	Puerto Rico	787-892-1860	www.hospitalconcepcion.org
Hospital Dr Cayetano Coll y Toste	Arecibo	Puerto Rico	787-650-7272	
Hospital Hima-San Pablo Bayamon	Bayamon	Puerto Rico	787-620-4747	
Hospital Dr Federico Trilla	Carolina	Puerto Rico	787-757-1800	
Iberia General Hospital and Medical Center	New Iberia	Louisiana	337-374-7104	www.iberiamedicalcenter.com
Indian River Medical Center	Vero Beach	Florida	772-567-4311	www.irmh.com
Integris Grove Hospital	Grove	Oklahoma	918-786-2243	www.integris-health.com
IU Health Goshen Hospital	Goshen	Indiana	574-533-2141	www.goshenhosp.com
Jane Phillips Medical Center	Bartlesville	Oklahoma	918-333-7200	www.jpmc.org
Jefferson County Health Center	Fairfield	Iowa	641-472-4111	www.jchospital.org
Jefferson Regional Medical Center	Pine Bluff	Arkansas	870-541-7100	www.jrmc.org
Jennie Edmundson Hospital	Council Bluffs	Iowa	712-396-6000	www.bestcare.org
Jennie Stuart Medical Center	Hopkinsville	Kentucky	270-887-0100	www.jsmc.org
Johnston Memorial Hospital	Abingdon	Virginia	276-676-7000	www.jmh.org
Kaweah Delta Medical Center	Visalia	California	559-624-2000	www.kaweahdelta.org
Lake Pointe Medical Center	Rowlett	Texas	972-412-2273	www.lakepointemedical.com
Laurens County Healthcare System	Clinton	South Carolina	864-833-9100	www.lchcs.org
Leesburg Regional Medical Center	Leesburg	Florida	352-323-5762	www.leesburgregional.org
Limestone Medical Center	Groesbeck	Texas	254-729-3281	lmchospital.com
Litzenberg Memorial County Hospital	Central City	Nebraska	308-946-3015	www.lmchealth.com
Lodi Memorial Hospital	Lodi	California	209-334-3411	www.lodihealth.org
Lompoc Valley Medical Center	Lompoc	California	805-737-3300	lompochospital.org
Madera Community Hospital	Madera	California	559-675-5555	www.maderahospital.org
Madison St Joseph Health Center	Madisonville	Texas	936-348-2631	www.st-joseph.org/madison
Manatee Memorial Hospital	Bradenton	Florida	941-746-5111	www.manateememorial.com
Manati Medical Center Dr Otero Lopez	Manati	Puerto Rico	787-621-3700	www.mmcaol.com
Margaret Mary Community Hospital	Batesville	Indiana	812-934-6624	www.mmch.org
Maria Parham Hospital	Henderson	North Carolina	252-438-4143	www.mphosp.org
Marshall County Hospital	Benton	Kentucky	270-527-4800	
Mary Hitchcock Memorial Hospital	Lebanon	New Hampshire	603-650-5000	www.dhmc.org
Massena Memorial Hospital	Massena	New York	315-764-1711	www.massenahospital.org
Maury Regional Hospital	Columbia	Tennessee	931-381-1111	www.maurgregional.com
McDuffie Regional Medical Center	Thomson	Georgia	706-595-1411	
Medical Center of Central Georgia	Macon	Georgia	478-633-6805	www.mccg.org
Medical Center South Arkansas	El Dorado	Arkansas	870-863-2000	www.themedcenter.net
Medical College of Georgia Hospitals and Clinics	Augusta	Georgia	706-721-6569	www.mcghealth.org
Memorial Community Hospital	Blair	Nebraska	402-426-2182	www.mchhs.org
Memorial Health System of East Texas - Lufkin	Lufkin	Texas	936-634-8111	www.mymemorialhealth.org
Memorial Healthcare	Owosso	Michigan	989-723-5211	www.memorialhealthcare.org
Memorial Hermann Baptist Beaumont Hospital	Beaumont	Texas	409-212-5012	www.mhbh.org
Memorial Medical Center	Springfield	Illinois	217-788-3000	www.memorialmedical.com
Mena Regional Health System	Mena	Arkansas	479-394-6100	
Menifee Valley Medical Center	Sun City	California	951-679-8888	www.valleyhealthsystem.com
Mercy Health Center	Oklahoma City	Oklahoma	405-755-1515	www.mercyok.net/mhc
Mercy Hospital of Defiance	Defiance	Ohio	419-782-8444	
Mercy Hospital of Kansas Independence	Independence	Kansas	620-331-2200	
Mercy Medical Center-North Iowa	Mason City	Iowa	641-422-7000	www.mercynorthiowa.com
Mercy Memorial Health Center	Ardmore	Oklahoma	405-223-5400	www.mercyok.com/mmhc
Methodist Healthcare Memphis Hospitals	Memphis	Tennessee	901-516-8274	www.methodisthealth.org
Midland Memorial Hospital	Midland	Texas	432-685-1111	www.midland-memorial.com
Milton S Hershey Medical Center	Hershey	Pennsylvania	717-531-8521	www.hmc.psu.edu
Morehead Memorial Hospital	Eden	North Carolina	336-623-9711	www.morehead.org
Morrow County Hospital	Mount Gilead	Ohio	419-949-3180	www.morrowcountyhospital.com
The Moses H Cone Memorial Hospital	Greensboro	North Carolina	336-832-7000	www.mosescone.com
Natchez Regional Medical Center	Natchez	Mississippi	601-443-2100	
Nemaha County Hospital	Auburn	Nebraska	402-274-4366	www.nchnet.org
North Carolina Baptist Hospital	Winston-Salem	North Carolina	336-716-2011	www.wfubmc.edu
Olympic Medical Center	Port Angeles	Washington	360-417-7000	www.olympicmedical.org
Oneida Healthcare Center	Oneida	New York	315-363-6000	www.oneidahealthcare.org
Oswego Hospital	Oswego	New York	315-349-5511	www.oswegohealth.org
Our Lady of the Lake Regional Medical Center	Baton Rouge	Louisiana	225-765-8902	www.ololrmc.com
Paris Regional Medical Center	Paris	Texas	903-785-4521	www.parisregional.com
Passavant Area Hospital	Jacksonville	Illinois	217-245-9551	www.passavanthospital.com
Penobscot Valley Hospital	Lincoln	Maine	207-794-3321	www.pvhhealthcare.org

Hospital	City	State	Phone	Web Site
Perry Memorial Hospital	Princeton	Illinois	815-875-2811	www.perry-memorial.org
Phelps County Regional Medical Center	Rolla	Missouri	573-458-8899	www.rollanet.org/~pcrmc
Phoebe Putney Memorial Hospital	Albany	Georgia	229-312-4053	www.phoebeputney.com
Phoenixville Hospital	Phoenixville	Pennsylvania	610-983-1000	www.pennhealth.com
Piedmont Medical Center	Rock Hill	South Carolina	803-329-1234	www.piedmontmedicalcenter.com
Pike Community Hospital	Waverly	Ohio	740-947-2186	
Pikeville Medical Center	Pikeville	Kentucky	606-437-3500	www.pikevillehospital.org
Pioneer Health Services of Patrick County	Stuart	Virginia	276-694-8678	www.rjrhospital.com
Pomerado Hospital	Poway	California	858-485-6511	www.pph.org
Ponca City Medical Center	Ponca City	Oklahoma	580-765-3321	www.poncamedcenter.com
Poplar Bluff Regional Medical Center	Poplar Bluff	Missouri	573-686-5313	www.poplarbluffregional.com
Pottstown Memorial Medical Center	Pottstown	Pennsylvania	610-327-7000	www.pmmctr.org
Proctor Hospital	Peoria	Illinois	309-691-1000	www.proctor.org
Putnam County Hospital	Greencastle	Indiana	765-655-2620	
Regional West Medical Center	Scottsbluff	Nebraska	308-635-3711	www.rwmc.net
River Parishes Hospital	Laplace	Louisiana	985-652-7000	www.riverparisheshospital.com
River Region Health System	Vicksburg	Mississippi	601-883-5000	www.riverregion.com
Riverside Medical Center	Waupaca	Wisconsin	715-258-1000	www.riversidemedical.org
Roane General Hospital	Spencer	West Virginia	304-927-4444	www.roanegeneralhospital.com
Rockcastle Regional Hospital & Respiratory Care Center	Mount Vernon	Kentucky	606-256-2195	www.rockcastlehospital.com
Rockdale Medical Center	Conyers	Georgia	770-918-3000	www.rockdalehospital.org
Russell County Medical Center	Lebanon	Virginia	276-883-8000	
Ryder Memorial Hospital	Humacao	Puerto Rico	787-852-0768	
Saint Agnes Medical Center	Fresno	California	559-450-3000	www.samc.com
Saint Mary's Regional Medical Center	Reno	Nevada	775-770-3000	www.saintmarysreno.com
Samaritan Hospital	Moses Lake	Washington	509-765-5606	www.samaritanhealthcare.com
Samaritan Medical Center	Watertown	New York	315-785-4121	www.samaritanhealth.com
San Gorgonio Memorial Hospital	Banning	California	951-769-2101	www.sgmh.org
San Luke's Memorial Hospital	Ponce	Puerto Rico	787-844-2080	www.ssepr.com/hospital_sanlucas.html
Scenic Mountain Medical Center	Big Spring	Texas	432-263-1211	www.smmccares.com
Selby General Hospital	Marietta	Ohio	740-568-2000	www.selbygeneralhospital.con
Self Regional Healthcare	Greenwood	South Carolina	864-227-4111	www.selfregional.org
Sentara Obici Hospital	Suffolk	Virginia	757-934-4000	www.sentara.com
Seven Rivers Regional Medical Center	Crystal River	Florida	352-795-6560	www.srrmc.com
Shands Live Oak Regional Medical Center	Live Oak	Florida	904-362-1413	www.shands.org
Sharp Memorial Hospital	San Diego	California	858-939-3400	www.sharp.com/memorial
Sierra View District Hospital	Porterville	California	559-784-1110	www.sierra-view.com
Simpson General Hospital	Mendenhall	Mississippi	601-847-2221	www.simpsongeneralhospital.com
Skagit Valley Hospital	Mount Vernon	Washington	360-424-4111	www.skagitvalleyhospital.org
Skyridge Medical Center	Cleveland	Tennessee	423-339-4132	www.skyridgemedcenter.com
South Central Regional Medical Center	Laurel	Mississippi	601-649-4000	www.scrmc.com
South Jersey Healthcare Regional Medical Center	Vineland	New Jersey	856-641-8000	www.sjhs.com
Southeast Georgia Health System - Brunswick Campus	Brunswick	Georgia	912-466-7000	www.sghs.org
Saint Bernards Medical Center	Jonesboro	Arkansas	870-972-4100	www.sbrmc.com
Saint Francis Hospital	Columbus	Georgia	706-596-4020	wecareforlife.com
Saint Francis Medical Center	Cape Girardeau	Missouri	573-331-3000	www.sfmc.net
Saint Helena Hosptial-Clearlake	Clearlake	California	707-994-6486	www.redbudhospital.org
Saint Johns Hospital	Springfield	Illinois	217-544-6464	www.st-johns.org
Saint Joseph Hospital	Orange	California	714-633-9111	www.sjo.org
Saint Joseph Regional Medical Center	Lewiston	Idaho	208-743-2511	www.sjrmc.org
Saint Josephs Medical Center of Stockton	Stockton	California	209-943-2000	www.stjospehscares.org
Saint Mary's Community Hospital	Nebraska City	Nebraska	402-873-3321	www.stmaryshospitalnecity.com
Saint Mary's Hospital - Passaic	Passaic	New Jersey	973-365-4300	www.smh-nj.com
Saint Mary's Medical Center	West Palm Beach	Florida	561-840-6202	www.stmarysmc.com
Saint Marys Regional Medical Center	Russellville	Arkansas	479-968-2841	www.saintmarysregional.com
Saint Peter's Hospital	Helena	Montana	406-442-2100	www.stpetes.org
Strong Memorial Hospital	Rochester	New York	585-275-2121	www.urmc.rochester.edu
Sturdy Memorial Hospital	Attleboro	Massachusetts	508-222-5200	
Sumner Regional Medical Center	Gallatin	Tennessee	615-452-4210	
Tanner Medical Center - Carrollton	Carrollton	Georgia	770-836-9580	www.tanner.org
Terrebonne General Medical Center	Houma	Louisiana	985-873-4141	www.tgmc.com
TLC Health Network	Gowanda	New York	716-532-3377	
Tri-City Medical Center	Oceanside	California	760-724-8411	www.tricitymed.org
Trinity Rock Island	Rock Island	Illinois	309-779-5000	www.trinityqc.com
Tulare Regional Medical Center	Tulare	California	559-688-0821	www.tdhs.org
United Hospital System	Kenosha	Wisconsin	262-656-2368	
Unity Health Center	Shawnee	Oklahoma	405-273-2270	www.unityhealthcenter.com

Hospital	City	State	Phone	Web Site
University Hospital	Augusta	Georgia	706-722-9011	www.universityhealth.org
University Hospital S U N Y Health Science Center	Syracuse	New York	315-473-4240	www.upstate.edu
University of Louisville Hospital	Louisville	Kentucky	502-562-3000	www.uoflhealthcare.org
Venice Regional Medical Center	Venice	Florida	941-485-7711	www.veniceregional.com
Washington County Hospital	Plymouth	North Carolina	252-793-4135	www.wchonline.com
Washington County Hospital	Washington	Iowa	319-653-5481	www.wchc.org
West Branch Regional Medical Center	West Branch	Michigan	989-345-6366	www.wbrmc.org
Western Plains Medical Complex	Dodge City	Kansas	620-225-8400	www.westernplainsmc.com
Wheeling Hospital	Wheeling	West Virginia	304-243-3000	www.wheelinghospital.com
Williamsburg Regional Hospital	Kingstree	South Carolina	843-355-0167	www.w-rh.org
Wilson Medical Center	Wilson	North Carolina	252-399-8040	www.wilmed.org/contact.asp
Yakima Valley Memorial Hospital	Yakima	Washington	509-575-8000	www.yakimamemorialhospital.org

Note: Table shows hospitals nationwide whose Pneumonia 30-day risk-adjusted mortality rate is worse (higher) than U.S. rate of 11.6%

Hospital Mortality from Heart Attack: State and National Summary

Area	Number of Hospitals			
	Better than U.S. National Rate[1]	Worse than U.S. National Rate[2]	No Different than U.S. National Rate[3]	Number of Cases Too Small[4]
U.S. and Territories	95	45	2744	1685
Alabama	0	0	60	40
Alaska	0	0	5	13
American Samoa	0	0	0	0
Arizona	2	0	43	26
Arkansas	1	5	37	32
California	4	2	228	99
Colorado	0	0	33	31
Connecticut	7	0	22	3
Delaware	1	0	4	0
District of Columbia	0	0	5	2
Florida	6	4	147	26
Georgia	1	1	84	58
Guam	0	0	1	0
Hawaii	0	0	12	4
Idaho	0	0	9	27
Illinois	5	0	121	56
Indiana	3	1	74	39
Iowa	0	0	41	70
Kansas	0	0	31	84
Kentucky	3	0	56	38
Louisiana	0	1	59	48
Maine	0	0	32	4
Maryland	1	0	42	2
Massachusetts	9	0	51	5
Michigan	6	2	83	38
Minnesota	2	0	42	81
Mississippi	0	2	36	49
Missouri	3	0	62	46
Montana	0	0	9	38
N. Mariana Islands	0	0	0	1
Nebraska	1	0	18	61
Nevada	0	0	17	13
New Hampshire	1	0	20	5
New Jersey	3	1	67	3
New Mexico	1	0	17	23
New York	10	5	154	19
North Carolina	3	2	82	22
North Dakota	0	0	11	30
Ohio	3	1	121	34
Oklahoma	1	2	37	69
Oregon	0	0	39	17
Pennsylvania	4	2	136	20
Puerto Rico	0	1	29	16
Rhode Island	0	0	10	0
South Carolina	0	1	43	13
South Dakota	1	0	10	36
Tennessee	1	2	70	43
Texas	7	3	200	134
Utah	0	0	13	24
Vermont	0	0	12	2
Virgin Islands	0	0	1	1
Virginia	1	2	71	5
Washington	0	3	41	41
West Virginia	0	1	34	16
Wisconsin	4	1	60	54
Wyoming	0	0	2	24

Note: (1) 30-day risk-adjusted mortality rate is better (lower) than U.S. rate of 16.2%; (2) 30-day risk-adjusted mortality rate is worse (higher) than U.S. rate of 16.2%; (3) 30-day risk-adjusted mortality rate is about the same as U.S. rate of 16.2%; (4) The number of cases is too small to classify the hospital

Hospital Mortality from Heart Failure: State and National Summary

Area	Number of Hospitals			
	Better than U.S. National Rate[1]	Worse than U.S. National Rate[2]	No Different than U.S. National Rate[3]	Number of Cases Too Small[4]
U.S. and Territories	199	140	3801	603
Alabama	3	0	93	5
Alaska	0	0	10	11
American Samoa	0	0	0	1
Arizona	0	0	61	17
Arkansas	0	10	62	4
California	13	11	267	55
Colorado	0	0	55	17
Connecticut	4	0	28	0
Delaware	0	0	5	0
District of Columbia	2	0	5	0
Florida	11	8	157	7
Georgia	6	3	122	15
Guam	0	0	1	0
Hawaii	0	0	13	5
Idaho	0	0	26	10
Illinois	21	7	150	5
Indiana	5	3	107	3
Iowa	0	1	101	14
Kansas	0	1	92	33
Kentucky	5	1	88	3
Louisiana	2	5	87	25
Maine	0	0	34	2
Maryland	5	0	40	1
Massachusetts	12	0	50	3
Michigan	14	3	107	8
Minnesota	3	0	94	33
Mississippi	0	4	82	8
Missouri	5	5	100	3
Montana	0	1	30	28
N. Mariana Islands	0	0	0	1
Nebraska	1	1	53	29
Nevada	0	0	26	7
New Hampshire	0	1	24	1
New Jersey	14	1	59	0
New Mexico	0	1	34	7
New York	19	7	158	6
North Carolina	1	1	100	8
North Dakota	0	0	28	14
Ohio	16	6	134	6
Oklahoma	1	2	81	33
Oregon	0	6	46	6
Pennsylvania	17	6	135	6
Puerto Rico	0	0	35	14
Rhode Island	0	1	9	0
South Carolina	0	4	53	2
South Dakota	0	0	29	25
Tennessee	1	8	104	4
Texas	12	5	296	58
Utah	0	2	23	15
Vermont	0	3	10	1
Virgin Islands	0	0	2	0
Virginia	1	3	74	4
Washington	0	11	55	20
West Virginia	1	2	45	4
Wisconsin	4	5	105	7
Wyoming	0	1	16	9

Note: (1) 30-day risk-adjusted mortality rate is better (lower) than U.S. rate of 11.2%; (2) 30-day risk-adjusted mortality rate is worse (higher) than U.S. rate of 11.2%; (3) 30-day risk-adjusted mortality rate is about the same as U.S. rate of 11.2%; (4) The number of cases is too small to classify the hospital

Hospital Mortality from Pneumonia: State and National Summary

Area	Number of Hospitals			
	Better than U.S. National Rate[1]	Worse than U.S. National Rate[2]	No Different than U.S. National Rate[3]	Number of Cases Too Small[4]
U.S. and Territories	222	221	3988	357
Alabama	2	0	95	4
Alaska	0	0	16	6
American Samoa	0	0	1	0
Arizona	2	0	65	11
Arkansas	1	7	67	1
California	16	26	258	53
Colorado	4	0	59	11
Connecticut	5	0	26	1
Delaware	0	0	5	0
District of Columbia	0	0	7	0
Florida	15	9	155	7
Georgia	5	12	121	6
Guam	0	1	0	0
Hawaii	0	1	13	6
Idaho	0	2	31	4
Illinois	18	10	149	6
Indiana	7	4	104	3
Iowa	3	6	104	3
Kansas	4	2	109	13
Kentucky	4	6	85	2
Louisiana	5	4	88	24
Maine	2	1	33	0
Maryland	8	0	37	1
Massachusetts	13	1	49	3
Michigan	11	3	114	4
Minnesota	5	0	113	13
Mississippi	0	6	81	8
Missouri	6	6	100	3
Montana	0	1	41	18
N. Mariana Islands	0	0	1	0
Nebraska	0	6	72	7
Nevada	0	3	27	3
New Hampshire	1	3	22	0
New Jersey	10	2	61	1
New Mexico	0	0	40	3
New York	17	14	155	6
North Carolina	2	10	96	2
North Dakota	0	0	41	3
Ohio	14	7	138	3
Oklahoma	3	7	97	10
Oregon	1	1	53	3
Pennsylvania	12	5	143	5
Puerto Rico	0	7	29	15
Rhode Island	0	0	10	0
South Carolina	2	6	50	1
South Dakota	0	0	47	8
Tennessee	2	10	101	5
Texas	18	14	300	43
Utah	0	0	36	4
Vermont	0	1	13	0
Virgin Islands	0	0	2	0
Virginia	0	6	73	6
Washington	2	4	71	11
West Virginia	1	3	48	0
Wisconsin	1	4	113	3
Wyoming	0	0	23	4

Note: (1) 30-day risk-adjusted mortality rate is better (lower) than U.S. rate of 11.6%; (2) 30-day risk-adjusted mortality rate is worse (higher) than U.S. rate of 11.6%; (3) 30-day risk-adjusted mortality rate is about the same as U.S. rate of 11.6%; (4) The number of cases is too small to classify the hospital

What Do These Mortality Categories Show?

These categories show how hospitals' risk-adjusted 30-Day Death (mortality) rates compare to the rate across the U.S., after making adjustments for how sick patients were before they were admitted to the hospital and taking into account differences in death rates that might be due to chance.

Hospitals are shown to be Better or Worse Than U.S. National Rate only if we can be 95% certain that the difference between their risk-adjusted death (mortality) rates and the U.S. National rate is not due to chance. All others are shown in the No Different Than U.S. National Rate and Number of Cases Too Small categories.

Better than U.S. National Rate. Hospitals in the Better Than U.S. National Rate category have risk-adjusted 30-day death (mortality) rates that are lower than the U.S. National rate, and we can be 95% certain that this difference is not due to chance.

No Different than U.S. National Rate. Many hospitals in the No Different Than U.S. National Rate category have risk-adjusted 30-day death (mortality) rates that are about the same as the U.S. National rate. Other hospitals in this category have rates that are higher or lower than the U.S. National rate, but we cannot be 95% certain that these differences are not due to chance.

Worse than U.S. National Rate. Hospitals in the Worse Than U.S. National Rate category have risk-adjusted 30-day death (mortality) rates that are higher than the U.S. National rate, and we can be 95% certain that this difference is not due to chance.

Number of Cases Too Small. The number of cases is too small to classify the hospital. One cannot be certain about differences when a hospital has very few relevant patients.

Why are Death Rates for Individual Hospitals Not Shown?

Comparisons based on estimated death (mortality) rates alone can be misleading. Risk-adjusted death (mortality) rates are estimated for individual hospitals based on information taken from a particular time period. If a slightly different time period had been chosen, chances are that each hospital's results would have been somewhat different.

Researchers almost always report a range ("confidence interval" or in this case an "interval estimate") around their estimates, to show how much variation might be due to this kind of chance. A confidence interval or interval estimate tells us we can be reasonably "confident" (in this case, 95% confident) that a hospital's death (mortality) rate fell somewhere within this specified range. The smaller the range, the more precise the estimate.

When hospitals treat a very large number of patients, chance differences will not have much effect on the overall rates. The range will be small, and the estimated death (mortality) rates will be more precise. In hospitals that treat smaller numbers of patients, however, even small chance differences could have a big impact on death (mortality) rates. The 95% confidence interval, or range, will be large, and the estimated death (mortality) rates will be much less precise.

Because the number of patients treated at U.S. hospitals varies widely, the precision of hospitals' estimated death (mortality) rates also varies.

Calculation of 30-Day Risk-Standardized Mortality Rates

The 30-day risk-standardized mortality measures for heart attack, heart failure, and pneumonia are produced from Medicare claims and enrollment data using sophisticated statistical modeling techniques that adjust for patient-level risk factors and account for the clustering of patients within hospitals.

The three mortality models estimate hospital-specific, risk-standardized, all-cause 30-day mortality rates for patients hospitalized with a principal diagnosis of heart attack, heart failure, and pneumonia. All-cause mortality is defined as death from any cause within 30 days after the add link here index admission date, regardless of whether the patient dies while still in the hospital or after discharge. For each condition, the risk-standardized ("adjusted" or "risk-adjusted") hospital mortality rate can be used to compare performance across hospitals. The mortality measures for heart attack, heart failure, and pneumonia have been endorsed by the National Quality Forum (NQF), the non-profit public-private partnership organization that endorses national healthcare performance measures.

Data Collection Methods

Cases Included in the Model. All admissions for people with Medicare aged 65 or over who were enrolled in Original Medicare (traditional fee-for-service Medicare) for the entire 12 months prior to their hospital admission for heart attack or heart failure or pneumonia, and for whom complete administrative data for that 12-month period are available, are included in the model. The model identifies (1) all short-stay acute-care hospital discharges for heart attack or heart failure or pneumonia in the reference year based on a principal discharge diagnosis on the Medicare beneficiary's inpatient claim, and (2) all deaths (for all causes) within 30 days of admission. Hospital stays that lasted one day or less are excluded, provided the patient was discharged alive and not against medical advice. The measure now excludes admissions for patients who enrolled into the Medicare Hospice program on the first day of the admission and continue to exclude patients enrolled any time in the 12 months prior to admission. Discharges for patients who left against medical advice (AMA) are excluded beginning in 2009. If a beneficiary had multiple admissions during a year, one admission is chosen randomly for inclusion in the model from each year. (For the publication of the rates in June 2009, the reference period used for calculating mortality rates is July 2005 through June 2008. Subsequent updates to the rates are expected to use the same July/June three-year reference period.)

Hospital mortality rates for heart attack are calculated based on all admissions for heart attack, even if an individual Medicare beneficiary was hospitalized more than once for this condition during the 12-month period. However, for purposes of calculating heart failure mortality rates, if a beneficiary had multiple admissions during the 12-month period, one admission is chosen randomly for inclusion in the model.

Use of a 30-Day Period to Assess Mortality

The model tracks deaths that occur within 30 days of a hospital admission, rather than inpatient mortality only, or mortality over some other post-discharge period. Thirty-day mortality was chosen over inpatient mortality because variability across hospitals in lengths of stay can make differences in inpatient mortality hard to interpret. For example, a heart attack patient hospitalized for 12 days may have a higher chance of dying during the hospital stay than a patient hospitalized for only 7 days, merely because the first patient's outcome is tracked for 5 days longer than the second patient's. Thirty-day mortality was chosen over longer windows (such as 90 days or one year), because mortality over longer periods may have less to do with the care received in the hospital and more to do with other complicating illnesses, patients' own behavior, or the care they received after discharge.

Use of Administrative Claims Data

Administrative claims data, rather than medical records data, are used to predict 30-day mortality. These data are widely available for Original Medicare (traditional fee-for-service) beneficiaries, are relatively inexpensive to acquire, and are timely. Using administrative data makes it possible to calculate mortality without having to do chart reviews or requiring hospitals to report additional data. Research conducted when the measures were being developed demonstrated that the administrative claims-based models perform well in predicting mortality compared with models based on chart reviews.

Risk-Adjustment and Covariates Included in the Model

Risk-Adjustment. The model adjusts for differences in patients' risks unrelated to their hospital care (risk-adjustment). The characteristics that Medicare patients bring with them when they arrive at a hospital with a heart attack or heart failure or pneumonia are not under the control of the hospital. However, some patient characteristics may make death more likely (increase the "risk" of death), no matter where the patient is treated or how good the care is. Moreover, some hospitals may treat people with a history of more severe disease. Therefore, when mortality rates are calculated for each hospital for a 12-month period, they are adjusted based on the unique mix of patients that hospital treated during that period. Factors included in the risk-adjustment model include age, gender, past medical history, and other diseases or conditions (comorbidities) that patients had when they arrived at the hospital that are known to increase their risk.

Past medical history and comorbidities are included in the model using CMS's condition categories (CCs) and a history of certain procedures. Medicare patients are assigned to one or more CCs based on diagnoses (ICD-9 codes) obtained from the patient's discharge claim, and from the hospital inpatient, hospital outpatient, and physician Medicare claims submitted for the patient one year prior to the admission. Secondary diagnoses from the patient's hospital discharge claim that might represent complications that occurred while the patient was in the hospital, rather than conditions that were present on admission, are not included in assigning the patient's CC. Research has shown that coding differences among providers affect CCs only slightly. Diagnoses from unreliable sources (such as laboratory or other claims that were not based on face-to-face encounters) are not included when assigning the CCs in the model.

To "risk-adjust" mortality rates for patient characteristics, the statistical model estimates the independent effects of age, gender, comorbidities, and a hospital-specific component of quality on mortality of patients within 30 days of hospital admission (the dependent variable). Using these estimates, the model calculates an adjusted mortality rate for each hospital that can be compared with those of other hospitals with different case mixes.

Covariates in 30-Day Mortality Risk-Adjustment Models		
Heart Attack	Heart Failure	Pneumonia
Age-65	Age-65	Age-65
Gender (male)	Gender (male)	Gender (male)
History of PTCA	History of PTCA	History of PTCA
History of CABG	History of CABG	History of CABG
History of heart failure	History of heart failure	History of heart failure
History of MI	History of MI	History of MI
AMI location (Group 1): anterior, anterolateral		
AMI location (Group 2): inferolateral, inferior, inferoposterior, other lateral, and true posterior		
Unstable angina	Unstable angina	Unstable angina
Chronic atherosclerosis	Chronic atherosclerosis	Chronic atherosclerosis
Cardiopulmonary-respiratory failure and shock	Cardiopulmonary-respiratory failure and shock	
Valvular heart disease	Valvular heart disease	Valvular heart disease
Hypertension	Hypertension	Hypertension
Stroke	Stroke	Stroke
Cerebrovascular disease		
Renal failure	Renal failure	Renal failure
COPD	COPD	COPD
Pneumonia	Pneumonia	Pneumonia
Diabetes	Diabetes	Diabetes
Protein-calorie malnutrition	Protein-calorie malnutrition	Protein-calorie malnutrition
Dementia	Dementia	Dementia
Functional disability	Functional disability	Functional disability
Peripheral vascular disease	Peripheral vascular disease	Peripheral vascular disease
Metastatic cancer	Metastatic cancer	Metastatic cancer
Trauma in last year	Trauma in last year	Trauma in last year
Major psych disorder	Major psych disorder	Major psych disorder
Chronic liver disease	Chronic liver disease	Chronic liver disease
		Severe hematological disorders
		Depression
		Seizure disorders/ convulsions
		Asthma
		Iron deficiency/anemias
		Parkinson's/Huntington's
		Lung fibrosis/chronic lung disorders
		Vertebral fractures

Statistical Methods Used to Calculate Mortality Rates

Hierarchical Regression Model. The statistical model for computing 30-day risk-adjusted mortality rate measures is a "hierarchical regression model." This type of model is based on the assumption that any heart attack or heart failure patients treated at a particular hospital will experience a level of quality of care that applies to all patients treated for the same condition in that hospital. In other words, the expected risk of death for two similar heart attack or heart failure patients treated in the same hospital would be more alike than the risk of death for the same two patients treated in two different hospitals. The likelihood that an individual patient will die is therefore a combination of (1) his or her individual risk characteristics (for example, gender, comorbidities, and past medical history) and 2) the hospital's unique quality of care for all patients treated for that condition in that hospital. The model estimates the effects of both of these components on mortality.

Calculating Mortality Rates. Each hospital's "30-day risk-adjusted mortality rate" (also called the "Risk Standardized Mortality Rate" or RSMR) is computed in several steps. First, the predicted 30-day mortality for a particular hospital obtained from the hierarchical regression model is divided by the expected mortality for that hospital, which is also obtained from the regression model. Predicted mortality is the rate of deaths from heart attack or heart failure that would be anticipated in the particular hospital during the 12-month period, given the patient case mix and the hospital's unique quality of care effect on mortality. Expected mortality is the rate of deaths from heart attack or heart failure that would be expected if the same patients with the same characteristics had instead been treated at an "average" hospital, given the "average" hospital's quality of care effect on mortality for patients with that condition. This ratio is then multiplied by the national unadjusted mortality rate for the condition for all hospitals to compute a "risk-adjusted mortality rate" for the hospital. So, the higher a hospital's predicted 30-day mortality rate, relative to expected mortality for the hospital's particular case mix of patients, the higher its adjusted mortality rate will be. Hospitals with better quality will have lower rates.

(Predicted 30-day mortality/Expected mortality) * U.S. National mortality rate = RSMR

For example, suppose the model predicts that 10 percent of Hospital A's heart attack patients would die within 30 days of admission in a given year, based on their ages, gender mix, and pre-existing health conditions, and based on the estimate of the hospital's specific quality of care. Then, suppose that the expected rate of 30-day deaths for those same patients were higher – say, 15 percent – if they had instead been treated at an "average" U.S. hospital. If the actual mortality rate for the 12-month period for all heart attack patients in all hospitals in the U.S. is 12 percent, then the hospital's risk-adjusted 30-day mortality rate would be 8 percent.

(10%/15%)* 12% = RSMR for Hospital A 8%

If, instead, 9 percent of these patients would be expected to have died if treated at the average hospital, then the hospital's mortality rate would be 13.3 percent.

(10%/9%)* 12% = RSMR for Hospital A 13.3%

In the first case, the hospital performed better than the average hospital and had a relatively low risk-adjusted mortality rate (8 percent); in the second case it performed worse and had a relatively high rate (13.3 percent).

Hospitals with relatively low-risk patients whose predicted mortality rate is the same as the expected mortality rate for the average hospital for the same group of low-risk patients would have an adjusted mortality rate equal to the national rate (12 percent in this example). Similarly, hospitals with high-risk patients whose predicted mortality rate is the same as the expected mortality rate for the average hospital for the same group of high-risk patients would also have an adjusted mortality rate equal to the national rate of 12 percent. Thus, each hospital's case mix should not affect the adjusted mortality rates used to compare hospitals.

Adjusting for Small Hospitals or a Small Number of Cases. The hierarchical regression model also adjusts mortality rates results for small hospitals or hospitals with few heart attack or heart failure cases in a given year. This reduces the chance that such hospitals' performance will fluctuate wildly from year to year or that they will be wrongly classified as either a worse or better performer. For these hospitals, the model not only considers deaths among patients treated for the condition in the small sample size of cases, but pools together patients from all hospitals treated for the given condition, to make the result more reliable. In essence, the predicted mortality rate for a hospital with a small number of cases is moved toward the overall U.S. National mortality rate for all hospitals. The estimates of mortality for hospitals with few patients will rely considerably on the pooled data for all hospitals, making it less likely that small hospitals will fall into either of the outlier categories. This pooling affords a "borrowing of statistical strength" that provides more confidence in the results.

Significance Testing, Interval Estimates, and Comparing Rates Among Hospitals

Significance Testing and Interval Estimates. The model also calculates how precise the estimates of the adjusted mortality rate are, and determines upper and lower bounds (Interval Estimates) for each hospital's risk-adjusted rate. Interval estimates, which are like confidence intervals, describe how much uncertainty there is around the rate—how much bigger or smaller the rate might really be. Larger hospitals typically have more precise estimates and smaller interval estimates, since more data are available to estimate mortality. The smaller the sample size, the greater the difference in mortality rates between a hospital and the national rate must be in order for that difference to be statistically meaningful.

Comparing Mortality Rates Among Hospitals. The risk-adjusted hospital rate with its interval estimate can be compared to the U.S. National crude mortality rate. If the interval estimate includes (overlaps with) the national crude mortality rate, the hospital's performance is in the "no different than U.S. National rate" category. If the entire interval estimate is below the national crude mortality rate, then the hospital is performing "better than U.S. National rate." If the entire interval estimate is above the national crude mortality rate, it is "worse than U.S. National rate."

Hospitals whose Heart Attack 30-Day Readmission Rate is Better (Lower) than the U.S. National Rate

Hospital	City	State	Phone	Web Site
Anmed Health	Anderson	South Carolina	864-261-1109	www.anmed.com
Avera Heart Hospital of South Dakota	Sioux Falls	South Dakota	605-977-7000	
Ball Memorial Hospital	Muncie	Indiana	765-747-3111	www.accesschs.org/baal-memorial-l
Boca Raton Regional Hospital	Boca Raton	Florida	561-362-5002	
Carilion Medical Center	Roanoke	Virginia	540-981-7000	www.carilion.com/crmh
Cox Medical Center	Springfield	Missouri	417-269-6000	www.coxhealth.com
Greenville Memorial Hospital	Greenville	South Carolina	864-455-7000	www.ghs.org
Indiana University Health	Indianapolis	Indiana	317-962-5900	
Lancaster General Hospital	Lancaster	Pennsylvania	717-299-5511	www.lancastergeneral.org
Lutheran Hospital of Indiana	Fort Wayne	Indiana	260-435-7001	www.lutheranhospital.com
Memorial Mission Hospital and Asheville Surgery Center	Asheville	North Carolina	828-213-1111	www.missionhospitals.org
Munson Medical Center	Traverse City	Michigan	231-935-5000	www.munsonhealthcare.org
Naples Community Hospital	Naples	Florida	239-436-5000	www.nchmd.org
Northeast Georgia Medical Center	Gainesville	Georgia	770-535-3553	www.nghs.com
Piedmont Hospital	Atlanta	Georgia	404-605-5000	www.piedmonthospital.org
Rogue Valley Medical Center	Medford	Oregon	541-789-7000	www.asante.org
Santa Barbara Cottage Hospital	Santa Barbara	California	805-682-7111	www.cottagehealthsystem.org
Santa Rosa Memorial Hospital	Santa Rosa	California	707-525-5300	www.stjosephhealth.org
Sarasota Memorial Hospital	Sarasota	Florida	941-917-9000	www.smh.com
Shannon Medical Center	San Angelo	Texas	325-653-6741	www.shannonhealth.com
Sisters of Charity Providence Hospitals	Columbia	South Carolina	803-256-5300	www.providencehospitals.com
Spectrum Health - Butterworth Campus	Grand Rapids	Michigan	616-391-1774	www.spectrum-health.org
Saint John's Regional Health Center	Springfield	Missouri	417-820-2000	www.stjohns.com
Saint Mary's Medical Center	Huntington	West Virginia	304-526-1234	www.st-marys.org
Saint Vincent Heart Center of Indiana	Indianapolis	Indiana	317-583-5000	www.theheartcenter.com
Stanford Hospital	Stanford	California	650-723-5708	www.stanfordhospital.com
Tri-City Medical Center	Oceanside	California	760-724-8411	www.tricitymed.org
Venice Regional Medical Center	Venice	Florida	941-485-7711	www.veniceregional.com
York Hospital	York	Pennsylvania	717-851-2345	www.wellspan.org

Note: Table shows hospitals nationwide whose Acute Myocardial Infarction 30-day readmission rate is better (lower) than U.S. rate of 19.9%

Hospitals whose Heart Attack 30-Day Readmission Rate is Worse (Higher) than the U.S. National Rate

Hospital	City	State	Phone	Web Site
Abington Memorial Hospital	Abington	Pennsylvania	215-481-2000	www.amh.org
Advocate South Suburban Hospital	Hazel Crest	Illinois	708-799-8000	www.advocatehealth.com
Albert Einstein Medical Center	Philadelphia	Pennsylvania	215-456-6090	www.einstein.edu
Banner Boswell Medical Center	Sun City	Arizona	623-977-7211	www.bannerhealth.com
Barnes Jewish Hospital	Saint Louis	Missouri	314-747-3000	www.barnesjewish.org
Beth Israel Deaconess Medical Center	Boston	Massachusetts	617-667-7000	www.bidmc.harvard.edu
Christian Hospital Northeast	Saint Louis	Missouri	314-653-5000	www.christianhospital.org
Cleveland Clinic	Cleveland	Ohio	216-444-2200	www.clevelandclinic.org
Duke University Hospital	Durham	North Carolina	919-684-8111	www.dukehealth.org
Easton Hospital	Easton	Pennsylvania	610-250-4076	www.easton-hospital.com
Fairfield Medical Center	Lancaster	Ohio	740-687-8009	www.fmchealth.org
Florida Hospital	Orlando	Florida	407-303-1976	www.floridahospital.com
Floyd Memorial Hospital and Health Services	New Albany	Indiana	812-949-5500	www.floydmedical.org
Franciscan St Margaret Health - Hammond	Hammond	Indiana	219-932-2300	www.smmhc.com
Hallmark Health System	Melrose	Massachusetts	781-979-3000	www.hallmarkhealth.org
Jacobi Medical Center	Bronx	New York	718-918-5000	www.ci.nyc.ny.us/html/hhc
Jamaica Hospital Medical Center	Jamaica	New York	718-262-6000	www.jamaicahospital.org
Johnson City Medical Center	Johnson City	Tennessee	423-431-6111	www.msha.com
Libertyhealth-Jersey City Medical Center Campus	Jersey City	New Jersey	201-915-2000	www.libertyhcs.org
Lutheran Medical Center	Brooklyn	New York	718-630-8000	www.lmcmc.com
Maimonides Medical Center	Brooklyn	New York	718-283-6000	www.maimonidesmed.org
Mary Washington Hospital	Fredericksburg	Virginia	540-741-1100	www.medicorp.org
Metrosouth Medical Center	Blue Island	Illinois	708-597-2000	www.stfrancisblueisland.com
Mount Sinai Hospital	New York	New York	212-241-7981	www.mountsinai.org
Nassau University Medical Center	East Meadow	New York	516-572-0123	www.numc.edu
New York Methodist Hospital	Brooklyn	New York	718-780-3000	www.nym.org
North Carolina Baptist Hospital	Winston-Salem	North Carolina	336-716-2011	www.wfubmc.edu
North Shore University Hospital	Manhasset	New York	516-562-0100	www.northshorelij.com
Our Lady of the Resurrection Medical Center	Chicago	Illinois	773-282-7000	www.reshealth.org
Raritan Bay Medical Center	Perth Amboy	New Jersey	732-442-3700	
Rochester General Hospital	Rochester	New York	585-922-4000	www.rochestergeneral.org
Saint Michael's Medical Center	Newark	New Jersey	973-877-5350	www.cathedralhealth.org
South Shore Hospital	South Weymouth	Massachusetts	781-340-8000	www.southshorehospital.org
Saint Elizabeth's Medical Center	Brighton	Massachusetts	617-789-3000	www.semc.org
Saint Francis Medical Center	Monroe	Louisiana	318-966-4141	www.stfran.com
Saint John Hospital and Medical Center	Detroit	Michigan	313-343-4000	www.stjohnprovidence.org
Trinity Medical Center East & Trinity Medical Center West	Steubenville	Ohio	740-264-7212	www.trinityhealth.com
Trinity Rock Island	Rock Island	Illinois	309-779-5000	www.trinityqc.com
Union Memorial Hospital	Baltimore	Maryland	410-554-2227	www.unionmemorial.org
University Hospital	Cincinnati	Ohio	513-584-1000	www.universityhospitalcincinnati.com
University of Iowa Hospital & Clinics	Iowa City	Iowa	319-356-1616	www.uihealthcare.com
Waterbury Hospital	Waterbury	Connecticut	203-573-6000	www.waterburyhospital.org
Wyckoff Heights Medical Center	Brooklyn	New York	718-963-7272	www.wyckoffhospital.org

Note: Table shows hospitals nationwide whose Acute Myocardial Infarction 30-day readmission rate is worse (higher) than U.S. rate of 19.9%

Hospitals whose Heart Failure 30-Day Readmission Rate is Better (Lower) than the U.S. National Rate

Hospital	City	State	Phone	Web Site
Allegiance Health	Jackson	Michigan	517-788-4800	www.footehealth.org
Allen Memorial Hospital	Waterloo	Iowa	319-235-3941	www.allenhospital.org
Alpena Regional Medical Center	Alpena	Michigan	989-356-7390	www.agh.org
Athens Regional Medical Center	Athens	Georgia	706-475-7000	www.armc.org
Aultman Hospital	Canton	Ohio	330-452-9911	www.aultman.com
Aurora St Lukes Medical Center	Milwaukee	Wisconsin	414-649-6000	www.aurorahealthcare.org
Ball Memorial Hospital	Muncie	Indiana	765-747-3111	www.accesschs.org/baal-memorial-l
Baptist Health Medical Center-Little Rock	Little Rock	Arkansas	501-202-2000	www.baptist-health.com
Baptist St Anthonys Health System-Baptist Campus	Amarillo	Texas	806-212-2000	www.bsahs.com
Bay Medical Center	Panama City	Florida	850-769-1511	www.baymedical.org
Baylor Heart and Vascular Hospital	Dallas	Texas	214-820-0670	
Baylor University Medical Center	Dallas	Texas	214-820-0111	www.baylorhealth.com
Bellin Memorial Hospital	Green Bay	Wisconsin	920-433-3500	www.bellin.org
Bethesda Memorial Hospital	Boynton Beach	Florida	561-737-7733	www.bethesdahealthcare.com
Bon Secours - Depaul Medical Center	Norfolk	Virginia	757-889-5000	www.bonsecourshamptonroads.com
Borgess Medical Center	Kalamazoo	Michigan	269-226-7000	www.borgess.com
Bromenn Healthcare	Normal	Illinois	309-454-1400	
Cape Coral Hospital	Cape Coral	Florida	239-574-2323	
Capital Regional Medical Center	Tallahassee	Florida	850-656-5000	www.capitalregionalmedicalcenter.com
Carolinas Medical Center-Behavioral Health	Charlotte	North Carolina	704-355-2000	www.carolinasmedicalcenter.org
Catholic Medical Center	Manchester	New Hampshire	603-668-3545	www.catholicmedicalcenter.org
Central Baptist Hospital	Lexington	Kentucky	859-260-6100	www.centralbap.com
Central Vermont Medical Center	Barre	Vermont	802-371-4100	www.cvmc.hitchcock.org
Central Washington Hospital	Wenatchee	Washington	509-662-1511	www.cwhs.com
Christus Schumpert Health System	Shreveport	Louisiana	318-681-4215	www.christusschumpert.org
Citrus Memorial Hospital	Inverness	Florida	352-726-1551	www.citrusmh.com
Citrus Valley Medical Center-IC Campus	Covina	California	626-814-2468	www.cvhp.org
Community Hospital of the Monterey Peninsula	Monterey	California	831-624-5311	www.chomp.org
Cookeville Regional Medical Center	Cookeville	Tennessee	931-646-2000	www.crmchealth.org
The Cooley Dickinson Hospital	Northampton	Massachusetts	413-582-2000	www.cooley-dickinson.org
The Corpus Christi Medical Center	Corpus Christi	Texas	361-761-1000	
Cox Medical Center	Springfield	Missouri	417-269-6000	www.coxhealth.com
Deborah Heart and Lung Center	Browns Mills	New Jersey	609-893-6611	
Dixie Regional Medical Center	Saint George	Utah	435-251-1000	intermountainhealthcare.org
Doctors Hospital at Renaissance	Edinburg	Texas	956-666-7100	www.dhr-rgv.com
Door County Memorial Hospital	Sturgeon Bay	Wisconsin	920-743-5566	www.doorcountymemorial.org
East Jefferson General Hospital	Metairie	Louisiana	504-454-4000	www.EastJeffHospital.org
Ephrata Community Hospital	Ephrata	Pennsylvania	717-733-0311	www.ephratahospital.org
Exempla Lutheran Medical Center	Wheat Ridge	Colorado	303-425-4500	www.exemlpa.org
Florida Hospital Waterman	Tavares	Florida	352-253-3300	www.fhwat.org
Flower Hospital	Sylvania	Ohio	419-824-1444	www.promedica.org
Flowers Hospital	Dothan	Alabama	334-793-5000	www.flowershospital.com
Gaston Memorial Hospital	Gastonia	North Carolina	704-834-2000	www.caromont.org
Geisinger Medical Center	Danville	Pennsylvania	570-271-6211	www.geisinger.org
Genesis Healthcare System	Zanesville	Ohio	740-454-5000	www.genesishcs.org
Greenville Memorial Hospital	Greenville	South Carolina	864-455-7000	www.ghs.org
Hamilton Medical Center	Dalton	Georgia	706-272-6105	www.hamilitonhealth.com
Hamot Medical Center	Erie	Pennsylvania	814-877-6000	www.hamot.org
Heart Hospital of Austin	Austin	Texas	512-407-7581	www.hearthospitalofaustin.com
Hendrick Medical Center	Abilene	Texas	325-670-2000	www.ehendrick.org
Hendricks Regional Health	Danville	Indiana	317-745-4451	www.hendricksregional.org
Henrico Doctors' Hospital	Richmond	Virginia	804-289-4500	www.henricodoctors.com
Immanuel-St Josephs-Mayo Health System	Mankato	Minnesota	507-625-4031	www.isj-mhs.org
Intermountain Medical Center	Murray	Utah	801-507-7000	intermountainhealthcare.org
Iowa Lutheran Hospital	Des Moines	Iowa	515-263-5612	ihsdesmoines.org
Johnston Memorial Hospital	Smithfield	North Carolina	919-934-8171	www.johnstanmemorial.org
Kadlec Regional Medical Center	Richland	Washington	509-946-4611	www.kadlecmed.org
Kalispell Regional Medical Center	Kalispell	Montana	406-752-1774	www.krmc.org
Kaweah Delta Medical Center	Visalia	California	559-624-2000	www.kaweahdelta.org
Lancaster General Hospital	Lancaster	Pennsylvania	717-299-5511	www.lancastergeneral.org
Lawrence & Memorial Hospital	New London	Connecticut	860-442-0711	www.lmhospital.org
Lee Memorial Hospital	Fort Myers	Florida	239-332-1111	www.leememorial.org
Manatee Memorial Hospital	Bradenton	Florida	941-746-5111	www.manateememorial.com
Martin Memorial Medical Center	Stuart	Florida	772-287-5200	www.mmhs.com

Hospital	City	State	Phone	Web Site
Mary Hitchcock Memorial Hospital	Lebanon	New Hampshire	603-650-5000	www.dhmc.org
Massachusetts General Hospital	Boston	Massachusetts	617-726-2000	www.massgeneral.org
McKay-Dee Hospital Center	Ogden	Utah	801-387-2800	intermountainhealthcare.org
Memorial Healthcare System	Chattanooga	Tennessee	423-495-2525	www.memorial.org
Memorial Hermann Hospital System	Houston	Texas	713-448-6796	www.memorialhermann.org
Memorial Hospital and Health Care Center	Jasper	Indiana	812-482-2345	www.mhhcc.org
Memorial Hospital of South Bend	South Bend	Indiana	574-647-3632	www.qualityoflife.org
Memorial Medical Center of West Michigan	Ludington	Michigan	231-843-2591	www.mmcwm.com
Memorial Mission Hospital and Asheville Surgery Center	Asheville	North Carolina	828-213-1111	www.missionhospitals.org
Mercy Health Partners - Mercy Campus	Muskegon	Michigan	231-672-3901	www.mghp.com
Mercy Medical Center-Cedar Rapids	Cedar Rapids	Iowa	319-398-6011	www.mercycare.org
Mercy Medical Center Redding	Redding	California	530-225-6102	www.redding.mercy.org
Methodist Hospital	San Antonio	Texas	210-575-4000	www.mh.sahealth.com
Mount Carmel Health	Columbus	Ohio	614-546-4533	www.mountcarmelhealth.com
Naples Community Hospital	Naples	Florida	239-436-5000	www.nchmd.org
Nebraska Heart Hospital	Lincoln	Nebraska	402-328-3000	www.neheart.com
North Kansas City Hospital	North Kansas City	Missouri	816-691-2000	www.nkch.org
Northeast Georgia Medical Center	Gainesville	Georgia	770-535-3553	www.nghs.com
Northern Michigan Regional Hospital	Petoskey	Michigan	231-487-4000	www.northernhealth.org
Our Lady of the Lake Regional Medical Center	Baton Rouge	Louisiana	225-765-8902	www.ololrmc.com
Park Nicollet Methodist Hospital	Saint Louis Park	Minnesota	952-993-5000	www.parknicollet.com/methodist
Parkview Hospital	Fort Wayne	Indiana	260-373-4000	www.parkview.com
Parkview Medical Center	Pueblo	Colorado	719-584-4000	www.parkviewmc.com
Peacehealth St Joseph Medical Center	Bellingham	Washington	360-734-5400	www.peacehealth.org
Peninsula Medical Center	Burlingame	California	650-696-5270	www.mills-peninsula.org
Peninsula Regional Medical Center	Salisbury	Maryland	410-543-7116	www.peninsula.org
Piedmont Hospital	Atlanta	Georgia	404-605-5000	www.piedmonthospital.org
Portneuf Medical Center	Pocatello	Idaho	208-239-1000	www.portmed.org
Presbyterian Hospital	Albuquerque	New Mexico	505-724-7281	www.phs.org
Providence Alaska Medical Center	Anchorage	Alaska	907-261-3675	www.providence.org
Providence Hospital	Mobile	Alabama	251-633-1000	www.providencehospital.org
Providence Regional Medical Center Everett	Everett	Washington	425-261-2000	www.providence.org
Providence Sacred Heart Medical Center	Spokane	Washington	509-474-3040	www.shmc.org
Providence St Vincent Medical Center	Portland	Oregon	503-216-1234	www.providence.org
Rapid City Regional Hospital	Rapid City	South Dakota	605-719-1000	www.rcrh.org
Reading Hospital Medical Center	Reading	Pennsylvania	610-988-8000	www.readinghospital.org
Redmond Regional Medical Center	Rome	Georgia	706-802-3012	
Regional Medical Center Bayonet Point	Hudson	Florida	727-819-2929	www.mchealth.com or www.heartoftampa.com
Riverside Regional Medical Center	Newport News	Virginia	757-594-2000	www.riversideonline.com
Rogue Valley Medical Center	Medford	Oregon	541-789-7000	www.asante.org
Rowan Regional Medical Center	Salisbury	North Carolina	704-210-5000	www.rowan.org
Sacred Heart Medical Center - University District	Eugene	Oregon	541-686-7274	www.peacehealth.org
Saint Joseph Regional Medical Center	Mishawaka	Indiana	574-335-5000	www.sjmed.com
Saint Joseph's Hospital of Atlanta	Atlanta	Georgia	678-843-5720	www.stjosephsatlanta.org
Saint Vincent Health Center	Erie	Pennsylvania	814-452-5000	www.svhs.org
Santa Barbara Cottage Hospital	Santa Barbara	California	805-682-7111	www.cottagehealthsystem.org
Santa Rosa Memorial Hospital	Santa Rosa	California	707-525-5300	www.stjosephhealth.org
Sarasota Memorial Hospital	Sarasota	Florida	941-917-9000	www.smh.com
Scott & White Memorial Hospital	Temple	Texas	254-724-2111	www.sw.org
Sentara Leigh Hospital	Norfolk	Virginia	757-261-6601	www.sentara.com
Sequoia Hospital	Redwood City	California	650-367-5551	www.sequoiahospital.org
Sisters of Charity Providence Hospitals	Columbia	South Carolina	803-256-5300	www.providencehospitals.com
Saint Clare Medical Center	Crawfordsville	Indiana	765-362-2800	www.stclaremedical.org
Saint Dominic-Jackson Memorial Hospital	Jackson	Mississippi	601-200-2000	stdom.com
Saint Francis Health Center	Topeka	Kansas	785-295-8000	www.stfrancistopeka.org
Saint Francis Hospital	Columbus	Georgia	706-596-4020	wecareforlife.com
Saint Francis-Downtown	Greenville	South Carolina	864-255-1000	www.stfrancishealth.org
Saint John's Regional Health Center	Springfield	Missouri	417-820-2000	www.stjohns.com
Saint Lukes Episcopal Hospital	Houston	Texas	832-355-1000	www.sleh.com
Saint Lukes Regional Medical Center	Boise	Idaho	208-381-2222	www.slrmc.org
Saint Marks Hospital	Salt Lake City	Utah	801-268-7700	www.stmarkshospital.com
Saint Patrick Hospital and Health Sciences Center	Missoula	Montana	406-543-7271	www.saintpatrick.org
Saint Vincent Heart Center of Indiana	Indianapolis	Indiana	317-583-5000	www.theheartcenter.com
Sutter Medical Center of Santa Rosa	Santa Rosa	California	707-576-4000	www.suttersantarosa.org
Tallahassee Memorial Healthcare	Tallahassee	Florida	850-431-1155	www.tmh.org
The Toledo Hospital	Toledo	Ohio	419-291-7463	www.promedica.org
Tucson Medical Center	Tucson	Arizona	520-327-5461	www.tmcaz.com

Hospital	City	State	Phone	Web Site
United Regional Health Care System	Wichita Falls	Texas	940-764-3055	www.urhcs.org
University Health Care - University Hospitals and Clinics	Salt Lake City	Utah	801-581-2121	www.healthcare.utah.edu
University Hospital	Augusta	Georgia	706-722-9011	www.universityhealth.org
UPMC Horizon	Greenville	Pennsylvania	724-588-2100	www.upmc.com
Upper Valley Medical Center	Troy	Ohio	937-440-7853	www.uvmc.com
Via Christi Hospitals Wichita	Wichita	Kansas	316-268-5000	www.via-christi.org
Virtua Memorial Hospital of Burlington County	Mount Holly	New Jersey	609-914-6200	www.virtua.org
Warren General Hospital	Warren	Pennsylvania	814-723-3300	
Wentworth-Douglass Hospital	Dover	New Hampshire	603-740-2580	
Wesley Medical Center	Wichita	Kansas	316-962-2000	www.wesleymc.com
Westerly Hospital	Westerly	Rhode Island	401-596-6000	
Wilkes-Barre General Hospital	Wilkes-Barre	Pennsylvania	570-829-8111	www.wvhcs.org
Williamsport Hospital & Medical Center	Williamsport	Pennsylvania	570-321-1000	www.susquehannahealth.org
Willis Knighton Bossier Health Center	Bossier City	Louisiana	318-212-7000	www.wkhs.com/Locations/Bossier.aspx
Woman's Christian Association	Jamestown	New York	716-487-0141	www.wcahospital.org
Yakima Valley Memorial Hospital	Yakima	Washington	509-575-8000	www.yakimamemorialhospital.org

Note: Table shows hospitals nationwide whose Heart Failure 30-day readmission rate is better (lower) than U.S. rate of 24.7%

Hospitals whose Heart Failure 30-Day Readmission Rate is Worse (Higher) than the U.S. National Rate

Hospital	City	State	Phone	Web Site
Advocate Trinity Hospital	Chicago	Illinois	773-967-2000	www.advocatehealth.com/trin
Albert Einstein Medical Center	Philadelphia	Pennsylvania	215-456-6090	www.einstein.edu
Alegent Health Midlands Hospital	Papillion	Nebraska	402-593-3000	www.alegent.com
Aria Health	Philadelphia	Pennsylvania	215-612-4129	www.ariahealth.com
Avoyelles Hospital	Marksville	Louisiana	318-240-6000	www.avoyelleshospital.com
Barnes Jewish Hospital	Saint Louis	Missouri	314-747-3000	www.barnesjewish.org
Bates County Memorial Hospital	Butler	Missouri	660-200-7000	www.bcmhospital.com
Bayshore Community Hospital	Holmdel	New Jersey	732-739-5900	www.bchs.com
Bellevue Hospital Center	New York	New York	212-561-4132	www.nyc.gov/html/hhc/html/facilities/bellevue.shtml
Beth Israel Deaconess Medical Center	Boston	Massachusetts	617-667-7000	www.bidmc.harvard.edu
Beth Israel Medical Center	New York	New York	212-420-2000	www.wehealny.org
Biloxi Regional Medical Center	Biloxi	Mississippi	228-436-1104	www.hmabrmc.com
Bolivar Medical Center	Cleveland	Mississippi	662-846-2551	www.bolivarmedical.com
Bronx-Lebanon Hospital Center	Bronx	New York	212-588-7000	www.bronx-leb.org
Brookdale Hospital Medical Center	Brooklyn	New York	718-240-5966	www.brookdalehospital.org
Caldwell Memorial Hospital	Columbia	Louisiana	318-649-6111	
Cambridge Health Alliance	Cambridge	Massachusetts	617-665-2300	
Carolina Pines Regional Medical Center	Hartsville	South Carolina	864-339-2100	www.cprmc.com
Centegra Health System - McHenry Hospital	Mchenry	Illinois	815-344-5000	www.centegra.org
Centrastate Medical Center	Freehold	New Jersey	732-431-2000	www.centrastate.com
Chicot Memorial Medical Center	Lake Village	Arkansas	870-265-5351	www.chicotmemorial.com
Christian Hospital Northeast	Saint Louis	Missouri	314-653-5000	www.christianhospital.org
Civista Medical Center	La Plata	Maryland	301-609-4265	www.civista.org
Cleveland Clinic	Cleveland	Ohio	216-444-2200	www.clevelandclinic.org
Cleveland Regional Medical Center	Cleveland	Texas	281-593-1811	www.clevelandregionalmedical.com
Coffee Regional Medical Center	Douglas	Georgia	229-384-1900	www.coffeeregional.org
Community Regional Medical Center	Fresno	California	559-459-6000	www.communitymedical.org
Community Regional Medical Center	Lorain	Ohio	440-960-3295	
Coney Island Hospital	Brooklyn	New York	718-616-3000	
Cooper University Hospital	Camden	New Jersey	856-342-2000	www.cooperhealth.org
Davis Regional Medical Center	Statesville	North Carolina	704-873-0281	
Detroit Receiving Hospital & Univ Health Center	Detroit	Michigan	313-745-3104	www.drhuhc.org
Doctors' Community Hospital	Lanham	Maryland	301-552-8085	www.DCHweb.org
East Orange General Hospital	East Orange	New Jersey	973-266-4401	www.evh.org
Eastern Oklahoma Medical Center	Poteau	Oklahoma	918-647-8161	www.eomchospital.com
Fleming County Hospital	Flemingsburg	Kentucky	606-849-2351	www.flemingcountyhospital.org
Flushing Hospital Medical Center	Flushing	New York	718-670-5000	www.flushinghospital.org
Forest Hills Hospital	Forest Hills	New York	718-830-4000	www.northshorelij.com
Forrest General Hospital	Hattiesburg	Mississippi	601-288-7000	www.forrestgeneral.com
Franklin Square Hospital Center	Baltimore	Maryland	443-777-7850	www.franklinsquare.org
Galichia Heart Hospital	Wichita	Kansas	316-858-2610	www.ghhospital.com
George Washington Univ Hospital	Washington	District of Columbia	202-716-4605	www.gwhospital.com
Georgiana Hospital	Georgiana	Alabama	334-376-2205	
Hackensack University Medical Center	Hackensack	New Jersey	201-996-2000	www.humed.com
Halifax Regional Medical Center	Roanoke Rapids	North Carolina	252-535-8005	www.halifaxmedicalcenter.org
Hallmark Health System	Melrose	Massachusetts	781-979-3000	www.hallmarkhealth.org
Harbor Hospital	Brooklyn	Maryland	410-350-3201	www.harborhospital.org
Harlan Appalachian Regional Healthcare Hospital	Harlan	Kentucky	606-573-8100	www.arh.org
Harris Hospital	Newport	Arkansas	870-523-8911	www.harrishospital.com
Hawaii Medical Center West	Ewa Beach	Hawaii	808-678-7000	
Henry Ford Hospital	Detroit	Michigan	313-916-2600	www.henryfordhospital.com
Highlands Medical Center	Scottsboro	Alabama	256-259-4444	www.highlandsmedcenter.com
Highlands Regional Medical Center	Prestonsburg	Kentucky	606-886-8511	www.hrmc.org
Hollywood Presbyterian Medical Center	Los Angeles	California	213-413-3000	www.qahpmc.com
Holy Cross Hospital	Chicago	Illinois	773-471-8000	www.holycrosshospital.org
Holy Name Medical Center	Teaneck	New Jersey	201-833-3000	www.holyname.org
Holy Redeemer Hospital and Medical Center	Meadowbrook	Pennsylvania	215-947-3000	www.holyredeemer.com
Holzer Medical Center	Gallipolis	Ohio	740-446-5000	www.holzer.org
Howard University Hospital	Washington	District of Columbia	202-745-6100	www.huhosp.org
Hugh Chatham Memorial Hospital	Elkin	North Carolina	336-527-7000	www.hughchatham.org
Ingalls Memorial Hospital	Harvey	Illinois	708-333-2300	www.ingalls.org
Integris Baptist Regional Health Center	Miami	Oklahoma	918-542-6611	www.integris-health.com
Jackson Health System	Miami	Florida	305-585-1111	www.jhsmiami.org
Jameson Memorial Hospital	New Castle	Pennsylvania	724-658-9001	

Hospital	City	State	Phone	Web Site
Jefferson Regional Medical Center	Crystal City	Missouri	636-933-1000	www.jeffersonmemorial.org
Jennersville Regional Hospital	West Grove	Pennsylvania	610-869-1000	www.jennersville.com
JFK Medical Center	Edison	New Jersey	732-321-7000	www.jfkmc.org
Johnson City Medical Center	Johnson City	Tennessee	423-431-6111	www.msha.com
Johnson Memorial Hospital	Stafford Springs	Connecticut	860-684-4251	www.johnsonhealthnetwork.com
Kennedy University Hospital	Stratford	New Jersey	856-346-6000	www.kennedyhealth.org
Kimball Medical Center	Lakewood	New Jersey	732-363-1900	www.sbhcs.com
King's Daughters' Medical Center	Ashland	Kentucky	606-327-4000	www.kdmc.com
Kings County Hospital Center	Brooklyn	New York	718-245-3901	www.nyc.gov/html/hhc/html/facilities/kings.shtml
Lake Wales Medical Center	Lake Wales	Florida	863-676-1433	www.lakewalesmedicalcenter.com
Lakeway Regional Hospital	Morristown	Tennessee	423-522-6000	
Lane Regional Medical Center	Zachary	Louisiana	225-658-4303	www.lanehospital.org
Lenox Hill Hospital	New York	New York	212-439-2345	www.lenoxhillhospital.org
Libertyhealth-Jersey City Medical Center Campus	Jersey City	New Jersey	201-915-2000	www.libertyhcs.org
Lincoln Medical & Mental Health Center	Bronx	New York	718-579-5000	
Livingston Regional Hospital	Livingston	Tennessee	931-823-5611	www.livingstonregionalhospital.com
Long Beach Medical Center	Long Beach	New York	516-897-1000	www.lbmc.org
Long Island College Hospital	Brooklyn	New York	718-780-4651	www.wehealny.org
Lower Bucks Hospital	Bristol	Pennsylvania	215-785-9200	www.lowerbuckshospital.org
Lutheran Medical Center	Brooklyn	New York	718-630-8000	www.lmcmc.com
Magee General Hospital	Magee	Mississippi	601-849-5070	www.mghosp.org
Magnolia Regional Health Center	Corinth	Mississippi	662-293-7660	www.mrhc.org
Mary Washington Hospital	Fredericksburg	Virginia	540-741-1100	www.medicorp.org
Medical Center of Southeastern Oklahoma	Durant	Oklahoma	405-924-3080	www.mcsohealth.com
Memorial Hermann Katy Hospital	Katy	Texas	281-392-1111	www.memorialhermann.org
Memorial Hospital	Manchester	Kentucky	606-598-5104	www.manchestermemorial.com
Memorial Hospital	Nacogdoches	Texas	936-564-4611	www.nacmem.org
Memorial Hospital of Rhode Island	Pawtucket	Rhode Island	401-729-2000	mhriweb.org
Memorial Hospital of Salem County	Salem	New Jersey	856-935-1000	www.mhshealth.com
Memorial Hospital of Stilwell	Stilwell	Oklahoma	918-696-3101	
Mercy Fitzgerald Hospital	Darby	Pennsylvania	215-237-4000	www.mercyhealth.org
Mercy Regional Medical Center	Ville Platte	Louisiana	337-363-5684	www.vpmc.com
Methodist Hospital	Henderson	Kentucky	270-827-7700	www.methodisthospital.net
Methodist Hospitals	Gary	Indiana	219-886-4601	www.methodisthospital.org
Metrosouth Medical Center	Blue Island	Illinois	708-597-2000	www.stfrancisblueisland.com
Monongahela Valley Hospital	Monongahela	Pennsylvania	724-258-1000	www.monvalleyhospital.com
Monroe County Medical Center	Tompkinsville	Kentucky	270-487-9231	www.mcmccares.com
Montefiore Medical Center	Bronx	New York	718-920-4321	www.montefiore.org
Montgomery General Hospital	Olney	Maryland	301-774-8771	www.montgomerygeneral.com
Mount Sinai Hospital	New York	New York	212-241-7981	www.mountsinai.org
New York Hospital Medical Center of Queens	Flushing	New York	718-670-1231	www.nyhq.org
New York Methodist Hospital	Brooklyn	New York	718-780-3000	www.nym.org
New York Westchester Square Medical Center	Bronx	New York	718-430-7300	www.nywsmc.org
New York-Presbyterian Hospital	New York	New York	212-746-4189	www.nyp.org
Newark Beth Israel Medical Center	Newark	New Jersey	973-926-7850	www.sbhcs.com
North Carolina Baptist Hospital	Winston-Salem	North Carolina	336-716-2011	www.wfubmc.edu
North Oaks Medical Center	Hammond	Louisiana	985-345-2700	www.northoaks.org
North Shore University Hospital	Manhasset	New York	516-562-0100	www.northshorelij.com
Northwest Community Hospital	Arlington Heights	Illinois	847-618-1000	www.nch.org
Northwestern Memorial Hospital	Chicago	Illinois	312-926-2000	www.nmh.org
NW Mississippi Regional Medical Center	Clarksdale	Mississippi	662-627-3211	www.nwmsregionalmedcenter.com
O'Connor Hospital	San Jose	California	408-947-2500	www.oconnorhospital.org
Oakdale Community Hospital	Oakdale	Louisiana	318-335-3700	www.oakdalecommunityhospital.com
Oakwood Annapolis Hospital	Wayne	Michigan	734-467-4175	www.oakwood.org
Oakwood Hospital and Medical Center	Dearborn	Michigan	313-593-7125	www.oakwood.org
Ocean Medical Center	Brick	New Jersey	732-840-2200	www.meridianhealth.com/mcoc.cfm/ind
Olympia Medical Center	Los Angeles	California	310-657-5900	www.olympiamc.com
Oroville Hospital	Oroville	California	530-533-8500	www.orovillehospital.com
Our Lady of the Resurrection Medical Center	Chicago	Illinois	773-282-7000	www.reshealth.org
Palisades Medical Center - NY Presbyterian Healthcare System	North Bergen	New Jersey	201-854-5000	www.palisadesmedical.org
Palos Community Hospital	Palos Heights	Illinois	708-923-4000	www.paloshospital.org
Paul B Hall Regional Medical Center	Paintsville	Kentucky	606-789-3511	www.pbhrmc.com
Perry Community Hospital	Linden	Tennessee	931-589-2121	
Pineville Community Hospital	Pineville	Kentucky	606-337-3051	
Pitt County Memorial Hospital	Greenville	North Carolina	252-847-4100	www.uhseast.com
Plainview Hospital	Plainview	New York	516-719-3000	www.nslij.com
Pleasant Valley Hospital	Point Pleasant	West Virginia	304-675-4340	

Hospital	City	State	Phone	Web Site
Prince Georges Hospital Center	Cheverly	Maryland	301-618-2000	www.princegeorgeshospital.org
Raleigh General Hospital	Beckley	West Virginia	304-256-4100	
Raritan Bay Medical Center	Perth Amboy	New Jersey	732-442-3700	
Regional Medical Center of San Jose	San Jose	California	408-259-5000	www.regionalmedicalsanjose.com
RHC St Francis Hospital	Evanston	Illinois	847-316-4000	www.reshealth.org
Ripley County Memorial Hospital	Doniphan	Missouri	573-996-2141	
Robert Packer Hospital	Sayre	Pennsylvania	570-888-6666	www.guthrie.org
Robert Wood Johnson University Hospital at Rahway	Rahway	New Jersey	732-381-4200	www.rwjuhr.com/about/history.html
Robert Wood Johnson University Hospital Hamilton	Hamilton	New Jersey	609-586-7900	www.rwjhamilton.org
Rush University Medical Center	Chicago	Illinois	312-942-5000	www.ruch.edu
Russell County Medical Center	Lebanon	Virginia	276-883-8000	
Saint Peter's University Hospital	New Brunswick	New Jersey	732-745-7944	www.saintpetersuh.com
San Gabriel Valley Medical Center	San Gabriel	California	626-289-5454	www.sangabrielvalleymedctr.org
Sandhills Regional Medical Center	Hamlet	North Carolina	910-958-2361	www.hma-corp.com
Seton Health System-St Mary's Campus	Troy	New York	518-272-5000	www.setonhealth.org
Silver Cross Hospital	Joliet	Illinois	815-740-1100	www.silvercross.org
Sinai Hospital of Baltimore	Baltimore	Maryland	410-601-5131	www.sinai-balt.com
Sinai-Grace Hospital	Detroit	Michigan	313-966-3300	www.sinaigrace.org
Somerset Medical Center	Somerville	New Jersey	908-685-2200	www.somersetmedicalcenter.com
South Bay Hospital	Sun City Center	Florida	813-634-3301	www.southbayhospital.com
Southern Tennessee Medical Center	Winchester	Tennessee	931-967-8295	www.southerntennessee.com
Southwest General Health Center	Middleburg Heights	Ohio	440-816-8000	www.swgeneral.com
Southwest Mississippi Regional Medical Center	Mccomb	Mississippi	601-249-5500	www.smrmc.com
SSM Depaul Health Center	Bridgeton	Missouri	314-344-6000	www.ssmdepaul.com
SSM St Marys Health Center	Richmond Heights	Missouri	314-768-8000	
Saint Barnabas Hospital	Bronx	New York	212-960-9000	www.stbarnabashospital.org
Saint Bernard Hospital	Chicago	Illinois	773-962-3900	www.stbernardhospital.com
Saint Catherine Hospital	East Chicago	Indiana	219-392-7004	www.comhs.org/stcatherine
Saint Clair Memorial Hospital	Pittsburgh	Pennsylvania	412-561-4900	www.stclair.org
Saint James Hospital & Health Center-Olympia Fields	Olympia Fields	Illinois	708-747-4000	
Saint John Hospital and Medical Center	Detroit	Michigan	313-343-4000	www.stjohnprovidence.org
Saint Joseph's Regional Medical Center	Paterson	New Jersey	973-754-2000	www.sjhmc.org
Saint Luke's Roosevelt Hospital	New York	New York	212-523-4000	www.wehealny.org
Saint Mary Mercy Hospital	Livonia	Michigan	734-655-4800	www.stmarymercy.org
Saint Mary's Hospital - Passaic	Passaic	New Jersey	973-365-4300	www.smh-nj.com
Saint Marys Hospital	Centralia	Illinois	618-436-8000	www.stmarys-goodsamaritan.com
Saint Tammany Parish Hospital	Covington	Louisiana	985-898-4000	www.stph.org
Staten Island University Hospital	Staten Island	New York	718-226-9000	www.siuh.edu
Swedish American Hospital	Rockford	Illinois	815-968-4400	www.swedishamerican.org
Teche Regional Medical Center	Morgan City	Louisiana	504-384-2200	www.techeregional.com
The Regional Medical Center of Acadiana	Lafayette	Louisiana	337-989-6700	www.medicalcentersw.com
Thomas Jefferson University Hospital	Philadelphia	Pennsylvania	215-955-6000	www.jeffersonhospital.org
Trinitas Regional Medical Center	Elizabeth	New Jersey	908-994-5000	www.trinitashospital.org
Trinity Medical Center East & Trinity Medical Center West	Steubenville	Ohio	740-264-7212	www.trinityhealth.com
Tufts Medical Center	Boston	Massachusetts	617-636-5000	www.tuftsmedicalcenter.org
UHHS Bedford Medical Center	Bedford	Ohio	440-735-3628	www.uhhsbmc.com
Unity Hospital	Fridley	Minnesota	763-236-5000	www.mercyunity.com
University Hospital	Cincinnati	Ohio	513-584-1000	www.universityhospitalcincinnati.com
University of Illinois Hospital	Chicago	Illinois	312-996-3900	www.uic.edu
Valley Baptist Medical Center	Harlingen	Texas	956-389-1100	www.vbmc.org
Valley Baptist Medical Center - Brownsville	Brownsville	Texas	956-544-1400	www.brownsvillemedical.com
Vassar Brothers Medical Center	Poughkeepsie	New York	845-454-8500	www.vasserbrothers.org
Western Pennsylvania Hospital - Forbes Regional Campus	Monroeville	Pennsylvania	412-858-2000	www.wpahs.org
Westlake Regional Hospital	Columbia	Kentucky	270-384-4753	www.westlake-healthcare.org
White County Medical Center	Searcy	Arkansas	501-278-3100	www.centralarkhospital.com
Williamson ARH Hospital	South Williamson	Kentucky	606-237-1700	www.arh.org
Williamson Memorial Hospital	Williamson	West Virginia	304-235-2500	www.hmawmh.com
Woodhull Medical and Mental Health Center	Brooklyn	New York	718-963-8100	www.ci.nyc.ny.us
Yakima Regional Medical and Cardiac Center	Yakima	Washington	509-575-5102	www.yakimaregional.org
Yale-New Haven Hospital	New Haven	Connecticut	203-688-4242	www.ynhh.org

Note: Table shows hospitals nationwide whose Heart Failure 30-day readmission rate is worse (higher) than U.S. rate of 24.7%

Hospitals whose Pneumonia 30-Day Readmission Rate is Better (Lower) than the U.S. National Rate

Hospital	City	State	Phone	Web Site
Alpena Regional Medical Center	Alpena	Michigan	989-356-7390	www.agh.org
Augusta Health	Fishersville	Virginia	540-932-4000	www.augustamed.com
Ball Memorial Hospital	Muncie	Indiana	765-747-3111	www.accesschs.org/baal-memorial-l
Bayfront Medical Center	Saint Petersburg	Florida	727-823-1234	www.bayfront.org
Bloomington Hospital	Bloomington	Indiana	812-353-9555	bloomingtonhospital.org
Boca Raton Regional Hospital	Boca Raton	Florida	561-362-5002	
Central Washington Hospital	Wenatchee	Washington	509-662-1511	www.cwhs.com
Cherokee Regional Medical Center	Cherokee	Iowa	712-225-5101	www.cherokeermc.org
Christus Santa Rosa Hospital	San Antonio	Texas	210-794-3336	www.christussantarosa.org
Christus Spohn Hospital Corpus Christi	Corpus Christi	Texas	361-902-4103	www.christusspohn.org
Citrus Memorial Hospital	Inverness	Florida	352-726-1551	www.citrusmh.com
Conroe Regional Medical Center	Conroe	Texas	936-539-1111	www.conroeregional.com
The Corpus Christi Medical Center	Corpus Christi	Texas	361-761-1000	
East Jefferson General Hospital	Metairie	Louisiana	504-454-4000	www.EastJeffHospital.org
Elmhurst Memorial Hospital	Elmhurst	Illinois	630-833-1400	www.emhc.org
Georgetown Memorial Hospital	Georgetown	South Carolina	843-527-7000	www.gmhsc.com
Gulf Breeze Hospital	Gulf Breeze	Florida	850-934-2000	www.ebaptisthealthcare.org/GulfBreezeHospital/Default
Hamot Medical Center	Erie	Pennsylvania	814-877-6000	www.hamot.org
Howard Regional Health System	Kokomo	Indiana	765-453-8371	www.howardcommunity.org
Intermountain Medical Center	Murray	Utah	801-507-7000	intermountainhealthcare.org
Kootenai Medical Center	Coeur D'alene	Idaho	208-666-2003	www.kootenaihealth.org
Lancaster General Hospital	Lancaster	Pennsylvania	717-299-5511	www.lancastergeneral.org
Logan Regional Hospital	Logan	Utah	435-716-1000	intermountainhealthcare.org
Marshalltown Medical & Surgical Center	Marshalltown	Iowa	641-754-5151	www.everydaychampions.org
McDonough District Hospital	Macomb	Illinois	309-833-4101	www.mdh.org
McAlester Regional Health Center	Mcalester	Oklahoma	918-426-1800	www.mrhcok.com
McKay-Dee Hospital Center	Ogden	Utah	801-387-2800	intermountainhealthcare.org
Memorial Healthcare System	Chattanooga	Tennessee	423-495-2525	www.memorial.org
Memorial Hermann Hospital System	Houston	Texas	713-448-6796	www.memorialhermann.org
Memorial Hermann Memorial City Medical Center	Houston	Texas	713-242-3000	www.mhhs.org
Mercy Medical Center-Cedar Rapids	Cedar Rapids	Iowa	319-398-6011	www.mercycare.org
Methodist Hospital	San Antonio	Texas	210-575-4000	www.mh.sahealth.com
Midmichigan Medical Center-Midland	Midland	Michigan	989-839-3000	www.midmichigan.org
Munson Medical Center	Traverse City	Michigan	231-935-5000	www.munsonhealthcare.org
Naples Community Hospital	Naples	Florida	239-436-5000	www.nchmd.org
National Park Medical Center	Hot Springs	Arkansas	501-321-1000	www.nationalparkmedical.com
Nor Lea General Hospital	Lovington	New Mexico	575-396-6611	www.nlgh.org
Northwest Hospital	Seattle	Washington	206-364-0500	www.nwhospital.org
Olympic Medical Center	Port Angeles	Washington	360-417-7000	www.olympicmedical.org
Parkview Hospital	Fort Wayne	Indiana	260-373-4000	www.parkview.com
Peacehealth St Joseph Medical Center	Bellingham	Washington	360-734-5400	www.peacehealth.org
Presbyterian Hospital	Albuquerque	New Mexico	505-724-7281	www.phs.org
Providence Hospital	Mobile	Alabama	251-633-1000	www.providencehospital.org
Providence Portland Medical Center	Portland	Oregon	503-215-1111	www.providence.org/oregon
Rapid City Regional Hospital	Rapid City	South Dakota	605-719-1000	www.rcrh.org
Reading Hospital Medical Center	Reading	Pennsylvania	610-988-8000	www.readinghospital.org
Salinas Valley Memorial Hospital	Salinas	California	831-757-4333	www.svmh.com
San Juan Regional Medical Center	Farmington	New Mexico	505-609-2000	www.sanjuanregional.com
Santa Barbara Cottage Hospital	Santa Barbara	California	805-682-7111	www.cottagehealthsystem.org
Sarasota Memorial Hospital	Sarasota	Florida	941-917-9000	www.smh.com
Shenandoah Memorial Hospital	Woodstock	Virginia	540-459-1100	www.valleyhealthlink.com
Skaggs Community Health Center	Branson	Missouri	417-335-7000	www.skaggs.net
Spartanburg Regional Medical Center	Spartanburg	South Carolina	864-560-6000	www.srhs.com
Saint Edward Mercy Medical Center	Fort Smith	Arkansas	479-314-6000	www.stedwardmercy.com
Saint Elizabeth East	Lafayette	Indiana	765-502-4000	www.ste.org
Saint John Medical Center	Tulsa	Oklahoma	918-744-2345	www.sjmc.org
Saint John's Regional Health Center	Springfield	Missouri	417-820-2000	www.stjohns.com
Saint Lukes Magic Valley RMC	Twin Falls	Idaho	208-737-2103	www.stlukesonline.org/magic_valley
Waverly Health Center	Waverly	Iowa	319-352-4120	www.waverlyhealthcenter.org
Wesley Medical Center	Wichita	Kansas	316-962-2000	www.wesleymc.com
Wheaton Franciscan Healthcare - Elmbrook Memorial	Brookfield	Wisconsin	262-785-2000	www.mywheaton.org
Williamsport Hospital & Medical Center	Williamsport	Pennsylvania	570-321-1000	www.susquehannahealth.org
Willis Knighton Medical Center	Shreveport	Louisiana	318-632-4000	www.wkhs.com//Locations/MedicalCenter.aspx
Wooster Community Hospital	Wooster	Ohio	330-263-8100	www.woosterhospital.org

Note: Table shows hospitals nationwide whose Pneumonia 30-day readmission rate is better (lower) than U.S. rate of 18.3%

Hospitals whose Pneumonia 30-Day Readmission Rate is Worse (Higher) than the U.S. National Rate

Hospital	City	State	Phone	Web Site
Adena Regional Medical Center	Chillicothe	Ohio	740-779-7778	www.adena.org
Advocate Christ Hospital & Medical Center	Oak Lawn	Illinois	708-684-8000	www.advocatehealth.com
Advocate Lutheran General Hospital	Park Ridge	Illinois	847-723-2210	www.advocatehealth.com
Allegheny General Hospital	Pittsburgh	Pennsylvania	412-359-3131	www.allhealth.edu
Aurora St Lukes Medical Center	Milwaukee	Wisconsin	414-649-6000	www.aurorahealthcare.org
Baptist Medical Center South	Montgomery	Alabama	334-288-2100	www.baptistfirst.org/south
Barnes Jewish Hospital	Saint Louis	Missouri	314-747-3000	www.barnesjewish.org
Baxter Regional Medical Center	Mountain Home	Arkansas	870-508-1000	www.baxterregional.org
Bayshore Community Hospital	Holmdel	New Jersey	732-739-5900	www.bchs.com
Beth Israel Deaconess Medical Center	Boston	Massachusetts	617-667-7000	www.bidmc.harvard.edu
Beth Israel Medical Center	New York	New York	212-420-2000	www.wehealny.org
Botsford Hospital	Farmington Hills	Michigan	248-471-8000	www.botsfordsystem.org
Bronx-Lebanon Hospital Center	Bronx	New York	212-588-7000	www.bronx-leb.org
Brookhaven Memorial Hospital Medical Center	Patchogue	New York	631-654-7100	www.brookhavenhospitalorg
Brooklyn Hospital Center at Downtown Campus	Brooklyn	New York	718-250-8000	www.tbh.org
Cameron Regional Medical Center	Cameron	Missouri	816-632-2101	www.cameronregional.org
Carolina Pines Regional Medical Center	Hartsville	South Carolina	864-339-2100	www.cprmc.com
Centegra Health System - McHenry Hospital	Mchenry	Illinois	815-344-5000	www.centegra.org
Centegra Health System - Woodstock Hospital	Woodstock	Illinois	815-788-5823	
Centinela Hospital Medical Center	Inglewood	California	310-673-4660	www.centinelafreeman.com
Centrastate Medical Center	Freehold	New Jersey	732-431-2000	www.centrastate.com
Choctaw Memorial Hospital	Hugo	Oklahoma	580-317-9500	
Christ Hospital	Jersey City	New Jersey	201-795-8200	www.christhospital.org
Crockett Hospital	Lawrenceburg	Tennessee	931-762-6571	www.crocketthospital.com
Crossroads Community Hospital	Mount Vernon	Illinois	618-244-5500	www.crossroadscommnityhospital.com
Doctors Memorial Hospital	Bonifay	Florida	850-547-1120	www.pahn.org/dmh.cfm
Dyersburg Regional Medical Center	Dyersburg	Tennessee	731-285-2410	
East Orange General Hospital	East Orange	New Jersey	973-266-4401	www.evh.org
Elmhurst Hospital Center	Elmhurst	New York	718-334-1141	nyc.gov
Enloe Medical Center	Chico	California	530-332-7300	www.enloe.org
Fairmont General Hospital	Fairmont	West Virginia	304-367-7100	www.fghi.com
Faxton-St Luke's Healthcare	Utica	New York	315-798-6000	
Fayette County Hospital	Vandalia	Illinois	618-283-1231	
Fleming County Hospital	Flemingsburg	Kentucky	606-849-2351	www.flemingcountyhospital.org
Forest Hills Hospital	Forest Hills	New York	718-830-4000	www.northshorelij.com
Forrest General Hospital	Hattiesburg	Mississippi	601-288-7000	www.forrestgeneral.com
Galesburg Cottage Hospital	Galesburg	Illinois	309-345-4555	www.cottagehospital.com
Garden City Hospital	Garden City	Michigan	734-421-3300	www.gchosp.org
Georgiana Hospital	Georgiana	Alabama	334-376-2205	
Harlan Appalachian Regional Healthcare Hospital	Harlan	Kentucky	606-573-8100	www.arh.org
Hazard Arh Regional Medical Center	Hazard	Kentucky	606-439-6600	www.arh.org/hazard
Henry Ford Hospital	Detroit	Michigan	313-916-2600	www.henryfordhospital.com
Highlands Regional Medical Center	Sebring	Florida	863-385-6101	www.highlandsregional.com
Highlands Regional Medical Center	Prestonsburg	Kentucky	606-886-8511	www.hrmc.org
Hoboken University Medical Center	Hoboken	New Jersey	201-418-1004	www.bonsecoursnj.com
Holy Cross Hospital	Silver Spring	Maryland	301-754-7010	www.holycrosshealth.org
Holzer Medical Center	Gallipolis	Ohio	740-446-5000	www.holzer.org
Hospital of St Raphael	New Haven	Connecticut	203-789-3000	www.srhs.org
Jennersville Regional Hospital	West Grove	Pennsylvania	610-869-1000	www.jennersville.com
Jennie Stuart Medical Center	Hopkinsville	Kentucky	270-887-0100	www.jsmc.org
Jewish Hospital	Cincinnati	Ohio	513-686-3003	www.jewishhospitalcincinnati.com
John Ed Chambers Memorial Hospital	Danville	Arkansas	479-495-2241	
Johns Hopkins Bayview Medical Center	Baltimore	Maryland	410-550-0123	www.hopkinsbayview.org
Jordan Hospital	Plymouth	Massachusetts	508-746-2000	www.jordanhospital.org
Kennedy University Hospital	Stratford	New Jersey	856-346-6000	www.kennedyhealth.org
Kimball Medical Center	Lakewood	New Jersey	732-363-1900	www.sbhcs.com
Kings County Hospital Center	Brooklyn	New York	718-245-3901	www.nyc.gov/html/hhc/html/facilities/kings.shtml
Kingston Hospital	Kingston	New York	914-331-3131	www.kingstonregionalhealth.org
Lake Cumberland Regional Hospital	Somerset	Kentucky	606-679-7441	
Laughlin Memorial Hospital	Greeneville	Tennessee	423-787-5000	
Lee Regional Medical Center	Pennington Gap	Virginia	276-546-1440	www.leeregional.com
Liberty Hospital	Liberty	Missouri	816-781-7200	www.libertyhospital.org
Little Company of Mary Hospital	Evergreen Park	Illinois	708-422-6200	www.lcmh.org
Magee General Hospital	Magee	Mississippi	601-849-5070	www.mghosp.org

Hospital	City	State	Phone	Web Site
Magnolia Regional Health Center	Corinth	Mississippi	662-293-7660	www.mrhc.org
Mary Washington Hospital	Fredericksburg	Virginia	540-741-1100	www.medicorp.org
Maryland General Hospital	Baltimore	Maryland	410-225-8996	www.marylandgeneral.org
Marymount Hospital	Garfield Heights	Ohio	216-581-0500	www.marymount.org
Massena Memorial Hospital	Massena	New York	315-764-1711	www.massenahospital.org
Medical Center of Southeastern Oklahoma	Durant	Oklahoma	405-924-3080	www.mcsohealth.com
Medical Park Hospital	Hope	Arkansas	870-777-2323	www.medicalparkhospitals.com
Memorial Hermann Baptist Beaumont Hospital	Beaumont	Texas	409-212-5012	www.mhbh.org
Memorial Hospital at Easton	Easton	Maryland	410-822-1000	www.shorehealth.org
Memorial Hospital of Rhode Island	Pawtucket	Rhode Island	401-729-2000	mhriweb.org
Memorial Hospital of Salem County	Salem	New Jersey	856-935-1000	www.mhshealth.com
Mercy Fitzgerald Hospital	Darby	Pennsylvania	215-237-4000	www.mercyhealth.org
Mercy Memorial Health Center	Ardmore	Oklahoma	405-223-5400	www.mercyok.com/mmhc
Mercy Regional Medical Center	Ville Platte	Louisiana	337-363-5684	www.vpmc.com
Methodist Hospital	Henderson	Kentucky	270-827-7700	www.methodisthospital.net
Methodist Hospital of Chicago	Chicago	Illinois	773-271-9040	www.methodistchicago.org
Metro Health Medical Center	Cleveland	Ohio	216-778-5700	www.metrohealth.org
Midstate Medical Center	Meriden	Connecticut	203-694-8200	www.midstatemedical.org
Montefiore Medical Center	Bronx	New York	718-920-4321	www.montefiore.org
Mount Sinai Hospital	New York	New York	212-241-7981	www.mountsinai.org
Nassau University Medical Center	East Meadow	New York	516-572-0123	www.numc.edu
New York Community Hospital of Brooklyn	Brooklyn	New York	718-692-5302	www.nych.com
New York Downtown Hospital	New York	New York	212-312-5000	www.downtownhospital.org
New York Hospital Medical Center of Queens	Flushing	New York	718-670-1231	www.nyhq.org
New York Westchester Square Medical Center	Bronx	New York	718-430-7300	www.nywsmc.org
North Arkansas Regional Medical Center	Harrison	Arkansas	870-414-4000	www.narmc.com
North Carolina Baptist Hospital	Winston-Salem	North Carolina	336-716-2011	www.wfubmc.edu
North Central Bronx Hospital	Bronx	New York	212-519-5000	www.nyc.gov/html/hhc/ncbh/home.html
Northside Medical Center	Youngstown	Ohio	330-884-1000	
Northwest Community Hospital	Arlington Heights	Illinois	847-618-1000	www.nch.org
Northwestern Memorial Hospital	Chicago	Illinois	312-926-2000	www.nmh.org
Norwegian-American Hospital	Chicago	Illinois	773-292-8200	www.nahospital.org
O'Bleness Memorial Hospital	Athens	Ohio	740-593-5551	www.obleness.org
Oakdale Community Hospital	Oakdale	Louisiana	318-335-3700	www.oakdalecommunityhospital.com
Orange Regional Medical Center	Goshen	New York	845-343-2424	
Oroville Hospital	Oroville	California	530-533-8500	www.orovillehospital.com
Our Lady of the Resurrection Medical Center	Chicago	Illinois	773-282-7000	www.reshealth.org
Palos Community Hospital	Palos Heights	Illinois	708-923-4000	www.paloshospital.org
Parkview Regional Hospital	Mexia	Texas	254-562-5332	www.parkviewregional.com
Paul B Hall Regional Medical Center	Paintsville	Kentucky	606-789-3511	www.pbhrmc.com
Pottstown Memorial Medical Center	Pottstown	Pennsylvania	610-327-7000	www.pmmctr.org
Presbyterian Hospital	Charlotte	North Carolina	704-384-4000	www.presbyterian.org
Princeton Community Hospital	Princeton	West Virginia	304-487-7260	www.pchonline.org
Raritan Bay Medical Center	Perth Amboy	New Jersey	732-442-3700	
Regional Hospital of Jackson	Jackson	Tennessee	731-661-2000	www.regionalhospitaljackson.com
RHC St Francis Hospital	Evanston	Illinois	847-316-4000	www.reshealth.org
Rhode Island Hospital	Providence	Rhode Island	401-444-4000	www.rhodeislandhospital.org
River Park Hospital	McMinnville	Tennessee	931-815-4101	www.riverparkhospital.com
Riverview Regional Medical Center	Gadsden	Alabama	256-543-5200	www.riverviewregional.com
Robert Packer Hospital	Sayre	Pennsylvania	570-888-6666	www.guthrie.org
Robert Wood Johnson University Hospital	New Brunswick	New Jersey	732-828-3000	www.rwjuh.edu
Robert Wood Johnson University Hospital Hamilton	Hamilton	New Jersey	609-586-7900	www.rwjhamilton.org
Russell County Medical Center	Lebanon	Virginia	276-883-8000	
Russellville Hospital	Russellville	Alabama	256-332-1611	
Saint Francis Hospital	Tulsa	Oklahoma	918-494-2200	www.saintfrancis.com
Schuylkill Medical Center - South Jackson Street	Pottsville	Pennsylvania	570-621-5000	www.pottsvillehospital.com
Sinai-Grace Hospital	Detroit	Michigan	313-966-3300	www.sinaigrace.org
South Nassau Communities Hospital	Oceanside	New York	516-632-3000	www.southnassau.org
Southeastern Ohio Regional Medical Center	Cambridge	Ohio	740-439-8111	www.seormc.org
Southern Maryland Hospital Center	Clinton	Maryland	301-877-4530	www.smhchealth.org
SSM Depaul Health Center	Bridgeton	Missouri	314-344-6000	www.ssmdepaul.com
Saint Barnabas Hospital	Bronx	New York	212-960-9000	www.stbarnabashospital.org
Saint Bernard Hospital	Chicago	Illinois	773-962-3900	www.stbernardhospital.com
Saint Elizabeth's Medical Center	Brighton	Massachusetts	617-789-3000	www.semc.org
Saint Francis Hospital & Medical Center	Hartford	Connecticut	860-714-4000	www.saintfranciscare.com
Saint James Hospital & Health Center-Olympia Fields	Olympia Fields	Illinois	708-747-4000	
Saint John's Episcopal Hospital at South Shore	Far Rockaway	New York	718-869-7000	

Hospital	City	State	Phone	Web Site
Saint Joseph's Regional Medical Center	Paterson	New Jersey	973-754-2000	www.sjhmc.org
Saint Luke's Cornwall Hospital	Newburgh	New York	845-561-4400	www.stlukeshospital.org
Saint Lukes Hospital	Chesterfield	Missouri	314-434-1500	www.goodhealthmatters.com
Saint Mary Mercy Hospital	Livonia	Michigan	734-655-4800	www.stmarymercy.org
Saint Mary's Medical Center of Campbell County	La Follette	Tennessee	423-907-1200	www.stmaryshealth.com
Saint Marys Hospital	Centralia	Illinois	618-436-8000	www.stmarys-goodsamaritan.com
Saint Vincent Hospital	Worcester	Massachusetts	508-363-5000	www.stvincenthospital.com
Saint Vincent's Medical Center	Jacksonville	Florida	904-308-7300	www.jaxhealth.com
Stonewall Jackson Memorial Hospital	Weston	West Virginia	304-269-8080	www.stonewallhospital.com
Sweetwater Hospital Association	Sweetwater	Tennessee	865-213-8200	www.sweetwaterhospital.org
The Medical Center at Bowling Green	Bowling Green	Kentucky	270-745-1000	www.mcbg.org
Three Rivers Medical Center	Louisa	Kentucky	606-638-9451	www.threeriversmedicalcenter.com
Trego County Lemke Memorial Hospital	Wa Keeney	Kansas	785-743-2182	
UHHS Bedford Medical Center	Bedford	Ohio	440-735-3628	www.uhhsbmc.com
Unity Hospital of Rochester	Rochester	New York	585-723-7000	www.unityhealth.org
University Hospital	Cincinnati	Ohio	513-584-1000	www.universityhospitalcincinnati.com
University of Kansas Hospital	Kansas City	Kansas	913-588-7332	www.kumc.edu
Valley Medical Center	Renton	Washington	425-228-3450	www.valleymed.org
Vanderbilt University Hospital	Nashville	Tennessee	615-322-3454	www.mc.vanderbilt.edu
Vassar Brothers Medical Center	Poughkeepsie	New York	845-454-8500	www.vasserbrothers.org
The Washington Hospital	Washington	Pennsylvania	724-225-7000	www.washingtonhospital.org
Webster General Hospital	Eupora	Mississippi	662-258-6221	
Westlake Regional Hospital	Columbia	Kentucky	270-384-4753	www.westlake-healthcare.org
White County Medical Center	Searcy	Arkansas	501-278-3100	www.centralarkhospital.com
Wyckoff Heights Medical Center	Brooklyn	New York	718-963-7272	www.wyckoffhospital.org
Yale-New Haven Hospital	New Haven	Connecticut	203-688-4242	www.ynhh.org

Note: Table shows hospitals nationwide whose Pneumonia 30-day readmission rate is worse (higher) than U.S. rate of 18.3%

Hospital Heart Attack Readmission Rates: State and National Summary

Area	Number of Hospitals			
	Better than U.S. National Rate[1]	Worse than U.S. National Rate[2]	No Different than U.S. National Rate[3]	Number of Cases Too Small[4]
U.S. and Territories	29	45	2403	1999
Alabama	0	0	44	56
Alaska	0	0	4	13
American Samoa	0	0	0	0
Arizona	0	1	43	25
Arkansas	0	0	30	44
California	4	0	200	122
Colorado	0	0	29	36
Connecticut	0	1	28	2
Delaware	0	0	5	0
District of Columbia	0	0	5	2
Florida	4	1	140	37
Georgia	2	0	63	75
Guam	0	0	1	0
Hawaii	0	0	10	6
Idaho	0	0	9	24
Illinois	0	4	103	73
Indiana	4	2	61	50
Iowa	0	1	26	82
Kansas	0	0	25	84
Kentucky	0	0	43	53
Louisiana	0	1	49	55
Maine	0	0	25	11
Maryland	0	1	39	5
Massachusetts	0	4	53	7
Michigan	2	1	76	49
Minnesota	0	0	30	91
Mississippi	0	0	28	54
Missouri	2	2	51	55
Montana	0	0	9	37
N. Mariana Islands	0	0	0	1
Nebraska	0	0	18	55
Nevada	0	0	16	13
New Hampshire	0	0	18	8
New Jersey	0	3	67	4
New Mexico	0	0	11	24
New York	0	12	139	35
North Carolina	1	2	69	36
North Dakota	0	0	7	33
Ohio	0	4	104	50
Oklahoma	0	0	33	72
Oregon	1	0	27	28
Pennsylvania	2	3	125	32
Puerto Rico	0	0	26	21
Rhode Island	0	0	10	0
South Carolina	3	0	33	21
South Dakota	1	0	8	33
Tennessee	0	1	61	54
Texas	1	0	185	151
Utah	0	0	14	20
Vermont	0	0	10	4
Virgin Islands	0	0	1	1
Virginia	1	1	65	12
Washington	0	0	42	38
West Virginia	1	0	25	24
Wisconsin	0	0	58	59
Wyoming	0	0	2	22

Note: (1) 30-day readmission rate is better (lower) than U.S. rate of 19.9%; (2) 30-day readmission rate is worse (higher) than U.S. rate of 19.9%; (3) 30-day readmission rate is about the same as U.S. rate of 19.9%; (4) The number of cases is too small to classify the hospital

Hospital Heart Failure Readmission Rates: State and National Summary

Area	Number of Hospitals			
	Better than U.S. National Rate[1]	Worse than U.S. National Rate[2]	No Different than U.S. National Rate[3]	Number of Cases Too Small[4]
U.S. and Territories	147	193	3869	550
Alabama	2	2	93	4
Alaska	1	0	9	12
American Samoa	0	0	0	1
Arizona	1	0	60	17
Arkansas	1	3	69	4
California	9	7	280	51
Colorado	2	0	53	16
Connecticut	1	2	29	0
Delaware	0	0	5	0
District of Columbia	0	2	5	0
Florida	13	3	162	6
Georgia	8	1	126	11
Guam	0	0	1	0
Hawaii	0	1	12	6
Idaho	2	0	24	10
Illinois	1	18	160	4
Indiana	8	2	105	3
Iowa	3	0	101	12
Kansas	3	1	90	32
Kentucky	1	11	83	2
Louisiana	4	9	85	21
Maine	0	0	35	1
Maryland	1	7	37	1
Massachusetts	2	4	56	3
Michigan	6	7	112	8
Minnesota	2	1	102	25
Mississippi	1	7	78	8
Missouri	3	7	100	4
Montana	2	0	29	28
N. Mariana Islands	0	0	1	0
Nebraska	1	1	54	28
Nevada	0	0	27	6
New Hampshire	3	0	22	1
New Jersey	2	22	50	0
New Mexico	1	0	33	8
New York	1	28	155	6
North Carolina	5	6	92	6
North Dakota	0	0	31	11
Ohio	6	7	145	4
Oklahoma	0	4	87	27
Oregon	3	0	50	5
Pennsylvania	10	12	138	5
Puerto Rico	0	0	35	13
Rhode Island	1	1	8	0
South Carolina	3	1	53	2
South Dakota	1	0	28	25
Tennessee	2	5	107	3
Texas	12	5	303	59
Utah	5	0	23	12
Vermont	1	0	12	1
Virgin Islands	0	0	2	0
Virginia	4	2	73	4
Washington	6	1	63	17
West Virginia	0	3	46	3
Wisconsin	3	0	112	6
Wyoming	0	0	18	8

Note: (1) 30-day readmission rate is better (lower) than U.S. rate of 24.7%; (2) 30-day readmission rate is worse (higher) than U.S. rate of 24.7%; (3) 30-day readmission rate is about the same as U.S. rate of 24.7%; (4) The number of cases is too small to classify the hospital

Hospital Pneumonia Readmission Rates: State and National Summary

Area	Number of Hospitals			
	Better than U.S. National Rate[1]	Worse than U.S. National Rate[2]	No Different than U.S. National Rate[3]	Number of Cases Too Small[4]
U.S. and Territories	64	163	4223	363
Alabama	1	4	92	4
Alaska	0	0	16	6
American Samoa	0	0	1	0
Arizona	0	0	68	10
Arkansas	2	5	69	2
California	2	3	296	54
Colorado	0	0	63	12
Connecticut	0	4	27	1
Delaware	0	0	5	0
District of Columbia	0	0	7	0
Florida	6	3	170	9
Georgia	0	0	140	5
Guam	0	0	1	0
Hawaii	0	0	15	6
Idaho	2	0	31	4
Illinois	3	18	158	5
Indiana	5	0	111	2
Iowa	4	0	109	3
Kansas	1	2	113	12
Kentucky	0	11	84	2
Louisiana	2	2	93	23
Maine	0	0	36	0
Maryland	0	5	40	1
Massachusetts	0	4	59	3
Michigan	3	5	120	4
Minnesota	0	0	118	13
Mississippi	0	4	84	8
Missouri	2	5	105	5
Montana	0	0	44	16
N. Mariana Islands	0	0	1	0
Nebraska	0	0	78	7
Nevada	0	0	30	3
New Hampshire	0	0	26	0
New Jersey	0	12	62	0
New Mexico	3	0	37	3
New York	0	30	156	5
North Carolina	0	2	105	3
North Dakota	0	0	42	2
Ohio	1	10	148	4
Oklahoma	2	4	102	11
Oregon	1	0	55	2
Pennsylvania	4	7	149	6
Puerto Rico	0	0	36	13
Rhode Island	0	2	8	1
South Carolina	2	1	55	1
South Dakota	1	0	48	6
Tennessee	1	8	103	6
Texas	7	4	322	52
Utah	3	0	33	4
Vermont	0	0	14	0
Virgin Islands	0	0	2	0
Virginia	2	3	74	7
Washington	4	1	74	9
West Virginia	0	3	49	1
Wisconsin	1	1	116	3
Wyoming	0	0	23	4

Note: (1) 30-day readmission rate is better (lower) than U.S. rate of 18.3%; (2) 30-day readmission rate is worse (higher) than U.S. rate of 18.3%; (3) 30-day readmission rate is about the same as U.S. rate of 18.3%; (4) The number of cases is too small to classify the hospital

What Do These Readmission Categories Show?

"Readmission" is when patients who have had a recent stay in the hospital go back into a hospital again. The information shows how often patients are readmitted within 30 days of discharge from a previous hospital stay for heart attack, heart failure, or pneumonia. Patients may have been readmitted back to the same hospital or to a different hospital or acute care facility. They may have been readmitted for the same condition as their recent hospital stay, or for a different reason.

This appendix shows how different hospitals' rates of readmission for heart attack, heart failure, and pneumonia patients compared to the U.S. National Rate. You can see whether the 30-day risk-adjusted rate of readmission for a hospital is lower (better) than the national rate, no different than the national rate, or higher (worse) than the national rate, given how sick patients were when they were admitted to the hospital. For some hospitals, the number of cases is too small (fewer than 25) to reliably tell how well the hospital is performing, so no comparison to the national rate is shown.

Better than U.S. National Rate. Hospitals in the Better Than U.S. National Rate category have risk-adjusted 30-day readmission rates that are lower than the U.S. National rate, and we can be 95% certain that this difference is not due to chance.

No Different than U.S. National Rate. Many hospitals in the No Different Than U.S. National Rate category have risk-adjusted 30-day readmission rates that are about the same as the U.S. National rate. Other hospitals in this category have rates that are higher or lower than the U.S. National rate, but we cannot be 95% certain that these differences are not due to chance.

Worse than U.S. National Rate. Hospitals in the Worse Than U.S. National Rate category have risk-adjusted 30-day readmission rates that are higher than the U.S. National rate, and we can be 95% certain that this difference is not due to chance.

Number of Cases Too Small. The number of cases is too small to classify the hospital. One cannot be certain about differences when a hospital has very few relevant patients.

Why are Readmission Rates for Individual Hospitals Not Shown?

Comparisons based on estimated readmission rates alone can be misleading. Risk-adjusted readmission rates are estimated for individual hospitals based on information taken from a particular time period. If a slightly different time period had been chosen, chances are that each hospital's results would have been somewhat different.

Researchers almost always report a range ("confidence interval" or in this case an "interval estimate") around their estimates, to show how much variation might be due to this kind of chance. A confidence interval or interval estimate tells us we can be reasonably "confident" (in this case, 95% confident) that a hospital's readmission rate fell somewhere within this specified range. The smaller the range, the more precise the estimate.

When hospitals treat a very large number of patients, chance differences will not have much effect on the overall rates. The range will be small, and the estimated readmission rates will be more precise. In hospitals that treat smaller numbers of patients, however, even small chance differences could have a big impact on readmission rates. The 95% confidence interval, or range, will be large, and the estimated readmission rates will be much less precise.

Because the number of patients treated at U.S. hospitals varies widely, the precision of hospitals' estimated readmission rates also varies.

Calculation of 30-Day Risk-Standardized Rates of Readmission

The three readmission models estimate hospital-specific, risk-standardized, all-cause 30-day readmission rates for patients discharged alive to a non-acute care setting with a principal diagnosis of heart attack, heart failure, and pneumonia. For each condition, the risk-standardized ("adjusted" or "risk-adjusted") hospital readmission rate can be used to compare performance across hospitals. The readmission measures for heart attack, heart failure, and pneumonia have been endorsed by the National Quality Forum (NQF).

Because of the way hospitals are paid under Medicare in Maryland, readmissions to hospital-owned rehabilitation and psychiatric facilities were counted as readmissions to acute care hospitals. This adversely impacted the 30-day readmission rates for some Maryland hospitals. CMS suppressed the readmission measures results for Maryland Hospitals in June 2009 due to these coding issues unique to Maryland.

CMS has resolved this coding issue to accurately reflect readmissions in Maryland for the June 2010 (and beyond) updates of the readmission data for Maryland hospitals and will no longer suppress readmission measures results for Maryland Hospitals.

Data Collection Methods

Cases Included in the Model. For each of the three principal discharge diagnoses (heart attack, heart failure, and pneumonia), the model includes admissions to all short-stay acute-care hospitals for people age 65 years or older who are enrolled in Original Medicare (traditional fee-for-service Medicare) and who have a complete claims history for 12 months prior to admission.

Excluded Admissions. For the heart attack, heart failure, and pneumonia readmission measures, admissions are excluded if they meet any of the following criteria:

- Admissions for patients with an in-hospital death are excluded because they are not eligible for readmission.
- Admissions for patients subsequently transferred to another acute care facility are excluded because we are focusing on discharges to non-acute care settings.
- Admissions for patients who are discharged against medical advice (AMA) are excluded because providers did not have the opportunity to deliver full care and prepare the patient for discharge.
- Admissions for patients without at least 30 days post-discharge enrollment in fee-for-service Medicare are excluded because the 30-day readmission outcome cannot be assessed in this group.
- If a patient has one or more additional admissions for the given condition (heart attack, heart failure, or pneumonia) within 30 days of discharge from an index admission- Opens in a new window, we do not consider the additional admissions as index admissions- Opens in a new window (they are considered as readmissions). Thus, any admission is either an index admission- Opens in a new window or a readmission, but not both.

For the heart attack readmission measure only, the following exclusion criterion also applies:

- Admissions are excluded for patients who are discharged alive on the same day that they are admitted because these patients are unlikely to have had a heart attack.

Admissions Not Counted As Readmissions

The measure does not count as readmissions claims for same-day readmissions to the same hospital for the same condition. This is done to put all hospitals on an even playing field, as CMS rules already require Prospective Payment System (PPS) acute-care hospitals to combine same-day, same condition readmissions into one claim (so the readmission would appear as part of the initial stay in the administrative data).

For the heart attack readmission measure only, readmissions within 30 days for percutaneous transluminal coronary angioplasty (PTCA) or coronary artery bypass graft (CABG) procedures are not counted as readmissions if they likely represent planned readmissions that are part of the same episode of care as the index admission.

Use of a 30-Day Period to Assess Readmissions

The model tracks readmissions that occur within 30 days of a hospital discharge, rather than readmission over some other post-discharge period. Thirty-day readmission was chosen over longer windows (such as 90 days), because readmission over longer periods may have less to do with the care received in the hospital and more to do with other complicating illnesses, patients' own behavior, or the care they received after discharge.

Use of Administrative Claims Data

Administrative claims data, rather than medical record data, are used to predict 30-day readmission. These data are widely available for people with Original Medicare (traditional fee-for-service), are relatively inexpensive to acquire, and are timely. Using administrative data makes it possible to calculate readmission without having to do chart reviews or requiring hospitals to report additional data. Research conducted when the measures were being developed demonstrated that the administrative claims-based models perform well in predicting readmission compared with models based on chart reviews.

Risk-Adjustment and Covariates Included in the Model

Risk-Adjustment. For each of the three principal discharge diagnoses (heart attack, heart failure, and pneumonia), the model adjusts for differences in patients' risks unrelated to their hospital care (risk-adjustment). The characteristics that Medicare patients bring with them when they arrive at a hospital with a heart attack, heart failure, or pneumonia are not under the control of the hospital. However, some patient characteristics may make readmission more likely (increase the "risk" of readmission), no matter where the patient is treated or how good the care is. Moreover, some hospitals may treat people with a history of more severe disease. Therefore, when readmission rates are calculated for each hospital, they are adjusted based on the unique mix of patients that the hospital treated during the study period. Factors included in the risk-adjustment model include age, gender, past medical history, and other diseases or conditions (comorbidities) that patients had when they arrived at the hospital and increase their risk of readmission.

Past medical history and comorbidities are included in the model using CMS's Condition Categories (CCs) and a history of certain procedures. Medicare patients are assigned to one or more CCs based on diagnoses (ICD-9 codes) obtained from the patient's discharge claim, and from the hospital inpatient, hospital outpatient, and physician Medicare claims submitted for the patient up to 12 months prior to the admission. Secondary diagnoses from the patient's hospital discharge claim that might represent complications that occurred while the patient was in the hospital, rather than conditions that were present on admission, are not included in assigning the patient's CCs. Research has shown that coding differences among providers affect CCs only slightly. Diagnoses from unreliable sources (such as laboratory or other claims that were not based on face-to-face encounters) are not included when assigning the CCs in the model.

To "risk-adjust" readmission rates for patient characteristics, the statistical model estimates the independent effects of age, gender, past medical history, comorbidities, and a hospital-specific component of quality on readmission of patients within 30 days of hospital discharge (the dependent variable). Using these estimates, the model calculates an adjusted readmission rate for each hospital that can be compared with those of other hospitals with different case mixes.

Statistical Methods Used to Calculate Readmission Rates

Hierarchical Regression Model. The statistical model for computing the 30-day risk-standardized readmission rates is a "hierarchical regression model." This type of model is based on the assumption that any heart attack, heart failure, or pneumonia patient treated at a particular hospital will experience a level of quality of care that applies to all patients treated for the same condition in that hospital. In other words, the expected risk of readmission for two similar heart attack, heart failure, or pneumonia patients treated in the same hospital would be more alike than the risk of readmission for the same two patients treated in two different hospitals. The likelihood that an individual patient will be readmitted is therefore a combination of:

- his or her individual risk characteristics (for example, gender, comorbidities, and past medical history) and
- the hospital's unique quality of care for all patients treated for that condition in that hospital.

The model estimates the effects of both of these components on on risk of readmission.

Calculating Readmission Rates. Each hospital's 30-day risk-standardized readmission rate (RSRR) is computed in several steps. First, the predicted 30-day readmission for a particular hospital obtained from the hierarchical regression model is divided by the expected readmission for that hospital, which is also obtained from the regression model. Predicted readmission is the number of readmissions (following discharge for heart attack, heart failure, or pneumonia) that would be anticipated in the particular hospital during the study period, given the patient case mix and the hospital's unique quality of

Covariates in 30-Day Risk-Standardized Readmission Models		
Heart Attack	Heart Failure	Pneumonia
Age, years over 65	Age, years over 65	Age, years over 65
Males	Males	Males
History of percutaneous transluminal coronary angioplasty (PTCA)		
History of coronary artery bypass graft (CABG) surgery	History of coronary artery bypass graft (CABG) surgery	History of coronary artery bypass graft (CABG) surgery
Anterior myocardial infarction		
Other location of myocardial infarction		
	Cardio-respiratory failure or shock	Cardio-respiratory failure or shock
History of congestive heart failure	History of congestive heart failure	History of congestive heart failure
Acute coronary syndrome	Acute coronary syndrome	Acute coronary syndrome
Angina pectoris/old myocardial infarction		
Coronary atherosclerosis		
	Coronary atherosclerosis or angina	Coronary atherosclerosis or angina
Valvular or rheumatic heart disease	Valvular or rheumatic heart disease	Valvular or rheumatic heart disease
Arrhythmias	Arrhythmias	Arrhythmias
	Other heart disorders	
Stroke	Stroke	Stroke
Cerebrovascular disease		
Hemiplegia, paraplegia, paralysis, functional disability	Hemiplegia, paraplegia, paralysis, functional disability	Hemiplegia, paraplegia, paralysis, functional disability
Vascular or circulatory disease	Vascular or circulatory disease	Vascular or circulatory disease
Diabetes or DM complications	Diabetes or DM complications	Diabetes or DM complications
Renal failure	Renal failure	Renal failure
End-stage renal disease or dialysis	End-stage renal disease or dialysis	End-stage renal disease or dialysis
Chronic obstructive pulmonary disease (COPD)	Chronic obstructive pulmonary disease (COPD)	Chronic obstructive pulmonary disease (COPD)
History of pneumonia	History of pneumonia	History of pneumonia
	Lung fibrosis or other chronic lung disorders	Lung fibrosis or other chronic lung disorders
Asthma	Asthma	Asthma
	Pleural effusion/pneumothorax	Pleural effusion/pneumothorax
	Other lung disorders	Other lung disorders
	Severe hematological disorders	Severe hematological disorders
Iron deficiency or other unspecified anemias and blood disease	Iron deficiency or other unspecified anemias and blood disease	Iron deficiency or other unspecified anemias and blood disease
Dementia or other specified brain disorders	Dementia or other specified brain disorders	Dementia or other specified brain disorders
	Drug/alcohol abuse/dependence/psychosis	Drug/alcohol abuse/dependence/psychosis
	Major psychiatric disorders	Major psychiatric disorders
	Depression	
	Other psychiatric disorders	Other psychiatric disorders
Metastatic cancer or acute leukemia	Metastatic cancer or acute leukemia	Metastatic cancer or acute leukemia
Cancer	Cancer	
		Lung or other severe cancers
		Other major cancers
Protein-calorie malnutrition	Protein-calorie malnutrition	Protein-calorie malnutrition
Disorders of fluid/electrolyte/acid-base	Disorders of fluid/electrolyte/acid-base	Disorders of fluid/electrolyte/acid-base
	End stage liver disease	
	Peptic ulcer, hemorrhage, other specified gastrointestinal disorders	
	Other gastrointestinal disorders	Other gastrointestinal disorders
History of infection		History of infection
		Septicemia/shock
	Nephritis	
		Urinary tract infection
Other urinary tract disorders	Other urinary tract disorders	Other urinary tract disorders
Decubitus ulcer or chronic skin ulcer	Decubitus ulcer or chronic skin ulcer	Decubitus ulcer or chronic skin ulcer
		Vertebral fractures
		Other injuries

care effect on readmission. Expected readmission is the number of readmissions (following discharge for heart attack, heart failure, or pneumonia) that would be expected if the same patients with the same characteristics had instead been treated at an "average" hospital, given the "average" hospital's quality of care effect on readmission for patients with that condition. This ratio is then multiplied by the national unadjusted readmission rate for the condition for all hospitals to compute an RSRR for the hospital. So, the higher a hospital's predicted 30-day readmission rate, relative to expected readmission for the hospital's particular case mix of patients, the higher its adjusted readmission rate will be. Hospitals with better quality will have lower rates.

(Predicted 30-day readmission/Expected readmission) * U.S. National readmission rate = RSRR

For example, suppose the model predicts that 10 of Hospital A's heart attack admissions would be readmitted within 30 days of discharge in a given year, based on their age, gender, and pre-existing health conditions, and based on the estimate of the hospital's specific quality of care. Then, suppose that the expected number of 30-day readmissions for those same patients were higher – say, 15 – if they had instead been treated at an "average" U.S. hospital. If the actual readmission rate for the study period for all heart attack admissions in all hospitals in the U.S. is 12 percent, then the hospital's 30-day risk-standardized readmission rate would be 8 percent.

RSRR for Hospital A = (10/15)* 12% = 8%

If, instead, 9 of these patients would be expected to have been readmitted if treated at the "average" hospital, then the hospital's readmission rate would be 13.3 percent.

RSRR for Hospital A = (10/9)* 12% = 13.3%

In the first case, the hospital performed better than the national average and had a relatively low risk-standardized readmission rate (8 percent); in the second case, it performed worse and had a relatively high rate (13.3 percent).

Hospitals with relatively low-risk patients whose predicted readmission is the same as the expected readmission for the average hospital for the same group of low-risk patients would have an adjusted readmission rate equal to the national rate (12 percent in this example). Similarly, hospitals with high-risk patients whose predicted readmission is the same as the expected readmission for the average hospital for the same group of high-risk patients would also have an adjusted readmission rate equal to the national rate of 12 percent. Thus, each hospital's case mix should not affect the adjusted readmission rates used to compare hospitals.

Adjusting for Small Hospitals or a Small Number of Cases. The hierarchical regression model also adjusts readmission rate results for small hospitals or hospitals with few heart attack, heart failure, or pneumonia cases in a given reference period. This reduces the chance that such hospitals' performance will fluctuate wildly from year to year or that they will be wrongly classified as either a worse or a better performer. For these hospitals, the model not only considers readmissions among patients treated for the condition in the small sample size of cases, but pools together patients from all hospitals treated for the given condition, to make the result more reliable. In essence, the predicted readmission rate for a hospital with a small number of cases is moved toward the overall U.S. National readmission rate for all hospitals. The estimates of readmission for hospitals with few patients will rely considerably on the pooled data for all hospitals, making it less likely that small hospitals will fall into either of the outlier categories. This pooling affords a "borrowing of statistical strength" that provides more confidence in the results.

Significance Testing and Interval Estimates

The model also calculates how precise the estimates of the adjusted readmission rate are, and determines upper and lower bounds (Interval Estimates) for each hospital's risk-standardized readmission rate. Interval estimates, which are like confidence intervals, describe how much uncertainty there is around the rate—how much bigger or smaller the rate might really be. Larger hospitals typically have more precise estimates and smaller interval estimates, since more data are available to estimate readmission. The smaller the sample size, the greater the difference in readmission rates between a hospital and the national rate must be in order for that difference to be statistically meaningful.

Comparing Readmission Rates Among Hospitals

The risk-standardized hospital rate with its interval estimate can be compared to the U.S. National crude readmission rate. If the interval estimate includes (overlaps with) the national crude readmission rate, the hospital's performance is in the "no different than U.S. National rate" category. If the entire interval estimate is below the national crude readmission rate, then the hospital is performing "better than U.S. National rate." If the entire interval estimate is above the national crude readmission rate, it is "worse than U.S. National rate." Hospitals with extremely few cases—those with fewer than 25 qualifying cases in the 3-year period—will be reported separately as: "number of cases too small (fewer than 25) to reliably tell how the hospital is performing."

Glossary of Terms

Accreditation
An evaluative process in which a healthcare organization undergoes an examination of its policies, procedures and performance by an external private sector organization ("accrediting body") to ensure that it is meeting predetermined criteria. It usually involves both on- and off-site surveys. Also see the terms AOA, The Joint Commission, and Medicare-Certified Hospitals.

Acute Care Hospital
A hospital that provides inpatient medical care and other related services for surgery, acute medical conditions or injuries (usually for a short term illness or condition).

Acute Myocardial Infarction (AMI)
A condition (also called a heart attack) that occurs when the arteries leading to the heart become blocked and the blood supply is slowed or stopped. When the heart muscle can't get the oxygen and nutrients it needs, the part of the heart tissue that is affected may die.

American Hospital Association (AHA)
The national organization that represents and serves all types of hospitals, health care networks, and their patients and communities. AHA takes part in national health policy development, legislative and regulatory debates, and legal matters. AHA provides education for health care leaders and is a source of information on health care issues and trends.

American Osteopathic Association (AOA)
A member association representing approximately 52,000 osteopathic physicians (D.O.s). The AOA serves as the primary certifying body for D.O.s, and is the accrediting agency for all osteopathic medical colleges and health care facilities. The AOA writes a performance report on each hospital that it checks. You can call or write to AOA to find out a hospital's level of accreditation.

Angioplasty
In angioplasty, a catheter is used to insert a balloon that is inflated to open a blocked blood vessel. Percutaneous transluminal coronary angioplasty (PTCA) is one of several procedures used to open a blocked blood vessel, known collectively as a percutaneous coronary intervention or PCI.

Angiotensin Converting Enzyme (ACE) Inhibitor
A medicine used to treat heart attacks, heart failure, or a decreased function of the left heart. They stop production of a hormone that can narrow blood vessels. This helps reduce the pressure in the heart and lower blood pressure.

Angiotensin Receptor Blocker (ARB)
A medicine used to treat patients with heart failure and a decreased function of the left heart. ARBs block the action of a hormone that can narrow blood vessels. This helps reduce the pressure in the heart and lower blood pressure.

Antibiotic
Medicine used to fight bacteria in the body.

Atherectomy
A procedure where a blade or laser on a catheter cuts through and removes blockages in blood vessels. It is one of several procedures used to open a blocked blood vessel (known as a Percutaneous Coronary Intervention or PCI).

Beta Blocker
A type of medicine that is used to lower blood pressure, treat chest pain (angina) and heart failure, and to help prevent a heart attack. Beta blockers relieve the stress on the heart by slowing the heart rate and reducing the force with which the heart muscles contract to pump blood. They also help keep blood vessels from constricting in the heart, brain, and body.

Blood Culture
A blood test that shows if there are bacteria in the blood, and what type of bacteria it is. It helps your doctor decide which antibiotic to use to treat a bacterial infection.

Centers for Medicare & Medicaid Services (CMS)
The federal agency that runs the Medicare program for the elderly aged and disabled. In addition, CMS works with the states to run the Medicaid program for low-income individuals. CMS works to make sure that the people in these programs are able to get high quality health care. Also see the term DHHS.

Certification (Medicare-Certified)
State government agencies inspect health care providers, including hospitals, nursing homes, dialysis facilities and home health agencies, as well as other health care providers. These providers are certified if they pass inspection. Being certified is not the same as being accredited. Medicare or Medicaid only pays for care provided by certified or accredited providers.

Critical Access Hospital (CAH)
A small, generally geographically remote facility that provides outpatient and inpatient hospital services to people in rural areas. The designation was established by law, for special payments under the Medicare program. To be designated as a CAH, a hospital must be located in a rural area, provide 24-hour emergency services; have an average length-of-stay for its patients of 96 hours or less; be located more than 35 miles (or more than 15 miles in areas with mountainous terrain) from the nearest hospital or be designated by its State as a "necessary provider". Hospitals may have no more than 25 beds.

Department of Health and Human Services (DHHS)
A division of the U.S. government that administers many of the social programs at the Federal level dealing with the health and welfare of the citizens of the United States. CMS is an agency within DHHS.

Diastolic Pressure
The lowest pressure in the artery when the heart is filling with blood. In a blood pressure reading, the diastolic pressure is the second number recorded.

Do hospitals that treat sicker patients have worse death rates? (Risk-adjustment)
Hospitals that treat sicker patients do not necessarily have worse death rates. The hospital-specific 30-day death (mortality) rates used in this report have been adjusted to account for differences in patients' health before their hospital admission.

Sicker patients or patients with more health-related risks may be more likely to die than healthier patients. Moreover, patients who are sicker may be more likely to be treated at particular hospitals while patients who are healthier may be more likely to be treated at other hospitals.

To compare hospitals fairly (and to avoid penalizing those that treat sicker patients) it is therefore important to consider differences in patients' health before they were admitted to the hospital. The statistical process of accounting for differences in patients' sickness before they were admitted to the hospital is called risk-adjustment. This statistical process aims to 'level the playing field' by accounting for health risks that patients have before they enter the hospital.

Fibrinolysis, Fibrinolytic Drugs
Fibrinolytic drugs are "clot-busting" medicines that can help dissolve blood clots in blood vessels and improve blood flow to your heart. They are important for treating heart attacks. If you have a heart attack, your doctor may give you a fibrinolytic drug, perform a percutaneous coronary intervention (PCI), or both.

Hospital Quality Alliance (HQA): Improving Care Through Information
In December 2002, the American Hospital Association (AHA), Federation of American Hospitals (FAH), and Association of American Medical Colleges (AAMC) launched the Hospital Quality Alliance (HQA), a national public-private collaboration to encourage hospitals to voluntarily collect and report hospital quality performance information. This effort is intended to make important information about hospital performance accessible to the public and to inform and invigorate efforts to improve quality. CMS and the Joint Commission participate in the HQA, along with the AHA, the FAH, the AAMC, the American Medical Association, the American Nurses Association, the National Association of Children's Hospitals and Related Organizations, American Association of Retired People, American Federation of Labor and Council of Industrial Organizations, the Consumer-Purchaser Disclosure Project, the Agency for Healthcare Research and Quality, the National Quality Forum, the Blue Cross and Blue Shield Association, the National Business Coalition on Health, General Electric, and the U.S. Chamber of Commerce.

Influenza
Influenza is a serious and sometimes deadly lung infection that can spread quickly in a community. Symptoms include fever-often a high temperature of more than 102° Fahrenheit (38.9° Celsius), headache, muscle aches and pains, chills, cough and chest pain when you take a breath ("pleuritic chest pain"). Although most people recover from the illness, the Centers for Disease Control and Prevention (the CDC) estimates that in the United States more than 200,000 people are hospitalized and about 36,000 people die from the flu and its complications every year.

Influenza Vaccination ("Flu Shot")
The main way to keep from getting flu is to get a yearly flu vaccination. Scientists make a different vaccine every year because the strains of flu viruses change from year to year. Nine to 10 months before the flu season begins, they prepare a new vaccine made from inactivated (killed) flu viruses. Because the viruses have been killed, they cannot cause infection. The vaccine preparation is based on the strains of the flu viruses that are in circulation at the time.

Hospitals should check to make sure that pneumonia patients get a flu shot during flu season to protect them from another lung infection and to help prevent the spread of influenza in the community. You can also get the vaccine at your doctor's office or a local clinic, and in many communities at workplaces, supermarkets, and drugstores. You must get the vaccine every year because it changes.

Inpatient Hospital Services
Services provided to patients admitted to a hospital that include bed and board, nursing services, diagnostic or therapeutic services, and medical or surgical services.

Left Ventricular Function Assessment
A test to check how well the heart is pumping.

Long-term Care Hospital
A facility, like a nursing home, that provides a variety of services that help people with health or personal needs and activities of daily living (like walking, eating, and going to the bathroom) over a period of time. Most long-term care is custodial care, for which Medicare does not pay.

Measurement
The process of collecting data to assess performance conducted at a single point in time or repeated over time.

Medicaid
A joint federal and state program that helps with medical costs for some people with low incomes and limited resources. Medicaid programs vary from state to state, but most health care costs are covered if you qualify for both Medicare and Medicaid.

Medicare-Certified Hospital
In order to receive any payment from either the Medicare or Medicaid programs, a hospital must meet a set of basic standards for quality of care, called "conditions of participation". Medicare-certified hospitals are reviewed periodically (every three years) to assure that they are continuing to provide services of acceptable quality.

Medicare also considers or "deems" hospitals as Medicare-certified that meet the accreditation requirements of the The Joint Commission or the American Osteopathic Association. Most short-term acute care hospitals in the United States choose to be Medicare-certified, either directly or through accreditation.

Medicare Provider Number
Medicare identifies the hospitals with which it works using a unique number. These numbers were used to identify the facilities that reported data for Hospital Compare. If hospitals share a Medicare Provider Number (for example, they bill Medicare for services as a single legal entity), the performance data for those hospitals are, in effect, combined into an aggregate rate representing all of the hospitals represented by the Medicare Provider Number. If you are interested in a hospital that is part of a system or network, you may not be able to find your specific hospital.

Medigap Policy
A Medicare supplement insurance policy sold by private insurance companies to fill "gaps" in Original Medicare Plan coverage. Except in Massachusetts, Minnesota and Wisconsin, there are 10 standardized plans labeled Plan A through Plan J. Medigap policies only work with the Original Medicare Plan.

Original Medicare Plan
A pay-per-visit health plan that lets you go to any doctor, hospital, or other health care supplier who accepts Medicare and is accepting new Medicare patients. You must pay the deductible. Medicare pays its share of the Medicare-approved amount, and you pay your share (coinsurance). In some cases you may be charged more than the Medicare-approved amount. The Original Medicare Plan has two parts: Part A (Hospital Insurance) and Part B (Medical Insurance).

Osteopathic Doctor
A licensed physician who can do surgery and prescribe drugs who has training in manipulative therapy. Also called a Doctor of Osteopathy or DO.

Outcome Measures
Measures designed to reflect the results of care, rather than how frequently a specific treatment or intervention was performed.

Oxygenation Assessment
Test that measures the amount of oxygen in your blood to see if you need oxygen therapy.

Percutaneous Coronary Interventions (PCI)
The procedures called Percutaneous Coronary Interventions (PCI), such as angioplasty and atherectomy are among those that are the most effective for opening blocked blood vessels that cause heart attacks. Doctors may perform a PCI, or give medicine to open the blockage, and in some cases, may do both.

Plan of Care
A written plan of care created with your physician and hospital staff. It tells what services you will get to reach and keep your best physical, mental, and social well being. The hospital staff keeps your doctor up-to-date on how you are doing and updates your care plan as needed.

Pneumonia
An inflammation of the lungs caused by a viral or bacterial infection. This fills your lungs with mucus and lowers the oxygen level in your blood. Symptoms can include fever, fatigue, difficulty breathing, chills, a "wet" cough, and chest pain.

Pneumonia (pneumococcal) Vaccination
Vaccine given to prevent pneumonia, estimated to protect against 80% of bacteria causing pneumonia.

Process of Care Measures
Measures that show, in percentage form or as a rate, how often a health care provider gives recommended care; that is, the treatment known to give the best results for most patients with a particular condition.

Provider
A doctor, hospital, health care professional, or health care facility.

Psychiatric Hospital
A facility that provides inpatient psychiatric services for the diagnosis and treatment of mental illness on a 24-hour basis, by or under the supervision of a physician.

Quality
Quality health care is how well a doctor, hospital, health plan, or other provider of health care, keeps its members healthy or treats them when they are sick. Good quality health care means doing the right thing at the right time, in the right way, for the right person and getting the best possible results.

Quality Assurance
The process of looking at how well a medical service is provided. The process may include formally reviewing health care given to a person, or group of persons, locating the problem, correcting the problem, and then checking to see if what you did worked.

Quality Improvement Organizations (QIOs)
Groups of practicing doctors and other health care experts who are paid by the federal government to check and improve the care given to Medicare patients. They must review your complaints about the quality of care given by: inpatient hospitals, hospital outpatient departments, hospital emergency rooms, skilled nursing facilities, home health agencies, Private Fee-for-Service plans, and ambulatory surgical centers.

Rehabilitation Hospital
A hospital that specializes in improving or restoring a patient's functional ability through therapies. Sometimes called a post-acute hospital.

Risk-Adjusted 30-Day Death (Mortality) Rates
The 30-day Risk-Adjusted Death (Mortality) Rates are produced using a complex statistical model, that relies on Medicare claims and enrollment information. The model predicts patient deaths for any cause within 30 days of hospital admission for heart attack or heart failure, whether the patients die while still in the hospital or after discharge. Thirty-day mortality is used because this is the time period when deaths are most likely to be related to the care patients received in the hospital. Deaths that occur outside the hospital within 30 days are included along with deaths that occur in the hospital, because some hospitals discharge patients sooner than others.

Stent
A small wire tube inserted in a blood vessel by a catheter to hold open a blocked blood vessel. One of several procedures to open a blocked blood vessel called a percutaneous coronary intervention (PCI).

The Joint Commission
An organization that evaluates and accredits health care organizations and programs in the United States. The Joint Commission is an independent, not-for-profit organization. The Joint Commission looks at how well a hospital treats patients and how good a hospital's staff and equipment are. A hospital is accredited by The Joint Commission if it meets certain quality standards. These checks are done at least every 3 years. Most hospitals take part in these accreditations.

The Joint Commission writes a "performance report" on each hospital that it checks. You can order these reports free of charge.

Thirty-Day Mortality Model Information
See Krumholtz, H., et al. "An Administrative Claims Model Suitable for Profiling Hospital Performance Based on 30-Day Mortality Rates Among Patients with an Acute Myocardial Infarction." Circulation. Vol. 113: 1683-1692, 2006, for details on the development of the AMI model. An accompanying article in the same volume discusses the heart failure model.

Treatment
Something done to help with a health problem. For example, medicine and surgery are treatments.

Treatment Options
The choices you have when there is more than one way to treat your health problem.

Grey House Publishing
2011 Title List

Visit **www.greyhouse.com** for Product Information, Table of Contents and Sample Pages

General Reference

American Environmental Leaders: From Colonial Times to the Present
An African Biographical Dictionary
An Encyclopedia of Human Rights in the United States
Encyclopedia of African-American Writing
Encyclopedia of Gun Control & Gun Rights
Encyclopedia of Invasions & Conquests
Encyclopedia of Prisoners of War & Internment
Encyclopedia of Religion & Law in America
Encyclopedia of Rural America
Encyclopedia of the United States Cabinet, 1789-2010
Encyclopedia of War Journalism
Encyclopedia of Warrior Peoples & Fighting Groups
From Suffrage to the Senate: America's Political Women
Nations of the World
Political Corruption in America
Speakers of the House of Representatives, 1789-2009
The Environmental Debate: A Documentary History
The Evolution Wars: A Guide to the Debates
The Religious Right: A Reference Handbook
The Value of a Dollar: 1860-2009
The Value of a Dollar: Colonial Era
University & College Museums, Galleries & Related Facilities
US Land & Natural Resource Policy
Weather America
Working Americans 1770-1869 Vol. IX: Revol. War to the Civil War
Working Americans 1880-1999 Vol. I: The Working Class
Working Americans 1880-1999 Vol. II: The Middle Class
Working Americans 1880-1999 Vol. III: The Upper Class
Working Americans 1880-1999 Vol. IV: Their Children
Working Americans 1880-2003 Vol. V: At War
Working Americans 1880-2005 Vol. VI: Women at Work
Working Americans 1880-2006 Vol. VII: Social Movements
Working Americans 1880-2007 Vol. VIII: Immigrants
Working Americans 1880-2009 Vol. X: Sports & Recreation
Working Americans 1880-2010 Vol. XI: Inventors & Entrepreneurs
Working Americans 1880-2011 Vol. XII: Musicians
World Cultural Leaders of the 20th & 21st Centuries

Business Information

Directory of Business Information Resources
Directory of Mail Order Catalogs
Directory of Venture Capital & Private Equity Firms
Environmental Resource Handbook
Food & Beverage Market Place
Grey House Homeland Security Directory
Grey House Performing Arts Directory
Hudson's Washington News Media Contacts Directory
New York State Directory
Sports Market Place Directory
The Rauch Guides – Industry Market Research Reports

Statistics & Demographics

America's Top-Rated Cities
America's Top-Rated Small Towns & Cities
America's Top-Rated Smaller Cities
Comparative Guide to American Hospitals
Comparative Guide to American Suburbs
Comparative Guide to Health in America
Profiles of... Series – State Handbooks

Health Information

Comparative Guide to American Hospitals
Comparative Guide to Health in America
Complete Directory for Pediatric Disorders
Complete Directory for People with Chronic Illness
Complete Directory for People with Disabilities
Complete Mental Health Directory
Directory of Health Care Group Purchasing Organizations
Directory of Hospital Personnel
HMO/PPO Directory
Medical Device Register
Older Americans Information Directory

Education Information

Charter School Movement
Comparative Guide to American Elementary & Secondary Schools
Complete Learning Disabilities Directory
Educators Resource Directory
Special Education

Financial Ratings Series

TheStreet.com Ratings Guide to Bond & Money Market Mutual Funds
TheStreet.com Ratings Guide to Common Stocks
TheStreet.com Ratings Guide to Exchange-Traded Funds
TheStreet.com Ratings Guide to Stock Mutual Funds
TheStreet.com Ratings Ultimate Guided Tour of Stock Investing
Weiss Ratings Consumer Box Set
Weiss Ratings Guide to Banks & Thrifts
Weiss Ratings Guide to Credit Unions
Weiss Ratings Guide to Health Insurers
Weiss Ratings Guide to Life & Annuity Insurers
Weiss Ratings Guide to Property & Casualty Insurers

Bowker's Books In Print® Titles

Books In Print®
Books In Print® Supplement
American Book Publishing Record® Annual
American Book Publishing Record® Monthly
Books Out Loud™
Bowker's Complete Video Directory™
Children's Books In Print®
Complete Directory of Large Print Books & Serials™
El-Hi Textbooks & Serials In Print®
Forthcoming Books®
Law Books & Serials In Print™
Medical & Health Care Books In Print™
Publishers, Distributors & Wholesalers of the US™
Subject Guide to Books In Print®
Subject Guide to Children's Books In Print®

Canadian General Reference

Associations Canada
Canadian Almanac & Directory
Canadian Environmental Resource Guide
Canadian Parliamentary Guide
Financial Services Canada
Governments Canada
Libraries Canada
The History of Canada

Grey House Publishing
4919 Route 22, PO Box 56, Amenia NY 12501-0056 | (800) 562-2139 | www.greyhouse.com | books@greyhouse.com

Grey House Publishing
2011 Title List

Visit www.greyhouse.com for Product Information, Table of Contents and Sample Pages

General Reference

American Environmental Leaders: From Colonial Times to the Present
An African Biographical Dictionary
An Encyclopedia of Human Rights in the United States
Encyclopedia of African-American Writing
Encyclopedia of Gun Control & Gun Rights
Encyclopedia of Invasions & Conquests
Encyclopedia of Prisoners of War & Internment
Encyclopedia of Religion & Law in America
Encyclopedia of Rural America
Encyclopedia of the United States Cabinet, 1789-2010
Encyclopedia of War Journalism
Encyclopedia of Warrior Peoples & Fighting Groups
From Suffrage to the Senate, America's Political Women
Nations of the World
Political Corruption in America
Speakers of the House of Representatives, 1789-2009
The Environmental Debate: A Documentary History
The Evolution Wars: A Guide to the Debates
The Religious Right: A Reference Handbook
The Value of a Dollar 1860-2009
The Value of a Dollar: Colonial Era
University & College Museums, Galleries & Related Facilities
US Land & Natural Resource Policy
Weather America
Working Americans 1770-1869 Vol. IX: Revolutionary War to the Civil War
Working Americans 1880-1999 Vol. I: The Working Class
Working Americans 1880-1999 Vol. II: The Middle Class
Working Americans 1880-1999 Vol. III: The Upper Class
Working Americans 1880-1999 Vol. IV: Their Children
Working Americans 1880-2003 Vol. V: At War
Working Americans 1880-2005 Vol. VI: Women at Work
Working Americans 1880-2006 Vol. VII: Social Movements
Working Americans 1880-2007 Vol. VIII: Immigrants
Working Americans 1880-2009 Vol. X: Sports & Recreation
Working Americans 1880-2010 Vol. XI: Inventors & Entrepreneurs
Working Americans 1880-2011 Vol. XII: Musicians
World Cultural Leaders of the 20th & 21st Centuries

Business Information

Directory of Business Information Resources
Directory of Mail Order Catalogs
Directory of Venture Capital & Private Equity Firms
Environmental Resource Handbook
Food & Beverage Market Place
Grey House Homeland Security Directory
Grey House Performing Arts Directory
Hudson's Washington News Media Contacts Directory
New York State Directory
Sports Market Place Directory
The Rauch Guides – Industry Market Research Reports

Statistics & Demographics

America's Top-Rated Cities
America's Top-Rated Small Towns & Cities
America's Top-Rated Smaller Cities
Comparative Guide to American Hospitals
Comparative Guide to American Suburbs
Comparative Guide to Health in America
Profiles of... Series – State Handbooks

Health Information

Comparative Guide to American Hospitals
Comparative Guide to Health in America
Complete Directory for Pediatric Disorders
Complete Directory for People with Chronic Illness
Complete Directory for People with Disabilities
Complete Mental Health Directory
Directory of Health Care Group Purchasing Organizations
Directory of Hospital Personnel
HMO/PPO Directory
Medical Device Register
Older Americans Information Directory

Education Information

Charter School Movement
Comparative Guide to American Elementary & Secondary Schools
Complete Learning Disabilities Directory
Educators Resource Directory
Special Education

Financial Ratings Series

TheStreet.com Ratings Guide to Bond & Money Market Mutual Funds
TheStreet.com Ratings Guide to Common Stocks
TheStreet.com Ratings Guide to Exchange-Traded Funds
TheStreet.com Ratings Guide to Stock Mutual Funds
TheStreet.com Ratings Ultimate Guided Tour of Stock Investing
Weiss Ratings Consumer Box Set
Weiss Ratings Guide to Banks & Thrifts
Weiss Ratings Guide to Credit Unions
Weiss Ratings Guide to Health Insurers
Weiss Ratings Guide to Life & Annuity Insurers
Weiss Ratings Guide to Property & Casualty Insurers

Bowker's Books in Print® Titles

Books In Print®
Books In Print® Supplement
American Book Publishing Record® Annual
American Book Publishing Record® Monthly
Books Out Loud™
Bowker's Complete Video Directory™
Children's Books In Print®
Complete Directory of Large Print Books & Serials™
El-Hi Textbooks & Serials In Print®
Forthcoming Books®
Law Books & Serials In Print™
Medical & Health Care Books In Print™
Publishers, Distributors & Wholesalers of the US™
Subject Guide to Books In Print®
Subject Guide to Children's Books In Print®

Canadian General Reference

Associations Canada
Canadian Almanac & Directory
Canadian Environmental Resource Guide
Canadian Parliamentary Guide
Financial Services Canada
Governments Canada
Libraries Canada
The History of Canada

Grey House Publishing
4919 Route 22, PO Box 56, Amenia NY 12501-0056 | (800) 562-2139 | www.greyhouse.com | books@greyhouse.com